WEBSTER'S
All-In-One
Dictionary
& Thesaurus

THIRD EDITION

Created in Cooperation with the Editors of
MERRIAM-WEBSTER

FEDERAL
STREET
PRESS

A Division of Merriam-Webster, Incorporated
Springfield, Massachusetts

This edition published by
Federal Street Press
A Division of Merriam-Webster, Incorporated
P.O. Box 281
Springfield, MA 01102

Federal Street Press books are available for bulk purchase for
sales promotion and premium use. For details write the manager of
special sales, Federal Street Press, P.O. Box 281, Springfield, MA 01102

ISBN 978-1-59695-184-6

1st Printing   Thomson Press India Ltd., Faridabad   July 2023   SRM

Printed in India

CONTENTS

PREFACE

Webster's All-in-One Dictionary and Thesaurus, Third Edition, combines the functions of a dictionary and a thesaurus in one integrated volume. In this work, the dictionary features of definitions, pronunciations, and grammatical information are presented along with the synonym and antonym features of a thesaurus. Rather than separating the dictionary and thesaurus into different sections of the book, here the thesaurus material for a word immediately follows its dictionary entry. Presenting the dictionary and thesaurus as a unified whole enables readers and writers to access both kinds of information quickly and to see the relationship between them easily.

This third edition of *Webster's All-in-One Dictionary and Thesaurus* is based on *Merriam-Webster's Dictionary and Thesaurus*. The dictionary entries for that book are based on *The Merriam-Webster Dictionary*, the highly popular paperback, and on *Merriam-Webster's Collegiate Dictionary, Eleventh Edition*, as well as on the dictionary on the award-winning website, Merriam-Webster. com. The thesaurus entries are drawn from Merriam-Webster's most up-to-date thesauruses. The dictionary and thesaurus entries were prepared in cooperation with the editors at Merriam-Webster to ensure correspondence between the indicated dictionary senses and the selection of similar and contrasting words offered in the thesaurus lists.

More than 68,000 dictionary definitions give coverage to the most frequently used words in the language. The definitions are based on examples of actual word use found in the Merriam-Webster citation files, which now contain more than 100 million words available through electronic searching. The thesaurus lists, which follow the definitions, are set off in tinted type. They offer nearly 130,000 synonyms and antonyms for the writer interested in finding a more appropriate or more colorful word choice.

The editors who worked on the project were Serenity H. Carr, who did the primary editing of the thesaurus entries, and Linda Wood, who did the primary editing of the dictionary entries. Credit for editing also goes to Susan L. Brady, who did the primary editing of *Merriam-Webster's Dictionary and Thesaurus*, upon which this edition is based. The entire project was supervised by Em Vezina, who also handled the task of cross-reference. Daniel Brandon and Anne E. McDonald handled data entry and data-file processing and contributed essential technical assistance in a number of other ways. Paul S. Wood served as editor in charge of production, guiding the book through its typesetting stages. Proofreading was capably performed by Faith A. Bell, Faith de Castro, Carin A. Helfer, Diana M. Jones, Benjamin T. Korzec, Michael D. Metivier, and Emily D. Villanueva.

USING THIS BOOK

This book contains so much information that it is necessary to condense much of it to accommodate the limitations of the printed page. This section provides information on the conventions used throughout this book, from the styling of entries and pronunciation to how we present information on usage and meaning. An understanding of the information contained in these notes will make this book both easier and more rewarding to use.

ENTRIES

A boldface letter or a combination of such letters, including punctuation marks and diacritics where needed, that is set flush with the left-hand margin of each column of type is a main entry. The main entry may consist of letters set solid, of letters joined by a hyphen or a diagonal, or of letters separated by spaces:

alone . . . *adj*
avant–garde . . . *n*
and/or . . . *conj*
assembly language . . . *n*

The material in lightface type that follows each main entry on the same line and on succeeding indented lines presents information about the main entry.

The main entries follow one another in alphabetical order letter by letter: *bird of prey* follows *birdlime*; *Day of Atonement* follows *daylight saving time*. Main entries containing an Arabic numeral are alphabetized as if the numeral were spelled out: *4-H* comes between *fourfold* and *Four Hundred*; *3-D* comes between *three* and *three-dimensional*. Those that often begin with the abbreviation *St.* in common usage have the abbreviation spelled out: *Saint Valentine's Day*. Main entries that begin with *Mc* are alphabetized just as they are spelled.

***

A pair of guide words is printed at the top of each page. These guide words indicate the range of entries that fall alphabetically on those pages.

The guide words are the alphabetically first and the alphabetically last main entries on the pages:

hotbed • however

***

When one main entry has exactly the same written form as another, the two are distinguished by superscript numerals preceding each word:

¹**melt** . . . *vb*
²**melt** *n*
¹**pine** . . . *n*
²**pine** *vb*

Full words come before parts of words made up of the same letters; solid compounds come before hyphenated compounds; hyphenated compounds come before open compounds; and lowercase entries come before those with an initial capital:

¹**su·per** . . . *n*
²**super** *adj*
super- . . . *prefix*
run·down . . . *n*
run–down . . . *adj*
run down *vb*
dutch . . . *adv*
Dutch . . . *n*

The centered dots within entry words indicate division points at which a hyphen may be put at the end of a line of print or writing. Thus the noun *cap·puc·ci·no* may be ended on one line and continued on the next in this manner:

cap-

puccino

cappuc-

cino

cappucci-

no

Centered dots are not shown after a single initial letter or before a single terminal letter because typesetters seldom cut off a single letter:

abyss . . . *n*
flighty . . . *adj*
idea . . . *n*

Centered dots are not usually shown at the second and succeeding homographs unless they differ among themselves:

¹**sig·nal** . . . *n*
²**signal** *vb*
³**signal** *adj*
   but
¹**min·ute** . . . *n*
²**mi·nute** . . . *adj*

There are acceptable alternative end-of-line divisions just as there are acceptable variant spellings and pronunciations, but no more than one pattern is shown for any entry in this dictionary.

A double hyphen (=) at the end of a line in this dictionary (as in the definition at **Bantustan**) stands for a hyphen that is retained when the word is written as a unit on one line. This kind of fixed hyphen is always represented in boldface words in this dictionary with an en dash, longer than an ordinary hyphen.

***

When a main entry is followed by the word *or* and another spelling, the two spellings are equal variants. Both are standard, and either one may be used according to personal inclination:

ocher *or* **ochre**

If two variants joined by *or* are out of alphabetical order, they remain equal variants. The one printed first is, however, slightly more common than the second:

¹plow *or* **plough**

When another spelling is joined to the main entry by the word *also*, the spelling after *also* is a secondary variant and occurs less frequently than the first:

ab·sinthe *also* **ab·sinth**

Secondary variants belong to standard usage and may be used according to personal inclination. Once the word *also* is used to signal a secondary variant, all following secondary variants are joined by *or*:

²wool·ly *also* **wool·ie** *or* **wooly**

Variants whose spelling puts them alphabetically more than a column away from the main entry are entered at their own alphabetical places as well as at the main entry:

²gage *var of* GAUGE

. . .

¹gauge *also* **gage**

To show all the stylings that are found for English compounds would require space that can be better used for other information. So this dictionary limits itself to a single styling for a compound:

peace·mak·er
pell–mell
boom box

When a compound is widely used and one styling predominates, that styling is shown. When a compound is uncommon or when the evidence indicates that two or three stylings are approximately equal in frequency, the styling shown is based on the comparison of other similar compounds.

***

A main entry may be followed by one or more derivatives or by a homograph with a different functional label. These are run-on entries. Each is introduced by a long dash, and each has a functional label. They are not defined, however, since their meanings are readily understood from the meaning of the root word:

ab·do·men . . . *n* . . . — **ab·dom·i·nal** . . . *adj* — **ab·dom·i·nal·ly** . . . *adv*
seis·mo·graph . . . *n* . . . — **seis·mo·graph·ic** . . . *adj* — **seis·mog·ra·phy** . . . *n*

A main entry may be followed by one or more phrases containing the entry word or an inflected form of it. These are also run-on entries. Each is introduced by a long dash but there is no functional label. They are, however, defined since their meanings are more than the sum of the meanings of their elements:

¹set . . . *vb* . . . — **set sail :** to begin a voyage
¹hand . . . *n* . . . — **at hand :** near in time . . .

Defined phrases of this sort are run on at the entry defining the first major word in the phrase. When there are variants, however, the run-on appears at the entry defining the first major invariable word in the phrase:

¹seed . . . *n* . . . **1 :** the grains of plants used for sowing . . . — **go to seed** *or* **run to seed 1 :** to develop seed **2 :** DECAY

PRONUNCIATION

The matter between a pair of reversed slashes \ \ following the entry word indicates the pronunciation. The symbols used are explained in the chart at the end of this section.

A hyphen is used in the pronunciation to show syllabic division. These hyphens sometimes coincide with the centered dots in the entry word that indicate end-of-line division, and sometimes they do not:

ab·sen·tee \ˌab-sən-ˈtē\
met·ric \ˈme-trik\

A high-set mark ˈ indicates major (primary) stress or accent; a low-set mark ˌ indicates minor (secondary) stress or accent:

heart·beat \ˈhärt-ˌbēt\

The stress mark stands at the beginning of the syllable that receives the stress.

A syllable with neither a high-set mark nor a low-set mark is unstressed:

¹struc·ture \ˈstrək-chər\

The presence of variant pronunciations indicates that not all educated speakers pronounce words the same way. A second-place variant is not to be regarded as less acceptable than the pronunciation that is given first. It may, in fact, be used by as many educated speakers as the first variant, but the requirements of the printed page are such that one must precede the other:

apri·cot \ˈa-prə-ˌkät, ˈā-\
fore·head \ˈfȯr-əd, ˈfȯr-ˌhed\

Symbols enclosed by parentheses represent elements that are present in the pronunciation of some speakers but are absent from the pronunciation of other speakers, or elements that are present in some but absent from other utterances of the same speaker:

¹om·ni·bus \'äm-ni-(ˌ)bəs\
ad·di·tion·al \ə-'di-sh(ə-)nəl\

Thus, the above parentheses indicate that some people say \'äm-ni-ˌbəs\ and others say \'äm-ni-bəs\; some \ə-'di-shə-nəl\, others \ə-'di-shnəl\.

When a main entry has less than a full pronunciation, the missing part is to be supplied from a pronunciation in a preceding entry or within the same pair of reversed slashes:

cham·pi·on·ship \-ˌship\
pa·la·ver \pə-'la-vər, -'lä-\

The pronunciation of the first three syllables of *championship* is found at the main entry **champion**. The hyphens before and after \'lä\ in the pronunciation of *palaver* indicate that both the first and the last parts of the pronunciation are to be taken from the immediately preceding pronunciation.

In general, no pronunciation is indicated for open compounds consisting of two or more English words that have own-place entry:

witch doctor *n*

Only the first entry in a sequence of numbered homographs is given a pronunciation if their pronunciations are the same:

¹re·ward \ri-'wȯrd\ *vb*
²reward *n*

The absent but implied pronunciation of derivatives and compounds run on after a main entry is a combination of the pronunciation at the main entry and the pronunciation of the other element as given at its alphabetical place in the vocabulary:

— **ab·ject·ness** *n*
— **bungee jumper** *n*

Thus, the pronunciation of *abjectness* is the sum of the pronunciations given at *abject* and *-ness*; that of *bungee jumper*, the sum of the pronunciations of the two elements that make up the phrase.

FUNCTIONAL LABELS

An italic label indicating a part of speech or another functional classification follows the pronunciation or, if no pronunciation is given, the main entry.

The eight traditional parts of speech are indicated as follows:

bold . . . *adj*
forth·with . . . *adv*
¹but . . . *conj*
ge·sund·heit . . . *interj*
bo·le·ro . . . *n*
²un·der . . . *prep*
¹it . . . *pron*
¹slap . . . *vb*

Other italicized labels used to indicate functional classifications that are not traditional parts of speech include:

AT *abbr*
self- *comb form*
un- . . . *prefix*
-ial *adj suffix*
²-ly *adv suffix*
²-er . . . *n suffix*
-ize . . . *vb suffix*
Fe *symbol*
may . . . *verbal auxiliary*

Functional labels are sometimes combined:

afloat . . . *adj or adv*

INFLECTED FORMS

NOUNS

The plurals of nouns are shown in this dictionary when suffixation brings about a change of final -*y* to -*i*-, when the noun ends in a consonant plus -*o* or in -*ey*, when the noun ends in -*oo*, when the noun has an irregular plural or an uninflected plural or a foreign plural, when the noun is a compound that pluralizes any element but the last, when a final consonant is doubled, when the noun has variant plurals, and when it is believed that the dictionary user might have

reasonable doubts about the spelling of the plural or when the plural is spelled in a way contrary to what is expected:

²spy *n, pl* **spies**
si·lo . . . *n, pl* **silos**
val·ley . . . *n, pl* **valleys**
²shampoo *n, pl* **shampoos**
mouse . . . *n, pl* **mice**
moose . . . *n, pl* **moose**

cri·te·ri·on . . . *n, pl* **-ria**
son–in–law . . . *n, pl* **sons–in–law**
¹**quiz** . . . *n, pl* **quiz·zes**
¹**fish** . . . *n, pl* **fish** *or* **fish·es**
pi . . . *n, pl* **pis**
³**dry** *n, pl* **drys**

Cutback inflected forms are used when the noun has three or more syllables:

ame·ni·ty . . . *n, pl* **-ties**

The plurals of nouns are usually not shown when the base word is unchanged by suffixation, when the noun is a compound whose second element is readily recognizable as a regular free form entered at its own place, or

when the noun is unlikely to occur in the plural:

¹**night** . . . *n*
fore·foot . . . *n*
mo·nog·a·my . . . *n*

Nouns that are plural in form and that are regularly construed as plural are labeled *n pl*:

munch·ies . . . *n pl*

Nouns that are plural in form but that are not always construed as plurals are appropriately labeled:

lo·gis·tics . . . *n sing or pl* : . . .
me·dia . . . *n, pl* **me·di·as** . . . *2 sing or pl in constr*
: MASS MEDIA

VERBS

The principal parts of verbs are shown in this dictionary when suffixation brings about a doubling of a final consonant or an elision of a final *-e* or a change of final *-y* to *-i-*, when final *-c* changes to *-ck* in suffixation, when the verb ends in *-ey*, when the inflection is irregular, when there are variant inflected forms, and when it is believed that the dictionary user might have reasonable doubts about the spelling of an inflected form or when the inflected form is spelled in a way contrary to what is expected:

²**snag** *vb* **snagged; snag·ging**
¹**move** . . . *vb* **moved; mov·ing**
¹**cry** . . . *vb* **cried; cry·ing**
¹**frol·ic** . . . *vb* **frol·icked; frol·ick·ing**
¹**sur·vey** . . . *vb* **sur·veyed; sur·vey·ing**
¹**drive** . . . *vb* **drove** . . . **driv·en** . . . **driv·ing**
²**bus** *vb* **bused** *or* **bussed; bus·ing** *or* **bus·sing**
²**visa** *vb* **vi·saed** . . . **vi·sa·ing**
²**chagrin** *vb* **cha·grined** . . . **cha·grin·ing**

The principal parts of a regularly inflected verb are shown when it is desirable to indicate the pronunciation of one of the inflected forms:

learn . . . *vb* **learned** \'lərnd, 'lərnt\; **learn·ing**
¹**al·ter** \'ȯl-tər\ *vb* **al·tered; al·ter·ing** \-t(ə-)riŋ\

Cutback inflected forms are usually used when the verb has three or more syllables, when it is a two-syllable word that ends in *-l* and has variant spellings, and when it is a compound whose second element is readily recognized as an irregular verb:

elim·i·nate . . . *vb* **-nat·ed; -nat·ing**
²**quarrel** *vb* **-reled** *or* **-relled; -rel·ing** *or* **-rel·ling**
¹**re·take** . . . *vb* **-took** . . . **-tak·en** . . . **-tak·ing**

The principal parts of verbs are usually not shown when the base word is unchanged by suffixation or when the verb is a compound whose second element is readily recognizable as a regular free form entered at its own place:

¹**jump** . . . *vb*
pre·judge . . . *vb*

Another inflected form of English verbs is the third person singular of the present tense, which is regularly formed by the addition of *-s* or *-es* to the base form of the verb. This inflected form is not shown except at a handful of entries (as *have* and *do*) for which it is in some way unusual.

ADJECTIVES & ADVERBS

The comparative and superlative forms of adjectives and adverbs are shown in this dictionary when suffixation brings about a doubling of a final consonant or an elision of a final *-e* or a change of final *-y* to *-i-*, when the word ends in *-ey*, when the inflection is irregular, and when there are variant inflected forms:

¹**red** . . . *adj* **red·der; red·dest**
¹**tame** . . . *adj* **tam·er; tam·est**
¹**kind·ly** . . . *adj* **kind·li·er; -est**
hors·ey *also* **horsy** . . . *adj* **hors·i·er; -est**

¹**good** . . . *adj* **bet·ter** . . . **best**
¹**far** . . . *adv* **far·ther** . . . *or* **fur·ther** . . . **far·thest** *or* **fur·thest**

The superlative forms of adjectives and adverbs of two or more syllables are usually cut back:

³**fancy** *adj* **fan·ci·er; -est**
¹**ear·ly** . . . *adv* **ear·li·er; -est**

The comparative and superlative forms of regularly inflected adjectives and adverbs are shown when it is desirable to indicate the pronunciation of the inflected forms:

¹young \\'yəŋ\ *adj* **youn·ger** \\'yəŋ-gər\; **youn·gest** \\'yəŋ-gəst\

The inclusion of inflected forms in *-er* and *-est* at adjective and adverb entries means nothing more about the use of *more* and *most* with these adjectives and adverbs than that their comparative and superlative degrees may be expressed in either way: *lazier* or *more lazy*; *laziest* or *most lazy*.

At a few adjective entries only the superlative form is shown:

²mere *adj, superlative* **mer·est**

The absence of the comparative form indicates that there is no evidence of its use.

The comparative and superlative forms of adjectives and adverbs are usually not shown when the base word is unchanged by suffixation, when the inflected forms of the word are identical with those of a preceding homograph, or when the word is a compound whose second element is readily recognizable as a regular free form entered at its own place:

¹near . . . *adv*
³good *adv*
un·wor·thy . . . *adj*

Inflected forms are not shown at run-in and undefined run-on entries.

CAPITALIZATION

Most entries in this dictionary begin with a lowercase letter. A few of these have an italicized label *often cap*, which indicates that the word is as likely to be capitalized as not and that it is as acceptable with an uppercase initial as it is with one in lowercase. Some entries begin with an uppercase letter, which indicates that the word is usually capitalized. The absence of an initial capital or of an *often cap* label indicates that the word is not ordinarily capitalized:

salm·on . . . *n*
gar·gan·tuan . . . *adj, often cap*
Mo·hawk . . . *n*

The capitalization of entries that are open or hyphenated compounds is similarly indicated by the form of the entry or by an italicized label:

dry goods . . . *n pl*
french fry *n, often cap 1st F*
un–Amer·i·can . . . *adj*
Par·kin·son's disease . . . *n*
lazy Su·san . . . *n*
Jack Frost *n*

A word that is capitalized in some senses and lowercase in others shows variations from the form of the main entry by the use of italicized labels at the appropriate senses:

Trin·i·ty . . . *n* . . . **2** *not cap*
To·ry . . . *n* . . . **3** *often not cap*
ti·tan . . . *n* **1** *cap*
re·nais·sance . . . *n* **1** *cap* . . . **2** *often cap*

USAGE

Three types of status labels are used in this dictionary—temporal, regional, and stylistic—to signal that a word or a sense of a word is not part of the standard vocabulary of English.

The temporal label *obs* (for *obsolete*) means that there is no evidence of use since 1755:

³post *n* **1** *obs* : COURIER

The label *obs* is a comment on the word being defined. When a thing, as distinguished from the word used to designate it, is obsolete, appropriate orientation is usually given in the definition:

cat·a·pult . . . *n* **1** : an ancient military machine for hurling missiles

The temporal label *archaic* means that a word or sense once in common use is found today only sporadically or in special contexts:

¹mete . . . *vb* . . . **1** *archaic*
¹thou . . . *pron, archaic*

A word or sense limited in use to a specific region of the U.S. has an appropriate label. The adverb *chiefly* precedes a label when the word has some currency outside the specified region, and a double label is used to indicate considerable currency in each of two specific regions:

²wash *n* . . . **5** *West*
do·gie . . . *n, chiefly West*
crul·ler . . . *n* . . . **2** *Northern & Midland*

Words current in all regions of the U.S. have no label.

A word or sense limited in use to one of the other countries of the English-speaking world has an appropriate regional label:

chem·ist . . . *n* . . . **2** *Brit*
loch . . . *n, Scot*
²wireless *n* . . . **2** *chiefly Brit*

The label *dial* for "dialect" indicates that the pattern of use of a word or sense is too complex for summary labeling: it usually includes several regional varieties of American English or of American and British English:

    ²mind *vb* **1** *chiefly dial*

The stylistic label *slang* is used with words or senses that are especially appropriate in contexts of extreme informality:

    ³can . . . *vb* . . . **2** *slang*
    ²grand *n* . . . *slang*

There is no satisfactory objective test for slang, especially with reference to a word out of context. No word, in fact, is invariably slang, and many standard words can be given slang applications.

The stylistic labels *offensive* and *disparaging* are used for those words or senses that in common use are intended to hurt or that are likely to give offense even when they are used without such an intent:

    dumb . . . *adj* **1** *often offensive*
    egg·head . . . *n, often disparaging*

Definitions are sometimes followed by verbal illustrations that show a typical use of the word in context. These illustrations are enclosed in angle brackets, and the word being illustrated is usually replaced by a lightface swung dash. The swung dash stands for the boldface entry word, and it may be followed by an italicized suffix:

    ¹jump . . . *vb* . . . **5** . . . ⟨~ the gun⟩
    all–around . . . *adj* **1** . . . ⟨best ~ performance⟩
    ¹can·on . . . *n* . . . **3** . . . ⟨the ~s of good taste⟩
    en·joy . . . *vb* . . . **2** . . . ⟨~ed the concert⟩

The swung dash is not used when the form of the boldface entry word is changed in suffixation, and it is not used for compounds:

    ²deal *vb* . . . **2** . . . ⟨*dealt* him a blow⟩
    drum up *vb* **1** . . . ⟨*drum up* business⟩

Definitions are sometimes followed by usage notes that give supplementary information about such matters as idiom, syntax, and semantic relationship. A usage note is introduced by a lightface dash:

    ²cry *n* . . . **5** . . . — usu. used in the phrase *a far cry*
    ²drum *vb* . . . **4** . . . — usu. used with *out*
    ¹jaw . . . *n* . . . **2** . . . — usu. used in pl.
    ¹ada·gio . . . *adv or adj* . . . — used as a direction in music
    hajji . . . *n* . . . — often used as a title

Sometimes a usage note is used in place of a definition. Some function words (as conjunctions and prepositions) have chiefly grammatical meaning and little or no lexical meaning; most interjections express feelings but are otherwise untranslatable into lexical meaning; and some other words (as honorific titles) are more amenable to comment than to definition:

    or . . . *conj* — used as a function word to indicate an alternative
    at . . . *prep* **1** — used to indicate a point in time or space
    auf Wie·der·seh·en . . . *interj* . . . — used to express farewell
    sir . . . *n* . . . **2** — used as a usu. respectful form of address

SENSE DIVISION

A boldface colon is used in this dictionary to introduce a definition:

    ¹equine . . . *adj* . . . : of or relating to the horse

It is also used to separate two or more definitions of a single sense:

    no·ti·fy . . . *vb* . . . **1** : to give notice of : report the occurrence of

Boldface Arabic numerals separate the senses of a word that has more than one sense:

    ad·judge . . . *vb* . . . **1** : to decide or rule upon as a judge : JUDGE, ADJUDICATE **2** : to hold or pronounce to be : DEEM **3** : . . .

A particular semantic relationship between senses is sometimes suggested by the use of an italic sense divider (as *esp* or *also*).

The sense divider *esp* (for *especially*) is used to introduce the most common meaning included in the more general preceding definition:

    crys·tal . . . *n* . . . **2** : something resembling crystal (as in transparency); *esp* : a clear glass used for table articles

The sense divider *also* is used to introduce a meaning related to the preceding sense by an easily understood extension of that sense:

    chi·na . . . *n* : porcelain ware; *also* : domestic pottery in general

The order of senses is historical: the sense known to have been first used in English is entered first. This is not to be taken to mean, however, that each sense of a multisense word developed from the immediately preceding sense. It is altogether possible that sense 1 of a word has given rise to sense 2 and sense 2 to sense 3, but frequently sense 2 and sense 3 may have developed independently of one another from sense 1.

When an italicized label follows a boldface numeral, the label applies only to that specific numbered sense. It does not apply to any other boldface numbered senses:

¹craft . . . *n* . . . **3** *pl usu* **craft**
¹fa·ther . . . *n* . . . **2** *cap* . . . **5** *often cap*

dul·ci·mer . . . *n* . . . **2** *or* **dul·ci·more** \-ˌmōr\
²lift *n* . . . **5** *chiefly Brit*

At *craft* the *pl* label applies to sense 3 but to none of the other numbered senses. At *father* the *cap label* applies only to sense 2 and the *often cap* label only to sense 5. At *dulcimer* the variant spelling and pronunciation apply only to sense 2, and the *chiefly Brit* label at *lift* applies only to sense 5.

THESAURUS LISTS

Thesaurus lists follow their dictionary entries and are set off in tinted text. Every dictionary sense that has a corresponding thesaurus list is marked with a black diamond, and the thesaurus list is likewise indicated.

bore·dom . . . *n* ♦ : the condition of being weary and restless because of dullness

♦ doldrums, ennui, listlessness, restlessness, tedium, tiredness, weariness

When there are multiple dictionary senses highlighted, the thesaurus lists are marked with the appropriate dictionary sense numbers in square brackets to make it easy for the user to choose the corresponding list of synonyms.

abide . . . *vb* . . . **1** ♦ : to bear patiently . . . **2 a** ♦ : to continue in a state or place **b** ♦ : to have one's abode . . .

♦ [1] bear, brook . . . ♦ [2a] continue, endure . . . ♦ [2b] dwell, live, reside

Thesaurus entries all show synonyms, and some lists also have common contrasting words (antonyms), which are introduced by a bold italic *Ant*.

fer·tile . . . *adj* **1** ♦ : producing plentifully . . .

♦ fecund, fruitful, luxuriant, productive, prolific, rich *Ant* barren, infertile, sterile, unfruitful, unproductive

CROSS-REFERENCE

Four different kinds of cross-references are used in this book: directional, synonymous, cognate, and inflectional. In each instance the cross-reference is readily recognized by the lightface small capitals in which it is printed.

A cross-reference following a lightface dash and beginning with *compare* is a directional cross-reference. It directs the user to look elsewhere for further information:

ordinal number . . . *n* . . . —compare CARDINAL NUMBER

A cross-reference following a boldface colon is a synonymous cross-reference. It may stand alone as the only definition for an entry or for a sense of an entry; it may follow an analytical definition; it may be one of two or more synonymous cross-references separated by commas:

fact . . . *n* . . . **1** : DEED . . .
²paper *adj* . . . **3** : existing only in theory : NOMINAL

A synonymous cross-reference indicates that an entry, a definition at the entry, or a specific sense at the entry

cross-referred to can be substituted as a definition for the entry or the sense in which the cross-reference appears.

A cross-reference following an italic *var of* (*variant of*) is a cognate cross-reference:

pick·a·back . . . *var of* PIGGYBACK

Occasionally a cognate cross-reference has a limiting label preceding *var of* as an indication that the variant is not standard American English:

cosy *chiefly Brit var of* COZY

A cross-reference following an italic label that identifies an entry as an inflected form (as of a noun or verb) is an inflectional cross-reference:

calves *pl of* CALF
woven *past part of* WEAVE

Inflectional cross-references appear only when the inflected form falls at least a column away from the entry cross-referred to.

COMBINING FORMS, PREFIXES, & SUFFIXES

An entry that begins or ends with a hyphen is an element that forms part of a compound:

-wise . . . *adv comb form* . . . ⟨slant*wise*⟩
ex- . . . *prefix* . . . **2** . . . ⟨*ex*-president⟩
-let . . . *n suffix* **1** . . . ⟨book*let*⟩

Combining forms, prefixes, and suffixes are entered in this dictionary for two reasons: to make understandable the meaning of many undefined run-ons and to make recognizable the meaningful elements of words that are not entered in the dictionary.

LISTS OF UNDEFINED WORDS

Many words that begin with the prefixes or combining forms *anti-*, *in-*, *non-*, *over-*, *re-*, *self-*, *semi-*, *sub-*, *super-*, and *un-* are self-explanatory combinations of the prefix or combining form and a word entered elsewhere in the dictionary, and these words are listed undefined immediately following the entry for the prefix.

ABBREVIATIONS & SYMBOLS

Abbreviations and symbols for chemical elements are included as main entries in the vocabulary:

RSVP *abbr* . . . please reply
Ca *symbol* calcium

Abbreviations have been normalized to one form. However, there is considerable variation in the use of periods and capitalization (as *vhf*, *v.h.f.*, *VHF*, and *V.H.F.*), and stylings other than those in this book are often acceptable.

BASIC ENGLISH PUNCTUATION

The English writing system uses punctuation marks to separate groups of words for meaning and emphasis; to convey an idea of the variations of pitch, volume, pauses, and intonations of speech; and to help avoid ambiguity. English punctuation marks, together with general rules and bracketed examples of their use, follow.

APOSTROPHE '

1. indicates the possessive case of nouns and indefinite pronouns

⟨the boy's mother⟩ ⟨the boys' mother⟩

2. marks omissions in contracted words

⟨didn't⟩ ⟨o'clock⟩

3. often forms plurals of letters, figures, and words referred to as words

⟨You should dot your *i*'s and cross your *t*'s.⟩

⟨several *8*'s⟩

BRACKETS [ ]

1. set off extraneous data such as editorial additions especially within quoted material

⟨wrote that the author was "trying to dazzle his readers with phrases like *jeu de mots* [play on words]"⟩

2. function as parentheses within parentheses

⟨Bowman Act (22 Stat., ch. 4, § [or sec.] 4, p. 50)⟩

COLON :

1. introduces a word, clause, or phrase that explains, illustrates, amplifies, or restates what has gone before

⟨The sentence was poorly constructed: it lacked both unity and coherence.⟩

2. introduces a series

⟨Three countries were represented: England, France, and Belgium.⟩

3. introduces lengthy quoted material set off from the rest of a text by indentation but not by quotation marks

⟨I quote from the text of Chapter One:⟩

4. separates data in time-telling and data in bibliographic and biblical references

⟨8:30 a.m.⟩

⟨New York: Smith Publishing Co.⟩

⟨John 4:10⟩

5. follows the salutation in formal correspondence

⟨Dear Sir:⟩

⟨Gentlemen:⟩

COMMA ,

1. separates main clauses joined by a coordinating conjunction (as *and*, *but*, *or*, *nor*, or *for*) and very short clauses not so joined

⟨She knew very little about him, and he volunteered nothing.⟩

⟨I came, I saw, I conquered.⟩

2. sets off an adverbial clause (or a long phrase) that precedes the main clause

⟨When she found that her friends had deserted her, she sat down and cried.⟩

3. sets off from the rest of the sentence transitional words and expressions (as *on the contrary*, *on the other hand*), conjunctive adverbs (as *consequently*, *furthermore*, *however*), and expressions that introduce an illustration or example (as *namely*, *for example*)

⟨Your second question, on the other hand, remains open.⟩

⟨She expects to travel through two countries, namely, France and England.⟩

4. separates words, phrases, or clauses in series and co-ordinate adjectives modifying a noun

⟨Men, women, and children crowded into the square.⟩

⟨The harsh, cold wind was strong.⟩

5. sets off from the rest of the sentence parenthetic elements (as nonrestrictive modifiers)

⟨Our guide, who wore a blue beret, was an experienced traveler.⟩

⟨We visited Gettysburg, the site of a famous battle.⟩

6. introduces a direct quotation, terminates a direct quotation that is neither a question nor an exclamation, and encloses split quotations

⟨John said, "I am leaving."⟩

⟨"I am leaving," John said.⟩

⟨"I am leaving," John said with determination, "even if you want me to stay."⟩

7. sets of words in direct address, absolute phrases, and mild interjections

⟨You may go, Mary, if you wish.⟩

⟨I fear the encounter, his temper being what it is.⟩

⟨Ah, that's my idea of an excellent dinner.⟩

8. separates a question from the rest of the sentence which it ends

⟨It's a fine day, isn't it?⟩

9. indicates the omission of a word or words, and especially a word or words used earlier in the sentence

⟨Common stocks are preferred by some investors; bonds, by others.⟩

10. is used to avoid ambiguity

⟨To Mary, Jane was someone special.⟩

11. is used to group numbers into units of three in separating thousands, millions, etc.; however, it is generally not used in numbers of four figures, in page numbers, in dates, or in street numbers

⟨Smithville, pop. 100,000⟩

but

⟨3600 rpm⟩

⟨the year 1973⟩

⟨page 1411⟩

⟨4507 Smith Street⟩

12. punctuates an inverted name

⟨Smith, John W., Jr.⟩

13. separates a proper name from a following academic, honorary, governmental, or military title

⟨John Smith, M.D.⟩

14. sets off geographical names (as state or country from city), items in dates, and addresses from the rest of a text

⟨Shreveport, Louisiana, is the site of a large air base.⟩

⟨On Sunday, June 23, 1940, he was wounded.⟩

⟨Number 10 Downing Street, London, is a famous address.⟩

but when only the year or the month and year are given, the comma is generally omitted

⟨October 1929 brought an end to all that.⟩

15. follows the salutation in informal correspondence and follows the closing line of a formal or informal letter

⟨Dear Mary,⟩

⟨Affectionately,⟩

⟨Very truly yours,⟩

DASH —

1. usually marks an abrupt change or break in the continuity of a sentence

⟨When in 1960 the stockpile was sold off—indeed, dumped as surplus—natural-rubber sales were hard hit. —Barry Commoner⟩

2. introduces a summary statement after a series

⟨Oil, steel, and wheat—these are the sinews of industrialization.⟩

3. often precedes the attribution of a quotation

⟨My foot is on my native heath. . . . —Sir Walter Scott⟩

ELLIPSES ... .

1. indicates the omission of one or more words within a quoted passage

⟨The head is not more native to the heart . . . than is the throne of Denmark to thy father. —Shakespeare⟩

2. indicates halting speech or an unfinished sentence in dialogue

⟨"I'd like to . . . that is . . . if you don't mind. . . ." He faltered and then stopped speaking.⟩

3. indicates the omission of one or more sentences within a quoted passage or the omission of words at the end of a sentence by using four spaced dots, the last of which represents the period

⟨That recovering the manuscripts would be worth almost any effort is without question. . . . The monetary value of a body of Shakespeare's manuscripts would be almost incalculable —Charlton Ogburn⟩

4. usually indicates omission of one or more lines of poetry when ellipsis is extended the length of the line

⟨When I heard the learned astronomer,

. . . .

How soon unaccountable I became tired and sick,

Til rising and gliding out I wandered off by myself,

—Walt Whitman⟩

EXCLAMATION POINT !

1. terminates an emphatic phrase or sentence

⟨Get out of here!⟩

2. terminates an emphatic interjection

⟨Encore!⟩

HYPHEN -

1. marks separation or division of a word at the end of a line

⟨Stanley's search came to an end at Lake Tanganyika, in the Arab settlement of Ujiji.⟩

2. is used between some prefix and word combinations, as prefix + proper name

⟨pre-Renaissance⟩;

prefix ending with a vowel + word beginning often with the same vowel

⟨co-opted⟩

⟨re-ink⟩;

stressed prefix + word, especially when this combination is similar to a different one

⟨re-cover a sofa⟩

but

⟨recover from an illness⟩

3. is used in some compounds, especially those containing prepositions

⟨president-elect⟩

⟨sister-in-law⟩

4. is often used between elements of a unit modifier in attributive position in order to avoid ambiguity

⟨He is a small-business man.⟩

⟨She has gray-green eyes.⟩

5. suspends the first part of a hyphenated compound when used with another hyphenated compound

⟨a six- or eight-cylinder engine⟩

6. is used in writing out compound numbers between 21 and 99

⟨thirty-four⟩

⟨one hundred twenty-eight⟩

7. is used between the numerator and the denominator in writing out fractions especially when they are used as modifiers

⟨a two-thirds majority of the vote⟩

8. serves instead of the phrase "(up) to and including" between numbers and dates

⟨pages 40-98⟩

⟨the decade 1960-69⟩

PARENTHESES ( )

1. set off supplementary, parenthetic, or explanatory material when the interruption is more marked than that usually indicated by commas

⟨Three old destroyers (all now out of commission) will be scrapped.⟩

⟨He is hoping (as we all are) that this time he will succeed.⟩

2. enclose numerals which confirm a written number in a text

⟨Delivery will be made in thirty (30) days.⟩

3. enclose numbers or letters in a series

⟨We must set forth (1) our long-term goals, (2) our immediate objectives, and (3) the means at our disposal.⟩

PERIOD .

1. terminates sentences or sentence fragments that are neither interrogatory nor exclamatory

⟨Obey the law.⟩

⟨He obeyed the law.⟩

2. follows some abbreviations and contractions

⟨Dr.⟩   ⟨Jr.⟩

⟨etc.⟩   ⟨cont.⟩

QUESTION MARK ?

1. terminates a direct question

⟨Who threw the bomb?⟩

⟨"Who threw the bomb?" he asked.⟩

2. indicates the writer's ignorance or uncertainty

⟨Omar Khayyám, Persian poet (?-?1123)⟩

QUOTATION MARKS, DOUBLE " "

1. enclose direct quotations in conventional usage

⟨He said, "I am leaving."⟩

2. enclose words or phrases borrowed from others, words used in a special way, and often slang when it is introduced into formal writing

⟨He called himself "emperor," but he was really just a dictator.⟩

⟨He was arrested for smuggling "smack."⟩

3. enclose titles of short poems, short stories, articles, lectures, chapters of books, songs, short musical compositions, and radio and TV programs

⟨Robert Frost's "Dust of Snow"⟩

⟨Pushkin's "Queen of Spades"⟩

⟨The third chapter of *Treasure Island* is entitled "The Black Spot."⟩

⟨"America the Beautiful"⟩

⟨Ravel's "Bolero"⟩

⟨NBC's "Today Show"⟩

4. are used with other punctuation marks in the following ways:

the period and the comma fall within the quotation marks

⟨"I am leaving," he said.⟩

⟨His camera was described as "waterproof," but "moisture-resistant" would have been a better description.⟩;

the semicolon falls outside the quotation marks

⟨He spoke of his "little cottage in the country"; he might have called it a mansion.⟩;

the dash, question mark, and exclamation point fall within the quotation marks when they refer to the quoted matter; they fall outside when they refer to the whole sentence

⟨He asked, "When did you leave?"⟩

⟨What is the meaning of "the open door"?⟩

⟨The sergeant shouted, "Halt!"⟩

⟨Save us from his "mercy"!⟩

QUOTATION MARKS, SINGLE ' '

enclose a quotation within a quotation in conventional usage

⟨The witness said, "I distinctly heard him say, 'Don't be late,' and then I heard the door close."⟩

SEMICOLON ;

1. links main clauses not joined by coordinating conjunctions

⟨Some people have the ability to write well; others do not.⟩

2. links main clauses joined by conjunctive adverbs (as *consequently, furthermore, however*

⟨Speeding is illegal; furthermore, it is very dangerous.⟩

3. links clauses which themselves contain commas even when such clauses are joined by coordinating conjunctions

⟨Mr. King, whom you met yesterday, will be our representative on the committee; but you should follow the proceedings carefully yourself, because they are vitally important to us.⟩

SLASH /

1. separates alternatives

⟨. . . intended for high-heat and/or high-speed applications —F. S. Badger, Jr.⟩

2. separates successive divisions (as months or years) of an extended period of time

⟨the fiscal year 1972/73⟩

3. serves as a dividing line between run-in lines of poetry

⟨Say, sages, what's the charm on earth/Can turn death's dart aside? —Robert Burns⟩

4. often represents *per* in abbreviations

⟨9 ft/sec⟩

⟨20 km/hr⟩

ABBREVIATIONS USED IN THIS WORK

ab	about	*Gk*	Greek	*OIt*	Old Italian
abbr	abbreviation	*Gmc*	Germanic	*ON*	Old Norse
abl	ablative	*Heb*	Hebrew	*OPer*	Old Persian
acc	accusative	*Hung*	Hungarian	*orig*	originally
A.D.	anno Domini	*Icel*	Icelandic	*part*	participle
adj	adjective	*imit*	imitative	*Per*	Persian
adv	adverb	*imper*	imperative	*perh*	perhaps
alter	alteration	*interj*	interjection	*Pg*	Portuguese
Am, Amer	American	*Ir*	Irish	*pl*	plural
AmerF	American French	*irreg*	irregular	*Pol*	Polish
AmerInd	American Indian	*It, Ital*	Italian	*pp*	past participle
AmerSp	American Spanish	*Jp*	Japanese	*prep*	preposition
Ant	Antonym(s)	*K*	Kelvin	*pres*	present, president
Ar	Arabic	*km*	kilometers	*prob*	probably
Aram	Aramaic	*L*	Latin	*pron*	pronoun, pronunciation
B.C.	before Christ	*LaF*	Louisiana French	*prp*	present participle
Brit	British	*LG*	Low German	*pseud*	pseudonym
C	Celsius	*LGk*	Late Greek	*r*	reigned
Calif	California	*LHeb*	Late Hebrew	*Russ*	Russian
Canad	Canadian	*lit*	literally	*Sc*	Scotch, Scots
CanF	Canadian French	*LL*	Late Latin	*Scand*	Scandinavian
cap	capital, capitalized	*m*	meters	*ScGael*	Scottish Gaelic
Celt	Celtic	*masc*	masculine	*Scot*	Scottish
cen	central	*MD*	Middle Dutch	*sing*	singular
cent	century	*ME*	Middle English	*Skt*	Sanskrit
Chin	Chinese	*MexSp*	Mexican Spanish	*Slav*	Slavic
comb	combining	*MF*	Middle French	*So*	South
compar	comparative	*MGk*	Middle Greek	*Sp, Span*	Spanish
conj	conjunction	*mi*	miles	*St*	Saint
D	Dutch	*ML*	Medieval Latin	*superl*	superlative
Dan	Danish	*modif*	modification	*Sw*	Swedish
dat	dative	*MS*	manuscript	*syn*	synonym, synonymy
deriv	derivative	*Mt*	Mount	*trans*	translation
dial	dialect	*n*	noun	*Turk*	Turkish
dim	diminutive	*neut*	neuter	*US*	United States
E	English	*NewEng*	New England	*USSR*	Union of Soviet Socialist
Egypt	Egyptian	*NGk*	New Greek		Republics
Eng	English	*NHeb*	New Hebrew	*usu*	usually
esp	especially	*NL*	New Latin	*var*	variant
F	Fahrenheit, French	*No*	North	*vb*	verb
fem	feminine	*Norw*	Norwegian	*vi*	verb intransitive
fl	flourished	*n pl*	noun plural	*VL*	Vulgar Latin
fr	from	*obs*	obsolete	*vt*	verb transitive
ft	feet	*OE*	Old English	*W*	Welsh
G, Ger	German	*OF*	Old French		

PRONUNCIATION SYMBOLS

ə	abut, collect, suppose	òr	boar, port
ˈə, ˌə	humdrum	œ	French bœuf, feu, German Hölle, Höhle
ᵊ	(in ᵊl, ᵊn) battle, cotton; (in lᵊ, mᵊ, rᵊ) French table, prisme, titre	òi	toy
		p	pepper, lip
ər	operation, further	r	rarity
a	map, patch	s	source, less
ā	day, fate	sh	shy, mission
ä	bother, cot, father	t	tie, attack
är	car, heart	th	thin, ether
aù	now, out	t̲h̲	then, either
b	baby, rib	ü	boot, few \ˈfyü\
ch	chin, catch	ù	put, pure \ˈpyùr\
d	did, adder	ùr	boor, tour
e	set, red	ue	French rue, German füllen, fühlen
er	bare, fair	v	vivid, give
ē	beat, easy	w	we, away
f	fifty, cuff	y	yard, cue \ˈkyü\
g	go, big	ʸ	indicates that a preceding \l\, \n\, or \w\ is modified by having the tongue approximate the position for \y\, as in French digne \dēnʸ\
h	hat, ahead		
hw	whale		
i	tip, banish		
ir	near, deer	z	zone, raise
ī	site, buy	zh	vision, pleasure
j	job, edge	\	slant line used in pairs to mark the beginning and end of a transcription: \ˈpen\
k	kin, cook		
k̲	German Bach, Scots loch	ˈ	mark at the beginning of a syllable that has primary (strongest) stress: \ˈshə-fəl-ˌbòrd\
l	lily, cool		
m	murmur, dim	ˌ	mark at the beginning of a syllable that has secondary (next-strongest) stress: \ˈshə-fəl-ˌbòrd\
n	nine, own		
ⁿ	indicates that a preceding vowel is pronounced through both nose and mouth, as in French bon \bōⁿ\	-	mark of a syllable division in pronunciations (the mark of end-of-line division in boldface entries is a centered dot •)
ŋ	sing, singer, finger, ink	( )	indicate that what is symbolized between sometimes occurs and sometimes does not occur in the pronunciation of the word: bakery \ˈbā-k(ə-)rē\ = \ˈbā-kə-rē, ˈbā-krē\
ō	bone, hollow		
ò	saw		

¹a \'ā\ *n, pl* **a's** *or* **as** \'āz\ *often cap* **1 :** the 1st letter of the English alphabet **2 :** a grade rating a student's work as superior

²a \ə, (')ā\ *indefinite article* **:** ONE, SOME — used to indicate an unspecified or unidentified individual ⟨there's ∼ man outside⟩

³a *abbr, often cap* **1** absent **2** acre **3** alto **4** answer **5** are **6** area

AA *abbr* **1** Alcoholics Anonymous **2** antiaircraft **3** associate in arts

AAA *abbr* American Automobile Association

A and M *abbr* agricultural and mechanical

A and R *abbr* artists and repertory

aard·vark \'ärd-ˌvärk\ *n* **:** a large burrowing African mammal that feeds on ants and termites with its long sticky tongue

¹ab \'ab\ *n* **:** an abdominal muscle

²ab *abbr* about

AB *abbr* **1** able-bodied seaman **2** airman basic **3** bachelor of arts

ABA *abbr* American Bar Association

aback \ə-'bak\ *adv* ♦ **:** by surprise ⟨taken ∼⟩

♦ suddenly, unaware, unawares

aba·cus \'a-bə-kəs\ *n, pl* **aba·ci** \-ˌsī, -ˌkē\ *or* **aba·cus·es :** an instrument for making calculations by sliding counters along rods or grooves

¹abaft \ə-'baft\ *prep* **:** to the rear of

²abaft *adv* **:** toward or at the stern **:** AFT

ab·a·lo·ne \ˌa-bə-'lō-nē, 'a-bə-ˌ\ *n* **:** any of a genus of large edible sea mollusks with a flattened slightly spiral shell with holes along the edge

¹aban·don \ə-'ban-dən\ *vb* ♦ **:** to give up completely **:** FORSAKE, DESERT

♦ desert, forsake, maroon, quit

²abandon *n* ♦ **:** a thorough yielding to natural impulses

♦ abandonment, ease, lightheartedness, naturalness, spontaneity, unrestraint *Ant* constraint, restraint

aban·doned \ə-'ban-dənd\ *adj* **1 :** morally unrestrained **2** ♦ **:** given up **:** FORSAKEN

♦ derelict, deserted, forsaken

aban·don·ment \ə-'ban-dən-mənt\ *n* **1** ♦ **:** the act of abandoning **2** ♦ **:** freedom from restraint

♦ [1] dereliction, desertion ♦ [2] abandon, ease, lightheartedness, naturalness, spontaneity, unrestraint

abase \ə-'bās\ *vb* **abased; abas·ing** ♦ **:** to lower in rank, office, prestige, or esteem **:** HUMBLE, DEGRADE — **abase·ment** *n*

♦ debase, degrade, demean, demoralize, humble, subvert, warp

abash \ə-'bash\ *vb* ♦ **:** to destroy the composure of **:** EMBARRASS

♦ confound, confuse, discomfit, disconcert, discountenance, embarrass, faze, fluster, mortify, rattle

abash·ment \ə-'bash-mənt\ *n* ♦ **:** the quality or state of being abashed

♦ confusion, discomfiture, embarrassment, fluster, mortification

abate \ə-'bāt\ *vb* **abat·ed; abat·ing** **1 :** to put an end to ⟨∼ a nuisance⟩ **2** ♦ **:** to decrease in amount, number, or degree

♦ decline, decrease, diminish, dwindle, ebb, fall, lessen, recede, subside, taper, wane

abate·ment \ə-'bāt-mənt\ *n* **1** ♦ **:** an amount of taking away; *esp* **:** a deduction from a tax **2** ♦ **:** an amount abated or lessened

♦ [1] deduction, discount, reduction ♦ [1, 2] decline, decrease, decrement, diminution, drop, fall, loss, reduction, shrinkage

ab·at·toir \'a-bə-ˌtwär\ *n* **:** SLAUGHTERHOUSE

ab·ba·cy \'a-bə-sē\ *n, pl* **-cies :** the office or term of office of an abbot or abbess

ab·bé \a-'bā, 'a-ˌ\ *n* **:** a member of the French secular clergy — used as a title

ab·bess \'a-bəs\ *n* **:** the superior of a convent for nuns

ab·bey \'a-bē\ *n, pl* **abbeys** **1** ♦ **:** a house for persons and esp. monks under religious vows **:** MONASTERY **2 :** CONVENT **3 :** an abbey church

♦ cloister, friary, monastery, priory

ab·bot \'a-bət\ *n* **:** the superior of a monastery for men

abbr *abbr* abbreviation

ab·bre·vi·ate \ə-'brē-vē-ˌāt\ *vb* **-at·ed; -at·ing** ♦ **:** to make briefer **:** SHORTEN, CURTAIL; *esp* **:** to reduce to an abbreviation

♦ abridge, curtail, cut back, shorten

ab·bre·vi·a·tion \ə-ˌbrē-vē-'ā-shən\ *n* **1** ♦ **:** the act or result of abbreviating **:** ABRIDGMENT **2 :** a shortened form of a word or phrase used for brevity esp. in writing

♦ abridgment, condensation, digest

¹ABC \ˌā-(ˌ)bē-'sē\ *n, pl* **ABC's** *or* **ABCs** \-'sēz\ **1 :** ALPHABET — usu. used in pl. **2 :** RUDIMENTS — usu. used in pl.

²ABC *abbr* American Broadcasting Company

Ab·di·as \ab-'dī-əs\ *n* **:** OBADIAH

ab·di·cate \'ab-di-ˌkāt\ *vb* **-cat·ed; -cat·ing** ♦ **:** to give up (as a throne) formally — **ab·di·ca·tion** \ˌab-di-'kā-shən\ *n*

♦ abnegate, cede, relinquish, renounce, resign, step down, surrender

ab·do·men \'ab-də-mən, ab-'dō-\ *n* **1** ♦ **:** the cavity in or area of the body between the chest and the pelvis **2 :** the part of the body posterior to the thorax in an arthropod — **ab·dom·i·nal** \ab-'dä-mən-³l\ *adj* — **ab·dom·i·nal·ly** *adv*

♦ belly, gut, solar plexus, stomach, tummy

ab·duct \ab-'dəkt\ *vb* **:** to take away (a person) by force **:** KIDNAP — **ab·duc·tion** \-'dək-shən\ *n* — **ab·duc·tor** \-tər\ *n*

abeam \ə-'bēm\ *adv or adj* **:** on a line at right angles to a ship's keel

abed \ə-'bed\ *adv or adj* **:** in bed

Abe·na·ki \ˌa-bə-'nä-kē\ *n, pl* **Abenaki** *or* **Abenakis :** a member of a group of Algonquian-speaking Indigenous peoples of northern New England and southern Quebec

ab·er·rant \a-'ber-ənt\ *adj* **1** ♦ **:** departing from the right or normal way **2** ♦ **:** departing from the usual or natural type **:** ATYPICAL

♦ [1] abnormal, anomalous, deviant, irregular, unnatural ♦ [2] abnormal, atypical, exceptional, extraordinary, freak, odd, peculiar, uncommon, uncustomary, unique, unusual, unwonted

ab·er·ra·tion \ˌa-bə-'rā-shən\ *n* **1 :** deviation esp. from a moral standard or normal state **2 :** failure of a mirror or lens to produce exact point-to-point correspondence between an object and its image **3 :** unsoundness of mind **:** DERANGEMENT

abet \ə-'bet\ *vb* **abet·ted; abet·ting** **1** ♦ **:** to actively second and encourage (as in wrongdoing) **:** INCITE **2** ♦ **:** to assist or support in the achievement of a purpose

♦ [1, 2] ferment, foment, incite, instigate, provoke, raise, stir, whip ♦ [2] aid, assist, back, help, prop, support

abet·tor *also* **abet·ter** \-'be-tər\ *n* ♦ **:** one that abets

♦ accessory, accomplice, cohort, confederate ♦ ally, backer, confederate, supporter, sympathizer

abey·ance \ə-'bā-əns\ *n* ♦ **:** a condition of suspended activity

♦ doldrums, dormancy, latency, quiescence, suspension *Ant* continuance, continuation

ab·hor \əb-'hȯr, ab-\ *vb* **ab·horred; ab·hor·ring** ♦ **:** to regard with extreme dislike **:** LOATHE, DETEST

♦ abominate, despise, detest, execrate, hate, loathe

ab·hor·rence \-əns\ *n* **1** ♦ **:** the feeling of one who abhors **2** ♦ **:** one that is abhorred

♦ [1] abomination, execration, hate, hatred, loathing ♦ [2] abomination, anathema, antipathy, aversion, bête noire, hate

ab·hor·rent \-ənt\ *adj* ♦ **:** causing or deserving strong dislike **:** LOATHSOME

♦ abominable, appalling, hideous, horrible, horrid, offensive, repellent, repugnant, repulsive, revolting, shocking

abid·ance \ə-'bī-dən(t)s\ *n* ♦ **:** an act or state of abiding

♦ ceaselessness, continuance, continuation, duration, endurance, persistence, subsistence

abide \ə-'bīd\ *vb* **abode** \-'bōd\ *or* **abid·ed; abid·ing** **1 ♦ :** to bear patiently **:** ENDURE **2 a ♦ :** to continue in a state or place **b ♦ :** to have one's abode — **abide by :** to conform or acquiesce to ⟨*abide by* the law⟩

♦ [1] bear, brook, countenance, endure, meet, stand, stick out, stomach, support, sustain, take, tolerate ♦ [2a] continue, endure, hold, keep up, last, persist, run on ♦ [2b] dwell, live, reside

abid·ing \ə-'bī-diŋ\ *adj* ♦ **:** lasting and unchanging **:** ENDURING, CONTINUING ⟨an ∼ interest in nature⟩

♦ ageless, continuing, dateless, enduring, eternal, everlasting, immortal, imperishable, lasting, perennial, perpetual, timeless, undying

abil·i·ty \ə-'bi-lə-tē\ *n, pl* **-ties** ♦ **:** the quality of being able

♦ capability, capacity, competence, faculty *Ant* inability, incapability, incapacity, incompetence, ineptitude

-ability *also* **-ibility** *n suffix* **:** capacity, fitness, or tendency to act or be acted on in a (specified) way ⟨flamm*ability*⟩

ab·ject \'ab-jekt, ab-'jekt\ *adj* **:** low in spirit or hope **:** CRINGING — **ab·jec·tion** \ab-'jek-shən\ *n* — **ab·ject·ly** *adv* — **ab·ject·ness** *n*

ab·jure \ab-'jùr\ *vb* **ab·jured; ab·jur·ing** **1 ♦ :** to renounce solemnly **:** RECANT **2 :** to abstain from — **ab·ju·ra·tion** \ab-jə-'rā-shən\ *n*

♦ recant, renounce, retract, take back, unsay, withdraw *Ant* adhere (to)

abl *abbr* ablative

ab·late \a-'blāt\ *vb* **ab·lat·ed; ab·lat·ing** **:** to remove or become removed esp. by cutting, abrading, or vaporizing

ab·la·tion \a-'blā-shən\ *n* **1 :** surgical cutting and removal **2 :** loss of a part (as the outside of a nose cone) by melting or vaporization

ab·la·tive \'ab-lə-tiv\ *adj* **:** of, relating to, or constituting a grammatical case (as in Latin) expressing typically the relation of separation and source — **ablative** *n*

ablaze \ə-'blāz\ *adj or adv* **1 ♦ :** being on fire **:** BLAZING **2 ♦ :** radiant with light

♦ [1] afire, burning, fiery ♦ [2] alight, bright, light

able \'ā-bəl\ *adj* **abler** \-b(ə-)lər\; **ablest** \-b(ə-)ləst\ **1 ♦ :** having sufficient power, skill, or resources to accomplish an object **2 ♦ :** marked by skill or efficiency

♦ [1, 2] capable, competent, fit, good, qualified, suitable

-able *also* **-ible** *adj suffix* **1 :** capable of, fit for, or worthy of (being so acted upon or toward) ⟨break*able*⟩ ⟨collect*ible*⟩ **2 :** tending, given, or liable to ⟨knowledge*able*⟩ ⟨perish*able*⟩

able–bod·ied \ā-bəl-'bä-dēd\ *adj* ♦ **:** having a sound strong body

♦ chipper, fit, hale, healthy, hearty, robust, sound, well, whole, wholesome

abloom \ə-'blüm\ *adj* **:** BLOOMING

ab·lu·tion \ə-'blü-shən, a-\ *n* **:** the washing of one's body or part of it

ably \'ā-blē\ *adv* ♦ **:** in an able manner

♦ adeptly, capably, expertly, masterfully, proficiently, skillfully, well

ABM \ā-(,)bē-'em\ *n, pl* **ABM's** *or* **ABMs :** ANTIBALLISTIC MISSILE

ab·ne·gate \'ab-ni-gāt\ *vb* **-gat·ed; -gat·ing** **1 :** DENY, RENOUNCE **2 ♦ :** to give up (as a right or privilege) **:** SURRENDER, RELINQUISH

♦ abdicate, cede, relinquish, renounce, resign, step down, surrender

ab·ne·ga·tion \ab-ni-'gā-shən\ *n* ♦ **:** restraint or denial of desire or self-interest

♦ renouncement, renunciation, repudiation, self-denial

ab·nor·mal \ab-'nȯr-məl\ *adj* ♦ **:** deviating from the normal or average — **ab·nor·mal·ly** *adv*

♦ aberrant, exceptional, extraordinary, rare, singular, uncommon, uncustomary, unique, unusual ♦ aberrant, anomalous, atypical, deviant, irregular, unnatural

ab·nor·mal·i·ty \ab-nȯr-'ma-lə-tē\ *n* ♦ **:** something abnormal

♦ freak, monster, monstrosity

¹**aboard** \ə-'bōrd\ *adv* **1 :** ALONGSIDE **2 :** on, onto, or within a car, ship, or aircraft **3 :** in or into a group or association ⟨welcome new workers ∼⟩

²**aboard** *prep* **:** ON, ONTO, WITHIN

abode \ə-'bōd\ *n* **1 :** STAY, SOJOURN **2 ♦ :** the place where one abides **:** HOME, RESIDENCE

♦ domicile, dwelling, home, house, lodging, quarters, residence

abol·ish \ə-'bä-lish\ *vb* ♦ **:** to do away with **:** ANNUL — **ab·o·li·tion** \a-bə-'li-shən\ *n*

♦ abrogate, annul, cancel, dissolve, invalidate, negate, nullify, quash, repeal, rescind, void

ab·o·li·tion·ism \a-bə-'li-shə-ni-zəm\ *n* **:** advocacy of the abolition of slavery — **ab·o·li·tion·ist** \-'li-sh(ə-)nist\ *n or adj*

A–bomb \'ā-bäm\ *n* **:** ATOMIC BOMB — **A–bomb** *vb*

abom·i·na·ble \ə-'bä-mə-nə-bəl\ *adj* ♦ **:** worthy of or causing disgust or hatred **:** ODIOUS

♦ abhorrent, appalling, awful, horrible, horrid, odious, offensive, repellent, repugnant, repulsive, revolting

abominable snow·man \-'snō-mən, -man\ *n, often cap A&S* **:** a mysterious creature with human or apelike characteristics reported to exist in the high Himalayas

abom·i·nate \ə-'bä-mə-nāt\ *vb* **-nat·ed; -nat·ing** ♦ **:** to hate or loathe intensely **:** LOATHE, DETEST

♦ abhor, despise, detest, execrate, hate, loathe

abom·i·na·tion \ə-bä-mə-'nā-shən\ *n* **1 ♦ :** something abominable **2 ♦ :** extreme disgust and hatred **:** LOATHING

♦ [1] abhorrence, anathema, antipathy, aversion, bête noire, hate ♦ [2] abhorrence, execration, hate, hatred, loathing

ab·orig·i·nal \a-bə-'ri-jə-nəl\ *adj* ♦ **:** being the first or earliest known of its kind present in a region **:** INDIGENOUS

♦ born, endemic, indigenous, native

ab·orig·i·ne \a-bə-'ri-jə-nē\ *n* **:** a member of the original people to inhabit a region esp. as contrasted with an invading or colonizing people

aborn·ing \ə-'bȯr-niŋ\ *adv* **:** while being born or produced

¹**abort** \ə-'bȯrt\ *vb* **1 :** to cause or undergo abortion **2 ♦ :** to terminate prematurely ⟨∼ a spaceflight⟩

♦ call, call off, cancel, drop, recall, repeal, rescind, revoke

²**abort** *n* **:** the premature termination of a mission or of a procedure relating to an aircraft or spacecraft

abor·tion \ə-'bȯr-shən\ *n* **1 :** the spontaneous or induced termination of a pregnancy after, accompanied by, resulting in, or closely followed by the death of the embryo or fetus **2 ♦ :** arrest of development (as of a part or process); *also* **:** a result of such arrest

♦ calling, cancellation, recall, repeal, rescission, revocation

abor·tion·ist \-sh(ə-)nist\ *n* **:** one who induces abortions

abor·tive \ə-'bȯr-tiv\ *adj* ♦ **:** not successful

♦ fruitless, futile, ineffective, unproductive, unsuccessful

abound \ə-'baund\ *vb* **1 ♦ :** to be plentiful **:** TEEM **2 :** to be fully supplied

♦ brim, bulge, burst, crawl, swarm, teem

¹**about** \ə-'baut\ *adv* **1 ♦ :** reasonably close to; *also* **:** on the verge of ⟨∼ to join the army⟩ **2 :** on all sides **3 :** in the vicinity **:** NEARBY **4 ♦ :** in the opposite direction

♦ [1] almost, most, much, near, nearly, next to, nigh, practically, some, virtually, well-nigh ♦ [4] around, back, round

²**about** *prep* **1 :** on every side of **2 ♦ :** near to **3 ♦ :** relating to **:** CONCERNING **4 ♦ :** over or in different parts of

♦ [2] around, by, near, next to ♦ [3] apropos of, concerning, of, on, regarding, respecting, toward ♦ [4] around, over, round, through, throughout

about–face \-'fās\ *n* **:** a reversal of direction or attitude — **about–face** *vb*

¹**above** \ə-'bəv\ *adv* **1 :** in the sky; *also* **:** in or to heaven **2 ♦ :** in or to a higher place; *also* **:** higher on the same page or on a preceding page

♦ aloft, over, overhead, skyward *Ant* below, beneath, under

²**above** *prep* **1 :** in or to a higher place than **:** OVER ⟨storm clouds ∼ the bay⟩ **2 :** superior to ⟨he thought her far ∼ him⟩ **3 :** more than **:** EXCEEDING **4 :** as distinct from ⟨∼ the noise⟩

above·board \-bȯrd\ *adv or adj* **:** without concealment or deception **:** OPENLY

abp *abbr* archbishop

abr *abbr* abridged; abridgment

ab·ra·ca·dab·ra \a-brə-kə-'da-brə\ *n* **1 ♦ :** a magical charm or incantation against calamity **2 ♦ :** unintelligible or meaningless language : GIBBERISH

♦ [1, 2] bewitchment, charm, conjuration, enchantment, incantation, spell

abrade \ə-'brād\ *vb* **abrad·ed; abrad·ing 1 a ♦ :** to wear away by friction **b ♦ :** to irritate or roughen by rubbing **2 :** to wear down in spirit : IRRITATE

♦ [1a] chafe, erode, fray, fret, gall, rub, wear ♦ [1b] graze, scrape, scratch, scuff

abra·sion \ə-'brā-zhən\ *n* **:** an abraded area of the skin or mucous membrane

¹**abra·sive** \ə-'brā-siv\ *n* **:** a substance (as pumice) for abrading, smoothing, or polishing

²**abrasive** *adj* **:** tending to abrade : causing irritation ⟨∼ relationships⟩ — **abra·sive·ly** *adv* — **abra·sive·ness** *n*

abreast \ə-'brest\ *adv or adj* **1 ♦ :** side by side **2 ♦ :** up to a standard or level esp. of knowledge

♦ conversant, familiar, informed, knowledgeable, up, up-to-date, versed

abridge \ə-'brij\ *vb* **abridged; abridg·ing ♦ :** to lessen in length or extent : SHORTEN

♦ abbreviate, curtail, cut back, shorten

abridg·ment *or* **abridge·ment** \ə-'brij-ment\ *n* **♦ :** a shortened form of a work

♦ abbreviation, condensation, digest

abroad \ə-'brȯd\ *adv or adj* **1 :** over a wide area **2 :** away from one's home **3 :** outside one's country

ab·ro·gate \'a-brə-ˌgāt\ *vb* **-gat·ed; -gat·ing ♦ :** to abolish by authoritative action : ANNUL — **ab·ro·ga·tion** \ˌa-brə-'gā-shən\ *n*

♦ abolish, annul, cancel, dissolve, invalidate, negate, nullify, quash, repeal, rescind, void

abrupt \ə-'brəpt\ *adj* **1 :** broken or as if broken off **2 :** SUDDEN, HASTY **3 ♦ :** so quick as to seem rude **4 :** DISCONNECTED **5 :** STEEP

♦ bluff, blunt, brusque, curt, snippy

abrupt·ly \-lē\ *adv* **:** in an abrupt manner

abs *abbr* absolute

ab·scess \'ab-ˌses\ *n, pl* **ab·scess·es :** a localized collection of pus surrounded by inflamed tissue — **ab·scessed** \-ˌsest\ *adj*

ab·scis·sa \ab-'si-sə\ *n, pl* **abscissas** *also* **ab·scis·sae** \-'si-(ˌ)sē\ **:** the horizontal coordinate of a point in a plane coordinate system obtained by measuring parallel to the x-axis

ab·scis·sion \ab-'si-zhən\ *n* **1 :** the act or process of cutting off **2 :** the natural separation of flowers, fruits, or leaves from plants — **ab·scise** \ab-'sīz\ *vb*

ab·scond \ab-'skänd\ *vb* **♦ :** to depart secretly and hide oneself

♦ clear out, escape, flee, fly, get out, lam, run away, run off

ab·sence \'ab-səns\ *n* **1 :** the state or time of being absent **2 ♦ :** failure to be present where needed, wanted, or normally expected : WANT, LACK **3 :** INATTENTION

♦ lack, need, want

¹**ab·sent** \'ab-sənt\ *adj* **1 ♦ :** not present **2 ♦ :** to be deficient or missing : LACKING **3 :** not paying attention : INATTENTIVE

♦ [1] away, missing, out *Ant* here, present ♦ [2] missing, nonexistent, wanting *Ant* existent, present

²**ab·sent** \ab-'sent\ *vb* **:** to keep (oneself) away

³**ab·sent** \'ab-sənt\ *prep* **:** in the absence of : WITHOUT

ab·sen·tee \ˌab-sən-'tē\ *n* **:** one that is absent or keeps away

absentee ballot *n* **:** a ballot submitted (as by mail) in advance of an election by a voter who is unable to be present at the polls

ab·sen·tee·ism \ˌab-sən-'tē-ˌi-zəm\ *n* **:** chronic absence (as from work or school)

ab·sent·mind·ed \ˌab-sənt-'mīn-dəd\ *adj* **♦ :** unaware of one's surroundings or actions : INATTENTIVE — **ab·sent·mind·ed·ly** *adv* — **ab·sent·mind·ed·ness** *n*

♦ abstracted, preoccupied *Ant* alert

ab·sinthe *also* **ab·sinth** \'ab-ˌsinth\ *n* **:** a liqueur flavored esp. with wormwood and anise

ab·so·lute \'ab-sə-ˌlüt, ˌab-sə-'lüt\ *adj* **1 ♦ :** free from imperfection or mixture **2 ♦ :** free from control, restriction, or qualification **3 :** lacking grammatical connection with any other word in a sentence ⟨∼ construction⟩ **4 ♦ :** not disputable : POSITIVE ⟨∼ proof⟩ **5 :** relating to the fundamental units of length, mass, and time **6 :** FUNDAMENTAL, ULTIMATE

♦ [1] faultless, flawless, ideal, impeccable, letter-perfect, perfect, unblemished ♦ [1] fine, neat, plain, pure, refined, straight, unadulterated, undiluted, unmixed ♦ [2] autocratic, despotic, dictatorial, tyrannical, tyrannous *Ant* limited ♦ [2] complete, consummate, perfect, total, unequivocal, unqualified, utter ♦ [4] clear, conclusive, decisive, definitive, positive

ab·so·lute·ly \-lē\ *adv* **♦ :** in an absolute manner or condition

♦ all, altogether, clean, completely, entirely, fully, quite, totally, utterly, wholly

absolute pitch *n* **1 :** the position of a tone in a standard scale independently determined by its rate of vibration **2 :** the ability to sing a note asked for or to name a note heard

absolute value *n* **:** a nonnegative number equal to a given real number with any negative sign removed

absolute zero *n* **:** a theoretical temperature marked by a complete absence of heat and motion and equivalent to exactly -273.15°C or -459.67°F

ab·so·lu·tion \ˌab-sə-'lü-shən\ *n* **♦ :** the act of absolving; *esp* **:** a remission of sins pronounced by a priest in the sacrament of reconciliation

♦ amnesty, forgiveness, pardon, remission

ab·so·lut·ism \'ab-sə-ˌlü-ˌti-zəm\ *n* **1 :** the theory that a ruler or government should have unlimited power **2 :** government by an absolute ruler or authority

ab·solve \ab-'zälv, -'sälv\ *vb* **ab·solved; ab·solv·ing ♦ :** to set free from an obligation or the consequences of guilt

♦ acquit, clear, exculpate, exonerate, vindicate

ab·sorb \ab-'sȯrb, -'zȯrb\ *vb* **1 :** to take in and make part of an existent whole **2 ♦ :** to suck up or take in in the manner of a sponge **3 ♦ :** to engage (one's attention) : ENGROSS **4 :** to receive without recoil or echo ⟨a ceiling that ∼s sound⟩ **5 :** ASSUME, BEAR ⟨∼ all costs⟩ **6 :** to transform (radiant energy) into a different form usu. with a resulting rise in temperature

♦ [2] drink, imbibe, soak, sponge, suck ♦ [3] busy, engage, engross, enthrall, fascinate, grip, immerse, interest, intrigue, involve, occupy

ab·sorbed \ab-'sȯrbd, -'zȯrbd\ *adj* **♦ :** obliviously engaged or occupied

♦ attentive, engrossed, intent, observant, rapt

ab·sor·bent *also* **ab·sor·bant** \ab-'sȯr-bənt, -'zȯr-\ *adj* **:** able to absorb ⟨∼ cotton⟩ — **ab·sor·ben·cy** \-bən-sē\ *n* — **absorbent** *also* **absorbant** *n*

ab·sorb·ing \ab-'sȯrb-iŋ, -'zȯrb-iŋ\ *adj* **♦ :** fully taking attention : ENGROSSING — **ab·sorb·ing·ly** *adv*

♦ engaging, engrossing, enthralling, fascinating, interesting, intriguing

ab·sorp·tion \ab-'sȯrp-shən, -'zȯrp-\ *n* **1 :** a process of absorbing or being absorbed **2 ♦ :** concentration of attention — **ab·sorp·tive** \-tiv\ *adj*

♦ attention, concentration

ab·stain \ab-'stān\ *vb* **1 ♦ :** to refrain from an action or practice **2 :** to choose not to vote — **ab·stain·er** *n* — **ab·sten·tion** \-'sten-chən\ *n*

♦ forbear, forgo, keep, refrain

ab·ste·mi·ous \ab-'stē-mē-əs\ *adj* **♦ :** sparing in use of food or drink : TEMPERATE — **ab·ste·mi·ous·ly** *adv* — **ab·ste·mi·ous·ness** *n*

♦ abstinent, sober, temperate *Ant* self-indulgent

ab·sti·nence \'ab-stə-nəns\ *n* **:** voluntary refraining esp. from eating certain foods, drinking liquor, or engaging in sexual intercourse

ab·sti·nent \'ab-stə-nənt\ *adj* **♦ :** practicing abstinence

♦ abstemious, sober, temperate

abstr *abbr* abstract

¹**ab·stract** \ab-'strakt, 'ab-ˌstrakt\ *adj* **1 :** considered apart from a particular instance **2 :** expressing a quality apart from an object ⟨*beauty* is an ∼ word⟩ **3 :** having only intrinsic form with little or no pictorial representation ⟨∼ painting⟩ — **ab·stract·ly** *adv* — **ab·stract·ness** *n*

²**ab·stract** \'ab-ˌstrakt; 2 *also* ab-'strakt\ *n* **1 ♦ :** a summary of points (as of a writing) : SUMMARY, EPITOME **2 :** an abstract thing or state

♦ digest, encapsulation, epitome, outline, précis, recapitulation, résumé (*or* resume), roundup, sum, summary, synopsis, wrap-up

³**ab·stract** \ab-'strakt, 'ab-ˌstrakt; 2 *usu* 'ab-ˌstrakt\ *vb* **1 :** REMOVE, SEPARATE **2 ♦ :** to make an abstract of : SUMMARIZE

3 : to draw away the attention of **4** : STEAL — **ab·stract·ed·ly** \ab-'strak-təd-lē, 'ab-ˌstrak-\ *adv*

♦ digest, encapsulate, epitomize, outline, recapitulate, sum up, summarize, wrap up

ab·stract·ed \ab-'strak-təd, 'ab-ˌstrak-\ *adj* ♦ : lost in thought and unaware of one's surroundings or actions

♦ absentminded, preoccupied

abstract expressionism *n* : art that expresses the artist's attitudes and emotions through abstract forms — **abstract expressionist** *n*

ab·strac·tion \ab-'strak-shən\ *n* **1** : the act of abstracting : the state of being abstracted **2** : an abstract idea **3** : an abstract work of art

ab·struse \ab-'strüs\ *adj* ♦ : hard to understand : RECONDITE — **ab·struse·ly** *adv* — **ab·struse·ness** *n*

♦ deep, esoteric, profound

ab·surd \əb-'sərd, -'zərd\ *adj* ♦ : ridiculously unreasonable, unsound, or incongruous — **ab·surd·ly** *adv*

♦ bizarre, fanciful, fantastic, foolish, nonsensical, preposterous, unreal, wild ♦ comical, derisive, farcical, laughable, ludicrous, preposterous, ridiculous, risible, silly

ab·sur·di·ty \-'sər-də-tē, -'zər-\ *n* **1** ♦ : the quality or state of being absurd **2** ♦ : something that is absurd

♦ [1] daftness, fatuity, folly, foolishness, inanity, silliness, zaniness ♦ [2] fatuity, folly, foolery, foolishness, idiocy, inanity, madness, stupidity

abun·dance \ə-'bən-dəns\ *n* ♦ : an ample quantity

♦ deal, gobs, heap, loads, lot, pile, plenty, quantity, scads ♦ plenty, superabundance, wealth

abun·dant \ə-'bən-dənt\ *adj* ♦ : more than enough : amply sufficient — **abun·dance** \-dəns\ *n* — **abun·dant·ly** *adv*

♦ ample, bountiful, comfortable, generous, liberal, plentiful

¹abuse \ə-'byüs\ *n* **1** : a corrupt practice **2** ♦ : incorrect or improper use : MISUSE ⟨drug ∼⟩ **3** ♦ : coarse and insulting speech ⟨verbal ∼⟩ **4** : MISTREATMENT ⟨child ∼⟩

♦ [2] misuse, perversion ♦ [3] fulmination, invective, vitriol, vituperation

²abuse \ə-'byüz\ *vb* **abused; abus·ing** **1** ♦ : to put to a wrong use : MISUSE **2** ♦ : to use so as to injure or damage : MISTREAT **3** ♦ : to attack in words **4** : to use to excess ⟨∼ alcohol⟩ — **abus·er** *n* — **abu·sive·ness** *n*

♦ [1] misapply, misuse, pervert, profane ♦ [1] capitalize, cash in, exploit, impose, play, use ♦ [2] ill-treat, maltreat, manhandle, mishandle, mistreat, misuse ♦ [3] assail, attack, belabor, blast, castigate, excoriate, jump, lambaste, slam, vituperate

abu·sive \ə-'byü-siv\ *adj* ♦ : characterized by or serving for abuse — **abu·sive·ly** *adv*

♦ opprobrious, scurrilous

abut \ə-'bət\ *vb* **abut·ted; abut·ting** ♦ : to touch along a border : border on

♦ adjoin, border (on), flank, fringe, join, skirt, touch, verge (on)

abut·ment \ə-'bət-mənt\ *n* : the part of a structure (as a bridge) that supports weight or withstands lateral pressure

abut·ter \ə-'bə-tər\ *n* : one that abuts; *esp* : the owner of a contiguous property

abys·mal \ə-'biz-məl\ *adj* **1** : immeasurably deep : BOTTOMLESS **2** : absolutely wretched ⟨∼ living conditions of the poor⟩ — **abys·mal·ly** *adv*

abyss \ə-'bis\ *n* **1** : the bottomless pit in old accounts of the universe **2** : an immeasurable depth

abys·sal \ə-'bi-səl\ *adj* : of or relating to the bottom waters of the ocean depths

ac *abbr* account

-ac *n suffix* : one affected with ⟨hypochondri*ac*⟩

Ac *symbol* actinium

AC *abbr* **1** air-conditioning **2** alternating current **3** before Christ **4** before meals **5** area code

aca·cia \ə-'kā-shə\ *n* : any of numerous leguminous trees or shrubs with round white or yellow flower clusters and often fernlike leaves

acad *abbr* academic; academy

ac·a·deme \'a-kə-ˌdēm, ˌa-kə-'\ *n* : SCHOOL; *also* : academic environment

¹ac·a·dem·ic \ˌa-kə-'de-mik\ *n* : a person who is academic in background, outlook, or methods

²academic *adj* **1** ♦ : of, relating to, or associated with schools or colleges **2** : literary or general rather than technical **3** : theoretical rather than practical — **ac·a·dem·i·cal·ly** \-mi-k(ə-)lē\ *adv*

♦ educational, scholarly, scholastic *Ant* nonacademic, unacademic

ac·a·de·mi·cian \ˌa-kə-də-'mi-shən, ə-ˌka-də-\ *n* **1** : a member of a society of scholars or artists **2** : ACADEMIC

ac·a·dem·i·cism \ˌa-kə-'de-mə-ˌsi-zəm\ *also* **acad·e·mism** \ə-'ka-də-ˌmi-zəm\ *n* **1** : a formal academic quality **2** : purely speculative thinking

acad·e·my \ə-'ka-də-mē\ *n, pl* **-mies** **1** : a school usu. above the elementary level; *esp* : a private high school **2** : a society of scholars or artists

acan·thus \ə-'kan-thəs\ *n, pl* **acanthus** **1** : any of a genus of prickly herbs of the Mediterranean region **2** : an ornamentation (as on a column) representing the leaves of the acanthus

a cap·pel·la *also* **a ca·pel·la** \ˌä-kə-'pe-lə\ *adv or adj* : without instrumental accompaniment

acc *abbr* accusative

ac·cede \ak-'sēd\ *vb* **ac·ced·ed; ac·ced·ing** **1** : to become a party to an agreement **2** ♦ : to express approval **3** : to enter upon an office

♦ acquiesce, agree, assent, come round, consent, subscribe (to) *Ant* dissent

ac·cel·er·ate \ik-'se-lə-ˌrāt, ak-\ *vb* **-at·ed; -at·ing** **1** : to bring about earlier **2** ♦ : to speed up : QUICKEN — **ac·cel·er·a·tion** \-ˌse-lə-'rā-shən\ *n*

♦ hasten, hurry, quicken, rush, speed (up), step up, whisk

ac·cel·er·a·tor \ik-'se-lə-ˌrā-tər, ak-\ *n* **1** : one that accelerates **2** : a pedal for controlling the speed of a motor-vehicle engine **3** : an apparatus for imparting high velocities to charged particles

ac·cel·er·om·e·ter \ik-ˌse-lə-'rä-mə-tər, ak-\ *n* : an instrument for measuring acceleration or vibrations

¹ac·cent \'ak-ˌsent, ak-'sent\ *vb* ♦ : to give prominence to : STRESS, EMPHASIZE

♦ accentuate, emphasize, feature, highlight, play, point, stress, underline, underscore

²ac·cent \'ak-ˌsent\ *n* **1** : a distinctive manner of pronunciation ⟨a foreign ∼⟩ **2** : prominence given to one syllable of a word esp. by stress **3** : a mark (as ´, `, ˆ) over a vowel used usu. to indicate a difference in pronunciation from a vowel not so marked **4** ♦ : special concern or attention : EMPHASIS — **ac·cen·tu·al** \ak-'sen-chə-wəl\ *adj*

♦ accentuation, emphasis, stress, weight

ac·cen·tu·ate \ak-'sen-chə-ˌwāt\ *vb* **-at·ed; -at·ing** ♦ : to give prominence to : ACCENT

♦ accent, emphasize, feature, highlight, play, point, stress, underline, underscore

ac·cen·tu·a·tion \-ˌsen-chə-'wā-shən\ *n* ♦ : the act or the result of accentuating

♦ accent, emphasis, stress, weight

ac·cept \ik-'sept, ak-\ *vb* **1** : to receive with consent **2** ♦ : to make a favorable response to **3** ♦ : to recognize as true **4** ♦ : to assume an obligation

♦ [2] approve, care, countenance, favor (*or* favour), OK, subscribe ♦ [3] believe, credit, swallow, trust ♦ [4] assume, bear, shoulder, take over, undertake

ac·cept·able \ik-'sep-tə-bəl, ak-\ *adj* ♦ : capable or worthy of being accepted — **ac·cept·abil·i·ty** \-ˌbi-lə-tē, ak-\ *n*

♦ adequate, all right, decent, fine, OK, passable, respectable, satisfactory, tolerable

ac·cep·tance \ik-'sep-təns, ak-\ *n* **1** : the act of accepting **2** : the state of being accepted or acceptable **3** : an accepted bill of exchange

ac·cep·ta·tion \ˌak-sep-'tā-shən\ *n* : the generally understood meaning of a word

¹ac·cess \'ak-ˌses\ *n* **1** ♦ : capacity to enter or approach **2** ♦ : a way of approach : ENTRANCE

♦ admission, doorway, entrance, entrée, entry, gateway

²access *vb* ♦ : to get at : gain access to

♦ enter, penetrate, pierce, probe

ac·ces·si·ble \ik-'se-sə-bəl, ak-, ek-\ *adj* **1** ♦ : capable of being reached ⟨∼ by train⟩ **2** ♦ : capable of being used, seen, or known : OBTAINABLE ⟨∼ information⟩ — **ac·ces·si·bil·i·ty** \-ˌse-sə-ˈbi-lə-tē\ n

♦ [1] convenient, handy, reachable ♦ [2] acquirable, attainable, available, obtainable, procurable

ac·ces·sion \ik-ˈse-shən, ak-\ n **1** : increase by something added **2** : something added **3** : the act of coming to a high office or position

¹**ac·ces·so·ry** also **ac·ces·sa·ry** \ik-ˈse-sə-rē, ak-\ n, pl **-ries 1** ♦ : a person who though not present abets or assists in the commission of an offense **2** ♦ : something helpful but not essential

♦ [1] abettor, accomplice, cohort, confederate ♦ [2] accoutrement (or accouterment), adjunct, appendage, attachment

²**accessory** adj ♦ : aiding or contributing in a secondary way

♦ auxiliary, peripheral, supplementary

ac·ci·dent \ˈak-sə-dənt\ n **1** ♦ : an esp. unfortunate event occurring by chance or unintentionally **2** ♦ : lack of intention or necessity : CHANCE ⟨met by ∼⟩ **3** : a nonessential property

♦ [1] casualty, mishap ♦ [2] chance, circumstance, hazard, luck

¹**ac·ci·den·tal** \ˌak-sə-ˈdent-ᵊl\ adj **1** ♦ : happening unexpectedly or by chance **2** : happening without intent or through carelessness — **ac·ci·den·tal·ly** \-ˈden-tə-lē\ also **ac·ci·dent·ly** \-ˈdent-lē\ adv

♦ casual, chance, fluky, fortuitous, incidental, unintended, unintentional, unplanned, unpremeditated, unwitting Ant deliberate, intended, intentional, planned, premeditated

²**accidental** n : a musical note foreign to a key indicated by a signature

¹**ac·claim** \ə-ˈklām\ vb **1** ♦ : to express a favorable judgment of : APPLAUD, PRAISE **2** : to declare by acclamation

♦ applaud, cheer, crack up, hail, laud, praise, salute, tout Ant knock, pan, slam

²**acclaim** n ♦ : the act of acclaiming

♦ accolade, credit, distinction, glory, homage, honor (or honour), laurels

ac·cla·ma·tion \ˌa-klə-ˈmā-shən\ n **1** ♦ : loud eager expression of approval, praise, or assent **2** : an overwhelming affirmative vote by shouting or applause rather than by ballot

♦ applause, ovation

ac·cli·mate \ˈa-klə-ˌmāt, ə-ˈklī-mət\ vb **-mat·ed; -mat·ing** ♦ : to accustom or become accustomed to a new environment or situation — **ac·cli·ma·tion** \ˌa-klə-ˈmā-shən, -ˌklī-\ n

♦ accommodate, adapt, adjust, condition, conform, fit, shape

ac·cli·ma·tize \ə-ˈklī-mə-ˌtīz\ vb **-tized; -tiz·ing** : ACCLIMATE — **ac·cli·ma·ti·za·tion** \-ˌklī-mə-tə-ˈzā-shən\ n

ac·cliv·i·ty \ə-ˈkli-və-tē\ n, pl **-ties** : an ascending slope

ac·co·lade \ˈa-kə-ˌlād\ n ♦ : an expression of praise

♦ citation, commendation, encomium, eulogy, homage, paean, panegyric, salutation, tribute ♦ acclaim, credit, distinction, glory, homage, honor (or honour), laurels

ac·com·mo·date \ə-ˈkä-mə-ˌdāt\ vb **-dat·ed; -dat·ing 1** ♦ : to make fit or suitable : ADAPT, ADJUST **2** ♦ : to bring into agreement or concord : HARMONIZE, RECONCILE **3** : to provide with something needed **4** ♦ : to hold without crowding **5** : to undergo visual accommodation

♦ [1] acclimate, adapt, adjust, condition, conform, fit, shape ♦ [2] conciliate, conform, coordinate, harmonize, key, reconcile ♦ [4] fit, hold, take

accommodating adj ♦ : willing to please : OBLIGING

♦ friendly, indulgent, obliging

ac·com·mo·da·tion \ə-ˌkä-mə-ˈdā-shən\ n **1** : something supplied to satisfy a need; esp : LODGINGS — usu. used in pl. **2** ♦ : the act of accommodating **3** : the automatic adjustment of the eye for seeing at different distances

♦ compromise, concession, give-and-take, negotiation

ac·com·pa·ni·ment \ə-ˈkəm-pə-nē-mənt, -ˈkəmp-nē-\ n : something that accompanies another; esp : subordinate music to support a principal voice or instrument

ac·com·pa·ny \-nē\ vb **-nied; -ny·ing 1** ♦ : to go or occur with : ATTEND **2** : to play an accompaniment for — **ac·com·pa·nist** \-nist\ n

♦ attend, convoy, escort, squire

ac·com·plice \ə-ˈkäm-pləs, -ˈkəm-\ n ♦ : an associate in crime

♦ abettor, accessory, cohort, confederate

ac·com·plish \ə-ˈkäm-plish, -ˈkəm-\ vb ♦ : to bring to completion — **ac·com·plish·er** n

♦ achieve, carry out, commit, compass, do, execute, follow through, fulfill, make, perform

ac·com·plished adj **1** ♦ : marked by proficiency : EXPERT, SKILLED **2** : established beyond doubt

♦ ace, adept, crack, experienced, expert, master, masterful, masterly, practiced, proficient, seasoned, skilled, skillful

ac·com·plish·ment \ə-ˈkäm-plish-mənt, -ˈkəm-\ n **1** ♦ : the act of accomplishing : COMPLETION **2** ♦ : something completed or effected : ACHIEVEMENT **3** : an acquired excellence or skill

♦ [1] achievement, actuality, attainment, consummation, fruition, fulfillment, realization ♦ [2] achievement, attainment, coup, success, triumph

¹**ac·cord** \ə-ˈkȯrd\ vb **1** ♦ : to grant or give esp. as appropriate, due, or earned : GRANT **2** ♦ : to be consistent or in harmony : AGREE, HARMONIZE — **ac·cor·dant** \-ˈkȯrd-ᵊnt\ adj

♦ [1] award, confer, grant ♦ [2] agree, coincide, comport, conform, correspond, fit, go, harmonize

²**accord** n **1** ♦ : the act or fact of agreeing or being in harmony : AGREEMENT, HARMONY **2** ♦ : willingness to act ⟨gave of their own ∼⟩

♦ [1] agreement, conformity, consonance, harmony, tune ♦ [1] agreement, concurrence, consensus, unanimity ♦ [1] agreement, bargain, compact, contract, convention, covenant, deal, pact, settlement, understanding ♦ [2] choice, free will, option, self-determination, volition, will

ac·cor·dance \ə-ˈkȯrd-ᵊns\ n **1** : the act or fact of agreeing or being in harmony : ACCORD **2** : the act of granting

ac·cord·ing·ly \ə-ˈkȯr-diŋ-lē\ adv **1** : in accordance **2** ♦ : as a result : CONSEQUENTLY, SO

♦ consequently, ergo, hence, so, therefore, thus, wherefore

according to prep **1** : in conformity with ⟨paid according to ability⟩ **2** : as stated or attested by ⟨according to you⟩

¹**ac·cor·di·on** \ə-ˈkȯr-dē-ən\ n : a portable keyboard instrument with a bellows and reeds — **ac·cor·di·on·ist** \-ə-nist\ n

²**accordion** adj : folding like the bellows of an accordion ⟨∼ pleats⟩

ac·cost \ə-ˈkȯst\ vb : to approach and speak to esp. aggressively

¹**ac·count** \ə-ˈkaȯnt\ n **1** ♦ : a statement of business transactions **2** : a formal business arrangement for regular dealings or services ⟨an advertising ∼⟩ ⟨an e-mail ∼⟩ **3** : a statement of reasons, causes, or motives **4** : value or importance esp. as attributed by others **5** ♦ : a sum of money deposited in a bank and subject to withdrawal by the depositor **6** ♦ : a description of facts, conditions, or events — **on account of** : BECAUSE OF — **on no account** : under no circumstances — **on one's own account** : on one's own behalf

♦ [1] bill, check, invoice, statement, tab ♦ [5] budget, deposit, fund, kitty, nest egg, pool ♦ [6] chronicle, history, narrative, record, report, story

²**account** vb **1** ♦ : to think of as : CONSIDER ⟨I ∼ him lucky⟩ **2** ♦ : to give an explanation — used with for

♦ [1] call, consider, count, esteem, hold, rate, reckon, regard, take ♦ usu account for [2] explain, rationalize

ac·count·able \ə-ˈkaȯn-tə-bəl\ adj **1** ♦ : subject to giving an account : ANSWERABLE, RESPONSIBLE **2** : EXPLICABLE — **ac·count·abil·i·ty** \-ˌkaȯn-tə-ˈbi-lə-tē\ n

♦ answerable, liable, responsible

ac·coun·tant \ə-ˈkaȯnt-ᵊnt\ n : a person skilled in accounting — **ac·coun·tan·cy** \-ᵊn-sē\ n

account executive n : a business executive in charge of a client's account

ac·count·ing \ə-ˈkaȯn-tiŋ\ n : the art or system of keeping and analyzing financial records

ac·cou·tre or **ac·cou·ter** \ə-ˈkü-tər\ vb **-cou·tred** or **-cou·tered; -cou·tring** or **-cou·ter·ing** \-ˈkü-t(ə-)riŋ\ ♦ : to provide with equipment or furnishings : EQUIP, OUTFIT

♦ equip, fit, furnish, outfit, rig, supply

ac·cou·tre·ment or **ac·cou·ter·ment** \ə-ˈkü-trə-mənt, -ˈkü-tər-\ n **1** ♦ : an accessory item — usu. used in pl. **2** : an identifying characteristic

♦ accessory, adjunct, appendage, attachment ♦ usu **accoutre-**

ments apparatus, equipment, gear, matériel, outfit, paraphernalia, tackle

ac·cred·it \ə-'kre-dət\ *vb* **1 ♦ :** to endorse or approve officially **2 ♦ :** to explain by indicating a cause : CREDIT — **ac·cred·i·ta·tion** \-ˌkre-də-'tā-shən\ *n*

♦ [1] authorize, certify, commission, empower, enable, invest, license, qualify ♦ [2] ascribe, attribute, credit, impute

ac·cre·tion \ə-'krē-shən\ *n* **1 :** growth or enlargement esp. by addition from without **2 ♦ :** a product of accretion

♦ addition, augmentation, boost, expansion, gain, increase, increment, plus, proliferation, raise, rise, supplement

ac·cru·al \ə-'krü-əl\ *n* **:** something that accrues or has accrued
ac·crue \ə-'krü\ *vb* **ac·crued; ac·cru·ing 1 :** to come by way of increase **2 :** to be added by periodic growth
acct *abbr* account; accountant
ac·cul·tur·a·tion \ə-ˌkəl-chə-'rā-shən\ *n* **:** cultural modification of an individual or group by borrowing and adapting traits from another culture
ac·cu·mu·late \ə-'kyü-myə-ˌlāt\ *vb* **-lat·ed; -lat·ing ♦ :** to gather or pile up — **ac·cu·mu·la·tive** \-'kyü-myə-lə-tiv\ *adj* — **ac·cu·mu·la·tor** \-'kyü-myə-ˌlā-tər\ *n*

♦ appreciate, build, increase, mount, multiply, proliferate, rise ♦ amass, assemble, collect, gather, group, lump, pile, round up

ac·cu·mu·la·tion \-ˌkyü-myə-'lā-shən\ *n* **1 ♦ :** something that has accumulated or has been accumulated **2 :** the action or process of accumulating

♦ assemblage, collection, gathering

ac·cu·ra·cy \-rə-sē\ *n* **♦ :** the quality, state, or degree of being accurate

♦ closeness, delicacy, exactness, fineness, precision, veracity

ac·cu·rate \'a-kyə-rət\ *adj* **1 ♦ :** free from error : EXACT, PRECISE **2 ♦ :** conforming exactly to truth or to a standard — **ac·cu·rate·ness** *n*

♦ [1] close, delicate, exact, fine, mathematical, pinpoint, precise, rigorous ♦ [2] correct, exact, precise, proper, right, so, true

ac·cu·rate·ly \'a-kyə-rət-lē\ *adv* **♦ :** in an accurate manner

♦ exactly, just, precisely, right, sharp, squarely

ac·cursed \ə-'kərst, -'kər-səd\ *or* **ac·curst** \ə-'kərst\ *adj* **1 :** being under a curse **2 ♦ :** DAMNABLE, EXECRABLE
ac·cus·al \ə-'kyü-zəl\ *n* **:** ACCUSATION
ac·cu·sa·tive \ə-'kyü-zə-tiv\ *adj* **:** of, relating to, or being a grammatical case marking the direct object of a verb or the object of a preposition — **accusative** *n*
ac·cu·sa·to·ry \ə-'kyü-zə-ˌtȯr-ē\ *adj* **:** expressing accusation ⟨an ∼ tone⟩
ac·cuse \ə-'kyüz\ *vb* **ac·cused; ac·cus·ing ♦ :** to charge with an offense : BLAME — **ac·cu·sa·tion** \ˌa-kyə-'zā-shən\ *n* — **ac·cus·er** *n*

♦ charge, incriminate, indict *Ant* absolve, acquit, clear, exculpate, exonerate, vindicate

ac·cused \ə-'kyüzd\ *n, pl* **accused :** the defendant in a criminal case
ac·cus·tom \ə-'kəs-təm\ *vb* **♦ :** to make familiar with through use or experience

♦ acquaint, familiarize, initiate, introduce, orient

ac·cus·tomed \ə-'kəs-təmd\ *adj* **1 :** USUAL, CUSTOMARY **2 ♦ :** being in the habit or custom

♦ given, used, wont *Ant* unaccustomed, unused

¹ace \'ās\ *n* **1 :** a playing card bearing a single large pip in its center **2 :** a very small amount or degree **3 :** a point (as in tennis) won on a serve that goes untouched **4 :** a golf score of one stroke on a hole **5 :** a combat pilot who has downed five or more enemy planes **6 ♦ :** one that excels in knowledge or skill

♦ authority, crackerjack, expert, maestro, master, virtuoso, whiz, wizard

²ace *vb* **aced; ac·ing 1 :** to score an ace against (an opponent) or on (a golf hole) **2 :** to defeat decisively
³ace *adj* **♦ :** of first or high rank or quality ⟨an ∼ mechanic⟩

♦ accomplished, adept, crack, experienced, expert, master, skilled, skillful

ACE in·hib·i·tor \ˌā-ˌsē-'in-'hi-bə-tər, 'ās-\ *n* **:** any of a group of drugs that lower blood pressure by relaxing the arteries
acer·bic \ə-'sər-bik, a-\ *adj* **:** acid in temper, mood, or tone

acer·bi·ty \ə-'sər-bə-tē\ *n, pl* **-ties :** SOURNESS, BITTERNESS
acet·amin·o·phen \ə-ˌsē-tə-'mi-nə-fən\ *n* **:** a crystalline compound used in chemical synthesis and in medicine to relieve pain and fever
ac·e·tate \'a-sə-ˌtāt\ *n* **1 :** a salt or ester of acetic acid **2 :** a textile fiber made from cellulose and acetic acid; *also* **:** a fabric or plastic made of this fiber
ace·tic acid \ə-'sē-tik-\ *n* **:** a colorless pungent liquid acid that is the chief acid of vinegar and is used esp. in making chemical compounds
ac·e·tone \'a-sə-ˌtōn\ *n* **:** a volatile flammable fragrant liquid compound used in making other chemical compounds and as a solvent
ace·tyl·cho·line \ə-ˌsēt-ᵊl-'kō-ˌlēn\ *n* **:** a compound that is released at nerve endings of the autonomic nervous system and is active in the transmission of nerve impulses
acet·y·lene \ə-'set-ᵊl-ən, -ᵊl-ˌēn\ *n* **:** a colorless flammable gas used as a fuel (as in welding and soldering)
acet·yl·sal·i·cyl·ic acid \ə-ˌsēt-ᵊl-ˌsa-lə-ˌsi-lik-\ *n* **:** ASPIRIN 1
¹ache \'āk\ *vb* **ached; ach·ing 1 ♦ :** to suffer a usu. dull persistent pain **2 ♦ :** to experience a painful eagerness or yearning **:** LONG, YEARN ⟨he *ached* for that new car⟩ — **ache** *n*

♦ [1] hurt, pain, smart ♦ [2] die, hanker, hunger, itch, long, pant, pine, sigh, thirst, yearn ♦ *usu* **ache for** [2] crave, desire, die for, hanker for, hunger for, long for, lust (for *or* after), pine for, repine for, thirst for, want, wish for, yearn for

²ache *n* **♦ :** a usu. dull persistent pain

♦ pain, pang, prick, smart, sting, stitch, tingle, twinge

achiev·able \-'chē-və-bəl\ *adj* **♦ :** capable of being achieved

♦ attainable, doable, feasible, possible, practicable, realizable, viable, workable

achieve \ə-'chēv\ *vb* **achieved; achiev·ing 1 ♦ :** to carry out successfully **:** ACCOMPLISH **2 ♦ :** to gain by work or effort — **achiev·er** *n*

♦ [1] accomplish, carry out, commit, compass, do, execute, follow through, fulfill, make, perform ♦ [2] attain, hit, make, score, win

achieve·ment \ə-'chēv-mənt\ *n* **1 ♦ :** the act of achieving **2 ♦ :** a result gained by effort

♦ [1] accomplishment, attainment, success ♦ [2] accomplishment, attainment, coup, success, triumph

Achil·les' heel \ə-ˌki-lēz-\ *n* **:** a vulnerable point
Achil·les tendon \ə-ˌki-lēz-\ *n* **:** the tendon joining the muscles in the calf of the leg to the bone of the heel
ach·ing *adj* **♦ :** afflicted with aches

♦ achy, nasty, painful, sore

ach·ro·mat·ic \ˌa-krə-'ma-tik\ *adj* **:** giving an image almost free from extraneous colors ⟨∼ lens⟩
achy \'ā-kē\ *adj* **ach·i·er; ach·i·est ♦ :** afflicted with aches — **ach·i·ness** *n*

♦ aching, nasty, painful, sore

¹ac·id \'a-səd\ *adj* **1 ♦ :** sour or biting to the taste **2 :** of or relating to an acid **3 ♦ :** sharp, biting, or sour in manner, disposition, or nature — **acid·ly** *adv*

♦ [1, 3] acidic, sour, tart, vinegary

²acid *n* **1 :** a sour substance **2 :** a usu. water-soluble chemical compound that has a sour taste, reacts with a base to form a salt, and reddens litmus **3 :** LSD
acid·ic \ə-'si-dik\ *adj* **♦ :** sour or biting to the taste; *also* **:** sharp or sour in manner

♦ acid, sour, tart, vinegary

acid·i·fy \ə-'si-də-ˌfī\ *vb* **-fied; -fy·ing 1 :** to make or become acid **2 :** to change into an acid — **acid·i·fi·ca·tion** \-ˌsi-də-fə-'kā-shən\ *n*
acid·i·ty \ə-'si-də-tē\ *n* **♦ :** the quality, state, or degree of being acid

♦ acrimony, asperity, bitterness, cattiness, tartness, virulence, vitriol

ac·i·do·sis \ˌa-sə-'dō-səs\ *n, pl* **-do·ses** \-ˌsēz\ **:** an abnormal state of reduced alkalinity of the blood and body tissues
acid precipitation *n* **:** precipitation with above normal acidity that is caused esp. by atmospheric pollutants
acid rain *n* **:** acid precipitation in the form of rain
acid test *n* **:** a severe or crucial test
acid·u·lous \ə-'si-jə-ləs\ *adj* **:** somewhat acid or harsh in taste or manner

ack *abbr* acknowledge; acknowledgment

ac·knowl·edge \ik-ˈnä-lij, ak-\ *vb* **-edged; -edg·ing** **1 :** to recognize the rights or authority of **2 :** to admit as true **3 :** to express thanks for; *also* **:** to report receipt of **4** ♦ **:** to recognize as genuine or valid

♦ admit, agree, allow, concede, confess, grant, own

ac·knowl·edg·ment *or* **ac·knowl·edge·ment** \-mənt\ *n* **1** ♦ **:** the act of acknowledging **2 :** recognition or favorable notice of an act or achievement

♦ admission, avowal, concession, confession

ACL \ˌā-ˌsē-ˈel\ *n* ANTERIOR CRUCIATE LIGAMENT

ACLU *abbr* American Civil Liberties Union

ac·me \ˈak-mē\ *n* ♦ **:** the highest point

♦ apex, climax, crown, culmination, head, height, meridian, peak, pinnacle, summit, tip-top, top, zenith

ac·ne \ˈak-nē\ *n* **:** a skin disorder marked by inflammation of skin glands and hair follicles and by pimple formation esp. on the face

ac·o·lyte \ˈa-kə-ˌlīt\ *n* **1 :** one who assists a member of the clergy in a liturgical service **2 :** FOLLOWER

ac·o·nite \ˈa-kə-ˌnīt\ *n* **1 :** MONKSHOOD **2 :** a drug obtained from a common Old World monkshood

acorn \ˈā-ˌkȯrn, -kərn\ *n* **:** the nut of the oak

acorn squash *n* **:** an acorn-shaped dark green winter squash with a ridged surface

acous·tic \ə-ˈkü-stik\ *or* **acous·ti·cal** \-sti-kəl\ *adj* **1** ♦ **:** of or relating to the sense or organs of hearing, to sound, or to the science of sounds **2 :** deadening sound ⟨∼ tile⟩ **3 :** operated by or utilizing sound waves — **acous·ti·cal·ly** \-k(ə-)lē\ *adv*

♦ auditory, aural, auricular

acous·tics \ə-ˈkü-stiks\ *n sing or pl* **1 :** the science of sound **2 :** the qualities in a room that make it easy or hard for a person in it to hear distinctly

ac·quaint \ə-ˈkwānt\ *vb* **1** ♦ **:** to cause to know personally **2** ♦ **:** to make familiar **:** to cause to know firsthand

♦ [1, 2] accustom, apprise, brief, clue, familiarize, fill in, inform, initiate, introduce, orient

ac·quain·tance \ə-ˈkwänt-ᵊns\ *n* **1** ♦ **:** personal knowledge **2 :** a person with whom one is acquainted — **ac·quain·tance·ship** *n*

♦ cognizance, familiarity *Ant* unfamiliarity

ac·qui·esce \ˌa-kwē-ˈes\ *vb* **-esced; -esc·ing** ♦ **:** to accept, comply, or submit without open opposition — **ac·qui·es·cence** \-ˈes-ᵊns\ *n* — **ac·qui·es·cent·ly** *adv*

♦ accede, agree, assent, come round, consent, subscribe (to)

ac·qui·es·cent \-ᵊnt\ *adj* ♦ **:** inclined to acquiesce

♦ passive, resigned, tolerant, unresistant, unresisting, yielding

ac·quir·able \-ˈkwī-rə-bəl\ *adj* ♦ **:** capable of being acquired

♦ accessible, attainable, available, obtainable, procurable

ac·quire \ə-ˈkwīr\ *vb* **ac·quired; ac·quir·ing** ♦ **:** to gain possession of

♦ cultivate, develop, form ♦ attain, capture, carry, draw, earn, gain, garner, get, land, make, obtain, procure, realize, secure, win

ac·quired \ə-ˈkwīrd\ *adj* **1 :** gained by or as a result of effort or experience **2 :** caused by environmental forces and not passed from parent to offspring in the genes ⟨∼ characteristics⟩

acquired immune deficiency syndrome *n* **:** AIDS

acquired immunodeficiency syndrome *n* **:** AIDS

ac·quire·ment \ə-ˈkwī-(ə)r-mənt\ *n* **1** ♦ **:** something that has been accomplished **:** ACHIEVEMENT, ACCOMPLISHMENT **2 :** the act of acquiring

♦ accomplishment, achievement, attainment, coup, success, triumph

ac·qui·si·tion \ˌa-kwə-ˈzi-shən\ *n* **1 :** ACQUIREMENT **2 :** something acquired

ac·quis·i·tive \ə-ˈkwi-zə-tiv\ *adj* ♦ **:** eager to acquire **:** GREEDY — **ac·quis·i·tive·ly** *adv*

♦ avaricious, avid, covetous, grasping, greedy, mercenary, rapacious

ac·quis·i·tive·ness \-nəs\ *n* ♦ **:** the quality or state of being acquisitive

♦ avarice, avidity, covetousness, cupidity, greed, rapaciousness

ac·quit \ə-ˈkwit\ *vb* **ac·quit·ted; ac·quit·ting** **1** ♦ **:** to pronounce not guilty **2** ♦ **:** to conduct (oneself) usu. satisfactorily

♦ [1] absolve, clear, exculpate, exonerate, vindicate ♦ [2] bear, behave, comport, conduct, demean, deport, quit

ac·quit·tal \ə-ˈkwit-ᵊl\ *n* ♦ **:** a setting free from the charge of an offense by verdict, sentence, or other legal process

♦ exculpation, exoneration, vindication *Ant* conviction

acre \ˈā-kər\ *n* **1** *pl* **:** an area of land under individual ownership **:** ESTATE **2 :** a unit of land measure equal to 43,560 square feet

acre·age \ˈā-k(ə-)rij\ *n* **:** area in acres

ac·rid \ˈa-krəd\ *adj* **1 :** sharp and biting in taste or odor **2** ♦ **:** deeply bitter **:** marked by incisive sarcasm **:** CAUSTIC — **acrid·i·ty** \a-ˈkri-də-tē\ *n* — **ac·rid·ly** *adv*

♦ acrimonious, bitter, hard, rancorous, resentful, sore ♦ biting, caustic, cutting, mordant, sarcastic, satiric, scathing, sharp

ac·rid·ness \-nəs\ *n* **:** the quality or state of being acrid

ac·ri·mo·ni·ous \ˌa-krə-ˈmō-nē-əs\ *adj* ♦ **:** caustic, biting, or rancorous esp. in feeling, language, or manner

♦ acrid, bitter, hard, rancorous, resentful, sore

ac·ri·mo·ni·ous·ness \-nəs\ *n* **:** the quality or state of being acrimonious

ac·ri·mo·ny \ˈa-krə-ˌmō-nē\ *n, pl* **-nies** ♦ **:** harsh or biting sharpness esp. of words, manner, or disposition — **ac·ri·mo·ni·ous·ly** *adv*

♦ acidity, asperity, bitterness, cattiness, tartness, virulence, vitriol

ac·ro·bat \ˈa-krə-ˌbat\ *n* **:** a performer of gymnastic feats — **ac·ro·bat·ic** \ˌa-krə-ˈba-tik\ *adj* — **ac·ro·bat·i·cal·ly** \-ti-k(ə-)lē\ *adv*

ac·ro·bat·ics \ˌa-krə-ˈba-tiks\ *n sing or pl* **:** the performance of an acrobat

ac·ro·nym \ˈa-krə-ˌnim\ *n* **:** a word (as *radar*) formed from the initial letter or letters of each of the successive parts or major parts of a compound term

ac·ro·pho·bia \ˌa-krə-ˈfō-bē-ə\ *n* **:** abnormal dread of being at a great height

acrop·o·lis \ə-ˈkrä-pə-ləs\ *n* **:** the upper fortified part of an ancient Greek city

¹across \ə-ˈkrȯs\ *adv* **1** ♦ **:** to or on the opposite side **2 :** so as to be understandable ⟨get the point ∼⟩

♦ over, through

²across *prep* **1** ♦ **:** to or on the opposite side of ⟨ran ∼ the street⟩ **2 :** on so as to cross or pass at an angle ⟨a log ∼ the road⟩

♦ athwart, over, through

across–the–board *adj* **1 :** placed to win if a competitor wins, places, or shows ⟨an ∼ bet⟩ **2 :** including all classes or categories ⟨an ∼ wage increase⟩

acros·tic \ə-ˈkrȯs-tik\ *n* **:** a composition usu. in verse in which the initial or final letters of the lines taken in order form a word or phrase — **acrostic** *adj*

acryl·ic \ə-ˈkri-lik\ *n* **1 :** ACRYLIC RESIN **2 :** a paint in which the vehicle is acrylic resin **3 :** a quick-drying synthetic textile fiber

acrylic resin *n* **:** a glassy thermoplastic used for cast and molded parts or as coatings and adhesives

¹act \ˈakt\ *n* **1** ♦ **:** a thing done **:** DEED **2** ♦ **:** the formal product of a legislative body **:** STATUTE; *also* **:** a decision or determination of a sovereign, a legislative council, or a court of justice **3 :** a main division of a play; *also* **:** an item on a variety program **4** ♦ **:** an instance of insincere behavior **:** PRETENSE

♦ [1] action, deed, doing, exploit, feat, thing ♦ [2] enactment, law, ordinance, statute ♦ [4] airs, facade, front, guise, masquerade, pose, pretense, put-on, semblance, show

²act *vb* **1 :** to perform by action esp. on the stage; *also* **:** to make a pretense of **:** FEIGN, SIMULATE, PRETEND **2 :** to take action **3** ♦ **:** to conduct oneself or behave in a certain manner ⟨how did she ∼ toward you⟩ **4** ♦ **:** to perform a specified function **5** ♦ **:** to produce an effect

♦ [1] impersonate, perform, play, portray ♦ *usu* **act toward** [3] be, deal, handle, serve, treat, use ♦ [4] function, perform, serve, work ♦ [5] appear, look, make, seem, sound ♦ [5] function, operate, perform, take, work

³act *abbr* **1** active **2** actual

ACT *abbr* Australian Capital Territory

actg *abbr* acting

ACTH \ˌā-(ˌ)sē-(ˌ)tē-ˈāch\ *n* **:** a protein hormone of the pituitary gland that stimulates the adrenal cortex

act·ing \ˈak-tiŋ\ *adj* ♦ **:** doing duty temporarily or for another ⟨∼ president⟩

♦ interim, provisional, temporary *Ant* long-term, permanent

ac·tin·i·um \ak-'ti-nē-əm\ *n* : a radioactive metallic chemical element

ac·tion \'ak-shən\ *n* **1** ♦ : a legal proceeding **2** : the manner or method of performing **3** : ACTIVITY **4** ♦ : a thing done : ACT, DEED **5** : the accomplishment of a thing usu. over a period of time, in stages, or with the possibility of repetition **6** *pl* ♦ : the deportment and expression of one that acts or speaks : CON·DUCT **7** : combat in war : BATTLE **8** : the events of a literary plot **9** : an operating mechanism ⟨the ∼ of a gun⟩; *also* : the way it operates ⟨stiff ∼⟩

♦ [1] lawsuit, proceeding, suit ♦ [4] act, deed, doing, exploit, feat, thing ♦ *usu* actions [6] bearing, behavior (*or* behaviour), comportment, conduct, demeanor (*or* demeanour), deportment

ac·tion·able \'ak-sh(ə-)nə-bəl\ *adj* : affording ground for an action or suit at law — **ac·tion·ably** \-blē\ *adv*

action figure *n* : a small-scale figure (as of a superhero) used esp. as a toy

ac·ti·vate \'ak-tə-₁vāt\ *vb* **-vat·ed; -vat·ing** **1** ♦ : to spur into action; *also* : to make active, reactive, or radioactive **2** : to treat (as carbon) so as to improve adsorptive properties **3** : to set up (a military unit) formally; *also* : to call to active duty — **ac·ti·va·tion** \₁ak-tə-'vā-shən\ *n* — **ac·ti·va·tor** \'ak-tə-₁vā-tər\ *n*

♦ actuate, crank, drive, move, propel, run, set off, spark, start, touch off, trigger, turn on *Ant* cut, deactivate, kill, shut off, turn off

ac·tive \'ak-tiv\ *adj* **1** : causing or involving action or change **2** : asserting that the grammatical subject performs the action represented by the verb ⟨∼ voice⟩ **3** ♦ : briskly alert and energetic : BRISK, LIVELY **4** ♦ : marked by vigorous activity : BUSY **5** : erupting or likely to erupt ⟨∼ volcano⟩ **6** ♦ : presently in operation or use **7** : tending to progress or to cause degeneration ⟨∼ tuberculosis⟩ — **active** *n* — **ac·tive·ly** *adv* — **ac·tive·ness** *n*

♦ [3] animate, animated, brisk, energetic, lively, spirited, sprightly, springy ♦ [4] assiduous, busy, diligent, engaged, laborious, occupied, sedulous, working ♦ [6] alive, functional, living, on, operational, operative, running, working *Ant* broken, dead, inactive, inoperative, nonfunctional

ac·tiv·ism \'ak-ti-₁vi-zəm\ *n* : a doctrine or practice that emphasizes vigorous action for political ends — **ac·tiv·ist** \-vist\ *n or adj*

ac·tiv·i·ty \ak-'ti-və-tē\ *n, pl* **-ties** **1** : the quality or state of being active **2** ♦ : forceful or energetic action **3** : an occupation in which one is engaged

♦ exercise, exertion

ac·tor \'ak-tər\ *n* ♦ : a person who acts (as in a play, movie, television show, etc.)

♦ impersonator, mummer, player, trouper

act out *vb* ♦ : to behave badly or in a socially unacceptable often self-defeating manner esp. as a means of venting painful emotions (as fear or frustration)

♦ act up, carry on, misbehave

ac·tress \'ak-trəs\ *n* : a woman or girl who is an actor

Acts \'akts\ *or* **Acts of the Apostles** *n* : a book of the New Testament of the Christian Scripture

ac·tu·al \'ak-chə-wəl, -shə-\ *adj* ♦ : really existing : REAL

♦ concrete, existent, factual, real, true, very *Ant* hypothetical, ideal, nonexistent, theoretical

ac·tu·al·i·ty \₁ak-chə-'wa-lə-tē, -shə-\ *n* : the quality or state of being actual

♦ existence, reality, subsistence ♦ accomplishment, achievement, attainment, consummation, fruition, fulfillment, realization

ac·tu·al·ize \'ak-chə-wə-₁līz, -shə-\ *vb* ♦ : to become actual — **ac·tu·al·iza·tion** \₁ak-chə-wə-lə-'zā-shən, -shə-\ *n*

♦ begin, commence, get off, launch, open, start

ac·tu·al·ly \'ak-chə-wə-lē, -shə-\ *adv* **1** ♦ : in fact or in truth : REALLY **2** ♦ : in point of fact — used to suggest something unexpected

♦ [1] admittedly, frankly, honestly, really, truly, truthfully, verily ♦ [2] authentically, genuinely, really, veritably, very

ac·tu·ary \'ak-chə-₁wer-ē, -shə-\ *n, pl* **-ar·ies** : a person who calculates insurance risks and premiums — **ac·tu·ar·i·al** \₁ak-chə-'wer-ē-əl, -shə-\ *adj*

ac·tu·ate \'ak-chə-₁wāt\ *vb* **-at·ed; -at·ing** **1** ♦ : to put into mechanical action **2** ♦ : to move to action — **ac·tu·a·tion** \₁ak-chə-'wā-shən, -shə-\ *n* — **ac·tu·a·tor** \'ak-chə-₁wā-tər, -shə-\ *n*

♦ [1] activate, crank, drive, move, propel, run, set off, spark, start, touch off, trigger, turn on ♦ [2] drive, impel, move, propel, work

act up *vb* **1 a** ♦ : to behave in an unruly, recalcitrant, or capricious manner : MISBEHAVE **b** ♦ : to seek to attract attention by conspicuous behavior **2** : to function improperly

♦ [1a] act out, carry on, misbehave ♦ [1b] clown (around), cut up, fool around, monkey, show off, skylark

acu·ity \ə-'kyü-ə-tē\ *n, pl* **-ities** ♦ : keenness of perception

♦ acuteness, delicacy, keenness, sensitiveness, sensitivity

acu·men \ə-'kyü-mən\ *n* ♦ : mental keenness and penetration

♦ astuteness, caginess, canniness, hardheadedness, intelligence, keenness, sharpness, shrewdness, wit

acu·pres·sure \'a-kyu̇-₁pre-shər\ *n* : the application of pressure (as with the thumbs or fingertips) to the same discrete points on the body stimulated in acupuncture that is used for its therapeutic effects (as the relief of tension or pain)

acu·punc·ture \-₁pəŋk-chər\ *n* : an orig. Chinese practice of puncturing the body (as with needles) at specific points to cure disease or relieve pain — **acu·punc·tur·ist** \₁a-kyu̇-'pəŋk-chə-rist\ *n*

acute \ə-'kyüt\ *adj* **acut·er; acut·est** **1** : SHARP, POINTED **2** : containing less than 90 degrees ⟨an ∼ angle⟩ **3** ♦ : sharply perceptive; *esp* : mentally keen **4 a** ♦ : characterized by sharpness or severity : SEVERE ⟨∼ distress⟩ **b** ♦ : having a sudden onset, sharp rise, and short duration ⟨∼ inflammation⟩ **5** ♦ : high in pitch **6** : of, marked by, or being an accent mark having the form ´ — **acute·ly** *adv* — *n*

♦ [3] delicate, keen, perceptive, sensitive, sharp ♦ [4a] agonizing, biting, excruciating, severe, sharp ♦ [4b] critical, dire, imperative, imperious, instant, pressing, urgent *Ant* noncritical ♦ [5] sharp, shrill, squeaky, treble

acute·ness \-nəs\ *n* ♦ : the quality or state of being acute

♦ acuity, delicacy, keenness, sensitiveness, sensitivity

acy·clo·vir \(₁)ā-'sī-klō-₁vir\ *n* : a drug used esp. to treat the genital form of herpes simplex

ad \'ad\ *n* : a public notice : ADVERTISEMENT

AD *abbr* **1** after date **2** in the year of our Lord — often printed in small capitals and often punctuated **3** assistant director **4** athletic director

ad·age \'a-dij\ *n* ♦ : an old familiar saying : PROVERB, MAXIM

♦ aphorism, byword, epigram, maxim, proverb, saying

¹ada·gio \ə-'dä-j(ē-₁)ō, -zh(ē-₁)ō\ *adv or adj* : at a slow tempo — used as a direction in music

²adagio *n, pl* **-gios** **1** : an adagio movement **2** : a ballet duet or trio displaying feats of lifting and balancing

¹ad·a·mant \'a-də-mənt, -₁mant\ *n* : a stone believed to be impenetrably hard

²adamant *adj* ♦ : unshakable or insistent esp. in maintaining a position or opinion : INFLEXIBLE, UNYIELDING — **ad·a·mant·ly** *adv*

♦ hard, immovable, implacable, inflexible, pat, rigid, unbending, uncompromising, unrelenting, unyielding

ad·a·man·tine \₁a-də-'man-₁tēn, -₁tīn\ *adj* : rigidly firm : UNYIELDING

Ad·am's apple \'a-dəmz-\ *n* : the projection in front of the neck formed by the largest cartilage of the larynx

adapt \ə-'dapt\ *vb* ♦ : to make suitable or fit (as for a new use or for different conditions) — **ad·ap·ta·tion** \₁a-₁dap-'tā-shən\ *n* — **ad·ap·ta·tion·al** \-sh(ə-)nəl\ *adj* — **adap·tive** \ə-'dap-tiv\ *adj* — **ad·ap·tiv·i·ty** \₁a-₁dap-'ti-və-tē\ *n*

♦ acclimate, accommodate, adjust, condition, conform, fit, shape

adapt·able \ə-'dap-tə-bəl\ *adj* ♦ : capable of being or becoming adapted — **adapt·abil·i·ty** \ə-₁dap-tə-'bi-lə-tē\ *n*

♦ protean, universal, versatile ♦ adjustable, changeable, elastic, flexible, fluid, malleable, variable

adapt·er *also* **adap·tor** \ə-'dap-tər\ *n* **1** : one that adapts **2** : a device for connecting two dissimilar parts of an apparatus **3** ♦ : an attachment for adapting an apparatus for uses not orig. intended

♦ *also* **adaptor** accessory, accoutrement (*or* accouterment), adjunct, appendage, attachment, option

ADC *abbr* **1** aide-de-camp **2** Aid to Dependent Children

add \'ad\ *vb* **1** ♦ : to join to something else so as to increase in number or amount **2** : to say further ⟨let me ～ this⟩ **3** ♦ : to combine (numbers) into one sum **4** ♦ : to serve as or make an addition ⟨the TV appearance *added* to his fame⟩ ⟨*added* to her savings⟩

♦ [1] adjoin, annex, append, tack *Ant* deduct, remove, subtract, take ♦ [3] foot, sum, total ♦ *usu* **add to** [4] aggrandize, amplify, augment, boost, compound, enlarge, escalate, expand, extend, increase, multiply, raise, swell, up

ADD *abbr* attention deficit disorder

ad·dend \'a-,dend\ *n* : a number to be added to another

ad·den·dum \a-'den-dəm\ *n, pl* **-da** \-də\ : something added; *esp* : a supplement to a book

¹ad·der \'a-dər\ *n* **1** : a poisonous European viper or a related snake **2** : any of various harmless No. American snakes (as the hognose snake)

²add·er \'a-dər\ *n* : one that adds; *esp* : a device that performs addition

¹ad·dict \ə-'dikt\ *vb* **1** : to devote or surrender (oneself) to something habitually or excessively **2** : to cause addiction to a substance in (as a person) — **ad·dic·tive** \-'dik-tiv\ *adj*

²ad·dict \'a-(,)dikt\ *n* **1** ♦ : one who is addicted esp. to a substance **2** ♦ : an ardent follower, supporter, or enthusiast

♦ [1] doper, fiend, user ♦ [2] aficionado, buff, bug, devotee, enthusiast, fan, fanatic, fancier, fiend, freak, lover, maniac, nut

ad·dic·tion \ə-'dik-shən\ *n* **1** : the quality or state of being addicted **2** : compulsive need for and use of a habit-forming substance (as heroin, nicotine, or alcohol) characterized by well-defined physiological symptoms upon withdrawal; *also* : persistent compulsive use of a substance known by the user to be harmful

ad·di·tion \ə-'di-shən\ *n* **1** ♦ : the act or process of adding; *also* : something added **2** : the operation of combining numbers to obtain their sum

♦ annex, extension, penthouse ♦ accretion, augmentation, boost, expansion, gain, increase, increment, plus, proliferation, raise, rise, supplement

ad·di·tion·al \ə-'di-sh(ə-)nəl\ *adj* ♦ : coming by way of addition : ADDED

♦ another, else, farther, further, more, other

ad·di·tion·al·ly \ə-'di-sh(ə-)nə-lē\ *adv* ♦ : in or by way of addition : FURTHERMORE

♦ again, also, besides, further, furthermore, likewise, more, moreover, then, too, withal, yet

¹ad·di·tive \'a-də-tiv\ *adj* **1** : of, relating to, or characterized by addition **2** : produced by addition — **ad·di·tiv·i·ty** \,a-də-'ti-və-tē\ *n*

²additive *n* : a substance added to another in small quantities to effect a desired change in properties ⟨food ～s⟩

ad·dle \'ad-²l\ *vb* **ad·dled; ad·dling** **1** ♦ : to throw into confusion : MUDDLE **2** : to become rotten ⟨*addled* eggs⟩

♦ baffle, befog, befuddle, bemuse, bewilder, confound, confuse, disorient, muddle, muddy, mystify, perplex, puzzle

addn *abbr* addition

addnl *abbr* additional

add-on \'ad-,òn, -,än\ *n* : something (as a feature or accessory) added esp. as an enhancement

¹ad·dress \ə-'dres\ *vb* **1** ♦ : to direct the attention of (oneself) **2** : to direct one's remarks to : deliver an address to **3** : to mark directions for delivery on **4** : to identify (as a memory location) by an address

♦ apply, bend, buckle, devote, give

²ad·dress \ə-'dres, 'a-,dres\ *n* **1** : skillful management **2** ♦ : a formal speech **3** : the place where a person or organization may be communicated with **4** : the directions for delivery placed on mail; *also* : the designation of a computer account for sending and receiving e-mail **5** : a location (as in a computer's memory) where particular data is stored

♦ declamation, harangue, oration, speech, talk

ad·dress·ee \,a-,dre-'sē, ə-,dre-'sē\ *n* : one to whom something is addressed

ad·duce \ə-'düs, -'dyüs\ *vb* **ad·duced; ad·duc·ing** ♦ : to offer as example, reason, or proof — **ad·duc·er** *n*

♦ cite, instance, mention, quote

add up *vb* **1** ♦ : to come to the expected total **2** ♦ : to reach in kind or quality — used with *to*

♦ *usu* **add up to** [1] amount (to), come, number, sum, total ♦ *usu* **add up to** [2] amount, come, correspond, equal

-ade *n suffix* **1** : act : action ⟨block*ade*⟩ **2** : product; *esp* : sweet drink ⟨lime*ade*⟩

ad·e·nine \'ad-²n-,ēn\ *n* : one of the purine bases that make up the genetic code of DNA and RNA

ad·e·noid \'ad-,nòid, -²n-,òid\ *n* : an enlarged mass of tissue near the opening of the nose into the throat — usu. used in pl. — **adenoid** *or* **ad·e·noi·dal** \,ad-'nòi-dəl, -²n-'òi-\ *adj*

aden·o·sine tri·phos·phate \ə-'de-nə-,sēn-trī-'fäs-,fāt\ *n* : ATP

¹ad·ept \'a-,dept\ *n* ♦ : a highly skilled or well-trained individual : EXPERT

♦ artist, authority, expert, master, virtuoso, whiz, wizard

²adept \ə-'dept\ *adj* ♦ : highly skilled : EXPERT

♦ accomplished, ace, crack, experienced, expert, master, masterful, masterly, practiced, proficient, seasoned, skilled, skillful, versed

adept·ly \ə-'dep(t)-lē\ *adv* ♦ : in an adept manner

♦ ably, capably, expertly, masterfully, proficiently, skillfully, well

adept·ness \-'dep(t)-nəs\ *n* ♦ : the quality or state of being adept

♦ adroitness, art, artfulness, artifice, artistry, cleverness, craft, cunning, deftness, masterfulness, skill

ad·e·qua·cy \'a-di-kwə-sē\ *n* : the quality or state of being adequate

ad·e·quate \'a-di-kwət\ *adj* ♦ : equal to or sufficient for a specific requirement — **ad·e·quate·ness** *n*

♦ acceptable, all right, decent, fine, OK, passable, respectable, satisfactory, tolerable *Ant* deficient, inadequate, lacking, unacceptable, unsatisfactory, wanting

ad·e·quate·ly \-lē\ *adv* ♦ : in an adequate manner

♦ enough, satisfactorily

ad·here \ad-'hir\ *vb* **ad·hered; ad·her·ing** **1** ♦ : to give support : maintain loyalty **2** ♦ : to stick fast : CLING

♦ *usu* **adhere to** [1] cling, hew, keep, stick *Ant* defect (from) ♦ [2] cling, hew, stick

ad·her·ence \-'hir-əns\ *n* ♦ : the act, action, or quality of adhering

♦ adhesion, cohesion

¹ad·her·ent \-ənt\ *adj* : able or tending to adhere

²ad·her·ent *n* ♦ : one that adheres: as **a** : a follower of a leader, party, or profession **b** : a believer in or advocate esp. of a particular idea or church

♦ convert, disciple, follower, partisan, pupil, votary

ad·he·sion \ad-'hē-zhən\ *n* **1** ♦ : the act or state of adhering **2** : the union of bodily tissues abnormally grown together after inflammation; *also* : the newly formed uniting tissue **3** : the molecular attraction between the surfaces of bodies in contact

♦ adherence, cohesion

¹ad·he·sive \-'hē-siv, -ziv\ *adj* **1** ♦ : tending to adhere : STICKY **2** : prepared for adhering

♦ gelatinous, gluey, glutinous, gooey, gummy, sticky, viscid, viscous

²adhesive *n* ♦ : an adhesive substance

♦ cement, glue, size

adhesive tape *n* : tape coated on one side with an adhesive mixture; *esp* : one used for covering wounds

¹ad hoc \'ad-'häk, -'hōk\ *adv* : for the case at hand apart from other applications

²ad hoc *adj* : concerned with or formed for a particular purpose ⟨an *ad hoc* committee⟩ ⟨*ad hoc* solutions⟩

adi·a·bat·ic \,a-dē-ə-'ba-tik\ *adj* : occurring without loss or gain of heat — **adi·a·bat·i·cal·ly** \-ti-k(ə-)lē\ *adv*

adieu \ə-'dü, -'dyü\ *n, pl* **adieus** *or* **adieux** \ə-'düz, -'dyüz\ ♦ : a wish of well-being at parting : FAREWELL — often used interjectionally

♦ au revoir, bon voyage, farewell, good-bye

ad in·fi·ni·tum \,ad-,in-fə-'nī-təm\ *adv or adj* : without end or limit

ad in·ter·im \ad-'in-tə-rəm, -,rim\ *adv* : for the intervening time — **ad interim** *adj*

adi·os \ˌa-dē-ˈōs, ˌä-\ *interj* — used to express farewell

ad·i·pose \ˈa-də-ˌpōs\ *adj* : of or relating to animal fat : FATTY

adj *abbr* **1** adjective **2** adjutant

ad·ja·cent \ə-ˈjās-ᵊnt\ *adj* ♦ : situated near or next — **ad·ja·cent·ly** *adv*

♦ adjoining, contiguous, touching *Ant* nonadjacent

ad·jec·tive \ˈa-jik-tiv\ *n* : a word that typically serves as a modifier of a noun — **ad·jec·ti·val** \ˌa-jik-ˈtī-vəl\ *adj* — **ad·jec·ti·val·ly** *adv*

ad·join \ə-ˈjȯin\ *vb* **1** ♦ : to add or attach by joining **2** ♦ : to be situated next to

♦ [1] add, annex, append, tack ♦ [2] abut, border (on), flank, fringe, join, skirt, touch, verge (on)

ad·join·ing *adj* ♦ : touching or bounding at a point or line

♦ adjacent, contiguous, touching

ad·journ \ə-ˈjərn\ *vb* **1** ♦ : to suspend indefinitely or until a stated time **2** : to transfer to another place — **ad·journ·ment** *n*

♦ break off, discontinue, interrupt, recess, suspend

ad·judge \ə-ˈjəj\ *vb* **ad·judged; ad·judg·ing 1** : to decide or rule upon as a judge : JUDGE, ADJUDICATE **2** : to hold or pronounce to be : DEEM **3** : to award by judicial decision

ad·ju·di·cate \ə-ˈjü-di-ˌkāt\ *vb* **-cat·ed; -cat·ing** ♦ : to pass judgment on : to settle judicially — **ad·ju·di·ca·tion** \ə-ˌjü-di-ˈkā-shən\ *n*

♦ arbitrate, decide, determine, judge, referee, rule, settle, umpire

ad·junct \ˈa-ˌjəŋkt\ *n* ♦ : something joined or added to another but not essentially a part of it

♦ accessory, accoutrement (*or* accouterment), adapter, appendage, attachment

ad·jure \ə-ˈjùr\ *vb* **ad·jured; ad·jur·ing** : to command solemnly : urge earnestly — **ad·ju·ra·tion** \ˌa-jə-ˈrā-shən\ *n*

ad·just \ə-ˈjəst\ *vb* **1** : to bring to agreement : SETTLE **2** ♦ : to cause to conform : ADAPT, FIT **3** : REGULATE ⟨~ a watch⟩ — **ad·just·er** *also* **ad·jus·tor** \ə-ˈjəs-tər\ *n* — **ad·just·ment** \ə-ˈjəst-mənt\ *n*

♦ acclimate, accommodate, adapt, condition, conform, fit, shape

ad·just·able \-ˈjəs-tə-bəl\ *adj* ♦ : capable of being adjusted

♦ adaptable, changeable, elastic, flexible, fluid, malleable, variable

ad·ju·tant \ˈa-jə-tənt\ *n* : one who assists; *esp* : an officer who assists a commanding officer by handling correspondence and keeping records

ad·ju·vant \ˈa-jə-vənt\ *n* : one that helps or facilitates; *esp* : something that enhances the effectiveness of medical treatment — **adjuvant** *adj*

¹**ad–lib** \ˈad-ˈlib\ *vb* **ad–libbed; ad–lib·bing** : to improvise (esp. lines or a speech) — **ad–lib** *n*

²**ad–lib** *adj* ♦ : spoken, composed, or performed without preparation

♦ extemporaneous, impromptu, offhand, snap, unplanned, unpremeditated, unprepared, unrehearsed

ad lib \ˈad-ˈlib\ *adv* **1** : at one's pleasure **2** : without limit

adm *abbr* administration; administrative

ADM *abbr* admiral

ad·man \ˈad-ˌman\ *n* : one who writes, solicits, or places advertisements

admin *abbr* administration; administrative

ad·min·is·ter \ad-ˈmi-nə-stər\ *vb* **1** ♦ : to manage or supervise the execution, use, or conduct of **2** ♦ : to mete out : DISPENSE **3** : to give ritually or remedially ⟨~ quinine for malaria⟩ **4** : to perform the office of administrator — **ad·min·is·tra·ble** \-strə-bəl\ *adj* — **ad·min·is·trant** \-strənt\ *n*

♦ [1] apply, enforce, execute, implement ♦ [1] carry on, conduct, control, direct, govern, guide, handle, manage, operate, oversee, regulate, run, superintend, supervise ♦ [2] allocate, apportion, deal, dispense, distribute, mete, parcel, portion, prorate

ad·min·is·tra·tion \ad-ˌmi-nə-ˈstrā-shən\ *n* **1** : the act or process of administering **2** ♦ : performance of executive duties **3** : the officials directing the government of a country **4** : the term of office of an administrative officer or body — **ad·min·is·tra·tive·ly** *adv*

♦ authority, government, jurisdiction, regime, rule ♦ conduct, control, direction, guidance, management, operation, oversight, regulation, running, superintendence, supervision

ad·min·is·tra·tive \ad-ˈmi-nə-ˌstrā-tiv\ *adj* : of or relating to administration

ad·min·is·tra·tor \ad-ˈmi-nə-ˌstrā-tər\ *n* ♦ : one that administers; *esp* : one who settles an intestate estate

♦ director, executive, manager, superintendent, supervisor

ad·mi·ra·ble \ˈad-m(ə-)rə-bəl\ *adj* ♦ : worthy of admiration : EXCELLENT — **ad·mi·ra·bil·i·ty** \ˌad-m(ə-)rə-ˈbi-lə-tē\ *n* — **ad·mi·ra·ble·ness** *n* — **ad·mi·ra·bly** \-blē\ *adv*

♦ applaudable, commendable, creditable, excellent, laudable, meritorious, praiseworthy *Ant* censurable, discreditable, reprehensible

ad·mi·ral \ˈad-m(ə-)rəl\ *n* : a commissioned officer in the navy ranking next below a fleet admiral

ad·mi·ral·ty \ˈad-m(ə-)rəl-tē\ *n* **1** *cap* : a British government department formerly having authority over naval affairs **2** : the court having jurisdiction over questions of maritime law

ad·mi·ra·tion \ˌad-mə-ˈrā-shən\ *n* ♦ : delighted or astonished approval

♦ appreciation, esteem, estimation, favor (*or* favour), regard, respect *Ant* disfavor

ad·mire \əd-ˈmīr\ *vb* **ad·mired; ad·mir·ing** ♦ : to regard with high esteem — **ad·mir·er** *n* — **ad·mir·ing·ly** \-ˈmī-riŋ-lē\ *adv*

♦ appreciate, esteem, regard, respect

ad·mis·si·ble \əd-ˈmi-sə-bəl\ *adj* ♦ : that can be or is worthy to be admitted or allowed : ALLOWABLE ⟨~ evidence⟩ — **ad·mis·si·bil·i·ty** \-ˌmi-sə-ˈbi-lə-tē\ *n*

♦ allowable, permissible, sufferable

ad·mis·sion \əd-ˈmi-shən\ *n* **1** ♦ : the act of admitting **2** : the privilege of being admitted **3** : a fee paid for admission **4** : the granting of an argument **5** : the acknowledgment of a fact

♦ [1] acknowledgment, avowal, concession, confession ♦ [2] access, doorway, entrance, entrée, entry, gateway

ad·mit \əd-ˈmit\ *vb* **ad·mit·ted; ad·mit·ting 1** : PERMIT, ALLOW **2** ♦ : to recognize as genuine or valid **3** : to allow to enter

♦ acknowledge, agree, allow, concede, confess, grant, own *Ant* deny

ad·mit·tance \əd-ˈmit-ᵊns\ *n* : permission to enter

ad·mit·ted·ly \əd-ˈmi-təd-lē\ *adv* **1** : as has been or must be admitted **2** ♦ : it must be admitted

♦ actually, frankly, honestly, indeed, really, truly, truthfully, verily

ad·mix \ad-ˈmiks\ *vb* : to mix in

ad·mix·ture \ad-ˈmiks-chər\ *n* **1** : something added in mixing **2** ♦ : a product of mixing : MIXTURE

♦ amalgam, blend, combination, composite, compound, fusion, intermixture, mix, mixture

ad·mon·ish \ad-ˈmä-nish\ *vb* ♦ : to express warning or disapproval to esp. in a gentle manner — **ad·mon·ish·er** *n* — **ad·mon·ish·ment** *n*

♦ chide, rebuke, reprimand, reproach, reprove

ad·mon·ish·ing \-iŋ\ *adj* ♦ : expressing admonition

♦ admonitory, cautionary, warning

ad·mo·ni·tion \ˌad-mə-ˈni-shən\ *n* ♦ : counsel or warning against fault or oversight

♦ alarm, alert, caution, notice, warning

ad·mon·i·to·ry \ad-ˈmä-nə-ˌtōr-ē\ *adj* ♦ : expressing admonition

♦ admonishing, cautionary, warning

ad nau·se·am \ad-ˈnȯ-zē-əm\ *adv* : to a sickening or excessive degree

ado \ə-ˈdü\ *n* **1** ♦ : bustling excitement : FUSS **2** : TROUBLE

♦ commotion, disturbance, furor, fuss, hubbub, hullabaloo, pandemonium, tumult, turmoil, uproar

ado·be \ə-ˈdō-bē\ *n* **1** : sun-dried brick; *also* : clay for making such bricks **2** : a structure made of adobe bricks

ad·o·les·cence \ˌad-ᵊl-ˈes-ᵊns\ *n* : the process or period of growth between childhood and maturity

¹**ad·o·les·cent** \-ᵊnt\ *n* : one that is in the state of adolescence

²**adolescent** *adj* **1** ♦ : of, relating to, or being in adolescence **2** ♦ : emotionally or intellectually immature

♦ [1] immature, juvenile, young, youthful ♦ [2] callow, green, immature, inexperienced, juvenile, raw

adopt \ə-'däpt\ *vb* **1** : to take (a child of other parents) as one's own child **2** ♦ : to take up and practice or use as one's own **3** : to accept formally and put into effect — **adopt·able** \-'däp-tə-bəl\ *adj* — **adopt·er** *n* — **adop·tion** \-'däp-shən\ *n*

♦ borrow, embrace, take up

adop·tive \ə-'däp-tiv\ *adj* : made or acquired by adoption ⟨∼ father⟩ — **adop·tive·ly** *adv*

ador·able \ə-'dȯr-ə-bəl\ *adj* **1** ♦ : worthy of adoration **2** : extremely charming — **ador·able·ness** *n* — **ador·ably** \-blē\ *adv*

♦ darling, dear, endearing, lovable, precious, sweet, winning

adore \ə-'dȯr\ *vb* **adored; ador·ing** **1** ♦ : to worship or honor as a deity or as divine : WORSHIP **2** ♦ : to regard with loving admiration ⟨∼s her family⟩ **3** ♦ : to be extremely fond of often to the point of excess — **ad·o·ra·tion** \ₐa-də-'rā-shən\ *n*

♦ [1] deify, glorify, revere, venerate, worship ♦ [2] cherish, love, worship ♦ [2] delight, enjoy, fancy, like, love, relish, revel ♦ [3] canonize, deify, dote on, idolize, worship

adorn \ə-'dȯrn\ *vb* ♦ : to enhance the appearance of esp. with ornaments

♦ array, beautify, deck, decorate, do, dress, embellish, enrich, garnish, grace, ornament, trim

adorn·ment \-mənt\ *n* ♦ : something that adorns

♦ caparison, decoration, embellishment, frill, garnish, ornament, trim

ad·re·nal \ə-'drēn-ᵊl\ *adj* : of, relating to, or being a pair of endocrine organs (**adrenal glands**) that are located near the kidneys and produce several hormones and esp. epinephrine

adren·a·line \ə-'dren-ᵊl-ən\ *n* : EPINEPHRINE

adrift \ə-'drift\ *adv or adj* **1** : afloat without motive power or moorings **2** : without guidance or purpose

adroit \ə-'drȯit\ *adj* ♦ : having or showing skill, cleverness, or resourcefulness in handling situations — **adroit·ly** *adv*

♦ artful, dexterous, masterful, practiced, skillful, virtuoso

adroit·ness \-nəs\ *n* ♦ : the quality or state of being adroit

♦ cleverness, craft, dexterity, finesse, sleight ♦ adeptness, art, artfulness, artifice, artistry, cleverness, craft, cunning, deftness, masterfulness, skill

ad·sorb \ad-'sȯrb, -'zȯrb\ *vb* : to take up (as molecules of gases) and hold on the surface of a solid or liquid — **ad·sorp·tion** \-'sȯrp-shən, -'zȯrp-\ *n*

ad·u·late \'a-jə-ˌlāt\ *vb* **-lat·ed; -lat·ing** : to flatter or admire excessively — **ad·u·la·tor** \'a-jə-ˌlā-tər\ *n*

ad·u·la·tion \ˌa-jə-'lā-shən\ *n* ♦ : extreme or excessive admiration or flattery

♦ deification, idolatry, worship ♦ blarney, flattery, overpraise

ad·u·la·to·ry \-lə-ˌtȯr-ē\ *adj* ♦ : characterized by or given to adulation

♦ fulsome, unctuous

¹**adult** \ə-'dəlt, 'a-ˌ\ *adj* ♦ : fully developed and mature

♦ full-blown, full-fledged, mature, ripe

²**adult** *n* : one that is adult; *esp* : a human being after an age (as 18) specified by law

adul·ter·ant \ə-'dəl-tə-rənt\ *n* ♦ : something used to adulterate another

♦ contaminant, defilement, impurity, pollutant

adul·ter·ate \ə-'dəl-tə-ˌrāt\ *vb* **-at·ed; -at·ing** ♦ : to make impure by mixing in a foreign or inferior substance — **adul·ter·a·tion** \-ˌdəl-tə-'rā-shən\ *n*

♦ dilute, thin, water, weaken *Ant* enrich, fortify, strengthen

adul·tery \ə-'dəl-t(ə-)rē\ *n, pl* **-ter·ies** : sexual unfaithfulness of a married person — **adul·ter·er** \-tər-ər\ *n* — **adul·ter·ess** \-t(ə-)rəs\ *n* — **adul·ter·ous** \-t(ə-)rəs\ *adj*

adult·hood \ə-'dəlt-ˌhu̇d\ *n* : the state or time of being an adult

ad·um·brate \'a-dəm-ˌbrāt\ *vb* **-brat·ed; -brat·ing** **1** : to foreshadow vaguely : INTIMATE **2** : to suggest or disclose partially **3** : SHADE, OBSCURE — **ad·um·bra·tion** \ₐa-dəm-'brā-shən\ *n*

adv *abbr* **1** adverb **2** advertisement

ad va·lor·em \ₐad-və-'lȯr-əm\ *adj* : imposed at a percentage of the value ⟨an *ad valorem* tax⟩

¹**ad·vance** \əd-'vans\ *vb* **ad·vanced; ad·vanc·ing** **1** ♦ : to assist the progress of **2** ♦ : to bring or move forward **3** ♦ : to promote in rank **4** : to make earlier in time **5** ♦ : to bring for-

ward for notice, consideration, or acceptance : PROPOSE **6** : to supply or furnish in expectation of repayment : LEND **7** : to raise in rate : INCREASE

♦ [1] cultivate, encourage, forward, foster, further, nourish, nurture, promote ♦ [2] fare, forge, get along, go, march, proceed, progress ♦ [3] elevate, promote, raise, upgrade ♦ [5] offer, pose, proffer, propose, propound, suggest, vote

²**advance** *n* **1** ♦ : a forward movement **2** ♦ : a progressive step : IMPROVEMENT **3** : a rise esp. in price or value **4** : OFFER — **in advance** : BEFOREHAND

♦ [1] advancement, furtherance, headway, march, onrush, passage, process, procession, progress, progression *Ant* recession, regression, retrogression ♦ [2] advancement, breakthrough, enhancement, improvement, refinement *Ant* setback

³**advance** *adj* : made, sent, or furnished ahead of time ⟨∼ sales⟩

ad·vanced \əd-'vanst\ *adj* **1** ♦ : far on in time or course ⟨a man ∼ in years⟩ **2** ♦ : being beyond others in progress ⟨a student with ∼ abilities⟩

♦ high, progressive, refined *Ant* backward, low, lower, primitive, rudimentary, undeveloped

ad·vance·ment \-mənt\ *n* ♦ : the action of advancing : the state of being advanced

♦ ascent, elevation, promotion, rise, upgrade *Ant* abasement, demotion, downgrade, reduction ♦ breakthrough, enhancement, improvement, refinement *Ant* setback

ad·van·tage \əd-'van-tij\ *n* **1** ♦ : superiority of position **2** ♦ : something that promotes well-being : BENEFIT **3** : the 1st point won in tennis after deuce — **ad·van·ta·geous·ly** *adv*

♦ [1] better, drop, edge, jump, upper hand, vantage *Ant* disadvantage, handicap, liability ♦ [2] aid, benefit, boon, help

ad·van·ta·geous \ₐad-van-'tā-jəs\ *adj* ♦ : giving an advantage

♦ beneficial, favorable (*or* favourable), helpful, profitable, salutary

ad·vent \'ad-ˌvent\ *n* **1** *cap* : a penitential period beginning four Sundays before Christmas **2** *cap* : the coming of Christ **3** : a coming into being or use

ad·ven·ti·tious \ₐad-vən-'ti-shəs\ *adj* **1** ♦ : coming from another source and not inherent or innate **2** : arising or occurring sporadically or in other than the usual location ⟨∼ buds⟩ — **ad·ven·ti·tious·ly** *adv*

♦ alien, extraneous, extrinsic, foreign

¹**ad·ven·ture** \əd-'ven-chər\ *n* **1** ♦ : a risky undertaking **2** ♦ : a remarkable and exciting experience

♦ experience, happening, time

²**adventure** *vb* **-ven·tured; -ven·tur·ing** \-'ven-ch(ə-)riŋ\ ♦ : to expose to danger or loss : RISK, HAZARD

♦ compromise, gamble with, hazard, imperil, jeopardize, menace, risk, venture

ad·ven·tur·er \əd-'ven-ch(ə-)rər\ *n* **1** : a person who seeks dangerous or exciting experiences **2** : a person who follows a military career for adventure or profit **3** : a person who tries to gain wealth by questionable means

ad·ven·ture·some \əd-'ven-chər-səm\ *adj* : inclined to take risks

ad·ven·tur·ess \əd-'ven-ch(ə-)rəs\ *n* : a woman who seeks dangerous or exciting experiences

ad·ven·tur·ous \-ch(ə-)rəs\ *adj* ♦ : disposed to seek adventure or to cope with the new and unknown

♦ audacious, bold, daring, enterprising, nervy, venturesome

ad·verb \'ad-ˌvərb\ *n* : a word that typically serves as a modifier of a verb, an adjective, or another adverb — **ad·ver·bi·al** \ad-'vər-bē-əl\ *adj* — **ad·ver·bi·al·ly** *adv*

¹**ad·ver·sary** \'ad-və(r)-ˌser-ē\ *n, pl* **-sar·ies** ♦ : one that contends with, opposes, or resists

♦ antagonist, enemy, foe, opponent

²**adversary** *adj* : involving antagonistic parties or interests

ad·verse \ad-'vərs, 'ad-ˌvərs\ *adj* **1** : acting against or in a contrary direction **2** ♦ : opposed to one's interests : UNFAVORABLE — **ad·verse·ly** *adv*

♦ counter, disadvantageous, hostile, inimical, negative, prejudicial, unfavorable (*or* unfavourable), unfriendly, unsympathetic *Ant* advantageous, favorable, friendly, positive, sympathetic, well-disposed

ad·ver·si·ty \ad-'vər-sə-tē\ *n, pl* **-ties** ♦ **:** hard times **:** occurrences of misfortune

♦ knock, misadventure, mischance, misfortune, mishap ♦ asperity, difficulty, hardness, hardship, rigor

ad·vert \ad-'vərt\ *vb* ♦ **:** to call attention in the course of speaking or writing **:** REFER

♦ cite, instance, mention, name, note, notice, quote, refer (to), specify, touch (*on* or *upon*)

ad·ver·tise \'ad-vər-ˌtīz\ *vb* **-tised; -tis·ing** **1 :** INFORM, NOTIFY **2** ♦ **:** to call public attention to esp. in order to sell — **ad·ver·tis·er** *n*

♦ announce, blaze, broadcast, declare, enunciate, placard, post, proclaim, promulgate, publicize, publish, sound

ad·ver·tise·ment \ˌad-vər-'tīz-mənt; əd-'vər-təs-mənt\ *n* **1 :** the act of advertising **2** ♦ **:** a public notice intended to advertise something

♦ announcement, bulletin, notice, notification, release

ad·ver·tis·ing \'ad-vər-ˌtī-ziŋ\ *n* **:** the business of preparing advertisements

ad·vice \əd-'vīs\ *n* **1** ♦ **:** recommendation with regard to a course of action **:** COUNSEL **2 :** INFORMATION, REPORT

♦ counsel, guidance, input

ad·vis·able \əd-'vī-zə-bəl\ *adj* ♦ **:** proper to be done **:** EXPEDIENT — **ad·vis·abil·i·ty** \-ˌvī-zə-'bi-lə-tē\ *n*

♦ desirable, expedient, judicious, politic, prudent, tactical, wise

ad·vise \əd-'vīz\ *vb* **ad·vised; ad·vis·ing** **1 a :** to give advice to **:** COUNSEL **b** ♦ **:** to recommend esp. as the best or most expedient act, course, or policy **2** ♦ **:** to give information or notice to **:** INFORM **3** ♦ **:** to take counsel **:** CONSULT, CONFER

♦ [1b] counsel, suggest ♦ [2] acquaint, apprise, brief, clue, enlighten, familiarize, fill in, inform, instruct, tell, wise ♦ [3] confer, consult, counsel, parley

ad·vised \əd-'vīzd\ *adj* ♦ **:** thought out **:** CONSIDERED ⟨well-*advised*⟩

♦ calculated, deliberate, measured, reasoned, studied, thoughtful, thought-out

ad·vis·ed·ly \əd-'vī-zəd-lē\ *adv* **:** with or after forethought or consideration

ad·vise·ment \əd-'vīz-mənt\ *n* **1** ♦ **:** careful consideration **2 :** the act of advising

♦ consideration, debate, deliberation, study, thought

ad·vis·er *or* **ad·vi·sor** \-'vī-zər\ *n* **:** one that gives advice

ad·vi·so·ry \əd-'vī-zə-rē\ *adj* **1 :** having or exercising power to advise **2 :** containing advice

¹ad·vo·cate \'ad-və-kət, -ˌkāt\ *n* **1** ♦ **:** one who pleads another's cause **2** ♦ **:** one who argues or pleads for a cause or proposal — **ad·vo·ca·cy** \-və-kə-sē\ *n*

♦ [1] attorney, counsel, lawyer ♦ [2] apostle, backer, booster, champion, exponent, friend, promoter, proponent, supporter

²ad·vo·cate \-ˌkāt\ *vb* **-cat·ed; -cat·ing** ♦ **:** to plead in favor of — **ad·vo·ca·tion** \ˌad-və-'kā-shən\ *n*

♦ back, champion, endorse, patronize, support

advt *abbr* advertisement

adze *also* **adz** \'adz\ *n* **:** a tool with a curved blade set at right angles to the handle that is used in shaping wood

AEC *abbr* Atomic Energy Commission

ae·gis \'ē-jəs\ *n* **1** ♦ **:** one that protects **:** SHIELD **2 :** PATRONAGE, SPONSORSHIP

♦ armor (*or* armour), cover, defense (*or* defence), guard, protection, safeguard, screen, security, shield, wall, ward

ae·o·li·an harp \ē-'ō-lē-ən-\ *n* **:** a box with strings that produce musical sounds when the wind blows on them

ae·on *chiefly Brit var of* EON

aer·ate \'a-(ə)r-ˌāt\ *vb* **aer·at·ed; aer·at·ing** **1 :** to supply (blood) with oxygen by respiration **2 :** to supply, impregnate, or combine with a gas and esp. air — **aer·a·tion** \ˌa-(ə)r-'ā-shən\ *n* — **aer·a·tor** \'a(-ə)r-ˌā-tər\ *n*

¹aer·i·al \'ar-ē-əl\ *adj* **1 :** inhabiting, occurring in, or done in the air **2 :** AIRY **3 :** of or relating to aircraft

²aer·i·al \'ar-ē-əl\ *n* **:** ANTENNA 2

ae·ri·al·ist \'ar-ē-ə-list\ *n* **:** a performer of feats above the ground esp. on a trapeze

ae·rie \'ar-ē, 'ir-ē\ *n* **:** a highly placed nest (as of an eagle)

aer·o·bat·ics \ˌar-ə-'ba-tiks\ *n sing or pl* **:** spectacular flying feats and maneuvers

aer·o·bic \ˌa(-ə)r-'rō-bik\ *adj* **1 :** living or active only in the presence of oxygen ⟨~ bacteria⟩ **2 :** involving or increasing oxygen consumption ⟨~ activity⟩; *also* **:** of or relating to aerobics — **aer·o·bi·cal·ly** \-bi-k(ə-)lē\ *adv*

aer·o·bics \-biks\ *n sing or pl* **:** strenuous exercises that produce a marked temporary increase in respiration and heart rate; *also* **:** a system of physical conditioning involving these

aero·drome \'ar-ə-ˌdrōm\ *n, chiefly Brit* **:** AIRPORT

aero·dy·nam·ics \ˌar-ō-dī-'na-miks\ *n* **:** the science dealing with the forces acting on bodies in motion in a gas (as air) — **aero·dy·nam·ic** \-mik\ *also* **aero·dy·nam·i·cal** \-mi-kəl\ *adj* — **aero·dy·nam·i·cal·ly** \-mi-k(ə-)lē\ *adv*

aero·naut \'ar-ə-ˌnȯt\ *n* **:** one who operates or travels in an airship or balloon

aero·nau·tics \ˌar-ə-'nȯ-tiks\ *n* **:** the science of aircraft operation — **aero·nau·ti·cal** \-ti-kəl\ *also* **aero·nau·tic** \-tik\ *adj*

aero·sol \'ar-ə-ˌsäl, -ˌsȯl\ *n* **1 :** a suspension of fine solid or liquid particles in a gas **2 :** a substance (as an insecticide) dispensed from a pressurized container as an aerosol

aero·space \'ar-ō-ˌspās\ *n* **:** the earth's atmosphere and the space beyond — **aerospace** *adj*

aery \'ar-ē\ *adj* **aer·i·er; -est :** having an aerial quality **:** ETHEREAL

aes·thete \'es-ˌthēt\ *n* **:** a person having or affecting sensitivity to beauty esp. in art

aes·thet·ic \es-'the-tik\ *adj* **1 :** of or relating to aesthetics **:** ARTISTIC **2 :** appreciative of the beautiful **3** ♦ **:** pleasing in appearance **:** ATTRACTIVE — **aes·thet·i·cal·ly** \-ti-k(ə-)lē\ *adv*

♦ attractive, beautiful, cute, fair, gorgeous, handsome, knockout, lovely, pretty, ravishing, stunning

aes·thet·ics \-tiks\ *n* **:** a branch of philosophy dealing with the nature, creation, and appreciation of beauty

AF *abbr* **1** air force **2** audio frequency

¹afar \ə-'fär\ *adv* **:** from, at, or to a great distance

²afar *n* **:** a great distance

AFB *abbr* air force base

AFC *abbr* **1** American Football Conference **2** automatic frequency control

AFDC *abbr* Aid to Families with Dependent Children

af·fa·bil·i·ty \ˌa-fə-'bi-lə-tē\ *n* **:** the quality or state of being affable

af·fa·ble \'a-fə-bəl\ *adj* ♦ **:** courteous and agreeable esp. in conversation — **af·fa·bly** \'a-fə-blē\ *adv*

♦ agreeable, amiable, genial, good-natured, gracious, nice, sweet, well-disposed ♦ cordial, genial, gracious, hospitable, sociable

af·fair \ə-'far\ *n* **1 :** something that relates to or involves one **:** MATTER **2 a** ♦ **:** a procedure, action, or occasion only vaguely specified ⟨the most important social ~ of the year⟩ **b :** an object or collection of objects only vaguely specified ⟨their house was a 2-story ~⟩ **3** ♦ **:** a romantic or sexual attachment of limited duration

♦ [2a] blowout, event, fete, function, get-together, party ♦ [2a] circumstance, episode, event, happening, incident, occasion, occurrence, thing ♦ [3] amour, love affair, romance

¹af·fect \ə-'fekt, a-\ *vb* **1 :** to be fond of using or wearing **2** ♦ **:** to put on a pretense of **:** SIMULATE, ASSUME, PRETEND

♦ assume, counterfeit, fake, feign, pretend, profess, put on, sham, simulate

²affect *vb* ♦ **:** to produce an effect on **:** INFLUENCE

♦ impact, impress, influence, move, strike, sway, tell, touch

af·fec·ta·tion \ˌa-ˌfek-'tā-shən\ *n* ♦ **:** an attitude or behavior that is assumed by a person but not genuinely felt

♦ pretense, pretension, pretentiousness

af·fect·ed \a-'fek-təd\ *adj* **1 :** given to affectation **2** ♦ **:** artificially assumed to impress others — **af·fect·ed·ly** *adv*

♦ [1] grandiose, highfalutin, ostentatious, pompous, pretentious ♦ [2] artificial, assumed, fake, false, feigned, phony, put= on, sham, unnatural

af·fect·ing \a-'fek-tiŋ\ *adj* ♦ **:** evoking a strong emotional response ⟨an ~ story⟩ — **af·fect·ing·ly** *adv*

♦ emotional, impressive, moving, poignant, stirring, touching

af·fec·tion \ə-'fek-shən\ *n* **1** ♦ **:** tender attachment **2 :** a condition of the living animal or plant body or of one of its parts that impairs normal function **:** DISEASE — **af·fec·tion·ate·ly** *adv*

♦ attachment, devotion, fondness, love, passion

af·fec·tion·ate \-sh(ə-)nət\ *adj* **1** ♦ : having affection or warm regard : LOVING **2** ♦ : motivated by affection : TENDER

♦ [1, 2] devoted, fond, loving, tender, tenderhearted

af·fer·ent \'a-fə-rənt, -ˌfer-ənt\ *adj* : bearing or conducting inward toward a more central part and esp. a nerve center (as the brain or spinal cord)

af·fi·ance \ə-'fī-əns\ *vb* **-anced; -anc·ing** : BETROTH, ENGAGE

af·fi·da·vit \ˌa-fə-'dā-vət\ *n* : a sworn statement in writing

¹**af·fil·i·ate** \ə-'fi-lē-ˌāt\ *vb* **-at·ed; -at·ing** : to associate as a member or branch

²**af·fil·i·ate** \ə-'fi-lē-ət\ *n* ♦ : an affiliated person or organization

♦ branch, chapter, local

af·fil·i·a·tion \-ˌfi-lē-'ā-shən\ *n* ♦ : the act of affiliating : the state or relation of being affiliated

♦ alliance, association, collaboration, confederation, connection, cooperation, hookup, liaison, partnership, relation, relationship, union

af·fin·i·ty \ə-'fi-nə-tē\ *n, pl* **-ties** **1** : KINSHIP, RELATIONSHIP **2** ♦ : an attraction to or liking for something

♦ bent, devices, disposition, genius, inclination, leaning, partiality, penchant, predilection, predisposition, proclivity, propensity, talent, tendency, turn

af·firm \ə-'fərm\ *vb* **1** : CONFIRM **2** ♦ : to assert positively **3** : to make a solemn and formal declaration or assertion in place of an oath

♦ allege, assert, aver, avouch, avow, claim, contend, declare, insist, maintain, profess, protest, warrant

af·fir·ma·tion \ˌa-fər-'mā-shən\ *n* ♦ : something affirmed : a positive assertion

♦ assertion, avowal, claim, declaration, profession, protestation

¹**af·fir·ma·tive** \ə-'fər-mə-tiv\ *adj* : asserting that the fact is so : POSITIVE

²**affirmative** *n* **1** : an expression of affirmation or assent **2** : the side that upholds the proposition stated in a debate

affirmative action *n* : an active effort to improve the employment or educational opportunities of members of minority groups and women

¹**af·fix** \ə-'fiks\ *vb* **1** ♦ : to attach physically ⟨∼ a stamp to a letter⟩ **2** : to attach in any way : ADD ⟨∼ a signature to the document⟩

♦ attach, fasten, fix

²**af·fix** \'a-ˌfiks\ *n* : one or more sounds or letters attached to the beginning or end of a word that produce a derivative word or an inflectional form

af·fla·tus \ə-'flā-təs\ *n* : divine inspiration

af·flict \ə-'flikt\ *vb* ♦ : to cause pain and distress to

♦ agonize, bedevil, curse, harrow, martyr, persecute, plague, rack, torment, torture

af·flic·tion \-'flik-shən\ *n* ♦ : great suffering

♦ agony, anguish, distress, misery, pain, torment, torture, tribulation, woe

af·flic·tive \ə-'flik-tiv\ *adj* : causing affliction : DISTRESSING — **af·flic·tive·ly** *adv*

af·flu·ence \'a-ˌflü-ən(t)s, a-'flü-\ *n* : abundant supply; *also* : WEALTH, RICHES

af·flu·ent \-ənt\ *adj* ♦ : having a generously sufficient and typically increasing supply of material possessions

♦ flush, loaded, moneyed, opulent, rich, wealthy, well-fixed, well-heeled, well-off, well-to-do

af·ford \ə-'fōrd\ *vb* **1** : to manage to bear or bear the cost of without serious harm or loss **2** : PROVIDE, FURNISH

af·ford·able \ə-'fōr-də-bəl\ *adj* ♦ : that can be afforded : of a cost that can be borne without serious harm or loss

♦ cheap, cut-rate, inexpensive, low, popular, reasonable

af·for·es·ta·tion \a-ˌfōr-ə-'stā-shən\ *n* : the act or process of establishing a forest — **af·for·est** \a-'fōr-əst, -'fär-\ *vb*

af·fray \ə-'frā\ *n, chiefly Brit* : a fight between two or more people in a public place that disturbs the peace : FRAY

af·fright \ə-'frīt\ *vb, archaic* : to make afraid : FRIGHTEN, ALARM — **affright** *n*

¹**af·front** \ə-'frənt\ *vb* **1** ♦ : to insult esp. to the face **2** : CONFRONT

♦ insult, offend, outrage, slight, wound

²**affront** *n* ♦ : a deliberate offense

♦ barb, dart, dig, indignity, insult, name, offense, outrage, put-down, sarcasm, slight, slur, wound

af·ghan \'af-ˌgan\ *n* **1** *cap* : a native or inhabitant of Afghanistan **2** : a blanket or shawl of colored wool knitted or crocheted in sections — **Afghan** *adj*

Afghan hound *n* : any of a breed of tall slim swift hunting dogs with a coat of silky thick hair and a long silky topknot

afi·cio·na·do \ə-ˌfish(ē-)ə-'nä-dō, -sē-ə-\ *n, pl* **-dos** ♦ : a person who likes, knows about, and appreciates a usu. fervently pursued interest or activity : DEVOTEE, FAN

♦ addict, buff, bug, devotee, enthusiast, fan, fanatic, fancier, fiend, freak, lover, maniac, nut

afield \ə-'fēld\ *adv* **1** : to, in, or on the field **2** : away from home **3** ♦ : out of the way : ASTRAY — **afield** *adj*

♦ amiss, astray, awry, wrong

afire \ə-'fīr\ *adj* ♦ : being on fire : BURNING — **afire** *adv*

♦ ablaze, burning, fiery

AFL *abbr* American Football League

aflame \ə-'flām\ *adj* : being on fire — **aflame** *adv*

AFL–CIO *abbr* American Federation of Labor and Congress of Industrial Organizations

afloat \ə-'flōt\ *adj or adv* **1** : borne on or as if on the water **2** : CIRCULATING ⟨rumors were ∼⟩ **3** : ADRIFT

aflut·ter \ə-'flə-tər\ *adj* **1** : FLUTTERING **2** ♦ : nervously excited

♦ anxious, edgy, jittery, jumpy, nervous, perturbed, tense, uneasy

afoot \ə-'fut\ *adv or adj* **1** : on foot **2** ♦ : in action : in progress

♦ ongoing, proceeding

afore·men·tioned \ə-'fōr-ˌmen-chənd\ *adj* : mentioned previously

afore·said \-ˌsed\ *adj* : said or named before

afore·thought \-ˌthôt\ *adj* : PREMEDITATED ⟨with malice ∼⟩

a for·ti·o·ri \ˌä-ˌfōr-tē-'ōr-ē\ *adv* : with even greater reason

afoul of \ə-'faul-əv\ *prep* **1** : in or into conflict with **2** : in or into collision or entanglement with

Afr *abbr* Africa; African

afraid \ə-'frād\ *adj* ♦ : filled with fear or apprehension : FRIGHTENED, FEARFUL

♦ aghast, fearful, scared, terrified *Ant* fearless, unafraid

A–frame \'ā-ˌfrām\ *n* : a building having triangular front and rear walls with the roof reaching to the ground

afresh \ə-'fresh\ *adv* : from a fresh beginning : ANEW, AGAIN

Af·ri·can \'a-fri-kən\ *n* **1** : a native or inhabitant of Africa **2** : a person and esp. a Black person of African ancestry — **African** *adj*

African American *n* : an American of African and esp. of Black African descent — **African American** *or* **Af·ri·can–Amer·i·can** \-ə-'mer-ə-kən\ *adj*

Af·ri·can·ized bee \'a-frə-kə-ˌnīzd-\ *n* : a highly aggressive hybrid honeybee accidentally produced from Brazilian and African stocks that has spread from So. America into Mexico and the southern U.S.

Africanized honeybee *n* : AFRICANIZED BEE

African violet *n* : a tropical African plant widely grown indoors for its velvety fleshy leaves and showy purple, pink, or white flowers

Af·ri·kaans \ˌa-fri-'käns\ *n* : a language developed from 17th century Dutch that is one of the official languages of the Republic of So. Africa

Afro \'a-frō\ *n, pl* **Afros** : a hairstyle of tight curls in a full evenly rounded shape

Af·ro–Amer·i·can \ˌa-frō-ə-'mer-ə-kən\ *n* : AFRICAN AMERICAN — **Afro–American** *adj*

aft \'aft\ *adv* : near, toward, or in the stern of a ship or the tail of an aircraft

AFT *abbr* American Federation of Teachers

¹**af·ter** \'af-tər\ *adv* ♦ : following in time or place : AFTERWARD, SUBSEQUENTLY

♦ afterward, later, subsequently, thereafter *Ant* before, beforehand, earlier, previously

²**after** *prep* **1** : behind in place **2** : later than **3** : in pursuit or search of ⟨he's ∼ your job⟩

³**after** *conj* : following the time when

⁴**after** *adj* **1** ♦ : later in time **2** : located toward the rear

♦ later, posterior, subsequent

after all *adv* **1** : in spite of considerations or expectations to the contrary : NEVERTHELESS **2** : in view of the circumstances

af·ter·birth \'af-tər-,bərth\ n : the placenta and membranes of the fetus that are expelled after childbirth

af·ter·burn·er \-,bər-nər\ n : a device incorporated in the tail pipe of a turbojet engine for injecting fuel into the hot exhaust gases and burning it to provide extra thrust

af·ter·care \-,ker\ n : the care, nursing, or treatment of a convalescent patient

af·ter·deck \-,dek\ n : the rear half of the deck of a ship

af·ter·ef·fect \-ə-,fekt\ n : an effect that follows its cause after an interval

af·ter·glow \-,glō\ n : a glow remaining where a light has disappeared

af·ter·im·age \-,im-ij\ n : a usu. visual sensation continuing after the stimulus causing it has ended

af·ter·life \-,līf\ n ♦ : an existence after death

♦ eternity, hereafter, immortality

af·ter·math \-,math\ n 1 : a second-growth crop esp. of hay 2 ♦ : something produced by a cause or necessarily following from a set of conditions : CONSEQUENCE, EFFECT

♦ consequence, effect, outcome, outgrowth, product, result, resultant, sequence, upshot

af·ter·noon \,af-tər-'nün\ n : the time between noon and evening

af·ter·shave \'af-tər-,shāv\ n : a usu. scented lotion for the face after shaving

af·ter·taste \-,tāst\ n : a sensation (as of flavor) continuing after the stimulus causing it has ended

af·ter–tax \'af-tər-'taks\ adj : remaining after payment of taxes and esp. of income tax ⟨an ∼ profit⟩

af·ter·thought \-,thót\ n : a later thought; also : something thought of later

af·ter·ward \-wərd\ or **af·ter·wards** \-wərdz\ adv ♦ : at a later time

♦ after, later, subsequently, thereafter

Ag symbol silver

AG abbr 1 adjutant general 2 attorney general

again \ə-'gen, -'gin\ adv 1 ♦ : once more : ANEW 2 : on the other hand 3 ♦ : in addition : BESIDES

♦ [1] anew, over Ant nevermore ♦ [3] additionally, also, besides, further, furthermore, likewise, more, moreover, then, too, withal, yet

against \ə-'genst\ prep 1 : in opposition to 2 : directly opposite to : FACING 3 : as defense from 4 a : in the direction of and into contact with ⟨threw him ∼ the ropes⟩ b : in contact with ⟨leaning ∼ the wall⟩

1aga·pe \ä-'gä-pā, 'ä-gə-,pā\ n : unselfish unconditional love for another

2agape \ə-'gāp\ adj or adv ♦ : being in a state of wonder or expectation

♦ agog, anticipatory, expectant

agar \'ä-,gär\ n 1 : a jellylike substance extracted from a red alga and used esp. as a gelling and stabilizing agent in foods 2 : a culture medium containing agar

agar–agar \,ä-,gär-'ä-,gär\ n : AGAR

ag·ate \'a-gət\ n 1 : a striped or clouded quartz 2 : a playing marble of agate or of glass

aga·ve \ə-'gä-vē\ n : any of a genus of spiny-leaved plants (as a century plant) related to the amaryllis

agcy abbr agency

1age \'āj\ n 1 ♦ : the length of time during which a being or thing has lived or existed 2 : the time of life at which some particular qualification is achieved; esp : MAJORITY 3 : the latter part of life 4 ♦ : a long time 5 : a period in history

♦ [1] epoch, era, period, time ♦ [4] cycle, eon (or aeon), eternity

2age vb aged; ag·ing or age·ing 1 : to grow old or cause to grow old 2 ♦ : to become or cause to become mature or mellow

♦ develop, grow, grow up, mature, progress, ripen

-age n suffix 1 : aggregate : collection ⟨trackage⟩ 2 : action : process ⟨haulage⟩ 3 : cumulative result of ⟨breakage⟩ 4 : rate of ⟨dosage⟩ 5 : house or place of ⟨orphanage⟩ 6 : state : rank ⟨vassalage⟩ 7 : fee : charge ⟨postage⟩

aged \'ā-jəd for 1; 'ājd for 2\ adj 1 : of advanced age 2 : having attained a specified age ⟨a man ∼ 40 years⟩

age·ism \'ā-ji-zəm\ n : discrimination against persons of a particular age and esp. the elderly

age·less \'āj-ləs\ adj 1 : not growing old or showing the effects of age 2 ♦ : not affected by time : having infinite duration : TIMELESS ⟨∼ truths⟩

♦ abiding, continuing, dateless, enduring, eternal, everlasting, immortal, imperishable, lasting, perennial, perpetual, timeless, undying

agen·cy \'ā-jən-sē\ n, pl **-cies** 1 ♦ : one through which something is accomplished : INSTRUMENTALITY 2 : the office or function of an agent 3 : an establishment doing business for another 4 : an administrative division (as of a government)

♦ agent, instrument, instrumentality, machinery, means, medium, organ, vehicle

agen·da \ə-'jen-də\ n ♦ : a list of things to be done : PROGRAM

♦ calendar, docket, program, schedule, timetable

agen·der \ā-'jen-dər\ adj : of, relating to, or being a person whose gender identity is genderless or neutral

agent \'ā-jənt\ n 1 : one that acts 2 ♦ : something that produces or is capable of producing an effect : MEANS, INSTRUMENT 3 ♦ : a person acting or doing business for another

♦ [2] agency, instrument, instrumentality, machinery, means, medium, organ, vehicle ♦ [3] attorney, commissary, delegate, deputy, envoy, factor, proxy, representative

Agent Orange n : an herbicide widely used in the Vietnam War that is composed of 2,4-D and 2,4,5-T and contains a toxic contaminant

agent pro·vo·ca·teur \'ä-,zhäⁿ-prō-,vä-kə-'tər, 'ä-jənt-\ n, pl **agents provocateurs** \'ä-,zhäⁿ-prō-,väk-ə-'tər, 'ä-jənts-prō-\ : a person hired to infiltrate a group and incite its members to illegal action

age–old \'āj-'ōld\ adj ♦ : having existed for ages : ANCIENT

♦ ancient, antediluvian, antique, dateless, old, venerable

ag·er·a·tum \,a-jə-'rā-təm\ n, pl **-tums** : any of a large genus of tropical American plants that are related to the daisies and have small showy heads of blue or white flowers

Ag·ge·us \a-'gē-əs\ n : HAGGAI

1ag·glom·er·ate \ə-'glä-mə-,rāt\ vb **-at·ed; -at·ing** ♦ : to gather into a mass : CLUSTER

♦ ball, cluster, conglomerate, roll, round, wad

2ag·glom·er·ate \-rət\ n : rock composed of volcanic fragments

ag·glom·er·a·tion \ə-,glä-mə-'rā-shən\ n ♦ : a cluster of disparate elements

♦ assortment, clutter, jumble, medley, mélange, miscellany, motley, muddle, variety, welter

ag·glu·ti·nate \ə-'glüt-ᵊn-,āt\ vb **-nat·ed; -nat·ing** 1 : to cause to adhere : gather into a group or mass 2 : to cause (as red blood cells or bacteria) to collect into clumps — **ag·glu·ti·na·tion** \-,glüt-ᵊn-'ā-shən\ n

ag·gran·dise Brit var of AGGRANDIZE

ag·gran·dize \ə-'gran-,dīz, 'a-grən-\ vb **-dized; -diz·ing** 1 ♦ : to make great or greater 2 ♦ : to enhance the power, wealth, position, or reputation of — **ag·gran·dize·ment** \ə-'gran-dəz-mənt, -,dīz-; ,a-grən-'dīz-\ n

♦ [1] add, amplify, augment, boost, compound, enlarge, escalate, expand, extend, increase, multiply, raise, swell, up ♦ [2] dignify, ennoble, exalt, glorify, magnify

ag·gra·vate \'a-grə-,vāt\ vb **-vat·ed; -vat·ing** 1 : to make more severe : INTENSIFY 2 ♦ : to rouse to displeasure or anger by usu. persistent and often petty goading : IRRITATE

♦ annoy, bother, bug, grate, irk, irritate, nettle, peeve, persecute, pique, put out, rile, vex

aggravating adj ♦ : arousing displeasure, impatience, or anger

♦ annoying, bothersome, frustrating, galling, irksome, irritating, pesty, vexatious

ag·gra·va·tion \,a-grə-'vā-shən\ n ♦ : the act, action, or result of aggravating

♦ annoyance, bother, harassment, vexation

1ag·gre·gate \'a-gri-gət\ adj : formed by the gathering of units into one mass

2ag·gre·gate \-,gāt\ vb **-gat·ed; -gat·ing** : to collect into one mass

3ag·gre·gate \-gət\ n 1 : a mass or body of units or parts somewhat loosely associated with one another 2 ♦ : the whole amount

♦ full, sum, total, totality, whole

ag·gre·ga·tion \,a-gri-'gā-shən\ n 1 : a group, body, or mass composed of many distinct parts 2 : the collecting of units or parts into a mass or whole

ag·gres·sion \ə-'gre-shən\ n 1 ♦ : an unprovoked attack

2 : the practice of making attacks   **3 ♦ :** hostile, injurious, or destructive behavior or outlook esp. when caused by frustration

♦ [1] assault, attack, charge, offense (or offence), offensive, onset, onslaught, raid, rush, strike ♦ [3] aggressiveness, belligerence, fight, militancy, pugnacity, truculence

ag·gres·sive \ə-'gre-siv\ adj   **1 ♦ :** tending toward or exhibiting aggression; esp : marked by combative readiness   **2 ♦ :** marked by driving energy or initiative : ENTERPRISING   **3 :** more intensive or comprehensive esp. in dosage or extent — **ag·gres·sive·ly** adv

♦ [1] argumentative, bellicose, belligerent, combative, contentious, militant, pugnacious, quarrelsome, scrappy, ·truculent, warlike ♦ [2] ambitious, assertive, enterprising, fierce, go-getting, high-pressure, militant, self-assertive Ant unaggressive, unambitious, unassertive, unenterprising

ag·gres·sive·ness n ♦ : the quality or state of being aggressive

♦ aggression, belligerence, fight, militancy, pugnacity, truculence ♦ ambition, drive, enterprise, go, hustle, initiative

ag·gres·sor \-'gre-sər\ n : one that commits or practices aggression

ag·grieve \ə-'grēv\ vb **ag·grieved; ag·griev·ing   1 :** to cause grief to   **2 :** to inflict injury on : WRONG

aggrieved adj ♦ : troubled or distressed in spirit

♦ discontent, discontented, dissatisfied, malcontent

aghast \ə-'gast\ adj ♦ : struck with amazement or horror

♦ afraid, terrified

ag·ile \'a-jəl\ adj ♦ : able to move quickly and easily

♦ graceful, light, lissome, lithe, nimble, spry

agil·i·ty \ə-'ji-lə-tē\ n ♦ : the quality or state of being agile

♦ deftness, dexterity, nimbleness, sleight

ag·i·tate \'a-jə-,tāt\ vb **-tat·ed; -tat·ing   1 ♦ :** to move or cause to move with an irregular rapid motion   **2 ♦ :** to excite and often trouble the mind or feelings of : DISTURB   **3 :** to discuss earnestly   **4 :** to attempt to arouse public feeling

♦ [1] convulse, jolt, jounce, quake, quiver, shake, shudder, vibrate, wobble ♦ [2] bother, concern, discompose, disquiet, distress, disturb, perturb, unsettle, upset, worry

agitated adj ♦ : troubled in mind

♦ feverish, frenzied, heated, hectic, overactive, overwrought

ag·i·ta·tion \,a-jə-'tā-shən\ n ♦ : the act or state of agitating or being agitated

♦ anxiety, apprehension, care, concern, disquiet, nervousness, perturbation, uneasiness, worry

ag·i·ta·tor \'a-jə-,tā-tər\ n ♦ : one that agitates

♦ demagogue, firebrand, incendiary, inciter, rabble-rouser

ag·it·prop \'a-jət-,präp\ n : political propaganda promulgated esp. through the arts

agleam \ə-'glēm\ adj : GLEAMING
aglit·ter \ə-'gli-tər\ adj : GLITTERING
aglow \ə-'glō\ adj ♦ : glowing esp. with warmth or excitement : GLOWING

♦ beaming, glowing, radiant, sunny

ag·nos·tic \ag-'näs-tik\ adj : of or relating to the belief that the existence of any ultimate reality (as God) is unknown and prob. unknowable — **agnostic** n — **ag·nos·ti·cism** \-'näs-tə-,si-zəm\ n

ago \ə-'gō\ adj or adv : earlier than the present time
agog \ə-'gäg\ adj ♦ : full of intense interest or excitement

♦ agape, anticipatory, expectant ♦ anxious, ardent, athirst, avid, eager, enthusiastic, keen

a–go–go \ä-'gō-,gō\ adj : GO-GO
ag·o·nise Brit var of AGONIZE
ag·o·nize \'a-gə-,nīz\ vb **-nized; -niz·ing** ♦ : to suffer or cause to suffer agony

♦ afflict, bedevil, curse, harrow, martyr, persecute, plague, rack, torment, torture ♦ bleed, feel, grieve, hurt, mourn, sorrow, suffer

agonizing adj ♦ : causing agony

♦ bitter, cruel, excruciating, galling, grievous, harrowing, harsh, hurtful, painful, tortuous

ag·o·niz·ing·ly \-lē\ adv ♦ : in a manner that is agonizing

♦ bitterly, grievously, hard, sorrowfully, unhappily, wretchedly

ag·o·ny \'a-gə-nē\ n, pl **-nies   1 ♦ :** extreme pain of mind or body   **2 :** a strong sudden display (as of joy or delight) : OUTBURST

♦ affliction, anguish, distress, misery, pain, torment, torture, tribulation, woe

ag·o·ra·pho·bia \,a-gə-rə-'fō-bē-ə\ n : abnormal fear of being in a helpless, embarrassing, or inescapable situation characterized esp. by avoidance of open or public places — **ag·o·ra·pho·bic** \-'fō-bik, -'fä-\ adj or n

agr abbr agricultural; agriculture
agrar·i·an \ə-'grer-ē-ən\ adj   **1 :** of or relating to land or its ownership ⟨∼ reforms⟩   **2 :** of or relating to farmers or farming interests — **agrarian** n — **agrar·i·an·ism** n

agree \ə-'grē\ vb **agreed; agree·ing   1 ♦ :** to concur in (as an opinion) : ADMIT, CONCEDE   **2 ♦ :** to be similar : CORRESPOND   **3 ♦ :** to express agreement or approval   **4 ♦ :** to be in harmony   **5 :** to settle by common consent   **6 :** to be fitting or healthful : SUIT

♦ [1, 3] acknowledge, admit, allow, concede, confess, grant, own ♦ [2] accord, check, coincide, comport, conform, correspond, dovetail, fit, go, harmonize, jibe, square, tally ♦ [3] accede, acquiesce, assent, consent, subscribe (to) ♦ [4] blend, conform, coordinate, harmonize

agree·able \ə-'grē-ə-bəl\ adj   **1 ♦ :** pleasing to the mind or senses esp. as according well with one's tastes or needs   **2 :** ready to consent   **3 :** being in harmony

♦ [1] all right, alright, fine, good, OK, palatable, satisfactory ♦ [1] congenial, delightful, enjoyable, felicitous, good, pleasant, pleasurable, satisfying ♦ [1] affable, amiable, genial, good-natured, gracious, nice, sweet, well-disposed ♦ [3] amicable, compatible, congenial, harmonious, kindred, unanimous, united

agree·able·ness \-nəs\ n ♦ : the quality or state of being agreeable

♦ amenity, amiability, geniality, graciousness, niceness, pleasantness, sweetness

agree·ably \-blē\ adv ♦ : in an agreeable manner

♦ delightfully, favorably (or favourably), felicitously, gloriously, nicely, pleasantly, pleasingly, satisfyingly, splendidly, well

agree·ment \ə-'grē-mənt\ n   **1 ♦ :** harmony of opinion or action   **2 ♦ :** mutual understanding or arrangement; also : a document containing such an arrangement

♦ [1] accord, conformity, consonance, harmony, tune ♦ [1] accord, concurrence, consensus, unanimity Ant disagreement, dissent ♦ [2] accord, bargain, compact, contract, convention, covenant, deal, pact, settlement, understanding

ag·ri·busi·ness \'a-grə-,biz-nəs, -,nəz\ n : an industry engaged in the manufacture and sale of farm equipment and supplies and in the production, processing, storage, and sale of farm commodities

agric abbr agricultural; agriculture
ag·ri·cul·tur·al \,a-gri-'kəl-ch(ə-)rəl\ adj : of, relating to, used in, or concerned with agriculture
ag·ri·cul·ture \'a-gri-,kəl-chər\ n : the science, art, or practice of cultivating the soil, producing crops, and raising livestock and in varying degrees the preparation and marketing of the resulting products : FARMING, HUSBANDRY
ag·ri·cul·tur·ist \-ch(ə-)rist\ or **ag·ri·cul·tur·al·ist** \-ch(ə-)rə-list\ n ♦ : one that is trained in or practices agriculture

♦ cultivator, farmer, grower, planter, tiller

agron·o·mist \ə-'grä-nə-mist\ n : one that is trained in or practices agronomy
agron·o·my \ə-'grä-nə-mē\ n : a branch of agriculture that deals with the raising of crops and the care of the soil — **ag·ro·nom·ic** \,a-grə-'nä-mik\ adj
aground \ə-'graünd\ adv or adj : on or onto the bottom or shore ⟨ran ∼⟩
agt abbr agent
ague \'ā-gyü\ n : a fever (as malaria) with recurrent chills and sweating
ahead \ə-'hed\ adv or adj   **1 ♦ :** in or toward the front   **2 ♦ :** into or for the future ⟨plan ∼⟩   **3 :** in or toward a more advantageous position   **4 ♦ :** at or to an earlier time

♦ [1, 2] along, forth, forward, on, onward ♦ [4] before, beforehand, previously Ant after, afterward, later

ahead of prep   **1 ♦ :** in front or advance of   **2 :** in excess of : ABOVE

♦ before, ere, of, previous to, prior to, to

AHL *abbr* American Hockey League

ahoy \ə-'hòi\ *interj* — used in hailing ⟨ship ∼⟩

AI *abbr* artificial intelligence

¹aid \'ād\ *vb* ♦ : to provide with what is useful in achieving an end : ASSIST

♦ abet, assist, back, help, prop, support

²aid *n* **1** ♦ : an act or instance of help given : ASSISTANCE **2** ♦ : an assisting person, group, or device : ASSISTANT

♦ [1] assist, assistance, backing, boost, help, lift, support ♦ [2] apprentice, assistant, deputy, helper, helpmate, mate, sidekick ♦ [2] advantage, benefit, boon, help

AID *abbr* Agency for International Development

aide \'ād\ *n* : a person who acts as an assistant; *esp* : a military officer assisting a superior

aide–de–camp \ˌād-di-'kamp, -'käⁿ\ *n, pl* **aides–de–camp** \ˌādz-di-\ : AIDE

AIDS \'ādz\ *n* : a serious disease of the human immune system that is characterized by severe reduction in the numbers of helper T cells and increased vulnerability to life-threatening illnesses and that is caused by infection with HIV commonly transmitted in infected blood and in bodily secretions

AIDS–related complex *n* : a group of symptoms (as fever, weight loss, and lymphadenopathy) that is associated with the presence of antibodies to HIV and is followed by the development of AIDS in a certain proportion of cases

AIDS virus *n* : HIV

ai·grette \ā-'gret, 'ā-\ *n* : a plume or decorative tuft for the head

ail \'āl\ *vb* **1** ♦ : to be the matter with : be trouble to **2** : to be unwell

♦ agitate, bother, concern, discompose, disquiet, distress, disturb, exercise, freak out, perturb, undo, unhinge, unsettle, upset, worry

ai·lan·thus \ā-'lan-thəs\ *n* : any of a genus of Asian trees or shrubs with pinnate leaves and ill-scented greenish flowers

ai·le·ron \'ā-lə-ˌrän\ *n* : a movable part of an airplane wing used in banking

ail·ment \'āl-mənt\ *n* ♦ : a bodily disorder

♦ bug, complaint, complication, condition, disease, disorder, fever, ill, illness, infirmity, malady, sickness, trouble

¹aim \'ām\ *vb* **1** : to point a weapon at an object **2** ♦ : to direct one's efforts : ASPIRE **3** ♦ : to direct to or toward a specified object or goal

♦ [2] aspire, contemplate, design, intend, mean, meditate, plan, propose ♦ [3] bend, cast, direct, head, level, set, train

²aim *n* **1** : the pointing of a weapon at an object **2** : the ability to hit a target **3** ♦ : a clearly directed intent or purpose : OBJECT, PURPOSE — **aim·less·ly** *adv* — **aim·less·ness** *n*

♦ ambition, aspiration, design, end, goal, intent, object, objective, plan, purpose

aim·less \-ləs\ *adj* ♦ : without aim or purpose

♦ arbitrary, desultory, erratic, haphazard, random, scattered, stray

AIM *abbr* American Indian Movement

ain't \'ānt\ **1** : are not **2** : is not **3** : am not — though disapproved by many and more common in less educated speech, used in both speech and writing to catch attention and to gain emphasis

Ai·nu \'ī-nü\ *n, pl* **Ainu** *or* **Ainus** **1** : a member of an Indigenous people of northern Japan **2** : the language of the Ainu people

¹air \'ar\ *n* **1** : the gaseous mixture surrounding the earth **2** ♦ : a light breeze **3** ♦ : a sweet or agreeable succession or arrangement of sounds : MELODY, TUNE **4** ♦ : the outward appearance of a person or thing : apparent character **5** *usu* **airs** ♦ : an artificial manner **6** : COMPRESSED AIR ⟨∼ sprayer⟩ **7** : AIRCRAFT ⟨∼ patrol⟩ **8** : AVIATION ⟨∼ safety⟩ **9** : the medium of transmission of radio waves; *also* : RADIO, TELEVISION

♦ [2] breath, breeze, puff, waft, zephyr ♦ [3] lay, melody, song, strain, tune, warble ♦ [4] atmosphere, aura, climate, flavor (*or* flavour), mood, note, temper ♦ **airs** [5] act, facade, front, guise, masquerade, pose, pretense, put-on, semblance, show

²air *vb* **1** : to expose to the air **2** ♦ : to expose to public view or bring to public notice **3** : to broadcast on radio or television

♦ express, give, look, sound, state, vent, voice

air·bag \'er-ˌbag\ *n* : a bag designed to inflate automatically to protect automobile occupants in case of collision

air·boat \'ar-ˌbōt\ *n* : a shallow-draft boat driven by an airplane propeller

air·borne \-ˌbȯrn\ *adj* : done or being in the air

air brake *n* **1** : a brake operated by a piston driven by compressed air **2** : a surface projected into the airflow to lower an airplane's speed

air·brush \'ar-ˌbrəsh\ *n* : a device for applying a fine spray (as of paint) by compressed air — **airbrush** *vb*

air–con·di·tion \ˌar-kən-'di-shən\ *vb* : to equip with an apparatus for filtering air and controlling its humidity and temperature — **air con·di·tion·er** \-'di-sh(ə-)nər\ *n*

air·craft \'ar-ˌkraft\ *n, pl* **aircraft** : a vehicle for traveling through the air

aircraft carrier *n* : a warship with a deck on which airplanes can be launched and landed

air·drop \'ar-ˌdräp\ *n* : delivery of cargo or personnel by parachute from an airplane in flight — **air–drop** *vb*

Aire·dale terrier \'ar-ˌdāl-\ *n* : any of a breed of large terriers with a hard wiry coat

air·fare \'ar-ˌfar\ *n* : fare for travel by airplane

air·field \-ˌfēld\ *n* : an area of land from which aircraft operate : AIRPORT

air·flow \-ˌflō\ *n* : the motion of air relative to a body in it

air·foil \-ˌfȯil\ *n* : an airplane surface designed to produce reaction forces from the air through which it moves

air force *n* : the military organization of a nation for air warfare

air·frame \'ar-ˌfrām\ *n* : the structure of an aircraft, rocket, or missile without the power plant

air·freight \-'frāt\ *n* : freight transport by aircraft in volume; *also* : the charge for this service

air gun *n* **1** : a gun operated by compressed air **2** : a hand tool that works by compressed air; *esp* : AIRBRUSH

air·head \'ar-ˌhed\ *n* : a mindless or stupid person

air lane *n* : AIRWAY 1

air·lift \'ar-ˌlift\ *n* : transportation (as of supplies or passengers) by aircraft — **airlift** *vb*

air·line \-ˌlīn\ *n* : a transportation system using airplanes

air·lin·er \-ˌlī-nər\ *n* : a large passenger airplane operated by an airline

air lock *n* : an airtight chamber separating areas of different pressure

air·mail \'ar-ˌmāl\ *n* : the system of transporting mail by aircraft; *also* : mail so transported — **airmail** *vb*

air·man \-mən\ *n* **1** ♦ : a civilian or military pilot, aviator, or aviation technician : AVIATOR, PILOT **2** : an enlisted person in the air force ranking next below an airman first class

♦ aviator, flier, pilot

airman basic *n* : an enlisted person of the lowest rank in the air force

airman first class *n* : an enlisted person in the air force ranking next below a senior airman

air mass *n* : a large horizontally homogeneous body of air

air·mo·bile \'ar-ˌmō-bəl, -ˌbēl\ *adj* : of, relating to, or being a military unit whose members are transported to combat areas usu. by helicopter

air·plane \-ˌplān\ *n* : a powered heavier-than-air aircraft that has fixed wings from which it derives lift

airplane mode *n* : an operating mode for an electronic device (as a smartphone) in which the device does not connect to wireless networks and cannot send or receive communications (as calls) or access the Internet but is usable for other functions

air·play \-ˌplā\ *n* : the playing of a musical recording on the air by a radio station

air pocket *n* : a condition of the atmosphere that causes an airplane to drop suddenly

air police *n* : the military police of an air force

air·port \'ar-ˌpȯrt\ *n* : a place from which aircraft operate that usu. has paved runways and a terminal

air raid *n* : an attack by armed airplanes on a surface target

air·ship \'ar-ˌship\ *n* : a lighter-than-air aircraft having propulsion and steering systems

air·sick \-ˌsik\ *adj* : affected with motion sickness associated with flying — **air·sick·ness** *n*

air·space \-ˌspās\ *n* : the space above a nation and under its jurisdiction

air·speed \-ˌspēd\ *n* : the speed of an object (as an airplane) with relation to the surrounding air

air·strip \-ˌstrip\ *n* : a runway without normal airport facilities

air·tight \'ar-'tīt\ *adj* **1** : so tightly sealed that no air can enter or escape **2** : leaving no opening for attack

air–to–air *adj* : launched from one airplane in flight at another; *also* : involving aircraft in flight

air·waves \'ar-ˌwāvz\ *n pl* : AIR 9

air·way \-ˌwā\ *n* **1** : a regular route for airplanes **2** : AIRLINE

air·wor·thy \-₁wər-_thē_\ *adj* : fit for operation in the air ⟨an ∼ plane⟩ — **air·wor·thi·ness** *n*

airy \'ar-ē\ *adj* **air·i·er; -est** **1** : high in the air : LOFTY **2** : lacking in reality : EMPTY **3** ♦ : exceptionally light, delicate, or refined **4** : BREEZY

♦ ethereal, fluffy, light *Ant* heavy, leaden

aisle \'īl\ *n* **1** : the side of a church nave separated by piers from the nave proper **2** : a passage between sections of seats

ajar \ə-'jär\ *adj or adv* : partly open

AK *abbr* Alaska

aka *abbr* also known as

AKC *abbr* American Kennel Club

akim·bo \ə-'kim-bō\ *adj or adv* : having the hand on the hip and the elbow turned outward

akin \ə-'kin\ *adj* **1** ♦ : related by blood **2** ♦ : essentially similar or related

♦ [1] kindred, related ♦ [2] alike, analogous, comparable, correspondent, like, parallel, similar

Al *symbol* aluminum

AL *abbr* **1** Alabama **2** American League **3** American Legion

¹-al *adj suffix* : of, relating to, or characterized by ⟨direction*al*⟩

²-al *n suffix* : action : process ⟨rehears*al*⟩

Ala *abbr* Alabama

al·a·bas·ter \'a-lə-₁bas-tər\ *n* **1** : a compact fine-textured usu. white and translucent gypsum often carved into objects (as vases) **2** : a hard translucent calcite

à la carte \₁a-lə-'kärt, ₁ä-\ *adv or adj* : with a separate price for each item on the menu

alac·ri·ty \ə-'la-krə-tē\ *n* ♦ : cheerful readiness

♦ gameness, goodwill, willingness

à la mode \₁a-lə-'mōd, ₁ä-\ *adj* **1** ♦ : conforming to the custom, fashion, or established mode : STYLISH **2** : topped with ice cream

♦ chic, fashionable, in, modish, sharp, smart, snappy, stylish

¹alarm \ə-'lärm\ *also* **ala·rum** \ə-'lär-əm, -'lar-\ *n* **1** ♦ : a warning signal or device **2** ♦ : the terror caused by sudden danger

♦ [1] admonition, alert, caution, notice, warning ♦ [2] anxiety, apprehension, dread, fear, fright, horror, panic, terror, trepidation

²alarm *also* **alarum** *vb* **1** : to warn of danger **2** ♦ : to strike with fear : FRIGHTEN

♦ frighten, horrify, panic, scare, shock, spook, startle, terrify, terrorize

alarm·ist \ə-'lär-mist\ *n* : a person who alarms others esp. needlessly

alas \ə-'las\ *interj* — used to express unhappiness, pity, or concern

al·ba·core \'al-bə-₁kōr\ *n, pl* **-core** *or* **-cores** : a large tuna that is a source of canned tuna

Al·ba·nian \al-'bā-nē-ən\ *n* : a native or inhabitant of Albania

al·ba·tross \'al-bə-₁trós, -₁träs\ *n, pl* **-tross** *or* **-tross·es** : any of a family of large web-footed seabirds

al·be·do \al-'bē-(₁)dō\ *n, pl* **-dos** : the fraction of incident radiation that is reflected by a body or surface

al·be·it \òl-'bē-ət, al-\ *conj* ♦ : even though : ALTHOUGH

♦ although, howbeit, though, when, while

al·bi·no \al-'bī-nō\ *n, pl* **-nos** : a person or nonhuman mammal lacking coloring matter in the skin, hair, and eyes — **al·bi·nism** \'al-bə-₁ni-zəm\ *n*

al·bum \'al-bəm\ *n* **1** : a book with blank pages used for making a collection (as of stamps) **2** : one or more recordings (as on tape or disk) produced as a single unit **3** ♦ : a collection usu. in book form of literary selections, musical compositions, or pictures : ANTHOLOGY

♦ anthology, compilation, miscellany

al·bu·men \al-'byü-mən\ *n* **1** : the white of an egg **2** : ALBUMIN

al·bu·min \al-'byü-mən\ *n* : any of numerous water-soluble proteins of blood, milk, egg white, and plant and animal tissues

al·bu·min·ous \al-'byü-mə-nəs\ *adj* : containing or resembling albumen or albumin

alc *abbr* alcohol

al·cal·de \al-'käl-dē\ *n* : the chief administrative and judicial officer of a Spanish or Spanish-American town

al·ca·zar \al-'kä-zər, -'ka-\ *n* : a Spanish fortress or palace

al·che·my \'al-kə-mē\ *n* : medieval chemistry chiefly concerned with efforts to turn base metals into gold — **al·che·mist** \'al-kə-mist\ *n*

al·co·hol \'al-kə-₁hól\ *n* **1** : a colorless flammable liquid that is the intoxicating agent in fermented and distilled liquors **2** : any of various carbon compounds similar to alcohol **3** ♦ : beverages containing alcohol

♦ booze, drink, intoxicant, liquor, moonshine, spirits

¹al·co·hol·ic \₁al-kə-'hò-lik, -'hä-\ *adj* **1** : of, relating to, caused by, or containing alcohol **2** : affected with alcoholism — **al·co·hol·i·cal·ly** \-li-k(ə-)lē\ *adv*

²alcoholic *n* ♦ : a person affected with alcoholism

♦ drunk, drunkard, inebriate, soak, sot, souse, tippler

al·co·hol·ism \'al-kə-₁hò-₁li-zəm\ *n* : continued excessive and usu. uncontrollable use of alcoholic drinks; *also* : a complex chronic psychological and nutritional disorder associated with such use

al·cove \'al-₁kōv\ *n* **1** : a nook or small recess opening off a larger room **2** ♦ : a niche or arched opening (as in a wall)

♦ niche, nook, recess

ald *abbr* alderman

al·der \'òl-dər\ *n* : a tree or shrub related to the birches and growing in wet areas

al·der·man \'òl-dər-mən\ *n* : a member of a city legislative body

ale \'āl\ *n* : an alcoholic beverage brewed from malt and hops that is usu. more bitter than beer

ale·a·tor·ic \₁ā-lē-ə-'tòr-ik\ *adj* : characterized by chance or random elements ⟨∼ music⟩

ale·a·to·ry \'ā-lē-ə-₁tōr-ē\ *adj* : ALEATORIC

alee \ə-'lē\ *adv* : on or toward the lee

ale·house \'āl-₁haùs\ *n* : a place where ale is sold to be drunk on the premises

¹alert \ə-'lərt\ *adj* **1** ♦ : watchful against danger **2** ♦ : quick to perceive and act — **alert·ly** *adv*

♦ [1] attentive, awake, vigilant, watchful, wide-awake ♦ [2] brainy, bright, brilliant, clever, intelligent, keen, nimble, quick, quick-witted, sharp, smart ♦ [2] expeditious, prompt, quick, ready, willing

²alert *n* **1** ♦ : a warning signal or device : ALARM **2** : the period during which an alert is in effect

♦ admonition, alarm, caution, notice, warning

³alert *vb* **1** ♦ : to call to a state of readiness : WARN **2** : to make aware of

♦ caution, forewarn, warn

alert·ness \-nəs\ *n* ♦ : the quality or state of being alert

♦ attentiveness, lookout, vigilance, watch

Aleut \₁a-lē-'üt, ə-'lüt\ *n* **1** : a member of a people of the Aleutian and Shumagin islands and the western part of Alaska Peninsula **2** : the language of the Aleuts

ale·wife \'āl-₁wīf\ *n, pl* **ale·wives** \-₁wīvz\ : a food fish of the herring family abundant esp. on the Atlantic coast

Al·ex·an·dri·an \₁al-ig-'zan-drē-ən\ *adj* **1** : of or relating to Alexander the Great **2** : HELLENISTIC

al·ex·an·drine \-'zan-drən\ *n, often cap* : a line of six iambic feet

al·fal·fa \al-'fal-fə\ *n* : a leguminous plant widely grown for hay and forage

al·fres·co \al-'fres-kō\ *adj or adv* : taking place in the open air

alg *abbr* algebra

al·ga \'al-gə\ *n, pl* **al·gae** \'al-(₁)jē\ : any of a group of lower plants having chlorophyll but no vascular system and including seaweeds and related freshwater plants — **al·gal** \-gəl\ *adj*

al·ge·bra \'al-jə-brə\ *n* : a branch of mathematics using symbols (as letters) to explore the relationships between numbers and the operations used to work with them — **al·ge·bra·ic** \₁al-jə-'brā-ik\ *adj* — **al·ge·bra·i·cal·ly** \-'brā-ə-k(ə-)lē\ *adv*

Al·ge·ri·an \al-'jir-ē-ən\ *n* : a native or inhabitant of Algeria — **Algerian** *adj*

Al·gon·qui·an \al-'gän-kwē-ən, -'gän-\ *or* **Al·gon·quin** \-kwən\ *n* **1** *usu* Algonquin : a First Nations people of the Ottawa River valley **2** *usu* Algonquian : a family of languages spoken by Indigenous peoples of eastern and central No. America

al·go·rithm \'al-gə-₁ri-_thəm_\ *n* : a procedure for solving a problem esp. in mathematics or computing — **al·go·rith·mic** \₁al-gə-'rith-mik\ *adj* — **al·go·rith·mi·cal·ly** \-mi-k(ə-)lē\ *adv*

¹ali·as \'ā-lē-əs, 'āl-yəs\ *adv* : otherwise called

²alias *n* ♦ : an assumed or additional name

♦ cognomen, nickname

¹al·i·bi \'a-lə-₁bī\ *n* **1** : a plea offered by an accused person of not having been at the scene of an offense **2** ♦ : an excuse (as for failure)

♦ defense (*or* defence), excuse, justification, plea, reason

²**alibi** *vb* **-bied; -bi·ing** **1** : to furnish an excuse for **2** : to offer an excuse

¹**alien** \'ā-lē-ən, 'āl-yən\ *adj* ♦ : belonging or relating to another person, place, or thing : FOREIGN

♦ adventitious, extraneous, extrinsic, foreign

²**alien** *n* **1** : a foreign-born resident who has not been naturalized **2** : EXTRATERRESTRIAL

alien·able \'āl-yə-nə-bəl, 'ā-lē-ə-nə-\ *adj* : transferable to the ownership of another ⟨~ property⟩

alien·ate \'ā-lē-ə-ˌnāt, 'āl-yə-\ *vb* **-at·ed; -at·ing** **1** ♦ : to make hostile : ESTRANGE **2** : to transfer (property) to another

♦ disaffect, disgruntle, estrange, sour

alien·ation \ˌā-lē-ə-'nā-shən, ˌāl-yə-\ *n* ♦ : a withdrawing or separation of a person or a person's affections from an object or position of former attachment

♦ disaffection, estrangement

alien·ist \'ā-lē-ə-nist, 'āl-yə-\ *n* : PSYCHIATRIST

¹**alight** \ə-'līt\ *vb* **alight·ed** *also* **alit** \ə-'lit\; **alight·ing** **1** : to get down (as from a vehicle) **2** ♦ : to come to rest from the air

♦ land, light, perch, roost, settle

²**alight** *adj* ♦ : lighted up

♦ ablaze, bright, light

align *also* **aline** \ə-'līn\ *vb* **1** : to bring into line **2** : to array on the side of or against a cause — **align·er** *n* — **align·ment** *also* **aline·ment** *n*

¹**alike** \ə-'līk\ *adv* ♦ : in the same manner, form, or degree

♦ also, correspondingly, likewise, similarly, so

²**alike** *adj* ♦ : exhibiting close resemblance without being identical : LIKE

♦ akin, analogous, comparable, correspondent, like, parallel, similar, such *Ant* different, dissimilar, diverse, unlike

al·i·ment \'a-lə-mənt\ *n* : NOURISHMENT 1 — **aliment** *vb*

al·i·men·ta·ry \ˌa-lə-'men-t(ə-)rē\ *adj* : of, relating to, or functioning in nourishment or nutrition

alimentary canal *n* : the tube that extends from the mouth to the anus and functions in the digestion and absorption of food and the elimination of residues

al·i·mo·ny \'a-lə-ˌmō-nē\ *n, pl* **-nies** : an allowance made to one spouse by the other for support pending or after legal separation or divorce

A–line \'ā-ˌlīn\ *adj* : having a flared bottom and a close-fitting top ⟨an ~ skirt⟩

alive \ə-'līv\ *adj* **1** ♦ : having life **2** ♦ : being in force or operation **3** ♦ : knowing or realizing the existence of ⟨~ to the danger⟩ **4** : ALERT, BRISK **5** ♦ : marked by much life, animation, or activity : ANIMATED ⟨streets ~ with traffic⟩ — **alive·ness** *n*

♦ [1] existent, extant, living ♦ [1] animate, live, living *Ant* dead, deceased, defunct, lifeless, nonliving ♦ [2] active, functional, living, on, operational, operative, running, working ♦ [3] aware, cognizant, conscious, mindful, sensible, sentient, witting ♦ [5] animated, astir, busy, lively, vibrant *Ant* asleep, dead, inactive, lifeless, sleepy

alk *abbr* alkaline

al·ka·li \'al-kə-ˌlī\ *n, pl* **-lies** *or* **-lis** **1** : a substance (as a hydroxide) that has a bitter taste and neutralizes acids **2** : a mixture of salts in the soil of some dry regions in such amount as to make ordinary farming impossible — **al·ka·line** \-kə-lən, -ˌlīn\ *adj* — **al·ka·lin·i·ty** \ˌal-kə-'li-nə-tē\ *n*

al·ka·loid \'al-kə-ˌlȯid\ *n* : any of various usu. basic and bitter organic compounds found esp. in seed plants

al·kane \'al-ˌkān\ *n* : a hydrocarbon in which each carbon atom is bonded to 4 other atoms

al·kyd \'al-kəd\ *n* : any of numerous synthetic resins used esp. for protective coatings and in paint

¹**all** \'ȯl\ *adj* **1** ♦ : the whole of **2** : every member of **3** : EVERY ⟨~ manner of problems⟩ **4** : any whatever ⟨beyond ~ doubt⟩ **5** : nothing but ⟨~ ears⟩ **6** : being more than one person or thing ⟨who ~ is coming⟩

♦ concentrated, entire, undivided, whole

²**all** *adv* **1** ♦ : to the full or entire extent : WHOLLY **2** : selected as the best — used in combination ⟨*all*-state champs⟩ **3** : so much ⟨~ the better for it⟩ **4** : for each side ⟨the score is two ~⟩

♦ absolutely, clean, completely, entirely, fully, quite, totally, utterly, wholly

³**all** *pron* **1** : the whole number, quantity, or amount ⟨~ of it is gone⟩ **2** : every person or thing ⟨that is ~⟩

⁴**all** *n* : the whole of one's resources ⟨gave his ~⟩

Al·lah \'ä-lä, 'ä-; ä-'lä\ *n* : the Being perfect in power, wisdom, and goodness who is worshipped as creator and ruler of the universe — used in Islam

all along *adv* : all the time ⟨knew it *all along*⟩

all–Amer·i·can \ˌȯl-ə-'mer-ə-kən\ *adj* **1** : selected as the best in the U.S. **2** : composed wholly of American elements **3** : typical of the U.S. — **all–American** *n*

all–around \ˌȯl-ə-'raund\ *adj* **1** ♦ : considered in or encompassing all aspects ⟨best ~ performance⟩ **2** : competent in many fields : VERSATILE ⟨an ~ athlete⟩

♦ general, unlimited, unqualified, unrestricted

all around \ˌȯl-ə-'raund\ *adv* ♦ : without concentration on one area or aspect

♦ altogether, collectively, overall, together

al·lay \ə-'lā\ *vb* **1** ♦ : to subdue or reduce in intensity or severity : ALLEVIATE **2** ♦ : to make quiet : CALM

♦ [1] alleviate, assuage, ease, help, mitigate, mollify, palliate, relieve, soothe ♦ [2] calm, compose, quiet, settle, soothe, still, tranquilize

all clear *n* : a signal that a danger has passed

al·lege \ə-'lej\ *vb* **al·leged; al·leg·ing** **1** ♦ : to assert without proof **2** : to offer as a reason — **al·le·ga·tion** \ˌa-li-'gā-shən\ *n* — **al·leg·ed·ly** \ə-'le-jəd-lē\ *adv*

♦ affirm, assert, aver, avouch, avow, claim, contend, declare, insist, maintain, profess, protest, warrant

al·le·giance \ə-'lē-jəns\ *n* **1** : loyalty owed by a citizen to a government **2** ♦ : loyalty to a person or cause

♦ constancy, dedication, devotion, faith, faithfulness, fastness, fealty, fidelity, loyalty, steadfastness

al·le·go·ry \'a-lə-ˌgȯr-ē\ *n, pl* **-ries** : the expression through symbolism of truths or generalizations about human experience; *also* : an instance (as in a story or painting) of such expression — **al·le·gor·i·cal** \ˌa-lə-'gȯr-i-kəl\ *adj* — **al·le·gor·i·cal·ly** \-k(ə-)lē\ *adv*

¹**al·le·gro** \ə-'le-grō, -'lā-\ *n, pl* **-gros** : an allegro movement

²**allegro** *adv or adj* : at a brisk lively tempo — used as a direction in music

al·le·lu·ia \ˌa-lə-'lü-yə\ *interj* : HALLELUJAH

Al·len wrench \'a-lən-\ *n* : an L-shaped hexagonal metal bar of which either end fits the socket of a screw or bolt

al·ler·gen \'a-lər-jən\ *n* : something that causes allergy — **al·ler·gen·ic** \ˌa-lər-'je-nik\ *adj*

al·ler·gic \ə-'lər-jik\ *adj* : of, relating to, affected with, or caused by allergy

al·ler·gist \'a-lər-jist\ *n* : a specialist in allergies

al·ler·gy \'a-lər-jē\ *n, pl* **-gies** **1** : exaggerated or abnormal reaction (as by sneezing) to substances or situations harmless to most people **2** ♦ : a feeling of antipathy or aversion

♦ aversion, disfavor (*or* disfavour), disinclination, dislike

al·le·vi·ate \ə-'lē-vē-ˌāt\ *vb* **-at·ed; -at·ing** ♦ : to remove or lessen (as suffering) : RELIEVE

♦ allay, assuage, ease, help, mitigate, mollify, palliate, relieve, soothe

al·le·vi·a·tion \ə-ˌlē-vē-'ā-shən\ *n* ♦ : the action of alleviating or of being alleviated

♦ comfort, ease, relief

al·ley \'a-lē\ *n, pl* **alleys** **1** : a garden or park walk **2** : a place for bowling **3** : a narrow passageway esp. between buildings

al·ley–oop \ˌa-lē-'yüp\ *n* : a basketball play in which a player catches a pass above the basket and immediately dunks the ball

al·ley·way \'a-lē-ˌwā\ *n* : ALLEY 3

All·hal·lows \ȯl-'ha-lōz\ *n, pl* **Allhallows** : ALL SAINTS' DAY

al·li·ance \ə-'lī-əns\ *n* **1** ♦ : a union to promote common interests **2** : union by relationship in qualities **3** : a treaty of alliance

♦ [1] bloc, coalition, combination, combine, confederacy, confederation, federation, league, union ♦ [2] affiliation, association, collaboration, confederation, connection, cooperation, hookup, liaison, partnership, relation, relationship, union

al·li·ga·tor \'a-lə-ˌgā-tər\ *n* : either of two large short-legged reptiles resembling crocodiles but having a shorter and broader snout

alligator pear *n* : AVOCADO

al·lit·er·ate \ə-'li-tə-ˌrāt\ *vb* **-at·ed; -at·ing** **1** : to form an alliteration **2** : to arrange so as to make alliteration

al·lit·er·a·tion \ə-ˌli-tə-ˈrā-shən\ *n* : the repetition of initial sounds in adjacent words or syllables — **al·lit·er·a·tive** \-ˈli-tə-ˌrā-tiv\ *adj*

al·lo·cate \ˈa-lə-ˌkāt\ *vb* **-cat·ed; -cat·ing** ♦ : to apportion for a specific purpose or to particular persons or things

♦ administer, apportion, deal, dispense, distribute, mete, parcel, portion, prorate ♦ allot, allow, apportion, ration

al·lo·ca·tion \ˌa-lə-ˈkā-shən\ *n* **1** ♦ : the act or action of allocating **2** ♦ : the amount allocated to one sharer

♦ [1] dispensation, distribution, division, issuance ♦ [2] allotment, appropriation, grant, subsidy

al·lot \ə-ˈlät\ *vb* **al·lot·ted; al·lot·ting** ♦ : to distribute as a share

♦ allocate, allow, apportion, ration

al·lot·ment \-mənt\ *n* **1** : the act of allotting **2** ♦ : something that is allotted

♦ allocation, appropriation, grant, subsidy ♦ allowance, cut, part, portion, proportion, quota, share

all–out \ˈȯl-ˈaut\ *adj* ♦ : marked by thoroughness or zeal : THOROUGHGOING

♦ clean, complete, comprehensive, exhaustive, full-scale, out-and-out, thorough, thoroughgoing, total

all out *adv* ♦ : with maximum effort

♦ full tilt

all over *adv* : in every place or part : EVERYWHERE

al·low \ə-ˈlau\ *vb* **1** ♦ : to assign as a share ⟨∼ time for rest⟩ **2** : to count as a deduction **3** : to make allowance ⟨∼ for expansion⟩ **4** ♦ : to accept as true, valid, or accurate usu. reluctantly : ADMIT, CONCEDE **5 a** : to give leave for or make possible : PERMIT ⟨∼s the dog to roam⟩ **b** ♦ : to give leave to

♦ [1] allocate, allot, apportion, ration ♦ [4] acknowledge, admit, agree, concede, confess, grant, own *Ant* ban, enjoin, forbid, prohibit, proscribe, veto ♦ [5b] let, permit, suffer *Ant* enjoin, forbid, prohibit

al·low·able \ə-ˈlau-ə-bəl\ *adj* ♦ : that may be permitted

♦ admissible, permissible, sufferable

al·low·ance \-əns\ *n* **1** ♦ : an allotted share **2** : money given regularly for expenses **3** ♦ : the act of allowing : PERMISSION **4** : a taking into account of extenuating circumstances

♦ [1] allotment, cut, part, portion, proportion, quota, share ♦ [3] authorization, clearance, concurrence, consent, leave, license (*or* licence), permission, sanction, sufferance

al·loy \ˈa-ˌlȯi, ə-ˈlȯi\ *n* **1** : a substance composed of metals melted together **2** : an admixture that lessens value — **al·loy** \ə-ˈlȯi, ˈa-ˌlȯi\ *vb*

¹**all right** *adj* **1** ♦ : giving satisfaction : SATISFACTORY **2** ♦ : free from harm or risk **3** : having qualities that tend to give pleasure — often used as a generalized term of approval

♦ [1] acceptable, adequate, decent, fine, OK, passable, respectable, satisfactory, tolerable ♦ [2] alright, safe, secure

²**all right** *adv* **1** — used interjectionally to express agreement or resignation or to indicate the resumption of a discussion ⟨all right, let's go⟩ **2** : beyond doubt **3** ♦ : well enough : SATISFACTORILY

♦ [1] alright, OK, yea, yes ♦ [3] adequately, fine, good, nicely, OK, passably, satisfactorily, so-so, tolerably, well

All Saints' Day *n* : a Christian feast on November 1 in honor of all the saints

All Souls' Day *n* : a day of prayer observed by some Christian churches on November 2 for the souls of the faithful departed

all·spice \ˈȯl-ˌspīs\ *n* : the berry of a West Indian tree related to the European myrtle; *also* : the mildly pungent and aromatic spice made from it

all–star \ˈȯl-ˌstär\ *n* : a member of a team of star performers — **all–star** *adj*

all–ter·rain vehicle *n* : a small motor vehicle for use on a wide range of terrain

all told *adv* : with everything counted

al·lude \ə-ˈlüd\ *vb* **al·lud·ed; al·lud·ing** ♦ : to refer indirectly — **al·lu·sion** \-ˈlü-zhən\ *n* — **al·lu·sive** \-ˈlü-siv\ *adj* — **al·lu·sive·ly** *adv* — **al·lu·sive·ness** *n*

♦ hint, imply, indicate, infer, insinuate, intimate, suggest

¹**al·lure** \ə-ˈlur\ *vb* **al·lured; al·lur·ing** ♦ : to entice by charm or attraction — **allure** *n* — **al·lur·ing·ly** *adv*

♦ beguile, bewitch, captivate, charm, enchant, fascinate, wile
♦ beguile, decoy, entice, lead on, lure, seduce, tempt

²**allure** *n* ♦ : power of attraction or fascination

♦ appeal, attractiveness, captivation, charisma, charm, enchantment, fascination, glamour, magic, magnetism

alluring *adj* ♦ : marked by allure

♦ attractive, captivating, charming, elfin, engaging, fascinating, fetching, glamorous, magnetic, seductive

al·lu·vi·um \ə-ˈlü-vē-əm\ *n, pl* **-vi·ums** *or* **-via** \-vē-ə\ : soil material (as clay) deposited by running water — **al·lu·vi·al** \-vē-əl\ *adj or n*

¹**al·ly** \ə-ˈlī, ˈa-ˌlī\ *vb* **al·lied; al·ly·ing** ♦ : to enter into an alliance

♦ associate, band, club, confederate, conjoin, cooperate, federate, league, unite *Ant* break up, disband

²**al·ly** \ˈa-ˌlī, ə-ˈlī\ *n* ♦ : one that is associated with another as a helper

♦ abettor, backer, confederate, supporter, sympathizer

-ally *adv suffix* : ²-LY ⟨specific*ally*⟩

al·ma ma·ter \ˌal-mə-ˈmä-tər\ *n* **1** : an educational institute that one has attended **2** : the song or hymn of an alma mater

al·ma·nac \ˈȯl-mə-ˌnak, ˈal-\ *n* **1** : a publication esp. of astronomical and meteorological data **2** : a usu. annual publication of miscellaneous information

al·man·dite \ˈal-mən-ˌdīt\ *n* : a deep red garnet

al·mighty \ȯl-ˈmī-tē\ *adj* **1** *often cap* : having absolute power over all ⟨*Almighty* God⟩ **2** : relatively unlimited in power — **al·might·i·ness** *n*

Almighty *n* ♦ : the Being worshipped as the creator and ruler of the universe

♦ deity, Jehovah, Supreme Being

al·mond \ˈä-mənd, ˈa-; ˈal-\ *n* : a small tree related to the peach; *also* : the edible nutlike kernel of its fruit

al·mo·ner \ˈal-mə-nər, ˈä-mə-\ *n* : a person who distributes alms

al·most \ˈȯl-ˌmōst, ȯl-ˈmōst\ *adv* ♦ : very nearly but not exactly

♦ about, most, much, near, nearly, next to, nigh, practically, some, virtually, well-nigh

alms \ˈämz, ˈälmz\ *n, pl* **alms** ♦ : something given freely to relieve the poor

♦ benefaction, beneficence, charity, contribution, donation, philanthropy

alms·house \-ˌhaus\ *n* : POORHOUSE

al·oe \ˈa-lō\ *n* **1** : any of a large genus of succulent chiefly southern African plants related to the lilies **2** *pl* : the dried juice of the leaves of an aloe used esp. formerly as a laxative

aloft \ə-ˈlȯft\ *adv* **1** : high in the air **2** : in flight

♦ above, over, overhead, skyward

alo·ha \ə-ˈlō-ə, ä-ˈlō-ˌhä\ *interj* — used to greet or bid farewell

¹**alone** \ə-ˈlōn\ *adj* **1** ♦ : separated from others **2** ♦ : not including anyone or anything else : ONLY — **alone** *adv*

♦ [1] lone, lonely, lonesome, solitary, unaccompanied *Ant* accompanied ♦ [2] lone, only, singular, sole, solitary, special, unique

²**alone** *adv* **1** ♦ : to the exclusion of all else : SOLELY **2** ♦ : without aid or support

♦ [1] exclusively, just, only, simply, solely ♦ [2] independently, singly, solely, unaided, unassisted

¹**along** \ə-ˈlȯng\ *prep* **1** : in line with the direction of ⟨sail ∼ the coast⟩ **2** : at a point on or during ⟨stopped ∼ the way⟩

²**along** *adv* **1** ♦ : FORWARD, ON **2** : as a companion ⟨bring her ∼⟩ **3** ♦ : at an advanced point ⟨plans are far ∼⟩

♦ ahead, forth, forward, on, onward

along·shore \ə-ˈlȯng-ˈshȯr\ *adv or adj* : along the shore or coast

¹**along·side** \-ˌsīd\ *adv* : along or by the side

²**alongside** *prep* **1** : along or by the side of **2** : in association with

alongside of *prep* : ALONGSIDE

aloof \ə-ˈlüf\ *adj* ♦ : removed or distant physically or emotionally — **aloof·ness** *n*

♦ antisocial, cold, cool, detached, distant, frosty, remote, standoffish, unsocial

al·o·pe·cia \ˌa-lə-ˈpē-sh(ē-)ə\ *n* : BALDNESS

aloud \ə-ˈlaud\ *adv* : with the speaking voice

alp \ˈalp\ *n* : a high rugged mountain

al·paca \al-ˈpa-kə\ *n* : a domesticated mammal esp. of Peru that is prob. descended from the vicuña; *also* : its woolly hair or cloth made from this

al·pha \'al-fə\ *n* **1** : the 1st letter of the Greek alphabet — A or α **2** : something first : BEGINNING

al·pha·bet \'al-fə-ˌbet\ *n* : the set of letters or characters used in writing a language

al·pha·bet·i·cal \ˌal-fə-'be-ti-kəl\ *or* **al·pha·bet·ic** \-'be-tik\ *adj* **1** : arranged in the order of the letters of the alphabet **2** : of or employing an alphabet — **al·pha·bet·i·cal·ly** \-ti-k(ə-)lē\ *adv*

al·pha·bet·ize \'al-fə-bə-ˌtīz\ *vb* **-ized; -iz·ing** : to arrange in alphabetical order — **al·pha·bet·iz·er** *n*

al·pha·nu·mer·ic \ˌal-fə-nú-'mer-ik, -nyú-\ *adj* : consisting of letters and numbers and often other symbols ⟨an ∼ code⟩; *also* : being a character in an alphanumeric system

alpha particle *n* : a positively charged particle identical with the nucleus of a helium atom that is ejected at high speed in certain radioactive transformations

alpha rhythm *n* : ALPHA WAVE

alpha wave *n* : an electrical rhythm of the brain often associated with a state of wakeful relaxation

Al·pine \'al-ˌpīn\ *adj* **1** : relating to, located in, or resembling the Alps mountains **2** *often not cap* : of, relating to, or growing on upland slopes above timberline **3** : of or relating to competitive ski events consisting of slalom and downhill racing

al·ready \òl-'re-dē\ *adv* : by this time : PREVIOUSLY

¹**al·right** \òl-'rīt\ *adv* : very well : ALL RIGHT — used interjectionally to express agreement or resignation or to indicate the resumption of a discussion ⟨alright, let's go⟩

²**alright** *adj* **1** ♦ : giving satisfaction : SATISFACTORY **2** ♦ : free from harm or risk **3** ♦ : having qualities that tend to give pleasure — often used as a generalized term of approval

♦ [1] agreeable, all right, fine, good, OK, palatable, satisfactory ♦ [2] all right, safe, secure ♦ [3] OK, yea, yes

al·so \'òl-sō\ *adv* **1** ♦ : in like manner : LIKEWISE **2** ♦ : in addition : TOO

♦ [1] alike, correspondingly, likewise, similarly, so *Ant* differently, otherwise ♦ [2] additionally, again, besides, further, furthermore, likewise, more, moreover, then, too, withal, yet

al·so-ran \-ˌran\ *n* **1** : a horse or dog that finishes out of the money in a race **2** : a contestant that does not win

alt *abbr* **1** alternate **2** altitude

Alta *abbr* Alberta

al·tar \'òl-tər\ *n* **1** : a structure on which sacrifices are offered or incense is burned **2** : a table used as a center of ritual or worship

altar server *n* : a boy or girl who assists the celebrant at a church service

¹**al·ter** \'òl-tər\ *vb* **al·tered; al·ter·ing** \-t(ə-)riŋ\ **1** ♦ : to make or become different **2** : to remove the sex organs of

♦ change, make over, modify, recast, redo, refashion, remake, remodel, revamp, revise, rework, vary

²**alter** *abbr* alteration

al·ter·a·tion \ˌòl-tə-'rā-shən\ *n* ♦ : the act, process, or result of altering

♦ change, difference, modification, revise, revision, variation

al·ter·ca·tion \ˌòl-tər-'kā-shən\ *n* ♦ : a noisy or angry dispute

♦ argument, disagreement, dispute, fight, hassle, misunderstanding, quarrel, row, scrap, spat, squabble, wrangle

al·ter ego \ˌòl-tər-'ē-gō\ *n* : a second self; *esp* : a trusted friend

¹**al·ter·nate** \'òl-tər-nət, 'al-\ *adj* **1** : arranged or succeeding by turns **2** : every other **3** : being an alternative ⟨an ∼ route⟩ — **al·ter·nate·ly** *adv*

²**al·ter·nate** \-ˌnāt\ *vb* **-nat·ed; -nat·ing** : to occur or cause to occur by turns — **al·ter·na·tion** \ˌòl-tər-'nā-shən, ˌal-\ *n*

³**alternate** *n* : SUBSTITUTE

alternating current *n* : an electric current that reverses its direction at regular intervals

¹**al·ter·na·tive** \òl-'tər-nə-tiv, al-\ *adj* : offering a choice

²**alternative** *n* ♦ : an opportunity for deciding between two or more courses or propositions

♦ choice, discretion, option, pick, preference, way

alternative medicine *n* : any of various systems of healing (as homeopathy) not typically practiced in conventional Western medicine

al·ter·na·tor \'òl-tər-ˌnā-tər, 'al-\ *n* : an electric generator for producing alternating current

al·though *also* **al·tho** \òl-'thō\ *conj* ♦ : in spite of the fact that : even though

♦ albeit, howbeit, though, when, while

al·tim·e·ter \al-'ti-mə-tər, 'al-tə-ˌmē-tər\ *n* : an instrument for measuring altitude

al·ti·tude \'al-tə-ˌtüd, -ˌtyüd\ *n* **1** : angular distance above the horizon **2** ♦ : vertical distance : HEIGHT **3** : the perpendicular distance in a geometric figure from the vertex to the base, from the vertex of an angle to the side opposite, or from the base to a parallel side or face

♦ elevation, height

al·to \'al-tō\ *n, pl* **altos** : the lower female voice part in a 4-part chorus; *also* : a singer having this voice or part

¹**al·to·geth·er** \ˌòl-tə-'ge-thər\ *adv* **1** ♦ : to the full or entire extent : WHOLLY **2** ♦ : in all **3** ♦ : on the whole

♦ [1] absolutely, all, clean, completely, dead, entirely, fast, flat, full, fully, perfectly, quite, thoroughly, well, wholly ♦ [2] all around, collectively, overall, together ♦ [3] chiefly, generally, largely, mainly, mostly, overall, predominantly, primarily, principally

²**altogether** *n* : NUDE ⟨posed in the ∼⟩

al·tru·ism \'al-trü-ˌi-zəm\ *n* : unselfish interest in the welfare of others — **al·tru·ist** \-ist\ *n* — **al·tru·is·ti·cal·ly** \-ti-k(ə-)lē\ *adv*

al·tru·is·tic \ˌal-trü-'is-tik\ *adj* ♦ : relating to or given to altruism

♦ beneficent, benevolent, charitable, humanitarian, philanthropic

al·um \'a-ləm\ *n* : either of two colorless crystalline aluminum-containing compounds used esp. as an emetic or as an astringent and styptic

alu·mi·na \ə-'lü-mə-nə\ *n* : the oxide of aluminum occurring in nature as corundum and in bauxite

al·u·min·i·um \ˌal-yə-'mi-nē-əm\ *n, chiefly Brit* : ALUMINUM

alu·mi·nize \ə-'lü-mə-ˌnīz\ *vb* **-nized; -niz·ing** : to treat with aluminum

alu·mi·num \ə-'lü-mə-nəm\ *n* : a silver-white malleable ductile light metallic element that is the most abundant metal in the earth's crust

alum·na \ə-'ləm-nə\ *n, pl* **-nae** \-(ˌ)nē\ : a woman or girl who is a graduate or former student of a college or school

alum·nus \ə-'ləm-nəs\ *n, pl* **-ni** \-ˌnī\ : a graduate or former student of a college or school

al·ways \'òl-wēz, -wəz, -(ˌ)wāz\ *adv* **1** ♦ : at all times : INVARIABLY **2** ♦ : for a limitless time : FOREVER

♦ [1] constantly, continually, ever, forever, incessantly, invariably, perpetually, unfailingly *Ant* ne'er, never ♦ [2] eternally, ever, everlastingly, forever, permanently, perpetually

Alz·hei·mer's disease \'älts-ˌhī-mərz-, 'alts-\ *n* : a degenerative brain disease characterized esp. by progressive mental deterioration and memory loss

am *pres 1st sing of* BE

¹**Am** *abbr* America; American

²**Am** *symbol* americium

¹**AM** \'ā-ˌem\ *n* : a broadcasting system using amplitude modulation; *also* : a radio receiver for broadcasts made by such a system

²**AM** *abbr* **1** ante meridiem — often not cap. and often punctuated **2** master of arts

AMA *abbr* American Medical Association

amah \'ä-(ˌ)mä\ *n* : a female servant in eastern Asia; *esp* : a Chinese nurse

amal·gam \ə-'mal-gəm\ *n* **1** : an alloy of mercury with another metal used in making dental cements **2** ♦ : a mixture of different elements

♦ admixture, blend, combination, composite, compound, fusion, intermixture, mix, mixture

amal·gam·ate \ə-'mal-gə-ˌmāt\ *vb* **-at·ed; -at·ing** ♦ : to unite or merge into one body

♦ blend, combine, commingle, fuse, incorporate, integrate, intermingle, merge, mingle, mix

amal·ga·ma·tion \-ˌmal-gə-'mā-shən\ *n* : the result of amalgamating

aman·u·en·sis \ə-ˌman-yə-'wen-səs\ *n, pl* **-en·ses** \-ˌsēz\ : one employed to write from dictation or to copy what another has written : SECRETARY

am·a·ranth \'a-mə-ˌranth\ *n* **1** : any of a large genus of coarse herbs sometimes grown for their showy flowers **2** : a flower that never fades

am·a·ran·thine \ˌa-mə-'ran-thən, -ˌthīn\ *adj* **1** : relating to or resembling an amaranth **2** : UNDYING

am·a·ryl·lis \ˌa-mə-'ri-ləs\ *n* : any of various plants related to the lilies; *esp* : any of several African herbs having bulbs and grown for their clusters of large showy flowers

amass \ə-'mas\ *vb* ♦ : to collect into a mass : ACCUMULATE

♦ accumulate, assemble, collect, concentrate, garner, gather, group, lump, pick up, round up, scrape

¹am·a·teur \'a-mə-(ˌ)tər, -ˌtu̇r, -ˌtyu̇r, -ˌchu̇r, -chər\ *n* **1 :** a person who engages in a pursuit for pleasure and not as a profession **2 :** a person who is not expert — **am·a·teur·ism** \'a-mə-(ˌ)tər-iˌzəm, -ˌtu̇r-, -ˌtyu̇r-, -ˌchu̇r-, -chər-\ *n*

²amateur *adj* ♦ **:** engaged in or performed by or as if by an amateur

    ♦ amateurish, inexperienced, inexpert, nonprofessional, unprofessional, unskilled, unskillful

am·a·teur·ish \ˌa-mə-'tər-ish, -'tu̇r-, -'tyu̇r-, -'chu̇r-, -'chər-\ *adj* ♦ **:** having the characteristics of an amateur **:** lacking professional finish

    ♦ amateur, inexperienced, inexpert, nonprofessional, unprofessional, unskilled, unskillful *Ant* ace, expert, masterful, professional

am·a·tive \'a-mə-tiv\ *adj* **:** indicative of love **:** AMOROUS — **am·a·tive·ly** *adv* — **am·a·tive·ness** *n*

am·a·to·ry \'a-mə-ˌtȯr-ē\ *adj* ♦ **:** of or expressing sexual love

    ♦ amorous, erotic, sexy

amaze \ə-'māz\ *vb* **amazed; amaz·ing** ♦ **:** to fill with wonder **:** ASTOUND — **amaz·ing·ly** *adv*

    ♦ astonish, astound, bowl, dumbfound, flabbergast, floor, shock, startle, stun, stupefy, surprise

amazed *adj* ♦ **:** filled with wonder or astonishment

    ♦ awestruck, stunned, thunderstruck

amaze·ment \-mənt\ *n* ♦ **:** the quality or state of being amazed

    ♦ admiration, astonishment, awe, wonder, wonderment

amazing *adj* ♦ **:** causing amazement, great wonder, or surprise

    ♦ astonishing, astounding, eye-opening, shocking, startling, stunning, surprising ♦ astonishing, astounding, awesome, fabulous, marvelous (*or* marvellous), miraculous, surprising, wonderful

am·a·zon \'a-mə-ˌzän, -zən\ *n* **1** *cap* **:** a member of a race of female warriors of Greek mythology **2 :** a tall strong often masculine woman — **am·a·zo·ni·an** \ˌa-mə-'zō-nē-ən\ *adj, often cap*

amb *abbr* ambassador

am·bas·sa·dor \am-'ba-sə-dər\ *n* ♦ **:** a representative esp. of a government — **am·bas·sa·do·ri·al** \-ˌba-sə-'dȯr-ē-əl\ *adj* — **am·bas·sa·dor·ship** *n*

    ♦ delegate, emissary, envoy, legate, minister, representative

am·ber \'am-bər\ *n* **:** a yellowish or brownish fossil resin used esp. for ornamental objects; *also* **:** the color of this resin

Amber Alert *n* **:** a widely publicized bulletin that alerts the public to a recently abducted or missing child

am·ber·gris \'am-bər-ˌgris, -ˌgrēs\ *n* **:** a waxy substance from the sperm whale used in making perfumes

am·bi·dex·trous \ˌam-bi-'dek-strəs\ *adj* **:** using both hands with equal ease — **am·bi·dex·trous·ly** *adv*

am·bi·ence *or* **am·bi·ance** \'am-bē-əns, äⁿ-'byäⁿs\ *n* **:** a pervading atmosphere

am·bi·ent \'am-bē-ənt\ *adj* **:** existing on all sides

am·bi·gu·i·ty \ˌam-bə-'gyü-ə-tē\ *n* ♦ **:** the quality or state of being ambiguous

    ♦ darkness, murkiness, obscurity, opacity

am·big·u·ous \am-'bi-gyə-wəs\ *adj* ♦ **:** capable of being understood in more than one way — **am·big·u·ous·ly** *adv*

    ♦ cryptic, enigmatic, equivocal, mysterious, nebulous, obscure

am·bi·tion \am-'bi-shən\ *n* **1** ♦ **:** eager desire for success or power **2** ♦ **:** the object of ambition

    ♦ [1] aspiration, go-getting ♦ [2] aim, aspiration, goal, mark, meaning, object, objective, plan, purpose

am·bi·tious \-shəs\ *adj* ♦ **:** characterized by ambition — **am·bi·tious·ly** *adv*

    ♦ go-getting, self-seeking

am·biv·a·lence \am-'bi-və-ləns\ *n* **:** simultaneous attraction toward and repulsion from a person, object, or action — **am·biv·a·lent** \-lənt\ *adj*

¹am·ble \'am-bəl\ *vb* **am·bled; am·bling** \-b(ə-)liŋ\ **:** to go at an amble

²amble *n* **:** an easy gait esp. of a horse

am·bro·sia \am-'brō-zh(ē-)ə\ *n* **:** the food of the Greek and Roman gods

am·bro·sial \-zh(ē-)əl\ *adj* ♦ **:** pleasing to the senses esp. of taste or smell

    ♦ aromatic, fragrant, redolent, savory, scented, sweet ♦ appetiz-

ing, delectable, delicious, flavorful (*or* flavourful), luscious, palatable, savory, scrumptious, tasty, toothsome, yummy

am·bu·lance \'am-byə-ləns\ *n* **:** a vehicle equipped for carrying the injured or sick

am·bu·lant \'am-byə-lənt\ *adj* **:** AMBULATORY

¹am·bu·la·to·ry \'am-byə-lə-ˌtȯr-ē\ *adj* **1 :** of, relating to, or adapted to walking **2 :** able to walk or move about

²ambulatory *n, pl* **-ries :** a sheltered place (as in a cloister) for walking

am·bus·cade \'am-bə-ˌskäd\ *n* **:** AMBUSH

¹am·bush \'am-ˌbu̇sh\ *n* ♦ **:** a trap in which concealed persons wait to attack by surprise

    ♦ net, snare, trap, web ♦ surprise, trap

²ambush *vb* ♦ **:** to attack from an ambush

    ♦ surprise, waylay

amdt *abbr* amendment

ameba, ameboid *var of* AMOEBA, AMOEBOID

ame·lio·rate \ə-'mēl-yə-ˌrāt\ *vb* **-rat·ed; -rat·ing** ♦ **:** to make or grow better **:** IMPROVE — **ame·lio·ra·tion** \-ˌmēl-yə-'rā-shən\ *n*

    ♦ amend, better, enhance, enrich, improve, perfect, refine

amen \(ˌ)ä-'men, (ˌ)ā-\ *interj* — used esp. at the end of prayers to affirm or express approval

ame·na·ble \ə-'mē-nə-bəl, -'me-\ *adj* **1 :** ANSWERABLE **2 a** ♦ **:** readily brought to yield, submit, or cooperate **:** COMPLIANT **b** ♦ **:** inclined or favorably disposed in mind **:** WILLING

    ♦ [2a] compliant, conformable, docile, obedient, submissive, tractable ♦ [2b] disposed, game, glad, inclined, ready, willing

amend \ə-'mend\ *vb* **1** ♦ **:** to change for the better **:** IMPROVE **2 :** to alter formally in phraseology — **amend·able** \-'men-də-bəl\ *adj*

    ♦ ameliorate, better, enhance, enrich, improve, perfect, refine ♦ correct, debug, emend, rectify, reform, remedy

amend·ment \ə-'mend-mənt\ *n* **1 :** the act of amending **2 :** the process of amending a parliamentary motion or a constitution; *also* **:** the alteration so proposed or made

amends \ə-'mendz\ *n sing or pl* **:** compensation for injury or loss

ame·ni·ty \ə-'me-nə-tē, -'mē-\ *n, pl* **-ties 1** ♦ **:** the quality of being pleasant or agreeable **:** AGREEABLENESS **2** ♦ **:** a gesture observed in social relationships **3** ♦ **:** something that serves as a comfort or convenience

    ♦ [1] agreeableness, amiability, geniality, graciousness, niceness, pleasantness, sweetness ♦ [2] civility, courtesy, formality, gesture ♦ [3] comfort, extra, frill, indulgence, luxury, superfluity

Amer *abbr* America; American

amerce \ə-'mərs\ *vb* **amerced; amerc·ing 1 :** to penalize by a fine determined by the court **2 :** PUNISH — **amerce·ment** *n*

Amer·i·can \ə-'mer-ə-kən\ *n* **1 :** a native or inhabitant of No. or So. America **2 :** a citizen of the U.S. — **American** *adj* — **Amer·i·can·ism** \-ə-kə-ˌni-zəm\ *n* — **Amer·i·can·iza·tion** \ə-ˌmer-ə-kə-nə-'zā-shən\ *n* — **Amer·i·can·ize** \ə-'mer-ə-kə-ˌnīz\ *vb* — **Amer·i·can·ness** *n*

Amer·i·ca·na \ə-ˌmer-ə-'ka-nə, -'kä-\ *n pl* **:** materials concerning or characteristic of America, its civilization, or its culture

American Indian *n* **:** a member of any of the Indigenous peoples of No. and So. America except certain peoples (such as the Yupik and Inuit) who live in arctic regions; *esp* **:** an American Indian of No. America and esp. the U.S.

American plan *n* **:** a hotel plan whereby the daily rates cover the cost of room and three meals

American Sign Language *n* **:** a sign language for the deaf in which meaning is conveyed by a system of hand gestures and placement

am·er·i·ci·um \ˌam-ə-'rish-ē-əm, -'ris-\ *n* **:** a radioactive metallic chemical element produced artificially from plutonium

AmerInd *abbr* American Indian

Am·er·in·di·an \ˌa-mə-'rin-dē-ən\ *n* **:** AMERICAN INDIAN — **Amerindian** *adj*

am·e·thyst \'a-mə-thəst\ *n* **:** a gemstone consisting of clear purple or bluish violet quartz

ami·a·bil·i·ty \ˌā-mē-ə-'bi-lə-tē\ *n* ♦ **:** the quality of being amiable

    ♦ agreeableness, amenity, geniality, graciousness, niceness, pleasantness, sweetness *Ant* disagreeableness, unpleasantness

ami·a·ble \'ā-mē-ə-bəl\ *adj* **1 :** pleasing to one's mind or senses **:** AGREEABLE **2** ♦ **:** having a friendly and sociable disposition — **ami·a·bly** \'ā-mē-ə-blē\ *adv*

♦ affable, agreeable, genial, good-natured, gracious, nice, sweet, well-disposed *Ant* disagreeable, ill-natured, ill-tempered, ungracious, unpleasant

ami·a·ble·ness \-nəs\ *n* : the quality of being amiable

am·i·ca·ble \'a-mi-kə-bəl\ *adj* ♦ : characterized by friendly goodwill — **am·i·ca·bil·i·ty** \,a-mi-kə-'bi-lə-tē\ *n* — **am·i·ca·bly** \'a-mi-kə-blē\ *adv*

♦ agreeable, compatible, congenial, harmonious, kindred, unanimous, united ♦ companionable, comradely, cordial, friendly, genial, hearty, neighborly, warm, warmhearted

amid \ə-'mid\ *or* **amidst** \-'midst\ *prep* ♦ : in or into the middle of : AMONG

♦ among, midst, through

amid·ships \ə-'mid-,ships\ *adv* : in or near the middle of a ship
ami·no acid \ə-'mē-nō-\ *n* : any of numerous nitrogen-containing acids that include some which are used by cells to build proteins
amir *var of* EMIR
¹**amiss** \ə-'mis\ *adv* 1 ♦ : in a mistaken way : WRONGLY 2 ♦ : off the right path or route : ASTRAY 3 : IMPERFECTLY

♦ [1] erroneously, faultily, improperly, inaptly, incorrectly, mistakenly, wrongly ♦ [2] afield, astray, awry, wrong

²**amiss** *adj* 1 : WRONG 2 ♦ : out of place under the circumstances 3 ♦ : marked by fault or defect : FAULTY, IMPERFECT

♦ [2] improper, inappropriate, inapt, infelicitous, unbecoming, unfit, unseemly, unsuitable, wrong ♦ [3] bad, defective, faulty, imperfect

am·i·ty \'a-mə-tē\ *n, pl* **-ties** ♦ : the quality or state of being friendly; *esp* : friendly relations between nations

♦ benevolence, cordiality, fellowship, friendliness, friendship, goodwill, kindliness

am·me·ter \'a-,mē-tər\ *n* : an instrument for measuring electric current in amperes
am·mo \'a-mō\ *n* : AMMUNITION
am·mo·nia \ə-'mō-nyə\ *n* 1 : a colorless gaseous compound of nitrogen and hydrogen used in refrigeration and in the making of fertilizers and explosives 2 : a solution (**ammonia water**) of ammonia in water
am·mo·ni·um \ə-'mō-nē-əm\ *n* : an ion or chemical group derived from ammonia by combination with hydrogen
ammonium chloride *n* : a white crystalline volatile salt used in batteries and as an expectorant
am·mu·ni·tion \,am-yə-'ni-shən\ *n* 1 : projectiles fired from guns 2 : explosive items used in war 3 : material for use in attack or defense
Amn *abbr* airman
am·ne·sia \am-'nē-zhə\ *n* 1 : abnormal loss of memory 2 : the selective overlooking of events or acts not favorable to one's purpose — **am·ne·si·ac** \-zhē-,ak, -zē-\ *or* **am·ne·sic** \-zik, -sik\ *adj or n*
am·nes·ty \'am-nə-stē\ *n, pl* **-ties** ♦ : an act granting a pardon to a group of individuals — **amnesty** *vb*

♦ absolution, forgiveness, pardon, remission

am·nio·cen·te·sis \,am-nē-ō-,sen-'tē-səs\ *n, pl* **-te·ses** \-,sēz\ : the surgical insertion of a hollow needle through the abdominal wall and uterus of a pregnant female esp. to obtain fluid used to check the fetus for chromosomal abnormality and to determine sex
amoe·ba \ə-'mē-bə\ *n, pl* **-bas** *or* **-bae** \-(,)bē\ : any of various tiny one-celled protozoans that lack permanent cell organs and occur esp. in water and soil — **amoe·bic** \-bik\ *adj*
amoe·boid \-,bȯid\ *adj* : resembling an amoeba esp. in moving or readily changing shape
amok \ə-'mək, -'mäk\ *or* **amuck** \-'mək\ *adv* ♦ : in a violent, frenzied, or uncontrolled manner ⟨run ∼⟩

♦ berserk, frantically, harum-scarum, hectically, helter-skelter, madly, pell-mell, wild, wildly

among \ə-'məŋ\ *also* **amongst** \-'məŋst\ *prep* 1 ♦ : in or through the midst of 2 : in the number, class, or company of 3 : in shares to each of 4 : by common action of

♦ amid, midst, through

amon·til·la·do \ə-,män-tə-'lä-dō\ *n, pl* **-dos** : a medium dry sherry
amor·al \ā-'mȯr-əl\ *adj* 1 : neither moral nor immoral; *esp* : being outside the sphere to which moral judgments apply 2 : lacking moral sensibility — **amor·al·ly** *adv*
am·o·rous \'a-mə-rəs\ *adj* 1 ♦ : strongly moved by love and

esp. sexual love 2 : being in love 3 ♦ : of or indicative of love and esp. sexual love — **am·o·rous·ly** *adv* — **am·o·rous·ness** *n*

♦ [1, 3] amatory, erotic, sexy

amor·phous \ə-'mȯr-fəs\ *adj* 1 ♦ : having no definite form : FORMLESS 2 : not crystallized

♦ formless, shapeless, unformed, unshaped, unstructured

am·or·tize \'a-mər-,tīz, ə-'mȯr-\ *vb* **-tized; -tiz·ing** : to extinguish (as a mortgage) usu. by payment on the principal at the time of each periodic interest payment — **amor·ti·za·tion** \,a-mər-tə-'zā-shən, ə-,mȯr-\ *n*
¹**amount** \ə-'maʉnt\ *vb* 1 ♦ : to be equivalent — usu. used with *to* 2 ♦ : to reach a total : add up — usu. used with *to*

♦ *usu* **amount to** [1] add up, come, correspond, equal ♦ *usu* **amount to** [2] add up, come, number, sum, total

²**amount** *n* 1 ♦ : the total number or quantity 2 : a principal sum plus the interest on it

♦ measure, quantity

amour \ə-'mʉr, ä-, a-\ *n* 1 ♦ : a love affair esp. when illicit 2 : LOVER

♦ affair, love affair, romance

amour pro·pre \,a-,mʉr-'prȯprᵊ, ä-, -'prȯprᵊ\ *n* : SELF-ESTEEM
¹**amp** \'amp\ *n* : AMPLIFIER; *also* : a unit consisting of an electronic amplifier and a loudspeaker
²**amp** *abbr* ampere
am·per·age \'am-p(ə-)rij\ *n* : the strength of a current of electricity expressed in amperes
am·pere \'am-,pir\ *n* : a unit of electric current equivalent to a steady current produced by one volt applied across a resistance of one ohm
am·per·sand \'am-pər-,sand\ *n* : a character & used for the word *and*
am·phet·amine \am-'fe-tə-,mēn, -mən\ *n* : a compound or one of its derivatives that stimulates the central nervous system and is used esp. to treat hyperactive children and to suppress appetite
am·phib·i·an \am-'fi-bē-ən\ *n* 1 : an amphibious organism; *esp* : any of a class of vertebrate animals (as frogs and salamanders) intermediate between fishes and reptiles 2 : an airplane that can land on and take off from either land or water
am·phib·i·ous \am-'fi-bē-əs\ *adj* 1 : able to live both on land and in water 2 : adapted for both land and water 3 : made by joint action of land, sea, and air forces invading from the sea; *also* : trained for such action
am·phi·bole \'am-fə-,bōl\ *n* : any of a group of rock-forming minerals of similar crystal structure
am·phi·the·ater \'am-fə-,thē-ə-tər\ *n* 1 : an oval or circular structure with rising tiers of seats around an arena 2 : a very large auditorium
am·pho·ra \'am-fə-rə\ *n, pl* **-rae** \-,rē\ *or* **-ras** : an ancient Greek jar or vase with two handles that rise almost to the level of the mouth
am·ple \'am-pəl\ *adj* **am·pler** \-plər\; **am·plest** \-pləst\ 1 ♦ : generous or more than adequate in size, scope, or capacity : CAPACIOUS 2 ♦ : enough to satisfy : ABUNDANT

♦ [1] capacious, commodious, roomy, spacious ♦ [2] abundant, bountiful, comfortable, generous, liberal, plentiful

am·pli·fy \'am-plə-,fī\ *vb* **-fied; -fy·ing** 1 ♦ : to expand by extended treatment 2 ♦ : to increase in magnitude or strength; *esp* : to make louder — **am·pli·fi·ca·tion** \,am-plə-fə-'kā-shən\ *n* — **am·pli·fi·er** \'am-plə-,fī(-ə)r\ *n*

♦ [1] develop, elaborate (on), enlarge (on), expand ♦ [2] add, aggrandize, augment, boost, compound, enlarge, escalate, expand, extend, increase, multiply, raise, swell, up ♦ [2] beef, boost, consolidate, deepen, enhance, heighten, intensify, magnify, redouble, step up, strengthen

am·pli·tude \-,tüd, -,tyüd\ *n* 1 ♦ : ample extent : FULLNESS 2 ♦ : the extent or range of a quality, property, process, or phenomenon: as : the extent of a vibratory movement (as of a pendulum) or of an oscillation (as of an alternating current or a radio wave)

♦ breadth, compass, extent, range, reach, realm, scope, sweep, width

amplitude modulation *n* : modulation of the amplitude of a radio carrier wave in accordance with the strength of the signal; *also* : a broadcasting system using such modulation
am·ply \'am-plē\ *adv* ♦ : in an ample manner

♦ bountifully, generously, handsomely, liberally, unstintingly, well

am·poule *or* **am·pule** *also* **am·pul** \'am-,pyül, -,pül\ *n* : a small sealed bulbous glass vessel used to hold a solution for hypodermic injection

am·pu·tate \'am-pyə-,tāt\ *vb* **-tat·ed; -tat·ing** : to cut off ⟨∼ a leg⟩ — **am·pu·ta·tion** \,am-pyə-'tā-shən\ *n*

am·pu·tee \,am-pyə-'tē\ *n* : one who has had a limb amputated

AMSLAN *abbr* American Sign Language

amt *abbr* amount

amuck *var of* AMOK

am·u·let \'am-yə-lət\ *n* ♦ : an ornament worn as a charm against evil

    ♦ charm, fetish, mascot, talisman

amuse \ə-'myüz\ *vb* **amused; amus·ing** ♦ : to entertain in a light or playful manner : DIVERT

    ♦ disport, divert, entertain, regale

amuse·ment \-mənt\ *n* ♦ : pleasurable diversion

    ♦ distraction, diversion, entertainment

amus·ing \ə-'myü-ziŋ\ *adj* ♦ : giving amusement

    ♦ delightful, diverting, enjoyable, entertaining, fun, pleasurable

AM·VETS \'am-,vets\ *abbr* American Veterans (of World War II)

am·y·lase \'a-mə-,lās, -,lāz\ *n* : any of several enzymes that accelerate the breakdown of starch and glycogen

an \ən, (')an\ *indefinite article* : A — used before words beginning with a vowel sound

¹**-an** *or* **-ian** *also* **-ean** *n suffix* **1** : one that belongs to ⟨American⟩ ⟨crustac*ean*⟩ **2** : one skilled in or specializing in ⟨phonetic*ian*⟩

²**-an** *or* **-ian** *also* **-ean** *adj suffix* **1** : of or belonging to ⟨American⟩ **2** : characteristic of : resembling ⟨Shakespear*ean*⟩

AN *abbr* airman (Navy)

an·a·bol·ic steroid \,a-nə-'bä-lik-\ *n* : any of a group of synthetic steroid hormones sometimes abused by athletes in training to increase temporarily the size of their muscles

anach·ro·nism \ə-'na-krə-,ni-zəm\ *n* **1** : the error of placing a person or thing in the wrong period **2** : one that is chronologically out of place — **anach·ro·nis·tic** \ə-,na-krə-'nis-tik\ *adj* — **anach·ro·nous** \-'na-krə-nəs\ *adj*

an·a·con·da \,a-nə-'kän-də\ *n* : a large So. American snake that suffocates and kills its prey by constriction

anad·ro·mous \ə-'na-drə-məs\ *adj* : ascending rivers from the sea for breeding ⟨∼ fish⟩

an·aer·obe \'a-nə-,rōb\ *n* : an anaerobic organism

an·aer·o·bic \,a-nə-'rō-bik\ *adj* : living, active, occurring, or existing in the absence of free oxygen

ana·gram \'a-nə-,gram\ *n* : a word or phrase made by transposing the letters of another word or phrase

¹**anal** \'ān-ºl\ *adj* **1** : of, relating to, or situated near the anus **2** : of, relating to, or characterized by the stage of psychosexual development in psychoanalytic theory during which one is concerned esp. with feces **3** : of, relating to, or characterized by personality traits (as parsimony and ill humor) considered typical of fixation at the anal stage of development — **anal·ly** *adv*

²**anal** *abbr* **1** analogy **2** analysis; analytic

an·al·ge·sia \,an-ºl-'jē-zhə\ *n* : insensibility to pain — **an·al·ge·sic** \-'jē-zik, -sik\ *adj*

an·al·ge·sic \-'jē-zik, -,sik\ *n* : an agent for producing analgesia

analog computer \'an-ºl-,óg-, -,äg-\ *n* : a computer that operates with numbers represented by directly measurable quantities (as voltages)

anal·o·gous \ə-'na-lə-gəs\ *adj* ♦ : similar in one or more respects

    ♦ akin, alike, comparable, correspondent, like, parallel, similar, such

an·a·logue *or* **an·a·log** \'an-ºl-,óg, -,ag\ *n* **1** : something that is analogous to something else **2** : an organ similar in function to one of another animal or plant but different in structure or origin

anal·o·gy \ə-'na-lə-jē\ *n, pl* **-gies 1** : inference that if two or more things agree in some respects they will probably agree in others **2** : a likeness in one or more ways between things otherwise unlike — **an·a·log·i·cal** \,an-ºl-'ä-ji-kəl\ *adj* — **an·a·log·i·cal·ly** \-k(ə-)lē\ *adv*

anal·y·sis \ə-'na-lə-səs\ *n, pl* **-y·ses** \-,sēz\ **1** ♦ : separation of a thing into the parts or elements of which it is composed **2 a** : an examination of a thing to determine its parts or elements **b** ♦ : a statement showing the results of a critical examination **3** : PSYCHOANALYSIS — **an·a·lyst** \'an-ºl-ist\ *n* — **an·a·lyt·i·cal·ly** *adv*

    ♦ [1] assay, breakdown, breakup, dissection ♦ [2b] comment, commentary, exposition

an·a·lyt·ic \,an-ºl-'i-tik\ *adj* *or* **an·a·lyt·i·cal** \-ti-kəl\ *adj* ♦ : of or

relating to analysis; *esp* : separating something into component parts or constituent elements

    ♦ coherent, good, logical, rational, reasonable, sensible, sober, sound, valid

an·a·lyze \'an-ºl-,īz\ *vb* **-lyzed; -lyz·ing** ♦ : to make an analysis of

    ♦ anatomize, assay, break down, break up, dissect

an·a·pest \'a-nə-,pest\ *n* : a metrical foot of two unaccented syllables followed by one accented syllable — **an·a·pes·tic** \,a-nə-'pes-tik\ *adj or n*

an·ar·chic \a-'när-kik\ *adj* ♦ : of, relating to, or advocating anarchy

    ♦ disorderly, lawless, unruly

an·ar·chism \'a-nər-,ki-zəm\ *n* : the theory that all government is undesirable — **an·ar·chist** \-kist\ *n or adj* — **an·ar·chis·tic** \,a-nər-'kis-tik\ *adj*

an·ar·chy \'an-ər-kē\ *n* **1 a** : a social structure without government or law and order **b** : a state of lawlessness or political disorder due to the absence of governmental authority **2** : utter confusion — **an·ar·chi·cal·ly** \-ki-k(ə-)lē\ *adv*

anas·to·mo·sis \ə-,nas-tə-'mō-səs\ *n, pl* **-mo·ses** \-,sēz\ **1** : the union of parts or branches (as of blood vessels) **2** : NETWORK

anat *abbr* anatomical; anatomy

anath·e·ma \ə-'na-thə-mə\ *n* **1 a** : a person or thing accursed **b** ♦ : one intensely disliked **2** ♦ : a solemn curse

    ♦ [1b] abhorrence, abomination, antipathy, aversion, bête noire, hate ♦ [2] curse, execration, imprecation, malediction

anath·e·ma·tize \-,tīz\ *vb* **-tized; -tiz·ing** : to pronounce an anathema against : CURSE

anat·o·mise *Brit var of* ANATOMIZE

anat·o·mize \ə-'na-tə-,mīz\ *vb* **-mized; -miz·ing 1** : to dissect so as to examine the structure and parts **2** ♦ : to study or determine the nature and relationship of the parts of by analysis : ANALYZE

    ♦ analyze, assay, break down, break up, dissect

anat·o·my \ə-'na-tə-mē\ *n, pl* **-mies 1** : a branch of science dealing with the structure of organisms **2** : structural makeup esp. of an organism or any of its parts **3** : a separating into parts for detailed study : ANALYSIS — **an·a·tom·ic** \,a-nə-'tä-mik\ *or* **an·a·tom·i·cal** \-mi-kəl\ *adj* — **an·a·tom·i·cal·ly** \-mi-k(ə-)lē\ *adv* — **anat·o·mist** \ə-'na-tə-mist\ *n*

anc *abbr* ancient

-ance *n suffix* **1** : action or process ⟨further*ance*⟩ : instance of an action or process ⟨perform*ance*⟩ **2** : quality or state : instance of a quality or state ⟨protuber*ance*⟩ **3** : amount or degree ⟨conduct*ance*⟩

an·ces·tor \'an-,ses-tər\ *n* **1** ♦ : one from whom an individual is descended **2** ♦ : an individual that exhibits the essential features of a later type

    ♦ [1] father, forebear, forefather, grandfather *Ant* descendant ♦ [2] antecedent, forerunner, precursor *Ant* descendant

an·ces·tress \'an-,ses-trəs\ *n* : a female ancestor

an·ces·try \'an-,ses-trē\ *n* **1** : line of descent : LINEAGE **2** : ANCESTORS — **an·ces·tral** \an-'ses-trəl\ *adj*

    ♦ birth, blood, bloodline, breeding, descent, extraction, family tree, genealogy, line, lineage, origin, parentage, pedigree, stock, strain *Ant* issue, posterity, progeny, seed

¹**an·chor** \'aŋ-kər\ *n* **1** : a heavy metal device attached to a ship that catches hold of the bottom and holds the ship in place **2** : a broadcaster who reads the news and introduces the reports of other broadcasters : ANCHORPERSON

²**anchor** *vb* ♦ : to hold or become held in place by or as if by an anchor

    ♦ catch, clamp, fasten, fix, hitch, moor, secure, set

an·chor·age \'aŋ-k(ə-)rij\ *n* ♦ : a place suitable for ships to anchor

    ♦ harbor (*or* harbour), haven, port

an·cho·rite \'aŋ-kə-,rīt\ *n* ♦ : one that retires from society and lives in solitude : HERMIT

    ♦ hermit, recluse, solitary

an·chor·man \'aŋ-kər-,man\ *n* **1** : the member of a team who competes last **2** : an anchorperson who is a man

an·chor·per·son \-,pər-sən\ *n* : a broadcaster who reads the news and introduces the reports of other broadcasters

an·chor·wom·an \-,wü-mən\ *n* : a woman who anchors a broadcast

an·cho·vy \'an-ˌchō-vē, an-'chō-\ *n, pl* **-vies** *or* **-vy** : a small herringlike fish used esp. for sauces and relishes

an·cien ré·gime \äⁿs-yaⁿ-rā-'zhēm\ *n* **1** : the political and social system of France before the Revolution of 1789 **2** : a system no longer prevailing

¹an·cient \'ān-shənt\ *adj* **1** ♦ : having existed for many years **2** ♦ : belonging to times long past; *esp* : belonging to the period before the Middle Ages

♦ [1] elderly, geriatric, old, senior ♦ [2] age-old, antediluvian, antique, dateless, hoary, old, venerable *Ant* modern, new, recent ♦ [2] early, primal, primeval, primitive

²ancient *n* **1** : an aged person **2** *pl* : the peoples of ancient Greece and Rome; *esp* : the classical authors of Greece and Rome

an·cil·lary \'an-sə-ˌler-ē\ *adj* **1** : SUBORDINATE, SUBSIDIARY **2** : AUXILIARY, SUPPLEMENTARY — **ancillary** *n*

-ancy *n suffix* : quality or state ⟨flamboyancy⟩

and \ənd, (')and\ *conj* **1** — used to indicate connection or addition esp. of items within the same class or type or to join words or phrases of the same grammatical rank or function **2** — used to join one finite verb to another so that together they are equivalent to an infinitive of purpose ⟨come ~ see me⟩

¹an·dan·te \än-'dän-ˌtā, -tē\ *adv or adj* : moderately slow — used as a direction in music

²andante *n* : an andante movement

and·iron \'an-ˌdī(-ə)rn\ *n* : one of a pair of metal supports for firewood in a fireplace

and/or \'and-'ȯr\ *conj* — used to indicate that either *and* or *or* may apply ⟨"apples ~ oranges" means that the possibilities include apples, oranges, or both⟩

An·dor·ran \an-'dȯr-ən\ *n* : a native or inhabitant of Andorra

an·dro·gen \'an-drə-jən\ *n* : a male sex hormone

an·drog·y·nous \an-'drä-jə-nəs\ *adj* **1** : having the characteristics of both male and female **2** : suitable for either sex ⟨~ clothing⟩

an·droid \'an-ˌdrȯid\ *n* : a mobile robot usu. with a human form

an·ec·dot·al \ˌa-nik-'dōt-ᵊl\ *adj* **1** : relating to or consisting of anecdotes **2** : based on reports of an unscientific nature — **an·ec·dot·al·ly** *adv*

an·ec·dote \'an-ik-ˌdōt\ *n, pl* **-dotes** *also* **-dota** \ˌa-nik-'dō-tə\ ♦ : a brief story of an interesting, amusing, or biographical incident

♦ story, tale

ane·mia \ə-'nē-mē-ə\ *n* **1** : a condition in which blood is deficient in quantity, in red blood cells, or in hemoglobin and which is marked by pallor, weakness, and irregular heart action **2** : lack of vitality — **ane·mic** \ə-'nē-mik\ *adj*

an·e·mom·e·ter \ˌa-nə-'mä-mə-tər\ *n* : an instrument for measuring the force or speed of the wind

anem·o·ne \ə-'ne-mə-nē\ *n* : any of a large genus of herbs related to the buttercups that have showy flowers without petals but with conspicuous often colored sepals

anent \ə-'nent\ *prep* : CONCERNING

an·es·the·sia *or Can and Brit* **an·aes·the·sia** \ˌa-nəs-'thē-zhə\ *n* : loss of bodily sensation

an·es·the·si·ol·o·gy *or chiefly Brit* **an·aes·the·si·ol·o·gy** \-ˌthē-zē-'ä-lə-jē\ *n* : a branch of medical science dealing with anesthesia and anesthetics — **an·es·the·si·ol·o·gist** \-jist\ *n*

¹an·es·thet·ic *or Can and Brit* **an·aes·thet·ic** \ˌa-nəs-'the-tik\ *adj* : of, relating to, or capable of producing anesthesia

²anesthetic *or Can and Brit* **anaesthetic** *n* : an agent that produces anesthesia — **anes·the·tist** \ə-'nes-thə-tist\ *n* — **anes·the·tize** \-ˌtīz\ *vb*

an·eu·rysm \'an-yə-ˌri-zəm\ *n* : an abnormal blood-filled bulge of a blood vessel

anew \ə-'nü, -'nyü\ *adv* **1** ♦ : over again **2** : in a new form

♦ again, over

an·gel \'ān-jəl\ *n* **1** : a spiritual being superior to humans **2** : an attendant spirit **3** : a winged figure of human form in art **4** ♦ : one that precedes and indicates the approach of another : HARBINGER **5** : a person held to resemble an angel (as in looks or behavior) **6** : a financial backer — **an·gel·ic** \an-'je-lik\ *or* **an·gel·i·cal** \-li-kəl\ *adj* — **an·gel·i·cal·ly** \-k(ə-)lē\ *adv*

♦ forerunner, harbinger, herald, precursor

an·gel·fish \'ān-jəl-ˌfish\ *n* : any of several bright-colored tropical fishes that are flattened from side to side

an·gel·i·ca \an-'je-li-kə\ *n* : a biennial herb related to the carrot whose roots and fruit furnish a flavoring oil

¹an·ger \'aŋ-gər\ *vb* ♦ : to make angry

♦ antagonize, enrage, incense, inflame, infuriate, madden, outrage, rankle, rile, roil *Ant* delight, gratify, please

²anger *n* ♦ : a strong feeling of displeasure

♦ furor, fury, indignation, ire, outrage, rage, spleen, wrath, wrathfulness *Ant* delight, pleasure

an·gi·na \an-'jī-nə\ *n* : a disorder (as of the heart) marked by attacks of intense pain; *esp* : ANGINA PECTORIS — **an·gi·nal** \an-'jīn-ᵊl\ *adj*

angina pec·to·ris \-'pek-t(ə-)rəs\ *n* : a heart disease marked by brief attacks of sharp chest pain caused by deficient oxygenation of heart muscles

an·gio·gram \'an-jē-ə-ˌgram\ *n* : an X-ray photograph made by angiography

an·gi·og·ra·phy \ˌan-jē-'ä-grə-fē\ *n* : the use of X-rays to make blood vessels visible (as by photography) after injection of a substance opaque to radiation

an·gio·plas·ty \'an-jē-ə-ˌplas-tē\ *n* : surgical repair of a blood vessel esp. by using an inflatable catheter to unblock arteries clogged by atherosclerotic deposits

an·gio·sperm \-ˌspərm\ *n* : FLOWERING PLANT

¹an·gle \'aŋ-gəl\ *n* **1** : a sharp projecting corner **2** : the figure formed by the meeting of two lines in a point **3 a** ♦ : a point of view **b** ♦ : the aspect seen from such an angle **4** : a special technique or plan : GIMMICK — **an·gled** *adj*

♦ [3a] outlook, perspective, point of view, slant, standpoint, viewpoint ♦ [3b] aspect, facet, hand, phase, side

²angle *vb* **an·gled; an·gling** \-g(ə-)liŋ\ ♦ : to turn, move, or direct at an angle

♦ cant, cock, heel, incline, lean, list, slant, slope, tilt, tip

³angle *vb* **an·gled; an·gling** \-g(ə-)liŋ\ : to fish with a hook and line — **an·gler** \-glər\ *n*

an·gle·worm \'aŋ-gəl-ˌwərm\ *n* : EARTHWORM

An·gli·can \'aŋ-gli-kən\ *adj* **1** : of or relating to the established episcopal Church of England **2** : of or relating to England or the English nation — **Anglican** *n* — **An·gli·can·ism** \-kə-ˌni-zəm\ *n*

an·gli·cize \'aŋ-glə-ˌsīz\ *vb* **-cized; -ciz·ing** *often cap* **1** : to make English (as in habits, speech, character, or outlook) **2** : to borrow (a foreign word or phrase) into English without changing form or spelling and sometimes without changing pronunciation — **an·gli·ci·za·tion** \ˌaŋ-glə-sə-'zā-shən\ *n, often cap*

an·gling \-gliŋ\ *n* : the action of one who angles; *esp* : the action or sport of fishing with hook and line

An·glo \'aŋ-glō\ *n, pl* **Anglos** : a non-Hispanic white inhabitant of the U.S.; *esp* : one of English origin and descent

An·glo–French \ˌaŋ-glō-'french\ *n* : the French language used in medieval England

An·glo·phile \'aŋ-glə-ˌfīl\ *also* **An·glo·phil** \-ˌfil\ *n* : one who greatly admires England and things English

An·glo·phobe \'aŋ-glə-ˌfōb\ *n* : one who is averse to England and things English

An·glo–Sax·on \ˌaŋ-glō-'sak-sən\ *n* **1** : a member of any of the Germanic peoples who invaded England in the 5th century A.D. **2** : a member of the English people **3** : the language of the English people before about 1100 — **Anglo–Saxon** *adj*

an·go·ra \aŋ-'gōr-ə, an-\ *n* **1** : yarn or cloth made from the hair of an Angora goat or rabbit **2** *cap* : any of a breed of cats, goats, or rabbits with a long silky coat

an·gry \'aŋ-grē\ *adj* **an·gri·er; -est** ♦ : feeling or showing anger — **an·gri·ly** \-grə-lē\ *adv*

♦ enraged, furious, irate, sore, wrathful *Ant* delighted, pleased

angst \'äŋst\ *n* : a feeling of anxiety

ang·strom \'aŋ-strəm\ *n* : a unit of length equal to one ten-billionth of a meter

an·guish \'aŋ-gwish\ *n* ♦ : extreme pain or distress esp. of mind

♦ affliction, agony, distress, misery, pain, torment, torture, tribulation, woe ♦ affliction, dolor, grief, heartache, sorrow, woe

an·guished \-gwisht\ *adj* **1** : suffering anguish ⟨the ~ martyrs⟩ **2** ♦ : expressing anguish ⟨~ cries⟩

♦ dolorous, lamentable, mournful, plaintive, sorrowful, sorry, woeful

an·gu·lar \'aŋ-gyə-lər\ *adj* **1** : sharp-cornered **2** : having one or more angles **3** : being thin and bony — **an·gu·lar·i·ty** \ˌaŋ-gyə-'lar-ə-tē\ *n*

An·gus \'aŋ-gəs\ *n* : any of a breed of usu. black hornless beef cattle originating in Scotland

an·hy·drous \an-'hī-drəs\ *adj* : free from water

an·i·line \'an-ᵊl-ən\ *n* : an oily poisonous liquid used in making dyes, medicines, and explosives

an·i·mad·vert \ˌa-nə-ˌmad-'vərt\ *vb* : to remark critically : express censure — **an·i·mad·ver·sion** \-'vər-zhən\ *n*

¹an·i·mal \'a-nə-məl\ *n* **1** : any of a kingdom of living things typically differing from plants in capacity for active movement, in rapid response to stimulation, and in lack of cellulose cell walls **2 ♦** : a lower animal as distinguished from human beings; *also* : MAMMAL

♦ beast, brute, creature, critter

²animal *adj* **1** : of, relating to, or derived from animals **2 ♦** : of or relating to the physical as distinguished from the mental or spiritual

♦ bodily, carnal, corporal, fleshly, material, physical, somatic

an·i·mal·cule \,a-nə-'mal-kyül\ *n* : a tiny animal usu. invisible to the naked eye

¹an·i·mate \'a-nə-mət\ *adj* **1 ♦** : having life : ALIVE **2 ♦** : full of vigor and spirit : LIVELY

♦ [1] alive, live, living ♦ [2] active, animated, energetic, lively, peppy, perky, spirited, sprightly, springy, vital, vivacious

²an·i·mate \-,māt\ *vb* **-mat·ed; -mat·ing** **1** : to impart life to **2 ♦** : to give spirit and vigor to **3** : to make appear to move ⟨∼ a cartoon for motion pictures⟩

♦ brace, energize, enliven, fire, invigorate, jazz up, liven up, pep up, quicken, stimulate, vitalize, vivify, zip (up) *Ant* damp, dampen, deaden, dull

an·i·mat·ed \-,mā-təd\ *adj* **1 ♦** : endowed with life or the qualities of life : ALIVE **2 ♦** : full of movement and activity ⟨an ∼ crowd⟩ **3 ♦** : full of vigor and spirit : LIVELY

♦ [1, 2] alive, astir, busy, lively, vibrant ♦ [3] active, animate, energetic, lively, peppy, perky, spirited, sprightly, springy, vital, vivacious

an·i·ma·tion \,a-nə-'mā-shən\ *n* **1 ♦** : the state of being animate or animated : LIVELINESS **2** : a motion picture made from a series of drawings, computer graphics, or stop-motion images simulating motions by means of slight progressive changes

♦ briskness, exuberance, liveliness, lustiness, robustness, sprightliness, vibrancy, vitality

an·i·mism \'a-nə-,mi-zəm\ *n* : attribution of conscious life to objects in and phenomena of nature or to inanimate objects — **an·i·mist** \-mist\ *n* — **an·i·mis·tic** \,a-nə-'mis-tik\ *adj*

an·i·mos·i·ty \,a-nə-'mä-sə-tē\ *n, pl* **-ties** **♦** : ill will or resentment tending toward active hostility

♦ antagonism, antipathy, bitterness, enmity, gall, grudge, hostility, rancor

an·i·mus \'a-nə-məs\ *n* : deep-seated resentment and hostility

an·ion \'a-,nī-ən, -,nī-,än\ *n* : a negatively charged ion

an·ise \'a-nəs\ *n* : an herb related to the carrot with aromatic seeds (**aniseed** \-sēd\) used in flavoring

an·is·ette \,a-nə-'set, -'zet\ *n* : a usu. colorless sweet liqueur flavored with aniseed

ankh \'äŋk\ *n* : a cross having a loop for its upper vertical arm and serving esp. in ancient Egypt as an emblem of life

an·kle \'aŋ-kəl\ *n* : the joint or region between the foot and the leg

an·kle·bone \'aŋ-kəl-,bōn\ *n* : the bone that in human beings bears the weight of the body and with the tibia and fibula forms the ankle joint

an·klet \'aŋ-klət\ *n* **1** : something (as an ornament) worn around the ankle **2** : a short sock reaching slightly above the ankle

ann *abbr* **1** annals **2** annual

an·nal·ist \'an-ᵊl-ist\ *n* : a writer of annals

an·nals \'an-ᵊlz\ *n pl* **1 ♦** : a record of events in chronological order **2** : historical records

♦ chronicle, history, record

an·neal \ə-'nēl\ *vb* **1** : to make (as glass or steel) less brittle by heating and then cooling **2** : STRENGTHEN, TOUGHEN

¹an·nex \ə-'neks, 'a-,neks\ *vb* **1 ♦** : to attach as an addition **2** : to incorporate (as a territory) within a political domain — **an·nex·a·tion** \,a-,nek-'sā-shən\ *n*

♦ add, adjoin, append, tack

²an·nex \'a-,neks, -niks\ *n* **♦** : a subsidiary or supplementary structure

♦ addition, extension, penthouse

an·ni·hi·late \ə-'nī-ə-,lāt\ *vb* **-lat·ed; -lat·ing** **♦** : to destroy completely

♦ blot out, demolish, eradicate, exterminate, liquidate, obliterate, root, rub out, snuff, stamp, wipe out

an·ni·hi·la·tion \-,nī-ə-'lā-shən\ *n* **♦** : the act of annihilating or state of being annihilated

♦ demolition, desolation, destruction, devastation, havoc, loss, obliteration, ruin, wastage, wreckage

an·ni·ver·sa·ry \,a-nə-'vər-sə-rē\ *n, pl* **-ries** : the annual return of the date of a notable event and esp. a wedding

an·no Do·mi·ni \,a-nō-'dä-mə-nē, -'dō-, -,nī\ *adv, often cap A* — used to indicate that a time division falls within the Christian era

an·no·tate \'a-nə-,tāt\ *vb* **-tat·ed; -tat·ing** : to furnish with notes — **an·no·ta·tion** \,a-nə-'tā-shən\ *n* — **an·no·ta·tor** \'a-nə-,tā-tər\ *n*

an·nounce \ə-'naůns\ *vb* **an·nounced; an·nounc·ing** **1 ♦** : to make known publicly **2** : to give notice of the arrival or presence of

♦ advertise, blaze, broadcast, declare, enunciate, placard, post, proclaim, promulgate, publicize, publish, sound

an·nounce·ment \-mənt\ *n* **♦** : a public notification or declaration

♦ advertisement, bulletin, notice, notification, release

an·nounc·er \ə-'naůn-sər\ *n* : a person who introduces radio or television programs, makes commercial announcements, or gives station identification

an·noy \ə-'nȯi\ *vb* **♦** : to disturb or irritate esp. by repeated acts : VEX — **an·noy·ing·ly** *adv*

♦ aggravate, bother, bug, chafe, exasperate, gall, get, grate, irk, irritate, nettle, peeve, rile, vex

an·noy·ance \ə-'nȯi-əns\ *n* **1 ♦** : the act of annoying **2 ♦** : the state of being annoyed **3 ♦** : one that is annoying, unpleasant, or obnoxious : NUISANCE

♦ [1] aggravation, disturbance, harassment, vexation ♦ [2] aggravation, bother, exasperation, frustration, vexation ♦ [3] bother, exasperation, frustration, hassle, headache, inconvenience, irritant, nuisance, peeve, pest, problem, thorn

an·noy·ing \-iŋ\ *adj* **♦** : causing vexation

♦ aggravating, bothersome, frustrating, galling, irksome, irritating, pesty, vexatious

¹an·nu·al \'an-yə-wəl\ *adj* **1** : covering the period of a year **2** : occurring once a year : YEARLY **3** : completing the life cycle in one growing season ⟨∼ plants⟩ — **an·nu·al·ly** *adv*

²annual *n* **1** : a publication appearing once a year **2** : an annual plant

annual ring *n* : the layer of wood produced by a single year's growth of a woody plant

an·nu·i·tant \ə-'nü-ə-tənt, -'nyü-\ *n* : a beneficiary of an annuity

an·nu·i·ty \ə-'nü-ə-tē, -'nyü-\ *n, pl* **-i·ties** **1** : an amount payable annually **2** : the right to receive an annual payment

an·nul \ə-'nəl\ *vb* **an·nulled; an·nul·ling** **1 ♦** : to make ineffective or inoperative **2 ♦** : to make legally void — **an·nul·ment** *n*

♦ [1, 2] abolish, abrogate, cancel, dissolve, invalidate, negate, nullify, quash, repeal, rescind, void

an·nu·lar \'an-yə-lər\ *adj* : ring-shaped

an·nun·ci·ate \ə-'nən-sē-,āt\ *vb* **-at·ed; -at·ing** : ANNOUNCE

an·nun·ci·a·tion \ə-,nən-sē-'ā-shən\ *n* **1** : ANNOUNCEMENT **2** *cap* : March 25 observed as a church festival commemorating the announcement of the Incarnation

an·nun·ci·a·tor \ə-'nən-sē-,ā-tər\ *n* : one that annunciates; *specif* : a usu. electrically controlled signal board or indicator

an·ode \'a-,nōd\ *n* **1** : the positive electrode of an electrolytic cell **2** : the negative terminal of a battery **3** : the electron-collecting electrode of an electron tube — **an·od·ic** \a-'nä-dik\ *also* **an·od·al** \-'nōd-ᵊl\ *adj*

an·od·ize \'a-nə-,dīz\ *vb* **-ized; -iz·ing** : to subject (a metal) to electrolytic action as the anode of a cell in order to coat with a protective or decorative film

an·o·dyne \'a-nə-,dīn\ *n* : something that relieves pain : a soothing agent

anoint \ə-'nȯint\ *vb* **1** : to apply oil to esp. as a sacred rite **2** : CONSECRATE — **anoint·ment** *n*

anom·a·lous \ə-'nä-mə-ləs\ *adj* **♦** : deviating from a general rule : ABNORMAL

♦ aberrant, abnormal, atypical, deviant, irregular, unnatural

anom·a·ly \ə-'nä-mə-lē\ *n, pl* **-lies** : something anomalous

¹anon \ə-'nän\ *adv* **♦** : in the near future

♦ momentarily, presently, shortly, soon

²anon *abbr* anonymous; anonymously

an·o·nym·i·ty \,a-nə-'ni-mə-tē\ *n* : the quality or state of being anonymous

anon·y·mous \ə-'nä-nə-məs\ *adj* ♦ : of unknown or undeclared origin or authorship — **anon·y·mous·ly** *adv*

♦ nameless, unbaptized, unchristened, unidentified, unnamed, untitled

anoph·e·les \ə-'nä-fə-ˌlēz\ *n* : any of a genus of mosquitoes that includes all mosquitoes which transmit malaria to human beings

an·o·rec·tic \ˌa-nə-'rek-tik\ *adj* : ANOREXIC — **anorectic** *n*

an·orex·ia \ˌa-nə-'rek-sē-ə\ *n* **1** : loss of appetite esp. when prolonged **2** : ANOREXIA NERVOSA

anorexia ner·vo·sa \-nər-'vō-sə\ *n* : a serious disorder in eating behavior marked esp. by a pathological fear of weight gain leading to faulty eating patterns, malnutrition, and usu. excessive weight loss

an·orex·ic \ˌa-nə-'rek-sik\ *adj* **1** : lacking or causing loss of appetite **2** : affected with or as if with anorexia nervosa — **an·orexic** *n*

¹an·oth·er \ə-'nə-thər\ *adj* **1** : some other **2** ♦ : being one in addition : one more

♦ additional, else, farther, further, more, other

²another *pron* **1** : an additional one : one more **2** : one that is different from the first or present one

ans *abbr* answer

¹an·swer \'an-sər\ *n* **1** ♦ : something spoken or written in reply to a question **2** : a solution of a problem

♦ comeback, reply, response, retort, return *Ant* inquiry, query, question

²answer *vb* **1** ♦ : to speak or write in reply to **2** ♦ : to be or make oneself responsible or accountable ⟨∼ for a debt⟩ **3** ♦ : to be in conformity or correspondence ⟨∼ed to the description⟩ **4** : to be adequate **5** ♦ : to offer a solution for — **an·swer·er** *n*

♦ [1] rejoin, reply, respond, retort, return *Ant* inquire, question ♦ [2] comply, fill, fulfill, keep, meet, redeem, satisfy ♦ [3] check, coincide, comport, conform, correspond, dovetail, fit, go, harmonize, jibe, square, tally ♦ [5] break, crack, dope, figure out, puzzle, resolve, riddle, solve, unravel, work, work out

an·swer·able \'an-sə-rə-bəl\ *adj* **1** ♦ : subject to taking blame or responsibility **2** : capable of being refuted

♦ accountable, liable, responsible

answering machine *n* : a machine that receives telephone calls by playing a recorded message and usu. by recording messages from callers

answering service *n* : a commercial service that answers telephone calls for its clients

¹ant \'ant\ *n* : any of a family of small social insects related to the bees and living in communities usu. in earth or wood

²ant *abbr* antonym

Ant *abbr* Antarctica

¹-ant *n suffix* **1** : one that performs or promotes (a specified action) ⟨cool*ant*⟩ **2** : thing that is acted upon (in a specified manner) ⟨inhal*ant*⟩

²-ant *adj suffix* **1** : performing (a specified action) or being (in a specified condition) ⟨propell*ant*⟩ **2** : promoting (a specified action or process) ⟨expector*ant*⟩

ant·ac·id \ant-'a-səd\ *n* : an agent that counteracts acidity — **antacid** *adj*

an·tag·o·nism \an-'ta-gə-ˌni-zəm\ *n* **1** ♦ : active opposition or hostility **2** : opposition in physiological action

♦ animosity, antipathy, bitterness, enmity, gall, grudge, hostility, rancor

an·tag·o·nist \-nist\ *n* ♦ : one that contends with or opposes another : ADVERSARY, OPPONENT

♦ adversary, enemy, foe, opponent

an·tag·o·nis·tic \-ˌta-gə-'nis-tik\ *adj* ♦ : marked by or resulting from antagonism

♦ hostile, inhospitable, inimical, jaundiced, negative, unfriendly, unsympathetic

an·tag·o·nize \an-'ta-gə-ˌnīz\ *vb* **-nized; -niz·ing** ♦ : to provoke the hostility of

♦ anger, enrage, incense, inflame, infuriate, madden, outrage, rankle, rile, roil

ant·arc·tic \ant-'ärk-tik, -'är-tik\ *adj, often cap* : of or relating to the south pole or the region near it

antarctic circle *n, often cap A&C* : the parallel of latitude that is approximately 66½ degrees south of the equator

¹an·te \'an-tē\ *n* : a poker stake put up before the deal to build the pot; *also* : an amount paid : PRICE

²ante *vb* **an·ted; an·te·ing** **1** : to put up (an ante) **2** : PAY

ant·eat·er \'ant-ˌē-tər\ *n* : any of several mammals (as an aardvark) that feed mostly on ants or termites

an·te·bel·lum \ˌan-ti-'be-ləm\ *adj* : existing before a war; *esp* : existing before the U.S. Civil War of 1861-65

¹an·te·ced·ent \ˌan-tə-'sēd-ᵊnt\ *n* **1** : a noun, pronoun, phrase, or clause referred to by a personal or relative pronoun **2** ♦ : a preceding event or cause **3** *pl* : the significant conditions of one's earlier life **4 a** ♦ : one that precedes : PREDECESSOR; *esp* : a model or stimulus for later developments **b** *pl* : ANCESTORS

♦ [2] cause, occasion, reason ♦ [4a] ancestor, forerunner, precursor

²antecedent *adj* ♦ : earlier in time or order

♦ anterior, foregoing, preceding, previous, prior

an·te·cham·ber \'an-ti-ˌchām-bər\ *n* : ANTEROOM

an·te·date \'an-ti-ˌdāt\ *vb* **1** : to date (a paper) as of an earlier day than that on which the actual writing or signing is done **2** ♦ : to precede in time

♦ forego, precede

an·te·di·lu·vi·an \ˌan-ti-də-'lü-vē-ən, -dī-\ *adj* **1** : of the period before the biblical flood **2** ♦ : made, evolved, or developed a long time ago **3** : extremely primitive or outmoded

♦ age-old, ancient, antique, dateless, hoary, old, venerable

an·te·lope \'ant-ᵊl-ˌōp\ *n, pl* **-lope** *or* **-lopes** **1** : any of various deerlike ruminant mammals that chiefly inhabit Africa and have a slender build and horns extending upward and backward **2** : PRONGHORN

an·te me·ri·di·em \ˌan-ti-mə-'ri-dē-əm\ *adj* : being before noon

an·ten·na \an-'te-nə\ *n, pl* **-nae** \-(ˌ)nē\ *or* **-nas** **1** : one of the long slender paired segmented sensory organs on the head of an arthropod (as an insect or crab) **2** *pl usu* **-nas** : a metallic device (as a rod or wire) for sending out or receiving radio waves

an·te·pe·nult \ˌan-ti-'pē-ˌnəlt\ *also* **an·te·pen·ul·ti·ma** \-pi-'nəl-tə-mə\ *n* : the 3d syllable of a word counting from the end — **an·te·pen·ul·ti·mate** \-pi-'nəl-tə-mət\ *adj or n*

an·te·ri·or \an-'tir-ē-ər\ *adj* **1** : situated before or toward the front **2** : situated near or nearer to the head **3** ♦ : coming before in time

♦ antecedent, foregoing, preceding, previous, prior

anterior cruciate ligament *n* : a cross-shaped ligament of the knee that connects the tibia and femur

an·te·room \'an-ti-ˌrüm, -ˌrum\ *n* : a room forming the entrance to another and often used as a waiting room

an·them \'an-thəm\ *n* **1** ♦ : a sacred vocal composition **2** ♦ : a song or hymn of praise or gladness

♦ [1, 2] canticle, carol, chorale, hymn, psalm, spiritual

an·ther \'an-thər\ *n* : the part of a stamen of a seed plant that produces and contains pollen

ant·hill \'ant-ˌhil\ *n* : a mound thrown up by ants or termites in digging their nest

an·thol·o·gy \an-'thä-lə-jē\ *n, pl* **-gies** ♦ : a collection of literary selections — **an·thol·o·gist** \-jist\ *n* — **an·thol·o·gize** \-ˌjīz\ *vb*

♦ album, compilation, miscellany

an·thra·cite \'an-thrə-ˌsīt\ *n* : a hard glossy coal that burns without much smoke

an·thrax \'an-ˌthraks\ *n* : an infectious and usu. fatal bacterial disease of warm-blooded animals (as cattle and sheep) that is transmissible to humans; *also* : a bacterium causing anthrax

an·thro·po·cen·tric \ˌan-thrə-pə-'sen-trik\ *adj* : interpreting or regarding the world in terms of human values and experiences

an·thro·poid \'an-thrə-ˌpȯid\ *n* **1** : any of several large tailless apes (as a gorilla) **2** : a person resembling an ape — **anthropoid** *adj*

an·thro·pol·o·gy \ˌan-thrə-'pä-lə-jē\ *n* : the science of human beings; *esp* : the study of human beings and their ancestors through time and space and in relation to physical character, environmental and social relations, and culture — **an·thro·po·log·i·cal** \-pə-'lä-ji-kəl\ *adj* — **an·thro·pol·o·gist** \-'pä-lə-jist\ *n*

an·thro·po·mor·phism \ˌan-thrə-pə-'mȯr-fi-zəm\ *n* : an interpretation of what is not human or personal in terms of human or personal characteristics : HUMANIZATION — **an·thro·po·mor·phic** \-fik\ *adj*

an·ti \'an-ˌtī, -tē\ *n, pl* **antis** : one who is opposed

anti- \ˌan-ti, -tē, -ˌtī\ *or* **ant-** *or* **anth-** *prefix* **1** : opposite in kind, position, or action **2** : opposing : hostile toward **3** : counteractive **4** : preventive of : curative of

antiaging
anti–AIDS
antiaircraft
antialcohol
anti–American
antiapartheid
antibacterial
anticapitalist
anti–Catholic
anticholesterol
anticlerical
anticolonial
anticommunism
anticommunist
antidemocratic
antiestablishment
antifascist

antigovernment
anti–imperialism
anti–imperialist
antiknock
antilabor
antimalarial
antimicrobial
antinausea
antipoverty
antislavery
antispasmodic
antistatic
antisubmarine
antitank
antitumor
antiviral
antiwar

an·ti·abor·tion \ˌan-tē-ə-'bȯr-shən, ˌan-ˌtī-\ *adj* : opposed to abortion

an·ti·bal·lis·tic missile \ˌan-ti-bə-'lis-tik-, ˌan-ˌtī-\ *n* : a missile for intercepting and destroying ballistic missiles

an·ti·bi·ot·ic \-'bī-'ä-tik, -bē-\ *n* : a substance produced by or derived by chemical alteration of a substance produced by a microorganism (as a fungus or bacterium) that in dilute solution inhibits or kills another microorganism — **antibiotic** *adj*

an·ti·body \'an-ti-ˌbä-dē\ *n* : any of a large number of proteins of high molecular weight produced normally by specialized B cells after stimulation by an antigen and acting specifically against the antigen in an immune response

¹**an·tic** \'an-tik\ *n* ♦ : an often wildly playful or funny act or action
   ♦ caper, escapade, frolic, monkeyshine, practical joke, prank, trick

²**antic** *adj* **1** *archaic* : GROTESQUE **2 a** ♦ : characterized by clownish extravagance or absurdity **b** ♦ : whimsically merry : PLAYFUL
   ♦ [2a] comic, comical, droll, farcical, funny, hilarious, humorous, hysterical, laughable, ludicrous, ridiculous, riotous ♦ [2b] coltish, elfish, fay, frisky, frolicsome, playful, sportive

an·ti·can·cer \ˌan-ti-'kan-sər, ˌan-ˌtī-\ *adj* : used against or tending to arrest cancer ⟨∼ drugs⟩

An·ti·christ \'an-ti-ˌkrīst\ *n* **1** : one who denies or opposes Christ **2** : a false Christ

an·tic·i·pate \an-'ti-sə-ˌpāt\ *vb* **-pat·ed; -pat·ing 1** ♦ : to foresee and provide for beforehand **2** ♦ : to look forward to —
an·tic·i·pa·tion \-ˌti-sə-'pā-shən\ *n*
   ♦ [1] divine, foreknow, foresee ♦ [2] await, expect, hope, watch

an·tic·i·pa·to·ry \-'ti-sə-pə-ˌtōr-ē\ *adj* ♦ : characterized by anticipation
   ♦ agape, agog, expectant

an·ti·cli·max \ˌan-ti-'klī-ˌmaks\ *n* : something closing a series that is strikingly less important than what has preceded it —
an·ti·cli·mac·tic \-klī-'mak-tik\ *adj*

an·ti·cline \'an-ti-ˌklīn\ *n* : an arch of layers of rock in the earth's crust

an·ti·co·ag·u·lant \ˌan-ti-kō-'a-gyə-lənt\ *n* : a substance that hinders the clotting of blood — **anticoagulant** *adj*

an·ti·cy·clone \ˌan-ti-'sī-ˌklōn\ *n* : a system of winds that rotates about a center of high atmospheric pressure — **an·ti·cy·clon·ic** \-sī-'klä-nik\ *adj*

¹**an·ti·de·pres·sant** \ˌan-ti-di-'pres-ᵊnt, ˌan-ˌtī-\ *adj* : used or tending to relieve or prevent depression ⟨∼ drugs⟩

²**antidepressant** *n* : an antidepressant drug

an·ti·dote \'an-ti-ˌdōt\ *n* : a remedy to counteract the effects of poison

an·ti·drug \'an-ˌtī-ˌdrəg\ *adj* : acting against or opposing illicit drugs

an·ti·fer·til·i·ty \ˌan-ti-fər-'ti-lə-tē\ *adj* : tending to reduce or destroy fertility : CONTRACEPTIVE ⟨∼ agents⟩

an·ti·freeze \'an-ti-ˌfrēz\ *n* : a substance added to a liquid to lower its freezing temperature

an·ti·gen \'an-ti-jən\ *n* : any substance (as a toxin or an enzyme) foreign to the body that induces an immune response —
an·ti·gen·ic \ˌan-ti-'je-nik\ *adj* — **an·ti·ge·nic·i·ty** \-jə-'ni-sə-tē\ *n*

an·ti·grav·i·ty \ˌan-ti-'gra-və-tē, ˌan-ˌtī-\ *adj* : reducing or canceling the effect of gravity

an·ti·he·ro \'an-ti-ˌhē-rō, 'an-ˌtī-\ *n* : a protagonist who is notably lacking in heroic qualities (as courage)

an·ti·his·ta·mine \ˌan-ti-'his-tə-ˌmēn, ˌan-ˌtī-, -mən\ *n* : any of various drugs used in treating allergies and colds

an·ti·hy·per·ten·sive \-ˌhī-pər-'ten-siv\ *n* : a substance that is effective against high blood pressure — **antihypertensive** *adj*

an·ti·in·flam·ma·to·ry \-in-'fla-mə-ˌtōr-ē\ *adj* : counteracting inflammation — **anti–inflammatory** *n*

an·ti·in·tel·lec·tu·al \-ˌint-ᵊl-'ek-chə-wəl\ *adj* : opposing or hostile to intellectuals or to an intellectual view or approach

an·ti·lock \'an-ti-ˌläk, 'an-ˌtī-\ *adj* : being a braking system designed to prevent the wheels from locking

an·ti·log·a·rithm \ˌan-ti-'lȯ-gə-ˌri-ᵺəm, ˌan-ˌtī-, -'lä-\ *n* : the number corresponding to a given logarithm

an·ti·ma·cas·sar \ˌan-ti-mə-'ka-sər\ *n* : a cover to protect the back or arms of furniture

an·ti·mat·ter \'an-ti-ˌma-tər, 'an-ˌtī-\ *n* : matter composed of antiparticles

an·ti·mo·ny \'an-tə-ˌmō-nē\ *n* : a brittle silvery white metallic chemical element used esp. in alloys

an·ti·neu·tron \ˌan-ti-'nü-ˌträn, ˌan-ˌtī-, -'nyü-\ *n* : the antiparticle of the neutron

an·ti·no·mi·an \ˌan-ti-'nō-mē-ən\ *n* : one who denies the validity of moral laws

an·tin·o·my \an-'ti-nə-mē\ *n, pl* **-mies** : a contradiction between two seemingly true statements

an·ti·nov·el \'an-ti-ˌnä-vəl, 'an-ˌtī-\ *n* : a work of fiction that lacks all or most of the traditional features of the novel

an·ti·nu·cle·ar \ˌan-ti-'nü-klē-ər, -'nyü-\ *adj* : opposing the use or production of nuclear power plants

an·ti·ox·i·dant \ˌan-tē-'äk-sə-dənt, ˌan-ˌtī-\ *n* : a substance that inhibits oxidation — **antioxidant** *adj*

an·ti·par·ti·cle \'an-ti-ˌpär-ti-kəl, 'an-ˌtī-\ *n* : a subatomic particle identical to another subatomic particle in mass but opposite to it in electric and magnetic properties

an·ti·pas·to \ˌan-ti-'pas-tō, ˌän-ti-'päs-\ *n, pl* **-ti** -(ˌ)tē\ : any of various typically Italian hors d'oeuvres

an·ti·pa·thet·ic \ˌan-ti-pə-'the-tik\ *adj* : having an aversion to or dislike of

an·tip·a·thy \an-'ti-pə-thē\ *n, pl* **-thies 1** ♦ : settled aversion or dislike **2** ♦ : an object of aversion
   ♦ [1] animosity, antagonism, bitterness, enmity, gall, grudge, hostility, rancor ♦ [2] abhorrence, abomination, anathema, aversion, bête noire, hate

an·ti·per·son·nel \ˌan-ti-ˌpərs-ᵊn-'el, ˌan-ˌtī-\ *adj* : designed for use against military personnel ⟨∼ mine⟩

an·ti·per·spi·rant \-'pər-spə-rənt\ *n* : a preparation used to check perspiration

an·tiph·o·nal \an-'ti-fən-ᵊl\ *adj* : performed by two alternating groups — **an·tiph·o·nal·ly** *adv*

an·tip·o·dal \an-'ti-pəd-ᵊl\ *adj* ♦ : diametrically opposite or opposed to
   ♦ antithetical, contradictory, contrary, diametric, opposite, polar

an·ti·pode \'an-tə-ˌpōd\ *n, pl* **an·tip·o·des** \an-'ti-pə-ˌdēz\ **1** : the parts of the earth diametrically opposite — usu. used in pl. **2** ♦ : the exact opposite or contrary
   ♦ antithesis, contrary, negative, opposite, reverse

an·tip·o·de·an \(ˌ)an-ˌti-pə-'dē-ən\ *adj* : diametrically opposite or opposed to

an·ti·pol·lu·tion \ˌan-ti-pə-'lü-shən\ *adj* : designed to prevent, reduce, or eliminate pollution ⟨∼ laws⟩

an·ti·pope \'an-ti-ˌpōp\ *n* : one elected or claiming to be pope in opposition to the pope canonically chosen

an·ti·pro·ton \ˌan-ti-'prō-ˌtän\ *n* : the antiparticle of the proton

an·ti·quar·i·an \ˌan-tə-'kwer-ē-ən\ *adj* **1** : of or relating to antiquities **2** : dealing in old books — **antiquarian** *n* —
an·ti·quar·i·an·ism *n*

an·ti·quary \'an-tə-ˌkwer-ē\ *n, pl* **-quar·ies** : a person who collects or studies antiquities

an·ti·quat·ed \'an-tə-ˌkwā-təd\ *adj* ♦ : outmoded or discredited by reason of age : OUT-OF-DATE
   ♦ archaic, dated, obsolete, outdated, outmoded, outworn, passé

¹**an·tique** \an-'tēk\ *n* : an object made in a bygone period

²**antique** *adj* **1** ♦ : belonging to antiquity **2** ♦ : being in the style or fashion of former times : OLD-FASHIONED **3** : of a bygone style or period
   ♦ [1] age-old, ancient, antediluvian, dateless, hoary, old, venerable ♦ [2] old-fashioned, old-time, quaint

³**antique** *vb* **-tiqued; -tiqu·ing 1** : to finish or refinish in antique style : give an appearance of age to **2** : to shop around for antiques — **an·tiqu·er** *n*

an·tiq·ui·ty \an-'ti-kwə-tē\ *n, pl* **-ties** **1** : ancient times **2** : great age **3** *pl* : relics of ancient times **4** *pl* : matters relating to ancient culture

antis *pl of* ANTI

an·ti–Sem·i·tism \ˌan-ti-'se-mə-ˌti-zəm, ˌan-ˌtī-\ *n* : hostility toward Jews as a religious or social minority — **an·ti–Se·mit·ic** \-sə-'mi-tik\ *adj*

an·ti·sep·tic \ˌan-tə-'sep-tik\ *adj* **1** : killing or checking the growth of germs that cause decay or infection **2** : scrupulously clean : ASEPTIC — **antiseptic** *n* — **an·ti·sep·ti·cal·ly** *adv*

an·ti·se·rum \'an-ti-ˌsir-əm, 'an-ˌtī-\ *n* : a serum containing antibodies

an·ti·so·cial \ˌan-ti-'sō-shəl\ *adj* **1** ♦ : disliking the society of others **2** : contrary or hostile to the well-being of society ⟨crime is ∼⟩ — **an·ti·so·cial·ly** *adv*

♦ aloof, cold, cool, detached, distant, frosty, remote, standoffish, unsociable

an·tith·e·sis \an-'ti-thə-səs\ *n, pl* **-eses** \-ˌsēz\ **1** : the opposition or contrast of ideas **2** ♦ : the direct opposite

♦ antipode, contrary, negative, opposite, reverse

an·ti·thet·i·cal \ˌan-tə-'the-ti-kəl\ *also* **an·ti·thet·ic** \-tik\ *adj* ♦ : constituting or marked by antithesis — **an·ti·thet·i·cal·ly** \-ti-k(ə-)lē\ *adv*

♦ antipodal, contradictory, contrary, diametric, opposite, polar

an·ti·tox·in \ˌan-ti-'täk-sən\ *n* : an antibody that is able to neutralize a particular toxin or disease-causing agent; *also* : an antiserum containing an antitoxin

an·ti·trust \ˌan-ti-'trəst\ *adj* : of or relating to legislation against trusts; *also* : consisting of laws to protect trade and commerce from unlawful restraints and monopolies or unfair business practices

an·ti·ven·in \-'ve-nən\ *n* : an antitoxin to a venom; *also* : a serum containing such antitoxin

ant·ler \'ant-lər\ *n* : one of the paired deciduous solid bone processes on the head of a deer; *also* : a branch of this — **ant·lered** \-lərd\ *adj*

ant lion *n* : any of various insects having a long-jawed larva that digs a conical pit in which it lies in wait for insects (as ants) on which it feeds

an·to·nym \'an-tə-ˌnim\ *n* : a word of opposite meaning

anus \'ā-nəs\ *n* : the lower or posterior opening of the alimentary canal

an·vil \'an-vəl\ *n* **1** : a heavy iron block on which metal is shaped **2** : INCUS

anx·i·ety \aŋ-'zī-ə-tē\ *n, pl* **-et·ies** **1** ♦ : painful uneasiness of mind usu. over an anticipated ill **2** : abnormal apprehension and fear often accompanied by physiological signs (as sweating and increased pulse), by doubt about the nature and reality of the threat itself, and by self-doubt

♦ agitation, apprehension, care, concern, disquiet, nervousness, perturbation, uneasiness, worry

anx·ious \'aŋk-shəs\ *adj* **1** ♦ : uneasy in mind : WORRIED ⟨∼ parents⟩ **2** ♦ : characterized by, resulting from, or causing anxiety ⟨an ∼ night⟩ **3** : earnestly wishing : EAGER — **anx·ious·ly** *adv*

♦ [1, 2] distressful, nervous, restless, tense, unsettling, upsetting, worrisome

¹any \'e-nē\ *adj* **1** : one chosen at random **2** : of whatever number or quantity

²any *pron* **1** : any one or ones ⟨take ∼ of the books you like⟩ **2** : any amount ⟨∼ of the money not used is to be returned⟩

³any *adv* : to any extent or degree : AT ALL ⟨could not walk ∼ farther⟩

any·body \-ˌbä-dē, -bə-\ *pron* : ANYONE

any·how \-ˌhau̇\ *adv* **1** : in any way **2** : in spite of that; *also* : in any case

any·more \ˌe-nē-'mōr\ *adv* **1** : any longer **2** ♦ : at the present time

♦ now, nowadays, presently, right now, today

any·one \'e-nē-(ˌ)wən\ *pron* : any person

any·place \-ˌplās\ *adv* : ANYWHERE

any·thing \-ˌthiŋ\ *pron* : any thing whatever

any·time \'e-nē-ˌtīm\ *adv* : at any time whatever

any·way \-ˌwā\ *adv* : in spite of that : ANYHOW

any·where \-ˌhwer\ *adv* : in or to any place

any·wise \-ˌwīz\ *adv* : in any way whatever

A–OK \ˌā-ō-'kā\ *adv or adj* : very definitely OK

A1 \'ā-'wən\ *adj* ♦ : of the finest quality

♦ excellent, fabulous, fine, grand, great, prime, sensational, splendid, superb, superior, unsurpassed, wonderful

aor·ta \ā-'ȯr-tə\ *n, pl* **-tas** *or* **-tae** \-tē\ : the main artery that carries blood from the heart — **aor·tic** \-tik\ *adj*

ap *abbr* **1** apostle **2** apothecaries'

AP *abbr* **1** American plan **2** Associated Press

apace \ə-'pās\ *adv* ♦ : at a quick pace : SWIFTLY

♦ briskly, fast, hastily, pronto, quick, quickly, rapidly, speedily, swift, swiftly

Apache \ə-'pa-chē\ *n, pl* **Apache** *or* **Apach·es** \-'pa-chēz, -'pa-shəz\ : a member of a group of Indigenous peoples of the southwestern U.S.; *also* : any of the languages of the Apache people — **Apach·e·an** \ə-'pa-chē-ən\ *adj or n*

apart \ə-'pärt\ *adv* **1** : separately in place or time **2** : ASIDE **3** : in two or more parts : to pieces

apart·heid \ə-'pär-ˌtāt, -ˌtīt\ *n* : racial segregation; *esp* : a former policy of racial segregation practiced in the Republic of So. Africa

apart·ment \ə-'pärt-mənt\ *n* : a room or set of rooms occupied as a dwelling; *also* : a building divided into individual dwelling units

ap·a·thet·ic \ˌa-pə-'the-tik\ *adj* ♦ : having or showing apathy

♦ casual, disinterested, indifferent, insouciant, nonchalant, perfunctory, unconcerned, uncurious, uninterested

ap·a·thy \'a-pə-thē\ *n* **1** ♦ : lack of emotion **2** ♦ : lack of interest : INDIFFERENCE — **ap·a·thet·i·cal·ly** \-ti-k(ə-)lē\ *adv*

♦ [1] impassivity, numbness, phlegm, stupor *Ant* emotion, feeling, sensibility ♦ [2] disinterestedness, disregard, indifference, insouciance, nonchalance

ap·a·tite \'a-pə-ˌtīt\ *n* : any of a group of minerals that are phosphates of calcium and occur esp. in phosphate rock and in bones and teeth

apato·sau·rus \ə-ˌpa-tə-'sȯr-əs\ *n* : any of a genus of very large 4-footed plant-eating dinosaurs of the Jurassic : BRONTOSAURUS

APB *abbr* all points bulletin

¹ape \'āp\ *n* **1** : any of the larger tailless primates (as a baboon or gorilla); *also* : MONKEY **2** : MIMIC, IMITATOR; *also* : a large uncouth person

²ape *vb* **aped; ap·ing** ♦ : to copy closely but often clumsily and ineptly : IMITATE, MIMIC

♦ copy, emulate, imitate, mime, mimic

ape–man \'āp-ˌman\ *n* : a primate intermediate in character between Homo sapiens and the higher apes

aper·çu \ˌä-per-sē, ˌa-pər-'sü\ *n, pl* **aperçus** \-sē(z), -'süz\ : an immediate impression; *esp* : INSIGHT

aper·i·tif \ˌä-per-ə-'tēf\ *n* : an alcoholic drink taken as an appetizer

ap·er·ture \'a-pər-ˌchu̇r, -chər\ *n* ♦ : an opening or open space : OPENING, HOLE

♦ hole, opening, orifice, perforation

apex \'ā-ˌpeks\ *n, pl* **apex·es** *or* **api·ces** \'ā-pə-ˌsēz, 'a-\ **1** ♦ : the highest point : PEAK **2** ♦ : the narrowed or pointed end

♦ [1] acme, climax, crown, culmination, head, height, meridian, peak, pinnacle, summit, tip-top, top, zenith ♦ [2] cusp, end, pike, point, tip

apha·sia \ə-'fā-zh(ē-)ə\ *n* : loss or impairment of the power to use or comprehend words — **apha·sic** \-zik\ *adj or n*

aph·elion \a-'fēl-yən\ *n, pl* **-elia** \-yə\ : the point in an object's orbit most distant from the sun

aphid \'ā-fəd\ *n* : any of numerous small insects that suck the juices of plants

aphis \'ā-fəs, 'a-\ *n, pl* **aphi·des** \-fə-ˌdēz\ : APHID

aph·o·rism \'a-fə-ˌri-zəm\ *n* ♦ : a short saying stating a general truth or sentiment : MAXIM

♦ adage, byword, epigram, maxim, proverb, saying

aph·o·ris·tic \ˌa-fə-'ris-tik\ *adj* : of, resembling, or characterized by aphorisms

aph·ro·di·si·ac \ˌa-frə-'di-zē-ˌak, -'dē-zē-\ *n* : an agent that excites sexual desire — **aphrodisiac** *adj*

api·ary \'ā-pē-ˌer-ē\ *n, pl* **-ar·ies** : a place where bees are kept — **api·a·rist** \-pē-ə-rist\ *n*

api·cal \'ā-pi-kəl, 'a-\ *adj* : of, relating to, or situated at an apex — **api·cal·ly** \-k(ə-)lē\ *adv*

apiece \ə-'pēs\ *adv* : for each one

aplen·ty \ə-'plen-tē\ *adj* : being in plenty or abundance

aplomb \ə-'pläm, -'pləm\ *n* ♦ : complete composure or self-assurance

♦ calmness, composure, coolness, equanimity, placidity, self-possession, serenity, tranquility ♦ confidence, self-assurance, self-confidence, self-esteem

APO *abbr* army post office

Apoc *abbr* **1** Apocalypse **2** Apocrypha

apoc·a·lypse \ə-'pä-kə-ˌlips\ *n* **1** : a writing prophesying a cataclysm in which evil forces are destroyed **2** *cap* : a book of the New Testament of the Christian Scripture — **apoc·a·lyp·tic** \-ˌpä-kə-'lip-tik\ *also* **apoc·a·lyp·ti·cal** \-ti-kəl\ *adj*

Apoc·ry·pha \ə-'pä-krə-fə\ *n* **1** *not cap* : writings of dubious authenticity **2** : books included in the Septuagint and Vulgate but excluded from the Jewish and Protestant canons of the Old Testament **3** : early Christian writings not included in the New Testament

apoc·ry·phal \-fəl\ *adj* **1** : not canonical : SPURIOUS **2** *often cap* : of or resembling the Apocrypha — **apoc·ry·phal·ly** *adv* — **apoc·ry·phal·ness** *n*

apo·gee \'a-pə-(ˌ)jē\ *n* : the point at which an orbiting object is farthest from the body being orbited

apo·lit·i·cal \ˌā-pə-'li-ti-kəl\ *adj* **1** : having an aversion for or no interest in political affairs **2** : having no political significance — **apo·lit·i·cal·ly** \-k(ə-)lē\ *adv*

apol·o·get·ic \ə-ˌpä-lə-'je-tik\ *adj* ♦ : expressing apology — **apol·o·get·i·cal·ly** \-ti-k(ə-)lē\ *adv*

♦ contrite, penitent, regretful, remorseful, repentant, rueful, sorry

ap·o·lo·gia \ˌa-pə-'lō-j(ē-)ə\ *n* : APOLOGY; *esp* : an argument in support or justification

apol·o·gise *Brit var of* APOLOGIZE

apol·o·gize \ə-'pä-lə-ˌjīz\ *vb* **-gized; -giz·ing** : to make an apology : express regret — **apol·o·gist** \-jist\ *n*

apol·o·gy \ə-'pä-lə-jē\ *n, pl* **-gies** **1** : a formal justification : DEFENSE **2** : an expression of regret for a wrong

ap·o·plexy \'a-pə-ˌplek-sē\ *n* : STROKE **3** — **ap·o·plec·tic** \ˌa-pə-'plek-tik\ *adj*

aport \ə-'pōrt\ *adv* : on or toward the left side of a ship

apos·ta·sy \ə-'päs-tə-sē\ *n, pl* **-sies** : a renunciation or abandonment of a former loyalty (as to a religion)

apos·tate \ə-'päs-ˌtāt, -tət\ *n* ♦ : one who commits apostasy — **apostate** *adj*

♦ betrayer, double-crosser, quisling, recreant, traitor, turncoat

a pos·te·ri·o·ri \ˌä-pō-ˌstir-ē-'ōr-ē\ *adj* : relating to or derived by reasoning from observed facts — **a posteriori** *adv*

apos·tle \ə-'pä-səl\ *n* **1** : one of the group composed of Jesus' 12 original disciples and Paul **2** : the first prominent missionary to a region or group **3 a** : a person who initiates or first advocates a great reform **b** ♦ : an ardent supporter — **apos·tle·ship** *n*

♦ advocate, backer, booster, champion, exponent, friend, promoter, proponent, supporter

ap·os·tol·ic \ˌa-pə-'stä-lik\ *adj* **1** : of or relating to an apostle or to the New Testament apostles **2** : of or relating to a succession of spiritual authority from the apostles **3** : PAPAL ⟨∼ authority⟩

¹apos·tro·phe \ə-'päs-trə-(ˌ)fē\ *n* : the rhetorical addressing of a usu. absent person or a usu. personified thing (as in "O grave, where is thy victory?")

²apostrophe *n* : a punctuation mark ' used esp. to indicate the possessive case or the omission of a letter or figure

apos·tro·phise *Brit var of* APOSTROPHIZE

apos·tro·phize \ə-'päs-trə-ˌfīz\ *vb* **-phized; -phiz·ing** : to address as if present or capable of understanding

apothecaries' weight *n* : a system of weights based on the troy pound and ounce and used chiefly by pharmacists

apoth·e·cary \ə-'pä-thə-ˌker-ē\ *n, pl* **-car·ies** : one who prepares and sells drugs or compounds for medicinal purposes : DRUGGIST

ap·o·thegm \'a-pə-ˌthem\ *or Can and Brit* **ap·o·phthegm** *n* : APHORISM

apo·the·o·sis \ə-ˌpä-thē-'ō-səs, ˌa-pə-'thē-ə-səs\ *n, pl* **-o·ses** \-ˌsēz\ **1** : DEIFICATION **2** : the perfect example

app *abbr* **1** apparatus **2** appendix

ap·pall *also* **ap·pal** \ə-'pȯl\ *vb* **ap·palled; ap·pall·ing** ♦ : to overcome with consternation, shock, or dismay

♦ bowl, floor, jolt, shake up, shock

ap·pall·ing *adj* ♦ : inspiring horror, dismay, or disgust

♦ abhorrent, abominable, awful, distasteful, horrible, horrid, nauseating, noisome, obnoxious, odious, offensive, repellent, revolting ♦ astonishing, awful, dreadful, frightful, ghastly, hideous, horrible, horrid, shocking, terrible

Ap·pa·loo·sa \ˌa-pə-'lü-sə\ *n* : any of a breed of saddle horses developed in western No. America and usu. having a white or solid-colored coat with small spots

ap·pa·nage \'a-pə-nij\ *n* **1** : provision (as a grant of land) made by a sovereign or legislative body for dependent members of the royal family **2** : something that is attached or associated in a natural or necessary way : a natural adjunct

ap·pa·ra·tus \ˌa-pə-'ra-təs, -'rā-\ *n, pl* **-tus·es** *or* **-tus** **1** ♦ : a set of materials or equipment for a particular use **2** : a complex machine or device : MECHANISM **3** : the organization of a political party or underground movement

♦ accoutrements (*or* accouterments), equipment, gear, matériel, outfit, paraphernalia, tackle

¹ap·par·el \ə-'par-əl\ *vb* **-eled** *or* **-elled; -el·ing** *or* **-el·ling** **1** : to put clothes on : CLOTHE **2** : ADORN

²apparel *n* ♦ : personal attire : CLOTHING, DRESS

♦ attire, clothing, dress, duds, raiment, wear

ap·par·ent \ə-'par-ənt\ *adj* **1** ♦ : open to view : VISIBLE **2** ♦ : clear or manifest to the understanding : EVIDENT, OBVIOUS **3** ♦ : appearing as real or true : SEEMING

♦ [1] observable, visible, visual ♦ [2] clear, distinct, evident, manifest, obvious, plain, transparent, unambiguous, unequivocal, unmistakable ♦ [3] assumed, evident, ostensible, reputed, seeming, supposed

ap·par·ent·ly \-lē\ *adv* ♦ : it seems apparent

♦ evidently, ostensibly, presumably, seemingly, supposedly

ap·pa·ri·tion \ˌa-pə-'ri-shən\ *n* ♦ : a supernatural appearance : GHOST

♦ bogey, ghost, phantasm, phantom, poltergeist, shade, shadow, specter, spirit, spook, vision, wraith

¹ap·peal \ə-'pēl\ *n* **1** ♦ : an earnest plea **2** ♦ : the power of arousing a sympathetic response

♦ [1] cry, entreaty, petition, plea, prayer, solicitation, suit, supplication ♦ [2] allure, attractiveness, captivation, charisma, charm, enchantment, fascination, glamour, magic, magnetism

²appeal *vb* **1** : to take steps to have (a case) reheard in a higher court **2** ♦ : to plead for help, corroboration, or decision **3** : to arouse a sympathetic response

♦ *usu* **appeal to** beg, beseech, entreat, implore, importune, petition, plead, pray, solicit, supplicate

ap·pear \ə-'pir\ *vb* **1** ♦ : to become visible **2** : to come formally before an authority **3** ♦ : to have an outward aspect : SEEM **4** : to become evident **5** : to come before the public

♦ [1] come out, materialize, show up, turn up *Ant* disappear, clear, dissolve, evaporate, fade, go (away), melt (away), vanish ♦ [3] act, look, make, seem, sound

ap·pear·ance \ə-'pir-əns\ *n* **1** ♦ : outward aspect : LOOK **2** : the act of appearing **3** : PHENOMENON

♦ aspect, look, mien, presence ♦ face, guise, name, semblance, show

ap·pease \ə-'pēz\ *vb* **ap·peased; ap·peas·ing** **1** : to cause to subside : ALLAY **2** ♦ : to bring to a state of peace or quiet : PACIFY, CONCILIATE; *esp* : to buy off by concessions — **ap·peas·able** \-'pē-zə-bəl\ *adj* — **ap·pease·ment** *n* — **ap·peas·er** *n*

♦ conciliate, disarm, mollify, pacify, placate, propitiate

ap·pel·lant \ə-'pe-lənt\ *n* : one who appeals esp. from a judicial decision

ap·pel·late \ə-'pe-lət\ *adj* : having power to review decisions of a lower court

ap·pel·la·tion \ˌa-pə-'lā-shən\ *n* ♦ : an identifying name or title : NAME, DESIGNATION

♦ cognomen, denotation, designation, handle, name, title

ap·pel·lee \ˌa-pə-'lē\ *n* : one against whom an appeal is taken

ap·pend \ə-'pend\ *vb* ♦ : to attach esp. as something additional

♦ add, adjoin, annex, tack

ap·pend·age \ə-'pen-dij\ *n* **1** ♦ : something appended to a principal or greater thing **2** : a projecting part of the body (as an antenna) esp. when paired with one on each side

♦ accessory, accoutrement (*or* accouterment), adjunct, attachment

ap·pen·dec·to·my \ˌa-pən-'dek-tə-mē\ *n, pl* **-mies** : surgical removal of the intestinal appendix

ap·pen·di·ci·tis \ə-ˌpen-də-'sī-təs\ *n* : inflammation of the intestinal appendix

ap•pen•dix \ə-'pen-diks\ *n, pl* **-dix•es** *or* **-di•ces** \-də-ˌsēz\ **1** : supplementary matter added at the end of a book **2** : a narrow blind tube usu. about three or four inches long that extends from the cecum in the lower right-hand part of the abdomen

ap•per•tain \ˌa-pər-'tān\ *vb* ♦ : to belong or be connected as a rightful part or privilege

♦ apply, bear, pertain, refer, relate

ap•pe•tite \'a-pə-ˌtīt\ *n* **1** ♦ : natural desire for satisfying some want or need esp. for food **2** ♦ : individual preference : TASTE

♦ [1] craving, desire, drive, hankering, hunger, itch, thirst, urge, yen ♦ [2] fancy, favor (*or* favour), fondness, like, liking, love, partiality, preference, relish, shine, taste, use

ap•pe•tiz•er \'a-pə-ˌtī-zər\ *n* : a food or drink taken just before a meal to stimulate the appetite

ap•pe•tiz•ing \-ziŋ\ *adj* ♦ : tempting to the appetite — **ap•pe•tiz•ing•ly** *adv*

♦ delectable, delicious, flavorful (*or* flavourful), palatable, tasty, toothsome

appl *abbr* applied

ap•plaud \ə-'plȯd\ *vb* ♦ : to show approval esp. by clapping

♦ acclaim, cheer, hail, laud, praise, salute, tout

ap•plaud•able \ə-'plȯ-də-bəl\ *adj* ♦ : worthy of being applauded

♦ admirable, commendable, creditable, laudable, meritorious, praiseworthy

ap•plause \ə-'plȯz\ *n* ♦ : approval publicly expressed (as by clapping)

♦ acclamation, ovation *Ant* hissing

ap•ple \'a-pəl\ *n* : a rounded fruit with firm white flesh and a seedy core; *also* : a tree that bears this fruit

ap•ple•jack \-ˌjak\ *n* : a liquor distilled from fermented cider

app•let \'a-ˌplət\ *n* : a short computer program esp. for performing a simple specific task

ap•pli•ance \ə-'plī-əns\ *n* **1** : an instrument or device designed for a particular use or function **2** : a piece of household equipment (as a stove or toaster) operated by gas or electricity

ap•pli•ca•bil•i•ty \ˌa-pli-kə-'bi-lə-tē, ə-ˌpli-kə-\ *n* ♦ : the quality or state of being applicable

♦ bearing, connection, pertinence, relevance

ap•pli•ca•ble \'a-pli-kə-bəl, ə-'pli-kə-\ *adj* ♦ : capable of being applied

♦ functional, practicable, practical, serviceable, usable, useful, workable, working ♦ appropriate, apt, felicitous, fit, fitting, good, happy, meet, proper, right, suitable ♦ apposite, apropos, germane, material, pertinent, pointed, relative, relevant

ap•pli•cant \'a-pli-kənt\ *n* ♦ : one who applies

♦ aspirant, campaigner, candidate, contender, hopeful, prospect, seeker

ap•pli•ca•tion \ˌa-plə-'kā-shən\ *n* **1** ♦ : the act of applying **2** : assiduous attention **3** : REQUEST; *also* : a form used in making a request **4** : something placed or spread on a surface **5** : capacity for use **6** : a program (as a word processor) that performs one of a computer's major tasks

♦ employment, exercise, operation, play, use

ap•pli•ca•tor \'a-plə-ˌkā-tər\ *n* : a device for applying a substance (as medicine or polish)

ap•plied \ə-'plīd\ *adj* : put to practical use ⟨∼ art⟩

ap•pli•qué \ˌa-plə-'kā\ *n* : a fabric decoration cut out and fastened to a larger piece of material — **appliqué** *vb*

ap•ply \ə-'plī\ *vb* **ap•plied; ap•ply•ing 1 a** ♦ : to put to practical use **b** ♦ : to bring into action **c** : to lay or spread on **d** ♦ : to put into operation or effect **2** : to place in contact : put or spread on a surface **3** ♦ : to employ with close attention **4** ♦ : to have reference or connection **5** : to submit a request

♦ [1a, 1b] employ, exercise, exploit, harness, operate, use, utilize ♦ [1d] administer, enforce, execute, implement ♦ [3] address, bend, buckle, devote, give ♦ [4] appertain, bear, pertain, refer, relate

ap•point \ə-'pȯint\ *vb* **1** ♦ : to fix or set officially ⟨∼ a day for trial⟩ **2** ♦ : to name officially **3** : to fit out : EQUIP

♦ [1] designate, fix, name, set ♦ [2] assign, attach, commission, constitute, designate, detail, name

ap•poin•tee \ə-ˌpȯin-'tē, ˌa-\ *n* : a person appointed

ap•point•ive \ə-'pȯin-tiv\ *adj* : subject to appointment

ap•point•ment \ə-'pȯint-mənt\ *n* **1** : the act of appointing **2** ♦ : an arrangement for a meeting **3** *pl* : articles of furniture for the interior of a building : FURNISHINGS **4** ♦ : a nonelective office or position

♦ [2] date, engagement, rendezvous, tryst ♦ *usu* **appointments** [4] billet, capacity, function, job, place, position, post, situation ♦ [4] assignment, commission, designation *Ant* discharge, dismissal, expulsion, firing

ap•por•tion \ə-'pōr-shən\ *vb* ♦ : to distribute proportionately

♦ allocate, allot, allow, ration ♦ administer, allocate, deal, dispense, distribute, mete, parcel, portion, prorate

ap•por•tion•ment \-mənt\ *n* : an act or result of apportioning

ap•po•site \'a-pə-zət\ *adj* ♦ : highly pertinent or appropriate : RELEVANT — **ap•po•site•ly** *adv* — **ap•po•site•ness** *n*

♦ applicable, apropos, germane, material, pertinent, pointed, relative, relevant

ap•po•si•tion \ˌa-pə-'zi-shən\ *n* : a grammatical construction in which a noun or pronoun is followed by another that has the same referent (as *the poet* and *Burns* in "a biography of the poet Burns")

ap•pos•i•tive \ə-'pä-zə-tiv, a-\ *adj* : of, relating to, or standing in grammatical apposition — **appositive** *n*

ap•prais•al \ə-'prā-zəl\ *n* ♦ : an act or instance of appraising

♦ assessment, estimate, estimation, evaluation, judgment (*or* judgement)

ap•praise \ə-'prāz\ *vb* **ap•praised; ap•prais•ing 1** : to set a value on **2** ♦ : to evaluate the worth, significance, or status of — **ap•prais•er** *n*

♦ assess, estimate, evaluate, rate, set, value

ap•pre•cia•ble \ə-'prē-shə-bəl\ *adj* ♦ : large enough to be recognized and measured — **ap•pre•cia•bly** *adv*

♦ detectable, discernible, distinguishable, palpable, perceptible, sensible

ap•pre•ci•ate \ə-'prē-shē-ˌāt\ *vb* **-at•ed; -at•ing 1** ♦ : to value justly **2** ♦ : to judge with understanding : be fully aware of **3** : to be grateful for **4** ♦ : to increase in value

♦ [1] cherish, prize, treasure, value ♦ [1] admire, esteem, regard, respect ♦ [2] apprehend, catch, catch on (to), comprehend, get, grasp, make, make out, perceive, see, seize, understand ♦ [4] accumulate, build, expand, increase, mount, multiply, proliferate, rise

ap•pre•ci•a•tion \ə-ˌprē-shē-'ā-shən\ *n* **1 a** ♦ : an opinion or estimate formed by discerning and comparing; *esp* : a favorable critical estimate **b** : sensitive awareness **2** ♦ : an expression of admiration, approval, or gratitude

♦ [1a] admiration, esteem, estimation, favor (*or* favour), regard, respect ♦ [1a] apprehension, comprehension, grasp, grip, perception, understanding ♦ [2] gratefulness, gratitude, thanks

ap•pre•cia•tive \ə-'prē-shə-tiv, -shē-ˌā-\ *adj* ♦ : having or showing appreciation — **ap•pre•cia•tive•ly** *adv*

♦ complimentary, favorable (*or* favourable), friendly, good, positive ♦ grateful, obliged, thankful

ap•pre•hend \ˌa-pri-'hend\ *vb* **1** ♦ : to take or keep in custody by authority of law : ARREST **2** : to become aware of **3** : to look forward to with dread **4** ♦ : to grasp with the understanding : UNDERSTAND

♦ [1] arrest, nab, pick up, restrain, seize ♦ [4] appreciate, catch, catch on (to), comprehend, get, grasp, make, make out, perceive, see, seize, understand

ap•pre•hen•sion \ˌa-pri-'hen-chən\ *n* **1 a** : the act or power of perceiving or comprehending **b** ♦ : the result of apprehending mentally **2** : seizure by legal process **3** ♦ : suspicion or fear esp. of future evil

♦ [1b] appreciation, comprehension, grasp, grip, perception, understanding ♦ [3] agitation, anxiety, care, concern, disquiet, nervousness, perturbation, uneasiness, worry

ap•pre•hen•sive \-'hen-siv\ *adj* : viewing the future with anxiety — **ap•pre•hen•sive•ly** *adv* — *n*

ap•pre•hen•sive•ness \-nəs\ *n* : the quality or state of being apprehensive

¹ap•pren•tice \ə-'pren-təs\ *n* **1** ♦ : a person learning a craft under a skilled worker **2** : BEGINNER — **ap•pren•tice•ship** *n*

♦ aid, assistant, helper

²apprentice *vb* **-ticed; -tic•ing** : to bind or set at work as an apprentice

ap·prise \ə-'prīz\ vb **ap·prised; ap·pris·ing** ♦ : to give notice to : INFORM

♦ acquaint, advise, brief, clue, enlighten, familiarize, fill in, inform, instruct, tell, wise

¹**ap·proach** \ə-'prōch\ vb **1** ♦ : to move nearer to **2** ♦ : to be almost the same as **3** : to make advances to esp. for the purpose of creating a desired result **4** : to take preliminary steps toward — **ap·proach·able** adj

♦ [1] advance, close, come, near Ant back (up or away), recede, retire, retreat, withdraw ♦ [2] approximate, compare, measure up, stack up

²**approach** n **1** ♦ : a means of access : AVENUE **2 a** : the taking of preliminary steps toward a particular purpose **b** ♦ : a particular manner of taking steps toward an end

♦ [1] avenue, passage, path, route, way ♦ [2b] fashion, form, manner, method, strategy, style, system, tack, tactics, technique, way

ap·pro·ba·tion \ˌa-prə-'bā-shən\ n ♦ : an act of commending : APPROVAL

♦ approval, blessing, favor (or favour), imprimatur, OK

¹**ap·pro·pri·ate** \ə-'prō-prē-ˌāt\ vb **-at·ed; -at·ing 1** ♦ : to take possession of **2** : to set apart for a particular use

♦ arrogate, commandeer, preempt, usurp

²**ap·pro·pri·ate** \ə-'prō-prē-ət\ adj ♦ : fitted to a purpose or use

♦ applicable, apt, felicitous, fit, fitting, good, happy, meet, proper, right, suitable

ap·pro·pri·ate·ly \-lē\ adv ♦ : in an appropriate manner

♦ correctly, fittingly, happily, properly, rightly, suitably

ap·pro·pri·ate·ness \-nəs\ n ♦ : the quality or state of being appropriate

♦ aptness, fitness, rightness, suitability Ant inaptness, infelicity, unfitness

ap·pro·pri·a·tion \ə-ˌprō-prē-'ā-shən\ n ♦ : something (as money) set aside by formal action for a specific use

♦ allocation, allotment, grant, subsidy

ap·prov·al \ə-'prü-vəl\ n ♦ : an act of approving — **on approval** : subject to a prospective buyer's acceptance or refusal

♦ approbation, blessing, favor (or favour), imprimatur, OK Ant disapprobation, disapproval, disfavor

ap·prove \ə-'prüv\ vb **ap·proved; ap·prov·ing 1** ♦ : to have or express a favorable opinion of **2** ♦ : to accept as satisfactory : RATIFY

♦ [1] authorize, clear, OK, ratify, sanction, warrant Ant decline, deny, disallow, disapprove, negative, reject, turn down ♦ usu **approve of** [2] accept, care, countenance, favor (or favour), OK, subscribe Ant disapprove (of), discountenance, disfavor, frown (on or upon)

approx abbr approximate; approximately

¹**ap·prox·i·mate** \ə-'präk-sə-mət\ adj ♦ : nearly correct or exact — **ap·prox·i·mate·ly** adv

♦ comparative, near, relative

²**ap·prox·i·mate** \-ˌmāt\ vb **-mat·ed; -mat·ing** ♦ : to come near : APPROACH — **ap·prox·i·ma·tion** \ə-ˌpräk-sə-'mā-shən\ n

♦ approach, compare, measure up, stack up

appt abbr appoint; appointed; appointment

ap·pur·te·nance \ə-'pərt-nəns, -ᵊn-əns\ n : something that belongs to or goes with another thing — **ap·pur·te·nant** \ə-'pərt-nənt, -ᵊn-ənt\ adj

Apr abbr April

APR abbr annual percentage rate

apri·cot \'a-prə-ˌkät, 'ā-\ n : an oval orange-colored fruit resembling the related peach and plum in flavor; also : a tree bearing apricots

April \'ā-prəl\ n : the 4th month of the year

a pri·o·ri \ˌä-prē-'ōr-ē\ adj **1** : characterized by or derived by reasoning from self-evident propositions **2** : independent of experience — **a priori** adv

apron \'ā-prən\ n **1** : a garment tied over the front of the body to protect the clothes **2** : a paved area for parking or handling airplanes — **aproned** adj

¹**ap·ro·pos** \ˌa-prə-'pō, 'a-prə-ˌpō\ adv **1** : OPPORTUNELY **2** : in passing : INCIDENTALLY

²**apropos** adj ♦ : being to the point

♦ applicable, apposite, germane, material, pertinent, pointed, relative, relevant

apropos of prep ♦ : with regard to

♦ about, concerning, of, on, regarding, respecting, toward

apse \'aps\ n : a projecting usu. semicircular and vaulted part of a building (as a church)

¹**apt** \'apt\ adj **1** ♦ : well adapted : SUITABLE **2** ♦ : having an habitual tendency **3** : quick to learn — **apt·ly** adv

♦ [1] applicable, appropriate, felicitous, fit, fitting, good, happy, meet, proper, right, suitable ♦ [2] given, inclined, prone

²**apt** abbr **1** apartment **2** aptitude

ap·ti·tude \'ap-tə-ˌtüd, -ˌtyüd\ n **1** ♦ : natural ability : TALENT **2** : capacity for learning **3** : APPROPRIATENESS

♦ endowment, faculty, flair, genius, gift, knack, talent

apt·ness \'apt-nəs\ n ♦ : the quality or state of being apt

♦ proneness, propensity, tendency, way ♦ appropriateness, fitness, rightness, suitability

aqua \'ä-kwə, 'ä-\ n : a light greenish blue color

aqua·cul·ture also **aqui·cul·ture** \'a-kwə-ˌkəl-chər, 'ä-\ n : the cultivation of aquatic plants or animals (as fish or shellfish) for human use

aqua·ma·rine \ˌa-kwə-mə-'rēn, ˌä-\ n **1** : a bluish green gem **2** : a pale blue to light greenish blue

aqua·naut \'a-kwə-ˌnot, 'ä-\ n : a person who lives in an underwater shelter for an extended period

aqua·plane \-ˌplān\ n : a board towed behind a motorboat and ridden by a person standing on it — **aquaplane** vb

aqua re·gia \ˌa-kwə-'rē-j(ē-)ə\ n : a mixture of nitric and hydrochloric acids that dissolves gold or platinum

aquar·i·um \ə-'kwar-ē-əm\ n, pl **-i·ums** or **-ia** \-ē-ə\ **1** : a container (as a glass tank) in which living aquatic animals or plants are kept **2** : a place where aquatic animals and plants are kept and shown

Aquar·i·us \ə-'kwar-ē-əs\ n **1** : a zodiacal constellation between Capricorn and Pisces usu. pictured as a man pouring water **2** : the 11th sign of the zodiac in astrology; also : one born under this sign

¹**aquat·ic** \ə-'kwä-tik, -'kwa-\ adj **1** : growing or living in or frequenting water **2** : performed in or on water

²**aquatic** n : an aquatic animal or plant

aqua·vit \'ä-kwə-ˌvēt\ n : a clear liquor flavored with caraway seeds

aqua vi·tae \ˌa-kwə-'vī-tē, ˌä-\ n : a strong alcoholic liquor (as brandy)

aq·ue·duct \'a-kwə-ˌdəkt\ n **1** ♦ : a conduit for carrying running water **2** : a structure carrying a canal over a river or hollow **3** : a passage in a bodily part

♦ canal, channel, conduit, flume, raceway, watercourse

aque·ous \'ā-kwē-əs, 'a-\ adj **1** : WATERY **2** : made of, by, or with water

aqueous humor n : a clear fluid occupying the space between the lens and the cornea of the eye

aqui·fer \'a-kwə-fər, 'ä-\ n : a water-bearing stratum of permeable rock, sand, or gravel

aq·ui·line \'a-kwə-ˌlīn, -lən\ adj **1** : of or resembling an eagle **2** : hooked like an eagle's beak ⟨an ∼ nose⟩

ar abbr arrival; arrive

Ar symbol argon

AR abbr Arkansas

-ar adj suffix **1** : of or relating to ⟨molecular⟩ : being ⟨spectacular⟩ **2** : resembling ⟨oracular⟩

Ar·ab \'ar-əb\ n **1** : a member of a Semitic people of the Arabian peninsula in southwestern Asia **2** : a member of an Arabic-speaking people — **Arab** adj — **Ara·bi·an** \ə-'rā-bē-ən\ adj or n

ar·a·besque \ˌar-ə-'besk\ n : a design of interlacing lines forming figures of flowers, foliage, and sometimes animals — **arabesque** adj

¹**Ar·a·bic** \'ar-ə-bik\ n : a Semitic language of southwestern Asia and northern Africa

²**Arabic** adj **1** : of or relating to the Arabs, Arabic, or the Arabian peninsula in southwestern Asia **2** : expressed in or making use of Arabic numerals

Arabic numeral n : any of the number symbols 0, 1, 2, 3, 4, 5, 6, 7, 8, 9

ar·a·ble \'ar-ə-bəl\ adj : fit for or used for the growing of crops

arach·nid \ə-'rak-nəd\ n : any of a class of usu. 8-legged arthropods comprising the spiders, scorpions, mites, and ticks — **arachnid** adj

Ar•a•ma•ic \ˌar-ə-ˈmā-ik\ *n* : an ancient Semitic language

ar•a•mid \ˈar-ə-məd, -ˌmid\ *n* : any of several light but very strong heat-resistant synthetic materials used esp. in textiles and plastics

Arap•a•ho *or* **Arap•a•hoe** \ə-ˈra-pə-ˌhō\ *n, pl* **-ho** *or* **-hos** *or* **-hoe** *or* **-hoes**   **1** : a member of an Algonquian-speaking Indigenous people of the Great Plains   **2** : the Algonquian language of the Arapaho people

ar•bi•ter \ˈär-bə-tər\ *n* ♦ : one having power to decide a dispute

 ♦ arbitrator, judge, referee, umpire ♦ arbitrator, broker, go-between, intercessor, intermediary, mediator, middleman, peacemaker

ar•bi•trage \ˈär-bə-ˌträzh\ *n* : the purchase and sale of the same or equivalent securities in different markets in order to profit from price discrepancies

ar•bi•tra•geur \ˌär-bə-(ˌ)trä-ˈzhər\ *or* **ar•bi•trag•er** \ˈär-bə-ˌträ-zhər\ *n* : one who practices arbitrage

ar•bit•ra•ment \är-ˈbi-trə-mənt\ *n*   **1** : the act of deciding a dispute   **2** : the judgment given by an arbitrator

ar•bi•trary \ˈär-bə-ˌtrer-ē\ *adj*   **1** ♦ : marked by or resulting from the unrestrained and often tyrannical exercise of power   **2** ♦ : determined by will or caprice : selected at random — **ar•bi•trari•ly** \ˌär-bə-ˈtrer-ə-lē\ *adv* — **ar•bi•trari•ness** \ˈär-bə-ˌtrer-ē-nəs\ *n*

 ♦ [1] dictatorial, high-handed, imperious, peremptory, willful ♦ [2] aimless, desultory, erratic, haphazard, random, scattered, stray

ar•bi•trate \ˈär-bə-ˌträt\ *vb* **-trat•ed; -trat•ing**   **1** : to act as arbitrator   **2** ♦ : to act on as arbitrator   **3** : to submit for decision to an arbitrator — **ar•bi•tra•tion** \ˌär-bə-ˈträ-shən\ *n*

 ♦ adjudicate, decide, determine, judge, referee, rule, settle, umpire

ar•bi•tra•tor \ˈär-bə-ˌträ-tər\ *n* ♦ : one chosen to settle differences between two parties in a controversy

 ♦ arbiter, judge, referee, umpire ♦ arbiter, broker, go-between, intercessor, intermediary, mediator, middleman, peacemaker

ar•bor *or Can and Brit* **ar•bour** \ˈär-bər\ *n* : a shelter formed of or covered with vines or branches

ar•bo•re•al \är-ˈbōr-ē-əl\ *adj*   **1** : of, relating to, or resembling a tree   **2** : living in trees ⟨∼ monkeys⟩

ar•bo•re•tum \ˌär-bə-ˈrē-təm\ *n, pl* **-retums** *or* **-re•ta** \-tə\ : a place where trees and plants are grown for scientific and educational purposes

ar•bor•vi•tae \ˌär-bər-ˈvī-tē\ *n* : any of various evergreen trees and shrubs with scalelike leaves that are related to the cypresses

ar•bu•tus \är-ˈbyü-təs\ *n* : TRAILING ARBUTUS

¹**arc** \ˈärk\ *n*   **1** : a sustained luminous discharge of electricity (as between two electrodes)   **2** ♦ : a continuous portion of a curved line (as part of the circumference of a circle)

 ♦ arch, bend, bow, crook, curve

²**arc** *vb* **arced** \ˈärkt\; **arc•ing** \ˈär-kiŋ\   **1** : to form an electric arc   **2** ♦ : to follow an arc-shaped course

 ♦ bend, bow, crook, curve, hook, round, sweep, swerve, wheel

ARC *abbr*   **1** AIDS-related complex   **2** American Red Cross

ar•cade \är-ˈkād\ *n*   **1** : an arched or covered passageway; *esp* : one lined with shops   **2** : a row of arches with their supporting columns   **3** : an amusement center having coin-operated games

ar•cane \är-ˈkān\ *adj* : SECRET, MYSTERIOUS

¹**arch** \ˈärch\ *n*   **1** : a curved structure spanning an opening (as a door)   **2** ♦ : something resembling an arch   **3** : ARCHWAY

 ♦ arc, bend, bow, crook, curve

²**arch** *vb*   **1** : to cover with an arch   **2** : to form or bend into an arch

³**arch** *adj*   **1** ♦ : most important : CHIEF   **2** ♦ : impertinently bold and impudent — **arch•ly** *adv* — **arch•ness** *n*

 ♦ [1] chief, dominant, foremost, key, main, predominant, primary, principal ♦ [2] bold, brash, cheeky, cocky, fresh, impertinent, impudent, insolent, nervy, sassy, saucy

⁴**arch** *abbr* architect; architectural; architecture

ar•chae•ol•o•gy *or* **ar•che•ol•o•gy** \ˌär-kē-ˈä-lə-jē\ *n* : the study of past human life as revealed by relics left by ancient peoples — **ar•chae•o•log•i•cal** \-ə-ˈlä-ji-kəl\ *adj* — **ar•chae•ol•o•gist** \-ˈä-lə-jist\ *n*

ar•cha•ic \är-ˈkā-ik\ *adj*   **1** : having the characteristics of the language of the past and surviving chiefly in specialized uses ⟨∼ words⟩   **2** ♦ : belonging to an earlier time : ANTIQUATED — **ar•cha•i•cal•ly** \-i-k(ə-)lē\ *adv*

 ♦ antiquated, dated, obsolete, outdated, outmoded, outworn, passé

arch•an•gel \ˈärk-ˌān-jəl\ *n* : a chief angel

arch•bish•op \ärch-ˈbi-shəp\ *n* : a bishop of high rank

arch•bish•op•ric \-shə-(ˌ)prik\ *n* : the jurisdiction or office of an archbishop

arch•con•ser•va•tive \(ˌ)ärch-kən-ˈsər-və-tiv\ *n* : an extreme conservative — **archconservative** *adj*

arch•dea•con \-ˈdē-kən\ *n* : a church official who assists a diocesan bishop in ceremonial or administrative functions

arch•di•o•cese \-ˈdī-ə-səs, -ˌsēz, -ˌsēz\ *n* : the diocese of an archbishop

arch•duke \-ˈdük, -ˈdyük\ *n*   **1** : a sovereign prince   **2** : a prince of the imperial family of Austria

Ar•che•an \är-ˈkē-ən\ *adj* : of, relating to, or being the earliest eon of geologic history — **Archean** *n*

arch•en•e•my \ärch-ˈe-nə-mē\ *n, pl* **-mies** : a principal enemy

Ar•cheo•zo•ic \ˌär-kē-ə-ˈzō-ik\ *adj* : ARCHEAN — **Archeozoic** *n*

ar•chery \ˈär-chə-rē\ *n* : the art or practice of shooting with bow and arrows — **ar•cher** \ˈär-chər\ *n*

arch•e•type \ˈär-ki-ˌtīp\ *n* : the original pattern or model of all things of the same type

arch•fiend \ˌärch-ˈfēnd\ *n* : a chief fiend; *esp* : SATAN

ar•chi•epis•co•pal \ˌär-kē-ə-ˈpis-kə-pəl\ *adj* : of or relating to an archbishop

ar•chi•man•drite \ˌär-kə-ˈman-ˌdrīt\ *n* : a dignitary in an Eastern church ranking below a bishop

ar•chi•pel•a•go \ˌär-kə-ˈpe-lə-ˌgō, ˌär-chə-\ *n, pl* **-goes** *or* **-gos** : a group of islands

ar•chi•tect \ˈär-kə-ˌtekt\ *n*   **1** : a person who plans buildings and oversees their construction   **2** : a person who designs and guides a plan or undertaking

ar•chi•tec•ture \ˈär-kə-ˌtek-chər\ *n*   **1** : the art or science of planning and building structures   **2** : a method or style of building   **3** : the manner in which the elements (as of a design) are arranged or organized — **ar•chi•tec•tur•al** \ˌär-kə-ˈtek-chə-rəl, -ˈtek-shrəl\ *adj* — **ar•chi•tec•tur•al•ly** *adv*

ar•chi•trave \ˈär-kə-ˌträv\ *n* : the supporting horizontal member just above the columns in a building in the classical style of architecture

ar•chive \ˈär-ˌkīv\ *n* : a place for keeping public records; *also* : public records — often used in pl.

ar•chi•vist \ˈär-kə-vist, -ˌkī-\ *n* : a person in charge of archives

ar•chon \ˈär-ˌkän, -kən\ *n* : a chief magistrate of ancient Athens

arch•way \ˈärch-ˌwā\ *n* : a passageway under an arch; *also* : an arch over a passage

arc lamp *n* : a gas-filled electric lamp that produces light when a current arcs between incandescent electrodes

¹**arc•tic** \ˈärk-tik, ˈär-tik\ *adj*   **1** *often cap* : of or relating to the north pole or the region near it   **2** ♦ : bitter cold : FRIGID

 ♦ bitter, cold, freezing, frigid, frosty, glacial, icy, polar

²**arc•tic** \ˈär-tik, ˈärk-tik\ *n* : a rubber overshoe that reaches to the ankle or above

arctic circle *n, often cap A&C* : the parallel of latitude that is approximately 66½ degrees north of the equator

-ard *also* **-art** *n suffix* : one that is characterized by performing some action, possessing some quality, or being associated with some thing esp. conspicuously or excessively ⟨brag*gart*⟩ ⟨dull-*ard*⟩

ar•dent \ˈär-dᵊnt\ *adj*   **1** ♦ : characterized by warmth of feeling typically expressed in eager zealous support or activity   **2** : FIERY, HOT   **3** ♦ : GLOWING — **ar•dent•ly** *adv*

 ♦ burning, charged, emotional, fervent, fiery, impassioned, passionate, vehement ♦ avid, eager, enthusiastic, gung ho, hot, hungry, keen

ar•dor *or Can and Brit* **ar•dour** \ˈär-dər\ *n*   **1 a** ♦ : warmth of feeling   ♦ : eagerness and ardent interest in pursuit of something   **2** : sexual excitement

 ♦ [1a] emotion, fervency, fervor, heat, intensity, passion, vehemence, warmth *Ant* impassivity ♦ [1b] avidity, eagerness, enthusiasm, excitement, hunger, impatience, keenness, thirst

ar•du•ous \ˈär-jə-wəs, -dyù-wəs\ *adj*   **1** ♦ : hard to accomplish or achieve : DIFFICULT   **2** ♦ : marked by great labor or effort — **ar•du•ous•ness** *n*

 ♦ [1, 2] demanding, difficult, exacting, formidable, grueling, hard, laborious, strenuous, toilsome, tough

ar•du•ous•ly \-lē\ *adv* : in an arduous manner

¹**are** *pres 2d sing or pres pl of* BE

²**are** \ˈar\ *n* : a metric measure equal to 100 square meters

ar•ea \ˈar-ē-ə\ *n*   **1** : a flat surface or space   **2** : the amount of surface included (as within the lines of a geometric figure)   **3** ♦ : range or extent of some thing or concept : FIELD   **4** ♦ : any particular extent of space or surface : REGION

♦ [3] arena, demesne, department, discipline, domain, field, line, province, realm, specialty, sphere ♦ [4] demesne, field, region, zone

area code *n* : a 3-digit number that identifies each telephone service area in a country (as the U.S. or Canada)

are·na \ə-'rē-nə\ *n* **1** ♦ : an enclosed area used for public entertainment **2** ♦ : a sphere of activity or competition

♦ [1] hall, theater ♦ [2] area, demesne, department, discipline, domain, field, line, province, realm, specialty, sphere

Ar·gen·tine \'är-jən-ˌtēn, -ˌtīn\ *or* **Ar·gen·tin·ean** *or* **Ar·gen·tin·i·an** \ˌär-jən-'ti-nē-ən\ *n* : a native or inhabitant of Argentina — **Argentine** *or* **Argentinean** *or* **Argentinian** *adj*

ar·gen·tite \'är-jən-ˌtīt\ *n* : a dark gray mineral that is an important ore of silver

ar·gon \'är-ˌgän\ *n* : a colorless odorless gaseous chemical element found in the air and used for filling electric lamps

ar·go·sy \'är-gə-sē\ *n, pl* **-sies** **1** : a large merchant ship **2** : FLEET

ar·got \'är-gət, -ˌgō\ *n* ♦ : the language of a particular group or class

♦ cant, jargon, language, lingo, slang, terminology, vocabulary

argu·able \'är-gyü-ə-bəl\ *adj* ♦ : open to argument, dispute, or question

♦ debatable, disputable, doubtful, moot, questionable

ar·gu·ably \'är-gyü-(ə-)blē\ *adv* : it can be argued

ar·gue \'är-gyü\ *vb* **ar·gued; ar·gu·ing** **1** ♦ : to give reasons for or against something **2** ♦ : to contend in words : DISPUTE ⟨*argued* about money⟩ **3** ♦ : to consider the pros and cons of **4** ♦ : to persuade by giving reasons

♦ [1] assert, contend, maintain, plead, reason ♦ [2] bicker, brawl, dispute, fall out, fight, hassle, quarrel, row, scrap, spat, squabble, wrangle ♦ [3] chew over, debate, discuss, dispute, hash, moot, talk over ♦ [4] convince, get, induce, move, persuade, prevail, satisfy, talk, win

ar·gu·er \'är-gyə-wər\ *n* ♦ : one who argues

♦ debater, disputant, disputer

ar·gu·ment \'är-gyə-mənt\ *n* **1** ♦ : a reason offered in proof **2** ♦ : discourse intended to persuade **3** ♦ : a usu. verbal conflict : QUARREL

♦ [1] assertion, contention, thesis ♦ [1] case, defense (*or* defence), explanation, rationale, reason ♦ [2] colloquy, conference, deliberation, discourse, discussion, give-and-take, parley, talk ♦ [3] altercation, bicker, brawl, disagreement, dispute, fight, hassle, misunderstanding, quarrel, row, scrap, spat, squabble, wrangle

ar·gu·men·ta·tion \ˌär-gyə-mən-'tā-shən\ *n* : the art of formal discussion

ar·gu·men·ta·tive \ˌär-gyə-'men-tə-tiv\ *adj* ♦ : inclined to argue

♦ contentious, disputatious, quarrelsome, scrappy

ar·gyle *also* **ar·gyll** \'är-ˌgīl\ *n, often cap* : a geometric knitting pattern of varicolored diamonds on a single background color; *also* : a sock knit in this pattern

aria \'är-ē-ə\ *n* : an accompanied elaborate vocal solo forming part of a larger work

ar·id \'ar-əd\ *adj* : very dry; *esp* ♦ : having insufficient rainfall to support agriculture — **arid·i·ty** \ə-'ri-də-tē\ *n*

♦ dry, sere, thirsty

Ar·ies \'ar-ˌēz, -ē-ˌēz\ *n* **1** : a zodiacal constellation between Pisces and Taurus pictured as a ram **2** : the 1st sign of the zodiac in astrology; *also* : one born under this sign

aright \ə-'rīt\ *adv* : RIGHT, CORRECTLY

arise \ə-'rīz\ *vb* **arose** \-'rōz\; **aris·en** \-'riz-ᵊn\; **aris·ing** \-'rī-ziŋ\ **1** : to get up **2 a** ♦ : to originate from a source **b** ♦ : to come into being or to attention **3** ♦ : to move upward : ASCEND

♦ [2a] begin, commence, dawn, form, materialize, originate, spring, start ♦ [2b] crop, emerge, materialize, spring, surface ♦ [3] ascend, climb, lift, mount, rise, soar, up

ar·is·toc·ra·cy \ˌar-ə-'stä-krə-sē\ *n, pl* **-cies** **1** : government by a noble or privileged class; *also* : a state so governed **2** : the governing class of an aristocracy **3** : UPPER CLASS

aris·to·crat \ə-'ris-tə-ˌkrat\ *n* ♦ : a member of an aristocracy

♦ gentleman, grandee, noble, patrician

aris·to·crat·ic \ə-ˌris-tə-'kra-tik\ *adj* ♦ : belonging to, having the qualities of, or favoring aristocracy

♦ genteel, gentle, grand, highborn, noble, patrician, wellborn

arith *abbr* arithmetic; arithmetical

arith·me·tic \ə-'rith-mə-ˌtik\ *n* **1** : a branch of mathematics that deals with computations usu. with nonnegative real numbers **2** ♦ : the process or an act of computing or calculating : COMPUTATION, CALCULATION — **ar·ith·met·ic** \ˌar-ith-'me-tik\ *or* **ar·ith·met·i·cal** \-ti-kəl\ *adj* — **ar·ith·met·i·cal·ly** \-ti-k(ə-)lē\ *adv* — **arith·me·ti·cian** \ə-ˌrith-mə-'ti-shən\ *n*

♦ calculation, computation, reckoning

arithmetic mean *n* : the sum of a set of numbers divided by the number of numbers in the set

Ariz *abbr* Arizona

ark \'ärk\ *n* **1** : a boat held to resemble that of Noah's at the time of the Flood **2** : the sacred chest in a synagogue representing to Hebrews the presence of God; *also* : the repository for the scrolls of the Torah

Ark *abbr* Arkansas

¹**arm** \'ärm\ *n* **1** : a human upper limb and esp. the part between the shoulder and wrist; *also* : a corresponding limb of a 2-footed vertebrate **2** : something resembling an arm in shape or position ⟨an ∼ of land⟩ ⟨an ∼ of a chair⟩ **3** ♦ : the power, authority, or resources wielded (as by an individual or group) ⟨the ∼ of the law⟩ — **armed** \'ärmd\ *adj* — **arm·less** *adj*

♦ authority, clutch, command, control, dominion, grip, hold, power, sway

²**arm** *vb* : to furnish with weapons

³**arm** *n* **1** ♦ : a means (as a weapon) of offense or defense; *esp* : FIREARM **2** : a branch of the military forces **3** *pl* : the hereditary heraldic devices of a family

♦ firearm, gun, piece

ar·ma·da \är-'mä-də, -'mā-\ *n* **1** : a fleet of warships **2** ♦ : a large force or group usu. of moving things ⟨an ∼ of trailers⟩

♦ caravan, cavalcade, fleet, motorcade, train

ar·ma·dil·lo \ˌär-mə-'di-lō\ *n, pl* **-los** : any of several small burrowing mammals with the head and body protected by an armor of bony plates

Ar·ma·ged·don \ˌär-mə-'ged-ᵊn\ *n* : a final conclusive battle between the forces of good and evil; *also* : the site or time of this

ar·ma·ment \'är-mə-mənt\ *n* **1** : military strength **2** : arms and equipment (as of a tank or combat unit) **3** : the process of preparing for war

ar·ma·ture \'är-mə-ˌchůr, -chər\ *n* **1** : a protective covering or structure (as the spines of a cactus) **2** : the rotating part of an electric generator or motor; *also* : the movable part in an electromagnetic device (as a loudspeaker)

arm·chair \'ärm-ˌcher\ *n* : a chair with armrests

armed forces *n pl* ♦ : the combined military, naval, and air forces of a nation

♦ military, services, troops

Ar·me·nian \är-'mē-nē-ən\ *n* : a native or inhabitant of Armenia

arm·ful \'ärm-ˌfůl\ *n, pl* **armfuls** *or* **arms·ful** \'ärmz-ˌfůl\ : as much as the arm or arms can hold

arm·hole \'ärm-ˌhōl\ *n* : an opening for the arm in a garment

ar·mi·stice \'är-mə-stəs\ *n* : temporary suspension of hostilities by mutual agreement : TRUCE

arm·let \'ärm-lət\ *n* : a band worn around the upper arm

ar·mor *or Can and Brit* **ar·mour** \'är-mər\ *n* **1** ♦ : protective covering **2** ♦ : a quality or circumstance that affords protection **3** : armored forces and vehicles — **ar·mored** \-mərd\ *adj*

♦ [1] capsule, case, casing, cocoon, cover, housing, husk, jacket, pod, sheath, shell ♦ [2] aegis, cover, defense (*or* defence), guard, protection, safeguard, screen, security, shield, wall, ward

ar·mor·er *or Can and Brit* **ar·mour·er** \'är-mər-ər\ *n* **1** : a person who makes arms and armor **2** : a person who services firearms

ar·mo·ri·al \är-'mōr-ē-əl\ *or Can and Brit* **ar·mou·ri·al** *adj* : of or bearing heraldic arms

ar·mory \'är-mə-rē\ *or Can and Brit* **ar·moury** *n, pl* **ar·mor·ies** *or* **ar·mour·ies** **1** ♦ : a place where arms are stored **2** : a factory where arms are made

♦ arsenal, depot, dump, magazine

arm·pit \'ärm-ˌpit\ *n* : the hollow under the junction of the arm and shoulder

arm·rest \-ˌrest\ *n* : a support for the arm

ar·my \'är-mē\ *n, pl* **armies** **1** ♦ : a body of armed personnel organized for war **2** *often cap* : the complete military organization of a country for land warfare **3** ♦ : a great number ⟨an ∼ of birds⟩ **4** : a body of persons organized to advance a cause

♦ [1] battalion, host, legion ♦ [3] crowd, crush, drove, flock, horde, host, legion, mob, multitude, press, swarm, throng

ar·my ant *n* : any of various nomadic social ants

ar·my·worm \ˈär-mē-ˌwərm\ *n* : any of numerous moths whose larvae move about destroying crops

aro·ma \ə-ˈrō-mə\ *n* ♦ : a usu. pleasing odor : FRAGRANCE

♦ bouquet, fragrance, incense, perfume, redolence, scent, spice

aro·ma·ther·a·py \ə-ˌrō-mə-ˈther-ə-pē\ *n* : massage with a preparation of fragrant oils extracted from herbs, flowers, and fruits

ar·o·mat·ic \ˌar-ə-ˈma-tik\ *adj* ♦ : of, relating to, or having aroma

♦ ambrosial, fragrant, redolent, savory, scented, sweet

arose *past of* ARISE

¹**around** \ə-ˈraund\ *adv* **1** : in a circle or in circumference ⟨a tree five feet ∼⟩ **2** : in or along a circuit ⟨the road goes ∼ by the lake⟩ **3 a** : on all sides ⟨nothing for miles ∼⟩ **b** ♦ : at all times : throughout the extent ⟨mild weather the year ∼⟩ **4** ♦ : in or near one's present place or situation : NEARBY ⟨wait ∼ awhile⟩ **5** : from one place to another ⟨travels ∼ on business⟩ **6** ♦ : in an opposite direction ⟨turn ∼⟩

♦ [3b] over, round, through, throughout ♦ [4] by, close, hard, in, near, nearby, nigh ♦ [6] about, back, round

²**around** *prep* **1 a** : on all sides of : SURROUNDING ⟨trees ∼ the house⟩ **b** : so as to encircle or enclose ⟨go ∼ the world⟩ **2** : to or on another side of ⟨∼ the corner⟩ **3** ♦ : at, within, or to a short distance or time : NEAR ⟨stayed right ∼ home⟩ **4** ♦ : here and there in or throughout ⟨barnstorming ∼ the country⟩

♦ [3] about, by, near, next to ♦ [4] about, over, round, through, throughout

arouse \ə-ˈrauz\ *vb* **aroused; arous·ing 1** ♦ : to awaken from sleep **2** ♦ : to stir up — **arous·al** \-ˈrau-zəl\ *n*

♦ [1] awake, rouse, wake ♦ [2] encourage, excite, fire, incite, instigate, move, pique, provoke, stimulate, stir

ar·peg·gio \är-ˈpe-jē-ˌō, -ˈpe-jō\ *n, pl* **-gios** : a chord whose notes are performed in succession and not simultaneously

arr *abbr* **1** arranged **2** arrival; arrive

ar·raign \ə-ˈrān\ *vb* **1** : to call before a court to answer to an indictment **2** : to accuse of wrong or imperfection — **ar·raign·ment** *n*

ar·range \ə-ˈrānj\ *vb* **ar·ranged; ar·rang·ing 1** ♦ : to put in order **2** : to make preparations for **3** : to adapt (a musical composition) to voices or instruments other than those for which it was orig. written **4** ♦ : to come to an agreement about : SETTLE — **ar·rang·er** *n*

♦ [1] array, classify, codify, dispose, draw up, marshal, order, organize, range, systematize ♦ [4] decide, fix, set, settle

ar·range·ment \-mənt\ *n* **1 a** ♦ : the state of being arranged **b** : the act of arranging **2** : something arranged: as **a** ♦ : a preparatory act or measure **b** : an adaptation of a musical composition **c** : an informal agreement or settlement **3** : something made by arranging parts or things together ⟨a floral ∼⟩

♦ [1a] composition, configuration, design, form, format, layout, makeup, pattern ♦ [1a] array, disposal, disposition, distribution, order, sequence, setup ♦ [2a] blueprint, design, game, plan, project, system

ar·rant \ˈar-ənt\ *adj* : being notoriously without moderation : EXTREME

ar·ras \ˈar-əs\ *n, pl* **arras 1** : TAPESTRY **2** : a wall hanging or screen of tapestry

¹**ar·ray** \ə-ˈrā\ *vb* **1** ♦ : to dress or decorate esp. splendidly **2** ♦ : to arrange in order

♦ [1] adorn, beautify, clothe, deck, decorate, do, dress, embellish, enrich, garnish, ornament, trim ♦ [2] arrange, classify, codify, dispose, draw up, marshal, order, organize, range, systematize

²**array** *n* **1** ♦ : a regular arrangement **2** ♦ : rich apparel **3** ♦ : an imposing group

♦ [1] arrangement, disposal, disposition, distribution, order, sequence, setup ♦ [2] attire, best, bravery, caparison, feather, finery, frippery, full dress, gaiety, regalia ♦ [3] assemblage, block, collection, group, lot

ar·rears \ə-ˈrirz\ *n pl* **1** : a state of being behind in the discharge of obligations ⟨in ∼ with the rent⟩ **2** : overdue debts

¹**ar·rest** \ə-ˈrest\ *vb* **1** ♦ : to bring to a stop **2** ♦ : to take into legal custody **3** ♦ : to catch suddenly and engagingly ⟨∼ attention⟩

♦ [1] catch, check, draw up, fetch up, halt, hold up, stall, stay, still, stop ♦ [2] apprehend, nab, pick up, restrain, seize *Ant* discharge ♦ [3] enchant, enthrall, fascinate, grip, hypnotize, mesmerize

²**arrest** *n* **1** : the act of stopping; *also* : the state of being stopped **2** : the taking into custody by legal authority

ar·riv·al \ə-ˈrī-vəl\ *n* **1** : the act of arriving **2** : one that arrives

ar·rive \ə-ˈrīv\ *vb* **ar·rived; ar·riv·ing 1** ♦ : to reach a destination **2** : to make an appearance ⟨the guests have *arrived*⟩ **3** : to attain success — **arrive at** : to reach by effort or thought ⟨*arrived at* a decision⟩

♦ come, land, show up, turn up

ar·ro·gance \ˈar-ə-gəns\ *n* ♦ : an attitude of superiority that shows itself in an overbearing manner or in presumptuous claims or assumptions

♦ haughtiness, loftiness, pretense, pretension, pretentiousness, self-importance, superiority *Ant* humility, modesty

ar·ro·gant \ˈar-ə-gənt\ *adj* ♦ : offensively exaggerating one's own importance — **ar·ro·gant·ly** *adv*

♦ cavalier, haughty, highfalutin, high-handed, high-hat, imperious, important, lofty, overweening, peremptory, pompous, presumptuous, pretentious, supercilious *Ant* humble, modest

ar·ro·gate \-ˌgāt\ *vb* **-gat·ed; -gat·ing** ♦ : to claim or seize without justification as one's right — **ar·ro·ga·tion** \ˌar-ə-ˈgā-shən\ *n*

♦ appropriate, commandeer, preempt, usurp

ar·row \ˈar-ō\ *n* **1** : a missile shot from a bow and usu. having a slender shaft, a pointed head, and feathers at the butt **2** : a pointed mark used to indicate direction

ar·row·head \ˈar-ō-ˌhed\ *n* : the pointed end of an arrow

ar·row·root \-ˌrüt, -ˌrut\ *n* : an edible starch from the roots of any of several tropical American plants; *also* : a plant yielding arrowroot

ar·royo \ə-ˈrȯi-ə, -ō\ *n, pl* **-royos 1** : a watercourse in a dry region **2** : a water-carved gully or channel

ar·se·nal \ˈärs-nəl, ˈärs-ᵊn-əl\ *n* **1** ♦ : a place for making and storing arms and military equipment **2** : STORE, REPERTORY

♦ armory, depot, dump, magazine

ar·se·nic \ˈärs-nik, ˈärs-ᵊn-ik\ *n* **1** : a solid brittle poisonous chemical element of grayish metallic luster **2** : a very poisonous oxygen compound of arsenic used in making insecticides

ar·son \ˈärs-ᵊn\ *n* : the willful or malicious burning of property — **ar·son·ist** \-ist\ *n*

¹**art** \ˈärt\ *n* **1** : skill acquired by experience or study **2** : a branch of learning; *esp* : one of the humanities **3** : an occupation requiring knowledge or skill **4** ♦ : the use of skill and imagination in the production of things of beauty; *also* : works so produced **5** : ARTFULNESS

♦ adeptness, adroitness, artfulness, artifice, artistry, cleverness, craft, cunning, deftness, masterfulness, skill

²**art** *abbr* **1** article **2** artificial **3** artillery

ar·te·ri·al \är-ˈtir-ē-əl\ *adj* **1** : of or relating to an artery; *also* : relating to or being the oxygenated blood found in most arteries **2** : of, relating to, or being a route for through traffic

ar·te·ri·ole \är-ˈtir-ē-ˌōl\ *n* : one of the small terminal branches of an artery that ends in capillaries — **ar·te·ri·o·lar** \-ˌtir-ē-ˈō-lər\ *adj*

ar·te·rio·scle·ro·sis \är-ˌtir-ē-ō-sklə-ˈrō-səs\ *n* : a chronic disease in which arterial walls are abnormally thickened and hardened — **ar·te·rio·scle·rot·ic** \-ˈrä-tik\ *adj or n*

ar·tery \ˈär-tə-rē\ *n, pl* **-ter·ies 1** : one of the tubular vessels that carry blood from the heart **2** ♦ : a main channel of transportation or communication

♦ avenue, highway, road, route, thoroughfare, turnpike, way

ar·te·sian well \är-ˈtē-zhən-\ *n* : a well from which the water flows to the surface by natural pressure; *also* : a deep well

art·ful \ˈärt-fəl\ *adj* **1** ♦ : performed with or showing art or skill ⟨an ∼ performance on the violin⟩ **2 a** ♦ : using or characterized by art and skill ⟨an ∼ writer⟩ **b** ♦ : adroit in attaining an end usu. by deceptive or indirect means : CRAFTY — **art·ful·ly** *adv*

♦ [1] adroit, dexterous, masterful, practiced, skillful, virtuoso ♦ [2a] clever, creative, imaginative, ingenious ♦ [2b] cagey, crafty, cunning, devious, foxy, guileful, slick, sly, subtle, wily *Ant* artless, ingenuous

art·ful·ness \-nəs\ *n* ♦ : the quality or state of being artful

♦ artifice, caginess, canniness, craft, craftiness, cunning, guile, slyness, wiliness ♦ adeptness, adroitness, art, artifice, artistry, cleverness, craft, cunning, deftness, masterfulness, skill

ar·thri·tis \är-'thrī-təs\ *n, pl* **-thri·ti·des** \-'thri-tə-ˌdēz\ : inflammation of the joints — **ar·thrit·ic** \-'thri-tik\ *adj or n*
ar·thro·pod \'är-thrə-ˌpäd\ *n* : any of a phylum of invertebrate animals comprising those (as insects, spiders, or crabs) with segmented bodies and jointed limbs — **arthropod** *adj*
ar·thros·co·py \är-'thräs-kə-pē\ *n, pl* **-pies** : visual examination of the interior of a joint (as the knee) with a special surgical instrument; *also* : joint surgery using arthroscopy — **ar·thro·scope** \'är-thrə-ˌskōp\ *n* — **ar·thro·scop·ic** \ˌär-thrə-'skä-pik\ *adj*
ar·ti·choke \'är-tə-ˌchōk\ *n* : a tall herb related to the daisies; *also* : its edible flower head
ar·ti·cle \'är-ti-kəl\ *n* **1** : a distinct part of a written document **2** ♦ : a nonfictional prose composition forming an independent part of a publication **3** : a word (as *an, the*) used with a noun to limit or give definiteness to its application **4** : a member of a class of things; *esp* : COMMODITY
♦ composition, essay, paper, theme
ar·tic·u·lar \är-'ti-kyə-lər\ *adj* : of or relating to a joint
¹ar·tic·u·late \är-'ti-kyə-lət\ *adj* **1** : divided into meaningful parts : INTELLIGIBLE **2** ♦ : able to speak; *also* : expressing oneself readily and effectively **3** : JOINTED — **ar·tic·u·late·ly** *adv*
♦ eloquent, fluent, well-spoken *Ant* inarticulate
²ar·tic·u·late \-ˌlāt\ *vb* **-lat·ed; -lat·ing** **1 a** ♦ : to give clear and effective utterance to ⟨~ their grievances⟩ **b** : to utter distinctly ⟨~ each note in the musical phrase⟩ **2** : to unite by or as if by joints
♦ clothe, couch, express, formulate, phrase, put, say, state, word
ar·tic·u·late·ness \-nəs\ *n* ♦ : the quality or state of being articulate
♦ eloquence, poetry, rhetoric
ar·tic·u·la·tion \-ˌti-kyə-'lā-shən\ *n* **1** ♦ : the act of giving utterance or expression **2** : the act or manner of articulating sounds
♦ expression, formulation, statement, utterance, voice
ar·ti·fact \'är-tə-ˌfakt\ *n* : something made or modified by humans usu. for a purpose; *esp* : an object remaining from another time or culture ⟨prehistoric ~s⟩
ar·ti·fice \'är-tə-fəs\ *n* **1 a** ♦ : clever or artful skill **b** : an ingenious device **2 a** ♦ : an artful stratagem : TRICK **b** ♦ : false or insincere behavior
♦ [1a] adeptness, adroitness, art, artfulness, artistry, cleverness, craft, cunning, deftness, masterfulness, skill ♦ [2a] device, dodge, gimmick, jig, ploy, scheme, sleight, stratagem, trick, wile ♦ [2b] craft, craftiness, crookedness, cunning, deceit, deceitfulness, dishonesty, dissimulation, double-dealing, duplicity, guile, wiliness
ar·ti·fic·er \är-'ti-fə-sər, 'är-tə-fə-sər\ *n* ♦ : a skilled worker
♦ artisan, craftsman, handicrafter
ar·ti·fi·cial \ˌär-tə-'fi-shəl\ *adj* **1** ♦ : produced by art rather than nature; *also* : made by humans to imitate nature **2** ♦ : not genuine : FEIGNED — **ar·ti·fi·ci·al·i·ty** \-ˌfi-shē-'a-lə-tē\ *n* — **ar·ti·fi·cial·ly** *adv* — **ar·ti·fi·cial·ness** *n*
♦ [1] fake, faux, imitation, mock, sham, synthetic ♦ [2] affected, assumed, bogus, contrived, false, feigned, insincere, mechanical, phony, put-on, spurious, unnatural *Ant* genuine, natural, spontaneous, unfeigned, unforced
artificial insemination *n* : introduction of semen into the uterus or oviduct by other than natural means
artificial intelligence *n* : the capability of a machine and esp. a computer to imitate intelligent human behavior
artificial respiration *n* : the rhythmic forcing of air into and out of the lungs of a person whose breathing has stopped
ar·til·lery \är-'ti-lə-rē\ *n, pl* **-ler·ies** **1** : crew-served mounted firearms (as guns) **2** : a branch of the army armed with artillery — **ar·til·ler·ist** \-rist\ *n*
ar·ti·san \'är-tə-zən, -sən\ *n* ♦ : a skilled manual worker
♦ artificer, craftsman, handicrafter
art·ist \'är-tist\ *n* **1** : one who practices an imaginative art; *esp* : one who creates objects of beauty **2** : ARTISTE **3** ♦ : one who is adept at something
♦ adept, authority, expert, master, virtuoso, whiz, wizard
ar·tiste \är-'tēst\ *n* : a skilled public performer
ar·tis·tic \är-'tis-tik\ *adj* **1** : of, relating to, or characteristic of art or artists **2** : showing taste and skill — **ar·tis·ti·cal·ly** \-ti-k(ə-)lē\ *adv*

art·ist·ry \'är-tə-strē\ *n* ♦ : artistic quality or ability
♦ adeptness, adroitness, art, artfulness, artifice, cleverness, craft, cunning, deftness, masterfulness, skill
art·less \'ärt-ləs\ *adj* **1** : lacking art or skill **2 a** ♦ : made without skill : CRUDE **b** : free from artificiality : NATURAL **3** ♦ : free from guile : SINCERE
♦ [2a] clumsy, crude, rough, rude, unrefined ♦ [3] genuine, honest, ingenuous, innocent, naive, natural, real, simple, sincere, true, unaffected, unpretentious
art·less·ly \-lē\ *adv* : in an artless manner
♦ ingenuously, naively, naturally, unaffectedly
art·less·ness \-nəs\ *n* ♦ : the quality or state of being artless
♦ greenness, ingenuousness, innocence, naïveté, naturalness, simplicity, unworldliness
art nou·veau \ˌär-nü-'vō, ˌärt-\ *n, often cap A&N* : a late 19th century design style characterized by sinuous lines and leaf⸗ shaped forms
arty \'är-tē\ *adj* **art·i·er; -est** : showily or pretentiously artistic — **art·i·ly** \'ärt-ᵊl-ē\ *adv* — **art·i·ness** *n*
ar·um \'ar-əm\ *n* : any of a family of plants (as the jack-in-the⸗ pulpit or a skunk cabbage) with flowers in a fleshy enclosed spike
ARV *abbr* American Revised Version
¹-ary *n suffix* : thing or person belonging to or connected with ⟨function*ary*⟩
²-ary *adj suffix* : of, relating to, or connected with ⟨budget*ary*⟩
Ary·an \'ar-ē-ən, 'er-; 'är-yən\ *adj* **1** : INDO-EUROPEAN **2** : NORDIC — **Aryan** *n*
¹as \əz, (ˌ)az\ *adv* **1** : to the same degree or amount : EQUALLY ⟨~ green as grass⟩ **2** : for instance ⟨various trees, ~ oak or pine⟩ **3** : when considered in a specified relation ⟨my opinion ~ distinguished from his⟩
²as *conj* **1** : in the same amount or degree in which ⟨green ~ grass⟩ **2** : in the same way that ⟨farmed ~ his father before him had farmed⟩ **3** : WHILE, WHEN ⟨spoke to me ~ I was leaving⟩ **4** : THOUGH ⟨improbable ~ it seems⟩ **5** : SINCE, BECAUSE ⟨~ I'm not wanted, I'll go⟩ **6** : that the result is ⟨so guilty ~ to leave no doubt⟩
³as *pron* **1** : THAT — used after *same* or *such* ⟨it's the same price ~ before⟩ **2** : a fact that ⟨he's rich, ~ you know⟩
⁴as *prep* : in the capacity or character of ⟨this will serve ~ a substitute⟩
As *symbol* arsenic
AS *abbr* **1** American Samoa **2** Anglo-Saxon **3** associate in science
asa·fet·i·da *or* **asa·foe·ti·da** \ˌa-sə-'fi-tə-dē, -'fe-tə-də\ *n* : an ill-smelling plant gum formerly used in medicine
ASAP *abbr* as soon as possible
as·bes·tos \as-'bes-təs, az-\ *n* : a noncombustible grayish mineral that occurs in fibrous form and has been used as a fireproof material
as·cend \ə-'send\ *vb* **1** ♦ : to move upward : MOUNT, CLIMB **2** : to succeed to : OCCUPY ⟨he ~ed the throne⟩
♦ arise, climb, lift, mount, rise, soar, up *Ant* decline, descend, dip, drop, fall (off)
as·cen·dan·cy *also* **as·cen·den·cy** \ə-'sen-dən-sē\ *n* ♦ : controlling influence
♦ dominance, dominion, predominance, preeminence, supremacy
¹as·cen·dant *also* **as·cen·dent** \ə-'sen-dənt\ *n* : a dominant position
²ascendant *also* **ascendent** *adj* **1** : moving upward **2** : DOMINANT
as·cen·sion \ə-'sen-chən\ *n* : the act or process of ascending
Ascension Day *n* : the Thursday 40 days after Easter observed in commemoration of Christ's ascension into heaven
as·cent \ə-'sent\ *n* **1 a** ♦ : the act of mounting upward : CLIMB **b** : an upward slope or rising grade **2** ♦ : an advance in social status or reputation
♦ [1a] climb, rise *Ant* descent, dip, drop, fall ♦ [2] advancement, elevation, promotion, rise, upgrade
as·cer·tain \ˌas-ər-'tān\ *vb* ♦ : to learn with certainty — **as·cer·tain·able** *adj*
♦ catch on, discover, find out, hear, learn, realize, see ♦ detect, determine, discover, ferret out, find, hit on, locate, track down
as·cet·ic \ə-'se-tik\ *adj* : practicing self-denial esp. for spiritual reasons : AUSTERE — **ascetic** *n* — **as·cet·i·cism** \-'se-tə-ˌsi-zəm\ *n*
ASCII \'as-kē\ *n* : a computer code for representing alphanumeric information

ascor·bic acid \ə-'skȯr-bik-\ n : VITAMIN C

as·cot \'as-kət, -ˌkät\ n : a broad neck scarf that is looped under the chin

as·cribe \ə-'skrīb\ vb **as·cribed; as·crib·ing** ♦ : to refer to a supposed cause, source, or author : ATTRIBUTE — **as·crib·able** adj — **as·crip·tion** \-'skrip-shən\ n

♦ accredit, attribute, credit, impute

asep·tic \ā-'sep-tik\ adj ♦ : free or freed from disease-causing germs

♦ hygienic, sanitary, sterile

asex·u·al \ā-'sek-shə-wəl\ adj 1 : lacking sex or functional sex organs 2 : occurring or formed without the production and union of two kinds of germ cells ⟨∼ reproduction⟩ 3 : devoid of sexuality 4 : neither male nor female — **asex·u·al·ly** adv

as for prep : with regard to : CONCERNING ⟨as for the others, they were late⟩

¹ash \'ash\ n 1 : any of a genus of trees related to the olive and having winged seeds and bark with grooves and ridges 2 : the tough elastic wood of an ash

²ash n 1 : the solid matter left when material is burned 2 : fine mineral particles from a volcano 3 pl : the remains of the dead human body after cremation or disintegration

ashamed \ə-'shāmd\ adj 1 ♦ : feeling shame 2 : restrained by anticipation of shame ⟨∼ to say anything⟩ — **asham·ed·ly** \-'shā-məd-lē\ adv

♦ contrite, guilty, hangdog, penitent, remorseful, repentant, shamefaced

ash·en \'a-shən\ adj ♦ : resembling ashes (as in color); esp : deadly pale

♦ cadaverous, livid, lurid, pale, pasty, peaked

ash·lar \'ash-lər\ n : hewn or squared stone; also : masonry of such stone

ashore \ə-'shȯr\ adv : on or to the shore

as how conj : THAT ⟨allowed as how she was glad to be here⟩

ash·ram \'äsh-rəm\ n : a religious retreat esp. of a Hindu sage

ash·tray \'ash-ˌtrā\ n : a receptacle for tobacco ashes

Ash Wednesday n : the 1st day of Lent

ashy \'a-shē\ adj **ash·i·er; -est** : resembling ashes (as in color); esp : deadly pale : ASHEN

Asian \'ā-zhən\ adj : of, relating to, or characteristic of the continent of Asia or its people — **Asian** n

¹aside \ə-'sīd\ adv 1 : to or toward the side ⟨stepped ∼⟩ 2 : out of the way : AWAY ⟨put ∼ some savings⟩

²aside n : an actor's words heard by the audience but supposedly not by other characters on stage

aside from prep 1 : BESIDES ⟨aside from being pretty, she's intelligent⟩ 2 ♦ : with the exception of ⟨aside from one D his grades are excellent⟩

♦ bar, barring, besides, but, except, outside (of), save

as if conj 1 : as it would be if ⟨it's as if nothing had changed⟩ 2 : as one would if ⟨he acts as if he'd never been away⟩ 3 : THAT ⟨it seems as if nothing ever happens around here⟩

as·i·nine \'as-ᵊn-ˌīn\ adj ♦ : extremely or utterly foolish

♦ absurd, cuckoo, fatuous, foolish, nonsensical, nutty, senseless, silly, stupid

as·i·nin·i·ty \ˌa-sə-'ni-nə-tē\ n 1 ♦ : the quality or state of being asinine 2 : something that is asinine

♦ daftness, folly, foolishness, inanity, silliness

ask \'ask\ vb **asked** \'askt\; **ask·ing** 1 ♦ : to call on for an answer ⟨∼ a question⟩ 2 : UTTER ⟨∼ a question⟩ 3 : to make a request of ⟨∼ him for help⟩ 4 ♦ : to make a request for ⟨∼ help of her⟩ 5 ♦ : to set as a price ⟨∼ed $800 for the car⟩ 6 : to increase the likelihood of : INVITE

♦ [1] inquire of, interrogate, query, question, quiz Ant answer, reply, respond ♦ usu **ask for** [4] call, plead, quest, request, seek, solicit, sue ♦ [5] charge, command, demand

askance \ə-'skans\ adv 1 : with a side glance 2 ♦ : with distrust

♦ distrustfully, dubiously, mistrustfully, suspiciously Ant trustfully

askew \ə-'skyü\ adj ♦ : being out of line : AWRY — **askew** adv

♦ awry, cockeyed, crooked, listing, lopsided, slantwise, uneven

ASL abbr American Sign Language

¹aslant \ə-'slant\ adv or adj : in a slanting direction

²aslant prep : over or across in a slanting direction

asleep \ə-'slēp\ adv or adj 1 ♦ : in or into a state of sleep 2 : DEAD 3 ♦ : lacking sensation : NUMB 4 : INACTIVE

♦ [1] dormant Ant awake, wakeful, wide-awake ♦ [3] dead, numb, unfeeling

as long as conj 1 : provided that ⟨do as you like as long as you get home on time⟩ 2 : INASMUCH AS, SINCE ⟨as long as you're up, turn on the light⟩

aso·cial \(ˌ)ā-'sō-shəl\ adj : ANTISOCIAL

as of prep : AT, DURING, FROM, ON ⟨takes effect as of July 1⟩

asp \'asp\ n : a small poisonous African snake

as·par·a·gus \ə-'spar-ə-gəs\ n : a tall branching perennial herb related to the lilies; also : its edible young stalks

as·par·tame \as-'pär-ˌtām\ n : a crystalline low-calorie sweetener

ASPCA abbr American Society for the Prevention of Cruelty to Animals

as·pect \'as-ˌpekt\ n 1 : a position facing a particular direction 2 ♦ : a particular appearance or countenance : APPEARANCE, LOOK 3 ♦ : a particular status or phase in which something appears or may be regarded

♦ [2] appearance, look, mien, presence ♦ [3] angle, facet, hand, phase, side

as·pen \'as-pən\ n : any of several poplars with leaves that flutter in the slightest breeze

as per \'az-ˌpər\ prep : in accordance with ⟨as per instructions⟩

as·per·i·ty \a-'sper-ə-tē\ n, pl **-ties** 1 ♦ : a characteristic making for hardship : RIGOR 2 : ROUGHNESS 3 ♦ : harshness of manner or temper

♦ [1] adversity, difficulty, hardness, hardship, rigor ♦ [3] acidity, acrimony, bitterness, cattiness, tartness, virulence, vitriol

as·per·sion \ə-'spər-zhən\ n : a slanderous or defamatory remark

as·phalt \'as-ˌfȯlt\ also **as·phal·tum** \as-'fȯl-təm\ n : a dark substance found in natural beds or obtained as a residue in petroleum refining and used esp. in paving streets

asphalt jungle n : a big city or a specified part of a big city

as·pho·del \'as-fə-ˌdel\ n : any of several Old World herbs related to the lilies and bearing flowers in long erect spikes

as·phyx·ia \as-'fik-sē-ə\ n : a lack of oxygen or excess of carbon dioxide in the body usu. caused by interruption of breathing and causing unconsciousness

as·phyx·i·ate \-sē-ˌāt\ vb **-at·ed; -at·ing** : SUFFOCATE — **as·phyx·i·a·tion** \-ˌfik-sē-'ā-shən\ n

as·pic \'as-pik\ n : a savory meat jelly

as·pi·rant \'as-pə-rənt, ə-'spī-rənt\ n ♦ : one who aspires

♦ applicant, campaigner, candidate, contender, hopeful, prospect, seeker

¹as·pi·rate \'as-pə-rət\ n 1 : an independent sound \h\ or a character (as the letter h) representing it 2 : a consonant having aspiration as its final component

²as·pi·rate \'as-pə-ˌrāt\ vb **-rat·ed; -rat·ing** : to draw, remove, or take up or into by suction

as·pi·ra·tion \ˌas-pə-'rā-shən\ n 1 : the pronunciation or addition of an aspirate; also : the aspirate or its symbol 2 : a drawing of something in, out, up, or through by or as if by suction 3 a : a strong desire to achieve something noble b ♦ : an object of strong desire

♦ aim, ambition, design, dream, end, goal, intent, object, objective, purpose

as·pire \ə-'spīr\ vb **as·pired; as·pir·ing** 1 ♦ : to seek to attain or accomplish a particular goal 2 : to rise aloft

♦ aim, contemplate, design, intend, plan, propose

as·pi·rin \'as-pə-rən\ n, pl **aspirin** or **aspirins** 1 : a white crystalline drug used to relieve pain and fever 2 : a tablet of aspirin

as regards also **as respects** prep : in regard to : with respect to

ass \'as\ n 1 : any of several long-eared mammals smaller than the related horses; esp : one of Africa ancestral to the donkey 2 impolite : a foolish or unlikeable person

♦ donkey, jackass

as·sail \ə-'sāl\ vb ♦ : to attack violently with blows or words — **as·sail·able** adj — **as·sail·ant** n

♦ abuse, attack, belabor, blast, castigate, excoriate, jump, lambaste, slam, vituperate ♦ assault, attack, beset, charge, descend, jump, pounce (on or upon), raid, rush, storm, strike

as·sas·sin \ə-'sas-ᵊn\ n : a murderer esp. for hire or fanatical reasons

as·sas·si·nate \ə-'sas-ᵊn-ˌāt\ vb **-nat·ed; -nat·ing** : to murder by sudden or secret attack — **as·sas·si·na·tion** \-ˌsas-ᵊn-'ā-shən\ n

¹as•sault \ə-'sȯlt\ *n* **1** ♦ : a violent attack **2** : an unlawful attempt or threat to do harm to another

♦ aggression, attack, charge, descent, offense (*or* offence), offensive, onset, onslaught, raid, rush, strike

²assault *vb* ♦ : to make an assault on

♦ assail, attack, beset, charge, descend, jump, pounce (on *or* upon), raid, rush, storm, strike

assault rifle *n* : a military automatic rifle with a large-capacity magazine

¹as•say \'a-ˌsā, a-'sā\ *n* ♦ : analysis to determine the quantity of one or more components present in a sample (as of an ore or drug)

♦ analysis, breakdown, breakup, dissection

²as•say \a-'sā, 'a-ˌsā\ *vb* **1** ♦ : to make an attempt at : TRY **2** ♦ : to subject (as an ore or drug) to an assay **3** : JUDGE 3

♦ [1] attempt, endeavor (*or* endeavour), essay, seek, strive, try ♦ [2] analyze, anatomize, break down, break up, dissect

as•sem•blage \ə-'sem-blij, *3 & 4 also* ˌas-ˌäm-'bläzh\ *n* **1** ♦ : a collection of persons or things **2** : the act of assembling **3** : an artistic composition made from scraps, junk, and odds and ends **4** : the art of making assemblages

♦ assembly, conference, congregation, convocation, gathering, meeting, muster ♦ accumulation, array, bunch, collection, group, lot, package, parcel

as•sem•ble \ə-'sem-bəl\ *vb* **-bled; -bling** **1** ♦ : to collect into one place **2** ♦ : to fit together the parts of **3** ♦ : to meet together : CONVENE

♦ [1] accumulate, amass, collect, concentrate, garner, gather, group, lump, pick up, round up, scrape ♦ [2] build, construct, erect, fabricate, make, make up, piece, put up, raise, rear, set up ♦ [3] cluster, collect, concentrate, conglomerate, congregate, convene, forgather, gather, meet, rendezvous *Ant* break up, disband, disperse, split up

as•sem•bly \ə-'sem-blē\ *n, pl* **-blies** **1** ♦ : a gathering of persons : MEETING **2** *cap* : a legislative body; *esp* : the lower house of a legislature **3** : a signal for troops to assemble **4** : the fitting together of parts (as of a machine)

♦ assemblage, conference, congregation, convocation, gathering, meeting, muster

assembly language *n* : a computer language consisting of mnemonic codes corresponding to machine-language instructions

assembly line *n* : an arrangement of machines, equipment, and workers in which work passes from operation to operation in a direct line

as•sem•bly•man \ə-'sem-blē-mən\ *n* : a member of an assembly

as•sem•bly•wom•an \-ˌwu̇-mən\ *n* : a woman who is a member of an assembly

as•sent \ə-'sent\ *vb* ♦ : to join with others in agreement : AGREE — **assent** *n*

♦ accede, acquiesce, agree, come round, consent, subscribe (to)

as•sert \ə-'sərt\ *vb* **1** ♦ : to state positively **2** : to demonstrate the existence of

♦ affirm, aver, avouch, avow, declare, lay down, profess ♦ argue, contend, maintain, plead, reason ♦ allege, aver, avouch, avow, claim, contend, declare, insist, maintain, profess, protest, warrant

as•ser•tion \ə-'sər-shən\ *n* ♦ : a positive statement

♦ argument, contention, thesis ♦ affirmation, avowal, claim, declaration, profession, protestation

as•ser•tive \ə-'sər-tiv\ *adj* ♦ : disposed to or characterized by bold or confident assertion

♦ aggressive, dynamic, emphatic, energetic, forceful, resounding, strenuous, vehement, vigorous

as•ser•tive•ness \-nəs\ *n* ♦ : the quality or state of being assertive

♦ emphasis, fierceness, intensity, vehemence

as•sess \ə-'ses\ *vb* **1** ♦ : to fix the rate or amount of **2** ♦ : to impose (as a tax) at a specified rate **3** : to evaluate for taxation **4** ♦ : to determine the importance, size, or value of ⟨~ the problem⟩ — **as•ses•sor** \-'se-sər\ *n*

♦ [1, 2] charge, exact, fine, impose, lay, levy, put ♦ [4] appraise, estimate, evaluate, rate, set, value

as•sess•ment \-mənt\ *n* **1** ♦ : the action or an instance of assessing : APPRAISAL **2** ♦ : the amount assessed

♦ [1] appraisal, estimate, estimation, evaluation, reckoning, valuation ♦ [2] duty, impost, levy, tax

as•set \'a-ˌset\ *n* **1** *pl* ♦ : the entire property of a person or company that may be used to pay debts **2** : ADVANTAGE, RESOURCE

♦ capital, fortune, means, opulence, riches, substance, wealth, wherewithal

as•sev•er•ate \ə-'se-və-ˌrāt\ *vb* **-at•ed; -at•ing** : to assert earnestly — **as•sev•er•a•tion** \-ˌse-və-'rā-shən\ *n*

as•si•du•i•ty \ˌa-sə-'dü-ə-tē, -'dyü-\ *n* ♦ : the quality or state of being assiduous

♦ diligence, industry

as•sid•u•ous \ə-'si-jə-wəs\ *adj* ♦ : marked by careful unremitting attention or persistent application : DILIGENT

♦ active, busy, diligent, engaged, laborious, occupied, sedulous, working

as•sid•u•ous•ly \ə-'si-jə-wəs-lē\ *adv* : in an assiduous manner

as•sid•u•ous•ness \-nəs\ *n* : the quality or state of being assiduous

as•sign \ə-'sīn\ *vb* **1** ♦ : to transfer (property) to another **2** ♦ : to appoint to or as a duty ⟨~ a lesson⟩ **3** : FIX, SPECIFY ⟨~ a limit⟩ **4** : ASCRIBE ⟨~ a reason⟩ — **as•sign•able** *adj*

♦ [1] cede, deed, make over, transfer ♦ [2] appoint, attach, commission, constitute, designate, detail, name

as•sig•na•tion \ˌa-sig-'nā-shən\ *n* : an appointment for a meeting; *esp* : TRYST

assigned risk *n* : a poor risk (as an accident-prone motorist) that an insurance company is forced to insure by state law

as•sign•ment \ə-'sīn-mənt\ *n* **1** : the act of assigning **2** ♦ : something assigned

♦ chore, duty, job, stint, task ♦ charge, job, mission, operation, post

as•sim•i•late \ə-'si-mə-ˌlāt\ *vb* **-lat•ed; -lat•ing** **1** ♦ : to take up and absorb as nourishment; *also* : to absorb into a cultural tradition **2** : COMPREHEND **3** : to make or become similar — **as•sim•i•la•tion** \-ˌsi-mə-'lā-shən\ *n*

♦ embody, incorporate, integrate

¹as•sist \ə-'sist\ *vb* ♦ : to give support or aid : HELP

♦ abet, aid, back, help, prop, support

²assist *n* **1** ♦ : an act of assistance **2** : the action of a player who enables a teammate to make a putout (as in baseball) or score a goal (as in hockey)

♦ aid, assistance, backing, boost, help, lift, support

as•sis•tance \-'sis-təns\ *n* ♦ : the act of assisting or the help supplied

♦ aid, assist, backing, boost, help, lift, support

as•sis•tant \ə-'sis-tənt\ *n* ♦ : a person who assists : HELPER

♦ aid, apprentice, deputy, helper, helpmate, mate, sidekick

as•sist•ed living \ə-'sis-təd-\ *n* : a system of housing and limited care for senior citizens who need assistance with daily activities but do not require care in a nursing home

as•size \ə-'sīz\ *n* **1** : a judicial inquest **2** *pl* : the former regular sessions of superior courts in English counties

assn *abbr* association

assoc *abbr* associate; associated; association

¹as•so•ci•ate \ə-'sō-shē-ˌāt, -sē-\ *vb* **-at•ed; -at•ing** **1** ♦ : to join in companionship or partnership **2** ♦ : to connect in thought

♦ [1] ally, band, club, confederate, conjoin, cooperate, federate, league, unite ♦ [1] chum, consort, fraternize, hang around, hobnob, pal ♦ [2] connect, correlate, identify, link, relate

²as•so•ci•ate \-shē-ət, -sē-; -shət\ *n* **1** : a fellow worker : PARTNER **2** ♦ : one that accompanies another : COMPANION **3** *often cap* : a degree conferred esp. by a junior college ⟨~ in arts⟩ — **associate** *adj*

♦ cohort, companion, comrade, crony, fellow, mate

as•so•ci•a•tion \ə-ˌsō-shē-'ā-shən, -sē-\ *n* **1 a** : the act of associating **b** ♦ : the state of being associated **2** ♦ : an organization of persons : SOCIETY

♦ [1b] affiliation, alliance, collaboration, confederation, connection, cooperation, hookup, liaison, partnership, relation, relationship, union *Ant* dissociation ♦ [2] brotherhood, club, college, congress, council, fellowship, fraternity, guild, institute, institution, league, order, organization, society

as•so•cia•tive \ə-'sō-shē-ˌā-tiv, -sē-; -shə-tiv\ *adj* : of, relating to, or involved in association esp. of ideas or images

as·so·nance \'a-sə-nəns\ *n* : repetition of vowels esp. as an alternative to rhyme in verse — **as·so·nant** \-nənt\ *adj or n*

as soon as *conj* : immediately at or shortly after the time that ⟨we'll start *as soon as* they arrive⟩

as·sort \ə-'sȯrt\ *vb* **1** ♦ : to distribute into like groups : CLASSIFY **2** : HARMONIZE

♦ break down, categorize, class, classify, grade, group, peg, place, range, rank, separate, sort

as·sort·ed \-'sȯr-təd\ *adj* ♦ : consisting of various kinds

♦ heterogeneous, miscellaneous, mixed, motley, varied

as·sort·ment \-'sȯrt-mənt\ *n* **1 a** : the act of assorting **b** ♦ : the state of being assorted **2** ♦ : a collection of assorted things or persons

♦ [1b] diversity, variety ♦ [2] clutter, jumble, medley, mélange, miscellany, motley, muddle, variety, welter

asst *abbr* assistant

as·suage \ə-'swāj\ *vb* **as·suaged; as·suag·ing 1** ♦ : to make (as pain or grief) less : EASE **2** ♦ : to put an end to by satisfying

♦ [1] allay, alleviate, ease, help, mitigate, mollify, palliate, relieve, soothe ♦ [2] quench, sate, satiate, satisfy

as·sume \ə-'süm\ *vb* **as·sumed; as·sum·ing 1** ♦ : to take upon oneself **2** ♦ : to pretend to have or be **3** ♦ : to take as granted or true though not proved

♦ [1] accept, bear, shoulder, take over, undertake *Ant* disavow, disclaim, disown, repudiate ♦ [2] affect, counterfeit, fake, feign, pretend, profess, put on, sham, simulate ♦ [3] postulate, premise, presume, presuppose, suppose

as·sumed \ə-'sümd\ *adj* **1** ♦ : not real or genuine ⟨an ∼ cheerfulness⟩ ⟨an ∼ name⟩ **2** ♦ : taken for granted : SUPPOSED

♦ [1] affected, artificial, bogus, contrived, fake, false, feigned, phony, put-on, sham ♦ [2] apparent, evident, ostensible, reputed, seeming, supposed

as·sump·tion \ə-'səmp-shən\ *n* **1** : the taking up of a person into heaven **2** *cap* : August 15 observed in commemoration of the Assumption of the Virgin Mary **3** : a taking upon oneself **4** : PRETENSION **5 a** : an assuming that something is true **b** ♦ : a fact or statement taken for granted : SUPPOSITION

♦ postulate, premise, presumption, supposition

as·sur·ance \ə-'shu̇r-əns\ *n* **1** : PLEDGE **2** *chiefly Brit* : INSURANCE **3** : the state of being assured: as **a** : SECURITY **b** ♦ : a being certain in the mind **c** ♦ : confidence of mind or manner; *also* : excessive self-confidence

♦ [3b] certainty, certitude, confidence, conviction, positiveness, sureness ♦ [3c] aplomb, confidence, self-assurance, self-confidence, self-esteem

as·sure \ə-'shu̇r\ *vb* **as·sured; as·sur·ing 1** ♦ : to make safe **2** : to give confidence to **3** : to state confidently to **4** : to make certain the coming or attainment of

♦ cinch, ensure, guarantee, guaranty, insure, secure

¹as·sured \ə-'shu̇rd\ *adj* **1** ♦ : sure of oneself **2** ♦ : satisfied as to the certainty or truth of a matter

♦ [1] confident, secure, self-assured, self-confident ♦ [2] certain, clear, cocksure, confident, doubtless, positive, sanguine, sure

²assured *n, pl* **assured** *or* **assureds** : INSURED

as·ta·tine \'as-tə-ˌtēn\ *n* : an unstable radioactive chemical element

as·ter \'as-tər\ *n* : any of various mostly fall-blooming leafy-stemmed composite herbs with daisylike purple, white, pink, or yellow flower heads

as·ter·isk \'as-tə-ˌrisk\ *n* : a character * used as a reference mark or as an indication of the omission of letters or words

astern \ə-'stərn\ *adv or adj* **1** : in, at, or toward the stern **2** : BACKWARD

as·ter·oid \'as-tə-ˌrȯid\ *n* : any of the numerous small celestial bodies found esp. between Mars and Jupiter

asth·ma \'az-mə\ *n* : a chronic lung disorder marked by recurrent episodes of labored breathing, a feeling of tightness in the chest, and coughing — **asth·mat·ic** \az-'ma-tik\ *adj or n*

as though *conj* : as it would be or as one would do it : AS IF

astig·ma·tism \ə-'stig-mə-ˌti-zəm\ *n* : a defect in a lens or an eye causing improper focusing — **as·tig·mat·ic** \ˌas-tig-'ma-tik\ *adj*

astir \ə-'stər\ *adj* **1** ♦ : exhibiting activity **2** : being out of bed

♦ alive, animated, busy, lively, vibrant

as to *prep* **1** : ABOUT, CONCERNING ⟨uncertain *as to* what went on⟩ **2** : ACCORDING TO ⟨graded *as to* size⟩

as·ton·ish \ə-'stä-nish\ *vb* ♦ : to strike with sudden and usu. great wonder : AMAZE

♦ amaze, astound, bowl, dumbfound, flabbergast, floor, shock, startle, stun, stupefy, surprise

as·ton·ish·ing \-iŋ\ *adj* ♦ : causing astonishment : SURPRISING — **as·ton·ish·ing·ly** *adv*

♦ amazing, astounding, eye-opening, shocking, startling, stunning, surprising

as·ton·ish·ment \-mənt\ *n* ♦ : the state of being astonished

♦ amazement, awe, wonder, wonderment

as·tound \ə-'staund\ *vb* ♦ : to fill with bewilderment or wonder — **as·tound·ing·ly** *adv*

♦ amaze, astonish, bowl, dumbfound, flabbergast, floor, shock, startle, stun, stupefy, surprise

as·tound·ing \-iŋ\ *adj* ♦ : causing astonishment or amazement

♦ amazing, astonishing, awesome, fabulous, marvelous (*or* marvellous), prodigious, stunning, stupendous, surprising, wonderful

¹astrad·dle \ə-'strad-ᵊl\ *adv* : on or above and extending onto both sides

²astraddle *prep* : ASTRIDE

as·tra·khan \'as-trə-kən, -ˌkan\ *n, often cap* **1** : karakul of Russian origin **2** : a cloth with a usu. wool, curled, and looped pile resembling karakul

as·tral \'as-trəl\ *adj* ♦ : of, relating to, or coming from the stars

♦ star, starry, stellar

astray \ə-'strā\ *adv or adj* **1** ♦ : off the right path or route **2** : into error

♦ afield, amiss, awry, wrong

¹astride \ə-'strīd\ *adv* **1** : with one leg on each side **2** : with legs apart

²astride *prep* : with one leg on each side of

¹as·trin·gent \ə-'strin-jənt\ *adj* : able or tending to shrink body tissues — **as·trin·gen·cy** \-jən-sē\ *n*

²astringent *n* : an astringent agent or substance

astrol *abbr* astrologer; astrology

as·tro·labe \'as-trə-ˌlāb\ *n* : an instrument formerly used for observing the positions of celestial bodies

as·trol·o·gy \ə-'strä-lə-jē\ *n* : divination based on the supposed influence of the stars upon human events — **as·trol·o·ger** \-jər\ *n* — **as·tro·log·i·cal** \ˌas-trə-'lä-ji-kəl\ *adj*

astron *abbr* astronomer; astronomy

as·tro·naut \'as-trə-ˌnȯt\ *n* : a traveler in a spacecraft

as·tro·nau·tics \ˌas-trə-'nȯ-tiks\ *n* : the science of the construction and operation of spacecraft — **as·tro·nau·tic** \-tik\ *or* **as·tro·nau·ti·cal** \-ti-kəl\ *adj*

as·tro·nom·i·cal \ˌas-trə-'nä-mi-kəl\ *also* **as·tro·nom·ic** \-mik\ *adj* **1** : of or relating to astronomy **2** ♦ : extremely large ⟨an ∼ amount of money⟩

♦ colossal, enormous, giant, gigantic, ginormous, huge, prodigious, titanic, tremendous, whopping

astronomical unit *n* : a unit of length used in astronomy equal to the mean distance of the earth from the sun or about 93 million miles (150 million kilometers)

as·tron·o·my \ə-'strä-nə-mē\ *n, pl* **-mies** : the science of objects and matter beyond the earth's atmosphere — **as·tron·o·mer** \-mər\ *n*

as·tro·phys·ics \ˌas-trə-'fi-ziks\ *n* : astronomy dealing esp. with the physical properties and dynamic processes of celestial objects — **as·tro·phys·i·cal** \-zi-kəl\ *adj* — **as·tro·phys·i·cist** \-'fi-zə-sist\ *n*

as·tute \ə-'stüt, -'styüt, a-\ *adj* ♦ : shrewdly discerning; *also* : WILY — **as·tute·ly** *adv*

♦ canny, hardheaded, knowing, sharp, shrewd, smart, wily

as·tute·ness *n* ♦ : the quality or state of being astute

♦ acumen, caginess, canniness, hardheadedness, intelligence, keenness, sharpness, shrewdness, wit

asun·der \ə-'sən-dər\ *adv or adj* **1** : into separate pieces ⟨torn ∼⟩ **2** : separated in position from each other

ASV *abbr* American Standard Version

¹as well as *conj* : and in addition : and moreover ⟨brave *as well as* loyal⟩

²as well as *prep* : in addition to : BESIDES ⟨the coach, *as well as* the team, is ready⟩

asy·lum \ə-'sī-ləm\ *n*   **1** ♦ : a place of refuge   **2** : protection given to esp. political fugitives   **3** : an institution for the care of the needy or sick and esp. of the mentally ill

  ♦ haven, refuge, retreat, sanctuary, shelter

asym·met·ri·cal \ˌā-sə-'me-tri-kəl\ *or* **asym·met·ric** \-'trik\ *adj* : not symmetrical — **asym·me·try** \(ˌ)ā-'si-mə-trē\ *n*

as·ymp·tote \'a-səmp-ˌtōt\ *n* : a straight line that is associated with a curve and tends to approximate it along an infinite branch — **as·ymp·tot·ic** \ˌa-səmp-'tä-tik\ *adj* — **as·ymp·tot·i·cal·ly** \-ti-k(ə-)lē\ *adv*

at \ət, (')at\ *prep*   **1** — used to indicate a point in time or space ⟨be here ∼ 3 o'clock⟩   **2** — used to indicate a goal ⟨swung ∼ the ball⟩   **3** — used to indicate position or condition ⟨∼ rest⟩   **4** — used to indicate means, cause, or manner ⟨sold ∼ auction⟩

At *symbol* astatine

AT *abbr* automatic transmission

at all *adv* : in any way : in any circumstances ⟨not *at all* likely⟩

at·a·vism \'a-tə-ˌvi-zəm\ *n* : appearance in an individual of a character typical of an ancestral form; *also* : such an individual or character — **at·a·vis·tic** \ˌa-tə-'vis-tik\ *adj*

atax·ia \ə-'tak-sē-ə\ *n* : an inability to coordinate muscular movements

ate *past of* EAT

¹-ate *n suffix*   **1** : one acted upon (in a specified way) ⟨distill*ate*⟩   **2** : chemical compound or complex derived from a (specified) compound or element ⟨acet*ate*⟩

²-ate *n suffix*   **1** : office : function : rank : group of persons holding a (specified) office or rank ⟨episcop*ate*⟩   **2** : state : dominion : jurisdiction ⟨emir*ate*⟩

³-ate *adj suffix*   **1** : acted on (in a specified way) : being in a (specified) state ⟨temper*ate*⟩ ⟨degener*ate*⟩   **2** : marked by having ⟨vertebr*ate*⟩

⁴-ate *vb suffix*   **1** : cause to be modified or affected by ⟨pollin*ate*⟩ : cause to become ⟨activ*ate*⟩   **2** : furnish with ⟨aer*ate*⟩

ate·lier \ˌat-ᵊl-'yā\ *n*   **1** : an artist's or designer's studio   **2** : WORKSHOP

athe·ist \'ā-thē-ist\ *n* : one who denies the existence of God — **athe·ism** \-ˌi-zəm\ *n* — **athe·is·tic** \ˌā-thē-'is-tik\ *adj*

ath·e·nae·um *or* **ath·e·ne·um** \ˌa-thə-'nē-əm\ *n* : LIBRARY 1

ath·ero·scle·ro·sis \ˌa-thə-rō-sklə-'rō-səs\ *n* : arteriosclerosis characterized by the deposition of fatty substances in and the hardening of the inner layer of the arteries — **ath·ero·scle·rot·ic** \-'rä-tik\ *adj*

athirst \ə-'thərst\ *adj*   **1** *archaic* : THIRSTY   **2** ♦ : having a strong eager desire

  ♦ eager, enthusiastic, gung ho, keen, raring

ath·lete \'ath-ˌlēt\ *n* : a person who is trained to compete in athletics

athlete's foot *n* : ringworm of the feet

ath·let·ic \ath-'le-tik\ *adj*   **1** : of or relating to athletes or athletics   **2** : VIGOROUS, ACTIVE   **3** : STURDY, MUSCULAR

ath·let·ics \ath-'le-tiks\ *n sing or pl* : exercises and games requiring physical skill, strength, and endurance

athletic supporter *n* : an elastic pouch used to support the male genitals and worn esp. during athletic activity

¹athwart \ə-'thwȯrt\ *prep*   **1** ♦ : to or on the opposite side of : ACROSS   **2** : in opposition to

  ♦ across, over, through

²athwart *adv* ♦ : obliquely across

  ♦ crosswise, obliquely, transversely

atilt \ə-'tilt\ *adv or adj*   **1** : in a tilted position   **2** : with lance in hand

-ation *n suffix* : action or process ⟨flirt*ation*⟩ : something connected with an action or process ⟨discolor*ation*⟩

Atl *abbr* Atlantic

at·las \'at-ləs\ *n* : a book of maps

atm *abbr* atmosphere; atmospheric

ATM *n* : a computerized electronic machine that performs basic banking functions

at·mo·sphere \'at-mə-ˌsfir\ *n*   **1** : the gaseous envelope of a celestial body; *esp* : the mass of air surrounding the earth   **2** ♦ : a surrounding influence or environment   **3** : a unit of pressure equal to the pressure of air at sea level or about 14.7 pounds per square inch (10 newtons per square centimeter)   **4** : a dominant effect — **at·mo·spher·ic** \ˌat-mə-'sfir-ik, -'sfer-\ *adj* — **at·mo·spher·i·cal·ly** \-i-k(ə-)lē\ *adv*

  ♦ air, aura, climate, flavor (*or* flavour), mood, note, temper ♦ climate, environment, environs, medium, milieu, setting, surroundings

at·mo·sphe·rics \ˌat-mə-'sfir-iks, -'sfer-\ *n pl* : radio noise from atmospheric electrical phenomena

atoll \'a-ˌtȯl, -ˌtäl, 'ā-\ *n* : a coral island consisting of a reef surrounding a lagoon

at·om \'a-təm\ *n*   **1** ♦ : a tiny particle : BIT   **2** : the smallest particle of a chemical element that can exist alone or in combination

  ♦ bit, grain, granule, molecule, particle

atom·ic \ə-'tä-mik\ *adj*   **1** : of or relating to atoms; *also* : NUCLEAR 2 ⟨∼ energy⟩   **2** ♦ : extremely small

  ♦ infinitesimal, microscopic, miniature, minute, tiny

atomic bomb *n* : a very destructive bomb utilizing the energy released by splitting the atom

atomic clock *n* : a very precise clock regulated by the natural vibration of atoms or molecules (as of cesium)

atomic number *n* : the number of protons in the nucleus of an element

atomic weight *n* : the mass of one atom of an element

at·om·ise, at·om·is·er *Brit var of* ATOMIZE, ATOMIZER

at·om·ize \'a-tə-ˌmīz\ *vb* **-ized; -iz·ing** ♦ : to reduce to minute particles

  ♦ crush, grind, powder, pulverize

at·om·iz·er \'a-tə-ˌmī-zər\ *n* : a device for dispensing a liquid (as perfume) as a mist

atom smasher *n* : ACCELERATOR 3

aton·al \ā-'tōn-ᵊl\ *adj* : marked by avoidance of traditional musical tonality — **ato·nal·i·ty** \ˌā-tō-'na-lə-tē\ *n* — **aton·al·ly** \ā-'tōn-ᵊl-ē\ *adv*

atone \ə-'tōn\ *vb* **atoned; aton·ing**   **1** : to make amends   **2** : EXPIATE ⟨∼ for sins⟩

atone·ment \ə-'tōn-mənt\ *n*   **1** : the reconciliation of God and humankind through the death of Jesus Christ   **2** : reparation for an offense : SATISFACTION

¹atop \ə-'täp\ *prep* : on top of

²atop *adv or adj* : on, to, or at the top

ATP \ˌā-tē-'pē\ *n* : a compound that occurs widely in living tissue and supplies energy for many cellular processes by undergoing enzymatic hydrolysis

atri·um \'ā-trē-əm\ *n, pl* **atria** \-trē-ə\ *also* **atri·ums**   **1** : the central room of a Roman house; *also* : an open patio or court in the center of a building (as a hotel)   **2** : an anatomical cavity or passage; *esp* : one of the chambers of the heart that receives blood from the veins — **atri·al** \-əl\ *adj*

atro·cious \ə-'trō-shəs\ *adj*   **1** : savagely brutal, cruel, or wicked   **2** ♦ : inspiring horror, dismay, or disgust : APPALLING   **3** ♦ : utterly revolting   **4** ♦ : of very poor quality — **atro·cious·ly** *adv*

  ♦ [2, 3] appalling, awful, dreadful, frightful, ghastly, hideous, horrible, horrid, shocking, terrible ♦ [4] awful, execrable, lousy, punk, rotten, terrible, wretched

atro·cious·ness \-nəs\ *n* ♦ : the quality or state of being atrocious

  ♦ atrocity, frightfulness, hideousness, horror, monstrosity, repulsiveness

atroc·i·ty \ə-'trä-sə-tē\ *n, pl* **-ties**   **1** ♦ : the quality or state of being atrocious : ATROCIOUSNESS   **2** : an atrocious act or object ⟨the *atrocities* of war⟩

  ♦ atrociousness, depravity, enormity, heinousness, monstrosity, vileness, wickedness

at·ro·phy \'a-trə-fē\ *n, pl* **-phies** : decrease in size or wasting away of a bodily part or tissue — **atrophy** *vb*

at·ro·pine \'a-trə-ˌpēn\ *n* : a drug from belladonna and related plants used esp. to relieve spasms and to dilate the pupil of the eye

att *abbr* **1** attached   **2** attention   **3** attorney

at·tach \ə-'tach\ *vb*   **1** : to seize legally in order to force payment of a debt   **2** ♦ : to assign (an individual or unit in the military) temporarily   **3** : to bind by personal ties   **4** ♦ : to make fast (as by tying or gluing) : FASTEN   **5** : to be fastened or connected

  ♦ [2] appoint, assign, commission, constitute, designate, detail, name ♦ [4] affix, fasten, fix

at·ta·ché \ˌa-tə-'shā, ˌa-ˌta-, ə-ˌta-\ *n* : a technical expert on the diplomatic staff of an ambassador

at·ta·ché case \ə-'ta-shā-, ˌa-tə-'shā-\ *n* : a small thin suitcase used esp. for carrying business papers; *also* : BRIEFCASE

at·tach·ment \ə-'tach-mənt\ *n*   **1** : legal seizure of property   **2** ♦ : connection by ties of affection and regard   **3** : a device attached to a machine or implement   **4** : a connection by which one thing is attached to another   **5** : a document or file included with an electronic message

♦ affection, devotion, fondness, love, passion

¹**at·tack** \ə-'tak\ *vb* **1** ♦ : to set upon with force or words : AS-SAIL **2** : to set to work on

♦ assail, assault, beset, charge, descend, jump, pounce (on *or* upon), raid, rush, storm, strike ♦ abuse, assail, belabor, blast, castigate, excoriate, jump, lambaste, slam, vituperate

²**attack** *n* **1** ♦ : the act or action of attacking with physical force or unfriendly words **2** ♦ : a fit of sickness

♦ [1] aggression, assault, charge, descent, offense (*or* offence), offensive, onset, onslaught, raid, rush, strike ♦ [2] bout, case, fit, seizure, siege, spell

at·tain \ə-'tān\ *vb* **1** ♦ : to reach as an end : ACHIEVE ⟨∼ a goal⟩ **2** : to come to as the end of a progression or course of movement ⟨∼ the top of the hill⟩ ⟨∼ a ripe old age⟩ — **at·tain·abil·i·ty** \-'tā-nə-'bi-lə-tē\ *n*

♦ achieve, hit, make, score, win

at·tain·able \ə-'tā-nə-bəl\ *adj* ♦ : capable of being attained

♦ achievable, doable, feasible, possible, practicable, realizable, viable, workable ♦ accessible, acquirable, available, obtainable, procurable

at·tain·der \ə-'tān-dər\ *n* : extinction of the civil rights of a person upon sentence of death or outlawry

at·tain·ment \ə-'tān-mənt\ *n* **1** ♦ : the act of attaining : the condition of being attained **2** ♦ : something that has been accomplished : ACCOMPLISHMENT

♦ [1] accomplishment, actuality, consummation, fruition, fulfillment, realization ♦ [2] accomplishment, achievement, coup, success, triumph

at·tar \'a-tər\ *n* : a fragrant floral oil

¹**at·tempt** \ə-'tempt\ *vb* ♦ : to make an effort toward

♦ assay, endeavor (*or* endeavour), essay, seek, strive, try

²**attempt** *n* ♦ : the act or an instance of attempting

♦ bid, crack, endeavor (*or* endeavour), essay, fling, go, pass, shot, stab, trial, try, whack, whirl

at·tend \ə-'tend\ *vb* **1** ♦ : to look after : TEND **2** ♦ : to go or stay with as a companion, nurse, or servant **3** : to be present at **4** : to apply oneself **5** ♦ : to pay attention **6** : to direct one's attention

♦ [1] care, mind, oversee, superintend, supervise, tend ♦ [2] accompany, convoy, escort, squire ♦ [5] hark, hear, heed, listen, mind

at·ten·dance \ə-'ten-dəns\ *n* **1** : the act or fact of attending **2** : the number of persons present; *also* : the number of times a person attends

¹**at·ten·dant** \ə-'ten-dənt\ *n* ♦ : one that attends another to render a service

♦ companion, escort, guard, guide

²**attendant** *adj* ♦ : accompanying or following as a consequence or result ⟨∼ circumstances⟩

♦ consequent, consequential, due, resultant ♦ coincident, concomitant, concurrent

at·ten·tion \ə-'ten-chən\ *n* **1** ♦ : the act or state of attending esp. through applying the mind to an object of sense or thought **2** : CONSIDERATION **3** : an act of courtesy **4** : a position of readiness assumed on command by a soldier

♦ absorption, concentration *Ant* inattention ♦ awareness, cognizance, ear, eye, heed, notice, observance, observation

attention deficit disorder *n* : a behavioral syndrome esp. of children that is marked by hyperactivity, impulsive behavior, and inattention

attention–deficit/hyperactivity disorder *n* : ATTENTION DEFICIT DISORDER

at·ten·tive \ə-'ten-tiv\ *adj* **1** ♦ : regarding with care or attention : OBSERVANT **2** ♦ : heedful of the comfort of others — **at·ten·tive·ly** *adv*

♦ [1] absorbed, engrossed, intent, observant, rapt *Ant* distracted, inattentive, unfocused, unobservant ♦ [1] alert, awake, vigilant, watchful, wide-awake ♦ [2] considerate, kind, solicitous, thoughtful

at·ten·tive·ness \-nəs\ *n* ♦ : the quality or state of being attentive

♦ alertness, lookout, vigilance, watch

at·ten·u·ate \ə-'ten-yə-ˌwāt\ *vb* **-at·ed; -at·ing** **1** : to make or become thin **2** : WEAKEN — **attenuate** \-wət\ *adj* — **at·ten·u·a·tion** \-ˌten-yə-'wā-shən\ *n*

at·test \ə-'test\ *vb* **1** ♦ : to certify as genuine by signing as a witness **2** : MANIFEST **3** ♦ : to bear witness : TESTIFY

♦ [1] authenticate, avouch, certify, testify, vouch, witness ♦ [3] depose, swear, testify, witness

at·tes·ta·tion \ˌa-ˌtes-'tā-shən\ *n* **1** : the act of attesting **2** ♦ : the proof or evidence by which something is attested

♦ confirmation, corroboration, documentation, evidence, proof, substantiation, testament, testimony, validation, witness

at·tic \'a-tik\ *n* : the space or room in a building immediately below the roof

¹**at·tire** \ə-'tīr\ *vb* **at·tired; at·tir·ing** ♦ : to put garments on : DRESS, ARRAY

♦ apparel, array, clothe, deck, dress, garb, rig, suit

²**attire** *n* ♦ : garments in general : DRESS, CLOTHES

♦ apparel, clothing, dress, duds, raiment, wear

at·ti·tude \'a-tə-ˌtüd, -ˌtyüd\ *n* **1** : POSTURE **2** : a mental position or feeling with regard to a fact or state **3** : the position of something in relation to something else **4** : a cocky, arrogant, or hostile manner

at·ti·tu·di·nise *Brit var of* ATTITUDINIZE

at·ti·tu·di·nize \ˌa-tə-'tüd-ᵊn-ˌiz, -'tyüd-\ *vb* **-nized; -niz·ing** : to assume an affected mental attitude : POSE

attn *abbr* attention

at·tor·ney \ə-'tər-nē\ *n, pl* **-neys** ♦ : one who is legally appointed to transact business on another's behalf; *esp* : one whose profession is to conduct lawsuits for clients or to advise as to legal rights and obligations in other matters : LAWYER

♦ commissary, delegate, deputy, envoy, factor, proxy, representative ♦ advocate, counsel, lawyer

attorney general *n, pl* **attorneys general** *or* **attorney generals** : the chief legal representative and adviser of a nation or state

at·tract \ə-'trakt\ *vb* **1** : to draw to or toward oneself : cause to approach **2** : to draw by emotional or aesthetic appeal

at·trac·tant \ə-'trak-tənt\ *n* : a substance (as a pheromone) used to attract insects or other animals

at·trac·tion \ə-'trak-shən\ *n* **1** : the act or power of attracting; *esp* : personal charm **2** ♦ : an attractive quality, object, or feature **3** : a force tending to draw particles together

♦ draw, lodestone, magnet

at·trac·tive \ə-'trak-tiv\ *adj* **1** ♦ : having or relating to the power to attract **2** ♦ : arousing interest or pleasure — **at·trac·tive·ly** *adv*

♦ [1] alluring, captivating, charming, elfin, engaging, fascinating, fetching, glamorous, magnetic, seductive ♦ [2] beautiful, cute, handsome, lovely, pretty

at·trac·tive·ness \-nəs\ *n* ♦ : the state or quality of being attractive

♦ allure, appeal, captivation, charisma, charm, enchantment, fascination, glamour, magic, magnetism ♦ beauty, comeliness, handsomeness, looks, loveliness, prettiness

¹**at·tri·bute** \'a-trə-ˌbyüt\ *n* **1** ♦ : an inherent characteristic **2** : a word ascribing a quality; *esp* : ADJECTIVE

♦ character, characteristic, feature, mark, peculiarity, point, property, quality, trait

²**at·trib·ute** \ə-'tri-ˌbyüt, -byət\ *vb* **-ut·ed; -ut·ing** **1** ♦ : to explain as to cause or origin ⟨∼ the illness to fatigue⟩ **2** : to regard as a characteristic — **at·trib·ut·able** *adj* — **at·tri·bu·tion** \ˌa-trə-'byü-shən\ *n*

♦ accredit, ascribe, credit, impute

at·trib·u·tive \ə-'trib-yə-tiv\ *adj* : joined directly to a modified noun without a linking verb ⟨*red* in *red hair* is an ∼ adjective⟩ — **attributive** *n*

at·tri·tion \ə-'tri-shən\ *n* **1** : the act of wearing away by or as if by rubbing **2** : the act of weakening or exhausting by constant harassment, abuse, or attack **3** : a reduction in numbers as a result of resignation, retirement, or death

at·tune \ə-'tün, -'tyün\ *vb* : to bring into harmony : TUNE — **at·tune·ment** *n*

atty *abbr* attorney

ATV *abbr* all-terrain vehicle

atyp·i·cal \ā-'ti-pi-kəl\ *adj* ♦ : not typical — **atyp·i·cal·ly** \-k(ə-)lē\ *adv*

♦ aberrant, abnormal, exceptional, extraordinary, irregular, odd, peculiar, uncommon, uncustomary, unique, unusual, unwonted

Au *symbol* gold

au·burn \'ȯ-bərn\ *adj* : reddish brown — **auburn** *n*

au cou·rant \ō-kü-'räⁿ\ *adj* : UP-TO-DATE, STYLISH

¹**auc·tion** \'ȯk-shən\ *n* : public sale of property to the highest bidder

²**auction** *vb* **auc·tioned; auc·tion·ing** \-shə-niŋ\ : to sell at auction

auc·tion·eer \‚ȯk-shə-'nir\ *n* : an agent who conducts an auction

aud *abbr* audit; auditor

au·da·cious \ȯ-'dā-shəs\ *adj* **1** ♦ : intrepidly daring **2** : contemptuous of law, religion, or decorum : INSOLENT — **au·da·cious·ly** *adv* — **au·da·cious·ness** *n*

   ♦ adventurous, bold, daring, enterprising, gutsy, hardy, nervy, venturesome

au·dac·i·ty \ȯ-'da-sə-tē\ *n* ♦ : the quality or state of being audacious; *also* : the quality of being bold to the point of rudeness

   ♦ brass, brazenness, cheek, chutzpah, effrontery, gall, nerve, presumption, sauce, sauciness, temerity

¹**au·di·ble** \'ȯ-də-bəl\ *adj* : capable of being heard — **au·di·bil·i·ty** \‚ȯ-də-'bi-lə-tē\ *n* — **au·di·bly** \'ȯ-də-blē\ *adv*

²**audible** *n* : a play called at the line of scrimmage

au·di·ence \'ȯ-dē-əns\ *n* **1** : a formal interview **2** : an opportunity of being heard **3** : an assembly of listeners or spectators

¹**au·dio** \'ȯ-dē-‚ō\ *adj* **1** : of or relating to frequencies (as of radio waves) corresponding to those of audible sound waves **2** : of or relating to sound or its reproduction and esp. high-fidelity reproduction **3** : relating to or used in the transmission or reception of sound

²**audio** *n* **1** : the transmission, reception, or reproduction of sound **2** : the section of television or motion-picture equipment that deals with sound

au·dio·book \'ȯ-dē-ō-‚bůk\ *n* : a recording of a book or magazine being read aloud

au·di·ol·o·gy \‚ȯ-dē-'ä-lə-jē\ *n* : a branch of science dealing with hearing and esp. with the treatment of individuals having trouble with hearing — **au·di·o·log·i·cal** \-ə-'lä-ji-kəl\ *adj* — **au·di·ol·o·gist** \-'ä-lə-jist\ *n*

au·dio·phile \'ȯ-dē-ō-‚fīl\ *n* : one who is enthusiastic about high-fidelity sound reproduction

au·dio·tape \'ȯ-dē-ō-‚tāp\ *n* : a tape recording of sound

au·dio·vi·su·al \‚ȯ-dē-ō-'vi-zhə-wəl\ *adj* : of, relating to, or making use of both hearing and sight

au·dio·vi·su·als \-wəlz\ *n pl* : audiovisual teaching materials (as videotapes)

¹**au·dit** \'ȯ-dət\ *n* **1** : a formal examination and verification of financial accounts **2** ♦ : a methodical examination and review

   ♦ check, checkup, examination, inspection, review, scan, scrutiny, survey

²**audit** *vb* **1** ♦ : to perform an audit on or for **2** : to attend (a course) without expecting formal credit

   ♦ check, examine, inspect, review, scan, scrutinize, survey

¹**au·di·tion** \ȯ-'di-shən\ *n* : HEARING; *esp* : a trial performance to appraise an entertainer's merits

²**audition** *vb* **-tioned; -tion·ing** \-'di-shə-niŋ\ : to give an audition to; *also* : to give a trial performance

au·di·tor \'ȯ-də-tər\ *n* **1** : LISTENER **2** : a person who audits

au·di·to·ri·um \‚ȯ-də-'tōr-ē-əm\ *n, pl* **-riums** *or* **-ria** \-rē-ə\ **1** : the part of a public building where an audience sits **2** : a hall or building used for public gatherings

au·di·to·ry \'ȯ-də-‚tōr-ē\ *adj* ♦ : of or relating to hearing or to the sense or organs of hearing

   ♦ acoustic, aural, auricular

auditory tube *n* : EUSTACHIAN TUBE

auf Wie·der·seh·en \auf-'vē-dər-‚zān\ *interj* — used to express farewell

Aug *abbr* August

au·ger \'ȯ-gər\ *n* : a tool for boring

aught \'ȯt, 'ät\ *n* **1** : the arithmetical symbol 0 denoting the absence of all magnitude or quantity : ZERO, CIPHER

   ♦ cipher, naught, nil, nothing, zero, zip

aug·ment \ȯg-'ment\ *vb* ♦ : to make greater, more numerous, larger, or more intense : ENLARGE, INCREASE

   ♦ add, aggrandize, amplify, boost, compound, enlarge, escalate, expand, extend, increase, multiply, raise, swell, up

aug·men·ta·tion \‚ȯg-mən-'tā-shən\ *n* **1 a** : the act or process of augmenting **b** : the state of being augmented **2** ♦ : something that augments : ADDITION

   ♦ accretion, addition, boost, expansion, gain, increase, increment, plus, proliferation, raise, rise, supplement

au gra·tin \ō-'grat-ᵊn, ȯ-, -'grät-\ *adj* : covered with bread crumbs or grated cheese and browned

¹**au·gur** \'ȯ-gər\ *n* ♦ : one held to foretell events by omens : DIVINER, SOOTHSAYER

   ♦ diviner, forecaster, fortune-teller, futurist, prognosticator, prophet, seer, soothsayer

²**augur** *vb* **1** ♦ : to foretell esp. from omens **2** ♦ : to give promise of : show potential for a good outcome

   ♦ [1] forecast, foretell, predict, presage, prognosticate, prophesy ♦ [2] bode, promise

au·gu·ry \'ȯ-gyə-rē, -gə-\ *n, pl* **-ries** **1** : divination from omens **2** ♦ : an occurrence or phenomenon believed to portend a future event : OMEN, PORTENT

   ♦ auspice, foreboding, omen, portent, presage

au·gust \ȯ-'gəst\ *adj* ♦ : marked by majestic dignity or grandeur — **au·gust·ly** *adv*

   ♦ dignified, grand, imposing, magnificent, majestic, regal, royal, splendid, stately

Au·gust \'ȯ-gəst\ *n* : the 8th month of the year

au·gust·ness \-nəs\ *n* ♦ : the quality or state of being august

   ♦ grandeur, grandness, magnificence, majesty, nobility, nobleness, stateliness

au jus \ō-'zhü, -'zhüs, -'jüs; ō-zhū̄ē\ *adj* : served in the juice obtained from roasting

auk \'ȯk\ *n* : any of several stocky black-and-white diving seabirds that breed in colder parts of the northern hemisphere

auld \'ȯl, 'ȯld, 'äl, 'äld\ *adj, chiefly Scot* : OLD

aunt \'ant, 'änt\ *n* **1** : the sister of one's father or mother **2** : the wife of one's uncle or aunt

au pair \ō-'par\ *n* : a usu. young foreign person who does domestic work for a family in return for room and board and to learn the family's language

au·ra \'ȯr-ə\ *n* **1** ♦ : a distinctive atmosphere surrounding a given source **2** : a luminous radiation

   ♦ air, atmosphere, climate, flavor (*or* flavour), mood, note, temper

au·ral \'ȯr-əl\ *adj* ♦ : of or relating to the ear or to the sense of hearing

   ♦ acoustic, auditory, auricular

au·re·ole \'ȯr-ē-‚ōl\ *or* **au·re·o·la** \ȯ-'rē-ə-lə\ *n* : HALO, NIMBUS

au re·voir \‚ō-rə-'vwär\ *n* ♦ : a concluding remark or gesture at parting : GOOD-BYE

   ♦ adieu, bon voyage, farewell, good-bye

au·ri·cle \'ȯr-i-kəl\ *n* : an atrium of the heart

au·ric·u·lar \ȯ-'ri-kyə-lər\ *adj* **1** : told privately ⟨~ confession⟩ **2** ♦ : known or recognized by the sense of hearing

   ♦ acoustic, auditory, aural

au·ro·ra \ə-'rōr-ə\ *n, pl* **auroras** *or* **au·ro·rae** \-(‚)ē\ **1** ♦ : the first appearance of light in the morning followed by sunrise **2** : a luminous phenomenon of streamers or arches of light appearing in the upper atmosphere esp. of a planet's polar regions — **au·ro·ral** \-əl\ *adj*

   ♦ cockcrow, dawn, morning, sunrise

aurora aus·tra·lis \-ȯ-'strā-ləs\ *n* : an aurora that occurs in earth's southern hemisphere

aurora bo·re·al·is \-‚bōr-ē-'a-ləs\ *n* : an aurora that occurs in earth's northern hemisphere

AUS *abbr* Army of the United States

aus·pice \'ȯ-spəs\ *n, pl* **aus·pic·es** \-spə-səz, -‚sēz\ **1** : observation of birds by an augur **2** *pl* : kindly patronage and protection **3** ♦ : a prophetic sign or omen

   ♦ augury, foreboding, omen, portent, presage

aus·pi·cious \ȯ-'spi-shəs\ *adj* **1** ♦ : promising success : PROPITIOUS **2** : FORTUNATE, PROSPEROUS — **aus·pi·cious·ly** *adv* — **aus·pi·cious·ness** *n*

   ♦ bright, encouraging, heartening, hopeful, likely, promising, propitious, rosy, upbeat

aus·tere \ȯ-'stir\ *adj* **1** ♦ : stern and cold in appearance or manner : STERN, SEVERE **2** : ABSTEMIOUS **3** : UNADORNED ⟨~ style⟩ — **aus·tere·ly** *adv* — **aus·ter·i·ty** \-'ster-ə-tē\ *n*

   ♦ authoritarian, flinty, hard, harsh, heavy-handed, ramrod, rigid, rigorous, severe, stern, strict

aus·tral \'ȯs-trəl\ *adj* : SOUTHERN

Aus·tra·lian \ȯ-'strāl-yən\ *n* : a native or inhabitant of Australia — **Australian** *adj*

Aus·tri·an \'ȯ-strē-ən\ *n* : a native or inhabitant of Austria — **Austrian** *adj*

Aus·tro·ne·sian \ˌȯs-trə-'nē-zhən\ *adj* : of, relating to, or constituting a family of languages spoken in the area extending from Madagascar eastward through the Malay Peninsula to Hawaii and Easter Island

auth *abbr* **1** authentic **2** author **3** authorized

au·then·tic \ə-'then-tik, ȯ-\ *adj* ♦ : not false or imitation — **au·then·tic·i·ty** \ˌȯ-ˌthen-'ti-sə-tē\ *n*

♦ bona fide, genuine, real, right, true *Ant* bogus, counterfeit, fake, false, mock, phony, pseudo, sham, spurious, unauthentic, unreal ♦ accurate, exact, faithful, precise, right, strict, true, veracious

au·then·ti·cal·ly \-ti-k(ə-)lē\ *adv* ♦ : in actual fact

♦ actually, genuinely, really, veritably, very

au·then·ti·cate \ə-'then-ti-ˌkāt, ȯ-\ *vb* **-cat·ed; -cat·ing** ♦ : to prove genuine — **au·then·ti·ca·tion** \-ˌthen-ti-'kā-shən\ *n*

♦ attest, avouch, certify, testify, vouch, witness

au·thor \'ȯ-thər\ *n* **1** ♦ : one that originates or creates **2** : one that writes or composes a literary work

♦ creator, father, founder, originator

au·thor·ess \'ȯ-thə-rəs\ *n* : a woman or girl who is an author

au·tho·ri·sa·tion, au·tho·rise *Brit var of* AUTHORIZATION, AUTHORIZE

au·thor·i·tar·i·an \ȯ-ˌthär-ə-'ter-ē-ən, ə-, -ˌthȯr-\ *adj* **1** ♦ : characterized by or favoring the principle of blind obedience to authority **2** : characterized by or favoring concentration of political power in an authority not responsible to the people — **authoritarian** *n*

♦ autocratic, bossy, despotic, dictatorial, domineering, imperious, overbearing, peremptory, tyrannical, tyrannous ♦ austere, flinty, hard, harsh, heavy-handed, ramrod, rigid, rigorous, severe, stern, strict

au·thor·i·ta·tive \ə-'thär-ə-ˌtā-tiv, ȯ-, -'thȯr-\ *adj* ♦ : supported by, proceeding from, or being an authority — **au·thor·i·ta·tive·ly** *adv* — **au·thor·i·ta·tive·ness** *n*

♦ forceful, influential, weighty

au·thor·i·ty \ə-'thär-ə-tē, ȯ-, -'thȯr-\ *n, pl* **-ties** **1** : a citation used in support of a statement or in defense of an action; *also* : the source of such a citation **2** ♦ : one appealed to as an expert **3** ♦ : power to influence thought or behavior **4** : freedom granted : RIGHT **5 a** : persons in command **b** ♦ : the office, authority, or function of governing : GOVERNMENT **6** ♦ : convincing force

♦ [2] ace, adept, expert, master, scholar, virtuoso, whiz, wizard ♦ [3] clout, influence, pull, sway, weight ♦ [5b] administration, government, jurisdiction, regime, rule ♦ [6] arm, clutch, command, control, dominion, grip, hold, power, sway

au·tho·ri·za·tion \ˌȯ-thə-rə-'zā-shən\ *n* ♦ : the act of authorizing

♦ allowance, clearance, concurrence, consent, leave, license (*or* licence), permission, sanction, sufferance ♦ commission, delegation, license (*or* licence), mandate

au·tho·rize \'ȯ-thə-ˌrīz\ *vb* **-rized; -riz·ing** **1** ♦ : to establish by or as if by authority : SANCTION **2** ♦ : to invest esp. with legal authority

♦ [1] approve, clear, OK, ratify, sanction, warrant ♦ [2] accredit, certify, commission, empower, enable, invest, license, qualify

au·tho·rized \'ȯ-thə-ˌrīzd\ *adj* : sanctioned by authority

au·thor·ship \'ȯ-thər-ˌship\ *n* **1** : the state of being an author **2** : the source of a piece of writing, music, or art

au·tism \'ȯ-ˌti-zəm\ *n* : a disorder that appears by age three and is characterized esp. by impaired ability to communicate with others and form normal social relationships and by repetitive patterns of behavior — **au·tis·tic** \ȯ-'tis-tik\ *adj or n*

¹**au·to** \'ȯ-tō\ *n, pl* **autos** : a usu. 4-wheeled automotive vehicle designed for passenger transportation : AUTOMOBILE

²**auto** *abbr* automatic

au·to·bahn \'ȯ-tō-ˌbän, 'au̇-\ *n* : a German, Swiss, or Austrian expressway

au·to·bi·og·ra·phy \ˌȯ-tə-bī-'ä-grə-fē\ *n* : the biography of a person narrated by that person — **au·to·bi·og·ra·pher** \-fər\ *n* — **au·to·bi·o·graph·i·cal** \-ˌbī-ə-'gra-fi-kəl\ *adj* — **au·to·bio·graph·i·cal·ly** \-k(ə-)lē\ *adv*

au·toch·tho·nous \ȯ-'täk-thə-nəs\ *adj* : INDIGENOUS, NATIVE

au·to·clave \'ȯ-tō-ˌklāv\ *n* : an apparatus (as for sterilizing) using superheated high-pressure steam

au·to·cor·rect \'ȯ-tō-kə-'rekt\ *n* : a computer feature that attempts to correct the spelling of a word as the user types — **autocorrect** *vb*

au·toc·ra·cy \ȯ-'tä-krə-sē\ *n, pl* **-cies** ♦ : government by one person having unlimited power

♦ despotism, dictatorship, totalitarianism, tyranny

au·to·crat \'ȯ-tə-ˌkrat\ *n* **1** ♦ : a person (as a monarch) ruling with unlimited authority **2** ♦ : one who has undisputed influence or power

♦ [1] monarch, ruler, sovereign ♦ [2] despot, dictator, oppressor, tyrant

au·to·crat·ic \ˌȯ-tə-'kra-tik\ *adj* **1** : of, relating to, or being an autocracy **2** ♦ : characteristic of or resembling an autocrat : DESPOTIC — **au·to·crat·i·cal·ly** \-ti-k(ə-)lē\ *adv*

♦ absolute, despotic, dictatorial, tyrannical, tyrannous ♦ authoritarian, bossy, domineering, imperious, overbearing, peremptory

¹**au·to·graph** \'ȯ-tə-ˌgraf\ *n* **1** : an original manuscript **2** : a person's signature written by hand

²**autograph** *vb* : to write one's signature on

au·to·im·mune \ˌȯ-tō-i-'myün\ *adj* : of, relating to, or caused by antibodies or lymphocytes that attack molecules, cells, or tissues of the organism producing them ⟨~ diseases⟩ — **au·to·im·mu·ni·ty** \-i-'myü-nə-tē\ *n*

au·to·mate \'ȯ-tə-ˌmāt\ *vb* **-mat·ed; -mat·ing** **1** : to operate automatically using mechanical or electronic devices **2** : to convert to automatic operation — **au·to·ma·tion** \ˌȯ-tə-'mā-shən\ *n*

automated teller machine *n* : a computer terminal allowing access to one's own bank accounts

¹**au·to·mat·ic** \ˌȯ-tə-'ma-tik\ *adj* **1** ♦ : largely or wholly involuntary **2** ♦ : made so that certain parts act in a desired manner at the proper time : SELF-ACTING — **au·to·mat·i·cal·ly** \-ti-k(ə-)lē\ *adv*

♦ [1] involuntary, mechanical, spontaneous ♦ [2] laborsaving (*or* laboursaving), robotic, self-acting

²**automatic** *n* **1** : an automatic device; *esp* : an automatic firearm **2** : an automobile with an automatic transmission

au·tom·a·ton \ȯ-'tä-mə-tən, -ˌtän\ *n, pl* **-atons** *or* **-a·ta** \-ə-tə, -ˌtä\ **1** : an automatic machine; *esp* : ROBOT **2** : an individual who acts mechanically

au·to·mo·bile \ˌȯ-tə-mō-ˌbēl, ˌȯ-tə-mə-'bēl\ *n* ♦ : a usu. 4-wheeled automotive vehicle for conveying passengers

♦ car, machine, motor vehicle

au·to·mo·tive \ˌȯ-tə-'mō-tiv\ *adj* **1** : of or relating to automobiles, trucks, or buses **2** : SELF-PROPELLED

au·to·nom·ic nervous system \ˌȯ-tə-'nä-mik-\ *n* : a part of the vertebrate nervous system that governs involuntary actions and that consists of the sympathetic nervous system and the parasympathetic nervous system

au·ton·o·mous \ȯ-'tä-nə-məs\ *adj* ♦ : having the right or power of self-government — **au·ton·o·mous·ly** *adv*

♦ free, independent, self-governing, separate, sovereign

au·ton·o·my \-mē\ *n* ♦ : the quality or state of being independent, free, and self-directing

♦ freedom, independence, liberty, self-government, sovereignty

au·top·sy \'ȯ-ˌtäp-sē, 'ȯ-təp-\ *n, pl* **-sies** : examination of a dead body usu. with dissection sufficient to determine the cause of death or extent of change produced by disease — **autopsy** *vb*

au·tumn \'ȯ-təm\ *n* : the season between summer and winter — **au·tum·nal** \ȯ-'təm-nəl\ *adj*

aux *abbr* auxiliary

¹**aux·il·ia·ry** \ȯg-'zil-yə-rē, -'zi-lə-rē\ *adj* **1** ♦ : providing help **2** : functioning in a subsidiary capacity **3** : accompanying a verb form to express person, number, mood, or tense ⟨~ verbs⟩

♦ accessory, peripheral, supplementary *Ant* chief, main, principal

²**auxiliary** *n, pl* **-ries** **1** : an auxiliary person, group, or device **2** : an auxiliary verb

aux·in \'ȯk-sən\ *n* : a plant hormone that stimulates growth in length

av *abbr* **1** avenue **2** average **3** avoirdupois

AV *abbr* **1** ad valorem **2** audiovisual **3** Authorized Version

¹**avail** \ə-'vāl\ *vb* ♦ : to produce or result in as a benefit or advantage

♦ benefit, profit, serve

²avail *n* ♦ : advantage toward attainment of a goal or purpose : USE ⟨effort was of no ∼⟩

♦ account, service, use, utility

avail•able \ə-'vā-lə-bəl\ *adj* **1** ♦ : present or ready for immediate use : USABLE **2** ♦ : capable of being reached : ACCESSIBLE **3** : free and able to do something ⟨∼ to meet⟩ **4** : qualified or willing to do something ⟨∼ workers⟩ — **avail•abil•i•ty** \-ˌvā-lə-'bi-lə-tē\ *n*

♦ [1] fit, functional, operable, practicable, serviceable, usable, useful ♦ [2] accessible, acquirable, attainable, obtainable, procurable *Ant* inaccessible, unattainable, unavailable, unobtainable

av•a•lanche \'a-və-ˌlanch\ *n* : a mass of snow, ice, earth, or rock sliding down a mountainside

avant–garde \ä-ˌvän-'gärd, -ˌvänt-\ *n* : those esp. in the arts who create or apply new or experimental ideas and techniques — **avant–garde** *adj*

av•a•rice \'a-və-rəs\ *n* ♦ : excessive desire for wealth : GREED

♦ acquisitiveness, avidity, covetousness, cupidity, greed, rapaciousness

av•a•ri•cious \ˌa-və-'ri-shəs\ *adj* ♦ : excessively acquisitive

♦ acquisitive, avid, covetous, grasping, greedy, mercenary, rapacious

avast \ə-'vast\ *vb imper* — a nautical command to stop or cease

av•a•tar \'a-və-ˌtär\ *n* **1** : INCARNATION **2** : an electronic image that represents and may be manipulated by a computer user (as in a game)

avaunt \ə-'vȯnt\ *adv* : AWAY, HENCE

avdp *abbr* avoirdupois

ave *abbr* avenue

Ave Ma•ria \ˌä-ˌvā-mə-'rē-ə\ *n* : HAIL MARY 1

avenge \ə-'venj\ *vb* **avenged; aveng•ing** ♦ : to take vengeance for

♦ requite, retaliate, revenge

aveng•er *n* ♦ : one that avenges

♦ castigator, nemesis, scourge

av•e•nue \'a-və-ˌnü, -ˌnyü\ *n* **1** ♦ : a way or route to a place or goal : PATH **2** ♦ : a broad street

♦ [1, 2] approach, passage, path, route, way ♦ [2] artery, road, route, street, way

aver \ə-'vər\ *vb* **averred; aver•ring 1 a** : to verify or prove to be true in pleading a cause **b** ♦ : to allege or assert in pleading **2** ♦ : to declare positively

♦ [1b, 2] affirm, allege, assert, avouch, avow, claim, contend, declare, insist, maintain, profess, protest, warrant

¹av•er•age \'a-və-rij, 'a-vrij\ *n* **1** : ARITHMETIC MEAN **2 a** : an estimation of or approximation to an arithmetic mean **b** : a level (as of intelligence) typical of a group, class, or series **3** : a ratio of successful tries to total tries esp. in athletics ⟨batting ∼ of .303⟩

♦ norm, normal, par, standard

²average *adj* **1** : equaling or approximating an arithmetic mean **2** ♦ : being about midway between extremes **3** ♦ : not out of the ordinary

♦ [2] intermediate, median, medium, middle, moderate, modest ♦ [3] common, commonplace, everyday, normal, ordinary, routine, run-of-the-mill, standard, typical, usual

³average *vb* **av•er•aged; av•er•ag•ing 1** : to be at or come to an average **2** : to be, do, or get usually **3** : to find the average of

averse \ə-'vərs\ *adj* : having an active feeling of dislike or reluctance ⟨∼ to exercise⟩

aver•sion \ə-'vər-zhən\ *n* **1** ♦ : a feeling of repugnance for something with a desire to avoid it **2** : something decidedly disliked

♦ disgust, distaste, loathing, nausea, repugnance, repulsion, revulsion ♦ allergy, disfavor (*or* disfavour), disinclination, dislike

avert \ə-'vərt\ *vb* **1** : to turn aside or away ⟨∼ the eyes⟩ **2** ♦ : to ward off

♦ forestall, help, obviate, preclude, prevent

avg *abbr* average

avi•an \'ā-vē-ən\ *adj* : of, relating to, or derived from birds

avi•ary \'ā-vē-ˌer-ē\ *n, pl* **-ar•ies** : a place for keeping birds confined

avi•a•tion \ˌā-vē-'ā-shən, ˌa-\ *n* **1** : the operation of heavier-

than-air aircraft **2** : aircraft manufacture, development, and design

avi•a•tor \'ā-vē-ˌā-tər, 'a-\ *n* ♦ : an airplane pilot

♦ airman, flier, pilot

avi•a•trix \ˌā-vē-'ā-triks, ˌa-\ *n, pl* **-trix•es** \-trik-səz\ *or* **-tri•ces** \-trə-ˌsēz\ : a woman who is an aviator

av•id \'a-vəd\ *adj* **1** ♦ : desirous to the point of greed : GREEDY **2** ♦ : enthusiastic in pursuit of an interest — **av•id•ly** *adv* — **av•id•ness** *n*

♦ [1] acquisitive, avaricious, covetous, grasping, greedy, mercenary, rapacious ♦ [2] ardent, eager, enthusiastic, keen, nuts, raring

avid•i•ty \ə-'vi-də-tē, a-\ *n* ♦ : the quality or state of being avid

♦ acquisitiveness, avarice, covetousness, cupidity, greed, rapaciousness ♦ eagerness, enthusiasm, excitement, keenness, thirst

avi•on•ics \ˌā-vē-'ä-niks, ˌa-\ *n pl* : electronics designed for use in aerospace vehicles — **avi•on•ic** \-nik\ *adj*

av•o•ca•do \ˌa-və-'kä-dō, ˌä-\ *n, pl* **-dos** *also* **-does** : a pulpy green to purple nutty-flavored edible fruit of a tropical American tree; *also* : this tree

av•o•ca•tion \ˌa-və-'kā-shən\ *n* : HOBBY

av•o•cet \'a-və-ˌset\ *n* : any of several long-legged shorebirds with webbed feet and slender upward-curving bills

avoid \ə-'vȯid\ *vb* **1** ♦ : to keep away from : SHUN **2** : to prevent the occurrence of **3** : to refrain from — **avoid•able** *adj* — **avoid•ably** *adv*

♦ dodge, duck, elude, escape, eschew, evade, shake, shirk, shun

avoid•ance \-ᵊns\ *n* ♦ : an act or practice of avoiding or withdrawing from something

♦ cop-out, escape, evasion, out

av•oir•du•pois \ˌa-vər-də-'pȯiz\ *n* **1** : AVOIRDUPOIS WEIGHT **2** : WEIGHT, HEAVINESS; *esp* : personal weight

avoirdupois weight *n* : a system of weights based on a pound of 16 ounces and an ounce of 16 drams (28 grams)

avouch \ə-'vau̇ch\ *vb* **1** ♦ : to declare positively : AVER **2** ♦ : to maintain as just or true : vouch for

♦ [1] affirm, allege, assert, aver, avow, claim, contend, declare, insist, maintain, profess, protest, warrant ♦ [2] attest, authenticate, certify, testify, vouch, witness

avow \ə-'vau̇\ *vb* ♦ : to declare openly

♦ affirm, allege, assert, aver, avouch, claim, contend, declare, insist, maintain, profess, protest, warrant

avow•al \-'vau̇(-ə)l\ *n* ♦ : an open declaration or acknowledgment

♦ acknowledgment, admission, concession, confession ♦ affirmation, assertion, claim, declaration, profession, protestation

avun•cu•lar \ə-'vəŋ-kyə-lər\ *adj* : of, relating to, or resembling an uncle

await \ə-'wāt\ *vb* ♦ : to wait for : EXPECT

♦ anticipate, expect, hope, watch ♦ bide, hold on, stay, wait

¹awake \ə-'wāk\ *vb* **awoke** \-'wōk\ *also* **awaked** \-'wākt\; **awo•ken** \-'wō-kən\ *or* **awaked** *also* **awoke; awak•ing** ♦ : to bring back to consciousness : wake up

♦ arouse, rouse, wake

²awake *adj* ♦ : fully conscious, alert, and aware

♦ sleepless, wakeful, wide-awake ♦ alert, attentive, vigilant, watchful, wide-awake

awak•en \ə-'wā-kən\ *vb* **awak•ened; awak•en•ing** \-'wā-kə-niŋ\ : to bring back to consciousness : wake up

¹award \ə-'wȯrd\ *vb* **1** : to give by judicial decision ⟨∼ damages⟩ **2** ♦ : to confer or bestow as being deserved, earned, or needed

♦ accord, confer, grant

²award *n* **1** : a final decision : JUDGMENT **2** ♦ : something awarded : PRIZE

♦ decoration, distinction, honor (*or* honour), plume, prize

aware \ə-'war\ *adj* ♦ : having perception or knowledge : CONSCIOUS

♦ alive, cognizant, conscious, mindful, sensible, sentient, witting

aware•ness \-nəs\ *n* ♦ : the quality or state of being aware

♦ attention, cognizance, ear, eye, heed, notice, observance, observation

awash \ə-'wȯsh, -'wäsh\ *adj* **1** : washed by waves or tide **2** : AFLOAT **3** : covered with water : FLOODED

¹away \ə-'wā\ *adv* **1** : from this or that place ⟨go ∼⟩ **2** : out of the way **3** : in another direction ⟨turn ∼⟩ **4** : out of existence ⟨fade ∼⟩ **5** : from one's possession ⟨give ∼⟩ **6** : without interruption ⟨chatter ∼⟩ **7** : at a distance in space or time ⟨far ∼⟩ ⟨∼ back in 1910⟩

²away *adj* **1** ♦ : absent from a place : ABSENT **2** ♦ : distant in space or time ⟨a lake 10 miles ∼⟩

   ♦ [1] absent, missing, out ♦ [2] distant, far, far-off, remote

¹awe \'ȯ\ *n* **1** ♦ : an emotion variously combining dread, veneration, and wonder that is inspired by authority or by the sacred or sublime **2** : respectful fear inspired by authority

   ♦ admiration, amazement, astonishment, wonder, wonderment

²awe *vb* **awed; aw•ing** : to inspire with awe

aweigh \ə-'wā\ *adj* : just clear of the bottom ⟨anchors ∼⟩

awe•some \'ȯ-səm\ *adj* **1** : expressive of awe **2** ♦ : inspiring awe

   ♦ amazing, astonishing, astounding, marvelous (*or* marvellous), stunning, surprising, wonderful

awe•struck \-,strək\ *also* **awe•strick•en** \-,stri-kən\ *adj* ♦ : filled with awe

   ♦ amazed, stunned, thunderstruck

aw•ful \'ȯ-fəl\ *adj* **1** : inspiring awe **2** ♦ : extremely disagreeable, unpleasant, or shoddy **3** : very great ⟨an ∼ lot of money⟩

   ♦ appalling, dreadful, frightful, ghastly, grisly, gruesome, hideous, horrible, horrid, repellent, repugnant, repulsive, revolting, shocking, terrible ♦ atrocious, execrable, lousy, punk, rotten, wretched

aw•ful•ly \'ȯ-fə-lē\ *adv* : to a great degree : VERY

awhile \ə-'hwīl\ *adv* : for a while

awhirl \ə-'hwərl\ *adj* : being in a whirl

awk•ward \'ȯ-kwərd\ *adj* **1** ♦ : lacking dexterity or skill (as in the use of hands) **2** ♦ : lacking ease or grace (as of movement or expression) **3** ♦ : difficult to explain : EMBARRASSING **4** ♦ : difficult to deal with — **awk•ward•ly** *adv* — **awk•ward•ness** *n*

   ♦ [1, 2] clumsy, gauche, gawky, graceless, inelegant, stiff, stilted, uncomfortable, uneasy, ungainly, ungraceful, wooden *Ant* graceful, suave, urbane ♦ [3] disconcerting, embarrassing, uncomfortable ♦ [4] clumsy, cranky, cumbersome, ungainly, unhandy, unwieldy

awl \'ȯl\ *n* : a pointed instrument for making small holes

aw•ning \'ȯ-niŋ\ *n* : a rooflike cover (as of canvas) extended over or in front of a place as a shelter

AWOL \'ā-,wȯl, ,ā-,də-bəl-yü-,ō-'el\ *n* : a person who is absent without leave — **AWOL** *adj or adv*

awry \ə-'rī\ *adv or adj* **1** ♦ : in a turned or twisted position or direction : ASKEW **2** ♦ : off the correct or expected course : AMISS ⟨the plans went ∼⟩

   ♦ [1] askew, cockeyed, crooked, listing, lopsided, slantwise, uneven *Ant* even, level, straight ♦ [2] afield, amiss, astray, wrong

ax *or* **axe** \'aks\ *n* : a chopping or cutting tool with an edged head fitted parallel to a handle

ax•i•al \'ak-sē-əl\ *adj* **1** : of, relating to, or functioning as an axis **2** : situated around, in the direction of, on, or along an axis — **ax•i•al•ly** *adv*

ax•i•om \'ak-sē-əm\ *n* **1** : a statement generally accepted as true : MAXIM **2** : a proposition regarded as a self-evident truth — **ax•i•om•at•ic** \,ak-sē-ə-'ma-tik\ *adj* — **ax•i•om•at•i•cal•ly** \-ti-k(ə-)lē\ *adv*

ax•is \'ak-səs\ *n, pl* **ax•es** \-,sēz\ **1** : a straight line around which a body rotates **2** : a straight line or structure with respect to which a body or figure is symmetrical **3** : one of the reference lines of a system of coordinates **4** : an alliance between major powers

ax•le \'ak-səl\ *n* : a shaft on which a wheel revolves

ayah \'ī-ə\ *n* : a nurse or maid native to India

aya•tol•lah \,ī-ə-'tō-lə\ *n* : an Islamic religious leader — used as a title of respect

¹aye *also* **ay** \'ā\ *adv* : for a limitless time : ALWAYS, EVER

²aye *also* **ay** \'ī\ *adv* : YES — used as a function word to express assent or agreement

³aye *also* **ay** \'ī\ *n, pl* **ayes** : an affirmative vote

AZ *abbr* Arizona

aza•lea \ə-'zāl-yə\ *n* : any of numerous rhododendrons with funnel-shaped blossoms and usu. deciduous leaves

az•i•do•thy•mi•dine \ə-,zi-dō-'thī-mə-,dēn\ *n* : AZT

az•i•muth \'a-zə-məth\ *n* : horizontal direction expressed as an angular distance from a fixed point

AZT \,ā-(,)zē-'tē\ *n* : an antiviral drug used to treat AIDS

Az•tec \'az-,tek\ *n* : a member of a Nahuatl-speaking people that founded the Mexican empire and were conquered by Hernán Cortés in 1519 — **Az•tec•an** *adj*

azure \'a-zhər\ *n* : the blue of the clear sky — **azure** *adj*

B

¹b \'bē\ *n, pl* **b's** *or* **bs** \'bēz\ *often cap* **1** : the 2d letter of the English alphabet **2** : a grade rating a student's work as good

²b *abbr, often cap* **1** bachelor **2** bass **3** bishop **4** book **5** born

B *symbol* boron

Ba *symbol* barium

BA *abbr* **1** bachelor of arts **2** batting average

bab•bitt \'ba-bət\ *n* : an alloy used for lining bearings; *esp* : one containing tin, copper, and antimony

¹bab•ble \'ba-bəl\ *vb* **bab•bled; bab•bling 1** ♦ : to talk enthusiastically or excessively **2** ♦ : to utter meaningless sounds

   ♦ chatter, drivel, gabble, gibber, jabber, prattle, sputter

²babble *n* **1** : foolish or idle talk **2** ♦ : continuous meaningless vocal sounds : a murmur or a continuity of confused sounds

   ♦ gabble, gibberish, gobbledygook, hogwash, nonsense, piffle, prattle

bab•bler \-b(ə-)lər\ *n* : one that babbles

babe \'bāb\ *n* **1** : an extremely young child : BABY **2** *slang* : GIRL, WOMAN **3** *slang* : a person who is physically attractive

ba•bel \'bā-bəl, 'ba-\ *n, often cap* : a place or scene of noise and confusion; *also* : a confused sound

ba•boon \ba-'bün\ *n* : any of several large apes of Asia and Africa with doglike muzzles

ba•bush•ka \bə-'büsh-kə, -'büsh-\ *n* ♦ : a kerchief for the head

   ♦ bandanna, do-rag, kerchief, mantilla

¹ba•by \'bā-bē\ *n, pl* **babies 1** ♦ : a very young child : INFANT **2** : the youngest or smallest of a group **3** : a childish person — **baby** *adj* — **ba•by•hood** *n*

   ♦ child, infant, newborn

²baby *vb* **ba•bied; ba•by•ing** ♦ : to tend or treat often with excessive care

   ♦ coddle, mollycoddle, nurse, pamper, spoil *Ant* abuse, ill-treat, ill-use, maltreat, mishandle, mistreat, misuse

baby boom *n* : a marked rise in birthrate — **baby boom•er** \-'bü-mər\ *n*

ba•by•ish *adj* ♦ : resembling a baby : CHILDISH, INFANTILE

   ♦ childish, immature, infantile, juvenile, kiddish

baby's breath *n* : any of a genus of herbs that are related to the pinks and have small delicate flowers

ba•by-sit \'bā-bē-,sit\ *vb* **-sat** \-,sat\; **-sit•ting** : to care for children usu. during a short absence of the parents

ba•by-sit•ter *n* : a person usu. hired for relatively short periods of time to take care of a child or children while the parents are away from the home

bac•ca•lau•re•ate \,ba-kə-'lȯr-ē-ət\ *n* **1** : the degree of bachelor conferred by colleges and universities **2** : a sermon delivered to a graduating class

bac•ca•rat \,bä-kə-'rä, ,ba-\ *n* : a card game in which three hands are dealt and players may bet either or both hands against the dealer's

bac·cha·nal \'ba-kən-°l, ˌba-kə-'nal, ˌbä-kə-'näl\ *n* **1** : ORGY **2** : REVELER
bac·cha·na·lia \ˌba-kə-'näl-yə\ *n, pl* **bacchanalia** : a drunken orgy — **bac·cha·na·lian** \-'näl-yən\ *adj or n*
bach·e·lor \'ba-chə-lər\ *n* **1** : a person who has received the usu. lowest degree conferred by a 4-year college **2** : an unmarried man — **bach·e·lor·hood** *n*
bach·e·lor·ette \ˌba-chə-lə-'ret\ *n* : a young unmarried woman
bachelor's button *n* : a European plant related to the daisies and having blue, pink, or white flower heads
ba·cil·lus \bə-'si-ləs\ *n, pl* **-li** \-ˌlī\ : any of numerous rod-shaped bacteria; *also* : a disease-producing bacterium — **bac·il·lary** \'ba-sə-ˌler-ē\ *adj*
¹back \'bak\ *n* **1** : the rear or dorsal part of the human body; *also* : the corresponding part of a lower animal **2** : the part or surface opposite the front **3** : a player in the backfield in football — **back·less** \-ləs\ *adj*
²back *adv* **1** ♦ : to, toward, or at the rear **2** : AGO **3** : so as to be restrained or delayed **4** ♦ : to, toward, or in a former place or state **5** : in return or reply
   ♦ [1, 4] about, around, round
³back *adj* **1** ♦ : located at or in the back **2** : OVERDUE **3** : moving or operating backward **4** : not current
   ♦ hind, hindmost, posterior, rear *Ant* anterior, fore, forward, front
⁴back *vb* **1** ♦ : to assist by material, moral, or financial assistance : SUPPORT **2** : to go or cause to go backward or in reverse **3** : to furnish with a back : form the back of
   ♦ advocate, champion, endorse, patronize, support ♦ abet, aid, assist, help, prop, support
back·ache \'ba-ˌkāk\ *n* : a pain in the lower back
back away *vb* ♦ : to move away (as from a stand on an issue or from a commitment)
   ♦ fall back, recede, retire, retreat, withdraw
back–bench·er \-'ben-chər\ *n* : a rank-and-file member of a British legislature
back·bite \-ˌbīt\ *vb* **-bit** \-ˌbit\; **-bit·ten** \-ˌbit-°n\; **-bit·ing** \-ˌbī-tiŋ\ : to say mean or spiteful things about someone who is absent — **back·bit·er** *n*
back·board \-ˌbōrd\ *n* : a board placed at or serving as the back of something
back·bone \-ˌbōn\ *n* **1** ♦ : the bony column in the back of a vertebrate that is the chief support of the trunk and consists of a jointed series of vertebrae enclosing and protecting the spinal cord **2** ♦ : firm resolute character
   ♦ [1] spine, vertebral column ♦ [2] fiber (*or* fibre), fortitude, grit, guts, pluck, spunk
back down *vb* ♦ : to withdraw from a commitment or position
   ♦ cop out, renege
back·drop \'bak-ˌdräp\ *n* **1** : a painted cloth hung across the rear of a stage **2** : the scenery or ground behind something : BACKGROUND
back·er \'ba-kər\ *n* ♦ : one that supports
   ♦ advocate, apostle, booster, champion, exponent, friend, promoter, proponent, supporter ♦ guarantor, patron, sponsor, surety
back·field \-ˌfēld\ *n* : the football players whose positions are behind the line
¹back·fire \-ˌfīr\ *n* : a loud noise caused by the improperly timed explosion of fuel in the cylinder of an internal combustion engine
²backfire *vb* **1** : to make or undergo a backfire **2** : to have a result opposite to what was intended
back·gam·mon \'bak-ˌga-mən\ *n* : a game played with pieces on a double board in which the moves are determined by throwing dice
back·ground \'bak-ˌgraund\ *n* **1** : the scenery behind something **2** : the setting within which something takes place; *also* : the sum of a person's experience, training, and understanding
back·hand \'bak-ˌhand\ *n* : a stroke (as in tennis) made with the back of the hand turned in the direction of movement; *also* : the side on which such a stroke is made — **back·hand** *vb*
back·hand·ed \'bak-ˈhan-dəd\ *adj* **1** : not straightforward and open : characterized by wiliness and trickery; *esp* : SARCASTIC ⟨a ~ compliment⟩ **2** : using or made with a backhand ⟨a ~ catch⟩
back·hoe \'bak-ˌhō\ *n* : an excavating machine having a bucket that is drawn toward the machine
back·ing \'ba-kiŋ\ *n* **1** : something forming a back **2** ♦ : the act or process of supporting : AID; *also* : a body of supporters
   ♦ aid, assist, assistance, boost, help, lift, support

back·lash \'bak-ˌlash\ *n* **1** : a sudden violent backward movement or reaction **2** : a strong adverse reaction
¹back·log \-ˌlog, -ˌläg\ *n* **1** : a large log at the back of a hearth fire **2** : an accumulation of tasks unperformed or materials not processed
²backlog *vb* : to accumulate in reserve
back of *prep* : in or to a place or situation to the rear of : BEHIND
back off *vb* : to withdraw from a commitment or position : BACK DOWN
back out *vb* : to withdraw esp. from a commitment or contest
¹back·pack \'bak-ˌpak\ *n* : a camping pack supported by a frame and carried on the back
²backpack *vb* : to hike with a backpack — **back·pack·er** *n*
back·ped·al \'bak-ˌped-°l\ *vb* : RETREAT
back·rest \-ˌrest\ *n* : a rest for the back
back·side \-ˌsīd\ *n* ♦ : the seat of the body : BUTTOCKS
   ♦ bottom, butt, buttocks, posterior, rear, rump, seat
back·slap \-ˌslap\ *vb* : to display excessive cordiality — **back·slap·per** *n*
back·slide \-ˌslīd\ *vb* **-slid** \-ˌslid\; **-slid** *or* **-slid·den** \-ˌslid-°n\; **-slid·ing** \-ˌslī-diŋ\ : to lapse morally or in religious practice
back·slid·er *n* : one that backslides ⟨a ~ who pleads his former righteousness⟩
back·spin \-ˌspin\ *n* : a backward rotary motion of a ball
¹back·stage \'bak-ˌstāj\ *adj* **1** : relating to or occurring in the area behind a stage **2** : of or relating to the private lives of theater people **3** : of or relating to the inner working or operation
²back·stage \'bak-'stāj\ *adv* **1** : in or to a backstage area **2** : SECRETLY
back·stairs \-ˌstarz\ *adj* : SECRET, FURTIVE; *also* : SORDID, SCANDALOUS
¹back·stop \-ˌstäp\ *n* : something serving as a stop behind something else; *esp* : a screen or fence to keep a ball from leaving the field of play
²backstop *vb* **1** : SUPPORT **2** : to serve as a backstop to
back·stretch \'bak-'strech\ *n* : the side opposite the homestretch on a racecourse
back·stroke \-ˌstrōk\ *n* : a swimming stroke executed on the back
back talk *n* ♦ : impudent, insolent, or argumentative replies
   ♦ cheek, impertinence, impudence, insolence, sauce
back·track \'bak-ˌtrak\ *vb* **1** : to retrace one's course **2** : to reverse a position or stand
back·up \-ˌəp\ *n* **1** : one that serves as a substitute or alternative **2** ♦ : an accumulation caused by a stoppage in the flow ⟨traffic ~⟩
   ♦ [1] pinch hitter, relief, replacement, reserve, stand-in, sub, substitute ♦ [2] bottleneck, jam, snarl
¹back·ward \'bak-wərd\ *or* **back·wards** \-wərdz\ *adv* **1** : toward the back **2** : with the back foremost **3** : in a reverse or contrary direction or way **4** : toward the past; *also* : toward a worse state
²backward *adj* **1** : directed, turned, or done backward **2** : DIFFIDENT, SHY **3** : slow in development or learning — **back·ward·ly** *adv* — **back·ward·ness** *n*
back·wash \'bak-ˌwosh, -ˌwäsh\ *n* : a backward flow or movement (as of water or air) produced by a propelling force (as the motion of oars)
back·wa·ter \-ˌwo-tər, -ˌwä-\ *n* **1** : water held or turned back in its course **2** : an isolated or backward place or condition
back·woods \-'wudz\ *n pl* **1** ♦ : wooded or partly cleared areas far from cities **2** : a remote or isolated place
   ♦ [1, 2] bush, frontier, hinterland, sticks, up-country
ba·con \'bā-kən\ *n* : salted and smoked meat from the sides or back of a pig
bac·te·ri·cid·al \bak-ˌtir-ə-'sīd-°l\ *adj* : destroying bacteria — **bac·te·ri·cide** \-'tir-ə-ˌsīd\ *n*
bac·te·ri·ol·o·gy \bak-ˌtir-ē-'ä-lə-jē\ *n* **1** : a science dealing with bacteria **2** : bacterial life and phenomena — **bac·te·ri·o·log·ic** \-ə-'lä-jik\ *or* **bac·te·ri·o·log·i·cal** \-ə-'lä-ji-kəl\ *adj* — **bac·te·ri·ol·o·gist** \-'ä-lə-jist\ *n*
bac·te·rio·phage \bak-'tir-ē-ə-ˌfāj\ *n* : any of various viruses that attack specific bacteria
bac·te·ri·um \bak-'tir-ē-əm\ *n, pl* **-ria** \-ē-ə\ : any of a group of single-celled microorganisms including some that are disease producers and others that are valued esp. for their chemical effects (as fermentation) — **bac·te·ri·al** \-ē-əl\ *adj*
bad \'bad\ *adj* **worse** \'wərs\; **worst** \'wərst\ **1** ♦ : below standard : POOR; *also* : UNFAVORABLE ⟨a ~ report⟩ **2** ♦ : having deteriorated because of spoiling **3 a** ♦ : morally unacceptable

or reprehensible : EVIL **b** : not well-behaved : NAUGHTY **4** **a** ♦ : causing discomfort : DISAGREEABLE ⟨a ∼ taste⟩ **b** ♦ : causing harm : HARMFUL **5** : having a defect : FAULTY ⟨∼ wiring⟩; *also* : not valid ⟨a ∼ check⟩ **6** : being in poor health : UNWELL, ILL **7** : full of regret : SORRY

♦ [1] deficient, inferior, lousy, off, poor, substandard, unacceptable, unsatisfactory, wanting, wretched, wrong *Ant* acceptable, satisfactory ♦ [2] putrid, rotten ♦ [3a] evil, immoral, iniquitous, nefarious, sinful, unethical, unsavory, vile, villainous, wicked *Ant* ethical, good, moral, right, righteous, virtuous ♦ [4a] disagreeable, distasteful, nasty, rotten, sour, unpleasant ♦ [4b] adverse, baleful, baneful, damaging, deleterious, detrimental, evil, harmful, hurtful, ill, injurious, mischievous, noxious, pernicious, prejudicial

bade *past and past part of* BID
badge \ˈbaj\ *n* : a device or token usu. worn as a sign of status
¹**bad·ger** \ˈba-jər\ *n* : any of several sturdy burrowing mammals with long claws on their forefeet
²**badger** *vb* : to harass or annoy persistently
ba·di·nage \ˌbad-ᵊn-ˈäzh\ *n* : playful talk back and forth : BANTER
bad·land \ˈbad-ˌland\ *n* : a region marked by intricate erosional sculpturing and scanty vegetation — usu. used in pl.
bad·ly *adv* : in a bad manner ⟨played ∼⟩
bad·min·ton \ˈbad-ˌmint-ᵊn\ *n* : a court game played with light rackets and a shuttlecock volleyed over a net
bad–mouth \ˈbad-ˌmau̇th\ *vb* : to criticize severely
bad·ness *n* : the quality or state of being bad
Bae·de·ker \ˈbā-di-kər, ˈbe-\ *n* : GUIDEBOOK
¹**baf·fle** \ˈba-fəl\ *vb* **baf·fled; baf·fling** \-fə-liŋ\ **1** ♦ : to interfere with or slow the progress of : FRUSTRATE, THWART **2** ♦ : to cause to be mentally confused : PERPLEX

♦ [1] balk, checkmate, foil, frustrate, thwart ♦ [2] addle, befog, befuddle, bemuse, bewilder, confound, confuse, disorient, muddle, muddy, mystify, perplex, puzzle

²**baffle** *n* : a device (as a wall or screen) to deflect, check, or regulate flow (as of liquid or sound) — **baf·fled** \ˈba-fəld\ *adj*
baf·fle·ment *n* ♦ : the state of being baffled

♦ bewilderment, confusion, distraction, muddle, mystification, perplexity, puzzlement, whirl

¹**bag** \ˈbag\ *n* ♦ : a flexible usu. closable container (as for storing or carrying)

♦ handbag, pocketbook, purse

²**bag** *vb* **bagged; bag·ging** **1** : to expand from internal pressure : BULGE **2** : to put in a bag **3** ♦ : to get possession of; *esp* : to take in hunting

♦ capture, catch, get, grab, nab, seize, snare, trap

ba·gasse \bə-ˈgas\ *n* : plant residue (as of sugarcane) left after a product (as juice) has been extracted
bag·a·telle \ˌba-gə-ˈtel\ *n* : TRIFLE
ba·gel \ˈbā-gəl\ *n* : a hard glazed doughnut-shaped roll
bag·gage \ˈba-gij\ *n* **1** : the traveling bags and personal belongings of a traveler : LUGGAGE **2** : things that get in the way
bag·gie \ˈba-gē\ *n* : a usu. small clear plastic bag
bag·gies \ˈba-gēz\ *n pl* : baggy pants or shorts
bag·gy \ˈba-gē\ *adj* **bag·gi·er; -est** : puffed out or hanging like a bag ⟨a ∼ sweater⟩ — **bag·gi·ly** \-gə-lē\ *adv* — **bag·gi·ness** \-gē-nəs\ *n*
bag·man \ˈbag-mən\ *n* : a person who collects or distributes illicitly gained money on behalf of another
ba·gnio \ˈban-yō\ *n, pl* **bagnios** : BROTHEL
bag·pipe \ˈbag-ˌpīp\ *n* : a musical wind instrument consisting of a bag, a tube with valves, and sounding pipes — often used in pl.
ba·guette \ba-ˈget\ *n* **1** : a gem having the shape of a narrow rectangle; *also* : the shape itself **2** : a long thin loaf of French bread
Ba·ha·mi·an \bə-ˈhä-mē-ən, -ˈhā-\ *n* : a native or inhabitant of the Bahama Islands
¹**bail** \ˈbāl\ *n* : a container for ladling water out of a boat
²**bail** *vb* : to dip and throw water from a boat — **bail·er** *n*
³**bail** *n* : security given to guarantee a prisoner's appearance when legally required; *also* : one giving such security or the release secured
⁴**bail** *vb* : to release under bail; *also* : to procure the release of by giving bail — **bail·able** \ˈbā-lə-bəl\ *adj*
⁵**bail** *n* : the arched handle (as of a pail or kettle)
bai·liff \ˈbā-ləf\ *n* **1** : an aide of a British sheriff who serves writs and makes arrests; *also* : a minor officer of a U.S. court **2** : an estate or farm manager esp. in Britain : STEWARD

bai·li·wick \ˈbā-li-ˌwik\ *n* : one's special province or domain
bail·out \ˈbāl-ˌau̇t\ *n* : a rescue from financial distress
bairn \ˈbarn\ *n, chiefly Scot* : CHILD
¹**bait** \ˈbāt\ *vb* **1** ♦ : to persecute by continued attacks **2** : to harass with dogs usu. for sport ⟨∼ a bear⟩ **3** : to furnish (as a hook) with bait **4** : ALLURE, ENTICE **5** : to give food and drink to (as an animal)

♦ bug, hassle, heckle, needle, ride, taunt, tease

²**bait** *n* **1** : a lure for catching animals (as fish) **2** : an inducement to pleasure or gain : LURE, TEMPTATION
baize \ˈbāz\ *n* : a coarse feltlike fabric
¹**bake** \ˈbāk\ *vb* **baked; bak·ing** **1** : to cook or become cooked in dry heat esp. in an oven **2** : to dry and harden by heat ⟨∼ bricks⟩ — **bak·er** *n*
²**bake** *n* : a social gathering featuring baked food
bak·er's dozen *n* : THIRTEEN
bak·ery \ˈbā-k(ə-)rē\ *n, pl* **-er·ies** : a place for baking or selling baked goods
bake sale *n* : a fund-raising event at which usu. homemade foods are sold
bake·shop \ˈbāk-ˌshäp\ *n* : BAKERY
baking powder *n* : a powder that consists of a carbonate, an acid, and a starch and that makes the dough rise in baking cakes and biscuits
baking soda *n* : SODIUM BICARBONATE
bak·sheesh \ˈbak-ˌshēsh\ *n* : payment (as a tip or bribe) to expedite service
bal *abbr* balance
bal·a·lai·ka \ˌba-lə-ˈlī-kə\ *n* : a triangular 3-stringed instrument of Russian origin played by plucking or strumming
¹**bal·ance** \ˈba-ləns\ *n* **1** : a weighing device : SCALE **2** ♦ : a weight, force, or influence counteracting the effect of another **3** : an oscillating wheel used to regulate a timepiece **4** ♦ : a state of equilibrium **5** ♦ : a remaining group, part, or trace : REST; *esp* : an amount in excess esp. on the credit side of an account **6** : mental and emotional steadiness **7** ♦ : an aesthetically pleasing integration of elements

♦ [2] canceler, counterbalance, counterweight, offset ♦ [4] equilibrium, equipoise, poise *Ant* imbalance ♦ [5] leavings, leftovers, odds and ends, remainder, remains, remnant, residue, rest ♦ [7] coherence, consonance, harmony, proportion, symmetry, symphony, unity

²**balance** *vb* **bal·anced; bal·anc·ing** **1** : to compute the balance of an account **2** ♦ : to arrange so that one set of elements equals another; *also* : to equal or equalize in weight, number, or proportions **3** : WEIGH **4** : to bring or come to a state or position of balance; *also* : to bring into harmony or proportion

♦ equalize, equate, even, level

bal·anced \-lənst\ *adj* ♦ : being in a state of balance (as physically, emotionally, or aesthetically)

♦ clearheaded, lucid, normal, right, sane, stable ♦ congruous, consonant, harmonious

bal·co·ny \ˈbal-kə-nē\ *n, pl* **-nies** **1** : a platform projecting from the side of a building and enclosed by a railing **2** : a gallery inside a building
bald \ˈbȯld\ *adj* **1** ♦ : lacking a natural or usual covering (as of hair) **2** ♦ : lacking embellishment or decoration : PLAIN **3** : having little or no tread ⟨∼ tires⟩ **4** : not disguised ⟨∼ hate⟩ — **bald·ly** *adv* — **bald·ness** *n*

♦ [1] bare, exposed, naked, open, uncovered ♦ [2] plain, simple, unadorned, undecorated, unvarnished

bal·da·chin \ˈbȯl-də-kən, ˈbal-\ *or* **bal·da·chi·no** \ˌbal-də-ˈkē-nō\ *n, pl* **-chins** *or* **-chinos** : a canopylike structure over an altar
bald cypress *n* : either of two large swamp trees of the southern U.S. with hard red wood
bald eagle *n* : an eagle of No. America that when mature has white head and neck feathers and a white tail
bal·der·dash \ˈbȯl-dər-ˌdash\ *n* : NONSENSE
bald·ing \ˈbȯl-diŋ\ *adj* : getting bald
bal·dric \ˈbȯl-drik\ *n* : a belt worn over the shoulder to carry a sword or bugle
¹**bale** \ˈbāl\ *n* : a large or closely packed bundle
²**bale** *vb* **baled; bal·ing** : to pack in a bale — **bal·er** *n*
ba·leen \bə-ˈlēn\ *n* : a horny substance attached in plates to the upper jaw of some large whales (**baleen whales**)
bale·ful \ˈbāl-fəl\ *adj* **1** ♦ : likely to cause or capable of producing harm or death **2** ♦ : foreboding or foreshadowing evil : OMINOUS

♦ [1] adverse, bad, baneful, damaging, deleterious, detrimental, evil, harmful, hurtful, pernicious ♦ [2] dire, foreboding, menacing, ominous, portentous, sinister

¹**balk** \'bȯk\ *n* **1** ♦ : something that makes movement or progress more difficult : HINDRANCE **2** : an illegal motion of the pitcher in baseball while in position

²**balk** *vb* **1** ♦ : to hinder the passage, progress, or accomplishment of : THWART **2** : to stop short and refuse to go on **3** : to commit a balk in sports

♦ baffle, beat, checkmate, foil, frustrate, thwart

balky \'bȯ-kē\ *adj* : refusing or likely to refuse to proceed, act, or function as directed or expected ⟨a ∼ mule⟩

¹**ball** \'bȯl\ *n* **1** ♦ : a rounded body or mass (as at the base of the thumb or for use as a missile or in a game) **2** : a game played with a ball **3** : a pitched baseball that misses the strike zone and is not swung at by the batter **4** : a hit or thrown ball in various games ⟨foul ∼⟩ — **on the ball** : COMPETENT, KNOWLEDGEABLE, ALERT

♦ orb, sphere

²**ball** *vb* ♦ : to form into a ball

♦ agglomerate, conglomerate, roll, round, wad

³**ball** *n* ♦ : a large formal dance

♦ dance, formal, prom

bal·lad \'ba-ləd\ *n* **1** : a narrative poem of strongly marked rhythm suitable for singing **2** : a simple song : AIR **3** : a slow romantic song

bal·lad·eer \ˌba-lə-'dir\ *n* : a singer of ballads

¹**bal·last** \'ba-ləst\ *n* **1** : heavy material used to stabilize a ship or control a balloon's ascent **2** : crushed stone laid in a railroad bed or used in making concrete

²**ballast** *vb* : to provide with ballast

ball bearing *n* : a bearing in which the revolving part turns upon steel balls that roll easily in a groove; *also* : one of the balls in such a bearing

ball·car·ri·er \'bȯl-ˌkar-ē-ər\ *n* : the football player carrying the ball in an offensive play

bal·le·ri·na \ˌba-lə-'rē-nə\ *n* : a woman or girl who is a ballet dancer

bal·let \'ba-ˌlā, ba-'lā\ *n* **1** : dancing in which fixed poses and steps are combined with light flowing movements often to convey a story; *also* : a theatrical art form using ballet dancing **2** : a company of ballet dancers

bal·let·o·mane \ba-'le-tə-ˌmān\ *n* : a devotee of ballet

bal·lis·tic missile \bə-'lis-tik-\ *n* : a missile that is guided during ascent and that falls freely during descent

bal·lis·tics \-tiks\ *n sing or pl* **1** : the science of the motion of projectiles (as bullets) in flight **2** : the flight characteristics of a projectile — **ballistic** *adj*

¹**bal·loon** \bə-'lün\ *n* **1** : a bag filled with gas or heated air so as to rise and float in the atmosphere **2** : a toy consisting of an inflatable bag — **bal·loon·ist** *n*

²**balloon** *vb* **1** ♦ : to swell or puff out **2** : to travel in a balloon **3** ♦ : to increase rapidly

♦ [1, 3] appreciate, build, burgeon, enlarge, escalate, expand, increase, mushroom, rise, swell, wax ♦ [1] belly, bulge, overhang, poke, project, protrude, start, stick out

¹**bal·lot** \'ba-lət\ *n* **1** : a piece of paper used to cast a vote **2** : the action or a system of voting; *also* : the right to vote

²**ballot** *vb* : to decide by ballot : VOTE

¹**ball·park** \'bȯl-ˌpärk\ *n* : a park in which ball games are played

²**ballpark** *adj* : approximately correct ⟨∼ estimate⟩

ball·point \'bȯl-ˌpȯint\ *n* : a pen whose writing point is a small rotating metal ball that inks itself from an inner container

ball·room \'bȯl-ˌrüm, -ˌrùm\ *n* : a large room for dances

¹**bal·ly·hoo** \'ba-lē-ˌhü\ *n, pl* **-hoos** : extravagant statements and claims made for publicity

²**ballyhoo** *vb* **bal·ly·hoo·ed; bal·ly·hoo·ing; bal·ly·hoos** ♦ : to drum up interest in by means of ballyhoo : PUBLICIZE

♦ boast, plug, promote, publicize, tout

balm \'bäm, 'bälm\ *n* **1** : a fragrant healing or soothing lotion or ointment **2** : any of several spicy fragrant herbs of the mint family **3** : something that comforts or soothes

balm·i·ness \'bä-mē-nəs, 'bäl-\ *n* ♦ : the quality or state of being balmy

♦ absurdity, asininity, daftness, fatuity, folly, foolishness, inanity, silliness, simplicity, zaniness

balmy \'bä-mē, 'bäl-\ *adj* **balm·i·er; -est** **1 a** ♦ : gently soothing : MILD **b** ♦ : being pleasant and not too cool or too hot **2 a** ♦ : disordered in mind **b** ♦ : lacking in judgment : FOOLISH

♦ [1a] benign, bland, delicate, gentle, light, mellow, mild, soft, soothing, tender ♦ [1b] clement, equable, gentle, mild, moderate, temperate ♦ [2a, 2b] absurd, cuckoo, fatuous, foolish, nonsensical, nutty, senseless, silly, stupid

ba·lo·ney \bə-'lō-nē\ *n* : NONSENSE

bal·sa \'bȯl-sə\ *n* : the extremely light strong wood of a tropical American tree; *also* : the tree

bal·sam \'bȯl-səm\ *n* **1** : a fragrant aromatic and usu. resinous substance oozing from various plants; *also* : a preparation containing or smelling like balsam **2** : a balsam-yielding tree (as balsam fir) **3** : a common garden ornamental plant — **bal·sam·ic** \bȯl-'sa-mik\ *adj*

balsam fir *n* : a resinous American evergreen tree that is widely used for pulpwood and as a Christmas tree

balsamic vinegar *n* : an aged Italian vinegar made from white grapes

Bal·ti·more oriole \'bȯl-tə-ˌmȯr-\ *n* : a common American oriole in which the male is brightly colored with orange, black, and white

bal·us·ter \'ba-lə-stər\ *n* : an upright support for a rail (as of a staircase)

bal·us·trade \'ba-lə-ˌsträd\ *n* : a row of balusters topped by a rail

bam·boo \bam-'bü\ *n, pl* **bamboos** : any of various woody mostly tall tropical grasses including some with strong hollow stems used for building, furniture, or utensils

bamboo curtain *n, often cap B&C* : a political, military, and ideological barrier in eastern Asia

bam·boo·zle \bam-'bü-zəl\ *vb* **-boo·zled; -boo·zling** : TRICK, HOODWINK

¹**ban** \'ban\ *vb* **banned; ban·ning** ♦ : to hinder or prevent by authority

♦ bar, enjoin, forbid, interdict, outlaw, prohibit, proscribe

²**ban** **1** : CURSE **2** ♦ : a legal or formal prohibition ⟨∼ remarks⟩

♦ embargo, interdict, interdiction, prohibition, proscription, veto

ba·nal \bə-'näl, -'nal; 'bān-ᵊl\ *adj* ♦ : lacking originality, freshness, or novelty : COMMONPLACE, TRITE

♦ commonplace, hackneyed, musty, stale, stereotyped, threadbare, tired, trite

ba·nal·i·ty \bā-'na-lə-tē\ *n* ♦ : something banal : COMMONPLACE

♦ cliché, commonplace, platitude, shibboleth

ba·nana \bə-'na-nə\ *n* : a treelike tropical plant bearing thick clusters of yellow or reddish finger-shaped fruit; *also* : this fruit

¹**band** \'band\ *n* **1** : something that binds, ties, or goes around **2** ♦ : a strip or stripe that can be distinguished (as by color or texture) from nearby matter **3** : a range of wavelengths (as in radio)

♦ [1] bond, chain, fetter, irons, ligature, manacle, shackle ♦ [2] circle, hoop, ring, round ♦ [2] bar, streak, stripe

²**band** *vb* **1** ♦ : to tie up, finish, or enclose with a band **2** ♦ : to gather together or unite esp. for some common end — used often with *together* **3** : to furnish or decorate with a band — **band·er** *n*

♦ [1] belt, gird, girdle, wrap ♦ [1] bind, gird, tie, truss ♦ *often* **band together** [2] ally, associate, club, confederate, conjoin, cooperate, federate, league, unite

³**band** *n* ♦ : a group of persons, animals, or things; *esp* : a group of musicians organized for playing together

♦ company, crew, gang, outfit, party, squad, team

¹**ban·dage** \'ban-dij\ *n* : a strip of material used esp. in dressing wounds

²**bandage** *vb* **ban·daged; ban·dag·ing** : to dress or cover with a bandage

ban·dan·na *or* **ban·dana** \ban-'da-nə\ *n* ♦ : a large colored figured handkerchief

♦ babushka, do-rag, kerchief, mantilla

B and B *abbr* bed-and-breakfast

band·box \'band-ˌbäks\ *n* : a usu. cylindrical box for carrying clothing

band·ed \'ban-dəd\ *adj* : having or marked with bands

ban·de·role *or* **ban·de·rol** \'ban-də-ˌrōl\ *n* : a long narrow forked flag or streamer

ban·dit \'ban-dət\ *n* **1** *pl also* **ban·dit·ti** \ban-'di-tē\ : an outlaw who lives by plunder; *esp* : a member of a band of marauders **2** : ROBBER — **ban·dit·ry** \'ban-də-trē\ *n*

ban·do·lier *or* **ban·do·leer** \ˌban-də-'lir\ *n* : a belt slung over the shoulder esp. to carry ammunition

band saw *n* : a saw in the form of an endless steel belt running over pulleys

band·stand \'band-ˌstand\ *n* : a usu. roofed platform on which a band or orchestra performs outdoors

b and w *abbr* black and white

band·wag·on \'band-ˌwa-gən\ *n* **1** : a wagon carrying musicians in a parade **2** ♦ : a movement that attracts growing support ⟨a political ∼⟩

♦ campaign, cause, crusade, drive, movement

¹**ban·dy** \'ban-dē\ *vb* **ban·died; ban·dy·ing** **1** : to exchange (as blows or quips) esp. in rapid succession **2** : to use in a glib or offhand way

²**bandy** *adj* : curved outward ⟨∼ legs⟩

bane \'bān\ *n* **1** ♦ : a substance that through its chemical action usu. kills, injures, or impairs an organism : POISON **2** : WOE, HARM; *also* : a source of this

♦ poison, toxin, venom

bane·ful \'bān-fəl\ *adj* ♦ : productive of destruction or woe : seriously harmful

♦ bad, baleful, damaging, deleterious, harmful, hurtful, injurious, noxious, pernicious

¹**bang** \'baŋ\ *vb* **1** ♦ : to knock against something with a forceful jolt : BUMP ⟨fell and ∼ed his knee⟩ **2** ♦ : to strike, thrust, or move vigorously and often with a loud noise

♦ [1, 2] bash, bump, collide, crash, hit, impact, knock, smash, strike

²**bang** *n* **1** : a resounding blow **2** ♦ : a sudden loud noise **3** ♦ : a sudden wave of emotion ⟨I get a ∼ out of all this⟩

♦ [2] blast, boom, clap, crack, crash, pop, report, slam, smash ♦ [3] exhilaration, kick, thrill, titillation

³**bang** *adv* : DIRECTLY, RIGHT

⁴**bang** *n* : a fringe of hair cut short (as across the forehead) — usu. used in pl.

⁵**bang** *vb* : to cut a bang in

Ban·gla·deshi \ˌbäŋ-glə-'de-shē\ *n* : a native or inhabitant of Bangladesh — **Bangladeshi** *adj*

ban·gle \'baŋ-gəl\ *n* : an ornamental band or chain worn around the wrist; *also* : a loose-hanging ornament

bang-up \'baŋ-ˌəp\ *adj* ♦ : being of the very best kind : FIRST-RATE, EXCELLENT ⟨a ∼ job⟩

♦ A1, banner, excellent, fabulous, fine, grand, great, prime, sensational, splendid, superb, superior, unsurpassed, wonderful

ban·ish \'ba-nish\ *vb* **1** ♦ : to require by authority to leave a country **2** ♦ : to drive out : EXPEL

♦ [1] deport, displace, exile, expatriate, transport ♦ [2] boot (out), bounce, cast, drum, eject, expel, oust, rout, run off, throw out

ban·ish·ment *n* ♦ : a legal expulsion from a country

♦ deportation, displacement, exile, expulsion

ban·is·ter \'ba-nə-stər\ *n* **1** : an upright often vase-shaped support for a rail **2** : a handrail with its supporting posts **3** : HANDRAIL

ban·jo \'ban-ˌjō\ *n, pl* **banjos** *also* **banjoes** : a musical instrument with a long neck, a drumlike body, and usu. five strings — **ban·jo·ist** \-ist\ *n*

¹**bank** \'baŋk\ *n* **1** ♦ : a piled-up mass (as of cloud or earth) **2** : an undersea elevation **3** : rising ground bordering a lake, river, or sea **4** : the sideways slope of a surface along a curve or of a vehicle as it rounds a curve

♦ bar, drift, mound

²**bank** *vb* **1** : to form a bank about **2** : to cover (as a fire) with fuel to keep inactive **3** : to build (a curve) with the roadbed or track inclined laterally upward from the inside edge **4** : to pile or heap in a bank; *also* : to arrange in a tier **5** : to incline (an airplane) laterally

³**bank** *n* **1** : an establishment concerned esp. with the custody, loan, exchange, or issue of money, the extension of credit, and the transmission of funds **2** : a stock of or a place for holding something in reserve ⟨a blood ∼⟩

⁴**bank** *vb* **1** : to conduct the business of a bank **2** : to deposit money or have an account in a bank — **bank·er** *n* — **bank·ing** *n*

⁵**bank** *n* : a group of objects arranged close together (as in a row or tier) ⟨a ∼ of file drawers⟩

bank·book \'baŋk-ˌbu̇k\ *n* : the depositor's book in which a bank records deposits and withdrawals

bank·card \-ˌkärd\ *n* : a credit card issued by a bank

bank·note \-ˌnōt\ *n* : a promissory note issued by a bank and circulating as money

bank·roll \-ˌrōl\ *n* : supply of money : FUNDS

¹**bank·rupt** \'baŋ-(ˌ)krəpt\ *n* : an insolvent person; *esp* : one whose property is turned over by court action to a trustee to be handled for the benefit of his or her creditors

²**bankrupt** *adj* **1** : reduced to financial ruin; *esp* : legally declared a bankrupt **2** : wholly lacking in or deprived of some essential ⟨morally ∼⟩ — **bank·rupt·cy** \'baŋ-(ˌ)krəpt-sē\ *n*

³**bankrupt** *vb* : to reduce to bankruptcy

¹**ban·ner** \'ba-nər\ *n* **1** ♦ : a piece of cloth attached to a staff and used by a leader as his or her standard **2** ♦ : a usu. rectangular piece of fabric of distinctive design that is used as a symbol (as of a nation), as a signaling device, or as a decoration : FLAG **3** : an advertisement that runs usu. across the top of a Web page

♦ [1, 2] colors (*or* colours), ensign, flag, jack, pennant, standard, streamer

²**banner** *adj* ♦ : distinguished from all others esp. in excellence ⟨a ∼ year⟩

♦ A1, boss, excellent, grand, great, stellar, superior, unsurpassed

ban·nock \'ba-nək\ *n* : a flat oatmeal or barley cake usu. cooked on a griddle

banns \'banz\ *n pl* : public announcement esp. in church of a proposed marriage

¹**ban·quet** \'baŋ-kwət\ *n* ♦ : a ceremonial dinner

♦ dinner, feast, feed, spread

²**banquet** *vb* : to partake of or treat with a banquet

ban·quette \baŋ-'ket\ *n* : a long upholstered bench esp. along a wall

ban·shee \'ban-shē\ *n* : a female spirit in Gaelic folklore whose wailing warns a family that one of them will soon die

ban·tam \'ban-təm\ *n* **1** : any of numerous small domestic fowls that are often miniatures of standard breeds **2** : a small but pugnacious person

¹**ban·ter** \'ban-tər\ *vb* : to speak to in a witty and teasing manner

²**banter** *n* ♦ : good-natured witty joking

♦ chaff, persiflage, raillery, repartee

Ban·tu \'ban-ˌtü\ *n, pl* **Bantu** *or* **Bantus** **1** : a family of languages spoken in central and southern Africa **2** : a member of any of a group of African peoples who speak Bantu languages

Ban·tu·stan \ˌban-tu̇-'stan, ˌbän-tu̇-'stän\ *n* : any of several all-Black enclaves formerly in the Republic of So. Africa that had a limited degree of self-government

ban·yan \'ban-yən\ *n* : a large tropical Asian tree whose aerial roots grow downward to the ground and form new trunks

ban·zai \bän-'zī\ *n* : a Japanese cheer or cry of triumph

bao·bab \'bau̇-ˌbab, 'bā-ə-\ *n* : a tropical African tree with a short swollen trunk and sour edible gourdlike fruits

bap·tism \'bap-ˌti-zəm\ *n* **1** : a Christian sacrament signifying spiritual rebirth and symbolized by the ritual use of water **2** : an act, experience, or ordeal by which one is purified, sanctified, initiated, or named — **bap·tis·mal** \bap-'tiz-məl\ *adj*

baptismal name *n* : GIVEN NAME

Bap·tist \'bap-tist\ *n* : a member of any of several Protestant denominations emphasizing baptism by immersion of believers only

bap·tis·tery *or* **bap·tis·try** \'bap-tə-strē\ *n, pl* **-ter·ies** *or* **-tries** : a place esp. in a church used for baptism

bap·tize \bap-'tīz, 'bap-ˌtīz\ *vb* **bap·tized; bap·tiz·ing** **1 a** : to administer baptism to **b** : to give a name to : CHRISTEN **2 a** : to purify esp. by an ordeal **b** ♦ : to induct into membership by or as if by special rites : INITIATE

♦ inaugurate, induct, initiate, install, invest

¹**bar** \'bär\ *n* **1** : a long narrow piece of material (as wood or metal) used esp. for a lever, fastening, or support **2 a** ♦ : something that blocks or is intended to block passage : OBSTACLE **b** : a submerged or partly submerged bank (as of sand) along a shore or in a river often obstructing navigation **3 a** : the railing in a law court at which prisoners are stationed **b** : the legal profession or the whole body of lawyers **4** ♦ : a stripe, band, or line much longer than wide **5** ♦ : a counter at which food or esp. drink is served; *also* : BARROOM **6** : a vertical line across the musical staff

♦ [2a] block, encumbrance, hindrance, inhibition, obstacle ♦ [4] band, streak, stripe ♦ [5] barroom, café, pub, public house, saloon, tavern

²**bar** *vb* **barred; bar·ring** **1** : to fasten, confine, or obstruct with or as if with a bar or bars **2** : to mark with bars : STRIPE **3** ♦ : to shut or keep out : EXCLUDE **4** ♦ : to command against : FORBID

♦ [3] ban, count out, debar, eliminate, except, exclude, rule out ♦ [4] ban, enjoin, forbid, interdict, outlaw, prohibit, proscribe

³bar *prep* ♦ : with the exclusion or exception of : EXCEPT

♦ aside from, barring, besides, but, except, outside (of), save

⁴bar *abbr* barometer; barometric
Bar *abbr* Baruch
barb \'bärb\ *n* **1** : a sharp projection extending backward (as from the point of an arrow) **2** ♦ : a biting critical remark — **barbed** \'bärbd\ *adj*

♦ affront, dart, dig, indignity, insult, name, offense, outrage, put-down, sarcasm, slight, slur, wound

¹bar•bar•ian \bär-'ber-ē-ən\ *adj* **1** : of, relating to, or being a land, culture, or people alien to and usu. believed to be inferior to another's **2** : lacking refinement, learning, or artistic or literary culture
²barbarian *n* : one that is barbarian
bar•bar•ic \bär-'bar-ik\ *adj* **1** : BARBARIAN **2** : marked by a lack of restraint : WILD **3** : mercilessly harsh or cruel : BARBAROUS ⟨a ∼ crime⟩
bar•ba•rism \'bär-bə-ˌri-zəm\ *n* **1** : the social condition of barbarians; *also* : the use or display of barbarian or barbarous acts, attitudes, or ideas **2** : a word or expression that offends standards of correctness or purity
bar•be•cue \'bär-'bar-ə-tē\ *n* ♦ : barbarous cruelty

♦ brutality, cruelty, inhumanity, sadism, savagery, viciousness, wantonness

bar•ba•rous \'bär-bə-rəs\ *adj* **1** ♦ : lacking culture or refinement **2** : using linguistic barbarisms **3** ♦ : mercilessly harsh or cruel — **bar•ba•rous•ly** *adv*

♦ [1] heathen, heathenish, Neanderthal, rude, savage, uncivil, uncivilized, uncultivated, wild ♦ [3] brutal, cruel, heartless, inhumane, sadistic, savage, vicious

¹bar•be•cue \'bär-bi-ˌkyü\ *n* : a social gathering at which barbecued food is served
²barbecue *vb* **-cued; -cu•ing** **1** : to cook over hot coals or on a revolving spit **2** : to cook in a highly seasoned vinegar sauce
bar•bell \'bär-ˌbel\ *n* : a bar with adjustable weights attached to each end used for exercise and in weight lifting
bar•ber \'bär-bər\ *n* : one whose business is cutting and dressing hair and shaving and trimming beards
bar•ber•ry \'bär-ˌber-ē\ *n* : any of a genus of spiny shrubs bearing yellow flowers and oblong red berries
bar•bi•tu•rate \bär-'bi-chə-rət\ *n* : any of various compounds (as a salt or ester) formed from an organic acid (**bar•bi•tu•ric acid** \ˌbär-bə-'tùr-ik-, -'tyùr-\); *esp* : one used as a sedative or hypnotic
bar•ca•role *or* **bar•ca•rolle** \'bär-kə-ˌrōl\ *n* : a Venetian boat song characterized by a beat suggesting a rowing rhythm; *also* : a piece of music imitating this
bar chart *n* : BAR GRAPH
bar•code \'bär-ˌkōd\ *n* : a set of printed and variously spaced bars and sometimes numerals that is designed to be scanned to identify the object it labels — **bar–cod•ed** \'bär-ˌkō-dəd\ *adj* — **bar coding** *n*
bard \'bärd\ *n* ♦ : one who writes poetry : a maker of verses : POET

♦ minstrel, poet, versifier

bard•ic \'bär-dik\ *adj* ♦ : being, belonging, or relating to a bard or the poetry of a bard

♦ lyric, lyrical, poetic

¹bare \'bar\ *adj* **bar•er; bar•est** **1** ♦ : devoid of customary or natural covering : NAKED **2** : open to view : UNCONCEALED, EXPOSED **3** ♦ : containing nothing : EMPTY ⟨the cupboard was ∼⟩ **4** : leaving nothing to spare : MERE **5** ♦ : lacking ornament : PLAIN, UNADORNED

♦ [1] bald, exposed, naked, nude, open, uncovered ♦ [3] blank, devoid, empty, stark, vacant, void ♦ [5] bald, naked, plain, simple, unadorned, undecorated, unvarnished

²bare *vb* **bared; bar•ing** ♦ : to make or lay bare : UNCOVER

♦ disclose, discover, divulge, expose, reveal, spill, tell, uncover, unmask, unveil

bare•back \-ˌbak\ *or* **bare•backed** \-'bakt\ *adv or adj* : without a saddle
bare•faced \-'fāst\ *adj* **1** : having the face uncovered; *esp* : BEARDLESS **2** : not concealed : OPEN — **bare•faced•ly** \-'fā-səd-lē, -'fāst-lē\ *adv*
bare•foot \-ˌfùt\ *or* **bare•foot•ed** \-'fù-təd\ *adv or adj* : with bare feet

bare–hand•ed \-'han-dəd\ *adv or adj* **1** : without gloves **2** : without tools or weapons
bare•head•ed \-'he-dəd\ *adv or adj* : without a hat
bare•ly \'bar-lē\ *adv* **1** : PLAINLY, MEAGERLY **2** ♦ : by a narrow margin : only just ⟨∼ enough money⟩

♦ hardly, just, marginally, scarcely, slightly

bare•ness *n* : the quality or state of being bare
barf \'bärf\ *vb* ♦ : to discharge the contents of the stomach through the mouth : VOMIT

♦ gag, heave, hurl, puke, retch, spit up, throw up, vomit

bar•fly \'bär-ˌflī\ *n* : a drinker who frequents bars
bar•gain \'bär-gən\ *n* **1** ♦ : an agreement between parties settling a transaction **2** ♦ : an advantageous purchase **3** : a transaction, situation, or event regarded in the light of its results

♦ [1] accord, agreement, compact, contract, convention, covenant, deal, pact, settlement, understanding ♦ [2] buy, deal, steal

²bargain *vb* **1** ♦ : to negotiate over the terms of an agreement; *also* : to come to terms : BARTER

♦ chaffer, deal, dicker, haggle, negotiate, palter

bar•gain–base•ment \'bär-gən-'bās-mənt\ *adj* : markedly inexpensive
¹barge \'bärj\ *n* **1** : a broad flat-bottomed boat usu. moved by towing **2** : a motorboat supplied to a flagship (as for an admiral) **3** : a ceremonial boat elegantly furnished — **barge•man** \-mən\ *n*
²barge *vb* **barged; barg•ing** **1** : to carry by barge **2** : to move or thrust oneself clumsily or rudely
bar graph *n* : a graphic technique for comparing amounts by rectangles whose lengths are proportional to the amounts they represent
ba•ris•ta \bə-'rēs-tə\ *n* : a person who makes and serves coffee to the public
bari•tone \'bar-ə-ˌtōn\ *n* : a male singing voice between bass and tenor; *also* : a person having this voice
bar•i•um \'bar-ē-əm\ *n* : a silver-white metallic chemical element that occurs only in combination
¹bark \'bärk\ *vb* **1** : to make the short loud cry of a dog **2** : to speak or utter in a curt loud tone : SNAP
²bark *n* : the sound made by a barking dog
³bark *n* : the tough corky outer covering of a woody stem or root
⁴bark *vb* **1** ♦ : to strip the bark from **2** ♦ : to rub the skin from

♦ [1, 2] flay, hull, husk, peel, shell, skin

⁵bark *n* : a ship of three or more masts with the aft mast fore-and-aft rigged and the others square-rigged
bar•keep \'bär-ˌkēp\ *also* **bar•keep•er** \-ˌkē-pər\ *n* : BARTENDER
bark•er \'bär-kər\ *n* : a person who stands at the entrance esp. to a show and tries to attract customers to it
bar•ley \'bär-lē\ *n* : a cereal grass with seeds used as food and in making malt liquors; *also* : its seed
bar mitz•vah \bär-'mits-və\ *n, often cap B&M* **1** : a Jewish boy who reaches his 13th birthday and assumes religious responsibilities **2** : the ceremony recognizing a boy as a bar mitzvah
barn \'bärn\ *n* : a building used esp. for storing hay and grain and for housing livestock or farm equipment
bar•na•cle \'bär-ni-kəl\ *n* : any of numerous small marine crustaceans free-swimming when young but permanently fixed (as to rocks, whales, or ships) when adult
barn•storm \'bärn-ˌstorm\ *vb* : to travel through the country making brief stops to entertain (as with shows or flying stunts) or to campaign for political office
barn•yard \-ˌyärd\ *n* : a usu. fenced area adjoining a barn
baro•graph \'bar-ə-ˌgraf\ *n* : a recording barometer
ba•rom•e•ter \bə-'räm-ə-tər\ *n* : an instrument for measuring atmospheric pressure — **baro•met•ric** \ˌbar-ə-'me-trik\ *adj*
bar•on \'bar-ən\ *n* **1** : a member of the lowest grade of the British peerage **2** ♦ : a man who possesses great power or influence in some field of activity — **bar•ony** \'bar-ə-nē\ *n*

♦ czar, king, magnate, mogul, prince, tycoon

bar•on•age \'bar-ə-nij\ *n* : PEERAGE
bar•on•ess \'bar-ə-nəs\ *n* **1** : the wife or widow of a baron **2** : a woman holding a baronial title in her own right
bar•on•et \'bar-ə-nət\ *n* : the holder of a rank of honor below a baron but above a knight — **bar•on•et•cy** \-sē\ *n*
ba•ro•ni•al \bə-'rō-nē-əl\ *adj* **1** : of or relating to a baron or the baronage **2** ♦ : generous or more than adequate in size, scope, or capacity : STATELY

♦ grand, grandiose, imposing, magnificent, majestic, monumental, stately

ba·roque \bə-'rōk, -'räk\ *adj* : marked by the use of complex forms, bold ornamentation, and the juxtapositioning of contrasting elements

ba·rouche \bə-'rüsh\ *n* : a 4-wheeled carriage with a high driver's seat in front and a folding top

bar·racks \'bar-əks\ *n sing or pl* : a building or group of buildings for lodging soldiers

bar·ra·cu·da \,bar-ə-'kü-də\ *n, pl* **-da** *or* **-das** : any of several large slender predaceous sea fishes including some used for food

bar·rage \bə-'räzh, -'räj\ *n* **1** : a heavy concentration of fire (as of artillery) **2** ♦ : vigorous or rapid outpouring of many things at once

♦ bombardment, cannonade, fusillade, hail, salvo, shower, storm, volley

barred \'bärd\ *adj* : marked by or divided off by bars : STRIPED

¹**bar·rel** \'bar-əl\ *n* **1** ♦ : a round bulging cask with flat ends of equal diameter **2 a** : the amount contained in a barrel **b** ♦ : a great quantity **3** : a drum or cylindrical part ⟨gun ∼⟩ — **bar·reled** \-əld\ *adj*

♦ [1] cask, hogshead, keg, pipe, puncheon ♦ [2b] abundance, deal, gobs, heap, loads, lot, pile, plenty, quantity, scads

²**barrel** *vb* **-reled** *or* **-relled; -rel·ing** *or* **-rel·ling** **1** : to pack in a barrel **2** ♦ : to travel at high speed

♦ dash, fly, hurry, hurtle, rush, speed, tear, zip, zoom

bar·rel·head \-,hed\ *n* : the flat end of a barrel — **on the barrelhead** : asking for or granting no credit ⟨paid cash *on the barrelhead*⟩

barrel roll *n* : an airplane maneuver in which a complete revolution about the longitudinal axis is made

¹**bar·ren** \'bar-ən\ *adj* **1** ♦ : not producing fruit, spores, or offspring : STERILE **2 a** : not productive ⟨a ∼ scheme⟩ **b** ♦ : producing little or no vegetation : DESOLATE **3** : lacking interest or charm **4** : DULL, STUPID — **bar·ren·ness** \-nəs\ *n*

♦ [1] impotent, infertile, sterile ♦ [2b] infertile, poor, stark, unproductive, waste *Ant* fertile, fruitful, lush, luxuriant, productive, rich

²**barren** *n* ♦ : a tract of barren land

♦ desert, desolation, waste, wasteland

bar·rette \bä-'ret, bə-\ *n* : a clasp or bar for holding the hair in place

¹**bar·ri·cade** \'bar-ə-,kād, ,bar-ə-'kād\ *vb* **-cad·ed; -cad·ing** **1** : to block, obstruct, or fortify with a barricade **2** ♦ : to prevent access to by means of a barricade

♦ besiege, block, cut off, dam, encircle, surround

²**barricade** *n* **1** : a hastily thrown-up obstruction or fortification **2** : something that impedes progress or achievement : BARRIER

bar·ri·er \'bar-ē-ər\ *n* ♦ : something that separates, demarcates, or serves as a barricade ⟨trade ∼s⟩ ⟨traffic ∼s⟩

♦ fence, hedge, wall

barrier island *n* : a long broad sandy island lying parallel to a shore

barrier reef *n* : a coral reef roughly parallel to a shore and separated from it by a lagoon

bar·ring \'bär-iŋ\ *prep* ♦ : excluding by exception

♦ aside from, bar, besides, but, except, outside (of), save

bar·rio \'bär-ē-,ō, 'bar-\ *n, pl* **-ri·os** **1** : a district of a city or town in a Spanish-speaking country **2** : a Spanish-speaking quarter in a U.S. city

bar·ris·ter \'bar-ə-stər\ *n* : a British counselor admitted to plead in the higher courts

bar·room \'bär-,rüm, -,rùm\ *n* ♦ : a room or establishment whose main feature is a bar for the sale of liquor

♦ bar, café, pub, public house, saloon, tavern

¹**bar·row** \'bar-ō\ *n* : a large burial mound of earth and stones

²**barrow** *n* **1** : WHEELBARROW **2** : a cart with a boxlike body and two shafts for pushing it

Bart *abbr* baronet

bar·tend·er \'bär-,ten-dər\ *n* : a person who serves liquor at a bar

¹**bar·ter** \'bär-tər\ *vb* : to trade by exchange of goods — **bar·ter·er** *n*

²**barter** *n* **1** ♦ : the act or practice of carrying on trade by bartering **2** : the thing given in exchange in bartering

♦ commutation, exchange, swap, trade, truck

Ba·ruch \'bär-,ük, bə-'rük\ *n* : homiletic book included in the Roman Catholic canon of the Old Testament and in the Protestant Apocrypha

bas·al \'bā-səl\ *adj* **1** : situated at or forming the base **2** : BASIC

basal metabolism *n* : the turnover of energy in a fasting and resting organism using energy solely to maintain vital cellular activity, respiration, and circulation as measured by the rate at which heat is given off

ba·salt \bə-'sòlt, 'bā-,sòlt\ *n* : a dark fine-grained igneous rock — **ba·sal·tic** \bə-'sòl-tik\ *adj*

¹**base** \'bās\ *n, pl* **bas·es** \'bā-səz\ **1 a** ♦ : the lowest part or place : BOTTOM **b** ♦ : the physical or philosophical foundation upon which something is based **2** : a side or face on which a geometrical figure stands; *also* : the length of a base **3** ♦ : a main ingredient or fundamental part **4** : the point of beginning an act or operation **5** : a place on which a force depends for supplies **6** : a number (as 5 in 5^7) that is raised to a power; *esp* : a number that when raised to a power equal to the logarithm of a number yields the number itself ⟨the logarithm of 100 to ∼ 10 is 2 since 10^2 = 100⟩ **7** : the number of units in a given digit's place of a number system that is required to give the numeral 1 in the next higher place ⟨the decimal system uses a ∼ of 10⟩; *also* : such a system using an indicated base ⟨convert from ∼ 10 to ∼ 2⟩ **8** : any of the four stations at the corners of a baseball diamond **9** : a chemical compound (as lime or ammonia) that reacts with an acid to form a salt, has a bitter taste, and turns litmus blue — **base·man** \'bās-mən\ *n*

♦ [1a] bottom, foot ♦ [1b] basis, bedrock, cornerstone, footing, foundation, ground, groundwork, keystone, underpinning ♦ [3] center (*or* centre), core, cynosure, eye, focus, heart, hub, mecca, nucleus, seat

²**base** *vb* **based; bas·ing** **1** ♦ : to form or serve as a base for **2** : ESTABLISH

♦ ground, rest

³**base** *adj* **1** : of inferior quality : DEBASED, ALLOYED **2** ♦ : characterized by baseness, lowness, or meanness : CONTEMPTIBLE, IGNOBLE **3** : MENIAL, DEGRADING **4** : of little value — **base·ly** *adv* — **base·ness** *n*

♦ contemptible, despicable, detestable, dirty, dishonorable (*or* dishonourable), ignoble, low, mean, snide, sordid, vile, wretched

base·ball \'bās-,bòl\ *n* : a game played with a bat and ball by two teams on a field with four bases arranged in a diamond; *also* : the ball used in this game

base·board \-,bòrd\ *n* : a line of boards or molding covering the joint of a wall and the adjoining floor

base·born \-'bòrn\ *adj* **1** : MEAN, IGNOBLE **2** : of humble birth **3** : born to parents who are not married to each other

base exchange *n* : a post exchange at a naval or air force base

base hit *n* : a hit in baseball that enables the batter to reach base safely with no error made and no base runner forced out

BASE jumping \'bās-\ *n* : the activity of parachuting from a high structure or cliff

base·less \-ləs\ *adj* ♦ : having no base or basis : GROUNDLESS

♦ groundless, invalid, unfounded, unreasonable, unsubstantiated, unsupported, unwarranted *Ant* reasonable, reasoned, substantiated, valid, well-founded

base·line \'bās-,līn\ *n* **1** : a line serving as a basis esp. to calculate or locate something **2** : the area within which a baseball player must keep when running between bases

base·ment \-mənt\ *n* **1** : the part of a building that is wholly or partly below ground level **2** : the lowest or fundamental part of something

base on balls : an advance to first base awarded a baseball player who during a turn at bat takes four pitches without swinging

base runner *n* : a baseball player who is on base or is attempting to reach a base

¹**bash** \'bash\ *vb* **1** ♦ : to strike violently : HIT **2** : to smash by a blow **3** ♦ : to attack physically or verbally

♦ [1] bang, collide, crash, hit, ram, slam, smash, strike ♦ [3] bat, batter, beat, hammer, lambaste, pelt, pound, thrash

²**bash** *n* **1** : a heavy blow **2** : a festive social gathering : PARTY

bash·ful \'bash-fəl\ *adj* ♦ : inclined to shrink from public attention — **bash·ful·ness** *n*

♦ coy, demure, diffident, introverted, modest, retiring, sheepish, shy

ba·sic \'bā-sik\ *adj* **1** ♦ : of, relating to, or forming the base or essence : FUNDAMENTAL **2** : of, relating to, or having the character of a chemical base — **ba·sic·i·ty** \bā-'si-sə-tē\ *n*

♦ elemental, elementary, essential, fundamental, rudimentary, underlying

BA·SIC \'bā-sik\ n : a simplified language for programming a computer

ba·si·cal·ly \'bā-si-k(ə-)lē\ adv **1** : at a basic level **2** ♦ : for the most part **3** : in a basic manner

♦ altogether, chiefly, generally, largely, mainly, mostly, overall, predominantly, primarily, principally

ba·sil \'bā-zəl, 'ba-, -səl\ n : any of several mints with fragrant leaves used in cooking

ba·sil·i·ca \bə-'si-li-kə, -'zi-\ n **1** : an early Christian church building consisting of nave and aisles with clerestory and apse **2** : a Roman Catholic church given ceremonial privileges

bas·i·lisk \'ba-sə-,lisk, 'ba-zə-\ n : a legendary reptile with fatal breath and glance

ba·sin \'bās-ᵊn\ n **1** : an open usu. circular vessel with sloping sides for holding liquid (as water) **2** : a hollow or enclosed place containing water; also : the region drained by a river

ba·sis \'bā-səs\ n, pl **ba·ses** \-,sēz\ **1** : the lowest part or place : FOUNDATION **2** ♦ : a fundamental principle

♦ base, bedrock, cornerstone, footing, foundation, ground, groundwork, keystone, underpinning

bask \'bask\ vb **1** ♦ : to lie or relax in comfortable warmth **2** : to enjoy something warmly comforting ⟨∼ing in his friends' admiration⟩

♦ loll, lounge, relax, repose, rest

bas·ket \'bas-kət\ n : a container made of woven material (as twigs or grasses); also : any of various lightweight usu. wood containers — **bas·ket·ful** n

bas·ket·ball \-,bȯl\ n : a game played on a court by two teams who try to throw an inflated ball through a raised goal; also : the ball used in this game

basket case n **1** : a person who has all four limbs amputated **2** : a person who is functionally incapacitated or worn out (as from nervous tension or mental or physical overwork)

basket weave n : a textile weave resembling the checkered pattern of a plaited basket

basmati rice \,bäz-'mä-tē-\ n : an aromatic long-grain rice originating in southern Asia

bas mitzvah var of BAT MITZVAH

Basque \'bask\ n **1** : a member of a people inhabiting a region bordering on the Bay of Biscay in northern Spain and southwestern France **2** : the language of the Basque people — **Basque** adj

bas–re·lief \,bä-ri-'lēf\ n : a sculpture in relief with the design raised very slightly from the background

¹**bass** \'bas\ n, pl **bass** or **bass·es** : any of numerous sport and food bony fishes (as a striped bass)

²**bass** \'bās\ adj ♦ : of low pitch

♦ deep, low, throaty

³**bass** \'bās\ n **1** : a deep sound or tone **2** : the lower half of the musical pitch range **3** : the lowest part in a 4-part chorus; also : a singer having this voice or part

bas·set hound \'ba-sət-\ n : any of an old breed of short-legged hunting dogs of French origin having long ears and a short smooth coat

bas·si·net \,ba-sə-'net\ n : a baby's bed that resembles a basket and often has a hood over one end

bas·so \'ba-sō, 'bä-\ n, pl **bassos** or **bas·si** \'bä-,sē\ : a bass singer

bas·soon \bə-'sün\ n : a musical wind instrument lower in pitch than the oboe

bass·wood \'bas-,wu̇d\ n : any of several New World lindens or their wood

bast \'bast\ n : BAST FIBER

¹**bas·tard** \'bas-tərd\ n **1** usu offensive : a child born to parents who are not married to each other **2** : an offensive or disagreeable person

²**bastard** adj **1** usu offensive : born to parents who are not married to each other **2** : of an inferior or nontypical kind, size, or form; also : SPURIOUS — **bas·tardy** n

bas·tard·ise Brit var of BASTARDIZE

bas·tard·ize \'bas-tər-,dīz\ vb **-ized; -iz·ing** : to reduce from a higher to a lower state : DEBASE

¹**baste** \'bāst\ vb **bast·ed; bast·ing** : to sew with long stitches so as to keep temporarily in place

²**baste** vb **bast·ed; bast·ing** : to moisten (as meat) at intervals with liquid while cooking

bast fiber n : a strong woody plant fiber obtained chiefly from phloem and used esp. in making ropes

bas·ti·na·do \,bas-tə-'nā-dō, -'nä-\ or **bas·ti·nade** \,bas-tə-'nād, -'näd\ n, pl **-na·does** or **-nades 1** : a blow or beating esp. with a stick **2** : a punishment consisting of beating the soles of the feet

bas·tion \'bas-chən\ n **1** : a projecting part of a fortification **2** ♦ : a fortified position

♦ citadel, fastness, fort, fortification, fortress, hold, stronghold

¹**bat** \'bat\ n **1** ♦ : a stout stick : CLUB **2** ♦ : a sharp blow **3** : an implement (as of wood) used to hit a ball (as in baseball) **4** : a turn at batting — usu. used with at

♦ [1] billy club, bludgeon, club, cudgel, staff, truncheon ♦ [2] belt, blow, box, clout, hit, punch, slug, wallop, whack

²**bat** vb **bat·ted; bat·ting** : to hit with or as if with a bat

³**bat** n : any of an order of night-flying mammals with forelimbs modified to form wings

⁴**bat** vb **bat·ted; bat·ting** : WINK, BLINK

batch \'bach\ n **1** : a quantity (as of bread) baked at one time **2** : a quantity of material for use at one time or produced at one operation **3** ♦ : a quantity (as of persons or things) considered as a group

♦ array, assemblage, block, bunch, collection, group, set

bate \'bāt\ vb **bat·ed; bat·ing** : MODERATE, REDUCE

bath \'bath, 'báth\ n, pl **baths** \'bathz, 'baths, 'báthz, 'báths\ **1** : a washing of the body **2** : water for washing the body **3** : a liquid in which objects are immersed so that it can act on them **4** : a room containing a bathtub or shower and usu. a sink and toilet : BATHROOM **5** : a financial loss ⟨took a ∼ in the market⟩

bathe \'bāth\ vb **bathed; bath·ing 1** ♦ : to wash in liquid and esp. water; also : to apply water or a medicated liquid to ⟨bathed her eyes⟩ **2** : to take a bath; also : to take a swim **3** ♦ : to wash along, over, or against so as to wet **4** : to suffuse with or as if with light — **bath·er** n

♦ [1, 3] douse, drench, soak, sop, souse, wash, water, wet

bath·house \'bath-,ha͝us, 'báth-\ n **1** : a building equipped for bathing **2** : a building containing dressing rooms for bathers

bathing suit n : SWIMSUIT

ba·thos \'bā-,thäs\ n **1** : the sudden appearance of the commonplace in otherwise elevated matter or style **2** : insincere or overdone pathos — **ba·thet·ic** \bə-'the-tik\ adj

bath·robe \'bath-,rōb, 'báth-\ n : a loose often absorbent robe worn before and after bathing or as a dressing gown

bath·room \-,rüm, -,ru̇m\ n ♦ : a room containing a bathtub or shower and usu. a sink and toilet

♦ lavatory, toilet

bathroom tissue n : TOILET PAPER

bath·tub \-,təb\ n : a usu. fixed tub for bathing

ba·tik \bə-'tēk, 'ba-tik\ n **1** : an Indonesian method of hand-printing textiles by coating with wax the parts not to be dyed; also : a design so executed **2** : a fabric printed by batik

ba·tiste \bə-'tēst\ n : a fine sheer fabric of plain weave

bat·man \'bat-mən\ n : an orderly of a British military officer

bat mitz·vah \bät-'mits-və\ also **bas mitz·vah** \bäs-\ n, often cap B&M **1** : a Jewish girl who at 12 or more years of age assumes religious responsibilities **2** : the ceremony recognizing a girl as a bat mitzvah

ba·ton \bə-'tän\ n : STAFF, ROD; esp : a stick with which the leader directs an orchestra or band

bats·man \'bats-mən\ n : a batter esp. in cricket

bat·tal·ion \bə-'tal-yən\ n **1** ♦ : a large body of troops organized to act together : ARMY **2** : a military unit composed of a headquarters and two or more units (as companies)

♦ army, host, legion

¹**bat·ten** \'bat-ᵊn\ vb **1** : to grow or make fat **2** : THRIVE

²**batten** n : a strip of wood used esp. to seal or strengthen a joint

³**batten** vb : to fasten with or as if with battens

¹**bat·ter** \'ba-tər\ vb ♦ : to beat or damage with repeated blows

♦ bash, beat, bludgeon, club, pound, thrash, thump, wallop

²**batter** n : a soft mixture (as for cake) basically of flour and liquid

³**batter** n : one that bats; esp : the player whose turn it is to bat

battering ram n **1** : an ancient military machine for battering down walls **2** : a heavy metal bar with handles used to batter down doors

bat·tery \'ba-tə-rē\ n, pl **-ter·ies 1** : BEATING; esp : unlawful beating or use of force on a person **2** : a grouping of artillery pieces for tactical purposes; also : the guns of a warship **3** : a group of electric cells for furnishing electric current; also : a single electric cell ⟨a flashlight ∿⟩ **4** : a number of similar items grouped or used as a unit ⟨a ∿ of tests⟩ **5** : the pitcher and catcher of a baseball team

bat·ting \'ba-tiŋ\ *n* : layers or sheets of cotton or wool (as for lining quilts)

¹bat·tle \'bat-ᵊl\ *n* **1** : a general military engagement **2 ♦** : an extended contest, struggle, or controversy

♦ fight, fray, scrabble, struggle ♦ combat, conflict, confrontation, contest, duel, rivalry, struggle, tug-of-war, warfare

²battle *vb* **bat·tled; bat·tling** **1 ♦** : to engage in battle : FIGHT **2 ♦** : to contend with full strength, vigor, skill, or resources

♦ [1] clash, combat, fight, scrimmage, skirmish, war ♦ [2] combat, contend, counter, fight, oppose

bat·tle–ax \'bat-ᵊl-,aks\ *n* **1** : a long-handled ax formerly used as a weapon **2** : an angry and domineering woman

battle fatigue *n* : COMBAT FATIGUE

bat·tle·field \'bat-ᵊl-,fēld\ *n* : a place where a battle is fought

bat·tle·ment \-mənt\ *n* : a decorative or defensive parapet on top of a wall

bat·tle·ship \-,ship\ *n* : a warship of the most heavily armed and armored class

bat·tle·wag·on \-,wa-gən\ *n* : BATTLESHIP

bat·ty \'ba-tē\ *adj* **bat·ti·er; -est** : mentally unstable : CRAZY

bau·ble \'bȯ-bəl\ *n* ♦ : a small ornament (as a jewel or ring) : TRINKET

♦ curiosity, gewgaw, knickknack, novelty, tchotchke, trinket

baud \'bȯd, *Brit* 'bȯd\ *n, pl* **baud** *also* **bauds** : a unit of data transmission speed

baux·ite \'bȯk-,sīt\ *n* : a clayey mixture that is the chief ore of aluminum

bawd \'bȯd\ *n* **1** : MADAM 2 **2** : PROSTITUTE

bawd·i·ness \-dē-nəs\ *n* ♦ : the quality or state of being bawdy ⟨his ribaldry and ∿⟩

♦ coarseness, indecency, lewdness, nastiness, obscenity, ribaldry, smut, vulgarity

bawdy \'bȯ-dē\ *adj* **bawd·i·er; -est** ♦ : offensive to morality or virtue : LEWD — **bawd·i·ly** \'bȯd-ᵊl-ē\ *adv*

♦ coarse, crude, indecent, obscene, smutty, unprintable, vulgar ♦ lewd, racy, ribald, risqué, spicy, suggestive

¹bawl \'bȯl\ *vb* ♦ : to cry or cry out loudly; *also* : to scold harshly

♦ blubber, cry, sob, weep ♦ call, cry, holler, shout, vociferate, yell

²bawl *n* : a long loud cry : BELLOW

bawl out *vb* ♦ : to reprimand loudly or severely

♦ admonish, chide, lecture, rail (at *or* against), rate, rebuke, reprimand, scold

¹bay \'bā\ *adj* : reddish brown

²bay *n* **1** : a bay-colored animal **2** : a reddish brown color

³bay *n* **1** : a section or compartment of a building or vehicle **2** : a compartment projecting outward from the wall of a building and containing a window (**bay window**)

⁴bay *vb* ♦ : to bark with deep long tones

♦ howl, keen, wail, yowl

⁵bay *n* **1** : the position of one unable to escape and forced to face danger **2** : a baying of dogs

⁶bay *n* ♦ : an inlet of a body of water (as the sea) usu. smaller than a gulf

♦ bight, cove, estuary, firth, fjord, gulf, inlet

⁷bay *n* : the European laurel; *also* : a shrub or tree resembling this

bay·ber·ry \'bā-,ber-ē\ *n* : a hardy deciduous shrub of coastal eastern No. America bearing small hard berries coated with a white wax used for candles; *also* : its fruit

bay leaf *n* : the dried leaf of the European laurel used in cooking

¹bay·o·net \'bā-ə-nət, ,bā-ə-'net\ *n* : a daggerlike weapon made to fit on the muzzle end of a rifle

²bayonet *vb* **-net·ed** *also* **-net·ted; -net·ing** *also* **-net·ting** : to use or stab with a bayonet

bay·ou \'bī-yü, -ō\ *n* : a marshy or sluggish body of water

bay rum *n* : a fragrant liquid used esp. as a cologne or aftershave lotion

ba·zaar \bə-'zär\ *n* **1** : a group of shops : MARKETPLACE **2** : a fair for the sale of articles usu. for charity

ba·zoo·ka \bə-'zü-kə\ *n* : a weapon consisting of a tube that launches a rocket able to pierce armor

¹BB \'bē-(,)bē\ *n* : a small round shot pellet

²BB *abbr* base on balls

BBB *abbr* Better Business Bureau

BBC *abbr* British Broadcasting Corporation

bbl *abbr* barrel; barrels

BC *abbr* **1** before Christ — often printed in small capitals and often punctuated **2** British Columbia

¹bcc \,bē-,sē-'sē\ *vb* **1** : to send a blind carbon copy to **2** : to send as a blind carbon copy

²bcc *abbr* blind carbon copy

B cell *n* : any of the lymphocytes that secrete antibodies when mature

B complex *n* : VITAMIN B COMPLEX

bd *abbr* **1** board **2** bound

bdl *or* **bdle** *abbr* bundle

bdrm *abbr* bedroom

be \'bē\ *vb, past 1st & 3d sing* **was** \'wəz, 'wäz\ *2d sing* **were** \'wər\ *pl* **were** *past subjunctive* **were** *past part* **been** \'bin\ *pres part* **be·ing** \'bē-iŋ\ *pres 1st sing* **am** \əm, 'am\ *2d sing* **are** \ər, 'är\ *3d sing* **is** \'iz, əz\ *pl* **are** *pres subjunctive* **be** **1** : to equal in meaning or symbolically ⟨God *is* love⟩; *also* : to have a specified qualification or relationship ⟨leaves *are* green⟩ ⟨this fish *is* a trout⟩ **2 a** ♦ : to have objective existence ⟨I think, therefore I *am*⟩ **b** ♦ : to have or occupy a particular place ⟨here *is* your pen⟩ **3** : to take place : OCCUR ⟨the meeting *is* tonight⟩ **4** — used with the past participle of transitive verbs as a passive voice auxiliary ⟨the door *was* opened⟩ **5** — used as the auxiliary of the present participle in expressing continuous action ⟨he *is* sleeping⟩ **6** — used as an auxiliary with the past participle of some intransitive verbs to form archaic perfect tenses **7** — used as an auxiliary with *to* and the infinitive to express futurity, prearrangement, or obligation ⟨you *are* to come when called⟩

♦ [2a] breathe, exist, live, subsist *Ant* depart, die, expire, pass away, perish, succumb ♦ [2b] lie, sit, stand

Be *symbol* beryllium

¹beach \'bēch\ *n* : a sandy or gravelly part of the shore of an ocean or lake

²beach *vb* : to run or drive ashore

beach buggy *n* : DUNE BUGGY

beach·comb·er \'bēch-,kō-mər\ *n* : a person who searches along a shore for something of use or value

beach·head \'bēch-,hed\ *n* : a small area on an enemy-held shore occupied in the initial stages of an invasion

bea·con \'bē-kən\ *n* **1** : a signal fire **2** : a guiding or warning signal (as a lighthouse) **3** : a radio transmitter emitting signals for guidance of aircraft

¹bead \'bēd\ *n* **1** *pl* : a series of prayers and meditations made with a rosary **2** : a small piece of material pierced for threading on a line (as in a rosary) **3** : a small globular body **4** : a narrow projecting rim or band — **bead·ing** *n* — **beady** *adj*

²bead *vb* : to form into a bead

bea·dle \'bēd-ᵊl\ *n* : a usu. English parish officer whose duties include keeping order in church

bea·gle \'bē-gəl\ *n* : a small short-legged smooth-coated hound

beak \'bēk\ *n* : the bill of a bird and esp. of a bird of prey; *also* : a pointed projecting part — **beaked** \'bēkt\ *adj*

bea·ker \'bē-kər\ *n* **1** : a large widemouthed drinking cup **2** : a widemouthed thin-walled laboratory vessel

¹beam \'bēm\ *n* **1** : a large long piece of timber or metal **2** : the bar of a balance from which the scales hang **3** : the breadth of a ship at its widest part **4** : a ray or shaft of light **5** : a collection of nearly parallel rays (as X-rays) or particles (as electrons) **6** : a constant radio signal transmitted for the guidance of pilots; *also* : the course indicated by this signal

²beam *vb* **1** : to send out light **2** : to aim (a broadcast) by directional antennas **3** : to smile with joy

beam·ing *adj* **1** ♦ : marked by, emitting, or reflecting strong or clear rays of light **2** ♦ : marked by or expressive of extreme and unreserved joy, happiness, or satisfaction

♦ [1] bright, brilliant, incandescent, luminous, shiny ♦ [2] aglow, glowing, radiant, sunny

¹bean \'bēn\ *n* : the edible seed borne in pods by some leguminous plants; *also* : a plant or a pod bearing these

²bean *vb* : to strike on the head with an object

bean·bag \'bēn-,bag\ *n* : a cloth bag partially filled typically with dried beans and used as a toy

bean·ball \'bēn-,bȯl\ *n* : a pitch thrown at a batter's head

bean curd *n* : TOFU

bean·ie \'bē-nē\ *n* : a small round tight-fitting skullcap

beano \'bē-nō\ *n, pl* **beanos** : BINGO

¹bear \'bar\ *n, pl* **bears** **1** *or pl* **bear** : any of a family of large heavy mammals with shaggy hair and small tails **2** ♦ : a gruff or sullen person　**3** : one who sells (as securities) in expectation of a price decline

　♦ complainer, crab, crank, curmudgeon, grouch, grumbler, whiner

²**bear** *vb* **bore** \ˈbōr\; **borne** \ˈbōrn\ *also* **born** \ˈbōrn\; **bear·ing　1** ♦ : to move while supporting : CARRY　**2** : to be equipped with　**3** : to give as testimony ⟨∼ witness to the facts of the case⟩　**4** : to give birth to; *also* : PRODUCE, YIELD ⟨a tree that ∼*s* regularly⟩　**5 a** ♦ : to support (as a weight or structure) ⟨*bore* the weight on piles⟩　**b** ♦ : to accept or allow oneself to be subject to : take on or endure ⟨∼ pain⟩　**6** : to go in an indicated direction ⟨∼ to the right⟩　**7** : to manage the actions of (oneself) in a particular way : CONDUCT　**8** ♦ : to hold in the mind or emotions　**9** : to exert pressure or influence　**10** ♦ : to have relevance or a valid connection : PERTAIN — often used with *on* or *upon* ⟨facts ∼*ing* on the question⟩ — **bear·er** *n*

　♦ [1] carry, cart, convey, ferry, haul, lug, pack, tote, transport ♦ [5a] bolster, brace, buttress, carry, prop, shore, stay, support, uphold ♦ [5b] accept, assume, shoulder, take over, undertake ♦ [5b] abide, brook, countenance, endure, meet, stand, stick out, stomach, support, sustain, take, tolerate ♦ [8] cherish, entertain, harbor (*or* harbour), have, hold, nurse ♦ *usu* **bear on** [10] appertain, apply, pertain, refer, relate

bear·able *adj* ♦ : capable of being borne

　♦ endurable, sufferable, supportable, sustainable, tolerable *Ant* insufferable, insupportable, intolerable, unbearable, unendurable, unsupportable

¹**beard** \ˈbird\ *n*　**1** : the hair that grows on the face of a man　**2** : a growth of bristly hairs (as on a goat's chin) — **beard·ed** \ˈbir-dəd\ *adj* — **beard·less** *adj*

²**beard** *vb* ♦ : to confront boldly

　♦ brave, brazen, confront, dare, defy, face

bear down *vb* : to exert full strength and concentrated attention — **bear down on** ♦ : to weigh heavily on

　♦ *usu* **bear down on** depress, press, shove, weigh

bear·ing \ˈbar-iŋ\ *n*　**1** ♦ : manner of carrying oneself : COMPORTMENT　**2** : a supporting object, purpose, or point　**3** : a machine part in which another part (as an axle or pin) turns　**4** : an emblem in a coat of arms　**5** : the position or direction of one point with respect to another or to the compass; *also* : a determination of position　**6** *pl* : comprehension of one's situation　**7** ♦ : connection with or influence on something; *also* : SIGNIFICANCE

　♦ [1] actions, behavior (*or* behaviour), comportment, conduct, demeanor (*or* demeanour), deportment ♦ [7] applicability, pertinence, relevance, significance ♦ [7] association, connection, linkage, relation, relationship

bear·ish *adj*　**1** ♦ : resembling a bear in build or in roughness, gruffness, or surliness ⟨a ∼ man⟩　**2** : marked by, tending to cause, or fearful of falling prices (as in a stock market)

　♦ bilious, cantankerous, disagreeable, dyspeptic, ill-humored, ill-tempered, ornery, splenetic, surly

bear market *n* : a market in which securities or commodities are persistently falling in value

bear out *vb* ♦ : to give new assurance of the validity of : CONFIRM, SUBSTANTIATE ⟨a theory *borne out* by data⟩

　♦ confirm, corroborate, substantiate, support, validate, verify, vindicate

bear·skin \ˈbar-ˌskin\ *n* : an article made of the skin of a bear

beast \ˈbēst\ *n*　**1** ♦ : any of a kingdom of living things typically differing from plants in capacity for active movement, in rapid response to stimulation, and in lack of cellulose cell walls : ANIMAL; *esp* : a 4-footed mammal　**2** ♦ : a contemptible person

　♦ [1] animal, creature, critter ♦ [2] brute, devil, fiend, monster, savage, villain

¹**beast·ly** \ˈbēst-lē\ *adj* **beast·li·er; -est　1** : BESTIAL　**2** : ABOMINABLE, DISAGREEABLE — **beast·li·ness** \-nəs\ *n*

²**beastly** *adv* : to a high degree : VERY, EXCEEDINGLY

¹**beat** \ˈbēt\ *vb* **beat; beat·en** \ˈbēt-ᵊn\ *or* **beat; beat·ing　1** ♦ : to strike repeatedly　**2** : TREAD　**3** ♦ : to affect or alter by beating ⟨∼ metal into sheets⟩　**4** : to sound (as an alarm) on a drum　**5 a** ♦ : to get the better of : OVERCOME　**b** ♦ : to become better, greater, or stronger than : SURPASS　**6** : to act or arrive before ⟨∼ his brother home⟩　**7** : to beat or vibrate rhythmically : THROB　**8** : to flap or thrash at vigorously　**9** : to glare or strike with oppressive intensity ⟨the sun ∼ down on the caravan⟩

　♦ [1] bash, bat, batter, club, drub, pound, thrash, thump, wallop, whale, whip ♦ [3] forge, hammer, pound ♦ [5a] best, conquer, crush, defeat, lick, overcome, prevail, rout, skunk, subdue, thrash, triumph, trounce, wallop, whip *Ant* lose (to) ♦ [5b] better, eclipse, excel, outdistance, outdo, outshine, outstrip, surpass, top, transcend

²**beat** *n*　**1 a** : a single stroke or blow esp. of a series　**b** ♦ : a rhythmic throbbing, contraction and expansion, or vibration : PULSATION　**2** ♦ : a rhythmic stress in poetry or music or the rhythmic effect of these　**3** : a regularly traversed course

　♦ [1b] palpitation, pulsation, pulse, throb ♦ [2] cadence, measure, meter (*or* metre), rhythm

³**beat** *adj*　**1** ♦ : consumed entirely : EXHAUSTED　**2** : of or relating to beatniks

　♦ bushed, dead, drained, exhausted, prostrate, spent, weary, worn-out

⁴**beat** *n* : BEATNIK

beat·er *n* : one that beats

be·a·tif·ic \ˌbē-ə-ˈti-fik\ *adj* : giving or indicative of great joy or bliss

be·at·i·fy \bē-ˈa-tə-ˌfī\ *vb* **-fied; -fy·ing　1** : to make supremely happy　**2** : to declare to have attained the blessedness of heaven and authorize the title "Blessed" for — **be·at·i·fi·ca·tion** \-ˌa-tə-fə-ˈkā-shən\ *n*

be·at·i·tude \bē-ˈa-tə-ˌtüd, -ˌtyüd\ *n*　**1** : a state of utmost bliss　**2** : any of the declarations made in the Sermon on the Mount (Mt 5:3–12) beginning "Blessed are"

beat·nik \ˈbēt-nik\ *n* : a person who rejects the mores of established society and indulges in exotic philosophizing and self-expression

beau \ˈbō\ *n, pl* **beaux** \ˈbōz\ *or* **beaus　1** : a man of fashion : DANDY　**2** ♦ : a male romantic companion : BOYFRIEND

　♦ boyfriend, fellow, man, swain

beau geste \bō-ˈzhest\ *n, pl* **beaux gestes** *or* **beau gestes** \bō-ˈzhest\ : a graceful or magnanimous gesture

beau ide·al \ˌbō-ī-ˈdē(-ə)l\ *n, pl* **beau ideals** ♦ : the perfect type or model

　♦ classic, epitome, exemplar, ideal, model, nonpareil, paragon, perfection, quintessence

Beau·jo·lais \ˌbō-zhō-ˈlā\ *n* : a French red table wine

beau monde \bō-ˈmänd, -ˈmōⁿd\ *n, pl* **beau mondes** \-ˈmänz, -ˈmändz\ *or* **beaux mondes** \bō-ˈmōⁿd\ : the world of high society and fashion

beau·te·ous \ˈbyü-tē-əs\ *adj* : having beauty : BEAUTIFUL — **beau·te·ous·ly** *adv*

beau·ti·cian \byü-ˈti-shən\ *n* : COSMETOLOGIST

beau·ti·ful \ˈbyü-ti-fəl\ *adj* ♦ : characterized by beauty : LOVELY — **beau·ti·ful·ly** \-f(ə-)lē\ *adv*

　♦ attractive, cute, fair, gorgeous, handsome, knockout, lovely, pretty, ravishing, stunning *Ant* homely, plain, ugly, unattractive, unhandsome, unlovely

beau·ti·ful·ness \ˈbyü-ti-fəl-nəs\ *n* : the quality or state of being beautiful

beautiful people *n pl, often cap B&P* : wealthy or famous people whose lifestyle is usu. expensive and well-publicized

beau·ti·fy \ˈbyü-tə-ˌfī\ *vb* **-fied; -fy·ing** ♦ : to make more beautiful — **beau·ti·fi·ca·tion** \ˌbyü-tə-fə-ˈkā-shən\ *n* — **beau·ti·fi·er** *n*

　♦ adorn, bedeck, deck, decorate, embellish, enrich, garnish, grace, ornament, trim

beau·ty \ˈbyü-tē\ *n, pl* **beauties　1** ♦ : qualities that give pleasure to the senses or exalt the mind : LOVELINESS　**2** ♦ : a beautiful person or thing; *esp* : a beautiful woman　**3** ♦ : an extreme or egregious example or instance

　♦ [1] attractiveness, comeliness, handsomeness, looks, loveliness, prettiness *Ant* homeliness, plainness, ugliness ♦ [2] enchantress, fox, goddess, knockout, queen ♦ [3] crackerjack, dandy, jim-dandy, knockout, pip

beauty shop *n* : an establishment where hairdressing, facials, and manicures are done

beaux arts \bō-ˈzär\ *n pl* : FINE ARTS

bea·ver \ˈbē-vər\ *n, pl* **beavers** : a large fur-bearing herbivorous rodent that builds dams and underwater houses of mud and sticks; *also* : its fur

be·calm \bi-ˈkäm, -ˈkälm\ *vb* : to keep (as a ship) motionless by lack of wind

be·cause \bi-ˈkȯz, -ˈkəz\ *conj* ♦ : for the reason that

　♦ for, now, since, whereas

because of *prep* ♦ : by reason of

♦ due to, owing to, through, with

beck \'bek\ *n* : a beckoning gesture; *also* : SUMMONS
beck·on \'be-kən\ *vb* : to summon or signal esp. by a nod or gesture; *also* : ATTRACT
be·cloud \bi-'klaúd\ *vb* ♦ : to prevent clear perception or realization of

♦ befog, blur, cloud, darken, dim, fog, haze, mist, obscure, overcast, overshadow, shroud

be·come \bi-'kəm\ *vb* **-came** \-'kām\; **-come; -com·ing 1** ♦ : to come to be ⟨~ tired⟩ **2** : to suit or be suitable to ⟨her dress ~s her⟩

♦ come, get, go, grow, run, turn, wax

be·com·ing *adj* : adapted to a use or purpose : SUITABLE, FIT; *also* : ATTRACTIVE — **be·com·ing·ly** *adv*
¹**bed** \'bed\ *n* **1** ♦ : an article of furniture to sleep on **2** : a plot of ground prepared for plants **3** : an underlying base or support : BOTTOM **4** : LAYER, STRATUM

♦ bunk, pad, sack

²**bed** *vb* **bed·ded; bed·ding 1** : to put or go to bed **2** : to fix in a foundation : EMBED **3** : to plant in beds **4** : to lay or lie flat or in layers
bed–and–breakfast *n* : an establishment offering lodging and breakfast
be·daub \bi-'dȯb\ *vb* : to spread or daub over a surface : SMEAR
be·daz·zle \bi-'da-zəl\ *vb* : to confuse by or as if by a strong light; *also* : FASCINATE — **be·daz·zle·ment** *n*
bed·bug \'bed-,bəg\ *n* : a wingless bloodsucking bug infesting houses and esp. beds
bed·clothes \'bed-,klō͟thz\ *n pl* : BEDDING 1
bed·ding \'be-diŋ\ *n* **1** : materials for making up a bed **2** : FOUNDATION
be·deck \bi-'dek\ *vb* ♦ : to furnish with something ornamental : ADORN

♦ adorn, array, beautify, deck, decorate, do, dress, embellish, enrich, garnish, grace, ornament, trim

be·dev·il \bi-'de-vəl\ *vb* **1** ♦ : to cause distress : TORMENT **2** : CONFUSE, MUDDLE

♦ afflict, agonize, curse, harrow, martyr, persecute, plague, rack, torment, torture

be·dew \bi-'dü, -'dyü\ *vb* : to wet with or as if with dew
bed·fast \'bed-,fast\ *adj* : BEDRIDDEN
bed·fel·low \-,fe-lō\ *n* **1** : one sharing the bed of another **2** : a close associate : ALLY
be·di·zen \bi-'dīz-ᵊn, -'diz-\ *vb* : to dress or adorn with showy or vulgar finery
bed·lam \'bed-ləm\ *n* **1** *often cap* : an asylum for the mentally ill **2** ♦ : a scene of uproar and confusion

♦ circus, hell, madhouse

bed·ou·in *or* **bed·u·in** \'be-də-wən\ *n, pl* **bedouin** *or* **bedouins** *or* **beduin** *or* **beduins** *often cap* : a nomadic Arab of the Arabian, Syrian, or northern African deserts
bed·pan \'bed-,pan\ *n* : a shallow vessel used by a bedridden person for urination or defecation
bed·post \-,pōst\ *n* : the post of a bed
be·drag·gled \bi-'dra-gəld\ *adj* : soiled and disordered as if by being drenched
bed·rid·den \'bed-,rid-ᵊn\ *adj* : kept in bed by illness or weakness
¹**bed·rock** \-'räk\ *n* **1** : the solid rock underlying surface materials (as soil) **2** : the bottom of something considered as its foundation

♦ base, basis, cornerstone, footing, foundation, ground, groundwork, keystone, underpinning

²**bedrock** *adj* : solidly fundamental, basic, or reliable ⟨traditional ~ values⟩
bed·roll \'bed-,rōl\ *n* : bedding rolled up for carrying
bed·room \-,rüm, -,rùm\ *n* : a room containing a bed and used esp. for sleeping
bed·side \-,sīd\ *n* : the place beside a bed esp. of a sick or dying person
bed·sore \-,sȯr\ *n* : an ulceration of tissue deprived of adequate blood supply by prolonged pressure
bed·spread \-,spred\ *n* ♦ : a usu. ornamental cloth cover for a bed

♦ counterpane, spread

bed·stead \-,sted\ *n* : the framework of a bed

bed·time \-,tīm\ *n* : time for going to bed
bed–wet·ting \-,we-tiŋ\ *n* : involuntary discharge of urine esp. in bed during sleep — **bed–wet·ter** *n*
¹**bee** \'bē\ *n* : any of numerous 4-winged insects (as honeybees or bumblebees) that feed on nectar and pollen and that sometimes produce honey or have a painful sting
²**bee** *n* : a gathering of people for a specific purpose ⟨quilting ~⟩
beech \'bēch\ *n, pl* **beech·es** *or* **beech** : any of a genus of deciduous hardwood trees with smooth gray bark and small sweet triangular nuts; *also* : the wood of a beech — **beech·en** \'bē-chən\ *adj*
beech·nut \'bēch-,nət\ *n* : the nut of a beech
¹**beef** \'bēf\ *n, pl* **beefs** \'bēfs\ *or* **beeves** \'bēvz\ **1** : the flesh of a steer, cow, or bull; *also* : the dressed carcass of a beef animal **2** : a steer, cow, or bull esp. when fattened for food **3** : MUSCLE, BRAWN **4** *pl* **beefs** ♦ : expression of grief, pain, or dissatisfaction : COMPLAINT

♦ complaint, fuss, grievance, gripe, grumble, murmur, plaint, squawk

²**beef** *vb* **1** ♦ : to increase or add substance, strength, or power to : STRENGTHEN — usu. used with *up* **2** ♦ : to express grief, pain, or discontent : COMPLAIN

♦ *usu* **beef up** [1] fortify, harden, strengthen, toughen ♦ *usu* **beef up** [1] amplify, boost, consolidate, deepen, enhance, heighten, intensify, magnify, redouble, step up ♦ [2] bellyache, carp, complain, crab, gripe, grouse, growl, grumble, kick, moan, squawk, wail, whine

beef·eat·er \'bē-,fē-tər\ *n* : a yeoman of the guard of an English monarch
beef·steak \-,stāk\ *n* : a slice of beef suitable for broiling or frying
beefy \'bē-fē\ *adj* **beef·i·er; -est** ♦ : heavily and powerfully built : BRAWNY ⟨a ~ wrestler⟩

♦ brawny, burly, husky

bee·hive \'bē-,hīv\ *n* : HIVE 1, 3
bee·keep·er \-,kē-pər\ *n* : a person who raises bees — **bee·keep·ing** *n*
bee·line \-,līn\ *n* : a straight direct course
been *past part of* BE
beep·er \'bē-pər\ *n* : a small radio receiver that beeps when signaled to alert the person carrying it
beer \'bir\ *n* : an alcoholic beverage brewed from malt and hops — **beery** *adj*
bees·wax \'bēz-,waks\ *n* : WAX 1
beet \'bēt\ *n* : a garden plant with edible leaves and a thick sweet root used as a vegetable, as a source of sugar, or as forage; *also* : its root
¹**bee·tle** \'bēt-ᵊl\ *n* : any of an order of insects having four wings of which the stiff outer pair covers the membranous inner pair when not in flight
²**beetle** *vb* **bee·tled; bee·tling** ♦ : to jut out : PROJECT

♦ bulge, overhang, poke, project, protrude, stick out

be·fall \bi-'fȯl\ *vb* **-fell** \-'fel\; **-fall·en** \-'fȯ-lən\; **-fall·ing** ♦ : to happen to : OCCUR

♦ be, betide, chance, come, go, happen, occur, pass, transpire

be·fit \bi-'fit\ *vb* ♦ : to be suitable to

♦ do, fit, go, serve, suit

be·fog \bi-'fȯg, -'fäg\ *vb* **1** ♦ : to make dark, dim, or indistinct : OBSCURE **2** ♦ : to make mentally unclear or uncertain : CONFUSE

♦ [1] becloud, blur, cloud, darken, dim, fog, haze, mist, obscure, overcast, overshadow, shroud ♦ [2] addle, baffle, befuddle, bemuse, bewilder, confound, confuse, disorient, muddle, muddy, mystify, perplex, puzzle

¹**be·fore** \bi-'fȯr\ *adv or adj* **1** : in front **2** ♦ : at an earlier time : PREVIOUSLY

♦ ahead, beforehand, previously

²**before** *prep* **1** : in front of ⟨stood ~ him⟩ **2** ♦ : earlier than ⟨got there ~ me⟩ **3** : in a more important category than ⟨put quality ~ quantity⟩

♦ ahead of, ere, of, previous to, prior to, to *Ant* after, following

³**before** *conj* **1** : earlier than the time that ⟨she started ~ I did⟩ **2** : more willingly than ⟨he'd starve ~ he'd steal⟩
be·fore·hand \bi-'fȯr-,hand\ *adv or adj* ♦ : in advance

♦ ahead, before, early, previously

be·foul \bi-'faúl\ *vb* ♦ : to make foul (as with dirt or waste)

♦ begrime, besmirch, blacken, dirty, muddy, smirch, soil, stain ♦ contaminate, defile, foul, poison, pollute, taint

be·friend \bi-'frend\ vb : to act as friend to

be·fud·dle \bi-'fəd-ᵊl\ vb ♦ : to muddle or stupefy with or as if with drink : CONFUSE

♦ addle, baffle, befog, bemuse, bewilder, confound, confuse, disorient, muddle, muddy, mystify, perplex, puzzle

beg \'beg\ vb **begged; beg·ging** 1 ♦ : to ask as a charity; also : ENTREAT 2 : EVADE; also : assume as established, settled, or proved ⟨∼ the question⟩

♦ appeal, beseech, entreat, implore, importune, petition, plead, pray, solicit, supplicate

be·get \bi-'get\ vb **-got** \-'gät\; **-got·ten** \-'gät-ᵊn\ or **-got; -get·ting** ♦ : to become the father of : SIRE

♦ father, get, produce, sire

¹beg·gar \'be-gər\ n : one that begs; esp : a person who begs as a way of life

²beggar vb : IMPOVERISH

beg·gar·ly \'be-gər-lē\ adj 1 : contemptibly mean or inadequate 2 : marked by unrelieved poverty ⟨a ∼ life⟩

beg·gary \'be-gə-rē\ n ♦ : extreme poverty

♦ destitution, impecuniousness, impoverishment, indigence, need, pauperism, penury, poverty, want

be·gin \bi-'gin\ vb **be·gan** \-'gan\; **be·gun** \-'gən\; **be·gin·ning** 1 ♦ : to do the first part of an action : COMMENCE 2 ♦ : to come into being : ARISE; also : FOUND ⟨they began the movement⟩ 3 : ORIGINATE, INVENT

♦ [1] commence, embark (on or upon), enter, get off, launch, open, start, strike *Ant* conclude, end, finish, terminate ♦ [2] arise, commence, dawn, form, found, materialize, originate, spring, start *Ant* cease, end, stop

be·gin·ner n ♦ : one that begins something; esp : an inexperienced person

♦ fledgling, freshman, greenhorn, neophyte, newcomer, novice, recruit, rookie, tenderfoot, tyro *Ant* old-timer, vet, veteran

be·gin·ning \bi-'gi-niŋ, bē-\ n ♦ : the point at which something starts : START

♦ birth, commencement, dawn, genesis, launch, morning, onset, outset, start, threshold *Ant* close, conclusion, end, ending

beg off vb : to ask to be excused from something

be·gone \bi-'gȯn\ vb : to go away : DEPART — used esp. in the imperative

be·go·nia \bi-'gō-nyə\ n : any of a genus of tropical herbs widely grown for their showy leaves and waxy flowers

be·grime \bi-'grīm\ vb **be·grimed; be·grim·ing** ♦ : to make dirty

♦ befoul, besmirch, blacken, dirty, foul, grime, mire, muddy, smirch, soil, stain

be·grudge \bi-'grəj\ vb 1 : to give or concede reluctantly 2 : to be reluctant to grant or allow

be·guile \-'gīl\ vb **be·guiled; be·guil·ing** 1 ♦ : to lead by deception 2 : to while away 3 ♦ : to engage the interest of by guile

♦ [1] deceive, dupe, fool, hoax, misinform, mislead, take in, trick ♦ [1] decoy, entice, lead on, lure, seduce, tempt ♦ [3] bewitch, captivate, charm, enchant, fascinate, wile

be·guine \bi-'gēn\ n : a vigorous popular dance of the islands of Saint Lucia and Martinique

be·gum \'bā-gəm, 'bē-\ n : a Muslim woman of high rank

be·half \bi-'haf, -'hȧf\ n : BENEFIT, SUPPORT, DEFENSE

be·have \bi-'hāv\ vb **be·haved; be·hav·ing** 1 ♦ : to bear, comport, or conduct oneself in a particular and esp. a proper way 2 : to act, function, or react in a particular way

♦ acquit, bear, comport, conduct, demean, deport, quit

be·hav·ior \bi-'hā-vyər\ or Can and Brit **be·hav·iour** n ♦ : way of behaving; esp : personal conduct — **be·hav·ior·al** \-vyə-rəl\ adj

♦ actions, bearing, comportment, conduct, demeanor (or demeanour), deportment

be·hav·ior·ism or Can and Brit **be·hav·iour·ism** \bi-'hā-vyə-ˌri-zəm\ n : a school of psychology concerned with the objective evidence of behavior without reference to conscious experience

be·head \bi-'hed\ vb : to remove the head from

be·he·moth \bi-'hē-məth, 'bē-ə-ˌmäth\ n 1 : a huge powerful animal described in Job 40:15–24 2 ♦ : something of monstrous size or power

♦ blockbuster, colossus, giant, jumbo, leviathan, mammoth, monster, titan, whale, whopper

be·hest \bi-'hest\ n 1 ♦ : an authoritative order : COMMAND 2 : an urgent prompting

♦ charge, command, commandment, decree, dictate, direction, directive, edict, instruction, order, word

¹be·hind \bi-'hīnd\ adv or adj 1 : BACK, BACKWARD ⟨look ∼⟩ 2 ♦ : later in time : LATE

♦ belated, delinquent, late, overdue, tardy

²behind prep 1 : in or to a place or situation in back of or to the rear of ⟨look ∼ you⟩ ⟨the staff stayed ∼ the troops⟩ 2 : inferior to (as in rank) ⟨three games ∼ the first-place team⟩ 3 : in support of : SUPPORTING ⟨we're ∼ you all the way⟩ 4 — used as a function word to indicate backwardness, delay, or deficiency ⟨∼ the times⟩

be·hind·hand \bi-'hīnd-ˌhand\ adj : being in arrears

be·hold \bi-'hōld\ vb **-held** \-'held\; **-hold·ing** 1 ♦ : to have in sight : SEE 2 — used imperatively to direct the attention — **be·hold·er** n

♦ descry, discern, distinguish, espy, eye, look, note, notice, observe, perceive, regard, remark, see, sight, spy, view, witness

be·hold·en \bi-'hōl-dən\ adj ♦ : owing gratitude or recognition to another : OBLIGATED, INDEBTED

♦ indebted, obligated, obliged

be·hoof \bi-'hüf\ n : ADVANTAGE, PROFIT

be·hoove \bi-'hüv\ vb **be·hooved; be·hoov·ing** : to be necessary, proper, or advantageous for

beige \'bāzh\ n : a pale dull yellowish brown — **beige** adj

be·ing \'bē-iŋ\ n 1 a : EXISTENCE b ♦ : something that actually exists 2 : the qualities or constitution of an existent thing 3 ♦ : a living thing; esp : PERSON

♦ [1b] entity, individual, object, substance, thing ♦ [3] body, creature, human, individual, man, mortal, person

be·la·bor of Can and Brit **be·la·bour** \bi-'lā-bər\ vb ♦ : to assail (as with words) tiresomely or at length

♦ abuse, assail, attack, blast, castigate, excoriate, jump, lambaste, slam, vituperate

be·lat·ed \bi-'lā-təd\ adj ♦ : delayed beyond the usual time : LATE ⟨∼ birthday wishes⟩

♦ behind, delinquent, late, overdue, tardy

be·lay \bi-'lā\ vb 1 : to wind (a rope) around a pin or cleat in order to hold secure 2 : QUIT, STOP — used in the imperative

belch \'belch\ vb 1 : to expel (gas) from the stomach through the mouth 2 ♦ : to gush forth ⟨a volcano ∼ing lava⟩ — **belch** n

♦ disgorge, eject, erupt, expel, jet, spew, spout, spurt

bel·dam or **bel·dame** \'bel-dəm\ n : an old woman

be·lea·guer \bi-'lē-gər\ vb 1 : to surround with armed forces : BESIEGE 2 : HARASS ⟨∼ed parents⟩

bel·fry \'bel-frē\ n, pl **belfries** : a tower for a bell (as on a church); also : the part of the tower in which the bell hangs

Belg abbr Belgian; Belgium

Bel·gian \'bel-jən\ n : a native or inhabitant of Belgium — **Belgian** adj

Belgian waffle n : a waffle with large depressions and often served with fruit topping

be·lie \bi-'lī\ vb **-lied; -ly·ing** 1 : to give a false impression of : MISREPRESENT 2 ♦ : to show (something) to be false 3 : to run counter to

♦ confute, disprove, rebut, refute

be·lief \bə-'lēf\ n 1 : CONFIDENCE, TRUST 2 ♦ : something (as a tenet or creed) believed

♦ conviction, eye, feeling, judgment (or judgement), mind, notion, opinion, persuasion, sentiment, verdict, view ♦ credence, credit, faith *Ant* disbelief, discredit, doubt, unbelief

be·liev·able \-'lē-və-bəl\ adj ♦ : capable of being believed esp. as within the range of known possibility or probability

♦ credible, likely, plausible, probable *Ant* implausible, improbable, incredible, unbelievable, unlikely

be·lieve \bə-'lēv\ vb **be·lieved; be·liev·ing** 1 : to have religious convictions 2 ♦ : to have a firm conviction about something : accept as true 3 ♦ : to hold as an opinion : SUPPOSE — **be·liev·er** n

♦ [2] accept, credit, swallow, trust *Ant* disbelieve, discredit, reject ♦ [3] consider, deem, feel, figure, guess, hold, imagine, suppose, think

be·like \bi-ˈlīk\ *adv, archaic* : PROBABLY

be·lit·tle \bi-ˈlit-ᵊl\ *vb* **-lit·tled; -lit·tling** **1** : to make seem little or less **2** ♦ : to speak slightingly about : DISPARAGE

♦ cry down, decry, deprecate, depreciate, diminish, discount, disparage, minimize, put down, write off

¹bell \ˈbel\ *n* **1** : a hollow metallic device that makes a ringing sound when struck **2** : the sounding or stroke of a bell (as on shipboard to tell the time); *also* : time so indicated **3** : something with the flared form of a bell

²bell *vb* : to provide with a bell

bel·la·don·na \ˌbe-lə-ˈdä-nə\ *n* : a medicinal extract (as atropine) from a poisonous European herb related to the potato; *also* : this herb

bell–bot·toms \ˈbel-ˈbä-təmz\ *n pl* : pants with wide flaring bottoms — **bell–bottom** *adj*

bell·boy \ˈbel-ˌbȯi\ *n* : BELLHOP

belle \ˈbel\ *n* : an attractive and popular girl or woman

belles let·tres \bel-ˈletrᵊ\ *n pl* : literature that is an end in itself and not practical or purely informative — **bel·le·tris·tic** \ˌbe-lə-ˈtris-tik\ *adj*

bell·hop \ˈbel-ˌhäp\ *n* : a hotel or club employee who takes guests to rooms, carries luggage, and runs errands

bel·li·cose \ˈbe-li-ˌkōs\ *adj* ♦ : favoring or inclined to start quarrels or wars : WARLIKE, PUGNACIOUS

♦ aggressive, argumentative, belligerent, combative, contentious, discordant, disputatious, militant, pugnacious, quarrelsome, scrappy, truculent, warlike

bel·li·cos·i·ty \ˌbe-li-ˈkä-sə-tē\ *n* : showy or extreme combativeness or aggressiveness

bel·lig·er·ence \-rəns\ *n* ♦ : an aggressive or truculent attitude, atmosphere, or disposition

♦ aggression, aggressiveness, fight, militancy, pugnacity, truculence *Ant* pacifism

bel·lig·er·en·cy \bə-ˈli-jə-rən-sē\ *n* **1** : the status of a nation engaged in war **2** : BELLIGERENCE, TRUCULENCE

bel·lig·er·ent \-rənt\ *adj* **1** : waging war **2** ♦ : inclined to or exhibiting assertiveness, hostility, or combativeness : TRUCULENT — **belligerent** *n*

♦ aggressive, argumentative, bellicose, combative, contentious, discordant, disputatious, militant, pugnacious, quarrelsome, scrappy, truculent, warlike *Ant* nonbelligerent, pacific, peaceable, peaceful

bel·low \ˈbe-lō\ *vb* **1** : to make the deep hollow sound characteristic of a bull **2** ♦ : to shout in a deep voice — **bellow** *n*

♦ boom, growl, roar, thunder

bel·lows \-lōz, -ləz\ *n sing or pl* : a closed device with sides that can be spread apart and then pressed together to draw in air and expel it through a tube

bell·weth·er \ˈbel-ˈwe-thər, -ˌwe-\ *n* : one that takes the lead or initiative

¹bel·ly \ˈbe-lē\ *n, pl* **bellies** **1** ♦ : the part of the body between the thorax and the pelvis : ABDOMEN **2** : the underpart of an animal's body

♦ abdomen, gut, solar plexus, stomach, tummy

²belly *vb* **bel·lied; bel·ly·ing** ♦ : to swell or fill beyond a point : BULGE

♦ billow, bulge, overhang, protrude, start, stick out

¹bel·ly·ache \ˈbe-lē-ˌāk\ *n* : pain in the abdomen

²bellyache *vb* ♦ : to find fault : COMPLAIN

♦ beef, carp, complain, crab, croak, fuss, gripe, grouse, growl, grumble, kick, moan, murmur, mutter, repine, squawk, wail, whine

bel·ly·ach·er \ˈbe-lē-ˌā-kər\ *n* ♦ : one who bellyaches

♦ bear, complainer, crab, crank, curmudgeon, grouch, grumbler, whiner

belly button *n* : the human navel

belly dance *n* : a usu. solo dance emphasizing movement of the belly — **belly dance** *vb* — **belly dancer** *n*

belly laugh *n* : a deep hearty laugh

be·long \bi-ˈlȯŋ\ *vb* **1** : to be suitable or appropriate; *also* : to be properly situated ⟨shoes ∼ in the closet⟩ **2** : to be the property ⟨this ∼s to me⟩; *also* : to be attached (as through birth or membership) ⟨∼ to a club⟩ **3** : to form an attribute or part ⟨this

wheel ∼s to the cart⟩ **4** : to be classified ⟨whales ∼ among the mammals⟩

be·long·ings \-ˈlȯŋ-iŋz\ *n pl* ♦ : moveable property : EFFECTS, POSSESSIONS

♦ chattels, effects, holdings, paraphernalia, possessions, things

¹be·loved \bi-ˈləvd, -ˈlə-vəd\ *adj* ♦ : dearly loved

♦ darling, dear, favorite (*or* favourite), loved, pet, precious, special, sweet

²beloved *n* : one who is loved; *esp* : SWEETHEART

¹be·low \bi-ˈlō\ *adv* **1** ♦ : in or to a lower place or rank **2** : on earth **3** : in hell

♦ down, downward, over ♦ beneath, under *Ant* up

²below *prep* **1** : lower than **2** : inferior to (as in rank)

be·low·decks \bi-ˈlō-ˈdeks, -ˈlō-ˌdeks\ *adv* : inside the superstructure of a boat or down to a lower deck

¹belt \ˈbelt\ *n* **1** ♦ : a strip (as of leather) worn about the waist **2** : a flexible continuous band to communicate motion or convey material **3** ♦ : a region marked by some distinctive feature; *esp* : one suited to a particular crop

♦ [1] cincture, cummerbund, girdle, sash ♦ [3] land, region, tract, zone

²belt *vb* **1** ♦ : to encircle or secure with a belt **2** : to beat with or as if with a belt **3** : to mark with an encircling band **4** : to sing loudly

♦ band, gird, girdle, wrap

³belt *n* **1** ♦ : a jarring blow : WHACK **2** : DRINK ⟨a ∼ of whiskey⟩

♦ bat, blow, box, clout, hit, punch, slug, thump, wallop, whack

belt–tightening *n* : a reduction in spending

belt·way \ˈbelt-ˌwā\ *n* : a highway around a city

be·lu·ga \bə-ˈlü-gə\ *n* **1** : a large white sturgeon of the Black Sea, Caspian Sea, and their tributaries that is a source of caviar; *also* : caviar from beluga roe **2** : a whale of arctic and subarctic waters that is white when mature

bel·ve·dere \ˈbel-və-ˌdir\ *n* : a structure (as a summerhouse) designed to command a view

be·mire \bi-ˈmīr\ *vb* : to cover or soil with or sink in mire

be·moan \bi-ˈmōn\ *vb* ♦ : to express deep grief or distress over : LAMENT, DEPLORE

♦ bewail, deplore, grieve, lament, mourn, wail

be·muse \bi-ˈmyüz\ *vb* ♦ : to make confused : BEWILDER

♦ addle, baffle, befog, befuddle, bewilder, confound, confuse, disorient, muddle, muddy, mystify, perplex, puzzle

¹bench \ˈbench\ *n* **1** : a long seat for two or more persons **2** : the seat of a judge in court; *also* : the office or dignity of a judge **3 a** : COURT **b** ♦ : the persons who sit as judges **4** : a table for holding work and tools ⟨a carpenter's ∼⟩

♦ court, judge, justice, magistrate

²bench *vb* **1** : to furnish with benches **2** : to seat on a bench **3** : to remove from or keep out of a game

bench mark *n* **1** : a mark on a permanent object serving as an elevation reference in topographical surveys **2** *usu* **bench·mark** : a point of reference for measurement; *also* : STANDARD

bench press *n* : a press in weight lifting performed by a lifter lying on a bench — **bench–press** *vb*

bench warrant *n* : a warrant issued by a presiding judge or by a court against a person guilty of contempt or indicted for a crime

¹bend \ˈbend\ *vb* **bent** \ˈbent\; **bend·ing** **1** : to draw (as a bow) taut **2** ♦ : to curve or cause a change of shape in ⟨∼ a bar⟩ **3** : to make fast **4** : to DEFLECT **5** ♦ : to turn in a certain direction ⟨bent his steps toward town⟩ **6** ♦ : to direct strenuously or with interest : APPLY ⟨bent themselves to the task⟩ **7** : SUBDUE **8** : to curve downward **9** : YIELD, SUBMIT

♦ [2] arc, arch, bow, crook, curve, hook, round, sweep, swerve, wheel ♦ [5] aim, cast, direct, head, level, set, train ♦ [6] address, apply, buckle, devote, give

²bend *n* **1** : an act or process of bending **2** ♦ : something bent; *esp* : CURVE **3** *pl* : a painful and sometimes fatal disorder caused by release of gas bubbles in the tissues upon too rapid decrease in air pressure after a stay in a compressed atmosphere

♦ angle, arc, arch, bow, crook, curve, turn, wind *Ant* straight line

³bend *n* : a knot by which a rope is fastened (as to another rope)

bend·er \ˈben-dər\ *n* : SPREE

¹**be·neath** \bi-'nēth\ adv ♦ : in or to a lower position : BELOW

♦ below, under

²**beneath** prep **1** : in or to a lower position than : BELOW, UNDER ⟨stood ~ a tree⟩ **2** : unworthy of ⟨considered such behavior ~ her⟩ **3** : concealed by

bene·dic·tion \,be-nə-'dik-shən\ n : the invocation of a blessing esp. at the close of a public worship service

ben·e·fac·tion \-'fak-shən\ n ♦ : a charitable donation

♦ alms, beneficence, charity, contribution, donation, philanthropy

ben·e·fac·tor \'ben-ə-,fak-tər\ n : one that confers a benefit and esp. a benefaction

ben·e·fac·tress \-,fak-trəs\ n : a woman who is a benefactor

ben·e·fice \'be-nə-fəs\ n : an ecclesiastical office to which the revenue from an endowment is attached

be·nef·i·cence \bə-'ne-fə-səns\ n **1** : beneficent quality **2** ♦ : a benefit conferred : BENEFACTION

♦ alms, benefaction, charity, contribution, donation, philanthropy

be·nef·i·cent \-sənt\ adj **1** ♦ : doing or producing good (as by acts of kindness or charity) **2** : BENEFICIAL

♦ benevolent, compassionate, good-hearted, humane, kind, kindly, sympathetic, tender, tenderhearted, warmhearted ♦ altruistic, benevolent, charitable, humanitarian, philanthropic

ben·e·fi·cial \,be-nə-'fi-shəl\ adj ♦ : being of benefit or help : HELPFUL — **ben·e·fi·cial·ly** adv

♦ advantageous, favorable (or favourable), helpful, profitable, salutary *Ant* disadvantageous, unfavorable, unhelpful

ben·e·fi·cia·ry \,be-nə-'fi-shē-,er-ē, -'fi-shə-rē\ n, pl **-ries** : one that receives a benefit (as the income of a trust or the proceeds of an insurance)

¹**ben·e·fit** \'be-nə-,fit\ n **1** ♦ : something that promotes well-being : ADVANTAGE ⟨the ~s of exercise⟩ **2 a** ♦ : a useful aid **b** : material aid provided or due (as in sickness or unemployment) as a right **3** : a performance or event to raise funds

♦ advantage, aid, boon, help

²**benefit** vb **-fit·ed** \-,fi-təd\ also **-fit·ted; -fit·ing** also **-fit·ting 1** ♦ : to be useful or profitable to **2** : to receive benefit

♦ avail, profit, serve

be·nev·o·lence \bə-'ne-və-ləns\ n **1** ♦ : charitable nature **2** : an act of kindness : CHARITY — **be·nev·o·lent·ly** adv

♦ amity, cordiality, fellowship, friendliness, friendship, goodwill, kindliness

be·nev·o·lent \-lənt\ adj ♦ : marked by or disposed to doing good

♦ beneficent, compassionate, good-hearted, humane, kind, kindly, sympathetic, tender, tenderhearted, warmhearted ♦ altruistic, beneficent, charitable, humanitarian, philanthropic

be·night·ed \bi-'nī-təd\ adj **1** : overtaken by darkness or night **2** : living in ignorance

be·nign \bi-'nīn\ adj **1** ♦ : of a gentle disposition; also : showing kindness of a mild kind; esp : not malignant ⟨~ tumors⟩ — **be·nig·ni·ty** \-'nig-nə-tē\ n

♦ balmy, bland, delicate, gentle, light, mellow, mild, soft, soothing, tender

be·nig·nant \-'nig-nənt\ adj : having a kind and gentle nature

ben·i·son \'be-nə-sən, -zən\ n : a prayer that blesses : BLESSING, BENEDICTION

bent \'bent\ n **1** ♦ : strong inclination or interest **2** : power of endurance

♦ affinity, devices, disposition, genius, inclination, leaning, partiality, penchant, predilection, predisposition, proclivity, propensity, talent, tendency, turn

ben·thic \'ben-thik\ adj : of, relating to, or occurring at the bottom of a body of water

ben·ton·ite \'bent-ᵊn-,īt\ n : an absorptive clay used esp. as a filler (as in paper)

bent·wood \'bent-,wüd\ adj : made of wood bent into shape ⟨a ~ rocker⟩

be·numb \bi-'nəm\ vb **1** : to make inactive : DULL, DEADEN **2** : to make numb esp. by cold

ben·zene \'ben-,zēn\ n : a colorless volatile flammable liquid hydrocarbon used in organic synthesis and as a solvent

ben·zine \'ben-,zēn\ n : any of various flammable petroleum distillates used as solvents or as motor fuels

ben·zo·ate \'ben-zə-,wāt\ n : a salt or ester of benzoic acid

ben·zo·ic acid \ben-'zō-ik-\ n : a white crystalline acid used as a preservative and antiseptic and in synthesizing chemicals

ben·zo·in \'ben-zə-wən, -,zóin\ n : a balsamlike resin from trees of southern Asia used esp. in medicine and perfumes

be·queath \bi-'kwēth, -'kwēth\ vb **1** : to leave by will **2** : to hand down

be·quest \bi-'kwest\ n **1** : the action of bequeathing **2** ♦ : something bequeathed : LEGACY

♦ birthright, heritage, inheritance, legacy

be·rate \-'rāt\ vb ♦ : to scold harshly

♦ admonish, chide, lecture, rail (at or against), rate, rebuke, reprimand, scold

Ber·ber \'bər-bər\ n : a member of any of various peoples living in northern Africa west of Tripoli

ber·ceuse \ber-'sœz, -'süz\ n, pl **berceuses** \same or -'sü-zəz\ **1** : LULLABY **2** : a musical composition that resembles a lullaby

¹**be·reaved** \bi-'rēvd\ adj : grieving the death of a loved one ⟨her ~ family⟩ — **be·reave·ment** n

²**bereaved** n, pl **bereaved** : one who is bereaved

be·reft \-'reft\ adj **1** ♦ : deprived of or lacking something — usu. used with of **2** : grieving the death of a loved one : BEREAVED

♦ destitute, devoid, void

be·ret \bə-'rā\ n : a round soft cap with no visor

berg \'bərg\ n : ICEBERG

beri·beri \,ber-ē-'ber-ē\ n : a deficiency disease marked by weakness, wasting, and nerve damage and caused by lack of thiamine

berke·li·um \'bər-klē-əm\ n : an artificially prepared radioactive chemical element

berm \'bərm\ n : a narrow shelf or path at the top or bottom of a slope; also : a mound or bank of earth

Ber·mu·das \bər-'myü-dəz\ n pl : BERMUDA SHORTS

Bermuda shorts n pl : knee-length walking shorts

ber·ry \'ber-ē\ n, pl **berries 1** : a small pulpy fruit (as a strawberry) **2** : a simple fruit (as a grape, tomato, or banana) with the wall of the ripened ovary thick and pulpy **3** : the dry seed of some plants (as coffee)

¹**ber·serk** \bər-'sərk, -'zərk\ adj : FRENZIED, CRAZED

²**berserk** adv ♦ : in a berserk manner

♦ amok, frantically, harum-scarum, hectically, helter-skelter, madly, pell-mell, wild, wildly

¹**berth** \'bərth\ n **1** : adequate distance esp. for a ship to maneuver **2** : the place where a ship is anchored or a vehicle rests **3** : ACCOMMODATIONS **4** : an employment for which one has been hired : JOB, POSITION

²**berth** vb **1** : to bring or come into a berth **2** : to allot a berth to

ber·yl \'ber-əl\ n : a hard silicate mineral occurring as green, yellow, pink, or white crystals

be·ryl·li·um \bə-'ri-lē-əm\ n : a light strong metallic chemical element used as a hardener in alloys

be·seech \bi-'sēch\ vb **-sought** \-'sót\ or **-seeched; -seech·ing** ♦ : to beg earnestly or urgently : ENTREAT

♦ appeal, beg, entreat, implore, importune, petition, plead, pray, solicit, supplicate

be·seem \bi-'sēm\ vb, archaic : BEFIT

be·set \-'set\ vb **-set; -set·ting 1** : TROUBLE, HARASS **2 a** ♦ : to set upon : ASSAIL ⟨~ by wild dogs⟩ **b** : SURROUND

♦ assail, assault, attack, charge, descend, jump, pounce (on or upon), raid, rush, storm, strike

be·set·ting adj : persistently present

¹**be·side** \bi-'sīd\ prep **1** : by the side of ⟨sit ~ me⟩ **2** : BESIDES: as **a** : other than **b** : together with **3** : not relevant to

²**beside** adv, archaic : BESIDES

¹**be·sides** \bi-'sīdz\ prep **1** ♦ : other than **2** : together with

♦ aside from, bar, barring, but, except, outside (of), save

²**besides** adv **1** : as well : ALSO **2** ♦ : in addition to what precedes : MOREOVER

♦ additionally, again, also, further, furthermore, likewise, more, moreover, then, too, withal, yet

be·siege \bi-'sēj\ vb **1** ♦ : to lay siege to **2** : to press with requests — **be·sieg·er** n

♦ barricade, block, cut off, dam, encircle, surround

be·smear \-'smir\ vb : to spread with something oily, thick, or sticky : SMEAR

be·smirch \-'smərch\ vb ♦ : to make soiled or tarnished : SMIRCH, SOIL

♦ befoul, begrime, blacken, dirty, foul, grime, mire, muddy, smirch, soil, stain

be·som \'bē-zəm\ *n* : BROOM

be·sot \bi-'sät\ *vb* **be·sot·ted; be·sot·ting** **1** : INFATUATE **2** : to make dull esp. by drinking

be·spat·ter \-'spa-tər\ *vb* : to splash with or as if with a liquid : SPATTER

be·speak \bi-'spēk\ *vb* **-spoke** \-'spōk\; **-spo·ken** \-'spō-kən\; **-speak·ing** **1** : to hire, engage, or claim beforehand : PREAR-RANGE **2** : ADDRESS **3** : REQUEST **4 ♦** : to be a sign or indication of ⟨~s considerable practice⟩ **5** : FORETELL

♦ betray, demonstrate, display, evince, expose, give away, manifest, reveal, show

be·sprin·kle \-'sprin-kəl\ *vb* : SPRINKLE

¹best \'best\ *adj, superlative of* GOOD **1** : excelling all others ⟨the ~ student⟩ **2** : most productive (as of good or satisfaction) **3** : LARGEST, MOST

²best *adv, superlative of* WELL **1** : in the best way **2** : MOST

³best *n* **1 ♦** : something that is best **2 ♦** : best clothes ⟨Sunday ~⟩

♦ [1] choice, cream, elect, elite, fat, flower, pick, prime ♦ [2] array, bravery, caparison, feather, finery, frippery, full dress, gaiety, regalia

⁴best *vb* **♦** : to get the better of

♦ beat, defeat, master, overcome, prevail, triumph, trounce, wallop, whip, win

best friend *n* : one's closest and dearest friend

bes·tial \'bes-chəl\ *adj* **1** : of or relating to beasts **2** : resembling a beast esp. in brutality or lack of intelligence

bes·ti·al·i·ty \,bes-chē-'a-lə-tē, ,bēs-\ *n, pl* **-ties** **1** : the condition or status of a lower animal **2** : display or gratification of bestial traits or impulses

bes·ti·ary \'bes-chē-,er-ē\ *n, pl* **-ar·ies** : a medieval allegorical or moralizing work on the appearance and habits of animals

best·ie \'be-stē\ *n* : BEST FRIEND

be·stir \bi-'stər\ *vb* : to rouse to action

best man *n* : the principal groomsman at a wedding

be·stow \bi-'stō\ *vb* **1** : PUT, PLACE, STOW **2 ♦** : to present as a gift

♦ contribute, donate, give, present

be·stow·al *n* **♦** : something bestowed or given

♦ donation, freebie, gift, lagniappe, present

be·stride \bi-'strīd\ *vb* **-strode** \-'strōd\; **-strid·den** \-'strid-ᵊn\; **-strid·ing** : to ride, sit, or stand astride

¹bet \'bet\ *n* **1 a** : something that is wagered, risked, or pledged usu. between two parties on the outcome of a contest **b** : the making of such a bet **2** : OPTION ⟨the back road is your best ~⟩

²bet *vb* **bet** *also* **bet·ted; bet·ting** **1 ♦** : to stake on the outcome of an issue or a contest ⟨~ $2 on the race⟩ **2** : to make a bet with **3** : to lay a bet

♦ gamble, go, lay, stake, wager

³bet *abbr* between

be·ta \'bā-tə\ *n* **1** : the 2d letter of the Greek alphabet — B or β **2** : a nearly complete version of a new product (as computer software)

beta–block·er \-,blä-kər\ *n* : any of a group of drugs that decrease the rate and force of heart contractions and lower high blood pressure

be·ta·car·o·tene \-'kar-ə-,tēn\ *n* : an isomer of carotene found in dark green and dark yellow vegetables and fruits

be·take \bi-'tāk\ *vb* **-took** \-'tùk\; **-tak·en** \-'tā-kən\; **-tak·ing** : to cause (oneself) to go

beta particle *n* : a high-speed electron; *esp* : one emitted by a radioactive nucleus

beta ray *n* **1** : BETA PARTICLE **2** : a stream of beta particles

beta test *n* : a field test of the beta version of a product prior to commercial release

be·tel \'bēt-ᵊl\ *n* : a climbing pepper of southeastern Asia whose leaves are chewed together with lime and betel nut as a stimulant

betel nut *n* : the astringent seed of an Asian palm that is chewed with betel leaves

bête noire \,bet-'nwär, ,bāt-\ *n, pl* **bêtes noires** *same or* -'nwärz\ **♦** : a person or thing strongly disliked, avoided, or feared

♦ bogey, bugbear, hobgoblin, ogre ♦ abhorrence, abomination, anathema, antipathy, aversion, hate

beth·el \'be-thəl\ *n* : a place of worship esp. for seamen

be·tide \bi-'tīd\ *vb* **♦** : to happen to

♦ be, befall, chance, come, go, happen, occur, pass, transpire

be·times \bi-'tīmz\ *adv* : in good time : EARLY

be·to·ken \bi-'tō-kən\ *vb* **1** : PRESAGE **2 ♦** : to give evidence of

♦ display, disport, exhibit, expose, flash, flaunt, parade, show, show off, sport, strut, unveil

be·tray \bi-'trā\ *vb* **1** : to lead astray; *esp* : SEDUCE **2** : to deliver to an enemy **3** : ABANDON **4** : to prove unfaithful to **5 ♦** : to reveal unintentionally; *also* : SHOW

♦ bespeak, demonstrate, display, evince, expose, give away, manifest, reveal, show

be·tray·al *n* **♦** : the act of betraying or fact of being betrayed

♦ disloyalty, double cross, faithlessness, falseness, falsity, infidelity, perfidy, treachery, treason, unfaithfulness

be·tray·er *n* **♦** : one who betrays (something or someone)

♦ blabbermouth, informer, rat, snitch, stool pigeon, tattler, tattletale ♦ apostate, double-crosser, quisling, recreant, traitor, turncoat

be·troth \bi-'trōth, -'trȯth\ *vb* : to promise to marry

be·troth·al *n* **♦** : the act of betrothing or fact of being betrothed; *also* : a mutual promise or contract for a future marriage

♦ engagement, espousal, troth

be·trothed *n* **♦** : the person to whom one is betrothed

♦ intended

¹bet·ter \'be-tər\ *adj, comparative of* GOOD **1** : greater than half **2** : improved in health **3** : more attractive, favorable, or commendable **4** : more advantageous or effective **5** : improved in accuracy or performance

²better *vb* **1 ♦** : to make or become better **2 ♦** : to surpass in excellence : EXCEL

♦ [1] ameliorate, amend, enhance, enrich, improve, perfect, refine ♦ [2] beat, eclipse, excel, outdistance, outdo, outshine, outstrip, surpass, top, transcend

³better *adv, comparative of* WELL **1** : in a superior manner **2** : to a higher or greater degree; *also* : MORE

⁴better *n* **1** : something better; *also* : a superior esp. in merit or rank **2** : superiority of position or condition : ADVANTAGE

⁵better *verbal auxiliary* : had better ⟨you ~ hurry⟩

better half *n* **♦** : the person to whom another is married : SPOUSE

♦ consort, mate, partner, spouse

bet·ter·ment \'be-tər-mənt\ *n* : IMPROVEMENT

bet·tor *or* **bet·ter** \'be-tər\ *n* : one that bets

¹be·tween \bi-'twēn\ *prep* **1** : by the common action of ⟨earned $10,000 ~ the two of them⟩ **2** : in the interval separating ⟨an alley ~ two buildings⟩; *also* : in intermediate relation to **3** : in point of comparison of ⟨choose ~ two cars⟩

²between *adv* : in an intervening space or interval

be·twixt \bi-'twikst\ *adv or prep* : BETWEEN

¹bev·el \'be-vəl\ *n* **1** : a device for adjusting the slant of the surfaces of a piece of work **2** : the angle or slant that one surface or line makes with another when not at right angles

²bevel *vb* **-eled** *or* **-elled; -el·ing** *or* **-el·ling** **1** : to cut or shape to a bevel **2** : INCLINE, SLANT

bev·er·age \'bev-rij\ *n* **♦** : a drinkable liquid

♦ drink, libation, quencher

bevy \'be-vē\ *n, pl* **bev·ies** **1** : a large group or collection **2** : a group of animals and esp. quail together

be·wail \bi-'wāl\ *vb* **♦** : to express deep sorrow for usu. by wailing and lamentation

♦ bemoan, deplore, grieve, lament, mourn, wail

be·ware \-'war\ *vb* **♦** : to be on one's guard : be wary of

♦ *usu* **beware of** guard (against), mind, watch out (for)

be·wil·der \bi-'wil-dər\ *vb* **♦** : to perplex or confuse esp. by complexity or variety

♦ addle, baffle, befog, befuddle, bemuse, confound, confuse, disorient, muddle, muddy, mystify, perplex, puzzle

be·wil·der·ment *n* **1 ♦** : the quality or state of being bewildered **2** : a bewildering tangle or confusion

♦ bafflement, confusion, distraction, muddle, mystification, perplexity, puzzlement, whirl

be·witch \-'wich\ *vb* **1 ♦** : to affect by witchcraft **2 ♦** : to attract as if by the power of witchcraft : CHARM, FASCINATE

♦ [1] charm, enchant, hex, spell ♦ [2] allure, beguile, captivate, charm, enchant, fascinate, wile

be·witch·ment *n* **1** ♦ : the act or power of bewitching; *also* : a spell that bewitches **2** : the state of being bewitched

♦ charm, conjuration, enchantment, incantation, spell ♦ enchantment, magic, necromancy, sorcery, witchcraft, wizardry

bey \'bā\ *n* **1** : a former Turkish provincial governor **2** : the former native ruler of Tunis or Tunisia

¹**be·yond** \bē-'änd\ *adv* **1** ♦ : on or to the farther side **2** : BESIDES

♦ farther, further, yonder

²**beyond** *prep* **1** : at a greater distance than **2** ♦ : past the reach or sphere of **3** : BESIDES

♦ outside, without *Ant* within

be·zel \'bē-zəl, 'be-\ *n* **1** : a rim that holds a transparent covering (as on a watch) **2** : the faceted part of a cut gem that rises above the setting

bf *abbr* boldface

BFF *abbr* best friends forever

BG *or* **B Gen** *abbr* brigadier general

Bh *symbol* bohrium

bhang \'baŋ\ *n* : a mildly intoxicating preparation of the leaves and flowering tops of uncultivated hemp

Bi *symbol* bismuth

BIA *abbr* Bureau of Indian Affairs

bi·an·nu·al \(ˌ)bī-'an-yə-wəl\ *adj* : occurring twice a year — **bi·an·nu·al·ly** *adv*

¹**bi·as** \'bī-əs\ *n* **1** : a line diagonal to the grain of a fabric **2** ♦ : a personal and sometimes unreasoned judgment : PREJUDICE

♦ favor (*or* favour), partiality, partisanship, prejudice *Ant* impartiality, neutrality, objectivity

²**bias** *adv* : on the bias : DIAGONALLY

³**bias** *vb* **bi·ased** *or* **bi·assed; bi·as·ing** *or* **bi·as·sing** : to give a settled and often prejudiced outlook to : PREJUDICE

bi·ased *adj* ♦ : exhibiting or characterized by bias

♦ one-sided, partial, partisan, prejudiced

bi·ath·lon \bī-'ath-lən, -ˌlän\ *n* : a composite athletic contest consisting of cross-country skiing and target shooting with a rifle

¹**bib** \'bib\ *n* : a cloth or plastic shield tied under the chin to protect the clothes while eating

²**bib** *abbr* Bible; biblical

bi·be·lot \'bē-bə-ˌlō\ *n, pl* **bibelots** *same or* -ˌlōz\ : a small household ornament or decorative object

bi·ble \'bī-bəl\ *n* **1** *cap* : the sacred scriptures of Christians comprising the Old and New Testaments **2** *cap* : the sacred scriptures of Judaism; *also* : those of some other religion **3** : a publication that is considered authoritative for its subject — **bib·li·cal** \'bi-bli-kəl\ *adj*

bib·li·og·ra·phy \ˌbi-blē-'ä-grə-fē\ *n, pl* **-phies** **1** : the history or description of writings or publications **2** : a list of writings (as on a subject or of an author) — **bib·li·og·ra·pher** \-fər\ *n* — **bib·li·o·graph·ic** \-ə-'gra-fik\ *also* **bib·li·o·graph·i·cal** \-fi-kəl\ *adj*

bib·lio·phile \'bi-blē-ə-ˌfīl\ *n* : a lover of books

bib·u·lous \'bi-byə-ləs\ *adj* **1** : highly absorbent **2** : fond of alcoholic beverages

bi·cam·er·al \'bī-'ka-mə-rəl\ *adj* : having or consisting of two legislative branches

bicarb \(ˌ)bī-'kärb, 'bī-ˌ\ *n* : SODIUM BICARBONATE

bi·car·bon·ate \(ˌ)bī-'kär-bə-ˌnāt, -nət\ *n* : an acid carbonate

bi·cen·te·na·ry \ˌbī-sen-'te-nə-rē, bī-'sent-ᵊn-ˌer-ē\ *n* : BICENTENNIAL *adj*

bi·cen·ten·ni·al \ˌbī-sen-'te-nē-əl\ *n* : a 200th anniversary or its celebration — **bicentennial** *adj*

bi·ceps \'bī-ˌseps\ *n, pl* **biceps** *also* **bicepses** : a muscle (as in the front of the upper arm) having two points of origin

¹**bick·er** \'bi-kər\ *n* : petulant quarreling : ALTERCATION

²**bicker** *vb* ♦ : to engage in a petty quarrel

♦ argue, brawl, dispute, fall out, fight, hassle, quarrel, row, scrap, spat, squabble, wrangle

bick·er·er \'bi-kə-rər\ *n* : one who bickers

bi·coast·al \bī-'kōst-ᵊl\ *adj* : living or working on both the East and West coasts of the U.S.

bi·con·cave \ˌbī-(ˌ)kän-'kāv, (ˌ)bī-'kän-ˌkāv\ *adj* : concave on both sides

bi·con·vex \ˌbī-(ˌ)kän-'veks, (ˌ)bī-'kän-ˌveks\ *adj* : convex on both sides

bi·cus·pid \bī-'kəs-pəd\ *n* : PREMOLAR

¹**bi·cy·cle** \'bī-si-kəl\ *n* : a light 2-wheeled vehicle with a steering handle, saddle, and pedals

²**bicycle** *vb* **-cy·cled; -cy·cling** \-ˌsi-k(ə-)liŋ, -ˌsī-\ : to ride a bicycle — **bi·cy·cler** \-k(ə-)lər\ *n* — **bi·cy·clist** \-k(ə-)list\ *n*

¹**bid** \'bid\ *vb* **bade** \'bad, 'bād\ *or* **bid; bid·den** \'bid-ᵊn\ *or* **bid** *also* **bade; bid·ding** **1** ♦ : to issue an order to : COMMAND, ORDER **2** : INVITE **3** : to give expression to **4** : to make a bid : OFFER — **bid·der** *n*

♦ boss, charge, command, direct, enjoin, instruct, order, tell

²**bid** *n* **1** : the act of one who bids; *also* : an offer for something **2** : INVITATION **3** : an announcement in a card game of what a player proposes to accomplish **4** ♦ : an attempt to win or gain ⟨a ∼ for mayor⟩

♦ attempt, crack, endeavor (*or* endeavour), essay, fling, go, pass, shot, stab, trial, try, whack, whirl

bid·da·ble \'bi-də-bəl\ *adj* **1** : OBEDIENT, DOCILE **2** : capable of being bid

bid·dy \'bi-dē\ *n, pl* **biddies** : HEN; *also* : a young chicken

bide \'bīd\ *vb* **bode** \'bōd\ *or* **bid·ed; bided; bid·ing** **1** : to wait for **2** ♦ : to wait awhile : TARRY **3** : DWELL

♦ await, hold on, stay, tarry, wait

bi·det \bi-'dā\ *n* : a bathroom fixture used esp. for bathing the external genitals and the posterior parts of the body

bi·di·rec·tion·al \ˌbī-də-'rek-sh(ə-)nəl\ *adj* : involving, moving, or taking place in two usu. opposite directions — **bi·di·rec·tion·al·ly** *adv*

bi·en·ni·al \bī-'e-nē-əl\ *adj* **1** : taking place once in two years **2** : lasting two years **3** : producing leaves the first year and fruiting and dying the second year — **biennial** *n* — **bi·en·ni·al·ly** *adv*

bi·en·ni·um \bī-'e-nē-əm\ *n, pl* **-niums** *or* **-nia** \-ə-\ : a period of two years

bier \'bir\ *n* : a stand bearing a coffin or corpse

bi·fo·cal \'bī-ˌfō-kəl\ *adj* : having two focal lengths

bifocals \-kəlz\ *n pl* : eyeglasses with lenses that have one part that corrects for near vision and one for distant vision

bi·fur·cate \'bī-fər-ˌkāt, bī-'fər-\ *vb* **-cat·ed; -cat·ing** : to divide into two branches or parts — **bi·fur·ca·tion** \ˌbī-fər-'kā-shən\ *n*

big \'big\ *adj* **big·ger; big·gest** **1** ♦ : large in size, amount, or scope **2** : PREGNANT; *also* : SWELLING **3** ♦ : of great importance or significance : IMPORTANT **4** ♦ : POPULAR

♦ [1] bumper, considerable, goodly, grand, great, large, sizable, substantial, voluminous ♦ [3] consequential, eventful, important, major, material, meaningful, momentous, significant, substantial, weighty

big·a·my \'bi-gə-mē\ *n* : the act of marrying one person while still legally married to another — **big·a·mist** \-mist\ *n* — **big·a·mous** \-məs\ *adj*

big bang theory *n* : a theory in astronomy: the universe originated in an explosion (**big bang**) from a single point of nearly infinite energy density

big brother *n* **1** : an older brother **2** : a man who serves as a friend, father figure, or role model for a boy **3** *cap both Bs* : the leader of an authoritarian state or movement **4** : a powerful government organization that watches people and controls their actions

Big Dipper *n* : the seven principal stars of Ursa Major in a form resembling a dipper

big·foot \'big-ˌfut\ *n* : SASQUATCH

big·horn \'big-ˌhorn\ *n, pl* **bighorn** *or* **bighorns** : a wild sheep of mountainous western No. America

bight \'bīt\ *n* **1** ♦ : a curve in a coast; *also* : the bay formed by such a curve **2** : a slack part in a rope

♦ bay, cove, estuary, fjord, gulf, inlet

big leaguer *n* ♦ : one who operates at the top rank of an activity or enterprise

♦ big shot, bigwig, kingpin, nabob, nawab, wheel

big–name \'big-ˌnām\ *adj* : widely popular ⟨a ∼ performer⟩ — **big name** *n*

big·ness *n* ♦ : quality or state of being big

♦ grandness, greatness, largeness

big·ot \'bi-gət\ *n* : one intolerantly devoted to his or her own prejudices or opinions — **big·ot·ry** \-trē\ *n*

big·ot·ed \-gə-təd\ *adj* ♦ : obstinately and blindly attached to some creed, opinion, or practice

♦ intolerant, narrow, narrow-minded, prejudiced

big shot \'big-ˌshät\ *n* ♦ : an important person

♦ big leaguer, bigwig, kingpin, nabob, nawab, wheel *Ant* lightweight, nobody, nonentity, nothing, shrimp, twerp, whippersnapper, zero, zilch

big sister *n* **1 :** an older sister **2 :** a woman who serves as a friend, mother figure, and role model for a girl

big time \-ˌtīm\ *n* **1 :** a high-paying vaudeville circuit requiring only two performances a day **2 :** the top rank of an activity or enterprise — **big–tim•er** *n*

big top *n* **1 :** the main tent of a circus **2 :** CIRCUS

big•wig \'big-ˌwig\ *n* ♦ **:** an important person

  ♦ big shot, big leaguer, kingpin, nabob, nawab, wheel

bike \'bīk\ *n* **1 :** BICYCLE **2 :** MOTORCYCLE

bik•er *n* **:** MOTORCYCLIST; *esp* **:** one who is a member of an organized gang

bike•way \'bīk-ˌwā\ *n* **:** a thoroughfare for bicycles

bi•ki•ni \bə-'kē-nē\ *n* **:** a woman's brief 2-piece bathing suit

bi•lat•er•al \bī-'la-tə-rəl\ *adj* **1 :** having or involving two sides **2 :** affecting reciprocally two sides or parties — **bi•lat•er•al•ly** *adv*

bile \'bīl\ *n* **1 :** a bitter greenish fluid secreted by the liver that aids in the digestion of fats **2** ♦ **:** an ill-humored mood

  ♦ acidity, acrimony, asperity, bitterness, cattiness, tartness, virulence, vitriol

bilge \'bilj\ *n* **1 :** the part of a ship that lies between the bottom and the point where the sides go straight up **2 :** stale or worthless remarks or ideas

bi•lin•gual \bī-'liŋ-gwəl\ *adj* **:** expressed in, knowing, or using two languages

bil•ious \'bil-yəs\ *adj* **1 :** marked by or suffering from disordered liver function **2** ♦ **:** of or indicative of a peevish ill-natured disposition **:** ILL-TEMPERED ⟨a ∼ disposition⟩

  ♦ bearish, cantankerous, disagreeable, dyspeptic, ill-humored, ill-tempered, ornery, splenetic, surly

bil•ious•ness *n* ♦ **:** an ill-natured disposition

  ♦ grumpiness, irritability, peevishness, perverseness, perversity

bilk \'bilk\ *vb* **:** CHEAT, SWINDLE

¹bill \'bil\ *n* **1 :** the jaws of a bird together with their horny covering; *also* **:** a mouth structure (as of a turtle) resembling these **2 :** the visor of a cap or hood — **billed** \'bild\ *adj*

²bill *vb* **:** to caress fondly

³bill *n* **1** ♦ **:** an itemized statement of particulars; *also* **:** INVOICE **2 :** a written document or note **3** ♦ **:** a printed advertisement (as a poster) announcing an event **4 :** a draft of a law presented to a legislature for enactment **5 :** a written statement of a legal wrong suffered or of some breach of law **6 :** a piece of paper money

  ♦ [1] account, check, invoice, statement, tab ♦ [3] placard, poster

⁴bill *vb* **1 :** to enter in or prepare a bill; *also* **:** to submit a bill or account to **2 :** to advertise by bills or posters

bill•board \-ˌbōrd\ *n* **:** a flat surface on which advertising bills are posted

¹bil•let \'bi-lət\ *n* **1 :** an order requiring a person to provide lodging for a soldier; *also* **:** quarters assigned by or as if by such an order **2** ♦ **:** a regular paying position **:** APPOINTMENT

  ♦ appointment, capacity, function, job, place, position, post, situation

²billet *vb* ♦ **:** to assign lodging to by billet

  ♦ accommodate, chamber, domicile, harbor (*or* harbour), house, lodge, put up, quarter, roof, shelter, take in

bil•let–doux \ˌbi-lā-'dü\ *n, pl* **billets–doux** *same or* -'düz\ **:** a love letter

bill•fold \'bil-ˌfōld\ *n* **:** WALLET

bil•liards \'bil-yərdz\ *n* **:** any of several games played on an oblong table by driving balls against each other or into pockets with a cue

bil•lings•gate \'bi-liŋz-ˌgāt, *Brit usu* -git\ *n* **:** coarsely abusive language

bil•lion \'bil-yən\ *n* **1 :** a thousand millions **2** *Brit* **:** a million millions — **billion** *adj* — **bil•lionth** \-yənth\ *adj or n*

¹bil•low \'bi-lō\ *n* **1** ♦ **:** a moving ridge or swell on the surface of a liquid **:** WAVE; *esp* **:** a great wave **2 :** a rolling mass (as of fog or flame) like a great wave — **bil•lowy** \'bi-lə-wē\ *adj*

  ♦ surge, swell, wave

²billow *vb* **1 :** to rise and roll in waves **2** ♦ **:** to swell out ⟨∼*ing* sails⟩

  ♦ balloon, beetle, belly, bulge, overhang, poke, project, protrude, start, stick out

bil•ly \'bi-lē\ *n, pl* **billies :** a heavy usu. wooden club **:** BILLY CLUB

billy club *n* ♦ **:** a heavy usu. wooden club; *esp* **:** a police officer's club

  ♦ bat, bludgeon, club, cudgel, nightstick, staff, truncheon

bil•ly goat \'bi-lē-\ *n* **:** a male goat

bi•met•al \'bī-ˌmet-ᵊl\ *adj* **:** BIMETALLIC — **bimetal** *n*

bi•me•tal•lic \ˌbī-mə-'ta-lik\ *adj* **:** made of two different metals — often used of devices having a bonded expansive part — **bimetallic** *n*

bi•met•al•lism \bī-'met-ᵊl-ˌi-zəm\ *n* **:** the use of two metals at fixed ratios to form a standard of value for a monetary system

¹bi•month•ly \bī-'mənth-lē\ *adj* **1 :** occurring every two months **2 :** occurring twice a month **:** SEMIMONTHLY — **bimonthly** *adv*

²bimonthly *n* **:** a bimonthly publication

bin \'bin\ *n* ♦ **:** a box, crib, or enclosure used for storage

  ♦ box, caddy, case, casket, chest, locker, trunk

bi•na•ry \'bī-nə-rē, -ˌner-ē\ *adj* **1 :** consisting of two things or parts **2 :** relating to, being, or belonging to a system of numbers having 2 as its base ⟨the ∼ digits 0 and 1⟩ **3 :** involving a choice between or condition of two alternatives only (as on-off, yes-no) — **binary** *n*

  ♦ bipartite, double, dual, duplex, twin

binary star *n* **:** a system of two stars revolving around each other

bin•au•ral \bī-'nȯr-əl\ *adj* **:** of or relating to sound reproduction involving the use of two separated microphones and two transmission channels to achieve a stereophonic effect

bind \'bīnd\ *vb* **bound** \'baȯnd\; **bind•ing 1 a :** to make secure by tying **b :** to restrain as if by tying **2 :** to put under an obligation; *also* **:** to constrain with legal authority **3 :** to dress or cover with a bandage **4** ♦ **:** to unite into a mass **5 :** to compel as if by a pledge ⟨a handshake ∼*s* the deal⟩ **6 :** to strengthen or decorate with a band **7 :** to fasten together and enclose in a cover ⟨∼ books⟩ **8 :** to exert a tying, restraining, or compelling effect — **bind•er** *n*

  ♦ band, gird, tie, truss

bind•ing \'bīn-diŋ\ *n* **:** something (as a ski fastening, a book cover, or an edging fabric) used to bind

¹binge \'binj\ *n* ♦ **:** an unrestrained and often excessive indulgence **:** SPREE

  ♦ fling, frolic, gambol, lark, revel, rollick, romp

²binge *vb* **binged; binge•ing** *or* **bing•ing :** to go on a binge and esp. an eating binge — **bing•er** *n*

bin•go \'biŋ-gō\ *n, pl* **bingos :** a game of chance played with cards having numbered squares corresponding to numbered balls drawn at random and won by covering five squares in a row

bin•na•cle \'bi-ni-kəl\ *n* **:** a container holding a ship's compass

¹bin•oc•u•lar \bī-'nä-kyə-lər, bə-\ *adj* **:** of, relating to, or adapted to the use of both eyes — **bin•oc•u•lar•ly** *adv*

²bin•oc•u•lar \bə-'nä-kyə-lər, bī-\ *n* **1 :** a binocular optical instrument (as a microscope) **2 :** a handheld optical instrument composed of two telescopes and a focusing device — usu. used in pl.

bi•no•mi•al \bī-'nō-mē-əl\ *n* **1 :** a mathematical expression consisting of two terms connected by the sign plus (+) or minus (−) **2 :** a biological species name consisting of two terms — **binomial** *adj*

bio•chem•is•try \ˌbī-ō-'ke-mə-strē\ *n* **:** chemistry that deals with the chemical compounds and processes occurring in living things — **bio•chem•i•cal** \-mi-kəl\ *adj or n* — **bio•chem•ist** \-mist\ *n*

bio•de•grad•able \-di-'grā-də-bəl\ *adj* **:** capable of being broken down esp. into innocuous products by the actions of living things (as microorganisms) ⟨a ∼ detergent⟩ — **bio•de•grad•abil•i•ty** \-ˌgrā-də-'bi-lə-tē\ *n* — **bio•deg•ra•da•tion** \-ˌde-grə-'dā-shən\ *n* — **bio•de•grade** \-di-'grād\ *vb*

bio•di•ver•si•ty \-də-'vər-sə-tē, -dī-\ *n* **:** biological diversity in an environment as indicated by numbers of different species of plants and animals

bio•en•gi•neer•ing *n* **1 :** the application of engineering principles to medicine and biology **2 :** GENETIC ENGINEERING

bio•eth•ics \-'e-thiks\ *n* **:** the ethics of biological research and its applications esp. in medicine — **bio•eth•i•cal** \-'e-thi-kəl\ *adj* — **bio•eth•i•cist** \-'e-thə-sist\ *n*

bio•feed•back \-'fēd-ˌbak\ *n* **:** the technique of making unconscious or involuntary bodily processes (as heartbeats or brain waves) objectively perceptible to the senses (as by use of an oscilloscope) in order to manipulate them by conscious mental control

biog *abbr* biographer; biographical; biography

bio•ge•og•ra•phy \ˌbī-ō-jē-'ä-grə-fē\ *n* **:** a science that deals with the geographic distribution of plants and animals — **bio•ge•og•ra•pher** *n*

bi•og•ra•phy \bī-'ä-grə-fē, bē-\ *n, pl* **-phies :** a written history of a person's life; *also* **:** such writings in general — **bi•og•ra•pher** *n*

— **bi·o·graph·i·cal** \ˌbī-ə-'gra-fi-kəl\ *also* **bi·o·graph·ic** \-fik\ *adj*

biol *abbr* biologic; biological; biologist; biology

bi·o·log·i·cal \ˌbī-ə-'lä-ji-kəl\ *also* **bi·o·log·ic** \-jik\ *adj* **1** : of, relating to, or produced by biology or life and living processes **2** : related by direct genetic relationship rather than by adoption or marriage ⟨∼ parents⟩ — **bi·o·log·i·cal·ly** \-ji-k(ə-)le\ *adv*

biological clock *n* : an inherent timing mechanism in a living system that is inferred to exist in order to explain the timing of various physiological and behavioral states and processes

biological warfare *n* : warfare in which harmful living organisms (**biological weapons**) are used against an enemy esp. to cause large-scale death and disease

bi·ol·o·gy \bī-'ä-lə-jē\ *n* **1** : a science that deals with living beings and life processes **2** : the life processes of an organism or group — **bi·ol·o·gist** \bī-'ä-lə-jist\ *n*

bio·mass \'bī-ō-ˌmas\ *n* **1** : the amount of living matter (as in a unit area) **2** : plant materials and animal waste used esp. as fuel

bio·med·i·cal \ˌbī-ō-'me-di-kəl\ *adj* : of, relating to, or involving biological, medical, and physical science

bi·on·ic \bī-'ä-nik\ *adj* : having normal biological capability or performance enhanced by or as if by electronic or mechanical devices

bio·phys·ics \ˌbī-ō-'fi-ziks\ *n* : a branch of science concerned with the application of physical principles and methods to biological problems — **bio·phys·i·cal** \-zi-kəl\ *adj* — **bio·phys·i·cist** \-'fi-zə-sist\ *n*

bi·op·sy \'bī-ˌäp-sē\ *n, pl* **-sies** : the removal of tissue, cells, or fluids from the living body for examination — **biopsy** *vb*

bio·rhythm \'bī-ō-ˌri-thəm\ *n* : an innately determined rhythmic biological process (as sleep); *also* : the internal mechanism controlling such a process

bio·sphere \'bī-ə-ˌsfir\ *n* **1** : the part of the world in which life can exist **2** : living beings together with their environment

bio·tech \'bī-ō-ˌtek\ *n* : BIOTECHNOLOGY

bio·tech·nol·o·gy \ˌbī-ō-tek-'nä-lə-jē\ *n* : biological science when applied esp. in genetic engineering and recombinant DNA technology

bio·ter·ror·ism \-'ter-ər-ˌi-zəm\ *n* : terrorism involving the use of biological weapons

bi·ot·ic \bī-'ä-tik\ *adj* : of or relating to life; *esp* : caused by living beings

bi·o·tin \'bī-ə-tən\ *n* : a vitamin of the vitamin B complex found esp. in yeast, liver, and egg yolk and active in growth promotion

bi·o·tite \'bī-ə-ˌtīt\ *n* : a dark mica containing iron, magnesium, potassium, and aluminum

bi·par·ti·san \bī-'pär-tə-zən\ *adj* : marked by or involving cooperation, agreement, and compromise between two major political parties — **bi·par·ti·san·ship** \-ˌship\ *n*

bi·par·tite \-'pär-ˌtīt\ *adj* **1** ♦ : being in two parts **2** : shared by two ⟨∼ treaty⟩

♦ binary, double, dual, duplex, twin

bi·ped \'bī-ˌped\ *n* : a 2-footed animal — **bi·ped·al** \(ˌ)bī-'ped-əl\ *adj*

bi·plane \'bī-ˌplān\ *n* : an aircraft with two wings placed one above the other

bi·po·lar \bī-'pō-lər\ *adj* : having or involving the use of two poles — **bi·po·lar·i·ty** \ˌbī-pō-'lar-ə-tē\ *n*

bipolar disorder *n* : any of several psychological disorders of mood characterized by usu. alternating episodes of depression and mania

bi·ra·cial \bī-'rā-shəl\ *adj* : of, relating to, or involving members of two races

¹**birch** \'bərch\ *n* **1** : any of a genus of mostly short-lived deciduous shrubs and trees with membranous outer bark and close-grained wood; *also* : this wood **2** : a birch rod or bundle of twigs for flogging — **birch** *or* **birch·en** \'bər-chən\ *adj*

²**birch** *vb* : to beat with or as if with a birch : WHIP

¹**bird** \'bərd\ *n* : any of a class of warm-blooded egg-laying vertebrates having the body feathered and the forelimbs modified to form wings

²**bird** *vb* : to observe or identify wild birds in their native habitat — **bird·er** *n*

bird·bath \'bərd-ˌbath, -ˌbath\ *n* : a usu. ornamental basin set up for birds to bathe in

bird·house \-ˌhaus\ *n* : an artificial nesting place for birds; *also* : AVIARY

bird·ie \'bər-dē\ *n* : a score of one under par on a hole in golf

bird·lime \-ˌlīm\ *n* : a sticky substance smeared on twigs to snare small birds

bird of prey : a carnivorous bird (as a hawk, falcon, or vulture) that feeds wholly or chiefly on meat taken by hunting or on carrion

bird·seed \'bərd-ˌsēd\ *n* : a mixture of small seeds (as of hemp or millet) used for feeding birds

bird's-eye \'bərdz-ˌī\ *adj* **1** : marked with spots resembling birds' eyes ⟨∼ maple⟩ **2 a** : seen from above as if by a flying bird ⟨∼ view⟩ **b** ♦ : having or involving a bird's-eye view : CURSORY

♦ broad, cursory, general, nonspecific, overall

bi·ret·ta \bə-'re-tə\ *n* : a square cap with three ridges on top worn esp. by Roman Catholic clergymen

birth \'bərth\ *n* **1** : the act or fact of being born or of bringing forth young **2** ♦ : descent in a line from a common progenitor : LINEAGE **3** ♦ : rise, beginning, or derivation from a source

♦ [2] ancestry, blood, bloodline, breeding, descent, extraction, family tree, genealogy, line, lineage, origin, parentage, pedigree, stock, strain ♦ [3] beginning, commencement, dawn, genesis, launch, morning, onset, outset, start, threshold

birth canal *n* : the channel formed by the cervix, vagina, and vulva through which the fetus passes during birth

birth control *n* : control of the number of children born esp. by preventing or lessening the frequency of conception

birth·day \'bərth-ˌdā\ *n* : the day or anniversary of one's birth

birth defect *n* : a physical or biochemical defect present at birth and inherited or environmentally induced

birth·mark \'bərth-ˌmärk\ *n* : an unusual mark or blemish on the skin at birth

birth·place \-ˌplās\ *n* ♦ : place of birth or origin

♦ cradle, home

birth·rate \-ˌrāt\ *n* : the number of births per number of individuals in a given area or group during a given time

birth·right \-ˌrīt\ *n* ♦ : a right, privilege, or possession to which one is entitled by birth

♦ prerogative, right

birth·stone \-ˌstōn\ *n* : a gemstone associated symbolically with the month of one's birth

bis·cuit \'bis-kət\ *n* **1** : a crisp flat cake; *esp, Brit* : CRACKER 2 **2** : a small quick bread made from dough that has been rolled and cut or dropped from a spoon

bi·sect \'bī-ˌsekt\ *vb* : to divide into two usu. equal parts; *also* : CROSS, INTERSECT — **bi·sec·tion** \'bī-ˌsek-shən\ *n* — **bi·sec·tor** \-tər\ *n*

bi·sex·u·al \bī-'sek-shə-wəl\ *adj* **1** : possessing characters of both sexes **2** : of, relating to, or characterized by sexual or romantic attraction to both sexes **3** : of, relating to, or involving both sexes — **bisexual** *n* — **bi·sex·u·al·i·ty** \ˌbī-ˌsek-shə-'wal-ə-tē\ *n*

bish·op \'bi-shəp\ *n* **1** : a member of the clergy ranking above a priest and typically governing a diocese **2** : any of various Protestant church officials who superintend other clergy **3** : a chess piece that can move diagonally across any number of adjoining unoccupied squares

bish·op·ric \'bi-shə-prik\ *n* **1** : DIOCESE **2** : the office of bishop

bis·muth \'biz-məth\ *n* : a heavy brittle grayish white metallic chemical element used in alloys and medicine

bi·son \'bīs-ᵊn, 'bīz-\ *n, pl* **bison** : BUFFALO 2

bisque \'bisk\ *n* : a thick cream soup

bis·tro \'bēs-trō, 'bis-\ *n, pl* **bistros** **1** : a small or unpretentious restaurant **2** : BAR; *also* : NIGHTCLUB

¹**bit** \'bit\ *n* **1** : the biting or cutting edge or part of a tool **2** : the part of a bridle that is placed in a horse's mouth

²**bit** *n* **1 a** : a morsel of food **b** ♦ : a small piece or quantity of something **2** : a small coin; *also* : a unit of value equal to 12½ cents **3** : SOMETHING small and trivial **4** ♦ : an indefinite usu. small degree or extent ⟨a ∼ tired⟩

♦ [1b] ace, crumb, dab, hint, lick, little, mite, nip, particle, shred, speck, spot, touch, trace ♦ [4] space, spell, stretch, while

³**bit** *n* : a unit of computer information equivalent to the result of a choice between two alternatives; *also* : its physical representation

¹**bitch** \'bich\ *n* **1** : a female canine; *esp* : a female dog **2** *often offensive* : a malicious, spiteful, and domineering woman **3** *informal* : something difficult or unpleasant

²**bitch** *vb* : COMPLAIN

¹**bite** \'bīt\ *vb* **bit** \'bit\; **bit·ten** \'bit-ᵊn\ *also* **bit**; **bit·ing** \'bī-tiŋ\ **1** : to grip with teeth or jaws; *also* : to wound or sting with or as if with fangs **2** : to cut or pierce with or as if with an edged instrument **3** : to cause to smart or sting **4** ♦ : to eat away by degrees as if by gnawing : CORRODE **5** : to take bait

♦ *usu* **bite on** [1] champ, chew, chomp, crunch, gnaw, nibble ♦ *usu* **bite at** [4] corrode, eat, erode, fret

²bite *n* **1** : the act or manner of biting **2** ♦ : a small amount of food **3 a** : a wound made by biting **b** ♦ : a penetrating effect or sensation

♦ [2] morsel, mouthful, nibble, taste, tidbit ♦ [3b] bitterness, harshness, pungency, sharpness, tartness

bit·ing \'bī-tiŋ\ *adj* ♦ : having the power to bite so as to cause physical or mental discomfort ⟨a ∼ wind⟩; *esp* : able to grip and impress deeply ⟨a ∼ wit⟩

♦ bitter, cutting, keen, penetrating, piercing, raw, sharp ♦ acute, agonizing, excruciating, sharp, smart ♦ acrid, caustic, cutting, mordant, pungent, sarcastic, satiric, scathing, sharp, tart

bit·mapped \'bit-ˌmapt\ *adj* : of, relating to, or being a digital image or display for which an array of binary data specifies the value of each pixel — **bit·map** \-ˌmap\ *n*

bit·ter \'bi-tər\ *adj* **1** : being or inducing the one of the basic taste sensations that is acrid, astringent, or disagreeable and is suggestive of hops **2** ♦ : marked by intensity or severity (as of distress or hatred) **3** ♦ : extremely harsh or cruel **4** ♦ : intensely unpleasant esp. in coldness or rawness

♦ [2] acrid, acrimonious, hard, rancorous, resentful, sore ♦ [3] agonizing, galling, harrowing, harsh, hurtful, painful, tortuous *Ant* gratifying, pleasing, sweet ♦ [3] brutal, burdensome, grim, hard, harsh, heavy, onerous, oppressive, severe, stiff, tough, trying ♦ [4] arctic, cold, freezing, frigid, frosty, glacial, icy, polar, raw, wintry

bit·ter·ly *adv* ♦ : in a bitter manner

♦ hard, sadly, sorrowfully, unhappily, wretchedly

bit·tern \'bi-tərn\ *n* : any of various small or medium-sized herons

bit·ter·ness *n* ♦ : the quality or state of being bitter; *also* : something that is bitter

♦ animosity, antagonism, antipathy, enmity, gall, grudge, hostility, rancor ♦ bite, harshness, pungency, sharpness, tartness

bit·ters \'bi-tərz\ *n sing or pl* : a usu. alcoholic solution of bitter and often aromatic plant products used in mixing drinks and as a mild tonic

¹bit·ter·sweet \'bi-tər-ˌswēt\ *n* **1** : a poisonous nightshade with purple flowers and orange-red berries **2** : a woody vine with yellow capsules that open when ripe and disclose scarlet seed coverings

²bittersweet *adj* : being at once both bitter and sweet

bi·tu·mi·nous coal \bə-'tü-mə-nəs-, bī-, -'tyü-\ *n* : a coal that when heated yields considerable volatile waste matter

bi·valve \'bī-ˌvalv\ *n* : any of a class of mollusks (as clams or scallops) with a shell composed of two separate parts that open and shut — **bivalve** *adj*

¹biv·ouac \'bi-və-ˌwak\ *n* ♦ : a temporary encampment or shelter

♦ camp, encampment

²bivouac *vb* **-ouacked; -ouack·ing** : to form a bivouac : CAMP

¹bi·week·ly \ˌbī-'wē-klē\ *adj* **1** : occurring twice a week **2** : occurring every two weeks : FORTNIGHTLY — **biweekly** *adv*

²biweekly *n* : a biweekly publication

bi·year·ly \-'yir-lē\ *adj* **1** : BIANNUAL **2** : BIENNIAL

bi·zarre \bə-'zär\ *adj* : strikingly out of the ordinary: as **a** ♦ : odd, extravagant, or eccentric in style or mode **b** ♦ : involving sensational contrasts or incongruities : FANTASTIC — **bi·zarre·ly** *adv*

♦ [a] curious, far-out, funny, odd, outlandish, peculiar, quaint, quirky, screwy, strange, weird ♦ [b] absurd, fanciful, fantastic, foolish, nonsensical, preposterous, unreal, wild

bi·zar·ro \bə-'zär-ō\ *adj* : characterized by a bizarre, fantastic, or unconventional approach ⟨a ∼ movie⟩

bk *abbr* **1** bank **2** book

Bk *symbol* berkelium

bkg *abbr* banking

bkgd *abbr* background

bks *abbr* barracks

bkt *abbr* **1** basket **2** bracket

bl *abbr* **1** bale **2** barrel **3** blue

blab \'blab\ *vb* **blabbed; blab·bing** **1** ♦ : to talk idly or thoughtlessly **2** : to reveal a secret esp. by indiscreet chatter : TATTLE, GOSSIP

♦ chat, converse, gab, jaw, palaver, patter, prattle, rattle, talk, visit

blab·ber·mouth \'bla-bər-ˌmaůth\ *n* ♦ : a person who talks too much; *esp* : TATTLETALE

♦ betrayer, informer, rat, snitch, stool pigeon, tattler, tattletale

blab·by \'bla-bē\ *adj* : given to talking

¹black \'blak\ *adj* **1** ♦ : of the color black; *also* : very dark **2** : having dark skin, hair, and eyes **3** *usu cap* : of or relating to any of various population groups esp. of African ancestry often considered as having dark pigmentation of the skin but in fact having a wide range of skin colors **4** *usu cap* : of or relating to Black people and often esp. to African American people or their culture **5** : SOILED, DIRTY ⟨hands ∼ with grime⟩ **6** : lacking light ⟨a ∼ night⟩ **7** : thoroughly sinister or evil : WICKED ⟨∼ magic⟩ **8** ♦ : very sad, gloomy, or calamitous : DISMAL ⟨a ∼ outlook⟩ **9** : SULLEN ⟨a ∼ mood⟩ — **black·ish** *adj* — **black·ly** *adv*

♦ [1] ebony, raven *Ant* white ♦ [8] bleak, dark, dismal, dreary, gloomy, gray (*or* grey), somber (*or* sombre), wretched

²black *n* **1** : a black pigment or dye; *also* : something (as clothing) that is black **2** : the characteristic color of soot or coal **3** *usu cap* : a person belonging to any of various population groups of esp. African ancestry often considered as having dark pigmentation of the skin but in fact having a wide range of skin colors — offensive in sing. **4** *usu cap* : AFRICAN AMERICAN — offensive in sing.

³black *vb* : BLACKEN

⁴black *n* ♦ : total or nearly total absence of light

♦ dark, darkness, dusk, gloaming, gloom, murk, night, semidarkness, shade, shadows, twilight

black–and–blue \ˌbla-kən-'blü\ *adj* : darkly discolored from blood effused by bruising

black·ball \'blak-ˌbȯl\ *vb* **1** ♦ : to vote against; *esp* : to exclude from membership by casting a negative vote **2** : OSTRACIZE — **black·ball** *n*

♦ kill, negative, veto

black bass *n* : any of several freshwater sunfishes native to eastern and central No. America

black bear *n* : a usu. black-furred bear of the No. American forests

¹black belt \'blak-ˌbelt\ *n, often cap both Bs* : an area densely populated by Black people

²black belt \-'belt\ *n* : one who holds the rating of expert (as in judo or karate); *also* : the rating itself

black·ber·ry \-ˌber-ē\ *n* : the usu. black or purple juicy but seedy edible fruit of various brambles; *also* : a plant bearing this fruit

black·bird \-ˌbərd\ *n* : any of various birds (as the red-winged blackbird) of which the male is largely or wholly black

black·board \-ˌbȯrd\ *n* : a smooth usu. dark surface used for writing or drawing on with chalk

black·body \-'bä-dē\ *n* : a body or surface that completely absorbs incident radiation with no reflection

black box *n* **1** : a usu. complicated electronic device whose components and workings are unknown or mysterious to the user **2** : a device used in aircraft to record cockpit conversations and flight data

black death *n* : an epidemic of bacterial plague and esp. bubonic plague that spread rapidly in Europe and Asia in the 14th century

black·en \'bla-kən\ *vb* **black·ened; black·en·ing** **1** ♦ : to make or become black or dark **2** ♦ : to speak evil of : DEFAME ⟨∼ed their reputation⟩

♦ [1] becloud, cloud, darken, dim, obscure, overcast, overshadow, shadow ♦ [1] befoul, begrime, besmirch, dirty, muddy, smirch, soil, stain ♦ [2] defame, libel, malign, slander, smear, traduce, vilify

black·ened *adj* : coated with spices and quickly seared in a very hot skillet ⟨∼ swordfish⟩

black eye *n* : a discoloration of the skin around the eye from bruising

black–eyed Su·san \ˌblak-ˌīd-'süz-ᵊn\ *n* : a coarse No. American plant that is related to the daisies and has deep yellow to orange flower heads with dark conical centers

Black·foot \'blak-ˌfůt\ *n, pl* **Black·feet** *or* **Blackfoot** : a member of an Algonquian-speaking Indigenous people of Montana, Alberta, and Saskatchewan

black·guard \'bla-gərd, -ˌgärd\ *n* : SCOUNDREL, RASCAL

black·head \'blak-ˌhed\ *n* : a small usu. dark oily mass plugging the outlet of a skin gland

black hole *n* : a hypothetical celestial object with a gravitational field so strong that light cannot escape from it

black ice *n* : a thin layer of ice on a paved road that is very difficult to see

black·ing \'bla-kiŋ\ *n* : a substance applied to something to make it black

¹black·jack \'blak-ˌjak\ *n* **1** : a leather-covered club with a flexible handle   **2 :** a card game in which the object is to be dealt cards having a higher count than the dealer but not exceeding 21

²blackjack \vb\ **:** to hit with or as if with a blackjack

black light n **:** invisible ultraviolet light

black•list \'blak-ˌlist\ n **:** a list of persons who are disapproved of and are to be punished or boycotted — **blacklist** vb

black•mail \'blak-ˌmāl\ n **:** extortion by threats esp. of public exposure; also **:** something so extorted — **blackmail** vb

black•mail•er n **:** one who blackmails another

black market n **:** illicit trade in goods; also **:** a place where such trade is carried on

Black Mass n **:** a travesty of the Christian mass ascribed to worshipers of Satan

Black Muslim n **:** a member of a chiefly Black group that professes Islamic religious belief

black nationalist n, often cap B&N **:** a member of a Black advocacy group esp. during the 1960's and 1970's that sought to empower Black people financially, promote a sense of Black community and identity, and form a separate self-governing Black nation — **black nationalism** n, often cap B&N

black•ness n **:** the quality or state of being black

black•out \'bla-ˌkau̇t\ n   **1 :** a period of darkness due to electrical power failure   **2 ♦ :** a transitory loss or dulling of vision or consciousness   **3 :** the prohibition or restriction of the telecasting of a sports event

♦ faint, knockout, swoon

black out vb ♦ **:** to temporarily lose vision, consciousness, or memory

♦ faint, pass out, swoon

black pepper n **:** a spice that consists of the dried berry of a pepper plant that is ground with the black husk still on

Black Power n **:** the mobilization of the political and economic power of Black Americans esp. to compel respect for their rights and improve their condition

black sheep n **:** a member of a group who is disreputable or who is not regarded favorably

black•smith \'blak-ˌsmith\ n **:** a smith who forges iron — **black•smith•ing** n

black•thorn \-ˌthȯrn\ n **:** a European thorny plum

black–tie \'blak-ˈtī\ adj **:** characterized by or requiring semiformal evening clothes consisting of a usu. black tie and tuxedo for men and a formal dress for women

black•top \'blak-ˌtäp\ n **:** a dark tarry material (as asphalt) used esp. for surfacing roads — **blacktop** vb

black widow n **:** a venomous New York spider having the female black with an hourglass-shaped red mark on the underside of the abdomen

blad•der \'bla-dər\ n **:** a sac in which liquid or gas is stored; esp **:** one in a vertebrate into which urine passes from the kidneys

blade \'blād\ n   **1 :** a leaf of a plant and esp. of a grass; also **:** the flat part of a leaf as distinguished from its stalk   **2 :** something (as the flat part of an oar or an arm of a propeller) resembling the blade of a leaf   **3 :** the cutting part of an instrument or tool   **4 :** a weapon (as a cutlass or rapier) with a long blade for cutting or thrusting that is often used as a symbol of honor or authority **:** SWORD; also **:** SWORDSMAN   **5 :** a dashing fellow   **6 :** the runner of an ice skate — **blad•ed** \'blā-dəd\ adj

blain \'blān\ n **:** an inflammatory swelling or sore

blam•able adj ♦ **:** deserving blame

♦ blameworthy, censurable, culpable, reprehensible

¹blame \'blām\ vb **blamed; blam•ing**   **1 ♦ :** to find fault with   **2 :** to hold responsible or responsible for

♦ censure, condemn, criticize, denounce, fault, knock, pan, reprehend

²blame n   **1 :** CENSURE, REPROOF   **2 ♦ :** responsibility for fault or error

♦ culpability, fault, guilt, rap Ant blamelessness

blame•less adj ♦ **:** free from blame or fault — **blame•less•ly** adv — **blame•less•ness** n

♦ clear, faultless, guiltless, impeccable, innocent, irreproachable

blame•wor•thy \-ˌwər-thē\ adj ♦ **:** deserving blame — **blame•wor•thi•ness** n

♦ blamable, censurable, culpable, reprehensible Ant blameless, faultless, impeccable, irreproachable

blanch \'blanch\ vb ♦ **:** to make or become white or pale **:** BLEACH

♦ bleach, blench, dull, fade, pale, wash out, whiten

blanc•mange \blə-ˈmänj, -ˈmänzh\ n **:** a dessert made from gelatin or a starchy substance and milk usu. sweetened and flavored

bland \'bland\ adj   **1 :** smooth in manner **:** SUAVE   **2 ♦ :** gently soothing ⟨a ∼ diet⟩; also **:** INSIPID — **bland•ly** adv — **bland•ness** n

♦ balmy, benign, delicate, gentle, insipid, light, mellow, mild, soft, soothing, tender

blan•dish•ment \'blan-dish-mənt\ n **:** flattering or coaxing speech or action **:** CAJOLERY

¹blank \'blaŋk\ adj   **1 a :** showing or causing an appearance of dazed dismay   **b ♦ :** lacking expression   **2 ♦ :** free from writing or marks; also **:** having spaces to be filled in   **3 :** DULL, EMPTY ⟨∼ moments⟩   **4 :** ABSOLUTE, DOWNRIGHT ⟨a ∼ refusal⟩   **5 :** not shaped in final form — **blank•ly** adv

♦ [1b] deadpan, expressionless, impassive, inexpressive, stolid, vacant Ant demonstrative, expressive ♦ [2] bare, devoid, empty, stark, vacant, void

²blank n   **1 ♦ :** an empty space   **2 ♦ :** a form with spaces for the entry of data   **3 :** an unfinished form (as of a key)   **4 :** a cartridge with propellant and a seal but no projectile

♦ [1] blankness, emptiness, vacancy, vacuity, void ♦ [2] document, form, paper

³blank vb   **1 :** to cover or close up **:** OBSCURE   **2 :** to keep from scoring

blank check n   **1 :** a signed check with the amount unspecified   **2 :** complete freedom of action

¹blan•ket \'blaŋ-kət\ n   **1 :** a heavy woven often woolen covering   **2 ♦ :** a covering layer ⟨a ∼ of snow⟩

♦ cloak, curtain, hood, mantle, mask, shroud, veil

²blanket vb   **1 ♦ :** to cover with or as if with a blanket   **2 ♦ :** to cover so as to obscure, interrupt, suppress, or extinguish

♦ [1] carpet, coat, cover, overlay, overlie, overspread ♦ [2] blot out, cloak, conceal, cover, curtain, enshroud, hide, mask, obscure, occlude, occult, screen, shroud, veil

³blanket adj ♦ **:** covering a group or class ⟨∼ insurance⟩; also **:** applicable in all instances ⟨∼ rules⟩

♦ common, general, generic, global, overall, universal

blank•ness n ♦ **:** the quality or state of being blank

♦ blank, emptiness, vacancy, vacuity, void

blank verse n **:** unrhymed iambic pentameter

blare \'blar\ vb **blared; blar•ing** **:** to sound loud and harsh; also **:** to proclaim loudly — **blare** n

blar•ney \'blär-nē\ n ♦ **:** skillful flattery **:** BLANDISHMENT

♦ adulation, flattery, overpraise

bla•sé \blä-ˈzā\ adj **:** apathetic to pleasure or excitement as a result of excessive indulgence; also **:** SOPHISTICATED

blas•pheme \blas-ˈfēm, ˈblas-ˌ\ vb **blas•phemed; blas•phem•ing**   **1 :** to speak of or address with irreverence   **2 :** to utter blasphemy — **blas•phem•er** n

blas•phe•mous \-məs\ adj ♦ **:** impiously irreverent

♦ irreverent, profane, sacrilegious

blas•phe•my \'blas-fə-mē\ n, pl **-mies**   **1 ♦ :** the act of expressing lack of reverence for God   **2 ♦ :** irreverence toward something considered sacred

♦ [1, 2] defilement, desecration, impiety, irreverence, sacrilege Ant adoration, glorification, worship

¹blast \'blast\ n   **1 ♦ :** a violent gust of wind; also **:** its effect   **2 :** sound made by a wind instrument   **3 :** a current of air forced at high pressure through a hole in a furnace (**blast furnace**)   **4 :** a sudden withering esp. of plants **:** BLIGHT   **5 ♦ :** an explosion or violent detonation; also **:** the often destructive shock wave of an explosion

♦ [1] blow, flurry, gust, williwaw ♦ [5] detonation, eruption, explosion

²blast vb   **1 ♦ :** to make a vigorous attack   **2 a :** to use an explosive   **b ♦ :** to discharge or propel something by means of an explosive **:** SHOOT   **3 ♦ :** to shatter by or as if by an explosive

♦ [1] abuse, assail, attack, belabor, castigate, excoriate, jump, lambaste, slam, vituperate ♦ [2b] discharge, fire, loose, shoot ♦ [3] blow up, burst, demolish, explode, pop, shatter, smash

blast off vb **:** TAKE OFF 4 — used esp. of rocket-propelled vehicles — **blast•off** \'blast-ˌȯf\ n

bla·tant \'blāt-ᵊnt\ *adj* ♦ : offensively obtrusive : vulgarly showy — **bla·tan·cy** \-ᵊn-sē\ *n* — **bla·tant·ly** *adv*

♦ conspicuous, egregious, flagrant, glaring, gross, obvious, patent, prominent, pronounced, rank, striking

blath·er \'bla-thər\ *vb* : to talk foolishly at length — **blather** *n*
blath·er·skite \'bla-thər-ˌskīt\ *n* : a person who blathers
¹**blaze** \'blāz\ *n* **1** : FIRE **2** ♦ : intense direct light often accompanied by heat ⟨the ∼ of TV lights⟩ **3** : something (as a dazzling display or sudden outburst) suggesting fire ⟨a ∼ of autumn leaves⟩

♦ flare, fluorescence, glare, gleam, glow, illumination, incandescence, light, luminescence, radiance, shine

²**blaze** *vb* **blazed**; **blaz·ing** **1** ♦ : to burn brightly; *also* : to flare up **2** ♦ : to be conspicuously bright

♦ [1] burn, flame, flare, glow ♦ [1, 2] beat, burn, flame, flare, glare

³**blaze** *vb* **blazed**; **blaz·ing** ♦ : to make public or conspicuous

♦ advertise, announce, broadcast, declare, enunciate, flash, herald, placard, post, proclaim, promulgate, publicize, publish, sound

⁴**blaze** *n* **1** : a usu. white stripe on the face of an animal **2** : a trail marker; *esp* : one made on a tree
⁵**blaze** *vb* **blazed**; **blaz·ing** : to mark (as a tree or trail) with blazes
blaz·er \'blā-zər\ *n* : a sports jacket often with notched collar and pockets that are stitched on
¹**bla·zon** \'blāz-ᵊn\ *n* **1** : COAT OF ARMS **2** : ostentatious display
²**blazon** *vb* **1** : to publish widely : PROCLAIM **2** : DECK, ADORN
bldg *abbr* building
bldr *abbr* builder
¹**bleach** \'blēch\ *vb* ♦ : to make or become white : BLANCH

♦ blanch, blench, dull, fade, pale, wash out, whiten

²**bleach** *n* : a preparation used in bleaching
bleach·ers \'blē-chərz\ *n sing or pl* : a usu. uncovered stand of tiered seats for spectators
bleak \'blēk\ *adj* **1** ♦ : desolately barren and often windswept **2** ♦ : lacking warm or cheering qualities — **bleak·ish** *adj* — **bleak·ly** *adv*

♦ [1] dirty, foul, inclement, nasty, raw, rough, squally, stormy, tempestuous, turbulent ♦ [2] dark, dismal, dreary, gloomy, gray (*or* grey), somber (*or* sombre), wretched

bleak·ness *n* ♦ : the quality or state of being bleak

♦ bite, bitterness, chill, nip, rawness, sharpness

blear \'blir\ *adj* : dim with water or tears ⟨∼ eyes⟩
bleary \'blir-ē\ *adj* **1** ♦ : dull or dimmed esp. from fatigue or sleep **2** ♦ : poorly outlined or defined

♦ dim, faint, foggy, fuzzy, hazy, indefinite, indistinct, unclear, undefined, undetermined

bleat \'blēt\ *n* : the cry of a sheep or goat or a sound like it — **bleat** *vb*
bleed \'blēd\ *vb* **bled** \'bled\; **bleed·ing** **1** : to lose or shed blood **2 a** : to be wounded **b** ♦ : to feel pain or distress **3 a** ♦ : to flow or ooze from a wounded surface **b** ♦ : to draw fluid from esp. in a controlled manner ⟨∼ steam from the pipes⟩ ⟨∼ a tire⟩ **4** : to extort money from

♦ [2b] agonize, feel, grieve, hurt, mourn, sorrow, suffer ♦ [3a] exude, ooze, percolate, seep, strain, sweat, weep ♦ [3b] drain, draw, pump, siphon, tap

bleed·er \'blē-dər\ *n* : one that bleeds; *esp* : HEMOPHILIAC
bleeding heart *n* **1** : a garden plant related to the poppies that has usu. deep pink drooping heart-shaped flowers **2** *disparaging* : a person who shows extreme sympathy esp. for an object of alleged persecution
¹**blem·ish** \'ble-mish\ *vb* ♦ : to spoil by a flaw : MAR

♦ mar, poison, spoil, stain, taint, tarnish, touch, vitiate

²**blemish** *n* ♦ : a noticeable flaw

♦ defect, deformity, disfigurement, fault, flaw, imperfection, mark, pockmark, scar

¹**blench** \'blench\ *vb* ♦ : to draw back or turn aside from lack of courage : FLINCH, QUAIL

♦ flinch, quail, recoil, shrink, wince

²**blench** *vb* ♦ : to grow or make pale

♦ blanch, bleach, dull, fade, pale, wash out, whiten

¹**blend** \'blend\ *vb* **blend·ed**; **blend·ing** **1** ♦ : to mix thoroughly **2** : to prepare (as coffee) by mixing different variet-

ies **3** ♦ : to combine into an integrated whole **4** : to produce a harmonious effect : HARMONIZE — **blend·er** *n*

♦ amalgamate, commingle, fuse, incorporate, intermingle, merge, mingle, mix *Ant* break down, break up, separate

²**blend** *n* ♦ : a product of blending

♦ admixture, amalgam, combination, composite, compound, fusion, intermixture, mix, mixture

bless \'bles\ *vb* **blessed** \'blest\ *also* **blest** \'blest\; **bless·ing** **1** ♦ : to consecrate by religious rite or word **2** : to sanctify with the sign of the cross **3** : to invoke divine care for **4** ♦ : to give glory to : PRAISE, GLORIFY **5** : to confer happiness upon

♦ [1] consecrate, hallow, sanctify ♦ [4] extol, glorify, laud, magnify, praise

bless·ed \'ble-səd\ *also* **blest** \'blest\ *adj* **1 a** ♦ : held in reverence **b** ♦ : venerated as or as if sacred : HOLY **2** : BEATIFIED **3** : DELIGHTFUL — **bless·ed·ly** *adv*

♦ [1a] hallowed, holy, sacred, sacrosanct, sanctified ♦ [1b] divine, godlike, heavenly, holy

bless·ed·ness *n* ♦ : the quality or state of being blessed

♦ bliss, felicity, gladness, happiness, joy ♦ devoutness, godliness, holiness, piety, sainthood, sanctity

bless·ing \'ble-siŋ\ *n* **1 a** ♦ : the act or words of one who blesses **b** ♦ : acknowledgment and support of something : APPROVAL ⟨gave their ∼ to the proposal⟩ **2** ♦ : a thing conducive to happiness **3** : grace said at a meal

♦ [1a] consecration, sanctification ♦ [1b] approbation, approval, favor (*or* favour), imprimatur, OK ♦ [2] benefit, boon, felicity, godsend, good, manna, windfall *Ant* affliction, bane, curse, evil, plague, scourge

blew *past of* BLOW
¹**blight** \'blīt\ *n* **1** ♦ : a plant disease or injury marked by withering; *also* : an organism causing a blight **2** : an impairing or frustrating influence; *also* : a deteriorated condition ⟨urban ∼⟩
²**blight** *vb* : to affect with or suffer from blight
blimp \'blimp\ *n* : a nonrigid airship
¹**blind** \'blīnd\ *adj* **1** : lacking or grossly deficient in ability to see; *also* : intended for blind persons **2** : not based on reason, evidence, or knowledge ⟨∼ faith⟩ **3** : not intelligently controlled or directed ⟨∼ chance⟩ **4** : performed solely by using aircraft instruments ⟨a ∼ landing⟩ **5** : hard to discern or make out : HIDDEN ⟨a ∼ seam⟩ **6** : lacking an opening or outlet ⟨a ∼ alley⟩ — **blind·ly** *adv* — **blind·ness** \'blīnd-nəs\ *n*
²**blind** *vb* **1** : to make blind **2** : to overpower with brightness : DAZZLE **3** : DARKEN; *also* : HIDE
³**blind** *n* **1** : something (as a shutter) to hinder vision or keep out light **2** : a place of concealment **3** : SUBTERFUGE
blind carbon copy *n* : a copy of a message (as an e-mail) that is sent without the knowledge of the other recipients
blind date *n* : a date between persons who have not previously met; *also* : either of these persons
blind·er \'blīn-dər\ *n* : either of two flaps on a horse's bridle to prevent it from seeing to the side
blind·fold \'blīnd-ˌfōld\ *vb* : to cover the eyes of with or as if with a bandage — **blindfold** *n*
¹**blink** \'bliŋk\ *vb* **1** : to close and open the eyes involuntarily : WINK **2** ♦ : to shine dimly or intermittently : TWINKLE **3** : EVADE, IGNORE — often used with *at* **4** ♦ : to cease resistance : YIELD

♦ [2] flash, twinkle, wink ♦ [4] bow, budge, capitulate, concede, give in, knuckle under, quit, submit, succumb, surrender, yield

²**blink** *n* **1** : GLIMMER, SPARKLE **2** : a usu. involuntary shutting and opening of the eye
blink·er \'bliŋ-kər\ *n* : a blinking light used as a signal
blin·tze \'blint-sə\ *or* **blintz** \'blints\ *n* : a thin rolled pancake with a filling usu. of cream cheese
blip \'blip\ *n* **1** : a spot on a radar screen **2** : ABERRATION 1
bliss \'blis\ *n* ♦ : complete happiness : JOY

♦ blessedness, felicity, gladness, happiness, joy

bliss·ful \-fəl\ *adj* ♦ : full of, marked by, or causing bliss — **bliss·ful·ly** *adv*

♦ delighted, glad, happy, joyful, pleased

¹**blis·ter** \'blis-tər\ *n* **1** : a raised area of skin containing watery fluid; *also* : an agent that causes blisters **2** : something (as a raised spot in paint) suggesting a blister **3** : a disease of plants marked by large swollen patches on the leaves

²**blister** vb : to develop a blister; also : to cause blisters

blithe \ˈblīth, ˈblīth\ adj **blith·er; blith·est** ♦ : happily light-hearted — **blithe·ly** adv

  ♦ bright, buoyant, cheerful, cheery, chipper, lightsome, sunny, upbeat ♦ boon, festive, gleeful, jocund, jolly, jovial, merry, mirthful, sunny

blithe·some \-səm\ adj : full of gaiety or high spirits

¹**blitz** \ˈblits\ n **1** : an intensive series of air raids **2** : a fast intensive campaign **3** : a rush of the passer by the defensive linebackers in football

²**blitz** vb ♦ : to subject to a blitz; esp : to damage by a blitz

  ♦ bombard, shell

blitz·krieg \-ˌkrēg\ n ♦ : a sudden violent enemy attack

  ♦ aggression, assault, attack, charge, descent, offense (or offence), offensive, onset, onslaught, raid, rush, strike

bliz·zard \ˈbli-zərd\ n : a long severe snowstorm

blk abbr **1** black **2** block

bloat \ˈblōt\ vb : to swell by or as if by filling with water or air

blob \ˈbläb\ n ♦ : a small lump or drop of a thick consistency

  ♦ chunk, clod, clump, glob, gob, hunk, lump, nub, wad

bloc \ˈbläk\ n ♦ : a combination of individuals or groups (as nations) working for a common purpose

  ♦ body, coalition, combination, combine, faction, party, sect, set, side, wing ♦ alliance, coalition, combination, combine, confederacy, confederation, federation, league, union

¹**block** \ˈbläk\ n **1** : a solid piece of substantial material (as wood or stone) **2** ♦ : something that impedes progress or achievement : HINDRANCE, OBSTRUCTION; also : interruption of normal function of body or mind ⟨heart ∼⟩ **3** : a frame enclosing one or more pulleys and having a hook or strap by which it may be attached **4** : a piece of material with a hand-cut design on its surface from which copies are to be made **5** : a large building divided into separate units (as apartments or offices) **6** : a row of houses or shops **7** : a city square; also : the distance along one of the sides of such a square **8** ♦ : a quantity of things considered as a unit ⟨a ∼ of seats⟩

  ♦ [2] bar, clog, crimp, drag, embarrassment, hindrance, let, obstacle, stop, stumbling block ♦ [8] array, assemblage, batch, bunch, cluster, collection, group, package, set, suite

²**block** vb **1** ♦ : to make unsuitable for passage or progress by obstruction : OBSTRUCT **2** : to outline roughly ⟨∼ out a design⟩ **3** : to provide or support with a block ⟨∼ up a wheel⟩ — **block·er** n

  ♦ dam, fill, pack, plug, stop, stuff ♦ choke, clog, close (off), congest, dam, jam, obstruct, plug (up), stop (up), stuff

¹**block·ade** \blä-ˈkād\ n : the isolation of a place usu. by troops or ships

²**blockade** vb : to subject to or isolate with a blockade — **block·ad·er** n

block·age \ˈblä-kij\ n : an act or instance of obstructing : the state of being blocked

block·bust·er \ˈbläk-ˌbəs-tər\ n ♦ : one that is very large, successful, or violent ⟨a ∼ of a movie⟩

  ♦ hit, smash, success, winner ♦ behemoth, colossus, giant, jumbo, leviathan, mammoth, monster, titan, whale, whopper

block·head \ˈbläk-ˌhed\ n ♦ : a slow-witted or stupid person : DOLT, DUNCE

  ♦ dope, dummy, idiot, imbecile, jackass, moron, numskull

block·house \-ˌhau̇s\ n : a small strong building used as a shelter (as from enemy fire) or observation post

blog \ˈblȯg, ˈbläg\ n : a website containing one's reflections, opinions, and comments; also : the contents of such a site — **blog** vb — **blog·ger** n — **blog·ging** n

¹**blond** or **blonde** \ˈbländ\ adj **1** : fair in complexion **2** ♦ : of a light or bleached color ⟨∼ mahogany⟩ — **blond·ish** \ˈblän-dish\ adj

  ♦ fair, flaxen, golden, sandy, straw Ant dark

²**blond** or **blonde** n : a person having blond hair

blood \ˈbləd\ n **1** : a usu. red liquid that circulates in the heart, arteries, and veins of animals **2** : LIFEBLOOD; also : LIFE **3** ♦ : human stock or lineage **4 a** : relationship by descent from a common ancestor **b** ♦ : persons related by means of a common ancestor : KINDRED **5** : the taking of life **6** : TEMPER, PASSION **7** : DANDY 1 — **blood·less** adj

  ♦ [3] ancestry, birth, bloodline, breeding, descent, extraction,

family tree, genealogy, line, lineage, origin, parentage, pedigree, stock, strain ♦ [4b] clan, family, folks, house, kin, kindred, kinfolk, line, lineage, people, race, stock, tribe

blood bank n : a place where blood or plasma is stored

blood·bath \ˈbləd-ˌbath, -ˌbäth\ n : MASSACRE

blood count n : the determination of the number of blood cells in a specific volume of blood; also : the number of cells so determined

blood·cur·dling \ˈbləd-kərd-liŋ, -ˌkər-dᵊl-iŋ\ adj : arousing fright or horror

blood·ed \ˈblə-dəd\ adj **1** : having blood of a specified kind ⟨warm-blooded animals⟩ **2** : entirely or largely purebred ⟨∼ horses⟩

blood group n : one of the classes into which human beings can be separated by the presence or absence in their blood of specific antigens

blood·hound \ˈbləd-ˌhau̇nd\ n : any of a breed of large powerful hounds with long drooping ears, a wrinkled face, and keen sense of smell

blood·let·ting \-ˌle-tiŋ\ n **1** : PHLEBOTOMY **2** : BLOODSHED

blood·line \-ˌlīn\ n ♦ : a sequence of direct ancestors esp. in a pedigree

  ♦ ancestry, birth, blood, breeding, descent, extraction, family tree, genealogy, line, lineage, origin, parentage, pedigree, stock, strain

blood·mo·bile \-mō-ˌbēl\ n : a motor vehicle equipped for collecting blood from donors

blood poisoning n : invasion of the bloodstream by virulent microorganisms from a focus of infection accompanied esp. by chills, fever, and prostration

blood pressure n : pressure of the blood on the walls of blood vessels and esp. arteries

blood·root \ˈbləd-ˌrüt, -ˌru̇t\ n : a plant related to the poppy that has a red root and sap, a solitary leaf, and a white flower in early spring

blood·shed \-ˌshed\ n : wounding or taking of life : CARNAGE, SLAUGHTER

blood·shot \-ˌshät\ adj : inflamed to redness ⟨∼ eyes⟩

blood·stain \-ˌstān\ n : a discoloration caused by blood

blood·stained \-ˌstānd\ adj : stained with blood; also : involved with slaughter

blood·stone \-ˌstōn\ n : a green quartz sprinkled with red spots

blood·stream \-ˌstrēm\ n : the flowing blood in a circulatory system

blood·suck·er \-ˌsə-kər\ n : an animal that sucks blood; esp : LEECH — **blood·suck·ing** adj

blood test n : a test of the blood; esp : one for disease or medical condition

blood·thirsty \ˈbləd-ˌthər-stē\ adj ♦ : eager to shed blood — **blood·thirst·i·ly** \-ˌthər-stə-lē\ adv — **blood·thirst·i·ness** \-stē-nəs\ n

  ♦ bloody, homicidal, murderous, sanguinary, sanguine

blood type n : BLOOD GROUP — **blood–typ·ing** n

blood vessel n : a vessel (as a vein or artery) in which blood circulates in the body

bloody adj **1** : containing or made up of blood; also : smeared or stained with blood **2** ♦ : accompanied by or involving bloodshed

  ♦ bloodthirsty, homicidal, murderous, sanguinary, sanguine

Bloody Mary \-ˈmer-ē\ n, pl **Bloody Marys** : a drink made essentially of vodka and tomato juice

¹**bloom** \ˈblüm\ n **1** : the part of a seed plant that normally bears reproductive organs : FLOWER 1; also : flowers or amount of flowers (as of a plant) **2** : the period or state of flowering **3** ♦ : a state or time of beauty and vigor **4** : a powdery coating esp. on fruits and leaves **5** : rosy color; also : an appearance of freshness or health — **bloomy** adj

  ♦ blossom, flower, flush, heyday, prime

²**bloom** vb ♦ **1** : to produce or yield flowers **2** : MATURE **3** : to glow esp. with healthy color

  ♦ blossom, blow, burgeon, flower, unfold

bloo·mers \ˈblü-mərz\ n pl : a woman's garment of short loose trousers gathered at the knee

bloop·er \ˈblü-pər\ n **1** : a fly ball hit barely beyond a baseball infield **2** : an embarrassing public blunder

¹**blos·som** \ˈblä-səm\ n **1** : the flower of a plant **2** ♦ : the period or state of flowering **3** : a peak period or stage of development

  ♦ bloom, flower, flush, heyday, prime

²blossom *vb* ♦ : to produce or yield flowers : BLOOM, FLOWER

♦ bloom, blow, burgeon, flower, unfold

¹blot \'blät\ *n* **1** : SPOT, STAIN ⟨ink ∼s⟩ **2** ♦ : a mark of reproach : moral flaw or blemish ⟨a ∼ on her record⟩

♦ brand, smirch, spot, stain, stigma, taint

²blot *vb* **blot·ted; blot·ting** **1** : SPOT, STAIN **2** : OBSCURE, ECLIPSE **3** *obs* : MAR; *esp* : DISGRACE **4** : to dry or remove with or as if with an absorbing material **5** : to make a blot

¹blotch \'bläch\ *n* : a usu. large and irregular spot or mark (as of ink or color) — **blotchy** *adj*

²blotch *vb* ♦ : to mark or mar with blotches

♦ mottle, spot

blot out *vb* **1** ♦ : to make obscure, insignificant, or inconsequential ⟨*blot out* the sun⟩ **2** ♦ : to destroy completely

♦ [1] blanket, cloak, conceal, cover, curtain, enshroud, hide, mask, obscure, occlude, occult, screen, shroud, veil ♦ [2] annihilate, demolish, destroy, exterminate, extinguish, obliterate, pulverize, ruin, smash, waste, wipe out, wreck

blot·ter \'blä-tər\ *n* **1** : a piece of blotting paper **2** : a book for preliminary records (as of sales or arrests)

blot·ting paper *n* : a spongy paper used to absorb ink

blouse \'blaüs, 'blaüz\ *n* **1** : a loose outer garment like a smock **2** : a usu. loose garment reaching from the neck to about the waist

¹blow \'blō\ *vb* **blew** \'blü\; **blown** \'blōn\; **blow·ing** **1** : to move forcibly ⟨the wind *blew*⟩ **2** : to send forth a current of gas (as air) **3** : to act on with a current of gas or vapor; *esp* : to drive with such a current **4** : to sound or cause to sound ⟨∼ a horn⟩ **5** ♦ : to breathe quickly or in a labored manner : PANT, GASP; *also* : to expel moist air in breathing ⟨the whale *blew*⟩ **6** : BOAST; *also* : BLUSTER **7** : MELT — used of an electrical fuse **8** : to shape or form by blown or injected air ⟨∼ glass⟩ **9** : to shatter or destroy by or as if by explosion **10** : to make breathless by exertion **11** ♦ : to spend recklessly **12** : to foul up hopelessly ⟨*blew* her lines⟩ — **blow·er** *n*

♦ [5] gasp, pant, puff, wheeze ♦ [11] dissipate, fritter, lavish, misspend, run through, spend, squander, throw away, waste

²blow *n* **1** : a usu. strong blowing of air : GALE **2** : BOASTING, BRAG **3** : an act or instance of blowing

³blow *vb* **blew** \'blü\; **blown** \'blōn\; **blow·ing** : to produce or yield flowers : FLOWER, BLOOM

⁴blow *n* **1** ♦ : a forcible stroke **2** : COMBAT ⟨come to ∼s⟩ **3** : a severe and usu. unexpected calamity

♦ bat, belt, box, clout, hit, punch, slug, thump, wallop, whack

blow–by–blow *adj* : minutely detailed ⟨∼ account⟩

blow–dry \-,drī\ *vb* : to dry and usu. style hair with a blow-dryer

blow–dry·er \-,drī-(-ə)r\ *n* : a handheld hair dryer

blow·fly \'blō-,flī\ *n* : any of a family of dipteran flies (as a bluebottle) that deposit their eggs or maggots on meat or in wounds

blow·gun \-,gən\ *n* : a tube from which an arrow or a dart may be shot by the force of the breath

blow·out \'blō-,aüt\ *n* **1** ♦ : a festive social affair **2** : a bursting of something (as a tire) because of pressure of the contents (as air)

♦ affair, event, fete, function, get-together, party

blow·sy *also* **blow·zy** \'blaü-zē\ *adj* : DISHEVELED, SLOVENLY

blow·torch \'blō-,tòrch\ *n* : a small portable burner whose flame is made hotter by a blast of air or oxygen

blow·up \'blō-,əp\ *n* **1** : EXPLOSION **2** ♦ : an outburst of temper **3** : a photographic enlargement

♦ dudgeon, explosion, fireworks, fit, huff, scene, tantrum

blow up *vb* **1** ♦ : to rend apart, shatter, or destroy by or as if by explosion **2** ♦ : to lose self-control; *esp* : to become violently angry **3** ♦ : to undergo or be destroyed by an explosion

♦ [1, 3] blast, burst, demolish, detonate, explode, pop, shatter, smash ♦ [2] flare, flip, fulminate, rant, vituperate *Ant* calm (down)

blowy \'blō-ē\ *adj* ♦ : marked by strong wind : WINDY

♦ blustery, breezy, gusty, windy

BLT \,bē-,el-'tē\ *n* : a bacon, lettuce, and tomato sandwich

¹blub·ber \'blə-bər\ *vb* ♦ : to cry noisily

♦ bawl, cry, sob, weep

²blubber *n* **1** : the fat of large sea mammals (as whales) **2** : a noisy crying

¹blud·geon \'blə-jən\ *n* ♦ : a short often loaded club

♦ bat, billy club, club, cudgel, staff, truncheon

²bludgeon *vb* ♦ : to strike with or as if with a bludgeon

♦ bash, bat, batter, beat, club, pound

¹blue \'blü\ *adj* **blu·er; blu·est** **1** : of the color blue; *also* : BLUISH **2** ♦ : low in spirits : MELANCHOLY; *also* : DEPRESSING **3** : PURITANICAL **4** : INDECENT **5** : tending to support Democratic candidates ⟨a ∼ state⟩ — **blue·ness** *n*

♦ depressed, down, downcast, glum, low, melancholy, miserable, sad, unhappy

²blue *n* **1** : a color between green and violet in the spectrum : the color of the clear daytime sky **2** ♦ : something (as clothing or the sky or ocean) that is blue

♦ high, sky ♦ brine, deep, ocean, sea

blue baby *n* : a baby with bluish skin due to faulty circulation caused by a heart defect

blue·bell \-,bel\ *n* : any of various plants with blue bell-shaped flowers

blue·ber·ry \'blü-,ber-ē, -bə-rē\ *n* : the edible blue or blackish berry of various shrubs of the heath family; *also* : one of these shrubs

blue·bird \-,bərd\ *n* : any of several small No. American thrushes that are blue above and reddish-brown or pale blue below

blue·bon·net \'blü-,bä-nət\ *n* : either of two low-growing annual lupines of Texas with silky foliage and blue flowers

blue·bot·tle \'blü-,bät-ᵊl\ *n* : any of several blowflies with iridescent blue bodies or abdomens

blue cheese *n* : cheese having veins of greenish blue mold

blue–col·lar \'blü-'kä-lər\ *adj* : of, relating to, or being the class of workers whose duties call for work clothes

blue·fish \-,fish\ *n* : a marine sport and food fish bluish above and silvery below

blue·grass \-,gras\ *n* **1** : KENTUCKY BLUEGRASS **2** : country music played on stringed instruments having free improvisation and close harmonies

blue jay \-,jā\ *n* : a crested bright blue No. American jay

blue jeans *n pl* : pants usu. made of blue denim

blue·nose \'blü-,nōz\ *n* : a person who advocates a rigorous moral code

blue·point \-,pòint\ *n* : a small oyster typically from the south shore of Long Island, New York

¹blue·print \-,print\ *n* **1** : a photographic print in white on a blue ground used esp. for copying mechanical drawings and architects' plans **2** ♦ : a detailed plan of action

♦ arrangement, design, game, plan, project, scheme, strategy, system

²blueprint *vb* **1** : to make a blueprint of **2** ♦ : to work out (as a program or plan) in detail

♦ arrange, calculate, chart, design, frame, lay out, map, plan, project, scheme

blues \'blüz\ *n pl* **1** ♦ : low spirits : MELANCHOLY **2** : music in a style marked by recurrent minor intervals and melancholy lyrics

♦ dejection, depression, doldrums, dumps, melancholy, sadness

blue screen *n* : a cinematic technique in which a subject is filmed in front of a blue background so as to allow the creation of a composite with other footage

blue·stock·ing \'blü-,stä-kiŋ\ *n* : a woman having intellectual interests

blu·et \'blü-ət\ *n* : a low No. American herb with dainty bluish flowers

blue whale *n* : a very large baleen whale that may reach a weight of 150 tons (135 metric tons) and a length of 100 feet (30 meters)

¹bluff \'bləf\ *adj* **1** : having a broad flattened front **2** : rising steeply with a broad flat front **3** : good-naturedly frank and outspoken

²bluff *n* ♦ : a high steep bank : CLIFF

♦ cliff, crag, escarpment, palisade, precipice, scarp

³bluff *vb* ♦ : to frighten or deceive by pretense or a mere show of strength

♦ deceive, dupe, fool, gull, misinform, mislead, trick

⁴bluff *n* : an act or instance of bluffing; *also* : one who bluffs

blu·ing *or* **blue·ing** \'blü-iŋ\ *n* : a preparation used in laundering to counteract yellowing of white fabrics

blu·ish \'blü-ish\ *adj* : somewhat blue

¹blun·der \'blən-dər\ *vb* **1** ♦ : to move clumsily or unsteadily **2** : to make a stupid or needless mistake

♦ flounder, limp, lumber, plod, stumble

²blunder *n* ♦ : an avoidable and usu. serious mistake

♦ error, fault, flub, fumble, goof, lapse, miscue, misstep, mistake, oversight, slip, stumble

blun·der·buss \'blən-dər-ˌbəs\ *n* **:** an obsolete short-barreled firearm with a flaring muzzle

¹**blunt** \'blənt\ *adj* **1** ♦ **:** not sharp **:** DULL **2** ♦ **:** lacking in tact **:** BLUFF — **blunt·ly** *adv* — **blunt·ness** *n*

♦ [1] dull, obtuse ♦ [2] abrupt, brusque, curt, snippy *Ant* circuitous, mealymouthed

²**blunt** *vb* ♦ **:** to make or become less sharp, definite, or forceful

♦ dampen, deaden, dull, numb

¹**blur** \'blər\ *n* **1** **:** a smear or stain that obscures **2** **:** something vaguely perceived; *esp* **:** something moving too quickly to be clearly perceived

²**blur** *vb* **blurred; blur·ring** ♦ **:** to make dim, imperfect, or confused **:** CLOUD, OBSCURE ⟨*blurred* vision⟩

♦ becloud, befog, cloud, confuse, dim, fog, haze, mist, obscure, shroud

blurb \'blərb\ *n* **:** a short publicity notice (as on a book jacket)

blur·ry \'blər-ē\ *adj* ♦ **:** lacking definition or focus

♦ bleary, dim, faint, foggy, fuzzy, hazy, indefinite, indistinct, indistinguishable, misty, murky, nebulous, obscure, opaque, shadowy, unclear, undefined, undetermined, vague

blurt \'blərt\ *vb* ♦ **:** to utter suddenly and impulsively

♦ *usu* **blurt out** bolt, cry, ejaculate, spout

¹**blush** \'bləsh\ *n* **1** **:** a reddening of the face (as from modesty or confusion) **:** FLUSH **2** **:** a cosmetic used to tint the face pink — **blush·ful** *adj*

²**blush** *vb* ♦ **:** to become red in the face esp. from shame, modesty, or confusion

♦ bloom, color (*or* colour), crimson, flush, glow, redden

¹**blus·ter** \'bləs-tər\ *vb* **1** **:** to blow in stormy noisy gusts **2** ♦ **:** to talk or act with noisy swaggering threats

♦ fulminate, rant, rave, spout

²**bluster** *n* **1** **:** a violent boisterous blowing **2** ♦ **:** violent commotion **3** ♦ **:** loudly boastful or threatening speech

♦ [2] cacophony, clamor (*or* clamour), din, noise, racket, roar ♦ [3] bombast, brag, gas, grandiloquence, rant

blus·tery \-tə-rē\ *adj* ♦ **:** blowing boisterously ⟨a ∼ day⟩

♦ blowy, breezy, gusty, windy

blvd *abbr* boulevard

B lymphocyte *n* **:** B CELL

BM *abbr* bowel movement

B movie *n* **:** a cheaply produced motion picture

BO *abbr* **1** best offer **2** body odor **3** box office **4** branch office

boa \'bō-ə\ *n* **1** **:** a large snake (as the **boa con·stric·tor** \-kən-ˈstrik-tər\ or the related anaconda) that suffocates and kills its prey by constriction **2** **:** a fluffy scarf usu. of fur or feathers

boar \'bōr\ *n* **:** a male swine; *also* **:** WILD BOAR

¹**board** \'bōrd\ *n* **1** **:** the side of a ship **2** **:** a thin flat length of sawed lumber; *also* **:** material (as cardboard) or a piece of material formed as a thin flat firm sheet **3** *pl* **:** a theater stage as representing the acting profession **4 a :** a table spread with a meal **b :** daily meals esp. when furnished for pay **5 :** a table at which a council or magistrates sit **6 :** a group or association of persons organized for a special responsibility (as the management of a business or institution); *also* **:** an organized commercial exchange **7 :** a sheet of insulating material carrying circuit elements and inserted in an electronic device

²**board** *vb* **1** **:** to go or put aboard ⟨∼ a boat⟩ **2** **:** to cover with boards **3** ♦ **:** to provide or be provided with meals and often lodging

♦ accommodate, billet, bunk, domicile, house, lodge, put up, quarter

board·er *n* ♦ **:** one that boards; *esp* **:** one that is provided with regular meals or regular meals and lodging

♦ lodger, renter, roomer, tenant

board game *n* **:** a game (as checkers, chess, or backgammon) played by placing or moving pieces on a board

board·ing·house \'bōr-diŋ-ˌhau̇s\ *n* **:** a house at which persons are boarded

board·walk \'bōrd-ˌwȯk\ *n* **:** a promenade (as of planking) along a beach

¹**boast** \'bōst\ *vb* **1** ♦ **:** to praise oneself **2** ♦ **:** to mention or assert with excessive pride **3** **:** to prize as a possession; *also*

: HAVE ⟨the house ∼s a fireplace⟩ — **boast·ful** \-fəl\ *adj* — **boast·ful·ly** *adv*

♦ [1, 2] brag, crow, plume, swagger

²**boast** *n* **1** **:** the act or an instance of boasting **2** ♦ **:** a cause for pride

♦ credit, glory, honor (*or* honour), jewel, pride, treasure

boast·er \'bō-stər\ *n* ♦ **:** one who boasts

♦ brag, braggadocio, braggart, bragger

¹**boat** \'bōt\ *n* ♦ **:** a small vessel for travel on water; *also* **:** SHIP

♦ bottom, craft, ship, vessel

²**boat** *vb* **:** to go by boat

boat·er \'bō-tər\ *n* **1** **:** one that travels in a boat **2** **:** a stiff straw hat

boat·load \'bōt-ˌlōd\ *n* ♦ **:** an indefinitely large number

♦ abundance, deal, gobs, heap, loads, lot, pile, plenty, quantity, scads

boat·man \'bōt-mən\ *n* **:** a man who operates, works on, or deals in boats

boat people *n pl* **:** refugees fleeing by boat

boat·swain \'bōs-ᵊn\ *n* **:** a subordinate officer of a ship in charge of the hull and related equipment

¹**bob** \'bäb\ *vb* **bobbed; bob·bing** **1** ♦ **:** to move up and down jerkily or repeatedly **2** **:** to emerge, arise, or appear suddenly or unexpectedly

♦ bobble, jog, jounce, nod, pump, seesaw

²**bob** *n* **:** a bobbing movement

³**bob** *n* **1** **:** a knob, knot, twist, or curl esp. of ribbons, yarn, or hair **2** **:** a short haircut of a woman or child **3** **:** FLOAT 2 **4** **:** a weight hanging from a line

⁴**bob** *vb* **bobbed; bob·bing** **:** to cut hair in a bob

⁵**bob** *n, pl* **bob** *slang Brit* **:** SHILLING

bob·bin \'bä-bən\ *n* **:** a cylinder or spindle for holding or dispensing thread (as in a sewing machine)

bob·ble \'bä-bəl\ *vb* **bob·bled; bob·bling** **1** ♦ **:** to move up and down in a short quick movement **2** ♦ **:** to make awkward attempts to do or find something; *also* **:** FUMBLE ⟨the catcher *bobbled* the ball⟩ — **bobble** *n*

♦ [1] bob, jog, jounce, nod, pump, seesaw ♦ [2] botch, bungle, butcher, flub, foul up, fumble, mangle, mess up, screw up

bob·by \'bä-bē\ *n, pl* **bobbies** *Brit* **:** a police officer

bobby pin *n* **:** a flat wire hairpin with prongs that press close together

bob·cat \'bäb-ˌkat\ *n* **:** a small usu. rusty-colored No. American lynx

bob·o·link \'bä-bə-ˌliŋk\ *n* **:** an American migratory songbird related to the meadowlarks

bob·sled \'bäb-ˌsled\ *n* **1** **:** a short sled usu. used as one of a joined pair **2** **:** a racing sled with two pairs of runners, a steering wheel, and a hand brake — **bobsled** *vb*

bob·white \(ˌ)bäb-ˈhwīt\ *n* **:** any of a genus of quail; *esp* **:** a popular game bird of eastern and central No. America

boc·cie *or* **boc·ci** *or* **boc·ce** \'bä-chē\ *n* **:** Italian lawn bowling played on a long narrow court

bock \'bäk\ *n* **:** a strong dark beer usu. sold in early spring

bod \'bäd\ *n* **:** BODY

¹**bode** \'bōd\ *vb* **bod·ed; bod·ing** ♦ **:** to indicate by signs **:** PRESAGE

♦ augur, promise

²**bode** *past of* BIDE

bo·de·ga \bō-ˈdä-gə\ *n* **:** a store specializing in Hispanic groceries

bod·ice \'bä-dəs\ *n* **:** the usu. close-fitting part of a dress above the waist

bodi·less \'bä-di-ləs\ *adj* ♦ **:** lacking a body or material form

♦ immaterial, incorporeal, insubstantial, nonmaterial, nonphysical, spiritual, unsubstantial

¹**bodi·ly** \'bä-dᵊl-ē\ *adj* ♦ **:** of or relating to the body ⟨∼ contact⟩

♦ animal, carnal, corporal, fleshly, material, physical, somatic

²**bodily** *adv* **1** **:** in the flesh **2** **:** as a whole ⟨lifted the crate up ∼⟩

bod·kin \'bäd-kən\ *n* **1** **:** DAGGER **2** **:** a pointed implement for punching holes in cloth **3** **:** a blunt needle for drawing tape or ribbon through a loop or hem

body \'bä-dē\ *n, pl* **bod·ies** **1** **:** the physical whole of a living or dead organism; *also* **:** the trunk or main mass of an organism as distinguished from its appendages **2** ♦ **:** a human being **:** PERSON **3** ♦ **:** the main part of something **4** **:** a mass of matter distinct from other masses **5** ♦ : a group of persons or things **6** : VISCOSITY, FIRMNESS **7** : richness of flavor — used esp. of wines — **bod·ied** \'bä-dēd\ *adj*

♦ [2] being, creature, human, individual, man, mortal, person ♦ [3] bulk, core, generality, main, mass, staple, weight ♦ [5] array, batch, bunch, cluster, crop, group, huddle, knot, lot, parcel, party

body·build·ing \'bä-dē-ˌbil-diŋ\ *n* : a developing of the body through exercise and diet — **body·build·er** \-dər\ *n*

body English *n* : bodily motions made in a usu. unconscious effort to influence the movement of a propelled object (as a ball)

body·guard \'bä-dē-ˌgärd\ *n* : a personal guard; *also* : RETINUE

body language *n* : body movements or postures interpreted as a means of communication

body stocking *n* : a sheer close-fitting one-piece garment for the torso that often has sleeves and legs

body·work \'bä-dē-ˌwərk\ *n* : the making or repairing of vehicle bodies

Boer \'bȯr, 'bu̇r\ *n* : a South African of Dutch or Huguenot descent

¹**bog** \'bäg, 'bȯg\ *n* ♦ : wet, spongy, poorly drained, and usu. acid ground — **bog·gy** *adj*

♦ fen, marsh, mire, morass, slough, swamp

²**bog** *vb* **bogged; bog·ging** : to sink into or as if into a bog

bo·gey *also* **bo·gie** *or* **bo·gy** \'bu̇-gē, 'bō- for 1; 'bō- for 2\ *n, pl* **bogeys** *also* **bogies 1 a** ♦ : a visible disembodied spirit : SPECTER **b** ♦ : a source of fear or annoyance **2** : a score of one over par on a hole in golf

♦ [1a] apparition, ghost, phantasm, phantom, poltergeist, shade, shadow, specter, spirit, spook, vision, wraith ♦ [1b] bête noire, bugbear, hobgoblin, ogre

bo·gey·man \'bu̇-gē-ˌman, 'bō-, 'bü-\ *n* : an imaginary monster used in threatening children

bog·gle \'bä-gəl\ *vb* **bog·gled; bog·gling** : to overwhelm or be overwhelmed with fright or amazement

bo·gus \'bō-gəs\ *adj* ♦ : not genuine : SHAM

♦ counterfeit, fake, false, inauthentic, phony, sham, spurious, unauthentic ♦ artificial, fake, faux, imitation, mock, sham, synthetic

Bo·he·mi·an \bō-'hē-mē-ən\ *n* **1** : a native or inhabitant of Bohemia **2** *often not cap* : VAGABOND, WANDERER **3** *often not cap* ♦ : a person (as a writer or artist) living an unconventional life — **bohemian** *adj, often cap*

♦ deviant, individualist, loner, maverick, nonconformist

bohr·i·um \'bȯr-ē-əm\ *n* : an artifically produced radioactive chemical element

¹**boil** \'bȯil\ *n* : an inflamed swollen bump on the skin resulting from an infected hair follicle

²**boil** *vb* **1 a** : to heat or become heated to a temperature (**boil·ing point**) at which vapor is formed and rises in bubbles ⟨water ∼s and changes to steam⟩ **b** ♦ : to act on or be acted on by a boiling liquid ⟨∼ eggs⟩ **2** ♦ : to be in a state of seething agitation **3** ♦ : to churn violently as if boiling

♦ [1b] coddle, stew ♦ [2, 3] burn, churn, fume, rage, seethe, steam

³**boil** *n* : the act or state of boiling

boil·er \'bȯi-lər\ *n* **1** : a container in which something is boiled **2** : a strong vessel used in making steam **3** : a tank holding hot water

boil·er·mak·er \'bȯi-lər-ˌmā-kər\ *n* : whiskey with a beer chaser

boil·ing *adj* ♦ : intensely agitated ⟨∼ with anger⟩

♦ angry, furious, irate, mad, rabid, sore

bois·ter·ous \'bȯi-st(ə-)rəs\ *adj* ♦ : noisily turbulent or exuberant — **bois·ter·ous·ly** *adv*

♦ rambunctious, raucous, rowdy *Ant* orderly

bok choy \'bäk-'chȯi\ *n* : a Chinese vegetable related to the mustards that forms a loose head of green leaves with long thick white stalks

bo·la \'bō-lə\ *or* **bo·las** \-ləs\ *n, pl* **bolas** \-ləz\ *also* **bo·las·es** : a cord with weights attached to the ends

bold \'bōld\ *adj* **1** ♦ : fearless before danger **2** ♦ : overstepping due bounds : IMPUDENT **3** : marked by great and continuous steepness : STEEP **4** : ADVENTUROUS, FREE ⟨a ∼ thinker⟩ **5** ♦ : standing out prominently **6** : being set in boldface — **bold·ly** *adv* — **bold·ness** \'bōld-nəs\ *n*

♦ [1] adventurous, audacious, daring, enterprising, gutsy, hardy, nervy, venturesome *Ant* unadventurous, unenterpris-

ing ♦ [2] arch, brash, brazen, cheeky, cocky, fresh, impertinent, impudent, insolent, nervy, sassy, saucy ♦ [2] familiar, forward, free, immodest, presumptuous ♦ [5] catchy, conspicuous, emphatic, marked, noticeable, prominent, pronounced, remarkable, striking

bold·face \'bōld-ˌfās\ *n* : a heavy-faced type; *also* : printing in boldface — **bold–faced** \-'fāst\ *adj*

bole \'bōl\ *n* : the trunk of a tree

bo·le·ro \bə-'ler-ō\ *n, pl* **-ros 1** : a Spanish dance or its music **2** : a short loose jacket open at the front

Bo·liv·i·an \bə-'li-vē-ən\ *n* : a native or inhabitant of Bolivia — **Bolivian** *adj*

boll \'bōl\ *n* : a seed pod (as of cotton)

boll weevil *n* : a small grayish weevil that infests the cotton plant both as a larva and as an adult

boll·worm \'bōl-ˌwərm\ *n* : any of several moths and esp. the corn earworm whose larvae feed on cotton bolls

bo·lo·gna \bə-'lō-nē\ *n* : a large smoked sausage of beef, veal, and pork

Bol·she·vik \'bōl-shə-ˌvik\ *n, pl* **Bolsheviks** *also* **Bol·she·vi·ki** \ˌbōl-shə-'vi-kē\ : a member of the party that seized power in Russia in the revolution of November 1917 **2** : COMMUNIST — **Bolshevik** *adj*

bol·she·vism \'bōl-shə-ˌvi-zəm\ *n, often cap* : the doctrine or program of the Bolsheviks advocating violent overthrow of capitalism

¹**bol·ster** \'bōl-stər\ *n* : a long pillow or cushion

²**bolster** *vb* ♦ : to support with or as if with a bolster; *also* : REINFORCE

♦ bear, brace, buttress, carry, prop, shore, stay, support, uphold

¹**bolt** \'bōlt\ *n* **1** : a missile (as an arrow) for a crossbow or catapult **2** : a flash of lightning : THUNDERBOLT **3** : a sliding bar used to fasten a door **4** : a roll of cloth or wallpaper of specified length **5** : a rod with a head at one end and a screw thread at the other used with a nut to fasten objects together **6** : a metal cylinder that drives the cartridge into the chamber of a firearm

²**bolt** *vb* **1 a** ♦ : to move suddenly (as in fright or hurry) : START **b** ♦ : to rush off or away (as in fleeing) ⟨he ∼ed out of the room⟩ **2** : to break away (as from association) ⟨∼ from a political platform⟩ **3** : to produce seed prematurely **4** : to secure or fasten with a bolt **5** : to swallow hastily or without chewing **6** ♦ : to say impulsively

♦ [1a] jump, start, startle ♦ [1b] break, flee, fly, retreat, run, run away, run off ♦ [6] blurt, cry, ejaculate, spout

³**bolt** *n* : an act of bolting

bo·lus \'bō-ləs\ *n* **1** : a large pill **2** : a soft mass of chewed food

¹**bomb** \'bäm\ *n* **1** : a fused explosive device designed to detonate under specified conditions (as impact) **2** : an aerosol or foam dispenser (as of insecticide) : SPRAY CAN **3** : a long pass in football **4** ♦ : one that has failed : FAILURE, FLOP

♦ bummer, bust, catastrophe, debacle, dud, failure, fiasco, fizzle, flop, lemon, loser, miss, turkey, washout

²**bomb** *vb* **1** : to attack with bombs **2** : to fail utterly

bom·bard \bäm-'bärd\ *vb* **1** ♦ : to attack esp. with artillery or bombers **2** : to assail persistently **3** : to subject to the impact of rapidly moving particles (as electrons)

♦ blitz, shell

bom·bar·dier \ˌbäm-bər-'dir\ *n* : a bomber-crew member who releases the bombs

bom·bard·ment *n* ♦ : the act or an instance of bombarding or the state of being bombarded

♦ barrage, cannonade, fusillade, hail, salvo, shower, storm, volley

bom·bast \'bäm-ˌbast\ *n* ♦ : pretentious wordy speech or writing — **bom·bas·ti·cal·ly** \-ti-k(ə-)lē\ *adv*

♦ bluster, brag, gas, grandiloquence, rant, rhetoric

bom·bas·tic \bäm-'bas-tik\ *adj* ♦ : marked by or given to bombast

♦ gaseous, grandiloquent, oratorical, rhetorical, windy

bom·ba·zine \ˌbäm-bə-'zēn\ *n* **1** : a twilled fabric with silk warp and worsted filling **2** : a silk fabric in twill weave dyed black

bomb·er \'bä-mər\ *n* : one that bombs; *esp* : an airplane for dropping bombs

bomb·proof \'bäm-ˌprüf\ *adj* : safe against the explosive force of bombs

bomb·shell \'bäm-ˌshel\ *n* **1** : BOMB 1 **2** ♦ : one that stuns, amazes, or completely upsets

♦ bolt, jar, jolt, surprise

bona fide \\'bō-nə-ˌfīd, 'bä-; ˌbō-nə-'fī-dē, -də\\ *adj* **1 :** made in good faith ⟨a *bona fide* agreement⟩ **2 ♦ :** neither specious nor counterfeit : GENUINE, REAL ⟨a *bona fide* bargain⟩

♦ authentic, genuine, real, right, true

bo·nan·za \\bə-'nan-zə\\ *n* **:** something yielding a rich return
bon·bon \\'bän-ˌbän\\ *n* **:** a candy with a creamy center and a soft covering (as of chocolate)
¹bond \\'bänd\\ *n* **1 ♦ :** something that binds or restrains : FETTER **2 ♦ :** a binding or uniting force or tie ⟨∼s of friendship⟩ **3 ♦ :** an agreement or obligation often made binding by a pledge of money or goods **4 :** a person who acts as surety for another **5 :** an interest-bearing certificate of public or private indebtedness **6 :** the state of goods subject to supervision pending payment of taxes or duties due

♦ [1] band, chain, fetter, irons, ligature, manacle, shackle ♦ [2] cement, knot, ligature, link, tie ♦ [3] contract, covenant, guarantee, guaranty, surety, warranty

²bond *vb* **1 :** to assure payment of duties or taxes on (goods) by giving a bond **2 :** to insure against losses caused by the acts of ⟨∼ a bank teller⟩ **3 :** to make or become firmly united as if by bonds ⟨∼ iron to copper⟩ **4 :** to form a close relationship ⟨gave them a chance to ∼ with their father⟩
bond·age \\'bän-dij\\ *n* **♦ :** a state of being bound usu. by compulsion : SLAVERY, SERVITUDE

♦ enslavement, servitude, slavery, thrall, yoke

bond·hold·er \\'bänd-ˌhōl-dər\\ *n* **:** one that owns a government or corporation bond
bond·ing *n* **1 :** the formation of a close personal relationship esp. through frequent or constant association **2 :** the attaching of a material (as porcelain) to a tooth surface esp. for cosmetic purposes
bond·man \\'bänd-mən\\ *n* **♦ :** a person held in forced servitude

♦ chattel, slave, thrall

¹bonds·man \\'bändz-mən\\ *n* **:** SURETY 3
²bondsman *n* **♦ :** a person held in forced servitude : BONDMAN

♦ bondman, chattel, slave, thrall

bond·wom·an \\'bänd-ˌwu̇-mən\\ *n* **:** a woman held in forced servitude
¹bone \\'bōn\\ *n* **1 :** a hard largely calcareous tissue forming most of the skeleton of a vertebrate animal; *also* **:** one of the pieces of bone making up a vertebrate skeleton **2 :** a hard animal substance (as ivory or baleen) similar to true bone **3 :** something made of bone — **bone·less** *adj* — **bony** *also* **bon·ey** \\'bō-nē\\ *adj*
²bone *vb* **boned; bon·ing :** to free from bones ⟨∼ a chicken⟩
bone black *n* **:** the black carbon residue from calcined bones used esp. as a pigment
bone meal *n* **:** crushed or ground bone used esp. as fertilizer or feed
bon·er \\'bō-nər\\ *n* **:** a stupid and ridiculous blunder
bone up *vb* **1 :** to try to master necessary information quickly **2 :** to refresh one's memory ⟨*boned* up on the speech before giving it⟩
bon·fire \\'bän-ˌfīr\\ *n* **:** a large fire built in the open air
bon·go \\'bäŋ-gō\\ *n, pl* **bongos** *also* **bongoes :** one of a pair of small tuned drums played with the hands
bon·ho·mie \\ˌbä-nə-'mē\\ *n* **:** good-natured easy friendliness
bo·ni·to \\bə-'nē-tō\\ *n, pl* **-tos** *or* **-to :** any of several medium-sized tunas
bon mot \\bōⁿ-'mō\\ *n, pl* **bons mots** *same*\\ *or* **bon mots** *same or* -'mōz\\ **:** a clever remark
bon·net \\'bä-nət\\ *n* **:** a covering (as a cap) for the head; *esp* **:** a hat for a woman or infant tied under the chin
bon·ny \\'bä-nē\\ *adj* **bon·ni·er; -est** *chiefly Brit* **♦ :** very pleasing to look at : ATTRACTIVE; *also* **:** FINE, EXCELLENT

♦ attractive, beautiful, cute, fair, gorgeous, handsome, knockout, lovely, pretty, ravishing, stunning

bon·sai \\bōn-'sī\\ *n, pl* **bonsai :** a potted plant (as a tree) dwarfed by special methods of culture; *also* **:** the art of growing such a plant
bo·nus \\'bō-nəs\\ *n* **♦ :** something in addition to what is expected

♦ dividend, extra, lagniappe, perquisite, tip

bon vi·vant \\ˌbän-vē-'vänt, ˌbōⁿ-vē-'väⁿ\\ *n, pl* **bons vivants** \\ˌbän-vē-'vänts, ˌbōⁿ-vē-'väⁿ\\ *or* **bon vivants** *same*\\ **:** a person having cultivated, refined, and sociable tastes esp. in food and drink
bon voy·age \\ˌbōⁿ-ˌvȯi-'äzh, ˌbän-; ˌbōⁿ-ˌvwä-'yäzh\\ *n* **♦ :** a

wish of well-being at parting : FAREWELL — often used as an interjection

♦ adieu, au revoir, farewell, good-bye

bony fish *n* **:** any of a very large group of fishes (as a salmon or marlin) with a bony rather than a cartilaginous skeleton
bonze \\'bänz\\ *n* **:** a Buddhist monk
boo \\'bü\\ *n, pl* **boos ♦ :** a shout of disapproval or contempt — **boo** *vb*

♦ catcall, hiss, hoot, jeer, raspberry, snort

boo·by \\'bü-bē\\ *n, pl* **boobies ♦ :** an awkward foolish person : DOPE

♦ dope, fool, goose, jackass, nitwit, nut, simpleton, turkey

booby prize *n* **:** an award for the poorest performance in a contest
booby trap *n* **♦ :** a trap for the unwary; *esp* **:** a concealed explosive device set to go off when some harmless-looking object is touched — **booby–trap** *vb*

♦ catch, pitfall, snag ♦ explosive

boo·dle \\'büd-ᵊl\\ *n* **1 :** bribe money **2 :** a large amount of money
¹book \\'bu̇k\\ *n* **1 :** a set of sheets bound into a volume **2 :** a long written or printed narrative or record **3 :** a major division of a long literary work **4** *cap* **:** BIBLE — **in one's book :** in one's opinion
²book *vb* **1 :** to engage, reserve, or schedule by or as if by writing in a book ⟨∼ seats on a plane⟩ **2 :** to enter charges against in a police register
book·case \\-ˌkās\\ *n* **:** a piece of furniture consisting of shelves to hold books
book·end \\-ˌend\\ *n* **:** a support to hold up a row of books
book·ie \\'bu̇-kē\\ *n* **:** BOOKMAKER
book·ish \\'bu̇-kish\\ *adj* **1 :** fond of books and reading **2 a :** inclined to rely unduly on book knowledge **b** *of words* **♦ :** literary and formal as opposed to colloquial and informal

♦ erudite, learned, literary *Ant* colloquial, nonliterary

book·keep·er \\'bu̇k-ˌkē-pər\\ *n* **:** one who records the accounts or transactions of a business — **book·keep·ing** *n*
book·let \\'bu̇k-lət\\ *n* **♦ :** a little book; *esp* **:** PAMPHLET

♦ brochure, circular, folder, leaflet, pamphlet

book·mak·er \\'bu̇k-ˌmā-kər\\ *n* **:** one who determines odds and receives and pays off bets — **book·mak·ing** *n*
book·mark \\-ˌmärk\\ *or* **book·mark·er** \\-ˌmär-kər\\ *n* **1 :** a marker for finding a place in a book **2 :** a shortcut to a previously viewed location (as on a website) on a computer
book·mo·bile \\'bu̇k-mō-ˌbēl\\ *n* **:** a truck that serves as a traveling library
book off *vi, chiefly Can* **:** to notify an employer that one is not reporting for work (as because of sickness)
book·plate \\'bu̇k-ˌplāt\\ *n* **:** a label pasted in a book to show who owns it
book·sell·er \\'bu̇k-ˌse-lər\\ *n* **:** one who sells books; *esp* **:** the proprietor of a bookstore
book·shelf \\-ˌshelf\\ *n* **:** a shelf for books
book·worm \\'bu̇k-ˌwərm\\ *n* **:** a person unusually devoted to reading and study
¹boom \\'büm\\ *vb* **1 :** to make a deep hollow sound **2 :** to grow or cause to grow rapidly esp. in value, esteem, or importance
²boom *n* **1 :** a booming sound or cry **2 :** a rapid expansion or increase esp. of economic activity

♦ bang, blast, clap, crack, crash, pop, report, slam, smash, snap, thwack, whack

³boom *n* **1 :** a long spar used to extend the bottom of a sail **2 :** a line of floating timbers used to obstruct passage or catch floating objects **3 :** a beam projecting from the upright pole of a derrick to support or guide the object lifted **4 :** a long supporting pole or arm (as for a microphone)
boom box *n* **:** a large portable radio and often CD or tape player
boo·mer·ang \\'bü-mə-ˌraŋ\\ *n* **:** a bent or angular club that can be so thrown as to return near the starting point
boom·ing *adj* **1 ♦ :** making a loud deep sound ⟨his ∼ voice⟩ **2 :** forcefully or powerfully executed ⟨hit a ∼ serve⟩

♦ clamorous (*or* clamourous), loud, resounding, roaring, sonorous, stentorian, thunderous

¹boon \\'bün\\ *n* **1 ♦ :** something that promotes well-being; *also* **:** useful aid **2 ♦ :** something given or granted as a favor

♦ [1] advantage, aid, benefit, help ♦ [1] benefit, blessing, felicity, godsend, good, manna, windfall ♦ [2] courtesy, favor (*or* favour), grace, indulgence, kindness, mercy, service, turn

²**boon** *adj* ♦ : enjoying companionship and the pleasures of feasting and drinking ⟨a ～ companion⟩

♦ companionable, convivial, extroverted, gregarious, outgoing, sociable, social

boon·docks \'bün-ˌdäks\ *n pl* **1** : rough country filled with dense brush **2** : a rural area

boon·dog·gle \'bün-ˌdä-gəl, -ˌdȯ-\ *n* : a useless or wasteful project or activity

boor \'bu̇r\ *n* **1** : YOKEL **2** ♦ : a rude or insensitive person

♦ beast, churl, clown, creep, cretin, cur, heel, jerk, joker, louse, lout, skunk, slob, snake

boor·ish *adj* ♦ : having the qualities or behavior of a boor

♦ churlish, clownish, loutish, uncouth

¹**boost** \'büst\ *vb* **1** ♦ : to push up from below **2** ♦ : to make or become greater : INCREASE, RAISE ⟨～ prices⟩ **3** : to enthusiastically promote or support (a cause) ⟨voted a bonus to ～ morale⟩

♦ [1] crane, elevate, heave, heft, heighten, hike, hoist, jack, lift, pick up, raise, up, uphold ♦ [2] add, aggrandize, amplify, augment, compound, enlarge, escalate, expand, extend, increase, multiply, raise, swell, up ♦ [2] amplify, beef, consolidate, deepen, enhance, heighten, intensify, magnify, redouble, step up, strengthen

²**boost** *n* **1** : a push upward **2** ♦ : an act that brings help or encouragement **3** ♦ : an increase in amount

♦ [2] aid, assist, assistance, backing, help, lift, support ♦ [3] accretion, addition, augmentation, expansion, gain, increase, increment, plus, proliferation, raise, rise, supplement

boost·er *n* ♦ : one that boosts; *esp* : an enthusiastic supporter

♦ advocate, apostle, backer, champion, exponent, friend, promoter, proponent, supporter

¹**boot** \'büt\ *n, chiefly dial* : something to equalize a trade — **to boot** : BESIDES

²**boot** *vb, archaic* : AVAIL, PROFIT

³**boot** *n* **1** : a covering for the foot and leg **2** : a protective sheath (as of a flower) **3** *Brit* : an automobile trunk **4** : KICK; *also* : a discharge from employment **5** : a navy or marine corps trainee

⁴**boot** *vb* **1** : KICK **2** ♦ : to eject or discharge summarily — often used with *out* **3** *of a computer* : to start or make ready for operation

♦ *usu* **boot out** banish, bounce, cast, chase, dismiss, drum, eject, expel, oust, rout, run off, throw out

boot·black \'büt-ˌblak\ *n* : a person who shines shoes

boot camp *n* **1** : a navy or marine corps training camp **2** : a facility with a rigorous disciplinary program for young offenders

boo·tee *or* **boo·tie** \'bü-tē\ *n* : an infant's knitted or crocheted sock

booth \'büth\ *n, pl* **booths** \'büthz, 'büths\ **1** : a small enclosed stall (as at a fair) **2** : a small enclosure giving privacy for a person ⟨voting ～⟩ ⟨telephone ～⟩ **3** : a restaurant accommodation having a table between backed benches

boot·leg \'büt-ˌleg\ *vb* : to make, transport, or sell (as liquor) illegally — **boot·leg** *adj or n* — **boot·leg·ger** *n*

boot·less \'büt-ləs\ *adj* : producing no gain, good, or result : USELESS — **boot·less·ly** *adv* — **boot·less·ness** *n*

♦ fruitless, futile, ineffective, unproductive, unsuccessful

¹**boo·ty** \'bü-tē\ *n, pl* **booties** ♦ : plunder taken (as in war) : SPOIL

♦ loot, plunder, spoil, swag

²**booty** \'bü-tē\ *n, pl* **booties** *slang* : BUTTOCK 2

¹**booze** \'büz\ *vb* **boozed; booz·ing** : to drink liquor to excess — **booz·er** *n*

²**booze** *n* ♦ : intoxicating liquor — **boozy** *adj*

♦ alcohol, drink, intoxicant, liquor, moonshine, spirits

¹**bop** \'bäp\ *vb* **bopped; bop·ping** : to reach with a blow : HIT, SOCK

²**bop** *n* : a blow esp. with the fist or a club

BOQ *abbr* bachelor officers' quarters

bor *abbr* borough

bo·rate \'bōr-ˌāt\ *n* : a salt or ester of boric acid

bo·rax \'bōr-ˌaks\ *n* : a crystalline borate of sodium that occurs as a mineral and is used as a flux and cleanser

bor·del·lo \bȯr-'de-lō\ *n, pl* **-los** : BROTHEL

¹**bor·der** \'bȯr-dər\ *n* **1** ♦ : an outer part or edge **2** ♦ : something that marks or fixes a limit : BOUNDARY

♦ [1] borderland, frontier, march ♦ [2] bound, boundary, circumference, compass, confines, edge, end, fringe, margin, perimeter, periphery, rim, skirt, verge

²**border** *vb* **bor·dered; bor·der·ing** **1** ♦ : to put a border on **2** ♦ : to touch at the edge or boundary : ADJOIN **3** : to approach the nature of a specified thing : VERGE ⟨～s on the ridiculous⟩

♦ *usu* **border on** [1] bound, fringe, margin, rim, skirt ♦ *usu* **border on** [2] abut, adjoin, flank, fringe, join, skirt, touch, verge (on)

border collie *n, often cap B* : any of a British breed of medium-sized long-haired sheepdogs

bor·der·land \'bȯr-dər-ˌland\ *n* **1** ♦ : territory at or near a border **2** : an outlying or intermediate region often not clearly defined

♦ border, frontier, march

bor·der·line \-ˌlīn\ *adj* : being in an intermediate position or state; *esp* : not quite up to what is standard or expected ⟨～ intelligence⟩

¹**bore** \'bȯr\ *vb* **bored; bor·ing** **1** ♦ : to make a hole in with or as if with a drill **2** : to make (as a well) by boring or digging away material — **bor·er** *n*

♦ drill, hole, perforate, pierce, punch, puncture

²**bore** *n* **1** : a hole made by or as if by boring **2** : a cylindrical cavity **3** : the diameter of a hole or tube; *esp* : the interior diameter of a gun barrel or engine cylinder

³**bore** *past of* BEAR

⁴**bore** *n* : a tidal flood with a high abrupt front

⁵**bore** *n* : one that causes boredom

⁶**bore** *vb* **bored; bor·ing** ♦ : to weary with tedious dullness

♦ jade, tire, weary *Ant* absorb, engage, engross, grip, interest, intrigue

bo·re·al \'bōr-ē-əl\ *adj* : of, relating to, or located in northern regions

bore·dom \'bȯr-dəm\ *n* ♦ : the condition of being weary and restless because of dullness

♦ doldrums, ennui, listlessness, restlessness, tedium, tiredness, weariness

bo·ric acid \'bȯr-ik-\ *n* : a white crystalline weak acid that contains boron and is used esp. as an antiseptic

born \'bȯrn\ *adj* **1** : brought into life by birth **2** ♦ : belonging by birth : NATIVE ⟨American-*born*⟩ **3** : having special natural abilities or character from birth ⟨a ～ leader⟩

♦ aboriginal, endemic, indigenous, native

born–again *adj* : having experienced a revival of a personal faith or conviction ⟨～ believer⟩ ⟨～ liberal⟩

borne *past part of* BEAR

bo·ron \'bȯr-ˌän\ *n* : a chemical element that occurs in nature only in combination (as in borax)

bor·ough \'bər-ō\ *n* **1** : a British town that sends one or more members to Parliament; *also* : an incorporated British urban area **2** : an incorporated town or village in some U.S. states; *also* : any of the five political divisions of New York City **3** : a civil division of the state of Alaska corresponding to a county in most other states

bor·row \'bär-ō\ *vb* **1** : to take or receive (something) temporarily and with intent to return **2** ♦ : to take into possession or use from another source ⟨～ a metaphor⟩

♦ adopt, embrace, take up

borscht \'bȯrsht\ *or* **borsch** \'bȯrsh\ *n* : a soup made mainly from beets

bosh \'bäsh\ *n* : foolish talk or action : NONSENSE

bosky \'bäs-kē\ *adj* : covered with trees or shrubs

¹**bos·om** \'bu̇-zəm, 'bü-\ *n* **1** : the front of the human chest; *esp* : the female breasts **2** : the seat of secret thoughts and feelings **3** : the part of a garment covering the breast — **bos·omed** \-zəmd\ *adj*

²**bosom** *adj* ♦ : closely acquainted : INTIMATE

♦ chummy, close, familiar, friendly, intimate, thick

¹**boss** \'bäs, 'bȯs\ *n* : a knoblike ornament : STUD

²**boss** *vb* : to ornament with bosses

³**boss** \'bȯs\ *n* **1** ♦ : one (as a foreman or manager) exercising control or supervision **2** : a politician who controls votes or dictates policies

♦ captain, chief, foreman, head, headman, helmsman, kingpin, leader, master, taskmaster

⁴**boss** \'bȯs\ *vb* **1** ♦ : to act as a boss : SUPERVISE **2** ♦ : to give usu. arbitrary orders to — usu. used with *around*

♦ [1] captain, head, oversee, superintend, supervise ♦ *usu*

boss around [2] bid, charge, command, direct, enjoin, instruct, order, tell

⁴**boss** adj, slang ♦ : very good of its kind : EXCELLENT, FIRST-RATE

♦ A1, bang-up, banner, excellent, fabulous, fine, grand, great, prime, sensational, splendid, superb, superior, unsurpassed, wonderful

bossy adj ♦ : inclined to issue orders

♦ authoritarian, autocratic, despotic, dictatorial, domineering, imperious, overbearing, peremptory, tyrannical, tyrannous

bosun var of BOATSWAIN

¹**bot** \'bät\ n 1 : ROBOT 2 : a computer program that performs automatic, repetitive, and sometimes harmful tasks 3 : a computer program or character that mimics human actions

²**bot** abbr botanical; botanist; botany

bot·a·ny \'bät-ᵊn-ē, 'bät-nē\ n, pl **-nies** 1 : a branch of biology dealing with plants and plant life 2 : plant life (as of a region); also : the biology of a plant or plant group — **bo·tan·i·cal** \bə-'ta-ni-kəl\ adj — **bot·a·nist** \'bät-ᵊn-ist, 'bät-nist\ n — **bot·a·nize** \-ᵊn-ˌīz\ vb

botch \'bäch\ vb ♦ : to foul up hopelessly : BUNGLE — **botch** n

♦ bobble, bungle, butcher, flub, foul up, fumble, mangle, mess up, screw up

¹**both** \'bōth\ pron : both ones : the one as well as the other

²**both** conj — used as a function word to indicate and stress the inclusion of each of two or more things specified by coordinated words, phrases, or clauses ⟨∼ New York and London⟩

³**both** adj : being the two : including the one and the other

¹**both·er** \'bä-thər\ vb 1 a ♦ : to annoy esp. by petty provocation b ♦ : to intrude upon : PESTER 2 a ♦ : to become concerned : become mentally troubled b ♦ : to cause to be anxious or concerned

♦ [1a] aggravate, annoy, bug, chafe, exasperate, gall, get, grate, irk, irritate, nettle, peeve, persecute, pique, put out, rasp, rile, vex ♦ [1b] bug, disturb, intrude, pester ♦ [2a] fear, fret, stew, sweat, trouble, worry ♦ [2b] concern, discompose, disquiet, distress, disturb, perturb, unsettle, upset, worry

²**bother** n 1 a : a state of petty discomfort, annoyance, or worry b ♦ : something that causes petty annoyance or worry 2 ♦ : needless bustle or excitement

♦ [1b] aggravation, annoyance, exasperation, frustration, hassle, headache, inconvenience, irritant, nuisance, peeve, pest, problem, thorn, vexation ♦ [2] bustle, commotion, disturbance, furor, fuss, pother, stew, stir

both·er·some \-səm\ adj ♦ : causing bother

♦ aggravating, annoying, frustrating, galling, irksome, irritating, pesty, vexatious

¹**bot·tle** \'bät-ᵊl\ n 1 : a container (as of glass) with a narrow neck and usu. no handles 2 : the quantity held by a bottle 3 : intoxicating liquor

²**bottle** vb **bot·tled; bot·tling** 1 : to confine as if in a bottle : RESTRAIN 2 : to put into a bottle

bot·tle·neck \'bät-ᵊl-ˌnek\ n 1 : a narrow passage or point of congestion 2 ♦ : something that obstructs or impedes

♦ backup, jam, snarl

¹**bot·tom** \'bä-təm\ n 1 a ♦ : an under or supporting surface b ♦ : the seat of the body : BUTTOCKS 2 : the surface on which a body of water lies 3 ♦ : the lowest part or place; also : an inferior position ⟨start at the ∼⟩ 4 : BOTTOMLAND 5 a : the part of a ship's hull lying below the water b ♦ : used for traveling on water : BOAT — **bottom** adj — **bot·tom·less** adj

♦ [1a] underbelly, underside Ant face, top ♦ [1b] backside, butt, buttocks, posterior, rear, rump, seat ♦ [3] base, foot Ant head, top ♦ [5b] boat, craft, ship, vessel

²**bottom** vb 1 : to furnish with a bottom 2 : to reach the bottom 3 : to reach a low point before rebounding — usu. used with out

bot·tom·land \'bä-təm-ˌland\ n : low land along a river

bottom line n 1 : the essential point : CRUX 2 : the final result : OUTCOME

bot·u·lism \'bä-chə-ˌli-zəm\ n : an acute paralytic disease caused by a bacterial toxin (**bot·u·li·num toxin** \ˌbä-chə-ˌlī-nəm-\) esp. in tainted food

bou·doir \'bü-ˌdwär, 'bü-, ˌbü-', ˌbü-'\ n : a woman's dressing room or bedroom

bouf·fant \bü-'fänt, 'bü-ˌfänt\ adj : puffed out ⟨∼ hairdos⟩

bough \'bau̇\ n : a usu. large or main branch of a tree

bought past and past part of BUY

bouil·la·baisse \ˌbü-yə-'bās\ n : a highly seasoned fish stew made with at least two kinds of fish

bouil·lon \'bü-ˌyän; 'bu̇l-ˌyän, -yən\ n : a clear soup made usu. from beef

boul·der \'bōl-dər\ n : a large detached rounded or worn mass of rock — **boul·dered** \-dərd\ adj

bou·le·vard \'bu̇-lə-ˌvärd, 'bü-\ n : a broad often landscaped thoroughfare

¹**bounce** \'bau̇ns\ vb **bounced; bounc·ing** 1 : to cause to rebound ⟨∼ a ball⟩ 2 : to rebound after striking 3 ♦ : to expel hastily from a place 4 : to issue (a check) on an account having insufficient funds 5 ♦ : to recover quickly from a blow or defeat — usu. used with back

♦ [2] carom, glance, rebound, ricochet, skim, skip ♦ [3] banish, boot (out), cast, chase, dismiss, drum, eject, expel, oust, rout, run off, throw out ♦ usu **bounce back** [5] rally, rebound, recover, snap back

²**bounce** n ♦ : the quality or state of being lively — **bouncy** \'bau̇n-sē\ adj

♦ dash, drive, esprit, pep, punch, snap, spirit, verve, vim, zing, zip

bounc·er \'bau̇n-sər\ n : a person employed in a public place to remove disorderly persons

¹**bound** \'bau̇nd\ adj ♦ : intending to go ⟨homeward ∼⟩

♦ decisive, determined, firm, intent, purposeful, resolute, set, single-minded

²**bound** n : something that limits or restrains : LIMIT, BOUNDARY

³**bound** vb 1 ♦ : to set limits to 2 ♦ : to form the boundary of 3 : to name the boundaries of

♦ [1] circumscribe, define, delimit, demarcate, limit, mark, terminate ♦ [2] border, fringe, margin, rim, skirt

⁴**bound** past and past part of BIND

⁵**bound** adj 1 : constrained by or as if by bonds : CONFINED, OBLIGED 2 : enclosed in a binding or cover 3 ♦ : firmly decided : RESOLVED, DETERMINED; also : SURE

♦ decisive, determined, firm, intent, purposeful, resolute, set, single-minded

⁶**bound** n 1 ♦ : the act or an instance of leaping into the air : JUMP 2 : REBOUND, BOUNCE

♦ hop, jump, leap, spring, vault

⁷**bound** vb : to move by leaping : SPRING, BOUNCE

bound·ary \'bau̇n-drē\ n, pl **-aries** ♦ : something that marks or fixes a limit (as of territory)

♦ bound, ceiling, confines, end, extent, limit, limitation, line, termination ♦ border, bound, circumference, compass, confines, edge, end, fringe, margin, perimeter, periphery, rim, skirt, verge

bound·en \'bau̇n-dən\ adj : BINDING

bound·less adj ♦ : having no boundaries — **bound·less·ness** n

♦ endless, illimitable, immeasurable, indefinite, infinite, limitless, measureless, unbounded, unfathomable, unlimited

boun·te·ous \'bau̇n-tē-əs\ adj 1 : bestowing gifts or favors freely : GENEROUS 2 : more than enough : ABUNDANT — **boun·te·ous·ly** adv — **boun·te·ous·ness** n

boun·ti·ful \'bau̇n-ti-fəl\ adj 1 ♦ : giving freely 2 ♦ : given or provided abundantly : PLENTIFUL

♦ [1] charitable, free, generous, liberal, munificent, openhanded, unselfish, unsparing ♦ [2] abundant, ample, comfortable, generous, liberal, plentiful

boun·ti·ful·ly adv ♦ : in a bountiful degree

♦ generously, handsomely, liberally, well

boun·ti·ful·ness n : the quality or state of being bountiful

boun·ty \'bau̇n-tē\ n, pl **bounties** 1 ♦ : liberality in giving : GENEROSITY 2 : something given liberally 3 : a reward, premium, or subsidy given usu. for doing something

♦ generosity, liberality, philanthropy, unselfishness

bou·quet \bō-'kā, bü-\ n 1 : flowers picked and fastened together in a bunch 2 ♦ : a distinctive aroma (as of wine)

♦ aroma, fragrance, incense, perfume, redolence, scent, spice

bour·bon \'bər-bən\ n : a whiskey distilled from a corn mash

bour·geois \'bu̇rzh-ˌwä, bu̇rzh-'wä\ n, pl **bourgeois** \same or -ˌwäz, -'wäz\ : a middle-class person — **bourgeois** adj

bour·geoi·sie \ˌbu̇rzh-wä-'zē\ n : a social order dominated by bourgeois

bourne also **bourn** \'bōrn, 'bu̇rn\ n : BOUNDARY; also : DESTINATION

bourse \'bu̇rs\ *n* : a European stock exchange
bout \'bau̇t\ *n* **1** ♦ : an athletic match : CONTEST **2 a** ♦ : a fit of sickness : ATTACK ⟨a ~ of measles⟩ **b** : OUTBREAK **3** : SESSION

♦ [1] competition, contest, event, game, match, meet, tournament ♦ [2a] attack, case, fit, seizure, siege, spell

bou·tique \bü-'tēk\ *n* : a small fashionable specialty shop
bou·ton·niere \ˌbüt-ᵊn-'iər\ *n* : a flower or bouquet worn in a buttonhole
¹**bo·vine** \'bō-ˌvīn, -ˌvēn\ *adj* **1** : of or relating to bovines **2** : having qualities (as placidity or dullness) characteristic of oxen or cows
²**bovine** *n* : any of a group of mammals including oxen, buffalo, and their close relatives
bovine spon·gi·form encephalopathy \-'spän-ji-ˌfȯrm-\ *n* : MAD COW DISEASE
¹**bow** \'bau̇\ *vb* **1** ♦ : to give oneself over to the will or authority of another : YIELD **2** : to bend the head or body (as in submission, courtesy, or assent)

♦ blink, budge, capitulate, concede, give in, knuckle under, quit, submit, succumb, surrender, yield

²**bow** *n* : an act or posture of bowing
³**bow** \'bō\ *n* **1 a** ♦ : something bent into a simple curve : BEND, ARCH **b** : RAINBOW **2** : a weapon for shooting arrows; *also* : ARCHER **3** : a knot formed by doubling a line into two or more loops **4** : a wooden rod strung with horsehairs for playing an instrument of the violin family

♦ angle, arc, arch, bend, crook, curve, turn, wind

⁴**bow** \'bō\ *vb* **1** : to bend into a curve **2** : to play (an instrument) with a bow
⁵**bow** \'bau̇\ *n* : the forward part of a ship — **bow** *adj*
bowd·ler·ise *Brit var of* BOWDLERIZE
bowd·ler·ize \'bōd-lə-ˌrīz, 'bau̇d-\ *vb* **-ized; -iz·ing** : to expurgate by omitting parts considered vulgar
bow·el \'bau̇(-ə)l\ *n* **1** : INTESTINE; *also* : one of the divisions of the intestine — usu. used in pl. **2** *pl* : the inmost parts ⟨the ~s of the earth⟩
bowel movement *n* : an act of passing usu. solid waste through the rectum and anus; *also* : STOOL 4
bow·er \'bau̇(-ə)r\ *n* : a shelter of boughs or vines : ARBOR
¹**bowl** \'bōl\ *n* **1** : a concave vessel used to hold liquids **2** : a drinking vessel **3** ♦ : a bowl-shaped part or structure; *esp* : an athletic stadium — **bowl·ful** \-ˌfu̇l\ *n*

♦ circus, coliseum, stadium

²**bowl** *n* **1** : a ball for rolling on a level surface in bowling **2** : a cast of the ball in bowling
³**bowl** *vb* **1** : to play a game of bowling; *also* : to roll a ball in bowling **2** ♦ : to travel (as in a vehicle) rapidly and smoothly **3** ♦ : to strike or knock down with a moving object

♦ [2] breeze, coast, drift, flow, glide, roll, sail, skim, slide, slip, stream, sweep, whisk ♦ *usu* **bowl down** [3] down, drop, fell, floor, knock, level

bow·legged \'bō-ˌle-gəd\ *adj* : having legs that bow outward at or below the knee — **bow·leg** \'bō-ˌleg\ *n*
¹**bowl·er** \'bō-lər\ *n* : a person who bowls
²**bowl·er** \'bō-lər\ *n* : DERBY 3
bow·line \'bō-lən, -ˌlīn\ *n* : a knot used to form a loop that neither slips nor jams
bowl·ing \'bō-liŋ\ *n* : any of various games in which balls are rolled on a green or alley at an object or a group of objects; *esp* : TENPINS
bowl over *vb* ♦ : to overwhelm with surprise; *also* : to make a vivid impression on

♦ amaze, astonish, astound, dumbfound, flabbergast, floor, shock, startle, stun, stupefy, surprise

bow·man \'bō-mən\ *n* : ARCHER
bow·sprit \'bau̇-ˌsprit\ *n* : a spar projecting forward from the prow of a ship
bow·string \'bō-ˌstriŋ\ *n* : the cord connecting the two ends of a shooting bow
¹**box** \'bäks\ *n, pl* **box** *or* **box·es** : an evergreen shrub or small tree used esp. for hedges
²**box** *n* **1** ♦ : a rigid typically rectangular receptacle often with a cover; *also* : the quantity held by a box **2** : a small compartment (as for a group of theater patrons); *also* : a boxlike receptacle or division **3** : any of six spaces on a baseball diamond where the batter, pitcher, coaches, and catcher stand **4** : a difficult situation : PREDICAMENT

♦ caddy, case, casket, chest, locker, trunk

³**box** *vb* : to enclose in or as if in a box
⁴**box** *n* ♦ : a punch or slap esp. on the ear

♦ belt, blow, buffet, hit, punch, slug

⁵**box** *vb* **1** : to strike with the hand **2** : to engage in boxing with
box·car \'bäks-ˌkär\ *n* : a roofed freight car usu. with sliding doors in the sides
box cutter *n* : a small cutting tool with a retractable razor blade
¹**box·er** \'bäk-sər\ *n* **1** ♦ : a person who engages in boxing **2** *pl* : BOXER SHORTS

♦ fighter, prizefighter, pugilist

²**boxer** *n* : any of a German breed of compact medium-sized dogs with a short usu. fawn or brindled coat
boxer shorts *n pl* : men's loose-fitting shorts worn as underwear
box·ing \'bäk-siŋ\ *n* : the sport of fighting with the fists
box office *n* : an office (as in a theater) where admission tickets are sold
box turtle *n* : any of several No. American land turtles able to withdraw completely into their shell
box·wood \'bäks-ˌwu̇d\ *n* : the tough hard wood of the box; *also* : a box tree or shrub
boy \'bȯi\ *n* **1** ♦ : a male child : YOUTH **2** : SON — **boy·hood** \-ˌhu̇d\ *n* — **boy·ish** *adj* — **boy·ish·ly** *adv* — **boy·ish·ness** *n*

♦ lad, nipper, shaver, stripling, youth

boy·cott \'bȯi-ˌkät\ *vb* : to refrain from having any dealings with — **boycott** *n*
boy·friend \'bȯi-ˌfrend\ *n* **1** : a male friend **2** ♦ : a frequent or regular male companion in a romantic or sexual relationship

♦ beau, fellow, man, swain

Boy Scout *n* : a member of any of various national scouting programs (as the Boy Scouts of America)
boy·sen·ber·ry \'bȯiz-ᵊn-ˌber-ē, 'bȯis-\ *n* : a large bramble fruit with a raspberry flavor; *also* : the hybrid plant bearing it developed by crossing blackberries and raspberries
bo·zo \'bō-ˌzō\ *n, pl* **bozos** : a foolish or incompetent person
bp *abbr* **1** bishop **2** birthplace
BP *abbr* **1** batting practice **2** blood pressure **3** boiling point
bpl *abbr* birthplace
BPOE *abbr* Benevolent and Protective Order of Elks
br *abbr* **1** branch **2** brass **3** brown
¹**Br** *abbr* Britain; British
²**Br** *symbol* bromine
BR *abbr* bedroom
bra \'brä\ *n* : BRASSIERE
¹**brace** \'brās\ *vb* **braced; brac·ing** **1** *archaic* : to make fast : BIND **2** : to tighten preparatory to use; *also* : to get ready for : prepare oneself **3** ♦ : to restore strength and activity to : INVIGORATE **4** ♦ : to furnish or support with a brace; *also* : STRENGTHEN **5** : to set firmly **6** ♦ : to gain courage or confidence

♦ [3] animate, energize, enliven, fire, invigorate, jazz up, liven up, pep up, quicken, stimulate, vitalize, vivify, zip (up) ♦ [4] bear, bolster, buttress, carry, prop, shore, stay, strengthen, support, uphold ♦ [6] forearm, fortify, nerve, psych (up), ready, steel

²**brace** *n, pl* **brac·es** **1** *or pl* **brace** ♦ : two of a kind ⟨a ~ of dogs⟩ **2** : a crank-shaped device for turning a bit **3** ♦ : something (as a tie, prop, or clamp) that distributes, directs, or resists pressure or weight **4** *pl* : SUSPENDERS **5** : an appliance for supporting a body part (as the shoulders) **6** *pl* : a dental appliance used to exert pressure to straighten misaligned teeth **7** : one of two marks { } used to connect words or items to be considered together

♦ [1] couple, duo, pair, twain, twosome ♦ [3] bulwark, buttress, mount, shore, stay, support, underpinning

brace·let \'brā-slət\ *n* **1** : an ornamental band or chain worn around the wrist **2** : something (as handcuffs) resembling a bracelet
bra·ce·ro \brä-'ser-ō\ *n, pl* **-ros** : a Mexican laborer admitted to the U.S. esp. for seasonal farm work
brac·ing *adj* ♦ : giving strength, vigor, or freshness

♦ invigorating, refreshing, restorative, stimulative, tonic

brack·en \'bra-kən\ *n* : a large coarse fern; *also* : a growth of such ferns
¹**brack·et** \'bra-kət\ *n* **1** : a projecting framework or arm designed to support weight; *also* : a shelf on such framework **2** : one of a pair of punctuation marks [ ] used esp. to enclose interpolated matter **3** ♦ : a continuous section of a series; *esp* : one of a graded series of income groups

♦ category, class, division, family, grade, group, kind, order, set, species, type

²bracket *vb* **1** : to furnish or fasten with brackets **2 a** : to place within brackets **b** : to separate or group with or as if with brackets

brack·ish \'bra-kish\ *adj* : somewhat salty — **brack·ish·ness** *n*

bract \'brakt\ *n* : an often modified leaf on or at the base of a flower stalk

brad \'brad\ *n* : a slender nail with a small head

brae \'brā\ *n, chiefly Scot* : a hillside esp. along a river

¹brag \'brag\ *vb* **bragged; brag·ging** ♦ : to talk or assert boastfully — **brag·ger** *n*

♦ boast, crow, plume, swagger

²brag *n* **1** ♦ : arrogant talk or manner **2** : one who brags : BRAGGART

♦ bluster, bombast, braggadocio, gas, grandiloquence, hot air, rant

brag·ga·do·cio \ˌbra-gə-'dō-shē-ˌō, -sē-, -chē-\ *n, pl* **-cios** **1** ♦ : one who brags : BRAGGART **2** ♦ : empty boasting **3** : arrogant pretension : COCKINESS

♦ [1] braggart, boaster, bragger ♦ [2] bluster, bombast, brag, gas, grandiloquence, hot air, rant

brag·gart \'bra-gərt\ *n* ♦ : one who brags

♦ boaster, braggadocio, bragger

brag·ger \'bra-gər\ *n* ♦ : one who brags

♦ braggart, boaster, braggadocio

Brah·man *or* **Brah·min** \'brä-mən *for 1;* 'brā-, 'brä-, 'bra- *for 2*\ *n* **1** : a Hindu of the highest caste traditionally assigned to the priesthood **2** : any of a breed of large vigorous humped cattle developed in the southern U.S. from the zebu **3** *usu* **Brahmin** : a person of high social standing and cultivated intellect and taste

Brah·man·ism \'brä-mə-ˌni-zəm\ *n* : orthodox Hinduism

¹braid \'brād\ *vb* **1** : to form (strands) into a braid : PLAIT; *also* : to make from braids **2** : to ornament with braid

²braid *n* **1** ♦ : a length of braided hair **2** ♦ : a cord or ribbon of three or more interwoven strands

♦ [1, 2] lace, plait

braille \'brāl\ *n, often cap* : a system of writing for the blind that uses characters made up of raised dots

¹brain \'brān\ *n* **1** : the part of the vertebrate central nervous system enclosed in the skull and continuous with the spinal cord that is composed of neurons and supporting structures and is the center of thought and nervous system control; *also* : a centralized mass of nerve tissue in an invertebrate **2 a** ♦ : INTELLECT, INTELLIGENCE — often used in pl. **b** ♦ : a very intelligent or intellectual person — **brained** \'brānd\ *adj*

♦ *often* **brains** [2a] gray matter (*or* grey matter), intellect, intelligence, reason, sense ♦ [2b] genius, intellect, thinker, whiz, wizard

²brain *vb* **1** : to kill by smashing the skull **2** : to hit on the head

brain·child \'brān-ˌchīld\ *n* : a product of one's creative imagination

brain death *n* : final cessation of activity in the central nervous system esp. as indicated by a flat electroencephalogram — **brain–dead** \-ˌded\ *adj*

brain drain *n* : the departure of educated or professional people from one country, sector, or field to another usu. for better pay or living conditions

brain·less *adj* : lacking intelligence

brain·storm \-ˌstȯrm\ *n* : a sudden inspiration or idea — **brainstorm** *vb*

brain·teas·er \-ˌtē-zər\ *n* : a challenging puzzle

brain·wash·ing \'brān-ˌwȯ-shiŋ, -ˌwä-\ *n* **1** : a forcible indoctrination to induce someone to give up basic political, social, or religious beliefs and attitudes and to accept contrasting regimented ideas **2** : persuasion by propaganda or salesmanship — **brain·wash** *vb*

brain wave *n* **1** : BRAINSTORM **2** : rhythmic fluctuations of voltage between parts of the brain; *also* : a current produced by brain waves

brainy *adj* ♦ : having or showing a well-developed intellect

♦ alert, bright, brilliant, clever, intelligent, keen, nimble, quick, quick-witted, sharp, smart

braise \'brāz\ *vb* **braised; brais·ing** : to cook (meat) slowly in fat and little moisture in a closed pot

¹brake \'brāk\ *n* : a common bracken fern

²brake *n* ♦ : rough or wet land heavily overgrown (as with thickets or reeds)

♦ brushwood, chaparral, coppice, covert, thicket

³brake *n* : a device for slowing or stopping motion esp. by friction — **brake·less** *adj*

⁴brake *vb* **braked; brak·ing** **1** ♦ : to slow or stop by or as if by a brake **2** : to apply a brake

♦ decelerate, retard, slow

brake·man \'brāk-mən\ *n* : a train crew member who inspects the train and assists the conductor

bram·ble \'bram-bəl\ *n* : any of a large genus of prickly shrubs (as a blackberry) related to the roses; *also* : any rough prickly shrub or vine

bram·bly \-b(ə-)lē\ *adj* ♦ : like or full of brambles

♦ prickly, scratchy, thorny

bran \'bran\ *n* : the edible broken husks of cereal grain sifted from flour or meal

¹branch \'branch\ *n* **1** : a natural subdivision (as a bough or twig) of a plant stem **2** : a division (as of an antler or a river) related to a whole like a plant branch to its stem **3** : a discrete element of a complex system: as **a** ♦ : a separate but dependent part of a central organization ⟨the executive ∼⟩ **b** : a division of a family descended from one ancestor — **branched** \'brancht\ *adj*

♦ affiliate, chapter, local

²branch *vb* **1** : to develop branches **2** ♦ : to spring out (as from a main stem) : DIVERGE **3** : to extend activities ⟨the business is ∼ing out⟩

♦ diverge, fan, radiate ♦ *usu* **branch out** diverge, divide, fork, separate

¹brand \'brand\ *n* **1** : a piece of charred or burning wood **2 a** : a mark made (as by burning) usu. to identify **b** ♦ : a mark of disgrace : STIGMA **3** : a class of goods identified as the product of a particular firm or producer **4** : a distinctive kind ⟨my own ∼ of humor⟩

♦ blot, smirch, spot, stain, stigma, taint

²brand *vb* **1** : to mark with a brand **2** : STIGMATIZE

bran·dish \'bran-dish\ *vb* : to shake or wave menacingly

brand–new \'bran-'nü, -'nyü\ *adj* ♦ : conspicuously new and unused

♦ fresh, pristine, virgin ♦ new, spick-and-span, unused

bran·dy \'bran-dē\ *n, pl* **brandies** : a liquor distilled from wine or fermented fruit juice — **brandy** *vb*

brash \'brash\ *adj* **1** ♦ : prone to act in a rash, impetuous manner **2** ♦ : aggressively self-assertive — **brash·ly** *adv* — **brash·ness** *n*

♦ [1] foolhardy, madcap, overbold, overconfident, reckless ♦ [2] arch, bold, brazen, cheeky, cocky, fresh, impertinent, impudent, insolent, nervy, sassy, saucy

brass \'bras\ *n* **1** : an alloy of copper and zinc; *also* : an object of brass **2** ♦ : brazen self-assurance **3** : persons of high rank (as in the military)

♦ audacity, brazenness, cheek, chutzpah, effrontery, gall, nerve, presumption, sauce, sauciness, temerity

bras·siere \brə-'zir\ *n* : a woman's close-fitting undergarment designed to support the breasts

brassy *adj* : shamelessly bold

brat \'brat\ *n* **1** *disparaging* : an ill-behaved child **2** : a child of a career military person — **brat·ti·ness** *n* — **brat·ty** *adj*

bra·va·do \brə-'vä-dō\ *n, pl* **-does** *or* **-dos** **1** : blustering swaggering conduct **2** : a show of bravery

¹brave \'brāv\ *adj* **brav·er; brav·est** **1** ♦ : showing courage **2** : EXCELLENT, SPLENDID — **brave·ly** *adv*

♦ courageous, dauntless, doughty, fearless, gallant, greathearted, heroic, intrepid, lionhearted, manful, stalwart, stout, undaunted, valiant, valorous **Ant** cowardly, craven, fainthearted, fearful, pusillanimous, timorous

²brave *vb* **braved; brav·ing** ♦ : to face or endure bravely

♦ beard, brazen, confront, dare, defy, face

³brave *n* : a person who is brave; *specif* : a No. American Indigenous warrior

brav·ery \'brā-və-rē\ *n, pl* **-er·ies** **1** ♦ : the quality or state of being brave : COURAGE **2** : fine clothes; *also* : showy display

♦ courage, daring, fearlessness, gallantry, guts, hardihood, heart, heroism, nerve, stoutness, valor

bra·vo \'brä-vō\ *n, pl* **bravos** : a shout of approval — often used as an interjection in applauding
bra·vu·ra \bra-'vyur-a, -'vur-\ *n* **1** : a florid brilliant musical style **2** : self-assured brilliant performance — **bravura** *adj*
¹**brawl** \'brȯl\ *n* ♦ : a noisy quarrel — **brawl·er** *n*

♦ altercation, argument, disagreement, dispute, fight, quarrel, row, wrangle ♦ fracas, fray, free-for-all, melee, row

²**brawl** *vb* ♦ : to quarrel or fight noisily

♦ argue, bicker, dispute, fall out, fight, hassle, quarrel, row, scrap, spat, squabble, wrangle

brawn \'brȯn\ *n* : strong muscles; *also* : muscular strength — **brawn·i·ness** *n*
brawny *adj* ♦ : having well-developed muscles

♦ muscular, rugged, sinewy, stalwart, stout, strong

bray \'brā\ *n* : the characteristic harsh cry of a donkey — **bray** *vb*
braze \'brāz\ *vb* **brazed; braz·ing** : to solder with an alloy (as brass) that melts at a lower temperature than the metals being joined — **braz·er** *n*
¹**bra·zen** \'brāz-ᵊn\ *adj* **1** : made of brass **2** : sounding harsh and loud **3** : of the color of brass **4** ♦ : marked by contemptuous boldness — **bra·zen·ly** *adv*

♦ arch, bold, brash, cheeky, cocky, fresh, impertinent, impudent, insolent, nervy, sassy, saucy

²**brazen** *vb* ♦ : to face boldly or defiantly

♦ beard, brave, confront, dare, defy, face

bra·zen·ness *n* ♦ : the quality or state of being brazen

♦ discourtesy, disrespect, impertinence, impudence, incivility, insolence, rudeness ♦ audacity, brass, cheek, chutzpah, effrontery, gall, nerve, presumption, sauce, sauciness, temerity

¹**bra·zier** \'brā-zhər\ *n* : a worker in brass
²**brazier** *n* **1** : a vessel holding burning coals (as for heating) **2** : a device on which food is grilled
Bra·zil·ian \bra-'zil-yən\ *n* : a native or inhabitant of Brazil — **Brazilian** *adj*
Bra·zil nut \bra-'zil-\ *n* : a triangular oily edible nut borne in large capsules by a tall So. American tree; *also* : the tree
¹**breach** \'brēch\ *n* **1** ♦ : a breaking of a law, obligation, tie (as of friendship), or standard (as of conduct) **2** ♦ : an interruption or opening made by or as if by breaking through

♦ [1] infraction, infringement, offense, transgression, trespass, violation *Ant* observance ♦ [2] break, discontinuity, gap, gulf, hole, interval, opening, rent, rift, separation

²**breach** *vb* **1** : to make a breach in **2** : to leap out of water ⟨whales ~*ing*⟩ **3** ♦ : to fail to keep or honor : violate a trust ⟨~*ed* the agreements⟩

♦ break, transgress, violate

¹**bread** \'bred\ *n* **1** : baked food made basically of flour or meal **2** : a substance with food value : FOOD
²**bread** *vb* : to cover with bread crumbs before cooking
bread·bas·ket \'bred-,bas-kət\ *n* : a major cereal-producing region
bread·fruit \-,früt\ *n* : a round usu. seedless fruit resembling bread in color and texture when baked; *also* : a tall tropical tree related to the mulberry and bearing breadfruit
bread·stuff \-,stəf\ *n* : GRAIN, FLOUR
breadth \'bredth, 'bretth\ *n* **1 a** : distance from side to side : WIDTH **b** ♦ : a wide expanse **2** ♦ : comprehensive quality : SCOPE ⟨~ of knowledge⟩

♦ [1b] expanse, extent, reach, spread, stretch ♦ [2] amplitude, compass, extent, range, reach, realm, scope, sweep, width

bread·win·ner \'bred-,wi-nər\ *n* : a member of a family whose wages supply its livelihood
¹**break** \'brāk\ *vb* **broke** \'brōk\; **bro·ken** \'brō-kən\; **break·ing** **1** ♦ : to separate into parts usu. suddenly or violently : come or force apart **2** ♦ : to violate a command or law : TRANSGRESS ⟨~ a law⟩ **3** : to force a way into, out of, or through **4 a** : to disrupt the order or unity of ⟨~ ranks⟩ ⟨~ up a gang⟩ **b** : to cause the destruction or loss of effectiveness of; *also* : to bring to submission or helplessness **5** : EXCEED, SURPASS ⟨~ a record⟩ **6 a** : to cause to suffer financial ruin **b** : to reduce in rank ⟨*broken* from sergeant to private⟩ **7 a** : to make known **b** ♦ : to find an explanation or solution for; *also* : to discover the essentials of (a code or cipher system) **8 a** ♦ : to stop or bring to an end suddenly : HALT **b** : to act or change abruptly (as a course or activity) **9** : to come esp. suddenly into being or notice ⟨as day ~s⟩ **10** ♦ : to fail under stress **11** : HAPPEN, DEVELOP **12** ♦ : to escape with sudden forceful effort

♦ [1] bust, fracture, fragment ♦ [2] breach, transgress, violate ♦ [6b] bust, degrade, demote, downgrade, reduce ♦ [7b] answer, crack, decode, dope, figure out, puzzle, resolve, riddle, solve, unravel, work, work out ♦ [8a] break off, cease, cut, desist, discontinue, drop, end, halt, knock off, lay off, leave off, quit, shut off, stop ♦ [10] break down, conk, crash, cut out, die, fail, stall ♦ [12] bolt, flee, fly, retreat, run, run away, run off

²**break** *n* **1** : an act of breaking **2** ♦ : a result of breaking; *esp* : an interruption of strength or continuity ⟨coffee ~⟩ ⟨a ~ in the wall⟩ **3** : a stroke of good luck

♦ breach, discontinuity, gap, gulf, hole, interval, opening, rent, rift, separation ♦ breath, breather, recess, respite

break·able *adj* ♦ : capable of being broken — **breakable** *n*

♦ delicate, fragile, frail

break·age \'brā-kij\ *n* **1** : the action of breaking **2** : articles or amount broken **3** : loss due to things broken
break·down \'brāk-,daun\ *n* **1** : functional failure; *esp* : a physical, mental, or nervous collapse **2** : DISINTEGRATION **3** ♦ : the process of decomposing : DECOMPOSITION **4** ♦ : division into categories : ANALYSIS

♦ [3] corruption, decay, decomposition, putrefaction, rot, spoilage ♦ [4] analysis, assay, dissection

break down *vb* **1** ♦ : to stop functioning because of breakage or wear **2** ♦ : to divide into parts or categories **3** ♦ : to undergo decomposition **4** ♦ : to succumb to mental or emotional stress

♦ [1] break, conk, crash, cut out, die, fail, stall ♦ [2] assort, categorize, class, classify, grade, group, peg, place, range, rank, separate, sort ♦ [3] corrupt, decay, decompose, disintegrate, molder, putrefy, rot, spoil ♦ [4] crack, flip, freak

break·er \'brā-kər\ *n* **1** : one that breaks **2** : a wave that breaks into foam (as against the shore)
break·fast \'brek-fəst\ *n* : the first meal of the day — **breakfast** *vb*
break in *vb* **1** : to enter a building by force **2** ♦ : to hinder by speaking when another is speaking : INTERRUPT; *also* : INTRUDE **3** : TRAIN — **break–in** \'brāk-,in\ *n*

♦ chime in, cut in, interpose, interrupt, intrude

break·neck \'brāk-'nek\ *adj* ♦ : very fast or dangerous ⟨~ speed⟩

♦ breathless, dizzy, fast, fleet, lightning, rapid, rattling, speedy, swift

break off *vb* ♦ : to stop abruptly : bring or come to an end

♦ break, cease, cut, desist, discontinue, drop, end, halt, knock off, lay off, leave off, quit, shut off, stop

break out *vb* **1** ♦ : to develop or erupt suddenly or with force **2** : to develop a skin rash

♦ burst, erupt, explode, flame, flare, go off

break·through \'brāk-,thrü\ *n* **1** : an act or instance of breaking through an obstruction or defensive line **2** ♦ : a sudden advance in knowledge or technique

♦ advance, advancement, enhancement, improvement, refinement

break·up \-,əp\ *n* **1** ♦ : the act or process of dissolving : DISSOLUTION **2** : a division into smaller units

♦ dissolution, division, partition, schism, separation, split

break up *vb* **1** ♦ : to cease to exist as a unified whole **2** ♦ : to break into pieces

♦ [1] disband, disperse, dissolve ♦ [2] disconnect, disjoint, dissever, dissociate, disunite, divide, divorce, part, resolve, separate, sever, split, sunder, unyoke

break·wa·ter \'brāk-,wȯ-tər, -,wä-\ *n* : a structure protecting a harbor or beach from the force of waves
bream \'brim, 'brēm\ *n, pl* **bream** *or* **breams** : any of various small freshwater sunfishes
breast \'brest\ *n* **1** : either of the pair of mammary glands extending from the front of the chest esp. in pubescent and adult human females **2** : the front part of the body between the neck and the abdomen **3** : the seat of emotion and thought
breast·bone \'brest-,bōn\ *n* : STERNUM
breast–feed \-,fēd\ *vb* : to feed (a baby) from a mother's breast rather than from a bottle
breast·plate \-,plāt\ *n* : a metal plate of armor for the breast
breast·stroke \-,strōk\ *n* : a swimming stroke executed by extending both arms forward and then sweeping them back with palms out while kicking backward and outward with both legs

breast·work \-ˌwərk\ *n* : a temporary fortification

breath \'breth\ *n* **1 a** : the act or power of breathing **b** ♦ : opportunity or time to breathe; *esp* : a pause in an activity **2** ♦ : a slight breeze **3** : air inhaled or exhaled in breathing **4** : spoken sound **5** : SPIRIT — **breath·less·ly** *adv* — **breath·less·ness** *n* — **breathy** \'bre-thē\ *adj*

♦ [1b] break, breather, pause, recess, respite ♦ [2] air, breeze, puff, waft, zephyr

breathe \'brēth\ *vb* **breathed; breath·ing 1** : to inhale and exhale **2** ♦ : to be alive : LIVE **3** : to halt for rest **4** : to utter softly or secretly — **breath·able** *adj*

♦ be, exist, live, subsist

breath·er \'brē-thər\ *n* **1** : one that breathes **2** ♦ : a short rest

♦ break, breath, recess, respite

breath·less *adj* **1 a** : panting or gasping for breath **b** ♦ : not breathing : not alive **2** ♦ : very rapid or strenuous **3** ♦ : oppressive because of no fresh air or breeze

♦ [1b] dead, deceased, defunct, gone, late, lifeless ♦ [2] breakneck, brisk, dizzy, fast, fleet, hasty, lightning, nippy, quick, rapid, rattling, snappy, speedy, swift ♦ [3] close, stuffy

breath·tak·ing \'breth-ˌtā-kiŋ\ *adj* **1** : making one out of breath **2** ♦ : producing excitement : EXCITING, THRILLING ⟨~ beauty⟩ — **breath·tak·ing·ly** *adv*

♦ electric, exciting, exhilarating, rousing, stirring, thrilling

brec·cia \'bre-chē-ə, -chə\ *n* : a rock consisting of sharp fragments held in fine-grained material

breech \'brēch\ *n* **1** *usu* **breech·es** *usu* 'bri-chəz\ ♦ : trousers ending near the knee; *also* : PANTS **2** : the hind end of the body : BUTTOCKS, RUMP **3** : the part of a firearm at the rear of the barrel

♦ britches, pantaloons, pants, slacks, trousers

¹breed \'brēd\ *vb* **bred** \'bred\; **breed·ing 1** : BEGET; *also* : ORIGINATE **2** ♦ : to propagate sexually; *also* : MATE **3** ♦ : to bring (a person) to maturity through nurturing care and education : BRING UP **4** : to produce (fissionable material) from material that is not fissionable — **breed·er** *n*

♦ [2] mate, multiply, procreate, propagate, reproduce ♦ [3] bring up, foster, raise, rear

²breed *n* **1** : a strain of similar and presumably related plants or animals usu. developed in domestication **2** ♦ : a group, set, or kind sharing common attributes : SORT, CLASS

♦ class, description, feather, ilk, kind, like, manner, nature, order, sort, species, type

breed·ing *n* **1** ♦ : line of descent : ANCESTRY **2** : training in polite social interaction **3** : sexual propagation of plants or animals

♦ ancestry, birth, blood, bloodline, descent, extraction, family tree, genealogy, line, lineage, origin, parentage, pedigree, stock, strain

¹breeze \'brēz\ *n* **1** ♦ : a light wind **2** ♦ : something easily done : CINCH, SNAP — **breeze·less** *adj*

♦ [1] air, breath, puff, waft, zephyr ♦ [2] child's play, cinch, picnic, pushover, snap

²breeze *vb* **breezed; breez·ing** ♦ : to progress quickly and easily; *also* : to move swiftly and airily

♦ bowl, coast, drift, flow, glide, roll, sail, skim, slide, slip, stream, sweep, whisk ♦ dash, fly, hasten, hurry, run, rush, speed, whirl, zip, zoom

breeze·way \'brēz-ˌwā\ *n* : a roofed open passage connecting two buildings (as a house and garage)

breezy \'brē-zē\ *adj* **1** ♦ : swept by breezes **2** ♦ : briskly informal — **breez·i·ly** \'brē-zə-lē\ *adv* — **breez·i·ness** \-zē-nəs\ *n*

♦ [1] blowy, blustery, gusty, windy ♦ [2] affable, easygoing, happy-go-lucky, laid-back

breth·ren \'breth-rən, 'bre-thə-; 'bre-thərn\ *pl of* BROTHER — used esp. in formal or solemn address

Brethren *n pl* : members of one of several Protestant denominations originating chiefly in a German religious movement and stressing personal religious experience

bre·via·ry \'brē-vyə-rē, -vē-ˌer-ē\ *n, pl* **-ries** *often cap* : a book of prayers, hymns, psalms, and readings used by Roman Catholic priests

brev·i·ty \'bre-və-tē\ *n, pl* **-ties 1** ♦ : shortness or conciseness of expression **2** ♦ : shortness of duration

♦ [1, 2] briefness, conciseness, shortness

brew \'brü\ *vb* **1** : to prepare (as beer) by steeping, boiling, and fermenting **2** : to prepare (as tea) by steeping in hot water — **brew** *n* — **brew·er** *n* — **brew·ery** \'brü-ə-rē, 'brü(-ə)r-ē\ *n*

¹briar *also* **brier** \'brī-ər\ *n* : a plant (as a bramble or rose) with a thorny or woody usu. woody stem

²briar *n* : a tobacco pipe made from the root or stem of a European heath

brib·able *adj* ♦ : capable of being bribed

♦ corruptible, purchasable, venal

¹bribe \'brīb\ *n* : something (as money or a favor) given or promised to a person to influence conduct

²bribe *vb* **bribed; brib·ing** : to influence by offering a bribe — **brib·er** *n* — **brib·ery** \'brī-bə-rē\ *n*

bric-a-brac \'bri-kə-ˌbrak\ *n pl* : small ornamental articles

¹brick \'brik\ *n* : a block molded from moist clay and hardened by heat used esp. for building

²brick *vb* : to close, cover, or pave with bricks

brick·bat \'brik-ˌbat\ *n* **1** : a piece of a hard material (as a brick) esp. when thrown as a missile **2** : an uncomplimentary remark

brick·lay·er \'brik-ˌlā-ər\ *n* : a person who builds or paves with bricks — **brick·lay·ing** *n*

¹brid·al \'brīd-ᵊl\ *n* : a marriage festival or ceremony : WEDDING

²bridal *adj* : of or relating to a bride or a wedding

bride \'brīd\ *n* : a woman just married or about to be married

bride·groom \'brīd-ˌgrüm, -ˌgrum\ *n* : a man just married or about to be married

brides·maid \'brīdz-ˌmād\ *n* : a woman who attends a bride at her wedding

¹bridge \'brij\ *n* **1** : a structure built over a depression or obstacle for use as a passageway **2** : something (as the upper part of the nose) resembling a bridge in form or function **3** : a curved piece raising the strings of a musical instrument **4** : the forward part of a ship's superstructure from which it is navigated **5** : an artificial replacement for missing teeth

²bridge *vb* **bridged; bridg·ing** : to build a bridge over — **bridge·able** *adj*

³bridge *n* : a card game for four players developed from whist

bridge·head \-ˌhed\ *n* : an advanced position seized in enemy territory

bridge·work \-ˌwərk\ *n* : dental bridges

¹bri·dle \'brīd-ᵊl\ *n* **1** : headgear with which a horse is controlled **2** : CURB, RESTRAINT

²bridle *vb* **bri·dled; bri·dling 1 a** : to put a bridle on **b** ♦ : to restrain with or as if with a bridle **2** : to show hostility or scorn usu. by tossing the head

♦ check, constrain, contain, control, curb, govern, inhibit, regulate, rein, restrain, tame

Brie \'brē\ *n* : a soft cheese with a whitish rind and a pale yellow interior

¹brief \'brēf\ *adj* **1** ♦ : short in duration or extent **2** ♦ : marked by brevity of expression or statement : CONCISE; *also* : CURT — **brief·ly** *adv*

♦ [1] little, short, short-lived ♦ [2] compact, compendious, concise, crisp, curt, epigrammatic, laconic, pithy, succinct, summary, terse

²brief *n* **1** : a concise statement or document; *esp* : one summarizing a law client's case or a legal argument **2** *pl* : short snug underpants

³brief *vb* ♦ : to give instructions or information to

♦ acquaint, advise, apprise, clue, enlighten, familiarize, fill in, inform, instruct, tell, wise

brief·case \'brēf-ˌkās\ *n* : a flat flexible case for carrying papers

brief·ness *n* ♦ : the quality or state of being brief

♦ brevity, conciseness, shortness ♦ brevity, compactness, conciseness, crispness, succinctness, terseness

bri·er *var of* BRIAR

¹brig \'brig\ *n* : a 2-masted square-rigged sailing ship

²brig *n* ♦ : the place of confinement for offenders on a naval ship

♦ hoosegow, jail, jug, lockup, pen, penitentiary, prison, stockade

³brig *abbr* brigade

bri·gade \bri-'gād\ *n* **1** : a military unit composed of a headquarters, one or more units of infantry or armored forces, and supporting units **2** : a group organized for a particular purpose (as fire fighting)

brig·a·dier general \ˌbri-gə-ˌdir-\ *n* : a commissioned officer (as in the army) ranking next below a major general

brig·and \'bri-gənd\ *n* : BANDIT — **brig·and·age** \-gən-dij\ *n*

brig·an·tine \'bri-gən-ˌtēn\ *n* : a 2-masted square-rigged ship with a fore-and-aft mainsail

Brig Gen *abbr* brigadier general

bright \'brīt\ *adj* **1** ♦ **:** radiating or reflecting light **2 :** ILLUSTRIOUS, GLORIOUS **3 a** ♦ **:** having a cheerful nature **b** ♦ **:** mentally quick and resourceful **:** INTELLIGENT, CLEVER ⟨a ∼ student⟩ **4** ♦ **:** conducive to cheer — **bright** *adv* — **bright·ly** *adv*

♦ [1] beaming, brilliant, effulgent, glowing, incandescent, lambent, lucent, lucid, luminous, lustrous, radiant, refulgent, shiny *Ant* dim, dull, lackluster ♦ [1] ablaze, alight, light *Ant* blackened, dark, darkened, darkling, dimmed, dusky ♦ [3a] blithe, buoyant, cheerful, cheery, chipper, lightsome, sunny, upbeat ♦ [3b] alert, brainy, brilliant, clever, intelligent, keen, nimble, quick, quick-witted, sharp, smart ♦ [4] auspicious, encouraging, fair, golden, heartening, hopeful, likely, promising, propitious, rosy, upbeat

bright·en \'brīt-ᵊn\ *vb* **:** to make or become bright or brighter — **bright·en·er** *n*

bright·ness *n* **:** the state or quality of being bright

bril·liance \-yəns\ *n* ♦ **:** the quality or state of being brilliant

♦ augustness, glory, grandeur, grandness, magnificence, majesty, nobility, nobleness, resplendence, splendor, stateliness ♦ dazzle, effulgence, illumination, lightness, lucidity, luminosity, radiance, refulgence, splendor *Ant* blackness, dark, darkness, duskiness

bril·lian·cy \-yən-sē\ *n* **:** the quality or state of being brilliant

¹**bril·liant** \'bril-yənt\ *adj* **1** ♦ **:** very bright **2 :** STRIKING, DISTINCTIVE **3** ♦ **:** very intelligent — **bril·liant·ly** *adv*

♦ [1] beaming, bright, effulgent, glowing, incandescent, lambent, lucent, lucid, luminous, lustrous, radiant, refulgent, shiny ♦ [3] alert, brainy, bright, clever, intelligent, keen, nimble, quick, quick-witted, sharp, smart

²**brilliant** *n* **:** a gem cut in a particular form with many facets

¹**brim** \'brim\ *n* **1 :** an upper or outer margin **:** EDGE, RIM **2 :** the projecting rim of a hat — **brim·less** *adj*

²**brim** *vb* **brimmed; brim·ming** ♦ **:** to be or become full often to overflowing

♦ abound, bulge, burst, crawl, swarm, teem

brim·ful \-'fúl\ *adj* ♦ **:** full to the brim

♦ chock-full, crowded, fat, fraught, full, loaded, packed, replete

brim·stone \'brim-ˌstōn\ *n* **:** SULFUR

brin·dled \'brin-dᵊld\ *adj* **:** having dark streaks or flecks on a gray or tawny ground ⟨a ∼ Great Dane⟩

brine \'brīn\ *n* **1 :** water saturated with salt **2** ♦ **:** the water of a sea or salt lake **:** OCEAN

♦ blue, deep, ocean, sea

bring \'briŋ\ *vb* **brought** \'brót\; **bring·ing** \'briŋ-iŋ\ **1 :** to cause to come with one **2 :** INDUCE, PERSUADE, LEAD **3 :** PRODUCE, EFFECT **4** ♦ **:** to sell for ⟨∼ a good price⟩ — **bring·er** *n*

♦ cost, fetch, go, sell

bring about *vb* ♦ **:** to cause to take place

♦ cause, create, effect, effectuate, generate, induce, make, produce, prompt, result, work, yield

bring up *vb* **1** ♦ **:** to give a parent's fostering care to **2 :** to come or bring to a sudden halt **3** ♦ **:** to call to notice

♦ [1] breed, foster, raise, rear ♦ [3] broach, introduce, moot, raise

brink \'briŋk\ *n* **1 :** an edge at the top of a steep place **2 :** the point of onset

briny \'brī-nē\ *adj* ♦ **:** of, relating to, or resembling brine or the sea — **brin·i·ness** *n*

♦ saline, salty

brio \'brē-ō\ *n* **:** VIVACITY, SPIRIT

bri·quette *or* **bri·quet** \bri-'ket\ *n* **:** a compacted often brick=shaped mass of fine material ⟨a charcoal ∼⟩

bris *also* **briss** \'bris\ *n* **:** the Jewish rite of circumcision

brisk \'brisk\ *adj* **1** ♦ **:** keenly alert **:** LIVELY **2 :** INVIGORATING **3 :** acting or capable of acting with speed

♦ active, animate, animated, energetic, jaunty, lively, peppy, perky, pert, spirited, sprightly, springy, vital, vivacious

bris·ket \'bris-kət\ *n* **:** the breast or lower chest of a quadruped; *also* **:** a cut of beef from the brisket

brisk·ly *adv* ♦ **:** in a brisk manner

♦ apace, fast, hastily, pronto, quick, quickly, rapidly, speedily, swift, swiftly

brisk·ness *n* ♦ **:** the quality or state of being brisk

♦ animation, exuberance, liveliness, lustiness, robustness, sprightliness, vibrancy, vitality

bris·ling \'briz-liŋ, 'bris-\ *n* **:** SPRAT

¹**bris·tle** \'bri-səl\ *n* **:** a short stiff coarse hair — **bris·tle·like** \'bri-səl-ˌlīk\ *adj*

²**bristle** *vb* **bris·tled; bris·tling** **1 :** to stand stiffly erect **2 :** to show angry defiance **3 :** to appear as if covered with bristles

bris·tly *adj* **:** consisting of or like bristles

Brit *abbr* Britain; British

Bri·tan·nic \bri-'ta-nik\ *adj* **:** BRITISH

britch·es \'bri-chəz\ *n pl* ♦ **:** an outer garment covering each leg separately from waist to ankle **:** BREECHES, TROUSERS

♦ breeches, pantaloons, pants, slacks, trousers

Brit·ish \'bri-tish\ *n pl* **:** the people of Great Britain or the Commonwealth — **British** *adj* — **Brit·ish·ness** *n*

British thermal unit *n* **:** the quantity of heat needed to raise the temperature of one pound of water one degree Fahrenheit

Brit·on \'brit-ᵊn\ *n* **1 :** a member of a people inhabiting Britain before the Anglo-Saxon invasion **2 :** a native or inhabitant of Great Britain

brit·tle \'brit-ᵊl\ *adj* **brit·tler; brit·tlest** ♦ **:** easily broken — **brit·tle·ness** *n*

♦ crisp, crumbly, flaky, friable, short

bro \'brō\ *n, pl* **bros** **1 :** BROTHER 1 **2 :** SOUL BROTHER

¹**broach** \'brōch\ *n* **:** a pointed tool

²**broach** *vb* **1 :** to pierce (as a cask) in order to draw the contents **2** ♦ **:** to introduce as a topic of conversation

♦ bring up, introduce, moot, raise

¹**broad** \'bród\ *adj* **1 :** having a specified extension from side to side **:** WIDE **2** ♦ **:** extending far and wide **3 :** CLEAR, OPEN **4** ♦ **:** easily understood **:** OBVIOUS ⟨a ∼ hint⟩ **5 :** COARSE, CRUDE ⟨∼ stories⟩ **6 :** tolerant in outlook **7 :** GENERAL **8** ♦ **:** dealing with main or essential points — **broad·ness** *n*

♦ [2] expansive, extended, extensive, far-flung, far-reaching, wide, widespread ♦ [4] apparent, clear, clear-cut, distinct, evident, lucid, manifest, obvious, palpable, patent, perspicuous, plain, transparent, unambiguous, unequivocal, unmistakable ♦ [8] bird's-eye, general, nonspecific, overall

²**broad** *n, slang, often offensive* **:** WOMAN

broad·band \'bród-ˌband\ *n* **:** a system of high-speed telecommunications in which a frequency range is divided into multiple independent channels for simultaneous transmission of signals

¹**broad·cast** \'bród-ˌkast\ *vb* **broadcast** *also* **broad·cast·ed; broad·cast·ing** **1 :** to scatter or sow broadcast **2** ♦ **:** to make widely known **3 :** to transmit a broadcast — **broad·cast·er** *n*

♦ circulate, disseminate, propagate, spread, strew ♦ advertise, announce, blaze, declare, enunciate, placard, post, proclaim, promulgate, publicize, publish, sound

²**broadcast** *adv* **:** to or over a wide area

³**broadcast** *n* **1 :** the transmission of sound or images by radio or television **2 :** a single radio or television program

broad·cloth \-ˌklóth\ *n* **1 :** a smooth dense woolen cloth **2 :** a fine soft cloth of cotton, silk, or synthetic fiber

broad·en \'bród-ᵊn\ *vb* **:** WIDEN

broad·loom \-ˌlüm\ *adj* **:** woven on a wide loom esp. in a solid color

broad·ly *adv* ♦ **:** in a broad manner; *esp* **:** to a great extent

♦ considerably, greatly, largely, much, sizably

broad–mind·ed \-'mīn-dəd\ *adj* ♦ **:** tolerant of varied opinions — **broad–mind·ed·ly** *adv* — **broad–mind·ed·ness** *n*

♦ liberal, nonorthodox, nontraditional, open-minded, progressive, radical, unconventional, unorthodox

¹**broad·side** \-ˌsīd\ *n* **1 :** a sheet of paper printed usu. on one side (as an advertisement) **2 :** all of the guns on one side of a ship; *also* **:** their simultaneous firing **3 :** a volley of abuse or denunciation

²**broadside** *adv* **1 :** with one side forward **:** SIDEWAYS **2 :** from the side ⟨the car was hit ∼⟩

broad–spectrum *adj* **:** effective against a wide range of organisms ⟨∼ antibiotics⟩

broad·sword \'bród-ˌsōrd\ *n* **:** a broad-bladed sword

broad·tail \-ˌtāl\ *n* **:** a karakul esp. with flat and wavy fur

bro·cade \brō-'kād\ *n* **:** a usu. silk fabric with a raised design

broc·co·li \'brä-kə-lē\ *n* **:** the stems and immature usu. green or purple flower heads of either of two garden vegetable plants closely related to the cabbage; *also* **:** either of the plants

bro·chette \brō-'shet\ *n* **:** SKEWER

bro·chure \brō-'shùr\ *n* ♦ : an unbound printed publication with no cover or with a paper cover : PAMPHLET, BOOKLET

♦ booklet, circular, folder, leaflet, pamphlet

bro·gan \'brō-gən, brō-'gan\ *n* : a heavy shoe

brogue \'brōg\ *n* : a dialect or regional pronunciation; *esp* : an Irish accent

broil \'bròil\ *vb* : to cook by exposure to radiant heat : GRILL — **broil** *n*

broil·er \'bròi-lər\ *n* **1** : a utensil for broiling **2** : a young chicken fit for broiling

broil·ing *adj* ♦ : extremely hot

♦ burning, fiery, hot, red-hot, scorching, sultry, torrid

¹broke \'brōk\ *past of* BREAK

²broke *adj* ♦ : having no money or assets : PENNILESS

♦ destitute, impecunious, indigent, needy, penniless, penurious, poor, poverty-stricken

¹bro·ken \'brō-kən\ *past part of* BREAK

²broken *adj* **1** : SHATTERED **2 a** : having gaps or breaks : INTERRUPTED, DISRUPTED **b** ♦ : being irregular, interrupted, or full of obstacles **3** : SUBDUED, CRUSHED **4** : BANKRUPT **5** : imperfectly spoken ⟨∼ English⟩ — **bro·ken·ly** *adv*

♦ bumpy, coarse, irregular, jagged, lumpy, pebbly, ragged, rough, rugged, uneven

bro·ken·heart·ed \ˌbrō-kən-'här-təd\ *adj* ♦ : overcome by grief or despair

♦ depressed, despondent, disconsolate, heartsick, miserable, mournful, sad, sorrowful, unhappy, wretched

bro·ker \'brō-kər\ *n* ♦ : an agent who negotiates contracts of purchase and sale — **broker** *vb*

♦ arbiter, arbitrator, go-between, intercessor, intermediary, mediator, middleman, peacemaker

bro·ker·age \'brō-kə-rij\ *n* **1** : the business of a broker **2** : the fee or commission charged by a broker

bro·mance \'brō-mans\ *n* : a close nonsexual friendship between men — **bro·man·tic** \brō-'man-tik\ *adj*

bro·mide \'brō-ˌmīd\ *n* : a compound of bromine and another element or chemical group including some (as potassium bromide) used as sedatives

bro·mid·ic \brō-'mi-dik\ *adj* : TRITE, UNORIGINAL

bro·mine \'brō-ˌmēn\ *n* : a deep red liquid corrosive chemical element that gives off an irritating vapor

bronc \'bränk\ *n* : an unbroken or partly broken range horse of western No. America; *also* : MUSTANG

bron·chi·al \'brän-kē-əl\ *adj* : of, relating to, or affecting the bronchi or their branches

bron·chi·tis \brän-'kī-təs, brän-\ *n* : inflammation of the bronchi and their branches — **bron·chit·ic** \-'ki-tik\ *adj*

bron·chus \'brän-kəs\ *n, pl* **bron·chi** \-ˌkī, -ˌkē\ : either of the main divisions of the windpipe each leading to a lung

bron·co \'brän-kō\ *n, pl* **broncos** : BRONC

bron·to·sau·rus \ˌbrän-tə-'sòr-əs\ *also* **bron·to·saur** \'brän-tə-ˌsòr\ *n* : any of a genus of very large 4-footed plant-eating dinosaurs of the Jurassic : APATOSAURUS

Bronx cheer \'bränks-\ *n* : RASPBERRY 2

¹bronze \'bränz\ *vb* **bronzed; bronz·ing** : to give the appearance of bronze to

²bronze *n* **1** : an alloy of copper and tin and sometimes other elements; *also* : something made of bronze **2** : a yellowish brown color — **bronzy** \'brän-zē\ *adj*

brooch \'brōch, 'brüch\ *n* : an ornamental clasp or pin

¹brood \'brüd\ *n* : a family of young animals or children and esp. of birds

²brood *adj* : kept for breeding ⟨a ∼ mare⟩

³brood *vb* **1** ♦ : to sit on eggs to hatch them; *also* : to shelter (hatched young) with the wings **2** : to think anxiously or gloomily about something — **brood·ing·ly** *adv*

♦ hatch, incubate, set, sit

brood·er \'brü-dər\ *n* **1** : one that broods **2** : a heated structure for raising young birds

¹brook \'brùk\ *n* ♦ : a small natural stream

♦ creek, rill, rivulet, streamlet

²brook *vb* ♦ : to stand for : TOLERATE, BEAR

♦ abide, bear, countenance, endure, meet, stand, stick out, stomach, support, sustain, take, tolerate

brook·let \'brùk-lət\ *n* : a small brook

brook trout *n* : a common speckled cold-water char of No. America

broom \'brüm, 'brùm\ *n* **1** : any of several shrubs of the legume family with long slender branches and usu. yellow flowers **2** : an implement with a long handle (**broom·stick** \-ˌstik\) used for sweeping

bros *pl of* BRO

broth \'bròth\ *n, pl* **broths** \'bròths, 'bròthz\ **1** : liquid in which meat or sometimes vegetable food has been cooked **2** : a fluid culture medium

broth·el \'brä-thəl, 'brò-\ *n* : a house of prostitution

broth·er \'brə-thər\ *n, pl* **brothers** *also* **breth·ren** \'breth-rən, 'bre-thə-; 'bre-thərn\ **1** : a male having one or both parents in common with another individual **2** : a man who is a religious but not a priest : KINSMAN; *also* : SOUL BROTHER — **broth·er·li·ness** \-lē-nəs\ *n* — **broth·er·ly** *adj*

broth·er·hood \'brə-thər-ˌhùd\ *n* **1** : the state of being brothers or a brother **2** ♦ : an association (as a labor union or monastic society) for a particular purpose : FRATERNITY **3** : the whole body of persons in a business or profession

♦ association, club, college, congress, council, fellowship, fraternity, guild, institute, institution, league, order, organization, society

broth·er–in–law \'brə-thə-rən-ˌlò, 'brə-thərn-ˌlò\ *n, pl* **brothers–in–law** \'brə-thər-zən-\ : the brother of one's spouse; *also* : the husband of one's sibling or of one's spouse's sibling

brougham \'brü-(ə)m, 'brō-(ə)m\ *n* : a light closed horse-drawn carriage with the driver outside in front

brought *past and past part of* BRING

brou·ha·ha \'brü-ˌhä-ˌhä\ *n* : HUBBUB, UPROAR

brow \'braù\ *n* **1** : the eyebrow or the ridge on which it grows; *also* : FOREHEAD **2** : the projecting upper part of a steep place

brow·beat \'braù-ˌbēt\ *vb* **-beat; -beat·en** \-'bēt-ən\ *or* **-beat; -beat·ing** ♦ : to intimidate by sternness or arrogance

♦ bully, cow, hector, intimidate

¹brown \'braùn\ *adj* **1** : of the color brown; *also* : having dark or tanned skin **2** *often cap* : of or relating to any of various population groups considered as having medium pigmentation of the skin

²brown *n* **1** : a color like that of coffee or chocolate that is a blend of red and yellow darkened by black **2** *pl often cap* : people belonging to any of various population groups considered as having medium pigmentation of the skin — **brown·ish** *adj*

³brown *vb* : to make or become brown

brown bag·ging \-'ba-giŋ\ *n* : the practice of carrying one's lunch usu. in a brown bag — **brown bag·ger** *n*

brown bear *n* : any of various large typically brown-furred bears including the grizzly bear

brown·ie \'braù-nē\ *n* **1** ♦ : a legendary cheerful elf who performs good deeds at night **2** *cap* : a member of a program of the Girl Scouts for girls in the first through third grades **3** : a small square or rectangle of chocolate cake

♦ dwarf, elf, fairy, fay, gnome, hobgoblin, leprechaun, pixie, puck, troll

brown·nose \'braùn-ˌnōz\ *vb, disparaging* : to ingratiate oneself with — **brownnose** *n*

brown·out \'braù-ˌnaùt\ *n* : a period of reduced voltage of electricity caused esp. by high demand and resulting in reduced illumination

brown rice *n* : hulled but unpolished rice that retains most of the bran layers

brown·stone \'braùn-ˌstōn\ *n* : a dwelling faced with reddish brown sandstone

¹browse \'braùz\ *vb* **browsed; brows·ing** **1** ♦ : to feed on browse; *also* : GRAZE **2** ♦ : to read or look over something in a casual way **3** : to access (as the World Wide Web) with a browser

♦ [1] forage, graze, pasture ♦ [2] dip, glance, glimpse, peek, skim

²browse *n* : tender shoots, twigs, and leaves fit for food for cattle

brows·er \'braù-zər\ *n* : a computer program for accessing sites or information on a network (as the World Wide Web)

bru·in \'brü-ən\ *n* : BEAR

¹bruise \'brüz\ *vb* **bruised; bruis·ing** **1** : to inflict a bruise on; *also* : to become bruised **2** : to break down (as leaves or berries) by pounding

²bruise *n* : a surface injury to flesh : CONTUSION

bruis·er \'brü-zər\ *n* : a big husky man

bruit \'brüt\ *vb* : to make widely known by common report

brunch \'brənch\ *n* : a meal that combines a late breakfast and an early lunch

bru·net *or* **bru·nette** \brü-'net\ *adj* : having brown hair — **brunet** *or* **brunette** *n*

brunt \'brənt\ *n* : the main shock, force, or stress esp. of an attack; *also* : the greater burden

bru•schet•ta \brü-'she-tə, -'ske-\ *n* : an appetizer of grilled bread with toppings

¹**brush** \'brəsh\ *n* **1** : BRUSHWOOD **2** : scrub vegetation or land covered with it

²**brush** *n* **1** : a device composed of bristles set in a handle and used esp. for cleaning or painting **2** : a bushy tail (as of a fox) **3** : an electrical conductor that makes contact between a stationary and a moving part (as of a motor) **4** : a quick light touch in passing

³**brush** *vb* **1** : to treat (as in cleaning or painting) with a brush **2 a** : to remove with or as if with a brush **b** ♦ : to dismiss in an offhand manner — usu. used with *aside* or *off* **3** ♦ : to touch gently in passing

♦ *usu* **brush aside** *or* **brush off** [2b] condone, disregard, excuse, gloss over, ignore, pardon, pass over, shrug off, wink at ♦ [3] graze, kiss, nick, shave, skim

⁴**brush** *n* ♦ : a brief encounter or skirmish : SKIRMISH

♦ encounter, run-in, scrape, skirmish

brush–off \'brəsh-ˌȯf\ *n* ♦ : a curt offhand dismissal

♦ cold shoulder, rebuff, repulse, snub

brush up *vb* : to renew one's skill

brush•wood \'brəsh-ˌwu̇d\ *n* **1** : small branches of wood esp. when cut **2** ♦ : a thicket of shrubs and small trees

♦ brake, chaparral, coppice, covert, thicket

brusque \'brəsk\ *adj* ♦ : blunt in manner or speech often to the point of ungracious harshness : CURT, BLUNT, ABRUPT — **brusque•ly** *adv*

♦ abrupt, blunt, curt, snippy

brus•sels sprout \'brəs-əlz-\ *n, often cap B* : one of the edible small heads borne on the stalk of a plant closely related to the cabbage; *also, pl* : this plant

bru•tal \'brüt-ᵊl\ *adj* **1** : befitting a brute : CRUEL **2** ♦ : physically discomforting : HARSH, SEVERE ⟨∼ weather⟩ **3** : unpleasantly accurate — **bru•tal•ly** *adv*

♦ [1] barbarous, cruel, heartless, inhumane, sadistic, savage, vicious, wanton ♦ [2] bitter, burdensome, cruel, excruciating, grievous, grim, hard, harsh, heavy, inhuman, murderous, onerous, oppressive, rough, rugged, severe, stiff, tough, trying

bru•tal•ise *Brit var of* BRUTALIZE

bru•tal•i•ty \brü-'ta-lə-tē\ *n* ♦ : the quality or state of being brutal

♦ barbarity, cruelty, inhumanity, sadism, savagery, viciousness, wantonness

bru•tal•ize \'brüt-ᵊl-ˌīz\ *vb* **-ized; -iz•ing** **1** : to make brutal **2** : to treat brutally

¹**brute** \'brüt\ *adj* **1** : of or relating to beasts **2** : BRUTAL **3** : UNREASONING; *also* : purely physical ⟨∼ strength⟩

²**brute** *n* **1** ♦ : a 4-footed animal : BEAST **2** ♦ : a brutal person

♦ [1] animal, beast, creature, critter ♦ [2] beast, devil, fiend, monster, savage, villain

brut•ish \'brü-tish\ *adj* **1** : BRUTE 1 **2** : strongly sensual; *also* : showing little intelligence

BS *abbr* bachelor of science

BSA *abbr* Boy Scouts of America

bskt *abbr* basket

Bt *abbr* baronet

btry *abbr* battery

Btu *abbr* British thermal unit

bu *abbr* bushel

¹**bub•ble** \'bə-bəl\ *n* **1** : a globule of gas in a liquid **2** : a thin film of liquid filled with gas **3** : something lacking firmness or solidity

²**bubble** *vb* **bub•bled; bub•bling** : to form, rise in, or give off bubbles

bub•bly *adj* ♦ : full of or showing good spirits

♦ buoyant, effervescent, exuberant, frolicsome, high-spirited, vivacious

bub•kes \'bəp-kəs, 'bu̇p-\ *n pl* : the least amount ⟨didn't win ∼⟩

bu•bo \'bü-bō, 'byü-\ *n, pl* **buboes** : an inflammatory swelling of a lymph gland

bu•bon•ic plague \bü-'bä-nik-, byü-\ *n* : plague caused by a bacterium transmitted to human beings by flea bites and marked esp. by chills and fever and by buboes usu. in the groin

buc•ca•neer \ˌbə-kə-'nir\ *n* ♦ : any of the freebooters preying on Spanish ships and settlements esp. in 17th century West Indies; *broadly* : PIRATE

♦ corsair, freebooter, pirate, rover

¹**buck** \'bək\ *n, pl* **bucks 1** *or pl* **buck** : a male animal (as a deer or antelope) **2 a** ♦ : a male human being **b** ♦ : a man with unusual consideration for personal appearance : DANDY **3** : DOLLAR

♦ [2a] chap, dude, fellow, gent, gentleman, guy, hombre, jack, joker, lad, male, man ♦ [2b] dandy, dude, fop, gallant

²**buck** *vb* **1** ♦ : to spring with an arching leap ⟨a ∼ing horse⟩ **2** : to charge against something; *also* : to strive for advancement sometimes without regard to ethical behavior **3** ♦ : to offer resistance to

♦ [1] hitch, jerk, jolt, twitch ♦ [3] defy, fight, oppose, repel, resist, withstand

buck•board \-ˌbȯrd\ *n* : a 4-wheeled horse-drawn wagon with a floor of long springy boards

buck•et \'bə-kət\ *n* **1** : a cylindrical open-top container with a handle : PAIL **2 a** : an object resembling a bucket in collecting, scooping, or carrying something **b** : as much as a bucket will hold; *broadly* ♦ : a large quantity — usu. used in pl. ⟨has *buckets* of money⟩ — **buck•et•ful** *n*

♦ *usu* **buckets** abundance, deal, gobs, heap, loads, lot, pile, plenty, quantity, scads

bucket list *n* : a list of things one has not done but wants to do before dying

bucket seat *n* : a low separate seat for one person (as in an automobile)

buck•eye \'bə-ˌkī\ *n* : any of various trees or shrubs related to the horse chestnut; *also* : the large nutlike seed of such a shrub or tree

buck fever *n* : nervous excitement of an inexperienced hunter at the sight of game

¹**buck•le** \'bə-kəl\ *n* : a clasp (as on a belt) for two loose ends

²**buckle** *vb* **buck•led; buck•ling** **1** : to fasten with a buckle **2** ♦ : to apply oneself with vigor **3** : to crumple up : BEND, COLLAPSE

♦ address, apply, bend, devote, give

³**buckle** *n* : BEND, FOLD, KINK

buck•ler \'bə-klər\ *n* : SHIELD

buck•ram \'bə-krəm\ *n* : a coarse stiff cloth used esp. for binding books

buck•saw \'bək-ˌsȯ\ *n* : a saw set in a usu. H-shaped frame for sawing wood

buck•shot \'bək-ˌshät\ *n* : lead shot that is from .24 to .33 inch (about 6.1 to 8.4 millimeters) in diameter

buck•skin \-ˌskin\ *n* **1** : the skin of a buck **2** : a soft usu. suede-finished leather — **buckskin** *adj*

buck•tooth \-ˈtüth\ *n* : a large projecting front tooth — **buck–toothed** \-ˈtütht\ *adj*

buck•wheat \-ˌhwēt\ *n* : either of two plants grown for their triangular seeds which are used as a cereal grain; *also* : these seeds

bu•col•ic \byü-'kä-lik\ *adj* ♦ : relating to or typical of rural life and esp. shepherds or herdsmen : PASTORAL

♦ country, pastoral, rural, rustic

¹**bud** \'bəd\ *n* **1** : an undeveloped plant shoot (as of a leaf or a flower); *also* : a partly opened flower **2** : an asexual reproductive structure that detaches from the parent and forms a new individual **3** : something not yet fully developed ⟨nipped in the ∼⟩

²**bud** *vb* **bud•ded; bud•ding** **1** : to form or put forth buds; *also* : to reproduce by asexual buds **2** : to be or develop like a bud **3** : to reproduce a desired variety (as of peach) by inserting a bud in a plant of a different variety

Bud•dhism \'bü-ˌdi-zəm, 'bu̇-\ *n* : a religion of eastern and central Asia growing out of the teachings of Gautama Buddha — **Bud•dhist** \'bü-dist, 'bu̇-\ *n or adj*

bud•dy \'bə-dē\ *n, pl* **buddies** **1** ♦ : one associated with another esp. in an action; *also* : FRIEND **2** : FELLOW

♦ chum, comrade, crony, familiar, friend, intimate, pal

budge \'bəj\ *vb* **budged; budg•ing** **1** ♦ : to change the place, position, or direction of : MOVE, SHIFT **2** ♦ : to give up resistance : YIELD

♦ [1] dislocate, displace, disturb, move, remove, shift, transfer ♦ [2] blink, bow, capitulate, concede, give in, knuckle under, quit, submit, succumb, surrender, yield

bud•ger•i•gar \'bə-jə-rē-ˌgär\ *n* : a small brightly colored Australian parrot often kept as a pet

¹**bud•get** \'bə-jət\ *n* **1** ♦ : a store or supply accumulated or avail-

able   **2** : a financial report containing estimates of income and expenses; *also* : a plan for coordinating income and expenses   **3 ♦** : the amount of money available for a particular use — **bud·get·ary** \'bə-jə-₁ter-ē\ *adj*

♦ [1, 3] account, deposit, fund, kitty, nest egg, pool, supply

²**budget** *vb*   **1** : to allow for in a budget   **2** : to draw up a budget
³**budget** *adj* : INEXPENSIVE
bud·gie \'bə-jē\ *n* : BUDGERIGAR
¹**buff** \'bəf\ *n*   **1** : a yellow to orange yellow color   **2 ♦** : one who is ardently attached to a cause, object, or pursuit : FAN, ENTHUSIAST

♦ addict, aficionado, bug, devotee, enthusiast, fan, fanatic, fancier, fiend, freak, lover, maniac, nut

²**buff** *adj* : of the color buff
³**buff** *vb* ♦ : to make smooth and glossy usu. by friction

♦ burnish, dress, gloss, grind, polish, rub, shine, smooth

buf·fa·lo \'bə-fə-₁lō\ *n, pl* **-lo** *or* **-loes** *also* **-los**   **1** : WATER BUFFALO   **2** : a large shaggy-maned No. American wild bovine mammal that has short horns and heavy forequarters with a large muscular hump
¹**buf·fer** \'bə-fər\ *n* ♦ : something or someone that protects or shields (as from physical damage or a financial blow)

♦ bumper, cushion, fender, pad

²**buffer** *n* : one that buffs
¹**buf·fet** \'bə-fət\ *n* : a blow esp. with the hand : SLAP
²**buffet** *vb*   **1 a** : to strike with the hand   **b** ♦ : to pound repeatedly   **2** : to struggle against or on

♦ bash, bat, batter, beat, hammer, pound, thump

³**buf·fet** \(₁)bə-'fā, bü-\ *n*   **1** : piece of dining-room furniture having compartments and shelves for holding articles of table service : SIDEBOARD   **2** : a counter for refreshments; *also* : a meal at which people serve themselves informally
buff leather *n* : a strong supple oil-tanned leather
buf·foon \(₁)bə-'fün\ *n* ♦ : a ludicrous figure : CLOWN — **buf·foon·ery** \-'fü-nə-rē\ *n*

♦ clown, harlequin, zany

¹**bug** \'bəg\ *n*   **1** : an insect or other creeping or crawling invertebrate animal; *esp* : an insect pest (as a bedbug)   **2** : any of an order of insects with sucking mouthparts and incomplete metamorphosis that includes many plant pests   **3** : an unexpected flaw or imperfection ⟨a ~ in a computer program⟩   **4 a** : a disease-producing germ   **b** ♦ : a disease caused by a germ   **5** : a concealed listening device   **6** ♦ : one who is ardently attached to a cause, object, or pursuit — **bug·gy** \'bə-gē\ *adj*

♦ [4b] ailment, complaint, complication, condition, disease, disorder, fever, ill, illness, infirmity, malady, sickness, trouble   ♦ [6] addict, aficionado, buff, devotee, enthusiast, fan, fanatic, fancier, fiend, freak, lover, maniac, nut

²**bug** *vb* **bugged; bug·ging**   **1** ♦ : to annoy esp. by petty provocation   **2** : to plant a concealed microphone in

♦ bait, hassle, heckle, needle, ride, taunt, tease   ♦ aggravate, annoy, bother, chafe, exasperate, gall, get, grate, irk, irritate, nettle, peeve, perplex, pique, put out, rasp, rile, vex

³**bug** *vb* **bugged; bug·ging** *of the eyes* : PROTRUDE, BULGE
bug·a·boo \'bə-gə-₁bü\ *n, pl* **-boos** : an imaginary object of fear : BOGEY
bug·bear \'bəg-₁bar\ *n* ♦ : an imaginary object of fear : BOGEY; *also* : a source of dread

♦ bête noire, bogey, hobgoblin, ogre

bug·gy \'bə-gē\ *n, pl* **buggies**   **1** : a light horse-drawn carriage   **2** : a carriage for a baby
bu·gle \'byü-gəl\ *n* : a valveless brass instrument resembling a trumpet and used esp. for military calls — **bu·gler** *n*
bug out *vb* : to depart in a hurry; *also* : to flee in panic
¹**build** \'bild\ *vb* **built** \'bilt\; **build·ing**   **1 a** ♦ : to form or have formed by ordering and uniting materials ⟨~ a house⟩   **b** ♦ : to develop or bring into being esp. according to a set plan   **2** ♦ : to produce or create gradually ⟨~ an argument on facts⟩   **3** ♦ : to become progressively greater : INCREASE, ENLARGE; *also* : ENHANCE   **4** : to engage in building — **build·er** *n*

♦ [1a, 1b] assemble, construct, erect, fabricate, make, make up, piece, put up, raise, rear, set up *Ant* disassemble, dismantle, take down   ♦ *usu* **build up** [2] carve, forge, grind, hammer, work out   ♦ *usu* **build up** [3] accumulate, appreciate, balloon, burgeon, enhance, enlarge, escalate, expand, increase, mount, multiply, mushroom, proliferate, rise, snowball, swell, wax

²**build** *n* ♦ : form or mode of structure; *esp* : PHYSIQUE

♦ constitution, figure, form, frame, physique, shape

build·ing \'bil-diŋ\ *n*   **1** : a usu. roofed and walled structure (as a house) for permanent use   **2** : the art or business of constructing buildings
building block *n* ♦ : a unit of construction or composition

♦ component, constituent, element, factor, ingredient, member

build-up \'bil-₁dəp\ *n* : the act or process of building up; *also* : something produced by this
built-in \'bilt-'tin\ *adj*   **1** : forming an integral part of a structure   **2** : INHERENT
bulb \'bəlb\ *n*   **1** : an underground resting stage of a plant (as a lily or an onion) consisting of a short stem base bearing one or more buds enclosed in overlapping leaves; *also* : a fleshy plant structure (as a tuber) resembling a bulb   **2** : a plant having or growing from a bulb   **3** : a rounded more or less bulb-shaped object or part (as for an electric lamp) — **bul·bous** \'bəl-bəs\ *adj*
Bul·gar·i·an \₁bəl-'gar-ē-ən, bùl-\ *n* : a native or inhabitant of Bulgaria — **Bulgarian** *adj*
¹**bulge** \'bəlj\ *vb* **bulged; bulg·ing** ♦ : to become or cause to become protuberant

♦ balloon, beetle, belly, billow, overhang, poke, project, protrude, start, stick out

²**bulge** *n* ♦ : a swelling projecting part

♦ overhang, projection, protrusion, protuberance *Ant* concavity, dent, depression, hollow, indentation, pit

bu·li·mia \bü-'lē-mē-ə, byü-, -'li-\ *n*   **1** : an abnormal and constant craving for food   **2** : a serious eating disorder chiefly of females that is characterized by compulsive overeating usu. followed by self-induced vomiting or laxative or diuretic abuse — **bu·lim·ic** \-'lē-mik, -'li-\ *adj or n*
¹**bulk** \'bəlk\ *n*   **1** : MAGNITUDE, VOLUME   **2** : material that forms a mass in the intestine; *esp* : FIBER 2   **3** : a large mass   **4** ♦ : the major portion

♦ body, core, generality, main, mass, staple, weight

²**bulk** *vb*   **1** : to cause to swell or bulge   **2** : to appear as a factor : LOOM
bulk·head \'bəlk-₁hed\ *n*   **1** : a partition separating compartments   **2** : a structure built to cover a shaft or a cellar stairway
bulky \'bəl-kē\ *adj* **bulk·i·er; -est** : having bulk; *esp* : being large and unwieldy
¹**bull** \'bùl\ *n*   **1** : a male bovine animal; *also* : a usu. adult male of various large animals (as the moose, elephant, or whale)   **2** : one who buys securities or commodities in expectation of a price increase — **bull·ish** *adj*
²**bull** *adj*   **1** : of, relating to, or suggestive of a bull : MALE   **2** : large of its kind
³**bull** *n*   **1** : a papal letter   **2** : DECREE
⁴**bull** *n, slang* : NONSENSE
⁵**bull** *abbr* bulletin
¹**bull·dog** \'bùl-₁dòg\ *n* : any of a breed of compact muscular short-haired dogs of English origin
²**bulldog** *vb* : to throw (a steer) by seizing the horns and twisting the neck
bull·doze \-₁dōz\ *vb*   **1** : to move, clear, or level with a tractor-driven machine (**bull·doz·er**) having a broad blade for pushing   **2** ♦ : to force as if by using a bulldozer

♦ elbow, muscle, press, push

bul·let \'bù-lət\ *n* : a missile to be shot from a firearm
bul·le·tin \'bù-lət-ᵊn\ *n*   **1** ♦ : a brief public report intended for immediate release on a matter of public interest   **2** : a periodical publication (as of a college) — **bulletin** *vb*

♦ advertisement, announcement, notice, notification, release

bulletin board *n*   **1** : a board (as of cork) for posting notices   **2** : a public forum on a computer network in which users write or read messages or download files
bul·let·proof \'bù-lət-₁prüf\ *adj*   **1** : impenetrable to bullets; *also* : INVINCIBLE   **2** : not subject to corrections, alteration, or modification
bull·fight \'bùl-₁fīt\ *n* : a spectacle in which people ceremonially fight with and usu. kill bulls in an arena — **bull·fight·er** *n*
bull·frog \-₁fròg, -₁fräg\ *n* : a large deep-voiced frog
bull·head \-₁hed\ *n* : any of several common freshwater catfishes of the U.S.
bull·head·ed \-'he-dəd\ *adj* : stupidly stubborn : HEADSTRONG
bull·head·ed·ness \-'he-dəd-nəs\ *n* ♦ : the quality or state of being bullheaded

♦ hardheadedness, mulishness, obduracy, obstinacy, peevishness, persistence, pertinacity, self-will, stubbornness, tenacity

bul·lion \'bùl-yən\ *n* : gold or silver esp. in bars or ingots

bull market *n* : a market in which securities or commodities are persistently rising in value

bull·ock \'bù-lək\ *n* : a young bull; *also* : STEER

bull pen *n* : a place on a baseball field where pitchers warm up; *also* : the relief pitchers of a baseball team

bull session *n* : an informal discussion

bull's-eye \'bùl-ˌzī\ *n, pl* **bull's-eyes** : the center of a target; *also* : a shot that hits the bull's-eye

¹**bul·ly** \'bù-lē\ *n, pl* **bullies** ♦ : a person habitually cruel to others who are weaker

♦ gangster, goon, hood, hoodlum, mobster, mug, punk, rowdy, ruffian, thug, tough

²**bully** *adj* : EXCELLENT, FIRST-RATE — often used interjectionally

³**bully** *vb* **bul·lied; bul·ly·ing** ♦ : to behave as a bully toward — **bul·ly·ing** *n*

♦ browbeat, cow, hector, intimidate

bul·rush \'bùl-ˌrəsh\ *n* : any of several large rushes or sedges of wetlands

bul·wark \'bùl-(ˌ)wərk, -ˌwörk; 'bəl-(ˌ)wərk\ *n* **1** : a wall-like defensive structure **2** ♦ : a strong support or protection

♦ brace, buttress, mount, shore, stay, support, underpinning

¹**bum** \'bəm\ *adj* **1** : of poor quality ⟨∼ advice⟩ **2** : DISABLED ⟨a ∼ knee⟩

²**bum** *vb* **bummed; bum·ming** **1** : to spend time unemployed and wandering; *also* : LOAF **2** : to obtain by begging

³**bum** *n* **1** : LOAFER **2** : a person who is devoted to a recreational activity ⟨a ski ∼⟩ **3** ♦ : a person who has no job and wanders from place to place : VAGRANT, TRAMP

♦ hobo, tramp, vagabond, vagrant

bum·ble·bee \'bəm-bəl-ˌbē\ *n* : any of numerous large hairy social bees

bum·mer \'bə-mər\ *n* **1** : an unpleasant experience **2** ♦ : something that fails or disappoints : FAILURE

♦ bust, catastrophe, debacle, dud, failure, fiasco, fizzle, flop, lemon, loser, turkey, washout

¹**bump** \'bəmp\ *n* **1** ♦ : a local bulge; *esp* : a swelling of tissue **2** ♦ : a sudden forceful blow or impact

♦ [1] knot, lump, nodule, swelling ♦ [2] collision, concussion, crash, impact, jar, jolt, shock, smash, strike, wallop

²**bump** *vb* **1** : to strike or knock forcibly; *also* : to move by or as if by bumping **2** ♦ : to collide with

♦ bang, bash, collide, crash, hit, impact, knock, ram, slam, smash, strike, swipe, thud

¹**bum·per** \'bəm-pər\ *n* **1** : a cup or glass filled to the brim **2** : something unusually large

²**bumper** *adj* ♦ : unusually large

♦ big, grand, great, large, outsize, oversize, whopping

³**bump·er** \'bəm-pər\ *n* ♦ : a device for absorbing shock or preventing damage; *esp* : a usu. metal bar at either end of an automobile

♦ buffer, cushion, fender, pad

bump·kin \'bəmp-kən\ *n* ♦ : an awkward and unsophisticated country person

♦ clodhopper, hick, rustic, yokel

bump·tious \'bəmp-shəs\ *adj* : obtusely and often noisily self-assertive

bumpy *adj* ♦ : having or covered with bumps; *also* : marked by bumps or jolts

♦ broken, coarse, irregular, jagged, lumpy, pebbly, ragged, rough, rugged, uneven

bun \'bən\ *n* : a sweet or plain round roll

¹**bunch** \'bənch\ *n* **1** : SWELLING **2** ♦ : a number of things of the same kind — **bunchy** *adj*

♦ array, assemblage, batch, block, clump, cluster, collection, group, huddle, knot, lot, package, parcel, set, suite

²**bunch** *vb* ♦ : to form into a group or bunch

♦ cluster, crowd, huddle, press

bun·co *or* **bun·ko** \'bəŋ-kō\ *n, pl* **buncos** *or* **bunkos** : a swindling scheme — **bunco** *vb*

¹**bun·dle** \'bən-dᵊl\ *n* **1** ♦ : several items bunched and fastened together; *also* : something wrapped for carrying **2** : a considerable amount : LOT **3** : a small band of mostly parallel nerve or muscle fibers

♦ pack, package, parcel

²**bundle** *vb* **bun·dled; bun·dling** : to gather or tie in a bundle

bun·dling \'bənd-(ᵊ-)liŋ\ *n* : a former custom of a courting couple's occupying the same bed without undressing

bung \'bəŋ\ *n* : the stopper in the bunghole of a cask

bun·ga·low \'bəŋ-gə-ˌlō\ *n* : a one-storied house with a low-pitched roof

bun·gee cord \'bən-jē-\ *n* : a long elastic cord used esp. as a fastening or shock-absorbing device

bungee jump *vb* : to jump for sport from a height (as from a bridge) while attached to a sturdy bungee cord — **bungee jumper** *n*

bung·hole \'bəŋ-ˌhōl\ *n* : a hole for emptying or filling a cask

bun·gle \'bəŋ-gəl\ *vb* **bun·gled; bun·gling** ♦ : to do badly : BOTCH — **bungle** *n* — **bun·gler** *n*

♦ bobble, botch, butcher, flub, foul up, fumble, mangle, mess up, screw up

bun·ion \'bən-yən\ *n* : an inflamed swelling of the first joint of the big toe

¹**bunk** \'bəŋk\ *n* ♦ : an article of furniture to sleep on : BED; *esp* : a built-in bed that is often one of a tier

♦ bed, pad, sack

²**bunk** *n* ♦ : insincere or foolish talk : BUNKUM, NONSENSE

♦ claptrap, drivel, folly, foolishness, fudge, hogwash, humbug, nonsense, piffle, rot, silliness, slush, stupidity, trash

bunk bed *n* : one of two single beds usu. placed one above the other

bun·ker \'bəŋ-kər\ *n* **1** : a bin or compartment for storage (as for coal on a ship) **2** : a protective embankment or dugout **3** : a sand trap or embankment constituting a hazard on a golf course

bun·kum *or* **bun·combe** \'bəŋ-kəm\ *n* : insincere or foolish talk

bun·ny \'bə-nē\ *n, pl* **bun·nies** : RABBIT

Bun·sen burner \'bən-sən-\ *n* : a gas burner usu. consisting of a straight tube with air holes at the bottom

¹**bunt** \'bənt\ *vb* **1** : ¹BUTT **2** : to push or tap a baseball lightly without swinging the bat

²**bunt** *n* : an act or instance of bunting; *also* : a bunted ball

¹**bun·ting** \'bən-tiŋ\ *n* : any of numerous small stout-billed finches

²**bunting** *n* : a thin fabric used esp. for flags; *also* : FLAGS

¹**buoy** \'bü-ē, 'böi\ *n* **1** : a floating object anchored in water to mark something (as a channel) **2** : a float consisting of a ring of buoyant material to support a person who has fallen into the water

²**buoy** *vb* **1** : to mark by a buoy **2** : to keep afloat **3** ♦ : to raise the spirits of — usu. used with *up*

♦ *usu* **buoy up** cheer, comfort, embolden, encourage, hearten, inspire, steel

buoy·an·cy \'böi-ən-sē, 'bü-yən-\ *n* **1** : the tendency of a body to float or rise when submerged in a fluid **2** : the power of a fluid to exert an upward force on a body placed in it **3** : resilience of spirit

buoy·ant \-ənt, -yənt\ *adj* : having buoyancy: as **a** : capable of floating **b** ♦ : having or inducing high spirits

♦ blithe, bright, cheerful, cheery, chipper, lightsome, sunny, upbeat ♦ bubbly, effervescent, exuberant, frolicsome, high-spirited, vivacious

¹**bur** \'bər\ *var of* BURR

²**bur** *abbr* bureau

¹**bur·den** \'bərd-ᵊn\ *n* **1 a** ♦ : something that is carried : LOAD **b** ♦ : a duty or obligation one must take care of : RESPONSIBILITY **2** : something oppressive : ENCUMBRANCE **3** ♦ : goods or merchandise loaded to be conveyed : CARGO; *also* : capacity for cargo

♦ [1a, 3] cargo, freight, haul, lading, load, payload, weight ♦ [1b] charge, commitment, duty, need, obligation, responsibility

²**burden** *vb* ♦ : to encumber or oppress with something heavy, laborious, or disheartening

♦ depress, oppress, sadden ♦ encumber, load, lumber, saddle, weight

³**burden** *n* **1** ♦ : a phrase or verse recurring regularly in a poem or song : REFRAIN, CHORUS **2** : a main theme or idea : GIST

♦ chorus, refrain

bur·den·some \-səm\ *adj* ♦ : imposing or constituting a burden

♦ grim, hard, harsh, heavy, oppressive, rough, rugged, severe, stiff, tough, trying ♦ arduous, challenging, demanding, exacting, grueling, laborious, onerous, taxing, toilsome

bur·dock \'bər-ˌdäk\ n : any of a genus of coarse composite herbs with globe-shaped flower heads surrounded by prickly bracts

bu·reau \'byu̇r-ō\ n, pl **bureaus** also **bu·reaux** \-ōz\ 1 : a chest of drawers 2 ♦ : an administrative unit (as of a government department) 3 : a branch of a publication or wire service in an important news center

♦ department, desk, division, office

bu·reau·cra·cy \byu̇-'rä-krə-sē\ n, pl **-cies** 1 : a body of appointive government officials 2 : government marked by specialization of functions under fixed rules and a hierarchy of authority; also : an unwieldy administrative system burdened with excessive complexity and lack of flexibility

bu·reau·crat \'byu̇r-ə-ˌkrat\ n : a member of a bureaucracy — **bu·reau·crat·ic** \ˌbyu̇r-ə-'kra-tik\ adj

bur·geon \'bər-jən\ vb 1 ♦ : to put forth fresh growth (as from buds) 2 ♦ : to grow and expand rapidly

♦ [1] bloom, blossom, blow, flower, unfold ♦ [2] accumulate, appreciate, balloon, build, enlarge, escalate, expand, increase, mount, multiply, mushroom, proliferate, rise, snowball, swell, wax ♦ [2] flourish, prosper, thrive

burgh \'bər-ō\ n : a Scottish town

bur·gher \'bər-gər\ n 1 ♦ : an inhabitant of a borough or a town 2 : a prosperous solid citizen

♦ townie

bur·glar·ize \'bər-glə-ˌrīz\ vb ♦ : to break into and steal from; also : to commit burglary

♦ rip off, rob, steal

bur·glary \'bər-glə-rē\ n, pl **-glar·ies** : forcible entry into a building esp. at night with the intent to commit a crime (as theft) — **bur·glar** \-glər\ n

bur·gle \'bər-gəl\ vb **bur·gled**; **bur·gling** : to commit burglary on

bur·go·mas·ter \'bər-gə-ˌmas-tər\ n : the chief magistrate of a town in some European countries

bur·gun·dy \'bər-gən-dē\ n, pl **-dies** often cap 1 : a red or white table wine from the Burgundy region of France 2 : an American red table wine

buri·al \'ber-ē-əl\ n ♦ : the act or process of burying

♦ entombment, interment, sepulture Ant exhumation, unearthing

bur·ka or **bur·qa** \'bur-kə\ n : a loose garment that covers the face and body and is worn in public by certain Muslim women

burl \'bərl\ n : a hard woody often flattened hemispherical outgrowth on a tree

bur·lap \'bər-ˌlap\ n : a coarse fabric usu. of jute or hemp used esp. for bags

¹**bur·lesque** \(ˌ)bər-'lesk\ n 1 ♦ : a witty or derisive literary or dramatic imitative work 2 : broadly humorous theatrical entertainment consisting of several items (as songs, skits, or dances)

♦ caricature, parody, spoof, takeoff

²**burlesque** vb **bur·lesqued**; **bur·lesqu·ing** ♦ : to make ludicrous by burlesque

♦ caricature, imitate, mimic, mock, parody, take off, travesty

bur·ly \'bər-lē\ adj **bur·li·er**; **-est** ♦ : strongly and heavily built : HUSKY

♦ beefy, brawny, husky

Bur·mese \ˌbər-'mēz, -'mēs\ n, pl **Burmese** : a native or inhabitant of Burma (Myanmar) — **Burmese** adj

¹**burn** \'bərn\ vb **burned** \'bərnd, 'bərnt\ or **burnt** \'bərnt\; **burn·ing** 1 ♦ : to be on fire 2 ♦ : to feel or look as if on fire 3 : to alter or become altered by or as if by the action of fire or heat 4 ♦ : to use as fuel ⟨∼ coal⟩; also : to destroy by fire ⟨∼ trash⟩ 5 : to cause or make by fire ⟨∼ a hole⟩; also : to affect as if by heat 6 ♦ : to become emotionally excited or agitated 7 : to record (as music or data) on by means of a laser ⟨∼ a CD⟩

♦ [1, 2] blaze, flame, flare, glow ♦ [4] fire, ignite, inflame, kindle, light Ant douse, extinguish, put out, quench, snuff (out) ♦ [6] boil, fume, rage, seethe, steam

²**burn** n : an injury or effect produced by or as if by burning

burn·er \'bər-nər\ n : the part of a fuel-burning or heat-producing device where the flame or heat is produced

burn·ing \'bər-niŋ\ adj 1 **a** ♦ : being on fire **b** ♦ : affecting with or as if with heat 2 ♦ : existing in an extreme degree ⟨a ∼ desire⟩

♦ [1a] ablaze, afire, fiery ♦ [1b] broiling, fiery, hot, red-hot, scorching, sultry, torrid ♦ [2] ardent, charged, emotional, fervent, hot-blooded, impassioned, passionate, red-hot, vehement

bur·nish \'bər-nish\ vb ♦ : to make shiny esp. by rubbing : POLISH — **bur·nish·er** n — **bur·nish·ing** adj or n

♦ buff, dress, gloss, grind, polish, rub, shine, smooth

bur·noose or **bur·nous** \(ˌ)bər-'nüs\ n : a hooded cloak worn esp. by Arabs

burn·out \'bər-ˌnau̇t\ n 1 : the cessation of operation of a jet or rocket engine 2 ♦ : exhaustion of one's physical or emotional strength; also : a person suffering from burnout

♦ collapse, exhaustion, fatigue, lassitude, prostration, tiredness, weariness

burn out vb 1 : to drive out or destroy the property of by fire 2 ♦ : to cause to fail, wear out, or become exhausted esp. from overwork or overuse; also : to suffer burnout

♦ do in, drain, exhaust, fag, fatigue, tire, tucker, wash out, wear, wear out, weary

burp \'bərp\ n : an act of belching — **burp** vb

burp gun n : a small submachine gun

burr \'bər\ n 1 usu **bur** : a rough or prickly envelope of a fruit; also : a plant that bears burs 2 : roughness left in cutting or shaping metal 3 : WHIRR — **bur·ry** adj

bur·ri·to \bə-'rē-tō\ n : a flour tortilla rolled around a filling and baked

bur·ro \'bər-ō, 'bu̇r-\ n, pl **burros** : a usu. small donkey

¹**bur·row** \'bər-ō\ n ♦ : a hole in the ground made by an animal (as a rabbit)

♦ den, hole, lair, lodge

²**burrow** vb 1 : to form by tunneling; also : to make a burrow 2 : to progress by or as if by digging — **bur·row·er** n

bur·sar \'bər-sər\ n : a treasurer esp. of a college

bur·si·tis \(ˌ)bər-'sī-təs\ n : inflammation of the serous sac (**bur·sa** \'bər-sə\) of a joint (as the elbow or shoulder)

¹**burst** \'bərst\ vb **burst** or **burst·ed**; **burst·ing** 1 ♦ : to fly apart or into pieces : to cause to burst 2 : to show one's feelings suddenly; also : PLUNGE ⟨∼ into song⟩ 3 ♦ : to enter or emerge suddenly 4 : to be filled to the breaking point

♦ [1] blast, blow up, demolish, explode, pop, shatter, smash ♦ usu **burst forth** [3] break out, erupt, explode, flame, flare, go off

²**burst** n 1 **a** ♦ : a sudden outbreak : SPURT **b** ♦ : a vehement outburst (as of emotion) 2 : EXPLOSION 3 : result of bursting

♦ [1a] flare, flare-up, flash, flurry, flutter, outbreak, outburst, spurt ♦ [1b] agony, eruption, explosion, fit, flare, flare-up, flash, flush, gale, gush, gust, outburst, paroxysm, spasm, storm

Bu·run·di·an \bu̇-'rün-dē-ən\ n : a native or inhabitant of Burundi

bury \'ber-ē\ vb **bur·ied**; **bury·ing** 1 : to deposit in the earth; also : to inter with funeral ceremonies 2 ♦ : to conceal from view or in obscurity : HIDE 3 : SUBMERGE, ENGROSS — usu. used with in

♦ cache, conceal, ensconce, hide, secrete

¹**bus** \'bəs\ n, pl **bus·es** or **bus·ses** : a large motor vehicle for carrying passengers

²**bus** vb **bused** or **bussed**; **bus·ing** or **bus·sing** 1 : to travel or transport by bus 2 : to work as a busboy

³**bus** abbr business

bus·boy \'bəs-ˌbȯi\ n : a waiter's helper

bus·by \'bəz-bē\ n, pl **busbies** : a military full-dress fur hat

bush \'bu̇sh\ n 1 : SHRUB 2 ♦ : rough uncleared country 3 : a thick tuft ⟨a ∼ of hair⟩ — **bushy** adj

♦ backwoods, frontier, hinterland, sticks, up-country

bushed \'bu̇sht\ adj ♦ : drained of strength and energy : TIRED, EXHAUSTED

♦ beat, dead, drained, effete, jaded, limp, prostrate, spent, tired, weary, worn-out

bush·el \'bu̇-shəl\ n 1 : a measure of dry capacity equal to 4 pecks 2 ♦ : a large quantity

♦ abundance, deal, gobs, heap, loads, lot, pile, plenty, quantity, scads

bush·ing \'bu̇-shiŋ\ n : a usu. removable cylindrical lining for an opening of a mechanical part to limit the size of the opening, re-sist wear, or serve as a guide

bush·mas·ter \'bush-ˌmas-tər\ *n* : a large venomous tropical American pit viper

bush·whack \-ˌhwak\ *vb* **1** : AMBUSH **2** : to clear a path through esp. by chopping down bushes and branches — **bush·whack·er** *n*

busi·ly \'bi-zə-lē\ *adv* : in a busy manner

busi·ness \'biz-nəs, -nəz\ *n* **1** : OCCUPATION; *also* : TASK, MIS-SION **2 a** ♦ : a commercial or industrial enterprise **b** ♦ : the dealings and transactions involved in buying and selling : TRADE ⟨∼ is good⟩ **3** : a subject under consideration : AFFAIR, MAT-TER **4** : personal concern

♦ [2a] company, concern, enterprise, establishment, firm, house, outfit ♦ [2b] commerce, marketplace, trade, traffic

busi·ness·man \-ˌman\ *n* : a man engaged in business esp. as an executive

busi·ness·per·son \-ˌpərs-ᵊn\ *n* : a businessman or business-woman

busi·ness·wom·an \-ˌwu̇-mən\ *n* : a woman engaged in busi-ness esp. as an executive

bus·kin \'bəs-kən\ *n* **1** : a laced boot reaching halfway to the knee **2** : tragic drama

buss \'bəs\ *n* : KISS — **buss** *vb*

¹**bust** \'bəst\ *n* **1** : sculpture representing the upper part of the human figure **2** : the part of the human torso between the neck and the waist; *esp* : the breasts of a woman

²**bust** *vb* **bust·ed** *also* **bust; bust·ing 1** ♦ : to break or smash esp. with force; *also* : BURST **2** ♦ : to ruin financially **3** : TAME **4** ♦ : to reduce to a lower grade or rank : DEMOTE **5** *slang* : ARREST; *also* : RAID **6** ♦ : to strike heavily with or as if with the fist or a bat

♦ [1] break, burst, fracture, fragment ♦ [2] ruin ♦ [4] break, degrade, demote, downgrade, reduce ♦ [6] bash, bat, clobber, clout, hammer, hit, pound, punch, slug, strike, thump

³**bust** *n* **1** : a drinking session **2** ♦ : a complete failure : FLOP **3** : a business depression **4** : a quick blow with or as if with the fist : PUNCH, SOCK **5** *slang* : a police raid; *also* : ARREST

♦ bummer, catastrophe, debacle, dud, failure, fiasco, fizzle, flop, lemon, loser, turkey, washout

¹**bus·tle** \'bə-səl\ *vb* **bus·tled; bus·tling** : to move or work in a brisk busy manner

²**bustle** *n* ♦ : briskly energetic activity

♦ commotion, disturbance, furor, hubbub, hullabaloo, pande-monium, tumult, turmoil

³**bustle** *n* : a pad or frame worn to support the fullness at the back of a woman's skirt

¹**busy** \'bi-zē\ *adj* **busi·er; -est 1** ♦ : engaged in action : not idle **2** : being in use ⟨∼ telephones⟩ **3** ♦ : full of activity ⟨∼ streets⟩ **4** : full of distracting detail ⟨a ∼ design⟩

♦ [1] active, assiduous, diligent, engaged, laborious, occupied, sedulous, working ♦ [3] alive, animated, astir, lively, vibrant

²**busy** *vb* **bus·ied; busy·ing** ♦ : to make or keep busy : OCCUPY

♦ absorb, engage, engross, enthrall, fascinate, grip, immerse, interest, intrigue, involve, occupy

busy·body \'bi-zē-ˌbä-dē\ *n* ♦ : an officious or inquisitive per-son : MEDDLER

♦ interloper, intruder, kibitzer, meddler

busy·work \-ˌwərk\ *n* : work that appears productive but only keeps one occupied

¹**but** \'bət\ *conj* **1** ♦ : except for the fact ⟨would have protested ∼ that he was afraid⟩ **2** : THAT ⟨there's no doubt ∼ he won⟩ **3** : without the certainty that ⟨never rains ∼ it pours⟩ **4** : on the contrary ⟨not one, ∼ two job offers⟩ **5** : YET ⟨poor ∼ proud⟩ **6** : with the exception of ⟨none ∼ the strongest attempt it⟩

♦ except, only, yet

²**but** *prep* ♦ : other than : EXCEPT ⟨this letter is nothing ∼ an in-sult⟩; *also* : with the exception of ⟨no one here ∼ me⟩

♦ aside from, bar, barring, besides, except, outside (of), save

³**but** *adv* **1** ♦ : being nothing more than **2** ♦ : to the contrary

♦ [1] just, merely, only, simply ♦ [2] howbeit, however, never-theless, nonetheless, notwithstanding, still, though, withal, yet

bu·tane \'byü-ˌtān\ *n* : either of two gaseous hydrocarbons used as a fuel

butch \'buch\ *adj* : notably masculine in appearance or manner

¹**butch·er** \'bu̇-chər\ *n* **1** : one who slaughters animals or dresses their flesh; *also* : a dealer in meat **2** : one that kills brutally or needlessly **3** : one that botches

²**butcher** *vb* **1** : to slaughter and dress for meat ⟨∼ hogs⟩ **2** ♦ : to kill barbarously **3** ♦ : to foul up hopelessly : BOTCH ⟨the singer ∼ed the song⟩

♦ [2] massacre, slaughter ♦ [3] bobble, botch, bungle, flub, foul up, fumble, mangle, mess up, screw up

butch·ery \-chə-rē\ *n* **1** : the preparation of meat for sale **2** ♦ : cruel and ruthless slaughter of human beings

♦ carnage, massacre, slaughter

but·ler \'bət-lər\ *n* : the chief male servant of a household

¹**butt** \'bət\ *vb* : to strike with the head or horns

²**butt** *n* : a blow or thrust with the head or horns

³**butt** *n* : a large cask

⁴**butt** *n* **1** : TARGET **2** ♦ : an object of abuse or ridicule **3** ♦ : the seat of the body : BUTTOCKS

♦ [2] laughingstock, mark, mock, mockery, target ♦ [3] back-side, bottom, buttocks, posterior, rear, rump, seat

⁵**butt** *n* **1** : a large, thicker, or bottom end of something **2** : BUT-TOCKS

⁶**butt** *vb* **1** : ABUT **2** : to place or join edge to edge without over-lapping

butte \'byüt\ *n* : an isolated steep hill

¹**but·ter** \'bə-tər\ *n* **1** : a solid edible emulsion of fat obtained from cream by churning **2** : a substance resembling butter — **but·tery** *adj*

²**butter** *vb* : to spread with or as if with butter

but·ter–and–eggs \ˌbə-tə-rə-ˈnegz\ *n sing or pl* : a common perennial herb related to the snapdragon that has showy yellow and orange flowers

butter bean *n* **1** : LIMA BEAN **2** : WAX BEAN **3** : a green shell bean

butter cream *n* : a sweet butter-based mixture used esp. as a fill-ing or frosting

but·ter·cup \'bə-tər-ˌkəp\ *n* : any of a genus of herbs having usu. yellow flowers with five petals and sepals

but·ter·fat \-ˌfat\ *n* : the natural fat of milk and chief constituent of butter

but·ter·fin·gered \-ˌfiŋ-gərd\ *adj* : likely to let things fall or slip through the fingers — **but·ter·fin·gers** \-gərz\ *n sing or pl*

but·ter·fly \-ˌflī\ *n* : any of a group of slender day-flying insects with broad often brightly-colored wings

but·ter·milk \-ˌmilk\ *n* : the liquid remaining after butter is churned

but·ter·nut \-ˌnət\ *n* : the sweet egg-shaped nut of an American tree related to the walnut; *also* : this tree

butternut squash *n* : a smooth buff-colored cylindrical winter squash

but·ter·scotch \-ˌskäch\ *n* : a candy made from brown sugar, corn syrup, and water; *also* : the flavor of such candy

butt in *vb* ♦ : to meddle in the affairs of others

♦ interfere, intrude, meddle, mess, nose, obtrude, poke, pry, snoop

but·tock \'bə-tək\ *n* **1** : the back of a hip that forms one of the fleshy parts on which a person sits **2** *usu* **but·tocks** ♦ : the seat of the body : RUMP

♦ **buttocks** backside, bottom, butt, posterior, rear, rump, seat

¹**but·ton** \'bət-ᵊn\ *n* **1** : a small knob secured to an article (as of clothing) and used as a fastener by passing it through a buttonhole or loop **2** : something that resembles a button **3** : PUSH BUT-TON **4** : a hidden sensitivity that can be manipulated to produce a desired response ⟨he is constantly pushing my ∼s⟩ **5** : a usu. box-shaped computer icon that when clicked initiates a software function

²**button** *vb* : to close or fasten with or as if with buttons

¹**but·ton·hole** \'bət-ᵊn-ˌhōl\ *n* : a slit or loop for a button to pass through

²**buttonhole** *vb* : to detain in conversation by or as if by holding on to the outer garments of

¹**but·tress** \'bə-trəs\ *n* **1** : a projecting structure to support a wall **2** ♦ : something that supports or strengthens : SUPPORT

♦ dependence, mainstay, pillar, reliance, standby, sup-port ♦ brace, bulwark, mount, shore, stay, support, underpinning

²**buttress** *vb* ♦ : to furnish or shore up with a buttress : SUPPORT

♦ bear, bolster, brace, carry, prop, shore, stay, support, uphold

bux·om \'bək-səm\ *adj* : healthily plump; *esp* : full-bosomed

¹**buy** \'bī\ *vb* **bought** \'bȯt\; **buy·ing 1 ♦** : to obtain for a price : PURCHASE; *also* : BRIBE **2** : to accept as true — **buy·er** *n*

  ♦ acquire, get, obtain, pick up, procure, purchase, secure, take

²**buy** *n* **1** : PURCHASE 1, 2 **2 ♦** : an exceptional value : BARGAIN

  ♦ bargain, deal, steal

¹**buzz** \'bəz\ *vb* **1** : to make a buzz **2 ♦** : to fly fast and close to

  ♦ drone, hum, whir, whish, whiz, zip, zoom

²**buzz** *n* **1 ♦** : a low humming sound **2** : RUMOR, GOSSIP

  ♦ drone, hum, purr, whir, whiz, zoom

buz·zard \'bə-zərd\ *n* : any of various usu. large birds of prey and esp. the turkey vulture

buzz·er \'bə-zər\ *n* : a device that signals with a buzzing sound

buzz saw *n* : CIRCULAR SAW

buzz·word \'bəz-ˌwərd\ *n* : a voguish word or phrase often from technical jargon

BV *abbr* Blessed Virgin

BVM *abbr* Blessed Virgin Mary

BWI *abbr* British West Indies

bx *abbr* box

BX *abbr* base exchange

¹**by** \'bī, bə\ *prep* **1 ♦** : in proximity to : NEAR ⟨stood ～ the window⟩ **2** : through or through the medium of ⟨left ～ the door⟩ **3** : into the vicinity of and beyond : PAST ⟨drove ～ the house⟩ **4** : DURING, AT ⟨studied ～ night⟩ **5** : no later than ⟨get here ～ 3 p.m.⟩ **6 ♦** : through the means or direct agency of ⟨～ force⟩ **7** : in conformity with; *also* : ACCORDING TO ⟨did it ～ the book⟩ **8** : with respect to ⟨a vet ～ profession⟩ **9** : to the amount or extent of ⟨won ～ a nose⟩ **10** — used to express relationship in multiplication, in division, and in measurements ⟨divide *a* ～ *b*⟩ ⟨multiply ～ 6⟩ ⟨15 feet ～ 20 feet⟩

  ♦ [1] about, around, near, next to ♦ [6] per, through, with

²**by** \'bī\ *adv* **1 a ♦** : near at hand   **b** : at or to another's house : IN ⟨stop ～⟩ **2** : PAST **3** : ASIDE, APART

  ♦ around, close, hard, in, near, nearby, nigh

bye \'bī\ *n* : a position of a participant in a tournament who advances to the next round without playing

by–elec·tion *also* **bye–elec·tion** \'bī-ə-ˌlek-shən\ *n* : a special election held between regular elections in order to fill a vacancy

by·gone \'bī-ˌgȯn\ *adj* **♦** : gone by — **bygone** *n*

  ♦ dead, defunct, extinct, gone

by·law *or* **bye·law** \'bī-ˌlȯ\ *n* : a rule adopted by an organization for managing its internal affairs

by–line \'bī-ˌlīn\ *n* : a line at the beginning of a news story or magazine article giving the writer's name

BYO *abbr* bring your own

BYOB *abbr* bring your own beer; bring your own booze; bring your own bottle

¹**by·pass** \'bī-ˌpas\ *n* : a passage to one side or around a blocked or congested area; *also* : a surgical procedure establishing this ⟨a coronary ～⟩

²**bypass** *vb* **♦** : to avoid by means of a bypass

  ♦ circumvent, detour, skirt

by·path \-ˌpath, -ˌpȧth\ *n* : BYWAY

by·play \'bī-ˌplā\ *n* : action engaged in on the side (as of a stage) while the main action proceeds

by–prod·uct \-ˌprä-(ˌ)dəkt\ *n* : a sometimes unexpected product or result produced in addition to the main product or result

by·stand·er \-ˌstan-dər\ *n* : one present but not participating

byte \'bīt\ *n* : a group of 8 bits that a computer processes as a unit

by·way \'bī-ˌwā\ *n* **1** : a little-traveled side road **2** : a secondary aspect

by·word \-ˌwərd\ *n* **1 ♦** : a proverbial saying : PROVERB **2** : one that is noteworthy or notorious

  ♦ adage, aphorism, epigram, maxim, proverb, saying

Byz·an·tine \'biz-ᵊn-ˌtēn, 'bī-, -ˌtīn; bə-'zan-, bī-\ *adj* **1** : of, relating to, or characteristic of the ancient city of Byzantium or the Byzantine Empire **2** *often not cap* : intricately involved and often devious

---

C

---

¹**c** \'sē\ *n, pl* **c's** *or* **cs** \'sēz\ *often cap* **1** : the 3d letter of the English alphabet **2** *slang* : a sum of $100 **3** : a grade rating a student's work as fair

²**c** *abbr, often cap* **1** calorie **2** carat **3** Celsius **4** cent **5** centigrade **6** centimeter **7** century **8** chapter **9** circa **10** cocaine **11** copyright

C *symbol* carbon

ca *abbr* circa

Ca *symbol* calcium

CA *abbr* **1** California **2** chartered accountant **3** chief accountant **4** chronological age

cab \'kab\ *n* **1** : a light closed horse-drawn carriage **2** : an automobile available on call to carry a passenger for a fare determined by a running meter or a flat rate : TAXICAB **3** : the covered compartment for the engineer and controls of a locomotive; *also* : a similar compartment (as on a truck)

CAB *abbr* Civil Aeronautics Board

ca·bal \kə-'bäl, -'bal\ *n* **♦** : a secret group of plotters or political conspirators

  ♦ conspiracy, gang, mob, ring, syndicate

cabala *var of* KABBALAH

ca·bana \kə-'ban-yə, -'ba-nə\ *n* : a shelter at a beach or swimming pool

cab·a·ret \ˌka-bə-'rā\ *n* : a place of entertainment open at night usu. serving food and liquor and often having a floor show : NIGHTCLUB

cab·bage \'ka-bij\ *n* : a vegetable related to the mustard with a dense head of leaves

cab·bie *or* **cab·by** \'ka-bē\ *n, pl* **cabbies** : a driver of a cab

cab·er·net sau·vi·gnon \ˌka-bər-'nā-sō-vē-'nyōⁿ\ *n* : a dry red wine made from a single variety of black grape

cab·in \'ka-bən\ *n* **1** : a private room on a ship; *also* : a compartment below deck on a boat for passengers or crew **2** : the passenger or cargo compartment of a vehicle (as an airplane or automobile) **3 ♦** : a small simple one-story house

  ♦ camp, cottage, hut, hutch, shack, shanty

cabin boy *n* : a boy working as a servant on a ship

cabin class *n* : a class of accommodations on a passenger ship superior to tourist class and inferior to first class

cabin cruiser *n* : CRUISER 3

cab·i·net \'kab-nit\ *n* **1 ♦** : a case or cupboard for holding or displaying articles **2** : the advisory council of a head of state (as a president or sovereign)

  ♦ buffet, closet, cupboard, hutch, locker, sideboard

cab·i·net·mak·er \-ˌmā-kər\ *n* : a woodworker who makes fine furniture — **cab·i·net·mak·ing** *n*

cab·i·net·work \-ˌwərk\ *n* : the finished work of a cabinetmaker

¹**ca·ble** \'kā-bəl\ *n* **1 ♦** : a very strong rope, wire, or chain **2** : a bundle of insulated wires usu. twisted around a central core **3** : CABLEGRAM **4** : CABLE TELEVISION

  ♦ cord, lace, line, rope, string, wire

²**cable** *vb* **ca·bled; ca·bling** : to telegraph by cable

cable car *n* : a vehicle moved by an endless cable

ca·ble·cast \'kā-bəl-ˌkast\ *n* : a cable television transmission — **cablecast** *vb*

ca·ble·gram \'kā-bəl-ˌgram\ *n* : a message sent by a submarine telegraph cable

cable modem *n* : a modem for connecting a computer to a network over a cable television line

cable television *n* : a system of television reception in which signals from distant stations are sent by cable to the receivers of paying subscribers

cab·o·chon \'ka-bə-ˌshän\ *n* : a gem or bead cut in convex form and highly polished but not given facets; *also* : this style of cutting — **cabochon** *adv*

ca·boose \kə-'büs\ *n* : a car usu. at the rear of a freight train for the use of the train crew and railroad workers

cab·ri·o·let \ˌka-brē-ə-'lā\ *n* **1** : a light 2-wheeled one-horse carriage **2** : a convertible coupe

cab·stand \'kab-ˌstand\ *n* : a place where cabs wait for passengers

ca·cao \kə-'kaù, -'kā-ō\ *n, pl* **cacaos** : a So. American tree whose seeds (**cacao beans**) are the source of cocoa and chocolate; *also* : its dried fatty seeds

cac·cia·to·re \ˌkä-chə-'tōr-ē\ *adj* : cooked with tomatoes and herbs 〈chicken ∼〉

¹**cache** \'kash\ *n* **1** : a hiding place esp. for preserving provisions **2** ♦ : something hidden or stored in a cache

♦ deposit, hoard, reserve, stash, stockpile, store

²**cache** *vb* ♦ : to place, hide, or store in a cache

♦ bury, conceal, ensconce, hide, secrete

ca·chet \ka-'shā\ *n* **1** : a seal used esp. as a mark of official approval **2** : a feature or quality conferring prestige; *also* : PRESTIGE **3** : a design, inscription, or advertisement printed or stamped on mail

¹**cack·le** \'ka-kəl\ *vb* **cack·led; cack·ling** **1** : to make the sharp broken cry characteristic of a hen **2** : to laugh or chatter noisily

²**cackle** *n* ♦ : the action or noise of cackling

♦ chortle, laugh, laughter, snicker, titter

cack·ler *n* : one that cackles

ca·coph·o·nous \ka-'kä-fə-nəs\ *adj* ♦ : marked by cacophony

♦ discordant, dissonant, inharmonious, unmelodious, unmusical

ca·coph·o·ny \ka-'kä-fə-nē\ *n, pl* **-nies** ♦ : harsh or discordant sound

♦ bluster, clamor (*or* clamour), din, noise, racket, roar

cac·tus \'kak-təs\ *n, pl* **cac·ti** \-ˌtī\ *or* **cac·tus·es** *also* **cactus** : any of a large family of drought-resistant flowering plants with succulent stems and with leaves replaced by scales or prickles

cad \'kad\ *n* : a man who deliberately disregards another's feelings — **cad·dish** \'ka-dish\ *adj* — **cad·dish·ly** *adv* — **cad·dish·ness** *n*

ca·dav·er \kə-'da-vər\ *n* : a dead body esp. of a human being

ca·dav·er·ous \kə-'da-və-rəs\ *adj* ♦ : suggesting a corpse esp. in gauntness or pallor — **ca·dav·er·ous·ly** *adv*

♦ ashen, livid, lurid, pale, pasty, peaked ♦ gaunt, haggard, skeletal, wasted

cad·die *or* **cad·dy** \'ka-dē\ *n, pl* **caddies** : a person who assists a golfer esp. by carrying the clubs — **caddie** *or* **caddy** *vb*

cad·dy \'ka-dē\ *n, pl* **caddies** ♦ : a small box, can, or chest; *esp* : one to keep tea in

♦ box, case, casket, chest, locker, trunk

ca·dence \'kād-ᵊns\ *n* ♦ : the measure or beat of a rhythmical flow : RHYTHM

♦ beat, measure, meter (*or* metre), rhythm

ca·denced \-ᵊnst\ *adj* ♦ : marked by cadence

♦ measured, metrical, rhythmic

ca·den·za \kə-'den-zə\ *n* : a brilliant sometimes improvised passage usu. toward the close of a musical composition

ca·det \kə-'det\ *n* **1** : a younger son or brother **2** : a student in a service academy

Ca·dette \kə-'det\ *n* : a member of a Girl Scout program for girls in sixth through ninth grades

cadge \'kaj\ *vb* **cadged; cadg·ing** : SPONGE, BEG 〈∼ a free meal〉 — **cadg·er** *n*

cad·mi·um \'kad-mē-əm\ *n* : a bluish-white metallic chemical element used esp. in protective platings

cad·re \'ka-ˌdrā, 'kä-, -drē\ *n* **1** : FRAMEWORK **2** : a central unit esp. of trained personnel able to assume control and train others **3** : a group of indoctrinated leaders active in promoting the interests of a revolutionary party

ca·du·ceus \kə-'dü-sē-əs, -'dyü-, -shəs\ *n, pl* **-cei** \-sē-ˌī\ **1** : the staff of a herald; *esp* : a representation of a staff with two entwined snakes and two wings at the top **2** : an insignia bearing a caduceus and symbolizing a physician

cae·cum *var of* CECUM

Cae·sar \'sē-zər\ *n* **1** : any of the Roman emperors succeeding Augustus Caesar — used as a title **2** *often not cap* : a powerful ruler : AUTOCRAT, DICTATOR; *also* : the civil or temporal power

caesarean *var of* CESAREAN

cae·su·ra \si-'zhùr-ə\ *n, pl* **-suras** *or* **-su·rae** \-'zhùr-(ˌ)ē\ : a break in the flow of sound usu. in the middle of a line of verse

ca·fé \ka-'fā\ *n* **1** : a usu. small and informal establishment serving various refreshments (as coffee) : RESTAURANT **2** ♦ : a room or establishment whose main feature is a bar for the sale of liquor : BARROOM **3** ♦ : a place of entertainment open at night usu. serving food and liquor and providing music and space for dancing and often having a floor show : NIGHTCLUB

♦ [2] bar, barroom, pub, public house, saloon, tavern ♦ [3] disco, discotheque, nightclub

ca·fé au lait \(ˌ)ka-ˌfā-ō-'lā\ *n* : coffee with hot milk in about equal parts

caf·e·te·ria \ˌka-fə-'tir-ē-ə\ *n* : a restaurant in which the customers serve themselves or are served at a counter

caf·fein·at·ed \'ka-fə-ˌnā-təd\ *adj* **1** : stimulated by or as if by caffeine **2** : containing caffeine

caf·feine \ka-'fēn, 'ka-ˌfēn\ *n* : a stimulating alkaloid found esp. in coffee and tea

caf·fe lat·te \ˌkä-fā-'lä-tā\ *n* : espresso mixed with hot or steamed milk

caf·tan \kaf-'tan, 'kaf-ˌtan\ *n* : an ankle-length garment with long sleeves worn in countries of the eastern Mediterranean

¹**cage** \'kāj\ *n* **1** ♦ : an openwork enclosure for confining an animal **2** : something resembling a cage

♦ coop, corral, pen, pound

²**cage** *vb* **caged; cag·ing** : to put or keep in or as if in a cage

ca·gey *also* **ca·gy** \'kā-jē\ *adj* **ca·gi·er; -est** **1** : wary of being trapped or deceived : SHREWD **2** ♦ : marked by cleverness — **ca·gi·ly** \-jə-lē\ *adv*

♦ artful, crafty, cunning, devious, foxy, guileful, slick, sly, subtle, wily

ca·gi·ness \-jē-nəs\ *n* ♦ : skill in devising or using indirect or subtle methods

♦ artfulness, artifice, canniness, craft, craftiness, cunning, guile, slyness, wiliness

CAGS *abbr* Certificate of Advanced Graduate Study

ca·hoot \kə-'hüt\ *n* : PARTNERSHIP, LEAGUE — usu. used in pl. 〈officials in ∼s with the underworld〉

cai·man \'kā-mən; kā-'man, kī-\ *n* : any of several Central and So. American reptiles closely related to alligators and crocodiles

cairn \'karn\ *n* : a heap of stones serving as a memorial or a landmark

cais·son \'kā-ˌsän, 'kās-ᵊn\ *n* **1** : a usu. 2-wheeled vehicle for artillery ammunition **2** : a watertight chamber used in underwater construction work or as a foundation

caisson disease *n* : ²BEND 2

cai·tiff \'kā-təf\ *adj* : being base, cowardly, or despicable — **caitiff** *n*

ca·jole \kə-'jōl\ *vb* **ca·joled; ca·jol·ing** ♦ : to persuade or coax esp. with flattery or false promises — **ca·jole·ment** *n* — **ca·jol·ery** \-'jō-lə-rē\ *n*

♦ coax, wheedle

Ca·jun \'kā-jən\ *n* : a Louisianian descended from French-speaking immigrants from Acadia (Nova Scotia) — **Cajun** *adj*

¹**cake** \'kāk\ *n* **1** : a baked or fried breadlike food usu. in a small flat shape **2** : a sweet baked food made from batter or dough usu. containing flour, sugar, or shortening, and a leaven (as baking powder) **3** : a hardened or compacted substance 〈a ∼ of soap〉 **4** : something easily done 〈the quiz was ∼〉

²**cake** *vb* **caked; cak·ing** **1** : to cover or overlay with or as if with a crust : ENCRUST **2** : to form or harden into a cake

cake·walk \'kāk-ˌwök\ *n* **1** : a stage dance typically involving a high prance with backward tilt **2** : a one-sided contest or an easy task

cal *abbr* **1** calendar **2** caliber

Cal *abbr* **1** California **2** calorie

cal·a·bash \'ka-lə-ˌbash\ *n* : the fruit of a gourd; *also* : a utensil made from its hard shell

cal·a·boose \'ka-lə-ˌbüs\ *n* : JAIL

cal·a·di·um \kə-'lā-dē-əm\ *n* : any of a genus of tropical American ornamental plants related to the arums

cal·a·mari \ˌkä-lə-'mär-ē\ *n* : squid used as food

cal·a·mine \'ka-lə-ˌmīn\ *n* : a lotion of oxides of zinc and iron

ca·lam·i·tous \-təs\ *adj* ♦ : being, causing, or accompanied by calamity — **ca·lam·i·tous·ly** *adv* — **ca·lam·i·tous·ness** *n*

♦ cataclysmic, catastrophic, destructive, disastrous, fatal, fateful, ruinous, unfortunate

ca·lam·i·ty \kə-'la-mə-tē\ *n, pl* **-ties** **1** : great distress or misfortune **2** ♦ : an event causing great harm or loss and affliction : DISASTER

♦ cataclysm, catastrophe, debacle, disaster, tragedy

calc *abbr* calculate; calculated

cal·car·e·ous \kal-'kar-ē-əs\ *adj* : resembling calcium carbonate in hardness; *also* : containing calcium or calcium carbonate

cal·cif·er·ous \kal-'si-fə-rəs\ *adj* : producing or containing calcium carbonate

cal·ci·fy \'kal-sə-ˌfī\ *vb* **-fied; -fy·ing** : to make or become calcareous — **cal·ci·fi·ca·tion** \ˌkal-sə-fə-'kā-shən\ *n*

cal·ci·mine \'kal-sə-ˌmīn\ *n* : a thin water paint used esp. on plastered surfaces — **calcimine** *vb*

cal·cine \kal-'sīn\ *vb* **cal·cined; cal·cin·ing** : to heat to a high temperature but without fusing to drive off volatile matter and often to reduce to powder — **cal·ci·na·tion** \ˌkal-sə-'nā-shən\ *n*

cal·cite \'kal-ˌsīt\ *n* : a crystalline mineral consisting of calcium carbonate — **cal·cit·ic** \kal-'si-tik\ *adj*

cal·ci·um \'kal-sē-əm\ *n* : a silver-white soft metallic chemical element occurring only in combination

calcium carbonate *n* : a substance found in nature as limestone and marble and in plant ashes, bones, and shells

cal·cu·late \'kal-kyə-ˌlāt\ *vb* **-lat·ed; -lat·ing** **1** ♦ : to determine by mathematical processes : COMPUTE **2** ♦ : to reckon by exercise of practical judgment : ESTIMATE **3** ♦ : to design or adapt for a purpose by forethought or careful plan **4** : COUNT, RELY — **cal·cu·la·ble** \-lə-bəl\ *adj* — **cal·cu·la·tor** \-ˌlā-tər\ *n*

♦ [1] compute, figure, reckon, work out ♦ [2] call, conjecture, estimate, figure, gauge, guess, judge, make, place, put, reckon, suppose ♦ [3] arrange, blueprint, chart, design, frame, lay out, map, plan, project, scheme

cal·cu·lat·ed \-ˌlā-təd\ *adj* **1** ♦ : undertaken after estimating the probability of success or failure ⟨a ∼ risk⟩ **2** ♦ : planned purposefully : DELIBERATE

♦ [1, 2] advised, deliberate, measured, reasoned, studied, thoughtful, thought-out

cal·cu·lat·ing \-ˌlā-tiŋ\ *adj* : marked by shrewd consideration esp. of self-interest — **cal·cu·lat·ing·ly** *adv*

cal·cu·la·tion \ˌkal-kyə-'lā-shən\ *n* **1** ♦ : the process or an act of calculating **2** : the result of an act of calculating **3** : studied care; *also* : cold heartless planning to promote self-interest

♦ arithmetic, computation, reckoning

cal·cu·lus \'kal-kyə-ləs\ *n, pl* **-li** \-ˌlī\ *also* **-lus·es** **1** : a method of computation or calculation in a special notation (as of logic) **2** : a branch of mathematics concerned with the rate of change of functions and with methods of finding lengths, areas, and volumes **3** : a concretion usu. of mineral salts esp. in hollow organs or ducts

cal·de·ra \kal-'der-ə, kȯl-, -'dir-\ *n* : a large crater usu. formed by the collapse of a volcanic cone

cal·dron *var of* CAULDRON

¹cal·en·dar \'ka-lən-dər\ *n* **1** : an arrangement of time into days, weeks, months, and years; *also* : a sheet or folder containing such an arrangement for a period **2** ♦ : an orderly list

♦ agenda, docket, program, schedule, timetable

²calendar *vb* : to enter in a calendar

¹cal·en·der \'ka-lən-dər\ *vb* : to press (as cloth or paper) between rollers or plates so as to make smooth or glossy or to thin into sheets

²calender *n* : a machine for calendering

ca·lends \'ka-ləndz, 'kā-\ *n sing or pl* : the first day of the ancient Roman month

ca·len·du·la \kə-'len-jə-lə\ *n* : any of a genus of yellow-flowered herbs related to the daisies

¹calf \'kaf, 'kȧf\ *n, pl* **calves** \'kavz, 'kȧvz\ **1** : the young of the domestic cow; *also* : the young of various large mammals (as the elephant or whale) **2** : CALFSKIN

²calf *n, pl* **calves** \'kavz, 'kȧvz\ : the fleshy back of the leg below the knee

calf·skin \'kaf-ˌskin, 'kȧf-\ *n* : leather made of the skin of a calf

cal·i·ber *or Can and Brit* **cal·i·bre** \'ka-lə-bər\ *n* **1** ♦ : degree of mental capacity, excellence, or importance **2** : the diameter of a projectile **3** : the diameter of the bore of a gun

♦ grade, quality, rate

cal·i·brate \'ka-lə-ˌbrāt\ *vb* **-brat·ed; -brat·ing** : to adjust precisely

cal·i·bra·tion \ˌka-lə-'brā-shən\ *n* : a set of graduated marks indicating values or positions

cal·i·co \'ka-li-ˌkō\ *n, pl* **-coes** *or* **-cos** **1** : printed cotton fabric **2** : a mottled or spotted animal — **calico** *adj*

Calif *abbr* California

Cal·i·for·nia poppy \ˌka-lə-'fȯr-nyə-\ *n* : a widely cultivated herb with usu. yellow or orange flowers that is related to the poppies

cal·i·for·ni·um \ˌka-lə-'fȯr-nē-əm\ *n* : an artificially prepared radioactive chemical element

cal·i·per \'ka-lə-pər\ *n* **1** : any of various instruments having two arms, legs, or jaws used esp. to measure diameter or thickness — usu. used in pl. **2** : a device for pressing a frictional material against the sides of a rotating wheel or disk

ca·liph \'kā-ləf, 'ka-\ *n* : a successor of Muhammad as head of Islam — used as a title — **ca·liph·ate** \-lə-ˌfāt, -fət\ *n*

cal·is·then·ics \ˌka-ləs-'the-niks\ *n sing or pl* : bodily exercises usu. done without apparatus — **cal·is·then·ic** *adj*

calk \'kȯk\ *var of* CAULK

¹call \'kȯl\ *vb* **1 a** ♦ : to speak in a loud distinct voice so as to be heard at a distance esp. in order to attract the attention of, summon, or make a request of another : SHOUT, CRY **b** : to utter a characteristic note or cry **2** : to utter in a loud clear voice **3** : to announce authoritatively **4** ♦ : to invite or command (a group) to meet : SUMMON **5** ♦ : to make a request or demand ⟨∼ for an investigation⟩ **6** : to halt (a baseball game or other public event) because of unsuitable conditions (as rain or darkness) **7** : to demand payment of (a loan); *also* : to demand surrender of (as a bond) for redemption **8** ♦ : to get or try to get in communication by telephone **9** ♦ : to make a brief stop or visit at a place ⟨called on a friend⟩ **10 a** ♦ : to speak of or address by name : give a name to **b** : regard as or characterize as of a certain kind : describe as **11** ♦ : to estimate or consider for practical purposes ⟨∼ it ten miles⟩ **12** : to temporarily transfer control of computer processing to (as a subroutine or procedure)

♦ [1a] bawl, cry, holler, shout, vociferate, yell ♦ [4] assemble, convene, convoke, muster, summon ♦ [5] ask, insist, plead, press, quest, request, seek, solicit, sue ♦ [5] claim, clamor (*or* clamour), command, demand, enjoin, exact, insist, press, quest, stipulate (for) ♦ [8] dial, telephone ♦ [9] drop (by *or* in), pop (in), stop (by *or* in), visit ♦ [10a] baptize, christen, denominate, designate, dub, entitle, label, name, style, term, title ♦ [11] calculate, conjecture, estimate, figure, gauge, guess, judge, make, place, put, reckon, suppose

²call *n* **1** : SHOUT **2** : the cry of an animal (as a bird) **3** : a request or a command to come or assemble : INVITATION, SUMMONS **4 a** ♦ : a calling on another for something due or supposed to be due : CLAIM **b** : an instance of asking for something : REQUEST **5** : a brief usu. formal visit **6** : an act of calling on the telephone **7** : DECISION ⟨a tough ∼⟩ **8** : a temporary transfer of control of computer processing to a particular set of instructions

♦ claim, pretense, pretension, right

cal·la lily \'ka-lə-\ *n* : a plant related to the arums and grown for its large white lilylike bract that surrounds a fleshy spike of small yellow flowers

call·back \'kȯl-ˌbak\ *n* : a calling back; *esp* : RECALL 5

call–board \-ˌbȯrd\ *n* : a board for posting notices (as of rehearsal calls)

call down *vb* : REPRIMAND

call·er *n* ♦ : one that calls : a person who makes a brief visit

♦ guest, visitor

call girl *n* : a prostitute with whom appointments are made by phone

cal·lig·ra·phy \kə-'li-grə-fē\ *n* : artistic or elegant handwriting; *also* : the art of producing such writing — **cal·lig·ra·pher** \-fər\ *n*

call–in \'kȯl-ˌin\ *adj* : allowing listeners to engage in broadcast telephone conversations ⟨a ∼ show⟩

call in *vb* **1** : to order to return or be returned **2** : to summon to one's aid **3** : to report by telephone

call·ing \'kȯ-liŋ\ *n* **1** : a strong inner impulse toward a particular course of action **2** ♦ : the activity in which one customarily engages as an occupation

♦ employment, line, occupation, profession, trade, vocation, work

cal·li·ope \kə-'lī-ə-(ˌ)pē, 'ka-lē-ˌōp\ *n* : a keyboard musical instrument similar to an organ and made up of a series of whistles

call number *n* : a combination of characters assigned to a library book to indicate its place on a shelf

call off *vb* ♦ : to give up (an undertaking or planned activity) : CANCEL

♦ abort, cancel, drop, recall, repeal, rescind, revoke

cal·los·i·ty \ka-'lä-sə-tē\ *n, pl* **-ties** **1** : the quality or state of being callous **2** : CALLUS 1

¹cal·lous \'ka-ləs\ *adj* **1** : being thickened and hardened ⟨∼ skin⟩ **2** ♦ : feeling no emotion or sympathy — **cal·lous·ly** *adv* — **cal·lous·ness** *n*

♦ hard, heartless, inhuman, inhumane, pitiless, soulless, unfeeling, unsympathetic

²**callous** *vb* : to make callous

cal·low \'ka-lō\ *adj* ♦ : lacking adult sophistication ⟨a ∼ youth⟩ — **cal·low·ness** *n*

♦ adolescent, green, immature, inexperienced, juvenile, raw *Ant* adult, experienced, grown-up, mature, ripe

call–up \'kȯl-ˌəp\ *n* : an order to report for active military service

call up *vb* : to summon for active military duty

cal·lus \'ka-ləs\ *n* **1** : a callous area on skin or bark **2** : tissue that is converted into bone in the healing of a bone fracture — **callus** *vb*

call–waiting *n* : a telephone service by which during a call in progress an incoming call is signaled (as by a click)

¹**calm** \'käm, 'kälm\ *n* **1** ♦ : a period or a condition free from storms, high winds, or rough water **2** : complete or almost complete absence of wind **3** ♦ : a state of tranquility

♦ [1, 3] calmness, hush, peace, placidity, quiet, quietness, repose, serenity, still, stillness, tranquility *Ant* bustle, commotion, hubbub, hurly-burly, pandemonium, tumult, turmoil, uproar

²**calm** *vb* **1** ♦ : to make or become calm **2** ♦ : to make peaceful : induce quietude and repose in instead of agitation, passion, or excitement — often used with *down*

♦ [1, 2] allay, compose, quiet, settle, soothe, still, tranquilize *Ant* agitate, discompose, disquiet, disturb, perturb, upset ♦ [2] collect, compose, control, settle ♦ *usu* **calm down** [2] cool (off *or* down), hush, quiet, settle (down)

³**calm** *adj* **1** ♦ : marked by calm : STILL **2** ♦ : free from agitation, excitement, or disturbance ⟨a ∼ manner⟩

♦ [1, 2] collected, composed, cool, placid, self-possessed, serene, still, tranquil, undisturbed, unperturbed, unruffled, unshaken, untroubled, unworried *Ant* agitated, discomposed, disturbed, perturbed, upset ♦ [1, 2] halcyon, hushed, peaceful, placid, quiet, serene, still, tranquil, untroubled *Ant* agitated, angry, stormy, turbulent

calm·ly *adv* ♦ : in a calm manner : with calm

♦ quiet, quietly, still

calm·ness *n* ♦ : the quality or state of being calm

♦ aplomb, composure, coolness, equanimity, placidity, self-possession, serenity, tranquility

cal·o·mel \'ka-lə-məl, -ˌmel\ *n* : a chloride of mercury used esp. as a fungicide

ca·lor·ic \kə-'lȯr-ik\ *adj* **1** : of or relating to heat **2** : of, relating to, or containing calories

cal·o·rie *also* **cal·o·ry** \'ka-lə-rē\ *n, pl* **-ries** : a unit for measuring heat; *esp* : one for measuring the value of foods for producing heat and energy in the human body equivalent to the amount of heat required to raise the temperature of one kilogram of water one degree Celsius

cal·o·rim·e·ter \ˌka-lə-'ri-mə-tər\ *n* : an apparatus for measuring quantities of heat — **cal·o·rim·e·try** \-trē\ *n*

cal·u·met \'kal-yə-ˌmet, -mət\ *n* : a ceremonial pipe used by some Indigenous American people

ca·lum·ni·ate \kə-'ləm-nē-ˌāt\ *vb* **-at·ed; -at·ing** : to make false and malicious statements about — **ca·lum·ni·a·tion** \-ˌləm-nē-'ā-shən\ *n* — **ca·lum·ni·a·tor** \-'ləm-nē-ˌā-tər\ *n*

cal·um·ny \'ka-ləm-nē\ *n, pl* **-nies** : false and malicious accusation — **ca·lum·ni·ous** \kə-'ləm-nē-əs\ *adj*

calve \'kav, 'kȧv\ *vb* **calved; calv·ing** : to give birth to a calf

calves *pl of* CALF

Cal·vin·ism \'kal-və-ˌni-zəm\ *n* : the theological system of John Calvin and his followers — **Cal·vin·ist** \-nist\ *n or adj* — **Cal·vin·is·tic** \ˌkal-və-'nis-tik\ *adj*

ca·lyp·so \kə-'lip-sō\ *n, pl* **-sos** : a style of music originating in the British West Indies and having lyrics that usu. satirize local personalities and events

ca·lyx \'kā-liks, 'ka-\ *n, pl* **ca·lyx·es** *or* **ca·ly·ces** \'kā-lə-ˌsēz, 'ka-\ : the usu. green or leaflike outer part of a flower consisting of sepals

cal·zo·ne \kal-'zōn, -'zō-nē\ *n* : a baked or fried turnover of pizza dough stuffed with cheese and various fillings

¹**cam** \'kam\ *n* : a rotating or sliding piece in a mechanical linkage by which rotary motion is transformed into linear motion or vice versa

²**cam** *n* : CAMERA

ca·ma·ra·de·rie \ˌkäm-'rä-də-rē, ˌkam-, -'ra-\ *n* ♦ : friendly feeling and goodwill among comrades

♦ companionship, company, comradeship, fellowship, society

cam·bi·um \'kam-bē-əm\ *n, pl* **-bi·ums** *or* **-bia** \-bē-ə\ : a thin cellular layer between xylem and phloem of most higher plants from which new tissues develop — **cam·bi·al** \-əl\ *adj*

Cam·bo·di·an \kam-'bō-dē-ən\ *n* : a native or inhabitant of Cambodia — **Cambodian** *adj*

Cam·bri·an \'kam-brē-ən, 'käm-\ *adj* : of, relating to, or being the earliest period of the Paleozoic era — **Cambrian** *n*

cam·bric \'kām-brik\ *n* : a fine thin white linen or cotton fabric

cam·cord·er \'kam-ˌkȯr-dər\ *n* : a small portable video camera and recorder

came *past of* COME

cam·el \'ka-məl\ *n* : either of two large hoofed cud-chewing mammals used esp. in desert regions of Asia and Africa for carrying and riding

camel hair *also* **camel's hair** *n* **1** : the hair of a camel or a substitute for it **2** : cloth made of camel hair or of camel hair and wool

ca·mel·lia \kə-'mēl-yə\ *n* : any of a genus of shrubs and trees related to the tea plant and grown in warm regions and greenhouses for their showy roselike flowers

Cam·em·bert \'ka-məm-ˌber\ *n* : a soft cheese with a grayish rind and yellow interior

cam·eo \'ka-mē-ˌō\ *n, pl* **-eos** **1** : a gem carved in relief; *also* : a small medallion with a profiled head in relief **2** : a brief appearance esp. by a well-known actor in a play or movie

cam·era \'kam-rə, 'ka-mər-ə\ *n* : a device with a lightproof chamber fitted with a lens through which the image of an object is projected onto a surface for recording (as on film) or for conversion into electrical signals (as for television broadcast) — **cam·era·man** \-ˌman, -mən\ *n* — **cam·era·wom·an** *n*

Cam·er·oo·ni·an \ˌka-mə-'rü-nē-ən\ *n* : a native or inhabitant of the Republic of Cameroon or the Cameroons region — **Camer·oonian** *adj*

cam·i·sole \'ka-mə-ˌsōl\ *n* : a short sleeveless garment for women

camomile *var of* CHAMOMILE

¹**cam·ou·flage** \'ka-mə-ˌfläzh, -ˌfläj\ *n* **1** : the disguising of military equipment with paint, nets, or foliage; *also* : the disguise itself **2** ♦ : concealment by means of disguise **3** : deceptive behavior

♦ disguise, guise

²**camouflage** *vb* ♦ : to conceal or disguise by camouflage

♦ cloak, disguise, dress up, mask

¹**camp** \'kamp\ *n* **1** ♦ : a place where tents or buildings are erected for usu. temporary shelter; *also* : a building in such a place for occasional use **2** : a collection of tents or other shelters **3** : a program offering recreational activities (as boating and hiking) for a limited time ⟨summer ∼⟩ **4** : a body of persons encamped **5** : a training session for athletes outside of the regular season

♦ cabin, chalet, cottage, lodge ♦ bivouac, encampment

²**camp** *vb* **1** : to make or occupy a camp **2** : to live in a camp or outdoors

³**camp** *n* **1** : exaggerated effeminate mannerisms **2** : something so outrageous, inappropriate, or theatrical as to be considered amusing — **camp** *adj* — **camp·i·ly** \'kam-pə-lē\ *adv* — **camp·i·ness** \-pē-nəs\ *n* — **campy** \-pē\ *adj*

⁴**camp** *vb* : to engage in camp : exhibit the qualities of camp

cam·paign \kam-'pān\ *n* **1** : a series of military operations forming one distinct stage in a war **2** ♦ : a series of activities designed to bring about a particular result ⟨advertising ∼⟩ — **campaign** *vb*

♦ bandwagon, cause, crusade, drive, movement

cam·paign·er *n* ♦ : one that goes on, engages in, or conducts a campaign

♦ applicant, aspirant, candidate, contender, hopeful, prospect, seeker

cam·pa·ni·le \ˌkam-pə-'nē-lē\ *n, pl* **-ni·les** *or* **-ni·li** \-'nē-lē\ : a usu. freestanding bell tower

cam·pa·nol·o·gy \ˌkam-pə-'nä-lə-jē\ *n* : the art of bell ringing — **cam·pa·nol·o·gist** \-jist\ *n*

camp·er \'kam-pər\ *n* **1** : one who camps **2** ♦ : a portable dwelling (as a specially equipped vehicle) for use during casual travel and camping

♦ caravan, motor home, trailer

Camp Fire Girl *n* : a member of a national organization of girls from ages 5 to 18

camp follower *n* **1** : a civilian (as a prostitute) who follows a military unit to attend or exploit its personnel **2** : a follower of a group who is not an adherent; *esp* : a politician who joins a movement solely for personal gain

camp·ground \-ˌgrau̇nd\ *n* : the area or place used for a camp, for camping, or for a camp meeting

cam·phor \ˈkam-fər\ *n* : a gummy volatile aromatic compound obtained from an evergreen Asian tree (**camphor tree**) and used esp. in medicine

camp meeting *n* : a series of evangelistic meetings usu. held outdoors

camp·o·ree \ˌkam-pə-ˈrē\ *n* : a gathering of Boy Scouts or Girl Scouts from a given geographic area

camp·site \-ˌsīt\ *n* : a place suitable for or used as the site of a camp

cam·pus \ˈkam-pəs\ *n* : the grounds and buildings of a college or school; *also* : grounds resembling a campus ⟨hospital ∼⟩

cam·shaft \ˈkam-ˌshaft\ *n* : a shaft to which a cam is fastened

¹**can** \kən, ˈkan\ *vb, past* **could** \kəd, ˈku̇d\ *pres sing & pl* **can** 1 : be able to   2 : may perhaps ⟨∼ he still be alive⟩   3 : be permitted by conscience or feeling to ⟨you ∼ hardly blame her⟩   4 : have permission to ⟨you ∼ go now⟩

²**can** \ˈkan\ *n* 1 ♦ : a usu. cylindrical container or receptacle ⟨garbage ∼⟩ ⟨coffee ∼⟩   2 : JAIL   3 : TOILET

♦ canister, drum, tin

³**can** \ˈkan\ *vb* **canned; can·ning** 1 : to put in a can : preserve by sealing in airtight cans or jars   2 *slang* : to discharge from employment   3 *slang* : to put a stop or an end to — **can·ner** *n*

Can *or* **Canad** *abbr* Canada; Canadian

Canada Day *n* : July 1 observed as a legal holiday in commemoration of the proclamation of dominion status in 1867

Can·a·da goose \ˈka-nə-də-\ *n* : a common wild goose of No. America

Ca·na·di·an \kə-ˈnā-dē-ən\ *n* : a native or inhabitant of Canada — **Canadian** *adj*

Canadian football *n* : a game resembling American football that is played on a turfed field between two teams of 12 players each

ca·naille \kə-ˈnī, -ˈnāl\ *n* : RABBLE, RIFFRAFF

ca·nal \kə-ˈnal\ *n* 1 : a tubular passage in the body : DUCT   2 ♦ : an artificial waterway (as for boats or irrigation)

♦ aqueduct, channel, conduit, flume, raceway, watercourse

can·a·lize \ˈkan-ᵊl-ˌīz\ *vb* **-lized; -liz·ing** 1 : to provide with a canal or make into or like a channel   2 : to provide with an outlet; *esp* : to direct into preferred channels — **ca·nal·i·za·tion** \ˌkan-ᵊl-ə-ˈzā-shən\ *n*

can·a·pé \ˈka-nə-pē, -ˌpā\ *n* : a piece of bread or toast or a cracker topped with a savory food

ca·nard \kə-ˈnärd\ *n* : a false or unfounded report or story

ca·nary \kə-ˈner-ē\ *n, pl* **ca·nar·ies** 1 : a usu. sweet wine similar to Madeira   2 : a usu. yellow or greenish finch often kept in a cage as a pet

ca·nas·ta \kə-ˈnas-tə\ *n* : rummy played with two full decks of cards plus four jokers

canc *abbr* canceled

can·can \ˈkan-ˌkan\ *n* : a woman's dance of French origin characterized by high kicking

¹**can·cel** \ˈkan-səl\ *vb* **-celed** *or* **-celled; -cel·ing** *or* **-cel·ling** 1 ♦ : to destroy the force or validity of ⟨∼ a magazine subscription⟩   2 ♦ : to match in force or effect — often used with *out*   3 : to cross out : DELETE   4 : to remove (a common divisor) from a numerator and denominator; *also* : to remove (equivalents) on opposite sides of an equation or account   5 : to mark (a postage stamp or check) so that it cannot be reused   6 : to neutralize each other's strength or effect

♦ [1] abort, call off, drop, recall, repeal, rescind, revoke *Ant* continue, keep ♦ *often* **cancel out** [2] annul, compensate, correct, counteract, counterbalance, make up, neutralize, offset

²**cancel** *n* 1 : CANCELLATION   2 : a deleted part

can·cel·er *or* **can·cel·ler** *n* ♦ : a force or influence that cancels out or offsets an opposing force

♦ balance, counterbalance, counterweight, equipoise, offset

can·cel·la·tion \ˌkan-sə-ˈlā-shən\ *n* ♦ : the act or an instance of canceling : the calling off of an arrangement

♦ abortion, calling, recall, repeal, rescission, revocation *Ant* continuation

can·cer \ˈkan-sər\ *n* 1 *cap* : a zodiacal constellation between Gemini and Leo usu. pictured as a crab   2 *cap* : the 4th sign of the zodiac in astrology; *also* : one born under this sign   3 : a malignant tumor that tends to spread in the body; *also* : an abnormal state marked by such tumors   4 : a malignant evil that spreads destructively — **can·cer·ous** \-sə-rəs\ *adj* — **can·cer·ous·ly** *adv*

can·de·la·bra \ˌkan-də-ˈlä-brə, -ˈla-\ *n* : an ornamental branched candlestick or lamp with several lights

can·de·la·brum \-brəm\ *n, pl* **-bra** *also* **-brums** : CANDELABRA

can·did \ˈkan-dəd\ *adj* 1 ♦ : marked by honest sincere expression : FRANK, STRAIGHTFORWARD   2 : relating to photography of subjects acting naturally or spontaneously without being posed — **can·did·ly** *adv*

♦ direct, forthright, foursquare, frank, honest, open, outspoken, plain, straight, straightforward, unguarded, unreserved

can·di·da·cy \ˈkan-də-də-sē\ *n, pl* **-cies** : the state of being a candidate

can·di·date \ˈkan-də-ˌdāt, ˈka-nə-, -dət\ *n* ♦ : one who seeks or is proposed for an office, honor, or membership

♦ applicant, aspirant, campaigner, contender, hopeful, prospect, seeker

can·di·da·ture \ˈkan-də-də-ˌchu̇r, ˈka-nə-\ *n, chiefly Brit* : CANDIDACY

can·did·ness \ˈkan-dəd-nəs\ *n* ♦ : the quality or state of being candid

♦ candor (*or* candour), directness, forthrightness, frankness, openness, outspokenness, plainness

can·died \ˈkan-dēd\ *adj* : preserved in or encrusted with sugar

¹**can·dle** \ˈkan-dᵊl\ *n* : a usu. slender mass of tallow or wax molded around a wick that is burned to give light

²**candle** *vb* **can·dled; can·dling** : to examine (as eggs) by holding between the eye and a light — **can·dler** *n*

can·dle·light \ˈkan-dᵊl-ˌlīt\ *n* 1 : the light of a candle; *also* : any soft artificial light   2 : the time when candles are lit : TWILIGHT

can·dle·lit \-ˌlit\ *adj* : illuminated by candlelight ⟨a ∼ dinner⟩

Can·dle·mas \ˈkan-dᵊl-məs\ *n* : February 2 observed as a church festival in commemoration of the presentation of Christ in the temple

can·dle·stick \-ˌstik\ *n* : a holder with a socket for a candle

can·dle·wick \-ˌwik\ *n* : a soft cotton yarn; *also* : embroidery made with this yarn usu. in tufts

can·dor \ˈkan-dər\ *or Can and Brit* **can·dour** *n* ♦ : unreserved, honest, or sincere expression : FRANKNESS

♦ candidness, directness, forthrightness, frankness, openness, plainness *Ant* dissembling, pretense

C and W *abbr* country and western

¹**can·dy** \ˈkan-dē\ *n, pl* **candies** 1 : a confection made from sugar often with flavoring and filling   2 : something that appeals in a light or frivolous way

²**candy** *vb* **can·died; can·dy·ing** : to encrust in sugar often by cooking in a syrup

candy floss *n, Can and Brit* : COTTON CANDY

candy strip·er \-ˈstrī-pər\ *n* : a teenage volunteer worker at a hospital

¹**cane** \ˈkān\ *n* 1 : a slender hollow or pithy stem (as of a reed or bramble)   2 : a tall woody grass or reed (as sugarcane)   3 **a** : a walking stick   **b** : a rod for flogging

²**cane** *vb* **caned; can·ing** 1 : to beat with a cane   2 : to weave or make with cane — **can·er** *n*

cane·brake \ˈkān-ˌbrāk\ *n* : a thicket of cane

¹**ca·nine** \ˈkā-ˌnīn\ *n* 1 : a pointed tooth between the outer incisor and the first premolar   2 : a canine mammal (as a domestic dog)

²**canine** *adj* : of or relating to dogs or to the family to which they belong

can·is·ter \ˈka-nə-stər\ *n* ♦ : an often cylindrical container

♦ can, drum, tin

can·ker \ˈkaŋ-kər\ *n* : a spreading sore that eats into tissue — **can·ker·ous** \-kə-rəs\ *adj*

can·ker·worm \-ˌwərm\ *n* : either of two moths and esp. their larvae that are pests of fruit and shade trees

can·na \ˈka-nə\ *n* : any of a genus of tropical herbs with large leaves and racemes of bright-colored flowers

can·na·bis \ˈka-nə-bəs\ *n* : any of the psychoactive preparations (as marijuana) or chemicals (as THC) derived from hemp; *also* : HEMP

canned \ˈkand\ *adj* : prepared in standardized form for general use or wide distribution

can·nery \ˈka-nə-rē\ *n, pl* **-ner·ies** : a factory for the canning of foods

can·ni·bal \ˈka-nə-bəl\ *n* : one that eats the flesh of its own kind — **can·ni·bal·ism** \-bə-ˌli-zəm\ *n* — **can·ni·bal·is·tic** \-bə-ˈlis-tik\ *adj*

can·ni·bal·ise *Brit var of* CANNIBALIZE

can·ni·bal·ize \ˈka-nə-bə-ˌlīz\ *vb* **-ized; -iz·ing** 1 : to take usable parts from (as an inoperative machine) to construct or repair another machine   2 : to practice cannibalism

can·ni·ness \'ka-nē-nəs\ *n* ♦ : skill in devising or using indirect or subtle methods

♦ artfulness, artifice, caginess, craft, craftiness, cunning, guile, slyness, wiliness ♦ acumen, astuteness, caginess, hardheadedness, intelligence, keenness, sharpness, shrewdness, wit

can·non \'ka-nən\ *n, pl* **cannons** *or* **cannon** : a large heavy gun; *esp* : one mounted on a carriage

can·non·ade \,ka-nə-'nād\ *n* **1** : a heavy fire of artillery **2** ♦ : an attack (as with words) likened to artillery fire : BOMBARDMENT — **cannonade** *vb*

♦ barrage, bombardment, fusillade, hail, salvo, shower, storm, volley

can·non·ball \'ka-nən-,bȯl\ *n* : a usu. round solid missile for a cannon

can·non·eer \,ka-nə-'nir\ *n* : an artillery gunner

can·not \'ka-,nät, kə-'nät\ : can not — **cannot but** : to be unable to do otherwise than ⟨we *cannot but* wonder why⟩

can·nu·la \'kan-yə-lə\ *n, pl* **-las** *or* **-lae** \-,lē\ : a small tube for insertion into a body cavity or into a duct or vessel

can·ny \'ka-nē\ *adj* **can·ni·er; -est** ♦ : marked by clever discerning awareness : SHREWD ⟨a *canny* lawyer⟩ — **can·ni·ly** \'kan-ᵊl-ē\ *adv*

♦ astute, hardheaded, knowing, sharp, shrewd, smart

ca·noe \kə-'nü\ *n* : a light narrow boat with sharp ends and curved sides that is usu. propelled by paddles — **canoe** *vb* — **ca·noe·ist** *n*

ca·no·la \kə-'nō-lə\ *n* : a rape plant producing seeds that are low in a toxic acid and yield an edible oil (**canola oil**) high in monounsaturated fatty acids; *also* : this oil

¹can·on \'ka-nən\ *n* **1** : a regulation decreed by a church council; *also* : a provision of canon law **2** : an official or authoritative list (as of works of literature) **3** : an accepted principle ⟨the ∼s of good taste⟩

²canon *n* : a member of the clergy on the staff of a cathedral

ca·non·i·cal \kə-'nä-ni-kəl\ *adj* **1** : of, relating to, or forming a canon **2** : conforming to a general rule or acceptable procedure : ORTHODOX **3** : of or relating to a canon of a cathedral — **ca·non·i·cal·ly** \-k(ə-)lē\ *adv*

can·on·ize \'ka-nə-,nīz\ *vb* **can·on·ized** \-,nīzd\; **can·on·iz·ing 1** : to declare (a deceased person) an officially recognized saint **2** ♦ : to treat as illustrious, preeminent, or sacred — **can·on·i·za·tion** \,ka-nə-nə-'zā-shən\ *n*

♦ adore, deify, dote on, idolize, worship

canon law *n* : the law governing a church

can·o·py \'ka-nə-pē\ *n, pl* **-pies 1** ♦ : an overhanging cover, shelter, or shade **2** : the uppermost spreading layer of a forest **3** : a transparent cover for an airplane cockpit **4** : the fabric part of a parachute — **canopy** *vb*

♦ ceiling, roof, tent

¹cant \'kant\ *vb* ♦ : to give a slant to

♦ angle, cock, heel, incline, lean, list, slant, slope, tilt, tip

²cant *n* **1** : an oblique or slanting surface **2** ♦ : upward or downward slant or inclination or degree of slope : TILT, SLANT

♦ diagonal, grade, inclination, incline, lean, pitch, slant, slope, tilt, upgrade

³cant *vb* **1** : to beg in a whining manner **2** : to talk hypocritically

⁴cant *n* **1** ♦ : the special idiom of a profession or trade : JARGON **2** ♦ : insincere speech; *esp* : insincerely pious words or statements

♦ [1] argot, jargon, language, lingo, slang, terminology, vocabulary ♦ [2] dissimulation, hypocrisy, piety

Cant *abbr* Canticle of Canticles

can·ta·bi·le \kän-'tä-bə-,lā\ *adv or adj* : in a singing manner — used as a direction in music

can·ta·loupe *also* **can·ta·loup** \'kant-ᵊl-,ōp\ *n* : MUSKMELON; *esp* : one with orange flesh and rough skin

can·tan·ker·ous \kan-'taŋ-kə-rəs\ *adj* ♦ : marked by ill humor, irritability, and determination to disagree : ILL-NATURED — **can·tan·ker·ous·ly** *adv* — **can·tan·ker·ous·ness** *n*

♦ bearish, bilious, disagreeable, dyspeptic, ill-humored, ill-tempered, ornery, splenetic, surly

can·ta·ta \kən-'tä-tə\ *n* : a choral composition usu. sung to instrumental accompaniment

canted *adj* ♦ : placed at an incline or given a degree of cant : SLANTED

♦ diagonal, inclined, listing, oblique, slantwise

can·teen \kan-'tēn\ *n* **1** : a flask for carrying liquids **2** : a place of recreation and entertainment for military personnel **3** : a small cafeteria or counter at which snacks are served

can·ter \'kan-tər\ *n* : a horse's 3-beat gait resembling but smoother and slower than a gallop — **canter** *vb*

Can·ter·bury bell \'kant-ər-,ber-ē-\ *n* : any of several plants related to the bluebell that are cultivated for their showy flowers

can·ti·cle \'kan-ti-kəl\ *n* **1** : SONG **2** ♦ : any of several liturgical songs taken from the Bible

♦ anthem, carol, chorale, hymn, psalm, spiritual

Canticle of Canticles *n* : SONG OF SONGS

¹can·ti·le·ver \'kant-ᵊl-,ē-vər\ *n* : a projecting beam or structure supported only at one end; *also* : either of a pair of such structures projecting toward each other so that when joined they form a bridge

²cantilever *vb* **1** : to support by a cantilever ⟨a ∼*ed* shelf⟩ **2** : to build as a cantilever **3** : to project as a cantilever

can·tle \'kant-ᵊl\ *n* : the upwardly projecting rear part of a saddle

can·to \'kan-,tō\ *n, pl* **cantos** : one of the major divisions of a long poem

can·ton \'kant-ᵊn, 'kan-,tän\ *n* : a small territorial division of a country; *esp* : one of the political divisions of Switzerland — **can·ton·al** \'kant-ᵊn-əl, kan-'tän-ᵊl\ *adj*

can·ton·ment \kan-'tōn-mənt, -'tän-\ *n* : usu. temporary quarters for troops

can·tor \'kan-tər\ *n* **1** : a choir leader **2** : a synagogue official who sings liturgical music and leads the congregation in prayer

Ca·nuck \kə-'nək *sometimes* -'nuk\ *n* : a Canadian and esp. a French Canadian

can·vas *also* **can·vass** \'kan-vəs\ *n* **1** : a strong cloth formerly much used for making tents and sails **2** : a set of sails **3** : a group of tents **4** : a piece of cloth prepared as a surface for painting; *also* : a painting on this surface **5** : the canvas-covered floor of a boxing or wrestling ring

can·vas·back \'kan-vəs-,bak\ *n* : a No. American wild duck with red head and gray back

¹can·vass *also* **can·vas** \'kan-vəs\ *vb* **can·vassed; can·vassing** ♦ : to go through (a district) or to (persons) to solicit votes or orders for goods or to determine public opinion or sentiment — **can·vass·er** *n*

♦ poll, solicit, survey

²canvass *n* : an act or instance of canvassing

can·yon \'kan-yən\ *n* ♦ : a deep narrow valley with high steep sides

♦ defile, flume, gap, gorge, gulch, notch, pass, ravine

¹cap \'kap\ *n* **1** ♦ : a covering for the head esp. with a visor and no brim **2** ♦ : something that serves as a cover or protection esp. for a tip, knob, or end ⟨a bottle ∼⟩ **3** : a container holding an explosive charge **4** : an upper limit (as on expenditures)

♦ [1] hat, headgear ♦ [2] cover, lid, top

²cap *vb* **capped; cap·ping 1** : to provide or protect with a cap **2** : to form a cap over : CROWN ⟨snow-*capped* mountains⟩ **3** : OUTDO, SURPASS **4** ♦ : to provide a culminating event for : CLIMAX — often used with *off*

♦ *often* **cap off** climax, crown

³cap *abbr* **1** capacity **2** capital **3** capitalize; capitalized

CAP *abbr* Civil Air Patrol

ca·pa·bil·i·ty \,kā-pə-'bi-lə-tē\ *n* **1** ♦ : the quality or state of being capable physically, intellectually, morally, or legally **2** ♦ : natural talent or acquired proficiency esp. in a particular work or activity

♦ [1] ability, capacity, competence, faculty ♦ [2] credentials, qualification, stuff

ca·pa·ble \'kā-pə-bəl\ *adj* ♦ : having ability, capacity, or power to do something : ABLE, COMPETENT

♦ able, competent, fit, good, qualified, suitable

ca·pa·bly *adv* ♦ : in a capable manner

♦ ably, adeptly, expertly, masterfully, proficiently, skillfully, well

ca·pa·cious \kə-'pā-shəs\ *adj* ♦ : able to contain much — **ca·pa·cious·ly** *adv* — **ca·pa·cious·ness** *n*

♦ ample, commodious, roomy, spacious

ca·pac·i·tance \kə-'pa-sə-təns\ *n* : the property of an electric nonconductor that permits the storage of energy

ca·pac·i·tor \kə-'pa-sə-tər\ *n* : an electronic circuit device for temporary storage of electrical energy

¹**ca·pac·i·ty** \kə-'pa-sə-tē\ n, pl **-ties** **1** : legal qualification or fitness **2** : the ability to contain, receive, or accommodate **3** : the maximum amount or number that can be contained **4** ♦ : an individual's mental or physical ability and skill in doing something : ABILITY **5** ♦ : position or character assigned or assumed ⟨is happy to serve in any ∼⟩

♦ [4] ability, capability, competence, faculty ♦ [5] appointment, billet, function, job, place, position, post, situation ♦ [5] function, job, part, place, position, purpose, role, task, work

²**capacity** adj : equaling maximum capacity ⟨a ∼ crowd⟩
cap–a–pie or **cap-à-pie** \ˌka-pə-'pē\ adv : from head to foot : at all points
¹**ca·par·i·son** \kə-'par-ə-sən\ n **1** : an ornamental covering for a horse **2** ♦ : rich clothing

♦ array, best, bravery, feather, finery, frippery, full dress, gaiety, regalia

²**caparison** vb : to dress richly
¹**cape** \'kāp\ n **1** ♦ : a point of land jutting out into water **2** often cap : CAPE COD COTTAGE

♦ headland, peninsula, point, promontory, spit

²**cape** n : a sleeveless garment hanging from the neck over the shoulders
Cape Cod cottage \'kāp-'käd-\ n : a compact rectangular dwelling of one or one-and-a-half stories usu. with a steep gable roof
¹**ca·per** \'kā-pər\ n : the flower bud or young berry of a Mediterranean shrub pickled for use as a relish; also : this shrub
²**caper** vb **ca·pered; ca·per·ing** ♦ : to leap about in a playful manner

♦ cavort, disport, frisk, frolic, gambol, lark, rollick, romp, sport

³**caper** n **1** : a frolicsome leap **2** ♦ : a capricious escapade **3** : an illegal or questionable act

♦ antic, escapade, frolic, monkeyshine, practical joke, prank, trick

cape·skin \'kāp-ˌskin\ n : a light flexible leather made from sheepskins
Cape Verd·ean \-'vər-dē-ən\ n : a native or inhabitant of the Republic of Cape Verde
cap·ful \'kap-ˌfùl\ n, pl **cap·fuls** also **caps·ful** \'kaps-\ : as much as a cap will hold
cap·il·lar·i·ty \ˌka-pə-'lar-ə-tē\ n, pl **-ties** : the action by which the surface of a liquid where it is in contact with a solid (as in a slender tube) is raised or lowered depending on the relative attraction of the molecules of the liquid for each other and for those of the solid
¹**cap·il·lary** \'ka-pə-ˌler-ē\ adj **1** : resembling a hair **2** : having a very small bore ⟨∼ tube⟩ **3** : of or relating to capillaries or to capillarity
²**capillary** n, pl **-lar·ies** : any of the tiny thin-walled blood vessels that carry blood between the smallest arteries and their corresponding veins
¹**cap·i·tal** \'ka-pət-ᵊl\ n : the top part or piece of an architectural column
²**capital** adj **1** : conforming to the series A, B, C rather than a, b, c ⟨∼ letters⟩ ⟨∼ G⟩ **2** : punishable by death ⟨a ∼ crime⟩ **3** : most serious ⟨a ∼ error⟩ **4** : first in importance or position : CHIEF; also : being the seat of government ⟨the ∼ city⟩ **5** : of or relating to capital ⟨∼ expenditures⟩; esp : relating to or being assets that add to the long-term net worth of a corporation **6** : of the first order of size, importance, or quality : FIRST-RATE, EXCELLENT
³**capital** n **1** ♦ : accumulated wealth esp. as used to produce more wealth **2** : the total face value of shares of stock issued by a company **3** : persons holding capital **4** : ADVANTAGE, GAIN **5** : a letter larger than the ordinary small letter and often different in form **6 a** : the capital city of a state, province, or country **b** : a city preeminent in some activity ⟨the fashion ∼⟩

♦ assets, fortune, means, opulence, riches, substance, wealth, wherewithal

capital gain n : the increase in value of an asset (as stock or real estate) between the time it is bought and the time it is sold
capital goods n pl : machinery, tools, factories, and commodities used in the production of goods
cap·i·tal·ise Brit var of CAPITALIZE
cap·i·tal·ism \'ka-pət-ᵊl-ˌi-zəm\ n : an economic system characterized by private or corporate ownership of capital goods and by prices, production, and distribution of goods that are determined mainly by competition in a free market

¹**cap·i·tal·ist** \-ist\ n **1** : a person who has capital esp. invested in business **2** : a person of great wealth : PLUTOCRAT **3** : a believer in capitalism
²**capitalist** or **cap·i·tal·is·tic** \ˌka-pət-ᵊl-'is-tik\ adj **1** : owning capital **2** : practicing or advocating capitalism **3** : marked by capitalism — **cap·i·tal·is·ti·cal·ly** \-ti-k(ə-)lē\ adv
cap·i·tal·iza·tion \ˌka-pət-ᵊl-ə-'zā-shən\ n **1** : the act or process of capitalizing **2** : the total amount of money used as capital in a business
cap·i·tal·ize or Brit **cap·i·tal·ise** \'ka-pət-ᵊl-ˌīz\ vb **-ized; -iz·ing** **1** : to write or print with an initial capital or in capitals **2** : to convert into or use as capital **3** ♦ : to supply capital for **4** ♦ : to gain by turning something to advantage ⟨∼ on an opponent's mistake⟩

♦ [3] endow, finance, fund, stake, subsidize, underwrite ♦ usu **capitalize on** [4] abuse, cash in, exploit, impose, play, use

cap·i·tal·ly \'ka-pət-ᵊl-ē\ adv : ADMIRABLY, EXCELLENTLY
cap·i·ta·tion \ˌka-pə-'tā-shən\ n : a direct uniform tax levied on each person
cap·i·tol \'ka-pət-ᵊl\ n : the building in which a legislature holds its sessions
ca·pit·u·late \kə-'pi-chə-ˌlāt\ vb **-lat·ed; -lat·ing** **1** ♦ : to surrender esp. on conditions agreed upon **2** ♦ : to cease resisting

♦ [1, 2] blink, bow, budge, concede, give in, give up, knuckle under, quit, submit, succumb, surrender, yield

ca·pit·u·la·tion \-ˌpi-chə-'lā-shən\ n **1** ♦ : the act of surrendering or yielding **2** : the terms of surrender

♦ relinquishment, submission, surrender

cap·let \'ka-plət\ n : a capsule-shaped medicinal tablet
ca·pon \'kā-ˌpän, -pən\ n : a castrated male chicken
cap·puc·ci·no \ˌka-pə-'chē-nō, ˌkä-\ n : espresso mixed with foamy hot milk or cream and often flavored with cinnamon
ca·pric·cio \kə-'prē-chē-ˌō, -chō\ n, pl **-cios** : an instrumental piece in free form usu. lively in tempo and brilliant in style
ca·price \kə-'prēs\ n **1** ♦ : a sudden whim or fancy **2** ♦ : an inclination to do things impulsively **3** : CAPRICCIO

♦ fancy, freak, notion, vagary, whim

ca·pri·cious \-'pri-shəs\ adj **1** ♦ : marked or guided by a sudden whim or fancy **2** ♦ : not guided by steady judgment or purpose — **ca·pri·cious·ly** adv — **ca·pri·cious·ness** n

♦ [1] impulsive, whimsical ♦ [2] changeable, fickle, fluid, inconstant, mercurial, mutable, temperamental, uncertain, unpredictable, unsettled, unstable, unsteady, variable, volatile

Cap·ri·corn \'ka-pri-ˌkorn\ n **1** : a zodiacal constellation between Sagittarius and Aquarius usu. pictured as a goat **2** : the 10th sign of the zodiac in astrology; also : one born under this sign
cap·ri·ole \'ka-prē-ˌōl\ n : ³CAPER 1; also : an upward leap of a horse with a backward kick at the height of the leap — **capriole** vb
caps abbr **1** capitals **2** capsule
cap·sa·i·cin \kap-'sā-ə-sən\ n : a colorless compound found in various capsicums that gives hot peppers their hotness
cap·si·cum \'kap-si-kəm\ n : PEPPER 2
cap·size \'kap-ˌsīz, kap-'sīz\ vb **cap·sized; cap·siz·ing** : to turn over : UPSET, OVERTURN
cap·stan \'kap-stən, -ˌstan\ n **1** : a machine for moving or raising heavy weights that consists of a vertical drum which can be rotated and around which cable is turned **2** : a rotating shaft that drives recorder tape
cap·su·lar \'kap-sə-lər\ adj : of, relating to, or resembling a capsule
cap·su·lat·ed \-ˌlā-təd\ adj : enclosed in a capsule
¹**cap·sule** \'kap-səl, -sül\ n **1 a** : a membrane or sac enclosing a body part (as of a joint) **b** ♦ : a surrounding saclike structure that protects something held inside **2** : a case bearing spores or seeds **3** ♦ : a gelatin shell for packaging something (as a drug or vitamins) **4** : a small pressurized compartment or vehicle (as for space flight)

♦ [1b] armor, case, casing, cocoon, cover, housing, husk, jacket, pod, sheath, shell ♦ [3] pill, tablet

²**capsule** adj **1** ♦ : very brief **2** : very compact

♦ brief, compact, compendious, concise, crisp, epigrammatic, laconic, pithy, succinct, summary, terse

Capt abbr captain
¹**cap·tain** \'kap-tən\ n **1** ♦ : a commander of a body of troops **2** : a commissioned officer in the army, air force, or marine corps ranking next below a major **3** : an officer in charge of a ship **4** : a commissioned officer in the navy ranking next below a rear admiral

or a commodore **5** ♦ : one who leads or supervises (as a sports team or work crew) **6** : a dominant figure — **cap·tain·cy** *n*

♦ [1] commander ♦ [5] boss, chief, foreman, head, headman, helmsman, kingpin, leader, taskmaster

²**captain** *vb* ♦ : to be or fill the role of captain ⟨∼ed the football team⟩

♦ boss, head, oversee, superintend, supervise ♦ boss, command, control, govern, preside, rule ♦ boss, command, dominate, head, lead, spearhead

cap·tion \'kap-shən\ *n* **1** : a heading esp. of an article or document : TITLE **2** : the explanatory matter accompanying an illustration **3** : a motion-picture subtitle — **cap·tion** *vb*

cap·tious \'kap-shəs\ *adj* ♦ : marked by an inclination to find fault — **cap·tious·ly** *adv* — **cap·tious·ness** *n*

♦ carping, critical, hypercritical, overcritical

cap·ti·vate \'kap-tə-ˌvāt\ *vb* **-vat·ed; -vat·ing** ♦ : to attract and hold irresistibly by some special charm or art — **cap·ti·va·tor** \'kap-tə-ˌvā-tər\ *n*

♦ allure, beguile, bewitch, charm, enchant, fascinate, wile

cap·ti·vat·ing *adj* ♦ : having the ability to captivate : CHARMING

♦ alluring, attractive, charming, elfin, engaging, fascinating, fetching, glamorous, magnetic, seductive

cap·ti·va·tion \ˌkap-tə-'vā-shən\ *n* ♦ : the action or power of influencing and dominating by some special charm or irresistible appeal

♦ allure, appeal, attractiveness, charisma, charm, enchantment, fascination, glamour, magic, magnetism

¹**cap·tive** \'kap-tiv\ *adj* **1** : made prisoner esp. in war **2** : kept within bounds : CONFINED **3** : held under control

²**captive** *n* ♦ : one captured and held prisoner

♦ capture, internee, prisoner *Ant* captor

cap·tiv·i·ty \kap-'ti-və-tē\ *n* ♦ : state or condition of being held captive esp. in war

♦ confinement, imprisonment, incarceration, internment

cap·tor \'kap-tər\ *n* : one that captures

¹**cap·ture** \'kap-chər\ *n* **1** : the act of capturing **2** : one that has been captured

²**capture** *vb* **cap·tured; cap·tur·ing** **1 a** ♦ : to take, seize, or catch esp. as captive or prize by effort or skill **b** : to take control of esp. by force **c** ♦ : to gain or win esp. through effort **2** : to preserve in a relatively permanent form

♦ [1a] bag, catch, collar, corral, get, grab, grapple, hook, land, nab, seize, snare, trap ♦ [1c] acquire, attain, carry, draw, earn, gain, garner, get, land, make, obtain, procure, realize, secure, win

Ca·pu·chin \'ka-pyə-shən\ *n* : a member of an austere branch of the order of St. Francis of Assisi engaged in missionary work and preaching

car \'kär\ *n* **1** ♦ : a vehicle moving on wheels **2** : the compartment of an elevator **3** : the part of a balloon or airship that carries passengers or equipment

♦ automobile, machine, motor vehicle

car·a·cole \'kar-ə-ˌkōl\ *n* : a half turn to right or left executed by a mounted horse — **caracole** *vb*

car·a·cul \'kar-ə-ˌkəl\ *n* : the pelt of a karakul lamb after the curl begins to loosen

ca·rafe \kə-'raf, -'räf\ *n* **1** : a bottle with a flaring lip used esp. to hold wine **2** : a usu. glass pitcher for pouring coffee

car·am·bo·la \ˌkar-əm-'bō-lə\ *n* **1** : a five-angled green to yellow edible tropical fruit of star-shaped cross section **2** : a tropical Asian tree widely cultivated for carambolas

car·a·mel \'kar-ə-məl, 'kär-məl\ *n* **1** : an amorphous substance obtained by heating sugar and used for flavoring and coloring **2** : a firm chewy candy

car·a·pace \'kar-ə-ˌpās\ *n* : a protective case or shell on the back of some animals (as turtles or crabs)

¹**carat** *var of* KARAT

²**car·at** \'kar-ət\ *n* : a unit of weight for precious stones equal to 200 milligrams

car·a·van \'kar-ə-ˌvan\ *n* **1** : a group of travelers journeying together through desert or hostile regions **2** ♦ : a group of vehicles traveling in a file **3** ♦ : a covered wagon or motortruck equipped as traveling living quarters

♦ [2] armada, cavalcade, fleet, motorcade, train ♦ [3] camper, motor home, trailer

car·a·van·sa·ry \ˌkar-ə-'van-sə-rē\ *or* **car·a·van·se·rai** \-sə-ˌrī\ *n, pl* **-ries** *or* **-rais** *or* **-rai** **1** : an inn in eastern countries where caravans rest at night **2** : an establishment that provides lodging and usu. meals for the public : HOTEL, INN

car·a·vel \'kar-ə-ˌvel\ *n* : a small 15th and 16th century ship with a broad bow, high narrow poop, and usu. three masts

car·a·way \'kar-ə-ˌwā\ *n* : an aromatic herb related to the carrot with fruits (**caraway seed**) used in seasoning and medicine; *also* : its fruit

car·bide \'kär-ˌbīd\ *n* : a compound of carbon with another element

car·bine \'kär-ˌbēn, -ˌbīn\ *n* : a short-barreled lightweight rifle

car·bo·hy·drate \ˌkär-bō-'hī-ˌdrāt, -drət\ *n* : any of various compounds composed of carbon, hydrogen, and oxygen (as sugars and starches)

car·bol·ic acid \ˌkär-'bä-lik-\ *n* : PHENOL

car·bon \'kär-bən\ *n* **1** : a nonmetallic chemical element occurring in nature esp. as diamond and graphite and as a constituent of coal, petroleum, and limestone **2** : a sheet of carbon paper; *also* : CARBON COPY 1 — **car·bon·less** \-ləs\ *adj*

car·bo·na·ceous \ˌkär-bə-'nā-shəs\ *adj* : relating to, containing, or composed of carbon

¹**car·bon·ate** \'kär-bə-ˌnāt, -nət\ *n* : a salt or ester of carbonic acid

²**car·bon·ate** \-ˌnāt\ *vb* **-at·ed; -at·ing** : to combine or infuse with carbon dioxide ⟨*carbonated* beverages⟩ — **car·bon·ation** \ˌkär-bə-'nā-shən\ *n*

carbon black *n* : any of various black substances consisting chiefly of carbon and used esp. as pigments

carbon copy *n* **1** : a copy made by carbon paper **2** ♦ : one that strongly resembles or closely corresponds to another : DUPLICATE

♦ counterpart, double, duplicate, duplication, facsimile, image, likeness, match, picture, replica, ringer, spit

carbon dating *n* : the determination of the age of old material (as an archaeological specimen) by its content of carbon 14

carbon dioxide *n* : a heavy colorless gas that does not support combustion and is formed in animal respiration and in the combustion and decomposition of organic substances

carbon footprint *n* : the amount of carbon dioxide emitted by something in a given period

carbon 14 *n* : a heavy radioactive form of carbon used esp. in dating archaeological materials

car·bon·ic acid \kär-'bä-nik-\ *n* : a weak acid that decomposes readily into water and carbon dioxide

car·bon·if·er·ous \ˌkär-bə-'ni-fə-rəs\ *adj* **1** : producing or containing carbon or coal **2** *cap* : of, relating to, or being the period of the Paleozoic era between the Devonian and the Permian — **Carboniferous** *n*

carbon monoxide *n* : a colorless odorless very poisonous gas formed by the incomplete burning of carbon

carbon paper *n* : a thin paper coated with a pigment and used for making copies

carbon tet·ra·chlo·ride \-ˌte-trə-'klōr-ˌīd\ *n* : a colorless nonflammable toxic liquid used esp. as a solvent

carbon 12 *n* : the most abundant isotope of carbon having a nucleus of 6 protons and 6 neutrons and used as a standard for measurements of atomic weight

car·boy \'kär-ˌbȯi\ *n* : a large container for liquids

car·bun·cle \'kär-ˌbəŋ-kəl\ *n* : a painful inflammation of the skin and underlying tissue that discharges pus from several openings

car·bu·re·tor \'kär-bə-ˌrā-tər, -byə-\ *n* : an apparatus for premixing vaporized fuel and air and supplying the mixture to an internal combustion engine

car·cass \'kär-kəs\ *n* : a dead body; *esp* : one of an animal dressed for food

car·cin·o·gen \kär-'si-nə-jən\ *n* : an agent causing or inciting cancer — **car·ci·no·gen·ic** \ˌkärs-ᵊn-ō-'je-nik\ *adj* — **car·ci·no·ge·nic·i·ty** \-jə-'ni-sə-tē\ *n*

car·ci·no·ma \ˌkärs-ᵊn-'ō-mə\ *n, pl* **-mas** *also* **-ma·ta** \-tə\ : a malignant tumor of epithelial origin — **car·ci·no·ma·tous** \-təs\ *adj*

¹**card** \'kärd\ *vb* : to comb with a card : cleanse and untangle before spinning — **card·er** *n*

²**card** *n* : an instrument for combing fibers (as wool or cotton)

³**card** *n* **1** : PLAYING CARD **2** *pl* : a game played with playing cards; *also* : card playing **3** : an emotional issue used to one's advantage (as in a political campaign) **4** ♦ : a usu. clownishly amusing person : WAG **5** : a flat stiff usu. small piece of paper, cardboard, or plastic often bearing pictures or information **6** : PROGRAM; *esp* : a sports program

♦ comedian, comic, humorist, jester, joker, wag, wit

⁴**card** *vb* **1** : to list or schedule on a card **2** : SCORE **3** : to ask for identification (as at a bar)

⁵card *abbr* cardinal

car·da·mom \ˈkär-də-məm\ *n* : the aromatic capsular fruit of an East Indian herb related to the ginger whose seeds are used as a spice or condiment and in medicine; *also* : this plant

card·board \ˈkärd-ˌbȯrd\ *n* : a material thicker than paper and made from cellulose fiber

card–car·ry·ing \ˈkärd-ˌkar-ē-iŋ\ *adj* : being a regularly enrolled member of an organization (as a political party)

card catalog *n* : a catalog (as of books) in which the entries are arranged systematically on cards

car·di·ac \ˈkär-dē-ˌak\ *adj* **1** : of, relating to, or located near the heart **2** : of, relating to, or affected with heart disease

car·di·gan \ˈkär-di-gən\ *n* : a sweater or jacket usu. without a collar and with a full-length opening in the front

¹car·di·nal \ˈkärd-nəl, ˈkär-dᵊn-əl\ *n* **1** : an ecclesiastical official of the Roman Catholic Church ranking next below the pope **2** : a crested No. American finch that is nearly completely red in the male

²cardinal *adj* **1** ♦ : of basic importance : CHIEF, MAIN, PRIMARY **2** : very serious ⟨a ∼ sin⟩ — **car·di·nal·ly** *adv*

    ♦ arch, central, chief, dominant, first, foremost, grand, key, main, paramount, predominant, preeminent, premier, primary, principal, sovereign, supreme

car·di·nal·ate \ˈkärd-nə-lət, ˈkär-dᵊn-ə-let, -ˌlāt\ *n* : the office, rank, or dignity of a cardinal

cardinal flower *n* : a No. American plant that bears a spike of brilliant red flowers

cardinal number *n* : a number (as 1, 5, 82, 357) that is used in simple counting and answers the question "how many?"

cardinal point *n* : one of the four principal compass points north, south, east, and west

car·dio \ˈkär-dē-ō\ *adj* : CARDIOVASCULAR 2

car·di·ol·o·gy \ˌkär-dē-ˈä-lə-jē\ *n* : the study of the heart and its action and diseases — **car·di·ol·o·gist** \-jist\ *n*

car·dio·pul·mo·nary resuscitation \ˌkär-dē-ō-ˈpu̇l-mə-ˌner-ē-\ *n* : a procedure to restore normal breathing after cardiac arrest that includes the clearance of air passages to the lungs, mouth-to-mouth method of artificial respiration, and heart massage by the exertion of pressure on the chest

car·dio·vas·cu·lar \-ˈvas-kyə-lər\ *adj* **1** : of or relating to the heart and blood vessels **2** : causing a temporary increase in heart rate ⟨a ∼ workout⟩

card·sharp·er \ˈkärd-ˌshär-pər\ *or* **card·sharp** \-ˌshärp\ *n* : a cheater at cards

¹care \ˈker\ *n* **1** : a disquieted state of uncertainty and responsibility : ANXIETY **2** ♦ : painstaking or watchful attention **3** ♦ : responsibility for the care of another ⟨under a doctor's ∼⟩ **4** : a person or thing that is an object of attention, anxiety, or solicitude

    ♦ [2] alertness, carefulness, caution, circumspection, heedfulness ♦ [2] carefulness, heed, heedfulness, pains, scrupulousness *Ant* carelessness, heedlessness ♦ [3] custody, guardianship, keeping, safekeeping, trust, ward ♦ [3] charge, guidance, headship, oversight, regulation, superintendence, supervision

²care *vb* **cared; car·ing** **1** : to feel trouble or anxiety **2** : to feel interest or concern ⟨∼ about freedom⟩ **3** ♦ : to give care — usu. used with *for* ⟨∼ for the sick⟩ **4 a** ♦ : to have a liking, fondness, taste, or inclination **b** : have regard or respect **5** : to be concerned about ⟨nobody ∼s what I do⟩ **6** : to have or express a wish for — usu. used with *for*

    ♦ usu **care for** [3] aid, minister, mother, nurse ♦ usu **care for** [3] attend, mind, oversee, superintend, supervise, tend ♦ usu **care for** [4a] accept, approve, countenance, favor (*or* favour), OK, subscribe

CARE *abbr* Cooperative for American Relief to Everywhere

ca·reen \kə-ˈrēn\ *vb* **1** : to put (a ship or boat) on a beach esp. in order to clean or repair its hull **2** ♦ : to sway from side to side **3** : CAREER

    ♦ lurch, pitch, rock, roll, seesaw, sway, toss, wobble

¹ca·reer \kə-ˈrir\ *n* **1** : COURSE, PASSAGE; *also* : speed in a course ⟨ran at full ∼⟩ **2** : an occupation or profession followed as a life's work

²career *vb* ♦ : to go at top speed esp. in a headlong manner

    ♦ barrel, bowl, fly, hurry, hurtle, pelt, race, rocket, rush, shoot, speed, tear, zip, zoom

care·free \ˈker-ˌfrē\ *adj* ♦ : free from care or worry

    ♦ careless, cavalier, easygoing, happy-go-lucky, insouciant, lighthearted, unconcerned *Ant* careworn

care·ful \-fəl\ *adj* **care·ful·ler; care·ful·lest** **1** ♦ : using or taking care **2** ♦ : marked by solicitude, caution, or prudence — **care·ful·ly** *adv*

    ♦ [1] conscientious, fussy, meticulous, painstaking ♦ [2] alert, cautious, circumspect, considerate, gingerly, guarded, heedful, safe, wary *Ant* careless, heedless, incautious, unguarded, unsafe, unwary

care·ful·ness *n* ♦ : the quality of being careful : close or steady attention (as to a task)

    ♦ alertness, care, caution, circumspection, heedfulness

care·giv·er \-ˌgi-vər\ *n* : a person who provides direct care (as for children, the disabled, or the chronically ill)

care·less \-ləs\ *adj* **1** : free from care : UNTROUBLED **2** ♦ : having no concern or interest ⟨∼ of the consequences⟩ **3** ♦ : not taking care esp. to avoid danger or harm **4 a** ♦ : not taking ordinary or proper care **b** : not showing or receiving care — **care·less·ly** *adv*

    ♦ [2, 3] heedless, mindless, unguarded, unsafe, unwary *Ant* alert, cautious, circumspect, gingerly, guarded, heedful, safe, wary ♦ [4a] derelict, lax, negligent, remiss, slack

care·less·ness *n* ♦ : failure to exercise the care that a reasonably prudent person would in like circumstances

    ♦ dereliction, heedlessness, laxness, negligence, remissness, slackness

¹ca·ress \kə-ˈres\ *n* : a tender or loving touch or embrace

²caress *vb* ♦ : to touch or stroke tenderly or lovingly — **ca·ress·er** *n*

    ♦ fondle, love, pat, pet, stroke

car·et \ˈkar-ət\ *n* : a mark ^ used to indicate the place where something is to be inserted

care·tak·er \ˈker-ˌtā-kər\ *n* **1** ♦ : one in charge usu. as occupant in place of an absent owner **2** : one temporarily fulfilling the functions of an office

    ♦ custodian, guardian, janitor, keeper, warden, watchman

care·worn \-ˌwȯrn\ *adj* : showing the effects of grief or anxiety

car·fare \ˈkär-ˌfar\ *n* : passenger fare (as on a streetcar or bus)

car·go \ˈkär-gō\ *n, pl* **cargoes** *or* **cargos** ♦ : the goods carried in a ship, airplane, or vehicle : FREIGHT

    ♦ freight, load, payload, shipment ♦ burden, freight, haul, lading, load, payload, weight

Ca·rib·be·an \ˌkar-ə-ˈbē-ən, kə-ˈri-bē-ən\ *adj* : of or relating to the eastern and southern West Indies or the Caribbean Sea

car·i·bou \ˈkar-ə-ˌbü\ *n, pl* **caribou** *or* **caribous** : a large circumpolar gregarious deer of northern taiga and tundra that usu. has palmate antlers in both sexes — used esp. for one of the New World

¹car·i·ca·ture \ˈkar-i-kə-ˌchu̇r\ *n* **1** ♦ : distorted representation to produce a ridiculous effect **2** ♦ : a representation esp. in literature or art having the qualities of caricature — **car·i·ca·tur·ist** \-ist\ *n*

    ♦ [1] farce, joke, mockery, parody, sham, travesty ♦ [2] burlesque, parody, spoof, takeoff

²caricature *vb* ♦ : to make or draw a caricature of : represent in caricature

    ♦ burlesque, imitate, mimic, mock, parody, take off, travesty

car·ies \ˈkar-ēz\ *n, pl* **caries** : tooth decay

car·il·lon \ˈkar-ə-ˌlän\ *n* : a set of tuned bells sounded by hammers controlled from a keyboard

car·i·ous \ˈkar-ē-əs\ *adj* : affected with caries

car·jack·ing \ˈkär-ˌja-kiŋ\ *n* : the theft of an automobile by force or intimidation — **car·jack·er** *n*

car·load \ˈkär-ˌlōd\ *n* : a load that fills a car

car·mi·na·tive \kär-ˈmi-nə-tiv\ *adj* : expelling gas from the alimentary canal — **carminative** *n*

car·mine \ˈkär-mən, -ˌmīn\ *n* : a vivid red

car·nage \ˈkär-nij\ *n* ♦ : great destruction of life : SLAUGHTER

    ♦ butchery, massacre, slaughter

car·nal \ˈkärn-ᵊl\ *adj* **1** ♦ : of or relating to the body **2** ♦ : relating to or given to sensual pleasures and appetites **3** ♦ : of or relating to this world : earthly rather than heavenly or spiritual — **car·nal·i·ty** \kär-ˈna-lə-tē\ *n* — **car·nal·ly** *adv*

    ♦ [1] animal, bodily, corporal, fleshly, material, physical, somatic ♦ [2] fleshly, luscious, sensual, sensuous, voluptuous ♦ [3] earthly, fleshly, material, mundane, temporal, terrestrial, worldly

car·na·tion \kär-'nā-shən\ *n* : a cultivated pink of any of numerous usu. double-flowered varieties derived from an Old World species

car·nau·ba wax \kär-'nȯ-bə-, -'naú-; ˌkär-nə-'ü-bə-\ *n* : a brittle yellowish wax from a Brazilian palm that is used esp. in polishes

car·ne·lian \kär-'nēl-yən\ *n* : a hard tough reddish quartz used as a gem

car·ni·val \'kär-nə-vəl\ *n* **1** : a festival of merrymaking just before Lent **2** : a boisterous merrymaking **3** : a traveling enterprise offering amusements **4** ♦ : an organized program of entertainment

♦ celebration, festival, festivity, fete, fiesta, gala, jubilee

car·niv·o·ra \kär-'ni-və-rə\ *n pl* : carnivorous mammals

car·ni·vore \'kär-nə-ˌvȯr\ *n* : a flesh-eating animal; *esp* : any of an order of mammals (as dogs, cats, bears, minks, and seals) feeding mostly on animal flesh

car·niv·o·rous \kär-'ni-və-rəs\ *adj* **1** : feeding on animal tissues **2** : of or relating to the carnivores — **car·niv·o·rous·ly** *adv* — **car·niv·o·rous·ness** *n*

car·ny *or* **car·ney** *or* **car·nie** \'kär-nē\ *n, pl* **carnies** *or* **car·neys 1** : CARNIVAL 3 **2** : one who works with a carnival

¹car·ol \'kar-əl\ *n* ♦ : a song of joy or devotion

♦ anthem, canticle, chorale, hymn, psalm, spiritual

²carol *vb* : to sing esp. in a cheerful manner

car·ol·er *or* **car·ol·ler** *n* ♦ : one that carols

♦ singer, songster, vocalist, voice

¹car·om \'kar-əm\ *n* **1** : a shot in billiards in which the cue ball strikes two other balls **2** : a rebounding esp. at an angle

²carom *vb* ♦ : to strike and rebound

♦ bounce, glance, rebound, ricochet, skim, skip

car·o·tene \'kar-ə-ˌtēn\ *n* : any of several orange to red pigments (as beta-carotene) formed esp. in plants and used as a source of vitamin A

ca·rot·en·oid \kə-'rä-tə-ˌnȯid\ *n* : any of various usu. yellow to red pigments (as carotenes) found widely in plants and animals

ca·rot·id \kə-'rä-təd\ *adj* : of, relating to, or being the chief artery or pair of arteries that pass up the neck and supply the head — **carotid** *n*

ca·rous·al \kə-'raú-zəl\ *n* : a period of heavy drinking : CAROUSE

ca·rouse \kə-'raúz\ *n* : a drunken revel — **carouse** *vb* — **ca·rous·er** *n*

car·ou·sel \ˌkar-ə-'sel, 'kar-ə-ˌsel\ *n* **1** : MERRY-GO-ROUND **2** : a circular conveyor ⟨a baggage ∼⟩

¹carp \'kärp\ *vb* ♦ : to find fault — **carp** *n*

♦ beef, bellyache, cavil, complain, crab, croak, fuss, gripe, grouse, growl, grumble, kick, moan, squawk, wail, whine

²carp *n, pl* **carp** *or* **carps** : a large variable Asian freshwater fish of sluggish waters often raised for food

¹car·pal \'kär-pəl\ *adj* : relating to the wrist or the bones of the wrist

²carpal *n* : a carpal element or bone

carpal tunnel syndrome *n* : a condition characterized esp. by weakness, pain, and disturbances of sensation (as numbness) in the hand and fingers and caused by compression of a nerve in the wrist

car park *n, chiefly Can and Brit* : a lot or garage for parking

car·pe di·em \'kär-pe-'dē-ˌem, -'dī-\ *n* : enjoyment of the present without concern for the future

car·pel \'kär-pəl\ *n* : one of the highly modified leaves that together form the ovary of a flower of a seed plant

car·pen·ter \'kär-pən-tər\ *n* : one who builds or repairs wooden structures — **carpenter** *vb* — **car·pen·try** \-trē\ *n*

carp·er *n* ♦ : an excessive faultfinder

♦ castigator, caviler, censurer, critic, faultfinder, nitpicker, railer, scold

¹car·pet \'kär-pət\ *n* : a heavy fabric used as a floor covering

²carpet *vb* ♦ : to cover with or as if with a carpet

♦ blanket, coat, cover, overlay, overlie, overspread

car·pet·bag \-ˌbag\ *n* : a traveling bag common in the 19th century

car·pet·bag·ger \-ˌba-gər\ *n* : a Northerner in the South after the American Civil War usu. seeking private gain under the reconstruction governments

car·pet·ing \'kär-pə-tin\ *n* : material for carpets; *also* : CARPETS

carping *adj* ♦ : marked by or inclined to querulous and often perverse criticism

♦ captious, critical, hypercritical, overcritical

car pool *n* : an arrangement in which a group of people commute together by car; *also* : a group having this arrangement — **car·pool** \-ˌpül\ *vb*

car·port \'kär-ˌpȯrt\ *n* : an open-sided automobile shelter

car·pus \'kär-pəs\ *n* : the wrist or its bones

car·ra·geen·an *or* **car·ra·geen·in** \ˌkar-ə-'gē-nən\ *n* : a colloid extracted esp. from a dark purple branching seaweed and used in foods esp. to stabilize and thicken them

car·rel \'kar-əl\ *n* : a table often partitioned or enclosed for individual study in a library

car·riage \'kar-ij\ *n* **1** : the act of carrying **2** : manner of holding the body **3** : a wheeled vehicle **4** *Brit* : a railway passenger coach **5** : a movable part of a machine for supporting some other moving part ⟨a typewriter ∼⟩

carriage trade *n* : trade from well-to-do or upper-class people

car·ri·er \'kar-ē-ər\ *n* **1** : one that carries **2** : a person or organization in the transportation business **3** : AIRCRAFT CARRIER **4** : one whose system carries the causative agents of a disease but who is immune to the disease **5** : an individual having a gene for a trait or condition that is not expressed outwardly **6** : an electromagnetic wave whose amplitude or frequency is varied in order to convey a radio or television signal

carrier pigeon *n* : a pigeon used esp. to carry messages

car·ri·on \'ker-ē-ən\ *n* : dead and decaying flesh

car·rot \'ker-ət\ *n* : the elongated usu. orange root of a common garden plant that is eaten as a vegetable; *also* : this plant

car·rou·sel *var of* CAROUSEL

¹car·ry \'ka-rē, 'ker-ē\ *vb* **car·ried; car·ry·ing 1** ♦ : to move while supporting : TRANSPORT, CONVEY **2** : to influence by mental or emotional appeal **3** : to get possession or control of : CAPTURE, WIN **4** : to transfer from one place (as a column) to another ⟨∼ a number in adding⟩ **5** : to have or wear on one's person; *also* : to bear within one **6** ♦ : to have within or as part of itself : INVOLVE, INCLUDE **7** : to hold or bear (oneself) in a specified way **8** : to keep in stock for sale **9** ♦ : to sustain the weight or burden of : SUPPORT **10** : to prolong in space, time, or degree **11** : to keep on one's books as a debtor **12** : to succeed in (an election) **13** : to win adoption (as in a legislature) **14 a** : to present to the public for use or as entertainment **b** : PUBLISH, PRINT **15** : to reach or penetrate to a distance

♦ [1] bear, cart, convey, ferry, haul, lug, pack, tote, transport ♦ [6] comprehend, contain, embrace, encompass, entail, include, involve, number, take in ♦ [9] bear, bolster, brace, buttress, prop, shore, stay, support, uphold

²carry *n* **1** : the range of a gun or projectile or of a struck or thrown ball **2** : PORTAGE **3** : an act or method of carrying ⟨fireman's ∼⟩

car·ry·all \'kar-ē-ˌȯl\ *n* ♦ : a large bag or carrying case

♦ grip, handbag, portmanteau, suitcase, traveling bag

carry away *vb* ♦ : to arouse to a high and often excessive degree of emotion

♦ enrapture, enthrall, entrance, ravish, transport

carrying charge *n* : a charge added to the price of merchandise sold on the installment plan

car·ry—on *n* : a piece of luggage suitable for being carried aboard an airplane by a passenger — **carry—on** *adj*

carry on *vb* **1** ♦ : to have the direction of : CONDUCT, MANAGE **2** ♦ : to behave in a foolish, excited, or improper manner **3** : to continue in spite of hindrance or discouragement

♦ [1] administer, conduct, control, direct, govern, guide, handle, manage, operate, oversee, regulate, run, superintend, supervise ♦ [2] act out, act up, misbehave

carry out *vb* **1** ♦ : to bring to a successful conclusion **2** : to put into execution

♦ accomplish, achieve, commit, compass, do, execute, follow through, fulfill, make, perform

car·sick \'kär-ˌsik\ *adj* : affected with motion sickness esp. in an automobile — **car sickness** *n*

¹cart \'kärt\ *n* **1** : a heavy 2-wheeled wagon **2** : a small wheeled vehicle

²cart *vb* ♦ : to convey in or as if in a cart — **cart·er** *n*

♦ bear, carry, convey, ferry, haul, lug, pack, tote, transport

cart·age \'kär-tij\ *n* : the act of or rate charged for carting

carte blanche \'kärt-'blänsh\ *n, pl* **cartes blanches** *same or* -'blänᵗ-shəz\ : full discretionary power

car·tel \kär-'tel\ *n* ♦ : a combination of independent business enterprises designed to limit competition

♦ combination, combine, syndicate, trust

car·ti·lage \'kär-tə-lij\ *n* : a usu. translucent somewhat elastic tissue that composes most of the skeleton of young vertebrate embryos and later is mostly converted to bone in higher vertebrates — **car·ti·lag·i·nous** \,kärt-ᵊl-'a-jə-nəs\ *adj*

cartilaginous fish *n* : any of a class of fishes (as a shark or ray) having the skeleton wholly or largely composed of cartilage

car·tog·ra·phy \kär-'tä-grə-fē\ *n* : the making of maps — **car·tog·ra·pher** *n* — **car·to·graph·ic** \,kär-tə-'gra-fik\ *adj*

car·ton \'kärt-ᵊn\ *n* : a cardboard box or container

car·toon \kär-'tün\ *n* **1** ♦ : a preparatory sketch (as for a painting)   **2** : a drawing intended as humor, caricature, or satire   **3** ♦ : a group of cartoons or drawings arranged in a narrative sequence : COMIC STRIP — **cartoon** *vb* — **car·toon·ist** *n*

 ♦ [1] delineation, drawing, sketch ♦ [3] comic strip

car·tridge \'kär-trij\ *n* **1** : a tube containing a complete charge for a firearm   **2** : a container of material for insertion into an apparatus   **3** : a small case containing a phonograph needle and transducer that is attached to a tonearm   **4** : a case containing a magnetic tape or disk   **5** : a case for holding integrated circuits containing a computer program

cart·wheel \'kärt-,hwēl\ *n* **1** : a large coin (as a silver dollar)   **2** : a lateral handspring with arms and legs extended

carve \kärv\ *vb* **carved; carv·ing**   **1** : to cut with care or precision : shape by cutting   **2** ♦ : to cut or hew out esp. with some effort : make or get by or as if by cutting — often used with *out* ⟨~ out a fortune⟩   **3** : to slice and serve meat at table — **carv·er** *n*

 ♦ *usu* **carve out** build, forge, grind, hammer, work out

cary·at·id \,kar-ē-'a-təd\ *n, pl* **-ids** *or* **-i·des** \-'a-tə-,dēz\ : a sculptured draped female figure used as an architectural column

CAS *abbr* certificate of advanced study

ca·sa·ba \kə-'sä-bə\ *n* : any of several muskmelons with a yellow rind and sweet flesh

¹cas·cade \,kas-'kād\ *n* **1** : a steep usu. small waterfall   **2** : something arranged in a series or succession of stages so that each stage derives from or acts upon the product of the preceding

²cascade *vb* **cas·cad·ed; cas·cad·ing** : to fall, pass, or connect in or as if in a cascade ⟨water *cascaded* over the rocks⟩

cas·cara \kas-'kar-ə\ *n* : the dried bark of a small Pacific coastal tree of the U.S. and southern Canada used as a laxative; *also* : this tree

¹case \'kās\ *n* **1 a** ♦ : a set of circumstances or conditions   **b** ♦ : a set of circumstances constituting a problem : a matter for consideration or decision   **2** : an inflectional form of a noun, pronoun, or adjective indicating its grammatical relation to other words; *also* : such a relation whether indicated by inflection or not   **3** : what actually exists or happens : FACT   **4** : a suit or action in law : CAUSE   **5** ♦ : a convincing argument   **6 a** : an instance of disease or injury   **b** : a sick individual esp. when awaiting medical care or treatment : PATIENT   **7** ♦ : an instance or example of a particular type : INSTANCE, EXAMPLE — **in case** : as a precaution — **in case of** : in the event of

 ♦ [1a] contingency, event, eventuality, possibility ♦ [1b] knot, matter, problem, trouble ♦ [5] argument, defense (*or* defence), explanation, rationale, reason ♦ [7] example, exemplar, illustration, instance, representative, sample, specimen

²case *n* **1** ♦ : a box or container for holding something; *also* : a box with its contents   **2** ♦ : an outer covering   **3** : a divided tray for holding printing type   **4** : CASING 2

 ♦ [1] box, caddy, casket, chest, locker, trunk ♦ [2] armor, capsule, casing, cocoon, cover, housing, husk, jacket, pod, sheath, shell

³case *vb* **cased; cas·ing**   **1** : to enclose in or cover with a case   **2** : to inspect esp. with intent to rob

ca·sein \'kā-,sēn, kā-'\ *n* : any of several phosphorus-containing proteins occurring in or produced from milk

case·ment \'kās-mənt\ *n* : a window that opens like a door

case·work \-,wərk\ *n* : social work that involves the individual person or family — **case·work·er** *n*

¹cash \'kash\ *n* **1** : ready money   **2** ♦ : money or its equivalent paid at the time of purchase or delivery

 ♦ currency, dough, lucre, money, pelf, tender

²cash *vb* : to pay or obtain cash for

ca·shew \'ka-shü, kə-'shü\ *n* : an edible kidney-shaped nut of a tropical American tree related to the sumacs; *also* : this tree

¹ca·shier \ka-'shir\ *vb* ♦ : to dismiss from service; *esp* : to dismiss in disgrace

 ♦ dismiss, fire, remove, retire, sack

²cash·ier \ka-'shir\ *n* **1** : a bank official responsible for moneys received and paid out   **2** : a person who receives and records payments

cashier's check *n* : a check drawn by a bank upon its own funds and signed by its cashier

cash in *vb* **1** : to convert into cash ⟨*cash in* bonds⟩   **2** : to settle accounts and withdraw from a gambling game or business deal   **3** ♦ : to obtain advantage or financial profit — often used with *on* ⟨*cash in* on a best seller⟩

 ♦ *usu* **cash in on** abuse, capitalize, exploit, impose, play, use

cash·less \'kash-ləs\ *adj* : relying on monetary transactions that use electronic means rather than cash

cash·mere \'kazh-,mir, 'kash-\ *n* : fine wool from the undercoat of an Indian goat (**cashmere goat**) or a yarn spun of this; *also* : a soft twilled fabric orig. woven from this yarn

cash out *vb* : to convert noncash assets into cash

cash register *n* : a business machine that usu. has a money drawer, indicates each sale, and records the money received

cash–strapped \'kash-,strapt\ *adj* : lacking sufficient money

cas·ing \'kā-siŋ\ *n* **1** ♦ : something that encases   **2** : the frame of a door or window

 ♦ armor, capsule, case, cocoon, cover, housing, husk, jacket, pod, sheath, shell

ca·si·no \kə-'sē-nō\ *n, pl* **-nos**   **1** : a building or room for social amusements; *esp* : one used for gambling   **2** *also* **cas·si·no** : a card game in which players win cards by matching those on the table

cask \'kask\ *n* ♦ : a barrel-shaped container usu. for liquids; *also* : the quantity held by such a container

 ♦ barrel, hogshead, keg, pipe, puncheon

cas·ket \'kas-kət\ *n* **1** ♦ : a small chest or box (as for jewels)   **2** : a usu. fancy coffin for burying a corpse : COFFIN

 ♦ box, caddy, case, chest, locker, trunk

casque \'kask\ *n* : HELMET

cas·sa·va \kə-'sä-və\ *n* : any of several tropical spurges with rootstocks yielding a nutritious starch from which tapioca is prepared; *also* : the rootstock or its starch

cas·se·role \'ka-sə-,rōl\ *n* **1** : a dish in which food may be baked and served   **2** : food cooked and served in a casserole

cas·sette *also* **ca·sette** \kə-'set\ *n* **1** : a lightproof container for photographic plates or film   **2** : a plastic case containing magnetic tape

cas·sia \'ka-shə\ *n* **1** : a coarse cinnamon bark   **2** : any of a genus of leguminous herbs, shrubs, and trees of warm regions including several which yield senna

cas·sit·er·ite \kə-'si-tə-,rīt\ *n* : a dark mineral that is the chief tin ore

cas·sock \'ka-sək\ *n* : an ankle-length garment worn esp. by Roman Catholic and Anglican clergy

cas·so·wary \'ka-sə-,wer-ē\ *n, pl* **-war·ies** : any of a genus of large flightless birds closely related to the emu

¹cast \'kast\ *vb* **cast; cast·ing**   **1** ♦ : to cause to move or send forth by throwing : THROW, FLING   **2** ♦ : to point, extend, or project in a specified line or course : DIRECT ⟨~ a glance⟩   **3** : to deposit (a ballot) formally   **4** ♦ : to throw off, out, or away : DISCARD, SHED   **5** : COMPUTE; *esp* : to add up   **6** : to assign the parts of (a play) to actors; *also* : to assign to a role or part   **7 a** : to shape (a substance) by pouring it in liquid or plastic form into a mold and letting it harden without pressure   **b** ♦ : to give form to : establish or create in a particular form ⟨the book is ~ in the form of an autobiography⟩   **8** : to make (as a knot or stitch) by looping or catching up

 ♦ [1] catapult, chuck, dash, fire, fling, heave, hurl, hurtle, launch, peg, pelt, pitch, sling, throw, toss ♦ [2] aim, bend, direct, head, level, set, train ♦ [4] discard, ditch, dump, fling, jettison, junk, lose, reject, scrap, shed, shuck, slough, throw away, throw out, unload ♦ [7b] compose, craft, draft, draw, formulate, frame, prepare

²cast *n* **1** : THROW, FLING   **2** : a throw of dice   **3** : the set of actors in a dramatic production   **4** : something formed in or as if in a mold; *also* : a rigid surgical dressing (as for protecting and supporting a fractured bone)   **5** ♦ : a slight change in the appearance of a substance by a trace of some added hue : a trace of a particular quality : TINGE, HUE   **6 a** : a turning of the eye in a particular direction   **b** ♦ : a physical form or character : SHAPE   **c** ♦ : facial aspect or vocal intonation as indicative of feeling : LOOK   **7** : something thrown out or off, shed, or expelled ⟨worm ~s⟩   **8** : a forecast or conjecture concerning future events or conditions

 ♦ [5] color (*or* colour), hue, shade, tinge, tint, tone ♦ [6b] configuration, conformation, figure, form, geometry, shape ♦ [6c] countenance, expression, face, look, visage

cast about *vb* ♦ : to seek here and there : look around

♦ cast around, forage, hunt, pursue, quest, search (for *or* out), seek

cas·ta·net \ˌkas-tə-ˈnet\ *n* : a rhythm instrument consisting of two small wooden, ivory, or plastic shells held in the hand and clicked together

cast around *vb* ♦ : to look around : SEEK

♦ cast about, forage, hunt, pursue, quest, search (for *or* out), seek

¹**cast·away** \ˈkas-tə-ˌwā\ *adj* **1** : thrown away : REJECTED **2** : cast adrift or ashore as a survivor of a shipwreck

²**castaway** *n* ♦ : one who has been cast away, cast off, or rejected

♦ outcast, reject

caste \ˈkast\ *n* **1** : one of the hereditary social classes in Hinduism **2** ♦ : a division of a society based on wealth, inherited rank, or occupation **3** : social position : PRESTIGE **4** : a system of rigid social stratification

♦ class, estate, folk, order, stratum

cas·tel·lat·ed \ˈkas-tə-ˌlā-təd\ *adj* : having battlements like a castle

cast·er \ˈkas-tər\ *n* **1** *or* **cas·tor** : a small container to hold salt or pepper at the table **2** : a small wheel that turns freely and is used to support and move furniture, trucks, and equipment

cas·ti·gate \ˈkas-tə-ˌgāt\ *vb* **-gat·ed; -gat·ing** ♦ : to punish or criticize severely

♦ admonish, chide, lecture, rail (at *or* against), rate, rebuke, reprimand, scold ♦ chasten, chastise, correct, discipline, penalize, punish

cas·ti·ga·tion \ˌkas-tə-ˈgā-shən\ *n* ♦ : severe punishment or criticism

♦ chastisement, correction, desert, discipline, nemesis, penalty, punishment, wrath

cas·ti·ga·tor \ˈkas-tə-ˌgā-tər\ *n* ♦ : one that castigates

♦ carper, caviler, censurer, critic, faultfinder, nitpicker, railer, scold

cast·ing \ˈkas-tiŋ\ *n* **1** : CAST 7 **2** : something cast in a mold

casting vote *n* : a deciding vote cast by a presiding officer to break a tie

cast iron *n* : a hard brittle alloy of iron, carbon, and silicon cast in a mold

cas·tle \ˈka-səl\ *n* **1** : a large fortified building or set of buildings **2** ♦ : a large or imposing house **3** : ³ROOK

♦ estate, hall, manor, mansion, palace, villa

cast–off \ˈkas-ˌtȯf\ *adj* : thrown away or aside — **cast·off** *n*

cas·tor oil \ˈkas-tər-\ *n* : a thick yellowish oil extracted from the poisonous seeds of an herb (**castor–oil plant**) and used as a lubricant and purgative

cast out *vb* ♦ : to banish, expel, or drive away (as from a former home or country)

♦ banish, boot (out), bounce, chase, dismiss, drum, eject, expel, oust, rout, run off, throw out

cas·trate \ˈkas-ˌtrāt\ *vb* **cas·trat·ed; cas·trat·ing** : to deprive of sex glands and esp. testes — **cas·tra·tion** \kas-ˈtrā-shən\ *n* — **cas·tra·tor** \-ər\ *n*

ca·su·al \ˈka-zhə-wəl\ *adj* **1** ♦ : resulting from or occurring by chance **2** ♦ : occurring without regularity : OCCASIONAL **3** ♦ : feeling or showing little concern : NONCHALANT **4** ♦ : designed for informal use ⟨∼ clothing⟩ — **ca·su·al·ly** *adv*

♦ [1] accidental, chance, fluky, fortuitous, incidental, unintended, unintentional, unplanned, unpremeditated, unwitting ♦ [2] choppy, discontinuous, erratic, fitful, intermittent, irregular, occasional, spasmodic, sporadic, spotty, unsteady ♦ [3] apathetic, disinterested, indifferent, insouciant, nonchalant, perfunctory, unconcerned, uncurious, uninterested ♦ [4] everyday, informal, workaday *Ant* dressy, formal

ca·su·al·ness *n* : the quality, state, or fact of being casual or disinterested

ca·su·al·ty \ˈka-zhəl-tē, ˈka-zhə-wəl-\ *n, pl* **-ties** **1** ♦ : a serious or fatal accident **2** : a military person lost through death, injury, sickness, or capture or through being missing in action **3** ♦ : a person or thing injured, lost, or destroyed

♦ [1] accident, mishap ♦ [3] fatality, loss, victim

ca·su·ist·ry \ˈka-zhə-wə-strē\ *n, pl* **-ries** : specious argument : RATIONALIZATION — **ca·su·ist** \-wist\ *n* — **ca·su·is·tic** \ˌka-zhə-ˈwis-tik\ *or* **ca·su·is·ti·cal** \-ti-kəl\ *adj*

ca·sus bel·li \ˌkä-səs-ˈbe-ˌlē, ˌkä-səs-be-ˌlī\ *n, pl* **ca·sus belli** \ˌkä-ˌsüs-, ˌkä-\ : a cause or pretext for a declaration of war

¹**cat** \ˈkat\ *n* **1** ♦ : a carnivorous mammal long domesticated as a pet and for catching rats and mice **2** : any of a family of animals (as the lion, lynx, or leopard) including the domestic cat **3** : a spiteful woman **4** : GUY

♦ feline, kitty, puss

²**cat** *abbr* catalog

ca·tab·o·lism \kə-ˈta-bə-ˌli-zəm\ *n* : destructive metabolism involving the release of energy and resulting in the breakdown of complex materials — **cat·a·bol·ic** \ˌka-tə-ˈbä-lik\ *adj*

cat·a·clysm \ˈka-tə-ˌkli-zəm\ *n* **1** ♦ : a surging flood of water : DELUGE **2** ♦ : a violent change or upheaval

♦ [1] cataract, deluge, flood, inundation, overflow, spate, torrent ♦ [2] calamity, catastrophe, debacle, disaster, tragedy ♦ [2] convulsion, paroxysm, storm, tempest, tumult, upheaval, uproar

cat·a·clys·mic \ˌka-tə-ˈkliz-mik\ *or* **cat·a·clys·mal** \-ˈkliz-məl\ *adj* ♦ : of, relating to, or having the characteristics of a cataclysm ⟨a ∼ nuclear war⟩

♦ calamitous, catastrophic, destructive, devastating, disastrous, fatal, fateful, ruinous, unfortunate

cat·a·comb \ˈka-tə-ˌkōm\ *n* : an underground burial place with galleries and recesses for tombs

cat·a·falque \ˈka-tə-ˌfalk, -ˌfȯlk, -ˌfȯk\ *n* : an ornamental structure sometimes used in solemn funerals to hold the body

cat·a·lep·sy \ˈka-tə-ˌlep-sē\ *n, pl* **-sies** : a trancelike nervous condition characterized esp. by loss of voluntary motion — **cat·a·lep·tic** \ˌka-tə-ˈlep-tik\ *adj or n*

¹**cat·a·log** *or* **cat·a·logue** \ˈkat-ᵊl-ˌȯg\ *n* **1** ♦ : a simple series of items (as the names of persons or objects) : LIST, REGISTER **2** : a systematic list of items with descriptive details; *also* : a book containing such a list

♦ checklist, list, listing, menu, register, registry, roll, roster, schedule, table

²**catalog** *or* **catalogue** *vb* **-loged** *or* **-logued; -log·ing** *or* **-logu·ing** **1** : to make a catalog of **2** ♦ : to enter in a catalog — **cat·a·log·er** *or* **cat·a·logu·er** *n*

♦ enroll, enter, index, inscribe, list, put down, record, register, schedule, slate

ca·tal·pa \kə-ˈtal-pə\ *n* : any of a genus of broad-leaved trees with showy flowers and long slim pods

ca·tal·y·sis \kə-ˈta-lə-səs\ *n, pl* **-y·ses** \-ˌsēz\ : a change and esp. increase in the rate of a chemical reaction brought about by a substance (**cat·a·lyst** \ˈkat-ᵊl-ist\) that is itself unchanged at the end of the reaction — **cat·a·lyt·ic** \ˌkat-ᵊl-ˈi-tik\ *adj* — **cat·a·lyt·i·cal·ly** \-ti-k(ə-)lē\ *adv*

catalytic converter *n* : an automobile exhaust-system component in which a catalyst changes harmful gases into mostly harmless products

cat·a·lyze \ˈkat-ᵊl-ˌīz\ *vb* **-lyzed; -lyz·ing** : to bring about the catalysis of (a chemical reaction)

cat·a·ma·ran \ˌka-tə-mə-ˈran\ *n* : a boat with twin hulls

cat·a·mount \ˈka-tə-ˌmaůnt\ *n* : a large powerful tawny-brown cat : COUGAR; *also* : LYNX

¹**cat·a·pult** \ˈka-tə-ˌpəlt, -ˌpůlt\ *n* **1** : an ancient military machine for hurling missiles **2** : a device for launching an airplane (as from an aircraft carrier)

²**catapult** *vb* ♦ : to throw or launch by or as if by a catapult

♦ cast, chuck, dash, fire, fling, heave, hurl, hurtle, launch, peg, pelt, pitch, sling, throw, toss

cat·a·ract \ˈka-tə-ˌrakt\ *n* **1** : a cloudiness of the lens of the eye obstructing vision **2 a** : a large waterfall; *also* : steep rapids in a river **b** ♦ : an overwhelming downpour or rush

♦ cataclysm, deluge, flood, inundation, overflow, spate, torrent

ca·tarrh \kə-ˈtär\ *n* : inflammation of a mucous membrane esp. of the nose and throat — **ca·tarrh·al** \-əl\ *adj*

ca·tas·tro·phe \kə-ˈtas-trə-(ˌ)fē\ *n* **1** ♦ : a great disaster or misfortune **2** : utter failure

♦ calamity, cataclysm, debacle, disaster, tragedy

cat·a·stroph·ic \ˌka-tə-ˈsträ-fik\ *adj* ♦ : of, relating to, resembling, or resulting in catastrophe — **cat·a·stroph·i·cal·ly** \-fi-k(ə-)lē\ *adv*

♦ calamitous, cataclysmic, destructive, disastrous, fatal, fateful, ruinous, unfortunate

cat·a·ton·ic \ˌka-tə-ˈtä-nik\ *adj* : of, relating to, or marked by schizophrenia characterized esp. by stupor, negativism, rigidity, purposeless excitement, and bizarre posturing — **catatonic** *n*

cat·bird \'kat-ˌbərd\ *n* : an American songbird with a catlike mewing call

cat·boat \'kat-ˌbōt\ *n* : a single-masted sailboat with a single large sail extended by a long boom

cat·call \-ˌkȯl\ *n* ♦ : a loud cry made esp. to express disapproval — **catcall** *vb*

♦ boo, hiss, hoot, jeer, raspberry *Ant* cheer

¹**catch** \'kach, 'kech\ *vb* **caught** \'kȯt\; **catch·ing** **1** : to capture esp. after pursuit **2** ♦ : to capture, take, or entangle in or as if in a snare **3** : TRAP **3** : to discover unexpectedly ⟨*caught* in the act⟩ **4** : to become suddenly aware of **5** : to take hold of : SNATCH ⟨~ at a straw⟩ **6** ♦ : stop or interrupt the progress or course of **7** : to get entangled **8** ♦ : to become affected with or by ⟨~ fire⟩ ⟨~ cold⟩ **9 a** ♦ : to seize and hold firmly **b** : to cause to be seized and held **10** : OVERTAKE **11** : to be in time for ⟨~ a train⟩ **12** : to take in and retain ⟨didn't ~ your name⟩ **13** : to look at or listen to ⟨~ a TV show⟩

♦ [2, 9a] bag, capture, collar, corral, get, grab, grapple, hook, land, nab, seize, snare, trap *Ant* miss ♦ [6] arrest, check, draw up, fetch up, halt, hold up, stall, stay, still, stop ♦ [8] come down, contract, get, sicken, take

²**catch** *n* **1 a** : something caught **b** ♦ : the total quantity caught at one time ⟨a good ~ of fish⟩ **2** : the act of catching; *also* : a game consisting of throwing and catching a ball **3** : something that catches or checks or holds immovable ⟨a door ~⟩ **4** ♦ : one that is worth catching or acquiring esp. as a mate **5** : FRAGMENT, SNATCH **6** ♦ : a concealed difficulty or complication

♦ [1b] haul, take, yield ♦ [4] gem, jewel, pearl, plum, prize, treasure ♦ [6] booby trap, pitfall, snag

catch·all \'ka-ˌchȯl, 'ke-\ *n* : something to hold a variety of odds and ends

catch–as–catch–can *adj* : using any means available

catch·er \'ka-chər, 'ke-\ *n* : one that catches; *esp* : a player positioned behind home plate in baseball

catch·ing *adj* **1** ♦ : communicable by infection : CONTAGIOUS ⟨the flu is ~⟩ **2** ♦ : spreading or capable of spreading rapidly to others ⟨their enthusiasm was ~⟩

♦ [1, 2] communicable, contagious, transmittable ♦ [2] contagious, infectious

catch·ment \'kach-mənt, 'kech-\ *n* **1** : something that catches water **2** : the action of catching water

catch on *vb* **1 a** ♦ : to become aware : LEARN **b** ♦ : to grasp the meaning of : UNDERSTAND **2** : to become popular

♦ [1a] ascertain, discover, find out, hear, learn, realize, see ♦ *usu* **catch on to** [1b] appreciate, apprehend, catch, comprehend, get, grasp, make, make out, perceive, see, seize, understand

catch·pen·ny \'kach-ˌpe-nē, 'kech-\ *adj* : using sensationalism or cheapness for appeal ⟨a ~ newspaper⟩

catch·phrase \-ˌfrāz\ *n* : a word or expression frequently used to represent or characterize a person, group, idea, or point of view

catch–22 \-ˌtwen-tē-ˈtü\ *n, pl* **catch–22's** *or* **catch–22s** *often cap* C : a problematic situation for which the only solution is denied by a circumstance inherent in the problem or by a rule; *also* : the circumstance or rule that denies a solution

catchup *var of* KETCHUP

catch up *vb* : to travel or work fast enough to overtake or complete

catch·word \'kach-ˌwərd, 'kech-\ *n* **1** : GUIDE WORD **2** : CATCHPHRASE

catchy \'ka-chē, 'ke-\ *adj* **catch·i·er; -est** **1** ♦ : likely to catch the interest or attention **2** ♦ : requiring skill or caution (as in doing or handling) : TRICKY

♦ [1] bold, conspicuous, emphatic, marked, noticeable, prominent, pronounced, remarkable, striking ♦ [2] delicate, difficult, knotty, problematic, spiny, thorny, ticklish, touchy, tough, tricky

cat·e·chism \'ka-tə-ˌki-zəm\ *n* : a summary or test (as of religious doctrine) usu. in the form of questions and answers — **cat·e·chist** \-ˌkist\ *n* — **cat·e·chize** \-ˌkīz\ *vb*

cat·e·chu·men \ˌka-tə-ˈkyü-mən\ *n* : a religious convert receiving training before baptism

cat·e·gor·i·cal \ˌka-tə-ˈgȯr-i-kəl\ *adj* **1** : not modified or restricted : ABSOLUTE, UNQUALIFIED ⟨a ~ denial⟩ **2** : of, relating to, or constituting a category — **cat·e·gor·i·cal·ly** \-i-k(ə-)lē\ *adv*

cat·e·go·rise *Brit var of* CATEGORIZE

cat·e·go·rize \'ka-ti-gə-ˌrīz\ *vb* **-rized; -riz·ing** ♦ : to put into a

category : CLASSIFY — **cat·e·go·ri·za·tion** \ˌka-ti-gə-rə-ˈzā-shən\ *n*

♦ assort, break down, class, classify, grade, group, peg, place, range, rank, separate, sort

cat·e·go·ry \'ka-tə-ˌgȯr-ē\ *n, pl* **-ries** ♦ : a division within a system of classification; *esp* : CLASS, GROUP, KIND

♦ bracket, class, division, family, grade, group, kind, order, set, species, type

ca·ter \'kā-tər\ *vb* **1** ♦ : to provide a supply of food **2** ♦ : to supply what is wanted — **ca·ter·er** *n*

♦ [1] board, feed, provision ♦ *usu* **cater to** [2] gratify, humor (*or* humour), indulge

catercorner *or* **cater–cornered** *var of* KITTY-CORNER

cat·er·pil·lar \'ka-tər-ˌpi-lər\ *n* : a wormlike often hairy insect larva esp. of a butterfly or moth

cat·er·waul \'ka-tər-ˌwȯl\ *vb* : to make a harsh cry — **caterwaul** *n*

cat·fish \'kat-ˌfish\ *n* : any of an order of chiefly freshwater stout-bodied fishes with slender tactile processes around the mouth

cat·gut \-ˌgət\ *n* : a tough cord made usu. from sheep intestines

ca·thar·sis \kə-ˈthär-səs\ *n, pl* **ca·thar·ses** \-ˌsēz\ **1** : an act of purging or purification **2** : elimination of a complex by bringing it to consciousness and affording it expression

¹**ca·thar·tic** \kə-ˈthär-tik\ *adj* : of, relating to, or producing catharsis

²**cathartic** *n* : PURGATIVE

ca·the·dral \kə-ˈthē-drəl\ *n* : the principal church of a diocese

cath·e·ter \'ka-thə-tər\ *n* : a tube for insertion into a bodily passage or cavity usu. for injecting or drawing off material or for keeping a passage open

cath·e·ter·i·za·tion \ˌka-thə-tə-rə-ˈzā-shən\ *n* : the use of or introduction of a catheter — **cath·e·ter·ize** \'ka-thə-tə-ˌrīz\ *vb*

cath·ode \'ka-ˌthōd\ *n* **1** : the negative electrode of an electrolytic cell **2** : the positive terminal of a battery **3** : the electron-emitting electrode of an electron tube — **cath·od·al** \'ka-ˌthō-dᵊl\ *adj* — **ca·thod·ic** \ka-ˈthä-dik\ *adj*

cathode–ray tube *n* : a vacuum tube in which a beam of electrons is projected on a fluorescent screen to produce a luminous spot

cath·o·lic \'kath-lik, 'ka-thə-\ *adj* **1** : of or relating to Catholics and esp. Roman Catholics **2** : GENERAL, UNIVERSAL

Cath·o·lic \'kath-lik, 'ka-thə-\ *n* : a member of a church claiming historical continuity from the ancient undivided Christian church; *esp* : a member of the Roman Catholic Church — **Ca·thol·i·cism** \kə-ˈthä-lə-ˌsi-zəm\ *n*

cath·o·lic·i·ty \ˌka-thə-ˈli-sə-tē\ *n, pl* **-ties** **1** *cap* : the character of being in conformity with a Catholic church **2** : liberality of sentiments or views **3** : comprehensive range

cat·ion \'kat-ˌī-ən\ *n* : the ion in an electrolyte that migrates to the cathode; *also* : a positively charged ion

cat·kin \'kat-kən\ *n* : a long flower cluster (as of a willow) bearing crowded flowers and prominent bracts

cat·like \-ˌlīk\ *adj* : resembling a cat or its behavior; *esp* : STEALTHY

¹**cat·nap** \-ˌnap\ *n* ♦ : a very short light nap

♦ doze, drowse, forty winks, nap, siesta, snooze, wink

²**catnap** *vb* : to sleep for a short period of time

cat·nip \-ˌnip\ *n* : an aromatic mint that is esp. attractive to cats

cat–o'–nine–tails \ˌka-tə-ˈnīn-ˌtālz\ *n, pl* **cat–o'–nine–tails** : a whip made of usu. nine knotted cords fastened to a handle

CAT scan \'kat-\ *n* : an image made by computed tomography

CAT scanner *n* : a medical instrument consisting of integrated X-ray and computing equipment that is used to make CAT scans

cat's cradle *n* : a game played with a string looped on the fingers in such a way as to resemble a small cradle

cat's–eye \'kats-ˌī\ *n, pl* **cat's–eyes** : any of various iridescent gems

cat's–paw \-ˌpȯ\ *n, pl* **cat's–paws** : a person used by another as a tool

cat·tail \'kat-ˌtāl\ *n* : any of a genus of tall reedlike marsh plants with furry brown spikes of tiny flowers

cat·ti·ly \'ka-tᵊl-ē\ *adv* : in a catty manner

cat·ti·ness *n* ♦ : the quality or state of being catty

♦ acidity, acrimony, asperity, bitterness, tartness, virulence, vitriol ♦ despite, hatefulness, malice, malignity, meanness, nastiness, spite, spleen, venom, viciousness

cat·tle \'kat-ᵊl\ *n pl* : LIVESTOCK; *esp* : domestic bovines (as cows, bulls, or calves) — **cat·tle·man** \-mən, -ˌman\ *n*

cat·ty \'ka-tē\ *adj* **cat·ti·er; -est** ♦ : slyly spiteful

♦ cruel, hateful, malevolent, malicious, malign, malignant, mean, nasty, spiteful, virulent

catty–corner *or* **catty–cornered** *var of* KITTY-CORNER

CATV *abbr* community antenna television

cat·walk \'kat-ˌwȯk\ *n* : a narrow walk (as along a bridge)

Cau·ca·sian \kȯ-'kā-zhən\ *adj* : of or relating to a group of people usu. having European ancestry and classified according to certain physical traits (as light skin pigmentation) — **Caucasian** *n* — **Cau·ca·soid** \'kȯ-kə-ˌsȯid\ *adj or n*

cau·cus \'kȯ-kəs\ *n* : a meeting of a group of persons belonging to the same political party or faction usu. to decide upon policies and candidates — **caucus** *vb*

cau·dal \'kȯ-dᵊl\ *adj* : of, relating to, or located near the tail or the hind end of the body — **cau·dal·ly** *adv*

cau·di·llo \kaù-'thē-(ˌ)yō, -'thēl-\ *n, pl* **-llos** : a Spanish or Latin-American military dictator

caught \'kȯt\ *past and past part of* CATCH

caul \'kȯl\ *n* : the inner fetal membrane of higher vertebrates esp. when covering the head at birth

caul·dron \'kȯl-drən\ *n* : a large kettle

cau·li·flow·er \'kȯ-li-ˌflaù(-ə)r\ *n* : a garden plant closely related to cabbage and grown for its compact edible head of undeveloped flowers; *also* : this head used as a vegetable

cauliflower ear *n* : an ear deformed from injury and excessive growth of scar tissue

¹**caulk** \'kȯk\ *vb* : to stop up and make tight against leakage (as a boat or its seams) — **caulk·er** *n*

²**caulk** *also* **caulk·ing** *n* : material used to caulk

caus·al \'kȯ-zəl\ *adj* **1** : expressing or indicating cause **2** : relating to or acting as a cause — **cau·sal·i·ty** \kȯ-'za-lə-tē\ *n* — **caus·al·ly** *adv*

cau·sa·tion \kȯ-'zā-shən\ *n* **1** : the act or process of causing **2** : the means by which an effect is produced

¹**cause** \'kȯz\ *n* **1** : REASON, MOTIVE **2 a** ♦ : something that brings about a result **b** ♦ : a person or thing that is the agent of bringing something about **3** : a suit or action in court : CASE **4** : a question or matter to be decided **5** : a principle or movement earnestly supported — **cause·less** *adj*

♦ [2a] bandwagon, campaign, crusade, drive, movement ♦ [2a, 2b] antecedent, occasion, reason *Ant* aftereffect, aftermath, consequence, corollary, development, effect, fate, fruit, issue, outcome, outgrowth, product, result, resultant, sequel, sequence, upshot

²**cause** *vb* **caused; caus·ing** ♦ : to be the cause or occasion of — **caus·a·tive** \'kȯ-zə-tiv\ *adj* — **caus·er** *n*

♦ bring about, create, effect, effectuate, generate, induce, make, produce, prompt, result, work, yield

cause cé·lè·bre \ˌkȯz-sā-'lebrᵊ, ˌkȯz-\ *n, pl* **causes célèbres** *same*\ **1** : a legal case that excites widespread interest **2** : a notorious person, thing, incident, or episode

cau·se·rie \ˌkȯz-'rē, ˌkō-zə-\ *n* **1** : an informal conversation : CHAT **2** : a short informal essay

cause·way \'kȯz-ˌwā\ *n* : a raised way or road across wet ground or water

¹**caus·tic** \'kȯ-stik\ *adj* **1** : CORROSIVE **2** ♦ : marked by incisive sarcasm : SHARP ⟨~ wit⟩

♦ acrid, biting, cutting, mordant, pungent, sarcastic, satiric, scathing, sharp, tart

²**caustic** *n* **1** : a substance that burns or destroys organic tissue by chemical action **2** : SODIUM HYDROXIDE

cau·ter·ize \'kȯ-tə-ˌrīz\ *vb* **-ized; -iz·ing** : to burn or sear usu. to prevent infection or bleeding — **cau·ter·i·za·tion** \ˌkȯ-tə-rə-'zā-shən\ *n*

¹**cau·tion** \'kȯ-shən\ *n* **1** ♦ : a warning or reminder of possible danger or risk : ADMONITION, WARNING **2** ♦ : prudent forethought to minimize risk **3** ♦ : one that astonishes

♦ [1] admonition, alarm, alert, notice, warning ♦ [2] alertness, care, carefulness, circumspection, heedfulness *Ant* carelessness, heedlessness, recklessness ♦ [3] flash, marvel, miracle, phenomenon, portent, prodigy, sensation, wonder

²**caution** *vb* ♦ : to advise caution to

♦ alert, forewarn, warn

cau·tion·ary \-shə-ˌner-ē\ *adj* ♦ : having the characteristics of or serving as a caution

♦ admonishing, admonitory, warning

cau·tious \'kȯ-shəs\ *adj* ♦ : marked by or given to caution : CAREFUL — **cau·tious·ly** *adv*

♦ alert, careful, circumspect, considerate, gingerly, guarded, heedful, safe, wary

cau·tious·ness *n* : the quality or state of being cautious

cav *abbr* **1** cavalry **2** cavity

cav·al·cade \ˌka-vəl-'kād\ *n* **1 a** : a procession of riders or carriages **b** ♦ : a procession of vehicles **2** : a dramatic sequence or procession

♦ armada, caravan, fleet, motorcade, train

¹**cav·a·lier** \ˌka-və-'lir\ *n* **1** : a mounted soldier : KNIGHT **2** *cap* : an adherent of Charles I of England **3** : a man who is esp. attentive to women : GALLANT

²**cavalier** *adj* **1** : DEBONAIR **2** ♦ : marked by or given to offhand dismissal of important matters **3** ♦ : marked by lofty disregard of others' interests or feelings : HAUGHTY — **cav·a·lier·ly** *adv*

♦ [2, 3] arrogant, haughty, highfalutin, high-handed, high-hat, imperious, important, lofty, lordly, overweening, peremptory, pompous, presumptuous, pretentious, supercilious, superior, uppity

cav·al·ry \'ka-vəl-rē\ *n, pl* **-ries** : troops mounted on horseback or moving in motor vehicles — **cav·al·ry·man** \-mən, -ˌman\ *n*

¹**cave** \'kāv\ *n* : a natural underground chamber open to the surface

²**cave** *vb* **caved; cav·ing** **1** ♦ : to collapse or cause to collapse — usu. used with *in* **2** : to cease to resist : SUBMIT — usu. used with *in*

♦ *usu* **cave in** collapse, crumple, give, go, yield

ca·ve·at \'ka-vē-ˌät, -ˌat; 'kä-vē-ˌät\ *n* : WARNING

caveat emp·tor \-'emp-tər, -ˌtȯr\ *n* : a principle in commerce: without a warranty the buyer takes a risk

cave–in \'kā-ˌvin\ *n* **1** : the action of caving in **2** : a place where earth has caved in

cave·man \'kāv-ˌman\ *n* **1** : a cave dweller esp. of the Stone Age **2** : a man who acts in a rough or crude manner

cav·ern \'ka-vərn\ *n* : a natural underground chamber or series of chambers open to the surface : CAVE; *esp* : one of large or unknown size — **cav·ern·ous** *adj* — **cav·ern·ous·ly** *adv*

cav·i·ar *also* **cav·i·are** \'ka-vē-ˌär, 'kä-\ *n* : the salted roe of a large fish (as sturgeon) used as an appetizer

cav·il \'ka-vəl\ *vb* **-iled** *or* **-illed; -il·ing** *or* **-il·ling** ♦ : to make frivolous objections or raise trivial objections to — **cavil** *n*

♦ carp, fuss, quibble

cav·il·er *or* **cav·il·ler** *n* ♦ : a person who complains and criticizes for trivial reasons

♦ carper, castigator, censurer, critic, faultfinder, nitpicker, railer, scold

cav·ing \'kā-viŋ\ *n* : the sport of exploring caves : SPELUNKING

cav·i·ta·tion \ˌka-və-'tā-shən\ *n* : the formation of partial vacuums in a liquid by a swiftly moving solid body (as a propeller) or by high-intensity sound waves

cav·i·ty \'ka-və-tē\ *n, pl* **-ties** **1** ♦ : an unfilled space within a mass : a hollow place **2** : an area of decay in a tooth

♦ concavity, dent, depression, hole, hollow, indentation, pit, recess

ca·vort \kə-'vȯrt\ *vb* ♦ : to bound, prance, or frisk about : CAPER

♦ caper, disport, frisk, frolic, gambol, lark, rollick, romp, sport

ca·vy \'kā-vē\ *n, pl* **cavies** : GUINEA PIG 1

caw \'kȯ\ *vb* : to utter the harsh call of the crow or a similar cry — **caw** *n*

cay \'kē, 'kā\ *n* ♦ : a small area of land surrounded by water : KEY

♦ island, isle, key

cay·enne pepper \ˌkī-'en-, ˌkā-\ *n* : a condiment consisting of ground dried fruits or seeds of a hot pepper

cayman *var of* CAIMAN

Ca·yu·ga \kā-'ü-gə, kī-\ *n, pl* **Cayuga** *or* **Cayugas** : a member of an Indigenous people of central New York; *also* : their language

Cay·use \'kī-ˌyüs, kī-'\ *n* **1** *pl* **Cayuse** *or* **Cayuses** : a member of a once-nomadic Indigenous people of Oregon and Washington **2** *pl* **cayuses**, *not cap, West* : a native range horse

Cb *symbol* columbium

CB \'sē-'bē\ *n* : CITIZENS BAND; *also* : the radio set used for citizens-band communications

CBC *abbr* Canadian Broadcasting Corporation

CBD *abbr* cash before delivery

CBS *abbr* Columbia Broadcasting System

CBW *abbr* chemical and biological warfare

¹**cc** \ˌsē-'sē\ *vb* **cc'd; cc'ing** : to send a copy of an e-mail, letter, etc., to someone ⟨~ an e-mail to a coworker⟩ ⟨~ me on your reply⟩

²**cc** *abbr* cubic centimeter

CC *abbr* **1** carbon copy **2** community college **3** country club

CCD \ˌsē-ˌsē-'dē\ *n* : CHARGE-COUPLED DEVICE
CCTV *abbr* closed-circuit television
CCU *abbr* **1** cardiac care unit **2** coronary care unit **3** critical care unit
ccw *abbr* counterclockwise
cd *abbr* cord
Cd *symbol* cadmium
¹**CD** \ˌsē-'dē\ *n* : CERTIFICATE OF DEPOSIT
²**CD** *n* : a small optical disk usu. containing recorded music or computer data; *also* : the content of a CD
³**CD** *abbr* Civil Defense
CDR *abbr* commander
CD–ROM \ˌsē-ˌdē-'räm\ *n* : a CD containing computer data that cannot be altered
CDT *abbr* central daylight (saving) time
Ce *symbol* cerium
CE *abbr* **1** chemical engineer **2** civil engineer **3** Corps of Engineers
cease \'sēs\ *vb* **ceased; ceas·ing** ♦ : to come or bring to an end : STOP

 ♦ break off, break up, close, conclude, desist, die, discontinue, end, expire, finish, halt, quit, stop, terminate *Ant* continue, hang on, persist

cease–fire \'sēs-'fī(-ə)r\ *n* : a suspension of active hostilities
cease·less \'sēs-ləs\ *adj* ♦ : being without pause or stop : continuing without interruption — **cease·less·ly** *adv*

 ♦ continual, continuous, incessant, unbroken, unceasing, uninterrupted ♦ dateless, deathless, endless, eternal, everlasting, immortal, permanent, perpetual, undying, unending

cease·less·ness *n* ♦ : the quality or state of being ceaseless

 ♦ abidance, continuance, duration, endurance, persistence, subsistence

ce·cum *also* **cae·cum** \'sē-kəm\ *n, pl* **ce·ca** \-kə\ : the blind pouch at the beginning of the large intestine into which the small intestine opens — **ce·cal** *also* **cae·cal** \-kəl\ *adj*
ce·dar \'sē-dər\ *n* : any of numerous coniferous trees (as a juniper) noted for their fragrant durable wood; *also* : this wood
cede \'sēd\ *vb* **ced·ed; ced·ing** **1** ♦ : to yield or give up **2** ♦ : to transfer (as property) to another : ASSIGN, TRANSFER — **ced·er** *n*

 ♦ [1] deliver, give up, hand over, leave, relinquish, render, surrender, turn over, yield ♦ [2] alienate, assign, deed, make over, transfer

ce·dil·la \si-'di-lə\ *n* : a mark placed under the letter *c* (as ç) to show that the *c* is to be pronounced like *s*
ceil·ing \'sē-liŋ\ *n* **1** : the overhead inside lining of a room **2** ♦ : something thought of as an overhanging shelter or canopy **3** : the height above the ground of the base of the lowest layer of clouds when over half of the sky is obscured **4** : the greatest height at which an airplane can operate efficiently **5** ♦ : a prescribed upper limit ⟨price ∼⟩

 ♦ [2] canopy, roof, tent ♦ [5] bound, boundary, confines, end, extent, limit, limitation, line, termination

cel·an·dine \'se-lən-ˌdīn, -ˌdēn\ *n* : a yellow-flowered herb related to the poppies
cel·e·brant \-brənt\ *n* ♦ : one who celebrates

 ♦ merrymaker, reveler, roisterer *Ant* killjoy

cel·e·brate \'se-lə-ˌbrāt\ *vb* **-brat·ed; -brat·ing** **1** : to perform (as a sacrament) with appropriate rites **2** ♦ : to honor (as a holiday) by solemn ceremonies or by refraining from ordinary business **3** : to observe a notable occasion with festivities **4** : EXTOL — **cel·e·bra·to·ry** \-brə-ˌtōr-ē, -ˌtòr-; ˌse-lə-'brā-tə-rē\ *adj*

 ♦ [1, 2] commemorate, keep, observe

cel·e·brat·ed *adj* ♦ : widely known and often referred to

 ♦ famed, famous, noted, notorious, prominent, renowned, star, well-known

cel·e·bra·tion \ˌse-lə-'brā-shən\ *n* ♦ : the act or process of celebrating

 ♦ carnival, festival, festivity, fete, fiesta, gala, jubilee

cel·e·bra·tor \'se-lə-brā-tər\ *n* : one that celebrates
ce·leb·ri·ty \sə-'le-brə-tē\ *n, pl* **-ties** **1** ♦ : the state of being celebrated **2** ♦ : a celebrated person

 ♦ [1] fame, notoriety, renown ♦ [2] figure, light, luminary, notable, personage, personality, somebody, star, superstar, VIP *Ant* nobody

ce·ler·i·ty \sə-'ler-ə-tē\ *n* ♦ : rapidity of motion or action : SPEED, RAPIDITY

 ♦ fastness, fleetness, haste, hurry, quickness, rapidity, speed, swiftness, velocity

cel·ery \'se-lə-rē\ *n, pl* **-er·ies** : a European herb related to the carrot and widely grown for the crisp edible stems of its leaves
celery cabbage *n* : CHINESE CABBAGE 2
ce·les·ta \sə-'les-tə\ *or* **ce·leste** \sə-'lest\ *n* : a keyboard instrument with hammers that strike steel plates
ce·les·tial \sə-'les-chəl\ *adj* **1** ♦ : of, relating to, or suggesting heaven or divinity : HEAVENLY **2** : of or relating to the sky ⟨∼ bodies⟩ — **ce·les·tial·ly** *adv*

 ♦ Elysian, empyrean, heavenly, supernal *Ant* hellish, infernal

celestial navigation *n* : navigation by observation of the positions of stars
celestial sphere *n* : an imaginary sphere of infinite radius against which the celestial bodies appear to be projected
cel·i·ba·cy \'se-lə-bə-sē\ *n* **1** : the state of being unmarried; *esp* : abstention by vow from marriage **2** : abstention from sexual intercourse
cel·i·bate \'se-lə-bət\ *n* : one who lives in celibacy — **celibate** *adj*
cell \'sel\ *n* **1 a** ♦ : a small room (as in a convent or prison) usu. for one person **1 b** ♦ : a small compartment, cavity, or bounded space **2** : a tiny mass of protoplasm that usu. contains a nucleus, is enclosed by a membrane, and forms the smallest structural unit of living matter capable of functioning independently **3** : a container holding an electrolyte either for generating electricity or for use in electrolysis **4** : a single unit in a device for converting radiant energy into electrical energy — **celled** \'seld\ *adj*

 ♦ [1a] chamber, closet, room ♦ [1a, 1b] bay, chamber, compartment, cubicle, room

cel·lar \'se-lər\ *n* **1** : the part of a building that is wholly or partly below ground level : BASEMENT **2** : the lowest position (as in an athletic league) **3** : a stock of wines
cel·lar·ette *or* **cel·lar·et** \ˌse-lə-'ret\ *n* : a case or cabinet for a few bottles of wine or liquor
cell body *n* : the nucleus-containing central part of a neuron
cel·lo \'che-lō\ *n, pl* **cellos** : a bass member of the violin family tuned an octave below the viola — **cel·list** \-list\ *n*
cel·lo·phane \'se-lə-ˌfān\ *n* : a thin transparent material made from cellulose and used as a wrapping
cell phone *n* : a portable cordless telephone for use in a cellular system
cel·lu·lar \'sel-yə-lər\ *adj* **1** : of, relating to, or consisting of cells **2** : of, relating to, or being a radiotelephone system in which a geographic area is divided into small sections each served by a transmitter of limited range
cel·lu·lite \'sel-yə-ˌlīt\ *n* : deposits of lumpy fat within connective tissue (as in the thighs, hips, and buttocks)
cel·lu·lose \'sel-yə-ˌlōs\ *n* : a complex carbohydrate of the cell walls of plants used esp. in making paper or rayon — **cel·lu·los·ic** \ˌsel-yə-'lō-sik\ *adj or n*
Cel·si·us \'sel-sē-əs\ *adj* : relating to or having a scale for measuring temperature on which the interval between the triple point and the boiling point of water is divided into 99.99 degrees with 0.01° being the triple point and 100.00° the boiling point
Celt \'kelt, 'selt\ *n* : a member of any of a group of peoples (as the Irish or Welsh) of western Europe — **Celt·ic** *adj*
cem·ba·lo \'chem-bə-ˌlō\ *n, pl* **-ba·li** \-ˌlē\ *or* **-balos** : HARPSICHORD
¹**ce·ment** \si-'ment\ *n* **1** : a powder that is produced from a burned mixture chiefly of clay and limestone and that is used in mortar and concrete; *also* : CONCRETE **2 a** ♦ : a binding element or substance (as glue, paste, or plaster) **b** ♦ : something serving to unite firmly **3** : CEMENTUM; *also* : a substance for filling cavities in teeth

 ♦ [2a] adhesive, glue, size ♦ [2b] bond, knot, ligature, link, tie

²**cement** *vb* **1** : to unite by or as if by cement **2** : to cover with concrete — **ce·ment·er** *n*
ce·men·tum \si-'men-təm\ *n* : a specialized external bony layer covering the dentin of the part of a tooth normally within the gum
cem·e·tery \'se-mə-ˌter-ē\ *n, pl* **-ter·ies** : a burial ground : GRAVEYARD
cen·o·bite \'se-nə-ˌbīt\ *n* : a member of a religious group living together in a monastic community — **cen·o·bit·ic** \ˌse-nə-'bi-tik\ *adj*
ceno·taph \'se-nə-ˌtaf\ *n* : a tomb or a monument erected in honor of a person whose body is elsewhere
Ce·no·zo·ic \ˌsē-nə-'zō-ik, ˌse-\ *adj* : of, relating to, or being the

era of geologic history that extends from about 65 million years ago to the present — **Cenozoic** n

cen•ser \'sen-sər\ n : a vessel for burning incense (as in a religious ritual)

¹**cen•sor** \'sen-sər\ n **1** : one of two early Roman magistrates whose duties included taking the census **2** : an official who inspects printed matter or sometimes motion pictures with power to suppress anything objectionable — **cen•so•ri•al** \sen-'sōr-ē-əl\ adj

²**censor** vb : to subject to censorship

cen•so•ri•ous \sen-'sōr-ē-əs\ adj : marked by or given to censure : CRITICAL — **cen•so•ri•ous•ly** adv — **cen•so•ri•ous•ness** n

cen•sor•ship \'sen-sər-ˌship\ n **1** : the action of a censor esp. in stopping the transmission or publication of matter considered objectionable **2** : the office of a Roman censor

cen•sur•able adj ♦ : deserving or open to censure

♦ blamable, blameworthy, culpable, reprehensible ♦ objectionable, obnoxious, offensive, reprehensible

¹**cen•sure** \'sen-chər\ n **1** : the act of blaming or condemning sternly **2** ♦ : an official reprimand

♦ denunciation, rebuke, reprimand, reproach, reproof, stricture Ant citation, commendation, endorsement

²**censure** vb **cen•sured; cen•sur•ing** ♦ : to find fault with and criticize as blameworthy

♦ condemn, damn, decry, denounce, reprehend, reprobate ♦ blame, condemn, criticize, denounce, fault, knock, pan, reprehend ♦ condemn, denounce, rebuke, reprimand, reproach, reprove Ant cite, commend, endorse

cen•sur•er n ♦ : one that censures

♦ carper, castigator, caviler, critic, faultfinder, nitpicker, railer, scold

cen•sus \'sen-səs\ n **1** : a periodic governmental count of population **2** : COUNT, TALLY — **cen•sus** vb

¹**cent** \'sent\ n **1** : a monetary unit equal to ¹/₁₀₀ of a basic unit of value (as of a dollar) **2** : a coin, token, or note representing one cent

²**cent** abbr **1** centigrade **2** central **3** century

cen•taur \'sen-ˌtȯr\ n : any of a race of creatures in Greek mythology half human and half horse

cen•te•nar•i•an \ˌsent-ᵊn-'er-ē-ən\ n : a person who is 100 or more years old

cen•te•na•ry \sen-'te-nə-rē, 'sent-ᵊn-ˌer-ē\ n, pl **-ries** : CENTENNIAL — **centenary** adj

cen•ten•ni•al \sen-'te-nē-əl\ n : a 100th anniversary or its celebration — **centennial** adj

¹**cen•ter** or Can and Brit **cen•tre** \'sen-tər\ n **1** ♦ : the point that is equally distant from all points on the circumference of a circle or surface of a sphere; also : MIDDLE **2** ♦ : the point about which an activity concentrates or from which something originates **3** : a region of concentrated population **4** : a middle part **5** often cap : political figures holding moderate views esp. between those of conservatives and liberals **6** : a player occupying a middle position (as in football or basketball)

♦ [1] core, midpoint, midst Ant perimeter, periphery ♦ [2] base, core, cynosure, eye, focus, heart, hub, mecca, nucleus, seat

²**center** or Can and Brit **cen•tre** vb **centered** or **centred; centering** or **centring 1** ♦ : to place or fix at or around a center or central area **2** ♦ : to give a central focus or basis : CONCENTRATE **3** : to have a center : FOCUS

♦ centralize, concentrate, consolidate, unify, unite

cen•ter•board or Can and Brit **cen•tre•board** \'sen-tər-ˌbōrd\ n : a retractable keel used esp. in sailboats

cen•ter•piece \-ˌpēs\ or Can and Brit **cen•tre•piece** n **1** : an object in a central position; esp : an adornment in the center of a table **2** : one that is of central importance or interest in a larger whole ⟨the ∼ of the speech⟩

cen•tes•i•mal \sen-'te-sə-məl\ adj : marked by or relating to division into hundredths

cen•ti•grade \'sen-tə-ˌgrād, 'sän-\ adj : relating to, conforming to, or having a thermometer scale on which the interval between the freezing and boiling points of water is divided into 100 degrees with 0° representing the freezing point and 100° the boiling point ⟨10° ∼⟩

cen•ti•gram \-ˌgram\ n : a metric unit of measure equal to ¹/₁₀₀ gram

cen•ti•li•ter \'sen-ti-ˌlē-tər\ or Can and Brit **cen•ti•li•tre** n : a metric unit of measure equal to ¹/₁₀₀ liter

cen•ti•me•ter \'sen-tə-ˌmē-tər, 'sän-\ or Can and Brit **cen•ti•me•tre** n : a metric unit of measure equal to ¹/₁₀₀ meter

centimeter–gram–second adj : of, relating to, or being a system of units based on the centimeter as the unit of length, the gram as the unit of mass, and the second as the unit of time

cen•ti•pede \'sen-tə-ˌpēd\ n : any of a class of long flattened segmented arthropods with one pair of legs on each segment except the first which has a pair of poison fangs

¹**cen•tral** \'sen-trəl\ adj **1** : constituting a center **2** ♦ : belonging to the center as the most important part : PRINCIPAL **3** : situated at, in, or near the center **4** : centrally placed and superseding separate units ⟨∼ heating⟩ — **cen•tral•ly** adv

♦ arch, cardinal, chief, dominant, first, foremost, grand, key, main, paramount, predominant, preeminent, premier, primary, principal, sovereign, supreme

²**central** n : a central controlling office

cen•tral•ise Brit var of CENTRALIZE

cen•tral•ize \'sen-trə-ˌlīz\ vb **-ized; -iz•ing** ♦ : to bring to a central point or under central control — **cen•tral•i•za•tion** \ˌsen-trə-lə-'zā-shən\ n — **cen•tral•iz•er** \'sen-trə-ˌlī-zər\ n

♦ center (or centre), concentrate, consolidate, unify, unite Ant decentralize, spread (out)

central nervous system n : the part of the nervous system which integrates nervous function and activity and which in vertebrates consists of the brain and spinal cord

cen•tre Can and Brit var of CENTER

cen•trif•u•gal \sen-'tri-fyə-gəl, -fi-\ adj **1** : proceeding or acting in a direction away from a center or axis **2** : using or acting by centrifugal force

centrifugal force n : the apparent force felt by an object moving in a curved path and acting outward from a center of rotation

cen•tri•fuge \'sen-trə-ˌfyüj\ n : a machine using centrifugal force (as for separating substances of different densities or for removing moisture)

cen•trip•e•tal \sen-'tri-pət-ᵊl\ adj : proceeding or acting in a direction toward a center or axis

centripetal force n : the force needed to keep an object revolving about a point moving in a circular path

cen•trist \'sen-trist\ n **1** often cap : a member of a center party **2** : one who holds moderate views

cen•tu•ri•on \sen-'tur-ē-ən, -'tyur-\ n : an officer commanding a Roman century

cen•tu•ry \'sen-chə-rē\ n, pl **-ries 1** : a subdivision of a Roman legion **2** : a group or sequence of 100 like things **3** : a period of 100 years

century plant n : a Mexican agave maturing and flowering only once in many years and then dying

CEO \ˌsē-(ˌ)ē-'ō\ n : the executive with the chief decision-making authority in an organization or business

ce•phal•ic \sə-'fa-lik\ adj **1** : of or relating to the head **2** : directed toward or situated on or in or near the head

ce•ram•ic \sə-'ra-mik\ n **1** pl : the art or process of making articles from a nonmetallic mineral (as clay) by firing **2** : a product produced by ceramics — **ceramic** adj

ce•ra•mist \sə-'ra-mist\ or **ce•ram•i•cist** \sə-'ra-mə-sist\ n : one who engages in ceramics

¹**ce•re•al** \'sir-ē-əl\ adj : relating to grain or to the plants that produce it; also : made of grain

²**cereal** n **1** : a grass (as wheat) yielding grain suitable for food; also : its grain **2** : a food and esp. a breakfast food prepared from the grain of a cereal

cer•e•bel•lum \ˌser-ə-'be-ləm\ n, pl **-bellums** or **-bel•la** \-lə\ : a part of the brain that projects over the medulla and is concerned esp. with coordination of muscular action and with bodily balance — **cer•e•bel•lar** \-lər\ adj

ce•re•bral \sə-'rē-brəl, 'ser-ə-\ adj **1** ♦ : of or relating to the brain, intellect, or cerebrum **2** ♦ : appealing to or involving the intellect — **ce•re•bral•ly** adv

♦ [1, 2] inner, intellectual, mental, psychological

cerebral cortex n : the surface layer of gray matter of the cerebrum that functions chiefly in coordination of sensory and motor information

cerebral palsy n : a disorder caused by brain damage usu. before, during, or shortly after birth and marked esp. by defective muscle control

cer•e•brate \'ser-ə-ˌbrāt\ vb **-brat•ed; -brat•ing** : THINK — **cer•e•bra•tion** \ˌser-ə-'brā-shən\ n

ce•re•brum \sə-'rē-brəm, 'ser-ə-\ n, pl **-brums** or **-bra** \-brə\ : the enlarged front and upper part of the brain that contains the higher nervous centers

cere•ment \'ser-ə-mənt, 'sir-mənt\ *n* : a shroud for the dead

¹cer•e•mo•ni•al \,ser-ə-'mō-nē-əl\ *adj* **1 ♦** : of, relating to, or forming a ceremony **2** : stressing careful attention to form and detail — **cer•e•mo•ni•al•ly** *adv*

♦ ceremonious, conventional, formal, orthodox, regular, routine

²ceremonial *n* : a ceremonial act or system : RITUAL, FORM

cer•e•mo•ni•ous \,ser-ə-'mō-nē-əs\ *adj* **1** : devoted to forms and ceremony **2** : of, relating to, or constituting a ceremony : CEREMONIAL **3 ♦** : according to formal usage or procedure **4 ♦** : marked by ceremony — **cer•e•mo•ni•ous•ly** *adv* — **cer•e•mo•ni•ous•ness** *n*

♦ [3, 4] correct, decorous, formal, proper, starchy *Ant* casual, easygoing, informal, laid-back

cer•e•mo•ny \'ser-ə-,mō-nē\ *n, pl* **-nies** **1 ♦** : a formal act or series of acts prescribed by law, ritual, or convention **2** : a conventional act of politeness **3** : a mere outward form with no deeper significance **4** : FORMALITY

♦ ceremonial, form, formality, observance, rite, ritual, solemnity

ce•re•us \'sir-ē-əs\ *n* : any of various cacti of the western U.S. and tropical America

ce•rise \sə-'rēs\ *n* : a moderate red color

ce•ri•um \'sir-ē-əm\ *n* : a malleable metallic chemical element used esp. in alloys

cer•met \'sər-,met\ *n* : a strong alloy of a heat-resistant compound and a metal used esp. for turbine blades

cert *abbr* certificate; certification; certified; certify

¹cer•tain \'sərt-ᵊn\ *adj* **1 ♦** : not subject to change or fluctuation : FIXED, SETTLED **2 ♦** : of a specific but unspecified character ⟨∼ people in authority⟩ **3 a ♦** : capable of being depended on : DEPENDABLE, RELIABLE **b ♦** : incapable of failing **4** : INDISPUTABLE, UNDENIABLE **5 ♦** : assured in mind or action ⟨I am ∼ that I am right⟩ **6 ♦** : INEVITABLE

♦ [1] determinate, final, firm, fixed, flat, frozen, hard, hard-and-fast, set, settled, stable ♦ [2] anonymous, one, some, unidentified, unnamed, unspecified ♦ [3b] sure, surefire, unfailing ♦ [5] assured, clear, cocksure, confident, doubtless, positive, sanguine, sure *Ant* doubtful, dubious, uncertain, unsure

²certain *pron* : certain ones

cer•tain•ly *adv* **1 ♦** : in a manner that is certain : with certainty **2** : it is certain that

♦ definitely, doubtless, incontestably, indeed, indisputably, really, surely, truly, undeniably, undoubtedly, unquestionably

cer•tain•ty \-tē\ *n, pl* **-ties** **1** : something that is certain **2 ♦** : the quality or state of being certain

♦ assurance, certitude, confidence, conviction, positiveness, sureness

cer•tif•i•cate \sər-'ti-fi-kət\ *n* **1** : a document testifying to the truth of a fact **2** : a document testifying that one has fulfilled certain requirements (as of a course or school) **3** : a document giving evidence of ownership or debt ⟨a stock ∼⟩

certificate of deposit : a money-market bond redeemable without penalty only on maturity

cer•ti•fi•ca•tion \,sər-tə-fə-'kā-shən\ *n* **1** : the act of certifying : the state of being certified **2** : a certified statement

certified mail *n* : first class mail for which proof of delivery may be secured but no indemnity value is claimed

certified public accountant *n* : an accountant who has met the requirements of a state law and has been granted a certificate

cer•ti•fy \'sər-tə-,fī\ *vb* **-fied; -fy•ing** **1 ♦** : to attest as being true **2** : to endorse officially **3** : to guarantee (a bank check) as good by a statement to that effect stamped on its face **4 ♦** : to provide with a usu. professional certificate or license — **cer•ti•fi•able** \-ə-bəl\ *adj* — **cer•ti•fi•ably** \-blē\ *adv* — **cer•ti•fi•er** *n*

♦ [1] attest, authenticate, avouch, testify, vouch, witness ♦ [4] accredit, authorize, commission, empower, enable, invest, license, qualify

cer•ti•tude \'sər-tə-,tüd, -,tyüd\ *n* **♦** : the state of being or feeling certain

♦ assurance, certainty, confidence, conviction, positiveness, sureness

ce•ru•le•an \sə-'rü-lē-ən\ *adj* : AZURE

ce•ru•men \sə-'rü-mən\ *n* : EARWAX

cer•vi•cal \'sər-vi-kəl\ *adj* : of or relating to a neck or cervix

cervical cap *n* : a contraceptive device in the form of a thimble-shaped molded cap that fits over the uterine cervix and blocks sperm from entering the uterus

cer•vix \'sər-viks\ *n, pl* **cer•vi•ces** \-və-,sēz\ *or* **cer•vix•es** **1** : NECK; *esp* : the back part of the neck **2** : a constricted portion of an organ or part; *esp* : the narrow outer end of the uterus

ce•sar•e•an *or* **ce•sar•i•an** *also* **cae•sar•e•an** \si-'zar-ē-ən\ *n, often cap* : CESAREAN SECTION — **cesarean** *or* **caesarean** *also* **cesarian** *adj, often cap*

cesarean section *also* **caesarean section** *n, often cap* C : surgical incision of the walls of the abdomen and uterus for delivery of offspring

ce•si•um \'sē-zē-əm\ *n* : a silver-white soft ductile chemical element

ces•sa•tion \se-'sā-shən\ *n* **♦** : a temporary or final ceasing (as of action)

♦ close, closure, conclusion, end, ending, expiration, finish, halt, lapse, shutdown, stop, stoppage, termination

ces•sion \'se-shən\ *n* : a yielding (as of rights) to another

cess•pool \'ses-,pül\ *n* : an underground pit or tank for receiving household sewage

ce•ta•cean \si-'tā-shən\ *n* : any of an order of aquatic mostly marine mammals that includes whales, porpoises, dolphins, and related forms — **cetacean** *adj*

cf *abbr* compare

Cf *symbol* californium

CF *abbr* cystic fibrosis

CFC *abbr* chlorofluorocarbon

CFL *abbr* compact fluorescent lamp; compact fluorescent light bulb

CFO *abbr* chief financial officer

cg *abbr* centigram

CG *abbr* **1** coast guard **2** commanding general

cgs *abbr* centimeter-gram-second

ch *abbr* **1** chain **2** champion **3** chapter **4** church

CH *abbr* **1** clearinghouse **2** courthouse **3** customhouse

Cha•blis \sha-'blē, shə-, shä-; 'sha-,blē\ *n, pl* **Cha•blis** \-'blēz, -(,)blē\ **1** : a dry sharp white Burgundy wine **2** : a white California wine

cha–cha \'chä-,chä\ *n* : a fast rhythmic ballroom dance of Latin American origin

Chad•i•an \'cha-dē-ən\ *n* : a native or inhabitant of Chad — **Chadian** *adj*

chafe \'chāf\ *vb* **chafed; chaf•ing** **1 ♦** : to bring trouble or distress to : cause agitation or anxiety to : IRRITATE, VEX **2** : FRET **3** : to warm by rubbing **4 ♦** : to rub so as to wear away **5 ♦** : to make sore by rubbing

♦ [1] aggravate, annoy, bother, bug, exasperate, gall, get, grate, irk, irritate, nettle, peeve, persecute, pique, put out, rasp, rile, vex ♦ [4] abrade, erode, fray, fret, gall, rub, wear ♦ [5] abrade, gall, irritate

cha•fer \'chā-fər\ *n* : any of various scarab beetles

¹chaff \'chaf\ *n* **1** : debris (as husks) separated from grain in threshing **2 ♦** : something relatively worthless

♦ deadwood, dust, garbage, junk, litter, refuse, riffraff, rubbish, scrap, trash, waste

²chaff *n* **♦** : light jesting talk : BANTER

♦ banter, persiflage, raillery, repartee

³chaff *vb* **♦** : to tease good-naturedly

♦ jive, josh, kid, rally, razz, rib, ride, roast, tease

chaf•fer \'cha-fər\ *vb* **♦** : to discuss terms : haggle esp. over a price — **chaf•fer•er** *n*

♦ bargain, deal, dicker, haggle, negotiate, palter

chaf•finch \'cha-,finch\ *n* : a common European finch with a cheerful song

chaffy *adj* **♦** : of little importance or worth

♦ empty, junky, no-good, null, valueless, worthless

chaf•ing dish \'chā-fiŋ-\ *n* : a utensil for cooking food at the table

¹cha•grin \shə-'grin\ *n* : mental uneasiness or annoyance caused by failure, disappointment, or humiliation

²chagrin *vb* **cha•grined** \-'grind\; **cha•grin•ing** : to cause to feel chagrin

¹chain \'chān\ *n* **1** : a flexible series of connected links **2** : a chainlike surveying instrument; *also* : a unit of length equal to 66 feet (about 20 meters) **3 ♦** : something that confines, restrains, or secures : BOND, FETTER **4 ♦** : a series of things linked, connected, or associated together ⟨a ∼ of events⟩ ⟨a mountain ∼⟩

♦ [3] band, bond, fetter, irons, ligature, manacle, shackle
♦ [4] progression, sequence, string, train

²**chain** vb **1 ♦** : to fasten, bind, or connect with a chain; also : FETTER **2 ♦** : to join together so as to make a chain

♦ [1] bind, enchain, fetter, handcuff, manacle, shackle, trammel ♦ [2] compound, connect, couple, hitch, hook, join, link, yoke

chain gang n : a gang of convicts chained together
chain letter n : a letter sent to several persons with a request that each send copies to an equal number of persons
chain mail n : flexible armor of interlocking metal rings
chain reaction n **1** : a series of events in which each event initiates the succeeding one **2** : a chemical or nuclear reaction yielding products that cause further reactions of the same kind
chain saw n : a portable power saw that has teeth linked together to form an endless chain — **chain-saw** \'chān-,sȯ\ vb
chain–smoke \'chān-'smōk\ vb : to smoke esp. cigarettes continuously
chain store n : any of numerous stores under the same ownership that sell the same lines of goods
¹**chair** \'cher\ n **1** : a seat with a back for one person **2** : ELECTRIC CHAIR **3 ♦** : an official seat or a seat of authority, state, or dignity; also : an office or position of authority or dignity **4** : the presiding officer of a meeting or event : CHAIRMAN

♦ head, headship, helm, rein

²**chair** vb : to act as chairman of
chair-lift \'cher-,lift\ n : a motor-driven conveyor for skiers consisting of seats hung from a moving cable
chair-man \-mən\ n **♦** : the presiding officer of a meeting or of a committee — **chair-man-ship** n

♦ chair, moderator, president, speaker

chair-per-son \-,pər-sən\ n : the presiding officer of a meeting or assembly : CHAIRMAN
chair-wom-an \-,wu̇-mən\ n : a woman who serves as chairman
chaise \'shāz\ n : a 2-wheeled horse-drawn carriage with a folding top
chaise longue \'shāz-'lȯŋ\ n, pl **chaise longues** \same or -'lȯŋz\ : a long reclining chair
chaise lounge \-'lau̇nj\ n : CHAISE LONGUE
chal-ced-o-ny \kal-'sed-ᵊn-ē\ n, pl **-nies** : a translucent pale blue or gray quartz
chal-co-py-rite \,kal-kə-'pī-,rīt\ n : a yellow mineral constituting an important ore of copper
cha-let \sha-'lā\ n **1** : a herdsman's cabin in the Swiss mountains **2 a** : a building in the style of a Swiss cottage with a wide roof overhang **b ♦** : a cottage or house in chalet style

♦ cabin, camp, cottage, lodge

chal-ice \'cha-ləs\ n : a drinking cup; esp : the eucharistic cup
¹**chalk** \'chȯk\ n **1** : a soft limestone **2** : chalk or chalky material esp. when used as a crayon — **chalky** adj
²**chalk** vb **1** : to rub or mark with chalk **2** : to record with or as if with chalk — usu. used with up
chalk-board \'chȯk-,bȯrd\ n : BLACKBOARD
chalk up vb **1** : ASCRIBE, CREDIT **2** : ATTAIN, ACHIEVE
¹**chal-lenge** \'cha-lənj\ vb **chal-lenged; chal-leng-ing 1** : to order to halt and prove identity **2 ♦** : to dispute esp. as being unjust, invalid, or untrue : to take exception to : DISPUTE **3 ♦** : to issue an invitation to compete against one esp. in single combat : DARE, DEFY

♦ [2] contest, dispute, query, question Ant accept, believe, embrace, swallow ♦ [3] dare, defy

²**challenge** n **1** : a summons to a duel **2** : an invitation to compete in a sport **3 ♦** : a calling to account or into question **4** : an exception taken to a juror **5** : a sentry's command to halt and prove identity **6** : a stimulating or interesting task or problem

♦ complaint, demur, expostulation, fuss, kick, objection, protest, question, remonstrance

challenged adj : presented with difficulties (as by a disability) : DISABLED
chal-leng-er n **♦** : one that challenges; specif : a contender for a championship (as boxing)

♦ competition, competitor, contender, contestant, rival

challenging adj **♦** : arousing competitive interest, thought, or action ⟨a ∼ course of study⟩

♦ arduous, burdensome, demanding, exacting, grueling, laborious, onerous, taxing, toilsome

chal-lis \'sha-lē\ n, pl **chal-lises** \-lēz\ : a lightweight clothing fabric of wool, cotton, or synthetic yarns
cham-ber \'chām-bər\ n **1 ♦** : a partitioned part of the inside of

a building : ROOM **2 ♦** : an enclosed space or cavity **3** : a hall for meetings of a legislative body **4** : a judge's consultation room — usu. used in pl. **5** : a legislative or judicial body; also : a council for a business purpose **6** : the part of a firearm that holds the cartridge or powder charge during firing — **cham-bered** \-bərd\ adj

♦ [1, 2] bay, cabin, cell, compartment, cubicle

cham-ber-lain \'chām-bər-lən\ n **1** : a chief officer in the household of a king or nobleman **2** : TREASURER
cham-ber-maid \-,mād\ n : a maid who takes care of bedrooms
chamber music n : music intended for performance by a few musicians before a small audience
cham-bray \'sham-,brā\ n : a lightweight clothing fabric of white and colored threads
cha-me-leon \kə-'mēl-yən\ n : a small lizard whose skin changes color esp. according to its surroundings
¹**cham-fer** \'cham-fər\ vb **1** : to cut a furrow in (as a column) : GROOVE **2** : to make a chamfer on : BEVEL
²**chamfer** n : a beveled edge
cham-ois \'sha-mē\ n, pl **cham-ois** \same or -mēz\ **1** : a small goatlike antelope of Europe and the Caucasus region of Russia **2** also **cham-my** \'sha-mē\ : a soft leather made esp. from the skin of the sheep or goat **3** : a cotton fabric made in imitation of chamois leather
cham-o-mile \'ka-mə-,mīl, -,mēl\ n : any of a genus of strong-scented herbs related to the daisies and having flower heads that yield a bitter substance used esp. in tonics and teas
¹**champ** \'champ, 'chämp\ vb **1** : to chew noisily **2** : to show impatience of delay or restraint
²**champ** \'champ\ n **♦** : a winner of first prize or first place in competition : CHAMPION; also : one who shows marked superiority

♦ champion, victor, winner

cham-pagne \sham-'pān\ n : a white effervescent wine
¹**cham-pi-on** \'cham-pē-ən\ n **1 ♦** : a militant advocate or defender **2 ♦** : one that wins first prize or place in a contest **3** : one that is acknowledged to be better than all others

♦ [1] advocate, apostle, backer, booster, exponent, friend, promoter, proponent, supporter ♦ [2] champ, victor, winner

²**champion** vb **♦** : to protect or fight for as a champion

♦ advocate, back, endorse, patronize, support

cham-pi-on-ship \-,ship\ n **1** : the position or title of a champion **2** : the act of championing : DEFENSE **3** : a contest held to determine a champion
¹**chance** \'chans\ n **1** : something that happens without apparent cause **2 ♦** : the unpredictable element in existence : LUCK **3 ♦** : a situation favoring some purpose : OPPORTUNITY **4 ♦** : the likelihood of a particular outcome in an uncertain situation : PROBABILITY **5 ♦** : a gamble or risk taken in hopes of a favorable outcome with a real possibility of loss **6** : a raffle ticket — **by chance** : in the haphazard course of events

♦ [2] accident, circumstance, hazard, luck ♦ [3] occasion, opening, opportunity, room ♦ [4] odds, percentage, probability ♦ [5] enterprise, flier, gamble, speculation, venture

²**chance** vb **chanced; chanc-ing 1 ♦** : to take place by chance : HAPPEN **2 ♦** : to encounter or discover by chance — used with upon **3** : to leave the outcome of to chance **4 ♦** : to accept the risk of

♦ [1] be, befall, betide, come, go, happen, occur, pass, transpire ♦ usu **chance upon** [2] encounter, find, happen (on or upon), hit, meet, stumble ♦ [4] gamble, hazard, risk, venture

³**chance** adj **♦** : happening, experienced, or encountered by chance, without forethought, plan, or intention

♦ accidental, casual, fluky, fortuitous, incidental, unintended, unintentional, unplanned, unpremeditated, unwitting

chan-cel \'chan-səl\ n : the part of a church including the altar and choir
chan-cel-lery or **chan-cel-lory** \'chan-sə-lə-rē\ n, pl **-ler-ies** or **-lor-ies 1** : the position or office of a chancellor **2** : the building or room where a chancellor works **3** : the office or staff of an embassy or consulate
chan-cel-lor \'chan-sə-lər\ n **1** : a high state official in various countries **2** : the head of a university **3** : a judge in the equity court in various states of the U.S. **4** : the chief minister of state in some European countries — **chan-cel-lor-ship** n
chan-cery \'chan-sə-rē\ n, pl **-cer-ies 1** : any of various courts of equity in the U.S. and Britain **2** : a record office for public or diplomatic archives **3** : a chancellor's court or office **4** : the office of an embassy

chan·cre \'shaŋ-kər\ *n* : a primary sore or ulcer at the site of entry of an infective agent (as of syphilis)

chan·croid \'chaŋ-ˌkrȯid\ *n* : a sexually transmitted disease caused by a bacterium and characterized by chancres that differ from those of syphilis in lacking hardened margins

chancy \'chan-sē\ *adj* **chanc·i·er; -est** **1** *Scot* : AUSPICIOUS **2** : RISKY

chan·de·lier \ˌshan-də-'lir\ *n* : a branched lighting fixture suspended from a ceiling

chan·dler \'chand-lər\ *n* : a dealer in provisions and supplies of a specified kind ⟨ship's ∼⟩ — **chan·dlery** *n*

¹change \'chānj\ *vb* **changed; chang·ing** **1** ♦ : to make or become different : ALTER **2** ♦ : to replace with another **3** : to give or receive an equivalent sum in notes or coins of usu. smaller denominations or of another currency **4** : to put fresh clothes or covering on ⟨∼ a bed⟩ **5** : to put on different clothes **6** ♦ : to switch to or with another : EXCHANGE ⟨neither liked his seat so they ∼ed with each other⟩ — **chang·er** *n*

♦ [1] alter, make over, modify, recast, redo, refashion, remake, remodel, revamp, revise, rework, vary *Ant* fix, freeze, set, stabilize ♦ [1] fluctuate, mutate, shift, vary *Ant* stabilize ♦ [2, 6] commute, exchange, shift, substitute, swap, switch, trade

²change *n* **1** ♦ : the act, process, or result of changing **2** : a fresh set of clothes **3** : money given in exchange for other money of higher denomination **4** : money returned when a payment exceeds the sum due **5** : coins esp. of small denominations

♦ alteration, difference, modification, revise, revision, variation *Ant* fixation, stabilization

change·able *adj* **1** ♦ : subject to change ⟨∼ plans⟩ **2** ♦ : able or apt to vary ⟨∼ weather⟩

♦ [1] adaptable, adjustable, elastic, flexible, fluid, malleable, variable ♦ [2] capricious, fickle, fluid, inconstant, mercurial, mutable, temperamental, uncertain, unpredictable, unsettled, unstable, unsteady, variable, volatile

change·ful *adj* : notably variable : UNCERTAIN

change·ling \'chānj-liŋ\ *n* : a child secretly exchanged for another in infancy

change·over \'chānj-ˌō-vər\ *n* ♦ : the action of changing over : CONVERSION

♦ conversion, metamorphosis, transfiguration, transformation

change ringing *n* : the art or practice of ringing a set of tuned bells in continually varying order

¹chan·nel \'chan-ᵊl\ *n* **1** : the bed of a stream **2** : the deeper part of a waterway **3** ♦ : a comparatively narrow passageway connecting two large bodies of water : STRAIT **4** : a means of passage or transmission **5** : a range of frequencies of sufficient width for a single radio or television transmission **6** ♦ : a usu. tubular enclosed passage : CONDUIT **7** ♦ : a long gutter, groove, or furrow usu. for the passage of water

♦ [3] narrows, sound, strait ♦ [6] conduit, duct, leader, line, penstock, pipe, tube ♦ [6, 7] aqueduct, canal, conduit, flume, raceway, watercourse

²channel *vb* **-neled** *or* **-nelled; -neling** *or* **-nel·ling** **1** : to make a channel in **2** ♦ : to direct into or through a channel

♦ conduct, direct, funnel, pipe, siphon

chan·nel·ize \'chan-ᵊl-ˌīz\ *vb* **-ized; -iz·ing** : to direct through or into a channel or restricted area : CHANNEL — **chan·nel·iza·tion** \ˌchan-ᵊl-ə-'zā-shən\ *n*

chan·son \shäⁿ-'sōⁿ\ *n, pl* **chan·sons** *same or* -'sōⁿz\ : SONG; *esp* : a cabaret song

¹chant \'chant\ *vb* **1** ♦ : to make melodic sounds with the voice : SING; *esp* : to sing a chant **2** : to utter or recite in the manner of a chant **3** : to celebrate or praise in song — **chant·er** *n*

♦ carol, descant, sing, vocalize

²chant *n* **1** : a repetitive melody in which several words are sung to one tone : SONG; *esp* : a liturgical melody **2** : a manner of singing or speaking in musical monotones

chan·te·relle \ˌshan-tə-'rel\ *n* : a fragrant edible mushroom

chan·teuse \shäⁿ-'tərz, shan-'tüz\ *n, pl* **chan·teuses** *same or* -'tər-zəz, -'tü-zəz\ : a woman who is a concert or nightclub singer

chan·tey *or* **chan·ty** \'shan-tē, 'chan-\ *n, pl* **chanteys** *or* **chan·ties** : a song sung by sailors in rhythm with their work

chan·ti·cleer \ˌchan-tə-'klir, ˌshan-\ *n* : ROOSTER

Chanukah *var of* HANUKKAH

cha·os \'kā-ˌäs\ *n* **1** *often cap* : the confused unorganized state existing before the creation of distinct forms **2** : the inherent unpredictability in the behavior of a natural system (as the atmosphere or the beating heart) **3** ♦ : a state of utter confusion or disorder

♦ confusion, disarray, disorder, disorganization, havoc, hell, jumble, mess, muddle, shambles *Ant* order, orderliness

chaos theory *n* : a branch of mathematical and physical theory concerned with chaotic systems

cha·ot·ic \kā-'ä-tik\ *adj* ♦ : completely confused or disordered — **cha·ot·i·cal·ly** \-ti-k(ə-)lē\ *adv*

♦ confused, disheveled, disordered, messy, muddled, sloppy, unkempt, untidy

¹chap \'chap\ *vb* **chapped; chap·ping** : to dry and crack open usu. from wind and cold ⟨*chapped* lips⟩

²chap *n* : a jaw with its fleshy covering — usu. used in pl.

³chap *n* ♦ : an adult male individual : FELLOW

♦ buck, dude, fellow, gent, gentleman, guy, hombre, jack, joker, lad, male, man

⁴chap *abbr* chapter

chap·ar·ral \ˌsha-pə-'ral\ *n* **1** ♦ : a dense impenetrable thicket of shrubs or dwarf trees **2** : an ecological community esp. of southern California composed of shrubby plants

♦ brake, brushwood, coppice, covert, thicket

chap·book \'chap-ˌbu̇k\ *n* : a small book of ballads, tales, or tracts

cha·peau \sha-'pō\ *n, pl* **cha·peaus** \-'pōz\ *or* **cha·peaux** \-'pō, -'pōz\ : HAT

chap·el \'cha-pəl\ *n* **1** : a private or subordinate place of worship **2** : an assembly at an educational institution usu. including devotional exercises **3** : a place of worship used by a Christian group other than an established church

¹chap·er·one *or* **chap·er·on** \'sha-pə-ˌrōn\ *n* **1** : a person (as a matron) who accompanies young unmarried women in public for propriety **2** : an older person who accompanies young people at a social gathering to ensure proper behavior

²chaperone *or* **chaperon** *vb* **-oned; -on·ing** **1** ♦ : to attend upon : ESCORT **2** ♦ : to act as a chaperone to or for ⟨∼ a dance⟩ — **chap·er·on·age** \-ˌrō-nij\ *n*

♦ [1, 2] accompany, attend, convoy, escort, squire

chap·fall·en \'chap-ˌfȯ-lən, 'chäp-\ *adj* **1** : having the lower jaw hanging loosely **2** : DEJECTED, DEPRESSED

chap·lain \'cha-plən\ *n* **1** : a member of the clergy officially attached to a special group (as the army) **2** : a person chosen to conduct religious exercises (as for a club) — **chap·lain·cy** \-sē\ *n*

chap·let \'cha-plət\ *n* **1** : a wreath for the head **2** : a string of beads : NECKLACE

chap·man \'chap-mən\ *n, Brit* : an itinerant dealer : PEDDLER

chaps \'shaps, 'chaps\ *n pl* : leather leggings resembling trousers without a seat that are worn esp. by western ranch hands

chap·ter \'chap-tər\ *n* **1** : a main division of a book **2** : a body of canons (as of a cathedral) **3** ♦ : a local branch of an organization

♦ affiliate, branch, local

¹char \'chär\ *n, pl* **char** *or* **chars** : any of a genus of trouts (as the common brook trout) with small scales

²char *vb* **charred; char·ring** **1** : to burn or become burned to charcoal **2** ♦ : to burn slightly or partly : SCORCH

♦ scorch, sear, singe

³char *vb* **charred; char·ring** : to work as a cleaning woman

char·ac·ter \'kar-ik-tər\ *n* **1** : a graphic symbol (as a letter) used in writing or printing **2** : a symbol that represents information; *also* : a representation of such a character that may be accepted by a computer **3** : a distinguishing feature : ATTRIBUTE **4** ♦ : the complex of mental and ethical traits marking a person or a group **5** ♦ : a person marked by conspicuous often peculiar traits **6** : one of the persons in a novel or play **7** ♦ : reputation esp. when good : good name : REPUTATION **8** ♦ : moral excellence

♦ [4] complexion, constitution, genius, identity, nature, personality, tone ♦ [5] crackpot, crank, eccentric, kook, nut, oddball, screwball, weirdo ♦ [7] mark, name, note, report, reputation ♦ [8] decency, goodness, honesty, honor (*or* honour), integrity, morality, probity, rectitude, righteousness, uprightness, virtue

¹char·ac·ter·is·tic \ˌkar-ik-tə-'ris-tik\ *n* ♦ : a distinguishing trait, quality, or property

♦ attribute, character, feature, mark, peculiarity, point, property, quality, trait

²**char·ac·ter·is·tic** *adj* ♦ : serving to mark individual character — **char·ac·ter·is·ti·cal·ly** \-ti-k(ə-)lē\ *adv*

♦ classic, distinct, distinctive, individual, peculiar, proper, symptomatic, typical *Ant* atypical, nontypical

char·ac·ter·ize \'kar-ik-tə-ˌrīz\ *vb* **-ized; -iz·ing** **1** ♦ : to describe the character of **2** : to be a characteristic of — **char·ac·ter·iza·tion** \ˌkar-ik-tə-rə-'zā-shən\ *n*

♦ define, depict, describe, portray, represent

cha·rades \shə-'rādz\ *n sing or pl* : a game in which some of the players try to guess a word or phrase from the actions of another player who may not speak

char·coal \'chär-ˌkōl\ *n* **1** : a porous carbon prepared from vegetable or animal substances **2** : a piece of fine charcoal used in drawing; *also* : a drawing made with charcoal

chard \'chärd\ *n* : SWISS CHARD

char·don·nay \ˌshard-ᵊn-'ā\ *n, often cap* : a dry white wine made from a single variety of white grape

¹**charge** \'chärj\ *n* **1** : a quantity (as of fuel or ammunition) required to fill something to capacity **2** : a store or accumulation of force **3** : an excess or deficiency of electrons in a body **4** : THRILL, KICK **5** ♦ : a task or duty imposed **6** : a person or thing committed to the care of another : CARE **7** ♦ : control of the acts, workings, or disposition of something **8 a** ♦ : a direction or order calling for compliance **b** : instructions from a judge to a jury **9** ♦ : the price demanded for something : COST, PRICE; *also* : a debit to an account **10** ♦ : a formal assertion of illegality : INDICTMENT **11** : a violent rush forward (as to attack) : ATTACK, ASSAULT

♦ [5] assignment, job, mission, operation, post ♦ [7] care, guidance, headship, oversight, regulation, superintendence, supervision ♦ [8a] behest, command, commandment, decree, dictate, direction, directive, edict, instruction, order, word ♦ [9] cost, fee, figure, price ♦ [10] complaint, count, indictment, rap

²**charge** *vb* **charged; charg·ing** **1** : to load or fill to capacity **2** : to give an electric charge to; *also* : to restore the activity of (a storage battery) by means of an electric current **3** ♦ : to impose a task or responsibility on **4** : to command, instruct, or exhort with authority : COMMAND, ORDER ⟨I ∼ you not to go⟩ **5** : to make an assertion against esp. by ascribing guilt or blame : ACCUSE **6** ♦ : to rush against : rush forward in assault **7** ♦ : to make liable for payment; *also* : to record a debt or liability against **8** ♦ : to fix as a price — **charge·able** *adj*

♦ [3] assign, commission, entrust, trust ♦ [6] assail, assault, attack, beset, descend, jump, pounce (on *or* upon), raid, rush, storm, strike ♦ [7] assess, exact, fine, impose, lay, levy, put ♦ [8] ask, command, demand

charge–coupled device *n* : a semiconductor device used esp. as an optical sensor

charged \'chärjd\ *adj* **1** ♦ : possessing or showing strong emotion **2** : capable of arousing strong emotion; *also* : EXCITING

♦ ardent, burning, emotional, fervent, fiery, hot-blooded, impassioned, passionate, red-hot, vehement

char·gé d'af·faires \shär-ˌzhā-də-'far\ *n, pl* **chargés d'affaires** \-ˌzhā-, -ˌzhāz-\ : a diplomat who substitutes for an ambassador or minister

¹**charg·er** \'chär-jər\ *n* : a large platter

²**charg·er** *n* **1** : a device or a worker that charges something **2** : WARHORSE

char·i·ness \'cher-ē-nəs\ *n* : the quality or state of being chary

char·i·ot \'char-ē-ət\ *n* : a 2-wheeled horse-drawn vehicle of ancient times used esp. in war and in races — **char·i·o·teer** \ˌchar-ē-ə-'tir\ *n*

cha·ris·ma \kə-'riz-mə\ *n* ♦ : a personal quality of leadership arousing popular loyalty or enthusiasm — **char·is·mat·ic** \ˌkar-əz-'ma-tik\ *adj*

♦ allure, appeal, attractiveness, captivation, charm, enchantment, fascination, glamour, magic, magnetism

char·i·ta·ble \'char-ə-tə-bəl\ *adj* **1** ♦ : liberal in giving to needy people **2** ♦ : merciful or lenient in judging others — **char·i·ta·ble·ness** *n* — **char·i·ta·bly** \-blē\ *adv*

♦ [1] bountiful, free, generous, liberal, munificent, openhanded, unselfish, unsparing ♦ [2] altruistic, beneficent, benevolent, humanitarian, philanthropic *Ant* self-centered, selfish

char·i·ty \'char-ə-tē\ *n, pl* **-ties** **1** : a disposition to goodwill, kindliness, and sympathy **2** ♦ : an act or feeling of generosity **3** ♦ : the giving of aid to the poor; *also* : ALMS **4** : an institution engaged in relief of the poor **5** : leniency in judging others

♦ [2, 3] alms, benefaction, beneficence, contribution, donation, philanthropy

char·la·tan \'shär-lə-tən\ *n* ♦ : a person making usu. showy pretenses to knowledge or ability : FRAUD

♦ fake, fraud, hoaxer, humbug, mountebank, phony, pretender, quack

Charles·ton \'chärl-stən\ *n* : a lively dance in which the knees are swung in and out and the heels are turned sharply outward on each step

char·ley horse \'chär-lē-ˌhors\ *n* : a muscular pain, cramping, or stiffness from a strain or bruise

¹**charm** \'chärm\ *n* **1** ♦ : a practice or expression believed to have magic power **2** ♦ : something worn about the person to ward off evil or bring good fortune : AMULET **3** : a trait that fascinates or allures **4** ♦ : physical grace or attraction **5** : a small ornament worn on a bracelet or chain **6** : a quark with a charge of +²/₃ and a measured energy of approximately 1.5 billion electron volts

♦ [1] bewitchment, conjuration, enchantment, incantation, spell ♦ [2] amulet, fetish, mascot, talisman *Ant* hoodoo, jinx ♦ [4] allure, appeal, attractiveness, captivation, charisma, enchantment, fascination, glamour, magic, magnetism *Ant* repulsion, repulsiveness

²**charm** *vb* **1** ♦ : to affect by or as if by a magic spell **2** : to protect by or as if by charms **3** : to please, soothe, or delight by compelling attraction : FASCINATE, ENCHANT ⟨∼s customers with his suave manner⟩ — **charm·er** *n*

♦ allure, beguile, bewitch, captivate, enchant, fascinate, wile ♦ bewitch, enchant, hex, spell

charmed \'chärmd\ *adj* : extremely lucky or prosperous ⟨a ∼ life⟩

charm·er *n* **1** : one that charms : ENCHANTER, MAGICIAN **2** : one that pleases, intrigues, or fascinates

charm·ing \'chär-miŋ\ *adj* ♦ : marked by compelling attraction or appeal — **charm·ing·ly** *adv*

♦ alluring, attractive, captivating, elfin, engaging, fascinating, fetching, glamorous, magnetic, seductive

char·nel house \'chärn-ᵊl-\ *n* : a building or chamber in which bodies or bones are deposited

¹**chart** \'chärt\ *n* **1** : an outline map detailing certain geographic aspects of an area : MAP **2** : a sheet giving information in the form of a table, list, or diagram; *also* : GRAPH

²**chart** *vb* **1** : to make a chart of **2** ♦ : to lay out a plan for : PLAN

♦ arrange, blueprint, calculate, design, frame, lay out, map, plan, project, scheme

¹**char·ter** \'chär-tər\ *n* **1** : an official document granting rights or privileges (as to a colony, town, or college) from a sovereign or a governing body **2** : CONSTITUTION **3** : a written instrument from a society creating a branch **4** : a mercantile lease of a ship

²**charter** *vb* **1** : to grant a charter to **2** *Brit* : CERTIFY ⟨∼ed engineer⟩ **3** : to hire, rent, or lease for temporary use — **char·ter·er** *n*

charter member *n* : an original member of an organization

char·treuse \shär-'trüz, -'trüs\ *n* : a brilliant yellow green

char·wom·an \'chär-ˌwu̇-mən\ *n* : a cleaning woman esp. in large buildings

chary \'char-ē\ *adj* **chari·er; -est** **1** : CAUTIOUS, CIRCUMSPECT **2** : SPARING — **char·i·ly** \-ə-lē\ *adv*

¹**chase** \'chās\ *n* **1 a** ♦ : the act of chasing : PURSUIT **b** : HUNTING **2** : something pursued : QUARRY **3** : a tract of unenclosed land used as a game preserve

♦ following, pursuit, tracing

²**chase** *vb* **chased; chas·ing** **1** ♦ : to follow rapidly : PURSUE **2** : to pursue for food or in sport : HUNT **3** : to seek out ⟨*chasing* down clues⟩ **4** ♦ : to cause to depart or flee : drive away **5** : RUSH, HASTEN

♦ [1] dog, follow, hound, pursue, shadow, tag, tail, trace, track, trail ♦ [4] banish, boot (out), bounce, dismiss, drum, eject, expel, oust, rout, run off

³**chase** *vb* **chased; chas·ing** : to decorate (a metal surface) by embossing or engraving

⁴**chase** *n* : FURROW, GROOVE

chas·er \'chā-sər\ *n* **1** : one that chases **2** : a mild drink (as beer) taken after hard liquor

chasm \'ka-zəm\ *n* : a deep cleft in the surface (as of a planet) : GORGE 2

chas·sis \'cha-sē, 'sha-sē\ *n, pl* **chas·sis** \-sēz\ : the supporting frame of a structure (as an automobile or television set)

chaste \'chāst\ *adj* **chast·er; chast·est 1** ♦ : innocent of unlawful sexual intercourse : VIRTUOUS, PURE **2** ♦ : CELIBATE **3** ♦ : pure in thought : MODEST **4** : severe or simple in design

♦ [1, 3] clean, decent, immaculate, modest, pure, virtuous *Ant* immodest, impure, indecent, unchaste, unclean

chaste·ly *adv* ♦ : in a chaste manner

♦ modestly, purely, righteously, virtuously

chas·ten \'chās-ᵊn\ *vb* **1** ♦ : to correct through punishment or suffering : DISCIPLINE **2** : PURIFY — **chas·ten·er** *n*

♦ castigate, chastise, correct, discipline, penalize, punish

chaste·ness *n* : the state or quality of being chaste
chas·tise \chas-'tīz\ *vb* **chas·tised; chas·tis·ing 1** ♦ : to punish esp. bodily **2** ♦ : to censure severely : CASTIGATE

♦ [1, 2] castigate, chasten, correct, discipline, penalize, punish

chas·tise·ment \-mənt, 'chas-təz-\ *n* ♦ : the action, an act, or the means of chastising; *esp* : PUNISHMENT

♦ castigation, correction, desert, discipline, nemesis, penalty, punishment, wrath

chas·ti·ty \'chas-tə-tē\ *n* ♦ : the quality or state of being chaste; *esp* : sexual purity

♦ modesty, purity *Ant* immodesty, impurity, unchastity

cha·su·ble \'cha-zə-bəl, -sə-\ *n* : the outer vestment of the priest at mass
¹chat \'chat\ *n* **1** ♦ : light familiar informal talk **2** : online discussion in a chat room — **chat** *vb*

♦ chatter, chitchat, gabfest, gossip, palaver, rap, talk

²chat *vb* ♦ : to talk in a light and familiar manner

♦ converse, gab, jaw, palaver, patter, prattle, rattle, talk, visit ♦ *usu* **chat with** speak, talk

châ·teau \sha-'tō\ *n, pl* **châ·teaus** \-'tōz\ *or* **châ·teaux** \-'tō, -'tōz\ **1** : a feudal castle in France **2** : a large country house **3** : a French vineyard estate
chat·e·laine \'shat-ᵊl-ˌān\ *n* **1** : the mistress of a chateau **2** : a clasp or hook for a watch, purse, or keys
chat room *n* : a real-time online interactive discussion group
chat·tel \'chat-ᵊl\ *n* **1** ♦ : an item of tangible property other than real estate **2** : an enslaved person held as the legal property of another : BONDMAN

♦ *usu* **chattels** effects, holdings, paraphernalia, possessions, things

¹chat·ter \'cha-tər\ *vb* **1** ♦ : to utter speechlike but meaningless sounds **2** ♦ : to talk idly, incessantly, or fast **3** : to click repeatedly or uncontrollably

♦ [1] babble, drivel, gabble, gibber, jabber, prattle, sputter ♦ [2] chat, converse, gab, jaw, palaver, patter, prattle, rattle, talk, visit

²chatter *n* : idle talk
chat·ter·box \'cha-tər-ˌbäks\ *n* ♦ : one who talks incessantly

♦ jabberer, magpie, talker

chat·ter·er *n* : a person who rambles on and on
chat·ty \'cha-tē\ *adj* **chat·ti·er; -est 1** ♦ : fond of chatting : TALKATIVE ⟨a ∼ neighbor⟩ **2** ♦ : having the style and manner of light familiar conversation ⟨a ∼ letter⟩ — **chat·ti·ly** \-tə-lē\ *adv* — **chat·ti·ness** \-tē-nəs\ *n*

♦ [1] conversational, gabby, garrulous, loquacious, talkative ♦ [2] colloquial, conversational, newsy *Ant* bookish, literary

¹chauf·feur \'shō-fər, shō-'fər\ *n* : a person employed to drive an automobile
²chauffeur *vb* **chauf·feured; chauf·feur·ing 1** : to do the work of a chauffeur **2** : to transport in the manner of a chauffeur
chau·vin·ism \'shō-və-ˌni-zəm\ *n* **1** : excessive or blind patriotism **2** : an attitude of superiority toward members of the opposite sex — **chau·vin·is·tic** \ˌshō-və-'nis-tik\ *adj* — **chau·vin·is·ti·cal·ly** \-ti-k(ə-)lē\ *adv*
chau·vin·ist *n or adj* : one who practices chauvinism
cheap \'chēp\ *adj* **1** : of small cost : INEXPENSIVE **2** : costing little effort to obtain **3** ♦ : of inferior quality or worth : SHODDY **4** : worthy of scorn **5** : not generous or liberal in using, giving, or spending : STINGY — **cheap** *adv* — **cheap·ly** *adv*

♦ [1] cut-rate, inexpensive, low, reasonable *Ant* costly, dear, expensive, high, premium ♦ [3] bad, bum, coarse, common, cut-rate, execrable, inferior, junky, lousy, mediocre, miserable,

poor, rotten, second-rate, shoddy, sleazy, terrible, trashy, wretched *Ant* excellent, fine, first-rate, good, superior, top-notch

cheap·en \'chē-pən\ *vb* **1** ♦ : to make or become cheap or cheaper in price or value **2** : to make tawdry

♦ depreciate, depress, mark down, write off

cheap·ness *n* ♦ : the quality or state of being cheap

♦ closeness, miserliness, parsimony, stinginess, tightness

cheap·skate \'chēp-ˌskāt\ *n* ♦ : a miserly or stingy person; *esp* : one who tries to avoid paying a fair share of costs

♦ miser, niggard, skinflint, tightwad

¹cheat \'chēt\ *vb* **1** ♦ : to deprive of something through fraud or deceit **2** : to practice fraud or trickery **3** : to violate rules (as of a game) dishonestly — **cheat·er** *n*

♦ bleed, chisel, cozen, defraud, fleece, hustle, mulct, rook, shortchange, skin, squeeze, stick, sting, swindle, victimize

²cheat *n* **1** : the act of deceiving : FRAUD, DECEPTION **2** ♦ : one that cheats : a dishonest person

♦ dodger, hoaxer, shark, sharper, swindler, trickster

¹check \'chek\ *n* **1** : exposure of a chess king to an attack **2** : a sudden stoppage of progress **3** : a sudden pause or break **4** ♦ : something that stops or restrains **5** : a standard for testing or evaluation **6** ♦ : a strict or close inspection : a study of by close examination : EXAMINATION **7** : the act of testing or verifying **8** *or Can and Brit* **cheque** : a written order directing a bank to pay money as instructed : DRAFT **9** : a ticket or token showing ownership or identity **10** ♦ : a slip indicating an amount due **11** : a pattern in squares; *also* : a fabric in such a pattern **12** : a mark typically ✓ placed beside an item to show that it has been noted **13** : CRACK, SPLIT

♦ [4] condition, constraint, curb, fetter, limitation, restraint, restriction ♦ [6] audit, checkup, examination, inspection, review, scan, scrutiny, survey ♦ [10] account, bill, invoice, statement, tab

²check *vb* **1** : to put (a chess king) in check **2** ♦ : to slow down or stop **3** ♦ : to restrain the action or force of : CURB **4** : to compare with a source, original, or authority : VERIFY — often used with *out* **5** ♦ : to inspect or test for satisfactory condition **6** : to mark with a check as examined **7** : to consign for shipment for one holding a passenger ticket **8** : to mark into squares **9** : to leave or accept for safekeeping in a checkroom **10** : to prove to be consistent or truthful **11** : CRACK, SPLIT **12** ♦ : to correspond often detail for detail

♦ [2] arrest, catch, draw up, fetch up, halt, hold up, stall, stay, still, stop ♦ [3] bridle, constrain, contain, control, curb, govern, inhibit, regulate, rein, restrain, tame ♦ *usu* **check out** [5] audit, examine, inspect, review, scan, scrutinize, survey ♦ [12] accord, agree, answer, coincide, comport, conform, correspond, dovetail, fit, go, harmonize, jibe, square, tally *Ant* differ (from), disagree (with)

check·book \'chek-ˌbu̇k\ *n* : a book containing blank checks
¹check·er \'che-kər\ *n* : a piece in the game of checkers
²checker *vb* **1** : to variegate with different colors or shades **2** : to vary with contrasting elements ⟨a ∼ed career⟩ **3** : to mark into squares
³checker *n* : one that checks; *esp* : one who checks out purchases in a supermarket
check·er·ber·ry \'che-kər-ˌber-ē\ *n* : WINTERGREEN 1; *also* : the spicy red fruit of this plant
check·er·board \-ˌbȯrd\ *n* : a board of 64 squares of alternate colors used in various games
check·ered \'che-kərd\ *adj* : marked by inconsistent fortune or recurring problems ⟨his ∼ past⟩
check·ers \'che-kərz\ *n* : a game for two played on a checkerboard with each player having 12 pieces
check in *vb* : to report one's presence or arrival (as at a hotel)
check·list \'chek-ˌlist\ *n* **1** ♦ : a list of things to be checked or done **2** ♦ : a comprehensive list

♦ [1, 2] catalog, list, listing, menu, register, registry, roll, roster, schedule, table

check·mate \'chek-ˌmāt\ *vb* **1** ♦ : to thwart completely : FRUSTRATE **2** : to attack (an opponent's king) in chess so that escape is impossible — **checkmate** *n*

♦ baffle, balk, beat, foil, frustrate, thwart

check·off \'chek-ˌȯf\ *n* : the deduction of union dues from a worker's paycheck by the employer
check·out \'che-ˌkau̇t\ *n* **1** : the action or an instance of

checking out **2** : a counter at which checking out is done **3** : the process of examining and testing something as to readiness for intended use

check out *vb* **1** : to settle one's account (as at a hotel) and leave **2** : to total or have totaled the cost of purchases in a store and to make or receive payment for them

check•point \'chek-ˌpȯint\ *n* : a point at which a check is performed

check•room \-ˌrüm, -ˌru̇m\ *n* : a room at which baggage, parcels, or clothing is left for safekeeping

checks and balances *n pl* : a system allowing each branch of a government to restrict the actions of another branch (as by a veto)

check•up \'che-ˌkəp\ *n* ♦ : the act of checking something or someone : EXAMINATION; *esp* : a general physical examination

♦ audit, check, examination, inspection, review, scan, scrutiny, survey

ched•dar \'che-dər\ *n, often cap* : a hard mild to sharp white or yellow cheese of smooth texture

cheek \'chēk\ *n* **1** : the fleshy side part of the face **2** ♦ : insolent boldness and self-assurance : IMPUDENCE, AUDACITY **3** : BUTTOCK 1 — **cheeked** \'chēkt\ *adj*

♦ audacity, brass, brazenness, chutzpah, effrontery, gall, impertinence, impudence, nerve, presumption, sauce, sauciness, temerity

cheek•bone \'chēk-ˌbōn\ *n* : the bone or bony ridge below the eye

cheek•i•ness \-kē-nəs\ *n* : insolence or impudence of speech or behavior

cheeky \'chē-kē\ *adj* **cheek•i•er; -est** ♦ : insolently bold : IMPUDENT, SAUCY — **cheek•i•ly** \-kə-lē\ *adv*

♦ arch, bold, brash, brazen, cocky, fresh, impertinent, impudent, insolent, nervy, sassy, saucy

cheep \'chēp\ *vb* ♦ : to utter faint shrill sounds : PEEP — **cheep** *n*

♦ chirp, peep, pipe, tweet, twitter

¹**cheer** \'chir\ *n* **1** ♦ : state of mind or heart : SPIRIT **2** ♦ : lightness of mind and feeling **3** : hospitable entertainment : WELCOME **4** : food and drink for a feast **5** : something that gladdens **6** : a shout of applause or encouragement

♦ [1] frame, humor (*or* humour), mode, mood, spirit, temper ♦ [2] comfort, consolation, relief, solace ♦ [2] cheerfulness, cheeriness, glee, hilarity, joviality, merriment, mirth

²**cheer** *vb* **1** ♦ : to give hope or courage to : COMFORT — usu. used with *up* **2** : to make glad **3** : to urge on esp. by shouts **4** ♦ : to applaud or show approval of esp. with shouts **5** : to grow or be cheerful — usu. used with *up* — **cheer•er** *n*

♦ *usu* cheer up [1] buoy (up), comfort, embolden, encourage, hearten, inspire, steel ♦ [4] acclaim, applaud, crack up, hail, laud, praise, salute, tout

cheer•ful \'chir-fəl\ *adj* **1** ♦ : having or showing good spirits **2** ♦ : conducive to good spirits : pleasant and bright

♦ [1] blithe, bright, buoyant, cheery, chipper, lightsome, sunny, upbeat *Ant* dour, gloomy, glum, morose, saturnine, sulky, sullen ♦ [2] bright, cheery, glad *Ant* bleak, cheerless, dark, depressing, dismal, dreary, gloomy, gray

cheer•ful•ly *adv* ♦ : in a cheerful manner

♦ gaily, happily, heartily, jovially, merrily, mirthfully

cheer•ful•ness *n* ♦ : the quality or state of being cheerful

♦ cheer, cheeriness, glee, hilarity, joviality, merriment, mirth

cheer•i•ness \-ē-nəs\ *n* ♦ : the quality or state of being cheery

♦ cheer, cheerfulness, glee, hilarity, joviality, merriment, mirth, mirthfulness

cheer•lead•er \'chir-ˌlē-dər\ *n* : a person who directs organized cheering esp. at a sports event

cheer•less \'chir-ləs\ *adj* : lacking qualities that cheer : BLEAK, DISPIRITING — **cheer•less•ly** *adv* — **cheer•less•ness** *n*

cheery \'chir-ē\ *adj* **cheer•i•er; -est** **1** ♦ : marked by cheerfulness or good spirits : CHEERFUL **2** ♦ : causing or suggesting cheerfulness ⟨~ music⟩ — **cheer•i•ly** \-ə-lē\ *adv*

♦ [1] blithe, bright, buoyant, cheerful, chipper, lightsome, sunny, upbeat ♦ [2] bright, cheerful, glad

cheese \'chēz\ *n* : the curd of milk usu. pressed into cakes and cured for use as food

cheese•burg•er \-ˌbər-gər\ *n* : a hamburger topped with cheese

cheese•cake \-ˌkāk\ *n* **1** : a dessert consisting of a creamy fill-

ing usu. containing cheese baked in a shell **2** : photographs of shapely scantily clad women

cheese•cloth \-ˌklȯth\ *n* : a lightweight coarse cotton gauze

cheese•par•ing \-ˌpar-iŋ\ *n* : miserly economizing — **cheese-paring** *adj*

cheese•steak \-ˌstāk\ *n* : a sandwich of thinly sliced beef topped with melted cheese

cheesy \'chē-zē\ *adj* **chees•i•er; -est** **1** : resembling, suggesting, or containing cheese **2** : CHEAP 3

chee•tah \'chē-tə\ *n* : a large long-legged swift-moving spotted cat of Africa and formerly Asia

chef \'shef\ *n* **1** : a cook who manages the kitchen (as of a restaurant) **2** : a person who prepares food for eating : COOK

chef d'oeu•vre \shā-'dœvrᵊ\ *n, pl* **chefs d'oeuvre** *same*\ : MASTERPIECE

chem *abbr* chemical; chemist; chemistry

¹**chem•i•cal** \'ke-mi-kəl\ *adj* **1** : of, relating to, used in, or produced by chemistry **2** : acting or operated or produced by chemicals — **chem•i•cal•ly** \-k(ə-)lē\ *adv*

²**chemical** *n* : a substance obtained by a chemical process or used for producing a chemical effect

chemical engineering *n* : engineering dealing with the industrial application of chemistry

chemical warfare *n* : warfare using incendiary mixtures, smokes, or irritant, burning, or asphyxiating gases

chemical weapon *n* : a weapon used in chemical warfare

che•mise \shə-'mēz\ *n* **1** : a woman's one-piece undergarment **2** : a loose straight-hanging dress

chem•ist \'ke-mist\ *n* **1** : one trained in chemistry **2** *Brit* : PHARMACIST

chem•is•try \'ke-mə-strē\ *n, pl* **-tries** **1** : the science that deals with the composition, structure, and properties of substances and of the changes they undergo **2** : chemical composition or properties ⟨the ~ of gasoline⟩ **3** : a strong mutual attraction; *also* : harmonious interaction among people (as on a team)

che•mo \'kē-mō\ *n* : CHEMOTHERAPY

che•mo•ther•a•py \ˌkē-mō-'ther-ə-pē\ *n* : the use of chemicals in the treatment or control of disease — **che•mo•ther•a•peu•tic** \-ˌther-ə-'pyü-tik\ *adj*

che•nille \shə-'nēl\ *n* : a fabric with a deep fuzzy pile often used for bedspreads and rugs

cheque *Can and Brit var of* ¹CHECK 8

cher•ish \'cher-ish\ *vb* **1** ♦ : to hold dear : feel or treat with care and affection **2** ♦ : to keep deeply in mind — **cher•ish•able** *adj* — **cher•ish•er** *n*

♦ [1] adore, love, worship ♦ [1] appreciate, love, prize, treasure, value ♦ [2] bear, entertain, harbor (*or* harbour), have, hold, nurse

Cher•o•kee \'cher-ə-(ˌ)kē\ *n, pl* **Cherokee** *or* **Cherokees** : a member of an Indigenous people orig. of Tennessee and No. Carolina; *also* : their language

che•root \shə-'rüt\ *n* : a cigar cut square at both ends

cher•ry \'cher-ē\ *n, pl* **cherries** **1** : the small fleshy pale yellow to deep blackish red fruit of a tree related to the roses; *also* : the tree or its wood **2** : a moderate red

chert \'chərt, 'chat\ *n* : a rock resembling flint and consisting essentially of fine crystalline quartz and fibrous chalcedony — **cherty** *adj*

cher•ub \'cher-əb\ *n* **1** *pl* **cher•u•bim** \'cher-ə-ˌbim\ : an angel of the 2d highest rank **2** *pl* **cherubs** : a chubby rosy person — **che•ru•bic** \chə-'rü-bik\ *adj*

chess \'ches\ *n* : a game for two played on a chessboard with each player having 16 pieces — **chess•man** \-ˌman, -mən\ *n*

chess•board \'ches-ˌbȯrd\ *n* : a checkerboard used in the game of chess

chest \'chest\ *n* **1** ♦ : a box, case, or boxlike receptacle for storage or shipping **2** : the part of the body enclosed by the ribs and sternum — **chest•ed** \'ches-təd\ *adj* — **chest•ful** \'chest-ˌfu̇l\ *n*

♦ box, caddy, case, casket, locker, trunk

ches•ter•field \'ches-tər-ˌfēld\ *n* **1** : an overcoat with a velvet collar **2** : a large sofa usu. with upright armrests

chest•nut \'ches-(ˌ)nət\ *n* **1** : the edible nut of any of a genus of trees related to the beech and oaks; *also* : this tree **2** : a grayish to reddish brown **3** : an old joke or story

che•val glass \shə-'val-\ *n* : a full-length mirror that may be tilted in a frame

che•va•lier \ˌshe-və-'lir, shə-'val-ˌyā\ *n* : a member of one of various orders of knighthood or of merit

chev•i•ot \'she-vē-ət\ *n, often cap* **1** : a twilled fabric with a rough nap **2** : a sturdy soft-finished cotton fabric

chev·ron \'she-vrən\ *n* : a sleeve badge of one or more V-shaped or inverted V-shaped stripes worn to indicate rank or service (as in the armed forces)

¹chew \'chü\ *vb* ♦ : to crush, grind, or gnaw (as food) with the teeth — **chew·able** *adj* — **chew·er** *n* — **chew on** : to think about : PONDER ⟨*chew on* the proposals⟩ — **chew the fat** : to make conversation : CHAT

   ♦ bite, champ, chomp, crunch, gnaw, nibble

²chew *n* **1** : an act of chewing **2** : something for chewing

chew out *vb* ♦ : to bawl out : to criticize severely

   ♦ admonish, chide, lecture, rail (at *or* against), rate, rebuke, reprimand, scold

chew over *vb* ♦ : to meditate on : think about reflectively

   ♦ cogitate, consider, contemplate, debate, deliberate, entertain, meditate, mull, ponder, question, ruminate, study, think, weigh

chewy \'chü-ē\ *adj* : requiring much chewing ⟨~ candy⟩

Chey·enne \shī-'an, -'en\ *n, pl* **Cheyenne** *or* **Cheyennes** : a member of an Indigenous people of the western Great Plains of the U.S.; *also* : their language

chg *abbr* **1** change **2** charge

chi \'kī\ *n* : the 22d letter of the Greek alphabet — X or χ

Chi·an·ti \kē-'än-tē, -'an-\ *n* : a dry usu. red wine

chiar·oscu·ro \kē-,är-ə-'skür-ō, -'skyur-\ *n, pl* **-ros** **1** : pictorial representation in terms of light and shade without regard to color **2** : the arrangement or treatment of light and dark parts in a pictorial work of art

¹chic \'shēk\ *n* : STYLISHNESS

²chic *adj* ♦ : cleverly stylish : SMART; *also* : currently fashionable

   ♦ à la mode, fashionable, in, modish, sharp, smart, snappy, stylish

Chi·ca·na \chi-'kä-nə *also* shi-\ *n* : an American woman or girl of Mexican descent — **Chicana** *adj*

chi·cane \shi-'kān\ *n* : CHICANERY

chi·ca·nery \-'kā-nə-rē\ *n, pl* **-ner·ies** ♦ : deception by artful subterfuge or sophistry : TRICKERY

   ♦ artifice, hanky-panky, subterfuge, trickery, wile

Chi·ca·no \chi-'kä-nō\ *n, pl* **-nos** : an American of Mexican descent — **Chicano** *adj*

chi·chi \'shē-(,)shē, 'chē-(,)chē\ *adj* **1** : SHOWY, FRILLY **2** : ARTY, PRECIOUS **3** : CHIC ⟨a ~ restaurant⟩ — **chichi** *n*

chick \'chik\ *n* **1** : a young chicken; *also* : a young bird **2** *sometimes offensive* : a young woman

chick·a·dee \'chi-kə-(,)dē\ *n* : any of several small grayish American birds with black or brown caps

Chick·a·saw \'chi-kə-,sò\ *n, pl* **Chickasaw** *or* **Chickasaws** : a member of an Indigenous people orig. of western Tennessee and adjacent states; *also* : their language

¹chick·en \'chi-kən\ *n* **1** : a common domestic fowl esp. when young; *also* : its flesh used as food **2** ♦ : one who is easily frightened and easily daunted : COWARD

   ♦ coward, craven, dastard, poltroon, recreant, sissy

²chicken *adj* **1** ♦ : being or behaving like a coward : COWARD-LY **2** *slang* : insistent on petty esp. military discipline

   ♦ cowardly, craven, dastardly, pusillanimous, recreant, spineless, yellow

chicken feed *n, slang* : an insignificant sum of money

chick·en·heart·ed \,chi-kən-'här-təd\ *adj* : being or behaving like a coward : COWARDLY

chicken out *vb* : to lose one's courage

chicken pox *n* : an acute contagious virus disease esp. of children characterized by a low fever and vesicles

chicken wire *n* : a light wire netting of hexagonal mesh

chick·pea \'chik-,pē\ *n* : an Asian herb of the legume family cultivated for its short pods with one or two edible seeds; *also* : its seed

chick·weed \'chik-,wēd\ *n* : any of several low-growing small-leaved weeds related to the pinks

chi·cle \'chi-kəl\ *n* : a gum from the latex of a tropical tree used as the chief ingredient of chewing gum

chic·o·ry \'chi-kə-rē\ *n, pl* **-ries** : a usu. blue-flowered herb related to the daisies and grown for its root and for use in salads; *also* : its dried ground root used to flavor or adulterate coffee

chide \'chīd\ *vb* **chid** \'chid\ *or* **chid·ed** \'chī-dəd\; **chid** *or* **chid·den** \'chid-ᵊn\ *or* **chided; chid·ing** ♦ : to speak disapprovingly to

   ♦ admonish, rebuke, reprimand, reproach, reprove ♦ admonish, lecture, rail (at *or* against), rate, rebuke, scold

¹chief \'chēf\ *adj* **1** ♦ : highest in rank **2** ♦ : most important

   ♦ [1] first, foremost, head, high, lead, preeminent, premier, primary, prime, principal, supreme ♦ [2] arch, cardinal, central, dominant, first, foremost, grand, key, main, paramount, predominant

²chief *n* **1** ♦ : the leader of a body or organization : HEAD **2** : the principal or most valuable part — **chief·dom** *n*

   ♦ boss, captain, foreman, head, headman, helmsman, kingpin, leader, taskmaster

chief·ly *adv* ♦ : for the most part : most importantly

   ♦ altogether, basically, generally, largely, mainly, mostly, overall, predominantly, primarily, principally

chief master sergeant *n* : a noncommissioned officer of the highest rank in the air force

chief petty officer *n* : an enlisted person in the navy ranking next below a senior chief petty officer

chief·tain \'chēf-tən\ *n* : a chief esp. of a band, tribe, or clan — **chief·tain·cy** \-sē\ *n* — **chief·tain·ship** *n*

chief warrant officer *n* : a warrant officer of senior rank

chif·fon \shi-'fän, 'shi-,\ *n* : a sheer fabric esp. of silk

chif·fo·nier \,shi-fə-'nir\ *n* : a high narrow chest of drawers

chig·ger \'chi-gər\ *n* : a larval mite that feeds on skin cells and causes intense itching

chi·gnon \'shēn-,yän\ *n* : a knot of hair worn at the back of the head

Chi·hua·hua \chə-'wä-,wä\ *n* : any of a breed of very small large-eared dogs that originated in Mexico

chil·blain \'chil-,blān\ *n* : a sore or inflamed swelling (as on the feet or hands) caused by exposure to cold

child \'chīld\ *n, pl* **chil·dren** \'chil-drən\ **1** ♦ : an unborn or recently born person **2** ♦ : a young person between the periods of infancy and youth **3** : a male or female offspring : SON, DAUGHTER **4** : one strongly influenced by another or by a place or state of affairs — **child·less** *adj* — **child·less·ness** *n* — **child·like** *adj*

   ♦ [1] baby, infant, newborn ♦ [2] cub, juvenile, kid, youngster, youth *Ant* adult, grown-up

child·bear·ing \'chīld-,bar-iŋ\ *n* : of or relating to the process of conceiving, being pregnant with, and giving birth to children : CHILDBIRTH — **childbearing** *adj*

child·birth \-,bərth\ *n* ♦ : the act or process of giving birth to offspring

   ♦ delivery, labor (*or* labour)

child·hood \-,hud\ *n* : the state or period of being a child

child·ish *adj* ♦ : marked by or suggestive of immaturity and lack of poise — **child·ish·ly** *adv* — **child·ish·ness** *n*

   ♦ adolescent, babyish, immature, infantile, juvenile, kiddish *Ant* adult, grown-up, mature

¹child·proof \-,prüf\ *adj* **1** : made to prevent opening or use by children ⟨~ lighters⟩ **2** : made safe for children

²childproof *vb* : to make childproof ⟨~ a house⟩

child's play *n* **1** ♦ : an extremely simple task or act **2** : something that is insignificant

   ♦ breeze, cinch, picnic, pushover, snap

Chil·ean \'chi-lē-ən, chə-'lā-ən\ *n* : a native or inhabitant of Chile — **Chilean** *adj*

chili *or* **chile** *or* **chil·li** \'chi-lē\ *n, pl* **chil·ies** *or* **chil·es** *or* **chil·lies** **1** : a pungent pepper related to the tomato **2** : a thick sauce of meat and chilies **3** : CHILI CON CARNE

chili con car·ne \,chi-lē-kän-'kär-nē\ *n* : a spiced stew of ground beef and chili peppers or chili powder usu. with beans

chili powder *n* : a seasoning made of ground chili peppers and other spices

chili sauce *n* : a spiced tomato sauce usu. made with red and green peppers

¹chill \'chil\ *n* **1** : a feeling of coldness accompanied by shivering **2** ♦ : moderate coldness **3** : a check to enthusiasm or warmth of feeling

   ♦ bite, bitterness, bleakness, nip, rawness, sharpness

²chill *adj* **1** : moderately cold **2** : affected by a penetrating cold : benumbed or shivering with cold : COLD, RAW **3** : cool in manner or feeling : lacking warmth : UNFRIENDLY ⟨a ~ reception⟩ **4** : DEPRESSING, DISPIRITING

³chill *vb* **1** : to make or become cold or chilly **2** : to make cool esp. without freezing — **chill·er** *n*

chill·i·ness *n* : the quality or state of being chilly

chill·ing \'chi-liŋ\ *adj* : gravely disturbing or frightening ⟨a ~ scene⟩

chill out *vb, slang* ♦ : to calm down : RELAX

♦ de-stress, relax, unwind

chilly \'chi-lē\ *adj* **chill·i·er; -est** **1** ♦ : noticeably cold **2** : unpleasantly affected by cold **3** ♦ : lacking warmth of feeling

♦ [1] bitter, bleak, chill, nippy, raw, sharp ♦ [3] chill, cold, cold-blooded, cool, frigid, frosty, glacial, icy, unfriendly, unsympathetic, wintry

¹**chime** \'chīm\ *n* **1** : a set of bells musically tuned **2** : the sound of a set of bells — usu. used in pl. **3** : a musical sound suggesting bells

²**chime** *vb* **chimed; chim·ing** **1** ♦ : to make bell-like sounds **2** : to indicate (as the time of day) by chiming **3** : to be or act in accord : be in harmony

♦ knell, peal, ring, toll

chime in *vb* ♦ : to break into or join in a conversation

♦ break, cut in, interpose, interrupt, intrude

chi·me·ra \kī-'mir-ə, kə-\ *n* **1** : an imaginary monster made up of incongruous parts **2 a** ♦ : an illusion or fabrication of the mind **b** : an impossible dream

♦ conceit, daydream, delusion, dream, fancy, fantasy, figment, hallucination, illusion, phantasm, pipe dream, unreality, vision

chi·mer·i·cal \ki-'mer-i-kəl\ *also* **chi·me·ric** \-ik\ *adj* **1** ♦ : existing only as the product of unchecked imagination : fantastically visionary or improbable **2** : given to fantastic schemes

♦ fabulous, fanciful, fantastic, fictitious, imaginary, made-up, mythical, phantom, pretend, unreal

chim·ney \'chim-nē\ *n, pl* **chimneys** **1** : a vertical structure extending above the roof of a building for carrying off smoke **2** : a glass tube around a lamp flame

chimp \'chimp\ *n* : CHIMPANZEE

chim·pan·zee \,chim-,pan-'zē, chim-'pan-zē\ *n* : an African ape related to the much larger gorilla

¹**chin** \'chin\ *n* : the part of the face below the lower lip including the prominence of the lower jaw — **chin·less** *adj*

²**chin** *vb* **chinned; chin·ning** : to raise (oneself) while hanging by the hands until the chin is level with the support

chi·na \'chī-nə\ *n* : porcelain ware; *also* : domestic pottery in general

Chi·na·town \-,taun\ *n* : the Chinese quarter of a city

chinch bug \'chinch-\ *n* : a small black and white bug destructive to cereal grasses

chin·chil·la \chin-'chi-lə\ *n* **1** : either of two small So. American rodents with soft pearl-gray fur; *also* : this fur **2** : a heavy long-napped woolen cloth

chine \'chīn\ *n* : the back or spine of an animal or human : BACKBONE, SPINE; *also* : a cut of meat including all or part of the backbone

Chi·nese \chī-'nēz, -'nēs\ *n, pl* **Chinese** **1** : a native or inhabitant of China **2** : any of a group of related languages of China — **Chinese** *adj*

Chinese cabbage *n* **1** : BOK CHOY **2** : an Asian garden plant related to the cabbage and widely grown in the U.S. for its tight elongate cylindrical heads of pale green to cream-colored leaves

Chinese checkers *n* : a game in which each player in turn transfers a set of marbles from a home point to the opposite point of a pitted 6-pointed star

Chinese gooseberry *n* : a subtropical vine that bears kiwifruit; *also* : KIWIFRUIT

Chinese lantern *n* : a collapsible translucent cover for a light

¹**chink** \'chiŋk\ *n* ♦ : a small crack or fissure

♦ cleft, crack, cranny, crevice, fissure, rift, split

²**chink** *vb* : to fill the chinks of : stop up

³**chink** *n* : a slight sharp metallic sound

⁴**chink** *vb* ♦ : to make a slight sharp metallic sound

♦ jingle, tinkle

chi·no \'chē-nō\ *n, pl* **chinos** **1** : a usu. khaki cotton twill **2** *pl* : an article of clothing made of chino

Chi·nook \shə-'nuk, chə-, -'nük\ *n, pl* **Chinook** *or* **Chinooks** : a member of an Indigenous people of Oregon; *also* : their language

chintz \'chints\ *n* : a usu. glazed printed cotton cloth

chintzy \'chint-sē\ *adj* **chintz·i·er; -est** **1** : decorated with or as if with chintz **2** : GAUDY, CHEAP **3** : STINGY

chin–up \'chi-,nəp\ *n* : the act of chinning oneself

¹**chip** \'chip\ *n* **1** ♦ : a small usu. thin and flat piece (as of wood) cut or broken off **2** : a thin crisp morsel of food **3** : a counter used in games (as poker) **4** *pl* : something generally accepted as

a means of payment : MONEY **5** ♦ : a flaw left after a chip is removed **6** : INTEGRATED CIRCUIT **7** : a very small slice of silicon containing electronic circuits

♦ [1] flake, splinter ♦ [5] hack, indentation, nick, notch

²**chip** *vb* **chipped; chip·ping** **1** : to cut or break chips from **2** : to break off in small pieces at the edges **3** : to play a chip shot

chip in *vb* ♦ : to give money or assistance to an enterprise : CONTRIBUTE

♦ contribute, kick in, pitch in

chip·munk \'chip-,məŋk\ *n* : any of a genus of small striped No. American and Asian rodents closely related to the squirrels and marmots

chi·pot·le \chə-'pōt-lā\ *n* : a smoked and usu. dried jalapeño pepper

chipped beef \'chipt-\ *n* : smoked and usu. dried beef sliced thin

¹**chip·per** \'chi-pər\ *n* : one that chips

²**chipper** *adj* **1** ♦ : being high in spirits : CHEERFUL **2** ♦ : being in good health : being in a state of physical well-being

♦ [1] blithe, bright, buoyant, cheerful, cheery, lightsome, sunny, upbeat ♦ [2] able-bodied, fit, hale, healthy, hearty, robust, sound, well, whole, wholesome

Chip·pe·wa \'chi-pə-,wò, -,wä, -,wā, -wə\ *n, pl* **Chippewa** *or* **Chippewas** : OJIBWA

chip shot *n* : a short usu. low shot to the green in golf

chi·rog·ra·phy \kī-'rä-grə-fē\ *n* : HANDWRITING, PENMANSHIP — **chi·ro·graph·ic** \,kī-rə-'gra-fik\ *adj*

chi·rop·o·dy \kə-'rä-pə-dē, shə-\ *n* : PODIATRY — **chi·rop·o·dist** \-dist\ *n*

chi·ro·prac·tic \'kī-rə-,prak-tik\ *n* : a system of therapy based esp. on manipulation of body structures — **chi·ro·prac·tor** \-tər\ *n*

¹**chirp** \'chərp\ *n* : a short sharp sound characteristic of a small bird or cricket

²**chirp** *vb* ♦ : to make a usu. repetitive short sharp sound

♦ cheep, peep, pipe, tweet, twitter

¹**chis·el** \'chi-zəl\ *n* : a metal tool with a sharpened edge at one end used to chip, carve, or cut into a solid material (as wood or stone)

²**chisel** *vb* **-eled** *or* **-elled; -el·ing** *or* **-el·ling** **1** : to work with or as if with a chisel **2 a** ♦ : to obtain something from by unfair practices : CHEAT **b** : to obtain by shrewd often unfair methods — **chis·el·er** *n*

♦ bleed, cheat, cozen, defraud, fleece, hustle, mulct, rook, short-change, skin, squeeze, stick, sting, swindle, victimize

¹**chit** \'chit\ *n* **1** : CHILD **2** : a pert young woman

²**chit** *n* : a signed voucher for a small debt

chit·chat \'chit-,chat\ *n* ♦ : casual or trifling conversation — **chitchat** *vb*

♦ chat, chatter, gabfest, gossip, palaver, rap, talk

chi·tin \'kīt-ᵊn\ *n* : a sugar polymer that forms part of the hard outer integument esp. of insects — **chi·tin·ous** *adj*

chit·ter·lings *or* **chit·lins** \'chit-lənz\ *n pl* : the intestines of hogs esp. when prepared as food

chi·val·ric \shə-'val-rik\ *adj* : relating to chivalry : CHIVALROUS

chiv·al·rous \'shi-vəl-rəs\ *adj* **1** : of or relating to chivalry **2** ♦ : marked by honor, courtesy, and generosity **3** : marked by gracious courtesy esp. to women — **chiv·al·rous·ly** *adv* — **chiv·al·rous·ness** *n*

♦ gallant, great, greathearted, high, high-minded, lofty, lordly, magnanimous, noble, sublime

chiv·al·ry \'shi-vəl-rē\ *n, pl* **-ries** **1** : mounted men-at-arms **2** : the system or practices of knighthood **3** : the spirit or character of the ideal knight

chive \'chīv\ *n* : an herb related to the onion that has leaves used for flavoring

chla·myd·ia \klə-'mi-dē-ə\ *n, pl* **-i·ae** \-dē-,ē\ **1** : any of a genus of bacteria that cause various diseases of the eye and urogenital tract **2** : a disease or infection caused by chlamydiae

chlo·ral hydrate \'klōr-əl-\ *n* : a white crystalline compound used as a hypnotic and sedative

chlor·dane \'klōr-,dān\ *n* : a highly chlorinated persistent insecticide

chlo·ride \'klōr-,īd\ *n* : a compound of chlorine with another element or group

chlo·ri·nate \'klōr-ə-,nāt\ *vb* **-nat·ed; -nat·ing** : to treat or combine with chlorine or a chlorine compound — **chlo·ri·na·tion** \,klōr-ə-'nā-shən\ *n* — **chlo·ri·na·tor** \'klōr-ə-,nā-tər\ *n*

chlo·rine \'klōr-,ēn\ *n* : a nonmetallic chemical element that is found alone as a strong-smelling greenish yellow irritating gas and is used as a bleach, oxidizing agent, and disinfectant

chlo·rite \'klōr-ˌīt\ *n* : a usu. green mineral found with and resembling mica

chlo·ro·flu·o·ro·car·bon \ˌklōr-ə-ˈflōr-ə-ˌkär-bən, -ˈflur-\ *n* : any of several gaseous compounds that contain carbon, chlorine, fluorine, and sometimes hydrogen and are used esp. as solvents, refrigerants, and aerosol propellants

¹**chlo·ro·form** \'klōr-ə-ˌfōrm\ *n* : a colorless heavy fluid with etherlike odor used as a solvent and anesthetic

²**chloroform** *vb* : to treat with chloroform to produce anesthesia or death

chlo·ro·phyll \-ˌfil\ *n* : the green coloring matter of plants that functions in photosynthesis

chm *abbr* chairman

chock \'chäk\ *n* : a wedge for steadying something or for blocking the movement of a wheel — **chock** *vb*

chock·a·block \'chä-kə-ˌbläk\ *adj* : very full : CROWDED

chock-full *or* **chock·ful** \'chək-ˈful, 'chäk-\ *adj* ♦ : full to the limit : CRAMMED

♦ brimful, crowded, fat, fraught, full, loaded, packed, replete

choc·o·late \'chä-k(ə-)lət, 'chó-\ *n* **1** : a food prepared from ground roasted cacao beans; *also* : a drink prepared from this **2** : a candy made of or with a coating of chocolate **3** : a dark brown color — **choc·o·laty** *or* **choc·o·lat·ey** \-k(ə-)lə-tē\ *adj*

Choc·taw \'chäk-ˌtò\ *n, pl* **Choctaw** *or* **Choctaws** : a member of an Indigenous people orig. of Mississippi and Alabama; *also* : their language

¹**choice** \'chòis\ *n* **1** ♦ : the act of choosing : SELECTION **2** ♦ : the power or opportunity of choosing : OPTION **3** ♦ : the best part **4** : a person or thing selected **5** : a variety offered for selection

♦ [1] election, selection ♦ [2] alternative, discretion, option, pick, preference, way ♦ [3] best, cream, elect, elite, fat, flower, pick, prime

²**choice** *adj* **choic·er; choic·est 1** : worthy of being chosen **2** : selected with care **3** ♦ : of high quality

♦ dainty, delicate, elegant, exquisite, rare, select

choir \'kwī(-ə)r\ *n* **1** ♦ : an organized company of singers (as in a church service) **2** : the part of a church occupied by the singers or by the clergy

♦ chorale, chorus

choir·boy \'kwī(-ə)r-ˌbòi\ *n* : a boy member of a church choir

choir·mas·ter \-ˌmas-tər\ *n* : the director of a choir (as in a church)

¹**choke** \'chōk\ *vb* **choked; chok·ing 1** ♦ : to hinder breathing (as by obstructing the trachea) : STRANGLE **2** : to check the growth or action of **3** ♦ : to obstruct by filling up or clogging : CLOG, OBSTRUCT **4** : to enrich the fuel mixture of (a motor) by restricting the carburetor air intake **5** : to perform badly in a critical situation

♦ [1] smother, stifle, strangle, suffocate ♦ [1] garrote, strangle, throttle ♦ [3] block, clog, close (off), congest, dam, jam, obstruct, plug (up), stop (up), stuff

²**choke** *n* **1** : the act of choking **2** : a narrowing in size toward the muzzle in the bore of a gun **3** : a valve for choking a gasoline engine

chok·er \'chō-kər\ *n* : something (as a necklace) worn tightly around the neck

chol·er \'kä-lər, 'kō-\ *n* : a tendency toward anger : IRASCIBILITY

chol·era \'kä-lə-rə\ *n* : any of several bacterial diseases usu. marked by severe vomiting and dysentery

chol·er·ic \'kä-lə-rik, kə-ˈler-ik\ *adj* **1** ♦ : easily moved to often unreasonable or excessive anger : hot-tempered **2** : ANGRY, IRATE

♦ crabby, cranky, cross, crotchety, grouchy, grumpy, irascible, irritable, peevish, perverse, petulant, short-tempered, snappish, snappy, snippy, testy, waspish

cho·les·ter·ol \kə-ˈles-tə-ˌròl\ *n* : a physiologically important waxy steroid alcohol found in animal tissues and in high concentrations implicated as a cause of arteriosclerosis

chomp \'chämp, 'chòmp\ *vb* ♦ : to chew or bite on something heavily

♦ bite, champ, chew, crunch, gnaw, nibble

choose \'chüz\ *vb* **chose** \'chōz\; **cho·sen** \'chōz-ᵊn\; **choos·ing** \'chü-ziŋ\ **1** ♦ : to select esp. after consideration **2** ♦ : to make a final choice or judgment about : DECIDE **3** : to have a preference for — **choos·er** *n*

♦ [1] cull, elect, handpick, name, opt, pick, prefer, select, single, take **Ant** decline, refuse, reject, turn down ♦ [2] conclude, decide, determine, figure, opt, resolve

choosy *or* **choos·ey** \'chü-zē\ *adj* **choos·i·er; -est** ♦ : very particular in making choices

♦ demanding, exacting, particular, picky, selective

¹**chop** \'chäp\ *vb* **chopped; chop·ping 1** ♦ : to cut or sever usu. by repeated blows **2** ♦ : to cut into small pieces : MINCE **3** : to strike (a ball) with a short quick downward stroke

♦ [1] cut, fell, hew ♦ [2] hash, mince

²**chop** *n* **1** : a sharp downward blow or stroke **2** : a small cut of meat often including part of a rib **3** : a short abrupt motion (as of a wave)

³**chop** *n* **1** : an official seal or stamp **2** : a mark on goods to indicate quality or kind; *also* : QUALITY, GRADE

chop·house \'chäp-ˌhaùs\ *n* : RESTAURANT

chop·per \'chä-pər\ *n* **1** : one that chops **2** *pl, slang* : TEETH **3** : HELICOPTER

chop·pi·ness \'chä-pē-nəs\ *n* : the quality or state of being choppy

¹**chop·py** \'chä-pē\ *adj* **chop·pi·er; -est 1** : rough with small waves ⟨a ∼ sea⟩ **2** ♦ : interrupted by ups and downs : moving along with fits and starts **3** ♦ : lacking orderly continuity, arrangement, or relevance : DISCONNECTED ⟨short ∼ sentences⟩ — **chop·pi·ly** \-pə-lē\ *adv*

♦ [2] casual, discontinuous, erratic, fitful, intermittent, irregular, occasional, spasmodic, sporadic, spotty, unsteady ♦ [3] disconnected, disjointed, unconnected

²**choppy** *adj* **chop·pi·er; -est** : CHANGEABLE, VARIABLE ⟨a ∼ wind⟩

chops \'chäps\ *n pl* **1** : the fleshy covering of the jaws **2** : expertise in a particular field or activity ⟨acting ∼⟩

chop·stick \'chäp-ˌstik\ *n* : one of a pair of sticks used chiefly in Asian countries for lifting food to the mouth

chop su·ey \chäp-ˈsü-ē\ *n, pl* **chop sueys** : a dish made of vegetables (as bean sprouts, bamboo shoots, water chestnuts, onions, mushrooms) and meat or fish and served with rice

cho·ral \'kōr-əl\ *adj* : of, relating to, or sung by a choir or chorus or in chorus — **cho·ral·ly** *adv*

cho·rale \kə-ˈral, -ˈräl\ *n* **1** ♦ : a hymn or psalm sung in church; *also* : a harmonization of a traditional melody **2** : a group formed to sing church music : CHORUS, CHOIR

♦ anthem, canticle, carol, hymn, psalm, spiritual

¹**chord** \'kòrd\ *n* : three or more musical tones sounded simultaneously

²**chord** *n* **1** : CORD 2 **2** : a straight line joining two points on a curve

chore \'chōr\ *n* **1** *pl* : the daily light work of a household or farm **2** ♦ : a routine task or job **3** : a difficult or disagreeable task

♦ assignment, duty, job, stint, task

cho·rea \kə-ˈrē-ə\ *n* : a nervous disorder marked by spasmodic uncontrolled movements

cho·re·og·ra·phy \ˌkōr-ē-ˈä-grə-fē\ *n, pl* **-phies** : the art of composing and arranging dances and esp. ballets — **cho·re·o·graph** \'kōr-ē-ə-ˌgraf\ *vb* — **cho·re·og·ra·pher** \ˌkōr-ē-ˈä-grə-fər\ *n* — **cho·reo·graph·ic** \ˌkōr-ē-ə-ˈgra-fik\ *adj* — **cho·reo·graph·i·cal·ly** \-fi-k(ə-)lē\ *adv*

cho·ris·ter \'kōr-ə-stər\ *n* : a singer in a choir

¹**chor·tle** \'chòrt-ᵊl\ *vb* **chor·tled; chor·tling** : to laugh or chuckle esp. in satisfaction or exultation

²**chortle** *n* ♦ : a sound expressive of pleasure or exultation

♦ cackle, laugh, laughter, snicker, titter

¹**cho·rus** \'kōr-əs\ *n* **1** ♦ : an organized company of singers : CHOIR **2** : a group of dancers and singers (as in a musical comedy) **3** : a part of a song repeated at intervals **4** : a composition to be sung by a chorus; *also* : group singing **5** : sounds uttered by a number of persons or animals together ⟨a ∼ of boos⟩

♦ choir, chorale

²**chorus** *vb* : to sing or utter in chorus

chose *past of* CHOOSE

cho·sen \'chōz-ᵊn\ *adj* ♦ : selected or marked for special favor or privilege

♦ elect, select

¹**chow** \'chaù\ *n* ♦ : material that is taken or absorbed into the body in order to sustain growth and to furnish energy : FOOD

♦ fare, food, grub, meat, provender, provisions, viands, victuals

²chow *vb* : EAT — often used with *down*

³chow *n* : CHOW CHOW

chow·chow \'chaü-ˌchaü\ *n* : chopped mixed pickles in mustard sauce

chow chow \'chaü-ˌchaü\ *n* : any of a breed of thick-coated straight-legged muscular dogs of Chinese origin with a blue= black tongue and a short tail curled close to the back

chow·der \'chaü-dər\ *n* : a soup or stew made from seafood or vegetables and containing milk or tomatoes

chow mein \'chaü-'mān\ *n* : a seasoned stew of shredded or diced meat, mushrooms, and vegetables that is usu. served with fried noodles

chrism \'kri-zəm\ *n* : consecrated oil used esp. in baptism, confirmation, and ordination

Christ \'krīst\ *n* : Jesus esp. as the Messiah — **Christ·like** *adj* — **Christ·ly** *adj*

chris·ten \'kris-ᵊn\ *vb* 1 : BAPTIZE 2 ♦ : to name at baptism 3 ♦ : to name or dedicate (as a ship) by a ceremony suggestive of baptism — **chris·ten·ing** *n*

  ♦ [2, 3] baptize, call, denominate, designate, dub, entitle, label, name, style, term, title

Chris·ten·dom \'kris-ᵊn-dəm\ *n* 1 : CHRISTIANITY 2 : the part of the world in which Christianity prevails

¹Chris·tian \'kris-chən\ *n* : an adherent of Christianity

²Christian *adj* 1 : of or relating to Christianity 2 : based on or conforming with Christianity 3 : of or relating to a Christian 4 : professing Christianity

chris·ti·a·nia \ˌkris-chē-'a-nē-ə, ˌkris-tē-\ *n* : CHRISTIE

Chris·ti·an·i·ty \ˌkris-chē-'a-nə-tē\ *n* : the religion derived from Jesus Christ, based on the Bible as sacred scripture, and professed by Christians

Chris·tian·ize \'kris-chə-ˌnīz\ *vb* **-ized; -iz·ing** : to make Christian

Christian name *n* : a name that precedes one's surname : GIVEN NAME

Christian Science *n* : a religion and system of healing founded by Mary Baker Eddy and taught by the Church of Christ, Scientist — **Christian Scientist** *n*

chris·tie *or* **chris·ty** \'kris-tē\ *n, pl* **christies** : a skiing turn made by shifting body weight forward and skidding into a turn with parallel skis

Christ·mas \'kris-məs\ *n* : December 25 celebrated as a church festival in commemoration of the birth of Christ and observed as a legal holiday

Christmas club *n* : a savings account in which regular deposits are made to provide money for Christmas shopping

Christ·mas·tide \'kris-məs-ˌtīd\ *n* ♦ : the season of Christmas

  ♦ Christmastime, Noel, yuletide

Christ·mas·time \-ˌtīm\ *n* ♦ : the Christmas season

  ♦ Christmastide, Noel, yuletide

chro·mat·ic \krō-'ma-tik\ *adj* 1 : of or relating to color 2 : proceeding by half steps of the musical scale — **chro·mat·i·cism** \-tə-ˌsi-zəm\ *n*

chro·mato·graph \krō-'ma-tə-ˌgraf\ *n* : an instrument used in chromatography

chro·ma·tog·ra·phy \ˌkrō-mə-'tä-grə-fē\ *n* : the separation of a complex mixture into its component compounds as a result of the different rates at which the compounds travel through or over a stationary substance due to differing affinities for the substance — **chro·mato·graph·ic** \krō-ˌma-tə-'gra-fik\ *adj* — **chro·mato·graph·i·cal·ly** \-fi-k(ə-)lē\ *adv*

chrome \'krōm\ *n* 1 : CHROMIUM 2 : a chromium pigment 3 : something plated with an alloy of chromium

chro·mi·um \'krō-mē-əm\ *n* : a bluish white metallic element used esp. in alloys and chrome plating

chro·mo·some \'krō-mə-ˌsōm, -ˌzōm\ *n* : any of the rod= shaped or threadlike DNA-containing structures of cellular organisms that contain most or all of the genes of the organism — **chro·mo·som·al** \ˌkrō-mə-'sō-məl, -'zō-\ *adj*

chro·mo·sphere \'krō-mə-ˌsfir\ *n* : the lower part of a star's atmosphere

chron *abbr* 1 chronicle 2 chronological; chronology

Chron *abbr* Chronicles

chron·ic \'krä-nik\ *adj* 1 : marked by long duration or frequent recurrence ⟨a ∼ disease⟩ 2 ♦ : being such habitually : HABITUAL ⟨a ∼ grumbler⟩ — **chron·i·cal·ly** \-ni-k(ə-)lē\ *adv*

  ♦ confirmed, habitual, inveterate

chronic fatigue syndrome *n* : a disorder of unknown cause that is characterized by persistent profound fatigue

¹chron·i·cle \'krä-ni-kəl\ *n* ♦ : an account of events arranged in the order of time : HISTORY, NARRATIVE

  ♦ account, history, narrative, record, report, story

²chronicle *vb* **-cled; -cling** : to record in or as if in a chronicle

chron·i·cler *n* : a writer or compiler of a chronicle

Chronicles *n* : either of two books of the Jewish and Christian Scripture

chro·no·graph \'krä-nə-ˌgraf\ *n* : an instrument for measuring and recording time intervals with accuracy — **chro·no·graph·ic** \ˌkrä-nə-'gra-fik\ *adj* — **chro·nog·ra·phy** \krə-'nä-grə-fē\ *n*

chro·nol·o·gy \krə-'nä-lə-jē\ *n, pl* **-gies** 1 : the science that deals with measuring time and dating events 2 : a chronological list or table 3 : arrangement of events in the order of their occurrence — **chro·no·log·i·cal** \ˌkrän-ᵊl-'ä-ji-kəl\ *adj* — **chro·no·log·i·cal·ly** \-k(ə-)lē\ *adv* — **chro·nol·o·gist** \krə-'nä-lə-jist\ *n*

chro·nom·e·ter \krə-'nä-mə-tər\ *n* : a very accurate timepiece

chrys·a·lid \'kri-sə-ləd\ *n* : CHRYSALIS

chrys·a·lis \'kri-sə-ləs\ *n, pl* **chry·sal·i·des** \kri-'sa-lə-ˌdēz\ *or* **chrys·a·lis·es** : an insect pupa in a firm case without a cocoon

chry·san·the·mum \kri-'san-thə-məm\ *n* : any of various plants related to the daisies including some grown for their showy flowers or for medicinal products or insecticides; *also* : a flower of a chrysanthemum

chub \'chəb\ *n, pl* **chub** *or* **chubs** : any of various small freshwater fishes related to the carp

chub·bi·ness *n* : the quality or state of being chubby

chub·by \'chə-bē\ *adj* **chub·bi·er; -est** ♦ : short, thick, and well-rounded : PLUMP

  ♦ corpulent, fat, fleshy, full, gross, obese, overweight, plump, portly, rotund, round

¹chuck \'chək\ *vb* 1 : to give a pat or tap 2 ♦ : to throw with a short action of the arm or hand : TOSS 3 : DISCARD; *also* : EJECT 4 : to have done with

  ♦ cast, catapult, dash, fire, fling, heave, hurl, hurtle, launch, peg, pelt, pitch, sling, throw, toss

²chuck *n* 1 : a light pat under the chin 2 : TOSS

³chuck *n* 1 : a cut of beef including most of the neck and the parts around the shoulder blade and the first three ribs 2 : a device for holding parts or a tool in a machine (as a lathe)

chuck·hole \'chək-ˌhōl\ *n* : POTHOLE

¹chuck·le \'chə-kəl\ *vb* **chuck·led; chuck·ling** : to laugh in a quiet hardly audible manner

²chuckle *n* : a quiet hardly audible laugh

chuck wagon *n* : a wagon equipped with a stove and food supplies

¹chug \'chəg\ *n* : a dull explosive sound made by or as if by a laboring engine

²chug *vb* **chugged; chug·ging** : to move or go with chugs

chuk·ka \'chə-kə\ *n* : a usu. ankle-length leather boot

chuk·ker \'chə-kər\ *also* **chuk·ka** \'chə-kə\ *n* : a playing period of a polo game

¹chum \'chəm\ *n* ♦ : a close friend

  ♦ buddy, comrade, crony, familiar, friend, intimate, pal

²chum *vb* **chummed; chum·ming** 1 : to room together 2 ♦ : to be a close friend

  ♦ associate, consort, fraternize, hang around, hobnob, pal

chum·mi·ness \-mē-nəs\ *n* : the quality or state of being chummy

chum·my \'chə-mē\ *adj* **chum·mi·er; -est** ♦ : quite friendly : INTIMATE — **chum·mi·ly** \-mə-lē\ *adv* — **chum·mi·ness** \-mē-nəs\ *n*

  ♦ bosom, close, familiar, friendly, intimate, thick

chump \'chəmp\ *n* : stupid lout : FOOL, BLOCKHEAD

chunk \'chəŋk\ *n* 1 ♦ : a short thick piece 2 : a sizable amount

  ♦ blob, clod, clump, glob, gob, hunk, lump, nub, wad

chunky \'chəŋ-kē\ *adj* **chunk·i·er; -est** 1 ♦ : compact, sturdy, and thick in build : STOCKY 2 : containing chunks

  ♦ dumpy, heavyset, squat, stocky, stout, stubby, stumpy, thickset

church \'chərch\ *n* 1 : a building for public and esp. Christian worship 2 *often cap* : the whole body of Christians 3 : DENOMINATION 4 : a group of persons assembled for worship : CONGREGATION 5 : public divine worship

church·go·er \'chərch-ˌgō-(ə)r\ *n* : one who habitually attends church — **church·go·ing** *adj or n*

church·less \'chərch-ləs\ *adj* : not affiliated with a church

church·man \'chərch-mən\ *n* **1** : CLERGYMAN **2** : a member of a church

church·war·den \'chərch-,word-ᵊn\ *n* : WARDEN 5

church·yard \-,yärd\ *n* : a yard that belongs to a church and is often used as a burial ground

churl \'chərl\ *n* **1** : a medieval peasant **2** : RUSTIC **3** ♦ : a rude ill-bred person — **churl·ish** *adj* — **churl·ish·ly** *adv* — **churl·ish·ness** *n*

♦ beast, boor, clown, creep, cretin, cur, heel, jerk, joker, louse, lout, skunk, slob, snake

churl·ish *adj* ♦ : marked by a lack of civility or graciousness — **churl·ish·ly** *adv* — **churl·ish·ness** *n*

♦ boorish, clownish, loutish, uncouth

¹churn \'chərn\ *n* : a container in which milk or cream is violently agitated in making butter

²churn *vb* **1** : to stir in a churn; *also* : to make (butter) by such stirring **2** ♦ : to stir or shake around esp. violently **3** ♦ : to experience violent motion or agitation

♦ [2] agitate, stir, swirl, whirl ♦ [3] boil, roil, seethe

churn out *vb* : to produce mechanically or in large quantity

chute \'shüt\ *n* **1** : an inclined surface, trough, or passage down or through which something may pass ⟨a coal ∼⟩ ⟨a mail ∼⟩ **2** : PARACHUTE

chut·ney \'chət-nē\ *n, pl* **chutneys** : a thick sauce containing fruits, vinegar, sugar, and spices

chutz·pah \'hut-spə, 'kut-, -(,)spä\ *n* ♦ : supreme self-confidence

♦ audacity, brass, brazenness, cheek, effrontery, gall, nerve, presumption, sauce, sauciness, temerity

CIA *abbr* Central Intelligence Agency

cía *abbr* company

cia·bat·ta \chə-'bä-tə\ *n* : a flat bread with a moist interior and a crispy crust

ciao \'chaù\ *interj* — used to express greeting or farewell

ci·ca·da \sə-'kā-də\ *n* : any of a family of stout-bodied insects related to the aphids and having wide blunt heads and large transparent wings

ci·ca·trix \'si-kə-,triks\ *n, pl* **ci·ca·tri·ces** \,si-kə-'trī-,sēz\ : a scar resulting from formation and contraction of fibrous tissue in a wound

ci·ce·ro·ne \,si-sə-'rō-nē, ,chē-chə-\ *n, pl* **-ni** \-(,)nē\ : a guide who conducts sightseers

CID *abbr* Criminal Investigation Department

ci·der \'sī-dər\ *n* : juice pressed from fruit (as apples) and used as a beverage, vinegar, or flavoring

cie *abbr* company

ci·gar \si-'gär\ *n* : a roll of tobacco for smoking

cig·a·rette \,si-gə-'ret, 'si-gə-,ret\ *n* : a slender roll of cut tobacco enclosed in paper for smoking

cig·a·ril·lo \,si-gə-'ri-lō, -'rē-ō\ *n, pl* **-los** **1** : a very small cigar **2** : a cigarette wrapped in tobacco rather than paper

ci·lan·tro \si-'län-trō, -'lan-\ *n* : leaves of coriander used as a flavoring or garnish; *also* : the coriander plant

cil·i·ate \'si-lē-,āt\ *n* : any of a group of protozoans characterized by cilia

cil·i·um \'si-lē-əm\ *n, pl* **-ia** \-lē-ə\ **1** : a minute short hairlike process; *esp* : one of a cell **2** : EYELASH

C in C *abbr* commander in chief

¹cinch \'sinch\ *n* **1** : a girth for a pack or saddle **2** ♦ : a thing done with ease

♦ breeze, child's play, picnic, pushover, snap *Ant* chore, headache, labor

²cinch *vb* ♦ : to make certain : ASSURE

♦ assure, ensure, guarantee, guaranty, insure, secure

cin·cho·na \sin-'kō-nə\ *n* : any of a genus of So. American trees related to the madder; *also* : the bitter quinine-containing bark of a cinchona

cinc·ture \'siŋk-chər\ *n* ♦ : an article of dress encircling the body usu. at the waist : BELT, SASH

♦ belt, cummerbund, girdle, sash

cin·der \'sin-dər\ *n* **1** : SLAG **2** *pl* : ASHES **3** : a hot piece of partly burned wood or coal **4** : a fragment of lava from an erupting volcano — **cinder** *vb* — **cin·dery** *adj*

cinder block *n* : a building block made of cement and coal cinders

cin·e·ma \'si-nə-mə\ *n* **1** : a motion-picture theater **2** : the film industry : MOVIES — **cin·e·mat·ic** \,si-nə-'ma-tik\ *adj*

cin·e·ma·theque \,si-nə-mə-'tek\ *n* : a small movie house specializing in avant-garde films

cin·e·ma·tog·ra·phy \,si-nə-mə-'tä-grə-fē\ *n* : motion-picture photography — **cin·e·ma·tog·ra·pher** *n* — **cin·e·mat·o·graph·ic** \-,ma-tə-'gra-fik\ *adj*

cin·e·plex \'si-nə-,pleks\ *n* : a complex that houses several movie theaters

cin·er·ar·i·um \,si-nə-'rer-ē-əm\ *n, pl* **-ia** \-ē-ə\ : a place to receive the ashes of the cremated dead — **cin·er·ary** \'si-nə-,rer-ē\ *adj*

cin·na·bar \'si-nə-,bär\ *n* : a red mineral that is the only important ore of mercury

cin·na·mon \'si-nə-mən\ *n* : a spice prepared from the highly aromatic bark of any of several trees related to the true laurel; *also* : a tree that yields cinnamon

cinque·foil \'siŋk-,fȯil, 'saŋk-\ *n* : any of a genus of plants related to the roses with leaves having five lobes

¹ci·pher \'sī-fər\ *n* **1** ♦ : the symbol 0 denoting the absence of all magnitude or quantity : ZERO, NAUGHT **2** : a method of secret writing

♦ aught, naught, nil, nothing, zero, zip

²cipher *vb* : to compute arithmetically

cir *or* **circ** *abbr* circular

cir·ca \'sər-kə\ *prep* : ABOUT ⟨∼ 1600⟩

cir·ca·di·an \,sər-'kā-dē-ən, ,sər-kə-'dī-ən\ *adj* : being, having, characterized by, or occurring in approximately 24-hour intervals (as of biological activity)

¹cir·cle \'sər-kəl\ *n* **1** ♦ : a closed curve every point of which is equally distant from a fixed point within it **2** ♦ : something circular **3** : an area of action or influence **4** : a series ending at its starting point : CYCLE **5** ♦ : a group bound by a common tie

♦ [1, 2] band, hoop, ring, round ♦ [5] clan, clique, coterie, crowd, fold, gang, ring, set

²circle *vb* **cir·cled; cir·cling** **1** ♦ : to enclose in a circle **2** ♦ : to move or revolve around; *also* : to move in a circle

♦ [1] encircle, enclose, encompass, ring, surround ♦ [2] circumnavigate, coil, compass, encircle, girdle, loop, orbit, ring, round

cir·clet \'sər-klət\ *n* : a small circle; *esp* : a circular ornament

cir·cuit \'sər-kət\ *n* **1** : a boundary around an enclosed space **2** : a course around a periphery **3** : a regular tour (as by a judge) around an assigned territory **4** : the complete path of an electric current; *also* : an assemblage of electronic components **5** : LEAGUE; *also* : a chain of theaters — **cir·cuit·al** \-ᵊl\ *adj*

circuit breaker *n* : a switch that automatically interrupts an electric circuit under an abnormal condition

circuit court *n* : a court that sits at two or more places within one judicial district

cir·cu·i·tous \,sər-'kyü-ə-təs\ *adj* **1** ♦ : having a circular or winding course **2** ♦ : not being forthright or direct in language or action

♦ [1] circular, indirect, roundabout ♦ [2] diffuse, long-winded, prolix, rambling, verbose, windy, wordy

cir·cuit·ry \'sər-kə-trē\ *n, pl* **-ries** : the plan or the components of an electric circuit

cir·cu·ity \,sər-'kyü-ə-tē\ *n, pl* **-ities** : INDIRECTION

¹cir·cu·lar \'sər-kyə-lər\ *adj* **1** : having the form of a circle : ROUND **2** : moving in or around a circle **3** ♦ : not forthright or direct in language or action : CIRCUITOUS **4** : intended for circulation ⟨a ∼ letter⟩ — **cir·cu·lar·i·ty** \'sər-kyə-'lar-ə-tē\ *n*

♦ circuitous, indirect, roundabout

²circular *n* ♦ : a paper (as a leaflet) intended for wide distribution

♦ booklet, brochure, folder, leaflet, pamphlet

cir·cu·lar·ise *Brit var of* CIRCULARIZE

cir·cu·lar·ize \'sər-kyə-lə-,rīz\ *vb* **-ized; -iz·ing** **1** : to send circulars to **2** : to poll by questionnaire

circular saw *n* : a power saw with a round cutting blade

cir·cu·late \'sər-kyə-,lāt\ *vb* **-lat·ed; -lat·ing** **1** : to move or cause to move in a circle, circuit, or orbit **2** ♦ : to pass from place to place or from person to person **3** ♦ : to become well≈ known or widespread — **cir·cu·la·tion** \,sər-kyə-'lā-shən\ *n*

♦ [2, 3] broadcast, disseminate, propagate, spread, strew

cir·cu·la·to·ry \'sər-kyə-lə-,tōr-ē\ *adj* : of or relating to circulation or the circulatory system

circulatory system *n* : the system of blood, blood vessels, lymphatic vessels, and heart concerned with the circulation of the blood and lymph

cir·cum·am·bu·late \,sər-kəm-'am-byə-,lāt\ *vb* **-lat·ed; -lat·ing** : to circle on foot esp. as part of a ritual

cir·cum·cise \'sər-kəm-ˌsīz\ *vb* **-cised; -cis·ing** : to cut off the foreskin of — **cir·cum·ci·sion** \ˌsər-kəm-'si-zhən\ *n*
cir·cum·fer·ence \sər-'kəm-f(ə-)rəns\ *n* **1** : the perimeter of a circle **2** ♦ : the external boundary or surface of a figure or object

♦ border, bound, boundary, compass, confines, edge, end, fringe, margin, perimeter, periphery, rim, skirt, verge

cir·cum·flex \'sər-kəm-ˌfleks\ *n* : the mark ^ over a vowel
cir·cum·lo·cu·tion \ˌsər-kəm-lō-'kyü-shən\ *n* ♦ : the use of an unnecessarily large number of words to express an idea

♦ prolixity, redundancy, verbiage, wordiness

cir·cum·lu·nar \-'lü-nər\ *adj* : revolving about or surrounding the moon
cir·cum·nav·i·gate \-'na-və-ˌgāt\ *vb* ♦ : to go completely around (as the earth) esp. by water — **cir·cum·nav·i·ga·tion** \-ˌna-və-'gā-shən\ *n*

♦ circle, coil, compass, encircle, girdle, loop, orbit, ring, round

cir·cum·po·lar \-'pō-lər\ *adj* **1** : continually visible above the horizon ⟨a ∼ star⟩ **2** : surrounding or found near a pole of the earth
cir·cum·scribe \'sər-kəm-ˌskrīb\ *vb* **1** ♦ : to constrict the range or activity of **2** : to draw a line around — **cir·cum·scrip·tion** \ˌsər-kəm-'skrip-shən\ *n*

♦ check, confine, control, curb, inhibit, limit, restrain, restrict ♦ bound, define, delimit, demarcate, limit, mark, terminate

cir·cum·spect \'sər-kəm-ˌspekt\ *adj* ♦ : careful to consider all circumstances and consequences : PRUDENT — **cir·cum·spec·tion** \ˌsər-kəm-'spek-shən\ *n*

♦ alert, careful, cautious, considerate, gingerly, guarded, heedful, prudent, safe, wary

cir·cum·spec·tion \ˌsər-kəm-'spek-shən\ *n* ♦ : careful consideration to minimize risk

♦ alertness, care, carefulness, caution, heedfulness

cir·cum·stance \'sər-kəm-ˌstans\ *n* **1** : a condition, fact, or event accompanying, conditioning, or determining another **2** : surrounding conditions **3 a** ♦ : an inevitable and often adverse end : FATE **b** ♦ : something that happens unpredictably : CHANCE **4** *pl* : situation with regard to wealth **5** : CEREMONY ⟨pomp and ∼⟩

♦ [3a] destiny, doom, fate, fortune, lot, portion ♦ [3b] accident, chance, hazard, luck

cir·cum·stan·tial \ˌsər-kəm-'stan-chəl\ *adj* **1** : consisting of or depending on circumstances **2** : INCIDENTAL **3** ♦ : containing full details — **cir·cum·stan·tial·ly** *adv*

♦ detailed, elaborate, full, minute, thorough

cir·cum·vent \ˌsər-kəm-'vent\ *vb* **1 a** ♦ : to go around : make a full circuit around or bypass without going through **b** ♦ : to manage to get around esp. by ingenuity or stratagem **2** : to check or defeat esp. by stratagem — **cir·cum·ven·tion** \-'vent-shən\ *n*

♦ [1a, 1b] dodge, sidestep, skirt *Ant* comply (with), follow, keep, obey, observe ♦ [1a, 1b] bypass, detour, skirt

cir·cus \'sər-kəs\ *n* **1** ♦ : a large arena enclosed by tiers of seats on three or all four sides and used esp. for sports or spectacles **2** : a usu. traveling show that features feats of physical skill, wild animal acts, and performances by clowns **3** : a circus performance; *also* : the equipment, livestock, and personnel of a circus **4** ♦ : something suggestive of a circus (as in frenzied activity or razzle-dazzle) ⟨a media ∼⟩

♦ [1] bowl, coliseum, stadium ♦ [4] bedlam, hell, madhouse

cirque \'sərk\ *n* : a deep steep-walled mountain basin usu. forming the blunt end of a valley
cir·rho·sis \sə-'rō-səs\ *n, pl* **-rho·ses** \-ˌsēz\ : fibrosis of the liver — **cir·rhot·ic** \-'rä-tik\ *adj or n*
cir·rus \'sir-əs\ *n, pl* **cir·ri** \'sir-ˌī\ : a wispy white cloud usu. of minute ice crystals at high altitudes
cis \'sis\ *adj* : CISGENDER
cis·gen·der \(ˌ)sis-'jen-dər\ *also* **cis·gen·dered** \-dərd\ *adj* : of, relating to, or being a person whose gender identity corresponds with the sex the person had or was identified as having at birth
cis·lu·nar \(ˌ)sis-'lü-nər\ *adj* : lying between the earth and the moon or the moon's orbit
cis·tern \'sis-tərn\ *n* : an often underground tank for storing water
cit *abbr* **1** citation; cited **2** citizen

cit·a·del \'si-tə-dəl, -ˌdel\ *n* **1** ♦ : a fortress commanding a city **2** ♦ : a place of security or survival : STRONGHOLD

♦ [1, 2] bastion, fastness, fort, fortification, fortress, hold, stronghold

ci·ta·tion \sī-'tā-shən\ *n* **1** : an official summons to appear (as before a court) **2 a** : something that is quoted **b** : a passage referred to or given as an example : QUOTATION **3** ♦ : a formal statement of the achievements of a person; *also* : a specific reference in a military dispatch to meritorious performance of duty

♦ accolade, commendation, encomium, eulogy, homage, paean, panegyric, salutation, tribute

cite \'sīt\ *vb* **cit·ed; cit·ing** **1** : to summon to appear before a court **2** ♦ : to quote by way of example, authority, or proof : QUOTE **3** : to refer to esp. in commendation or praise **4** ♦ : to bring forward or call to another's attention esp. as an example

♦ [2] advert (to), instance, mention, name, note, notice, quote, refer (to), specify, touch (*on* or *upon*) ♦ [4] adduce, instance, mention, quote

cit·i·fied \'si-ti-ˌfīd\ *adj* : of, relating to, or characterized by an urban style of living
cit·i·zen \'si-tə-zən\ *n* **1** : an inhabitant of a city or town **2** : a person who owes allegiance to a government and is entitled to its protection — **cit·i·zen·ship** *n*
cit·i·zen·ry \-rē\ *n, pl* **-ries** : a whole body of citizens
citizens band *n* : a range of radio frequencies set aside for private radio communications
cit·ric acid \'si-trik-\ *n* : a sour organic acid obtained from lemon and lime juices or by fermentation of sugars and used as a flavoring
cit·ron \'si-trən\ *n* **1** : the oval lemonlike fruit of an Asian citrus tree; *also* : the tree **2** : a small hard-fleshed watermelon used esp. in pickles and preserves
cit·ro·nel·la \ˌsi-trə-'ne-lə\ *n* : a lemon-scented oil obtained from a fragrant grass of southern Asia and used in perfumes and as an insect repellent
cit·rus \'si-trəs\ *n, pl* **citrus** *or* **cit·rus·es** : any of a genus of often thorny evergreen trees or shrubs grown for their fruits (as the orange, lemon, lime, and grapefruit); *also* : the fruit
city \'si-tē\ *n, pl* **cit·ies** **1** ♦ : an inhabited place larger or more important than a town **2** : a municipality in the U.S. governed under a charter granted by the state; *also* : an incorporated municipal unit of the highest class in Canada

♦ metropolis, municipality

city manager *n* : an official employed by an elected council to direct the administration of a city government
city–state \'si-tē-ˌstāt\ *n* : an autonomous state consisting of a city and surrounding territory
civ *abbr* **1** civil; civilian **2** civilization
civ·et \'si-vət\ *n* : a yellowish strong-smelling substance obtained from a catlike mammal (**civet cat**) of Africa or Asia and used in making perfumes
civ·ic \'si-vik\ *adj* : of or relating to a city, citizenship, or civil affairs
civ·ics \-viks\ *n* : a social science dealing with the rights and duties of citizens
civ·il \'si-vəl\ *adj* **1** ♦ : of or relating to citizens or to the state as a political body **2** ♦ : adequate in courtesy and politeness : COURTEOUS, POLITE **3** : of or relating to legal proceedings in connection with private rights and obligations ⟨the ∼ code⟩ **4** : of or relating to the general population : not military or ecclesiastical

♦ [1] national, public, state ♦ [2] courteous, genteel, gracious, mannerly, polite, well-bred

civil defense *n* : protective measures and emergency relief activities conducted by civilians in case of enemy attack or natural disaster
civil disobedience *n* : refusal to obey governmental commands esp. as a nonviolent means of protest
civil engineer *n* : an engineer whose training or occupation is in the design and construction esp. of public works (as roads or harbors) — **civil engineering** *n*
ci·vil·ian \sə-'vil-yən\ *n* : a person not on active duty in a military, police, or fire-fighting force
ci·vil·i·ty \sə-'vi-lə-tē\ *n, pl* **-ties** **1** ♦ : civilized conduct : POLITENESS, COURTESY **2** ♦ : a polite act or expression

♦ [1] courtesy, gentility, graciousness, mannerliness, politeness ♦ [2] amenity, courtesy, formality, gesture

civ·i·li·za·tion \ˌsi-və-lə-'zā-shən\ *n* **1** ♦ : a relatively high level of cultural and technological development **2** ♦ : the culture characteristic of a time or place — **civ·i·li·za·tion·al** \-shə-nᵊl\ *adj*

♦ [1] cultivation, culture, polish, refinement ♦ [2] culture, life, lifestyle, society

civ·i·lize \'si-və-ˌlīz\ *vb* **-lized; -liz·ing 1** : to raise from a primitive state to an advanced and ordered stage of cultural development **2** : REFINE

civ·i·lized *adj* **1** : characteristic of a state of civilization **2** ♦ : characterized by taste, refinement, or restraint

♦ cultivated, cultured, genteel, polished, refined

civil liberty *n* : freedom from arbitrary governmental interference specifically by denial of governmental power — usu. used in pl.

civ·il·ly \'si-vəl-lē\ *adv* **1** : in terms of civil rights, matters, or law ⟨~ dead⟩ **2** : in a civil manner : POLITELY

civil rights *n pl* : the nonpolitical rights of a citizen; *esp* : those guaranteed by the 13th and 14th amendments to the Constitution and by acts of Congress

civil servant *n* : a member of a civil service

civil service *n* : the administrative service of a government

civil war *n* : a war between opposing groups of citizens of the same country

civ·vies \'si-vēz\ *n pl* : civilian clothes as distinguished from a military uniform

CJ *abbr* chief justice

ck *abbr* **1** cask **2** check

cl *abbr* **1** centiliter **2** class

Cl *symbol* chlorine

¹**clack** \'klak\ *vb* **1** : CHATTER, PRATTLE **2** : to make an abrupt striking sound or series of sounds

²**clack** *n* **1** : rapid continuous talk : CHATTER **2** : a sound of clacking ⟨the ~ of a typewriter⟩

clad \'klad\ *adj* **1** : CLOTHED, COVERED **2** : being or consisting of coins made of outer layers of one metal bonded to a core of a different metal

¹**claim** \'klām\ *vb* **1** ♦ : to ask for esp. as a right **2** : to call for : REQUIRE **3** ♦ : to state as a fact : MAINTAIN

♦ [1] call, clamor (*or* clamour), command, demand, enjoin, exact, insist, press, quest, stipulate (for) ♦ [3] affirm, allege, assert, aver, avouch, avow, contend, declare, insist, maintain, profess, protest, warrant *Ant* deny, gainsay

²**claim** *n* **1** ♦ : a demand for something due or believed to be due **2** ♦ : a right to something usu. in another's possession **3** ♦ : an assertion open to challenge **4** ♦ : something claimed (as a tract of land)

♦ [1] demand, dun, requisition ♦ [2] call, pretense, pretension, right ♦ [3] affirmation, assertion, avowal, declaration, profession, protestation ♦ [4] interest, share, stake

claim·ant \'klā-mənt\ *n* : a person making a claim

clair·voy·ance \-əns\ *n* : the power or faculty of discerning objects not present to the senses

clair·voy·ant \klar-'vȯi-ənt\ *adj* **1** : unusually perceptive **2** : having the power of discerning objects not present to the senses — **clairvoyant** *n*

clam \'klam\ *n* **1** : any of numerous bivalve mollusks including many that are edible **2** : DOLLAR

clam·bake \-ˌbāk\ *n* : a party or gathering (as at the seashore) at which food is cooked usu. on heated rocks covered by seaweed

clam·ber \'klam-bər\ *vb* : to climb awkwardly — **clam·ber·er** *n*

clam·my \'kla-mē\ *adj* **clam·mi·er; -est** : being damp, soft, sticky, and usu. cool — **clam·mi·ness** *n*

¹**clam·or** \'kla-mər\ *or Can and Brit* **clam·our** *n* **1** ♦ : a noisy shouting **2** ♦ : a loud continuous noise **3** : insistent public expression (as of support or protest)

♦ [1] howl, hubbub, hue and cry, hullabaloo, noise, outcry, roar, tumult, uproar ♦ [2] bluster, cacophony, din, noise, racket, roar

²**clamor** *or Can and Brit* **clamour** *vb* ♦ : to appeal, demand, or protest by sustained noisy outcry : to become loudly insistent — usu. used with *for*

♦ usu **clamor for** call, claim, demand, enjoin, exact, insist, press, quest, stipulate (for)

clam·or·ous *or Can and Brit* **clamourous** *adj* **1** ♦ : marked by confused din or outcry **2** ♦ : full of noise : noisily insistent

♦ [1] blatant, obstreperous, vociferous ♦ [2] booming, deafening, earsplitting, loud, piercing, resounding, ringing, roaring, sonorous, stentorian, thunderous

¹**clamp** \'klamp\ *n* : a device that holds or presses parts together firmly

²**clamp** *vb* ♦ : to fasten with or as if with a clamp

♦ anchor, fasten, fix, hitch, moor, secure, set

clamp down *vb* ♦ : to impose restrictions : become repressive — **clamp·down** \'klamp-ˌdau̇n\ *n*

♦ usu **clamp down on** crack down, crush, put down, quash, quell, repress, silence, snuff, squash, squelch, subdue, suppress

clam·shell \'klam-ˌshel\ *n* **1** : the shell of a clam **2** : a bucket or grapnel (as on a dredge) having two hinged jaws

clam up *vb* ♦ : to become silent

♦ hush, pipe down, quiet (down), shut up

clan \'klan\ *n* **1** ♦ : a group of people tracing descent from a common ancestor **2** ♦ : a group united by a common interest or common characteristics — **clan·nish** *n* — **clan·nish·ness** *n*

♦ [1] blood, family, folks, house, kin, kindred, kinfolk, line, lineage, people, race, stock, tribe ♦ [2] circle, clique, coterie, crowd, fold, gang, ring, set

clan·des·tine \klan-'des-tən\ *adj* ♦ : held in or conducted with secrecy

♦ covert, furtive, hugger-mugger, private, secret, sneak, sneaky, stealthy, surreptitious, undercover, underground, underhanded

clang \'klaŋ\ *n* ♦ : a loud metallic ringing sound — **clang** *vb*

♦ clash

clan·gor *or Can and Brit* **clan·gour** \'klaŋ-ər, -gər\ *n* : a loud deeply resounding sound made esp. by metal objects struck together

clank \'klaŋk\ *n* : a sharp brief metallic ringing sound — **clank** *vb*

clan·nish *n* : tending to associate only with a select group of similar background or status — **clan·nish·ness** *n*

¹**clap** \'klap\ *vb* **clapped; clap·ping 1** ♦ : to strike noisily **2** : APPLAUD

²**clap** *n* **1** ♦ : a loud noisy crash **2** : a sudden sometimes resounding blow or stroke **3** : the noise made by clapping the hands

♦ bang, blast, boom, crack, crash, pop, report, slam, smash, snap, thwack, whack

³**clap** *n* : GONORRHEA

clap·board \'kla-bərd, -ˌbȯrd; 'klap-ˌbȯrd\ *n* : a narrow board thicker at one edge than the other used for siding — **clap·board** *vb*

clap·per \'kla-pər\ *n* : one that claps; *esp* : the tongue of a bell

clap·trap \'klap-ˌtrap\ *n* ♦ : pretentious nonsense

♦ bunk, drivel, fiddlesticks, folly, foolishness, fudge, hogwash, humbug, nonsense, piffle, rot, silliness, slush, stupidity, trash

claque \'klak\ *n* **1** : a group hired to applaud at a performance **2** : a group of sycophants

clar·et \'klar-ət\ *n* : a dry red wine

clar·i·fi·ca·tion \ˌklar-ə-fə-'kā-shən\ *n* ♦ : the act or process of clarifying; *also* : something that clarifies

♦ construction, elucidation, explanation, explication, exposition, illumination, illustration, interpretation

clar·i·fy \'klar-ə-ˌfī\ *vb* **-fied; -fy·ing** ♦ : to make or become clear

♦ clear (up), construe, demonstrate, elucidate, explain, explicate, expound, illuminate, illustrate, interpret, spell out ♦ clear, distill, filter, purify

clar·i·net \ˌklar-ə-'net\ *n* : a single-reed woodwind instrument in the form of a cylindrical tube with a moderately flaring end — **clar·i·net·ist** *or* **clar·i·net·tist** \-'ne-tist\ *n*

clar·i·on \'klar-ē-ən\ *adj* : brilliantly clear ⟨a ~ call⟩

clar·i·ty \'klar-ə-tē\ *n* ♦ : the quality or state of being clear : LUCIDITY

♦ explicitness, lucidity, perspicuity, simplicity

¹**clash** \'klash\ *vb* **1** : to make or cause to make a clash **2** ♦ : to be incompatible **3** ♦ : to come into conflict

♦ [2] collide, conflict, jar *Ant* blend, harmonize, match ♦ usu **clash with** [3] battle, combat, fight, scrimmage, skirmish, war

²**clash** *n* **1** ♦ : a noisy usu. metallic sound of collision **2** ♦ : a hostile encounter; *also* : a conflict of opinion

♦ [1] clang ♦ [2] battle, combat, conflict, contest, fight, fracas, fray, hassle, scrap, scrimmage, scuffle, skirmish, struggle, tussle

¹**clasp** \'klasp\ *n* **1** : a device (as a hook) for holding objects or parts together **2** : a holding or enveloping with or as if with the hands or arms : EMBRACE, GRASP

²**clasp** *vb* ♦ : to enclose and hold with the arms or hands

♦ caress, embrace, enfold, grasp, hug ♦ grasp, grip, hold, take

¹**class** \'klas\ *n* **1** : a group of students meeting regularly in a course; *also* : a group graduating together **2** : a course of instruction; *also* : the period when such a course is taught **3 a** ♦ : social rank; *esp* : high social rank **b** ♦ : high quality : ELEGANCE **4** ♦ : a group of the same general status or nature; *esp* : a major category in biological classification that is above the order and below the phylum **5** ♦ : a division or rating based on grade or quality — **class·less** *adj*

♦ [3a] caste, estate, folk, order, place, position, rank, standing, status, stratum ♦ [3b] elegance, grace, handsomeness, majesty, refinement, stateliness ♦ [4] breed, description, feather, ilk, kind, like, manner, nature, order, sort, species, type ♦ [5] bracket, category, division, family, grade, group, kind, order, set, species, type

²**class** *vb* ♦ : to arrange in classes : CLASSIFY

♦ assort, break down, categorize, classify, grade, group, peg, place, range, rank, separate, sort

class action *n* : a legal action undertaken in behalf of the plaintiffs and all others having an identical interest in the alleged wrong

¹**clas·sic** \'kla-sik\ *adj* **1** ♦ : serving as a standard of excellence; *also* : TRADITIONAL **2** : CLASSICAL 2 **3** : notable esp. as the best example **4** : AUTHENTIC **5** ♦ : typical or regarded as typical : ideally illustrative

♦ [1] model, paradigmatic, quintessential, traditional ♦ [5] characteristic, distinct, distinctive, individual, peculiar, proper, symptomatic, typical

²**classic** *n* **1** : a work of enduring excellence and esp. of ancient Greece or Rome; *also* : its author **2** ♦ : a typical or perfect example **3** : a traditional event

♦ beau ideal, epitome, exemplar, ideal, perfection, quintessence

clas·si·cal \'kla-si-kəl\ *adj* **1** : CLASSIC **2** : of or relating to the ancient Greek and Roman classics **3** : of or relating to a form or system of primary significance before modern times ⟨∼ economics⟩ **4** : concerned with a general study of the arts and sciences **5** ♦ : handed down (as beliefs or customs) by example from one generation to another — **clas·si·cal·ly** \-k(ə-)lē\ *adv*

♦ conventional, customary, traditional

clas·si·cism \'kla-sə-ˌsi-zəm\ *n* **1** : the principles or style of the literature or art of ancient Greece and Rome **2** : adherence to traditional standards believed to be universally valid — **clas·si·cist** \-sist\ *n*

clas·si·fi·ca·tion \ˌkla-sə-fə-'kā-shən\ *n* ♦ : a group of the same general status or nature : CLASS, CATEGORY

♦ bracket, category, class, division, family, grade, group, kind, order, rank, set, species, type

clas·si·fied \'kla-sə-ˌfīd\ *adj* : withheld from general circulation for reasons of national security

clas·si·fieds \-ˌfīdz\ *n pl* : advertisements grouped by subject

clas·si·fy \'kla-sə-ˌfī\ *vb* **-fied; -fy·ing** ♦ : to arrange in or assign to classes — **clas·si·fi·able** *adj* — **clas·si·fi·ca·tion** \ˌkla-sə-fə-'kā-shən\ *n* — **clas·si·fi·er** *n*

♦ arrange, array, codify, dispose, draw up, marshal, order, organize, range, systematize ♦ assort, break down, categorize, class, grade, group, peg, place, range, rank, separate, sort

class·less \'klas-ləs\ *adj* ♦ : having the qualities or behavior of a boor : BOORISH

♦ boorish, churlish, clownish, loutish, uncouth

class·mate \'klas-ˌmāt\ *n* : a member of the same class (as in a college)

class·room \-ˌrüm, -ˌrum\ *n* : a place where classes meet

classy \'kla-sē\ *adj* **class·i·er; -est** : ELEGANT, STYLISH — **class·i·ness** *n*

¹**clat·ter** \'kla-tər\ *n* **1** : a rattling sound ⟨the ∼ of dishes⟩ **2** : an agitated disturbance or noisy confusion

²**clatter** *vb* : to make a rattling sound

clause \'kloz\ *n* **1** : a group of words having its own subject and predicate but forming only part of a compound or complex sentence **2** : a separate part of an article or document

claus·tro·pho·bia \ˌklo-strə-'fō-bē-ə\ *n* : abnormal dread of being in closed or narrow spaces — **claus·tro·pho·bic** \-bik\ *adj*

clav·i·chord \'kla-və-ˌkord\ *n* : an early keyboard instrument in use before the piano

clav·i·cle \'kla-vi-kəl\ *n* : COLLARBONE

cla·vier \klə-'vir; 'klā-vē-ər\ *n* **1** : the keyboard of a musical instrument **2** : an early keyboard instrument

¹**claw** \'klo\ *n* **1** : a sharp usu. curved nail on the toe of an animal **2** : a sharp curved process (as on the foot of an insect); *also* : a pincerlike organ at the end of a limb of some arthropods (as a lobster) — **clawed** \'klod\ *adj*

²**claw** *vb* : to rake, seize, or dig with or as if with claws

clay \'klā\ *n* **1** : an earthy material that is plastic when moist but hard when fired and is used in making pottery; *also* : finely divided soil consisting largely of such clay **2** : EARTH, MUD **3** : a plastic substance used for modeling **4** : the mortal human body — **clay·ey** \'klā-ē\ *adj*

clay·more \'klā-ˌmōr\ *n* : a large 2-edged sword formerly used by Scottish Highlanders

clay pigeon *n* : a saucer-shaped target thrown from a trap in trapshooting

¹**clean** \'klēn\ *adj* **1** ♦ : free from dirt or disease **2 a** ♦ : free from moral taint or corruption : PURE **b** ♦ : observing the rules : FAIR **3** ♦ : so decisive and complete as to leave no loose ends or uncertainty : THOROUGH ⟨made a ∼ break with the past⟩ **4** : TRIM ⟨a ship with ∼ lines⟩; *also* : EVEN **5** : habitually neat — **clean·ly** \'klēn-lē\ *adv* — **clean·ness** \'klēn-nəs\ *n*

♦ [1] immaculate, spick-and-span, spotless, stainless, unsoiled, unsullied *Ant* dirty, filthy, foul, grubby, soiled, spotted, stained, sullied, unclean ♦ [2a] chaste, decent, immaculate, modest, pure ♦ [2b] fair, legal, sportsmanlike ♦ [3] all-out, complete, comprehensive, exhaustive, full-scale, out-and-out, thorough, thoroughgoing, total

²**clean** *adv* ♦ : all the way : COMPLETELY

♦ absolutely, all, altogether, completely, entirely, fully, quite, totally, utterly, wholly

³**clean** *vb* **1** : to make or become clean **2** ♦ : to remove the entrails from **3** ♦ : to exhaust the stock of — usu. used with *out*

♦ [2] draw, eviscerate, gut ♦ *usu* **clean out** [3] consume, deplete, drain, exhaust, expend, spend, use up

clean–cut \'klēn-'kət\ *adj* **1** : cut so that the surface or edge is smooth and even **2** : sharply defined or outlined **3** : giving an effect of wholesomeness

clean·er *n* ♦ : a preparation for cleaning

♦ detergent, soap

clean·ly \'klen-lē\ *adj* **clean·li·er; -est** **1** : careful to keep clean **2** : habitually kept clean — **clean·li·ness** *n*

clean room \'klēn-ˌrüm, -ˌrum\ *n* : an uncontaminated room maintained for the manufacture or assembly of objects (as precision parts)

cleanse \'klenz\ *vb* **cleansed; cleans·ing** **1** : to make clean **2** : to rid of impurities by or as if by washing

cleans·er *vb* : a preparation (as a scouring powder or a skin cream) used for cleaning

cleans·ing *n* : the action or an act of cleansing esp. morally or spiritually

¹**clean·up** \'klē-ˌnəp\ *n* **1** : an act or instance of cleaning **2** : a very large profit

²**cleanup** *adj* : being 4th in the batting order of a baseball team

clean up *vb* **1** : to make a spectacular business profit **2** : rid of debasing or harmful features or elements

¹**clear** \'klir\ *adj* **1 a** : shining brightly : entirely light **b** : UNTROUBLED, SERENE **2** ♦ : having the sky free from clouds : CLOUDLESS **3 a** : CLEAN, PURE **b** ♦ : easily seen through : TRANSPARENT **4 a** ♦ : easily heard, seen, or understood **b** : easy to perceive or determine with certainty **5 a** : capable of sharp discernment **b** : free from doubt **6** ♦ : free from guile or guilt : INNOCENT **7** ♦ : free from restriction, obstruction, or entanglement — **clear** *adv* — **clear·ly** \'klir-lē\ *adv* — **clear·ness** *n*

♦ [2] cloudless, fair, sunny, sunshiny, unclouded ♦ [3b] limpid, liquid, lucent, pellucid, transparent *Ant* cloudy, opaque ♦ [4a] apparent, broad, clear-cut, distinct, evident, lucid, manifest, obvious, palpable, patent, perspicuous, plain, transparent, unambiguous, unequivocal, unmistakable *Ant* dark, enigmatic, indistinct, mysterious, obscure, unclear; ambiguous, equivocal ♦ [6] blameless, faultless, guiltless, impeccable, innocent, irreproachable ♦ [7] free, open, unobstructed

²**clear** *vb* **1** ♦ : to make or become clear **2** : to go away : DISPERSE **3 a** ♦ : to free from accusation or blame **b** ♦ : to accept officially as satisfactory **c** : to certify as trustworthy **4** ♦ : to explain or make understandable — often used with *up* **5** : to get free from obstruction **6** ♦ : to make clear or free from debt or obligation : SETTLE **7** : NET **8** : to get rid of : REMOVE ⟨∼ed

snow off the roof⟩ **9 a ♦ :** to free (as from contact or entanglement) **:** DISENTANGLE **b :** to jump or go by without touching; *also* **:** PASS

♦ [1] clarify, distill, filter, purify ♦ [3a] absolve, acquit, exculpate, exonerate, vindicate ♦ [3b] approve, authorize, OK, ratify, sanction, warrant ♦ *usu* **clear up** [4] clarify, construe, demonstrate, elucidate, explain, explicate, expound, illuminate, illustrate, interpret, spell out ♦ [6] discharge, foot, liquidate, pay, pay off, quit, recompense, settle, spring, stand ♦ [9a] disengage, disentangle, extricate, free, liberate, release, untangle

³**clear** *n* **:** a clear space or part
clear·ance \'klir-əns\ *n* **1 :** an act or process of clearing **2 :** the distance by which one object clears another **3 ♦ :** certification as clear of objection **:** AUTHORIZATION

♦ allowance, authorization, concurrence, consent, leave, license (*or* licence), permission, sanction, sufferance

clear–cut \'klir-'kət\ *adj* **1 :** sharply outlined **:** DISTINCT **2 ♦ :** free from ambiguity or uncertainty **:** DEFINITE, UNEQUIVOCAL

♦ definite, definitive, explicit, express, specific, unambiguous, unequivocal

clear·head·ed \-'he-dəd\ *adj* ♦ **:** having a clear understanding **:** able to think clearly

♦ balanced, lucid, normal, right, sane, stable

clear·ing \'klir-iŋ\ *n* **1 :** a tract of land cleared of wood and brush **2 :** the passage of checks and claims through a clearinghouse **3 :** the act or process of becoming clear
clear·ing·house \-ˌhaus\ *n* **:** an institution maintained by banks for making an exchange of checks and claims held by each bank against other banks; *also* **:** an informal channel for information or assistance
clear out *vb* **1 ♦ :** to drive out or away usu. by force **2 ♦ :** to go away or run from **:** DEPART

♦ [1] disband, disperse, dissipate, scatter ♦ [2] abscond, escape, flee, fly, get out, lam, run away, run off ♦ [2] depart, exit, get off, go, move, pull, quit, sally, shove, take off

cleat \'klēt\ *n* **:** a piece of wood or metal fastened on or projecting from something to give strength, provide a grip, or prevent slipping
cleav·age \'klē-vij\ *n* **1 :** a splitting apart **:** SPLIT **2 :** the depression between a woman's breasts esp. when exposed by a low-cut neckline
¹**cleave** \'klēv\ *vb* **cleaved** \'klēvd\ *or* **clove** \'klōv\; **cleaved; cleav·ing :** to adhere firmly and closely or loyally and unwaveringly **:** ADHERE, CLING
²**cleave** *vb* **cleaved** \'klēvd\ *also* **cleft** \'kleft\ *or* **clove** \'klōv\; **cleaved** *also* **cleft** *or* **clo·ven** \'klō-vən\; **cleav·ing 1 :** to divide by force **:** split asunder **2 :** DIVIDE
cleav·er \'klē-vər\ *n* **:** a heavy chopping knife for cutting meat
clef \'klef\ *n* **:** a sign placed on the staff in music to show what pitch is represented by each line and space
cleft \'kleft\ *n* ♦ **:** a space or opening made by or as if by splitting **:** FISSURE, CRACK

♦ chink, crack, cranny, crevice, fissure, rift, split

cleft palate *n* **:** a split in the roof of the mouth that appears as a birth defect
clem·a·tis \'kle-mə-təs; kli-'ma-təs\ *n* **:** any of a genus of vines or herbs related to the buttercups that have showy usu. white or purple flowers
clem·en·cy \'kle-mən-sē\ *n, pl* **-cies 1 ♦ :** disposition to be merciful **2 :** mildness of weather

♦ charity, leniency, mercy, quarter

clem·ent \'kle-mənt\ *adj* **1 :** MERCIFUL, LENIENT **2 ♦ :** not severe in temperature **:** TEMPERATE, MILD

♦ balmy, equable, gentle, mild, moderate, temperate *Ant* harsh, inclement, intemperate, severe

clem·en·tine \'kle-mən-ˌtēn\ *n* **:** a small citrus fruit that is probably a hybrid between a tangerine and an orange
clench \'klench\ *vb* **1 :** CLINCH 1 **2 ♦ :** to hold fast **:** CLUTCH **3 :** to set or close tightly

♦ cling, clutch, grip, hang on, hold, hold on

clere·sto·ry \'klir-ˌstōr-ē\ *n* **:** an outside wall of a room or building that rises above an adjoining roof and contains windows
cler·gy \'klər-jē\ *n* **:** a body of religious officials authorized to conduct services
cler·gy·man \-mən\ *n* ♦ **:** a member of the clergy

♦ divine, ecclesiastic, father, minister, preacher, priest, reverend *Ant* layman

cler·ic \'kler-ik\ *n* **:** a member of the clergy
cler·i·cal \'kler-i-kəl\ *adj* **1 ♦ :** of or relating to the clergy ⟨∼ vestments⟩ **2 :** of or relating to a clerk

♦ ministerial, pastoral, priestly, sacerdotal *Ant* lay, nonclerical

cler·i·cal·ism \'kler-i-kə-ˌli-zəm\ *n* **:** a policy of maintaining or increasing the power of a religious hierarchy
clerk \'klərk, *Brit* 'klärk\ *n* **1 :** CLERIC **2 a ♦ :** an official responsible for correspondence, records, and accounts **b :** a person employed to perform general office work **3 :** a store salesperson — **clerk** *vb* — **clerk·ship** *n*

♦ register, registrar, scribe

clev·er \'kle-vər\ *adj* **1 ♦ :** showing skill or resourcefulness **2 ♦ :** marked by wit or ingenuity — **clev·er·ly** *adv*

♦ [1] alert, brainy, bright, intelligent, keen, nimble, quick, quick-witted, sharp, smart ♦ [1] adroit, artful, creative, deft, imaginative, ingenious, innovative *Ant* uncreative, unimaginative ♦ [2] facetious, humorous, jocular, smart, witty

clev·er·ness *n* ♦ **:** the quality of being clever

♦ adeptness, adroitness, art, artfulness, artifice, artistry, craft, cunning, deftness, masterfulness, skill

clev·is \'kle-vəs\ *n* **:** a U-shaped shackle used for fastening
¹**clew** \'klü\ *n* **1 :** CLUE **2 :** a metal loop on a lower corner of a sail
²**clew** *vb* **:** to haul (a sail) up or down by ropes through the clews
cli·ché \kli-'shā\ *n* ♦ **:** a trite phrase or expression — **cli·chéd** \-'shād\ *adj*

♦ banality, commonplace, platitude, shibboleth

¹**click** \'klik\ *vb* **1 :** to make or cause to make a click **2 :** to fit together **:** hit it off **3 ♦ :** to function or operate smoothly or successfully **4 :** to select or make a selection on a computer by pressing a button on a control device (as a mouse) — **click·able** \'kli-kə-bəl\ *adj*

♦ deliver, go over, pan out, succeed, work out

²**click** *n* **:** a slight sharp noise
click·er \'kli-kər\ *n* **:** a remote control device (as for a television)
cli·ent \'klī-ənt\ *n* **1 :** DEPENDENT **2 :** a person who engages the professional services of another; *also* **:** PATRON, CUSTOMER **3 :** a computer in a network that uses the services (as access to files) provided by a server
cli·en·tele \ˌklī-ən-'tel, ˌklē-\ *n* **:** a body of clients and esp. customers
cliff \'klif\ *n* ♦ **:** a high steep face of rock, earth, or ice

♦ bluff, crag, escarpment, palisade, precipice, scarp

cliff–hang·er \-ˌhaŋ-ər\ *n* **1 :** an adventure serial or melodrama usu. presented in installments each of which ends in suspense **2 :** a contest whose outcome is in doubt up to the very end
cli·mac·ter·ic \klī-'mak-tə-rik\ *n* **1 :** a major turning point or critical stage **2 :** MENOPAUSE; *also* **:** a corresponding period in the male
cli·mate \'klī-mət\ *n* **1 :** a region having specific climatic conditions **2 :** the average weather conditions at a place over a period of years **3 :** the prevailing set of conditions (as temperature and humidity) indoors **4 ♦ :** a prevailing atmosphere or environment ⟨the ∼ of opinion⟩ — **cli·mat·ic** \klī-'ma-tik\ *adj* — **cli·mat·i·cal·ly** \-ti-k(ə-)lē\ *adv*

♦ air, atmosphere, aura, flavor (*or* flavour), mood, note, temper ♦ atmosphere, environment, environs, medium, milieu, setting, surroundings

cli·ma·tol·o·gy \ˌklī-mə-'tä-lə-jē\ *n* **:** the science that deals with climates — **cli·ma·to·log·i·cal** \-mət-ᵊl-'ä-ji-kəl\ *adj* — **cli·ma·to·log·i·cal·ly** \-k(ə-)lē\ *adv* — **cli·ma·tol·o·gist** \-mə-'tä-lə-jist\ *n*
¹**cli·max** \'klī-ˌmaks\ *n* **1 :** a series of ideas or statements so arranged that they increase in force and power from the first to the last; *also* **:** the last member of such a series **2 ♦ :** the highest point ⟨the ∼ of her career⟩ **3 :** ORGASM — **cli·mac·tic** \klī-'mak-tik\ *adj*

♦ acme, apex, crown, culmination, head, height, meridian, peak, pinnacle, summit, tip-top, top, zenith

²**climax** *vb* **:** to come or bring to a climax **:** provide a culminating event for
¹**climb** \'klīm\ *vb* **1 ♦ :** to rise to a higher point **2 ♦ :** to go up or down esp. by use of hands and feet; *also* **:** to ascend in growing — **climb·er** *n*

♦ [1, 2] arise, ascend, lift, mount, rise, soar, up

²**climb** n **1** : a place where climbing is necessary **2** ♦ : the act of climbing : ascent by climbing

♦ ascent, rise, soar

clime \'klīm\ n : CLIMATE ⟨prefers a warmer ∼⟩
¹**clinch** \'klinch\ vb **1** : to turn over or flatten the end of something sticking out ⟨∼ a nail⟩; also : to fasten by clinching **2** : to make final : SETTLE ⟨∼ a deal⟩ **3** : to hold fast or firmly
²**clinch** n **1** : a fastening by means of a clinched nail, rivet, or bolt **2** : an act or instance of clinching in boxing
clinch·er \'klin-chər\ n : one that clinches; esp : a decisive fact, argument, act, or remark
cling \'kliŋ\ vb **clung** \'kləŋ\; **cling·ing** **1 a** ♦ : to adhere as if glued **b** ♦ : to hold or hold on tightly **2** : to have a strong emotional attachment **3** ♦ : to give support or maintain loyalty

♦ [1a] adhere, hew, stick ♦ usu **cling to** [1b] clench, clutch, grip, hang on, hold, hold on ♦ usu **cling to** [3] adhere, hew, keep, stick

cling·stone \'kliŋ-ˌstōn\ n : any of various fruits (as some peaches) whose flesh adheres strongly to the pit
clin·ic \'kli-nik\ n **1** : a medical class in which patients are examined and discussed **2** : a group meeting for teaching a certain skill and working on individual problems ⟨a reading ∼⟩ **3** : a facility (as of a hospital) for diagnosis and treatment of outpatients
clin·i·cal \'kli-ni-kəl\ adj **1** : of, relating to, or typical of a clinic; esp : involving direct observation of the patient **2** : scientifically dispassionate — **clin·i·cal·ly** \-k(ə-)lē\ adv
cli·ni·cian \kli-'ni-shən\ n : a person qualified in the clinical practice of medicine, psychiatry, or psychology as distinguished from one specializing in laboratory or research techniques or in theory
¹**clink** \'kliŋk\ vb : to make or cause to make a sharp short metallic sound
²**clink** n : a clinking sound
clin·ker \'kliŋ-kər\ n : stony matter fused together : SLAG
¹**clip** \'klip\ vb **clipped; clip·ping** : to fasten with a clip
²**clip** n **1** : a device that grips, clasps, or hooks **2** : a cartridge holder for a rifle
³**clip** vb **clipped; clip·ping 1** ♦ : to cut or cut off with shears **2** : CURTAIL, DIMINISH **3** : HIT, PUNCH **4** : to illegally block (an opponent) in football

♦ bob, crop, cut, cut back, dock, lop, nip, prune, shave, shear, trim

⁴**clip** n **1** : a 2-bladed instrument for cutting esp. the nails **2** : a sharp blow **3** : a rapid pace ⟨moving at a good ∼⟩
clip·board \'klip-ˌbȯrd\ n : a small writing board with a spring clip at the top for holding papers
clip joint n, slang : an establishment (as a nightclub) that makes a practice of defrauding its customers
clip·per \'kli-pər\ n **1** : an implement for clipping esp. the hair or nails — usu. used in pl. **2** : a fast sailing ship
clip·ping \'kli-piŋ\ n : a piece clipped from something (as a newspaper)
clique \'klēk, 'klik\ n ♦ : a small exclusive group of people : COTERIE — **cli·quey** \'klē-kē, 'kli-\ adj — **cli·quish** \-kish\ adj

♦ circle, clan, community, coterie, crowd, fold, gang, ring, set

cli·to·ris \'kli-tə-rəs\ n, pl **cli·to·ris·es** : a small erectile organ at the anterior or ventral part of the vulva homologous to the penis — **cli·to·ral** \-rəl\ adj
clk abbr clerk
clo abbr clothing
¹**cloak** \'klōk\ n **1** : a loose outer garment **2** ♦ : something that conceals

♦ curtain, hood, mantle, mask, shroud, veil

²**cloak** vb ♦ : to cover or hide with a cloak

♦ blanket, blot out, conceal, cover, curtain, enshroud, hide, mask, obscure, occult, screen, shroud, veil

cloak–and–dagger adj : involving or suggestive of espionage
clob·ber \'klä-bər\ vb **1** : to pound mercilessly **2** : to hit with force **3** ♦ : to defeat overwhelmingly

♦ drub, rout, skunk, thrash, trim, trounce, wallop, whip

cloche \'klōsh\ n : a woman's small close-fitting hat
¹**clock** \'kläk\ n : a timepiece not intended to be carried on the person
²**clock** vb **1** : to time (a person or a performance) by a timing device **2** : to register (as speed) on a mechanical recording device — **clock·er** n

³**clock** n : an ornamental figure on a stocking or sock
clock·wise \'kläk-ˌwīz\ adv : in the direction in which the hands of a clock move — **clockwise** adj
clock·work \-ˌwərk\ n **1** : the machinery that runs a mechanical device (as a clock or toy) **2** : the precision or regularity associated with a clock
clod \'kläd\ n **1** ♦ : a lump esp. of earth or clay **2** ♦ : a dull or insensitive person

♦ [1] blob, chunk, clump, glob, gob, hunk, lump, nub, wad ♦ [2] hulk, lout, lubber, lug, oaf

clod·hop·per \-ˌhä-pər\ n **1** ♦ : an uncouth rustic **2** : a large heavy shoe

♦ bumpkin, hick, rustic, yokel

¹**clog** \'kläg\ n **1 a** : a weight attached to an animal to impede motion **b** : something that shackles or impedes **2** : a thick-soled shoe
²**clog** vb **clogged; clog·ging 1 a** : to impede with a clog : HINDER **b** ♦ : to halt or slow the progress, operation, or growth of : ENCUMBER **2** ♦ : to obstruct passage through **3** : to become filled with extraneous matter

♦ [1b] encumber, hamper, hinder, hold up, impede, inhibit, interfere with, obstruct, tie up ♦ [2] block, choke, close (off), congest, dam, jam, obstruct, plug (up), stop (up), stuff Ant clear, free, open (up), unclog

cloi·son·né \ˌklȯiz-ən-'ā\ adj : a colored decoration made of enamels poured into the divided areas in a design outlined with wire or metal strips
¹**clois·ter** \'klȯi-stər\ n **1** ♦ : a monastic establishment **2** : a covered usu. colonnaded passage on the side of a court — **clois·tral** \-strəl\ adj

♦ abbey, friary, monastery, priory

²**cloister** vb : to shut away from the world
clois·tered \'klȯi-stərd\ adj **1** : being or living in or as if in a cloister **2** ♦ : providing shelter from contact with the outside world

♦ covert, isolated, quiet, remote, secluded, secret

clone \'klōn\ n **1** : the collection of genetically identical cells or organisms produced asexually from a single ancestral cell or organism; also : an individual grown from a single cell and genetically identical to it ⟨a sheep ∼⟩ **2** : a group of replicas of a biological molecule (as DNA) **3** : one that appears to be a copy of an original form — **clon·al** \'klō-nᵊl\ adj — **clone** vb
clop \'kläp\ n : a sound made by or as if by a hoof or wooden shoe against pavement — **clop** vb
¹**close** \'klōz\ vb **closed; clos·ing 1** : to bar passage through : SHUT **2** : to suspend the operations (as of a school) **3** ♦ : to bring or come to an end or period : END, TERMINATE **4** : to bring together the parts or edges of; also : to fill up **5** ♦ : to come near or approach close **6** : GRAPPLE ⟨∼ with the enemy⟩ **7** : to enter into an agreement — **clos·able** or **close·able** adj

♦ [3] conclude, end, finish, round, terminate, wind up, wrap up Ant begin, commence, inaugurate, open, start ♦ [5] approach, near

²**close** \'klōz\ n ♦ : a coming or bringing of something to a conclusion or an end : CONCLUSION, END

♦ conclusion, consummation, end, ending, finale, finis, finish, windup ♦ cessation, closure, conclusion, end, ending, expiration, finish, halt, lapse, shutdown, stop, stoppage, termination

³**close** \'klōs\ n ♦ : an enclosed space

♦ court, courtyard, quadrangle, yard

⁴**close** \'klōs\ adj **clos·er; clos·est 1** : having no openings : CLOSED **2** : narrowly restricting or restricted **3** : limited to a privileged class **4 a** : SECLUDED **b** ♦ : marked by a disposition to secrecy or extreme discreetness about divulging information : SECRETIVE **5** : RIGOROUS **6** ♦ : hot and stuffy : causing a sensation of being slightly smothered or stifled **7** : not generous in giving or spending : STINGY **8** ♦ : having little space between items or units **9** : fitting tightly; also : SHORT ⟨∼ haircut⟩ **10** ♦ : being near in time, space, effect, or degree : NEAR **11** ♦ : marked by a warm friendship developing through long association : INTIMATE ⟨∼ friends⟩ **12** : very precise and attentive to details : ACCURATE **13** ♦ : decided by a narrow margin ⟨a ∼ game⟩ — **close·ly** adv

♦ [4b] closemouthed, dark, reticent, secretive, uncommunicative ♦ [6] breathless, stuffy ♦ [8] compact, crowded, dense, packed, serried, thick, tight Ant loose, uncrowded ♦ [10] immediate, near, nearby, nigh Ant distant, far, faraway, far-off, remote ♦ [11] bosom, chummy, familiar, friendly, intimate, thick ♦ [13] narrow, neck and neck, nip and tuck, tight

⁵**close** *adv* ♦ : in proximity of space or time

♦ around, by, hard, in, near, nearby, nigh

closed–cir·cuit \'klōzd-'sər-kət\ *adj* : used in, shown on, or being a television installation in which the signal is transmitted by wire to a limited number of receivers
closed shop *n* : an establishment having only members of a labor union on the payroll
close-fist·ed \'klōz-'fis-təd, 'klōs-\ *adj* : not openhanded or liberal esp. in giving : STINGY
close–knit \'klōs-'nit\ *adj* : closely bound together by social, cultural, economic, or political ties
close·mouthed \'klōz-'maût͟hd, 'klōs-'maûtht\ *adj* 1 ♦ : cautious or reticent in speaking 2 ♦ : disposed to secrecy about one's personal affairs

♦ [1] laconic, reserved, reticent, silent, taciturn, uncommunicative ♦ [2] close, dark, reticent, secretive, uncommunicative

close·ness *n* ♦ : the quality or state of being close

♦ familiarity, intimacy, nearness ♦ contiguity, immediacy, nearness, proximity

close·out \'klō-zaût\ *n* : a sale of a business's entire stock at low prices
close out *vb* 1 : to dispose of by a closeout 2 : to dispose of a business : SELL OUT
¹**clos·et** \'klä-zət, 'klȯ-\ *n* 1 ♦ : a small room for privacy 2 ♦ : a small compartment for household utensils or clothing 3 : a state or condition of secrecy ⟨came out of the ∼⟩

♦ [1] cell, chamber, room ♦ [2] buffet, cabinet, cupboard, hutch, locker, sideboard

²**closet** *vb* 1 : to shut up in or as if in a closet 2 : to take into a private room for an interview
close–up \'klō-ˌsəp\ *n* 1 : a photograph or movie shot taken at close range 2 : an intimate view or examination
clo·sure \'klō-zhər\ *n* 1 ♦ : an act of closing : the condition of being closed 2 : a bringing to a point of completion 3 : something that closes 4 : CLOTURE

♦ cessation, close, conclusion, end, ending, expiration, finish, halt, lapse, shutdown, stop, stoppage, termination

¹**clot** \'klät\ *n* : a mass formed by a portion of liquid (as blood) thickening and sticking together
²**clot** *vb* ♦ : to become a clot

♦ coagulate, congeal, gel, jell, set

cloth \'klȯth\ *n, pl* **cloths** \'klȯt͟hz, 'klȯths\ 1 : a pliable fabric made usu. by weaving or knitting natural or synthetic fibers and filaments 2 : TABLECLOTH 3 : distinctive dress of the clergy; *also* : CLERGY
clothe \'klōt͟h\ *vb* **clothed** *or* **clad** \'klad\; **cloth·ing** 1 ♦ : to provide with clothes : cover with clothes : DRESS 2 ♦ : to express by suitably significant language

♦ [1] apparel, array, attire, caparison, deck, dress, garb, invest, rig, suit *Ant* disrobe, strip, unclothe, undress ♦ [2] articulate, couch, express, formulate, phrase, put, say, state, word

clothes \'klōt͟hz, 'klōz\ *n pl* 1 : covering for the human body or garments in general : CLOTHING 2 : BEDCLOTHES
clothes·horse \-ˌhȯrs\ *n* 1 : a frame on which to hang clothes 2 : a conspicuously dressy person
clothes·line \-ˌlīn\ *n* : a rope or cord on which clothes are hung to dry
clothes moth *n* : any of several small pale moths whose larvae eat wool, fur, and feathers
clothes·pin \'klōt͟hz-ˌpin, 'klōz-\ *n* : a device for fastening clothes on a line
clothes·press \-ˌpres\ *n* : a receptacle for clothes
cloth·ier \'klōt͟h-yər, 'klōt͟h-ē-ər\ *n* : a maker or seller of clothing
cloth·ing \'klō-t͟hiŋ\ *n* ♦ : garments in general

♦ apparel, attire, dress, duds, raiment, wear

clo·ture \'klō-chər\ *n* : the closing or limitation (as by calling for a vote) of debate in a legislative body
¹**cloud** \'klaûd\ *n* 1 : a visible mass of particles of condensed vapor (as water or ice) suspended in the atmosphere 2 : a usu. visible mass of minute airborne particles; *also* : a mass of obscuring matter in interstellar space 3 : CROWD, SWARM ⟨a ∼ of mosquitoes⟩ 4 : something having a dark or threatening aspect ⟨a ∼ of suspicion⟩ 5 : something that obscures or blemishes ⟨a ∼ of ambiguity⟩ 6 : the computers and networks that support cloud computing — **cloud·i·ness** \'klaû-dē-nəs\ *n*

²**cloud** *vb* 1 ♦ : to darken or hide with or as if with a cloud : OBSCURE 2 ♦ : to make unclear or confused : CONFUSE 3 : TAINT, SULLY

♦ [1] becloud, befog, blur, darken, dim, fog, haze, mist, obscure, overshadow, shroud *Ant* brighten, illuminate, illumine, lighten ♦ [2] becloud, befog, blur, confuse, fog, muddy

cloud·burst \-ˌbərst\ *n* ♦ : a sudden heavy rainfall

♦ deluge, downpour, rain, rainstorm, storm, wet

cloud computing *n* : the practice of storing regularly used computer data on multiple servers that can be accessed through the Internet
cloud·less *adj* ♦ : free from any cloud

♦ clear, fair, sunny, sunshiny, unclouded

cloud·let \-lət\ *n* : a small cloud
cloud nine *n* : a feeling of extreme well-being or elation — usu. used with *on*
cloudy *adj* 1 ♦ : having a cloudy or overcast sky 2 ♦ : dimmed or dulled as if by clouds 3 ♦ : having visible material in suspension : MURKY

♦ [1] dull, hazy, heavy, overcast ♦ [2] foggy, hazy, misty, murky, smoggy, soupy ♦ [3] muddy, murky, turbid *Ant* clear

¹**clout** \'klaût\ *n* 1 ♦ : a blow esp. with the hand 2 ♦ : the power to sway people : special influence

♦ [1] bat, belt, blow, box, hit, punch, slug, thump, wallop, whack ♦ [2] authority, influence, pull, sway, weight

²**clout** *vb* : to hit forcefully
¹**clove** \'klōv\ *n* : one of the small bulbs that grows at the base of the scales of a large bulb ⟨a ∼ of garlic⟩
²**clove** *past of* CLEAVE
³**clove** *n* : the dried flower bud of an East Indian tree used esp. as a spice
clo·ven \'klō-vən\ *past part of* CLEAVE
cloven foot *n* : CLOVEN HOOF — **cloven–foot·ed** \-'fu̇-təd\ *adj*
cloven hoof *n* : a foot (as of a sheep) with the front part divided into two parts — **cloven–hoofed** \-'hu̇ft, -'hu̇vd\ *adj*
clo·ver \'klō-vər\ *n* : any of a genus of leguminous herbs with usu. 3-parted leaves and dense flower heads
clo·ver·leaf \-ˌlēf\ *n, pl* **cloverleafs** \-ˌlēfs\ *or* **clo·ver·leaves** \-ˌlēvz\ : an interchange between two major highways that from above resembles a four-leaf clover
¹**clown** \'klaûn\ *n* 1 ♦ : a rude ill-bred person : BOOR 2 ♦ : a fool or comedian in an entertainment (as a circus)

♦ [1] beast, boor, churl, creep, cretin, cur, heel, jerk, joker, louse, lout, skunk, slob, snake ♦ [2] buffoon, harlequin, zany

²**clown** *vb* ♦ : to act like a clown ⟨always ∼*ing* around⟩

♦ *usu* **clown around** act up, cut up, fool around, monkey, show off, skylark

clown·ish *adj* ♦ : resembling or befitting a clown (as in ignorance and lack of sophistication) — **clown·ish·ly** *adv* — **clown·ish·ness** *n*

♦ boorish, churlish, loutish, uncouth *Ant* cultivated, polished, refined, well-bred; courtly, genteel, gentlemanly, ladylike; civil, courteous, polite

cloy \'klȯi\ *vb* : to disgust or nauseate with excess of something orig. pleasing — **cloy·ing·ly** *adv*
clr *abbr* clear
¹**club** \'kləb\ *n* 1 ♦ : a heavy wooden stick or staff used as a weapon; *also* : BAT 2 : any of a suit of playing cards marked with a black figure resembling a clover leaf 3 a : a group of persons associated for a common purpose b : the meeting place of a group or association

♦ [1] bat, billy club, bludgeon, cudgel, nightstick, staff, truncheon ♦ [3a] association, brotherhood, college, congress, council, fellowship, fraternity, guild, institute, institution, league, order, organization, society

²**club** *vb* **clubbed; club·bing** 1 : to strike with a club 2 ♦ : to unite or combine for a common cause

♦ ally, associate, band, confederate, conjoin, cooperate, federate, league, unite

club·foot \'kləb-'fut\ *n* : a misshapen foot twisted out of position from birth; *also* : this deformed condition — **club·foot·ed** \-'fu̇-təd\ *adj*
club·house \'kləb-ˌhaûs\ *n* 1 : a house occupied by a club 2 : locker rooms used by an athletic team 3 : a building at a golf course with locker rooms and usu. a pro shop and a restaurant

club sandwich *n* : a sandwich of three slices of bread with two layers of meat (as turkey) and lettuce, tomato, and mayonnaise

club soda *n* : SODA WATER

cluck \'klək\ *n* : the call of a hen esp. to her chicks — **cluck** *vb*

¹**clue** \'klü\ *n* **1** ♦ : something that guides through an intricate procedure or maze; *esp* : a piece of evidence leading to the solution of a problem **2** ♦ : an indication that properly interpreted may lead to full understanding of something : IDEA, NOTION ⟨has no ∼ what he's doing⟩

     ♦ [1, 2] cue, hint, idea, indication, inkling, intimation, lead, notion, suggestion

²**clue** *vb* **clued; clue·ing** *or* **clu·ing** **1** : to provide with a clue **2** ♦ : to give information to ⟨∼ me in⟩

     ♦ *usu* **clue in** acquaint, advise, apprise, brief, enlighten, familiarize, fill in, inform, instruct, tell, wise

¹**clump** \'kləmp\ *n* **1** ♦ : a group of things clustered together **2** ♦ : a compact mass **3** : a heavy tramping sound

     ♦ array, assemblage, bank, batch, block, bunch, cluster, collection, group, huddle, knot, lot, package, parcel, set, suite

²**clump** *vb* : to tread clumsily and noisily

clum·sy \'kləm-zē\ *adj* **clum·si·er; -est** **1** ♦ : lacking dexterity, nimbleness, or grace **2** ♦ : not tactful or subtle ⟨a ∼ attempt at a joke⟩ **3** ♦ : awkward or inefficient in use or construction : UNWIELDY — **clum·si·ly** \-zə-lē\ *adv* — **clum·si·ness** \-zē-nəs\ *n*

     ♦ [1] awkward, gawky, graceless, heavy-handed, lubberly, lumpish, ungainly, unhandy *Ant* deft, dexterous, graceful, handy ♦ [2] awkward, inept, inexpert, maladroit ♦ [3] awkward, cranky, cumbersome, ungainly, unhandy, unwieldy

clung *past and past part of* CLING

clunk·er \'kləŋ-kər\ *n* **1** : a dilapidated automobile **2** : a notable failure

¹**clus·ter** \'kləs-tər\ *n* ♦ : a number of similar things that occur together : GROUP, BUNCH

     ♦ array, assemblage, bank, batch, block, bunch, clump, collection, group, huddle, knot, lot, package, parcel, set, suite

²**cluster** *vb* ♦ : to grow or gather in a cluster

     ♦ assemble, collect, concentrate, conglomerate, congregate, convene, forgather, gather, meet, rendezvous ♦ bunch, crowd, huddle, press

¹**clutch** \'kləch\ *vb* ♦ : to grasp with or as if with the hand

     ♦ clench, cling, grip, hang on, hold, hold on

²**clutch** *n* **1 a** : the claws or a hand in the act of grasping **b** ♦ : an often cruel or unrelenting control, power, or possession : CONTROL, POWER **2** : a device for gripping an object **3** : a coupling used to connect and disconnect a driving and a driven part of a mechanism; *also* : a lever or pedal operating such a coupling **4** ♦ : a crucial situation

     ♦ [1b] arm, authority, command, control, dominion, grip, hold, power, sway ♦ [4] crisis, crunch, emergency, head, juncture

³**clutch** *adj* : made, done, or successful in a crucial situation

⁴**clutch** *n* **1** : a nest or batch of eggs; *also* : a brood of chicks **2** : GROUP, BUNCH

¹**clut·ter** \'klə-tər\ *vb* ♦ : to fill or cover with a disorderly scattering of things

²**clutter** *n* ♦ : a crowded mass

     ♦ assortment, jumble, medley, mélange, miscellany, motley, muddle, variety, welter

cm *abbr* centimeter

Cm *symbol* curium

CM *abbr* Northern Mariana Islands

cmdr *abbr* commander

cml *abbr* commercial

CMSgt *abbr* chief master sergeant

Cn *symbol* copernicium

CNO *abbr* chief of naval operations

CNS *abbr* central nervous system

co *abbr* **1** company **2** county

Co *symbol* cobalt

CO *abbr* **1** Colorado **2** commanding officer **3** conscientious objector

c/o *abbr* care of

¹**coach** \'kōch\ *n* **1** : a large closed 4-wheeled carriage with an elevated outside front seat for the driver **2** : a railroad passenger car esp. for day travel **3** : BUS **4 a** : a private tutor **b** : one who instructs or trains; *esp* : one who instructs players in a sport ⟨a soccer ∼⟩

²**coach** *vb* ♦ : to instruct, direct, or prompt as a coach

     ♦ counsel, guide, lead, mentor, pilot, shepherd, show, tutor

coach·man \-mən\ *n* : a man who drives a coach or carriage

co·ad·ju·tor \ˌkō-ə-'jü-tər, kō-'a-jə-tər\ *n* : one who works together with another : ASSISTANT; *esp* : an assistant bishop having the right of succession

co·ag·u·lant \kō-'a-gyə-lənt\ *n* : something that produces coagulation

co·ag·u·late \-ˌlāt\ *vb* **-lat·ed; -lat·ing** ♦ : to cause to become viscous or thickened into a coherent mass : CLOT — **co·ag·u·la·tion** \kō-ˌa-gyə-'lā-shən\ *n*

     ♦ clot, congeal, gel, jell, set

¹**coal** \'kōl\ *n* **1** : EMBER **2** : a black solid combustible mineral used as fuel

²**coal** *vb* **1** : to supply with coal **2** : to take in coal

co·a·lesce \ˌkō-ə-'les\ *vb* **co·a·lesced; co·a·lesc·ing** **1** : to grow together **2** ♦ : to unite into a whole : FUSE — **co·a·les·cence** \-'ns\ *n*

     ♦ associate, combine, conjoin, connect, couple, fuse, join, link, marry, unify, unite

coal·field \'kōl-ˌfēld\ *n* : a region rich in coal deposits

coal gas *n* : gas from coal; *esp* : gas distilled from bituminous coal and used for heating

co·a·li·tion \ˌkō-ə-'li-shən\ *n* **1** : UNION **2** ♦ : a temporary alliance of distinct parties, persons, or states for a common purpose — **co·a·li·tion·ist** *n*

     ♦ alliance, bloc, combination, combine, confederacy, confederation, federation, league, union ♦ bloc, body, combination, combine, faction, party, sect, set, side, wing

coal oil *n* : KEROSENE

coal tar *n* : tar distilled from bituminous coal and used in dyes and drugs

co·an·chor \'kō-ˌaŋ-kər\ *n* : a newscaster who shares the duties of head broadcaster

coarse \'kȯrs\ *adj* **coars·er; coars·est** **1** ♦ : of ordinary or inferior quality **2** ♦ : composed of large parts or particles ⟨∼ sand⟩ **3** ♦ : crude or unrefined in taste, manners, or language : CRUDE ⟨∼ manners⟩ **4** : harsh or rough in tone or texture : ROUGH, HARSH — **coarse·ly** *adv*

     ♦ [1] bad, bum, cheap, common, cut-rate, inferior, junky, lousy, mediocre, poor, second-rate, shoddy, sleazy, trashy ♦ [2] grainy, granular *Ant* dusty, fine, floury, powdery ♦ [3] common, crass, crude, gross, ill-bred, low, rough, rude, tasteless, uncouth, uncultivated, uncultured, unpolished, unrefined, vulgar *Ant* cultivated, cultured, genteel, polished, refined, smooth, tasteful, well-bred

coars·en \'kȯr-sᵊn\ *vb* : to make or become coarse

coarse·ness *n* ♦ : the quality or state of being coarse

     ♦ grossness, indelicacy, lowness, rudeness, vulgarity

¹**coast** \'kōst\ *n* **1** : SEASHORE **2** : a slide down a slope **3** : the immediate area of view — used in the phrase *the coast is clear* — **coast·al** *adj*

²**coast** *vb* **1** : to sail along the shore **2** ♦ : to move (as downhill on a sled) without effort

     ♦ bowl, breeze, drift, flow, glide, roll, sail, skim, slide, slip, stream, sweep, whisk

coast·er *n* **1** : one that coasts **2** : a shallow container or a plate or mat to protect a surface

coaster brake *n* : a brake in the hub of the rear wheel of a bicycle

coast guard *n* : a military force employed in guarding or patrolling a coast — **coast·guards·man** \'kōst-ˌgärdz-mən\ *n*

coast·line \'kōst-ˌlīn\ *n* : the outline or shape of a coast

¹**coat** \'kōt\ *n* **1** : an outer garment for the upper part of the body **2** ♦ : an external growth (as of fur or feathers) on an animal **3** : a covering layer ⟨a ∼ of paint⟩ — **coat·ed** \'kō-təd\ *adj*

     ♦ fleece, fur, hair, pelage, pile, wool

²**coat** *vb* ♦ : to cover usu. with a finishing or protective coat or layer

     ♦ blanket, carpet, cover, overlay, overlie, overspread

coat·ing \'kō-tiŋ\ *n* : COAT, COVERING

coat of arms *n* : a shield or similar device for displaying the insignia of a family or group

co·au·thor \'kō-'ȯ-thər\ *n* : a joint or associate author — **coau·thor** *vb*

coax \'kōks\ *vb* ♦ : to gain by gentle urging or flattery : WHEEDLE

     ♦ cajole, wheedle

co·ax·i·al \'kō-'ak-sē-əl\ *adj* : having coincident axes — **co·ax·i·al·ly** *adv*

coaxial cable *n* : a cable that consists of a tube of electrically conducting material surrounding a central conductor

cob \'käb\ *n* **1** : a male swan **2** : CORNCOB **3** : a short-legged stocky horse

co·balt \'kō-ˌbolt\ *n* : a tough shiny silver-white magnetic metallic chemical element found with iron and nickel

cob·ble \'kä-bəl\ *vb* **cob·bled; cob·bling** : to make or put together roughly or hastily — often used with *together* or *up* ⟨~ together a solution⟩

cob·bler \'kä-blər\ *n* **1** : a mender or maker of shoes **2** : a deep-dish fruit pie with a thick crust

cob·ble·stone \'kä-bəl-ˌstōn\ *n* : a naturally rounded stone larger than a pebble and smaller than a boulder

co·bra \'kō-brə\ *n* : any of several venomous snakes of Asia and Africa that when excited expand the skin of the neck into a broad hood

cob·web \'käb-ˌweb\ *n* **1** : SPIDERWEB; *also* : a thread spun by a spider or insect larva **2** : something flimsy or entangling — **cob·web·by** \-ˌwe-bē\ *adj*

co·caine \kō-'kān, 'kō-ˌkān\ *n* : a drug obtained from the leaves of a So. American shrub (**co·ca** \'kō-kə\) that can result in severe psychological dependence and is sometimes used in medicine as a local anesthetic and illegally as a stimulant of the central nervous system

coc·cus \'kä-kəs\ *n, pl* **coc·ci** \'käk-ˌsī\ : a spherical bacterium

coc·cyx \'käk-siks\ *n, pl* **coc·cy·ges** \'käk-sə-ˌjēz\ *also* **coc·cyx·es** \'käk-sik-səz\ : the end of the spinal column beyond the sacrum esp. in humans

co·chi·neal \'kä-chə-ˌnēl\ *n* : a red dye made from the dried bodies of females of a tropical American insect (**cochineal insect**)

co·chlea \'kō-klē-ə, 'kä-\ *n, pl* **co·chle·as** *or* **co·chle·ae** \-klē-ˌē, -ˌī\ : the usu. spiral part of the inner ear containing nerve endings which carry information about sound to the brain — **co·chle·ar** \-klē-ər\ *adj*

¹cock \'käk\ *n* **1** : the adult male of a bird and esp. of the common domestic chicken **2** ♦ : a device (as a faucet or valve) for regulating the flow of a liquid : VALVE, FAUCET **3** : LEADER **4 a** : the hammer of a firearm **b** : the position of the hammer when ready for firing

♦ faucet, gate, spigot, tap, valve

²cock *vb* **1** : to draw back the hammer of a firearm **2** : to set or draw back in readiness for some action ⟨~ your arm to throw⟩ **3** ♦ : to turn or tilt usu. to one side

♦ angle, cant, heel, incline, lean, list, slant, slope, tilt, tip

³cock *n* ♦ : the act of tilting : the state or position of being tilted

♦ bend, inclination, list, slant, tilt, tip

⁴cock *n* : a small pile (as of hay)

cock·ade \kä-'kād\ *n* : an ornament worn on the hat as a badge

cock·a·tiel \ˌkä-kə-'tēl\ *n* : a small crested gray parrot often kept as a cage bird

cock·a·too \'kä-kə-ˌtü\ *n, pl* **-toos** : any of various large noisy crested parrots chiefly of Australia

cock·a·trice \'kä-kə-trəs, -ˌtrīs\ *n* : a legendary serpent with a deadly glance

cock·crow \'käk-ˌkrō\ *n* ♦ : the first appearance of light in the morning followed by sunrise : DAWN

♦ aurora, dawn, morning, sunrise

cocked hat \'käkt-\ *n* : a hat with the brim turned up on two or three sides

cock·er·el \'kä-kə-rəl\ *n* : a young male domestic chicken

cock·er spaniel \'kä-kər-\ *n* : any of a breed of small spaniels with long ears, square muzzle, and silky coat

cock·eyed \'kä-ˌkīd\ *adj* **1** ♦ : turned or tilted to one side **2** : slightly crazy : FOOLISH

♦ askew, awry, crooked, listing, lopsided, slantwise, uneven

cock·fight \'käk-ˌfīt\ *n* : a contest of gamecocks usu. fitted with metal spurs

¹cock·le \'kä-kəl\ *n* : any of several weedy plants related to the pinks

²cockle *n* : a bivalve mollusk with a heart-shaped shell

cock·le·shell \-ˌshel\ *n* **1** : the shell of a cockle **2** : a light flimsy boat

cock·ney \'käk-nē\ *n, pl* **cockneys** : a native of London and esp. of the East End of London; *also* : the dialect of a cockney

cock·pit \'käk-ˌpit\ *n* **1** : a pit for cockfights **2** : a space or compartment in a vehicle from which it is steered, piloted, or driven

cock·roach \'käk-ˌrōch\ *n* : any of an order or suborder of active nocturnal insects including some which infest houses and ships

cock·sure \'käk-'shùr\ *adj* **1** ♦ : perfectly sure : CERTAIN **2** : COCKY

♦ assured, certain, clear, confident, doubtless, positive, sanguine, sure

cock·tail \'käk-ˌtāl\ *n* **1** : an iced drink made of liquor and flavoring ingredients **2** : an appetizer (as tomato juice) served as a first course of a meal

cocky \'kä-kē\ *adj* **cock·i·er; -est** ♦ : boldly and brashly self-confident — **cock·i·ly** \-kə-lē\ *adv* — **cock·i·ness** \-kē-nəs\ *n*

♦ arch, bold, brash, brazen, cheeky, fresh, impertinent, impudent, insolent, nervy, sassy, saucy

co·coa \'kō-kō\ *n* **1** : CACAO **2** : chocolate deprived of some of its fat and powdered; *also* : a drink made of this heated with water or milk

cocoa butter *n* : a pale vegetable fat obtained from cacao beans

co·co·nut \'kō-kə-(ˌ)nət\ *n* : a large edible nut produced by a tall tropical palm (**coconut palm**)

co·coon \kə-'kün\ *n* **1** : a case usu. of silk formed by some insect larvae for protection during the pupal stage **2** ♦ : something suggesting a cocoon esp. in providing protection or in producing isolation

♦ armor, capsule, case, casing, cover, housing, husk, jacket, pod, sheath, shell

cod \'käd\ *n, pl* **cod** *also* **cods** : a bottom-dwelling bony fish of the No. Atlantic that is an important food fish; *also* : a related fish of the Pacific Ocean

COD *abbr* **1** cash on delivery **2** collect on delivery

co·da \'kō-də\ *n* : a closing section in a musical composition that is formally distinct from the main structure

cod·dle \'käd-ᵊl\ *vb* **cod·dled; cod·dling** **1** : to cook slowly in water below the boiling point **2** ♦ : to treat with extreme or excessive care or kindness : PAMPER

♦ baby, mollycoddle, nurse, pamper, spoil

¹code \'kōd\ *n* **1** : a systematic statement of a body of law **2** : a system of principles or rules ⟨moral ~⟩ **3** : a system of signals **4** : a system of symbols (as in secret communication) with special meanings **5** : GENETIC CODE

²code *vb* **cod·ed; cod·ing** : to put into the form or symbols of a code

co·deine \'kō-ˌdēn\ *n* : a narcotic drug obtained from opium and used esp. as an analgesic and cough suppressant

co·dex \'kō-ˌdeks\ *n, pl* **co·di·ces** \'kō-də-ˌsēz, 'kä-\ : a manuscript book (as of the Scriptures or classics)

cod·fish \'käd-ˌfish\ *n* : COD

cod·ger \'kä-jər\ *n* : an odd or cranky and usu. elderly fellow

cod·i·cil \'kä-də-səl, -ˌsil\ *n* : a legal instrument modifying an earlier will

cod·i·fy \'kä-də-ˌfī, 'kō-\ *vb* **-fied; -fy·ing** ♦ : to arrange in a systematic form — **cod·i·fi·ca·tion** \ˌkä-də-fə-'kā-shən, ˌkō-\ *n*

♦ arrange, array, classify, dispose, draw up, marshal, order, organize, range, systematize

co·ed \'kō-ˌed\ *n* : a female student in a coeducational institution — **coed** *adj*

co·ed·u·ca·tion \ˌkō-ˌe-jə-'kā-shən\ *n* : the education of male and female students at the same institution — **co·ed·u·ca·tion·al** \-shə-nəl\ *adj* — **co·ed·u·ca·tion·al·ly** *adv*

co·ef·fi·cient \ˌkō-ə-'fi-shənt\ *n* **1** : a constant factor as distinguished from a variable in a mathematical term **2** : a number that serves as a measure of some property (as of a substance, device, or process)

coe·len·ter·ate \si-'len-tə-ˌrāt, -rət\ *n* : any of a phylum of radially symmetrical invertebrate animals including the corals, sea anemones, and jellyfishes

co·equal \kō-'ē-kwəl\ *adj* : equal with another — **coequal** *n* — **co·equal·i·ty** \ˌkō-ē-'kwä-lə-tē\ *n* — **co·equal·ly** *adv*

co·erce \kō-'ərs\ *vb* **co·erced; co·erc·ing** **1** : RESTRAIN, REPRESS **2** ♦ : to compel to an act or choice **3** : ENFORCE — **co·er·cive** \-'ər-siv\ *adj*

♦ compel, constrain, drive, force, make, muscle, obligate, oblige, press, pressure

co·er·cion \-'ər-zhən, -shən\ *n* ♦ : the act, process, or power of coercing

♦ compulsion, constraint, duress, force, pressure

¹co·e·val \kō-'ē-vəl\ *adj* ♦ : of the same age

♦ concurrent, contemporary, simultaneous, synchronous

²**coeval** *n* : one of the same age

co·ex·ist \ˌkō-ig-ˈzist\ *vb* **1** : to exist together or at the same time **2** : to live in peace with each other

co·ex·is·tence \-ˈzis-təns\ *n* : the quality or state of coexisting

co·ex·ten·sive \ˌkō-ik-ˈsten-siv\ *adj* : having the same scope or extent in space or time

C of C *abbr* Chamber of Commerce

cof·fee \ˈkȯ-fē\ *n* : a drink made from the roasted and ground seeds of a fruit of a tropical shrub or tree; *also* : these seeds (**coffee beans**) or a plant producing them

cof·fee·house \-ˌhau̇s\ *n* : a place where refreshments (as coffee) are sold

coffee klatch \-ˌklach\ *n* : KAFFEEKLATSCH

cof·fee·pot \-ˌpät\ *n* : a pot for brewing or serving coffee

coffee shop *n* : a small restaurant

coffee table *n* : a low table customarily placed in front of a sofa

cof·fer \ˈkȯ-fər\ *n* : a chest or box used esp. for valuables

cof·fer·dam \-ˌdam\ *n* : a watertight enclosure from which water is pumped to expose the bottom of a body of water and permit construction

cof·fin \ˈkȯ-fən\ *n* : a box or chest for a corpse to be buried in

C of S *abbr* chief of staff

¹**cog** \ˈkäg\ *n* : a tooth on the rim of a wheel or gear — **cogged** \ˈkägd\ *adj*

²**cog** *abbr* cognate

co·gen·cy \-jən-sē\ *n* ♦ : the quality or state of being cogent

♦ effectiveness, force, impact, persuasiveness, pertinence, punch, relevance, soundness, strength *Ant* ineffectiveness

co·gen·er·a·tion \ˌkō-je-nə-ˈrā-shən\ *n* : the simultaneous generation of electricity and heat from the same fuel

co·gent \ˈkō-jənt\ *adj* ♦ : having power to compel or constrain : CONVINCING

♦ compelling, conclusive, convincing, decisive, effective, forceful, persuasive, pertinent, relevant, satisfying, sound, strong, telling, valid *Ant* inconclusive, indecisive, ineffective, unconvincing

cog·i·tate \ˈkä-jə-ˌtāt\ *vb* **-tat·ed; -tat·ing** ♦ : to ponder or meditate on usu. intently : THINK, PONDER — **cog·i·ta·tion** \ˌkä-jə-ˈtā-shən\ *n* — **cog·i·ta·tive** \ˈkä-jə-ˌtā-tiv\ *adj*

♦ chew over, consider, contemplate, debate, deliberate, entertain, meditate, mull, ponder, question, ruminate, study, think, weigh

cog·nac \ˈkōn-ˌyak\ *n* : a French brandy

cog·nate \ˈkäg-ˌnāt\ *adj* **1** : of the same or similar nature **2** : RELATED; *esp* : related by descent from the same ancestral language — **cognate** *n*

cog·ni·tive \ˈkäg-nə-tiv\ *adj* : of, relating to, or being conscious intellectual activity (as thinking, remembering, reasoning, or using language) — **cog·ni·tion** \käg-ˈni-shən\ *n* — **cog·ni·tive·ly** *adv*

cog·ni·zance \ˈkäg-nə-zəns\ *n* **1** ♦ : apprehension by the mind : AWARENESS **2** : NOTICE, HEED **3** : particular knowledge : conscious recognition

♦ attention, awareness, ear, eye, heed, notice, observance, observation

cog·ni·zant \ˈkäg-nə-zənt\ *adj* ♦ : knowledgeable of something esp. through personal experience

♦ alive, aware, conscious, mindful, sensible, sentient, witting

cog·no·men \käg-ˈnō-mən, ˈkäg-nə-\ *n, pl* **cognomens** *or* **cog·no·mi·na** \käg-ˈnä-mə-nə, -ˈnō-\ ♦ : a word or phrase that constitutes the distinctive designation of a person or thing : NAME; *esp* : NICKNAME

♦ alias, nickname ♦ appellation, denotation, designation, handle, name, title

co·gno·scen·te \ˌkän-yə-ˈshen-tē\ *n, pl* **-scen·ti** \-tē\ : CONNOISSEUR

cog·wheel \ˈkäg-ˌhwēl\ *n* : a wheel with cogs or teeth

co·hab·it \kō-ˈha-bət\ *vb* : to live together as a couple — **co·hab·i·ta·tion** \-ˌha-bə-ˈtā-shən\ *n*

co·here \kō-ˈhir\ *vb* **co·hered; co·her·ing** **1** : to stick together **2** : to become united in principles, relationships, or interests

co·her·ence \-əns\ *n* ♦ : the quality or state of being coherent

♦ balance, consonance, harmony, proportion, symmetry, symphony, unity

co·her·ent \kō-ˈhir-ənt\ *adj* **1** : having the quality of cohering **2** ♦ : logically consistent — **co·her·ent·ly** *adv*

♦ analytic, good, logical, rational, reasonable, sensible, sober, sound, valid

co·he·sion \kō-ˈhē-zhən\ *n* **1** ♦ : a sticking together **2** : molecular attraction by which the particles of a body are united — **co·he·sive** \-siv\ *adj* — **co·he·sive·ly** *adv* — **co·he·sive·ness** *n*

♦ adherence, adhesion

co·ho \ˈkō-ˌhō\ *n, pl* **cohos** *or* **coho** : a rather small Pacific salmon with light-colored flesh

co·hort \ˈkō-ˌhȯrt\ *n* **1** : a group of warriors or followers **2** ♦ : one that keeps company with another : COMPANION, ACCOMPLICE

♦ accomplice, associate, companion, comrade, crony, fellow, mate

coif \ˈkȯif; 2 usu ˈkwäf\ *n* **1** : a close-fitting hat **2** : COIFFURE

coif·feur \kwä-ˈfər\ *n* : HAIRDRESSER

coif·feuse \kwä-ˈfərz, -ˈfəz, -ˈfüz, -ˈfyüz\ *n* : a female hairdresser

coif·fure \kwä-ˈfyu̇r\ *n* : a manner of arranging the hair

¹**coil** \ˈkȯil\ *vb* ♦ : to wind in a spiral shape

♦ curl, entwine, spiral, twine, twist, wind

²**coil** *n* : a series of rings or loops (as of coiled rope, wire, or pipe) : RING, LOOP

¹**coin** \ˈkȯin\ *n* **1** : a piece of metal issued by government authority as money **2** : metal money

²**coin** *vb* **1** : to make (a coin) esp. by stamping : MINT **2** : CREATE, INVENT ⟨~ a phrase⟩ — **coin·er** *n*

coin·age \ˈkȯi-nij\ *n* **1** : the act or process of coining **2 a** ♦ : something that has been coined **b** : COINS

♦ concoction, contrivance, creation, innovation, invention, wrinkle

co·in·cide \ˌkō-ən-ˈsīd, ˈkō-ən-ˌsīd\ *vb* **-cid·ed; -cid·ing** **1** : to occupy the same place in space or time **2** ♦ : to correspond or agree exactly

♦ accord, agree, answer, check, comport, conform, correspond, dovetail, fit, go, harmonize, jibe, square, tally

co·in·ci·dence \kō-ˈin-sə-dəns\ *n* **1** : exact agreement **2** : occurrence together apparently without reason; *also* : an event that so occurs

co·in·ci·dent \-sə-dənt\ *adj* **1** : of similar nature **2** ♦ : occupying the same space or time

♦ attendant, concomitant, concurrent

co·in·ci·den·tal \kō-ˌin-sə-ˈdent-ᵊl\ *adj* : occurring or existing at the same time

co·i·tus \ˈkō-ə-təs\ *n* : physical union of male and female genitalia : SEXUAL INTERCOURSE — **co·i·tal** \-ᵊl\ *adj*

¹**coke** \ˈkōk\ *n* : a hard gray porous fuel made by heating soft coal to drive off most of its volatile material

²**coke** *n* : COCAINE

¹**col** *abbr* **1** colonial; colony **2** column

²**col** *or* **coll** *abbr* **1** collect, collected, collection **2** college, collegiate

Col *abbr* **1** colonel **2** Colorado **3** Colossians

COL *abbr* **1** colonel **2** cost of living

co·la \ˈkō-lə\ *n* : a carbonated soft drink usu. containing sugar, caffeine, caramel, and special flavoring

col·an·der \ˈkə-lən-dər, ˈkä-\ *n* : a perforated utensil for draining food

¹**cold** \ˈkōld\ *adj* **1** ♦ : having a low or decidedly subnormal temperature **2** ♦ : lacking warmth of feeling **3** : suffering or uncomfortable from lack of warmth **4** : giving the appearance of being dead : UNCONSCIOUS — **cold·ly** *adv* — **cold·ness** *n* — **in cold blood** : with premeditation : DELIBERATELY

♦ [1] arctic, bitter, chill, chilly, cool, freezing, frigid, frosty, glacial, icy, nippy, polar, raw, snappy, wintry *Ant* broiling, burning, fiery, hot, piping hot, red-hot, roasting, scalding, scorching, searing, sultry, summery, sweltering, torrid, tropical, warm, warming ♦ [2] aloof, antisocial, cool, detached, distant, frosty, remote, standoffish, unsociable ♦ [2] chill, chilly, cold-blooded, cool, frigid, frosty, glacial, icy, unfriendly, unsympathetic, wintry *Ant* cordial, friendly, genial, hearty, sympathetic, warm, warm-blooded, warmhearted

²**cold** *n* **1 a** : a condition marked by low temperature **b** : cold weather **2** : a chilly feeling **3** : a bodily disorder popularly associated with chilling; *esp* : COMMON COLD

³**cold** *adv* **1** : TOTALLY, FINALLY ⟨stopped them ~⟩ **2** : without notice or preparation ⟨performed the song ~⟩

cold–blood·ed \ˈkōld-ˈblə-dəd\ *adj* **1** ♦ : lacking normal human feelings **2** : having a body temperature not internally regulated but close to that of the environment **3** : sensitive to cold

♦ callous, hard, heartless, inhuman, inhumane, pitiless, soulless, unfeeling, unsympathetic ♦ apathetic, impassive, phlegmatic, stoic, stolid, unemotional

cold feet *n pl* : doubt or fear that prevents action

cold front *n* : an advancing edge of a cold air mass

cold shoulder *n* ♦ : cold or unsympathetic behavior — **cold–shoul·der** *vb*

♦ brush-off, rebuff, repulse, snub

cold sore *n* : a group of fluid-filled blisters appearing in or about the mouth in the oral form of herpes simplex

cold sweat *n* : concurrent perspiration and chill usu. associated with fear, pain, or shock

¹**cold turkey** *n* : abrupt complete cessation of the use of an addictive drug

²**cold turkey** *adv* **1** : without a period of adjustment **2** : without preparation

cold war *n* : a conflict characterized by the use of means short of sustained overt military action

cole·slaw \'kōl-ˌslo\ *n* : a salad made of raw cabbage

col·ic \'kä-lik\ *n* **1** : sharp sudden abdominal pain **2** : a condition marked by recurrent episodes of crying and irritability in an otherwise healthy infant — **col·icky** \'kä-li-kē\ *adj*

col·i·se·um \ˌkä-lə-'sē-əm\ *n* ♦ : a large structure esp. for athletic contests

♦ bowl, circus, stadium

co·li·tis \kō-'lī-təs\ *n* : inflammation of the colon

col·lab·o·rate \kə-'la-bə-ˌrāt\ *vb* **-rat·ed; -rat·ing** **1** ♦ : to work jointly with others (as in writing a book) **2** : to cooperate with an enemy force occupying one's country — **col·lab·o·ra·tive** \-'la-bə-ˌrā-tiv, -b(ə-)rə-\ *adj* — **col·lab·o·ra·tor** \-'la-bə-ˌrā-tər\ *n*

♦ concert, cooperate, join, team

col·lab·o·ra·tion \-ˌla-bə-'rā-shən\ *n* ♦ : the act of collaborating or a situation marked by collaborating

♦ affiliation, alliance, association, confederation, connection, cooperation, hookup, liaison, partnership, relation, relationship, union ♦ cooperation, coordination, teamwork

col·lage \kə-'läzh\ *n* : an artistic composition of fragments (as of printed matter) pasted on a surface

col·la·gen \'kä-lə-jən\ *n* : any of a group of fibrous proteins widely found in vertebrate connective tissue

¹**col·lapse** \kə-'laps\ *vb* **col·lapsed; col·laps·ing** **1** ♦ : to fall or shrink together abruptly **2** : to break down completely : DISINTEGRATE; *also* : to fall in : give way **3 a** : to break down physically or mentally; *esp* : to fall helpless or unconscious **b** : to suddenly lose force, significance, effectiveness, or worth **4** : to fold down compactly — **col·laps·ible** *adj*

♦ cave in, crumple, give, go, yield

²**collapse** *n* ♦ : sudden failure : a failure to function

♦ burnout, exhaustion, fatigue, lassitude, prostration, tiredness, weariness ♦ crash, cropper, defeat, failure, fizzle, nonsuccess

¹**col·lar** \'kä-lər\ *n* **1** : a band, strip, or chain worn around the neck or the neckline of a garment **2** : something resembling a collar — **col·lar·less** *adj*

²**collar** *vb* **1** : to seize by the collar **2** ♦ : to take or seize by or as if by a sudden motion or grasp : GRAB **3** ♦ : to take or get control of

♦ [2, 3] bag, capture, catch, corral, get, grab, grapple, hook, land, nab, seize, snare, trap

col·lar·bone \-ˌbōn\ *n* : the bone of the shoulder that joins the breastbone and the shoulder blade

col·lard \'kä-lərd\ *n* : a stalked smooth-leaved kale — usu. used in pl.

col·late \kə-'lāt; 'kä-ˌlāt, 'kō-\ *vb* **col·lat·ed; col·lat·ing** **1** : to compare (as two texts) carefully and critically **2** : to assemble in proper order

¹**col·lat·er·al** \kə-'la-tə-rəl\ *adj* **1** : associated but of secondary importance **2** : descended from the same ancestors but not in the same line **3** : PARALLEL **4** : of, relating to, or being collateral used as security; *also* : secured by collateral

²**collateral** *n* : property (as stocks) used as security for the repayment of a loan

col·la·tion \kä-'lā-shən, kō-\ *n* **1** : a light meal **2** : the act, process, or result of collating

col·league \'kä-ˌlēg\ *n* : an associate esp. in a profession

¹**col·lect** \'kä-likt, -ˌlekt\ *n* : a short prayer comprising an invocation, petition, and conclusion

²**col·lect** \kə-'lekt\ *vb* **1 a** ♦ : to bring or come together into one body or place : GATHER **b** : to gather or exact from a number of persons or sources **2** ♦ : to gain control of ⟨∼ his thoughts⟩ **3** : to receive payment of **4** ♦ : to form a layer, heap, or mass — **col·lect·ible** *or* **col·lect·able** *adj or n* — **col·lec·tor** \-'lek-tər\ *n*

♦ [1a] accumulate, amass, assemble, concentrate, garner, gather, group, lump, pick up, round up, scrape ♦ [2] calm, compose, control, settle ♦ [4] accumulate, conglomerate, gather, heap, pile up

³**col·lect** \kə-'lekt\ *adv or adj* : to be paid for by the receiver

col·lect·ed \kə-'lek-təd\ *adj* ♦ : possessed of calmness and composure often through concentrated effort : SELF-POSSESSED, CALM

♦ calm, composed, cool, placid, self-possessed, serene, tranquil, undisturbed, unperturbed, unshaken, untroubled, unworried

col·lec·tion \kə-'lek-shən\ *n* **1** : the act or process of collecting ⟨garbage ∼⟩ **2** ♦ : something collected ⟨a stamp ∼⟩ **3** ♦ : a number of individuals or objects brought together as a unit : GROUP

♦ [2, 3] accumulation, assemblage, gathering ♦ [3] array, assemblage, bank, batch, block, bunch, clump, cluster, group, huddle, knot, lot, package, parcel, set, suite

¹**col·lec·tive** \kə-'lek-tiv\ *adj* **1** : of, relating to, or denoting a group of individuals considered as a whole **2** ♦ : involving all members of a group as distinct from its individuals **3** ♦ : shared or assumed by all members of the group

♦ [2, 3] common, communal, concerted, conjoint, joint, mutual, public, united *Ant* individual, single, sole

²**collective** *n* **1** : GROUP **2** : a cooperative unit or organization

collective bargaining *n* : negotiation between an employer and a labor union

col·lec·tive·ly \kə-'lek-tiv-lē\ *adv* ♦ : in a collective sense or manner

♦ all around, altogether, overall, together

col·lec·tiv·ise *chiefly Brit var of* COLLECTIVIZE

col·lec·tiv·ism \kə-'lek-ti-ˌvi-zəm\ *n* : a political or economic theory advocating collective control esp. over production and distribution

col·lec·tiv·ize \-ˌvīz\ *vb* **-ized; -iz·ing** : to organize under collective control — **col·lec·tiv·i·za·tion** \-ˌlek-ti-və-'zā-shən\ *n*

col·leen \kä-'lēn, 'kä-ˌlēn\ *n* : an Irish girl

col·lege \'kä-lij\ *n* **1** : a building used for an educational or religious purpose **2** : an institution of higher learning or division of a university granting a bachelor's degree; *also* : an institution offering instruction esp. in a vocational or technical field ⟨barber ∼⟩ **3** ♦ : an organized body of persons having common interests or duties ⟨∼ of cardinals⟩ — **col·le·giate** \kə-'lē-jət\ *adj*

♦ association, brotherhood, club, congress, council, fellowship, fraternity, guild, institute, institution, league, order, organization, society

col·le·gi·al·i·ty \kə-ˌlē-jē-'a-lə-tē\ *n* : the relationship of colleagues

col·le·gian \kə-'lē-jən\ *n* : a college student or recent college graduate

col·le·gi·um \kə-'le-gē-əm, -'lā-\ *n, pl* **-gia** \-gē-ə\ *or* **-giums** : a group in which each member has approximately equal power

col·lide \kə-'līd\ *vb* **col·lid·ed; col·lid·ing** **1** ♦ : to come together with solid impact **2** ♦ : to come into conflict : CLASH

♦ [1] bang, bash, bump, crash, hit, impact, knock, ram, slam, smash, strike, swipe, thud ♦ [2] clash, conflict, jar

col·lid·er \kə-'lī-dər\ *n* : a particle accelerator in which two beams of particles are made to collide

col·lie \'kä-lē\ *n* : any of a breed of large dogs developed in Scotland for herding sheep that occur in rough-coated and smooth‗ coated varieties

col·lier \'käl-yər\ *n* **1** : a coal miner **2** : a ship for carrying coal

col·liery \'käl-yə-rē\ *n, pl* **-lier·ies** : a coal mine and its associated buildings

col·li·mate \'kä-lə-ˌmāt\ *vb* **-mat·ed; -mat·ing** : to make (as light rays) parallel

col·li·sion \kə-'li-zhən\ *n* ♦ : an act or instance of colliding

♦ bump, concussion, crash, impact, jar, jolt, shock, smash, strike, wallop ♦ crack-up, crash, smash, wreck

col·lo·ca·tion \ˌkä-lə-'kā-shən\ *n* : the act or result of placing or arranging together; *esp* : a noticeable arrangement or conjoining of linguistic elements (as words)

col·loid \'kä-,loid\ *n* : a substance in the form of submicroscopic particles that when in solution or suspension do not settle out; *also* : such a substance together with the medium in which it is dispersed — **col·loi·dal** \kə-'loid-ᵊl\ *adj*

colloq *abbr* colloquial

col·lo·qui·al \kə-'lō-kwē-əl\ *adj* ♦ : of, relating to, or characteristic of conversation and esp. of familiar and informal conversation

♦ conversational, informal, nonliterary, vernacular, vulgar *Ant* bookish, formal, learned, literary

col·lo·qui·al·ism \-'lō-kwē-ə-,li-zəm\ *n* : a colloquial expression

col·lo·qui·um \kə-'lō-kwē-əm\ *n, pl* **-qui·ums** *or* **-quia** \-ə\ : CONFERENCE, SEMINAR

col·lo·quy \'kä-lə-kwē\ *n, pl* **-quies** ♦ : a usu. formal conversation or conference

♦ forum, panel, parley, seminar, symposium ♦ argument, conference, deliberation, discourse, discussion, give-and-take, parley, talk

col·lu·sion \kə-'lü-zhən\ *n* ♦ : secret agreement or cooperation for an illegal or deceitful purpose — **col·lu·sive** \-siv\ *adj*

♦ connivance, conspiracy

Colo *abbr* Colorado

co·logne \kə-'lōn\ *n* : a perfumed liquid — **co·logned** \-'lōnd\ *adj*

Co·lom·bi·an \kə-'ləm-bē-ən\ *n* : a native or inhabitant of Colombia — **Colombian** *adj*

¹**co·lon** \'kō-lən\ *n, pl* **colons** *or* **co·la** \-lə\ : the part of the large intestine extending from the cecum to the rectum — **co·lon·ic** \kō-'lä-nik\ *adj*

²**colon** *n, pl* **colons** : a punctuation mark : used esp. to direct attention to following matter (as a list)

col·o·nel \'kərn-ᵊl\ *n* : a commissioned officer (as in the army) ranking next below a brigadier general

¹**co·lo·nial** \kə-'lō-nē-əl\ *adj* **1** : of, relating to, or characteristic of a colony; *also* : possessing or composed of colonies **2** *often cap* : of or relating to the original 13 colonies forming the U.S.

²**colonial** *n* : a member or inhabitant of a colony

co·lo·nial·ism \-nē-ə-,li-zəm\ *n* : control by one power over a dependent area or people; *also* : a policy advocating or based on such control — **co·lo·nial·ist** \-list\ *n or adj*

col·o·nise *Brit var of* COLONIZE

col·o·nist \'kä-lə-nist\ *n* **1** ♦ : a member or inhabitant of a colony : COLONIAL **2** ♦ : one that colonizes or settles in a new country

♦ [1, 2] frontiersman, homesteader, pioneer, settler

col·o·nize \'kä-lə-,nīz\ *vb* **-nized; -niz·ing 1** : to establish a colony in or on **2** : SETTLE — **col·o·ni·za·tion** \,kä-lə-nə-'zā-shən\ *n*

col·o·niz·er *n* : one that colonizes or settles in a new country

col·on·nade \,kä-lə-'nād\ *n* : an evenly spaced row of columns usu. supporting the base of a roof structure

co·lo·nos·co·py \,kō-lə-'näs-kə-pē\ *n, pl* **-pies** : endoscopic examination of the colon — **co·lon·o·scope** \kō-'lä-nə-,skōp\ *n*

col·o·ny \'kä-lə-nē\ *n, pl* **-nies 1** : a body of people living in a new territory; *also* : the territory inhabited by these people **2** : a localized population of organisms ⟨a ∼ of bees⟩ **3** : a group with common interests situated in close association ⟨a writers' ∼⟩; *also* : the area occupied by such a group

col·o·phon \'kä-lə-fən, -,fän\ *n* **1** : an inscription placed at the end of a book with facts relative to its production **2** : a distinctive symbol used by a printer or publisher

¹**col·or** *or Can and Brit* **col·our** \'kə-lər\ *n* **1** ♦ : a phenomenon of light (as red or blue) or visual perception that enables one to differentiate otherwise identical objects; *also* : a hue as contrasted with black, white, or gray **2** : APPEARANCE **3** : complexion tint **4** *pl* ♦ : an identifying badge, pennant, or flag; *also* : military service ⟨a call to the ∼s⟩ **5** : VIVIDNESS, INTEREST **6** ♦ : something used to give color

♦ [1] cast, hue, shade, tinge, tint, tone ♦ *usu* colors [4] banner, ensign, flag, jack, pennant, standard, streamer ♦ [6] dye, pigment, stain

²**color** *or Can and Brit* **colour** *vb* **1 a** ♦ : to give color to **b** ♦ : to change the color of (as by dyeing, staining, or painting) **2** ♦ : to become red in the face : BLUSH **3** ♦ : to give a false or misleading representation of the facts

♦ [1a, 1b] dye, paint, stain, tinge, tint ♦ [2] bloom, blush, crimson, flush, glow, redden ♦ [3] distort, falsify, garble, misinter-

pret, misrepresent, misstate, pervert, twist, warp ♦ [3] elaborate, embroider, exaggerate, magnify, pad, stretch

Col·o·ra·do potato beetle \,kä-lə-'ra-dō-, -'rä-\ *n* : a black= and-yellow striped beetle that feeds on the leaves of the potato

col·or·ation \,kə-lə-'rā-shən\ *n* : use or arrangement of colors

col·o·ra·tu·ra \,kə-lə-rə-'túr-ə, -'tyúr-\ *n* **1** : elaborate ornamentation in vocal music **2** : a soprano specializing in coloratura

col·or–blind *or Can and Brit* **col·our–blind** \'kə-lər-,blīnd\ *adj* **1** : partially or totally unable to distinguish one or more chromatic colors **2** : not influenced by differences of race — **col·or blind·ness** *n*

col·ored *or Can and Brit* **col·oured** \'kə-lərd\ *adj* **1** : having color **2** : SLANTED, BIASED

col·or·fast *or Can and Brit* **col·our·fast** \'kə-lər-,fast\ *adj* : having color that does not fade or run — **col·or·fast·ness** *n*

col·or·ful *or Can and Brit* **col·our·ful** *adj* ♦ : having striking colors

♦ multicolored (*or* multicoloured), variegated *Ant* colorless; monochromatic

col·or·ize *or Can* **col·our·ize** *or Brit* **-ise** \'kə-lə-,rīz\ *vb* **-ized; -iz·ing** : to add color to by means of a computer — **col·or·i·za·tion** \,kə-lə-rə-'zā-shən\ *n*

col·or·less *or Can and Brit* **col·our·less** *adj* ♦ : lacking color

♦ uncolored (*or* uncoloured), unpainted, white *Ant* colored, dyed, painted, stained, tinged, tinted

co·los·sal \kə-'lä-səl\ *adj* ♦ : of very great size or degree

♦ astronomical, enormous, giant, gigantic, ginormous, grand, huge, mammoth, massive, monumental, tremendous

Co·los·sians \kə-'lä-shənz\ *n* : a book of the New Testament of Christian Scripture

co·los·sus \kə-'lä-səs\ *n, pl* **co·los·si** \-,sī\ **1** : a gigantic statue **2** ♦ : something of great size or scope

♦ behemoth, blockbuster, giant, jumbo, leviathan, mammoth, monster, titan, whale, whopper

col·our *Can and Brit var of* COLOR

col·por·teur \'käl-,pōr-tər\ *n* : a peddler of religious books

colt \'kōlt\ *n* **1** : FOAL; *also* : a young male horse, ass, or zebra **2** : a young untried person

colt·ish *adj* : full of play : inclined to friskiness or liveliness

♦ antic, elfish, fay, frisky, frolicsome, playful, sportive

col·um·bine \'kä-ləm-,bīn\ *n* : any of a genus of plants with showy spurred flowers that are related to the buttercups

co·lum·bi·um \kə-'ləm-bē-əm\ *n* : NIOBIUM

Columbus Day \kə-'ləm-bəs-\ *n* : the 2d Monday in October or formerly October 12 observed as a legal holiday in many states in commemoration of the landing of Columbus in the Bahamas in 1492

col·umn \'kä-ləm\ *n* **1** : one of two or more vertical sections of a printed page; *also* : one in a usu. regular series of articles (as in a newspaper) **2** ♦ : a supporting pillar; *esp* : one consisting of a usu. round shaft, a capital, and a base **3** : something resembling a column ⟨a ∼ of water⟩ **4** ♦ : a long row (as of soldiers) — **co·lum·nar** \kə-'ləm-nər\ *adj*

♦ [2] pier, pillar, post, stanchion ♦ [4] cue, file, line, queue, range, string, train

col·um·nist \'kä-ləm-nist\ *n* : a person who writes a newspaper or magazine column

com *abbr* **1** comedy; comic **2** comma **3** commercial organization

co·ma \'kō-mə\ *n* : a state of deep unconsciousness caused by disease, injury, or poison — **co·ma·tose** \'kō-mə-,tōs, 'kä-\ *adj*

Co·man·che \kə-'man-chē\ *n, pl* **Comanche** *or* **Comanches** : a member of a nation of Indigenous peoples ranging from Wyoming and Nebraska south into New Mexico and Texas; *also* : their language

¹**comb** \'kōm\ *n* **1** : a toothed instrument for arranging the hair or for separating and cleaning textile fibers **2** : a fleshy crest on the head of a fowl **3** : HONEYCOMB — **combed** \'kōmd\ *adj*

²**comb** *vb* **1** : to draw a comb through for the purpose of arranging or cleaning **2** : to pass across with a scraping or raking action **3** : to eliminate (as with a comb) by a thorough going-over **4** : to search or examine systematically

³**comb** *abbr* combination; combining

¹**com·bat** \'käm-,bat\ *n* ♦ : a fight or contest between individuals or groups

♦ battle, conflict, confrontation, contest, duel, face-off, rivalry, struggle, tug-of-war, warfare ♦ battle, clash, conflict, contest, fight, fracas, fray, hassle, scrap, scrimmage, scuffle, skirmish, struggle, tussle

²combat \kəm-'bat, 'käm-ˌbat\ *vb* **-bat·ed** *or* **-bat·ted; -bat·ing** *or* **-bat·ting** **1** ♦ : to fight with : FIGHT, CONTEND **2** ♦ : to struggle against : OPPOSE **3** : to engage in battle during war — **com·bat·ant** \kəm-'bat-ᵊnt, 'käm-bə-tənt\ *n*

♦ battle, contend, counter, fight, oppose

combat fatigue *n* : a traumatic psychological reaction occurring under wartime conditions (as combat) that cause intense stress
com·bat·ive \kəm-'ba-tiv\ *adj* ♦ : marked by eagerness to fight or contend

♦ aggressive, argumentative, bellicose, belligerent, contentious, discordant, disputatious, militant, pugnacious, quarrelsome, scrappy, truculent, warlike

comb·er \'kō-mər\ *n* **1** : one that combs **2** : a long curling wave of the sea
com·bi·na·tion \ˌkäm-bə-'nā-shən\ *n* **1 a** ♦ : a result or product of combining **b** ♦ : an alliance of individuals, corporations, or states united to achieve a social, political, or economic end **c** ♦ : two or more persons working as a team **2** : a sequence of letters or numbers chosen in setting a lock **3 a** ♦ : the act or process of combining **b** : the quality or state of being combined

♦ [1a] admixture, amalgam, blend, composite, compound, fusion, intermixture, mix, mixture ♦ [1b] alliance, bloc, coalition, combine, confederacy, confederation, federation, league, union ♦ [1b, 1c] bloc, body, coalition, combine, faction, party, sect, set, side, wing ♦ [3a] connection, consolidation, coupling, junction, unification, union

¹com·bine \kəm-'bīn\ *vb* **com·bined; com·bin·ing** **1** ♦ : to become one : UNITE **2** ♦ : to cause (as two or more things or ideas) to mix together

♦ [1] associate, coalesce, conjoin, connect, couple, fuse, join, link, marry, unify, unite ♦ [2] amalgamate, blend, commingle, fuse, incorporate, integrate, intermingle, merge, mingle, mix

²com·bine \'käm-ˌbīn\ *n* **1** ♦ : a combination esp. of business or political interests **2** : a machine that harvests and threshes grain while moving over a field

♦ alliance, bloc, coalition, combination, confederacy, confederation, federation, league, union ♦ cartel, combination, syndicate, trust ♦ bloc, body, coalition, combination, faction, party, sect, set, side, wing

comb·ings \'kō-miŋz\ *n pl* : loose hairs or fibers removed by a comb
combining form *n* : a linguistic form that occurs only in compounds or derivatives
com·bo \'käm-bō\ *n, pl* **combos** : a small jazz or dance band
com·bus·ti·ble \kəm-'bəs-tə-bəl\ *adj* ♦ : capable of being burned — **com·bus·ti·bil·i·ty** \-ˌbəs-tə-'bi-lə-tē\ *n* — **combustible** *n*

♦ flammable, ignitable, inflammable *Ant* fireproof, incombustible, noncombustible, nonflammable, noninflammable

com·bus·tion \kəm-'bəs-chən\ *n* **1** : an act or instance of burning **2** : slow oxidation (as in the animal body)
comdg *abbr* commanding
comdr *abbr* commander
comdt *abbr* commandant
come \'kəm\ *vb* **came** \'käm\; **come; com·ing** \'kə-miŋ\ **1** ♦ : to move toward something : APPROACH **2** ♦ : to arrive at a particular place, end, result, or conclusion : ARRIVE **3** : to reach the point of being or becoming ⟨~ to a boil⟩ **4 a** ♦ : to reach a total : add up : AMOUNT ⟨the bill came to $10⟩ **b** ♦ : to be equal or nearly equal in or at the end **5** : to come to pass : take place **6** : ORIGINATE, ARISE **7** : to be available **8** : REACH, EXTEND — **come across 1** : to make a specified impression ⟨came across as rude⟩ **2** : to find esp. by chance ⟨came across an intriguing story⟩ — **come clean** : CONFESS — **come into** : ACQUIRE, ACHIEVE — **come of age** : MATURE — **come to grips with** : to meet or deal with frankly — **come to pass** : HAPPEN — **come to terms** : to reach an agreement

♦ [1] advance, approach, near *Ant* go, retreat, withdraw ♦ [2] arrive, land, show up, turn up *Ant* go ♦ *usu* **come to** [4a, 4b] add up, amount, equal, number, sum, total ♦ [5] be, befall, betide, chance, go, happen, occur, pass, transpire

come around *vb* **1** : to come round **2** ♦ : to recover consciousness

♦ come round, come to, revive

come·back \'kəm-ˌbak\ *n* **1** ♦ : a sharp or witty reply : RE-

TORT **2** ♦ : a return to a former position or condition — **come back** *vb*

♦ [1] repartee, retort, riposte ♦ [1] answer, reply, response, retort, return ♦ [2] convalescence, rally, recovery, recuperation, rehabilitation

come by *vb* ♦ : to make a brief visit

♦ call, drop (by *or* in), pop (in), stop (by *or* in), visit

co·me·di·an \kə-'mē-dē-ən\ *n* **1** : an actor in comedy **2** ♦ : a comic person; *esp* : an entertainer specializing in comedy

♦ card, comic, humorist, jester, joker, wag, wit

co·me·di·enne \-ˌmē-dē-'en\ *n* : a woman who is a comedian
come·down \'kəm-ˌdaun\ *n* ♦ : a descent in rank or dignity

♦ decline, descent, down, downfall, fall *Ant* aggrandizement, ascent, exaltation, rise

come down *vb* **1** : to lose or fall in estate or condition **2 a** : to pass by tradition **b** : to pass from a usu. high source **3** : to reduce itself : AMOUNT ⟨it *comes down* to this⟩ **4** ♦ : to become ill ⟨*come down* with measles⟩

♦ catch, contract, get, sicken, take

com·e·dy \'kä-mə-dē\ *n, pl* **-dies** **1** : a light amusing play with a happy ending **2** : a literary work treating a comic theme or written in a comic style **3** ♦ : humorous entertainment — **co·me·dic** \kə-'mē-dik\ *adj*

♦ farce, humor (*or* humour), slapstick

come·li·ness *n* ♦ : the condition of being comely esp. with respect to grace or beauty of external form

♦ attractiveness, beauty, handsomeness, looks, loveliness, prettiness

come·ly \'kəm-lē\ *adj* **come·li·er; -est** : having a pleasing appearance : ATTRACTIVE, HANDSOME
come off *vb* : SUCCEED
come-on \'kə-ˌmȯn, -ˌmän\ *n* : INDUCEMENT, LURE
come out *vb* **1 a** ♦ : to come into view **b** ♦ : to become public **2** : to declare oneself **3** ♦ : to turn out in an outcome : end up : TURN OUT **5** ⟨everything *came out* all right⟩ — **come out with** : SAY 1

♦ [1a] appear, materialize, show up, turn up ♦ [1b] get out, leak out, out, spread ♦ [3] pan out, prove, turn out

com·er \'kə-mər\ *n* **1** : one that comes ⟨all ~s⟩ **2** : a promising beginner
come round *vb* **1** : to change direction **2** ♦ : to recover consciousness **3** ♦ : to accede to a particular opinion or course of action

♦ [2] come around, come to, revive ♦ [3] accede, acquiesce, agree, assent, consent, subscribe (to)

¹co·mes·ti·ble \kə-'mes-tə-bəl\ *adj* : EDIBLE
²comestible *n* : FOOD — usu. used in pl.
com·et \'kä-mət\ *n* : a small bright celestial body that develops a long tail when near the sun
come to *vb* ♦ : to regain consciousness

♦ come around, come round, revive

come·up·pance \kə-'mə-pəns\ *n* : a deserved rebuke or penalty
com·fit \'kəm-fət\ *n* : a candied fruit or nut
¹com·fort \'kəm-fərt\ *vb* **1** ♦ : to give strength and hope to **2** ♦ : to ease the grief or trouble of : CONSOLE

♦ [1] buoy (up), cheer, embolden, encourage, hearten, inspire, steel ♦ [2] assure, cheer, console, reassure, solace, soothe *Ant* distress, torment, torture, trouble

²comfort *n* **1** : the act or an instance of consoling : the state of being consoled **2** ♦ : freedom from pain, trouble, or anxiety **3** ♦ : something that consoles : something that gives freedom or ease **4** ♦ : one that gives or brings comfort ⟨all the ~s of home⟩

♦ [2] alleviation, ease, relief ♦ [2] cheer, consolation, relief, solace ♦ [3, 4] amenity, convenience, luxury *Ant* burden, millstone, weight

com·fort·able \'kəm-fər-tə-bəl, 'kəmf-tər-\ *adj* **1** ♦ : providing comfort or security **2** ♦ : feeling at ease **3** ♦ : affording an ease with money and a secure way of living without great wealth — **com·fort·ably** \-blē\ *adv*

♦ [1] easy, snug, soft *Ant* uncomfortable ♦ [2] content, contented, peaceful, pleased, relaxed, untroubled *Ant* uncomfortable ♦ [3] abundant, ample, bountiful, generous, liberal, plentiful

com·fort·er \'kəm-fər-tər\ *n* **1** : one that comforts **2** : QUILT

comforting *adj* ♦ : providing or intended to provide comfort

♦ encouraging, gratifying, heartening, heartwarming, rewarding, satisfying ♦ dreamy, narcotic, sedative, soothing

com·fy \'kəm-fē\ *adj* : COMFORTABLE

¹**com·ic** \'kä-mik\ *adj* **1** : relating to comedy or comic strips **2** : provoking laughter or amusement

²**comic** *n* **1** ♦ : a comical individual esp. a professional entertainer who uses any of various physical or verbal means to be amusing : COMEDIAN **2** *pl* : the part of a newspaper devoted to comic strips

♦ card, comedian, humorist, jester, joker, wag, wit

com·i·cal *adj* ♦ : causing laughter

♦ antic, comic, droll, farcical, funny, hilarious, humorous, hysterical, laughable, ludicrous, ridiculous, riotous, risible, screaming, uproarious ♦ absurd, derisive, farcical, laughable, ludicrous, preposterous, ridiculous, risible, silly

comic book *n* : a magazine containing sequences of comic strips

comic strip *n* ♦ : a group of cartoons in narrative sequence

♦ cartoon

coming \'kə-miŋ\ *adj* **1** ♦ : immediately due in sequence or development : APPROACHING, NEXT **2** : gaining importance

♦ forthcoming, imminent, impending, oncoming, pending ♦ following, next, succeeding

co·mi·ty \'kä-mə-tē, 'kō-\ *n, pl* **-ties** : friendly civility : COURTESY

coml *abbr* commercial

comm *abbr* **1** command; commander **2** commerce; commercial **3** commission; commissioner **4** committee **5** common **6** commonwealth

com·ma \'kä-mə\ *n* : a punctuation mark, used esp. as a mark of separation within the sentence

¹**com·mand** \kə-'mand\ *vb* **1** ♦ : to direct authoritatively : ORDER **2** ♦ : to exercise a dominating influence over : have command of **3** : to overlook from a strategic position **4** ♦ : to demand or receive as one's due ⟨~s a high fee⟩

♦ [1] bid, boss, charge, direct, enjoin, instruct, order, tell *Ant* mind, obey ♦ [2] boss, captain, control, govern, preside, rule ♦ [2] dominate, head, lead, spearhead ♦ [4] ask, charge, demand

²**command** *n* **1** ♦ : an order given **2 a** ♦ : ability to control : MASTERY **b** : facility in use ⟨a good ~ of French⟩ **3** : the act of commanding **4** : a signal that actuates a device (as a computer); *also* : the activation of a device by means of a signal **5 a** : a body of troops under a commander **b** : an area or position that one commands **6** : a position of highest authority

♦ [1] behest, charge, commandment, decree, dictate, direction, directive, edict, instruction, order, word ♦ [2a] arm, authority, clutch, control, dominion, grip, hold, power, sway

com·man·dant \'kä-mən-,dant, -,dänt\ *n* : an officer in command

com·man·deer \,kä-mən-'dir\ *vb* ♦ : to take possession of by force

♦ appropriate, arrogate, preempt, usurp

com·mand·er \kə-'man-dər\ *n* **1 a** ♦ : one in an official position of command or control **b** ♦ : an officer commanding an army or subdivision of an army **2** : a commissioned officer in the navy ranking next below a captain

♦ [1a, 1b] captain

com·mand·ment \kə-'mand-mənt\ *n* ♦ : something that is commanded : COMMAND, ORDER; *esp* : any of the Ten Commandments

♦ behest, charge, command, decree, dictate, direction, directive, edict, instruction, order, word

command module *n* : a space vehicle module designed to carry the crew and reentry equipment

com·man·do \kə-'man-dō\ *n, pl* **-dos** *or* **-does** : a member of a military unit trained for surprise raids

command sergeant major *n* : a noncommissioned officer in the army ranking above a sergeant major

com·mem·o·rate \kə-'me-mə-,rāt\ *vb* **-rat·ed; -rat·ing 1** : to call or recall to mind **2** : to serve as a memorial of **3** ♦ : to mark by some ceremony or observation : OBSERVE — **com·mem·o·ra·tion** \-,me-mə-'rā-shən\ *n*

♦ celebrate, keep, observe

com·mem·o·ra·tive \kə-'mem-rə-tiv, -'me-mə-,rā-tiv\ *adj* : intended to commemorate an event

com·mence \kə-'mens\ *vb* **com·menced; com·menc·ing** ♦ : to have or make a beginning : BEGIN, START

♦ arise, begin, dawn, form, materialize, originate, spring, start ♦ begin, embark (on *or* upon), enter, get off, launch, open, start, strike

com·mence·ment \-mənt\ *n* **1** ♦ : the act or time of a beginning **2** : the graduation exercises of a school or college

♦ beginning, birth, dawn, genesis, launch, morning, onset, outset, start, threshold

com·mend \kə-'mend\ *vb* **1** ♦ : to entrust for care or preservation **2** : RECOMMEND **3** : PRAISE — **com·mend·ably** \-blē\ *adv* — **com·men·da·tion** \,kä-mən-'dā-shən, -,men-\ *n* — **com·mend·er** *n*

♦ commit, consign, delegate, deliver, entrust, give, hand over, leave, pass, transfer, transmit, trust, turn over, vest

com·mend·able \-'men-də-bəl\ *adj* ♦ : worthy of being commended

♦ admirable, creditable, laudable, meritorious, praiseworthy

com·men·da·tion \,kä-mən-'dā-shən, -,men-\ *n* ♦ : the act of commending : the expression of approval

♦ accolade, citation, encomium, eulogy, homage, paean, panegyric, salutation, tribute

com·men·su·ra·ble \kə-'men-sə-rə-bəl\ *adj* : having a common measure or a common divisor

com·men·su·rate \kə-'men-sə-rət, -'men-chə-\ *adj* : equal in measure or extent; *also* : PROPORTIONAL, CORRESPONDING ⟨a job ~ with her abilities⟩

¹**com·ment** \'kä-,ment\ *n* **1** ♦ : an expression of opinion **2** ♦ : an explanatory, illustrative, or critical note or observation : REMARK

♦ note, observation, reflection, remark

²**comment** *vb* ♦ : to explain or interpret something by comment : OBSERVE — **com·men·ter** *n*

♦ note, observe, opine, remark

com·men·tary \'kä-mən-,ter-ē\ *n, pl* **-tar·ies** ♦ : a systematic series of comments

♦ analysis, comment, exposition

com·men·ta·tor \-,tā-tər\ *n* : one who comments; *esp* : a person who discusses news events on radio or television

com·merce \'kä-(,)mərs\ *n* ♦ : the buying and selling of commodities : TRADE

♦ business, marketplace, trade, traffic

¹**com·mer·cial** \kə-'mər-shəl\ *adj* **1** : having to do with commerce **2** : designed for profit or for mass appeal — **com·mer·cial·ly** *adv*

²**commercial** *n* : an advertisement broadcast on radio or television

com·mer·cial·ise *Brit var of* COMMERCIALIZE

com·mer·cial·ism \kə-'mər-shə-,li-zəm\ *n* **1** : a spirit, method, or practice characteristic of business **2** : excessive emphasis on profit

com·mer·cial·ize *or Brit* **com·mer·cial·ise** \-,līz\ *vb* **-ized; -iz·ing 1** : to manage on a business basis for profit **2** : to exploit for profit

com·mi·na·tion \,kä-mə-'nā-shən\ *n* : DENUNCIATION — **com·mi·na·to·ry** \kə-'mi-nə-,tōr-ē\ *adj*

com·min·gle \kə-'miŋ-gəl\ *vb* ♦ : to mingle or mix together : MINGLE, BLEND

♦ amalgamate, blend, combine, fuse, incorporate, integrate, intermingle, merge, mingle, mix

com·mis·er·ate \kə-'mi-zə-,rāt\ *vb* **-at·ed; -at·ing** ♦ : to feel or express pity : SYMPATHIZE

♦ bleed, feel, pity, sympathize

com·mis·er·a·tion \-,mi-zə-'rā-shən\ *n* ♦ : the act of commiserating : the feeling or showing of sorrow or the expression of condolence for the wants or distresses of another

♦ charity, compassion, feeling, heart, humanity, kindliness, kindness, mercy, pity, sympathy

com·mis·sar \'kä-mə-,sär\ *n* : a Communist party official

com·mis·sar·i·at \,kä-mə-'ser-ē-ət\ *n* **1** : a system for supplying troops with food **2** : a department headed by a commissar

com·mis·sary \'kä-mə-,ser-ē\ *n, pl* **-sar·ies 1** : a store for equipment and provisions esp. for military personnel **2** ♦ : one delegated by a superior to execute a duty or an office

♦ agent, attorney, delegate, deputy, envoy, factor, proxy, representative

[1]com·mis·sion \kə-'mi-shən\ *n* **1** ♦ : a warrant granting certain powers and imposing certain duties; *also* : the fact of granting these powers or duties **2** : a certificate conferring military rank and authority **3** ♦ : authority to act as agent for another; *also* : something to be done by an agent **4** : a body of persons charged with performing a duty **5** ♦ : the doing of some act; *also* : the thing done **6** : the allowance made to an agent for transacting business for another

♦ [1] authorization, delegation, license (*or* licence), mandate ♦ [3] appointment, assignment, designation ♦ [5] accomplishment, achievement, discharge, enactment, execution, fulfillment, implementation, performance *Ant* nonfulfillment, nonperformance

[2]commission *vb* **1** ♦ : to give a commission to **2** : to order to be made **3** : to put (a ship) into a state of readiness for service

♦ assign, charge, entrust, trust ♦ accredit, authorize, certify, delegate, empower, enable, invest, license, qualify ♦ appoint, assign, attach, constitute, designate, detail, name

commissioned officer *n* : an officer of the armed forces holding rank by a commission from the president
com·mis·sion·er \kə-'mi-shə-nər\ *n* **1** : a member of a commission **2** : an official in charge of a department of public service **3** : the administrative head of a professional sport — **com·mis·sion·er·ship** *n*
com·mit \kə-'mit\ *vb* **com·mit·ted; com·mit·ting** **1 a** : to put into charge or trust : ENTRUST **b** ♦ : to put in a place for disposal or safekeeping **2** ♦ : to put in a prison or mental institution **3** : TRANSFER, CONSIGN **4** ♦ : to carry into action ⟨~ a crime⟩ **5** ♦ : to pledge or assign to some particular course or use — **com·mit·tal** *n*

♦ [1b] commend, consign, delegate, deliver, entrust, give, hand over, leave, pass, transfer, transmit, trust, turn over, vest ♦ [2] confine, immure, imprison, jail ♦ [4] accomplish, achieve, carry out, compass, do, execute, follow through, fulfill, make, perform ♦ [5] engage, pledge, troth

com·mit·ment *n* ♦ : an agreement or pledge to do something in the future

♦ burden, charge, duty, need, obligation, responsibility

com·mit·tee \kə-'mi-tē\ *n* : a body of persons selected to consider and act or report on some matter — **com·mit·tee·man** \-mən\ *n* — **com·mit·tee·wom·an** \-ˌwu̇-mən\ *n*
commo *abbr* commodore
com·mode \kə-'mōd\ *n* **1** : a movable washstand with cupboard below **2** : TOILET 3
com·mo·di·ous \kə-'mō-dē-əs\ *adj* ♦ : comfortably spacious : ROOMY

♦ ample, capacious, roomy, spacious

com·mod·i·ty \kə-'mä-də-tē\ *n, pl* **-ties** **1** : a product of agriculture or mining **2** ♦ : an article of commerce — often used in pl. **3** : something useful or valued ⟨that valuable ~ patience⟩

♦ *usu* **commodities** merchandise, wares

com·mo·dore \'kä-mə-ˌdōr\ *n* **1** : a commissioned officer in the navy ranking next below a rear admiral **2** : an officer commanding a group of merchant ships **3** : the chief officer of a yacht club
[1]com·mon \'kä-mən\ *adj* **1** ♦ : belonging to or serving the community : PUBLIC **2** ♦ : shared by a number in a group **3** ♦ : widely or generally known, found, or observed : FAMILIAR **4** : VERNACULAR 3 ⟨~ names of plants⟩ **5** ♦ : not above the average esp. in social status **6** ♦ : lacking refinement : COARSE **7** ♦ : falling below ordinary standards

♦ [1] blanket, general, generic, global, overall, public, universal ♦ [2] collective, communal, concerted, conjoint, joint, mutual, public, united ♦ [3] commonplace, customary, everyday, familiar, frequent, normal, ordinary, regular, routine, standard, usual *Ant* extraordinary, infrequent, rare, uncommon, unfamiliar, unusual ♦ [5] humble, ignoble, inferior, low, lowly, mean, plebeian, vulgar ♦ [6] coarse, crass, crude, gross, ill-bred, low, rough, rude, tasteless, uncouth, uncultivated, uncultured, unpolished, unrefined, vulgar ♦ [7] fair, indifferent, mediocre, medium, middling, ordinary, passable, run-of-the-mill, second-rate, so-so

[2]common *n* **1** *pl* : the common people **2** *pl* : a dining hall **3** *pl, cap* : the lower house of the British and Canadian parliaments **4** : a piece of land subject to common use — **in common** : shared together
com·mon·al·ty \'kä-mən-əl-tē\ *n, pl* **-ties** : the common people
common cold *n* : a contagious respiratory disease caused by a

virus and characterized by a sore, swollen, and inflamed nose and throat, usu. by much mucus, and by coughing and sneezing
common denominator *n* **1** : a common multiple of the denominators of a group of fractions **2** : a common trait or theme
common divisor *n* : a number or expression that divides two or more numbers or expressions without remainder
com·mon·er \'kä-mə-nər\ *n* ♦ : one of the common people : a person having no rank of nobility

♦ *usu* **commoners** herd, masses, mob, people, plebeians, populace, rank and file

common fraction *n* : a fraction (as $1/2$ or $3/4$) in which the numerator and denominator are both integers and are separated by a horizontal or slanted line
common law *n* : a group of legal practices and traditions based on judges' decisions and social customs and usu. having the same force as laws passed by legislative bodies
common logarithm *n* : a logarithm whose base is 10
com·mon·ly *adv* ♦ : as a general thing : often in the usual course of events

♦ generally, ordinarily, typically, usually

common market *n* : an economic association formed to remove trade barriers among members
common multiple *n* : a multiple of each of two or more numbers or expressions
[1]com·mon·place \'kä-mən-ˌplās\ *n* ♦ : something that is ordinary or trite

♦ banality, cliché, platitude, shibboleth

[2]commonplace *adj* ♦ : commonly found or seen : ORDINARY

♦ average, common, everyday, normal, ordinary, prosaic, routine, run-of-the-mill, standard, unexceptional, unremarkable, usual, workaday

common sense *n* ♦ : ordinary good sense and judgment — **com·mon·sen·si·cal** \ˌkä-mən-'sen-si-kəl\ *adj*

♦ horse sense, sense, wisdom, wit

com·mon·weal \'kä-mən-ˌwēl\ *n* **1** *archaic* : COMMONWEALTH **2** : the general welfare
com·mon·wealth \-ˌwelth\ *n* **1** ♦ : the body of people politically organized into a state **2** : a state esp. conceived as a body politic founded on law and united by compact or by tacit agreement of the people for the common good; *also* : an association or federation of autonomous states

♦ country, land, nation, sovereignty, state

com·mo·tion \kə-'mō-shən\ *n* **1** ♦ : violent or sharp disturbance : noisy, unruly, or tumultuous stir **2** : mental excitement, uncertainty, or confusion

♦ disturbance, furor, fuss, hubbub, hullabaloo, pandemonium, tumult, turmoil, uproar

com·mu·nal \kə-'myün-ᵊl, 'käm-yən-ᵊl\ *adj* **1** : of or relating to a commune or community **2** : marked by collective ownership and use of property **3** ♦ : shared or used in common

♦ collective, common, concerted, conjoint, joint, mutual, public, united

[1]com·mune \kə-'myün\ *vb* **com·muned; com·mun·ing** : to communicate intimately
[2]com·mune \'käm-ˌyün; kə-'myün\ *n* **1** : the smallest administrative district in some European countries **2** : a community organized on a communal basis
com·mu·ni·ca·ble \kə-'myü-ni-kə-bəl\ *adj* ♦ : capable of being communicated ⟨~ diseases⟩ — **com·mu·ni·ca·bil·i·ty** \-ˌmyü-ni-kə-'bi-lə-tē\ *n*

♦ catching, contagious, transmittable

com·mu·ni·cant \-'myü-ni-kənt\ *n* **1** : a church member entitled to receive Communion **2** : one that communicates; *esp* : INFORMANT
com·mu·ni·cate \kə-'myü-nə-ˌkāt\ *vb* **-cat·ed; -cat·ing** **1** : to make known **2** ♦ : to pass from one to another : TRANSMIT **3** : to receive Communion **4** : to be in communication **5** : JOIN, CONNECT — **com·mu·ni·ca·tor** \-ˌkā-tər\ *n*

♦ convey, impart, spread, transfer, transfuse, transmit

com·mu·ni·ca·tion \kə-ˌmyü-nə-'kā-shən\ *n* **1** : an act of transmitting **2** : information communicated : a verbal or written message **3** : exchange of information or opinions **4** : a means of communicating — **com·mu·ni·ca·tive** \-'myü-nə-ˌkā-tiv, -ni-kə-tiv\ *adj*
com·mu·nion \kə-'myü-nyən\ *n* **1** : a sharing of something with others **2** *cap* : a Christian sacrament in which bread and

wine are consumed as the substance or symbols of Christ's body and blood in commemoration of the death of Christ **3** : intimate fellowship or rapport **4** : a body of Christians having a common faith and discipline

com·mu·ni·qué \kə-'myü-nə-ˌkā, -ˌmyü-nə-'kā\ *n* ♦ : a brief public report intended for immediate release on a matter of public interest : BULLETIN

♦ advertisement, announcement, bulletin, notice, notification, release

com·mu·nism \'käm-yə-ˌni-zəm\ *n* **1** : social organization in which goods are held in common **2** : a theory of social organization advocating common ownership of means of production and a distribution of products of industry based on need **3** *cap* : a political doctrine based on revolutionary Marxist socialism that was; the official ideology of the U.S.S.R. and some other countries; *also* : a system of government in which one party controls state-owned means of production — **com·mu·nist** \-nist\ *n or adj, often cap* — **com·mu·nis·tic** \ˌkäm-yə-'nis-tik\ *adj, often cap*

com·mu·ni·ty \kə-'myü-nə-tē\ *n, pl* **-ties** **1** : a body of people living in the same place under the same laws; *also* : a natural population of plants and animals that interact ecologically and live in one place (as a pond) **2** : society at large **3** : joint ownership **4** ♦ : common character : SIMILARITY, LIKENESS **5** : the people with common interests living in a particular area **6** ♦ : a body of persons of common and esp. professional interests scattered through a larger society

♦ [4] correspondence, likeness, parallelism, resemblance, similarity, similitude ♦ [6] brotherhood, corps, fellowship, fraternity

community college *n* : a 2-year government-supported college that offers an associate degree

community property *n* : property held jointly by a married couple

com·mu·ta·tion \ˌkäm-yə-'tā-shən\ *n* ♦ : substitution of one form of payment or penalty for another

♦ barter, exchange, swap, trade, truck

com·mu·ta·tive \'käm-yə-ˌtā-tiv, kə-'myü-tə-\ *adj* : of, having, or being the property that the result obtained using a mathematical operation on any two elements of a set does not differ with the order in which the elements are used ⟨*a* × *b* = *b* × *a* because multiplication is ∼⟩ — **com·mu·ta·tiv·i·ty** \kə-ˌmyü-tə-'ti-və-tē, ˌkäm-yə-tə-\ *n*

com·mu·ta·tor \'käm-yə-ˌtā-tər\ *n* : a device (as on a generator or motor) for changing the direction of electric current

¹**com·mute** \kə-'myüt\ *vb* **com·mut·ed; com·mut·ing** **1** ♦ : to give in exchange for another : EXCHANGE **2** : to revoke (a sentence) and impose a milder penalty **3** : to travel back and forth regularly — **com·mut·er** *n*

♦ change, exchange, shift, substitute, swap, switch, trade

²**commute** *n* : a trip made in commuting

comp *abbr* **1** comparative; compare **2** compensation **3** compiled; compiler **4** composition; compositor **5** compound **6** comprehensive **7** comptroller

¹**com·pact** \kəm-'pakt, 'käm-ˌpakt\ *adj* **1** ♦ : having a dense structure or parts or units closely packed or joined : SOLID, DENSE **2** ♦ : not diffuse or verbose : BRIEF, SUCCINCT **3** ♦ : occupying a small volume by efficient use of space ⟨a ∼ formation of troops⟩

♦ [1] dense, firm, hard, rigid, solid, stiff, unyielding ♦ [2] brief, compendious, concise, crisp, epigrammatic, laconic, pithy, succinct, summary, terse ♦ [3] close, crowded, dense, packed, serried, thick, tight

²**compact** *vb* **1** ♦ : to pack together : COMPRESS **2** : to knit or draw together : CONSOLIDATE — **com·pac·tor** \kəm-'pak-tər, 'käm-ˌpak-\ *n*

♦ compress, condense, constrict, contract, squeeze

³**com·pact** \'käm-ˌpakt\ *n* **1** : a small case for cosmetics **2** : a small automobile

⁴**com·pact** \'käm-ˌpakt\ *n* ♦ : an agreement or covenant between two or more parties

♦ accord, agreement, bargain, contract, convention, covenant, deal, pact, settlement, understanding

compact disc \'käm-ˌpakt-\ *n* : CD

com·pact·ly *adv* ♦ : in a compact manner

♦ concisely, crisply, laconically, shortly, succinctly, summarily, tersely

com·pact·ness *n* ♦ : the quality or state of being compact

♦ brevity, briefness, conciseness, crispness, succinctness, terseness

com·pa·dre \kəm-'pä-drā\ *n* ♦ : a close friend : BUDDY

♦ buddy, chum, comrade, crony, familiar, friend, intimate, pal

¹**com·pan·ion** \kəm-'pan-yən\ *n* **1 a** ♦ : one that accompanies another : COMRADE **b** ♦ : an intimate friend or associate **2** ♦ : one that is closely connected with something similar

♦ [1a, 1b] associate, cohort, comrade, crony, fellow, mate ♦ [2] half, match, mate, twin

²**companion** *n* : COMPANIONWAY

com·pan·ion·able *adj* ♦ : marked by, conducive to, or suggestive of companionship

♦ amicable, comradely, cordial, friendly, genial, hearty, neighborly, warm, warmhearted ♦ boon, convivial, extroverted, gregarious, outgoing, sociable, social

com·pan·ion·ship *n* ♦ : the fellowship existing among companions : COMPANY

♦ camaraderie, company, comradeship, fellowship, society

com·pan·ion·way *n* : a ship's stairway from one deck to another

com·pa·ny \'kəm-pə-nē\ *n, pl* **-nies** **1** ♦ : association with another or others : FELLOWSHIP; *also* : COMPANIONS **2** : GUESTS **3** ♦ : a group of persons or things **4** : an infantry unit consisting of two or more platoons and normally commanded by a captain **5** : a group of musical or dramatic performers **6** : the officers and crew of a ship **7** ♦ : an association of persons for carrying on a business

♦ [1] camaraderie, companionship, comradeship, fellowship, society ♦ [3] band, crew, gang, outfit, party, squad, team ♦ [7] business, concern, enterprise, establishment, firm, house, outfit

com·pa·ra·ble \'käm-pə-rə-bəl, -prə-\ *adj* ♦ : capable of being compared — **com·pa·ra·bil·i·ty** \ˌkäm-pə-rə-'bi-lə-tē\ *n*

♦ akin, alike, analogous, correspondent, like, parallel, similar, such

¹**com·par·a·tive** \kəm-'par-ə-tiv\ *adj* **1** : of, relating to, or constituting the degree of grammatical comparison that denotes increase in quality, quantity, or relation **2** ♦ : considered as if in comparison to something else as a standard not quite attained : RELATIVE ⟨a ∼ stranger⟩ — **com·par·a·tive·ly** *adv*

♦ approximate, near, relative *Ant* absolute, complete, downright, out-and-out, outright, perfect, pure, unqualified

²**comparative** *n* : the comparative degree or form in a language

¹**com·pare** \kəm-'par\ *vb* **com·pared; com·par·ing** **1** ♦ : to represent as similar : LIKEN **2 a** : to examine for likenesses and differences **b** ♦ : to view in relation to **3** : to inflect or modify (an adjective or adverb) according to the degrees of comparison

♦ [1] bracket, equate, liken *Ant* contrast ♦ *usu* **compare with** [2b] approach, approximate, measure up, stack up

²**compare** *n* : the possibility of comparing ⟨beauty beyond ∼⟩

com·par·i·son \kəm-'par-ə-sən\ *n* **1** : the act of comparing **2** : change in the form of an adjective or adverb to show different levels of quality, quantity, or relation

com·part·ment \kəm-'pärt-mənt\ *n* **1** : a separate division **2** ♦ : a section of an enclosed space

♦ bay, cabin, cell, chamber, cubicle

com·part·men·tal·ise *Brit var of* COMPARTMENTALIZE

com·part·men·tal·ize \kəm-ˌpärt-'ment-ᵊl-ˌīz\ *vb* **-ized; -iz·ing** : to separate into compartments

¹**com·pass** \'kəm-pəs, 'käm-\ *vb* **1** : CONTRIVE, PLOT **2** ♦ : to lie around : ENCIRCLE **3** ♦ : to bring about : ACHIEVE

♦ [2] circle, circumnavigate, coil, encircle, girdle, loop, orbit, ring, round ♦ [3] accomplish, achieve, carry out, commit, do, execute, follow through, fulfill, make, perform

²**compass** *n* **1** ♦ : an often rounded or curved boundary limit : BOUNDARY, CIRCUMFERENCE **2** : an enclosed space **3** ♦ : range or limit of perception, knowledge, interest, or concern : RANGE, SCOPE **4** : a device for determining direction by means of a magnetic needle swinging freely and pointing to the magnetic north; *also* : a nonmagnetic device that indicates direction **5** : an instrument for drawing circles or transferring measurements consisting of two legs joined by a pivot

♦ [1] border, bound, boundary, circumference, confines, edge, end, fringe, margin, perimeter, periphery, rim, skirt, verge ♦ [3] amplitude, breadth, extent, range, reach, realm, scope, sweep, width

com·pas·sion \kəm-'pa-shən\ *n* ♦ : sympathetic feeling : PITY, MERCY

♦ charity, commiseration, feeling, heart, humanity, kindliness, kindness, mercy, pity, sympathy

com·pas·sion·ate \-shə-nət\ *adj* ♦ : having or showing compassion — **com·pas·sion·ate·ly** *adv*

♦ beneficent, benevolent, good-hearted, humane, kind, kindly, sympathetic, tender, tenderhearted, warmhearted

com·pat·i·bil·i·ty \-ˌpa-tə-'bi-lə-tē\ *n* ♦ : the quality or state of being compatible

♦ concord, harmony, peace

com·pat·i·ble \kəm-'pa-tə-bəl\ *adj* ♦ : able to exist or act together harmoniously ⟨∼ colors⟩ ⟨∼ drugs⟩

♦ agreeable, amicable, congenial, harmonious, kindred, unanimous, united ♦ conformable (to), congruous, consistent, consonant, correspondent, harmonious

com·pa·tri·ot \kəm-'pā-trē-ət, -ˌät\ *n* : a fellow countryman

com·peer \'käm-ˌpir\ *n* : EQUAL, PEER

com·pel \kəm-'pel\ *vb* **com·pelled; com·pel·ling** ♦ : to drive or urge with force

♦ coerce, constrain, drive, force, make, muscle, obligate, oblige, press, pressure

compelling *adj* **1** : demanding and holding one's attention ⟨a ∼ novel⟩ **2** ♦ : tending to convince or convert by or as if by forcefulness of evidence

♦ cogent, conclusive, convincing, decisive, effective, forceful, persuasive, satisfying, strong, telling

com·pen·di·ous \kəm-'pen-dē-əs\ *adj* **1** ♦ : marked by brief expression of a comprehensive matter : concise and comprehensive **2** ♦ : covering completely or broadly : COMPREHENSIVE

♦ [1] brief, compact, concise, crisp, epigrammatic, laconic, pithy, succinct, summary, terse ♦ [2] complete, comprehensive, encyclopedic, full, global, inclusive, omnibus, panoramic, universal

com·pen·di·um \kəm-'pen-dē-əm\ *n, pl* **-di·ums** *or* **-dia** \-ə\ **1** : a brief summary of a larger work or of a field of knowledge **2** : COLLECTION

com·pen·sate \'käm-pən-ˌsāt\ *vb* **-sat·ed; -sat·ing 1 a** : to be equivalent to **b** ♦ : to make up for : COUNTERBALANCE **2** ♦ : to make an appropriate and usu. counterbalancing payment to : PAY, REMUNERATE — **com·pen·sa·to·ry** \kəm-'pen-sə-ˌtōr-ē\ *adj*

♦ *usu* **compensate for** [1b] annul, cancel, correct, counteract, counterbalance, make up, neutralize, offset ♦ [2] indemnify, pay, recompense, recoup, remunerate, requite

com·pen·sa·tion \ˌkäm-pən-'sā-shən\ *n* **1** ♦ : the act or action of making up, making good, or counterbalancing : rendering equal **2** ♦ : something that constitutes an equivalent or recompense

♦ [1] disbursement, payment, remittance, remuneration ♦ [2] damages, indemnity, quittance, recompense, redress, remuneration, reparation, requital, restitution, satisfaction ♦ [2] consideration, pay, payment, remittance, remuneration, requital

com·pete \kəm-'pēt\ *vb* **com·pet·ed; com·pet·ing** ♦ : to seek or strive for something (as a position, possession, reward) for which others are also contending : CONTEND, VIE

♦ battle, contend, fight, race, vie

com·pe·tence \'käm-pə-təns\ *n* **1** : adequate means for subsistence **2** ♦ : the quality or state of being functionally adequate or of having sufficient knowledge, judgment, skill, or strength : ABILITY

♦ ability, capability, capacity, faculty

com·pe·ten·cy \-tən-sē\ *n, pl* **-cies** : the quality or state of being competent

com·pe·tent \-tənt\ *adj* ♦ : having requisite or adequate ability or qualities : CAPABLE, FIT, QUALIFIED

♦ able, capable, fit, good, qualified, suitable *Ant* incompetent, inept, poor, unfit, unqualified

com·pe·ti·tion \ˌkäm-pə-'ti-shən\ *n* **1** : the act of competing : RIVALRY **2 a** ♦ : a contest between rivals : CONTEST, MATCH **b** : one that competes; *also* : one's competitors — **com·pet·i·tive** \kəm-'pe-tə-tiv\ *adj* — **com·pet·i·tive·ly** *adv* — **com·pet·i·tive·ness** *n*

♦ bout, contest, event, game, match, meet, tournament

com·pet·i·tor \kəm-'pe-tə-tər\ *n* ♦ : one that competes : RIVAL

♦ challenger, competition, contender, contestant, rival

com·pi·la·tion \ˌkäm-pə-'lā-shən\ *n* ♦ : something that is a product of the putting together of two or more items

♦ album, anthology, miscellany

com·pile \kəm-'pīl\ *vb* **com·piled; com·pil·ing 1** : to compose out of materials from other documents **2** : to collect and edit into a volume **3** : to translate (a computer program) with a compiler **4** : to build up gradually ⟨∼ a record of four wins and two losses⟩

com·pil·er \kəm-'pī-lər\ *n* **1** : one that compiles **2** : a computer program that translates any program correctly written in a specific programming language into machine language

com·pla·cence \kəm-'plās-ᵊns\ *n* ♦ : the quality or state of being self-satisfied

♦ conceit, ego, egotism, pride, self-conceit, self-esteem, self-importance, self-satisfaction, smugness, vainglory, vanity *Ant* humbleness, humility, modesty

com·pla·cen·cy \-ᵊn-sē\ *n, pl* **-cies 1** : SATISFACTION **2** : the quality or state of being self-satisfied

com·pla·cent \-ᵊnt\ *adj* ♦ : marked by complacency : SELF-SATISFIED — **com·pla·cent·ly** *adv*

♦ conceited, egotistic, important, overweening, pompous, prideful, proud, self-important, self-satisfied, smug, stuck-up, vain

com·plain \kəm-'plān\ *vb* **1** ♦ : to express grief, pain, or discontent **2** : to make a formal accusation

♦ beef, bellyache, carp, crab, croak, fuss, gripe, grouse, growl, grumble, kick, moan, murmur, mutter, repine, squawk, wail, whine *Ant* rejoice

com·plain·ant *n* **1** : the party who makes the complaint in a legal action or proceeding : **2** : one who complains

com·plain·er *n* ♦ : one that complains

♦ bear, crab, crank, curmudgeon, grouch, grumbler, whiner

com·plaint \kəm-'plānt\ *n* **1** ♦ : expression of grief, pain, or dissatisfaction **2** ♦ : a bodily ailment or disease **3** ♦ : a formal accusation against a person

♦ [1] challenge, demur, expostulation, fuss, kick, objection, protest, question, remonstrance ♦ [1] beef, fuss, grievance, gripe, grumble, murmur, plaint, squawk ♦ [2] ailment, complication, condition, disease, disorder, fever, ill, illness, infirmity, malady, sickness, trouble ♦ [3] charge, count, indictment, rap

com·plai·sance \kəm-'plās-ᵊns, ˌkäm-plā-'zans\ *n* : disposition to please — **com·plai·sant** \-ᵊnt, -'zant\ *adj*

com·pleat \kəm-'plēt\ *adj* : PROFICIENT

com·plect·ed \kəm-'plek-təd\ *adj* : having a specified facial complexion ⟨dark-*complected*⟩

¹**com·ple·ment** \'käm-plə-mənt\ *n* **1 a** : something that fills up or completes **b** : the full quantity, number, or amount that makes a thing complete **2** : an added word by which a predicate is made complete **3** : a group of proteins in blood that combines with antibodies to destroy antigens

²**com·ple·ment** \-ˌment\ *vb* : to be complementary to : fill out

com·ple·men·ta·ry \ˌkäm-plə-'men-t(ə-)rē\ *adj* : serving to fill out or complete : being complements of each other

complementary medicine *n* : ALTERNATIVE MEDICINE

¹**com·plete** \kəm-'plēt\ *adj* **com·plet·er; -est 1** ♦ : having all parts or elements **2** ♦ : brought to an end **3** ♦ : fully carried out **4** : fully realized : carried to the ultimate : ABSOLUTE **2** ⟨∼ silence⟩ — **com·plete·ness** *n* — **com·ple·tion** \-'plē-shən\ *n*

♦ [1] compendious, comprehensive, encyclopedic, full, global, inclusive, omnibus, panoramic, universal ♦ [1] comprehensive, entire, full, grand, intact, integral, perfect, plenary, total, whole *Ant* imperfect, incomplete, partial ♦ [2] done, down, over, through, up *Ant* continuing, incomplete, ongoing, unfinished ♦ [3] all-out, clean, comprehensive, exhaustive, full-scale, out-and-out, thorough, thoroughgoing, total

²**complete** *vb* **com·plet·ed; com·plet·ing 1** ♦ : to bring to an end and esp. into a perfected state : FINISH **2** ♦ : to make whole or perfect ⟨the hat ∼s the outfit⟩

♦ [1, 2] consummate, finalize, finish, perfect

com·plete·ly *adv* **1** ♦ : so as to be complete : FULLY **2** ♦ : to a complete degree

♦ [1, 2] altogether, dead, entirely, fast, flat, full, fully, perfectly, quite, thoroughly, well, wholly

¹**com·plex** \'käm-ˌpleks\ *n* **1** : a whole made up of or involving intricately interrelated elements **2** : a group of repressed desires

and memories that exert a dominating influence on one's personality and behavior ⟨a guilt ∼⟩ **3 ♦ :** a building or group of buildings housing related units

♦ establishment, facility, installation

²**com·plex** \käm-ˈpleks, ˈkäm-ˌpleks\ *adj* **1 ♦ :** composed of two or more parts **2 :** consisting of a main clause and one or more subordinate clauses ⟨∼ sentence⟩ **3 ♦ :** hard to separate, analyze, solve, or do **4 ♦ :** marked by an involvement of many parts, aspects, or details necessitating careful study or attention — **com·plex·ly** *adv*

♦ [1, 4] complicated, convoluted, elaborate, intricate, involved, knotty, sophisticated *Ant* plain, simple ♦ [3] complicated, detailed, elaborate, fancy, intricate, involved, sophisticated

complex fraction *n* **:** a fraction with a fraction or mixed number in the numerator or denominator or both
com·plex·ion \kəm-ˈplek-shən\ *n* **1 ♦ :** the hue or appearance of the skin esp. of the face **2 ♦ :** overall aspect or character — **com·plex·ioned** \-shənd\ *adj*

♦ character, constitution, genius, nature, personality, tone

com·plex·i·ty \käm-ˈplek-sə-tē\ *n* **1 ♦ :** something complex **2 ♦ :** the quality or state of being complex

♦ [1] complication, difficulty, intricacy ♦ [2] elaborateness, intricacy, sophistication *Ant* plainness, simpleness, simplicity

complex number *n* **:** a number of the form $a + b\sqrt{-1}$ where *a* and *b* are real numbers
com·pli·ance \kəm-ˈplī-əns\ *n* **1 ♦ :** the act of complying to a demand or proposal **2 ♦ :** a disposition to yield

♦ [1] conformity, obedience, observance, submission, subordination ♦ [2] deference, docility, obedience *Ant* defiance, disobedience, recalcitrance

com·pli·ant \-ənt\ *adj* ♦ **:** ready or disposed to comply

♦ amenable, conformable, docile, obedient, submissive, tractable

com·pli·cate \ˈkäm-plə-ˌkāt\ *vb* **-cat·ed; -cat·ing :** to make or become complex or intricate
com·pli·cat·ed \ˈkäm-plə-ˌkā-təd\ *adj* **1 ♦ :** consisting of parts intricately combined **2 :** difficult to analyze, understand, or explain **3 :** not simple or easy to fabricate or comprehend ⟨a ∼ issue⟩ — **com·pli·cat·ed·ly** *adv*

♦ complex, convoluted, detailed, elaborate, intricate, involved, knotty, sophisticated

com·pli·ca·tion \ˌkäm-plə-ˈkā-shən\ *n* **1 a :** the quality or state of being complicated **b ♦ :** a complex feature **2 ♦ :** a disease or condition that develops during and affects the course of a primary disease or condition

♦ [1b] complexity, difficulty, intricacy ♦ [2] ailment, bug, complaint, condition, disease, disorder, fever, ill, illness, infirmity, malady, sickness, trouble

com·plic·i·ty \kəm-ˈpli-sə-tē\ *n, pl* **-ties :** the state of being an accomplice
¹**com·pli·ment** \ˈkäm-plə-mənt\ *n* **1 :** an expression of approval or admiration; *esp* **:** a flattering remark **2** *pl* ♦ **:** best wishes **:** REGARDS

♦ *usu* **compliments** greetings, regards, respects

²**com·pli·ment** \-ˌment\ *vb* **:** to pay a compliment to
com·pli·men·ta·ry \ˌkäm-plə-ˈmen-t(ə-)rē\ *adj* **1 ♦ :** containing or expressing a compliment **2 ♦ :** given free as a courtesy ⟨∼ ticket⟩

♦ [1] appreciative, favorable (*or* favourable), friendly, good, positive ♦ [2] free, gratuitous

com·ply \kəm-ˈplī\ *vb* **com·plied; com·ply·ing ♦ :** to conform, submit, or adapt (as to a regulation or to another's wishes) as required or requested

♦ *usu* **comply with** conform, follow, mind, obey, observe ♦ *usu* **comply with** answer, fill, fulfill, keep, meet, redeem, satisfy

¹**com·po·nent** \kəm-ˈpō-nənt, ˈkäm-ˌpō-\ *n* ♦ **:** a component part

♦ constituent, element, factor, ingredient, member

²**component** *adj* **:** serving to form a part of **:** CONSTITUENT
com·port \kəm-ˈpōrt\ *vb* **1 ♦ :** to be fitting **:** AGREE, ACCORD **2 ♦ :** to behave in a manner conformable to what is right, proper, or expected **:** CONDUCT

♦ [1] accord, agree, answer, check, coincide, conform, corre-

spond, dovetail, fit, go, harmonize, jibe, square, tally ♦ [2] acquit, bear, behave, conduct, demean, deport, quit

com·port·ment *n* ♦ **:** manner of bearing **:** DEMEANOR

♦ actions, bearing, behavior (*or* behaviour), conduct, demeanor (*or* demeanour), deportment

com·pose \kəm-ˈpōz\ *vb* **com·posed; com·pos·ing 1 a :** to form by putting together **b ♦ :** to form the substance of **2 ♦ :** to produce (as pages of type) by composition **3 :** ADJUST, ARRANGE **4 ♦ :** to free from agitation **:** CALM, QUIET **5 :** to practice composition ⟨∼ music⟩

♦ [1b] comprise, constitute, form, make up ♦ [2] cast, craft, draft, draw, formulate, frame, prepare ♦ [4] allay, calm, quiet, settle, soothe, still, tranquilize ♦ [4] calm, collect, control, settle

composed *adj* ♦ **:** free from agitation

♦ calm, collected, cool, placid, self-possessed, serene, tranquil, undisturbed, unperturbed, unshaken, untroubled, unworried

com·pos·er *n* **:** one that composes **:** a person who writes music
¹**com·pos·ite** \käm-ˈpä-zət\ *adj* **1 ♦ :** made up of distinct parts or elements **2 :** of, relating to, or being a large family of flowering plants (as a daisy or aster) that bear many small flowers united into compact heads resembling single flowers
²**composite** *n* **1 ♦ :** something composite **2 :** a plant of the composite family

♦ admixture, amalgam, blend, combination, compound, fusion, intermixture, mix, mixture

com·po·si·tion \ˌkäm-pə-ˈzi-shən\ *n* **1 a :** the act or process of composing **b ♦ :** arrangement esp. in artistic form **2 :** the arrangement or production of type for printing **3 :** general make-up **4 ♦ :** a product of mixing various elements or ingredients **5 a ♦ :** a literary, musical, or artistic product **b ♦ :** a brief piece of writing **:** ESSAY

♦ [1b] arrangement, configuration, design, form, format, layout, makeup, pattern ♦ [5a] opus, piece, work ♦ [5b] article, essay, paper, theme

com·pos·i·tor \kəm-ˈpä-zə-tər\ *n* **:** one who sets type
com·post \ˈkäm-ˌpōst\ *n* **:** a fertilizing material consisting largely of decayed organic matter
com·po·sure \kəm-ˈpō-zhər\ *n* ♦ **:** a calmness or repose esp. of mind, bearing, or appearance **:** CALMNESS, SELF-POSSESSION

♦ aplomb, calmness, coolness, equanimity, placidity, self-possession, serenity, tranquility

com·pote \ˈkäm-ˌpōt\ *n* **1 :** fruits cooked in syrup **2 :** a bowl (as of glass) usu. with a base and stem for serving esp. fruit or compote
¹**com·pound** \käm-ˈpau̇nd, ˈkäm-ˌ\ *vb* **1 ♦ :** to put together (parts) so as to form a whole **:** COMBINE **2 :** to form by combining parts ⟨∼ a medicine⟩ **3 :** SETTLE ⟨∼ a dispute⟩; *also* **:** to refrain from prosecuting (an offense) in return for a consideration **4 a :** to increase (as interest) by an amount that can itself vary **b ♦ :** to add to

♦ [1] chain, combine, connect, couple, hitch, hook, join, link, yoke ♦ [4b] add, aggrandize, amplify, augment, boost, enlarge, escalate, expand, extend, increase, multiply, raise, swell, up

²**com·pound** \ˈkäm-ˌpau̇nd\ *adj* **1 :** made up of individual parts **2 :** composed of united similar parts esp. of a kind usu. independent ⟨a ∼ plant ovary⟩ **3 :** formed by the combination of two or more otherwise independent elements ⟨∼ sentence⟩
³**com·pound** \ˈkäm-ˌpau̇nd\ *n* **1 :** a word consisting of parts that are words **2 ♦ :** something formed from a union of elements or parts; *esp* **:** a distinct substance formed by the union of two or more chemical elements

♦ admixture, amalgam, blend, combination, composite, fusion, intermixture, mix, mixture

⁴**com·pound** \ˈkäm-ˌpau̇nd\ *n* **:** an enclosure containing buildings
compound interest *n* **:** interest computed on the sum of an original principal and accrued interest
com·pre·hend \ˌkäm-pri-ˈhend\ *vb* **1 ♦ :** to grasp the nature, significance, or meaning of **:** UNDERSTAND **2 ♦ :** to contain or hold within a total scope, significance, or amount **:** INCLUDE — **com·pre·hen·si·ble** \-ˈhen-sə-bəl\ *adj*

♦ [1] appreciate, apprehend, catch, catch on (to), get, grasp, make, make out, perceive, see, seize, understand *Ant* miss ♦ [2] carry, contain, embrace, encompass, entail, include, involve, number, take in

com·pre·hen·sion \-'hen-chən\ *n* ♦ : knowledge gained by comprehending

♦ appreciation, apprehension, grasp, grip, perception, understanding

com·pre·hen·sive \-siv\ *adj* ♦ : covering completely or broadly : covering all possibilities — **com·pre·hen·sive·ly** *adv* — **com·pre·hen·sive·ness** *n*

♦ compendious, complete, encyclopedic, full, global, inclusive, omnibus, panoramic, universal ♦ complete, entire, full, grand, intact, integral, perfect, plenary, total, whole

¹**com·press** \kəm-'pres\ *vb* **1** ♦ : to press or squeeze together **2** ♦ : to reduce in size, quantity, or volume as if by squeezing — **com·pres·sor** \-'pre-sər\ *n*

♦ [1] condense, constrict, contract, shrink ♦ [2] compact, condense, constrict, contract, squeeze *Ant* expand, open, outspread

²**com·press** \'käm-ˌpres\ *n* : a folded pad or cloth used to press upon a body part

compressed air *n* : air under pressure greater than that of the atmosphere

com·pres·sion \-'pre-shən\ *n* **1** ♦ : the act or process of compressing **2** : the process of compressing the fuel mixture in an internal combustion engine **3** : conversion (as of data) in order to reduce the space occupied or the bandwidth required

♦ condensation, constriction, contraction *Ant* expansion

com·prise \kəm-'prīz\ *vb* **com·prised; com·pris·ing 1** : IN-CLUDE, CONTAIN **2** : to consist of : to be made up of **3** ♦ : to make up : COMPOSE, CONSTITUTE

♦ compose, constitute, form, make up

¹**com·pro·mise** \'käm-prə-ˌmīz\ *n* ♦ : a settlement of differences reached by mutual concessions

♦ accommodation, concession, give-and-take, negotiation

²**compromise** *vb* **-mised; -mis·ing 1** : to settle by compromise **2 a** : to expose to suspicion or loss of reputation **b** ♦ : to put in jeopardy : endanger by some act that cannot be recalled

♦ adventure, gamble with, hazard, imperil, jeopardize, menace, risk, venture

comp·trol·ler \kən-'trō-lər, 'kämp-ˌtrō-\ *n* : an official who audits and supervises expenditures and accounts

com·pul·sion \kəm-'pəl-shən\ *n* **1** ♦ : an act of compelling **2** : a force that compels **3** : an irresistible persistent impulse to perform an act

♦ coercion, constraint, duress, force, pressure

com·pul·sive \-siv\ *adj* : of, having to do with, caused by, or suggestive of psychological compulsion or obsession

com·pul·so·ry \-sə-rē\ *adj* ♦ : demanded, directed, or designated by authority

♦ imperative, incumbent, involuntary, mandatory, necessary, nonelective, obligatory, peremptory

com·punc·tion \kəm-'pəŋk-shən\ *n* ♦ : anxiety arising from guilt

♦ misgiving, qualm, scruple

com·pu·ta·tion \ˌkäm-pyů-'tā-shən\ *n* ♦ : the act or action of computing — **com·pu·ta·tion·al** *adj*

♦ arithmetic, calculation, reckoning

com·pute \kəm-'pyüt\ *vb* **com·put·ed; com·put·ing** ♦ : to determine or ascertain esp. by mathematical means : arrive at an answer to or sum for : CALCULATE, RECKON

♦ calculate, figure, reckon, work out

computed tomography *n* : radiography in which a three-dimensional image of a body structure is constructed by computer from a series of plane cross-sectional images made along an axis

com·put·er \kəm-'pyü-tər\ *n* : a programmable electronic device that can store, retrieve, and process data

com·put·er·ise *chiefly Brit var of* COMPUTERIZE

com·put·er·ize \kəm-'pyü-tə-ˌrīz\ *vb* **-ized; -iz·ing 1** : to carry out, control, or produce by means of a computer **2** : to provide with computers **3** : to store in a computer; *also* : put into a form that a computer can use — **com·put·er·iza·tion** \-ˌpyü-tə-rə-'zā-shən\ *n*

computerized axial tomography *n* : COMPUTED TOMOGRAPHY

com·rade \'käm-ˌrad\ *n* ♦ : an intimate friend or associate : COMPANION, ASSOCIATE

♦ associate, cohort, companion, crony, fellow, mate ♦ buddy, chum, crony, familiar, friend, intimate, pal

com·rade·ly *adj* ♦ : of or like a comrade or partner

♦ amicable, companionable, cordial, friendly, genial, hearty, neighborly, warm, warmhearted

com·rade·ship *n* ♦ : association as comrades

♦ camaraderie, companionship, company, fellowship, society

¹**con** \'kän\ *vb* **conned; con·ning 1** : to commit to memory by vocal or mental repetition : MEMORIZE **2** : STUDY

²**con** *adv* : in opposition : AGAINST

³**con** *n* : an opposing argument, person, or position ⟨pros and ∼s⟩

⁴**con** *vb* **conned; con·ning 1** : SWINDLE **2** : PERSUADE, CAJOLE

⁵**con** *n* : CONVICT

conc *abbr* concentrated

con·cat·e·nate \kän-'ka-tə-ˌnāt\ *vb* **-nat·ed; -nat·ing** : to link together in a series or chain — **con·cat·e·na·tion** \(ˌ)kän-ˌka-tə-'nā-shən\ *n*

con·cave \kän-'kāv, 'kän-ˌ\ *adj* ♦ : curved or rounded inward like the inside of a bowl

♦ depressed, hollow, sunken

con·cav·i·ty \kän-'ka-və-tē\ *n* ♦ : a concave line, surface, or space

♦ cavity, dent, depression, hole, hollow, indentation, pit, recess

con·ceal \kən-'sēl\ *vb* ♦ : to place out of sight : HIDE

♦ bury, cache, ensconce, hide, secrete

con·ceal·ment *n* **1** ♦ : the act or practice of concealing **2** ♦ : a hiding place

♦ [1] secretion *Ant* display, exhibition, exposure, parading, showing ♦ [2] covert, den, hideout, lair, nest

con·cede \kən-'sēd\ *vb* **con·ced·ed; con·ced·ing 1** ♦ : to admit to be true **2** ♦ : to make concession : GRANT, YIELD

♦ [1] acknowledge, admit, agree, allow, confess, grant, own ♦ [2] blink, bow, budge, capitulate, give in, grant, knuckle under, quit, submit, succumb, surrender, yield

con·ceit \kən-'sēt\ *n* **1** ♦ : excessively high opinion of one's self or ability : VANITY **2** : an elaborate or strained metaphor **3** ♦ : a fanciful idea

♦ [1] complacence, ego, egotism, pride, self-conceit, self-esteem, self-importance, self-satisfaction, smugness, vainglory, vanity ♦ [3] chimera, daydream, delusion, dream, fancy, fantasy, figment, hallucination, illusion, phantasm, pipe dream, unreality, vision

con·ceit·ed *adj* ♦ : having or showing an excessively high opinion of oneself — **con·ceit·ed·ly** *adv* — **con·ceit·ed·ness** *n*

♦ complacent, egotistic, important, overweening, pompous, prideful, proud, self-important, self-satisfied, smug, stuck-up, vain *Ant* humble, modest

con·ceiv·ably \-blē\ *adv* ♦ : it may be conceived : POSSIBLY

♦ maybe, perchance, perhaps, possibly

con·ceive \kən-'sēv\ *vb* **con·ceived; con·ceiv·ing 1** : to become pregnant or pregnant with ⟨∼ a child⟩ **2** ♦ : to form an idea of : IMAGINE — **con·ceiv·able** \-'sē-və-bəl\ *adj*

♦ dream, envisage, fancy, imagine, picture, vision, visualize

con·cel·e·brant \kən-'se-lə-brənt\ *n* : one that jointly participates in celebrating the Eucharist

¹**con·cen·trate** \'kän-sən-ˌtrāt\ *vb* **-trat·ed; -trat·ing 1** ♦ : to gather into one body, mass, or force **2** : to make less dilute **3** ♦ : to fix one's powers, efforts, or attentions

♦ [1] center (*or* centre), centralize, consolidate, unify, unite ♦ [1] accumulate, amass, assemble, collect, garner, gather, group, lump, pick up, round up, scrape ♦ [3] fasten, focus, rivet, train

²**concentrate** *n* : something concentrated

concentrated *adj* **1** ♦ : rich in respect to a particular or essential element **2** ♦ : not scattered or dispersed

♦ [1] full, full-bodied, potent, rich, robust, strong ♦ [2] all, entire, undivided, whole

con·cen·tra·tion \ˌkän-sən-'trā-shən\ *n* **1** ♦ : the act or process of concentrating : the state of being concentrated; *esp* : direction of attention on a single object **2** : the amount of a component in a given area or volume

♦ absorption, attention

concentration camp *n* : a camp where persons (as prisoners of war or political prisoners) are confined

con·cen·tric \kən-'sen-trik\ *adj* **1 :** having a common center ⟨~ circles⟩ **2 :** COAXIAL

¹con·cept \'kän-‚sept\ *n* ♦ **:** something conceived in the mind **:** THOUGHT, NOTION, IDEA

♦ idea, image, impression, notion, picture, thought

²concept *adj* **1 :** organized around a main idea or theme ⟨a ~ album⟩ **2 :** created to illustrate a concept ⟨a ~ car⟩

con·cep·tion \kən-'sep-shən\ *n* **1 :** the process of conceiving or being conceived **2 :** the power to form or understand ideas or concepts **3 :** a general idea **:** CONCEPT **4 :** the originating of something

con·cep·tu·al \kən-'sep-chə-wəl\ *adj* **:** of, relating to, or consisting of concepts — **con·cep·tu·al·ly** *adv*

con·cep·tu·al·ise *Brit var of* CONCEPTUALIZE

con·cep·tu·al·ize \-'sep-chə-wə-‚līz\ *vb* **-ized; -iz·ing :** to form a conception of

¹con·cern \kən-'sərn\ *vb* **1 :** to relate to **:** be about ⟨the novel ~s three soldiers⟩ **2 :** to be the business of **:** INVOLVE **3 :** ENGAGE, OCCUPY **4** ♦ **:** to be a care, trouble, or distress to

♦ [1] cover, deal, pertain, treat ♦ [2] affect, interest, involve, touch ♦ [4] agitate, bother, discompose, disquiet, distress, disturb, exercise, freak out, perturb, undo, unhinge, unsettle, upset, worry

²concern *n* **1** ♦ **:** an uneasy state of blended interest, uncertainty, and apprehension **:** ANXIETY **2 :** AFFAIR, MATTER **3** ♦ **:** a business organization

♦ [1] agitation, anxiety, apprehension, care, disquiet, nervousness, perturbation, uneasiness, worry ♦ [3] business, company, enterprise, establishment, firm, house, outfit

con·cerned *adj* **1 :** ANXIOUS, UNEASY **2 :** INVOLVED

con·cern·ing *prep* ♦ **:** relating to **:** REGARDING

♦ about, apropos of, of, on, regarding, respecting, toward

con·cern·ment \kən-'sərn-mənt\ *n* **1 :** something in which one is concerned **2 :** IMPORTANCE, CONSEQUENCE

¹con·cert \'kän-(‚)sərt\ *n* **1 :** agreement in a plan or design **2 :** a concerted action **3 :** a public performance (as of music)

²con·cert \kən-'sərt\ *vb* **1** ♦ **:** to plan together **2** ♦ **:** to settle or adjust by conferring and reaching an agreement

♦ [1] collaborate, cooperate, join, team ♦ [2] arrange, conclude, negotiate

con·cert·ed \kən-'sər-təd\ *adj* **1 :** mutually agreed on **2** ♦ **:** performed in unison

♦ collective, common, communal, conjoint, joint, mutual, public, united

con·cer·ti·na \‚kän-sər-'tē-nə\ *n* **:** an instrument of the accordion family

concertina wire *n* **:** a coiled wire with sharp points for use as an obstacle

con·cert·mas·ter \'kän-sərt-‚mas-tər\ *or* **con·cert·meis·ter** \-‚mī-stər\ *n* **:** the leader of the first violins of an orchestra and assistant to the conductor

con·cer·to \kən-'cher-tō\ *n, pl* **-ti** \-(‚)tē\ *or* **-tos :** a piece for one or more solo instruments and orchestra in three movements

con·ces·sion \kən-'se-shən\ *n* **1** ♦ **:** an act of conceding or yielding **2** ♦ **:** something yielded **3 :** a grant by a government of land or of a right to use it **4 :** a grant of a portion of premises for some specific purpose; *also* **:** the activities or enterprise carried on — **con·ces·sion·ary** \-'se-shə-‚ner-ē\ *adj*

♦ [1] acknowledgment, admission, avowal, confession ♦ [1, 2] accommodation, compromise, give-and-take, negotiation

con·ces·sion·aire \kən-‚se-shə-'nar, -'ner\ *n* **:** one that owns or operates a concession

conch \'käŋk, 'känch\ *n, pl* **conchs** \'käŋks\ *or* **conch·es** \'kän-chəz\ **:** a large spiral-shelled marine gastropod mollusk; *also* **:** its shell

con·cierge \kōⁿ-'syerzh\ *n, pl* **con·cierges** *same or* -'syerzhəz\ **1 :** a resident in an apartment building who performs services for the tenants **2 :** a usu. multilingual hotel staff member who usu. handles mail and reservations

con·cil·i·ate \kən-'si-lē-‚āt\ *vb* **-at·ed; -at·ing 1** ♦ **:** to bring into agreement **:** RECONCILE **2 :** to gain the goodwill of — **con·cil·i·a·tion** \-‚si-lē-'ā-shən\ *n*

♦ accommodate, conform, coordinate, harmonize, key, reconcile

con·cil·ia·to·ry \-'si-lē-ə-‚tōr-ē\ *adj* ♦ **:** tending to conciliate

♦ pacific, propitiatory

con·cise \kən-'sīs\ *adj* ♦ **:** expressing much in few words **:** BRIEF

♦ brief, compact, compendious, crisp, epigrammatic, laconic, pithy, succinct, summary, terse *Ant* diffuse, long-winded, prolix, rambling, verbose, wordy

con·cise·ly *adv* ♦ **:** in a concise manner

♦ compactly, crisply, laconically, shortly, succinctly, summarily, tersely

con·cise·ness *n* ♦ **:** the quality or state of being concise

♦ brevity, briefness, compactness, crispness, succinctness, terseness

con·clave \'kän-‚klāv\ *n* **:** a private gathering; *also* **:** CONVENTION

con·clude \kən-'klüd\ *vb* **con·clud·ed; con·clud·ing 1** ♦ **:** to bring or come to a close **:** END **2 a** ♦ **:** to reach as a logically necessary end by reasoning **:** JUDGE **b** ♦ **:** to make a decision about **:** DECIDE **3 :** to bring about as a result

♦ [1] close, end, finish, round, terminate, wind up, wrap up ♦ [2a] deduce, extrapolate, gather, infer, judge, reason, understand ♦ [2b] choose, decide, determine, figure, opt, resolve

con·clu·sion \kən-'klü-zhən\ *n* **1** ♦ **:** the logical consequence of a reasoning process **2** ♦ **:** the last part of anything **:** END **3** ♦ **:** a final decision or settlement **:** OUTCOME, RESULT

♦ [1, 3] aftermath, consequence, corollary, development, effect, issue, outcome, outgrowth, product, result, resultant, sequence, upshot ♦ [2] close, consummation, end, ending, finale, finis, finish, windup

con·clu·sive \-siv\ *adj* ♦ **:** putting an end to debate or question esp. by reason of irrefutability — **con·clu·sive·ly** *adv*

♦ absolute, clear, decisive, definitive *Ant* inconclusive, indecisive, unclear

con·clu·sive·ness *adj* ♦ **:** the quality or state of being conclusive

♦ authority, cogency, effectiveness, force, persuasion, persuasiveness

con·coct \kən-'käkt, kän-\ *vb* **1 :** to prepare by combining raw materials **2 a** ♦ **:** to formulate by thought **b :** to put together usu. for the purposes of deception **:** DEVISE

♦ contrive, cook up, devise, fabricate, invent, make up, manufacture, think up

con·coc·tion \-'käk-shən\ *n* **1** ♦ **:** something that is concocted (as a food or scheme) **2 :** something that suggests origin by concoction (as by mingling of diverse elements)

♦ coinage, contrivance, creation, innovation, invention, wrinkle

¹con·com·i·tant \-'kä-mə-tənt\ *adj* ♦ **:** accompanying esp. in a subordinate or incidental way

♦ attendant, coincident, concurrent

²concomitant *n* **:** something that accompanies or is collaterally connected with something else

con·cord \'kän-‚kȯrd, 'käŋ-\ *n* ♦ **:** a state of agreement **:** HARMONY

♦ compatibility, harmony, peace

con·cor·dance \kən-'kȯr-dᵊns\ *n* **1 :** an alphabetical index of words in a book or in an author's works with the passages in which they occur **2 :** AGREEMENT, COVENANT

con·cor·dant \-dᵊnt\ *adj* ♦ **:** marked by accord in sentiment or action **:** HARMONIOUS

♦ compatible, conformable (to), congruous, consistent, consonant, correspondent, harmonious

con·cor·dat \kän-'kȯr-‚dat\ *n* **:** CONCORDANCE 2

con·course \'kän-‚kȯrs\ *n* **1 :** a spontaneous coming together **:** GATHERING **2 :** an open space or hall (as in a bus terminal) where crowds gather

¹con·crete \kän-'krēt, 'kän-‚krēt\ *adj* **1 :** naming a real thing or class of things **:** not abstract **2** ♦ **:** not theoretical **:** ACTUAL **3 :** made of or relating to concrete **4** ♦ **:** formed by coalition of particles into one solid mass

♦ [2] actual, existent, factual, real, true, very ♦ [4] material, physical, substantial

²con·crete \'kän-‚krēt, kän-'krēt\ *vb* **con·cret·ed; con·cret·ing 1 :** to form into a solid mass **:** SOLIDIFY **2 :** to cover with concrete

³con·crete \'kän-‚krēt, kän-'krēt\ *n* **:** a hard building material made by mixing cement, sand, and gravel with water

con·cre·tion \kän-'krē-shən\ *n* **:** a hard mass esp. when formed abnormally in the body

con·cu·bine \'käŋ-kyù-‚bīn\ *n* **:** a woman who is not legally a wife but lives with a man and sometimes has a recognized position in his household; *also* : MISTRESS — **con·cu·bi·nage** \kän-'kyü-bə-nij\ *n*

con·cu·pis·cence \kän-'kyü-pə-səns\ *n* : ardent sexual desire : LUST

con·cur \kən-'kər\ *vb* **con·curred; con·cur·ring** **1** : to act together **2** : to express agreement : AGREE **3** : to happen together : COINCIDE

con·cur·rence \-'kər-əns\ *n* **1** ♦ : agreement in action or opinion **2** : occurrence together

♦ accord, agreement, consensus, unanimity

con·cur·rent \-'kər-ənt\ *adj* **1** ♦ : happening or operating at the same time **2** : joint and equal in authority

♦ coeval, contemporary, simultaneous, synchronous ♦ attendant, coincident, concomitant

con·cus·sion \kən-'kə-shən\ *n* **1** ♦ : a hard blow or collision; *also* : bodily injury (as to the brain) resulting from a sudden jar **2** : AGITATION, SHAKING

♦ bump, collision, crash, impact, jar, jolt, shock, smash, strike, wallop

con·demn \kən-'dem\ *vb* **1** ♦ : to declare to be wrong, reprehensible, or evil **2** : to pronounce guilty **3** ♦ : to sentence judicially **4** ♦ : to pronounce unfit for use or consumption ⟨∼ a building⟩ **5** : to declare forfeited or taken for public use **6** ♦ : to pronounce judgment on the faults of — **con·dem·na·tion** \kən-dem-'nā-shən\ *n*

♦ [1] censure, damn, decry, denounce, reprehend, reprobate *Ant* bless ♦ [3] damn, doom, sentence ♦ [4] censure, denounce, rebuke, reprimand, reproach, reprove ♦ [6] blame, censure, criticize, denounce, fault, knock, pan, reprehend

con·den·sate \'kän-dən-sāt, kən-'den-\ *n* : a product of condensation

con·den·sa·tion \kän-den-'sā-shən\ *n* **1** ♦ : the act or process of condensing **2** ♦ : abridgment and usu. compression of a literary work

♦ [1] compression, constriction, contraction ♦ [2] abbreviation, digest

con·dense \kən-'dens\ *vb* **con·densed; con·dens·ing** **1** ♦ : to make or become more compact or dense : compress or concentrate into a smaller scope or volume **2** : to change from vapor to liquid

♦ compact, compress, constrict, contract, squeeze

condensed *adj* : reduced to a more compact form

con·dens·er \kən-'den-sər\ *n* **1** : one that condenses **2** : CAPACITOR

con·de·scend \kän-di-'send\ *vb* **1** : to descend to a less formal or dignified level **2** : to assume an air of superiority — **con·de·scend·ing·ly** \-'sen-diŋ-lē\ *adv* — **con·de·scen·sion** \-'sen-chən\ *n*

con·dign \kən-'dīn, 'kän-dīn\ *adj* : DESERVED, APPROPRIATE ⟨∼ punishment⟩

con·di·ment \'kän-də-mənt\ *n* : something used to make food savory; *esp* : a pungent seasoning (as pepper)

¹**con·di·tion** \kən-'di-shən\ *n* **1** ♦ : something essential to the occurrence of some other thing **2** ♦ : state of being **3** : social status **4** *pl* : state of affairs : CIRCUMSTANCES **5** : a bodily state in which something is wrong ⟨a heart ∼⟩ **6** ♦ : a state of health, fitness, or working order ⟨in good ∼⟩ **7** ♦ : a restricting or modifying factor

♦ [1] essential, must, necessity, provision, proviso, qualification, requirement, stipulation ♦ [2, 6] estate, fettle, form, order, repair, shape, trim ♦ [7] check, constraint, curb, fetter, limitation, restraint, restriction

²**condition** *vb* **1** ♦ : to put into proper condition for action or use **2** ♦ : to adapt, modify, or mold to respond in a particular way **3** : to modify so that an act or response previously associated with one stimulus becomes associated with another

♦ [1, 2] acclimate, accommodate, adapt, adjust, conform, fit, shape

con·di·tion·al \kən-'di-shə-nəl\ *adj* ♦ : containing, implying, or depending on a condition — **con·di·tion·al·ly** *adv*

♦ contingent, dependent, subject

con·di·tioned *adj* : determined or established by conditioning

con·di·tion·er \-'di-shə-nər\ *n* : a preparation used to improve the condition of hair

con·do \'kän-(ˌ)dō\ *n* : CONDOMINIUM 3

con·dole \kən-'dōl\ *vb* **con·doled; con·dol·ing** : to express sympathetic sorrow — **con·do·lence** \kən-'dō-ləns\ *n*

con·dom \'kän-dəm, 'kən-\ *n* : a usu. rubber sheath worn over the penis (as to prevent pregnancy or venereal infection during sexual intercourse)

con·do·min·i·um \kän-də-'mi-nē-əm\ *n, pl* **-ums** **1** : joint sovereignty (as by two or more nations) **2** : a politically dependent territory under condominium **3** : individual ownership of a unit (as an apartment) in a multiunit structure; *also* : a unit so owned

con·done \kən-'dōn\ *vb* **con·doned; con·don·ing** ♦ : to overlook or forgive esp. by treating (an offense) as harmless or trivial — **con·do·na·tion** \kän-də-'nā-shən\ *n*

♦ disregard, excuse, gloss over, ignore, pardon, pass over, shrug off, wink at

con·dor \'kän-dər, -ˌdȯr\ *n* : a very large American vulture of the high Andes; *also* : a related nearly extinct vulture of southern California

con·duce \kən-'düs, -'dyüs\ *vb* **con·duced; con·duc·ing** : to lead or contribute to a particular result — **con·du·cive** *adj*

¹**con·duct** \'kän-(ˌ)dəkt\ *n* **1** ♦ : the act, manner, or process of carrying on : MANAGEMENT, DIRECTION **2** ♦ : a mode or standard of personal behavior esp. as based on moral principles : BEHAVIOR

♦ [1] administration, control, direction, government, guidance, management, operation, oversight, regulation, running, superintendence, supervision ♦ [2] actions, bearing, behavior (*or* behaviour), comportment, demeanor (*or* demeanour), deportment

²**con·duct** \kən-'dəkt\ *vb* **1** ♦ : to bring by or as if by leading : GUIDE **2** ♦ : to direct or take part in the operation or management of : MANAGE, DIRECT **3** ♦ : to convey in a channel **4** ♦ : to cause (oneself) to act or behave in a particular and esp. in a controlled manner : BEHAVE — **con·duc·tion** \-'dək-shən\ *n*

♦ [1] direct, guide, lead, marshal, pilot, route, show, steer, usher ♦ [2] administer, carry on, control, direct, govern, guide, handle, manage, operate, oversee, regulate, run, superintend, supervise ♦ [3] channel, direct, funnel, pipe, siphon ♦ [4] acquit, bear, behave, comport, demean, deport, quit

con·duc·tance \kən-'dək-təns\ *n* : the readiness with which a conductor transmits an electric current

con·duc·tive \kən-'dək-tiv\ *adj* : having the power to conduct (as heat or electricity) — **con·duc·tiv·i·ty** \kän-dək-'ti-və-tē\ *n*

con·duc·tor \kən-'dək-tər\ *n* **1** : one that conducts; *esp* : a material that permits an electric current to flow easily **2** : a collector of fares in a public conveyance **3** : the leader of a musical ensemble

con·duit \'kän-dü-ət, -ˌdyü-, -dwət\ *n* **1** ♦ : a natural or artificial channel through which something (as a fluid) is conveyed **2** : a tube or trough for protecting electric wires or cables **3** : a means of transmitting or distributing

♦ channel, duct, leader, line, penstock, pipe, tube ♦ aqueduct, canal, channel, flume, raceway, watercourse

con·dyle \'kän-dīl, -dᵊl\ *n* : an articular prominence of a bone — **con·dy·lar** \-də-lər\ *adj*

cone \'kōn\ *n* **1** : the scaly fruit of trees of the pine family **2** : a solid figure formed by rotating a right triangle about one of its legs **3** : a solid figure that slopes evenly to a point from a usu. circular base **4** : any of the conical light-sensitive receptor cells of the retina that function in color vision **5** : something shaped like a cone

Con·es·to·ga wagon \kä-nə-'stō-gə-\ *n* : a broad-wheeled covered wagon used esp. for transporting freight across the prairies

co·ney \'kō-nē\ *n, pl* **coneys** **1** : RABBIT; *also* : its fur **2** : PIKA

conf *abbr* **1** conference **2** confidential

con·fab \'kän-ˌfab, kən-'fab\ *n* : CONFABULATION 1

con·fab·u·la·tion \kən-ˌfab-yə-'lā-shən\ *n* **1** : CHAT; *also* : CONFERENCE **2** : a filling in of gaps in memory by fabrication

con·fec·tion \kən-'fek-shən\ *n* : a fancy dish or sweet; *also* : CANDY

con·fec·tion·er \-shə-nər\ *n* : a maker of or dealer in confections

con·fec·tion·ery \-shə-ˌner-ē\ *n, pl* **-er·ies** **1** : sweet foods **2** : a confectioner's place of business

Confed *abbr* Confederate

con·fed·er·a·cy \kən-'fe-də-rə-sē\ *n, pl* **-cies** **1** ♦ : a league or compact for mutual support or common action : LEAGUE, ALLIANCE **2** *cap* : the 11 southern states that seceded from the U.S. in 1860 and 1861

♦ alliance, bloc, coalition, combination, combine, confederation, federation, league, union

¹**con·fed·er·ate** \kən-'fe-də-rət\ *adj* **1** : united in a league : ALLIED **2** *cap* : of or relating to the Confederacy

²confederate *n* **1** ♦ : one that is associated with another as a helper **2** *cap* : an adherent of the Confederacy

  ♦ abettor, accessory, accomplice, cohort ♦ abettor, ally, backer, supporter, sympathizer

³con·fed·er·ate \-'fe-də-ˌrāt\ *vb* **-at·ed; -at·ing** ♦ : to unite in a confederacy

  ♦ ally, associate, band, club, conjoin, cooperate, federate, league, unite

con·fed·er·a·tion \kən-ˌfe-də-'rā-shən\ *n* **1** : an act of confederating : ALLIANCE **2** ♦ : as association of parties for mutual assistance : LEAGUE

  ♦ alliance, bloc, coalition, combination, combine, confederacy, federation, league, union

con·fer \kən-'fər\ *vb* **con·ferred; con·fer·ring** **1** ♦ : to give or grant from or as if from a position of superiority : BE-STOW **2** ♦ : to exchange views : CONSULT — **con·fer·ee** \ˌkän-fə-'rē\ *n*

  ♦ [1] accord, award, bestow, give, grant ♦ [2] advise, consult, counsel, parley

con·fer·ence \'kän-f(ə-)rəns\ *n* **1 a** ♦ : an interchange of views **b** ♦ : a meeting for an exchange of views **2** : an association of athletic teams

  ♦ [1a] argument, colloquy, deliberation, discourse, discussion, give-and-take, parley, talk ♦ [1b] assembly, congress, convention, convocation, council, gathering, get-together, huddle, meeting, seminar

con·fer·enc·ing \'kän-f(ə-)rən-siŋ\ *n* : the holding of conferences esp. by means of electronic devices
con·fess \kən-'fes\ *vb* **1** ♦ : to tell or make known (as something wrong or damaging to oneself) **2** : to acknowledge one's sins to God or to a priest **3** : to receive the confession of (a penitent)

  ♦ acknowledge, admit, agree, allow, concede, grant, own

con·fess·ed·ly \-'fe-səd-lē\ *adv* : by confession : ADMITTEDLY
con·fes·sion \-'fe-shən\ *n* **1** ♦ : an act of confessing (as in the sacrament of penance) **2** ♦ : an acknowledgment of guilt **3** : a formal statement of religious beliefs **4** : a religious body having a common creed — **con·fes·sion·al** *adj*

  ♦ [1, 2] acknowledgment, admission, avowal, concession

con·fes·sion·al \-'fe-shə-nəl\ *n* : a place where a priest hears confessions
con·fes·sor \kən-'fe-sər\ *n* **1** : one that confesses **2** : a priest who hears confessions
con·fet·ti \kən-'fe-tē\ *n* : bits of colored paper or ribbon for throwing (as at weddings)
con·fi·dant \'kän-fə-ˌdänt, -ˌdant\ *n* : one to whom secrets are confided
con·fi·dante \-ˌdänt, -ˌdant\ *n* : CONFIDANT; *esp* : one who is a woman
con·fide \kən-'fīd\ *vb* **con·fid·ed; con·fid·ing** **1** : to have or show faith : TRUST ⟨∼ in a friend⟩ **2** : to tell confidentially ⟨∼ a secret⟩ **3** : ENTRUST
¹con·fi·dence \'kän-fə-dəns\ *n* **1** : faith or belief that one will act in a right, proper, or effective way : TRUST **2** ♦ : a feeling or consciousness of one's powers or of reliance on one's circumstances : SELF-ASSURANCE **3** ♦ : a state of trust or intimacy **4** : a communication made in confidence : SECRET **2** **5** ♦ : the quality or state of being certain : CERTITUDE

  ♦ [2] aplomb, assurance, self-assurance, self-confidence, self-esteem *Ant* diffidence, self-doubt ♦ [3] credence, faith, stock, trust ♦ [5] assurance, certainty, certitude, conviction, positiveness, sureness *Ant* doubt, incertitude, uncertainty

²confidence *adj* : of or relating to swindling by false promises ⟨a ∼ game⟩
con·fi·dent \-dənt\ *adj* **1** ♦ : full of conviction : CERTAIN **2** ♦ : having or showing assurance and self-reliance — **con·fi·dent·ly** *adv*

  ♦ [1] assured, certain, clear, cocksure, doubtless, positive, sanguine, sure ♦ [2] assured, secure, self-assured, self-confident *Ant* diffident, insecure

con·fi·den·tial \ˌkän-fə-'den-shəl\ *adj* **1** ♦ : known only to a limited few : SECRET, PRIVATE **2** : entrusted with confidences ⟨∼ clerk⟩ — **con·fi·den·tial·ly** \-'den-shə-lē\ *adv*

  ♦ hushed, inside, intimate, private, secret

con·fig·u·ra·tion \kən-ˌfi-gyə-'rā-shən\ *n* ♦ : relative arrangement of parts or elements : SHAPE

  ♦ arrangement, composition, design, form, format, layout, makeup, pattern, shape

con·fig·ure \kən-'fi-gyər\ *vb* **-ured; -ur·ing** : to set up for operation esp. in a particular way
con·fine \kən-'fīn\ *vb* **con·fined; con·fin·ing** **1** ♦ : to hold within a location; *also* : IMPRISON **2** ♦ : to keep within limits ⟨will ∼ my remarks to one subject⟩ — **con·fin·er** *n*

  ♦ [1] commit, immure, imprison, jail ♦ [2] check, circumscribe, control, curb, inhibit, limit, restrain, restrict

con·fine·ment *n* ♦ : an act of confining : the state of being confined

  ♦ captivity, imprisonment, incarceration, internment

con·fines \'kän-ˌfīnz\ *n pl* ♦ : something (as borders or walls) that encloses : something that restrains

  ♦ boundary, ceiling, end, extent, limit, limitation, line, termination ♦ border, boundary, circumference, compass, edge, end, fringe, margin, perimeter, periphery, rim, skirt, verge

con·firm \kən-'fərm\ *vb* **1** : to give approval to : RATIFY **2** : to make firm or firmer **3** : to administer the rite of confirmation to **4** ♦ : to give new assurance of the validity of : VERIFY, CORROBORATE

  ♦ bear out, corroborate, substantiate, support, validate, verify, vindicate *Ant* disprove, rebut, refute

con·fir·ma·tion \ˌkän-fər-'mā-shən\ *n* **1** : a religious ceremony admitting a person to full membership in a church or synagogue **2** ♦ : an act of ratifying or corroborating; *also* : PROOF

  ♦ attestation, corroboration, documentation, evidence, proof, substantiation, testament, testimony, validation, witness

con·fir·ma·to·ry \-'fər-mə-ˌtōr-ē\ *adj* ♦ : serving to confirm

  ♦ corroborative

confirmed *adj* **1** ♦ : marked by long continuance and likely to persist **2** ♦ : fixed in habit and unlikely to change

  ♦ [1] deep-rooted, deep-seated, inveterate, settled ♦ [2] chronic, habitual, inveterate

con·fis·cate \'kän-fə-ˌskāt\ *vb* **-cat·ed; -cat·ing** : to take possession of by or as if by public authority — **con·fis·ca·tion** \ˌkän-fə-'skā-shən\ *n* — **con·fis·ca·to·ry** \kən-'fis-kə-ˌtōr-ē\ *adj*
con·fit \kōn-'fē\ *n* : a garnish of fruit or vegetables cooked in a seasoned liquid
con·fla·gra·tion \ˌkän-flə-'grā-shən\ *n* ♦ : FIRE; *esp* : a large disastrous fire

  ♦ fire, holocaust, inferno

¹con·flict \'kän-ˌflikt\ *n* **1** ♦ : prolonged fighting esp. with weapons : WAR **2** ♦ : a clash between hostile or opposing elements, ideas, or forces

  ♦ [1] battle, clash, combat, contest, fight, fracas, fray, hassle, scrap, scrimmage, scuffle, skirmish, struggle, war, warfare ♦ [1, 2] battle, combat, confrontation, contest, duel, face-off, rivalry, struggle, tug-of-war, warfare ♦ [2] discord, dissension, dissent, disunity, friction, schism, strife, variance, war, warfare

²con·flict \kən-'flikt\ *vb* ♦ : to show opposition or irreconcilability : CLASH

  ♦ clash, collide, jar

con·flu·ence \'kän-ˌflü-əns, kən-'flü-\ *n* **1** ♦ : a coming together at one point **2** : the meeting or place of meeting of two or more streams — **con·flu·ent** \-ənt\ *adj*

  ♦ conjunction, convergence, meeting

con·flux \'kän-ˌfləks\ *n* : CONFLUENCE
con·form \kən-'fōrm\ *vb* **1 a** ♦ : to be similar or identical **b** ♦ : to be in agreement or harmony : AGREE **2** ♦ : to be obedient or compliant — usu. used with *to; also* : COMPLY **3** ♦ : to make like : shape to fit — **con·form·ist** \-'fōr-mist\ *adj*

  ♦ [1b] accord, agree, answer, check, coincide, comport, correspond, dovetail, fit, go, harmonize, jibe, square, tally ♦ *usu* **conform to** [2] comply, follow, mind, obey, observe ♦ [3] acclimate, accommodate, adapt, adjust, condition, fit, shape

con·form·able *adj* **1** ♦ : corresponding or consistent in form or character **2** ♦ : giving compliance or obedience

  ♦ *usu* **conformable to** [1] compatible, congruous, consistent, consonant, correspondent, harmonious ♦ [2] amenable, compliant, docile, obedient, submissive, tractable

con·for·mance \kən-'fȯr-məns\ *n* : CONFORMITY
con·for·ma·tion \ˌkän-fȯr-'mā-shən\ *n* ♦ : formation of something by appropriate arrangement of parts or elements : an assembling into a whole

♦ arrangement, configuration, format, layout, setup

con·for·mi·ty \kən-'fȯr-mə-tē\ *n, pl* **-ties** **1** ♦ : correspondence in form, manner, or character : HARMONY, AGREEMENT **2** ♦ : action in accordance with some specified standard or authority : COMPLIANCE, OBEDIENCE

♦ [1] accord, agreement, consonance, harmony, tune *Ant* conflict, disagreement ♦ [2] compliance, obedience, observance, submission, subordination

con·found \kən-'faȯnd, kän-\ *vb* **1** ♦ : to throw (a person) into confusion or perplexity **2** ♦ : to put to shame : CONFUSE 2

♦ [1] addle, baffle, befog, befuddle, bemuse, bewilder, confuse, disorient, muddle, muddy, mystify, perplex, puzzle ♦ [2] abash, confuse, discomfit, disconcert, discountenance, embarrass, faze, fluster, mortify, rattle

con·fra·ter·ni·ty \ˌkän-frə-'tər-nə-tē\ *n* : a society devoted esp. to a religious or charitable cause
con·frere \'kän-ˌfrer, 'kōⁿ-\ *n* : COLLEAGUE, COMRADE
con·front \kən-'frənt\ *vb* **1 a** ♦ : to face esp. in challenge **b** ♦ : to deal unflinchingly with ⟨~ed the issue⟩ **2** : to cause to face or meet

♦ [1a, 1b] beard, brave, brazen, dare, defy, face

con·fron·ta·tion \ˌkän-frən-'tā-shən\ *n* ♦ : the act of confronting : the state of being confronted — **con·fron·ta·tion·al** \-shə-nᵊl\ *adj*

♦ battle, combat, conflict, contest, duel, face-off, rivalry, struggle, tug-of-war, warfare

Con·fu·cian \kən-'fyü-shən\ *adj* : of or relating to the Chinese philosopher Confucius or his teachings — **Con·fu·cian·ism** \-shə-ˌni-zəm\ *n*
con·fuse \kən-'fyüz\ *vb* **con·fused; con·fus·ing** **1 a** ♦ : to make mentally unclear or uncertain **b** ♦ : to disturb the composure of **2** : to mix up : JUMBLE **3** ♦ : to fail to make clear or distinct — **con·fus·ed·ly** \-'fyü-zəd-lē\ *adv*

♦ [1a] addle, baffle, befog, befuddle, bemuse, bewilder, confound, disorient, muddle, muddy, mystify, perplex, puzzle ♦ [1b] abash, confound, discomfit, disconcert, discountenance, embarrass, faze, fluster, mortify, rattle ♦ [3] becloud, befog, blur, cloud, fog, muddy *Ant* clarify

confused *adj* **1** ♦ : being perplexed or disconcerted **2** ♦ : being disordered or mixed up

♦ [1] dizzy, stunned ♦ [2] chaotic, disheveled, disordered, messy, muddled, sloppy, unkempt, untidy

con·fu·sion \-'fyü-zhən\ *n* **1** : an act or instance of confusing **2** ♦ : the quality or state of being confused **3** ♦ : a confused mass or mixture

♦ [2] bafflement, bewilderment, distraction, muddle, mystification, perplexity, puzzlement, whirl ♦ [3] chaos, disarray, disorder, disorganization, havoc, hell, jumble, mess, muddle, shambles

con·fu·ta·tion \ˌkän-fyü-'tā-shən\ *n* ♦ : something (as an argument or statement) that refutes

♦ rebuttal, refutation *Ant* proof

con·fute \kən-'fyüt\ *vb* **con·fut·ed; con·fut·ing** ♦ : to overwhelm by argument : refute conclusively

♦ belie, disprove, rebut, refute

cong *abbr* congress; congressional
con·ga \'käŋ-gə\ *n* : a Cuban dance of African origin performed by a group usu. in single file
con·geal \kən-'jēl\ *vb* **1** ♦ : to change from a fluid to a solid state by or as if by cold : FREEZE **2** ♦ : to make or become hard or thick

♦ [1] clot, coagulate, gel, jell, set ♦ [1, 2] concrete, firm, freeze, harden, set, solidify

con·gee \'kän-jē\ *n* : porridge made from rice
con·ge·ner \'kän-jə-nər\ *n* : one related to another; *esp* : a plant or animal of the same taxonomic genus as another — **con·ge·ner·ic** \ˌkän-jə-'ner-ik\ *adj*
con·ge·nial \kən-'jē-nyəl\ *adj* **1** ♦ : having the same nature, disposition, or tastes : KINDRED **2** ♦ : agreeably suited to one's nature, tastes, or outlook : AGREEABLE — **con·ge·ni·al·i·ty** \-ˌjē-nē-'a-lə-tē\ *n* — **con·ge·nial·ly** *adv*

♦ [1] agreeable, amicable, compatible, harmonious, kindred, unanimous, united ♦ [2] agreeable, delectable, delicious, delightful, dreamy, felicitous, good, grateful, gratifying, nice, palatable, pleasant, pleasurable, satisfying

con·gen·i·tal \kən-'je-nə-tᵊl\ *adj* : existing at or dating from birth
con·ger eel \'kän-gər-\ *n* : a large edible marine eel of the Atlantic
con·ge·ries \'kän-jə-(ˌ)rēz\ *n, pl* **congeries** : AGGREGATION, COLLECTION
con·gest \kən-'jest\ *vb* **1** : to cause excessive fullness of the blood vessels of (as a lung) **2** ♦ : to obstruct by overcrowding **3** : to concentrate in a small or narrow space — **con·ges·tion** \-'jes-chən\ *n* — **con·ges·tive** \-'jes-tiv\ *adj*

♦ block, choke, clog, close (off), dam, jam, obstruct, plug (up), stop (up), stuff

congestive heart failure *n* : heart failure in which the heart is unable to keep enough blood circulating in the tissues or is unable to pump out the blood returned to it by the veins
¹con·glom·er·ate \kən-'glä-mə-rət\ *adj* : made up of parts from various sources
²con·glom·er·ate \-ˌrāt\ *vb* **-at·ed; -at·ing** ♦ : to gather into a mass : form a coherent whole — **con·glom·er·a·tion** \-ˌglä-mə-'rā-shən\ *n*

♦ accumulate, collect, gather, heap, pile up

³con·glom·er·ate \-rət\ *n* **1** : a mass formed of fragments from various sources; *esp* : a rock composed of fragments varying from pebbles to boulders held together by a cementing material **2** : a widely diversified corporation
Con·go·lese \ˌkäŋ-gə-'lēz, -'lēs\ *n* : a native or inhabitant of Congo — **Congolese** *adj*
con·grat·u·late \kən-'gra-chə-ˌlāt\ *vb* **-lat·ed; -lat·ing** : to express sympathetic pleasure to on account of success or good fortune : FELICITATE — **con·grat·u·la·to·ry** \-'gra-chə-lə-ˌtȯr-ē\ *adj*
con·grat·u·la·tion \-ˌgra-chə-'lā-shən\ *n* **1** : the act of congratulating **2** : a congratulatory expression — usu. used in pl.
con·gre·gate \'käŋ-gri-ˌgāt\ *vb* **-gat·ed; -gat·ing** ♦ : to collect into a group or crowd : ASSEMBLE

♦ assemble, cluster, collect, concentrate, conglomerate, convene, forgather, gather, meet, rendezvous

con·gre·ga·tion \ˌkäŋ-gri-'gā-shən\ *n* **1** ♦ : an assembly of persons met esp. for worship; *also* : a group that habitually so meets **2** : a religious community or order **3** : the act or an instance of congregating

♦ assemblage, assembly, conference, convocation, gathering, meeting, muster

con·gre·ga·tion·al \-shə-nəl\ *adj* **1** : of or relating to a congregation **2** *cap* : observing the faith and practice of certain Protestant churches which recognize the independence of each congregation in church matters — **con·gre·ga·tion·al·ism** \-shə-nə-ˌli-zəm\ *n, often cap* — **con·gre·ga·tion·al·ist** \-list\ *n, often cap*
con·gress \'käŋ-grəs\ *n* **1** ♦ : an assembly esp. of delegates for discussion and usu. action on some question **2** : the body of senators and representatives constituting a nation's legislature **3** : the body of persons coming together for a common purpose — **con·gres·sio·nal** \kən-'gre-shə-nəl\ *adj*

♦ assembly, conference, convention, convocation, council, gathering, get-together, huddle, meeting, seminar

con·gress·man \'käŋ-grəs-mən\ *n* : a member of a congress
con·gress·wom·an \-ˌwu̇-mən\ *n* : a woman who is a member of a congress
con·gru·ence \kən-'grü-əns, 'käŋ-grü-\ *n* : the quality of agreeing or coinciding : CONGRUITY — **con·gru·ent** \kən-'grü-ənt, 'käŋ-grü-\ *adj*
con·gru·en·cy \-sē\ *n, pl* **-cies** : CONGRUENCE
con·gru·ity \kän-'grü-ə-tē\ *n, pl* **-ities** : correspondence between things
con·gru·ous \'käŋ-grü-əs\ *adj* ♦ : being in agreement, harmony, or correspondence

♦ balanced, consonant, harmonious ♦ compatible, conformable (to), consistent, consonant, correspondent, harmonious

con·ic \'kä-nik\ *adj* **1** : of or relating to a cone **2** : CONICAL
con·i·cal \'kä-ni-kəl\ *adj* : resembling a cone esp. in shape
co·ni·fer \'kä-nə-fər, 'kō-\ *n* : any of an order of shrubs or trees (as the pines) that usu. are evergreen and bear cones — **co·nif·er·ous** \kō-'ni-fə-rəs\ *adj*

conj *abbr* conjunction

con·jec·tur·al \-chə-rəl\ *adj* ♦ : of the nature of or involving or based on conjecture

    ♦ hypothetical, speculative, theoretical

¹**con·jec·ture** \kən-ˈjek-chər\ *n* **1** ♦ : a conclusion deduced by surmise or guesswork : GUESS, SURMISE **2** ♦ : inference from defective or presumptive evidence

    ♦ [1, 2] guess, supposition, surmise ♦ [2] hypothesis, proposition, supposition, theory

²**conjecture** *vb* ♦ : to arrive at or deduce by conjecture : GUESS

    ♦ calculate, call, estimate, figure, gauge, guess, judge, make, place, put, reckon, suppose ♦ assume, guess, presume, speculate, suppose, surmise, suspect

con·join \kən-ˈjoin\ *vb* ♦ : to join together — **con·joint** \-ˈjoint\ *adj*

    ♦ associate, coalesce, combine, connect, couple, fuse, join, link, marry, unify, unite

con·joint \-ˈjoint\ *adj* ♦ : related to, made up of, or carried on by two or more in combination

    ♦ collective, common, communal, concerted, joint, mutual, public, united

con·ju·gal \ˈkän-ji-gəl\ *adj* ♦ : of or relating to marriage : MATRIMONIAL

    ♦ connubial, marital, matrimonial, nuptial

¹**con·ju·gate** \ˈkän-ji-gət, -jə-ˌgāt\ *adj* **1** : united esp. in pairs : COUPLED **2** : of kindred origin and meaning ⟨*sing* and *song* are ∼⟩ — **con·ju·gate·ly** *adv*

²**con·ju·gate** \-jə-ˌgāt\ *vb* **-gat·ed; -gat·ing 1** : INFLECT ⟨∼ a verb⟩ **2** : to join together : COUPLE

con·ju·ga·tion \ˌkän-jə-ˈgā-shən\ *n* **1** : an arrangement of the inflectional forms of a verb **2** : the act of conjugating : the state of being conjugated

con·junct \kän-ˈjəŋkt\ *adj* : JOINED, UNITED

con·junc·tion \kən-ˈjəŋk-shən\ *n* **1** ♦ : the act or an instance of conjoining : the state of being combined **2** : occurrence at the same time **3** : a word that joins together sentences, clauses, phrases, or words

    ♦ confluence, convergence, meeting

con·junc·ti·va \ˌkän-jəŋk-ˈtī-və\ *n, pl* **-vas** *or* **-vae** \-(ˌ)vē\ : the mucous membrane lining the inner surface of the eyelids and continuing over the forepart of the eyeball

con·junc·tive \kən-ˈjəŋk-tiv\ *adj* **1** : CONNECTIVE **2** : CONJUNCT **3** : being or functioning like a conjunction

con·junc·ti·vi·tis \kən-ˌjəŋk-ti-ˈvī-təs\ *n* : inflammation of the conjunctiva

con·junc·ture \kən-ˈjəŋk-chər\ *n* **1** : CONJUNCTION, UNION **2** : JUNCTURE 3

con·jun·to \kōn-ˈhün-tō\ *n* : Mexican-American music influenced by the music of German immigrants to Texas

con·ju·ra·tion \ˌkän-jú-ˈrā-shən, ˌkən-\ *n* ♦ : a magic expression used in conjuring

    ♦ bewitchment, charm, enchantment, incantation, spell

con·jure \ˈkän-jər, ˈkən- *for 1, 2*; kən-ˈjúr *for 3*\ *vb* **con·jured; con·jur·ing 1** : to implore earnestly or solemnly **2** : to practice magic; *esp* : to summon (as a devil) by sorcery **3** : to practice sleight of hand **4 a** : to summon by or as if by invocation or incantation **b** : to affect or effect by or as if by magic

con·jur·er *or* **con·ju·ror** \ˈkän-jər-ər, ˈkən-\ *n* **1** ♦ : one that practices magic arts : WIZARD **2** ♦ : one that performs feats of sleight of hand and illusion : MAGICIAN

    ♦ [1] enchanter, magician, necromancer, sorcerer, voodoo, witch, wizard ♦ [2] illusionist, magician, trickster

conk \ˈkäŋk\ *vb* ♦ : to become inoperative or ineffective : BREAK DOWN; *esp* : STALL ⟨the motor ∼*ed* out⟩

    ♦ break, break down, crash, cut out, die, fail, stall

Conn *abbr* Connecticut

con·nect \kə-ˈnekt\ *vb* **1** ♦ : to join or fasten together in a single relationship often by something intervening : JOIN, LINK **2** ♦ : to associate in one's mind **3** : to establish a communications connection ⟨∼ to the Internet⟩ — **con·nect·able** *adj* — **con·nec·tor** *n*

    ♦ [1] chain, compound, couple, hitch, hook, join, link, yoke *Ant* disconnect, disjoin, separate, unchain, uncouple, unhitch, unyoke ♦ [2] associate, correlate, identify, link, relate

con·nec·tion \kə-ˈnek-shən\ *n* **1 a** ♦ : the act of connecting : a coming into or being put in contact : JUNCTION, UNION **b** ♦ : the state of being connected or linked **c** ♦ : the place where a connection occurs **2** ♦ : logical relationship; *esp* : relation of a word to other words in a sentence **3** : family relationship **4** : something that connects or the point of the connecting **5** : a person related by blood or marriage **6** ♦ : relationship in social affairs or in business **7** : a set or group of persons connected or associated together in a common interest; *esp* : a religious denomination

    ♦ [1a] combination, consolidation, coupling, junction, unification, union ♦ [1b] association, bearing, kinship, liaison, linkage, relation, relationship ♦ [1c] coupling, joint, junction, juncture ♦ [2] applicability, bearing, pertinence, relevance ♦ [6] affiliation, alliance, association, collaboration, confederation, cooperation, hookup, liaison, partnership, relation, relationship, union

¹**con·nec·tive** \kə-ˈnek-tiv\ *adj* : serving to connect — **con·nec·tiv·i·ty** \ˌkä-ˌnek-ˈti-və-tē\ *n*

²**connective** *n* : a word (as a conjunction) that connects words or word groups

connective tissue *n* : a tissue (as bone or cartilage) that forms a supporting framework for the body or its parts

con·nex·ion *chiefly Brit var of* CONNECTION

con·ning tower \ˈkä-niŋ-\ *n* : a raised structure on the deck of a submarine

con·nip·tion \kə-ˈnip-shən\ *n* : a fit of rage, hysteria, or alarm

con·niv·ance *n* ♦ : knowledge of and active or passive consent to wrongdoing

    ♦ collusion, conspiracy

con·nive \kə-ˈnīv\ *vb* **con·nived; con·niv·ing 1** : to pretend ignorance of something one ought to oppose as wrong **2** : to cooperate secretly : give secret aid — **con·niv·er** *n*

con·nois·seur \ˌkä-nə-ˈsər\ *n* : a critical judge in matters of art or taste

con·no·ta·tion \ˌkä-nə-ˈtā-shən\ *n* : a meaning in addition to or apart from the thing explicitly named or described by a word

con·no·ta·tive \ˈkä-nə-ˌtā-tiv, kə-ˈnō-tə-\ *adj* **1** : connoting or tending to connote **2** : relating to connotation

con·note \kə-ˈnōt\ *vb* **con·not·ed; con·not·ing** : to suggest or mean as a connotation

con·nu·bi·al \kə-ˈnü-bē-əl, -ˈnyü-\ *adj* ♦ : of or relating to the married state : CONJUGAL

    ♦ conjugal, marital, matrimonial, nuptial

con·quer \ˈkäŋ-kər\ *vb* **1** ♦ : to gain by force of arms : WIN **2** ♦ : to get the better of : OVERCOME

    ♦ [1] prevail, triumph, win ♦ [2] beat, crush, defeat, dominate, overcome, overpower, subdue, subject, vanquish

con·quer·or \-ər\ *n* ♦ : one that conquers

    ♦ master, victor, winner

con·quest \ˈkän-ˌkwest, ˈkäŋ-\ *n* **1** ♦ : an act of conquering **2** : something conquered

    ♦ domination, subjection

con·quis·ta·dor \kōn-ˈkēs-tə-ˌdór, kän-ˈkwis-\ *n, pl* **-do·res** \-ˌkēs-tə-ˈdór-ēz, -ˌkwis-\ *or* **-dors** : CONQUEROR; *esp* : a leader in the Spanish conquest of the Americas in the 16th century

cons *abbr* consonant

con·san·guin·i·ty \ˌkän-ˌsan-ˈgwi-nə-tē, -ˌsaŋ-\ *n, pl* **-ties** : blood relationship — **con·san·guin·e·ous** \-nē-əs\ *adj*

con·science \ˈkän-chəns\ *n* : consciousness of the moral right and wrong of one's own acts or motives — **con·science·less** *adj*

con·sci·en·tious \ˌkän-chē-ˈen-chəs\ *adj* **1** ♦ : guided by one's own sense of right and wrong **2** ♦ : marked by or done with exact or thoughtful attention — **con·sci·en·tious·ly** *adv*

    ♦ [1] ethical, honest, honorable (*or* honourable), just, moral, principled, scrupulous *Ant* cutthroat, dishonest, dishonorable, immoral, unethical, unjust, unprincipled, unscrupulous ♦ [2] careful, fussy, meticulous, painstaking

conscientious objector *n* : a person who refuses to serve in the armed forces or to bear arms on moral or religious grounds

¹**con·scious** \ˈkän-chəs\ *adj* **1** ♦ : perceiving, apprehending, or noticing with a degree of controlled thought or observation : AWARE **2** : known or felt by one's inner self **3** : mentally awake or alert : not asleep or unconscious **4** : INTENTIONAL — **con·scious·ness** *n*

    ♦ alive, aware, cognizant, mindful, sensible, sentient, witting *Ant* insensible, unaware, unconscious, unmindful

²**conscious** *n* : the upper level of mental life of which a person is aware : CONSCIOUSNESS

con·scious·ly adv ♦ : in a conscious manner

♦ deliberately, intentionally, knowingly, purposely, willfully

¹**con·script** \kən-'skript\ vb : to enroll by compulsion for military or naval service — **con·scrip·tion** \kən-'skrip-shən\ n

²**con·script** \'kän-ˌskript\ n : a conscripted person (as a military recruit)

con·se·crate \'kän-sə-ˌkrāt\ vb **-crat·ed; -crat·ing 1 :** to induct (as a bishop) into an office with a religious rite **2 ♦ :** to make or declare sacred ⟨~ a church⟩ **3 ♦ :** to devote solemnly to a purpose

♦ [2] bless, hallow, sanctify ♦ [3] allocate, dedicate, devote, earmark, reserve, save

con·se·cra·tion \ˌkän-sə-'krā-shən\ n ♦ : the act or ceremony of consecrating

♦ blessing, sanctification

con·sec·u·tive \kən-'se-kyə-tiv\ adj ♦ : following in regular order : SUCCESSIVE — **con·sec·u·tive·ly** adv

♦ sequential, successive

con·sen·su·al \kən-'sen-chə-wəl\ adj : involving or based on mutual consent

con·sen·sus \kən-'sen-səs\ n **1 ♦ :** agreement in opinion, testimony, or belief **2 :** collective opinion

♦ accord, agreement, concurrence, unanimity

¹**con·sent** \kən-'sent\ vb ♦ : to give assent or approval

♦ accede, acquiesce, agree, assent, come round, subscribe (to)

²**consent** n ♦ : approval or acceptance of something done or proposed by another

♦ allowance, authorization, clearance, concurrence, leave, license (or licence), permission, sanction, sufferance

con·se·quence \'kän-sə-ˌkwens\ n **1 :** something produced by a cause or necessarily following from a set of conditions : RESULT **2 ♦ :** importance with respect to power to produce an effect

♦ [1] aftermath, conclusion, corollary, development, effect, issue, outcome, outgrowth, product, result, resultant, sequence, upshot ♦ [2] import, magnitude, moment, significance, weight

con·se·quent \-kwənt, -ˌkwent\ adj ♦ : following as a result or effect

♦ attendant, consequential, due, resultant

con·se·quen·tial \ˌkän-sə-'kwen-chəl\ adj **1 ♦ :** having significant consequences : IMPORTANT **2 :** showing self-importance **3 :** following as a result

♦ big, eventful, important, major, material, meaningful, momentous, significant, substantial, weighty

con·se·quent·ly \'kän-sə-ˌkwent-lē, -kwənt-\ adv ♦ : as a result : ACCORDINGLY

♦ accordingly, ergo, hence, so, therefore, thus, wherefore

con·ser·van·cy \kən-'sər-vən-sē\ n, pl **-cies :** an organization or area designated to conserve natural resources

con·ser·va·tion \ˌkän-sər-'vā-shən\ n ♦ : a careful preservation and protection of something : PRESERVATION; esp : planned management of natural resources

♦ maintenance, preservation, upkeep

con·ser·va·tion·ist \-shə-nist\ n : a person who advocates conservation esp. of natural resources

con·ser·va·tism \kən-'sər-və-ˌti-zəm\ n : disposition to keep to established ways : opposition to change

¹**con·ser·va·tive** \kən-'sər-və-tiv\ adj **1 :** PRESERVATIVE **2 ♦ :** disposed to maintain existing views, conditions, or institutions **3 :** MODERATE, CAUTIOUS **4 ♦ :** marked by or relating to traditional norms of taste, elegance, style, or manners — **con·ser·va·tive·ly** adv

♦ [2] old-fashioned, orthodox, reactionary, traditional Ant liberal, nonorthodox, nontraditional, progressive, unorthodox ♦ [4] muted, quiet, restrained, subdued, unpretentious

²**conservative** n ♦ : a person who is conservative esp. in politics

♦ reactionary, rightist, Tory Ant leftist, liberal, progressive

con·ser·va·tor \kən-'sər-və-tər, 'kän-sər-ˌvā-\ n **1 :** PROTECTOR, GUARDIAN **2 :** one named by a court to protect the interests of an incompetent (as a child)

con·ser·va·to·ry \kən-'sər-və-ˌtōr-ē\ n, pl **-ries 1 :** a greenhouse for growing or displaying plants **2 :** a place of instruction in one of the fine arts (as music)

¹**con·serve** \kən-'sərv\ vb **con·served; con·serv·ing ♦ :** to keep from losing or wasting : preserve in a sound state

♦ keep up, maintain, preserve, save

²**con·serve** \'kän-ˌsərv\ n **1 :** CONFECTION; esp : a candied fruit **2 :** PRESERVE; esp : one prepared from a mixture of fruits

con·sid·er \kən-'si-dər\ vb **1 ♦ :** to reflect on : think about with a degree of care or caution **2 ♦ :** to be of the opinion : REGARD **3 ♦ :** to think of : come to view, judge, or classify — **con·sid·ered** adj

♦ [1] chew over, cogitate, contemplate, debate, deliberate, entertain, meditate, mull, ponder, question, ruminate, study, think, weigh ♦ [2, 3] account, count, esteem, hold, rate, reckon, regard, take

con·sid·er·able \-'si-dər-ə-bəl, -'si-drə-bəl\ adj **1 :** worthy of consideration : of consequence or distinction **2 ♦ :** large in extent, amount, or degree

♦ good, goodly, healthy, respectable, significant, sizable, substantial, tidy Ant inconsiderable, insignificant, insubstantial

con·sid·er·ably \-blē\ adv ♦ : to a notable extent or degree

♦ broadly, greatly, hugely, largely, massively, monstrously, much, sizably, stupendously, tremendously, utterly, vastly

con·sid·er·ate \kən-'si-də-rət\ adj **1 ♦ :** observant of the rights and feelings of others **2 ♦ :** marked by or given to careful consideration

♦ [1] attentive, kind, solicitous, thoughtful ♦ [2] alert, careful, cautious, circumspect, gingerly, guarded, heedful, safe, wary

con·sid·er·ation \kən-ˌsi-də-'rā-shən\ n **1 ♦ :** careful thought : DELIBERATION **2 :** a matter taken into account **3 :** thoughtful attention **4 :** JUDGMENT, OPINION **5 ♦ :** something given as recompense

♦ [1] debate, deliberation, thought ♦ [5] compensation, pay, payment, recompense, remittance, remuneration, requital

con·sid·er·ing prep : in view of : taking into account

con·sign \kən-'sīn\ vb **1 ♦ :** to give over to another's charge, custody, or care : ENTRUST, COMMIT **2 :** to deliver formally **3 :** to send (goods) to an agent for sale — **con·sign·ee** \ˌkän-sə-'nē, -ˌsī-; kən-ˌsī-\ n — **con·sign·or** \ˌkän-sə-'nòr, -ˌsī-; kən-ˌsī-\ n

♦ commend, commit, delegate, deliver, entrust, give, hand over, leave, pass, transfer, transmit, trust, turn over, vest

con·sign·ment \kən-'sīn-mənt\ n : something consigned esp. in a single shipment

con·sist \kən-'sist\ vb **1 :** to be inherent : LIE — usu. used with in **2 :** to be composed or made up — usu. used with of

con·sis·tence \kən-'sis-təns\ n : CONSISTENCY

con·sis·ten·cy \-tən-sē\ n, pl **-cies 1 :** COHESIVENESS, FIRMNESS **2 :** agreement or harmony in parts or of different things **3 :** UNIFORMITY ⟨~ of behavior⟩ **4 ♦ :** degree of firmness, density, viscosity, or resistance to movement or separation of constituent particles

♦ thickness, viscosity

con·sis·tent \-tənt\ adj ♦ : marked by agreement

♦ compatible, conformable (to), congruous, consonant, correspondent, harmonious Ant conflicting, incompatible, incongruous, inconsistent, inharmonious

con·sis·tent·ly adv : in a consistent manner

con·sis·to·ry \kən-'sis-tə-rē\ n, pl **-ries :** a solemn assembly (as of Roman Catholic cardinals)

consol abbr : CONSOLIDATED

con·so·la·tion \ˌkän-sə-'lā-shən\ n ♦ : the act or an instance of consoling : the state of being consoled

♦ cheer, comfort, relief, solace ♦ comforting, solace

¹**con·sole** \'kän-ˌsōl\ n **1 :** the desklike part of an organ at which the organist sits **2 :** the combination of displays and controls of a device or system **3 :** a cabinet for a radio or television set resting directly on the floor **4 :** a small storage cabinet between bucket seats in an automobile

²**con·sole** \kən-'sōl\ vb **con·soled; con·sol·ing ♦ :** to soothe the grief of : COMFORT, SOLACE — **con·so·la·to·ry** \kən-'sō-lə-ˌtōr-ē, -'sä-\ adj

♦ assure, cheer, comfort, reassure, solace, soothe

con·sol·i·date \kən-'sä-lə-ˌdāt\ vb **-dat·ed; -dat·ing 1 ♦ :** to unite or become united into one whole : COMBINE **2 :** to make stronger or more secure **3 ♦ :** to form into a compact mass

♦ [1, 3] center (or centre), centralize, combine, compact, concentrate, unify, unite

con·sol·i·da·tion \-ˌsä-lə-'dā-shən\ *n* ♦ : the act or process of consolidating : the state of being consolidated

♦ combination, connection, coupling, junction, unification, union

con·som·mé \ˌkän-sə-'mā\ *n* : a clear soup made from well-seasoned stock

con·so·nance \'kän-sə-nəns\ *n* 1 ♦ : harmony or agreement among components 2 : repetition of consonants esp. as an alternative to rhyme in verse

♦ balance, coherence, harmony, proportion, symmetry, symphony, unity

¹**con·so·nant** \-nənt\ *adj* ♦ : having consonance, harmony, or agreement — **con·so·nant·ly** *adv*

♦ compatible, conformable (to), congruous, consistent, correspondent, harmonious

²**consonant** *n* 1 : a speech sound (as p, g, n, l, s, r) characterized by constriction or closure at one or more points in the breath channel 2 : a letter other than *a, e, i, o,* and *u* — **con·so·nan·tal** \ˌkän-sə-'nant-ᵊl\ *adj*

¹**con·sort** \'kän-ˌsȯrt\ *n* 1 : a ship accompanying another 2 : a wife or husband : SPOUSE, MATE

²**con·sort** \kən-'sȯrt\ *vb* 1 ♦ : to spend time in the company of 2 : ACCORD, HARMONIZE

♦ associate, chum, fraternize, hang around, hobnob, pal

con·sor·tium \kən-'sȯr-shəm; -shē-əm, -tē-\ *n, pl* **-sor·tia** \-shə-; -shē-ə, -tē-\ : an agreement or combination (as of companies) formed to undertake a large enterprise

con·spec·tus \kən-'spek-təs\ *n* 1 : a brief survey or summary 2 : SUMMARY

con·spic·u·ous \kən-'spi-kyə-wəs\ *adj* 1 ♦ : obvious to the eye or mind : PROMINENT 2 ♦ : attracting attention : STRIKING 3 ♦ : marked by a noticeable violation of good taste — **con·spic·u·ous·ly** *adv*

♦ [1, 2] bold, catchy, emphatic, marked, noticeable, prominent, pronounced, remarkable, striking ♦ [3] blatant, egregious, flagrant, glaring, gross, obvious, patent, prominent, pronounced, rank, striking

con·spir·a·cy \kən-'spir-ə-sē\ *n, pl* **-cies** 1 ♦ : an agreement among conspirators : PLOT 2 ♦ : a group of conspirators

♦ [1] design, intrigue, machination, plot, scheme ♦ [2] cabal, gang, mob, ring, syndicate

con·spir·a·tor \kən-'spir-ə-tər\ *n* : one that conspires — **con·spir·a·to·ri·al** \-ˌspir-ə-'tȯr-ē-əl\ *adj*

con·spire \kən-'spīr\ *vb* **con·spired; con·spir·ing** ♦ : to plan secretly an unlawful act : PLOT

♦ contrive, intrigue, machinate, plot, scheme

const *abbr* 1 constant 2 constitution; constitutional

con·sta·ble \'kän-stə-bəl, 'kən-\ *n* ♦ : a public officer responsible for keeping the peace

♦ cop, officer, police officer

con·stab·u·lary \kən-'sta-byə-ˌler-ē\ *n, pl* **-lar·ies** 1 : the police of a particular district or country 2 : a police force organized like the military

con·stan·cy \'kän-stən-sē\ *n, pl* **-cies** 1 ♦ : firmness of mind 2 ♦ : a state of being constant or unchanging

♦ [1] allegiance, dedication, devotion, faith, faithfulness, fastness, fealty, fidelity, loyalty, steadfastness ♦ [2] fixedness, immutability, stability, steadiness *Ant* instability, mutability, unsteadiness, variability

¹**con·stant** \-stənt\ *adj* 1 ♦ : marked by firm steadfast resolution or faithfulness : STEADFAST, FAITHFUL 2 ♦ : fixed and invariable : remaining unchanged : UNCHANGING 3 ♦ : continually recurring : REGULAR

♦ [1] devoted, faithful, fast, good, loyal, pious, staunch, steadfast, steady, true, true-blue ♦ [2] stable, stationary, steady, unchanging, unvarying *Ant* changeful, changing, fluctuating, inconstant, varying, unstable, unsteady ♦ [3] frequent, habitual, periodic, regular, repeated, steady

²**constant** *n* : something unchanging

con·stant·ly *adv* ♦ : with regular occurrence

♦ continually, frequently, often, repeatedly ♦ always, continually, ever, forever, incessantly, invariably, perpetually, unfailingly

con·stel·la·tion \ˌkän-stə-'lā-shən\ *n* : any of 88 groups of stars forming patterns

con·ster·na·tion \ˌkän-stər-'nā-shən\ *n* : amazement or dismay that hinders or throws into confusion

con·sti·pa·tion \ˌkän-stə-'pā-shən\ *n* : abnormally difficult or infrequent bowel movements — **con·sti·pate** \'kän-stə-ˌpāt\ *vb*

con·stit·u·en·cy \kən-'sti-chə-wən-sē\ *n, pl* **-cies** : a body of constituents; *also* : an electoral district

¹**con·stit·u·ent** \-wənt\ *n* 1 : a person entitled to vote for a representative for a district 2 ♦ : a component part

♦ component, element, factor, ingredient, member

²**constituent** *adj* 1 : COMPONENT 2 : having power to create a government or frame or amend a constitution

con·sti·tute \'kän-stə-ˌtüt, -ˌtyüt\ *vb* **-tut·ed; -tut·ing** 1 ♦ : to appoint to an office or duty 2 ♦ : to set up : ESTABLISH ⟨∼ a law⟩ 3 ♦ : to make up (the element or elements of which a thing, person, or idea is made up) : COMPOSE

♦ [1] appoint, assign, attach, commission, designate, detail, name ♦ [2] establish, found, inaugurate, initiate, innovate, institute, introduce, launch, pioneer, set up, start ♦ [3] compose, comprise, form, make up

con·sti·tu·tion \ˌkän-stə-'tü-shən, -'tyü-\ *n* 1 : an established law or custom 2 ♦ : the physical makeup of the individual 3 ♦ : the structure, composition, or makeup of something ⟨∼ of the sun⟩ 4 : the basic law in a politically organized body; *also* : a document containing such law

♦ [2] build, figure, form, frame, physique, shape ♦ [3] character, complexion, genius, nature, personality, tone

¹**con·sti·tu·tion·al** \-shə-nəl\ *adj* 1 : of or relating to the constitution of body or mind 2 : being in accord with the constitution of a state or society; *also* : of or relating to such a constitution

²**constitutional** *n* : an exercise (as a walk) taken for one's health

con·sti·tu·tion·al·i·ty \-ˌtü-shə-'na-lə-tē, -ˌtyü-\ *n* : the quality or state of being constitutional

con·sti·tu·tion·al·ly *adv* ♦ : with respect to mental or spiritual makeup : with respect to bodily makeup

♦ inherently, innately, intrinsically, naturally

con·sti·tu·tive \'kän-stə-ˌtü-tiv, -ˌtyü-; kən-'sti-chə-tiv\ *adj* 1 : CONSTRUCTIVE 2 : CONSTITUENT, ESSENTIAL

constr *abbr* construction

con·strain \kən-'strān\ *vb* 1 ♦ : to force by imposed stricture, restriction, or limitation : COMPEL 2 : CONFINE 3 ♦ : to withhold or restrain by force

♦ [1] coerce, compel, drive, force, make, muscle, obligate, oblige, press, pressure ♦ [3] bridle, check, contain, control, curb, govern, inhibit, regulate, rein, restrain, tame

con·straint \-'strānt\ *n* **1 a** : the state of being checked, restricted, or compelled to avoid or perform some action : COMPULSION **b** ♦ : the act or action of using force or threat of force to prevent or condition an action **c** ♦ : a constraining condition, agency, or force : RESTRAINT 2 ♦ : repression of one's natural feelings

♦ [1b] coercion, compulsion, duress, force, pressure ♦ [1c] check, condition, curb, fetter, limitation, restraint, restriction ♦ [2] reserve, restraint, self-control

con·strict \kən-'strikt\ *vb* 1 ♦ : to draw together : SQUEEZE 2 ♦ : to become constricted — **con·stric·tion** \-'strik-shən\ *n* — **con·stric·tive** \-'strik-tiv\ *adj*

♦ [1, 2] compact, compress, condense, contract, squeeze

con·stric·tion \-'strik-shən\ *n* ♦ : the act or product of constricting

♦ compression, condensation, contraction

con·stric·tor \kən-'strik-tər\ *n* : a snake that coils around and compresses its prey

con·struct \kən-'strəkt\ *vb* ♦ : to make or form by combining or arranging parts or elements : BUILD, MAKE — **con·struc·tor** \-'strək-tər\ *n*

♦ assemble, build, erect, fabricate, make, make up, piece, put up, raise, rear, set up

con·struc·tion \kən-'strək-shən\ *n* 1 ♦ : the act or result of construing, interpreting, or explaining **2 a** : the art, process, or manner of building **b** : something built, created, or established : STRUCTURE 3 : syntactical arrangement of words in a sentence

♦ clarification, elucidation, explanation, explication, exposition, illumination, illustration, interpretation

con·struc·tion·ist \-shə-nist\ *n* : a person who construes a legal document (as the U.S. Constitution) in a specific way ⟨a strict ∼⟩

con·struc·tive \-tiv\ *adj* : of or relating to construction or creation

con·strue \kən-'strü\ *vb* **con·strued; con·stru·ing** **1** : to analyze the mutual relations of words in a sentence; *also* : TRANSLATE **2** ♦ : to understand or explain the sense or intention of usu. in a particular way or with respect to a given set of circumstances : EXPLAIN, INTERPRET — **con·stru·able** *adj*

♦ clarify, clear (up), demonstrate, elucidate, explain, explicate, expound, illuminate, illustrate, interpret, spell out

con·sub·stan·ti·a·tion \ˌkän-səb-ˌstan-chē-'ā-shən\ *n* : the actual substantial presence and combination of the body and blood of Christ with the eucharistic bread and wine

con·sul \'kän-səl\ *n* **1** : a chief magistrate of the Roman republic **2** : a government official who resides in a foreign country to care for the commercial interests of the appointing government's citizens — **con·sul·ar** \-s-lər\ *adj* — **con·sul·ate** \-lət\ *n* — **con·sul·ship** *n*

con·sult \kən-'səlt\ *vb* **1** : to ask the advice or opinion of **2** ♦ : to deliberate together : CONFER — **con·sul·ta·tion** \ˌkän-səl-'tā-shən\ *n*

♦ advise, confer, counsel, parley

con·sul·tant \-ᵊnt\ *n* : one who gives professional advice or services

con·sume \kən-'süm\ *vb* **con·sumed; con·sum·ing** **1** : to do away with completely ⟨*consumed* by fire⟩ **2 a** : to spend wastefully **b** ♦ : to use up **3** : to eat up : DEVOUR **4** : to absorb the attention of : ENGROSS **5** : to utilize as a customer — **con·sum·able** *adj* — **con·sum·er** *n*

♦ clean, deplete, drain, exhaust, expend, spend, use up

con·sum·er·ism \kən-'sü-mə-ˌri-zəm\ *n* : the promotion of consumers' interests (as against false advertising)

consumer price index *n* : an index measuring the change in the cost of widely purchased goods and services from the cost in some base period

¹**con·sum·mate** \'kän-sə-mət, kən-'sə-\ *adj* **1** : complete in every detail : PERFECT **2** ♦ : extremely skilled and accomplished **3** ♦ : of the highest degree

♦ [2] accomplished, adept, crack, crackerjack, expert, good, great, master, masterful, masterly, proficient, skilled, skillful, virtuoso ♦ [3] maximum, most, nth, paramount, supreme, top, ultimate, utmost

²**con·sum·mate** \'kän-sə-ˌmāt\ *vb* **-mat·ed; -mat·ing** ♦ : to make complete : FINISH

♦ complete, finalize, finish, perfect

con·sum·ma·tion \ˌkän-sə-'mā-shən\ *n* ♦ : the ultimate end

♦ close, conclusion, end, ending, finale, finis, finish, windup ♦ accomplishment, achievement, actuality, attainment, fruition, fulfillment, realization

con·sump·tion \kən-'səmp-shən\ *n* **1** : progressive bodily wasting away; *also* : TUBERCULOSIS **2** : the act of consuming or using up **3** : the use of economic goods

¹**con·sump·tive** \-'səmp-tiv\ *adj* **1** : tending to consume **2** : relating to or affected with consumption

²**consumptive** *n* : a person who has consumption

cont *abbr* **1** containing **2** contents **3** continent; continental **4** continued **5** control

¹**con·tact** \'kän-ˌtakt\ *n* **1** : a touching or meeting of bodies **2** : association or relationship (as in physical or mental or business or social meeting or communication) : CONNECTION **3** : a person serving as a go-between or source of information **4** : CONTACT LENS

²**contact** *vb* **1** : to come or bring into contact : TOUCH **2** : to get in communication with

contact lens *n* : a thin lens fitting over the cornea usu. to correct vision

con·ta·gion \kən-'tā-jən\ *n* **1** : a contagious disease; *also* : the transmission of such a disease **2** : a disease-producing agent (as a virus) **3** : transmission of an influence on the mind or emotions

con·ta·gious \-jəs\ *adj* **1** ♦ : able to be passed by contact between individuals ⟨colds are ∼⟩ ⟨∼ disease⟩; *also* : capable of passing on a contagious disease **2** ♦ : communicated or transmitted like a contagious disease; *esp* : exciting similar emotion or conduct in others

♦ [1] catching, communicable, transmittable ♦ [2] catching, infectious

con·tain \kən-'tān\ *vb* **1** ♦ : to keep within limits : hold back or hold down **2** : to have within : HOLD **3** ♦ : to consist of wholly or in part : COMPRISE, INCLUDE — **con·tain·able** \-'tā-nə-bəl\ *adj* — **con·tain·ment** *n*

♦ [1] bridle, check, constrain, control, curb, govern, inhibit,

regulate, rein, restrain, tame ♦ [3] carry, comprehend, comprise, embrace, encompass, entail, include, involve, number, take in

con·tain·er \kən-'tā-nər\ *n* ♦ : a receptacle (as a box or jar) for holding goods; *esp* : one for shipment of goods

♦ holder, receptacle, vessel

con·tam·i·nant \kən-'ta-mə-nənt\ *n* ♦ : something that contaminates

♦ adulterant, defilement, impurity, pollutant

con·tam·i·nate \kən-'ta-mə-ˌnāt\ *vb* **-nat·ed; -nat·ing** ♦ : to soil, stain, or infect by contact or association — **con·tam·i·na·tion** \-ˌta-mə-'nā-shən\ *n*

♦ befoul, defile, foul, poison, pollute, taint *Ant* decontaminate, purify

contd *abbr* continued

con·temn \kən-'tem\ *vb* : to view or treat with contempt : DESPISE

con·tem·plate \'kän-təm-ˌplāt\ *vb* **-plat·ed; -plat·ing** **1** ♦ : to view or consider with continued attention **2** ♦ : to view as contingent or probable or as an end or intention : INTEND

♦ [1] chew over, cogitate, consider, debate, deliberate, entertain, meditate, mull, ponder, question, ruminate, study, think, weigh ♦ [2] aim, aspire, design, intend, mean, meditate, plan, propose

con·tem·pla·tion \ˌkän-təm-'plā-shən\ *n* : an act of considering with attention

con·tem·pla·tive \kən-'tem-plə-tiv, 'kän-təm-ˌplā-\ *adj* ♦ : marked by or given to contemplation

♦ meditative, melancholy, pensive, reflective, ruminant, thoughtful *Ant* unreflective

con·tem·po·ra·ne·ous \kən-ˌtem-pə-'rā-nē-əs\ *adj* : existing, occurring, or originating during the same time : CONTEMPORARY

¹**con·tem·po·rary** \kən-'tem-pə-ˌrer-ē\ *adj* **1** ♦ : occurring or existing at the same time **2** ♦ : marked by characteristics of the present period

♦ [1] coeval, concurrent, simultaneous, synchronous ♦ [2] current, hot, mod, modern, new, newfangled, red-hot, space-age, ultramodern, up-to-date

²**contemporary** *n* : one of the same or nearly the same age as another

con·tempt \kən-'tempt\ *n* **1** ♦ : the act of despising : the state of mind of one who despises **2** : the state of being despised **3** : disobedience to or open disrespect of a court or legislature

♦ despite, disdain, scorn *Ant* admiration, esteem, regard, respect

con·tempt·ible \kən-'temp-tə-bəl\ *adj* ♦ : deserving contempt : DESPICABLE — **con·tempt·ibly** \-blē\ *adv*

♦ base, despicable, detestable, dirty, dishonorable (*or* dishonourable), ignoble, low, mean, snide, sordid, vile, wretched ♦ despicable, lousy, nasty, pitiful, scabby, scurvy, sorry, wretched *Ant* admirable

con·temp·tu·ous \-'temp-chə-wəs\ *adj* ♦ : manifesting, feeling, or expressing contempt — **con·temp·tu·ous·ly** *adv*

♦ degrading, derogatory, disdainful, scornful, uncomplimentary

con·tend \kən-'tend\ *vb* **1** ♦ : to strive or vie in contest or rivalry or against difficulties — often used with *with* **2** : to strive in debate : ARGUE **3** ♦ : to affirm in or as if in argument : MAINTAIN, ASSERT

♦ [1] battle, compete, fight, race, vie ♦ *usu* **contend with** [1] cope with, grapple with, handle, manage, maneuver (*or* manoeuvre), negotiate, swing, treat ♦ [3] affirm, allege, argue, assert, aver, avouch, avow, claim, declare, insist, maintain, profess, protest, warrant

con·tend·er *n* ♦ : one that contends

♦ applicant, aspirant, campaigner, candidate, hopeful, prospect, seeker ♦ challenger, competition, competitor, contestant, rival

¹**con·tent** \kən-'tent\ *adj* ♦ : having desires limited to whatever one has : SATISFIED

♦ contented, happy, pleased *Ant* discontent, discontented, displeased, dissatisfied, malcontent, unhappy

²**content** *vb* ♦ : to appease the desires of : SATISFY; *esp* : to limit (oneself) in requirements or actions

♦ delight, gladden, gratify, please, rejoice, satisfy, suit, warm

³**content** *n* : the quality or state of being contented : CONTENTMENT

[4]**con·tent** \'kän-ˌtent\ *n* **1** : something contained ⟨~s of a room⟩ **2** ♦ : subject matter or topics treated (as in a book) **3** : material (as text or music) offered by a website **4** : essential meaning or significance **5** : the amount of material contained **6** : the ability to hold, receive, or accommodate

    ♦ matter, motif, question, subject, theme, topic

con·tent·ed \kən-'ten-təd\ *adj* ♦ : easy in mind : satisfied esp. with one's lot in life — **con·tent·ed·ly** *adv*

    ♦ content, happy, pleased

con·tent·ed·ness *n* ♦ : the quality or state of being contented

    ♦ content, contentment, gratification, happiness, pleasure, satisfaction

con·ten·tion \kən-'ten-chən\ *n* **1** : CONTEST, STRIFE **2** ♦ : an idea or point for which a person argues

    ♦ argument, assertion, thesis

con·ten·tious \-chəs\ *adj* ♦ : exhibiting an often perverse and wearisome tendency to quarrels and disputes — **con·ten·tious·ly** *adv*

    ♦ argumentative, disputatious, quarrelsome, scrappy

con·tent·ment \kən-'tent-mənt\ *n* ♦ : ease of mind : SATISFACTION

    ♦ delectation, delight, enjoyment, gladness, gratification, pleasure, relish, satisfaction

con·ter·mi·nous \kän-'tər-mə-nəs\ *adj* : having the same or a common boundary — **con·ter·mi·nous·ly** *adv*
[1]**con·test** \kən-'test\ *vb* **1** : to engage in a struggle or competition : COMPETE, VIE **2** ♦ : to make the subject of dispute, contention, or litigation : CHALLENGE, DISPUTE

    ♦ challenge, dispute, query, question

[2]**con·test** \'kän-ˌtest\ *n* ♦ : a struggle for superiority or victory

    ♦ bout, competition, event, game, match, meet, tournament ♦ battle, combat, conflict, confrontation, duel, face-off, rivalry, struggle, tug-of-war, warfare

con·tes·tant \-'tes-tənt\ *n* ♦ : one that participates in a contest

    ♦ challenger, competition, competitor, contender, rival

con·text \'kän-ˌtekst\ *n* : the parts of a discourse that surround a word or passage and help to explain its meaning; *also* : the circumstances surrounding an act or event — **con·tex·tu·al·ly** *adv*
con·ti·gu·i·ty \ˌkän-tə-'gyü-ə-tē\ *n* ♦ : the quality or state of being contiguous

    ♦ closeness, immediacy, nearness, proximity

con·tig·u·ous \kən-'ti-gyə-wəs\ *adj* ♦ : being in contact : TOUCHING; *also* : ADJOINING

    ♦ adjacent, adjoining, touching

con·ti·nence \'känt-ᵊn-əns\ *n* **1** : SELF-RESTRAINT; *esp* : a refraining from sexual intercourse **2** : the ability to retain urine or feces voluntarily
[1]**con·ti·nent** \'känt-ᵊn-ənt\ *adj* : exercising continence
[2]**continent** *n* **1** : any of the great divisions of land on the globe **2** *cap* : the continent of Europe
[1]**con·ti·nen·tal** \ˌkän-tə-'nent-ᵊl\ *adj* **1** : of or relating to a continent; *esp, often cap* : of or relating to the continent of Europe **2** *often cap* : of or relating to the colonies later forming the U.S. **3** : of or relating to cuisine based on classical European cooking
[2]**continental** *n* **1** *often cap* : a soldier in the Continental army **2** : EUROPEAN
continental drift *n* : a hypothetical slow movement of the continents over a fluid layer deep within the earth
continental shelf *n* : a shallow submarine plain forming a border to a continent
continental slope *n* : a usu. steep slope from a continental shelf to the ocean floor
con·tin·gen·cy \kən-'tin-jən-sē\ *n, pl* **-cies** ♦ : a chance or possible event

    ♦ case, event, eventuality, possibility

[1]**con·tin·gent** \-jənt\ *adj* **1** : liable but not certain to happen : POSSIBLE **2** : happening by chance : not planned **3** ♦ : dependent on something that may or may not occur — used with *on* or *upon*

    ♦ *usu* **contingent on** *or* **contingent upon** conditional, dependent, subject

[2]**contingent** *n* : a quota (as of troops) supplied from an area or group
con·tin·u·al \kən-'tin-yə-wəl\ *adj* **1** ♦ : continuing indefinitely in time without interruption : CONTINUOUS, UNBROKEN **2** ♦ : steadily recurring

    ♦ [1] ceaseless, continuous, incessant, unbroken, unceasing, uninterrupted ♦ [2] intermittent, periodic, recurrent

con·tin·u·al·ly *adv* ♦ : in a continual way : in an unceasing or regular way

    ♦ always, constantly, ever, forever, incessantly, invariably, perpetually, unfailingly

con·tin·u·ance \-yə-wəns\ *n* **1** : unbroken succession **2** : the extent of continuing : DURATION **3** : adjournment of legal proceedings

    ♦ continuation, duration, endurance, persistence, subsistence

con·tin·u·a·tion \kən-ˌtin-yə-'wā-shən\ *n* **1** ♦ : extension or prolongation of a state or activity **2** : resumption after an interruption; *also* : something that carries on after a pause or break

    ♦ continuance, duration, endurance, persistence, subsistence *Ant* ending, termination

con·tin·ue \kən-'tin-yü\ *vb* **-tin·ued; -tinu·ing** **1** : to maintain without interruption **2** ♦ : to remain in existence : ENDURE, LAST **3** : to remain in a place or condition **4** ♦ : to resume (as a story) after an intermission **5** : EXTEND; *also* : to persist in **6** : to allow to remain **7** : to keep (a legal case) on the calendar or undecided

    ♦ [2] abide, endure, hold, keep up, last, persist, run on *Ant* cease, desist, discontinue, quit, stop ♦ [4] renew, reopen, restart, resume

con·tin·u·ing *adj* ♦ : needing no renewal : ENDURING

    ♦ abiding, ageless, dateless, enduring, eternal, everlasting, immortal, imperishable, lasting, perennial, perpetual, timeless, undying

con·ti·nu·i·ty \ˌkän-tə-'nü-ə-tē, -'nyü-\ *n, pl* **-ties** **1** : the state of being continuous **2** : something that has or provides continuity
con·tin·u·ous \kən-'tin-yə-wəs\ *adj* ♦ : continuing without interruption — **con·tin·u·ous·ly** *adv*

    ♦ ceaseless, continual, incessant, unbroken, unceasing, uninterrupted *Ant* noncontinuous

con·tin·u·um \-yə-wəm\ *n, pl* **-ua** \-yə-wə\ *also* **-u·ums** : something that is the same throughout or consists of a series of variations or of a sequence of things in regular order
con·tort \kən-'tȯrt\ *vb* ♦ : to twist out of shape

    ♦ deform, distort, screw, warp

con·tor·tion \-'tȯr-shən\ *n* ♦ : a twisting into abnormal or grotesque shape

    ♦ deformation, distortion

con·tor·tion·ist \-'tȯr-shə-nist\ *n* : an acrobat able to twist the body into unusual postures
con·tour \'kän-ˌtu̇r\ *n* **1** ♦ : an outline esp. of a curving or irregular figure : OUTLINE **2** : SHAPE, FORM — often used in pl. ⟨the ~s of a statue⟩

    ♦ outline, silhouette

contr *abbr* contract; contraction
con·tra·band \'kän-trə-ˌband\ *n* : goods legally prohibited in trade; *also* : smuggled goods
con·tra·cep·tion \ˌkän-trə-'sep-shən\ *n* : intentional prevention of conception and pregnancy — **con·tra·cep·tive** \-'sep-tive\ *adj or n*
[1]**con·tract** \'kän-ˌtrakt\ *n* **1** ♦ : a binding agreement **2** : an undertaking to win a specified number of tricks in bridge — **con·trac·tu·al** \kən-'trak-chə-wəl\ *adj* — **con·trac·tu·al·ly** *adv*

    ♦ bond, covenant, guarantee, guaranty, surety, warranty ♦ accord, agreement, bargain, compact, convention, covenant, deal, pact, settlement, understanding

[2]**con·tract** \kən-'trakt, *2 usu* 'kän-ˌtrakt\ *vb* **1** ♦ : to become affected with ⟨~ a disease⟩ **2** : to establish or undertake by contract **3 a** ♦ : to reduce to smaller size by or as if by squeezing or forcing together : SHRINK, LESSEN; *esp* : to draw together esp. so as to shorten ⟨~ a muscle⟩ **b** ♦ : to become reduced in size or volume **4** : to shorten (a word) by omitting letters or sounds in the middle — **con·tract·ible** \kən-'trak-tə-bəl, 'kän-ˌ\ *adj* — **con·trac·tor** \'kän-ˌtrak-tər, kən-'trak-\ *n*

    ♦ [1] catch, come down, get, sicken, take ♦ [3a, 3b] compress, condense, constrict, lessen, shrink *Ant* expand, swell

con·trac·tile \kən-'trakt-ᵊl\ *adj* : able to contract — **con·trac·til·i·ty** \ˌkän-ˌtrak-'ti-lə-tē\ *n*

con·trac·tion \kən-'trak-shən\ *n* ♦ : the action or process of contracting

♦ compression, condensation, constriction

con·tra·dict \ˌkän-trə-'dikt\ *vb* ♦ : to assert the contrary of : deny the truth of

♦ deny, disallow, disavow, disclaim, gainsay, negate, negative, reject, repudiate

con·tra·dic·tion \-'dik-shən\ *n* ♦ : the act or an instance of contradicting

♦ denial, disallowance, disavowal, disclaimer, negation, rejection, repudiation

con·tra·dic·to·ry \-'dik-tə-rē\ *adj* ♦ : involving, causing, or constituting a contradiction

♦ antipodal, antithetical, contrary, diametric, opposite, polar

con·tra·dis·tinc·tion \ˌkän-trə-dis-'tiŋk-shən\ *n* : distinction by contrast

con·trail \'kän-ˌtrāl\ *n* : a streak of condensed water vapor created by an airplane or rocket at high altitudes

con·tra·in·di·cate \ˌkän-trə-'in-də-ˌkāt\ *vb* : to make (a treatment or procedure) inadvisable — **con·tra·in·di·ca·tion** \-ˌin-də-'kā-shən\ *n*

con·tral·to \kən-'tral-tō\ *n, pl* **-tos** : the lowest female voice; *also* : a singer having such a voice

con·trap·tion \kən-'trap-shən\ *n* ♦ : something devised or contrived : CONTRIVANCE

♦ contrivance, gadget, gimmick, gizmo, jigger

con·tra·pun·tal \ˌkän-trə-'pənt-ᵊl\ *adj* : of or relating to counterpoint

con·tra·ri·ety \ˌkän-trə-'rī-ə-tē\ *n, pl* **-eties** : the state of being contrary : DISAGREEMENT, INCONSISTENCY

con·trari·wise \'kän-ˌtrer-ē-ˌwīz, kən-'trer-\ *adv* **1** : on the contrary **2** : VICE VERSA

con·trary \'kän-ˌtrer-ē; *4 often* kən-'trer-ē\ *adj* **1** ♦ : opposite in nature or position **2** : COUNTER, OPPOSED **3** : UNFAVORABLE — used of wind or weather **4** ♦ : unwilling to accept control or advice — **con·trari·ly** \-ˌtrer-ə-lē, -'trer-\ *adv* — **con·trar·i·ness** \'kän-ˌtrer-ē-nəs, -'trer-\ *n* — **contrary** \n is 'kän-ˌtrer-ē, *adv* is like adj\ *n or adv*

♦ [1] antipodal, antithetical, contradictory, diametric, opposite, polar ♦ [4] defiant, disobedient, froward, intractable, rebellious, recalcitrant, refractory, unruly, untoward, wayward, willful

¹**con·trast** \kən-'trast\ *vb* **1** : to show differences when compared **2** : to compare in such a way as to show differences

²**con·trast** \'kän-ˌtrast\ *n* **1** : diversity of adjacent parts in color, emotion, tone, or brightness ⟨the ∼ of a photograph⟩ **2** ♦ : unlikeness as shown when things are compared : DIFFERENCE

♦ difference, disagreement, discrepancy, disparity, distinction, diversity, unlikeness

con·tra·vene \ˌkän-trə-'vēn\ *vb* **-vened; -ven·ing** **1** : to go or act contrary to ⟨∼ a law⟩ **2** : CONTRADICT

con·tre·temps \'kän-trə-ˌtäⁿ, kōⁿ-trə-'täⁿ\ *n, pl* **con·tre·temps** \-ˌtäⁿ, -ˌtäⁿz\ : an inopportune or embarrassing occurrence

contrib *abbr* contribution; contributor

con·trib·ute \kən-'tri-byət\ *vb* **-ut·ed; -ut·ing** **1** ♦ : to give along with others (as to a fund) **2** : HELP, ASSIST — **con·trib·u·tor** \kən-'tri-byə-tər\ *n* — **con·trib·u·to·ry** \-byə-ˌtōr-ē\ *adj*

♦ bestow, chip in, donate, give, kick in, pitch in, present

con·tri·bu·tion \ˌkän-trə-'byü-shən\ *n* **1** : the act of contributing **2** ♦ : the thing contributed

♦ alms, benefaction, beneficence, charity, donation, philanthropy

con·trite \'kän-ˌtrīt, kən-'trīt\ *adj* ♦ : feeling or showing sorrow and remorse for a sin or shortcoming : PENITENT, REPENTANT — **con·trite·ly** *adv*

♦ apologetic, penitent, regretful, remorseful, repentant, rueful, sorry *Ant* impenitent, remorseless, unapologetic, unrepentant

con·tri·tion \kən-'tri-shən\ *n* ♦ : the state of being contrite

♦ guilt, penitence, remorse, repentance, self-reproach, shame

con·triv·ance \kən-'trī-vəns\ *n* **1** ♦ : a mechanical device; *broadly* : something contrived, invented, or devised **2** : SCHEME, PLAN **3** : the act or faculty of contriving : the state of being contrived

♦ contraption, creation, gadget, gimmick, gizmo, invention, jigger

con·trive \kən-'trīv\ *vb* **con·trived; con·triv·ing** **1** ♦ : to form or create in an artistic or ingenious manner : PLAN, DEVISE **2** ♦ : to make devices : form plans, schemes, or designs **3** : to bring about with difficulty

♦ [1] concoct, cook up, devise, fabricate, invent, make up, manufacture, plan, think up ♦ [2] conspire, intrigue, machinate, plot, scheme

con·trived \-'trīvd\ *adj* ♦ : lacking in natural or spontaneous quality

♦ affected, artificial, assumed, bogus, factitious, fake, false, feigned, mechanical, mock, phony, put-on, sham, spurious, unnatural

con·triv·er *n* : one that contrives

¹**con·trol** \kən-'trōl\ *vb* **con·trolled; con·trol·ling** **1** ♦ : to exercise restraining or directing influence over : REGULATE **2** ♦ : to have power over : RULE

♦ [1] bridle, check, constrain, contain, curb, govern, inhibit, regulate, rein, restrain, tame ♦ [1] check, circumscribe, confine, curb, inhibit, limit, restrain, restrict ♦ [2] boss, captain, command, govern, preside, rule ♦ [2] administer, carry on, conduct, direct, govern, guide, handle, manage, operate, oversee, regulate, run, superintend, supervise

²**control** *n* **1** ♦ : power to direct or regulate **2** : the condition of being restrained, checked, or controlled; *also* : RESERVE, RESTRAINT **3** : a device for regulating a mechanism

♦ arm, authority, clutch, command, dominion, grip, hold, power, sway

con·trol·ler \kən-'trō-lər, 'kän-ˌtrō-lər\ *n* **1** : COMPTROLLER **2** : one that controls

con·tro·ver·sy \'kän-trə-ˌvər-sē\ *n, pl* **-sies** **1** ♦ : a clash of opposing views **2** : strife through expression of opposing views or claims : DISPUTE — **con·tro·ver·sial** \ˌkän-trə-ˌvər-shəl, -sē-əl\ *adj*

♦ difference, disagreement, dispute, dissension

con·tro·vert \'kän-trə-ˌvərt, ˌkän-trə-'vərt\ *vb* : DENY, CONTRADICT — **con·tro·vert·ible** *adj*

con·tu·ma·cious \ˌkän-tü-'mā-shəs, -tyü-\ *adj* : stubbornly disobedient — **con·tu·ma·cy** \kən-'tü-mə-sē, -'tyü-; 'kän-tyə-\ *n* — **con·tu·ma·cious·ly** *adv*

con·tu·me·ly \kən-'tü-mə-lē, -'tyü-; 'kän-tə-ˌmē-lē, -tyə-\ *n, pl* **-lies** : contemptuous treatment : INSULT

con·tu·sion \kən-'tü-zhən, -'tyü-\ *n* : BRUISE — **con·tuse** \-'tüz, -'tyüz\ *vb*

co·nun·drum \kə-'nən-drəm\ *n* ♦ : an intricate and difficult problem : RIDDLE

♦ enigma, mystery, mystification, puzzle, puzzlement, riddle, secret

conv *abbr* **1** convention **2** convertible

con·va·lesce \ˌkän-və-'les\ *vb* **-lesced; -lesc·ing** ♦ : to recover health gradually — **con·va·les·cent** \-ᵊnt\ *adj or n*

♦ gain, heal, mend, rally, recover, recuperate, snap back

con·va·les·cence \-ᵊns\ *n* ♦ : gradual recovery of health and strength after disease

♦ comeback, rally, recovery, recuperation, rehabilitation

con·vec·tion \kən-'vek-shən\ *n* : circulatory motion in a fluid due to warmer portions rising and cooler denser portions sinking; *also* : the transfer of heat by such motion — **con·vec·tion·al** \-shə-nəl\ *adj* — **con·vec·tive** \-'vek-tiv\ *adj*

convection oven *n* : an oven with a fan that circulates hot air uniformly and continuously around the food

con·vene \kən-'vēn\ *vb* **con·vened; con·ven·ing** **1** ♦ : to come together, meet, or assemble in a group or body : ASSEMBLE, MEET **2** ♦ : to cause (persons) to assemble in a group or body : call or gather together

♦ [1] assemble, cluster, collect, concentrate, conglomerate, congregate, forgather, gather, meet, rendezvous ♦ [2] assemble, call, convoke, muster, summon

con·ve·nience \kən-'vē-nyəns\ *n* **1** : SUITABLENESS **2** : a labor-saving device **3** : a suitable time ⟨at your ∼⟩ **4** ♦ : personal comfort : EASE

♦ amenity, comfort, luxury

convenience store *n* : a small market that is open long hours

con·ve·nient \-nyənt\ *adj* **1** : suited to personal comfort or ease **2** ♦ : placed near at hand — **con·ve·nient·ly** *adv*

♦ accessible, handy, reachable *Ant* inaccessible, inconvenient, unhandy, unreachable

con·vent \'kän-vənt, -₁vent\ *n* : a local community or house of a religious order esp. of nuns — **con·ven·tu·al** \kän-'ven-chə-wəl\ *adj*

con·ven·ti·cle \kən-'ven-ti-kəl\ *n* : MEETING; *esp* : a secret meeting for worship

con·ven·tion \kən-'ven-chən\ *n* 1 ♦ : an agreement esp. between states on a matter of common concern 2 : MEETING, ASSEMBLY 3 ♦ : an assembly of delegates convened for some purpose 4 : generally accepted custom, practice, or belief

 ♦ [1] accord, agreement, bargain, compact, contract, covenant, deal, pact, settlement, understanding ♦ [3] assembly, conference, congress, convocation, council, gathering, get-together, huddle, meeting, seminar

con·ven·tion·al \-chə-nəl\ *adj* 1 ♦ : sanctioned by general custom 2 : COMMONPLACE, ORDINARY — **con·ven·tion·al·i·ty** \-₁ven-chə-'na-lə-tē\ *n* — **con·ven·tion·al·ize** \-'ven-chə-nə-₁līz\ *vb* — **con·ven·tion·al·ly** *adv*

 ♦ current, customary, popular, standard, stock, usual ♦ classical, customary, traditional

con·verge \kən-'vərj\ *vb* **con·verged; con·verg·ing** : to approach one common center or single point — **con·ver·gent** \-jənt\ *adj*

con·ver·gence \kən-'vər-jəns\ *n* ♦ : the act of converging

 ♦ confluence, conjunction, meeting *Ant* divergence

con·ver·sant \kən-'vərs-ᵊnt\ *adj* ♦ : having knowledge and experience — used with *with*

 ♦ *usu* **conversant with** abreast, familiar, informed, knowledgeable, up, up-to-date, versed

con·ver·sa·tion \₁kän-vər-'sā-shən\ *n* ♦ : an informal talking together — **con·ver·sa·tion·al·ly** *adv*

 ♦ colloquy, dialogue, discourse, discussion, exchange

con·ver·sa·tion·al \-shə-nəl\ *adj* 1 ♦ : inclined to converse : fond of or given to conversation 2 ♦ : of, for, characteristic of, or suited to conversation or oral communication

 ♦ [1] chatty, gabby, garrulous, loquacious, talkative ♦ [2] colloquial, informal, nonliterary, vernacular, vulgar

con·ver·sa·tion·al·ist \-shə-nᵊl-ist\ *n* : a person who converses a great deal or who excels in conversation

¹**con·verse** \'kän-₁vərs\ *n* : CONVERSATION

²**con·verse** \kən-'vərs\ *vb* **con·versed; con·vers·ing** : to engage in conversation

³**con·verse** \'kän-₁vərs\ *n* : a statement related to another statement by having its hypothesis and conclusion or its subject and predicate reversed or interchanged

⁴**con·verse** \kən-'vərs, 'kän-₁vers\ *adj* : reversed in order or relation — **con·verse·ly** *adv*

con·ver·sion \kən-'vər-zhən\ *n* 1 ♦ : a change in nature or form 2 : an experience associated with a decisive adoption of religion

 ♦ changeover, metamorphosis, transfiguration, transformation

¹**con·vert** \kən-'vərt\ *vb* 1 : to turn from one belief or party to another 2 ♦ : to change from one form or function to another : TRANSFORM 3 : MISAPPROPRIATE 4 : EXCHANGE — **con·vert·er** *or* **con·ver·tor** \-'vər-tər\ *n*

 ♦ make over, metamorphose, transfigure, transform

²**con·vert** \'kän-₁vərt\ *n* ♦ : one that is converted

 ♦ adherent, disciple, follower, partisan, pupil, votary

¹**con·vert·ible** \kən-'vər-tə-bəl\ *adj* : capable of being converted

²**convertible** *n* : an automobile with a top that may be lowered or removed

con·vex \kän-'veks, 'kän-₁veks\ *adj* : curved or rounded like the exterior of a sphere or circle — **con·vex·i·ty** \kän-'vek-sə-tē\ *n*

con·vey \kən-'vā\ *vb* 1 ♦ : to bear from one place to another : CARRY, TRANSPORT 2 ♦ : to transfer or deliver (as property) to another : TRANSMIT, TRANSFER — **con·vey·or** *also* **con·vey·er** \-ər\ *n*

 ♦ [1] bear, carry, cart, ferry, haul, lug, pack, tote, transport ♦ [2] communicate, impart, spread, transfer, transfuse, transmit

con·vey·ance \-'vā-əns\ *n* 1 : the act of conveying 2 : a legal paper transferring ownership of property 3 ♦ : a means of transport : VEHICLE

 ♦ transport, vehicle

¹**con·vict** \kən-'vikt\ *vb* : to prove or find guilty

²**con·vict** \'kän-₁vikt\ *n* : a person serving a prison sentence

con·vic·tion \kən-'vik-shən\ *n* 1 : the act of convicting esp. in a court 2 ♦ : the state of being convinced 3 ♦ : a strong persuasion or belief

 ♦ [2] assurance, certainty, certitude, confidence, positiveness, sureness ♦ [3] belief, eye, feeling, judgment (*or* judgement), mind, notion, opinion, persuasion, sentiment, verdict, view

con·vince \kən-'vins\ *vb* **con·vinced; con·vinc·ing** ♦ : to bring (as by argument) to belief or action — **con·vinc·ing·ly** *adv*

 ♦ argue, get, induce, move, persuade, prevail, satisfy, talk, win

con·vinc·ing *adj* ♦ : satisfying or assuring by argument or proof

 ♦ cogent, compelling, conclusive, decisive, effective, forceful, persuasive, satisfying, strong, telling

con·viv·ial \kən-'vi-vē-əl\ *adj* ♦ : enjoying companionship and the pleasures of feasting and drinking — **con·viv·ial·ly** *adv*

 ♦ boon, companionable, extroverted, gregarious, outgoing, sociable, social *Ant* antisocial, introverted, unsociable

con·viv·i·al·i·ty \-₁vi-vē-'a-lə-tē\ *n* ♦ : convivial activities or behavior

 ♦ festivity, gaiety, jollification, merriment, merrymaking, revelry

con·vo·ca·tion \₁kän-və-'kā-shən\ *n* 1 a : a ceremonial assembly (as of the clergy) b ♦ : an assembly of persons convoked 2 : the act of convoking

 ♦ assemblage, assembly, conference, congregation, gathering, meeting, muster

con·voke \kən-'vōk\ *vb* **con·voked; con·vok·ing** ♦ : to call together to a meeting

 ♦ assemble, call, convene, muster, summon

con·vo·lut·ed \'kän-və-₁lü-təd\ *adj* 1 : folded in curved or tortuous windings 2 ♦ : marked by extreme and often needless or excessive complexity : INVOLVED, INTRICATE

 ♦ complex, complicated, elaborate, intricate, involved, knotty, sophisticated

con·vo·lu·tion \₁kän-və-'lü-shən\ *n* : a tortuous or sinuous structure; *esp* : one of the ridges of the brain

¹**con·voy** \'kän-₁vȯi, kən-'vȯi\ *vb* ♦ : to accompany for protection

 ♦ accompany, attend, escort, squire

²**con·voy** \'kän-₁vȯi\ *n* 1 : one that convoys; *esp* : a protective escort (as for ships) 2 : the act of convoying 3 : a group of moving vehicles

con·vulse \kən-'vəls\ *vb* **con·vulsed; con·vuls·ing** ♦ : to agitate violently

 ♦ agitate, jolt, jounce, quake, quiver, shake, shudder, vibrate, wobble

con·vul·sion \kən-'vəl-shən\ *n* 1 : an abnormal and violent involuntary contraction or series of contractions of muscle 2 ♦ : a violent disturbance

 ♦ cataclysm, paroxysm, storm, tempest, tumult, upheaval, uproar

con·vul·sive \-siv\ *adj* ♦ : resembling a convulsion in being violent, sudden, frantic, or spasmodic — **con·vul·sive·ly** *adv*

 ♦ stormy, tempestuous, tumultuous

cony *var of* CONEY

coo \'kü\ *n* : a soft low sound made by doves or pigeons; *also* : a sound like this — **coo** *vb*

COO *abbr* chief operating officer

¹**cook** \'kuk\ *n* : a person who prepares food for eating

²**cook** *vb* 1 : to prepare food for eating 2 : to subject to heat or fire 3 ♦ : to devise by thinking : FABRICATE — usu. used with *up* — **cook·er** *n* — **cook·ware** \-₁war\ *n*

 ♦ *usu* **cook up** concoct, contrive, devise, fabricate, invent, make up, manufacture, think up

cook·book \-₁buk\ *n* : a book of cooking directions and recipes

cook·ery \'ku-kə-rē\ *n, pl* **-er·ies** : the art or practice of cooking

cook·ie *or* **cooky** \'ku-kē\ *n, pl* **cook·ies** 1 : a small sweet flat cake 2 *cookie* : a file containing information about a website user created and read by a website server and stored on the user's computer

cookie–cutter *adj* : marked by a lack of originality or distinction ⟨~ malls⟩

cook·out \'kuk-₁aut\ *n* : an outing at which a meal is cooked and served in the open

¹**cool** \'kül\ *adj* 1 : moderately cold 2 ♦ : not excited

: CALM **3** ♦ : not friendly **4** : IMPUDENT **5** : protecting from heat **6** *slang* : very good — **cool•ly** *adv*

♦ [2] calm, collected, composed, placid, self-possessed, serene, tranquil, undisturbed, unperturbed, unshaken, untroubled, unworried ♦ [3] aloof, antisocial, chilly, cold, detached, distant, frosty, remote, standoffish, unfriendly, unsociable *Ant* cordial, friendly, sociable, warm

²**cool** *vb* ♦ : to make or become cool : lose or cause to lose heat, warmth, or passion — sometimes used with *off* or *down*

♦ *sometimes* **cool off** or **cool down** calm (down), hush, quiet, settle (down)

³**cool** *n* **1** : a cool time or place **2** : INDIFFERENCE; *also* : SELF-ASSURANCE, COMPOSURE ⟨kept his ∼⟩
cool•ant \'kü-lənt\ *n* : a usu. fluid cooling agent
cool•er \'kü-lər\ *n* **1** : a container for keeping food or drink cool **2** : JAIL, PRISON **3** : a tall iced drink
coo•lie \'kü-lē\ *n, usu offensive* : an unskilled laborer usu. in or from the Far East
cool•ness *n* ♦ : the quality or state of being cool

♦ aplomb, calmness, composure, equanimity, placidity, self= possession, serenity, tranquility

coon \'kün\ *n* : RACCOON
coon•hound \-ˌhau̇nd\ *n* : a sporting dog trained to hunt raccoons
coon•skin \-ˌskin\ *n* : the pelt of a raccoon; *also* : something (as a cap) made of this
¹**coop** \'küp, 'ku̇p\ *n* ♦ : a small enclosure or building usu. for poultry

♦ cage, corral, pen, pound

²**coop** *vb* ♦ : to confine in or as if in a coop — usu. used with *up*

♦ *usu* **coop up** cage, closet, corral, encase, enclose, envelop, fence, hedge, hem, house, immure, pen, wall

co—op \'kō-ˌäp\ *n* : COOPERATIVE
coo•per \'kü-pər, 'ku̇-\ *n* : one who makes or repairs barrels or casks — **cooper** *vb* — **coo•per•age** \-pə-rij\ *n*
co•op•er•ate \kō-'ä-pə-ˌrāt\ *vb* ♦ : to act jointly with another or others — **co•op•er•a•tor** \-'ä-pə-ˌrā-tər\ *n*

♦ affiliate, ally, associate, band, collaborate, combine, concert, confederate, join, league, team, unite

co•op•er•a•tion \-ˌä-pə-'rā-shən\ *n* ♦ : the act of cooperating : a condition marked by cooperating

♦ collaboration, coordination, teamwork

¹**co•op•er•a•tive** \kō-'ä-prə-tiv, -'ä-pə-ˌrā-\ *adj* **1** : willing to work with others **2** : of or relating to an association formed to enable its members to buy or sell to better advantage by eliminating middlemen's profits **3** ♦ : marked by cooperation

♦ collective, common, communal, concerted, conjoint, joint, mutual, public, united

²**cooperative** *n* : a cooperative association
co—opt \kō-'äpt\ *vb* **1** : to choose or elect as a colleague **2** : ABSORB, ASSIMILATE; *also* : TAKE OVER
¹**co•or•di•nate** \kō-'o̅rd-°n-ət\ *adj* **1** : equal in rank or order **2** : of equal rank in a compound sentence ⟨∼ clause⟩ **3** : joining words or word groups of the same rank — **co•or•di•nate•ly** *adv*
²**co•or•di•nate** \-'o̅rd-°n-ˌāt\ *vb* **-nat•ed; -nat•ing 1** ♦ : to make or become coordinate **2** ♦ : to work or act together harmoniously — **co•or•di•na•tor** \-'o̅rd-°n-ˌā-tər\ *n*

♦ accommodate, agree, blend, conciliate, conform, harmonize, key, reconcile

³**co•or•di•nate** \-'o̅rd-°n-ət\ *n* **1** : one of a set of numbers used in specifying the location of a point on a surface or in space **2** *pl* : articles (as of clothing) designed to be used together and to attain their effect through pleasing contrast **3** ♦ : one who is of equal rank, authority, or importance with another

♦ counterpart, equal, equivalent, fellow, like, match, parallel, peer, rival

co•or•di•na•tion \-ˌo̅rd-°n-'ā-shən\ *n* ♦ : the harmonious functioning of parts for effective results

♦ collaboration, cooperation, teamwork

coot \'küt\ *n* **1** : a dark-colored ducklike bird related to the rails **2** : any of several No. American sea ducks **3** : a harmless simple person
coo•tie \'kü-tē\ *n* : a body louse
¹**cop** \'käp\ *n* ♦ : a member of a police force : POLICE OFFICER

♦ constable, officer, police officer

²**cop** *vb* **1** *slang* : to take surreptitiously ⟨∼ a glance⟩ **2** *slang* : ADMIT — used with *to* ⟨∼ to the charges⟩ **3** : to take up and practice or use : ADOPT ⟨∼ an attitude⟩
co—pay \'kō-ˌpā\ *n* : CO-PAYMENT
co—pay•ment \'kō-ˌpā-mənt, ˌkō-'\ *n* : a fixed fee required of a patient by a health insurer (as an HMO) at the time of each outpatient service or filling of a prescription
¹**cope** \'kōp\ *n* : a long cloaklike ecclesiastical vestment
²**cope** *vb* **coped; cop•ing** : to struggle to overcome problems or difficulties — usu. used with *with*

♦ do, fare, get along, make out, manage, shift ♦ *usu* **cope with** contend with, grapple with, handle, manage, maneuver (*or* manoeuvre), negotiate, swing, treat

co•per•nic•i•um \ˌkō-pər-'ni-sē-əm\ *n* : a short-lived artificially produced radioactive element
cop•i•er \'kä-pē-ər\ *n* : one that copies; *esp* : a machine for making copies
co•pi•lot \'kō-ˌpī-lət\ *n* : an assistant pilot of an aircraft or spacecraft
cop•ing \'kō-piŋ\ *n* : the top layer of a wall
co•pi•ous \'kō-pē-əs\ *adj* ♦ : present in large quantity : LAVISH — **co•pi•ous•ly** *adv* — **co•pi•ous•ness** *n*

♦ lavish, profuse, riotous

cop—out \'käp-ˌau̇t\ *n* ♦ : an excuse for copping out; *also* : an act of copping out

♦ avoidance, escape, evasion, out

cop out *vb* : to back out (as of an unwanted responsibility)

♦ back down, renege

cop•per \'kä-pər\ *n* **1** : a malleable reddish metallic chemical element that is one of the best conductors of heat and electricity **2** : a coin or token made of copper — **cop•pery** *adj*
cop•per•head \'kä-pər-ˌhed\ *n* : a largely coppery brown pit viper esp. of the eastern and central U.S.
cop•pice \'kä-pəs\ *n* ♦ : a thicket, grove, or growth of small trees : THICKET

♦ brake, brushwood, chaparral, covert, thicket

co•pra \'kō-prə\ *n* : dried coconut meat yielding coconut oil
copse \'käps\ *n* : a thicket, grove, or growth of small trees : THICKET
cop•ter \'käp-tər\ *n* : HELICOPTER
cop•u•la \'kä-pyə-lə\ *n* : LINKING VERB — **cop•u•la•tive** \-lə-tiv, -ˌlā-\ *adj*
cop•u•late \'kä-pyə-ˌlāt\ *vb* **-lat•ed; -lat•ing** : to engage in sexual intercourse — **cop•u•la•to•ry** \'kä-pyə-lə-ˌtȯr-ē\ *adj*
cop•u•la•tion \ˌkä-pyə-'lā-shən\ *n* ♦ : sexual union

♦ intercourse, sexual intercourse

¹**copy** \'kä-pē\ *n, pl* **cop•ies 1** ♦ : an imitation or reproduction of an original work **2** : material to be set in type

♦ carbon copy, duplicate, duplication, facsimile, imitation, replica, replication, reproduction *Ant* original

²**copy** *vb* **cop•ied; copy•ing 1** ♦ : to make a copy of **2** ♦ : to attempt to resemble : IMITATE — **copy•ist** *n*

♦ [1] duplicate, imitate, replicate, reproduce *Ant* originate
♦ [2] ape, emulate, imitate, mime, mimic

copy•book \'kä-pē-ˌbu̇k\ *n* : a book formerly used to teach handwriting containing examples to be copied
copy•boy \-ˌbȯi\ *n* : a person who carries copy and runs errands (as in a newspaper office)
copy•cat \-ˌkat\ *n* : one who imitates another
copy•desk \-ˌdesk\ *n* : the desk at which newspaper copy is edited
copy editor *n* : one who edits newspaper copy and writes headlines; *also* : one who reads and corrects manuscript copy in a publishing house
copy•read•er \-ˌrē-dər\ *n* : COPY EDITOR
¹**copy•right** \-ˌrīt\ *n* : the sole right to reproduce, publish, and sell a literary or artistic work
²**copyright** *vb* : to secure a copyright on
copy•writ•er \'kä-pē-ˌrī-tər\ *n* : a writer of advertising copy
co•quet *or* **co•quette** \kō-'ket\ *vb* **co•quet•ted; co•quet•ting** : FLIRT — **co•quet•ry** \'kō-kə-trē, kō-'ke-trē\ *n*
co•quette \kō-'ket\ *n* : FLIRT
co•quett•ish *adj* ♦ : having the air or nature of a coquette

♦ coy, demure, kittenish

cor *abbr* corner
Cor *abbr* Corinthians

cor·a·cle \'kȯr-ə-kəl\ *n* : a boat made of a frame covered usu. with hide or tarpaulin

cor·al \'kȯr-əl\ *n* **1** : a stony or horny material that forms the skeleton of colonies of tiny sea polyps and includes a red form used in jewelry; *also* : a coral-forming polyp or polyp colony **2** : a deep pink color — **coral** *adj*

coral snake *n* : any of several venomous chiefly tropical New World snakes brilliantly banded in red, black, and yellow or white

cor·bel \'kȯr-bəl\ *n* : a bracket-shaped architectural member that projects from a wall and supports a weight

¹cord \'kȯrd\ *n* **1** ♦ : a usu. heavy string consisting of several strands woven or twisted together **2** : a long slender anatomical structure (as a tendon or nerve) **3** : a small flexible insulated electrical cable used to connect an appliance with a receptacle **4** : a cubic measure used esp. for firewood and equal to a stack 4×4×8 feet **5** : a rib or ridge on cloth

♦ cable, lace, line, rope, string, wire

²cord *vb* **1** : to tie or furnish with a cord **2** : to pile (wood) in cords

cord·age \'kȯr-dij\ *n* : ROPES, CORDS; *esp* : ropes in the rigging of a ship

¹cor·dial \'kȯr-jəl\ *adj* ♦ : warmly receptive or welcoming — **cor·dial·ly** *adv*

♦ amicable, companionable, comradely, friendly, genial, hearty, neighborly, warm, warmhearted ♦ affable, genial, gracious, hospitable, sociable

²cordial *n* **1** : a stimulating medicine or drink **2** : LIQUEUR

cor·di·al·i·ty \ˌkȯr-jē-'a-lə-tē, kȯr-'ja-\ *n* ♦ : sincere affection and kindness

♦ amity, benevolence, fellowship, friendliness, friendship, goodwill, kindliness

cor·dil·le·ra \ˌkȯr-dəl-'yer-ə, -də-'ler-\ *n* : a series of parallel mountain ranges

cord·less \'kȯrd-ləs\ *adj* : having no cord; *esp* : powered by a battery ⟨a ∼ phone⟩ — **cord·less** *n*

cor·don \'kȯrd-ᵊn\ *n* **1** : an ornamental cord or ribbon **2** : an encircling line (as of troops or police) — **cordon** *vb*

cor·do·van \'kȯr-də-vən\ *n* : a soft fine-grained leather

cor·du·roy \'kȯr-də-ˌrȯi\ *n, pl* -**roys** : a heavy ribbed fabric; *also, pl* : trousers of this material

cord·wain·er \'kȯrd-ˌwā-nər\ *n* : SHOEMAKER

¹core \'kȯr\ *n* **1 a** : the central usu. inedible part of some fruits (as the apple) **b** ♦ : an inmost part of something **2** ♦ : the essential meaning : GIST **3** ♦ : a central or most important part distinct from the enveloping part

♦ [1b, 2] crux, gist, heart, nub, pith, pivot ♦ [3] base, center (*or* centre), cynosure, eye, focus, heart, hub, mecca, nucleus, seat ♦ [3] body, bulk, generality, main, mass ♦ [3] center (*or* centre), midpoint

²core *vb* **cored; cor·ing** : to take out the core of — **cor·er** *n*

CORE \'kȯr\ *abbr* Congress of Racial Equality

co·re·op·sis \ˌkȯr-ē-'äp-səs\ *n, pl* **coreopsis** : any of a genus of widely cultivated composite herbs with showy often yellow flower heads

co·re·spon·dent \ˌkō-ri-'spän-dənt\ *n* : a person named as guilty of adultery with the defendant in a divorce suit

cor·i·an·der \'kȯr-ē-ˌan-dər\ *n* : an herb related to the carrot; *also* : its aromatic dried fruit used as a flavoring

Cor·in·thi·ans \kə-'rin-thē-ənz\ *n* : either of two letters written by St. Paul to the Christians of Corinth and included as books in the New Testament

¹cork \'kȯrk\ *n* **1** : the tough elastic bark of a European oak (**cork oak**) used esp. for stoppers and insulation; *also* : a stopper of this **2** : a tissue of a woody plant making up most of the bark — **corky** *adj*

²cork *vb* : to furnish with or stop up with cork or a cork

cork·screw \'kȯrk-ˌskrü\ *n* : a device for drawing corks from bottles

corm \'kȯrm\ *n* : a solid bulblike underground part of a stem (as of the crocus or gladiolus)

cor·mo·rant \'kȯr-mə-rənt, -ˌrant\ *n* : any of a family of dark-colored water birds with a long neck, hooked bill, and distensible throat pouch

¹corn \'kȯrn\ *n* **1** *Brit* : the seeds of a cereal grass and esp. of the chief cereal crop of a region (as wheat in Britain); *also* : a cereal grass **2 a** : a tall widely cultivated cereal grass grown for its large ears of starchy seeds **b** : the typically yellow or whitish seeds of corn esp. used as a food **c** : an ear of corn

²corn *vb* : to salt (as beef) in brine and preservatives

³corn *n* : a local hardening and thickening of skin (as on a toe)

¹corn·ball \'kȯrn-ˌbȯl\ *n* : an unsophisticated person; *also* : something corny

²cornball *adj* : CORNY

corn bread *n* : bread made with cornmeal

corn·cob \-ˌkäb\ *n* : the woody core on which the kernels of corn are arranged

corn·crib \-ˌkrib\ *n* : a crib for storing ears of corn

cor·nea \'kȯr-nē-ə\ *n* : the transparent part of the coat of the eyeball covering the iris and the pupil — **cor·ne·al** *adj*

corn ear·worm \-'ir-ˌwərm\ *n* : a moth whose larva is destructive esp. to corn

¹cor·ner \'kȯr-nər\ *n* **1** : the point or angle formed by the meeting of lines, edges, or sides **2** ♦ : the place where two streets come together **3** : a quiet secluded place **4** ♦ : a position from which retreat or escape is impossible **5** : control of enough of the available supply (as of a commodity) to permit manipulation of the price — **cor·nered** *adj* — **around the corner** : ready to take place : about to happen ⟨has a birthday just *around the corner*⟩

♦ [2] crossing, crossroad, intersection ♦ [4] fix, hole, jam, pickle, predicament, spot

²cor·ner *vb* **1** : to drive into a corner **2** : to get a corner on ⟨∼ the wheat market⟩ **3** : to turn a corner

cor·ner·stone \'kȯr-nər-ˌstōn\ *n* **1** : a stone forming part of a corner in a wall; *esp* : such a stone laid at a formal ceremony **2** ♦ : something of basic importance

♦ base, basis, bedrock, footing, foundation, ground, groundwork, keystone, underpinning

cor·net \kȯr-'net\ *n* : a brass band instrument resembling the trumpet

corn flour *n, Brit* : CORNSTARCH

corn·flow·er \'kȯrn-ˌflau̇(-ə)r\ *n* : BACHELOR'S BUTTON

cor·nice \'kȯr-nəs\ *n* : the horizontal projecting part crowning the wall of a building

corn·meal \'kȯrn-ˌmēl\ *n* : meal ground from corn

corn·row \-ˌrō\ *n* : a section of hair braided flat to the scalp in rows — **cornrow** *vb*

corn·stalk \-ˌstȯk\ *n* : a stalk of corn

corn·starch \-ˌstärch\ *n* : a starch made from corn and used in cookery as a thickening agent

corn syrup *n* : a sweet syrup obtained from cornstarch

cor·nu·co·pia \ˌkȯr-nə-'kō-pē-ə, -nyə-\ *n* : a horn-shaped container filled with fruits and grain emblematic of abundance

corny \'kȯr-nē\ *adj* **corn·i·er; -est** ♦ : tiresomely simple or sentimental

♦ maudlin, mawkish, mushy, saccharine, sappy, schmaltzy, sentimental *Ant* unsentimental

co·rol·la \kə-'rä-lə, -'rō-\ *n* : the petals of a flower

cor·ol·lary \'kȯr-ə-ˌler-ē\ *n, pl* -**lar·ies** **1** : a deduction from a proposition already proved true **2** ♦ : something that naturally follows : CONSEQUENCE, RESULT

♦ aftermath, conclusion, consequence, development, effect, issue, outcome, outgrowth, product, result, resultant, sequence, upshot

co·ro·na \kə-'rō-nə\ *n* **1** : a colored circle often seen around and close to a luminous body (as the sun or moon) **2** : the outermost part of the atmosphere of a star (as the sun) — **co·ro·nal** \'kȯr-ən-ᵊl, kə-'rōn-ᵊl\ *adj*

cor·o·nal \'kȯr-ən-ᵊl\ *n* : a circlet for the head

¹cor·o·nary \'kȯr-ə-ˌner-ē\ *adj* : of or relating to the heart or its blood vessels

²coronary *n, pl* -**nar·ies** **1** : a coronary blood vessel **2** : CORONARY THROMBOSIS; *also* : HEART ATTACK

coronary thrombosis *n* : the blocking by a thrombus of one of the arteries supplying the heart tissues

cor·o·na·tion \ˌkȯr-ə-'nā-shən\ *n* : the act or ceremony of crowning a monarch

co·ro·na·vi·rus \kə-'rō-nə-ˌvī-rəs\ *n* **1** : any of a family of viruses that infect birds and many mammals including humans and include the causative agent of COVID-19 **2** : an illness caused by a coronavirus; *esp* : COVID-19

cor·o·ner \'kȯr-ə-nər\ *n* : a public official who investigates causes of deaths possibly not due to natural causes

cor·o·net \ˌkȯr-ə-'net\ *n* **1** : a small crown **2** : an ornamental band worn around the temples

corp *abbr* **1** corporal **2** corporation

¹cor·po·ral \'kȯr-p(ə-)rəl\ *adj* ♦ : of or relating to the body ⟨∼ punishment⟩

♦ animal, bodily, carnal, fleshly, material, physical, somatic

²**cor·po·ral** *n* : a noncommissioned officer (as in the army) ranking next below a sergeant

cor·po·rate \'kȯr-p(ə-)rət\ *adj* **1** : INCORPORATED; *also* : belonging to an incorporated body **2** : combined into one body

cor·po·ra·tion \ˌkȯr-pə-'rā-shən\ *n* **1** : the municipal authorities of a town or city **2** : a legal creation authorized to act with the rights and liabilities of a person ⟨a business ~⟩

cor·po·rat·ize \'kȯr-pə-rə-ˌtīz\ *vb* **-ized; -iz·ing** : to subject to corporate control ⟨~ education⟩

cor·po·re·al \kȯr-'pōr-ē-əl\ *adj* **1** : having, consisting of, or relating to a physical material body : PHYSICAL, MATERIAL **2** *archaic* : BODILY — **cor·po·re·al·i·ty** \kȯr-ˌpōr-ē-'a-lə-tē\ *n* — **cor·po·re·al·ly** *adv*

corps \'kȯr\ *n, pl* **corps** \'kȯrz\ **1** : an organized subdivision of a country's military forces **2** ♦ : a group acting under common direction

   ♦ brotherhood, community, fellowship, fraternity

corpse \'kȯrps\ *n* : a dead body

corps·man \'kȯr-mən, 'kȯrz-\ *n* : an enlisted person trained to give first aid

cor·pu·lence \'kȯr-pyə-ləns\ *n* ♦ : excessive fatness : OBESITY

   ♦ fatness, grossness, obesity, plumpness *Ant* leanness, thinness

cor·pu·lent \-lənt\ *adj* ♦ : having a large bulky body : OBESE

   ♦ chubby, fat, fleshy, full, gross, obese, overweight, plump, portly, rotund, round

cor·pus \'kȯr-pəs\ *n, pl* **cor·po·ra** \-pə-rə\ **1** : BODY; *esp* : CORPSE **2** : a body of writings or works

cor·pus·cle \'kȯr-pə-səl, -ˌpə-\ *n* **1** : a minute particle **2** : a living cell (as in blood or cartilage) not aggregated into continuous tissues — **cor·pus·cu·lar** \kȯr-'pəs-kyə-lər\ *adj*

cor·pus de·lic·ti \ˌkȯr-pəs-di-'lik-ˌtī, -tē\ *n, pl* **corpora delicti** **1** : the substantial fact proving that a crime has been committed **2** : the body of a victim of murder

corr *abbr* **1** correct; corrected; correction **2** correspondence; correspondent; corresponding

¹**cor·ral** \kə-'ral\ *n* **1** ♦ : an enclosure for confining or capturing animals **2** : an enclosure of wagons for defending a camp

   ♦ cage, coop, pen, pound

²**corral** *vb* **corralled; corralling** **1** ♦ : to enclose in a corral **2** ♦ : to gain or regain control of

   ♦ [1] cage, closet, coop up, encase, enclose, envelop, fence, hedge, hem, house, immure, pen, wall ♦ [2] bag, capture, catch, collar, get, grab, grapple, hook, land, nab, seize, snare, trap

¹**cor·rect** \kə-'rekt\ *vb* **1** ♦ : to make right **2** ♦ : to punish (as a child) with a view to reforming or improving : CHASTISE **3** ♦ : to counteract the activity or effect of — **cor·rect·able** \-'rek-tə-bəl\ *adj*

   ♦ [1] amend, debug, emend, rectify, reform, remedy ♦ [2] castigate, chasten, chastise, discipline, penalize, punish ♦ [3] annul, cancel, compensate, counteract, counterbalance, make up, neutralize, offset

²**correct** *adj* **1** ♦ : conforming to a conventional standard **2** ♦ : agreeing with fact or truth **3** : conforming to the standards of a specific ideology ⟨environmentally ~⟩ — **cor·rect·ness** *n*

   ♦ [1] decent, decorous, genteel, nice, polite, proper, respectable, seemly ♦ [2] accurate, exact, precise, proper, right, so, true *Ant* false, improper, inaccurate, incorrect, inexact, untrue, wrong

cor·rec·tion \-'rek-shən\ *n* **1** ♦ : the action or an instance of correcting **2** ♦ : a reproving or punishing of faults or deviations from proper actions

   ♦ [1, 2] castigation, chastisement, desert, discipline, nemesis, penalty, punishment, wrath

cor·rec·tion·al \-'rek-sh(ə-)nəl\ *adj* : of or relating to correction

cor·rec·tive \-'rek-tiv\ *adj* ♦ : tending to correct

   ♦ disciplinary, penal, punitive ♦ reformative, remedial

cor·rect·ly *adv* ♦ : in a correct manner

   ♦ appropriately, fittingly, happily, properly, rightly, suitably

cor·re·late \'kȯr-ə-ˌlāt\ *vb* **-lat·ed; -lat·ing** ♦ : to connect in a systematic way : establish the mutual relations of — **cor·re·late** \-lət, -ˌlāt\ *n* — **cor·re·la·tion** \ˌkȯr-ə-'lā-shən\ *n*

   ♦ associate, connect, identify, link, relate

cor·rel·a·tive \kə-'re-lə-tiv\ *adj* **1** : reciprocally related **2**

: regularly used together (as *either* and *or*) — **correlative** *n* — **cor·rel·a·tive·ly** *adv*

cor·re·spond \ˌkȯr-ə-'spänd\ *vb* **1** ♦ : to be in agreement **2** : to communicate by letter **3** ♦ : to compare closely — usu. used with *to* or *with*

   ♦ [1] accord, agree, answer, check, coincide, comport, conform, dovetail, fit, go, harmonize, jibe, square, tally ♦ *usu* **correspond to** [3] equal, match, parallel

cor·re·spon·dence \-'spän-dəns\ *n* **1** ♦ : agreement between particular things **2** : communication by letters; *also* : the letters exchanged

   ♦ community, likeness, parallelism, resemblance, similarity, similitude

¹**cor·re·spon·dent** \-dənt\ *adj* **1** ♦ : having or participating in the same relationship (as kind, degree, position, correspondence, or function) : SIMILAR **2** ♦ : of a kind appropriate to the situation — used with *with* or *to*

   ♦ [1] akin, alike, analogous, comparable, like, parallel, similar, such ♦ *usu* **correspondent with** *or* **correspondent to** [2] compatible, conformable (to), congruous, consistent, consonant, harmonious

²**correspondent** *n* **1** : something that corresponds **2** : a person with whom one communicates by letter **3** ♦ : a person employed to contribute news regularly from a place

   ♦ journalist, newsman, reporter

cor·re·spond·ing·ly *adv* ♦ : in a corresponding manner

   ♦ alike, also, likewise, similarly, so

cor·ri·dor \'kȯr-ə-dər, -ˌdȯr\ *n* **1** ♦ : a passageway into which compartments or rooms open (as in a hotel or school) **2** : a narrow strip of land esp. through foreign-held territory **3** : a densely populated strip of land including two or more major cities

   ♦ gallery, hall, hallway, passage

cor·ri·gen·dum \ˌkȯr-ə-'jen-dəm\ *n, pl* **-da** \-də\ : an error in a printed work discovered after printing and shown with its correction on a separate sheet

cor·ri·gi·ble \'kȯr-ə-jə-bəl\ *adj* : CORRECTABLE

cor·rob·o·rate \kə-'rä-bə-ˌrāt\ *vb* **-rat·ed; -rat·ing** ♦ : to support with evidence : CONFIRM

   ♦ bear out, confirm, substantiate, support, validate, verify, vindicate

cor·rob·o·ra·tion \-ˌrä-bə-'rā-shən\ *n* ♦ : something that corroborates

   ♦ attestation, confirmation, documentation, evidence, proof, substantiation, testament, testimony, validation, witness

cor·rob·o·ra·tive \-'rä-bə-ˌrā-tiv, -'rä-brə-\ *adj* ♦ : serving or tending to corroborate

   ♦ confirmatory *Ant* confuting, disproving, refuting

cor·rob·o·ra·to·ry \-'rä-bə-rə-ˌtōr-ē\ *adj* : serving or tending to corroborate

cor·rode \kə-'rōd\ *vb* **cor·rod·ed; cor·rod·ing** ♦ : to wear or be worn away gradually (as by chemical action) — **cor·ro·sion** \-'rō-zhən\ *n* — **cor·ro·sive** \-'rō-siv\ *adj or n*

   ♦ bite, eat, erode, fret

cor·ru·gate \'kȯr-ə-ˌgāt\ *vb* **-gat·ed; -gat·ing** : to form into wrinkles or ridges and grooves — **cor·ru·gat·ed** *adj* — **cor·ru·ga·tion** \ˌkȯr-ə-'gā-shən\ *n*

¹**cor·rupt** \kə-'rəpt\ *vb* **1 a** ♦ : to make evil : DEPRAVE **b** : BRIBE **2** ♦ : to undergo decomposition from the action of bacteria or fungi : ROT, SPOIL

   ♦ [1a] debase, degrade, demean, demoralize, humble, subvert, warp ♦ [2] break down, decay, decompose, disintegrate, molder, putrefy, rot, spoil

²**corrupt** *adj* ♦ : morally degenerate; *also* : characterized by improper conduct ⟨~ officials⟩

   ♦ debauched, decadent, degenerate, dissolute, perverse, perverted, reprobate

cor·rupt·ible *adj* ♦ : capable of being corrupted

   ♦ bribable, purchasable, venal

cor·rup·tion \-'rəp-shən\ *n* **1** ♦ : impairment of integrity, virtue, or moral principle **2** : the process of rotting

   ♦ [1] debasement, debauchery, decadence, degeneracy, degeneration, degradation, demoralization, depravity, dissipation, dissoluteness, perversion ♦ [2] breakdown, decay, decomposition, putrefaction, rot, spoilage

cor·sage \kòr-'säzh, -'säj\ *n* **1** : the waist or bodice of a dress **2** : a bouquet to be worn or carried
cor·sair \'kòr-,sar\ *n* ♦ : one who commits or practices piracy : PIRATE

♦ buccaneer, freebooter, pirate, rover

cor·set \'kòr-sət\ *n* : a stiffened undergarment worn for support or to give shape to the waist and hips
cor·tege *also* **cor·tège** \kòr-'tezh, 'kòr-,tezh\ *n* **1** : PROCESSION; *esp* : a funeral procession **2** ♦ : a train of attendants

♦ following, retinue, suite, train

cor·tex \'kòr-,teks\ *n, pl* **cor·ti·ces** \'kòr-tə-,sēz\ *or* **cor·tex·es** : an outer or covering layer of an organism or one of its parts ⟨the adrenal ∼⟩ ⟨∼ of a plant stem⟩; *esp* : CEREBRAL CORTEX — **cor·ti·cal** \'kòr-ti-kəl\ *adj*
cor·ti·co·ste·roid \,kòr-ti-kō-'stir-,òid, -'ster-\ *n* : any of various steroids made in the adrenal cortex and used medically as anti-inflammatory agents
cor·ti·sone \'kòr-tə-,sōn, -,zōn\ *n* : an adrenal hormone used in treating rheumatoid arthritis
co·run·dum \kə-'rən-dəm\ *n* : a very hard aluminum-containing mineral used as an abrasive or as a gem
cor·us·cate \'kòr-ə-,skāt\ *vb* **-cat·ed; -cat·ing** : FLASH, SPARKLE — **cor·us·ca·tion** \,kòr-ə-'skā-shən\ *n*
cor·vette \kòr-'vet\ *n* **1** : a naval sailing ship smaller than a frigate **2** : an armed escort ship smaller than a destroyer
co·ry·za \kə-'rī-zə\ *n* : an inflammatory disorder of the upper respiratory tract; *esp* : COMMON COLD
cos *abbr* cosine
COS *abbr* **1** cash on shipment **2** chief of staff
co·sig·na·to·ry \kō-'sig-nə-,tōr-ē\ *n* : a joint signer
co·sign·er \'kō-,sī-nər\ *n* : COSIGNATORY; *esp* : a joint signer of a promissory note
co·sine \'kō-,sīn\ *n* : the trigonometric function that is the ratio between the side next to an acute angle in a right triangle and the hypotenuse
¹**cos·met·ic** \käz-'me-tik\ *adj* **1** : intended to beautify the hair or complexion **2** : correcting physical defects esp. to improve appearance ⟨∼ dentistry⟩ **3** : SUPERFICIAL
²**cosmetic** *n* : a cosmetic preparation
cos·me·tol·o·gist \,käz-mə-'tä-lə-jist\ *n* : one who gives beauty treatments — **cos·me·tol·o·gy** \-jē\ *n*
cos·mic \'käz-mik\ *also* **cos·mi·cal** \-mi-kəl\ *adj* **1** : of or relating to the cosmos **2** : characterized by greatness esp. in extent, intensity, or comprehensiveness : VAST, GRAND — **cos·mi·cal·ly** *adv*
cosmic ray *n* : a stream of very penetrating atomic nuclei that enter the earth's atmosphere from outer space
cos·mog·o·ny \käz-'mä-gə-nē\ *n, pl* **-nies** : the origin or creation of the world or universe
cos·mol·o·gy \-'mä-lə-jē\ *n, pl* **-gies** : a branch of astronomy dealing with the origin and structure of the universe — **cos·mo·log·i·cal** \,käz-mə-'lä-ji-kəl\ *adj* — **cos·mol·o·gist** \käz-'mä-lə-jist\ *n*
cos·mo·naut \'käz-mə-,nòt\ *n* : a Soviet or Russian astronaut
cos·mo·pol·i·tan \,käz-mə-'pä-lət-ᵊn\ *adj* ♦ : belonging to all the world : not local — **cosmopolitan** *n*

♦ smart, sophisticated, worldly, worldly-wise

cos·mos \'käz-məs, *1 also* -,mōs, -,mäs\ *n* **1** ♦ : the whole body of things and phenomena observed or postulated : UNIVERSE **2** : a tall garden herb related to the daisies

♦ creation, macrocosm, nature, universe, world

co·spon·sor \'kō-,spän-sər, -'spän-\ *n* : a joint sponsor — **cosponsor** *vb*
Cos·sack \'kä-,sak, -sək\ *n* : a member of one of several autonomous communities drawn from various ethnic groups in southern Russia; *also* : a mounted soldier from one of these communities
¹**cost** \'kòst\ *n* **1** ♦ : the amount paid or charged for something **2** : the loss or penalty incurred in gaining something ⟨knowledge is gained at the ∼ of innocence⟩ **3** *pl* : expenses incurred in a lawsuit — **at all costs** : regardless of consequences ⟨win *at all costs*⟩

♦ disbursement, expenditure, expense, outgo, outlay ♦ charge, fee, figure, price

²**cost** *vb* **cost; cost·ing** **1** : to require a specified amount in payment **2** : to cause to pay, suffer, or lose **3** ♦ : to have a price of

♦ bring, fetch, go, sell

co–star \'kō-,stär\ *n* : one of two leading players in a motion picture or play — **co–star** *vb*

Cos·ta Ri·can \,käs-tə-'rē-kən\ *n* : a native or inhabitant of Costa Rica — **Costa Rican** *adj*
cos·tive \'käs-tiv\ *adj* : affected with or causing constipation
cost·ly \'kòst-lē\ *adj* **cost·li·er; -est** **1** ♦ : of great cost or value : not cheap **2** : done at great expense or sacrifice ⟨a ∼ error⟩ — **cost·li·ness** *n*

♦ dear, expensive, high, precious, valuable *Ant* cheap, inexpensive

cos·tume \'käs-,tüm, -,tyüm\ *n* **1** : the style of attire characteristic of a period or country **2** : an outfit worn to create the appearance characteristic of a particular period, person, place, or thing ⟨Halloween ∼s⟩ — **cos·tum·er** \'käs-,tü-mər, -,tyü-\ *n*
costume jewelry *n* : inexpensive jewelry
cosy *chiefly Brit var of* COZY
¹**cot** \'kät\ *n* : a small house : COTTAGE
²**cot** *n* : a small often collapsible bed
cote \'kōt, 'kät\ *n* : a small shed or coop (as for sheep or doves)
co·te·rie \'kō-tə-,rē, ,kō-tə-'rē\ *n* ♦ : an intimate often exclusive group of persons with a common interest

♦ circle, clan, clique, crowd, fold, gang, ring, set

co·ter·mi·nous \,kō-'tər-mə-nəs\ *adj* : having the same scope or duration
co·til·lion \kō-'til-yən, kə-\ *n* : a formal ball
cot·tage \'kä-tij\ *n* ♦ : a small house — **cot·tag·er** *n*

♦ cabin, camp, chalet, lodge

cottage cheese *n* : a soft uncured cheese made from soured skim milk
cot·ter *or* **cot·tar** \'kä-tər\ *n* : a peasant or farm laborer occupying a cottage and often a small holding
cotter pin *n* : a metal strip bent into a pin whose ends can be spread apart after insertion through a hole or slot
cot·ton \'kä-tᵊn\ *n* **1** : a soft fibrous usu. white substance composed of hairs attached to the seeds of various tropical plants related to the mallow; *also* : this plant **2** : thread or cloth made of cotton
cotton candy *n* : a candy made of spun sugar
cot·ton·mouth \'kät-ᵊn-,mauth\ *n* : WATER MOCCASIN
cot·ton·seed \-,sēd\ *n* : the seed of the cotton plant yielding a protein-rich meal and a fatty oil (**cottonseed oil**) used esp. in cooking
cot·ton·tail \-,tāl\ *n* : a No. American rabbit with a white-tufted tail
cot·ton·wood \-,wud\ *n* : a poplar having seeds with cottony hairs
cot·tony *adj* ♦ : resembling cotton in appearance or character

♦ downy, satiny, silken, soft, velvety

cot·y·le·don \,kä-tə-'lēd-ᵊn\ *n* : the first leaf or one of the first pair or whorl of leaves developed by a seed plant
¹**couch** \'kauch\ *vb* **1** : to lie or place on a couch **2** ♦ : to phrase in a specified manner

♦ articulate, clothe, express, formulate, phrase, put, say, state, word

²**couch** *n* ♦ : a piece of furniture (as a bed or sofa) that one can sit or lie on

♦ davenport, divan, lounge, settee, sofa

couch·ant \'kau-chənt\ *adj* : lying down with the head raised ⟨coat of arms with lion ∼⟩
couch potato *n* : one who spends a great deal of time watching television
cou·gar \'kü-gər\ *n, pl* **cougars** *also* **cougar** ♦ : a large powerful tawny brown wild American cat

♦ mountain lion, panther

cough \'kòf\ *vb* : to force air from the lungs with short sharp noises; *also* : to expel by coughing — **cough** *n*
could \kəd, 'kud\ *past of* CAN — used as an auxiliary in the past or as a polite or less forceful alternative to *can* in the present
cou·lee \'kü-lē\ *n* **1** : a small stream **2** : a dry streambed **3** : GULLY
cou·lomb \'kü-,läm, -,lōm\ *n* : a unit of electric charge equal to the electricity transferred by a current of one ampere in one second
coun·cil \'kaun-səl\ *n* **1** ♦ : an assembly or meeting for consultation, advice, or discussion **2** : an official body of lawmakers ⟨city ∼⟩ **3** ♦ : an association of persons for some common object usu. jointly supported and meeting periodically — **coun·cil·lor** *or* **coun·cil·or** \-sə-lər\ *n* — **coun·cil·man** \-səl-mən\ *n* — **coun·cil·wom·an** \-,wu-mən\ *n*

♦ [1] assembly, conference, congress, convention, convocation, gathering, get-together, huddle, meeting, seminar ♦ [3] association, brotherhood, club, college, congress, fellowship, fraternity, guild, institute, institution, league, order, organization, society

¹**coun·sel** \'kaún-səl\ n **1 :** ADVICE **2 :** a plan of action **3 :** deliberation together **4** pl **counsel** ♦ **:** one who gives professional advice or services : LAWYER

♦ advocate, attorney, lawyer

²**counsel** vb **-seled** or **-selled; -sel·ing** or **-sel·ling 1** ♦ **:** to give advice to **2** ♦ **:** to ask the advice or opinion of : CONSULT

♦ [1] coach, guide, lead, mentor, pilot, shepherd, show, tutor ♦ [2] advise, confer, consult, parley

coun·sel·or or **coun·sel·lor** \'kaún-sə-lər\ n **1 :** a person who gives advice or counseling : ADVISER **2 :** one that gives advice in law and manages cases for clients in court : LAWYER **3 :** one who has supervisory duties at a summer camp

¹**count** \'kaúnt\ vb **1** ♦ **:** to name or indicate one by one in order to find the total number **2 :** to recite numbers in order **3** ♦ **:** to take into account : CONSIDER, ACCOUNT **4** ♦ **:** to rely or depend on someone or something : RELY — used with on ⟨you can ∼ on me⟩ **5** ♦ **:** to be of value or account **6** ♦ **:** to exclude by or as if by counting — used with out ⟨∼ him out⟩ **7 :** to include by or as if by counting — used with in ⟨∼ me in⟩ — **count·able** adj

♦ [1] enumerate, number, tell ♦ [3] account, consider, esteem, hold, rate, reckon, regard, take ♦ usu **count on** [4] depend, lean, reckon, rely ♦ [5] import, matter, mean, signify, weigh ♦ usu **count out** [6] ban, bar, debar, eliminate, except, exclude, rule out

²**count** n **1 :** the act of counting; also **:** the total obtained by counting **2** ♦ **:** a particular charge in an indictment or legal declaration

♦ charge, complaint, indictment, rap

³**count** n **:** a European nobleman whose rank corresponds to that of a British earl

count·down \'kaúnt-,daún\ n **:** a backward counting in fixed units (as seconds) to indicate the time remaining before an event (as the launching of a rocket) — **count down** vb

¹**coun·te·nance** \'kaúnt-²n-əns\ n **1** ♦ **:** the human face **2 :** FAVOR, APPROVAL **3** ♦ **:** the expression of the face

♦ [1] face, mug, visage ♦ [3] cast, expression, face, look, visage

²**countenance** vb **-nanced; -nanc·ing** ♦ **:** to extend approval or toleration to : SANCTION, TOLERATE

♦ accept, approve, care, favor (or favour), OK, sanction, subscribe ♦ abide, bear, brook, endure, meet, stand, stick out, stomach, support, sustain, take, tolerate

¹**count·er** \'kaún-tər\ n **1 :** a piece (as of metal or plastic) used in reckoning or in games **2 :** a level surface over which business is transacted, food is served, or work is conducted

²**count·er** n **:** a device for recording a number or amount

³**count·er** vb ♦ **:** to act in opposition to

♦ battle, combat, contend, fight, oppose

⁴**count·er** adv **:** in an opposite direction : CONTRARY

⁵**count·er** n **1 :** OPPOSITE, CONTRARY **2 :** an answering or offsetting force or blow

⁶**count·er** adj **:** marked by or tending toward or in an opposite direction or effect : CONTRARY, OPPOSITE

coun·ter·act \,kaún-tər-'akt\ vb ♦ **:** to lessen the force of : OFFSET — **coun·ter·ac·tive** \-'ak-tiv\ adj

♦ annul, cancel, compensate, correct, counterbalance, make up, neutralize, offset

coun·ter·at·tack \'kaún-tər-ə-,tak\ n **:** an attack made to oppose an enemy's attack — **counterattack** vb

¹**coun·ter·bal·ance** \'kaún-tər-,ba-ləns\ n ♦ **:** a weight or influence that balances another

♦ balance, canceler, counterweight, equipoise, offset

²**counterbalance** \,kaún-tər-'ba-ləns\ vb **:** to oppose with equal weight or influence

coun·ter·claim \'kaún-tər-,klām\ n **:** an opposing claim esp. in law

coun·ter·clock·wise \,kaún-tər-'kläk-,wīz\ adv **:** in a direction opposite to that in which the hands of a clock rotate — **counterclockwise** adj

coun·ter·cul·ture \'kaún-tər-,kəl-chər\ n **:** a culture esp. of the young with values and mores that run counter to those of established society

coun·ter·es·pi·o·nage \,kaún-tər-'es-pē-ə-,näzh, -,nij\ n **:** activities intended to discover and defeat enemy espionage

¹**coun·ter·feit** \'kaún-tər-,fit\ adj **1** ♦ **:** not genuine or real **2** ♦ **:** made in imitation of something else with intent to deceive

♦ bogus, fake, false, inauthentic, phony, sham, spurious, unauthentic Ant authentic, bona fide, genuine, real

²**counterfeit** vb **1 :** to copy or imitate in order to deceive **2** ♦ **:** to imitate or feign esp. with intent to deceive : PRETEND, FEIGN — **coun·ter·feit·er** n

♦ affect, assume, fake, feign, pretend, profess, put on, sham, simulate

³**counterfeit** n ♦ **:** something counterfeit : FORGERY

♦ fake, forgery, hoax, humbug, phony, sham

coun·ter·in·sur·gen·cy \,kaún-tər-in-'sər-jən-sē\ n **:** military activity designed to deal with insurgents

coun·ter·in·tel·li·gence \-in-'te-lə-jəns\ n **:** organized activities of an intelligence service designed to counter the activities of an enemy's intelligence service

coun·ter·in·tu·i·tive \-in-'tü-ə-tiv, -'tyü-\ adj **:** contrary to what would intuitively be expected

count·er·man \'kaún-tər-,man, -mən\ n **:** one who tends a counter

coun·ter·mand \'kaúnt-ər-,mand\ vb **:** to withdraw (an order already given) by a contrary order

coun·ter·mea·sure \-,me-zhər\ n **:** an action or device designed to counter another

coun·ter·of·fen·sive \-ə-,fen-siv\ n **:** a large-scale counterattack

coun·ter·pane \-,pān\ n ♦ **:** a usu. ornamental cloth cover for a bed : BEDSPREAD

♦ bedspread, spread

coun·ter·part \-,pärt\ n ♦ **:** a person or thing very closely like or corresponding to another person or thing

♦ coordinate, equal, equivalent, fellow, like, match, parallel, peer, rival ♦ carbon copy, double, duplicate, duplication, facsimile, image, likeness, match, picture, replica, ringer, spit

coun·ter·point \-,póint\ n **:** music in which one melody is accompanied by one or more other melodies all woven into a harmonious whole

coun·ter·poise \-,póiz\ n **:** a force or influence that offsets or checks an opposing force : COUNTERBALANCE

coun·ter·rev·o·lu·tion \,kaún-tər-,re-və-'lü-shən\ n **:** a revolution opposed to a current or earlier one — **coun·ter·rev·o·lu·tion·ary** \-shə-,ner-ē\ adj or n

coun·ter·sign \'kaún-tər-,sīn\ n **1 :** a confirmatory signature added to a writing already signed by another person **2 :** a military secret signal that must be given by a person who wishes to pass a guard — **countersign** vb

coun·ter·sink \-,siŋk\ vb **-sunk** \-,səŋk\; **-sink·ing 1 :** to form a funnel-shaped enlargement at the outer end of a drilled hole **2 :** to set the head of (as a screw) at or below the surface — **countersink** n

coun·ter·spy \-,spī\ n **:** a spy engaged in counterespionage

coun·ter·ten·or \-,te-nər\ n **:** a tenor with an unusually high range

coun·ter·vail \,kaún-tər-'vāl\ vb **:** COUNTERACT

coun·ter·weight \'kaún-tər-,wāt\ n ♦ **:** a force or influence that offsets or checks an opposing force : COUNTERBALANCE

♦ balance, canceler, counterbalance, equipoise, offset

count·ess \'kaún-təs\ n **1 :** the wife or widow of a count or an earl **2 :** a woman holding the rank of a count or an earl in her own right

count·ing·house \'kaún-tiŋ-,haús\ n **:** a building or office for keeping books and conducting business

count·less \'kaúnt-ləs\ adj ♦ **:** too numerous to be counted : INNUMERABLE

♦ innumerable, numberless, uncountable, unnumbered, untold Ant countable

coun·tri·fied also **coun·try·fied** \'kən-tri-,fīd\ adj **1 :** RURAL, RUSTIC **2 :** UNSOPHISTICATED **3 :** played or sung in the manner of country music

¹**coun·try** \'kən-trē\ n, pl **countries 1 :** REGION, DISTRICT **2** ♦ **:** the land of a person's birth, residence, or citizenship : FATHERLAND **3** ♦ **:** a nation or its territory **4 :** rural regions as opposed to towns and cities **5 :** COUNTRY MUSIC

♦ [2] fatherland, home, homeland, motherland, sod ♦ [3] commonwealth, land, nation, sovereignty, state

²**country** *adj* **1** ♦ : of, relating to, or characteristic of the country : RURAL **2** : of or relating to country music ⟨a ∼ singer⟩

♦ bucolic, pastoral, rural, rustic

country and western *n* : COUNTRY MUSIC

country club *n* : a suburban club for social life and recreation; *esp* : one having a golf course — **country–club** *adj*

coun·try–dance \'kən-trē-₁dans\ *n* : an English dance in which partners face each other esp. in rows

coun·try·man \'kən-trē-mən, 2 often -₁man\ *n* **1** : an inhabitant of a specified country **2** : COMPATRIOT **3** : one raised or living in the country : RUSTIC

country music *n* : music derived from or imitating the folk style of the southern U.S. or of the Western cowboy

coun·try·side \'kən-trē-₁sīd\ *n* : a rural area or its people

coun·ty \'kaùn-tē\ *n, pl* **counties** : the domain of a count **2** : a territorial division of a country or state for purposes of local government

coup \'kü\ *n, pl* **coups** \'küz\ **1** ♦ : a highly successful stroke, action, plan, or stratagem **2** : COUP D'ÉTAT

♦ accomplishment, achievement, attainment, success, triumph

coup de grace \₁kü-də-'gräs\ *n, pl* **coups de grace** *same*\ : DEATHBLOW; *also* : a final decisive stroke or event

coup d'état \₁kü-də-'tä\ *n, pl* **coups d'état** *same*\ : a sudden violent overthrow of a government by a small group

cou·pé *or* **coupe** \kü-'pā, 2 often 'küp\ **1** ♦ : a closed horse-drawn carriage for two persons inside with an outside seat for the driver **2** *usu* coupe : a 2-door automobile with an enclosed body

¹**cou·ple** \'kə-pəl\ *n* **1** : two persons closely associated; *esp* : two persons married, engaged, or otherwise romantically paired **2** ♦ : two of the same kind considered together : PAIR **3** : BOND, TIE **4** : an indefinite small number : FEW ⟨a ∼ of days ago⟩

♦ brace, duo, pair, twain, twosome

²**couple** *vb* **cou·pled; cou·pling** ♦ : to link together

♦ associate, combine, conjoin, connect, hitch, hook, join, link, marry, unify, unite, yoke

cou·plet \'kə-plət\ *n* : two successive rhyming lines of verse

cou·pling \'kə-pliŋ (*usual for 2*), -pə-liŋ\ *n* **1** ♦ : the act of bringing or coming together : CONNECTION; *also* : the point at which things are connected **2** : a device for connecting two parts or things

♦ combination, connection, consolidation, junction, unification, union

cou·pon \'kü-₁pän, 'kyü-\ *n* **1** : a statement attached to a bond showing interest due and designed to be cut off and presented for payment **2** : a form surrendered in order to obtain an article, service, or accommodation **3** : a printed document or slip used to submit orders or inquiries or to obtain a discount on merchandise or services

cour·age \'kər-ij\ *n* ♦ : ability to conquer fear or despair : BRAVERY, VALOR

♦ bravery, daring, fearlessness, gallantry, guts, hardihood, heart, heroism, nerve, stoutness, valor *Ant* cowardice

cou·ra·geous \kə-'rā-jəs\ *adj* ♦ : having or characterized by courage — **cou·ra·geous·ly** *adv*

♦ brave, dauntless, doughty, fearless, gallant, greathearted, heroic, intrepid, lionhearted, manful, stalwart, stout, undaunted, valiant, valorous

cou·ri·er \'kúr-ē-ər, 'kər-ē-\ *n* ♦ : one who bears messages or information esp. for the diplomatic or military services

♦ go-between, messenger, page, runner

¹**course** \'kōrs\ *n* **1 a** : the act or action of moving in a path from point to point : PROGRESS, PASSAGE **b** ♦ : direction of progress **2** : the ground or path over which something moves **3 a** ♦ : method of procedure **b** : CONDUCT, BEHAVIOR **4** ♦ : an ordered series of acts or proceedings : sequence of events **5** : a series of instruction periods dealing with a subject **6** : the series of studies leading to graduation from a school or college **7** : the part of a meal served at one time — **of course** : as might be expected

♦ [1b] line, path, route, track, way ♦ [3a] line, policy, procedure, program ♦ [4] operation, procedure, proceeding, process

²**course** *vb* **coursed; cours·ing** **1** : to hunt with dogs **2** ♦ : to run or go speedily

♦ barrel, career, dash, fly, hurry, pelt, race, rip, rocket, run, rush, shoot, speed, tear, zip, zoom

cours·er \'kōr-sər\ *n* : a swift or spirited horse

¹**court** \'kōrt\ *n* **1** : the residence of a sovereign or similar dignitary **2** : a sovereign's formal assembly of officials and advisers as a governing power **3** : an assembly of the retinue of a sovereign **4** ♦ : an open space enclosed by a building or buildings **5** : a space walled or marked off for playing a game (as tennis or basketball) **6** : the place where justice is administered; *also* : a judicial body or a meeting of a judicial body **7** : attention intended to win favor **8** ♦ : a judge or judges in session

♦ [4] close, courtyard, quadrangle, yard ♦ [8] bench, judge, justice, magistrate

²**court** *vb* **1** : to try to gain the favor of **2** ♦ : to seek to gain or achieve : WOO **3** : ATTRACT, TEMPT

♦ ask, woo

cour·te·ous \'kər-tē-əs\ *adj* ♦ : marked by respect for others : CIVIL, POLITE

♦ civil, genteel, gracious, mannerly, polite, well-bred

cour·te·ous·ly *adv* ♦ : in a courteous manner

♦ kindly, nicely, thoughtfully, well

cour·te·san \'kōr-tə-zən, -₁zan\ *n* : PROSTITUTE

cour·te·sy \'kər-tə-sē\ *n, pl* **-sies** **1** ♦ : courteous behavior **2** ♦ : a favor courteously performed

♦ [1] amenity, civility, formality, gesture ♦ [1] civility, gentility, graciousness, mannerliness, politeness ♦ [2] boon, favor (*or* favour), grace, indulgence, kindness, mercy, service, turn

court·house \'kōrt-₁haùs\ *n* : a building in which courts of law are held or county offices are located

court·ier \'kōr-tē-ər\ *n* : a person in attendance at a royal court

court·li·ness *n* ♦ : the quality of being courtly

♦ class, elegance, grace, gracefulness, handsomeness, majesty, refinement, stateliness

court·ly \'kōrt-lē\ *adj* **court·li·er; -est** : of a quality befitting the court : REFINED, ELEGANT

court–mar·tial \'kōrt-₁mär-shəl\ *n, pl* **courts–martial** : a military or naval court for trial of offenses against military or naval law; *also* : a trial by this court — **court–martial** *vb*

court·room \-₁rüm, -₁rùm\ *n* : a room in which a court of law is held

court·ship \-₁ship\ *n* : the act of courting : the act of wooing

court·yard \-₁yärd\ *n* ♦ : an enclosure next to a building

♦ close, court, quadrangle, yard

cous·cous \'küs-₁küs\ *n* : a No. African dish of steamed semolina usu. served with meat or vegetables; *also* : the semolina itself

cous·in \'kə-zən\ *n* : a child of one's uncle or aunt

cou·ture \kü-'túr, -'tür\ *n* : the business of designing fashionable custom-made women's clothing; *also* : the designers and establishments engaged in this business

cou·tu·ri·er \kü-'túr-ē-ər, -ē-₁ā\ *n* : the owner of an establishment engaged in couture

cove \'kōv\ *n* ♦ : a small sheltered inlet or bay

♦ bay, bight, estuary, fjord, gulf, inlet

co·ven \'kə-vən\ *n* : an assembly or band of witches

¹**cov·e·nant** \'kə-və-nənt\ *n* ♦ : a formal binding agreement : COMPACT

♦ accord, agreement, bargain, compact, contract, convention, deal, pact, settlement, understanding ♦ bond, contract, guarantee, surety, warranty

²**cov·e·nant** \-nənt, -₁nant\ *vb* ♦ : to promise by a covenant

♦ pledge, promise, swear, vow

¹**cov·er** \'kə-vər\ *vb* **1** : to bring or hold within range of a firearm **2** ♦ : to afford protection or security to : PROTECT, SHIELD **3** ♦ : to hide from sight or knowledge : HIDE, CONCEAL **4** ♦ : to place something over or upon **5** : INCLUDE, COMPRISE **6** : to have as one's field of activity ⟨one salesman ∼s the state⟩ **7** : to buy (stocks) in order to have them for delivery on a previous short sale **8** ♦ : to deal with **9** ♦ : to pass over **10** ♦ : to act as a substitute or replacement during an absence

♦ [2] defend, guard, protect, safeguard, screen, secure, shield, ward ♦ [3] blanket, blot out, cloak, conceal, curtain, enshroud, hide, mask, obscure, occult, screen, shroud, veil ♦ [4] blanket, carpet, coat, overlay, overlie, overspread ♦ [8] concern, deal, pertain, treat ♦ [9] crisscross, cross, cut, follow, go, pass, proceed, travel, traverse ♦ [10] fill in, pinch-hit, stand in, sub, substitute, take over

²**cover** *n* **1** ♦ : something that protects or shelters **2** ♦ : a mov-

able cover for the opening of a hollow container : LID, TOP **3** : CASE, BINDING **4** : TABLECLOTH **5** : a cloth used on a bed **6** : SCREEN, DISGUISE **7** : an envelope or wrapper for mail

♦ [1] aegis, armor, defense (*or* defence), guard, protection, safeguard, screen, security, shield, wall, ward ♦ [1] armor, capsule, case, casing, cocoon, housing, husk, jacket, pod, sheath, shell ♦ [2] cap, lid, top

cov•er•age \ˈkə-və-rij\ *n* **1** : the act or fact of covering **2** : the total group covered : SCOPE

cov•er•all \ˈkə-vər-ˌȯl\ *n* : a one-piece outer garment worn to protect one's clothes — usu. used in pl.

cover charge *n* : a charge made by a restaurant or nightclub in addition to the charge for food and drink

cover crop *n* : a crop planted to prevent soil erosion and to provide humus

cov•er•ing *n* : something that covers or conceals

cov•er•let \ˈkə-vər-lət\ *n* : a usu. ornamental cloth cover for a bed : BEDSPREAD

¹co•vert \ˈkō-ˌvərt, ˈkə-vərt\ *adj* **1** ♦ : not openly shown, engaged in, or avowed : SECRET **2** : SHELTERED — **co•vert•ly** *adv*

♦ cloistered, isolated, quiet, remote, secluded, secret ♦ clandestine, furtive, hugger-mugger, private, secret, sneak, sneaky, stealthy, surreptitious, undercover, underground, underhanded

²co•vert \ˈkə-vərt, ˈkō-\ *n* **1** ♦ : a secret or sheltered place; *esp* : a thicket sheltering game **2** : a feather covering the bases of the quills of the wings and tail of a bird

♦ concealment, den, hideout, lair, nest ♦ brake, brushwood, chaparral, coppice, thicket

cov•er–up \ˈkə-vər-ˌəp\ *n* **1** : a device for masking or concealing **2** : a usu. concerted effort to keep an illegal or unethical act or situation from being made public

cov•et \ˈkə-vət\ *vb* ♦ : to desire enviously (what belongs to another)

♦ ache for, crave, desire, die for, hanker for, hunger for, long for, lust (for *or* after), pine for, repine for, thirst for, want, wish for, yearn for

cov•et•ous *adj* ♦ : marked by inordinate desire for wealth or possessions or for another's possessions

♦ acquisitive, avaricious, avid, grasping, greedy, mercenary, rapacious

cov•et•ous•ness *n* ♦ : the state of being covetous

♦ acquisitiveness, avarice, avidity, cupidity, greed, rapaciousness

cov•ey \ˈkə-vē\ *n, pl* **coveys** **1** : a bird with her brood of young **2** : a small flock (as of quail)

COVID-19 \ˈkō-vid-nīn-tēn\ *also* **Co•vid-19** *or* **COVID** \ˈkō-vid\ *or* **Co•vid** *n* **1** : a mild to severe respiratory illness that is caused by a coronavirus, is transmitted chiefly by contact with infected material (as respiratory droplets), and is characterized esp. by fever, cough, and shortness of breath and may progress to pneumonia and respiratory failure **2** : the coronavirus that causes COVID-19

¹cow \ˈkau̇\ *n* **1** : the mature female of cattle or of an animal (as the moose, elephant, or whale) of which the male is called *bull* **2** : any domestic bovine animal irrespective of sex or age

²cow *vb* ♦ : to destroy the resolve or courage of : INTIMIDATE

♦ browbeat, bully, hector, intimidate

cow•ard \ˈkau̇(-ə)rd\ *n* ♦ : one who lacks courage or shows shameful fear or timidity — **coward** *adj* — **cow•ard•ice** \ˈkau̇-ər-dəs\ *n*

♦ chicken, craven, dastard, poltroon, recreant, sissy *Ant* hero, stalwart, valiant

cow•ard•ly *adv or adj* ♦ : being, resembling, or befitting a coward

♦ chicken, craven, dastardly, pusillanimous, recreant, spineless, yellow *Ant* brave, courageous, daring, dauntless, doughty, fearless, gallant, greathearted, gutsy, hardy, heroic, intrepid, lionhearted, stalwart, stout, valiant, valorous

cow•bird \ˈkau̇-ˌbərd\ *n* : a small No. American blackbird that lays its eggs in the nests of other birds

cow•boy \-ˌbȯi\ *n* : one (as a mounted ranch hand) who tends cattle or horses

cow•er \ˈkau̇(-ə)r\ *vb* ♦ : to shrink or crouch down from fear or cold : QUAIL

♦ cringe, grovel, quail

cow•girl \ˈkau̇-ˌgərl\ *n* : a girl or woman who tends cattle or horses

cow•hand \ˈkau̇-ˌhand\ *n* : one who tends cattle or horses : COWBOY

cow•hide \-ˌhīd\ *n* **1** : the hide of a cow; *also* : leather made from it **2** : a coarse whip of braided rawhide

cowl \ˈkau̇l\ *n* : a monk's hood

cow•lick \ˈkau̇-ˌlik\ *n* : a turned-up tuft of hair that resists control

cowl•ing \ˈkau̇-liŋ\ *n* : a usu. metal covering for the engine or another part of an airplane

cow•man \ˈkau̇-mən, -ˌman\ *n* : one who tends cattle or horses : COWBOY; *also* : a cattle owner or rancher

co•work•er \ˈkō-ˌwər-kər\ *n* : a fellow worker

cow•poke \ˈkau̇-ˌpōk\ *n* : one who tends cattle or horses : COWBOY

cow pony *n* : a strong and agile horse trained for herding cattle

cow•pox \ˈkau̇-ˌpäks\ *n* : a mild disease of the cow that when communicated to humans protects against smallpox

cow•punch•er \-ˌpən-chər\ *n* : one who tends cattle or horses : COWBOY

cow•slip \ˈkau̇-ˌslip\ *n* **1** : a yellow-flowered European primrose **2** : MARSH MARIGOLD

cox•comb \ˈkäks-ˌkōm\ *n* : a conceited foolish person : FOP

cox•swain \ˈkäk-sən, -ˌswān\ *n* : the steersman of a ship's boat or a racing shell

coy \ˈkȯi\ *adj* **1** ♦ : shrinking from contact or familiarity : BASHFUL, SHY **2** ♦ : marked by artful playfulness : COQUETTISH — **coy•ly** *adv* — **coy•ness** *n*

♦ [1] bashful, demure, diffident, introverted, modest, retiring, sheepish, shy ♦ [2] coquettish, demure, kittenish

coy•ote \ˈkī-ˌōt, kī-ˈō-tē\ *n, pl* **coyotes** *or* **coyote** : a mammal of No. America smaller than the related wolves

coy•pu \ˈkȯi-pü\ *n* : NUTRIA 2

coz•en \ˈkəz-ᵊn\ *vb* ♦ : to deceive, win over, or induce to do something by artful coaxing and wheedling or shrewd trickery — **coz•en•age** \-ij\ *n* — **coz•en•er** *n*

♦ beguile, bluff, deceive, delude, dupe, fool, gull, have, hoax, hoodwink, humbug, misinform, mislead, string along, take in, trick ♦ bleed, cheat, chisel, defraud, fleece, hustle, mulct, rook, shortchange, skin, squeeze, stick, sting, swindle, victimize

¹co•zy \ˈkō-zē\ *adj* **co•zi•er; -est** : enjoying or affording warmth and ease : SNUG, COMFORTABLE — **co•zi•ly** \-zə-lē\ *adv* — **co•zi•ness** \-zē-nəs\ *n*

²cozy *n, pl* **co•zies** : a padded covering for a vessel (as a teapot) to keep the contents hot

cp *abbr* **1** compare **2** coupon

CP *abbr* **1** cerebral palsy **2** chemically pure **3** command post **4** communist party

CPA *abbr* certified public accountant

CPB *abbr* Corporation for Public Broadcasting

cpd *abbr* compound

CPI *abbr* consumer price index

Cpl *abbr* corporal

CPO *abbr* chief petty officer

CPOM *abbr* master chief petty officer

CPOS *abbr* senior chief petty officer

CPR *abbr* cardiopulmonary resuscitation

CPT *abbr* captain

CPU \ˌsē-ˌpē-ˈyü\ *n* : the part of a computer that performs its basic operations, manages its components, and exchanges data with memory or peripherals

CQ *abbr* charge of quarters

cr *abbr* credit; creditor

Cr *symbol* chromium

¹crab \ˈkrab\ *n* : any of various crustaceans with a short broad shell and small abdomen

²crab *n* ♦ : an ill-natured person

♦ bear, complainer, crank, grouch, grumbler, whiner

³crab *vb* **crabbed; crab•bing** ♦ : to complain about peevishly : COMPLAIN, GROUSE

♦ beef, bellyache, carp, complain, croak, fuss, gripe, grouse, growl, grumble, kick, moan, murmur, mutter, repine, squawk, wail, whine

crab apple *n* : a small often highly colored sour apple; *also* : a tree that produces crab apples

crab•bed \ˈkra-bəd\ *adj* **1** : MOROSE, PEEVISH **2** : CRAMPED, IRREGULAR

crab•by \ˈkra-bē\ *adj* **crab•bi•er; -est** ♦ : marked by typically transitory bad temper : CROSS

♦ choleric, cranky, cross, crotchety, grouchy, grumpy, irascible, irritable, peevish, perverse, petulant, short-tempered, snappish, snappy, snippy, testy, waspish

crab·grass \'krab-ˌgras\ *n* : a weedy grass with creeping or sprawling stems that root freely at the nodes

crab louse *n* : a louse infesting the pubic region in humans

¹crack \'krak\ *vb* **1** : to break with a sharp sudden sound **2** : to break with or without completely separating into parts **3** : to fail in tone or become harsh ⟨her voice ∼*ed*⟩ **4** : to subject (as a petroleum oil) to heat for breaking down into lighter products (as gasoline) **5** : to strike with a sharp noise **6** ♦ : to puzzle out and expose, solve, or reveal the mystery of **7** ♦ : to lose control or effectiveness under pressure

♦ [6] answer, break, decode, dope, figure out, puzzle, resolve, riddle, solve, unravel, work, work out ♦ [7] break, flip, freak

²crack *n* **1** ♦ : a sudden sharp noise **2** ♦ : a witty or sharp remark **3** ♦ : a narrow break or opening : FISSURE **4** ♦ : a sharp blow **5** ♦ : an attempt or opportunity to do something **6** : a potent form of cocaine in small chips used illicitly for smoking

♦ [1] bang, blast, boom, clap, crash, pop, report, slam, smash, snap, thwack, whack ♦ [2] gag, jest, joke, laugh, pleasantry, quip, sally, waggery, wisecrack, witticism ♦ [3] chink, cleft, cranny, crevice, fissure, rift, split ♦ [4] bat, belt, blow, box, clout, hit, punch, slug, thump, wallop, whack ♦ [5] attempt, bid, endeavor (*or* endeavour), essay, fling, go, pass, shot, stab, trial, try, whack, whirl

³crack *adj* ♦ : extremely proficient

♦ accomplished, adept, consummate, crackerjack, expert, good, great, master, masterful, masterly, proficient, skilled, skillful, virtuoso

crack·down \'krak-ˌdau̇n\ *n* : an act or instance of taking positive disciplinary action ⟨a ∼ on gambling⟩

crack down *vb* ♦ : to take positive regulatory or disciplinary action — used with *on*

♦ *usu* **crack down on** clamp down, crush, put down, quash, quell, repress, silence, snuff, squash, squelch, subdue, suppress

cracked *adj* : mentally disturbed : CRAZY

crack·er \'kra-kər\ *n* **1** : FIRECRACKER **2** : a dry thin crispy baked bread product made of flour and water

¹crack·er·jack \-ˌjak\ *n* ♦ : a person or thing of marked excellence

♦ ace, adept, artist, authority, expert, maestro, master, scholar, shark, virtuoso, whiz, wizard

²crackerjack *adj* ♦ : of striking ability or excellence

♦ accomplished, adept, consummate, crack, expert, good, great, master, masterful, masterly, proficient, skilled, skillful, virtuoso

crack·le \'kra-kəl\ *vb* **crack·led; crack·ling** **1** : to make small sharp snapping noises **2** : to develop fine cracks in a surface — **crackle** *n* — **crack·ly** \-k(ə-)lē\ *adj*

crack·pot \'krak-ˌpät\ *n* ♦ : an eccentric person

♦ character, crank, eccentric, kook, nut, oddball, screwball, weirdo

crack–up \'krak-ˌəp\ *n* **1** ♦ : a wrecking or smashing esp. of a vehicle : CRASH, WRECK **2** : BREAKDOWN

♦ collision, crash, smash, wreck

crack up *vb* **1** ♦ : to express a favorable judgment of : PRAISE ⟨isn't all it's *cracked up* to be⟩ **2** : to laugh or cause to laugh out loud **3** : to crash a vehicle

♦ acclaim, applaud, cheer, hail, laud, praise, salute, tout

¹cra·dle \'krād-ᵊl\ *n* **1** : a baby's bed or cot **2** : a framework or support (as for a telephone receiver) **3** : INFANCY ⟨from ∼ to the grave⟩ **4** ♦ : a place of origin

♦ birthplace, home

²cradle *vb* **cra·dled; cra·dling** **1** : to place in or as if in a cradle **2** : SHELTER, REAR

¹craft \'kraft\ *n* **1 a** ♦ : skill in planning, making, or executing **b** ♦ : an occupation requiring special skill **2** ♦ : skill in deceiving to gain an end : CUNNING, GUILE **3** *pl usu* **craft** ♦ : a boat esp. of small size; *also* : AIRCRAFT, SPACECRAFT

♦ [1a] adeptness, adroitness, art, artfulness, artifice, artistry, cleverness, cunning, deftness, masterfulness, skill ♦ [1b] handicraft, trade ♦ [2] artfulness, artifice, caginess, canniness, craftiness, cunning, guile, slyness, wiliness ♦ [3] boat, bottom, vessel

²craft *vb* ♦ : to make or produce with care, skill, or ingenuity — **craft·er** *n*

♦ cast, compose, draft, draw, formulate, frame, prepare

craft·i·ness \-tē-nəs\ *n* ♦ : the quality or state of being crafty

♦ artfulness, artifice, caginess, canniness, craft, cunning, guile, slyness, wiliness

crafts·man \'krafts-mən\ *n* ♦ : a skilled artisan — **crafts·man·ship** *n*

♦ artificer, artisan, handicrafter

crafty \'kraf-tē\ *adj* **craft·i·er; -est** ♦ : adept in the use of subtlety and cunning : CUNNING, SUBTLE — **craft·i·ly** \-tə-lē\ *adv*

♦ artful, cagey, cunning, devious, foxy, guileful, slick, sly, subtle, wily

crag \'krag\ *n* ♦ : a steep rugged cliff or rock

♦ bluff, cliff, escarpment, palisade, precipice, scarp

crag·gy *adj* ♦ : having a broken, uneven, or bumpy surface

♦ broken, jagged, ragged, scraggly

cram \'kram\ *vb* **crammed; cram·ming** **1** ♦ : to pack in tight : JAM **2** : to eat greedily **3** : to study rapidly under pressure for an examination

♦ crowd, jam, ram, sandwich, squeeze, stuff, wedge ♦ charge, fill, heap, jam, jam-pack, load, pack, stuff

¹cramp \'kramp\ *n* **1** ♦ : a sudden painful contraction of muscle **2** : sharp abdominal pain — usu. used in pl.

♦ spasm

²cramp *vb* **1** : to affect with a cramp or cramps **2** ♦ : to restrain from free action : HAMPER

♦ encumber, hamper, hinder, hold up, impede, inhibit, interfere with, obstruct, tie up

cran·ber·ry \'kran-ˌber-ē, -bə-rē\ *n* : the red acid berry of any of several trailing plants related to the heaths; *also* : one of these plants

¹crane \'krān\ *n* **1** : any of a family of tall wading birds related to the rails; *also* : any of several herons **2** : a machine for lifting and carrying heavy objects

²crane *vb* **craned; cran·ing** **1** : to stretch one's neck to see better **2** ♦ : to raise or lift by or as if by a crane

♦ boost, elevate, heave, heft, heighten, hike, hoist, jack, lift, pick up, raise, up, uphold

crane fly *n* : any of a family of long-legged slender dipteran flies that resemble large mosquitoes but do not bite

cranial nerve *n* : any of the nerves that arise in pairs from the lower surface of the brain and pass through openings in the skull to the periphery of the body

cra·ni·um \'krā-nē-əm\ *n, pl* **-ni·ums** *or* **-nia** \-ə\ : SKULL; *esp* : the part enclosing the brain — **cra·ni·al** \-əl\ *adj*

¹crank \'kraŋk\ *n* **1** : a bent part of an axle or shaft or an arm at right angles to the end of a shaft by which circular motion is imparted to or received from it **2** ♦ : an eccentric person **3** ♦ : a bad-tempered person : GROUCH

♦ [2] character, crackpot, eccentric, kook, nut, oddball, screwball, weirdo ♦ [3] bear, complainer, crab, curmudgeon, grouch, grumbler, whiner

²crank *vb* ♦ : to start or operate by or as if by turning a crank — usu. used with *up*

♦ *usu* **crank up** activate, actuate, drive, move, propel, run, set off, spark, start, touch off, trigger, turn on

crank·case \'kraŋk-ˌkās\ *n* : the housing of a crankshaft

crank out *vb* : to produce in a mechanical manner

crank·shaft \'kraŋk-ˌshaft\ *n* : a shaft turning or driven by a crank

cranky \'kraŋ-kē\ *adj* **crank·i·er; -est** **1** ♦ : given to fretful fussiness : IRRITABLE **2** ♦ : operating uncertainly or imperfectly

♦ [1] choleric, crabby, cross, crotchety, fussy, grouchy, grumpy, irascible, irritable, peevish, perverse, petulant, short-tempered, snappish, snappy, snippy, testy, waspish ♦ [2] awkward, clumsy, cumbersome, ungainly, unhandy, unwieldy

cran·ny \'kra-nē\ *n, pl* **crannies** ♦ : a small break or slit : CREVICE, CHINK

♦ chink, cleft, crack, crevice, fissure, rift, split

craps \'kraps\ *n* : a gambling game played with two dice

crap·shoot·er \'krap-ˌshü-tər\ *n* : a person who plays craps

¹crash \'krash\ *vb* **1** ♦ : to break noisily : SMASH **2** : to damage an airplane in landing **3** : to enter or attend without invitation or without paying ⟨∼ a party⟩ **4** : to decline suddenly and steeply **5** ♦ : to suffer a sudden major failure usu. with loss of data ⟨my computer ∼*ed*⟩

♦ [1] bang, bash, bump, collide, hit, impact, knock, ram, slam, smash, strike, swipe, thud ♦ [5] break, break down, conk, cut out, die, fail, stall

²**crash** n 1 ♦ : a loud sound (as of things smashing) 2 ♦ : an instance of crashing ⟨a plane ∼⟩; *also* : COLLISION 3 ♦ : a sudden failure (as of a business)

♦ [1] bang, blast, boom, clap, crack, pop, report, slam, smash, snap, thwack, whack ♦ [2] collision, crack-up, smash, wreck ♦ [3] collapse, cropper, defeat, failure, fizzle, nonsuccess

³**crash** adj : marked by concerted effort over the shortest possible time

⁴**crash** n : coarse linen fabric used for towels and draperies

crash–land \'krash-ˌland\ vb : to land an aircraft or spacecraft under emergency conditions usu. with damage to the craft — **crash landing** n

crass \'kras\ adj ♦ : coarse in nature or behavior : GROSS — **crass•ly** adv

♦ coarse, common, crude, gross, ill-bred, low, rough, rude, tasteless, uncouth, uncultivated, uncultured, unpolished, unrefined, vulgar

crate \'krāt\ n : a container often of wooden slats — **crate** vb

cra•ter \'krā-tər\ n 1 : the depression around the opening of a volcano 2 : a depression formed by the impact of a meteorite or by the explosion of a bomb or shell

cra•vat \krə-'vat\ n : NECKTIE

crave \'krāv\ vb **craved; crav•ing** 1 : to ask for earnestly : BEG 2 ♦ : to long for : DESIRE

♦ ache for, covet, desire, die for, hanker for, hunger for, long for, lust (for *or* after), pine for, repine for, thirst for, want, wish for, yearn for

¹**cra•ven** \'krā-vən\ adj ♦ : lacking the least bit of courage : contemptibly fainthearted

♦ chicken, cowardly, dastardly, pusillanimous, recreant, spineless, yellow

²**craven** n : an avowed coward

crav•ing \'krā-viŋ\ n ♦ : an urgent or abnormal desire

♦ appetite, desire, drive, hankering, hunger, itch, longing, lust, passion, thirst, urge, yearning, yen

craw•fish \'krȯ-ˌfish\ n 1 : CRAYFISH 1 2 : SPINY LOBSTER

¹**crawl** \'krȯl\ vb 1 : to move slowly by drawing the body along the ground 2 ♦ : to advance feebly, cautiously, or slowly 3 ♦ : to be swarming with or feel as if swarming with creeping things ⟨a place ∼ing with ants⟩ ⟨her flesh ∼ed⟩

♦ [1] creep, grovel, slither, snake, worm ♦ [2] creep, drag, inch, plod, poke *Ant* fly, race, speed, whiz, zip ♦ [3] abound, brim, bulge, burst, swarm, teem

²**crawl** n 1 : a very slow pace 2 : a prone speed swimming stroke

cray•fish \'krā-ˌfish\ n 1 : any of numerous freshwater crustaceans usu. much smaller than the related lobsters 2 : SPINY LOBSTER

cray•on \'krā-ˌän, -ən\ n : a stick of chalk or wax used for writing, drawing, or coloring; *also* : a drawing made with such material — **crayon** vb

¹**craze** \'krāz\ vb **crazed; craz•ing** ♦ : to make or become insane

♦ derange, madden, unhinge

²**craze** n ♦ : an exaggerated and often transient enthusiasm : FAD

♦ fad, mode, rage, style, trend, vogue

cra•zi•ness \-zē-nəs\ n ♦ : the quality or state of being crazy

♦ absurdity, asininity, balminess, daftness, fatuity, folly, foolishness, inanity, silliness, simplicity, zaniness

cra•zy \'krā-zē\ adj **cra•zi•er; -est** 1 : mentally disordered : INSANE — not used technically 2 ♦ : not characterized by common sense : wildly impractical; *also* : ERRATIC 3 ♦ : distracted with desire or excitement 4 ♦ : absurdly fond — usu. used with *about* or *over* — **cra•zi•ly** \-zə-lē\ adv

♦ [2] absurd, cuckoo, fatuous, foolish, nonsensical, nutty, senseless, silly, stupid ♦ [3] agog, anxious, ardent, athirst, avid, eager, enthusiastic, gung ho, hot, hungry, keen, nuts, raring, solicitous, thirsty, voracious ♦ usu **crazy about** or **crazy over** [4] mad, nuts

CRC abbr Civil Rights Commission

creak \'krēk\ vb : to make a prolonged squeaking or grating sound — **creak** n — **creaky** adj

¹**cream** \'krēm\ n 1 : the yellowish fat-rich part of milk 2 : a

thick smooth sauce, confection, or cosmetic 3 ♦ : the choicest part 4 : a pale yellow color — **creamy** adj

♦ best, choice, elect, elite, fat, flower, pick, prime

²**cream** vb 1 : to prepare with a cream sauce 2 : to beat or blend into creamy consistency 3 : to defeat decisively

cream cheese n : a cheese made from whole milk enriched with cream

cream•ery \'krē-mə-rē\ n, pl **-er•ies** : an establishment where butter and cheese are made or milk and cream are prepared for sale

¹**crease** \'krēs\ n ♦ : a mark or line made by or as if by folding

♦ crimp, crinkle, furrow, wrinkle

²**crease** vb : to become creased

cre•ate \krē-'āt\ vb **cre•at•ed; cre•at•ing** ♦ : to bring into being : cause to exist

♦ bring about, cause, effect, effectuate, generate, induce, make, produce, prompt, result, work, yield ♦ engender, generate, induce, make, produce, spawn

cre•a•tion \krē-'ā-shən\ n 1 : the act of creating or producing ⟨∼ of the world⟩ 2 ♦ : something that is created 3 ♦ : all created things : WORLD

♦ [2] coinage, concoction, contrivance, innovation, invention, wrinkle ♦ [3] cosmos, macrocosm, nature, universe, world

cre•a•tion•ism \krē-'ā-shə-ˌni-zəm\ n : a doctrine or theory holding that matter, the various forms of life, and the world were created by God out of nothing — **cre•a•tion•ist** \-nist\ n or adj

cre•a•tive \-'ā-tiv\ adj ♦ : marked by the ability or power to create — **cre•a•tive•ness** n

♦ artful, clever, imaginative, ingenious, innovative, inventive, original *Ant* uncreative, unimaginative, unoriginal

cre•a•tiv•i•ty \ˌkrē-(ˌ)ā-'ti-və-tē\ n ♦ : the ability to create

♦ ingenuity, invention, inventiveness, originality

cre•a•tor \krē-'ā-tər\ n 1 ♦ : one that creates : MAKER, AUTHOR 2 cap : GOD 1

♦ author, father, founder, originator

crea•ture \'krē-chər\ n 1 ♦ : a lower animal 2 ♦ : a human being

♦ [1] animal, beast, brute, critter ♦ [2] being, body, human, individual, man, mortal, person

crèche \'kresh\ n : a representation of the Nativity scene

cre•dence \'krēd-ᵊns\ n ♦ : mental acceptance as true or real

♦ confidence, faith, stock, trust ♦ belief, credit, faith

cre•den•tial \kri-'den-chəl\ n ♦ : something that gives a basis for credit or confidence — used in pl.

♦ usu **credentials** capability, qualification, stuff

cre•den•za \kri-'den-zə\ n : a sideboard, buffet, or bookcase usu. without legs

cred•i•ble \'kre-də-bəl\ adj ♦ : offering reasonable grounds for being believed : BELIEVABLE — **cred•i•bil•i•ty** \ˌkre-də-'bi-lə-tē\ n

♦ believable, likely, plausible, probable

¹**cred•it** \'kre-dət\ vb 1 ♦ : to trust in the truth of : BELIEVE 2 ♦ : to give credit to

♦ [1] accept, believe, swallow, trust ♦ [2] accredit, ascribe, attribute, impute

²**credit** n 1 : the balance (as in a bank) in a person's favor 2 : time given for payment for goods sold on trust 3 : an accounting entry of payment received 4 ♦ : reliance on the truth or reality of something : BELIEF, FAITH 5 : financial trustworthiness 6 ♦ : good name 7 ♦ : a source of honor or distinction 8 : a unit of academic work

♦ [4] belief, credence, faith ♦ [6] acclaim, accolade, distinction, glory, homage, honor (*or* honour), laurels ♦ [7] boast, glory, honor (*or* honour), jewel, pride, treasure

cred•it•able \'kre-də-tə-bəl\ adj ♦ : worthy of esteem or praise ⟨a ∼ performance⟩ — **cred•it•ably** \-blē\ adv

♦ admirable, commendable, laudable, meritorious, praiseworthy

credit card n : a card authorizing purchases on credit

cred•i•tor \'kre-də-tər\ n : a person to whom money is owed

cre•do \'krē-dō, 'krā-\ n, pl **credos** 1 : a set of fundamental beliefs : CREED 2 : a guiding principle

cred•u•lous \'kre-jə-ləs\ adj : inclined to believe esp. on slight evidence — **cre·du·li·ty** \kri-'dü-lə-tē, -'dyü-\ *n* — **cred·u·lous·ly** *adv*

Cree \'krē\ *n, pl* **Cree** *or* **Crees** : a member of an Algonquian-speaking First Nations people of Quebec, Ontario, Manitoba, and Saskatchewan

creed \'krēd\ *n* **1** ♦ : a statement of the essential beliefs of a religious faith; *also* : the body of such beliefs **2** ♦ : a guiding principle

♦ [1] cult, faith, persuasion, religion ♦ [2] doctrine, gospel, ideology, philosophy

creek \'krēk, 'krik\ *n* **1** *chiefly Brit* : a small inlet **2** ♦ : a stream smaller than a river

♦ brook, rill, rivulet, streamlet

Creek \'krēk\ *n* : a member of any of a group of Indigenous American peoples that formed a confederacy in Georgia and eastern Alabama in the eighteenth and early nineteenth centuries

creel \'krēl\ *n* : a wicker basket esp. for carrying fish

¹**creep** \'krēp\ *vb* **crept** \'krept\; **creep·ing** **1** ♦ : to move along with the body prone and close to the ground : CRAWL **2** : to feel as though insects were crawling on the skin **3** : to grow over a surface like ivy **4** ♦ : to go very slowly **5** : to enter, advance, or progress gradually so as to be almost unnoticed ⟨the cost of living keeps ∼*ing* up⟩ — **creep·er** *n*

♦ [1] crawl, grovel, slither, snake, worm ♦ [4] crawl, drag, inch, plod, poke

²**creep** *n* ♦ : an unpleasant or obnoxious person

♦ beast, boor, churl, clown, cretin, cur, heel, jerk, joker, louse, lout, skunk, slob, snake

creep·ing \'krē-piŋ\ *adj* ♦ : developing or advancing by imperceptible degrees

♦ dilatory, laggard, languid, poky, slow, sluggish, tardy

creepy \'krē-pē\ *adj* **creep·i·er; -est** ♦ : having or producing a nervous shivery fear

♦ eerie, haunting, spooky, uncanny, unearthly, weird

cre·mate \'krē-ˌmāt\ *vb* **cre·mat·ed; cre·mat·ing** : to reduce (a dead body) to ashes with fire — **cre·ma·tion** \kri-'mā-shən\ *n*

cre·ma·to·ry \'krē-mə-ˌtōr-ē, 'krē-\ *n, pl* **-ries** : a furnace for cremating; *also* : a structure containing such a furnace

crème \'krem, 'krēm\ *n, pl* **crèmes** *same or* 'kremz, 'krēmz\ : a sweet liqueur

cren·el·lat·ed *or* **cren·el·at·ed** \'kren-ᵊl-ˌā-təd\ *adj* : having battlements — **cren·el·la·tion** \ˌkren-ᵊl-'ā-shən\ *n*

Cre·ole \'krē-ˌōl\ *n* **1** : a descendant of early French or Spanish settlers of the U.S. Gulf states preserving their speech and culture; *also* : a person of mixed French or Spanish and Black descent speaking a dialect of French or Spanish **2** *not cap* : a language that has evolved from a pidgin but serves as the native language of a speech community

cre·o·sote \'krē-ə-ˌsōt\ *n* : an oily liquid obtained by distillation of coal tar and used in preserving wood

crepe *or* **crêpe** \'krāp\ *n* : a light crinkled fabric of any of various fibers

crêpe su·zette \ˌkrāp-sù-'zet\ *n, pl* **crêpes suzette** *same or* ˌkrāps-\ *or* **crêpe suzettes** \-sù-'zets\ *often cap S* : a thin folded or rolled pancake in a hot orange-butter sauce that is sprinkled with a liqueur and set ablaze for serving

cre·pus·cu·lar \kri-'pəs-kyə-lər\ *adj* **1** : of, relating to, or resembling twilight **2** : occurring or active during twilight ⟨∼ insects⟩

cre·scen·do \krə-'shen-dō\ *adv or adj* : increasing in loudness — used as a direction in music — **crescendo** *n*

cres·cent \'kres-ᵊnt\ *n* : the moon at any stage between new moon and first quarter and between last quarter and new moon; *also* : something shaped like the figure of the crescent moon with a convex and a concave edge — **cres·cen·tic** \kre-'sen-tik\ *adj*

cress \'kres\ *n* : any of several salad plants related to the mustards

¹**crest** \'krest\ *n* **1** : a tuft or process on the head of an animal (as a bird) **2** : a heraldic device **3** : an upper part, edge, or limit ⟨the ∼ of a hill⟩ — **crest·ed** \'kres-təd\ *adj* — **crest·less** *adj*

²**crest** *vb* **1** : CROWN **2** : to reach the crest of **3** : to rise to a crest

crest·fall·en \'krest-ˌfò-lən\ *adj* : feeling shame or humiliation; *also* : feeling low in spirit : DISPIRITED, DEJECTED

Cre·ta·ceous \kri-'tā-shəs\ *adj* : of, relating to, or being the latest period of the Mesozoic era marked by great increase in flowering plants, diversification of mammals, and extinction of the dinosaurs — **Cretaceous** *n*

cre·tin \'krēt-ᵊn\ *n* **1** *often offensive* : one affected with cretinism **2** ♦ : a stupid, vulgar, or insensitive person

♦ blockhead, dope, dummy, idiot, imbecile, jackass, moron, numskull

cre·tin·ism \-ˌi-zəm\ *n* : a usu. congenital condition characterized by physical stunting and intellectual disability

cre·tonne \'krē-ˌtän\ *n* : a strong unglazed cotton cloth for curtains and upholstery

cre·vasse \kri-'vas\ *n* : a deep fissure esp. in a glacier

crev·ice \'kre-vəs\ *n* ♦ : a narrow fissure

♦ chink, cleft, crack, cranny, fissure, rift, split

¹**crew** \'krü\ *chiefly Can and Brit past of* CROW

²**crew** *n* **1** ♦ : a body of people trained to work together for certain purposes **2** : a group of people who operate a ship, train, aircraft, or spacecraft **3** : the rowers and coxswain of a racing shell; *also* : the sport of rowing engaged in by a crew — **crew·man** \-mən\ *n*

♦ band, company, gang, outfit, party, squad, team

crew cut *n* : a very short bristly haircut

crewed \'krüd\ *adj* : having a crew : carrying or performed by people **crew·el** \'krü-əl\ *n* : slackly twisted worsted yarn used for embroidery — **crew·el·work** \-ˌwərk\ *n*

¹**crib** \'krib\ *n* **1** : a manger for feeding animals **2** : a child's bedstead with high sides **3** : a building or bin for storage (as of grain) **4** : something used for cheating in an exam

²**crib** *vb* **cribbed; crib·bing** **1** : to put in a crib **2** : STEAL, PLAGIARIZE — **crib·ber** *n*

crib·bage \'kri-bij\ *n* : a card game usu. played by two players and scored on a board (**cribbage board**)

crib death *n* : SUDDEN INFANT DEATH SYNDROME

crick \'krik\ *n* : a painful spasm of muscles (as of the neck)

¹**crick·et** \'kri-kət\ *n* : any of a family of leaping insects related to the grasshoppers and noted for the chirping noises of the male

²**cricket** *n* : a game played with a bat and ball by two teams on a field centering upon two wickets each defended by a batsman

cri·er \'krī-(ə)r\ *n* : one who calls out proclamations and announcements

crime \'krīm\ *n* **1** ♦ : a serious offense against the public law **2** ♦ : something reprehensible, foolish, or disgraceful

♦ [1] error, malefaction, misdeed, misdoing, offense, sin, transgression, violation, wrongdoing ♦ [2] disgrace, outrage, pity, scandal, shame, sin

¹**crim·i·nal** \'kri-mən-ᵊl\ *adj* **1** ♦ : involving or being a crime **2** : relating to crime or its punishment — **crim·i·nal·i·ty** \ˌkri-mə-'na-lə-tē\ *n* — **crim·i·nal·ly** *adv*

♦ illegal, illegitimate, illicit, unlawful, wrongful

²**criminal** *n* ♦ : one who has committed a crime

♦ crook, culprit, felon, lawbreaker, malefactor, offender

crim·i·nol·o·gy \ˌkri-mə-'nä-lə-jē\ *n* : the scientific study of crime and criminals — **crim·i·nol·o·gist** \ˌkri-mə-'nä-lə-jist\ *n*

¹**crimp** \'krimp\ *vb* : to cause to become crinkled, wavy, or bent

²**crimp** *n* **1** : something (as a curl in hair) produced by or as if by crimping **2** ♦ : a bend or crease formed in something **3** ♦ : something that cramps or inhibits

♦ [2] crease, crinkle, furrow, wrinkle ♦ [3] bar, block, encumbrance, hindrance, inhibition, obstacle

¹**crim·son** \'krim-zən\ *n* : a deep purplish red color — **crimson** *adj*

²**crimson** *vb* ♦ : to make or become crimson

♦ bloom, blush, color (*or* colour), flush, glow, redden

cringe \'krinj\ *vb* **cringed; cring·ing** : to shrink in fear : COWER

♦ cower, grovel, quail

¹**crin·kle** \'kriŋ-kəl\ *vb* **crin·kled; crin·kling** ♦ : to form many short bends or curves; *also* : WRINKLE — **crin·kly** \-kə-lē\ *adj*

♦ crease, furrow, rumple, wrinkle

²**crinkle** *n* : a line, mark, or ridge made by or as if by folding a pliable substance

crin·o·line \'krin-ᵊl-ən\ *n* **1** : an open-weave cloth used for stiffening and lining **2** : a full stiff skirt or underskirt made of crinoline

¹**crip·ple** \'kri-pəl\ *n* : one that is disabled or deficient in a specified manner ⟨a social ∼⟩

²**cripple** *vb* **crip·pled; crip·pling** **1** ♦ : to make lame **2** ♦ : to make useless or imperfect

♦ [1] disable, lame, maim, mutilate ♦ [2] blemish, break, damage, deface, disfigure, flaw, harm, hurt, injure, mar, spoil, vitiate ♦ [2] disable, hamstring, immobilize, incapacitate, paralyze, prostrate

cri·sis \'krī-səs\ *n, pl* **cri·ses** \-ˌsēz\   **1** : the turning point for better or worse in an acute disease or fever   **2** ♦ : a decisive or critical moment

♦ clutch, crunch, emergency, head, juncture

crisp \'krisp\ *adj*   **1** : CURLY, WAVY   **2** ♦ : easily crumbled : BRITTLE   **3** : FIRM, FRESH ⟨∼ lettuce⟩   **4** ♦ : being sharp and clear; *also* : concise and to the point   **5** : LIVELY, SPARKLING   **6** : FROSTY, SNAPPY; *also* : INVIGORATING   **7** ♦ : noticeably neat — **crisp** *vb*

♦ [2] brittle, crumbly, flaky, friable ♦ [4] brief, compact, compendious, concise, epigrammatic, laconic, pithy, succinct, summary, terse ♦ [7] neat, orderly, shipshape, snug, tidy, trim, uncluttered

crisp·ly *adv* ♦ : in a crisp manner

♦ compactly, concisely, laconically, shortly, succinctly, summarily, tersely

crisp·ness *n* ♦ : the quality or state of being crisp

♦ brevity, briefness, compactness, conciseness, succinctness, terseness

crispy *adj* : easily crumbled
¹criss·cross \'kris-ˌkrös\ *vb*   **1** : to mark with crossed lines   **2** ♦ : to go or pass back and forth through or over

♦ cover, cross, cut, follow, go, pass, proceed, travel, traverse

²crisscross *adj* : marked or characterized by crisscrossing — **crisscross** *adv*
³crisscross *n* : a pattern formed by crossed lines
crit *abbr* critical; criticism
cri·te·ri·on \krī-'tir-ē-ən\ *n, pl* **-ria** \-ē-ə\ ♦ : a standard on which a judgment may be based

♦ grade, mark, measure, par, standard, touchstone, yardstick

crit·ic \'kri-tik\ *n*   **1** : a person who judges literary or artistic works   **2** ♦ : one inclined to find fault

♦ carper, castigator, caviler, censurer, faultfinder, nitpicker, railer, scold

crit·i·cal \'kri-ti-kəl\ *adj*   **1** : being or relating to a condition or disease involving danger of death   **2** ♦ : being a crisis   **3** ♦ : inclined to criticize   **4** : relating to criticism or critics   **5** : requiring careful judgment   **6** : UNCERTAIN   **7** ♦ : marked by or indicative of significant worth or consequence — **crit·i·cal·ly** \-k(ə-)lē\ *adv*

♦ [2] acute, dire, imperative, imperious, instant, pressing, urgent ♦ [3] captious, carping, hypercritical, overcritical *Ant* uncritical ♦ [7] crucial, key, pivotal, vital

crit·i·cise *Brit var of* CRITICIZE
crit·i·cism \'kri-tə-ˌsi-zəm\ *n*   **1** : the act of criticizing; *esp* : CENSURE   **2** : a judgment or review   **3** : the art of judging works of literature or art
crit·i·cize \'kri-tə-ˌsīz\ *vb* **-cized; -ciz·ing**   **1** : to judge as a critic : EVALUATE   **2** ♦ : to find fault : express criticism

♦ blame, censure, condemn, denounce, fault, knock, pan, reprehend *Ant* extol, laud, praise

cri·tique \krə-'tēk\ *n* : a critical estimate or discussion
crit·ter \'kri-tər\ *n* ♦ : a lower animal : CREATURE

♦ animal, beast, brute, creature

¹croak \'krōk\ *n* : a hoarse harsh cry (as of a frog)
²croak *vb* ♦ : to mutter in discontent

♦ beef, bellyache, carp, complain, crab, fuss, gripe, grouse, growl, grumble, kick, moan, murmur, mutter, repine, squawk, wail, whine

Croat \'krō-ˌat\ *n* : CROATIAN
Cro·atian \krō-'ā-shən\ *n* : a native or inhabitant of Croatia — **Croatian** *adj*
cro·chet \krō-'shā\ *n* : needlework done with a single thread and hooked needle — **crochet** *vb*
crock \'kräk\ *n* : a thick earthenware pot or jar
crock·ery \'krä-kə-rē\ *n* : EARTHENWARE
croc·o·dile \'krä-kə-ˌdīl\ *n* : any of several thick-skinned long-bodied carnivorous reptiles of tropical and subtropical waters
cro·cus \'krō-kəs\ *n, pl* **cro·cus·es** *also* **crocus** *or* **cro·ci** \-ˌkī\ : any of a large genus of low herbs related to the irises and having brightly colored flowers borne singly in early spring
Crohn's disease \'krōnz\ *n* : a chronic inflammatory disease of the gastrointestinal tract and esp. the ileum

crois·sant \krȯ-'sänt, krwä-'säⁿ\ *n, pl* **croissants** *same or* -'sänts, -'säⁿz\ : a rich crescent-shaped roll
Cro-Ma·gnon \krō-'mag-nən, -'man-yən\ *n* : any of a tall erect human race known from skeletal remains found chiefly in southern France and usu. classified as the same species as present-day human beings — **Cro–Magnon** *adj*
crone \'krōn\ *n* ♦ : a withered old woman : HAG

♦ hag, witch

cro·ny \'krō-nē\ *n, pl* **cronies** ♦ : a close friend esp. of long standing

♦ associate, cohort, companion, comrade, fellow, mate ♦ buddy, chum, comrade, familiar, friend, intimate, pal

¹crook \'kru̇k\ *vb* ♦ : to curve or bend sharply

♦ arc, arch, bend, bow, curve, hook, round, sweep, swerve, wheel

²crook *n*   **1** : a bent or curved implement   **2** : a bent or curved part; *also* : BEND, CURVE   **3** : a person who engages in fraudulent or criminal practices : SWINDLER, THIEF
crook·ed \'kru̇-kəd\ *adj*   **1** ♦ : having a crook   **2** ♦ : characterized by lack of truth, honesty, or trustworthiness : DISHONEST — **crook·ed·ly** *adv*

♦ [1] devious, serpentine, sinuous, tortuous, winding *Ant* straight, straightaway ♦ [2] deceptive, dishonest, fast, fraudulent, shady, sharp, shifty, underhanded

crook·ed·ness *n* ♦ : the quality or state of being crooked

♦ artifice, craft, craftiness, cunning, deceit, deceitfulness, dishonesty, dissimulation, double-dealing, duplicity, guile, wiliness

croon \'krün\ *vb* : to sing or hum in a gentle murmuring voice — **croon·er** *n*
¹crop \'kräp\ *n*   **1** : the handle of a whip; *also* : a short riding whip   **2** : a pouch in the throat of many birds and insects where food is received   **3** : something that can be harvested; *also* : the yield at harvest   **4** : two or more figures forming a complete unit in a composition
²crop *vb* **cropped; crop·ping**   **1** ♦ : to remove the tips of : cut off short; *also* : TRIM   **2** : to feed on by cropping   **3 a** : to devote (land) to crops   **b** ♦ : to grow as a crop : yield a crop   **4** ♦ : to appear unexpectedly — often used with *up*

♦ [1] bob, clip, cut, cut back, dock, lop, nip, prune, shave, shear, trim ♦ [3b] cultivate, grow, promote, raise, rear, tend ♦ *usu* **crop up** [4] arise, emerge, materialize, spring, surface

crop duster *n* : a person who uses an airplane to spray crops with insecticidal dusts; *also* : an airplane so used
crop·land \-ˌland\ *n* : land devoted to the production of plant crops
¹crop·per \'krä-pər\ *n* : a raiser of crops; *esp* : SHARECROPPER
²cropper *n* ♦ : a sudden or violent failure or collapse

♦ collapse, crash, defeat, failure, fizzle, nonsuccess

cro·quet \krō-'kā\ *n* : a game in which mallets are used to drive wooden balls through a series of wickets set out on a lawn
cro·quette \krō-'ket\ *n* : a small often rounded mass of minced meat, fish, or vegetables fried in deep fat
cro·sier \'krō-zhər\ *n* : a staff carried by bishops and abbots
¹cross \'krös\ *n*   **1** : a structure consisting of an upright beam and a crossbar used esp. by the ancient Romans for execution   **2** : a figure of the cross on which Christ was crucified used as a Christian symbol; *also* : a product of this   **3** : a hybridizing of unlike individuals or strains; *also* : a product of this   **4** : a punch delivered with a circular motion over an opponent's lead   **5** ♦ : an affliction that tries one's virtue, steadfastness, or patience

♦ gauntlet, ordeal, trial

²cross *vb*   **1** : to lie or place across; *also* : INTERSECT   **2** : to cancel by marking a cross on or by lining through   **3** : THWART, OBSTRUCT   **4** ♦ : to go or extend across : TRAVERSE   **5** : HYBRIDIZE   **6** : to meet and pass on the way

♦ cover, crisscross, cut, follow, go, pass, proceed, travel, traverse

³cross *adj*   **1** : lying across   **2** : CONTRARY, OPPOSED   **3** ♦ : marked by bad temper   **4** : HYBRID — **cross·ly** *adv*

♦ choleric, crabby, cranky, crotchety, grouchy, grumpy, irascible, irritable, peevish, perverse, petulant, short-tempered, snappish, snappy, snippy, testy, waspish

cross·bar \'krös-ˌbär\ *n* : a transverse bar or piece
cross·bow \-ˌbō\ *n* : a short bow mounted crosswise at the end of a wooden stock that shoots short arrows

cross·breed \'kros-ˌbrēd, -'brēd\ vb **-bred** \-'bred\; **-breed·ing** : HYBRIDIZE

cross–coun·try \-'kən-trē\ adj **1** : extending or moving across a country **2** : proceeding over the countryside (as fields and woods) and not by roads **3** : of or relating to racing or skiing over the countryside instead of over a track or run — **cross–country** adv

cross–cur·rent \-'kər-ənt\ n **1** : a current running counter to another **2** : a conflicting tendency — usu. used in pl.

¹**cross·cut** \-ˌkət\ vb : to cut or saw crosswise esp. of the grain of wood

²**crosscut** adj **1** : made or used for crosscutting ⟨a ∼ saw⟩ **2** : cut across the grain

³**crosscut** n : something that cuts through transversely

cross–ex·am·ine \ˌkro-sig-'za-mən\ vb : to examine with questions to check the answers to previous questions — **cross–ex·am·i·na·tion** \-ˌza-mə-'nā-shən\ n

cross–eyed \'kro-ˌsīd\ adj : having one or both eyes turned inward toward the nose

cross–fer·til·i·za·tion \-ˌfərt-ᵊl-ə-'zā-shən\ n **1** : fertilization between sex cells produced by separate individuals or sometimes by individuals of different kinds; also : CROSS-POLLINATION **2** : a broadening or productive interchange (as between cultures) — **cross–fer·til·ize** \-'fərt-ᵊl-ˌīz\ vb

cross fire n **1** : crossing lines of fire in combat **2** : rapid or angry interchange

cross·hair \'kros-ˌhar\ n : a fine wire or thread in the eyepiece of an optical instrument used as a reference line

cross·hatch \'kros-ˌhach\ vb : to mark with two series of parallel lines that intersect — **cross·hatch·ing** n

cross·ing \'kro-siŋ\ n **1** : a place or structure for crossing something (as a river) **2** ♦ : a point of intersection (as of a street and a railroad track) **3** ♦ : the act or action of crossing

♦ [2] corner, crossroad, intersection ♦ [3] cruise, passage, sail, voyage

cross·over \'kros-ˌō-vər\ n **1** : CROSSING **2** : a member of a political party who votes in the primary of the other party **3** : a broadening of the popular appeal of an artist (as a musician) by a change in the artist's style, genre, or medium **4** : an instance of breaking into another category

cross over vb : to achieve broader popularity by a change of medium or style

cross·piece \'kros-ˌpēs\ n : a horizontal member

cross–pol·li·na·tion \ˌkros-ˌpä-lə-'nā-shən\ n : transfer of pollen from one flower to the stigma of another — **cross–pol·li·nate** \'kros-ˌpä-lə-ˌnāt\ vb

cross–pur·pose \'kros-'pər-pəs\ n : a purpose contrary to another purpose ⟨working at *cross-purposes*⟩

cross–ques·tion \-'kwes-chən\ vb : CROSS-EXAMINE — **cross–question** n

cross–re·fer \ˌkros-ri-'fər\ vb : to refer by a notation or direction from one place to another (as in a book or list) — **cross–ref·er·ence** \'kros-'re-frəns\ n

cross·road \'kros-ˌrōd\ n **1** : a road that crosses a main road or runs between main roads **2** ♦ : a place where roads meet — usu. used in pl. **3** : a crucial point where a decision must be made

♦ *usu* **crossroads** corner, crossing, intersection

cross section n **1** : a section cut across something; also : a representation made by or as if by such cutting **2** : a number of persons or things selected from a group that show the general nature of the whole group — **cross–sec·tion·al** adj

cross·walk \'kros-ˌwok\ n : a marked path for pedestrians crossing a street

cross·ways \-ˌwāz\ adv : so as to cross something : CROSSWISE

cross·wind \-ˌwind\ n : a wind not parallel to a course (as of an airplane)

cross·wise \-ˌwīz\ adv ♦ : so as to cross something — **cross·wise** adj

♦ athwart, obliquely, transversely

cross·word \'kros-ˌwərd\ n : a puzzle in which words are put into a pattern of numbered squares in answer to clues

cros·ti·ni \kro-'stē-nē\ n pl : small slices of toasted bread served with a topping

crotch \'kräch\ n : an angle formed by the parting of two legs, branches, or members

crotch·et \'krä-chət\ n **1** : an odd notion : WHIM **2** ♦ : a highly individual and usu. eccentric opinion or preference

♦ eccentricity, idiosyncrasy, mannerism, oddity, peculiarity, quirk, singularity, trick

crotch·ety adj ♦ : given to crotchets : subject to whims, crankiness, or ill temper

♦ choleric, crabby, cranky, cross, grouchy, grumpy, irascible, irritable, peevish, perverse, petulant, short-tempered, snappish, snappy, snippy, testy, waspish

crouch \'kraůch\ vb **1** ♦ : to stoop or bend low **2** : CRINGE, COWER — **crouch** n

♦ huddle, hunch, squat

croup \'krüp\ n : laryngitis esp. of infants marked by a hoarse ringing cough and difficult breathing — **croupy** adj

crou·pi·er \'krü-pē-ər, -pē-ˌā\ n : an employee of a gambling casino who collects and pays bets at a gaming table

crou·ton \'krü-ˌtän\ n : a small cube of bread toasted or fried crisp

¹**crow** \'krō\ n **1** : any of various large glossy black birds related to the jays **2** cap : a member of an Indigenous people of the Great Plains; also : their language

²**crow** vb **1** : to make the loud shrill sound characteristic of the cock **2** ♦ : to utter a sound expressive of pleasure **3** ♦ : to exult gloatingly esp. over the distress of another : EXULT **4** ♦ : to brag exultantly or blatantly : BRAG, BOAST

♦ [2, 3] delight, exult, glory, joy, rejoice, triumph ♦ [4] boast, brag, plume, swagger

³**crow** n : the cry of the cock

crow·bar \'krō-ˌbär\ n : a metal bar usu. wedge-shaped at the end for use as a pry or lever

¹**crowd** \'kraůd\ vb **1** ♦ : to press close **2** ♦ : to gather in numbers : THRONG **3** ♦ : to press, force, or thrust into a small space : CRAM, STUFF

♦ [1, 3] cram, jam, ram, sandwich, squeeze, stuff, wedge ♦ [2] flock, mob, swarm, throng

²**crowd** n **1** ♦ : a large number of people gathered together at random : THRONG **2** ♦ : a group of people having something (as a habit, interest, or occupation) in common

♦ [1] army, crush, drove, flock, horde, host, legion, mob, multitude, press, swarm, throng ♦ [2] circle, clan, clique, coterie, fold, gang, ring, set

crowd·ed adj **1** ♦ : filled with numerous things or people often overly compacted or concentrated **2** ♦ : pressed together

♦ [1] brimful, chock-full, fat, fraught, full, loaded, packed, replete ♦ [2] close, compact, dense, packed, serried, thick, tight

crowd·fund·ing \'kraůd-ˌfən-diŋ\ n : the practice of obtaining funding (as for a business) by seeking contributions from a large group of people esp. from the online community

crowd·sourc·ing \'kraůd-ˌsòr-siŋ\ n : the practice of obtaining needed services, ideas, or content by seeking contributions from a large group of people and esp. from the online community

¹**crown** \'kraůn\ n **1** : a mark of victory or honor; esp : the title of a champion in a sport **2** : a royal headdress **3** : the top of the head **4** ♦ : the highest part (as of a tree or tooth) **5** often cap : sovereign power; also : MONARCH **6** : a formerly used British silver coin — **crowned** \'kraůnd\ adj

♦ acme, apex, climax, culmination, head, height, meridian, peak, pinnacle, summit, tip-top, top, zenith

²**crown** vb **1** : to place a crown on **2** : HONOR **3** : TOP, SURMOUNT **4** : to fit (a tooth) with an artificial crown

crown vetch n : a European leguminous herb with umbels of pink-and-white flowers and sharp-angled pods

crow's–foot \'krōz-ˌfút\ n, pl **crow's–feet** \-ˌfēt\ : any of the wrinkles around the outer corners of the eyes — usu. used in pl.

crow's nest n : a partly enclosed platform high on a ship's mast for use as a lookout

crozier var of CROSIER

¹**CRT** \ˌsē-(ˌ)är-'tē\ n, pl **CRTs** or **CRT's** : CATHODE-RAY TUBE; also : a display device incorporating a cathode-ray tube

²**CRT** abbr carrier route

cru·cial \'krü-shəl\ adj **1** ♦ : important or essential as resolving a crisis : DECISIVE **2** : IMPORTANT, SIGNIFICANT

♦ critical, decisive, essential, indispensable, key, necessary, pivotal, pressing, requisite, urgent, vital

cru·ci·ate \'krü-shē-ˌāt\ adj : CRUCIFORM

cru·ci·ble \'krü-sə-bəl\ n **1** : a heat-resistant container in which material can be subjected to great heat **2** : a severe test

cru·ci·fix \'krü-sə-ˌfiks\ n : a representation of Christ on the cross

cru·ci·fix·ion \ˌkrü-sə-'fik-shən\ n **1** cap : the crucifying of Christ **2** : the act of crucifying

cru·ci·form \'krü-sə-ˌfórm\ *adj* : shaped like a cross
cru·ci·fy \'krü-sə-ˌfī\ *vb* **-fied; -fy·ing 1** : to put to death by nailing or binding the hands and feet to a cross **2** : MORTIFY 1 **3** : TORTURE, PERSECUTE
¹**crude** \'krüd\ *adj* **crud·er; crud·est 1** ♦ : not refined : RAW ⟨~ oil⟩ ⟨~ statistics⟩ **2** ♦ : lacking grace, taste, tact, or polish **3** ♦ : rough or inexpert in plan or execution — **crude·ly** *adv* — **cru·di·ty** \'krü-də-tē\ *n*

   ♦ [1] native, natural, raw, undressed, unprocessed, unrefined, untreated *Ant* processed, refined, treated ♦ [2] coarse, common, crass, gross, ill-bred, low, rough, rude, tasteless, uncouth, uncultivated, uncultured, unpolished, unrefined, vulgar ♦ [3] artless, clumsy, rough, rude, unrefined

²**crude** *n* : unrefined petroleum
cru·el \'krü-əl\ *adj* **cru·el·er** *or* **cru·el·ler; cru·el·est** *or* **cru·el·lest 1** ♦ : causing pain and suffering to others **2** ♦ : extremely painful — **cru·el·ly** *adv*

   ♦ [1] barbarous, brutal, heartless, inhumane, sadistic, savage, vicious, wanton *Ant* benign, benignant, compassionate, goodhearted, humane, kind, kindhearted, sympathetic, tenderhearted ♦ [2] agonizing, bitter, excruciating, galling, grievous, harrowing, harsh, hurtful, painful, tortuous

cru·el·ty \-tē\ *n* ♦ : the quality or state of being cruel

   ♦ barbarity, brutality, inhumanity, sadism, savagery, viciousness, wantonness *Ant* benignity, compassion, humanity, kindness, sympathy

cru·et \'krü-ət\ *n* : a small usu. glass bottle for vinegar, oil, or sauce
¹**cruise** \'krüz\ *vb* **cruised; cruis·ing 1** : to sail about touching at a series of ports **2** : to travel for pleasure **3** : to travel about the streets at random **4** : to travel at the most efficient operating speed ⟨the airplane's *cruising* speed⟩
²**cruise** *n* ♦ : an act or an instance of cruising; *esp* : a tour by ship

   ♦ crossing, passage, sail, voyage

cruis·er \'krü-zər\ *n* **1** : SQUAD CAR **2** : a large fast moderately armored and gunned warship **3** : a motorboat equipped for living aboard
crul·ler \'krə-lər\ *n* **1** : a small sweet cake in the form of a twisted strip fried in deep fat **2** *Northern & Midland* : an unraised doughnut
¹**crumb** \'krəm\ *n* **1** ♦ : a small fragment **2** ♦ : a small piece or quantity of some material thing

   ♦ atom, bit, fleck, flyspeck, grain, granule, molecule, morsel, mote, particle, patch, scrap, scruple, speck, tittle

²**crumb** *vb* **1** : to break into crumbs **2** : to cover with crumbs
crum·ble \'krəm-bəl\ *vb* **crum·bled; crum·bling 1** : to break into small pieces : DISINTEGRATE **2** : to break down completely
crum·bly *adj* ♦ : easily crumbled

   ♦ brittle, crisp, flaky, friable

crum·my \'krə-mē\ *adj* **crum·mi·er; -est** ♦ : very poor or inferior : LOUSY

   ♦ bad, deficient, inferior, lousy, off, poor, punk, rotten, substandard, unacceptable, wanting, wretched, wrong

crum·pet \'krəm-pət\ *n* : a small round unsweetened bread cooked on a griddle
crum·ple \'krəm-pəl\ *vb* **crum·pled; crum·pling 1** ♦ : to crush together : RUMPLE **2** ♦ : fall into a jumbled or flattened mass through the force of external pressure : COLLAPSE

   ♦ [1] crinkle, rumple, wrinkle *Ant* iron out, smooth ♦ [2] cave in, collapse, give, go, yield

¹**crunch** \'krənch\ *vb* **1** ♦ : to chew with a grinding noise **2** ♦ : to grind or press with a crushing noise

   ♦ *usu* **crunch on** [1] bite, champ, chew, chomp, gnaw, nibble ♦ [2] gnash, grate, grind, grit, scrape

²**crunch** *n* **1** : an act of or a sound made by crunching **2** ♦ : a tight or critical situation — **crunchy** *adj*

   ♦ clutch, crisis, emergency, head, juncture

cru·sade \krü-'sād\ *n* **1** *cap* : any of the expeditions in the 11th, 12th, and 13th centuries undertaken by Christian countries to take the Holy Land from the Muslims **2** ♦ : a reforming enterprise undertaken with zeal — **crusade** *vb*

   ♦ bandwagon, campaign, cause, drive, movement

cru·sad·er *n* ♦ : one engaged in a crusade

   ♦ fanatic, militant, partisan, zealot

cruse \'krüz, 'krüs\ *n* : a jar for water or oil
¹**crush** \'krəsh\ *vb* **1** ♦ : to squeeze out of shape **2** : HUG, EMBRACE **3** ♦ : to grind or pound to small bits **4** ♦ : to suppress or overwhelm as if by pressure or weight : SUPPRESS **5** ♦ : to subdue completely

   ♦ [1] mash, squash ♦ [3] atomize, grind, powder, pulverize ♦ [4, 5] clamp down, crack down, put down, quash, quell, repress, silence, snuff, squash, squelch, subdue, suppress ♦ [4, 5] carry away, devastate, floor, oppress, overcome, overpower, overwhelm, prostrate, snow under, swamp

²**crush** *n* **1** : an act of crushing **2** ♦ : a violent crowding **3** : INFATUATION

   ♦ army, crowd, drove, flock, horde, host, legion, mob, multitude, press, swarm, throng

crust \'krəst\ *n* **1** : the outside part of bread; *also* : a piece of old dry bread **2** : the cover of a pie **3** : a hard surface layer — **crust·al** *adj*
crus·ta·cean \ˌkrəs-'tā-shən\ *n* : any of a large class of mostly aquatic arthropods (as lobsters or crabs) having a firm crustlike shell — **crustacean** *adj*
crusty *adj* **crust·i·er; -est 1** : having or being a crust **2** : giving an effect of surly incivility in address or disposition : CROSS, GRUMPY
crutch \'krəch\ *n* : a supporting device; *esp* : a support fitting under the armpit for use by the disabled in walking
crux \'krəks, 'krùks\ *n, pl* **crux·es 1** : a puzzling or difficult problem **2** ♦ : a crucial point

   ♦ core, gist, heart, nub, pith, pivot

¹**cry** \'krī\ *vb* **cried; cry·ing 1** ♦ : to call out : SHOUT **2** : to proclaim publicly : ADVERTISE **3** ♦ : to shed tears often noisily : WEEP **4** ♦ : to protest or complain loudly or vigorously — often used with *out*

   ♦ [1] bawl, call, holler, shout, vociferate, yell ♦ [3] bawl, blubber, sob, weep ♦ *usu* **cry out** [4] blurt, bolt, ejaculate, spout

²**cry** *n, pl* **cries 1** ♦ : a loud outcry **2** ♦ : an earnest plea : APPEAL, ENTREATY **3** : a fit of weeping **4** : the characteristic sound uttered by an animal **5** : DISTANCE — usu. used in the phrase *a far cry* **6** ♦ : a loud shout **7** ♦ : a word or motto that embodies a principle or guide to action of an individual or group

   ♦ [1, 6] holler, hoot, howl, shout, whoop, yell, yowl ♦ [2] appeal, entreaty, petition, plea, prayer, solicitation, suit, supplication ♦ [7] shibboleth, slogan, watchword

cry·ba·by \'krī-ˌbā-bē\ *n* ♦ : one who cries or complains easily or often

   ♦ complainer, grumbler, whiner

cry down *vb* ♦ : to lower in rank or reputation

   ♦ belittle, decry, deprecate, depreciate, diminish, discount, disparage, minimize, put down, write off

cryo·gen·ic \ˌkrī-ə-'je-nik\ *adj* : of or relating to the production of very low temperatures; *also* : involving the use of a very low temperature — **cryo·gen·i·cal·ly** \-ni-k(ə-)lē\ *adv*
cryo·gen·ics \-niks\ *n* : a branch of physics that relates to the production and effects of very low temperatures
cryo·lite \'krī-ə-ˌlīt\ *n* : a usu. white mineral used in making aluminum
crypt \'kript\ *n* : a chamber wholly or partly underground
cryp·tic \'krip-tik\ *adj* **1** ♦ : meant to be puzzling or mysterious **2** ♦ : having or seeming to have a hidden or ambiguous meaning

   ♦ ambiguous, dark, darkling, deep, enigmatic, equivocal, inscrutable, murky, mysterious, mystic, nebulous, obscure, occult

cryp·to·gram \'krip-tə-ˌgram\ *n* : a communication in cipher or code
cryp·tog·ra·phy \krip-'tä-grə-fē\ *n* : the coding and decoding of secret messages — **cryp·tog·ra·pher** \-fər\ *n*
crys·tal \'krist-ᵊl\ *n* **1** : transparent quartz **2** : something resembling crystal (as in transparency); *esp* : a clear glass used for table articles **3** : a body that is formed by solidification of a substance and has a regular repeating arrangement of atoms and often of external plane faces ⟨a salt ~⟩ **4** : the transparent cover of a watch dial
crystal clear *adj* : perfectly or transparently clear
crys·tal·line \'kris-tə-lən\ *adj* **1** : made of or resembling crystal **2** : very clear or sparkling
crys·tal·lise *Brit var of* CRYSTALLIZE
crys·tal·lize \'kris-tə-ˌlīz\ *vb* **-lized; -liz·ing 1** : to assume or

cause to assume a crystalline form **2** ♦ : to take or cause to take a definite form — **crys·tal·li·za·tion** \ˌkris-tə-lə-ˈzā-shən\ *n*

♦ form, jell, shape, solidify

crys·tal·log·ra·phy \ˌkris-tə-ˈlä-grə-fē\ *n* : the science dealing with the forms and structures of crystals — **crys·tal·log·ra·pher** *n*

cs *abbr* case; cases

Cs *symbol* cesium

CS *abbr* **1** civil service **2** county seat

CSA *abbr* Confederate States of America

C–section \ˈsē-ˌsek-shən\ *n* : CESAREAN SECTION

CSM *abbr* command sergeant major

CST *abbr* central standard time

ct *abbr* **1** carat **2** cent **3** count **4** county **5** court

CT *abbr* **1** central time **2** Connecticut

ctn *abbr* carton

ctr *abbr* **1** center **2** counter

CT scan \ˌsē-ˈtē-\ *n* : CAT SCAN

cu *abbr* cubic

Cu *symbol* copper

cub \ˈkəb\ *n* **1** : a young individual of some animals (as a fox, bear, or lion) **2** ♦ : a young person

♦ child, juvenile, kid, kiddo, moppet, whelp, youngster, youth

Cu·ban \ˈkyü-bən\ *n* : a native or inhabitant of Cuba — **Cuban** *adj*

Cu·ban sandwich \ˈkyü-bən-\ *n* : a usu. grilled and pressed sandwich served on a long split roll

cub·by·hole \ˈkə-bē-ˌhōl\ *n* : a snug place (as for storing things)

¹cube \ˈkyüb\ *n* **1** : a solid having 6 equal square sides **2** : the product obtained by taking a number 3 times as a factor ⟨27 is the ~ of 3⟩

²cube *vb* **cubed; cub·ing** **1** : to raise to the third power **2** : to form into a cube **3** : to cut into cubes

cube root *n* : a number whose cube is a given number

cu·bic \ˈkyü-bik\ *also* **cu·bi·cal** *adj* **1** : having the form of a cube **2** : being the volume of a cube whose edge is a specified unit **3** : having length, width, and height

cu·bi·cle \ˈkyü-bi-kəl\ *n* ♦ : a small separate space (as for sleeping or studying)

♦ bay, cabin, cell, chamber, compartment

cubic measure *n* : a unit (as cubic inch) for measuring volume

cubic zir·co·nia \-ˌzər-ˈkō-nē-ə\ *also* **cubic zirconium** *n* : a synthetic gemstone resembling a diamond made from an oxide of zirconium

cub·ism \ˈkyü-ˌbi-zəm\ *n* : a style of art characterized by the abstraction of natural forms into fragmented geometric shapes — **cub·ist** \-bist\ *n or adj*

cu·bit \ˈkyü-bət\ *n* : an ancient unit of length equal to about 18 inches (46 centimeters)

Cub Scout *n* : a member of the program of the Boy Scouts for boys in the first through fifth grades in school

cuck·old \ˈkə-kəld, ˈku̇-\ *n* : a man whose wife is unfaithful — **cuckold** *vb*

¹cuck·oo \ˈkü-kü, ˈku̇-\ *n, pl* **cuckoos** : a largely grayish brown European bird that lays its eggs in the nests of other birds for them to hatch

²cuckoo *n* : a silly or foolish person

³cuckoo *adj* ♦ : being one that is silly or foolish

♦ absurd, fatuous, foolish, nonsensical, nutty, senseless, silly, stupid

cu·cum·ber \ˈkyü-(ˌ)kəm-bər\ *n* : the long fleshy many-seeded fruit of a vine of the gourd family that is grown as a garden vegetable; *also* : this vine

cud \ˈkəd\ *n* : food brought up into the mouth by some animals (as cows) from the rumen to be chewed again

cud·dle \ˈkəd-ᵊl\ *vb* **cud·dled; cud·dling** **1** ♦ : to lie close : SNUGGLE **2** ♦ : to hold close for warmth or comfort or in affection

♦ nestle, nuzzle, snug, snuggle

cud·gel \ˈkə-jəl\ *n* ♦ : a short heavy club — **cudgel** *vb*

♦ bat, billy club, bludgeon, club, staff, truncheon

¹cue \ˈkyü\ *n* **1** : a word, phrase, or action in a play serving as a signal for the next actor to speak or act **2** ♦ : a hint, intimation, or suggestion as to what course of action to take or when to take it : HINT — **cue** *vb*

♦ clue, hint, indication, inkling, intimation, lead, suggestion

²cue *n* : a tapered rod for striking the balls in billiards or pool

³cue *n* : a waiting line esp. of persons or vehicles

cue ball *n* : the ball a player strikes with a cue in billiards or pool

¹cuff \ˈkəf\ *n* **1** : a part (as of a sleeve or glove) encircling the wrist **2** : the folded hem of a trouser leg

²cuff *vb* : to strike esp. with the open hand : SLAP

³cuff *n* : to strike esp. with or as if with the palm of the hand

cui·sine \kwi-ˈzēn\ *n* : style of cooking; *also* : the food prepared

cuke \ˈkyük\ *n* : CUCUMBER

cul–de–sac \ˌkəl-di-ˈsak, ˌku̇l-\ *n, pl* **culs–de–sac** *same or* ˌkəlz-, ˌku̇lz-\ *also* **cul–de–sacs** \ˌkəl-də-ˈsaks, ˌku̇l-\ : a street or passage closed at one end

cu·li·nary \ˈkə-lə-ˌner-ē, ˈkyü-\ *adj* : of or relating to the kitchen or cookery

¹cull \ˈkəl\ *vb* **1** ♦ : to pick out from a group **2** : to reduce or control the size of something (as a herd) by removal (as by hunting or slaughter) of esp. weak or sick individuals ⟨~*ing* a herd of cattle⟩

♦ choose, elect, handpick, name, opt, pick, prefer, select, single, take

²cull *n* ♦ : something rejected from a group or lot as worthless or inferior

♦ discard, reject, rejection

cul·mi·nate \ˈkəl-mə-ˌnāt\ *vb* **-nat·ed; -nat·ing** : to reach the highest point

cul·mi·na·tion \ˌkəl-mə-ˈnā-shən\ *n* ♦ : culminating position

♦ acme, apex, climax, crown, head, height, meridian, peak, pinnacle, summit, tip-top, top, zenith

cu·lotte \ˈkü-ˌlät, ˌkyü-, kü-ˌlät, kyü-\ *n* : a divided skirt; *also* : a garment having a divided skirt — often used in pl.

cul·pa·bil·i·ty \ˌkəl-pə-ˈbi-lə-tē\ *n* ♦ : the quality or state of being culpable

♦ blame, fault, guilt, rap

cul·pa·ble \ˈkəl-pə-bəl\ *adj* ♦ : deserving blame

♦ blamable, blameworthy, censurable, reprehensible

cul·prit \ˈkəl-prət\ *n* ♦ : one accused or guilty of a crime

♦ criminal, crook, felon, lawbreaker, malefactor, offender

cult \ˈkəlt\ *n* **1** : formal religious veneration **2** ♦ : a religious system or its adherents **3** : faddish devotion; *also* : a group of persons showing such devotion — **cult·ish** \ˈkəl-tish\ *adj* — **cult·ist** \-tist\ *n*

♦ creed, faith, persuasion, religion

cul·ti·va·ble \ˈkəl-tə-və-bəl\ *adj* : capable of being cultivated

cul·ti·var \ˈkəl-tə-ˌvär, -ˌver\ *n* : a plant variety originating and persisting under cultivation

cul·ti·vate \ˈkəl-tə-ˌvāt\ *vb* **-vat·ed; -vat·ing** **1** ♦ : to prepare for the raising of crops **2** ♦ : to foster the growth of by tilling or by labor and care ⟨~ vegetables⟩ **3** ♦ : to improve by labor, care, or study **4** : to help forward : ENCOURAGE, FURTHER ⟨~ the arts⟩ **5** : to seek the friendship of

♦ [1] farm, tend ♦ [2] advance, encourage, forward, foster, further, nourish, nurture, promote ♦ [3] crop, grow, promote, raise, rear, tend

cul·ti·vat·ed \ˈkəl-tə-ˌvāt-əd\ *adj* ♦ : having an education; *esp* : trained in the arts and social graces

♦ civilized, cultured, genteel, polished, refined *Ant* philistine, uncivilized, uncultured, unpolished, unrefined

cul·ti·va·tion \ˌkəl-tə-ˈvā-shən\ *n* ♦ : enlightenment and excellence of taste acquired by intellectual and aesthetic training

♦ civilization, culture, polish, refinement

cul·ti·va·tor \ˈkəl-tə-ˌvā-tər\ *n* ♦ : one that cultivates

♦ agriculturist, farmer, grower, planter, tiller

cul·ture \ˈkəl-chər\ *n* **1** : TILLAGE, CULTIVATION **2** : the act of developing by education and training **3** ♦ : refinement of intellectual and artistic taste **4** ♦ : the customary beliefs, social forms, and material traits of a racial, religious, or social group — **cul·tur·al** \ˈkəl-chə-rəl\ *adj* — **cul·tur·al·ly** *adv*

♦ [3] civilization, cultivation, polish, refinement ♦ [4] civilization, life, lifestyle, society

cul·tured \-chərd\ *adj* ♦ : having an education; *esp* : having an education beyond the average

♦ civilized, cultivated, genteel, polished, refined

cul·vert \ˈkəl-vərt\ *n* : a drain crossing under a road or railroad

cum *abbr* cumulative

cum·ber \ˈkəm-bər\ *vb* : to weigh down : BURDEN, HINDER

cum·ber·some \ˈkəm-bər-səm\ *adj* ♦ : hard to handle or manage because of size or weight

♦ awkward, clumsy, cranky, ungainly, unhandy, unwieldy *Ant* handy

cum·brous \'kəm-brəs\ *adj* : unwieldy because of heaviness and bulk : CUMBERSOME — **cum·brous·ly** *adv* — **cum·brous·ness** *n*
cum·in \'kə-mən, 'kyü-\ *n* : the seedlike fruit of a small annual herb related to the carrot that is used as a spice; *also* : this herb
cum·mer·bund \'kə-mər-ˌbənd, 'kəm-bər-\ *n* ♦ : a broad sash worn as a waistband

♦ belt, cincture, girdle, sash

cu·mu·la·tive \'kyü-myə-lə-tiv, -ˌlā-\ *adj* : increasing in force or value by successive additions
cu·mu·lo·nim·bus \ˌkyü-myə-lō-'nim-bəs\ *n* : an anvil-shaped cumulus cloud extending to great heights
cu·mu·lus \'kyü-myə-ləs\ *n, pl* **-li** \-ˌlī, -ˌlē\ : a massive cloud having a flat base and rounded outlines
cu·ne·i·form \kyù-'nē-ə-ˌfȯrm\ *adj* **1** : wedge-shaped **2** : composed of wedge-shaped characters
cun·ni·lin·gus \ˌkə-ni-'liŋ-gəs\ *also* **cun·ni·linc·tus** \-'liŋk-təs\ *n* : oral stimulation of the vulva or clitoris
¹**cun·ning** \'kə-niŋ\ *adj* **1** ♦ : dexterous or crafty in the use of special resources (as skill or knowledge) or in attaining an end : DEXTEROUS **2** ♦ : marked by wiliness and trickery **3** : CUTE — **cun·ning·ly** *adv*

♦ [1] clever, deft, dexterous, handy ♦ [2] artful, cagey, crafty, devious, foxy, guileful, slick, sly, subtle, wily

²**cunning** *n* **1** ♦ : skill in planning, making, or executing : SKILL **2** ♦ : skill in deceiving to gain an end

♦ [1] adeptness, adroitness, art, artfulness, artifice, artistry, cleverness, craft, deftness, masterfulness, skill ♦ [2] artfulness, artifice, caginess, canniness, craft, craftiness, guile, slyness, wiliness

¹**cup** \'kəp\ *n* **1** : a small bowl-shaped drinking vessel **2** : the contents of a cup **3** : the consecrated wine of the Communion **4** : something resembling a cup : a small bowl or hollow **5** : a half pint — **cup·ful** *n* — **cup·like** \-ˌlīk\ *adj*
²**cup** *vb* **cupped; cup·ping** : to curve into the shape of a cup
cup·board \'kə-bərd\ *n* ♦ : a small closet with shelves for food or dishes

♦ buffet, cabinet, closet, hutch, locker, sideboard

cup·cake \'kəp-ˌkāk\ *n* : a small cake baked in a cuplike mold
cu·pid \'kyü-pəd\ *n* : a winged naked figure of an infant often with a bow and arrow that represents the god Cupid
cu·pid·i·ty \kyù-'pi-də-tē\ *n, pl* **-ties** ♦ : excessive desire for money

♦ acquisitiveness, avarice, avidity, covetousness, greed, rapaciousness

cu·po·la \'kyü-pə-lə, -ˌlō\ *n* : a small structure on top of a roof or building
¹**cur** \'kər\ *n* **1** : a mongrel dog **2** ♦ : a surly or cowardly fellow

♦ beast, boor, churl, clown, creep, cretin, heel, jerk, joker, louse, lout, skunk, slob, snake

²**cur** *abbr* **1** currency **2** current
cu·rate \'kyùr-ət\ *n* **1** : a member of the clergy who is in charge of a parish **2** : a member of the clergy who assists a rector or vicar — **cu·ra·cy** \-ə-sē\ *n*
cu·ra·tive \-ə-tiv\ *adj* : relating to or used in the cure of diseases — **curative** *n*
cu·ra·tor \'kyùr-ˌā-tər, kyù-'rā-\ *n* : CUSTODIAN; *esp* : one in charge of a place of exhibit (as a museum or zoo)
¹**curb** \'kərb\ *n* **1** : a bit that exerts pressure on a horse's jaws **2** ♦ : one that arrests, limits, or restrains : CHECK, RESTRAINT **3** : a raised edging (as of stone or concrete) along a paved street

♦ check, condition, constraint, fetter, limitation, restraint, restriction

²**curb** *vb* ♦ : to hold in or back : RESTRAIN

♦ bridle, check, constrain, contain, control, govern, inhibit, regulate, rein, restrain, tame

curb·ing \'kər-biŋ\ *n* **1** : the material for a curb **2** : CURB
curd \'kərd\ *n* : the thick protein-rich part of coagulated milk
cur·dle \'kərd-ᵊl\ *vb* **cur·dled; cur·dling** : to form curds; *also* : SPOIL, SOUR
¹**cure** \'kyùr\ *n* **1** : spiritual care **2** : recovery or relief from disease **3** ♦ : a curative agent : REMEDY **4** : a course or period of treatment

♦ drug, medicine, pharmaceutical, remedy, specific

²**cure** *vb* **cured; cur·ing** **1** ♦ : to restore to health : HEAL; *also* : to

become cured **2** : to process for storage or use ⟨∼ bacon⟩ — **cur·able** *adj*

♦ heal, mend, rehabilitate

cu·ré \kyù-'rā\ *n* : a parish priest
cure–all \'kyùr-ˌȯl\ *n* : a remedy for all ills : PANACEA
cu·ret·tage \ˌkyùr-ə-'täzh\ *n* : a surgical scraping or cleaning of a body part (as the uterus)
cur·few \'kər-ˌfyü\ *n* : a regulation that specified persons (as children) be off the streets at a set hour of the evening; *also* : the sounding of a signal (as a bell) at this hour
cu·ria \'kyùr-ē-ə, 'kùr-\ *n, pl* **cu·ri·ae** \'kyùr-ē-ˌē, 'kùr-ē-ˌī\ *often cap* : the body of congregations, tribunals, and offices through which the pope governs the Roman Catholic Church
cu·rie \'kyùr-ē\ *n* : a unit of radioactivity equal to 37 billion disintegrations per second
cu·rio \'kyùr-ē-ˌō\ *n, pl* **cu·ri·os** : an object or article valued because it is strange or rare
cu·ri·os·i·ty \ˌkyùr-ē-'ä-sə-tē\ *n* **1** ♦ : one that arouses interest esp. for uncommon or exotic characteristics **2** ♦ : an unusual knickknack

♦ [1] exotic, oddity, rarity ♦ [2] bauble, gewgaw, knickknack, novelty, tchotchke, trinket

cu·ri·ous \'kyùr-ē-əs\ *adj* **1** ♦ : having a desire to investigate and learn **2** ♦ : exciting attention as strange, novel, or unexpected : STRANGE, UNUSUAL, ODD

♦ [1] inquisitive, nosy, prying *Ant* incurious, uncurious ♦ [2] extraordinary, funny, odd, peculiar, rare, singular, strange, unaccustomed, uncommon, uncustomary, unique, unusual, weird

cu·ri·ous·ly *adv* **1** : in a curious manner **2** : as is curious
cu·ri·um \'kyùr-ē-əm\ *n* : a metallic radioactive element produced artificially
¹**curl** \'kərl\ *vb* **1** : to form into ringlets **2** ♦ : to move or progress in curves or spirals : COIL — **curl·er** *n*

♦ coil, entwine, spiral, twine, twist, wind

²**curl** *n* **1** : a lock of hair that coils : RINGLET **2** : something having a spiral or twisted form — **curly** *adj*
cur·lew \'kər-lü, 'kərl-yü\ *n, pl* **curlews** *or* **curlew** : any of various long-legged brownish birds that have a down-curved bill and are related to the sandpipers and snipes
curli·cue \'kər-li-ˌkyü\ *n* : a fancifully curved or spiral figure
curl up *vb* ♦ : to arrange oneself in or as if in a ball or curl

♦ nestle, snug, snuggle

cur·mud·geon \(ˌ)kər-'mə-jən\ *n* ♦ : a crusty, ill-tempered, and usu. old man

♦ bear, complainer, crab, crank, grouch, grumbler, whiner

cur·rant \'kər-ənt\ *n* **1** : a small seedless raisin **2** : the acid berry of a shrub related to the gooseberry; *also* : this plant
cur·ren·cy \'kər-ən-sē\ *n, pl* **-cies** **1** : general use or acceptance **2** ♦ : something that is in circulation as a medium of exchange : MONEY

♦ cash, dough, lucre, money, pelf, tender

¹**cur·rent** \'kər-ənt\ *adj* **1** ♦ : occurring in or belonging to the present **2** : used as a medium of exchange **3** ♦ : generally accepted or practiced

♦ [1] contemporary, hot, mod, modern, new, newfangled, redhot, space-age, ultramodern, up-to-date ♦ [3] conventional, customary, popular, standard, stock, usual *Ant* nonstandard, unconventional, unpopular, unusual

²**current** *n* **1** : the part of a body of fluid moving continuously in a certain direction; *also* : the swiftest part of a stream **2** : a flow of electric charge; *also* : the rate of such flow **3** ♦ : a tendency or course of events that is usu. the result of an interplay of forces

♦ drift, leaning, run, tendency, tide, trend, wind

cur·ric·u·lum \kə-'ri-kyə-ləm\ *n, pl* **-la** \-lə\ *also* **-lums** : the courses offered by an educational institution
¹**cur·ry** \'kər-ē\ *vb* **cur·ried; cur·ry·ing** **1** : to clean the coat of (a horse) with a currycomb **2** : to treat (tanned leather) esp. by incorporating oil or grease — **curry favor** : to seek to gain favor by flattery or attention
²**cur·ry** *n, pl* **cur·ries** : a powder of pungent spices used in cooking; *also* : a food seasoned with curry
cur·ry·comb \-ˌkōm\ *n* : a comb used esp. to curry horses — **currycomb** *vb*
¹**curse** \'kərs\ *n* **1** ♦ : a prayer for harm to come upon one **2**

: something that is cursed **3** : evil or misfortune coming as if in response to a curse

♦ anathema, execration, imprecation, malediction *Ant* benediction, benison, blessing

²**curse** *vb* **cursed; curs•ing 1** : to call on divine power to send injury upon **2** : BLASPHEME **3** ♦ : to bring great evil upon : AFFLICT

♦ afflict, agonize, bedevil, harrow, martyr, persecute, plague, rack, torment, torture

cur•sive \'kər-siv\ *adj* : written with the strokes of the letters joined together and the angles rounded

cur•sor \'kər-sər\ *n* : a visual cue (as a pointer) on a computer screen that indicates position (as for data entry)

cur•so•ri•ly \-rə-lē\ *adj* ♦ : in a cursory manner

♦ hastily, headlong, hurriedly, pell-mell, precipitately, rashly

cur•so•ry \'kər-sə-rē\ *adj* ♦ : rapidly and often superficially done : HASTY

♦ hasty, headlong, pell-mell, precipitate, precipitous, rash

curt \'kərt\ *adj* ♦ : rudely short or abrupt — **curt•ly** *adv* — **curt•ness** *n*

♦ abrupt, bluff, blunt, brusque, snippy

cur•tail \(ˌ)kər-'tāl\ *vb* ♦ : to cut off the end of : SHORTEN — **cur•tail•ment** *n*

♦ abbreviate, abridge, cut back, shorten

¹**cur•tain** \'kərt-ᵊn\ *n* **1** : a hanging screen that can be drawn back esp. at a window **2** : the screen between the stage and auditorium of a theater

²**curtain** *vb* ♦ : to veil with or as if with a curtain

♦ blanket, blot out, cloak, conceal, cover, enshroud, hide, mask, obscure, occult, screen, shroud, veil

curt•sy *also* **curt•sey** \'kərt-sē\ *n, pl* **curtsies** *or* **curtseys** : a courteous bow made by women chiefly by bending the knees — **curtsy** *also* **curtsey** *vb*

cur•va•ceous *also* **cur•va•cious** \ˌkər-'vā-shəs\ *adj* : having curves suggestive of a well-proportioned feminine figure

cur•va•ture \'kər-və-ˌchủr\ *n* **1** : a measure or amount of curving : BEND **2** : curved part

¹**curve** \'kərv\ *vb* **curved; curv•ing** ♦ : to bend from a straight line or course

♦ arc, arch, bend, bow, crook, hook, round, sweep, swerve, wheel *Ant* straighten

²**curve** *n* **1** : a line esp. when curved **2** ♦ : something that bends or curves without angles ⟨a ∼ in the road⟩ **3** : a baseball pitch thrown so that it swerves esp. downward and to one side — **curvy** \'kər-vē\ *adj*

♦ angle, arc, arch, bend, bow, crook, turn, wind

cur•vet \(ˌ)kər-'vet\ *n* : a prancing leap of a horse — **curvet** *vb*

¹**cush•ion** \'kủ-shən\ *n* **1** : a soft pillow or pad to rest on or against **2** : the springy pad inside the rim of a billiard table **3** ♦ : something soft that prevents discomfort or protects against injury

♦ buffer, bumper, fender, pad

²**cushion** *vb* **1** : to provide (as a seat) with a cushion **2** ♦ : to soften or lessen the force or shock of

♦ buffer, gentle, soften

cusp \'kəsp\ *n* ♦ : a pointed end or part (as of a tooth)

♦ apex, end, pike, point, tip

cus•pid \'kəs-pəd\ *n* : a canine tooth

cus•pi•dor \'kəs-pə-ˌdȯr\ *n* : SPITTOON

cus•tard \'kəs-tərd\ *n* : a sweetened cooked mixture of milk and eggs

cus•to•di•al \ˌkəs-'tō-dē-əl\ *adj* : marked by watching and protecting rather than seeking to cure ⟨∼ care⟩

cus•to•di•an \ˌkəs-'tō-dē-ən\ *n* ♦ : one that protects and maintains; *esp* : one who has custody (as of a building)

♦ caretaker, guardian, janitor, keeper, warden, watchman ♦ defender, defense (*or* defence), guard, protection, protector

cus•to•dy \'kəs-tə-dē\ *n, pl* **-dies** ♦ : immediate charge and control

♦ care, guardianship, keeping, safekeeping, trust, ward

¹**cus•tom** \'kəs-təm\ *n* **1** ♦ : habitual course of action : recognized usage **2** *pl* : taxes levied on imports **3** : business patronage

♦ fashion, habit, pattern, practice, trick, way, wont

²**custom** *adj* **1** : made to personal order **2** : doing work only on order

cus•tom•ary \'kəs-tə-ˌmer-ē\ *adj* **1** ♦ : based on or established by custom **2** ♦ : commonly practiced or observed — **cus•tom•ar•i•ly** *adv*

♦ [1] classical, conventional, traditional ♦ [2] conventional, current, popular, standard, stock, usual

cus•tom–built \'kəs-təm-'bilt\ *adj* : built to individual order

cus•tom•er \'kəs-tə-mər\ *n* **1** ♦ : one that purchases a commodity or service; *esp* : a regular or frequent buyer **2** : an individual usu. having some specified distinctive trait

♦ guest, patron

cus•tom•house \'kəs-təm-ˌhaủs\ *n* : the building where customs are paid

cus•tom•ise *Brit var of* CUSTOMIZE

cus•tom•ize \'kəs-tə-ˌmīz\ *vb* **-ized; -iz•ing** : to build, fit, or alter according to individual specifications

cus•tom–made \'kəs-təm-'mād\ *adj* ♦ : made to individual order

♦ custom, tailored *Ant* mass-produced, ready-made

¹**cut** \'kət\ *vb* **cut; cut•ting 1** ♦ : to penetrate or divide with a sharp edge : CLEAVE, GASH; *also* : to experience the growth of (a tooth) through the gum **2** : to hurt the feelings of **3** : to strike sharply **4** ♦ : to diminish or reduce by or as if by paring : SHORTEN, REDUCE **5** : to remove by severing or paring **6** : INTERSECT, CROSS **7** : to divide into parts **8 a** : to go quickly or change direction abruptly **b** : to veer from a direct line **9** : to cause to stop **10** ♦ : to proceed obliquely from a straight course — often used with *across* **11** : to remove (text, etc.) from a computer document for pasting elsewhere

♦ [1] rip, slash, slice, slit ♦ [4] bob, clip, crop, cut back, dock, lop, nip, prune, reduce, shave, shear, shorten, trim ♦ *usu* **cut across** [10] cover, crisscross, cross, follow, go, pass, proceed, travel, traverse

²**cut** *n* **1** : something made by cutting : GASH, CLEFT **2** ♦ : a portion belonging to, due to, or contributed by an individual or group : SHARE **3** : a segment or section of a meat carcass **4** : an excavated channel or roadway **5** : a sharp stroke or blow **6** : REDUCTION ⟨∼ in wages⟩ **7** : the shape or manner in which a thing is cut **8** ♦ : a grade or step

♦ [2] allotment, allowance, part, portion, proportion, quota, share ♦ [8] degree, grade, inch, notch, peg, phase, point, stage, step

cut–and–dried \ˌkət-ᵊn-'drīd\ *also* **cut–and–dry** \-'drī\ *adj* : according to a plan, set procedure, or formula

cu•ta•ne•ous \kyủ-'tā-nē-əs\ *adj* : of, relating to, or affecting the skin

cut•back \'kət-ˌbak\ *n* **1** : something cut back **2** : REDUCTION

cut back 1 ♦ : to shorten by cutting **2** ♦ : to remake in a smaller size

♦ [1] bob, clip, crop, cut, dock, lop, nip, prune, shave, shear, trim ♦ [2] abbreviate, abridge, curtail, shorten

cut down *vb* ♦ : to strike to the ground with or as if with a sharp blow

♦ chop, fell, hew

cute \'kyüt\ *adj* **cut•er; cut•est 1** : CLEVER, SHREWD **2** ♦ : daintily attractive : PRETTY

♦ attractive, beautiful, bonny, fair, pretty

cu•ti•cle \'kyü-ti-kəl\ *n* **1** : an outer layer (as of skin or a leaf) **2** : dead or horny epidermis esp. around a fingernail — **cu•tic•u•lar** \kyủ-'ti-kyə-lər\ *adj*

cut in *vb* **1** ♦ : to thrust oneself between others **2** : to interrupt a dancing couple and take one as one's partner

♦ break, chime in, interpose, interrupt, intrude

cut•lass \'kət-ləs\ *n* : a short heavy curved sword

cut•ler \'kət-lər\ *n* : one who makes, deals in, or repairs cutlery

cut•lery \'kət-lə-rē\ *n* : edged or cutting tools; *esp* : implements for cutting and eating food

cut•let \'kət-lət\ *n* **1** : a slice of meat (as veal) for broiling or frying **2** ♦ : a flat croquette of chopped meat or fish

♦ fritter, patty

cut•off \'kət-ˌȯf\ *n* **1** : the channel formed when a stream cuts through the neck of an oxbow; *also* : SHORTCUT **2** : a device for cutting off **3** *pl* : shorts orig. made from jeans with the legs cut off at the knees or higher

cut off *vb* ♦ : to set apart from others

♦ insulate, isolate, seclude, segregate, separate, sequester

cut·out \'kət-ˌaut\ *n* : something cut out or prepared for cutting out from something else ⟨a page of animal ∼s⟩

cut out *vb* **1** : to determine or assign through necessity ⟨had her work *cut out* for her⟩ **2** : DISCONNECT **3** ♦ : to cease operating ⟨the engine *cut out*⟩ **4** : ELIMINATE ⟨*cut out* unnecessary expense⟩ **5** : to put an end to

♦ break, break down, conk, crash, die, fail, stall

cut–rate \'kət-'rāt\ *adj* **1** ♦ : relating to or dealing in goods sold at reduced rates **2** ♦ : of second or inferior quality or value

♦ [1] cheap, low, reasonable ♦ [2] bad, bum, cheap, coarse, common, execrable, inferior, junky, lousy, mediocre, miserable, poor, rotten, second-rate, shoddy, sleazy, terrible, trashy, wretched

cut·ter \'kə-tər\ *n* **1** : a tool or a machine for cutting **2** : a ship's boat for carrying stores and passengers **3** : a small armed vessel in government service **4** : a light sleigh

¹**cut·throat** \'kət-ˌthrōt\ *n* : MURDERER

²**cutthroat** *adj* **1** : MURDEROUS, CRUEL **2** ♦ : marked by unprincipled practices ⟨∼ competition⟩

♦ immoral, Machiavellian, unconscionable, unethical, unprincipled, unscrupulous

cutthroat trout *n* : a large American trout with a red mark under the jaw

¹**cut·ting** \'kə-tiŋ\ *n* : a piece of a plant able to grow into a new plant

²**cutting** *adj* **1** ♦ : made for cutting, severing, or dividing : SHARP, EDGED **2** ♦ : marked by piercing cold **3** ♦ : likely to hurt the feelings : SARCASTIC ⟨a ∼ remark⟩

♦ [1] edgy, ground, keen, sharp ♦ [2] biting, bitter, keen, penetrating, piercing, raw, sharp ♦ [3] acrid, biting, caustic, mordant, pungent, sarcastic, satiric, scathing, sharp, tart

cut·tle·fish \'kə-tᵊl-ˌfish\ *n* : any of various marine mollusks having eight arms and two usu. longer tentacles and an internal shell (**cut·tle·bone** \-ˌbōn\) composed of calcium compounds

cut·up \'kət-ˌəp\ *n* : a person who clowns or acts boisterously

cut up *vb* ♦ : to behave in a comic, boisterous, or unruly manner

♦ act up, clown, fool, monkey, show off, skylark

cut·worm \-ˌwərm\ *n* : any of various smooth-bodied moth larvae that feed on plants at night

cw *abbr* clockwise

CWO *abbr* **1** cash with order **2** chief warrant officer

cwt *abbr* hundredweight

-cy \sē\ *n suffix* **1** : action : practice ⟨mendican*cy*⟩ **2** : rank : office ⟨chaplain*cy*⟩ **3** : body : class ⟨constituen*cy*⟩ **4** : state : quality ⟨accura*cy*⟩

cy·an \'sī-ˌan, -ən\ *n* : a greenish blue color

cy·a·nide \'sī-ə-ˌnīd, -nəd\ *n* : a poisonous compound of carbon and nitrogen with another element (as potassium)

cy·ber \'sī-bər\ *adj* : of, relating to, or involving computers or computer networks

cyber- *comb form* : computer : computer network

cy·ber·at·tack \'sī-bər-ə-ˌtak\ *n* : an attempt to gain illegal access to a computer or computer system for the purpose of causing damage or harm

cy·ber·bul·ly·ing \-ˌbú-lē-iŋ\ *n* : the electronic posting of mean-spirited messages about a person

cy·ber·ca·fe \'sī-bər-ka-ˌfā\ *n* : a small restaurant offering use of computers with Internet access

cy·ber·crime \-ˌkrīm\ *n* : criminal activity (as fraud or theft) committed using a computer

cy·ber·net·ics \ˌsī-bər-'ne-tiks\ *n* : the science of communication and control theory that is concerned esp. with the comparative study of automatic control systems — **cy·ber·net·ic** *adj*

cy·ber·punk \'sī-bər-ˌpəŋk\ *n* **1** : science fiction dealing with computer-dominated future societies **2** : HACKER 3

cy·ber·se·cu·ri·ty \-si-ˌkyùr-ə-tē\ *n* : protection of a computer or computer system against unauthorized access or attack

cy·ber·sex \'sī-bər-ˌseks\ *n* **1** : online sex-oriented conversations **2** : sex-oriented material available on a computer

cy·ber·space \'sī-bər-ˌspās\ *n* : the online world of computer networks

cy·ber·ter·ror·ism \-ˌter-ər-ˌi-zəm\ *n* : terrorist activities intended to damage or disrupt computer systems

cy·cla·men \'sī-klə-mən\ *n* : any of a genus of plants related to the primroses and grown for their showy nodding flowers

¹**cy·cle** \'sī-kəl\ *n* **1** : a period of time occupied by a series of events that repeat themselves regularly and in the same order **2** : a recurring round of operations or events **3** : one complete occurrence of a periodic process (as a vibration or current alternation) **4** : a circular or spiral arrangement **5** ♦ : a long period of time : AGE **6** : BICYCLE **7** : MOTORCYCLE — **cy·clic** \'sī-klik, 'si-\ *or* **cy·cli·cal** \-kli-kəl\ *adj* — **cy·cli·cal·ly** \-k(ə-)lē\ *also* **cy·clic·ly** *adv*

♦ age, eon (*or* aeon), eternity

²**cycle** *vb* **cy·cled; cy·cling** : to ride a cycle — **cy·clist** \'sī-klist, -klə-list\ *n*

cy·clone \'sī-ˌklōn\ *n* **1** : a storm or system of winds that rotates about a center of low atmospheric pressure and advances at 20 to 30 miles (about 30 to 50 kilometers) an hour **2** : TORNADO — **cy·clon·ic** \sī-'klä-nik\ *adj*

cy·clo·pe·dia *or* **cy·clo·pae·dia** \ˌsī-klə-'pē-dē-ə\ *n* : ENCYCLOPEDIA

cy·clo·tron \'sī-klə-ˌträn\ *n* : a device for giving high speed to charged particles by magnetic and electric fields

cyg·net \'sig-nət\ *n* : a young swan

cyl *abbr* cylinder

cyl·in·der \'si-lən-dər\ *n* : the solid figure formed by turning a rectangle about one side as an axis; *also* : a body or space of this form ⟨an engine ∼⟩ ⟨a bullet in the ∼ of a revolver⟩ — **cy·lin·dri·cal** \sə-'lin-dri-kəl\ *adj*

cyn·ic \'si-nik\ *n* : one who attributes all actions to selfish motives — **cyn·i·cal** \-ni-kəl\ *adj* — **cyn·i·cal·ly** \-k(ə-)lē\ *adv* — **cyn·i·cism** \si-nə-ˌsi-zəm\ *n*

cy·no·sure \'sī-nə-ˌshùr, 'si-\ *n* ♦ : a center of attraction or attention

♦ base, center (*or* centre), core, eye, focus, heart, hub, mecca, nucleus, seat

CYO *abbr* Catholic Youth Organization

cy·pher *chiefly Brit var of* CIPHER

cy·press \'sī-prəs\ *n* **1** : any of a genus of scaly-leaved evergreen trees and shrubs **2** : BALD CYPRESS **3** : the wood of a cypress

Cyp·ri·ot \'si-prē-ət, -ˌät\ *or* **Cyp·ri·ote** \-ˌōt, -ət\ *n* : a native or inhabitant of Cyprus — **Cypriot** *adj*

cyst \'sist\ *n* : an abnormal closed bodily sac usu. containing liquid — **cys·tic** \'sis-tik\ *adj*

cystic fibrosis *n* : a common hereditary disease marked esp. by deficiency of pancreatic enzymes, by respiratory symptoms, and by excessive loss of salt in the sweat

cy·tol·o·gy \sī-'tä-lə-jē\ *n* : a branch of biology dealing with cells — **cy·to·log·i·cal** \ˌsīt-ᵊl-'ä-ji-kəl\ *or* **cy·to·log·ic** \-jik\ *adj* — **cy·tol·o·gist** \sī-'tä-lə-jist\ *n*

cy·to·plasm \'sī-tə-ˌpla-zəm\ *n* : the protoplasm of a cell that lies external to the nucleus — **cy·to·plas·mic** \ˌsī-tə-'plaz-mik\ *adj*

cy·to·sine \'sī-tə-ˌsēn\ *n* : a chemical base that is a pyrimidine coding genetic information in DNA and RNA

CZ *abbr* **1** Canal Zone **2** cubic zirconia

czar \'zär, 'tsär\ *n* **1** : the ruler of Russia until 1917 **2** ♦ : one having great authority — **czar·ist** \-ist\ *n or adj*

♦ baron, king, magnate, mogul, prince, tycoon

cza·ri·na \zä-'rē-nə\ *n* : the wife of a czar

Czech \'chek\ *n* **1** : a native or inhabitant of Czechoslovakia or the Czech Republic **2** : the language of the Czechs — **Czech** *adj*

¹d \'dē\ *n, pl* **d's** *or* **ds** \'dēz\ *often cap* **1** : the 4th letter of the English alphabet **2** : a grade rating a student's work as poor

²d *abbr, often cap* **1** date **2** daughter **3** day **4** dead **5** deceased **6** degree **7** Democrat **8** penny; pence **9** depart; departure **10** diameter

D *symbol* deuterium

DA *abbr* **1** deposit account **2** district attorney **3** don't answer

¹dab \'dab\ *n* **1 a** ♦ : a sudden blow or thrust : POKE **b** : PECK **2** ♦ : a small amount **3** : a gentle touch or stroke : PAT **4** : DAUB

♦ [1a] dig, jab, poke ♦ [2] bit, hint, lick, little, particle, spot, touch

²dab *vb* **dabbed; dab·bing** **1** : to strike or touch gently : PAT **2** : to apply lightly or irregularly : DAUB — **dab·ber** *n*

dab·ble \'da-bəl\ *vb* **dab·bled; dab·bling** **1** : to wet by splashing **2** : to paddle or play in or as if in water **3** : to work or involve oneself without serious effort — **dab·bler** *n*

da ca·po \dä-'kä-(ˌ)pō\ *adv or adj* : from the beginning — used as a direction in music to repeat

dace \'dās\ *n, pl* **dace** : any of various small No. American freshwater fishes related to the carp

da·cha \'dä-chə\ *n* : a Russian country house

dachs·hund \'däks-ˌhunt\ *n, pl* **dachshunds** : any of a breed of long-bodied short-legged dogs of German origin

dac·tyl \'dakt-ᵊl\ *n* : a metrical foot of one accented syllable followed by two unaccented syllables — **dac·tyl·ic** \dak-'ti-lik\ *adj or n*

dad \'dad\ *n* : a male parent : FATHER 1

Da·da \'dä-(ˌ)dä\ *n* : a movement in art and literature based on deliberate irrationality and negation of traditional artistic values — **da·da·ism** \-ˌi-zəm\ *n, often cap* — **da·da·ist** \-ˌist\ *n or adj, often cap*

dad·dy \'da-dē\ *n, pl* **daddies** ♦ : a male human parent : FATHER 1

♦ father, papa, pop

dad·dy long·legs \ˌda-dē-'lȯŋ-ˌlegz\ *n, pl* **daddy longlegs** : any of an order of arachnids resembling the true spiders but having small rounded bodies and long slender legs

daemon *var of* DEMON

daf·fo·dil \'da-fə-ˌdil\ *n* : any of various bulbous herbs with usu. large flowers having a trumpetlike center

daf·fy \'da-fē\ *adj* **daf·fi·er; -est** **1** : exhibiting or indicative of a lack of common sense or sound judgment : FOOLISH **2** : disordered in mind : INSANE — not used technically

daft \'daft\ *adj* **1** ♦ : exhibiting or indicative of a lack of common sense or sound judgment : FOOLISH **2** *chiefly Brit* : disordered in mind : INSANE — not used technically

♦ absurd, cuckoo, fatuous, foolish, nonsensical, nutty, senseless, silly, stupid

daft·ness \-nəs\ *n* ♦ : the quality or state of being daft

♦ absurdity, asininity, balminess, fatuity, folly, foolishness, inanity, silliness, simplicity, zaniness

dag *abbr* dekagram

dag·ger \'da-gər\ *n* **1** : a sharp pointed knife for stabbing **2** : a character † used as a reference mark or to indicate a death date

da·guerre·o·type \də-'ger-(ē-)ə-ˌtīp\ *n* : an early photograph produced on a silver or a silver-covered copper plate

dahl·ia \'dal-yə, 'däl-\ *n* : any of a genus of tuberous herbs related to the daisies and having showy flowers

¹dai·ly \'dā-lē\ *adj* **1** : occurring, done, or used every day or every weekday **2** : of or relating to every day ⟨~ visitors⟩ **3** : computed in terms of one day ⟨~ wages⟩ — **dai·li·ness** \-lē-nəs\ *n* — **daily** *adv*

²daily *n, pl* **dailies** : a newspaper published every weekday

daily double *n* : a system of betting on races in which the bettor must pick the winners of two stipulated races in order to win

dain·ti·ness \'dān-tē-nəs\ *n* ♦ : the quality or state of being dainty

♦ delicacy, fineness, fragility

¹dain·ty \'dān-tē\ *n, pl* **dainties** ♦ : something delicious or pleasing to the taste : DELICACY

♦ delicacy, goody, tidbit, treat

²dainty *adj* **dain·ti·er; -est** **1** ♦ : pleasing to taste **2** : delicately pretty **3** ♦ : marked by fastidious discrimination or finicky taste — **dain·ti·ly** \-ti-lē\ *adv*

♦ [1] choice, delicate, elegant, exquisite, rare, select ♦ [3] choosy, delicate, demanding, exacting, fastidious, finicky, fussy, nice, old= maidish, particular, picky

dai·qui·ri \'dī-kə-rē, 'da-kə-rē\ *n* : a cocktail made of usu. rum, lime juice, and sugar

dairy \'der-ē\ *n, pl* **dair·ies** **1** : CREAMERY **2** : a farm specializing in milk production **3** : food made primarily of or from milk

dairy·ing \'der-ē-iŋ\ *n* : the business of operating a dairy

dairy·maid \-ˌmād\ *n* : a woman employed in a dairy

dairy·man \-mən, -ˌman\ *n* : a person who operates a dairy farm or works in a dairy

da·is \'dā-əs\ *n* ♦ : a raised platform usu. above the floor of a hall or large room

♦ platform, podium, rostrum, stage, stand

dai·sy \'dā-zē\ *n, pl* **daisies** : any of numerous composite plants having flower heads in which the marginal flowers resemble petals

dai·sy-chain \-ˌchān\ *vb* : to link (as computer components) together in series — **daisy chain** *n*

daisy wheel *n* : a disk with spokes bearing type that serves as the printing element of an electric typewriter or printer; *also* : a printer that uses such a disk

Da·ko·ta \də-'kō-tə\ *n, pl* **Dakotas** *also* **Dakota** : a member of an Indigenous people of the northern Mississippi valley; *also* : their language

dal *abbr* dekaliter

dale \'dāl\ *n* ♦ : a long depression between ranges of hills or mountains : VALLEY

♦ hollow, valley

dal·li·ance \'da-lē-əns\ *n* ♦ : an act of dallying

♦ frolic, fun, play, relaxation, sport

dal·ly \'da-lē\ *vb* **dal·lied; dal·ly·ing** **1** ♦ : to act playfully; *esp* : to play amorously **2** ♦ : to waste time **3** : to move slowly : LINGER

♦ [1] disport, frolic, play, recreate, rollick, sport ♦ [2] dawdle, dillydally, hang around, hang out, idle, loaf, loll, lounge

dal·ma·tian \dal-'mā-shən\ *n, often cap* : any of a breed of medium-sized dogs having a white short-haired coat with many black or brown spots

¹dam \'dam\ *n* : the female parent of an animal and esp. of a domestic animal

²dam *n* ♦ : a barrier (as across a stream) to stop the flow of water

♦ dike, embankment, levee

³dam *vb* **1** : to provide or restrain with a dam **2** ♦ : to stop up : BLOCK

♦ block, choke, clog, close (off), congest, jam, obstruct, plug (up), stop (up), stuff

⁴dam *abbr* dekameter

¹dam·age \'da-mij\ *n* **1** ♦ : loss or harm due to injury to persons, property, or reputation **2** *pl* ♦ : compensation in money imposed by law for loss or injury ⟨sued for ~s⟩

♦ [1] detriment, harm, hurt, injury ♦ *usu* **damages** [2] fine, forfeit, mulct, penalty ♦ *usu* **damages** [2] compensation, indemnity, quittance, recompense, redress, remuneration, reparation, requital, restitution, satisfaction

²damage *vb* **dam·aged; dam·ag·ing** ♦ : to cause damage to

♦ blemish, break, cripple, deface, disfigure, flaw, harm, hurt, injure, mar, spoil, vitiate *Ant* fix, mend, patch, rebuild, recondition, reconstruct, renovate, repair, revamp

dam·ag·ing *adj* ♦ : causing or able to cause damage

♦ adverse, bad, baleful, baneful, deleterious, detrimental, evil, harmful, hurtful, ill, injurious, mischievous, noxious, pernicious, prejudicial

dam·a·scene \'da-mə-ˌsēn\ *vb* **-scened; -scen·ing** : to ornament (as iron or steel) with wavy patterns or with inlaid work of precious metals

dam·ask \'da-məsk\ *n* **1** : a firm lustrous reversible figured fabric used for household linen **2** : a tough steel having decorative wavy lines

dame \'dām\ *n* **1** ♦ : a woman of rank, station, or authority **2** ♦ : an elderly woman **3** : WOMAN

  ♦ [1] gentlewoman, lady, noblewoman ♦ [2] dowager, matriarch, matron

damn \'dam\ *vb* **1** : to condemn to a punishment or fate; *esp* : to condemn esp. to hell **2** ♦ : to condemn as invalid, illegal, immoral, bad, or harmful **3** : CURSE — **damned** *adj*

  ♦ censure, condemn, decry, denounce, reprehend, reprobate

dam·na·ble \'dam-nə-bəl\ *adj* **1** : liable to or deserving punishment **2** : DETESTABLE ⟨~ weather⟩ — **dam·na·bly** \-blē\ *adv*

dam·na·tion \dam-'nā-shən\ *n* **1** : the act of damning **2** : the state of being damned

¹**damp** \'damp\ *n* **1** : a noxious gas **2** : the small amount of liquid that causes dampness : MOISTURE

²**damp** *vb* : to check or diminish the activity or vigor of : DAMPEN

³**damp** *adj* : MOIST

damp·en \'dam-pən\ *vb* **1** ♦ : to check or diminish in activity or vigor **2** : to make or become damp

  ♦ blunt, deaden, dull, numb

damp·er \'dam-pər\ *n* **1** : a dulling or deadening influence ⟨put a ~ on the party⟩ *esp* : a valve or movable plate (as in the flue of a stove, furnace, or fireplace) to regulate the draft

damp·ness \'damp-nəs\ *n* : the quality or state of being damp

dam·sel \'dam-zəl\ *n* : a young woman : MAIDEN

dam·sel·fly \-ˌflī\ *n* : any of a group of insects that are closely related to the dragonflies but fold their wings above the body when at rest

dam·son \'dam-zən\ *n* : a plum with acid purple fruit; *also* : its fruit

Dan *abbr* Daniel

¹**dance** \'dans\ *vb* **danced; danc·ing** **1** ♦ : to glide, step, or move through a set series of movements usu. to music **2** ♦ : to move quickly up and down or about **3** : to perform or take part in as a dancer — **danc·er** *n*

  ♦ [1] foot, step ♦ [2] dart, flit, flutter, zip

²**dance** *n* **1** : an act or instance of dancing **2** ♦ : a social gathering for dancing **3** : a piece of music (as a waltz) by which dancing may be guided **4** : the art of dancing

  ♦ ball, formal, hop, prom

D & C *n* : a surgical procedure that involves stretching the cervix and scraping the inside walls of the uterus (as to test for cancer or to perform an abortion)

dan·de·li·on \'dan-də-ˌlī-ən, -dē-\ *n* : any of a genus of common yellow-flowered composite herbs

dan·der \'dan-dər\ *n* : ANGER, TEMPER

dan·di·fy \'dan-di-ˌfī\ *vb* **-fied; -fy·ing** : to cause to resemble a dandy

dan·dle \'dand-ᵊl\ *vb* **dan·dled; dan·dling** **1** : to move up and down in one's arms or on one's knee in affectionate play **2** : to treat with extreme or excessive care and attention

dan·druff \'dan-drəf\ *n* : scaly white or grayish flakes of dead skin cells that come off the scalp — **dan·druffy** \-drə-fē\ *adj*

¹**dan·dy** \'dan-dē\ *n, pl* **dandies** **1** ♦ : a man unduly attentive to personal appearance **2** ♦ : something excellent in its class

  ♦ [1] buck, dude, fop, gallant ♦ [2] beauty, crackerjack, jim-dandy, knockout, pip

²**dandy** *adj* **dan·di·er; -est** : very good : FIRST-RATE

Dane \'dān\ *n* **1** : a native or inhabitant of Denmark **2** : GREAT DANE

dan·ger \'dān-jər\ *n* **1** ♦ : exposure or liability to injury, harm, or evil **2** ♦ : something that may cause injury or harm

  ♦ [1] distress, jeopardy, peril, risk, trouble *Ant* safety, security ♦ [2] hazard, menace, peril, pitfall, risk, threat, trouble

dan·ger·ous \'dān-jə-rəs\ *adj* **1** ♦ : exposing to or involving danger : HAZARDOUS **2** : able or likely to inflict injury — **dan·ger·ous·ly** *adv*

  ♦ grave, grievous, hazardous, menacing, parlous, perilous, risky, serious, unhealthy, unsafe, venturesome *Ant* harmless, innocent, innocuous, safe

dan·gle \'daŋ-gəl\ *vb* **dan·gled; dan·gling** **1** ♦ : to hang

loosely esp. with a swinging motion : SWING **2** : to be a hanger-on or dependent **3** : to be left without proper grammatical connection in a sentence **4** : to keep hanging uncertainly **5** : to offer as an inducement

  ♦ hang, sling, suspend, swing

Dan·iel \'dan-yəl\ *n* : a book of Jewish and Christian Scripture

Dan·ish \'dā-nish\ *n* **1** : the language of the Danes **2** *pl* **Danish** : a piece of Danish pastry — **Danish** *adj*

Danish pastry *n* : a pastry made of a rich yeast-raised dough

dank \'daŋk\ *adj* : disagreeably wet or moist : DAMP — **dank·ness** *n*

dan·seuse \dän-'sərz, -'səz; dän-'süz\ *n* : a female ballet dancer

dap·per \'da-pər\ *adj* **1** ♦ : neat and trim in style or appearance : SPRUCE **2** : being alert and lively in movement and manners : JAUNTY

  ♦ natty, sharp, smart, spruce

dap·ple \'da-pəl\ *vb* **dap·pled; dap·pling** ♦ : to mark with different-colored spots

  ♦ blotch, dot, fleck, freckle, mottle, pepper, speck, spot, sprinkle, stipple

dap·pled *adj* ♦ : marked with small spots or patches contrasting with the background

  ♦ mottled, piebald, pied, spotted ♦ mottled, spotted, spotty, variegated

DAR *abbr* Daughters of the American Revolution

¹**dare** \'der\ *vb* **dared; dar·ing** **1** : to have sufficient courage : be bold enough to **2** ♦ : to challenge to perform an action esp. as a proof of courage **3** ♦ : to confront boldly

  ♦ [2] challenge, defy ♦ [3] beard, brave, brazen, confront, defy, face

²**dare** *n* : an act or instance of daring : CHALLENGE

dare·dev·il \-ˌde-vəl\ *n* ♦ : a recklessly bold person — **daredevil** *adj*

  ♦ devil, madcap

¹**dar·ing** \'der-iŋ\ *adj* ♦ : venturesomely bold in action or thought — **dar·ing·ly** *adv*

  ♦ adventurous, audacious, bold, enterprising, gutsy, hardy, nervy, venturesome

²**dar·ing** *n* ♦ : venturesome boldness

  ♦ bravery, courage, fearlessness, gallantry, guts, hardihood, heart, heroism, nerve, stoutness, valor

¹**dark** \'därk\ *adj* **1** ♦ : being without light or without much light **2** : not light in color ⟨a ~ suit⟩ **3 a** : showing or causing gloom or depression : GLOOMY **b** ♦ : lacking knowledge or culture **4** ♦ : not clear to the understanding **5** *often cap* : being a period of stagnation or decline ⟨the *Dark* Ages⟩ **6** : tending to keep secrets or to act secretly : SECRETIVE — **dark·ly** *adv*

  ♦ [1] darkling, dim, dusky, gloomy, murky, obscure, somber (*or* sombre) *Ant* bright, brightened, brilliant, illuminated, illumined, light, lighted, lucent, lucid, luminous ♦ [3b] ignorant, illiterate, simple, uneducated, unlearned, untaught ♦ [4] ambiguous, cryptic, darkling, deep, enigmatic, equivocal, inscrutable, murky, mysterious, mystic, nebulous, obscure, occult

²**dark** *n* **1 a** ♦ : a place or time of little or no light **b** ♦ : absence of light : DARKNESS; *esp* : NIGHT **2** : a dark or deep color — **in the dark** **1** : in secrecy **2** : in ignorance ⟨kept *in the dark* about the plans⟩

  ♦ darkness, dusk, gloaming, gloom, murk, night, semidarkness, shade, shadows, twilight *Ant* blaze, brightness, brilliance, day, daylight, glare, glow, light, lightness

dark·en \'där-kən\ *vb* **1 a** ♦ : to make or grow dark or darker **b** ♦ : to make or become less clear : DIM **3** : BESMIRCH, TARNISH **4** ♦ : to make or become gloomy or forbidding

  ♦ [1a, 1b] becloud, befog, blur, cloud, dim, fog, haze, mist, obscure, overcast, overshadow, shroud ♦ [4] gloom, glower, lower *Ant* brighten, cheer (up), lighten, perk (up)

dark horse *n* : a contestant or a political figure whose abilities and chances as a contender are not known

dark·ling \'där-kliŋ\ *adj* **1** : DARK: as **a** : devoid or partially devoid of light **b** ♦ : not clear to the understanding : MYSTERIOUS **2** : done or taking place in the dark

  ♦ ambiguous, cryptic, dark, deep, enigmatic, equivocal, inscrutable, murky, mysterious, mystic, nebulous, obscure, occult

dark·ness \-nəs\ *n* ♦ : the quality or state of being dark

♦ dark, dusk, gloaming, gloom, murk, night, semidarkness, shade, shadows, twilight ♦ ambiguity, murkiness, obscurity, opacity

dark·room \'därk-ˌrüm, -ˌrum\ *n* : a lightproof room in which photographic materials are processed

¹dar·ling \'där-liŋ\ *n* **1** ♦ : a dearly loved person **2** ♦ : one that is treated or regarded with special favor or liking : FAVORITE

♦ [1] beloved, dear, flame, honey, love, sweet, sweetheart ♦ [2] favorite (*or* favourite), minion, pet, preference

²darling *adj* **1** ♦ : dearly loved : FAVORITE **2** ♦ : very pleasing : CHARMING

♦ [1] adorable, dear, endearing, lovable, precious, sweet, winning ♦ [2] agreeable, charming, delectable, delicious, delightful, enjoyable, heavenly, luscious, pleasurable

darm·stadt·i·um \ˌdärm-'sta-tē-əm\ *n* : a short-lived radioactive chemical element produced artificially

¹darn \'därn\ *vb* : to mend with interlacing stitches — **darn·er** *n*

²darn *or* **darned** \'därnd\ *adv* : VERY, EXTREMELY ⟨a ∼ good job⟩

darning needle *n* **1** : a needle for darning **2** : DRAGONFLY

¹dart \'därt\ *n* **1** : a small missile with a point on one end and feathers on the other; *also*, *pl* : a game in which darts are thrown at a target **2** ♦ : something causing a sudden pain or distress **3** : a stitched tapering fold in a garment **4** : a quick movement

♦ affront, barb, dig, indignity, insult, name, offense, outrage, put-down, sarcasm, slight, slur, wound

²dart *vb* **1** : to throw with a sudden movement **2** ♦ : to thrust or move suddenly or rapidly **3** : to shoot with a dart containing a usu. tranquilizing drug

♦ dance, flit, flutter, zip

dart·er \'där-tər\ *n* : any of numerous small No. American freshwater fishes related to the perches

Dar·win·ism \'där-wə-ˌni-zəm\ *n* : a theory explaining the origin and continued existence of new species of plants and animals by means of natural selection acting on chance variations — **Dar·win·ist** \-nist\ *n or adj*

¹dash \'dash\ *vb* **1** : SMASH **2** ♦ : to knock, hurl, or thrust violently **3** : to soil or stain with splashed liquid : SPLASH **4** : RUIN **5** : DEPRESS, SADDEN **6** : to perform or finish hastily **7** ♦ : to move with sudden speed : move rapidly

♦ [2] cast, catapult, chuck, fire, fling, heave, hurl, hurtle, launch, peg, pelt, pitch, sling, throw, toss ♦ [7] career, course, fly, hasten, hurry, race, rip, rocket, run, rush, shoot, speed, tear, zip, zoom

²dash *n* **1** : a sudden burst or splash **2** : a stroke of a pen **3** : a punctuation mark — that is used esp. to indicate a break in the thought or structure of a sentence **4** : a small addition ⟨a ∼ of salt⟩ **5** : flashy showiness **6** ♦ : animation in style and action **7** : a sudden rush or attempt ⟨made a ∼ for the door⟩ **8** : a short foot race **9** : DASHBOARD

♦ energy, life, pep, vigor (*or* vigour), vim, vitality

dash·board \-ˌbord\ *n* : a panel in an automobile or aircraft below the windshield usu. containing dials and controls

dash·er \'da-shər\ *n* : a device (as in a churn) for agitating something

da·shi·ki \də-'shē-kē\ *also* **dai·shi·ki** \dī-\ *n* : a usu. brightly colored loose-fitting pullover garment

dash·ing \'da-shiŋ\ *adj* **1** : marked by vigorous action **2** : marked by smartness esp. in dress and manners

das·tard \'das-tərd\ *n* **1** : one who shows disgraceful fear or timidity : COWARD **2** : a person who acts treacherously

♦ chicken, coward, craven, poltroon, recreant, sissy

das·tard·ly \-lē\ *adj* ♦ : showing disgraceful fear or timidity : COWARDLY

♦ chicken, cowardly, craven, pusillanimous, recreant, spineless, yellow

dat *abbr* dative

da·ta \'dā-tə, 'da-, 'dä-\ *n sing or pl* : factual information (as measurements or statistics) used as a basis for reasoning, discussion, or calculation

da·ta·base \-ˌbās\ *n* : a usu. large collection of data organized esp. for rapid search and retrieval (as by a computer) — **database** *vb*

data processing *n* : the action or process of supplying a computer with information and having the computer use it to produce a desired result

¹date \'dāt\ *n* : the oblong edible fruit of a tall palm; *also* : this palm

²date *n* **1** : the day, month, or year of an event **2** : a statement giving the time of execution or making (as of a coin or check) **3** ♦ : the period to which something belongs **4** ♦ : an appointment to meet at a specified time; *esp* : a social engagement between two persons that often has a romantic character **5** : a person with whom one has a usu. romantic date — **to date** : up to the present moment

♦ [3] duration, life, lifetime, run, standing, time ♦ [4] appointment, engagement, rendezvous, tryst

³date *vb* **dat·ed; dat·ing** **1** : to record the date of or on **2** : to determine, mark, or reveal the date, age, or period of **3** : to make or have a date with **4** : ORIGINATE ⟨∼s from ancient times⟩ **5** : EXTEND ⟨*dating* back to childhood⟩ **6** : to show qualities typical of a past period

dat·ed \'dā-təd\ *adj* **1** : provided with a date **2** ♦ : no longer acceptable, stylish, current, or usable

♦ antiquated, archaic, obsolete, outdated, outmoded, outworn, passé

date·less \'dāt-ləs\ *adj* **1** : being or seeming to be without end : ENDLESS **2** : having no date **3** ♦ : too ancient to be dated **4** : not limited or affected by time : TIMELESS

♦ age-old, ancient, antediluvian, antique, hoary, old, venerable

date·line \-ˌlīn\ *n* : a line in a publication giving the date and place of composition or issue — **dateline** *vb*

date rape *n* : rape committed by the victim's date

da·tive \'dā-tiv\ *adj* : of, relating to, or constituting a grammatical case marking typically the indirect object of a verb — **dative** *n*

da·tum \'dā-təm, 'da-, 'dä-\ *n, pl* **da·ta** \-tə\ *or* **datums** : a single piece of data : FACT

dau *abbr* daughter

¹daub \'dob\ *vb* **1** ♦ : to cover or smear with something sticky or dirty **2** : to apply paint or color crudely — **daub·er** *n*

♦ smear

²daub *n* **1** : something daubed on : SMEAR **2** : a crude picture

daugh·ter \'do-tər\ *n* **1** : a female offspring esp. of human beings **2** : a female adopted child **3** : a human female descendant — **daughter** *adj* — **daugh·ter·less** \-ləs\ *adj*

daugh·ter–in–law \'do-tə-rən-ˌlo\ *n, pl* **daugh·ters–in–law** \-tər-zən-\ : the wife of one's son or daughter

daunt \'dont\ *vb* ♦ : to lessen the courage of

♦ demoralize, discourage, dishearten, dismay, dispirit, unman, unnerve

daunt·ing \'don-tiŋ\ *adj* : tending to overwhelm or intimidate ⟨a ∼ task⟩

daunt·less \-ləs\ *adj* ♦ : marked by courageous resolution : FEARLESS — **daunt·less·ly** *adv*

♦ brave, courageous, doughty, fearless, gallant, greathearted, heroic, intrepid, lionhearted, manful, stalwart, stout, undaunted, valiant, valorous

dau·phin \'do-fən\ *n, often cap* : the eldest son of a king of France

DAV *abbr* Disabled American Veterans

dav·en·port \'da-vən-ˌport\ *n* ♦ : a large upholstered sofa

♦ couch, divan, lounge, settee, sofa

da·vit \'dā-vət, 'da-\ *n* : a small crane on a ship used in pairs esp. to raise or lower boats

daw·dle \'dod-ᵊl\ *vb* **daw·dled; daw·dling** **1** ♦ : to spend time wastefully or idly **2** ♦ : to move lackadaisically — **daw·dler** *n*

♦ [1] dally, dillydally, hang around, hang out, idle, loaf, loll, lounge ♦ [2] crawl, creep, dally, delay, dillydally, drag, lag, linger, loiter, poke, tarry

¹dawn \'don\ *vb* **1** : to begin to grow light as the sun rises **2** ♦ : to begin to appear or develop **3** : to begin to be understood ⟨the solution ∼ed on him⟩

♦ arise, begin, commence, form, materialize, originate, spring, start

²dawn *n* **1** ♦ : the first appearance of light in the morning **2** ♦ : a first appearance : BEGINNING ⟨the ∼ of a new era⟩

♦ [1] aurora, cockcrow, morning, sunrise *Ant* nightfall, sundown, sunset ♦ [2] beginning, birth, commencement, genesis, launch, morning, onset, outset, start, threshold

day \'dā\ *n* **1** : the period of light between one night and the next; *also* : DAYLIGHT, DAYTIME **2** : the period of rotation of a planet (as earth) or a moon on its axis **3** : a period of 24 hours beginning at midnight **4** : a specified day or date ⟨wedding ∼⟩ **5** : a specified time or period : AGE ⟨in olden ∼s⟩ **6** : the conflict or contention of the day **7** : the time set apart by usage or law for work ⟨the 8-hour ∼⟩

day·bed \'dā-ˌbed\ *n* : a couch that can be converted into a bed

day·book \-ˌbùk\ *n* : DIARY, JOURNAL

day·break \-ˌbrāk\ *n* : the first appearance of light in the morning followed by sunrise : DAWN

day care *n* : supervision of and care for children or disabled adults provided during the day; *also* : a program offering day care

day·dream \'dā-ˌdrēm\ *n* ♦ : a pleasant reverie — **daydream** *vb*

♦ chimera, conceit, delusion, dream, fancy, fantasy, figment, hallucination, illusion, phantasm, pipe dream, unreality, vision

day·light \'dā-ˌlīt\ *n* **1** : the light of day **2** : the time during which there is daylight : DAYTIME **3** : the first appearance of light in the morning followed by sunrise : DAWN **4** : understanding of something that has been obscure **5** *pl* : CONSCIOUSNESS; *also* : WITS **6** : a perceptible space, gap, or difference

daylight saving time *n* : time usu. one hour ahead of standard time

Day of Atonement : YOM KIPPUR

day school *n* : a private school without boarding facilities

day student *n* : a student who attends regular classes at a college or preparatory school but does not live there

day·time \'dā-ˌtīm\ *n* : the period of daylight

¹daze \'dāz\ *vb* **dazed; daz·ing 1** : to stupefy esp. by a blow **2** : to dazzle with light : DAZZLE — **da·zed·ly** \'dā-zəd-lē\ *adv*

²daze *n* ♦ : the state of being dazed

♦ fog, haze, muddle, spin

¹daz·zle \'da-zəl\ *vb* **daz·zled; daz·zling 1** ♦ : to overpower with light **2** : to impress greatly or confound with brilliance

♦ daze

²dazzle *n* ♦ : the action of dazzling

♦ brilliance, effulgence, illumination, lightness, lucidity, luminosity, radiance, refulgence, splendor

dB *abbr* decibel

Db *symbol* dubnium

d/b/a *abbr* doing business as

dbl *or* **dble** *abbr* double

DC *abbr* **1** from the beginning **2** direct current **3** District of Columbia **4** doctor of chiropractic

DD *abbr* **1** days after date **2** demand draft **3** dishonorable discharge **4** doctor of divinity

D–day *n* : a day set for launching an operation (as an invasion)

DDS *abbr* doctor of dental surgery

DDT \ˌdē-(ˌ)dē-'tē\ *n* : a persistent insecticide poisonous to many higher animals

DE *abbr* Delaware

dea·con \'dē-kən\ *n* : a subordinate officer in a Christian church

dea·con·ess \'dē-kə-nəs\ *n* : a woman chosen to assist in the church ministry

de·ac·ti·vate \dē-'ak-tə-ˌvāt\ *vb* ♦ : to make inactive or ineffective

♦ kill, shut off, turn off *Ant* activate, actuate, crank (up), drive, move, propel, run, set off, spark, start, touch off, trigger, turn on

¹dead \'ded\ *adj* **1** ♦ : deprived of life : LIFELESS **2** : having the appearance of death : DEATHLIKE ⟨in a ∼ faint⟩ **3** : lacking power to move, feel, or respond : NUMB **4** ♦ : very tired **5** : UNRESPONSIVE **6** : EXTINGUISHED ⟨∼ coals⟩ **7** : INANIMATE, INERT **8** ♦ : no longer active or functioning ⟨a ∼ battery⟩ **9** : lacking power, significance, or effect ⟨a ∼ custom⟩ **10** ♦ : no longer in use ⟨a ∼ language⟩ **11** : lacking in gaiety or animation ⟨a ∼ party⟩ **12** : QUIET, IDLE, UNPRODUCTIVE ⟨∼ capital⟩ **13** : lacking elasticity ⟨a ∼ tennis ball⟩ **14** : not circulating : STAGNANT ⟨∼ air⟩ **15** : lacking warmth, vigor, or taste ⟨∼ wine⟩ **16** : absolutely uniform ⟨∼ level⟩ **17** : UNERRING, EXACT ⟨a ∼ shot⟩ **18** : ABRUPT ⟨a ∼ stop⟩ **19** : having no exceptions or restrictions : COMPLETE ⟨a ∼ loss⟩

♦ [1] breathless, deceased, defunct, gone, late, lifeless *Ant* alive, breathing, living ♦ [4] beat, bushed, drained, effete, jaded, limp, prostrate, spent, tired, weary, worn-out ♦ [8] dormant, fallow, free, idle, inactive, inert, inoperative, latent, off, vacant ♦ [10] bygone, defunct, extinct, gone

²dead *n, pl* **dead 1** : one that is dead — usu. used collectively ⟨the living and the ∼⟩ **2** : the time of greatest quiet ⟨the ∼ of the night⟩

³dead *adv* **1** ♦ : in an absolute manner or condition ⟨∼ right⟩ **2** : in a sudden and complete manner ⟨stopped ∼⟩ **3** : in a direct manner : DIRECTLY ⟨∼ ahead⟩

♦ altogether, completely, entirely, fast, flat, full, fully, perfectly, quite, thoroughly, well, wholly

dead·beat \-ˌbēt\ *n* : a person who persistently fails to pay personal debts or expenses

dead duck *n* : GONER

dead·en \'ded-ᵊn\ *vb* **1** ♦ : to impair in vigor or sensation : BLUNT ⟨∼ pain⟩ **2** : to lessen the luster or spirit of **3** : to make (as a wall) soundproof

♦ blunt, dampen, dull, numb

dead end *n* **1** : an end (as of a street) without an exit **2** : a position, situation, or course of action that leads to nothing further — **dead–end** \ˌded-ˌend\ *adj*

dead heat *n* ♦ : a contest in which two or more contestants tie (as by crossing the finish line simultaneously)

♦ draw, stalemate, standoff, tie

dead horse *n* : an exhausted topic or issue

dead letter *n* **1** : something that has lost its force or authority without being formally abolished **2** : a letter that cannot be delivered or returned

dead·line \'ded-ˌlīn\ *n* : a date or time before which something must be done

dead·lock \'ded-ˌläk\ *n* **1** ♦ : a stoppage of action because neither faction in a struggle will give in **2** : a tie score — **deadlock** *vb*

♦ halt, impasse, stalemate, standstill

¹dead·ly \'ded-lē\ *adj* **dead·li·er; -est 1** ♦ : likely to cause or capable of causing death **2** : HOSTILE, IMPLACABLE **3** : very accurate : UNERRING **4** : tending to deprive of force or vitality ⟨a ∼ habit⟩ **5** : suggestive of death **6** : very great : EXTREME — **dead·li·ness** *n*

♦ baleful, deathly, fatal, fell, lethal, mortal, murderous, pestilent, vital *Ant* healthful, healthy, nonfatal, nonlethal, wholesome

²deadly *adv* **1** : suggesting death ⟨∼ pale⟩ **2** : to a high degree : EXTREMELY ⟨∼ dull⟩

deadly sin *n* : one of seven sins of pride, covetousness, lust, anger, gluttony, envy, and sloth held to be fatal to spiritual progress

dead meat *n* : one that is doomed

¹dead·pan \'ded-ˌpan\ *adj* ♦ : marked by an impassive manner or expression — **deadpan** *vb* — **deadpan** *adv*

♦ blank, expressionless, impassive, inexpressive, stolid, vacant

²deadpan *n* : a completely expressionless face

dead reckoning *n* : the determination of the position of a ship or aircraft solely from the record of the direction and distance of its course

dead·weight \'ded-'wāt\ *n* **1** : the unrelieved weight of an inert mass **2** : a ship's load including the weight of cargo, fuel, crew, and passengers

dead·wood \-ˌwùd\ *n* **1** : wood dead on the tree **2** ♦ : useless personnel or material

♦ chaff, dust, garbage, junk, litter, refuse, riffraff, rubbish, scrap, trash, waste

deaf \'def\ *adj* **1** : unable to hear **2** : unwilling to hear or listen ⟨∼ to all suggestions⟩ — **deaf·ness** *n*

deaf·en \'de-fən\ *vb* : to make deaf

deaf·en·ing \-iŋ\ *adj* ♦ : very loud

♦ booming, clamorous (*or* clamourous), earsplitting, loud, piercing, resounding, ringing, roaring, sonorous, stentorian, thunderous

deaf–mute \'def-ˌmyüt\ *n, often offensive* : a deaf person who cannot speak

¹deal \'dēl\ *n* **1** : a usu. large or indefinite quantity or degree ⟨a great ∼ of support⟩ **2** : the act or right of distributing cards to players in a card game; *also* : HAND

²deal *vb* **dealt** \'dēlt\; **deal·ing 1 a** ♦ : to give as one's portion : DISTRIBUTE **b** : to distribute playing cards to players in a game **2** : ADMINISTER, DELIVER ⟨*dealt* him a blow⟩ **3** ♦ : to concern itself : TREAT ⟨the book ∼s with crime⟩ **4** : to take action in regard to something ⟨∼ with offenders⟩ **5 a** : TRADE **b** ♦ : to sell or distribute something as a business ⟨∼ in used cars⟩ **6** : to reach a state of acceptance ⟨∼ with her child's death⟩ **7** : to engage in bargaining

♦ [1a] administer, allocate, apportion, dispense, distribute, mete, parcel, portion, prorate ♦ [3] concern, cover, pertain, treat ♦ [5b] market, merchandise, put up, retail, sell, vend

³deal *n* **1** ♦ : an act of buying and selling : TRANSACTION **2** : treatment received ⟨a raw ∼⟩ **3** ♦ : an often secret agreement or arrangement for mutual advantage **4** ♦ : something acquired by or as if by bargaining; *esp* : an advantageous purchase : BARGAIN

♦ [1] sale, trade, transaction ♦ [3] accord, agreement, bargain, compact, contract, convention, covenant, pact, settlement, understanding ♦ [4] bargain, buy, steal

⁴deal *n* : wood or a board of fir or pine
deal·er \ˈdē-lər\ *n* ♦ : one that deals; *esp* : a person who makes a business of buying and selling goods

   ♦ merchant, trader, trafficker ♦ seller, vendor

deal·er·ship \ˈdē-lər-ˌship\ *n* : an authorized sales agency
deal·ing \ˈdē-liŋ\ *n* **1** : a way of acting or of doing business **2** *pl* ♦ : friendly or business transactions

   ♦ *usu* **dealings** intercourse, relations

dean \ˈdēn\ *n* **1** : a clergyman who is head of a group of canons or of joint pastors of a church **2** : the head of a division, faculty, college, or school of a university **3** : a college or secondary school administrator in charge of counseling and disciplining students **4** ♦ : the senior member of a body or group ⟨the ∼ of a diplomatic corps⟩ — **dean·ship** *n*

   ♦ elder, senior *Ant* baby

dean·ery \ˈdē-nə-rē\ *n, pl* **-er·ies** : the office, jurisdiction, or official residence of a clerical dean
¹dear \ˈdir\ *adj* **1** ♦ : highly valued : PRECIOUS **2** : AFFECTIONATE, FOND **3** ♦ : high in price : EXPENSIVE **4** : HEARTFELT — **dear·ly** *adv* — **dear·ness** *n*

   ♦ [1] beloved, darling, favorite (*or* favourite), loved, pet, precious, special, sweet ♦ [3] costly, expensive, high, precious, valuable

²dear *n* ♦ : a loved one : DARLING

   ♦ beloved, darling, honey, love, sweet, sweetheart

Dear John \-ˈjän\ *n* : a letter (as to a soldier) in which a woman breaks off a marital or romantic relationship
dearth \ˈdərth\ *n* **1** ♦ : scarcity that makes dear : FAMINE **2** ♦ : an inadequate supply : LACK

   ♦ deficiency, deficit, failure, famine, inadequacy, insufficiency, lack, paucity, poverty, scantiness, scarcity, shortage, want

death \ˈdeth\ *n* **1** ♦ : the end of life **2** : the cause of loss of life **3** : the state of being dead **4** ♦ : the passing or destruction of something inanimate **5** : SLAUGHTER

   ♦ [1] decease, demise, doom, end, passing, quietus *Ant* birth ♦ [4] demise, expiration, termination *Ant* beginning, creation, start

death·bed \-ˌbed\ *n* **1** : the bed in which a person dies **2** : the last hours of life
death·blow \-ˌblō\ *n* : a destructive or killing stroke or event
death grip *n* : an extremely tight grip or hold
death·less \-ləs\ *adj* ♦ : not subject to death or destruction : IMMORTAL ⟨∼ fame⟩

   ♦ ceaseless, dateless, endless, eternal, everlasting, immortal, permanent, perpetual, undying, unending

death·like \-līk\ *adj* : of, relating to, or suggestive of death : DEATHLY
death·ly \-lē\ *adj* **1** ♦ : causing death : FATAL **2** ♦ : of, relating to, or suggesting death ⟨a ∼ pallor⟩ — **deathly** *adv*

   ♦ [1] baleful, deadly, fatal, fell, lethal, mortal, murderous, pestilent, vital ♦ [2] dead, mortal

death rattle *n* : a sound produced by air passing through mucus in the lungs and air passages of a dying person
death's–head \ˈdeths-ˌhed\ *n* : a human skull emblematic of death
death·watch \ˈdeth-ˌwäch\ *n* : a vigil kept over the dead or dying
deb \ˈdeb\ *n* : DEBUTANTE
de·ba·cle \di-ˈbä-kəl, -ˈba-\ *also* **dé·bâ·cle** *same or* dā-ˈbäk\ *n* **1** ♦ : a great disaster **2** ♦ : a complete failure : FIASCO ⟨a financial ∼⟩

   ♦ [1] calamity, cataclysm, catastrophe, disaster, tragedy ♦ [2] bummer, bust, catastrophe, dud, failure, fiasco, fizzle, flop, lemon, loser, turkey, washout

de·bar \di-ˈbär\ *vb* ♦ : to bar from having or doing something

   ♦ ban, bar, count out, eliminate, except, exclude, rule out

de·bark \di-ˈbärk\ *vb* : DISEMBARK — **de·bar·ka·tion** \ˌdē-ˌbär-ˈkā-shən\ *n*
de·base \di-ˈbās\ *vb* ♦ : to lower in character, quality, or value

   ♦ abase, corrupt, debauch, degrade, demean, demoralize, deprave, pervert, poison, profane, subvert, vitiate, warp *Ant* elevate, ennoble, uplift ♦ discredit, disgrace, dishonor (*or* dishonour), humble, humiliate, lower, shame, smirch, take down

de·base·ment \-mənt\ *n* **1** ♦ : the act or process of debasing **2** : the state of being debased

   ♦ corruption, debauchery, decadence, degeneracy, degeneration, degradation, demoralization, depravity, dissipation, dissoluteness, perversion

de·bat·able \di-ˈbā-tə-bəl\ *adj* ♦ : open to dispute : giving reason for being doubted, questioned, or challenged

   ♦ arguable, disputable, doubtful, moot, questionable *Ant* incontestable, incontrovertible, indisputable, indubitable, undeniable, unquestionable ♦ doubtful, equivocal, problematic, questionable, suspect, suspicious

¹de·bate \di-ˈbāt\ *n* **1** ♦ : a contention by words or arguments **2** ♦ : consideration of or reflection upon a problem ⟨after a moment of ∼, she went forward⟩

   ♦ [1] controversy, disagreement, dissension ♦ [2] consideration, deliberation, thought

²debate *vb* **de·bat·ed; de·bat·ing** **1** ♦ : to discuss a question by considering opposed arguments **2** : to take part in a debate **3** ♦ : to reflect upon (a question or problem)

   ♦ [1] argue, chew over, discuss, dispute, hash, moot, talk over ♦ [3] chew over, cogitate, consider, contemplate, deliberate, entertain, meditate, mull, ponder, question, ruminate, study, think, weigh

de·bat·er \-ˈbā-tər\ *n* ♦ : one that debates

   ♦ arguer, contender, disputant, disputer

de·bauch \di-ˈboch\ *vb* ♦ : to lead away from virtue or excellence : CORRUPT

   ♦ debase, degrade, demean, demoralize, humble, subvert, warp

de·bauched \-ˈbocht\ *adj* ♦ : having or showing looseness in morals or conduct

   ♦ corrupt, decadent, degenerate, dissolute, perverse, perverted, reprobate

de·bauch·ery \-ˈbo-chə-rē\ *n* ♦ : extreme indulgence in sensuality

   ♦ corruption, debasement, decadence, degeneracy, degeneration, degradation, demoralization, depravity, dissipation, dissoluteness, perversion ♦ corruption, depravity, immorality, iniquity, licentiousness, sin, vice

de·ben·ture \di-ˈben-chər\ *n* : BOND; *esp* : one secured by the general credit of the issuer rather than a lien on particular assets
de·bil·i·tate \di-ˈbi-lə-ˌtāt\ *vb* **-tat·ed; -tat·ing** ♦ : to impair the health or strength of

   ♦ enervate, enfeeble, prostrate, sap, soften, tire, waste, weaken

de·bil·i·ty \di-ˈbi-lə-tē\ *n, pl* **-ties** ♦ : an infirm or weakened state

   ♦ delicacy, enfeeblement, faintness, feebleness, frailty, infirmity, languor, lowness, weakness

¹deb·it \ˈde-bət\ *vb* : to enter as a debit : charge with or as a debit
²debit *n* **1** : an entry in an account showing money paid out or owed **2** ♦ : DISADVANTAGE, SHORTCOMING
debit card *n* : a card by which money may be withdrawn or the cost of purchases paid directly from the holder's bank account
deb·o·nair \ˌde-bə-ˈnar\ *adj* **1** ♦ : smoothly gracious and sophisticated : SUAVE **2** : LIGHTHEARTED

   ♦ smooth, sophisticated, suave, urbane

de·bouch \di-ˈbauch, -ˈbüsh\ *vb* : to come out into an open area : EMERGE
de·brief \di-ˈbrēf\ *vb* **1** : to question (as a pilot back from a mission) in order to obtain useful information **2** : to review carefully upon completion
de·bris \də-ˈbrē, dā-; ˈdā-ˌbrē\ *n, pl* **debris** \-ˈbrēz, -ˌbrēz\ **1** ♦ : the remains of something broken down or destroyed **2** : an accumulation of rock fragments **3** : RUBBISH

   ♦ remains, rubble, ruins, wreck, wreckage

debt \ˈdet\ *n* **1** : an offense against religious or moral law : SIN **2** : something owed : OBLIGATION **3** : a condition of owing
debt·or \ˈde-tər\ *n* **1** : one guilty of neglect or violation of duty **2** : one that owes a debt
de·bug \(ˌ)dē-ˈbəg\ *vb* ♦ : to eliminate errors in

   ♦ amend, correct, emend, rectify, reform, remedy

de·bunk \dē-ˈbəŋk\ *vb* ♦ : to expose the sham or falseness of ⟨∼ a legend⟩

   ♦ expose, show up, uncloak, uncover, unmask

¹de·but \'dā-ˌbyü, dā-'byü\ *n* **1 :** a first appearance **2 :** a formal entrance into society
²debut *vb* **:** to make a debut; *also* **:** INTRODUCE
deb·u·tante \'de-byu̇-ˌtänt\ *n* **:** a young woman making her formal entrance into society
dec *abbr* **1** deceased **2** decrease
Dec *abbr* December
de·cade \'de-ˌkād, de-'kād\ *n* **:** a period of 10 years
dec·a·dence \'de-kə-dəns, di-'kād-ᵊns\ *n* **1 ♦ :** the process of becoming decadent **:** the quality or state of being decadent **2 ♦ :** a period of decline

♦ [1, 2] corruption, debasement, debauchery, degeneracy, degeneration, degradation, demoralization, depravity, dissipation, dissoluteness, perversion

¹dec·a·dent \'de-kə-dənt, di-'kād-ᵊnt\ *adj* **1 ♦ :** marked by decay or decline **2 ♦ :** characterized by or appealing to self-indulgence

♦ [1] degenerate, effete, overripe ♦ [1, 2] corrupt, debauched, degenerate, dissolute, perverse, perverted, reprobate

²decadent *n* **♦ :** one that is decadent

♦ degenerate, libertine, pervert, profligate

de·caf \'dē-ˌkaf\ *n* **:** decaffeinated coffee
de·caf·fein·at·ed \(ˌ)dē-'ka-fə-nā-təd\ *adj* **:** having the caffeine removed ⟨∼ coffee⟩
deca·gon \'de-kə-ˌgän\ *n* **:** a plane polygon of 10 angles and 10 sides
de·cal \'dē-ˌkal\ *n* **:** a picture, design, or label made to be transferred (as to glass) from specially prepared paper
Deca·logue \'de-kə-ˌlȯg\ *n* **:** TEN COMMANDMENTS
de·camp \di-'kamp\ *vb* **1 :** to break up a camp **2 :** to depart suddenly
de·cant \di-'kant\ *vb* **:** to pour (as wine) gently from one vessel into another
de·cant·er \di-'kan-tər\ *n* **:** an ornamental glass bottle for serving wine
de·cap·i·tate \di-'ka-pə-ˌtāt\ *vb* **-tat·ed; -tat·ing :** BEHEAD — **de·cap·i·ta·tion** \-ˌka-pə-'tā-shən\ *n* — **de·cap·i·ta·tor** \-'ka-pə-ˌtā-tər\ *n*
deca·syl·lab·ic \ˌde-kə-sə-'la-bik\ *adj* **:** having or composed of verses having 10 syllables — **decasyllabic** *n*
de·cath·lon \di-'kath-lən, -ˌlän\ *n* **:** a 10-event athletic contest
¹de·cay \di-'kā\ *vb* **1 ♦ :** to decline from a sound or prosperous condition **2 ♦ :** to cause or undergo decomposition ⟨radium ∼s slowly⟩; *esp* **:** to break down while spoiling **:** ROT

♦ [1] decline, degenerate, descend, deteriorate, ebb, rot, sink, worsen ♦ [2] break down, corrupt, decompose, disintegrate, molder, putrefy, rot, spoil

²decay *n* **1 ♦ :** gradual decline in strength, soundness, or prosperity or in degree of excellence or perfection **2 :** the process of rotting **:** the state of being rotten

♦ [1] decline, degeneration, deterioration ♦ [2] breakdown, corruption, decomposition, putrefaction, rot, spoilage

decd *abbr* deceased
de·cease \di-'sēs\ *n* **♦ :** a permanent cessation of all vital functions **:** DEATH

♦ death, demise, doom, end, passing, quietus

¹de·ceased \-'sēst\ *adj* **♦ :** no longer alive; *esp* **:** recently dead

♦ breathless, dead, defunct, gone, late, lifeless

²deceased *n, pl* **deceased :** a dead person
de·ce·dent \di-'sēd-ᵊnt\ *n* **:** a deceased person
de·ceit \di-'sēt\ *n* **1 :** the act or practice of deceiving **:** DECEPTION **2 :** an attempt or device to deceive **:** TRICK **3 ♦ :** the quality of being deceitful **:** DECEITFULNESS

♦ artifice, craft, craftiness, crookedness, cunning, deceitfulness, dishonesty, dissimulation, double-dealing, duplicity, guile, wiliness *Ant* artlessness, forthrightness, good faith, guilelessness, sincerity

de·ceit·ful \-fəl\ *adj* **1 ♦ :** practicing or tending to practice deceit **2 ♦ :** tending or having power to deceive **:** DECEPTIVE ⟨a ∼ answer⟩ — **de·ceit·ful·ly** *adv*

♦ [1] crooked, dishonest, double-dealing, false, fraudulent ♦ [2] deceptive, delusive, fallacious, false, misleading, specious

de·ceit·ful·ness \-nəs\ *n* **♦ :** the quality or state of being deceitful

♦ artifice, craft, craftiness, crookedness, cunning, deceit, dishonesty, dissimulation, double-dealing, duplicity, guile, wiliness

de·ceive \di-'sēv\ *vb* **de·ceived; de·ceiv·ing 1 ♦ :** to cause to believe an untruth **2 :** to use or practice deceit — **de·ceiv·er** *n*

♦ beguile, bluff, cozen, delude, dupe, fool, gull, have, hoax, hoodwink, humbug, misinform, mislead, string along, take in, trick *Ant* undeceive

de·cel·er·ate \dē-'se-lə-ˌrāt\ *vb* **-at·ed; -at·ing ♦ :** to slow down

♦ brake, retard, slow

De·cem·ber \di-'sem-bər\ *n* **:** the 12th month of the year
de·cen·cy \'dēs-ᵊn-sē\ *n, pl* **-cies 1 ♦ :** the quality or state of being decent **:** PROPRIETY **2 ♦ :** conformity to standards of taste, propriety, or quality **3 :** a standard of propriety — usu. used in pl.

♦ [1] decorum, form, propriety *Ant* impropriety, indecency ♦ [2] character, goodness, honesty, honor (*or* honour), integrity, morality, probity, rectitude, righteousness, uprightness, virtue

de·cen·ni·al \di-'se-nē-əl\ *adj* **1 :** consisting of 10 years **2 :** happening every 10 years ⟨∼ census⟩
de·cent \'dē-sᵊnt\ *adj* **1 ♦ :** conforming to standards of propriety, good taste, or morality **2 :** modestly clothed **3 ♦ :** free from immodesty or obscenity **4 ♦ :** ADEQUATE ⟨∼ housing⟩ — **de·cent·ly** *adv*

♦ [1] ethical, good, honest, honorable (*or* honourable), just, moral, right, righteous, straight, upright, virtuous ♦ [1] correct, decorous, genteel, nice, polite, proper, respectable, seemly ♦ [3] chaste, clean, immaculate, modest, pure ♦ [4] acceptable, adequate, all right, fine, OK, passable, respectable, satisfactory, tolerable

de·cen·tral·i·za·tion \dē-ˌsen-trə-lə-'zā-shən\ *n* **1 :** the distribution of powers from a central authority to regional and local authorities **2 :** the redistribution of population and industry from urban centers to outlying areas — **de·cen·tral·ize** \-'sen-trə-ˌlīz\ *vb*
de·cep·tion \di-'sep-shən\ *n* **1 :** the act of deceiving **2 :** the fact or condition of being deceived **3 :** FRAUD, TRICK
de·cep·tive \di-'sep-tiv\ *adj* **♦ :** tending or having power to deceive — **de·cep·tive·ly** *adv* — **de·cep·tive·ness** *n*

♦ deceitful, delusive, fallacious, false, misleading, specious *Ant* aboveboard, forthright, straightforward

deci·bel \'de-sə-ˌbel, -bəl\ *n* **:** a unit for measuring the relative loudness of sounds
de·cide \di-'sīd\ *vb* **de·cid·ed; de·cid·ing 1 ♦ :** to arrive at a solution that ends uncertainty or dispute about **2 :** to bring to a definitive end ⟨one blow *decided* the fight⟩ **3 :** to induce to come to a choice **4 ♦ :** to make a choice or judgment

♦ [1] arrange, fix, set, settle ♦ [4] choose, conclude, determine, figure, opt, resolve ♦ [4] adjudicate, arbitrate, determine, judge, referee, rule, settle, umpire

de·cid·ed \di-'sī-dəd\ *adj* **1 :** UNQUESTIONABLE **2 :** FIRM, DETERMINED — **de·cid·ed·ly** *adv*
de·cid·u·ous \di-'si-jə-wəs\ *adj* **1 :** falling off or out usu. at the end of a period of growth or function ⟨∼ leaves⟩ ⟨a ∼ tooth⟩ **2 :** having deciduous parts ⟨∼ trees⟩
deci·gram \'de-sə-ˌgram\ *n* **:** a metric unit of measure equal to ¹/₁₀ gram
deci·li·ter \-ˌlē-tər\ *n* **:** a metric unit of measure equal to ¹/₁₀ liter
¹dec·i·mal \'de-sə-məl\ *adj* **:** based on the number 10 **:** reckoning by tens
²decimal *n* **:** any number expressed in base 10; *esp* **:** DECIMAL FRACTION
decimal fraction *n* **:** a fraction or mixed number in which the denominator is a power of 10 and thus usu. expressed with a decimal point ⟨the *decimal fraction* .25 is equivalent to the common fraction ²⁵/₁₀₀⟩
decimal place *n* **:** the position of a digit as counted to the right of the decimal point in a decimal fraction
decimal point *n* **:** a period, centered dot, or in some countries a comma at the left of a decimal fraction (as .678) less than one or between a whole number and a decimal fraction in a mixed number (as 3.678)
dec·i·mate \'de-sə-ˌmāt\ *vb* **-mat·ed; -mat·ing 1 :** to take or destroy the 10th part of **2 :** to cause great destruction or harm to
deci·me·ter \'de-sə-ˌmē-tər\ *n* **:** a metric unit of measure equal to ¹/₁₀ meter
de·ci·pher \di-'sī-fər\ *vb* **1 :** to convert (as a coded message) into intelligible form **:** DECODE **2 :** to make out the meaning of despite indistinctness — **de·ci·pher·able** *adj*
de·ci·sion \di-'si-zhən\ *n* **1 ♦ :** the act or result of deciding **2 ♦ :** promptness and firmness in deciding

♦ [1] conclusion, determination, diagnosis, judgment (*or* judgement), opinion, resolution, verdict ♦ [2] decisiveness, determination, firmness, granite, resolution, resolve

de·ci·sive \-'sī-siv\ *adj* **1** : having the power to decide ⟨the ~ vote⟩ **2** ♦ : marked by firm determination : RESOLUTE **3** ♦ : not questionable : CONCLUSIVE ⟨a ~ victory⟩ — **de·ci·sive·ly** *adv*

♦ [2] bound, determined, firm, intent, purposeful, resolute, set, single-minded ♦ [3] absolute, clear, conclusive, definitive

de·ci·sive·ness \-nəs\ *n* ♦ : the quality or state of being decisive

♦ decision, determination, firmness, granite, resolution, resolve

¹**deck** \'dek\ *n* **1** : a floorlike platform of a ship; *also* : something resembling the deck of a ship **2** : a pack of playing cards
²**deck** *vb* **1** ♦ : to clothe in a striking or elegant manner : ARRAY **2** ♦ : to furnish with something ornamental : DECORATE **3** : to furnish with a deck **4** : KNOCK DOWN, FLOOR

♦ [1] apparel, array, attire, caparison, clothe, dress, garb, invest, rig, suit ♦ [2] adorn, array, beautify, bedeck, decorate, do, dress, embellish, enrich, garnish, grace, ornament, trim

deck·hand \'dek-ˌhand\ *n* : a sailor who performs manual duties
de·claim \di-'klām\ *vb* ♦ : to speak or deliver in the manner of a formal speech — **de·clam·a·to·ry** \di-'kla-mə-ˌtȯr-ē\ *adj*

♦ descant, discourse, harangue, lecture, orate, speak, talk

dec·la·ma·tion \ˌde-klə-'mā-shən\ *n* ♦ : the act or art of declaiming

♦ address, harangue, oration, speech, talk

dec·la·ra·tion \ˌde-klə-'rā-shən\ *n* **1** ♦ : the act of declaring **2** : something that is declared

♦ affirmation, assertion, avowal, claim, profession, protestation

de·clar·a·tive \di-'klar-ə-tiv\ *adj* : making a declaration ⟨~ sentence⟩
de·clare \di-'klar\ *vb* **de·clared; de·clar·ing** **1** ♦ : to make known formally, officially, or explicitly : ANNOUNCE ⟨~ war⟩ **2** ♦ : to state emphatically : AFFIRM **3** : to make a full statement of — **de·clar·a·to·ry** \di-'klar-ə-ˌtȯr-ē\ *adj* — **de·clar·er** *n*

♦ [1] advertise, announce, blaze, broadcast, enunciate, placard, post, proclaim, promulgate, publicize, publish, sound ♦ [2] affirm, allege, assert, aver, avouch, avow, claim, contend, insist, maintain, profess, protest, warrant

de·clas·si·fy \dē-'kla-sə-ˌfī\ *vb* : to remove the security classification of — **de·clas·si·fi·ca·tion** \-ˌkla-sə-fə-'kā-shən\ *n*
de·clen·sion \di-'klen-chən\ *n* **1** : the inflectional forms of a noun, pronoun, or adjective **2** : a falling off or away esp. from a standard or a high point of development **3** : a bending or sloping downward
¹**de·cline** \di-'klīn\ *vb* **de·clined; de·clin·ing** **1** ♦ : to slope downward : DESCEND **2** : DROOP **3** : WANE **4** ♦ : to tend toward an inferior state or weaker condition **5** ♦ : to withhold consent; *also* : REFUSE **6** : INFLECT 2 ⟨~ a noun⟩ — **de·clin·able** *adj* — **dec·li·na·tion** \ˌde-klə-'nā-shən\ *n*

♦ [1] descend, dip, drop, fall, lower, plummet, plunge, sink, tumble ♦ [4] decay, degenerate, descend, deteriorate, ebb, rot, sink, worsen ♦ [5] disallow, disapprove, negative, refuse, reject, repudiate, spurn, turn down *Ant* accept, agree (to), approve

²**decline** *n* **1** ♦ : a gradual sinking and wasting away **2** ♦ : a change to a lower state or level **3** : the time when something is approaching its end **4** : a descending slope

♦ [1] decay, degeneration, deterioration *Ant* improvement, recovery, revitalization ♦ [2] degradation, fall *Ant* ascent, rise, upswing

de·cliv·i·ty \di-'kli-və-tē\ *n, pl* **-ties** : a steep downward slope
de·code \dē-'kōd\ *vb* ♦ : to convert (a coded message) into ordinary language — **de·cod·er** *n*

♦ break, crack *Ant* cipher, code, encode

dé·col·le·tage \ˌdā-ˌkä-lə-'täzh\ *n* : the low-cut neckline of a dress
dé·col·le·té \ˌdā-ˌkäl-'tā\ *adj* **1** : wearing a strapless or low-necked gown **2** : having a low-cut neckline
de·com·mis·sion \ˌdē-kə-'mi-shən\ *vb* : to remove from service
de·com·pose \ˌdē-kəm-'pōz\ *vb* **1** : to separate into constituent parts **2** ♦ : to break down in decay : ROT

♦ break down, corrupt, decay, disintegrate, molder, putrefy, rot, spoil

de·com·po·si·tion \dē-ˌkäm-pə-'zi-shən\ *n* ♦ : the act or process of decomposing

♦ breakdown, corruption, decay, putrefaction, rot, spoilage

de·com·press \ˌdē-kəm-'pres\ *vb* : to release from pressure or compression — **de·com·pres·sion** \-'pre-shən\ *n*
de·con·ges·tant \ˌdē-kən-'jes-tənt\ *n* : an agent that relieves congestion (as of mucous membranes)
de·con·struc·tion \ˌdē-kən-'strək-shən\ *n* : the analysis of something (as language or literature) by the separation and individual examination of its basic elements — **de·con·struct** \-'strəkt\ *vb*
de·con·tam·i·nate \ˌdē-kən-'ta-mə-ˌnāt\ *vb* : to rid of contamination (as radioactive material) — **de·con·tam·i·na·tion** \-ˌta-mə-ˌnā-shən\ *n*
de·con·trol \ˌdē-kən-'trōl\ *vb* : to end control of ⟨~ prices⟩ — **decontrol** *n*
de·cor *or* **dé·cor** \dā-'kȯr, 'dā-ˌkȯr\ *n* : DECORATION; *esp* : the style and layout of interior furnishings
dec·o·rate \'de-kə-ˌrāt\ *vb* **-rat·ed; -rat·ing** **1** ♦ : to furnish with something ornamental ⟨~ a room⟩ **2** : to award a mark of honor (as a medal) to

♦ adorn, array, beautify, bedeck, deck, do, dress, embellish, enrich, garnish, grace, ornament, trim *Ant* blemish, deface, disfigure, mar, scar, spoil

dec·o·ra·tion \ˌde-kə-'rā-shən\ *n* **1** : the act or process of decorating **2** ♦ : something that adorns, enriches, or beautifies : ORNAMENT **3** ♦ : a badge of honor

♦ [2] adornment, caparison, embellishment, frill, garnish, ornament, trim ♦ [3] award, distinction, honor (*or* honour), plume, prize

dec·o·ra·tive \'de-kə-rə-tiv\ *adj* : serving to decorate : ORNAMENTAL
dec·o·ra·tor \'de-kə-ˌrā-tər\ *n* : one that decorates; *esp* : a person who designs or executes interiors and their furnishings
dec·o·rous \'de-kə-rəs, di-'kōr-əs\ *adj* ♦ : marked by propriety and good taste : PROPER

♦ correct, decent, genteel, nice, polite, proper, respectable, seemly

de·co·rum \di-'kōr-əm\ *n* **1** ♦ : conformity to accepted standards of conduct **2** : ORDERLINESS

♦ decency, form, propriety

¹**de·coy** \'dē-ˌkȯi, di-'kȯi\ *n* **1** : something that lures or entices; *esp* : an artificial bird used to attract live birds within shot **2** : something used to draw attention away from another
²**de·coy** \di-'kȯi, 'dē-ˌkȯi\ *vb* ♦ : to lure by or as if by a decoy : ENTICE

♦ allure, beguile, entice, lead on, lure, seduce, tempt

¹**de·crease** \di-'krēs\ *vb* **de·creased; de·creas·ing** ♦ : to grow or cause to grow less : DIMINISH

♦ abate, decline, de-escalate, die, diminish, dwindle, ebb, fall, lessen, let up, lower, moderate, recede, relent, shrink, subside, taper, wane *Ant* accumulate, balloon, build, burgeon, enlarge, escalate, expand, grow, increase, intensify, mount, mushroom, pick up, rise, snowball, soar, swell, wax

²**de·crease** \'dē-ˌkrēs\ *n* **1** : the process of decreasing **2** ♦ : an amount of diminution : REDUCTION

♦ abatement, decline, decrement, diminution, drop, fall, loss, reduction, shrinkage *Ant* boost, enlargement, gain, increase, increment, raise, rise

¹**de·cree** \di-'krē\ *n* **1** ♦ : an order usu. having the force of law : EDICT **2** : a judicial decision

♦ behest, charge, command, commandment, dictate, direction, directive, edict, instruction, order, word

²**decree** *vb* **de·creed; de·cree·ing** **1** ♦ : to direct authoritatively : COMMAND **2** : to determine or order judicially

♦ command, dictate, direct, ordain, order

dec·re·ment \'de-krə-mənt\ *n* **1** : gradual decrease **2** ♦ : the quantity lost by diminution or waste

♦ abatement, decline, decrease, diminution, drop, fall, loss, reduction, shrinkage

de·crep·it \di-'kre-pət\ *adj* : broken down with age : WORN-OUT — **de·crep·i·tude** \-pə-ˌtüd, -ˌtyüd\ *n*
de·cre·scen·do \ˌdā-krə-'shen-dō\ *adv or adj* : with a decrease in volume — used as a direction in music
de·crim·i·nal·ize \dē-'kri-mən-ᵊl-ˌīz\ *vb* : to remove or reduce the criminal status of
de·cry \di-'krī\ *vb* ♦ : to express strong disapproval of

♦ belittle, cry down, deprecate, depreciate, diminish, discount, disparage, minimize, put down, write off *Ant* acclaim, applaud, exalt, extol, glorify, laud, magnify, praise

ded·i·cate \'de-di-ˌkāt\ *vb* **-cat·ed; -cat·ing 1 :** to devote to the worship of a divine being esp. with sacred rites **2 ♦ :** to set apart for a definite purpose **3 :** to inscribe or address as a compliment — **ded·i·ca·tor** \'de-di-ˌkā-tər\ *n* — **ded·i·ca·to·ry** \-kə-ˌtōr-ē\ *adj*

♦ allocate, consecrate, devote, earmark, reserve, save

ded·i·ca·tion \ˌde-di-'kā-shən\ *n* **1 :** an act or rite of dedicating esp. to a sacred use **2 :** a setting aside for a particular purpose **3 ♦ :** self-sacrificing devotion

♦ allegiance, constancy, devotion, faith, faithfulness, fastness, fealty, fidelity, loyalty, steadfastness

de·duce \di-'düs, -'dyüs\ *vb* **de·duced; de·duc·ing 1 ♦ :** to derive by reasoning : INFER **2 :** to trace the course of

♦ conclude, extrapolate, gather, infer, judge, reason, understand

de·duct \di-'dəkt\ *vb* : SUBTRACT — **de·duct·ible** *adj*
de·duc·tion \di-'dək-shən\ *n* **1 :** an act of taking away : SUBTRACTION **2 ♦ :** something that is or may be subtracted **3 :** the deriving of a conclusion by reasoning : the conclusion so reached — **de·duc·tive** \-'dək-tiv\ *adj* — **de·duc·tive·ly** *adv*

♦ abatement, discount, reduction *Ant* accession, addition

¹deed \'dēd\ *n* **1 ♦ :** something done **2 ♦ :** a usu. illustrious act or action : FEAT **3 :** a document containing some legal transfer, bargain, or contract

♦ exploit, feat, thing

²deed *vb* **♦ :** to convey or transfer by deed

♦ alienate, assign, cede, make over, transfer

dee·jay \'dē-ˌjā\ *n* : DISC JOCKEY
deem \'dēm\ *vb* **♦ :** to come to think or judge

♦ believe, consider, feel, figure, guess, hold, imagine, suppose, think

de–em·pha·size \dē-'em-fə-ˌsīz\ *vb* : to reduce in relative importance; *also* : to attach little importance to — **de–em·pha·sis** \-səs\ *n*

¹deep \'dēp\ *adj* **1 :** extending far down, back, within, or outward **2 :** having a specified extension downward or backward **3 ♦ :** difficult to understand; *also* : MYSTERIOUS ⟨a ∼ dark secret⟩ **4 :** WISE **5 :** ENGROSSED, INVOLVED ⟨∼ in thought⟩ **6 ♦ :** characterized by profundity of feeling or quality : INTENSE ⟨∼ grief⟩ ⟨∼ sleep⟩ **7 :** dark and rich in color ⟨a ∼ red⟩ **8 ♦ :** having a low musical pitch or range ⟨a ∼ voice⟩ **9 :** situated well within **10 :** covered, enclosed, or filled often to a specified degree — **deep·ly** *adv*

♦ [3] ambiguous, cryptic, dark, darkling, enigmatic, equivocal, inscrutable, murky, mysterious, mystic, nebulous, obscure, occult ♦ [6] explosive, exquisite, fearful, ferocious, fierce, furious, hard, heavy, intense, profound, terrible, vehement, vicious, violent ♦ [8] bass, low, throaty *Ant* acute, high, piping, sharp, shrill, treble

²deep *adv* **1 :** DEEPLY **2 :** far on : LATE ⟨∼ in the night⟩
³deep *n* **1 ♦ :** an extremely deep place or part; *esp* : the whole body of salt water that covers nearly three fourths of the surface of the earth : OCEAN **2 ♦ :** the middle or most intense part ⟨the ∼ of winter⟩

♦ [1] blue, brine, ocean, sea ♦ [2] depth, height, middle, midst, thick

deep·en \'dē-pən\ *vb* **♦ :** to make or become deep or deeper

♦ amplify, beef, boost, consolidate, enhance, heighten, intensify, magnify, redouble, step up, strengthen

deep–freeze \'dēp-'frēz\ *vb* **-froze** \-'frōz\; **-fro·zen** \-'frōz-ᵊn\; **-freez·ing :** QUICK-FREEZE
deep–fry *vb* : to cook in enough oil to cover the food being fried
deep pocket *n* **1 :** one having substantial financial resources **2** *pl* : substantial financial resources
deep–root·ed \'dēp-'rü-təd, -'rü-\ *adj* **♦ :** deeply implanted or established

♦ confirmed, deep-seated, inveterate, settled

deep–sea \'dēp-'sē\ *adj* : of, relating to, or occurring in the deeper parts of the sea ⟨∼ fishing⟩
deep–seat·ed \'dēp-'sē-təd\ *adj* **1 :** situated far below the surface **2 ♦ :** firmly established ⟨∼ convictions⟩

♦ confirmed, deep-rooted, inveterate, settled

deer \'dir\ *n, pl* **deer :** any of numerous ruminant mammals with cloven hoofs and usu. antlers esp. in the males

deer·fly \-ˌflī\ *n* : any of numerous small horseflies
deer·skin \-ˌskin\ *n* : leather made from the skin of a deer; *also* : a garment of such leather
deer tick *n* : a tick that transmits the bacterium causing Lyme disease
de·es·ca·late \dē-'es-kə-ˌlāt\ *vb* **♦ :** to decrease in extent, volume, or scope — **de·es·ca·la·tion** \-ˌes-kə-'lā-shən\ *n*

♦ abate, decline, decrease, die, diminish, dwindle, ebb, fall, lessen, let up, lower, moderate, recede, relent, shrink, subside, taper, wane

deet \'dēt\ *n, often all cap* : a colorless oily liquid insect and tick repellent
def *abbr* **1** defendant **2** definite **3** definition
de·face \di-'fās\ *vb* **♦ :** to destroy or mar the appearance of — **de·face·ment** *n* — **de·fac·er** *n*

♦ blemish, break, cripple, damage, disfigure, flaw, harm, hurt, injure, mar, spoil, vitiate

de fac·to \di-'fak-tō, dā-\ *adj or adv* **1 :** actually existing ⟨*de facto* segregation⟩ **2 :** actually exercising power ⟨*de facto* government⟩
de·fal·ca·tion \ˌdē-ˌfal-'kā-shən, -ˌfȯl-; ˌde-fəl-\ *n* : EMBEZZLEMENT
def·a·ma·tion \ˌde-fə-'mā-shən\ *n* **♦ :** the act of defaming another

♦ libel, slander, vilification

de·fam·a·to·ry \di-'fa-mə-ˌtōr-ē\ *adj* **♦ :** containing defamation : injurious to reputation

♦ libelous, scandalous, slanderous

de·fame \di-'fām\ *vb* **de·famed; de·fam·ing ♦ :** to injure or destroy the reputation of by libel or slander

♦ blacken, libel, malign, slander, smear, traduce, vilify

de·fault \di-'fȯlt\ *n* **1 ♦ :** failure to do something required by duty or law; *also* : failure to appear for a legal proceeding **2 :** failure to compete in or to finish an appointed contest ⟨lose a race by ∼⟩ **3 :** a choice made without active consideration due to lack of viable alternatives **4 :** a selection made automatically by a computer in the absence of a choice by the user — **default** *vb* — **de·fault·er** *n*

♦ delinquency, dereliction, failure, neglect, negligence, oversight

¹de·feat \di-'fēt\ *vb* **1 :** FRUSTRATE, NULLIFY **2 ♦ :** to win victory over : BEAT

♦ beat, conquer, master, overcome, prevail, rout, subdue, surmount, triumph, win

²defeat *n* **1 ♦ :** frustration by nullification or by prevention of success : the state or face of being defeated ⟨the bill suffered ∼ in the Senate⟩ **2 :** an overthrow of an army in battle **3 ♦ :** loss of a contest

♦ [1] collapse, crash, cropper, failure, fizzle, nonsuccess ♦ [3] loss, rout, shellacking *Ant* success, triumph, victory, win

de·feat·ism \-'fē-ˌti-zəm\ *n* : acceptance of or resignation to defeat — **de·feat·ist** \-tist\ *n*
defeatist *adj* **♦ :** characterized by defeatism

♦ despairing, hopeless, pessimistic

def·e·cate \'de-fi-ˌkāt\ *vb* **-cat·ed; -cat·ing 1 :** to free from impurity or corruption **2 :** to discharge feces from the bowels — **def·e·ca·tion** \ˌde-fi-'kā-shən\ *n*
¹de·fect \'dē-ˌfekt, di-'fekt\ *n* **♦ :** an imperfection that impairs worth or utility : BLEMISH

♦ blemish, deformity, disfigurement, fault, flaw, imperfection, mark, pockmark, scar

²de·fect \di-'fekt\ *vb* : to desert a cause or party esp. in order to espouse another — **de·fec·tion** \-'fek-shən\ *n*
de·fec·tive \di-'fek-tiv\ *adj* **♦ :** imperfect in form or function : FAULTY — **defective** *n*

♦ bad, faulty, imperfect

de·fec·tor \di-'fek-tər\ *n* **♦ :** one that defects

♦ deserter, recreant, renegade

de·fence *Can and Brit var of* DEFENSE
de·fend \di-'fend\ *vb* **1 ♦ :** to repel danger or attack from **2 :** to act as attorney for **3 :** to oppose the claim of another in a lawsuit : CONTEST **4 ♦ :** to maintain against opposition ⟨∼ an idea⟩

♦ [1] cover, guard, protect, safeguard, screen, secure, shield, ward *Ant* assail, assault, attack ♦ [4] justify, maintain, support, uphold

de·fen·dant \di-ˈfen-dənt\ *n* : a person required to make answer in a legal action or suit
de·fend·er \di-ˈfen-dər\ *n* ♦ : one that defends

♦ custodian, defense (*or* defence), guard, protection, protector

de·fense *or Can and Brit* **de·fence** \di-ˈfens\ *n* **1** : the act of defending : resistance against attack **2** ♦ : means, method, or capability of defending **3** ♦ : an argument in support or justification **4** : the answer made by the defendant in a legal action **5** : a defending party, group, or team

♦ [2] aegis, armor, cover, guard, protection, safeguard, screen, security, shield, wall, ward ♦ [3] alibi, excuse, justification, plea, reason

de·fense·less *or Can and Brit* **de·fence·less** \-ləs\ *adj* ♦ : being without defense

♦ exposed, helpless, susceptible, undefended, unguarded, unprotected, unresistant, vulnerable

defense mechanism *n* : an often unconscious mental process (as repression) that assists in reaching compromise solutions to personal problems
de·fen·si·ble \di-ˈfen(t)-si-bəl\ *adj* ♦ : capable of being defended

♦ justifiable, maintainable, supportable, sustainable, tenable

¹**de·fen·sive** \di-ˈfen-siv\ *adj* **1** : serving or intended to defend or protect **2** : of or relating to the attempt to keep an opponent from scoring (as in a game) — **de·fen·sive·ly** *adv* — **de·fen·sive·ness** *n*
²**defensive** *n* : a defensive position
¹**de·fer** \di-ˈfər\ *vb* **de·ferred; de·fer·ring** ♦ : to put off to a later time : POSTPONE

♦ delay, hold up, postpone, put off, shelve

²**defer** *vb* **deferred; deferring** : to submit or yield to the opinion or wishes of another
def·er·ence \ˈde-fər-əns\ *n* ♦ : courteous, respectful, or ingratiating regard for another's wishes

♦ compliance, docility, obedience

def·er·en·tial \ˌde-fə-ˈren-chəl\ *adj* ♦ : showing or expressing deference

♦ dutiful, regardful, respectful

de·fer·ment \di-ˈfər-mənt\ *n* : the act of delaying; *esp* : official postponement of military service
de·fi·ance \di-ˈfī-əns\ *n* **1** ♦ : the act or an instance of defying **2** : disposition to resist or contend

♦ disobedience, insubordination, rebelliousness, recalcitrance, refractoriness, unruliness

de·fi·ant \-ənt\ *adj* ♦ : full of defiance — **de·fi·ant·ly** *adv*

♦ contrary, disobedient, froward, intractable, rebellious, recalcitrant, refractory, unruly, untoward, wayward, willful

de·fi·bril·la·tor \dē-ˈfi-brə-ˌlā-tər\ *n* : an electronic device that applies an electric shock to restore the rhythm of a fibrillating heart — **de·fi·bril·late** \-ˌlāt\ *vb* — **de·fi·bril·la·tion** \-ˌfi-brə-ˈlā-shən\ *n*
de·fi·cien·cy \di-ˈfi-shən-sē\ *n* ♦ : the quality or state of being deficient

♦ dearth, deficit, failure, famine, inadequacy, insufficiency, lack, paucity, poverty, scantiness, scarcity, shortage, want *Ant* abundance, adequacy, amplitude, plenitude, plenty, sufficiency

deficiency disease *n* : a disease (as scurvy or beriberi) caused by a lack of essential dietary elements and esp. a vitamin or mineral
de·fi·cient \di-ˈfi-shənt\ *adj* ♦ : lacking in something necessary; *also* : not up to a normal standard

♦ inadequate, insufficient, scarce, short, shy, wanting ♦ bad, inferior, lousy, off, poor, punk, rotten, substandard, unacceptable, unsatisfactory, wanting, wretched, wrong

def·i·cit \ˈde-fə-sət\ *n* ♦ : a deficiency in amount; *esp* : an excess of expenditures over revenue

♦ dearth, deficiency, failure, famine, inadequacy, insufficiency, lack, paucity, poverty, scantiness, scarcity, shortage, want

¹**de·file** \di-ˈfīl\ *vb* **de·filed; de·fil·ing** **1** ♦ : to corrupt the purity or perfection of **2** ♦ : to make physically unclean esp. with something unpleasant or contaminating **3** : to violate the chastity of **4** ♦ : to violate the sanctity of : DESECRATE **5** : DISHONOR

♦ [1, 2] befoul, contaminate, foul, poison, pollute, taint ♦ [4] desecrate, profane, violate

²**de·file** \di-ˈfīl, ˈdē-ˌfīl\ *n* ♦ : a narrow passage or gorge

♦ canyon, flume, gap, gorge, gulch, notch, pass, ravine

de·file·ment \-mənt\ *n* **1** ♦ : the act of defiling or state of being defiled **2** ♦ : something that defiles

♦ [1] blasphemy, desecration, impiety, irreverence, sacrilege ♦ [2] adulterant, contaminant, impurity, pollutant

de·fine \di-ˈfīn\ *vb* **de·fined; de·fin·ing** **1** ♦ : to set forth the meaning of ⟨∼ a word⟩ **2** ♦ : to fix or mark the limits of **3** ♦ : to clarify in outline or character — **de·fin·able** *adj* — **de·fin·er** *n*

♦ [2] bound, circumscribe, delimit, demarcate, limit, mark, terminate ♦ [3] delineate, outline, silhouette, sketch, trace ♦ [3] characterize, depict, describe, portray, represent

def·i·nite \ˈde-fə-nət\ *adj* **1** ♦ : having distinct limits **2** ♦ : clear in meaning **3** : typically designating an identified or immediately identifiable person or thing — **def·i·nite·ness** *n*

♦ [1] determinate, finite, limited, measured, narrow, restricted ♦ [2] clear-cut, definitive, explicit, express, specific, unambiguous, unequivocal

def·i·nite·ly \-lē\ *adv* ♦ : in a definite way or manner

♦ certainly, doubtless, incontestably, indeed, indisputably, really, surely, truly, undeniably, undoubtedly, unquestionably

def·i·ni·tion \ˌde-fə-ˈni-shən\ *n* **1** : an act of determining or settling **2** : a statement of the meaning of a word or word group; *also* : the action or process of defining **3** : the action or the power of making definite and clear : CLARITY, DISTINCTNESS
de·fin·i·tive \di-ˈfi-nə-tiv\ *adj* **1** ♦ : serving to provide a final solution or to end a situation : DECISIVE **2** : authoritative and apparently exhaustive **3** : serving to define or specify precisely

♦ [1] absolute, clear, conclusive, decisive ♦ [3] clear-cut, definite, explicit, express, specific, unambiguous, unequivocal

de·flate \di-ˈflāt\ *vb* **de·flat·ed; de·flat·ing** **1** : to release air or gas from **2** : to reduce in size, importance, or effectiveness; *also* : to reduce from a state of inflation **3** : to become deflated
de·fla·tion \-ˈflā-shən\ *n* **1** : an act or instance of deflating : the state of being deflated **2** : reduction in the volume of available money or credit resulting in a decline of the general price level
de·flect \di-ˈflekt\ *vb* ♦ : to turn aside — **de·flec·tion** \-ˈflek-shən\ *n*

♦ divert, swerve, swing, turn, veer, wheel, whip

de·flo·ra·tion \ˌdē-flə-ˈrā-shən\ *n* : rupture of the hymen
de·flow·er \dē-ˈflau̇(-ə)r\ *vb* : to deprive of virginity
de·fog \dē-ˈfȯg, -ˈfäg\ *vb* : to remove fog or condensed moisture from — **de·fog·ger** *n*
de·fo·li·ant \dē-ˈfō-lē-ənt\ *n* : a chemical spray or dust used to defoliate plants
de·fo·li·ate \-ˌāt\ *vb* : to deprive of leaves esp. prematurely — **de·fo·li·a·tion** \dē-ˌfō-lē-ˈā-shən\ *n* — **de·fo·li·a·tor** \dē-ˈfō-lē-ˌā-tər\ *n*
de·for·es·ta·tion \dē-ˌfȯr-ə-ˈstā-shən\ *n* : the action or process of clearing an area of forests; *also* : the state of having been cleared of forests — **de·for·est** \(ˌ)dē-ˈfȯr-əst, -ˈfär-\ *vb*
de·form \di-ˈfȯrm\ *vb* **1** : DISFIGURE, DEFACE **2** ♦ : to make or become misshapen or changed in shape

♦ contort, distort, screw, warp

de·for·ma·tion \ˌdē-ˌfȯr-ˈmā-shən, ˌde-fər-\ *n* ♦ : the action of deforming

♦ contortion, distortion

de·formed *adj* ♦ : distorted or unshapely in form

♦ distorted, malformed, misshapen, monstrous, shapeless

de·for·mi·ty \di-ˈfȯr-mə-tē\ *n, pl* **-ties** **1** : the state of being deformed **2** ♦ : a physical blemish or distortion

♦ blemish, defect, disfigurement, fault, flaw, imperfection, mark, pockmark, scar

de·fraud \di-ˈfrȯd\ *vb* ♦ : to deprive of something by deception or fraud : CHEAT

♦ bleed, cheat, chisel, cozen, fleece, hustle, mulct, rook, shortchange, skin, squeeze, stick, sting, swindle, victimize

de·fray \di-ˈfrā\ *vb* : to provide for the payment of : PAY — **de·fray·al** *n*
de·frock \(ˌ)dē-ˈfräk\ *vb* : to deprive (as a priest) of the right to exercise the functions of office

de·frost \di-'fròst\ *vb* **1** : to thaw out **2** : to free from ice — **de·frost·er** *n*

deft \'deft\ *adj* ♦ : characterized by facility and skill — **deft·ly** *adv*

♦ clever, cunning, dexterous, handy

deft·ness \-nəs\ *n* ♦ : the quality or state of being deft

♦ agility, dexterity, nimbleness, sleight ♦ adeptness, adroitness, art, artfulness, artifice, artistry, cleverness, craft, cunning, masterfulness, skill

de·funct \di-'fəŋkt\ *adj* ♦ : no longer living, existing, or functioning

♦ bygone, dead, extinct, gone

de·fuse \dē-'fyüz\ *vb* **1** : to remove the fuse from (as a bomb) **2** : to make less harmful, potent, or tense

de·fy \di-'fī\ *vb* **de·fied; de·fy·ing** **1** ♦ : to challenge to do something considered impossible : DARE **2** ♦ : to refuse boldly to obey or to yield to ⟨~ the law⟩ **3** ♦ : to resist attempts at : WITHSTAND ⟨a scene that *defies* description⟩

♦ [1] challenge, dare ♦ [2] beard, brave, brazen, confront, dare, face ♦ [3] buck, fight, oppose, repel, resist, withstand

deg *abbr* degree

de·gas \dē-'gas\ *vb* : to remove gas from

de·gen·er·a·cy \di-'je-nə-rə-sē\ *n, pl* **-cies** **1** : the state of being degenerate **2** ♦ : the process of becoming degenerate **3** : PERVERSION

♦ corruption, debasement, debauchery, decadence, degeneration, degradation, demoralization, depravity, dissipation, dissoluteness, perversion

¹de·gen·er·ate \di-'je-nə-rət\ *adj* ♦ : fallen or deteriorated from a former, higher, or normal condition — **de·gen·er·a·tive** \-'je-nə-ˌrā-tiv\ *adj*

♦ corrupt, debauched, decadent, dissolute, perverse, perverted, reprobate

²de·gen·er·ate \di-'je-nə-ˌrāt\ *vb* ♦ : to undergo deterioration (as in morality, intelligence, structure, or function)

♦ decay, decline, descend, deteriorate, ebb, rot, sink, worsen

³de·gen·er·ate \-rət\ *n* ♦ : a degenerate person; *esp* : a sexual pervert

♦ decadent, libertine, pervert, profligate

de·gen·er·a·tion \di-ˌje-nə-'rā-shən\ *n* ♦ : the process of passing from a higher to a lower type

♦ decay, decline, deterioration ♦ corruption, debasement, debauchery, decadence, degeneracy, degradation, demoralization, depravity, dissipation, dissoluteness, perversion

de·grad·able \di-'grā-də-bəl\ *adj* : capable of being chemically degraded

deg·ra·da·tion \ˌde-grə-'dā-shən\ *n* **1** : the act or process of degrading **2 a** ♦ : decline to a low, destitute, or demoralized state **b** ♦ : moral or intellectual decadence

♦ [2a] decline, fall ♦ [2b] corruption, debasement, debauchery, decadence, degeneracy, degeneration, demoralization, depravity, dissipation, dissoluteness, perversion

de·grade \di-'grād\ *vb* **1** ♦ : to reduce from a higher to a lower rank or degree **2 a** ♦ : to bring to low esteem or into disrepute **b** ♦ : to drag down in moral or intellectual character : DEBASE **3** : DECOMPOSE

♦ [1] break, bust, demote, downgrade, reduce ♦ [2a] abase, debase, demean, discredit, disgrace, dishonor (*or* dishonour), humble, humiliate, lower, shame, smirch, take down ♦ [2b] debase, demean, demoralize, humble, subvert, warp

de·grad·ing *adj* ♦ : that degrades

♦ contemptuous, derogatory, disdainful, scornful, uncomplimentary

de·gree \di-'grē\ *n* **1** ♦ : a step in a series **2** ♦ : a rank or grade of official, ecclesiastical, or social position; *also* : the civil condition of a person **3** : the extent, intensity, or scope of something esp. as measured by a graded series **4** : one of the forms or sets of forms used in the comparison of an adjective or adverb **5** : a title conferred upon students by a college, university, or professional school on completion of a program of study **6** : a line or space of the musical staff; *also* : a note or tone of a musical scale **7** : a unit of measure for angles that is equal to an angle with its vertex at the center of a circle and its sides cutting off $1/360$ of the circumference; *also* : a unit of measure for arcs of a circle that is equal to the amount of arc extending $1/360$ of the circumference **8** : any of various units for measuring temperature

♦ [1] cut, grade, inch, notch, peg, phase, point, stage, step ♦ [2] footing, level, place, position, rank, situation, standing, station, status

de·horn \dē-'hòrn\ *vb* : to deprive of horns

de·hu·man·ize \dē-'hyü-mə-ˌnīz\ *vb* : to deprive of human qualities, personality, or spirit — **de·hu·man·i·za·tion** \ˌdē-ˌhyü-mə-nə-'zā-shən\ *n*

de·hu·mid·i·fy \ˌdē-hyü-'mi-də-ˌfī\ *vb* : to remove moisture from (as the air) — **de·hu·mid·i·fi·er** *n*

de·hy·drate \dē-'hī-ˌdrāt\ *vb* ♦ : to remove water from; *also* : to lose liquid — **de·hy·dra·tion** \ˌdē-hī-'drā-shən\ *n*

♦ dry, parch, sear

de·hy·dro·ge·na·tion \ˌdē-(ˌ)hī-ˌdrä-jə-'nā-shən, -drə-\ *n* : the removal of hydrogen from a chemical compound — **de·hy·dro·ge·nate** \ˌdē-(ˌ)hī-'drä-jə-ˌnāt, dē-'hī-drə-jə-\ *vb*

de·ice \dē-'īs\ *vb* : to keep free or rid of ice ⟨~ a plane⟩ — **de·ic·er** *n*

de·i·fi·ca·tion \ˌdē-ə-fə-'kā-shən\ *n* ♦ : the act or an instance of deifying

♦ adulation, idolatry, worship

de·i·fy \'dē-ə-ˌfī\ *vb* **-fied; -fy·ing** **1 a** : to make a god of **b** ♦ : to treat as an object of worship **2** ♦ : to glorify as of supreme worth; *also* : WORSHIP

♦ [1b] adore, canonize, dote on, idolize, worship ♦ [2] adore, glorify, revere, venerate, worship

deign \'dān\ *vb* : CONDESCEND

de·ion·ize \dē-'ī-ə-ˌnīz\ *vb* : to remove ions from

de·ism \'dē-ˌi-zəm\ *n, often cap* : a system of thought advocating natural religion based on human morality and reason rather than divine revelation — **de·ist** \'dē-ist\ *n, often cap* — **de·is·tic** \dē-'is-tik\ *adj*

de·i·ty \'dē-ə-tē, 'dā-\ *n, pl* **-ties** **1** ♦ : the quality or state of being divine : DIVINITY **2** *cap* ♦ : the Being worshipped as the creator and ruler of the universe : GOD 1 **3** : a god or goddess

♦ [1] divinity, godhead ♦ **Deity** [2] Almighty, Jehovah, Supreme Being

dé·jà vu \ˌdā-ˌzhä-'vü\ *n* : the feeling that one has seen or heard something before

de·ject·ed \di-'jek-təd\ *adj* ♦ : low in spirits : SAD — **de·ject·ed·ly** *adv*

♦ bad, blue, depressed, despondent, disconsolate, down, forlorn, gloomy, glum, low, melancholy, miserable, mournful, sad, unhappy

de·jec·tion \di-'jek-shən\ *n* ♦ : lowness of spirits

♦ blues, depression, desolation, despondency, doldrums, dumps, forlornness, gloom, heartsickness, melancholy, sadness

de ju·re \dē-'jùr-ē\ *adv or adj* : by legal right

deka·gram \'de-kə-ˌgram\ *n* : a metric unit of measure equal to 10 grams

deka·li·ter \-ˌlē-tər\ *n* : a metric unit of measure equal to 10 liters

deka·me·ter \-ˌmē-tər\ *n* : a metric unit of measure equal to 10 meters

del *abbr* delegate; delegation

Del *abbr* Delaware

Del·a·ware \'de-lə-ˌwar\ *n, pl* **Delaware** *or* **Delawares** : a member of an Indigenous people orig. of the Delaware valley; *also* : the Algonquian language of the Delaware people

¹de·lay \di-'lā\ *n* **1** : the act of delaying : the state of being delayed **2** : the time for which something is delayed

²delay *vb* **1** ♦ : to put off to a later time : POSTPONE **2** ♦ : to stop, detain, or hinder for a time **3** ♦ : to move or act slowly

♦ [1] defer, hold up, postpone, put off, shelve ♦ [2] encumber, hamper, hinder, hold up, impede, inhibit, interfere with, obstruct, tie up ♦ [3] crawl, creep, dally, dawdle, dillydally, drag, lag, linger, loiter, poke, tarry *Ant* hurry, run, rush, speed

de·lec·ta·ble \di-'lek-tə-bəl\ *adj* **1** ♦ : highly pleasing : DELIGHTFUL **2** ♦ : very pleasing to the taste or smell : DELICIOUS

♦ [1] agreeable, congenial, delicious, delightful, dreamy, felicitous, good, grateful, gratifying, nice, palatable, pleasant, pleasurable, satisfying ♦ [2] ambrosial, appetizing, delicious, flavorful (*or* flavourful), luscious, palatable, savory, scrumptious, tasty, toothsome, yummy

de·lec·ta·tion \ˌdē-ˌlek-'tā-shən\ *n* **1** ♦ : a high degree of gratification **2** ♦ : something that gives great pleasure : DELIGHT

♦ contentment, delight, enjoyment, gladness, gratification, pleasure, relish, satisfaction

¹del·e·gate \'de-li-gət, -ˌgāt\ *n* **1** ♦ **:** a person acting for another **2 :** a member of the lower house of the legislature of Maryland, Virginia, or West Virginia

♦ ambassador, emissary, envoy, legate, minister, representative ♦ agent, attorney, commissary, deputy, envoy, factor, proxy, representative

²del·e·gate \-ˌgāt\ *vb* **-gat·ed; -gat·ing** **1 :** to assign (as responsibility or power to act or make decisions) to another ⟨∼ authority⟩ **2** ♦ **:** to appoint as one's delegate

♦ commission, deputize

del·e·ga·tion \ˌde-li-'gā-shən\ *n* **1** ♦ **:** the act of delegating **2 :** one or more persons chosen to represent others

♦ authorization, commission, license (*or* licence), mandate

de·lete \di-'lēt\ *vb* **de·let·ed; de·let·ing :** to eliminate esp. by blotting out, cutting out, or erasing — **de·le·tion** \-'lē-shən\ *n*
del·e·te·ri·ous \ˌde-lə-'tir-ē-əs\ *adj* ♦ **:** harmful often in a subtle or unexpected way **:** NOXIOUS

♦ adverse, bad, baleful, baneful, damaging, detrimental, evil, harmful, hurtful, ill, injurious, mischievous, noxious, pernicious, prejudicial

delft \'delft\ *n* **1 :** a Dutch pottery with an opaque white glaze and predominantly blue decoration **2 :** glazed pottery esp. when blue and white
delft·ware \-ˌwer\ *n* **:** DELFT
deli \'de-lē\ *n, pl* **del·is :** DELICATESSEN
¹de·lib·er·ate \di-'li-bə-ˌrāt\ *vb* **-at·ed; -at·ing** ♦ **:** to consider carefully — **de·lib·er·a·tive** \-'li-bə-ˌrā-tiv, -brə-tiv\ *adj* — **de·lib·er·a·tive·ly** *adv*

♦ chew over, cogitate, consider, contemplate, debate, entertain, meditate, mull, ponder, question, ruminate, study, think, weigh

²de·lib·er·ate \di-'li-bə-rət, -'li-brət\ *adj* **1** ♦ **:** determined after careful thought **2** ♦ **:** done or said intentionally **3 :** UNHURRIED, SLOW — **de·lib·er·ate·ness** *n*

♦ [1] advised, calculated, measured, reasoned, studied, thoughtful, thought-out *Ant* casual ♦ [2] freewill, intentional, purposeful, voluntary, willful, willing *Ant* coerced, forced, involuntary, unintentional

de·lib·er·ate·ly \-lē\ *adv* ♦ **:** in a deliberate manner

♦ consciously, intentionally, knowingly, purposely, willfully

de·lib·er·a·tion \di-ˌli-bə-'rā-shən\ *n* **1** ♦ **:** the act of deliberating **2 :** the quality or state of being deliberate

♦ consideration, debate, thought ♦ argument, colloquy, conference, discourse, discussion, give-and-take, parley, talk

del·i·ca·cy \'de-li-kə-sē\ *n, pl* **-cies** **1 :** something pleasing to eat and considered rare or luxurious **2 a** ♦ **:** the quality or state of being dainty **:** FINENESS **b :** the quality or state of being frail **:** FRAILTY **3 :** nicety or expressiveness of touch **4 a :** precise perception and discrimination **b** ♦ **:** extreme sensitivity and precision **5 :** sensibility in feeling or conduct; *also* **:** SQUEAMISH-NESS **6 :** the quality or state of requiring delicate handling

♦ [1] dainty, goody, tidbit, treat ♦ [2a] daintiness, fineness, fragility *Ant* coarseness, crudity, roughness, rudeness ♦ [4b] accuracy, closeness, exactness, fineness, precision, veracity

del·i·cate \'de-li-kət\ *adj* **1 :** pleasing to the senses of taste or smell esp. in a mild or subtle way **2** ♦ **:** marked by daintiness or charm **:** EXQUISITE **3 a :** difficult to please **:** FASTIDIOUS **b :** SQUEAMISH **4 a** ♦ **:** easily damaged **:** FRAGILE **b :** not robust in health or constitution **:** SICKLY **5** ♦ **:** requiring skill or tact **6** ♦ **:** marked by care, skill, or tact **7** ♦ **:** marked by minute precision **:** very sensitive — **del·i·cate·ly** *adv*

♦ [2] dainty, exquisite, gentle, mild, refined, subtle *Ant* robust, strong, sturdy ♦ [2] choice, dainty, elegant, exquisite, rare, select ♦ [4a] breakable, fragile, frail ♦ [5] catchy, difficult, knotty, problematic, spiny, thorny, ticklish, touchy, tough, tricky ♦ [6] exact, fine, minute, nice, refined, subtle ♦ [7] acute, keen, perceptive, sensitive, sharp

del·i·ca·tes·sen \ˌde-li-kə-'tes-ᵊn\ *n pl* **1 :** ready-to-eat food products (as cooked meats and prepared salads) **2** *sing, pl* **delicatessens :** a store where delicatessen are sold
de·li·cious \di-'li-shəs\ *adj* **1 :** affording great pleasure **:** DELIGHTFUL **2** ♦ **:** appealing to one of the bodily senses esp. of taste or smell

♦ ambrosial, appetizing, delectable, flavorful (*or* flavourful),

luscious, palatable, savory, scrumptious, tasty, toothsome, yummy *Ant* flat, flavorless, insipid, stale, tasteless, unappetizing, unpalatable

de·li·cious·ly \-lē\ *adv* **1 :** in a delicious manner **2 :** so as to produce delight
de·li·cious·ness \-nəs\ *n* ♦ **:** the quality or state of being delicious

♦ lusciousness, palatability, savor, tastiness

¹de·light \di-'līt\ *n* **1** ♦ **:** great pleasure or satisfaction **2** ♦ **:** something that gives great pleasure

♦ [1] delectation, joy, kick, manna, pleasure, treat ♦ [1, 2] contentment, delectation, enjoyment, gladness, gratification, pleasure, relish, satisfaction

²delight *vb* **1** ♦ **:** to take great pleasure **2** ♦ **:** to satisfy greatly **:** PLEASE

♦ [1] crow, exult, glory, joy, rejoice, triumph ♦ *usu* **delight in** [1] adore, dig, enjoy, fancy, groove, like, love, relish, revel ♦ [2] content, gladden, gratify, please, rejoice, satisfy, suit, warm

de·light·ed *adj* ♦ **:** highly pleased **:** GRATIFIED — **de·light·ed·ly** *adv*

♦ blissful, glad, happy, joyful, pleased

de·light·ful \-fəl\ *adj* ♦ **:** affording great pleasure and satisfaction

♦ agreeable, congenial, delectable, delicious, dreamy, felicitous, good, grateful, gratifying, nice, palatable, pleasant, pleasurable, satisfying ♦ amusing, diverting, enjoyable, entertaining, fun, pleasurable

de·light·ful·ly \-fə-lē\ *adv* ♦ **:** in a delightful manner

♦ agreeably, favorably (*or* favourably), felicitously, gloriously, nicely, pleasantly, pleasingly, satisfyingly, splendidly, well

de·lim·it \di-'li-mət\ *vb* ♦ **:** to mark the limits of

♦ bound, circumscribe, define, demarcate, limit, mark, terminate

de·lin·eate \di-'li-nē-ˌāt\ *vb* **-eat·ed; -eat·ing** **1** ♦ **:** to mark the outline of **:** SKETCH **2** ♦ **:** to picture in words **:** DESCRIBE

♦ [1] define, outline, silhouette, sketch, trace ♦ [2] depict, describe, draw, image, paint, picture, portray, sketch

de·lin·ea·tion \di-ˌli-nē-'ā-shən\ *n* **1 :** the act of delineating **2** ♦ **:** something made by delineating

♦ cartoon, drawing, sketch ♦ depiction, description, picture, portrait, portrayal, sketch

de·lin·quen·cy \di-'liŋ-kwən-sē\ *n, pl* **-cies** ♦ **:** the quality or state of being delinquent

♦ default, dereliction, failure, neglect, negligence, oversight

¹de·lin·quent \-kwənt\ *n* **:** a delinquent person
²delinquent *adj* **1 :** offending by neglect or violation of duty or of law **2** ♦ **:** being overdue in payment

♦ behind, belated, late, overdue, tardy

del·i·quesce \ˌde-li-'kwes\ *vb* **-quesced; -quesc·ing** ♦ **:** to dissolve or melt away — **del·i·ques·cent** \-'kwes-ᵊnt\ *adj*

♦ flux, fuse, liquefy, melt, run, thaw

de·lir·i·ous \-ē-əs\ *adj* **1 :** of, relating to, or characteristic of delirium **2** ♦ **:** affected with or marked by delirium — **de·lir·i·ous·ly** *adv*

♦ feverish, fierce, frantic, frenetic, frenzied, furious, mad, rabid, violent, wild

de·lir·i·um \di-'lir-ē-əm\ *n* **1 :** mental disturbance marked by confusion, disordered speech, and hallucinations **2** ♦ **:** frenzied excitement

♦ agitation, distraction, frenzy, furor, fury, hysteria, rage, rampage, uproar

delirium tre·mens \-'trē-mənz, -'tre-\ *n* **:** a violent delirium with tremors that is induced by excessive and prolonged use of alcoholic liquors
de·liv·er \di-'li-vər\ *vb* **-ered; -er·ing** **1** ♦ **:** to set free **:** rescue from actual or feared evil **:** SAVE **2** ♦ **:** to take and hand over to or leave for another **:** TRANSFER ⟨∼ a letter⟩ **3 :** to assist in giving birth or at the birth of; *also* **:** to give birth to **4 :** UTTER, COMMUNICATE **5 :** to send to an intended target or destination **6** ♦ **:** to produce the promised, desired, or expected results — **de·liv·er·able** \-'li-v(ə-)rə-bəl\ *adj*

♦ [1] rescue, save ♦ [2] commend, commit, consign, entrust,

give, hand over, leave, pass, transfer, transmit, trust, turn over, vest ♦ [6] click, go over, pan out, succeed, work out

de·liv·er·ance \di-'li-v(ə-)rən(t)s\ *n* **1 :** the act of delivering someone or something **:** the state of being delivered **2 :** something delivered; *esp* **:** an opinion or decision (as the verdict of a jury) expressed publicly

♦ rescue, salvation

de·liv·er·er \-ər\ *n* ♦ **:** one that delivers

♦ redeemer, rescuer, savior

de·liv·ery \di-'li-və-rē\ *n, pl* **-er·ies** ♦ **:** the act or manner of delivering something; *also* **:** something delivered — **de·liv·ery·man** \-ˌman\ *n*

♦ discharge, quietus, quittance, release ♦ childbirth, labor (*or* labour)

dell \'del\ *n* **:** a small secluded valley
de·louse \dē-'laus\ *vb* **:** to remove lice from
del·phin·i·um \del-'fi-nē-əm\ *n* **:** any of a genus of mostly perennial herbs related to the buttercups with tall branching spikes of irregular flowers
del·ta \'del-tə\ *n* **1 :** the 4th letter of the Greek alphabet — Δ or δ **2 :** something shaped like a capital Δ; *esp* **:** the triangular silt-formed land at the mouth of a river — **del·ta·ic** \del-'tā-ik\ *adj*
del·toid \'del-ˌtoid\ *n* **:** a large triangular muscle that covers the shoulder joint and raises the arm laterally
de·lude \di-'lüd\ *vb* **de·lud·ed; de·lud·ing** ♦ **:** to mislead the mind or judgment of **:** DECEIVE

♦ beguile, bluff, cozen, deceive, dupe, fool, gull, have, hoax, hoodwink, humbug, misinform, mislead, string along, take in, trick

¹del·uge \'del-yüj\ *n* **1** ♦ **:** a flooding of land by water **2** ♦ **:** a drenching rain **3 :** a great amount or number

♦ [1] cataclysm, cataract, flood, inundation, overflow, spate, torrent ♦ [2] cloudburst, downpour, rain, rainstorm, storm, wet

²deluge *vb* **del·uged; del·ug·ing 1** ♦ **:** to overflow with water **:** INUNDATE **2 :** to overwhelm as if with a deluge

♦ drown, engulf, flood, inundate, overflow, overwhelm, submerge, swamp

de·lu·sion \di-'lü-zhən\ *n* ♦ **:** a deluding or being deluded; *esp* **:** a persistent false psychotic belief — **de·lu·sion·al** \-'lü-zhə-nəl\ *adj*

♦ chimera, conceit, daydream, dream, fancy, fantasy, figment, hallucination, illusion, phantasm, pipe dream, unreality, vision

de·lu·sive \di-'lü-siv\ *adj* **1** ♦ **:** likely to delude **2 :** constituting a delusion

♦ deceitful, deceptive, fallacious, false, misleading, specious

de·luxe \di-'luks, -'ləks, -'lüks\ *adj* ♦ **:** notably luxurious or elegant

♦ lavish, luxuriant, luxurious, opulent, palatial, plush, sumptuous

delve \'delv\ *vb* **delved; delv·ing 1 :** to dig or labor with or as if with a spade **2** ♦ **:** to seek laboriously for information

♦ *usu* **delve into** dig, explore, go, inquire into, investigate, look, probe, research

dely *abbr* delivery
Dem *abbr* Democrat; Democratic
de·mag·ne·tize \dē-'mag-nə-ˌtīz\ *vb* **:** to cause to lose magnetic properties — **de·mag·ne·ti·za·tion** \dē-ˌmag-nə-tə-'zā-shən\ *n*
dem·a·gogue *also* **dem·a·gog** \'de-mə-ˌgäg\ *n* ♦ **:** a person who appeals to the emotions and prejudices of people esp. in order to gain political power — **dem·a·gogu·ery** \-ˌgä-gə-rē\ *n* — **dem·a·gogy** \-ˌgä-gē, -ˌgä-jē\ *n*

♦ agitator, firebrand, incendiary, inciter, rabble-rouser

¹de·mand \di-'mand\ *n* **1** ♦ **:** an act of demanding; *also* **:** something claimed as due or just **2 :** the ability and desire to buy goods or services; *also* **:** the quantity of goods wanted at a stated price **3 :** a seeking or being sought after **:** urgent need **4** ♦ **:** a pressing need or requirement

♦ [1] claim, dun, requisition ♦ [4] condition, essential, must, necessity, need, requirement, requisite

²demand *vb* **1** ♦ **:** to ask for with authority **:** claim as due or just **2 :** to ask earnestly or in the manner of a command **3** ♦ **:** to call for as useful or necessary **:** REQUIRE ⟨a patient who ∼s constant care⟩

♦ [1] call, claim, clamor (*or* clamour), command, enjoin, exact,

insist, press, quest, stipulate (for) ♦ [3] necessitate, need, require, take, want, warrant

de·mand·ing *adj* **1** ♦ **:** requiring much time, effort, or attention **2** ♦ **:** difficult in making demands

♦ [1] arduous, burdensome, challenging, exacting, grueling, laborious, onerous, taxing, toilsome *Ant* light, undemanding ♦ [2] choosy, dainty, delicate, exacting, fastidious, finicky, fussy, nice, old-maidish, particular, picky

de·mar·cate \di-'mär-ˌkāt, 'dē-ˌmär-\ *vb* **-cat·ed; -cat·ing 1** ♦ **:** to fix or define the limits of **:** DELIMIT **2 :** to set apart **:** DISTINGUISH

♦ bound, circumscribe, define, delimit, limit, mark, terminate

de·mar·ca·tion \ˌdē-ˌmär-'kā-shən\ *n* ♦ **:** the act or process of demarcating; *also* **:** the result of demarcating

♦ discrimination, distinction, separation

dé·marche *or* **de·marche** \dā-'märsh\ *n* **:** a course of action **:** MANEUVER
¹de·mean \di-'mēn\ *vb* **de·meaned; de·mean·ing** ♦ **:** to behave or conduct (oneself) usu. in a proper manner

♦ acquit, bear, behave, comport, conduct, deport, quit

²demean *vb* **de·meaned; de·mean·ing** ♦ **:** to lower in character, status, or reputation **:** DEGRADE

♦ debase, degrade, demoralize, humble, subvert, warp

de·mean·or *or Can and Brit* **de·mean·our** \di-'mē-nər\ *n* ♦ **:** behavior toward others **:** BEARING

♦ actions, bearing, behavior (*or* behaviour), comportment, conduct, deportment

de·ment·ed \di-'men-təd\ *adj* **:** disordered in mind **:** INSANE — not used technically — **de·ment·ed·ly** *adv*
de·men·tia \di-'men-chə\ *n* **1 :** deterioration of cognitive functioning (as in Alzheimer's disease) **2 :** a deranged state of the mind **:** INSANITY ⟨fanaticism bordering on ∼⟩
de·mer·it \di-'mer-ət\ *n* **1** ♦ **:** a quality that deserves blame or lacks merit **:** FAULT **2 :** a mark placed against a person's record for some fault or offense

♦ failing, fault, foible, frailty, shortcoming, vice, weakness

de·mesne \di-'mān, -'mēn\ *n* **1 :** manorial land actually possessed by the lord and not held by free tenants **2 a** ♦ **:** the land attached to a mansion **b :** ESTATE **3** ♦ **:** an indeterminate geographic area **:** REGION **4 :** a sphere of knowledge, influence, or activity **:** REALM

♦ [2a] grounds, park, premises, yard ♦ [3] area, field, region, zone

demi·god \'de-mi-ˌgäd\ *n* **:** a mythological being with more power than a mortal but less than a god
demi·john \'de-mi-ˌjän\ *n* **:** a large narrow-necked bottle usu. enclosed in wickerwork
de·mil·i·ta·rize \dē-'mi-lə-tə-ˌrīz\ *vb* **:** to strip of military forces, weapons, or fortifications — **de·mil·i·tar·i·za·tion** \dē-ˌmi-lə-tə-rə-'zā-shən\ *n*
demi·mon·daine \ˌde-mi-ˌmän-'dān\ *n* **:** a woman of the demimonde
demi·monde \'de-mi-ˌmänd\ *n* **1 :** a class of women on the fringes of respectable society supported by wealthy lovers **2 :** a distinct isolated group having low reputation or prestige
de·min·er·al·ize \dē-'mi-nə-rə-ˌlīz\ *vb* **:** to remove the mineral matter from — **de·min·er·al·i·za·tion** \-ˌmi-nə-rə-lə-'zā-shən\ *n*
de·mise \di-'mīz\ *n* **1 :** LEASE **2 :** transfer of sovereignty to a successor ⟨∼ of the crown⟩ **3 a** ♦ **:** a permanent cessation of all vital functions **:** DEATH **b** ♦ **:** a cessation of existence or activity **4 :** loss of status

♦ [3a] death, expiration, termination ♦ [3b] death, decease, doom, end, passing, quietus

demi·tasse \'de-mi-ˌtas\ *n* **:** a small cup of black coffee; *also* **:** the cup used to serve it
demo \'de-mō\ *n, pl* **dem·os 1 :** DEMONSTRATION **2 :** a product used to show performance or merits to prospective buyers **3 :** a recording used to show off a song or performer
de·mo·bi·lize \di-'mō-bə-ˌlīz, dē-\ *vb* **1 :** DISBAND **2 :** to discharge from military service — **de·mo·bi·li·za·tion** \di-ˌmō-bə-lə-'zā-shən, dē-\ *n*
de·moc·ra·cy \di-'mä-krə-sē\ *n, pl* **-cies 1 :** government by the people; *esp* **:** rule of the majority **2 :** a government in which the supreme power is held by the people **3 :** a political unit that has a democratic government **4** *cap* **:** the principles and policies of

the Democratic party in the U.S. **5** : the common people esp. when constituting the source of political authority **6** : the absence of hereditary or arbitrary class distinctions or privileges

dem·o·crat \'de-mə-ˌkrat\ *n* **1** : one who believes in or practices democracy **2** *cap* : a member of the Democratic party of the U.S.

dem·o·crat·ic \ˌde-mə-'kra-tik\ *adj* **1** ♦ : of, relating to, or favoring democracy **2** *often cap* : of or relating to one of the two major political parties in the U.S. associated in modern times with policies of broad social reform and internationalism **3** : relating to or appealing to the common people ⟨~ art⟩ **4** : not snobbish — **dem·o·crat·i·cal·ly** \-ti-k(ə-)lē\ *adv*

♦ popular, republican, self-governing *Ant* undemocratic

de·moc·ra·tize \di-'mä-krə-ˌtīz\ *vb* **-tized; -tiz·ing** : to make democratic

dé·mo·dé \ˌdā-mō-'dā\ *adj* : no longer fashionable : OUT-OF-DATE

de·mo·graph·ics \ˌde-mə-'gra-fiks, ˌdē-\ *n pl* : the statistical characteristics of human populations

de·mog·ra·phy \di-'mä-grə-fē\ *n* : the statistical study of human populations and esp. their size and distribution and the number of births and deaths — **de·mog·ra·pher** \-fər\ *n* — **de·mo·graph·ic** \ˌde-mə-'gra-fik, ˌdē-\ *adj* — **de·mo·graph·i·cal·ly** \-fi-k(ə-)lē\ *adv*

dem·oi·selle \ˌdem-wə-'zel\ *n* : a young woman

de·mol·ish \di-'mä-lish\ *vb* **1** ♦ : to destroy to the ground : RAZE **2** ♦ : to break to pieces : SMASH **3** ♦ : to put an end to

♦ [1, 3] annihilate, blot out, desolate, destroy, devastate, do in, exterminate, extinguish, obliterate, pulverize, ruin, shatter, smash, tear down, waste, wipe out, wreck ♦ [2] blast, blow up, burst, explode, pop, shatter, smash

de·mo·li·tion \ˌde-mə-'li-shən, ˌdē-\ *n* ♦ : the act of demolishing; *esp* : destruction by means of explosives

♦ annihilation, desolation, destruction, devastation, havoc, loss, obliteration, ruin, wastage, wreckage

de·mon *or* **dae·mon** \'dē-mən\ *n* **1** ♦ : an evil spirit : DEVIL **2** *usu daemon* : an attendant power or spirit **3** : one that has unusual drive or effectiveness

♦ devil, fiend, ghoul, imp

de·mon·e·tize \dē-'mä-nə-ˌtīz, -'mə-\ *vb* : to stop using as money or as a monetary standard ⟨~ silver⟩ — **de·mon·e·ti·za·tion** \dē-ˌmä-nə-tə-'zā-shən, -mə-\ *n*

de·mo·ni·ac \di-'mō-nē-ˌak\ *also* **de·mo·ni·a·cal** \ˌdē-mə-'nī-ə-kəl\ *adj* **1** : possessed or influenced by a demon **2** : of, relating to, or suggestive of a demon : DEVILISH

de·mon·ic \di-'mä-nik\ *also* **de·mon·i·cal** \-ni-kəl\ *adj* ♦ : of, relating to, or suggestive of a demon : FIENDISH

♦ devilish, diabolical, fiendish, satanic

de·mon·ize \'dē-mə-ˌnīz\ *vb* **-ized; -iz·ing** **1** : to convert into a demon **2** : to characterize or treat as evil or harmful

de·mon·ol·o·gy \ˌdē-mə-'nä-lə-jē\ *n* **1** : the study of demons **2** : belief in demons

de·mon·stra·ble \di-'män-strə-bəl\ *adj* **1** ♦ : capable of being demonstrated **2** : APPARENT, EVIDENT — **de·mon·stra·bly** \-blē\ *adv*

♦ provable, supportable, sustainable, verifiable

dem·on·strate \'de-mən-ˌstrāt\ *vb* **-strat·ed; -strat·ing** **1** ♦ : to show clearly **2** ♦ : to prove or make clear by reasoning or evidence **3** ♦ : to explain esp. with many examples **4** : to show publicly ⟨~ a new car⟩ **5** : to make a public display ⟨~ in protest⟩ — **dem·on·stra·tor** \'de-mən-ˌstrā-tər\ *n*

♦ [1] establish, prove, show, substantiate ♦ [2] document, establish, prove, substantiate, validate ♦ [3] clarify, clear (up), construe, elucidate, explain, explicate, expound, illuminate, illustrate, interpret, spell out

dem·on·stra·tion \ˌde-mən-'strā-shən\ *n* **1** : an act, process, or means of demonstrating to the intelligence **2** ♦ : an outward expression or display

♦ display, exhibition, show

¹de·mon·stra·tive \di-'män-strə-tiv\ *adj* **1** : demonstrating as real or true **2** : characterized by demonstration **3** : pointing out the one referred to and distinguishing it from others of the same class ⟨~ pronoun⟩ **4** ♦ : marked by display of feeling : EFFUSIVE — **de·mon·stra·tive·ly** *adv* — **de·mon·stra·tive·ness** *n*

♦ effusive, emotional, uninhibited, unreserved, unrestrained *Ant* inhibited, reserved, restrained, undemonstrative, unemotional

²demonstrative *n* : a demonstrative word and esp. a pronoun

de·mor·al·i·za·tion \di-ˌmȯr-ə-lə-'zā-shən\ *n* ♦ : the act or process of demoralizing : a demoralized state

♦ corruption, debasement, debauchery, decadence, degeneracy, degeneration, degradation, depravity, dissipation, dissoluteness, perversion ♦ despair, despondency, discouragement, dismay

de·mor·al·ize \di-'mȯr-ə-ˌlīz\ *vb* **1** ♦ : to corrupt in morals **2** ♦ : to weaken in discipline or spirit

♦ [1] debase, degrade, demean, humble, subvert, warp ♦ [2] daunt, discourage, dishearten, dismay, dispirit, unman, unnerve

de·mote \di-'mōt\ *vb* **de·mot·ed; de·mot·ing** ♦ : to reduce to a lower grade or rank — **de·mo·tion** \-'mō-shən\ *n*

♦ break, bust, degrade, downgrade, reduce *Ant* advance, elevate, promote, raise

de·mot·ic \di-'mä-tik\ *adj* : COMMON, POPULAR

¹de·mur \di-'mər\ *vb* **de·murred; de·mur·ring** ♦ : to take exception : OBJECT

♦ kick, object, protest, remonstrate

²demur *n* **1** : hesitation (as in doing or accepting) usu. based on doubt of the acceptability of something offered or proposed **2** ♦ : the act or an instance of objecting — **de·mur·ral** \-əl\ *n*

♦ challenge, complaint, expostulation, fuss, kick, objection, protest, question, remonstrance

de·mure \di-'myu̇r\ *adj* **1** ♦ : quietly modest **2** ♦ : affectedly modest, reserved, or serious — **de·mure·ly** *adv*

♦ [1] humble, lowly, meek, modest, retiring, shy, unassuming, unpretentious ♦ [2] coquettish, coy, kittenish

de·mur·rer \di-'mər-ər\ *n* : a claim by the defendant in a legal action that the plaintiff does not have sufficient grounds to proceed

den \'den\ *n* **1** ♦ : the lair of a wild usu. predatory animal **2** ♦ : a refuge or place for hiding : HIDEOUT ⟨a robber's ~⟩; *also* : a place like a hideout or a center of secret activity ⟨opium ~⟩ ⟨a ~ of iniquity⟩ **3** : a cozy private little room

♦ [1] burrow, hole, lair, lodge ♦ [2] concealment, covert, hideout, lair, nest

Den *abbr* Denmark

de·na·ture \dē-'nā-chər\ *vb* **de·na·tured; de·na·tur·ing** : to remove or change the natural qualities of; *esp* : to make (alcohol) unfit for drinking

den·drol·o·gy \den-'drä-lə-jē\ *n* : the study of trees — **den·drol·o·gist** \-jist\ *n*

den·gue \'deŋ-gē, -gā\ *n* : an acute infectious disease characterized by headache, severe joint pain, and rash

de·ni·al \di-'nī-əl\ *n* **1** ♦ : rejection of a request **2** ♦ : refusal to admit the truth of a statement or charge; *also* : assertion that something alleged is false **3** : DISAVOWAL **4** : restriction on one's own activity or desires

♦ [1] disallowance, nay, no, refusal, rejection *Ant* allowance, grant ♦ [2] contradiction, disallowance, disavowal, disclaimer, negation, rejection, repudiation *Ant* acknowledgment, admission, avowal, confirmation

de·ni·er \'den-yər\ *n* : a unit of fineness for yarn

den·i·grate \'de-ni-ˌgrāt\ *vb* **-grat·ed; -grat·ing** ♦ : to cast aspersions on : DEFAME — **den·i·gra·tion** \ˌde-ni-'grā-shən\ *n*

den·im \'de-nəm\ *n* **1** : a firm durable twilled usu. cotton fabric woven with colored warp and white filling threads **2** *pl* : overalls or pants of usu. blue denim

den·i·zen \'de-nə-zən\ *n* ♦ : one that occupies a particular place regularly, routinely, or for a period of time : INHABITANT

♦ dweller, inhabitant, occupant, resident

de·nom·i·nate \di-'nä-mə-ˌnāt\ *vb* ♦ : to assign a name to : DESIGNATE

♦ baptize, call, christen, designate, dub, entitle, label, name, style, term, title

de·nom·i·na·tion \di-ˌnä-mə-'nā-shən\ *n* **1** : an act of denominating **2** : a value or size of a series of related values (as of money) **3** : a word or phrase that constitutes the distinctive designation of a person or thing : NAME; *esp* : a general name for a category **4** : a religious organization uniting local congregations in a single body — **de·nom·i·na·tion·al** \-shə-nəl\ *adj*

de·nom·i·na·tor \di-'nä-mə-ˌnā-tər\ *n* : the part of a fraction that is below the line indicating division

de·no·ta·tion \ˌdē-nō-'tā-shən\ *n* **1** : an act or process of denoting **2** ♦ : the thing one conveys or intends to convey esp. by language; *esp* : a direct specific meaning as distinct from an implied or associated idea **3** ♦ : a denoting term : NAME

♦ [2] drift, import, intent, meaning, purport, sense, significance, signification ♦ [3] appellation, cognomen, designation, handle, name, title

de·no·ta·tive \'dē-nō-,tā-tiv, di-'nō-tə-tiv\ *adj* **1** ♦ : denoting or tending to denote **2** : relating to denotation

♦ indicative, significant, telltale

de·note \di-'nōt\ *vb* **1** : to mark out plainly : INDICATE **2** : to make known **3** ♦ : to serve as a linguistic expression of the notion of : MEAN

♦ express, import, mean, signify, spell

de·noue·ment \,dā-,nü-'mäⁿ\ *n* : the final outcome of the dramatic complications in a literary work
de·nounce \di-'naùns\ *vb* **de·nounced; de·nounc·ing 1** ♦ : to pronounce esp. publicly to be blameworthy or evil **2** : to inform against : ACCUSE **3** : to announce formally the termination of (as a treaty) — **de·nounce·ment** *n*

♦ censure, condemn, damn, decry, reprehend, reprobate ♦ blame, criticize, fault, knock, pan

de no·vo \di-'nō-vō\ *adv or adj* : over again : ANEW
dense \'dens\ *adj* **dens·er; dens·est 1** ♦ : marked by compactness or crowding together of parts : THICK ⟨~ forest⟩ ⟨a ~ fog⟩ **2** ♦ : slow to understand : STUPID — **dense·ly** *adv*

♦ [1] close, compact, crowded, packed, serried, thick, tight ♦ [2] dull, dumb, obtuse, simple, slow, stupid, thick

dense·ness \-nəs\ *n* ♦ : the quality or state of being dense

♦ dopiness, obtuseness, stupidity

den·si·ty \'den-sə-tē\ *n, pl* **-ties 1** : the quality or state of being dense **2** : the quantity of something per unit volume, unit area, or unit length
dent \'dent\ *n* **1** ♦ : a small depressed place made by a blow or by pressure **2** : an impression or weakening effect made usu. against resistance **3** : initial progress — **dent** *vb*

♦ cavity, concavity, depression, hole, hollow, indentation, pit, recess

den·tal \'dent-ᵊl\ *adj* : of or relating to teeth or dentistry — **den·tal·ly** *adv*
dental floss *n* : a thread used to clean between the teeth
dental hygienist *n* : a person licensed to clean and examine teeth
den·tate \'den-,tāt\ *adj* : having pointed projections : NOTCHED
den·ti·frice \'den-tə-frəs\ *n* : a powder, paste, or liquid for cleaning the teeth
den·tin \'dent-ᵊn\ *or* **den·tine** \'den-,tēn, den-'tēn\ *n* : a calcareous material like bone but harder and denser that composes the principal mass of a tooth
den·tist \'den-tist\ *n* : a person licensed in the care, treatment, and replacement of teeth — **den·tist·ry** *n*
den·ti·tion \den-'ti-shən\ *n* : the number, kind, and arrangement of teeth (as of a person or animal); *also* : TEETH
den·ture \'den-chər\ *n* : a set of teeth; *esp* : a partial or complete set of false teeth
de·nude \di-'nüd, -'nyüd\ *vb* **de·nud·ed; de·nud·ing** : to strip the covering from — **de·nu·da·tion** \,dē-nü-'dā-shən, -nyü-\ *n*
de·nun·ci·a·tion \di-,nən-sē-'ā-shən\ *n* ♦ : the act of denouncing; *esp* : a public condemnation

♦ censure, rebuke, reprimand, reproach, reproof, stricture

de·ny \di-'nī\ *vb* **de·nied; de·ny·ing 1** ♦ : to declare untrue **2** : to refuse to recognize or acknowledge : DISAVOW **3** ♦ : to refuse to grant ⟨~ a request⟩ **4** : to reject as false ⟨~ a theory⟩

♦ [1] contradict, disallow, disavow, disclaim, gainsay, negate, negative, reject, repudiate *Ant* acknowledge, admit, allow, avow, concede, confirm, own ♦ [3] decline, disallow, refuse, reject, withhold *Ant* allow, concede, grant, let, permit

de·o·dar \'dē-ə-,där\ *n* : a Himalayan cedar
de·odor·ant \dē-'ō-də-rənt\ *n* : a preparation that destroys or masks unpleasant odors
de·odor·ize \dē-'ō-də-,rīz\ *vb* : to eliminate the offensive odor of
de·ox·i·dize \dē-'äk-sə-,dīz\ *vb* : to remove oxygen from
de·oxy·ri·bo·nu·cle·ic acid \dē-,äk-si-,rī-bō-nù-,klē-ik-, -nyü-\ *n* : DNA
de·oxy·ri·bose \dē-,äk-si-'rī-,bōs\ *n* : a sugar with five carbon and four oxygen atoms in each molecule that is part of DNA
dep *abbr* **1** depart; departure **2** deposit **3** deputy
de·part \di-'pärt\ *vb* **1** ♦ : to go away : go away from **2** : to cease living : DIE **3** : to turn aside : DEVIATE

♦ clear out, exit, get off, go, move, pull, quit, sally, shove, take off

de·part·ment \di-'pärt-mənt\ *n* **1** ♦ : a distinct sphere or category esp. of an activity or attribute **2** ♦ : a functional or territorial division (as of a government, business, or college) — **de·part·men·tal** \di-,pärt-'ment-ᵊl, ,dē-\ *adj* — **de·part·men·tal·ly** *adv*

♦ [1] area, arena, demesne, discipline, domain, field, line, province, realm, specialty, sphere ♦ [2] bureau, desk, division, office

department store *n* : a store having separate sections for a wide variety of goods
de·par·ture \di-'pär-chər\ *n* **1** ♦ : the act of going away **2** : a starting out (as on a journey) **3** : DIVERGENCE

♦ exit, farewell, leave-taking, parting *Ant* arrival

de·pend \di-'pend\ *vb* **1** ♦ : to be determined, based, or contingent ⟨life ~s on food⟩ **2** ♦ : to place reliance or trust ⟨you can ~ on me⟩ **3** : to be dependent esp. for financial support **4** : to hang down ⟨a vine ~ing from a tree⟩

♦ [1] base, hang, rest ♦ [2] count, lean, reckon, rely

de·pend·abil·i·ty \di-,pen-də-'bi-lə-tē\ *n* ♦ : the quality or state of being dependable

♦ reliability, solidity, sureness, trustworthiness

de·pend·able \di-'pen-də-bəl\ *adj* ♦ : capable of being depended on : RELIABLE

♦ good, reliable, responsible, safe, solid, steady, sure, tried, true, trustworthy *Ant* irresponsible, undependable, unreliable, untrustworthy

de·pen·dence *also* **de·pen·dance** \di-'pen-dəns\ *n* **1** : the quality or state of being dependent; *esp* : the quality or state of being influenced by or subject to another **2** : RELIANCE, TRUST **3** ♦ : something on which one relies **4** : drug addiction; *also* : HABITUATION 2

♦ buttress, mainstay, pillar, reliance, standby, support

de·pen·den·cy \-dən-sē\ *n, pl* **-cies 1** : DEPENDENCE **2** : a territory under the jurisdiction of a nation but not formally annexed by it
¹**de·pen·dent** \-dənt\ *adj* **1** ♦ : hanging down **2 a** ♦ : determined or conditioned by another **b** : affected with drug dependence **3** : relying on another for support **4** : subject to another's jurisdiction **5** : SUBORDINATE 4

♦ [1] pendulous ♦ [2a] conditional, contingent, subject *Ant* independent

²**dependent** *also* **de·pen·dant** \-dənt\ *n* : one that is dependent; *esp* : a person who relies on another for support
de·pict \di-'pikt\ *vb* **1** ♦ : to represent by a picture **2** ♦ : to describe in words

♦ [1] image, picture, portray, represent ♦ [2] delineate, describe, draw, image, paint, picture, portray, sketch

de·pic·tion \di-'pik-shən\ *n* ♦ : a descriptive statement

♦ delineation, description, picture, portrait, portrayal, sketch

de·pil·a·to·ry \di-'pi-lə-,tōr-ē\ *n, pl* **-ries** : a preparation for removing hair, wool, or bristles
de·plane \dē-'plān\ *vb* : to get out of an airplane
de·plete \di-'plēt\ *vb* **de·plet·ed; de·plet·ing** ♦ : to exhaust esp. of strength or resources — **de·ple·tion** \-'plē-shən\ *n*

♦ clean, consume, drain, exhaust, expend, spend, use up *Ant* renew, replace

de·plor·able \di-'plōr-ə-bəl\ *adj* **1** ♦ : that is to be regretted or lamented : LAMENTABLE **2** : deserving censure or contempt : WRETCHED — **de·plor·ably** *adv*

♦ distressful, grievous, heartbreaking, lamentable, regrettable, unfortunate, woeful

de·plore \-'plōr\ *vb* **de·plored; de·plor·ing 1** ♦ : to feel or express grief for **2** ♦ : to regret strongly **3** : to consider unfortunate or deserving of disapproval

♦ [1] bemoan, bewail, grieve, lament, mourn, wail ♦ [2] bemoan, lament, regret, repent, rue

de·ploy \di-'ploi\ *vb* : to spread out (as troops or ships) in order for battle — **de·ploy·ment** \-mənt\ *n*
de·po·nent \di-'pō-nənt\ *n* : one who gives evidence
de·pop·u·late \dē-'pä-pyə-,lāt\ *vb* : to reduce greatly the population of — **de·pop·u·la·tion** \-,pä-pyə-'lā-shən\ *n*
de·port \di-'pōrt\ *vb* **1** ♦ : to behave or comport (oneself) esp.

in accord with a code : CONDUCT **2** ♦ : to send out of the country : BANISH

♦ [1] acquit, bear, behave, comport, conduct, demean, quit ♦ [2] banish, displace, exile, expatriate, transport

de·por·ta·tion \ˌdē-ˌpȯr-ˈtā-shən\ *n* ♦ : an act or instance of deporting

♦ banishment, displacement, exile, expulsion

de·port·ment \di-ˈpȯrt-mənt\ *n* ♦ : the manner in which one conducts oneself : BEHAVIOR

♦ actions, bearing, behavior (*or* behaviour), comportment, conduct, demeanor (*or* demeanour)

de·pose \di-ˈpōz\ *vb* **de·posed; de·pos·ing 1** ♦ : to remove from high office (as of king) **2** ♦ : to testify under oath or by affidavit

♦ oust *Ant* crown, enthrone, throne ♦ [2] attest, swear, testify, witness

¹**de·pos·it** \di-ˈpä-zət\ *vb* **de·pos·it·ed** \-zə-təd\; **de·pos·it·ing 1** ♦ : to place for safekeeping or as a pledge; *esp* : to put money in a bank **2** ♦ : to lay down : PLACE **3** : to let fall or sink ⟨silt ∼ed by a flood⟩ — **de·pos·i·tor** \-zə-tər\ *n*

♦ [1] bank, cache, lay away, store *Ant* withdraw ♦ [2] dispose, fix, lay, place, position, put, set, set up, stick

²**deposit** *n* **1** : the state of being deposited ⟨money on ∼⟩ **2** ♦ : something placed for safekeeping; *esp* : money deposited in a bank **3** : money given as a pledge **4** : an act of depositing **5** ♦ : something laid down ⟨a ∼ of silt⟩ **6** : a natural accumulation (as of a mineral)

♦ [2] cache, hoard, reserve, store ♦ [2] account, budget, fund, kitty, nest egg, pool ♦ [5] dregs, grounds, lees, precipitate, sediment

de·po·si·tion \ˌde-pə-ˈzi-shən, ˌdē-\ *n* **1** : an act of removing from a position of authority **2** : TESTIMONY **3** : the process of depositing **4** : something deposited : DEPOSIT

de·pos·i·to·ry \di-ˈpä-zə-ˌtȯr-ē\ *n, pl* **-ries** ♦ : a place where something is deposited esp. for safekeeping

♦ repository, storage, storehouse, warehouse

de·pot *1, 2 usu* ˈde-pō, *3 usu* ˈdē-\ *n* **1** : a place for storing goods or motor vehicles : STOREHOUSE **2** ♦ : a place where military supplies or replacements are kept or assembled **3** : a building for railroad or bus passengers

♦ armory, arsenal, dump, magazine

depr *abbr* depreciation

de·prave \di-ˈprāv\ *vb* **de·praved; de·prav·ing** ♦ : to make bad : CORRUPT

♦ debase, degrade, demean, demoralize, humble, subvert, warp

de·praved *adj* : marked by corruption or evil

de·prav·i·ty \di-ˈpra-və-tē\ *n* **1** ♦ : a corrupt act or practice **2** ♦ : the quality or state of being depraved

♦ [1] corruption, debasement, debauchery, decadence, degeneracy, degeneration, degradation, demoralization, dissipation, dissoluteness, perversion ♦ [1] immorality, iniquity, licentiousness, sin, vice ♦ [2] atrociousness, atrocity, enormity, heinousness, monstrosity, vileness, wickedness

dep·re·cate \ˈde-pri-ˌkāt\ *vb* **-cat·ed; -cat·ing 1** ♦ : to express disapproval of **2** ♦ : to speak slightingly of : BELITTLE

♦ [1] disapprove, discountenance, disfavor (*or* disfavour), dislike, frown, reprove ♦ [2] belittle, cry down, decry, depreciate, diminish, discount, disparage, minimize, put down, write off

dep·re·ca·tion \ˌde-pri-ˈkā-shən\ *n* ♦ : an act of deprecating

♦ disapproval, disfavor (*or* disfavour), dislike, displeasure

dep·re·ca·to·ry \ˈde-pri-kə-ˌtȯr-ē\ *adj* **1** : APOLOGETIC **2** : serving to deprecate : DISAPPROVING

de·pre·ci·ate \di-ˈprē-shē-ˌāt\ *vb* **-at·ed; -at·ing 1** ♦ : to speak slightingly of : DISPARAGE **2** ♦ : to lessen in price or value

♦ cheapen, depress, mark down, write off *Ant* appreciate, mark up

de·pre·ci·a·tion \di-ˌprē-shē-ˈā-shən\ *n* ♦ : the act of reducing in value or esteem

♦ deprecation, detraction, disparagement, put-down *Ant* aggrandizement, ennoblement, exaltation, glorification, magnification

dep·re·da·tion \ˌde-prə-ˈdā-shən\ *n* : a laying waste or plundering — **dep·re·date** \ˈde-prə-ˌdāt\ *vb*

de·press \di-ˈpres\ *vb* **1** ♦ : to press down : cause to sink to a lower position **2** : to lessen the activity or force of **3** ♦ : to make sad : SADDEN **4** ♦ : to lessen in price or value — **de·pres·sor** \-ˈpre-sər\ *n*

♦ [1] bear, press, shove, weigh ♦ [3] burden, oppress, sadden *Ant* brighten, buoy, cheer, gladden ♦ [4] cheapen, depreciate, mark down, write off

de·pres·sant \di-ˈpre-sᵊnt\ *n* : one that depresses; *esp* : a chemical substance (as a drug) that reduces bodily functional activity — **depressant** *adj*

de·pressed *adj* **1** ♦ : low in spirits; *also* : affected with psychological depression **2** ♦ : having the central part lower than the margin **3** : suffering from economic depression

♦ [1] bad, blue, down, gloomy, glum, low, melancholy, miserable, mournful, sad, sorrowful, sorry, unhappy ♦ [2] concave, hollow, sunken

de·press·ing *adj* ♦ : that depresses; *esp* : causing emotional depression

♦ bleak, dark, dismal, dreary, gloomy, gray (*or* grey), somber (*or* sombre), wretched

de·pres·sion \di-ˈpre-shən\ *n* **1** : an act of depressing : a state of being depressed **2** : a pressing down : LOWERING **3** ♦ : a state of feeling sad **4** : a psychological disorder marked esp. by sadness, inactivity, difficulty in thinking and concentration, and feelings of dejection **5** ♦ : a depressed area or part **6** : a period of low general economic activity with widespread unemployment

♦ [3] blues, dejection, desolation, despondency, doldrums, dumps, forlornness, gloom, heartsickness, melancholy, sadness ♦ [5] cavity, concavity, dent, hole, hollow, indentation, pit, recess

¹**de·pres·sive** \di-ˈpre-siv\ *adj* **1** : tending to depress **2** : characterized or affected by psychological depression

²**depressive** *n* : a person affected with or prone to psychological depression

de·pres·sur·ize \(ˌ)dē-ˈpre-shə-ˌrīz\ *vb* : to release pressure from

dep·ri·va·tion \ˌde-prə-ˈvā-shən\ *n* **1** : an act or instance of depriving : LOSS **2** : PRIVATION 2

de·prive \di-ˈprīv\ *vb* **de·prived; de·priv·ing 1** : to take something away from **2** : to stop from having something

deprived *adj* : marked by deprivation esp. of the necessities of life

de·pro·gram \(ˌ)dē-ˈprō-ˌgram, -grəm\ *vb* : to dissuade from convictions usu. of a religious nature often by coercive means

dept *abbr* department

depth \ˈdepth\ *n, pl* **depths** \ˈdepths\ **1** : something that is deep; *esp* : the deep part of a body of water **2** : a part that is far from the outside or surface; *also* : the middle or innermost part **3** : ABYSS **4** ♦ : a profound or intense state ⟨the ∼s of reflection⟩; *also* : the worst part ⟨during the ∼s of the depression⟩ **5** : a reprehensibly low condition **6** : the distance from top to bottom or from front to back **7** : the quality of being deep **8** : the degree of intensity

♦ deep, height, middle, midst, thick

depth charge *n* : an explosive device for use underwater esp. against submarines

dep·u·ta·tion \ˌde-pyə-ˈtā-shən\ *n* **1** : the act of appointing a deputy **2** : DELEGATION

de·pute \di-ˈpyüt\ *vb* **de·put·ed; de·put·ing** : to appoint as one's representative : DELEGATE

dep·u·tize \ˈde-pyə-ˌtīz\ *vb* **-tized; -tiz·ing** ♦ : to appoint or act as deputy

♦ commission, delegate

dep·u·ty \ˈde-pyə-tē\ *n, pl* **-ties 1** ♦ : a person appointed to act for or in place of another **2** : a second in command or assistant who usu. takes charge when his or her superior is absent **3** : a member of a lower house of a legislative assembly

♦ agent, attorney, commissary, delegate, envoy, factor, proxy, representative

der *or* **deriv** *abbr* derivation; derivative

de·rail \di-ˈrāl\ *vb* : to leave or cause to leave the rails — **de·rail·ment** *n*

de·rail·leur \di-ˈrā-lər\ *n* : a device for shifting gears on a bicycle by moving the chain from one set of exposed gears to another

de·range \di-ˈrānj\ *vb* **de·ranged; de·rang·ing 1** : to disturb the arrangement or order of : DISARRANGE **2** : to make mentally unsound

deranged *adj* : mentally unsound

de·range·ment \-mənt\ *n* : the state of being deranged

der·by \'dər-bē, *Brit* 'där-\ *n, pl* **derbies** **1** : a horse race usu. for three-year-olds held annually **2** : a race or contest open to all **3** : a stiff felt hat with dome-shaped crown and narrow brim

de·re·cho \də-'rā-chō\ *n, pl* **-chos** : a complex of thunderstorms with powerful winds

de·reg·u·la·tion \(ˌ)dē-ˌre-gyù-'lā-shən\ *n* : the act of removing restrictions or regulations — **de·reg·u·late** \-'re-gyù-ˌlāt\ *vb*

¹**der·e·lict** \'der-ə-ˌlikt\ *adj* **1** ◆ : abandoned by the owner or occupant **2** ◆ : failing to exercise the care expected : NEGLIGENT ⟨~ in his duty⟩

◆ [1] abandoned, deserted, forsaken ◆ [2] careless, lax, negligent, remiss, slack

²**derelict** *n* **1** : something voluntarily abandoned; *esp* : a ship abandoned on the high seas **2** : a destitute homeless social misfit : VAGRANT, BUM

der·e·lic·tion \ˌder-ə-'lik-shən\ *n* **1** ◆ : the act of abandoning : the state of being abandoned **2** ◆ : a failure in duty

◆ [1] abandonment, desertion *Ant* reclamation ◆ [2] default, delinquency, failure, neglect, negligence, oversight

de·ride \di-'rīd\ *vb* **de·rid·ed; de·rid·ing** ◆ : to laugh at scornfully : RIDICULE

◆ gibe, jeer, laugh, mock, ridicule, scout

de ri·gueur \də-rē-'gər\ *adj* : prescribed or required by fashion, etiquette, or custom : PROPER

de·ri·sion \də-'ri-zhən\ *n* **1** : RIDICULE **2** : an object of ridicule or scorn

de·ri·sive \də-'rī-siv\ *adj* ◆ : expressing or causing derision — **de·ri·sive·ly** *adv* — **de·ri·sive·ness** *n*

◆ absurd, comical, farcical, laughable, ludicrous, preposterous, ridiculous, risible, silly

de·ri·so·ry \də-'rī-sə-rē\ *adj* : worthy of derision

der·i·va·tion \ˌder-ə-'vā-shən\ *n* **1** : the formation of a word from an earlier word or root; *also* : an act of ascertaining or stating the derivation of a word **2** : ETYMOLOGY **3** : SOURCE, ORIGIN; *also* : DESCENT **4** : an act or process of deriving

de·riv·a·tive \di-'ri-və-tiv\ *n* **1** : a word formed by derivation **2** ◆ : something derived — **derivative** *adj*

◆ offshoot, outgrowth, spin-off *Ant* origin, root, source

de·rive \di-'rīv\ *vb* **de·rived; de·riv·ing** **1** : to receive or obtain from a source **2** : to obtain from a parent substance **3** ◆ : to come to as a conclusion from facts or premises : INFER, DEDUCE **4** : to trace the derivation of **5** : to come from a certain source

◆ conclude, deduce, extrapolate, gather, infer, judge, reason, understand

der·mal \'dər-məl\ *adj* : of or relating to the skin : CUTANEOUS

der·ma·ti·tis \ˌdər-mə-'tī-təs\ *n, pl* **-tit·i·des** \-'ti-tə-ˌdēz\ *or* **-ti·tis·es** : inflammation of the skin

der·ma·tol·o·gy \ˌdər-mə-'tä-lə-jē\ *n* : a branch of medical science dealing with the structure, functions, and diseases of the skin — **der·ma·tol·o·gist** \-jist\ *n*

der·mis \'dər-məs\ *n* : the sensitive vascular inner layer of the skin

der·o·gate \'der-ə-ˌgāt\ *vb* **-gat·ed; -gat·ing** **1** : to cause to seem inferior : DISPARAGE **2** : DETRACT — **der·o·ga·tion** \ˌder-ə-'gā-shən\ *n* — **de·rog·a·tive** \di-'rä-gə-tiv\ *adj*

de·rog·a·to·ry \di-'rä-gə-ˌtōr-ē\ *adj* ◆ : intended to lower the reputation of a person or thing : DISPARAGING — **de·rog·a·to·ri·ly** \-ˌrä-gə-'tōr-ə-lē\ *adv*

◆ contemptuous, degrading, disdainful, scornful, uncomplimentary *Ant* complimentary

der·rick \'der-ik\ *n* **1** : a hoisting apparatus : CRANE **2** : a framework over a drill hole (as for oil) for supporting machinery

der·ri·ere *or* **der·ri·ère** \ˌder-ē-'er\ *n* : BUTTOCKS

der·ring-do \ˌder-iŋ-'dü\ *n* : DARING

der·rin·ger \'der-ən-jər\ *n* : a short-barreled pocket pistol

der·vish \'dər-vish\ *n* : a member of a Muslim religious order noted for devotional exercises (as bodily movements leading to a trance)

de·sal·i·nate \dē-'sa-lə-ˌnāt\ *vb* **-nat·ed; -nat·ing** : DESALT — **de·sal·i·na·tion** \-ˌsa-lə-'nā-shən\ *n*

de·sal·i·nize \dē-'sa-lə-ˌnīz\ *vb* **-nized; -niz·ing** : DESALT — **de·sal·i·ni·za·tion** \-ˌsa-lə-nə-'zā-shən\ *n*

de·salt \dē-'sȯlt\ *vb* : to remove salt from ⟨~ seawater⟩ — **de·salt·er** *n*

des·cant \'des-ˌkant\ *vb* **1** ◆ : to sing or play part music : SING **2** : to discourse or write at length

◆ carol, chant, sing, vocalize

de·scend \di-'send\ *vb* **1** ◆ : to pass from a higher to a lower place or level : pass, move, or climb down or down along **2** : DERIVE ⟨~ed from royalty⟩ **3** : to pass by inheritance or transmission **4** ◆ : to incline, lead, or extend downward **5** ◆ : to swoop down or appear suddenly (as in an attack)

◆ [1, 4] decline, dip, drop, fall, plunge *Ant* ascend, climb, rise ◆ [5] assail, assault, attack, beset, charge, jump, pounce (on *or* upon), raid, rush, storm, strike

¹**de·scen·dant** *also* **de·scen·dent** \di-'sen-dənt\ *adj* **1** : moving or directed downward **2** : proceeding from an ancestor or source

²**descendant** *also* **descendent** *n* **1** : one descended from another or from a common stock **2** : one deriving directly from a precursor or prototype

de·scent \di-'sent\ *n* **1** ◆ : derivation from an ancestor : LINEAGE **2** ◆ : the act or process of descending **3** : SLOPE **4** : a descending way (as a downgrade) **5** ◆ : a sudden hostile raid or assault **6** ◆ : a downward step (as in station or value) : DECLINE

◆ [1] ancestry, birth, blood, bloodline, breeding, extraction, family tree, genealogy, line, lineage, origin, parentage, pedigree, stock, strain ◆ [2] dip, dive, down, drop, fall, plunge *Ant* ascent, climb, rise, upswing, upturn ◆ [5] aggression, assault, attack, charge, offense (*or* offence), offensive, onset, onslaught, raid, rush, strike ◆ [6] comedown, decline, down, downfall, fall

de·scribe \di-'skrīb\ *vb* **de·scribed; de·scrib·ing** **1 a** ◆ : to represent or give an account of in words **b** ◆ : to communicate an account of salient identifying features of **2** : to trace the outline of — **de·scrib·able** *adj*

◆ delineate, depict, draw, image, narrate, paint, picture, portray, recount, sketch

de·scrip·tion \di-'skrip-shən\ *n* **1** ◆ : an account of something; *esp* : an account that presents a picture to a person who reads or hears it **2** ◆ : kind or character esp. as determined by prominent features : SORT — **de·scrip·tive** \-'skrip-tiv\ *adj*

◆ [1] delineation, depiction, picture, portrait, portrayal, sketch ◆ [2] breed, class, feather, ilk, kind, like, manner, nature, order, sort, species, type

de·scry \di-'skrī\ *vb* **de·scried; de·scry·ing** **1** ◆ : to catch sight of **2** : to discover by observation or investigation

◆ behold, discern, distinguish, espy, eye, look, note, notice, observe, perceive, regard, remark, see, sight, spy, view, witness

des·e·crate \'de-si-ˌkrāt\ *vb* **-crat·ed; -crat·ing** ◆ : to violate the sanctity of : PROFANE

◆ defile, profane, violate

des·e·cra·tion \ˌde-si-'krā-shən\ *n* ◆ : an act or instance of desecrating

◆ blasphemy, defilement, impiety, irreverence, sacrilege

de·seg·re·gate \dē-'se-gri-ˌgāt\ *vb* : to eliminate segregation in; *esp* : to free of any law or practice requiring isolation on the basis of race — **de·seg·re·ga·tion** \-ˌse-gri-'gā-shən\ *n*

de·sen·si·tize \dē-'sen-sə-ˌtīz\ *vb* : to make (a sensitized or hypersensitive individual) insensitive or nonreactive to a sensitizing agent — **de·sen·si·ti·za·tion** \-ˌsen-sə-tə-'zā-shən\ *n*

¹**des·ert** \'de-zərt\ *n* ◆ : dry land with few plants and little rainfall

◆ barren, desolation, waste, wasteland

²**des·ert** \'de-zərt\ *adj* : of, relating to, or resembling a desert; *esp* : being barren and without life ⟨a ~ island⟩

³**de·sert** \di-'zərt\ *n* **1** : the quality or fact of deserving reward or punishment **2** ◆ : a just reward or punishment

◆ castigation, chastisement, correction, discipline, nemesis, penalty, punishment, wrath

⁴**de·sert** \di-'zərt\ *vb* **1** ◆ : to withdraw from and leave esp. permanently **2** ◆ : to leave in the lurch : ABANDON

◆ [1, 2] abandon, forsake, maroon, quit

de·sert·ed \di-'zər-təd\ *adj* ◆ : left without the accustomed occupants, company, or support

◆ abandoned, derelict, forsaken

de·sert·er \di-'zər-tər\ *n* ◆ : one who forsakes a duty or cause

◆ defector, recreant, renegade

de·ser·tion \di-'zər-shən\ *n* ◆ : an act of deserting

◆ abandonment, dereliction

de·serve \di-'zərv\ *vb* **de·served; de·serv·ing** ◆ : to be worthy of : MERIT

♦ earn, merit, rate

de·serv·ed·ly \-'zər-vəd-lē\ *adv* : according to merit : JUSTLY
deserving *adj* ♦ : meriting honor or esteem

♦ good, meritorious, worthy

des·ic·cate \'de-si-ˌkāt\ *vb* **-cat·ed; -cat·ing** : DRY, DEHYDRATE — **des·ic·ca·tion** \ˌde-si-'kā-shən\ *n* — **des·ic·ca·tor** \'de-si-ˌkā-tər\ *n*

de·sid·er·a·tum \di-ˌsi-də-'rä-təm, -ˌzi-, -'rā-\ *n, pl* **-ta** \-tə\ : something desired as essential

¹**de·sign** \di-'zīn\ *vb* **1** ♦ : to conceive and plan out in the mind **2** ♦ : to have as a purpose : INTEND **3** : to devise for a specific function or end **4** : to make a pattern or sketch of **5** : to conceive and draw the plans for

♦ [1] arrange, blueprint, calculate, chart, frame, lay out, map, plan, project, scheme ♦ [2] aim, aspire, contemplate, intend, mean, meditate, plan, propose

²**design** *n* **1** ♦ : a particular purpose : deliberate planning **2** ♦ : a mental project or scheme : PLAN **3** ♦ : a secret project or scheme : PLOT **4** *pl* : aggressive or evil intent — used with *on* or *against* **5** : a preliminary sketch or plan **6** : an underlying scheme that governs functioning, developing, or unfolding : MOTIF **7** ♦ : the arrangement of elements or details in a product or a work of art **8** ♦ : a decorative pattern **9** : the art of executing designs

♦ [1] arrangement, blueprint, game, plan, project, scheme, strategy, system ♦ [2] aim, ambition, aspiration, dream, end, goal, intent, mark, meaning, object, objective, plan, pretension, purpose, thing ♦ [3] conspiracy, intrigue, machination, plot, scheme ♦ [7] arrangement, composition, configuration, form, format, layout, makeup, pattern ♦ [8] figure, motif, motive, pattern

¹**des·ig·nate** \'de-zig-ˌnāt, -nət\ *adj* : chosen but not yet installed ⟨ambassador ∼⟩
²**des·ig·nate** \-ˌnāt\ *vb* **-nat·ed; -nat·ing** **1** ♦ : to appoint and set apart for a special purpose **2** ♦ : to mark or point out : INDICATE; *also* : SPECIFY, STIPULATE **3** ♦ : to call by a name or title

♦ [1] appoint, assign, attach, commission, constitute, detail, name ♦ [3] baptize, call, christen, denominate, dub, entitle, label, name, style, term, title

designated driver *n* : a person chosen to abstain from alcohol so as to transport others safely
designated hitter *n* : a baseball player designated at the start of the game to bat in place of the pitcher without causing the pitcher to be removed from the game
des·ig·na·tion \ˌde-zig-'nā-shən\ *n* **1** : the act of indicating or identifying **2** ♦ : appointment to or selection for an office, post, or service **3** ♦ : a distinguishing name, sign, or title

♦ [2] appointment, assignment, commission ♦ [3] appellation, cognomen, denotation, handle, name, title

de·sign·er \di-'zī-nər\ *n* ♦ : one that designs: as **a** : one who creates plans for a project or structure **b** : one who designs and manufactures a new product style or design; *esp* : one who designs and manufactures high-fashion clothing — **designer** *adj*

♦ developer, innovator, inventor, originator

designer drug *n* : a synthetic version of an illicit drug that has been chemically altered to avoid its prohibition
de·sign·ing \di-'zī-niŋ\ *adj* ♦ : adept in the use of subtlety and cunning : CRAFTY, SCHEMING

♦ artful, cagey, crafty, cunning, devious, foxy, guileful, scheming, slick, sly, subtle, wily

de·sir·able \di-'zī-rə-bəl\ *adj* **1** : PLEASING, ATTRACTIVE **2** ♦ : worth seeking or doing as advantageous, beneficial, or wise : ADVISABLE ⟨∼ legislation⟩ — **de·sir·abil·i·ty** \-ˌzī-rə-'bi-lə-tē\ *n* — **de·sir·able·ness** *n*

♦ advisable, expedient, judicious, politic, prudent, tactical, wise

¹**de·sire** \di-'zīr\ *vb* **de·sired; de·sir·ing** **1** ♦ : to long or hope for : exhibit or feel desire for **2** : REQUEST

♦ ache for, covet, crave, die for, hanker for, hunger for, long for, lust (for *or* after), pine for, repine for, thirst for, want, wish for, yearn for

²**desire** *n* **1** ♦ : a strong wish : LONGING **2** : sexual urge or appetite **3** : a usu. formal request for action **4** : something desired

♦ appetite, craving, drive, hankering, hunger, itch, longing, lust, passion, thirst, urge, yearning, yen

de·sir·ous \di-'zī-rəs\ *adj* : impelled or governed by desire
de·sist \di-'zist, -'sist\ *vb* ♦ : to cease to proceed, act, or continue

♦ *usu* **desist from** break, break off, cease, cut, discontinue, drop, end, halt, knock off, layoff, leave off, quit, shut off, stop

desk \'desk\ *n* **1** : a table, frame, or case esp. for writing and reading **2** : a counter, stand, or booth at which a person performs duties **3** ♦ : a specialized division of an organization (as a newspaper) ⟨city ∼⟩

♦ bureau, department, division, office

desk·top publishing \'desk-ˌtäp-\ *n* : the production of printed matter by means of a microcomputer
¹**des·o·late** \'de-sə-lət, -zə-\ *adj* **1** : DESERTED, ABANDONED **2** ♦ : joyless, disconsolate, and sorrowful through or as if through separation from a loved one : LONELY **3** : DILAPIDATED **4** : BARREN, LIFELESS **5** ♦ : devoid of warmth, comfort, or hope : CHEERLESS — **des·o·late·ly** *adv* — **des·o·late·ness** *n*

♦ [2] forlorn, lonely, lonesome ♦ [5] bleak, dark, dismal, dreary, gloomy, gray (*or* grey), somber (*or* sombre), wretched

²**des·o·late** \-ˌlāt\ *vb* **-lat·ed; -lat·ing** : to make desolate : destroy the activity, vitality, or sound condition or contentment of : make wretched
des·o·la·tion \ˌde-sə-'lā-shən, -zə-\ *n* **1** ♦ : the action of desolating : state of being desolated **2** : the quality or state of being sad : SADNESS **3** : LONELINESS **4** ♦ : a condition of neglect leading to confusion and disintegration or of natural barrenness and bleakness **5** ♦ : barren wasteland

♦ [1] annihilation, demolition, destruction, devastation, havoc, loss, obliteration, ruin, wastage, wreckage ♦ [4] dilapidation, disrepair, neglect ♦ [5] barren, desert, waste, wasteland

des·oxy·ri·bo·nu·cle·ic acid \de-ˌzäk-sē-'rī-bō-nü-ˌklē-ik-, -nyü-\ *n* : DNA
¹**de·spair** \di-'spar\ *vb* : to lose all hope or confidence
²**despair** *n* **1** ♦ : utter destruction of hope **2** : a cause of hopelessness

♦ desperation, despondency, forlornness, hopelessness *Ant* hope, hopefulness

de·spair·ing *adj* ♦ : given to, arising from, or marked by despair : having no hope — **de·spair·ing·ly** *adv*

♦ defeatist, hopeless, pessimistic

des·per·a·do \ˌdes-pə-'rä-dō, -'rā-\ *n, pl* **-does** *or* **-dos** : a bold or reckless criminal
des·per·ate \'des-pə-rət, -prət\ *adj* **1** : being beyond or almost beyond hope : causing despair **2** : RASH ⟨a ∼ attempt⟩ **3** : extremely intense — **des·per·ate·ly** *adv* — **des·per·ate·ness** *n*
des·per·a·tion \ˌdes-pə-'rā-shən\ *n* **1** ♦ : a loss of hope and surrender to despair **2** : a state of hopelessness leading to rashness

♦ despair, despondency, forlornness, hopelessness

de·spi·ca·ble \di-'spi-kə-bəl, 'des-pi-\ *adj* ♦ : deserving to be despised — **de·spi·ca·bly** \-blē\ *adv*

♦ contemptible, lousy, nasty, pitiful, scabby, scurvy, sorry, wretched ♦ base, contemptible, detestable, dirty, dishonorable (*or* dishonourable), ignoble, low, mean, snide, sordid, vile, wretched

de·spise \di-'spīz\ *vb* **de·spised; de·spis·ing** **1** ♦ : to look down on with contempt or aversion : DETEST **2** ♦ : to regard as negligible, worthless, or distasteful

♦ [1] abhor, abominate, detest, execrate, hate, loathe ♦ [2] disregard, flout, scorn

¹**de·spite** \di-'spīt\ *prep* ♦ : in spite of

♦ notwithstanding, regardless of, with

²**despite** *n* : the act of despising : CONTEMPT
de·spoil \di-'spȯil\ *vb* ♦ : to strip of belongings, possessions, or value — **de·spoil·er** *n* — **de·spoil·ment** *n*

♦ loot, maraud, pillage, plunder, ransack, sack, strip

de·spo·li·a·tion \di-ˌspō-lē-'ā-shən\ *n* : the act of plundering : the state of being despoiled
¹**de·spond** \di-'spänd\ *vb* : to become discouraged or disheartened
²**despond** *n* : DESPONDENCY
de·spon·den·cy \-'spän-dən-sē\ *n* ♦ : the state of being despondent

♦ blues, dejection, depression, desolation, doldrums, dumps, forlornness, gloom, heartsickness, melancholy, sadness ♦ despair, desperation, forlornness, hopelessness

de·spon·dent \-dənt\ *adj* ♦ : feeling or showing extreme discouragement, dejection, or depression — **de·spon·dent·ly** *adv*

♦ brokenhearted, dejected, depressed, disconsolate, heartsick, miserable, sad, wretched

des·pot \'des-pət, -ˌpät\ *n* **1 :** a ruler with absolute power and authority **2** ♦ **:** a person exercising power tyrannically

♦ autocrat, dictator, oppressor, tyrant

des·pot·ic \des-'pä-tik\ *adj* ♦ **:** of, relating to, or characteristic of a despot

♦ authoritarian, autocratic, bossy, dictatorial, domineering, imperious, overbearing, peremptory, tyrannical, tyrannous

des·po·tism \'des-pə-ˌti-zəm\ *n* ♦ **:** a system of government in which the ruler has unlimited power

♦ autocracy, dictatorship, totalitarianism, tyranny

des·sert \di-'zərt\ *n* **:** a course of sweet food, fruit, or cheese served at the close of a meal

des·ti·na·tion \ˌdes-tə-'nā-shən\ *n* **1 :** a purpose for which something is destined **2 :** an act of appointing, setting aside for a purpose, or predetermining **3 :** a place to which one is journeying or to which something is sent

des·tine \'des-tən\ *vb* **des·tined; des·tin·ing 1 :** to settle in advance **2** ♦ **:** to designate, assign, or dedicate in advance **3 :** to direct or set apart for a specific purpose or place

♦ doom, foredoom, foreordain, ordain, predestine

des·ti·ny \'des-tə-nē\ *n, pl* **-nies 1** ♦ **:** something to which a person or thing is destined **:** FATE **2 :** a predetermined course of events

♦ circumstance, doom, fate, fortune, lot, portion

des·ti·tute \'des-tə-ˌtüt, -ˌtyüt\ *adj* **1 :** lacking something needed or desirable **2** ♦ **:** suffering extreme poverty

♦ broke, devoid, impecunious, indigent, needy, penniless, penurious, poor, poverty-stricken

des·ti·tu·tion \ˌdes-tə-'tü-shən, -'tyü-\ *n* ♦ **:** the state of being destitute

♦ beggary, impecuniousness, impoverishment, indigence, need, pauperism, penury, poverty, want

de–stress \dē-'stres\ *vb* ♦ **:** to release bodily or mental tension **:** UNWIND

♦ chill out, relax, unwind

de·stroy \di-'stròi\ *vb* **1** ♦ **:** to put an end to **:** RUIN **2** ♦ **:** to deprive of life **:** KILL

♦ [1] annihilate, blot out, demolish, desolate, devastate, do in, exterminate, extinguish, obliterate, pulverize, ruin, shatter, smash, tear down, waste, wipe out, wreck *Ant* build, construct, erect, put up, raise ♦ [2] dispatch, do in, fell, kill, slay

de·stroy·er \di-'stròi-ər\ *n* **1 :** one that destroys **2 :** a small speedy warship

de·struc·ti·ble \di-'strək-tə-bəl\ *adj* **:** capable of being destroyed — **de·struc·ti·bil·i·ty** \-ˌstrək-tə-'bi-lə-tē\ *n*

de·struc·tion \di-'strək-shən\ *n* **1** ♦ **:** the state or fact of being destroyed **:** RUIN **2 :** the action or process of destroying something **3 :** a destroying agency

♦ annihilation, demolition, desolation, devastation, havoc, loss, obliteration, ruin, wastage, wreckage *Ant* building, construction, erection, raising

de·struc·tive \di-'strək-tiv\ *adj* **1** ♦ **:** causing destruction **:** RUINOUS **2** ♦ **:** designed or tending to destroy — **de·struc·tive·ly** *adv* — **de·struc·tive·ness** *n*

♦ calamitous, devastating, disastrous, ruinous *Ant* constructive

de·sue·tude \'de-swi-ˌtüd, -ˌtyüd\ *n* **:** DISUSE

des·ul·to·ry \'de-səl-ˌtòr-ē\ *adj* ♦ **:** passing aimlessly from one thing or subject to another

♦ aimless, arbitrary, erratic, haphazard, random, scattered, stray

det *abbr* **1** detached; detachment **2** detail

de·tach \di-'tach\ *vb* **1 :** to separate esp. from a larger mass **2 :** DISENGAGE, WITHDRAW — **de·tach·able** *adj*

de·tached \di-'tacht\ *adj* **1** ♦ **:** not joined or connected **:** SEPARATE **2** ♦ **:** exhibiting an aloof objectivity ⟨a ∼ attitude⟩

♦ [1] disconnected, discrete, freestanding, separate, single, unattached, unconnected ♦ [2] aloof, antisocial, cold, cool, distant, frosty, remote, standoffish, unsociable

de·tach·ment \di-'tach-mənt\ *n* **1 :** SEPARATION **2 :** the dispatching of a body of troops or part of a fleet from the main body for special service; *also* **:** the portion so dispatched **3 :** a small permanent military unit of special composition **4 :** indifference

to worldly concerns **:** ALOOFNESS **5** ♦ **:** freedom from bias or prejudice **:** IMPARTIALITY

♦ disinterestedness, impartiality, neutrality, objectivity *Ant* bias, favor, favoritism, partiality, partisanship, prejudice

1de·tail \di-'tāl, 'dē-ˌtāl\ *n* **1 :** a dealing with something item by item ⟨go into ∼⟩ **2** ♦ **:** a part of a whole ⟨the ∼s of a story⟩ **3 :** selection (as of soldiers) for special duty; *also* **:** the persons thus selected

♦ fact, particular, point

2detail *vb* **1** ♦ **:** to report minutely and distinctly **2** ♦ **:** to assign to a special duty

♦ [1] enumerate, itemize, list, numerate, rehearse, tick (off) ♦ [2] appoint, assign, attach, commission, constitute, designate, name

de·tailed \di-'tāld, 'dē-ˌtāld\ *adj* ♦ **:** marked by abundant detail

♦ circumstantial, elaborate, full, minute, thorough *Ant* compendious, summary ♦ complex, complicated, elaborate, fancy, intricate, involved, sophisticated

de·tail·ing \'dē-ˌtāl-iŋ\ *n* **:** the meticulous cleaning and refurbishing of an automobile

de·tain \di-'tān\ *vb* **1 :** to hold in or as if in custody **2 :** STOP, DELAY

de·tect \di-'tekt\ *vb* ♦ **:** to discover the nature, existence, presence, or fact of — **de·tec·tor** \-'tek-tər\ *n*

♦ determine, dig up, discover, ferret out, find, hit on, locate, track down

de·tect·able \di-tek-tə-bəl\ *adj* ♦ **:** capable of being detected

♦ appreciable, discernible, distinguishable, palpable, perceptible, sensible

de·tec·tion \di-'tek-shən\ *n* ♦ **:** the act of detecting

♦ discovery, finding

1de·tec·tive \di-'tek-tiv\ *adj* **1 :** fitted or used for detection **2 :** of or relating to detectives

2detective *n* ♦ **:** a person employed or engaged in detecting lawbreakers or getting information that is not readily accessible

♦ investigator, operative, shadow, sleuth, tail

dé·tente *or* **de·tente** \dā-'tänt\ *n* **:** a relaxation of strained relations or tensions (as between nations)

de·ten·tion \di-'ten-chən\ *n* **1 :** the act or fact of detaining **:** CONFINEMENT; *esp* **:** a period of temporary custody prior to disposition by a court **2 :** a forced delay

de·ter \di-'tər\ *vb* **de·terred; de·ter·ring 1** ♦ **:** to turn aside, discourage, or prevent from acting (as by fear) **2 :** INHIBIT

♦ discourage, dissuade, inhibit

de·ter·gent \di-'tər-jənt\ *n* ♦ **:** a cleansing agent; *esp* **:** a chemical product similar to soap in its cleaning ability

♦ cleaner, soap

de·te·ri·o·rate \di-'tir-ē-ə-ˌrāt\ *vb* **-rat·ed; -rat·ing** ♦ **:** to make or become worse in quality or condition

♦ decay, decline, degenerate, descend, ebb, rot, sink, worsen *Ant* ameliorate, improve, meliorate

de·te·ri·o·ra·tion \di-ˌtir-ē-ə-'rā-shən\ *n* ♦ **:** the action or process of deteriorating

♦ decay, decline, degeneration

de·ter·min·able \-'tər-mə-nə-bəl\ *adj* **:** capable of being determined; *esp* **:** ASCERTAINABLE

de·ter·mi·nant \-mə-nənt\ *n* **1 :** something that determines or conditions **2 :** GENE

de·ter·mi·nate \di-'tər-mə-nət\ *adj* **1** ♦ **:** having fixed limits **:** DEFINITE **2** ♦ **:** definitely settled — **de·ter·mi·nate·ness** *n*

♦ [1] definite, finite, limited, measured, narrow, restricted ♦ [2] certain, final, firm, fixed, flat, frozen, hard, hard-and-fast, set, settled, stable

de·ter·mi·na·tion \di-ˌtər-mə-'nā-shən\ *n* **1 a :** the act of coming to a decision **b** ♦ **:** the decision or conclusion reached **2 :** a fixing of the extent, position, or character of something **3 :** accurate measurement (as of length or volume) **4** ♦ **:** firm or fixed purpose

♦ [1b] conclusion, decision, deliverance, diagnosis, judgment (*or* judgement), opinion, resolution, verdict ♦ [4] decision, decisiveness, firmness, granite, resolution, resolve *Ant* hesitation, indecision, irresolution, vacillation

de·ter·mine \di-'tər-mən\ *vb* **-mined; -min·ing 1** ♦ **:** to fix conclusively or authoritatively **2 ♦** : to come to a decision : RE-SOLVE **3** : to fix the form or character of beforehand : ORDAIN; *also* : REGULATE **4** : to find out the limits, nature, dimensions, or scope of ⟨∼ a position at sea⟩ **5** : to find out or come to a decision about by investigation, reasoning, or calculation **6** : to bring about as a result

♦ [1] adjudicate, arbitrate, decide, judge, referee, rule, settle, umpire ♦ [2] choose, conclude, decide, figure, opt, resolve

de·ter·mined \-'tər-mənd\ *adj* **1 ♦** : firmly resolved **2 ♦** : characterized by or showing determination — **de·ter·mined·ness** \-mənd-nəs\ *n*

♦ [1] bound, decisive, firm, intent, purposeful, resolute, set, single-minded *Ant* faltering, hesitant, indecisive, irresolute, undetermined, unresolved, vacillating, wavering ♦ [2] dogged, grim, implacable, relentless, unflinching, unrelenting, unyielding

de·ter·mined·ly \di-'tər-mənd-lē, -mə-nəd-lē\ *adv* ♦ : in a determined manner

♦ diligently, hard, hardly, laboriously, mightily, strenuously, tirelessly

de·ter·min·ism \di-'tər-mə-ˌni-zəm\ *n* : a doctrine that acts of the will, natural events, or social changes are determined by preceding events or natural causes — **de·ter·min·ist** \-nist\ *n or adj*
de·ter·rence \di-'tər-əns\ *n* : the inhibition of criminal behavior by fear esp. of punishment
de·ter·rent \-ənt\ *adj* **1** : serving to deter ⟨the law's ∼ effect⟩ **2** : relating to deterrence — **deterrent** *n*
de·test \di-'test\ *vb* ♦ : to feel intense and often violent antipathy toward : LOATHE — **de·tes·ta·tion** \ˌdē-tes-'tā-shən\ *n*

♦ abhor, abominate, despise, execrate, hate, loathe

de·test·able \di-'tes-tə-bəl\ *adj* ♦ : arousing or meriting intense dislike

♦ base, contemptible, despicable, dirty, dishonorable (*or* dishonourable), ignoble, low, mean, snide, sordid, vile, wretched

de·throne \di-'thrōn\ *vb* : to remove from a throne : DEPOSE — **de·throne·ment** *n*
det·o·nate \'det-ᵊn-ˌāt\ *vb* **-nat·ed; -nat·ing** ♦ : to explode or cause to explode with violence

♦ blow up, burst, explode, go off, pop

det·o·na·tion \ˌdet-ᵊn-'ā-shən\ *n* ♦ : the action or process of detonating

♦ blast, eruption, explosion

det·o·na·tor \'det-ᵊn-ˌā-tər\ *n* : a device for detonating an explosive
¹**de·tour** \'dē-ˌtu̇r\ *n* : an indirect way replacing part of a route
²**detour** *vb* ♦ : to go by detour

♦ bypass, circumvent, skirt ♦ deviate, sheer, swerve, swing, turn, turn off, veer

de·tox \'dē-ˌtäks, di-'täks\ *n* : detoxification from an intoxicating or addictive substance — **detox** *vb*
de·tox·i·fy \dē-'täk-sə-ˌfī\ *vb* **-fied; -fy·ing** **1** : to remove a poison or toxin or the effect of such from **2** : to free (someone) from an intoxicating or addictive substance or from dependence on it — **de·tox·i·fi·ca·tion** \dē-ˌtäk-sə-fə-'kā-shən\ *n*
de·tract \di-'trakt\ *vb* **1** : to take away or diminish the value or effect of something **2** : DIVERT — **de·trac·tor** \-'trak-tər\ *n*
de·trac·tion \di-'trak-shən\ *n* ♦ : a lessening of reputation or esteem esp. by envious, malicious, or petty criticism

♦ deprecation, depreciation, disparagement, put-down

de·train \dē-'trān\ *vb* : to leave or cause to leave a railroad train
det·ri·ment \'de-trə-mənt\ *n* **1** : hurt, damage, or loss sustained **2 ♦** : a cause of injury or damage

♦ damage, harm, hurt, injury

det·ri·men·tal \ˌde-trə-'ment-ᵊl\ *adj* ♦ : obviously harmful — **det·ri·men·tal·ly** *adv*

♦ adverse, bad, baleful, baneful, damaging, deleterious, evil, harmful, hurtful, ill, injurious, mischievous, noxious, pernicious, prejudicial

de·tri·tus \di-'trī-təs\ *n, pl* **de·tri·tus** : fragments resulting from disintegration (as of rocks) : DEBRIS
deuce \'düs, 'dyüs\ *n* **1** : a two in cards or dice **2** : a tie in a tennis game with both sides at 40 **3** : DEVIL — used chiefly as a mild oath
Deut *abbr* Deuteronomy
deu·te·ri·um \dü-'tir-ē-əm, dyü-\ *n* : an isotope of hydrogen that has twice the mass of ordinary hydrogen

Deu·ter·on·o·my \ˌdü-tə-'rä-nə-mē, ˌdyü-\ *n* : a book of Jewish and Christian Scripture
deut·sche mark \'dȯi-chə-ˌmärk\ *n* : a former monetary unit of Germany
dev *abbr* deviation
de·val·ue \dē-'val-yü\ *vb* : to reduce the international exchange value of ⟨∼ a currency⟩ — **de·val·u·a·tion** \-ˌval-yə-'wā-shən\ *n*
dev·as·tate \'de-və-ˌstāt\ *vb* **-tat·ed; -tat·ing** **1 ♦** : to bring to ruin **2 ♦** : to reduce to chaos or helplessness

♦ [1] destroy, ravage, ruin, scourge ♦ [2] carry away, crush, floor, oppress, overcome, overpower, overwhelm, prostrate, snow under, swamp

devastating *adj* ♦ : serving, tending, or having the power to devastate

♦ calamitous, destructive, disastrous, ruinous

dev·as·ta·tion \ˌde-və-'stā-shən\ *n* ♦ : the action of devastating or state of being devastated

♦ annihilation, demolition, desolation, destruction, havoc, loss, obliteration, ruin, wastage, wreckage

de·vel·op \di-'ve-ləp\ *vb* **1 ♦** : to unfold gradually or in detail **2** : to place (exposed photographic material) in chemicals to produce a visible image **3** : to bring out the possibilities of **4** : to make more available or usable ⟨∼ land⟩ **5 ♦** : to acquire gradually ⟨∼ a taste for olives⟩ **6 ♦** : to go through a natural process of growth, differentiation, or evolution **7** : to come into being gradually

♦ [1] amplify, elaborate (on), enlarge (on), expand ♦ [5] acquire, cultivate, form *Ant* lose ♦ [6] age, grow, grow up, mature, progress, ripen

de·vel·op·er \-lə-pər\ *n* ♦ : one that develops something new

♦ designer, innovator, inventor, originator

de·vel·op·ment \-ləp-mənt\ *n* ♦ : the act, process, or result of developing — **de·vel·op·men·tal** \-ˌve-ləp-'ment-ᵊl\ *adj* — **de·vel·op·men·tal·ly** \-t²l-ē\ *adv*

♦ elaboration, evolution, expansion, growth, maturation, progress, progression *Ant* regression, retrogression ♦ aftermath, conclusion, consequence, corollary, effect, issue, outcome, outgrowth, product, result, resultant, sequence, upshot

¹**de·vi·ant** \'dē-vē-ənt\ *adj* ♦ : deviating esp. from some accepted norm ⟨∼ behavior⟩ — **de·vi·ance** \-əns\ *n* — **de·vi·an·cy** \-ən-sē\ *n*

♦ aberrant, abnormal, anomalous, atypical, irregular, unnatural *Ant* natural, normal, regular, standard, typical

²**deviant** *n* ♦ : one that is deviant

♦ bohemian, individualist, loner, maverick, nonconformist

de·vi·ate \'dē-vē-ˌāt\ *vb* **-at·ed; -at·ing** ♦ : to turn aside from a course, standard, principle, or topic — **de·vi·ate** \-vē-ət, -vē-ˌāt\ *n* — **de·vi·a·tion** \ˌdē-vē-'ā-shən\ *n*

♦ detour, sheer, swerve, swing, turn, turn off, veer

de·vice \di-'vīs\ *n* **1 ♦** : a scheme to deceive : STRATA-GEM **2 ♦** : a piece of equipment or a mechanism for a special purpose **3 ♦** : a particular disposition of mind or character : INCLINA-TION — used in pl. ⟨left to my own ∼s⟩ **4** : an emblematic design

♦ [1] artifice, dodge, gimmick, jig, ploy, scheme, sleight, stratagem, trick, wile ♦ [2] implement, instrument, tool, utensil ♦ *usu* **devices** [3] affinity, bent, disposition, genius, inclination, leaning, partiality, penchant, predilection, predisposition, proclivity, propensity, talent, tendency, turn

¹**dev·il** \'de-vəl\ *n* **1** *often cap* : the personal supreme spirit of evil **2 ♦** : an evil spirit : DEMON **3 ♦** : a wicked person **4 a ♦** : an energetic, reckless, or dashing person **b ♦** : a person prone to mischief **5** : an individual human : FELLOW ⟨poor ∼⟩ ⟨lucky ∼⟩

♦ [2] demon, fiend, ghoul, imp ♦ [3] beast, evildoer, fiend, no-good, reprobate, rogue, varlet, villain, wretch ♦ [4a] daredevil, madcap ♦ [4b] hellion, imp, mischief, monkey, rapscallion, rascal, rogue, scamp, urchin

²**devil** *vb* **-iled** *or* **-illed; -il·ing** *or* **-il·ling** **1** : to season highly ⟨∼ed eggs⟩ **2** : TEASE, ANNOY
dev·il·ish \'de-və-lish\ *adj* **1 ♦** : befitting a devil : EVIL; *also* : MISCHIEVOUS **2** : exceeding the ordinary, usual, or expected : EXTREME

♦ demonic, diabolical, evil, fiendish, satanic ♦ impish, knavish, mischievous, rascally, roguish, sly, waggish, wicked

dev·il·ish·ly \-lē\ *adv* ♦ : in a devilish manner

♦ excessively, inordinately, monstrously, overly, overmuch, too

dev·il·ish·ness \-nəs\ *n* ♦ : the quality or state of being devilish

♦ impishness, knavery, mischief, mischievousness, rascality, shenanigans, waggery, wickedness

dev·il·ment \'dev-əl-mənt, -ˌment\ *n* : MISCHIEF

dev·il·ry \-rē\ *or* **dev·il·try** \-trē\ *n, pl* **-il·ries** *or* **-il·tries**   **1** : action performed with the help of the devil   **2** : action that annoys or irritates : MISCHIEF

de·vi·ous \'dē-vē-əs\ *adj*   **1** ♦ : deviating from a straight line   **2** : ERRANT 3   **3 a** : deviating from a right, accepted, or common course   **b** ♦ : not straightforward : CUNNING ⟨a ∼ politician⟩; *also* : tending or having power to deceive ⟨a ∼ trick⟩

♦ [1] crooked, serpentine, sinuous, tortuous, winding ♦ [3b] artful, cagey, crafty, cunning, foxy, guileful, slick, sly, subtle, wily

¹**de·vise** \di-'vīz\ *vb* **de·vised; de·vis·ing**   **1** ♦ : to form in the mind by new combinations or applications of ideas or principles : INVENT   **2** : PLOT   **3** : to give (real estate) by will

♦ concoct, contrive, cook up, fabricate, invent, make up, manufacture, think up

²**devise** *n*   **1** : a disposing of real property by will   **2** : a will or clause of a will disposing of real property   **3** : property given by will

de·vi·tal·ize \dē-'vīt-ᵊl-ˌīz\ *vb* : to deprive of life or vitality

de·void \di-'void\ *adj* ♦ : being without : VOID ⟨a book ∼ of interest⟩

♦ bare, blank, empty, stark, vacant, void ♦ bereft, destitute, empty, void *Ant* replete

de·voir \də-'vwär\ *n*   **1** : DUTY   **2** : a formal act of civility or respect

de·volve \di-'välv\ *vb* **de·volved; de·volv·ing** : to pass (as rights or responsibility) from one to another usu. by succession or transmission — **dev·o·lu·tion** \ˌde-və-'lü-shən, ˌdē-\ *n*

De·vo·ni·an \di-'vō-nē-ən\ *adj* : of, relating to, or being the period of the Paleozoic era between the Silurian and the Mississippian — **Devonian** *n*

de·vote \di-'vōt\ *vb* **de·vot·ed; de·vot·ing**   **1** ♦ : to commit to wholly or chiefly ⟨∼s herself to serving the poor⟩   **2** ♦ : to set apart for a special purpose : DEDICATE

♦ [1] address, apply, bend, buckle, give ♦ [2] allocate, consecrate, dedicate, earmark, reserve, save

de·vot·ed \-'vō-təd\ *adj* ♦ : characterized by loyalty and devotion : FAITHFUL

♦ constant, faithful, fast, good, loyal, pious, staunch, steadfast, steady, true, true-blue

dev·o·tee \ˌde-və-'tē, -'tā\ *n* ♦ : an ardent follower, supporter, or enthusiast

♦ addict, aficionado, buff, bug, enthusiast, fan, fanatic, fancier, fiend, freak, lover, maniac, nut

de·vo·tion \di-'vō-shən\ *n*   **1** ♦ : religious fervor   **2** : an act of prayer or private worship — usu. used in pl.   **3** : a religious exercise for private use   **4** ♦ : the fact or state of being dedicated and loyal ⟨∼ to the cause⟩; *also* : the act of devoting

♦ [1] faith, piety, religion ♦ [4] allegiance, constancy, dedication, faith, faithfulness, fastness, fealty, fidelity, loyalty, steadfastness ♦ [4] affection, attachment, fondness, love, passion

de·vo·tion·al \-shə-nəl\ *adj* ♦ : of, relating to, or characterized by devotion

♦ religious, sacred, spiritual

de·vour \di-'vaür\ *vb*   **1** ♦ : to eat up greedily or ravenously   **2** : WASTE, ANNIHILATE   **3** : to enjoy avidly ⟨∼ a book⟩ — **de·vour·er** *n*

♦ bolt, gobble, gorge, gormandize, gulp, scarf

de·vout \di-'vaüt\ *adj*   **1** ♦ : devoted to religion : PIOUS   **2** : expressing devotion or piety   **3** : EARNEST, SERIOUS — **de·vout·ly** *adv*

♦ faithful, godly, holy, pious, religious, sainted, saintly

de·vout·ness \-nəs\ *n* ♦ : the quality or state of being devout

♦ blessedness, godliness, holiness, piety, sainthood, sanctity

dew \'dü, 'dyü\ *n* : moisture that condenses on the surfaces of cool bodies at night — **dewy** *adj*

dew·ber·ry \'dü-ˌber-ē, 'dyü-\ *n* : any of several sweet edible berries related to and resembling blackberries; *also* : a trailing bramble bearing these

dew·claw \-ˌklȯ\ *n* : a digit on the foot of a mammal that does not reach the ground; *also* : its claw or hoof

dew·lap \-ˌlap\ *n* : loose skin hanging under the neck of an animal

dew point *n* : the temperature at which the moisture in the air begins to condense

dex·ter·i·ty \dek-'ster-ə-tē\ *n, pl* **-ties**   **1** ♦ : quickness and skill in managing any complicated or difficult affair   **2** ♦ : readiness and grace in physical activity; *esp* : skill and ease in using the hands

♦ [1] adroitness, cleverness, craft, finesse, sleight ♦ [2] agility, deftness, nimbleness, sleight *Ant* awkwardness, clumsiness

dex·ter·ous *also* **dex·trous** \'dek-strəs\ *adj*   **1** : CLEVER   **2** ♦ : done with skillfulness   **3** ♦ : skillful and competent with the hands — **dex·ter·ous·ly** *adv*

♦ [2] adroit, artful, masterful, practiced, skillful, virtuoso ♦ [3] clever, cunning, deft, handy *Ant* butterfingered, heavy-handed, unhandy

dex·trose \'dek-ˌstrōs\ *n* : the naturally occurring form of glucose found in plants and blood

DFC *abbr* Distinguished Flying Cross

dg *abbr* decigram

DG *abbr*   **1** by the grace of God   **2** director general

DH \ˌdē-'āch\ *n* : DESIGNATED HITTER

dhow \'daü\ *n* : an Arab sailing ship usu. having a long overhang forward and a high poop

DI *abbr* drill instructor

dia *abbr* diameter

di·a·be·tes \ˌdī-ə-'bē-tēz, -təs\ *n* : an abnormal state marked by passage of excessive amounts of urine; *esp* : one (**diabetes mel·li·tus** \-'me-lə-təs\) characterized by deficient insulin, by excess sugar in the blood and urine, and by thirst, hunger, and loss of weight — **di·a·bet·ic** \-'be-tik\ *adj or n*

di·a·bol·i·cal \ˌdī-ə-'bä-li-kəl\ *or* **di·a·bol·ic** \-lik\ *adj* ♦ : of, relating to, or characteristic of the devil : DEVILISH — **di·a·bol·i·cal·ly** \-k(ə-)lē\ *adv*

♦ demonic, devilish, fiendish, satanic

di·a·bol·i·cal·ness \ˌdī-ə-'bä-li-kəl-nəs\ *n* : the quality or state of being diabolical

di·a·crit·ic \ˌdī-ə-'kri-tik\ *n* : a mark accompanying a letter and indicating a sound value different from that of the same letter when unmarked — **di·a·crit·i·cal** \-ti-kəl\ *adj*

di·a·dem \'dī-ə-ˌdem\ *n* : CROWN; *esp* : a royal headband

di·aer·e·sis *or* **di·er·e·sis** \dī-'er-ə-səs\ *n, pl* **-e·ses** \-ˌsēz\ : a mark ¨ placed over a vowel to show that it is pronounced in a separate syllable (as in *naïve*)

diag *abbr*   **1** diagonal   **2** diagram

di·ag·no·sis \ˌdī-ig-'nō-səs\ *n, pl* **-no·ses** \-ˌsēz\   **1** : the art or act of identifying a disease from its signs and symptoms; *also* : the decision reached by diagnosis   **2 a** : investigation or analysis of the cause or nature of a condition, situation, or problem   **b** ♦ : a statement or conclusion from an investigation or analysis — **di·ag·nose** \'dī-ig-ˌnōs\ *vb* — **di·ag·nos·tic** \ˌdī-ig-'näs-tik\ *adj* — **di·ag·nos·ti·cian** \-ˌnäs-'ti-shən\ *n*

♦ conclusion, decision, deliverance, determination, judgment (*or* judgement), opinion, resolution, verdict

¹**di·ag·o·nal** \dī-'a-gə-nəl\ *adj*   **1** : extending from one corner to the opposite corner in a 4-sided figure   **2** ♦ : running in a slanting direction ⟨∼ stripes⟩   **3** : having slanting markings or parts ⟨a ∼ weave⟩ — **di·ag·o·nal·ly** *adv*

♦ canted, inclined, listing, oblique, slantwise

²**diagonal** *n*   **1** : a diagonal line or plane   **2** : a diagonal row, pattern, or direction   **3** : a mark / used esp. to mean "or," "and or," or "per"

¹**di·a·gram** \'dī-ə-ˌgram\ *n* ♦ : a design and esp. a drawing that makes something easier to understand — **di·a·gram·ma·ble** \-ˌgra-mə-bəl\ *adj* — **di·a·gram·mat·ic** \ˌdī-ə-grə-'ma-tik\ *adj* — **di·a·gram·mat·i·cal·ly** \-ti-k(ə-)lē\ *adv*

♦ figure, graphic, illustration, plate

²**diagram** *vb* **-grammed** *or* **-gramed** \-ˌgramd\; **-gram·ming** *or* **-gram·ing** : to represent by a diagram

¹**di·al** \'dī(-ə)l\ *n*   **1** : the face of a sundial   **2** : the face of a timepiece   **3** : a face with a pointer and numbers that indicate something ⟨the ∼ of a gauge⟩   **4** : a device used for making electrical connections or for regulating operation (as of a radio)

²**dial** *vb* **di·aled** *or* **di·alled; di·al·ing** *or* **di·al·ling**   **1** : to manipulate a dial so as to operate or select   **2** ♦ : to make a telephone call or connection

♦ call, telephone

³**dial** *abbr* dialect

di·a·lect \'dī-ə-ˌlekt\ *n* ♦ : a regional variety of a language

  ♦ argot, cant, jargon, language, lingo, patois, patter, slang, vocabulary

di·a·lec·tic \ˌdī-ə-'lek-tik\ *n* : the process or art of reasoning by discussion of conflicting ideas; *also* : the tension between opposing elements — **di·a·lec·ti·cal** \-ti-kəl\ *adj*

dialog box *n* : a window on a computer screen for choosing options or inputting information

di·a·logue \'dī-ə-ˌlóg\ *also* **di·a·log** *n* **1** ♦ : a conversation between two or more parties **2** : the parts of a literary or dramatic work that represent conversation

  ♦ colloquy, conversation, discourse, discussion, exchange

di·al·y·sis \dī-'a-lə-səs\ *n, pl* **-y·ses** \-ˌsēz\ **1** : the separation of substances from solution by means of their unequal diffusion through semipermeable membranes **2** : the medical procedure of removing blood from an artery, purifying it by dialysis, and returning it to a vein

diam *abbr* diameter

di·am·e·ter \dī-'a-mə-tər\ *n* **1** : a straight line passing through the center of a figure or body; *esp* : one that divides a circle in half **2** : the length of a diameter

di·a·met·ric \ˌdī-ə-'me-trik\ *or* **di·a·met·ri·cal** \-tri-kəl\ *adj* **1** : of, relating to, or constituting a diameter **2** ♦ : completely opposed or opposite — **di·a·met·ri·cal·ly** \-k(ə-)lē\ *adv*

  ♦ antipodal, antithetical, contradictory, contrary, opposite, polar

di·a·mond \'dī-mənd, 'dī-ə-\ *n* **1** : a hard brilliant mineral that consists of crystalline carbon and is used as a gem **2** : a flat figure having four equal sides, two acute angles, and two obtuse angles **3** : any of a suit of playing cards marked with a red diamond **4** : INFIELD; *also* : the entire playing field in baseball

di·a·mond·back rattlesnake \-ˌbak-\ *n* : either of two large and deadly rattlesnakes of the southern U.S.

di·an·thus \dī-'an-thəs\ *n* : ¹PINK 1

di·a·pa·son \ˌdī-ə-'pāz-ᵊn, -'pās-\ *n* **1** : the organ stop governing the flue pipes that form the primary basis of organ tone **2** : the entire range of musical tones

¹**di·a·per** \'dī-pər, 'dī-ə-\ *n* **1** : a cotton or linen fabric woven in a simple geometric pattern **2** : a garment for a baby drawn up between the legs and fastened about the waist

²**diaper** *vb* **1** : to ornament with diaper designs **2** : to put a diaper on

di·aph·a·nous \dī-'a-fə-nəs\ *adj* : of so fine a texture as to be transparent

di·a·pho·ret·ic \ˌdī-ə-fə-'re-tik\ *adj* : having the power to increase perspiration — **diaphoretic** *n*

di·a·phragm \'dī-ə-ˌfram\ *n* **1** : a sheet of muscle between the chest and abdominal cavities of a mammal **2** : a vibrating disk (as in a microphone) **3** : a cup-shaped device usu. of thin rubber fitted over the uterine cervix to act as a mechanical contraceptive barrier — **di·a·phrag·mat·ic** \ˌdī-ə-frəg-'ma-tik, -ˌfrag-\ *adj*

di·a·rist \'dī-ə-rist\ *n* : one who keeps a diary

di·ar·rhea *or chiefly Brit* **di·ar·rhoea** \ˌdī-ə-'rē-ə\ *n* : abnormally frequent and watery bowel movements

di·a·ry \'dī-ə-rē\ *n, pl* **-ries** : a daily record esp. of personal experiences; *also* : a book used as a diary

di·as·po·ra \dī-'as-pə-rə\ *n* **1** *cap* : the settling of scattered colonies of Jews outside Palestine after the Babylonian exile **2** *cap* : the Jews living outside Palestine or modern Israel **3** : the migration or scattering of a people away from an ancestral homeland

di·as·to·le \dī-'as-tə-(ˌ)lē\ *n* : the stretching of the chambers of the heart during which they fill with blood — **di·a·stol·ic** \ˌdī-ə-'stä-lik\ *adj*

di·a·ther·my \'dī-ə-ˌthər-mē\ *n* : the generation of heat in tissue by electric currents for medical purposes

di·a·tom \'dī-ə-ˌtäm\ *n* : any of a class of planktonic one-celled or colonial algae with skeletons of silica

di·atom·ic \ˌdī-ə-'tä-mik\ *adj* : having two atoms in the molecule

di·a·tribe \'dī-ə-ˌtrīb\ *n* ♦ : biting or abusive speech or writing

  ♦ harangue, rant, tirade

di·az·e·pam \dī-'a-zə-ˌpam\ *n* : a tranquilizer used esp. to relieve anxiety, tension, and muscle spasms

dib·ble \'di-bəl\ *n* : a pointed hand tool for making holes (as for planting bulbs) in the ground — **dibble** *vb*

¹**dice** \'dīs\ *n, pl* **dice** : DIE 1

²**dice** *vb* **diced; dic·ing** **1** : to cut into small cubes ⟨∼ carrots⟩ **2** : to play games with dice

di·chot·o·my \dī-'kä-tə-mē\ *n, pl* **-mies** : a division or the process of dividing into two esp. mutually exclusive or contradictory groups — **di·chot·o·mous** \-məs\ *adj*

dick·er \'di-kər\ *vb* ♦ : to negotiate over the terms of a purchase, agreement, or contract : BARGAIN

  ♦ bargain, chaffer, deal, haggle, negotiate, palter

dick·ey *or* **dicky** \'di-kē\ *n, pl* **dickeys** *or* **dick·ies** : a small fabric insert worn to fill in the neckline

di·cot·y·le·don \ˌdī-ˌkät-ᵊl-'ēd-ᵊn\ *n* : any of a group of seed plants having an embryo with two cotyledons — **di·cot·y·le·don·ous** *adj*

dict *abbr* dictionary

¹**dic·tate** \'dik-ˌtāt\ *vb* **dic·tat·ed; dic·tat·ing** **1** : to speak or read for a person to transcribe or for a machine to record **2** : to issue as an order : COMMAND — **dic·ta·tion** \dik-'tā-shən\ *n*

²**dic·tate** \'dik-ˌtāt\ *n* ♦ : an authoritative rule, prescription, or injunction : COMMAND ⟨the ∼s of conscience⟩

  ♦ behest, charge, command, commandment, decree, direction, directive, edict, instruction, order, word

dic·ta·tor \'dik-ˌtā-tər\ *n* **1** ♦ : a person ruling absolutely and often brutally and oppressively **2** : one that dictates

  ♦ autocrat, despot, oppressor, tyrant

dic·ta·to·ri·al \ˌdik-tə-'tōr-ē-əl\ *adj* ♦ : of, relating to, or characteristic of a dictator or a dictatorship

  ♦ arbitrary, authoritarian, autocratic, bossy, despotic, domineering, imperious, overbearing, peremptory, tyrannical, tyrannous

dic·ta·tor·ship \dik-'tā-tər-ˌship, 'dik-ˌtā-\ *n* **1** : the office of a dictator **2** : autocratic rule, control, or leadership **3** ♦ : a government or country in which absolute power is held by a dictator or a small clique

  ♦ autocracy, despotism, totalitarianism, tyranny

dic·tion \'dik-shən\ *n* **1** ♦ : choice of words esp. with regard to correctness, clearness, or effectiveness : WORDING **2** : ENUNCIATION

  ♦ language, phraseology, phrasing, wording

dic·tio·nary \'dik-shə-ˌner-ē\ *n, pl* **-nar·ies** : a reference book containing words usu. alphabetically arranged along with information about their forms, pronunciations, functions, etymologies, meanings, and syntactical and idiomatic uses

dic·tum \'dik-təm\ *n, pl* **dic·ta** \-tə\ *also* **dictums** : a noteworthy, formal, or authoritative statement or observation

did *past of* DO

di·dac·tic \dī-'dak-tik\ *adj* **1** : intended to instruct, inform, or teach a moral lesson **2** : making moral observations

di·do \'dī-dō\ *n, pl* **didoes** *or* **didos** : a mischievous act : PRANK

¹**die** \'dī\ *vb* **died; dy·ing** \'dī-iŋ\ **1** ♦ : to cease living : EXPIRE **2** ♦ : to pass out of existence ⟨a *dying* language⟩ **3** ♦ : to disappear or subside gradually ⟨the wind *died* down⟩ **4** ♦ : to long keenly — usu. used with *to* or *for* ⟨*dying* to go⟩ ⟨*dying* for a snack⟩ **5** : to cease functioning : STOP ⟨the motor *died*⟩

  ♦ [1] depart, expire, pass, pass away, perish, succumb *Ant* breathe, live ♦ [2] break off, break up, cease, close, conclude, discontinue, elapse, end, expire, finish, halt, lapse, leave off, let up, pass, quit, stop, terminate, wind up ♦ *usu* **die down** [3] abate, decline, decrease, de-escalate, diminish, dwindle, ebb, fall, lessen, let up, lower, moderate, recede, relent, shrink, subside, taper, wane ♦ *usu* **die for** [4] ache for, crave, desire, hanker for, hunger for, long for, lust (for *or* after), pine for, repine, thirst for, want, wish for, yearn for

²**die** \'dī\ *n* **1** *pl* **dice** \'dīs\ : a small cube marked on each face with one to six spots and used usu. in pairs in games and gambling **2** *pl* **dies** \'dīz\ : a device used to shape, finish, or impress an object

die·hard \'dī-ˌhärd\ *n* : one who is strongly devoted or determined

die·re·sis *var of* DIAERESIS

die·sel \'dē-zəl, -səl\ *n* **1** : DIESEL ENGINE **2** : a vehicle driven by a diesel engine **3** : DIESEL FUEL

diesel engine *n* : an internal combustion engine in whose cylinders air is compressed to a temperature sufficiently high to ignite the fuel

diesel fuel *n* : a heavy mineral oil used as fuel in diesel engines

die·sel·ing \'dē-zə-liŋ\ *n* : the continued operation of an internal combustion engine after the ignition has been turned off

¹**di·et** \'dī-ət\ *n* **1** : food and drink regularly consumed : FARE **2** : an allowance of food prescribed for a special reason (as to lose weight) — **di·e·tary** \-ə-ˌter-ē\ *adj or n*

²**diet** *vb* : to eat or cause to eat or drink less or according to a prescribed rule — **di·et·er** *n*

dietary supplement *n* : a product taken orally that contains ingredients (as vitamins or amino acids) intended to supplement one's diet

di·e·tet·ics \ˌdī-ə-ˈte-tiks\ *n sing or pl* : the science or art of applying the principles of nutrition to diet — **di·e·tet·ic** *adj*

di·e·ti·tian *or* **di·e·ti·cian** \ˌdī-ə-ˈti-shən\ *n* : a specialist in dietetics

dif *or* **diff** *abbr* difference

dif·fer \ˈdi-fər\ *vb* **dif·fered; dif·fer·ing** **1** : to be unlike **2** : VARY **3** : DISAGREE

dif·fer·ence \ˈdi-frəns, ˈdi-fə-rəns\ *n* **1** ♦ : the quality or state of being different : UNLIKENESS ⟨∼ in their looks⟩ **2** : distinction or discrimination in preference **3** ♦ : disagreement in opinion; *also* : an instance or cause of disagreement ⟨unable to settle their ∼s⟩ **4** : the amount by which one number or quantity differs from another

♦ [1] contrast, disagreement, discrepancy, disparity, distinction, diversity, unlikeness *Ant* community, likeness, resemblance, sameness, similarity ♦ [3] controversy, disagreement, dispute, dissension

dif·fer·ent \ˈdi-frənt, ˈdi-fə-rənt\ *adj* **1** ♦ : unlike in nature or quality **2** ♦ : not the same ⟨∼ age groups⟩; *also* : VARIOUS ⟨∼ members of the club⟩ **3** : ANOTHER ⟨try a ∼ channel⟩ **4** : UNUSUAL, SPECIAL ⟨a quite ∼ style⟩

♦ disparate, dissimilar, distinct, distinctive, distinguishable, diverse, other, unalike, unlike *Ant* alike, indistinguishable, like, parallel, same, similar

¹dif·fer·en·tial \ˌdi-fə-ˈren-chəl\ *adj* : showing, creating, or relating to a difference

²differential *n* **1** : the amount or degree by which things differ **2** : DIFFERENTIAL GEAR

differential gear *n* : an arrangement of gears in an automobile that allows one wheel to turn faster than another (as in rounding curves)

dif·fer·en·ti·ate \ˌdi-fə-ˈren-chē-ˌāt\ *vb* **-at·ed; -at·ing** **1** : to make or become different **2** : to attain a specialized adult form and function during development **3** ♦ : to recognize or state the difference ⟨∼ between them⟩ — **dif·fer·en·ti·a·tion** \-ˌren-chē-ˈā-shən\ *n*

♦ discern, discriminate, distinguish, separate

dif·fer·ent·ly \-lē\ *adv* ♦ : in a different manner

♦ else, other, otherwise

dif·fi·cult \ˈdi-fi-(ˌ)kəlt\ *adj* **1** ♦ : hard to do or make **2** ♦ : hard to understand or deal with ⟨∼ reading⟩ ⟨a ∼ child⟩

♦ [1] arduous, demanding, exacting, formidable, grueling, hard, herculean, laborious, rough, stiff, strenuous, tall, toilsome, tough ♦ [2] catchy, delicate, knotty, problematic, spiny, thorny, ticklish, touchy, tough, tricky

dif·fi·cul·ty \-(ˌ)kəl-tē\ *n, pl* **-ties** **1** : difficult nature ⟨the ∼ of a task⟩ **2** : DISAGREEMENT ⟨settled their *difficulties*⟩ **3** ♦ : something that is difficult or serves to impede ⟨overcome *difficulties*⟩ **4** : an instance of trouble ⟨in financial *difficulties*⟩

♦ adversity, asperity, hardness, hardship, rigor ♦ complexity, complication, intricacy

dif·fi·dent \ˈdi-fə-dənt\ *adj* **1** ♦ : lacking confidence **2** : RESERVED 1 — **dif·fi·dence** \-dəns\ *n* — **dif·fi·dent·ly** *adv*

♦ bashful, coy, demure, introverted, modest, retiring, sheepish, shy

dif·frac·tion \di-ˈfrak-shən\ *n* : the bending or spreading of waves (as of light) esp. when passing through narrow slits

¹dif·fuse \di-ˈfyüs\ *adj* **1** ♦ : being at once verbose and ill-organized ⟨∼ writing⟩ **2** : not concentrated or localized ⟨∼ light⟩

♦ circuitous, long-winded, prolix, rambling, verbose, windy, wordy

²dif·fuse \di-ˈfyüz\ *vb* **dif·fused; dif·fus·ing** **1** : to pour out or spread widely **2** : to undergo or cause to undergo diffusion **3** : to break up light by diffusion

dif·fu·sion \di-ˈfyü-zhən\ *n* **1** : a diffusing or a being diffused **2** : movement of particles (as of a gas) from a region of high to one of lower concentration **3** : the reflection of light from a rough surface or the passage of light through a translucent material

¹dig \ˈdig\ *vb* **dug** \ˈdəg\; **dig·ging** **1** : to turn up the soil (as with a spade) **2** : to hollow out or form by removing earth ⟨∼ a hole⟩ **3 a** : to uncover or seek by turning up earth ⟨∼ potatoes⟩ **b** ♦ : to penetrate below the surface in search of something hidden or buried — used with *into* **c** ♦ : to advance by or as if by removing or pushing aside material ⟨∼ through the toy box⟩ **4** ♦ : to come upon by searching or effort : DISCOVER ⟨∼

up information⟩ **5** : POKE, THRUST ⟨∼ a person in the ribs⟩ **6** : to work hard **7 a** : UNDERSTAND, APPRECIATE **b** ♦ : to feel attraction toward or take pleasure in : LIKE

♦ *usu* **dig into** [3b] delve, explore, go, inquire into, investigate, look, probe, research ♦ *usu* **dig through** [3c] dredge, hunt, rake, ransack, rifle, rummage, scour, search ♦ *usu* **dig up** [4] detect, determine, discover, ferret out, find, hit on, locate, track down ♦ [7b] adore, delight, enjoy, fancy, groove, like, love, relish, revel

²dig *n* **1 a** : a quick thrust : POKE **b** ♦ : a cutting remark **2** *pl* : living accommodations

♦ affront, barb, dart, indignity, insult, name, offense, outrage, put-down, sarcasm, slight, slur, wound

³dig *abbr* digest

¹di·gest \ˈdī-ˌjest\ *n* ♦ : a summation or condensation of a body of information; *esp* : a summarized or shortened version esp. of a literary work

♦ abbreviation, condensation ♦ abstract, encapsulation, epitome, outline, précis, recapitulation, résumé (*or* resume), roundup, sum, summary, synopsis, wrap-up

²di·gest \dī-ˈjest, də-\ *vb* **1** : to think over and arrange in the mind **2** : to convert (food) into simpler forms that can be absorbed by the body **3** ♦ : to compress into a short summary — **di·gest·ibil·i·ty** \-ˌjes-tə-ˈbi-lə-tē\ *n* — **di·gest·ible** *adj* — **di·ges·tion** \-ˈjes-chən\ *n* — **di·ges·tive** \-ˈjes-tiv\ *adj*

♦ abstract, encapsulate, epitomize, outline, recapitulate, sum up, summarize, wrap up

di·ges·tif \ˌdē-zhes-ˈtēf\ *n* : an alcoholic drink taken after a meal

dig in *vb* **1** : to take a defensive stand esp. by digging trenches **2** : to firmly set to work **3** : to begin eating

dig·it \ˈdi-jət\ *n* **1** ♦ : any of the Arabic numerals 1 to 9 and usu. the symbol 0 **2** : FINGER, TOE

♦ figure, integer, number, numeral, whole number

dig·i·tal \ˈdi-jə-t°l\ *adj* **1** : of, relating to, or done with a finger or toe **2** : of, relating to, or using calculation by numerical methods or by discrete units **3** : relating to or employing communications signals in the form of binary digits ⟨a ∼ broadcast⟩ **4** : providing a readout in numerical digits ⟨a ∼ watch⟩ **5** : ELECTRONIC; *also* : characterized by computerized technology ⟨the ∼ age⟩ — **dig·i·tal·ly** *adv*

digital camera *n* : a camera that records images as digital data instead of on film

dig·i·tal·is \ˌdi-jə-ˈta-ləs\ *n* : a drug from the common foxglove that is a powerful heart stimulant; *also* : FOXGLOVE

digital versatile disc *n* : DVD

digital video disc *n* : DVD

dig·ni·fied \ˈdig-nə-ˌfīd\ *adj* ♦ : showing or expressing dignity

♦ august, imposing, solemn, staid, stately *Ant* flighty, frivolous, giddy, goofy, silly, undignified

dig·ni·fy \-ˌfī\ *vb* **-fied; -fy·ing** ♦ : to give dignity, distinction, or attention to

♦ aggrandize, ennoble, exalt, glorify, magnify

dig·ni·tary \ˈdig-nə-ˌter-ē\ *n, pl* **-tar·ies** : a person of high position or honor

dig·ni·ty \ˈdig-nə-tē\ *n, pl* **-ties** **1** : the quality or state of being worthy, honored, or esteemed **2** : high rank, office, or position **3** : formal reserve of manner, language, or appearance

di·graph \ˈdī-ˌgraf\ *n* : a group of two successive letters whose phonetic value is a single sound (as *ea* in *bread*)

di·gress \dī-ˈgres, də-\ *vb* : to turn aside esp. from the main subject or argument — **di·gres·sion** \dī-ˈgre-shən\ *n*

di·gres·sive \dī-ˈgre-siv\ *adj* ♦ : characterized by digressions

♦ desultory, discursive, rambling

Di·jon mustard \ˈdē-ˌzhän-, di-ˈzhän-\ *n* : a mustard made from dark mustard seeds, white wine, and spices

dike \ˈdīk\ *n* **1** ♦ : an artificial watercourse : DITCH **2** ♦ : a bank of earth constructed to control water : LEVEE

♦ [1] ditch, gutter, trench ♦ [2] dam, embankment, levee

dil *abbr* dilute

di·lap·i·dat·ed \də-ˈla-pə-ˌdā-təd\ *adj* ♦ : fallen into partial ruin or decay

♦ grungy, mean, neglected, ratty, seedy, shabby

di·lap·i·da·tion \də-ˌla-pə-ˈdā-shən\ *n* ♦ : the act of dilapidating or the state of being dilapidated

♦ desolation, disrepair, neglect

di·late \dī-'lāt, 'dī-ˌlāt\ *vb* **di·lat·ed; di·lat·ing** : SWELL, DISTEND, EXPAND — **dil·a·ta·tion** \ˌdi-lə-'tā-shən\ *n* — **di·la·tion** \dī-'lā-shən\ *n*

dil·a·to·ry \'di-lə-ˌtōr-ē\ *adj* **1** : DELAYING **2** ♦ : characterized by procrastination : TARDY

 ♦ creeping, laggard, languid, poky, slow, sluggish, tardy

di·lem·ma \də-'le-mə\ *n* **1** : a usu. undesirable or unpleasant choice; *also* : a situation involving such a choice **2** : PREDICAMENT

dil·et·tante \ˌdi-lə-'tänt, -'tant\ *n, pl* **-tantes** *or* **-tan·ti** \-'tän-tē, -'tan-\ : a person having a superficial interest in an art or a branch of knowledge

dil·i·gence \'di-lə-jəns\ *n* ♦ : persevering application

 ♦ assiduity, industry

dil·i·gent \'di-lə-jənt\ *adj* ♦ : characterized by steady, earnest, and energetic effort

 ♦ active, assiduous, busy, engaged, laborious, occupied, sedulous, working

dil·i·gent·ly \-lē\ *adv* ♦ : in a diligent manner

 ♦ determinedly, hard, laboriously, strenuously, tirelessly

dill \'dil\ *n* : an herb related to the carrot with aromatic leaves and seeds used as seasoning and in pickles

dil·ly \'di-lē\ *n, pl* **dil·lies** : one that is remarkable or outstanding

dil·ly-dal·ly \'di-lē-ˌda-lē\ *vb* ♦ : to waste time by loitering or delaying

 ♦ crawl, creep, dally, dawdle, delay, drag, lag, linger, loiter, poke, tarry

¹**di·lute** \dī-'lüt, də-\ *vb* **di·lut·ed; di·lut·ing** ♦ : to lessen the consistency or strength of by mixing with something else — **di·lu·tion** \-'lü-shən\ *n*

 ♦ adulterate, thin, water, weaken

²**dilute** *adj* ♦ : having the consistency or strength of lessened by mixing with something else

 ♦ impure, polluted ♦ thin, watery, weak

¹**dim** \'dim\ *adj* **dim·mer; dim·mest** **1** ♦ : lacking brilliance or luster : DULL **2** ♦ : not bright or distinct : OBSCURE **3** : not seeing or understanding clearly **4** ♦ : perceived by the senses or mind indistinctly or weakly — **dim·ly** *adv* — **dim·ness** *n*

 ♦ [1] dull, flat, lusterless ♦ [2] dark, darkling, dusky, gloomy, murky, obscure, somber (*or* sombre) ♦ [4] bleary, faint, foggy, fuzzy, hazy, indefinite, indistinct, indistinguishable, murky, nebulous, obscure, opaque, shadowy, unclear, undefined, undetermined, vague

²**dim** *vb* **dimmed; dim·ming** **1** ♦ : to make or become dim or lusterless **2** ♦ : to reduce the light from

 ♦ becloud, befog, blur, cloud, darken, fog, haze, mist, obscure, overcast, overshadow, shroud

³**dim** *abbr* **1** dimension **2** diminished **3** diminutive

dime \'dīm\ *n* : a U.S. or Canadian coin worth ten cents

di·men·sion \də-'men-chən, dī-\ *n* **1** : the physical property of length, breadth, or thickness; *also* : a measure of this **2 a** ♦ : the quality of spatial extension : EXTENT **b** : the range over which or the degree to which something extends : SCOPE — usu. used in pl. — **di·men·sion·al** \-'men-chə-nəl\ *adj* — **di·men·sion·al·i·ty** \-ˌmen-chə-'na-lə-tē\ *n*

 ♦ extent, magnitude, measure, measurement, proportion, size

di·min·ish \də-'mi-nish\ *vb* **1** : to make less or cause to appear less **2** ♦ : to lessen the authority, dignity, or reputation of : BELITTLE **3** ♦ : to become gradually less (as in size or importance) : DWINDLE **4** : to diminish gradually : TAPER

 ♦ [2] belittle, cry down, decry, deprecate, depreciate, discount, disparage, minimize, put down, write off ♦ [3, 4] abate, decline, decrease, de-escalate, die, dwindle, ebb, fall, lessen, let up, lower, moderate, recede, relent, shrink, subside, taper, wane

di·min·u·en·do \də-ˌmin-yə-'wen-dō\ *adv or adj* : DECRESCENDO

dim·i·nu·tion \ˌdi-mə-'nü-shən, -'nyü-\ *n* ♦ : the act, process, or an instance of diminishing

 ♦ abatement, decline, decrease, decrement, drop, fall, loss, reduction, shrinkage

¹**di·min·u·tive** \də-'min-yə-tiv\ *n* **1** : a diminutive word or affix ⟨the word "kitchenette" is a ∼⟩ **2** : a diminutive individual

²**diminutive** *adj* **1** : indicating small size and sometimes the state or quality of being lovable, pitiable, or contemptible ⟨the ∼ suffixes *-ette* and *-ling*⟩ **2** : extremely small : TINY

dim·i·ty \'di-mə-tē\ *n, pl* **-ties** : a thin usu. corded cotton fabric

dim·mer \'di-mər\ *n* : a device for controlling the amount of light from an electric lighting unit

di·mor·phic \(ˌ)dī-'mȯr-fik\ *adj* : occurring in two distinct forms — **di·mor·phism** \-ˌfi-zəm\ *n*

¹**dim·ple** \'dim-pəl\ *n* : a small depression esp. in the cheek or chin

²**dimple** *vb* **dim·pled; dim·pling** : to form dimples (as in smiling)

din \'din\ *n* ♦ : a loud confused mixture of noises

 ♦ bluster, cacophony, clamor (*or* clamour), noise, racket, roar

dine \'dīn\ *vb* **dined; din·ing** **1** ♦ : to eat dinner **2** ♦ : to give a dinner to

 ♦ [1] eat, fare, feed ♦ [2] banquet, feast, junket, regale

din·er \'dī-nər\ *n* **1** : one that dines **2** : a railroad dining car **3** ♦ : a restaurant usu. resembling a dining car

 ♦ café, grill, restaurant

di·nette \dī-'net\ *n* : an alcove or small room used for dining

ding \'diŋ\ *vb* : to cause minor damage to a surface — **ding** *n*

din·ghy \'diŋ-ē\ *n, pl* **dinghies** **1** : a small boat **2** : LIFE RAFT

din·gi·ness \'din-jē-nəs\ *n* ♦ : the quality or state of being dingy

 ♦ dirtiness, filthiness, foulness, grubbiness, nastiness, uncleanliness

din·gle \'diŋ-gəl\ *n* : a small wooded valley

din·go \'diŋ-gō\ *n, pl* **dingoes** : a reddish brown wild dog of Australia

din·gus \'diŋ-gəs, -əs\ *n* : DOODAD

din·gy \'din-jē\ *adj* **din·gi·er; -est** **1** : not clean or pure : DIRTY **2** : SHABBY

dink \'diŋk\ *n, often all cap* : a couple with two incomes and no children; *also* : a member of such a couple

din·ky \'diŋ-kē\ *adj* **din·ki·er; -est** : overly or unattractively small

din·ner \'di-nər\ *n* **1** : the main meal of the day **2** ♦ : a formal banquet

 ♦ banquet, feast, feed, spread

din·ner·ware \'di-nər-ˌwar\ *n* : tableware other than flatware

di·no \'dī-nō\ *n, pl* **dinos** : DINOSAUR

di·no·fla·gel·late \ˌdī-nō-'fla-jə-lət, -ˌlāt\ *n* : any of an order of planktonic plantlike unicellular flagellates of which some cause red tide

di·no·saur \'dī-nə-ˌsȯr\ *n* : any of a group of extinct long-tailed Mesozoic reptiles often of huge size

dint \'dint\ *n* **1** : FORCE ⟨by ∼ of sheer grit⟩ **2** : a depression or hollow made by a blow or by pressure : DENT

di·o·cese \'dī-ə-səs, -ˌsēz, -ˌsēs\ *n, pl* **-ces·es** \-sə-səz, -ˌsē-zəz, -ˌsē-səz\ : the territorial jurisdiction of a bishop — **di·oc·e·san** \dī-'ä-sə-sən, ˌdī-ə-'sēz-ᵊn\ *adj or n*

di·ode \'dī-ˌōd\ *n* : an electronic device with two electrodes or terminals used esp. as a rectifier

di·ox·in \dī-'äk-sən\ *n* : a persistent toxic hydrocarbon that occurs esp. as a by-product of industrial processes and waste incineration

¹**dip** \'dip\ *vb* **dipped; dip·ping** **1** ♦ : to plunge temporarily or partially under the surface (as of a liquid) **2** : to thrust in a way to suggest immersion **3** ♦ : to scoop up or out : LADLE **4** : to lower and then raise quickly ⟨∼ a flag in salute⟩ **5** ♦ : to drop or slope down esp. suddenly ⟨the moon *dipped* below the crest⟩ **6** ♦ : to decrease moderately and usu. temporarily ⟨prices *dipped*⟩ **7** : to reach inside or as if inside or below a surface ⟨*dipped* into their savings⟩ **8** ♦ : to examine or read something casually or superficially ⟨∼ into a book⟩

 ♦ [1] douse, duck, dunk, immerse, souse, submerge ♦ [3] ladle, scoop, spoon ♦ [5, 6] decline, descend, drop, fall, lower, plummet, plunge, sink, tumble ♦ [8] browse, glance, glimpse, peek, skim

²**dip** *n* **1** : an act of dipping; *esp* : a short swim **2** ♦ : inclination downward : DROP **3** : something obtained by or used in dipping **4** : a sauce or soft mixture into which food may be dipped **5** : a liquid into which something may be dipped (as for cleansing or coloring)

 ♦ descent, dive, down, drop, fall, plunge

diph·the·ria \dif-'thir-ē-ə\ *n* : an acute contagious bacterial disease marked by fever and by coating of the air passages with a membrane that interferes with breathing

diph·thong \'dif-ˌthȯŋ\ *n* : two vowel sounds joined in one syllable to form one speech sound (as *ou* in *out*)

dip·loid \'di-ˌplȯid\ *adj* : having two haploid sets of chromosomes ⟨∼ somatic cells⟩ — **diploid** *n*

di·plo·ma \də-ˈplō-mə\ *n, pl* **diplomas** : an official record of graduation from or of a degree conferred by a school

di·plo·ma·cy \də-ˈplō-mə-sē\ *n* **1** : the art and practice of conducting negotiations between nations **2** : TACT

dip·lo·mat \ˈdi-plə-ˌmat\ *n* : one employed or skilled in diplomacy — **dip·lo·mat·ic** \ˌdi-plə-ˈma-tik\ *adj*

di·plo·ma·tist \də-ˈplō-mə-tist\ *n* : DIPLOMAT

dip·per \ˈdi-pər\ *n* **1** : any of a genus of birds that are related to the thrushes and are skilled in diving **2** : something (as a ladle or scoop) that dips or is used for dipping **3** *cap* : BIG DIPPER **4** *cap* : LITTLE DIPPER

dip·so·ma·nia \ˌdip-sə-ˈmā-nē-ə\ *n* : an uncontrollable craving for alcoholic liquors — **dip·so·ma·ni·ac** \-nē-ˌak\ *n*

dip·stick \ˈdip-ˌstik\ *n* : a graduated rod for indicating depth

dip·ter·an \ˈdip-tə-rən\ *adj* : of, relating to, or being a fly (sense 2) — **dipteran** *n* — **dip·ter·ous** \-rəs\ *adj*

dir *abbr* **1** direction **2** director

¹dire \ˈdīr\ *adj* **dir·er; dir·est 1** ♦ : very horrible : DREADFUL **2** ♦ : warning of disaster **3** : EXTREME **4** ♦ : demanding immediate action to fend off disastrous consequences

♦ [1] dreadful, fearful, fearsome, forbidding, formidable, frightful, hair-raising, horrible, redoubtable, scary, shocking, terrible, terrifying ♦ [2] baleful, foreboding, menacing, ominous, portentous, sinister ♦ [4] acute, critical, imperative, imperious, instant, pressing, urgent

¹di·rect \də-ˈrekt, dī-\ *vb* **1** ♦ : ADDRESS ⟨~ a letter⟩; *also* : to impart orally : AIM ⟨~ a remark to the gallery⟩ **2** ♦ : to regulate the activities or course of : guide the supervision, organizing, or performance of **3** ♦ : to cause to turn, move, or point or to follow a certain course **4** : to point, extend, or project in a specified line or course **5** ♦ : to request or instruct with authority **6** ♦ : to show or point out the way

♦ [2] administer, carry on, conduct, control, govern, guide, handle, manage, operate, oversee, regulate, run, superintend, supervise ♦ [3] aim, bend, cast, head, level, set, train ♦ [5] command, decree, dictate, ordain, order ♦ [5] bid, boss, charge, command, enjoin, instruct, order, tell ♦ [6] conduct, guide, lead, marshal, pilot, route, show, steer, usher

²direct *adj* **1** ♦ : stemming immediately from a source ⟨~ result⟩ **2** : being or passing in a straight line of descent : LINEAL ⟨~ ancestor⟩ **3** : leading from one point to another in time or space without turn or stop : STRAIGHT **4** ♦ : free from evasiveness or obscurity : STRAIGHTFORWARD ⟨a ~ manner⟩ **5** : operating without an intervening agency or step ⟨~ action⟩ **6** : effected by the action of the people or the electorate and not by representatives ⟨~ democracy⟩ **7** : consisting of or reproducing the exact words of a speaker or writer

♦ [1] firsthand, immediate, primary *Ant* indirect, secondhand ♦ [4] candid, forthright, foursquare, frank, honest, open, outspoken, plain, straight, straightforward, unguarded, unreserved

³direct *adv* ♦ : in a direct way

♦ dead, directly, due, plump, right, straight

direct broadcast satellite *n* : a television broadcasting system in which satellite transmissions are received at the viewing location

direct current *n* : an electric current flowing in one direction only

direct deposit *n* : a method of payment in which money is transferred to the payee's account without the use of checks or cash

di·rec·tion \də-ˈrek-shən, dī-\ *n* **1** ♦ : guidance or supervision of action or conduct : MANAGEMENT **2** : an explicit instruction : COMMAND **3** : the course or line along which something moves, lies, or points **4** : TENDENCY, TREND — **di·rec·tion·al** \-shə-nəl\ *adj*

♦ administration, conduct, control, government, guidance, management, operation, oversight, regulation, running, superintendence, supervision

di·rec·tive \də-ˈrek-tiv, dī-\ *n* ♦ : something that directs and usu. impels toward an action or goal; *esp* : an order issued by a high-level body or official

♦ decree, edict, fiat, ruling ♦ behest, charge, command, commandment, decree, dictate, direction, edict, instruction, order, word

di·rect·ly \-lē\ *adv* **1** ♦ : in a direct manner **2** ♦ : without delay

♦ [1] dead, direct, due, plump, right, straight *Ant* indirectly ♦ [2] forthwith, immediately, instantly, now, promptly, pronto, right away, right now

direct mail *n* : printed matter used for soliciting business or contributions and mailed direct to individuals

di·rect·ness \-nəs\ *n* **1** : the character of being accurate in course or aim **2** ♦ : strict pertinence : FORTHRIGHTNESS

♦ candor (*or* candour), forthrightness, frankness, openness, plainness

di·rec·tor \də-ˈrek-tər, dī-\ *n* **1** ♦ : one that directs : MANAGER **2** : one of a group of persons who direct the affairs of an organized body — **di·rec·tor·ship** *n*

♦ administrator, executive, manager, superintendent, supervisor

di·rec·tor·ate \-tə-rət\ *n* **1** : the office or position of director **2** : a board of directors; *also* : membership on such a board **3** : an executive staff

di·rec·to·ri·al \də-ˌrek-ˈtōr-ē-əl\ *adj* ♦ : serving to direct

♦ executive, managerial, supervisory

director's cut *n* : a version of a motion picture that is edited according to the director's wishes

di·rec·to·ry \-tə-rē\ *n, pl* **-ries** : an alphabetical or classified list esp. of names and addresses

dire·ful \ˈdīr-fəl\ *adj* **1** : causing great and oppressive fear : DREADFUL ⟨a ~ disease⟩ **2** : OMINOUS

dirge \ˈdərj\ *n* ♦ : a song of lamentation; *also* : a slow mournful piece of music

♦ elegy, lament, requiem, threnody

di·ri·gi·ble \ˈdir-ə-jə-bəl, də-ˈri-jə-\ *n* : AIRSHIP

dirk \ˈdərk\ *n* : DAGGER 1

dirndl \ˈdərnd-ᵊl\ *n* : a full skirt with a tight waistband

dirt \ˈdərt\ *n* **1** ♦ : a filthy or soiling substance (as mud, dust, or grime) **2** ♦ : loose or packed earth : SOIL **3** : moral uncleanness **4** : scandalous gossip **5** : embarrassing or incriminating information

♦ [1] filth, grime, muck, smut, soil ♦ [2] earth, ground, soil

dirt·i·ness \ˈdər-tē-nəs\ *n* ♦ : the quality or state of being dirty

♦ dinginess, filthiness, foulness, grubbiness, nastiness, uncleanliness *Ant* cleanliness

¹dirty \ˈdər-tē\ *adj* **dirt·i·er; -est 1** ♦ : not clean : SOILED **2** ♦ : morally unclean or corrupt : INDECENT ⟨~ jokes⟩ **3 a** ♦ : lacking honor : BASE ⟨a ~ trick⟩ **b** ♦ : not characteristic of or exhibiting good sportsmanship **4** ♦ : relating to, characterized by, or indicative of a storm ⟨~ weather⟩ **5** : not clear in color : DULL ⟨a ~ red⟩ — **dirty** *adv*

♦ [1] dusty, filthy, foul, grubby, grungy, mucky, muddy, nasty, smutty, sordid, unclean *Ant* clean, cleanly, immaculate, spick-and-span, spotless, stainless, unsoiled, unstained, unsullied ♦ [2] bawdy, coarse, crude, filthy, foul, gross, indecent, lascivious, lewd, nasty, obscene, pornographic, ribald, smutty, unprintable, vulgar, wanton ♦ [3a] base, contemptible, despicable, detestable, dishonorable (*or* dishonourable), ignoble, low, mean, snide, sordid, vile, wretched ♦ [3b] foul, illegal, unfair, unsportsmanlike ♦ [4] bleak, foul, inclement, nasty, raw, rough, squally, stormy, tempestuous, turbulent

²dirty *vb* **dirt·ied; dirty·ing** ♦ : to make or become dirty

♦ befoul, begrime, besmirch, blacken, foul, grime, mire, muddy, smirch, soil, stain *Ant* clean, cleanse

dis·able \di-ˈsā-bəl\ *vb* **dis·abled; dis·abling 1** : to disqualify legally **2** ♦ : to make unable to perform by or as if by illness, injury, or malfunction — **dis·abil·i·ty** \ˌdi-sə-ˈbi-lə-tē\ *n*

♦ cripple, hamstring, immobilize, incapacitate, paralyze, prostrate

dis·abled *adj* : incapacitated by illness, injury, or wounds; *also* : physically or mentally impaired

dis·abuse \ˌdi-sə-ˈbyüz\ *vb* : to free from error, fallacy, or misconception

dis·ad·van·tage \ˌdi-səd-ˈvan-tij\ *n* **1** : loss or damage esp. to reputation or finances **2 a** : an unfavorable, inferior, or prejudicial condition **b** ♦ : a quality or circumstance that makes achievement unusually difficult : HANDICAP

♦ drawback, handicap, liability, minus, penalty, strike *Ant* advantage, asset, edge, plus

dis·ad·van·taged \-tijd\ *adj* : lacking in basic resources or conditions believed necessary for an equal position in society

dis·ad·van·ta·geous \di-ˌsad-ˌvan-ˈtā-jəs, -vən-\ *adj* ♦ : constituting a disadvantage

♦ adverse, counter, hostile, inimical, negative, prejudicial, unfavorable (*or* unfavourable), unfriendly, unsympathetic

dis·af·fect \ˌdi-sə-ˈfekt\ *vb* ♦ : to alienate the affection or loyalty of

♦ alienate, disgruntle, estrange, sour ♦ discontent, disgruntle, displease, dissatisfy

dis·af·fec·tion \ˌdi-sə-ˈfek-shən\ *n* ♦ : alienation of affection

♦ alienation, estrangement

dis·agree \ˌdi-sə-ˈgrē\ *vb* **1** : to fail to agree **2** : to differ in opinion **3** : to cause discomfort or distress ⟨fried foods ∼ with her⟩
dis·agree·able \-ə-bəl\ *adj* **1** ♦ : causing discomfort : UNPLEAS-ANT **2** ♦ : marked by ill temper : ILL-TEMPERED — **dis·agree·able·ness** *n* — **dis·agree·ably** \-blē\ *adv*

♦ [1] bad, distasteful, nasty, rotten, sour, uncongenial, unlovely, unpleasant, unwelcome ♦ [2] bearish, bilious, cantankerous, dyspeptic, ill-humored, ill-tempered, ornery, splenetic, surly

dis·agree·ment \-mənt\ *n* **1** ♦ : the act or instance of disagreeing **2 a** ♦ : the state of being at variance : DISPARITY **b** ♦ : a usu. verbal conflict between antagonists : QUARREL

♦ [1] controversy, difference, dispute, dissension *Ant* accord, agreement, harmony ♦ [2a] contrast, difference, discrepancy, disparity, distinction, diversity, unlikeness ♦ [2b] altercation, argument, bicker, brawl, dispute, fight, hassle, misunderstanding, quarrel, row, scrap, spat, squabble, wrangle

dis·al·low \ˌdi-sə-ˈlau̇\ *vb* **1** ♦ : to deny the force, truth, or validity of : REJECT ⟨∼ a claim⟩ **2** ♦ : to refuse to allow

♦ contradict, deny, disavow, disclaim, gainsay, negate, negative, reject, repudiate

dis·al·low·ance \ˌdi-sə-ˈlau̇-ən(t)s\ *n* ♦ : the act of disallowing

♦ contradiction, denial, disavowal, disclaimer, negation, rejection, repudiation

dis·ap·pear \ˌdi-sə-ˈpir\ *vb* **1** ♦ : to pass out of sight **2** : to cease to exist : become lost — **dis·ap·pear·ance** *n*

♦ dissolve, evaporate, fade, flee, go, melt, vanish *Ant* appear, materialize

dis·ap·point \ˌdi-sə-ˈpȯint\ *vb* ♦ : to fail to fulfill the expectation or hope of

♦ cheat, dissatisfy, fail, let down *Ant* satisfy

dis·ap·point·ment \-mənt\ *n* ♦ : the act or an instance of disappointing : the state or emotion of being disappointed

♦ dismay, dissatisfaction, frustration, letdown *Ant* contentment, gratification, satisfaction

dis·ap·pro·ba·tion \di-ˌsa-prə-ˈbā-shən\ *n* : the act or state of disapproving : the state of being disapproving : DISAPPROVAL
dis·ap·prov·al \ˌdi-sə-ˈprü-vəl\ *n* ♦ : the act or state of disapproving : the state of being disapproved

♦ deprecation, disfavor (*or* disfavour), dislike, displeasure *Ant* approbation, approval, favor

dis·ap·prove \-ˈprüv\ *vb* **1** ♦ : to pass unfavorable judgment on **2** : to feel or express disapproval ⟨∼s of smoking⟩ **3** ♦ : to refuse approval to : REJECT — **dis·ap·prov·ing·ly** \-ˈprü-viŋ-lē\ *adv*

♦ *usu* disapprove of [1] deprecate, discountenance, disfavor (*or* disfavour), dislike, frown, reprove *Ant* approve, favor, like ♦ [3] decline, disallow, negative, refuse, reject, repudiate, spurn, turn down

dis·arm \di-ˈsärm\ *vb* **1** : to take arms or weapons from **2** : to reduce the size and strength of the armed forces of a country **3** ♦ : to make harmless, peaceable, or friendly : win over ⟨a ∼ing smile⟩ — **dis·ar·ma·ment** \-ˈsär-mə-mənt\ *n*

♦ appease, conciliate, mollify, pacify, placate, propitiate

dis·ar·range \ˌdi-sə-ˈrānj\ *vb* : to disturb the arrangement or order of
dis·ar·range·ment \-mənt\ *n* : the act of disarranging or the state of being disarranged
dis·ar·ray \-ˈrā\ *n* **1** ♦ : a lack of order or sequence : DISORDER **2** : disorderly or careless dress

♦ chaos, confusion, disorder, disorganization, havoc, hell, jumble, mess, muddle, shambles

dis·as·sem·ble \ˌdi-sə-ˈsem-bəl\ *vb* ♦ : to take apart

♦ dismantle, knock down, strike, take down *Ant* assemble, construct, put together

dis·as·so·ci·ate \-ˈsō-shē-ˌāt, -sē-\ *vb* : to detach from association

dis·as·ter \di-ˈzas-tər, -ˈsas-\ *n* ♦ : a sudden or great misfortune — **dis·as·trous·ly** *adv*

♦ calamity, cataclysm, catastrophe, debacle, tragedy

di·sas·trous \di-ˈzas-trəs\ *adj* ♦ : attended by or causing suffering or disaster

♦ calamitous, catastrophic, destructive, fatal, fateful, ruinous, unfortunate

dis·avow \ˌdi-sə-ˈvau̇\ *vb* **1** ♦ : to deny responsibility for : RE-PUDIATE **2** ♦ : to refuse to acknowledge or accept : DISCLAIM

♦ [1, 2] contradict, deny, disallow, disclaim, gainsay, negate, negative, reject, repudiate

dis·avow·al \ˌdi-sə-ˈvau̇-əl\ *n* ♦ : the act or an instance of disavowing

♦ contradiction, denial, disallowance, disclaimer, negation, rejection, repudiation

dis·band \dis-ˈband\ *vb* ♦ : to break up the organization of : DIS-PERSE

♦ break up, disperse, dissolve *Ant* band, join, unite

dis·bar \dis-ˈbär\ *vb* : to expel from the legal profession — **dis·bar·ment** *n*
dis·be·lieve \ˌdis-bə-ˈlēv\ *vb* **1** : to hold not worthy of belief : not believe **2** : to withhold or reject belief — **dis·be·lief** \-ˈlēf\ *n*
dis·be·liev·er \ˌdis-bə-ˈlē-vər\ *n* ♦ : one that is not a believer

♦ doubter, questioner, skeptic, unbeliever

dis·bur·den \dis-ˈbərd-ᵊn\ *vb* ♦ : to rid of a burden

♦ clear, disencumber, free, relieve, rid, unburden

dis·burse \dis-ˈbərs\ *vb* **dis·bursed; dis·burs·ing** **1** ♦ : to pay out : EXPEND **2** : DISTRIBUTE

♦ expend, give, lay out, pay, spend

dis·burse·ment \-mənt\ *n* **1** ♦ : the act of disbursing **2** ♦ : funds paid out

♦ [1] compensation, payment, remittance, remuneration ♦ [2] cost, expenditure, expense, outgo, outlay

¹disc *var of* DISK
²disc *abbr* discount
¹dis·card \dis-ˈkärd, ˈdis-ˌkärd\ *vb* **1** : to let go a playing card from one's hand; *also* : to play (a card) from a suit other than a trump but different from the one led **2** ♦ : to get rid of as unwanted

♦ cast, ditch, dump, fling, jettison, junk, lose, reject, scrap, shed, shuck, slough, throw away, throw out, unload

²discard \ˈdis-ˌkärd\ *n* ♦ : one that is cast off or rejected

♦ cull, reject, rejection

disc brake *n* : a brake that operates by the friction of a pair of plates pressing against the sides of a rotating disc
dis·cern \di-ˈsərn, -ˈzərn\ *vb* **1** ♦ : to detect with the eyes : DIS-TINGUISH **2** ♦ : to recognize or identify as separate and distinct : DISCRIMINATE **3** : to come to know or recognize mentally ⟨∼ right from wrong⟩

♦ [1] behold, descry, distinguish, espy, eye, look, note, notice, observe, perceive, regard, remark, see, sight, spy, view, witness ♦ [2] differentiate, discriminate, distinguish, separate

dis·cern·ible \di-ˈsər-nə-bəl, -ˈzər-\ *n* ♦ : capable of being discerned

♦ appreciable, detectable, distinguishable, palpable, perceptible, sensible

dis·cern·ing *adj* ♦ : revealing insight and understanding

♦ insightful, perceptive, sagacious, sage, sapient, wise

dis·cern·ment \-mənt\ *n* ♦ : the ability to grasp and comprehend what is obscure

♦ insight, perception, sagacity, sapience, wisdom

¹dis·charge \dis-ˈchärj, ˈdis-ˌchärj\ *vb* **1** ♦ : to relieve of a charge, load, or burden : UNLOAD; *esp* : to remove the electrical energy from ⟨∼ a storage battery⟩ **2** ♦ : to let or put off ⟨∼ passengers⟩ **3** ♦ : to drive (as an arrow or bullet) forward quickly or forcibly : SHOOT **4** : to set free ⟨∼ a prisoner⟩ **5** ♦ : to give outlet or vent to ⟨∼ emotions⟩ ⟨∼ fumes⟩ **6** : to dismiss from service or employment, service, or duty ⟨∼ a soldier⟩ **7** ♦ : to get rid of by paying or doing ⟨∼ a debt⟩ **8** ♦ : to give forth fluid ⟨the river ∼s into the ocean⟩

♦ [1, 2] disburden, disencumber, unburden, unload ♦ [3] blast, fire, loose, shoot ♦ [5] cast, emit, exhale, expel, issue, release, shoot, vent ♦ [7] clear, foot, liquidate, pay, pay off, quit, recompense, settle, spring, stand

²**dis·charge** \'dis-ˌchärj, dis-'chärj\ *n* **1** ♦ : the act of discharging, unloading, releasing, or relieving **2** : something that discharges; *esp* : a certification of release or payment **3** : a firing off (as of a gun) **4** : a flowing out (as of blood from a wound); *also* : something that is emitted ⟨a purulent ∼⟩ **5** ♦ : release or dismissal esp. from an office or employment; *also* : complete separation from military service **6** : a flow of electricity (as through a gas)

♦ [1] delivery, quietus, quittance, release ♦ [5] dismissal, layoff

dis·ci·ple \di-'sī-pəl\ *n* **1** ♦ : one who accepts and helps to spread the teachings of another; *also* : a convinced adherent **2** *cap* : a member of the Disciples of Christ

♦ adherent, convert, follower, partisan, pupil, votary

dis·ci·pli·nar·i·an \ˌdi-sə-plə-'ner-ē-ən\ *n* : one who enforces order
dis·ci·plin·ary \'di-sə-plə-ˌner-ē\ *adj* ♦ : of or relating to discipline; *also* : CORRECTIVE ⟨take ∼ action⟩

♦ corrective, penal, punitive

¹**dis·ci·pline** \'di-sə-plən\ *n* **1** : suffering, pain, or loss that serves as retribution : PUNISHMENT **2** ♦ : a field of study **3** : training that corrects, molds, or perfects **4** : control gained by obedience or training : orderly conduct **5** : a system of rules governing conduct

♦ area, arena, demesne, department, domain, field, line, province, realm, specialty, sphere

²**discipline** *vb* **-plined; -plin·ing** **1** ♦ : to punish or penalize for the sake of discipline : PUNISH **2** : to train or develop by instruction and exercise esp. in self-control **3** : to bring under control ⟨∼ troops⟩; *also* : to impose order upon

♦ castigate, chasten, chastise, correct, penalize, punish

disc jockey *or* **disk jockey** *n* : an announcer of a radio show of popular recorded music
dis·claim \dis-'klām\ *vb* **1** : to declare untrue : DENY **2** ♦ : to refuse to admit or acknowledge : DISAVOW

♦ disavow, disown, repudiate *Ant* acknowledge, avow, claim, own, recognize

dis·claim·er \dis-'klā-mər\ *n* **1** : a denial or disavowal of legal claim; *also* : a writing that embodies a legal disclaimer **2** ♦ : a refusal to acknowledge or accept

♦ contradiction, denial, disallowance, disavowal, negation, rejection, repudiation

dis·close \dis-'klōz\ *vb* **1** : to expose to view **2** ♦ : to make known or public — **dis·clo·sure** \-'klō-zhər\ *n*

♦ bare, discover, divulge, expose, reveal, spill, tell, unbosom, uncloak, uncover, unmask, unveil

dis·co \'dis-kō\ *n, pl* **discos** **1** ♦ : a nightclub for dancing to live or recorded music **2** : popular dance music characterized by hypnotic rhythm, repetitive lyrics, and electronically produced sounds

♦ café, discotheque, nightclub

dis·col·or *or Can and Brit* **dis·col·our** \dis-'kə-lər\ *vb* : to alter or change in hue or color esp. for the worse — **dis·col·or·ation** \-ˌkə-lə-'rā-shən\ *n*
dis·com·bob·u·late \ˌdis-kəm-'bä-byü-ˌlāt\ *vb* **-lat·ed; -lat·ing** ♦ : to disturb the composure of : CONFUSE

♦ addle, baffle, befog, befuddle, bemuse, bewilder, confound, confuse, disorient, muddle, muddy, mystify, perplex, puzzle

dis·com·fit \dis-'kəm-fət, *esp Southern* ˌdis-kəm-'fit\ *vb* ♦ : to put into a state of perplexity and embarrassment

♦ abash, confound, confuse, disconcert, discountenance, embarrass, faze, fluster, mortify, rattle

dis·com·fi·ture \dis-'kəm-fə-ˌchúr\ *n* ♦ : the act of discomfiting : the state of being discomfited

♦ abashment, confusion, embarrassment, fluster, mortification

¹**dis·com·fort** \dis-'kəm-fərt\ *vb* : to make uncomfortable or uneasy
²**discomfort** *n* : mental or physical uneasiness
dis·com·mode \ˌdis-kə-'mōd\ *vb* **-mod·ed; -mod·ing** ♦ : to cause inconvenience to : TROUBLE

♦ disoblige, disturb, inconvenience, trouble

¹**dis·com·pose** \-kəm-'pōz\ *vb* **1** ♦ : to destroy the composure of : AGITATE **2** : to disturb the order of : DISARRANGE — **dis·com·po·sure** \-'pō-zhər\ *n*

♦ agitate, bother, concern, disquiet, distress, disturb, exercise, freak out, perturb, undo, unhinge, unsettle, upset, worry

dis·con·cert \ˌdis-kən-'sərt\ *vb* ♦ : to disturb the composure of : CONFUSE ⟨the bad news ∼ed us⟩

♦ abash, confound, confuse, discomfit, discountenance, embarrass, faze, fluster, mortify, rattle

dis·con·cert·ing *adj* ♦ : causing loss of composure or self-possession

♦ awkward, embarrassing, uncomfortable

dis·con·nect \ˌdis-kə-'nekt\ *vb* ♦ : to undo the connection of — **dis·con·nec·tion** \-'nek-shən\ *n*

♦ break up, disjoint, dissever, dissociate, disunite, divide, divorce, part, resolve, separate, sever, split, sunder, unyoke

dis·con·nect·ed *adj* **1** ♦ : not connected : SEPARATE **2** ♦ : lacking orderly continuity, arrangement, or relevance : INCOHERENT — **dis·con·nect·ed·ly** *adv* — **dis·con·nect·ed·ness** *n*

♦ [1] detached, discrete, freestanding, separate, single, unattached, unconnected ♦ [2] disjointed, incoherent, unconnected

dis·con·so·late \dis-'kän-sə-lət\ *adj* **1** : CHEERLESS **2** ♦ : hopelessly sad — **dis·con·so·late·ly** *adv*

♦ brokenhearted, despondent, forlorn, heartsick, miserable, sad, unhappy, wretched

¹**dis·con·tent** \ˌdis-kən-'tent\ *n* ♦ : uneasiness of mind : DISSATISFACTION

♦ displeasure, disquiet, dissatisfaction *Ant* contentedness, contentment, pleasure, satisfaction

²**discontent** *vb* ♦ : to make dissatisfied or displeased

♦ disaffect, disgruntle, displease, dissatisfy *Ant* content, gratify, please, satisfy

dis·con·tent·ed *adj* ♦ : expressing or showing lack of satisfaction

♦ aggrieved, discontent, dissatisfied, malcontent *Ant* content, contented, gratified, pleased, satisfied

dis·con·tin·u·ance \ˌdis-kən-'tin-yə-wəns\ *n* : the act or an instance of discontinuing
dis·con·tin·ue \ˌdis-kən-'tin-yü\ *vb* **1** ♦ : to break the continuity of : cease to operate, use, or take **2** ♦ : to come or bring to an end

♦ [1, 2] break, break off, cease, cut, desist, drop, end, halt, knock off, lay off, leave off, quit, shut off, stop

dis·con·ti·nu·ity \dis-ˌkän-tə-'nü-ə-tē, -'nyü-\ *n* **1** : lack of continuity or cohesion **2** ♦ : a break in continuity : GAP

♦ gap, hiatus, interim, interlude, intermission, interruption, interval

dis·con·tin·u·ous \ˌdis-kən-'tin-yə-wəs\ *adj* ♦ : not continuous

♦ casual, choppy, erratic, fitful, intermittent, irregular, occasional, spasmodic, sporadic, spotty, unsteady

dis·cord \'dis-ˌkórd\ *n* **1** ♦ : lack of agreement or harmony : DISSENSION **2** : a harsh combination of musical sounds **3** : a harsh or unpleasant sound

♦ conflict, dissent, disunity, friction, schism, strife, variance, war, warfare *Ant* accord, agreement, concord, concordance, harmony, peace

dis·cor·dant \dis-'kórd-ᵊnt\ *adj* **1 a** ♦ : being at variance ⟨∼ opinions⟩ **b** : apt or disposed to quarrel in an often petty manner : QUARRELSOME **2** ♦ : relating to a discord ⟨a ∼ tone⟩ — **dis·cor·dant·ly** *adv*

♦ [1a] discrepant, incompatible, incongruous, inharmonious ♦ [2] dissonant, inharmonious, unmelodious, unmusical

dis·co·theque *or* **discothèque** \'dis-kə-ˌtek\ *n* ♦ : a nightclub for dancing to live or recorded music : DISCO 1

♦ café, disco, nightclub

¹**dis·count** \'dis-ˌkaunt\ *n* **1** ♦ : a reduction made from a regular or list price **2** : a deduction of interest in advance when lending money

♦ [1, 2] abatement, deduction, reduction

²**dis·count** \'dis-ˌkaunt, dis-'kaunt\ *vb* **1** ♦ : to deduct from the amount of a bill, debt, or charge usu. for cash or prompt payment; *also* : to sell or offer for sale at a discount **2** : to lend money after deducting the discount ⟨∼ a note⟩ **3 a** : DISREGARD **b** ♦ : to minimize the importance of **4** : to make allowance for bias or

exaggeration **5 :** to take into account (as a future event) in present calculations — **dis·count·able** *adj* — **dis·count·er** *n*

♦ belittle, cry down, decry, deprecate, depreciate, diminish, disparage, minimize, put down, write off

³**dis·count** \'dis-ˌkaunt\ *adj* : selling goods or services at a discount; *also* : sold at or reflecting a discount

dis·coun·te·nance \dis-'kaunt-ᵊn-ənts\ *vb* **1 ♦ :** to disturb the composure of : DISCONCERT **2 ♦ :** to look with disfavor on

♦ [1] abash, confound, confuse, discomfit, disconcert, embarrass, faze, fluster, mortify, rattle ♦ [2] deprecate, disapprove, disfavor (*or* disfavour), dislike, frown, reprove

dis·cour·age \dis-'kər-ij\ *vb* **-aged; -ag·ing** **1 ♦ :** to deprive of courage or confidence : DISHEARTEN **2 :** to hinder by disfavoring **3 ♦ :** to dissuade or attempt to dissuade — **dis·cour·ag·ing·ly** *adv*

♦ [1] daunt, demoralize, dishearten, dismay, dispirit, unman, unnerve *Ant* embolden, encourage, hearten, nerve, steel ♦ [3] deter, dissuade, inhibit *Ant* encourage, persuade

dis·cour·age·ment \-mənt\ *n* **♦ :** the act of discouraging : the state of being discouraged

♦ demoralization, despair, despondency, dismay *Ant* encouragement

¹**dis·course** \'dis-ˌkōrs\ *n* **1 ♦ :** verbal interchange of ideas **2 :** formal and usu. extended expression of thought on a subject

♦ colloquy, conversation, dialogue, discussion, exchange

²**dis·course** \dis-'kōrs\ *vb* **dis·coursed; dis·cours·ing** **1 ♦ :** to express oneself in esp. oral discourse **2 :** TALK, CONVERSE

♦ declaim, descant, harangue, lecture, orate, speak, talk

dis·cour·te·ous \(ˌ)dis-'kər-tē-əs\ *adj* **♦ :** lacking courtesy : RUDE — **dis·cour·te·ous·ly** *adv*

♦ ill-bred, ill-mannered, impertinent, impolite, inconsiderate, rude, thoughtless, uncivil, ungracious, unmannerly

dis·cour·te·sy \-'kər-tə-sē\ *n* **♦ :** the quality or state of being rude : RUDENESS; *also* : a rude act

♦ brazenness, disrespect, impertinence, impudence, incivility, insolence, rudeness *Ant* civility, consideration, courtesy, genteelness, gentility, graciousness, politeness, thoughtfulness

dis·cov·er \dis-'kə-vər\ *vb* **1 ♦ :** to make known or visible **2 a ♦ :** to obtain sight or knowledge of for the first time **b ♦ :** to learn by study, observation, or search : FIND OUT — **dis·cov·er·er** *n*

♦ [1] bare, disclose, divulge, expose, reveal, spill, tell, unbosom, uncloak, uncover, unmask, unveil ♦ [2a] ascertain, catch on, find out, hear, learn, realize, see ♦ [2b] detect, determine, dig up, ferret out, find, hit on, locate, track down

dis·cov·ery \dis-'kə-və-rē\ *n, pl* **-er·ies** **1 ♦ :** the act or process of discovering **2 :** something discovered **3 :** the disclosure usu. before a civil trial of pertinent facts or documents

♦ detection, finding

¹**dis·cred·it** \(ˌ)dis-'kre-dət\ *vb* **1 :** DISBELIEVE **2 :** to cause disbelief in the accuracy or authority of **3 ♦ :** to deprive of good repute : DISGRACE

♦ abase, debase, degrade, demean, disgrace, dishonor (*or* dishonour), humble, humiliate, lower, shame, smirch, take down

²**discredit** *n* **1 ♦ :** loss of reputation **2 :** lack or loss of belief or confidence

♦ disgrace, dishonor (*or* dishonour), disrepute, ignominy, infamy, odium, opprobrium, reproach, shame

dis·cred·it·able \-tə-bəl\ *adj* **♦ :** not reputable or decent : injurious to a reputation for decency

♦ disgraceful, dishonorable (*or* dishonourable), disreputable, ignominious, infamous, notorious, shameful

dis·creet \dis-'krēt\ *adj* : showing good judgment; *esp* : capable of observing prudent silence — **dis·creet·ly** *adv*

dis·crep·an·cy \dis-'kre-pən-sē\ *n, pl* **-cies** **1 ♦ :** the quality or state of being discrepant : DIFFERENCE **2 :** an instance of being discrepant

♦ contrast, difference, disagreement, disparity, distinction, diversity, unlikeness

dis·crep·ant \-pənt\ *adj* **♦ :** being at variance

♦ discordant, incompatible, incongruous, inharmonious

dis·crete \dis-'krēt, 'dis-ˌkrēt\ *adj* **1 ♦ :** individually distinct **2 :** NONCONTINUOUS

♦ detached, disconnected, freestanding, separate, single, unattached, unconnected

dis·cre·tion \dis-'kre-shən\ *n* **1 ♦ :** the quality of being discreet : PRUDENCE **2 ♦ :** individual choice or judgment **3 :** power of free decision or latitude of choice

♦ [1] common sense, horse sense, prudence ♦ [2] alternative, choice, option, pick, preference, way

dis·cre·tion·ary \-'kre-shə-ˌner-ē\ *adj* **1 ♦ :** left to discretion : exercised at one's own discretion **2 :** available for discretionary use

♦ elective, optional, voluntary

dis·crim·i·nate \dis-'kri-mə-ˌnāt\ *vb* **-nat·ed; -nat·ing** **1 ♦ :** to recognize or give expression to a difference : DISTINGUISH **2 :** to make a difference in treatment on a basis other than individual merit

♦ differentiate, discern, distinguish, separate

dis·crim·i·nat·ing *adj* : marked by discrimination; *esp* : DISCERNING, JUDICIOUS

dis·crim·i·na·tion \dis-ˌkri-mə-'nā-shən\ *n* **1 a :** the quality or power of finely distinguishing **b ♦ :** recognition, perception, or identification esp. of differences **2 a :** the act, practice, or an instance of discriminating categorically rather than individually **b :** prejudiced or prejudicial outlook, action, or treatment

♦ demarcation, distinction, separation

dis·crim·i·na·to·ry \dis-'kri-mə-nə-ˌtōr-ē\ *adj* : marked by esp. unjust discrimination ⟨∼ treatment⟩

dis·cur·sive \dis-'kər-siv\ *adj* **♦ :** moving from topic to topic without order : RAMBLING ⟨a ∼ speech⟩ — **dis·cur·sive·ly** *adv* — **dis·cur·sive·ness** *n*

♦ desultory, digressive, rambling

dis·cus \'dis-kəs\ *n, pl* **dis·cus·es** : a disk that is hurled for distance in a track-and-field contest

dis·cuss \di-'skəs\ *vb* **1 ♦ :** to argue or consider carefully by presenting the various sides **2 :** to talk about

♦ argue, chew over, debate, dispute, hash, moot, talk over

dis·cus·sant \di-'skəs-ᵊnt\ *n* : one who takes part in a formal discussion

dis·cus·sion \di-'skə-shən\ *n* **♦ :** consideration of a question in open and usu. informal debate

♦ argument, colloquy, conference, deliberation, discourse, give-and-take, parley, talk

¹**dis·dain** \dis-'dān\ *n* **♦ :** a feeling of contempt for someone or something regarded as unworthy or inferior : SCORN

♦ contempt, despite, scorn

²**disdain** *vb* **1 ♦ :** to look on with scorn **2 :** to reject or refrain from because of disdain ⟨∼ed gambling⟩

♦ high-hat, scorn, slight, sniff at, snub

dis·dain·ful \dis-'dān-fəl\ *adj* **♦ :** full of or expressing disdain — **dis·dain·ful·ly** *adv*

♦ haughty, highfalutin, lofty, lordly, prideful, proud, superior ♦ contemptuous, degrading, derogatory, scornful, uncomplimentary

dis·ease \di-'zēz\ *n* **♦ :** an abnormal bodily condition that impairs normal functioning and can usu. be recognized by signs and symptoms : SICKNESS — **dis·eased** \-'zēzd\ *adj*

♦ ailment, bug, complaint, complication, condition, disorder, fever, ill, illness, infirmity, malady, sickness, trouble *Ant* health, wellness

dis·em·bark \ˌdi-səm-'bärk\ *vb* **♦ :** to go or put ashore from a ship — **dis·em·bar·ka·tion** \di-ˌsem-ˌbär-'kā-shən\ *n*

♦ dock, land, moor, tie up

dis·em·body \ˌdi-səm-'bä-dē\ *vb* : to deprive of bodily existence

dis·em·bow·el \-'bau-əl\ *vb* : to take out the bowels of : EVISCERATE — **dis·em·bow·el·ment** *n*

dis·em·pow·er \ˌdis-im-'pau(-ə)r\ *vb* : to deprive of power, authority, or influence

dis·en·chant \ˌdis-ᵊn-'chant\ *vb* **♦ :** to free from illusion : DISILLUSION — **dis·en·chant·ment** *n*

♦ disillusion, undeceive

dis·en·chant·ed \-'chan-təd\ *adj* : DISAPPOINTED, DISSATISFIED

dis·en·cum·ber \ˌdis-ᵊn-'kəm-bər\ *vb* **♦ :** to free from something that burdens

♦ disburden, discharge, unburden, unload

dis·en·fran·chise \ˌdis-in-ˈfran-ˌchīz\ *vb* : to deprive of a franchise, a legal right, or a privilege; *esp* : to deprive of the right to vote — **dis·en·fran·chise·ment** *n*
dis·en·gage \ˌdis-ᵊn-ˈgāj\ *vb* ♦ : to release from something that engages or involves : EXTRICATE ⟨∼ from a harness⟩ ⟨∼ the clutch⟩ — **dis·en·gage·ment** *n*

♦ clear, disentangle, extricate, free, liberate, release, untangle

dis·en·gaged \-ˈgājd\ *adj* : IMPARTIAL, DETACHED ⟨a ∼ observer⟩
dis·en·tan·gle \ˌdis-ᵊn-ˈtaŋ-gəl\ *vb* ♦ : to free from entanglement

♦ unravel, untangle, untwine

dis·equi·lib·ri·um \di-ˌsē-kwə-ˈli-brē-əm\ *n* : loss or lack of equilibrium
dis·es·tab·lish \ˌdi-sə-ˈsta-blish\ *vb* : to end the establishment of; *esp* : to deprive of the status of an established church — **dis·es·tab·lish·ment** *n*
dis·es·teem \ˌdi-sə-ˈstēm\ *n* : lack of esteem : DISFAVOR, DISREPUTE
dis·fa·vor *or Can and Brit* **dis·fa·vour** \(ˌ)dis-ˈfā-vər\ *n* 1 ♦ : a feeling of aversion or disapproval : DISLIKE 2 : the state or fact of being no longer favored

- ♦ aversion, disinclination, dislike ♦ deprecation, disapproval, dislike, displeasure

dis·fig·ure \dis-ˈfi-gyər\ *vb* ♦ : to spoil the appearance of ⟨*disfigured* by a scar⟩

♦ blemish, break, cripple, damage, deface, flaw, harm, hurt, injure, mar, spoil, vitiate

dis·fig·ure·ment \-mənt\ *n* 1 : the act of disfiguring or the state of being disfigured 2 ♦ : something that disfigures

♦ blemish, defect, deformity, fault, flaw, imperfection, mark, pockmark, scar

dis·fran·chise \dis-ˈfran-ˌchīz\ *vb* : DISENFRANCHISE — **dis·fran·chise·ment** *n*
disfunction *var of* DYSFUNCTION
dis·gorge \-ˈgórj\ *vb* 1 : to discharge by the throat and mouth : VOMIT 2 ♦ : to discharge forcefully or confusedly

♦ belch, eject, erupt, expel, jet, spew, spout, spurt

¹dis·grace \di-ˈskrās, dis-ˈgrās\ *vb* ♦ : to bring reproach or shame to

♦ abase, debase, degrade, demean, discredit, dishonor (*or dishonour*), humble, humiliate, lower, shame, smirch, take down

²disgrace *n* 1 a ♦ : the condition of one fallen from grace or honor : SHAME b ♦ : a source of shame 2 : the condition of being out of favor : loss of respect

♦ [1a] discredit, dishonor (*or dishonour*), disrepute, ignominy, infamy, odium, opprobrium, reproach, shame *Ant* esteem, honor, respect ♦ [1b] dishonor, reflection, reproach, scandal *Ant* credit, honor

dis·grace·ful \-fəl\ *adj* ♦ : bringing or involving disgrace — **dis·grace·ful·ly** *adv*

♦ discreditable, dishonorable (*or dishonourable*), disreputable, ignominious, infamous, notorious, shameful

dis·grun·tle \dis-ˈgrənt-ᵊl\ *vb* **dis·grun·tled; dis·grun·tling** ♦ : to put in bad humor — usu. used as a participial adjective ⟨a *disgruntled* employee⟩

♦ alienate, disaffect, estrange, sour ♦ disaffect, discontent, displease, dissatisfy

¹dis·guise \dis-ˈgīz\ *vb* **dis·guised; dis·guis·ing** 1 ♦ : to change the appearance of to conceal the identity or to resemble another 2 : HIDE, CONCEAL

♦ camouflage, cloak, dress up, mask

²disguise *n* 1 ♦ : clothing put on to conceal one's identity or counterfeit another's 2 : an outward appearance that hides what something really is

♦ camouflage, guise

¹dis·gust \dis-ˈgəst\ *n* ♦ : marked aversion aroused by something highly distasteful : REPUGNANCE — **dis·gust·ful** \-fəl\ *adj*

♦ distaste, loathing, nausea, repugnance, repulsion, revulsion

²disgust *vb* ♦ : to provoke to loathing, repugnance, or aversion : be offensive to — **dis·gust·ing** \-ˈgəs-tiŋ\ *adj* — **dis·gust·ing·ly** *adv*

♦ nauseate, repel, repulse, revolt, sicken, turn off

dis·gust·ed *adj* ♦ : affected by disgust — **dis·gust·ed·ly** *adv*

♦ sick, squeamish

¹dish \ˈdish\ *n* 1 : a vessel used for serving food 2 : the food served in a dish ⟨a ∼ of berries⟩ 3 : food prepared in a particular way 4 : something resembling a dish esp. in being shallow and concave 5 : SATELLITE DISH 6 : GOSSIP 2
²dish *vb* 1 : to put into a dish 2 : to make concave like a dish 3 : GOSSIP
dis·ha·bille \ˌdi-sə-ˈbēl\ *n* : the state of being dressed in a casual or careless manner
dis·har·mo·ny \(ˌ)dis-ˈhär-mə-nē\ *n* : lack of harmony — **dis·har·mo·ni·ous** \ˌdis-(ˌ)här-ˈmō-nē-əs\ *adj*
dish·cloth \ˈdish-ˌklȯth\ *n* : a cloth for washing dishes
dis·heart·en \dis-ˈhärt-ᵊn\ *vb* ♦ : to cause to lose spirit or morale : DISCOURAGE

♦ daunt, demoralize, discourage, dismay, dispirit, unman, unnerve

dished \ˈdisht\ *adj* : CONCAVE
di·shev·el \di-ˈshe-vəl\ *vb* **-shev·eled** *or* **-shev·elled; -shev·el·ing** *or* **-shev·el·ling** ♦ : to throw into disorder or disarray

♦ derange, disarray, disorder, disrupt, disturb, mess, mix, muddle, rumple, upset

di·shev·eled *or* **di·shev·elled** *adj* ♦ : marked by disorder or disarray

♦ disordered, messy, muddled, unkempt, untidy

dis·hon·est \di-ˈsä-nəst\ *adj* ♦ : not honest — **dis·hon·est·ly** *adv*

♦ lying, mendacious *Ant* honest, truthful, veracious ♦ crooked, deceptive, fast, fraudulent, shady, sharp, shifty, underhanded *Ant* aboveboard, honest, straight

dis·hon·es·ty \di-ˈsä-nə-stē\ *n* ♦ : lack of honesty or integrity

♦ artifice, craft, craftiness, crookedness, cunning, deceit, deceitfulness, dissimulation, double-dealing, duplicity, guile, wiliness

¹dis·hon·or *or Can and Brit* **dis·hon·our** \di-ˈsä-nər\ *vb* 1 ♦ : to bring reproach or shame on : DISGRACE 2 : to refuse to accept or pay ⟨∼ a check⟩

♦ abase, debase, degrade, demean, discredit, disgrace, humble, humiliate, lower, shame, smirch, take down

²dishonor *or Can and Brit* **dishonour** *n* 1 : lack or loss of honor 2 ♦ : the state of one who has lost honor or prestige : SHAME 3 ♦ : a cause of disgrace 4 : the act of dishonoring a negotiable instrument when presented for payment

♦ [2] discredit, disgrace, disrepute, ignominy, infamy, odium, opprobrium, reproach, shame ♦ [3] disgrace, reflection, reproach, scandal

dis·hon·or·able *or Can and Brit* **dis·hon·our·able** \di-ˈsä-nə-rə-bəl\ *adj* ♦ : lacking honor — **dis·hon·or·ably** \-blē\ *adv*

♦ base, contemptible, despicable, detestable, dirty, ignoble, low, mean, snide, sordid, vile, wretched ♦ discreditable, disgraceful, disreputable, ignominious, infamous, notorious, shameful

dish out *vb* : to give freely
dish·rag \ˈdish-ˌrag\ *n* : DISHCLOTH
dish·wash·er \-ˌwȯ-shər, -ˌwä-\ *n* : a person or machine that washes dishes
dish·wa·ter \-ˌwȯ-tər, -ˌwä-\ *n* : water used for washing dishes
dis·il·lu·sion \ˌdi-sə-ˈlü-zhən\ *vb* ♦ : to leave without illusion or naive faith and trust — **dis·il·lu·sion·ment** *n*

♦ disenchant, undeceive

dis·il·lu·sioned *adj* : DISAPPOINTED, DISSATISFIED
dis·in·cli·na·tion \ˌdi-ˌsin-klə-ˈnā-shən\ *n* ♦ : a preference for avoiding something : slight aversion

♦ hesitancy, reluctance, reticence

dis·in·cline \ˌdis-ᵊn-ˈklīn\ *vb* : to make unwilling
dis·in·clined *adj* : unwilling because of dislike or disapproval
dis·in·fect \ˌdis-ᵊn-ˈfekt\ *vb* : to cleanse of infection-causing germs — **dis·in·fec·tant** \-ˈfek-tənt\ *n* — **dis·in·fec·tion** \-ˈfek-shən\ *n*
dis·in·for·ma·tion \-ˌin-fər-ˈmā-shən\ *n* : false information deliberately and often covertly spread
dis·in·gen·u·ous \ˌdis-ᵊn-ˈjen-yə-wəs\ *adj* : lacking in candor; *also* : giving a false appearance of simple frankness
dis·in·her·it \ˌdis-ᵊn-ˈher-ət\ *vb* : to deprive of the right to inherit
dis·in·te·grate \di-ˈsin-tə-ˌgrāt\ *vb* 1 ♦ : to break or decompose

into constituent parts or small particles **2** : to destroy the unity or integrity of — **dis·in·te·gra·tion** \-ˌsin-tə-ˈgrā-shən\ *n*

♦ break down, corrupt, decay, decompose, molder, putrefy, rot, spoil

dis·in·ter \ˌdis-ᵊn-ˈtər\ *vb* **1** : to take from the grave or tomb **2** : UNEARTH

dis·in·ter·est·ed \(ˌ)dis-ˈin-tə-rəs-təd, -ˌres-\ *adj* **1** ♦ : not interested **2** ♦ : free from selfish motive or interest : UNBIASED

♦ [1] apathetic, casual, indifferent, insouciant, nonchalant, perfunctory, unconcerned, uncurious, uninterested ♦ [2] dispassionate, equal, equitable, fair, impartial, just, nonpartisan, objective, square, unbiased, unprejudiced

dis·in·ter·est·ed·ness \(ˌ)dis-ˈin-tə-rəs-təd-nəs, -ˌres-\ *n* ♦ : the quality or state of being objective or impartial

♦ detachment, impartiality, neutrality, objectivity

dis·join \(ˌ)dis-ˈjȯin\ *vb* : to end the joining of : SEPARATE
dis·joint \(ˌ)dis-ˈjȯint\ *vb* **1** : to disturb the orderly arrangement of **2** ♦ : to separate at the joints

♦ break up, disconnect, dissever, dissociate, disunite, divide, divorce, part, resolve, separate, sever, split, sunder, unyoke

dis·joint·ed *adj* **1** ♦ : lacking coherence or orderly sequence **2** : separated at or as if at the joint

♦ disconnected, incoherent, unconnected

disk *or* **disc** \ˈdisk\ *n* **1** : something round and flat; *esp* : a flat rounded anatomical structure (as the central part of the flower head of a composite plant or a pad of cartilage between vertebrae) **2** *usu disc* : a phonograph record **3** : a round flat plate coated with a magnetic substance on which data for a computer is stored **4** *usu disc* : OPTICAL DISK

disk drive *n* : a device for accessing or storing data on a magnetic disk

dis·kette \ˌdis-ˈket\ *n* : FLOPPY DISK

disk jockey *var of* DISC JOCKEY

¹dis·like \(ˌ)dis-ˈlīk\ *n* ♦ : a feeling of aversion or disapproval

♦ deprecation, disapproval, disfavor (*or* disfavour), displeasure ♦ aversion, disfavor (*or* disfavour), disinclination *Ant* appetite, fondness, like, liking, partiality, preference, taste

²dislike *vb* ♦ : to regard with dislike : DISAPPROVE

♦ deprecate, disapprove, discountenance, disfavor (*or* disfavour), frown, reprove

dis·lo·cate \ˈdis-lō-ˌkāt, dis-ˈlō-\ *vb* **1** ♦ : to put out of place; *esp* : to displace (a bone or joint) from normal connections ⟨~ a shoulder⟩ **2** : to force a change in the usual status, relationship, or order of : DISRUPT

♦ budge, displace, disturb, move, remove, shift, transfer

dis·lo·ca·tion \ˌdis-(ˌ)lō-ˈkā-shən\ *n* ♦ : the act of dislocating : the state of being dislocated

♦ disruption, disturbance, upset

dis·lodge \(ˌ)dis-ˈläj\ *vb* : to force out of a place esp. of rest, hiding, or defense

dis·loy·al \(ˌ)dis-ˈlȯi-əl\ *adj* ♦ : lacking in loyalty

♦ faithless, false, fickle, inconstant, loose, perfidious, recreant, traitorous, treacherous, unfaithful, untrue

dis·loy·al·ty \(ˌ)dis-ˈlȯi-əl-tē\ *n* ♦ : lack of loyalty

♦ betrayal, double cross, faithlessness, falseness, falsity, infidelity, perfidy, treachery, treason, unfaithfulness

dis·mal \ˈdiz-məl\ *adj* **1** ♦ : showing or causing gloom or depression **2** : lacking merit ⟨a ~ performance⟩ — **dis·mal·ly** *adv*

♦ bleak, dark, dreary, gloomy, gray (*or* grey), somber (*or* sombre), wretched

dis·man·tle \(ˌ)dis-ˈmant-ᵊl\ *vb* **-tled; -tling** **1** ♦ : to take apart **2** : to strip of furniture and equipment — **dis·man·tle·ment** *n*

♦ disassemble, knock down, strike, take down

¹dis·may \dis-ˈmā\ *vb* ♦ : to cause to lose courage or resolution from alarm or fear : DAUNT — **dis·may·ing·ly** *adv*

♦ daunt, demoralize, discourage, dishearten, dispirit, unman, unnerve

²dismay *n* **1** ♦ : sudden loss of courage or resolution from alarm or fear **2** ♦ : sudden disappointment

♦ [1] demoralization, despair, despondency, discouragement ♦ [2] disappointment, dissatisfaction, frustration, letdown

dis·mem·ber \dis-ˈmem-bər\ *vb* **1** : to cut off or separate the limbs or parts of **2** : to break up or tear into pieces — **dis·mem·ber·ment** *n*

dis·miss \dis-ˈmis\ *vb* **1** ♦ : to send away **2** ♦ : to dismiss from service or employment **3** : to put aside or out of mind **4** : to put out of judicial consideration ⟨~ed all charges⟩ — **dis·mis·sive** \-ˈmi-siv\ *adj* — **dis·mis·sive·ly** *adv*

♦ [1] banish, boot (out), bounce, cast, chase, drum, eject, expel, oust, rout, run off, throw out ♦ [2] cashier, fire, remove, retire, sack *Ant* employ, hire

dis·miss·al \ˈmi-səl\ *n* ♦ : the act of dismissing : the fact or state of being dismissed

♦ discharge, layoff

dis·mount \dis-ˈmaȯnt\ *vb* **1** : to get down from something (as a horse or bicycle) **2** : UNHORSE **3** : DISASSEMBLE

dis·obe·di·ence \ˌdi-sə-ˈbē-dē-əns\ *n* ♦ : neglect or refusal to obey

♦ defiance, insubordination, rebelliousness, recalcitrance, refractoriness, unruliness *Ant* compliance, docility, obedience

dis·obe·di·ent \-ənt\ *adj* ♦ : refusing or neglecting to obey

♦ contrary, defiant, froward, intractable, rebellious, recalcitrant, refractory, unruly, untoward, wayward, willful *Ant* amenable, compliant, docile, obedient, tractable

dis·obey \ˌdi-sə-ˈbā\ *vb* : to fail to obey : be disobedient

dis·oblige \ˌdi-sə-ˈblīj\ *vb* **1** : to go counter to the wishes of **2** ♦ : to subject to inconvenience

♦ discommode, disturb, inconvenience, trouble

¹dis·or·der \di-ˈsȯr-dər\ *vb* **1** ♦ : to disturb the order of **2** : to disturb the regular or normal functions of

♦ confuse, derange, disarray, discompose, dishevel, dislocate, disrupt, disturb, jumble, mess, mix, muddle, rumple, scramble, shuffle, tumble, upset *Ant* arrange, array, draw up, marshal, order, organize, range, regulate, straighten (up), tidy

²disorder *n* **1** ♦ : lack of order : CONFUSION **2** : breach of the peace or public order : TUMULT **3** ♦ : an abnormal physical or mental condition : AILMENT

♦ [1] chaos, confusion, disarray, disorganization, havoc, hell, jumble, mess, muddle, shambles ♦ [3] ailment, bug, complaint, condition, disease, fever, ill, illness, infirmity, malady, sickness, trouble

dis·or·dered *adj* **1** ♦ : marked by disorder **2** : not functioning in a normal orderly healthy way

♦ chaotic, confused, disheveled, messy, muddled, sloppy, unkempt, untidy

dis·or·der·ly \-lē\ *adj* **1** ♦ : offensive to public order **2** : marked by disorder ⟨a ~ desk⟩ — **dis·or·der·li·ness** *n*

♦ anarchic, lawless, unruly

dis·or·ga·ni·za·tion \di-ˌsȯr-gə-nə-ˈzā-shən\ *n* ♦ : the act of disorganizing or the quality or state of being disorganized

♦ chaos, confusion, disarray, disorder, havoc, hell, jumble, mess, muddle, shambles

dis·or·ga·nize \di-ˈsȯr-gə-ˌnīz\ *vb* : to break up the regular system of : throw into disorder

dis·ori·ent \di-ˈsȯr-ē-ˌent\ *vb* ♦ : to cause to be confused or lost — **dis·ori·en·ta·tion** \di-ˌsȯr-ē-ən-ˈtā-shən\ *n*

♦ addle, baffle, befog, befuddle, bemuse, bewilder, confound, confuse, muddle, muddy, mystify, perplex, puzzle

dis·own \di-ˈsōn\ *vb* ♦ : to repudiate any connection or identification with : DISCLAIM ⟨her parents ~ed her⟩

♦ disavow, disclaim, repudiate

dis·par·age \di-ˈspar-ij\ *vb* **-aged; -ag·ing** **1** : to lower in rank or reputation : DEGRADE **2** ♦ : to depreciate by indirect means (as invidious comparison) : BELITTLE — **dis·par·ag·ing·ly** *adv*

♦ belittle, cry down, decry, deprecate, depreciate, diminish, discount, minimize, put down, write off

dis·par·age·ment \-mənt\ *n* ♦ : diminution of esteem or standing

♦ deprecation, depreciation, detraction, put-down

dis·pa·rate \ˈdis-pə-rət, dis-ˈpar-ət\ *adj* ♦ : distinct in quality or character

♦ different, dissimilar, distinct, distinctive, distinguishable, diverse, other, unalike, unlike

dis·par·i·ty \di-'spar-ə-tē\ *n* ♦ : the state of being disparate

♦ contrast, difference, disagreement, discrepancy, distinction, diversity, unlikeness

dis·pas·sion·ate \(͵)dis-'pa-shə-nət\ *adj* ♦ : not influenced by strong feeling : IMPARTIAL — **dis·pas·sion** \-'pa-shən\ *n* — **dis·pas·sion·ate·ly** *adv*

♦ disinterested, equal, equitable, fair, impartial, just, nonpartisan, objective, square, unbiased, unprejudiced

¹**dis·patch** \di-'spach\ *vb* **1** ♦ : to send off or away with promptness or speed esp. on official business **2** ♦ : to put to death **3** : to attend to rapidly or efficiently **4** : DEFEAT — **dis·patch·er** *n*

♦ [1] consign, pack, send, ship, transfer, transmit, transport ♦ [2] do in, execute, kill, liquidate, murder, slay

²**dis·patch** \di-'spach, 'dis-͵pach\ *n* **1** ♦ : a message sent with speed **2** : a news item sent in by a correspondent to a newspaper **3** : the act of dispatching; *esp* : SHIPMENT **4** : the act of putting to death **5** : promptness and efficiency in performing a task

♦ letter, memorandum, missive, note

dis·pel \di-'spel\ *vb* **dis·pelled; dis·pel·ling** : to drive away by scattering : DISSIPATE ⟨∼ a rumor⟩

dis·pens·able \di-'spen-sə-bəl\ *adj* : capable of being dispensed with

dis·pen·sa·ry \di-'spen-sə-rē\ *n, pl* **-ries** : a place where medicine or medical or dental aid is dispensed

dis·pen·sa·tion \͵dis-pən-'sā-shən\ *n* **1** : a system of rules for ordering affairs **2** : a particular arrangement or provision esp. of nature **3** : an exemption from a rule or from a vow or oath **4** ♦ : the act of dispensing **5** : something dispensed or distributed

♦ allocation, distribution, division, issuance

dis·pense \di-'spens\ *vb* **dis·pensed; dis·pens·ing** **1** ♦ : to portion out **2** : ADMINISTER ⟨∼ justice⟩ **3** : EXEMPT **4** : to make up and give out (remedies) — **dis·pens·er** *n* — **dispense with** **1** : SUSPEND **2** : to do without

♦ administer, allocate, apportion, deal, distribute, mete, parcel, portion, prorate

dis·per·sal \-'spər-səl\ *n* : the act or result of dispersing

dis·perse \di-'spərs\ *vb* **dis·persed; dis·pers·ing** ♦ : to break up and scatter about

♦ clear out, disband, dissipate, scatter ♦ break up, disband, dissolve

dis·per·sion \-'spər-zhən\ *n* : the act or process of dispersing : the state of being dispersed

dis·pir·it \dis-'pir-ət\ *vb* ♦ : to deprive of morale or enthusiasm : DISCOURAGE

♦ daunt, demoralize, discourage, dishearten, dismay, unman, unnerve

dis·place \dis-'plās\ *vb* **1** ♦ : to remove from the usual or proper place; *esp* : to expel or force to flee from home or native land ⟨*displaced* persons⟩ **2** : to move out of position ⟨water *displaced* by a floating object⟩ **3** ♦ : to take the place of : REPLACE

♦ [1] budge, dislocate, disturb, move, remove, shift, transfer ♦ [1] banish, deport, exile, expatriate, transport ♦ [3] replace, substitute, supersede, supplant

dis·place·ment \-mənt\ *n* **1** ♦ : the act of displacing : the state of being displaced **2** : the volume or weight of a fluid (as water) displaced by a floating body (as a ship) **3** : the difference between the initial position of an object and a later position

♦ banishment, deportation, exile, expulsion

¹**dis·play** \di-'splā\ *vb* ♦ : to present to view : make evident

♦ disport, exhibit, expose, flash, flaunt, parade, show, show off, sport, strut, unveil

²**display** *n* **1** ♦ : a displaying of something **2** : an electronic device (as a cathode-ray tube) that gives information in visual form; *also* : the visual information

♦ demonstration, exhibition, show ♦ exhibit, exhibition, exposition, fair, show

dis·please \(͵)dis-'plēz\ *vb* **1** ♦ : to arouse the disapproval and dislike of **2** : to be offensive to : give displeasure

♦ disaffect, discontent, disgruntle, dissatisfy

dis·plea·sure \-'ple-zhər\ *n* ♦ : a feeling of dislike and irritation : a display of disapproval

♦ deprecation, disapproval, disfavor (*or* disfavour), dislike

dis·port \di-'spōrt\ *vb* **1** ♦ : to entertain or occupy in a light,

playful, or pleasant manner : AMUSE **2** ♦ : to amuse oneself in light or lively fashion : FROLIC **3** : to make evident : DISPLAY

♦ [1] amuse, divert, entertain, regale ♦ [2] caper, cavort, frisk, frolic, gambol, lark, rollick, romp, sport

dis·pos·able \di-'spō-zə-bəl\ *adj* **1** : remaining after deduction of taxes ⟨∼ income⟩ **2** : designed to be used once and then thrown away ⟨∼ diapers⟩ — **disposable** *n*

dis·pos·al \di-'spō-zəl\ *n* **1** : CONTROL, COMMAND **2** ♦ : an orderly arrangement **3** ♦ : a getting rid of **4** : MANAGEMENT, ADMINISTRATION **5** : presenting or bestowing something ⟨∼ of favors⟩ **6** : a device used to reduce waste matter (as by grinding)

♦ [2] arrangement, array, disposition, distribution, order, sequence, setup ♦ [3] disposition, dumping, jettison, removal, riddance

dis·pose \di-'spōz\ *vb* **dis·posed; dis·pos·ing** **1** : to give a tendency to : INCLINE ⟨*disposed* to accept⟩ **2** ♦ : to put in place ⟨troops *disposed* for withdrawal⟩ **3** : SETTLE — **dis·pos·er** *n* — **dispose of** **1** : to transfer to the control of another **2** : to get rid of **3** : to deal with conclusively

♦ deposit, fix, lay, place, position, put, set, set up, stick ♦ arrange, array, classify, codify, draw up, marshal, order, organize, range, systematize

dis·posed *adj* ♦ : having a particular temperament, disposition, or tendency : being in a particular frame of mind

♦ amenable, game, glad, inclined, ready, willing

dis·po·si·tion \͵dis-pə-'zi-shən\ *n* **1** : the act or power of disposing : DISPOSAL **2** : RELINQUISHMENT **3** ♦ : orderly arrangement **4** ♦ : prevailing tendency, mood, or inclination **5** : natural attitude toward things ⟨a cheerful ∼⟩

♦ [3] arrangement, array, disposal, distribution, order, sequence, setup ♦ [4] affinity, bent, devices, genius, inclination, leaning, partiality, penchant, predilection, predisposition, proclivity, propensity, talent, tendency, turn ♦ [4] grain, nature, temper, temperament

dis·pos·sess \͵dis-pə-'zes\ *vb* : to put out of possession or occupancy — **dis·pos·ses·sion** \-'ze-shən\ *n*

dis·praise \dis-'prāz\ *vb* : DISPARAGE — **dispraise** *n* — **dis·prais·er** *n*

dis·proof \(͵)dis-'prüf\ *n* : evidence that disproves

dis·pro·por·tion \͵dis-prə-'pōr-shən\ *n* : lack of proportion, symmetry, or proper relation — **dis·pro·por·tion·ate** \-shə-nət\ *adj*

dis·prove \(͵)dis-'prüv\ *vb* ♦ : to prove to be false or wrong

♦ belie, confute, rebut, refute *Ant* confirm, prove, verify

dis·put·able \di-'spyü-tə-bəl, 'dis-pyə-tə-bəl\ *adj* ♦ : capable of being disputed or contested

♦ arguable, debatable, doubtful, moot, questionable

dis·pu·tant \di-'spyüt-ᵊnt, 'dis-pyə-tənt\ *n* ♦ : one that is engaged in a dispute

♦ arguer, contender, debater, disputer

dis·pu·ta·tion \͵dis-pyù-'tā-shən\ *n* **1** : the action of disputing : DEBATE **2** : an oral defense of an academic thesis

dis·pu·ta·tious \-shəs\ *adj* ♦ : inclined to dispute : ARGUMENTATIVE

♦ argumentative, contentious, quarrelsome, scrappy

¹**dis·pute** \di-'spyüt\ *vb* **dis·put·ed; dis·put·ing** **1** ♦ : to engage in argument : ARGUE **2** : WRANGLE **3** ♦ : to question the truth or rightness of **4** : to struggle against or over : OPPOSE

♦ [1] argue, chew over, debate, discuss, hash, moot, talk over ♦ [3] challenge, contest, query, question

²**dis·pute** *n* **1** ♦ : verbal controversy **2** ♦ : a usu. verbal conflict between antagonists : QUARREL

♦ [1] controversy, difference, disagreement, dissension ♦ [2] altercation, argument, bicker, brawl, disagreement, fight, hassle, misunderstanding, quarrel, row, scrap, spat, squabble, wrangle

dis·put·er *n* ♦ : one that disputes

♦ arguer, contender, debater, disputant

dis·qual·i·fy \(͵)dis-'kwä-lə-͵fī\ *vb* : to make or declare unfit or not qualified — **dis·qual·i·fi·ca·tion** \-͵kwä-lə-fə-'kā-shən\ *n*

¹**dis·qui·et** \(͵)dis-'kwī-ət\ *vb* ♦ : to make uneasy or restless : DISTURB ⟨was ∼ed by the news⟩

♦ agitate, bother, concern, discompose, distress, disturb, exercise, freak out, perturb, undo, unhinge, unsettle, upset, worry

²dis·quiet *n* ♦ : lack of peace or tranquility
- ♦ agitation, anxiety, apprehension, care, concern, nervousness, perturbation, uneasiness, worry

dis·qui·e·tude \(ˌ)dis-ˈkwī-ə-ˌtüd, -ˌtyüd\ *n* : AGITATION, ANXIETY

dis·qui·si·tion \ˌdis-kwə-ˈzi-shən\ *n* : a formal inquiry or discussion

¹dis·re·gard \ˌdis-ri-ˈgärd\ *vb* ♦ : to pay no attention to : treat as unworthy of notice or regard
- ♦ forget, ignore, neglect, overlook, pass over, slight, slur ♦ condone, excuse, gloss over, ignore, pardon, pass over, shrug off, wink at

²disregard *n* ♦ : the act of disregarding : the state of being disregarded — **dis·re·gard·ful** *adj*
- ♦ apathy, disinterestedness, indifference, insouciance, nonchalance

dis·re·pair \ˌdis-ri-ˈpar\ *n* ♦ : the state of being in need of repair
- ♦ desolation, dilapidation, neglect

dis·rep·u·ta·ble \dis-ˈre-pyu̇-tə-bəl\ *adj* ♦ : having a bad reputation
- ♦ discreditable, disgraceful, dishonorable (*or* dishonourable), ignominious, infamous, notorious, shameful *Ant* honorable, reputable, respectable

dis·re·pute \ˌdis-ri-ˈpyüt\ *n* ♦ : lack or decline of reputation : a state of being held in low esteem
- ♦ discredit, disgrace, dishonor (*or* dishonour), ignominy, infamy, odium, opprobrium, reproach, shame

dis·re·spect \ˌdis-ri-ˈspekt\ *n* ♦ : lack of respect : DISCOURTESY
- ♦ brazenness, discourtesy, impertinence, impudence, incivility, insolence, rudeness

dis·re·spect·ful \ˌdis-ri-ˈspekt-fəl\ *adj* ♦ : lacking proper respect in speech or action
- ♦ discourteous, ill-bred, ill-mannered, impertinent, impolite, inconsiderate, rude, thoughtless, uncivil, ungracious, unmannerly

dis·robe \dis-ˈrōb\ *vb* : to strip of clothing or covering : UNDRESS

dis·rupt \dis-ˈrəpt\ *vb* **1** : to break apart **2** ♦ : to throw into disorder **3** : INTERRUPT — **dis·rup·tive** \-ˈrəp-tiv\ *adj*
- ♦ discompose, disorder, disturb, upset

dis·rup·tion \-ˈrəp-shən\ *n* ♦ : the act or process of disrupting : the state of being disrupted
- ♦ dislocation, disturbance, upset

dis·sat·is·fac·tion \di-ˌsa-təs-ˈfak-shən\ *n* ♦ : the quality or state of being dissatisfied
- ♦ disappointment, dismay, frustration, letdown

dis·sat·is·fied \-fīd\ *adj* ♦ : expressing or showing lack of satisfaction : not pleased or satisfied
- ♦ aggrieved, discontent, discontented, malcontent

dis·sat·is·fy \di-ˈsa-təs-ˌfī\ *vb* ♦ : to fail to satisfy
- ♦ disappoint, fail, let down

dis·sect \di-ˈsekt\ *vb* **1** ♦ : to divide into parts esp. for examination and study **2** ♦ : to analyze and interpret minutely — **dis·sec·tor** \-ˈsek-tər\ *n*
- ♦ analyze, anatomize, assay, break down, break up

dis·sect·ed *adj* : cut deeply into narrow lobes ⟨a ∼ leaf⟩

dis·sec·tion \-ˈsek-shən\ *n* ♦ : the act or process of dissecting : the state of being dissected
- ♦ analysis, assay, breakdown, breakup

dis·sem·ble \di-ˈsem-bəl\ *vb* **-bled; -bling** **1** ♦ : to hide under or put on a false appearance : conceal facts, intentions, or feelings under some pretense **2** : SIMULATE — **dis·sem·bler** *n*
- ♦ dissimulate, let on, pretend

dis·sem·i·nate \di-ˈse-mə-ˌnāt\ *vb* **-nat·ed; -nat·ing** ♦ : to spread abroad as if sowing seed ⟨∼ ideas⟩ — **dis·sem·i·na·tion** \-ˌse-mə-ˈnā-shən\ *n*
- ♦ broadcast, circulate, propagate, spread, strew

dis·sen·sion \di-ˈsen-chən\ *n* ♦ : disagreement in opinion
- ♦ controversy, difference, disagreement, dispute

¹dis·sent \di-ˈsent\ *vb* **1** : to withhold assent **2** : to differ in opinion

²dissent *n* **1 a** ♦ : difference of opinion; *esp* : religious noncon-

formity **b** ♦ : contentious quarreling **2** : a written statement in which a justice disagrees with the opinion of the majority
- ♦ [1a] heresy, heterodoxy, nonconformity ♦ [1a, 1b] conflict, discord, disunity, friction, schism, strife, variance, war, warfare

dis·sent·er \di-ˈsen-tər\ *n* **1** ♦ : one that dissents **2** *cap* : an English Nonconformist
- ♦ dissident, heretic, nonconformist

dis·ser·ta·tion \ˌdi-sər-ˈtā-shən\ *n* : an extended usu. written treatment of a subject; *esp* : one submitted for a doctorate

dis·ser·vice \di-ˈsər-vəs\ *n* ♦ : ill service : INJURY
- ♦ injury, injustice, raw deal, wrong *Ant* justice

dis·sev·er \di-ˈse-vər\ *vb* ♦ : to set or keep apart : SEPARATE
- ♦ break up, disconnect, disjoint, dissociate, disunite, divide, divorce, part, resolve, separate, sever, split, sunder, unyoke

dis·si·dence \ˈdi-sə-dəns\ *n* : difference of opinion : DISSENT

¹dis·si·dent \-dənt\ *adj* ♦ : disagreeing esp. with an established religious or political system, organization, or belief
- ♦ heretical, heterodox, nonconforming, nonconformist, nonorthodox, unconventional, unorthodox

²dissident *n* : one that is dissident

dis·sim·i·lar \di-ˈsi-mə-lər\ *adj* ♦ : not like : UNLIKE
- ♦ different, disparate, distinct, distinctive, distinguishable, diverse, other, unalike, unlike

dis·sim·i·lar·i·ty \di-ˌsi-mə-ˈlar-ə-tē\ *n* : the quality or state of being dissimilar

dis·sim·u·late \di-ˈsi-myə-ˌlāt\ *vb* ♦ : to hide under a false appearance : DISSEMBLE
- ♦ dissemble, let on, pretend

dis·sim·u·la·tion \di-ˌsi-myə-ˈlā-shən\ *n* ♦ : the act of dissembling or the fact of being dissembled
- ♦ artifice, craft, craftiness, crookedness, cunning, deceit, deceitfulness, dishonesty, double-dealing, duplicity, guile, wiliness

dis·si·pate \ˈdi-sə-ˌpāt\ *vb* **-pat·ed; -pat·ing** **1** ♦ : to break up and drive off : DISPERSE ⟨the breeze *dissipated* the fog⟩ **2** ♦ : to spend or use up wastefully or foolishly : SQUANDER **3** : to break up and vanish **4** : to be dissolute; *esp* : to drink alcoholic beverages to excess — **dis·si·pat·ed** *adj*
- ♦ [1] clear out, disband, disperse, scatter ♦ [2] blow, fritter, lavish, misspend, run through, spend, squander, throw away, waste

dis·si·pa·tion \ˌdi-sə-ˈpā-shən\ *n* **1** : the action or process of dissipating : the state of being dissipated **2** ♦ : self-indulgence and intemperate living
- ♦ corruption, debasement, debauchery, decadence, degeneracy, degeneration, degradation, demoralization, depravity, dissoluteness, perversion

dis·so·ci·ate \di-ˈsō-shē-ˌāt\ *vb* **-at·ed; -at·ing** ♦ : to set or keep apart : DISCONNECT — **dis·so·ci·a·tion** \di-ˌsō-shē-ˈā-shən\ *n* — **dis·so·cia·tive** \di-ˈsō-shē-ˌā-tiv\ *adj*
- ♦ break up, disconnect, disjoint, dissever, disunite, divide, divorce, part, resolve, separate, sever, split, sunder, unyoke

dis·so·lute \ˈdi-sə-ˌlüt\ *adj* ♦ : loose in morals or conduct — **dis·so·lute·ly** *adv*
- ♦ corrupt, debauched, decadent, degenerate, perverse, perverted, reprobate

dis·so·lute·ness \-nəs\ *n* ♦ : the quality or state of being dissolute
- ♦ corruption, debasement, debauchery, decadence, degeneracy, degeneration, degradation, demoralization, depravity, dissipation, perversion

dis·so·lu·tion \ˌdi-sə-ˈlü-shən\ *n* **1** : the action or process of dissolving **2** ♦ : separation of a thing into its parts **3** : DECAY *also* : DEATH **4** : the termination or breaking up of (as an assembly)
- ♦ breakup, division, partition, schism, separation, split

dis·solve \di-ˈzälv\ *vb* **1** ♦ : to separate into component parts **2** : to pass or cause to pass into solution ⟨sugar ∼s in water⟩ **3** ♦ : to bring or come to an end ⟨∼ parliament⟩ ⟨the organization *dissolved*⟩ **4** : to waste or fade away ⟨his courage *dissolved*⟩ **5** : to be overcome emotionally ⟨∼ in tears⟩ **6** : to resolve itself as if by dissolution **7** ♦ : to disperse or disappear or cause to disperse or disappear
- ♦ [1] break up, disband, disperse ♦ [3] abolish, abrogate, an-

nul, cancel, invalidate, negate, nullify, quash, repeal, rescind, void ♦ [7] disappear, evaporate, fade, flee, go, melt, vanish

dis·so·nance \'di-sə-nəns\ *n* : DISCORD
dis·so·nant \-nənt\ *adj* ♦ : marked by dissonance : DISCORDANT
 ♦ discordant, inharmonious, unmelodious, unmusical *Ant* harmonious, harmonizing, melodious, musical

dis·suade \di-'swād\ *vb* **dis·suad·ed; dis·suad·ing** ♦ : to advise against a course of action : persuade or try to persuade not to do something — **dis·sua·sion** \-'swā-zhən\ *n* — **dis·sua·sive** \-'swā-siv\ *adj*
 ♦ deter, discourage, inhibit

dist *abbr* **1** distance **2** district
¹**dis·taff** \'dis-ˌtaf\ *n, pl* **distaffs** \-ˌtafs, -ˌtavz\ **1** : a staff for holding the flax, tow, or wool in spinning **2** : a woman's work or domain **3** : the female branch or side of a family
²**distaff** *adj* **1** : MATERNAL 2 **2** : FEMALE 1
dis·tal \'dist-ᵊl\ *adj* **1** : situated away from the point of attachment or origin esp. on the body **2** : of, relating to, or being the surface of a tooth that is farthest from the middle of the front of the jaw — **dis·tal·ly** *adv*
¹**dis·tance** \'dis-təns\ *n* **1** ♦ : measure of separation in space or time **2** : EXPANSE **3** : the full length ⟨go the ∼⟩ **4** : spatial remoteness **5** : COLDNESS, RESERVE **6** : DIFFERENCE, DISPARITY **7** : a distant point
 ♦ lead, length, remove, spread, stretch, way
²**distance** *vb* **dis·tanced; dis·tanc·ing** : to leave far behind : OUTSTRIP
³**distance** *adj* : taking place via electronic media linking instructors and students ⟨∼ learning⟩
dis·tant \'dis-tənt\ *adj* **1** : separate in space : AWAY **2** ♦ : situated at a great distance : FAR-OFF **3** : far apart or behind **4** : not close in relationship ⟨a ∼ cousin⟩ **5** : different in kind **6** ♦ : reserved or aloof in personal relationship : COLD ⟨∼ politeness⟩ **7** : going a long distance — **dis·tant·ly** *adv* — **dis·tant·ness** *n*
 ♦ [2] away, far, far-off, remote *Ant* close, near, nearby, nigh ♦ [6] aloof, antisocial, cold, cool, detached, frosty, remote, standoffish, unsociable

dis·taste \(ˌ)dis-'tāst\ *n* ♦ : a settled dislike
 ♦ disgust, loathing, nausea, repugnance, repulsion, revulsion
dis·taste·ful \-fəl\ *adj* **1** ♦ : objectionable because inappropriate, unethical, or offensive to taste **2** ♦ : unpleasant to the sense of taste ⟨∼ fruit⟩
 ♦ [1] bad, disagreeable, nasty, offensive, rotten, sour, uncongenial, unlovely, unpleasant, unwelcome ♦ [2] unappetizing, unsavory *Ant* appetizing, delectable, delicious, palatable, savory, tasty

dis·tem·per \(ˌ)dis-'tem-pər\ *n* : a bodily disorder usu. of a domestic animal; *esp* : a contagious often fatal virus disease of dogs
dis·tend \di-'stend\ *vb* : EXPAND, SWELL — **dis·ten·si·ble** \-'sten-sə-bəl\ *adj* — **dis·ten·sion** *or* **dis·ten·tion** \-chən\ *n*
dis·tich \'dis-(ˌ)tik\ *n* : a unit of two lines of poetry
dis·till *also* **dis·til** \di-'stil\ *vb* **dis·tilled; dis·till·ing** **1** : to fall or let fall in drops **2** ♦ : to obtain or purify by distillation — **dis·till·er** *n* — **dis·till·ery** \-'sti-lə-rē\ *n*
 ♦ clarify, clear, filter, purify
dis·til·late \'dis-tə-ˌlāt, -lət\ *n* : a liquid product condensed from vapor during distillation
dis·til·la·tion \ˌdis-tə-'lā-shən\ *n* : the process of purifying a liquid by successive evaporation and condensation
dis·tinct \di-'stiŋkt\ *adj* **1** : distinguishable to the eye or mind as discrete : SEPARATE **2** ♦ : presenting a clear unmistakable impression — **dis·tinct·ly** *adv*
 ♦ apparent, broad, clear, clear-cut, evident, lucid, manifest, obvious, palpable, patent, perspicuous, plain, transparent, unambiguous, unequivocal, unmistakable

dis·tinc·tion \di-'stiŋk-shən\ *n* **1** ♦ : the distinguishing of a difference; *also* : the difference distinguished **2** : something that distinguishes **3** ♦ : special honor or recognition **4** ♦ : the quality or state of being distinguished or worthy
 ♦ [1] contrast, difference, disagreement, discrepancy, disparity, diversity, unlikeness ♦ [1] demarcation, discrimination, separation ♦ [3] acclaim, accolade, award, credit, glory, homage, honor (*or* honour), laurels ♦ [4] excellence, merit, value, virtue

dis·tinc·tive \di-'stiŋk-tiv\ *adj* **1 a** ♦ : serving to distinguish **b** ♦ : set apart from others **2** ♦ : having or giving style or distinction — **dis·tinc·tive·ly** *adv*

 ♦ [1a, 2] characteristic, classic, distinct, individual, peculiar, proper, symptomatic, typical ♦ [1b] different, disparate, dissimilar, distinct, distinguishable, diverse, other, unalike, unlike

dis·tinc·tive·ness \-nəs\ *n* : the quality or state of being distinctive
dis·tinct·ness \-nəs\ *n* : the quality or state of being distinct
dis·tin·guish \di-'stiŋ-gwish\ *vb* **1** ♦ : to recognize by some mark or characteristic **2** ♦ : to hear or see clearly : DISCERN **3** ♦ : to make distinctions ⟨∼ between right and wrong⟩ **4** : to give prominence or distinction to; *also* : to take special notice of
 ♦ [1] behold, descry, discern, espy, eye, look, note, notice, observe, perceive, regard, remark, see, sight, spy, view, witness ♦ [2, 3] differentiate, discern, discriminate, separate *Ant* confuse, mistake, mix (up)

dis·tin·guish·able \di-'stiŋ-gwi-shə-bəl\ *adj* ♦ : capable of being distinguished
 ♦ appreciable, detectable, discernible, palpable, perceptible, sensible

dis·tin·guished \-gwisht\ *adj* **1** ♦ : marked by eminence or excellence **2** : befitting an eminent person
 ♦ eminent, illustrious, noble, notable, noteworthy, outstanding, preeminent, prestigious, signal, star, superior

dis·tort \di-'stȯrt\ *vb* **1** ♦ : to twist out of the true meaning **2** ♦ : to twist out of a natural, normal, or original shape or condition **3** : to cause to be perceived unnaturally
 ♦ [1] color (*or* colour), falsify, garble, misinterpret, misrepresent, misstate, pervert, twist, warp ♦ [2] contort, deform, screw, warp

distorted *adj* ♦ : twisted or deformed in shape or condition
 ♦ deformed, malformed, misshapen, monstrous, shapeless

dis·tor·tion \di-'stȯr-shən\ *n* **1** ♦ : the act of distorting **2** : the quality or state of being distorted : a product of distorting
 ♦ contortion, deformation

distr *abbr* distribute; distribution
dis·tract \di-'strakt\ *vb* **1** ♦ : to draw (the attention or mind) to a different object : DIVERT **2** : to stir up or confuse with conflicting emotions or motives
dis·tract·ed \di-'strakt-əd\ *adj* ♦ : mentally confused, troubled, or remote
 ♦ absent, absentminded, abstracted, preoccupied

dis·trac·tion \-'strak-shən\ *n* **1** ♦ : the act of distracting or the state of being distracted; *esp* : mental confusion ⟨driven to ∼⟩ **2** ♦ : something that distracts; *esp* : AMUSEMENT ⟨a harmless ∼⟩
 ♦ [1] bafflement, bewilderment, confusion, muddle, mystification, perplexity, puzzlement, whirl ♦ [2] amusement, diversion, entertainment

dis·trait \di-'strā\ *adj* : apprehensively divided or withdrawn in attention
dis·traught \di-'strȯt\ *adj* **1** ♦ : agitated with doubt or mental conflict **2** : driven mad
 ♦ agitated, delirious, frantic, frenzied, hysterical

¹**dis·tress** \di-'stres\ *n* **1** ♦ : suffering of body or mind : PAIN **2** : TROUBLE, MISFORTUNE **3** ♦ : a condition of danger or desperate need
 ♦ [1] affliction, agony, anguish, misery, pain, torment, torture, tribulation, woe ♦ [3] danger, jeopardy, peril, risk, trouble

²**distress** *vb* **1** : to subject to great strain or difficulties **2** ♦ : to cause to worry or be troubled : UPSET
 ♦ agitate, bother, concern, discompose, disquiet, disturb, exercise, freak out, perturb, undo, unhinge, unsettle, upset, worry

dis·tressed \-'strest\ *adj* : experiencing economic decline or difficulty
dis·tress·ful \-fəl\ *adj* ♦ : causing distress : full of distress
 ♦ anxious, nervous, restless, tense, unsettling, upsetting, worrisome

dis·trib·ute \di-'stri-byüt\ *vb* **-ut·ed; -ut·ing** **1** ♦ : to divide among several or many **2** : to spread out : SCATTER; *also* : DELIVER **3** : CLASSIFY
 ♦ administer, allocate, apportion, deal, dispense, mete, parcel, portion, prorate

dis·tri·bu·tion \ˌdis-trə-'byü-shən\ *n* **1** ♦ : the act or process of distributing **2** ♦ : the position, arrangement, or frequency of occurrence (as of the members of a group) over an area or throughout a space or unit of time

♦ [1] allocation, dispensation, division, issuance ♦ [2] arrangement, array, disposal, disposition, order, sequence, setup

dis·trib·u·tive \di-'stri-byù-tiv\ *adj* **1** : of or relating to distribution **2** : of, having, or being the property of producing the same value when an operation is carried out on a whole expression and when it is carried out on each part of an expression with the results then collected together ⟨$a(b + c) = ab + ac$ because multiplication is ∼⟩ — **dis·trib·u·tive·ly** *adv*

dis·trib·u·tor \di-'stri-byù-tər\ *n* **1** : one that distributes **2** : one that markets goods **3** : a device for directing current to the spark plugs of an engine

dis·trict \'dis-(‚)trikt\ *n* **1** ♦ : a fixed territorial division (as for administrative or electoral purposes) **2** ♦ : an area, region, or section with a distinguishing character

♦ neighborhood (*or* neighbourhood), quarter, section

district attorney *n* : the prosecuting attorney of a judicial district

¹**dis·trust** \dis-'trəst\ *n* ♦ : a lack or absence of trust

♦ doubt, incertitude, misgiving, mistrust, skepticism, suspicion, uncertainty

²**distrust** *vb* ♦ : to hold as untrustworthy or unreliable

♦ doubt, mistrust, question, suspect *Ant* trust

dis·trust·ful \-fəl\ *adj* ♦ : having or showing distrust

♦ incredulous, leery, mistrustful, skeptical, suspicious ♦ doubtful, dubious, mistrustful, skeptical, suspicious, uncertain, undecided, unsettled, unsure

dis·trust·ful·ly \-fə-lē\ *adv* ♦ : in a distrustful manner

♦ askance, dubiously, mistrustfully, suspiciously

dis·turb \di-'stərb\ *vb* **1** : to interfere with : INTERRUPT **2** ♦ : to alter the position or arrangement of; *also* : to upset the natural and esp. the ecological balance of **3** ♦ : to destroy the tranquility or composure of : make uneasy **4** : to throw into disorder **5** ♦ : to put to inconvenience — **dis·turb·er** *n* — **dis·turb·ing·ly** \-'stər-biŋ-lē\ *adv*

♦ [2] budge, dislocate, displace, move, remove, shift, transfer ♦ [3] agitate, bother, concern, discompose, disquiet, distress, exercise, freak out, perturb, undo, unhinge, unsettle, upset, worry *Ant* calm, compose, quiet, settle, soothe, tranquilize ♦ [5] discommode, disoblige, inconvenience, trouble

dis·tur·bance \-'stər-bəns\ *n* ♦ : the act of disturbing : the state of being disturbed

♦ dislocation, disruption, upset ♦ commotion, furor, fuss, hubbub

dis·turbed \-'stərbd\ *adj* : showing symptoms of emotional illness

dis·unite \‚dis-yü-'nīt\ *vb* ♦ : to destroy the unity of : DIVIDE

♦ break up, disconnect, disjoint, dissever, dissociate, divide, divorce, part, resolve, separate, sever, split, sunder, unyoke

dis·uni·ty \dis-'yü-nə-tē\ *n* ♦ : lack of unity; *esp* : DISSENSION

♦ conflict, discord, dissent, friction, schism, strife, variance, war, warfare

dis·use \-'yüs\ *n* : a cessation of use or practice

dis·used \-'yüzd\ *adj* : no longer used or occupied

¹**ditch** \'dich\ *n* ♦ : a long narrow channel or trench dug in the earth

♦ dike, gutter, trench

²**ditch** *vb* **1** : to enclose with a ditch; *also* : to dig a ditch in **2** ♦ : to get rid of : DISCARD **3** : to make a forced landing of an airplane on water

♦ cast, discard, dump, fling, jettison, junk, lose, reject, scrap, shed, shuck, slough, throw away, throw out, unload

dith·er \'di-thər\ *n* ♦ : a highly nervous, excited, or agitated state

♦ fluster, fret, fuss, huff, lather, pother, stew, tizzy, twitter

dit·sy *or* **dit·zy** \'dit-sē\ *adj* **dits·i·er** *or* **ditz·i·er; -est** : eccentrically silly, giddy, or inane

dit·to \'di-tō\ *n, pl* **dittos** **1** : a thing mentioned previously or above — used to avoid repeating a word **2** : a mark " or ″ used as a symbol for the word *ditto*

dit·ty \'di-tē\ *n, pl* **ditties** : a short simple song

dit·zy *or* **dit·sy** \'dit-sē\ *adj* **ditz·i·er** *or* **dits·i·er; -est** : eccentrically silly, giddy, or inane

di·uret·ic \‚dī-yə-'re-tik\ *adj* : tending to increase urine flow — **diuretic** *n*

di·ur·nal \dī-'ərn-°l\ *adj* **1** : DAILY **2** : of, relating to, occurring, or active in the daytime

div *abbr* **1** divided **2** dividend **3** division **4** divorced

di·va \'dē-və\ *n, pl* **divas** *or* **di·ve** \-‚vä\ **1** : PRIMA DONNA **2** : a usu. glamorous and successful female performer or personality ⟨the current ∼ of the popular music world⟩

di·va·gate \'dī-və-‚gāt\ *vb* **-gat·ed; -gat·ing** : to wander or stray from a course or subject : DIVERGE — **di·va·ga·tion** \‚dī-və-'gā-shən\ *n*

di·van \'dī-‚van, di-'van\ *n* ♦ : a large couch usu. without back or arms often designed for use as a bed

♦ couch, davenport, lounge, settee, sofa

¹**dive** \'dīv\ *vb* **dived** \'dīvd\ *or* **dove** \'dōv\; **dived; div·ing** **1** ♦ : to plunge into water headfirst **2** : SUBMERGE **3** : to come or drop down precipitously **4** : to descend in an airplane at a steep angle **5** : to plunge into some matter or activity **6** : DART, LUNGE — **div·er** *n*

♦ pitch, plunge, sound

²**dive** *n* **1** ♦ : the act or an instance of diving **2** ♦ : a sharp decline **3** : a disreputable bar or place of amusement

♦ descent, dip, down, drop, fall, plunge

di·verge \də-'vərj, dī-\ *vb* **di·verged; di·verg·ing** **1** ♦ : to move or extend in different directions from a common point : draw apart **2** : to differ in character, form, or opinion **3** : DEVIATE **4** : DEFLECT — **di·ver·gence** \-'vər-jəns\ *n* — **di·ver·gent** \-jənt\ *adj*

♦ branch, fan, radiate ♦ branch, divide, fork, separate

di·vers \'dī-vərz\ *adj* : of differing kinds : VARIOUS

di·verse \dī-'vərs, də-, 'dī-‚vərs\ *adj* **1** ♦ : differing from one another : UNLIKE **2** : composed of distinct forms or qualities — **di·verse·ly** *adv*

♦ different, disparate, dissimilar, distinct, distinctive, distinguishable, other, unalike, unlike

di·ver·si·fy \də-'vər-sə-‚fī, dī-\ *vb* **-fied; -fy·ing** : to make different or various in form or quality — **di·ver·si·fi·ca·tion** \-‚vər-sə-fə-'kā-shən\ *n*

di·ver·sion \də-'vər-zhən, dī-\ *n* **1** : a turning aside from a course, activity, or use : DEVIATION **2** ♦ : something that diverts or amuses

♦ delight, entertainment, fun, pleasure ♦ amusement, distraction, entertainment

di·ver·si·ty \də-'vər-sə-tē, dī-\ *n, pl* **-ties** **1** ♦ : the condition of being diverse **2** : an instance of being diverse

♦ assortment, variety ♦ contrast, difference, disagreement, discrepancy, disparity, distinction, unlikeness

di·vert \də-'vərt, dī-\ *vb* **1** ♦ : to turn from a course or purpose : DEFLECT **2** : DISTRACT **3** ♦ : to give pleasure to esp. by distracting the attention from what burdens or distresses : ENTERTAIN

♦ [1] deflect, swerve, swing, turn, veer, wheel, whip ♦ [3] amuse, disport, entertain, regale

di·vert·ing \də-'vər-tiŋ, dī-\ *adj* ♦ : providing amusement or entertainment

♦ amusing, delightful, enjoyable, entertaining, fun, pleasurable

di·vest \dī-'vest, də-\ *vb* **1** : to deprive or dispossess esp. of property, authority, or rights **2** : to strip esp. of clothing, ornament, or equipment

¹**di·vide** \də-'vīd\ *vb* **di·vid·ed; di·vid·ing** **1 a** : to separate into two or more parts, areas, or groups **b** : CLASSIFY **2** : CLEAVE, PART **3** : DISTRIBUTE, APPORTION **4** : to possess or make use of in common : share in **5** ♦ : to cause to be separate, distinct, or apart from one another **6** : to separate into opposing sides or parties **7** : to mark divisions on **8** : to subject to or use in mathematical division; *also* : to be used as a divisor with respect to **9** ♦ : to branch out

♦ [5] break up, disconnect, disjoint, dissever, dissociate, disunite, divorce, part, resolve, separate, sever, split, sunder, unyoke ♦ [9] branch, diverge, fork, separate

²**divide** *n* : WATERSHED 1

div·i·dend \'di-və-‚dend\ *n* **1** : an individual share of something distributed **2** ♦ : something in addition to what is expected or strictly due : BONUS **3** : a number to be divided **4** : a sum or fund to be divided or distributed

♦ bonus, extra, lagniappe, perquisite, tip

di·vid·er \də-'vī-dər\ *n* **1** : one that divides (as a partition) ⟨room ~⟩ **2** *pl* : COMPASS 5

div·i·na·tion \ˌdi-və-'nā-shən\ *n* **1** : the art or practice of using omens or magic powers to foretell the future **2** : unusual insight or intuitive perception

¹**di·vine** \də-'vīn\ *adj* **di·vin·er; -est** **1** ♦ : of, relating to, or being God or a god **2** : supremely good : SUPERB; *also* : HEAVENLY — **di·vine·ly** *adv*

   ♦ blessed, godlike, heavenly, holy

²**divine** *n* **1** : a member of the clergy : CLERGYMAN **2** : THEOLOGIAN

³**divine** *vb* **di·vined; di·vin·ing** **1** : INFER, CONJECTURE **2** ♦ : to predict with assurance or on the basis of mystic knowledge **3** : DOWSE

   ♦ anticipate, foreknow, foresee

di·vin·er \də-'vī-nər\ *n* ♦ : a person who practices divination

   ♦ augur, forecaster, fortune-teller, futurist, prognosticator, prophet, seer, soothsayer

divining rod *n* : a forked rod believed to reveal the presence of water or minerals by dipping downward when held over a vein

di·vin·i·ty \də-'vi-nə-tē\ *n, pl* **-ties** **1** : THEOLOGY **2** ♦ : the quality or state of being divine **3** : a divine being; *esp* : GOD 1

   ♦ deity, godhead

di·vis·i·ble \də-'vi-zə-bəl\ *adj* : capable of being divided — **di·vis·i·bil·i·ty** \-ˌvi-zə-'bi-lə-tē\ *n*

di·vi·sion \də-'vi-zhən\ *n* **1 a** ♦ : the act or process of dividing : SEPARATION **b** ♦ : the act, process, or an instance of distributing among a number : DISTRIBUTION **2** ♦ : one of the parts or groupings into which a whole is divided **3** : DISAGREEMENT, DISUNITY **4** : something that divides or separates **5** : the mathematical operation of finding how many times one number is contained in another **6** : a large self-contained military unit **7** ♦ : an administrative or operating unit of a governmental, business, or educational organization — **di·vi·sion·al** \-'vi-zhə-nəl\ *adj*

   ♦ [1a] breakup, dissolution, partition, schism, separation, split ♦ [1b] allocation, dispensation, distribution, issuance ♦ [2] bracket, category, class, family, grade, group, kind, order, set, species, type ♦ [7] bureau, department, desk, office

di·vi·sive \də-'vī-siv, -'vi-ziv\ *adj* : creating disunity or dissension — **di·vi·sive·ly** *adv* — **di·vi·sive·ness** *n*

di·vi·sor \də-'vī-zər\ *n* : the number by which a dividend is divided

¹**di·vorce** \də-'vōrs\ *n* **1** : an act or instance of legally dissolving a marriage **2** : SEPARATION, SEVERANCE — **di·vorce·ment** *n*

²**divorce** *vb* **1** : to end marriage with (one's spouse) by divorce ⟨*divorced* his wife⟩ **2** : to dissolve the marriage contract between ⟨they were *divorced* last year⟩ **3** ♦ : to make or keep separate

   ♦ break up, disconnect, disjoint, dissever, dissociate, disunite, divide, part, resolve, separate, sever, split, sunder, unyoke

di·vor·cé \də-ˌvōr-'sā\ *n* : a divorced man

di·vor·cée \də-ˌvōr-'sā, -'sē\ *n* : a divorced woman

div·ot \'di-vət\ *n* : a piece of turf dug from a golf fairway in making a stroke

di·vulge \də-'vəlj, dī-\ *vb* **di·vulged; di·vulg·ing** ♦ : to make known (as a confidence or secret) : REVEAL

   ♦ bare, disclose, discover, expose, reveal, spill, tell, unbosom, uncloak, uncover, unmask, unveil

Dix·ie·land \'dik-sē-ˌland\ *n* : jazz music in duple time played in a style developed in New Orleans

diz·zy \'di-zē\ *adj* **diz·zi·er; -est** **1** : FOOLISH, SILLY **2** ♦ : having a sensation of whirling : GIDDY **3 a** : causing or caused by giddiness **b** ♦ : confusing or feeling confused mentally **4** ♦ : extremely rapid — **diz·zi·ly** \-zə-lē\ *adv* — **diz·zi·ness** \-zē-nəs\ *n*

   ♦ [2] giddy, light-headed ♦ [3b] confused, stunned *Ant* clearheaded ♦ [4] breakneck, breathless, brisk, fast, fleet, hasty, lightning, nippy, quick, rapid, rattling, snappy, speedy, swift

DJ *n, often not cap* : DISC JOCKEY

dk *abbr* **1** dark **2** deck **3** dock

dl *abbr* deciliter

DLitt *or* **DLit** *abbr* doctor of letters; doctor of literature

DLO *abbr* dead letter office

dm *abbr* decimeter

DMD *abbr* doctor of dental medicine

DMZ *abbr* demilitarized zone

dn *abbr* down

DNA \ˌdē-(ˌ)en-'ā\ *n* : any of various nucleic acids that are usu. the molecular basis of heredity and are localized esp. in cell nuclei

DNR *abbr* do not resuscitate

¹**do** \'dü\ *vb* **did** \'did\; **done** \'dən\; **do·ing; does** \'dəz\ **1** ♦ : to bring to pass : ACCOMPLISH **2** : ACT, BEHAVE ⟨~ as I say⟩ **3** : to be active or busy ⟨up and ~ing⟩ **4** : HAPPEN ⟨what's ~*ing*?⟩ **5** : to be engaged in the study or practice of : work at ⟨he *does* tailoring⟩ **6** : COOK ⟨steak *done* rare⟩ **7** : to put in order (as by cleaning or arranging) ⟨~ the dishes⟩ **8** : to furnish with something ornamental : DECORATE ⟨*did* the hall in blue⟩ **9** : GET ALONG ⟨~ well in school⟩ **10** ♦ : to deal with something successfully : MANAGE **11** : RENDER ⟨sleep will ~ you good⟩ **12** : to bring to an end : FINISH ⟨when he had *done*⟩ **13** : EXERT ⟨*did* my best⟩ **14** : PRODUCE ⟨*did* a poem⟩ **15** : to play the part of **16** : CHEAT ⟨*did* him out of his share⟩ **17** : TRAVERSE, TOUR **18** : TRAVEL **19** : to spend or serve out a period of time ⟨*did* ten years in prison⟩ **20** ♦ : to serve the needs of **21** ♦ : to be fitting or proper **22** : USE ⟨doesn't ~ drugs⟩ **23** — used as an auxiliary verb (1) before the subject in an interrogative sentence ⟨*does* he work?⟩ and after some adverbs ⟨never *did* she say so⟩, (2) in a negative statement ⟨I *don't* know⟩, (3) for emphasis ⟨you ~ know⟩, and (4) as a substitute for a preceding predicate ⟨he works harder than I ~⟩ — **do away with** **1** : to put an end to **2** : DESTROY, KILL — **do by** : to deal with : TREAT ⟨*did* right *by* her⟩ — **do for** : to bring about the death or ruin of — **do the trick** : to produce a desired result

   ♦ [1] accomplish, achieve, carry out, commit, compass, execute, follow through, make, perform ♦ [10] cope, fare, get along, make out, manage, shift ♦ [20, 21] befit, fit, go, serve, suit

²**do** *n* **1** : AFFAIR, PARTY **2** : a command or entreaty to do something ⟨list of ~s and don'ts⟩ **3** : HAIRDO

³**do** *abbr* ditto

DOA *abbr* dead on arrival

do·able \'dü-ə-bəl\ *adj* ♦ : that can be done : PRACTICABLE

   ♦ achievable, attainable, feasible, possible, practicable, realizable, viable, workable

DOB *abbr* date of birth

dob·bin \'dä-bən\ *n* **1** : a farm horse **2** : a quiet plodding horse

Do·ber·man pin·scher \'dō-bər-mən-'pin-chər\ *n* : any of a German breed of short-haired medium-sized dogs

¹**doc** \'däk\ *n* : DOCTOR

²**doc** *abbr* document

do·cent \'dōs-ᵊnt, dōt-'sent\ *n* : TEACHER, LECTURER; *also* : a person who leads a guided tour

doc·ile \'dä-səl\ *adj* ♦ : easily taught, led, or managed : TRACTABLE

   ♦ amenable, compliant, conformable, obedient, submissive, tractable

do·cil·i·ty \dä-'si-lə-tē\ *n* ♦ : the quality or state of being docile

   ♦ compliance, deference, obedience

¹**dock** \'däk\ *n* : any of a genus of coarse weedy herbs related to buckwheat

²**dock** *vb* **1** : to cut off the end of : cut short **2** : to take away a part of : deduct from ⟨~ a worker's wages⟩

³**dock** *n* **1** : an artificial basin to receive ships **2** : ²SLIP 2 **3** ♦ : a wharf or platform for loading or unloading materials

   ♦ float, jetty, landing, levee, pier, quay, wharf

⁴**dock** *vb* **1** ♦ : to bring or come into dock **2** : to join (as two spacecraft) mechanically in space

   ♦ disembark, land, moor, tie up

⁵**dock** *n* : the place in a court where a prisoner stands or sits during trial

dock·age \'dä-kij\ *n* : docking facilities

dock·et \'dä-kət\ *n* **1** : a formal abridged record of the proceedings in a legal action; *also* : a register of such records **2** : a list of legal causes to be tried **3** ♦ : a calendar of matters to be acted on : AGENDA **4** : a label attached to a document containing identification or directions — **docket** *vb*

   ♦ agenda, calendar, program, schedule, timetable

dock·hand \'däk-ˌhand\ *n* : LONGSHOREMAN

dock·work·er \-ˌwər-kər\ *n* : LONGSHOREMAN

dock·yard \-ˌyärd\ *n* : SHIPYARD

¹**doc·tor** \'däk-tər\ *n* **1** : a person holding one of the highest academic degrees (as a PhD) conferred by a university **2** : a person skilled in healing arts; *esp* : one (as a physician, dentist, or

veterinarian) academically and legally qualified to practice **3** : a person who restores or repairs things — **doc·tor·al** \-tə-rəl\ *adj*
²**doctor** *vb* **1** : to give medical treatment to **2** : to practice medicine **3** ♦ : to restore to good condition : REPAIR **4** : to adapt or modify for a desired end **5** : to alter deceptively

♦ fix, mend, patch, recondition, renovate, repair, revamp

doc·tor·ate \'däk-tə-rət\ *n* : the degree, title, or rank of a doctor
doc·tri·naire \,däk-trə-'nar\ *n* : one who attempts to put an abstract theory into effect without regard to practical difficulties — **doctrinaire** *adj*
doc·trine \'däk-trən\ *n* **1** : something that is taught **2** ♦ : a principle or position or the body of principles in a branch of knowledge or system of belief — **doc·tri·nal** \-trən-ᵊl\ *adj*

♦ creed, gospel, ideology, philosophy

docu·dra·ma \'dä-kyə-,drä-mə, -,dra-\ *n* : a drama for television, motion pictures, or theater that deals freely with historical events
¹**doc·u·ment** \'dä-kyə-mənt\ *n* **1** : a paper that furnishes information, proof, or support of something else **2** : a computer file containing information input by a computer user usu. via a word processor
²**doc·u·ment** \-,ment\ *vb* ♦ : to furnish documentary evidence of — **doc·u·ment·er** *n*

♦ demonstrate, establish, prove, substantiate, validate

doc·u·men·ta·ry \,dä-kyə-'men-tə-rē\ *adj* **1** : consisting of documents; *also* : being in writing ⟨~ proof⟩ **2 a** : giving a factual presentation in artistic form ⟨a ~ movie⟩ **b** ♦ : of or relating to facts — **documentary** *n*

♦ factual, hard, historical, literal, matter-of-fact, nonfictional, objective, true

doc·u·men·ta·tion \,dä-kyə-mən-'tā-shən\ *n* **1** : the act or an instance of furnishing or authenticating with documents **2 a** : the provision of documents in substantiation **b** ♦ : documentary evidence

♦ attestation, confirmation, corroboration, evidence, proof, substantiation, testament, testimony, validation, witness

DOD *abbr* Department of Defense
¹**dod·der** \'dä-dər\ *n* : any of a genus of leafless parasitic twining vines that are highly deficient in chlorophyll
²**dodder** *vb* **dod·dered; dod·der·ing 1** : to tremble or shake usu. from age **2** ♦ : to progress feebly and unsteadily

♦ careen, lurch, reel, stagger, teeter, totter

¹**dodge** \'däj\ *n* **1** : an act of evading by sudden bodily movement **2** ♦ : an artful device to evade, deceive, or trick **3** : EXPEDIENT

♦ artifice, device, gimmick, jig, ploy, scheme, sleight, stratagem, trick, wile

²**dodge** *vb* **dodged; dodg·ing 1** ♦ : to evade usu. by trickery **2** ♦ : to move suddenly aside; *also* : to avoid or evade by so doing

♦ [1] avoid, duck, elude, escape, eschew, evade, shake, shirk, shun ♦ [2] duck, sidestep

dodg·er \'dä-jər\ *n* ♦ : one that dodges; *esp* : one who uses tricky devices

♦ cheat, hoaxer, shark, sharper, swindler, trickster

do·do \'dō-dō\ *n, pl* **dodoes** *or* **dodos 1** : an extinct heavy flightless bird of the island of Mauritius related to the pigeons and larger than a turkey **2** ♦ : one hopelessly behind the times **3** ♦ : a stupid person

♦ [2] antediluvian, fogy, fossil, fuddy-duddy, reactionary ♦ [3] blockhead, dope, dummy, idiot, imbecile, jackass, moron, numskull

doe \'dō\ *n, pl* **does** *or* **doe** : an adult female of various mammals (as a deer, rabbit, or kangaroo) of which the male is called *buck*
DOE *abbr* Department of Energy
do·er \'dü-ər\ *n* : one that does
does *pres 3d sing of* DO *pl of* DOE
doff \'däf\ *vb* **1** : to take off (the hat) in greeting or as a sign of respect **2** : to rid oneself of **3** ♦ : to remove (an article of wear) from the body

♦ peel, put off, remove, take off

¹**dog** \'dȯg\ *n* **1** : a flesh-eating domestic mammal related to the wolves; *esp* : a male of this animal **2** : a worthless or contemptible person **3** : FELLOW, CHAP ⟨you lucky ~⟩ **4** : a mechanical

device for holding something **5** : uncharacteristic or affected stylishness or dignity ⟨put on the ~⟩ **6** *pl* : RUIN ⟨gone to the ~s⟩
²**dog** *vb* **dogged; dog·ging 1** ♦ : to hunt or track like a hound **2** : to worry as if by pursuit with dogs : PLAGUE

♦ chase, follow, hound, pursue, shadow, tag, tail, trace, track, trail

dog·bane \'dȯg-,bān\ *n* : any of a genus of mostly poisonous herbs with milky juice and often showy flowers
dog·cart \-,kärt\ *n* : a light one-horse carriage with two seats back to back
dog·catch·er \-,ka-chər, -,ke-\ *n* : a community official assigned to catch and dispose of stray dogs
dog·ear \'dȯg-,ir\ *n* : the turned-down corner of a leaf of a book — **dog·ear** *vb*
dog·eared \'dȯg-,ird\ *adj* : ill-kept : SHABBY
dog·fight \'dȯg-,fīt\ *n* : a fight between fighter planes at close range
dog·fish \-,fish\ *n* : any of various small usu. bottom-dwelling sharks
dog·ged \'dȯ-gəd\ *adj* ♦ : stubbornly determined — **dog·ged·ly** *adv*

♦ insistent, patient, persevering, persistent, pertinacious, tenacious ♦ determined, grim, implacable, relentless, unflinching, unrelenting, unyielding

dog·ged·ness \-nəs\ *n* : the quality or state of being dogged
dog·ger·el \'dȯ-gə-rəl\ *n* : verse that is loosely styled and irregular in measure esp. for comic effect
dog·gie bag *or* **doggy bag** \'dȯ-gē-\ *n* : a container for carrying home leftover food from a restaurant meal
¹**dog·gy** *or* **dog·gie** \'dȯ-gē\ *n, pl* **doggies** : a usu. small dog
²**dog·gy** *adj* **dog·gi·er; -est** : of or resembling a dog ⟨a ~ odor⟩
dog·house \'dȯg-,haus\ *n* : a shelter for a dog — **in the dog-house** : in a state of disfavor
do·gie \'dō-gē\ *n, chiefly West* : a motherless calf in a range herd
dog·leg \'dȯg-,leg\ *n* : a sharp bend or angle (as in a road or a golf fairway) — **dogleg** *vb*
dog·ma \'dȯg-mə\ *n, pl* **dogmas** *also* **dog·ma·ta** \-mə-tə\ **1** : a tenet or code of tenets **2** : a doctrine or body of doctrines formally proclaimed by a church
dog·ma·tism \'dȯg-mə-,ti-zəm\ *n* : positiveness in stating matters of opinion esp. when unwarranted or arrogant — **dog·mat·ic** \dȯg-'ma-tik\ *adj* — **dog·mat·i·cal·ly** \-ti-k(ə-)lē\ *adv*
do–good·er \'dü-,gu̇-dər\ *n* : an earnest often naive humanitarian or reformer
dog·tooth violet \'dȯg-,tüth-\ *n* : any of a genus of small spring-flowering bulbous herbs related to the lilies
dog·trot \'dȯg-,trät\ *n* : a gentle trot — **dogtrot** *vb*
dog·wood \'dȯg-,wu̇d\ *n* : any of a genus of trees and shrubs having heads of small flowers often with showy white, pink, or red bracts
doi·ly \'dȯi-lē\ *n, pl* **doilies** : a small often decorative mat
do in *vb* **1** : to bring about the defeat or destruction of : RUIN **2** ♦ : to deprive of life : KILL **3** ♦ : to tire extremely or completely : EXHAUST ⟨the climb *did* him *in*⟩ **4** : CHEAT

♦ [2] destroy, dispatch, fell, kill, slay ♦ [3] burn out, drain, exhaust, fag, fatigue, tire, tucker, wash out, wear, wear out, weary

do·ing \'dü-iŋ\ *n* **1** ♦ : the act or result of performing, executing, or creating ⟨to achieve those plans will take some ~⟩ **2**
do·ings \'dü-iŋz\ *pl* : things that go on or occur ⟨the daily ~s in the market⟩

♦ deed, exploit, feat, thing

do–it–yourself *n* : the activity of doing or making something without professional training or help — **do–it–your·self·er** *n*
dol *abbr* dollar
dol·drums \'dōl-drəmz, 'däl-\ *n pl* **1** ♦ : a spell of listlessness or despondency **2** *often cap* : a part of the ocean near the equator known for calms **3** : a state or period of inactivity, stagnation, or slump

♦ blues, dejection, depression, desolation, despondency, dumps, forlornness, gloom, heartsickness, melancholy, sadness ♦ boredom, ennui, listlessness, restlessness, tedium, tiredness, weariness

¹**dole** \'dōl\ *n* **1** ♦ : a distribution esp. of food, money, or clothing to the needy; *also* : something so distributed **2** : a grant of government funds to the unemployed

♦ charity, philanthropy

²**dole** *vb* **doled; dol·ing** : to give or distribute as a charity — usu. used with *out*

dole·ful \'dōl-fəl\ *adj* : full of grief : SAD — **dole·ful·ly** *adv*

dole out *vb* **1** ♦ : to give or deliver in small portions **2** : to give or dispense freely : DISH OUT

♦ administer, allocate, apportion, deal, dispense, distribute, mete, parcel, portion, prorate

doll \'däl, 'dȯl\ *n* **1** : a small figure of a human being used esp. as a child's plaything **2** ♦ : a pretty woman **3** : an attractive person — **doll·ish** \'dä-lish, 'dȯ-\ *adj*

♦ girl, lass, maid, maiden, miss

dol·lar \'dä-lər\ *n* **1** : a basic monetary unit of any of several countries (as the U.S., Canada, Australia, and Singapore) **2** : a coin, note, or token representing one dollar

dol·lop \'dä-ləp\ *n* **1** : LUMP, GLOB **2** : PORTION 1 — **dollop** *vb*

doll up *vb* **1** : to dress elegantly or extravagantly **2** : to make more attractive **3** : to get dolled up

dol·ly \'dä-lē\ *n, pl* **dollies** : a small cart or wheeled platform (as for a television or movie camera)

dol·men \'dōl-mən, 'däl-\ *n* : a prehistoric monument consisting of two or more upright stones supporting a horizontal stone slab

do·lo·mite \'dō-lə-ˌmīt, 'dä-\ *n* : a mineral found in broad layers as a compact limestone

do·lor *or Can and Brit* **do·lour** \'dō-lər, 'dä-\ *n* ♦ : mental suffering or anguish : SORROW

♦ affliction, anguish, grief, heartache, sorrow, woe

do·lor·ous \'dō-lə-rəs, 'dä-\ *adj* ♦ : causing, marked by, or expressing misery or grief — **do·lor·ous·ly** *adv*

♦ funeral, lugubrious, mournful, plaintive, regretful, rueful, sorrowful, weeping, woeful

dol·phin \'däl-fən\ *n* **1** : any of various small whales with conical teeth and an elongated beaklike snout **2** : either of two active food fishes of tropical and temperate seas

dolt \'dōlt\ *n* ♦ : a stupid individual

♦ blockhead, dope, dummy, idiot, imbecile, jackass, moron, numskull

dolt·ish \'dōl-tish\ *adj* : like a dolt : STUPID

dolt·ish·ness \-nəs\ *n* : the quality or state of being doltish : STUPIDITY

dom *abbr* **1** domestic **2** dominant **3** dominion

-dom *n suffix* **1** : dignity : office ⟨duke*dom*⟩ **2** : realm : jurisdiction ⟨king*dom*⟩ **3** : state or fact of being ⟨free*dom*⟩ **4** : those having a (specified) office, occupation, interest, or character ⟨official*dom*⟩

do·main \dō-'mān\ *n* **1** : complete and absolute ownership of land **2** : land completely owned **3** : a territory over which dominion is exercised **4** ♦ : a sphere of knowledge, influence, or activity ⟨the ∼ of science⟩ **5** : a subdivision of the Internet made up of computers whose URLs share a characteristic abbreviation (as *com* or *gov*)

♦ area, arena, demesne, department, discipline, field, line, province, realm, specialty, sphere

domain name *n* : a sequence of characters (as Merriam-Webster. com) that specifies a group of online resources and forms part of its URL

dome \'dōm\ *n* **1** : a large hemispherical roof or ceiling **2** : a structure or natural formation that resembles the dome of a building **3** : a roofed sports stadium — **dome** *vb*

¹**do·mes·tic** \də-'mes-tik\ *adj* **1** : living near or about human habitations **2** : reduced from a state of native wildness esp. so as to be tractable and useful to humans : DOMESTICATED **3** : relating and limited to one's own country or the country under consideration **4** : of or relating to the household or the family **5** : devoted to home duties and pleasures **6** : INDIGENOUS 1 — **do·mes·ti·cal·ly** \-ti-k(ə-)lē\ *adv*

²**domestic** *n* ♦ : a household servant

♦ girl, housemaid, maid, maidservant

do·mes·ti·cate \də-'mes-ti-ˌkāt\ *vb* **-cat·ed; -cat·ing** : to adapt to life in association with and to the use of humans — **do·mes·ti·ca·tion** \-ˌmes-ti-'kā-shən\ *n*

do·mes·tic·i·ty \ˌdō-ˌmes-'ti-sə-tē, ˌdä-\ *n, pl* **-ties** **1** : the quality or state of being domestic or domesticated **2** : domestic activities or life

domestic violence *n* : the inflicting of injury by one family or household member on another

¹**do·mi·cile** \'dä-mə-ˌsīl, 'dō-; 'dä-mə-səl\ *n* ♦ : a dwelling place : HOME — **dom·i·cil·i·ary** \ˌdä-mə-'si-lē-ˌer-ē, ˌdō-\ *adj*

♦ abode, dwelling, home, house, lodging, quarters, residence

²**domicile** *vb* ♦ : to establish in or provide with a domicile

♦ accommodate, billet, chamber, harbor (*or* harbour), house, lodge, put up, quarter, roof, shelter, take in

dom·i·nance \'dä-mə-nəns\ *n* **1** ♦ : dominant position esp. in a social hierarchy **2** : the property of one of a pair of alleles or traits that suppresses expression of the other when both are present

♦ ascendancy, dominion, predominance, preeminence, supremacy

¹**dom·i·nant** \-nənt\ *adj* **1** ♦ : controlling or prevailing over all others **2** : overlooking from a high position **3** : exhibiting genetic dominance

♦ arch, cardinal, central, chief, first, foremost, grand, key, main, paramount, predominant, preeminent, premier, primary, principal, sovereign, supreme

²**dominant** *n* : a dominant gene or trait

dom·i·nate \'dä-mə-ˌnāt\ *vb* **-nat·ed; -nat·ing** **1** ♦ : to exert control, direction, or influence on **2** ♦ : to have a commanding position or controlling power over **3** : to rise high above in a position suggesting power to dominate — **dom·i·na·tor** \-ˌnā-tər\ *n*

♦ [1] conquer, overpower, subdue, subject, vanquish ♦ [2] boss, captain, command, head, lead, spearhead

dom·i·na·tion \ˌdä-mə-'nā-shən\ *n* **1** : supremacy or preeminence over another **2** ♦ : exercise of mastery, ruling power, or preponderant influence

♦ conquest, subjection

dom·i·na·trix \ˌdä-mə-'nā-triks\ *n, pl* **-tri·ces** \-'nā-trə-ˌsēz, -nə-'trī-sēz\ : a woman who dominates her partner in a sexual encounter; *also* : a dominating woman

dom·i·neer \ˌdä-mə-'nir\ *vb* **1** : to rule in an arrogant manner **2** : to be overbearing

dom·i·neer·ing \-'nir-iŋ\ *adj* ♦ : inclined to exercise arbitrary and overbearing control over others

♦ authoritarian, autocratic, bossy, despotic, dictatorial, imperious, overbearing, peremptory, tyrannical, tyrannous

do·mi·nie *1 usu* 'dä-mə-nē, *2 usu* 'dō-\ *n* **1** *chiefly Scot* : SCHOOLMASTER **2** : a member of the clergy : CLERGYMAN

do·min·ion \də-'min-yən\ *n* **1** : DOMAIN **2** ♦ : supreme authority **3** *often cap* : a self-governing nation of the Commonwealth

♦ ascendancy, dominance, predominance, preeminence, supremacy

dom·i·no \'dä-mə-ˌnō\ *n, pl* **-noes** *or* **-nos** **1** : a long loose hooded cloak usu. worn with a half mask as a masquerade costume **2** : a flat rectangular block used as a piece in a game (**dominoes**)

¹**don** \'dän\ *vb* **donned; don·ning** ♦ : to put on (as clothes)

♦ put on, slip, throw

²**don** *n* **1** : a Spanish nobleman or gentleman — used as a title prefixed to the first name **2** : a head, tutor, or fellow in an English university

do·ña \'dō-nyə\ *n* : a Spanish woman of rank — used as a title prefixed to the first name

do·nate \'dō-ˌnāt\ *vb* **do·nat·ed; do·nat·ing** **1** ♦ : to make a gift of : CONTRIBUTE **2** : to make a donation

♦ bestow, contribute, give, present

do·na·tion \dō-'nā-shən\ *n* **1** : the making of a gift esp. to a charity **2** ♦ : a free contribution

♦ alms, benefaction, beneficence, charity, contribution, philanthropy ♦ bestowal, freebie, gift, lagniappe, largesse, present

¹**done** \'dən\ *past part of* DO

²**done** *adj* **1** : doomed to failure, defeat, or death **2** ♦ : gone by : OVER ⟨when day is ∼⟩ **3** : cooked sufficiently **4** : conformable to social convention

♦ complete, down, over, through, up

done deal *n* : FAIT ACCOMPLI

don·key \'däŋ-kē, 'dəŋ-\ *n, pl* **donkeys** **1** ♦ : a sturdy and patient domestic mammal classified with the asses **2** : a stupid or obstinate person

♦ ass, jackass

don·ny·brook \'dä-nē-ˌbrůk\ *n, often cap* : an uproarious brawl

do·nor \'dō-nər\ *n* : one that gives, donates, or presents

donut *var of* DOUGHNUT

doo·dad \'dü-ˌdad\ *n* : an often small article whose common name is unknown or forgotten

doo•dle \'dü-d°l\ *vb* **doo•dled; doo•dling :** to draw or scribble aimlessly while occupied with something else — **doodle** *n* — **doo•dler** *n*

¹**doom** \'düm\ *n* **1 ♦ :** a judicial decision; *esp* **:** a judicial condemnation or sentence **2 ♦ :** something to which a person or thing is destined **:** DESTINY **3 a :** RUIN **b :** a permanent cessation of all vital functions **:** DEATH

♦ [1] finding, holding, judgment (*or* judgement), ruling, sentence ♦ [2] circumstance, destiny, fate, fortune, lot, portion

²**doom** *vb* **1 ♦ :** to give judgment against **:** CONDEMN **2 ♦ :** to fix the fate of **:** DESTINE

♦ [1] condemn, damn, sentence ♦ [2] destine, foredoom, foreordain, ordain, predestine

dooms•day \'dümz-ˌdā\ *n* **:** JUDGMENT DAY

door \'dōr\ *n* **1 ♦ :** a usu. swinging or sliding barrier by which an entry is closed and opened; *also* **:** a similar part of a piece of furniture **2 ♦ :** the opening that a door closes **:** DOORWAY **3 :** a means of access or participation **:** OPPORTUNITY

♦ [1] gate, hatch, portal ♦ [2] doorway, entrance, gate, gateway, way

door•keep•er \-ˌkē-pər\ *n* **♦ :** a person who tends a door

♦ gatekeeper, janitor

door•knob \-ˌnäb\ *n* **:** a knob that when turned releases a door latch

door•man \-ˌman, -mən\ *n* **:** a usu. uniformed attendant at the door of a building (as a hotel)

door•mat \-ˌmat\ *n* **:** a mat placed before or inside a door for wiping dirt from the shoes

door•plate \-ˌplāt\ *n* **:** a nameplate on a door

door•step \-ˌstep\ *n* **:** a step or series of steps before an outer door

door•way \-ˌwā\ *n* **1 ♦ :** the opening that a door closes **2 ♦ :** a means of access or participation

♦ [1] door, entrance, gate, gateway, way ♦ [2] access, admission, entrance, entrée, gateway

do•pa \'dō-pə\ *n* **:** a form of an amino acid that is used esp. in the treatment of Parkinson's disease

do•pa•mine \'dō-pə-ˌmēn\ *n* **:** an organic compound that occurs esp. as a neurotransmitter in the brain

¹**dope** \'dōp\ *n* **1 :** a preparation for giving a desired quality **2 :** an illicit, habit-forming, or narcotic drug; *esp* **:** MARIJUANA **3 ♦ :** a stupid person **4 ♦ :** information esp. from a reliable source

♦ [3] blockhead, dummy, idiot, imbecile, jackass, moron, numskull ♦ [4] lowdown, scoop, tip

²**dope** *vb* **doped; dop•ing 1 :** to treat with dope; *esp* **:** to give a narcotic to **2 ♦ :** to find a solution, explanation, or answer for **:** FIGURE OUT — usu. used with *out* **3 :** to take dope

♦ *usu* **dope out** answer, break, crack, figure out, puzzle, resolve, riddle, solve, unravel, work, work out

dop•er *n* **♦ :** an habitual or frequent drug user

♦ addict, fiend, user

dop•ey *also* **dopy** \'dō-pē\ *adj* **dop•i•er; -est 1 :** dulled by alcohol or a narcotic **2 :** SLUGGISH **3 :** slow of mind **:** STUPID; *also* **:** complacently or inanely foolish

dop•i•ness \-nəs\ *n* **♦ :** the quality or state of being dopey

♦ denseness, foolishness, imbecility, mindlessness, obtuseness, stupidity, vacuity

doping *n* **:** the use of a substance or technique to illegally improve athletic performance

Dopp•ler effect \'dä-plər-\ *n* **:** a change in the frequency at which waves (as of sound) reach an observer from a source in motion with respect to the observer

do–rag \'dü-ˌrag\ *n* **:** a kerchief worn esp. to cover the hair

♦ babushka, bandanna, kerchief, mantilla

dork \'dȯrk\ *n, slang* **:** NERD 2; *also* **:** JERK 2

dorm \'dȯrm\ *n* **:** DORMITORY

dor•man•cy \-mən-sē\ *n* **♦ :** the quality or state of being dormant

♦ abeyance, doldrums, latency, quiescence, suspension ♦ idleness, inaction, inactivity, inertness, quiescence

dor•mant \'dȯr-mənt\ *adj* **1 ♦ :** marked by a suspension of activity **2 ♦ :** sleeping or drowsing

♦ [1] dead, fallow, free, idle, inactive, inert, inoperative, latent, off, vacant ♦ [2] asleep

dor•mer \'dȯr-mər\ *n* **:** a window built upright in a sloping roof; *also* **:** the roofed structure containing such a window

dor•mi•to•ry \'dȯr-mə-ˌtȯr-ē\ *n, pl* **-ries 1 :** a room for sleeping; *esp* **:** a large room containing a number of beds **2 :** a residence hall providing sleeping rooms

dor•mouse \'dȯr-ˌmaús\ *n* **:** any of numerous Old World rodents that resemble small squirrels

dor•sal \'dȯr-səl\ *adj* **:** of, relating to, or located near or on the surface of the body that in humans is the back but in most other animals is the upper surface — **dor•sal•ly** *adv*

do•ry \'dȯr-ē\ *n, pl* **dories :** a flat-bottomed boat with high flaring sides and a sharp bow

DOS *abbr* disk operating system

¹**dose** \'dōs\ *n* **1 :** a measured quantity (as of medicine) to be taken or administered at one time **2 :** the quantity of radiation administered or absorbed — **dos•age** \'dō-sij\ *n*

²**dose** *vb* **dosed; dos•ing 1 :** to give in doses **2 :** to give medicine to

do•sim•e•ter \dō-'si-mə-tər\ *n* **:** a device for measuring doses of radiations (as X-rays) — **do•sim•e•try** \-mə-trē\ *n*

dos•sier \'dȯs-ˌyā, 'dȯ-sē-ˌā\ *n* **:** a file containing detailed records on a particular person or subject

¹**dot** \'dät\ *n* **1 ♦ :** a small spot **:** SPECK **2 :** a small round mark **3 :** a precise point esp. in time ⟨be here on the ∼⟩

♦ blotch, fleck, mottle, patch, point, speck, spot

²**dot** *vb* **dot•ted; dot•ting 1 :** to mark with a dot ⟨∼ an *i*⟩ **2 ♦ :** to cover with or as if with dots — **dot•ter** *n*

♦ blotch, dapple, fleck, freckle, mottle, pepper, speck, spot, sprinkle, stipple

DOT *abbr* Department of Transportation

dot•age \'dō-tij\ *n* **:** feebleness of mind esp. in old age **:** SENILITY

dot•ard \-tərd\ *n* **:** a person in dotage

dot–com \'dät-ˌkäm\ *n* **:** a company that markets its products or services usu. exclusively via a website

dote \'dōt\ *vb* **dot•ed; dot•ing 1 :** to be feebleminded esp. from old age **2 ♦ :** to be lavish or excessive in one's attention, affection, or fondness ⟨doted on her niece⟩

♦ *usu* **dote on** adore, canonize, deify, idolize, worship

dot matrix *n* **:** a rectangular arrangement of dots from which alphanumeric characters can be formed (as by a computer printer)

Dou•ay Version \dü-'ā-\ *n* **:** an English translation of the Vulgate used by Roman Catholics

¹**dou•ble** \'də-bəl\ *adj* **1 :** TWOFOLD, DUAL **2 ♦ :** consisting of two members or parts **3 :** being twice as great or as many **4 :** folded in two **5 :** having more than one whorl of petals ⟨∼ roses⟩

♦ binary, bipartite, dual, duplex, twin *Ant* single

²**double** *vb* **dou•bled; dou•bling 1 :** to make, be, or become twice as great or as many **2 :** to make a call in bridge that increases the trick values and penalties of (an opponent's bid) **3 :** FOLD **4 :** CLENCH **5 :** to be or cause to be bent over **6 :** to take the place of another **7 :** to hit a double **8 :** to turn sharply and suddenly; *esp* **:** to turn back on one's course

³**double** *adv* **1 :** DOUBLY **2 :** two together

⁴**double** *n* **1 :** something twice another in size, strength, speed, quantity, or value **2 :** a base hit that enables the batter to reach second base **3 ♦ :** one that is the counterpart of another **:** DUPLICATE; *esp* **:** a person who closely resembles another **4 :** UNDERSTUDY, SUBSTITUTE **5 :** a sharp turn **:** REVERSAL **6 :** FOLD **7 :** a combined bet placed on two different contests **8** *pl* **:** a game between two pairs of players **9 :** an act of doubling in a card game

♦ carbon copy, counterpart, duplicate, duplication, facsimile, image, likeness, match, picture, replica, ringer, spit

double bond *n* **:** a chemical bond in which two atoms in a molecule share two pairs of electrons

double cross *n* **♦ :** an act of betraying or cheating esp. an associate — **dou•ble–cross** \ˌdə-bəl-'krȯs\ *vb*

♦ betrayal, disloyalty, faithlessness, falseness, falsity, infidelity, perfidy, treachery, treason, unfaithfulness

dou•ble–cross•er *n* **♦ :** one that double-crosses

♦ apostate, betrayer, quisling, recreant, traitor, turncoat

¹**dou•ble–deal•ing** \ˌdə-bəl-'dē-liŋ\ *n* **♦ :** action contradictory to a professed attitude **:** DUPLICITY — **dou•ble–deal•er** \-'dē-lər\ *n*

♦ artifice, craft, craftiness, crookedness, cunning, deceit, deceitfulness, dishonesty, dissimulation, duplicity, guile, wiliness

²**double–dealing** *adj* **♦ :** given to or marked by duplicity

♦ crooked, deceitful, dishonest, false, fraudulent

dou•ble–deck•er \-'de-kər\ *n* **:** something having two decks, levels, or layers — **dou·ble–deck** \-ˌdek\ *or* **dou·ble–decked** \-ˌdekt\ *adj*

dou·ble–dig·it \ˌdə-bəl-ˈdi-jət\ *adj* : amounting to 10 percent or more

dou·ble–dip \-ˈdip\ *vb* **1** : to obtain money from two sources at the same time or by two separate accounting methods; *esp* : to draw a pension from one government department while working for another **2** : to repeat the action of dipping a chip or other snack into a shared dipping sauce or mixture after taking a bite — **dou·ble–dip·per** *n* — **dou·ble–dip·ping** *n*

double down *vb* : to become more tenacious, zealous, or resolute

dou·ble en·ten·dre \ˌdüb²l-än-ˈtänd, ˌdə-bəl-, -ˈtänd-r²\ *n, pl* **double entendres** *same or* -ˈtän-drəz\ : a word or expression capable of two interpretations with one usu. risqué

dou·ble·head·er \ˌdə-bəl-ˈhe-dər\ *n* : two games played consecutively on the same day

double helix *n* : a helix or spiral consisting of two strands (as of DNA) in the surface of a cylinder which coil around its axis

dou·ble–hung \ˌdə-bəl-ˈhəŋ\ *adj, of a window* : having an upper and a lower sash that can slide past each other

dou·ble–joint·ed \-ˈjȯin-təd\ *adj* : having a joint that permits an exceptional degree of freedom of motion of the parts joined ⟨a ∼ finger⟩

dou·ble–park \ˌdə-bəl-ˈpärk\ *vb* : to park a vehicle beside a row of vehicles already parked parallel to the curb

double play *n* : a play in baseball by which two players are put out

double pneumonia *n* : pneumonia affecting both lungs

double standard *n* : a set of principles that applies differently and usu. more rigorously to one group of people or circumstances than to another

dou·blet \ˈdə-blət\ *n* **1** : a man's close-fitting jacket worn in Europe esp. in the 16th century **2** : one of two similar or identical things

dou·ble take \ˈdə-bəl-ˌtāk\ *n* : a delayed reaction to a surprising or significant situation after an initial failure to notice anything unusual

dou·ble–talk \-ˌtȯk\ *n* ♦ : language that appears to be meaningful but in fact is a mixture of sense and nonsense

   ♦ babble, bunk, claptrap, drivel, fudge, gabble, gibberish, gobbledygook, hogwash, jabber, jabberwocky, jazz, moonshine, mumbo jumbo, nonsense, piffle, prattle

double up *vb* : to share accommodations designed for one

double whammy *n* : a combination of two usu. adverse forces, circumstances, or effects

dou·bloon \ˌdə-ˈblün\ *n* : a former gold coin of Spain and Spanish America

dou·bly \ˈdə-blē\ *adv* **1** : in a twofold manner **2** : to twice the degree

¹**doubt** \ˈdau̇t\ *vb* **1** : to be uncertain about **2** ♦ : to lack confidence in : DISTRUST **3** : to consider unlikely

   ♦ distrust, mistrust, question, suspect

²**doubt** *n* **1** : uncertainty of belief or opinion **2** : a condition causing uncertainty, hesitation, or suspense ⟨the outcome was in ∼⟩ **3** ♦ : a lack of confidence : DISTRUST **4** : an inclination not to believe or accept

   ♦ distrust, incertitude, misgiving, mistrust, skepticism, suspicion, uncertainty *Ant* assurance, belief, certainty, certitude, confidence, conviction, sureness, surety, trust

doubt·able \ˈdau̇t-ə-bəl\ *adj* : capable of being doubted : QUESTIONABLE

doubt·er \ˈdau̇-tər\ *n* ♦ : one that doubts

   ♦ disbeliever, questioner, skeptic, unbeliever

doubt·ful \ˈdau̇t-fəl\ *adj* **1** ♦ : giving rise to doubt : open to question **2 a** : lacking a definite opinion, conviction, or determination **b** : uncertain in outcome ⟨company's future is ∼⟩ **3** ♦ : marked by qualities that raise doubts about worth, honesty, or validity — **doubt·ful·ness** *n*

   ♦ [1, 3] debatable, disputable, dubious, equivocal, fishy, problematic, questionable, shady, shaky, suspect, suspicious *Ant* certain, incontestable, indisputable, indubitable, sure, undeniable, undoubted, unquestionable ♦ [3] distrustful, dubious, mistrustful, skeptical, suspicious, uncertain, undecided, unsettled, unsure *Ant* certain, convinced, positive, sure

doubt·ful·ly \-fə-lē\ *adv* : in a doubtful manner

¹**doubt·less** \ˈdau̇t-ləs\ *adv* **1** ♦ : without doubt **2** : without much doubt : PROBABLY

   ♦ certainly, definitely, incontestably, indeed, indisputably, really, surely, truly, undeniably, undoubtedly, unquestionably

²**doubtless** *adj* ♦ : free from doubt : CERTAIN — **doubt·less·ly** *adv*

   ♦ assured, certain, clear, cocksure, confident, positive, sanguine, sure

douche \ˈdüsh\ *n* **1** : a jet of fluid (as water) directed against a part or into a cavity of the body; *also* : a cleansing with a douche **2** : a device for giving douches — **douche** *vb*

dough \ˈdō\ *n* **1** : a mixture that consists of flour or meal and a liquid (as milk or water) and is stiff enough to knead or roll **2** : something resembling dough esp. in consistency **3** ♦ : something generally accepted as a medium of exchange, a measure of value, or a means of payment : MONEY — **dough·y** \ˈdō-ē\ *adj*

   ♦ cash, currency, lucre, money, pelf, tender

dough·boy \-ˌbȯi\ *n* : an American infantryman esp. in World War I

dough·nut *also* **do·nut** \-(ˌ)nət\ *n* : a small usu. ring-shaped cake fried in fat

dough·ty \ˈdau̇-tē\ *adj* **dough·ti·er; -est** ♦ : marked by fearless resolution : VALIANT

   ♦ brave, courageous, dauntless, fearless, gallant, greathearted, heroic, intrepid, lionhearted, manful, stalwart, stout, undaunted, valiant, valorous

Doug·las fir \ˈdə-gləs-\ *n* : a tall evergreen timber tree of the western U.S.

dou·la \ˈdü-lə\ *n* : a person trained to provide assistance to a mother before, during, and just after childbirth

do up *vb* **1** : to prepare (as by cleaning) for use **2** : to wrap up **3** : CLOTHE, DECORATE **4** : FASTEN

dour \ˈdau̇(-ə)r, ˈdu̇r\ *adj* **1** ♦ : marked by harsh sternness or severity **2** : OBSTINATE **3** : SULLEN — **dour·ly** *adv*

   ♦ austere, fierce, flinty, forbidding, grim, gruff, rough, rugged, severe, stark, steely, stern

douse \ˈdau̇s, ˈdau̇z\ *vb* **doused; dous·ing** **1** ♦ : to plunge into water **2** ♦ : to throw a liquid on : DRENCH **3** ♦ : to cause to cease burning : EXTINGUISH

   ♦ [1] dip, duck, dunk, immerse, souse, submerge ♦ [2] bathe, drench, soak, sop, souse, water, wet ♦ [3] extinguish, put out, quench, snuff

¹**dove** \ˈdəv\ *n* **1** : any of numerous pigeons; *esp* : a small wild pigeon **2** : an advocate of peace or of a peaceful policy **3** ♦ : a gentle woman or child — **dov·ish** \ˈdə-vish\ *adj*

   ♦ angel, innocent, lamb, sheep

²**dove** \ˈdōv\ *past of* DIVE

¹**dove·tail** \ˈdəv-ˌtāl\ *n* : something that resembles a dove's tail; *esp* : a flaring tenon and a mortise into which it fits tightly

²**dovetail** *vb* **1** : to join by means of dovetails **2** ♦ : to fit skillfully together to form a whole ⟨our plans ∼ nicely⟩

   ♦ accord, agree, answer, check, coincide, comport, conform, correspond, fit, go, harmonize, jibe, square, tally

dow·a·ger \ˈdau̇-i-jər\ *n* **1** : a widow owning property or a title from her deceased husband **2** ♦ : a dignified elderly woman

   ♦ dame, matriarch, matron

dowdy \ˈdau̇-dē\ *adj* **dowd·i·er; -est** **1** ♦ : lacking neatness and charm : UNTIDY **2** ♦ : lacking smartness or taste

   ♦ [1] frowsy, sloppy, slovenly, unkempt, untidy ♦ [2] inelegant, tacky, tasteless, trashy, unfashionable, unstylish

dow·el \ˈdau̇(-ə)l\ *n* **1** : a pin used for fastening together two pieces of wood **2** : a round rod (as of wood) — **dowel** *vb*

¹**dow·er** \ˈdau̇(-ə)r\ *n* **1** : the part of a deceased husband's real estate which the law gives for life to his widow **2** : DOWRY

²**dower** *vb* : to supply with a dower or dowry : ENDOW

dow·itch·er \ˈdau̇-i-chər\ *n* : any of several long-billed wading birds related to the sandpipers

¹**down** \ˈdau̇n\ *adv* **1** ♦ : toward or in a lower physical position **2** : to a lying or sitting position **3** : toward or to the ground, floor, or bottom **4** : as a down payment ⟨paid $5 ∼⟩ **5** : on paper ⟨put ∼ what he says⟩ **6** : in a direction that is the opposite of up **7** : SOUTH **8** : to or in a lower or worse condition or status **9** : from a past time **10** : to or in a state of less activity **11** : into defeat ⟨voted the motion ∼⟩

   ♦ below, downward, over *Ant* up, upward, upwardly

²**down** *prep* : down in, on, along, or through : toward the bottom of

³**down** *vb* **1** ♦ : to go or cause to go or come down **2** : DEFEAT **3** : to cause (a football) to be out of play

   ♦ bowl, drop, fell, floor, knock, level

⁴down *adj* **1 :** occupying a low position; *esp* **:** lying on the ground **2 ♦ :** directed or going downward **3 :** being in a state of reduced or low activity **4 :** low in spirits : DEJECTED **5 ♦ :** affected with disease or ill health : SICK ⟨∼ with a cold⟩ **6 :** arrived at or brought to an end : DONE **7 :** completely mastered ⟨got her lines ∼⟩ **8 :** being on record ⟨you're ∼ for two tickets⟩

♦ [2] downcast, downward ♦ [5] bad, ill, indisposed, peaked, punk, sick, unhealthy, unsound, unwell

⁵down *n* **1 ♦ :** a low or falling period (as in activity, emotional life, or fortunes) **2 :** one of a series of attempts to advance a football **3 :** an instance of putting down **4 :** a quark with a charge of -¹/₃ that is one of the constituents of the proton and neutron

♦ comedown, decline, descent, downfall, fall

⁶down *n* ♦ **:** a rolling usu. treeless upland with sparse soil — usu. used in pl.

♦ *usu* **downs** grassland, plain, prairie, savanna, steppe, veld

⁷down *n* **1 :** a covering of soft fluffy feathers; *also* **:** such feathers **2 ♦ :** a downlike covering or material

♦ floss, fluff, fur, fuzz, lint, nap, pile

down·beat \'daún-,bēt\ *n* **:** the downward stroke of a conductor indicating the principally accented note of a measure of music
down·burst \-,bərst\ *n* **:** a powerful downdraft esp. associated with a thunderstorm that is a hazard for low-flying aircraft; *also* **:** MICROBURST
down·cast \-,kast\ *adj* **1 :** low on spirit : DEJECTED **2 ♦ :** directed down ⟨a ∼ glance⟩

♦ down, downward

down·draft \-,draft\ *n* **:** a downward current of gas (as air)
down·er \'daú-nər\ *n* **1 :** a depressant drug; *esp* **:** BARBITURATE **2 :** someone or something depressing
down·fall \'daún-,fól\ *n* **1 ♦ :** a sudden fall (as from high rank) **2 :** something that causes a downfall — **down·fall·en** \-,fó-lən\ *adj*

♦ comedown, decline, descent, down, fall

¹down·grade \'daún-,grād\ *n* **1 :** a downward slope (as of a road) **2 :** a decline toward a worse condition
²downgrade *vb* ♦ **:** to lower in quality, value, extent, or status

♦ break, bust, degrade, demote, reduce

down·heart·ed \-'här-təd\ *adj* **:** low in spirit : DEJECTED
¹down·hill \'daún-'hil\ *adv* **:** toward the bottom of a hill — **down·hill** \-,hil\ *adj*
²down·hill \-,hil\ *n* **:** the sport of skiing downhill usu. in a race against time
¹down·load \'daún-,lōd\ *n* **:** an act or instance of downloading something; *also* **:** the item downloaded
²download *vb* **:** to transfer (data) from a computer to another device — **down·load·able** \-,lō-də-bəl\ *adj*
down payment *n* **:** a part of the full price paid at the time of purchase or delivery with the balance to be paid later
down·play \'daún-,plā\ *vb* **:** DE-EMPHASIZE ⟨∼ed the allegations⟩
down·pour \'daún-,pōr\ *n* ♦ **:** a heavy rain

♦ cloudburst, deluge, rain, rainstorm, storm, wet

down·range \-'rānj\ *adv* **:** away from a launching site
¹down·right \-,rīt\ *adv* **:** THOROUGHLY
²downright *adj* **1 :** being completely or exactly what is stated : ABSOLUTE ⟨a ∼ lie⟩ **2 :** abrupt in speech or manner : BLUNT ⟨a ∼ man⟩
down·shift \-,shift\ *vb* **:** to shift an automotive vehicle into a lower gear
down·size \-,sīz\ *vb* ♦ **:** to reduce or undergo reduction in size or numbers

♦ abate, decrease, de-escalate, diminish, dwindle, lessen, lower, reduce

down·spout \-,spaút\ *n* **:** a vertical pipe used to drain rainwater from a roof
Down's syndrome \'daúnz-\ *or* **Down syndrome** \'daún-\ *n* **:** a congenital condition characterized esp. by developmental delays, impairment of cognitive functioning, upward slanting eyes, a flattened nasal bridge, broad hands with short fingers, decreased muscle tone, and the presence of an extra chromosome
down·stage \'daún-'stāj\ *adv or adj* **:** toward or at the front of a theatrical stage
down·stairs \-'starz\ *adv* **:** on or to a lower floor and esp. the main or ground floor — **down·stairs** \-,starz\ *adj or n*

down·stream \-'strēm\ *adv or adj* **:** in the direction of flow of a stream
down·stroke \-,strōk\ *n* **:** a downward stroke
down·swing \-,swing\ *n* **1 :** a swing downward **2 :** DOWNTURN
down—to—earth *adj* ♦ **:** having or showing concern for fact or reality and rejection of the impractical and visionary

♦ earthy, hardheaded, matter-of-fact, practical, pragmatic, realistic

down·town \'daún-,taún\ *n* **:** the main business district of a town or city — **downtown** \'daún-'taún\ *adj or adv*
down·trod·den \'daún-'trä-dᵊn\ *adj* **:** suffering oppression
down·turn \-,tərn\ *n* **:** a downward turn esp. in economic activity
¹down·ward \'daún-wərd\ *or* **down·wards** \-wərdz\ *adv* **1 ♦ :** from a higher to a lower place or condition **2 :** from an earlier time **3 :** from an ancestor or predecessor

♦ below, down, over

²downward *adj* ♦ **:** directed toward or situated in a lower place or condition

♦ down, downcast

down·wind \'daún-'wind\ *adv or adj* **:** in the direction that the wind is blowing
downy \'daú-nē\ *adj* **down·i·er; -est** ♦ **:** resembling or covered with down

♦ cottony, satiny, silken, soft, velvety

downy mildew *n* **:** any of various parasitic fungi producing whitish masses esp. on the underside of plant leaves; *also* **:** a plant disease caused by downy mildew
downy woodpecker *n* **:** a small black-and-white woodpecker of No. America
dow·ry \'daú-rē\ *n, pl* **dowries :** the property that a woman brings to her husband in marriage
dowse \'daúz\ *vb* **dowsed; dows·ing :** to use a divining rod esp. to find water — **dows·er** *n*
dox·ol·o·gy \däk-'sä-lə-jē\ *n, pl* **-gies :** a usu. short hymn of praise to God
doy·en \'dói-ən, 'dwä-,yaⁿ\ *n* **:** the senior or most experienced person in a group
doy·enne \dói-'yen, dwä-'yen\ *n* **:** a woman who is a doyen
doy·ley *chiefly Brit var of* DOILY
doz *abbr* dozen
¹doze \'dōz\ *vb* **dozed; doz·ing** ♦ **:** to sleep lightly

♦ catnap, drowse, nap, slumber, snooze

²doze *n* ♦ **:** a light sleep

♦ catnap, drowse, forty winks, nap, siesta, snooze, wink

doz·en \'də-zᵊn\ *n, pl* **dozens** *or* **dozen :** a group of twelve — **doz·enth** \-zᵊnth\ *adj*
¹DP \,dē-'pē\ *n, pl* **DP's** *or* **DPs 1 :** a displaced person **2 :** DOUBLE PLAY
²DP *abbr* data processing
dpt *abbr* department
DPT *abbr* diphtheria-pertussis-tetanus (vaccines)
dr *abbr* **1** debtor **2** dram **3** drive **4** drum
Dr *abbr* doctor
DR *abbr* **1** dead reckoning **2** dining room
drab \'drab\ *adj* **drab·ber; drab·best 1 :** being of a light olive-brown color **2 ♦ :** characterized by dullness and monotony — **drab·ly** *adv* — **drab·ness** *n*

♦ dreary, dry, dull, monotonous, uninteresting

dra·co·ni·an \drā-'kō-nē-ən, drə-\ *adj, often cap* **:** CRUEL; *also* **:** SEVERE
¹draft \'draft, 'dráft\ *n* **1 :** the act of drawing or hauling **2 a :** the act or an instance of drinking or inhaling **b ♦ :** the portion drunk or inhaled in one such act **3 :** DOSE, POTION **4 :** DELINEATION, PLAN, DESIGN; *also* **:** a preliminary sketch, outline, or version ⟨a rough ∼ of a speech⟩ **5 :** the act of drawing (as from a cask); *also* **:** a portion of liquid so drawn **6 :** the depth of water a ship draws esp. when loaded **7 :** a system for or act of selecting persons (as for compulsory military service or sports teams); *also* **:** the persons so selected **8 :** an order for the payment of money drawn by one person or bank on another **9 :** a heavy demand : STRAIN **10 :** a current of air; *also* **:** a device to regulate air supply (as in a stove) — **on draft :** ready to be drawn from a receptacle ⟨beer *on draft*⟩

♦ drag, drink, nip, quaff, shot, slug, snort, swallow, swig

²draft *adj* **1 :** used or adapted for drawing loads ⟨∼ horses⟩ **2 :** being or having been on draft ⟨∼ beer⟩
³draft *vb* **1 :** to select usu. on a compulsory basis; *esp* **:** to conscript

for military service **2** : to draw the preliminary sketch, version, or plan of **3** ♦ : to put into written form : COMPOSE **4** : to draw off or away — **draft·ee** \draf-'tē, dráf-\ *n*

♦ cast, compose, craft, draw, formulate, frame, prepare

draft·ee \draf-'tē, 'dráf-\ *n* : a person who is drafted
drafts·man \'draft-smən, 'dráft-\ : a person who draws plans (as for buildings or machinery)
drafty \'draf-tē, 'dráf-\ *adj* **draft·i·er; -est** : exposed to or abounding in drafts of air
¹**drag** \'drag\ *n* **1** : a device pulled along under water for detecting or gathering **2** : something (as a harrow or sledge) that is dragged along over a surface **3 a** : the act or an instance of dragging **b** : a draft of liquid **4** ♦ : something that hinders progress; *also* : something boring **5** : an open way for vehicles, persons, and animals : STREET ⟨the main ∼⟩ **6** : clothing typical of one sex worn by a member of the opposite sex

♦ bar, block, clog, crimp, embarrassment, hindrance, let, obstacle, stop, stumbling block

²**drag** *vb* **dragged; drag·ging** **1** ♦ : to draw slowly or heavily : HAUL **2** ♦ : to move with painful or undue slowness or difficulty **3** : to force into or out of some situation, condition, or course of action **4** : PROTRACT ⟨∼ a story out⟩ **5** : to hang or lag behind **6** : to explore, search, or fish with a drag **7** : to trail along on the ground **8** : DRAW, PUFF ⟨∼ on a cigarette⟩ **9** : to move (items on a computer screen) esp. by using a mouse — **drag·ger** *n* — **drag one's feet** *also* **drag one's heels** : to act slowly or with hesitation

♦ [1] draw, hale, haul, lug, pull, tow, tug ♦ [2] crawl, creep, dally, dawdle, delay, dillydally, lag, linger, loiter, poke, tarry

drag·net \-ˌnet\ *n* **1** : NET, TRAWL **2** : a network of planned actions for pursuing and catching ⟨a police ∼⟩
drag·o·man \'dra-gə-mən\ *n, pl* **-mans** *or* **-men** \-mən\ : an interpreter employed esp. in the Near East
drag·on \'dra-gən\ *n* : a fabulous animal usu. represented as a huge winged scaly serpent with a crested head and large claws
drag·on·fly \-ˌflī\ *n* : any of a group of large harmless 4-winged insects that hold the wings horizontal and unfolded in repose
¹**dra·goon** \drə-'gün, dra-\ *n* : a heavily armed mounted soldier
²**dragoon** *vb* : to force or attempt to force into submission : COERCE
drag race *n* : an acceleration contest between vehicles — **drag racer** *n*
drag·ster \'drag-stər\ *n* : a usu. high-powered vehicle used in a drag race
drag strip *n* : a site for drag races
¹**drain** \'drān\ *vb* **1** : to draw off or flow off gradually or completely **2** ♦ : to exhaust physically or emotionally **3** : to make or become gradually dry or empty **4** ♦ : to carry away the surface water : discharge surface or surplus water **5** ♦ : to deplete or empty by or as if by drawing off by degrees or in increments : EXHAUST — **drain·er** *n*

♦ [2] burn out, do in, exhaust, fag, fatigue, tire, tucker, wash out, wear, wear out, weary ♦ [4] bleed, draw off, pump, siphon, tap *Ant* fill ♦ [5] clean, consume, deplete, exhaust, expend, spend, use up

²**drain** *n* **1** : a means (as a channel or sewer) of draining **2** : the act of draining **3** : a gradual outflow; *also* : something causing an outflow ⟨a ∼ on our savings⟩
drain·age \'drā-nij\ *n* **1** : the act or process of draining; *also* : something that is drained off **2** : a means for draining : DRAIN, SEWER **3** : an area drained
drained *adj* ♦ : exhausted physically or emotionally

♦ beat, bushed, dead, effete, jaded, limp, prostrate, spent, tired, weary, worn-out

drain·pipe \'drān-ˌpīp\ *n* : a pipe for drainage
drake \'drāk\ *n* : a male duck
dram \'dram\ *n* **1** : a unit of measure equal to ¹/₁₆ ounce **2** : FLUID DRAM **3** : a small drink
dra·ma \'drä-mə, 'dra-\ *n* **1 a** : a literary composition designed for theatrical presentation **b** : a play, movie, or television production with a serious tone or subject **2** : dramatic art, literature, or affairs **3** : a series of events involving conflicting forces — **dra·ma·tist** \'drä-mə-tist, 'drä-\ *n*
dra·mat·ic \drə-'ma-tik\ *adj* **1** : of or relating to the drama **2 a** ♦ : suitable to or characteristic of the drama **b** ♦ : striking in appearance or effect — **dra·mat·i·cal·ly** \-ti-k(ə-)lē\ *adv*

♦ [2a] histrionic, melodramatic, theatrical ♦ [2b] catchy, conspicuous, flamboyant, showy, striking

dram·a·ti·sa·tion, dram·a·tise *Brit var of* DRAMATIZATION, DRAMATIZE

dra·ma·tize \'dra-mə-ˌtīz, 'drä-\ *vb* **-tized; -tiz·ing** **1** : to adapt for or be suitable for theatrical presentation **2** : to present or represent in a dramatic manner — **dram·a·ti·za·tion** \ˌdra-mə-tə-'zā-shən, ˌdrä-\ *n*
dra·me·dy \'drä-mə-dē, 'dra-\ *n* : a comedy having dramatic moments
drank *past and past part of* DRINK
¹**drape** \'drāp\ *vb* **draped; drap·ing** **1** : to cover or adorn with or as if with folds of cloth **2** : to cause to hang or stretch out loosely or carelessly **3** : to arrange or become arranged in flowing lines or folds
²**drape** *n* **1** : CURTAIN **2** : arrangement in or of folds **3** : the cut or hang of clothing
drap·er \'drā-pər\ *n, chiefly Brit* : a dealer in cloth and sometimes in clothing and dry goods
drap·ery \'drā-pə-rē\ *n, pl* **-er·ies** **1** *Brit* : DRY GOODS **2** : a decorative fabric when hung loosely and in folds; *also* : hangings of heavy fabric used as a curtain
dras·tic \'dras-tik\ *adj* : HARSH, RIGOROUS, SEVERE ⟨∼ punishment⟩ — **dras·ti·cal·ly** \-ti-k(ə-)lē\ *adv*
draught \'draft\, **draughty** \'dráf-tē\ *chiefly Brit var of* DRAFT, DRAFTY
draughts \'dráfts\ *n, Brit* : CHECKERS
¹**draw** \'drȯ\ *vb* **drew** \'drü\; **drawn** \'drȯn\; **draw·ing** **1** ♦ : to cause to move toward a force exerted **2** : to cause to go in a certain direction ⟨*drew* him aside⟩ **3** : to move or go steadily or gradually ⟨∼ near⟩ **4** : ATTRACT, ENTICE **5** : PROVOKE, ROUSE ⟨*drew* enemy fire⟩ **6** : INHALE ⟨∼ a deep breath⟩ **7** : to bring or pull out ⟨*drew* a gun⟩ **8** : to cause to come out of a container ⟨∼ water for a bath⟩ **9** : to take out the entrails of : EVISCERATE **10** : to require (a specified depth) to float in **11** : ACCUMULATE, GAIN ⟨∼*ing* interest⟩ **12** : to take money from a place of deposit : WITHDRAW **13** ♦ : to receive regularly ⟨∼ a salary⟩ **14** : to take (cards) from a stack or the dealer **15** : to receive or take at random ⟨∼ a winning number⟩ **16** : to bend (a bow) by pulling back the string **17** : WRINKLE, SHRINK **18** : to change shape by or as if by pulling or stretching ⟨a face *drawn* with sorrow⟩ **19** : to leave (a contest) undecided : TIE **20** ♦ : to give a portrayal of : DELINEATE **21** : to write out in due form : DRAFT ⟨∼ up a will⟩ **22** : FORMULATE ⟨∼ comparisons⟩ **23** : INFER ⟨∼ a conclusion⟩ **24** : to spread or elongate (metal) by hammering or by pulling through dies **25** : to produce or allow a draft or current of air ⟨the chimney ∼s well⟩ **26** : to swell out in a wind ⟨all sails ∼*ing*⟩ — **draw the line** *or* **draw a line** : to fix an arbitrary boundary usu. between two things

♦ [1] drag, hale, haul, lug, pull, tow, tug ♦ [13] acquire, attain, capture, carry, earn, gain, garner, get, land, make, obtain, procure, realize, secure, win ♦ [20] delineate, depict, describe, image, paint, picture, portray, sketch

²**draw** *n* **1** ♦ : the act, process, or result of drawing **2** : a lot or chance drawn at random **3** ♦ : a contest left undecided or deadlocked : TIE **4** ♦ : one that draws attention or patronage

♦ [1] haul, jerk, pluck, pull, tug, wrench ♦ [3] dead heat, stalemate, standoff, tie ♦ [4] attraction, lodestone, magnet

draw·back \'drȯ-ˌbak\ *n* ♦ : an unfavorable, inferior, or prejudicial condition : DISADVANTAGE

♦ disadvantage, handicap, liability, minus, penalty, strike

draw·bridge \-ˌbrij\ *n* : a bridge made to be raised, lowered, or turned to permit or deny passage
draw·er \'drȯr, 'drȯ-ər\ *n* **1** : one that draws **2** *pl* : an undergarment for the lower part of the body **3** : a sliding boxlike compartment (as in a table or desk)
draw·ing \'drȯ-iŋ\ *n* **1** : an act or instance of drawing; *esp* : an occasion when something is decided by drawing lots ⟨tonight's lottery ∼⟩ **2** : the act or art of making a figure, plan, or sketch by means of lines **3** ♦ : a representation made by drawing : SKETCH

♦ cartoon, delineation, sketch

drawing card *n* : DRAW 4
drawing room *n* : a formal reception room
drawl \'drȯl\ *vb* : to speak or utter slowly with vowels greatly prolonged — **drawl** *n*
draw off *vb* ♦ : to remove esp. from an environment or container

♦ bleed, drain, pump, siphon, tap

draw on *vb* : to draw nearer : APPROACH ⟨night *draws on*⟩
draw out *vb* **1** ♦ : to extend beyond a minimum in time : PROLONG **2** : to cause to speak freely

♦ elongate, extend, lengthen, prolong, protract, stretch

draw·string \'drò-ˌstriŋ\ *n* : a string, cord, or tape for use in closing a bag or controlling fullness in garments or curtains

draw up *vb* **1** ♦ : to prepare a draft or version of **2** : to pull oneself erect **3** ♦ : to bring or come to a stop **4** ♦ : to bring (as troops) into array

♦ [1] cast, compose, craft, draft, formulate, frame, prepare ♦ [3] arrest, catch, check, fetch up, halt, hold up, stall, stay, still, stop ♦ [4] arrange, array, classify, codify, dispose, marshal, order, organize, range, systematize

dray \'drā\ *n* : a strong low cart for carrying heavy loads

¹dread \'dred\ *vb* **1** : to fear greatly **2** : to feel extreme reluctance to meet or face

²dread *n* ♦ : great fear esp. of some harm to come

♦ alarm, anxiety, apprehension, fear, fright, horror, panic, terror, trepidation

³dread *adj* **1** : causing great fear or anxiety ⟨a ∼ disease⟩ **2** : inspiring awe

dread·ful \'dred-fəl\ *adj* **1** ♦ : inspiring dread or awe : FRIGHTENING **2** ♦ : extremely distasteful, unpleasant, or shocking ⟨a ∼ accident⟩ — **dread·ful·ly** *adv*

♦ [1] dire, fearful, fearsome, forbidding, formidable, frightful, hair-raising, horrible, redoubtable, scary, shocking, terrible, terrifying ♦ [2] appalling, atrocious, awful, frightful, ghastly, grisly, gruesome, hideous, horrible, horrid, lurid, macabre, monstrous, nightmarish, shocking, terrible

dread·locks \'dred-ˌläks\ *n pl* : long braids of hair over the entire head

dread·nought \'dred-ˌnòt\ *n* : BATTLESHIP

¹dream \'drēm\ *n* **1** : a series of thoughts, images, or emotions occurring during sleep **2** ♦ : a dreamlike vision **3** ♦ : something notable for its beauty, excellence, or enjoyable quality **4 a** ♦ : a strongly desired goal or purpose **b** : IDEAL — **dream·like** \-ˌlīk\ *adj*

♦ [2] chimera, conceit, daydream, delusion, fancy, fantasy, figment, hallucination, illusion, phantasm, pipe dream, unreality, vision ♦ [3] beauty, enchantress, fox, goddess, knockout, queen ♦ [4a] aim, ambition, aspiration, design, end, goal, intent, mark, meaning, object, objective, plan, pretension, purpose, thing

²dream \'drēm\ *vb* **dreamed** \'dremt, 'drēmd\ *or* **dreamt** \'dremt\; **dream·ing** **1** : to have a dream of **2** : to indulge in daydreams or fantasies : pass (time) in reverie or inaction **3** ♦ : to consider as a possibility : IMAGINE

♦ conceive, envisage, fancy, imagine, picture, vision, visualize

dream·boat \'drēm-ˌbōt\ *n, slang* : something highly desirable; *esp* : a very attractive person

dream·er \'drē-mər\ *n* **1** : one that dreams **2** ♦ : one who lives in a world of fancy and imagination **3** ♦ : one who has ideas or conceives projects regarded as impractical

♦ idealist, romantic, utopian, visionary

dream·land \'drēm-ˌland\ *n* : an unreal delightful country that exists in imagination or in dreams

dream up *vb* : INVENT, CONCOCT

dream·world \-ˌwərld\ *n* : a world of illusion or fantasy

dreamy \'drē-mē\ *adj* ♦ : quiet and soothing; *also* : pleasant

♦ comforting, narcotic, sedative, soothing ♦ agreeable, congenial, delectable, delicious, delightful, felicitous, good, grateful, gratifying, nice, palatable, pleasant, pleasurable, satisfying

drear \'drir\ *adj* : DREARY

drear·y \'drir-ē\ *adj* **drea·ri·er; -est** **1** : feeling, displaying, or reflecting listlessness or discouragement **2** ♦ : having nothing likely to provide cheer, comfort, or interest — **drea·ri·ly** \-ə-lē\ *adv*

♦ bleak, dark, dismal, gloomy, gray (*or* grey), somber (*or* sombre), wretched

¹dredge \'drej\ *vb* **dredged; dredg·ing** ♦ : to gather or search with or as if with a dredge; *esp* : to bring to light or gather by deep searching — often used with *up* — **dredg·er** *n*

♦ dig, hunt, rake, ransack, rifle, rummage, scour, search ♦ *often* **dredge up** detect, determine, dig up, discover, ferret out, find, hit on, locate, track down

²dredge *n* : a machine or barge for removing earth or silt

³dredge *vb* **dredged; dredg·ing** : to coat (food) by sprinkling (as with flour)

dregs \'dregz\ *n pl* **1** ♦ : the matter that settles to the bottom of a liquid : SEDIMENT **2** : the most undesirable part ⟨the ∼ of humanity⟩

♦ deposit, grounds, lees, precipitate, sediment

drench \'drench\ *vb* ♦ : to wet thoroughly

♦ bathe, douse, soak, sop, souse, wash, water, wet

¹dress \'dres\ *vb* **1** : to make or set straight : ALIGN **2** : to prepare for use; *esp* : BUTCHER **3** ♦ : to add decorative details or accessories to : EMBELLISH ⟨∼ a store window⟩ **4** ♦ : to put clothes on : CLOTHE; *also* : to put on or wear formal or fancy clothes **5** : to apply dressings or medicine to **6** : to arrange (the hair) by combing, brushing, or curling **7** : to apply fertilizer to **8** ♦ : to put through a finishing process : SMOOTH ⟨∼ leather⟩

♦ [3] adorn, array, beautify, bedeck, deck, decorate, do, embellish, enrich, garnish, grace, ornament, trim ♦ [4] apparel, array, attire, caparison, clothe, deck, garb, invest, rig, suit ♦ [8] buff, burnish, gloss, grind, polish, rub, shine, smooth

²dress *n* **1** ♦ : personal attire : CLOTHING **2** ♦ : a garment usu. consisting of a one-piece bodice and skirt **3** ♦ : covering, adornment, or appearance appropriate or peculiar to a particular time — **dress·mak·er** \-ˌmā-kər\ *n* — **dress·mak·ing** \-ˌmā-kiŋ\ *n*

♦ [1] apparel, attire, clothing, duds, raiment, wear ♦ [3] garb, getup, guise, outfit

³dress *adj* : suitable for a formal occasion; *also* : requiring formal dress

dres·sage \drə-'säzh\ *n* : the execution by a trained horse of complex movements in response to barely perceptible signals from its rider

dress down *vb* ♦ : to scold severely

♦ admonish, chide, lecture, rail (at *or* against), rate, rebuke, reprimand, scold

¹dress·er \'dre-sər\ *n* : a chest of drawers or bureau with a mirror

²dresser *n* : one that dresses

dress·ing \'dre-siŋ\ *n* **1** : the act or process of one who dresses **2** : a sauce for adding to a dish (as a salad) **3** : a seasoned mixture usu. used as stuffing **4** : material used to cover an injury

dressing gown *n* : a loose robe worn esp. while dressing or resting

dress rehearsal *n* : a full rehearsal of a play or other show done with all its costumes, scenery, lighting, etc., shortly before the first performance

dress up *vb* **1** : to change the customary dress or appearance of **2** ♦ : furnish with a false appearance

♦ camouflage, cloak, disguise, mask

dressy \'dre-sē\ *adj* **dress·i·er; -est** **1** : showy in dress **2** : STYLISH, SMART

drew *past of* DRAW

¹drib·ble \'dri-bəl\ *vb* **drib·bled; drib·bling** **1** ♦ : to fall or flow in drops : TRICKLE **2** ♦ : to let saliva trickle from the corner of the mouth : DROOL **3** : to propel by successive slight taps or bounces

♦ [1] gurgle, lap, plash, ripple, slosh, splash, trickle, wash ♦ [2] drivel, drool, salivate, slaver, slobber

²dribble *n* **1** : a small trickling stream or flow **2** : a drizzling shower **3** : the dribbling of a ball or puck

drib·let \'dri-blət\ *n* **1** : a trifling amount **2** ♦ : a drop of liquid

♦ blob, drip, drop, droplet, glob

dri·er *or* **dry·er** \'drī-ər\ *n* **1** : a substance that speeds drying (as of paint or ink) **2** *usu* **dryer** : a device for drying

¹drift \'drift\ *n* **1** ♦ : the motion or course of something drifting; *also* : a gradual shift of position **2** ♦ : a mass of matter (as snow or sand) piled up by wind **3** : earth, gravel, and rock deposited by a glacier **4** ♦ : a general underlying design or tendency : MEANING ⟨if you catch my ∼⟩

♦ [1] current, leaning, run, tendency, tide, trend, wind ♦ [2] bank, bar, mound ♦ [4] denotation, import, intent, meaning, purport, sense, significance, signification

²drift *vb* **1** ♦ : to float or be driven along by or as if by a current of water or air; *also* : to move along smoothly as if drifting on a current of water or air **2** : to become piled up by wind or water

♦ float, glide, hang, hover, poise, ride, sail, waft

drift·er \'drif-tər\ *n* ♦ : a person without aim, ambition, or initiative

♦ nomad, rambler, rover, stroller, vagabond, wanderer

drift net *n* : a fishing net often miles in extent arranged to drift with the tide or current

drift·wood \'drift-ˌwùd\ *n* : wood drifted or floated by water

¹drill \'dril\ *n* **1** : a tool for boring holes **2** : the training of soldiers in marching and the handling of arms **3** ♦ : a regularly practiced exercise

♦ exercise, practice, routine, training, workout

²drill vb **1 :** to instruct and exercise by repetition **2 :** to train in or practice military drill **3 ♦ :** to bore or drive a hole in **4 :** to shoot with or as if with a gun — **drill•er** n

♦ bore, hole, perforate, pierce, punch, puncture

³drill n **1 :** a shallow furrow or trench in which seed is sown **2 :** an agricultural implement for making furrows and dropping seed into them

⁴drill n **:** a firm cotton twilled fabric

drill•mas•ter \'dril-ˌmas-tər\ n **:** an instructor in military drill

drill press n **:** an upright drilling machine in which the drill is pressed to the work usu. by a hand lever

drily var of DRYLY

¹drink \'driŋk\ vb **drank** \'draŋk\; **drunk** \'drəŋk\ or **drank**; **drink•ing 1 ♦ :** to swallow liquid **:** IMBIBE **2 ♦ :** to take in or suck up **:** ABSORB **3 :** to take in through the senses ⟨∼ in the beautiful scenery⟩ **4 :** to give or join in a toast **5 :** to drink alcoholic beverages esp. to excess — **drink•able** adj — **drink•er** n

♦ [1] guzzle, imbibe, quaff, sup, swig, toss ♦ [2] absorb, imbibe, soak, sponge, suck

²drink n **1 a ♦ :** a liquid suitable for swallowing **:** BEVERAGE **b ♦ :** an alcoholic beverage **2 ♦ :** a draft or portion of liquid **3 :** excessive consumption of alcoholic beverages

♦ [1a] beverage, libation, quencher ♦ [1b] alcohol, booze, intoxicant, liquor, moonshine, spirits ♦ [2] draft, drag, nip, quaff, shot, slug, snort, swallow, swig

¹drip \'drip\ vb **dripped; drip•ping 1 :** to fall or let fall in drops **2 :** to let fall drops of moisture or liquid ⟨a dripping faucet⟩ **3 :** to overflow with or as if with moisture

²drip n **1 :** a falling in drops **2 ♦ :** liquid that falls, overflows, or is extruded in drops **3 :** the sound made by or as if by falling drops

♦ blob, driblet, drop, droplet, glob

¹drive \'drīv\ vb **drove** \'drōv\; **driv•en** \'dri-vən\; **driv•ing 1 ♦ :** to urge, push, or force onward **2 :** to carry through strongly ⟨∼ a bargain⟩ **3 ♦ :** to set or keep in motion or operation **4 :** to direct the movement or course of **5 :** to convey in a vehicle **6 :** to bring into a specified condition ⟨the noise ∼s me crazy⟩ **7 ♦ :** to exert inescapable or coercive pressure on **:** FORCE ⟨driven by hunger to steal⟩ **8 :** to project, inject, or impress forcefully ⟨drove the lesson home⟩ **9 :** to produce by opening a way ⟨∼ a well⟩ **10 :** to progress with strong momentum ⟨a driving rain⟩ **11 :** to propel an object of play (as a golf ball) by a hard blow — **driv•er** n

♦ [1] propel, push, shove, thrust ♦ [1] herd, punch, run ♦ [3] activate, actuate, crank, move, propel, run, set off, spark, start, touch off, trigger, turn on ♦ [7] coerce, compel, constrain, force, make, muscle, obligate, oblige, press, pressure

²drive n **1 :** a trip in a carriage or automobile **2 :** a driving or collecting of animals ⟨a cattle ∼⟩ **3 :** the guiding of logs downstream to a mill **4 :** the act of driving a ball; also **:** the flight of a ball **5 :** DRIVEWAY **6 :** a public road for driving (as in a park) **7 :** the state of being hurried and under pressure **8 ♦ :** a strong systematic group effort ⟨membership ∼⟩ **9 :** the apparatus by which motion is imparted to a machine **10 :** an offensive or aggressive move **:** a military attack **11 a ♦ :** an urgent, basic, or instinctual need **b ♦ :** an impelling culturally acquired concern, interest, or longing **12 ♦ :** dynamic quality **13 :** a device for reading and writing on magnetic media (as magnetic tape or disks)

♦ [8] bandwagon, campaign, cause, crusade, movement ♦ [11a, 11b] appetite, craving, desire, hankering, hunger, itch, longing, lust, passion, thirst, urge, yearning, yen ♦ [12] aggressiveness, ambition, enterprise, go, hustle, initiative

drive–in \'drī-ˌvin\ adj **:** accommodating patrons while they remain in their automobiles — **drive–in** n

¹driv•el \'dri-vəl\ vb **-eled** or **-elled; -el•ing** or **-el•ling 1 :** to let saliva dribble from the mouth **:** DROOL **2 ♦ :** to talk or utter stupidly, carelessly, or in an infantile way — **driv•el•er** n

♦ babble, chatter, gabble, gibber, jabber, prattle, sputter

²drivel n **♦ :** language, conduct, or an idea that is absurd or contrary to good sense **:** NONSENSE

♦ bunk, claptrap, fiddlesticks, folly, foolishness, fudge, hogwash, humbug, nonsense, piffle, rot, silliness, slush, stupidity, trash

drive•shaft \'drīv-ˌshaft\ n **:** a shaft that transmits mechanical power

drive–through also **drive–thru** \'drīv-ˌthrü\ adj **:** designed for

the service of patrons remaining in their automobiles — **drive–through** also **drive–thru** n

drive•way \-ˌwā\ n **:** a short private road leading from the street to a house, garage, or parking lot

¹driz•zle \'dri-zəl\ n **:** a fine misty rain

²drizzle vb **driz•zled; driz•zling :** to rain in very small drops

drogue \'drōg\ n **:** a small parachute for slowing down or stabilizing something (as a space capsule)

droid \'dróid\ n **:** ANDROID

droll \'drōl\ adj **♦ :** having a humorous, whimsical, or odd quality ⟨a ∼ expression⟩ — **droll•ery** \'drō-lə-rē\ n — **droll•ly** adv

♦ antic, comic, comical, farcical, funny, hilarious, humorous, hysterical, laughable, ludicrous, ridiculous, riotous, risible, screaming, uproarious

drom•e•dary \'drä-mə-ˌder-ē\ n, pl **-dar•ies :** CAMEL; esp **:** a domesticated one-humped camel of western Asia and northern Africa

drone \'drōn\ n **1 :** a male honeybee **2 :** one that lives on the labors of others **:** PARASITE **3 :** an uncrewed aircraft or ship guided by remote control **4 :** one whose work is menial or monotonous

²drone vb **droned; dron•ing ♦ :** to sound with a low dull monotonous murmuring sound; also **:** speak monotonously

♦ buzz, hum, whir, whish, whiz, zip, zoom

³drone n **♦ :** a deep monotonous sound

♦ buzz, hum, purr, whir, whiz, zoom

drool \'drül\ vb **1 ♦ :** to let liquid flow from the mouth **2 :** to talk foolishly

♦ dribble, drivel, salivate, slaver, slobber

¹droop \'drüp\ vb **1 ♦ :** to hang or incline downward **2 :** to sink gradually **3 ♦ :** to become depressed or weakened **:** LANGUISH

♦ [1] flag, hang, loll, sag, wilt ♦ [3] decay, fail, flag, go, lag, languish, sag, waste, weaken, wilt

²droop n **♦ :** the condition or appearance of drooping — **droopy** adj

♦ sag, slack, slackness

droopy \'drü-pē\ adj **1 :** low in spirits **2 ♦ :** drooping or tending to droop

♦ pendulous ♦ flaccid, floppy, lank, limp, slack, yielding

¹drop \'dräp\ n **1 ♦ :** the quantity of fluid that falls in one spherical mass **2** pl **:** a dose of medicine measured by drops **3 :** a small quantity of drink **4 :** the smallest practical unit of liquid measure **5 :** something (as a pendant or a small round candy) that resembles a liquid drop **6 ♦ :** the act or an instance of dropping **:** FALL **7 ♦ :** a decline in quantity or quality **8 :** a descent by parachute **9 :** the distance through which something drops **10 :** a slot into which something is to be dropped **11 :** something that drops or has dropped **12 ♦ :** an advantage or superiority over an opponent — usu. used in the phrase get the drop on

♦ [1] blob, driblet, drip, droplet, glob ♦ [6] descent, dip, dive, down, fall, plunge ♦ [7] abatement, decline, decrease, decrement, diminution, fall, loss, reduction, shrinkage ♦ [12] advantage, better, edge, jump, upper hand, vantage

²drop vb **dropped; drop•ping 1 :** to fall or let fall in drops **2 :** to let fall **:** LOWER ⟨∼ a glove⟩ ⟨dropped his voice⟩ **3 :** SEND ⟨∼ me a note⟩ **4 :** to let go **:** DISMISS ⟨∼ the subject⟩ **5 :** to knock down **:** cause to fall **6 ♦ :** to go lower **:** become less ⟨prices dropped⟩ **7 :** to come or go unexpectedly or informally ⟨∼ in to call⟩ **8 :** to pass from one state into a less active one ⟨∼ off to sleep⟩ **9 ♦ :** to move downward or with a current **10 ♦ :** to desist from **:** QUIT **11 :** to give birth to — **drop back :** to move toward the rear — **drop behind :** to fail to keep up

♦ [6] decline, descend, dip, fall, lower, plummet, plunge, sink, tumble Ant arise, lift, rise, soar ♦ [9] decline, descend, dip, fall, plunge ♦ [10] discontinue, give up, knock off, lay off, quit

drop by vb **♦ :** to pay a brief casual visit

♦ drop by or drop in call, pop (in), stop (by or in), visit

drop in vb **:** to pay an unexpected or casual visit

♦ call, pop (in), stop (by or in), visit

drop•kick \-ˈkik\ n **:** a kick made by dropping a ball to the ground and kicking it at the moment it starts to rebound — **drop–kick** vb

drop•let \'drä-plət\ n **♦ :** a tiny drop

♦ blob, driblet, drip, drop, glob

drop·off \\'dräp-ˌȯf\ *n* **1** : a steep or perpendicular descent **2** : a marked decline ⟨a ∼ in attendance⟩

drop off *vb* : to fall asleep

drop out *vb* : to withdraw from participation or membership; *esp* : to leave school before graduation — **drop·out** \\'dräp-ˌau̇t\ *n*

drop·per \\'drä-pər\ *n* **1** : one that drops **2** : a short glass tube with a rubber bulb used to measure out liquids by drops

drop·pings *n pl* ♦ : the feces of an animal : DUNG

♦ dung, slops, waste

drop·sy \\'dräp-sē\ *n* : EDEMA — **drop·si·cal** \-si-kəl\ *adj*

dross \\'dräs\ *n* **1** : the scum that forms on the surface of a molten metal **2** : waste matter : REFUSE

drought \\'drau̇t\ *also* **drouth** \\'drau̇th\ *n* : a long spell of dry weather

¹drove \\'drōv\ *n* **1** : a group of animals driven or moving in a body **2** ♦ : a large number : CROWD — usu. used in pl. ⟨tourists arriving in ∼s⟩

♦ *usu* **droves** army, crowd, crush, flock, horde, host, legion, mob, multitude, press, swarm, throng

²drove *past of* DRIVE

drov·er \\'drō-vər\ *n* : one that drives domestic animals usu. to market

drown \\'drau̇n\ *vb* **drowned** \\'drau̇nd\; **drown·ing** **1** : to suffocate by submersion esp. in water **2** : to become drowned **3** ♦ : to cover with water; *also* : to soak, drench, or cover with a liquid **4** : to cause to be muted (as a sound) by a loud noise **5** : OVERPOWER, OVERWHELM

♦ deluge, engulf, flood, inundate, overflow, overwhelm, submerge, swamp ♦ drench, impregnate, saturate, soak, sop, souse, steep

¹drowse \\'drau̇z\ *vb* **drowsed; drows·ing** ♦ : to fall into a light slumber : DOZE

♦ catnap, doze, nap, slumber, snooze

²drowse *n* ♦ : the act or an instance of drowsing

♦ catnap, doze, forty winks, nap, siesta, snooze, wink

drowsy \\'drau̇-zē\ *adj* **drows·i·er; -est** **1** ♦ : ready to fall asleep **2** ♦ : making one sleepy — **drows·i·ly** \-zə-lē\ *adv* — **drows·i·ness** \-zē-nəs\ *n*

♦ [1] sleepy, slumberous ♦ [2] hypnotic, narcotic, opiate, slumberous

drub \\'drəb\ *vb* **drubbed; drub·bing** **1** ♦ : to beat severely **2** ♦ : to defeat decisively

♦ [1] bash, bat, batter, beat, pound ♦ [2] clobber, rout, skunk, thrash, trim, trounce, wallop, whip

¹drudge \\'drəj\ *vb* **drudged; drudg·ing** ♦ : to do hard, menial, or monotonous work

♦ endeavor (*or* endeavour), grub, hustle, labor (*or* labour), peg, plod, plug, slog, strain, strive, struggle, sweat, toil, work

²drudge *n* ♦ : one whose work is menial or routine and boring

♦ peon, toiler, worker

drudg·ery \\'drə-jə-rē\ *n* ♦ : dull, irksome, and fatiguing work

♦ grind, labor (*or* labour), sweat, toil, travail

¹drug \\'drəg\ *n* **1** ♦ : a substance used as or in medicine **2** : a substance (as heroin or marijuana) that can cause addiction, habituation, or a marked change in mental status

♦ cure, medicine, pharmaceutical, remedy, specific

²drug *vb* **drugged; drug·ging** : to affect with or as if with drugs; *esp* : to stupefy with a narcotic

drug·gist \\'drə-gist\ *n* : a dealer in drugs and medicines; *also* : PHARMACIST

drug·store \\'drəg-ˌstȯr\ *n* : a retail shop where medicines and miscellaneous articles are sold

dru·id \\'drü-əd\ *n, often cap* : one of an ancient Celtic priesthood appearing in Irish, Welsh, and Christian legends as magicians and wizards

¹drum \\'drəm\ *n* **1** : a percussion instrument usu. consisting of a hollow cylinder with a skin or plastic head stretched over one or both ends that is beaten with the hands or with a stick **2** : the sound of a drum; *also* : a similar sound **3** ♦ : a drum-shaped object

♦ can, canister, tin

²drum *vb* **drummed; drum·ming** **1** : to beat a drum **2** : to sound rhythmically : THROB, BEAT **3** : to summon or enlist by or as if by beating a drum ⟨*drummed* into service⟩ **4** ♦ : to dismiss igno-

miniously : EXPEL — usu. used with *out* **5** : to drive or force by steady effort ⟨∼ the facts into memory⟩ **6** ♦ : to strike or tap repeatedly so as to produce rhythmic sounds

♦ [4] banish, boot (out), bounce, cast, chase, dismiss, eject, expel, oust, rout, run off, throw out ♦ [6] beat, rap, tap

drum·beat \\'drəm-ˌbēt\ *n* : a stroke on a drum or its sound

drum major *n* : the leader of a marching band

drum ma·jor·ette \-ˌmā-jə-'ret\ *n* : a girl or woman who leads a marching band; *also* : a baton twirler who accompanies a marching band

drum·mer \\'drə-mər\ *n* **1** : one that plays a drum **2** : a traveling salesman

drum·stick \\'drəm-ˌstik\ *n* **1** : a stick for beating a drum **2** : the lower segment of a fowl's leg

drum up *vb* **1** : to bring about by persistent effort ⟨*drum up* business⟩ **2** : INVENT, ORIGINATE ⟨*drum up* a new method⟩

¹drunk *past part of* DRINK

²drunk \\'drəŋk\ *adj* **1** ♦ : having the faculties impaired by alcohol ⟨∼ drivers⟩ **2** : dominated by an intense feeling ⟨∼ with power⟩ **3** : of, relating to, or caused by intoxication

♦ high, inebriate, intoxicated, tipsy *Ant* sober

³drunk *n* **1** : a period of excessive drinking **2** ♦ : a drunken person

♦ inebriate, soak, sot, souse, tippler

drunk·ard \\'drəŋ-kərd\ *n* : one who is habitually drunk

♦ inebriate, soak, sot, souse, tippler

drunk·en \\'drəŋ-kən\ *adj* **1** : being under the influence of alcohol : DRUNK **2** : given to habitual excessive use of alcohol **3** : of, relating to, or resulting from intoxication ⟨a ∼ brawl⟩ **4** : unsteady or lurching as if from intoxication — **drunk·en·ly** *adv* — **drunk·en·ness** *n*

drupe \\'drüp\ *n* : a partly fleshy fruit (as a plum or cherry) having one seed enclosed in a hard inner shell

¹dry \\'drī\ *adj* **dri·er** \-ər\; **dri·est** \-əst\ **1** : free or freed from water or liquid ⟨∼ fruits⟩; *also* : not being in or under water **2** ♦ : characterized by lack of water or moisture ⟨∼ climate⟩ **3** : lacking freshness : STALE **4** : devoid of natural moisture; *also* : THIRSTY **5** : no longer liquid or sticky ⟨the ink is ∼⟩ **6** : not giving milk ⟨a ∼ cow⟩ **7** : marked by the absence of alcoholic beverages **8** : prohibiting the making or distributing of alcoholic beverages **9** : not sweet ⟨∼ wine⟩ **10** : solid as opposed to liquid ⟨∼ groceries⟩ **11** : containing or employing no liquid **12 a** : not showing or communicating warmth, enthusiasm, or tender feeling : SEVERE **b** : causing weariness or lack of interest : UNINTERESTING **13** : not productive **14** : marked by a matter-of-fact, ironic, or terse manner of expression ⟨∼ humor⟩ — **dry·ly** or **dri·ly** *adv* — **dry·ness** *n*

♦ arid, sere, thirsty *Ant* damp, dank, humid, moist, wet

²dry *vb* **dried; dry·ing** ♦ : to make or become dry

♦ dehydrate, parch, sear *Ant* hydrate, wet

³dry *n, pl* **drys** : PROHIBITIONIST

dry·ad \\'drī-əd, -ˌad\ *n* : WOOD NYMPH

dry cell *n* : a battery whose contents are not spillable

dry–clean \\'drī-ˌklēn\ *vb* : to clean (fabrics) chiefly with solvents other than water — **dry cleaning** *n*

dry dock \\'drī-ˌdäk\ *n* : a dock that can be kept dry during ship construction or repair

dryer *var of* DRIER

dry farm·ing *n* : farming without irrigation in areas of limited rainfall — **dry–farm** *vb* — **dry farm·er** *n*

dry goods \\'drī-ˌgu̇dz\ *n pl* : cloth goods (as fabrics, ribbon, and ready-to-wear clothing)

dry ice *n* : solid carbon dioxide

dry measure *n* : a series of units of capacity for dry commodities

dry rot *n* : decay of timber in which fungi consume the wood's cellulose

dry run *n* ♦ : a practice exercise : REHEARSAL

♦ practice, rehearsal, trial

dry·wall \\'drī-ˌwȯl\ *n* : a wallboard consisting of fiberboard, paper, or felt over a plaster core

Ds *symbol* darmstadtium

DSC *abbr* **1** Distinguished Service Cross **2** doctor of surgical chiropody

DSM *abbr* Distinguished Service Medal

DST *abbr* daylight saving time

DTP *abbr* diphtheria, tetanus, pertussis (vaccines)

d.t.'s \ˌdē-'tēz\ *n pl, often cap* D&T : DELIRIUM TREMENS

du·al \\'dü-əl, 'dyü-\ *adj* **1** ♦ : consisting of two parts or elements or having two like parts : DOUBLE **2** : having a double character or nature — **du·al·ism** \-ə-ˌli-zəm\ *n* — **du·al·i·ty** \dü-ˈa-lə-tē, dyü-\ *n*

♦ binary, bipartite, double, duplex, twin

du·ath·lon \dü-ˈath-lən, -ˌlän, dyü-\ *n* : a long-distance race involving running and bicycling — **du·ath·lete** \-ˌlēt\ *n*

¹dub \ˈdəb\ *vb* **dubbed; dub·bing 1** : to confer knighthood upon **2** ♦ : to call by a distinctive title, epithet, or nickname : NAME

♦ baptize, call, christen, denominate, designate, entitle, label, name, style, term, title

²dub *n* : a clumsy person : DUFFER

³dub *vb* **dubbed; dub·bing** : to add (sound effects) to a motion picture or to a radio or television production

du·bi·ety \dü-ˈbī-ə-tē, dyü-\ *n, pl* **-eties 1** : UNCERTAINTY **2** : a matter of doubt

du·bi·ous \ˈdü-bē-əs, ˈdyü-\ *adj* **1** ♦ : of doubtful promise or outcome **2** ♦ : questionable or suspect as to true nature or quality : QUESTIONABLE **3** ♦ : feeling doubt — **du·bi·ous·ness** *n*

♦ [1] doubtful, flimsy, improbable, questionable, unlikely ♦ [2] debatable, disputable, doubtful, equivocal, fishy, problematic, questionable, shady, shaky, suspect, suspicious ♦ [3] distrustful, doubtful, mistrustful, skeptical, suspicious, uncertain, undecided, unsettled, unsure

du·bi·ous·ly \-lē\ *adv* ♦ : in a manner expressive of doubt, hesitation, or suspicion

♦ askance, distrustfully, mistrustfully, suspiciously

dub·ni·um \ˈdüb-nē-əm, ˈdəb-\ *n* : a short-lived radioactive chemical element produced artificially

du·cal \ˈdü-kəl, ˈdyü-\ *adj* : of or relating to a duke or dukedom

duc·at \ˈdə-kət\ *n* : a gold coin formerly used in various European countries

duch·ess \ˈdə-chəs\ *n* **1** : the wife or widow of a duke **2** : a woman holding the rank of duke in her own right

duchy \ˈdə-chē\ *n, pl* **duch·ies** : the territory of a duke or duchess : DUKEDOM

¹duck \ˈdək\ *n, pl* **ducks** : any of various swimming birds related to but smaller than geese and swans

²duck *vb* **1** ♦ : to thrust or plunge under water **2 a** : to lower the head or body suddenly : BOW **b** ♦ : to make a sudden movement in a new direction : DODGE **3** ♦ : to evade a duty, question, or responsibility ⟨~ the issue⟩

♦ [1] dip, douse, dunk, immerse, souse, submerge ♦ [2b] dodge, sidestep ♦ [3] avoid, dodge, elude, escape, eschew, evade, shake, shirk, shun

³duck *n* **1** : a durable closely woven usu. cotton fabric **2** *pl* : light clothes made of duck

duck·bill \ˈdək-ˌbil\ *n* : PLATYPUS

duck·ling \-liŋ\ *n* : a young duck

duck·pin \-ˌpin\ *n* **1** : a small bowling pin shorter and wider in the middle than a tenpin **2** *pl but sing in constr* : a bowling game using duckpins

duck sauce *n* : a thick sweet sauce made with fruits and seasonings and used in Chinese cuisine

duct \ˈdəkt\ *n* **1** : a tube or canal for conveying a bodily fluid **2** ♦ : a pipe or tube through which a fluid (as air) flows — **duct·less** *adj*

♦ channel, conduit, leader, line, penstock, pipe, tube

duc·tile \ˈdək-tᵊl\ *adj* **1** : capable of being drawn out into wire or thread **2** : easily led : DOCILE — **duc·til·i·ty** \ˌdək-ˈti-lə-tē\ *n*

ductless gland *n* : an endocrine gland

duct tape *n* : a cloth adhesive tape orig. designed for sealing certain ducts and joints — **duct–tape** *vb*

dud \ˈdəd\ *n* **1** *pl* ♦ : personal attire : CLOTHING **2** ♦ : one that fails completely; *also* : a bomb or missile that fails to explode

♦ [1] apparel, attire, clothing, dress, raiment, wear ♦ [2] bummer, bust, catastrophe, debacle, failure, fiasco, fizzle, flop, lemon, loser, turkey, washout

dude \ˈdüd, ˈdyüd\ *n* **1** ♦ : a man who gives exaggerated attention to personal appearance : DANDY **2** : a city dweller; *esp* : an Easterner in the West **3** ♦ : a male human : GUY — sometimes used as an informal form of address

♦ [1] buck, dandy, fop, gallant ♦ [3] buck, chap, fellow, gent, gentleman, guy, hombre, jack, joker, lad, male, man

dude ranch *n* : a vacation resort offering activities (as horseback riding) typical of western ranches

dud·geon \ˈdə-jən\ *n* ♦ : a fit or state of indignation ⟨in high ~⟩

♦ huff, offense, peeve, pique, resentment, umbrage

¹due \ˈdü, ˈdyü\ *adj* **1** : owed or owing as a debt **2** : owed or owing as a right **3** : APPROPRIATE, FITTING **4** : SUFFICIENT, ADEQUATE **5** ♦ : being in accordance with some established rule, law, or principle ⟨~ process of law⟩ **6** ♦ : capable of being attributed — used with *to* ⟨~ to negligence⟩ **7** : PAYABLE ⟨a bill ~ today⟩ **8** : SCHEDULED ⟨~ to arrive soon⟩

♦ [5] just, right ♦ *usu* **due to** [6] attendant, consequent, consequential, resultant

²due *n* **1** : something that rightfully belongs to one ⟨give everyone their ~⟩ **2** : DEBT **3** *pl* : FEES, CHARGES

³due *adv* ♦ : in a direct manner : DIRECTLY ⟨~ north⟩

♦ dead, direct, directly, plump, right, straight

du·el \ˈdü-əl, ˈdyü-\ *n* **1** : a combat between two persons; *esp* : one fought with weapons in the presence of witnesses **2** ♦ : a conflict between antagonistic persons, ideas, or forces; *also* : a hard-fought contest between two opponents — **duel** *vb* — **du·el·ist** \-ə-list\ *n*

♦ battle, combat, conflict, confrontation, contest, face-off, rivalry, struggle, tug-of-war, warfare

du·en·de \dü-ˈen-dā\ *n* : the power to attract through personal magnetism and charm

du·en·na \dü-ˈe-nə, dyü-\ *n* **1** : an elderly woman in charge of the younger ladies in a Spanish or Portuguese family **2** : CHAPERONE

du·et \dü-ˈet, dyü-\ *n* : a musical composition for two performers

due to *prep* ♦ : as a result of : BECAUSE OF

♦ because of, owing to, through, with

duf·fel bag \ˈdə-fəl-\ *n* : a large cylindrical bag for personal belongings

duf·fer \ˈdə-fər\ *n* : an incompetent or clumsy person

dug *past and past part of* DIG

dug·out \ˈdəg-ˌaut\ *n* **1** : a boat made by hollowing out a log **2** : a shelter dug in the ground **3** : a low shelter facing a baseball diamond that contains the players' bench

DUI *n* : the act or crime of driving while under the influence of alcohol

duke \ˈdük, ˈdyük\ *n* **1** : a sovereign ruler of a continental European duchy **2** : a nobleman of the highest rank; *esp* : a member of the highest grade of the British peerage **3** *slang* : FIST 1 ⟨put up your ~s⟩ — **duke·dom** *n*

dul·cet \ˈdəl-sət\ *adj* **1** : pleasing to the ear **2** : AGREEABLE, SOOTHING

dul·ci·mer \ˈdəl-sə-mər\ *n* **1** : a stringed instrument of trapezoidal shape played with light hammers held in the hands **2** *or* **dul·ci·more** \-ˌmȯr\ : an American folk instrument with three or four strings that is held on the lap and played by plucking or strumming

¹dull \ˈdəl\ *adj* **1** : mentally slow : STUPID **2** : slow in perception or sensibility **3** : LISTLESS **4** : slow in action : SLUGGISH ⟨a ~ market⟩ **5** : lacking in force or intensity; *also* : not resonant or ringing **6** ♦ : lacking sharpness of edge or point : BLUNT **7** ♦ : lacking brilliance or luster **8** ♦ : low in saturation and lightness ⟨~ color⟩ **9** : overcast with clouds : CLOUDY **10** ♦ : causing weariness or lack of interest : UNINTERESTING — **dul·ly** *adv*

♦ [6] blunt, obtuse *Ant* keen, pointed, sharp, whetted ♦ [7] dim, flat, lusterless ♦ [8] light, pale, pastel, washed-out ♦ [10] dry, flat, monotonous, uninteresting, weary

²dull *vb* ♦ : to make or become dull

♦ blunt, dampen, deaden, numb *Ant* sharpen, whet

dull·ard \ˈdə-lərd\ *n* : a stupid person

dull·ness *also* **dul·ness** \ˈdəl-nəs\ *n* : the quality or state of being dull

du·ly \ˈdü-lē, ˈdyü-\ *adv* : in a due manner or time

dumb \ˈdəm\ *adj* **1** *often offensive* : lacking the power of speech **2** ♦ : making no utterance : SILENT **3** ♦ : not having or showing intelligence : STUPID — **dumb·ly** *adv*

♦ [2] mum, mute, silent, speechless, uncommunicative ♦ [3] mindless, senseless, simple, stupid, unintelligent

dumb·bell \ˈdəm-ˌbel\ *n* **1** : a bar with weights at the end used for exercise **2** : one who is stupid : DUMMY

dumb down *vb* : to lower the level of difficulty or intellectual content of

dumb·found *also* **dum·found** \dəm-ˈfaúnd\ *vb* ♦ : to confound briefly and usu. with astonishment : ASTONISH

♦ amaze, astonish, astound, bowl, flabbergast, floor, shock, startle, stun, stupefy, surprise

dumb·wait·er \ˈdəm-ˌwā-tər\ *n* : a small elevator for conveying food and dishes from one floor to another

dum·my \ˈdə-mē\ *n, pl* **dummies** **1** ♦ : a stupid person **2** *dated, offensive* : a person who cannot speak **3** : the exposed hand in bridge played by the declarer in addition to that player's own hand; *also* : a bridge player whose hand is a dummy **4 a** : an imitative substitute for something **b** ♦ : a form representing the human figure used esp. for displaying clothes : MANNEQUIN **5** : one seeming to act alone but really acting for another **6** : a mock-up of matter to be reproduced esp. by printing

♦ [1] blockhead, dope, idiot, imbecile, jackass, moron, numskull ♦ [4b] figure, form, manikin, mannequin

¹**dump** \ˈdəmp\ *vb* **1** : to let fall in a pile **2** ♦ : to get rid of unceremoniously

♦ cast, discard, ditch, fling, jettison, junk, lose, reject, scrap, shed, shuck, slough, throw away, throw out, unload

²**dump** *n* **1** : a place for dumping something (as refuse) **2 a** : a reserve supply **b** ♦ : a place where reserve supplies are kept ⟨an ammunition ∼⟩ **3** : a messy or objectionable place

♦ armory, arsenal, depot, magazine

dump·ing \ˈdəm-piŋ\ *n* : the act of one that dumps; *esp* : the selling of goods in quantity at below market price

♦ disposal, disposition, jettison, removal, riddance

dump·ling \ˈdəm-pliŋ\ *n* **1** : a small mass of boiled or steamed dough **2** : a dessert of fruit baked in biscuit dough

dumps \ˈdəmps\ *n pl* ♦ : a gloomy state of mind : low spirits ⟨in the ∼⟩

♦ blues, dejection, depression, desolation, despondency, doldrums, forlornness, gloom, heartsickness, melancholy, sadness

dump·ster \ˈdəmp-stər\ *n, often cap* : a large trash receptacle

dump truck *n* : a truck for transporting and dumping bulk material

dumpy \ˈdəm-pē\ *adj* **dump·i·er; -est** **1** ♦ : short and thick in build **2** : SHABBY

♦ chunky, heavyset, squat, stocky, stout, stubby, stumpy, thickset

¹**dun** \ˈdən\ *n* : a brownish dark gray

²**dun** *vb* **dunned; dun·ning** **1** : to make persistent demands for payment : PLAGUE, PESTER — **dun** *n*

³**dun** *n* ♦ : an urgent request

♦ claim, demand, requisition

dunce \ˈdəns\ *n* ♦ : a slow stupid person

♦ blockhead, dope, dummy, idiot, imbecile, jackass, moron, numskull

dun·der·head \ˈdən-dər-ˌhed\ *n* : DUNCE, BLOCKHEAD

dune \ˈdün, ˈdyün\ *n* : a hill or ridge of sand piled up by the wind

dune buggy *n* : a motor vehicle with oversize tires for use on sand

¹**dung** \ˈdəŋ\ *n* ♦ : the feces of an animal : MANURE

♦ droppings, slops, waste

²**dung** *vb* : to dress (land) with dung

dun·ga·ree \ˌdəŋ-gə-ˈrē\ *n* **1** : a heavy coarse cotton twill; *esp* : blue denim **2** *pl* : clothes made of blue denim

dun·geon \ˈdən-jən\ *n* : a dark prison commonly underground

dung·hill \ˈdəŋ-ˌhil\ *n* : a manure pile

dunk \ˈdəŋk\ *vb* **1** ♦ : to dip or submerge temporarily in liquid **2** : to submerge oneself in water **3** : to shoot a basketball into the basket from above the rim

♦ dip, douse, duck, immerse, souse, submerge

duo \ˈdü-(ˌ)ō, ˈdyü-\ *n, pl* **du·os** **1** : DUET **2** ♦ : two similar or associated things : PAIR

♦ brace, couple, pair, twain, twosome

duo·dec·i·mal \ˌdü-ə-ˈde-sə-məl, ˌdyü-\ *adj* : of, relating to, or being a system of numbers with a base of 12

du·o·de·num \ˌdü-ə-ˈdē-nəm, ˌdyü-, dü-ˈäd-ᵊn-əm, dyü-\ *n, pl* **-de·na** \-ˈdē-nə, -ᵊn-ə\ *or* **-denums** : the first part of the small intestine extending from the stomach to the jejunum — **du·o·de·nal** \-ˈdēn-ᵊl, -ᵊn-əl\ *adj*

dup *abbr* **1** duplex **2** duplicate

¹**dupe** \ˈdüp, ˈdyüp\ *n* ♦ : one who is easily deceived or cheated

♦ gull, pigeon, sap, sucker, tool

²**dupe** *vb* **duped; dup·ing** ♦ : to make a dupe of : DECEIVE

♦ beguile, bluff, cozen, deceive, delude, fool, gull, have, hoax, hoodwink, humbug, misinform, mislead, string along, take in, trick

du·ple \ˈdü-pəl, ˈdyü-\ *adj* : having two beats or a multiple of two beats to the measure ⟨∼ time⟩

¹**du·plex** \ˈdü-ˌpleks, ˈdyü-\ *adj* ♦ : having two principal elements or parts : DOUBLE

♦ binary, bipartite, double, dual, twin

²**duplex** *n* : something duplex; *esp* : a 2-family house

¹**du·pli·cate** \ˈdü-pli-kət, ˈdyü-\ *adj* **1** : consisting of or existing in two corresponding or identical parts or examples **2** ♦ : being the same as another

♦ equal, even, identical, indistinguishable, same

²**du·pli·cate** \ˈdü-pli-ˌkāt, ˈdyü-\ *vb* **-cat·ed; -cat·ing** **1** : to make double or twofold **2** ♦ : to make a copy of

♦ copy, imitate, replicate, reproduce

³**du·pli·cate** \-kət\ *n* ♦ : a thing that exactly resembles another in appearance, pattern, or content : COPY

♦ carbon copy, copy, duplication, facsimile, imitation, replica, replication, reproduction

du·pli·ca·tion \ˌdü-pli-ˈkā-shən, ˌdyü-\ *n* **1** : the act or process of duplicating **2** ♦ : a thing that exactly resembles another in appearance, pattern, or content

♦ carbon copy, counterpart, double, duplicate, facsimile, image, likeness, match, picture, replica, ringer, spit

du·pli·ca·tor \ˈdü-pli-ˌkā-tər, ˈdyü-\ *n* : COPIER

du·plic·i·ty \dü-ˈpli-sə-tē, dyü-\ *n, pl* **-ties** ♦ : the disguising of true intentions by deceptive words or action — **du·plic·i·tous** \-təs\ *adj* — **du·plic·i·tous·ly** *adv*

♦ artifice, craft, craftiness, crookedness, cunning, deceit, deceitfulness, dishonesty, dissimulation, double-dealing, guile, wiliness

du·ra·bil·i·ty \ˌdúr-ə-ˈbi-lə-tē, ˌdyúr-\ *n* ♦ : the quality or state of being durable

♦ endurance, persistence

du·ra·ble \ˈdúr-ə-bəl, ˈdyúr-\ *adj* : able to exist for a long time without significant deterioration of qualities or capabilities ⟨∼ goods⟩

du·rance \ˈdúr-əns, ˈdyúr-\ *n* : restraint by or as if by physical force ⟨held in ∼ vile⟩

du·ra·tion \dú-ˈrā-shən, dyú-\ *n* **1** ♦ : continuance in time **2** ♦ : the time during which something exists or lasts

♦ [1] continuance, continuation, endurance, persistence, subsistence ♦ [2] date, life, lifetime, run, standing, time

du·ress \dú-ˈres, dyú-\ *n* ♦ : compulsion by threat ⟨confession made under ∼⟩

♦ coercion, compulsion, constraint, force, pressure

dur·ing \ˈdúr-iŋ, ˈdyúr-\ *prep* **1** ♦ : throughout the duration of ⟨swims every day ∼ the summer⟩ **2** : at some point in ⟨broke in ∼ the night⟩

♦ over, through, throughout

dusk \ˈdəsk\ *n* **1** ♦ : the darker part of twilight esp. at night **2** : partial darkness

♦ evening, gloaming, nightfall, sundown, sunset, twilight *Ant* aurora, cockcrow, dawn, dawning, daybreak, daylight, morn, morning, sunrise, sunup

dusky \ˈdəs-kē\ *adj* **dusk·i·er; -est** **1** : somewhat dark in color **2** ♦ : marked by slight or deficient light — **dusk·i·ness** *n*

♦ dark, darkling, dim, gloomy, murky, obscure, somber (*or* sombre)

¹**dust** \ˈdəst\ *n* **1** : fine particles of matter **2** : the particles into which something disintegrates **3** ♦ : something worthless **4** ♦ : the surface of the ground — **dust·less** *adj*

♦ [3] chaff, deadwood, garbage, junk, litter, refuse, riffraff, rubbish, scrap, trash, waste ♦ [4] dirt, earth, ground, land, soil

²**dust** *vb* **1** : to make free of or remove dust **2** : to sprinkle with fine particles **3** : to sprinkle in the form of dust

dust bowl *n* : a region suffering from long droughts and dust storms

dust devil *n* : a small whirlwind containing sand or dust

dust·er \ˈdəs-tər\ *n* **1** : one that removes dust **2** : a dress-length housecoat **3** : one that scatters fine particles; *esp* : a device for applying insecticides to crops

dust·pan \'dəst-ˌpan\ *n* : a flat-ended pan for sweepings
dust storm *n* : a violent wind carrying dust across a dry region
dusty \'dəs-tē\ *adj* **1** ♦ : consisting of dust : POWDERY **2** : covered or abounding with dust

♦ fine, floury, powdery

dutch \'dəch\ *adv, often cap* : with each person paying his or her own way ⟨go ∼⟩
Dutch \'dəch\ *n* **1 Dutch** *pl* : the people of the Netherlands **2** : the language of the Netherlands — **Dutch** *adj* — **Dutch·man** \-mən\ *n*
Dutch elm disease *n* : a fungus disease of elms characterized by yellowing of the foliage, defoliation, and death
dutch treat *n, often cap D* : an entertainment (as a meal) for which each person pays his or her own way — **dutch treat** *adv, often cap D*
du·te·ous \'dü-tē-əs, 'dyü-\ *adj* : DUTIFUL, OBEDIENT
du·ti·able \'dü-tē-ə-bəl, 'dyü-\ *adj* : subject to a duty ⟨∼ imports⟩
du·ti·ful \'dü-ti-fəl, 'dyü-\ *adj* **1** : motivated by a sense of duty ⟨a ∼ son⟩ **2** ♦ : coming from or showing a sense of duty ⟨∼ affection⟩ — **du·ti·ful·ly** *adv* — **du·ti·ful·ness** *n*

♦ deferential, regardful, respectful

du·ty \'dü-tē, 'dyü-\ *n, pl* **duties 1** ♦ : conduct or action required by one's occupation or position; *also* : obligatory tasks, conduct, or functions required by order or usage **2** : assigned service or business; *esp* : active military service **3** ♦ : a moral or legal obligation **4** ♦ : a charge usu. of money imposed by authority on persons or property for public purposes : TAX **5** : the service required (as of a machine) : USE ⟨a heavy-*duty* tire⟩

♦ [1] assignment, chore, job, stint, task ♦ [3] burden, charge, commitment, need, obligation, responsibility ♦ [4] assessment, impost, levy, tax

DV *abbr* **1** God willing **2** Douay Version
DVD \ˌdē-ˌvē-'dē\ *n* : a high-capacity optical disk format; *also* : an optical disk using such a format
DVM *abbr* doctor of veterinary medicine
DVR \ˌdē-ˌvē-'är\ *n* : a device that records and plays back television programs
¹**dwarf** \'dwȯrf\ *n, pl* **dwarfs** \'dwȯrfs\ *also* **dwarves** \'dwȯrvz\ **1** : a person of unusually small stature **2** ♦ : an animal or plant that is much below normal size **3** ♦ : a small legendary manlike being who is usu. misshapen and ugly and skilled as a craftsman

♦ [2] midget, mite, peewee, pygmy, runt *Ant* behemoth, colossus, giant, jumbo, leviathan, mammoth, monster, titan ♦ [3] brownie, elf, fairy, fay, gnome, hobgoblin, leprechaun, pixie, puck, sprite

²**dwarf** *vb* **1** : to restrict the growth or development of : STUNT **2** : to cause to appear smaller ⟨*dwarfed* by comparison⟩
³**dwarf** *adj* : characterized by smallness or insignificance of size, proportion, scope, strength, or power
dwarf·ish \'dwȯr-fish\ *adj* ♦ : of or like a dwarf

♦ dwarf, fine, little, pocket, pygmy, slight, small, undersized

dwarf planet *n* : a spherical celestial body that orbits the sun but is too small to disturb other objects from its orbit
dwell \'dwel\ *vb* **dwelt** \'dwelt\ *or* **dwelled** \'dweld, 'dwelt\; **dwell·ing 1** ♦ : to remain for a time : ABIDE **2** ♦ : to live as a resident : RESIDE **3** : to keep the attention directed **4** : to write or speak insistently — used with *on* or *upon*

♦ [1] abide, hang around, remain, stay, stick around, tarry ♦ [2] abide, live, reside

dwell·er \'dwe-lər\ *n* ♦ : one that dwells : INHABITANT

♦ denizen, inhabitant, occupant, resident

dwell·ing \'dwe-liŋ\ *n* ♦ : a shelter (as a house) in which people live : RESIDENCE

♦ abode, domicile, home, house, lodging, quarters, residence

DWI \ˌdē-ˌdəb-əl-(ˌ)yü-'ī\ *n* : DUI
dwin·dle \'dwin-dᵊl\ *vb* **dwin·dled; dwin·dling** ♦ : to make or become steadily less

♦ abate, decline, decrease, de-escalate, die, diminish, ebb, fall, lessen, let up, lower, moderate, recede, relent, shrink, subside, taper, wane

dwt *abbr* pennyweight
Dy *symbol* dysprosium
dyb·buk \'di-bək\ *n, pl* **dyb·bu·kim** \ˌdi-bù-'kēm\ *also* **dyb·buks** : a wandering soul believed in Jewish folklore to enter and possess a person
¹**dye** \'dī\ *n* **1** : color produced by dyeing **2** ♦ : material used for coloring or staining

♦ color (*or* colour), pigment, stain

²**dye** *vb* **dyed; dye·ing 1** ♦ : to impart a new color to esp. by impregnating with a dye **2** : to take up or impart color in dyeing — **dy·er** \'dī-(-ə)r\ *n*

♦ color (*or* colour), paint, stain, tinge, tint

dye·stuff \'dī-ˌstəf\ *n* : material used for coloring or staining : DYE
dying *pres part of* DIE
dy·nam·ic \dī-'na-mik\ *also* **dy·nam·i·cal** \-mi-kəl\ *adj* **1** : of or relating to physical force producing motion **2** ♦ : operating with or marked by vigor or effect : ENERGETIC

♦ energetic, flush, lusty, peppy, robust, strenuous, vigorous, vital ♦ aggressive, assertive, emphatic, forceful, resounding, vehement

dy·nam·i·cal·ly \dī-'na-mi-kə-lē\ *adv* ♦ : in a dynamic manner

♦ energetically, firmly, forcefully, forcibly, hard, mightily, powerfully, stiffly, stoutly, strenuously, strongly, sturdily, vigorously

¹**dy·na·mite** \'dī-nə-ˌmīt\ *n* **1** : an explosive made of nitroglycerin absorbed in a porous material; *also* : an explosive made without nitroglycerin **2** : one that has a powerful effect
²**dynamite** *vb* **-mit·ed; -mit·ing** : to blow up with dynamite
³**dynamite** *adj* : TERRIFIC, WONDERFUL
dy·na·mo \'dī-nə-ˌmō\ *n, pl* **-mos 1** : an electrical generator **2** : a forceful energetic individual
dy·na·mom·e·ter \ˌdī-nə-'mä-mə-tər\ *n* : an instrument for measuring mechanical power (as of an engine)
dy·nas·ty \'dī-nəs-tē, -ˌnas-\ *n, pl* **-ties 1** : a succession of rulers of the same family **2** : a powerful group or family that maintains its position for a long time — **dy·nas·tic** \dī-'nas-tik\ *adj*
dys·en·tery \'dis-ᵊn-ˌter-ē\ *n, pl* **-ter·ies** : a disease marked by diarrhea with blood and mucus in the feces; *also* : DIARRHEA
dys·func·tion *also* **dis·func·tion** \dis-'fəŋk-shən\ *n* **1** : impaired or abnormal functioning ⟨liver ∼⟩ **2** : abnormal or unhealthy behavior within a group ⟨family ∼⟩ — **dys·func·tion·al** \-shə-nəl\ *adj*
dys·lex·ia \dis-'lek-sē-ə\ *n* : a learning disability marked by difficulty in reading, writing, and spelling — **dys·lex·ic** \-sik\ *adj or n*
dys·pep·sia \dis-'pep-shə, -sē-ə\ *n* : INDIGESTION — **dys·pep·tic** \-'pep-tik\ *n*
dys·pep·tic *adj* ♦ : having or showing ill humor

♦ bearish, bilious, cantankerous, disagreeable, ill-humored, ill-tempered, ornery, splenetic, surly

dys·pla·sia \dis-'plā-zh(ē-)ə\ *n* : abnormal growth or development
dys·pro·si·um \dis-'prō-zē-əm\ *n* : a metallic chemical element that forms highly magnetic compounds
dys·to·pia \dis-'tō-pē-ə\ *n* : an imaginary place where people lead dehumanized and often fearful lives; *also* : a work of literature about such a place — **dys·to·pi·an** \-ən\ *adj*
dys·tro·phy \'dis-trə-fē\ *n, pl* **-phies** : a disorder involving atrophy of muscular tissue; *esp* : MUSCULAR DYSTROPHY
dz *abbr* dozen

¹**e** \'ē\ *n, pl* **e's** *or* **es** \'ēz\ *often cap* **1** : the 5th letter of the English alphabet **2** : the base of the system of natural logarithms having the approximate value 2.71828 **3** : a grade rating a student's work as poor or failing

²**e** *abbr, often cap* **1** east; eastern **2** error **3** excellent

e- *comb form* : electronic ⟨*e*-commerce⟩

ea *abbr* each

¹**each** \'ēch\ *adj* : being one of the class named ⟨~ player⟩

²**each** *pron* : every individual one

³**each** *adv* : to or for each : APIECE ⟨cost five cents ~⟩

each other *pron* : each of two or more in reciprocal action or relation ⟨looked at *each other*⟩

ea·ger \'ē-gər\ *adj* ♦ : marked by urgent or enthusiastic desire or interest ⟨~ to learn⟩ — **ea·ger·ly** *adv*

♦ avid, enthusiastic, hungry, keen, raring, thirsty *Ant* apathetic, indifferent

ea·ger·ness *n* ♦ : the quality or state of being eager; *also* : an act or instance of being eager

♦ alacrity, ambition, appetite, ardor, avidity, enthusiasm, excitement, hunger, impatience, keenness, quickness, thirst *Ant* apathy, indifference

¹**ea·gle** \'ē-gəl\ *n* **1** : a large bird of prey related to the hawks **2** : a score of two under par on a hole in golf

²**eagle** *vb* **ea·gled; ea·gling** : to score an eagle on a golf hole

ea·glet \'ē-glət\ *n* : a young eagle

-ean — see -AN

E and OE *abbr* errors and omissions excepted

¹**ear** \'ir\ *n* **1** : the organ of hearing; *also* : the outer part of this in a vertebrate **2** : something resembling a mammal's ear in shape, position, or function **3** : an ability to understand and appreciate something heard ⟨a good ~ for music⟩ **4** ♦ : sympathetic attention

♦ attention, awareness, cognizance, eye, heed, notice, observance, observation

²**ear** *n* : the fruiting spike of a cereal (as wheat or corn)

ear·ache \-ˌāk\ *n* : an ache or pain in the ear

ear·drum \-ˌdrəm\ *n* : a thin membrane that receives and transmits sound waves in the ear

eared \'ird\ *adj* : having ears esp. of a specified kind or number ⟨a long-*eared* dog⟩

ear·ful \'ir-ˌfu̇l\ *n* : a verbal outpouring (as of news, gossip, anger, or complaint)

earl \'ərl\ *n* : a member of the British peerage ranking below a marquess and above a viscount — **earl·dom** \-dəm\ *n*

ear·lobe \'ir-ˌlōb\ *n* : the pendent part of the ear

¹**ear·ly** \'ər-lē\ *adv* **ear·li·er; -est** ♦ : at an early time

♦ beforehand, precociously, prematurely, unseasonably *Ant* late

²**early** *adj* **ear·li·er; -est 1** : of, relating to, or occurring near the beginning; *also* : ANCIENT, PRIMITIVE **2** ♦ : occurring before the usual time ⟨an ~ breakfast⟩; *also* : occurring in the near future

♦ [1] ancient, primal, primeval, primitive *Ant* late ♦ [2] precocious, premature, unseasonable, untimely *Ant* late

¹**ear·mark** \'ir-ˌmärk\ *n* : an identification mark (as on the ear of an animal); *also* : a distinguishing mark ⟨~s of poverty⟩

²**earmark** *vb* **1** : to mark with an earmark **2** ♦ : to designate for a specific purpose

♦ allocate, consecrate, dedicate, devote, reserve, save

ear·muff \-ˌməf\ *n* : one of a pair of ear coverings worn to protect against cold

earn \'ərn\ *vb* **1** ♦ : to receive as a return for service **2** ♦ : to make or come to be duly worthy of : DESERVE, MERIT — **earn·er** *n*

♦ [1] acquire, attain, draw, gain, garner, get, land, make, secure, win *Ant* forfeit, lose ♦ [2] deserve, merit, rate

earned run *n* : a run in baseball that scores without benefit of an error before the fielding team has had a chance to make the third putout of the inning

earned run average *n* : the average number of earned runs per game scored against a pitcher in baseball

¹**ear·nest** \'ər-nəst\ *n* ♦ : an intensely serious state of mind ⟨spoke in ~⟩

♦ earnestness, gravity, intentness, seriousness, sobriety, solemnity

²**earnest** *adj* **1** ♦ : seriously intent and sober ⟨an ~ face⟩ ⟨an ~ attempt⟩ **2** ♦ : marked by importance : GRAVE — **ear·nest·ly** *adv*

♦ [1, 2] grave, humorless (*or* humourless), serious, severe, sober, solemn, staid, unsmiling, weighty

³**earnest** *n* **1** : something of value given by a buyer to a seller to bind a bargain **2** : PLEDGE

ear·nest·ness *n* ♦ : intent and serious state or quality (as of mind)

♦ gravity, intentness, seriousness, sobriety, solemnity *Ant* frivolity, levity, lightheartedness

earn·ings \'ər-niŋz\ *n pl* **1** ♦ : something (as wages) earned **2** ♦ : the balance of revenue after deduction of costs and expenses

♦ [1] income, proceeds, profit, return, revenue, yield ♦ [2] gain, lucre, net, payoff, proceeds, profit, return

ear·phone \'ir-ˌfōn\ *n* : a device that reproduces sound and is worn over or in the ear

ear·piece \-ˌpēs\ *n* : a part of an instrument which is placed against or in the ear; *esp* : EARPHONE

ear·plug \-ˌpləg\ *n* : a protective device for insertion into the opening of the ear

ear·ring \-ˌriŋ\ *n* : an ornament for the earlobe

ear·shot \-ˌshät\ *n* ♦ : range of hearing

♦ hail, hearing, sound

ear·split·ting \-ˌspli-tiŋ\ *adj* ♦ : intolerably loud or shrill

♦ booming, clamorous (*or* clamourous), deafening, loud, piercing, roaring, thunderous

earth \'ərth\ *n* **1** ♦ : the fragmental material composing part of the surface of the globe : SOIL, DIRT **2** ♦ : areas of land as distinguished from sea and air : LAND, GROUND **3** *often cap* ♦ : the planet on which we live that is 3d in order from the sun

♦ [1, 2] dirt, dust, ground, land, soil ♦ [3] planet, world

earth·en \'ər-thən\ *adj* : made of earth or baked clay

earth·en·ware \-ˌwar\ *n* : slightly porous opaque pottery fired at low heat

earth·ling \'ərth-liŋ\ *n* : an inhabitant of the earth

earth·ly \'ərth-lē\ *adj* ♦ : characteristic of or belonging to this earth; *also* : relating to the human race's actual life on this earth — **earth·li·ness** *n*

♦ material, mundane, temporal, terrestrial, worldly *Ant* heavenly, nontemporal

earth·quake \-ˌkwāk\ *n* : a shaking or trembling of a portion of the earth

earth science *n* : any of the sciences (as geology or meteorology) that deal with the earth or one of its parts

earth·shak·ing \'ərth-ˌshā-kiŋ\ *adj* : of great importance : MOMENTOUS

earth·ward \-wərd\ *also* **earth·wards** \-wərdz\ *adv* : toward the earth

earth·work \'ərth-ˌwərk\ *n* : an embankment or fortification of earth

earth·worm \-ˌwərm\ *n* : a long segmented worm found in damp soil

earthy \'ər-thē\ *adj* **earth·i·er; -est 1** : of, relating to, or consisting of earth; *also* : suggesting earth ⟨~ flavors⟩ **2** ♦ : not theoretical or ideal : PRACTICAL **3** : COARSE, GROSS — **earth·i·ness** *n*

♦ down-to-earth, hardheaded, matter-of-fact, practical, pragmatic, realistic

ear·wax \'ir-ˌwaks\ *n* : the yellow waxy secretion from the ear

ear·wig \-ˌwig\ *n* : any of numerous insects with slender many-jointed antennae and a pair of appendages resembling forceps at the end of the body

¹ease \'ēz\ *n* ♦ : comfort of body or mind : freedom from pain, discomfort, or concern **2** : naturalness of manner **3** ♦ : freedom from difficulty or effort

♦ [1] alleviation, comfort, decrease, relief ♦ [3] leisure, relaxation, repose, rest

²ease *vb* **eased; eas·ing 1** ♦ : to relieve from distress **2** ♦ : to lessen the pressure or tension of **3** ♦ : to make or become less difficult ⟨~ credit⟩

♦ [1] allay, alleviate, assuage, help, mitigate, mollify, palliate, relieve, soothe ♦ [2] loosen, relax, slack, slacken ♦ [3] assist, facilitate, further, hasten, help, improve, loosen, promote *Ant* complicate

ea·sel \'ē-zəl\ *n* : a frame for supporting something (as an artist's canvas)

eas·i·ly \'ē-zə-lē\ *adv* ♦ : in an easy manner : without difficulty

♦ effortlessly, fluently, freely, handily, lightly, painlessly, readily, smoothly *Ant* arduously, laboriously

¹east \'ēst\ *adv* : to or toward the east

²east *adj* **1** : situated toward or at the east **2** : coming from the east

³east *n* **1** : the general direction of sunrise **2** : the compass point directly opposite to west **3** *cap* : regions or countries east of a specified or implied point — **east·er·ly** \'ē-stər-lē\ *adv or adj* — **east·ward** *adv or adj* — **east·wards** *adv*

Eas·ter \'ē-stər\ *n* : a church feast observed on a Sunday in March or April in commemoration of Christ's resurrection

east·ern \'ē-stərn\ *adj* **1** *often cap* : of, relating to, or characteristic of a region designated East **2** *cap* : of, relating to, or being the Christian churches originating in the Church of the Eastern Roman Empire **3** : lying toward or coming from the east — **East·ern·er** *n*

easy \'ē-zē\ *adj* **eas·i·er; -est 1** ♦ : marked by ease ⟨an ~ life⟩; *esp* : not causing distress or difficulty ⟨~ tasks⟩ **2** : MILD, LENIENT ⟨be ~ on him⟩ **3** : GRADUAL ⟨an ~ slope⟩ **4** : free from pain, trouble, or worry ⟨felt ~⟩ **5** : LEISURELY ⟨an ~ pace⟩ **6** : NATURAL ⟨an ~ manner⟩ **7** ♦ : giving ease, comfort, or relaxation : COMFORTABLE ⟨an ~ chair⟩ **8** ♦ : readily taken advantage of — **eas·i·ness** \-zē-nəs\ *n*

♦ [1] effortless, facile, fluent, fluid, light, painless, ready, simple, smooth, snap, soft *Ant* arduous, difficult, hard, labored ♦ [7] comfortable, snug, soft ♦ [8] gullible, susceptible

easy–go·ing \,ē-zē-'gō-iŋ\ *adj* ♦ : relaxed and casual in style or manner

♦ affable, breezy, carefree, happy-go-lucky, informal, laid-back *Ant* uptight ♦ flexible, lax, loose, relaxed, slack, unrestrained, unrestricted *Ant* rigorous ♦ carefree, careless, cavalier, happy-go-lucky, insouciant, lighthearted, unconcerned

eat \'ēt\ *vb* **ate** \'āt\; **eat·en** \'ēt-ᵊn\; **eat·ing 1** : to take in as food : take food **2** : to use up : DEVOUR **3** ♦ : to consume gradually : CORRODE — **eat·able** *adj or n* — **eat·er** *n*

♦ [1] dine, fare, feed ♦ [3] bite, corrode, erode, fret

eat·ery \'ē-tə-rē\ *n, pl* **-ies** : LUNCHEONETTE, RESTAURANT

eaves \'ēvz\ *n pl* : the overhanging lower edge of a roof

eaves·drop \'ēvz-,dräp\ *vb* : to listen secretly — **eaves·drop·per** *n*

¹ebb \'eb\ *n* **1** : the flowing back from shore of water brought in by the tide **2** : a point or state of decline

²ebb *vb* **1** : to recede from the flood **2** ♦ : to fall from a higher to a lower level or from a better to a worse state : DECLINE ⟨his fortunes ~ed⟩

♦ abate, decline, decrease, diminish, dwindle, fall, lessen, recede, subside, taper

EBCDIC \'eb-sə-,dik\ *n* : a computer code for representing alphanumeric information

Ebo·la \ē-'bō-lə\ *n* : an often fatal hemorrhagic fever caused by a virus (**Ebola virus**) of African origin

¹eb·o·ny \'e-bə-nē\ *n, pl* **-nies** : a hard heavy wood of Old World tropical trees related to the persimmon

²ebony *adj* **1** : made of or resembling ebony **2** ♦ : of the color black

♦ black, raven

e–book \'ē-,bu̇k\ *n* : a book in digital form for displaying on a computer screen or a handheld device

ebul·lient \i-'bu̇l-yənt, -'bəl-\ *adj* **1** : BOILING, AGITATED **2** : EXUBERANT — **ebul·lience** \-yəns\ *n*

EC *abbr* European Community

¹ec·cen·tric \ik-'sen-trik\ *adj* **1** : deviating from a usual or ac-

cepted pattern **2** : deviating from a circular path ⟨~ orbits⟩ **3** : set with axis or support off center ⟨an ~ cam⟩; *also* : being off center — **ec·cen·tri·cal·ly** \-tri-k(ə-)lē\ *adv*

²eccentric *n* ♦ : an eccentric person

♦ character, crackpot, crank, kook, nut, oddball, screwball, weirdo

ec·cen·tric·i·ty \,ek-,sen-'tri-sə-tē\ *n* ♦ : the quality or state of being eccentric; *also* : odd or whimsical behavior

♦ crotchet, idiosyncrasy, mannerism, oddity, peculiarity, quirk, singularity, trick

Eccles *abbr* Ecclesiastes

Ec·cle·si·as·tes \i-,klē-zē-'as-tēz\ *n* : a book of wisdom literature in canonical Jewish and Christian Scripture

ec·cle·si·as·tic \i-,klē-zē-'as-tik\ *n* ♦ : a member of the clergy : CLERGYMAN

♦ clergyman, divine, father, minister, preacher, priest, reverend

ec·cle·si·as·ti·cal \-ti-kəl\ *or* **ec·cle·si·as·tic** \-tik\ *adj* : of or relating to a church esp. as an institution ⟨~ art⟩ — **ec·cle·si·as·ti·cal·ly** \-ti-k(ə-)lē\ *adv*

Ec·cle·si·as·ti·cus \i-,klē-zē-'as-ti-kəs\ *n* : a didactic book included in the Protestant Apocrypha and as Sirach in the Roman Catholic canon of the Old Testament

Ecclus *abbr* Ecclesiasticus

ECG *abbr* electrocardiogram

ech·e·lon \'e-shə-,län\ *n* **1** : a steplike arrangement (as of troops or airplanes) **2** ♦ : a level (as of authority or responsibility) within an organization

♦ degree, footing, level, place, position, rank, situation, standing, station, status

ech·i·na·cea \,e-ki-'nā-sē-ə, -shə\ *n* : the dried root of three composite herbs that is used primarily in herbal remedies to boost the immune system; *also* : any of these herbs

echi·no·derm \i-'kī-nə-,dərm\ *n* : any of a phylum of marine animals (as starfishes and sea urchins) having similar body parts (as the arms of a starfish) arranged around a central axis and often having a calcium-containing outer skeleton

¹echo \'e-kō\ *n, pl* **ech·oes** *also* **ech·os 1** : repetition of a sound caused by a reflection of the sound waves; *also* : the reflection of a radar signal by an object **2** : one who closely imitates or repeats another's words, ideas, or acts — **echo·ic** \e-'kō-ik\ *adj*

²echo *vb* ♦ : to produce an echo; *also* : to repeat or imitate (as a sound)

♦ repeat, resonate, resound, reverberate

echo·lo·ca·tion \,e-kō-lō-'kā-shən\ *n* : a process for locating distant or invisible objects by sound waves reflected back to the sender (as by a bat) from the objects

echt \'ekt\ *adj* : TRUE, GENUINE ⟨an ~ New Yorker⟩

éclair \ā-'klar\ *n* : an oblong shell of light pastry with whipped cream or custard filling

éclat \ā-'klä\ *n* **1** : a dazzling effect or success **2** : ACCLAIM

eclec·tic \e-'klek-tik\ *adj* **1** : selecting or made up of what seems best of varied sources **2** ♦ : composed of elements drawn from various sources; *also* : consisting of dissimilar ingredients or constituents — **eclectic** *n* — **eclec·ti·cism** \-'klek-tə-,si-zəm\ *n*

♦ assorted, heterogeneous, miscellaneous, mixed, motley, varied

¹eclipse \i-'klips\ *n* **1** : the total or partial obscuring of one celestial body by another; *also* : a passing into the shadow of a celestial body **2** : a falling into obscurity or decline ⟨a career in ~⟩

²eclipse *vb* **eclipsed; eclips·ing 1** : to cause an eclipse of **2** ♦ : to go beyond in accomplishment : SURPASS

♦ beat, better, excel, outdistance, outdo, outshine, outstrip, surpass, top, transcend

eclip·tic \i-'klip-tik\ *n* : the great circle of the celestial sphere that is the apparent path of the sun

ec·logue \'ek-,lȯg, -,läg\ *n* : a pastoral poem

ECM *abbr* European Common Market

ecol *abbr* ecological; ecology

E. coli \,ē-'kō-,lī\ *n, pl* **E. coli** : a rod-shaped bacterium that sometimes causes intestinal illness

ecol·o·gy \i-'kä-lə-jē, e-\ *n, pl* **-gies 1** : a branch of science concerned with the relationships between organisms and their environment **2** : the pattern of relations between one or more organisms and the environment — **eco·log·i·cal** \,ē-kə-'lä-ji-kəl, ,e-\ *also* **eco·log·ic** \-jik\ *adj* — **eco·log·i·cal·ly** \-ji-k(ə-)lē\ *adv* — **ecol·o·gist** \i-'kä-lə-jist, e-\ *n*

e–com·merce \'ē-,kä-(,)mərs\ *n* : commerce conducted via the Internet

econ *abbr* economics; economist; economy

eco·nom·ic \ˌe-kə-ˈnä-mik, ˌē-\ *adj* : of or relating to the production, distribution, and consumption of goods and services

eco·nom·i·cal \-ˈnä-mi-kəl\ *adj* **1** ♦ : marked by careful use of resources : THRIFTY **2** : operating with little waste or at a saving — **ec·o·nom·i·cal·ly** \-k(ə-)lē\ *adv*

  ♦ frugal, provident, sparing, thrifty

eco·nom·ics \ˌe-kə-ˈnä-miks, ˌē-\ *n sing or pl* : a social science dealing with the production, distribution, and consumption of goods and services — **econ·o·mist** \i-ˈkä-nə-mist\ *n*

econ·o·mise *Brit var of* ECONOMIZE

econ·o·mize \i-ˈkä-nə-ˌmīz\ *vb* **-mized; -miz·ing** ♦ : to practice economy : be frugal — **econ·o·miz·er** *n*

  ♦ save, scrimp, skimp *Ant* waste

¹**econ·o·my** \i-ˈkä-nə-mē\ *n, pl* **-mies** **1** ♦ : thrifty and efficient use of resources; *also* : an instance of this **2** : manner of arrangement or functioning : ORGANIZATION **3** : an economic system ⟨a money ~⟩

  ♦ frugality, husbandry, providence, thrift *Ant* wastefulness

²**economy** *adj* : ECONOMICAL ⟨~ cars⟩

eco·sys·tem \ˈē-kō-ˌsis-təm, ˈe-\ *n* : the complex of an ecological community and its environment functioning as a unit in nature

eco·tour·ism \ˌē-kō-ˈtu̇r-ˌi-zəm, ˌe-\ *n* : the touring of natural habitats in a manner meant to minimize ecological impact — **eco·tour·ist** \-ˈtu̇r-ist\ *n*

ecru \ˈe-krü, ˈā-\ *n* : BEIGE — **ecru** *adj*

ec·sta·sy \ˈek-stə-sē\ *n, pl* **-sies** **1** ♦ : extreme and usu. rapturous emotional excitement **2** *often cap* : an illicit drug with hallucinogenic properties that is chemically related to amphetamine

  ♦ elation, euphoria, exhilaration, heaven, intoxication, paradise, rapture, rhapsody, transport *Ant* depression

ec·stat·ic \ek-ˈsta-tik, ik-\ *adj* ♦ : of, relating to, or marked by ecstasy — **ec·stat·i·cal·ly** \-ti-k(ə-)lē\ *adv*

  ♦ elated, euphoric, intoxicated, rapturous, rhapsodic *Ant* depressed

Ecua *abbr* Ecuador

Ec·ua·dor·an \ˌe-kwə-ˈdȯr-ən\ *or* **Ec·ua·dor·ean** *or* **Ec·ua·dor·ian** \-ē-ən\ *n* : a native or inhabitant of Ecuador — **Ecuadorean** *or* **Ecuadorian** *adj*

ec·u·men·i·cal \ˌe-kyu̇-ˈme-ni-kəl\ *adj* : general in extent or influence; *esp* : promoting or tending toward worldwide Christian unity — **ec·u·men·i·cal·ly** \-k(ə-)lē\ *adv*

ec·ze·ma \ig-ˈzē-mə, ˈeg-zə-mə, ˈek-sə-\ *n* : an itching skin inflammation with oozing and then crusted lesions — **ec·zem·a·tous** \ig-ˈze-mə-təs\ *adj*

ed *abbr* **1** edited; edition; editor **2** education

¹**-ed** \d *after a vowel or* b, g, j, l, m, n, ŋ, r, th, v, z, zh; əd, id *after* d, t; t *after other sounds*\ *vb suffix or adj suffix* **1** — used to form the past participle of regular weak verbs ⟨end*ed*⟩ ⟨fad*ed*⟩ ⟨tri*ed*⟩ ⟨patt*ed*⟩ **2** : having : characterized by ⟨cultur*ed*⟩ ⟨2-legg*ed*⟩; *also* : having the characteristics of ⟨bigot*ed*⟩

²**-ed** *vb suffix* — used to form the past tense of regular weak verbs ⟨judg*ed*⟩ ⟨deni*ed*⟩ ⟨dropp*ed*⟩

Edam \ˈē-dəm, -ˌdam\ *n* : a yellow Dutch pressed cheese made in balls

ed·a·ma·me \ˌe-də-ˈmä-mā\ *n* : immature green soybeans usu. in the pod

ed·dy \ˈe-dē\ *n, pl* **eddies** : WHIRLPOOL — **eddy** *vb*

edel·weiss \ˈād-ᵊl-ˌwīs, -ˌvīs\ *n* : a small perennial woolly composite herb that grows high in the Alps

ede·ma \i-ˈdē-mə\ *n* : abnormal accumulation of watery fluid in connective tissue or in a serous cavity — **edem·a·tous** \-ˈde-mə-təs\ *adj*

Eden \ˈēd-ᵊn\ *n* ♦ : a place or state of bliss or delight : PARADISE

  ♦ Elysium, heaven, paradise, utopia

¹**edge** \ˈej\ *n* **1** : the cutting side of a blade **2** : a noticeably harsh or sharp quality; *also* : FORCE, EFFECTIVENESS **3** ♦ : the line where something begins or ends; *also* : the area adjoining such an edge **4** ♦ : a favorable margin : ADVANTAGE — **edged** \ˈejd\ *adj*

  ♦ [3] border, bound, boundary, fringe, margin, perimeter, periphery, rim, skirt, verge ♦ [4] advantage, better, drop, jump, upper hand, vantage

²**edge** *vb* **edged; edg·ing** **1** ♦ : to give or form an edge **2** : to move or force gradually ⟨~ into a crowd⟩ **3** : to defeat by a small margin ⟨*edged* out her opponent⟩ — **edg·er** *n*

  ♦ grind, hone, sharpen, strop, whet

edge·wise \ˈej-ˌwīz\ *adv* : SIDEWAYS

edg·ing \ˈe-jiŋ\ *n* : something that forms an edge or border ⟨a lace ~⟩

edgy \ˈe-jē\ *adj* **edg·i·er; -est** **1** ♦ : having an edge : SHARP ⟨an ~ tone⟩ **2** ♦ : being on edge : TENSE, NERVOUS **3** : having a bold, provocative, or unconventional quality — **edg·i·ness** *n*

  ♦ [1] cutting, ground, keen, sharp ♦ [2] aflutter, anxious, jittery, jumpy, nervous, nervy, tense, troubled, upset, worried

ed·i·ble \ˈe-də-bəl\ *adj* : fit or safe to be eaten — **ed·i·bil·i·ty** \ˌe-də-ˈbi-lə-tē\ *n* — **edible** *n*

edict \ˈē-ˌdikt\ *n* ♦ : a proclamation having the force of law; *also* : ORDER, DECREE

  ♦ decree, directive, fiat, order, ruling

ed·i·fi·ca·tion \ˌe-də-fə-ˈkā-shən\ *n* : instruction and improvement esp. in morality

ed·i·fice \ˈe-də-fəs\ *n* : a usu. large building

ed·i·fy \ˈe-də-ˌfī\ *vb* ♦ : to instruct and improve esp. in moral and religious knowledge

  ♦ educate, enlighten, nurture

ed·it \ˈe-dət\ *vb* **1** ♦ : to revise, assemble, or prepare for publication or release (as a motion picture) **2** : to direct the publication and policies of (as a newspaper) **3** : DELETE — **ed·i·tor** \ˈe-də-tər\ *n* — **ed·i·tor·ship** *n* — **ed·i·tress** \-trəs\ *n*

  ♦ redraft, revamp, revise, rework

edi·tion \i-ˈdi-shən\ *n* **1** : the form in which a text is published **2** : the total number of copies (as of a book) published at one time **3** : VERSION

¹**ed·i·to·ri·al** \ˌe-də-ˈtȯr-ē-əl\ *adj* **1** : of or relating to an editor or editing **2** : being or resembling an editorial — **ed·i·to·ri·al·ly** *adv*

²**editorial** *n* : an article (as in a newspaper) giving the views of the editors or publishers; *also* : an expression of opinion resembling an editorial ⟨a television ~⟩

ed·i·to·ri·al·ize \ˌe-də-ˈtȯr-ē-ə-ˌlīz\ *vb* **-ized; -iz·ing** **1** : to express an opinion in an editorial **2** : to introduce opinions into factual reporting — **ed·i·to·ri·al·i·za·tion** \-ˌtȯr-ē-ə-lə-ˈzā-shən\ *n* — **ed·i·to·ri·al·iz·er** *n*

EDP *abbr* electronic data processing

EDT *abbr* Eastern daylight (saving) time

educ *abbr* education; educational

ed·u·ca·ble \ˈe-jə-kə-bəl\ *adj* : capable of being educated

ed·u·cate \ˈe-jə-ˌkāt\ *vb* **-cat·ed; -cat·ing** **1** ♦ : to provide with schooling **2** ♦ : to develop mentally and morally; *also* : to provide with information

  ♦ [1] indoctrinate, instruct, school, teach, train, tutor ♦ [2] edify, enlighten, nurture

educated *adj* ♦ : having an education; *esp* : having an education beyond the average

  ♦ erudite, knowledgeable, learned, literate, scholarly, well-read *Ant* ignorant, illiterate, uneducated

ed·u·ca·tion \ˌe-jə-ˈkā-shən\ *n* **1** ♦ : the action or process of educating or being educated; *also* : the knowledge and development resulting from an educational process **2** : a field of study dealing with methods of teaching and learning

  ♦ instruction, teaching, training, tutelage ♦ erudition, knowledge, learning, scholarship, science

ed·u·ca·tion·al \-shə-nəl\ *adj* ♦ : of, relating to, or concerned with education; *also* : serving to further education — **ed·u·ca·tion·al·ly** *adv*

  ♦ informative, instructive

educational television *n* : PUBLIC TELEVISION

ed·u·ca·tor \-ˌkā-tər\ *n* ♦ : one skilled in teaching

  ♦ instructor, pedagogue, schoolteacher, teacher

educe \i-ˈdüs, -ˈdyüs\ *vb* **educed; educ·ing** **1** : to bring out (as something latent) : ELICIT, EVOKE **2** : DEDUCE

ed·u·tain·ment \ˌe-jə-ˈtān-mənt\ *n* : entertainment that is designed to be educational

¹**-ee** \ˈē, (ˌ)ē\ *n suffix* **1** : one that receives or benefits from (a specified action or thing) ⟨grant*ee*⟩ ⟨patent*ee*⟩ **2** : a person who does (a specified action) ⟨escap*ee*⟩

²**-ee** *n suffix* **1** : a particular esp. small kind of ⟨boot*ee*⟩ **2** : one resembling or suggestive of ⟨goat*ee*⟩

EE *abbr* electrical engineer

EEC *abbr* European Economic Community

EEG *abbr* **1** electroencephalogram **2** electroencephalograph

eel \ˈēl\ *n* : any of numerous snakelike bony fishes with a smooth slimy skin

EEO *abbr* equal employment opportunity

ee·rie *also* **ee·ry** \'ir-ē\ *adj* **ee·ri·er; -est** ♦ : so mysterious, strange, or unexpected as to send a chill up the spine : WEIRD, UNCANNY — **ee·ri·ly** \'ir-ə-lē\ *adv*

　♦ creepy, haunting, odd, spooky, strange, uncanny, unearthly, weird

eff *abbr* efficiency

ef·face \i-'fās, e-\ *vb* **ef·faced; ef·fac·ing** : to obliterate or obscure by or as if by rubbing out — **ef·face·able** *adj* — **ef·face·ment** *n*

¹**ef·fect** \i-'fekt\ *n* **1** : MEANING, INTENT **2** ♦ : something that inevitably follows an antecedent : RESULT **3** : APPEARANCE **4** ♦ : power to bring about a result : INFLUENCE **5** *pl* ♦ : movable property : GOODS, POSSESSIONS **6** : the quality or state of being operative : OPERATION

　♦ [2] aftermath, conclusion, consequence, issue, outcome, outgrowth, product, result, upshot *Ant* antecedent, cause, occasion, reason ♦ [4] impact, influence, mark, repercussion, sway ♦ *usu* **effects** [5] belongings, chattels, holdings, paraphernalia, possessions, things

²**effect** *vb* ♦ : to cause to happen ⟨∼ repairs⟩ ⟨∼ changes⟩

　♦ bring about, cause, create, effectuate, generate, induce, make, produce, prompt, result

ef·fec·tive \i-'fek-tiv\ *adj* **1** ♦ : producing a decisive or desired effect; *also* : marked by the quality of being influential or exerting positive influence ⟨an ∼ presentation⟩ **2** : IMPRESSIVE, STRIKING **3** : ready for service or action **4** : being in effect — **ef·fec·tive·ly** *adv*

　♦ convincing, decisive, effectual, efficacious, efficient, forceful, fruitful, persuasive, potent, productive *Ant* ineffective, ineffectual, inefficient, fruitless, unproductive

ef·fec·tive·ness *n* ♦ : the quality or state of being effective; *also* : power to be effective

　♦ efficacy, efficiency, force, impact, productiveness

ef·fec·tu·al \i-'fek-chə-wəl\ *adj* ♦ : producing an intended effect — **ef·fec·tu·al·ly** *adv*

　♦ effective, efficacious, efficient, fruitful, potent, productive

ef·fec·tu·ate \i-'fek-chə-ˌwāt\ *vb* **-at·ed; -at·ing** ♦ : to cause to come into being : BRING ABOUT, EFFECT

　♦ bring about, cause, create, effect, generate, induce, make, produce, prompt, result, work, yield

ef·fem·i·nate \ə-'fe-mə-nət\ *adj* ♦ : marked by qualities more typical of women than men — **ef·fem·i·na·cy** \-nə-sē\ *n*

　♦ feminine, girlish, unmanly, womanly *Ant* manly, mannish, masculine

ef·fen·di \e-'fen-dē\ *n* : a man of property, authority, or education in an eastern Mediterranean country

ef·fer·ent \'e-fə-rənt\ *adj* : bearing or conducting outward from a more central part ⟨∼ nerves⟩

ef·fer·vesce \ˌe-fər-'ves\ *vb* **-vesced; -vesc·ing** **1** : to bubble and hiss as gas escapes **2** : to show liveliness or exhilaration — **ef·fer·ves·cence** \-'ve-s³ns\ *n*

ef·fer·ves·cent \-³nt\ *adj* ♦ : impossible or difficult to restrain or suppress — **ef·fer·ves·cent·ly** *adv*

　♦ bubbly, buoyant, exuberant, frolicsome, high-spirited, vivacious

ef·fete \e-'fēt\ *adj* **1** ♦ : having lost character, vitality, or strength; *also* : DECADENT **2** : EFFEMINATE

　♦ decadent, degenerate, soft, weak

ef·fi·ca·cious \ˌe-fə-'kā-shəs\ *adj* ♦ : producing an intended effect ⟨∼ remedies⟩

　♦ effective, effectual, efficient, fruitful, potent, productive

ef·fi·ca·cy \'e-fi-kə-sē\ *n* ♦ : the power to produce an effect

　♦ effectiveness, efficiency, productiveness *Ant* ineffectiveness, inefficiency

ef·fi·cien·cy \-shən-sē\ *n* ♦ : the quality or degree of being efficient; *also* : efficient operation

　♦ effectiveness, efficacy, productiveness

ef·fi·cient \i-'fi-shənt\ *adj* ♦ : productive of desired effects esp. without waste — **ef·fi·cient·ly** *adv*

　♦ effective, effectual, efficacious, fruitful, potent, productive

ef·fi·gy \'e-fə-jē\ *n, pl* **-gies** : IMAGE; *esp* : a crude figure of a hated person

ef·flo·res·cence \ˌe-flə-'res-³ns\ *n* **1** : the period or state of flowering **2** : the action or process of developing **3** : fullness of development : FLOWERING

ef·flu·ence \'e-ˌflü-əns\ *n* : something that flows out

ef·flu·ent \'e-ˌflü-ənt\ *n* : something that flows out; *esp* : a fluid (as sewage) discharged as waste — **effluent** *adj*

ef·flu·vi·um \e-'flü-vē-əm\ *n, pl* **-via** \-vē-ə\ *also* **-vi·ums** **1** : a usu. unpleasant emanation **2** : a by-product usu. in the form of waste

ef·fort \'e-fərt\ *n* **1** ♦ : hard work : EXERTION; *also* : a product of effort **2** : active or applied force

　♦ exertion, expenditure, labor (*or* labour), pains, sweat, trouble, work

ef·fort·less *adj* ♦ : showing or requiring little or no effort

　♦ easy, facile, fluent, fluid, light, painless, ready, smooth, snap

ef·fort·less·ly *adv* ♦ : in an effortless manner

　♦ easily, fluently, freely, handily, lightly, painlessly, readily, smoothly

ef·fron·tery \i-'frən-tə-rē\ *n, pl* **-ter·ies** ♦ : shameless and offensive boldness

　♦ audacity, brass, brazenness, cheek, chutzpah, gall, nerve, presumption, temerity

ef·ful·gence \i-'fúl-jəns, -'fəl-\ *n* ♦ : radiant splendor : BRILLIANCE

　♦ brilliance, dazzle, illumination, luminosity, radiance, splendor

ef·ful·gent \-jənt\ *adj* ♦ : extremely radiant

　♦ beaming, bright, brilliant, glowing, incandescent, luminous, lustrous, radiant

ef·fu·sion \i-'fyü-zhən, e-\ *n* : a gushing forth; *also* : unrestrained utterance — **ef·fuse** \i-'fyüz, e-\ *vb*

ef·fu·sive \i-'fyü-siv, e-\ *adj* ♦ : marked by the expression of great or excessive emotion or enthusiasm — **ef·fu·sive·ly** *adv*

　♦ demonstrative, emotional, uninhibited, unreserved, unrestrained

eft \'eft\ *n* : NEWT

EFT *or* **EFTS** *abbr* electronic funds transfer (system)

e.g. *abbr* for example

Eg *abbr* Egypt; Egyptian

egal·i·tar·i·an·ism \i-ˌga-lə-'ter-ē-ə-ˌni-zəm\ *n* : a belief in human equality esp. in social, political, and economic affairs — **egal·i·tar·i·an** *adj or n*

¹**egg** \'eg\ *vb* ♦ : to urge to action — usu. used with *on*

　♦ *usu* **egg on** encourage, exhort, goad, press, prod, prompt, urge

²**egg** *n* **1** : a rounded usu. hard-shelled reproductive body esp. of birds and reptiles from which the young hatches; *also* : the egg of the common domestic chicken as an article of food **2** : a germ cell produced by a female

egg·beat·er \'eg-ˌbē-tər\ *n* : a hand-operated kitchen utensil for beating, stirring, or whipping

egg cell *n* : EGG 2

egg·head \-ˌhed\ *n, often disparaging* : an intellectual person : INTELLECTUAL, HIGHBROW

egg·nog \-ˌnäg\ *n* : a drink consisting of eggs beaten with sugar, milk or cream, and often alcoholic liquor

egg·plant \-ˌplant\ *n* : the edible usu. large and purplish fruit of a plant related to the potato; *also* : the plant

egg roll *n* : a thin egg-dough casing filled with minced vegetables and often bits of meat and usu. deep-fried

egg·shell \'eg-ˌshel\ *n* : the hard exterior covering of an egg

egis *var of* AEGIS

eg·lan·tine \'e-glən-ˌtīn, -ˌtēn\ *n* : SWEETBRIER

ego \'ē-gō\ *n, pl* **egos** **1** : the self as distinguished from others **2** : the one of the three divisions of the psyche in psychoanalytic theory that is the organized conscious mediator between the person and reality **3** ♦ : an exaggerated sense of self-importance; *also* : a confidence and satisfaction in oneself

　♦ complacence, conceit, pride, self-importance, self-regard, self-respect, self-satisfaction, smugness, vainglory, vanity

ego·cen·tric \ˌē-gō-'sen-trik\ *adj* ♦ : concerned or overly concerned with the self; *esp* : SELF-CENTERED

　♦ egotistic, selfish, self-seeking *Ant* selfless

ego·ism \'ē-gō-ˌi-zəm\ *n* **1** : a doctrine holding self-interest to be the motive or the valid end of action **2** ♦ : excessive concern for oneself with or without exaggerated feelings of self-importance — **ego·ist** \-ist\ *n*

♦ egotism, self-centeredness, self-interest, selfishness, self-regard *Ant* selflessness

ego·is·tic \ˌē-gō-ˈis-tik\ *adj* : having an exaggerated sense of self-importance — **ego·is·ti·cal·ly** *adv*

ego·tism \ˈē-gə-ˌti-zəm\ *n* 1 : the practice of talking about oneself too much 2 ♦ : an exaggerated sense of self-importance : CONCEIT — **ego·tist** \-tist\ *n*

♦ complacence, conceit, pride, self-esteem, self-importance, self-satisfaction, smugness, vainglory, vanity

ego·tis·tic \ˌē-gə-ˈtis-tik\ *or* **ego·tis·ti·cal** \-ti-kəl\ *adj* ♦ : an exaggerated sense of self-importance — **ego·tis·ti·cal·ly** *adv*

♦ complacent, conceited, important, prideful, proud, self-important, self-satisfied, smug, stuck-up, vain

ego trip *n* : an act that enhances and satisfies one's ego

egre·gious \i-ˈgrē-jəs\ *adj* ♦ : notably bad : FLAGRANT — **egre·gious·ly** *adv* — **egre·gious·ness** *n*

♦ blatant, flagrant, glaring, gross, obvious, patent, pronounced, rank, striking

egress \ˈē-ˌgres\ *n* ♦ : a way out : EXIT

♦ exit, issue, outlet

egret \ˈē-grət, i-ˈgret\ *n* : any of various herons that bear long plumes during the breeding season

Egyp·tian \i-ˈjip-shən\ *n* 1 : a native or inhabitant of Egypt 2 : the language of the ancient Egyptians from earliest times to about the 3d century A.D. — **Egyptian** *adj*

ei·der \ˈī-dər\ *n* : any of several northern sea ducks that yield a soft down

ei·der·down \-ˌdau̇n\ *n* 1 : the down of the eider 2 : a comforter filled with eiderdown

ei·do·lon \ī-ˈdō-lən\ *n, pl* **-lons** *or* **-la** \-lə\ 1 : PHANTOM 2 : IDEAL

eight \ˈāt\ *n* 1 : one more than seven 2 : the 8th in a set or series 3 : something having eight units — **eight** *adj or pron* — **eighth** \ˈātth\ *adj or adv or n*

eight ball *n* : a black pool ball numbered 8 — **behind the eight ball** : in a highly disadvantageous position

eigh·teen \ˈāt-ˈtēn\ *n* : one more than 17 — **eighteen** *adj or pron* — **eigh·teenth** \-ˈtēnth\ *adj or n*

eighty \ˈā-tē\ *n, pl* **eight·ies** : eight times 10 — **eight·i·eth** \ˈā-tē-əth\ *adj or n* — **eighty** *adj or pron*

ein·stei·ni·um \īn-ˈstī-nē-əm\ *n* : an artificially produced radioactive element

¹ei·ther \ˈē-thər, ˈī-\ *adj* 1 : being the one and the other of two : EACH ⟨trees on ~ side⟩ 2 : being the one or the other of two ⟨take ~ road⟩

²either *pron* : the one or the other

³either *conj* — used as a function word before the first of two or more words or word groups of which the last is preceded by *or* to indicate that they represent alternatives ⟨a statement is ~ true or false⟩

ejac·u·late \i-ˈja-kyə-ˌlāt\ *vb* **-lat·ed; -lat·ing** 1 : to eject a fluid (as semen) 2 ♦ : to utter suddenly : EXCLAIM — **ejac·u·la·to·ry** \-ˈja-kyə-lə-ˌtȯr-ē\ *adj*

♦ blurt, bolt, cry, spout

ejac·u·la·tion \i-ˌja-kyə-ˈlā-shən\ *n* : something ejaculated; *esp* ♦ : a short sudden emotional utterance

♦ cry, exclamation, interjection

eject \i-ˈjekt\ *vb* ♦ : to drive or throw out or off — **ejec·tion** \-ˈjek-shən\ *n*

♦ banish, boot (out), bounce, cast, expel, oust, rout, run off, throw out ♦ belch, disgorge, erupt, jet, spew, spout, spurt

eke \ˈēk\ *vb* **eked; ek·ing** ♦ : to gain, supplement, or extend usu. with effort — usu. used with *out* ⟨~ out a living⟩

♦ usu **eke out** scrape, squeeze, wrest, wring

EKG *abbr* electrocardiogram; electrocardiograph

el *abbr* elevation

¹elab·o·rate \i-ˈla-bə-rət, -ˈla-brət\ *adj* 1 ♦ : planned or carried out with great care 2 ♦ : being complex and usu. ornate — **elab·o·rate·ly** *adv*

♦ [1, 2] complex, complicated, detailed, fancy, intricate, involved, sophisticated *Ant* simple

²elab·o·rate \i-ˈla-bə-ˌrāt\ *vb* **-rat·ed; -rat·ing** 1 : to build up from simpler ingredients 2 ♦ : to work out in detail : develop fully

♦ usu **elaborate on** amplify, develop, embellish, enlarge (on), expand

elab·o·rate·ness *n* ♦ : the state or quality of being elaborate

♦ complexity, intricacy, sophistication

elab·o·ra·tion \-ˌla-bə-ˈrā-shən\ *n* 1 ♦ : the act or process of elaborating 2 : something produced by elaborating

♦ development, evolution, expansion, growth, progress, progression

élan \ā-ˈlän\ *n* : ARDOR, SPIRIT

eland \ˈē-lənd, -ˌland\ *n, pl* **eland** *also* **elands** : either of two large African antelopes with spirally twisted horns in both sexes

elapse \i-ˈlaps\ *vb* **elapsed; elaps·ing** ♦ : to slip by : PASS

♦ cease, end, expire, finish, pass, quit, stop, terminate, wind up

¹elas·tic \i-ˈlas-tik\ *adj* 1 ♦ : capable of recovering size and shape after deformation : SPRINGY 2 ♦ : capable of ready change or easy expansion or contraction : FLEXIBLE; *also* : ADAPTABLE — **elas·tic·i·ty** \-ˌlas-ˈti-sə-tē, ˌē-ˌlas-\ *n*

♦ [1] flexible, resilient, rubbery, springy, stretch, supple *Ant* inelastic, inflexible, rigid, stiff ♦ [2] adaptable, adjustable, changeable, flexible, fluid, malleable, variable

²elastic *n* 1 : elastic material 2 : a rubber band

elate \i-ˈlāt\ *vb* **elat·ed; elat·ing** ♦ : to fill with joy

♦ elevate, enrapture, exhilarate, transport *Ant* depress

elated *adj* ♦ : marked by high spirits

♦ ecstatic, euphoric, intoxicated, rapturous, rhapsodic

ela·tion \-ˈlā-shən\ *n* ♦ : the quality or state of being elated

♦ ecstasy, euphoria, exhilaration, heaven, intoxication, paradise, rapture, rhapsody, transport

¹el·bow \ˈel-ˌbō\ *n* 1 : the joint of the arm; *also* : the outer curve of the bent arm 2 : a bend or joint resembling an elbow in shape

²elbow *vb* ♦ : to push aside with the elbow; *also* : to make one's way by elbowing

♦ bulldoze, muscle, press, push

elbow room \ˈel-bō-ˌrüm, -ˌru̇m\ *n* : enough space for work or operation

¹el·der \ˈel-dər\ *n* : ELDERBERRY 2

²elder *adj* 1 : being the older one 2 : EARLIER, FORMER 3 : of higher rank : SENIOR

³elder *n* 1 : an older individual : SENIOR 2 ♦ : one having authority by reason of age and experience 3 : a church officer

♦ [1] ancient, golden-ager, oldster, senior citizen ♦ [2] dean, senior

el·der·ber·ry \ˈel-dər-ˌber-ē\ *n* 1 : the edible black or red fruit of a shrub or tree related to the honeysuckle and bearing flat clusters of small white or pink flowers 2 : a tree or shrub bearing elderberries

el·der·ly \ˈel-dər-lē\ *adj* 1 ♦ : rather old; *esp* : past middle age 2 : of, relating to, or characteristic of later life

♦ ancient, geriatric, old, senior *Ant* young, youthful

el·dest \ˈel-dəst\ *adj* : of the greatest age

El Do·ra·do \ˌel-də-ˈrä-dō, -ˈrā-\ *n* : a place of vast riches, abundance, or opportunity

elec *abbr* electric; electrical; electricity

¹elect \i-ˈlekt\ *adj* 1 ♦ : carefully selected : CHOSEN 2 : elected but not yet installed in office ⟨the president-*elect*⟩

♦ chosen, select

²elect *n, pl* **elect** 1 : a selected person 2 *pl* ♦ : a select or exclusive group

♦ best, choice, cream, elite, fat, flower, pick, prime

³elect *vb* 1 : to select by vote (as for office or membership) 2 ♦ : to select or choose esp. by preference : PICK

♦ choose, cull, handpick, name, opt, pick, prefer, select, single, take

elec·tion \i-ˈlek-shən\ *n* 1 ♦ : an act or process of electing 2 : the fact of being elected

♦ choice, selection

elec·tion·eer \i-ˌlek-shə-ˈnir\ *vb* : to work for the election of a candidate or party

¹elec·tive \i-ˈlek-tiv\ *adj* 1 : chosen or filled by election 2 ♦ : permitting a choice : OPTIONAL

♦ discretionary, optional, voluntary

²elective *n* : an elective course or subject of study

elec·tor \i-ˈlek-tər\ *n* 1 : one qualified to vote in an election 2 : one elected to an electoral college — **elec·tor·al** \i-ˈlek-tə-rəl\ *adj*

electoral college *n* : a body of electors who elect the president and vice president of the U.S.

elec·tor·ate \i-ˈlek-tə-rət\ *n* : a body of persons entitled to vote

elec·tric \i-ˈlek-trik\ *adj* **1** *or* **elec·tri·cal** \-tri-kəl\ : of, relating to, operated by, or produced by electricity **2** ♦ : exciting as if by electric shock : ELECTRIFYING, THRILLING; *also* : charged with strong emotion — **elec·tri·cal·ly** *adv*

♦ breathtaking, exciting, exhilarating, rousing, stirring, thrilling

electrical storm *n* : THUNDERSTORM

electric chair *n* : a chair used to carry out the death penalty by electrocution

electric eye *n* : PHOTOELECTRIC CELL

elec·tri·cian \i-ˌlek-ˈtri-shən\ *n* : a person who installs, operates, or repairs electrical equipment

elec·tric·i·ty \i-ˌlek-ˈtri-sə-tē\ *n, pl* **-ties 1** : a form of energy that occurs naturally (as in lightning) or is produced (as in a generator) and that is expressed in terms of the movement and interaction of electrons **2** : electric current

elec·tri·fy \i-ˈlek-trə-ˌfī\ *vb* **-fied; -fy·ing 1** : to charge with electricity **2** : to equip for use of electric power **3** ♦ : to excite intensely or suddenly : THRILL — **elec·tri·fi·ca·tion** \i-ˌlek-trə-fə-ˈkā-shən\ *n*

♦ excite, exhilarate, galvanize, intoxicate, thrill, titillate, turn on

elec·tro·car·dio·gram \i-ˌlek-trō-ˈkär-dē-ə-ˌgram\ *n* : the tracing made by an electrocardiograph

elec·tro·car·dio·graph \-ˌgraf\ *n* : a device for recording the changes of electrical potential occurring during the heartbeat — **elec·tro·car·dio·graph·ic** \-ˌkär-dē-ə-ˈgra-fik\ *adj* — **elec·tro·car·di·og·ra·phy** \-dē-ˈä-grə-fē\ *n*

elec·tro·chem·is·try \-ˈke-mə-strē\ *n* : a branch of chemistry that deals with the relation of electricity to chemical changes — **elec·tro·chem·i·cal** \-ˈke-mi-kəl\ *adj*

elec·tro·cute \i-ˈlek-trə-ˌkyüt\ *vb* **-cut·ed; -cut·ing 1** : to kill (a criminal) by electricity **2** : to kill by electric shock — **elec·tro·cu·tion** \-ˌlek-trə-ˈkyü-shən\ *n*

elec·trode \i-ˈlek-ˌtrōd\ *n* : a conductor used to establish electrical contact with a nonmetallic part of a circuit

elec·tro·en·ceph·a·lo·gram \i-ˌlek-trō-in-ˈse-fə-lə-ˌgram\ *n* : the tracing made by an electroencephalograph

elec·tro·en·ceph·a·lo·graph \-ˌgraf\ *n* : an apparatus for detecting and recording brain waves — **elec·tro·en·ceph·a·lo·graph·ic** \-ˌse-fə-lə-ˈgra-fik\ *adj* — **elec·tro·en·ceph·a·log·ra·phy** \-ˈlä-grə-fē\ *n*

elec·trol·o·gist \i-ˌlek-ˈträ-lə-jist\ *n* : one that uses electrical means to remove hair, warts, moles, and birthmarks from the body

elec·trol·y·sis \i-ˌlek-ˈträ-lə-səs\ *n* **1** : the production of chemical changes by passage of an electric current through an electrolyte **2** : the destruction of hair roots with an electric current — **elec·tro·lyt·ic** \-trə-ˈli-tik\ *adj*

elec·tro·lyte \i-ˈlek-trə-ˌlīt\ *n* : a nonmetallic electric conductor in which current is carried by the movement of ions; *also* : a substance whose solution or molten form is such a conductor

elec·tro·mag·net \i-ˌlek-trō-ˈmag-nət\ *n* : a core of magnetic material (as iron) surrounded by a coil of wire through which an electric current is passed to magnetize the core

elec·tro·mag·net·ic \-ˈmag-ˈne-tik\ *adj* : of, relating to, or produced by electromagnetism — **elec·tro·mag·net·i·cal·ly** *adv*

electromagnetic radiation *n* : energy in the form of electromagnetic waves; *also* : a series of electromagnetic waves

electromagnetic wave *n* : a wave (as a radio wave, an X-ray, or a wave of visible light) that consists of associated electric and magnetic effects and that travels at the speed of light

elec·tro·mag·ne·tism \i-ˌlek-trō-ˈmag-nə-ˌti-zəm\ *n* **1** : magnetism developed by a current of electricity **2** : a natural force responsible for interactions between charged particles which result from their charge

elec·tro·mo·tive force \i-ˌlek-trə-ˈmō-tiv-\ *n* : the potential difference derived from an electrical source per unit quantity of electricity passing through the source

elec·tron \i-ˈlek-ˌträn\ *n* : a negatively charged elementary particle

elec·tron·ic \i-ˌlek-ˈträ-nik\ *adj* **1** : of or relating to electrons or electronics **2** : involving a computer — **elec·tron·i·cal·ly** \-ni-k(ə-)lē\ *adv*

electronic mail *n* : E-MAIL

elec·tron·ics \i-ˌlek-ˈträ-niks\ *n* **1** : the physics of electrons and electronic devices **2** : electronic components, devices, or equipment

electron microscope *n* : an instrument in which a beam of electrons is used to produce an enlarged image of a minute object

electron tube *n* : a device in which electrical conduction by elec-trons takes place within a sealed container and which is used for the controlled flow of electrons

electron volt *n* : a unit of energy equal to 1.60×10^{-19} joule

elec·tro·pho·re·sis \i-ˌlek-trə-fə-ˈrē-səs\ *n* : the movement of suspended particles through a medium (as paper or gel) by an electromotive force — **elec·tro·pho·ret·ic** \-ˈre-tik\ *adj*

elec·tro·plate \i-ˈlek-trə-ˌplāt\ *vb* : to coat (as with metal) by electrolysis

elec·tro·shock therapy \i-ˈlek-trō-ˌshäk-\ *n* : the treatment of mental illness by applying electric current to the head and inducing convulsions

elec·tro·stat·ics \i-ˌlek-trə-ˈsta-tiks\ *n* : physics dealing with the interactions of stationary electric charges

el·ee·mos·y·nary \ˌe-li-ˈmäs-ᵊn-ˌer-ē\ *adj* : CHARITABLE

el·e·gance \ˈe-li-gəns\ *n* **1 a** ♦ : refined gracefulness **b** ♦ : tasteful richness (as of design) **2** : something marked by elegance — **el·e·gant·ly** *adv*

♦ [1a, 1b] class, grace, handsomeness, majesty, refinement, stateliness

el·e·gant \-gənt\ *adj* ♦ : marked by elegance; *also* : of a high grade or quality

♦ graceful, handsome, majestic, refined, stately, tasteful *Ant* graceless, inelegant, tasteless, unhandsome ♦ choice, dainty, delicate, exquisite, rare, select

ele·gi·ac \ˌe-lə-ˈjī-ək, -ˌak\ *adj* : of or relating to an elegy

el·e·gy \ˈe-lə-jē\ *n, pl* **-gies** ♦ : a song, poem, or speech expressing grief for one who is dead; *also* : a reflective poem usu. melancholy in tone

♦ dirge, lament, requiem, threnody

elem *abbr* elementary

el·e·ment \ˈe-lə-mənt\ *n* **1** *pl* : weather conditions; *esp* : severe weather ⟨boards exposed to the ∼s⟩ **2** : natural environment ⟨in her ∼⟩ **3** ♦ : a constituent part **4** *pl* ♦ : the simplest principles (as of an art or science) : RUDIMENTS **5** : a member of a mathematical set **6** : any of more than 100 fundamental substances that consist of atoms of only one kind

♦ [3] component, constituent, factor, ingredient, member *Ant* whole ♦ *usu* **elements** [4] essentials, principles, rudiments

el·e·men·tal \ˌe-lə-ˈment-ᵊl\ *adj* ♦ : of, relating to, or being an element

♦ basic, elementary, essential, fundamental, rudimentary, underlying

el·e·men·ta·ry \ˌe-lə-ˈmen-trē, -tə-rē\ *adj* **1** ♦ : of, relating to, or dealing with the simplest elements or principles of something : RUDIMENTARY **2** : of, relating to, or teaching the basic subjects of education

♦ basic, elemental, essential, fundamental, rudimentary, underlying *Ant* advanced

elementary particle *n* : a subatomic particle of matter and energy that does not appear to be made up of other smaller particles

elementary school *n* : a school usu. including the first six or the first eight grades

el·e·phant \ˈe-lə-fənt\ *n, pl* **elephants** *also* **elephant** : any of a family of huge thickset nearly hairless mammals that have the snout lengthened into a trunk and two long curving pointed ivory tusks

el·e·phan·ti·a·sis \ˌe-lə-fən-ˈtī-ə-səs\ *n, pl* **-a·ses** \-ˌsēz\ : enlargement and thickening of tissues in response esp. to infection by minute parasitic worms

el·e·phan·tine \ˌe-lə-ˈfan-ˌtēn, -ˌtīn, ˈe-lə-fən-\ *adj* **1** ♦ : of great size or strength **2** : CLUMSY, PONDEROUS

♦ enormous, giant, gigantic, ginormous, huge, jumbo, mammoth, monumental, titanic, tremendous, vast, whopping

elev *abbr* elevation

el·e·vate \ˈe-lə-ˌvāt\ *vb* **-vat·ed; -vat·ing 1** ♦ : to lift up : RAISE **2** ♦ : to raise in rank or status **3** ♦ : to raise the spirits of : ELATE

♦ [1] boost, hike, hoist, jack, lift, raise ♦ [2] advance, promote, raise, upgrade ♦ [3] elate, enrapture, exhilarate, transport

el·e·va·tion \ˌe-lə-ˈvā-shən\ *n* **1** : the height to which something is raised (as above sea level) **2** ♦ : a lifting up **3** ♦ : something (as a hill or swelling) that is elevated

♦ [2] advancement, ascent, promotion, rise, upgrade ♦ [3] eminence, height, highland, hill, mound, prominence, rise

el·e·va·tor \ˈe-lə-ˌvā-tər\ *n* **1** : a cage or platform for conveying people or things from one level to another **2** : a building for storing and discharging grain **3** : a movable surface on an airplane to produce motion up or down

elev·en \i-'le-vən\ n **1** : one more than 10 **2** : the 11th in a set or series **3** : something having 11 units; *esp* : a football team — **eleven** *adj or pron* — **elev·enth** \-vənth\ *adj or n*

elf \'elf\ n, pl **elves** \'elvz\ ♦ : a mischievous fairy

 ♦ brownie, dwarf, fairy, fay, gnome, hobgoblin, leprechaun, pixie, puck, troll

ELF *abbr* extremely low frequency

elf·in \'el-fən\ *adj* **1** : of, relating to, or resembling an elf **2** ♦ : having an otherworldly or magical quality or charm

 ♦ alluring, attractive, charming, engaging, fascinating, fetching

elf·ish \'el-fish\ *adj* ♦ : of, relating to, or like an elf; *also* : irresponsibly playful

 ♦ antic, coltish, fay, frisky, frolicsome, playful, sportive

elic·it \i-'li-sət\ *vb* ♦ : to draw out or forth

 ♦ evoke, raise

elide \i-'līd\ *vb* **elid·ed; elid·ing** : to suppress or alter by elision

el·i·gi·ble \'e-lə-jə-bəl\ *adj* : qualified to participate or to be chosen — **el·i·gi·bil·i·ty** \ˌe-lə-jə-'bi-lə-tē\ n — **eligible** n

elim·i·nate \i-'li-mə-ˌnāt\ *vb* **-nat·ed; -nat·ing** **1** : REMOVE, ERADICATE **2** : to pass (wastes) from the body **3** : to leave out **4** ♦ : to bar from participation, enjoyment, consideration, or inclusion — **elim·i·na·tion** \-ˌli-mə-'nā-shən\ n

 ♦ ban, bar, count out, debar, except, exclude, rule out

eli·sion \i-'li-zhən\ n : the omission of a final or initial sound or a word; *esp* : the omission of an unstressed vowel or syllable in a verse to achieve a uniform rhythm

elite \ā-'lēt, ē-\ n **1** ♦ : the choice part; *also* : a superior group **2** : a typewriter type providing 12 characters to the inch — **elite** *adj*

 ♦ best, choice, cream, elect, fat, flower, pick, prime

elit·ism \-'lē-ˌti-zəm\ n : leadership or rule by an elite; *also* : advocacy of such elitism — **elit·ist** \-tist\ n or adj

elix·ir \i-'lik-sər\ n **1** : a substance held capable of prolonging life indefinitely; *also* : PANACEA **2** : a sweetened alcoholic medicinal solution

Eliz·a·be·than \i-ˌli-zə-'bē-thən\ *adj* : of, relating to, or characteristic of Elizabeth I of England or her times

elk \'elk\ n, pl **elk** *or* **elks** **1** : MOOSE — used for one of the Old World **2** : a large gregarious deer of No. America, Europe, Asia, and northwestern Africa with curved antlers having many branches

ell n : an extension at right angles to a building

el·lipse \i-'lips, e-\ n : a closed curve of oval shape

el·lip·sis \i-'lip-səs, e-\ n, pl **el·lip·ses** \-ˌsēz\ **1** : omission from an expression of a word clearly implied **2** : marks (as . . .) to show omission

el·lip·soid \i-'lip-ˌsȯid, e-\ n : a surface all plane sections of which are circles or ellipses — **el·lip·soi·dal** \-ˌlip-'sȯid-ᵊl\ *also* **ellipsoid** *adj*

el·lip·ti·cal \i-'lip-ti-kəl, e-\ *or* **el·lip·tic** \-tik\ *adj* **1** : of, relating to, or shaped like an ellipse **2** : of, relating to, or marked by ellipsis — **el·lip·ti·cal·ly** \-ti-k(ə-)lē\ *adv*

elm \'elm\ n : any of a genus of large trees that have toothed leaves and nearly circular one-seeded winged fruits and are often grown as shade trees; *also* : the wood of an elm

El Ni·ño \el-'nē-nyō\ n : a flow of unusually warm Pacific Ocean water moving toward and along the west coast of So. America

el·o·cu·tion \ˌe-lə-'kyü-shən\ n : the art of effective public speaking — **el·o·cu·tion·ist** \-shə-nist\ n

elon·gate \i-'lȯŋ-ˌgāt\ *vb* **-gat·ed; -gat·ing** ♦ : to make or grow longer

 ♦ draw out, extend, lengthen, prolong, protract, stretch

elon·ga·tion \(ˌ)ē-ˌlȯŋ-'gā-shən\ n ♦ : the state of being elongated or lengthened; *also* : the process of growing or increasing in length

 ♦ extension, prolongation

elope \i-'lōp\ *vb* **eloped; elop·ing** : to run away esp. to be married — **elope·ment** n — **elop·er** n

el·o·quence \-kwəns\ n ♦ : forceful and persuasive expression; *also* : the art or power of using such expression

 ♦ articulateness, persuasiveness, poetry, power, rhetoric

el·o·quent \'e-lə-kwənt\ *adj* **1** ♦ : having or showing clear and forceful expression ⟨an ~ speaker⟩ **2** ♦ : clearly showing some feeling or meaning — **el·o·quent·ly** *adv*

 ♦ [1] articulate, fluent, well-spoken ♦ [2] expressive, meaning, meaningful, pregnant, significant, suggestive

¹**else** \'els\ *adv* **1** ♦ : in a different or additional manner or place or at a different or additional time ⟨where ~ can we meet⟩ **2** : if not ⟨obey or ~ you'll be sorry⟩

 ♦ differently, other, otherwise

²**else** *adj* ♦ : being another : OTHER; *esp* : being in addition ⟨what ~ do you want⟩

 ♦ additional, another, farther, further, more, other

else·where \-ˌhwer\ *adv* : in or to another place

elu·ci·date \i-'lü-sə-ˌdāt\ *vb* **-dat·ed; -dat·ing** ♦ : to make clear usu. by explanation

 ♦ clarify, clear (up), demonstrate, explain, explicate, expound, illuminate, illustrate, interpret, spell out

elu·ci·da·tion \-ˌlü-sə-'dā-shən\ n ♦ : the act, process, or means of elucidating

 ♦ clarification, explanation, explication, exposition, illumination, illustration, interpretation

elude \ē-'lüd\ *vb* **elud·ed; elud·ing** **1** ♦ : to avoid adroitly : EVADE **2** : to escape the notice of

 ♦ avoid, dodge, duck, escape, eschew, evade, shake, shirk, shun

elu·sive \ē-'lü-siv\ *adj* ♦ : tending to elude : EVASIVE ⟨the solution remains ~⟩ — **elu·sive·ly** *adv* — **elu·sive·ness** n

 ♦ evasive, fugitive, slippery

el·ver \'el-vər\ n : a young eel

elves *pl of* ELF

Ely·sian \-'li-zhən\ *adj* ♦ : of or relating to Elysium; *esp* : full of bliss or delight

 ♦ celestial, empyrean, heavenly, supernal

Ely·si·um \i-'li-zhē-əm, -zē-\ n, pl **-si·ums** *or* **-sia** \-zhē-ə, -zē-\ ♦ : a place or state of bliss or delight : PARADISE

 ♦ Eden, heaven, paradise, utopia

em \'em\ n : a length approximately the width of the letter *M*

EM *abbr* **1** electromagnetic **2** electron microscope **3** enlisted man

ema·ci·ate \i-'mā-shē-ˌāt\ *vb* **-at·ed; -at·ing** : to become or cause to become very thin — **ema·ci·a·tion** \-ˌmā-shē-'ā-shən, -sē-\ n

e–mail *or* **email** \'ē-ˌmāl\ n **1** : a system for transmitting messages between computers on a network **2** : a message or messages sent and received through an e-mail system — **e–mail** *or* **email** *vb*

em·a·nate \'e-mə-ˌnāt\ *vb* **-nat·ed; -nat·ing** : to come out from a source — **em·a·na·tion** \ˌe-mə-'nā-shən\ n

eman·ci·pate \i-'man-sə-ˌpāt\ *vb* **-pat·ed; -pat·ing** ♦ : to set free — **eman·ci·pa·tor** \-'man-sə-ˌpā-tər\ n

 ♦ discharge, enfranchise, free, liberate, loose, loosen, manumit, release, spring, unbind, unchain, unfetter

eman·ci·pa·tion \-ˌman-sə-'pā-shən\ n ♦ : the act or process of emancipating

 ♦ enfranchisement, liberation, manumission

emas·cu·late \i-'mas-kyù-ˌlāt\ *vb* **-lat·ed; -lat·ing** **1** : to deprive of virility : CASTRATE **2** : to deprive of strength or spirit : WEAKEN — **emas·cu·la·tion** \-ˌmas-kyù-'lā-shən\ n

em·balm \im-'bäm, -'bälm\ *vb* : to treat (a corpse) so as to protect from decay — **em·balm·er** n

em·bank·ment \im-'baŋk-mənt\ n ♦ : a raised structure (as of earth) to hold back water or carry a roadway

 ♦ dam, dike, levee

em·bar·go \im-'bär-gō\ n, pl **-goes** ♦ : a prohibition on commerce — **embargo** *vb*

 ♦ ban, interdict, interdiction, prohibition, proscription, veto

em·bark \im-'bärk\ *vb* **1** : to put or go on board a ship or airplane **2** ♦ : to make a start — **em·bar·ka·tion** \ˌem-ˌbär-'kā-shən\ n

 ♦ begin, commence, enter, launch, open, start

em·bar·rass \im-'bar-əs\ *vb* **1** : CONFUSE, DISCONCERT **2** : to involve in financial difficulties **3** ♦ : to cause to experience self-conscious distress **4** ♦ : to hamper or impede the movement or freedom of movement of : HINDER, IMPEDE — **em·bar·rass·ing·ly** *adv*

 ♦ [3] abash, confound, confuse, discomfit, disconcert, discountenance, faze, fluster, mortify, rattle ♦ [4] encumber, hamper, hinder, hold up, impede, inhibit, interfere with, obstruct, tie up

em·bar·rass·ing *adj* ♦ : causing embarrassment

 ♦ awkward, disconcerting, uncomfortable

em·bar·rass·ment *n* **1 :** something that embarrasses; *esp* : a burden that impedes action or renders it difficult **2 :** the state of being embarrassed: as **a** ♦ : confusion or disturbance of mind **b** ♦ : difficulty in making progress or functioning (as from lack of resources or disease)

♦ [2a] abashment, confusion, discomfiture, fluster, mortification ♦ [2b] bar, block, encumbrance, hindrance, inhibition, obstacle

em·bas·sy \'em-bə-sē\ *n, pl* **-sies** **1 :** a group of representatives headed by an ambassador **2 :** the function, position, or mission of an ambassador **3 :** the official residence and offices of an ambassador

em·bat·tle \im-'bat-ᵊl\ *vb* **:** to arrange in order for battle; *also* : FORTIFY

em·bat·tled *adj* **1 :** engaged in battle, conflict, or controversy **2 :** being a site of battle, conflict, or controversy **3 :** characterized by conflict or controversy

em·bed \im-'bed\ *vb* **em·bed·ded; em·bed·ding** **1** ♦ : to enclose closely in a surrounding mass **2 :** to make something an integral part of

♦ entrench, fix, implant, ingrain, lodge, root

em·bel·lish \im-'be-lish\ *vb* **1** ♦ : to make beautiful with ornamentation : DECORATE **2** ♦ : to heighten the attractiveness of by adding decorative or fanciful details

♦ [1, 2] adorn, array, beautify, decorate, dress, enrich, garnish, grace, ornament, trim ♦ [2] color (*or* colour), elaborate, embroider, exaggerate, magnify, pad, stretch

em·bel·lish·ment *n* ♦ : the act or process of embellishing; *also* : something serving to embellish

♦ adornment, caparison, decoration, frill, garnish, ornament, trim ♦ elaboration, exaggeration, hyperbole, overstatement, padding

em·ber \'em-bər\ *n* **1 :** a glowing or smoldering fragment from a fire **2** *pl* **:** the smoldering remains of a fire

em·bez·zle \im-'be-zəl\ *vb* **-zled; -zling :** to steal (as money) by falsifying records — **em·bez·zle·ment** *n* — **em·bez·zler** *n*

em·bit·ter \im-'bi-tər\ *vb* **1 :** to arouse bitter feelings in **2 :** to make bitter

em·bla·zon \im-'blāz-ᵊn\ *vb* **1 :** to adorn with heraldic devices **2 :** to display conspicuously

em·blem \'em-bləm\ *n* ♦ : something (as an object or picture) suggesting another object or an idea : SYMBOL — **em·blem·at·ic** \ˌem-blə-'ma-tik\ *also* **em·blem·at·i·cal** \-ti-kəl\ *adj*

♦ hallmark, logo, symbol, trademark

em·bodi·ment \-di-mənt\ *n* **1** ♦ : a thing in which something (as a soul, idea, principle, or type) is embodied **2 :** the act of embodying; *also* : the state of being embodied

♦ epitome, incarnation, manifestation, personification

em·body \im-'bä-dē\ *vb* **em·bod·ied; em·body·ing** **1 :** INCARNATE **2 :** to express in definite form **3** ♦ : to incorporate into a system or body **4** ♦ : to represent in human or animal form : PERSONIFY

♦ [3] assimilate, incorporate, integrate ♦ [4] epitomize, manifest, materialize, personify, substantiate

em·bold·en \im-'bōl-dən\ *vb* ♦ : to inspire with courage

♦ buoy (up), cheer, comfort, encourage, hearten, inspire, steel

em·bo·lism \'em-bə-ˌli-zəm\ *n* **:** the obstruction of a blood vessel by a foreign or abnormal particle

em·bon·point \äⁿ-bōⁿ-'pwäⁿ\ *n* **:** plumpness of person : STOUTNESS

em·boss \im-'bäs, -'bòs\ *vb* **:** to ornament with raised work

em·bou·chure \'äm-bu̇-ˌshu̇r, ˌäm-bu̇-'shu̇r\ *n* **:** the position and use of the lips, tongue, and teeth in playing a wind instrument

em·bow·er \im-'bau̇(-ə)r\ *vb* **:** to shelter or enclose in a bower

¹em·brace \im-'brās\ *vb* **em·braced; em·brac·ing** **1** ♦ : to clasp in the arms; *also* : CHERISH, LOVE **2 :** to surround or close in **3** ♦ : to take up esp. readily or gladly : ADOPT ⟨*embraced* the cause⟩; *also* : WELCOME ⟨*embraced* the opportunity⟩ **4** ♦ : to take in or include as a part of a whole **5 :** to participate in an embrace

♦ [1] caress, clasp, enfold, grasp, hug ♦ [3] adopt, borrow, take up ♦ [4] carry, comprehend, contain, encompass, entail, include, involve, number, take in

²embrace *n* **:** an encircling with the arms

em·bra·sure \im-'brā-zhər\ *n* **1 :** an opening in a wall through which a cannon is fired **2 :** a recess of a door or window

em·bro·ca·tion \ˌem-brə-'kā-shən\ *n* **:** LINIMENT

em·broi·der \im-'brói-dər\ *vb* **1 :** to ornament with or do needlework **2** ♦ : to elaborate with exaggerated detail

♦ color (*or* colour), elaborate, embellish, exaggerate, magnify, stretch

em·broi·dery \im-'brói-də-rē\ *n, pl* **-der·ies** **1 :** the forming of decorative designs with needlework **2 :** something embroidered

em·broil \im-'brói l\ *vb* **1 :** to throw into confusion or disorder **2 :** to involve in conflict or difficulties ⟨∼ed in a dispute⟩ — **em·broil·ment** *n*

em·bryo \'em-brē-ˌō\ *n, pl* **embryos :** a living thing in its earliest stages of development — **em·bry·on·ic** \ˌem-brē-'ä-nik\ *adj*

em·bry·ol·o·gy \ˌem-brē-'ä-lə-jē\ *n* **:** a branch of biology dealing with embryos and their development — **em·bry·o·log·i·cal** \-brē-ə-'lä-ji-kəl\ *adj* — **em·bry·ol·o·gist** \-brē-'ä-lə-jist\ *n*

em·cee \'em-ˌsē\ *n* **:** MASTER OF CEREMONIES — **emcee** *vb*

emend \ē-'mend\ *vb* **:** to correct usu. by altering the text of — **emen·da·tion** \ˌē-ˌmen-'dā-shən\ *n*

♦ amend, correct, debug, rectify, reform, remedy

emer *abbr* emeritus

¹em·er·ald \'em-rəld, 'e-mə-\ *n* **:** a green beryl prized as a gem

²emerald *adj* **:** brightly or richly green

emerge \i-'mərj\ *vb* **emerged; emerg·ing** ♦ : to rise, come forth, or come out into view — **emer·gence** \-'mər-jəns\ *n* — **emer·gent** \-jənt\ *adj*

♦ arise, crop, materialize, spring, surface

emer·gen·cy \i-'mər-jən-sē\ *n, pl* **-cies** ♦ : an unforeseen event or condition requiring prompt action

♦ clutch, crisis, crunch, fix, hole, jam

emergency room *n* **:** a hospital room for receiving and treating persons needing immediate medical care

emer·i·ta \i-'mer-ə-tə\ *adj* **:** EMERITUS — used of a woman

emer·i·tus \i-'mer-ə-təs\ *adj* **:** retired from active duty ⟨professor ∼⟩

em·ery \'e-mə-rē\ *n, pl* **em·er·ies :** a dark granular mineral consisting primarily of corundum and used as an abrasive

emet·ic \i-'me-tik\ *n* **:** an agent that induces vomiting — **emetic** *adj*

emf *n* **:** POTENTIAL DIFFERENCE

em·i·grant \-mi-grənt\ *n* ♦ : one who emigrates

♦ émigré, immigrant, migrant, settler

em·i·grate \'e-mə-ˌgrāt\ *vb* **-grat·ed; -grat·ing :** to leave a place (as a country) to settle elsewhere — **em·i·gra·tion** \ˌe-mə-'grā-shən\ *n*

émi·gré *also* **emi·gré** \'e-mi-ˌgrā, ˌe-mi-'grā\ *n* ♦ : a person who emigrates esp. because of political conditions

♦ emigrant, evacuee, exile, expatriate, refugee

em·i·nence \'e-mə-nəns\ *n* **1** ♦ : high rank or position; *also* : a person of high rank or attainments **2** ♦ : a lofty place

♦ [1] distinction, dominance, preeminence, superiority ♦ [2] elevation, height, highland, hill, mound, prominence, rise

em·i·nent \'e-mə-nənt\ *adj* **1 :** CONSPICUOUS, EVIDENT **2** ♦ : exhibiting eminence esp. in standing above others in some quality or position : DISTINGUISHED, PROMINENT — **em·i·nent·ly** *adv*

♦ distinguished, illustrious, noble, notable, noteworthy, outstanding, preeminent, prestigious, prominent, superior

eminent domain *n* **:** a right of a government to take private property for public use

emir *or* **amir** \ə-'mir, ā-\ *n* **:** a ruler, chief, or commander in Islamic countries — **emir·ate** \'e-mər-ət\ *n*

em·is·sary \'e-mə-ˌser-ē\ *n, pl* **-sar·ies** **1** ♦ : one designated as the agent of another **2 :** a secret agent

♦ ambassador, delegate, envoy, legate, minister, representative

emis·sion \ē-'mi-shən\ *n* **:** something emitted; *esp* : substances discharged into the air

emit \ē-'mit\ *vb* **emit·ted; emit·ting** **1** ♦ : to give off or out ⟨∼ light⟩; *esp* : EJECT **2 :** EXPRESS, UTTER — **emit·ter** *n*

♦ cast, discharge, eject, exhale, expel, issue, release, shoot, vent

emo·ji \ē-'mō-jē\ *n, pl* **emoji** *or* **emo·jis :** any of various small images, symbols, or icons used in text fields in electronic communications to express something (as an emotion) without using words

emol·lient \i-'mäl-yənt\ *adj* **:** making soft or supple; *also* : soothing esp. to the skin or mucous membrane — **emollient** *n*

emol·u·ment \i-'mäl-yə-mənt\ *n* ♦ : the product (as salary or fees) of an employment

♦ hire, pay, payment, salary, stipend, wage

emote \i-'mōt\ *vb* **emot·ed; emot·ing** : to give expression to emotion in or as if in a play

emo·ti·con \i-'mō-ti-ˌkän\ *n* : a group of keyboard characters (as :-)) that often represents a facial expression and that is used esp. in electronic communications

emo·tion \i-'mō-shən\ *n* ♦ : a usu. intense feeling (as of love, hate, or despair)

♦ feeling, passion, sentiment ♦ ardor, fervency, fervor, heat, intensity, passion, vehemence, warmth

emo·tion·al \-shə-nəl\ *adj* **1** : of or relating to emotion **2** ♦ : dominated by or prone to emotion **3** ♦ : appealing to or arousing emotion **4** ♦ : markedly aroused or agitated in feeling or sensibilities — **emo·tion·al·ly** *adv*

♦ [2] demonstrative, effusive, uninhibited, unreserved, unrestrained ♦ [3] affecting, impressive, moving, poignant, stirring, touching ♦ [4] ardent, burning, charged, fervent, fiery, impassioned, passionate, red-hot, vehement

emot·ive \i-'mō-tiv\ *adj* **1** : of or relating to the emotions **2** : appealing to or expressing emotion

emp *abbr* emperor; empress

empanel *var of* IMPANEL

em·pa·thy \'em-pə-thē\ *n* : the experiencing as one's own of the feelings of another; *also* : the capacity for this — **em·path·ic** \em-'pa-thik\ *adj*

em·pen·nage \ˌäm-pə-'näzh, ˌem-\ *n* : the tail assembly of an airplane

em·per·or \'em-pər-ər\ *n* : the sovereign male ruler of an empire

em·pha·sis \'em-fə-səs\ *n, pl* **-pha·ses** \-ˌsēz\ ♦ : a forcefulness of expression that gives special significance or prominence (as to a syllable in speaking or to a phase of action)

♦ accent, accentuation, stress, weight

em·pha·sise *Brit var of* EMPHASIZE

em·pha·size \-ˌsīz\ *vb* **-sized; -siz·ing** ♦ : to place emphasis on : STRESS

♦ accent, accentuate, feature, highlight, play, point, stress, underline, underscore *Ant* play (down)

em·phat·ic \im-'fa-tik, em-\ *adj* **1** ♦ : uttered with emphasis **2** ♦ : attracting special attention ⟨an ~ refusal⟩ — **em·phat·i·cal·ly** \-'ti-k(ə-)lē\ *adv*

♦ [1] aggressive, assertive, dynamic, energetic, forceful, resounding, strenuous, vehement, vigorous *Ant* unemphatic ♦ [2] bold, catchy, conspicuous, marked, noticeable, prominent, pronounced, remarkable, striking

em·phy·se·ma \ˌem-fə-'zē-mə, -'sē-\ *n* : a condition marked esp. by abnormal expansion of the air spaces of the lungs and often by impairment of heart action

em·pire \'em-ˌpī(-ə)r\ *n* **1** : a large state or a group of states under a single sovereign who is usu. an emperor; *also* : something resembling a political empire **2** : imperial sovereignty or dominion

em·pir·i·cal \im-'pir-i-kəl\ *also* **em·pir·ic** \-ik\ *adj* : based on observation; *also* : subject to verification by observation or experiment ⟨~ laws⟩ — **em·pir·i·cal·ly** \-i-k(ə-)lē\ *adv*

em·pir·i·cism \im-'pir-ə-ˌsi-zəm, em-\ *n* : the practice of relying on observation and experiment esp. in the natural sciences — **em·pir·i·cist** \-sist\ *n*

em·place·ment \im-'plās-mənt\ *n* **1** : a prepared position for weapons or military equipment **2** : PLACEMENT

¹em·ploy \im-'ploi\ *vb* **1** ♦ : to make use of **2** ♦ : to use the services of **3** : OCCUPY, DEVOTE — **em·ploy·er** *n*

♦ [1] apply, exercise, exploit, harness, operate, use, utilize ♦ [2] engage, hire, retain, take on *Ant* discharge, dismiss, fire, sack

²em·ploy \im-'ploi; 'im-ˌploi, 'em-\ *n* ♦ : the state of being employed : EMPLOYMENT

♦ employment, engagement, hire

em·ploy·ee *also* **em·ploye** \im-ˌploi-'ē, ˌem-; im-'ploi-ˌē, em-\ *n* ♦ : a person who works for another

♦ hand, hireling, jobholder, worker *Ant* employer

em·ploy·ment \im-'ploi-mənt\ *n* **1** ♦ : activity in which one engages or is employed : OCCUPATION **2** ♦ : the act of employing : the condition of being employed

♦ [1] calling, line, occupation, profession, trade, vocation, work ♦ [2] application, exercise, operation, play, use ♦ [2] employ, engagement, hire

em·po·ri·um \im-'pȯr-ē-əm, em-\ *n, pl* **-ri·ums** *also* **-ria** \-ē-ə\ ♦ : a commercial center; *esp* : a store carrying varied articles

♦ shop, store

em·pow·er \im-'paủ(-ə)r\ *vb* ♦ : to give authority or power to; *also* : ENABLE — **em·pow·er·ment** \-mənt\ *n*

♦ accredit, authorize, certify, commission, enable, invest, license, qualify

em·press \'em-prəs\ *n* **1** : the wife or widow of an emperor **2** : a woman who is the sovereign ruler of an empire

emp·ti·ness *n* ♦ : the quality or state of being empty

♦ blank, blankness, vacancy, vacuity, void

¹emp·ty \'emp-tē\ *adj* **emp·ti·er; -est** **1** ♦ : containing nothing **2** : UNOCCUPIED, UNINHABITED **3** ♦ : lacking value, force, sense, or purpose **4** ♦ : feeling the need for food

♦ [1] bare, blank, devoid, stark, vacant, void *Ant* full ♦ [3] meaningless, pointless, senseless, worthless ♦ [3] fruitless, futile, ineffective, unproductive, unsuccessful ♦ [4] famished, hungry

²empty *vb* **emp·tied; emp·ty·ing** **1** : to make or become empty **2** ♦ : to discharge contents; *also* : to remove from what holds or encloses

♦ clear, evacuate, vacate, void *Ant* fill, load

³empty *n, pl* **empties** : an empty bottle or can

emp·ty–hand·ed \ˌemp-tē-'han-dəd\ *adj* **1** : having or bringing nothing **2** : having acquired or gained nothing

¹em·py·re·an \ˌem-ˌpī-'rē-ən, -pə-\ *n* **1** : the highest heaven; *also* : FIRMAMENT **2** : an ideal place or state

²empyrean *adj* ♦ : of or relating to the empyrean

♦ celestial, Elysian, heavenly, supernal

EMT \ˌē-(ˌ)em-'tē\ *n* : a specially trained medical technician certified to provide basic medical services before and during transport to a hospital

¹emu \'ē-myü, -mü\ *n* : a swift-running flightless Australian bird smaller than the related ostrich

²emu *abbr* electromagnetic unit

em·u·late \'em-yủ-ˌlāt\ *vb* **-lat·ed; -lat·ing** ♦ : to strive to equal or excel : IMITATE — **em·u·la·tion** \ˌem-yủ-'lā-shən\ *n* — **em·u·lous** \'em-yủ-ləs\ *adj*

♦ ape, copy, imitate, mime, mimic

emul·si·fi·er \i-'məl-sə-ˌfī(-ə)r\ *n* : a substance (as a soap) that helps to form and stabilize an emulsion

emul·si·fy \-ˌfī\ *vb* **-fied; -fy·ing** : to disperse (as an oil) in an emulsion — **emul·si·fi·ca·tion** \i-ˌməl-sə-fə-'kā-shən\ *n*

emul·sion \i-'məl-shən\ *n* **1** : a mixture of mutually insoluble liquids in which one is dispersed in droplets throughout the other ⟨an ~ of oil in water⟩ **2** : a light-sensitive coating on photographic film or paper

en \'en\ *n* : a length approximately half the width of the letter *M*

¹-en *also* **-n** *adj suffix* : made of : consisting of ⟨earthen⟩

²-en *vb suffix* **1** : become or cause to be ⟨sharpen⟩ **2** : cause or come to have ⟨lengthen⟩

en·able \i-'nā-bəl\ *vb* **en·abled; en·abling** **1** ♦ : to make able or feasible **2** ♦ : to give legal power, capacity, or sanction to

♦ [1] allow, let, permit *Ant* prevent ♦ [2] accredit, authorize, certify, commission, empower, invest, license, qualify

en·act \i-'nakt\ *vb* **1** ♦ : to make into law **2** : to act out

♦ lay down, legislate, make, pass *Ant* repeal, rescind, revoke

en·act·ment *n* ♦ : the act of enacting; *also* : something (as a law) that has been enacted

♦ act, law, ordinance, statute ♦ accomplishment, achievement, commission, discharge, execution, fulfillment, implementation, performance

enam·el \i-'na-məl\ *n* **1** : a glasslike substance used to coat the surface of metal or pottery **2** : the hard outer layer of a tooth **3** : a usu. glossy paint that forms a hard coat — **enamel** *vb*

enam·el·ware \-ˌwer\ *n* : metal utensils coated with enamel

en·am·or *or Can and Brit* **en·am·our** \i-'na-mər\ *vb* : to inflame with love

en bloc \äⁿ-'bläk\ *adv or adj* : as a whole : in a mass

enc *or* **encl** *abbr* enclosure

en·camp \in-'kamp\ *vb* : to make camp

en·camp·ment *n* ♦ : the place where a group (as a body of troops) is encamped

♦ bivouac, camp

en·cap·su·late \in-'kap-sə-ˌlāt\ *vb* **-lat·ed; -lat·ing** **1** : to en-

case or become encased in a capsule **2 ♦** : to give an abstract of
: SUMMARIZE

♦ abstract, digest, outline, recapitulate, sum up, summarize,
wrap up

en·cap·su·la·tion \-ˌkap-sə-ˈlā-shən\ *n* ♦ : an act, instance, or
result of encapsulating

♦ abstract, digest, outline, précis, résumé (*or* resume), summary, synopsis, wrap-up

en·case \in-ˈkās\ *vb* ♦ : to enclose in or as if in a case — **encase·ment** \-ˈkā-smənt\ *n*

♦ cage, coop up, corral, enclose, fence, hedge, hem, house, pen,
wall

-ence *n suffix* **1** : action or process ⟨emerg*ence*⟩ : instance of an
action or process ⟨refer*ence*⟩ **2** : quality or state ⟨depend*ence*⟩
en·ceinte \än-ˈsant\ *adj* : PREGNANT 1
en·ceph·a·li·tis \in-ˌse-fə-ˈlī-təs\ *n, pl* **-lit·i·des** \-ˈli-tə-ˌdēz\
: inflammation of the brain — **en·ceph·a·lit·ic** \-ˈli-tik\ *adj*
en·ceph·a·lop·a·thy \in-ˌse-fə-ˈlä-pə-thē\ *n, pl* **-thies** : a disease
of the brain
en·chain \in-ˈchān\ *vb* ♦ : to bind or hold with or as if with
chains : FETTER, CHAIN

♦ bind, chain, fetter, handcuff, manacle, shackle, trammel

en·chant \in-ˈchant\ *vb* **1** ♦ : to influence by or as if by charms
and incantation : BEWITCH **2** ♦ : to attract and move deeply —
en·chant·ing·ly *adv*

♦ [1] allure, beguile, bewitch, captivate, charm, fascinate, wile
♦ [2] arrest, enthrall, fascinate, grip, hypnotize, mesmerize

en·chant·er *n* ♦ : one that enchants

♦ conjurer, magician, necromancer, sorcerer, voodoo, witch,
wizard

en·chant·ment *n* **1** ♦ : the act or art of enchanting; *also* : the
quality or state of being enchanted **2** ♦ : something that enchants

♦ [1] allure, appeal, attractiveness, captivation, charisma,
charm, fascination, glamour, magic, magnetism ♦ [2] bewitchment, charm, conjuration, incantation, spell

en·chant·ress \-ˈchan-trəs\ *n* **1** ♦ : a woman who practices
magic **2** ♦ : a fascinating or beautiful woman

♦ [1] hag, hex, witch ♦ [2] beauty, fox, goddess, knockout,
queen

en·chi·la·da \ˌen-chə-ˈlä-də\ *n* : a rolled filled tortilla covered
with chili sauce and usu. baked
en·ci·pher \in-ˈsī-fər, en-\ *vb* : ENCODE
en·cir·cle \in-ˈsər-kəl\ *vb* ♦ : to pass completely around : SUR
ROUND — **en·cir·cle·ment** *n*

♦ circle, circumnavigate, coil, compass, enclose, encompass,
girdle, ring, round, surround

en·clave \ˈen-ˌklāv\ *n* : a distinct territorial, cultural,
or social unit enclosed within or as if within foreign territory
en·close \in-ˈklōz\ *vb* **1** ♦ : to shut up or in; *esp* : to surround
with a fence **2** : to include along with something else in a parcel
or envelope ⟨~ a check⟩ — **en·clo·sure** \-ˈklō-zhər\ *n*

♦ cage, coop up, corral, encase, envelop, fence, hedge, hem, pen
♦ circle, encircle, encompass, ring, surround

en·code \in-ˈkōd, en-\ *vb* : to convert (a message) into code
en·co·mi·um \en-ˈkō-mē-əm\ *n, pl* **-mi·ums** *also* **-mia** \-mē-ə\
n ♦ : high or glowing praise

♦ accolade, citation, commendation, eulogy, homage, paean,
panegyric, salutation, tribute

en·com·pass \in-ˈkəm-pəs\ *vb* **1** ♦ : to form a circle about
: ENCIRCLE **2** : to enclose or enfold completely with or as if with
a covering : ENVELOP, INCLUDE **3** ♦ : to contain or hold within a
total scope, significance, or amount

♦ [1] circle, encircle, enclose, ring, surround ♦ [3] carry, comprehend, contain, embrace, entail, include, involve, number, take
in

en·core \ˈän-ˌkȯr\ *n* **1** : a demand for repetition or reappearance **2** : a further performance or appearance demanded by an
audience **3** : a second achievement that usu. surpasses the first
— **encore** *vb*
¹**en·coun·ter** \in-ˈkau̇n-tər\ *vb* **1** : to meet as an enemy
: FIGHT **2** ♦ : to meet usu. unexpectedly

♦ chance, find, happen (on *or* upon), hit, meet, stumble (on *or*
upon)

²**encounter** *n* **1** ♦ : a hostile meeting : COMBAT **2** : a chance
meeting **3** : an experience shared with another ⟨a romantic ~⟩

♦ brush, run-in, scrape, skirmish

en·cour·age \in-ˈkər-ij\ *vb* **-aged; -ag·ing** **1** ♦ : to inspire with
courage and hope **2** ♦ : to spur on : STIMULATE, INCITE; *also* : to
attempt to persuade **3** ♦ : to give help or patronage to : FOSTER

♦ [1] buoy (up), cheer, comfort, embolden, hearten, inspire,
steel *Ant* daunt, discourage, dishearten, dispirit ♦ [2] arouse,
excite, fire, incite, instigate, move, pique, provoke, stimulate, stir
♦ [2] egg on, exhort, goad, press, prod, prompt, urge ♦ [3] advance, cultivate, forward, foster, further, nourish, nurture, promote

en·cour·age·ment *n* ♦ : the act of encouraging : the state of being encouraged; *also* : something that encourages

♦ boost, goad, impetus, impulse, incentive, instigation, motivation, provocation, spur, stimulus

en·cour·ag·ing \-i-jiŋ, -ri-jiŋ\ *adj* ♦ : giving hope or promise —
en·cour·ag·ing·ly *adv*

♦ auspicious, bright, fair, golden, heartening, hopeful, likely,
promising, propitious, rosy, upbeat ♦ comforting, gratifying,
heartening, heartwarming, rewarding, satisfying

en·croach \in-ˈkrōch\ *vb* : to enter gradually or stealthily upon
another's property or rights — **en·croach·er** *n* — **en·croachment** *n*
en·crust *also* **in·crust** \in-ˈkrəst\ *vb* : to provide with or form a
crust
en·crus·ta·tion \(ˌ)in-ˌkrəs-ˈtā-shən, ˌen-\ *var of* INCRUSTATION
en·crypt \in-ˈkript, en-\ *vb* : to change (information) from one
form to another esp. to hide its meaning
en·cum·ber \in-ˈkəm-bər\ *vb* **1** ♦ : to weigh down : BURDEN **2**
♦ : to hinder the function or activity of

♦ [1] burden, load, lumber, saddle, weight ♦ [2] hamper, hinder, hobble, hold back, hold up, impede, inhibit, interfere with,
obstruct, tie up

en·cum·brance \-brəns\ *n* **1** ♦ : something that encumbers **2**
: a claim (as a mortgage) against property

♦ bar, block, hindrance, inhibition, obstacle

ency *or* **encyc** *abbr* encyclopedia
-en·cy *n suffix* : quality or state ⟨despond*ency*⟩
¹**en·cyc·li·cal** \in-ˈsi-kli-kəl, en-\ *adj* : addressed to all the individuals of a group
²**encyclical** *n* : an encyclical letter; *esp* : a papal letter to the bishops of the church
en·cy·clo·pe·dia *also* **en·cy·clo·pae·dia** \in-ˌsī-klə-ˈpē-dē-ə\ *n*
: a work treating the various branches of learning
en·cy·clo·pe·dic *also* **en·cy·clo·pae·dic** \-ˈpē-dik\ *adj* ♦ : of,
relating to, or suggestive of an encyclopedia or its methods of
treating or covering a subject

♦ compendious, complete, comprehensive, full, global, inclusive, omnibus, panoramic, universal

en·cyst \in-ˈsist, en-\ *vb* : to form or become enclosed in a cyst
— **en·cyst·ment** *n*
¹**end** \ˈend\ *n* **1** ♦ : the part of an area that lies at the boundary;
also : a point which marks the extent or limit of something or at
which something ceases to exist **2** ♦ : a ceasing of a course (as
of action or activity); *also* : DEATH **3** : the ultimate state; *also*
: RESULT, ISSUE **4** ♦ : something incomplete, fragmentary, or undersized : REMNANT **5** : an outcome worked toward : PURPOSE,
OBJECTIVE **6** : a player stationed at the extremity of a line (as in
football) **7** : a share, operation, or aspect of an undertaking

♦ [1] bound, boundary, ceiling, confines, extent, limit, limitation, line, termination ♦ [2] death, decease, demise, doom,
passing, quietus ♦ [2] cessation, close, closure, conclusion, finish, halt, lapse, shutdown, stop, stoppage, termination *Ant* continuation ♦ [4] fag end, leftover, remainder, remnant, scrap
♦ [5] aim, ambition, aspiration, goal, intent, mark, meaning,
object, objective, plan, purpose

²**end** *vb* **1** ♦ : to bring or come to an end **2** : DESTROY; *also*
: DIE **3** : to form or be at the end of

♦ close, conclude, finish, round, terminate, wind up, wrap up
♦ break, break off, cease, cut, desist, discontinue, drop, halt,
knock off, layoff, leave off, quit, shut off, stop

en·dan·ger \in-ˈdān-jər\ *vb* ♦ : to bring into danger; *also* : to
create danger

♦ compromise, gamble with, hazard, imperil, jeopardize, menace, risk, venture

en·dan·gered *adj* : being or relating to an endangered species
endangered species *n* : a species threatened with extinction
en·dear \in-'dir\ *vb* : to cause to become beloved or admired
endearing *adj* ♦ : arousing affection, tenderness, or admiration

♦ adorable, darling, dear, lovable, precious, sweet, winning

en·dear·ment \-mənt\ *n* : a sign of affection : CARESS
¹**en·deav·or** *or Can and Brit* **en·deav·our** \in-'de-vər\ *vb* ♦ : to attempt (as the fulfillment of an obligation) by exertion of effort; *also* : to work with set purpose

♦ assay, attempt, essay, seek, strive, try

²**endeavor** *or Can and Brit* **endeavour** *n* ♦ : serious determined effort; *also* : activity directed toward a goal

♦ attempt, bid, crack, essay, fling, go, pass, shot, stab, trial, try, whack, whirl

en·dem·ic \en-'de-mik, in-\ *adj* ♦ : restricted to a particular place ⟨∼ plants⟩ ⟨an ∼ disease⟩ — **endemic** *n*

♦ aboriginal, born, indigenous, native

end·ing \'en-diŋ\ *n* **1** ♦ : something that forms an end **2** : SUFFIX

♦ close, conclusion, consummation, end, finale, finis, finish, windup

en·dive \'en-ˌdīv\ *n* **1** : an herb related to chicory and grown as a salad plant **2** : the blanched shoot of chicory
end·less \'end-ləs\ *adj* **1** ♦ : having or seeming to have no end : ETERNAL **2** : united at the ends : CONTINUOUS ⟨an ∼ belt⟩ — **end·less·ly** *adv*

♦ boundless, illimitable, immeasurable, indefinite, infinite, limitless, measureless, unbounded, unfathomable, unlimited ♦ ceaseless, dateless, deathless, eternal, everlasting, immortal, permanent, perpetual, undying, unending

end·most \-ˌmōst\ *adj* : situated at the very end
end·note \-ˌnōt\ *n* : a note placed at the end of a text
en·do·crine \'en-də-krən, -ˌkrīn, -ˌkrēn\ *adj* : producing secretions that are distributed by way of the bloodstream ⟨∼ glands⟩ — **endocrine** *n* — **en·do·cri·nol·o·gist** \-kri-'nä-lə-jist\ *n* — **en·do·cri·nol·o·gy** \-jē\ *n*
en·dog·e·nous \en-'dä-jə-nəs\ *adj* : caused or produced by factors inside the organism or system ⟨∼ psychic depression⟩ — **en·dog·e·nous·ly** *adv*
en·do·me·tri·um \ˌen-dō-'mē-trē-əm\ *n, pl* **-tria** \-trē-ə\ : the mucous membrane lining the uterus — **en·do·me·tri·al** \-trē-əl\ *adj*
en·dor·phin \en-'dȯr-fən\ *n* : any of a group of endogenous morphinelike proteins found esp. in the brain
en·dorse *also* **in·dorse** \in-'dȯrs\ *vb* **en·dorsed; en·dors·ing 1** : to sign one's name on the back of (as a check) **2** ♦ : to express support or approval of publicly and definitely; *esp* : to recommend (as a product) usu. for financial compensation — **en·dorse·ment** *also* **in·dorse·ment** *n*

♦ advocate, back, champion, patronize, support

en·do·scope \'en-də-ˌskōp\ *n* : an illuminated usu. fiber-optic instrument for visualizing the interior of a hollow organ or part (as the colon or esophagus) — **en·do·scop·ic** \ˌen-də-'skä-pik\ *adj* — **en·dos·co·py** \en-'däs-kə-pē\ *n*
en·do·ther·mic \ˌen-də-'thər-mik\ *adj* : characterized by or formed with absorption of heat
en·dow \in-'daů\ *vb* **1** ♦ : to furnish with funds for support ⟨∼ a school⟩ **2** ♦ : to furnish with something freely or naturally ⟨∼ed with intellect⟩

♦ [1] finance, fund, subsidize ♦ [2] invest

en·dow·ment *n* : something that is endowed: as **a** : the part of an institution's income derived from donations **b** ♦ : natural capacity, power, or ability

♦ aptitude, faculty, flair, genius, gift, knack, talent

en·due \in-'dü, -'dyü\ *vb* **en·dued; en·du·ing** : PROVIDE, ENDOW
en·dur·able *adj* ♦ : capable of being borne or endured

♦ bearable, sufferable, supportable, sustainable, tolerable

en·dur·ance \in-'dúr-əns, -'dyúr-\ *n* **1** ♦ : continuation in the same state : DURATION **2** : the ability to withstand hardship or stress : FORTITUDE

♦ continuance, continuation, duration, persistence, subsistence

en·dure \in-'dúr, -'dyúr\ *vb* **en·dured; en·dur·ing 1** ♦ : to continue in the same state : LAST, PERSIST **2** ♦ : to suffer firmly or patiently : BEAR **3** : TOLERATE

♦ [1] abide, continue, hold, keep up, last, persist, run on

♦ [2] abide, bear, brook, countenance, meet, stand, stick out, stomach, support, sustain, take, tolerate

enduring *adj* ♦ : existing or continuing a long while : LASTING

♦ abiding, ageless, continuing, dateless, eternal, everlasting, immortal, imperishable, lasting, perennial, perpetual, timeless, undying

end·ways \'end-ˌwāz\ *adv or adj* **1** : LENGTHWISE **2** : with the end forward **3** : on end
end·wise \-ˌwīz\ *adv or adj* : ENDWAYS
ENE *abbr* east-northeast
en·e·ma \'e-nə-mə\ *n, pl* **enemas** *also* **ene·ma·ta** \ˌe-nə-'mä-tə, 'e-nə-mə-tə\ : injection of liquid into the rectum; *also* : material so injected
en·e·my \'e-nə-mē\ *n, pl* **-mies** ♦ : one that attacks or tries to harm another : FOE; *esp* : a military opponent

♦ adversary, antagonist, foe, opponent *Ant* friend

en·er·get·ic \ˌe-nər-'je-tik\ *adj* ♦ : marked by energy : ACTIVE, VIGOROUS

♦ active, animated, jaunty, lively, peppy, spirited, sprightly, springy, vigorous, vital, vivacious

en·er·get·i·cal·ly \-ti-k(ə-)lē\ *adv* ♦ : in an energetic manner

♦ forcefully, powerfully, strongly, sturdily, vigorously

en·er·gise *chiefly Brit var of* ENERGIZE
en·er·gize \'e-nər-ˌjīz\ *vb* **-gized; -giz·ing** ♦ : to give energy to

♦ animate, brace, enliven, fire, invigorate, jazz up, liven up, pep up, quicken, stimulate, vitalize, vivify, zip (up)

en·er·gy \'e-nər-jē\ *n, pl* **-gies 1** : vigorous action : EFFORT **2** ♦ : capacity for action **3** ♦ : capacity for performing work **4** : usable power (as heat or electricity); *also* : the resources for producing such power

♦ [2] force, main, might, muscle, potency, power, strength, vigor (*or* vigour) ♦ [2, 3] force, main, might, muscle, potency, power, strength, vigor (*or* vigour) ♦ [3] dash, life, pep, vigor (*or* vigour), vim, vitality

energy level *n* : one of the stable states of constant energy that may be assumed by a physical system (as the electrons in an atom)
en·er·vate \'e-nər-ˌvāt\ *vb* **-vat·ed; -vat·ing** ♦ : to lessen the strength or vigor of : weaken in mind or body — **en·er·vat·ing·ly** \-ˌvā-tiŋ-lē\ *adv* — **en·er·va·tion** \ˌe-nər-'vā-shən\ *n*

♦ debilitate, enfeeble, prostrate, sap, soften, tire, waste, weaken

en·er·vat·ed \'e-nər-ˌvāt-əd\ *adj* ♦ : lacking physical, mental, or moral vigor

♦ lackadaisical, languid, languorous, limp, listless, spiritless

en·fee·ble \in-'fē-bəl\ *vb* **-bled; -bling** ♦ : to make feeble

♦ debilitate, enervate, prostrate, sap, soften, tire, waste, weaken

en·fee·ble·ment *n* ♦ : the action of enfeebling; *also* : the quality or state of being enfeebled

♦ debility, delicacy, faintness, feebleness, frailty, infirmity, languor, lowness, weakness

en·fi·lade \'en-fə-ˌlād, -ˌläd\ *n* : gunfire directed along the length of an enemy battle line — **enfilade** *vb*
en·fold \in-'fōld\ *vb* **1** ♦ : to cover with or as if with folds : ENVELOP **2** ♦ : to clasp within the arms : EMBRACE

♦ [1] caress, clasp, embrace, grasp, hug ♦ [2] enclose, encompass, enshroud, envelop, invest, lap, mantle, shroud, swathe, veil, wrap

en·force \in-'fȯrs\ *vb* **1** : COMPEL ⟨∼ obedience by threats⟩ **2** ♦ : to execute effectively ⟨∼ the law⟩ — **en·force·able** *adj* — **en·force·ment** *n*

♦ administer, apply, execute, implement

en·forc·er \in-'fȯr-sər\ *n* : one that enforces; *esp* : an aggressive player (as in ice hockey) known for rough play
en·fran·chise \in-'fran-ˌchīz\ *vb* **-chised; -chis·ing 1** ♦ : to set free (as from slavery) **2** : to admit to the rights of citizenship; *also* : to grant the vote to

♦ discharge, emancipate, free, liberate, loose, loosen, manumit, release, spring, unbind, unchain, unfetter

en·fran·chise·ment \-ˌchīz-mənt, -chəz-\ *n* : the act or result of enfranchising: as **a** ♦ : the releasing from slavery or custody **b** ♦ : admission to citizenship and its rights

♦ [a] emancipation, liberation, manumission ♦ [b] franchise, suffrage, vote

eng *abbr* engine; engineer; engineering

Eng *abbr* England; English

en·gage \in-'gāj\ *vb* **en·gaged; en·gag·ing 1 ♦** : to bind (as oneself) by a pledge to do something; *esp* : to bind by a pledge to marry **2 ♦** : to use the services of : EMPLOY, HIRE **3 ♦** : to attract and hold esp. by interesting; *also* : to cause to participate **4** : to commence or take part in a venture **5 ♦** : to bring or enter into conflict **6** : to connect or interlock with : MESH; *also* : to cause to mesh

   ♦ [1] commit, pledge, troth ♦ [2] employ, hire, retain, take on ♦ [3] absorb, busy, engross, enthrall, fascinate, grip, immerse, interest, intrigue, involve, occupy ♦ [5] battle, encounter, face, meet, take on

en·gaged \in-'gājd, en-\ *adj* **1 ♦** : involved in activity **2** : pledged to be married

   ♦ active, assiduous, busy, diligent, laborious, occupied, sedulous, working

en·gage·ment \in-'gāj-mənt\ *n* **1 ♦** : an arrangement to meet or be present at a specified time and place **2 ♦** : a job or period of employment esp. as a performer **3 ♦** : a mutual promise to marry **4** : a hostile encounter

   ♦ [1] appointment, date, rendezvous, tryst ♦ [2] employ, employment, hire ♦ [3] espousal, troth *Ant* disengagement

en·gag·ing *adj* ♦ : tending to draw favorable attention or interest : ATTRACTIVE — **en·gag·ing·ly** *adv*

   ♦ alluring, attractive, captivating, charming, fascinating, fetching, glamorous ♦ absorbing, engrossing, enthralling, fascinating, interesting, intriguing

en·gen·der \in-'jen-dər\ *vb* **1** : BEGET **2 ♦** : to cause to exist or to develop : CREATE

   ♦ create, generate, induce, make, produce, spawn

en·gine \'en-jən\ *n* **1** : a mechanical device **2** : a machine for converting energy into mechanical motion **3** : LOCOMOTIVE **4** : software that performs a fundamental function esp. of a larger program — **en·gine·less** *adj*

¹**en·gi·neer** \ˌen-jə-'nir\ *n* **1** : a member of a military unit specializing in engineering work **2** : a designer or builder of engines **3** : one trained in engineering **4** : one that operates an engine

²**engineer** *vb* **1** : to lay out or manage as an engineer **2** : to guide the course of

en·gi·neer·ing *n* : the practical applications of scientific and mathematical principles

En·glish \'iŋ-glish\ *n* **1** : the language of England, the U.S., and many areas now or formerly under British rule **2 English** *pl* : the people of England **3** : spin imparted to a ball that is driven or rolled — **English** *adj* — **En·glish·man** \-mən\ *n* — **En·glish·wom·an** \-ˌwu̇-mən\ *n*

English horn *n* : a woodwind instrument longer than and having a range lower than the oboe

English setter *n* : any of a breed of hunting dogs with a flat silky coat of white or white with color

English sparrow *n* : HOUSE SPARROW

English system *n* : a system of weights and measures in which the foot is the principal unit of length and the pound is the principal unit of weight

engr *abbr* **1** engineer **2** engraved

en·gram \'en-ˌgram\ *n* : a hypothetical change in neural tissue postulated in order to account for persistence of memory

en·grave \in-'grāv\ *vb* **en·graved; en·grav·ing 1 ♦** : to produce (as letters or lines) by incising a surface **2 ♦** : to cut figures, letters, or designs on for printing; *also* : to print from an engraved plate **3** : PHOTOENGRAVE **4 ♦** : to impress deeply as if with an engraving tool — **en·grav·er** *n*

   ♦ [1] etch, grave, inscribe ♦ [4] etch, impress, imprint, ingrain, inscribe

en·grav·ing \in-'grā-viŋ\ *n* **1** : the art of one who engraves **2** : an engraved plate; *also* : a print made from it

en·gross \in-'grōs\ *vb* ♦ : to take up the whole interest or attention of

   ♦ absorb, busy, engage, enthrall, grip, immerse, interest, intrigue, involve, occupy

en·grossed \in-'grōst\ *adj* ♦ : completely occupied or absorbed

   ♦ absorbed, attentive, intent, observant, rapt

en·gross·ing *adj* ♦ : taking up the time or attention completely

   ♦ absorbing, engaging, enthralling, fascinating, interesting, intriguing

en·gulf \in-'gəlf\ *vb* ♦ : to flow over and enclose

   ♦ deluge, drown, flood, inundate, overflow, overwhelm, submerge, swamp

en·hance \in-'hans\ *vb* **en·hanced; en·hanc·ing** ♦ : to increase or improve (as in value or desirability)

   ♦ ameliorate, amend, better, enrich, improve, perfect, refine

en·hance·ment *n* ♦ : the act of enhancing or state of being enhanced

   ♦ advance, advancement, breakthrough, improvement, refinement

enig·ma \i-'nig-mə\ *n* ♦ : something obscure or hard to understand

   ♦ conundrum, mystery, mystification, puzzle, puzzlement, riddle, secret

enig·mat·ic \ˌen-ig-'ma-tik\ *adj* ♦ : resembling an enigma — **en·ig·mat·i·cal·ly** \-ti-k(ə-)lē\ *adv*

   ♦ ambiguous, cryptic, deep, equivocal, inscrutable, murky, mysterious, mystic, nebulous, obscure, occult

en·join \in-'jȯin\ *vb* **1 ♦** : to direct or impose by authoritative order or with urgent warning : COMMAND **2 ♦** : to forbid by authority

   ♦ [1] call, charge, command, demand, direct, exact, insist, instruct, order, press, stipulate (for) ♦ [1, 2] ban, bar, forbid, interdict, outlaw, prohibit, proscribe

en·joy \in-'jȯi\ *vb* **1 ♦** : to have for one's benefit or use ⟨∼ good health⟩ **2 ♦** : to take pleasure or satisfaction in ⟨∼ed the concert⟩

   ♦ [1] command, have, hold, occupy, own, possess, retain ♦ [2] adore, delight, dig, fancy, like, love, relish, revel

en·joy·able *adj* ♦ : being a source of pleasure or enjoyment

   ♦ agreeable, amusing, delectable, delicious, delightful, entertaining, fun, heavenly, luscious, pleasurable

en·joy·ment *n* **1 ♦** : the action or state of enjoying **2** : something that gives keen satisfaction

   ♦ contentment, delectation, delight, gladness, gratification, pleasure, relish, satisfaction

enl *abbr* **1** enlarged **2** enlisted

en·large \in-'lärj\ *vb* **en·larged; en·larg·ing 1 ♦** : to make or grow larger **2 ♦** : to give greater scope to; *also* : to speak or write at length : ELABORATE — often used with *on* or *upon* — **en·large·ment** *n*

   ♦ [1] add, aggrandize, amplify, augment, boost, compound, escalate, expand, extend, increase, multiply, raise, swell, up ♦ *usu* enlarge on [2] amplify, develop, elaborate (on), expand

en·light·en \in-'līt-ᵊn\ *vb* **1 ♦** : to give knowledge to : INSTRUCT. INFORM **2 ♦** : to give spiritual insight to — **en·light·en·ment** *n*

   ♦ [1] acquaint, advise, apprise, brief, clue, familiarize, fill in, inform, instruct, tell, wise ♦ [2] edify, educate, nurture

en·list \in-'list\ *vb* **1** : to secure the aid or support of **2 ♦** : to engage for service in the armed forces **3 ♦** : to participate heartily (as in a cause or effort) ⟨∼ed in the cause of world peace⟩ — **en·list·ee** \-ˌlis-'tē\ *n* — **en·list·ment** \-'list-mənt\ *n*

   ♦ *usu* enlist in [2, 3] enroll, enter, join, sign on, sign up

en·list·ed \in-'lis-təd\ *adj* : of, relating to, or forming the part of a military force below commissioned or warrant officers

enlisted man *n* : a man or woman in the armed forces ranking below a commissioned or warrant officer

en·liv·en \in-'lī-vən\ *vb* ♦ : to give life, action, or spirit to : ANIMATE

   ♦ animate, brace, energize, fire, invigorate, jazz up, liven up, pep up, quicken, stimulate, vitalize, vivify, zip (up)

en masse \äⁿ-'mas\ *adv* : in a body : as a whole

en·mesh \in-'mesh\ *vb* ♦ : to catch or entangle in or as if in meshes

   ♦ ensnare, entangle, entrap, mesh, snare, tangle, trap

en·mi·ty \'en-mə-tē\ *n, pl* **-ties** ♦ : positive, active, and typically mutual hatred or ill will

   ♦ animosity, antagonism, antipathy, bitterness, gall, grudge, hostility, rancor *Ant* amity

en·no·ble \i-'nō-bəl\ *vb* **-bled; -bling** ♦ : to raise in rank or status : EXALT; *esp* : to raise to noble rank — **en·no·ble·ment** *n*

   ♦ aggrandize, dignify, exalt, glorify, magnify

en·nui \ˌän-'wē\ *n* ♦ : a feeling of weariness and dissatisfaction : BOREDOM

♦ boredom, doldrums, listlessness, restlessness, tedium, tiredness, weariness

enor·mi·ty \i-'nȯr-mə-tē\ *n, pl* **-ties** **1** : an outrageous, vicious, or immoral act **2** ♦ : great wickedness **3** ♦ : the quality or state of being huge : IMMENSITY

♦ [2] atrociousness, atrocity, depravity, heinousness, monstrosity, vileness, wickedness ♦ [3] hugeness, immensity, magnitude, massiveness, vastness

enor·mous \i-'nȯr-məs\ *adj* **1** : exceedingly wicked **2** ♦ : great in size, number, or degree : HUGE — **enor·mous·ly** *adv*

♦ astronomical, colossal, elephantine, giant, gigantic, ginormous, huge, jumbo, mammoth, massive, prodigious, titanic, tremendous, whopping

¹**enough** \i-'nəf\ *adj* : SUFFICIENT

²**enough** *adv* **1** ♦ : in or to a degree or quantity that suffices : SUFFICIENTLY **2** : FULLY, QUITE **3** ♦ : in a tolerable degree

♦ [1] adequately, satisfactorily *Ant* inadequately, insufficiently
♦ [3] fairly, kind of, moderately, so-so, somewhat, sort of

³**enough** *pron* : a sufficient number, quantity, or amount

en·quire \in-'kwī(-ə)r\, **en·qui·ry** \'in-ˌkwī(-ə)r-ē, in-'; 'in-kwə-rē, 'iŋ-\ *chiefly Brit var of* INQUIRE, INQUIRY

en·rage \in-'rāj\ *vb* ♦ : to fill with rage

♦ anger, antagonize, incense, inflame, infuriate, madden, outrage, rankle, rile, roil

en·raged \in-'rājd\ *adj* ♦ : full of fury or rage

♦ angry, boiling, furious, irate

en·rap·ture \in-'rap-chər\ *vb* **en·rap·tured**; **en·rap·tur·ing** ♦ : to fill with delight

♦ carry away, elate, elevate, enthrall, exhilarate, transport

en·rich \in-'rich\ *vb* **1 a** : to make rich or richer **b** ♦ : to add to or improve with additions **2** ♦ : to add beauty to : ORNAMENT, ADORN — **en·rich·ment** *n*

♦ [1b] ameliorate, amend, better, enhance, improve, perfect, refine ♦ [2] adorn, array, beautify, bedeck, deck, decorate, do, dress, embellish, garnish, grace, ornament, trim

en·roll *or Can and Brit* **en·rol** \in-'rōl\ *vb* **en·rolled**; **en·roll·ing** **1** ♦ : to enter or register on a roll or list **2** ♦ : to offer (oneself) for enrolling — **en·roll·ment** *n*

♦ [1] inscribe, itemize, list, matriculate, register ♦ [1] catalog, enter, index, inscribe, list, put down, record ♦ [2] enlist, enter, join, sign on, sign up

en·roll·ment *or chiefly Can and Brit* **en·rol·ment** *n* **1** : the act or process of enrolling (as at enlistment or registration) **2** : the number enrolled

en route \än-'rüt, en-\ *adv or adj* : on or along the way

ENS *abbr* ensign

en·sconce \in-'skäns\ *vb* **en·sconced**; **en·sconc·ing** **1** ♦ : to place out of sight : CONCEAL **2** ♦ : to settle snugly or securely

♦ [1] bury, cache, conceal, hide, secrete ♦ [2] install, lodge, perch, roost, settle

en·sem·ble \än-'säm-bəl\ *n* : a group (as of singers, dancers, or players) or a set (as of clothes) producing a single effect

en·sheathe \in-'shēth\ *vb* : to cover with or as if with a sheath

en·shrine \in-'shrīn\ *vb* **1** : to enclose in or as if in a shrine **2** : to cherish as sacred — **en·shrine·ment** \-mənt\ *n*

en·shroud \in-'shraùd\ *vb* ♦ : to cover or enclose with or as if with a shroud : OBSCURE

♦ blanket, blot out, cloak, conceal, cover, curtain, hide, mask, obscure, occult, screen, shroud, veil

en·sign \'en-sən, *1 also* 'en-ˌsīn\ *n* **1** ♦ : a flag that is flown (as by a ship) as the symbol of nationality and that may also be flown with a distinctive badge added to its design; *also* : BADGE, EMBLEM **2** : a commissioned officer in the navy ranking next below a lieutenant junior grade

♦ banner, colors (*or* colours), flag, jack, pennant, standard, streamer

en·slave \in-'slāv\ *vb* : to force into slavery

en·slave·ment *n* **1** : the act or process of enslaving **2** ♦ : the state of being enslaved

♦ bondage, servitude, slavery, thrall, yoke

en·snare \in-'snar\ *vb* ♦ : to take in or as if in a snare : TRAP

♦ enmesh, entangle, entrap, mesh, snare, tangle, trap

en·sue \in-'sü\ *vb* **en·sued**; **en·su·ing** : to follow in time or as a result ⟨the birds escaped and chaos *ensued*⟩

en·sure \in-'shùr\ *vb* **en·sured**; **en·sur·ing** ♦ : to give security to : INSURE, GUARANTEE

♦ assure, cinch, guarantee, guaranty, insure, secure

en·tail \in-'tāl\ *vb* **1** : to limit the inheritance of (property) to the owner's lineal descendants or to a class thereof **2** ♦ : to include or involve as a necessary step or result — **en·tail·ment** *n*

♦ carry, comprehend, contain, embrace, encompass, include, involve, number, take in

en·tan·gle \in-'taŋ-gəl\ *vb* **1** ♦ : to wrap or twist together : TANGLE; *also* : to make complicated **2** ♦ : to take in or as if in a snare; *also* : to involve in a perplexing or troublesome situation

♦ [1] interlace, intertwine, interweave, knot, snarl, tangle
♦ [2] enmesh, ensnare, entrap, mesh, snare, tangle, trap *Ant* disentangle

en·tan·gle·ment *n* **1** : the action of entangling : the state of being entangled **2** ♦ : something that entangles, confuses, or ensnares

♦ net, snare, web

en·tente \än-'tänt\ *n* : an understanding providing for joint action; *also* : parties linked by such an entente

en·ter \'en-tər\ *vb* **1** : to go or come in or into **2** ♦ : to become a member of : JOIN ⟨~ the ministry⟩ **3** : to make a beginning : to begin to consider a subject — usu. used with *into* or *upon* **4** : to take part in : CONTRIBUTE **5** : to go into or upon and take possession **6** ♦ : to set down (as in a list) : REGISTER ⟨~ the data⟩ **7** : to place (a complaint) before a court; *also* : to put on record ⟨~ a complaint⟩

♦ [2] enlist, enroll, join, sign on, sign up ♦ usu **enter into** *or* **enter upon** [3] begin, commence, embark (on *or* upon), get off, launch, open, start, strike ♦ [6] catalog, enroll, index, inscribe, list, put down, record, register, schedule, slate

en·ter·i·tis \ˌen-tə-'rī-təs\ *n* : intestinal inflammation; *also* : a disease marked by this

en·ter·prise \'en-tər-ˌprīz\ *n* **1** ♦ : a project or undertaking that is esp. difficult, complicated, or risky **2** ♦ : readiness for daring action : INITIATIVE **3** ♦ : a business organization

♦ [1] chance, flier, gamble, speculation, venture ♦ [2] aggressiveness, ambition, drive, go, hustle, initiative ♦ [3] business, company, concern, establishment, firm, house, outfit

en·ter·pris·ing \-ˌprī-ziŋ\ *adj* ♦ : bold and vigorous in action

♦ adventurous, audacious, bold, daring, gutsy, hardy, nervy, venturesome

en·ter·tain \ˌen-tər-'tān\ *vb* **1** : to treat or receive as a guest **2** ♦ : to provide entertainment for : AMUSE, DIVERT **3** ♦ : to hold in mind; *also* : to receive and take into consideration — **en·ter·tain·er** *n*

♦ [2] amuse, disport, divert, regale ♦ [3] consider, contemplate, debate, deliberate, meditate, mull, ponder, question, ruminate, study, think, weigh

en·ter·tain·ing \-'tā-niŋ\ *adj* ♦ : providing entertainment

♦ amusing, delightful, diverting, enjoyable, fun, pleasurable

en·ter·tain·ment *n* **1** ♦ : the act of entertaining **2** ♦ : amusement or diversion provided esp. by performers; *also* : something or someone diverting or engaging

♦ [1] amusement, distraction, diversion ♦ [2] delight, diversion, fun, pleasure

en·thrall *or* **en·thral** \in-'thrȯl\ *vb* **en·thralled**; **en·thrall·ing** **1** : ENSLAVE **2** ♦ : to hold the attention of as if under a spell : hold spellbound

♦ arrest, enchant, fascinate, grip, hypnotize, interest, intrigue, involve, mesmerize

en·thrall·ing *adj* ♦ : capable of holding spellbound : intensely absorbing or interesting

♦ absorbing, engaging, engrossing, fascinating, interesting, intriguing

en·throne \in-'thrōn\ *vb* **1** : to seat on or as if on a throne **2** : EXALT

en·thuse \in-'thüz, -'thyüz\ *vb* **en·thused**; **en·thus·ing** **1** : to make enthusiastic **2** ♦ : to show enthusiasm

♦ fuss, gush, rave, rhapsodize

en·thu·si·asm \in-'thü-zē-ˌa-zəm, -'thyü-\ *n* **1** ♦ : strong warmth of feeling : keen interest : FERVOR **2** ♦ : something that inspires or is pursued or regarded with ardent zeal or fervor

♦ [1] appetite, ardor, avidity, eagerness, excitement, fervor, hunger, impatience, keenness, thirst ♦ [2] craze, fad, fashion, go, mode, rage, sensation, style, trend, vogue

en•thu•si•ast \-,ast, -əst\ *n* ♦ : a person filled with enthusiasm

♦ addict, aficionado, buff, bug, devotee, fan, fancier, lover, nut

en•thu•si•as•tic \in-,thü-zē-'as-tik, -,thyü-\ *adj* ♦ : filled with or marked by enthusiasm — **en•thu•si•as•ti•cal•ly** \-ti-k(ə-)lē\ *adv*

♦ ardent, athirst, avid, eager, gung ho, keen, nuts, raring, thirsty

en•tice \in-'tīs\ *vb* **en•ticed; en•tic•ing** ♦ : to attract cunningly or by arousing hope or desire : ALLURE, TEMPT

♦ allure, beguile, decoy, lead on, lure, seduce, tempt

en•tice•ment *n* **1** ♦ : the act of enticing **2** ♦ : something that entices : a means or method of enticing

♦ lure, seduction, solicitation, temptation

en•tire \in-'tī(-ə)r\ *adj* ♦ : having no element or part left out : COMPLETE, WHOLE

♦ complete, comprehensive, full, grand, intact, integral, perfect, plenary, total, undivided, whole

en•tire•ly *adv* ♦ : to the full or entire extent

♦ altogether, completely, dead, fast, flat, full, fully, perfectly, quite, thoroughly, well, wholly

en•tire•ty \in-'tī-rə-tē, -'tī(-ə)r-tē\ *n, pl* **-ties** **1** : COMPLETE-NESS **2** : WHOLE, TOTALITY

en•ti•tle \in-'tī-t°l\ *vb* **en•ti•tled; en•ti•tling** **1** ♦ : to give a title to : DESIGNATE **2** ♦ : to furnish with proper grounds for seeking or claiming something ⟨*entitled* to a fair trial⟩

♦ [1] baptize, call, christen, denominate, designate, dub, label, name, style, term, title ♦ [2] authorize, qualify *Ant* disqualify

en•ti•tle•ment \in-'tīt-°l-mənt\ *n* : a government program providing benefits to members of a specified group

en•ti•ty \'en-tə-tē\ *n, pl* **-ties** **1** : EXISTENCE, BEING **2** ♦ : something with separate and real existence

♦ being, individual, object, substance, thing

en•tomb \in-'tüm\ *vb* : to place in a tomb : BURY

en•tomb•ment *n* ♦ : the act or process of entombing

♦ burial, interment, sepulture

en•to•mol•o•gy \,en-tə-'mä-lə-jē\ *n* : a branch of zoology that deals with insects — **en•to•mo•log•i•cal** \-mə-'lä-ji-kəl\ *adj* — **en•to•mol•o•gist** \-jist\ *n*

en•tou•rage \,än-tü-'räzh\ *n* : RETINUE

en•tr'acte \'än-,trakt\ *n* **1** : something (as a dance) performed between two acts of a play **2** : the interval between two acts of a play

en•trails \'en-,trālz\ *n pl* : the internal organs esp. in the trunk of the body : VISCERA; *esp* : the tubular part of the alimentary canal that extends from the stomach to the anus

¹en•trance \'en-trəns\ *n* **1** ♦ : permission or right to enter **2** : the act of entering **3** ♦ : a means or place of entry

♦ [1] access, admission, doorway, entrée, entry, gateway ♦ [3] door, doorway, gate, gateway, way

²en•trance \in-'trans\ *vb* **en•tranced; en•tranc•ing** ♦ : to carry away with delight, wonder, or rapture

♦ carry away, enrapture, enthrall, ravish, transport

en•trant \'en-trənt\ *n* : one that enters esp. as a competitor

en•trap \in-'trap\ *vb* ♦ : to catch in or as if in a trap : ENSNARE, TRAP — **en•trap•ment** *n*

♦ enmesh, ensnare, entangle, mesh, snare, tangle, trap

en•treat \in-'trēt\ *vb* ♦ : to ask urgently : BESEECH

♦ appeal, beg, beseech, implore, importune, petition, plead, pray, solicit, supplicate

en•treaty \-'trē-tē\ *n* ♦ : an act of entreating

♦ appeal, cry, petition, plea, prayer, solicitation, suit, supplication

en•trée *or* **en•tree** \'än-,trā\ *n* **1** ♦ : freedom of entry or access **2** : the main course of a meal in the U.S.

♦ access, admission, doorway, entrance, entry, gateway

en•trench \in-'trench\ *vb* **1 a** ♦ : to place within or surround with a trench esp. for defense **b** ♦ : to establish solidly ⟨∼ed customs⟩ **2** : ENCROACH, TRESPASS — **en•trench•ment** *n*

♦ embed, fix, implant, ingrain, lodge, root *Ant* dislodge, root (out), uproot

en•tre•pre•neur \,än-trə-prə-'nər, -'nür, -'nyür\ *n* : one who organizes and assumes the risk of a business or enterprise — **en•tre•pre•neur•ial** \-'nür-ē-əl, -'nyür-, -'nər-\ *adj* — **en•tre•pre•neur•ship** \-,ship\ *n*

en•tro•py \'en-trə-pē\ *n, pl* **-pies** **1** : the degree of disorder in a system **2** : an ultimate state of inert uniformity

en•trust \in-'trəst\ *vb* **1** ♦ : to commit something to as a trust **2** ♦ : to commit to another with confidence

♦ [1] assign, charge, commission, trust ♦ [2] commend, commit, consign, delegate, deliver, give, hand over, leave, pass, transfer, transmit, trust, turn over, vest

en•try \'en-trē\ *n, pl* **entries** **1** ♦ : a place of entrance; *also* : the act, means, right, or privilege of entering **2** : an entering in a record; *also* : an item so entered **3** : a headword with its definition or identification; *also* : VOCABULARY ENTRY **4** : one entered in a contest

♦ foyer, hall, lobby, vestibule ♦ access, admission, doorway, entrée, entrance, gateway

en•twine \in-'twīn\ *vb* ♦ : to twine together or around

♦ coil, curl, spiral, twine, twist, wind

enu•mer•ate \i-'nü-mə-,rāt, -'nyü-\ *vb* **-at•ed; -at•ing** **1** ♦ : to determine the number of : COUNT **2** ♦ : to specify one after another : LIST — **enu•mer•a•tion** \-,nü-mə-'rā-shən, -,nyü-\ *n*

♦ [1] count, number, tell ♦ [2] detail, itemize, list, numerate, rehearse, tick (off)

enun•ci•ate \ē-'nən-sē-,āt\ *vb* **-at•ed; -at•ing** **1 a** : to state definitely **b** ♦ : to make known publicly : ANNOUNCE, PROCLAIM **2** : to say clearly and effectively : PRONOUNCE, ARTICULATE — **enun•ci•a•tion** \-,nən-sē-'ā-shən\ *n*

♦ advertise, announce, blaze, broadcast, declare, placard, post, proclaim, promulgate, publicize, publish, sound

en•ure•sis \,en-yù-'rē-səs\ *n* : involuntary discharge of urine : BED-WETTING

env *abbr* envelope

en•vel•op \in-'ve-ləp\ *vb* ♦ : to enclose completely with or as if with a covering — **en•vel•op•ment** *n*

♦ embrace, enclose, encompass, enfold, enshroud, invest, lap, mantle, shroud, swathe, veil, wrap

en•ve•lope \'en-və-,lōp, 'än-\ *n* **1** : a usu. paper container for a letter **2** : WRAPPER, COVERING **3** : a conventionally accepted limit ⟨fashions that push the ∼⟩

en•ven•om \in-'ve-nəm\ *vb* **1** : to make poisonous **2** : EMBITTER

en•vi•able \'en-vē-ə-bəl\ *adj* : highly desirable — **en•vi•ably** \-blē\ *adv*

en•vi•ous \'en-vē-əs\ *adj* ♦ : feeling or showing envy — **en•vi•ous•ly** *adv*

♦ covetous, jaundiced, jealous, resentful

en•vi•ous•ness *n* ♦ : the quality or state of being envious

♦ covetousness, envy, jealousy, resentment

en•vi•ron•ment \in-'vī-rən-mənt, -'vī(-ə)rn-\ *n* **1** ♦ : the circumstances, objects, or conditions surrounding someone or something : SURROUNDINGS **2** : the whole complex of factors (as soil, climate, and living things) that influence the form and the ability to survive of a plant or animal or ecological community — **en•vi•ron•men•tal** \-,vī-rən-'ment-°l, -,vī(-ə)rn-\ *adj* — **en•vi•ron•men•tal•ly** \-t°l-ē\ *adv*

♦ atmosphere, climate, environs, medium, milieu, setting, surroundings

en•vi•ron•men•tal•ist \-,vī-rən-'ment-°l-ist, -,vīrn-\ *n* : a person concerned about environmental quality esp. with respect to control of pollution

en•vi•rons \in-'vī-rənz\ *n pl* **1** ♦ : the districts around a city **2** ♦ : the circumstances, conditions, or objects by which one is surrounded : SURROUNDINGS; *also* : VICINITY

♦ [1] exurbia, outskirts, suburbia ♦ [2] atmosphere, climate, environment, medium, milieu, setting, surroundings

en•vis•age \in-'vi-zij\ *vb* **-aged; -ag•ing** ♦ : to have a mental picture of

♦ conceive, dream, fancy, imagine, picture, vision, visualize

en•vi•sion \in-'vi-zhən, en-\ *vb* : to picture to oneself ⟨∼s world peace⟩

en•voy \'en-,vòi, 'än-\ *n* **1** ♦ : a diplomatic agent **2** ♦ : one who bears a message or does an errand : REPRESENTATIVE

♦ [1] ambassador, delegate, emissary, legate, minister, representative ♦ [2] agent, attorney, commissary, delegate, deputy, factor, proxy, representative

¹**en·vy** \'en-vē\ *n, pl* **envies** ♦ : painful or resentful awareness of another's advantages; *also* : an object of envy

♦ covetousness, enviousness, jealousy, resentment

²**envy** *vb* **en·vied; en·vy·ing** : to feel envy toward or on account of
en·zyme \'en-ˌzīm\ *n* : any of various complex proteins produced by living cells that catalyze specific biochemical reactions at body temperatures — **en·zy·mat·ic** \ˌen-zə-'ma-tik\ *adj*
Eo·cene \'ē-ə-ˌsēn\ *adj* : of, relating to, or being the epoch of the Tertiary between the Paleocene and the Oligocene — **Eocene** *n*
EOE *abbr* equal opportunity employer
eo·lian \ē-'ō-lē-ən\ *adj* : borne, deposited, or produced by the wind
EOM *abbr* end of month
eon \'ē-ən, -ˌän\ *n* ♦ : an indefinitely long time : AGE

♦ age, cycle, eternity

EP *abbr* European plan
EPA *abbr* Environmental Protection Agency
ep·au·let *also* **ep·au·lette** \ˌe-pə-'let\ *n* : a shoulder ornament esp. on a coat or military uniform
épée \'e-ˌpā, ā-'pā\ *n* : a fencing or dueling sword
Eph *or* **Ephes** *abbr* Ephesians
ephed·rine \i-'fe-drən\ *n* : a stimulant drug used to treat asthma and nasal congestion
ephem·era \i-'fe-mər-ə\ *n pl* : collectibles (as posters or tickets) not intended to have lasting value
ephem·er·al \i-'fe-mə-rəl\ *adj* ♦ : lasting a very short time : SHORT-LIVED, TRANSITORY — **ephem·er·al·i·ty** \i-ˌfe-mə-'ra-lə-tē\ *n*

♦ evanescent, flash, fleeting, impermanent, momentary, short-lived, transient

Ephe·sians \i-'fē-zhənz\ *n* : a letter addressed to early Christians and included as a book in the New Testament
ep·ic \'e-pik\ *n* : a long poem in elevated style narrating the deeds of a hero — **epic** *adj*
epi·cen·ter *or Can and Brit* **epi·cen·tre** \'e-pi-ˌsen-tər\ *n* : the point on the earth's surface directly above the point of origin of an earthquake
epi·cure \'e-pi-ˌkyūr\ *n* ♦ : a person with sensitive and discriminating tastes esp. in food and wine

♦ epicurean, gourmand, gourmet

ep·i·cu·re·an \ˌe-pi-kyū-'rē-ən, -'kyūr-ē-\ *n* ♦ : a person with sensitive and discriminating tastes esp. in food and wine : EPICURE — **epicurean** *adj*

♦ epicure, gourmand, gourmet

¹**ep·i·dem·ic** \ˌe-pə-'de-mik\ *adj* : affecting many persons at one time ⟨~ disease⟩; *also* : excessively prevalent
²**epidemic** *n* : an epidemic outbreak esp. of disease
ep·i·de·mi·ol·o·gy \ˌep-ə-ˌdē-mē-'ä-lə-jē\ *n* : the study of the incidence, distribution, and control of disease in a population — **ep·i·de·mio·log·i·cal** \-ˌdē-mē-ə-'lä-ji-kəl\ *also* **ep·i·de·mi·o·log·ic** \-jik\ *adj* — **ep·i·de·mi·ol·o·gist** \-'ä-lə-jist\ *n*
epi·der·mis \ˌe-pə-'dər-məs\ *n* : an outer layer esp. of skin — **epi·der·mal** \-məl\ *adj*
epi·du·ral \ˌe-pi-'d(y)ūr-əl\ *adj* : administered into the space outside the membrane that envelops the spinal cord ⟨~ anesthesia⟩ — **epidural** *n*
epi·glot·tis \ˌe-pə-'glä-təs\ *n* : a thin plate of flexible tissue protecting the tracheal opening during swallowing
ep·i·gram \'e-pə-ˌgram\ *n* **1** : a short often satirical poem **2** ♦ : a terse, sage, or witty often paradoxical saying

♦ adage, aphorism, byword, maxim, proverb, saying

ep·i·gram·mat·ic \ˌe-pə-grə-'ma-tik\ *adj* ♦ : of, relating to, or resembling an epigram; *also* : marked by or given to the use of epigrams

♦ brief, compact, compendious, concise, crisp, laconic, pithy, succinct, summary, terse

ep·i·lep·sy \'e-pə-ˌlep-sē\ *n, pl* **-sies** : a disorder marked by abnormal electrical discharges in the brain and typically manifested by sudden periods of diminished consciousness or by convulsions — **ep·i·lep·tic** \ˌe-pə-'lep-tik\ *adj or n*
ep·i·logue *also* **ep·i·log** \'e-pə-ˌlóg, -ˌläg\ *n* **1** : a concluding section of a literary work **2** : a speech addressed to the spectators by an actor at the end of a play
epi·neph·rine \ˌe-pə-'ne-frən\ *n* : an adrenal hormone used me-

dicinally esp. as a heart stimulant, a muscle relaxant, and a vaso-constrictor
epiph·a·ny \i-'pi-fə-nē\ *n, pl* **-nies** **1** *cap* : January 6 observed as a church festival in commemoration of the coming of the Magi to Jesus at Bethlehem **2** : a sudden striking understanding of something
epis·co·pa·cy \i-'pis-kə-pə-sē\ *n, pl* **-cies** **1** : government of a church by bishops **2** : EPISCOPATE
epis·co·pal \i-'pis-kə-pəl\ *adj* **1** : of or relating to a bishop or episcopacy **2** *cap* : of or relating to the Protestant Episcopal Church
Epis·co·pa·lian \i-ˌpis-kə-'pāl-yən\ *n* : a member of the Protestant Episcopal Church
epis·co·pate \i-'pis-kə-pət, -ˌpāt\ *n* **1** : the rank, office, or term of a bishop **2** : a body of bishops
ep·i·sode \'e-pə-ˌsōd\ *n* **1** : a unit of action in a dramatic or literary work **2** ♦ : an incident in a course of events : OCCURRENCE ⟨a feverish ~⟩

♦ affair, circumstance, event, happening, incident, occasion, occurrence, thing

ep·i·sod·ic \ˌe-pə-'sä-dik\ *adj* ♦ : made up of separate esp. loosely connected episodes

♦ periodic, serial

epis·tle \i-'pi-səl\ *n* **1** *cap* : one of the letters of the New Testament **2** : a direct or personal written or printed message addressed to a person or organization : LETTER; *esp* : a formal or elegant letter — **epis·to·lary** \i-'pis-tə-ˌler-ē\ *adj*
ep·i·taph \'e-pə-ˌtaf\ *n* : an inscription in memory of a dead person
ep·i·tha·la·mi·um \ˌe-pə-thə-'lä-mē-əm\ *or* **ep·i·tha·la·mi·on** \-mē-ən\ *n, pl* **-mi·ums** *or* **-mia** \-mē-ə\ : a song or poem in honor of a bride and bridegroom
ep·i·the·li·um \ˌe-pə-'thē-lē-əm\ *n, pl* **-lia** \-lē-ə\ : a cellular membrane covering a bodily surface or lining a cavity — **ep·i·the·li·al** \-lē-əl\ *adj*
ep·i·thet \'e-pə-ˌthet, -thət\ *n* : a characterizing and often abusive word or phrase
epit·o·me \i-'pi-tə-mē\ *n* **1** ♦ : a brief presentation or statement of something : ABSTRACT, SUMMARY **2** ♦ : a typical or ideal example : EMBODIMENT

♦ [1] abstract, digest, encapsulation, outline, précis, recapitulation, résumé (*or* resume), roundup, sum, summary, synopsis, wrap-up ♦ [2] embodiment, exemplar, ideal, incarnation, manifestation, personification, quintessence

epit·o·mize \-ˌmīz\ *vb* **1** ♦ : to make or give an epitome of **2** ♦ : to serve as the typical or ideal example of

♦ [1] abstract, digest, encapsulate, outline, recapitulate, sum up, summarize, wrap up ♦ [2] embody, manifest, materialize, personify

ep·och \'e-pək, -ˌpäk\ *n* ♦ : a usu. extended period : ERA, AGE — **ep·och·al** \-pə-kəl, -ˌpä-\ *adj*

♦ age, era, period, time

ep·onym \'e-pə-ˌnim\ *n* **1** : one for whom something is or is believed to be named **2** : a name (as of a disease) based on or derived from an eponym — **epon·y·mous** \i-'pä-nə-məs\ *adj*
ep·oxy \i-'päk-sē\ *vb* **ep·ox·ied** *or* **ep·oxyed; ep·oxy·ing** : to glue, fill, or coat with epoxy resin
epoxy resin *n* : a synthetic resin used in coatings and adhesives
ep·si·lon \'ep-sə-län, -lən\ *n* : the 5th letter of the Greek alphabet — E or ε
Ep·som salts \'ep-səm-\ *n* : a bitter colorless or white magnesium salt with cathartic properties
eq *abbr* **1** equal **2** equation
equa·ble \'e-kwə-bəl, 'ē-\ *adj* ♦ : showing regular or consistent movement, occurrence, operation, or character; *esp* : free from unpleasant extremes — **eq·ua·bil·i·ty** \ˌe-kwə-'bi-lə-tē, ˌē-\ *n* — **eq·ua·bly** \'e-kwə-blē, 'ē-\ *adv*

♦ balmy, clement, gentle, mild, moderate, temperate

¹**equal** \'ē-kwəl\ *adj* **1** ♦ : of the same measure, quantity, value, quality, number, degree, or status as another **2** ♦ : regarding or affecting all objects in the same way : IMPARTIAL ⟨~ justice⟩ **3** : free from extremes **4** : able to cope with a situation or task — **equal·ly** *adv*

♦ [1] duplicate, even, identical, indistinguishable, same ♦ [2] disinterested, dispassionate, equitable, fair, impartial, just, nonpartisan, objective, square, unbiased, unprejudiced

²**equal** *vb* **equaled** *or* **equalled; equal·ing** *or* **equal·ling** **1** ♦ : to

be or become equal to; *also* : to be identical in value to   **2 ♦** : to make or produce something equal to

   ♦ [1, 2] correspond, match, parallel ♦ [1, 2] add up, amount, come, correspond, meet, rival, tie, touch

³**equal** *n* ♦ : one that is equal

   ♦ coordinate, counterpart, equivalent, fellow, like, match, parallel, peer, rival

equal•ise, equal•is•er *Brit var of* EQUALIZE, EQUALIZER
equal•i•ty \i-ˈkwä-lə-tē\ *n* ♦ : the quality or state of being equal

   ♦ equivalence, par, parity, sameness

equal•ize \ˈē-kwə-ˌlīz\ *vb* **-ized; -iz•ing** ♦ : to make equal, uniform, or constant — **equal•i•za•tion** \ˌē-kwə-lə-ˈzā-shən\ *n* — **equal•iz•er** *n*

   ♦ balance, equate, even, level

equals sign *or* **equal sign** *n* : a sign = indicating equivalence
equa•nim•i•ty \ˌē-kwə-ˈni-mə-tē, ˌe-\ *n, pl* **-ties** ♦ : evenness of mind esp. under stress : COMPOSURE

   ♦ aplomb, calmness, composure, coolness, placidity, self-possession, serenity, tranquility *Ant* agitation, discomposure, perturbation

equate \i-ˈkwāt\ *vb* **equat•ed; equat•ing   1** ♦ : to make, treat, or regard as equal or comparable   **2** : show the relationship between

   ♦ balance, equalize, even, level ♦ bracket, compare, liken

equa•tion \i-ˈkwā-zhən\ *n*   **1** : an act of equating : the state of being equated   **2** : a usu. formal statement of equivalence esp. of mathematical expressions
equa•tor \i-ˈkwā-tər, ˈē-ˌ\ *n* : an imaginary circle around the earth that is everywhere equally distant from the two poles — **equa•to•ri•al** \ˌē-kwə-ˈtōr-ē-əl, ˌe-\ *adj*
equer•ry \ˈe-kwə-rē, i-ˈkwer-ē\ *n, pl* **-ries   1** : an officer in charge of the horses of a prince or noble   **2** : a personal attendant of a member of the British royal family
¹**eques•tri•an** \i-ˈkwes-trē-ən\ *adj* : of or relating to horseback riding; *also* : representing a person on horseback ⟨an ∼ statue⟩
²**equestrian** *n* : one who rides a horse
eques•tri•enne \i-ˌkwes-trē-ˈen\ *n* : a female rider on horseback
equi•dis•tant \ˌē-kwə-ˈdis-tənt\ *adj* : equally distant
equi•lat•er•al \ˌē-kwə-ˈla-tə-rəl\ *adj* : having all sides or faces equal ⟨∼ triangles⟩
equi•lib•ri•um \ˌē-kwə-ˈli-brē-əm, ˌe-\ *n, pl* **-ri•ums** *or* **-ria** \-brē-ə\   **1** : a state of intellectual or emotional balance   **2** ♦ : a state of balance between opposing forces or actions

   ♦ balance, equipoise, poise

¹**equine** \ˈē-ˌkwīn, ˈe-\ *adj* : of or relating to the horse
²**equine** *n* : a member of the family of hoofed mammals consisting of the horses, asses, and zebras and extinct related animals; *specif* : HORSE
equi•noc•tial \ˌē-kwə-ˈnäk-shəl, ˌe-\ *adj* : relating to an equinox
equi•nox \ˈē-kwə-ˌnäks, ˈe-\ *n* : either of the two times each year when the sun appears directly overhead at the equator and day and night are everywhere of equal length
equip \i-ˈkwip\ *vb* **equipped; equip•ping   1** ♦ : to supply with needed resources   **2** ♦ : to make ready : PREPARE

   ♦ [1] accoutre, fit, furnish, outfit, rig, supply ♦ [2] fit, prepare, qualify, ready, season

eq•ui•page \ˈe-kwə-pij\ *n* : a horse-drawn carriage usu. with its servants
equip•ment \i-ˈkwip-mənt\ *n*   **1** ♦ : things used in equipping : OUTFIT   **2** : the equipping of a person or thing : the state of being equipped

   ♦ accoutrements (*or* accouterments), apparatus, gear, matériel, outfit, paraphernalia, tackle

equi•poise \ˈe-kwə-ˌpȯiz, ˈē-\ *n*   **1** ♦ : a state of equilibrium : BALANCE   **2** ♦ : a weight or force that offsets another : COUNTERBALANCE

   ♦ [1] balance, equilibrium, poise ♦ [2] balance, counterbalance, counterweight, offset

eq•ui•ta•ble \ˈe-kwə-tə-bəl\ *adj* ♦ : having or exhibiting equity : JUST, FAIR — **eq•ui•ta•bly** \-blē\ *adv*

   ♦ disinterested, dispassionate, equal, fair, impartial, just, nonpartisan, objective, square, unbiased, unprejudiced

eq•ui•ta•tion \ˌe-kwə-ˈtā-shən\ *n* : the act or art of riding on horseback
eq•ui•ty \ˈe-kwə-tē\ *n, pl* **-ties   1** : JUSTNESS, IMPARTIALITY

2 : value of a property or of an interest in it in excess of claims against it
equiv *abbr* equivalent
equiv•a•lence \-ləns\ *n* ♦ : the state or property of being equivalent

   ♦ equality, par, parity, sameness *Ant* inequality

¹**equiv•a•lent** \i-ˈkwi-və-lənt\ *adj* : EQUAL; *also* : virtually identical
²**equivalent** *n* ♦ : one that is equivalent (as in value, meaning, or effect)

   ♦ coordinate, counterpart, equal, fellow, like, match, parallel, peer, rival

equiv•o•cal \i-ˈkwi-və-kəl\ *adj*   **1** ♦ : subject to two or more interpretations and usu. used to mislead or confuse : AMBIGUOUS   **2** : UNCERTAIN, UNDECIDED   **3** ♦ : of doubtful advantage, genuineness, or morality : SUSPICIOUS, DUBIOUS ⟨∼ behavior⟩ — **equiv•o•cal•ly** *adv*

   ♦ [1] ambiguous, cryptic, enigmatic, inscrutable, mysterious, mystic, nebulous, obscure, occult ♦ [3] debatable, disputable, doubtful, dubious, fishy, problematic, questionable, shady, shaky, suspect, suspicious

equiv•o•cate \i-ˈkwi-və-ˌkāt\ *vb* **-cat•ed; -cat•ing   1** : to use misleading language   **2** ♦ : to avoid committing oneself in what one says

   ♦ fudge, hedge, pussyfoot

equiv•o•ca•tion \-ˌkwi-və-ˈkā-shən\ *n* : an equivocal state or character; *esp* : the state of having more than one meaning
¹**-er** \ər\ *adj suffix or adv suffix* — used to form the comparative degree of adjectives and adverbs of one or two syllables ⟨hott*er*⟩ ⟨dri*er*⟩ ⟨silli*er*⟩ and sometimes of longer ones
²**-er** \ər\ *also* **-ier** \ē-ər, yər\ *or* **-yer** \yər\ *n suffix*   **1** : a person occupationally connected with ⟨hatt*er*⟩ ⟨lawy*er*⟩   **2** : a person or thing belonging to or associated with ⟨old-tim*er*⟩   **3** : a native of : resident of ⟨New Zealand*er*⟩   **4** : one that has ⟨double-deck*er*⟩   **5** : one that produces or yields ⟨pork*er*⟩   **6** : one that does or performs (a specified action) ⟨report*er*⟩   **7** : one that is a suitable object of (a specified action) ⟨broil*er*⟩   **8** : one that is ⟨foreign*er*⟩
Er *symbol* erbium
ER *abbr* emergency room
era \ˈir-ə, ˈer-ə, ˈē-rə\ *n*   **1** : a chronological order or system of notation reckoned from a given date as basis   **2** ♦ : a period identified by some special feature   **3** : any of the four major divisions of geologic time

   ♦ age, epoch, period, time

ERA *abbr*   **1** earned run average   **2** Equal Rights Amendment
erad•i•cate \i-ˈra-də-ˌkāt\ *vb* **-cat•ed; -cat•ing   1** : to pull up (as a weed) by the roots : UPROOT   **2** ♦ : destroy completely : ELIMINATE — **erad•i•ca•ble** \-di-kə-bəl\ *adj* — **erad•i•ca•tion** \-ˌra-də-ˈkā-shən\ *n*

   ♦ annihilate, blot out, demolish, eliminate, exterminate, liquidate, obliterate, root, rub out, snuff, stamp, wipe out

erase \i-ˈrās\ *vb* **erased; eras•ing** : to rub or scratch out (as written words); *also* : OBLITERATE — **eras•er** *n* — **era•sure** \i-ˈrā-shər\ *n*
er•bi•um \ˈər-bē-əm\ *n* : a rare metallic element found with yttrium
¹**ere** \ˌer\ *prep* ♦ : preceding in time : BEFORE

   ♦ ahead of, before, of, previous to, prior to, to

²**ere** *conj* : BEFORE
e–read•er \ˈē-ˌrē-dər\ *n* : a handheld electronic device used esp. for reading e-books
¹**erect** \i-ˈrekt\ *adj*   **1** ♦ : not leaning or lying down : UPRIGHT   **2** : being in a state of physiological erection

   ♦ perpendicular, standing, upright, upstanding, vertical *Ant* flat, recumbent

²**erect** *vb*   **1** ♦ : to put up by the fitting together of materials or parts : BUILD   **2** ♦ : to fix or set in an upright position   **3** : SET UP; *also* : ESTABLISH, DEVELOP

   ♦ [1] assemble, build, construct, fabricate, make, make up, piece, put up, raise ♦ [2] pitch, put up, raise, rear, set up

erec•tile \i-ˈrekt-ᵊl, -ˈrek-ˌtīl\ *adj* : capable of becoming erect ⟨∼ tissue⟩ ⟨∼ feathers of a bird⟩
erec•tion \i-ˈrek-shən\ *n*   **1** : the turgid state of a previously flaccid bodily part when it becomes dilated with blood   **2** : CONSTRUCTION ⟨the ∼ of a building⟩

ere·long \er-'lȯŋ\ *adv* : before long

er·e·mite \'er-ə-ˌmīt\ *n* : a religious recluse : HERMIT

er·go \'er-gō, 'ər-\ *adv* ♦ : because of a preceding fact or premise : THEREFORE

♦ accordingly, consequently, hence, so, therefore, thus, wherefore

er·go·nom·ics \ˌər-gə-'nä-miks\ *n sing or pl* : an applied science concerned with designing and arranging things people use in order to improve efficiency and safety — **er·go·nom·ic** \-mik\ *adj*

er·got \'ər-gət, -ˌgät\ *n* **1** : a disease of rye and other cereals caused by a fungus; *also* : this fungus **2** : a medicinal compound or preparation derived from an ergot fungus

Er·i·tre·an \ˌer-ə-'trē-ən, -'trā-\ *n* : a native or inhabitant of Eritrea — **Eritrean** *adj*

er·mine \'ər-mən\ *n, pl* **ermines** **1** : any of several weasels with winter fur mostly white; *also* : this white fur **2** : a rank or office whose official robe is ornamented with ermine

erode \i-'rōd\ *vb* **erod·ed; erod·ing** ♦ : to diminish or destroy by degrees; *esp* : to gradually eat into or wear away ⟨soil *eroded* by wind and water⟩ — **erod·ible** *also* **erod·able** \-'rō-də-bəl\ *adj*

♦ abrade, bite, chafe, corrode, eat, fray, fret, gall, rub, wear

erog·e·nous \i-'rä-jə-nəs\ *adj* **1** : sexually sensitive ⟨~ zones⟩ **2** : of, relating to, or arousing sexual feelings

ero·sion \i-'rō-zhən\ *n* : the process or state of being eroded — **ero·sion·al** \-'rō-zhə-nəl\ *adj* — **ero·sion·al·ly** *adv*

ero·sive \i-'rō-siv\ *adj* : tending to erode — **ero·sive·ness** *n*

erot·ic \i-'rä-tik\ *adj* ♦ : relating to or dealing with sexual love : AMATORY — **erot·i·cal·ly** \-ti-k(ə-)lē\ *adv* — **erot·i·cism** \-tə-ˌsi-zəm\ *n*

♦ amatory, amorous, sexy

err \'ər, 'er\ *vb* ♦ : to be or do wrong

♦ offend, sin, transgress, trespass

er·rand \'er-ənd\ *n* : a short trip taken to do something; *also* : the object or purpose of such a trip

er·rant \'er-ənt\ *adj* **1** ♦ : traveling or given to traveling : WANDERING ⟨an ~ knight⟩ **2** : straying outside proper bounds ⟨an ~ throw⟩ **3** ♦ : deviating from an accepted pattern or standard (as of behavior) ⟨an ~ child⟩

♦ [1] itinerant, nomad, nomadic, peripatetic, roaming, vagabond, vagrant ♦ [3] bad, contrary, froward, mischievous, naughty

er·ra·ta \e-'rä-tə\ *n* : a list of corrigenda

er·rat·ic \i-'ra-tik\ *adj* **1** : having no fixed course **2 a** ♦ : characterized by lack of consistency, regularity, or uniformity : INCONSISTENT **b** : ECCENTRIC ⟨~ behavior⟩ — **er·rat·i·cal·ly** \-ti-k(ə-)lē\ *adv*

♦ aimless, arbitrary, desultory, haphazard, random, scattered, stray ♦ choppy, discontinuous, fitful, intermittent, irregular, occasional, spasmodic, sporadic, spotty, uneven, unsteady

er·ra·tum \e-'rä-təm\ *n, pl* **-ta** \-tə\ : CORRIGENDUM

er·ro·ne·ous \i-'rō-nē-əs, e-'rō-\ *adj* ♦ : containing or characterized by error : INCORRECT

♦ false, inaccurate, incorrect, inexact, invalid, off, unsound, untrue, wrong

er·ro·ne·ous·ly *adv* ♦ : in an erroneous manner

♦ amiss, faultily, improperly, inaptly, incorrectly, mistakenly, wrongly

er·ror \'er-ər\ *n* **1** ♦ : a usu. ignorant or unintentional deviating from accuracy or truth ⟨made an ~ in adding⟩ **2** : a defensive misplay in baseball **3** : the state of one that errs ⟨to be in ~⟩ **4** : a product of mistake ⟨a typographical ~⟩ **5** ♦ : an act or condition of ignorant or imprudent deviation from a code of behavior **6** ♦ : an instance of false belief : a mistaken idea or system of ideas

♦ [1] blunder, fault, flub, fumble, goof, lapse, misstep, mistake, oversight, slip, stumble ♦ [5] crime, malefaction, misdeed, misdoing, offense, sin, transgression, violation, wrongdoing ♦ [6] fallacy, falsehood, falsity, illusion, misconception, untruth

er·ror·less *adj* : done, played, or performed without an error

er·satz \'er-ˌzäts\ *adj* : being usu. an artificial and inferior substitute

erst \'ərst\ *adv, archaic* : ERSTWHILE

¹**erst·while** \-ˌhwī(-ə)l\ *adv* : in the past : FORMERLY

²**erstwhile** *adj* ♦ : having been or existed at some past time : FORMER ⟨~ friends⟩

♦ former, late, old, onetime, past, sometime, whilom

er·u·dite \'er-ə-ˌdīt, 'er-yə-\ *adj* ♦ : possessing or displaying erudition

♦ educated, knowledgeable, learned, literate, scholarly, well-read ♦ bookish, learned, literary

er·u·di·tion \ˌer-ə-'di-shən, ˌer-yə-\ *n* ♦ : extensive knowledge acquired chiefly from books : SCHOLARSHIP, LEARNING

♦ education, knowledge, learning, scholarship, science

erupt \i-'rəpt\ *vb* **1 a** ♦ : to burst forth : emerge with a sudden often violent rush **b** ♦ : to cause to burst forth : force out or release usu. suddenly and violently **2** : to break through a surface ⟨teeth ~*ing* through the gum⟩ **3** : to break out with or as if with a skin rash — **erup·tive** \-tiv\ *adj*

♦ [1a] break out, burst, explode, flame, flare, go off ♦ [1b] belch, disgorge, eject, expel, jet, spew, spout, spurt

erup·tion \-'rəp-shən\ *n* ♦ : an act, process, or instance of erupting; *also* : a product of erupting (as a skin rash)

♦ agony, burst, explosion, fit, flare, flush, gush, outburst, paroxysm, spasm, storm ♦ blast, detonation, explosion

-ery *n suffix* **1** : qualities collectively : character : -NESS ⟨snobb*ery*⟩ **2** : art : practice ⟨cook*ery*⟩ **3** : place of doing, keeping, producing, or selling (the thing specified) ⟨fish*ery*⟩ ⟨bak*ery*⟩ **4** : collection : aggregate ⟨fin*ery*⟩ **5** : state or condition ⟨brav*ery*⟩

ery·sip·e·las \ˌer-ə-'si-pə-ləs, ˌir-\ *n* : an acute bacterial disease marked by fever and severe skin inflammation

er·y·the·ma \ˌer-ə-'thē-mə\ *n* : abnormal redness of the skin due to capillary congestion (as in inflammation)

eryth·ro·cyte \i-'ri-thrə-ˌsīt\ *n* : RED BLOOD CELL

Es *symbol* einsteinium

¹**-es** \əz, iz *after* s, z, sh, ch; z *after* v *or a vowel*\ *n pl suffix* — used to form the pl. of most nouns that end in s ⟨glass*es*⟩, z ⟨fuzz*es*⟩, sh ⟨bush*es*⟩, ch ⟨peach*es*⟩, or a final y that changes to i ⟨ladi*es*⟩ and of some nouns ending in f that changes to v ⟨loav*es*⟩

²**-es** *vb suffix* — used to form the third person singular present of most verbs that end in s ⟨bless*es*⟩, z ⟨fizz*es*⟩, sh ⟨hush*es*⟩, ch ⟨catch*es*⟩, or a final y that changes to i ⟨defi*es*⟩

es·ca·late \'es-kə-ˌlāt\ *vb* **-lat·ed; -lat·ing** ♦ : to increase in extent, volume, number, intensity, or scope ⟨the violence *escalated*⟩ — **es·ca·la·tion** \ˌes-kə-'lā-shən\ *n*

♦ accumulate, appreciate, balloon, build, burgeon, enlarge, expand, increase, mount, multiply, mushroom, proliferate, rise, snowball, swell, wax

es·ca·la·tor \'es-kə-ˌlā-tər\ *n* : a moving set of stairs

es·ca·pade \'es-kə-ˌpād\ *n* ♦ : a mischievous adventure

♦ antic, caper, frolic, monkeyshine, practical joke, prank, trick

¹**es·cape** \is-'kāp\ *vb* **es·caped; es·cap·ing** **1** ♦ : to get free or away **2** : to avoid a threatening evil **3** ♦ : miss or succeed in averting : AVOID **2** ⟨~ injury⟩ ⟨*escaped* punishment⟩ **4** : to fail to be noticed or recallable by : ELUDE ⟨his name ~s me⟩ **5** : to be produced or uttered involuntarily by ⟨let a sob ~ him⟩

♦ [1] abscond, clear out, flee, fly, get out, lam, run away, run off ♦ [3] avoid, dodge, duck, elude, eschew, evade, shake, shirk, shun

²**escape** *n* **1** ♦ : flight from or avoidance of something unpleasant **2** : LEAKAGE **3** ♦ : a means of escape

♦ [1] avoidance, cop-out, evasion, out ♦ [3] flight, getaway, lam, slip

³**escape** *adj* : providing a means or way of escape

es·cap·ee \is-ˌkā-'pē, ˌes-(ˌ)kā-\ *n* : one that has escaped esp. from prison

escape velocity *n* : the minimum velocity needed by a body (as a rocket) to escape from the gravitational field of a celestial body (as the earth)

es·cap·ism \is-'kā-ˌpi-zəm\ *n* : diversion of the mind to imaginative activity as an escape from routine — **es·cap·ist** \-pist\ *adj or n*

es·car·got \ˌes-ˌkär-'gō\ *n, pl* **-gots** \-'gō(z)\ : a snail prepared for use as food

es·ca·role \'es-kə-ˌrōl\ *n* : ENDIVE 1

es·carp·ment \es-'kärp-mənt\ *n* **1** : a steep slope in front of a fortification **2** ♦ : a long cliff

♦ bluff, cliff, crag, palisade, precipice, scarp

es·chew \is-'chü\ *vb* ♦ : to avoid habitually esp. on moral or practical grounds : SHUN, AVOID

♦ avoid, dodge, duck, elude, escape, evade, shake, shirk, shun

¹**es·cort** \'es-ˌkȯrt\ *n* ♦ : one (as a person or warship) accompanying another esp. as a protection or courtesy

♦ attendant, companion, guard, guide

²**es·cort** \is-'kȯrt, es-\ *vb* ♦ : to accompany as an escort

♦ accompany, attend, convoy, squire

es·crow \'es-ˌkrō\ *n* : something (as a deed or a sum of money) delivered by one person to another to be delivered to a third party only upon the fulfillment of a condition; *also* : a fund or deposit serving as an escrow

es·cutch·eon \is-'kə-chən\ *n* : the usu. shield-shaped surface on which a coat of arms is shown

Esd *abbr* Esdras

Es·dras \'ez-drəs\ *n* 1 : either of two books of the Roman Catholic canon of the Old Testament: **a** : a narrative book of canonical Jewish and Christian Scripture **b** : narrative and historical book of canonical Jewish and Christian Scripture 2 : either of two uncanonical books of Scripture included in the Protestant Apocrypha

ESE *abbr* east-southeast

Es·ki·mo \'es-kə-ˌmō\ *n* 1 *now sometimes offensive* : a member of a group of peoples of northern Canada, Greenland, Alaska, and eastern Siberia 2 : any of the languages of the Eskimo peoples

Eskimo dog *n* : a sled dog of American origin

ESL *abbr* English as a second language

esoph·a·gus \i-'sä-fə-gəs\ *n, pl* **-gi** \-ˌgī, -ˌjī\ : a muscular tube that leads from the cavity behind the mouth to the stomach — **esoph·a·geal** \-ˌsä-fə-'jē-əl\ *adj*

es·o·ter·ic \ˌe-sə-'ter-ik\ *adj* 1 ♦ : designed for or understood only by the specially initiated; *broadly* : difficult to understand 2 : PRIVATE, SECRET

♦ abstruse, deep, profound

esp *abbr* especially

ESP \ˌē-(ˌ)es-'pē\ *n* : EXTRASENSORY PERCEPTION

es·pa·drille \'es-pə-ˌdril\ *n* : a flat sandal usu. having a fabric upper and a flexible sole

es·pal·ier \is-'pal-yər, -ˌyā\ *n* : a plant (as a fruit tree) trained to grow flat against a support — **espalier** *vb*

es·pe·cial \is-'pe-shəl\ *adj* ♦ : being distinctive : SPECIAL

♦ distinct, express, precise, set, special, specific

es·pe·cial·ly *adv* 1 : in a special manner; *also* : in particular 2 ♦ : in a particularly strong or good way — used as an intensive

♦ extra, extremely, greatly, highly, hugely, mightily, mighty, mostly, most, much, real, right, so, very

Es·pe·ran·to \ˌes-pə-'ran-tō, -'rän-\ *n* : an artificial international language based esp. on words common to the chief European languages

es·pi·o·nage \'es-pē-ə-ˌnäzh, -nij\ *n* : the practice of spying

es·pla·nade \'es-plə-ˌnäd\ *n* : a level open stretch or area; *esp* : one for walking or driving along a shore

es·pous·al \i-'spaù-zəl\ *n* 1 ♦ : the act of betrothing or fact of being betrothed : BETROTHAL; *also* : WEDDING 2 : a taking up (as of a cause) as a supporter — **es·pouse** \-'spaùz\ *vb*

♦ marriage, wedding ♦ betrothal, engagement, troth

espres·so \e-'spre-sō\ *n, pl* **-sos** : coffee brewed by forcing steam through finely ground darkly roasted coffee beans

es·prit \i-'sprē\ *n* ♦ : sprightly wit

♦ bounce, dash, drive, pep, punch, snap, spirit, verve, vim, zing, zip

es·prit de corps \i-ˌsprē-də-'kȯr\ *n* : the common spirit existing in the members of a group

es·py \i-'spī\ *vb* **es·pied; es·py·ing** ♦ : to catch sight of

♦ discern, eye, notice, observe, perceive, regard, see, sight, spy, view

Esq *or* **Esqr** *abbr* esquire

es·quire \'es-ˌkwī(-ə)r\ *n* 1 : a man of the English gentry ranking next below a knight 2 : a candidate for knighthood serving as attendant to a knight 3 — used as a title of courtesy

-ess \əs, ˌes\ *n suffix* : female ⟨authoress⟩

¹**es·say** \e-'sā, 'e-ˌsā\ *vb* ♦ : to make an often tentative or experimental effort to perform : ATTEMPT, TRY

♦ assay, attempt, endeavor (*or* endeavour), seek, strive, try

²**es·say** \'e-ˌsā, e-'sā\ *n* 1 ♦ : an initial tentative effort : ATTEMPT 2 \'e-ˌsā\ ♦ : a literary composition usu. dealing with a subject from a limited or personal point of view — **es·say·ist** \'e-ˌsā-ist\ *n*

♦ [1] attempt, bid, crack, endeavor (*or* endeavour), fling, go,

pass, shot, stab, trial, try, whack, whirl ♦ [2] article, composition, paper, theme

es·sence \'es-ᵊns\ *n* 1 ♦ : fundamental nature or quality 2 : a substance distilled or extracted from another substance (as a plant or drug) and having the special qualities of the original substance 3 : PERFUME 4 ♦ : the most significant element or aspect of something ⟨the ∼ of the issue⟩

♦ [1, 4] nature, quintessence, soul, stuff, substance

¹**es·sen·tial** \i-'sen-chəl\ *adj* 1 ♦ : of, relating to, or constituting an essence ⟨voting is an ∼ right of citizenship⟩ ⟨∼ oils⟩ 2 ♦ : of the utmost importance : INDISPENSABLE ⟨water is ∼ for life⟩; *also* : of, relating to, or forming the base or essence 3 : being a substance that must be obtained from the diet because it is not sufficiently produced by the body ⟨∼ amino acids⟩ — **es·sen·tial·ly** *adv*

♦ [1] ingrained, inherent, innate, integral, intrinsic, natural ♦ [1] basic, elemental, elementary, fundamental, underlying ♦ [2] imperative, indispensable, integral, necessary, needful, requisite, vital *Ant* dispensable, needless, nonessential

²**essential** *n* ♦ : something indispensable

♦ condition, demand, must, necessity, need, requirement, requisite *Ant* nonessential ♦ *usu* **essentials** elements, principles, rudiments

est *abbr* 1 established 2 estimate; estimated

EST *abbr* eastern standard time

¹**-est** \əst, ist\ *adj suffix or adv suffix* — used to form the superlative degree of adjectives and adverbs of one or two syllables ⟨fatt*est*⟩ ⟨lat*est*⟩ ⟨lucki*est*⟩ ⟨often*est*⟩ and less often of longer ones

²**-est** \əst, ist\ *or* **-st** \st\ *vb suffix* — used to form the archaic second person singular of English verbs (with *thou*) ⟨did*st*⟩

es·tab·lish \i-'sta-blish\ *vb* 1 : to institute permanently ⟨∼ a law⟩ 2 : to bring into existence : FOUND ⟨∼ a settlement⟩; *also* : EFFECT 3 : to make firm or stable 4 : to put on a firm basis : SET UP ⟨∼ a son in business⟩ 5 ♦ : to gain acceptance or recognition of ⟨the movie ∼ed her as a star⟩; *also* : PROVE ⟨∼ed his innocence⟩

♦ [2] constitute, effect, found, inaugurate, initiate, innovate, institute, introduce, launch, pioneer, set up, start ♦ [5] demonstrate, prove, substantiate *Ant* disprove

es·tab·lish·ment \-mənt\ *n* 1 : something established: as **a** ♦ : a permanent civil or military organization **b** ♦ : a public or private institution 2 : a place of residence or business with its furnishings and staff 3 : an established ruling or controlling group ⟨the literary ∼⟩ 4 : the act or state of establishing or being established

♦ [1a, 1b] foundation, institute, institution ♦ [1b] business, company, concern, enterprise, firm, house, outfit

es·tate \i-'stāt\ *n* 1 **a** ♦ : mode or condition of being : STATE **b** : social standing : STATUS 2 ♦ : a social or political class ⟨the three ∼s of nobility, clergy, and commons⟩ 3 : a person's possessions : FORTUNE 4 ♦ : a landed property

♦ [1a] condition, fettle, form, order, repair, shape, state, trim ♦ [2] caste, class, folk, order, stratum ♦ [4] castle, hall, manor, mansion, palace, villa

¹**es·teem** \i-'stēm\ *n* ♦ : high regard

♦ admiration, appreciation, estimation, favor (*or* favour), regard, respect

²**esteem** *vb* 1 ♦ : to view as : REGARD ⟨was highly ∼ed⟩ 2 ♦ : to set a high value on

♦ [1] account, call, consider, count, hold, rate, reckon, regard, take ♦ [2] admire, appreciate, regard, respect

es·ter \'es-tər\ *n* : an often fragrant organic compound formed by the reaction of an acid and an alcohol

Esth *abbr* Esther

Es·ther \'es-tər\ *n* : a narrative book of canonical Jewish and Christian Scripture

esthete, esthetic esthetically esthetics *var of* AESTHETE, AESTHETIC, AESTHETICALLY, AESTHETICS

es·ti·ma·ble \'es-tə-mə-bəl\ *adj* : worthy of esteem

¹**es·ti·mate** \'es-tə-ˌmāt\ *vb* **-mat·ed; -mat·ing** 1 ♦ : to give or form an approximation (as of value, size, or cost) 2 : JUDGE, CONCLUDE — **es·ti·ma·tor** \-ˌmā-tər\ *n*

♦ appraise, assess, evaluate, rate, set, value ♦ calculate, call, conjecture, figure, gauge, guess, judge, make, place, put, reckon, suppose

²**es·ti·mate** \'es-tə-mət\ *n* 1 ♦ : an opinion or judgment of the

nature, character, or quality of a person or thing **2 ♦ :** a rough or approximate calculation **3 :** a statement of the cost of work to be done

♦ [1] appraisal, assessment, estimation, evaluation, judgment (*or* judgement) ♦ [2] calculation, computation, measurement, reckoning, valuation

es·ti·ma·tion \ˌes-tə-ˈmā-shən\ *n* **1 ♦ :** a view, judgment, or appraisal formed in the mind about a particular matter **:** JUDG-MENT **2 ♦ :** the value, amount, or size arrived at in an estimate **:** ESTIMATE; *also* **:** the act of estimating something **3 ♦ :** high regard **:** ESTEEM

♦ [1] appraisal, assessment, estimate, evaluation, judgment (*or* judgement), reckoning, valuation ♦ [2] appraisal, assessment, estimate, evaluation, judgment (*or* judgement) ♦ [3] admiration, appreciation, esteem, favor (*or* favour), regard, respect

es·ti·vate \ˈes-tə-ˌvāt\ *vb* **-vat·ed; -vat·ing :** to pass the summer in an inactive or resting state ⟨creatures *estivating* in the cool mud⟩ — **es·ti·va·tion** \ˌes-tə-ˈvā-shən\ *n*
Es·to·nian \e-ˈstō-nē-ən\ *n* **:** a native or inhabitant of Estonia — **Estonian** *adj*
es·trange \i-ˈstrānj\ *vb* **es·tranged; es·trang·ing ♦ :** to alienate the affections or confidence of

♦ alienate, disaffect, disgruntle, sour *Ant* reconcile

es·trange·ment *n* **♦ :** the act of estranging or the condition of being estranged **:** alienation esp. in friendship

♦ alienation, disaffection *Ant* reconciliation

es·tro·gen \ˈes-trə-jən\ *n* **:** a steroid (as a sex hormone) that tends to cause estrus and the development of female secondary sex characteristics — **es·tro·gen·ic** \ˌes-trə-ˈje-nik\ *adj*
estrous cycle *n* **:** the cycle of changes in the endocrine and reproductive systems of a female mammal from the beginning of one period of estrus to the beginning of the next
es·trus \ˈes-trəs\ *n* **:** a periodic state of sexual excitability during which the female of most mammals is willing to mate with the male and is capable of becoming pregnant **:** HEAT — **es·trous** \-trəs\ *adj*
es·tu·ary \ˈes-chù-ˌwer-ē\ *n, pl* **-ar·ies ♦ :** an arm of the sea at the mouth of a river

♦ bay, bight, cove, gulf, inlet

ET *abbr* eastern time
eta \ˈā-tə\ *n* **:** the 7th letter of the Greek alphabet — H or η
ETA *abbr* estimated time of arrival
et al. \et-ˈal\ *abbr* and others
etc. et cetera
et cet·era \et-ˈset-ə-rə\ **:** and others esp. of the same kind — used to imply that other items are to be understood
etch \ˈech\ *vb* **1 ♦ :** to produce (as a design) on a hard material by corroding its surface (as by acid) **2 ♦ :** to delineate or impress clearly — **etch·er** *n*

♦ [1] engrave, grave, inscribe ♦ [2] engrave, impress, imprint, ingrain, inscribe

etch·ing *n* **1 :** the action, process, or art of etching **2 :** a design produced on or print made from an etched plate
ETD *abbr* estimated time of departure
eter·nal \i-ˈtərn-əl\ *adj* **♦ :** having infinite duration **:** EVERLAST-ING, PERPETUAL

♦ ceaseless, dateless, deathless, endless, everlasting, immortal, permanent, perpetual, undying, unending

eter·nal·ly *adv* **♦ :** throughout eternity

♦ always, ever, everlastingly, forever, permanently, perpetually

eter·ni·ty \i-ˈtər-nə-tē\ *n, pl* **-ties 1 :** infinite duration **2 ♦ :** the state after death **:** IMMORTALITY **3 ♦ :** a seemingly endless or immeasurable time

♦ [2] afterlife, hereafter, immortality ♦ [3] age, cycle, eon (*or* aeon)

-eth \əth, ith\ *or* **-th** \th\ *vb suffix* — used to form the archaic third person singular present of verbs ⟨do*th*⟩
eth·ane \ˈe-ˌthān\ *n* **:** a colorless odorless gaseous hydrocarbon found in natural gas and used esp. as a fuel
eth·a·nol \ˈe-thə-ˌnól\ *n* **:** ALCOHOL 1
ether \ˈē-thər\ *n* **1 :** the upper regions of space; *also* **:** the gaseous element formerly held to fill these regions **2 :** a light flammable liquid used as an anesthetic and solvent
ethe·re·al \i-ˈthir-ē-əl\ *adj* **1 :** CELESTIAL, HEAVENLY **2 ♦ :** exceptionally delicate **:** AIRY, DAINTY ⟨∼ flaky pastry⟩ — **ethe·re·al·ly** *adv* — **ethe·re·al·ness** *n*

♦ airy, dainty, fluffy, light

Ether·net \ˈē-thər-ˌnet\ *n* **:** a computer network architecture for local area networks
eth·i·cal \ˈe-thi-kəl\ *adj* **1 :** of or relating to ethics **2 ♦ :** conforming to accepted and esp. professional standards of conduct — **eth·i·cal·ly** *adv*

♦ decent, good, honest, honorable (*or* honourable), just, moral, principled, right, straight, upright, virtuous ♦ conscientious, honest, honorable (*or* honourable), just, moral, principled, scrupulous

eth·ics \ˈe-thiks\ *n sing or pl* **1 :** a discipline dealing with good and evil and with moral duty **2 ♦ :** moral principles or practice

♦ morality, morals, principles, standards

Ethi·o·pi·an \ˌē-thē-ˈō-pē-ən\ *n* **:** a native or inhabitant of Ethiopia — **Ethiopian** *adj*
¹eth·nic \ˈeth-nik\ *adj* **:** of or relating to large groups of people classed according to common traits and customs — **eth·ni·cal·ly** *adv*
²ethnic *n* **:** a member of a minority ethnic group who retains its customs, language, or social views
eth·nol·o·gy \eth-ˈnä-lə-jē\ *n* **:** anthropology dealing chiefly with the comparative and analytic study of cultures — **eth·no·log·i·cal** \ˌeth-nə-ˈlä-ji-kəl\ *adj* — **eth·nol·o·gist** \eth-ˈnä-lə-jist\ *n*
ethol·o·gy \ē-ˈthä-lə-jē\ *n* **:** the scientific and objective study of animal behavior — **etho·log·i·cal** \ˌē-thə-ˈlä-ji-kəl, ˌe-\ *adj* — **ethol·o·gist** \ē-ˈthä-lə-jist\ *n*
ethos \ˈē-ˌthäs\ *n* **:** the distinguishing character, sentiment, moral nature, or guiding beliefs of a person, group, or institution
ethyl alcohol *n* **:** ALCOHOL 1
eth·yl·ene \ˈe-thə-ˌlēn\ *n* **:** a colorless flammable gas found in coal gas or obtained from petroleum
eti·ol·o·gy \ˌē-tē-ˈä-lə-jē\ *n* **:** the causes of a disease or abnormal condition; *also* **:** a branch of medicine concerned with the causes and origins of diseases — **eti·o·log·ic** \ˌē-tē-ə-ˈlä-jik\ *or* **eti·o·log·i·cal** \-ji-kəl\ *adj*
et·i·quette \ˈe-ti-kət, -ˌket\ *n* **♦ :** the forms prescribed by custom or authority to be observed in social, official, or professional life

♦ manners, mores

Etrus·can \i-ˈtrəs-kən\ *n* **1 :** the language of the Etruscans **2 :** an inhabitant of ancient Etruria — **Etruscan** *adj*
et seq *abbr* and the following one; and the following ones
-ette \ˈet, ˌet, ət, it\ *n suffix* **1 :** little one ⟨din*ette*⟩ **2 :** female ⟨usher*ette*⟩
étude \ˈā-ˌtüd, -ˌtyüd\ *n* **:** a musical composition for practice to develop technical skill
et·y·mol·o·gy \ˌe-tə-ˈmä-lə-jē\ *n, pl* **-gies 1 :** the history of a linguistic form (as a word) shown by tracing its development and relationships **2 :** a branch of linguistics dealing with etymologies — **et·y·mo·log·i·cal** \-mə-ˈlä-ji-kəl\ *adj* — **et·y·mol·o·gist** \-ˈmä-lə-jist\ *n*
Eu *symbol* europium
EU *abbr* European Union
eu·ca·lyp·tus \ˌyü-kə-ˈlip-təs\ *n, pl* **-ti** \-ˌtī\ *or* **-tus·es :** any of a genus of mostly Australian evergreen trees widely grown for shade or their wood, oils, resins, and gums
Eu·cha·rist \ˈyü-kə-rəst\ *n* **:** COMMUNION 2 — **eu·cha·ris·tic** \ˌyü-kə-ˈris-tik\ *adj, often cap*
¹eu·chre \ˈyü-kər\ *n* **:** a card game in which the side naming the trump must take three of five tricks to win
²euchre *vb* **eu·chred; eu·chring :** CHEAT, TRICK
eu·clid·e·an *also* **eu·clid·i·an** \yù-ˈkli-dē-ən\ *adj, often cap* **:** of or relating to the geometry of Euclid or a geometry based on similar axioms
eu·gen·ics \yù-ˈje-niks\ *n* **:** a science dealing with the improvement (as by selective breeding) of hereditary qualities esp. of human beings — **eu·gen·ic** \-nik\ *adj*
eu·lo·gy \ˈyü-lə-jē\ *n, pl* **-gies 1 ♦ :** a speech in praise of some person or thing esp. in honor of a deceased person **2 :** high praise — **eu·lo·gis·tic** \ˌyü-lə-ˈjis-tik\ *adj* — **eu·lo·gize** \ˈyü-lə-ˌjīz\ *vb*

♦ accolade, citation, commendation, encomium, homage, paean, panegyric, salutation, tribute

eu·nuch \ˈyü-nək\ *n* **:** a castrated man
eu·phe·mism \ˈyü-fə-ˌmi-zəm\ *n* **:** the substitution of a mild or pleasant expression for one offensive or unpleasant; *also* **:** the expression substituted — **eu·phe·mis·tic** \ˌyü-fə-ˈmis-tik\ *adj* — **eu·phe·mis·ti·cal·ly** \-ti-k(ə-)lē\ *adv*
eu·pho·ni·ous \yù-ˈfō-nē-əs\ *adj* **♦ :** pleasing to the ear — **eu·pho·ni·ous·ly** *adv*

♦ harmonious, lyric, melodious, musical, symphonic, tuneful

eu·pho·ny \\'yü-fə-nē\\ *n, pl* **-nies** : the effect produced by words so combined as to please the ear

eu·pho·ria \\yu̇-'fȯr-ē-ə\\ *n* ♦ : a marked feeling of well-being or elation

♦ ecstasy, elation, exhilaration, heaven, intoxication, paradise, rapture, rhapsody, transport

eu·phor·ic \\-'fȯr-ik\\ *adj* ♦ : characterized by or based on euphoria

♦ ecstatic, elated, intoxicated, rapturous, rhapsodic

Eur *abbr* Europe; European

Eur·asian \\yu̇-'rā-zhən, -shən\\ *adj* **1** : of mixed European and Asian origin **2** : of or relating to Europe and Asia — **Eurasian** *n*

eu·re·ka \\yu̇-'rē-kə\\ *interj* — used to express triumph on a discovery

eu·ro \\'yu̇r-ō\\ *n, pl* **euros** : the common basic monetary unit of most countries of the European Union

Eu·ro-Amer·i·can \\,yu̇r-ō-ə-'mer-ə-kən\\ *n* **1** : a person of mixed European and American ancestry **2** : an American of European and esp. white European descent

Eu·ro·bond \\'yu̇r-ō-,bänd\\ *n* : a bond of a U.S. corporation that is sold outside the U.S. but that is valued and paid for in dollars and yields interest in dollars

Eu·ro·cur·ren·cy \\,yu̇r-ō-'kər-ən-sē\\ *n* : moneys (as of the U.S. and Japan) held outside their countries of origin and used in the money markets of Europe

Eu·ro·dol·lar \\'yu̇r-ō-,dä-lər\\ *n* : a U.S. dollar held as Eurocurrency

Eu·ro·pe·an \\,yu̇r-ə-'pē-ən\\ *n* **1** : a native or inhabitant of Europe **2** : a person of European descent — **European** *adj* — **Eu·ro·pe·an·ize** \\-ə-,nīz\\ *vb*

European–American *n* : EURO-AMERICAN

Eu·ro·pe·an·ism \\,yu̇r-ō-'pē-ə-ni-zəm\\ *n* **1** : allegiance to the traditions, interests, or ideals of Europeans **2** : advocacy of political and economic integration of Europe — **eu·ro·pe·an·ist** \\-nist\\ *n*

European plan *n* : a hotel plan whereby the daily rates cover only the cost of the room

eu·ro·pi·um \\yu̇-'rō-pē-əm\\ *n* : a rare metallic chemical element

eu·sta·chian tube \\yu̇-'stā-shən-\\ *n, often cap E* : a tube connecting the inner cavity of the ear with the throat and equalizing air pressure on both sides of the eardrum

eu·tha·na·sia \\,yü-thə-'nā-zhə\\ *n* : the act or practice of killing or permitting the death of hopelessly sick or injured persons or animals with as little pain as possible for reasons of mercy

EVA *abbr* extravehicular activity

evac·u·ate \\i-'va-kyə-,wāt\\ *vb* **-at·ed; -at·ing** **1** ♦ : to make empty : empty out **2** : to discharge wastes from the body **3** : to remove or withdraw from : VACATE — **evac·u·a·tion** \\-,va-kyə-'wā-shən\\ *n*

♦ clear, empty, vacate, void

evac·u·ee \\i-,va-kyə-'wē\\ *n* ♦ : a person removed from a dangerous place

♦ émigré, exile, expatriate, refugee

evade \\i-'vād\\ *vb* **evad·ed; evad·ing** ♦ : to manage to avoid esp. by dexterity or slyness : ELUDE, ESCAPE

♦ avoid, dodge, duck, elude, escape, eschew, shake, shirk, shun

eval·u·ate \\i-'val-yü-,wāt\\ *vb* **-at·ed; -at·ing** ♦ : to determine or fix the value of : APPRAISE, VALUE; *also* : to determine the significance, worth, or condition of usu. by careful appraisal and study

♦ appraise, assess, estimate, rate, set, value

eval·u·a·tion \\-,val-yü-'wā-shən\\ *n* ♦ : the act or result of evaluating

♦ appraisal, assessment, estimate, estimation, judgment (*or* judgement)

ev·a·nes·cent \\,e-və-'nes-ᵊnt\\ *adj* ♦ : tending to vanish like vapor — **ev·a·nes·cence** \\-ᵊns\\ *n*

♦ ephemeral, flash, fleeting, impermanent, momentary, short-lived, transient

evan·gel·i·cal \\,ē-,van-'je-li-kəl, ,e-vən-\\ *adj* **1** : of or relating to the Christian gospel esp. as presented in the four Gospels **2** : of or relating to certain Protestant churches emphasizing the authority of Scripture and the importance of preaching as contrasted with ritual **3** : ZEALOUS ⟨∼ fervor⟩ — **Evangelical** *n* — **Evan·gel·i·cal·ism** \\-kə-,li-zəm\\ *n* — **evan·gel·i·cal·ly** *adv*

evan·ge·lism \\i-'van-jə-,li-zəm\\ *n* **1** : the winning or revival of personal commitments to Christ **2** : militant or crusading zeal —

evan·ge·lis·tic \\-,van-jə-'lis-tik\\ *adj* — **evan·ge·lis·ti·cal·ly** *adv*

evan·ge·list \\i-'van-jə-list\\ *n* **1** *often cap* : the writer of any of the four Gospels **2** : a person who evangelizes; *esp* : a Protestant minister or layman who preaches at special services

evan·ge·lize \\i-'van-jə-,līz\\ *vb* **-lized; -liz·ing** **1** : to preach the gospel **2** : to convert to Christianity

evap *abbr* evaporate

evap·o·rate \\i-'va-pə-,rāt\\ *vb* **-rat·ed; -rat·ing** **1** : to pass off or cause to pass off in vapor **2** ♦ : to disappear quickly **3** : to drive out the moisture from (as by heat) — **evap·o·ra·tion** \\-,va-pə-'rā-shən\\ *n* — **evap·o·ra·tor** \\-,rā-tər\\ *n*

♦ disappear, dissolve, fade, flee, go, melt, vanish

evap·o·rite \\i-'va-pə-,rīt\\ *n* : a sedimentary rock that originates by the evaporation of seawater in an enclosed basin

eva·sion \\i-'vā-zhən\\ *n* **1** ♦ : a means of evading **2** ♦ : an act or instance of evading ⟨tax ∼⟩ — **eva·sive·ness** *n*

♦ [1, 2] avoidance, cop-out, escape, out

eva·sive \\i-'vā-siv\\ *adj* ♦ : tending or intended to evade; *also* : not easily caught

♦ elusive, fugitive, slippery

eve \\'ēv\\ *n* **1** : EVENING **2** : the period just before some important event

¹even \\'ē-vən\\ *adj* **1** ♦ : having a horizontal surface : LEVEL, FLAT ⟨∼ grounds⟩ **2** : REGULAR, SMOOTH **3** : EQUAL, FAIR **4** : BALANCED; *also* : fully revenged **5** : divisible by two **6** ♦ : having no fraction either lacking or in excess : EXACT ⟨an ∼ dollar⟩ — **even·ly** *adv* — **even·ness** *n*

♦ [1] flat, flush, level, plane, smooth ♦ [6] exact, flat, precise, round

²even *adv* **1** : EXACTLY, PRECISELY **2** : FULLY, QUITE **3** : at the very time **4** ♦ — used as an intensive to stress the identity or character of something ⟨∼ I know that⟩ ⟨he looked content, ∼ happy⟩ **5** — used as an intensive to emphasize something extreme or highly unlikely ⟨so simple ∼ a child can do it⟩ **6** — used as an intensive to stress the comparative degree ⟨did ∼ better⟩ **7** — used as an intensive to indicate a small or minimum degree ⟨didn't ∼ try⟩

♦ indeed, nay, truly, verily, yea

³even *vb* ♦ : to make or become even

♦ balance, equalize, equate, level ♦ level, plane, smooth *Ant* rough, roughen

even·hand·ed \\,ē-vən-'han-dəd\\ *adj* ♦ : marked by justice, honesty, and freedom from bias : FAIR, IMPARTIAL ⟨an ∼ assessment⟩ — **even·hand·ed·ly** *adv*

♦ disinterested, dispassionate, equal, equitable, fair, impartial, just, nonpartisan, objective, square, unbiased, unprejudiced

eve·ning \\'ēv-niŋ\\ *n* **1** ♦ : the end of the day and early part of the night **2** *chiefly Southern & Midland* : AFTERNOON

♦ dusk, gloaming, nightfall, sundown, sunset, twilight

evening primrose *n* : a coarse biennial herb with yellow flowers that open in the evening

evening star *n* : a bright planet (as Venus) seen esp. in the western sky at or after sunset

even·song \\'ē-vən-,sȯŋ\\ *n, often cap* **1** : VESPERS **2** : evening prayer esp. when sung

event \\i-'vent\\ *n* **1** ♦ : something that happens : OCCURRENCE **2** ♦ : a noteworthy happening; *also* : a social occasion or activity **3** ♦ : a postulated outcome, condition, or eventuality : CONTINGENCY ⟨in the ∼ of rain⟩ **4** ♦ : a contest in a program of sports

♦ [1] affair, circumstance, deed, episode, experience, occurrence ♦ [2] affair, fete, function, get-together, party ♦ [3] case, contingency, eventuality, possibility ♦ [4] bout, competition, contest, game, match, meet, tournament

event·ful *adj* **1** : full of or rich in events **2** ♦ : very important

♦ big, consequential, important, major, material, meaningful, momentous, significant, substantial, weighty

even·tide \\'ē-vən-,tīd\\ *n* : the time of evening : EVENING

even·tu·al \\i-'ven-chü-wəl\\ *adj* : coming at some later time : ULTIMATE

even·tu·al·i·ty \\i-,ven-chü-'wa-lə-tē\\ *n, pl* **-ties** ♦ : a possible event or outcome

♦ case, contingency, event, possibility

even·tu·al·ly *adv* ♦ : at an unspecified later time : in the end

♦ someday, sometime, ultimately, yet

even·tu·ate \i-'ven-chú-ˌwāt\ vb **-at·ed; -at·ing :** to result finally
ev·er \'e-vər\ adv **1 ♦ :** at all times **:** ALWAYS **2 ♦ :** at any time **3 :** in any way **:** AT ALL ⟨how can I ∼ thank you⟩

♦ [1] always, eternally, everlastingly, forever, permanently, perpetually *Ant* never, nevermore ♦ [2] always, invariably, unfailingly

ev·er·glade \'e-vər-ˌglād\ n **:** a low-lying tract of swampy or marshy land
ev·er·green \-ˌgrēn\ adj **:** having foliage that remains green ⟨most coniferous trees are ∼⟩ — **evergreen** n
¹ev·er·last·ing \ˌe-vər-'las-tiŋ\ adj **1 ♦ :** enduring forever **:** ETERNAL **2 :** having or being flowers or foliage that retain form or color for a long time when dried

♦ ceaseless, dateless, deathless, endless, eternal, immortal, permanent, perpetual, undying, unending *Ant* impermanent, mortal, temporary

²everlasting n **1 :** ETERNITY ⟨from ∼⟩ **2 :** a plant with everlasting flowers; *also* **:** its flower
ev·er·last·ing·ly adv **♦ :** in an everlasting manner

♦ always, eternally, éver, forever, permanently, perpetually

ev·er·more \ˌe-vər-'mōr\ adv **:** for a limitless time **:** FOREVER
ev·ery \'ev-rē\ adj **1 :** being each one of a group **2 :** all possible ⟨given ∼ chance⟩; *also* **:** COMPLETE ⟨have ∼ confidence⟩
ev·ery·body \'ev-ri-ˌbä-dē, -bə-\ pron **:** every person
ev·ery·day \'ev-rē-ˌdā\ adj **♦ :** encountered or used routinely **:** ORDINARY

♦ average, common, commonplace, customary, familiar, normal, ordinary, prosaic, routine, run-of-the-mill, standard, unexceptional, unremarkable, usual, workaday

ev·ery·one \-(ˌ)wən\ pron **:** every person **:** EVERYBODY
ev·ery·thing \'ev-rē-ˌthiŋ\ pron **1 :** all that exists **2 :** all that is relevant
ev·ery·where \'ev-rē-ˌhwer\ adv **:** in every place or part
evg abbr evening
evict \i-'vikt\ vb **1 :** to put (a person) out from a property by legal process **2 :** EXPEL — **evic·tion** \-'vik-shən\ n
¹ev·i·dence \'e-və-dəns\ n **1 :** an outward sign **2 ♦ :** something that furnishes proof **:** PROOF, TESTIMONY; *esp* **:** matter submitted in court to determine the truth of alleged facts

♦ attestation, confirmation, corroboration, documentation, proof, substantiation, testament, testimony, validation, witness

²evidence vb **:** PROVE, EVINCE
ev·i·dent \-dənt\ adj **♦ :** clear to the vision and understanding

♦ apparent, broad, clear, clear-cut, distinct, lucid, manifest, obvious, palpable, patent, perspicuous, plain, transparent, unambiguous, unequivocal, unmistakable

ev·i·dent·ly \'e-və-dənt-lē, ˌe-və-'dent-\ adv **1 :** in an evident manner **2 ♦ :** on the basis of available evidence ⟨he was born ∼ in Texas⟩

♦ apparently, ostensibly, presumably, seemingly, supposedly

¹evil \'ē-vəl\ adj **evil·er** or **evil·ler; evil·est** or **evil·lest**
1 ♦ : morally reprehensible **:** WICKED **2 ♦ :** causing or threatening distress or harm **:** PERNICIOUS — **evil·ly** adv

♦ [1] bad, immoral, iniquitous, nefarious, rotten, sinful, vicious, vile, villainous, wicked, wrong ♦ [2] bad, damaging, deleterious, detrimental, harmful, hurtful, injurious, noxious, pernicious

²evil n **1 ♦ :** the fact of suffering, misfortune, and wrongdoing; *also* **:** evil actions or deeds **2 :** a source of sorrow, distress, or calamity

♦ bad, ill, immorality, iniquity, sin, villainy, wrong *Ant* good, morality, right, virtue

evil–do·er \ˌē-vəl-'dü-ər\ n **♦ :** one who does evil

♦ beast, devil, fiend, no-good, reprobate, rogue, varlet, villain, wretch ♦ malefactor, sinner, wrongdoer

evil–mind·ed \-'mīn-dəd\ adj **:** having an evil disposition or evil thoughts — **evil–mind·ed·ly** adv
evince \i-'vins\ vb **evinced; evinc·ing ♦ :** to constitute outward evidence of **:** SHOW, REVEAL

♦ bespeak, betray, demonstrate, display, expose, give away, manifest, reveal, show

evis·cer·ate \i-'vi-sə-ˌrāt\ vb **-at·ed; -at·ing 1 ♦ :** to remove the entrails of **2 :** to deprive of vital content or force — **evis·cer·a·tion** \-ˌvi-sə-ˌrā-shən\ n

♦ clean, draw, gut

evoke \i-'vōk\ vb **evoked; evok·ing ♦ :** to call forth or up —
evo·ca·tion \ˌē-vō-'kā-shən, ˌe-və-\ n — **evoc·a·tive** \i-'vä-kə-tiv\ adj

♦ elicit, raise

evo·lu·tion \ˌe-və-'lü-shən\ n **1 :** one of a set of prescribed movements (as in a dance) **2 ♦ :** a process of change in a particular direction **3 :** a theory that the various kinds of plants and animals are descended from other kinds that lived in earlier times and that the differences are due to inherited changes that occurred over many generations — **evo·lu·tion·ary** \-shə-ˌner-ē\ adj — **evo·lu·tion·ist** \-shə-nist\ n

♦ development, elaboration, expansion, growth, progress, progression

evolve \i-'välv\ vb **evolved; evolv·ing :** to develop or change by or as if by evolution
EW abbr enlisted woman
e—waste \'ē-ˌwāst\ n **:** waste consisting of discarded electronic products
ewe \'yü\ n **:** a female sheep
ew·er \'yü-ər\ n **♦ :** a water pitcher

♦ flagon, jug, pitcher

¹ex \'eks\ prep **:** out of **:** FROM
²ex n **:** a former spouse
³ex abbr **1** example **2** express **3** extra
Ex abbr Exodus
ex- \e also occurs in this prefix where only i is shown below (as in "express") and ks sometimes occurs where only gz is shown (as in "exact")\ prefix **1 :** out of **:** outside **2 :** former ⟨ex-president⟩
ex·ac·er·bate \ig-'za-sər-ˌbāt\ vb **-bat·ed; -bat·ing :** to make more violent, bitter, or severe ⟨comments that ∼ the dispute⟩ — **ex·ac·er·ba·tion** \-ˌza-sər-'bā-shən\ n
¹ex·act \ig-'zakt\ vb **1 ♦ :** to demand and force or compel (as payment, surrender, concession, performance, or compliance) **2 :** to call for or establish as suitable or necessary — **ex·ac·tion** \-'zak-shən\ n

♦ call, claim, command, demand, enjoin, extort, insist, press
♦ assess, charge, fine, impose, lay, levy, put

²exact adj **♦ :** precisely accurate or correct

♦ accurate, correct, precise, proper, right, so, true ♦ delicate, fine, minute, nice, refined, subtle

ex·act·ing \ig-'zak-tiŋ\ adj **1 ♦ :** greatly demanding ⟨an ∼ supervisor⟩ **2 ♦ :** requiring close attention and precision

♦ [1] choosy, demanding, fastidious, finicky, particular, picky
♦ [1] inflexible, rigid, rigorous, strict, stringent, uncompromising ♦ [2] arduous, burdensome, challenging, demanding, grueling, laborious, onerous, taxing, toilsome

ex·ac·ti·tude \ig-'zak-tə-ˌtüd, -ˌtyüd\ n **:** the quality or state of being exact
ex·act·ly adv **1 ♦ :** in a manner or measure or to a degree or number that strictly conforms to a fact or condition; *also* **:** in every respect **2 :** quite so **:** as you say or state — used to express agreement

♦ accurately, just, precisely, right, sharp, squarely, strictly

ex·act·ness n **♦ :** the quality or an instance of being exact

♦ accuracy, closeness, delicacy, fineness, precision, veracity

ex·ag·ger·ate \ig-'za-jə-ˌrāt\ vb **-at·ed; -at·ing ♦ :** to enlarge (as a statement) beyond normal — **ex·ag·ger·at·ed·ly** adv — **ex·ag·ger·a·tor** \-'za-jə-ˌrā-tər\ n

♦ color (or colour), elaborate, embellish, embroider, magnify, pad, stretch

ex·ag·ger·a·tion \-ˌza-jə-'rā-shən\ n **♦ :** the act of exaggerating; *also* **:** the state or an instance of being exaggerated

♦ elaboration, embellishment, hyperbole, magnification, overstatement, padding *Ant* understatement

ex·alt \ig-'zolt\ vb **1 ♦ :** to raise up esp. in rank, power, or dignity **2 ♦ :** to elevate in estimation **:** GLORIFY — **ex·al·ta·tion** \ˌeg-ˌzol-'tā-shən, ˌek-ˌsol-\ n

♦ [1, 2] aggrandize, dignify, ennoble, glorify, magnify *Ant* abase, debase, degrade, demean, humble, humiliate

ex·am \ig-'zam\ n **:** an exercise or a series of exercises designed to examine progress or test qualification **:** EXAMINATION
ex·am·i·na·tion \-ˌza-mə-'nā-shən\ n **1 ♦ :** the act or process of examining; *also* **:** the state of being examined **2 ♦ :** an exercise designed to examine progress or test qualification or knowledge **3 :** a formal interrogation

♦ [1] check, checkup, inspection, review, scan, scrutiny, survey
♦ [1] exploration, inquiry, investigation, probe, research, study
♦ [2] quiz, test

ex·am·ine \ig-'za-mən\ *vb* **ex·am·ined; ex·am·in·ing 1** ♦ : to inspect closely **2** ♦ : to attempt to determine or test by questioning

♦ [1] audit, check, inspect, review, scan, scrutinize, survey
♦ [2] grill, interrogate, pump, query, question, quiz

ex·am·ple \ig-'zam-pəl\ *n* **1** : something forming a model to be followed or avoided **2** ♦ : a representative sample **3** : a problem to be solved in order to show the application of some rule

♦ case, exemplar, illustration, instance, representative, sample, specimen

ex·as·per·ate \ig-'zas-pə-ˌrāt\ *vb* **-at·ed; -at·ing** ♦ : to excite the anger of : VEX, IRRITATE

♦ aggravate, annoy, bother, bug, grate, irk, irritate, vex

ex·as·per·at·ing *adj* ♦ : causing irritation : ANNOYING

♦ aggravating, annoying, frustrating, irksome, irritating, pesty, vexatious

ex·as·per·a·tion \ig-ˌzas-pə-'rā-shən\ *n* ♦ : the state of being exasperated; *also* : the act or source of being exasperated

♦ aggravation, annoyance, bother, frustration, hassle, headache, irritant, nuisance, problem, thorn, vexation

exc *abbr* **1** excellent **2** except
ex·ca·vate \'ek-skə-ˌvāt\ *vb* **-vat·ed; -vat·ing 1** : to hollow out; *also* : to form by hollowing out **2** : to dig out and remove (as earth) **3** : to reveal to view by digging away a covering — **ex·ca·va·tion** \ˌek-skə-'vā-shən\ *n* — **ex·ca·va·tor** \'ek-skə-ˌvā-tər\ *n*
ex·ceed \ik-'sēd\ *vb* **1** ♦ : to go or be beyond the limit of **2** ♦ : to be greater than or superior to : SURPASS

♦ [1, 2] overreach, overrun, overshoot, overstep, surpass

ex·ceed·ing \-'sē-diŋ\ *adj* ♦ : exceptional in amount, quality, or degree

♦ aberrant, abnormal, atypical, exceptional, extraordinary, freak, odd, peculiar, phenomenal, rare, singular, uncommon, uncustomary, unique, unusual, unwonted

ex·ceed·ing·ly \-'sē-diŋ-lē\ *also* **ex·ceed·ing** *adv* : to an extreme degree : EXTREMELY, VERY
ex·cel \ik-'sel\ *vb* **ex·celled; ex·cel·ling** ♦ : to be superior to : SURPASS, OUTDO

♦ beat, better, eclipse, outdistance, outdo, outshine, outstrip, surpass, top, transcend

ex·cel·lence \'ek-sə-ləns\ *n* **1** ♦ : the quality of being excellent **2** ♦ : an excellent or valuable quality : VIRTUE **3** : EXCELLENCY 2

♦ [1] distinction, greatness, preeminence, superiority, supremacy ♦ [2] distinction, merit, value, virtue *Ant* deficiency

ex·cel·len·cy \-lən-sē\ *n, pl* **-cies 1** : outstanding or valuable quality : EXCELLENCE **2** — used as a title of honor
ex·cel·lent \-lənt\ *adj* ♦ : very good of its kind — **ex·cel·lent·ly** *adv*

♦ A1, bang-up, banner, fabulous, fine, grand, great, marvelous (*or* marvellous), prime, sensational, splendid, superb, superior, unsurpassed, wonderful *Ant* poor

ex·cel·si·or \ik-'sel-sē-ər\ *n* : fine curled wood shavings used esp. for packing fragile items
¹**ex·cept** \ik-'sept\ *also* **ex·cept·ing** *prep* ♦ : with the exclusion or exception of ⟨daily ∼ Sundays⟩

♦ aside from, bar, barring, besides, but, except for, exclusive of, outside (of), save

²**except** *vb* **1** ♦ : to take or leave out **2** : OBJECT

♦ ban, bar, count out, debar, eliminate, exclude, rule out

³**except** *also* **excepting** *conj* **1** : UNLESS ⟨∼ you repent⟩ **2** ♦ : were it not that : ONLY ⟨I'd go, ∼ it's too far⟩

♦ but, only, yet

except for *prep* **1** ♦ : with the exception of ⟨everyone was gone *except for* me⟩ **2** : were it not for ⟨*except for* you I would be dead⟩

♦ aside from, bar, barring, besides, but, exclusive of, other than, outside (of), save

ex·cep·tion \ik-'sep-shən\ *n* **1** : the act of excepting **2** : something excepted **3** : OBJECTION

ex·cep·tion·able \ik-'sep-shə-nə-bəl\ *adj* : being likely to cause objection : OBJECTIONABLE
ex·cep·tion·al \ik-'sep-shə-nəl\ *adj* **1** ♦ : forming an exception : UNUSUAL ⟨an ∼ number of rainy days⟩ **2** : SUPERIOR ⟨∼ skill⟩ — **ex·cep·tion·al·ly** *adv*

♦ abnormal, atypical, rare, singular, uncommon, uncustomary, unique, unusual, unwonted *Ant* common, customary, normal, ordinary, typical

ex·cerpt \'ek-ˌsərpt, 'eg-ˌzərpt\ *n* : a passage selected or copied : EXTRACT — **excerpt** \ek-'sərpt, eg-'zərpt; 'ek-ˌsərpt, 'eg-ˌzərpt\ *vb*
¹**ex·cess** \ik-'ses, 'ek-ˌses\ *n* **1** ♦ : the state or an instance of surpassing usual, proper, or specified limits : SUPERFLUITY, SURPLUS **2** : the amount by which one quantity exceeds another **3** : INTEMPERANCE; *also* : an instance of intemperance ⟨the dictator's ∼es⟩

♦ fat, overabundance, overflow, superfluity, surfeit, surplus *Ant* deficiency, deficit, insufficiency

²**excess** *adj* ♦ : more than the usual, proper, or specified amount

♦ extra, spare, superfluous, supernumerary, surplus

ex·ces·sive \ik-'se-siv\ *adj* ♦ : exceeding what is usual, proper, necessary, or normal

♦ extravagant, extreme, immoderate, inordinate, lavish, overmuch, steep, stiff *Ant* moderate, modest, reasonable, temperate

ex·ces·sive·ly *adv* ♦ : to an exceptional or even improper degree

♦ inordinately, overly, overmuch, too

exch *abbr* exchange; exchanged
¹**ex·change** \iks-'chānj\ *n* **1** ♦ : the giving or taking of one thing in return for another : TRADE **2** : a substituting of one thing for another **3** : interchange of valuables and esp. of bills of exchange or money of different countries **4** : a place where things and services are exchanged; *esp* : a marketplace for securities **5** : a central office in which telephone lines are connected for communication **6** ♦ : a reciprocal interchange (as of things or ideas); *also* : the act of such an interchange

♦ [1] barter, commutation, swap, trade, truck ♦ [6] colloquy, conversation, dialogue, discourse, discussion

²**exchange** *vb* **ex·changed; ex·chang·ing** ♦ : to transfer in return for some equivalent : SWAP — **ex·change·able** \iks-'chān-jə-bəl\ *adj*

♦ change, commute, shift, substitute, swap, switch, trade

ex·che·quer \'eks-ˌche-kər\ *n* : TREASURY; *esp* : a national treasury
ex·cise \'ek-ˌsīz\ *n* : a tax on the manufacture, sale, or consumption of a commodity
ex·ci·sion \ik-'si-zhən\ *n* : removal by or as if by cutting out esp. by surgical means — **ex·cise** \ik-'sīz\ *vb*
ex·cit·able \ik-'sī-tə-bəl\ *adj* ♦ : easily excited — **ex·cit·abil·i·ty** \-ˌsī-tə-'bi-lə-tē\ *n*

♦ flighty, fluttery, high-strung, jittery, jumpy, nervous, skittish, spooky *Ant* unflappable

ex·cite \ik-'sīt\ *vb* **ex·cit·ed; ex·cit·ing 1** ♦ : to stir up the emotions of **2** ♦ : to increase the activity of : STIMULATE — **ex·ci·ta·tion** \ˌek-ˌsī-'tā-shən, ˌek-sə-\ *n* — **ex·cit·ed·ly** *adv* — **ex·cit·ing·ly** *adv*

♦ [1] electrify, exhilarate, galvanize, intoxicate, thrill, titillate, turn on ♦ [2] arouse, encourage, fire, incite, instigate, move, pique, provoke, stimulate, stir

ex·cite·ment \ik-'sīt-mənt\ *n* **1** ♦ : something that excites or rouses **2** ♦ : the action of exciting : the state of being excited

♦ [1] incitement, instigation, provocation, stimulus ♦ [2] appetite, ardor, avidity, eagerness, enthusiasm, hunger, impatience, keenness, thirst

ex·cit·ing *adj* ♦ : producing excitement

♦ breathtaking, electric, exhilarating, rousing, stirring, thrilling *Ant* unexciting

ex·claim \iks-'klām\ *vb* : to cry out, speak, or utter sharply or vehemently — **ex·clam·a·to·ry** \iks-'kla-mə-ˌtōr-ē\ *adj*
ex·cla·ma·tion \ˌeks-klə-'mā-shən\ *n* ♦ : a sharp or sudden utterance

♦ cry, ejaculation, interjection

exclamation point *n* : a punctuation mark ! used esp. after an interjection or exclamation
ex·clude \iks-'klüd\ *vb* **ex·clud·ed; ex·clud·ing 1** ♦ : to pre-

vent from using or participating : BAR **2 :** to put out : EXPEL — **ex·clu·sion** \-'klü-zhən\ *n*

♦ ban, bar, count out, debar, eliminate, except, rule out *Ant* admit, include

ex·clud·ing *adj* : being prevented from using or participating
ex·clu·sive \iks-'klü-siv\ *adj* **1 :** reserved for particular persons **2 :** snobbishly aloof; *also* : STYLISH **3 :** having no sharer : SOLE ⟨∼ rights⟩; *also* : UNDIVIDED — **exclusive** *n* — **ex·clu·sive·ness** *n* — **ex·clu·siv·i·ty** \,eks-,klü-si-və-tē, iks-, -zi-\ *n*

ex·clu·sive·ly *adv* ♦ : in an exclusive manner

♦ alone, just, only, simply, solely

exclusive of *prep* ♦ : not taking into account

♦ aside from, bar, barring, besides, but, except for, other than, outside (of), save

ex·cog·i·tate \ek-'skä-jə-,tāt\ *vb* : to think out : DEVISE
ex·com·mu·ni·cate \,ek-skə-'myü-nə-,kāt\ *vb* : to cut off officially from the rites of the church — **ex·com·mu·ni·ca·tion** \-,myü-nə-'kā-shən\ *n*
ex·co·ri·ate \ek-'skōr-ē-,āt\ *vb* **-at·ed; -at·ing** ♦ : to criticize severely

♦ abuse, assail, attack, belabor, blast, castigate, jump, lambaste, slam, vituperate

ex·co·ri·a·tion \(,)ek-,skōr-ē-'ā-shən\ *n* ♦ : a harsh and usu. public criticism

♦ denunciation, rebuke, reprimand, reproach, reproof, stricture

ex·cre·ment \'ek-skrə-mənt\ *n* : waste discharged from the body and esp. from the alimentary canal; *esp* : FECES — **ex·cre·men·tal** \,ek-skrə-'ment-ᵊl\ *adj*
ex·cres·cence \ik-'skres-ᵊns\ *n* : OUTGROWTH; *esp* ♦ : an abnormal outgrowth (as a wart)

♦ growth, lump, neoplasm, tumor

ex·cre·ta \ik-'skrē-tə\ *n pl* : waste matter separated or eliminated from an organism
ex·crete \ik-'skrēt\ *vb* **ex·cret·ed; ex·cret·ing** : to separate and eliminate wastes from the body esp. in urine or sweat — **ex·cre·tion** \-'skrē-shən\ *n* — **ex·cre·to·ry** \'ek-skrə-,tōr-ē\ *adj*
ex·cru·ci·at·ing \ik-'skrü-shē-,ā-tiŋ\ *adj* ♦ : intensely painful, distressing, or difficult to bear — **ex·cru·ci·at·ing·ly** *adv*

♦ agonizing, harrowing

ex·cul·pate \'ek-(,)skəl-,pāt\ *vb* **-pat·ed; -pat·ing** ♦ : to clear from alleged fault or guilt

♦ absolve, acquit, clear, exonerate, vindicate *Ant* incriminate

ex·cul·pa·tion \,ek-(,)skəl-'pā-shən\ *n* ♦ : the act or fact of exculpating from alleged fault or crime

♦ acquittal, exoneration, vindication

ex·cur·sion \ik-'skər-zhən\ *n* **1 a :** EXPEDITION **b** ♦ : a pleasure trip **2 :** deviation from a direct, definite, or proper course : DIGRESSION

♦ jaunt, junket, outing, sally

ex·cur·sion·ist \-zhə-nist\ *n* ♦ : a person who goes on an excursion

♦ sightseer, tourist, traveler

ex·cur·sive \-'skər-siv\ *adj* : constituting or characterized by digression
ex·cus·able *adj* ♦ : capable of or fit for being excused, forgiven, justified, or acquitted of blame

♦ forgivable, pardonable, venial

¹**ex·cuse** \ik-'skyüz\ *vb* **ex·cused; ex·cus·ing** **1 a :** to make excuse for : offer apology for **b :** to try to remove blame from **2** ♦ : to forgive entirely or overlook as of little consequence : PARDON **3 :** to release from an obligation **4 :** JUSTIFY

♦ disregard, forgive, gloss over, pardon, pass over, shrug off, wink at

²**excuse** \ik-'skyüs\ *n* **1 :** an act of excusing **2** ♦ : something that excuses or is a reason for excusing : JUSTIFICATION

♦ alibi, defense (*or* defence), justification, plea, reason

exec *n* : EXECUTIVE
ex·e·cra·ble \'ek-si-krə-bəl\ *adj* **1 :** DETESTABLE **2** ♦ : very bad ⟨∼ spelling⟩

♦ atrocious, awful, lousy, punk, rotten, terrible, wretched

ex·e·crate \'ek-sə-,krāt\ *vb* **-crat·ed; -crat·ing** ♦ : to denounce as evil or detestable; *also* : DETEST

♦ condemn, damn, denounce *Ant* bless ♦ abhor, abominate, despise, detest, hate, loathe

ex·e·cra·tion \,ek-sə-'krā-shən\ *n* **1** ♦ : the act of cursing or denouncing; *also* : the curse so uttered **2 :** an object of curses : something detested

♦ anathema, curse, imprecation, malediction

ex·e·cute \'ek-si-,kyüt\ *vb* **-cut·ed; -cut·ing** **1** ♦ : to carry out fully : put completely into effect **2** ♦ : to do what is called for by (as a law) **3** ♦ : to put to death esp. in accordance with a legal sentence **4 :** to produce by carrying out a design **5 :** to do what is needed to give validity to ⟨∼ a deed⟩ — **ex·e·cu·tion·er** *n*

♦ [1] accomplish, achieve, carry out, commit, compass, do, follow through, make, perform ♦ [1, 2] administer, apply, enforce, implement ♦ [3] dispatch, do in, liquidate, murder, slay

ex·e·cu·tion \,ek-si-'kyü-shən\ *n* ♦ : the act or process of executing

♦ accomplishment, achievement, commission, discharge, enactment, fulfillment, implementation, performance, perpetration

¹**ex·ec·u·tive** \ig-'ze-kyə-tiv\ *adj* **1** ♦ : of or relating to the enforcement of laws and the conduct of affairs **2 :** designed for or related to carrying out plans or purposes

♦ directorial, managerial, supervisory

²**executive** *n* **1 :** the branch of government with executive duties **2** ♦ : one having administrative or managerial responsibility

♦ administrator, director, manager, superintendent, supervisor

ex·ec·u·tor \ig-'ze-kyə-tər\ *n* : the person named in a will to execute it
ex·ec·u·trix \ig-'ze-kyə-,triks\ *n, pl* **ex·ec·u·tri·ces** \-,ze-kyə-'trī-,sēz\ *or* **ex·ec·u·trix·es** \-'ze-kyə-,trik-səz\ : a woman who is an executor
ex·e·ge·sis \,ek-sə-'jē-səs\ *n, pl* **-ge·ses** \-'jē-,sēz\ : explanation or critical interpretation of a text
ex·e·gete \'ek-sə-,jēt\ *n* : one who practices exegesis — **ex·e·get·i·cal** \,ek-sə-'je-ti-kəl\ *adj*
ex·em·plar \ig-'zem-,plär, -plər\ *n* **1** ♦ : one that serves as a model or example; *esp* : an ideal model ⟨an ∼ of courage⟩ **2** ♦ : a typical instance or example

♦ [1] beau ideal, classic, epitome, ideal, model, nonpareil, paragon, perfection, quintessence ♦ [2] case, example, illustration, instance, representative, sample, specimen

ex·em·pla·ry \ig-'zem-plə-rē\ *adj* : serving as a pattern; *also* : COMMENDABLE
ex·em·pli·fy \ig-'zem-plə-,fī\ *vb* **-fied; -fy·ing** ♦ : to illustrate by example : serve as an example of — **ex·em·pli·fi·ca·tion** \-,zem-plə-fə-'kā-shən\ *n*

♦ illustrate, instance

¹**ex·empt** \ig-'zempt\ *adj* : free from some liability to which others are subject
²**exempt** *vb* : to make exempt : EXCUSE — **ex·emp·tion** \ig-'zemp-shən\ *n*
¹**ex·er·cise** \'ek-sər-,sīz\ *n* **1** ♦ : the act of bringing into play or realizing in action : EMPLOYMENT, USE ⟨∼ of authority⟩ **2** ♦ : exertion made for the sake of training or physical fitness **3** ♦ : a task or problem done to develop skill **4** *pl* : a public exhibition or ceremony

♦ [1] application, employment, operation, play, use ♦ [2] activity, exertion ♦ [3] drill, practice, routine, training, workout

²**exercise** *vb* **-cised; -cis·ing** **1** ♦ : to make effective in action; *also* : to bring to bear : EXERT ⟨∼ control⟩ **2 :** to train by or engage in exercise **3 :** to cause anxiety, alarm, or indignation in : WORRY, DISTRESS — **ex·er·cis·er** *n*

♦ [1] apply, exert, put out, wield ♦ [1] apply, employ, exploit, harness, operate, use, utilize

ex·ert \ig-'zert\ *vb* ♦ : to bring or put into action ⟨∼ influence⟩ ⟨∼*ed* himself⟩

♦ apply, exercise, put out, wield

ex·er·tion \-'zər-shən\ *n* ♦ : the act or an instance of exerting; *esp* : a laborious or perceptible effort

♦ activity, exercise ♦ effort, labor (*or* labour), pains, sweat, trouble, work

ex·fo·li·ate \eks-'fō-lē-,āt\ *vb* **-at·ed; -at·ing** : to cast off in scales, layers, or splinters — **ex·fo·li·a·tion** \-,fō-lē-'ā-shən\ *n*
ex·hale \eks-'hāl\ *vb* **ex·haled; ex·hal·ing** **1** ♦ : to breathe

out   **2 ♦ :** to give or pass off in the form of vapor — **ex·ha·la·tion** \ˌeks-hə-ˈlā-shən\ *n*

♦ [1] blow, breathe, expire *Ant* inhale, inspire ♦ [2] cast, discharge, emit, expel, issue, release, shoot, vent

¹**ex·haust** \ig-ˈzȯst\ *vb*   **1 ♦ :** to use up wholly   **2 ♦ :** to tire or wear out   **3 :** to draw off or let out completely; *also* : EMPTY   **4 :** to develop (a subject) completely

♦ [1] clean, consume, deplete, drain, expend, spend, use up
♦ [2] burn out, do in, drain, fag, fatigue, tire, tucker, wash out, wear, wear out, weary

²**exhaust** *n*   **1 :** the escape of used vapor or gas from an engine; *also* : the gas that escapes   **2 :** a system of pipes through which exhaust escapes

ex·haust·ed *adj* **:** being tired, worn out, or completely used up

♦ bushed, dead, drained, prostrate, spent, weary, worn-out

ex·haus·tion \ig-ˈzȯs-chən\ *n* ♦ **:** extreme weariness : FATIGUE

♦ burnout, collapse, fatigue, lassitude, prostration, tiredness, weariness

ex·haus·tive \ig-ˈzȯ-stiv\ *adj* ♦ **:** covering all possibilities : THOROUGH

♦ all-out, clean, complete, comprehensive, full-scale, out-and-out, thorough, thoroughgoing, total

ex·haus·tive·ly *adv* ♦ **:** in a thorough or exhaustive manner

♦ completely, fully, minutely, roundly, thoroughly, totally

¹**ex·hib·it** \ig-ˈzi-bət\ *vb*   **1 :** to display esp. publicly   **2 :** to present to a court in legal form — **ex·hib·i·tor** \ig-ˈzi-bə-tər\ *n*

²**exhibit** *n*   **1 ♦ :** an act or instance of exhibiting; *also* : something exhibited   **2 :** something produced and identified in court for use as evidence

♦ display, exhibition, exposition, fair, show

ex·hi·bi·tion \ˌek-sə-ˈbi-shən\ *n* ♦ **:** an act or instance of exhibiting; *also* : a public showing (as of works of art, objects of manufacture, or athletic skill)

♦ demonstration, display, show ♦ display, exhibit, exposition, fair, show

ex·hi·bi·tion·ism \ˌek-sə-ˈbi-shə-ˌni-zəm\ *n*   **1 :** a perversion marked by a tendency to indecently expose one's genitals   **2 :** the act or practice of behaving so as to attract attention to oneself — **ex·hi·bi·tion·ist** \-nist\ *n or adj*

ex·hil·a·rate \ig-ˈzi-lə-ˌrāt\ *vb* **-rat·ed; -rat·ing** ♦ **:** to make cheerful and excited

♦ elate, elevate, enrapture, thrill, transport

exhilarating *adj* ♦ **:** serving to exhilarate

♦ breathtaking, exciting, rousing, stirring, thrilling

ex·hil·a·ra·tion \-ˌzi-lə-ˈrā-shən\ *n*   **1 :** the action of exhilarating   **2 ♦ :** the feeling or the state of being exhilarated

♦ ecstasy, elation, euphoria, heaven, intoxication, paradise, rapture, rhapsody, thrill, transport

ex·hort \ig-ˈzȯrt\ *vb* ♦ **:** to urge, advise, or warn earnestly — **ex·hor·ta·tion** \ˌek-ˌsȯr-ˈtā-shən, ˌeg-ˌzȯr-, -zər-\ *n*

♦ egg on, encourage, goad, press, prod, prompt, urge

ex·hume \ig-ˈzüm, iks-ˈhyüm\ *vb* **ex·humed; ex·hum·ing** **:** DISINTER — **ex·hu·ma·tion** \ˌeks-hyü-ˈmā-shən, ˌeg-zü-\ *n*

ex·i·gen·cy \ˈek-sə-jən-sē, ig-ˈzi-jən-\ *n, pl* **-cies**   **1** *pl* : REQUIREMENTS   **2 :** urgent need — **ex·i·gent** \ˈek-sə-jənt\ *adj*

ex·ig·u·ous \ig-ˈzi-gyə-wəs\ *adj* **:** scanty in amount — **ex·i·gu·i·ty** \ˌeg-zi-ˈgyü-ə-tē\ *n*

¹**ex·ile** \ˈeg-ˌzīl, ˈek-ˌsīl\ *n*   **1 ♦ :** the state or a period of forced absence from one's country or home : BANISHMENT; *also* : voluntary absence from one's country or home   **2 ♦ :** a person who is in exile

♦ [1] banishment, deportation, displacement, expulsion
♦ [2] émigré, evacuee, expatriate, refugee

²**exile** *vb* **ex·iled; ex·il·ing** ♦ **:** to expel from one's own country or home : BANISH

♦ banish, deport, displace, expatriate, transport

ex·ist \ig-ˈzist\ *vb*   **1 :** to have being   **2 ♦ :** to continue to be : LIVE

♦ be, breathe, live, subsist

ex·is·tence \ig-ˈzis-təns\ *n*   **1 :** continuance in living   **2 ♦ :** actual or present occurrence ⟨~ of a state of war⟩   **3 :** something existing

♦ actuality, reality, subsistence *Ant* nonexistence

ex·is·tent \-tənt\ *adj* ♦ **:** having being; *also* : existing now

♦ actual, concrete, factual, real, true, very ♦ alive, extant, living

ex·is·ten·tial \ˌeg-zis-ˈten-chəl, ˌek-sis-\ *adj*   **1 :** of or relating to existence   **2 :** EMPIRICAL   **3 :** having being in time and space   **4 :** of or relating to existentialism or existentialists

ex·is·ten·tial·ism \ˌeg-zis-ˈten-chə-ˌli-zəm\ *n* **:** a philosophy centered on individual existence and personal responsibility for acts of free will in the absence of certain knowledge of what is right or wrong — **ex·is·ten·tial·ist** \-list\ *adj or n*

¹**ex·it** \ˈeg-zət, ˈek-sət\ *n*   **1 :** a departure from a stage   **2 ♦ :** a going out or away; *also* : DEATH   **3 ♦ :** a way out of an enclosed space   **4 :** a point of departure from an expressway

♦ [2] departure, farewell, leave-taking, parting ♦ [3] egress, issue, outlet *Ant* entrance, entry; ingress

²**exit** *vb* ♦ **:** to go out or away from

♦ clear out, depart, get off, go, move, pull, quit, sally, shove, take off

exo·bi·ol·o·gy \ˌek-sō-bī-ˈä-lə-jē\ *n* **:** biology concerned with life originating or existing outside the earth or its atmosphere — **exo·bi·ol·o·gist** \-jist\ *n*

exo·crine gland \ˈek-sə-krən\, -ˌkrīn-, -ˌkrēn-\ *n* **:** a gland (as a salivary gland) that releases a secretion externally by means of a canal or duct

Exod *abbr* Exodus

ex·o·dus \ˈek-sə-dəs\ *n*   **1** *cap* : the mainly narrative second book of canonical Jewish and Christian Scripture   **2 :** a mass departure : EMIGRATION

ex of·fi·cio \ˌek-sə-ˈfi-shē-ˌō\ *adv or adj* **:** by virtue of or because of an office ⟨*ex officio* chairman⟩

ex·og·e·nous \ek-ˈsä-jə-nəs\ *adj* **:** caused or produced by factors outside the organism or system — **ex·og·e·nous·ly** *adv*

ex·on·er·ate \ig-ˈzä-nə-ˌrāt\ *vb* **-at·ed; -at·ing** ♦ **:** to free from blame

♦ absolve, acquit, clear, exculpate, vindicate

ex·on·er·a·tion \-ˌzä-nə-ˈrā-shən\ *n* ♦ **:** the act or state of exonerating

♦ acquittal, exculpation, vindication

exo·plan·et \ˈek-sō-ˌpla-nət\ *n* **:** a planet orbiting a star that is not our sun

ex·or·bi·tant \ig-ˈzȯr-bə-tənt\ *adj* ♦ **:** exceeding what is usual or proper

♦ excessive, extravagant, extreme, immoderate, inordinate, lavish, steep, stiff

ex·or·cise \ˈek-ˌsȯr-ˌsīz, -sər-\ *vb* **-cised; -cis·ing**   **1 :** to get rid of by or as if by solemn command   **2 :** to free of an evil spirit — **ex·or·cism** \-ˌsi-zəm\ *n* — **ex·or·cist** \-ˌsist\ *n*

exo·sphere \ˈek-sō-ˌsfir\ *n* **:** the outermost region of the atmosphere

exo·ther·mic \ˌek-sō-ˈthər-mik\ *adj* **:** characterized by or formed with evolution of heat

ex·ot·ic \ig-ˈzä-tik\ *adj*   **1 :** introduced from another country   **2 ♦ :** strikingly, excitingly, or mysteriously different or unusual

♦ fantastic glamorous, marvelous (*or* marvellous), outlandish, romantic, strange

exp *abbr*   **1** expense   **2** experiment   **3** export   **4** express

ex·pand \ik-ˈspand\ *vb*   **1 ♦ :** to open up : UNFOLD   **2 ♦ :** to increase in extent, number, volume, or scope : ENLARGE   **3 ♦ :** to develop in detail — **ex·pand·er** *n*

♦ [1] extend, fan, flare, open, spread, stretch, unfold ♦ [2] add, aggrandize, amplify, augment, boost, compound, enlarge, escalate, extend, increase, multiply, raise, swell, up ♦ [3] amplify, develop, elaborate (on), enlarge (on) *Ant* abbreviate, abridge, condense, shorten

ex·panse \ik-ˈspans\ *n* ♦ **:** a broad extent (as of land or sea)

♦ breadth, extent, reach, spread, stretch

ex·pan·sion \ik-ˈspan-chən\ *n*   **1 ♦ :** the act or process of expanding   **2 :** the quality or state of being expanded   **3 ♦ :** an expanded part or thing

♦ [1] development, elaboration, evolution, growth, progress, progression ♦ [3] accretion, addition, augmentation, boost, gain, increase, increment, plus, proliferation, raise, rise, supplement

expansion slot *n* **:** a socket on a motherboard for a circuit board (**expansion card**) offering additional capabilities

ex·pan·sive \ik-ˈspan-siv\ *adj*   **1 :** tending to expand or to cause expansion   **2 :** warmly benevolent, generous, or ready to talk

3 ♦ : of large extent or scope — **ex·pan·sive·ly** *adv* — **ex·pan·sive·ness** *n*

♦ broad, extended, extensive, far-flung, far-reaching, wide, widespread

ex par·te \eks-'pär-tē\ *adv or adj* : from a one-sided point of view

ex·pa·ti·ate \ek-'spā-shē-ˌāt\ *vb* **-at·ed; -at·ing** : to talk or write at length — **ex·pa·ti·a·tion** \ek-ˌspā-shē-'ā-shən\ *n*

¹ex·pa·tri·ate \ek-'spā-trē-ˌāt\ *vb* **-at·ed; -at·ing 1** : to leave one's native country to live elsewhere : EXILE **2 ♦** : to drive into exile

♦ banish, deport, displace, exile, transport

²ex·pa·tri·ate \ek-'spā-trē-ˌāt, -trē-ət\ *adj* : living in a foreign country

³expatriate *n* : one who lives in a foreign country

ex·pa·tri·a·tion \ek-ˌspā-trē-'ā-shən\ *n* : the act or action of expatriating

ex·pect \ik-'spekt\ *vb* **1** : SUPPOSE, THINK **2 ♦** : to look forward to : ANTICIPATE **3** : to consider reasonable, due, or necessary **4** : to consider to be obliged

♦ anticipate, await, hope, watch

ex·pec·tan·cy \-'spek-tən-sē\ *n, pl* **-cies 1** : EXPECTATION **2** : the expected amount (as of years of life)

ex·pec·tant \-tənt\ *adj* ♦ : marked by expectation; *esp* : expecting the birth of a child — **ex·pec·tant·ly** *adv*

♦ agape, agog, anticipatory

ex·pec·ta·tion \ˌek-ˌspek-'tā-shən\ *n* **1** : the act or state of expecting **2** : prospect of good or bad fortune — usu. used in pl. **3** : something expected

ex·pec·to·rant \ik-'spek-tə-rənt\ *n* : an agent that promotes the discharge or expulsion of mucus from the respiratory tract — **expectorant** *adj*

ex·pec·to·rate \-ˌrāt\ *vb* **-rat·ed; -rat·ing** : SPIT — **ex·pec·to·ra·tion** \-ˌspek-tə-'rā-shən\ *n*

ex·pe·di·ence \ik-'spē-dē-əns\ *n* : EXPEDIENCY

ex·pe·di·en·cy \-ən-sē\ *n, pl* **-cies 1** : fitness to some end **2** : use of expedient means and methods; *also* : something expedient

¹ex·pe·di·ent \-ənt\ *adj* **1 ♦** : adapted for achieving a particular end **2** : marked by concern with what is advantageous; *esp* : governed by self-interest

♦ advisable, desirable, judicious, politic, prudent, tactical, wise *Ant* imprudent, inadvisable, inexpedient, injudicious, unwise

²expedient *n* ♦ : something expedient; *esp* : a temporary means to an end

♦ measure, move, shift, step ♦ recourse, resort, resource

ex·pe·dite \'ek-spə-ˌdīt\ *vb* **-dit·ed; -dit·ing** : to carry out promptly; *also* : to speed up ⟨~ a lawsuit⟩

ex·pe·dit·er \-ˌdī-tər\ *n* : one that expedites; *esp* : one employed to ensure efficient movement of goods or supplies in a business

ex·pe·di·tion \ˌek-spə-'di-shən\ *n* **1 ♦** : a journey for a particular purpose; *also* : the persons making it **2** : efficient promptness

♦ journey, passage, peregrination, trek, trip

ex·pe·di·tion·ary \-'di-shə-ˌner-ē\ *adj* : of, relating to, or constituting an expedition; *also* : sent on military service abroad

ex·pe·di·tious \-'di-shəs\ *adj* ♦ : marked by or acting with prompt efficiency

♦ alert, prompt, quick, ready, willing

ex·pel \ik-'spel\ *vb* **ex·pelled; ex·pel·ling** ♦ : to drive or force out

♦ banish, boot (out), bounce, cast, chase, dismiss, drum, eject, oust, rout, run off, throw out ♦ belch, disgorge, eject, erupt, jet, spew, spout, spurt

ex·pend \ik-'spend\ *vb* **1 ♦** : to pay out : SPEND **2 ♦** : to make use of ⟨~ energy⟩; *also* : USE UP — **ex·pend·able** *adj*

♦ [1] disburse, give, lay out, pay, spend ♦ [2] clean, consume, deplete, drain, exhaust, spend, use up

ex·pen·di·ture \ik-'spen-di-chər, -ˌchùr\ *n* **1** : the act or process of expending **2 ♦** : something expended

♦ cost, disbursement, expense, outgo, outlay

ex·pense \ik-'spens\ *n* **1 ♦** : something expended to secure a benefit or bring about a result : EXPENDITURE **2** : COST **3** : a cause of expenditure **4** : a loss, detriment, or embarrassment that results from some action or gain ⟨had a laugh at my ~⟩

♦ cost, disbursement, expenditure, outgo, outlay

ex·pen·sive \ik-'spen-siv\ *adj* ♦ : involving high cost or sacrifice : COSTLY, DEAR

♦ costly, dear, high, precious, valuable

ex·pen·sive·ly *adv* ♦ : in an expensive manner

♦ extravagantly, grandly, high, lavishly, luxuriously, opulently, richly

¹ex·pe·ri·ence \ik-'spir-ē-əns\ *n* **1** : observation of or participation in events resulting in or tending toward knowledge **2 ♦** : knowledge, practice, or skill derived from observation or participation in events; *also* : the length of such participation **3 ♦** : something encountered, undergone, or lived through (as by a person or community)

♦ [2] expertise, know-how, proficiency, savvy *Ant* inexperience
♦ [3] adventure, happening, time

²experience *vb* **-enced; -enc·ing 1** : FIND OUT, DISCOVER **2 ♦** : to have experience of : UNDERGO

♦ endure, feel, have, know, see, suffer, sustain, taste, undergo

ex·pe·ri·enced *adj* ♦ : made capable through experience

♦ accomplished, adept, expert, masterful, masterly, practiced, proficient, seasoned, skilled, skillful, versed *Ant* amateurish, inexperienced, inexpert, unseasoned, unskilled

¹ex·per·i·ment \ik-'sper-ə-mənt\ *n* ♦ : a controlled procedure carried out to discover, test, or demonstrate something; *also* : the process of testing

♦ test, trial

²ex·per·i·ment \-ˌment\ *vb* : to make experiments — **ex·per·i·ment·er** *n*

ex·per·i·men·tal \-ˌsper-ə-'ment-ᵊl\ *adj* : of, relating to, or based on experience or experiment; *also* : serving the ends of or used as a means of experimentation — **ex·per·i·men·tal·ly** \-'men-tᵊl-ē\ *adv*

ex·per·i·men·ta·tion \ik-ˌsper-ə-mən-'tā-shən\ *n* : the act, process, or practice of making experiments; *also* : an instance of experimentation

¹ex·pert \'ek-ˌspərt\ *adj* ♦ : showing special skill or knowledge ⟨~ advice⟩ — **ex·pert·ness** *n*

♦ accomplished, ace, adept, crack, experienced, master, masterful, masterly, practiced, proficient, seasoned, skilled, skillful, versed

²ex·pert \'ek-ˌspərt\ *n* ♦ : an expert person

♦ ace, artist, authority, master, scholar, shark, virtuoso, whiz, wizard *Ant* amateur

ex·per·tise \ˌek-(ˌ)spər-'tēz\ *n* ♦ : the skill of an expert

♦ experience, know-how, proficiency, savvy

ex·pert·ly *adv* ♦ : in an expert manner

♦ ably, adeptly, capably, masterfully, proficiently, skillfully, well

expert system *n* : computer software that attempts to mimic the reasoning of a human specialist

ex·pi·ate \'ek-spē-ˌāt\ *vb* **-at·ed; -at·ing** : to give satisfaction for : ATONE ⟨~ sin⟩ — **ex·pi·a·tion** \ˌek-spē-'ā-shən\ *n*

ex·pi·a·to·ry \'ek-spē-ə-ˌtōr-ē\ *adj* : serving to expiate

ex·pi·ra·tion \ˌek-spə-'rā-shən\ *n* **1** : the last emission of breath; *also* : the act or process of releasing air from the lungs through the nose or mouth **2 ♦** : the fact of coming to an end or the point at which something ends

♦ death, demise, termination ♦ cessation, close, conclusion, end, ending, finish, shutdown, stop, stoppage, termination

expiration date *n* **1** : the date after which something is no longer in effect **2** : the date after which a product is expected to decline in quality or effectiveness

ex·pire \ik-'spīr, ek-\ *vb* **ex·pired; ex·pir·ing 1 ♦** : to breathe one's last breath : DIE **2 ♦** : to come to an end **3 ♦** : to breathe out from or as if from the lungs

♦ [1] decease, depart, die, pass, pass away, perish, succumb
♦ [2] cease, close, conclude, die, discontinue, end, finish, halt, pass, quit, stop, terminate ♦ [3] blow, breathe, exhale

ex·plain \ik-'splān\ *vb* **1 ♦** : to make clear **2 ♦** : to give the reason for — **ex·plan·a·to·ry** \ik-'spla-nə-ˌtōr-ē\ *adj*

♦ [1] clarify, clear (up), construe, demonstrate, elucidate, explicate, expound, illuminate, illustrate, interpret, spell out *Ant* obscure ♦ [2] account, rationalize

explain away *vb* : to get rid of by or as if by explanation; *also* : to minimize the significance of by or as if by explanation

ex·pla·na·tion \,ek-splə-'nā-shən\ *n* **1 :** the act or process of explaining **2 ♦ :** something that explains

♦ clarification, construction, elucidation, explication, exposition, illumination, illustration, interpretation ♦ argument, case, defense (*or* defence), rationale, reason

ex·ple·tive \'ek-splə-tiv\ *n* : a usu. profane exclamation

ex·pli·ca·ble \ek-'spli-kə-bəl, 'ek-(,)spli-\ *adj* ♦ : capable of being explained

♦ answerable, resolvable, soluble, solvable

ex·pli·cate \'ek-splə-,kāt\ *vb* **-cat·ed; -cat·ing** ♦ : to give a detailed explanation of; *esp* : to interpret the meaning or sense of

♦ clarify, clear (up), construe, demonstrate, elucidate, explain, expound, illuminate, illustrate, interpret, spell out

ex·pli·ca·tion \,ek-spli-'kā-shən\ *n* **1 :** the act or process of explicating **2 ♦ :** something that explicates or that results from the act or process of explicating

♦ clarification, construction, elucidation, explanation, exposition, illumination, illustration, interpretation

ex·plic·it \ik-'spli-sət\ *adj* ♦ : clearly and precisely expressed ⟨~ directions⟩ — **ex·plic·it·ly** *adv*

♦ clear-cut, definite, definitive, express, specific, unambiguous, unequivocal *Ant* implicit, implied, inferred; ambiguous, circuitous

ex·plic·it·ness *n* ♦ : the quality or state of being explicit

♦ clarity, lucidity, perspicuity, simplicity

ex·plode \ik-'splōd\ *vb* **ex·plod·ed; ex·plod·ing** **1 :** DISCREDIT ⟨~ a belief⟩ **2 ♦ :** to burst or cause to burst violently and noisily ⟨~ a bomb⟩ ⟨the boiler *exploded*⟩ **3 :** to undergo a rapid chemical or nuclear reaction with production of heat and violent expansion of gas ⟨dynamite ~s⟩ **4 :** to give forth a sudden strong and noisy outburst of emotion **5 :** to increase rapidly ⟨the city's population *exploded*⟩ **6 ♦ :** to suggest an explosion (as in appearance or effect)

♦ [2] blow up, burst, detonate, go off, pop *Ant* implode
♦ [6] break out, burst, erupt, flame, flare, go off

ex·plod·ed *adj* : showing the parts separated but in correct relationship to each other ⟨an ~ view of a carburetor⟩

¹ex·ploit \'ek-,splȯit\ *n* ♦ : something that is done; *esp* : a notable or heroic act

♦ deed, feat, stunt, trick

²ex·ploit \ik-'splȯit\ *vb* **1 ♦ :** to make productive use of : UTILIZE **2 ♦ :** to use unfairly for one's own advantage ⟨~ migrant workers⟩ — **ex·ploi·ta·tion** \,ek-,splȯi-'tā-shən\ *n*

♦ [1] apply, employ, exercise, harness, operate, use, utilize
♦ [2] abuse, capitalize, cash in, impose, play, use

ex·plo·ra·tion \,ek-splə-'rā-shən\ *n* ♦ : the act or an instance of exploring

♦ examination, inquiry, investigation, probe, research, study

ex·plore \ik-'splōr\ *vb* **ex·plored; ex·plor·ing** **1 ♦ :** to look into or travel over thoroughly **2 ♦ :** to examine carefully ⟨~ a wound⟩ — **ex·plor·a·to·ry** \ik-'splōr-ə-,tōr-ē\ *adj* — **ex·plor·er** *n*

♦ [1] hunt, probe, prospect, search ♦ [2] delve, dig, go, inquire into, investigate, look, probe, research

ex·plo·sion \ik-'splō-zhən\ *n* ♦ : the act or an instance of exploding

♦ agony, burst, fit, flash, flush, outburst, paroxysm, spasm, storm ♦ blast, detonation, eruption *Ant* implosion

ex·plo·sive \ik-'splō-siv\ *adj* **1 a :** relating to or able to cause explosion **b :** characterized by or like an explosion **2 ♦ :** tending to explode; *also* : likely to erupt in or produce hostile reaction or violence ⟨an ~ temper⟩ — **explosive** *n* — **ex·plo·sive·ly** *adv*

♦ ferocious, fierce, furious, hot, rabid, rough, stormy, tempestuous, turbulent, violent, volcanic

ex·po \'ek-,spō\ *n, pl* **expos** : EXPOSITION 2

ex·po·nent \ik-'spō-nənt, 'ek-,spō-\ *n* **1 :** a symbol written above and to the right of a mathematical expression (as ^{3} in a^3) to signify how many times it is to be used as a factor **2 :** INTERPRETER, EXPOUNDER **3 ♦ :** one that champions, practices, or exemplifies — **ex·po·nen·tial** \,ek-spə-'nen-chəl\ *adj* — **ex·po·nen·tial·ly** *adv*

♦ advocate, apostle, backer, booster, champion, friend, promoter, proponent, supporter *Ant* adversary, antagonist, opponent

ex·po·nen·ti·a·tion \,ek-spə-,nen-chē-'ā-shen\ *n* : the mathematical operation of raising a quantity to a power

¹ex·port \ek-'spōrt, 'ek-,spōrt\ *vb* : to send (as merchandise) to foreign countries — **ex·por·ta·tion** \,ek-spōr-'tā-shən, -spər-\ *n* — **ex·port·er** *n*

²ex·port \'ek-,spōrt\ *n* **1 :** something exported esp. for trade **2 :** the act of exporting

ex·pose \ik-'spōz\ *vb* **ex·posed; ex·pos·ing** **1 :** to deprive of shelter or protection **2 :** to submit or subject to an action or influence; *esp* : to subject (as photographic film) to radiant energy (as light) **3 ♦ :** to bring to light; *esp* : to disclose or reveal the true nature of ⟨~ a scam⟩ **4 ♦ :** to cause to be open to view

♦ [3] bare, disclose, discover, divulge, reveal, spill, tell
♦ debunk, show up, uncloak, uncover, unmask *Ant* camouflage, cloak, disguise, mask ♦ [4] display, exhibit, show, unveil

ex·po·sé \,ek-spō-'zā\ *n* : an exposure of something discreditable

ex·posed \ik-'spōzd\ *adj* ♦ : open to view; *also* : not shielded or protected

♦ liable, open, sensitive, subject, susceptible, unprotected, vulnerable ♦ bald, bare, naked, open, uncovered

ex·po·si·tion \,ek-spə-'zi-shən\ *n* **1 ♦ :** a setting forth of the meaning or purpose (as of a writing); *also* : discourse designed to convey information **2 ♦ :** a public exhibition

♦ [1] clarification, construction, elucidation, explanation, explication, illumination, illustration, interpretation ♦ [1] analysis, comment, commentary ♦ [2] display, exhibit, exhibition, fair, show

ex·pos·i·tor \ik-'spä-zə-tər\ *n* : one who explains : COMMENTATOR

ex·pos·i·tory \ik-'spä-zə-tə-rē\ *adj* : serving to explain

ex post fac·to \,eks-'pōst-,fak-tō\ *adv or adj* : after the fact

ex·pos·tu·late \ik-'späs-chə-,lāt\ *vb* : to reason earnestly with a person esp. in dissuading : REMONSTRATE

ex·pos·tu·la·tion \-,späs-chə-'lā-shən\ *n* ♦ : an act or an instance of expostulating

♦ challenge, complaint, demur, fuss, kick, objection, protest, question, remonstrance

ex·po·sure \ik-'spō-zhər\ *n* **1 ♦ :** the fact or condition of being exposed **2 :** the act or an instance of exposing **3 :** the length of time for which a film is exposed **4 :** a section of a photographic film for one picture

♦ liability, openness, vulnerability

ex·pound \ik-'spaund\ *vb* **1 :** STATE **2 ♦ :** to explain by setting forth in careful and often elaborate detail : INTERPRET — **ex·pound·er** *n*

♦ clarify, clear (up), construe, demonstrate, elucidate, explain, explicate, illuminate, illustrate, interpret, spell out

¹ex·press \ik-'spres\ *adj* **1 ♦ :** directly, firmly, and explicitly stated; *also* : EXACT, PRECISE **2 ♦ :** of a particular sort : SPECIFIC ⟨this ~ purpose⟩ **3 :** traveling at high speed and esp. with few stops ⟨an ~ train⟩; *also* : adapted to high speed use ⟨~ roads⟩ — **ex·press·ly** *adv*

♦ [1] clear-cut, definite, definitive, explicit, specific, unambiguous, unequivocal ♦ [1, 2] distinct, especial, exact, precise, set, special, specific *Ant* nonspecific

²express *adv* : by express ⟨ship it ~⟩

³express *n* **1 :** a system for the prompt transportation of goods; *also* : a company operating such a service or the shipments so transported **2 :** an express vehicle

⁴express *vb* **1 ♦ :** to make known : STATE ⟨~ regret⟩; *also* : to represent by a sign or symbol **2 ♦ :** to squeeze out : extract by pressing **3 :** to send by express **4 :** to manifest or produce by a genetic process

♦ [1] denote, import, mean, signify, spell ♦ [1] articulate, clothe, couch, formulate, phrase, put, say, state, word ♦ [1] air, give, sound, state, voice *Ant* stifle, suppress ♦ [2] crush, mash, press, squeeze

ex·pres·sion \ik-'spre-shən\ *n* **1 ♦ :** an act, process, or instance of representing in a medium (as words) : UTTERANCE **2 :** something that represents or symbolizes; *esp* : a mathematical symbol or combination of signs and symbols representing a quantity or operation **3 :** a significant word or phrase; *also* : manner of expressing (as in writing or music) : SIGN; *esp* : facial aspect or vocal intonation indicative of feeling

♦ [1] articulation, formulation, statement, utterance, voice
♦ [4] cast, countenance, face, look, visage

ex·pres·sion·ism \ik-'spre-shə-ˌni-zəm\ *n* : a theory or practice in art of seeking to depict the artist's subjective responses to objects and events — **ex·pres·sion·ist** \-nist\ *n or adj* — **ex·pres·sion·is·tic** \-ˌspre-shə-'nis-tik\ *adj*

ex·pres·sion·less *adj* ♦ : lacking expression

♦ blank, deadpan, impassive, inexpressive, stolid, vacant

ex·pres·sive \ik-'spre-siv\ *adj* **1** : of or relating to expression **2** ♦ : serving to express ⟨an ∼ gesture⟩ — **ex·pres·sive·ly** *adv* — **ex·pres·sive·ness** *n*

♦ eloquent, meaning, meaningful, pregnant, significant, suggestive

ex·pres·sway \ik-'spres-ˌwā\ *n* : a divided superhighway with limited access

ex·pro·pri·ate \ek-'sprō-prē-ˌāt\ *vb* **-at·ed; -at·ing** : to deprive of possession or the right to own — **ex·pro·pri·a·tion** \(ˌ)ek-ˌsprō-prē-'ā-shən\ *n*

expt *abbr* experiment

ex·pul·sion \ik-'spəl-shən\ *n* ♦ : an expelling or being expelled

♦ banishment, deportation, displacement, exile

ex·punge \ik-'spənj\ *vb* **ex·punged; ex·pung·ing** : to efface completely : OBLITERATE

ex·pur·gate \'ek-spər-ˌgāt\ *vb* **-gat·ed; -gat·ing** : to clear (as a book) of objectionable passages — **ex·pur·ga·tion** \ˌek-spər-'gā-shən\ *n*

ex·qui·site \ek-'skwi-zət, 'ek-(ˌ)skwi-\ *adj* **1** : marked by flawless form or workmanship **2** : keenly appreciative or sensitive **3** ♦ : pleasingly beautiful or delicate **4** : characterized by sharpness or severity : INTENSE ⟨∼ pain⟩

♦ dainty, delicate, refined, subtle

ext *abbr* **1** extension **2** exterior **3** external **4** extra **5** extract

ex·tant \'ek-stənt; ek-'stant\ *adj* ♦ : currently or actually existing; *esp* : not lost or destroyed

♦ current, ongoing, present ♦ alive, existent, living *Ant* dead, extinct

ex·tem·po·ra·ne·ous \ek-ˌstem-pə-'rā-nē-əs\ *adj* ♦ : not planned beforehand : IMPROMPTU — **ex·tem·po·ra·ne·ous·ly** *adv*

♦ ad-lib, impromptu, informal, offhand, spontaneous, unplanned, unprepared, unrehearsed *Ant* considered, planned, premeditated, prepared, rehearsed

ex·tem·po·rary \ik-'stem-pə-ˌrer-ē\ *adj* : EXTEMPORANEOUS

ex·tem·po·re \ik-'stem-pə-(ˌ)rē\ *adv* : EXTEMPORANEOUSLY

ex·tem·po·rise *chiefly Brit var of* EXTEMPORIZE

ex·tem·po·rize \ik-'stem-pə-ˌrīz\ *vb* **-rized; -riz·ing** : to do something extemporaneously ⟨∼ a speech⟩

ex·tend \ik-'stend\ *vb* **1** ♦ : to spread or stretch forth or out (as in reaching) **2** : to exert or cause to exert to full capacity **3** ♦ : to make the offer of : PROFFER ⟨∼ credit⟩ **4** : PROLONG ⟨∼ a note⟩ **5** : to make greater or broader ⟨∼ knowledge⟩ ⟨∼ a business⟩ **6** : to stretch out or reach across a distance, space, or time — **ex·tend·able** *also* **ex·tend·ible** \-'sten-də-bəl\ *adj*

♦ [1] expand, fan, flare, open, spread, stretch, unfold ♦ [1] draw out, elongate, lengthen, prolong, protract, stretch *Ant* abbreviate, abridge, curtail, cut, cut back, shorten ♦ [3] give, offer, proffer, tender

ex·tend·ed *adj* **1** ♦ : drawn out in length esp. of time **2** : fully stretched out **3** ♦ : having wide or considerable extent

♦ [1] far, great, lengthy, long, marathon ♦ [3] broad, expansive, extensive, far-flung, far-reaching, wide, widespread

ex·ten·sion \ik-'sten-chən\ *n* **1** ♦ : an extending or being extended **2** : a program that geographically extends the educational resources of an institution **3** ♦ : an additional part; *also* : an extra telephone connected to a line

♦ [1] elongation, prolongation *Ant* abbreviation, abridgment, curtailment, cutback, shortening ♦ [3] addition, annex, penthouse

ex·ten·sive \ik-'sten-siv\ *adj* ♦ : of considerable extent : FAR-REACHING, BROAD ⟨∼ training⟩ — **ex·ten·sive·ly** *adv*

♦ broad, expansive, extended, far-flung, far-reaching, wide, widespread *Ant* narrow

ex·tent \ik-'stent\ *n* **1** ♦ : the range or space over which something extends ⟨a property of large ∼⟩ **2** ♦ : the point or degree to which something extends ⟨to the fullest ∼ of the law⟩ ⟨exerting the full ∼ of his power⟩

♦ [1] amplitude, breadth, compass, range, reach, realm, scope, sweep, width ♦ [1] dimension, magnitude, measure, measure-

ment, proportion, size ♦ [2] bound, boundary, ceiling, confines, end, limit, limitation, line, termination

ex·ten·u·ate \ik-'sten-yü-ˌwāt\ *vb* **-at·ed; -at·ing** : to lessen the seriousness of — **ex·ten·u·a·tion** \-ˌsten-yü-'wā-shən\ *n*

¹ex·te·ri·or \ek-'stir-ē-ər\ *adj* **1** ♦ : being on an outside surface : EXTERNAL **2** : suitable for use on an outside surface ⟨∼ paint⟩

♦ external, outer, outside, outward

²exterior *n* ♦ : an exterior part or surface

♦ face, outside, skin, surface, veneer *Ant* inside, interior

ex·ter·mi·nate \ik-'stər-mə-ˌnāt\ *vb* **-nat·ed; -nat·ing** ♦ : to get rid of completely usu. by killing off — **ex·ter·mi·na·tor** \-'stər-mə-ˌnā-tər\ *n*

♦ annihilate, blot out, demolish, eradicate, liquidate, obliterate, root, rub out, snuff, stamp, wipe out

ex·ter·mi·na·tion \-ˌstər-mə-'nā-shən\ *n* : the act of exterminating or the condition of being exterminated

¹ex·ter·nal \ek-'stərn-ᵊl\ *adj* **1** : outwardly perceivable; *also* : SUPERFICIAL **2** ♦ : of, relating to, or located on the outside or an outer part **3** : arising or acting from without; *also* : FOREIGN ⟨∼ affairs⟩ — **ex·ter·nal·ly** *adv*

♦ exterior, outer, outside, outward

²external *n* : an external feature

ex·tinct \ik-'stiŋkt\ *adj* **1** : EXTINGUISHED; *also* : no longer active ⟨an ∼ volcano⟩ **2** ♦ : no longer existing or in use ⟨dinosaurs are ∼⟩ ⟨∼ languages⟩

♦ bygone, dead, defunct, gone *Ant* alive, existent, existing, extant, living

ex·tinc·tion \ik-'stiŋk-shən\ *n* **1** : the act of making extinct or causing to be extinguished **2** : the condition or fact of being extinct or extinguished; *also* : the process of becoming extinct

ex·tin·guish \ik-'stiŋ-gwish\ *vb* **1** ♦ : to cause to stop burning **2** ♦ : to bring to an end **3** : cause to die out ⟨disease that *extinguished* an entire population⟩ ⟨*extinguishing* the last glimmer of hope⟩ — **ex·tin·guish·able** *adj* — **ex·tin·guish·er** *n*

♦ [1] douse, put out, quench, snuff *Ant* fire, ignite, inflame, kindle ♦ [2] annihilate, blot out, demolish, desolate, destroy, devastate, do in, obliterate, ruin, shatter, smash, wipe out, wreck

ex·tir·pate \'ek-stər-ˌpāt\ *vb* **-pat·ed; -pat·ing** **1** : to destroy completely ⟨∼ a heresy⟩ **2** : UPROOT — **ex·tir·pa·tion** \ˌek-stər-'pā-shən\ *n*

ex·tol *also* **ex·toll** \ik-'stōl\ *vb* **ex·tolled; ex·tol·ling** ♦ : to praise highly : GLORIFY

♦ bless, glorify, laud, magnify, praise

ex·tort \ik-'stòrt\ *vb* ♦ : to obtain by force or improper pressure ⟨∼ a bribe⟩ — **ex·tor·tion** \-'stòr-shən\ *n* — **ex·tor·tion·er** *n*

♦ exact, wrest, wring

ex·tor·tion·ate \ik-'stòr-shə-nət\ *adj* : EXCESSIVE, EXORBITANT — **ex·tor·tion·ate·ly** *adv*

ex·tor·tion·ist *n* ♦ : one that practices or is given to extortion

♦ racketeer

¹ex·tra \'ek-strə\ *adj* **1** ♦ : more than is due, usual, or necessary **2** : SUPERIOR

♦ excess, spare, superfluous, supernumerary, surplus

²extra *n* ♦ : one that is extra or additional: as **a** : a special edition of a newspaper **b** : an added charge **c** : an additional worker or performer (as in a motion picture)

♦ amenity, comfort, frill, indulgence, luxury, superfluity ♦ bonus, dividend, lagniappe, perquisite, tip

³extra *adv* ♦ : beyond what is usual

♦ extremely, greatly, highly, hugely, mightily, mighty, mortally, most, much, real, right, so, very

¹ex·tract \ik-'strakt, *esp for 3* 'ek-ˌstrakt\ *vb* **1** ♦ : to draw out; *esp* : to pull out forcibly ⟨∼ a tooth⟩ **2** : to withdraw (as a juice or a constituent) by a physical or chemical process **3** : to select for citation : QUOTE — **ex·tract·able** *adj* — **ex·trac·tor** \-tər\ *n*

♦ prize, pry, pull, root, tear, uproot, wrest

²ex·tract \'ek-ˌstrakt\ *n* **1** : EXCERPT, CITATION **2** : a product (as a juice or concentrate) obtained by extracting

ex·trac·tion \ik-'strak-shən\ *n* **1** : the act or process of extracting something **2** ♦ : line of descent

♦ ancestry, birth, descent, line, lineage, origin, parentage

ex·tra·cur·ric·u·lar \ˌek-strə-kə-'ri-kyə-lər\ *adj* : lying outside the regular curriculum; *esp* : of or relating to school-connected activities (as sports) usu. carrying no academic credit

ex·tra·dite \'ek-strə-ˌdīt\ *vb* **-dit·ed; -dit·ing** : to obtain by or deliver up to extradition

ex·tra·di·tion \ˌek-strə-'di-shən\ *n* : the surrender of an alleged criminal to a different jurisdiction for trial

ex·tra·mar·i·tal \ˌek-strə-'mar-ət-ᵊl\ *adj* : of or relating to sexual intercourse by a married person with someone other than his or her spouse

ex·tra·mu·ral \-'myu̇r-əl\ *adj* : existing or functioning beyond the bounds of an organized unit

ex·tra·ne·ous \ek-'strā-nē-əs\ *adj* **1** : coming from without **2** : not forming a vital part; *also* : IRRELEVANT — **ex·tra·ne·ous·ly** *adv*

♦ immaterial, irrelevant

ex·tra·net \'ek-strə-ˌnet\ *n* : a network like an intranet but also allowing access by certain outside parties

ex·traor·di·nary \ik-'stror-də-ˌner-ē, ˌek-strə-'or-\ *adj* **1** ♦ : notably unusual or exceptional ⟨did ~ work on the project⟩ **2** : employed on special service ⟨an ambassador ~⟩ — **ex·traor·di·nar·i·ly** \-ˌstror-də-'ner-ə-lē, ˌek-strə-ˌor-\ *adv*

♦ atypical, exceptional, phenomenal, rare, uncustomary, unique, unusual

ex·trap·o·late \ik-'stra-pə-ˌlāt\ *vb* **-lat·ed; -lat·ing** ♦ : to infer (unknown data) from known data — **ex·trap·o·la·tion** \-ˌstra-pə-'lā-shən\ *n*

♦ conclude, deduce, gather, infer, judge, reason, understand

ex·tra·sen·so·ry \ˌek-strə-'sen-sə-rē\ *adj* : not acting or occurring through the known senses

extrasensory perception *n* : perception (as in telepathy) of events external to the self not gained through the senses and not deducible from previous experience

ex·tra·ter·res·tri·al \-tə-'res-trē-əl\ *adj* : originating or existing outside the earth or its atmosphere ⟨~ life⟩ — **extraterrestrial** *n*

ex·tra·ter·ri·to·ri·al \-ˌter-ə-'tōr-ē-əl\ *adj* : existing or taking place outside the territorial limits of a jurisdiction

ex·tra·ter·ri·to·ri·al·i·ty \-ˌtōr-ē-'a-lə-tē\ *n* : exemption from the application or jurisdiction of local law or tribunals ⟨diplomats enjoy ~⟩

ex·trav·a·gance \-gəns\ *n* ♦ : an instance of excess or prodigality; *specif* : an excessive outlay of money

♦ lavishness, prodigality, wastefulness *Ant* economy, frugality

ex·trav·a·gant \ik-'stra-vi-gənt\ *adj* **1** ♦ : exceeding the limits of reason or necessity : EXCESSIVE ⟨~ claims⟩ **2** ♦ : spending or tending to spend much more than necessary : spending lavishly, recklessly, or wastefully **3** : too costly

♦ [1] excessive, extreme, immoderate, inordinate, lavish, overmuch, steep, stiff ♦ [2] prodigal, profligate, spendthrift, thriftless, unthrifty, wasteful

ex·trav·a·gant·ly *adv* ♦ : in an extravagant manner

♦ expensively, grandly, high, lavishly, luxuriously, opulently, richly

ex·trav·a·gan·za \ik-ˌstra-və-'gan-zə\ *n* **1** : a literary or musical work marked by extreme freedom of style and structure **2** : a spectacular show

ex·tra·ve·hic·u·lar \ˌek-strə-vē-'hi-kyə-lər\ *adj* : taking place outside a vehicle (as a spacecraft) ⟨~ activity⟩

¹**ex·treme** \ik-'strēm\ *adj* **1** : very great or intense ⟨~ cold⟩ **2** : very severe or radical ⟨~ measures⟩ **3** ♦ : going to great lengths or beyond normal limits ⟨politically ~⟩ **4** ♦ : most remote ⟨the ~ end⟩ **5** : UTMOST; *also* : MAXIMUM

♦ [3] excessive, immoderate, inordinate, overmuch, unconscionable ♦ [3] extremist, fanatic, rabid, radical, revolutionary, ultra *Ant* middle-of-the-road ♦ [4] farthest, furthest, outermost, ultimate, utmost *Ant* inmost, innermost

²**extreme** *n* **1** : something located at one end or the other of a range or series **2** : EXTREMITY 4

ex·treme·ly *adv* ♦ : in an extreme manner : to an extreme extent

♦ extra, greatly, highly, hugely, mightily, mighty, mortally, most, much, real, right, so, very

extremely low frequency *n* : a radio frequency in the lowest range of the radio spectrum

ex·trem·ism \ik-'strē-ˌmi-zəm\ *n* : the quality or state of being extreme; *esp* : advocacy of extreme political measures

¹**ex·trem·ist** \-mist\ *n* ♦ : an adherent or advocate of extremism

♦ radical, revolutionary

²**extremist** *adj* ♦ : of, relating to, or favoring extremism or extremists

♦ extreme, fanatic, rabid, radical, revolutionary, ultra

ex·trem·i·ty \ik-'stre-mə-tē\ *n, pl* **-ties 1** ♦ : the most remote part or point **2** : a limb of the body; *esp* : a human hand or foot **3** : the greatest need or danger **4** : the utmost degree; *also* : a drastic or desperate measure

♦ height, limit

ex·tri·cate \'ek-strə-ˌkāt\ *vb* **-cat·ed; -cat·ing** ♦ : to free from an entanglement or difficulty — **ex·tri·ca·ble** \ik-'stri-kə-bəl, ek-; 'ek-ˌstri-\ *adj* — **ex·tri·ca·tion** \ˌek-strə-'kā-shən\ *n*

♦ clear, disengage, disentangle, free, liberate, release, untangle *Ant* embroil, entangle

ex·trin·sic \ek-'strin-zik, -sik\ *adj* **1** ♦ : not forming part of or belonging to a thing **2** : EXTERNAL — **ex·trin·si·cal·ly** \-zi-k(ə-)lē, -si-\ *adv*

♦ adventitious, alien, extraneous, foreign *Ant* inherent, innate, intrinsic

ex·tro·vert *also* **ex·tra·vert** \'ek-strə-ˌvərt\ *n* : a gregarious and unreserved person — **ex·tro·ver·sion** *or* **ex·tra·ver·sion** \ˌek-strə-'vər-zhən\ *n*

ex·tro·vert·ed *also* **ex·tra·vert·ed** *adj* ♦ : having the characteristics of an extrovert : marked by extroversion

♦ boon, companionable, convivial, gregarious, outgoing, sociable, social

ex·trude \ik-'strüd\ *vb* **ex·trud·ed; ex·trud·ing 1** : to force, press, or push out **2** : to shape (as plastic) by forcing through a die — **ex·tru·sion** \-'strü-zhən\ *n* — **ex·trud·er** *n*

ex·u·ber·ance \-rəns\ *n* **1** ♦ : the quality or state of being exuberant **2** : an exuberant act or expression

♦ [1] animation, briskness, liveliness, lustiness, robustness, sprightliness, vibrancy, vitality

ex·u·ber·ant \ig-'zü-bə-rənt\ *adj* **1** ♦ : unrestrained in enthusiasm or style **2** : PROFUSE

♦ bubbly, buoyant, effervescent, frolicsome, high-spirited, vivacious *Ant* sullen

ex·u·ber·ant·ly *adv* ♦ : in an exuberant manner

♦ gaily, jauntily, sprightly

ex·ude \ig-'züd\ *vb* **ex·ud·ed; ex·ud·ing 1** ♦ : to discharge slowly through pores or cuts : OOZE **2** : to display conspicuously or abundantly ⟨~s charm⟩ — **ex·u·date** \'ek-sù-ˌdāt, -syù-\ *n* — **ex·u·da·tion** \ˌek-sù-'dā-shən, -syù-\ *n*

♦ bleed, ooze, percolate, seep, strain, sweat, weep

ex·ult \ig-'zəlt\ *vb* ♦ : to be extremely joyful : REJOICE, GLORY ⟨~ed in their victory⟩ — **ex·ul·tant·ly** *adv* — **ex·ul·ta·tion** \ˌek-(ˌ)səl-'tā-shən, ˌeg-(ˌ)zəl-\ *n*

♦ crow, delight, glory, joy, rejoice, triumph

ex·ul·tant \-'zəlt-ᵊnt\ *adj* ♦ : filled with or expressing great joy or triumph

♦ jubilant, rejoicing, triumphant

ex·urb \'ek-ˌsərb, 'eg-ˌzərb\ *n* : a region outside a city and its suburbs inhabited chiefly by well-to-do families — **ex·ur·ban** \ek-'sər-bən, eg-'zər-\ *adj*

ex·urb·an·ite \ek-'sər-bə-ˌnīt; eg-'zər-\ *n* : one who lives in an exurb

ex·ur·bia \ek-'sər-bē-ə, eg-'zer-\ *n* ♦ : the generalized region of exurbs

♦ environs, outskirts, suburbia

-ey — see -Y

¹**eye** \'ī\ *n* **1** : an organ of sight typically consisting in vertebrates of a globular structure that is located in a socket of the skull, is lined with a sensitive retina, and is normally paired **2** : skill or ability dependent upon eyesight : VISION, PERCEPTION; *also* : faculty of discrimination ⟨an ~ for bargains⟩ **3 a** ♦ : a way of looking at or thinking about something : JUDGMENT — often used in pl. ⟨in the ~s of the law⟩ **b** ♦ : an attentive or critical observation **4 a** : something having an appearance suggesting an eye ⟨the ~ of a needle⟩ **b** : an undeveloped bud (as on a potato) **5 a** : the calm center of a cyclone **b** ♦ : an important or pivotal point — **eyed** \'īd\ *adj*

♦ [3a] belief, conviction, feeling, judgment (*or* judgement), mind, notion, opinion, persuasion, sentiment, verdict, view
♦ [3b] cast, gander, glance, glimpse, look, regard, sight, view
♦ [5b] base, center (*or* centre), core, cynosure, focus, heart, hub, mecca, nucleus, seat

²**eye** *vb* **eyed; eye·ing** *or* **ey·ing** ♦ : to look at

♦ distinguish, espy, look, note, notice, observe, perceive, regard, remark, see, sight, spy, view, witness

¹**eye·ball** \'ī-₁bȯl\ *n* : the globular capsule of the vertebrate eye

²**eyeball** *vb* : to look at intently

eye·brow \-₁braủ\ *n* : the ridge over the eye or the hair growing on it

eye·drop·per \-₁drä-pər\ *n* : DROPPER 2

eye·glass \-₁glas\ *n* ♦ : a lens worn to aid vision; *also, pl* : GLASS-ES

♦ **eyeglasses** glasses, spectacles

eye·lash \-₁lash\ *n* **1** : the fringe of hair edging the eyelid — usu. used in pl. **2** : a single hair of the eyelashes

eye·let \-lət\ *n* **1** : a small hole intended for ornament or for passage of a cord or lace **2** : a typically metal ring for reinforcing an eyelet : GROMMET

eye·lid \-₁lid\ *n* : either of the movable folds of skin and muscle that can be closed over the eyeball

eye·lin·er \-₁lī-nər\ *n* : makeup used to emphasize the contour of the eyes

eye–open·er \-₁ō-pə-nər\ *n* : something startling or surprising

eye–open·ing *adj* ♦ : that which opens the eyes (as with astonishment) : surprising or enlightening

♦ amazing, astonishing, astounding, startling, stunning, surprising

eye·piece \-₁pēs\ *n* : the lens or combination of lenses at the eye end of an optical instrument

eye shadow *n* : a colored cosmetic applied to the eyelids to accent the eyes

eye·sight \-₁sīt\ *n* : the process, power, or function of seeing : SIGHT, VISION

eye·sore \-₁sȯr\ *n* ♦ : something offensive to view

♦ fright, horror, mess, monstrosity, sight

eye·strain \-₁strān\ *n* : weariness or a strained state of the eye

eye·tooth \-'tüth\ *n* : a canine tooth of the upper jaw

eye·wash \-₁wȯsh, -₁wäsh\ *n* **1** : an eye lotion **2** : misleading or deceptive statements, actions, or procedures

eye·wit·ness \-'wit-nəs\ *n* : a person who actually sees something happen

Ez *or* **Ezr** *abbr* Ezra

Ezech *abbr* Ezechiel

Eze·chiel \i-'zē-kyəl\ *n* : EZEKIEL

Ezek *abbr* Ezekiel

Eze·kiel \i-'zē-kyəl\ *n* : a book of Jewish and Christian Scripture

e-zine \'ē-₁zēn\ *n* : an online magazine

Ez·ra \'ez-rə\ *n* : a book of Jewish and Christian Scripture

F

¹**f** \'ef\ *n, pl* **f's** *or* **fs** \'efs\ *often cap* **1** : the 6th letter of the English alphabet **2** : a grade rating a student's work as failing

²**f** *abbr, often cap* **1** Fahrenheit **2** false **3** family **4** farad **5** female **6** feminine **7** forte **8** French **9** frequency **10** Friday

³**f** *symbol* focal length

F *symbol* fluorine

FAA *abbr* Federal Aviation Administration

fab \'fab\ *adj* : FABULOUS

Fa·bi·an \'fā-bē-ən\ *adj* : of, relating to, or being a society of socialists organized in England in 1884 to spread socialist principles gradually — **Fabian** *n* — **Fa·bi·an·ism** *n*

fa·ble \'fā-bəl\ *n* **1** : a legendary story of supernatural happenings **2** : a narration intended to teach a lesson; *esp* : one in which animals speak and act like people **3** : FALSEHOOD **4** : the plot, story, or connected series of events forming the theme of a literary work

fa·bled \'fā-bəld\ *adj* **1** : FICTITIOUS **2** ♦ : told or celebrated in fable ⟨~ deeds⟩

♦ fabulous, legendary, mythical

fab·ric \'fa-brik\ *n* **1** : STRUCTURE, FRAMEWORK ⟨the ~ of society⟩ **2** : CLOTH; *also* : a material that resembles cloth

fab·ri·cate \'fa-bri-₁kāt\ *vb* **-cat·ed; -cat·ing** **1** ♦ : to think up or imagine : concoct mentally : INVENT **2** ♦ : to make up for the sake of deception **3** : to form, make, or create by combining parts or elements : CONSTRUCT ⟨~ tools⟩ **4** ♦ : to form by art and labor

♦ [1] concoct, contrive, cook up, devise, invent, make up, manufacture, think up ♦ [2] fib, lie, prevaricate ♦ [4] fashion, form, frame, make, manufacture, produce

fab·ri·ca·tion *n* **1** ♦ : the invention or utterance of something calculated to deceive **2** ♦ : a product of the imagination

♦ [1] falsehood, fib, lie, story, tale, untruth, whopper ♦ [2] fantasy, fiction, figment, invention

fab·u·lous \'fa-byə-ləs\ *adj* **1** : resembling a fable **2** ♦ : told in or based on fable **3** : like the contents of fables in being so marvelous, incredible, absurd, extreme, exaggerated, or approaching the impossible **4** : not real, actual, or historical **5** ♦ : outstanding or remarkable esp. in some acceptable or pleasing quality — **fab·u·lous·ly** *adv*

♦ [2] fabled, legendary, mythical ♦ [5] excellent, grand, great, sensational, splendid, superb, superior, swell, terrific, unsurpassed, wonderful

fac *abbr* **1** facsimile **2** faculty

fa·cade *also* **fa·çade** \fə-'säd\ *n* **1** : the principal face or front of a building **2** ♦ : a false, superficial, or artificial appearance or effect ⟨a ~ of composure⟩ **3** ♦ : a surface or front

♦ [2] act, airs, front, guise, masquerade, pose, pretense, put-on, semblance, show ♦ [3] face, front

¹**face** \'fās\ *n* **1** : the front part of the head **2** : PRESENCE ⟨in the ~ of danger⟩ **3** ♦ : facial expression : LOOK ⟨put a sad ~ on⟩ **4** ♦ : a deliberate or involuntary distortion of the countenance expressive of some feeling : GRIMACE ⟨made a ~⟩ **5** : outward appearance ⟨looks easy on the ~ of it⟩ **6** : CONFIDENCE; *also* : BOLDNESS **7** : DIGNITY, PRESTIGE ⟨afraid to lose ~⟩ **8** ♦ : a front, upper, or outer surface or a surface presented to view or regarded as principal : SURFACE; *esp* : a front, principal, or bounding surface ⟨~ of a cliff⟩ ⟨the ~s of a cube⟩ — **faced** \'fāst, 'fā-səd\ *adj*

♦ [3] cast, countenance, expression, look, visage ♦ [4] frown, grimace, pout, scowl ♦ [8] facade, front ♦ [8] exterior, outside, skin, surface, veneer

²**face** *vb* **faced; fac·ing** **1** ♦ : to confront brazenly **2** : to line near the edge esp. with a different material; *also* : to cover the front or surface of ⟨~ a building with marble⟩ **3** ♦ : to meet or bring in direct contact or confrontation ⟨faced the problem⟩ **4** ♦ : to stand or sit with the face toward ⟨~ the sun⟩ **5** : to have the front oriented toward ⟨a house *facing* the park⟩ **6** : to have as or be a prospect ⟨~ a grim future⟩ **7** : to turn the face or body in a specified direction **8** : to bring directly to the attention of — **face the music** : to meet the unpleasant consequences of one's actions

♦ [1] beard, brave, brazen, confront, dare, defy ♦ [3] battle, encounter, engage, meet, take on ♦ [4] front, look, point

face·down \₁fās-'daủn\ *adv* : with the face downward

face·less \-ləs\ *n* **1** : lacking a face **2** : lacking character or individuality

face–lift \'fās-₁lift\ *n* **1** : plastic surgery on the face and neck to remove defects (as wrinkles) typical of aging : a cosmetic surgical operation for removal of facial defects (as wrinkles) typical of aging **2** : MODERNIZATION — **face–lift** *vb*

face–off \'fās-₁ȯf\ *n* **1** : a method of beginning play by dropping a ball or puck (as in hockey) between two opposing players each of whom attempts to control it **2** ♦ : the clashing of forces or ideas : CONFRONTATION

♦ battle, combat, conflict, contest, duel, rivalry, struggle

face off *vb* ♦ : to be or come into opposition or competition

♦ battle, compete, contend, fight, race, vie

fac·et \'fa-sət\ *n* **1 :** a small plane surface of a cut gem **2 ♦ :** any of the definable aspects that make up a subject (as of contemplation) or an object (as of consideration) : ASPECT, PHASE

♦ [2] angle, aspect, hand, phase, side

fa·ce·tious \fə-'sē-shəs\ *adj* **1 ♦ :** joking often inappropriately ⟨∼ remarks⟩ **2 ♦ :** characterized by pleasantry or levity : exciting laughter : JOCULAR — **fa·ce·tious·ly** *adv*

♦ [1] flip, flippant, pert, smart ♦ [2] clever, humorous, jocular, smart, witty

fa·ce·tious·ness *n* ♦ **:** the quality or state of being facetious

♦ flightiness, flippancy, frivolity, levity, lightness

¹**fa·cial** \'fā-shəl\ *adj* **1 :** of or relating to the face **2 :** used to improve the appearance of the face
²**facial** *n* **:** a facial treatment
fac·ile \'fa-səl\ *adj* **1 ♦ :** easily accomplished, handled, or attained **2 :** SIMPLISTIC **3 :** readily manifested and often insincere ⟨∼ prose⟩ **4 :** READY, FLUENT ⟨a ∼ writer⟩

♦ easy, effortless, fluent, fluid, light, painless, ready, simple, smooth, snap, soft

fa·cil·i·tate \fə-'si-lə-ˌtāt\ *vb* **-tat·ed; -tat·ing** ♦ **:** to make easier — **fa·cil·i·ta·tion** \-ˌsi-lə-'tā-shən\ *n* — **fa·cil·i·ta·tor** \-'si-lə-ˌtā-tər\ *n*

♦ ease, loosen, smooth, unclog

fa·cil·i·ty \fə-'si-lə-tē\ *n, pl* **-ties** **1 :** the quality of being easily performed **2 :** ease in performance : APTITUDE **3 :** PLIANCY **4 :** something that makes easier an action, operation, or course of conduct; *also* : REST ROOM — often used in pl. **5 ♦ :** something (as a hospital) built or installed for a particular purpose

♦ complex, establishment, installation

fac·ing \'fā-siŋ\ *n* **1 :** a lining at the edge esp. of a garment **2** *pl* **:** the collar, cuffs, and trimmings of a uniform coat **3 :** an ornamental or protective layer **4 :** material for facing
fac·sim·i·le \fak-'si-mə-lē\ *n* **1 ♦ :** an exact copy **2 :** a system of transmitting and reproducing printed matter or pictures by means of signals sent over telephone lines

♦ carbon copy, double, duplicate, image, match, replica, reproduction

fact \'fakt\ *n* **1 :** DEED; *esp* : CRIME ⟨accessory after the ∼⟩ **2 :** the quality of being actual **3 :** something that exists or occurs **4 ♦ :** a piece of information — **in fact :** in truth

♦ detail, particular, point

fac·tion \'fak-shən\ *n* ♦ **:** a group or combination (as in a government) acting together within and usu. against a larger body — **fac·tion·al·ism** \-shə-nə-ˌli-zəm\ *n*

♦ bloc, body, coalition, combination, combine, party, sect, set, side, wing

fac·tious \'fak-shəs\ *adj* **1 :** of, relating to, or caused by faction **2 :** inclined to faction or the formation of factions : causing dissension
fac·ti·tious \fak-'ti-shəs\ *adj* **1 a ♦ :** produced by human art, skill, or effort **b :** not natural or real : SHAM ⟨a ∼ display of grief⟩ **2 :** not natural or spontaneous

♦ artificial, fake, faux, imitation, mock, sham, synthetic

fac·toid \'fak-ˌtóid\ *n* **1 :** an invented fact believed to be true because of its appearance in print **2 :** a brief usu. trivial fact
¹**fac·tor** \'fak-tər\ *n* **1 :** a person that acts or transacts business for another : AGENT **2 ♦ :** something that actively contributes to a result ⟨a ∼ in her decision⟩ **3 :** GENE **4 :** any of the numbers or symbols in mathematics that when multiplied together form a product; *esp* : any of the integers that divide a given integer without a remainder

♦ [1] agent, attorney, delegate, deputy, representative ♦ [2] component, constituent, element, ingredient, member

²**factor** *vb* **1 :** to work as a factor **2 :** to find the mathematical factors of and esp. the prime mathematical factors of
¹**fac·to·ri·al** \fak-'tōr-ē-əl\ *adj* **:** of, relating to, or being a factor
²**factorial** *n* **:** the product of all the positive integers from 1 to a given integer *n*
fac·to·ry \'fak-trē, -tə-rē\ *n, pl* **-ries** **1 :** a trading post where resident brokers trade **2 ♦ :** a building or group of buildings used for manufacturing

♦ mill, plant, shop, works, workshop

fac·to·tum \fak-'tō-təm\ *n* **:** a person (as a servant) having numerous or varied duties

facts of life : the physiological processes and behavior involved in sex and reproduction
fac·tu·al \'fak-chə-wəl\ *adj* **1 ♦ :** of or relating to facts **2 ♦ :** based on fact — **fac·tu·al·ly** *adv*

♦ [1] actual, concrete, existent, real, true, very ♦ [2] documentary, literal, nonfictional, objective, true

fac·ul·ty \'fa-kəl-tē\ *n, pl* **-ties** **1 a ♦ :** ability to act or do **b ♦ :** natural aptitude **2 :** one of the powers of the mind or body ⟨the ∼ of hearing⟩ **3 :** the teachers in a school or college or one of its divisions

♦ [1a] ability, capability, capacity, competence ♦ [1b] aptitude, endowment, flair, genius, gift, knack, talent

fad \'fad\ *n* ♦ **:** a practice or interest followed for a time with exaggerated zeal : CRAZE — **fad·dist** *n*

♦ craze, mode, rage, style, trend, vogue

fad·dish \'fa-dish\ *adj* ♦ **:** constituting or resembling a fad — **fad·dish·ly** *adv*

♦ fashionable, hot, in, modish, popular, vogue

¹**fade** \'fād\ *vb* **fad·ed; fad·ing** **1 :** WITHER **2 ♦ :** to lose or cause to lose freshness or brilliance of color **3 ♦ :** to sink away : VANISH **4 :** to grow dim or faint

♦ [2] blanch, bleach, blench, dull, pale, wash out, whiten ♦ [3] disappear, dissolve, evaporate, flee, go, melt, vanish

²**fade** *n* **:** a short haircut in which hair on top of the head stands high
FADM *abbr* fleet admiral
fae·cal, fae·ces *chiefly Brit var of* FECAL, FECES
fae·rie *also* **fa·ery** \'fā-rē, 'far-ē\ *n, pl* **fa·er·ies** **1 :** FAIRYLAND **2 :** FAIRY
¹**fag** \'fag\ *vb* **fagged; fag·ging** **1 :** to work hard : DRUDGE **2 ♦ :** to tire by strenuous activity : TIRE, EXHAUST

♦ burn out, do in, drain, exhaust, fatigue, tire, tucker, wash out, wear, wear out, weary

²**fag** *n* ♦ **:** one who is obliged to do menial work : DRUDGE

♦ drudge, peon, toiler, worker

³**fag** *n* **:** an English public-school boy who acts as servant to another
⁴**fag** *vb* **:** to act as a servant to another esp. in an English public school
⁵**fag** *n* **:** CIGARETTE
fag end *n* **1 ♦ :** a worn, poor, or useless ending or remnant unlikely to afford either pleasure or profit : REMNANT **2 :** the extreme end **3 :** the last part or coarser end of a web of cloth **4 :** the untwisted end of a rope

♦ end, leftover, remainder, remnant, scrap

fag·ot *or* **fag·got** \'fa-gət\ *n* **:** a bundle of sticks or twigs
fag·ot·ing *or* **fag·got·ing** *n* **:** an embroidery produced by tying threads in hourglass-shaped clusters
Fah *or* **Fahr** *abbr* Fahrenheit
Fahr·en·heit \'far-ən-ˌhīt\ *adj* **:** relating to, conforming to, or having a thermometer scale with the boiling point of water at 212 degrees and the freezing point at 32 degrees above zero
fa·ience *or* **fa·ïence** \fä-'äns\ *n* **:** earthenware decorated with opaque colored glazes
¹**fail** \'fāl\ *vb* **1 ♦ :** to become feeble; *esp* : to decline in health **2 :** to die away **3 :** to stop functioning **4 ♦ :** to fall short ⟨∼ed in his duty⟩ **5 :** to be or become absent or inadequate **6 ♦ :** to be unsuccessful **7 :** to become bankrupt **8 ♦ :** to disappoint the expectations or trust of **9 :** NEGLECT

♦ [1] decay, droop, flag, go, lag, languish, sag, waste, weaken, wilt ♦ [3] break, break down, conk, crash, cut out, die, stall *Ant* start (up) ♦ [4, 8] cheat, disappoint, dissatisfy, let down ♦ [6] collapse, flop, flunk, fold, wash out *Ant* succeed

²**fail** *n* **:** FAILURE ⟨without ∼⟩
¹**fail·ing** \'fā-liŋ\ *n* ♦ **:** a usu. slight or insignificant defect in character, conduct, or ability : WEAKNESS, SHORTCOMING

♦ demerit, fault, foible, frailty, shortcoming, vice, weakness

²**failing** *prep* **:** in the absence or lack of
faille \'fī(-ə)l\ *n* **:** a somewhat shiny closely woven ribbed fabric (as silk)
fail–safe \'fāl-ˌsāf\ *adj* **1 :** incorporating a counteractive feature for a possible source of failure **2 :** having no chance of failure — **fail–safe** *n*
fail·ure \'fāl-yər\ *n* **1 ♦ :** a failing to do or perform **2 :** a state of inability to perform a normal function adequately ⟨heart ∼⟩; *also* : an abrupt cessation of functioning ⟨a power ∼⟩ **3 :** a fracturing or giving way under stress **4 ♦ :** a lack of success

5 : BANKRUPTCY **6** ♦ : a falling short : DEFICIENCY ⟨crop ～⟩ **7** : DETERIORATION, DECAY **8** ♦ : one that has failed

♦ [1] default, delinquency, dereliction, neglect, negligence, oversight ♦ [4] collapse, crash, cropper, defeat, fizzle, nonsuccess *Ant* accomplishment, achievement, success ♦ [6] dearth, deficiency, deficit, famine, inadequacy, insufficiency, lack, paucity, poverty, scantiness, scarcity, shortage, want ♦ [8] bust, catastrophe, debacle, dud, fiasco, fizzle, flop, loser, washout *Ant* hit, smash, success, winner

¹**fain** \ˈfān\ *adj* **1** *archaic* : GLAD; *also* : INCLINED **2** : being obliged or compelled
²**fain** *adv* **1** : with pleasure **2** : by preference
¹**faint** \ˈfānt\ *adj* **1** : COWARDLY, SPIRITLESS **2** : weak, dizzy, and likely to faint **3** ♦ : lacking vigor or strength : FEEBLE ⟨～ praise⟩ **4** ♦ : hardly perceptible : INDISTINCT, DIM — **faint·ly** *adv*

♦ [3] delicate, feeble, frail, infirm, slight, soft, wasted, weak ♦ [4] bleary, dim, foggy, fuzzy, hazy, indistinct, obscure, opaque, shadowy, unclear, vague *Ant* clear, definite

²**faint** *vb* ♦ : to lose consciousness

♦ black out, pass out, swoon *Ant* come around, come round, come to, revive

³**faint** *n* **1** : the action of fainting **2** ♦ : the condition of one who has fainted

♦ blackout, knockout, swoon

faint·heart·ed \ˌfānt-ˈhär-təd\ *adj* ♦ : lacking courage : TIMID

♦ fearful, mousy, shy, skittish, timid

faint·ness *n* ♦ : the quality or state of being faint; *esp* : a loss of strength or near loss of consciousness

♦ debility, feebleness, frailty, infirmity, languor, weakness

¹**fair** \ˈfer\ *adj* **1** ♦ : pleasing in appearance : BEAUTIFUL **2** : superficially pleasing : SPECIOUS **3** : CLEAN, PURE **4** : CLEAR, LEGIBLE **5** ♦ : not stormy or cloudy **6** ♦ : marked by impartiality and honesty : free from self-interest, prejudice, or favoritism : JUST **7** : conforming with the rules : ALLOWED; *also* : being within the foul lines ⟨～ ball⟩ **8** : open to legitimate pursuit or attack ⟨～ game⟩ **9** : giving promise of success or excellence : PROMISING, LIKELY ⟨a ～ chance of winning⟩ **10** : favorable to a ship's course ⟨a ～ wind⟩ **11** ♦ : light colored **12** ♦ : of middling quality **13** : significant in size ⟨a ～ amount of traffic⟩ — **fair·ness** *n*

♦ [1] attractive, beautiful, cute, handsome, lovely, pretty ♦ [5] clear, cloudless, sunny, sunshiny, unclouded *Ant* bleak, cloudy, overcast, stormy, sunless ♦ [6] disinterested, dispassionate, equal, equitable, impartial, just, nonpartisan, objective, square, unbiased, unprejudiced *Ant* biased, partisan, prejudiced, unequal, unjust ♦ [11] blond, flaxen, golden, sandy, straw ♦ [12] common, indifferent, mediocre, medium, middling, ordinary, passable, run-of-the-mill, second-rate, so-so

²**fair** *adv* **1** : in a fair manner ⟨play ～⟩ **2** *chiefly Brit* : FAIRLY 4
³**fair** *n* **1** ♦ : a gathering of buyers and sellers at a stated time and place for trade **2** ♦ : a competitive exhibition (as of farm products) **3** ♦ : a sale of assorted articles usu. for a charitable purpose **4** ♦ : an exhibition designed to promote available or planned products or services ⟨a book ～⟩ ⟨a job ～⟩

♦ [1, 2, 3, 4] display, exhibit, exhibition, exposition, show

fair·ground \ˌ-ˌgraund\ *n* : an area where outdoor fairs, circuses, or exhibitions are held
fair·ing \ˈfar-iŋ\ *n* : a structure for producing a smooth outline and reducing drag (as on an airplane)
fair·ly \ˈfar-lē\ *adv* **1** : HANDSOMELY **2** : in a manner of speaking ⟨～ bursting with pride⟩ **3** : without bias **4** : to a full degree or extent : PLAINLY, DISTINCTLY **5** ♦ : moderately well : SOMEWHAT, RATHER ⟨a ～ easy job⟩

♦ enough, kind of, moderately, pretty, quite, rather, somewhat, sort of, so-so

fair–spo·ken \ˈfar-ˈspō-kən\ *adj* : pleasant and courteous in speech
fair–trade \ˌ-ˈtrād\ *adj* : of, relating to, or being an agreement between a producer and a seller that branded merchandise will be sold at or above a specified price — **fair–trade** *vb*
fair·way \ˌ-ˌwā\ *n* : the mowed part of a golf course between tee and green
fairy \ˈfer-ē\ *n, pl* **fair·ies** ♦ : an imaginary being of folklore and romance usu. having diminutive human form and magic powers — **fairy** *adj*

♦ brownie, dwarf, elf, fay, gnome, hobgoblin, leprechaun, pixie, puck, troll

fairy·land \ˌ-ˌland\ *n* **1** : the land of fairies **2** : a beautiful or charming place
fairy tale *n* **1** : a children's story usu. about mythical beings (as fairies) **2** ♦ : an implausible, incredible, or lying story : a statement designed to delude or mislead : FIB

♦ fabrication, falsehood, falsity, fib, lie, story, untruth

fait ac·com·pli \ˈfāt-ˌä-ˌkōⁿ-ˈplē\ *n, pl* **faits accomplis** *same or* -ˈplēz\ : a thing accomplished and presumably irreversible
faith \ˈfāth\ *n, pl* **faiths** \ˈfāths, ˈfāthz\ **1** ♦ : allegiance to duty or a person : LOYALTY **2** ♦ : belief and trust in God **3** ♦ : complete trust **4** ♦ : a system of religious beliefs

♦ [1] allegiance, constancy, dedication, devotion, faithfulness, fastness, fealty, fidelity, loyalty, steadfastness ♦ [2] devotion, piety, religion *Ant* atheism, godlessness ♦ [3] confidence, credence, stock, trust ♦ [4] creed, cult, persuasion, religion

faith·ful \ˌ-fəl\ *adj* **1** ♦ : true and constant in affection or allegiance **2** ♦ : conforming to the facts or to an original — **faith·ful·ly** *adv*

♦ [1] constant, devoted, loyal, pious, staunch, steadfast, steady, true, true-blue *Ant* disloyal, false, fickle, inconstant, perfidious, traitorous, treacherous ♦ [2] accurate, authentic, exact, precise, right, strict, true, veracious *Ant* false, imprecise, inaccurate, inexact

faith·ful·ness *n* ♦ : the quality or state of being faithful

♦ allegiance, constancy, dedication, devotion, fealty, fidelity, loyalty, steadfastness

faith·less \ˈfāth-ləs\ *adj* **1** ♦ : false to promises or agreements : DISLOYAL **2** : not to be relied on — **faith·less·ly** *adv*

♦ disloyal, false, fickle, inconstant, perfidious, traitorous, treacherous, unfaithful, untrue *Ant* constant, devoted, loyal, staunch, steadfast, steady, true

faith·less·ness *n* ♦ : the quality or condition of being faithless

♦ betrayal, disloyalty, falsity, infidelity, perfidy, treachery, treason

fa·ji·ta \fə-ˈhē-tə\ *n* : a marinated strip usu. of beef or chicken grilled or broiled and served usu. with a flour tortilla and savory fillings
¹**fake** \ˈfāk\ *adj* ♦ : one that is not what it purports to be : SHAM

♦ bogus, counterfeit, false, inauthentic, phony, sham, spurious ♦ artificial, faux, imitation, mock, sham, synthetic

²**fake** *n* **1 a** ♦ : someone or something that is not genuine **b** ♦ : one that assumes false identity or title for the purpose of deception **2** : a simulated move in sports (as a pretended pass)

♦ [1a] counterfeit, forgery, hoax, humbug, phony, sham ♦ [1b] charlatan, fraud, hoaxer, humbug, phony, pretender, quack

³**fake** *vb* **faked; fak·ing 1** : to treat so as to falsify **2** ♦ : to counterfeit or make a counterfeit of in order to deceive **3** : to deceive (an opponent) in a sports contest by making a fake — **fak·er** *n*

♦ affect, assume, counterfeit, feign, pretend, profess, put on, sham, simulate

fa·kir \fə-ˈkir\ *n* **1** : a Muslim mendicant : DERVISH **2** : a wandering Hindu ascetic
fal·con \ˈfal-kən, ˈfol-\ *n* **1** : a hawk trained for use in falconry **2** : any of various swift long-winged long-tailed hawks having a notched beak and often inhabiting open areas
fal·con·ry \ˈfal-kən-rē, ˈfol-\ *n* **1** : the art of training hawks to hunt in cooperation with a person **2** : the sport of hunting with hawks — **fal·con·er** *n*
¹**fall** \ˈfol\ *vb* **fell** \ˈfel\; **fall·en** \ˈfo-lən\; **fall·ing 1** ♦ : to descend freely by the force of gravity **2** : to hang freely **3** : to come or go as if by falling ⟨darkness *fell*⟩ **4** : to become uttered **5** ♦ : to lower or become lowered : DROP ⟨her eyes *fell*⟩ **6** ♦ : to leave an erect position suddenly and involuntarily **7** : STUMBLE, STRAY **8** : to drop down wounded or dead esp. in battle **9** ♦ : to become captured ⟨the city *fell* to the enemy⟩ **10** : to suffer ruin, defeat, or failure **11** : to commit an immoral act **12** : to move or extend in a downward direction **13** ♦ : to become quiet or less : SUBSIDE, ABATE **14** : to decline in quality, activity, quantity, or value **15** : to assume a look of shame or dejection ⟨her face *fell*⟩ **16** : to occur at a certain time **17** : to come by chance **18** : DEVOLVE ⟨the duties *fell* to him⟩ **19** : to have the proper place or station ⟨the accent ～s on the first syllable⟩ **20** : to come within the scope of something **21** : to pass

from one condition to another ⟨*fell* ill⟩ **22** : to set about heartily or actively ⟨∼ to work⟩ — **fall all over oneself** *or* **fall over backward** : to display excessive eagerness — **fall flat** : to produce no response or result — **fall for 1** : to fall in love with **2** : to become a victim of — **fall foul** : to have a quarrel : CLASH — **fall from grace** : BACKSLIDE — **fall into line** : to comply with a certain course of action — **fall short 1** : to be deficient **2** : to fail to attain

♦ [1, 5] decline, descend, drop, lower, settle, sink *Ant* rise ♦ [6] slip, stumble, topple, trip, tumble *Ant* get up, rise, stand (up) ♦ [9] capitulate, give up, knuckle under, submit, succumb, surrender *Ant* stand ♦ [13] abate, decline, decrease, diminish, dwindle, ebb, lessen, recede, subside, wane

²**fall** *n* **1** ♦ : the act of falling **2** : a falling out, off, or away : DROPPING **3** : AUTUMN **4** : a thing or quantity that falls ⟨a light ∼ of snow⟩ ⟨a ∼ of 20% in the value of the stock⟩ **5** ♦ : loss of greatness, power, status, influence, or dominion **6** : the surrender or capture of a besieged place **7** : departure from virtue or goodness **8** : SLOPE **9** : WATERFALL — usu. used in pl. **10** ♦ : a decrease in size, quantity, degree, or value ⟨a ∼ in price⟩ **11** : the distance which something falls **12** : an act of forcing a wrestler's shoulders to the mat; *also* : a bout of wrestling

♦ [1] descent, dip, dive, down, drop, plunge ♦ [1] slip, spill, stumble, tumble ♦ [5] comedown, decline, descent, down, downfall ♦ [5] decline, degradation ♦ [10] decline, decrease, drop, loss, reduction, shrinkage

fal·la·cious \fə-ˈlā-shəs\ *adj* **1** ♦ : embodying a fallacy ⟨a ∼ argument⟩ **2** ♦ : tending to deceive or mislead

♦ [1] illogical, invalid, irrational, unsound, weak ♦ [2] deceptive, false, misleading, specious

fal·la·cy \ˈfa-lə-sē\ *n, pl* **-cies 1** ♦ : a false or mistaken idea **2** : an often plausible argument using false or illogical reasoning **3** : erroneous or fallacious character

♦ error, falsehood, falsity, illusion, misconception, myth, untruth *Ant* truth, verity

fall back *vb* ♦ : to give way : RETREAT, RECEDE

♦ back, recede, retire, retreat, withdraw

fall guy *n* **1** : one that is easily duped **2** : one who assumes or on whom is placed the blame or responsibility : SCAPEGOAT
fal·li·ble \ˈfa-lə-bəl\ *adj* **1** : liable to be erroneous **2** : capable of making a mistake — **fal·li·bly** \-blē\ *adv*
fall·ing–out \ˌfȯ-liŋ-ˈau̇t\ *n, pl* **fallings–out** *or* **falling–outs** : QUARREL
falling star *n* : METEOR
fal·lo·pi·an tube \fə-ˈlō-pē-ən-\ *n, often cap F* : either of the pair of anatomical tubes that carry the eggs from the ovary to the uterus
fall·out \ˈfȯ-ˌlau̇t\ *n* **1** : the often radioactive particles that result from a nuclear explosion and descend through the air **2** : a secondary and often lingering effect or result
fall out *vb* ♦ : to have a quarrel : QUARREL

♦ argue, bicker, dispute, quarrel, row, scrap, spat, squabble, wrangle

¹**fal·low** \ˈfa-(ˌ)lō\ *n* : fallow land; *also* : the state or period of being fallow — **fallow** *vb*
²**fallow** *adj* **1** : left without tilling or sowing after plowing **2** : characterized by a state of creative or recuperative rest or dormancy : DORMANT, INACTIVE ⟨a writer's ∼ period⟩

♦ dead, dormant, idle, inactive, inert, inoperative

false \ˈfȯls\ *adj* **fals·er; fals·est 1** ♦ : not genuine : artificially made or assumed **2** : intentionally untrue **3** ♦ : adjusted or made so as to deceive ⟨∼ scales⟩ **4 a** ♦ : tending to mislead : DECEPTIVE ⟨∼ promises⟩ **b** ♦ : assumed or designed to deceive ⟨∼ not true ⟨∼ concepts⟩ **6** ♦ : not faithful or loyal : TREACHEROUS **7** : not essential or permanent ⟨∼ front⟩ **8** : inaccurate in pitch **9** : based on mistaken ideas — **false·ly** *adv*

♦ [1] artificial, bogus, fake, imitation, mechanical, mock, phony, sham, synthetic, unnatural ♦ [3, 4b] counterfeit, crooked, deceitful, dishonest, fraudulent, phony, sham, spurious ♦ [4a] deceitful, deceptive, misleading, specious ♦ [5] erroneous, inaccurate, incorrect, inexact, untrue, wrong *Ant* accurate, correct, right, sound, true ♦ [6] disloyal, faithless, traitorous, treacherous, unfaithful

false·hood \ˈfȯls-ˌhu̇d\ *n* **1** ♦ : something that is untrue; *esp* : an untrue statement : LIE **2** : absence of truth or accuracy **3** : the practice of lying

♦ error, fallacy, falsity, illusion, misconception, myth, untruth

♦ fabrication, fairy tale, falsity, fib, lie, mendacity, prevarication, story, tale, untruth, whopper

false·ness *n* **1** ♦ : the quality or state of being false **2** ♦ : an instance of treachery : an act of perfidy or treason

♦ [1] fallacy, falseness, falsity, untruth ♦ [2] betrayal, disloyalty, infidelity, perfidy, treachery, treason, unfaithfulness

fal·set·to \fȯl-ˈse-tō\ *n, pl* **-tos** : an artificially high voice; *esp* : an artificial singing voice that overlaps and extends above the range of the full voice esp. of a tenor
fal·si·fy \ˈfȯl-sə-ˌfī\ *vb* **-fied; -fy·ing 1** : to prove to be false **2** ♦ : to alter so as to deceive **3** : LIE; *also* : MISREPRESENT — **fal·si·fi·able** \ˌfȯl-sə-ˈfī-ə-bəl\ *adj* — **fal·si·fi·ca·tion** \ˌfȯl-sə-fə-ˈkā-shən\ *n*

♦ color (*or* colour), distort, garble, misinterpret, misrepresent, misstate, pervert, twist, warp

fal·si·ty \ˈfȯl-sə-tē\ *n* **1** ♦ : something false **2** ♦ : the quality or state of being false

♦ [1] fallacy, falsehood, fib, lie, myth, tale, untruth ♦ [2] betrayal, disloyalty, infidelity, perfidy, treachery, treason, unfaithfulness

fal·ter \ˈfȯl-tər\ *vb* **1** ♦ : to move unsteadily : TOTTER **2** : to hesitate in speech : STAMMER **3** ♦ : to hesitate in purpose or action : WAVER **4** : to lose effectiveness ⟨a ∼ing business⟩ — **fal·ter·ing·ly** *adv*

♦ [1] seesaw, sway, teeter, totter, waver, wobble ♦ [3] hesitate, shilly-shally, teeter, vacillate, waver

fam *abbr* **1** familiar **2** family
fame \ˈfām\ *n* ♦ : public reputation : RENOWN

♦ celebrity, notoriety, renown *Ant* anonymity, obscurity

famed \ˈfāmd\ *adj* ♦ : known widely and well

♦ celebrated, famous, noted, prominent, renowned, well-known

fa·mil·ial \fə-ˈmil-yəl\ *adj* **1** : of, relating to, or suggestive of a family **2** : tending to occur in more members of a family than expected by chance alone ⟨a ∼ disorder⟩
¹**fa·mil·iar** \fə-ˈmil-yər\ *n* **1** ♦ : an intimate associate **2** : a spirit held to attend and serve or guard a person **3** : one who frequents a place

♦ comrade, friend, intimate

²**familiar** *adj* **1** ♦ : closely acquainted : INTIMATE **2** : of or relating to a family **3** : INFORMAL ⟨a ∼ style⟩ **4** ♦ : overly free and unrestrained : PRESUMPTUOUS **5** ♦ : frequently seen or experienced ⟨a ∼ face⟩ **6** : of everyday occurrence **7** ♦ : having personal or intimate knowledge — often used with *with* — **fa·mil·iar·ly** *adv*

♦ [1] chummy, close, friendly, intimate, thick *Ant* distant ♦ [4] bold, forward, free, immodest, presumptuous ♦ [5] common, customary, everyday, frequent, ordinary, routine, usual ♦ [7] conversant, informed, knowledgeable, up-to-date *Ant* ignorant, unacquainted, unfamiliar, uninformed

fa·mil·iar·ise *Brit var of* FAMILIARIZE
fa·mil·iar·i·ty \fə-ˌmil-ˈyar-ə-tē, -ˌmi-lē-ˈar-\ *n, pl* **-ties 1** ♦ : close friendship : INTIMACY **2** : INFORMALITY **3** ♦ : an unduly bold or forward act or expression : IMPROPRIETY **4** : close acquaintance with something

♦ [1] closeness, intimacy, nearness *Ant* distance ♦ [3] gaffe, impropriety, indiscretion

fa·mil·iar·ize \fə-ˈmil-yə-ˌrīz\ *vb* **-ized; -iz·ing 1** : to make known through experience or repetition : remove strangeness from **2** : to make (someone) thoroughly acquainted

♦ acquaint, apprise, brief, clue, enlighten, fill in, inform, instruct, tell

fam·i·ly \ˈfam-lē, ˈfa-mə-\ *n, pl* **-lies 1** : a group of individuals living under one roof and under one head : HOUSEHOLD **2** : a group of persons of common ancestry : CLAN **3** ♦ : a group of things having common characteristics; *esp* : a group of related plants or animals ranking in biological classification above a genus and below an order **4** : a social unit usu. consisting of one or two parents and their children

♦ [2] blood, clan, folks, house, kin, kindred, kinfolk, line, lineage, people, race, stock, tribe ♦ [3] category, class, division, group, kind, set, type

family planning *n* : planning intended to determine the number and spacing of one's children by using birth control
family tree *n* ♦ : an account or history of the descent of a person,

family, or group from an ancestor or ancestors or from older forms : GENEALOGY; *also* : a genealogical diagram

♦ ancestry, bloodline, descent, genealogy, lineage, origin

fam·ine \'fa-mən\ *n* **1 :** an extreme scarcity of food **2** ♦ : a great shortage

♦ dearth, deficiency, deficit, failure, inadequacy, insufficiency, lack, paucity, poverty, scantiness, scarcity, shortage, want

fam·ish \'fa-mish\ *vb* **1 :** STARVE **2 :** to suffer for lack of something necessary

fam·ished *adj* ♦ : intensely hungry

♦ empty, hungry

fa·mous \'fā-məs\ *adj* **1** ♦ : widely known **2 :** honored for achievement **3 :** EXCELLENT, FIRST-RATE

♦ celebrated, famed, noted, notorious, prominent, renowned, well-known *Ant* anonymous, obscure, unknown

fa·mous·ly *adv* : SPLENDIDLY, EXCELLENTLY ⟨got along ∼⟩

¹**fan** \'fan\ *n* : a device (as a hand-waved triangular piece or a mechanism with blades) for producing a current of air

²**fan** *vb* **fanned; fan·ning** **1 :** to drive away the chaff from grain by winnowing **2 :** to move (air) with or as if with a fan **3 :** to direct a current of air upon ⟨∼ a fire⟩ **4 :** to stir up to activity : STIMULATE **5** ♦ : to spread like a fan — often used with *out* **6 :** to strike out in baseball

♦ *usu* **fan out** expand, extend, flare, open, radiate, spread, unfold

³**fan** *n* ♦ : an enthusiastic follower or admirer

♦ addict, aficionado, buff, devotee, enthusiast, fancier, lover

¹**fa·nat·ic** \fə-'na-tik\ *or* **fa·nat·i·cal** \-ti-kəl\ *adj* ♦ : marked by excessive enthusiasm and often intense uncritical devotion — **fa·nat·i·cism** \-tə-ˌsi-zəm\ *n*

♦ extreme, extremist, rabid, radical, revolutionary, ultra

²**fa·nat·ic** *n* ♦ : a person who is ardently attached to a cause, object, or pursuit; *esp* : a person exhibiting excessive enthusiasm and intense uncritical devotion usu. toward some controversial matter

♦ crusader, militant, partisan, zealot

fan·ci·er \'fan-sē-ər\ *n* **1** ♦ : one that has a special liking or interest **2 :** a person who breeds or grows some kind of animal or plant for points of excellence

♦ aficionado, buff, devotee, enthusiast, fan, lover

fan·ci·ful \'fan-si-fəl\ *adj* **1** ♦ : marked by, existing in, or given to unrestrained imagination or whim rather than reason **2 :** curiously made or shaped — **fan·ci·ful·ly** *adv*

♦ fantastic, fictitious, imaginary, made-up, pretend, unreal

¹**fan·cy** \'fan-sē\ *vb* **fan·cied; fan·cy·ing** **1** ♦ : to be pleased with esp. on account of external appearance or manners : LIKE **2** ♦ : to form a conception of : IMAGINE **3 :** to believe without evidence or certainty **4 :** to visualize or interpret as

♦ [1] delight, enjoy, like, love, relish ♦ [2] conceive, imagine, picture, visualize

²**fancy** *n, pl* **fancies** **1** ♦ : amorous fondness : love or desire; *also* : LOVE **2** ♦ : an opinion or notion formed without much reflection : WHIM, NOTION ⟨a passing ∼⟩ **3** ♦ : an image or representation of something formed in the mind

♦ [1] favor (*or* favour), fondness, like, liking, love, partiality, preference ♦ [2] caprice, notion, whim ♦ [3] chimera, conceit, delusion, dream, fantasy, figment, hallucination, illusion, phantasm, pipe dream, unreality, vision

³**fancy** *adj* **fan·ci·er; -est** **1 :** WHIMSICAL **2 :** not plain : ornamented and often elegant **3 :** of particular excellence **4 :** bred esp. for a showy appearance **5 :** EXCESSIVE **6** ♦ : executed with technical skill and style — **fan·ci·ly** \'fan-sə-lē\ *adv*

♦ complex, complicated, detailed, elaborate, intricate

fancy dress *n* : a costume (as for a masquerade) chosen to suit a fancy

fan·cy-free \ˌfan-sē-'frē\ *adj* : free from amorous attachment; *also* : free to imagine

fan·cy·work \'fan-sē-ˌwərk\ *n* : ornamental needlework (as embroidery)

fan·dan·go \fan-'daŋ-gō\ *n, pl* **-gos** **1 :** a lively Spanish or Spanish-American dance **2 :** TOMFOOLERY

fane \'fān\ *n* **1 :** TEMPLE **2 :** CHURCH

fan·fare \'fan-ˌfar\ *n* **1 :** a flourish of trumpets **2 :** a showy display

fan fiction *n* : stories involving fictional characters that are written by fans

fang \'faŋ\ *n* : a long sharp tooth; *esp* : a grooved or hollow tooth of a venomous snake — **fanged** \'faŋd\ *adj*

fan·light \'fan-ˌlīt\ *n* : a semicircular window with radiating bars like a fan that is set over a door or window

fan·ny \'fa-nē\ *n, pl* **fannies** : BUTTOCKS

fan·tail \'fan-ˌtāl\ *n* **1 :** a fan-shaped tail or end **2 :** an overhang at the stern of a ship

fan·ta·sia \fan-'tā-zhə, -zhē-ə, -zē-ə; ˌfan-tə-'zē-ə\ *n* : a musical composition free and fanciful in form

fan·ta·sise *chiefly Brit var of* FANTASIZE

fan·ta·size \'fan-tə-ˌsīz\ *vb* **-sized; -siz·ing** : IMAGINE, DAYDREAM

fan·tas·tic \fan-'tas-tik\ *also* **fan·tas·ti·cal** \-ti-kəl\ *adj* **1** ♦ : based on fantasy rather than reason : IMAGINARY, UNREAL **2** ♦ : conceived by unrestrained fancy **3** ♦ : exceedingly or unbelievably great **4** ♦ : exhibiting strange, grotesque, inappropriate, or startlingly novel characteristics — **fan·tas·ti·cal·ly** \-ti-k(ə-)lē\ *adv*

♦ [1] fanciful, imaginary, made-up, unreal ♦ [2] absurd, bizarre, fanciful, foolish, preposterous, unreal *Ant* realistic, reasonable ♦ [3] inconceivable, incredible, unbelievable, unimaginable ♦ [4] exotic, glamorous, marvelous (*or* marvellous), outlandish, romantic, strange

fan·ta·sy *also* **phan·ta·sy** \'fan-tə-sē\ *n, pl* **-sies** **1** ♦ : the free play of creative imagination as it affects perception and productivity usu. as expressed in an art form or as elicited by projective techniques of formal psychology : IMAGINATION, FANCY **2** ♦ : a product of the imagination : ILLUSION **3** ♦ : a chimerical or fantastic notion — **fantasy** *vb*

♦ [1] creativity, fancy, imagination, invention ♦ [2, 3] chimera, conceit, delusion, dream, fancy, figment, hallucination, illusion, phantasm, pipe dream, unreality, vision

FAQ \'fak, ˌef-ˌā-'kyü\ *n* : a document (as on a website) that provides answers to a list of typical user questions

¹**far** \'fär\ *adv* **far·ther** \-thər\ *or* **fur·ther** \'fər-\; **far·thest** *or* **fur·thest** \-thəst\ **1 :** at or to a considerable distance in space or time ⟨∼ from home⟩ **2 :** by a broad interval : WIDELY, MUCH ⟨∼ better⟩ **3 :** to or at a definite distance, point, or degree ⟨as ∼ as I know⟩ **4 :** to an advanced point or extent ⟨go ∼ in his field⟩ **5 :** to a great extent — **by far :** by a considerable margin — **far and away :** DECIDEDLY — **so far :** until now

²**far** *adj* **farther; farthest** **1** ♦ : remote in space or time **2 :** DIFFERENT **3 :** involving a long distance ⟨a ∼ journey⟩ **4 :** being the more distant of two ⟨on the ∼ side of the lake⟩

♦ distant, far-off, remote *Ant* close, near, nearby

far·ad \'far-ˌad, -əd\ *n* : a unit of capacitance equal to the capacitance of a capacitor having a potential difference of one volt between its plates when it is charged with one coulomb of electricity

far·away \'fär-ə-ˌwā\ *adj* **1 :** distant in space or time : DISTANT, REMOTE **2 :** DREAMY

farce \'färs\ *n* **1** ♦ : a broadly satirical comedy with an improbable plot **2 :** the humor characteristic of farce or pretense **3** ♦ : a ridiculous or empty display

♦ [1] comedy, humor (*or* humour), slapstick ♦ [3] caricature, joke, mockery, parody, sham, travesty

far·ci·cal \'fär-si-kəl\ *adj* ♦ : of, relating to, or resembling farce

♦ absurd, comical, funny, humorous, laughable, ludicrous, ridiculous, silly

far cry *n* **1 :** a long distance **2 :** something notably different ⟨a *far cry* from what we expected⟩

¹**fare** \'far\ *vb* **fared; far·ing** **1** ♦ : to go or travel : GO, TRAVEL **2** ♦ : to get along : make out or turn out : GET ALONG **3 :** to consume food : EAT, DINE

♦ [1] advance, go, proceed, progress, travel ♦ [2] cope, do, get along, make out, manage

²**fare** *n* **1 a** ♦ : a range or stock of food **b :** material provided for use, consumption, or enjoyment ⟨fine theatrical ∼⟩ **2 :** the price charged to transport a person **3 :** a person paying a fare : PASSENGER

♦ food, provender, provisions, viands, victuals

¹**fare·well** \far-'wel\ *vb imper* : get along well — used interjectionally to or by one departing

²**farewell** *n* **1** ♦ : a wish of well-being at parting : GOOD-BYE **2** ♦ : act of departure : LEAVE-TAKING

♦ [1] adieu, au revoir, bon voyage, good-bye ♦ [2] departure, leave-taking, parting

³fare·well \'far-ˌwel\ *adj* : PARTING, FINAL ⟨a ∼ concert⟩

far·fetched \'fär-'fecht\ *adj* : not easily or naturally deduced or introduced : IMPROBABLE ⟨∼ story⟩

far–flung \-'fləŋ\ *adj* ♦ : widely spread or distributed

♦ broad, expansive, extensive, far-reaching, widespread

fa·ri·na \fə-'rē-nə\ *n* : a fine meal (as of wheat) used in puddings or as a breakfast cereal

far·i·na·ceous \ˌfar-ə-'nā-shəs\ *adj* **1** : having a mealy texture or surface **2** : containing or rich in starch

¹farm \'färm\ *n* **1** : a tract of land used for raising crops or livestock **2** : a minor-league subsidiary of a major-league team

²farm *vb* ♦ : to use (land) as a farm ⟨∼ed 200 acres⟩; *also* : to raise crops or livestock

♦ cultivate, tend

farm·er *n* ♦ : a person who cultivates land or crops or raises livestock

♦ agriculturist, cultivator, grower, planter, tiller

farm·hand \'färm-ˌhand\ *n* : a farm laborer

farm·house \-ˌhaüs\ *n* : a dwelling on a farm

farm·ing \'fär-miŋ\ *n* : the occupation or business of a person who farms

farm·land \'färm-ˌland\ *n* : land used or suitable for farming

farm out *vb* : to turn over (as a task) to another

farm·stead \'färm-ˌsted\ *n* : a farm with its buildings

farm·yard \-ˌyärd\ *n* : land around or enclosed by farm buildings

far–off \'fär-'òf\ *adj* ♦ : remote in time or space : DISTANT

♦ distant, remote

fa·rouche \fə-'rüsh\ *adj* **1** : WILD **2** : marked by shyness and lack of polish

far–out \'fär-'aüt\ *adj* ♦ : very unconventional ⟨∼ clothes⟩

♦ bizarre, odd, outlandish, outré, peculiar, strange, wacky, weird, wild

far·ra·go \fə-'rä-gō, -'rä-\ *n, pl* **-goes** : a confused collection : MIXTURE

far·reach·ing \'fär-'rē-chiŋ\ *adj* ♦ : having a wide range or effect

♦ broad, extensive, widespread

far·ri·er \'fer-ē-ər\ *n* : a person who shoes horses

¹far·row \'far-ō\ *vb* : to give birth to a litter of pigs

²farrow *n* : a litter of pigs

far·see·ing \'fär-ˌsē-iŋ\ *adj* **1** : FARSIGHTED 1 **2** : FARSIGHTED 2

far·sight·ed \'fär-ˌsī-təd\ *adj* **1 a** : seeing or able to see to a great distance **b** ♦ : having foresight : able to anticipate and plan for the future **2** : JUDICIOUS, WISE, SHREWD **3** : affected with an eye condition in which vision is better for distant than near objects — **far·sight·ed·ness** *n*

♦ foresighted, prescient, provident

¹far·ther \'fär-<u>th</u>ər\ *adv* **1** ♦ : at or to a greater distance or more advanced point **2** : to a greater degree or extent

♦ beyond, further, yonder

²farther *adj* **1** : more distant **2** ♦ : going or extending beyond what exists : ADDITIONAL

♦ additional, another, more

far·ther·most \-ˌmōst\ *adj* : most remote : FARTHEST

¹far·thest \'fär-<u>th</u>əst\ *adj* ♦ : most distant

♦ extreme, outermost, ultimate, utmost

²farthest *adv* **1** : to or at the greatest distance : REMOTEST ⟨hit the ball ∼⟩ **2** : to the most advanced point **3** : by the greatest degree or extent : MOST

fas·cia *1 is usu* 'fä-sh(ē-)ə, *2 is usu* 'fa-\ *n, pl* **-ci·ae** \-shē-ˌē\ *or* **-cias 1** : a flat usu. horizontal part (as a band or board) of or on a building **2** : a sheet of connective tissue covering body structures (as muscles)

fas·ci·cle \'fa-si-kəl\ *n* **1** : a small or slender bundle (as of pine needles or nerve fiber) **2** : one of the divisions of a book published in parts — **fas·ci·cled** \-kəld\ *adj*

fas·ci·nate \'fas-ᵊn-ˌāt\ *vb* **-nat·ed; -nat·ing 1** : to transfix and hold spellbound by an irresistible power **2 a** ♦ : to have or exercise the power of charming, alluring, or enthralling **b** ♦ : engage and powerfully hold the attention or interest **3** : to be irresistibly attractive

♦ [2a, 2b] allure, beguile, captivate, charm, enchant, enthrall

♦ [2b] engage, engross, grip, interest, intrigue, involve, occupy

fascinating *adj* ♦ : holding the interest as if by a spell

♦ alluring, attractive, captivating, charming, engaging, enthralling, interesting, intriguing *Ant* repellant, repelling, repugnant

fas·ci·na·tion \ˌfas-ᵊn-'ā-shən\ *n* ♦ : the quality of fascinating : the ability to enthrall

♦ allure, appeal, attractiveness, charisma, charm, enchantment, glamour

fas·cism \'fa-ˌshi-zəm\ *n, often cap* : a political philosophy, movement, or regime that exalts nation and often race and stands for a centralized autocratic often militaristic government — **fas·cist** \-shist\ *n or adj, often cap* — **fas·cis·tic** \fa-'shis-tik\ *adj, often cap*

¹fash·ion \'fa-shən\ *n* **1** : the make or form of something **2** ♦ : a distinctive or peculiar and often habitual manner or way : MANNER, WAY **3** ♦ : a prevailing usu. short-lived custom, usage, or style **4** : the prevailing style (as in dress)

♦ [2] custom, habit, manner, pattern, practice, way ♦ [3] craze, enthusiasm, fad, mode, rage, sensation, style, trend, vogue

²fashion *vb* **1** ♦ : to make or construct usu. with the use of imagination and ingenuity **2** : FIT, ADAPT

♦ fabricate, form, frame, make, manufacture, produce

fash·ion·able \'fa-shə-nə-bəl\ *adj* **1** ♦ : dressing or behaving according to fashion **2** ♦ : of, relating to, or being something in fashion ⟨∼ resorts⟩ — **fash·ion·ably** \-blē\ *adv*

♦ [1] à la mode, chic, in, modish, sharp, smart, snappy, stylish ♦ [2] hot, in, popular

¹fast \'fast\ *adj* **1** ♦ : firmly fixed **2** : tightly shut **3** : adhering firmly **4** : STUCK **5** ♦ : firmly loyal : STAUNCH ⟨∼ friends⟩ **6 a** ♦ : characterized by quick motion, operation, or effect ⟨a ∼ trip⟩ ⟨a ∼ track⟩ **b** ♦ : unusually quick and ingenious or cunning in finding or recognizing and profiting by easy and often shady ways of making or acquiring money **7** : indicating ahead of the correct time ⟨the clock is ∼⟩ **8** ♦ : not easily disturbed : SOUND ⟨a ∼ sleep⟩ **9** : permanently dyed; *also* : being proof against fading ⟨colors ∼ to sunlight⟩ **10** : DISSIPATED, WILD ⟨a ∼ crowd⟩ **11** : sexually promiscuous

♦ [1, 8] firm, secure, set, snug, sound, stable, tight ♦ [5] constant, devoted, faithful, loyal, staunch, steadfast, steady, true ♦ [6a] brisk, fleet, hasty, quick, rapid, speedy, swift *Ant* slow ♦ [6b] deceptive, dishonest, shady, sharp, shifty

²fast *adv* **1** ♦ : in a fast manner ⟨stuck ∼ in the mud⟩ ⟨∼ asleep⟩ **2** ♦ : in a rapid manner : SWIFTLY **3** : RECKLESSLY

♦ [1] completely, entirely, fully, thoroughly, well, wholly ♦ [2] briskly, hastily, presto, pronto, quick, quickly, rapidly, speedily, swiftly *Ant* slow, slowly

³fast *vb* **1** : to abstain from food **2** : to eat sparingly or abstain from some foods

⁴fast *n* **1** : the act or practice of fasting **2** : a time of fasting

fast·back \'fast-ˌbak\ *n* : an automobile having a roof with a long slope to the rear

fast·ball \-ˌbòl\ *n* : a baseball pitch thrown at full speed

fas·ten \'fas-ᵊn\ *vb* **1** ♦ : to attach or join by or as if by pinning, tying, or nailing **2** ♦ : to make fast : fix securely **3** : to become fixed or joined **4** ♦ : to focus attention ⟨∼ed onto the newest trends⟩ — **fas·ten·er** *n*

♦ [1, 2] attach, fix, secure, tie *Ant* detach, loose, loosen, undo ♦ [4] concentrate, focus, rivet, train

fas·ten·ing *n* : something that fastens : FASTENER

fast–food \'fast-'füd\ *adj* : specializing in food that is prepared and served quickly ⟨a ∼ restaurant⟩

fast–for·ward \-'fòr-wərd\ *n* **1** : a function of an electronic device that advances a recording rapidly **2** : a state of rapid advancement — **fast–forward** *vb*

fas·tid·i·ous \fa-'sti-dē-əs\ *adj* **1** ♦ : overly difficult to please **2** ♦ : showing a meticulous or demanding attitude ⟨∼ workmanship⟩ — **fas·tid·i·ous·ly** *adv* — **fas·tid·i·ous·ness** *n*

♦ [1, 2] choosy, demanding, exacting, finicky, fussy, particular, picky

fast·ness \'fast-nəs\ *n* **1 a** : the quality or state of being fast **b** : fixed attachment **c** ♦ : the quality or state of being swift **2** ♦ : a fortified or secure place : STRONGHOLD

♦ [1c] celerity, fleetness, haste, hurry, quickness, rapidity, speed, swiftness, velocity ♦ [2] bastion, citadel, fort, fortification, fortress, stronghold

fast–talk \'fast-ˌtòk\ *vb* : to influence by persuasive and usu. deceptive talk

fast–track \'fast-,trak\ *vb* ♦ : to speed up the processing or production of

♦ accelerate, hasten, hurry, quicken, rush, speed (up), whisk

fast track *n* : a course leading to rapid advancement or success

¹**fat** \'fat\ *adj* **fat·ter; fat·test** **1** ♦ : notable for having an unusual amount of fat : PLUMP, OBESE **2** : OILY, GREASY **3** ♦ : well filled out : unusually large **4** ♦ : well furnished, filled, or stocked : ABUNDANT **5** ♦ : richly rewarding **6** ♦ : having the quality or power of producing esp. in abundance

♦ [1] chubby, corpulent, obese, overweight, plump, portly, rotund, round *Ant* lean, slender, slim, spare, thin ♦ [3] broad, thick, wide ♦ [4] abundant, chock-full, full, packed, replete ♦ [5] gainful, lucrative, profitable, remunerative ♦ [6] fertile, fruitful, productive, prolific, rich

²**fat** *n* **1** : animal tissue rich in greasy or oily matter **2** : any of various energy-rich esters that occur naturally in animal fats and in plants and are soluble in organic solvents (as ether) but not in water **3** ♦ : the best or richest portion ⟨lived on the ~ of the land⟩ **4** : OBESITY **5** ♦ : something in excess or expendable

♦ [3] best, choice, elite, pick, prime ♦ [5] excess, overflow, surfeit, surplus

fa·tal \'fāt-ᵊl\ *adj* **1** : FATEFUL ⟨that ~ day⟩ **2** ♦ : causing death or ruin ⟨a ~ mistake⟩ — **fa·tal·ly** *adv*

♦ deadly, deathly, lethal, mortal, murderous, pestilent ♦ calamitous, catastrophic, destructive, disastrous, fateful, ruinous

fa·tal·ism \-,i-zəm\ *n* : the belief that events are determined by fate — **fa·tal·ist** \-ist\ *n* — **fa·tal·is·tic** \,fāt-ᵊl-'is-tik\ *adj* — **fa·tal·is·ti·cal·ly** \-ti-k(ə-)lē\ *adv*

fa·tal·i·ty \fā-'ta-lə-tē, fə-\ *n, pl* **-ties** **1** : DEADLINESS **2** : FATE **3 a** : death resulting from a disaster or accident **b** ♦ : one who suffers a death from a disaster or accident

♦ casualty, loss, victim

fat·back \'fat-,bak\ *n* : a fatty strip from the back of the hog usu. cured by salting and drying

fat cat *n* **1** : a wealthy contributor to a political campaign **2** : a wealthy privileged person

fate \'fāt\ *n* **1** ♦ : the cause or will that is held to determine events : DESTINY **2** ♦ : LOT, FORTUNE **3** : DISASTER; *esp* : DEATH **4** : ultimate lot or disposition : final outcome **5** *cap, pl* : the three goddesses of classical mythology who determine the course of human life

♦ [1, 2] circumstance, destiny, doom, fortune, lot

fat·ed \'fā-təd\ *adj* : decreed, controlled, or marked by fate

fate·ful \'fāt-fəl\ *adj* **1** : OMINOUS, PROPHETIC **2** : IMPORTANT, DECISIVE **3** ♦ : bringing on adverse fate : DESTRUCTIVE **4** : determined by fate — **fate·ful·ly** *adv*

♦ calamitous, catastrophic, destructive, disastrous, fatal, ruinous

fath *abbr* fathom

fat·head \'fat-,hed\ *n* ♦ : a stupid person — **fat·head·ed** \-'he-dəd\ *adj*

♦ blockhead, dope, dummy, idiot, imbecile, jackass, moron, numskull

¹**fa·ther** \'fä-thər\ *n* **1** ♦ : a male parent **2** *cap* : God esp. as the first person of the Trinity **3** ♦ : a male ancestor more remote than a parent : FOREFATHER **4** : one deserving the respect and love given to a father **5** *often cap* : an early Christian writer accepted by the church as an authoritative witness to its teaching and practice **6** ♦ : one that originates or institutes : ORIGINATOR ⟨the ~ of modern radio⟩; *also* : SOURCE **7** ♦ : a priest of the regular clergy : PRIEST — used esp. as a title **8** : one of the leading men ⟨city ~s⟩ — **fa·ther·hood** \-,hu̇d\ *n* — **fa·ther·less** *adj* — **fa·ther·ly** *adj*

♦ [1] daddy, papa, pop ♦ [3] ancestor, forefather, grandfather ♦ [6] author, creator, founder, originator ♦ [7] clergyman, minister, preacher, priest, reverend

²**father** *vb* **1** ♦ : to make oneself the father of : BEGET **2** : to be the founder, producer, or author of **3** : to treat or care for as a father

♦ beget, get, produce, sire

father–in–law \'fä-thə-rən-,lȯ\ *n, pl* **fa·thers–in–law** \-thər-zən-\ : the father of one's spouse

fa·ther·land \'fä-thər-,land\ *n* **1** : the native land of one's ancestors **2** ♦ : one's native land

♦ country, home, homeland

¹**fath·om** \'fa-thəm\ *n* : a unit of length equal to 6 feet (about 1.8 meters) used esp. for measuring the depth of water

²**fathom** *vb* **1** : to measure by a sounding line **2** : PROBE **3** : to penetrate and come to understand ⟨~ the problem⟩ — **fath·om·able** \'fa-thə-mə-bəl\ *adj*

fath·om·less \'fa-thəm-ləs\ *adj* : incapable of being fathomed

¹**fa·tigue** \fə-'tēg\ *n* **1** : manual or menial work performed by military personnel **2** *pl* : the uniform or work clothing worn on fatigue and in the field **3** ♦ : weariness from labor or stress **4** : the tendency of a material to break under repeated stress

♦ burnout, collapse, exhaustion, lassitude, prostration, tiredness, weariness *Ant* refreshment, rejuvenation, revitalization

²**fatigue** *vb* **fa·tigued; fa·tigu·ing** ♦ : to weary with labor or exertion : WEARY, TIRE

♦ burn out, do in, drain, exhaust, tire, wear out, weary

fat·ness *n* ♦ : the quality or state of being fat or rich in fats : fullness of flesh

♦ corpulence, obesity, plumpness

fat·ten \'fat-ᵊn\ *vb* : to make or grow fat

Fat Tuesday *n* : MARDI GRAS

¹**fat·ty** \'fa-tē\ *adj* **fat·ti·er; -est** **1** : containing fat esp. in unusual amounts **2** : GREASY

²**fatty** *n, pl* **fat·ties** *offensive* : an overweight person

fatty acid *n* : any of numerous acids that contain only carbon, hydrogen, and oxygen and that occur naturally in fats and various oils

fa·tu·ity \fə-'tü-ə-tē, -'tyü-\ *n, pl* **-ities** **1** ♦ : something foolish or stupid **2** ♦ : the quality or state of being stupid

♦ [1] absurdity, folly, foolery, foolishness, idiocy, inanity, madness, stupidity ♦ [2] absurdity, foolishness, inanity, silliness, simplicity, stupidity

fat·u·ous \'fa-chü-wəs\ *adj* ♦ : marked by lack of intelligence and rational consideration — **fat·u·ous·ly** *adv*

♦ dense, dull, dumb, obtuse, stupid, unintelligent, vacuous, witless

fau·bourg \fō-'bu̇r\ *n* **1** : a suburb esp. of a French city **2** : a city quarter

fau·ces \'fȯ-,sēz\ *n pl* : the narrow passage located between the soft palate and the base of the tongue that joins the mouth to the pharynx

fau·cet \'fȯ-sət, 'fä-\ *n* ♦ : a fixture for drawing off a liquid (as from a pipe)

♦ cock, gate, spigot, tap, valve

¹**fault** \'fȯlt\ *n* **1** ♦ : a weakness in character : FAILING **2** ♦ : a physical or electrical imperfection or impairment : IMPERFECTION, DEFECT **3** : an error esp. in service in a net or racket game **4** ♦ : a failure to do what is right : an unintentional error : MISTAKE **5** ♦ : responsibility for something wrong **6** : a fracture in the earth's crust accompanied by a displacement of one side relative to the other

♦ [1] demerit, failing, foible, frailty, shortcoming, vice, weakness *Ant* merit, virtue ♦ [2] blemish, defect, flaw, imperfection ♦ [4] blunder, error, fumble, goof, misstep, mistake, oversight, slip ♦ [5] blame, culpability, guilt, rap

²**fault** *vb* **1** : to commit a fault : ERR **2** : to fracture so as to produce a geologic fault **3** ♦ : to find a fault in **4** : to hold responsible or responsible for

♦ blame, condemn, criticize, denounce, knock, pan

fault·find·er \'fȯlt-,fīn-dər\ *n* ♦ : a person who tends to find fault or complain — **fault·find·ing** *n or adj*

♦ carper, castigator, censurer, critic, nitpicker, scold

fault·i·ly \'fȯl-tə-lē\ *adv* ♦ : in a faulty or blamable manner

♦ erroneously, improperly, incorrectly, wrongly

fault·less *adj* ♦ : having no fault : free from defect, imperfection, failing, blemish, or error

♦ flawless, impeccable, perfect, unblemished ♦ blameless, innocent, irreproachable

fault·less·ly *adv* ♦ : in a manner having no fault

♦ flawlessly, ideally, impeccably, perfectly

faulty *adj* ♦ : marked by a fault : having a fault, blemish, or defect

♦ bad, defective, imperfect *Ant* faultless, flawless, perfect

faun \'fȯn\ *n* : a Roman god similar to but gentler than a satyr

fau·na \'fȯ-nə\ *n, pl* **faunas** *also* **fau·nae** \-,nē, -,nī\ : animals or animal life esp. of a region, period, or environment — **fau·nal** \-nəl\ *adj*

fau·vism \'fō-ˌvi-zəm\ *n, often cap* : a movement in painting characterized by vivid colors, free treatment of form, and a vibrant and decorative effect — **fau·vist** \-vist\ *n, often cap*

faux \'fō\ *adj* 1 ♦ : resembling something else that is usu. genuine and of better quality 2 : not sincere ⟨a gesture of ∼ humility⟩

♦ artificial, fake, imitation, mock, sham, synthetic

faux pas \'fō-ˌpä, fo-'\ *n, pl* **faux pas** *same or* -ˌpäz, -'päz\ : BLUNDER; *esp* : a social blunder

fa·va bean \'fä-və-\ *n* : the large flat edible seed of an Old World vetch; *also* : this plant

¹**fa·vor** *or Can and Brit* **fa·vour** \'fā-vər\ *n* 1 ♦ : friendly regard shown toward another esp. by a superior 2 ♦ : the act of approving or the state of being approved of : APPROVAL 3 ♦ : bias in favor : PARTIALITY 4 : POPULARITY 5 : gracious kindness; *also* : an act of such kindness 6 *pl* ♦ : effort in one's behalf : ATTENTION 7 : a token of love (as a ribbon) usu. worn conspicuously 8 : a small gift or decorative item given out at a party 9 : a special privilege 10 : sexual privileges — usu. used in pl. 11 : BEHALF, INTEREST

♦ [1] admiration, appreciation, esteem, estimation, regard, respect ♦ [2] approbation, approval, blessing, imprimatur, OK ♦ [3] bias, partiality, partisanship, prejudice ♦ [6] boon, courtesy, grace, indulgence, kindness, mercy, service, turn

²**favor** *or Can and Brit* **favour** *vb* 1 ♦ : to regard or treat with favor 2 : to do a kindness for or oblige esp. with a gift : OBLIGE 3 : ENDOW ⟨∼ed by nature⟩ 4 : to treat gently or carefully : SPARE ⟨∼ a lame leg⟩ 5 ♦ : to show partiality toward : PREFER 6 : SUPPORT, SUSTAIN 7 : FACILITATE ⟨darkness ∼s attack⟩ 8 : RESEMBLE ⟨he ∼s his father⟩

♦ [1] accept, approve, care, countenance, OK, subscribe ♦ [5] lean, like, prefer

fa·vor·able *or Can and Brit* **fa·vour·able** \'fā-və-rə-bəl\ *adj* 1 ♦ : expressing approval : APPROVING ⟨a ∼ response⟩ 2 ♦ : tending to promote or facilitate : HELPFUL, ADVANTAGEOUS ⟨∼ weather⟩ 3 ♦ : marked by success

♦ [1] appreciative, complimentary, friendly, good, positive *Ant* adverse, disapproving, negative ♦ [2] advantageous, beneficial, helpful, profitable, salutary ♦ [3] auspicious, bright, encouraging, hopeful, promising, propitious *Ant* discouraging, inauspicious, unfavorable, unpromising

fa·vor·ably *or Can and Brit* **fa·vour·ably** \-blē\ *adv* ♦ : in a favorable manner

♦ agreeably, nicely, pleasantly, pleasingly, satisfyingly, well

¹**fa·vor·ite** *or Can and Brit* **fa·vour·ite** \'fā-və-rət, -vrət\ *n* 1 ♦ : a person or a thing that is favored above others 2 : a competitor regarded as most likely to win

♦ darling, pet, preference, prize, treasure

²**favorite** *or Can and Brit* **favourite** *adj* ♦ : being a favorite

♦ dear, loved, precious, special

favorite son *n* : a candidate supported by the delegates of his state at a presidential nominating convention

fa·vor·it·ism \'fā-və-rə-ˌti-zəm\ *or Can and Brit* **fa·vour·it·ism** *n* : PARTIALITY, BIAS

¹**fawn** \'fȯn, 'fän\ *vb* 1 : to show affection ⟨a dog ∼ing on its master⟩ 2 ♦ : to court favor by a cringing or flattering manner

♦ fuss, kowtow, toady

²**fawn** *n* 1 : a young deer 2 : a light grayish brown — **fawny** \'fȯ-nē, 'fä-\ *adj*

fax \'faks\ *n* 1 : FACSIMILE 2 2 : a device used to send or receive facsimile communications; *also* : such a communication — **fax** *vb*

¹**fay** \'fā\ *n* ♦ : a mythical being of folklore and romance usu. having diminutive human form and magic powers and given to beneficial or mischievous interference in human affairs

♦ brownie, dwarf, elf, fairy, gnome, hobgoblin, leprechaun, pixie, puck, troll

²**fay** *adj* ♦ : like an elf

♦ antic, elfish, frisky, frolicsome, playful

faze \'fāz\ *vb* **fazed; faz·ing** ♦ : to disturb the composure or courage of

♦ confound, confuse, disconcert, embarrass, fluster, rattle

FBI *abbr* Federal Bureau of Investigation
FCC *abbr* Federal Communications Commission
FD *abbr* fire department
FDA *abbr* Food and Drug Administration

FDIC *abbr* Federal Deposit Insurance Corporation
Fe *symbol* iron
fe·al·ty \'fēl-tē\ *n, pl* **-ties** ♦ : intense fidelity : LOYALTY, ALLEGIANCE

♦ allegiance, constancy, dedication, devotion, faith, faithfulness, fastness, fidelity, loyalty, steadfastness

¹**fear** \'fir\ *vb* 1 : to have a reverent awe of ⟨∼ God⟩ 2 : to be afraid of : have fear ⟨∼s spiders⟩ 3 ♦ : to be apprehensive

♦ bother, fret, stew, sweat, trouble, worry

²**fear** *n* 1 ♦ : an unpleasant often strong emotion caused by expectation or awareness of danger; *also* : an instance of or a state marked by this emotion 2 : anxious concern : SOLICITUDE 3 : profound reverence esp. toward God

♦ alarm, anxiety, apprehension, dread, fright, trepidation

fear·ful \-fəl\ *adj* 1 ♦ : causing fear 2 ♦ : filled with fear 3 ♦ : showing or caused by fear 4 ♦ : extremely bad, intense, or large ⟨paid a ∼ price⟩ — **fear·ful·ly** *adv*

♦ [1] dire, dreadful, fearsome, forbidding, formidable, frightful, hair-raising, horrible, redoubtable, scary, shocking, terrible, terrifying ♦ [2, 3] afraid, scared, skittish, timid ♦ [4] deep, fierce, furious, hard, intense, profound, terrible, violent

fear·less \-ləs\ *adj* ♦ : free from fear : BRAVE — **fear·less·ly** *adv*

♦ brave, courageous, heroic, intrepid, lionhearted, stalwart, stout, undaunted, valiant

fear·less·ness *n* ♦ : the quality or state of being without fear

♦ bravery, courage, daring, heroism, nerve, stoutness, valor

fear·some \-səm\ *adj* 1 ♦ : causing fear 2 : TIMID 3 : INTENSE ⟨∼ determination⟩

♦ fearful, formidable, hair-raising, scary, shocking, terrifying

fea·si·ble \'fē-zə-bəl\ *adj* 1 ♦ : capable of being done or carried out ⟨a ∼ plan⟩ 2 : SUITABLE 3 : REASONABLE, LIKELY — **fea·si·bil·i·ty** \ˌfē-zə-'bi-lə-tē\ *n* — **fea·si·bly** \'fē-zə-blē\ *adv*

♦ achievable, attainable, doable, possible, practicable, viable, workable

¹**feast** \'fēst\ *n* 1 ♦ : an elaborate meal : BANQUET 2 : ABUNDANCE ⟨a ∼ of good books⟩ 3 : FESTIVAL 1

♦ banquet, dinner, feed, spread

²**feast** *vb* 1 **a** : to take part in a feast **b** ♦ : to give a feast for 2 : to enjoy some unusual pleasure or delight 3 : DELIGHT, GRATIFY

♦ banquet, dine, junket, regale

feat \'fēt\ *n* ♦ : a deed notable esp. for courage : a heroic achievement; *esp* : an act notable for courage, skill, endurance, or ingenuity

♦ deed, exploit, stunt, trick

¹**feath·er** \'fe-thər\ *n* 1 : any of the light horny outgrowths that form the external covering of the body of a bird 2 : the vane of an arrow 3 : the entire clothing of feathers of a bird : PLUMAGE 4 ♦ : a group united by common traits or interests ⟨birds of a ∼⟩ 5 ♦ : elaborate, showy, or ceremonial dress ⟨in full ∼⟩ 6 : CONDITION, MOOD ⟨in fine ∼⟩ — **feath·ered** \-thərd\ *adj* — **feath·er·less** *adj* — **a feather in one's cap** : a mark of distinction : HONOR

♦ [4] class, ilk, kind, like, sort, type ♦ [5] array, best, finery, full dress, regalia

feather *vb* 1 : to furnish with a feather ⟨∼ an arrow⟩ 2 : to cover, clothe, line, or adorn with or as if with feathers — **feather one's nest** : to provide for oneself financially esp. while exploiting a position of trust

feath·er·bed·ding \'fe-thər-ˌbe-diŋ\ *n* : the requiring of an employer usu. under a union rule or safety statute to employ more workers than are needed

feath·er·edge \-ˌej\ *n* : a very thin sharp edge

feath·er·weight \-ˌwāt\ *n* : one that is very light in weight; *esp* : a boxer weighing more than 118 but not over 126 pounds

feath·ery *adj* ♦ : light and delicate

♦ airy, light

¹**fea·ture** \'fē-chər\ *n* 1 : the shape or appearance of the face or its parts 2 : a part of the face ⟨his eyes are his best ∼⟩ 3 ♦ : a prominent part or characteristic 4 : a special attraction (as in a newspaper) 5 : something offered to the public or advertised as particularly attractive ⟨a car's new ∼s⟩ — **fea·ture·less** *adj*

♦ attribute, character, characteristic, mark, peculiarity, point, property, quality, trait

²**feature** *vb* **1** : to picture in the mind : IMAGINE **2** ♦ : to give special prominence to ⟨the show ∼s new artists⟩ **3** : to play an important part

♦ accent, accentuate, emphasize, highlight, stress, underline, underscore

Feb *abbr* February

fe·brile \'fe-ˌbrī(-ə)l\ *adj* : FEVERISH

Feb·ru·ary \'fe-b(y)ə-ˌwer-ē, 'fe-brə-\ *n* : the 2d month of the year

fe·ces \'fē-ˌsēz\ *n pl* : bodily waste discharged from the intestine : EXCREMENT — **fe·cal** \-kəl\ *adj*

feck·less \'fek-ləs\ *adj* **1** : WEAK, INEFFECTIVE ⟨∼ behavior⟩ **2** : WORTHLESS, IRRESPONSIBLE

fe·cund \'fe-kənd, 'fē-\ *adj* ♦ : fruitful in offspring or vegetation : FRUITFUL, PROLIFIC ⟨∼ fields⟩ — **fe·cun·di·ty** \fi-'kən-də-tē, fe-\ *n*

♦ fat, fertile, fruitful, luxuriant, productive, prolific, rich

fed *abbr* federal; federation

fed·er·al \'fe-də-rəl, -drəl\ *adj* **1** : formed by a compact between political units that surrender individual sovereignty to a central authority but retain certain limited powers **2** : of or constituting a form of government in which power is distributed between a central authority and constituent territorial units **3** : of or relating to the central government of a federation **4** *cap* : FEDERALIST **5** *often cap* : of, relating to, or loyal to the federal government or the Union armies of the U.S. in the American Civil War — **fed·er·al·ly** *adv*

Federal *n* : a supporter of the U.S. government in the Civil War; *esp* : a soldier in the federal armies

federal district *n* : a district (as the District of Columbia) set apart as the seat of the central government of a federation

fed·er·al·ism \'fe-də-rə-ˌli-zəm, -drə-\ *n* **1** *often cap* : the distribution of power in an organization (as a government) between a central authority and the constituent units **2** : support or advocacy of federalism **3** *cap* : the principles of the Federalists

fed·er·al·ist \-list\ *n* **1** : an advocate of federalism **2** *often cap* : an advocate of a federal union between the American colonies after the Revolution and of adoption of the U.S. Constitution **3** *cap* : a member of a major political party in the early years of the U.S. favoring a strong centralized national government — **federalist** *adj, often cap*

fed·er·al·ize \'fe-də-rə-ˌlīz, -drə-\ *vb* **-ized; -iz·ing 1** : to unite in or under a federal system **2** : to bring under the jurisdiction of a federal government

fed·er·ate \'fe-də-ˌrāt\ *vb* **-at·ed; -at·ing** ♦ : to join in a federation

♦ ally, associate, band, club, confederate, conjoin, cooperate, league, unite

fed·er·a·tion \ˌfe-də-'rā-shən\ *n* **1** : a political or societal entity formed by uniting smaller entities **2** : a federal government **3** ♦ : a union of organizations **4** : the forming of a federal union

♦ alliance, bloc, coalition, combination, combine, confederacy, confederation, league, union

fedn *abbr* federation

fe·do·ra \fi-'dōr-ə\ *n* : a low soft felt hat with the crown creased lengthwise

fed up *adj* ♦ : satiated, tired, or disgusted beyond endurance ⟨*fed up* with bureaucracy⟩

♦ jaded, sick, tired, weary

fee \'fē\ *n* **1** : an estate in land held from a feudal lord **2** : an inherited or heritable estate in land **3** ♦ : a fixed charge; *also* : a charge for a service

♦ charge, cost, figure, price

fee·ble \'fē-bəl\ *adj* **fee·bler** \-bə-lər\; **fee·blest** \-bə-ləst\ **1** ♦ : markedly lacking in strength : FRAIL **2** : INEFFECTIVE, INADEQUATE ⟨a ∼ protest⟩ — **fee·bly** \-blē\ *adv*

♦ faint, frail, infirm, wasted, weak

fee·ble·mind·ed \ˌfē-bəl-'mīn-dəd\ *adj* : lacking normal intelligence — **fee·ble·mind·ed·ness** *n*

fee·ble·ness *n* ♦ : the quality or state of being feeble

♦ debility, frailty, infirmity, weakness

¹**feed** \'fēd\ *vb* **fed** \'fed\; **feed·ing 1** ♦ : to give food to; *also* : to give as food **2 a** ♦ : to consume food : EAT 1 **b** : to seize and devour prey — used with *on, upon,* or *off* **3** : to furnish what is necessary to the growth or function of **4** : to supply for use or consumption — **feed·er** *n*

♦ [1] board, cater, provision, victual ♦ [2a] dine, eat, fare

²**feed** *n* **1 a** ♦ : a usu. large meal; *esp* : a sumptuous meal **b** ♦ : the portion or serving of food eaten at a meal **2** : food for livestock **3** : a mechanism for feeding material to a machine **4** : a continuous series of electronic information updates (as to a blog or social media account)

♦ [1a] banquet, dinner, feast, spread ♦ [1b] board, chow, meal, mess, repast, table

feed·back \'fēd-ˌbak\ *n* **1** : the return to the input of a part of the output of a machine, system, or process **2** : response esp. to one in authority about an activity or policy **3** : sound (as whistling) resulting from the retransmission of an amplified or broadcast signal

feed·lot \'fēd-ˌlät\ *n* : land on which cattle are fattened for market

feed·stuff \-ˌstəf\ *n* : FEED 2

¹**feel** \'fēl\ *vb* **felt** \'felt\; **feel·ing 1** : to perceive or examine through physical contact : TOUCH, HANDLE **2** ♦ : to undergo passive experience of : EXPERIENCE; *also* : to suffer from **3** : to ascertain by cautious trial ⟨∼ out public sentiment⟩ **4** ♦ : to be aware of **5** : to be conscious of an inward impression, state of mind, or physical condition **6** ♦ : to be aware of by instinct or inference : BELIEVE, THINK ⟨say what you ∼⟩ **7** ♦ : to search for something with the fingers : GROPE **8** : SEEM ⟨it ∼s like spring⟩ **9** ♦ : to have sympathy or pity ⟨I ∼ for you⟩

♦ [2] endure, experience, have, know, see, suffer, sustain, taste, undergo ♦ [4] perceive, scent, see, sense, smell, taste ♦ [6] believe, consider, deem, figure, guess, hold, imagine, suppose, think ♦ [7] fish, fumble, grope ♦ *usu* **feel for** [9] commiserate, pity, sympathize

²**feel** *n* **1** : the sense of touch **2** ♦ : a sensation experienced through the sense of feeling **3** : the quality of a thing as imparted through touch

♦ [2] feeling, sensation, sense

feel·er \'fē-lər\ *n* **1** : one that feels; *esp* : a tactile organ (as on the head of an insect) **2** : a proposal or remark made to find out the views of other people

¹**feel·ing** \'fē-liŋ\ *n* **1 a** : the sense of touch **b** ♦ : a sensation perceived by touch **2** ♦ : a state of mind ⟨a ∼ of loneliness⟩ **3** *pl* : general emotional condition : SENSIBILITIES ⟨hurt their ∼s⟩ **4** ♦ : often unreasoned opinion or belief : OPINION, BELIEF **5** ♦ : capacity to respond emotionally

♦ [1b] feel, sensation, sense ♦ [2] emotion, sentiment ♦ [4] belief, conviction, eye, judgment (*or* judgement), mind, notion, opinion, persuasion, sentiment, verdict, view ♦ [5] compassion, heart, humanity, kindness, sympathy

²**feeling** *adj* **1** : having the capacity to feel or respond emotionally : SENSITIVE; *esp* : easily moved emotionally **2** : expressing emotion or sensitivity — **feel·ing·ly** *adv*

feet *pl of* FOOT

feign \'fān\ *vb* **1** ♦ : to give a false appearance of : SHAM ⟨∼ illness⟩ **2** : to assert as if true : PRETEND

♦ affect, assume, fake, pretend, put on, sham, simulate

feigned \'fānd\ *adj* **1** : not genuine or real **2** ♦ : not genuinely felt

♦ artificial, hypocritical, insincere, two-faced

feint \'fānt\ *n* : something feigned; *esp* : a mock blow or attack intended to distract attention from the real point of attack — **feint** *vb*

feisty \'fī-stē\ *adj* **feist·i·er; -est** : having or showing a lively aggressiveness ⟨a ∼ heroine⟩

feld·spar \'feld-ˌspär\ *n* : any of a group of crystalline minerals consisting of silicates of aluminum with another element (as potassium or sodium)

fe·lic·i·tate \fi-'li-sə-ˌtāt\ *vb* **-tat·ed; -tat·ing** : to offer congratulations to : CONGRATULATE ⟨*felicitated* the winner⟩

fe·lic·i·ta·tion \fi-ˌli-sə-'tā-shən\ *n* : the act or an instance of congratulating : CONGRATULATION

fe·lic·i·tous \fi-'li-sə-təs\ *adj* **1** ♦ : suitably expressed : APT **2** ♦ : highly pleasing : affording great pleasure and satisfaction : PLEASANT, DELIGHTFUL

♦ [1] applicable, appropriate, apt, fit, fitting, proper, right, suitable ♦ [2] agreeable, congenial, delightful, pleasant, pleasurable, satisfying

fe·lic·i·tous·ly *adv* ♦ : in a felicitous manner

♦ agreeably, favorably (*or* favourably), nicely, pleasantly, pleasingly, satisfyingly, splendidly, well

fe·lic·i·ty \fi-'li-sə-tē\ *n, pl* **-ties 1** ♦ : the quality or state of being happy; *esp* : great happiness **2** ♦ : something that causes happiness **3** : a pleasing manner or quality esp. in art or language **4** : an apt expression

♦ [1] blessedness, bliss, gladness, happiness, joy ♦ [2] benefit, blessing, boon, godsend, good, manna, windfall

¹fe·line \'fē-ˌlīn\ *adj* **1** : of or relating to cats or their kin **2** : sleekly graceful **3** : SLY, TREACHEROUS **4** : STEALTHY
²feline *n* ♦ : a feline animal

♦ cat, kitty, puss

¹fell \'fel\ *n* : SKIN, HIDE, PELT
²fell *vb* **1 a** ♦ : to cut, beat, or knock down **b** : to deprive of life **2** : to sew (a seam) by folding one raw edge under the other

♦ chop, cut, hew

³fell *past of* FALL
⁴fell *adj* **1** ♦ : violently hostile or aggressive in temperament : FIERCE **2** ♦ : killing or markedly sickening or destroying : DEADLY — **in one fell swoop** *also* **at one fell swoop** : all at once : with a single effort

♦ [1] ferocious, fierce, grim, savage, vicious ♦ [2] deadly, fatal, lethal, mortal, murderous, pestilent, vital

fel·lah \'fe-lə, fə-'lä\ *n, pl* **fel·la·hin** *or* **fel·la·heen** \ˌfe-lə-'hēn\ : a peasant or agricultural laborer in Arab countries (as Egypt or Syria)
fel·la·tio \fə-'lā-shē-ˌō\ *also* **fel·la·tion** \-shən\ *n* : oral stimulation of the penis
fel·low \'fe-lō\ *n* **1** ♦ : one that accompanies or is in the company of another : one much in the company of another **2** ♦ : an equal in rank, power, or character : EQUAL, PEER **3** : one of a pair : MATE **4** : a member of an incorporated literary or scientific society **5** ♦ : an individual human : an adult male human : MAN **6** ♦ : a frequent, regular, or favorite escort or male companion : BOYFRIEND **7** : a person granted a stipend for advanced study

♦ [1] associate, cohort, companion, comrade, crony, mate ♦ [2] equal, like, match, parallel, peer ♦ [5] buck, chap, dude, gent, gentleman, guy, hombre, jack, joker, lad, male, man ♦ [6] beau, boyfriend, man, swain

fel·low man \ˌfe-lō-'man\ *n* : a kindred human being
fel·low·ship \'fe-lō-ˌship\ *n* **1** ♦ : the condition of friendly relationship existing among persons **2** ♦ : a community of interest or feeling **3** ♦ : a group with similar interests **4** : the position of a fellow (as of a university) **5** : the stipend granted a fellow

♦ [1] camaraderie, companionship, company, comradeship, society ♦ [2] brotherhood, community, corps, fraternity ♦ [3] association, club, college, congress, council, fraternity, league, order, organization, society

fellow traveler *n* : a sympathetic supporter of another's cause; *esp* : a person who sympathizes with and often furthers the ideals and program of an organized group (as the Communist party) without joining it
fel·on \'fe-lən\ *n* **1** ♦ : one who has committed a felony **2** : WHITLOW

♦ criminal, crook, culprit, lawbreaker, malefactor, offender

fe·lo·ni·ous \fə-'lō-nē-əs\ *adj* : of, relating to, or having the nature of a felony
fel·o·ny \'fe-lə-nē\ *n, pl* **-nies** : a serious crime punishable by a heavy sentence
fel·spar *chiefly Brit var of* FELDSPAR
¹felt \'felt\ *n* **1** : a cloth made of wool and fur often mixed with natural or synthetic fibers **2** : a material resembling felt
²felt *past and past part of* FEEL
fem *abbr* **1** female **2** feminine
FEMA \'fē-mə\ *abbr* Federal Emergency Management Agency
¹fe·male \'fē-ˌmāl\ *adj* **1** : of, relating to, or being the sex that typically bears young; *also* : PISTILLATE **2** ♦ : of, relating to, or characteristic of girls or women ⟨∼ voices⟩

♦ feminine, womanly

²female *n* : a female individual
¹fem·i·nine \'fe-mə-nən\ *adj* **1 a** : of the female sex **b** ♦ : characteristic of or appropriate or unique to women **2** ♦ : of, relating to, or constituting the gender that includes most words or grammatical forms referring to females — **fem·i·nin·i·ty** \ˌfe-mə-'ni-nə-tē\ *n*

♦ female, womanly *Ant* male, manly, mannish, masculine

²feminine *n* : a noun, pronoun, adjective, or inflectional form or class of the feminine gender; *also* : the feminine gender
fem·i·nism \'fe-mə-ˌni-zəm\ *n* **1** : the theory of the political, economic, and social equality of the sexes **2** : organized activity on behalf of women's rights and interests — **fem·i·nist** \-nist\ *n or adj*

femme fa·tale \ˌfem-fə-'tal\ *n, pl* **femmes fa·tales** *same or* -'talz\ : a seductive woman
fe·mur \'fē-mər\ *n, pl* **fe·murs** *or* **fem·o·ra** \'fe-mə-rə\ : the long leg bone extending from the hip to the knee — **fem·o·ral** \'fe-mə-rəl\ *adj*
fen \'fen\ *n* ♦ : low swampy land

♦ bog, marsh, mire, morass, slough, swamp

¹fence \'fens\ *n* **1** ♦ : a barrier (as of wood or wire) to prevent escape or entry or to mark a boundary **2** : a person who receives stolen goods; *also* : a place where stolen goods are disposed of — **on the fence** : in a position of neutrality or indecision

♦ barrier, hedge, wall

²fence *vb* **fenced; fenc·ing** **1** ♦ : to enclose with a fence **2** : to keep in or out with a fence **3** : to practice fencing **4** : to use tactics of attack and defense esp. in debate — **fenc·er** *n*

♦ *usu* **fence in** cage, corral, enclose, hedge, pen

fenc·ing *n* **1** : the art or practice of attack and defense with the foil, épée, or saber **2** : the fences of a property or region **3** : material used for building fences
fend \'fend\ *vb* **1** ♦ : to keep or ward off : REPEL **2** : SHIFT ⟨∼ for yourself⟩

♦ *usu* **fend off** repel, repulse, stave off

fend·er \'fen-dər\ *n* ♦ : a protective device (as a guard over the wheel of an automobile)

♦ buffer, bumper, cushion, pad

fen·es·tra·tion \ˌfe-nə-'strā-shən\ *n* : the arrangement and design of windows and doors in a building
Fe·ni·an \'fē-nē-ən\ *n* : a member of a secret 19th century Irish and Irish-American organization dedicated to overthrowing British rule in Ireland
fen·nel \'fen-ᵊl\ *n* : a garden plant related to the carrot and grown for its aromatic foliage and seeds
FEPC *abbr* Fair Employment Practices Commission
fe·ral \'fir-əl, 'fer-\ *adj* **1** : SAVAGE **2** ♦ : not domesticated or cultivated : WILD 1 **3** : having escaped from domestication and become wild

♦ savage, unbroken, undomesticated, untamed, wild

fer·de·lance \'fer-də-'lans\ *n, pl* **fer·de·lance** : a large venomous pit viper of Central and So. America
¹fer·ment \fər-'ment\ *vb* **1** : to cause or undergo fermentation **2** : to be or cause to be in a state of agitation or intense activity
²fer·ment \'fər-ˌment\ *n* **1** : a living organism (as a yeast) causing fermentation by its enzymes; *also* : ENZYME **2** ♦ : a state of unrest

♦ restlessness, turmoil, uneasiness, unrest

fer·men·ta·tion \ˌfər-mən-'tā-shən, -ˌmen-\ *n* **1** : chemical decomposition of an organic substance (as in the souring of milk or the formation of alcohol from sugar) by enzymatic action in the absence of oxygen often with formation of gas **2** : FERMENT 2
fer·mi·um \'fer-mē-əm, 'fər-\ *n* : an artificially produced radioactive metallic chemical element
fern \'fərn\ *n* : any of an order of vascular plants resembling seed plants in having roots, stems, and leaflike fronds but reproducing by spores instead of by flowers and seeds
fern·ery \'fər-nə-rē\ *n, pl* **-er·ies** **1** : a place for growing ferns **2** : a collection of growing ferns
fe·ro·cious \fə-'rō-shəs\ *adj* **1** ♦ : exhibiting or given to extreme fierceness and unrestrained violence and brutality **2** ♦ : extremely intense — **fe·ro·cious·ly** *adv* — **fe·ro·cious·ness** *n*

♦ [1] fell, fierce, grim, savage, vicious ♦ [2] deep, fearful, heavy, intense, profound

fe·roc·i·ty \fə-'rä-sə-tē\ *n* : the quality or state of being ferocious
¹fer·ret \'fer-ət\ *n* : a partially domesticated usu. white European mammal related to the weasels
²ferret *vb* **1** : to hunt game with ferrets **2** : to drive out of a hiding place **3** ♦ : to find and bring to light by searching — usu. used with *out* ⟨∼ out the truth⟩

♦ *usu* **ferret out** detect, determine, dig up, discover, find, hit on, locate, track down

fer·ric \'fer-ik\ *adj* : of, relating to, or containing iron
ferric oxide *n* : an oxide of iron found in nature as hematite and as rust and used esp. as a pigment, for polishing, and in magnetic materials
Fer·ris wheel \'fer-əs-\ *n* : an amusement device consisting of a

large upright power-driven wheel with seats that remain horizontal around its rim

fer·ro·mag·net·ic \ˌfer-ō-mag-'ne-tik\ *adj* : of or relating to substances that are easily magnetized

fer·rous \'fer-əs\ *adj* : of, relating to, or containing iron

fer·rule \'fer-əl\ *n* : a metal ring or cap around a slender wooden shaft to prevent splitting

¹**fer·ry** \'fer-ē\ *vb* **fer·ried; fer·ry·ing** **1** : to carry by boat across a body of water **2** : to cross by a ferry **3** ♦ : to convey from one place to another

♦ bear, carry, convey, haul, transport

²**ferry** *n, pl* **ferries** **1** : a place where persons or things are ferried **2** : FERRYBOAT

fer·ry·boat \'fer-ē-ˌbōt\ *n* : a boat used in ferrying

fer·tile \'fərt-ᵊl\ *adj* **1** ♦ : producing plentifully : PRODUCTIVE ⟨~ soils⟩ ⟨a ~ mind⟩ **2** : capable of developing or reproducing ⟨~ seed⟩ ⟨a ~ bull⟩ — **fer·til·i·ty** \(ˌ)fər-'ti-lə-tē\ *n*

♦ fecund, fruitful, luxuriant, productive, prolific, rich *Ant* barren, infertile, sterile, unfruitful, unproductive

fer·til·ize \'fərt-ᵊl-ˌīz\ *vb* **-ized; -iz·ing** **1** : to unite with in the process of fertilization ⟨a sperm ~s an egg⟩ **2** : to apply fertilizer to — **fer·til·iza·tion** \ˌfərt-ᵊl-ə-'zā-shən\ *n*

fer·til·iz·er \-ˌī-zər\ *n* : material (as manure or a chemical mixture) for enriching land

fer·ule \'fer-əl\ *n* : a rod or ruler used to punish children

fer·ven·cy \'fər-vən-sē\ *n, pl* **-cies** ♦ : deep interest in or enthusiasm for something : FERVOR

♦ ardor, emotion, fervor, heat, intensity, passion, vehemence, warmth

fer·vent \'fər-vənt\ *adj* **1** : very hot : GLOWING **2** ♦ : marked by great intensity of feeling — **fer·vent·ly** *adv*

♦ ardent, burning, charged, emotional, fiery, hot-blooded, impassioned, passionate, red-hot, vehement *Ant* cold, cool, dispassionate, impassive, unemotional

fer·vid \-vəd\ *adj* **1** : very hot **2** ♦ : marked by often extreme fervor : ARDENT — **fer·vid·ly** *adv*

♦ ardent, burning, charged, emotional, fervent, fiery, hot-blooded, impassioned, intense, passionate, red-hot, vehement

fer·vor *or Can and Brit* **fer·vour** \'fər-vər\ *n* **1** : intense heat **2** ♦ : intensity of feeling or expression

♦ ardor, emotion, fervency, heat, intensity, passion, vehemence, warmth

fes·cue \'fes-kyü\ *n* : any of a genus of tufted perennial grasses

fes·tal \'fest-ᵊl\ *adj* : FESTIVE

fester \'fes-tər\ *vb* **1** : to form pus **2** : PUTREFY, ROT **3** : RANKLE

fes·ti·val \'fes-tə-vəl\ *n* **1** ♦ : a time of celebration marked by special observances; *esp* : an occasion marked with religious ceremonies **2** : a periodic season or program of cultural events or entertainment ⟨a dance ~⟩

♦ carnival, celebration, festivity, fete, fiesta, gala, jubilee

fes·tive \'fes-tiv\ *adj* **1** : of, relating to, or suitable for a feast or festival **2** ♦ : marked by gaiety, conviviality, or revelry — **fes·tive·ly** *adv*

♦ gleeful, jolly, jovial, merry, mirthful, sunny

fes·tiv·i·ty \fes-'ti-və-tē\ *n, pl* **-ties** **1** ♦ : a time of celebration marked by special observances : FESTIVAL 1 **2** : the quality or state of being festive **3** ♦ : festive activity

♦ [1] carnival, celebration, festival, fete, fiesta, gala, jubilee ♦ [3] conviviality, gaiety, jollification, merriment, merrymaking, revelry

¹**fes·toon** \fes-'tün\ *n* **1** : a decorative chain or strip hanging between two points **2** : a carved, molded, or painted ornament representing a decorative chain

²**festoon** *vb* **1** : to hang or form festoons on **2** : to shape into festoons

fe·ta \'fe-tə\ *n* : a white crumbly Greek cheese made from sheep's or goat's milk

fe·tal \'fēt-ᵊl\ *adj* : of, relating to, or being a fetus

fetch \'fech\ *vb* **1** : to go or come after and bring or take back ⟨teach a dog to ~ a stick⟩ **2** ♦ : to have as a price **3** : to cause to come : bring out ⟨~ed tears from the eyes⟩ **4** : to give by striking ⟨~ him a blow⟩

♦ bring, cost, go, sell

fetch·ing *adj* ♦ : tending to win interest or admiration : ATTRACTIVE — **fetch·ing·ly** *adv*

♦ alluring, attractive, charming, engaging, fascinating

fetch up *vb* ♦ : to bring to a stop

♦ draw up, halt, hold up, stay, still, stop

¹**fete** *or* **fête** \'fāt, 'fet\ *n* **1** ♦ : a festive celebration or entertainment : FESTIVAL **2** ♦ : a large elaborate entertainment or party

♦ [1] carnival, celebration, festival, festivity, fiesta, gala, jubilee ♦ [2] affair, blowout, event, function, get-together, party

²**fete** *or* **fête** *vb* **fet·ed** *or* **fêt·ed; fet·ing** *or* **fêt·ing** **1** : to honor or commemorate with a fete **2** : to pay high honor to

fet·id \'fe-təd\ *adj* ♦ : having an offensive smell

♦ foul, malodorous, noisome, rank, reeky, smelly, strong

fe·tish *also* **fe·tich** \'fe-tish\ *n* **1** ♦ : an object (as an idol or image) believed to have magical powers (as in curing disease) **2** ♦ : an object of unreasoning devotion or concern **3** : an object whose real or fantasied presence is psychologically necessary for sexual gratification

♦ [1] amulet, charm, mascot, talisman ♦ [2] fixation, mania, obsession, preoccupation, prepossession

fe·tish·ism \-ti-ˌshi-zəm\ *n* **1** : belief in or devotion to fetishes **2** : the pathological transfer of sexual interest and gratification to a fetish — **fe·tish·ist** \-shist\ *n* — **fe·tish·is·tic** \ˌfe-ti-'shis-tik\ *adj*

fe·tish·ize \-ti-ˌshīz\ *vb* **-ized; -iz·ing** : to make a fetish of

fet·lock \'fet-ˌläk\ *n* : a projection on the back of a horse's leg above the hoof; *also* : a tuft of hair on this

¹**fet·ter** \'fe-tər\ *n* **1** ♦ : a chain or shackle for the feet **2** ♦ : something that confines

♦ [1] band, bond, chain, irons, ligature, manacle, shackle ♦ [2] check, condition, constraint, curb, limitation, restraint, restriction

²**fetter** *vb* **1** ♦ : to put fetters on **2** ♦ : to restrain from motion, action, or progress

♦ [1] bind, chain, enchain, handcuff, manacle, shackle, trammel ♦ [2] delay, encumber, hamper, handicap, hinder, hobble, hold back, impede, inhibit, interfere with, obstruct

fet·tle \'fet-ᵊl\ *n* ♦ : a state of fitness or order : CONDITION ⟨in fine ~⟩

♦ condition, form, order, repair, shape, trim

fe·tus \'fē-təs\ *n* : an unborn or unhatched vertebrate esp. after its basic structure is laid down; *esp* : a developing human in the uterus from usu. three months after conception to birth

feud \'fyüd\ *n* : a prolonged quarrel; *esp* : a lasting conflict between families or clans marked by violent attacks made for revenge — **feud** *vb*

feu·dal \'fyü-dᵊl\ *adj* **1** : of, relating to, or having the characteristics of a medieval fee **2** : of, relating to, or characteristic of feudalism

feu·dal·ism \'fyü-də-ˌli-zəm\ *n* : a system of political organization prevailing in medieval Europe in which a vassal renders service to a lord and receives protection and land in return; *also* : a similar political or social system — **feu·dal·is·tic** \ˌfyü-də-ᵊl-'is-tik\ *adj*

¹**feu·da·to·ry** \'fyü-də-ˌtōr-ē\ *adj* : owing feudal allegiance

²**feudatory** *n, pl* **-ries** **1** : FIEF **2** : a person who holds lands by feudal law or usage

fe·ver \'fē-vər\ *n* **1 a** : a rise in body temperature above the normal **b** ♦ : an abnormal bodily condition characterized by increased heat, accelerated pulse, and systemic debility **c** ♦ : a disease of which a high body temperature is a chief symptom **2** : a state of heightened emotion or activity **3** : CRAZE ⟨baseball ~⟩ — **fe·ver·ish·ly** *adv*

♦ [1b, 1c] ailment, bug, complaint, condition, disease, disorder, ill, illness, infirmity, malady, sickness, trouble

fe·ver·ish *adj* ♦ : marked by intense emotion, activity, or instability

♦ agitated, frenzied, heated, hectic, overactive, overwrought ♦ delirious, fierce, frantic, frenetic, frenzied, furious, mad, violent, wild

¹**few** \'fyü\ *pron* : not many : a small number

²**few** *adj* **1** : consisting of or amounting to a small number **2** : not many but some ⟨caught a ~ fish⟩ — **few·ness** *n* — **few and far between** : RARE 3

³**few** *n* **1** ♦ : a small number of units or individuals ⟨a ~ of them⟩ **2** : a special limited number ⟨among the ~⟩

♦ handful, smattering, sprinkle, sprinkling *Ant* crowd, horde, many

few·er \'fyü-ər\ *pron* : a smaller number of persons or things

fey \ˈfā\ *adj* **1** *chiefly Scot* : fated to die; *also* : marked by a foreboding of death or calamity **2** : able to see into the future : VISIONARY **3** : marked by an otherworldly air or attitude **4** : mentally unsound — not used technically

fez \ˈfez\ *n, pl* **fez·zes** *also* **fez·es** : a round red felt hat that has a flat top and a tassel but no brim

ff *abbr* **1** folios 2 and the following ones **3** fortissimo

FHA *abbr* Federal Housing Administration

fi·an·cé \ˌfē-ˌän-ˈsā\ *n* : a man engaged to be married

fi·an·cée \ˌfē-ˌän-ˈsā\ *n* : a woman engaged to be married

fi·as·co \fē-ˈas-kō\ *n, pl* **-coes** ◆ : a complete failure

◆ bust, catastrophe, debacle, failure, flop, washout

fi·at \ˈfē-ət, -ˌat, -ˌät; ˈfī-ət, -ˌat\ *n* ◆ : an authoritative and often arbitrary order or decree

◆ decree, directive, edict, ruling

¹**fib** \ˈfib\ *n* ◆ : a trivial or childish lie

◆ fabrication, falsehood, falsity, lie, story, tale, untruth

²**fib** *vb* **fibbed; fib·bing** ◆ : to tell a fib

◆ fabricate, lie, prevaricate

fib·ber *n* ◆ : one that tells fibs

◆ liar, prevaricator

fi·ber *or Can and Brit* **fi·bre** \ˈfī-bər\ *n* **1** : a threadlike substance or structure (as a muscle cell or fine root); *esp* : a natural (as wool or flax) or artificial (as rayon) filament capable of being spun or woven **2** : indigestible material in human food that stimulates the intestine to move its contents along **3** : an element that gives texture or substance **4** ◆ : basic toughness : STRENGTH ⟨moral ∼⟩ — **fi·brous** \-brəs\ *adj*

◆ backbone, fortitude, grit, guts, pluck, spunk

fi·ber·board *or Can and Brit* **fi·bre·board** \ˈfī-bər-ˌbōrd\ *n* : a material made by compressing fibers (as of wood) into stiff sheets

fi·ber·fill *or Can and Brit* **fi·bre·fill** \-ˌfil\ *n* : synthetic fibers used as a filling material (as for cushions)

fi·ber·glass *or Can and Brit* **fi·bre·glass** \-ˌglas\ *n* : glass in fibrous form used in making various products (as insulation)

fiber optics *n* **1** *pl* : thin transparent fibers of glass or plastic that are enclosed by a less refractive material and that transmit light by internal reflection; *also* : a bundle of such fibers used in an instrument **2** : the technique of the use of fiber optics — **fiber–optic** *adj*

fi·bril \ˈfī-brəl, ˈfi-\ *n* : a small fiber

fi·bril·la·tion \ˌfi-brə-ˈlā-shən, ˌfī-\ *n* : rapid irregular contractions of the heart muscle fibers resulting in a lack of synchronism between heartbeat and pulse — **fib·ril·late** \ˈfi-brə-ˌlāt, ˈfī-\ *vb*

fi·brin \ˈfī-brən\ *n* : a white insoluble fibrous protein formed in the clotting of blood

fi·broid \ˈfī-ˌbroid, ˈfi-\ *adj* : resembling, forming, or consisting of fibrous tissue ⟨∼ tumors⟩

fi·bro·my·al·gia \ˌfī-brō-ˌmī-ˈal-jə\ *n* : any of a group of rheumatic disorders affecting soft tissues (as muscles or tendons)

fi·bro·sis \fī-ˈbrō-səs\ *n* : a condition marked by abnormal increase of fiber-containing tissue

fib·u·la \ˈfi-byə-lə\ *n, pl* **-lae** \-ˌlē, -ˌlī\ *or* **-las** : the outer and usu. the smaller of the two bones between the knee and ankle — **fib·u·lar** \-lər\ *adj*

FICA *abbr* Federal Insurance Contributions Act

-fication *n comb form* : making : production ⟨simpli*fication*⟩

fiche \ˈfēsh\ *n, pl* **fiche** : MICROFICHE

fi·chu \ˈfi-shü\ *n* : a woman's light triangular scarf draped over the shoulders and fastened in front

fick·le \ˈfi-kəl\ *adj* ◆ : not firm or steadfast in disposition or character : INCONSTANT ⟨∼ friends⟩ — **fick·le·ness** *n*

◆ capricious, changeable, inconstant, mercurial, uncertain, unpredictable, unsteady, variable *Ant* certain, constant, steady, unchangeable ◆ disloyal, faithless, false, inconstant, unfaithful, untrue

fic·tion \ˈfik-shən\ *n* **1** ◆ : something (as a story) invented by the imagination **2** ◆ : fictitious literature (as novels)

◆ [1, 2] fabrication, fantasy, figment, invention *Ant* fact

fic·tion·al \ˈfik-shə-nəl\ *adj* : of, relating to, or characteristic of fiction — **fic·tion·al·ly** *adv*

fic·ti·tious \fik-ˈti-shəs\ *adj* **1** ◆ : of, relating to, or characteristic of fiction : IMAGINARY **2** : FALSE, ASSUMED ⟨a ∼ name⟩ **3** : FEIGNED

◆ imaginary, made-up, mythical, pretend, unreal

¹**fid·dle** \ˈfid-ᵊl\ *n* : VIOLIN

²**fiddle** *vb* **fid·dled; fid·dling** **1** : to play on a fiddle **2** ◆ : to move the hands or fingers restlessly **3** ◆ : to move or act aimlessly or idly — often used with *around* **4** ◆ : to interest oneself in what is not one's concern — **fid·dler** *n*

◆ [2] fidget, jerk, squirm, twitch, wiggle ◆ *usu* **fiddle around** [3] fool, mess, monkey, play, putter ◆ *usu* **fiddle with** [4] fool, mess, monkey, play, tamper, tinker

fid·dle·head \ˈfid-ᵊl-ˌhed\ *n* : one of the young unfurling fronds of some ferns that are often eaten as greens

fiddler crab *n* : any of a genus of burrowing crabs with one claw much enlarged in the male

fid·dle·stick \ˈfid-ᵊl-ˌstik\ *n* **1** *archaic* : a violin bow **2** *pl* ◆ : language, conduct, or an idea that is absurd or contrary to good sense : NONSENSE — used as an interjection

fiddlesticks ◆ foolishness, hogwash, humbug, nonsense, silliness

fi·del·i·ty \fə-ˈde-lə-tē, fī-\ *n, pl* **-ties** **1** ◆ : the quality or state of being faithful **2** : ACCURACY ⟨∼ in sound reproduction⟩

◆ allegiance, constancy, dedication, devotion, faith, faithfulness, fastness, fealty, loyalty, steadfastness *Ant* disloyalty, infidelity, perfidy, treachery

¹**fidg·et** \ˈfi-jət\ *n* **1** : uneasiness or restlessness as shown by nervous movements — usu. used in pl. **2** : one that fidgets — **fidg·ety** *adj*

²**fidget** *vb* ◆ : to move or cause to move or act restlessly or nervously

◆ fiddle, jerk, squirm, twitch, wiggle

fi·du·cia·ry \fə-ˈdü-shē-ˌer-ē, -ˈdyü-, -shə-rē\ *adj* **1** : involving a confidence or trust **2** : held or holding in trust for another ⟨∼ accounts⟩ — **fiduciary** *n*

fie \ˈfī\ *interj* — used to express disgust or disapproval

fief \ˈfēf\ *n* : a feudal estate : FEE

¹**field** \ˈfēld\ *n* **1** ◆ : open country **2** : a piece of cleared land for cultivation or pasture **3** : a piece of land yielding some special product **4** : the place where a battle is fought; *also* : BATTLE **5** ◆ : an area, division, or sphere of activity ⟨the ∼ of science⟩ ⟨sales reps in the ∼⟩ **6** : an area for military exercises **7** : an area for sports **8** : a background on which something is drawn or projected ⟨a flag with white stars on a ∼ of blue⟩ **9** : a region or space in which a given effect (as magnetism) exists **10** : a particular area (as of a record in a database) in which the same type of information is regularly recorded — **field** *adj*

◆ [1] ground, lot, parcel, plat, plot, tract ◆ [5] area, arena, department, discipline, domain, line, province, realm, specialty, sphere

²**field** *vb* **1** : to handle a batted or thrown baseball while on defense **2** : to put into the field **3** : to answer satisfactorily ⟨∼ a tough question⟩ — **field·er** *n*

field day *n* **1** : a day devoted to outdoor sports and athletic competition **2** : a time of extraordinary pleasure or opportunity

field event *n* : a track-and-field event (as weight-throwing) other than a race

field glass *n* : a handheld binocular telescope — usu. used in pl.

field guide *n* : a manual for identifying natural objects, plants, or animals

field hockey *n* : a field game played between two teams of 11 players each whose object is to knock a ball into the opponent's goal with a curved stick

field marshal *n* : an officer (as in the British army) of the highest rank

field–test \-ˌtest\ *vb* : to test (as a new product) in actual situations reflecting intended use — **field test** *n*

fiend \ˈfēnd\ *n* **1** : DEVIL 1 **2** ◆ : an infernal being : DEMON **3** ◆ : an extremely wicked or cruel person **4** ◆ : a person excessively devoted to a pursuit ⟨a golf ∼⟩ **5** ◆ : one who is addicted esp. to a substance : ADDICT ⟨dope ∼⟩

◆ [2] demon, devil, ghoul, imp ◆ [3] beast, devil, evildoer, no-good, reprobate, rogue, varlet, villain, wretch ◆ [4] addict, enthusiast, fan, fanatic, freak, lover, maniac, nut ◆ [5] addict, doper, user

fiend·ish *adj* ◆ : perversely diabolical — **fiend·ish·ly** *adv*

◆ demonic, devilish, diabolical, satanic *Ant* angelic

fierce \ˈfirs\ *adj* **fierc·er; fierc·est** **1** ◆ : violently hostile or aggressive in temperament **2** : given to fighting or killing : PUGNACIOUS **3** ◆ : marked by unrestrained zeal or vehemence : INTENSE **4** ◆ : furiously active or determined **5** ◆ : wild or menacing in appearance — **fierce·ly** *adv*

♦ [1] fell, ferocious, grim, savage, vicious *Ant* gentle, mild
♦ [3] explosive, ferocious, furious, intense, terrible, vehement, vicious, violent ♦ [4] aggressive, ambitious, assertive, enterprising, go-getting, high-pressure, militant, self-assertive
♦ [5] austere, forbidding, grim, rough, rugged, severe, steely, stern

fierce·ness *n* ♦ : the quality or state of being fierce

♦ aggressiveness, assertiveness, emphasis, intensity, vehemence

fi·ery \'fī-ə-rē\ *adj* **fi·er·i·er; -est** 1 : consisting of fire 2 ♦ : on fire : BURNING, BLAZING 3 : FLAMMABLE 4 ♦ : hot like a fire 5 : RED ⟨a ~ sunset⟩ 6 ♦ : full of emotion or spirit 7 : IRRITABLE — **fi·eri·ness** \-rē-nəs\ *n*

♦ [2] ablaze, afire, burning ♦ [4] broiling, burning, hot, torrid
♦ [6] ardent, emotional, fervent, feverish, hot-blooded, impassioned, passionate, red-hot, vehement

fi·es·ta \fē-'es-tə\ *n* ♦ : a time of celebration marked by special observances : FESTIVAL

♦ carnival, celebration, festival, festivity, fete, gala, jubilee

fife \'fīf\ *n* : a small flute
FIFO *abbr* first in, first out
fif·teen \fif-'tēn\ *n* : one more than 14 — **fifteen** *adj or pron* — **fif·teenth** \-'tēnth\ *adj or n*
fifth \'fifth\ *n* 1 : one that is number five in a countable series 2 : one of five equal parts of something 3 : a unit of measure for liquor equal to ⅕ U.S. gallon — **fifth** *adj or adv*
fifth column *n* : a group of secret supporters of a nation's enemy that engage in espionage or sabotage within the country — **fifth columnist** *n*
fifth wheel *n* : one that is unnecessary and often burdensome
fif·ty \'fif-tē\ *n, pl* **fifties** : five times 10 — **fif·ti·eth** \-tē-əth\ *adj or n* — **fifty** *adj or pron*
fif·ty–fif·ty \,fif-tē-'fif-tē\ *adj* 1 : shared equally ⟨a ~ proposition⟩ 2 : half favorable and half unfavorable
¹**fig** \'fig\ *n* : a soft usu. pear-shaped edible fruit of a tree related to the mulberry; *also* : a tree bearing figs
²**fig** *abbr* 1 figurative; figuratively 2 figure
¹**fight** \'fīt\ *vb* **fought** \'fȯt\; **fight·ing** 1 ♦ : to contend against another in battle or physical combat 2 : BOX 3 : to put forth a determined effort 4 ♦ : to contend in disagreement or competition 5 ♦ : to attempt to prevent the success or effectiveness of 6 : WAGE ⟨~ a war⟩ 7 : to gain by struggle

♦ [1] battle, clash, combat, scrimmage, skirmish, war
♦ [4] battle, compete, contend, race, vie ♦ [4] argue, brawl, dispute, quarrel, row, scrap, spat, squabble ♦ [5] battle, combat, contend, counter, oppose *Ant* advance, encourage, promote

²**fight** *n* 1 ♦ : a hostile encounter : BATTLE 2 : a boxing match 3 ♦ : a verbal disagreement 4 ♦ : a struggle for a goal or an objective 5 ♦ : strength or disposition for fighting ⟨full of ~⟩

♦ [1] battle, clash, combat, conflict, contest, skirmish, struggle
♦ [3] argument, brawl, disagreement, dispute, quarrel, row, scrap, spat, squabble ♦ [4] battle, fray, scrabble, struggle
♦ [5] aggression, aggressiveness, belligerence, militancy, pugnacity, truculence

fight·er \'fī-tər\ *n* 1 ♦ : one that fights; *esp* : WARRIOR 2 ♦ : one that engages in the sport of boxing : BOXER 3 : a fast maneuverable warplane for destroying enemy aircraft

♦ [1] legionnaire, man-at-arms, regular, serviceman, soldier, warrior ♦ [2] boxer, prizefighter, pugilist

fig·ment \'fig-mənt\ *n* ♦ : something imagined or made up

♦ chimera, conceit, delusion, dream, fancy, fantasy, hallucination, illusion, phantasm, pipe dream, unreality, vision

fig·u·ra·tion \,fi-gyə-'rā-shən, -gə-\ *n* 1 : FORM, OUTLINE 2 : an act or instance of representation in figures and shapes
fig·u·ra·tive \'fi-gyə-rə-tiv, -gə-\ *adj* 1 : EMBLEMATIC 2 : expressing one thing in terms normally denoting another with which it may be regarded as analogous : SYMBOLIC, METAPHORICAL ⟨~ language⟩ — **fig·u·ra·tive·ly** *adv*
¹**fig·ure** \'fi-gyər, -gər\ *n* 1 ♦ : a number symbol : NUMERAL 2 : a written or printed character 3 ♦ : value esp. as expressed in numbers : PRICE 4 : a combination of points, lines, or surfaces in geometry ⟨a circle is a closed plane ~⟩ 5 ♦ : a body apparent chiefly in outline : an object significant or noticeable only in its form : SHAPE, FORM, OUTLINE 6 a : the graphic representation of a form esp. of a person b : a representation of the human figure used esp. for displaying clothes 7 ♦ : a diagram or pictorial illustration of textual matter 8 : an often repetitive pattern or design in a manufactured article (as cloth) or natural product (as

wood) : PATTERN, DESIGN 9 : appearance made or impression produced ⟨they cut quite a ~⟩ 10 : a series of movements (as in a dance) 11 ♦ : a prominent personality : PERSONAGE 12 ♦ : the shape of the human body

♦ [1] digit, integer, number, numeral, whole number
♦ [3] charge, cost, fee, price ♦ [5] cast, configuration, form, outline, shape ♦ [7] diagram, graphic, illustration, plate
♦ [11] celebrity, notable, personage, personality ♦ [12] build, constitution, form, frame, physique, shape

²**figure** *vb* **fig·ured; fig·ur·ing** 1 : to represent by or as if by a figure or outline 2 : to decorate with a pattern 3 : to indicate or represent by numerals 4 ♦ : to think of esp. with regard to taking some action 5 : to be or appear important or conspicuous 6 ♦ : to determine esp. by mathematical means : COMPUTE, CALCULATE ⟨*figured* the cost⟩ 7 : to reckon by exercise of practical judgment 8 ♦ : to take as granted or true

♦ [4] choose, conclude, decide, determine, opt, resolve
♦ [6] calculate, compute, reckon, work out ♦ [8] believe, consider, feel, imagine, suppose, think

fig·ure·head \'fi-gyər-,hed, -gər-\ *n* 1 : a figure on the bow of a ship 2 : a head or chief in name only
figure of speech : a form of expression (as a simile or metaphor) that often compares or identifies one thing with another to convey meaning or heighten effect
figure out *vb* 1 : FIND OUT, DISCOVER 2 ♦ : to find a solution, explanation, or answer for : SOLVE

♦ answer, puzzle, resolve, riddle, solve, unravel, work, work out

figure skating *n* : skating that includes various jumps, spins, and dance movements
fig·u·rine \,fi-gyə-'rēn, -gə-\ *n* : a small carved or molded figure
Fi·ji·an \'fē-jē-ən, fi-'jē-ən\ *n* : a native or inhabitant of the Pacific island country of Fiji — **Fijian** *adj*
fil·a·ment \'fi-lə-mənt\ *n* : a fine thread or threadlike object, part, or process — **fil·a·men·tous** \,fi-lə-'men-təs\ *adj*
fil·bert \'fil-bərt\ *n* : the sweet thick-shelled nut of either of two European hazels; *also* : a shrub or small tree bearing filberts
filch \'filch\ *vb* ♦ : to steal furtively

♦ appropriate, pilfer, pocket, steal, swipe, thieve

¹**file** \'fīl\ *n* : a usu. steel tool with a ridged or toothed surface used esp. for smoothing a hard substance
²**file** *vb* **filed; fil·ing** ♦ : to rub, smooth, or cut away with a file

♦ buff, grind, hone, rasp, rub, sand

³**file** *vb* **filed; fil·ing** 1 : to arrange in order 2 : to enter or record officially or as prescribed by law ⟨~ a lawsuit⟩ 3 : to send (copy) to a newspaper
⁴**file** *n* 1 : a device (as a folder or cabinet) by means of which papers may be kept in order 2 : a collection of papers or publications usu. arranged or classified 3 : a collection of data (as text) treated by a computer as a unit
⁵**file** *n* ♦ : a row of persons, animals, or things arranged one behind the other

♦ column, cue, line, queue, range, string, train

⁶**file** *vb* **filed; fil·ing** ♦ : to march or proceed in file

♦ march, pace, parade, stride

fi·let mi·gnon \,fi-(,)lā-mēn-'yōⁿ, fi-,lā-\ *n, pl* **filets mignons** \-(,)lā-mēn-'yōⁿz, -,lā-\ : a thick slice of beef cut from the narrow end of a beef tenderloin
fil·ial \'fi-lē-əl, 'fil-yəl\ *adj* : of, relating to, or befitting a son or daughter
fil·i·bus·ter \'fi-lə-,bəs-tər\ *n* 1 : a military adventurer; *esp* : an American engaged in fomenting 19th century Latin American uprisings 2 : the use of delaying tactics (as extremely long speeches) esp. in a legislative assembly; *also* : an instance of this practice — **filibuster** *vb* — **fil·i·bus·ter·er** *n*
fil·i·gree \'fi-lə-,grē\ *n* : ornamental openwork (as of fine wire) — **fil·i·greed** \-,grēd\ *adj*
fil·ing \'fī-liŋ\ *n* 1 : the act or instance of using a file 2 : a small piece scraped off by a file ⟨iron ~s⟩
Fil·i·pi·no \,fi-lə-'pē-nō\ *n, pl* **Filipinos** : a native or inhabitant of the Philippines — **Filipino** *adj*
¹**fill** \'fil\ *vb* 1 ♦ : to make or become full 2 ♦ : to stop up : PLUG ⟨~ a cavity⟩ 3 : FEED, SATIATE 4 ♦ : to carry out the terms of (as a contract) : SATISFY, FULFILL ⟨~ all requirements⟩ 5 : to occupy fully 6 : to spread through ⟨laughter ~ed the room⟩ 7 : OCCUPY ⟨~ the office of president⟩ 8 : to put a person in ⟨~ a vacancy⟩ 9 : to supply as directed ⟨~ a prescription⟩

♦ [1] charge, cram, heap, jam, jam-pack, load, pack, stuff *Ant* empty ♦ [2] block, dam, pack, plug, stop, stuff ♦ [4] answer, comply, fulfill, keep, meet, redeem, satisfy

²fill *n* **1** ♦ : a full supply; *esp* : a quantity that satisfies or satiates **2** : material used esp. for filling a low place

fill·er \'fi-lər\ *n* **1** ♦ : one that fills **2** ♦ : a substance added to another substance (as to increase bulk or weight) **3** : a material used for filling cracks and pores in wood before painting

♦ fill, filling, padding, stuffing

¹fil·let \'fi-lət, *in sense 2* fi-'lā, 'fi-(,)lā\ *also* **fi·let** \'fi-'lā, 'fi-(,)lā\ *n* **1** : a narrow band, strip, or ribbon **2** : a piece or slice of boneless meat or fish; *esp* : the tenderloin of beef

²fil·let \'fi-lət, *in sense 2 also* fi-'lā, 'fi-(,)lā\ *vb* **1** : to bind or adorn with or as if with a fillet **2** : to cut into fillets

fill in *vb* **1** ♦ : to provide necessary or recent information **2** ♦ : to serve as a temporary substitute

♦ [1] acquaint, brief, enlighten, familiarize, inform, instruct ♦ [2] cover, pinch-hit, stand in, sub, substitute, take over

fill·ing \'fi-liŋ\ *n* **1** ♦ : material used to fill something ⟨a ∼ for a tooth⟩ **2** : the yarn interlacing the warp in a fabric **3** : a food mixture used to fill pastry or sandwiches

♦ fill, filler, padding, stuffing

filling station *n* : a retail station for servicing motor vehicles esp. with gasoline and oil

fil·lip \'fi-ləp\ *n* **1** : a blow or gesture made by a flick or snap of the finger across the thumb **2** : something that serves to arouse or excite — **fillip** *vb*

fill-up \'fil-,əp\ *n* : an act or instance of filling something

fil·ly \'fi-lē\ *n, pl* **fillies** : a young female horse usu. less than four years old

¹film \'film\ *n* **1** : a thin skin or membrane **2** : a thin coating or layer **3** : a flexible strip of chemically treated material used in taking pictures **4** ♦ : a representation (as of a story) by means of motion pictures

♦ motion picture, movie, picture

²film *vb* **1** : to cover with a film **2** : to make a motion picture of

film·dom \'film-dəm\ *n* : the motion-picture industry

film·og·ra·phy \fil-'mä-grə-fē\ *n, pl* **-phies** : a list of motion pictures featuring the work of a film figure or a particular topic

film·strip \'film-,strip\ *n* : a strip of film bearing a sequence of images for projection as still pictures

filmy *adj* : light, transparent, and fluffy

fils \'fēs\ *n* : SON — used after a family name to distinguish a son from his father

¹fil·ter \'fil-tər\ *n* **1** : a porous material through which a fluid is passed to separate out matter in suspension; *also* : a device containing such material **2** : a device for suppressing waves of certain frequencies; *esp* : one (as for a camera) that absorbs light of certain colors **3** : software for sorting or blocking certain online material

²filter *vb* **1** ♦ : to remove by means of a filter **2** : to pass through a filter — **fil·ter·able** *also* **fil·tra·ble** \-tə-rə-bəl, -trə-\ *adj* — **fil·tra·tion** \fil-'trā-shən\ *n*

♦ clarify, clear, distill, purify

filth \'filth\ *n* **1** ♦ : foul matter; *esp* : loathsome dirt or refuse **2** ♦ : moral corruption **3** : something that tends to corrupt or disgust : OBSCENITY

♦ [1] dirt, grime, muck, refuse, smut, soil ♦ [2] coarseness, dirt, grossness, indecency, lewdness, obscenity, smut, vulgarity

filth·i·ness *n* ♦ : the quality or state of being filthy

♦ dinginess, dirtiness, foulness, grubbiness, nastiness, uncleanliness

¹filthy \'fil-thē\ *adj* **1** ♦ : covered with, having the appearance of, or containing filth : very dirty **2** ♦ : abhorrent to morality or virtue : designed to incite to lust or depravity

♦ [1] dirty, grubby, grungy, mucky, muddy, unclean ♦ [2] bawdy, coarse, crude, dirty, gross, indecent, lewd, obscene, pornographic, vulgar

²filthy *adv* : VERY, EXTREMELY ⟨∼ dirty⟩ ⟨∼ rich⟩

fil·trate \'fil-,trāt\ *n* : fluid that has passed through a filter

¹fin \'fin\ *n* **1** : one of the thin external processes by which an aquatic animal (as a fish) moves through water **2** : a fin-shaped part (as on an airplane) **3** : FLIPPER 2 — **finned** \'find\ *adj*

²fin *abbr* **1** finance; financial **2** finish

fi·na·gle \fə-'nā-gəl\ *vb* **-gled; -gling** **1** ♦ : to obtain by indirect or dishonest means : WANGLE **2** ♦ : to use devious dishonest methods to achieve one's ends — **fi·na·gler** *n*

♦ [1, 2] contrive, finesse, frame, machinate, maneuver, wangle

¹fi·nal \'fīn-ᵊl\ *adj* **1** ♦ : not to be altered or undone **2** ♦ : coming at the end : being the last in a series, process, or progress **3** : relating to or occurring at the end or conclusion — **fi·nal·i·ty** \fī-'na-lə-tē, fə-\ *n* — **fi·nal·ly** *adv*

♦ [1] certain, firm, fixed, hard, hard-and-fast, set, settled, stable ♦ [2] hindmost, last, latter, terminal, ultimate

²final *n* **1** : a deciding match or game — usu. used in pl. **2** : the last examination in a course — often used in pl.

fi·na·le \fə-'na-lē, fi-'nä-\ *n* ♦ : the close or end of something; *esp* : the last section of a musical composition

♦ close, conclusion, consummation, end, ending, finis, finish, windup *Ant* beginning, dawn, opening, start

fi·nal·ise *Brit var of* FINALIZE

fi·nal·ist \'fīn-ᵊl-əst\ *n* : a contestant in the finals of a competition

fi·nal·ize \'fīn-ᵊl-,īz\ *vb* **-ized; -iz·ing** ♦ : to put in final or finished form

♦ complete, consummate, finish, perfect

¹fi·nance \fə-'nans, 'fī-,nans\ *n* **1** *pl* ♦ : money resources available esp. to a government or business **2** : management of money affairs

♦ *usu* **finances** funds, resources, wherewithal

²finance *vb* **fi·nanced; fi·nanc·ing** **1** ♦ : to raise or provide funds for **2** ♦ : to furnish with necessary funds **3** : to sell or supply on credit

♦ [1] capitalize, endow, fund, stake, subsidize, underwrite ♦ [1, 2] endow, fund, subsidize

finance company *n* : a company that makes usu. small short-term loans usu. to individuals

fi·nan·cial \fə-'nan-chəl, fī-\ *adj* ♦ : relating to finance or financiers ⟨∼ problems⟩ — **fi·nan·cial·ly** *adv*

♦ fiscal, monetary, pecuniary

fi·nan·cials \-shəlz\ *n pl* : financial statistics

fi·nan·cier \,fi-nən-'sir, ,fī-nan-\ *n* **1** : a person skilled in managing public moneys **2** : a person who deals with large-scale finance and investment

finch \'finch\ *n* : any of numerous songbirds with strong conical bills

¹find \'fīnd\ *vb* **found** \'faund\; **find·ing** **1** ♦ : to meet with either by chance or by searching or study **2** : to obtain by effort or management ⟨∼ time to read⟩ **3** : to arrive at : REACH ⟨the bullet *found* its mark⟩ **4** : EXPERIENCE, FEEL ⟨*found* happiness⟩ **5** : to gain or regain the use of ⟨*found* his voice again⟩ **6** : to determine and make a statement about ⟨∼ a verdict⟩

♦ detect, determine, dig up, discover, ferret out, hit on, locate, track down *Ant* miss, overlook, pass over

²find *n* **1** : an act or instance of finding **2** : something found; *esp* : a valuable item of discovery

find·er \'fīn-dər\ *n* : one that finds; *esp* : VIEWFINDER

fin de siè·cle \,fa[n]-də-sē-'ekl²\ *adj* **1** : of, relating to, or characteristic of the close of the 19th century **2** : of or relating to the end of a century

find·ing \'fīn-diŋ\ *n* **1** ♦ : the act of finding **2** : FIND 2 **3** : the result of a judicial proceeding or inquiry

♦ detection, discovery

find out *vb* ♦ : to learn by study, observation, or search : DISCOVER

♦ ascertain, catch on, discover, hear, learn, realize, see

¹fine \'fīn\ *n* ♦ : money exacted as a penalty for an offense

♦ damages, forfeit, mulct, penalty

²fine *vb* **fined; fin·ing** ♦ : to impose a fine on : punish by a fine

♦ assess, charge, exact, impose, lay, levy, put

³fine *adj* **fin·er; fin·est** **1** ♦ : free from impurity **2 a** ♦ : very thin in gauge or texture **b** ♦ : very small **3** : not coarse **4** : SUBTLE, SENSITIVE ⟨a ∼ distinction⟩ **5** ♦ : superior in quality or appearance : eminently good **6** ♦ : very precise or accurate : REFINED **7** ♦ : very well — **fine·ly** *adv*

♦ [1] pure, refined, unadulterated, undiluted ♦ [2a] dusty, floury, powdery *Ant* coarse, grainy, granular ♦ [2b] narrow, skinny, slender, slim, thin ♦ [5] A1, excellent, grand, great, heavenly, prime, splendid, superb, superior, unsurpassed, wonderful ♦ [6] delicate, exact, minute, precise, refined, subtle *Ant* coarse, inexact, rough ♦ [7] agreeable, all right, alright, good, OK, satisfactory

⁴fine *adv* **1** ♦ : very well **2** — used to express agreement

♦ all right, good, nicely, OK, satisfactorily, well

fine art *n* : art (as painting, sculpture, or music) concerned esp. with the creation of beautiful objects — usu. used in pl.

fine·ness *n* **1 ♦** : exquisite perfection or elaborateness of form, texture, or construction : superior quality **2 ♦** : delicate, subtle, or sensitive in quality, perception, or discrimination

♦ [1] accuracy, closeness, delicacy, exactness, precision, veracity ♦ [2] daintiness, delicacy, fragility

fin·ery \'fī-nə-rē\ *n, pl* **-er·ies 1** : ORNAMENT, DECORATION **2 ♦** : showy clothing and jewels

♦ array, best, feather, frippery, full dress, regalia

fine·spun \'fīn-'spən\ *adj* : developed with extremely or excessively fine delicacy or detail

¹**fi·nesse** \fə-'nes\ *n* **1** : refinement or delicacy of workmanship, structure, or texture **2 ♦** : skillful handling of a situation : adroit maneuvering

♦ adroitness, cleverness, craft, dexterity, sleight

²**finesse** *vb* **♦** : to bring about, direct, or manage by adroit maneuvering

♦ finagle, maneuver, mastermind, negotiate, wangle

fine–tune \'fīn-'tün\ *vb* : to adjust so as to bring to the highest level of performance or effectiveness

fin·fish \'fin-,fish\ *n* : FISH 2

¹**fin·ger** \'fiŋ-gər\ *n* **1** : any of the five divisions at the end of the hand; *esp* : one other than the thumb **2** : something that resembles or does the work of a finger **3** : a part of a glove into which a finger is inserted

²**finger** *vb* **fin·gered; fin·ger·ing 1** : to touch or feel with the fingers : HANDLE **2** : to perform with the fingers or with a certain fingering **3** : to mark the notes of a piece of music as a guide in playing **4** : to point out

fin·ger·board \'fiŋ-gər-,bōrd\ *n* : the part of a stringed instrument against which the fingers press the strings to vary the pitch

finger bowl *n* : a small water bowl for rinsing the fingers at the table

fin·ger·ing \'fiŋ-gə-riŋ\ *n* **1** : handling or touching with the fingers **2** : the act or method of using the fingers in playing an instrument **3** : the marking of the method of fingering

fin·ger·ling \'fiŋ-gər-liŋ\ *n* : a small fish

fin·ger·nail \'fiŋ-gər-,nāl\ *n* : the nail of a finger

fin·ger·print \-,print\ *n* : the pattern of marks made by pressing the tip of a finger or thumb on a surface; *esp* : an ink impression of such a pattern taken for the purpose of identification — **fingerprint** *vb*

fin·ger·tip \-,tip\ *n* : the tip of a finger

fin·i·al \'fi-nē-əl\ *n* : an ornamental projection or end (as on a spire)

fin·ick·ing \'fi-ni-kiŋ\ *adj* : FINICKY

fin·icky \'fi-ni-kē\ *adj* **♦** : excessively particular in taste or standards ⟨a ∼ eater⟩

♦ choosy, dainty, delicate, demanding, exacting, fastidious, fussy, particular, picky *Ant* undemanding, unfussy

fi·nis \'fi-nəs\ *n* **1** : a point that marks the extent of something **2 ♦** : cessation of a course of action, pursuit, or activity : END, CONCLUSION

♦ close, conclusion, consummation, end, ending, finale, finish, windup

¹**fin·ish** \'fi-nish\ *vb* **1 ♦** : to come to an end : TERMINATE **2** : to use or dispose of entirely **3 ♦** : to bring to completion **4** : to put a final coat or surface on — **fin·ish·er** *n*

♦ [1] break off, cease, close, conclude, die, end, expire, quit, stop, terminate ♦ [3] complete, consummate, finalize, perfect

²**finish** *n* **1 ♦** : final stage : END, CONCLUSION **2** : something that completes or perfects **3** : the final treatment or coating of a surface

♦ close, conclusion, consummation, end, ending, finale, finis, windup

fi·nite \'fī-,nīt\ *adj* **1 ♦** : having definite or definable limits; *also* : having a limited nature or existence **2** : being less than some positive integer in number or measure and greater than its negative **3** : showing distinction of grammatical person and number ⟨a ∼ verb⟩

♦ definite, determinate, limited, measured, narrow, restricted

fink \'fiŋk\ *n* **1** : a contemptible person **2** : STRIKEBREAKER **3** : INFORMER

Finn \'fin\ *n* : a native or inhabitant of Finland

fin·nan had·die \,fi-nən-'ha-dē\ *n* : smoked haddock

¹**Finn·ish** \'fi-nish\ *adj* : of or relating to Finland, the Finns, or Finnish

²**Finnish** *n* : the language of the Finns

fin·ny \'fi-nē\ *adj* **1** : having or characterized by fins **2** : relating to or being fish

fiord *var of* FJORD

fir \'fər\ *n* : any of a genus of usu. large evergreen trees related to the pines; *also* : the light soft wood of a fir

¹**fire** \'fīr\ *n* **1** : the light or heat and esp. the flame of something burning **2** : ENTHUSIASM, ZEAL **3** : fuel that is burning (as in a stove or fireplace) **4 ♦** : destructive burning (as of a house) **5** : the firing of weapons — **fire·less** *adj*

♦ conflagration, holocaust, inferno

²**fire** *vb* **fired; fir·ing 1 ♦** : to set on fire : set fire to : KINDLE, IGNITE ⟨∼ a house⟩ **2 a ♦** : to give life or spirit to : STIR, ENLIVEN ⟨∼ the imagination⟩ **b ♦** : to become irritated : become angry or inflamed with passion **3 ♦** : to dismiss from employment **4 ♦** : to cause to be driven forward with force from a bow, sling, or similar device or from a firearm : SHOOT ⟨∼ a gun⟩ ⟨∼ an arrow⟩ **5** : BAKE ⟨firing pottery in a kiln⟩ **6** : to apply fire or fuel to something ⟨∼ a furnace⟩ **7 ♦** : to throw with speed or force

♦ [1] burn, ignite, inflame, kindle, light ♦ [2a] animate, brace, energize, enliven, invigorate, jazz up, liven up, pep up, quicken, stimulate, vitalize, vivify, zip (up) ♦ *usu* **fire (up)** [2b] arouse, encourage, excite, incite, instigate, move, pique, provoke, stimulate, stir ♦ [3] cashier, dismiss, remove, retire, sack ♦ [4] blast, discharge, loose, shoot ♦ [7] dash, fling, heave, hurl, hurtle, launch, pitch, sling, throw, toss

fire ant *n* : either of two small fiercely stinging So. American ants introduced into the southeastern U.S. where they are agricultural pests

fire·arm \'fī(-ə)r-,ärm\ *n* **♦** : a weapon (as a pistol) from which a shot is discharged by gunpowder

♦ arm, gun, piece

fire·ball \-,bȯl\ *n* **1** : a ball of fire **2** : a very bright meteor **3** : the highly luminous cloud of vapor and dust created by a nuclear explosion **4** : a highly energetic person

fire·boat \-,bōt\ *n* : a boat equipped for fighting fires

fire·bomb \-,bäm\ *n* : an incendiary bomb — **firebomb** *vb*

fire·box \-,bäks\ *n* **1** : a chamber (as of a furnace) that contains a fire **2** : a box containing a fire alarm

fire·brand \-,brand\ *n* **1** : a piece of burning wood **2 ♦** : a person who creates unrest or strife : AGITATOR

♦ agitator, demagogue, incendiary, inciter, rabble-rouser

fire·break \-,brāk\ *n* : a barrier of cleared or plowed land intended to check a forest or grass fire

fire·bug \-,bəg\ *n* : a person who deliberately sets destructive fires

fire·crack·er \-,kra-kər\ *n* : a paper tube containing an explosive and a fuse and set off to make a noise

fire department *n* : an organization for preventing or extinguishing fires; *also* : its members

fire engine *n* : a motor vehicle with equipment for extinguishing fires

fire escape *n* : a stairway or ladder for escape from a burning building

fire·fight·er \'fī(-ə)r-,fī-tər\ *n* : a person who fights fires; *esp* : a member of a fire department

fire·fly \-,flī\ *n* : any of various small night-flying beetles that produce flashes of light for courtship purposes

fire·house \-,haůs\ *n* : FIRE STATION

fire irons *n pl* : tools for tending a fire esp. in a fireplace

fire·man \'fī(-ə)r-mən\ *n* **1** : STOKER **2** : FIREFIGHTER

fire off *vb* : to write and send

fire·place \-,plās\ *n* **1** : a framed opening made in a chimney to hold an open fire **2** : an outdoor structure of brick or stone for an open fire

fire·plug \-,pləg\ *n* : HYDRANT

fire·pow·er \-,paů-(-ə)r\ *n* : the ability to deliver gunfire or warheads on a target

¹**fire·proof** \-'prüf\ *adj* **♦** : resistant to fire

♦ noncombustible, nonflammable, noninflammable

²**fireproof** *vb* : to make fireproof

fire–sale \-,sāl\ *adj* : heavily discounted ⟨∼ prices⟩

fire screen *n* : a protective screen before a fireplace

¹**fire·side** \'fī(-ə)r-,sīd\ *n* **1** : a place near the fire or hearth **2 ♦** : one's place of residence : HOME

♦ abode, domicile, dwelling, home, house, lodging

²fire·side *adj* : having an informal or intimate quality

fire station *n* : a building housing fire engines and usu. firefighters

fire·storm \'fī(-ə)r-ˌstȯrm\ *n* **1** : a large destructive very hot fire **2** : a sudden or violent outburst ⟨∼ of criticism⟩

fire tower *n* : a tower (as in a forest) from which a watch for fires is kept

fire·trap \'fī(-ə)r-ˌtrap\ *n* : a building or place apt to catch on fire or difficult to escape from in case of fire

fire truck *n* : FIRE ENGINE

fire·wall \-ˌwȯl\ *n* : computer hardware or software for preventing unauthorized access to data

fire·wa·ter \'fī(-ə)r-ˌwȯ-tər, -ˌwä-\ *n* : intoxicating liquor

fire·wood \-ˌwu̇d\ *n* : wood used for fuel

fire·work \-ˌwərk\ *n* **1** : a device designed to produce a striking display by the burning of explosive or flammable materials — usu. used in pl. ⟨a display of ∼s at the end of the festival⟩ **2** ♦ : *pl* a display of temper or intense conflict

♦ *usu* **fireworks** blowup, dudgeon, explosion, fit, huff, scene, tantrum

firing line *n* **1** : a line from which fire is delivered against a target **2** : the forefront of an activity

¹firm \'fərm\ *adj* **1** ♦ : securely fixed in place **2** : SOLID, VIGOROUS ⟨a ∼ handshake⟩ **3** ♦ : having a solid or compact texture **4** ♦ : not subject to change or fluctuation : STEADY ⟨∼ prices⟩ **5** ♦ : not easily moved or disturbed : STEADFAST **6** ♦ : indicating firmness or resolution

♦ [1] fast, frozen, secure, set, snug, tight ♦ [3] compact, hard, rigid, solid, stiff, unyielding *Ant* flabby, soft, spongy ♦ [4] certain, fixed, hard, hard-and-fast, set, settled, stable ♦ [5] fast, sound, stable, stalwart, steady, strong, sturdy ♦ [6] decisive, determined, intent, purposeful, resolute, set, single-minded

²firm *vb* ♦ : to make or become firm

♦ *usu* **firm up** concrete, congeal, freeze, harden, set, solidify

³firm *n* **1** : the name under which a company transacts business **2** : a business partnership of two or more persons **3** ♦ : a business enterprise

♦ business, company, concern, enterprise, establishment, house, outfit

fir·ma·ment \'fər-mə-mənt\ *n* : the arch of the sky : HEAVENS

firm·ly *adv* ♦ : in a firm manner

♦ forcefully, forcibly, hard, stoutly, strenuously, strongly, vigorously

firm·ness *n* ♦ : the quality or state of being firm

♦ decision, decisiveness, determination, resolution, resolve, stability, strength

firm·ware \'firm-ˌwer\ *n* : computer programs contained permanently in a hardware device

¹first \'fərst\ *adj* ♦ : preceding all others as in time, order, or importance

♦ chief, dominant, foremost, key, paramount, predominant, primary, principal ♦ initial, original, pioneer, premier *Ant* final, last, terminal, ultimate

²first *adv* **1** : before any other **2** : for the first time **3** ♦ : in preference to something else

♦ preferably, rather, readily, soon

³first *n* **1** : number one in a countable series **2** : something that is first **3** : the lowest forward gear in an automotive vehicle **4** : the winning or highest place in a competition or examination

first aid *n* : emergency care or treatment given an injured or ill person

first·born \'fərst-ˌbȯrn\ *adj* : ELDEST — **firstborn** *n*

first class *n* : the best or highest group in a classification — **first-class** *adj or adv*

first·hand \'fərst-ˌhand\ *adj* ♦ : coming from direct personal observation or experience — **firsthand** *adv*

♦ direct, immediate, primary

first lady *n, often cap F&L* : the wife or hostess of the chief executive of a political unit (as a country)

first lieutenant *n* : a commissioned officer (as in the army) ranking next below a captain

first·ling \'fərst-liŋ\ *n* : one that comes or is produced first

first·ly \-lē\ *adv* ♦ : in the first place : FIRST

♦ first, initially, originally, primarily

First Nation *n* : any of a number of peoples esp. of Canada who are Indigenous to the No. American continent

¹first–rate \-ˈrāt\ *adj* ♦ : of the first order of size, importance, or quality

♦ excellent, fabulous, fantastic, great, superb, terrific, wonderful

²first–rate *adv* : very well

first sergeant *n* **1** : a noncommissioned officer serving as the chief assistant to the commander of a military unit **2** : a rank in the army below a sergeant major and in the marine corps below a master gunnery sergeant

first strike *n* : a preemptive nuclear attack

first–string \'fərst-ˈstriŋ\ *adj* : being a regular as distinguished from a substitute — **first–string·er** \-ˈstriŋ-ər\ *n*

firth \'fərth\ *n* : a narrow arm of the sea : the opening of a river into the sea : ESTUARY

fis·cal \'fis-kəl\ *adj* **1** : of or relating to taxation, public revenues, or public debt **2** ♦ : of or relating to financial matters — **fis·cal·ly** *adv*

♦ financial, monetary, pecuniary

¹fish \'fish\ *n, pl* **fish** *or* **fish·es** **1** : a water-dwelling animal — usu. used in combination ⟨star*fish*⟩ ⟨shell*fish*⟩ **2** : any of numerous cold-blooded water-breathing vertebrates with fins, gills, and usu. scales that include the bony fishes and usu. the cartilaginous and jawless fishes **3** : the flesh of fish used as food

²fish *vb* **1** : to attempt to catch fish **2** : to seek something by roundabout means ⟨∼ for praise⟩ **3** : to search for something underwater **4** ♦ : to engage in a search by groping **5** : to draw forth

♦ feel, fumble, grope

fish–and–chips *n pl* : fried fish and french fried potatoes

fish·bowl \'fish-ˌbōl\ *n* **1** : a bowl for the keeping of live fish **2** : a place or condition that affords no privacy

fish·er \'fi-shər\ *n* **1** : one that fishes **2** : a dark brown No. American carnivorous mammal related to the weasels

fish·er·man \-mən\ *n* **1** : a person engaged in fishing **2** : a fishing boat

fish·ery \'fi-shə-rē\ *n, pl* **-er·ies** **1** : the business of catching fish **2** : a place for catching fish

fish farm *n* : a commercial facility for raising aquatic animals for human food — **fish–farm** *vb*

fish·hook \'fish-ˌhu̇k\ *n* : a usu. barbed hook for catching fish

fish ladder *n* : an arrangement of pools in steps by which fish can pass over a dam in going upstream

fish·net \'fish-ˌnet\ *n* **1** : netting for catching fish **2** : a coarse open-mesh fabric

fish·tail \-ˌtāl\ *vb* : to have the rear end slide from side to side out of control while moving forward

fish·wife \-ˌwīf\ *n* **1** : a woman who sells fish **2** : a vulgar abusive woman

fishy \'fi-shē\ *adj* **fish·i·er; -est** **1** : of or resembling fish **2** ♦ : inspiring doubt or suspicion : QUESTIONABLE ⟨the story sounds ∼ to me⟩

♦ debatable, doubtful, problematic, questionable, shady, shaky, suspect, suspicious

fis·sion \'fi-shən, -zhən\ *n* **1** : a cleaving into parts **2** : a method of reproduction in which a living cell or body divides into two or more parts each of which grows into a whole new individual **3** : the splitting of an atomic nucleus resulting in the release of large amounts of energy — **fis·sion·able** \'fi-shə-nə-bəl, -zhə-\ *adj*

fis·sure \'fi-shər\ *n* ♦ : a narrow opening or crack

♦ chink, cleft, crack, cranny, crevice, rift, split

fist \'fist\ *n* **1** : the hand with fingers folded into the palm **2** : INDEX 6

fist bump *n* : a gesture in which two people bump their fists together — **fist–bump** *vb*

fist·ful \'fist-ˌfu̇l\ *n* : HANDFUL

fist·i·cuffs \'fis-ti-ˌkəfs\ *n pl* : a fight with the fists

fist pump *n* : a celebratory gesture in which the fist is raised and lowered quickly and vigorously — **fist–pump** *vb*

fis·tu·la \'fis-chə-lə\ *n, pl* **-las** *or* **-lae** : an abnormal passage leading from an abscess or hollow organ — **fis·tu·lous** \-ləs\ *adj*

¹fit \'fit\ *adj* **fit·ter; fit·test** **1** ♦ : adapted to a purpose **2** : PROPER, RIGHT ⟨a movie ∼ for children⟩ **3** ♦ : put into a suitable state : made ready **4** ♦ : physically and mentally sound — **fit·ly** *adv*

♦ [1] appropriate, apt, good, happy, proper, right, suitable *Ant* inapplicable, inappropriate, unsuitable, wrong ♦ [1, 3] go, ready, set ♦ [3] available, functional, operable, practicable, serviceable, usable, useful ♦ [4] able-bodied, hale, healthy, hearty, robust, sound, well

²fit n **1 ♦** : a sudden violent attack (as in epilepsy) **2 ♦** : a sudden outburst

♦ [1] attack, bout, case, seizure, siege, spell ♦ [2] blowup, dudgeon, explosion, fireworks, huff, outburst, scene, tantrum

³fit vb **fit·ted** also **fit; fit·ting 1 ♦** : to be suitable for or to **2** : to be correctly adjusted to or shaped for **3 ♦** : to insert or adjust until correctly in place **4 ♦** : to make a place or room for **5 ♦** : to be in agreement or accord with **6 ♦** : to put into a condition of readiness : PREPARE **7 ♦** : to make or adjust to the right shape and size : ADJUST **8** : to supply with something that is adjusted or designed for the use required — usu. used with out **9** : to be in harmony or accord : BELONG — **fit·ter** n

♦ [1] befit, do, go, serve, suit ♦ [1, 6] equip, prepare, qualify, ready, season ♦ usu **fit in** or **fit into** [3] inject, insert, insinuate, interject, interpose, introduce ♦ [4] accommodate, hold, take ♦ [5] agree, answer, check, conform, correspond, dovetail, go, harmonize ♦ [7] acclimate, accommodate, adapt, adjust, condition, conform, shape

⁴fit n : the fact, condition, or manner of fitting or being fitted
fit·ful \'fit-fəl\ adj ♦ : not regular : INTERMITTENT ⟨~ sleep⟩ — **fit·ful·ly** adv

♦ erratic, intermittent, irregular, occasional, spasmodic, sporadic, spotty, unsteady **Ant** constant, continuous, regular, steady

fit·ness n ♦ : the quality or state of being fit

♦ health, robustness, soundness, wellness ♦ appropriateness, aptness, rightness, suitability

¹fit·ting \'fi-tiŋ\ adj ♦ : of a kind appropriate to the situation : APPROPRIATE, SUITABLE ⟨a ~ tribute⟩

♦ applicable, appropriate, apt, fit, proper, right, suitable

²fitting n **1** : the action or act of one that fits; esp : a trying on of clothes being made or altered **2** : a small often standardized part ⟨a plumbing ~⟩
fit·ting·ly adv ♦ : in a fitting manner

♦ appropriately, correctly, happily, properly, rightly, suitably

fit·ting·ness n : the quality or state of being appropriate to the situation
five \'fīv\ n **1** : one more than four **2** : the 5th in a set or series **3** : something having five units; esp : a basketball team **4** : a 5-dollar bill — **five** adj or pron
¹fix \'fiks\ vb **1** : to make firm, stable, or fast **2** : to give a permanent or final form to **3 ♦** : to attach physically : AFFIX, ATTACH **4** : to hold or direct steadily ⟨~es his eyes on the horizon⟩ **5 ♦** : to set or place definitely : SET **6** : ASSIGN ⟨~ the blame⟩ **7** : to set in order : ADJUST **8** : to get ready : PREPARE **9 ♦** : to make whole or sound again **10** : to get even with **11** : to influence by improper or illegal methods ⟨~ a race⟩ **12 ♦** : to assign precisely : settle on : arrange — **fix·er** n

♦ [3] affix, attach, fasten ♦ [5] deposit, place, position, put, set, set up, stick ♦ [9] doctor, mend, patch, recondition, renovate, repair, revamp ♦ [12] arrange, decide, set, settle

²fix n **1 ♦** : a position of difficulty or embarrassment : PREDICAMENT **2** : a determination of position (as of a ship) **3** : an accurate determination or understanding **4** : an act of improper influence **5** : a supply or dose of something (as an addictive drug) strongly desired or craved **6** : something that fixes or restores

♦ corner, hole, jam, pickle, predicament, spot

fix·a·tion \fik-'sā-shən\ n ♦ : an obsessive or unhealthy preoccupation or attachment — **fix·ate** \'fik-ˌsāt\ vb

♦ fetish, mania, obsession, preoccupation, prepossession

fix·a·tive \'fik-sə-tiv\ n : something that stabilizes or sets
fixed \'fikst\ adj **1** : securely placed or fastened : STATIONARY **2** : not volatile **3 ♦** : not subject to change or fluctuation **4** : INTENT, CONCENTRATED ⟨a ~ stare⟩ **5** : supplied with a definite amount of something needed (as money) — **fixed·ly** \'fik-səd-lē\ adv

♦ certain, determinate, final, firm, flat, frozen, hard, hard-and-fast, set, settled, stable ♦ fast, hard-and-fast, immutable, inflexible, unalterable, unchangeable

fixed·ness \'fik-səd-nəs\ n ♦ : the quality or state of being fixed

♦ constancy, immutability, stability, steadiness

fix·i·ty \'fik-sə-tē\ n, pl **-ties** : the quality or state of being fixed or stable

fix·ture \'fiks-chər\ n **1** : something firmly attached as a permanent part of some other thing **2** : a familiar feature in a particular setting; esp : a person associated with a place or activity
¹fizz \'fiz\ vb ♦ : to make a hissing or sputtering sound

♦ hiss, sizzle, swish, whish, whiz

²fizz n **1** : a hissing sound **2** : an effervescent beverage
fiz·zle \'fi-zəl\ vb **fiz·zled; fiz·zling 1** : FIZZ **2** : to fail after a good start — often used with out
²fizzle n ♦ : lack of satisfactory performance or effect : FAILURE

♦ collapse, crash, cropper, defeat, failure, nonsuccess

fjord or **fiord** \fē-'ȯrd\ n ♦ : a narrow inlet of the sea between cliffs or steep slopes

♦ bay, bight, cove, estuary, gulf, inlet

fl abbr **1** flourished **2** fluid
Fl symbol flerovium
FL or **Fla** abbr Florida
flab \'flab\ n : soft flabby body tissue
flab·ber·gast \'fla-bər-ˌgast\ vb ♦ : to overwhelm with shock, surprise, or wonder : ASTOUND

♦ amaze, astonish, astound, bowl, dumbfound, floor, shock, startle, stun, stupefy, surprise

flab·by \'fla-bē\ adj **flab·bi·er; -est** ♦ : lacking firmness : FLACCID ⟨~ muscles⟩ — **flab·bi·ness** \-bē-nəs\ n

♦ flaccid, mushy, pliable, soft, spongy

flac·cid \'flak-səd\ adj ♦ : lacking firmness ⟨~ muscles⟩

♦ droopy, floppy, lank, limp, slack, yielding

¹flag \'flag\ n : any of various irises; esp : a wild iris
²flag n **1** : a usu. rectangular piece of fabric of distinctive design that is used as a symbol (as of a nation) or as a signaling device **2 ♦** : something used like a flag to signal or attract attention **3** : one of the cross strokes of a musical note less than a quarter note in value

♦ banner, colors (or colours), ensign, pennant, standard, streamer

³flag vb **flagged; flag·ging 1 ♦** : to signal with or as if with a flag; esp : to signal to stop ⟨~ a taxi⟩ **2** : to mark or identify with or as if with a flag **3** : to call a penalty on

♦ gesture, motion, signal, wave

⁴flag vb **flagged; flag·ging 1 ♦** : to hang loose or limp **2 ♦** : to become unsteady, feeble, or spiritless **3** : to decline in interest or attraction ⟨the topic flagged⟩

♦ [1] droop, hang, loll, sag, wilt ♦ [2] decay, droop, fail, go, lag, languish, sag, waste, weaken, wilt

⁵flag n : a hard flat stone suitable for paving
flag·el·late \'fla-jə-ˌlāt\ vb **-lat·ed; -lat·ing** : to punish by whipping — **flag·el·la·tion** \ˌfla-jə-'lā-shən\ n
fla·gel·lum \flə-'je-ləm\ n, pl **-la** \-lə\ also **-lums** : a long whiplike process that is the primary organ of motion of many microorganisms — **fla·gel·lar** \-lər\ adj
fla·geo·let \ˌfla-jə-'let, -'lā\ n : a small woodwind instrument belonging to the flute class
fla·gi·tious \flə-'ji-shəs\ adj : grossly wicked : VILLAINOUS
flag·on \'fla-gən\ n ♦ : a container for liquids usu. with a handle, spout, and lid

♦ ewer, jug, pitcher

flag·pole \'flag-ˌpōl\ n : a pole on which to raise a flag
fla·grant \'flā-grənt\ adj ♦ : conspicuously bad ⟨~ abuse of power⟩ — **fla·grant·ly** adv

♦ blatant, conspicuous, egregious, gross, pronounced, rank, striking

fla·gran·te de·lic·to \flə-ˌgran-tē-di-'lik-tō\ adv : the act of committing a misdeed — used in the phrase in flagrante delicto
flag·ship \'flag-ˌship\ n **1** : the ship that carries the commander of a fleet or subdivision thereof and flies the commander's flag **2** : the most important one of a group
flag·staff \-ˌstaf\ n : FLAGPOLE
flag·stone \-ˌstōn\ n : ⁵FLAG
¹flail \'flāl\ n : a tool for threshing grain by hand
²flail vb ♦ : to strike or swing with or as if with a flail

♦ flog, hide, lash, switch, thrash, whale, whip

flair \'flar\ n **1 ♦** : ability to appreciate or make good use of something : TALENT **2** : a unique style

♦ aptitude, endowment, faculty, genius, gift, knack, talent

flak \'flak\ n, pl **flak 1** : antiaircraft guns or bursting shells fired from them **2** : CRITICISM, OPPOSITION

¹flake \'flāk\ *n* **1** : a small loose mass or bit **2** ♦ : a thin flattened piece or layer : CHIP

♦ chip, splinter

²flake *vb* **flaked; flak·ing** : to form or separate into flakes
³flake *n* : a markedly eccentric person : ODDBALL — **flak·i·ness** \'flā-kē-nəs\ *n* — **flaky** *adj*
flaky *adj* ♦ : tending to flake

♦ brittle, crisp, crumbly, friable

flam·beau \'flam-ˌbō\ *n, pl* **flambeaux** \-ˌbōz\ *or* **flambeaus** : a flaming torch
flam·boy·ance \flam-'bȯi-əns\ *n* ♦ : the quality or state of being flamboyant — **flam·boy·an·cy** \-ən-sē\ *n*

♦ flashiness, gaudiness, glitz, ostentation, pretentiousness, showiness, swank

flam·boy·ant \-ənt\ *adj* ♦ : marked by or given to strikingly elaborate or colorful display or behavior

♦ flashy, garish, gaudy, glitzy, loud, ostentatious, swank, tawdry

flam·boy·ant·ly *adv* ♦ : in a flamboyant manner : with flamboyance

♦ flashily, gaily, jauntily, rakishly

¹flame \'flām\ *n* **1** : the glowing gaseous part of a fire **2** : a state of blazing combustion **3** : a flamelike condition **4** : burning zeal or passion **5** : BRILLIANCE **6** ♦ : a person beloved : SWEETHEART **7** : an angry, hostile, or abusive electronic message

♦ beloved, darling, dear, honey, love, sweet, sweetheart

²flame *vb* **1** ♦ : to burn with a flame **2** ♦ : to burst or break out violently or passionately **3** ♦ : to shine brightly

♦ [1] blaze, burn, glow ♦ [2] break out, burst, erupt, explode, flare, go off ♦ [3] beat, blaze, burn, glare

fla·men·co \flə-'men-kō\ *n, pl* **-cos** : a vigorous rhythmic dance style of the Spanish Romani
flame·throw·er \'flām-ˌthrō-ər\ *n* : a device that expels from a nozzle a burning stream of liquid or semiliquid fuel under pressure
fla·min·go \flə-'miŋ-gō\ *n, pl* **-gos** *also* **-goes** : any of several long-legged long-necked tropical water birds with scarlet wings and a broad bill bent downward
flam·ma·ble \'fla-mə-bəl\ *adj* ♦ : easily ignited and quick-burning — **flam·ma·bil·i·ty** \ˌfla-mə-'bi-lə-tē\ *n* — **flammable** *n*

♦ combustible, ignitable, inflammable

flan \'flan, 'flän\ *n* **1** : an open pie with a sweet or savory filling **2** : custard baked with a caramel glaze
flange \'flanj\ *n* : a rim used for strengthening or guiding something or for attachment to another object
¹flank \'flaŋk\ *n* **1** : the fleshy part of the side between the ribs and the hip; *also* : the side of a quadruped **2** : SIDE **3** : the right or left of a formation
²flank *vb* **1** : to attack or threaten the flank of **2** ♦ : to be situated on the side of

♦ abut, adjoin, border (on), fringe, join, skirt, touch, verge (on)

flank·er \'flaŋ-kər\ *n* : a football player stationed wide of the formation slightly behind the line of scrimmage as a pass receiver
flan·nel \'flan-ᵊl\ *n* **1** : a soft twilled wool or worsted fabric with a napped surface **2** : a stout cotton fabric napped on one side **3** *pl* : flannel underwear or pants
¹flap \'flap\ *n* **1** : a stroke with something broad : SLAP **2** : something broad, limber, or flat and usu. thin that hangs loose **3** : the motion or sound of something broad and limber as it swings to and fro **4** : a state of excitement or confusion
²flap *vb* **flapped; flap·ping** **1** : to beat with something broad and flat **2** : FLING **3** ♦ : to move (as wings) with a beating motion **4** : to sway loosely usu. with a noise of striking

♦ beat, flail, flop, flutter, whip

flap·jack \'flap-ˌjak\ *n* ♦ : a flat cake made of thin batter and cooked (as on a griddle) on both sides : PANCAKE

♦ griddle cake, pancake

flap·per \'fla-pər\ *n* **1** : one that flaps **2** : a young woman of the 1920s who showed freedom from conventions (as in conduct)
¹flare \'flar\ *n* **1** ♦ : a blaze of light used esp. to signal or illuminate; *also* : a device for producing such a blaze **2** : an unsteady glaring light **3** ♦ : a sudden outburst (as of sound, excitement, or anger)

♦ [1] blaze, illumination, incandescence, light, luminescence, radiance, shine ♦ [3] agony, burst, eruption, explosion, fit, flare-up, flash, outburst, spasm, storm

²flare *vb* **flared; flar·ing** **1** ♦ : to flame with a sudden unsteady light **2** ♦ : to spread outward ⟨her skirt *flaring* at the bottom⟩ ⟨a boat with the gunwales *flaring* out⟩ **3** : to become suddenly excited or angry — usu. used with *up* ⟨she ~s up at the slightest provocation⟩ **4** ♦ : to break out or intensify usu. suddenly or violently — often used with *up* ⟨fighting *flared* up after a 2-week lull⟩

♦ [1] beat, blaze, burn, flame, glare ♦ usu **flare out** [2] expand, extend, fan, open, spread, stretch, unfold ♦ usu **flare up** [4] break out, burst, erupt, explode, flame, go off

flare-up \-ˌəp\ *n* ♦ : a sudden outburst or intensification

♦ burst, flare, flash, outbreak, outburst, spurt

¹flash \'flash\ *vb* **1** : to break forth in or like a sudden flame **2** : to appear or pass suddenly or with great speed **3** ♦ : to send out in or as if in flashes ⟨~ a message⟩ **4** : to make a sudden display (as of brilliance or feeling) **5** : to gleam or glow intermittently **6** : to fill by a sudden rush of water **7** : to expose to view very briefly ⟨~ a badge⟩ — **flash·er** *n*

♦ flame, gleam, glimmer, glisten, glitter, shimmer, sparkle, twinkle, wink

²flash *n* **1** : a sudden burst of light **2** : a movement of a flag or light in signaling **3** : a sudden and brilliant burst (as of wit) **4** ♦ : a brief time : SHOW, DISPLAY; *esp* : ostentatious display **6** ♦ : something or someone that attracts notice; *esp* : an outstanding athlete **7** : GLIMPSE, LOOK **8** : a first brief news report **9** : FLASHLIGHT **10** : a device for producing a brief and very bright flash of light for taking photographs **11** : a quick-spreading flame or momentary intense outburst of radiant heat

♦ [4] instant, jiffy, minute, moment, second, shake, twinkling, wink ♦ [6] marvel, miracle, phenomenon, prodigy, sensation, wonder

³flash *adj* : of sudden origin and short duration ⟨a ~ flood⟩

♦ fleeting, momentary, short-lived, transient

⁴flash *adv* : by very brief exposure to an intense agent (as heat or cold) ⟨~ freeze⟩
flash·back \'flash-ˌbak\ *n* **1** : interruption of the chronological sequence (as of a film or literary work) by an event of earlier occurrence **2** : a past event remembered vividly
flash back *vb* **1** : to vividly remember a past incident **2** : to employ a flashback
flash·bulb \-ˌbəlb\ *n* : an electric bulb that can be used only once to produce a brief and very bright flash of light for taking photographs
flash card *n* : a card bearing words, numbers, or pictures briefly displayed usu. as a learning aid
flash drive *n* : a data storage device that uses flash memory
flash·gun \-ˌgən\ *n* : a device for producing a bright flash of light for photography
flash·i·ly \-shə-lē\ *adv* ♦ : in a flashy manner or style

♦ flamboyantly, gaily, jauntily, rakishly

flash·i·ness \-shē-nəs\ *n* ♦ : the quality or state of being flashy

♦ flamboyance, gaudiness, glitz, ostentation, pretentiousness, showiness, swank

flash·ing \'fla-shiŋ\ *n* : sheet metal used in waterproofing (as at the angle between a chimney and a roof)
flash·light \'flash-ˌlīt\ *n* : a battery-operated portable electric light
flash memory *n* : a computer memory chip not requiring connection to a power source to retain its data
flashy \'fla-shē\ *adj* **flash·i·er; -est** **1** : momentarily dazzling **2** ♦ : superficially attractive or impressive : SHOWY

♦ flamboyant, garish, gaudy, glitzy, loud, ostentatious, showy, swank, tawdry

flask \'flask\ *n* : a flattened bottle-shaped container ⟨a whiskey ~⟩
¹flat \'flat\ *adj* **flat·ter; flat·test** **1** : spread out along a surface; *also* : being or characterized by a horizontal line **2** ♦ : having a smooth, level, or even surface **3** : having a broad smooth surface and little thickness **4** : clearly unmistakable : DOWNRIGHT ⟨a ~ refusal⟩ **5** : not varying : FIXED ⟨charge a ~ rate⟩ **6** ♦ : having no fraction either lacking or in excess : EXACT, PRECISE ⟨in four minutes ~⟩ **7 a** ♦ : lacking in animation, zest, or vigor : DULL, UNINTERESTING **b** ♦ : lacking savor : INSIPID **8** : DEFLATED ⟨a ~ tire⟩ **9** : lower than the true pitch; *also* : lower by a half step **10** ♦ : free from gloss ⟨a ~ paint⟩ **11** : lacking depth of characterization — **flat·ly** *adv* — **flat·ness** *n*

♦ [2] even, flush, level, plane, smooth ♦ [6] even, exact, precise, round ♦ [7a] dull, monotonous, uninteresting ♦ [7b] flavorless (or flavourless), insipid, tasteless ♦ [10] dim, dull, lusterless

²**flat** n **1** : a level surface of land : PLAIN **2** : a flat part or surface **3** : a character ♭ that indicates that a specified note is to be lowered by a half step; also : the resulting note **4** : something flat **5** : an apartment on one floor **6** : a deflated tire

³**flat** adv **1** : FLATLY **2** ♦ : without qualification or reservation : COMPLETELY ⟨~ broke⟩ **3** : below the true musical pitch

♦ completely, entirely, fully, perfectly, quite, thoroughly, wholly

⁴**flat** vb **flat·ted; flat·ting 1** : FLATTEN **2** : to lower in pitch esp. by a half step

flat·bed \'flat-ˌbed\ n : a truck or trailer with a body in the form of a platform or shallow box

flat·boat \-ˌbōt\ n : a flat-bottomed boat used esp. for carrying bulky freight

flat·car \-ˌkär\ n : a railroad freight car without sides or roof

flat·fish \-ˌfish\ n : any of an order of flattened marine bony fishes with both eyes on the upper side

flat·foot \-ˌfu̇t, -'fu̇t\ n, pl **flat·feet** \-ˌfēt, -'fēt\ : a condition in which the arch of the foot is flattened so that the entire sole rests upon the ground — **flat–foot·ed** \-'fu̇-tǝd\ adj

Flat·head \-ˌhed\ n, pl **Flatheads** or **Flathead** : a member of an Indigenous people of Montana

flat·iron \-ˌī(-ǝ)rn\ n : IRON 3

flat·land \-ˌland\ n : land lacking significant variation in elevation

flat–out \'flat-ˌau̇t\ adj **1** : being or going at maximum effort or speed **2** : OUT-AND-OUT, DOWNRIGHT ⟨it was a ~ lie⟩

flat out adv **1** : BLUNTLY, DIRECTLY **2** : at top speed **3** usu **flat–out** : to the greatest degree : COMPLETELY ⟨is just flat-out confusing⟩

flat–pan·el \-'pa-nᵊl\ adj : relating to or being a thin flat video display

flat–screen \-ˌskrēn\ adj : FLAT-PANEL

flat·ten \'flat-ᵊn\ vb : to make or become flat

flat·ter \'fla-tǝr\ vb **1** ♦ : to praise too much or without sincerity **2** : to represent too favorably ⟨the portrait ~s him⟩ **3** : to display to advantage **4** : to judge (oneself) favorably or too favorably — **flat·ter·er** n

♦ blarney, overpraise

flat·tery \'fla-tǝ-rē\ n, pl **-ter·ies** ♦ : flattering speech or attentions : insincere or excessive praise

♦ adulation, blarney, overpraise

flat·top \'flat-ˌtäp\ n **1** : AIRCRAFT CARRIER **2** : CREW CUT

flat·u·lent \'fla-chǝ-lǝnt\ adj **1** : full of gas ⟨a ~ stomach⟩ **2** : INFLATED, POMPOUS — **flat·u·lence** \-lǝns\ n

fla·tus \'flā-tǝs\ n : gas formed in the intestine or stomach

flat·ware \'flat-ˌwer\ n ♦ : eating and serving utensils

♦ silver, tableware

flat·worm \-ˌwǝrm\ n : any of a phylum of flattened mostly parasitic segmented worms (as trematodes and tapeworms)

flaunt \'flȯnt\ vb **1** ♦ : to display oneself to public notice **2** : to wave or flutter showily **3** : to display ostentatiously or impudently : PARADE — **flaunt** n

♦ display, disport, exhibit, flash, parade, show, show off

flau·ta \'flau̇-tǝ\ n : a tortilla rolled around a filling and deep-fried

flau·tist \'flȯ-tist, 'flau̇-\ n : FLUTIST

¹**fla·vor** or Can and Brit **fla·vour** \'flā-vǝr\ n **1** : the quality of something that affects the sense of taste or of taste and smell **2** ♦ : a substance that adds flavor **3** ♦ : characteristic or predominant quality — **fla·vored** \-vǝrd\ adj — **fla·vor·some** adj

♦ [2] seasoning, spice ♦ [3] air, atmosphere, aura, climate, mood, note, temper

²**flavor** or Can and Brit **flavour** vb ♦ : to give or add flavor to

♦ savor, season, spice

fla·vor·ful or Can and Brit **flavourful** adj ♦ : full of flavor

♦ appetizing, delectable, delicious, savory, tasty, toothsome, yummy

fla·vor·ing or Can and Brit **flavouring** n : a substance that flavors : FLAVOR 2

fla·vor·less or Can and Brit **flavourless** adj ♦ : lacking in flavor

♦ flat, insipid, tasteless

flaw \'flȯ\ n ♦ : a small often hidden defect — **flaw·less·ness** n

♦ blemish, defect, fault, imperfection, mark

flaw·less adj ♦ : lacking any flaw or imperfection

♦ absolute, faultless, ideal, impeccable, letter-perfect, perfect, unblemished

flaw·less·ly \-lē\ adv ♦ : in a flawless manner

♦ faultlessly, ideally, impeccably, perfectly

flax \'flaks\ n : a fiber that is the source of linen; also : a blue-flowered plant grown for this fiber and its oily seeds

flax·en \'flak-sǝn\ adj **1** : made of flax **2** ♦ : resembling flax esp. in pale soft straw color

♦ blond, fair, golden, sandy, straw

flay \'flā\ vb **1** ♦ : to strip off the skin or surface of **2** ♦ : to criticize harshly

♦ [1] bark, hull, husk, peel, shell, skin ♦ [2] admonish, chide, lecture, rail (at or against), rate, rebuke, reprimand, scold

fl dr abbr fluid dram

flea \'flē\ n : any of an order of small wingless leaping bloodsucking insects

flea·bane \'flē-ˌbān\ n : any of various plants of the daisy family once believed to drive away fleas

flea–bit·ten \-ˌbit-ᵊn\ adj : bitten by or infested with fleas

flea market n : a usu. open-air market for secondhand articles and antiques

¹**fleck** \'flek\ vb : to mark in or with spots : STREAK, SPOT

²**fleck** n **1** ♦ : a small area visibly different (as in color, finish, or material) from the surrounding area : SPOT, MARK **2** ♦ : a small loose mass or bit : PARTICLE

♦ [1] blotch, dapple, dot, mark, speck, spot ♦ [2] atom, bit, crumb, grain, granule, molecule, particle, speck

fledge \'flej\ vb **fledged; fledg·ing** : to develop the feathers necessary for flying or independent activity

fledg·ling \'flej-liŋ\ n **1** : a young bird with flight feathers newly developed **2** ♦ : an immature or inexperienced person

♦ beginner, greenhorn, neophyte, newcomer, novice, tyro

flee \'flē\ vb **fled** \'fled\; **flee·ing 1** ♦ : to run away often from danger or evil **2** ♦ : to pass away swiftly from perception

♦ [1] clear out, escape, fly, get out, lam, run away, run off ♦ [2] disappear, dissolve, evaporate, fade, go, melt, vanish

¹**fleece** \'flēs\ n **1** ♦ : the woolly coat of an animal and esp. a sheep **2** : a soft or woolly covering

♦ coat, fur, hair, pelage, pile, wool

²**fleece** vb **fleeced; fleec·ing 1** ♦ : to strip of money or property by fraud or extortion **2** : SHEAR

♦ cheat, defraud, rook, shortchange, skin, squeeze, stick, sting, swindle, victimize

fleecy adj ♦ : covered with, made of, or resembling fleece

♦ furry, hairy, unshorn, woolly

¹**fleet** \'flēt\ vb : to pass rapidly

²**fleet** n **1** : a group of warships under one command **2** ♦ : a group (as of ships, planes, or trucks) under one management

♦ armada, caravan, cavalcade, motorcade, train

³**fleet** adj **1** ♦ : swift in motion : SWIFT, NIMBLE **2** : not enduring : FLEETING

♦ breakneck, fast, hasty, lightning, nimble, nippy, quick, rapid, speedy, swift

fleet admiral n : an admiral of the highest rank in the navy

fleet·ing \'flē-tiŋ\ adj ♦ : passing swiftly

♦ ephemeral, evanescent, momentary, short-lived, transient

fleet·ness n ♦ : the quality or state of being fleet

♦ celerity, fastness, haste, hurry, quickness, rapidity, speed, swiftness, velocity

Flem·ing \'fle-miŋ\ n : a member of a Germanic people inhabiting chiefly northern Belgium

Flem·ish \'fle-mish\ n **1** : the Dutch language as spoken by the Flemings **2 Flemish** pl : FLEMINGS — **Flemish** adj

fle·ro·vi·um \flǝ-'rō-vē-ǝm\ n : a short-lived artifically produced radioactive chemical element

¹**flesh** \'flesh\ n **1** : the soft parts of an animal's body; esp : muscular tissue **2** : MEAT **3** : the physical nature of humans as distinguished from the soul **4** : human beings; also : living beings **5** : STOCK, KINDRED **6** : fleshy plant tissue (as fruit pulp) — **fleshed** \'flesht\ adj

²**flesh** vb ♦ : to make fuller or more nearly complete — usu. used with out

♦ *usu* **flesh out** amplify, develop, elaborate (on), enlarge (on), expand

flesh fly *n* : a dipteran fly whose maggots feed on flesh
flesh·ly \'flesh-lē\ *adj* **1** ♦ : of or relating to the flesh or body : CORPOREAL, BODILY **2** ♦ : not spiritual : WORLDLY **3** ♦ : of or relating to bodily appetites : CARNAL, SENSUAL

♦ [1] animal, bodily, carnal, corporal, material, physical, somatic ♦ [2] carnal, earthly, material, mundane, temporal, terrestrial, worldly ♦ [3] carnal, luscious, sensual, sensuous, voluptuous

flesh·pot \'flesh-ˌpät\ *n* **1** *pl* : bodily comfort : LUXURY **2** : a place of lascivious entertainment — usu. used in pl.
fleshy \'fle-shē\ *adj* **flesh·i·er; -est** **1** : consisting of or resembling animal flesh **2** ♦ : marked by abundant flesh : PLUMP, FAT **3** ♦ : full of juice

♦ [2] chubby, fat, plump, portly, rotund, round ♦ [3] juicy, pulpy, succulent

flew *past of* ¹FLY
flex \'fleks\ *vb* : to bend esp. repeatedly — **flex** *n*
flex·i·ble \'flek-sə-bəl\ *adj* **1** ♦ : capable of being flexed **2** ♦ : yielding to influence **3** ♦ : readily changed or changing — **flex·i·bil·i·ty** \ˌflek-sə-'bi-lə-tē\ *n*

♦ [1] limber, lissome, lithe, pliable, supple, willowy ♦ [1] elastic, resilient, rubbery, springy, stretch, supple ♦ [2, 3] easygoing, relaxed, unrestrained, unrestricted ♦ [3] adaptable, adjustable, changeable, elastic, fluid, malleable, variable *Ant* established, fixed, immutable

flex·or \'flek-sər, -ˌsòr\ *n* : a muscle serving to bend a body part
flex·ure \'flek-shər\ *n* : TURN, FOLD
flib·ber·ti·gib·bet \ˌfli-bər-tē-'ji-bət\ *n* : a silly flighty person
¹**flick** \'flik\ *n* **1** : a light sharp jerky stroke or movement **2** : a sound produced by a flick : ²FLICKER
²**flick** *vb* **1** : to strike lightly with a quick sharp motion **2** : FLUTTER, FLIT
³**flick** *n* : MOVIE ⟨can't wait to catch the new *flick* at the theater⟩
¹**flick·er** \'fli-kər\ *vb* **1** : to move irregularly or unsteadily : FLUTTER **2** : to burn fitfully or with a fluctuating light — **flick·er·ing·ly** *adv*
²**flicker** *n* **1** : an act of flickering **2** : a sudden brief movement ⟨a ∼ of an eyelid⟩ **3** : a momentary stirring ⟨a ∼ of interest⟩ **4** : a slight indication : HINT **5** : a wavering light
³**flicker** *n* : a large barred and spotted No. American woodpecker with a brown back that occurs as an eastern form with yellow on the underside of the wings and tail and a western form with red in these areas
flied *past and past part of* ³FLY
fli·er \'flī-ər\ *n* **1** : one that flies; *esp* : PILOT **2** ♦ : a reckless or speculative undertaking **3** *usu* **fly·er** ♦ : an advertising circular

♦ [1] airman, aviator, pilot ♦ [2] chance, enterprise, gamble, speculation, venture ♦ *usu* **flyer** [3] circular, leaflet, pamphlet

¹**flight** \'flīt\ *n* **1** : an act or instance of flying **2** : the ability to fly **3** : a passing through air or space **4** : the distance covered in a flight **5** : swift movement **6** : a trip made by or in an airplane or spacecraft **7** : a group of similar individuals (as birds or airplanes) flying as a unit **8** : a passing (as of the imagination) beyond ordinary limits **9** : a series of stairs from one landing to another — **flight·less** *adj*
²**flight** *n* ♦ : an act or instance of running away

♦ escape, getaway, lam, slip

flight bag *n* **1** : a lightweight traveling bag with zippered outside pockets **2** : a small canvas satchel
flight·i·ness \-tē-nəs\ *n* ♦ : the quality or state of being flighty

♦ facetiousness, flippancy, frivolity, levity, lightness

flight line *n* : a parking and servicing area for airplanes
flighty \'flī-tē\ *adj* **flight·i·er; -est** **1** ♦ : easily upset : VOLATILE **2** ♦ : easily excited : SKITTISH **3** ♦ : governed or characterized by caprice : CAPRICIOUS, SILLY

♦ [2] excitable, fluttery, high-strung, jittery, jumpy, nervous, skittish, spooky ♦ [3] capricious, frivolous, giddy, harebrained, scatterbrained, silly

flim·flam \'flim-ˌflam\ *n* : DECEPTION, FRAUD — **flim·flam·mery** \-ˌfla-mə-rē\ *n*
flim·sy \'flim-zē\ *adj* **flim·si·er; -est** **1** ♦ : lacking strength or substance **2** ♦ : of inferior materials and workmanship **3** ♦ : having little worth or plausibility ⟨a ∼ excuse⟩ — **flim·si·ly** \-zə-lē\ *adv* — **flim·si·ness** \-zē-nəs\ *n*

♦ [1, 2] gauzy, insubstantial, unsubstantial *Ant* sturdy, substantial ♦ [3] doubtful, dubious, improbable, questionable, unlikely

flinch \'flinch\ *vb* ♦ : to shrink from or as if from pain : WINCE — **flinch** *n*

♦ blench, quail, recoil, shrink, wince

¹**fling** \'fliŋ\ *vb* **flung** \'fləŋ\; **fling·ing** **1** : to move hastily, brusquely, or violently ⟨*flung* out of the room⟩ **2** : to kick or plunge vigorously **3 a** : to throw with force or recklessness **b** ♦ : to cast as if by throwing **4** : to put suddenly into a state or condition

♦ cast, catapult, chuck, hurl, hurtle, launch, pitch, sling, throw, toss

²**fling** *n* **1** : an act or instance of flinging **2** ♦ : a casual try : ATTEMPT **3** ♦ : a period of self-indulgence

♦ [2] attempt, bid, endeavor (*or* endeavour), essay, go, pass, shot, stab, trial, try, whack, whirl ♦ [3] frolic, gambol, lark, revel, rollick, romp

flint \'flint\ *n* **1** : a hard quartz that produces a spark when struck by steel **2** : an alloy used for producing a spark in lighters
flint glass *n* : heavy glass containing an oxide of lead and used in lenses and prisms
flint·lock \'flint-ˌläk\ *n* **1** : a lock for a gun using a flint to ignite the charge **2** : a firearm fitted with a flintlock
flinty *adj* ♦ : harsh and unyielding : rigorous and stern

♦ austere, authoritarian, hard, harsh, rigorous, severe, stern, strict

¹**flip** \'flip\ *vb* **flipped; flip·ping** **1** : to turn by tossing ⟨∼ a coin⟩ **2** ♦ : to turn over; *also* : to leaf through **3** : FLICK, JERK ⟨∼ a light switch⟩ **4** ♦ : to lose self-control — **flip** *n*

♦ [2] reverse, turn ♦ [4] break, crack, freak

²**flip** *adj* : glib or pert in speech : FLIPPANT
flip·pan·cy \'fli-pən-sē\ *n* ♦ : the quality or state of being flippant

♦ facetiousness, flightiness, frivolity, levity, lightness

flip·pant \'fli-pənt\ *adj* ♦ : lacking proper respect or seriousness

♦ facetious, flip, pert, smart *Ant* earnest, sincere

flip·per \'fli-pər\ *n* **1** : a broad flat limb (as of a seal) adapted for swimming **2** : a paddlelike shoe used in skin diving
flip side *n* : the reverse and usu. less popular side of a phonograph record
¹**flirt** \'flərt\ *vb* **1** : to move erratically : FLIT **2** : to behave amorously without serious intent **3** : to show casual interest ⟨∼ed with the idea⟩; *also* : to come close to ⟨∼ with danger⟩ — **flir·ta·tion** \ˌflər-'tā-shən\ *n* — **flir·ta·tious** \-shəs\ *adj*
²**flirt** *n* **1** : an act or instance of flirting **2** : a person who flirts
flit \'flit\ *vb* **flit·ted; flit·ting** ♦ : to pass or move quickly or abruptly from place to place : DART — **flit** *n*

♦ dance, dart, flutter, zip

flitch \'flich\ *n* : a side of cured meat; *esp* : a side of bacon
fliv·ver \'fli-vər\ *n* : a small cheap usu. old automobile
¹**float** \'flōt\ *n* **1** ♦ : something (as a raft) that floats; *also* : a floating platform anchored near a shoreline for use by swimmers or boats **2** : a cork buoying up the baited end of a fishing line **3** : a hollow ball that floats at the end of a lever in a cistern or tank and regulates the liquid level **4** : a vehicle with a platform to carry an exhibit **5** : a soft drink with ice cream floating in it

♦ dock, jetty, landing, levee, pier, quay, wharf

²**float** *vb* **1** : to rest on the surface of or be suspended in a fluid **2** ♦ : to move gently on or through a fluid **3** : to cause to float **4** : WANDER **5** : to offer (securities) in order to finance an enterprise **6** : to finance by floating an issue of stocks or bonds **7** : to arrange for ⟨∼ a loan⟩ — **float·er** *n*

♦ drift, glide, hang, hover, poise, ride, sail, waft *Ant* settle, sink

¹**flock** \'fläk\ *n* **1** : a group of birds or mammals assembled or herded together **2** : a group of people under the guidance of a leader; *esp* : CONGREGATION **3** ♦ : a large number ⟨a ∼ of tourists⟩

♦ army, crowd, crush, drove, horde, host, legion, mob, multitude, press, swarm, throng

²**flock** *vb* ♦ : to gather or move in a flock ⟨people ∼ed to the beach⟩

♦ crowd, mob, swarm, throng

floe \'flō\ *n* : a flat mass of floating ice

flog \'fläg\ *vb* **flogged; flog·ging 1 ♦ :** to beat with or as if with a rod or whip **2 :** SELL ⟨~ encyclopedias⟩ — **flog·ger** *n*

♦ bash, bat, batter, beat, belt, bludgeon, buffet, club, drub, hammer, hide, lace, lambaste, lick, maul, pelt, pound, thrash, thump, wallop, whale, whip

¹**flood** \'fləd\ *n* **1 ♦ :** a great flow of water over the land **2 :** the flowing in of the tide **3 ♦ :** an overwhelming volume

♦ [1, 3] cataclysm, cataract, deluge, inundation, overflow, spate, torrent *Ant* drought

²**flood** *vb* **1 ♦ :** to cover or become filled with a flood **2 :** to fill abundantly or excessively; *esp* : to supply an excess of fuel to ⟨~ed the engine⟩ **3 :** to pour forth in a flood — **flood·er** *n*

♦ deluge, drown, engulf, inundate, overflow, overwhelm, submerge, swamp *Ant* drain

flood·gate \'fləd-ˌgāt\ *n* : a gate for controlling a body of water : SLUICE

flood·light \-ˌlīt\ *n* : a lamp that throws a broad beam of light; *also* : the beam itself — **floodlight** *vb*

flood·plain \-ˌplān\ *n* : a plain along a river or stream subject to periodic flooding

flood tide *n* **1 :** a rising tide **2 :** an overwhelming quantity **3 :** a high point

flood·wa·ter \'fləd-ˌwȯ-tər, -ˌwä-\ *n* : the water of a flood

¹**floor** \'flȯr\ *n* **1 :** the bottom of a room on which one stands **2 :** a ground surface **3 :** a story of a building **4 :** a main level space (as in a legislative chamber) distinguished from a platform or gallery **5 :** AUDIENCE **6 :** the right to address an assembly **7 :** a lower limit ⟨put a ~ under wheat prices⟩ — **floor·ing** *n*

²**floor** *vb* **1 :** to furnish with a floor **2 ♦ :** to knock down **3 ♦ :** to overwhelm with shock, surprise, or wonder ⟨was ~ed by the news⟩ **4 :** to press (a vehicle's accelerator) to the floorboard esp. rapidly

♦ [2] bowl, down, drop, fell, knock, level ♦ [3] amaze, astonish, astound, bowl, dumbfound, flabbergast, overwhelm, shock, startle, stun, surprise

floor·board \-ˌbȯrd\ *n* **1 :** a board in a floor **2 :** the floor of an automobile

floor leader *n* : a member of a legislative body who has charge of a party's organization and strategy on the floor

floor show *n* : a series of acts presented in a nightclub

floor·walk·er \'flȯr-ˌwȯ-kər\ *n* : a person employed in a retail store to oversee the sales force and aid customers

floo·zy *or* **floo·zie** \'flü-zē\ *n, pl* **floozies** : a usu. young woman of loose morals

¹**flop** \'fläp\ *vb* **flopped; flop·ping 1 ♦ :** to swing or move loosely : FLAP **2 ♦ :** to throw oneself down heavily, clumsily, or in a relaxed manner ⟨*flopped* into a chair⟩ **3 ♦ :** to fall short of success : FAIL ⟨the show *flopped*⟩ — **flop** *adv* — **flop·per** *n*

♦ [1] beat, flail, flap, flutter, whip ♦ [2] plop, plump, plunk ♦ [3] collapse, fail, flunk, fold, wash out

²**flop** *n* **♦ :** something that is a failure

♦ bust, debacle, dud, failure, fiasco, fizzle, loser, washout

flop·house \'fläp-ˌhaús\ *n* : a cheap hotel

¹**flop·py** \'flä-pē\ *adj* **flop·pi·er; -est ♦ :** tending to flop; *esp* : soft and flexible — **flop·pi·ly** \-pə-lē\ *adv*

♦ droopy, flaccid, lank, limp, slack, yielding

²**floppy** *n, pl* **flop·pies** : FLOPPY DISK

floppy disk *n* : a thin plastic disk with a magnetic coating on which computer data can be stored

flop sweat *n* : sweat caused by the fear of failing

flo·ra \'flȯr-ə\ *n, pl* **floras** *also* **flo·rae** \-ˌē, -ˌī\ **♦ :** plants or plant life esp. of a region or period

♦ foliage, green, greenery, herbage, leafage, vegetation, verdure

flo·ral \'flȯr-əl\ *adj* : of, relating to, or depicting flowers ⟨a ~ design⟩

flo·res·cence \flȯ-'res-ᵊns, flə-\ *n* : a state or period of being in bloom or flourishing — **flo·res·cent** \-ᵊnt\ *adj*

flor·id \'flȯr-əd\ *adj* **1 ♦ :** very flowery in style ⟨~ prose⟩ **2 ♦ :** tinged with red : RUDDY **3 :** marked by emotional or sexual fervor ⟨a ~ love letter⟩

♦ [1] flowery, grandiloquent, highfalutin, high-flown ♦ [2] flush, glowing, rosy, ruddy, sanguine

flo·rin \'flȯr-ən\ *n* **1 :** an old gold coin first struck at Florence, Italy, in 1252 **2 :** a gold coin of a European country patterned after the florin of Florence **3 :** any of several modern silver coins issued in Commonwealth countries

flo·rist \'flȯr-ist\ *n* : a person who sells flowers or ornamental plants

¹**floss** \'fläs\ *n* **1 :** soft thread of silk or mercerized cotton for embroidery **2 :** DENTAL FLOSS **3 ♦ :** fluffy fibrous material

♦ down, fluff, fur, fuzz, lint, nap, pile

²**floss** *vb* : to use dental floss on (one's teeth)

flossy \'flä-sē\ *adj* **floss·i·er; -est 1 :** of, relating to, or having the characteristics of floss **2 :** STYLISH, GLAMOROUS — **floss·i·ly** \-sə-lē\ *adv*

flo·ta·tion \flō-'tā-shən\ *n* : the process or an instance of floating

flo·til·la \flō-'ti-lə\ *n* : a fleet esp. of small ships

flot·sam \'flät-səm\ *n* : floating wreckage of a ship or its cargo

¹**flounce** \'flaúns\ *vb* **flounced; flounc·ing 1 :** to move with exaggerated jerky or bouncy motions **2 :** to go with sudden determination

²**flounce** *n* : an act or instance of flouncing — **flouncy** \'flaún-sē\ *adj*

³**flounce** *n* **♦ :** a strip of fabric attached by one edge; *also* : a wide ruffle

♦ frill, furbelow, ruffle

¹**floun·der** \'flaún-dər\ *n, pl* **flounder** *or* **flounders** : FLATFISH; *esp* : any of various important marine food fishes

²**flounder** *vb* **1 :** to struggle to move or obtain footing **2 ♦ :** to proceed clumsily ⟨~ed through the speech⟩

♦ limp, lumber, plod, stumble

¹**flour** \'flaúr\ *n* : finely ground and sifted meal of a grain (as wheat); *also* : a fine soft powder

²**flour** *vb* : to coat with or as if with flour

¹**flour·ish** \'flər-ish\ *vb* **1 ♦ :** to grow luxuriantly : THRIVE, PROSPER **2 :** to be in a state of activity or production ⟨~ed about 1850⟩ **3 ♦ :** to reach a height of development or influence **4 :** to make bold and sweeping gestures **5 :** BRANDISH ⟨~ed his sword⟩

♦ [1] burgeon, prosper, thrive ♦ [3] prosper, succeed, thrive

²**flourish** *n* **1 :** a florid bit of speech or writing; *also* : an ornamental touch or decorative detail **2 :** FANFARE **3 :** WAVE ⟨with a ~ of his cane⟩ **4 :** showiness in doing something

floury *adj* **♦ :** of or resembling flour esp. in fine powdery texture

♦ dusty, fine, powdery

¹**flout** \'flaút\ *vb* **♦ :** to treat with contemptuous disregard ⟨~ the law⟩ — **flout·er** *n*

♦ despise, disregard, scorn

²**flout** *n* : TAUNT

¹**flow** \'flō\ *vb* **1 ♦ :** to issue or move in a stream **2 :** RISE ⟨the tide ebbs and ~s⟩ **3 :** ABOUND **4 ♦ :** to proceed smoothly and readily **5 :** to have a smooth continuity **6 :** to hang loose and billowing **7 :** COME, ARISE **8 :** MENSTRUATE

♦ [1] pour, roll, run, stream *Ant* back up ♦ [4] breeze, coast, glide, roll, sail, slide, slip, stream, sweep *Ant* flounder, struggle

²**flow** *n* **1 :** an act of flowing **2 :** FLOOD 1 2 **3 :** a smooth uninterrupted movement **4 :** STREAM; *also* : a mass of material that has flowed when molten **5 :** the quantity that flows in a certain time **6 :** MENSTRUATION **7 :** a continuous transfer of energy — **flow·age** \'flō-ij\ *n*

flow·chart \'flō-ˌchärt\ *n* : a symbolic diagram showing step-by-step progression through a procedure

flow diagram *n* : FLOWCHART

¹**flow·er** \'flaú(-ə)r\ *n* **1 :** a plant shoot modified for reproduction and bearing leaves specialized into floral organs; *esp* : one of a seed plant consisting of a calyx, corolla, stamens, and carpels **2 :** a plant cultivated for its blossoms **3 ♦ :** the best part or example **4 ♦ :** the finest most vigorous period **5 :** a state of blooming or flourishing — **flow·ered** \'flaú(-ə)rd\ *adj* — **flow·er·less** *adj* — **flow·er·like** \-ˌlīk\ *adj*

♦ [3] best, choice, cream, elite, pick, prime ♦ [4] bloom, blossom, flush, heyday, prime

²**flower** *vb* **1 :** DEVELOP; *also* : FLOURISH **2 ♦ :** to produce flowers : BLOOM

♦ bloom, blossom, blow, burgeon, unfold

flower girl *n* : a little girl who carries flowers at a wedding

flower head *n* : a compact cluster of small flowers without stems suggesting a single flower

flowering plant *n* : any of a major group of vascular plants (as magnolias, grasses, or roses) that produce flowers and fruit and have the seeds enclosed in an ovary

flow·er·pot \'flaú(-ə)r-ˌpät\ *n* : a pot in which to grow plants

flow·ery \ˈflau̇(-ə)r-ē\ *adj* **1** : of, relating to, or resembling flowers **2** ♦ : full of fine words or phrases ⟨a ~ speech⟩ — **flow·er·i·ly** \-ə-lē\ *adv* — **flow·er·i·ness** \-ē-nəs\ *n*
   ♦ florid, grandiloquent, highfalutin, high-flown

flown \ˈflōn\ *past part of* ¹FLY
fl oz *abbr* fluid ounce
flu \ˈflü\ *n* **1** : INFLUENZA **2** : any of several virus diseases marked esp. by respiratory or intestinal symptoms — **flu–like** \-ˌlīk\ *adj*
¹**flub** \ˈfləb\ *vb* **flubbed; flub·bing** ♦ : to make a mess of : BOTCH
   ♦ bobble, botch, bungle, foul up, fumble, mangle, mess up, screw up

²**flub** *n* ♦ : a clumsy or stupid failure
   ♦ blunder, error, fault, fumble, goof, mistake, slip, stumble

fluc·tu·ate \ˈflək-chə-ˌwāt\ *vb* **-at·ed; -at·ing 1** ♦ : to become wavering, unsteady, irresolute, or undetermined **2** : to move up and down or back and forth — **fluc·tu·a·tion** \ˌflək-chə-ˈwā-shən\ *n*
   ♦ change, mutate, shift, vary

flue \ˈflü\ *n* : a passage (as in a chimney) for directing a current (as of smoke or gases)
flu·ent \ˈflü-ənt\ *adj* **1** : capable of flowing : FLUID **2** ♦ : ready or facile in speech ⟨~ in French⟩; *also* : having or showing mastery in a subject or skill **3** ♦ : effortlessly smooth and rapid ⟨~ speech⟩ — **flu·en·cy** \-ən-sē\ *n*
   ♦ [2] articulate, eloquent, well-spoken ♦ [3] easy, effortless, facile, fluid, ready, simple, smooth

flu·ent·ly \-lē\ *adv* ♦ : in a fluent manner
   ♦ easily, effortlessly, freely, handily, lightly, painlessly, readily, smoothly

flue pipe *n* : an organ pipe whose tone is produced by an air current striking the beveled opening of the pipe
¹**fluff** \ˈfləf\ *n* **1** : ⁷DOWN 1 ⟨~ from a pillow⟩ **2** ♦ : something fluffy **3** : something inconsequential **4** : BLUNDER; *esp* : an actor's lapse of memory
   ♦ down, floss, fur, fuzz, lint, nap, pile

²**fluff** *vb* **1** : to make or become fluffy ⟨~ up a pillow⟩ **2** : to make a mistake
fluffy \ˈflə-fē\ *adj* **fluff·i·er; -est 1** : covered with or resembling fluff **2** ♦ : being light and soft or airy **3** : lacking in meaning or substance — **fluff·i·ly** \-fə-lē\ *adv*
   ♦ airy, ethereal, light

¹**flu·id** \ˈflü-əd\ *adj* **1** ♦ : capable of flowing **2** ♦ : subject to change or movement **3** ♦ : showing a smooth easy style ⟨~ movements⟩ **4** : available for a different use; *esp* : LIQUID 5 ⟨~ assets⟩ — **flu·id·i·ty** \flü-ˈi-də-tē\ *n* — **flu·id·ly** *adv*
   ♦ [1] fluent, liquid, runny *Ant* hard, solid ♦ [2] adaptable, adjustable, changeable, elastic, flexible, malleable, variable
   ♦ [3] easy, effortless, facile, fluent, light, ready, smooth

²**fluid** *n* : a substance (as a liquid or gas) tending to flow or take the shape of its container
fluid dram *or* **flu·i·dram** \ˌflü-ə-ˈdram\ *n* : a unit of liquid measure equal to ⅛ fluid ounce
fluid ounce *n* : a unit of liquid measure equal to 1/16 pint in the U.S. or 1/20 pint in the U.K.
¹**fluke** \ˈflük\ *n* : any of various trematode flatworms
²**fluke** *n* **1** : the part of an anchor that fastens in the ground **2** : a lobe of a whale's tail
³**fluke** *n* : a stroke of luck
fluky *also* **fluk·ey** \ˈflü-kē\ *adj* **1** ♦ : happening or depending on chance rather than skill **2** : light and uncertain
   ♦ accidental, casual, chance, fortuitous, incidental, unplanned

flume \ˈflüm\ *n* **1** ♦ : an inclined channel for carrying water **2** ♦ : a ravine or gorge with a stream running through it
   ♦ [1] aqueduct, canal, channel, conduit, raceway, watercourse
   ♦ [2] canyon, defile, gap, gorge, gulch, notch, pass, ravine

flung *past and past part of* FLING
flunk \ˈfləŋk\ *vb* ♦ : to fail esp. in an examination or course — **flunk** *n*
   ♦ collapse, fail, flop, fold, wash out

flun·ky *also* **flun·key** *or* **flun·kie** \ˈflən-kē\ *n, pl* **flunkies** *also* **flunkeys 1 a** : a liveried servant **b** ♦ : one performing menial or miscellaneous duties **2** : YES-MAN
   ♦ domestic, lackey, menial, retainer, servant, steward

fluo·res·cence \flȯ-ˈres-ᵊns\ *n* **1** : luminescence caused by radiation absorption that ceases almost immediately after the incident radiation has stopped **2** ♦ : visible emitted radiation — **fluo·resce** \-ˈres\ *vb* — **fluo·res·cent** \-ˈres-ᵊnt\ *adj*
   ♦ glow, illumination, incandescence, light, luminescence, radiance, shine

fluorescent lamp *n* : a tubular electric lamp in which light is produced by the action of ultraviolet light on a fluorescent material that coats the inner surface of the lamp
fluo·ri·date \ˈflȯr-ə-ˌdāt\ *vb* **-dat·ed; -dat·ing** : to add a fluoride to (as drinking water) to reduce tooth decay — **fluo·ri·da·tion** \ˌflȯr-ə-ˈdā-shən\ *n*
fluo·ride \ˈflȯr-ˌīd\ *n* : a compound of fluorine
fluo·ri·nate \ˈflȯr-ə-ˌnāt\ *vb* **-nat·ed; -nat·ing** : to treat or cause to combine with fluorine or a compound of fluorine — **fluo·ri·na·tion** \ˌflȯr-ə-ˈnā-shən\ *n*
fluo·rine \ˈflȯr-ˌēn, -ən\ *n* : a pale yellowish flammable irritating toxic gaseous chemical element
fluo·rite \ˈflȯr-ˌīt\ *n* : a mineral that consists of the fluoride of calcium used as a flux and in making glass
fluo·ro·car·bon \ˌflȯr-ō-ˈkär-bən\ *n* : a compound containing fluorine and carbon used chiefly as a lubricant, refrigerant, or nonstick coating; *also* : CHLOROFLUOROCARBON
fluo·ro·scope \ˈflȯr-ə-ˌskōp\ *n* : an instrument for observing the internal structure of an opaque object (as the living body) by means of X-rays — **fluo·ro·scop·ic** \ˌflȯr-ə-ˈskä-pik\ *adj* — **fluo·ros·co·py** \-ˈä-skə-pē\ *n*
fluo·ro·sis \ˌflu̇-ˈrō-səs, ˌflȯ-\ *n* : an abnormal condition (as spotting of the teeth) caused by fluorine or its compounds
flu·ox·e·tine \flü-ˈäk-sə-ˌtēn\ *n* : an antidepressant drug that enhances serotonin activity
flur·ry \ˈflər-ē\ *n, pl* **flurries 1** ♦ : a gust of wind **2** : a brief light snowfall **3** : COMMOTION, BUSTLE **4** ♦ : a brief outburst of activity ⟨a ~ of trading⟩ — **flurry** *vb*
   ♦ [1] blast, blow, gust, williwaw ♦ [4] burst, flash, outbreak, outburst, spurt

¹**flush** \ˈfləsh\ *vb* : to cause (a bird) to fly away suddenly
²**flush** *n* : a hand of cards all of the same suit
³**flush** *n* **1** : a sudden flow (as of water) **2** : a surge esp. of emotion ⟨a ~ of triumph⟩ **3** : a tinge of red : BLUSH **4** ♦ : a fresh and vigorous state ⟨in the ~ of youth⟩ **5** : a passing sensation of extreme heat
   ♦ bloom, blossom, flower, heyday, prime

⁴**flush** *vb* **1** : to flow and spread suddenly and freely **2** : to glow brightly **3** ♦ : to become red in the face esp. from shame, modesty, or confusion : BLUSH **4** ♦ : to wash out with a rush of fluid **5** : INFLAME, EXCITE ⟨was ~ed with anger⟩ **6** : to cause to blush
   ♦ [3] bloom, blush, color (*or* colour), crimson, glow, redden
   ♦ [4] irrigate, rinse, sluice, wash

⁵**flush** *adj* **1** ♦ : of a ruddy healthy color **2** : full of life and vigor **3** ♦ : filled to overflowing **4** ♦ : fully or generously supplied usu. with money **5** ♦ : readily available : ABUNDANT **6** ♦ : having an unbroken or even surface **7** : directly abutting : immediately adjacent **8** : set even with an edge of a type page or column — **flush·ness** *n*
   ♦ [1] florid, glowing, rosy, ruddy ♦ [3] fraught, replete, rife, thick ♦ [4] affluent, loaded, moneyed, opulent, rich, wealthy, well-fixed, well-heeled, well-off, well-to-do ♦ [6] even, flat, level, plane, smooth

⁶**flush** *adv* **1** : in a flush manner **2** : SQUARELY ⟨a blow ~ on the chin⟩
⁷**flush** *vb* : to make flush
¹**flus·ter** \ˈfləs-tər\ *vb* ♦ : to put into a state of agitated confusion
   ♦ abash, confound, confuse, discomfit, disconcert, embarrass, rattle

²**fluster** *n* ♦ : a state of agitated confusion
   ♦ abashment, confusion, discomfiture, dither, embarrassment, fret

flute \ˈflüt\ *n* **1** : a hollow pipelike musical instrument **2** : a grooved pleat **3** : GROOVE — **flute** *vb* — **flut·ed** *adj*
flut·ing *n* : fluted decoration
flut·ist \ˈflü-tist\ *n* : a flute player
¹**flut·ter** \ˈflə-tər\ *vb* **1** : to flap the wings rapidly **2** ♦ : to move with quick wavering or flapping motions **3** : to vibrate in irregular spasms **4** : to move about or behave in an agitated aimless manner
   ♦ beat, flail, flap, flop, whip

²flutter *n* **1** : an act of fluttering **2** : a state of nervous confusion **3** : a sudden but usu. slight stir : FLURRY

flut•tery \-tə-rē\ *adj* ♦ : given to or characterized by fluttering

♦ excitable, flighty, high-strung, jittery, jumpy, nervous, skittish, spooky

¹flux \'fləks\ *n* **1** : an act of flowing **2** : a state of continuous change **3** : a substance used to aid in fusing metals

²flux *vb* ♦ : to become or cause to become fluid

♦ deliquesce, fuse, liquefy, melt, run, thaw

¹fly \'flī\ *vb* **flew** \'flü\; **flown** \'flōn\; **fly•ing** **1** ♦ : to move in or pass through the air with wings **2** : to move through the air or before the wind **3** : to float or cause to float, wave, or soar in the air **4** ♦ : to take flight : FLEE **5** : to fade and disappear : VANISH **6** ♦ : to move or pass swiftly **7** : to become expended or dissipated rapidly **8** : to operate or travel in an aircraft or spacecraft **9** : to journey over by flying **10** : AVOID, SHUN **11** : to transport by flying

♦ [1] glide, plane, soar, wing ♦ [4] abscond, clear out, escape, flee, get out, lam, run away, run off ♦ [6] barrel, bolt, career, course, dash, hasten, hurry, pelt, race, run, rush, speed, tear, zip, zoom

²fly *n, pl* **flies** **1** : the action or process of flying : FLIGHT **2** *pl* : the space over a theater stage **3** : a garment closing concealed by a fold of cloth **4** : the length of an extended flag from its staff or support **5** : a baseball hit high into the air **6** : the outer canvas of a tent with a double top — **on the fly** : while still in the air

³fly *vb* **flied; fly•ing** : to hit a fly in baseball

⁴fly *n, pl* **flies** **1** : a winged insect — usu. used in combination ⟨butter*fly*⟩ **2** : any of a large order of insects mostly with one pair of functional wings and another pair that if present are reduced to balancing organs and often with larvae without a head, eyes, or legs; *esp* : one (as a housefly) that is large and stout-bodied **3** : a fishhook dressed to suggest an insect

fly•able \'flī-ə-bəl\ *adj* : suitable for flying or being flown

fly ball *n* : ²FLY 5

fly•blown \'flī-ˌblōn\ *adj* : not pure : TAINTED, CORRUPT

fly•by \-ˌbī\ *n, pl* **flybys** **1** : a usu. low-altitude flight by an aircraft over a public gathering **2** : a flight of a spacecraft past a celestial body (as Jupiter) close enough to obtain scientific data

fly–by–night \-bī-ˌnīt\ *adj* **1** : seeking a quick profit usu. by shady acts **2** : TRANSITORY, PASSING

fly casting *n* : the casting of artificial flies in fly-fishing or as a competitive sport

fly•catch•er \-ˌka-chər, -ˌke-\ *n* : any of various passerine birds that feed on insects caught in flight

flyer *var of* FLIER

fly–fish•ing \'flī-ˌfi-shiŋ\ *n* : a method of fishing in which an artificial fly is used for bait

flying boat *n* : a seaplane with a hull designed for floating

flying buttress *n* : a projecting arched structure to support a wall or building

flying fish *n* : any of numerous marine bony fishes capable of long gliding flights out of water by spreading their large fins like wings

flying saucer *n* : an unidentified flying object reported to be saucer-shaped or disk-shaped

flying squirrel *n* : either of two small nocturnal No. American squirrels with folds of skin connecting the forelegs and hind legs that enable them to make long gliding leaps

fly•leaf \'flī-ˌlēf\ *n, pl* **fly•leaves** \-ˌlēvz\ : a blank leaf at the beginning or end of a book

fly•pa•per \-ˌpā-pər\ *n* : paper poisoned or coated with a sticky substance for killing or catching flies

fly•speck \-ˌspek\ *n* **1** : a speck of fly dung **2** ♦ : something small and insignificant

♦ atom, bit, crumb, fleck, grain, particle, speck

fly•way \-ˌwā\ *n* : an established air route of migratory birds

fly•wheel \-ˌhwēl\ *n* : a heavy wheel for regulating the speed of machinery

fm *abbr* fathom

Fm *symbol* fermium

FM \'ef-ˌem\ *n* : a broadcasting system using frequency modulation; *also* : a radio receiver of such a system

fn *abbr* footnote

fo *or* **fol** *abbr* folio

FO *abbr* foreign office

¹foal \'fōl\ *n* : a young horse or related animal; *esp* : one under one year

²foal *vb* : to give birth to a foal

¹foam \'fōm\ *n* **1** ♦ : a mass of bubbles formed on the surface of a liquid : FROTH, SPUME **2** : material (as rubber) in a lightweight cellular form — **foamy** *adj*

♦ froth, head, lather, spume

²foam *vb* : to form foam : FROTH

fob \'fäb\ *n* **1** : a short strap, ribbon, or chain attached esp. to a pocket watch **2** : a small ornament worn on a fob **3** *or* **key fob** : an object attached to a key chain or key ring; *esp* : a small electronic device used typically in place of a key (as to unlock a door) or to remotely work another device

FOB *abbr* free on board

fob off *vb* **1** : to put off with a trick, excuse, or inferior substitute **2** : to pass or offer as genuine **3** : to put aside

FOC *abbr* free of charge

focal length *n* : the distance of a focus from a lens or curved mirror

fo'c'sle *var of* FORECASTLE

¹fo•cus \'fō-kəs\ *n, pl* **fo•ci** \-ˌsī\ *also* **fo•cus•es** **1** : a point at which rays (as of light, heat, or sound) meet or diverge or appear to diverge; *esp* : the point at which an image is formed by a mirror, lens, or optical system **2** : FOCAL LENGTH **3** : adjustment (as of eyes or eyeglasses) that gives clear vision **4** ♦ : a central point : CENTER — **fo•cal** \'fō-kəl\ *adj* — **fo•cal•ly** *adv*

♦ base, center (*or* centre), core, heart, hub, nucleus, seat

²focus *vb* **-cused** *also* **-cussed; -cus•ing** *also* **-cus•sing** **1** : to bring or come to a focus ⟨~ rays of light⟩ **2** ♦ : to cause to be concentrated ⟨~ attention on a problem⟩ **3** : to adjust the focus of

♦ concentrate, fasten, rivet, train

fod•der \'fä-dər\ *n* **1** : coarse dry food (as cornstalks) for livestock **2** : available material to supply a heavy demand

foe \'fō\ *n* ♦ : one who has personal enmity for another : ENEMY

♦ adversary, antagonist, enemy, opponent

FOE *abbr* Fraternal Order of Eagles

foehn *or* **föhn** \'fərn, 'fœn, 'fān\ *n* : a warm dry wind blowing down a mountainside

foe•man \'fō-mən\ *n* : FOE

foe•tal, foe•tus *chiefly Brit var of* FETAL, FETUS

¹fog \'fog, 'fäg\ *n* **1** ♦ : fine particles of water suspended in the lower atmosphere **2** : mental confusion

♦ [1] haze, murk, smog, soup ♦ [2] daze, haze, muddle, spin

²fog *vb* **fogged; fog•ging** ♦ : to obscure or be obscured with or as if with fog

♦ blur, cloud, confuse, dim, haze, mist, obscure ♦ becloud, befog, blur, cloud, confuse, muddy

fog•gy \'fo-gē, 'fä-\ *adj* **1 a** : filled or abounding with fog **b** ♦ : covered or made opaque by moisture or grime **2** ♦ : blurred or obscured as if by fog

♦ [1b] cloudy, hazy, misty, murky, smoggy, soupy ♦ [2] bleary, dim, faint, fuzzy, hazy, indefinite, indistinct, murky, obscure, unclear

fog•horn \'fog-ˌhorn, 'fäg-\ *n* : a horn sounded in a fog to give warning

fo•gy *also* **fo•gey** \'fō-gē\ *n, pl* **fogies** *also* **fogeys** ♦ : a person with old-fashioned ideas ⟨an old ~⟩

♦ antediluvian, dodo, fossil, fuddy-duddy, reactionary *Ant* modern

foi•ble \'foi-bəl\ *n* ♦ : a minor failing or weakness in character or behavior

♦ demerit, failing, fault, frailty, shortcoming, vice, weakness

foie gras \'fwä-ˈgrä\ *n* : the fattened liver of an animal and esp. of a goose usu. served as a pâté

¹foil \'foil\ *vb* **1** ♦ : to prevent from attaining an end **2** ♦ : to bring to naught : THWART

♦ [1, 2] baffle, balk, beat, checkmate, frustrate, thwart

²foil *n* **1** : a very thin sheet of metal ⟨aluminum ~⟩ **2** : one that serves as a contrast to another ⟨acted as a ~ for a comedian⟩

³foil *n* : a light fencing sword with a flexible blade tapering to a blunt point

foist \'foist\ *vb* : to pass off (something false or worthless) as genuine

¹fold \'fōld\ *n* **1** : an enclosure for sheep **2** ♦ : a group of people with a common faith, belief, or interest

♦ body, circle, clan, clique, community, coterie, set

²fold *vb* : to house (sheep) in a fold

³fold *vb* **1** : to lay one part over or against another part **2** : to clasp together **3** : EMBRACE **4** : to bend (as a layer of rock) into folds **5** : to incorporate into a mixture by overturning repeatedly without stirring or beating **6** : to become doubled or pleated **7** ♦ : to fail completely : FAIL, COLLAPSE

♦ collapse, fail, flop, flunk, wash out

⁴fold *n* **1** : a doubling or folding over **2** : a part doubled or laid over another part
fold·away \ˈfōl-də-ˌwā\ *adj* : designed to fold out of the way or out of sight
fold·er \ˈfōl-dər\ *n* **1** : one that folds **2** ♦ : a folded printed circular **3** : a folded cover or large envelope for loose papers **4** : an object in a computer operating system used to organize files or other folders

♦ booklet, brochure, circular, leaflet, pamphlet

fol·de·rol \ˈfäl-də-ˌräl\ *n* **1** : a useless trifle **2** : NONSENSE
fold·out \ˈfōl-ˌdaut\ *n* : a folded leaf (as in a magazine) larger in some dimension than the page
fo·liage \ˈfō-lē-ij\ *n* ♦ : a mass of leaves (as of a plant or forest)

♦ flora, green, greenery, herbage, leafage, vegetation, verdure

fo·li·at·ed \ˈfō-lē-ˌā-təd\ *adj* : composed of or separable into layers
fo·lic acid \ˌfō-lik-\ *n* : a vitamin of the vitamin B complex used esp. to treat nutritional anemias
fo·lio \ˈfō-lē-ˌō\ *n, pl* **fo·li·os** **1** : a leaf of a book; *also* : a page number **2** : the size of a piece of paper cut two from a sheet **3** : a book printed on folio pages
¹folk \ˈfōk\ *n, pl* **folk** *or* **folks** **1** : the largest number or most characteristic part of a group of people forming a tribe or nation **2 a** *pl* ♦ : a certain kind, class, or group of people : PEOPLE, PERSONS ⟨country ∼⟩ ⟨old ∼s⟩ **b** ♦ : people generally **3** *folks pl* ♦ : the persons of one's own family

♦ *usu* **folks** [2a, 2b] humanity, humankind, people, persons, public, society, world ♦ *usu* **folks** [3] blood, clan, family, house, kin, kindred, kinfolk, line, lineage, people, race, stock, tribe

²folk *adj* : of, relating to, or originating among the common people ⟨∼ music⟩
folk art *n* : the traditional anonymous art of usu. untrained people
folk·lore \ˈfōk-ˌlȯr\ *n* ♦ : customs, beliefs, stories, and sayings of a people handed down from generation to generation — **folk·lor·ic** \-ˌlȯr-ik\ *adj* — **folk·lor·ist** \-ist\ *n*

♦ legend, lore, myth, mythology, tradition

folk mass *n* : a mass in which traditional liturgical music is replaced by folk music
folk·sing·er \ˈfōk-ˌsiŋ-ər\ *n* : a singer of folk songs — **folk·sing·ing** *n*
folksy \ˈfōk-sē\ *adj* **folks·i·er; -est** **1** : SOCIABLE, FRIENDLY **2** : informal, casual, or familiar in manner or style
folk·way \ˈfōk-ˌwā\ *n* : a way of thinking, feeling, or acting common to a given group of people; *esp* : a traditional social custom
fol·li·cle \ˈfä-li-kəl\ *n* **1** : a small anatomical cavity or gland ⟨a hair ∼⟩ **2** : a small fluid-filled cavity in the ovary of a mammal enclosing a developing egg
fol·low \ˈfä-lō\ *vb* **1** ♦ : to go or come after **2** ♦ : to proceed along **3** : to engage in as a way of life ⟨∼ the sea⟩ ⟨∼ a profession⟩ **4** ♦ : to be or act in accordance with : to accept as authority : OBEY **5** ♦ : to pursue in an effort to overtake : PURSUE **6** : to come after in order or rank or natural sequence **7** ♦ : to keep one's attention fixed on **8** : to result from **9** : to understand the sense or logic of **10** : to subscribe to the social media feed of — **follow suit** **1** : to play a card of the same suit as the card led **2** : to follow an example set

♦ [1] succeed *Ant* antedate, precede, predate ♦ [2] go, pass, proceed, travel, traverse ♦ [4] comply, conform, mind, obey, observe ♦ [5] chase, pursue, tail, trace, track, trail *Ant* guide, lead, pilot ♦ [7] heed, listen, mind, note, observe, regard, watch

fol·low·er *n* **1** ♦ : one that follows the opinions or teachings of another **2** : one who subscribes to a feed esp. on social media

♦ adherent, convert, disciple, partisan, pupil, votary *Ant* leader

¹fol·low·ing \ˈfä-lə-wiŋ\ *adj* **1** ♦ : next after : SUCCEEDING ⟨the ∼ day⟩ **2** : that immediately follows ⟨trains will leave at the ∼ times⟩

♦ coming, next, succeeding

²following *n* ♦ : a group of followers, adherents, or partisans

♦ cortege, retinue, suite, train

³following *prep* : subsequent to : AFTER

follow through *vb* ♦ : to press on in an activity or process esp. to a conclusion

♦ accomplish, achieve, carry out, commit, compass, do, execute, fulfill, make, perform

fol·low–up \ˈfä-lə-ˌwəp\ *n* : a system or instance of pursuing an initial effort by supplementary action
fol·ly \ˈfä-lē\ *n, pl* **follies** **1** : lack of good sense **2** ♦ : a foolish act or idea **3** : an excessively costly or unprofitable undertaking

♦ absurdity, fatuity, foolery, foolishness, idiocy, inanity, madness, stupidity

fo·ment \fō-ˈment\ *vb* ♦ : to promote the growth or development of : INCITE

♦ abet, ferment, incite, instigate, provoke, raise, stir, whip

fo·men·ta·tion \ˌfō-mən-ˈtā-shən, -ˌmen-\ *n* **1** : a hot moist material (as a damp cloth) applied to the body to ease pain **2** : the act of fomenting : INSTIGATION
fond \ˈfänd\ *adj* **1** : FOOLISH, SILLY ⟨∼ pride⟩ **2** : prizing highly : DESIROUS ⟨∼ of praise⟩ **3** ♦ : strongly attracted or predisposed ⟨∼ of music⟩ **4 a** ♦ : foolishly tender : INDULGENT **b** : feeling or expressing love : LOVING, AFFECTIONATE **5** : CHERISHED, DEAR ⟨his ∼est hopes⟩ — **fond·ly** *adv*

♦ [3] inclined, partial *Ant* averse, disinclined ♦ [4b] affectionate, devoted, loving, tender, tenderhearted

fon·dant \ˈfän-dənt\ *n* : a creamy preparation of sugar used as a basis for candies or icings
fon·dle \ˈfänd-ᵊl\ *vb* **fon·dled; fon·dling** ♦ : to touch or handle lovingly : CARESS

♦ caress, love, pat, pet, stroke

fond·ness \ˈfän(d)-nəs\ *n* **1** ♦ : tender affection **2** ♦ : enjoyment of or delight in something that satisfies one's tastes, inclinations, or desires

♦ [1] affection, attachment, devotion, love, passion ♦ [1, 2] appetite, fancy, favor (*or* favour), like, liking, love, partiality, preference

fon·due *also* **fon·du** \fän-ˈdü, -ˈdyü\ *n* : a preparation of melted cheese often flavored with white wine
¹font \ˈfänt\ *n* **1** : a receptacle for baptismal or holy water **2** : FOUNTAIN, SOURCE
²font *n* : an assortment of printing type of one size and style
food \ˈfüd\ *n* **1** : material taken into an organism and used for growth, repair, and vital processes and as a source of energy; *also* : organic material produced by green plants and used by them as food **2** ♦ : nourishment in solid form **3** : something that nourishes, sustains, or supplies ⟨∼ for thought⟩

♦ chow, fare, meat, provisions, viands, victuals

food bank *n* : a usu. nonprofit organization that collects donated food and distributes it to people in need
food·borne \ˈfüd-ˌbȯrn\ *adj* : caused by contaminated food ⟨a ∼ illness⟩
food chain *n* **1** : a hierarchical arrangement of organisms in an ecological community such that each uses the next usu. lower member as a food source **2** : a hierarchy based on power or importance
food court *n* : an area (as within a shopping mall) set apart for food concessions
food poisoning *n* : a digestive illness caused by bacteria or by chemicals in food
food·stuff \ˈfüd-ˌstəf\ *n* : a substance with food value; *esp* : a specific nutrient (as fat or protein)
¹fool \ˈfül\ *n* **1** ♦ : a person who lacks sense or judgment **2** : JESTER **3** : DUPE **4** : IDIOT

♦ booby, goose, jackass, nitwit, simpleton

²fool *vb* **1** ♦ : to meddle or tamper thoughtlessly or ignorantly **2** ♦ : to speak in jest : JOKE **3** ♦ : to make a fool of : DECEIVE **4** : FRITTER ⟨∼ed away his time⟩

♦ [1] fiddle (around), mess, monkey, play, tamper, tinker ♦ [2] banter, fun, jest, jive, joke, josh, kid, quip, wisecrack ♦ [3] deceive, delude, dupe, gull, hoodwink, mislead, take in, trick

fool around *vb* **1** ♦ : to spend time idly, aimlessly, or frivolously **2** : to engage in casual sexual activity

♦ fiddle (around), monkey, play, trifle

fool·ery \ˈfü-lə-rē\ *n, pl* **-er·ies** **1** : a foolish act, utterance, or belief **2** ♦ : foolish behavior

♦ [1] absurdity, fatuity, folly, foolishness, idiocy, inanity, madness, stupidity ♦ [2] high jinks, horseplay, monkeyshines, shenanigans, tomfoolery

fool·har·dy \'fül-₁här-dē\ *adj* ♦ : foolishly daring : RASH — **fool·har·di·ness** \-dē-nəs\ *n*

♦ brash, madcap, overbold, overconfident, rash, reckless *Ant* careful, cautious, heedful, prudent

fool·ish \'fü-lish\ *adj* **1** ♦ : showing or arising from folly or lack of judgment **2** ♦ : ridiculously unreasonable, unsound, or incongruous : ABSURD **3** : ABASHED — **fool·ish·ly** *adv*

♦ [1] absurd, bizarre, fanciful, fantastic, nonsensical, preposterous, unreal, wild ♦ [2] absurd, asinine, cuckoo, daft, fatuous, kooky, nonsensical, nutty, preposterous, senseless, silly, stupid *Ant* judicious, prudent, sensible, sound, wise

fool·ish·ness *n* **1** ♦ : foolish behavior **2** ♦ : a foolish act or idea

♦ folly, nonsense, piffle, rot, silliness

fool·proof \'fül-₁prüf\ *adj* : so simple or reliable as to leave no opportunity for error, misuse, or failure ⟨a ～ plan⟩
fools·cap \'fül-₁skap\ *n* : a size of paper typically 16×13 inches
fool's gold *n* : PYRITE
¹**foot** \'füt\ *n, pl* **feet** \'fēt\ *also* **foot** **1** : the end part of a leg below the ankle of a vertebrate animal **2** : a unit of measure equal to 12 inches **3** : a group of syllables forming the basic unit of verse meter **4** : something resembling an animal's foot in position or use **5** ♦ : the lowest part : BOTTOM **6** : the part at the opposite end from the head **7** : the part (as of a stocking) that covers the foot

♦ base, bottom

²**foot** *vb* **1** ♦ : to tread to music : DANCE **2** ♦ : to go on foot **3** : to add up **4** ♦ : to pay or provide for paying

♦ *usu* **foot it** [1] dance, step ♦ *usu* **foot it** [2] leg, pad, step, traipse, tread, walk ♦ [4] clear, discharge, liquidate, pay, recompense, settle, spring, stand

foot·age \'fü-tij\ *n* **1** : length expressed in feet **2** : the length of film used for a scene; *also* : the material contained on such footage
foot–and–mouth disease *n* : an acute contagious viral disease esp. of cattle
foot·ball \'füt-₁bȯl\ *n* **1** : any of several games played by two teams on a rectangular field with goalposts at each end in which the object is to get the ball over the goal line or between goalposts by running, passing, or kicking **2** : the ball used in football
foot·board \-₁bȯrd\ *n* **1** : a narrow platform on which to stand or brace the feet **2** : a board forming the foot of a bed
foot·bridge \-₁brij\ *n* : a bridge for pedestrians
foot·ed \'fü-təd\ *adj* : having a foot or feet of a specified kind or number ⟨flat-*footed*⟩ ⟨four-*footed*⟩
-foot·er \'fü-tər\ *comb form* : one that is a specified number of feet in height, length, or breadth ⟨a six-*footer*⟩
foot·fall \'füt-₁fȯl\ *n* : the sound of a footstep
foot·hill \-₁hil\ *n* : a hill at the foot of higher hills or mountains
foot·hold \-₁hōld\ *n* **1** : a hold for the feet : FOOTING **2** : a position usable as a base for further advance
foot·ing *n* **1** : the placing of one's feet in a stable position **2** : the act of moving on foot **3** : a place or space for standing : FOOTHOLD **4** ♦ : position with respect to one another : STATUS **5** ♦ : an underlying condition or state of affairs : BASIS

♦ [4] degree, level, place, position, rank, situation, standing, station, status ♦ [5] base, basis, bedrock, cornerstone, foundation, ground, groundwork, keystone, underpinning

foot·less \'füt-ləs\ *adj* **1** : having no feet **2** : INEPT, INEFFECTUAL
foot·lights \-₁līts\ *n pl* **1** : a row of lights along the front of a stage floor **2** : the stage as a profession
foo·tling \'füt-liŋ\ *adj* **1** : INEPT **2** : TRIVIAL
foot·lock·er \'füt-₁lä-kər\ *n* : a small trunk designed to be placed at the foot of a bed (as in a barracks)
foot·loose \-₁lüs\ *adj* ♦ : having no ties : FREE

♦ free, loose, unbound, unconfined, unrestrained

foot·man \-mən\ *n* : a male servant who attends a carriage or waits on table, admits visitors, and runs errands
foot·note \-₁nōt\ *n* **1** : a note of reference, explanation, or comment placed usu. at the bottom of a page **2** : COMMENTARY
foot·pad \-₁pad\ *n* : a round somewhat flat foot on the leg of a spacecraft for distributing weight to minimize sinking into a surface
foot·path \-₁path, -₁pȧth\ *n* ♦ : a narrow path for pedestrians

♦ path, trace, track, trail

foot·print \-₁print\ *n* **1** : an impression of the foot **2** : the area on a surface covered by something
foot·race \-₁rās\ *n* : a race run on foot
foot·rest \-₁rest\ *n* : a support for the feet
foot·sore \-₁sȯr\ *adj* : having sore or tender feet (as from much walking)
foot·step \-₁step\ *n* **1** : the mark of the foot : TRACK **2** : TREAD **3** : distance covered by a step : PACE **4** : a step on which to ascend or descend **5** : a way of life, conduct, or action
foot·stool \-₁stül\ *n* : a low stool to support the feet
foot·wear \-₁war\ *n* : apparel (as shoes or boots) for the feet
foot·work \-₁wərk\ *n* : the management of the feet (as in boxing)
fop \'fäp\ *n* ♦ : a man who is devoted to or vain about his appearance or dress : DANDY — **fop·pery** \'fä-pə-rē\ *n* — **fop·pish** *adj*

♦ buck, dandy, dude, gallant

¹**for** \fər, 'fȯr\ *prep* **1** : as a preparation toward ⟨dress ～ dinner⟩ **2** : toward the purpose or goal of ⟨need time ～ study⟩ ⟨money ～ a trip⟩ **3** : so as to reach or attain ⟨run ～ cover⟩ **4** : as being characteristic of ⟨took him ～ a fool⟩ **5** : because of ⟨cry ～ joy⟩ **6** — used to indicate a recipient ⟨a letter ～ you⟩ **7** : in support of ⟨fought ～ his country⟩ **8** : directed at : AFFECTING ⟨a cure ～ what ails you⟩ **9** — used with a noun or pronoun followed by an infinitive to form the equivalent of a noun clause ⟨～ you to go would be silly⟩ **10** : in exchange as equal to : so as to return the value of ⟨a lot of trouble ～ nothing⟩ ⟨pay $10 ～ a hat⟩ **11** : CONCERNING ⟨a stickler ～ detail⟩ **12** : CONSIDERING ⟨tall ～ her age⟩ **13** : through the period of ⟨served ～ three years⟩ **14** : in honor of
²**for** *conj* ♦ : for the reason that : BECAUSE

♦ because, now, since, whereas

³**for** *abbr* **1** foreign **2** forestry
fora *pl of* FORUM
¹**for·age** \'fȯr-ij\ *n* **1** : food for animals esp. when taken by browsing or grazing **2** : a search for food or supplies
²**forage** *vb* **for·aged; for·ag·ing** **1** : to collect forage from **2** : to search for food or supplies **3** : to get by foraging **4** ♦ : to make a search : RUMMAGE

♦ *usu* **forage for** cast about, hunt, pursue, quest, rummage, search (for *or* out), seek

¹**for·ay** \'fȯr-₁ā, fȯ-'rā\ *vb* ♦ : to raid esp. in search of plunder

♦ *usu* **foray into** invade, overrun, raid

²**foray** *n* ♦ : a sudden or irregular incursion for war or spoils

♦ descent, incursion, invasion, irruption, raid

¹**for·bear** \fȯr-'ber\ *vb* **-bore** \-'bȯr\; **-borne** \-'bȯrn\; **-bear·ing** **1** : to refrain from : ABSTAIN **2** : to be patient

♦ abstain (from), forgo, keep, refrain *Ant* give in (to), succumb (to), yield (to)

²**forbear** *var of* FOREBEAR
for·bear·ance \-'ber-əns\ *n* ♦ : the act of forbearing

♦ long-suffering, patience, sufferance, tolerance

forbearing *adj* ♦ : marked by calm patience

♦ long-suffering, patient, stoic, tolerant, uncomplaining

for·bid \fər-'bid\ *vb* **-bade** \-'bad, -'bād\ *also* **-bad** \-'bad\; **-bid·den** \-'bi-dᵊn\; **-bid·ding** **1** ♦ : to command against : PROHIBIT **2** : HINDER, PREVENT

♦ ban, bar, enjoin, interdict, outlaw, prohibit, proscribe *Ant* allow, let, permit, suffer

forbidden *adj* ♦ : not allowed : not permitted

♦ impermissible, taboo

forbidding *adj* **1** : causing discomfort **2** ♦ : presenting, suggesting, or constituting a menace

♦ austere, grim, menacing, scary, severe

¹**force** \'fȯrs\ *n* **1** ♦ : strength or energy esp. of an exceptional degree : active power **2** ♦ : capacity to persuade or convince **3** : military strength; *also, pl* : the whole military strength (as of a nation) **4** ♦ : a body (as of persons or ships) available for a particular purpose **5** ♦ : violence, compulsion, or constraint used on or against a person or thing : COMPULSION **6** : an influence (as a push or pull) that causes motion or a change of motion — **in force 1** : in great numbers **2** : VALID, OPERATIVE

♦ [1] energy, main, might, muscle, potency, power, strength, vigor (*or* vigour) ♦ [2] cogency, effectiveness, persuasiveness ♦ [4] help, personnel, pool, staff ♦ [5] coercion, compulsion, constraint, duress, pressure

²force *vb* **forced; forc•ing** **1** ♦ : to compel by physical, moral, or intellectual means : COERCE **2** : to cause through necessity ⟨*forced* to admit defeat⟩ **3** : to press, attain to, or effect against resistance or inertia ⟨~ your way through⟩ **4** : to raise or accelerate to the utmost ⟨~ the pace⟩ **5** : to produce with unnatural or unwilling effort ⟨*forced* a smile⟩ **6** : to hasten (as in growth) by artificial means

♦ coerce, compel, constrain, drive, make, muscle, obligate, oblige, press, pressure

force•ful \\'fōrs-fəl\\ *adj* ♦ : possessing or filled with force — **force•ful•ness** \\-nəs\\ *n*

♦ cogent, compelling, convincing, decisive, emphatic, persuasive, strong ♦ authoritative, influential, weighty

force•ful•ly \\-fə-lē\\ *adv* ♦ : in a forceful manner

♦ firmly, forcibly, hard, mightily, powerfully, strongly, vigorously

for•ceps \\'fōr-səps\\ *n, pl* **forceps** : a handheld instrument for grasping, holding, or pulling objects esp. for delicate operations (as by a surgeon)

forc•ible \\'fōr-sə-bəl\\ *adj* **1** : obtained or done by force **2** : showing force or energy : POWERFUL

forc•i•bly \\-blē\\ *adv* ♦ : in a forcible manner

♦ energetically, firmly, forcefully, hard, mightily, powerfully, vigorously

¹ford \\'fōrd\\ *n* : a place where a stream may be crossed by wading
²ford *vb* : to cross (a body of water) by wading
¹fore \\'fōr\\ *adv* : in, toward, or adjacent to the front : FORWARD
²fore *adj* : being or coming before in time, order, or space
³fore *n* : something that occupies a front position
⁴fore *interj* — used by a golfer to warn anyone within range of the probable line of flight of the ball
fore–and–aft \\,fōr-ə-'naft\\ *adj* : lying, running, or acting along the length of a structure (as a ship)
¹fore•arm \\(,)fōr-'ärm\\ *vb* ♦ : to arm in advance : PREPARE

♦ brace, fortify, nerve, prepare, psych (up), ready, steel, strengthen

²fore•arm \\'fōr-,ärm\\ *n* : the part of the arm between the elbow and the wrist
fore•bear \\-,bar\\ *n* ♦ : one from whom a person is descended and who is usu. more remote in the line of descent than a grandparent : ANCESTOR, FOREFATHER

♦ ancestor, father, forefather, grandfather

fore•bode \\fōr-'bōd\\ *vb* **1** : to give promise of **2** : FORETELL, PREDICT
fore•bod•ing *n* ♦ : an omen, prediction, or presentiment esp. of coming evil — **fore•bod•ing•ly** *adv*

♦ omen, portent, premonition, presage, presentiment ♦ alarm, apprehension, dread, misgiving

¹fore•cast \\'fōr-,kast\\ *vb* **-cast** *also* **-cast•ed; -cast•ing** **1** ♦ : to calculate or predict (some future event or condition) : PREDICT ⟨~ weather conditions⟩ **2** ♦ : to indicate as likely to occur

♦ [1, 2] augur, foretell, predict, presage, prognosticate, prophesy

²forecast *n* ♦ : a prophecy, estimate, or prediction of a future happening or condition

♦ prediction, prognostication, prophecy

fore•cast•er *n* ♦ : one that forecasts

♦ diviner, fortune-teller, futurist, prognosticator, prophet, seer

fore•cas•tle *or* **fo'c'sle** \\'fōk-səl\\ *n* **1** : the forward part of the upper deck of a ship **2** : the crew's quarters usu. in a ship's bow
fore•close \\fōr-'klōz\\ *vb* **1** : to shut out : PRECLUDE **2** : to take legal measures to terminate a mortgage and take possession of the mortgaged property
fore•clo•sure \\-'klō-zhər\\ *n* : the act of foreclosing; *esp* : the legal procedure of foreclosing a mortgage
fore•doom \\fōr-'düm\\ *vb* ♦ : to doom beforehand

♦ destine, doom, foreordain, ordain, predestine

fore•fa•ther \\'fōr-,fä-thər\\ *n* **1** ♦ : one from whom a person is descended and who is usu. more remote in the line of descent than a grandparent : ANCESTOR **2** : a person of an earlier period and common heritage

♦ ancestor, father, forebear, grandfather

forefend *var of* FORFEND
fore•fin•ger \\-,fiŋ-gər\\ *n* : INDEX FINGER

fore•foot \\-,fut\\ *n* : either of the front feet of a quadruped; *also* : the front part of the human foot
fore•front \\-,frənt\\ *n* : the foremost part or place
foregather *var of* FORGATHER
¹fore•go \\fōr-'gō\\ *vb* **-went** \\-'went\\; **-gone** \\-'gon\\; **-go•ing** ♦ : to go before : PRECEDE

♦ antedate, precede

²forego *var of* FORGO
fore•go•ing *adj* ♦ : listed, mentioned, or occurring before : PRECEDING

♦ antecedent, anterior, preceding, previous, prior

fore•gone \\'fōr-,gon\\ *adj* : determined in advance ⟨a ~ conclusion⟩
fore•ground \\-,graund\\ *n* **1** : the part of a scene or representation that appears nearest to and in front of the spectator **2** : a position of prominence
fore•hand \\-,hand\\ *n* : a stroke (as in tennis) made with the palm of the hand turned in the direction in which the hand is moving; *also* : the side on which such a stroke is made — **forehand** *adj*
fore•hand•ed \\(,)fōr-'han-dəd\\ *adj* ♦ : mindful of the future : PRUDENT

♦ farsighted, foresighted, prescient, provident, prudent

fore•head \\'fōr-əd, 'fōr-,hed\\ *n* : the part of the face above the eyes
for•eign \\'fōr-ən\\ *adj* **1** : situated outside a place or country and esp. one's own country **2** : born in, belonging to, or characteristic of some place or country other than the one under consideration ⟨~ language⟩ **3** ♦ : not connected, pertinent, or characteristically present **4** : related to or dealing with other nations ⟨~ affairs⟩ **5** : occurring in an abnormal situation in the living body ⟨a ~ body in the eye⟩

♦ alien, extraneous, extrinsic

for•eign•er \\'fōr-ə-nər\\ *n* : a person belonging to or owing allegiance to a foreign country
foreign minister *n* : a governmental minister for foreign affairs
fore•know \\fōr-'nō\\ *vb* **-knew** \\-'nü, -'nyü\\; **-known** \\-'nōn\\; **-know•ing** ♦ : to have previous knowledge of — **fore•knowl•edge** \\'fōr-,nä-lij, fōr-'nä-\\ *n*

♦ anticipate, divine, foresee

fore•la•dy \\'fōr-,lā-dē\\ *n* : FOREWOMAN
fore•leg \\-,leg\\ *n* : a front leg
fore•limb \\-,lim\\ *n* : a front or upper limb (as a wing, arm, fin, or leg)
fore•lock \\-,läk\\ *n* : a lock of hair growing from the front part of the head
fore•man \\-mən\\ *n* **1** : a spokesperson of a jury **2** ♦ : a person in charge of a group of workers

♦ boss, captain, chief, head, headman, leader, taskmaster

fore•mast \\-,mast\\ *n* : the mast nearest the bow of a ship
fore•most \\-,mōst\\ *adj* ♦ : first in time, place, or order : most important : PREEMINENT — **foremost** *adv*

♦ chief, dominant, first, key, main, predominant, preeminent, primary, principal *Ant* last, least

fore•name \\-,nām\\ *n* : a first name
fore•named \\-,nāmd\\ *adj* : previously named : AFORESAID
fore•noon \\-,nün\\ *n* : MORNING
¹fo•ren•sic \\fə-'ren-sik\\ *adj* **1** : belonging to, used in, or suitable to courts of law or to public speaking or debate **2** : relating to the application of scientific knowledge to legal problems ⟨~ medicine⟩
²forensic *n* **1** : an argumentative exercise **2** *pl* : the art or study of argumentative discourse **3** *pl* : scientific analysis of physical evidence (as from a crime scene)
fore•or•dain \\,fōr-ōr-'dān\\ *vb* ♦ : to ordain or decree beforehand : PREDESTINE

♦ destine, doom, foredoom, ordain, predestine

fore•part \\'fōr-,pärt\\ *n* **1** : the anterior part of something **2** : the earlier part of a period of time
fore•quar•ter \\-,kwor-tər\\ *n* : the front half of a lateral half of the body or carcass of a quadruped ⟨a ~ of beef⟩
fore•run•ner \\-,rə-nər\\ *n* **1** ♦ : one that goes before to give notice of the approach of others : HARBINGER **2** ♦ : something belonging to a relatively early developmental period of a contemporary or fully developed object or phenomenon : PREDECESSOR, ANCESTOR

♦ [1] angel, harbinger, herald, precursor ♦ [2] ancestor, antecedent, precursor

fore·sail \-ˌsāl, -səl\ *n* **1** : the lowest sail on the foremast of a square-rigged ship or schooner **2** : the principal sail forward of the foremast (as of a sloop)

fore·see \fōr-'sē\ *vb* **-saw** \-'sò\; **-seen** \-'sēn\; **-see·ing** ♦ : to see or realize beforehand — **fore·see·able** *adj*

♦ anticipate, divine, foreknow

fore·shad·ow \-'sha-dō\ *vb* ♦ : to give a hint or suggestion of beforehand

♦ harbinger, prefigure

fore·short·en \fōr-'shòrt-²n\ *vb* : to shorten (a detail) in a drawing or painting so that it appears to have depth

fore·sight \'fōr-ˌsīt\ *n* **1** : the act or power of foreseeing **2** ♦ : care or provision for the future : PRUDENCE **3** : an act of looking forward; *also* : a view forward

♦ forethought, prescience, providence, prudence *Ant* improvidence, shortsightedness

fore·sight·ed \-ˌsī-təd\ *adj* ♦ : having foresight — **fore·sight·ed·ness** *n*

♦ farsighted, prescient, provident, prudent *Ant* improvident, shortsighted

fore·skin \-ˌskin\ *n* : a fold of skin enclosing the end of the penis

fore·st \'fòr-əst\ *n* ♦ : a large thick growth of trees and underbrush — **for·est·ed** \'fòr-ə-stəd\ *adj* — **for·est·land** \'fòr-əst-ˌland\ *n*

♦ timberland, woodland

fore·stall \fōr-'stòl\ *vb* ♦ : to keep out, hinder, or prevent by measures taken in advance

♦ avert, help, obviate, preclude, prevent

forest ranger *n* : a person in charge of the management and protection of a portion of a forest

for·est·ry \'fòr-ə-strē\ *n* : the science of growing and caring for forests — **for·est·er** \'fòr-ə-stər\ *n*

foreswear *var of* FORSWEAR

¹fore·taste \'fōr-ˌtāst\ *n* : an advance indication, warning, or notion ⟨a ~ of winter⟩

²fore·taste \fōr-'tāst\ *vb* : to taste beforehand : ANTICIPATE

fore·tell \fōr-'tel\ *vb* **-told** \-'tōld\; **-tell·ing** ♦ : to tell of beforehand : PREDICT

♦ augur, forecast, predict, presage, prognosticate, prophesy

fore·thought \'fōr-ˌthòt\ *n* **1** : PREMEDITATION **2** ♦ : consideration for the future

♦ foresight, prescience, providence

fore·to·ken \fōr-'tō-kən\ *vb* : to indicate in advance

fore·top \'fōr-ˌtäp\ *n* : a platform near the top of a ship's foremast

for·ev·er \fòr-'e-vər\ *adv* **1** ♦ : for a limitless time **2** ♦ : at all times : ALWAYS

♦ [1] always, eternally, ever, everlastingly, permanently, perpetually ♦ [2] always, constantly, continually, incessantly, invariably, unfailingly

for·ev·er·more \-ˌe-vər-'mōr\ *adv* : for a limitless time or endless ages : FOREVER

fore·warn \fōr-'wòrn\ *vb* ♦ : to warn beforehand — **fore·warn·ing** *n*

♦ alert, caution, warn

forewent *past of* FOREGO

fore·wing \'fōr-ˌwiŋ\ *n* : either of the anterior wings of a 4-winged insect

fore·wom·an \'fōr-ˌwu̇-mən\ *n* : a woman who is a foreman

fore·word \-ˌwərd\ *n* ♦ : prefatory comments (as for a book) esp. when written by someone other than the author : PREFACE

♦ introduction, preamble, preface, prologue

¹for·feit \'fòr-fət\ *n* **1** ♦ : something forfeited : PENALTY, FINE **2** : FORFEITURE **3** : something deposited and then redeemed on payment of a fine **4** *pl* : a game in which forfeits are exacted

♦ damages, fine, mulct, penalty

²forfeit *vb* : to lose or lose the right to by some error, offense, or crime

for·fei·ture \'fòr-fə-ˌchu̇r\ *n* **1** : the act of forfeiting **2** : something forfeited : PENALTY

for·fend \fòr-'fend\ *vb* **1** : PREVENT **2** : PROTECT, PRESERVE

for·gath·er \fòr-'ga-thər\ *vb* **1** ♦ : to come together : ASSEMBLE **2** : to meet someone usu. by chance

♦ assemble, collect, congregate, convene, gather, meet, rendezvous

¹forge \'fōrj\ *n* : a furnace or shop with its furnace where metal is heated and worked

²forge *vb* **forged; forg·ing** **1** ♦ : to form (metal) by heating and hammering **2** ♦ : to form or bring into being esp. by an expenditure of effort : FASHION, SHAPE ⟨~ an agreement⟩ **3** : to make or imitate falsely esp. with intent to defraud ⟨~ a signature⟩ — **forg·er** *n*

♦ [1] beat, hammer, pound ♦ [2] build, carve, fashion, grind, hammer, shape, work out

³forge *vb* **forged; forg·ing** ♦ : to move ahead steadily but gradually

♦ advance, fare, get along, go, march, proceed, progress

forg·ery \'fōr-jə-rē\ *n* ♦ : something forged

♦ counterfeit, fake, hoax, humbug, phony, sham

for·get \fər-'get\ *vb* **-got** \-'gät\; **-got·ten** \-'gät-²n\ *or* **-got**; **-get·ting** **1** : to be unable to think of or recall **2** ♦ : to fail to become mindful of at the proper time **3** ♦ : to treat with inattention or disregard : NEGLECT, DISREGARD ⟨*forgot* an old friend⟩ **4** : to give up hope for or expectation of

♦ [2] fail, neglect, omit ♦ [3] disregard, ignore, neglect, overlook, pass over, slight, slur

for·get·ful \-'get-fəl\ *adj* : likely to forget — **for·get·ful·ly** *adv* — **for·get·ful·ness** *n*

for·get–me–not \fər-'get-mē-ˌnät\ *n* : any of a genus of small herbs with bright blue or white flowers

forg·ing *n* : a piece of forged work

for·giv·able *adj* ♦ : being of a kind that can be forgiven

♦ excusable, pardonable, venial

for·give \fər-'giv\ *vb* **-gave** \-'gāv\; **-giv·en** \-'gi-vən\; **-giv·ing** **1** : to give up resentment of or claim to requital for **2** : to give up resentment of : PARDON, ABSOLVE **3** : to grant relief from payment of ⟨~ a debt⟩

for·give·ness *n* ♦ : an act of forgiving or state of being forgiven

♦ absolution, amnesty, pardon, remission

for·giv·ing *adj* **1** : willing or able to forgive **2** : allowing room for error or weakness ⟨a ~ recipe⟩

for·go \fòr-'gō\ *vb* **-went** \-'went\; **-gone** \-'gòn\; **-go·ing** ♦ : to give up the enjoyment or advantage of : do without

♦ abstain (from), forbear, keep, refrain

¹fork \'fòrk\ *n* **1** : an implement with two or more prongs for taking up (as in eating), pitching, or digging **2** : a forked part, tool, or piece of equipment **3** : a dividing into branches or a place where something branches; *also* : a branch of such a fork

²fork *vb* **1** ♦ : to divide into two or more branches **2** : to give the form of a fork to ⟨~*ing* her fingers⟩ **3** : to raise or pitch with a fork ⟨~ hay⟩ **4** : to make a disposal or transfer of : PAY — used with *over, out,* or *up*

♦ [1] branch, diverge, divide, separate ♦ *usu* **fork over** *or* **fork out** [4] disburse, expend, give, lay out, pay

forked \'fòrkt, 'fòr-kəd\ *adj* : having a fork : shaped like a fork ⟨~ lightning⟩

fork·lift \'fòrk-ˌlift\ *n* : a machine for lifting heavy objects by means of steel fingers inserted under the load

for·lorn \fər-'lòrn, fòr-\ *adj* **1** ♦ : sad and lonely because of isolation or desertion **2** : being in poor condition : WRETCHED **3** : nearly hopeless — **for·lorn·ly** *adv*

♦ desolate, lonely, lonesome, sad

for·lorn·ness *n* ♦ : forlorn quality or state

♦ blues, dejection, desolation, melancholy, sadness

¹form \'fòrm\ *n* **1** : SHAPE, STRUCTURE **2** ♦ : a body esp. of a person : FIGURE **3** : the essential nature of a thing **4** ♦ : an established manner of doing or saying something **5** : FORMULA **6** ♦ : a document with blank spaces for insertion of information ⟨tax ~⟩ **7** ♦ : conduct regulated by extraneous controls (as of custom or etiquette) : CEREMONY **8** : manner of performing according to recognized standards **9** : a long seat : BENCH **10** ♦ : a model of the human figure used for displaying clothes **11** : MOLD ⟨a ~ for concrete⟩ **12** : type or plates in a frame ready for printing **13** : one of the different modes of existence, action, or manifestation of a particular thing or substance : MODE, KIND, VARIETY ⟨coal is a ~ of carbon⟩ **14** : orderly method of arrangement; *also* : a particular kind or instance of such arrangement ⟨the sonnet ~ in poetry⟩ **15** ♦ : the structural element, plan, or design of a work of art **16** : a bounded surface or volume **17** : a grade in a British school or in some American private schools **18** : RACING FORM **19 a** : known ability to perform **b** ♦ : condition (as of an athlete) suitable for performing **20** : one of the ways in which a word is changed to show difference in use ⟨the plural ∼ of a noun⟩

♦ [2] build, constitution, figure, frame, physique, shape ♦ [4] manner, method, style, system, technique, way ♦ [6] blank, document, paper ♦ [7] ceremonial, ceremony, formality, observance, rite ♦ [10] dummy, figure, mannequin ♦ [15] arrangement, composition, configuration, design, format, layout, makeup, pattern ♦ [19b] condition, estate, fettle, order, repair, shape, trim

²**form** *vb* **1** ♦ : to give form or shape to : FASHION, MAKE **2** : TRAIN, INSTRUCT **3** ♦ : to serve to make up or constitute : CONSTITUTE, COMPOSE **4** ♦ : to acquire gradually : DEVELOP, ACQUIRE ⟨∼ a habit⟩ **5** : to arrange in order ⟨∼ a battle line⟩ **6** ♦ : to take form : ARISE ⟨clouds are ∼ing⟩ **7** : to take a definite form, shape, or arrangement

♦ [1] fabricate, fashion, frame, make, manufacture, produce ♦ [3] compose, comprise, constitute, make up ♦ [4] acquire, cultivate, develop ♦ [6] arise, begin, materialize, originate

¹**for·mal** \ˈfȯr-məl\ *adj* **1** ♦ : according with conventional forms and rules ⟨a ∼ dinner party⟩ **2** : done in due or lawful form ⟨a ∼ contract⟩ **3** ♦ : rigidly ceremonious : CEREMONIOUS ⟨a ∼ manner⟩ **4** ♦ : having the appearance without the substance : NOMINAL — **for·mal·ly** *adv*

♦ [1, 3] ceremonial, ceremonious, conventional, correct, decorous, proper, regular *Ant* informal, irregular, unceremonious ♦ [4] nominal, paper, titular

²**formal** *n* ♦ : something (as a social event) formal in character

♦ ball, dance, prom

form·al·de·hyde \fȯr-ˈmal-də-ˌhīd\ *n* : a colorless pungent gas used in water solution as a preservative and disinfectant

for·mal·ise *chiefly Brit var of* FORMALIZE

for·mal·ism \ˈfȯr-mə-ˌli-zəm\ *n* : strict adherence to set forms

for·mal·i·ty \fȯr-ˈma-lə-tē\ *n, pl* **-ties** **1** ♦ : compliance with formal or conventional rules **2** : the quality or state of being formal **3** ♦ : an established form that is required or conventional

♦ [1, 3] ceremonial, ceremony, form, observance, rite, ritual, solemnity ♦ [3] amenity, civility, courtesy, gesture

for·mal·ize \ˈfȯr-mə-ˌlīz\ *vb* **-ized; -iz·ing** **1** ♦ : to give a certain or definite form to **2** : to make formal; *also* : to give formal status or approval to

♦ homogenize, normalize, regularize, standardize

¹**for·mat** \ˈfȯr-ˌmat\ *n* **1** ♦ : the general composition or style of a publication **2** : the general plan or arrangement of something **3** ♦ : a method of organizing data ⟨various file ∼s⟩

♦ arrangement, composition, configuration, design, form, layout, makeup, pattern

²**format** *vb* **for·mat·ted; for·mat·ting** : to arrange (as material to be printed) in a particular format — **for·mat·ter** *n*

for·ma·tion \fȯr-ˈmā-shən\ *n* **1** : an act of giving form to something : DEVELOPMENT **2** : something that is formed **3** : the manner in which a thing is formed : STRUCTURE, SHAPE **4** : an arrangement of persons or things in a prescribed manner or for a certain purpose

for·ma·tive \ˈfȯr-mə-tiv\ *adj* **1** : giving or capable of giving form : CONSTRUCTIVE **2** : of, relating to, or characterized by important growth or formation ⟨a child's ∼ years⟩

for·mer \ˈfȯr-mər\ *adj* **1** : PREVIOUS, EARLIER **2** : FOREGOING **3** : being first mentioned or in order of two or more things **4** ♦ : having been previously

♦ erstwhile, late, old, onetime, past, sometime

for·mer·ly \-lē\ *adv* : in time past : PREVIOUSLY

form-fit·ting \ˈfȯrm-ˌfi-tiŋ\ *adj* : conforming to the outline of the body

for·mi·da·ble \ˈfȯr-mə-də-bəl, fȯr-ˈmi-\ *adj* **1** ♦ : exciting fear, dread, or awe **2** ♦ : imposing serious difficulties — **for·mi·da·bly** \-blē\ *adv*

♦ [1] dreadful, fearful, fearsome, forbidding, frightful, redoubtable, scary ♦ [2] arduous, demanding, difficult, exacting, hard, strenuous, tall, toilsome, tough

form·less *adj* ♦ : having no regular form or shape

♦ amorphous, shapeless, unformed, unshaped, unstructured *Ant* formed, shaped, structured

form letter *n* **1** : a letter on a frequently recurring topic that can be sent to different people at different times **2** : a letter for mass circulation sent out in many printed copies

for·mu·la \ˈfȯr-myə-lə\ *n, pl* **-las** *or* **-lae** \-ˌlē, -ˌlī\ **1** : a set form of words for ceremonial use **2** : RECIPE, PRESCRIPTION **3** : a milk mixture or substitute for a baby **4** : a group of symbols or figures joined to express information concisely **5** : a customary or set form or method

for·mu·late \-ˌlāt\ *vb* **-lat·ed; -lat·ing** **1** : to express in a formula **2** ♦ : to put into a systematized statement or expression ⟨∼ a policy⟩ **3** : to prepare according to a formula

♦ articulate, clothe, couch, express, phrase, put, say, state, word ♦ cast, compose, craft, draft, draw, frame, prepare

for·mu·la·tion \ˌfȯr-myə-ˈlā-shən\ *n* ♦ : an act or the product of formulating

♦ articulation, expression, statement, utterance, voice

for·ni·ca·tion \ˌfȯr-nə-ˈkā-shən\ *n* : consensual sexual intercourse between two persons not married to each other — **for·ni·cate** \ˈfȯr-nə-ˌkāt\ *vb* — **for·ni·ca·tor** \-ˌkā-tər\ *n*

for·sake \fər-ˈsāk, fȯr-\ *vb* **for·sook** \-ˈsuk\; **for·sak·en** \-ˈsā-kən\; **for·sak·ing** ♦ : to renounce or turn away from entirely

♦ abandon, desert, leave, quit

forsaken *adj* ♦ : left desolate or empty

♦ abandoned, derelict, deserted

for·swear \fȯr-ˈswar\ *vb* **-swore** \-ˈswȯr\; **-sworn** \-ˈswȯrn\; **-swear·ing** **1** : to swear falsely : commit perjury **2** : to renounce earnestly or under oath **3** : to deny under oath

for·syth·ia \fər-ˈsi-thē-ə\ *n, pl* **-ias** *also* **-ia** : any of a genus of shrubs related to the olive and having yellow bell-shaped flowers appearing before the leaves in early spring

fort \ˈfȯrt\ *n* **1** ♦ : a fortified place **2** : a permanent army post

♦ bastion, bulwark, citadel, fastness, fortification, fortress, hold, stronghold

¹**forte** \ˈfȯrt, ˈfȯr-ˌtā\ *n* : one's strong point

²**for·te** \ˈfȯr-ˌtā\ *adv or adj* : LOUD — used as a direction in music

forth \ˈfȯrth\ *adv* **1** ♦ : onward in time, place, or order : FORWARD, ONWARD ⟨from that day ∼⟩ **2** : out into view or notice ⟨put ∼ leaves⟩

♦ ahead, along, forward, on, onward

forth·com·ing \ˈfȯrth-ˈkə-miŋ\ *adj* **1** ♦ : coming or available soon ⟨the ∼ holidays⟩ **2** : marked by openness and candor : OUTGOING

♦ coming, imminent, impending, oncoming, pending *Ant* late, recent

forth·right \ˈfȯrth-ˌrīt\ *adj* **1** ♦ : free from ambiguity or evasiveness **2** ♦ : going straight to the point ⟨a ∼ answer⟩

♦ candid, direct, frank, honest, open, plain, straight, straightforward, unreserved

forth·right·ly *adv* ♦ : in a forthright manner

♦ directly, foursquare, plain, plainly, straight, straightforward

forth·right·ness *n* ♦ : the quality or state of being forthright

♦ candor (*or* candour), directness, frankness, openness, plainness

forth·with \ˌfȯrth-ˈwith\ *adv* ♦ : with dispatch : without delay : IMMEDIATELY

♦ directly, immediately, instantly, now, promptly, pronto, right away, right now

for·ti·fi·ca·tion \ˌfȯr-tə-fə-ˈkā-shən\ *n* ♦ : something that fortifies, defends, or strengthens; *esp* : works erected to defend a place or position

♦ bastion, citadel, fastness, fort, fortress, hold, stronghold

for·ti·fy \ˈfȯr-tə-ˌfī\ *vb* **-fied; -fy·ing** **1** : to strengthen by military defenses **2** ♦ : to give physical strength or endurance to **3** ♦ : to add mental or moral strength to : ENCOURAGE **4** : to strengthen or enrich with a material ⟨∼ bread with vitamins⟩

♦ [2] harden, season, steel, strengthen, toughen ♦ [3] brace, encourage, forearm, nerve, psych (up), ready, steel, strengthen

for·tis·si·mo \fȯr-ˈti-sə-ˌmō\ *adv or adj* : very loud — used as a direction in music

for·ti·tude \ˈfȯr-tə-ˌtüd, -ˌtyüd\ *n* ♦ : strength of mind that enables one to meet danger or bear pain or adversity with courage

♦ backbone, fiber (*or* fibre), grit, guts, pluck, spunk

fort·night \ˈfȯrt-ˌnīt\ *n* : two weeks — **fort·night·ly** \-lē\ *adj or adv*

for·tress \ˈfȯr-trəs\ *n* ♦ : a fortified place : FORT

♦ bastion, citadel, fastness, fort, fortification, hold, stronghold

for·tu·itous \fȯr-'tü-ə-təs, -'tyü-\ *adj* **1** ♦ : happening by chance ⟨a ∼ discovery⟩ **2** ♦ : producing or resulting in good by chance : FORTUNATE

♦ [1] accidental, casual, chance, fluky, unplanned ♦ [2] fortunate, happy, lucky, providential

for·tu·ity \-ə-tē\ *n, pl* **-ities 1** : the quality or state of being fortuitous **2** : a chance event or occurrence

for·tu·nate \'fȯr-chə-nət\ *adj* **1** ♦ : bringing some good thing not foreseen **2** : receiving some unforeseen or unexpected good

♦ fluky, fortuitous, happy, lucky, providential *Ant* luckless, unfortunate, unhappy, unlucky

for·tu·nate·ly \-lē\ *adv* **1** : in a fortunate manner **2** : it is fortunate that

for·tune \'fȯr-chən\ *n* **1** : prosperity attained partly through luck; *also* : CHANCE, LUCK **2** : what happens to a person : good or bad luck **3** ♦ : a predetermined course of events often held to be an irresistible power or agency : FATE, DESTINY **4** ♦ : abundance of valuable material possessions or resources : RICHES, WEALTH

♦ [3] circumstance, destiny, doom, fate, lot, portion ♦ [4] assets, capital, means, opulence, riches, substance, wealth, wherewithal

fortune hunter *n* : a person who seeks wealth esp. by marriage
for·tune–tell·er \-ˌte-lər\ *n* ♦ : a person who professes to foretell future events — **for·tune–tell·ing** *n or adj*

♦ augur, diviner, forecaster, futurist, prognosticator, prophet, seer, soothsayer

for·ty \'fȯr-tē\ *n, pl* **forties** : four times 10 — **for·ti·eth** \'fȯr-tē-əth\ *adj or n* — **forty** *adj or pron*
for·ty–five \ˌfȯr-tē-'fīv\ *n* **1** : a .45 caliber handgun — usu. written .45 **2** : a phonograph record designed to be played at 45 revolutions per minute
for·ty–nin·er \-'nī-nər\ *n* : a person in the rush to California for gold in 1849
forty winks *n sing or pl* ♦ : a short sleep

♦ catnap, doze, drowse, nap, siesta, snooze, wink

fo·rum \'fȯr-əm\ *n, pl* **forums** *also* **fo·ra** \-ə\ **1** : the marketplace or central meeting place of an ancient Roman city **2** : a medium (as a publication or online service) of open discussion **3** : COURT **4** ♦ : a public assembly, lecture, or program involving audience or panel discussion

♦ colloquy, panel, parley, seminar, symposium

¹**for·ward** \'fȯr-wərd\ *adj* **1** : being near or at or belonging to the front **2** : EAGER, READY **3** ♦ : lacking modesty or reserve : BOLD **4** : notably advanced or developed : PRECOCIOUS **5** : moving, tending, or leading toward a position in front **6** : EXTREME, RADICAL **7** : of, relating to, or getting ready for the future — **for·ward·ness** *n*

♦ bold, familiar, free, immodest, presumptuous

²**forward** *adv* ♦ : to or toward what is ahead or in front

♦ ahead, along, forth, on, onward

³**forward** *vb* **1** ♦ : to help onward : ADVANCE **2** : to send forward : TRANSMIT **3** : to send or ship onward

♦ advance, cultivate, encourage, foster, further, nourish, nurture, promote

⁴**forward** *n* : a player who plays at the front of a team's offensive formation near the opponent's goal
for·ward·er \-wər-dər\ *n* : one that forwards; *esp* : an agent who forwards goods
for·wards \'fȯr-wərdz\ *adv* : to or toward what is ahead or in front : FORWARD
forwent *past of* FORGO
¹**fos·sil** \'fä-səl\ *adj* **1** : preserved from a past geologic age ⟨∼ plants⟩ **2** : of or relating to fossil fuels
²**fossil** *n* **1** : a trace or impression or the remains of a plant or animal of a past geologic age preserved in the earth's crust **2** ♦ : a person whose ideas are out-of-date — **fos·sil·ize** \'fä-sə-ˌlīz\ *vb*

♦ antediluvian, dodo, fogy, fuddy-duddy, reactionary

fossil fuel *n* : a fuel (as coal or oil) that is formed in the earth from plant or animal remains
¹**fos·ter** \'fȯs-tər\ *adj* : affording, receiving, or sharing nourishment or parental care though not related by blood or legal ties ⟨∼ parent⟩ ⟨∼ child⟩
²**foster** *vb* **1** ♦ : to give parental care to **2** ♦ : to promote the growth or development of : ENCOURAGE

♦ [1] breed, bring up, raise, rear ♦ [2] advance, cultivate, en-

courage, forward, further, nourish, nurture, promote *Ant* discourage, frustrate, hinder, inhibit

foster home *n* : a household in which an orphaned, neglected, or delinquent child is placed for care
fos·ter·ling \-tər-liŋ\ *n* : a foster child
Fou·cault pendulum \ˌfü-'kō-\ *n* : a device that consists of a heavy weight hung by a long wire and that swings in a constant direction which appears to change showing that the earth rotates
fought *past and past part of* FIGHT
¹**foul** \'faú(-ə)l\ *adj* **1 a** ♦ : offensive to the senses **b** ♦ : clogged with dirt **2** ♦ : arousing or deserving hatred or repugnance : ODIOUS **3** ♦ : abhorrent to morality or virtue : OBSCENE **4** ♦ : being wet and stormy : STORMY ⟨∼ weather⟩ **5** : characterized by or manifesting treachery : DISHONORABLE, UNFAIR ⟨by fair means or ∼⟩ **6** : marking the bounds of a playing field ⟨∼ lines⟩; *also* : being outside the foul line ⟨∼ ball⟩ ⟨∼ territory⟩ **7** : containing marked-up corrections **8** : ENTANGLED — **foul·ly** *adv*

♦ [1a] fetid, malodorous, noisome, rank, reeky, smelly, strong ♦ [1b] dirty, filthy, muddy, unclean ♦ [2, 3] abhorrent, awful, distasteful, obnoxious, odious, offensive, repellent, repugnant, repulsive ♦ [4] bleak, dirty, inclement, nasty, raw, rough, squally, stormy, tempestuous, turbulent *Ant* clement, fair

²**foul** *n* **1** : an entanglement or collision in fishing or sailing **2** : an infraction of the rules in a game or sport; *also* : a baseball hit outside the foul line
³**foul** *vb* **1** ♦ : to make or become foul or filthy **2** : to entangle or become entangled **3** : OBSTRUCT, BLOCK **4** : to collide with **5** : to make or hit a foul

♦ befoul, blacken, contaminate, dirty, muddy, smirch, soil, stain, taint

⁴**foul** *adv* : in a foul manner
fou·lard \fù-'lärd\ *n* : a lightweight silk of plain or twill weave usu. decorated with a printed pattern
foul·mouthed \'faú(-ə)l-ˌmaúthd, -ˌmaútht\ *adj* : given to the use of obscene, profane, or abusive language
foul·ness *n* ♦ : the quality or state of being foul

♦ dirtiness, filth, filthiness, grossness, nastiness, obscenity, smut, vulgarity

foul play *n* **1** : unfair, dishonest, or treacherous conduct or dealing : VIOLENCE **2** : the crime of unlawfully killing a person esp. with malice aforethought : MURDER
foul–up \'faú(-ə)l-ˌəp\ *n* **1** : a state of being fouled up **2** : a mechanical difficulty
foul up *vb* **1** ♦ : to spoil by mistakes or poor judgment **2** : to cause a foul-up : BUNGLE

♦ bobble, botch, bungle, butcher, flub, fumble, mangle, mess up, screw up

¹**found** \'faúnd\ *past and past part of* FIND
²**found** *vb* **1** : to take the first steps in building **2** : to set or ground on something solid : BASE **3** ♦ : to establish (as an institution) often with provision for future maintenance

♦ establish, inaugurate, initiate, institute, introduce, launch, pioneer, set up, start *Ant* close (down), phase out, shut (up)

foun·da·tion \faún-'dā-shən\ *n* **1** : the act of founding **2** ♦ : a basis upon which something stands or is supported ⟨suspicions without ∼⟩ **3** **a** : funds given for the permanent support of an institution or cause : ENDOWMENT **b** ♦ : an endowed institution **4** : supporting structure : BASE **5** : CORSET — **foun·da·tion·al** \-shə-nəl\ *adj*

♦ [2] base, basis, bedrock, cornerstone, footing, ground, groundwork, keystone, underpinning ♦ [3b] establishment, institute, institution

¹**foun·der** \'faún-dər\ *vb* **1** : to make or become lame ⟨the horse ∼ed⟩ **2** : COLLAPSE **3** : SINK ⟨a ∼ing ship⟩ **4** : FAIL
²**found·er** *n* ♦ : one that founds or establishes

♦ author, creator, father, originator

found·ling \'faúnd-liŋ\ *n* : an infant found after its unknown parents have abandoned it
found·ry \'faún-drē\ *n, pl* **foundries** : a building or works where metal is cast
fount \'faúnt\ *n* : SOURCE, FOUNTAIN
foun·tain \'faún-ᵊn\ *n* **1** : a spring of water **2** : SOURCE **3** : an artificial jet of water **4** : a container for liquid that can be drawn off as needed
foun·tain·head \-ˌhed\ *n* : SOURCE
fountain pen *n* : a pen with a reservoir that feeds the writing point with ink
four \'fȯr\ *n* **1** : one more than three **2** : the 4th in a set or series **3** : something having four units — **four** *adj or pron*

4x4 *also* **four–by–four** \'fȯr-bī-ˌfȯr\ *n* : a four-wheel automobile with four-wheel drive

four–flush \-ˌfləsh\ *vb* : to make a false claim : BLUFF — **four–flush•er** *n*

four•fold \-ˌfōld, -ˈfōld\ *adj* **1** : being four times as great or as many **2** : having four units or members — **four•fold** \-ˈfōld\ *adv*

4–H \'fōr-ˈāch\ *adj* : of or relating to a program set up by the U.S. Department of Agriculture to help young people become productive citizens — **4–H'er** *n*

Four Hundred *or* **400** *n* : the exclusive social set of a community — used with *the*

four–in–hand \'fȯr-ən-ˌhand\ *n* **1** : a team of four horses driven by one person; *also* : a vehicle drawn by such a team **2** : a necktie tied in a slipknot with long ends overlapping vertically in front

four–o'clock \'fōr-ə-ˌkläk\ *n* : a garden plant with fragrant yellow, red, or white flowers without petals that open late in the afternoon

four–poster \-ˌfȯr-ˈpō-stər\ *n* : a bed with tall corner posts orig. designed to support curtains or a canopy

four•score \'fōr-ˈskȯr\ *adj* : being four times twenty : EIGHTY

four•some \'fōr-səm\ *n* **1** : a group of four persons or things **2** : a golf match between two pairs of partners

¹**four•square** \-ˈskwer\ *adj* **1** : SQUARE **2** ♦ : marked by boldness and conviction : FORTHRIGHT
   ♦ candid, direct, forthright, frank, honest, open, outspoken, plain, straightforward, unreserved

²**foursquare** *adv* ♦ : in a foursquare manner
   ♦ directly, forthrightly, plain, plainly, straight, straightforward

four•teen \fȯr-ˈtēn\ *n* : one more than 13 — **fourteen** *adj or pron* — **four•teenth** \-ˈtēnth\ *adj or n*

fourth \'fōrth\ *n* **1** : one that is number four in a countable series **2** : one of four equal parts of something — **fourth** *adj or adv*

fourth estate *n, often cap F&E* : the public press

fourth wall *n* : an imaginary wall that keeps performers from recognizing or directly addressing their audience

4WD *abbr* four-wheel drive

four–wheel \'fōr-ˌhwēl\ *or* **four•wheeled** \-ˌhwēld\ *adj* : acting on or by means of four wheels of a motor vehicle

four–wheel drive *n* : an automotive drive mechanism that acts on all four wheels of the vehicle; *also* : a vehicle with such a drive

¹**fowl** \'faủ(-ə)l\ *n, pl* **fowl** *or* **fowls** **1** : BIRD **2** : a cock or hen of the domestic chicken; *also* : the flesh of these used as food

²**fowl** *vb* : to hunt wildfowl

¹**fox** \'fäks\ *n, pl* **fox•es** *or* **fox** **1** : any of various flesh-eating mammals related to the wolves but smaller and with shorter legs and a more pointed muzzle; *also* : the fur of a fox **2** : a clever crafty person **3** *cap* : a member of an Indigenous people formerly living in what is now Wisconsin **4** ♦ : a good-looking young woman
   ♦ beauty, dream, enchantress, knockout, queen

²**fox** *vb* ♦ : to trick by ingenuity or cunning : OUTWIT
   ♦ outfox, outmaneuver, outsmart, outwit, overreach

fox•glove \'fäks-ˌgləv\ *n* : a common plant related to the snapdragons that is grown for its showy spikes of dotted white or purple tubular flowers and as a source of digitalis

fox•hole \-ˌhōl\ *n* : a pit dug for protection against enemy fire

fox•hound \-ˌhaủnd\ *n* : any of various large swift powerful hounds used in hunting foxes

fox•ing \'fäk-siŋ\ *n* : brownish spots on old paper

fox terrier *n* : a small lively terrier that occurs in varieties with smooth dense coats or with harsh wiry coats

fox–trot \'fäks-ˌträt\ *n* **1** : a short broken slow trotting gait **2** : a ballroom dance in duple time

foxy \'fäk-sē\ *adj* **fox•i•er; -est** **1** : resembling or suggestive of a fox **2** ♦ : cunningly shrewd : WILY **3** : physically attractive
   ♦ artful, cagey, crafty, cunning, devious, guileful, slick, sly, subtle, wily

foy•er \'fȯi-ər, 'fȯi-ˌyā\ *n* **1** ♦ : an anteroom or lobby esp. of a theater **2** ♦ : an entrance hallway
   ♦ [1, 2] entry, hall, lobby, vestibule

fpm *abbr* feet per minute
FPO *abbr* fleet post office
fps *abbr* feet per second
fr *abbr* **1** father **2** franc **3** friar **4** from
¹**Fr** *abbr* **1** France; French **2** Friday

²**Fr** *symbol* francium

fra•cas \'frā-kəs, 'fra-\ *n, pl* **fra•cas•es** \-kə-səz\ ♦ : a noisy quarrel
   ♦ brawl, fray, free-for-all, melee, row

frack•ing \'fra-kiŋ\ *n* : the injection of fluid into shale beds so as to free up petroleum — **frack** \'frak\ *vb*

frac•tal \'frak-t³l\ *n* : an irregular curve or shape that repeats itself at any scale on which it is examined — **fractal** *adj*

frac•tion \'frak-shən\ *n* **1** : a numerical representation (as ¹/₂, ³/₄, or 3.323) indicating the quotient of two numbers **2** : FRAGMENT **3** : PORTION — **frac•tion•al** \-shə-nəl\ *adj* — **frac•tion•al•ly** *adv*

frac•tious \'frak-shəs\ *adj* **1** : tending to be troublesome : hard to handle or control **2** : QUARRELSOME, IRRITABLE

¹**frac•ture** \'frak-chər\ *n* **1** : a breaking of something and esp. a bone **2** : CRACK, CLEFT

²**fracture** *vb* ♦ : to break or cause to break
   ♦ break, bust, fragment

frag•ile \'fra-jəl, -ˌjīl\ *adj* ♦ : easily broken : DELICATE
   ♦ breakable, delicate, frail *Ant* nonbreakable, strong, sturdy, tough, unbreakable

fra•gil•i•ty \frə-ˈji-lə-tē\ *n* ♦ : the quality or state of being fragile
   ♦ daintiness, delicacy, fineness

¹**frag•ment** \'frag-mənt\ *n* ♦ : a part broken off, detached, or incomplete
   ♦ piece, scrap

²**frag•ment** \-ˌment\ *vb* ♦ : to break into fragments — **frag•men•ta•tion** \ˌfrag-mən-ˈtā-shən, -ˌmən-\ *n*
   ♦ break, bust, fracture

frag•men•tary \'frag-mən-ˌter-ē\ *adj* ♦ : made up of fragments : INCOMPLETE
   ♦ deficient, halfway, incomplete, partial

fra•grance \-grəns\ *n* ♦ : a sweet or delicate odor
   ♦ aroma, bouquet, incense, perfume, redolence, scent, spice *Ant* reek, stench, stink

fra•grant \'frā-grənt\ *adj* ♦ : sweet or agreeable in smell — **fra•grant•ly** *adv*
   ♦ ambrosial, aromatic, redolent, savory, scented *Ant* fetid, foul, malodorous, noisome, putrid, smelly, stinking

frail \'frāl\ *adj* **1** ♦ : morally or physically weak **2** ♦ : easily broken or destroyed : FRAGILE, DELICATE
   ♦ [1] delicate, feeble, infirm, tender, wasted, weak ♦ [2] breakable, delicate, fragile

frail•ty \'frāl-tē\ *n, pl* **frailties** **1** ♦ : the quality or state of being frail **2** ♦ : a fault due to weakness
   ♦ [1] debility, delicacy, faintness, feebleness, infirmity, weakness ♦ [2] demerit, failing, fault, foible, shortcoming, vice, weakness

¹**frame** \'frām\ *vb* **framed; fram•ing** **1** ♦ : to make plans **2** ♦ : to form, make, or create by combining parts or elements : SHAPE, CONSTRUCT **3** ♦ : to give expression to : FORMULATE **4** ♦ : to make a draft of or draw up ⟨~ a constitution⟩ **5** : to make appear guilty **6** : to fit or adjust for a purpose : ARRANGE **7** : to provide with or enclose in a frame — **fram•er** *n*
   ♦ [1] arrange, blueprint, calculate, chart, design, lay out, map, plan, project, scheme ♦ [2] construct, fabricate, fashion, form, make, manufacture, produce, shape ♦ [3, 4] cast, compose, craft, draft, draw, formulate, prepare

²**frame** *n* **1** : something made of parts fitted and joined together **2** ♦ : the physical makeup of the body **3** ♦ : an arrangement of structural parts that gives form or support **4** : a supporting or enclosing border or open case (as for a window or picture) **5** : one picture of a series (as on a length of film) **6** : FRAME-UP
   ♦ [2] build, constitution, figure, form, physique, shape
   ♦ [3] configuration, framework, shell, skeleton, structure

³**frame** *adj* : having a wood frame

frame of mind *n* : mental attitude or outlook : MOOD

frame–up \'frā-ˌməp\ *n* **1** : an act or series of actions in which someone is framed **2** : an action that is planned, contrived, or formulated

frame•work \'frām-ˌwərk\ *n* ♦ : a basic supporting part or structure
   ♦ configuration, frame, shell, skeleton, structure

franc \'fraŋk\ *n*　**1 :** any of various former basic monetary units (as of Belgium, France, and Luxembourg)　**2 :** a basic monetary unit of any of several countries esp. in Africa

fran·chise \'fran-ˌchīz\ *n*　**1 :** a right or license granted to an individual or group ⟨a ～ to operate a ferry⟩　**2 a :** a constitutional or statutory right or privilege　**b ♦ :** the right to vote　**3 :** the right of membership in a professional sports league; *also* : a team having such membership

　♦ enfranchisement, suffrage, vote

fran·chi·see \ˌfran-ˌchī-'zē, -chə-\ *n* : one granted a franchise

fran·chis·er \'fran-ˌchī-zər\ *n*　**1 :** FRANCHISEE　**2 :** FRANCHISOR

fran·chi·sor \ˌfran-ˌchī-'zȯr, -chə-\ *n* : one that grants a franchise

fran·ci·um \'fran-sē-əm\ *n* : a radioactive metallic chemical element

Fran·co–Amer·i·can \ˌfraŋ-kō-ə-'mer-ə-kən\ *n* : an American of French or esp. French-Canadian descent — **Franco–American** *adj*

fran·gi·ble \'fran-jə-bəl\ *adj* : BREAKABLE — **fran·gi·bil·i·ty** \ˌfran-jə-'bi-lə-tē\ *n*

¹frank \'fraŋk\ *adj ♦ :* marked by free, forthright, and sincere expression

　♦ candid, direct, forthright, honest, open, outspoken, plain, straight, straightforward *Ant* dissembling

²frank *vb* : to mark (a piece of mail) with an official sign so that it can be mailed free; *also* : to mail free

³frank *n*　**1 :** the signature or mark on a piece of mail indicating free or paid postage　**2 :** the privilege of sending mail free

⁴frank *n* : FRANKFURTER

Fran·ken·stein \'fraŋ-kən-ˌstīn\ *n*　**1 :** a monstrous creation that usu. ruins its originator　**2 :** a monster in the shape of a man

frank·furt·er \'fraŋk-fər-tər, -ˌfər-\ *or* **frank·furt** \-fərt\ *n* : a seasoned sausage (as of beef or beef and pork)

frank·in·cense \'fraŋ-kən-ˌsens\ *n* : a fragrant resin burned as incense

frank·ly \'fraŋ-klē\ *adv*　**1 :** in a frank manner　**2 ♦ :** in truth

　♦ actually, honestly, really, truly, truthfully, verily

frank·ness *n ♦ :* the quality or state of being frank

　♦ candor (*or* candour), directness, forthrightness, openness, plainness

fran·tic \'fran-tik\ *adj ♦ :* marked by or showing uncontrolled emotion or disordered anxious activity

　♦ agitated, distraught, feverish, frenetic, frenzied, hysterical *Ant* collected, composed, self-possessed

fran·ti·cal·ly \-ti-k(ə-)lē\ *adv ♦ :* in a frantic manner

　♦ berserk, hectically, helter-skelter, madly, pell-mell, wild, wildly

frap·pé \fra-'pā\ *or* **frappe** *same or* 'frap\ *n*　**1 :** an iced or frozen drink　**2 :** a thick milk shake — **frap·pé** \fra-'pā\ *adj*

fra·ter·nal \frə-'tərn-ᵊl\ *adj*　**1 :** of, relating to, or involving brothers　**2 :** of, relating to, or being a fraternity or society　**3 :** derived from two ova ⟨～ twins⟩　**4 :** FRIENDLY, BROTHERLY — **fra·ter·nal·ly** *adv*

fra·ter·ni·ty \frə-'tər-nə-tē\ *n, pl* **-ties**　**1 ♦ :** a social, honorary, or professional group; *esp* : a men's student organization formed chiefly for social purposes　**2 :** BROTHERLINESS　**3 :** persons of the same class, profession, or tastes

　♦ association, brotherhood, club, council, fellowship, guild, league, order, organization, society

frat·er·nize \'fra-tər-ˌnīz\ *vb* **-nized; -niz·ing**　**1 ♦ :** to mingle as friends　**2 :** to associate on close terms with members of a hostile group — **frat·er·ni·za·tion** \ˌfra-tər-nə-'zā-shən\ *n*

　♦ associate, chum, consort, hang around, hobnob, pal

frat·ri·cide \'fra-trə-ˌsīd\ *n*　**1 :** one that kills a sibling or countryman　**2 :** the act of a fratricide — **frat·ri·cid·al** \ˌfra-trə-'sīd-ᵊl\ *adj*

fraud \'frȯd\ *n*　**1 :** DECEIT, TRICKERY　**2 :** TRICK　**3 ♦ :** a person who is not what he or she pretends to be : IMPOSTOR

　♦ charlatan, fake, hoaxer, humbug, impostor, mountebank, phony, pretender, quack

fraud·ster \'frȯd-stər\ *n, chiefly Brit* : a person who engages in fraud

fraud·u·lent \'frȯ-jə-lənt\ *adj ♦ :* characterized by, based on, or done by fraud — **fraud·u·lent·ly** *adv*

　♦ crooked, deceitful, deceptive, dishonest, double-dealing, false, misleading, specious *Ant* aboveboard, honest, truthful

fraught \'frȯt\ *adj ♦ :* full of or accompanied by something specified ⟨～ with danger⟩

　♦ flush, replete, rife

¹fray \'frā\ *n ♦ :* a usu. disorderly or protracted fight, struggle, or dispute : FIGHT, STRUGGLE

　♦ battle, clash, combat, conflict, contest, fight, fracas, hassle, struggle

²fray *vb*　**1 ♦ :** to wear (as an edge of cloth) by rubbing　**2 :** to separate the threads at the edge of　**3 :** STRAIN, IRRITATE ⟨～ed nerves⟩

　♦ abrade, chafe, erode, fret, gall, rub, wear

fraz·zle \'fra-zəl\ *vb* **fraz·zled; fraz·zling**　**1 :** FRAY　**2 :** to put in a state of extreme physical or nervous fatigue — **frazzle** *n*

¹freak \'frēk\ *n*　**1 ♦ :** a sudden and odd or seemingly pointless idea or turn of the mind : a seemingly capricious action or event　**2 ♦ :** a strange, abnormal, or unusual person or thing　**3** *slang* : a person who uses an illicit drug　**4 ♦ :** an ardent enthusiast — **freaky** \'frē-kē\ *adj*

　♦ [1] caprice, fancy, notion, vagary, whim ♦ [2] abnormality, monster, monstrosity *Ant* average, norm ♦ [4] addict, aficionado, buff, bug, devotee, fan, fanatic, fancier, fiend, lover, maniac, nut

²freak *vb*　**1 :** to experience the effects (as hallucinations) of taking illicit drugs — often used with *out*　**2 ♦ :** to distress or become distressed — often used with *out* — **freak–out** \'frē-ˌkau̇t\ *n*

　♦ *usu* **freak out** agitate, bother, concern, distress, disturb, exercise, perturb, unsettle, upset, worry

³freak *adj ♦ :* having the character of a freak

　♦ aberrant, abnormal, atypical, exceeding, exceptional, extraordinary, odd, peculiar, phenomenal, rare, singular, uncommon, uncustomary, unique, unusual, unwonted

¹freck·le \'fre-kəl\ *n* : a brownish spot on the skin

²freckle *vb ♦ :* to sprinkle or mark with freckles or small spots

　♦ dot, fleck, pepper, speck, spot, sprinkle

¹free \'frē\ *adj* **fre·er; fre·est**　**1 :** having liberty　**2 ♦ :** enjoying political or personal independence; *also* : not subject to or allowing slavery　**3 :** made or done voluntarily : SPONTANEOUS　**4 :** relieved from or lacking something unpleasant　**5 :** not subject to a duty, tax, or charge　**6 ♦ :** not obstructed : CLEAR　**7 :** not being used or occupied　**8 :** not fastened　**9 :** LAVISH　**10 :** OPEN, FRANK ⟨a ～ exchange of ideas⟩　**11 a ♦ :** given without charge　**b ♦ :** done, or given voluntarily or spontaneously　**12 :** not literal or exact　**13 :** not restricted by conventional forms　**14 ♦ :** overly familiar or forward in action or attitude

　♦ [1] footloose, loose, unbound, unconfined, unrestrained *Ant* bound, confined, restrained, unfree ♦ [2] autonomous, independent, self-governing, separate, sovereign *Ant* dependent, subject, unfree ♦ [6] clear, open, unobstructed ♦ [11a] complimentary, gratuitous ♦ [11b] bountiful, charitable, generous, liberal, munificent, openhanded, unselfish, unsparing ♦ [14] bold, familiar, forward, immodest, presumptuous

²free *vb* **freed; free·ing**　**1 ♦ :** to set free　**2 ♦ :** to relieve or rid of what restrains, confines, restricts, or embarrasses　**3 ♦ :** to clear from what obstructs or is unneeded : CLEAR

　♦ [1, 2] discharge, emancipate, enfranchise, liberate, manumit, release, unchain, unfetter *Ant* bind, confine, enchain, fetter, restrain ♦ [2] clear, disburden, disencumber, relieve, rid, unburden ♦ [2, 3] clear, disengage, disentangle, extricate, liberate, release, untangle ♦ [3] clear, open, unclog, unstop

³free *adv*　**1 :** FREELY　**2 :** without charge

free·base \'frē-ˌbās\ *n* : purified cocaine smoked as crack or heated to produce vapors for inhalation — **freebase** *vb*

free·bie *or* **free·bee** \'frē-bē\ *n ♦ :* something given without charge

　♦ bestowal, donation, gift, lagniappe, present

free·board \'frē-ˌbōrd\ *n* : the vertical distance between the waterline and the upper edge of the side of a boat

free·boo·ter \-ˌbü-tər\ *n ♦ :* one who commits or practices piracy : PIRATE

　♦ buccaneer, corsair, pirate, rover

free·born \-'bȯrn\ *adj*　**1 :** not born in vassalage or slavery　**2 :** of, relating to, or befitting one that is freeborn

freed·man \'frēd-mən, -ˌman\ *n* : a person freed from slavery

free·dom \'frē-dəm\ *n*　**1 ♦ :** the quality or state of being free : INDEPENDENCE　**2 :** EXEMPTION, RELEASE　**3 :** EASE, FACILITY

4 : FRANKNESS **5 :** unrestricted use **6 :** a political right; *also* : FRANCHISE, PRIVILEGE **7 ♦ :** the ability or capacity to act without undue hindrance or restraint

♦ [1] autonomy, independence, liberty, self-government, sovereignty *Ant* dependence, subjection ♦ [7] authorization, latitude, license (*or* licence), run

freedom fighter *n* **:** a person who takes part in a resistance movement against an oppressive political or social establishment

free enterprise *n* **:** freedom of private business to operate with little regulation by the government

¹**free–for–all** \'frē-fə-,rȯl\ *adj* ♦ **:** unrestricted as to entries, participants, or users

♦ open, public, unrestricted

²**free–for–all** *n* ♦ **:** a competition or fight open to all comers and usu. with no rules **:** BRAWL

♦ brawl, fracas, fray, melee, row

free·hand \-,hand\ *adj* **:** done without mechanical aids or devices ⟨a ∼ drawing⟩

free·hold \'frē-,hōld\ *n* **:** ownership of an estate for life usu. with the right to bequeath it to one's heirs; *also* **:** an estate thus owned — **free·hold·er** *n*

free·lance \-,lans\ *n* **:** one who pursues a profession (as writing) without a long-term commitment to any one employer — **free·lance** *adj or vb*

free–liv·ing \'frē-'li-viŋ\ *adj* **1 :** unrestricted in pursuing personal pleasures **2 :** being neither parasitic nor symbiotic ⟨∼ organisms⟩

free·load \'frē-,lōd\ *vb* **:** to impose upon another's hospitality — **free·load·er** *n*

free love *n* **1 :** the practice of living openly with a sexual partner without marriage **2 :** sexual relations without any commitments by either partner

free·ly *adv* ♦ **:** in a free manner

♦ easily, effortlessly, fluently, handily, lightly, painlessly, readily, smoothly

free·man \'frē-mən, -,man\ *n* **1 :** one who has civil or political liberty **2 :** one having the full rights of a citizen

Free·ma·son \-,mā-s⁰n\ *n* **:** a member of a secret fraternal society called Free and Accepted Masons — **Free·ma·son·ry** \-rē\ *n*

free radical *n* **:** an esp. reactive atom or group of atoms with one or more unpaired electrons; *esp* **:** one that can cause bodily damage (as by altering the chemical structure of cells)

free–range \'frē-,rānj\ *adj* **:** allowed to range and forage with relative freedom ⟨∼ chickens⟩; *also* **:** produced by free-range animals ⟨∼ eggs⟩

free speech *n* **:** speech that is protected by the First Amendment to the U.S. Constitution

free spirit *n* **:** NONCONFORMIST

free·stand·ing \'frē-'stan-diŋ\ *adj* ♦ **:** standing alone or on its own foundation free of support

♦ detached, disconnected, discrete, separate, single, unattached, unconnected

free·stone \'frē-,stōn\ *n* **1 :** a stone that may be cut freely without splitting **2 :** a fruit stone to which the flesh does not cling; *also* **:** a fruit (as a peach or cherry) having such a stone

free·think·er \-'thiŋ-kər\ *n* **:** one who forms opinions on the basis of reason independently of authority; *esp* **:** one who doubts or denies religious dogma — **free·think·ing** *n or adj*

free trade *n* **:** trade between nations without restrictions (as high taxes on imports)

free verse *n* **:** verse whose meter is irregular or whose rhythm is not metrical

free·ware \'frē-,wer\ *n* **:** software that is free or that has a small usu. optional cost

free·way \'frē-,wā\ *n* **:** an expressway without tolls

free·wheel \-'hwēl\ *vb* **:** to move, live, or play freely or irresponsibly

free·wheel·ing \,frē-'hwē-liŋ\ *adj* **:** free and loose in form or manner

free·will \'frē-,wil\ *adj* ♦ **:** produced in or by an act of choice

♦ deliberate, intentional, purposeful, voluntary, willful, willing

free will *n* ♦ **:** voluntary choice or decision

♦ accord, choice, option, self-determination, volition, will

¹**freeze** \'frēz\ *vb* **froze** \'frōz\; **fro·zen** \'frōz-⁰n\; **freez·ing** **1 ♦ :** to harden or cause to harden into a solid (as ice) by loss of heat **2 :** to withstand freezing **3 :** to chill or become chilled with cold **4 :** to damage by frost **5 :** to adhere solidly by or as if by freezing **6 :** to become fixed, motionless, or incapable of

speech **7 :** to cause to grip tightly **8 :** to become clogged with ice **9 :** to fix at a certain stage or level

♦ concrete, congeal, firm, harden, set, solidify

²**freeze** *n* **1 :** an act or instance of freezing **2 :** the state of being frozen **3 :** a state of weather marked by low temperature

freeze–dry \'frēz-'drī\ *vb* **:** to dry in a frozen state under vacuum esp. for preservation — **freeze–dried** *adj*

freez·er \'frē-zər\ *n* **:** a compartment, device, or room for freezing food or keeping it frozen

freez·ing *adj* ♦ **:** very cold

♦ arctic, cold, frigid, frosty, glacial, icy, polar, wintry

¹**freight** \'frāt\ *n* **1 :** payment for carrying goods **2 ♦ :** something that is loaded for transportation **:** CARGO **3 :** BURDEN **4 :** the carrying of goods by a common carrier **5 :** a train that carries freight

♦ burden, cargo, haul, lading, load, payload, weight

²**freight** *vb* **1 :** to load with goods for transportation **2 :** BURDEN, CHARGE **3 :** to ship or transport by freight

freight·er \'frā-tər\ *n* **:** a ship or airplane used chiefly to carry freight

French \'french\ *n* **1 :** the language of France **2 French** *pl* **:** the people of France **3 :** strong language — **French** *adj* — **French·man** \-mən\ *n* — **French·wom·an** \-,wu̇-mən\ *n*

French Canadian *n* **:** one of the descendants of French settlers in Lower Canada — **French–Canadian** *adj*

French door *n* **:** a door with small panes of glass extending the full length

French dressing *n* **1 :** a thin salad dressing usu. made of vinegar and oil with spices **2 :** a creamy salad dressing flavored with tomatoes

french fry *n, often cap 1st F* **:** a strip of potato fried in deep fat until brown — **french fry** *vb, often cap 1st F*

French horn *n* **:** a curved brass instrument with a funnel-shaped mouthpiece and a flaring bell

French press *n* **:** a coffeepot in which ground beans are infused and then pressed by a plunger

French toast *n* **:** bread dipped in a mixture of eggs and milk and fried at a low heat

French twist *n* **:** a woman's hairstyle in which the hair is coiled at the rear and secured in place

fren·e·my \'fre-nə-mē\ *n, pl* **-mies :** one who pretends to be a friend but is actually an enemy

fre·net·ic \fri-'ne-tik\ *adj* ♦ **:** marked by fast and nervous, disordered, or anxiety-driven activity **:** FRANTIC — **fre·net·i·cal·ly** \-ti-k(ə-)lē\ *adv*

♦ delirious, feverish, fierce, frantic, frenzied, furious, mad, rabid, violent, wild

fren·zied \'fren-zēd\ *adj* ♦ **:** feeling or showing great or abnormal excitement or emotional disturbance

♦ delirious, feverish, frantic, frenetic, furious, hectic, hysterical

fren·zy \'fren-zē\ *n, pl* **frenzies 1 ♦ :** temporary madness or a violently agitated state **2 ♦ :** intense often disordered activity

♦ [1, 2] agitation, chaos, confusion, disorder, furor, fury, hysteria, rage, rampage, tumult, turmoil, uproar

freq *abbr* frequency; frequent; frequently

fre·quen·cy \'frē-kwən-sē\ *n, pl* **-cies 1 :** the fact or condition of occurring frequently **2 :** rate of occurrence **3 :** the number of cycles per second of an alternating current **4 :** the number of waves (as of sound or electromagnetic energy) that pass a fixed point each second

frequency modulation *n* **:** variation of the frequency of a carrier wave according to another signal; *also* **:** FM

¹**fre·quent** \frē-'kwent, 'frē-kwənt\ *vb* ♦ **:** to associate with, be in, or resort to habitually

♦ hang around, hang out, haunt, resort, visit *Ant* avoid, shun

²**fre·quent** \'frē-kwənt\ *adj* **1 ♦ :** happening often or at short intervals **2 ♦ :** done or happening on a regular or recurring basis

♦ [1] common, commonplace, customary, everyday, familiar, ordinary, routine, usual ♦ [2] constant, habitual, periodic, regular, repeated, steady

fre·quent·er *n* **:** one that frequents

fre·quent–fli·er \'frē-kwənt-'flī-ər\ *adj* **:** of, relating to, or being an airline program offering awards for specified numbers of air miles traveled

fre·quent·ly *adv* ♦ **:** at frequent or short intervals

♦ constantly, continually, often, repeatedly

fres·co \'fres-kō\ *n, pl* **frescoes** : the art of painting on fresh plaster; *also* : a painting done by this method

fresh \'fresh\ *adj* **1** : VIGOROUS, REFRESHED **2** : not containing salt **3** : not altered by processing (as freezing or canning) **4** : free from taint : PURE **5** : fairly strong : BRISK ⟨~ breeze⟩ **6** ♦ : not stale, sour, or decayed ⟨~ bread⟩ **7** : not faded **8** ♦ : not worn or rumpled **9** ♦ : experienced, made, or received newly or anew **10** : ADDITIONAL, ANOTHER ⟨made a ~ start⟩ **11** : ORIGINAL, VIVID **12** : INEXPERIENCED **13** : newly come or arrived ⟨~ from school⟩ **14** ♦ : disposed to take liberties : IM-PUDENT

♦ [6, 8] brand-new, pristine, virgin *Ant* stale ♦ [9] new, novel, original, unfamiliar ♦ [14] bold, brash, brazen, cheeky, impudent, insolent, nervy, sassy, saucy

fresh·en \'fre-shən\ *vb* ♦ : to make, grow, or become fresh

♦ refresh, rejuvenate, renew, restore, revitalize, revive

fresh·et \'fre-shət\ *n* : an overflowing of a stream (as by heavy rains)

fresh·ly *adv* ♦ : in a fresh manner

♦ just, late, lately, new, newly, now, only, recently

fresh·man \'fresh-mən\ *n* **1** : a 1st-year student **2** ♦ : one that begins something; *esp* : an inexperienced person

♦ beginner, greenhorn, neophyte, newcomer, novice, recruit, rookie, tenderfoot, tyro

fresh·ness *n* ♦ : the quality or state of being fresh

♦ newness, novelty, originality

fresh·wa·ter \-ˌwȯ-tər, -ˌwä-\ *n* : water that is not salty — **fresh-water** *adj*

¹fret \'fret\ *vb* **fret·ted; fret·ting 1** : to eat or gnaw into **2** ♦ : to chafe with or as if with friction : RUB **3** : to make by wearing away **4** ♦ : to become irritated : WORRY ⟨*fretted* over his taxes⟩ **5** : GRATE; *also* : AGITATE

♦ [2] abrade, chafe, erode, fray, gall, rub, wear ♦ [4] bother, fear, stew, sweat, trouble, worry

²fret *n* ♦ : an irritated or worried state ⟨in a ~ about the interview⟩

♦ dither, fluster, fuss, huff, lather, pother, stew, tizzy, twitter

³fret *n* : ornamental work esp. of straight lines in symmetrical patterns

⁴fret *n* : one of a series of ridges across the fingerboard of a stringed musical instrument — **fret·ted** *adj*

fret·ful \'fret-fəl\ *adj* : IRRITABLE — **fret·ful·ly** *adv* — **fret·ful·ness** *n*

fret·saw \-ˌsȯ\ *n* : a narrow-bladed saw used for cutting curved outlines

fret·work \-ˌwərk\ *n* **1** : decoration consisting of frets **2** : ornamental openwork or work in relief

Fri *abbr* Friday

fri·a·ble \'frī-ə-bəl\ *adj* ♦ : easily crumbled or pulverized ⟨~ soil⟩

♦ brittle, crisp, crumbly, flaky

fri·ar \'frī-ər\ *n* : a member of a religious order that orig. lived by alms

fri·ary \'frī-ər-ē\ *n, pl* **-ar·ies** ♦ : a monastery of friars

♦ abbey, cloister, monastery, priory

¹fric·as·see \'fri-kə-ˌsē, ˌfri-kə-'sē\ *n* : a dish made of meat (as chicken) cut into pieces, stewed in stock, and served in sauce

²fricassee *vb* **-seed; -see·ing** : to cook as a fricassee

fric·tion \'frik-shən\ *n* **1** : the rubbing of one body against another **2** : the force that resists motion between bodies in contact **3** ♦ : clash in opinions between persons or groups : DIS-AGREEMENT — **fric·tion·al** *adj*

♦ conflict, discord, dissent, disunity, schism, strife, variance

friction tape *n* : a usu. cloth adhesive tape impregnated with insulating material and used esp. to protect and insulate electrical conductors

Fri·day \'frī-dē, -(ˌ)dā\ *n* : the sixth day of the week

fridge \'frij\ *n* : REFRIGERATOR

fried·cake \'frīd-ˌkāk\ *n* : DOUGHNUT, CRULLER

fried rice *n* : a dish of boiled or steamed rice that is stir-fried with soy sauce and typically includes egg, meat, and vegetables

¹friend \'frend\ *n* **1** ♦ : one attached to another by respect or affection **2** : ACQUAINTANCE **3** : one who is not hostile **4** : one who supports or favors something ⟨~ of art⟩ **5** *cap* : a member of the Society of Friends : QUAKER — **friend·less** *adj*

♦ [1] buddy, chum, comrade, crony, familiar, intimate, pal *Ant*

enemy, foe ♦ [4] advocate, apostle, backer, booster, champion, exponent, promoter, proponent, supporter

²friend *vb* **1** : BEFRIEND **2** : to include (someone) in a list of designated friends on a person's social networking site

friend·li·ness \-lē-nəs\ *n* ♦ : the quality or state of being friendly

♦ amity, benevolence, cordiality, fellowship, friendship, goodwill, kindliness

friend·ly \'fren(d)-lē\ *adj* ♦ : of, relating to, or befitting a friend

♦ appreciative, complimentary, favorable (*or* favourable), good, positive ♦ amicable, companionable, comradely, cordial, genial, hearty, neighborly, warm, warmhearted *Ant* antagonistic, hostile, unfriendly

friend·ship \-ˌship\ *n* ♦ : the state of being friends

♦ amity, benevolence, cordiality, fellowship, friendliness, goodwill, kindliness

frieze \'frēz\ *n* : an ornamental often sculptured band extending around something (as a building or room)

frig·ate \'fri-gət\ *n* **1** : a square-rigged warship **2** : a warship smaller than a destroyer

fright \'frīt\ *n* **1** : sudden terror : ALARM **2** ♦ : something that is ugly or shocking

♦ [1] alarm, anxiety, apprehension, dread, fear, horror, panic, terror, trepidation ♦ [2] eyesore, horror, mess, monstrosity, sight

fright·en \'frīt-ᵊn\ *vb* **1** ♦ : to make afraid **2** : to drive away or out by frightening **3** : to become frightened — **fright·en·ing** *adj* — **fright·en·ing·ly** *adv*

♦ alarm, horrify, panic, scare, shock, spook, startle, terrify, terrorize *Ant* reassure

fright·ful \'frīt-fəl\ *adj* **1** ♦ : causing intense fear or alarm : TER-RIFYING **2** : startling esp. in being bad or objectionable **3** : EX-TREME ⟨~ thirst⟩

♦ fearful, fearsome, forbidding, formidable, hair-raising, scary, shocking, terrifying

fright·ful·ly *adv* ♦ : in a frightful manner

♦ especially, extremely, greatly, highly, hugely, mightily, mighty, mortally, most, much, real, right, so, very

fright·ful·ness *n* ♦ : the quality or state of being frightful

♦ atrociousness, atrocity, hideousness, horror, monstrosity, repulsiveness

frig·id \'fri-jəd\ *adj* **1** ♦ : intensely cold **2** ♦ : lacking warmth or ardor : INDIFFERENT **3** : abnormally averse to or unable to achieve orgasm during sexual intercourse — used esp. of women — **fri·gid·i·ty** \fri-'ji-də-tē\ *n*

♦ [1] arctic, bitter, cold, freezing, frosty, glacial, icy, polar, wintry ♦ [2] chill, chilly, cold, cool, frosty, icy, indifferent, unfriendly, wintry

frigid zone *n* : the area or region between the arctic circle and the north pole or between the antarctic circle and the south pole

frill \'fril\ *n* **1** ♦ : a gathered, pleated, or ruffled edging **2** ♦ : something unessential — **frilly** *adj*

♦ [1] flounce, furbelow, ruffle ♦ [2] amenity, comfort, extra, indulgence, luxury, superfluity

¹fringe \'frinj\ *n* **1** : an ornamental border consisting of short threads or strips hanging from an edge or band **2** ♦ : something that resembles a fringe : EDGE **3** : something that is additional or secondary to an activity, process, or subject

♦ border, boundary, edge, margin, perimeter, periphery

²fringe *vb* **1** : to furnish or adorn with a fringe **2** ♦ : to serve as a border or fringe for

♦ border, bound, margin, rim, skirt

fringe benefit *n* **1** : an employment benefit paid for by an employer without affecting basic wage rates **2** : any additional benefit

frip·pery \'fri-pə-rē\ *n, pl* **-per·ies 1 a** ♦ : dressy or showy clothing and jewels : FINERY **b** ♦ : something showy, frivolous, or nonessential **2** : pretentious display

♦ [1a] array, best, bravery, caparison, feather, finery, full dress, gaiety, regalia ♦ [1b] child's play, nothing, trifle, triviality

frisk \'frisk\ *vb* **1** ♦ : to leap, skip, or dance in a lively or playful way : GAMBOL **2** : to search (a person) esp. for concealed weapons by running the hand rapidly over the clothing

♦ caper, cavort, disport, frolic, gambol, lark, rollick, romp, sport

frisk·i·ness \-kē-nəs\ *n* ♦ : the quality or state of being inclined to frisk

♦ impishness, mischief, mischievousness, playfulness

frisky \'fris-kē\ *adj* **frisk·i·er; -est** ♦ : inclined to frisk : PLAYFUL — **frisk·i·ly** \-kə-lē\ *adv*

♦ antic, coltish, elfish, fay, frolicsome, playful, sportive ♦ active, animated, energetic, lively, peppy, perky, spirited, sprightly

¹**frit·ter** \'fri-tər\ *n* : a small lump of fried batter often containing fruit or meat

²**fritter** *vb* **1** ♦ : to reduce or waste piecemeal — usu. used with *away* **2** : to break into small fragments

♦ *usu* **fritter away** blow, dissipate, lavish, misspend, run through, spend, squander, throw away, waste

fritz \'frits\ *n* : a state of disorder or disrepair — used in the phrase *on the fritz*

fri·vol·i·ty \fri-'vä-lə-tē\ *n* ♦ : the quality or state of being frivolous

♦ facetiousness, flightiness, flippancy, levity, lightness *Ant* gravity, seriousness, soberness, sobriety

friv·o·lous \'fri-və-ləs\ *adj* **1** ♦ : of little importance : TRIVIAL **2** ♦ : lacking in seriousness — **friv·o·lous·ly** *adv*

♦ [1] insignificant, little, minor, minute, negligible, slight, small, trifling, trivial, unimportant ♦ [2] flighty, giddy, goofy, harebrained, light-headed, scatterbrained, silly

frizz \'friz\ *vb* : to form into small tight curls — **frizz** *n* — **frizzy** *adj*

friz·zies \'fri-zēz\ *n pl* : hair which has become difficult to manage (as due to humidity)

¹**friz·zle** \'fri-zəl\ *vb* **friz·zled; friz·zling** : FRIZZ, CURL — **frizzle** *n*

²**frizzle** *vb* **friz·zled; friz·zling** **1** : to fry until crisp and curled **2** : to cook with a sizzling noise

fro \'frō\ *adv* : BACK, AWAY — used in the phrase *to and fro*

frock \'fräk\ *n* **1** : an outer garment worn by monks and friars **2** : an outer garment worn esp. by men **3** : a woman's or girl's dress

frock coat *n* : a man's knee-length usu. double-breasted coat with knee-length skirts

frog \'frȯg, 'fräg\ *n* **1** : any of various largely aquatic smooth-skinned tailless leaping amphibians **2** : an ornamental braiding for fastening the front of a garment by a loop through which a button passes **3** : a condition in the throat causing hoarseness **4** : a small holder (as of metal, glass, or plastic) with perforations or spikes that is placed in a bowl or vase to keep cut flowers in position

frog·man \'frȯg-,man, 'fräg-, -mən\ *n* : a swimmer equipped to work underwater for long periods of time

¹**frol·ic** \'frä-lik\ *vb* **frol·icked; frol·ick·ing** **1** ♦ : to make merry **2** ♦ : to play about happily : ROMP

♦ caper, cavort, disport, frisk, gambol, lark, play, rollick, romp, sport

²**frolic** *n* **1** ♦ : a playful or mischievous action **2** ♦ : an occasion or scene of fun

♦ [1] dalliance, fun, play, relaxation, sport ♦ [1] antic, caper, escapade, monkeyshine, practical joke, prank, trick ♦ [2] binge, fling, gambol, lark, revel, rollick, romp

frol·ic·some \-səm\ *adj* ♦ : full of gaiety

♦ antic, coltish, elfish, fay, frisky, playful, sportive

from \'frəm, 'främ\ *prep* **1** — used to show a starting point ⟨a letter ~ home⟩ **2** — used to show removal or separation ⟨subtract 3 ~ 9⟩ **3** — used to show a material, source, or cause ⟨suffering ~ a cold⟩

frond \'fränd\ *n* : a usu. large divided leaf esp. of a fern or palm tree

¹**front** \'frənt\ *n* **1** : FOREHEAD; *also* : the whole face **2** ♦ : external and often feigned appearance **3** : a region of active fighting; *also* : a sphere of activity **4** : a political coalition **5** : the side of a building containing the main entrance **6** ♦ : the forward part or surface **7** : FRONTAGE **8** : a boundary between two dissimilar air masses **9** : a position directly before or ahead of something else **10** : a person, group, or thing used to mask the identity of the actual controlling agent

♦ [2] act, airs, facade, guise, pose, pretense, put-on, semblance, show ♦ [6] facade, face *Ant* back, rear, reverse

²**front** *vb* **1** : to have the principal side adjacent to something **2** : to serve as a front **3** : CONFRONT

front·age \'frən-tij\ *n* **1** : a piece of land lying adjacent (as to a

street or the ocean) **2** : the length of a frontage **3** : the front side of a building

front·al \'frənt-ᵊl\ *adj* **1** : of, relating to, or next to the forehead **2** : of, relating to, or directed at the front ⟨a ~ attack⟩ — **front·al·ly** *adv*

fron·tier \,frən-'tir\ *n* **1** ♦ : a border between two countries **2** ♦ : a region that forms the margin of settled territory **3** : the outer limits of knowledge or achievement ⟨the ~s of science⟩

♦ [1] border, borderland, march ♦ [2] backwoods, bush, hinterland, sticks, up-country

fron·tiers·man \-'tirz-mən\ *n* ♦ : a person who lives or works on a frontier

♦ colonist, homesteader, pioneer, settler

fron·tis·piece \'frən-tə-,spēs\ *n* : an illustration preceding and usu. facing the title page of a book

front man *n* : a person serving as a front or figurehead

front·ward \'frənt-wərd\ *or* **front·wards** \-wərdz\ *adv or adj* : toward the front

¹**frost** \'frȯst\ *n* **1** : freezing temperature **2** : a covering of tiny ice crystals on a cold surface

²**frost** *vb* **1** : to cover with frost **2** : to put icing on (as a cake) **3** : to produce a slightly roughened surface on (as glass) **4** : to injure or kill by frost

¹**frost·bite** \'frȯst-,bīt\ *vb* **-bit** \-,bit\; **-bit·ten** \-,bit-ᵊn\; **-bit·ing** : to injure by frost or frostbite

²**frostbite** *n* : the freezing or the local effect of a partial freezing of some part of the body

frost heave *n* : an upthrust of pavement caused by freezing of moist soil

frost·ing \'frȯ-stiŋ\ *n* **1** : ICING **2** : dull finish on metal or glass

frosty *adj* **1** ♦ : briskly cold **2** : covered or appearing as if covered with frost **3** ♦ : marked by coolness or extreme reserve in manner

♦ [1] chill, chilly, cold, cool, nippy, raw, snappy, wintry ♦ [3] aloof, antisocial, cold, cool, detached, distant, remote, standoffish, unfriendly, unsociable

froth \'frȯth\ *n, pl* **froths** \'frȯths, 'frȯthz\ **1** ♦ : bubbles formed in or on a liquid **2** : something light or worthless — **frothy** *adj*

♦ foam, head, lather, spume

frou-frou \'frü-,frü\ *n* **1** : a rustling esp. of a woman's skirts **2** : showy or frilly ornamentation

fro·ward \'frō-wərd\ *adj* ♦ : habitually disposed to disobedience and opposition

♦ contrary, defiant, disobedient, headstrong, intractable, rebellious, unruly, untoward, wayward, willful

¹**frown** \'fraun\ *vb* **1** : to wrinkle the forehead (as in displeasure or thought) **2** ♦ : to look with disapproval — usu. used with *on* in transitive senses **3** : to express with a frown

♦ glare, gloom, glower, lower, scowl *Ant* beam, smile ♦ *usu* **frown on** deprecate, disapprove, discountenance, disfavor (*or* disfavour), dislike, reprove

²**frown** *n* ♦ : a wrinkling of the brow esp. in a severe, reproving, or stern look

♦ face, grimace, lower, mouth, pout, scowl

frow·sy *or* **frow·zy** \'frau-zē\ *adj* **frow·si·er** *or* **frow·zi·er; -est** ♦ : having a slovenly or uncared-for appearance

♦ dowdy, sloppy, slovenly, unkempt, untidy

froze *past of* FREEZE

fro·zen \'frōz-ᵊn\ *adj* **1** : treated, affected, or crusted over by freezing **2** : subject to long and severe cold **3** ♦ : incapable of being changed, moved, or undone ⟨~ wages⟩ **4** : not available for present use ⟨~ capital⟩ **5** : expressing or characterized by cold unfriendliness

♦ certain, determinate, final, firm, fixed, flat, hard, hard-and-fast, set, settled, stable

FRS *abbr* Federal Reserve System

frt *abbr* freight

fruc·ti·fy \'frək-tə-,fī, 'frük-\ *vb* **-fied; -fy·ing** **1** : to bear fruit **2** : to make fruitful or productive

fruc·tose \'frək-,tōs, 'frük-\ *n* : a very sweet soluble sugar that occurs esp. in fruit juices and honey

fru·gal \'frü-gəl\ *adj* ♦ : characterized by or reflecting economy in the use of resources : ECONOMICAL, THRIFTY — **fru·gal·ly** *adv*

♦ economical, provident, sparing, thrifty *Ant* prodigal, wasteful

fru·gal·i·ty \frü-'ga-lə-tē\ *n* ♦ : the quality or state of being frugal

♦ economy, husbandry, providence, thrift

¹**fruit** \'früt\ *n* **1** : a product of plant growth; *esp* : a usu. edible and sweet reproductive body (as a strawberry or apple) of a seed plant **2** : a product of fertilization in a plant; *esp* : the ripe ovary of a seed plant with its contents and appendages **3** : the effect or consequence of an action or operation — **fruit·ed** \'frü-təd\ *adj*

²**fruit** *vb* : to bear or cause to bear fruit

fruit·cake \'früt-ˌkāk\ *n* : a rich cake containing nuts, dried or candied fruits, and spices

fruit fly *n* : any of various small dipteran flies whose larvae feed on fruit or decaying vegetable matter

fruit·ful \'früt-fəl\ *adj* **1** ♦ : yielding or producing fruit **2** ♦ : very productive ⟨a ∼ soil⟩; *also* : bringing results ⟨a ∼ idea⟩ — **fruit·ful·ly** *adv* — **fruit·ful·ness** *n*

♦ [1] fat, fecund, fertile, luxuriant, productive, prolific, rich ♦ [2] effective, effectual, efficacious, efficient, potent, productive

fru·ition \frü-'i-shən\ *n* **1** : ENJOYMENT **2** : the state of bearing fruit **3** ♦ : the state of being realized : REALIZATION, ACCOMPLISHMENT

♦ accomplishment, achievement, actuality, attainment, consummation, fulfillment, realization *Ant* naught, nonfulfillment

fruit·less \'früt-ləs\ *adj* **1** : not bearing fruit **2** ♦ : not successful : UNSUCCESSFUL ⟨a ∼ attempt⟩ — **fruit·less·ly** *adv*

♦ futile, ineffective, unproductive, unsuccessful

fruity \'frü-tē\ *adj* **fruit·i·er; -est** : resembling a fruit esp. in flavor

frumpy \'frəm-pē\ *adj* **frump·i·er; -est** : DOWDY, DRAB

frus·trate \'frəs-ˌtrāt\ *vb* **frus·trat·ed; frus·trat·ing 1** ♦ : to balk or defeat in an endeavor **2** : to induce feelings of insecurity, discouragement, or dissatisfaction in **3** : to bring to nothing — **frus·trat·ing·ly** *adv*

♦ baffle, balk, beat, checkmate, foil, thwart

frus·trat·ing *adj* ♦ : tending to produce or characterized by frustration

♦ aggravating, annoying, bothersome, galling, irksome, irritating, pesty, vexatious

frus·tra·tion \ˌfrəs-'trā-shən\ *n* **1** ♦ : the state or an instance of being frustrated **2** ♦ : something that frustrates

♦ [1] disappointment, dismay, dissatisfaction, letdown ♦ [2] aggravation, annoyance, bother, exasperation, vexation

frus·tum \'frəs-təm\ *n, pl* **frustums** *or* **frus·ta** \-tə\ : the part of a cone or pyramid formed by cutting off the top by a plane parallel to the base

frwy *abbr* freeway

¹**fry** \'frī\ *vb* **fried; fry·ing 1** : to cook in a pan or on a griddle over heat esp. with the use of fat **2** : to undergo frying

²**fry** *n, pl* **fries 1** : a social gathering where fried food is eaten **2** : a dish of something fried; *esp, pl* : FRENCH FRIES

³**fry** *n, pl* **fry 1** : recently hatched fishes; *also* : very small adult fishes **2** : members of a group or class ⟨small ∼⟩

fry·er \'frī-ər\ *n* **1** : something (as a young chicken) suitable for frying **2** : a deep utensil for frying foods

FSLIC *abbr* Federal Savings and Loan Insurance Corporation

ft *abbr* **1** feet; foot **2** fort

FTC *abbr* Federal Trade Commission

FTP \ˌef-ˌtē-'pē\ *n* : a system for transferring computer files esp. via the Internet — **FTP** *vb*

fuch·sia \'fyü-shə\ *n* **1** : any of a genus of shrubs related to the evening primrose and grown for their showy nodding often red or purple flowers **2** : a vivid reddish purple color

fud·dle \'fəd-ᵊl\ *vb* **fud·dled; fud·dling** : MUDDLE, CONFUSE

fud·dy–dud·dy \'fə-dē-ˌdə-dē\ *n, pl* **-dies** ♦ : one that is old-fashioned, unimaginative, or conservative

♦ antediluvian, dodo, fogy, fossil, reactionary

¹**fudge** \'fəj\ *vb* **fudged; fudg·ing 1** : to exceed the proper bounds of something **2** : to act dishonestly : CHEAT; *also* : FALSIFY **3** ♦ : to fail to come to grips with

♦ equivocate, hedge, pussyfoot

²**fudge** *n* **1** ♦ : a piece of foolish nonsense **2** : a soft candy of milk, sugar, butter, and flavoring

♦ bunk, folly, foolishness, hogwash, humbug, nonsense, piffle, rot, silliness

¹**fu·el** \'fyü-əl, 'fyül\ *n* : a material used to produce heat or power by burning; *also* : a material from which nuclear energy can be liberated

²**fuel** *vb* **-eled** *or* **-elled; -el·ing** *or* **-el·ling** : to provide with or take in fuel

fuel cell *n* : a device that continuously changes the chemical energy of a fuel directly into electrical energy

fuel injection *n* : a system for injecting a precise amount of atomized fuel into an internal combustion engine — **fuel–in·ject·ed** \'fyül-in-ˌjek-təd\ *adj*

¹**fu·gi·tive** \'fyü-jə-tiv\ *n* **1** : one who flees or tries to escape **2** : something elusive or hard to find

²**fugitive** *adj* **1** : running away or trying to escape **2** ♦ : likely to vanish suddenly : not fixed or lasting

♦ ephemeral, evanescent, flash, fleeting, impermanent, momentary, short-lived, transient

fugue \'fyüg\ *n* **1** : a musical composition in which different parts successively repeat the theme **2** : a disturbed state of consciousness characterized by acts that are not recalled upon recovery

füh·rer *or* **fueh·rer** \'fyu̇r-ər, 'fir-\ *n* : LEADER; *esp* : TYRANT

¹**-ful** \fəl\ *adj suffix, sometimes* **-ful·er** *sometimes* **-ful·est 1** : full of ⟨pride*ful*⟩ **2** : characterized by ⟨peace*ful*⟩ **3** : having the qualities of ⟨master*ful*⟩ **4** : tending, given, or liable to ⟨help*ful*⟩

²**-ful** \ˌfu̇l\ *n suffix* : number or quantity that fills or would fill ⟨room*ful*⟩

ful·crum \'fu̇l-krəm, 'fəl-\ *n, pl* **ful·crums** *or* **ful·cra** \-krə\ : the support on which a lever turns

ful·fill *or* **ful·fil** \fu̇l-'fil\ *vb* **ful·filled; ful·fill·ing 1** : to put into effect **2** ♦ : to bring to an end **3** ♦ : to meet the requirements of : SATISFY ⟨∼ed expectations⟩

♦ [2] accomplish, achieve, carry out, commit, compass, do, execute, follow through, make, perform ♦ [3] answer, comply, fill, keep, meet, redeem, satisfy *Ant* breach, break, violate

ful·fill·ment *n* ♦ : the act or process of fulfilling

♦ accomplishment, achievement, actuality, attainment, consummation, fruition, realization

¹**full** \'fu̇l\ *adj* **1** ♦ : containing as much or as many as is possible or normal : FILLED **2** ♦ : complete esp. in detail, number, or duration **3** ♦ : having all the distinguishing characteristics ⟨a ∼ member⟩ **4** : being at the highest or greatest degree : MAXIMUM **5** : rounded in outline : being full or plump in form ⟨a ∼ figure⟩ **6** : possessing or containing an abundance ⟨∼ of wrinkles⟩ **7** : having an abundance of material ⟨a ∼ skirt⟩ **8** ♦ : satisfied esp. with food or drink **9** : having volume or depth of sound **10** : completely occupied with a thought or plan — **full·ness** *also* **ful·ness** *n*

♦ [1] brimful, crowded, loaded, packed, replete, rife *Ant* bare, empty, stark, vacant ♦ [2] complete, comprehensive, detailed, encyclopedic, inclusive, universal ♦ [3] complete, comprehensive, entire, total, whole ♦ [4] maximum, top, utmost *Ant* least, lowest, minimal, minimum ♦ [8] sated, satiate, satiated *Ant* empty, hungry, starving

²**full** *adv* **1** : to a high degree : VERY, EXTREMELY **2** ♦ : to a complete degree : ENTIRELY **3** : STRAIGHT, SQUARELY ⟨hit him ∼ in the face⟩

♦ altogether, completely, entirely, fully, perfectly, quite, thoroughly, well, wholly

³**full** *n* **1** : the highest or fullest state or degree **2** : the utmost extent **3** ♦ : the requisite or complete amount

♦ aggregate, sum, total, totality, whole

⁴**full** *vb* : to shrink and thicken (woolen cloth) by moistening, heating, and pressing — **full·er** *n*

full·back \'fu̇l-ˌbak\ *n* : a football back stationed between the halfbacks

full–blood·ed \'fu̇l-'blə-dəd\ *adj* ♦ : of unmixed ancestry : PUREBRED

♦ purebred, thoroughbred

full–blown \-'blōn\ *adj* **1** : being at the height of bloom **2** ♦ : fully mature or developed

♦ adult, full-fledged, mature, ripe

full–bod·ied \-'bä-dēd\ *adj* ♦ : marked by richness and fullness

♦ concentrated, full, potent, rich, robust, strong *Ant* light, mild, thin, weak

full dress *n* ♦ : the style of dress worn for ceremonial or formal occasions

♦ array, best, bravery, caparison, feather, finery, frippery, gaiety, regalia

full–fledged \'fùl-'flejd\ *adj* **1** ♦ : fully developed **2** : having attained complete status ⟨a ∼ lawyer⟩

♦ adult, full-blown, mature, ripe

full house *n* : a poker hand containing three of a kind and a pair
full moon *n* : the moon with its whole disk illuminated
full–on \-,ón, -,än\ *adj* : COMPLETE, FULL-FLEDGED
full–scale \'fùl-'skāl\ *adj* **1** : identical to an original in proportion and size ⟨∼ drawing⟩ **2** ♦ : involving full use of available resources ⟨a ∼ revolt⟩

♦ all-out, clean, complete, comprehensive, exhaustive, out-and-out, thorough, thoroughgoing, total

full–term \-,tərm\ *adj* : retained in the uterus for the normal period of gestation before birth ⟨a ∼ baby⟩
full tilt *adv* ♦ : at high speed : with a rush

♦ fast, hastily, posthaste, rapidly, speedily, swiftly

full–time \'fùl-'tīm\ *adj or adv* : involving or working a normal or standard schedule
ful·ly \'fù-lē\ *adv* **1** ♦ : in a full manner or degree : COMPLETE-LY **2** : at least

♦ altogether, chiefly, completely, entirely, generally, largely, mainly, mostly, perfectly, primarily, principally, quite, thoroughly, well, wholly *Ant* partially, partly

ful·mi·nate \'fùl-mə-,nāt, 'fəl-\ *vb* **-nat·ed; -nat·ing** ♦ : to utter or send out censure or invective : condemn severely

♦ bluster, rant, rave, spout

ful·mi·na·tion \,fùl-mə-'nā-shən, ,fəl-\ *n* ♦ : vehement menace or censure

♦ abuse, invective, vitriol, vituperation

ful·some \'fùl-səm\ *adj* **1** : COPIOUS, ABUNDANT ⟨∼ detail⟩ **2** : generous in amount or extent ⟨a ∼ victory⟩ **3** ♦ : excessively flattering ⟨∼ praise⟩

♦ adulatory, unctuous

fu·ma·role \'fyü-mə-,rōl\ *n* : a hole in a volcanic region from which hot gases issue
¹fum·ble \'fəm-bəl\ *vb* **fum·bled; fum·bling 1 a** ♦ : to grope about clumsily **b** : make awkward attempts to do or find something **2** ♦ : to fail to hold, catch, or handle properly

♦ [1a] feel, fish, grope ♦ [2] bobble, botch, bungle, flub, foul up, mangle, mess up, screw up

²fumble *n* : an act or instance of fumbling
¹fume \'fyüm\ *n* : a usu. irritating smoke, vapor, or gas
²fume *vb* **fumed; fum·ing 1** : to treat with fumes **2** : to give off fumes **3 a** ♦ : to express anger or annoyance **b** ♦ : to be in a state of excited irritation or anger

♦ [3a] rage, storm ♦ [3b] boil, burn, rage, seethe, steam

fu·mi·gant \'fyü-mi-gənt\ *n* : a substance used for fumigation
fu·mi·gate \'fyü-mə-,gāt\ *vb* **-gat·ed; -gat·ing** : to treat with fumes to disinfect or destroy pests — **fu·mi·ga·tion** \,fyü-mə-'gā-shən\ *n* — **fu·mi·ga·tor** \'fyü-mə-,gā-tər\ *n*
¹fun \'fən\ *n* **1** ♦ : something that provides amusement or enjoyment **2** : the action or state of enjoying : ENJOYMENT **3** ♦ : a mood for finding or making amusement

♦ [1] delight, diversion, entertainment, pleasure *Ant* bore, bummer, downer, drag ♦ [3] frolic, play, relaxation, sport ♦ [3] game, jest, play, sport *Ant* earnest

²fun *adj* ♦ : full of fun ⟨a ∼ person⟩ ⟨had a ∼ time⟩

♦ amusing, delightful, diverting, enjoyable, entertaining, pleasurable

¹func·tion \'fəŋk-shən\ *n* **1** ♦ : professional or official position of employment **2** : special purpose **3** ♦ : the particular purpose for which a person or thing is specially fitted or used or for which a thing exists ⟨the ∼ of a hammer⟩; *also* : the natural or proper action of a bodily part in a living thing ⟨the ∼ of the heart⟩ **4** ♦ : a formal ceremony or social affair **5** : a mathematical relationship that assigns to each element of a set one and only one element of the same or another set **6** : a variable (as a quality, trait, or measurement) that depends on and varies with another ⟨height is a ∼ of age in children⟩ **7** : a computer subroutine that performs a calculation with variables provided by a program — **func·tion·al·ly** *adv*

♦ [1] appointment, billet, capacity, job, place, position, post, situation ♦ [3] capacity, job, part, place, position, purpose, role, task, work ♦ [4] affair, blowout, event, fete, get-together, party

²function *vb* ♦ : to have or carry on a function

♦ act, perform, serve, work

func·tion·al \-shə-nəl\ *adj* **1** ♦ : performing or able to perform a regular function **2** : of, connected with, or being a function

♦ active, alive, living, on, operational, operative, running, working ♦ applicable, practicable, practical, serviceable, usable, useful, workable

func·tion·ary \'fəŋk-shə-,ner-ē\ *n, pl* **-ar·ies** ♦ : one who performs a certain function; *esp* : one who holds a public office

♦ officeholder, officer, official, public servant

function word *n* : a word (as a preposition, auxiliary verb, or conjunction) expressing the grammatical relationship between other words
¹fund \'fənd\ *n* **1** ♦ : a sum of money or resources intended for a special purpose ⟨∼ing research⟩ **2** : STORE, SUPPLY **3 a** *pl* ♦ : available money **b** ♦ : an available quantity of material or intangible resources **4** : an organization administering a special fund

♦ [1] account, budget, deposit, kitty, nest egg, pool ♦ *usu* **funds** [3a] finances, pocket, resources, wherewithal ♦ [3b] budget, pool, supply

²fund *vb* **1** ♦ : to provide funds for **2** : to convert (a short-term obligation) into a long-term interest-bearing debt — **fund·er** *n*

♦ capitalize, endow, finance, stake, subsidize, underwrite

fun·da·men·tal \,fən-də-'men-təl\ *adj* **1** : serving as an origin : PRIMARY **2** ♦ : serving as a basis supporting existence or determining essential structure or function : BASIC, ESSENTIAL **3** : RADICAL ⟨∼ change⟩ **4** : of central importance : PRINCIPAL — **fundamental** *n* — **fun·da·men·tal·ly** *adv*

♦ basic, elemental, elementary, essential, rudimentary, underlying

fun·da·men·tal·ism \-tə-,i-zəm\ *n* **1** *often cap* : a Protestant religious movement emphasizing the literal infallibility of the Bible **2** : a movement or attitude stressing strict adherence to a set of basic principles — **fun·da·men·tal·ist** \-ist\ *adj or n*
¹fu·ner·al \'fyü-nə-rəl\ *adj* **1** : of, relating to, or constituting a funeral **2** ♦ : befitting or suggesting a funeral : FUNEREAL

♦ dolorous, funereal, lugubrious, mournful, plaintive, sorrowful, woeful

²funeral *n* : the ceremonies held for a dead person usu. before burial
fu·ner·ary \'fyü-nə-,rer-ē\ *adj* : of, used for, or associated with burial ⟨∼ rites⟩
fu·ne·re·al \fyù-'nir-ē-əl\ *adj* **1** : of or relating to a funeral **2** ♦ : suggesting a funeral ⟨a ∼ mood⟩

♦ bleak, dark, dismal, dreary, gloomy, gray (*or* grey), somber (*or* sombre), wretched

fun·gi·cide \'fən-jə-,sīd, 'fəŋ-gə-\ *n* : an agent that kills or checks the growth of fungi — **fun·gi·cid·al** \,fən-jə-'sīd-²l, ,fəŋ-gə-\ *adj*
fun·gus \'fəŋ-gəs\ *n, pl* **fun·gi** \'fən-,jī, 'fəŋ-,gī\ *also* **fun·gus·es** \'fəŋ-gə-səz\ : any of a kingdom of parasitic spore-producing organisms (as molds, mildews, and mushrooms) formerly classified as plants — **fun·gal** \-gəl\ *adj* — **fun·gous** \-gəs\ *adj*
fu·nic·u·lar \fyù-'ni-kyə-lər, fə-\ *n* : a cable railway ascending a mountain
¹funk \'fəŋk\ *n* : a strong offensive smell
²funk *n* : a depressed state of mind
³funk *n* **1** : music that combines elements of rhythm and blues and soul music and that has a strong beat **2** : the quality or state of being funky
funky \'fəŋ-kē\ *adj* **funk·i·er; -est 1** : having the style and feeling of older African American music (as blues) or of funk **2** : odd or quaint in appearance or style ⟨a ∼ restaurant⟩
¹fun·nel \'fən-²l\ *n* **1** : a cone-shaped utensil with a tube used for catching and directing a downward flow (as of liquid) **2** : FLUE, SMOKESTACK
²funnel *vb* **-neled** *also* **-nelled; -nel·ing** *also* **-nel·ling 1** : to pass through or as if through a funnel **2** ♦ : to move to a central point or into a central channel

♦ channel, conduct, direct, pipe, siphon

fun·nies \'fə-nēz\ *n pl* : a comic strip or a comic section (as of a newspaper) — used with *the*
¹fun·ny \'fə-nē\ *adj* **fun·ni·er; -est 1** ♦ : affording light mirth and laughter **2** ♦ : seeking or intended to amuse **3** ♦ : differing from the ordinary in a suspicious, perplexing, quaint, or eccentric way : PECULIAR **4** : UNDERHANDED — **funny** *adv*

♦ [1, 2] amusing, antic, comic, comical, droll, farcical, hilarious, humorous, laughable, ludicrous, mirthful, risible *Ant* humorless, lame, uncomic, unfunny ♦ [3] bizarre, curious, odd, peculiar, quaint, quirky, strange, weird

²**funny** *n, pl* **funnies** : a comic strip or a comic section (as of a newspaper)

funny bone *n* : a place at the back of the elbow where a blow easily compresses a nerve and causes a painful tingling sensation

fun·plex \'fən-ˌpleks\ *n* : a center containing various entertainment facilities

¹**fur** \'fər\ *n* **1** : an article of clothing made of or with fur **2** ♦ : the hairy coat of a mammal esp. when fine, soft, and thick **3** ♦ : an animal's coat dressed for use **4** : a coating resembling fur — **fur** *adj* — **furred** \'fərd\ *adj*

♦ [2] coat, fleece, hair, pelage, pile, wool ♦ [3] hide, pelt, skin

²**fur** *abbr* furlong

fur·be·low \'fər-bə-ˌlō\ *n* **1** ♦ : a pleated or gathered piece of material **2** : showy trimming

♦ flounce, frill, ruffle

fur·bish \'fər-bish\ *vb* **1** : to make lustrous : POLISH **2** : to give a new look to : RENOVATE

fu·ri·ous \'fyür-ē-əs\ *adj* **1** ♦ : exhibiting or goaded by anger : indicative of or proceeding from anger **2** ♦ : BOISTEROUS **3** ♦ : existing in an extreme degree : INTENSE **4** ♦ : full of activity — **fu·ri·ous·ly** *adv*

♦ [1] angry, enraged, irate ♦ [3] deep, ferocious, fierce, hard, heavy, intense, profound, terrible ♦ [4] delirious, excessive, extreme, feverish, fierce, frantic, frenetic, frenzied, inordinate, intense, irrational, rabid, vehement, violent, wild *Ant* relaxed

furl \'fərl\ *vb* **1** : to wrap or roll (as a sail or a flag) close to or around something **2** : to curl in furls — **furl** *n*

fur·long \'fər-ˌlȯŋ\ *n* : a unit of distance equal to 220 yards (about 201 meters)

fur·lough \'fər-lō\ *n* **1** : a leave of absence from duty granted esp. to a soldier **2** : a leave of absence granted by an employer to an employee — **furlough** *vb*

fur·nace \'fər-nəs\ *n* : an enclosed structure in which heat is produced

fur·nish \'fər-nish\ *vb* **1** ♦ : to provide with what is needed : EQUIP **2** ♦ : to make available for use : SUPPLY, GIVE

♦ [1] accoutre, allocate, allot, assign, bestow, deal, dispense, distribute, donate, equip, fit, give, outfit, present, rig, store, supply ♦ [2] deliver, feed, give, hand, hand over, provide, supply *Ant* hold (back), keep (back), reserve, retain, withhold

fur·nish·ings \-ni-shiŋz\ *n pl* **1** : articles or accessories of dress **2** : an object that tends to increase comfort or utility; *esp* : an article of furniture

fur·ni·ture \'fər-ni-chər\ *n* **1** : equipment that is necessary or desirable **2** : movable articles (as chairs or beds) for a room

fu·ror \'fyür-ˌȯr\ *n* **1** ♦ : an angry or maniacal fit : RAGE **2** : a contagious excitement; *esp* : a fashionable craze **3** ♦ : furious or hectic activity : UPROAR

♦ [1] anger, fury, indignation, ire, outrage, rage, spleen, wrath, wrathfulness ♦ [3] commotion, disturbance, pandemonium, tumult, turmoil, uproar

fu·rore \-ˌȯr\ *n* **1** : a contagious excitement; *esp* : a fashionable craze **2** : furious or hectic activity : UPROAR

fur·ri·er \'fər-ē-ər\ *n* : one who prepares or deals in fur

fur·ring \'fər-iŋ\ *n* : wood or metal strips applied to a wall or ceiling to form a level surface or an air space

¹**fur·row** \'fər-ō\ *n* **1** : a trench in the earth made by a plow **2** ♦ : a narrow groove or wrinkle

♦ crease, crimp, crinkle, wrinkle

²**furrow** *vb* : to make or form furrows, grooves, wrinkles, or lines

fur·ry \'fər-ē\ *adj* **fur·ri·er; -est 1** ♦ : resembling or consisting of fur **2** ♦ : covered with fur

♦ [1] fuzzy, hairy, rough, shaggy, woolly ♦ [2] fleecy, hairy, hirsute, rough, shaggy, unshorn, woolly

¹**fur·ther** \'fər-thər\ *adv* **1** ♦ : at or to a greater distance or more advanced point : FARTHER **2** ♦ : in addition : MOREOVER **3** : to a greater extent or degree

♦ [1] beyond, farther, yonder ♦ [2] additionally, again, also, besides, more, moreover, then, too

²**further** *vb* ♦ : to promote or help advance

♦ advance, cultivate, encourage, forward, foster, nourish, nurture, promote

³**further** *adj* **1** : FARTHER 1 **2** ♦ : going or extending beyond what exists : ADDITIONAL

♦ additional, another, else, farther, more, other

fur·ther·ance \'fər-thə-rəns\ *n* ♦ : the act of furthering

♦ advance, advancement, passage, process, procession, progress, progression

fur·ther·more \'fər-thər-ˌmȯr\ *adv* ♦ : in addition to what precedes : BESIDES

♦ additionally, again, also, besides, more, too, withal, yet

fur·ther·most \-ˌmōst\ *adj* : most distant : FARTHEST

fur·thest \'fər-thəst\ *adv or adj* ♦ : to or at the greatest distance in space : FARTHEST

♦ extreme, farthest, outermost, ultimate, utmost

fur·tive \'fər-tiv\ *adj* ♦ : done by stealth ⟨a ∼ glance⟩ — **fur·tive·ly** *adv* — **fur·tive·ness** *n*

♦ clandestine, covert, secret, sneaky, stealthy, surreptitious, undercover

fu·ry \'fyür-ē\ *n, pl* **furies 1** ♦ : intense and often destructive rage **2** : extreme fierceness or violence **3** ♦ : a state of inspired exaltation : FRENZY **4** ♦ : one who resembles an avenging spirit; *esp* : a spiteful woman

♦ [1] anger, furor, indignation, ire, outrage, rage, spleen, wrath, wrathfulness ♦ [3] agitation, delirium, distraction, frenzy, furor, hysteria, rage, rampage, uproar ♦ [4] harpy, shrew, termagant, virago

furze \'fərz\ *n* : GORSE

¹**fuse** \'fyüz\ *vb* **fused; fus·ing 1** ♦ : to reduce to a liquid or plastic state by heat : MELT **2** ♦ : to unite by or as if by melting together — **fus·ible** *adj*

♦ [1] deliquesce, flux, liquefy, melt, run, thaw ♦ [2] associate, coalesce, combine, couple, join, link, marry, unify, unite ♦ [2] amalgamate, blend, commingle, merge, mingle

²**fuse** *n* : an electrical safety device having a metal wire or strip that melts and interrupts the circuit when the current becomes too strong

³**fuse** *n* **1** : a cord or cable that is set afire to ignite an explosive charge **2** *usu* **fuze** : a mechanical or electrical device for setting off the explosive charge of a projectile, bomb, or torpedo

⁴**fuse** *also* **fuze** \'fyüz\ *vb* **fused** *or* **fuzed; fus·ing** *or* **fuz·ing** : to equip with a fuse

fu·se·lage \'fyü-sə-ˌläzh, -zə-\ *n* : the central body portion of an aircraft

fu·sil·lade \'fyü-sə-ˌläd, -ˌlād\ *n* **1** : a number of shots fired simultaneously or in rapid succession **2** ♦ : something that gives the effect of a fusillade

♦ barrage, bombardment, cannonade, hail, salvo, shower, storm, volley

fu·sion \'fyü-zhən\ *n* **1** : the act or process of melting or making plastic by heat **2** ♦ : union by or as if by melting **3** : the union of light atomic nuclei to form heavier nuclei with the release of huge quantities of energy

♦ [2] admixture, amalgam, blend, combination, composite, compound, intermixture, mix, mixture

¹**fuss** \'fəs\ *n* **1** ♦ : needless bustle or excitement : COMMOTION **2** : effusive praise **3** : a state of agitation **4** ♦ : an act of objecting **5** : DISPUTE

♦ [1] bother, bustle, commotion, furor, hubbub, hullabaloo, pandemonium, stir, tumult, turmoil, uproar ♦ [3] dither, fluster, fret, huff, lather, pother, stew, tizzy, twitter ♦ [4] challenge, complaint, demur, expostulation, kick, objection, protest, question, remonstrance

²**fuss** *vb* **1** : to make a fuss **2 a** ♦ : to give flattering or doting attention to **b** : to pay close or undue attention to small details **3** ♦ : to express annoyance or complaint

♦ [2a] enthuse, fawn, gush, rave, rhapsodize, slobber ♦ [3] beef, carp, complain, crab, gripe, grouse, moan, squawk

fuss·bud·get \'fəs-ˌbə-jət\ *n* : one who fusses or is fussy about trifles

fussy \'fə-sē\ *adj* **fuss·i·er; -est 1** ♦ : nervous or easily upset **2** : overly decorated **3** ♦ : requiring or giving close attention or concern to details or niceties; *also* : overly difficult to please ⟨a ∼ customer⟩ — **fuss·i·ly** \-sə-lē\ *adv* — **fuss·i·ness** \-sē-nəs\ *n*

♦ [1] crabby, cranky, grouchy, grumpy, querulous *Ant* uncomplaining ♦ [3] choosy, dainty, delicate, demanding, exacting, fastidious, finicky, meticulous, painstaking, particular, picky

fus·tian \ˈfəs-chən\ *n* **1 :** a strong usu. cotton fabric **2 :** pretentious writing or speech — **fustian** *adj*

fus·ty \ˈfəs-tē\ *adj* **fus·ti·er; -est** **1** ♦ **:** saturated with dust and stale odors : MUSTY **2 :** OLD-FASHIONED ⟨∼ notions⟩

♦ malodorous, musty, smelly

fut *abbr* future

fu·tile \ˈfyüt-ᵊl, ˈfyü-ˌtīl\ *adj* **1** ♦ **:** serving no useful purpose : USELESS, VAIN **2 :** FRIVOLOUS, TRIVIAL — **fu·tile·ly** *adv* — **fu·til·i·ty** \fyü-ˈti-lə-tē\ *n*

♦ empty, fruitless, hopeless, ineffective, meaningless, pointless, unproductive, unsuccessful, useless, vain *Ant* effective, fruitful, productive, profitable, successful

fu·ton \ˈfü-ˌtän\ *n* **:** a usu. cotton-filled mattress used on the floor or in a frame as a bed, couch, or chair

¹**fu·ture** \ˈfyü-chər\ *adj* **1 :** of, relating to, or constituting a verb tense that expresses time yet to come **2 :** coming after the present

²**future** *n* **1** ♦ **:** time that is to come **2 :** what is going to happen **3 :** an expectation of advancement or progressive development **4 :** the future tense; *also* : a verb form in it

♦ hereafter *Ant* past

fu·tur·ism \ˈfyü-chə-ˌri-zəm\ *n* **:** a modern movement in art, music, and literature that tries esp. to express the energy and activity of mechanical processes

fu·tur·ist \ˈfyü-chə-rist\ *n* ♦ **:** one who studies and predicts the future esp. on the basis of current trends

♦ augur, diviner, forecaster, fortune-teller, prognosticator, prophet, seer, soothsayer

fu·tur·is·tic \ˌfyü-chə-ˈris-tik\ *adj* **:** of or relating to the future or to futurism; *also* : very modern

fu·tur·i·ty \fyu̇-ˈtu̇r-ə-tē, -ˈtyu̇r-\ *n, pl* **-ties** **1 :** time that is to come : FUTURE **2 :** the quality or state of being future **3** *pl* : future events or prospects

fuze *var of* FUSE

fuzz \ˈfəz\ *n* ♦ **:** fine light particles or fibers (as of down or fluff)

♦ down, floss, fluff, fur, lint, nap, pile

fuzzy \ˈfə-zē\ *adj* **fuzz·i·er; -est** **1** ♦ **:** having or resembling fuzz **2** ♦ **:** lacking in clarity or definition **3 :** being or relating to pleasant usu. sentimental emotions ⟨∼ feelings⟩ — **fuzz·i·ness** \-zē-nəs\ *n*

♦ [1] furry, hairy, rough, shaggy, woolly ♦ [2] indefinite, unclear, vague

fuzzy logic *n* **:** a system of logic in which a statement can be true, false, or any of a continuum of values in between

fwd *abbr* forward

FWD *abbr* front-wheel drive

FY *abbr* fiscal year

-fy *vb suffix* **:** make : form into ⟨dandi*fy*⟩

FYI *abbr* for your information

¹**g** \ˈjē\ *n, pl* **g's** *or* **gs** \ˈjēz\ *often cap* **1 :** the 7th letter of the English alphabet **2 :** a unit of force equal to the force exerted by gravity on a body at rest and used to indicate the force to which a body is subjected when accelerated **3** *slang* : a sum of $1000

²**g** *abbr, often cap* **1** game **2** gauge **3** good **4** gram **5** gravity

ga *abbr* gauge

¹**Ga** *abbr* Georgia

²**Ga** *symbol* gallium

GA *abbr* **1** general assembly **2** general average **3** general of the army **4** Georgia

gab \ˈgab\ *vb* **gabbed; gab·bing** ♦ **:** to talk in a rapid or thoughtless manner : CHATTER — **gab** *n*

♦ chat, converse, jaw, palaver, patter, prattle, rattle, talk, visit

gab·ar·dine \ˈga-bər-ˌdēn\ *n* **1 :** GABERDINE 1 **2 :** a firm durable twilled fabric having diagonal ribs and made of various fibers; *also* : a garment of gabardine

gab·ble \ˈga-bəl\ *vb* **gab·bled; gab·bling** ♦ **:** to talk fast or foolishly : JABBER, BABBLE — **gab·bler** \-b(ə-)lər\ *n*

♦ babble, chatter, drivel, gibber, jabber, prattle, sputter

gab·by \ˈga-bē\ *adj* **gab·bi·er; -est** ♦ **:** pointlessly or annoyingly talkative : GARRULOUS

♦ chatty, conversational, garrulous, loquacious, talkative

gab·er·dine \ˈga-bər-ˌdēn\ *n* **1 :** a long loose outer garment worn in medieval times and associated esp. with Jews **2 :** GABARDINE 2

gab·fest \ˈgab-ˌfest\ *n* **1 :** an informal gathering for general talk **2** ♦ **:** an extended conversation

♦ chat, chatter, chitchat, gossip, palaver, rap, talk

ga·ble \ˈgā-bəl\ *n* **:** the vertical triangular end of a building formed by the sides of the roof sloping from the ridge down to the eaves — **ga·bled** \-bəld\ *adj*

Gab·o·nese \ˌga-bə-ˈnēz, -ˈnēs\ *n* **:** a native or inhabitant of Gabon — **Gabonese** *adj*

gad \ˈgad\ *vb* **gad·ded; gad·ding** ♦ **:** to be constantly active without specific purpose — usu. used with *about* ⟨*gadded* about Europe for a year⟩ — **gad·der** *n*

♦ *usu* **gad about** gallivant, knock, meander, rove, traipse, wander

gad·about \ˈga-də-ˌbau̇t\ *n* **:** a person who flits about in social activity

gad·fly \ˈgad-ˌflī\ *n* **1 :** a fly that bites or harasses livestock **2** ♦ **:** a person who annoys esp. by persistent criticism

♦ annoyance, bother, nuisance, persecutor, pest, tease

gad·get \ˈga-jət\ *n* ♦ **:** an often small mechanical or electronic device with a practical use but often thought of as a novelty : CONTRIVANCE — **gad·get·ry** \ˈga-jə-trē\ *n*

♦ contraption, contrivance, gimmick, gizmo, jigger

gad·o·lin·i·um \ˌga-də-ˈli-nē-əm\ *n* **:** a magnetic metallic chemical element

¹**Gael** \ˈgāl\ *n* **:** a Celtic inhabitant of Ireland or Scotland

²**Gael** *abbr* Gaelic

Gael·ic \ˈgā-lik\ *adj* **:** of or relating to the Gaels or their languages — **Gaelic** *n*

gaff \ˈgaf\ *n* **1 :** a spear used in taking fish or turtles; *also* : a metal hook for holding or lifting heavy fish **2 :** the spar supporting the top of a fore-and-aft sail **3 :** rough treatment : ABUSE — **gaff** *vb*

gaffe \ˈgaf\ *n* **1** ♦ **:** a usu. social blunder **2** ♦ **:** a noticeable mistake

♦ [1] familiarity, impropriety, indiscretion ♦ [2] blunder, error, fault, flub, fumble, goof, lapse, miscue, misstep, mistake, oversight, screwup, slip, stumble, trip

gaf·fer \ˈga-fər\ *n* **1 :** an old man **2 :** a lighting electrician on a motion-picture or television set

¹**gag** \ˈgag\ *vb* **gagged; gag·ging** **1 :** to restrict use of the mouth with a gag **2 :** to prevent from speaking freely **3** ♦ **:** to retch or cause to retch **4 :** OBSTRUCT, CHOKE **5 :** BALK **6 :** to make quips — **gag·ger** *n*

♦ heave, spit up, throw up, vomit

²**gag** *n* **1 :** something thrust into the mouth esp. to prevent speech or outcry **2 :** an official check or restraint on free speech **3** ♦ **:** a laugh-provoking remark or act **4 :** PRANK, TRICK

♦ crack, jest, joke, laugh, pleasantry, quip, sally, waggery, wisecrack, witticism

¹**gage** \ˈgāj\ *n* **1 :** a token of defiance; *esp* : a glove or cap cast on the ground as a pledge of combat **2** ♦ **:** something deposited as a pledge of performance : SECURITY

♦ guarantee, guaranty, pawn, pledge, security

²**gage** *var of* GAUGE

gag·gle \'ga-gəl\ *n* **1 :** a flock of geese **2 :** an unorganized group

gai·ety \'gā-ə-tē\ *n, pl* **-eties 1 ♦ :** festive activity : MERRYMAKING **2 :** MERRIMENT **3 ♦ :** dressy or showy clothing and jewels : FINERY

♦ [1] conviviality, festivity, jollification, merriment, merrymaking, revelry ♦ [3] array, best, bravery, caparison, feather, finery, frippery, full dress, regalia

gai·ly \'gā-lē\ *adv* ♦ **:** in a cheerful or happy manner ⟨chatting ∼⟩

♦ cheerfully, happily, heartily, jovially, merrily, mirthfully *Ant* bleakly, cheerlessly, darkly, heavily, miserably, morosely, unhappily ♦ exuberantly, jauntily, sprightly *Ant* dully, inanimately, sluggishly, tardily ♦ flamboyantly, flashily, jauntily, rakishly *Ant* conservatively, plain, quietly

¹gain \'gān\ *n* **1 ♦ :** resources or advantage acquired or increased : PROFIT **2 :** ACQUISITION, ACCUMULATION **3 ♦ :** an increase in amount, magnitude, or degree

♦ [1] earnings, lucre, net, payoff, proceeds, profit, return ♦ [3] accretion, addition, augmentation, boost, expansion, increase, increment, plus, proliferation, raise, rise, supplement

²gain *vb* **1 ♦ :** to get possession of usu. by effort, merit, or craft : EARN **2 :** WIN ⟨∼ a victory⟩ **3 ♦ :** to increase in ⟨∼ momentum⟩ **4 :** PERSUADE **5 :** to arrive at **6 :** ACHIEVE ⟨∼ strength⟩ **7 :** to run fast ⟨the watch ∼s a minute a day⟩ **8 :** PROFIT **9 :** INCREASE **10 ♦ :** to improve in health — **gain·er** *n*

♦ [1] acquire, attain, capture, carry, draw, earn, garner, get, land, make, obtain, procure, realize, secure, win ♦ [3] build, gather, grow, pick up *Ant* decrease (in), lose ♦ [10] convalesce, heal, mend, rally, recover, recuperate, snap back

gain·ful \'gān-fəl\ *adj* ♦ **:** productive of gain : PROFITABLE — **gain·ful·ly** *adv*

♦ fat, lucrative, profitable, remunerative

gain·say \,gān-'sā\ *vb* **-said** \-'sād, -'sed\; **-say·ing; -says** \-'sāz, -'sez\ **1 ♦ :** to declare to be untrue or invalid : DENY **2 :** to speak against — **gain·say·er** *n*

♦ contradict, deny, disallow, disavow, disclaim, negate, negative, reject, repudiate

gait \'gāt\ *n* **:** manner of moving on foot; *also* **:** a particular pattern or style of such moving — **gait·ed** *adj*

gai·ter \'gā-tər\ *n* **1 :** a leg covering reaching from the instep to ankle, mid-calf, or knee **2 :** an overshoe with a fabric upper **3 :** an ankle-high shoe with elastic gores in the sides

¹gal \'gal\ *n* **:** GIRL, WOMAN

²gal *abbr* gallon

Gal *abbr* Galatians

ga·la \'gā-lə, 'ga-, 'gä-\ *n* ♦ **:** a festive celebration : FESTIVITY — **gala** *adj*

♦ carnival, celebration, festival, festivity, fete, fiesta, jubilee

ga·lac·tic \gə-'lak-tik\ *adj* **:** of or relating to a galaxy

Ga·la·tians \gə-'lā-shənz\ *n* **:** an argumentative letter of St. Paul written to the Christians of Galatia and included as a book in the New Testament

gal·axy \'ga-lək-sē\ *n, pl* **-ax·ies 1** *often cap* **:** MILKY WAY GALAXY — used with *the* **2 :** a very large group of stars **3 :** an assemblage of brilliant or famous persons or things

gale \'gāl\ *n* **1 :** a strong wind **2 ♦ :** an emotional outburst ⟨∼s of laughter⟩

♦ agony, burst, eruption, explosion, fit, flare, flare-up, flash, flush, gush, gust, outburst, paroxysm, spasm, storm

ga·le·na \gə-'lē-nə\ *n* **:** a lustrous bluish gray mineral that consists of the sulfide of lead and is the chief ore of lead

¹gall \'gol\ *n* **1 :** BILE **2 :** something bitter to endure **3 ♦ :** bitterness of spirit : RANCOR **4 ♦ :** brazen boldness coupled with impudent assurance and insolence : IMPUDENCE

♦ [3] animosity, antagonism, antipathy, bitterness, enmity, grudge, hostility, rancor ♦ [4] audacity, brass, brazenness, cheek, chutzpah, effrontery, impudence, nerve, presumption, sauce, sauciness, temerity

²gall *n* **:** a skin sore caused by chafing

³gall *vb* **1 ♦ :** to make or become sore or worn by rubbing : CHAFE **2 ♦ :** to provoke impatience, anger, or displeasure in : VEX

♦ [1] abrade, chafe, erode, fray, fret, rub, wear ♦ [2] aggravate, annoy, bother, bug, chafe, exasperate, get, grate, irk, irritate, nettle, peeve, persecute, pique, put out, rasp, rile, vex

⁴gall *n* **:** an abnormal outgrowth of plant tissue usu. due to parasites

¹gal·lant \gə-'lant, -'länt; 'ga-lənt\ *n* **1 :** a young man of fashion **2 :** a man who shows a marked fondness for the company of women and who is esp. attentive to them **3 :** one who courts a woman or seeks to marry her : SUITOR

♦ buck, dandy, dude, fop

²gal·lant \'ga-lənt (*usual for 2, 3, 4*); gə-'lant, -'länt (*usual for 5*)\ *adj* **1 :** showy in dress or bearing : SMART **2 :** impressive in size or splendor : SPLENDID, STATELY **3 ♦ :** full of energy, animation, or courage : SPIRITED, BRAVE **4 ♦ :** nobly chivalrous and often self-sacrificing **5 :** polite and attentive to women

♦ [3] brave, courageous, dauntless, doughty, fearless, heroic, intrepid, spirited, stalwart, stout, undaunted, valiant, valorous ♦ [4] chivalrous, great, greathearted, high, high-minded, lofty, lordly, magnanimous, noble, sublime

gal·lant·ly *adv* ♦ **:** in a gallant manner

♦ grandly, greatly, heroically, honorably (*or* honourably), magnanimously, nobly

gal·lant·ry \'ga-lən-trē\ *n, pl* **-ries 1** *archaic* **:** gallant appearance **2 :** an act of marked courtesy **3 :** courteous attention to a woman **4 ♦ :** conspicuous bravery

♦ bravery, courage, daring, fearlessness, guts, hardihood, heart, heroism, nerve, stoutness, valor

gall·blad·der \'gol-,bla-dər\ *n* **:** a membranous muscular sac attached to the liver and serving to store bile

gal·le·on \'ga-lē-ən\ *n* **:** a large square-rigged sailing ship formerly used esp. by the Spanish

gal·le·ria \,ga-lə-'rē-ə\ *n* **:** a roofed and usu. glass-enclosed promenade or court

gal·lery \'ga-lə-rē\ *n, pl* **-ler·ies 1 :** an outdoor balcony; *also* **:** PORCH, VERANDA **2 :** a long narrow passage, apartment, or hall **3 :** a narrow passage (as one made underground by a miner or through wood by an insect) **4 :** a room where works of art are exhibited; *also* **:** an organization dealing in works of art **5 :** a balcony in a theater, auditorium, or church; *esp* **:** the highest one in a theater **6 :** the spectators at a tennis or golf match **7 :** a photographer's studio — **gal·ler·ied** \-rēd\ *adj*

♦ corridor, hall, hallway, passage

gal·ley \'ga-lē\ *n, pl* **galleys 1 :** a long low ship propelled esp. by oars and formerly used esp. in the Mediterranean Sea **2 :** the kitchen esp. of a ship or airplane **3 :** a proof of typeset matter esp. in a single column

Gal·lic \'ga-lik\ *adj* **:** of or relating to Gaul or France

gal·li·mau·fry \,ga-lə-'mo-frē\ *n, pl* **-fries :** HODGEPODGE

gall·ing \'go-liŋ\ *adj* ♦ **:** markedly irritating

♦ aggravating, annoying, bothersome, frustrating, irksome, irritating, pesty, vexatious

gal·li·nule \'ga-lə-,nül, -,nyül\ *n* **:** any of several aquatic birds related to the rails

gal·li·um \'ga-lē-əm\ *n* **:** a bluish white metallic chemical element

gal·li·vant \'ga-lə-,vant\ *vb* ♦ **:** to travel, roam, or move about for pleasure

♦ gad, knock, maunder, meander, mope, ramble, range, roam, rove, traipse, wander

gal·lon \'ga-lən\ *n* **:** a unit of liquid capacity equal to 231 cubic inches or four quarts

¹gal·lop \'ga-ləp\ *vb* **1 :** to go or cause to go at a gallop **2 ♦ :** to run fast — **gal·lop·er** *n*

♦ dash, jog, run, scamper, sprint, trip

²gallop *n* **1 :** a bounding gait of a quadruped; *esp* **:** a fast 3-beat gait of a horse **2 :** a ride or run at a gallop

gal·lows \'ga-lōz\ *n, pl* **gallows** *or* **gal·lows·es :** a frame usu. of two upright posts and a crosspiece from which criminals are hanged; *also* **:** the punishment of hanging

gall·stone \'gol-,stōn\ *n* **:** an abnormal concretion occurring in the gallbladder or bile passages

gal·lus·es \'ga-lə-səz\ *n pl* **:** SUSPENDERS

ga·lore \gə-'lōr\ *adj* **:** amply supplied : characterized by, constituting, or existing in plenty

ga·losh \gə-'läsh\ *n* **:** a high overshoe

galv *abbr* galvanized

gal·va·nise *chiefly Brit var of* GALVANIZE

gal·va·nize \'gal-və-,nīz\ *vb* **-nized; -niz·ing 1 ♦ :** to stimulate as if by an electric shock **2 :** to coat (iron or steel) with zinc — **gal·va·ni·za·tion** \,gal-və-nə-'zā-shən\ *n* — **gal·va·niz·er** *n*

♦ electrify, excite, exhilarate, intoxicate, thrill, titillate, turn on

gal·va·nom·e·ter \ˌgal-və-ˈnä-mə-tər\ *n* : an instrument for detecting or measuring a small electric current

Gam·bi·an \ˈgam-bē-ən\ *n* : a native or inhabitant of Gambia — **Gambian** *adj*

gam·bit \ˈgam-bət\ *n* **1** : a chess opening in which a player risks one or more minor pieces to gain an advantage in position **2** : a calculated move : STRATAGEM

¹**gam·ble** \ˈgam-bəl\ *vb* **gam·bled; gam·bling 1** : to play a game for money or property **2** ♦ : to bet on an uncertain outcome : WAGER **3** ♦ : to expose to hazard : VENTURE, HAZARD

♦ [2] bet, go, lay, stake, wager ♦ *usu* **gamble on** [2] chance, hazard, risk, venture ♦ *usu* **gamble with** [3] adventure, compromise, hazard, imperil, jeopardize, menace, risk, venture

²**gamble** *n* ♦ : something chancy

♦ chance, enterprise, flier, speculation, venture

¹**gam·bol** \ˈgam-bəl\ *vb* **-boled** *or* **-bolled; -bol·ing** *or* **-bol·ling** ♦ : to skip about in play : FRISK

♦ caper, cavort, disport, frisk, frolic, lark, rollick, romp, sport

²**gambol** *n* : a skipping or leaping about in play

gam·brel roof \ˈgam-brəl-\ *n* : a roof with a lower steeper slope and an upper flatter one on each side

¹**game** \ˈgām\ *n* **1** : AMUSEMENT, DIVERSION **2** ♦ : often derisive or mocking jesting : SPORT, FUN **3** ♦ : a procedure or strategy for gaining an end : SCHEME, PROJECT **4** : a line of work : PROFESSION **5** ♦ : a physical or mental competition conducted according to rules with the participants in direct opposition to each other : CONTEST **6** : animals hunted for sport or food; *also* : the flesh of a game animal

♦ [2] fun, jest, play, sport ♦ [3] arrangement, blueprint, design, plan, project, scheme, strategy, system ♦ [5] bout, competition, contest, event, match, meet, tournament

²**game** *vb* **gamed; gam·ing** : to play for a stake : GAMBLE

³**game** *adj* ♦ : having or showing a resolute unyielding spirit; *also* : willing or ready to proceed — **game·ly** *adv*

♦ amenable, disposed, glad, inclined, ready, willing

⁴**game** *adj* : LAME ⟨a ∼ leg⟩

game·cock \ˈgām-ˌkäk\ *n* : a rooster trained for fighting

game fish *n* : SPORT FISH

game·keep·er \ˈgām-ˌkē-pər\ *n* : a person in charge of the breeding and protection of game animals or birds on a private preserve

game·ness *n* ♦ : the state or quality of being game

♦ alacrity, goodwill, willingness

game·some \ˈgām-səm\ *adj* : MERRY

game·ster \ˈgām-stər\ *n* : a person who gambles

gam·ete \ˈga-ˌmēt\ *n* : a mature germ cell — **ga·met·ic** \gə-ˈme-tik\ *adj*

game theory *n* : the analysis of a situation involving conflicting interests (as in business) in terms of gains and losses among opposing players

gam·in \ˈga-mən\ *n* **1** : a boy who loiters on the streets **2** : GAMINE 2

ga·mine \ga-ˈmēn\ *n* **1** : a girl who loiters on the streets **2** : a small playfully mischievous girl

gam·ma \ˈga-mə\ *n* : the 3d letter of the Greek alphabet — Γ or γ

gamma globulin *n* : a blood protein fraction rich in antibodies; *also* : a solution of this from human blood donors that is given to provide immunity against some infectious diseases (as measles)

gamma ray *n* : a photon emitted by a radioactive substance; *also* : a high-energy photon — usu. used in pl.

gam·mer \ˈga-mər\ *n, archaic* : an old woman

gam·mon \ˈga-mən\ *n, chiefly Brit* : a cured ham or side of bacon

gam·ut \ˈga-mət\ *n* ♦ : an entire range or series

♦ range, scale, spectrum, spread, stretch

gamy *or* **gam·ey** \ˈgā-mē\ *adj* **gam·i·er; -est 1** : GAME, PLUCKY **2** : having the flavor of game esp. when near tainting ⟨∼ meats⟩ **3** : SCANDALOUS; *also* : DISREPUTABLE — **gam·i·ness** \-mē-nəs\ *n*

¹**gan·der** \ˈgan-dər\ *n* : a male goose

²**gander** *n* ♦ : the act of looking : GLANCE

♦ cast, eye, glance, glimpse, look, peek, peep, regard, sight, view

¹**gang** \ˈgaŋ\ *n* **1** : a set of implements or devices arranged to operate together **2 a** ♦ : a group of persons working or associated together **b** ♦ : a group of esp. young people working to unlawful or antisocial ends

♦ [2a] band, company, crew, outfit, party, squad, team

♦ [2a] circle, clan, clique, coterie, crowd, fold, ring, set ♦ [2b] cabal, conspiracy, mob, ring, syndicate

²**gang** *vb* **1** : to attack in a gang — usu. used with *up* **2** : to form into or move or act as a gang

gang·land \ˈgaŋ-ˌland\ *n* : the world of organized crime

gan·gling \ˈgaŋ-gliŋ\ *adj* ♦ : loosely and awkwardly built : LANKY

♦ lanky, rangy, spindly

gan·gli·on \ˈgaŋ-glē-ən\ *n, pl* **-glia** \-ə\ *also* **-gli·ons** : a mass of nerve tissue containing cell bodies of neurons outside the central nervous system; *also* : NUCLEUS 3 — **gan·gli·on·ic** \ˌgaŋ-glē-ˈä-nik\ *adj*

gan·gly \ˈgaŋ-glē\ *adj* : GANGLING

gang·plank \ˈgaŋ-ˌplaŋk\ *n* : a movable bridge from a ship to the shore

gang·plow \-ˌplau̇\ *n* : a plow that turns two or more furrows at one time

gan·grene \ˈgaŋ-ˌgrēn, gaŋ-ˈgrēn\ *n* : the death of soft tissues in a local area of the body due to loss of the blood supply — **gan·grene** *vb* — **gan·gre·nous** \ˈgaŋ-grə-nəs\ *adj*

gang·ster \ˈgaŋ-stər\ *n* ♦ : a member of a gang of criminals : RACKETEER

♦ bully, goon, hood, hoodlum, mobster, mug, punk, rowdy, ruffian, thug, tough

gang·way \ˈgaŋ-ˌwā\ *n* **1** : PASSAGEWAY; *also* : GANGPLANK **2** : clear passage through a crowd

gan·net \ˈga-nət\ *n, pl* **gannets** *also* **gannet** : any of several large fish-eating usu. white and black seabirds that breed chiefly on offshore islands

gantlet *var of* GAUNTLET

gan·try \ˈgan-trē\ *n, pl* **gantries** : a frame structure on side supports over or around something

GAO *abbr* General Accounting Office

gaol \ˈjāl\, **gaol·er** \ˈjā-lər\ *chiefly Brit var of* JAIL, JAILER

gap \ˈgap\ *n* **1** : BREACH, CLEFT **2** ♦ : a mountain pass **3** ♦ : a blank space; *also* : an incomplete or deficient area **4** : a wide difference in character or attitude **5** : a problem caused by a disparity ⟨credibility ∼⟩

♦ [2] canyon, defile, flume, gorge, gulch, notch, pass, ravine ♦ [3] breach, break, gulf, hole, opening, rent, rift, separation ♦ [3] discontinuity, hiatus, interim, interlude, intermission, interruption, interval *Ant* continuation, continuity

gape \ˈgāp\ *vb* **gaped; gap·ing 1** : to open the mouth wide **2** : to open or part widely **3** ♦ : to stare with mouth open **4** : YAWN — **gape** *n*

♦ gawk, gaze, goggle, peer, rubberneck, stare

¹**gar** \ˈgär\ *n* : any of several fishes that have a long body resembling that of a pike and long narrow jaws

²**gar** *abbr* garage

GAR *abbr* Grand Army of the Republic

¹**ga·rage** \gə-ˈräzh, -ˈräj\ *n* : a shelter or repair shop for automobiles

²**garage** *vb* **ga·raged; ga·rag·ing** : to keep or put in a garage

garage sale *n* : a sale of used household or personal articles held on the seller's own premises

¹**garb** \ˈgärb\ *n* **1** ♦ : style of dress **2** : outward form : APPEARANCE

♦ dress, getup, guise, outfit

²**garb** *vb* ♦ : to cover with or as if with clothing

♦ apparel, array, attire, caparison, clothe, deck, dress, invest, rig, suit

gar·bage \ˈgär-bij\ *n* **1** : food waste **2** ♦ : unwanted or useless material

♦ chaff, deadwood, dust, junk, litter, refuse, riffraff, rubbish, scrap, trash, waste *Ant* find, prize

gar·bage·man \-ˌman\ *n* : a person who collects and removes garbage

gar·ble \ˈgär-bəl\ *vb* **gar·bled; gar·bling** ♦ : to distort the meaning of ⟨∼ a story⟩

♦ color (*or* colour), distort, falsify, misinterpret, misrepresent, misstate, pervert, twist, warp

gar·çon \gär-ˈsōⁿ\ *n, pl* **garçons** *same or* -ˈsōⁿz\ : WAITER

¹**gar·den** \ˈgär-dᵊn\ *n* **1** : a plot for growing fruits, flowers, or vegetables **2** : a public recreation area; *esp* : one for displaying plants or animals

²**garden** *vb* : to lay out or work in a garden — **gar·den·er** *n*

gar·de·nia \gär-ˈdē-nyə\ *n* : any of a genus of tropical trees or

shrubs that are related to the madder and have fragrant white or yellow flowers; *also* **:** one of these trees
gar·den–va·ri·e·ty *adj* **:** COMMONPLACE, ORDINARY
gar·fish \'gär-ˌfish\ *n* **:** GAR
gar·gan·tuan \gär-'gan-chə-wən\ *adj, often cap* ♦ **:** of tremendous size or volume

♦ colossal, enormous, giant, ginormous, huge, jumbo, mammoth, massive, prodigious, titanic, tremendous

gar·gle \'gär-gəl\ *vb* **gar·gled; gar·gling :** to rinse the throat with liquid agitated by air forced through it from the lungs — **gargle** *n*
gar·goyle \'gär-ˌgȯ(-ə)il\ *n* **1 :** a waterspout in the form of a grotesque human or animal figure projecting from the roof or eaves of a building **2 :** a grotesquely carved figure
gar·ish \'gar-ish\ *adj* **1 :** clothed in vivid colors **:** excessively or disturbingly vivid **2** ♦ **:** tastelessly showy **:** FLASHY, GAUDY

♦ flamboyant, flashy, gaudy, glitzy, loud, ostentatious, swank, tawdry

gar·ish·ness *n* **:** the quality or state of being garish
¹gar·land \'gär-lənd\ *n* **:** a decorative wreath or rope (as of leaves)
²garland *vb* **:** to form into or deck with a garland
gar·lic \'gär-lik\ *n* **:** an herb related to the lilies and grown for its pungent bulbs used in cooking; *also* **:** its bulb — **gar·licky** \-li-kē\ *adj*
gar·ment \'gär-mənt\ *n* **:** an article of clothing
gar·ner \'gär-nər\ *vb* **1 :** to gather into storage **2** ♦ **:** to acquire by effort **3** ♦ **:** to pick up **:** ACCUMULATE, COLLECT

♦ [2] acquire, attain, capture, carry, draw, earn, gain, get, land, make, obtain, procure, realize, secure, win ♦ [3] accumulate, amass, assemble, collect, concentrate, gather, group, lump, pick up, round up, scrape

gar·net \'gär-nət\ *n* **:** a transparent deep red mineral sometimes used as a gem
¹gar·nish \'gär-nish\ *vb* **1** ♦ **:** to furnish with something ornamental **:** DECORATE, EMBELLISH **2 :** to add decorative or savory touches to (food) **3 :** GARNISHEE

♦ adorn, array, beautify, bedeck, deck, decorate, do, dress, embellish, enrich, grace, ornament, trim

²garnish *n* **1** ♦ **:** something that lends grace or beauty **2 :** something (as lemon wedges or parsley) used to garnish food or drink

♦ adornment, caparison, decoration, embellishment, frill, ornament, trim

gar·nish·ee \ˌgär-nə-'shē\ *vb* **-eed; -ee·ing 1 :** to serve with a garnishment **2 :** to take (as a debtor's wages) by legal authority
gar·nish·ment \'gär-nish-mənt\ *n* **1 :** GARNISH **2 :** a legal warning concerning the attachment of property to satisfy a debt; *also* **:** the attachment of such property
gar·ni·ture \-ni-chər, -ˌchu̇r\ *n* **:** EMBELLISHMENT, TRIMMING
gar·ret \'gar-ət\ *n* **:** the part of a house just under the roof **:** ATTIC
gar·ri·son \'gar-ə-sən\ *n* **1 :** a military post; *esp* **:** a permanent military installation **2 :** the troops stationed at a garrison — **garrison** *vb*
garrison state *n* **:** a state organized on a primarily military basis
¹gar·rote *or* **ga·rotte** \gə-'rät, -'rōt\ *n* **1 :** a method of execution by strangulation; *also* **:** the apparatus used **2 :** an implement (as a wire with handles) for strangulation
²garrote *or* **garotte** *vb* ♦ **:** to strangle with or as if with a garrote

♦ choke, strangle, throttle

gar·ru·lous \'gar-ə-ləs\ *adj* **1 :** WORDY **2** ♦ **:** pointlessly or annoyingly talkative — **gar·ru·li·ty** \gə-'rü-lə-tē\ *n* — **gar·ru·lous·ly** *adv* — **gar·ru·lous·ness** *n*

♦ chatty, conversational, gabby, loquacious, talkative

gar·ter \'gär-tər\ *n* **:** a band or strap worn to hold up a stocking or sock
garter snake *n* **:** any of a genus of harmless American snakes with longitudinal stripes on the back
¹gas \'gas\ *n, pl* **gas·es** *also* **gas·ses 1 :** a fluid (as hydrogen or air) that tends to expand indefinitely **2 :** a gas or mixture of gases used as a fuel or anesthetic **3 :** a substance that can be used to produce a poisonous, asphyxiating, or irritant atmosphere **4 :** GASOLINE **5** ♦ **:** empty talk

♦ bombast, grandiloquence, hot air, rhetoric, wind

²gas *vb* **gassed; gas·sing 1 :** to treat with gas; *also* **:** to poison with gas **2 :** to fill with gasoline ⟨~ up the car⟩ **3 :** to talk idly or garrulously
gas·eous \'ga-sē-əs, -shəs\ *adj* **1 :** having the form of or being gas **2 :** characterized by many words but little content

♦ bombastic, grandiloquent, oratorical, rhetorical, windy

¹gash \'gash\ *n* ♦ **:** a deep long cut

♦ laceration, rent, rip, slash, slit, tear

²gash *vb* **:** to make a gash in
gas·ket \'gas-kət\ *n* **:** material (as rubber) or a part used to seal a joint
gas·light \'gas-ˌlīt\ *n* **1 :** light made by burning illuminating gas **2 :** a gas flame; *also* **:** a gas lighting fixture
gas mask *n* **:** a mask with a chemical air filter used to protect the face and lungs against poison gas
gas·o·line \'ga-sə-ˌlēn, ˌga-sə-'lēn\ *n* **:** a flammable liquid mixture made from petroleum and used esp. as a motor fuel
gasp \'gasp\ *vb* **1 :** to catch the breath audibly (as with shock) **2** ♦ **:** to breathe laboriously **:** PANT **3 :** to utter in a gasping manner — **gasp** *n*

♦ blow, pant, puff, wheeze

gas·tric \'gas-trik\ *adj* **:** of or relating to the stomach
gastric juice *n* **:** the acid digestive secretion of the stomach
gas·tri·tis \gas-'trī-təs\ *n* **:** inflammation of the lining of the stomach
gas·tro·en·ter·ol·o·gy \ˌgas-trō-ˌen-tə-'rä-lə-jē\ *n* **:** a branch of medicine concerned with the structure, functions, and diseases of the stomach and intestines — **gas·tro·en·ter·ol·o·gist** \-jist\ *n*
gas·tro·in·tes·ti·nal \ˌgas-trō-in-'tes-tən-ᵊl\ *adj* **:** of, relating to, affecting, or including both the stomach and intestine ⟨~ tract⟩ ⟨~ distress⟩
gas·tron·o·my \gas-'trä-nə-mē\ *n* **:** the art of good eating — **gas·tro·nom·ic** \ˌgas-trə-'nä-mik\ *also* **gas·tro·nom·i·cal** \-mi-kəl\ *adj*
gas·tro·pod \'gas-trə-ˌpäd\ *n* **:** any of a large class of mollusks (as snails and slugs) with a muscular foot and a spiral shell or none — **gastropod** *adj*
gas·works \'gas-ˌwərks\ *n sing or pl* **:** a plant for manufacturing gas
gate \'gāt\ *n* **1** ♦ **:** an opening for passage in a wall or fence **2 :** a city or castle entrance often with defensive structures **3 :** the frame or door that closes a gate **4** ♦ **:** a device (as a valve) for controlling the passage of a fluid or signal **5 :** the total admission receipts or the number of people at an event

♦ [1] door, hatch, portal ♦ [1] door, doorway, entrance, way
♦ [4] cock, faucet, spigot, tap, valve

-gate \ˌgāt\ *n comb form* **:** usu. political scandal often involving the concealment of wrongdoing
gate–crash·er \'gāt-ˌkra-shər\ *n* **:** a person who enters without paying admission or attends without invitation
gat·ed \'gāt-əd\ *adj* **1 :** having or controlled by a gate **2 :** designed to restrict entrance usu. by means of barriers, a private security fence, and a controlled gate ⟨a ~ community⟩
gate·keep·er \'gāt-ˌkē-pər\ *n* ♦ **:** a person who tends or guards a gate

♦ doorkeeper, janitor

gate·post \-ˌpōst\ *n* **:** the post to which a gate is hung or the one against which it closes
gate·way \-ˌwā\ *n* **1 :** an opening for a gate **2** ♦ **:** a means of entrance or exit

♦ access, admission, doorway, entrance, entry, entrée

gateway drug *n* **:** a drug (as marijuana) whose use is thought to lead to the use of and dependence on a harder drug
¹gath·er \'ga-thər\ *vb* **1** ♦ **:** to bring or come together **:** COLLECT **2** ♦ **:** to bring in a crop **:** PICK, HARVEST **3** ♦ **:** to pick up little by little **4 :** to gain or win by gradual increase **:** ACCUMULATE ⟨~ speed⟩ **5 :** to summon up ⟨~ courage to dive⟩ **6 :** to draw or close to something **7 :** to pull (fabric) along a line of stitching into puckers **8** ♦ **:** to reach a conclusion often intuitively from hints or through inferences **:** DEDUCE, INFER **9 :** ASSEMBLE **10 :** to swell out and fill with pus **11 :** GROW, INCREASE — **gath·er·er** *n*

♦ [1] accumulate, amass, assemble, collect, concentrate, garner, group, lump, pick up, round up, scrape *Ant* dispel, disperse, dissipate, scatter ♦ [1] assemble, congregate, convene, forgather, meet, rendezvous ♦ [2] harvest, pick, reap ♦ [3] build, gain, grow, pick up ♦ [8] conclude, deduce, extrapolate, infer, judge, reason, understand

²gather *n* **:** a puckering in cloth made by gathering
gathering *n* **1** ♦ **:** a company of persons gathered for deliberation and legislation, worship, or entertainment **2** ♦ **:** something compiled

♦ [1] assemblage, assembly, conference, congregation, convocation, meeting, muster ♦ [2] accumulation, assemblage, collection

GATT \\'gat\ *abbr* General Agreement on Tariffs and Trade
gauche \\'gōsh\ *adj* **1** ♦ : lacking social experience or grace; *also* : not tactful **2** : crudely made or done

♦ awkward, clumsy, graceless, inelegant, stiff, stilted, uncomfortable, uneasy, ungraceful, wooden

gau•che•rie \\ˌgō-shə-'rē\ *n* : a tactless or awkward action
gau•cho \\'gaù-chō\ *n, pl* **gauchos** : a cowboy of the So. American pampas
gaud \\'gòd\ *n* : a small ornament (as a jewel or ring)
gaud•i•ness \\-dē-nəs\ *n* ♦ : the quality or state of being gaudy

♦ flamboyance, flashiness, glitz, ostentation, pretentiousness, showiness, swank

gaudy \\'gò-dē\ *adj* **gaud•i•er; -est** **1** ♦ : ostentatiously or tastelessly ornamented **2** : marked by showiness or extravagance — **gaud•i•ly** \\-də-lē\ *adv*

♦ flamboyant, flashy, garish, glitzy, loud, ostentatious, swank, tawdry *Ant* conservative, quiet, understated

¹gauge *also* **gage** \\'gāj\ *n* **1** : measurement according to some standard or system **2** : DIMENSIONS, SIZE **3** *usu* gage : an instrument for measuring, testing, or registering
²gauge *also* **gage** *vb* **gauged** *also* **gaged; gaug•ing** *also* **gag•ing** **1** ♦ : to measure precisely the size, dimensions, or other measurable quantity of **2** : to determine the capacity or contents of **3** ♦ : to determine roughly the size, extent, or nature of : ESTIMATE, JUDGE

♦ [1] measure, scale, span ♦ [3] calculate, call, conjecture, estimate, figure, guess, judge, make, place, put, reckon, suppose

gaunt \\'gònt\ *adj* **1** ♦ : excessively thin and angular **2** : BARREN, DESOLATE — **gaunt•ness** *n*

♦ cadaverous, haggard, skeletal, wasted

¹gaunt•let \\'gònt-lət\ *n* **1** : a protective glove **2** : an open challenge (as to combat) **3** : a dress glove extending above the wrist
²gauntlet *n* **1** ♦ : a severe trial : ORDEAL **2** : a double file of men armed with weapons (as clubs) with which to strike at an individual who is made to run between them

♦ cross, ordeal, trial

gauze \\'gòz\ *n* : a very thin often transparent fabric used esp. for draperies and surgical dressings
gauzy *adj* **gauz•i•er; -est** ♦ : made of or resembling gauze; *also* : marked by vagueness, elusiveness, or fuzziness

♦ flimsy, insubstantial, sheer, unsubstantial

gave *past of* GIVE
gav•el \\'ga-vəl\ *n* : the mallet of a presiding officer or auctioneer
ga•votte \\gə-'vät\ *n* : a dance of French peasant origin marked by the raising rather than sliding of the feet
gawk \\'gòk\ *vb* ♦ : to gape or stare stupidly — **gawk•er** *n*

♦ gape, gaze, goggle, peer, rubberneck, stare

gawky \\'gò-kē\ *adj* **gawk•i•er; -est** ♦ : lacking ease or grace (as of movement or expression) : AWKWARD, CLUMSY — **gawk•i•ly** \\-kə-lē\ *adv*

♦ awkward, clumsy, graceless, heavy-handed, lubberly, lumpish, ungainly, unhandy

gay \\'gā\ *adj* **1** : happily excited : MERRY **2** : bright and lively in appearance **3** : brilliant in color **4** : given to social pleasures; *also* : LICENTIOUS **5** : of, relating to, or characterized by sexual or romantic attraction to people of one's same sex — often used to refer to men only
gayety, gayly *var of* GAIETY, GAILY
gaz *abbr* gazette
gaze \\'gāz\ *vb* **gazed; gaz•ing** ♦ : to fix the eyes in a steady intent look — **gaze** *n* — **gaz•er** *n*

♦ gape, gawk, goggle, peer, rubberneck, stare

ga•ze•bo \\gə-'zē-bō\ *n, pl* **-bos** **1** : BELVEDERE **2** : a freestanding roofed structure usu. open on the sides
ga•zelle \\gə-'zel\ *n, pl* **gazelles** *also* **gazelle** : any of numerous small swift graceful antelopes
ga•zette \\gə-'zet\ *n* **1** : NEWSPAPER **2** : an official journal
gaz•et•teer \\ˌga-zə-'tir\ *n* : a geographic dictionary
ga•zil•lion \\gə-'zil-yən\ *n* : ZILLION — **gazillion** *adj* — **ga•zil•lionth** \\-yənth\ *adj*
gaz•pa•cho \\gəz-'pä-(ˌ)chō, gə-'spä-\ *n, pl* **-chos** : a spicy soup usu. made from raw vegetables and served cold
GB *abbr* Great Britain
GCA *abbr* ground-controlled approach
gd *abbr* good
Gd *symbol* gadolinium

GDR *abbr* German Democratic Republic
Ge *symbol* germanium
gear \\'gir\ *n* **1** : CLOTHING **2** : movable property : GOODS **3** ♦ : the implements used in an operation or activity : EQUIPMENT ⟨fishing ∼⟩ **4** : a mechanism that performs a specific function ⟨steering ∼⟩ **5** : a toothed wheel **6** : working adjustment of gears ⟨in ∼⟩ **7** : an adjustment of transmission gears (as of an automobile or bicycle) that determines speed and direction of travel — **gear** *vb*

♦ accoutrements (*or* accouterments), apparatus, equipment, matériel, outfit, paraphernalia, tackle

gear•box \\'gir-ˌbäks\ *n* : TRANSMISSION 3
gear•shift \\-ˌshift\ *n* : a mechanism by which transmission gears are shifted
gear•wheel \\-ˌhwēl\ *n* : GEAR 5
gecko \\'ge-kō\ *n, pl* **geck•os** *also* **geck•oes** : any of numerous small chiefly tropical insect-eating lizards
GED *abbr* general equivalency diploma
geek \\'gēk\ *n* : a person of an intellectual bent who is often disliked — **geeky** *adj*
geese *pl of* GOOSE
gee•zer \\'gē-zər\ *n* : an odd or eccentric person usu. of old age
Gei•ger counter \\'gī-gər-\ *n* : an electronic instrument for detecting the presence of cosmic rays or radioactive substances
gei•sha \\'gā-shə, 'gē-\ *n, pl* **geisha** *or* **geishas** : a Japanese girl or woman who is trained to provide entertaining company for men
¹gel \\'jel\ *n* : a solid jellylike colloid (as gelatin dessert)
²gel *vb* ♦ : to change into or take on the form of a gel

♦ clot, coagulate, congeal, jell, set

gel•a•tin *also* **gel•a•tine** \\'je-lət-ᵊn\ *n* : glutinous material and esp. protein obtained from animal tissues by boiling and used as a food, in dyeing, and in photography; *also* : an edible jelly formed with gelatin
ge•lat•i•nous \\jə-'lat-ᵊn-əs\ *adj* ♦ : resembling gelatin or jelly

♦ adhesive, gluey, glutinous, gooey, gummy, sticky, viscid, viscous

geld \\'geld\ *vb* : CASTRATE
geld•ing *n* : a castrated male horse
gel•id \\'je-ləd\ *adj* : extremely cold
gem \\'jem\ *n* **1** ♦ : a usu. valuable stone cut and polished for ornament **2** ♦ : something valued for beauty or perfection ⟨a ∼ of colonial architecture⟩

♦ [1] brilliant, gemstone, jewel ♦ [2] catch, jewel, pearl, plum, prize, treasure

Gem•i•ni \\'je-mə-(ˌ)nē, -ˌnī; 'ge-mə-ˌnē\ *n* **1** : a zodiacal constellation between Taurus and Cancer usu. pictured as twins sitting together **2** : the 3d sign of the zodiac in astrology; *also* : one born under this sign
gem•ol•o•gy *or* **gem•mol•o•gy** \\je-'mä-lə-jē, jə-\ *n* : the science of gems — **gem•olog•i•cal** \\ˌje-mə-'lä-ji-kəl\ *adj* — **gem•ol•o•gist** *also* **gem•mol•o•gist** \\je-'mä-lə-jist\ *n*
gem•stone \\'jem-ˌstōn\ *n* : a mineral or petrified material that when cut and polished can be used in jewelry
gen *abbr* **1** general **2** genitive
Gen *abbr* Genesis
Gen AF *abbr* general of the air force
gen•darme \\'zhän-ˌdärm, 'jän-\ *n* : a member of a body of soldiers esp. in France serving as an armed police force
gen•der \\'jen-dər\ *n* **1** : any of two or more divisions within a grammatical class that determine agreement with and selection of other words or grammatical forms **2** : SEX 1 — **gen•der•less** *adj*
gender identity *n* : a person's internal sense of being male, female, or a combination of male and female, or neither male nor female
gene \\'jēn\ *n* : a part of DNA or RNA that contains chemical information needed to make a particular protein (as an enzyme) controlling or influencing an inherited bodily trait (as eye color) or activity or that influences or controls the activity of another gene or genes — **gen•ic** \\'jē-nik, 'je-\ *adj*
ge•ne•al•o•gy \\ˌjē-nē-'ä-lə-jē, ˌje-, -'a-\ *n, pl* **-gies** ♦ : an ancestral line : PEDIGREE, LINEAGE; *also* : the study of family pedigrees — **ge•ne•a•log•i•cal** \\ˌjē-nē-ə-'lä-ji-kəl, ˌje-\ *adj* — **ge•ne•a•log•i•cal•ly** \\-k(ə-)lē\ *adv* — **ge•ne•al•o•gist** \\ˌjē-nē-'ä-lə-jist, ˌje-; -'a-\ *n*

♦ ancestry, birth, blood, bloodline, breeding, descent, extraction, family tree, line, lineage, origin, parentage, pedigree, stock, strain

genera *pl of* GENUS

¹gen·er·al \'je-nə-rəl, 'jen-rəl\ *adj* **1 ♦** : of or relating to the whole **2** : taken as a whole **3** : relating to or covering all instances **4 ♦** : not special or specialized **5 ♦** : common to many ⟨a ∼ custom⟩ **6** : not limited in meaning : not specific **7** : holding superior rank ⟨inspector ∼⟩

♦ [1] blanket, common, generic, global, overall, universal *Ant* individual, particular ♦ [4] broad, nonspecific, overall, unlimited, wide *Ant* delineated, detailed, particularized, specific ♦ [5] characteristic, common, communal, contemporary, current, dominant, everyday, familiar, household, popular, predominant, present, public, rife, typical, universal, usual, well-known, widespread *Ant* uncommon, unpopular

²general *n* **1** : something that involves or is applicable to the whole **2** : a commissioned officer ranking next below a general of the army or a general of the air force **3** : a commissioned officer of the highest rank in the marine corps — **in general** : for the most part

general assembly *n* **1** : a legislative assembly; *esp* : a U.S. state legislature **2** *cap G&A* : the supreme deliberative body of the United Nations

gen·er·al·i·sa·tion, gen·er·al·ise *chiefly Brit var of* GENERALIZATION, GENERALIZE

gen·er·a·lis·si·mo \,je-nə-rə-'li-sə-,mō\ *n, pl* **-mos** : the chief commander of an army

gen·er·al·i·ty \,je-nə-'ra-lə-tē\ *n, pl* **-ties** **1** : the quality or state of being general **2** : a general statement, law, principle, or proposition : GENERALIZATION 2 **3** : a vague or inadequate statement **4 ♦** : the greatest part : BULK

♦ body, bulk, core, main, mass, staple, weight

gen·er·al·i·za·tion \,je-nə-rə-lə-'zā-shən, ,jen-rə-\ *n* **1** : the act or process of generalizing **2** : a general statement, law, principle, or proposition

gen·er·al·ize \'je-nə-rə-,līz, 'jen-rə-\ *vb* **-ized; -iz·ing** **1** : to make general **2** : to draw general conclusions from **3** : to reach a general conclusion esp. on the basis of particular instances **4** : to extend throughout the body

gen·er·al·ly \'jen-rə-lē, 'je-nə-\ *adv* **1** : in a general manner **2 ♦** : as a rule

♦ commonly, ordinarily, typically, usually ♦ altogether, basically, chiefly, largely, mainly, mostly, overall, predominantly, primarily, principally

general of the air force : a commissioned officer of the highest rank in the air force

general of the army : a commissioned officer of the highest rank in the army

general practitioner *n* : a physician or veterinarian whose practice is not limited to a specialty

gen·er·al·ship \'je-nə-rəl-,ship, 'jen-rəl-\ *n* **1** : office or tenure of office of a general **2** : LEADERSHIP **3** : military skill as a high commander

general store *n* : a retail store that carries a wide variety of goods but is not divided into departments

gen·er·ate \'je-nə-,rāt\ *vb* **-at·ed; -at·ing ♦** : to bring into existence : PRODUCE

♦ create, engender, induce, make, produce, spawn

gen·er·a·tion \,je-nə-'rā-shən\ *n* **1** : a body of living beings constituting a single step in the line of descent from an ancestor; *also* : the average period between generations **2** : PRODUCTION

Generation X *n* : the generation of Americans born in the 1960s and 1970s

gen·er·a·tive \'je-nə-rə-tiv, -,rā-tiv\ *adj* : having the power or function of generating, originating, producing, or reproducing ⟨∼ organs⟩

gen·er·a·tor \'je-nə-,rā-tər\ *n* **1** : one that generates **2** : a machine by which mechanical energy is changed into electrical energy

ge·ner·ic \jə-'ner-ik\ *adj* **1 ♦** : not specific : GENERAL **2** : not protected by a trademark ⟨a ∼ drug⟩ **3** : of or relating to a biological genus — **generic** *n* — **ge·ner·i·cal·ly** \-i-k(ə-)lē\ *adv*

♦ blanket, common, general, global, overall, universal

gen·er·os·i·ty \,je-nə-'rä-sə-tē\ *n* **1 ♦** : the quality or fact of being generous **2** : a generous act

♦ bounty, liberality, philanthropy, unselfishness

gen·er·ous \'je-nə-rəs\ *adj* **1 ♦** : free in giving or sharing **2** : HIGH-MINDED, NOBLE **3 ♦** : marked by abundance or ample proportions : COPIOUS — **gen·er·ous·ness** *n*

♦ [1] bountiful, charitable, free, liberal, munificent, openhanded, unselfish, unsparing *Ant* cheap, close, closefisted, miserly,

niggardly, parsimonious, penurious, selfish, stingy, tight, tightfisted, uncharitable ♦ [3] abundant, ample, bountiful, comfortable, copious, liberal, plentiful

gen·er·ous·ly \'je-nə-rəs-lē\ *adv* **♦** : in a generous manner

♦ bountifully, handsomely, liberally, well

gen·e·sis \'je-nə-səs\ *n, pl* **-e·ses** \-,sēz\ **♦** : the origin or coming into existence of something

♦ beginning, birth, commencement, dawn, launch, morning, onset, outset, start, threshold

Genesis *n* : the mainly narrative first book of canonical Jewish and Christian Scriptures

gene–splic·ing \-,splī-siŋ\ *n* : the process of preparing recombinant DNA

gene therapy *n* : the insertion of normal or altered genes into cells usu. to replace defective genes esp. in the treatment of genetic disorders

ge·net·ic \jə-'ne-tik\ *adj* **1** : of or relating to the origin, development, or causes of something **2 a** : of or relating to genetics **b ♦** : of, relating to, caused by, or controlled by genes — **ge·net·i·cal·ly** \-ti-k(ə-)lē\ *adv*

♦ hereditary, heritable, inborn, inherited

genetic code *n* : the chemical code that is the basis of genetic inheritance and consists of units of three linked chemical groups in DNA and RNA which specify particular amino acids used to make proteins or which start or stop the process of making proteins

genetic engineering *n* : the alteration of genetic material esp. by cutting up and joining together DNA from one or more species of organism and inserting the result into an organism — **genetically engineered** *adj*

ge·net·ics \jə-'ne-tiks\ *n* : a branch of biology dealing with heredity and variation — **ge·net·i·cist** \-tə-sist\ *n*

ge·nial \'jē-nyəl, 'jē-nē-əl\ *adj* **1** : favorable to growth or comfort ⟨∼ sunshine⟩ **2 ♦** : marked by or diffusing sympathy or friendliness ⟨a ∼ host⟩ — **ge·nial·ly** *adv*

♦ affable, agreeable, amiable, good-natured, gracious, nice, sweet, well-disposed ♦ amicable, companionable, comradely, cordial, friendly, hearty, hospitable, neighborly, sociable, warm, warmhearted

ge·nial·i·ty \,jē-nē-'a-lə-tē, jēn-'ya-\ *n* **♦** : the quality of being genial; *esp* : warmth of disposition and manners

♦ agreeableness, amenity, amiability, graciousness, niceness, pleasantness, sweetness

-gen·ic \'je-nik\ *adj comb form* **1** : producing : forming **2** : produced by : formed from **3** : suitable for production or reproduction by (such) a medium

ge·nie \'jē-nē\ *n, pl* **ge·nies** *also* **ge·nii** \-nē-,ī\ : a supernatural spirit that often takes human form usu. serving the person who calls on it

gen·i·tal \'je-nə-tᵊl\ *adj* **1** : concerned with reproduction ⟨∼ organs⟩ **2** : of, relating to, or characterized by the stage of psychosexual development in psychoanalytic theory in which oral and anal impulses are subordinated to adaptive interpersonal mechanisms — **gen·i·tal·ly** *adv*

gen·i·ta·lia \,je-nə-'tāl-yə\ *n pl* : reproductive organs; *esp* : the external genital organs — **gen·i·ta·lic** \-'ta-lik, -'tā-\ *adj*

gen·i·tals \'je-nə-tᵊlz\ *n pl* : GENITALIA

gen·i·tive \'je-nə-tiv\ *adj* : of, relating to, or constituting a grammatical case marking typically a relationship of possessor or source — **genitive** *n*

gen·i·to·uri·nary \,je-nə-tō-'yu̇r-ə-,ner-ē\ *adj* : of or relating to the genital and urinary organs or functions

ge·nius \'jē-nyəs\ *n, pl* **ge·nius·es** *or* **ge·nii** \-nē-,ī\ **1** *pl genii* : an attendant spirit of a person or place; *also* : a person who influences another for good or evil **2 ♦** : a strong leaning or inclination **3 ♦** : a peculiar or distinctive character or spirit (as of a nation or a language) **4** *pl usu genii* : SPIRIT, GENIE **5** *pl usu geniuses* **♦** : a single strongly marked capacity or aptitude **6 a** : extraordinary intellectual power **b ♦** : a person having extraordinary intellectual power

♦ [2] affinity, bent, devices, disposition, inclination, leaning, partiality, penchant, predilection, predisposition, proclivity, propensity, talent, tendency, turn ♦ [3] character, complexion, constitution, nature, personality, tone ♦ [5] aptitude, endowment, faculty, flair, gift, knack, talent ♦ [6b] brain, intellect, thinker, whiz, wizard *Ant* dumbbell, dummy, dunce, imbecile, moron

genl *abbr* general

geno•cide \'je-nə-ˌsīd\ *n* : the deliberate and systematic destruction of a racial, political, or cultural group

ge•nome \'jē-ˌnōm\ *n* **1** : one haploid set of chromosomes **2** : the genetic material of an organism

ge•no•mics \jē-'nō-miks\ *n* : a branch of biotechnology concerned esp. with investigating and collecting data about the structure and function of all or part of an organism's genome

-genous \jə-nəs\ *adj comb form* **1** : producing : yielding ⟨*erogenous*⟩ **2** : having (such) an origin ⟨*endogenous*⟩

genre \'zhän-rə, 'zhä°-; 'zhä°r; 'jän-rə\ *n* **1** : a distinctive type or category esp. of literary composition **2** : a style of painting in which everyday subjects are treated realistically

gens \'jenz, 'gens\ *n, pl* **gen•tes** \'jen-ˌtēz, 'gen-ˌtās\ : a Roman clan embracing the families of the same stock in the male line

gent *n* ♦ : a man of any social class or condition : GENTLEMAN

♦ buck, chap, dude, fellow, gentleman, guy, hombre, jack, joker, lad, male, man

gen•teel \jen-'tēl\ *adj* **1** ♦ : having an aristocratic quality or flavor; *also* : of or relating to the gentry or upper class **2** : ELEGANT, STYLISH **3** ♦ : free from vulgarity or rudeness : POLITE **4** : maintaining the appearance of superior social status **5** : marked by false delicacy, prudery, or affectation — **gen•teel•ly** *adv* — **gen•teel•ness** *n*

♦ [1] aristocratic, gentle, grand, highborn, noble, patrician, wellborn ♦ [1] civilized, cultivated, cultured, polished, refined ♦ [3] civil, courteous, gracious, mannerly, polite, well-bred ♦ [3] correct, decent, decorous, nice, polite, proper, respectable, seemly

gen•tian \'jen-chən\ *n* : any of numerous herbs with opposite leaves and showy usu. blue flowers in the fall

gen•tile \'jen-ˌtī(-ə)l\ *n* **1** *often cap* : a person who is not Jewish; *esp* : a Christian as distinguished from a Jew **2** : a person who does not acknowledge the God of the Bible : HEATHEN, PAGAN — **gentile** *adj, often cap*

gen•til•i•ty \jen-'ti-lə-tē\ *n, pl* **-ties** **1** : good birth and family **2** ♦ : the qualities characteristic of a well-bred person **3** : good manners **4** : superior social status shown in manners or mode of life

♦ civility, courtesy, graciousness, mannerliness, politeness

¹**gen•tle** \'jen-t°l\ *adj* **gen•tler** \'jent-lər, -t°l-ər\; **gen•tlest** \'jent-ləst, -t°l-əst\ **1** ♦ : belonging to a family of high social station **2** : of, relating to, or characteristic of a gentleman **3** : KIND, AMIABLE **4** : TRACTABLE, DOCILE **5** ♦ : not harsh, stern, or violent **6** : SOFT, DELICATE **7** ♦ : marked by moderation : MODERATE — **gen•tle•ness** *n* — **gen•tly** *adv*

♦ [1] aristocratic, genteel, grand, highborn, noble, patrician, wellborn ♦ [5] balmy, benign, bland, delicate, light, mellow, mild, soft, soothing, tender *Ant* abrasive, caustic, coarse, hard, harsh, rough ♦ [7] balmy, clement, equable, mild, moderate, temperate

²**gentle** *vb* **gen•tled; gen•tling** **1** : to make or become mild, docile, soft, or moderate **2** : MOLLIFY, PLACATE

gen•tle•folk \'jen-t°l-ˌfōk\ *also* **gen•tle•folks** \-ˌfōks\ *n* : persons of good family and breeding

gen•tle•man \-mən\ *n* **1** ♦ : a man of good family **2** : a well-bred man **3** ♦ : an adult male human being : MAN — used in pl. as a form of address — **gen•tle•man•ly** *adv*

♦ [1] aristocrat, grandee, noble, patrician ♦ [3] buck, chap, dude, fellow, gent, guy, hombre, jack, joker, lad, male, man

gen•tle•wom•an \-ˌwu̇-mən\ *n* **1** ♦ : a woman of good family **2** : a woman attending a lady of rank **3** : a woman with very good manners : LADY

♦ dame, lady, noblewoman

gen•tri•fi•ca•tion \ˌjen-trə-fə-'kā-shən\ *n* : the process of renewal accompanying the influx of middle-class people into deteriorating areas that often displaces earlier usu. poorer residents — **gen•tri•fy** \'jen-trə-fī\ *vb*

gen•try \'jen-trē\ *n, pl* **gentries** **1** : people of good birth, breeding, and education : ARISTOCRACY **2** : the class of English people between the nobility and the yeomanry **3** : persons of a designated class

gen•u•flect \'jen-yu̇-ˌflekt\ *vb* : to bend the knee esp. in worship — **gen•u•flec•tion** \ˌjen-yu̇-'flek-shən\ *n*

gen•u•ine \'jen-yə-wən\ *adj* **1** ♦ : actually having the reputed or apparent qualities or character : AUTHENTIC, REAL **2** ♦ : free from hypocrisy or pretense : SINCERE, HONEST — **gen•u•ine•ness** *n*

♦ [1] authentic, bona fide, real, right, true ♦ [2] artless, honest, ingenuous, innocent, naive, natural, real, simple, sincere, true, unaffected, unpretentious

gen•u•ine•ly *adv* ♦ : in a genuine manner : ACTUALLY

♦ actually, authentically, really, veritably, very

ge•nus \'jē-nəs\ *n, pl* **gen•era** \'je-nə-rə\ : a category of biological classification that ranks between the family and the species and contains related species

geo•cen•tric \ˌjē-ō-'sen-trik\ *adj* **1** : relating to or measured from the earth's center **2** : having or relating to the earth as a center

geo•chem•is•try \-'ke-mə-strē\ *n* : a branch of geology that deals with the chemical composition of and chemical changes in the earth — **geo•chem•i•cal** \-mi-kəl\ *adj* — **geo•chem•ist** \-'mist\ *n*

ge•ode \'jē-ˌōd\ *n* : a nodule of stone having a cavity lined with mineral matter

¹**geo•de•sic** \ˌjē-ə-'de-sik\ *adj* : made of light straight structural elements ⟨a ∼ dome⟩

²**geodesic** *n* : the shortest line between two points on a surface

geo•det•ic \ˌjē-ə-'de-tik\ *adj* : of, relating to, or being precise measurement of the earth and its features ⟨a ∼ survey⟩

geog *abbr* geographic; geographical; geography

ge•og•ra•phy \jē-'ä-grə-fē\ *n, pl* **-phies** **1** : a science that deals with the natural features of the earth and its climate, products, and inhabitants **2** : the natural features of a region — **ge•og•ra•pher** \-fər\ *n* — **geo•graph•ic** \ˌjē-ə-'gra-fik\ *or* **geo•graph•i•cal** \-fi-kəl\ *adj* — **geo•graph•i•cal•ly** \-fi-k(ə-)lē\ *adv*

geol *abbr* geologic; geological; geology

ge•ol•o•gy \jē-'ä-lə-jē\ *n, pl* **-gies** **1** : a science that deals with the history of the earth and its life esp. as recorded in rocks; *also* : a study of the features of a celestial body (as the moon) **2** : the geologic features of an area — **geo•log•ic** \ˌjē-ə-'lä-jik\ *or* **geo•log•i•cal** \-ji-kəl\ *adj* — **geo•log•i•cal•ly** \-ji-k(ə-)lē\ *adv* — **ge•ol•o•gist** \jē-'ä-lə-jist\ *n*

geom *abbr* geometric; geometrical; geometry

geo•mag•net•ic \ˌjē-ō-mag-'ne-tik\ *adj* : of or relating to the magnetism of the earth — **geo•mag•ne•tism** \-'mag-nə-ˌti-zəm\ *n*

geometric mean *n* : the *n*th root of the product of *n* numbers; *esp* : a number that is the second term of three consecutive terms of a geometric progression ⟨the *geometric mean* of 9 and 4 is 6⟩

geometric progression *n* : a progression (as 1, $\frac{1}{2}$, $\frac{1}{4}$) in which the ratio of a term to its predecessor is always the same

ge•om•e•try \jē-'ä-mə-trē\ *n, pl* **-tries** **1** : a branch of mathematics dealing with the relations, properties, and measurements of solids, surfaces, lines, points, and angles **2** : relative arrangement of parts or elements — **ge•om•e•ter** \-tər\ *n* — **ge•o•met•ric** \ˌjē-ə-'me-trik\ *or* **ge•o•met•ri•cal** \-tri-kəl\ *adj*

♦ cast, configuration, conformation, figure, form, shape

geo•phys•ics \ˌjē-ō-'fi-ziks\ *n* : the physics of the earth — **geo•phys•i•cal** \-zi-kəl\ *adj* — **geo•phys•i•cist** \-zə-sist\ *n*

geo•pol•i•tics \-'pä-lə-ˌtiks\ *n* : a combination of political and geographic factors relating to a state — **geo•po•lit•i•cal** \-pə-'li-ti-kəl\ *adj*

geo•ther•mal \ˌjē-ō-'thər-məl\ *adj* : of, relating to, or using the heat of the earth's interior ⟨∼ energy⟩

ger *abbr* gerund

Ger *abbr* German; Germany

ge•ra•ni•um \jə-'rā-nē-əm\ *n* : any of a genus of herbs with usu. deeply cut leaves and typically pink, purple, or white flowers; *also* : any of a related genus of herbs that are native to southern Africa and are widely grown for their clusters of showy usu. red, pink, or white flowers

ger•bil *also* **ger•bile** \'jər-bəl\ *n* : any of numerous Old World burrowing desert rodents with long hind legs

ge•ri•at•ric \ˌjer-ē-'a-trik\ *adj* **1** : of or relating to geriatrics or the process of aging **2** : of, relating to, or appropriate for elderly people **3** ♦ : advanced in years or age : OLD

♦ ancient, elderly, old, senior

ge•ri•at•rics \-triks\ *n* : a branch of medicine dealing with the problems and diseases of old age and aging

germ \'jərm\ *n* **1** : a bit of living matter capable of growth and development (as into an organism) **2** : SOURCE, RUDIMENTS **3** : MICROORGANISM; *esp* : one causing disease

Ger•man \'jər-mən\ *n* **1** : a native or inhabitant of Germany **2** : the language of Germany, Austria, and parts of Switzerland — **German** *adj* — **Ger•man•ic** \jər-'ma-nik\ *adj*

ger•mane \jər-'mān\ *adj* ♦ : being at once relevant and appropriate

♦ applicable, apposite, apropos, material, pertinent, pointed, relative, relevant

ger•ma•ni•um \jər-ˈmā-nē-əm\ *n* : a grayish white hard chemical element used esp. in semiconductors

German measles *n sing or pl* : an acute contagious virus disease milder than typical measles but damaging to the fetus when occurring early in pregnancy

German shepherd *n* : any of a breed of intelligent responsive working dogs of German origin often used in police work and as guide dogs for the blind

germ cell *n* : an egg or sperm or one of their antecedent cells

ger•mi•cide \ˈjər-mə-ˌsīd\ *n* : an agent that destroys germs — **ger•mi•cid•al** \ˌjər-mə-ˈsīd-ᵊl\ *adj*

ger•mi•nal \ˈjər-mə-nəl\ *adj* : of or relating to a germ or germ cell; *also* : EMBRYONIC

ger•mi•nate \ˈjər-mə-ˌnāt\ *vb* **-nat•ed; -nat•ing** **1** : to cause to develop : begin to develop : SPROUT **2** : to come into being : EVOLVE — **ger•mi•na•tion** \ˌjər-mə-ˈnā-shən\ *n*

ger•on•tol•o•gy \ˌjer-ən-ˈtä-lə-jē\ *n* : a scientific study of aging and the problems of the aged — **ger•on•to•log•i•cal** \jə-ˌränt-ᵊl-ˈä-ji-kəl\ *adj* — **ger•on•tol•o•gist** \ˌjer-ən-ˈtä-lə-jist\ *n*

ger•ry•man•der \ˈjer-ē-ˌman-dər\ *vb* : to divide into election districts so as to give one political party an advantage — **gerrymander** *n*

ger•und \ˈjer-ənd\ *n* : a word having the characteristics of both verb and noun

ge•sta•po \gə-ˈstä-pō\ *n, pl* **-pos** : a usu. terrorist secret-police organization operating against persons suspected of disloyalty

ges•ta•tion \je-ˈstā-shən\ *n* : PREGNANCY, INCUBATION — **ges•tate** \ˈjes-ˌtāt\ *vb*

ges•tic•u•late \je-ˈsti-kyə-ˌlāt\ *vb* **-lat•ed; -lat•ing** : to make gestures esp. when speaking

ges•tic•u•la•tion \-ˌsti-kyə-ˈlā-shən\ *n* : the act of making gestures; *also* : an expressive gesture made in showing strong feeling or in enforcing an argument

¹**ges•ture** \ˈjes-chər\ *n* **1** ♦ : a movement usu. of the body or limbs that expresses or emphasizes an idea, sentiment, or attitude **2** ♦ : something said or done by way of formality or courtesy, as a symbol or token, or for its effect on the attitudes of others — **ges•tur•al** \-chə-rəl\ *adj*

♦ [1] pantomime, sign, signal ♦ [2] amenity, civility, courtesy, formality

²**gesture** *vb* ♦ : to make a gesture; *also* : to express or direct by a gesture

♦ flag, motion, signal, wave

ge•sund•heit \gə-ˈzùnt-ˌhīt\ *interj* — used to wish good health esp. to one who has just sneezed

¹**get** \ˈget\ *vb* **got** \ˈgät\; **got** *or* **got•ten** \ˈgät-ᵊn\; **get•ting** **1** ♦ : to gain possession of (as by receiving, acquiring, earning, buying, or winning) : PROCURE, OBTAIN **2** : to succeed in coming or going ⟨*got* away to the lake⟩ **3** : to cause to come or go ⟨*got* the car to the station⟩ **4** ♦ : to become the father of : BEGET **5** : to cause to be in a certain condition or position ⟨don't ~ wet⟩ **6** ♦ : to undergo change or development : BECOME ⟨~ sick⟩ **7** : to make ready : PREPARE **8** ♦ : to take possession of : SEIZE **9** : to move emotionally; *also* : IRRITATE **10** : BAFFLE, PUZZLE **11** : KILL **12** : HIT **13** ♦ : to be subjected to ⟨~ the measles⟩ **14** : to receive as punishment **15** ♦ : to find out esp. by calculation **16 a** : HEAR **b** ♦ : to grasp the meaning of : UNDERSTAND **17** : to prevail on : PERSUADE, INDUCE **18** : HAVE ⟨he's *got* no money⟩ **19** : to have as an obligation or necessity ⟨you have *got* to go⟩ **20** : to establish communication with **21** : to be able ⟨finally *got* to go to med school⟩ **22** : to come to be ⟨*got* talking about old times⟩ **23** : to leave at once

♦ [1] acquire, attain, capture, carry, draw, earn, gain, garner, land, make, obtain, procure, realize, secure, win ♦ [4] beget, father, produce, sire ♦ [6] become, come, go, grow, run, turn, wax ♦ [8] bag, capture, catch, collar, corral, grab, grapple, hook, land, nab, seize, snare, trap ♦ [13] catch, come down, contract, sicken, take ♦ [15] detect, determine, dig up, discover, ferret out, find, hit on, locate, track down ♦ [16b] appreciate, apprehend, catch, catch on (to), comprehend, grasp, make, make out, perceive, see, seize, understand

²**get** \ˈget\ *n* : OFFSPRING, PROGENY

get across *vb* ♦ : to make clear or convincing

♦ clarify, clear (up), construe, demonstrate, elucidate, explain, explicate, expound, illuminate, illustrate, interpret, spell out

get along *vb* **1** ♦ : to meet one's needs **2** : to be on friendly terms **3** ♦ : to proceed toward a destination

♦ [1] cope, do, fare, make out, manage, shift ♦ [3] advance, fare, forge, go, march, proceed, progress

get around *vb* **1** ♦ : to manage to avoid the intent, effect, or force of something esp. by ingenuity or stratagem : CIRCUMVENT **2** ♦ : to become known or current

♦ [1] circumvent, dodge, shortcut, sidestep, skirt ♦ [2] circulate, come out, get out, leak out, out, spread

get•away \ˈge-tə-ˌwā\ *n* **1** ♦ : an act or instance of getting away : ESCAPE **2** : START

♦ escape, flight, lam, slip

get by *vb* : to meet one's needs : GET ALONG

get off *vb* ♦ : to go away from; *also* : to do or experience the first stages or actions of ⟨*got off* on the trip early⟩

♦ clear out, depart, exit, go, move, pull, quit, sally, shove, take off ♦ begin, commence, embark (on *or* upon), enter, launch, open, start, strike

get on *vb* **1** : to proceed toward a destination **2** : to meet one's needs : GET ALONG

get out *vb* **1** ♦ : to become known; *also* : to produce or release for distribution **2** ♦ : to get away (as by flight); *also* : to cause to leave or escape

♦ [1] come out, leak out, out, spread ♦ [1] issue, print, publish ♦ [2] abscond, clear out, escape, flee, fly, lam, run away, run off

get–to•geth•er \ˈget-tə-ˌge-thər\ *n* ♦ : an assembly for a common purpose; *esp* : an informal social gathering

♦ assembly, conference, congress, convention, convocation, council, gathering, huddle, meeting, seminar

get•up \ˈget-ˌəp\ *n* **1** ♦ : a clothing ensemble often for a special occasion or activity : OUTFIT, COSTUME **2** : general composition or structure

♦ dress, garb, guise, outfit

get up *vb* **1** : to arise from bed **2** : to rise to one's feet **3** : PREPARE, ORGANIZE **4** : to produce in oneself by effort ⟨*get up* the courage⟩

gew•gaw \ˈgü-ˌgò, ˈgyü-\ *n* ♦ : a showy trifle : BAUBLE, TRINKET

♦ bauble, curiosity, knickknack, novelty, tchotchke, trinket

gey•ser \ˈgī-zər\ *n* : a spring that intermittently shoots up hot water and steam

g–force \ˈjē-ˌfòrs\ *n* : the force of gravity or acceleration on a body

Gha•na•ian \gä-ˈnä-ən\ *n* : a native or inhabitant of Ghana — **Ghanaian** *adj*

ghast•ly \ˈgast-lē\ *adj* **ghast•li•er; -est** **1** ♦ : terrifyingly horrible to the senses : SHOCKING **2** : resembling a ghost : DEATHLIKE, PALE

♦ appalling, atrocious, awful, dreadful, frightful, horrible, horrid, nightmarish, shocking, terrible

ghat \ˈgòt\ *n* : a broad flight of steps on an Indian riverbank that provides access to the water

gher•kin \ˈgər-kən\ *n* **1** : a small prickly fruit of a vine related to the cucumber used to make pickles **2** : an immature cucumber

ghet•to \ˈge-tō\ *n, pl* **ghettos** *or* **ghettoes** : a quarter of a city in which members of a minority group live because of social, legal, or economic pressure

¹**ghost** \ˈgōst\ *n* **1** : the seat of life : SOUL **2** ♦ : a disembodied soul; *esp* : the soul of a dead person believed to be an inhabitant of the unseen world or to appear in bodily form to living people **3** : SPIRIT, DEMON **4** : a faint trace ⟨a ~ of a smile⟩ **5** : a false image in a photographic negative or on a television screen — **ghost•ly** *adv*

♦ apparition, bogey, phantasm, phantom, poltergeist, shade, shadow, specter, spirit, spook, vision, wraith

²**ghost** *vb* : GHOSTWRITE

ghost•write \-ˌrīt\ *vb* **-wrote** \-ˌrōt\; **-writ•ten** \-ˌri-tᵊn\ : to write for and in the name of another — **ghost•writ•er** *n*

ghoul \ˈgül\ *n* ♦ : a legendary evil being that robs graves and feeds on corpses — **ghoul•ish** *adj*

♦ demon, devil, fiend, imp

GHQ *abbr* general headquarters

gi *abbr* gill

¹**GI** \ˌjē-ˈī\ *adj* **1** : provided by an official U.S. military supply department ⟨~ shoes⟩ **2** : of, relating to, or characteristic of U.S. military personnel **3** : conforming to military regulations or customs ⟨a ~ haircut⟩

²**GI** *n, pl* **GIs** *or* **GI's** \-ˈīz\ : a member or former member of the U.S. armed forces; *esp* : an enlisted person

³GI *abbr* **1** galvanized iron **2** gastrointestinal **3** general issue **4** government issue

¹gi·ant \'jī-ənt\ *n* **1** : a legendary humanlike being of great size and strength **2** ♦ : a living being or thing of extraordinary size or powers

♦ behemoth, blockbuster, colossus, jumbo, leviathan, mammoth, monster, titan, whale, whopper **Ant** dwarf, midget, mini, miniature, peewee, pygmy, runt, shrimp

²giant *adj* ♦ : having extremely large size, proportion, or power

♦ astronomical, colossal, enormous, gigantic, ginormous, grand, huge, jumbo, mammoth, massive, monumental, prodigious, titanic, tremendous

gi·ant·ess \'jī-ən-təs\ *n* : a female giant
giant panda *n* : PANDA 2
gib·ber \'ji-bər\ *vb* ♦ : to speak rapidly, inarticulately, and often foolishly

♦ babble, chatter, drivel, gabble, jabber, prattle, sputter

gib·ber·ish \'ji-bə-rish\ *n* ♦ : unintelligible or confused speech or language

♦ babble, bunk, claptrap, drivel, gabble, gobbledygook, hogwash, nonsense, piffle, prattle, rot

¹gib·bet \'ji-bət\ *n* : GALLOWS
²gibbet *vb* **1** : to hang on a gibbet **2** : to expose to public scorn **3** : to execute by hanging
gib·bon \'gi-bən\ *n* : any of several tailless apes of southeastern Asia
gib·bous \'ji-bəs, 'gi-\ *adj* **1** : rounded like the exterior of a sphere or circle **2** : seen with more than half but not all of the apparent disk illuminated ⟨~ moon⟩ **3** : having a hump : HUMP-BACKED
gibe *or* **jibe** \'jīb\ *vb* **gibed** *or* **jibed; gib·ing** *or* **jib·ing** ♦ : to utter taunting words : SNEER — **gibe** *or* **jibe** *n*

♦ deride, jeer, laugh, mock, ridicule, scout

gib·lets \'jib-ləts\ *n pl* : the edible viscera of a fowl
Gib·son girl \'gib-sən-\ *adj* : of or relating to a style in women's clothing characterized by high necks, full sleeves, and slender waistlines
gid·dy \'gi-dē\ *adj* **gid·di·er; -est 1** ♦ : having a whirling sensation in the head with a tendency to fall : DIZZY **2** : causing dizziness **3** ♦ : not serious : FRIVOLOUS, SILLY — **gid·di·ness** \-dē-nəs\ *n*

♦ [1] dizzy, light-headed ♦ [3] flighty, frivolous, goofy, harebrained, light-headed, scatterbrained, silly **Ant** earnest, serious, sober

GIF \'gif, 'jif\ *n* : a computer file format for digital images; *also* : the image itself
gift \'gift\ *n* **1** ♦ : a special ability : TALENT **2** ♦ : something given : PRESENT **3** : the act or power of giving

♦ [1] aptitude, endowment, faculty, flair, genius, knack, talent
♦ [2] bestowal, donation, freebie, lagniappe, present

gift card *n* : a card entitling the recipient to goods or services of a specified value from the issuer
gift·ed \'gif-təd\ *adj* : TALENTED
¹gig \'gig\ *n* **1** : a long light ship's boat **2** : a light 2-wheeled one-horse carriage
²gig *n* : a pronged spear for catching fish — **gig** *vb*
³gig *n* : a job for a specified time; *esp* : an entertainer's engagement
⁴gig *n* : a military demerit — **gig** *vb*
giga·byte \'ji-gə-ˌbīt, 'gi-\ *n* : 1024 megabytes or 1,073,741,824 bytes; *also* : one billion bytes
gi·gan·tic \jī-'gan-tik\ *adj* ♦ : exceeding the usual (as in size or force)

♦ colossal, enormous, giant, ginormous, huge, jumbo, mammoth, massive, prodigious, titanic, tremendous

¹gig·gle \'gi-gəl\ *vb* **gig·gled; gig·gling** : to laugh with repeated short catches of the breath — **gig·gly** \-gə-lē\ *adj*
²giggle *n* : the act of giggling
GIGO *abbr* garbage in, garbage out
gig·o·lo \'ji-gə-ˌlō\ *n, pl* **-los 1** : a man supported by a woman usu. in return for his attentions **2** : a professional dancing partner or male escort
Gi·la monster \'hē-lə-\ *n* : a large orange and black venomous lizard of the southwestern U.S.
¹gild \'gild\ *vb* **gild·ed** *or* **gilt** \'gilt\; **gild·ing 1** : to overlay with or as if with a thin covering of gold **2** : to give an attractive but often deceptive appearance to
²gild *var of* GUILD

¹gill \'jil\ *n* : a British measure of capacity equal to 5 fluid ounces; *also* : a U.S. measure of capacity equal to 5 fluid ounces
²gill \'gil\ *n* : an organ (as of a fish) for obtaining oxygen from water
¹gilt \'gilt\ *adj* : of the color of gold
²gilt *n* : gold or a substance resembling gold laid on the surface of an object
³gilt *n* : a young female swine
¹gim·crack \'jim-ˌkrak\ *n* : a showy object of little use or value
²gimcrack *adj* : CHEAP, SHODDY
gim·let \'gim-lət\ *n* : a small tool with screw point and cross handle for boring holes
gim·mick \'gi-mik\ *n* **1** ♦ : an ingenious or novel mechanical device : CONTRIVANCE, GADGET **2** : an important feature that is not immediately apparent : CATCH **3** ♦ : a new and ingenious scheme — **gim·micky** \-mi-kē\ *adj*

♦ [1] contraption, contrivance, gadget, gizmo, jigger ♦ [3] artifice, device, dodge, jig, ploy, scheme, sleight, stratagem, trick, wile

gim·mick·ry \'gi-mi-krē\ *n, pl* **-ries** : an array of or the use of gimmicks
gimpy \'gim-pē\ *adj* : LAME 1
¹gin \'jin\ *n* **1** : TRAP, SNARE **2** : a machine to separate seeds from cotton — **gin** *vb*
²gin *n* : a liquor distilled from a grain mash and flavored with juniper berries
gin·ger \'jin-jər\ *n* **1** : the pungent aromatic rootstock of a tropical plant used esp. as a spice and in medicine; *also* : the spice or the plant **2** : brisk energy or initiative and high spirits
ginger ale *n* : a carbonated soft drink flavored with ginger
gin·ger·bread \'jin-jər-ˌbred\ *n* **1** : a cake made with molasses and flavored with ginger **2** : lavish or superfluous ornament
gin·ger·ly \'jin-jər-lē\ *adj* ♦ : very cautious or careful — **gingerly** *adv*

♦ alert, careful, cautious, circumspect, considerate, guarded, heedful, safe, wary

gin·ger·snap \-ˌsnap\ *n* : a thin brittle molasses cookie flavored with ginger
ging·ham \'giŋ-əm\ *n* : a cotton cloth that is often marked with a pattern of colored squares
gin·gi·vi·tis \ˌjin-jə-'vī-təs\ *n* : inflammation of the gums
gink·go *also* **ging·ko** \'giŋ-(ˌ)kō\ *n, pl* **ginkgoes** *or* **ginkgos** : a tree of eastern China with fan-shaped leaves often grown as a shade tree
ginkgo bi·lo·ba \-ˌbī-'lō-bə\ *n* : an extract of the leaves of ginkgo that is held to enhance mental functioning
gi·nor·mous \jī-'nȯr-məs\ *adj* ♦ : extremely large : HUGE

♦ colossal, enormous, giant, huge, jumbo, mammoth, massive, prodigious, titanic, tremendous

gin·seng \'jin-ˌseŋ\ *n* : an aromatic root of a Chinese or No. American herb used esp. in Chinese medicine; *also* : one of these herbs
Gip·sy *chiefly Brit var of* GYPSY
gi·raffe \jə-'raf\ *n, pl* **giraffes** : an African ruminant mammal with a very long neck and a short coat with dark blotches
gird \'gərd\ *vb* **gird·ed** *or* **girt** \'gərt\; **gird·ing 1** : to encircle or fasten (as a sword) with or as if with a belt **2** : to invest esp. with power or authority **3** : PREPARE, BRACE

♦ band, belt, girdle, wrap **Ant** unwrap ♦ band, bind, tie, truss

gird·er \'gər-dər\ *n* : a horizontal main supporting beam
¹gir·dle \'gər-dᵊl\ *n* **1** : something (as a belt or sash) that encircles or confines **2** : a woman's supporting undergarment that extends from the waist to below the hips
²girdle *vb* **gir·dled gir·dling** \'gər-dᵊl-iŋ\ **1** ♦ : to encircle with or as if with a girdle **2** ♦ : to move around

♦ [1] band, belt, gird, wrap ♦ [2] circle, circumnavigate, coil, compass, encircle, loop, orbit, ring, round

girl \'gərl\ *n* **1** : a female child **2** ♦ : a young woman **3** : SWEETHEART — **girl·hood** \-ˌhu̇d\ *n*

♦ doll, lass, maid, maiden, miss

girl Friday *n* : a female assistant (as in an office) entrusted with a wide variety of tasks
girl·friend \'gərl-ˌfrend\ *n* **1** : a female friend **2** : a frequent or regular female companion in a romantic or sexual relationship
girl·ish *adj* ♦ : of, relating to, or having the characteristics of a girl or girlhood

♦ effeminate, feminine, unmanly, womanly

Girl Scout *n* : a member of any of the scouting programs of the Girl Scouts of the United States of America

girth \\'gərth\ *n* **1** : a band around an animal by which something (as a saddle) may be fastened on its back **2** : a measure around something

gist \\'jist\ *n* ♦ : the main point or part ⟨the ∼ of the speech⟩

   ♦ core, crux, heart, nub, pith, pivot

git *dial var of* GET

¹**give** \\'giv\ *vb* **gave** \\'gāv\; **giv•en** \\'gi-vən\; **giv•ing** **1** ♦ : to make a present of **2** : to bestow by formal action **3** : to accord or yield to another **4** ♦ : to yield to force, strain, or pressure **5** ♦ : to put into the possession or keeping of another **6** ♦ : to offer to the action of another : PROFFER **7** : to put into the possession of another : DELIVER **8** ♦ : to present in public performance or to view **9** : PROVIDE ⟨∼ a party⟩ **10** : ATTRIBUTE **11** : to make, form, or yield as a product or result ⟨cows ∼ milk⟩ **12** : to yield possession of by way of exchange : PAY **13** : to deliver by some bodily action ⟨*gave* me a push⟩ **14** : to offer as a pledge ⟨I ∼ you my word⟩ **15** : to apply freely or fully : DEVOTE **16** : to cause to have or receive ⟨∼ me time⟩

   ♦ [1] bestow, contribute, donate, present ♦ [4] cave in, collapse, crumple, go, yield ♦ [5] commend, commit, consign, delegate, deliver, entrust, hand over, leave, pass, transfer, transmit, trust, turn over, vest *Ant* hold, keep, retain ♦ [6] extend, offer, proffer, tender ♦ [8] carry, mount, offer, present, stage

²**give** *n* **1** : capacity or tendency to yield to force or strain **2** : the quality or state of being springy

give–and–take \\,giv-ən-'tāk\ *n* **1** ♦ : the practice of making mutual concessions : COMPROMISE **2** ♦ : a usu. good-natured exchange (as of remarks or ideas)

   ♦ [1] accommodation, compromise, concession, negotiation ♦ [2] argument, colloquy, conference, deliberation, discourse, discussion, parley, talk

give•away \\'gi-və-,wā\ *n* **1** : an unintentional revelation or betrayal **2** : something given away free; *esp* : PREMIUM

give away *vb* **1** : to make a present of **2** : to deliver (a bride) ceremonially to the bridegroom at a wedding **3** : to reveal or make known sometimes unintentionally

   ♦ bespeak, betray, demonstrate, display, evince, expose, manifest, reveal, show

give in *vb* ♦ : to yield under insistence or entreaty : SUBMIT, SURRENDER

   ♦ blink, bow, budge, capitulate, concede, knuckle under, quit, submit, succumb, surrender, yield

¹**giv•en** \\'gi-vən\ *adj* **1** ♦ : having a tendency or inclination : INCLINED ⟨∼ to swearing⟩ **2** : SPECIFIED, PARTICULAR ⟨at a ∼ time⟩

   ♦ apt, inclined, prone ♦ accustomed, used, wont

²**given** *prep* : CONSIDERING

given name *n* : a name that precedes one's surname

give out *vb* **1** : EMIT **2** : BREAK DOWN **3** : to become exhausted : COLLAPSE

give up *vb* **1** ♦ : to yield control or possession of : SURRENDER **2** : to abandon (oneself) to a feeling, influence, or activity **3** ♦ : to cease doing or attempting something esp. as an admission of defeat : QUIT ⟨*gave up* his job⟩

   ♦ [1] cede, deliver, hand over, leave, relinquish, render, surrender, turn over, yield ♦ [3] discontinue, drop, knock off, lay off, quit

giz•mo *also* **gis•mo** \\'giz-mō\ *n, pl* **gizmos** *also* **gismos** ♦ : an often small mechanical or electronic device with a practical use but often thought of as a novelty : GADGET

   ♦ contraption, contrivance, gadget, gimmick, jigger

giz•zard \\'gi-zərd\ *n* : the muscular usu. horny-lined enlargement of the alimentary canal of a bird used for churning and grinding up food

gla•cial \\'glā-shəl\ *adj* **1** : suggestive of ice: as **a** ♦ : extremely cold **b** ♦ : devoid of warmth and cordiality **2** : of or relating to glaciers **3** : being or relating to a past period of time when a large part of the earth was covered by glaciers **4** *cap* : PLEISTOCENE **5** : very slow ⟨a ∼ pace⟩ — **gla•cial•ly** *adv*

   ♦ [1a] arctic, bitter, cold, freezing, frigid, polar, raw, wintry ♦ [1b] chill, chilly, cold, cold-blooded, cool, frigid, frosty, icy, unfriendly, unsympathetic, wintry

gla•ci•ate \\'glā-shē-,āt\ *vb* **-at•ed; -at•ing** **1** : to subject to glacial action **2** : to produce glacial effects in or on — **gla•ci•a•tion** \\,glā-shē-'ā-shən, -sē-\ *n*

gla•cier \\'glā-shər\ *n* : a large body of ice moving slowly down a slope or spreading outward on a land surface

¹**glad** \\'glad\ *adj* **glad•der; glad•dest** **1** ♦ : experiencing pleasure, joy, or delight **2** : PLEASED **3** ♦ : very willing **4** : PLEASANT, JOYFUL **5** ♦ : causing happiness and joy : CHEERFUL — **glad•ly** *adv*

   ♦ [1] blissful, delighted, happy, joyful, pleased *Ant* displeased, joyless, sad, unhappy, unsatisfied ♦ [3] amenable, disposed, game, inclined, ready, willing ♦ [5] bright, cheerful, cheery

²**glad** *n* : GLADIOLUS

glad•den \\'glad-ᵊn\ *vb* ♦ : to make glad

   ♦ content, delight, gratify, please, rejoice, satisfy, suit, warm

glade \\'glād\ *n* : a grassy open space surrounded by woods

glad•i•a•tor \\'gla-dē-,ā-tər\ *n* **1** : a person engaged in a fight to the death for public entertainment in ancient Rome **2** : a person engaging in a public fight or controversy; *also* : PRIZEFIGHTER

glad•i•a•to•ri•al \\,gla-dē-ə-'tōr-ē-əl\ *adj* **1** : of, relating to, or suggestive of gladiators or the combats of gladiators **2** : inclined toward controversy or contention

glad•i•o•lus \\,gla-dē-'ō-ləs\ *n, pl* **-o•li** \-(ˌ)ō-(ˌ)lē, -ˌlī\ *or* **-olus** : any of a genus of chiefly African plants related to the irises and having erect sword-shaped leaves and stalks of bright colored flowers

glad•ness *n* ♦ : the quality or state of being glad

   ♦ blessedness, bliss, felicity, happiness, joy ♦ contentment, delectation, delight, enjoyment, gratification, pleasure, relish, satisfaction

glad•some \\'glad-səm\ *adj* : giving or showing joy : CHEERFUL

glam \\'glam\ *n* : extravagantly showy glamour — **glam** *adj*

glam•or•ise *chiefly Brit var of* GLAMORIZE

glam•or•ize *also* **glam•our•ize** \\'gla-mə-,rīz\ *vb* **-ized; -iz•ing** ♦ : to make or look upon as glamorous; *also* : treat as idealized or heroic

   ♦ dream, glorify, idealize

glam•or•ous \-mə-rəs\ *adj* ♦ : full of glamour : excitingly attractive

   ♦ exotic, fantastic, marvelous (*or* marvellous), outlandish, romantic, strange ♦ alluring, attractive, captivating, charming, elfin, engaging, fascinating, fetching, magnetic, seductive

glam•our \\'gla-mər\ *n* ♦ : an exciting and often illusory and romantic attractiveness; *esp* : alluring personal attraction

   ♦ allure, appeal, attractiveness, captivation, charisma, charm, enchantment, fascination, magic, magnetism

¹**glance** \\'glans\ *vb* **glanced; glanc•ing** **1** ♦ : to strike and fly off to one side **2** ♦ : to flash or gleam with quick intermittent rays of light **3** ♦ : to give a quick look

   ♦ [1] bounce, carom, rebound, ricochet, skim, skip ♦ [2] flame, flash, gleam, glimmer, glisten, glitter, scintillate, shimmer, sparkle, twinkle, wink ♦ [3] browse, dip, glimpse, peek, skim *Ant* stare, gaze

²**glance** *n* **1** : a quick intermittent flash or gleam **2** : a deflected impact or blow **3** ♦ : a quick look

   ♦ cast, eye, gander, glimpse, look, peek, peep, regard, sight, view

gland \\'gland\ *n* : a cell or group of cells that prepares and secretes a substance (as saliva or sweat) for further use in or discharge from the body

glan•du•lar \\'glan-jə-lər\ *adj* : of, relating to, or involving glands

glans \\'glanz\ *n, pl* **glan•des** \\'glan-,dēz\ : a conical vascular body forming the extremity of the penis or clitoris

¹**glare** \\'gler\ *vb* **glared; glar•ing** **1** ♦ : to shine with a harsh dazzling light **2** ♦ : to stare fiercely or angrily

   ♦ [1] beat, blaze, burn, flame, flare ♦ [2] frown, gloom, glower, lower, scowl

²**glare** *n* **1** : a harsh dazzling light **2** : an angry or fierce stare

glaring *adj* ♦ : very conspicuous ⟨a ∼ error⟩ — **glar•ing•ly** *adv*

   ♦ blatant, conspicuous, egregious, flagrant, gross, obvious, patent, prominent, pronounced, rank, striking

glass \\'glas\ *n* **1** : a hard brittle amorphous usu. transparent or translucent material consisting typically of silica **2** : something made of glass; *esp* : TUMBLER 2 **3** *pl* ♦ : a pair of lenses used to correct defects of vision : SPECTACLES **4** : the quantity held by a glass container — **glass** *adj* — **glass•ful** \-,ful\ *n* — **glassy** *adj*

   ♦ **glasses** eyeglasses, spectacles

glass•blow•ing \-,blō-iŋ\ *n* : the art of shaping a mass of glass that has been softened by heat by blowing air into it through a tube — **glass•blow•er** *n*

glass·ware \-ˌwer\ *n* : articles made of glass

glau·co·ma \glaů-ˈkō-mə, glȯ-\ *n* : a disease of the eye marked by increased pressure within the eyeball resulting in damage to the retina and gradual loss of vision

¹**glaze** \ˈglāz\ *vb* **glazed; glaz·ing 1** : to furnish (as a window frame) with glass **2** : to apply glaze to

²**glaze** *n* : a glassy coating or surface

gla·zier \ˈglā-zhər\ *n* : a person who sets glass in window frames

¹**gleam** \ˈglēm\ *n* **1** : a transient subdued or partly obscured light **2 a** ♦ : a small bright light **b** : GLINT **3** : a faint trace ⟨a ~ of hope⟩

♦ blaze, flare, fluorescence, glare, glow, illumination, incandescence, light, luminescence, radiance, shine

²**gleam** *vb* **1** ♦ : to shine with subdued light or moderate brightness **2** : to appear briefly or faintly

♦ flame, flash, glance, glimmer, glisten, glitter, scintillate, shimmer, sparkle, twinkle, wink

glean \ˈglēn\ *vb* **1** : to gather grain left by reapers **2** : to collect little by little or with patient effort ⟨antiques ~ed from flea markets⟩ — **glean·able** *adj* — **glean·er** *n*

glean·ings \ˈglē-niŋz\ *n pl* : things acquired by gleaning

glee \ˈglē\ *n* **1** ♦ : exultant high-spirited joy : HILARITY **2** : a part-song for three usu. male voices

♦ cheer, cheerfulness, hilarity, joviality, merriment, mirth

glee club *n* : a chorus organized for singing usu. short choral pieces

glee·ful *adj* ♦ : full of glee

♦ blithe, boon, festive, jocund, jolly, jovial, merry, mirthful, sunny

glen \ˈglen\ *n* : a narrow hidden valley

glen·gar·ry \glen-ˈga-rē\ *n, pl* **-ries** *often cap* : a woolen cap of Scottish origin

glib \ˈglib\ *adj* **glib·ber; glib·best** : speaking or spoken with careless ease — **glib·ly** *adv*

glide \ˈglīd\ *vb* **glid·ed; glid·ing 1** ♦ : to move smoothly and effortlessly **2** ♦ : to descend gradually without engine power ⟨~ in an airplane⟩ — **glide** *n*

♦ [1] bowl, breeze, coast, drift, flow, roll, sail, skim, slide, slip, stream, sweep, whisk ♦ [2] fly, plane, soar, wing

glid·er \ˈglī-dər\ *n* **1** : one that glides **2** : an aircraft resembling an airplane but having no engine **3** : a porch seat suspended from an upright frame

¹**glim·mer** \ˈgli-mər\ *vb* ♦ : to shine faintly or unsteadily

♦ flame, flash, glance, gleam, glisten, glitter, scintillate, shimmer, sparkle, twinkle, wink

²**glimmer** *n* **1** : a faint unsteady light **2** : INKLING **3** ♦ : a small amount : HINT

♦ hint, little, mite, particle, touch, trace

¹**glimpse** \ˈglimps\ *vb* **glimpsed; glimps·ing** ♦ : to take a brief look : see momentarily or incompletely

♦ browse, dip, glance, peek, skim

²**glimpse** *n* **1** : a faint idea : GLIMMER **2** ♦ : a short hurried look

♦ cast, eye, gander, glance, look, peek, peep, regard, sight, view

¹**glint** \ˈglint\ *vb* **1** : to shine by reflection : SPARKLE, GLEAM **2** : to appear briefly or faintly — **glint** *n*

glis·san·do \gli-ˈsän-(ˌ)dō\ *n, pl* **-di** \-(ˌ)dē\ *or* **-dos** : a rapid sliding up or down the musical scale

¹**glis·ten** \ˈgli-sᵊn\ *vb* ♦ : to shine by reflection with a soft luster or sparkle

♦ flame, flash, glance, gleam, glimmer, glitter, scintillate, shimmer, sparkle, twinkle, wink

²**glisten** *n* : GLITTER, SPARKLE

glis·ter \ˈglis-tər\ *vb* : to shine by reflection with many small flashes of brilliant light : GLITTER

glitch \ˈglich\ *n* : MALFUNCTION; *also* : SNAG 2

¹**glit·ter** \ˈgli-tər\ *vb* **1** : to shine with brilliant or metallic luster : SPARKLE **2** : to shine with strong emotion : FLASH ⟨eyes ~ing in anger⟩ **3** : to be brilliantly attractive esp. in a superficial way

♦ flame, flash, glance, gleam, glimmer, glisten, scintillate, shimmer, sparkle, twinkle, wink

²**glitter** *n* **1** : sparkling brilliancy, showiness, or attractiveness **2** : small glittering objects used for ornamentation — **glit·tery** \ˈg-li-tə-rē\ *adj*

glitz \ˈglits\ *n* ♦ : extravagant showiness

♦ flamboyance, flashiness, gaudiness, ostentation, pretentiousness, showiness, swank

glitzy \ˈglit-sē\ *adj* ♦ : having glitz

♦ flamboyant, flashy, garish, gaudy, loud, ostentatious, swank, tawdry

gloam·ing \ˈglō-miŋ\ *n* ♦ : the light from the sky between full night and sunrise or between sunset and full night : TWILIGHT, DUSK

♦ dusk, evening, nightfall, sundown, sunset, twilight

gloat \ˈglōt\ *vb* : to think about something with triumphant and often malicious delight ⟨~ing over their victory⟩

glob \ˈgläb\ *n* **1** ♦ : a small drop **2** ♦ : a large rounded mass

♦ [1] blob, driblet, drip, drop, droplet ♦ [2] blob, chunk, clod, clump, gob, hunk, lump, nub, wad

glob·al \ˈglō-bəl\ *adj* **1** : of, relating to, or involving the entire world : WORLDWIDE **2** ♦ : of, relating to, or applying to a whole : COMPREHENSIVE, GENERAL — **glob·al·ly** *adv*

♦ blanket, common, general, generic, overall, universal ♦ compendious, complete, comprehensive, encyclopedic, full, inclusive, omnibus, panoramic, universal

glob·al·i·za·tion \ˌglō-bə-lə-ˈzā-shən\ *n* : the development of an increasingly integrated global economy

Global Positioning System *n* : GPS

global warming *n* : an increase in the earth's atmospheric and oceanic temperatures due to an increase in the greenhouse effect

globe \ˈglōb\ *n* **1** : a round body : BALL, SPHERE **2** : the planet on which we live that is third in order from the sun : EARTH; *also* : a spherical representation of the earth

globe–trot·ter \ˈglōb-ˌträ-tər\ *n* : a person who travels widely — **globe–trot·ting** *n or adj*

glob·u·lar \ˈglä-byə-lər\ *adj* : having the shape of a globe or globule

glob·ule \ˈglä-(ˌ)byül\ *n* : a tiny globe or ball esp. of a liquid

glob·u·lin \ˈglä-byə-lən\ *n* : any of a class of simple proteins insoluble in pure water but soluble in dilute salt solutions that occur widely in plant and animal tissues

glock·en·spiel \ˈglä-kən-ˌshpēl, -ˌspēl\ *n* : a percussion musical instrument consisting of a series of metal bars played with two hammers

gloom \ˈglüm\ *n* **1** ♦ : partial or total darkness **2** ♦ : lowness of spirits : DEJECTION **3** : an atmosphere of despondency ⟨a ~ fell over the household⟩

♦ [1] dark, darkness, dusk, gloaming, murk, night, semidarkness, shade, shadows, twilight ♦ [2] blues, dejection, depression, doldrums, dumps, melancholy, sadness

gloom·i·ness \-mē-nəs\ *n* : the quality or state of being gloomy

gloomy \ˈglü-mē\ *adj* **gloom·i·er; -est 1** ♦ : partially or totally dark **2** ♦ : causing gloom; *also* : lacking in promise or hopefulness **3** ♦ : low in spirits — **gloom·i·ly** \ˈglü-mə-lē\ *adv*

♦ [1] dark, darkling, dim, dusky, murky, obscure, somber (*or* sombre) ♦ [2] bleak, dark, depressing, desolate, dismal, dreary, glum, gray (*or* grey), miserable, murky, somber (*or* sombre) *Ant* bright, cheerful, festive, friendly, heartwarming, sunshiny ♦ [3] blue, dejected, depressed, down, downcast, forlorn, glum, low, melancholy, miserable, sad, sorrowful, unhappy

Gloomy Gus \-ˈgəs\ *n, pl* **Gloomy Gus·es** : a person who is habitually gloomy

glop \ˈgläp\ *n* : a messy mass or mixture

glo·ri·fy \ˈglȯr-ə-ˌfī\ *vb* **-fied; -fy·ing 1** : to raise to heavenly glory **2** : to light up brilliantly **3** ♦ : to represent as glorious : EXTOL **4** ♦ : to give glory to (as in worship) **5** ♦ : to cause to be or seem to be better than the actual condition **6** ♦ : to make glorious by bestowing honor, praise, or admiration — **glo·ri·fi·ca·tion** \ˌglȯr-ə-fə-ˈkā-shən\ *n*

♦ [3] bless, extol, laud, magnify, praise ♦ [4] adore, deify, revere, venerate, worship ♦ [5] dream, glamorize, idealize ♦ [6] aggrandize, dignify, ennoble, exalt, magnify

glo·ri·ous \ˈglȯr-ē-əs\ *adj* **1** : possessing or deserving glory : PRAISEWORTHY **2** : conferring glory **3** ♦ : marked by great beauty or splendor : MAGNIFICENT **4** : DELIGHTFUL, WONDERFUL

♦ august, baronial, gallant, grand, grandiose, heroic, imposing, magnificent, majestic, monumental, noble, proud, regal, royal, splendid, stately

glo·ri·ous·ly *adv* ♦ : in a glorious manner

♦ agreeably, delightfully, favorably (*or* favourably), felicitously, nicely, pleasantly, pleasingly, satisfyingly, splendidly, well

¹**glo·ry** \ˈglȯr-ē\ *n, pl* **glories** **1** ♦ : praise, honor, or distinction extended by common consent : RENOWN **2** : honor and praise rendered in worship **3** ♦ : something that secures praise or renown **4** : a distinguishing quality or asset **5** ♦ : great beauty and splendor : RESPLENDENCE, MAGNIFICENCE **6** : heavenly bliss **7** : a height of prosperity or achievement

♦ [1] acclaim, accolade, credit, distinction, fame, homage, honor (*or* honour), laurels, praise, renown ♦ [3] boast, credit, honor (*or* honour), jewel, pride, treasure ♦ [5] augustness, brilliance, grandeur, grandness, magnificence, majesty, nobility, nobleness, resplendence, splendor, stateliness

²**glory** *vb* **glo·ried; glo·ry·ing** ♦ : to rejoice proudly : EXULT

♦ crow, delight, exult, joy, rejoice, triumph

¹**gloss** \ˈgläs, ˈglȯs\ *n* **1** ♦ : a surface luster or brightness : SHEEN **2** : outward show

♦ luster (*or* lustre), polish, sheen, shine

²**gloss** *vb* **1** ♦ : to give a false appearance of acceptableness to ⟨~ over inadequacies⟩ **2** ♦ : to deal with too lightly or not at all — usu. used with *over* ⟨~ed over the problem⟩ **3** ♦ : to give a gloss to

♦ *usu* **gloss over** [1] excuse, palliate, whitewash ♦ *usu* **gloss over** [2] condone, disregard, excuse, forgive, ignore, pardon, pass over, shrug off, wink at ♦ [3] buff, burnish, dress, grind, polish, rub, shine, smooth

³**gloss** *n* **1** : an explanatory note (as in the margin of a text) **2** : GLOSSARY **3** : an interlinear translation **4** : a continuous commentary accompanying a text

⁴**gloss** *vb* : to furnish glosses for

glos·sa·ry \ˈglä-sə-rē, ˈglȯ-\ *n, pl* **-ries** : a collection of difficult or specialized terms with their meanings — **glos·sar·i·al** \glä-ˈser-ē-əl, glȯ-\ *adj*

glos·so·la·lia \ˌglä-sə-ˈlā-lē-ə, ˌglȯ-\ *n* : TONGUE 6

¹**glossy** \ˈglä-sē, ˈglȯ-\ *adj* **gloss·i·er; -est** ♦ : having a surface luster or brightness — **gloss·i·ly** \-sə-lē\ *adv* — **gloss·i·ness** \-sē-nəs\ *n*

♦ lustrous, polished, satiny, sleek *Ant* dim, dull, flat, lusterless, matte

²**glossy** *n, pl* **gloss·ies** : a photograph printed on smooth shiny paper

glot·tis \ˈglä-təs\ *n, pl* **glot·tis·es** *or* **glot·ti·des** \-tə-ˌdēz\ : the slitlike opening between the vocal cords in the larynx — **glot·tal** \ˈglä-t²l\ *adj*

glove \ˈgləv\ *n* **1** : a covering for the hand having separate sections for each finger **2** : a padded leather covering for the hand for use in a sport

¹**glow** \ˈglō\ *vb* **1** ♦ : to shine with or as if with intense heat **2** ♦ : to have a rich warm usu. ruddy color : FLUSH, BLUSH **3** : to feel hot **4** : to show exuberance or elation ⟨~ with pride⟩

♦ [1] blaze, burn, flame ♦ [2] bloom, blush, color (*or* colour), crimson, flush, redden

²**glow** *n* **1** : brightness or warmth of color; *esp* : REDNESS **2** : warmth of feeling or emotion **3** : a sensation of warmth **4** ♦ : light such as is emitted from a heated substance

♦ blaze, flare, fluorescence, glare, gleam, illumination, incandescence, light, luminescence, radiance, shine

glow·er \ˈglau̇(-ə)r\ *vb* ♦ : to stare angrily : SCOWL — **glower** *n*

♦ frown, glare, gloom, lower, scowl

glowing *adj* **1** ♦ : giving off light esp. because of heat **2** ♦ : marked by a rich warm coloration; *also* : marked by a radiant healthfully ruddy coloration **3** : highly enthusiastic

♦ [1] beaming, bright, brilliant, effulgent, incandescent, lambent, lucent, lucid, luminous, lustrous, radiant, refulgent, shiny ♦ [2] florid, flush, rosy, ruddy, sanguine

glow·worm \ˈglō-ˌwərm\ *n* : any of various insect larvae or adults that give off light

glox·in·ia \gläk-ˈsi-nē-ə\ *n* : any of a genus of tropical herbs related to the African violets; *esp* : one with showy bell-shaped or slipper-shaped flowers

gloze \ˈglōz\ *vb* **glozed; gloz·ing** : to make appear right or acceptable : GLOSS

glu·cose \ˈglü-ˌkōs\ *n* **1** : a form of crystalline sugar; *esp* : DEXTROSE **2** : a sweet light-colored syrup made from cornstarch

glue \ˈglü\ *n* ♦ : a jellylike protein substance made from animal materials and used for sticking things together; *also* : any of various other strong adhesives — **glue** *vb*

♦ adhesive, cement, size

glu·ey \ˈglü-ē\ *adj* **1** ♦ : having the quality of glue; *also* : resembling or suggestive of glue (as in stickiness or consistency) **2** : daubed, smeared, or covered with glue

♦ adhesive, gelatinous, glutinous, gooey, gummy, sticky, viscid, viscous

glum \ˈgləm\ *adj* **glum·mer; glum·mest** **1** ♦ : broodingly morose : SULLEN **2** ♦ : having nothing likely to provide cheer, comfort, or interest : DREARY, GLOOMY

♦ [1] moody, morose, sulky, sullen, surly ♦ [1; 2] bleak, dark, dismal, dreary, gloomy, gray (*or* grey), somber (*or* sombre), wretched

¹**glut** \ˈglət\ *vb* **glut·ted; glut·ting** **1** : to supply with more than is needed or than can be handled **2** ♦ : to fill esp. with food to satiety : SATIATE

♦ gorge, sate, satiate, stuff, surfeit

²**glut** *n* : an excessive supply

glu·ten \ˈglüt-²n\ *n* : a gluey protein substance that causes dough to be sticky

glu·ti·nous \ˈglü-tə-nəs\ *adj* ♦ : having the quality of glue : STICKY

♦ adhesive, gelatinous, gluey, gooey, gummy, sticky, viscid, viscous

glut·ton \ˈglə-t²n\ *n* : one that eats to excess — **glut·tony** \ˈglə-tə-nē\ *n*

glut·ton·ous \ˈglət-²n-əs\ *adj* ♦ : marked by or given to excessive eating or drinking

♦ greedy, hoggish, piggish, rapacious, ravenous, voracious

glyc·er·in *or* **glyc·er·ine** \ˈgli-sə-rən\ *n* : GLYCEROL

glyc·er·ol \ˈgli-sə-ˌrȯl, -ˌrōl\ *n* : a sweet syrupy alcohol usu. obtained from fats and used esp. as a solvent

gly·co·gen \ˈglī-kə-jən\ *n* : a white tasteless substance that is the chief storage carbohydrate of animals

gm *abbr* gram

GM *abbr* **1** general manager **2** guided missile

G–man \ˈjē-ˌman\ *n* : a special agent of the Federal Bureau of Investigation

GMT *abbr* Greenwich mean time

gnarled \ˈnärld\ *adj* **1** : KNOTTY **2** : GLOOMY, SULLEN

gnash \ˈnash\ *vb* ♦ : to grind (as teeth) together

♦ crunch, grate, grind, grit, scrape

gnat \ˈnat\ *n* : any of various small usu. biting dipteran flies

gnaw \ˈnȯ\ *vb* **1** ♦ : to consume, wear away, or make by persistent biting or nibbling **2** : to affect as if by gnawing

♦ *usu* **gnaw on** bite, champ, chew, chomp, crunch, nibble

gnaw·er *n* : one that gnaws

gneiss \ˈnīs\ *n* : a layered rock similar in composition to granite

gnome \ˈnōm\ *n* ♦ : a dwarf of folklore who lives inside the earth and guards precious ore or treasure — **gnom·ish** *adj*

♦ brownie, dwarf, elf, fairy, fay, hobgoblin, leprechaun, pixie, puck, troll

GNP *abbr* gross national product

gnu \ˈnü\ *n, pl* **gnu** *or* **gnus** : WILDEBEEST

¹**go** \ˈgō\ *vb* **went** \ˈwent\; **gone** \ˈgȯn, ˈgän\; **go·ing; goes** \ˈgōz\ **1** ♦ : to move on a course : PROCEED ⟨~ slow⟩ **2** ♦ : to move out of or away from a place expressed or implied : LEAVE, DEPART **3** : to take a certain course or follow a certain procedure ⟨reports ~ through department channels⟩ **4** : to extend from point to point or in a certain direction : RUN ⟨his land ~es to the river⟩; *also* : LEAD ⟨that door ~es to the cellar⟩ **5** : to be habitually in a certain state ⟨~es armed after dark⟩ **6** : to become lost, consumed, or spent; *also* : DIE **7** : ELAPSE, PASS **8** ♦ : to pass by sale ⟨went for a good price⟩ **9** : to become impaired or weakened **10** : to give way under force or pressure **11** : to move along in a specified manner ⟨it went well⟩ **12** : to be in general or on an average ⟨cheap, as yachts ~⟩ **13** : to become esp. as the result of a contest ⟨the decision went against him⟩ **14** : to put or subject oneself ⟨~ to great expense⟩ **15** ♦ : to have recourse to another ⟨went to court to recover damages⟩ **16** : to begin or maintain an action or motion ⟨here ~es⟩ **17** : to function properly ⟨the clock doesn't ~⟩ **18** : to be known ⟨~es by an alias⟩ **19** : to be or act in accordance ⟨a good rule to ~ by⟩ **20** : to come to be applied **21** : to pass by award, assignment, or lot **22** : to contribute to a result ⟨qualities that ~ to make a hero⟩ **23** : to be about, intending, or expecting something ⟨is ~ing to leave town⟩ **24** : to arrive at a certain state or condition ⟨~ to sleep⟩ **25** : to come to be ⟨the tire went flat⟩ **26** : to be capable of being sung or played ⟨the tune ~es

like this⟩ **27** : to be suitable or becoming : HARMONIZE **28** : to be capable of passing, extending, or being contained or inserted ⟨this coat will ∼ in the trunk⟩ **29** : to have a usual or proper place or position : BELONG ⟨these books ∼ on that shelf⟩ **30** : to be capable of being contained in ⟨3 ∼es into 6 twice⟩ **31** : to have a tendency ⟨that ∼es to show that he is honest⟩ **32** : to be acceptable, satisfactory, or adequate **33** : to empty the bladder or bowels **34** : to proceed along or according to : FOLLOW **35** ♦ : to travel through or along : TRAVERSE **36** : to make a wager or offer of : BET, BID ⟨willing to ∼ $50⟩ **37** : to assume the function or obligation of ⟨∼ bail for a friend⟩ **38** : to participate to the extent of ⟨∼ halves⟩ **39** : WEIGH **40** : ENDURE, TOLERATE **41** : AFFORD ⟨can't ∼ the price⟩ **42** : SAY — used chiefly in oral narration of speech **43** : to engage in ⟨don't ∼ telling everyone⟩ — **go at 1** : ATTACK, ATTEMPT **2** : UNDERTAKE — **go back on 1** : ABANDON **2** : BETRAY **3** : FAIL — **go by the board** : to be discarded — **go for 1** : to pass for or serve as **2** : to try to secure **3** : FAVOR — **go one better** : OUTDO, SURPASS — **go over 1** : EXAMINE **2** : REPEAT **3** : STUDY, REVIEW — **go places** : to be on the way to success — **go steady** : to date one person exclusively — **go to bat for** : DEFEND, CHAMPION — **go to town 1** : to work or act efficiently **2** : to be very successful

♦ [1] advance, fare, forge, get along, march, proceed, progress **Ant** remain, stand, stay, stop ♦ [2] clear out, depart, exit, get off, leave, move, pull, quit, sally, shove, take off **Ant** arrive, come, show up, turn up ♦ [4] extend, head, lead, lie, run ♦ usu **go for** [8] bring, cost, fetch, sell ♦ usu **go to** [15] refer, resort, turn ♦ [35] cover, crisscross, cross, cut, follow, pass, proceed, travel, traverse

²**go** n, pl **goes 1** : the act or manner of going **2** : the height of fashion ⟨boots are all the ∼⟩ **3** : a turn of affairs : OCCURRENCE **4** : active bodily or mental strength or force : ENERGY, VIGOR **5** ♦ : an experimental trial or attempt **6** : a spell of activity — **no go** : USELESS, HOPELESS — **on the go** : constantly active

♦ attempt, bid, crack, endeavor (or endeavour), essay, fling, pass, shot, stab, trial, try, whack, whirl

³**go** adj ♦ : functioning properly

♦ fit, ready, set

¹**goad** \'gōd\ n **1** : a pointed rod used to urge on an animal **2** ♦ : something that urges

♦ boost, encouragement, impetus, impulse, incentive, incitement, instigation, momentum, motivation, provocation, spur, stimulus, yeast

²**goad** vb ♦ : to incite or rouse as if with a goad

♦ egg on, encourage, exhort, press, prod, prompt, urge

go–ahead \'gō-ə-ˌhed\ n : authority to proceed
goal \'gōl\ n **1** : the mark set as limit to a race; also : an area to be reached safely in children's games **2** ♦ : the end toward which effort is directed : AIM, PURPOSE **3** : an area or object toward which play is directed to score; also : a successful attempt to score

♦ aim, ambition, aspiration, design, dream, end, intent, mark, meaning, object, objective, plan, pretension, purpose, thing

goal·ie \'gō-lē\ n : GOALKEEPER
goal·keep·er \'gōl-ˌkē-pər\ n : a player who defends the goal in various games
goal·post \-ˌpōst\ n : one of the two vertical posts with a crossbar that constitute the goal in various games
goat \'gōt\ n, pl **goats** or **goat** : any of various hollow-horned ruminant mammals related to the sheep that have backward-curving horns, a short tail, and usu. straight hair
goa·tee \gō-'tē\ n : a small trim pointed or tufted beard on a man's chin
goat·herd \'gōt-ˌhərd\ n : a person who tends goats
goat·skin \-ˌskin\ n : the skin of a goat or a leather made from it
¹**gob** \'gäb\ n **1** ♦ : a piece or mass of indefinite size and shape : LUMP, MASS **2** ♦ : a large amount — usu. used in pl. ⟨∼s of money⟩

♦ [1] blob, chunk, clod, clump, glob, hunk, lump, mass, nub, wad ♦ usu **gobs** [2] abundance, deal, heap, loads, lot, pile, plenty, quantity, scads

²**gob** n ♦ : a member of a ship's crew : SAILOR

♦ jack, jack-tar, mariner, sailor, seaman, swab, tar

gob·bet \'gä-bət\ n : a piece or mass of indefinite size and shape : LUMP, MASS
¹**gob·ble** \'gä-bəl\ vb **gob·bled**; **gob·bling 1** ♦ : to swallow or eat greedily **2** : to take eagerly : GRAB

♦ bolt, devour, gorge, gormandize, gulp, scarf, scoff, wolf

²**gobble** vb **gob·bled**; **gob·bling** : to make the natural guttural noise of a male turkey
gob·ble·dy·gook also **gob·ble·de·gook** \'gä-bəl-dē-ˌgúk, -ˌgük\ n ♦ : generally unintelligible jargon

♦ babble, gabble, gibberish, hogwash, jabber, jabberwocky, nonsense

gob·bler \'gä-blər\ n : a male turkey
go–be·tween \'gō-bə-ˌtwēn\ n ♦ : an intermediate agent : BROKER

♦ arbiter, arbitrator, broker, intercessor, intermediary, mediator, middleman, peacemaker

gob·let \'gä-blət\ n : a drinking glass with a foot and stem
gob·lin \'gä-blən\ n : an ugly or grotesque sprite that is mischievous and sometimes evil and malicious
go·by \'gō-bē\ n, pl **gobies** also **goby** : any of numerous spiny-finned fishes usu. having the pelvic fins united to form a ventral sucking disk
god \'gäd, 'gód\ n **1** cap : the supreme reality; esp : the Being worshiped as the creator and ruler of the universe **2** : a being or object believed to have supernatural attributes and powers and to require worship **3** : a thing of supreme value **4** : an extraordinarily attractive person
god·child \'gäd-ˌchīld, 'gód-\ n : a person for whom another person stands as sponsor at baptism
god·daugh·ter \-ˌdò-tər\ n : a female godchild
god·dess \'gä-dəs, 'gó-\ n **1** : a female god **2** ♦ : a woman whose charm or beauty arouses adoration

♦ beauty, enchantress, fox, knockout, queen

god·fa·ther \'gäd-ˌfä-thər, 'gód-\ n **1** : a man who sponsors a person at baptism **2** : the leader of an organized crime syndicate
god·head \-ˌhed\ n **1** ♦ : divine nature or essence **2** cap : GOD 1; also : the nature of God esp. as existing in three persons

♦ deity, divinity

god·hood \-ˌhúd\ n : the quality or state of being a god : DIVINITY
god·less \-ləs\ adj : not acknowledging a deity or divine law — **god·less·ness** n
god·like \-ˌlīk\ adj ♦ : resembling or having the qualities of God or a god

♦ blessed, divine, heavenly, holy

god·li·ness n ♦ : the quality or state of living a godly life

♦ blessedness, devoutness, holiness, piety, sainthood, sanctity

god·ly \-lē\ adj **god·li·er; -est 1** : DIVINE **2** ♦ : marked by or showing reverence for deity and devotion to divine worship : PIOUS, DEVOUT

♦ devout, faithful, holy, pious, religious, sainted, saintly

god·moth·er \-ˌmə-thər\ n : a woman who sponsors a person at baptism
god·par·ent \-ˌpar-ənt\ n : a sponsor at baptism
god·send \-ˌsend\ n ♦ : a desirable or needed thing or event that comes unexpectedly

♦ benefit, blessing, boon, felicity, good, manna, windfall

god·son \-ˌsən\ n : a male godchild
God·speed \-'spēd\ n : a prosperous journey : SUCCESS ⟨bade him ∼⟩
go·fer or **go·pher** \'gō-fər\ n : an employee whose duties include running errands
go–get·ter \'gō-ˌge-tər\ n ♦ : an aggressively enterprising person — adj or n

♦ hustler, live wire, powerhouse, self-starter

go–get·ting adj ♦ : marked by driving forceful energy, ambition, or initiative — **go-getting** n

♦ aggressive, ambitious, assertive, enterprising, fierce, high-pressure, militant, self-assertive

gog·gle \'gä-gəl\ vb **gog·gled**; **gog·gling** ♦ : to stare with wide or protuberant eyes

♦ gape, gawk, gaze, peer, rubberneck, stare

gog·gles \'gä-gəlz\ n pl : protective glasses set in a flexible frame that fits snugly against the face
go–go \'gō-ˌgō\ adj **1** : related to, being, or employed to entertain in a disco ⟨∼ dancers⟩ **2** : aggressively enterprising and energetic ⟨∼ entrepreneurs⟩
go·ings–on \ˌgō-iŋ-'zón, -'zän\ n pl : ACTIONS, EVENTS
goi·ter or Can and Brit **goi·tre** \'gói-tər\ n : an abnormally enlarged thyroid gland visible as a swelling at the base of the neck — **goi·trous** \-trəs, -tə-rəs\ adj

go–kart \'gō-ˌkärt\ *n* : a small motorized vehicle used esp. for racing

gold \'gōld\ *n* **1** : a malleable yellow metallic chemical element used esp. for coins and jewelry **2** : gold coins; *also* : MONEY **3** : a yellow color

gold·brick \'gōld-ˌbrik\ *n* : a person who shirks assigned work — **goldbrick** *vb*

gold coast *n, often cap G&C* : an exclusive residential district

gold digger *n* : a person who uses charm to extract money or gifts from others

gold·en \'gōl-dən\ *adj* **1** : made of or relating to gold **2** ♦ : having the color of gold; *also* : BLOND **3** : SHINING, LUSTROUS **4** : SUPERB **5** ♦ : marked by success or economic well‑being : PROSPEROUS **6** : radiantly youthful and vigorous **7** ♦ : tending to promote or facilitate : FAVORABLE, ADVANTAGEOUS ⟨a ~ opportunity⟩ **8** : rich and full but free from garishness or stridency : MELLOW, RESONANT

♦ [2] blond, fair, flaxen, sandy, straw ♦ [5] booming, palmy, prosperous, roaring, successful ♦ [7] advantageous, auspicious, bright, encouraging, favorable (*or* favourable), heartening, hopeful, promising, propitious

gold·en·ag·er \'gōl-dən-ˌā-jər\ *n* ♦ : an elderly and often retired person usu. engaging in club activities

♦ ancient, elder, oldster, senior citizen

golden hamster *n* : a small tawny hamster often kept as a pet

golden handcuffs *n pl* : special benefits offered to an employee as an inducement to continue service

golden handshake *n* : a generous severance agreement given esp. as an inducement to early retirement

golden retriever *n* : any of a breed of retrievers with a flat golden coat

gold·en·rod \'gōl-dən-ˌräd\ *n* : any of numerous herbs related to the daisies that have tall slender stalks with many tiny usu. yellow flower heads

golden years *n pl* : the advanced years in a lifetime

gold·finch \-ˌfinch\ *n* **1** : a small largely red, black, and yellow Old World finch often kept in a cage **2** : any of three small related American finches of which the males usu. become bright yellow and black in summer

gold·fish \-ˌfish\ *n* : a small usu. golden-orange carp often kept as an aquarium or pond fish

gold·smith \-ˌsmith\ *n* : a person who makes or deals in articles of gold

golf \'gälf, 'gȯlf\ *n* : a game played with a small ball and various clubs on a course having 9 or 18 holes — **golf** *vb* — **golf·er** *n*

-gon \ˌgän\ *n comb form* : figure having (so many) angles ⟨hexa*gon*⟩

go·nad \'gō-ˌnad\ *n* : a sperm- or egg-producing gland : OVARY, TESTIS — **go·nad·al** \gō-'na-dᵊl\ *adj*

go·nad·o·trop·ic \gō-ˌna-də-'trä-pik\ *also* **go·nad·o·tro·phic** \-'trō-fik, -'trä-\ *adj* : acting on or stimulating the gonads

go·nad·o·tro·pin \-'trō-pən\ *also* **go·nad·o·tro·phin** \-fən\ *n* : a gonadotropic hormone

gon·do·la \'gän-də-lə (*usual for 1*), gän-'dō-\ *n* **1** : a long narrow boat used on the canals of Venice **2** : a railroad car used for hauling loose freight (as coal) **3** : an enclosure beneath an airship or balloon **4** : an enclosed car suspended from a cable and used esp. for transporting skiers

gon·do·lier \ˌgän-də-'lir\ *n* : a person who propels a gondola

¹**gone** \'gȯn\ *past part of* GO

²**gone** *adj* **1** ♦ : no longer alive : DEAD **2** : no longer possessed : LOST, RUINED **3** : SINKING, WEAK **4** : INVOLVED, ABSORBED **5** : INFATUATED **6** : PREGNANT **7** : having existed or taken place in a period before the present : PAST

♦ bygone, dead, deceased, defunct, extinct

gon·er \'gȯ-nər\ *n* : one whose case is hopeless

gong \'gäŋ, 'gȯŋ\ *n* : a metallic disk that produces a resounding tone when struck

gono·coc·cus \ˌgä-nə-'kä-kəs\ *n, pl* **-coc·ci** \-'käk-ˌsī, -(ˌ)sē, -'kä-ˌkī, -(ˌ)kē\ : a pus-producing bacterium causing gonorrhea — **gono·coc·cal** \-'kä-kəl\ *adj*

gon·or·rhea \ˌgä-nə-'rē-ə\ *n* : a contagious sexually transmitted inflammation of the genital tract caused by the gonococcus — **gon·or·rhe·al** \-'rē-əl\ *adj*

goo \'gü\ *n* **1** : a viscid or sticky substance **2** : sentimental tripe

goo·ber \'gü-bər, 'gü-bə\ *n, Southern & Midland* : PEANUT

¹**good** \'gu̇d\ *adj* **bet·ter** \'be-tər\; **best** \'best\ **1** ♦ : of a favorable character or tendency **2** : BOUNTIFUL, FERTILE **3** : COMELY, ATTRACTIVE **4** ♦ : adapted to a use or purpose : SUITABLE, FIT **5** : SOUND, WHOLE **6** ♦ : having qualities that tend to give plea-

sure : AGREEABLE, PLEASANT **7** : SALUTARY, WHOLESOME **8** : of a noticeably large size or quantity : CONSIDERABLE **9** : FULL **10** ♦ : based on excellent reasoning, information, judgment, or grounds **11** : TRUE ⟨holds ~ for everybody⟩ **12** : legally valid or effectual **13** : sufficient for a specific requirement : SATISFACTORY **14** ♦ : conforming to a standard **15** : DISCRIMINATING **16** : worthy of being commended **17** : KIND **18** : UPPERCLASS **19** ♦ : having or displaying competence or skill **20** : unswerving in allegiance : LOYAL, CLOSE ⟨a ~ friend⟩ — **good·ish** *adj* — **good–look·ing** \-'lu̇-kiŋ\ *adj*

♦ [1] appreciative, complimentary, favorable (*or* favourable), friendly, positive ♦ [4] applicable, appropriate, apt, felicitous, fit, fitting, happy, meet, proper, right, suitable ♦ [6] agreeable, congenial, delightful, felicitous, grateful, gratifying, nice, palatable, pleasant, pleasurable, satisfying ♦ [10] hard, informed, just, logical, rational, reasonable, reasoned, sensible, solid, valid, well-founded *Ant* baseless, illogical, invalid, unfounded, uninformed, unreasonable, unsound ♦ [14] decent, ethical, honest, honorable (*or* honourable), just, moral, right, straight, virtuous *Ant* bad, evil, unethical, wrong ♦ [19] accomplished, adept, capable, competent, proficient, skilled, skillful

²**good** *n* **1** ♦ : something good **2** : GOODNESS **3** ♦ : advancement of prosperity or well-being : BENEFIT, WELFARE ⟨for the ~ of humankind⟩ **4** : something that has economic utility **5** *pl* : personal property **6** *pl* : CLOTH **7** *pl* : something manufactured or produced for sale : WARES, MERCHANDISE **8** : good persons ⟨the ~ die young⟩ **9** *pl* : proof of wrongdoing — **for good** : FOREVER, PERMANENTLY — **to the good** : in a position of net gain or profit ⟨$10 *to the good*⟩

♦ [1] blessing, boon, felicity, godsend, manna, windfall
♦ [3] benefit, interest, weal, welfare, well-being

³**good** *adv* ♦ : in a good or proper manner : WELL

♦ OK, adequately, all right, fine, nicely, passably, satisfactorily, so-so, tolerably, well

good–bye *or* **good–by** \gu̇d-'bī, gə-\ *n* ♦ : a concluding remark at parting

♦ adieu, au revoir, bon voyage, farewell *Ant* hello

good cholesterol *n* : HDL

good–for–noth·ing \'gu̇d-fər-ˌnə-thiŋ\ *adj* : of no use or value — **good–for–nothing** *n*

Good Friday *n* : the Friday before Easter observed as the anniversary of the crucifixion of Christ

good–heart·ed \-'här-təd\ *adj* ♦ : having a kindly generous disposition

♦ beneficent, benevolent, compassionate, humane, kind, kindly, sympathetic, tender, tenderhearted, warmhearted

good·ly \'gu̇d-lē\ *adj* **good·li·er; -est** **1** : of pleasing appearance **2** ♦ : significantly large : CONSIDERABLE

♦ considerable, good, healthy, respectable, significant, sizable, substantial, tidy

good·man \'gu̇d-mən\ *n, archaic* : MR.

good–na·tured \'gu̇d-'nā-chərd\ *adj* ♦ : of a cheerful disposition — **good–na·tured·ly** \-chərd-lē\ *adv*

♦ affable, agreeable, amiable, genial, gracious, nice, sweet, well-disposed

good·ness \-nəs\ *n* ♦ : the quality or state of being good : VIRTUE

♦ character, decency, honesty, honor (*or* honour), integrity, morality, probity, rectitude, righteousness, uprightness, virtue

good–tem·pered \-'tem-pərd\ *adj* : not easily angered or upset

good·wife \-ˌwīf\ *n, archaic* : MRS.

good·will \-'wil\ *n* **1** : kindly feeling of approval and support : BENEVOLENCE **2** : the value of the trade a business has built up over time **3** : cheerful consent **4** ♦ : willing effort

♦ [1] amity, benevolence, cordiality, fellowship, friendliness, friendship, kindliness *Ant* ill will, malevolence ♦ [4] alacrity, gameness, willingness

goody *or* **good·ie** \'gu̇-dē\ *n, pl* **good·ies** ♦ : something that is good esp. to eat

♦ dainty, delicacy, tidbit, treat

goody–goody \ˌgu̇-dē-'gu̇-dē\ *adj* : affectedly good — **goody–goody** *n*

goo·ey \'gü-ē\ *adj* ♦ : having a sticky or thick quality

♦ adhesive, gelatinous, gluey, glutinous, gummy, sticky, viscid, viscous

¹goof \'güf\ *vb* **1** ♦ : to spend time idly or foolishly — usu. used with *off* **2** : BLUNDER — usu. used with *up*

♦ *usu* **goof off** dally, dawdle, dillydally, hang around, hang out, idle, loaf, loll, lounge

²goof *n* **1** : a silly or stupid person **2** ♦ : a gross error or mistake resulting usu. from stupidity, ignorance, or carelessness

♦ blunder, error, fault, flub, fumble, lapse, miscue, misstep, mistake, oversight, slip, stumble

goof·ball \'güf-ˌbȯl\ *n* **1** *slang* : a barbiturate sleeping pill **2** : a goofy person

go off *vb* **1** ♦ : to burst forth with sudden violence or noise from internal energy : EXPLODE **2** : to follow a course ⟨the party *went off* well⟩

♦ blow up, burst, detonate, explode, pop

goof–off \'gü-ˌfȯf\ *n* : one who evades work or responsibility
goofy \'gü-fē\ *adj* **goof·i·er; -est** ♦ : being crazy, ridiculous, or mildly ludicrous : SILLY — **goof·i·ness** \-fē-nəs\ *n*

♦ flighty, frivolous, giddy, harebrained, light-headed, scatterbrained, silly

goo·gle \'gü-gəl\ *vb* **goo·gled; goo·gling** : to use the Google search engine to obtain information on the World Wide Web
goon \'gün\ *n* **1** ♦ : a man hired to terrorize or kill opponents **2** ♦ : a stupid person

♦ [1] bully, gangster, hood, hoodlum, mobster, mug, punk, rowdy, ruffian, thug, tough ♦ [2] blockhead, dope, dummy, idiot, imbecile, jackass, moron, numskull

go on *vb* **1** : to continue in a course of action **2** ♦ : to take place : HAPPEN

♦ be, befall, betide, chance, come, happen, occur, pass, transpire

goose \'güs\ *n, pl* **geese** \'gēs\ **1** : any of numerous long-necked web-footed birds related to the swans and ducks; *also* : a female goose as distinguished from a gander **2** ♦ : a foolish person **3** *pl* **goos·es** : a tailor's smoothing iron

♦ booby, fool, half-wit, jackass, nitwit, nut, simpleton, turkey

goose·ber·ry \'güs-ˌber-ē, 'güz-, -bə-rē\ *n* : the acid berry of any of several shrubs related to the currant and used esp. in jams and pies
goose bumps *n pl* : roughening of the skin caused usu. by cold, fear, or a sudden feeling of excitement
goose·flesh \-ˌflesh\ *n* : GOOSE BUMPS
goose pimples *n pl* : GOOSE BUMPS
go out *vb* **1** : to become extinguished **2** : to become a candidate ⟨*went out* for the football team⟩
go over *vb* ♦ : to win approval : SUCCEED

♦ click, deliver, pan out, succeed, work out

GOP *abbr* Grand Old Party (Republican)
¹go·pher \'gō-fər\ *n* **1** : a burrowing American land tortoise **2** : any of a family of No. American burrowing rodents with large cheek pouches opening beside the mouth **3** : any of several small ground squirrels of the prairie region of No. America
²gopher *var of* GOFER
¹gore \'gȯr\ *n* **1** : BLOOD **2** : vivid gruesomeness
²gore *n* : a tapering or triangular piece (as of cloth in a skirt)
³gore *vb* **gored; gor·ing** ♦ : to pierce or wound with something pointed

♦ harpoon, impale, lance, pierce, puncture, skewer, spear, spike, stab, stick, transfix

¹gorge \'gȯrj\ *n* **1** : THROAT **2** ♦ : a narrow ravine **3** : a mass of matter that chokes up a passage

♦ canyon, defile, flume, gap, gulch, notch, pass, ravine

²gorge *vb* **gorged; gorg·ing** ♦ : to eat greedily, hurriedly, or to capacity

♦ glut, sate, stuff, surfeit ♦ bolt, devour, gobble, gormandize, gulp, scarf, scoff, wolf

gor·geous \'gȯr-jəs\ *adj* ♦ : resplendently beautiful

♦ attractive, beautiful, cute, fair, handsome, knockout, lovely, pretty, ravishing, stunning

Gor·gon·zo·la \ˌgȯr-gən-'zō-lə\ *n* : a blue cheese of Italian origin
go·ril·la \gə-'ri-lə\ *n* : an African anthropoid ape related to but much larger than the chimpanzee
gor·man·dise *chiefly Brit var of* GORMANDIZE
gor·man·dize \'gȯr-mən-ˌdīz\ *vb* **-dized; -diz·ing** ♦ : to eat ravenously

♦ bolt, devour, gobble, gorge, gulp, scarf, scoff, wolf

gor·man·diz·er \ˌdī-zə(r)\ *n* : one who eats gluttonously or ravenously
gorp \'gȯrp\ *n* : a snack consisting of high-calorie food (as raisins and nuts)
gorse \'gȯrs\ *n* : a spiny yellow-flowered European evergreen shrub of the legume family
gory \'gȯr-ē\ *adj* **gor·i·er; -est** **1** : BLOODSTAINED **2** : HORRIBLE, SENSATIONAL ⟨∼ details⟩
gos·hawk \'gäs-ˌhȯk\ *n* : any of several long-tailed hawks with short rounded wings
gos·ling \'gäz-liŋ, 'gȯz-\ *n* : a young goose
¹gos·pel \'gäs-pəl\ *n* **1** : the teachings of Christ and the apostles **2** *cap* : any of the first four books of the New Testament **3** ♦ : something accepted as infallible truth

♦ creed, doctrine, ideology, philosophy

²gospel *adj* **1** : of, relating to, or emphasizing the gospel **2** : relating to or being American religious songs associated with evangelism
gos·sa·mer \'gä-sə-mər\ *n* **1** : a film of cobwebs floating in the air **2** : something light, delicate, or tenuous
¹gos·sip \'gä-səp\ *n* **1** : a person who habitually reveals personal or sensational facts **2** : rumor or report of an intimate nature **3** ♦ : an informal conversation

♦ chat, chatter, chitchat, gabfest, palaver, rap, talk

²gossip *vb* ♦ : to spread gossip

♦ blab, talk, tattle

gos·sipy *adj* : characterized by, full of, or given to gossip
got *past and past part of* GET
Goth \'gäth\ *n* : a member of a Germanic people that early in the Christian era overran the Roman Empire
¹Goth·ic \'gä-thik\ *adj* **1** : of or relating to the Goths **2** : of or relating to a style of architecture prevalent in western Europe from the middle 12th to the early 16th century
²Gothic *n* **1** : the Germanic language of the Goths **2** : the Gothic architectural style or decoration
gotten *past part of* GET
Gou·da \'gü-də\ *n* : a mild Dutch milk cheese shaped in balls
¹gouge \'gauj\ *n* **1** : a rounded troughlike chisel **2** : a hole or groove made with or as if with a gouge
²gouge *vb* **gouged; goug·ing** **1** : to cut holes or grooves in with or as if with a gouge **2** ♦ : to charge too much or too fully

♦ overcharge, soak, sting

gou·lash \'gü-ˌläsh, -ˌlash\ *n* : a stew made with meat, assorted vegetables, and paprika
go under *vb* : to be overwhelmed, defeated, or destroyed : FAIL
gourd \'gȯrd, 'gurd\ *n* **1** : any of a family of tendril-bearing vines including the cucumber, squash, and melon **2** : the fruit of a gourd; *esp* : any of various inedible hard-shelled fruits used esp. for ornament or implements
gour·mand \'gur-ˌmänd\ *n* **1** : one who is excessively fond of eating and drinking **2** ♦ : a connoisseur of food and drink : GOURMET

♦ epicure, epicurean, gourmet

gour·met \'gur-ˌmā, gur-'mā\ *n* ♦ : a connoisseur of food and drink

♦ epicure, epicurean, gourmand

gout \'gaut\ *n* : a metabolic disease marked by painful inflammation and swelling of the joints — **gouty** *adj*
gov *abbr* **1** government **2** governor
gov·ern \'gə-vərn\ *vb* **1** ♦ : to control and direct the making and administration of policy in : RULE **2** ♦ : to prevail or have decisive influence over : CONTROL, DIRECT **3** : DETERMINE, REGULATE **4** ♦ : to hold in check : RESTRAIN

♦ [1] boss, captain, command, control, preside, rule ♦ [2] administer, carry on, conduct, control, direct, guide, handle, manage, operate, oversee, regulate, run, superintend, supervise ♦ [4] bridle, check, constrain, contain, control, curb, inhibit, regulate, rein, restrain, tame

gov·er·nance \-vər-nəns\ *n* : the act or process of governing; *specif* : authoritative direction or control
gov·ern·ess \'gə-vər-nəs\ *n* : a woman who teaches and trains a child esp. in a private home
gov·ern·ment \'gə-vərn-mənt\ *n* **1** ♦ : authoritative direction or control : RULE **2** ♦ : the making of policy **3** : the organization or agency through which a political unit exercises authority **4** : the complex of institutions, laws, and customs through which a political unit is governed **5** : the governing body — **gov·ern·men·tal** \ˌgə-vərn-'ment-ᵊl\ *adj*

♦ [1] administration, authority, jurisdiction, regime, rule
♦ [2] conduct, control, direction, guidance, management, operation, oversight, regulation, running, superintendence, supervision

gov·er·nor \'gə-vər-nər\ n 1 : one that governs; *esp* : a ruler, chief executive, or head of a political unit (as a state) 2 : an attachment to a machine for automatic control of speed — **gov·er·nor·ship** n

govt *abbr* government

¹**gown** \'gaun\ n 1 : a loose flowing outer garment 2 : an official robe worn esp. by a judge, clergyman, or teacher 3 : a woman's dress ⟨evening ∼s⟩ 4 : a loose robe 5 : an academic community within a town or city

²**gown** vb : to dress in or invest with a gown

gp *abbr* group

GP *abbr* general practitioner

GPO 1 general post office 2 Government Printing Office

GPS \ǰē-ˌpē-'es\ n : a navigation system that uses satellite signals to fix location; *also* : the signal receiver itself

GQ *abbr* general quarters

gr *abbr* 1 grade 2 grain 3 gram 4 gravity 5 gross

¹**grab** \'grab\ vb **grabbed; grab·bing** ♦ : to take hastily : SNATCH

♦ bag, capture, catch, collar, corral, get, grapple, hook, land, nab, seize, snare, trap

²**grab** n 1 : something grabbed; *also* : an act or instance of grabbing 2 ♦ : an unlawful or unscrupulous seizure

♦ rip-off, theft

¹**grace** \'grās\ n 1 : unmerited help given to people by God (as in overcoming temptation) 2 : freedom from sin through divine grace 3 : a virtue coming from God 4 — used as a title for a duke, a duchess, or an archbishop 5 : a short prayer at a meal 6 : a temporary respite (as from the payment of a debt) 7 : APPROVAL, ACCEPTANCE ⟨in his good ∼s⟩ 8 : CHARM 9 : ATTRACTIVENESS, BEAUTY 10 ♦ : fitness or proportion of line or expression 11 : ease of movement 12 : a musical trill or ornament 13 ♦ : disposition to or an act or instance of kindness, courtesy, or clemency — **grace·ful·ly** adv — **grace·ful·ness** n

♦ [10] class, elegance, handsomeness, majesty, refinement, stateliness ♦ [13] boon, courtesy, favor (*or* favour), indulgence, kindness, mercy, service, turn

²**grace** vb **graced; grac·ing** 1 : HONOR 2 ♦ : to endow with grace : ADORN, EMBELLISH

♦ adorn, array, beautify, bedeck, deck, decorate, do, dress, embellish, enrich, garnish, ornament, trim

grace·ful \-fəl\ adj ♦ : displaying grace in form or action : pleasing or attractive in line, proportion, or movement

♦ elegant, handsome, majestic, refined, stately, tasteful ♦ agile, light, lissome, lithe, nimble, spry *Ant* awkward, clumsy, gawky, graceless, lumbering, ungainly, ungraceful

grace·ful·ness n : the quality or state of being graceful

grace·less adj 1 : artistically inept or unbeautiful 2 ♦ : lacking a sense of propriety

♦ [1] awkward, clumsy, gawky, heavy-handed, lubberly, lumpish, ungainly, unhandy ♦ [1] gauche, inelegant, stiff, stilted, uncomfortable, uneasy, ungraceful, wooden ♦ [2] improper, inappropriate, inapt, infelicitous, unbecoming, unfit, unseemly, unsuitable, wrong

gra·cious \'grā-shəs\ adj 1 ♦ : marked by kindness and courtesy 2 : GRACEFUL 3 : characterized by charm and good taste 4 : MERCIFUL — **gra·cious·ly** adv

♦ affable, agreeable, amiable, congenial, convivial, cordial, friendly, genial, hospitable, kind, kindly, sociable *Ant* inhospitable, ungracious, unsociable ♦ civil, courteous, genteel, mannerly, polite, well-bred

gra·cious·ness n ♦ : the quality or state of being gracious

♦ civility, courtesy, gentility, mannerliness, politeness ♦ agreeableness, amenity, amiability, geniality, niceness, pleasantness, sweetness

grack·le \'gra-kəl\ n : any of several large American blackbirds with glossy iridescent plumage

grad *abbr* graduate; graduated

gra·da·tion \grā-'dā-shən, grə-\ n 1 : a series forming successive stages 2 : a step, degree, or stage in a series 3 : an advance by regular degrees 4 : the act or process of grading

¹**grade** \'grād\ vb **grad·ed; grad·ing** 1 ♦ : to arrange in grades : SORT; *also* : to arrange in a scale or series 2 : to make level or

evenly sloping ⟨∼ a highway⟩ 3 : to give a grade to ⟨∼ a pupil in history⟩ 4 : to assign to a grade

♦ assort, break down, categorize, class, classify, group, peg, place, range, rank, rate, separate, sort

²**grade** n 1 ♦ : a degree or stage in a series, order, or ranking 2 ♦ : a position in a scale of rank, quality, or order 3 ♦ : a class of persons or things of the same rank or quality 4 : a division of the school course representing one year's work; *also* : the pupils in such a division 5 *pl* : the elementary school system 6 : a mark or rating esp. of accomplishment in school 7 ♦ : the degree of slope (as of a road); *also* : SLOPE 8 ♦ : a reference level or starting point used for measuring or calculating

♦ [1] cut, degree, inch, notch, peg, phase, point, stage, step ♦ [2] caliber (*or* calibre), class, quality, rate ♦ [3] bracket, category, class, division, family, group, kind, order, set, species, type ♦ [7] cant, diagonal, inclination, incline, lean, pitch, slant, slope, tilt, upgrade ♦ [8] criterion, mark, measure, par, standard, touchstone, yardstick

grad·er \'grā-dər\ n : a machine for leveling earth

grade school n : ELEMENTARY SCHOOL

gra·di·ent \'grā-dē-ənt\ n : the rate of regular or graded ascent or descent : SLOPE, GRADE

grad·u·al \'gra-jə-wəl\ adj ♦ : proceeding or changing by steps or degrees ⟨∼ improvements⟩ — **grad·u·al·ly** adv

♦ imperceptible, progressive *Ant* sudden

grad·u·al·ism \-wə-ˌli-zəm\ n : the policy of approaching a desired end gradually

¹**grad·u·ate** \'gra-jə-wət\ n 1 : a holder of an academic degree or diploma 2 : a graduated container for measuring contents

²**graduate** adj 1 : holding an academic degree or diploma 2 : of or relating to studies beyond the first or bachelor's degree ⟨∼ school⟩

³**grad·u·ate** \'gra-jə-ˌwāt\ vb **-at·ed; -at·ing** 1 : to grant or receive an academic degree or diploma 2 : to divide into grades, classes, or intervals 3 : to admit to a particular standing or grade

grad·u·a·tion \ˌgra-jə-'wā-shən\ n 1 : a mark that graduates something 2 ♦ : arrangement in degrees or ranks 3 : COMMENCEMENT 2

♦ ladder, scale

graf·fi·ti \grə-'fē-(ˌ)tē\ n : unauthorized writing or drawing on a public surface

graf·fi·to \gra-'fē-tō, grə-\ n, pl **-ti** \-(ˌ)tē\ : an inscription or drawing made on a public surface (as a wall)

¹**graft** \'graft\ n 1 : a grafted plant; *also* : the point of union in this 2 : material (as skin) used in grafting 3 : the getting of money or advantage dishonestly; *also* : the money or advantage so gained

²**graft** vb 1 : to insert a shoot from one plant into another so that they join and grow; *also* : to join one thing to another as in plant grafting ⟨∼ skin over a burn⟩ 2 : to get (as money) dishonestly — **graft·er** n

gra·ham cracker \'grā-əm-, 'gram-\ n : a slightly sweet cracker made chiefly of whole wheat flour

Grail \'grāl\ n : the cup or platter used according to medieval legend by Christ at the Last Supper and thereafter the object of knightly quests

grain \'grān\ n 1 : a seed or fruit of a cereal grass 2 : seeds or fruits of various food plants and esp. cereal grasses; *also* : a plant (as wheat) producing grain 3 ♦ : a small hard particle 4 : a unit of weight based on the weight of a grain of wheat 5 : TEXTURE; *also* : the arrangement of fibers in wood 6 ♦ : natural disposition — **grained** \'grānd\ adj

♦ [3] bit, granule, molecule, particle ♦ [6] disposition, nature, temper, temperament

grain alcohol n : ALCOHOL 1

grainy \'grā-nē\ adj **grain·i·er; -est** 1 ♦ : resembling or having some characteristic of grain : not smooth or fine 2 : appearing to be composed of grain-like particles ⟨a ∼ photograph⟩

♦ coarse, granular

¹**gram** \'gram\ n : a metric unit of mass and weight equal to ¹/₁₀₀₀ kilogram

²**gram** *abbr* grammar; grammatical

-gram \ˌgram\ n comb form : drawing : writing : record ⟨telegram⟩

gram·mar \'gra-mər\ n 1 : the study of the classes of words, their inflections, and their functions and relations in the sentence 2 : a study of what is to be preferred and what avoided in inflection and syntax 3 : speech or writing evaluated according to its conformity to grammatical rules — **gram·mar·i·an** \grə-ˈmer-ē-ən, -ˈmar-\ *n* — **gram·mat·i·cal** \-ˈma-ti-kəl\ *adj* — **gram·mat·i·cal·ly** \-k(ə-)lē\ *adv*

grammar school *n* **1** : a secondary school emphasizing Latin and Greek in preparation for college; *also* : a British college preparatory school **2** : a school intermediate between the primary grades and high school **3** : ELEMENTARY SCHOOL

gramme \ˈgram\ *chiefly Brit var of* GRAM

gram·o·phone \ˈgra-mə-ˌfōn\ *n* : PHONOGRAPH

gra·na·ry \ˈgrā-nə-rē, ˈgra-\ *n, pl* **-ries** **1** : a storehouse for grain **2** : a region producing grain in abundance

¹grand \ˈgrand\ *adj* **1** ♦ : higher in rank or importance : FOREMOST, CHIEF **2** ♦ : large and striking in size, scope, extent, or conception **3** ♦ : covering or intended to cover all items, costs, or services : COMPLETE ⟨a ∼ total⟩ **4** : MAGNIFICENT, SPLENDID **5** ♦ : showing wealth or high social standing **6** : fine or imposing in appearance or impression : IMPRESSIVE, STATELY **7** : very good : FINE

♦ [1] chief, dominant, first, foremost, key, main, paramount, predominant, preeminent, premier, primary, principal ♦ [2] august, baronial, gallant, glorious, grandiose, heroic, imposing, magnificent, majestic, monumental, noble, proud, regal, royal, splendid, stately *Ant* humble, unheroic, unimposing, unimpressive ♦ [3] big, considerable, goodly, great, large, outsize, oversize, sizable, substantial ♦ [3] complete, comprehensive, entire, full, intact, integral, perfect, plenary, total, whole ♦ [5] aristocratic, genteel, gentle, highborn, noble, patrician, wellborn

²grand *n, pl* **grand** *slang* : a thousand dollars

gran·dam \ˈgran-ˌdam, -dəm\ *or* **gran·dame** \-ˌdām, -dəm\ *n* : an old woman

grand·child \ˈgrand-ˌchī(-ə)ld\ *n* : a child of one's son or daughter

grand·daugh·ter \ˈgran-ˌdȯ-tər\ *n* : a daughter of one's son or daughter

grande dame \ˈgrän-ˈdäm\ *n, pl* **grandes dames** : a usu. elderly woman of great prestige or ability

gran·dee \gran-ˈdē\ *n* ♦ : a high-ranking Spanish or Portuguese nobleman

♦ aristocrat, gentleman, noble, patrician

gran·deur \ˈgran-jər\ *n* **1** ♦ : the quality or state of being grand : MAGNIFICENCE **2** : something that is grand

♦ augustness, brilliance, glory, grandness, magnificence, majesty, nobility, nobleness, resplendence, splendor, stateliness

grand·fa·ther \ˈgrand-ˌfä-thər\ *n* ♦ : the father of one's father or mother; *also* : ANCESTOR

♦ ancestor, father, forebear, forefather

grandfather clock *n* : a tall clock that stands on the floor

gran·dil·o·quence \gran-ˈdi-lə-kwəns\ *n* ♦ : pompous eloquence

♦ bombast, gas, hot air, rhetoric, wind

gran·dil·o·quent \-kwənt\ *adj* ♦ : marked by a lofty, extravagantly colorful, pompous, or bombastic style, manner, or quality esp. in language

♦ florid, flowery, highfalutin, high-flown ♦ bombastic, gaseous, oratorical, rhetorical, windy

gran·di·ose \ˈgran-dē-ˌōs, ˌgran-dē-ˈōs\ *adj* ♦ : impressive because of uncommon largeness, scope, effect, or grandeur : IMPOSING; *also* : affectedly splendid — **gran·di·ose·ly** *adv*

♦ august, baronial, gallant, glorious, grand, heroic, imposing, magnificent, majestic, monumental, noble, proud, regal, royal, splendid, stately ♦ affected, highfalutin, ostentatious, pompous, pretentious

gran·di·os·i·ty \ˌgran-dē-ˈä-sə-tē\ *n* : the quality or state of being grandiose

grand jury *n* : a jury that examines accusations of crime against persons and makes formal charges on which the persons are later tried

grand·ly \-ndlē, -lī\ *adv* ♦ : in a grand manner

♦ expensively, extravagantly, high, lavishly, luxuriously, opulently, richly ♦ gallantly, greatly, heroically, honorably (*or* honourably), magnanimously, nobly

grand mal \ˈgrän-ˌmäl; ˈgrand-ˌmal\ *n* : severe epilepsy

grand·moth·er \ˈgrand-ˌmə-thər\ *n* **1** : the mother of one's father or mother; *also* : a female ancestor

grand·ness \ˈgran(d)nəs\ *n* ♦ : the quality or state of being grand

♦ augustness, brilliance, glory, grandeur, magnificence, majes-

ty, nobility, nobleness, resplendence, splendor, stateliness ♦ bigness, greatness, largeness

grand·par·ent \-ˌpar-ənt\ *n* : a parent of one's father or mother

grand piano *n* : a piano with horizontal frame and strings

grand prix \ˈgränᵖ-ˈprē\ *n, pl* **grand prix** *same as* -ˈprēz\ *often cap G&P* : a long-distance auto race over a road course

grand slam *n* **1** : a total victory or success **2** : a home run hit with three runners on base

grand·son \ˈgrand-ˌsən\ *n* : a son of one's son or daughter

grand·stand \-ˌstand\ *n* : a usu. roofed stand for spectators at a racecourse or stadium

grange \ˈgrānj\ *n* **1** : a farm or farmhouse with its various buildings **2** *cap* : one of the lodges of a national association originally made up of farmers; *also* : the association itself — **grang·er** \ˈgrān-jər\ *n*

gran·ite \ˈgra-nət\ *n* **1** : a hard granular igneous rock used esp. for building **2** ♦ : unyielding firmness or endurance — **gra·nit·ic** \gra-ˈni-tik\ *adj*

♦ decision, decisiveness, determination, firmness, resolution, resolve

gran·ite·ware \ˈgra-nət-ˌwar\ *n* : ironware with mottled enamel

gra·no·la \grə-ˈnō-lə\ *n* : a cereal made of rolled oats and usu. raisins and nuts

¹grant \ˈgrant\ *vb* **1** : to consent to : ALLOW, PERMIT **2** ♦ : to bestow or transfer formally : GIVE **3** ♦ : to admit as true — **grant·er** *n* — **grant·or** \ˈgran-tər, -ˌtȯr\ *n*

♦ [2] accord, award, confer, give ♦ [3] acknowledge, admit, agree, allow, concede, confess, own

²grant *n* **1** : the act of granting **2** ♦ : something granted; *esp* : a gift for a particular purpose ⟨a ∼ for study abroad⟩ **3** : a transfer of property by deed or writing; *also* : the instrument by which such a transfer is made **4** : the property transferred by grant — **grant·ee** \gran-ˈtē\ *n*

♦ allocation, allotment, appropriation, subsidy

gran·u·lar \ˈgra-nyə-lər\ *adj* ♦ : consisting of or appearing to consist of granules — **gran·u·lar·i·ty** \ˌgra-nyə-ˈlar-ə-tē\ *n*

♦ coarse, grainy

gran·u·late \ˈgra-nyə-ˌlāt\ *vb* **-lat·ed; -lat·ing** : to form into grains or crystals — **gran·u·la·tion** \ˌgra-nyə-ˈlā-shən\ *n*

gran·ule \ˈgra-nyül\ *n* ♦ : a small grain or particle

♦ bit, grain, molecule, particle

grape \ˈgrāp\ *n* **1** : a smooth-skinned juicy edible greenish white, deep red, or purple berry that is the chief source of wine **2** : any of numerous woody vines widely grown for their bunches of grapes

grape·fruit \ˈgrāp-ˌfrüt\ *n* **1** *pl* **grapefruit** *or* **grapefruits** : a large edible yellow-skinned citrus fruit **2** : a tree bearing grapefruit

grape hyacinth *n* : any of several small bulbous spring-flowering herbs with clusters of usu. blue flowers that are related to the lilies

grape·shot \ˈgrāp-ˌshät\ *n* : a cluster of small iron balls formerly fired at people from short range by a cannon

grape·vine \-ˌvīn\ *n* **1** : GRAPE 2 ♦ : RUMOR; *also* : an informal means of circulating information or gossip

graph \ˈgraf\ *n* : a diagram that usu. by means of dots and lines shows change in one variable factor in comparison with one or more other factors — **graph** *vb*

-graph \ˌgraf\ *n comb form* **1** : something written ⟨auto*graph*⟩ **2** : instrument for making or transmitting records ⟨seismo*graph*⟩

¹graph·ic \ˈgra-fik\ *also* **graph·i·cal** \-fi-kəl\ *adj* **1** : of or relating to the arts (**graphic arts**) of representation, decoration, and printing on flat surfaces **2** : being written, drawn, or engraved **3** : vividly described ⟨∼ details⟩ — **graph·i·cal·ly** \-fi-k(ə-)lē\ *adv*

²graphic *n* **1** ♦ : a picture, map, or graph used for illustration **2** *pl* : a pictorial image displayed on a computer screen

♦ diagram, figure, illustration, plate

graphical user interface *n* : a computer program designed to allow easy user interaction esp. by having graphic menus or icons

graphic design *n* : the art or practice of using design elements (as typography and images) to convey information or create an effect; *also* : a product of this art — **graphic designer** *n*

graph·ics tablet \-fiks\ *n* : a computer input device for entering pictorial information by drawing or tracing

graph·ite \ˈgra-ˌfīt\ *n* : a soft black form of carbon used esp. for lead pencils and lubricants

grap·nel \'grap-nəl\ *n* : a small anchor with usu. four claws used esp. in dragging or grappling operations

¹grap·ple \'gra-pəl\ *n* ♦ : the act of grappling

♦ clasp, grasp, grip, hold

²grapple *vb* **grap·pled; grap·pling** **1** ♦ : to seize or hold with or as if with a hooked implement **2** ♦ : to engage in a hand-to-hand struggle : WRESTLE **3** ♦ : to attempt to deal with something — used with *with*

♦ [1] bag, capture, catch, collar, corral, get, grab, hook, land, nab, seize, snare, trap ♦ [2] scuffle, tussle, wrestle ♦ *usu* **grapple with** [3] contend with, cope with, handle, manage, maneuver (*or* manoeuvre), negotiate, swing, treat

¹grasp \'grasp\ *vb* **1** : to make the motion of seizing **2** : to take or seize firmly **3** ♦ : to enclose and hold with the fingers or arms **4** ♦ : to lay hold of with the mind : COMPREHEND

♦ [3] clasp, grip, hold, take ♦ [4] appreciate, apprehend, catch, catch on (to), comprehend, get, make, make out, perceive, see, seize, understand

²grasp *n* **1** : HANDLE **2** : EMBRACE **3** : HOLD, CONTROL **4** : the reach of the arms **5 a** ♦ : the act or manner of holding **b** : the power of seizing and holding **6** ♦ : mental hold or comprehension esp. when broad

♦ [5a] clasp, grapple, grip, hold ♦ [6] appreciation, apprehension, comprehension, grip, perception, understanding

grasp·ing *adj* ♦ : desiring material possessions urgently and excessively and often to the point of ruthlessness : GREEDY, AVARICIOUS

♦ acquisitive, avaricious, avid, covetous, greedy, mercenary, rapacious

grass \'gras\ *n* **1** : herbage for grazing animals **2** : any of a large family of plants (as wheat, bamboo, or sugarcane) with jointed stems and narrow leaves **3** : grass-covered land **4** : MARIJUANA — **grassy** *adj*

grass·hop·per \-ˌhä-pər\ *n* : any of numerous leaping plant-eating insects

grass·land \-ˌland\ *n* ♦ : land covered naturally or under cultivation with grasses and low-growing herbs

♦ down, plain, prairie, savanna, steppe, veld

grass roots *n pl* : society at the local level as distinguished from the centers of political leadership

¹grate \'grāt\ *vb* **grat·ed; grat·ing** **1** : to pulverize by rubbing against something rough **2** ♦ : to grind or rub against with a rasping noise **3** ♦ : to provoke impatience, anger, or displeasure in : IRRITATE — **grat·er** *n* — **grat·ing·ly** *adv*

♦ [2] grind, rasp, scrape, scratch ♦ [3] aggravate, annoy, bother, exasperate, irk, irritate, nettle, peeve, put out, vex

²grate *n* **1** : GRATING **2** : a frame of iron bars for holding fuel while it burns

grate·ful \'grāt-fəl\ *adj* **1** ♦ : appreciative of benefits received : THANKFUL; *also* : expressing gratitude **2** : giving pleasure or contentment : PLEASING — **grate·ful·ly** *adv*

♦ appreciative, obliged, thankful *Ant* thankless, unappreciative, ungrateful

grate·ful·ness *n* ♦ : the quality or state of being grateful

♦ appreciation, gratitude, thanks

grat·i·fi·ca·tion \ˌgra-tə-fə-'kā-shən\ *n* ♦ : the act of gratifying : the state of being gratified

♦ contentment, delectation, delight, enjoyment, gladness, pleasure, relish, satisfaction

grat·i·fy \'gra-tə-ˌfī\ *vb* **-fied; -fy·ing** **1** ♦ : to afford pleasure to **2** ♦ : to give in to

♦ [1] content, delight, gladden, please, rejoice, satisfy, suit, warm ♦ [2] cater to, humor (*or* humour), indulge

grat·i·fy·ing *adj* ♦ : giving pleasure or satisfaction

♦ agreeable, felicitous, good, grateful, pleasant, pleasurable, satisfying ♦ comforting, encouraging, heartening, heartwarming, rewarding, satisfying

grat·ing \'grā-tiŋ\ *n* : a framework with parallel bars or crossbars

gra·tis \'gra-təs, 'grā-\ *adv or adj* : without charge or recompense : FREE

grat·i·tude \'gra-tə-ˌtüd, -ˌtyüd\ *n* ♦ : the state of being grateful : THANKFULNESS

♦ appreciation, gratefulness, thanks

gra·tu·itous \grə-'tü-ə-təs, -'tyü-\ *adj* **1** ♦ : done or provided without recompense : FREE **2** : UNWARRANTED

♦ complimentary, free

gra·tu·ity \-ə-tē\ *n, pl* **-ities** : something given voluntarily or beyond obligation usu. for some service : TIP

gra·va·men \grə-'vā-mən\ *n, pl* **-va·mens** *or* **-vam·i·na** \-'va-mə-nə\ : the basic or significant part of a grievance or complaint

¹grave \'grāv\ *vb* **graved; grav·en** \'grā-vən\ *or* **graved; grav·ing** **1** : to carve or shape with a chisel : SCULPTURE **2** : to carve or cut (as letters or figures) into a hard surface : ENGRAVE

²grave *n* : an excavation in the earth as a place of burial; *also* : TOMB

³grave \'grāv; *5 also* 'gräv\ *adj* **1** ♦ : deserving serious consideration **2** ♦ : threatening great harm or danger **3** ♦ : having a serious and dignified quality or demeanor : SOLEMN **4** : drab in color : SOMBER **5** : of, marked by, or being an accent mark having the form ` — **grave·ly** *adv* — **grave·ness** *n*

♦ [1] heavy, serious, weighty ♦ [2] dangerous, grievous, hazardous, menacing, parlous, perilous, risky, serious, unhealthy, unsafe, venturesome ♦ [3] earnest, humorless (*or* humourless), serious, severe, sober, solemn, staid, unsmiling, weighty

grav·el \'gra-vəl\ *n* : pebbles and small pieces of rock larger than grains of sand

grav·el·ly *adj* **1** : of, containing, or covered with gravel **2** ♦ : having a rough or grating sound

♦ coarse, gruff, hoarse, husky, scratchy, throaty

Graves' disease \'grāvz-\ *n* : hyperthyroidism characterized by goiter and often protrusion of the eyeballs

grave·stone \'grāv-ˌstōn\ *n* ♦ : a burial monument

♦ headstone, monument, tombstone

grave·yard \-ˌyärd\ *n* : CEMETERY

grav·id \'gra-vəd\ *adj* : PREGNANT

gra·vi·me·ter \gra-'vi-mə-tər, 'gra-və-ˌmē-\ *n* : a device for measuring variations in a gravitational field

grav·i·tate \'gra-və-ˌtāt\ *vb* **-tat·ed; -tat·ing** : to move or tend to move toward something

grav·i·ta·tion \ˌgra-və-'tā-shən\ *n* **1** : a natural force of attraction that tends to draw bodies together and that occurs because of the mass of the bodies **2** : the action or process of gravitating — **grav·i·ta·tion·al** \-shə-nəl\ *adj* — **grav·i·ta·tion·al·ly** *adv*

grav·i·ty \'gra-və-tē\ *n, pl* **-ties** **1** ♦ : IMPORTANCE **2** ♦ : the quality or state of being serious **2** : ²MASS 5 **3** : the gravitational attraction of the mass of a celestial object (as earth) for bodies close to it; *also* : GRAVITATION 1

♦ earnest, earnestness, intentness, seriousness, sobriety, solemnity

gra·vure \grə-'vyu̇r\ *n* : PHOTOGRAVURE

gra·vy \'grā-vē\ *n, pl* **gravies** **1** : a sauce made from the thickened and seasoned juices of cooked meat **2** : unearned or illicit gain : GRAFT

¹gray *or chiefly Can and Brit* **grey** \'grā\ *adj* **1** ♦ : of the color gray; *also* : dull in color **2** : having gray hair **3** ♦ : lacking cheer or brightness in mood, outlook, style, or flavor : CHEERLESS, DISMAL **4** : intermediate in position or character — **gray·ness** *n*

♦ [1] leaden, pewter, silver, silvery, slate, steely ♦ [3] bleak, dark, dismal, dreary, gloomy, somber (*or* sombre), wretched

²gray *or chiefly Can and Brit* **grey** *n* **1** : something of a gray color **2** : a neutral color ranging between black and white

³gray *or chiefly Can and Brit* **grey** *vb* : to make or become gray

gray·beard *or chiefly Can and Brit* **greybeard** \'grā-ˌbird\ *n* : an old man

gray·ish *or chiefly Can and Brit* **grey·ish** *adj* : somewhat gray

gray·ling \'grā-liŋ\ *n, pl* **grayling** *also* **graylings** : any of several slender freshwater food and sport fishes related to the trouts

gray matter *n* **1** : the grayish part of nervous tissue consisting mostly of nerve cell bodies **2** ♦ : capacity for knowledge and learning : INTELLIGENCE

♦ brains, intellect, intelligence, reason, sense

gray wolf *n* : a large wolf of northern No. America and Asia that is usu. gray

¹graze \'grāz\ *vb* **grazed; graz·ing** **1** ♦ : to feed on herbage or pasture **2** : to feed (livestock) on grass or pasture — **graz·er** *n*

♦ browse, forage, pasture

²graze *vb* **grazed; graz·ing** **1** ♦ : to touch lightly in passing **2** ♦ : to irritate or roughen by rubbing : SCRATCH, ABRADE

♦ [1] brush, kiss, nick, shave, skim ♦ [2] abrade, scrape, scratch, scuff

¹**grease** \'grēs\ n 1 : rendered animal fat 2 : oily material 3 : a thick lubricant
²**grease** \'grēs, 'grēz\ vb **greased; greas·ing** ♦ : to smear or lubricate with grease

♦ lubricate, oil, slick, wax

grease·paint \'grēs-ˌpānt\ n : theater makeup
greasy \'grē-sē, -zē\ adj 1 : smeared or soiled with grease; also : oily in appearance, texture, or manner 2 ♦ : causing or tending to cause something to slide or fall 3 : containing an unusual amount of grease

♦ slick, slippery, slithery

great \'grāt\ adj 1 ♦ : large in size : BIG 2 : ELABORATE, AMPLE 3 : large in number : NUMEROUS 4 : being beyond the average : MIGHTY, INTENSE ⟨a ~ weight⟩ ⟨in ~ pain⟩ 5 : EMINENT, GRAND 6 ♦ : long continued ⟨a ~ while⟩ 7 : MAIN, PRINCIPAL 8 : more distant in a family relationship by one generation ⟨a great-grandfather⟩ 9 ♦ : markedly superior in character, quality, or skill ⟨~ at bridge⟩ 10 ♦ : very good of its kind : EXCELLENT, FINE ⟨had a ~ time⟩

♦ [1] big, hefty, large, outsize, oversize, sizable, substantial ♦ [6] extended, far, lengthy, long, marathon ♦ [9] accomplished, adept, consummate, crack, crackerjack, expert, good, master, masterly, masterful, proficient, skilled, skillful, virtuoso ♦ [10] excellent, fabulous, fine, grand, splendid, superb, superior, swell, terrific, wonderful

great ape n : any of a family of primates including the gorilla, orangutan, and chimpanzees
great blue heron n : a large crested grayish blue American heron
great circle n : a circle on the surface of a sphere that has the same center as the sphere; esp : one on the surface of the earth an arc of which is the shortest travel distance between two points
great·coat \'grāt-ˌkōt\ n : a heavy overcoat
Great Dane n : any of a breed of tall massive powerful smooth-coated dogs
great·er \'grā-tər\ adj, often cap : consisting of a central city together with adjacent areas ⟨the ~ metropolitan area⟩
great·heart·ed \'grāt-'här-təd\ adj 1 ♦ : characterized by bravery : COURAGEOUS 2 : characterized by a noble or forbearing spirit : MAGNANIMOUS

♦ brave, courageous, dauntless, doughty, fearless, gallant, heroic, intrepid, lionhearted, manful, stalwart, stout, undaunted, valiant, valorous

great·ly adv 1 ♦ : to a great extent or degree : very much 2 ♦ : in a great manner

♦ [1] broadly, considerably, extremely, highly, hugely, largely, much, sizably, tremendously, very Ant slightly ♦ [2] gallantly, grandly, heroically, honorably (or honourably), magnanimously, nobly Ant basely, dishonorably, ignobly

great·ness n ♦ : the quality or state of being great

♦ distinction, excellence, preeminence, superiority, supremacy ♦ bigness, grandness, largeness

great power n, often cap G&P : one of the nations that figure most decisively in international affairs
great white shark n : a large and dangerous shark of warm seas that has large saw-edged teeth and is whitish below and bluish or brownish above
grebe \'grēb\ n : any of a family of lobe-toed diving birds related to the loons
Gre·cian \'grē-shən\ adj : GREEK
greed \'grēd\ n ♦ : acquisitive or selfish desire beyond reason — **greed·i·ly** \'grē-də-lē\ adv

♦ acquisitiveness, avarice, avidity, covetousness, cupidity, rapaciousness

greed·i·ness \-dē-nəs\ n : the quality or state of being greedy; esp : extreme or excessive desire for wealth or gain
greedy \'grē-dē\ adj 1 ♦ : having a strong desire for food or drink 2 ♦ : marked by greed : having or showing a selfish desire for wealth and possessions

♦ [1] gluttonous, hoggish, piggish, rapacious, ravenous, voracious ♦ [2] acquisitive, avaricious, avid, covetous, grasping, mercenary, rapacious

¹**Greek** \'grēk\ n 1 : a native or inhabitant of Greece 2 : the ancient or modern language of Greece
²**Greek** adj 1 : of, relating to, or characteristic of Greece, the Greeks, or Greek 2 : ORTHODOX 3
¹**green** \'grēn\ adj 1 : of the color green 2 ♦ : covered with verdure; also : consisting of green plants or of the leafy parts of

plants ⟨a ~ salad⟩ 3 : UNRIPE; also : IMMATURE 4 ♦ : having a sickly appearance 5 : not fully processed or treated ⟨~ liquor⟩ ⟨~ hides⟩ 6 ♦ : lacking in training, knowledge, or experience : INEXPERIENCED; also : NAIVE 7 : concerned with or supporting environmentalism ⟨~ companies⟩ — **green·ish** adj

♦ [2] leafy, lush, luxuriant, verdant ♦ [4] cadaverous, lurid, pale, pasty, peaked, sallow, sickly ♦ [6] adolescent, callow, immature, inexperienced, juvenile, raw ♦ [6] ingenuous, innocent, naive, simple, unknowing, unsophisticated, unwary, unworldly

²**green** vb : to make or become green
³**green** n 1 : a color between blue and yellow in the spectrum : the color of growing fresh grass or of the emerald 2 : something of a green color 3 : green vegetation; esp, pl : leafy herbs or leafy parts of a vegetable ⟨collard ~s⟩ ⟨beet ~s⟩ 4 : a grassy plot; esp : a smooth grassy area around the hole into which the ball must be played in golf
green·back \'grēn-ˌbak\ n : a U.S. legal-tender note
green bean n : a kidney bean that is used as a snap bean when the pods are colored green
green·belt \'grēn-ˌbelt\ n : a belt of parks or farmlands around a community
green card n : an identity card attesting the permanent resident status of an alien in the U.S.
green·ery \'grē-nə-rē\ n, pl **-er·ies** ♦ : green foliage or plants

♦ flora, foliage, green, herbage, leafage, vegetation, verdure

green–eyed \'grē-ˌnīd\ adj : JEALOUS
green·gro·cer \'grēn-ˌgrō-sər\ n : a retailer of fresh vegetables and fruit
green·horn \-ˌhȯrn\ n ♦ : an inexperienced person; also : NEWCOMER

♦ beginner, fledgling, freshman, neophyte, newcomer, novice, recruit, rookie, tenderfoot, tyro

green·house \-ˌhaus\ n : a glass structure for the growing of tender plants
greenhouse effect n : warming of a planet's atmosphere that occurs when the sun's radiation passes through the atmosphere, is absorbed by the planet, and is reradiated as radiation of longer wavelength that can be absorbed by atmospheric gases
green manure n : an herbaceous crop (as clover) plowed under when green to enrich the soil
green·ness n ♦ : the quality or state of being green; esp : being unaffectedly simple and candid

♦ artlessness, ingenuousness, innocence, naturalness, naïveté, simplicity, unworldliness

green onion n : a young onion pulled before the bulb has enlarged and used esp. in salads : SCALLION
green pepper n : a sweet pepper before it turns red at maturity
green·room \'grēn-ˌrüm, -ˌrum\ n : a room in a theater or concert hall where actors or musicians relax before, between, or after appearances
green·sward \-ˌswȯrd\ n : turf that is green with growing grass
green thumb n : an unusual ability to make plants grow
green·wash·ing \'grēn-ˌwȯ-shiŋ, -ˌwä-\ n : expressions of environmentalist concerns as a cover for products, policies, or activities deleterious to the environment
Green·wich mean time \'gri-nij-, 'gre-, -nich-\ n : the time of the meridian of Greenwich used as the basis of worldwide standard time
Greenwich time n : GREENWICH MEAN TIME
green·wood \'grēn-ˌwud\ n : a forest green with foliage
greet \'grēt\ vb 1 : to address with expressions of kind wishes 2 : to meet or react to in a specified manner 3 : to be perceived by — **greet·er** n
greet·ing n 1 ♦ : a salutation on meeting 2 pl ♦ : best wishes : REGARDS

♦ [1] hello, salutation, salute ♦ **greetings** [2] compliments, regards, respects

greeting card n : a card that bears a message usu. sent on a special occasion
gre·gar·i·ous \gri-'gar-ē-əs\ adj 1 ♦ : marked by or indicating a liking for companionship : SOCIAL, COMPANIONABLE 2 : tending to flock together — **gre·gar·i·ous·ly** adv — **gre·gar·i·ous·ness** n

♦ boon, companionable, convivial, extroverted, outgoing, sociable, social

grem·lin \'grem-lən\ n : a cause of error or equipment malfunction conceived of as a small gnome
gre·nade \grə-'nād\ n : a small bomb that is thrown by hand or launched (as by a rifle)

gren·a·dier \\,gre-nə-'dir\\ *n* : a member of a European regiment formerly armed with grenades

gren·a·dine \\,gre-nə-'dēn, 'gre-nə-,dēn\\ *n* : a syrup flavored with pomegranates and used in mixed drinks

grew *past of* GROW

grey *var of* GRAY

grey·hound \\'grā-,haůnd\\ *n* : any of a breed of tall slender dogs noted for speed and keen sight

grid \\'grid\\ *n* **1** : GRATING **2** : a network of conductors for distributing electric power **3** : a network of horizontal and perpendicular lines (as for locating points on a map) **4** : GRIDIRON 2; *also* : FOOTBALL

grid·dle \\'grid-ᵊl\\ *n* : a flat usu. metal surface for cooking food

griddle cake *n* ♦ : a flat cake made of thin batter and cooked (as on a griddle) on both sides : PANCAKE

♦ flapjack, pancake

grid·iron \\'grid-,īrn, -,ī-ərn\\ *n* **1** : a grate for broiling food **2** : a football field

grid·lock \\-,läk\\ *n* : a traffic jam in which an intersection is so blocked that vehicles cannot move

grief \\'grēf\\ *n* **1** ♦ : emotional distress caused by or as if by bereavement; *also* : a cause of such distress **2** : DISASTER ⟨the expedition came to ~⟩; *also* : MISHAP

♦ affliction, anguish, dolor, heartache, sorrow, woe

griev·ance \\'grē-vəns\\ *n* **1** ♦ : a cause of distress affording reason for complaint or resistance **2** ♦ : the formal expression of a grievance : COMPLAINT

♦ [1] grudge, resentment, score ♦ [2] beef, complaint, fuss, gripe, grumble, murmur, plaint, squawk

grieve \\'grēv\\ *vb* **grieved; griev·ing 1** : to cause grief or sorrow to : DISTRESS **2** ♦ : to feel grief

♦ agonize, bleed, feel, hurt, mourn, sorrow, suffer ♦ *usu* **grieve for** bemoan, bewail, deplore, lament, mourn, wail

griev·ous \\'grē-vəs\\ *adj* **1** ♦ : causing or characterized by severe suffering, grief, or sorrow : SEVERE ⟨a ~ wound⟩ **2** ♦ : unreasonably burdensome or severe : OPPRESSIVE, ONEROUS **3** ♦ : having important or dangerous possible consequences : SERIOUS, GRAVE

♦ [1, 2] bitter, brutal, burdensome, cruel, excruciating, grim, hard, harsh, heavy, onerous, oppressive, rough, rugged, severe, stiff, tough, trying ♦ [3] dangerous, grave, hazardous, menacing, parlous, perilous, risky, serious, unhealthy, unsafe, venturesome

griev·ous·ly *adv* **1** ♦ : in a grievous manner : in a manner characterized by sorrow or grief **2** : to a grievous degree

♦ agonizingly, bitterly, hard, hardly, sadly, sorrowfully, unhappily, woefully, wretchedly

¹grill \\'gril\\ *vb* **1** : to broil on a grill; *also* : to fry or toast on a griddle **2** ♦ : to question intensely

♦ examine, interrogate, pump, query, question, quiz

²grill *n* **1** : a cooking utensil of parallel bars on which food is grilled **2** ♦ : an informal restaurant

♦ café, diner, restaurant

grille *or* **grill** \\'gril\\ *n* : a grating that forms a barrier or screen

grill·work \\'gril-,wərk\\ *n* : work constituting or resembling a grille

grim \\'grim\\ *adj* **grim·mer; grim·mest 1** ♦ : fierce in disposition or action : CRUEL **2** ♦ : harsh and forbidding in appearance **3** : ghastly or repellent in character **4** ♦ : not flinching or shrinking : RELENTLESS — **grim·ly** *adv* — **grim·ness** *n*

♦ [1] cruel, fell, ferocious, fierce, savage, vicious ♦ [2] austere, dour, fierce, flinty, forbidding, gruff, rough, rugged, severe, stark, steely, stern *Ant* benign, benignant, gentle, mild, tender ♦ [4] determined, dogged, implacable, relentless, unflinching, unrelenting, unyielding

gri·mace \\'gri-məs, gri-'mās\\ *n* ♦ : a facial expression usu. of disgust or disapproval — **grimace** *vb*

♦ face, frown, lower, mouth, pout, scowl

grime \\'grīm\\ *n* ♦ : soot, smut, or dirt adhering to or embedded in a surface; *also* : accumulated dirtiness and disorder

♦ dirt, filth, muck, smut, soil

grimy *adj* : full of or covered with grime

grin \\'grin\\ *vb* **grinned; grin·ning** : to draw back the lips so as to show the teeth esp. in amusement — **grin** *n*

¹grind \\'grīnd\\ *vb* **ground** \\'graůnd\\; **grind·ing 1** ♦ : to reduce to small particles **2** ♦ : to wear down, polish, or sharpen by friction **3** : OPPRESS **4** ♦ : to press with a grating noise : GRIT ⟨~ the teeth⟩ **5** : to operate or produce by turning a crank **6** : DRUDGE; *esp* : to study hard **7** : to move with difficulty or friction ⟨gears ~ing⟩

♦ [1] atomize, crush, powder, pulverize ♦ [2] buff, burnish, edge, file, hone, plane, polish, rasp, rub, sand, sharpen, whet ♦ [4] crunch, gnash, grate, grit, rasp, scrape, scratch

²grind *n* **1** ♦ : dreary monotonous labor, routine, or study **2** : one who works or studies excessively **3** ♦ : the act or sound of grinding

♦ [1] drudgery, labor (*or* labour), sweat, toil, travail ♦ [3] rasp, scrape, scratch

grind·er \\'grīn-dər\\ *n* **1** ♦ : MOLAR **2** *pl* : TEETH **3** : one that grinds **4** ♦ : a large sandwich on a long split roll : SUBMARINE 2

♦ hoagie, poor boy, sub, submarine

grind out *vb* ♦ : to produce in a mechanical way

♦ build, carve, forge, hammer, work out

grind·stone \\'grīnd-,stōn\\ *n* : a flat circular stone of natural sandstone that revolves on an axle and is used for grinding, shaping, or smoothing

¹grip \\'grip\\ *vb* **gripped; grip·ping 1** ♦ : to seize or hold firmly **2** ♦ : to hold the interest of strongly

♦ [1] clasp, clench, cling, clutch, grasp, hang on, hold, hold on ♦ [2] absorb, busy, engage, engross, enthrall, fascinate, immerse, interest, intrigue, involve, occupy

²grip *n* **1** : GRASP; *also* : strength in gripping **2** ♦ : a firm tenacious hold typically giving control, mastery, or understanding **3** ♦ : mental grasp : UNDERSTANDING **4** : a device for gripping **5** ♦ : portable case designed to hold a traveler's clothing and personal articles : TRAVELING BAG

♦ [2] arm, authority, clutch, command, control, dominion, hold, power, sway ♦ [3] appreciation, apprehension, comprehension, grasp, perception, understanding ♦ [5] carryall, handbag, portmanteau, suitcase, traveling bag

¹gripe \\'grīp\\ *vb* **griped; grip·ing 1** : IRRITATE, VEX **2** : to cause or experience spasmodic pains in the bowels **3** ♦ : to complain with grumbling

♦ beef, bellyache, carp, complain, crab, croak, fuss, grouse, growl, grumble, kick, moan, murmur, mutter, repine, squawk, wail, whine

²gripe *n* ♦ : expression of grief, pain, or dissatisfaction

♦ beef, complaint, fuss, grievance, grumble, murmur, plaint, squawk

grippe \\'grip\\ *n* : INFLUENZA

gris–gris \\'grē-,grē\\ *n, pl* **gris–gris** \\-,grēz\\ : an amulet or incantation believed capable of warding off evil and bringing good luck to oneself or misfortune to another

gris·ly \\'griz-lē\\ *adj* **gris·li·er; -est** ♦ : inspiring horror, intense fear, disgust, or distaste : HORRIBLE, GRUESOME

♦ appalling, atrocious, awful, dreadful, frightful, ghastly, gruesome, hideous, horrible, horrid, lurid, macabre, monstrous, nightmarish, shocking, terrible

grist \\'grist\\ *n* : grain to be ground or already ground

gris·tle \\'gri-səl\\ *n* : CARTILAGE — **gris·tly** \\'gris-lē\\ *adj*

grist·mill \\'grist-,mil\\ *n* : a mill for grinding grain

¹grit \\'grit\\ *n* **1** : a hard sharp granule (as of sand); *also* : material composed of such granules **2** ♦ : unyielding courage ⟨the pioneers' ~⟩ — **grit·ty** *adj*

♦ backbone, fiber (*or* fibre), fortitude, guts, pluck, spunk

²grit *vb* **grit·ted; grit·ting** : to give forth a grating sound : GRIND, GRATE

grits \\'grits\\ *n pl* : coarsely ground hulled grain ⟨hominy ~⟩

griz·zled \\'gri-zəld\\ *adj* : streaked or mixed with gray

griz·zly \\'griz-lē\\ *adj* **griz·zli·er; -est** : GRIZZLED

grizzly bear *n* : a large pale-coated bear of western No. America

gro *abbr* gross

groan \\'grōn\\ *vb* **1** ♦ : to utter a deep moan indicative of pain, grief, or annoyance : MOAN **2** : to make a harsh sound under sudden or prolonged strain ⟨the chair ~ed under his weight⟩ — **groan** *n*

♦ howl, keen, lament, moan, plaint, wail

groat \\'grōt\\ *n* : an old British coin worth four pennies

gro·cer \\'grō-sər\\ *n* : a dealer esp. in staple foodstuffs — **grocery** \\'grōs-rē, 'grōsh-, 'grō-sə-\\ *n*

grog \\'gräg\\ *n* : alcoholic liquor; *esp* : liquor (as rum) mixed with water

grog·gy \\'grä-gē\\ *adj* **grog·gi·er; -est** : weak and unsteady on the feet or in action — **grog·gi·ly** \\-gə-lē\\ *adv* — **grog·gi·ness** \\-gē-nəs\\ *n*

groin \\'gròin\\ *n* **1** : the juncture of the lower abdomen and inner part of the thigh; *also* : the region of this juncture **2** : the curved line or rib on a ceiling along which two vaults meet

grok \\'gräk\\ *vb* **grokked; grok·king** : to understand profoundly and intuitively

grom·met \\'grä-mət, 'grə-\\ *n* **1** : a ring of rope **2** : an eyelet of firm material to strengthen or protect an opening

¹groom \\'grüm, 'grüm\\ *n* **1** : a person responsible for the care of horses **2** : BRIDEGROOM

²groom *vb* **1** : to clean and care for (an animal) **2** : to make neat or attractive **3** : PREPARE

grooms·man \\'grümz-mən, 'grümz-\\ *n* : a male friend who attends a bridegroom at his wedding

¹groove \\'grüv\\ *n* **1** : a long narrow channel **2** ♦ : a fixed routine

♦ pattern, rote, routine, rut, treadmill

²groove *vb* **1** ♦ : to make a groove in; *also* : to form a groove **2** ♦ : to enjoy oneself intensely

♦ [1] score, scribe ♦ *usu* **groove on** [2] adore, delight, dig, enjoy, fancy, like, love, relish, revel

groovy \\'grü-vē\\ *adj* **groov·i·er; -est** **1** : unusually good : EXCELLENT **2** : HIP

grope \\'grōp\\ *vb* **groped; grop·ing** **1** ♦ : to feel about or search for blindly or uncertainly ⟨~ for the right word⟩ **2** : to feel one's way by groping

♦ feel, fish, fumble

gros·beak \\'grōs-ˌbēk\\ *n* : any of several finches of Europe or America with large stout conical bills

gros·grain \\'grō-ˌgrān\\ *n* : a silk or rayon fabric with crosswise cotton ribs

¹gross \\'grōs\\ *adj* **1** ♦ : glaringly noticeable **2** : OUT-AND-OUT, UTTER **3** ♦ : physically large : BIG, BULKY; *esp* : excessively fat **4** : GENERAL, BROAD **5** : consisting of an overall total exclusive of deductions ⟨~ earnings⟩ **6** : CARNAL, EARTHY ⟨~ pleasures⟩ **7** ♦ : coarse in nature or behavior : UNREFINED; *also* : crudely vulgar **8** : lacking knowledge — **gross·ly** *adv*

♦ [1] blatant, conspicuous, egregious, flagrant, glaring, obvious, patent, prominent, pronounced, rank, striking ♦ [3] chubby, corpulent, fat, fleshy, full, obese, overweight, plump, portly, rotund, round ♦ [7] coarse, common, crass, crude, ill-bred, low, rough, rude, tasteless, uncouth, uncultivated, uncultured, unpolished, unrefined, vulgar

²gross *n* : an overall total exclusive of deductions — **gross** *vb*

³gross *n, pl* **gross** : a total of 12 dozen things ⟨a ~ of pencils⟩

gross domestic product *n* : the gross national product excluding the value of net income earned abroad

gross national product *n* : the total value of the goods and services produced in a nation during a year

gross·ness *n* ♦ : the quality or state of being gross

♦ corpulence, fatness, obesity, plumpness ♦ coarseness, indelicacy, lowness, rudeness, vulgarity

grot \\'grät\\ *n* : a natural underground chamber or series of chambers open to the surface : GROTTO

gro·tesque \\grō-'tesk\\ *adj* **1** : FANCIFUL, BIZARRE **2** ♦ : absurdly incongruous **3** ♦ : departing markedly from the natural, the expected, or the typical — **gro·tesque·ly** *adv*

♦ [2] harsh, unaesthetic ♦ [3] hideous, ugly, unappealing, unattractive

grot·to \\'grä-tō\\ *n, pl* **grottoes** *also* **grottos** **1** : a natural underground chamber or series of chambers open to the surface : CAVE **2** : an artificial cavelike structure

grouch \\'graùch\\ *n* **1** : a fit of bad temper **2** ♦ : an habitually irritable or complaining person — **grouch** *vb*

♦ bear, complainer, crab, crank, curmudgeon, grumbler, whiner

grouchy *adj* ♦ : given to grumbling : marked by ill temper

♦ choleric, cross, crotchety, irascible, irritable, peevish, snappy, snippy, testy, waspish ♦ crabby, cranky, fussy, grumpy, querulous

¹ground \\'graùnd\\ *n* **1** : the bottom of a body of water **2** *pl* ♦ : sediment at the bottom of a liquid **3** ♦ : a basis for belief, action, or argument **4** : a surrounding area : BACKGROUND **5** ♦ : the surface of the earth; *also* : SOIL **6** : an area with a particular use ⟨fishing ~s⟩ **7** *pl* ♦ : the area about and belonging to a building **8** : a conductor that makes electrical connection with the earth

♦ **grounds** [2] deposit, dregs, lees, precipitate, sediment ♦ [3] base, basis, bedrock, cornerstone, footing, foundation, groundwork, keystone, underpinning ♦ *usu* **grounds** [3] motive, reason, wherefore, why ♦ [5] dirt, earth, soil ♦ **grounds** [7] demesne, park, premises, yard

²ground *vb* **1** : to bring to or place on the ground **2** : to run or cause to run aground **3** ♦ : to provide a reason or justification for **4** : to furnish with a foundation of knowledge **5** : to connect electrically with a ground **6** : to restrict to the ground; *also* : prohibit from some activity

♦ base, rest

³ground *past and past part of* GRIND

ground ball *n* : a batted baseball that rolls or bounces along the ground

ground cover *n* : low plants that grow over and cover the soil; *also* : a plant suitable for use as ground cover

ground·ed \\'graùn-dəd\\ *adj* : mentally and emotionally stable

ground·er \\'graùn-dər\\ *n* : GROUND BALL

ground·hog \\'graùnd-ˌhòg, -ˌhäg\\ *n* : WOODCHUCK

ground·less \\'graùn(d)-ləs\\ *adj* ♦ : having no ground or foundation

♦ baseless, invalid, unfounded, unreasonable, unsubstantiated, unsupported, unwarranted

ground·ling \\'graùnd-liŋ\\ *n* : a spectator in the pit of an Elizabethan theater

ground rule *n* **1** : a sports rule adopted to modify play on a particular field, court, or course **2** : a rule of procedure

ground squirrel *n* : any of various burrowing rodents of No. America and Eurasia that are related to the squirrels and live in colonies in open areas

ground swell *n* **1** : a broad deep ocean swell caused by an often distant gale or earthquake **2** *usu* **ground·swell** : a rapid spontaneous growth (as of political opinion)

ground·wa·ter \\'graùnd-ˌwò-tər, -ˌwä-\\ *n* : water within the earth that supplies wells and springs

ground·work \\-ˌwərk\\ *n* ♦ : something that forms a foundation or support : BASIS; *also* : preparation made beforehand

♦ base, basis, bedrock, footing, foundation, ground, keystone, underpinning

ground zero *n* **1** : the point above, below, or at which a nuclear explosion occurs **2** : the center or origin of rapid, intense, or violent activity

¹group \\'grüp\\ *n* **1** ♦ : a number of individuals related by a common factor (as physical association, community of interests, or blood) **2** : a combination of atoms commonly found together in a molecule ⟨a methyl ~⟩

♦ bracket, category, class, division, family, grade, kind, order, set, species, type

²group *vb* ♦ : to associate in groups

♦ assort, break down, categorize, class, classify, grade, peg, place, range, rank, separate, sort ♦ accumulate, amass, assemble, collect, concentrate, garner, gather, lump, pick up, round up, scrape

grou·per \\'grü-pər\\ *n, pl* **groupers** *also* **grouper** : any of numerous large solitary bottom fishes of warm seas

group home *n* : a residence for persons requiring care or supervision

group·ie \\'grü-pē\\ *n* : a fan of a rock group who usu. follows the group around on concert tours; *also* : ENTHUSIAST, FAN

group·ing \\'grü-piŋ\\ *n* **1** : the act or process of combining in groups **2** : a set of objects combined in a group

group therapy *n* : therapy in the presence of a therapist in which several patients discuss their personal problems

groupware \\'grüp-ˌwer\\ *n* : software that enables users to work jointly via a network on projects or files

¹grouse \\'graùs\\ *n, pl* **grouse** *or* **grouses** : any of numerous ground-dwelling game birds that have feathered legs and are usu. of reddish brown or other protective color

²grouse *vb* **groused; grous·ing** ♦ : to mutter in discontent : COMPLAIN, GRUMBLE

♦ beef, bellyache, carp, complain, crab, fuss, gripe, grumble, kick, moan, squawk, wail, whine

grout \\'graùt\\ *n* : material (as mortar) used for filling spaces — **grout** *vb*

grove \\'grōv\\ *n* : a small wood usu. without underbrush

grov·el \\'grä-vəl, 'grə-\\ *vb* **-eled** *or* **-elled; -el·ing** *or* **-el·ling** **1** ♦ : to creep or lie with the body prostrate in fear or humility **2** : to abase oneself

♦ crawl, creep, slither, snake, worm

grow \\'grō\\ *vb* **grew** \\'grü\\; **grown** \\'grōn\\; **grow·ing** **1** ♦ : to spring up and develop to maturity **2** : to be able to grow : THRIVE **3** : to take on some relation through or as if through growth ⟨tree limbs *grown* together⟩ **4** ♦ : to become progressively greater **5** : to develop from a parent source **6** ♦ : to pass into a condition : BECOME **7** : to have an increasing influence **8** ♦ : to cause to grow

♦ [1] age, develop, grow up, mature, progress, ripen ♦ *usu* **grow in** [4] build, gain, gather, pick up ♦ [6] become, come, get, go, run, turn, wax ♦ [8] crop, cultivate, culture, promote, raise, rear, tend

grow·er *n* **1** : one that grows esp. in a specified way **2** ♦ : a person who grows a specified fruit or other product

♦ agriculturist, cultivator, farmer, planter, tiller

growing pains *n pl* **1** : pains in the legs of growing children having no known relation to growth **2** : the stresses and strains attending a new project or development

growl \\'graul\\ *vb* **1** : RUMBLE **2** ♦ : to utter a deep throaty sound **3** : to complain angrily : GRUMBLE — **growl** *n*

♦ bellow, boom, roar, thunder

grown–up \\'grō-,nəp\\ *adj* : not childish : ADULT — **grown–up** *n*
growth \\'grōth\\ *n* **1** : stage or condition attained in growing **2** ♦ : a process of growing esp. through progressive development or increase **3 a** : a result or product of growing ⟨a fine ∼ of hair⟩ **b** ♦ : an abnormal mass of tissue (as a tumor)

♦ [2] development, elaboration, evolution, expansion, maturation, progress, progression ♦ [3b] excrescence, lump, neoplasm, tumor

growth hormone *n* : a vertebrate hormone that is secreted by the pituitary gland and regulates growth
growth industry *n* : a business, interest, or activity that is increasingly popular, profitable, or trendy
grow up *vb* ♦ : to grow toward or arrive at full stature or physical or mental maturity

♦ age, develop, grow, mature, progress, ripen

¹**grub** \\'grəb\\ *vb* **grubbed; grub·bing** **1** : to clear or root out by digging **2** : to dig in the ground usu. for a hidden object **3** : to search about **4** : to work hard and long
²**grub** *n* **1** : a soft thick wormlike insect larva ⟨beetle ∼s⟩ **2** : DRUDGE; *also* : a slovenly person **3** ♦ : nourishment in solid form : FOOD

♦ chow, fare, food, meat, provender, provisions, viands, victuals

grub·bi·ness \\-bē-nəs\\ *n* ♦ : the state of being grubby

♦ dinginess, dirtiness, filthiness, foulness, nastiness, uncleanliness

grub·by \\'grə-bē\\ *adj* **grub·bi·er; -est** ♦ : full of or covered with grime : DIRTY, SLOVENLY ⟨∼ clothes⟩

♦ dirty, filthy, foul, grungy, mucky, muddy, slovenly, unclean

grub·stake \\'grəb-,stāk\\ *n* : supplies or funds furnished a mining prospector in return for a share in his finds
¹**grudge** \\'grəj\\ *vb* **grudged; grudg·ing** : to be reluctant to give : BEGRUDGE
²**grudge** *n* ♦ : a feeling of deep-seated resentment or ill will

♦ animosity, antagonism, antipathy, bitterness, enmity, gall, hostility, rancor ♦ grievance, resentment, score

gru·el \\'grü-əl\\ *n* : a thin porridge
gru·el·ing *or* **gru·el·ling** \\'grü-liŋ, 'grü-ə-\\ *adj* ♦ : requiring extreme effort : EXHAUSTING ⟨a ∼ schedule⟩

♦ arduous, demanding, difficult, exacting, formidable, hard, herculean, laborious, murderous, rough, stiff, strenuous, tall, toilsome, tough

grue·some \\'grü-səm\\ *adj* ♦ : inspiring horror or repulsion

♦ appalling, atrocious, awful, dreadful, frightful, ghastly, grisly, hideous, horrible, horrid, lurid, macabre, monstrous, nightmarish, shocking, terrible

gruff \\'grəf\\ *adj* **1** ♦ : rough in speech or manner **2** ♦ : being deep and harsh : HOARSE — **gruff·ly** *adv*

♦ [1] flinty, grim, rough, rugged, severe, stark, steely, stern ♦ [2] coarse, gravelly, hoarse, husky, scratchy, throaty

grum·ble \\'grəm-bəl\\ *vb* **grum·bled; grum·bling** **1** ♦ : to mutter in discontent **2** ♦ : to utter a growl : GROWL, RUMBLE

♦ [1] beef, bellyache, complain, fuss, gripe, grouse, kick, moan, squawk, wail, whine ♦ [2] growl, lumber, roll, rumble

grum·bler *n* ♦ : one that grumbles

♦ bear, complainer, crab, crank, curmudgeon, grouch, whiner

grump·i·ness \\-pē-nəs\\ *n* ♦ : the quality or state of being grumpy

♦ biliousness, irritability, peevishness, perverseness, perversity

grumpy \\'grəm-pē\\ *adj* **grump·i·er; -est** ♦ : moodily cross : SURLY — **grump·i·ly** \\-pə-lē\\ *adv*

♦ choleric, crabby, cranky, cross, crotchety, grouchy, irascible, irritable, peevish, petulant, short-tempered, surly, testy, waspish

grunge \\'grənj\\ *n* **1** : one that is grungy **2** : heavy metal rock music expressing alienation and discontent **3** : untidy or tattered clothing typically worn by grunge fans
grun·gy \\'grən-jē\\ *adj* **grun·gi·er; -est** ♦ : shabby or dirty in character or condition

♦ dirty, grubby, mucky, muddy, unclean ♦ dilapidated, mean, neglected, ratty, seedy, shabby

grun·ion \\'grən-yən\\ *n* : a fish of the California coast which comes inshore to spawn at nearly full moon
¹**grunt** \\'grənt\\ *n* : a deep throaty sound (as that of a hog)
²**grunt** *vb* : to utter a grunt; *also* : to utter with a grunt
GSA *abbr* **1** General Services Administration **2** Girl Scouts of America
G suit *n* : a suit for a pilot or astronaut designed to counteract the physiological effects of acceleration
GSUSA *abbr* Girl Scouts of the United States of America
gt *abbr* great
Gt Brit *abbr* Great Britain
gtd *abbr* guaranteed
GU *abbr* Guam
gua·ca·mo·le \\,gwä-kə-'mō-lē\\ *n* : mashed and seasoned avocado
gua·nine \\'gwä-,nēn\\ *n* : a purine base that codes genetic information in the molecular chain of DNA and RNA
gua·no \\'gwä-nō\\ *n* : excrement esp. of seabirds or bats; *also* : a fertilizer composed chiefly of this excrement
¹**guar·an·tee** \\,gar-ən-'tē\\ *n* **1** : GUARANTOR **2** : GUARANTY] **3** ♦ : an agreement by which one person undertakes to secure another in the possession or enjoyment of something **4** : an assurance of the quality of or of the length of use to be expected from a product offered for sale **5** ♦ : something given as security : GUARANTY

♦ [3] bond, contract, covenant, guaranty, surety, warranty ♦ [5] gage, guaranty, pawn, pledge, security

²**guarantee** *vb* **-teed; -tee·ing** **1** : to undertake to answer for the debt, failure to perform, or faulty performance of (another) **2** : to undertake an obligation to establish, perform, or continue **3** ♦ : to give security to

♦ assure, cinch, ensure, guaranty, insure, secure

guar·an·tor \\,gar-ən-'tor\\ *n* ♦ : one who gives a guarantee

♦ backer, patron, sponsor, surety

¹**guar·an·ty** \\'gar-ən-tē\\ *n, pl* **-ties** **1** : an undertaking to answer for another's failure to pay a debt or perform a duty **2** ♦ : an agreement by which one person undertakes to secure another in the possession or enjoyment of something : GUARANTEE **3** : GUARANTOR **4** ♦ : something given as security : PLEDGE

♦ [2] bond, contract, covenant, guarantee, surety, warranty ♦ [4] gage, guarantee, pawn, pledge, security

²**guaranty** *vb* **-tied; -ty·ing** : to give security to : GUARANTEE
¹**guard** \\'gärd\\ *n* **1** ♦ : a person or a body of persons on sentinel duty **2** *pl* : troops assigned to protect a sovereign **3** : a defensive position (as in boxing) **4** ♦ : the act or duty of protecting or defending **5** ♦ : one that protects : PROTECTION **6** : a protective or safety device **7** : a football lineman playing between center and tackle; *also* : a basketball player stationed toward the rear — **on guard** : WATCHFUL, ALERT

♦ [1] custodian, guardian, keeper, lookout, picket, sentry, warden, warder, watch, watchman ♦ [4] aegis, armor, cover, defense (*or* defence), protection, safeguard, screen, security, shield, wall, ward ♦ [5] custodian, defender, defense (*or* defence), protection, protector

²**guard** *vb* **1** ♦ : to protect from danger esp. by watchful attention : DEFEND **2** : to watch over **3** ♦ : to be on guard

♦ [1] cover, defend, protect, safeguard, screen, secure, shield, ward ♦ *usu* **guard against** [3] beware (of), mind, watch out (for)

guard·ed \'gär-dəd\ *adj* ♦ : careful to consider all circumstances and possible consequences

♦ alert, careful, cautious, circumspect, considerate, gingerly, heedful, safe, wary

guard·house \'gärd-,haús\ *n* **1** : a building occupied by a guard or used as a headquarters by soldiers on guard duty **2** : a military jail

guard·ian \'gär-dē-ən\ *n* **1** ♦ : one that guards : CUSTODIAN **2** ♦ : one who has the care of the person or property of another

♦ caretaker, custodian, janitor, keeper, warden, watchman

guard·ian·ship *n* ♦ : supervision or support of one that is smaller and weaker; *specif* : the relationship existing between guardian and ward

♦ care, custody, keeping, safekeeping, trust, ward

guard·room \'gärd-,rüm\ *n* **1** : a room used by a military guard while on duty **2** : a room where military prisoners are confined
guards·man \'gärdz-mən\ *n* : a member of a military body called *guard* or *guards*
Gua·te·ma·lan \,gwä-tə-'mä-lən\ *n* : a native or inhabitant of Guatemala — **Guatemalan** *adj*
gua·va \'gwä-və\ *n* : the sweet yellow or pink acid fruit of a shrubby tropical American tree used esp. for making jam and jelly; *also* : the tree
gu·ber·na·to·ri·al \,gü-bər-nə-'tōr-ē-əl\ *adj* : of or relating to a governor
guer·don \'gərd-ᵊn\ *n* : REWARD, RECOMPENSE
Guern·sey \'gərn-zē\ *n, pl* **Guernseys** : any of a breed of usu. reddish brown and white dairy cattle that produce rich yellowish milk
guer·ril·la *or* **gue·ril·la** \gə-'ri-lə\ *n* : one who engages in irregular warfare esp. as a member of an independent unit
¹**guess** \'ges\ *vb* **1** ♦ : to form an opinion from little or no evidence **2** ♦ : to hold as an opinion : BELIEVE, SUPPOSE **3** ♦ : to conjecture correctly about

♦ [1] assume, conjecture, presume, speculate, suppose, surmise, suspect ♦ [2] believe, consider, deem, feel, figure, hold, imagine, suppose, think ♦ [3] calculate, call, conjecture, estimate, figure, gauge, judge, make, place, put, reckon, suppose

²**guess** *n* ♦ : a conclusion deduced by surmise or guesswork

♦ conjecture, supposition, surmise

guest \'gest\ *n* **1** : a person to whom hospitality (as of a house or a club) is extended **2** ♦ : a patron of a commercial establishment (as a hotel) **3** : a person not a regular member of a cast who appears on a program

♦ customer, patron

guest·house \'gest-,haús\ *n* : a house run as a boarding house or bed-and-breakfast
guf·faw \(,)gə-'fò\ *n* : a loud burst of laughter — **guffaw** *vb*
guid·ance \'gīd-ᵊns\ *n* **1** ♦ : the act or process of guiding **2** : the direction provided by a guide : ADVICE

♦ administration, conduct, control, direction, government, management, operation, oversight, regulation, running, superintendence, supervision

¹**guide** \'gīd\ *n* **1** ♦ : one who leads or directs another's course **2** ♦ : one who shows and explains points of interest **3** : something that provides guiding information; *also* : SIGNPOST **4** : a device to direct the motion of something

♦ [1, 2] attendant, companion, escort, guard

²**guide** *vb* **guid·ed; guid·ing** **1** ♦ : to act as a guide to **2** ♦ : to direct, supervise, or influence usu. to a particular end **3** : to superintend the training of — **guid·able** \'gī-də-bəl\ *adj*

♦ [1] conduct, direct, lead, marshal, pilot, route, show, steer, usher ♦ [1, 2] administer, carry on, conduct, control, direct, govern, handle, manage, operate, oversee, regulate, run, superintend, supervise ♦ [2] coach, counsel, lead, mentor, pilot, shepherd, show, tutor

guide·book \'gīd-,búk\ *n* : a book of information for travelers
guided missile *n* : a missile whose course may be altered during flight
guide dog *n* : a dog trained to lead the blind
guide·line \'gīd-,līn\ *n* : an indication or outline of policy or conduct
guide word *n* : a term at the head of a page of an alphabetical

reference work that indicates the alphabetically first or last word on that page

gui·don \'gī-,dän, -dᵊn\ *n* : a small flag (as of a military unit)
guild \'gild\ *n* ♦ : an association of people with common aims and interests; *esp* : a medieval association of merchants or craftsmen — **guild·hall** \-,hòl\ *n*

♦ association, brotherhood, club, college, congress, council, fellowship, fraternity, institute, institution, league, order, organization, society

guile \'gīl\ *n* ♦ : deceitful cunning : DUPLICITY

♦ artfulness, artifice, caginess, canniness, craft, craftiness, cunning, slyness, wiliness ♦ craft, craftiness, crookedness, deceit, deceitfulness, dishonesty, dissimulation, double-dealing, duplicity

guile·ful *adj* ♦ : full of guile : characterized by cunning, deceit, or treachery

♦ artful, cagey, crafty, cunning, devious, foxy, slick, sly, subtle, wily

guil·lo·tine \'gi-lə-,tēn, ,gē-ə-'tēn\ *n* : a machine for beheading persons — **guillotine** *vb*
guilt \'gilt\ *n* **1** : the fact of having committed an offense esp. against the law **2** ♦ : the state of one who has committed an offense esp. consciously **3** ♦ : a feeling of responsibility for wrongdoing

♦ [2] blame, culpability, fault, rap ♦ [3] contrition, penitence, remorse, repentance, self-reproach, shame

guilt·less *adj* ♦ : free from guilt or evil

♦ blameless, clear, faultless, impeccable, innocent, irreproachable

guilt-trip \'gilt-,trip\ *vb* : to cause feelings of guilt in
guilty \'gil-tē\ *adj* **guilt·i·er; -est** **1** ♦ : having committed a breach of conduct or a crime **2** : suggesting or involving guilt **3** ♦ : aware of or suffering from guilt — **guilt·i·ly** \-tə-lē\ *adv* — **guilt·i·ness** \-tē-nəs\ *n*

♦ [1] accountable, answerable, blamable, blameworthy, censurable, culpable, reprehensible *Ant* blameless, guiltless, innocent ♦ [3] ashamed, contrite, hangdog, penitent, remorseful, repentant, shamefaced *Ant* impenitent, remorseless, shameless, unashamed, unrepentant

guin·ea \'gi-nē\ *n* **1** : a British gold coin no longer issued worth 21 shillings **2** : a unit of value equal to 21 shillings
guinea fowl *n* : a gray and white spotted West African bird related to the pheasants and widely raised for food; *also* : any of several related birds
guinea hen *n* : a female guinea fowl; *also* : GUINEA FOWL
Guin·ean \'gi-nē-ən\ *n* : a native or inhabitant of Guinea — **Guinean** *adj*
guinea pig *n* **1** : a small stocky short-eared and nearly tailless So. American rodent often kept as a pet or used in lab research **2** : a subject of research or testing
guise \'gīz\ *n* **1** : a form or style of dress : COSTUME **2** ♦ : external appearance : SEMBLANCE

♦ [1] dress, garb, getup, outfit ♦ [2] appearance, face, name, semblance, show

gui·tar \gi-'tär\ *n* : a musical instrument with usu. six strings plucked with a pick or the fingers
gulch \'gəlch\ *n* ♦ : a deep or precipitous cleft : RAVINE

♦ canyon, defile, flume, gap, gorge, notch, pass, ravine

gulf \'gəlf\ *n* **1** ♦ : a part of an ocean or sea partly or mostly surrounded by land **2** : ABYSS, CHASM **3** : a wide separation

♦ bay, bight, cove, estuary, fjord, inlet

¹**gull** \'gəl\ *n* : any of numerous mostly white or gray long-winged web-footed seabirds
²**gull** *vb* ♦ : to make a dupe of : DECEIVE

♦ deceive, delude, dupe, fool, misinform, mislead, take in, trick

³**gull** *n* : a person who is easily deceived or cheated : DUPE
gul·let \'gə-lət\ *n* : ESOPHAGUS; *also* : THROAT
gull·ible \'gə-lə-bəl\ *adj* ♦ : easily duped or cheated

♦ easy, susceptible

gul·ly \'gə-lē\ *n, pl* **gullies** : a trench worn in the earth by and often filled with running water after rains
¹**gulp** \'gəlp\ *vb* **1** ♦ : to swallow hurriedly or greedily **2** : SUPPRESS ⟨~ down a sob⟩ **3** : to catch the breath as if in taking a long drink

♦ bolt, devour, gobble, gorge, gormandize, scarf, scoff, wolf

²**gulp** n **1 :** the act or an instance of gulping **2 :** the amount taken in a single large swallow

¹**gum** \'gəm\ n **:** the oral tissue that surrounds the necks of the teeth

²**gum** n **1 :** a sticky plant exudate; esp **:** one that hardens on drying **2 :** a sticky substance **3 :** a preparation usu. of a plant gum sweetened and flavored and used for chewing

gum arabic n **:** a water-soluble gum obtained from several acacias and used esp. in making inks, adhesives, confections, and pharmaceuticals

gum·bo \'gəm-bō\ n **:** a rich thick soup usu. thickened with okra

gum·drop \'gəm-ˌdräp\ n **:** a candy made usu. from corn syrup with gelatin and coated with sugar crystals

gum·my adj ♦ **:** having a thick or sticky quality; also **:** consisting, containing, or covered with gum

♦ adhesive, gelatinous, gluey, glutinous, gooey, sticky, viscid, viscous

gump·tion \'gəmp-shən\ n **1 :** shrewd common sense **2 :** ENTERPRISE, INITIATIVE

gum·shoe \'gəm-ˌshü\ n **:** DETECTIVE — **gumshoe** vb

¹**gun** \'gən\ n **1 :** CANNON **2 ♦ :** a portable firearm **3 :** a discharge of a gun **4 :** something suggesting a gun in shape or function **5 :** THROTTLE — **gunned** \'gənd\ adj

♦ arm, firearm, piece

²**gun** vb **gunned; gun·ning 1 :** to hunt with a gun **2 :** to hit with a missile (as a bullet) from a gun **:** SHOOT **3 :** to open up the throttle of so as to increase speed

gun·boat \'gən-ˌbōt\ n **:** a small lightly armed ship for use in shallow waters

gun·fight \-ˌfīt\ n **:** a duel with guns — **gun·fight·er** n

gun·fire \-ˌfīr\ n **:** the firing of guns

gung ho \'gəŋ-'hō\ adj ♦ **:** extremely zealous or enthusiastic

♦ avid, eager, enthusiastic, keen, nuts, raring

gun·man \-mən\ n **:** a man armed with a gun; esp **:** a professional killer

gun·ner \'gə-nər\ n **1 :** a soldier or airman who operates or aims a gun **2 :** one who hunts with a gun

gun·nery \'gə-nə-rē\ n **:** the use of guns; esp **:** the science of the flight of projectiles and effective use of guns

gunnery sergeant n **:** a noncommissioned officer in the marine corps ranking next below a master sergeant

gun·ny·sack \'gə-nē-ˌsak\ n **:** a sack made of a coarse heavy fabric (as burlap)

gun·point \'gən-ˌpȯint\ n **:** the muzzle of a gun — **at gunpoint :** under a threat of death by being shot

gun·pow·der \-ˌpau̇-dər\ n **:** an explosive powder used in guns and blasting

gun·shot \-ˌshät\ n **1 :** shot fired from a gun **2 :** the range of a gun ⟨within ∼⟩

gun–shy \-ˌshī\ adj **1 :** afraid of a loud noise **2 :** markedly distrustful

gun·sling·er \-ˌsliŋ-ər\ n **:** a skilled gunman esp. in the old West

gun·smith \-ˌsmith\ n **:** one who designs, makes, or repairs firearms

gun·wale also **gun·nel** \'gən-ᵊl\ n **:** the upper edge of a ship's or boat's side

gup·py \'gə-pē\ n, pl **guppies :** a small brightly colored tropical fish

gur·gle \'gər-gəl\ vb **gur·gled; gur·gling 1 :** to make a sound like that of an irregularly flowing or gently splashing liquid **2 ♦ :** to flow in a broken irregular current — **gurgle** n

♦ dribble, lap, plash, ripple, slosh, splash, trickle, wash Ant roll, pour, stream

Gur·kha \'gu̇r-kə, 'gər-\ n **:** a soldier from Nepal in the British or Indian army

gur·ney \'gər-nē\ n, pl **gurneys :** a wheeled cot or stretcher

gu·ru \'gu̇r-ü\ n, pl **gurus 1 :** a personal religious and spiritual teacher in Hinduism **2 :** a teacher in matters of fundamental concern **3 ♦ :** a person who has knowledge or skills acquired through practice **:** EXPERT ⟨a fitness ∼⟩

♦ ace, adept, artist, authority, crackerjack, expert, hand, hotshot, maestro, master, scholar, shark, virtuoso, whiz, wizard

gush \'gəsh\ vb **1 ♦ :** to issue or pour forth copiously or violently **:** SPOUT **2 ♦ :** to make an effusive display of affection or enthusiasm

♦ [1] jet, pour, rush, spew, spout, spurt, squirt Ant dribble, drip, drop, trickle ♦ [2] enthuse, fuss, rave, rhapsodize, slobber

gush·er \'gə-shər\ n **:** one that gushes; esp **:** an oil well with a large natural flow

gushy \'gə-shē\ adj **gush·i·er; -est :** marked by effusive sentimentality

gus·set \'gə-sət\ n **:** a triangular insert (as in a seam of a sleeve) to give width or strength — **gusset** vb

gus·sy up \'gə-sē-\ vb **1 :** to dress up in best or formal clothes **2 :** to make more attractive, glamorous or fancy

¹**gust** \'gəst\ n **1 ♦ :** a sudden brief rush of wind **2 :** a sudden outburst **:** SURGE

♦ blast, blow, flurry, williwaw

²**gust** vb **:** to blow in gusts ⟨winds ∼ing up to 40 mph⟩

gus·ta·to·ry \'gəs-tə-ˌtȯr-ē\ adj **:** relating to or associated with the sense of taste

gus·to \'gə-ˌstō\ n **:** enthusiastic and vigorous enjoyment, appreciation, or delight

gusty adj ♦ **:** blowing in gusts

♦ blowy, blustery, breezy, windy

¹**gut** \'gət\ n **1** pl **:** internal organs of the body **:** BOWELS, ENTRAILS **2 ♦ :** the alimentary canal or a part of it (as the intestine); also **:** BELLY, ABDOMEN **3** pl **:** the inner essential parts **4** pl ♦ **:** fortitude and stamina in coping with what alarms, repels, or discourages **:** COURAGE, PLUCK

♦ [2] abdomen, belly, solar plexus, stomach, tummy ♦ **guts** [4] bravery, courage, daring, fearlessness, hardihood, nerve, stoutness ♦ **guts** [4] backbone, fiber (or fibre), fortitude, grit, pluck, spunk

²**gut** vb **gut·ted; gut·ting 1 ♦ :** to take out the entrails of **:** EVISCERATE **2 :** to destroy the inside of

♦ clean, draw, eviscerate

gut check n **:** a test of courage, character, or determination

gutsy \'gət-sē\ adj **guts·i·er; -est** ♦ **:** marked by courage and determination

♦ adventurous, audacious, bold, daring, enterprising, hardy, nervy, venturesome

gut·ter \'gə-tər\ n ♦ **:** a groove or channel for carrying off esp. rainwater

♦ dike, ditch, trench

gut·ter·snipe \-ˌsnīp\ n **:** a street urchin

gut·tur·al \'gə-tə-rəl\ adj **1 :** sounded in the throat **2 :** being or marked by an utterance that is strange, unpleasant, or disagreeable — **guttural** n

gut·ty \'gə-tē\ adj **gut·ti·er; -est 1 :** GUTSY **2 :** having a vigorous challenging quality

gut–wrench·ing \'gət-ˌren-chiŋ\ adj **:** causing emotional anguish

¹**guy** \'gī\ n **:** a rope, chain, or rod attached to something as a brace or guide

²**guy** vb **:** to steady or reinforce with a guy

³**guy** n ♦ **:** an adult male human **:** MAN, FELLOW; also, pl **:** PERSONS ⟨all the ∼s came⟩

♦ buck, chap, dude, fellow, gent, gentleman, hombre, jack, joker, lad, male, man

⁴**guy** vb **:** to make fun of **:** RIDICULE

Guy·a·nese \ˌgī-ə-'nēz\ n, pl **Guyanese :** a native or inhabitant of Guyana — **Guyanese** adj

guz·zle \'gə-zəl\ vb **guz·zled; guz·zling** ♦ **:** to drink greedily

♦ drink, imbibe, quaff, sup, swig, toss

gym \'jim\ n **:** GYMNASIUM

gym·kha·na \jim-'kä-nə\ n **:** a meet featuring sports contests; esp **:** a contest of automobile-driving skill

gym·na·si·um \for 1 jim-'nä-zē-əm, -zhəm, for 2 gim-'nä-zē-əm\ n, pl **-na·si·ums** or **-na·sia** \-'nä-zē-ə, -'nä-zhə; -'nä-zē-ə\ **1 :** a room or building for indoor sports **2 :** a European secondary school that prepares students for the university

gym·nas·tics \jim-'nas-tiks\ n **:** physical exercises designed to demonstrate strength and coordination; also **:** a sport in which individuals perform acrobatic feats mostly on special equipment — **gym·nast** \'jim-ˌnast\ n — **gym·nas·tic** adj

gym·no·sperm \'jim-nə-ˌspərm\ n **:** any of a class or subdivision of woody vascular seed plants (as conifers) that produce naked seeds not enclosed in an ovary

gyn or **gynecol** abbr gynecology

gy·nae·col·o·gy chiefly Brit var of GYNECOLOGY

gy·ne·col·o·gy \ˌgī-nə-'kä-lə-jē\ n **:** a branch of medicine that deals with the diseases and routine care of the reproductive system of women — **gy·ne·co·log·ic** \-ni-kə-'lä-jik\ or **gy·ne·co·log·i·cal** \-ji-kəl\ adj — **gy·ne·col·o·gist** \-nə-'kä-lə-jist\ n

gy·no·cen·tric \ˌgī-nə-ˈsen-trik\ *adj* : emphasizing feminine interests or a feminine point of view

¹**gyp** \ˈjip\ *n*   **1** *offensive* : CHEAT, SWINDLER   **2** *offensive* : FRAUD, SWINDLE

²**gyp** *vb, offensive* : to deprive of something valuable by the use of deceit or fraud

gyp·sum \ˈjip-səm\ *n* : a calcium-containing mineral used in making plaster of paris

Gyp·sy \ˈjip-sē\ *n, pl* **Gypsies**   **1** *usually offensive* : a member of a traditionally traveling people coming orig. from India and now living chiefly in Europe and in smaller numbers throughout the world : ROMANI   **2** *usually offensive* : the language of the Romani people

gypsy moth *n* : SPONGY MOTH

gy·rate \ˈjī-ˌrāt\ *vb* **gy·rat·ed; gy·rat·ing**   **1** ♦ : to revolve around a point or axis   **2** : to oscillate with or as if with a circular or spiral motion

  ♦ pirouette, revolve, roll, rotate, spin, turn, twirl, wheel, whirl

gy·ra·tion \jī-ˈrā-shən\ *n* : an act or instance of gyrating

  ♦ pirouette, reel, revolution, roll, rotation, spin, twirl, wheel, whirl

gyr·fal·con \ˈjər-ˌfal-kən, -ˌföl-\ *n* : an arctic falcon with several color forms that is the largest of all falcons

¹**gy·ro** \ˈjī-rō\ *n, pl* **gyros** : GYROSCOPE

²**gy·ro** \ˈyē-ˌrō, ˈzhir-ō\ *n, pl* **gyros** : a sandwich esp. of lamb and beef, tomato, onion, and yogurt sauce on pita bread

gy·ro·scope \ˈjī-rō-ˌskōp\ *n* : a wheel or disk mounted to spin rapidly about an axis that is free to turn in various directions

Gy Sgt *abbr* gunnery sergeant

gyve \ˈjīv, ˈgīv\ *n* : FETTER — **gyve** *vb*

¹**h** \ˈāch\ *n, pl* **h's** *or* **hs** \ˈā-chəz\ *often cap* : the 8th letter of the English alphabet

²**h** *abbr, often cap*   **1** hard; hardness   **2** heroin   **3** hit   **4** husband

H *symbol* hydrogen

¹**ha** \ˈhä\ *interj* — used esp. to express surprise or joy

²**ha** *abbr* hectare

Hab *abbr* Habacuc; Habakkuk

Ha·ba·cuc \ˈha-bə-ˌkək, hə-ˈba-kək\ *n* : HABAKKUK

Ha·bak·kuk \ˈha-bə-ˌkək, hə-ˈba-kək\ *n* : a book of the canonical Jewish and Christian Scriptures

ha·ba·ne·ra \ˌhä-bə-ˈner-ə\ *n* : a Cuban dance in slow time; *also* : the music for this dance

ha·ba·ne·ro *also* **ha·ba·ñe·ro** \ˌ(h)ä-bə-ˈn(y)er-ō\ *n* : a very hot chili pepper that is usu. orange when mature

ha·be·as cor·pus \ˈhā-bē-əs-ˈkör-pəs\ *n* : a writ issued to bring a party before a court

hab·er·dash·er \ˈha-bər-ˌda-shər\ *n* : a dealer in men's clothing and accessories

hab·er·dash·ery \-ˌda-shə-rē\ *n, pl* **-er·ies**   **1** : goods sold by a haberdasher   **2** : a haberdasher's shop

ha·bil·i·ment \hə-ˈbi-lə-mənt\ *n*   **1** *pl* : TRAPPINGS, EQUIPMENT   **2** : DRESS; *esp* : the dress characteristic of an occupation or occasion — usu. used in pl.

hab·it \ˈha-bət\ *n*   **1** : DRESS, GARB   **2** : BEARING, CONDUCT   **3** : PHYSIQUE   **4** : mental makeup   **5** ♦ : a usual manner of behavior : CUSTOM   **6** : a behavior pattern acquired by frequent repetition   **7** : ADDICTION   **8** : mode of growth or occurrence ⟨trees with a spreading ∼⟩

  ♦ custom, fashion, pattern, practice, trick, way, wont

hab·it·able \ˈha-bə-tə-bəl\ *adj* : capable of being lived in —
hab·it·abil·i·ty \ˌha-bə-tə-ˈbi-lə-tē\ *n*

hab·i·tat \ˈha-bə-ˌtat\ *n* ♦ : the place or environment where a plant or animal naturally occurs

  ♦ home, niche, range, territory

hab·i·ta·tion \ˌha-bə-ˈtā-shən\ *n*   **1** : OCCUPANCY   **2** ♦ : a dwelling place : RESIDENCE   **3** : SETTLEMENT

  ♦ abode, domicile, dwelling, home, house, lodging, quarters, residence

hab·it·form·ing \ˈha-bət-ˌför-miŋ\ *adj* : causing addiction : ADDICTIVE

ha·bit·u·al \hə-ˈbi-chə-wəl\ *adj*   **1** ♦ : having the nature of a habit   **2** ♦ : doing, practicing, or acting by force of habit ⟨∼ drunkards⟩   **3** : inherent in an individual — **ha·bit·u·al·ly** *adv* — **ha·bit·u·al·ness** *n*

  ♦ [1] constant, frequent, periodic, regular, repeated, steady   ♦ [2] chronic, confirmed, inveterate

ha·bit·u·ate \hə-ˈbi-chə-ˌwāt\ *vb* **-at·ed; -at·ing**   **1** : ACCUSTOM   **2** : to cause or undergo habituation

ha·bit·u·a·tion \hə-ˌbi-chə-ˈwā-shən\ *n*   **1** : the process of becoming or state of being accustomed to or dependent on something   **2** : psychological dependence on a drug after a period of use

ha·bi·tué *also* **ha·bi·tue** \hə-ˈbi-chə-ˌwā\ *n* : one who may be regularly found in or at (as a place of entertainment)

ha·ci·en·da \ˌhä-sē-ˈen-də\ *n*   **1** : a large estate in a Spanish-speaking country   **2** : the main building of a farm or ranch

¹**hack** \ˈhak\ *vb*   **1** : to cut or sever with repeated irregular blows   **2** : to cough in a short dry manner   **3** : to manage successfully; *also* : TOLERATE   **4** : to gain access to a computer or computer system illegally

²**hack** *n*   **1** : an implement for hacking   **2** : a short dry cough   **3** : a hacking blow   **4** ♦ : a V-shaped indentation   **5** : an act or instance of gaining access to a computer or computer system illegally   **6** : a clever tip or technique for doing or improving something

  ♦ chip, indentation, nick, notch

³**hack** *n*   **1** : a horse hired or used for varied work   **2** : a horse worn out in service   **3** : a light easy often 3-gaited saddle horse   **4 a** : HACKNEY   **b** : an automobile that carries passengers for a fare usu. determined by the distance traveled : TAXICAB   **5** : a person who works solely for mercenary reasons; *esp* : a writer working solely for commercial success — **hack** *adj*

⁴**hack** *vb* : to operate a taxicab

hack·er \ˈha-kər\ *n*   **1** : one that hacks; *also* : a person unskilled at something   **2** : an expert at using a computer   **3** : a person who illegally gains access to and sometimes tampers with information in a computer system

hack·ie \ˈha-kē\ *n* : a taxicab driver

hack·le \ˈha-kəl\ *n*   **1** : one of the long feathers on the neck or back of a bird   **2** : hairs (as on a dog's neck) that can be erected   **3** *pl* : TEMPER, DANDER

hack·man \ˈhak-mən\ *n* : HACKIE

¹**hack·ney** \ˈhak-nē\ *n, pl* **hackneys**   **1** : a horse for riding or driving   **2** : a carriage or automobile kept for hire

²**hackney** *vb* : to make trite

hack·neyed \ˈhak-nēd\ *adj* ♦ : lacking in freshness or originality

  ♦ banal, commonplace, musty, stale, stereotyped, threadbare, tired, trite

hack·saw \ˈhak-ˌsö\ *n* : a fine-tooth saw in a frame for cutting metal

hack·work \-ˌwərk\ *n* : work done on order usu. according to a formula

had *past and past part of* HAVE

had·dock \ˈha-dək\ *n, pl* **haddock** *also* **haddocks** : an Atlantic food fish usu. smaller than the related cod

Ha·des \ˈhā-ˌdēz\ *n*   **1** : the abode of the dead in Greek mythology   **2** *often not cap* : HELL

hae·ma·tite *chiefly Brit var of* HEMATITE

haf·ni·um \ˈhaf-nē-əm\ *n* : a gray metallic chemical element

haft \ˈhaft\ *n* : the handle of a weapon or tool

hag \ˈhag\ *n*   **1** ♦ : an ugly or evil-looking old woman   **2** : a woman that is credited with usu. malignant supernatural powers

  ♦ crone, witch

Hag *abbr* Haggai

Hag·gai \ˈha-gē-ˌī, ˈha-ˌgī\ *n* : a book of the canonical Jewish and Christian Scriptures

hag·gard \'ha-gərd\ *adj* ♦ : having a worn or emaciated appearance — **hag·gard·ly** *adv* — **hag·gard·ness** *n*

♦ cadaverous, gaunt, skeletal, wasted

hag·gis \'ha-gəs\ *n* : a traditionally Scottish dish made of the heart, liver, and lungs of a sheep or a calf minced with suet, onions, oatmeal, and seasonings

hag·gle \'ha-gəl\ *vb* **hag·gled; hag·gling** ♦ : to argue in bargaining — **hag·gler** *n*

♦ bargain, chaffer, deal, dicker, negotiate, palter

Ha·gi·og·ra·pha \,ha-gē-'ä-grə-fə, ,hä-jē-\ *n pl* : the third part of the Jewish Scriptures

ha·gio·graph·ic \,ha-gē-ə-'gra-fik, ,hä-, -jē-\ *adj* : of or relating to hagiography; *esp* : excessively flattering

ha·gi·og·ra·phy \,ha-gē-'ä-grə-fē, ,hä-jē-\ *n* **1** : biography of saints or venerated persons **2** : idealizing or idolizing biography — **ha·gi·og·ra·pher** \-fər\ *n*

hai·ku \'hī-(,)kü\ *n, pl* **haiku** : an unrhymed Japanese verse form of three lines containing usu. 5, 7, and 5 syllables respectively; *also* : a poem in this form

¹**hail** \'hāl\ *n* **1** : precipitation in the form of small lumps of ice **2** ♦ : something that gives the effect of falling hail

♦ rain, shower, storm ♦ barrage, bombardment, cannonade, fusillade, salvo, shower, storm, volley

²**hail** *vb* **1** : to precipitate hail **2** : to pour down and strike like hail

³**hail** *interj* — used to express acclamation

⁴**hail** *vb* **1 a** : SALUTE, GREET **b** ♦ : to greet with enthusiastic approval : ACCLAIM **2** : SUMMON

♦ acclaim, applaud, cheer, crack up, laud, praise, salute, tout

⁵**hail** *n* **1** : an expression of greeting, approval, or praise **2** ♦ : hearing distance

♦ earshot, hearing, sound

Hail Mary *n* **1** : a salutation and prayer to the Virgin Mary **2** : a long forward pass in football thrown as a final attempt to score

hail·stone \'hāl-,stōn\ *n* : a pellet of hail

hail·storm \-,storm\ *n* : a storm accompanied by hail

hair \'har\ *n* **1 a** : a threadlike outgrowth esp. from the skin of a mammal **b** ♦ : a covering or growth of hairs of an animal or a body part **2** ♦ : a minute distance or amount — **haired** \'hard\ *adj* — **hair·less** *adj*

♦ [1b] coat, fleece, fur, pelage, pile, wool ♦ [2] ace, inch, step, stone's throw

hair·breadth \'har-,bredth\ *or* **hairs·breadth** \'harz-\ *n* ♦ : a very small distance or margin

♦ ace, hair, inch, step, stone's throw

hair·brush \-,brəsh\ *n* : a brush for the hair

hair·cloth \-,klȯth\ *n* : a stiff wiry fabric used esp. for upholstery

hair·cut \-,kət\ *n* : the act, process, or style of cutting and shaping the hair

hair·do \-,dü\ *n, pl* **hairdos** : a way of wearing the hair

hair·dress·er \-,dre-sər\ *n* : one who dresses or cuts hair — **hair·dress·ing** *n*

hair·line \-,līn\ *n* **1** : a very thin line **2** : the outline of the hair on the head

hair·piece \-,pēs\ *n* **1** : supplementary hair (as a switch) used in some women's hairdos **2** : TOUPEE

hair·pin \-,pin\ *n* **1** : a U-shaped pin to hold the hair in place **2** : a sharp U-shaped turn in a road — **hairpin** *adj*

hair–rais·ing \'har-,rā-ziŋ\ *adj* ♦ : causing terror or astonishment

♦ fearful, fearsome, forbidding, formidable, frightful, scary, shocking, terrible, terrifying

hair·split·ter \-,spli-tər\ *n* : a person who makes excessively fine distinctions in reasoning — **hair·split·ting** \-,spli-tiŋ\ *n*

hair·split·ting *adj* : made or done with extreme care and accuracy

hair·spray \'her-,sprā\ *n* : a liquid sprayed onto the hair to hold it in place

hair·style \-,stī(-ə)l\ *n* : HAIRDO — **hair·styl·ing** *n*

hair·styl·ist \-,stī-list\ *n* : HAIRDRESSER

hair–trigger *adj* : immediately responsive to the slightest stimulus

hairy \'har-ē\ *adj* **hair·i·er; -est** **1** ♦ : covered with or as if with hair **2** : tending to cause nervous tension ⟨a few ∼ moments⟩ **3** ♦ : composed of or being like hair — **hair·i·ness** \-ē-nəs\ *n*

♦ [1] fleecy, furry, hirsute, rough, shaggy, unshorn, woolly *Ant* bald, hairless, shorn, smooth ♦ [3] furry, fuzzy, rough, shaggy, woolly

hairy woodpecker *n* : a common No. American woodpecker with a white back that is larger than the similarly marked downy woodpecker

Hai·tian \'hā-shən\ *n* : a native or inhabitant of Haiti — **Haitian** *adj*

hajj \'haj\ *n* : a pilgrimage to Mecca prescribed as a religious duty for Muslims

hajji \'ha-jē\ *n* : one who has made a pilgrimage to Mecca — often used as a title

hake \'hāk\ *n* : any of several marine food fishes related to the cod

hal·berd \'hal-bərd, 'hȯl-\ *also* **hal·bert** \-bərt\ *n* : a weapon esp. of the 15th and 16th centuries consisting of a battle-ax and pike on a long handle

hal·cy·on \'hal-sē-ən\ *adj* ♦ : marked by calm : PEACEFUL

♦ calm, hushed, peaceful, placid, quiet, serene, still, tranquil, untroubled

¹**hale** \'hāl\ *adj* ♦ : free from defect, disease, or infirmity

♦ able-bodied, chipper, fit, healthy, hearty, robust, sound, well, whole, wholesome

²**hale** *vb* **haled; hal·ing** **1** ♦ : to exert force upon so as to cause or tend to cause motion toward the force : HAUL, PULL **2** : to compel to go

♦ drag, draw, haul, lug, pull, tow, tug

¹**half** \'haf, 'håf\ *n, pl* **halves** \'havz, 'håvz\ **1** : either of two equal parts that compose something **2** ♦ : one of a pair

♦ companion, match, mate, twin

²**half** *adj* **1** : being one of two equal parts **2** : amounting to nearly half **3** : PARTIAL, INCOMPLETE

³**half** *adv* **1 a** : in an equal part or degree **b** : not completely **2** : by any means : AT ALL

half–and–half \,haf-ᵊn-'haf, ,håf-ᵊn-'håf\ *n* : something that is half one thing and half another

half·back \'haf-,bak, 'håf-\ *n* **1** : a football back stationed on or near the flank **2** : a player stationed immediately behind the forward line

half–baked \-'bākt\ *adj* **1** : not thoroughly baked **2** ♦ : poorly planned; *also* : lacking common sense

♦ absurd, cuckoo, fatuous, foolish, nonsensical, nutty, senseless, silly, stupid

half–breed \-,brēd\ *n, offensive* : one of mixed racial descent — **half–breed** *adj, offensive*

half brother *n* : a brother related through one parent only

half–caste \'haf-,kast, 'håf-\ *n, offensive* : one of mixed racial descent : HALF-BREED — **half–caste** *adj, offensive*

half–dol·lar \-'dä-lər\ *n* **1** : a coin representing one half of a dollar **2** : the sum of fifty cents

half·heart·ed \-'här-təd\ *adj* ♦ : lacking spirit or interest — **half·heart·ed·ly** *adv* — **half·heart·ed·ness** *n*

♦ tepid, uneager, unenthusiastic

half–life \-,līf\ *n* : the time required for half of something (as atoms or a drug) to undergo a process

half–mast \-'mast\ *n* : a point about halfway down from the top of a mast or staff

half note *n* : a musical note equal in time to one half of a whole note

half·pen·ny \'hāp-nē\ *n, pl* **half·pence** \'hā-pəns\ *or* **halfpennies** : a formerly used British coin representing one half of a penny

half–pint \'haf-,pīnt, 'håf-\ *adj* : of less than average size — **half–pint** *n*

half sister *n* : a sister related through one parent only

half sole *n* : a shoe sole extending from the shank forward — **half–sole** *vb*

half–staff \'haf-'staf, 'håf-\ *n* : HALF-MAST

half step *n* : a musical interval equivalent to one twelfth of an octave

half·time \'haf-,tīm, 'håf-\ *n* : an intermission between halves of a game

half–track \-,trak\ *n* : a motor vehicle propelled by an endless chain-track drive system; *esp* : such a vehicle lightly armored for military use

half–truth \-,trüth\ *n* : a statement that is only partially true; *esp* : one that deliberately mixes truth and falsehood

half·way \-'wā\ *adj* **1** ♦ : midway between two points **2** : of or relating to a part rather than the whole : not general or total : PARTIAL — **halfway** *adv*

♦ intermediary, intermediate, median, medium, middle, midmost

half–wit \-ˌwit\ *n* ♦ : a foolish or imbecilic person

♦ booby, fool, goose, jackass, nitwit, nut, simpleton, turkey
♦ blockhead, dope, dummy, idiot, imbecile, jackass, moron, numskull

half–wit·ted \-ˈwi-təd\ *adj* : exhibiting or indicative of a lack of common sense or sound judgment — **half–wit·ted·ness** *n*

hal·i·but \ˈha-lə-bət\ *n, pl* **halibut** *also* **halibuts** : any of several large edible marine flatfishes

ha·lite \ˈha-ˌlīt, ˈhā-\ *n* : ROCK SALT

hal·i·to·sis \ˌha-lə-ˈtō-səs\ *n* : the condition of having fetid breath

hall \ˈhȯl\ *n* **1** : the residence of a medieval king or noble; *also* : the house of a landed proprietor **2** : a large public building **3** : a college or university building; *also* : DORMITORY **4 a** ♦ : the entrance room of a building : LOBBY **b** ♦ : a corridor or passage in a building **5** : a large room for assembly : AUDITORIUM **6** ♦ : a place used for public entertainment

♦ [4a] entry, foyer, lobby, vestibule ♦ [4b] corridor, gallery, hallway, passage ♦ [6] arena, theater

hal·le·lu·jah \ˌha-lə-ˈlü-yə\ *interj* — used to express praise, joy, or thanks

hall·mark \ˈhȯl-ˌmärk\ *n* **1** ♦ : a mark put on an article to indicate origin, purity, or genuineness **2** : a distinguishing characteristic

♦ emblem, logo, symbol, trademark

hal·low \ˈha-lō\ *vb* **1** ♦ : to make holy or set apart for holy use **2** : REVERE

♦ bless, consecrate, sanctify

hal·lowed \ˈha-lōd, -lə-wəd\ *adj* **1** ♦ : made or declared sacred **2** ♦ : regarded as worthy of great honor

♦ [1] blessed, holy, sacred, sacrosanct, sanctified ♦ [2] reverend, venerable

Hal·low·een *also* **Hal·low·e'en** \ˌha-lə-ˈwēn, ˌhä-\ *n* : the evening of October 31 observed esp. by children in merrymaking and masquerading

hal·lu·ci·nate \hə-ˈlüs-ᵊn-ˌāt\ *vb* **-nat·ed; -nat·ing** : to have hallucinations or experience as a hallucination

hal·lu·ci·na·tion \hə-ˌlüs-ᵊn-ˈā-shən\ *n* **1** : perception of objects with no reality due usu. to use of drugs or to disorder of the nervous system **2** ♦ : something perceived by hallucination — **hal·lu·ci·na·to·ry** \-ᵊn-ə-ˌtȯr-ē\ *adj*

♦ chimera, conceit, daydream, delusion, dream, fancy, fantasy, figment, illusion, phantasm, pipe dream, unreality, vision

hal·lu·ci·no·gen \hə-ˈlüs-ᵊn-ə-jən\ *n* : a substance that induces hallucinations — **hal·lu·ci·no·gen·ic** \-ˌlüs-ᵊn-ə-ˈje-nik\ *adj or n*

hall·way \ˈhȯl-ˌwā\ *n* **1** : an entrance hall **2** ♦ : a passageway into which compartments or rooms open : CORRIDOR

♦ corridor, gallery, hall, passage

ha·lo \ˈhā-lō\ *n, pl* **halos** *or* **haloes** **1** : a circle of light appearing to surround a shining body (as the sun) **2** : the aura of glory surrounding an idealized person or thing

¹hal·o·gen \ˈha-lə-jən\ *n* : any of the five elements fluorine, chlorine, bromine, iodine, and astatine

²halogen *adj* : containing, using, or being a halogen ⟨a ∼ lamp⟩

¹halt \ˈhȯlt\ *adj* : LAME

²halt *n* ♦ : a stop in an action or process

♦ cessation, close, closure, conclusion, end, ending, expiration, finish, lapse, shutdown, stop, stoppage, termination

³halt *vb* **1** : to stop marching or traveling **2** ♦ : to come or bring to an end : DISCONTINUE

♦ break, break off, cease, cut, desist, discontinue, drop, end, knock off, lay off, leave off, quit, shut off, stop ♦ arrest, catch, check, draw up, fetch up, hold up, stall, stay, still, stop

¹hal·ter \ˈhȯl-tər\ *n* **1** : a rope or strap for leading or tying an animal; *also* : HEADSTALL **2** : NOOSE **3** : a brief blouse held in place by straps around the neck and across the back

²halter *vb* **hal·tered; hal·ter·ing** **1** : to catch with or as if with a halter; *also* : to put a halter on (as a horse) **2** : HANG **3** : IMPEDE, RESTRAIN

halt·ing \ˈhȯl-tiŋ\ *adj* : UNCERTAIN, FALTERING — **halt·ing·ly** *adv*

halve \ˈhav, ˈhäv\ *vb* **halved; halv·ing** **1** : to divide into two equal parts **2** : to reduce to one half

halv·ers \ˈha-vərz, ˈhä-\ *n pl* : half shares : HALVES

halves *pl of* HALF

hal·yard \ˈhal-yərd\ *n* : a rope or tackle for hoisting and lowering (as sails)

¹ham \ˈham\ *n* **1** : a buttock with its associated thigh — usu. used in pl. **2** : a cut of meat and esp. pork from the thigh **3** : a showy performer **4** : an operator of an amateur radio station — **ham** *adj*

²ham *vb* **hammed; ham·ming** : to overplay a part : OVERACT

ham·burg·er \ˈham-ˌbər-gər\ *or* **ham·burg** \-ˌbərg\ *n* **1** : ground beef **2** : a sandwich consisting of a ground-beef patty in a round roll

ham·let \ˈham-lət\ *n* : a small village

¹ham·mer \ˈha-mər\ *n* **1** : a hand tool used for pounding; *also* : something resembling a hammer in form or function **2** : the part of a gun whose striking action causes explosion of the charge **3** : a metal sphere hurled for distance in a track-and-field event (**hammer throw**) **4** : ACCELERATOR 2

²hammer *vb* **1** ♦ : to beat, drive, or shape with or as if with repeated blows of a hammer : POUND **2** : to produce or bring about as if by repeated blows — usu. used with *out* **3** : to criticize severely

♦ beat, forge, pound

ham·mer·head \ˈha-mər-ˌhed\ *n* **1** : the striking part of a hammer **2** : any of a family of medium-sized sharks with eyes at the ends of lateral extensions of the flattened head

ham·mer·lock \-ˌläk\ *n* : a wrestling hold in which an opponent's arm is held bent behind the back

hammer out *vb* ♦ : to produce or bring about as if by repeated blows

♦ build, carve, forge, grind, work out

ham·mer·toe \-ˌtō\ *n* : a toe deformed by having one or more joints permanently flexed

¹ham·mock \ˈha-mək\ *n* : a swinging couch hung by cords at each end

²hammock *n* : a fertile elevated area of the southern U.S. and esp. Florida with hardwood vegetation and soil rich in humus

¹ham·per \ˈham-pər\ *vb* **1** ♦ : to restrict the movement or operation of : IMPEDE **2** : RESTRAIN

♦ clog, cramp, delay, embarrass, encumber, fetter, handicap, hinder, hobble, hold back, hold up, impede, inhibit, interfere with, manacle, obstruct, shackle, tie up, trammel *Ant* aid, assist, facilitate, help

²hamper *n* : a large usu. lidded basket

ham·ster \ˈham-stər\ *n* : any of a subfamily of small Old World rodents with large cheek pouches

¹ham·string \ˈham-ˌstriŋ\ *n* : any of several muscles at the back of the thigh or tendons at the back of the knee

²hamstring *vb* **-strung** \-ˌstrəŋ\; **-string·ing** **1** : to cripple by cutting the leg tendons **2** ♦ : to make ineffective or powerless

♦ cripple, disable, immobilize, incapacitate, paralyze, prostrate

¹hand \ˈhand\ *n* **1** : the end of a front limb when modified (as in humans) for grasping **2** ♦ : an indicator or pointer on a dial **3** ♦ : personal possession — usu. used in pl. and in the phrase *in one's hands; also* : CONTROL **4** ♦ : a position regarded as opposite to another : SIDE — usu. used in the phrase *on the other hand* **5** : a pledge esp. of betrothal **6** : style of penmanship : HANDWRITING **7** : SKILL, ABILITY; *also* : a significant part **8** : ASSISTANCE; *also* : PARTICIPATION **9** : an outburst of applause **10** : a single round in a card game; *also* : the cards held by a player after a deal **11** ♦ : one employed by another usu. for wages or salary and in a position below the executive level : WORKER, EMPLOYEE; *also* : a member of a ship's crew — **hand·less** *adj* — **at hand** : near in time or place — **on hand** : in present possession or readily available

♦ [2] index, indicator, needle, pointer ♦ *usu* **hands** [3] control, keeping, possession ♦ [4] angle, aspect, facet, phase, side ♦ [11] employee, hireling, jobholder, worker

²hand *vb* **1** : to lead, guide, or assist with the hand **2** ♦ : to give, pass, or transmit with the hand ⟨∼ed her a spoon⟩

♦ deliver, feed, furnish, give, hand over, provide, supply ♦ hand over, pass, reach, transfer

hand·bag \ˈhand-ˌbag\ *n* ♦ : a bag for carrying small personal articles and money

♦ bag, pocketbook, purse

hand·ball \-ˌbȯl\ *n* : a game played by striking a small rubber ball against a wall with the hand

hand·bill \-ˌbil\ *n* : a small printed sheet for distribution by hand

hand·book \-ˌbük\ *n* ♦ : a concise reference book : MANUAL

♦ manual, primer, textbook

hand•car \-ˌkär\ *n* : a small 4-wheeled railroad car propelled by hand or by a small motor

hand•clasp \-ˌklasp\ *n* : HANDSHAKE

hand•craft \-ˌkraft\ *vb* : to fashion by manual skill

¹**hand•cuff** \-ˌkəf\ *n* : a metal fastening that can be locked around a wrist and is usu. connected with another such fastening — usu. used in pl.

²**handcuff** *vb* **1 ♦** : to apply handcuffs to : MANACLE **2 ♦** : to hold in check : make ineffective or powerless

♦ [1, 2] bind, chain, enchain, fetter, manacle, shackle, trammel

hand•ed \ˈhan-dəd\ *adj* : having or using such or so many hands ⟨a left-*handed* person⟩ — **hand•ed•ness** *n*

hand•ful \ˈhand-ˌfu̇l\ *n, pl* **hand•fuls** \-ˌfu̇lz\ *also* **hands•ful** \ˈhandz-ˌfu̇l\ **1** : as much or as many as the hand will grasp **2 ♦** : a small number **3** : as much as one can manage

♦ few, smattering, sprinkle, sprinkling

hand•gun \-ˌgən\ *n* : a firearm held and fired with one hand

hand•held \ˈhand-ˌheld\ *adj* : designed for use while being held in the hand — **handheld** *n*

¹**hand•i•cap** \ˈhan-di-ˌkap\ *n* **1** : a contest in which an artificial advantage is given or disadvantage imposed on a contestant to equalize chances of winning; *also* : the advantage given or disadvantage imposed **2 ♦** : a disadvantage that makes achievement difficult

♦ disadvantage, drawback, liability, minus, penalty, strike

²**handicap** *vb* **-capped; -cap•ping 1** : to give a handicap to **2 ♦** : to put at a disadvantage

♦ encumber, hamper, hinder, hold up, impede, inhibit, interfere with, obstruct, tie up

hand•i•capped *adj, sometimes offensive* : having a physical or mental disability; *also* : of or for disabled persons

hand•i•cap•per \-ˌka-pər\ *n* : a person who predicts the winners in a horse race usu. for a publication

hand•i•craft \ˈhan-di-ˌkraft\ *n* **1** : manual skill **2 ♦** : an occupation requiring manual skill **3** : the articles fashioned by those engaged in handicraft — **hand•i•crafts•man** \-ˌkrafts-mən\ *n*

♦ craft, trade

hand•i•craft•er \ˈhan-di-ˌkraf-tər\ *n* **♦** : one that engages in a handicraft usu. as a hobby or avocation

♦ artificer, artisan, craftsman

hand•i•ly \ˈhan-də-lē\ *adv* **♦** : in an easy manner : without difficulty

♦ easily, effortlessly, fluently, freely, lightly, painlessly, readily, smoothly

hand in glove *or* **hand and glove** *adv* : in an extremely close relationship

hand•i•work \ˈhan-di-ˌwərk\ *n* **1** : work done personally or by the hands **2 ♦** : the product of handiwork

♦ affair, fruit, output, produce, product, thing, work, yield

hand•ker•chief \ˈhaŋ-kər-chəf, -ˌchēft\ *n, pl* **-chiefs** \-chəfs, -ˌchēfs\ *also* **-chieves** \-chēvz\ : a small piece of cloth used for various personal purposes (as the wiping of the face)

¹**han•dle** \ˈhand-ᵊl\ *n* **1** : a part (as of a tool) designed to be grasped by the hand **2** : a word or phrase that constitutes the distinctive designation of a person or thing : NAME — **han•dled** \-ᵊld\ *adj* — **off the handle** : into a state of sudden and violent anger — usu. used with *fly*

²**handle** *vb* **han•dled; han•dling 1** : to touch, hold, or manage with the hands **2 ♦** : to have responsibility for **3** : to deal or trade in **4** : to behave in a certain way when managed or directed ⟨a car that ~s well⟩ **5 ♦** : to act on or perform a required function with regard to — **han•dler** *n*

♦ [2] contend with, cope with, grapple with, manage, maneuver (*or* manoeuvre), negotiate, swing, treat *Ant* fumble, muddle (through) ♦ [2] administer, carry on, conduct, control, direct, govern, guide, manage, operate, oversee, regulate, run, superintend, supervise ♦ [5] act, be, deal, serve, treat, use

han•dle•bar \ˈhand-ᵊl-ˌbär\ *n* : a usu. bent bar with a grip at each end (as for steering a bicycle) — usu. used in pl.

hand•made \ˈhand-ˈmād\ *adj* : made by hand or by a hand process

hand•maid•en \-ˌmād-ᵊn\ *also* **hand•maid** \-ˌmād\ *n* : a female attendant

hand–me–down \-me-ˌdau̇n\ *adj* : used by one person after having been used by another — **hand–me–down** *n*

hand•out \ˈhand-ˌau̇t\ *n* **1** : a portion (as of food) given to a beggar **2** : a piece of printed information for free distribution; *also* : a prepared statement released to the press

hand over *vb* **♦** : to yield control of

♦ cede, deliver, give up, leave, relinquish, render, surrender, turn over, yield ♦ hand, pass, reach, transfer

hand•pick \ˈhand-ˈpik\ *vb* **♦** : to select personally ⟨a ~ed candidate⟩

♦ choose, cull, elect, name, opt, pick, prefer, select, single, take

hand•rail \-ˌrāl\ *n* : a narrow rail for grasping as a support

hand•saw \-ˌsȯ\ *n* : a saw designed to be used with one hand

hands down *adv* **1** : with little effort **2** : without question

hand•sel \ˈhan-səl\ *n* **1** : a gift made as a token of good luck **2** : a first installment : earnest money

hand•set \ˈhand-ˌset\ *n* : a combined telephone transmitter and receiver mounted on a handle

hand•shake \-ˌshāk\ *n* : a clasping usu. of right hands by two people

hands–off \ˈhandz-ˈȯf\ *adj* : characterized by noninterference

hand•some \ˈhan-səm\ *adj* **hand•som•er; -est 1** : moderately large : SIZABLE ⟨a ~ profit⟩ **2** : GENEROUS, LIBERAL **3 ♦** : pleasing and usu. impressive in appearance

♦ attractive, beautiful, fair, gorgeous, knockout, lovely, pretty, ravishing, stunning

hand•some•ly \-lē\ *adv* **♦** : in a handsome manner

♦ bountifully, generously, liberally, well

hand•some•ness \-nəs\ *n* **♦** : the quality or state of being handsome

♦ class, elegance, grace, majesty, refinement, stateliness ♦ attractiveness, beauty, comeliness, looks, loveliness, prettiness

hands–on \ˈhandz-ˈȯn, -ˈän\ *adj* **1** : being or providing direct practical experience in the operation of something **2** : characterized by active personal involvement ⟨~ management⟩

hand•spring \ˈhand-ˌspriŋ\ *n* : an acrobatic feat in which the body turns in a full circle from a standing position and lands first on the hands and then on the feet

hand•stand \-ˌstand\ *n* : an act of supporting the body on the hands with the trunk and legs balanced in the air

hand–to–hand *adj* : involving physical contact or very close range ⟨~ fighting⟩ — **hand to hand** *adv*

hand–to–mouth *adj* : having or providing nothing to spare

hand•wo•ven \ˈhand-ˈwō-vən\ *adj* : produced on a hand-operated loom

hand•writ•ing \-ˌrī-tiŋ\ *n* **1 ♦** : writing done by hand **2 ♦** : the form of writing peculiar to a person — **hand•writ•ten** \-ˌrit-ᵊn\ *adj*

♦ [1] manuscript, penmanship, script *Ant* print, type ♦ [2] hand, penmanship, script

handy \ˈhan-dē\ *adj* **hand•i•er; -est 1 ♦** : conveniently near **2** : easily used ⟨a ~ tool⟩ **3 ♦** : clever in using the hands : DEXTEROUS — **hand•i•ness** \-dē-nəs\ *n*

♦ [1] accessible, convenient, reachable ♦ [3] clever, cunning, deft, dexterous

handy•man \-ˌman\ *n* **1** : one who does odd jobs **2** : one competent in a variety of small skills or repair work

¹**hang** \ˈhaŋ\ *vb* **hung** \ˈhəŋ\ *also* **hanged; hang•ing 1 ♦** : to fasten or remain fastened to an elevated point without support from below; *also* : to fasten or be fastened so as to allow free motion on the point of suspension ⟨~ a door⟩ **2** : to suspend by the neck until dead; *also* : to die by hanging **3** : to hold or bear in a suspended or inclined manner : DROOP ⟨*hung* his head in shame⟩ **4** : to fasten to a wall ⟨~ wallpaper⟩ **5** : to prevent (a jury) from coming to a decision **6** : to display (pictures) in a gallery **7** : to remain stationary in the air **8 ♦** : to be imminent : IMPEND ⟨doom *hung* over the nation⟩ **9** : DEPEND **10** : to take hold for support **11** : to be burdensome **12** : to undergo delay **13** : to incline downward; *also* : to fit or fall from the figure in easy lines **14** : to be raptly attentive **15** : LINGER, LOITER — **hang•er** *n*

♦ [1] dangle, sling, suspend, swing ♦ [7] drift, float, glide, hover, poise, ride, sail, waft ♦ *usu* **hang over** [8] hover, menace, overhang, threaten

²**hang** *n* **1** : the manner in which a thing hangs **2** : an understanding of something

han•gar \ˈhaŋ-ər\ *n* : a covered and usu. enclosed area for housing and repairing aircraft

hang around *vb* **1 ♦ :** to pass time or stay aimlessly in or at **2 ♦ :** to spend one's time in company esp. idly

♦ *usu* **hang around in** [1] frequent, hang out, haunt, resort, visit ♦ [1] abide, dwell, remain, stay, stick around, tarry ♦ [2] associate, chum, consort, fraternize, hobnob, pal

hang back *vb* ♦ **:** to be reluctant

♦ falter, hesitate, shilly-shally, stagger, teeter, vacillate, waver, wobble

hang·dog \'haŋ-ˌdȯg\ *adj* **1 ♦ :** affected by or showing embarrassment caused by consciousness of a fault **:** ASHAMED, GUILTY **2 :** ABJECT, COWED

♦ ashamed, contrite, guilty, penitent, remorseful, repentant, shamefaced

hang·er \'haŋ-ər\ *n* **1 :** one that hangs **2 :** a device that fits inside or around a garment for hanging from a hook or rod

hang·er–on \'haŋ-ər-ˈȯn, -ˈän\ *n, pl* **hangers–on** ♦ **:** one who hangs around a person or place esp. for personal gain

♦ leech, parasite, sponge

hang in *vb* **:** to persist tenaciously

hang·ing *n* **1 :** an execution by strangling or snapping the neck by a suspended noose **2 :** something hung

hang·man \'haŋ-mən\ *n* **1 :** a public executioner **2 :** a game in which players must identify an unknown word by guessing the letters that comprise it within a designated number of chances

hang·nail \-ˌnāl\ *n* **:** a bit of skin hanging loose at the edge of a fingernail

hang on *vb* **1 :** HANG IN **2 :** to keep a telephone connection open **3 ♦ :** to keep hold onto something

♦ *usu* **hang on to** hold, keep, reserve, retain, withhold ♦ *usu* **hang on to** clench, cling, clutch, grip, hold, hold on

hang·out \'haŋ-ˌau̇t\ *n* ♦ **:** a favorite place for spending time

♦ haunt, rendezvous, resort

hang out *vb* ♦ **:** to spend time idly or in loitering around or in a particular place

♦ *usu* **hang out at** frequent, hang around, haunt, resort, visit ♦ dally, dawdle, dillydally, hang around, idle, loaf, loll, lounge

hang·over \-ˌō-vər\ *n* **1 :** something that remains from what is past **2 :** disagreeable physical effects following heavy drinking or the use of drugs

hang·up \'haŋ-ˌəp\ *n* **:** a source of mental or emotional difficulty

hang up *vb* **1 :** to place on a hook or hanger **2 :** to end a telephone conversation by breaking the connection **3 :** to keep delayed or suspended

hank \'haŋk\ *n* **:** COIL, LOOP ⟨a ∼ of rope⟩

han·ker \'haŋ-kər\ *vb* ♦ **:** to desire strongly or persistently — often used with *for* or *after*

♦ *usu* **hanker for** *or* **hanker after** ache for, covet, crave, desire, die for, hunger for, long for, lust (for *or* after), pine for, repine for, thirst for, want, wish for, yearn for

han·ker·ing *n* ♦ **:** the experience of one that hankers **:** strong desire

♦ appetite, craving, desire, drive, hunger, itch, longing, lust, passion, thirst, urge, yearning, yen

han·kie *or* **han·ky** \'haŋ-kē\ *n, pl* **hankies :** HANDKERCHIEF

han·ky–pan·ky \ˌhaŋ-kē-ˈpaŋ-kē\ *n* **1 ♦ :** questionable or underhanded activity **2 :** sexual dalliance

♦ artifice, chicanery, subterfuge, trickery, wile

hansel *var of* HANDSEL

han·som \'han-səm\ *n* **:** a 2-wheeled covered carriage with the driver's seat elevated at the rear

han·ta·virus \'hän-tə-ˌvī-rəs, 'hȯn-, 'han-\ *n* **:** any of a genus of viruses including some transmitted by rodents that cause pneumonia or hemorrhagic fevers

Ha·nuk·kah \'kä-nə-kə, 'hä-\ *n* **:** an 8-day Jewish holiday commemorating the rededication of the Temple of Jerusalem after its defilement by Antiochus of Syria

hap \'hap\ *n* **1 :** something that happens **:** HAPPENING **2 :** a force which shapes events unpredictably **:** CHANCE

¹**hap·haz·ard** \hap-ˈha-zərd\ *n* **:** CHANCE

²**haphazard** *adj* ♦ **:** marked by lack of plan or order — **hap·haz·ard·ly** *adv* — **hap·haz·ard·ness** *n*

♦ aimless, arbitrary, desultory, erratic, random, scattered, stray

hap·less \'hap-ləs\ *adj* ♦ **:** having no luck **:** UNFORTUNATE — **hap·less·ly** *adv* — **hap·less·ness** *n*

♦ ill-fated, ill-starred, luckless, unfortunate, unhappy, unlucky

hap·loid \'hap-ˌlȯid\ *adj* **:** having the number of chromosomes characteristic of gametic cells — **haploid** *n*

hap·ly \'hap-lē\ *adv* **:** by chance

hap·pen \'ha-pən\ *vb* **1 :** to occur by chance **2 ♦ :** to come into being or occur as an event, process, or result **3 ♦ :** to come casually or unexpectedly **:** CHANCE 2 — used with *on* or *upon*

♦ [2] be, befall, betide, chance, come, go, occur, pass, transpire ♦ *usu* **happen on** *or* **happen upon** [3] chance, encounter, find, hit, meet, stumble

¹**hap·pen·ing** *n* **1 ♦ :** something that happens **:** OCCURRENCE **2 ♦ :** an event that is esp. interesting, entertaining, or important

♦ [1] affair, circumstance, episode, event, incident, occasion, occurrence, thing ♦ [2] adventure, experience, time

²**happening** *adj* **1 :** very fashionable **2 :** offering much stimulating activity ⟨a ∼ nightclub⟩

hap·pi·ly \'ha-pə-lē\ *adv* **1 :** LUCKILY **2 ♦ :** in a happy manner or state ⟨lived ∼ ever after⟩ **3 ♦ :** in an adequate or fitting manner

♦ [2] cheerfully, gaily, heartily, jovially, merrily, mirthfully ♦ [3] appropriately, correctly, fittingly, properly, rightly, suitably

hap·pi·ness \'ha-pē-nəs\ *n* **1 a ♦ :** a state of well-being and contentment **b ♦ :** a pleasurable satisfaction **2 :** APTNESS

♦ [1a] blessedness, bliss, felicity, gladness, joy *Ant* misery, sadness, unhappiness, wretchedness ♦ [1b] content, contentedness, contentment, gratification, pleasure, satisfaction

hap·py \'ha-pē\ *adj* **hap·pi·er; -est 1 ♦ :** favored by luck or fortune **:** FORTUNATE **2 ♦ :** notably fitting, effective, or well adapted **:** APT, FELICITOUS **3 :** enjoying well-being and contentment **4 a :** PLEASANT **b ♦ :** made pleased, satisfied, or grateful

♦ [1] fluky, fortuitous, fortunate, lucky, providential ♦ [2] applicable, appropriate, apt, felicitous, fit, fitting, good, meet, proper, right, suitable ♦ [4b] blissful, content, delighted, glad, joyful, pleased

hap·py–go–lucky \ˌha-pē-gō-ˈlə-kē\ *adj* ♦ **:** blithely unconcerned

♦ carefree, careless, cavalier, easygoing, insouciant, lighthearted, unconcerned

happy hour *n* **:** a period of time when the price of drinks at a bar is reduced

hap·tics \'hap-tiks\ *n* **1 :** the use of electronically or mechanically generated movement that a user experiences through the sense of touch as part of an interface (as on a gaming console) **2 :** a science concerned with the sense of touch

hara–kiri \ˌhar-i-ˈkir-ē, -ˈkar-ē\ *n* **:** ritual suicide by disembowelment

¹**ha·rangue** \hə-ˈraŋ\ *n* **1 ♦ :** a ranting speech or writing **2 ♦ :** a speech addressed to a public assembly

♦ [1] diatribe, rant, tirade ♦ [2] address, declamation, oration, speech, talk

²**harangue** *vb* ♦ **:** to make a harangue — **ha·rangu·er** *n*

♦ declaim, descant, discourse, lecture, orate, speak, talk

ha·rass \hə-ˈras, 'har-əs\ *vb* **1 :** EXHAUST, FATIGUE **2 :** to worry and impede by repeated raids **3 :** to annoy continually

ha·rass·ment \-mənt\ *n* **1 ♦ :** the act or an instance of harassing **2 :** the condition of being harassed

♦ aggravation, annoyance, disturbance, vexation

¹**har·bin·ger** \'här-bən-jər\ *n* **1 ♦ :** one that announces or foreshadows what is coming **:** PRECURSOR **2 :** PORTENT

♦ angel, forerunner, herald, precursor

²**harbinger** *vb* ♦ **:** to be a harbinger of

♦ foreshadow, prefigure

¹**har·bor** *or Can and Brit* **har·bour** \'här-bər\ *n* **1 ♦ :** a place of security and comfort **2 ♦ :** a part of a body of water protected and deep enough to furnish anchorage **:** PORT

♦ [1] asylum, haven, refuge, retreat, sanctuary, shelter ♦ [2] anchorage, haven, port

²**harbor** *or Can and Brit* **harbour** *vb* **1 :** to give or take refuge **:** SHELTER **2 a ♦ :** to be the home or habitat of **b :** LIVE **3 ♦ :** to hold a thought or feeling ⟨∼ a grudge⟩

♦ [2a] accommodate, billet, chamber, domicile, house, lodge, put up, quarter, roof, shelter, take in ♦ [3] bear, cherish, entertain, have, hold, nurse

har·bor·age *or Can and Brit* **har·bour·age** \'här-bə-rij\ *n* **1** : a place of security and comfort **2** : a part of a body of water protected and deep enough to furnish anchorage : HARBOR

¹**hard** \'härd\ *adj* **1** ♦ : not easily penetrated : not easily yielding to pressure **2** : high in alcoholic content **3** : containing salts that prevent lathering with soap ⟨~ water⟩ **4** : stable in value ⟨~ currency⟩ **5 a** : physically fit **b** ♦ : resistant to stress or disease **6 a** ♦ : not subject to change or revision : FIRM ⟨~ agreement⟩ **b** ♦ : based on clear fact ⟨~ evidence⟩ **7** : CLOSE, SEARCHING ⟨~ look⟩ **8** : free from sentimentality or illusion : REALISTIC ⟨good ~ sense⟩ **9** ♦ : lacking in responsiveness : OBDURATE, UNFEELING ⟨~ heart⟩ **10** : difficult to bear ⟨~ times⟩; *also* : HARSH, SEVERE **11** ♦ : caused or marked by resentment : RESENTFUL ⟨~ feelings⟩ **12 a** ♦ : making no concession : STRICT **b** : rigidly firm in will or purpose : UNRELENTING **13** : INCLEMENT ⟨~ winter⟩ **14** : intense in force, manner, or degree ⟨~ blow⟩ **15** ♦ : demanding the exertion of considerable effort : ARDUOUS, STRENUOUS ⟨~ work⟩ **16** : sounding as in *arcing* and *geese* respectively — used of *c* and *g* **17** : TROUBLESOME ⟨~ problem⟩ **18** : having difficulty in doing something ⟨~ of hearing⟩ **19** : addictive and gravely detrimental to health ⟨~ drugs⟩ **20** : of or relating to the natural sciences and esp. the physical sciences

♦ [1] compact, firm, rigid, solid, stiff, unyielding ♦ [5b] hard-bitten, hardy, rugged, stout, strong, sturdy, tough, vigorous ♦ [6a] certain, determinate, final, firm, fixed, flat, frozen, hard-and-fast, set, settled, stable ♦ [6b] documentary, factual, historical, literal, matter-of-fact, nonfictional, objective, true ♦ [9] callous, cold-blooded, heartless, inhuman, merciless, obdurate, pitiless, ruthless, soulless, stony, uncharitable, unfeeling, unsparing, unsympathetic *Ant* charitable, compassionate, humane, merciful, sensitive, sympathetic, tender, tenderhearted, warm, warmhearted ♦ [11] acrid, acrimonious, bitter, rancorous, resentful, sore ♦ [12a] austere, authoritarian, flinty, harsh, heavy-handed, ramrod, rigid, rigorous, severe, stern, strict ♦ [15] arduous, demanding, difficult, exacting, formidable, grueling, herculean, laborious, murderous, rough, stiff, strenuous, tall, toilsome, tough *Ant* easy, effortless, facile, simple, soft, undemanding

²**hard** *adv* **1 a** ♦ : with great or utmost effort or energy **b** ♦ : in a fierce or violent manner **2 a** ♦ : in such a manner as to cause hardship, difficulty, or pain **b** ♦ : with rancor, bitterness, or grief **3** ♦ : close in time or space

♦ [1a] determinedly, diligently, hardly, laboriously, mightily, strenuously, tirelessly ♦ [1b] energetically, firmly, forcefully, forcibly, mightily, powerfully, stiffly, stoutly, strenuously, strongly, sturdily, vigorously *Ant* feebly, gently, softly, weakly ♦ [2a] hardly, harshly, ill, oppressively, roughly, severely, sternly, stiffly ♦ [2b] agonizingly, bitterly, grievously, hardly, sadly, sorrowfully, unhappily, woefully, wretchedly *Ant* gladly, happily, joyfully, joyously ♦ [3] around, by, close, in, near, nearby, nigh

hard–and–fast *adj* ♦ : rigidly binding ⟨a ~ rule⟩

♦ certain, determinate, final, firm, fixed, flat, frozen, hard, set, settled, stable ♦ fast, fixed, immutable, inflexible, unalterable, unchangeable

hard·back \'härd-ˌbak\ *n* : a hardcover book
hard·ball \-ˌbȯl\ *n* **1** : BASEBALL **2** : forceful uncompromising methods
hard–bit·ten \-'bit-ᵊn\ *adj* ♦ : seasoned or steeled by difficult experience : TOUGH ⟨~ campaigners⟩

♦ hard, hardy, rugged, stout, strong, sturdy, tough, vigorous

hard·board \-ˌbȯrd\ *n* : a very dense fiberboard
hard–boiled \-'bȯi(-ə)ld\ *adj* **1** : boiled until both white and yolk have solidified ⟨~ eggs⟩ **2 a** : lacking sentiment **b** : HARDHEADED 2
hard·bound \-ˌbau̇nd\ *adj* : HARDCOVER
hard copy *n* : a copy of textual or graphic information (as from computer storage) produced on paper
hard–core \'härd-'kȯr\ *adj* **1** : extremely resistant to solution or improvement **2** : being the most determined or dedicated members of a specified group **3** : containing explicit depictions of sex acts — **hard core** *n*
hard·cov·er \-'kə-vər\ *adj* : having rigid boards on the sides covered in cloth or paper ⟨~ books⟩
hard disk *n* : a sealed rigid metal disk used as a computer storage device
hard–drive *n* : a data-storage device consisting of a drive and one or more hard disks

hard–driv·ing \'härd)-'drī-vin\ *adj* ♦ : intensely ambitious, energetic, or hardworking

♦ ambitious, go-getting, self-seeking

hard·en \'härd-ᵊn\ *vb* **1** ♦ : to make or become hard or harder **2** : to confirm or become confirmed in disposition or action **3** ♦ : to make hardy or robust — **hard·en·er** *n*

♦ [1] concrete, congeal, firm, freeze, set, solidify *Ant* soften ♦ [3] fortify, season, steel, strengthen, toughen *Ant* soften

hard·hack \'härd-ˌhak\ *n* : an American spirea with dense clusters of pink or white flowers and leaves having a hairy rusty yellow underside
hard hat *n* **1** : a protective hat worn esp. by construction workers **2** : a construction worker
hard·head·ed \'härd-'he-dəd\ *adj* **1** ♦ : unreasonably or perversely unyielding : STUBBORN, WILLFUL **2** ♦ : concerned with or involving practical considerations — **hard·head·ed·ly** *adv*

♦ [1] dogged, headstrong, mulish, obdurate, obstinate, opinionated, peevish, pertinacious, perverse, pigheaded, stubborn, unyielding, willful ♦ [2] astute, canny, knowing, sharp, shrewd, smart ♦ [2] down-to-earth, earthy, matter-of-fact, practical, pragmatic, realistic

hard·head·ed·ness \-nəs\ *n* ♦ : the quality or state of being hardheaded

♦ mulishness, obduracy, obstinacy, peevishness, pertinacity, self-will, stubbornness, tenacity

hard–heart·ed \-'här-təd\ *adj* : PITILESS, CRUEL — **hard–heart·ed·ly** *adv* — **hard–heart·ed·ness** *n*
har·di·hood \'här-dē-ˌhu̇d\ *n* **1** : resolute courage and fortitude **2** : active bodily or mental strength or force : VIGOR

♦ bravery, courage, daring, fearlessness, gallantry, guts, heart, heroism, nerve, stoutness, valor

hard–line \'härd-'līn\ *adj* : advocating or involving a rigidly uncompromising course of action ⟨a ~ conservative⟩ — **hard–lin·er** \-'lī-nər\ *n*
hard–luck \-ˌlək\ *adj* ♦ : marked by or relating to bad luck ⟨~ losing teams⟩

♦ hapless, ill-fated, ill-starred, luckless, unfortunate, unhappy, unlucky

hard·ly \'härd-lē\ *adv* **1** : with force **2 a** ♦ : in a severe manner : HARSHLY **b** : with great or excessive grief or resentment **3** ♦ : with difficulty : by hard work or struggle **4** ♦ : only just : BARELY **5** ♦ : certainly not

♦ [2a] hard, harshly, ill, oppressively, roughly, severely, sternly, stiffly *Ant* gently, leniently, lightly, mildly, softly ♦ [3] determinedly, diligently, hard, laboriously, mightily, strenuously, tirelessly ♦ [4] barely, just, marginally, scarcely, slightly ♦ [5] no, none, scarcely *Ant* absolutely, certainly, completely, definitely, positively, surely

hard·ness \-nəs\ *n* **1** ♦ : the quality or state of being hard **2** ♦ : a condition that makes life difficult, challenging, or uncomfortable

♦ [1] harshness, inflexibility, rigidity, severity, sternness, strictness ♦ [2] adversity, asperity, difficulty, hardship, rigor

hard–nosed \'härd-'nōzd\ *adj* : TOUGH, UNCOMPROMISING; *also* : HARDHEADED 2
hard palate *n* : the bony anterior part of the palate forming the roof of the mouth
hard·pan \'härd-ˌpan\ *n* : a compact layer in soil that is impenetrable by roots
hard–pressed \-'prest\ *adj* : HARD PUT; *esp* : being under financial strain
hard put *adj* **1** : barely able **2** : faced with difficulty or perplexity
hard rock *n* : rock music marked by a heavy beat, high amplification, and usu. frenzied performances
hard–shell \'härd-ˌshel\ *adj* : HIDEBOUND, UNCOMPROMISING ⟨a ~ conservative⟩
hard·ship \-ˌship\ *n* **1** : SUFFERING, PRIVATION **2** ♦ : something that causes suffering or privation

♦ adversity, asperity, difficulty, hardness, rigor

hard·tack \-ˌtak\ *n* : a saltless hard biscuit, bread, or cracker
hard·top \-ˌtäp\ *n* : an automobile having a permanent rigid top
hard up *adj* ♦ : short of money

♦ broke, destitute, impecunious, impoverished, indigent, needy, penniless, penurious, poor, poverty-stricken

hard·ware \-ˌwar\ *n* **1** : ware (as cutlery or tools) made of metal **2 ♦ :** major items of equipment or their components used for a particular purpose **3 :** the physical components (as electronic devices) of a vehicle (as a spacecraft) or an apparatus (as a computer)

♦ accoutrements (*or* accouterments), apparatus, equipment, gear, matériel, outfit, paraphernalia, stuff, tackle

hard·wired \-ˌwī(-ə)rd\ *adj* **1 :** connected or incorporated by or as if by permanent electrical connections **2 :** genetically or innately determined or predisposed ⟨∼ reactions⟩ ⟨is ∼ to avoid change⟩

hard·wood \-ˌwu̇d\ *n* **:** the wood of a broad-leaved usu. deciduous tree as distinguished from that of a conifer; *also* **:** such a tree — **hardwood** *adj*

hard·work·ing \-ˈwər-kiŋ\ *adj* **:** INDUSTRIOUS

har·dy \ˈhär-dē\ *adj* **har·di·er; -est 1 :** BOLD, BRAVE ⟨∼ pioneers⟩ **2 ♦ :** intrepidly daring **:** AUDACIOUS **3 a :** ROBUST **b ♦ :** able to withstand adverse conditions ⟨∼ shrubs⟩ — **har·di·ly** \-də-lē\ *adv* — **har·di·ness** \-dē-nəs\ *n*

♦ [2] adventurous, audacious, bold, daring, enterprising, gutsy, nervy, venturesome ♦ [3b] hard, hard-bitten, rugged, stout, strong, sturdy, tough, vigorous *Ant* delicate, soft, tender, weak

hare \ˈhar\ *n, pl* **hare** *or* **hares :** any of various swift timid long-eared mammals like the related rabbits but born with open eyes and fur

hare·bell \ˈhar-ˌbel\ *n* **:** a slender herb with bright blue bell-shaped flowers

hare·brained \-ˈbrānd\ *adj* **♦ :** lacking in sense, judgment, or discretion ⟨a ∼ scheme⟩ ⟨∼ notions⟩

♦ absurd, cuckoo, fatuous, foolish, nonsensical, nutty, senseless, silly, stupid

hare·lip \-ˈlip\ *n, sometimes offensive* **:** a birth defect characterized by one or more clefts in the upper lip

ha·rem \ˈhar-əm\ *n* **1 :** a house or part of a house allotted to women in a Muslim household **2 :** the women and servants occupying a harem **3 :** a group of females associated with one male

hark \ˈhärk\ *vb* **♦ :** to pay close attention **:** LISTEN

♦ attend, hear, heed, listen, mind

harken *var of* HEARKEN

har·le·quin \ˈhär-li-kən, -kwən\ *n* **1** *cap* **:** a character (as in comedy) with a shaved head, masked face, variegated tights, and wooden sword **2 ♦ :** a fool or comedian in an entertainment (as a circus) **:** CLOWN

♦ buffoon, clown, zany

har·lot \ˈhär-lət\ *n, disparaging* **:** a woman who engages in sexual activities esp. for money **:** PROSTITUTE

¹**harm** \ˈhärm\ *n* **1 ♦ :** physical or mental damage **:** INJURY **2 :** MISCHIEF, HURT

♦ damage, detriment, hurt, injury

²**harm** *vb* **♦ :** to cause harm to **:** INJURE

♦ damage, hurt, injure, wound

harm·ful \-fəl\ *adj* **♦ :** of a kind likely to be damaging — **harm·ful·ly** *adv* — **harm·ful·ness** *n*

♦ adverse, bad, baleful, baneful, damaging, deleterious, detrimental, evil, hurtful, ill, injurious, mischievous, noxious, pernicious, prejudicial *Ant* harmless, innocent, innocuous, inoffensive, safe

harm·less \-ləs\ *adj* **♦ :** lacking capacity or intent to injure — **harm·less·ly** *adv* — **harm·less·ness** *n*

♦ innocent, innocuous, safe *Ant* adverse, bad, harmful, hurtful, ill, injurious

¹**har·mon·ic** \här-ˈmä-nik\ *adj* **1 :** of or relating to musical harmony or harmonics **2 :** pleasing to the ear — **har·mon·i·cal·ly** \-ni-k(ə-)lē\ *adv*

²**harmonic** *n* **:** a musical overtone

har·mon·i·ca \här-ˈmä-ni-kə\ *n* **:** a small wind instrument in which the sound is produced by metal reeds

har·mo·ni·ous \här-ˈmō-nē-əs\ *adj* **1 ♦ :** musically concordant **2 ♦ :** having the parts agreeably related **:** CONGRUOUS **3 ♦ :** marked by accord in sentiment or action ⟨a ∼ relationship⟩ — **har·mo·ni·ous·ly** *adv* — **har·mo·ni·ous·ness** *n*

♦ [1] euphonious, melodious, musical, symphonic, tuneful *Ant* discordant, dissonant, inharmonious, unmelodious, unmusical ♦ [2] balanced, congruous, consonant *Ant* incongruous, inharmonious, unbalanced ♦ [3] agreeable, amicable, compatible,

congenial, kindred, unanimous, united *Ant* disagreeable, disunited, incompatible, inharmonious, uncongenial

har·mo·nise *chiefly Brit var of* HARMONIZE

har·mo·ni·um \här-ˈmō-nē-əm\ *n* **:** a keyboard wind instrument in which the wind acts on a set of metal reeds

har·mo·nize \ˈhär-mə-ˌnīz\ *vb* **-nized; -niz·ing 1 :** to play or sing in harmony **2 ♦ :** to be in harmony **3 ♦ :** to bring into consonance or accord — **har·mo·ni·za·tion** \ˌhär-mə-nə-ˈzā-shən\ *n*

♦ [2, 3] agree, blend, conform, coordinate *Ant* clash, collide, conflict ♦ [3] accommodate, conciliate, conform, coordinate, key, reconcile *Ant* alienate, disjoin

har·mo·ny \ˈhär-mə-nē\ *n, pl* **-nies 1 :** musical agreement of sounds; *esp* **:** the combination of tones into chords and progressions of chords **2 a ♦ :** a pleasing arrangement of parts **b ♦ :** balanced interrelationship **3 :** internal calm

♦ [2a] balance, coherence, consonance, proportion, symmetry, symphony, unity *Ant* asymmetry, disproportion, disunity, imbalance, incoherence ♦ [2b] compatibility, concord, peace *Ant* conflict, discord, dissension

¹**har·ness** \ˈhär-nəs\ *n* **1 :** the gear other than a yoke of a draft animal **2 :** something that resembles a harness

²**harness** *vb* **1 :** to put a harness on; *also* **:** YOKE **2 ♦ :** to make use of **:** UTILIZE

♦ apply, employ, exercise, exploit, operate, use, utilize

¹**harp** \ˈhärp\ *n* **:** a musical instrument consisting of a triangular frame set with strings plucked by the fingers — **harp·ist** \ˈhär-pist\ *n*

²**harp** *vb* **1 :** to play on a harp **2 :** to dwell on a subject tiresomely — **harp·er** *n*

¹**har·poon** \här-ˈpün\ *n* **:** a barbed spear used esp. in hunting whales

²**harpoon** *vb* **♦ :** to strike or capture with or as if with a harpoon — **har·poon·er** *n*

♦ gore, impale, lance, pierce, puncture, skewer, spear, spike, stab, stick, transfix

harp·si·chord \ˈhärp-si-ˌkȯrd\ *n* **:** a keyboard instrument producing tones by the plucking of its strings with quills or with leather or plastic points

har·py \ˈhär-pē\ *n, pl* **harpies 1 :** a predatory person **:** LEECH **2 ♦ :** a shrewish woman

♦ fury, shrew, termagant, virago

har·ri·dan \ˈhar-əd-ᵊn\ *n* **:** SHREW 2

¹**har·ri·er** \ˈhar-ē-ər\ *n* **1 :** any of a breed of medium-sized foxhounds **2 :** a runner on a cross-country team

²**harrier** *n* **:** a slender long-legged hawk

¹**har·row** \ˈhar-ō\ *n* **:** a cultivating tool that has spikes, spring teeth, or disks and is used esp. to pulverize and smooth the soil

²**harrow** *vb* **1 :** to cultivate with a harrow **2 ♦ :** to cause distress or suffering to **:** TORMENT

♦ afflict, agonize, bedevil, curse, martyr, persecute, plague, rack, torment, torture

harrowing *adj* **♦ :** acutely distressing or painful

♦ agonizing, bitter, cruel, excruciating, galling, grievous, harsh, hurtful, painful, tortuous

har·rumph \hə-ˈrəmf\ *vb* **:** to comment disapprovingly as though clearing the throat

har·ry \ˈhar-ē\ *vb* **har·ried; har·ry·ing 1 :** RAID, PILLAGE **2 :** to torment by or as if by constant attack

harsh \ˈhärsh\ *adj* **1 :** disagreeably rough **2 ♦ :** causing discomfort or pain **3 ♦ :** unduly exacting **:** SEVERE **4 ♦ :** lacking in aesthetic appeal or refinement

♦ [2] bitter, brutal, burdensome, cruel, excruciating, grievous, grim, hard, heavy, inhuman, murderous, onerous, oppressive, rough, rugged, severe, stiff, tough, trying *Ant* easy, light, soft ♦ [3] austere, authoritarian, flinty, hard, heavy-handed, ramrod, rigid, rigorous, severe, stern, strict ♦ [4] grotesque, unaesthetic *Ant* aesthetic

harsh·en \ˈhär-shən\ *vb* **:** to make or become harsh ⟨∼ed his voice⟩

harsh·ly \-lē\ *adv* **♦ :** in a harsh manner

♦ hard, hardly, ill, oppressively, roughly, severely, sternly, stiffly

harsh·ness \-nəs\ *n* **♦ :** the quality or state of being harsh

♦ bite, bitterness, pungency, sharpness, tartness ♦ hardness, inflexibility, rigidity, severity, sternness, strictness

hart \ˈhärt\ *n, chiefly Brit* **:** STAG

¹har·um–scar·um \ˌhar-əm-ˈskar-əm\ *adj* ♦ : having or showing a lack of concern for the consequences of one's actions : RECKLESS, IRRESPONSIBLE

♦ daredevil, foolhardy, irresponsible, reckless

²harum–scarum *adv* ♦ : in a rash or heedless way

♦ amok, berserk, frantically, hectically, helter-skelter, madly, pell-mell, wild, wildly

¹har·vest \ˈhär-vəst\ *n* **1** : the season for gathering in crops; *also* : the act of gathering in a crop **2** : a mature crop **3** : the product or reward of effort

²harvest *vb* **1** ♦ : to gather in a crop : REAP **2** : to gather, hunt, or kill (as deer) for human use or population control — **har·vest·er** *n*

♦ gather, pick, reap

has *pres 3d sing of* HAVE

has–been \ˈhaz-ˌbin\ *n* : one that has passed the peak of ability, power, effectiveness, or popularity

¹hash \ˈhash\ *vb* **1** ♦ : to chop into small pieces **2** ♦ : to talk about — often used with *over* or *out* **3** : to make a confused muddle of

♦ [1] chop, mince ♦ *usu* **hash over** [2] argue, chew over, debate, discuss, dispute, moot, talk over

²hash *n* **1** : chopped meat mixed with potatoes and browned **2** ♦ : a mass of things mingled together without order or plan : HODGEPODGE, JUMBLE

♦ assortment, clutter, jumble, medley, mélange, miscellany, motley, muddle, variety, welter

³hash *n* : HASHISH

hash browns *n pl* : boiled potatoes that have been diced, mixed with chopped onions and shortening, and fried

hash·ish \ˈha-ˌshēsh, ha-ˈshēsh\ *n* : the intoxicating concentrated resin from the flowering tops of the female hemp plant

hash·tag \ˈhash-ˌtag\ *n* : a word or phrase preceded by the symbol # that classifies the accompanying text

hasp \ˈhasp\ *n* : a fastener (as for a door) consisting of a hinged metal strap that fits over a staple and is secured by a pin or padlock

has·si·um \ˈha-sē-əm\ *n* : an artificially produced radioactive metallic chemical element

¹has·sle \ˈha-səl\ *n* **1 a** ♦ : a heated often protracted argument **b** : a violent skirmish : FIGHT **2** ♦ : an annoying or troublesome concern

♦ [1a] altercation, argument, bicker, brawl, disagreement, dispute, fight, misunderstanding, quarrel, row, scrap, spat, squabble, wrangle ♦ [2] aggravation, annoyance, bother, exasperation, frustration, headache, inconvenience, irritant, nuisance, peeve, pest, problem, thorn

²hassle *vb* **1** : to contend or disagree in words **2** : to annoy persistently or acutely

♦ argue, bicker, brawl, dispute, fall out, fight, quarrel, row, scrap, spat, squabble, wrangle

has·sock \ˈha-sək\ *n* : a cushion that serves as a seat or leg rest; *also* : a cushion to kneel on in prayer

haste \ˈhāst\ *n* **1** ♦ : rapidity of motion or action : SPEED **2** ♦ : rash or headlong action **3** : excessive eagerness

♦ [1] celerity, fastness, fleetness, hurry, quickness, rapidity, speed, swiftness, velocity ♦ [2] hurry, hustle, precipitation, rush

has·ten \ˈhās-ᵊn\ *vb* **1** : to urge on **2** ♦ : to move or act quickly : HURRY; *also* : to cause to move or act faster

♦ accelerate, hurry, quicken, rush, speed (up), step up, whisk

hast·i·ly \ˈhā-stə-lē\ *adv* ♦ : in haste

♦ cursorily, headlong, hurriedly, pell-mell, precipitately, rashly *Ant* deliberately ♦ apace, briskly, fast, full tilt, posthaste, presto, pronto, quick, quickly, rapidly, soon, speedily, swift, swiftly

hast·i·ness \ˈhā-stē-nəs\ *n* : the quality or state of being hasty

hasty \ˈhā-stē\ *adj* ♦ : made, done, or acting in haste

♦ cursory, headlong, pell-mell, precipitate, precipitous, rash *Ant* deliberate, unhurried

hat \ˈhat\ *n* ♦ : a covering for the head usu. having a shaped crown and brim

♦ cap, headgear

hat·box \ˈhat-ˌbäks\ *n* : a round piece of luggage esp. for carrying hats

¹hatch \ˈhach\ *n* **1** ♦ : a small door or opening **2** : a door or cover for access down into a compartment of a ship

♦ door, gate, portal

²hatch *vb* **1 a** : to produce by incubation **b** ♦ : to incubate eggs **2** : to emerge from an egg or pupa; *also* : to give forth young **3** : ORIGINATE — **hatch·ery** \ˈha-chə-rē\ *n*

♦ brood, incubate, set, sit

hatch·back \ˈhach-ˌbak\ *n* : an automobile with a rear hatch that opens upward

hatch·et \ˈha-chət\ *n* **1** : a short-handled ax with a hammerlike part opposite the blade **2** : TOMAHAWK

hatchet man *n* : a person hired for murder, coercion, or unscrupulous attack

hatch·ing \ˈha-chiŋ\ *n* : the engraving or drawing of closely spaced fine lines chiefly to give an effect of shading; *also* : the pattern so created

hatch·way \ˈhach-ˌwā\ *n* : a hatch giving access usu. by a ladder or stairs

¹hate \ˈhāt\ *n* **1** ♦ : intense hostility and aversion **2** ♦ : an object of hatred

♦ [1] abhorrence, abomination, execration, hatred, loathing *Ant* affection, love, devotion, fondness ♦ [2] abhorrence, abomination, anathema, antipathy, aversion, bête noire *Ant* love

²hate *vb* **hat·ed; hat·ing** **1** ♦ : to express or feel extreme enmity **2** : to find distasteful — **hat·er** *n*

♦ abhor, abominate, despise, detest, execrate, loathe *Ant* love

hate·ful \-fəl\ *adj* ♦ : full of hate : MALICIOUS

♦ catty, cruel, malevolent, malicious, malign, malignant, mean, nasty, spiteful, virulent *Ant* benevolent, benign, benignant, loving, unmalicious

hate·ful·ly \-fə-lē\ *adv* ♦ : in a hateful manner

♦ maliciously, meanly, nastily, spitefully, viciously, wickedly

hate·ful·ness \-nəs\ *n* ♦ : the quality or state of being hateful

♦ cattiness, despite, malice, malignity, meanness, nastiness, spite, spleen, venom, viciousness

ha·tred \ˈhā-trəd\ *n* ♦ : intense hostility and aversion : HATE; *also* : prejudiced hostility or animosity

♦ abhorrence, abomination, execration, hate, loathing

hat·ter \ˈha-tər\ *n* : one that makes, sells, or cleans and repairs hats

hau·berk \ˈhȯ-bərk\ *n* : a coat of mail

haugh·ti·ness \ˈhȯ-tē-nəs\ *n* ♦ : the quality or state of being haughty

♦ arrogance, loftiness, pretense, pretension, pretentiousness, self-importance, superiority

haugh·ty \ˈhȯ-tē\ *adj* **haugh·ti·er; -est** ♦ : disdainfully proud — **haugh·ti·ly** \-tə-lē\ *adv*

♦ disdainful, highfalutin, lofty, lordly, prideful, proud, superior

¹haul \ˈhȯl\ *vb* **1** ♦ : to exert traction on : DRAW, PULL **2** ♦ : to furnish transportation : CART — **haul·er** *n*

♦ [1] drag, draw, hale, lug, pull, tow, tug ♦ [2] bear, carry, cart, convey, ferry, lug, pack, tote, transport

²haul *n* **1** : the act or process of hauling : PULL, TUG **2** ♦ : the result of an effort to obtain, collect, or win **3 a** : the length or course of a transportation route **b** ♦ : a quantity transported : LOAD

♦ [2] catch, take, yield ♦ [3b] burden, cargo, freight, lading, load, payload, weight

haul·age \ˈhȯ-lij\ *n* **1** : the act or process of hauling **2** : a charge for hauling

haunch \ˈhȯnch\ *n* **1** : ²HIP 1 **2** : HINDQUARTER 2 — usu. used in pl. **3** : HINDQUARTER 1

¹haunt \ˈhȯnt\ *vb* **1** ♦ : to visit often : FREQUENT **2** : to have a disquieting effect on; *also* : to reappear continually in **3** : to visit or inhabit as a ghost — **haunt·er** *n*

♦ frequent, hang around, hang out, resort, visit

²haunt \ˈhȯnt, *2 is usu* ˈhant\ *n* **1** ♦ : a place habitually frequented **2** *chiefly dial* : GHOST

♦ hangout, rendezvous, resort

haunting *adj* ♦ : having a disquieting effect — **haunt·ing·ly** *adv*

♦ creepy, eerie, spooky, uncanny, unearthly, weird

haute cou·ture \ˌōt-ku̇-ˈtu̇r\ *n* : the establishments or designers that create exclusive and often trend-setting fashions for women; *also* : the fashions created

haute cui•sine \-kwi-'zēn\ *n* : artful or elaborate cuisine

hau•teur \hȯ-'tər, ō-, hō-\ *n* : ARROGANCE, HAUGHTINESS

¹have \'hav, həv, v; *in sense 2 before "to" usu* 'haf\ *vb* **had** \'had, həd\; **hav•ing; has** \'haz, həz, *in sense 2 before "to" usu* 'has\ **1 ♦** : to hold in possession; *also* : to hold in one's use, service, or regard **2 ♦** : to be compelled or forced — usu. used with an infinitive with *to* ⟨~ to go now⟩ **3** : to stand in relationship to ⟨*has* many enemies⟩ **4** : OBTAIN; *also* : RECEIVE, ACCEPT **5** : to be marked by **6** : SHOW; *also* : USE, EXERCISE **7 a ♦** : to experience esp. by submitting to, undergoing, or suffering ⟨~ a cold⟩ **b** : TAKE ⟨~ a look⟩ **8 ♦** : to entertain in the mind ⟨~ an idea⟩ **9** : to cause to **10** : to consent to : ALLOW ⟨I won't ~ you jumping on the bed⟩ **11** : to be competent in **12 a** : to hold in a disadvantageous position **b ♦** : to take advantage of : TRICK **13** : to give birth to **14** : to partake of **15** — used as an auxiliary with the past participle to form the present perfect, past perfect, or future perfect — **have at** : ATTACK — **have coming** : DESERVE — **have done with** : to be finished with — **have had it** : to have endured all one will permit or can stand — **have to do with** : to have in the way of relation with or effect on

♦ [1] command, enjoy, hold, occupy, own, possess, retain *Ant* lack, want ♦ *usu* **have to** [2] must, need, ought, shall, should ♦ [7a] endure, experience, feel, know, see, suffer, sustain, taste, undergo ♦ [8] bear, cherish, entertain, harbor (*or* harbour), hold, nurse ♦ [12b] beguile, bluff, cozen, deceive, delude, dupe, fool, gull, hoax, hoodwink, humbug, misinform, mislead, string along, take in, trick

²have \'hav\ *n* : one that has material wealth

ha•ven \'hā-vən\ *n* **1 ♦** : a part of a body of water protected and deep enough to furnish anchorage : HARBOR, PORT **2 ♦** : a place of safety **3** : a place offering favorable conditions ⟨a tourist's ~⟩

♦ [1] anchorage, harbor (*or* harbour), port ♦ [2] asylum, refuge, retreat, sanctuary, shelter

have–not \'hav-ˌnät, -'nät\ *n* : one that is poor in material wealth

hav•er•sack \'ha-vər-ˌsak\ *n* : a bag similar to a knapsack but worn over one shoulder

hav•oc \'ha-vək\ *n* **1 ♦** : wide and general destruction **2 ♦** : great confusion and disorder

♦ [1] annihilation, demolition, desolation, destruction, devastation, loss, obliteration, ruin, wastage, wreckage ♦ [2] chaos, confusion, disarray, disorder, disorganization, hell, jumble, mess, muddle, shambles

haw \'hȯ\ *n* : a hawthorn berry; *also* : HAWTHORN

Ha•wai•ian \hə-'wä-yən\ *n* : the Polynesian language of Hawaii

¹hawk \'hȯk\ *n* **1** : any of numerous mostly small or medium-sized day-flying birds of prey (as a falcon or kite) **2** : a supporter of a war or a warlike policy — **hawk•ish** *adj*

²hawk *vb* : to offer goods for sale by calling out in the street — **hawk•er** *n*

³hawk *vb* : to make a harsh coughing sound in or as if in clearing the throat; *also* : to raise by hawking

hawk•weed \'hȯk-ˌwēd\ *n* : any of several plants related to the daisies usu. having yellow flowers

haw•ser \'hȯ-zər\ *n* : a large rope for towing, mooring, or securing a ship

haw•thorn \'hȯ-ˌthȯrn\ *n* : any of a genus of spiny spring-flowering shrubs or small trees related to the apple

¹hay \'hā\ *n* **1** : herbage (as grass) mowed and cured for fodder **2** : REWARD **3** *slang* : BED ⟨hit the ~⟩ **4** : a small amount of money

²hay *vb* : to cut, cure, and store for hay

hay•cock \'hā-ˌkäk\ *n* : a small conical pile of hay

hay fever *n* : an acute allergic reaction esp. to plant pollen that resembles a cold

hay•loft \'hā-ˌlȯft\ *n* : a loft for hay

hay•mow \-ˌmau̇\ *n* : a mow of or for hay

hay•rick \-ˌrik\ *n* : a large sometimes thatched outdoor stack of hay

hay•seed \-ˌsēd\ *n, pl* **hayseed** *or* **hayseeds** **1** : clinging bits of straw or chaff from hay **2** : BUMPKIN, YOKEL

hay•stack \-ˌstak\ *n* : a stack of hay

hay•wire \-ˌwī-(-ə)r\ *adj* : being out of order or control : CRAZY ⟨things went ~⟩

¹haz•ard \'ha-zərd\ *n* **1 ♦** : a source of danger **2 ♦** : the assumed impersonal purposeless determiner of unaccountable hap-

penings : CHANCE; *also* : ACCIDENT **3** : an obstacle on a golf course

♦ [1] danger, menace, peril, pitfall, risk, threat, trouble ♦ [2] accident, chance, circumstance, luck

²hazard *vb* **1** : to expose to possible risk of loss or damage : VENTURE, RISK **2 ♦** : to undertake the risks and dangers of **3** : to offer at the risk of rebuff, rejection, or censure

♦ chance, gamble, risk, venture

haz•ard•ous \'ha-zər-dəs\ *adj* ♦ : involving or exposing one to risk (as of loss or harm)

♦ dangerous, grave, grievous, menacing, parlous, perilous, risky, serious, unhealthy, unsafe, venturesome

¹haze \'hāz\ *n* **1 ♦** : fine dust, smoke, or light vapor causing lack of transparency in the air **2 ♦** : vagueness of mind or perception

♦ [1] fog, murk, smog, soup ♦ [2] daze, fog, muddle, spin

²haze *vb* : to make or become hazy, dull, or cloudy

³haze *vb* **hazed; haz•ing** : to harass by abusive and humiliating tricks usu. by way of initiation

ha•zel \'hā-zəl\ *n* **1** : any of a genus of shrubs or small trees related to the birches and bearing edible brown nuts (**ha•zel•nuts** \-ˌnəts\) **2** : a light brown color

hazy \'hā-zē\ *adj* **haz•i•er; -est** **1 ♦** : obscured or darkened by haze **2 ♦** : not clearly perceived or understood : VAGUE, INDEFINITE — **haz•i•ly** \-zə-lē\ *adv* — **haz•i•ness** \-zē-nəs\ *n*

♦ [1] cloudy, foggy, misty, murky, smoggy, soupy *Ant* clear, cloudless, limpid, pellucid, unclouded ♦ [2] bleary, dim, faint, foggy, fuzzy, indefinite, indistinct, indistinguishable, murky, nebulous, obscure, opaque, shadowy, unclear, undefined, undetermined, vague

Hb *abbr* hemoglobin

HBM *abbr* Her Britannic Majesty; His Britannic Majesty

H–bomb \'āch-ˌbäm\ *n* : HYDROGEN BOMB

HC *abbr* **1** Holy Communion **2** House of Commons

hd *abbr* head

HD *abbr* **1** heavy-duty **2** high definition

hdbk *abbr* handbook

hdkf *abbr* handkerchief

HDL \ˌāch-(ˌ)dē-'el\ *n* : a cholesterol-poor protein-rich lipoprotein of blood plasma correlated with reduced risk of atherosclerosis

hdwe *abbr* hardware

he \'hē\ *pron* **1** : that male one **2** : a person : the person ⟨~ who hesitates is lost⟩

He *symbol* helium

HE *abbr* **1** Her Excellency **2** His Eminence **3** His Excellency

¹head \'hed\ *n* **1 ♦** : the front or upper part of the body containing the brain, the chief sense organs, and the mouth **2 a ♦** : the seat of the intellect : MIND; *also* : mental or emotional control **b** : natural aptitude **3** : POISE ⟨a level ~⟩ **4** : the obverse of a coin **5** : a single human being : INDIVIDUAL; *also, pl* **head** : one of a number (as of cattle) **6** : the end that is upper or higher or opposite the foot; *also* : either end of something (as a drum) whose two ends need not be distinguished **7** : the source of a stream **8 ♦** : a person who leads : LEADER; *also* : a leading element (as of a procession) **9** : a projecting part; *also* : the striking part of a weapon **10** : the place of leadership or honor **11** : a separate part or topic **12 ♦** : the foam on a fermenting or effervescing liquid **13** : culminating point of action : CRISIS ⟨events came to a ~⟩ — **head•ed** \'he-dəd\ *adj* — **head•less** *adj*

♦ [1] noggin, pate, poll ♦ [2a] mind, reason, sanity, wit ♦ [8] boss, captain, chief, foreman, headman, helmsman, kingpin, leader, taskmaster ♦ [10] chair, headship, helm, rein ♦ [12] foam, froth, lather, spume

²head *adj* ♦ : most important, consequential, or influential : PRINCIPAL, CHIEF

♦ chief, first, foremost, high, lead, preeminent, premier, primary, prime, principal, supreme

³head *vb* **1** : to provide with or form a head; *also* : to form the head of **2 ♦** : to act as leader or head to **3** : to get in front of esp. so as to stop; *also* : SURPASS **4** : to put or stand at the head **5 ♦** : to point or proceed in a certain direction

♦ [2] boss, captain, command, dominate, lead, spearhead, supervise ♦ [5] extend, go, lead, lie, run

head•ache \'he-ˌdāk\ *n* **1** : pain in the head **2 ♦** : a vexatious or baffling situation or problem

♦ aggravation, annoyance, bother, exasperation, frustration, hassle, inconvenience, irritant, nuisance, peeve, pest, problem, thorn

head·band \'hed-ˌband\ *n* : a band worn on or around the head

head·bang·er \-ˌbaŋ-ər\ *n* : one who performs or enjoys hard rock

head·board \-ˌbȯrd\ *n* : a board forming the head (as of a bed)

head cold *n* : a common cold centered in the nasal passages and adjacent mucous tissues

head·dress \'hed-ˌdres\ *n* : an often elaborate covering for the head

head·first \-'fərst\ *adv* : HEADLONG 1 — **headfirst** *adj*

head·gear \-ˌgir\ *n* ♦ : a covering or protective device for the head

♦ cap, hat

head–hunt·ing \-ˌhən-tiŋ\ *n* : the practice of seeking out and decapitating enemies and preserving their heads as trophies — **head·hunt·er** \-tər\ *n*

head·ing \'he-diŋ\ *n* **1** : the compass direction in which the longitudinal axis of a ship or airplane points **2** ♦ : something that forms or serves as a head; *esp* : an inscription, headline, or title standing at the top or beginning (as of a letter or chapter)

♦ title

head·land \'hed-lənd, -ˌland\ *n* ♦ : a high point of land or rock projecting into a body of water : PROMONTORY

♦ cape, peninsula, point, promontory, spit

head·light \-ˌlīt\ *n* : a light mounted on the front of a vehicle to illuminate the road ahead

¹**head·line** \-ˌlīn\ *n* : a head of a newspaper story or article usu. printed in large type

²**headline** *vb* **1** : to provide with a headline **2** : to publicize highly **3** : to be a leading performer

head·lock \-ˌläk\ *n* : a wrestling hold in which one encircles the opponent's head with one arm

¹**head·long** \-'lȯŋ\ *adv* **1** : with the head foremost **2** ♦ : without deliberation : RASHLY **3** : without delay

♦ cursorily, hastily, hurriedly, pell-mell, precipitately, rashly

²**head·long** \-ˌlȯŋ\ *adj* **1** ♦ : lacking in calmness or restraint : PRECIPITATE, RASH **2** : plunging with the head foremost

♦ cursory, hasty, pell-mell, precipitate, precipitous, rash

head·man \'hed-'man, -ˌman\ *n* ♦ : one who is a leader

♦ boss, captain, chief, foreman, head, helmsman, kingpin, leader, taskmaster

head·mas·ter \-ˌmas-tər\ *n* : a man who is head of a private school

head·mis·tress \-ˌmis-trəs\ *n* : a woman who is head of a private school

head of steam : strong driving force : MOMENTUM

head–on \'hed-'ȯn, -'än\ *adj* : having the front facing in the direction of initial contact or line of sight ⟨~ collision⟩ — **head–on** *adv*

head·phone \-ˌfōn\ *n* : an earphone held on by a band over the head

head·piece \-ˌpēs\ *n* : a covering for the head

head·pin \-ˌpin\ *n* : a bowling pin that stands foremost in the arrangement of pins

head·quar·ters \-ˌkwȯr-tərz\ *n sing or pl* **1** : a place from which a commander exercises command **2** : the administrative center of an enterprise

head·rest \-ˌrest\ *n* **1** : a support for the head **2** : a pad at the top of the back of an automobile seat

head·room \-ˌrüm, -ˌru̇m\ *n* : vertical space in which to stand, sit, or move

head–scratcher \-ˌskra-chər\ *n* : PUZZLE, MYSTERY

head·set \-ˌset\ *n* : a pair of headphones

head·ship \-ˌship\ *n* ♦ : the position, office, or dignity of a head

♦ care, charge, guidance, oversight, regulation, superintendence, supervision ♦ chair, head, helm, rein

heads·man \'hedz-mən\ *n* : EXECUTIONER

head·stall \'hed-ˌstȯl\ *n* : a part of a bridle or halter that encircles the head

head start *n* **1** : an advantage allowed at the start of a race **2** : a favorable or promising beginning

head·stone \-ˌstōn\ *n* ♦ : a memorial stone at the head of a grave

♦ gravestone, monument, tombstone

head·strong \-ˌstrȯŋ\ *adj* **1** ♦ : not easily restrained **2** ♦ : directed by ungovernable will

♦ [1] froward, intractable, recalcitrant, refractory, uncontrollable, unmanageable, unruly, untoward, wayward, willful ♦ [2] dogged, hardheaded, mulish, obdurate, obstinate, opinionated, peevish, pertinacious, perverse, pigheaded, stubborn, unyielding, willful

heads–up \'hedz-ˌəp\ *n* : WARNING

head·wait·er \-'wā-tər\ *n* : the head of the dining-room staff of a restaurant or hotel

head·wa·ter \-ˌwȯ-tər, -ˌwä-\ *n* : the source of a stream — usu. used in pl.

head·way \-ˌwā\ *n* ♦ : forward motion; *also* : PROGRESS

♦ advance, advancement, furtherance, march, onrush, passage, process, procession, progress, progression

head wind *n* : a wind blowing in a direction opposite to a course esp. of a ship or aircraft

head·word \'hed-ˌwərd\ *n* **1** : a word or term placed at the beginning **2** : a word qualified by a modifier

head·work \-ˌwərk\ *n* : mental work or effort : THINKING

heady \'he-dē\ *adj* **head·i·er; -est 1** : WILLFUL, RASH; *also* : IMPETUOUS **2** : INTOXICATING ⟨a ~ wine⟩ **3** : SHREWD

heal \'hēl\ *vb* **1** ♦ : to make or become healthy, sound, or whole **2** ♦ : to restore to health : CURE — **heal·er** *n*

♦ [1] convalesce, gain, mend, rally, recover, recuperate, snap back ♦ [2] cure, mend, rehabilitate

health \'helth\ *n* **1** ♦ : sound physical or mental condition; *also* : overall condition of the body ⟨in poor ~⟩ **2** : WELL-BEING **3** : a toast to someone's health or prosperity

♦ fitness, heartiness, robustness, soundness, wellness, wholeness, wholesomeness *Ant* illness, sickness, unsoundness

health care *n* : efforts made to maintain or restore health — usu. hyphenated when used attributively

health club *n* : a commercial establishment providing health and fitness facilities and equipment for members

health·ful \'helth-fəl\ *adj* **1** ♦ : beneficial to health **2** : in good health — **health·ful·ly** *adv* — **health·ful·ness** *n*

♦ healthy, restorative, salubrious, salutary, wholesome *Ant* insalubrious, noxious, unhealthful, unhealthy, unwholesome

health·i·ness \'hel-thē-nəs\ *n* : the quality or state of being healthy

health maintenance organization *n* : HMO

healthy \'hel-thē\ *adj* **health·i·er; -est 1** ♦ : enjoying or typical of good health : WELL **2** ♦ : evincing or conducive to health **3 a** : PROSPEROUS **b** ♦ : not small or feeble : CONSIDERABLE — **health·i·ly** \-thə-lē\ *adv*

♦ [1] able-bodied, chipper, fit, hale, hearty, robust, sound, well, whole, wholesome *Ant* ailing, diseased, ill, sick, unfit, unhealthy, unsound, unwell ♦ [2] healthful, restorative, salubrious, salutary, wholesome ♦ [3b] considerable, good, goodly, respectable, significant, sizable, substantial, tidy

¹**heap** \'hēp\ *n* **1** ♦ : a collection of things thrown one on another : PILE **2** ♦ : a great number or large quantity : LOT

♦ [1] cock, hill, mound, mountain, pile, rick, stack ♦ [2] abundance, deal, gobs, loads, lot, pile, plenty, quantity, scads

²**heap** *vb* **1** ♦ : to throw or lay in a heap : pile or collect in great quantity **2 a** ♦ : to give in large quantities **b** ♦ : to load heavily

♦ [1] accumulate, collect, conglomerate, gather, pile up ♦ [1] hill, mound, pile, stack ♦ [2a] lavish, pour, rain, shower ♦ [2b] charge, cram, fill, jam, jam-pack, load, pack, stuff

hear \'hir\ *vb* **heard** \'hərd\; **hear·ing 1** : to perceive by the ear **2** ♦ : to gain knowledge of by hearing : LEARN **3** ♦ : to listen to with attention : HEED; *also* : ATTEND **4** : to give a legal hearing to or take testimony from — **hear·er** *n*

♦ [2] ascertain, catch on, discover, find out, learn, realize, see ♦ [3] attend, hark, heed, listen, mind

hear·ing *n* **1** : the process, function, or power of perceiving sound; *esp* : the special sense by which noises and tones are received as stimuli **2** ♦ : range of hearing : EARSHOT **3** : opportunity to be heard **4** : a listening to arguments (as in a court); *also* : a session (as of a legislative committee) in which testimony is taken from witnesses

♦ earshot, hail, sound

hear·ken \'här-kən\ *vb* : to give attention : LISTEN

hear·say \'hir-ˌsā\ *n* : RUMOR

hearse \'hərs\ *n* : a vehicle for carrying the dead to the grave

heart \'härt\ *n* **1** : a hollow muscular organ that by rhythmic contraction keeps up the circulation of the blood in the body; *also*

: something resembling a heart in shape   **2 :** any of a suit of playing cards marked with a red figure of a heart; *also, pl* : a card game in which the object is to avoid taking tricks containing hearts   **3 a :** the whole personality   **b :** the emotional or moral as distinguished from the intellectual nature   **c ♦ :** generous disposition : COMPASSION   **4 ♦ :** mental or moral strength to venture, persevere, and withstand danger, fear, or difficulty : COURAGE   **5 ♦ :** one's innermost being   **6 a :** CENTER   **b :** the essential part   **7 :** the younger central part of a compact leafy cluster (as of lettuce)   **8 :** a single human being ⟨dear ∼⟩ — **heart•ed** \'här-təd\ *adj* — **by heart :** by rote or from memory

♦ [3c] charity, commiseration, compassion, feeling, humanity, kindliness, kindness, mercy, pity, sympathy *Ant* inhumanity ♦ [4] bravery, courage, daring, fearlessness, gallantry, guts, hardihood, heroism, nerve, stoutness, valor ♦ [5] core, quick, soul ♦ [6b] core, crux, gist, nub, pith, pivot

heart•ache \-,āk\ *n* ♦ : anguish of mind

♦ affliction, anguish, dolor, grief, sorrow, woe

heart attack *n* : an acute episode of heart disease due to insufficient blood supply to the heart muscle
heart•beat \'härt-,bēt\ *n* : one complete pulsation of the heart
heart•break \-,brāk\ *n* : crushing grief
heart•break•ing \-,brā-kiŋ\ *adj* ♦ : causing extreme sorrow or distress — **heart•break•er** \-,brā-kər\ *n*

♦ depressing, dismal, dreary, melancholy, pathetic, sad, sorry, tearful ♦ deplorable, distressful, grievous, lamentable, regrettable, unfortunate, woeful

heart•bro•ken \-,brō-kən\ *adj* : overcome by sorrow
heart•burn \-,bərn\ *n* : a burning distress behind the sternum due to the backward flow of acid from the stomach to the esophagus
heart disease *n* : an abnormal organic condition of the heart or of the heart and circulation
heart•en \'härt-ᵊn\ *vb* ♦ : to give heart to : ENCOURAGE, CHEER ⟨were ∼ed by the victory⟩

♦ buoy (up), cheer, comfort, embolden, encourage, inspire, steel

heartening *adj* ♦ : tending or serving to hearten, inspire, or give fresh courage

♦ auspicious, bright, encouraging, fair, golden, hopeful, likely, promising, propitious, rosy, upbeat ♦ comforting, encouraging, gratifying, heartwarming, rewarding, satisfying

heart•felt \'härt-,felt\ *adj* : deeply felt : SINCERE ⟨∼ thanks⟩
hearth \'härth\ *n* **1 :** an area (as of brick) in front of a fireplace; *also* : the floor of a fireplace   **2 ♦ :** one's place of residence : HOME

♦ abode, domicile, dwelling, home, house, lodging, quarters, residence

hearth•stone \'härth-,stōn\ *n* **1 :** stone forming a hearth   **2** : one's place of residence : HOME
heart•i•ly \'här-tə-lē\ *adv* ♦ : in a hearty manner

♦ cheerfully, gaily, happily, jovially, merrily, mirthfully

heart•i•ness \'här-tē-nəs\ *n* ♦ : the quality or state of being hearty

♦ fitness, health, robustness, soundness, wellness, wholeness, wholesomeness

heart•less \'härt-ləs\ *adj* ♦ : lacking feeling or affection

♦ callous, hard, inhuman, inhumane, pitiless, soulless, unfeeling, unsympathetic

heart•rend•ing \-,ren-diŋ\ *adj* : causing extreme sorrow or distress : HEARTBREAKING
heart•sick \-,sik\ *adj* ♦ : very despondent

♦ bad, blue, brokenhearted, dejected, depressed, despondent, disconsolate, miserable, mournful, sad, wretched

heart•sick•ness \-nəs\ *n* ♦ : the quality or state of being heartsick

♦ blues, dejection, depression, desolation, despondency, doldrums, dumps, forlornness, gloom, melancholy, sadness

heart–stop•ping \-,stä-piŋ\ *adj* : extremely shocking or exciting
heart•strings \-,striŋz\ *n pl* : the deepest emotions or affections
heart•throb \-,thräb\ *n* **1 :** the throb of a heart   **2 :** sentimental emotion   **3 :** SWEETHEART   **4 :** an entertainer noted for his sex appeal
heart–to–heart *adj* : SINCERE, FRANK
heart•warm•ing \'härt-,wor-miŋ\ *adj* ♦ : inspiring sympathetic feeling

♦ comforting, encouraging, gratifying, heartening, rewarding,

satisfying *Ant* depressing, discouraging, disheartening, dispiriting

heart•wood \-,wud\ *n* : the older harder nonliving and usu. darker wood of the central part of a tree trunk
¹hearty \'här-tē\ *adj* **heart•i•er; -est** **1 a :** giving full support   **b ♦ :** enthusiastically or exuberantly cordial   **2 ♦ :** vigorously healthy   **3 :** ABUNDANT; *also* : NOURISHING ⟨a ∼ soup⟩   **4 ♦ :** carried out forcefully and energetically

♦ [1b] amicable, companionable, comradely, cordial, friendly, genial, neighborly, warm, warmhearted ♦ [2] able-bodied, chipper, fit, hale, healthy, robust, sound, well, whole, wholesome ♦ [4] firm, forceful, lusty, robust, solid, stout, strong, sturdy, vigorous

²hearty *n, pl* **heart•ies :** an enthusiastic jovial fellow; *also* : SAILOR
¹heat \'hēt\ *vb* **1 :** to make or become warm or hot   **2 :** EXCITE — **heat•ed•ly** *adv* — **heat•er** *n*
²heat *n* **1 :** a condition of being hot : WARMTH   **2 :** a form of energy that when added to a body causes the body to rise in temperature, to fuse, to evaporate, or to expand   **3 :** high temperature   **4 a ♦ :** intensity of feeling   **b :** sexual excitement esp. in a female mammal   **5 :** a preliminary race for narrowing the competition   **6 :** pungency of flavor   **7** *slang* : POLICE   **8 :** PRESSURE, COERCION; *also* : ABUSE, CRITICISM

♦ ardor, emotion, fervency, fervor, intensity, passion, vehemence, warmth

heat•ed \'hē-təd\ *adj* ♦ : marked by anger or passion

♦ agitated, feverish, frenzied, hectic, overactive, overwrought

heat exchanger *n* : a device (as an automobile radiator) for transferring heat from one fluid to another without allowing them to mix
heat exhaustion *n* : a condition marked by weakness, nausea, dizziness, and profuse sweating resulting from physical exertion in a hot environment
heath \'hēth\ *n* **1 :** any of a large family of often evergreen shrubby plants (as a blueberry or heather) of wet acid soils   **2 :** a tract of wasteland — **heathy** *adj*
¹hea•then \'hē-thən\ *adj* **1 :** of or relating to heathens, their religions, or their customs   **2 ♦ :** not civilized

♦ Neanderthal, barbarous, heathenish, rude, savage, uncivil, uncivilized, uncultivated, wild

²heathen *n, pl* **heathens** *or* **heathen** **1 :** an unconverted member of a people or nation that does not acknowledge the God of the Bible   **2 :** an uncivilized or irreligious person — **hea•then•dom** *n* — **hea•then•ism** *n*
hea•then•ish \'hē-thə-nish\ *adj* ♦ : resembling or characteristic of heathens : BARBAROUS

♦ Neanderthal, barbarous, heathen, rude, savage, uncivil, uncivilized, uncultivated, wild

heath•er \'he-thər\ *n* : a northern and alpine evergreen heath with usu. lavender flowers — **heath•ery** *adj*
heat lightning *n* : flashes of light without thunder ascribed to distant lightning reflected by high clouds
heat•stroke \'hēt-,strōk\ *n* : a disorder marked esp. by high body temperature without sweating and by collapse that follows prolonged exposure to excessive heat
¹heave \'hēv\ *vb* **heaved** *or* **hove** \'hōv\; **heav•ing** **1 ♦ :** to rise or lift upward   **2 ♦ :** to propel through the air by a forward motion of the hand and arm : THROW   **3 :** to rise and fall rhythmically; *also* : PANT   **4 :** to disgorge the stomach contents through the mouth; *also* : to make an effort to vomit   **5 :** PULL, PUSH — **heav•er** *n*

♦ [1] boost, heft, hoist, jack ♦ [2] cast, catapult, chuck, dash, fire, fling, hurl, hurtle, launch, peg, pelt, pitch, sling, throw, toss

²heave *n* **1 :** an effort to lift or raise   **2 :** THROW, CAST   **3 :** an upward motion   **4** *pl* : a chronic lung disease of horses marked by difficult breathing and persistent cough
heav•en \'he-vən\ *n* **1 :** FIRMAMENT — usu. used in pl.   **2** *often cap* : the abode of the Deity and of the blessed dead; *also* : a spiritual state of everlasting communion with God   **3** *cap* : GOD 1   **4 ♦ :** a place or condition of supreme happiness — **heav•en•ward** *adv or adj*

♦ Eden, Elysium, paradise, utopia ♦ ecstasy, elation, euphoria, exhilaration, intoxication, paradise, rapture, rhapsody, transport

heav•en•ly \-lē\ *adj* **1 ♦ :** of or relating to heaven or the heavens   **2 a :** suggesting the blessed state of heaven   **b ♦ :** highly pleasing

♦ [1] Elysian, celestial, empyrean, supernal ♦ [2b] agreeable, darling, delectable, delicious, delightful, enjoyable, luscious, pleasurable

heav·i·ly \'he-və-lē\ *adv* : to a large degree

¹heavy \'he-vē\ *adj* **heavi·er; -est** **1** ♦ : having great weight **2** ♦ : hard to bear **3** : of weighty import : SERIOUS **4** : characterized by intensity of quality : DEEP, PROFOUND **5** : burdened with something oppressive; *also* : PREGNANT **6** : SLUGGISH **7 a** : lacking sparkle or vivacity : DRAB **b** : DOLEFUL **8** : DROWSY **9** : greater than the average of its kind or class **10** : very rich and hard to digest; *also* : not properly raised or leavened **11** : producing goods (as steel) used in the production of other goods **12** ♦ : threatening to rain or snow — **heavi·ness** \-vē-nəs\ *n*

♦ [1] hefty, massive, ponderous, weighty *Ant* light, lightweight, weightless ♦ [2] bitter, brutal, burdensome, cruel, excruciating, grievous, grim, hard, harsh, inhuman, murderous, onerous, oppressive, rough, rugged, severe, stiff, tough, trying ♦ [12] cloudy, dull, hazy, overcast

²heavy *n, pl* **heav·ies** **1** : a theatrical role representing a dignified or imposing person **2** : a villain esp. in a story

heavy–du·ty \,he-vē-'dü-tē, -'dyü-\ *adj* : able to withstand unusual strain

heavy–hand·ed \-'han-dəd\ *adj* **1** ♦ : lacking dexterity, nimbleness, or grace : CLUMSY **2** ♦ : unduly exacting : HARSH

♦ [1] awkward, clumsy, gawky, graceless, lubberly, lumpish, ungainly, unhandy ♦ [2] austere, authoritarian, flinty, hard, harsh, ramrod, rigid, rigorous, severe, stern, strict

heavy·heart·ed \-'här-təd\ *adj* : SADDENED, DESPONDENT

heavy lifting *n* : a burdensome or laborious duty

heavy metal *n* : energetic and highly amplified electronic rock music

heavy·set \,he-vē-'set\ *adj* ♦ : stocky and compact in build

♦ chunky, dumpy, squat, stocky, stout, stubby, stumpy, thickset

heavy water *n* : water enriched in deuterium

heavy·weight \'he-vē-,wāt\ *n* : one above average in weight; *esp* : a boxer weighing over 175 pounds

Heb *abbr* Hebrews

He·bra·ism \'hē-brā-,i-zəm\ *n* : the thought, spirit, or practice characteristic of the Hebrews — **He·bra·ic** \hi-'brā-ik\ *adj*

He·bra·ist \'hē-,brā-ist\ *n* : a specialist in Hebrew and Hebraic studies

He·brew \'hē-brü\ *n* **1** : the language of the Hebrews **2** : a member of or descendant from a group of Semitic peoples; *esp* : ISRAELITE — **Hebrew** *adj*

He·brews \'hē-(,)brüz\ *n* : a book of the New Testament in Christian Scriptures

hec·a·tomb \'he-kə-,tōm\ *n* : an ancient Greek and Roman sacrifice of 100 oxen or cattle

heck·le \'he-kəl\ *vb* **heck·led; heck·ling** ♦ : to harass with questions or gibes

♦ bait, bug, hassle, needle, ride, taunt, tease

heck·ler \'he-k(ə-)lər\ *n* ♦ : one that heckles

♦ oppressor, persecutor, taunter, tormentor, torturer

hect·are \'hek-,tar\ *n* : a metric measure equal to 10,000 square meters

hec·tic \'hek-tik\ *adj* **1** : being hot and flushed **2** ♦ : filled with excitement, activity, or confusion

♦ agitated, feverish, frenzied, heated, overactive, overwrought

hec·ti·cal·ly \'hek-ti-k(ə-)lē\ *adv* ♦ : in a hectic manner

♦ amok, berserk, frantically, harum-scarum, helter-skelter, madly, pell-mell, wild, wildly

hec·to·gram \'hek-tə-,gram\ *n* : a metric measure equal to 100 grams

hec·to·li·ter \'hek-tə-,lē-tər\ *n* : a metric measure equal to 100 liters

hec·to·me·ter \'hek-tə-,mē-tər, hek-'tä-mə-tər\ *n* : a metric measure equal to 100 meters

hec·tor \'hek-tər\ *vb* **1** : SWAGGER **2** ♦ : to intimidate by bluster or personal pressure

♦ browbeat, bully, cow, intimidate

¹hedge \'hej\ *n* **1** : a fence or boundary formed of shrubs or small trees **2** ♦ : something that impedes or separates : BARRIER **3** : a means of protection (as against financial loss)

♦ barrier, fence, wall

²hedge *vb* **hedged; hedg·ing** **1** ♦ : to enclose or protect with or as if with a hedge **2** : HINDER **3** : to protect oneself financially by a counterbalancing action **4** ♦ : to evade the risk of commitment — **hedg·er** *n*

♦ [1] cage, closet, coop up, corral, encase, enclose, envelop, fence, hem, house, immure, pen, wall ♦ [4] equivocate, fudge, pussyfoot

hedge·hog \'hej-,hog, -,häg\ *n* : a small Old World insect-eating mammal covered with spines; *also* : PORCUPINE

hedge·hop \-,häp\ *vb* : to fly an airplane very close to the ground

hedge·row \-,rō\ *n* : a row of shrubs or trees bounding or separating fields

he·do·nism \'hēd-ᵊn-,i-zəm\ *n* : the doctrine that pleasure is the chief good in life; *also* : a way of life based on this — **he·do·nist** \-ist\ *n* — **he·do·nis·tic** \,hēd-ᵊn-'i-stik\ *adj*

¹heed \'hēd\ *vb* ♦ : to pay attention

♦ attend, hark, hear, listen, mind ♦ follow, listen, mind, note, observe, regard, watch *Ant* disregard, ignore, tune out

²heed *n* ♦ : the act or state of attending or noticing

♦ attention, awareness, cognizance, ear, eye, notice, observance, observation

heed·ful \'hēd-fəl\ *adj* ♦ : taking heed — **heed·ful·ly** *adv*

♦ alert, careful, cautious, circumspect, considerate, gingerly, guarded, safe, wary

heed·ful·ness \-nəs\ *n* ♦ : the quality or state of being heedful

♦ alertness, care, carefulness, caution, circumspection ♦ care, carefulness, heed, pains, scrupulousness

heed·less \-ləs\ *adj* ♦ : not taking heed — **heed·less·ly** *adv*

♦ careless, mindless, unguarded, unsafe, unwary

heed·less·ness \-ləs-nəs\ *n* ♦ : the quality or state of being heedless

♦ carelessness, dereliction, laxness, negligence, remissness, slackness

¹heel \'hēl\ *n* **1** : the hind part of the foot **2** : one of the crusty ends of a loaf of bread **3** : a solid attachment forming the back of the sole of a shoe **4** : a rear, low, or bottom part **5** ♦ : a contemptible person

♦ beast, boor, churl, clown, creep, cretin, cur, jerk, joker, louse, lout, skunk, slob, snake

²heel *vb* : to tilt to one side : LIST

¹heft \'heft\ *n* : WEIGHT, HEAVINESS

²heft *vb* **1** ♦ : to heave up : HOIST **2** : to test the weight of by lifting

♦ boost, heave, hoist, jack

hefty \'hef-tē\ *adj* **heft·i·er; -est** **1** : marked by bigness, bulk, and usu. strength **2** ♦ : impressively large **3** ♦ : quite heavy

♦ [2] big, large, outsize, oversize, sizable, substantial ♦ [3] heavy, massive, ponderous, weighty

he·ge·mo·ny \hi-'je-mə-nē\ *n* : preponderant influence or authority over others : DOMINATION

he·gi·ra \hi-'jī-rə\ *n* : a journey esp. when undertaken to escape a dangerous or undesirable environment

heif·er \'he-fər\ *n* : a young cow; *esp* : one that has not had a calf

height \'hīt\ *n* **1** ♦ : the highest or most advanced part or point **2** ♦ : the distance from the bottom to the top of something standing upright : ALTITUDE **4** ♦ : an extent of land rising to a considerable degree above the surrounding country

♦ [1] acme, apex, climax, crown, culmination, head, meridian, peak, pinnacle, summit, tip-top, top, zenith *Ant* bottom, nadir ♦ [1] extremity, limit ♦ [2] altitude, elevation ♦ [4] elevation, eminence, highland, hill, mound, prominence, rise *Ant* lowland

height·en \'hīt-ᵊn\ *vb* **1** ♦ : to increase in amount or degree **2** ♦ : to make or become high or higher

♦ [1] amplify, beef, boost, consolidate, deepen, enhance, intensify, magnify, redouble, step up, strengthen ♦ [2] boost, crane, elevate, heave, heft, hike, jack, lift, pick up, raise, up, uphold

Heim·lich maneuver \'hīm-lik-\ *n* : the manual application of sudden upward pressure on the upper abdomen of a choking victim to force a foreign object from the trachea

hei·nous \'hā-nəs\ *adj* : hatefully or shockingly evil — **hei·nous·ly** *adv*

hei·nous·ness \-nəs\ *n* ♦ : the state or quality of being heinous

♦ atrociousness, atrocity, depravity, enormity, monstrosity, vileness, wickedness

heir \'ar\ *n* : one who inherits or is entitled to inherit property, rank, title, or office — **heir·ship** *n*

heir apparent *n, pl* **heirs apparent** : an heir whose right to succeed (as to a title) cannot be taken away if he or she survives the present holder

heir·ess \'ar-əs\ *n* : a female heir esp. to great wealth

heir·loom \'ar-ˌlüm\ *n* **1** : a piece of personal property that descends by inheritance **2** : something handed on from one generation to another

heir presumptive *n, pl* **heirs presumptive** : an heir whose present right to inherit could be lost through the birth of a nearer relative

heist \'hīst\ *vb* : to commit armed robbery on; *also* : STEAL — **heist** *n*

held *past and past part of* HOLD

he·li·cal \'he-li-kəl, 'hē-\ *adj* ♦ : of, relating to, or having the form of a helix : SPIRAL

♦ spiral, winding

he·li·cop·ter \'he-lə-ˌkäp-tər, 'hē-\ *n* : an aircraft that is supported in the air by one or more rotors revolving on substantially vertical axes

he·lio·cen·tric \ˌhē-lē-ō-'sen-trik\ *adj* : having or relating to the sun as center

he·li·o·sphere \'hē-lē-ə-ˌsfir, -ō-\ *n* : the region in space influenced by the sun or solar wind

he·lio·trope \'hē-lē-ə-ˌtrōp\ *n* : any of a genus of herbs or shrubs related to the forget-me-not that have small white or purple flowers

he·li·port \'he-lə-ˌpōrt\ *n* : a landing and takeoff place for a helicopter

he·li·um \'hē-lē-əm\ *n* : a very light nonflammable gaseous chemical element occurring in various natural gases

he·lix \'hē-liks\ *n, pl* **he·li·ces** \'he-lə-ˌsēz, 'hē-\ *also* **he·lix·es** \'hē-lik-səz\ : something spiral in form

hell \'hel\ *n* **1** : a nether world in which the dead continue to exist **2** : the realm of the devil in which the damned suffer everlasting punishment **3** ♦ : a place or state of torment or wickedness **4** ♦ : a place or state of turmoil, disorder, or destruction — **hell·ish** *adj*

♦ [3] agony, horror, misery, murder, nightmare, torment, torture *Ant* heaven, paradise ♦ [4] bedlam, circus, madhouse ♦ [4] chaos, confusion, disarray, disorder, disorganization, havoc, jumble, mess, muddle, shambles

hel·la·cious \ˌhe-'lā-shəs\ *adj* **1** : exceptionally powerful or violent ⟨~ winds⟩ **2** : remarkably good **3** : extremely difficult ⟨a ~ schedule⟩ **4** : extraordinarily large

hell-bent \'hel-ˌbent\ *adj* ♦ : stubbornly determined

♦ bound, decisive, determined, firm, intent, purposeful, resolute, set, single-minded

hell·cat \-ˌkat\ *n* **1** : WITCH 2 **2** : a violently temperamental person; *esp* : an ill-tempered woman

hel·le·bore \'he-lə-ˌbōr\ *n* **1** : any of a genus of poisonous herbs related to the buttercups; *also* : the dried root of a hellebore **2** : a poisonous plant related to the lilies; *also* : its dried roots used in medicine and insecticides

Hel·lene \'he-ˌlēn\ *n* : GREEK

Hel·le·nism \'he-lə-ˌni-zəm\ *n* : a body of humanistic and classical ideals associated with ancient Greece — **Hel·len·ic** \he-'le-nik\ *adj* — **Hel·le·nist** \'he-lə-nist\ *n*

Hel·le·nis·tic \ˌhe-lə-'nis-tik\ *adj* : of or relating to Greek history, culture, or art after Alexander the Great

hell-for-leather *adv* : at full speed

hell·gram·mite \'hel-grə-ˌmīt\ *n* : an aquatic insect larva that is used as bait in fishing

hell·hole \'hel-ˌhōl\ *n* : a place of extreme misery or squalor

hel·lion \'hel-yən\ *n* ♦ : a troublesome or mischievous person

♦ devil, imp, mischief, monkey, rapscallion, rascal, rogue, scamp, urchin

hel·lo \hə-'lō, he-\ *n, pl* **hellos** ♦ : an expression of greeting — used interjectionally

♦ greeting, salutation, salute *Ant* adieu, bon voyage, farewell, Godspeed, good-bye

helm \'helm\ *n* **1** : a lever or wheel for steering a ship **2** ♦ : a position of control

♦ chair, head, headship, rein

hel·met \'hel-mət\ *n* : a protective covering for the head

helms·man \'helmz-mən\ *n* ♦ : the person at the helm

♦ boss, captain, chief, foreman, head, headman, kingpin, leader, taskmaster

hel·ot \'he-lət\ *n* : an enslaved person or serf

¹help \'help\ *vb* **1** ♦ : to give assistance or support to : AID **2** ♦ : to make more pleasant or bearable **3** : to be of use; *also* : PROMOTE **4** : to change for the better **5 a** : to refrain from **b** : to keep from occurring : PREVENT **6** : to serve with food or drink ⟨~ yourself⟩

♦ [1] abet, aid, assist, back, prop, support *Ant* hinder ♦ [2] allay, alleviate, assuage, ease, mitigate, mollify, palliate, relieve, soothe *Ant* aggravate

²help *n* **1 a** ♦ : the act of helping : help given **b** ♦ : a source of aid **2** : REMEDY, RELIEF **3** : one who assists another **4** ♦ : one employed by another usu. for wages or salary and in a position below the executive level — often used collectively

♦ [1a] aid, assist, assistance, backing, boost, lift, support *Ant* hindrance ♦ [1b] advantage, aid, benefit, boon *Ant* disadvantage, drawback, hindrance, impediment ♦ [4] force, personnel, pool, staff

help·er \'hel-pər\ *n* ♦ : one that helps

♦ aid, apprentice, assistant, deputy, helpmate, mate, sidekick

helper T cell *n* : a T cell that participates in the immune response by recognizing foreign antigens and has a protein on its surface to which HIV attaches

help·ful \-fəl\ *adj* ♦ : of service or assistance — **help·ful·ly** *adv* — **help·ful·ness** *n*

♦ advantageous, beneficial, favorable (*or* favourable), profitable, salutary

help·ing *n* : a portion of food

help·less \-ləs\ *adj* **1** ♦ : lacking protection or support : DEFENSELESS **2** ♦ : marked by an inability to act or react — **help·less·ly** *adv* — **help·less·ness** *n*

♦ [1] defenseless (*or* defenceless), exposed, susceptible, undefended, unguarded, unprotected, unresistant, vulnerable *Ant* guarded, invulnerable, protected, resistant, shielded ♦ [2] impotent, powerless, weak

help·mate \'help-ˌmāt\ *n* **1** ♦ : one that helps : HELPER **2** ♦ : a female partner in a marriage : WIFE

♦ [1] aid, apprentice, assistant, deputy, helper, mate, sidekick ♦ [2] lady, old lady, wife

help·meet \-ˌmēt\ *n* **1** : one that helps : HELPMATE **2** : a female partner in a marriage : WIFE

hel·ter-skel·ter \ˌhel-tər-'skel-tər\ *adv* **1** : in undue haste or disorder **2** ♦ : in a haphazard manner

♦ amok, berserk, frantically, harum-scarum, hectically, madly, pell-mell, wild, wildly

helve \'helv\ *n* : a handle of a tool or weapon

Hel·ve·tian \hel-'vē-shən\ *adj* : SWISS — **Helvetian** *n*

¹hem \'hem\ *n* **1** : a border of an article (as of cloth) doubled back and stitched down **2** : RIM, MARGIN

²hem *vb* **hemmed; hem·ming 1** : to make a hem in sewing; *also* : BORDER, EDGE **2** ♦ : to surround restrictively

♦ cage, closet, coop up, corral, encase, enclose, envelop, fence, hedge, house, immure, pen, wall

he-man \'hē-ˌman\ *n* : a strong virile man

he·ma·tite \'hē-mə-ˌtīt\ *n* : a mineral that consists of an oxide of iron and that constitutes an important iron ore

he·ma·tol·o·gy \ˌhē-mə-'tä-lə-jē\ *n* : a branch of biology that deals with the blood and blood-forming organs — **he·ma·to·log·ic** \-tə-'lä-jik\ *also* **he·ma·to·log·i·cal** \-ji-kəl\ *adj* — **he·ma·tol·o·gist** \-'tä-lə-jist\ *n*

he·ma·to·ma \-'tō-mə\ *n, pl* **mas** *also* **-ma·ta** \-mə-tə\ : a usu. clotted mass of blood forming as a result of a broken blood vessel

heme \'hēm\ *n* : the deep red iron-containing part of hemoglobin

hemi·sphere \'he-mə-ˌsfir\ *n* **1** : one of the halves of the earth as divided by the equator into northern and southern parts or by a meridian into eastern and western parts **2** : either of two half spheres formed by a plane through the sphere's center — **hemi·spher·ic** \ˌhe-mə-'sfir-ik, -'sfer-\ *or* **hemi·spher·i·cal** \-'sfir-i-kəl, -'sfer-i-kəl\ *adj*

hem·line \'hem-ˌlīn\ *n* : the line formed by the lower edge of a garment

hem·lock \'hem-ˌläk\ *n* **1** : any of several poisonous herbs related to the carrot **2** : an evergreen tree related to the pines; *also* : its soft light wood

he·mo·glo·bin \'hē-mə-ˌglō-bən\ *n* : an iron-containing compound found in red blood cells that carries oxygen from the lungs to the body tissues

he·mo·phil·ia \ˌhē-mə-'fi-lē-ə\ *n* : a hereditary blood defect usu.

of males that slows blood clotting with resulting difficulty in stopping bleeding — **he·mo·phil·i·ac** \-lē-,ak\ *adj or n*

hem·or·rhage \'hem-rij, 'he-mə-\ *n* : a large discharge of blood from the blood vessels — **hemorrhage** *vb* — **hem·or·rhag·ic** \,he-mə-'ra-jik\ *adj*

hem·or·rhoid \'hem-,rȯid, 'he-mə-\ *n* : a swollen mass of dilated veins at or just within the anus — usu. used in pl.

hemp \'hemp\ *n* : a tall widely grown Asian herb related to the mulberry that is the source of a tough fiber used in rope and of marijuana and hashish from its flowers and leaves; *also* : the fiber — **hemp·en** \'hem-pən\ *adj*

hem·stitch \'hem-,stich\ *vb* : to embroider (fabric) by drawing out parallel threads and stitching the exposed threads in groups to form designs

hen \'hen\ *n* : a female chicken esp. over a year old; *also* : a female bird

hence \'hens\ *adv* **1** : AWAY **2** : from this time **3** ♦ : because of a preceding fact or premise : CONSEQUENTLY **4** : from this source or origin

♦ accordingly, consequently, ergo, so, therefore, thus, wherefore

hence·forth \hens-,fȯrth\ *adv* : from this point on
hence·for·ward \-'fȯr-wərd\ *adv* : HENCEFORTH
hench·man \'hench-mən\ *n* : a trusted follower or supporter
hen·na \'he-nə\ *n* **1** : an Old World tropical shrub with fragrant white flowers; *also* : a reddish brown dye obtained from its leaves and used esp. on hair **2** : the color of henna dye
hen·peck \'hen-,pek\ *vb* ♦ : to nag and boss one's husband

♦ hound, nag, needle

hep \'hep\ *adj* : HIP
hep·a·rin \'he-pə-rən\ *n* : a compound found esp. in liver that slows the clotting of blood and is used medically
he·pat·ic \hi-'pa-tik\ *adj* : of, relating to, or associated with the liver
he·pat·i·ca \hi-'pa-ti-kə\ *n* : any of a genus of herbs related to the buttercups that have lobed leaves and delicate white, pink, or bluish flowers
hep·a·ti·tis \,he-pə-'tī-təs\ *n, pl* **-tit·i·des** \-'ti-tə-,dēz\ : inflammation of the liver; *also* : a virus disease of which this is a feature
hep·tam·e·ter \hep-'ta-mə-tər\ *n* : a line of verse containing seven metrical feet
hep·tath·lon \hep-'tath-lən, -,län\ *n* : a 7-event athletic contest for women

¹**her** \'hər\ *adj* : of or relating to her or herself
²**her** *pron, objective case of* SHE
¹**her·ald** \'her-əld\ *n* **1** : an official crier or messenger **2** ♦ : one that precedes or foreshadows : HARBINGER **3** : ANNOUNCER **4** : ADVOCATE

♦ angel, forerunner, harbinger, precursor

²**herald** *vb* **1** : to give notice of **2** : HAIL, GREET; *also* : PUBLICIZE
he·ral·dic \he-'ral-dik, hə-\ *adj* : of or relating to heralds or heraldry
her·ald·ry \'her-əl-drē\ *n, pl* **-ries** **1** : the practice of devising and granting armorial insignia and of tracing genealogies **2** : INSIGNIA **3** : PAGEANTRY
herb \'ərb, 'hərb\ *n* **1** : a seed plant that lacks woody tissue and dies to the ground at the end of a growing season **2** : a plant or plant part valued for medicinal or savory qualities — **her·ba·ceous** \,ər-'bā-shəs, ,hər-\ *adj*
herb·age \'ər-bij, 'hər-\ *n* ♦ : green plants esp. when used or fit for grazing

♦ flora, foliage, green, greenery, leafage, vegetation, verdure

herb·al \'ər-bəl, 'hər-\ *adj* : of, relating to, utilizing, or made of herbs
herb·al·ist \'ər-bə-list, 'hər-\ *n* **1** : a person who practices healing by the use of herbs **2** : a person who collects or grows herbs
her·bar·i·um \,ər-'bar-ē-əm, ,hər-\ *n, pl* **-ia** \-ē-ə\ **1** : a collection of dried plant specimens **2** : a place that houses an herbarium
her·bi·cide \'ər-bə-,sīd, 'hər-\ *n* : an agent used to destroy or inhibit plant growth — **her·bi·cid·al** \,ər-bə-'sīd-ᵊl, ,hər-\ *adj*
her·biv·o·rous \,ər-'bi-və-rəs, ,hər-\ *adj* : feeding on plants — **her·bi·vore** \'ər-bə-,vȯr, 'hər-\ *n*
her·cu·le·an \,hər-kyə-'lē-ən, ,hər-'kyü-lē-\ *adj, often cap* ♦ : of extraordinary power, size, or difficulty ⟨a ∼ task⟩

♦ arduous, demanding, difficult, exacting, formidable, grueling, hard, laborious, murderous, rough, stiff, strenuous, tall, toilsome, tough

¹**herd** \'hərd\ *n* **1** : a group of animals of one kind kept or living

together **2** : a group of people with a common bond **3** ♦ : the undistinguished masses : MOB

♦ commoners, masses, mob, people, plebeians, populace, rank and file

²**herd** *vb* ♦ : to assemble or move in or as if in a herd — **herd·er** *n*

♦ drive, punch, run

herds·man \'hərdz-mən\ *n* : one who manages, breeds, or tends livestock
¹**here** \'hir\ *adv* **1** : in or at this place; *also* : NOW **2** : at or in this point, particular, or case **3** : in the present life or state **4** : to this place
²**here** *n* : this place ⟨get away from ∼⟩
here·abouts \'hir-ə-,baùts\ *or* **here·about** \-,baùt\ *adv* : in this vicinity
¹**here·af·ter** \hir-'af-tər\ *adv* **1** : after this in sequence or in time **2** : in some future time or state
²**hereafter** *n, often cap* **1** : time that is to come : FUTURE **2** ♦ : an existence beyond earthly life

♦ afterlife, eternity, immortality

here·by \hir-'bī\ *adv* : by means of this
he·red·i·tary \hə-'re-də-,ter-ē\ *adj* **1** ♦ : genetically passed or passable from parent to offspring **2** : passing by inheritance; *also* : having title or possession through inheritance **3** : of a kind established by tradition

♦ genetic, heritable, inborn, inherited

he·red·i·ty \-də-tē\ *n* : the characteristics and potentialities genetically derived from one's ancestors; *also* : the passing of these from ancestor to descendant
Her·e·ford \'hər-fərd\ *n* : any of a breed of red-coated beef cattle with white faces and markings
here·in \hir-'in\ *adv* : in this
here·of \-'əv, -'äv\ *adv* : of this
here·on \-'ȯn, -'än\ *adv* : on this
her·e·sy \'her-ə-sē\ *n, pl* **-sies** **1** : adherence to a religious opinion contrary to church dogma **2** : an opinion or doctrine contrary to church dogma **3** ♦ : dissent from a dominant theory, opinion, or practice

♦ dissent, heterodoxy, nonconformity *Ant* conformity, orthodoxy

her·e·tic \'her-ə-,tik\ *n* ♦ : one who dissents from an accepted belief or doctrine

♦ dissenter, dissident, nonconformist

he·ret·i·cal \hə-'re-ti-kəl\ *adj* ♦ : of, relating to, or characterized by departure from accepted beliefs or standards

♦ dissident, heterodox, nonconforming, nonconformist, nonorthodox, unconventional, unorthodox *Ant* conforming, conventional, orthodox

here·to \hir-'tü\ *adv* : to this document
here·to·fore \'hir-tə-,fȯr\ *adv* ♦ : up to this time

♦ hitherto, yet

here·un·der \hir-'ən-dər\ *adv* : under this or according to this writing
here·un·to \hir-'ən-tü\ *adv* : to this
here·upon \'hir-ə-,pȯn, -,pän\ *adv* : on this or immediately after this
here·with \'hir-'with, -'with\ *adv* **1** : with this **2** : HEREBY
her·i·ta·ble \'her-ə-tə-bəl\ *adj* ♦ : capable of being inherited

♦ genetic, hereditary, inborn, inherited

her·i·tage \'her-ə-tij\ *n* **1** : property that descends to an heir **2** ♦ : something transmitted by or acquired from a predecessor : LEGACY **3** : BIRTHRIGHT

♦ bequest, birthright, inheritance, legacy

her·maph·ro·dite \(,)hər-'ma-frə-,dīt\ *n* : an animal or plant having both male and female reproductive organs — **hermaphrodite** *adj* — **her·maph·ro·dit·ic** \(,)hər-,ma-frə-'di-tik\ *adj*
her·met·ic \hər-'me-tik\ *also* **her·met·i·cal** \-ti-kəl\ *adj* : AIRTIGHT — **her·met·i·cal·ly** \-ti-k(ə-)lē\ *adv*
her·mit \'hər-mət\ *n* ♦ : one who lives in solitude esp. for religious reasons

♦ anchorite, recluse, solitary

her·mit·age \-mə-tij\ *n* **1** : the dwelling of a hermit **2** : a secluded dwelling
hermit crab *n* : any of numerous crabs that occupy empty mollusk shells
her·nia \'hər-nē-ə\ *n, pl* **-ni·as** *or* **-ni·ae** \-nē-,ē, -nē-,ī\ : a pro-

trusion of a bodily part (as a loop of intestine) into a pouch of the weakened wall of a cavity in which it is normally enclosed — **her·ni·ate** \-nē-ˌāt\ *vb* — **her·ni·a·tion** \ˌhər-nē-ˈā-shən\ *n*

he·ro \ˈhē-rō\ *n, pl* **heroes** **1** : a mythological or legendary figure of great strength or ability **2** : a person admired for his or her achievements and qualities **3** : the principal character in a literary or dramatic work **4** *pl usu* **heros** : a large sandwich on a long split roll : SUBMARINE 2

he·ro·ic \hi-ˈrō-ik\ *adj* **1** : of, relating to, resembling, or suggesting heroes esp. of antiquity **2** ♦ : exhibiting or marked by courage and daring **3** ♦ : of impressive size, power, extent, or effect

♦ [2] brave, courageous, dauntless, doughty, fearless, gallant, greathearted, intrepid, lionhearted, manful, stalwart, stout, undaunted, valiant, valorous ♦ [3] august, baronial, gallant, glorious, grand, grandiose, imposing, magnificent, majestic, monumental, noble, proud, regal, royal, splendid, stately

he·ro·i·cal·ly \hi-ˈrō-i-k(ə-)lē\ *adv* ♦ : in a heroic manner

♦ gallantly, grandly, greatly, honorably (*or* honourably), magnanimously, nobly

heroic couplet *n* : a rhyming couplet in iambic pentameter
he·ro·ics \hi-ˈrō-iks\ *n pl* : heroic or showy behavior
her·o·in \ˈher-ə-wən\ *n* : an illicit addictive narcotic drug made from morphine
her·o·ine \ˈher-ə-wən\ *n* **1** : a woman admired for her achievements and qualities **2** : the principal female character in a literary or dramatic work
her·o·ism \ˈher-ə-ˌwi-zəm\ *n* **1** ♦ : heroic conduct **2** : the qualities of a hero

♦ bravery, courage, daring, fearlessness, gallantry, guts, hardihood, heart, nerve, stoutness, valor

her·on \ˈher-ən\ *n, pl* **herons** *also* **heron** : any of various long-legged long-billed wading birds with soft plumage
her·pes \ˈhər-ˌpēz\ *n* : any of several virus diseases characterized by the formation of blisters on the skin or mucous membranes
herpes sim·plex \-ˈsim-ˌpleks\ *n* : either of two virus diseases marked in one by watery blisters above the waist (as on the mouth and lips) and in the other on the sex organs
herpes zos·ter \-ˈzäs-tər\ *n* : SHINGLES
her·pe·tol·o·gy \ˌhər-pə-ˈtä-lə-jē\ *n* : a branch of zoology dealing with reptiles and amphibians — **her·pe·tol·o·gist** \ˌhər-pə-ˈtä-lə-jist\ *n*
her·ring \ˈher-iŋ\ *n, pl* **herring** *or* **herrings** : a valuable narrow-bodied food fish of the north Atlantic; *also* : a related fish of the north Pacific harvested esp. for its roe
her·ring·bone \ˈher-iŋ-ˌbōn\ *n* : a pattern made up of rows of parallel lines with adjacent rows slanting in reverse directions; *also* : a twilled fabric with this pattern
hers \ˈhərz\ *pron* : one or the ones belonging to her
her·self \hər-ˈself\ *pron* : SHE, HER — used reflexively, for emphasis, or in absolute constructions
hertz \ˈhərts, ˈherts\ *n, pl* **hertz** : a unit of frequency equal to one cycle per second
hes·i·tance \ˈhe-zə-təns\ *n* : HESITANCY
hes·i·tan·cy \ˈhe-zə-tən-sē\ *n* **1** ♦ : the quality or state of being hesitant **2** ♦ : an act or instance of hesitating

♦ [1] disinclination, reluctance, reticence ♦ [2] hesitation, indecision, irresolution, vacillation

hes·i·tant \ˈhe-zə-tənt\ *adj* ♦ : tending to hesitate — **hes·i·tant·ly** *adv*

♦ afraid, dubious, indisposed, reluctant *Ant* disposed, inclined

hes·i·tate \ˈhe-zə-ˌtāt\ *vb* **-tat·ed; -tat·ing** **1** ♦ : to hold back (as in doubt) **2** : PAUSE

♦ falter, hang back, shilly-shally, stagger, teeter, vacillate, waver, wobble *Ant* dive (in), plunge (in)

hes·i·ta·tion \ˌhe-zə-ˈtā-shən\ *n* ♦ : an act or instance of hesitating

♦ hesitancy, indecision, irresolution, vacillation

het·ero·dox \ˈhe-tə-rə-ˌdäks\ *adj* **1** ♦ : differing from an acknowledged standard **2** ♦ : holding unorthodox opinions

♦ [1, 2] dissident, heretical, nonconforming, nonconformist, nonorthodox, unconventional, unorthodox

het·er·o·doxy \ˈhe-tə-rə-ˌdäk-sē\ *n* ♦ : the quality or state of being heterodox

♦ dissent, heresy, nonconformity

het·er·o·ge·neous \ˌhe-tə-rə-ˈjē-nē-əs, -nyəs\ *adj* ♦ : consist-

ing of dissimilar ingredients or constituents : MIXED — **het·er·o·ge·ne·i·ty** \-jə-ˈnē-ə-tē\ *n* — **het·er·o·ge·neous·ly** *adv*

♦ assorted, miscellaneous, mixed, motley, varied

het·ero·glos·sia \ˌhe-tə-rō-ˈglä-sē-ə, -ˈglò-\ *n* : a diversity of voices, styles of discourse, or points of view in a literary work
het·ero·sex·ism \ˌhe-tə-rō-ˈsek-si-zəm\ *n* : discrimination or prejudice against people who are not heterosexual
het·ero·sex·u·al \ˌhe-tə-rō-ˌsek-shə-wəl\ *adj* **1** : of, relating to, or characterized by sexual or romantic attraction to the opposite sex **2** : of or relating to different sexes — **heterosexual** *n* — **het·ero·sex·u·al·i·ty** \-ˌsek-shə-ˈwa-lə-tē\ *n*
hew \ˈhyü\ *vb* **hewed; hewed** *or* **hewn** \ˈhyün\; **hew·ing** **1** ♦ : to cut or fell with blows (as of an ax) **2** : to give shape to with or as if with an ax **3** ♦ : to conform or adhere strictly ⟨~ to tradition⟩ — **hew·er** *n*

♦ [1] chop, cut, fell ♦ *usu* **hew to** [3] adhere, cling, stick

HEW *abbr* Department of Health, Education, and Welfare
¹hex \ˈheks\ *vb* **1** : to practice witchcraft **2** : JINX **3** ♦ : to put a hex on

♦ bewitch, charm, enchant, spell

²hex *n* **1** ♦ : a person who practices witchcraft : WITCH **2** : SPELL, JINX

♦ enchantress, hag, witch

³hex *adj* : HEXAGONAL
⁴hex *abbr* hexagon
hexa·gon \ˈhek-sə-ˌgän\ *n* : a polygon having six angles and six sides — **hex·ag·o·nal** \hek-ˈsa-gən-ᵊl\ *adj*
hex·am·e·ter \hek-ˈsa-mə-tər\ *n* : a line of verse containing six metrical feet
hey \ˈhā\ *interj* — used esp. to call attention or to express doubt, surprise, or joy
hey·day \ˈhā-ˌdā\ *n* ♦ : a period of greatest strength, vigor, or prosperity

♦ bloom, blossom, flower, flush, prime

hf *abbr* half
Hf *symbol* hafnium
HF *abbr* high frequency
hg *abbr* hectogram
Hg *symbol* mercury
hgt *abbr* height
hgwy *abbr* highway
HH *abbr* **1** Her Highness **2** His Highness **3** His Holiness
HHS *abbr* Department of Health and Human Services
HI *abbr* **1** Hawaii **2** humidity index
hi·a·tus \hī-ˈā-təs\ *n* **1** : a break in an object : GAP **2** ♦ : a lapse in continuity

♦ discontinuity, gap, interim, interlude, intermission, interruption, interval

hi·ba·chi \hi-ˈbä-chē\ *n* : a charcoal brazier
hi·ber·nate \ˈhī-bər-ˌnāt\ *vb* **-nat·ed; -nat·ing** : to pass the winter in a torpid or resting state — **hi·ber·na·tion** \ˌhī-bər-ˈnā-shən\ *n* — **hi·ber·na·tor** \ˈhī-bər-ˌnā-tər\ *n*
hi·bis·cus \hī-ˈbis-kəs, hə-\ *n* : any of a genus of herbs, shrubs, and trees related to the mallows and noted for large showy flowers
hic·cup *also* **hic·cough** \ˈhi-(ˌ)kəp\ *n* **1** : a spasmodic breathing movement checked by sudden closing of the glottis accompanied by a peculiar sound; *also, pl* : an attack of hiccuping **2** : a slight irregularity, error, or malfunction **3** : a brief minor interruption or change — **hiccup** *vb*
hick \ˈhik\ *n* ♦ : an awkward provincial person — **hick** *adj*

♦ bumpkin, clodhopper, rustic, yokel *Ant* cosmopolitan

hick·o·ry \ˈhi-kə-rē\ *n, pl* **-ries** : any of a genus of No. American hardwood trees related to the walnuts; *also* : the wood of a hickory — **hickory** *adj*
hi·dal·go \hi-ˈdal-gō\ *n, pl* **-gos** *often cap* : a member of the lower nobility of Spain
hidden tax *n* **1** : a tax ultimately paid by someone other than the person on whom it is formally levied **2** : an economic injustice that reduces one's income or buying power
¹hide \ˈhīd\ *vb* **hid** \ˈhid\; **hid·den** \ˈhid-ᵊn\ *or* **hid; hid·ing** **1** ♦ : to put or remain out of sight **2** : to conceal for shelter or protection; *also* : to seek protection **3** ♦ : to keep secret **4** : to turn away in shame or anger — **hid·er** *n*

♦ [1] bury, cache, conceal, ensconce, secrete *Ant* display, exhibit ♦ [3] blanket, blot out, cloak, conceal, cover, curtain, enshroud, mask, obscure, occult, screen, shroud, veil *Ant* bare, disclose, display, divulge, expose, reveal, show, uncloak, uncover, unmask, unveil

²**hide** *n* ♦ : the skin of an animal

♦ fur, pelt, skin

³**hide** *vb* : to give a beating to

hide–and–seek \ˌhīd-ᵊn-ˈsēk\ *n* : a children's game in which everyone hides from one player who tries to find them

hide·away \ˈhī-də-ˌwā\ *n* : a place of refuge, retreat, or concealment : HIDEOUT

hide·bound \ˈhīd-ˌbau̇nd\ *adj* ♦ : being inflexible or conservative

♦ conservative, old-fashioned, orthodox, reactionary, traditional

hid·eous \ˈhi-dē-əs\ *adj* **1** ♦ : offensive to one of the senses : UGLY **2** ♦ : morally offensive : SHOCKING — **hid·eous·ly** *adv*

♦ [1] grotesque, ugly, unappealing, unattractive, unlovely, unsightly, vile ♦ [2] appalling, atrocious, awful, dreadful, frightful, ghastly, grisly, gruesome, horrible, horrid, lurid, macabre, monstrous, nightmarish, shocking, terrible

hid·eous·ness \-nəs\ *n* ♦ : the quality or state of being hideous

♦ atrociousness, atrocity, frightfulness, horror, monstrosity, repulsiveness

hide·out \ˈhī-ˌdau̇t\ *n* ♦ : a place of refuge or concealment

♦ concealment, covert, den, lair, nest

hie \ˈhī\ *vb* **hied; hy·ing** *or* **hie·ing** ♦ : to move or act quickly : HASTEN

♦ accelerate, fast-track, hasten, hurry, quicken, rush, speed, whisk

hi·er·ar·chy \ˈhī-ə-ˌrär-kē\ *n, pl* **-chies** **1** : a ruling body of clergy organized into ranks **2** : persons or things arranged in a graded series — **hi·er·ar·chi·cal** \ˌhī-ə-ˈrär-ki-kəl\ *adj* — **hi·er·ar·chi·cal·ly** \-k(ə-)lē\ *adv*

hi·er·o·glyph·ic \ˌhī-ə-rə-ˈgli-fik\ *n* **1** : a character in a system of picture writing (as of the ancient Egyptians) **2** : a symbol or sign difficult to decipher

hi–fi \ˈhī-ˈfī\ *n* **1** : HIGH FIDELITY **2** : equipment for reproduction of sound with high fidelity

¹**hig·gle·dy–pig·gle·dy** \ˌhi-gəl-dē-ˈpi-gəl-dē\ *adv* : in confusion

²**higgledy–piggledy** *adj* ♦ : lacking order

♦ chaotic, disheveled, disordered, disorderly, hugger-mugger, messy, pell-mell, topsy-turvy, unkempt, untidy

¹**high** \ˈhī\ *adj* **1 a** ♦ : having large extension upward ⟨a ~ wall⟩ **b** : having a specified elevation : TALL ⟨six feet ~⟩ **2** : advanced toward fullness or culmination; *also* : slightly tainted **3** : advanced esp. in complexity ⟨~er mathematics⟩ **4** : long past **5** : SHRILL, SHARP **6** : far from the equator ⟨~ latitudes⟩ **7** : exalted in character **8** ♦ : of greater degree, size, or amount than average ⟨~ in cholesterol⟩ ⟨~ prices⟩ **9** ♦ : of relatively great importance **10** : FORCIBLE, STRONG ⟨~ winds⟩ **11** : showing elation or excitement **12** ♦ : excited or stupefied by alcohol or a drug : INTOXICATED; *also* : excited or stupefied as if by a drug **13** ♦ : dear in price : EXPENSIVE

♦ [1a] lofty, tall, towering *Ant* low, short, squat ♦ [8] advanced, up *Ant* down, low ♦ [9] chief, first, foremost, head, lead, preeminent, premier, primary, prime, principal, supreme ♦ [12] drunk, inebriate, intoxicated, tipsy ♦ [13] costly, dear, expensive, precious, valuable

²**high** *adv* **1** : at or to a high place or degree **2** ♦ : in a luxurious manner ⟨living ~⟩

♦ expensively, extravagantly, grandly, lavishly, luxuriously, opulently, richly *Ant* austerely, humbly, modestly, plainly, simply

³**high** *n* **1 a** : an elevated place **b** : the space overhead : SKY **2** : a region of high barometric pressure **3** : a high point or level **4** : the gear of a vehicle giving the highest speed **5** : an excited or stupefied state produced by or as if by a drug

high·ball \ˈhī-ˌbȯl\ *n* : a usu. tall drink of liquor mixed with water or a carbonated beverage

high beam *n* : a vehicle headlight with a long-range focus

high·born \ˈhī-ˈbȯrn\ *adj* ♦ : of noble birth

♦ aristocratic, genteel, gentle, grand, noble, patrician, wellborn

high·boy \-ˌbȯi\ *n* : a high chest of drawers mounted on a base with legs

high·bred \-ˈbred\ *adj* : coming from superior stock

high·brow \-ˌbrau̇\ *n* ♦ : a person of superior learning or culture — **highbrow** *adj* — **high·brow·ism** \-ˌbrau̇-ˌi-zəm\ *n*

♦ intellectual, nerd

high–def \ˈhī-ˈdef\ *also* **hi–def** *adj* : HIGH-DEFINITION — **high–def** *also* **hi–def** *n*

high–definition *adj* : being or relating to a television system with twice as many scan lines per frame as a conventional system — **high definition** *n*

high–density li·po·pro·tein \-ˌlī-pō-ˈprō-tēn, -ˌli-\ *n* : HDL

high·er–up \ˌhī-ər-ˈəp\ *n* : a superior officer or official

high·fa·lu·tin \ˌhī-fə-ˈlüt-ᵊn\ *adj* **1** ♦ : characterized by or reflecting an attitude of self-importance or superciliousness **2** ♦ : expressed in or marked by the use of high-flown bombastic language

♦ [1] disdainful, haughty, lofty, lordly, prideful, proud, superior ♦ [1, 2] affected, grandiose, ostentatious, pompous, pretentious ♦ [2] florid, flowery, grandiloquent, high-flown

high fashion *n* **1** : HIGH STYLE **2** : HAUTE COUTURE

high fidelity *n* : the reproduction of sound or image with a high degree of faithfulness to the original

high five *n* : a slapping of upraised right hands by two people (as in celebration) — **high–five** *vb*

high–flown \ˈhī-ˈflōn\ *adj* **1** ♦ : exceedingly or excessively high or favorable **2** ♦ : having an excessively embellished or inflated character

♦ [1] eloquent, formal, lofty, majestic, stately, towering ♦ [2] florid, flowery, grandiloquent, highfalutin

high frequency *n* : a radio frequency between 3 and 30 megahertz

high gear *n* **1** : HIGH 4 **2** : a state of intense or maximum activity

high–hand·ed \ˈhī-ˈhan-dəd\ *adj* ♦ : having or showing no regard for the rights, concerns, or feelings of others — **high–hand·ed·ly** *adv* — **high–hand·ed·ness** *n*

♦ arbitrary, dictatorial, imperious, peremptory, willful

¹**high–hat** \-ˈhat\ *adj* ♦ : assuming an attitude of superiority : SUPERCILIOUS

♦ arrogant, cavalier, haughty, highfalutin, high-handed, imperious, important, lofty, lordly, overweening, peremptory, pompous, presumptuous, pretentious, supercilious, superior, uppity

²**high–hat** *vb* ♦ : to treat snobbishly

♦ disdain, scorn, slight, sniff at, snub

high jinks \ˈhī-ˌjinks\ *n pl* ♦ : boisterous or rambunctious carryings-on

♦ foolery, horseplay, monkeyshines, roughhouse, shenanigans, tomfoolery

high·land \ˈhī-lənd\ *n* ♦ : elevated or mountainous land

♦ elevation, eminence, height, hill, mound, prominence, rise

high·land·er \-lən-dər\ *n* **1** : an inhabitant of a highland **2** *cap* : an inhabitant of the Scottish Highlands

high·lev·el \ˈhī-ˈle-vəl\ *adj* **1** : being of high importance or rank **2** : being or relating to highly concentrated and environmentally hazardous nuclear waste

¹**high·light** \-ˌlīt\ *n* : an event or detail of major importance

²**highlight** *vb* **1** ♦ : to center attention on : EMPHASIZE **2** : to constitute a highlight of

♦ accent, accentuate, emphasize, feature, play, point, stress, underline, underscore

high·light·er \-ˌlī-tər\ *n* : a pen with transparent ink used for marking text passages

high·ly \ˈhī-lē\ *adv* **1** : in or to a high place, level, or rank **2** ♦ : in or to a high degree or amount **3** : with approval : FAVORABLY

♦ especially, extremely, greatly, hugely, mightily, mighty, mortally, most, much, real, right, so, very

high–mind·ed \-ˈmīn-dəd\ *adj* ♦ : marked by elevated principles and feelings — **high–mind·ed·ness** *n*

♦ chivalrous, gallant, great, greathearted, high, lofty, lordly, magnanimous, noble, sublime

high·ness \ˈhī-nəs\ *n* **1** : the quality or state of being high **2** — used as a title (as for kings)

high–pres·sure \-ˈpre-shər\ *adj* ♦ : using or involving aggressive and insistent sales techniques

♦ aggressive, ambitious, assertive, enterprising, fierce, go-getting, militant, self-assertive

high–rise \-ˈrīz\ *adj* : having several stories and being equipped with elevators ⟨~ apartments⟩; *also* : of or relating to high-rise buildings

high road *n* : HIGHWAY

high school *n* : a school usu. including grades 9 to 12 or 10 to 12

high sea *n* : the open sea outside territorial waters — usu. used in pl.

high–sound·ing \'hī-'saun-diŋ\ *adj* : POMPOUS, IMPOSING

high–spir·it·ed \-'spir-ə-təd\ *adj* ♦ : characterized by a bold or energetic spirit

   ♦ bubbly, buoyant, effervescent, exuberant, frolicsome, vivacious ♦ fiery, mettlesome, peppery, spirited, spunky

high–strung \-'strəŋ\ *adj* ♦ : having an extremely nervous or sensitive temperament

   ♦ excitable, flighty, fluttery, jittery, jumpy, nervous, skittish, spooky

high style *n* : the newest in fashion or design

high·tail \'hī-,tāl\ *vb* : to retreat at full speed

high tech \-'tek\ *n* : HIGH TECHNOLOGY

high technology *n* : technology involving the use of advanced devices

high–ten·sion \'hī-'ten-chən\ *adj* : having or using a high voltage

high–test \-'test\ *adj* : having a high octane number

high–tick·et \-'ti-kət\ *adj* : EXPENSIVE

high–toned \-'tōnd\ *adj* **1** : high in social, moral, or intellectual quality **2** : PRETENTIOUS, POMPOUS

high·way \'hī-,wā\ *n* ♦ : a main direct road

   ♦ artery, pike, road, thoroughfare, turnpike, way

high·way·man \'hī-,wā-mən\ *n* : a person who robs travelers on a road

hi·jab \hē-'jäb, -'jab\ *n* : the covering for the hair and neck that is worn by Muslim women

hi·jack *also* **high·jack** \'hī-,jak\ *vb* : to steal esp. by stopping a vehicle on the highway; *also* : to commandeer a flying airplane — **hijack** *n* — **hi·jack·er** *n*

¹hike \'hīk\ *vb* **hiked; hik·ing** **1** ♦ : to move or raise with a sudden motion **2** : to take a long walk — **hik·er** *n*

   ♦ boost, crane, elevate, heave, heft, heighten, hoist, jack, lift, pick up, raise, up, uphold

²hike *n* **1** : a long walk **2** : RISE, INCREASE

hi·lar·i·ous \hi-'lar-ē-əs, hī-\ *adj* ♦ : marked by or providing boisterous merriment — **hi·lar·i·ous·ly** *adv*

   ♦ antic, comic, comical, droll, farcical, funny, humorous, hysterical, laughable, ludicrous, ridiculous, riotous, risible, screaming, uproarious

hi·lar·i·ty \hi-'lar-ə-tē, hī-\ *n* ♦ : boisterous and high-spirited merriment or laughter

   ♦ cheer, cheerfulness, cheeriness, glee, joviality, merriment, mirth

hill \'hil\ *n* **1** ♦ : a usu. rounded elevation of land **2** ♦ : a little heap or mound (as of earth) — **hilly** *adj*

   ♦ [1] elevation, eminence, height, highland, mound, prominence, rise ♦ [2] cock, heap, mound, mountain, pile, rick, stack

hill·bil·ly \'hil-,bi-lē\ *n, pl* **-lies** *often offensive* : a person from a backwoods area

hill·ock \'hi-lək\ *n* : a small hill

hill·side \'hil-,sīd\ *n* : the part of a hill between the summit and the foot

hill·top \-,täp\ *n* : the top of a hill

hilt \'hilt\ *n* : a handle esp. of a sword or dagger

him \'him\ *pron, objective case of* HE

Hi·ma·la·yan \,hi-mə-'lā-ən, hi-'mäl-yən\ *adj* : of, relating to, or characteristic of the Himalaya mountains or the people living there

him·self \him-'self\ *pron* : HE, HIM — used reflexively, for emphasis, or in absolute constructions

¹hind \'hīnd\ *n, pl* **hinds** *also* **hind** : a female of a common Eurasian deer

²hind *adj* ♦ : of or forming the part that follows or is behind : REAR

   ♦ back, hindmost, posterior, rear

¹hin·der \'hin-dər\ *vb* **1** ♦ : to impede the progress of **2** : to hold back

   ♦ encumber, hamper, hold up, impede, inhibit, interfere with, obstruct, tie up

²hind·er \'hīn-dər\ *adj* : HIND

Hin·di \'hin-dē\ *n* : a literary and official language of northern India

hind·most \'hīnd-,mōst\ *adj* ♦ : farthest to the rear

   ♦ final, last, latter, terminal, ultimate

hind·quar·ter \-,kwor-tər\ *n* **1** : one side of the back half of the

carcass of a quadruped **2** *pl* : the part of the body of a quadruped behind the junction of hind limbs and trunk

hin·drance \'hin-drəns\ *n* **1** : the state of being hindered; *also* : the action of hindering **2** ♦ : something that impedes : IMPEDIMENT

   ♦ bar, block, encumbrance, inhibition, obstacle

hind·sight \'hīnd-,sīt\ *n* : understanding of an event after it has happened

Hin·du–Arabic *adj* : relating to, being, or composed of Arabic numerals

Hin·du·ism \'hin-dü-,i-zəm\ *n* : a body of religious beliefs and practices native to India — **Hin·du** *n or adj*

hind wing *n* : either of the posterior wings of a 4-winged insect

¹hinge \'hinj\ *n* : a jointed device on which a swinging part (as a door, gate, or lid) turns

²hinge *vb* **hinged; hing·ing** **1** : to attach by or furnish with hinges **2** : to be contingent on a single consideration

¹hint \'hint\ *n* **1** ♦ : an indirect or summary suggestion **2** ♦ : a slight indication of the existence, approach, or nature of something : CLUE **3** ♦ : a very small amount

   ♦ [1, 2] clue, cue, indication, inkling, intimation, lead, suggestion ♦ [3] bit, dab, little, particle, suspicion, touch, trace

²hint *vb* ♦ : to give a hint

   ♦ allude, imply, indicate, infer, insinuate, intimate, suggest

hin·ter·land \'hin-tər-,land\ *n* **1** : a region behind a coast **2** ♦ : a region remote from cities

   ♦ backwoods, bush, frontier, sticks, up-country

¹hip \'hip\ *n* : the fruit of a rose

²hip *n* **1** : the part of the body on either side below the waist consisting of the side of the pelvis and the upper thigh **2** : HIP JOINT

³hip *adj* **hip·per; hip·pest** : keenly aware of or interested in the newest developments or styles — **hip·ness** *n*

⁴hip *vb* **hipped; hip·ping** : TELL, INFORM

hip·bone \'hip-'bōn, -,bōn\ *n* : the large flaring bone that makes a lateral half of the pelvis in mammals

hip–hop \'hip-,häp\ *n* **1** : a subculture esp. of inner-city youths who are devotees of rap music **2** : the stylized rhythmic music that accompanies rap

hip–hug·gers \'hip-,hə-gərz\ *n pl* : low-slung close-fitting pants that rest on the hips

hip joint *n* : the articulation between the femur and the hipbone

hipped \'hipt\ *adj* : having hips esp. of a specified kind ⟨broad= *hipped*⟩

hip·pie *or* **hip·py** \'hi-pē\ *n, pl* **hippies** : a usu. young person who rejects established mores and advocates nonviolence; *also* : a long-haired unconventionally dressed young person

hip·po \'hi-pō\ *n, pl* **hippos** : HIPPOPOTAMUS

hip·po·drome \'hi-pə-,drōm\ *n* : an arena for equestrian performances

hip·po·pot·a·mus \,hi-pə-'pä-tə-məs\ *n, pl* **-mus·es** *or* **-mi** \-,mī\ : a large thick-skinned aquatic mammal of sub-Saharan Africa that is related to the swine

¹hire \'hīr\ *n* **1** : payment for labor or personal services : WAGES **2** ♦ : the state of being hired : EMPLOYMENT **3** : one who is hired

   ♦ employ, employment, engagement *Ant* unemployment

²hire *vb* **hired; hir·ing** **1** ♦ : to employ for pay **2** ♦ : to engage the temporary use of for pay **3** : to take employment

   ♦ [1] employ, engage, retain, take on ♦ [2] engage, lease, let, rent

hire·ling \'hīr-liŋ\ *n* ♦ : a hired person; *esp* : one with mercenary motives

   ♦ employee, hand, jobholder, worker

hir·sute \'hər-,süt, 'hir-\ *adj* ♦ : covered with hair or hairlike material : HAIRY

   ♦ fleecy, furry, hairy, rough, shaggy, unshorn, woolly

¹his \'hiz\ *adj* : of or relating to him or himself

²his *pron* : one or the ones belonging to him

His·pan·ic \hi-'spa-nik\ *adj* : of, relating to, or being a person of Latin-American descent living in the U.S. — **Hispanic** *n*

¹hiss \'his\ *vb* : to make a sharp sibilant sound; *also* : to express disapproval of by hissing

²hiss *n* **1** ♦ : a prolonged sibilant sound **2** ♦ : a hiss used to express disapproval

   ♦ [1] fizz, sizzle, swish, whish, whiz ♦ [2] boo, catcall, hoot, jeer, raspberry, snort

hissy fit \'hi-sē-\ *n* ♦ : a fit of bad temper : TANTRUM

♦ blowup, explosion, fireworks, fit, huff, scene, tantrum

hist *abbr* historian; historical; history

his·ta·mine \'his-tə-ˌmēn, -mən\ *n* : a compound widespread in animal tissues that plays a major role in allergic reactions (as hay fever)

his·to·gram \'his-tə-ˌgram\ *n* : a representation of statistical data by rectangles whose widths represent class intervals and whose heights usu. represent corresponding frequencies

his·tol·o·gy \his-'tä-lə-jē\ *n, pl* **-gies** **1** : a branch of anatomy dealing with tissue structure **2** : tissue structure or organization — **his·to·log·i·cal** \ˌhis-tə-'lä-ji-kəl\ *or* **his·to·log·ic** \-'lä-jik\ *adj* — **his·tol·o·gist** \-'tä-lə-jist\ *n*

his·to·ri·an \hi-'stȯr-ē-ən\ *n* : a student or writer of history

his·tor·i·cal \hi-'stȯr-i-kəl\ *adj* **1** : of, relating to, or having the character of history **2** ♦ : based on history — **his·tor·i·cal·ly** \-k(ə-)lē\ *adv*

♦ documentary, factual, hard, literal, matter-of-fact, nonfictional, objective, true

his·to·ric·i·ty \ˌhis-tə-'ri-sə-tē\ *n* : historical actuality

his·to·ri·og·ra·pher \hi-ˌstȯr-ē-'ä-grə-fər\ *n* : HISTORIAN

his·to·ry \'his-tə-rē\ *n, pl* **-ries** **1** ♦ : a chronological record of significant events often with an explanation of their causes **2** : a branch of knowledge that records and explains past events **3** ♦ : events that form the subject matter of history **4** : an established record ⟨a convict's ∼ of violence⟩ — **his·tor·ic** \hi-'stȯr-ik\ *adj*

♦ [1] annals, chronicle, record ♦ [1] account, chronicle, narrative, record, report, story ♦ [3] past, yesteryear, yore

his·tri·on·ic \ˌhis-trē-'ä-nik\ *adj* **1** ♦ : deliberately affected **2** : of or relating to actors, acting, or the theater — **his·tri·on·i·cal·ly** \-ni-k(ə-)lē\ *adv*

♦ dramatic, melodramatic, theatrical

his·tri·on·ics \-niks\ *n pl* **1** : theatrical performances **2** : deliberate display of emotion for effect

¹hit \'hit\ *vb* **hit; hit·ting** **1** ♦ : to reach with a blow : STRIKE; *also* : to arrive with a force like a blow ⟨the storm ∼⟩ **2** ♦ : to make or bring into contact : COLLIDE **3** : to affect detrimentally ⟨was ∼ by the flu⟩ **4** : to make a request of **5** ♦ : to come upon : to discover or meet esp. by chance **6** : to accord with : SUIT **7** ♦ : to reach as an end : ATTAIN **8** : to indulge in often to excess **9** ♦ : to succeed in attaining or coming up with something — often used with *on* or *upon* — **hit·ter** *n*

♦ [1] bang, bash, bat, belt, clout, crack, knock, pound, punch, slug, strike, swat, wallop, whack ♦ [2] bang, bash, bump, collide, crash, impact, knock, ram, slam, smash, strike, swipe, thud ♦ *usu* **hit upon** [5] chance, encounter, find, happen (on *or* upon), meet, stumble (on *or* upon) ♦ [7] achieve, attain, make, score, win ♦ *often* **hit on** *or* **hit upon** [9] detect, determine, dig up, discover, ferret out, find, locate, track down

²hit *n* **1** ♦ : an act or instance of hitting or being hit **2** ♦ : a great success **3** : BASE HIT **4** : a dose of a drug **5** : a murder committed by a gangster **6** : an instance of connecting to a particular website **7** : a successful match in a search (as of the Internet)

♦ [1] bat, blow, box, clout, punch, slug, thump, wallop, whack ♦ [2] blockbuster, smash, success, winner *Ant* bummer, bust, catastrophe, debacle, dud, failure, fiasco, flop, turkey, washout

¹hitch \'hich\ *vb* **1** ♦ : to move by jerks **2** ♦ : to catch or fasten esp. by a hook or knot **3** : HITCHHIKE

♦ [1] buck, jerk, jolt, twitch ♦ [2] anchor, catch, clamp, fasten, fix, moor, secure, set

²hitch *n* **1** : JERK, PULL **2** : a sudden halt **3** : a connection between something towed and its mover **4** : KNOT **5** ♦ : a delimited period esp. of military service

♦ stint, tenure, term, tour

hitch·hike \'hich-ˌhīk\ *vb* : to travel by securing free rides from passing vehicles — **hitch·hik·er** *n*

¹hith·er \'hi-thər\ *adv* : to this place

²hither *adj* : being on the near or adjacent side

hith·er·to \-ˌtü\ *adv* ♦ : up to this time

♦ heretofore, yet *Ant* henceforth, henceforward, hereafter, thenceforth, thenceforward, thereafter

HIV \ˌāch-(ˌ)ī-'vē\ *n* : any of several retroviruses that infect and destroy helper T cells causing the great reduction in their numbers that is diagnostic of AIDS

hive \'hīv\ *n* **1** : a container for housing honeybees **2** : a colony of bees **3** : a place swarming with busy occupants — **hive** *vb*

hives \'hīvz\ *n sing or pl* : an allergic disorder marked by raised itching patches on the skin or mucous membranes

hl *abbr* hectoliter

HL *abbr* House of Lords

hm *abbr* hectometer

HM *abbr* **1** Her Majesty; Her Majesty's **2** His Majesty; His Majesty's

HMO \ˌāch-(ˌ)em-'ō\ *n* : a comprehensive health-care organization financed by periodic fixed payments by voluntarily enrolled individuals and families

HMS *abbr* **1** Her Majesty's ship **2** His Majesty's ship

Ho *symbol* holmium

hoa·gie *also* **hoa·gy** \'hō-gē\ *n, pl* **hoagies** ♦ : a large sandwich on a long split roll : SUBMARINE

♦ grinder, poor boy, sub, submarine

¹hoard \'hȯrd\ *n* ♦ : a hidden accumulation

♦ cache, reserve, stash, stockpile, store

²hoard *vb* ♦ : to lay up a hoard — **hoard·er** *n*

♦ cache, lay away, lay up, put by, salt away, stash, stockpile, store

hoar·frost \'hȯr-ˌfrȯst\ *n* : FROST 2

hoarse \'hȯrs\ *adj* **hoars·er; hoars·est** **1** ♦ : rough and harsh in sound **2** : having a grating voice — **hoarse·ly** *adv* — **hoarse·ness** *n*

♦ coarse, gravelly, gruff, husky, scratchy, throaty

hoary \'hȯr-ē\ *adj* **hoar·i·er; -est** **1** : gray or white with or as if with age **2** ♦ : extremely old : ANCIENT — **hoar·i·ness** \'hȯr-ē-nəs\ *n*

♦ age-old, ancient, antediluvian, antique, dateless, old, venerable

¹hoax \'hōks\ *vb* ♦ : to trick into believing or accepting as genuine something that is false

♦ beguile, bluff, cozen, deceive, delude, dupe, fool, gull, have, hoodwink, humbug, misinform, mislead, string along, take in, trick

²hoax *n* **1** : an act intended to trick or dupe **2** ♦ : something accepted or established by fraud

♦ counterfeit, fake, forgery, humbug, phony, sham

hoax·er *n* ♦ : one that hoaxes another

♦ cheat, dodger, shark, sharper, swindler, trickster ♦ charlatan, fake, fraud, humbug, mountebank, phony, pretender, quack

hob \'häb\ *n* : action that annoys or irritates : MISCHIEF — used with *play* and *raise* ⟨always raising ∼⟩

¹hob·ble \'hä-bəl\ *vb* **hob·bled; hob·bling** **1** : to limp along; *also* : to make lame **2** : to fasten together the legs of (as a horse) to prevent straying : FETTER **3** ♦ : to place under handicap : HAMPER

♦ encumber, hamper, hinder, hold up, impede, inhibit, interfere with, obstruct, tie up

²hobble *n* **1** : a hobbling movement **2** : something used to hobble an animal

hob·by \'hä-bē\ *n, pl* **hobbies** : a pursuit or interest engaged in for relaxation — **hob·by·ist** \-ist\ *n*

hob·by·horse \'hä-bē-ˌhȯrs\ *n* **1** : a stick with a horse's head on which children pretend to ride **2** : a toy horse mounted on rockers **3** : a topic to which one constantly reverts

hob·gob·lin \'häb-ˌgäb-lən\ *n* **1** ♦ : a mischievous goblin **2** ♦ : a source of fear, perplexity, or harassment : BOGEY

♦ [1] brownie, dwarf, elf, fairy, fay, gnome, leprechaun, pixie, puck, troll ♦ [2] bête noire, bogey, bugbear, ogre

hob·nail \-ˌnāl\ *n* : a short large-headed nail for studding shoe soles — **hob·nailed** \-ˌnāld\ *adj*

hob·nob \-ˌnäb\ *vb* **hob·nobbed; hob·nob·bing** ♦ : to associate familiarly

♦ associate, chum, consort, fraternize, hang around, pal ♦ associate, fraternize, mingle, mix, socialize

ho·bo \'hō-bō\ *n, pl* **hoboes** *also* **hobos** ♦ : a homeless and usu. penniless vagabond : TRAMP

♦ bum, tramp, vagabond, vagrant

¹hock \'häk\ *n* : a joint or region in the hind limb of a quadruped just above the foot and corresponding to the human ankle

²hock *n* : PAWN; *also* : DEBT 3 — **hock** *vb*

hock·ey \'hä-kē\ *n* **1** : FIELD HOCKEY **2** : ICE HOCKEY

ho·cus–po·cus \ˌhō-kəs-ˈpō-kəs\ *n* **1** : SLEIGHT OF HAND **2** : nonsense or sham used to conceal deception

hod \ˈhäd\ *n* : a long-handled carrier for mortar or bricks

hodge·podge \ˈhäj-ˌpäj\ *n* ♦ : a heterogeneous mixture : JUMBLE

  ♦ assortment, clutter, jumble, medley, mélange, miscellany, motley, muddle, variety, welter

Hodgkin's disease \ˈhäj-kinz-\ *n* : a neoplastic disease of lymphoid tissue characterized esp. by enlargement of lymph nodes, spleen, and liver

hoe \ˈhō\ *n* : a long-handled implement with a thin flat blade used esp. for cultivating, weeding, or loosening the earth around plants — **hoe** *vb*

hoe·cake \ˈhō-ˌkāk\ *n* : a small cornmeal cake

hoe·down \-ˌdau̇n\ *n* **1** : SQUARE DANCE **2** : a gathering featuring hoedowns

¹hog \ˈhȯg, ˈhäg\ *n, pl* **hogs** *also* **hog** **1** : a domestic swine esp. when grown **2** : a selfish, gluttonous, or filthy person

²hog *vb* **hogged; hog·ging** : to take or hold selfishly

ho·gan \ˈhō-ˌgän\ *n* : a Navajo dwelling usu. made of logs and mud

hog·back \ˈhȯg-ˌbak, ˈhäg-\ *n* : a ridge with a sharp summit and steep sides

hog·gish \ˈhȯ-gish, ˈhä-\ *adj* ♦ : grossly selfish, gluttonous, or filthy

  ♦ gluttonous, greedy, piggish, rapacious, ravenous, voracious

hog·nose snake \ˈhȯg-ˌnōz-, ˈhäg-\ *or* **hog·nosed snake** \-ˌnōzd-\ *n* : any of a genus of rather small harmless stout-bodied No. American snakes that seldom bite but hiss wildly and often play dead when disturbed

hogs·head \ˈhȯgz-ˌhed, ˈhägz-\ *n* ♦ : a large cask or barrel

  ♦ barrel, cask, keg, pipe, puncheon

hog–tie \ˈhȯg-ˌtī, ˈhäg-\ *vb* **1** : to tie together the feet of ⟨~ a calf⟩ **2** : to make helpless

hog·wash \-ˌwȯsh, -ˌwäsh\ *n* **1** : SWILL, SLOP **2** ♦ : language, conduct, or an idea that is absurd or contrary to good sense : NONSENSE

  ♦ bunk, claptrap, drivel, fiddlesticks, folly, foolishness, fudge, humbug, nonsense, piffle, rot, silliness, slush, stupidity, trash

hog–wild \-ˈwīld\ *adj* : lacking in restraint

hoi pol·loi \ˌhȯi-pə-ˈlȯi\ *n pl* : the general populace

hoi·sin sauce \ˈhȯi-ˌsin-\ *n* : a thick reddish sauce of soybeans, spices, and garlic used in Asian cookery

¹hoist \ˈhȯist\ *vb* ♦ : to raise from a lower to a higher position

  ♦ boost, crane, elevate, heave, heft, heighten, hike, jack, lift, pick up, raise, up, uphold

²hoist *n* **1** : LIFT **2** : an apparatus for hoisting

hoke \ˈhōk\ *vb* **hoked; hok·ing** : FAKE — usu. used with *up*

hok·ey \ˈhō-kē\ *adj* **hok·i·er; -est** : CORNY; *also* : PHONY

ho·kum \ˈhō-kəm\ *n* : NONSENSE

¹hold \ˈhōld\ *vb* **held** \ˈheld\; **hold·ing** **1** ♦ : to have possession or ownership of or have at one's disposal **2** : RESTRAIN **3** ♦ : to have a grasp on **4** : to support, remain, or keep in a particular situation or position **5** : SUSTAIN; *also* : RESERVE **6** : BEAR, COMPORT **7** : to maintain in being or action : PERSIST **8** : to enclose and keep in a container or within bounds : ACCOMMODATE **9 a** ♦ : to have in the mind or express as a judgment, opinion, or belief **b** : to think of in a particular way : CONSIDER, REGARD **10** : to carry on by concerted action; *also* : CONVOKE **11** : to occupy esp. by appointment or election **12** : to be valid **13** : HALT, PAUSE — **hold forth** : to speak at length — **hold to** : to adhere to : MAINTAIN — **hold with** : to agree with or approve of

  ♦ [1] hang on, keep, reserve, retain, withhold ♦ [1] command, enjoy, have, occupy, own, possess, retain ♦ [3] clench, cling, clutch, grip, hang on, hold on ♦ [9a] believe, consider, deem, feel, figure, guess, imagine, suppose, think ♦ [9a] bear, cherish, entertain, harbor (*or* harbour), have, nurse ♦ [9b] account, call, consider, count, esteem, rate, reckon, regard, take

²hold *n* **1** ♦ : a fortified place : STRONGHOLD **2** : CONFINEMENT; *also* : PRISON **3** ♦ : the act or manner of holding : GRIP **4** ♦ : a restraining, dominating, or controlling influence **5** : something that may be grasped as a support **6** : an order or indication that something is to be reserved or delayed — **on hold** : in a temporary state of waiting (as during a phone call); *also* : in a state of postponement ⟨plans *on hold*⟩

  ♦ [1] bastion, citadel, fastness, fort, fortification, fortress, stronghold ♦ [3] clasp, grapple, grasp, grip ♦ [4] arm, authority, clutch, command, control, dominion, grip, power, sway

³hold *n* **1** : the interior of a ship below decks; *esp* : a ship's cargo deck **2** : an airplane's cargo compartment

hold back *vb* ♦ : to hinder the progress or achievement of

  ♦ encumber, hamper, hinder, hold up, impede, inhibit, interfere with, obstruct, tie up

hold·er *n* **1** ♦ : a person that holds **2** ♦ : a device that holds

  ♦ [1] owner, possessor, proprietor ♦ [2] container, receptacle, vessel

hold·ing *n* **1** ♦ : land or other property owned — usu. used in pl. **2** ♦ : a ruling of a court esp. on an issue of law

  ♦ usu **holdings** [1] belongings, chattels, effects, paraphernalia, possessions, things ♦ [2] doom, finding, judgment (*or* judgement), ruling, sentence

holding pattern *n* **1** : a course flown by an aircraft waiting to land **2** ♦ : a state of waiting or suspended activity or progress

  ♦ abeyance, doldrums, dormancy, latency, moratorium, quiescence, suspension

hold on *vb* **1** ♦ : to maintain a condition or position : PERSIST **2** ♦ : to maintain a grasp on something **3** ♦ : to await something (as a telephone connection) desired or requested

  ♦ [1] endure, hold, last, persist ♦ usu **hold on to** [2] clench, cling, clutch, grip, hang on, hold ♦ [3] await, bide, stay, wait

hold out *vb* **1** ♦ : to continue to fight or work **2** : to refuse to come to an agreement — **hold·out** \ˈhōl-ˌdau̇t\ *n*

  ♦ hold, keep up, last, prevail, survive *Ant* fail, fizzle, give out, go out, peter (out), run out

hold·over \ˈhōl-ˌdō-vər\ *n* : one that is held over

hold·up \ˈhōl-ˌdəp\ *n* **1** : DELAY **2** : robbery at the point of a gun

hold up *vb* **1** : to rob at gunpoint **2** ♦ : to stop, delay, or impede the course or advance of **3** : to call attention to **4** ♦ : to continue in the same condition without failing or losing effectiveness or force

  ♦ [2] arrest, catch, check, draw up, fetch up, halt, stall, stay, still, stop ♦ [2] encumber, hamper, hinder, impede, inhibit, interfere with, obstruct, tie up ♦ [4] abide, continue, endure, keep up, last, persist, run on

¹hole \ˈhōl\ *n* **1** ♦ : an opening into or through something **2** ♦ : a hollow place (as a pit or cave) **3** : the resting or living place of a wild animal : DEN, BURROW **4** : a wretched or dingy place **5** : a unit of play from tee to cup in golf **6** ♦ : an awkward position

  ♦ [1] breach, break, discontinuity, gap, gulf, interval, opening, rent, rift, separation ♦ [1] aperture, opening, orifice, perforation ♦ [2] cavity, concavity, dent, depression, hollow, indentation, pit, recess *Ant* bulge, convexity, protrusion, protuberance ♦ [6] corner, fix, jam, pickle, predicament, spot

²hole *vb* ♦ : to make a hole in

  ♦ bore, drill, perforate, pierce, punch, puncture

hol·i·day \ˈhä-lə-ˌdā\ *n* **1** : a day set aside for special religious observance **2** : a day of freedom from work; *esp* : one in commemoration of an event **3** : VACATION — **holiday** *vb*

ho·li·ness \ˈhō-lē-nəs\ *n* ♦ : the quality or state of being holy — used as a title for various high religious officials

  ♦ blessedness, devoutness, godliness, piety, sainthood, sanctity *Ant* godlessness, impiety, ungodliness, unholiness

ho·lis·tic \hō-ˈlis-tik\ *adj* : relating to or concerned with integrated wholes or complete systems rather than with the analysis or treatment of separate parts ⟨~ medicine⟩ ⟨~ ecology⟩

hol·lan·daise \ˌhä-lən-ˈdāz\ *n* : a rich sauce made basically of butter, egg yolks, and lemon juice or vinegar

¹hol·ler \ˈhä-lər\ *vb* : to cry out : SHOUT

²holler *n* ♦ : a loud cry or call

  ♦ cry, hoot, howl, shout, whoop, yell, yowl

¹hol·low \ˈhä-lō\ *n* **1** : CAVITY, HOLE **2** ♦ : a surface depression

  ♦ dale, valley ♦ cavity, concavity, dent, depression, hole, indentation, pit, recess

²hollow *adj* **hol·low·er** \ˈhä-lə-wər\; **hol·low·est** \-lə-wəst\ **1** ♦ : having an indentation or inward curve : CONCAVE, SUNKEN **2** : having a cavity within **3** : lacking in real value, sincerity, or substance; *also* : FALSE **4** : MUFFLED ⟨a ~ sound⟩ — **hol·low·ness** *n*

♦ concave, depressed, sunken *Ant* convex, bulging, protruding, protuberant

³**hollow** *vb* : to make or become hollow

hol·low·ware *or* **hol·lo·ware** \'hä-lə-ˌwar\ *n* : vessels (as bowls or cups) with a significant depth and volume

hol·ly \'hä-lē\ *n, pl* **hollies** : either of two trees or shrubs with branches of usu. evergreen glossy spiny-margined leaves and red berries

hol·ly·hock \'hä-lē-ˌhäk, -ˌhȯk\ *n* : a biennial or perennial herb related to the mallows that is widely grown for its tall stalks of showy flowers

hol·mi·um \'hōl-mē-əm\ *n* : a metallic chemical element

ho·lo·caust \'hä-lə-ˌkȯst, 'hō-\ *n* **1** ♦ : a thorough destruction esp. by fire **2** *often cap* : the killing of European Jews by the Nazis during World War II; *also* : GENOCIDE

♦ conflagration, fire, inferno

Ho·lo·cene \'hō-lə-ˌsēn\ *adj* : of, relating to, or being the present geologic epoch — **Holocene** *n*

ho·lo·gram \'hō-lə-ˌgram, 'hä-\ *n* : a three-dimensional image produced by an interference pattern of light (as laser light)

ho·lo·graph \'hō-lə-ˌgraf, 'hä-\ *n* : a document wholly in the handwriting of its author

ho·log·ra·phy \hō-'lä-grə-fē\ *n* : the process of making a hologram — **ho·lo·graph·ic** \ˌhō-lə-'gra-fik, ˌhä-\ *adj*

Hol·stein \'hōl-ˌstēn, -ˌstīn\ *n* : any of a breed of large black-and-white dairy cattle that produce large quantities of comparatively low-fat milk

Hol·stein–Frie·sian \-'frē-zhən\ *n* : HOLSTEIN

hol·ster \'hōl-stər\ *n* : a usu. leather case for a firearm

ho·ly \'hō-lē\ *adj* **ho·li·er; -est 1** ♦ : worthy of absolute devotion **2** ♦ : to be treated with veneration or the utmost respect : SACRED **3** ♦ : having a divine quality **4** ♦ : devoted to the deity or the work of the deity — **ho·li·ly** \-lə-lē\ *adv*

♦ [1, 2] inviolable, sacred, sacrosanct ♦ [1, 2] blessed, hallowed, sacred, sacrosanct, sanctified *Ant* unconsecrated, unhallowed ♦ [3] blessed, divine, godlike, heavenly ♦ [4] devout, faithful, godly, pious, religious, sainted, saintly *Ant* faithless, godless, impious, irreligious, ungodly, unholy

Holy Spirit *n* : the third person of the Christian Trinity

ho·ly·stone \'hō-lē-ˌstōn\ *n* : a soft sandstone used to scrub a ship's wooden decks — **holystone** *vb*

hom·age \'ä-mij, 'hä-\ *n* ♦ : expression of high regard; *also* : TRIBUTE

♦ accolade, citation, commendation, encomium, eulogy, paean, panegyric, salutation, tribute ♦ acclaim, accolade, credit, distinction, glory, honor (*or* honour), laurels

hom·bre \'äm-brē, 'əm-, -ˌbrā\ *n* ♦ : an adult male human : GUY, FELLOW

♦ buck, chap, dude, fellow, gent, gentleman, guy, jack, joker, lad, male, man

hom·burg \'häm-ˌbərg\ *n* : a man's felt hat with a stiff curled brim and a high crown creased lengthwise

¹**home** \'hōm\ *n* **1** ♦ : one's residence; *also* : HOUSE **2** : the social unit formed by a family living together **3** : a congenial environment; *also* : HABITAT **4** ♦ : a place of origin **5** : the objective in various games **6** ♦ : the place or environment where a plant or animal naturally or normally lives and grows

♦ [1] abode, domicile, dwelling, fireside, habitation, hearth, house, lodging, pad, place, quarters, residence, roof ♦ [4] country, fatherland, homeland, motherland, sod ♦ [6] habitat, niche, range, territory

²**home** *vb* **homed; hom·ing 1** : to go or return home **2** : to proceed to or toward a source of radiated energy used as a guide

home·body \'hōm-ˌbä-dē\ *n* : one whose life centers on home

home·boy \-ˌbȯi\ *n* **1** *slang* : a boy or man from one's neighborhood, hometown, or region; *also* : a male friend **2** *slang* : a boy or man who is a member of one's peer group; *also* : a member of one's gang **3** *slang* : an inner-city youth

home·bred \-'bred\ *adj* : produced at home : INDIGENOUS

home·com·ing \-ˌkə-miŋ\ *n* **1** : a return home **2** : an annual celebration for alumni at a college or university

home computer *n* : a small inexpensive microcomputer

home economics *n* : the theory and practice of homemaking

home·girl \'hōm-gərl\ *n* **1** *slang* : a girl or woman from one's neighborhood, hometown, or region; *also* : a female friend **2** *slang* : a girl or woman who is a member of one's peer group **3** *slang* : an inner-city girl or woman

home·grown \'hōm-'grōn\ *adj* **1** : grown domestically **2** : LOCAL, INDIGENOUS

home·land \-ˌland\ *n* **1** ♦ : native land **2** : an area set aside to be a state for a people of a particular national, cultural, or racial origin

♦ country, fatherland, home, motherland, sod

¹**home·less** \-ləs\ *adj* : having no home or permanent residence

²**homeless** *n pl* : persons esp. in urban areas that have no home

home·ly \'hōm-lē\ *adj* **home·li·er; -est 1** : FAMILIAR **2** : unaffectedly natural **3** : lacking beauty or proportion — **home·li·ness** \-lē-nəs\ *n*

home·made \'hōm-ˌmād\ *adj* : made in the home, on the premises, or by one's own efforts

home·mak·er \-ˌmā-kər\ *n* : one who manages a household esp. as a spouse and a parent — **home·mak·ing** \-kiŋ\ *n*

ho·me·op·a·thy \ˌhō-mē-'ä-pə-thē\ *n* : a system of medical practice that treats disease esp. with minute doses of a remedy that would in larger amounts produce symptoms similar to those of the disease in healthy persons — **ho·meo·path** \'hō-mē-ə-ˌpath\ *n* — **ho·meo·path·ic** \ˌhō-mē-ə-'pa-thik\ *adj*

ho·meo·sta·sis \ˌhō-mē-ō-'stā-səs\ *n* : the maintenance of a relatively stable state of equilibrium between interrelated physiological, psychological, or social factors characteristic of an individual or group — **ho·meo·stat·ic** \-'sta-tik\ *adj*

home page *n* : the page usu. encountered first on a website that usu. contains hyperlinks to the other pages of the site

home plate *n* : a slab at the apex of a baseball diamond that a base runner must touch in order to score

hom·er \'hō-mər\ *n* : HOME RUN — **homer** *vb*

home·room \'hōm-ˌrüm, -ˌrüm\ *n* : a classroom where pupils report at the beginning of each school day

home run *n* : a hit in baseball that enables the batter to go around all the bases and score a run

home·school \'hōm-ˌskül\ *vb* : to teach school subjects to one's children at home — **home·school·er** \-ˌskü-lər\ *n*

home·sick \'hōm-ˌsik\ *adj* : longing for home and family while absent from them — **home·sick·ness** *n*

home·spun \-ˌspən\ *adj* **1** : spun or made at home; *also* : made of a loosely woven usu. woolen or linen fabric **2** : SIMPLE, HOMELY

¹**home·stead** \-ˌsted\ *n* : the home and land occupied by a family

²**homestead** *vb* : to acquire or settle on public land

home·stead·er \-ˌste-dər\ *n* : one who seeks, establishes, or possesses a homestead under a homestead law

♦ colonist, frontiersman, pioneer, settler

home·stretch \-'strech\ *n* **1** : the part of a racecourse between the last curve and the winning post **2** ♦ : a final stage (as of a project)

♦ close, conclusion, consummation, end, ending, finale, finis, finish, windup

home theater *n* : an entertainment system (as a television with surround sound and a DVD player) for the home

home video *n* : prerecorded videocassettes or videodiscs for home viewing

¹**home·ward** \-wərd\ *or* **home·wards** \-wərdz\ *adv* : toward home

²**homeward** *adj* : being or going toward home

home·work \-ˌwərk\ *n* **1** : an assignment given a student to be completed outside the classroom **2** : preparatory reading or research

¹**hom·ey** \'hō-mē\ *adj* **hom·i·er; -est** : characteristic of home

²**homey** *or* **hom·ie** \'hō-mē\ *n, pl* **homeys** *or* **homies** : HOMEBOY

hom·i·cid·al \ˌhä-mə-'sīd-ᵊl\ *adj* ♦ : of, relating to, or tending toward homicide

♦ bloodthirsty, bloody, murderous, sanguinary, sanguine

ho·mi·cide \'hä-mə-ˌsīd, 'hō-\ *n* **1** : a person who kills another **2** ♦ : a killing of one human being by another

♦ murder

hom·i·ly \'hä-mə-lē\ *n, pl* **-lies** : SERMON — **hom·i·let·ic** \ˌhä-mə-'le-tik\ *adj*

homing pigeon *n* : a racing pigeon trained to return home

hom·i·nid \'hä-mə-nəd, -ˌnid\ *n* : any of a family of primate mammals that comprise all living humans and extinct ancestral and related forms — **hominid** *adj*

hom·i·ny \'hä-mə-nē\ *n* : hulled corn with the germ removed

ho·mo·cys·te·ine \ˌhō-mō-'sis-tə-ˌēn\ *n* : an amino acid associated with an increased risk of heart disease when occurring at high levels in the blood

ho·mo·erot·ic \ˌhō-mō-i-'rä-tik\ *adj* : marked by or portraying sexual desire between people of the same sex — **ho·mo·erot·i·cism** \-'rä-tə-ˌsi-zəm\ *n*

ho·mo·ge·neous \ˌhō-mə-ˈjē-nē-əs, -nyəs\ *adj* : of the same or a similar kind; *also* : of uniform structure — **ho·mo·ge·ne·i·ty** \-jə-ˈnē-ə-tē\ *n* — **ho·mo·ge·neous·ly** *adv*

ho·mog·e·ni·sa·tion, ho·mog·e·nise *chiefly Brit var of* HOMOGENIZATION, HOMOGENIZE

ho·mog·e·nize \hō-ˈmä-jə-ˌnīz, hə-\ *vb* **-nized; -niz·ing 1** ♦ : to make homogeneous **2** : to reduce the particles in (as milk) to uniform size and distribute them evenly throughout the liquid — **ho·mog·e·ni·za·tion** \-ˌmä-jə-nə-ˈzā-shən\ *n* — **ho·mog·e·niz·er** *n*

♦ formalize, normalize, regularize, standardize

ho·mo·graph \ˈhä-mə-ˌgraf, ˈhō-\ *n* : one of two or more words spelled alike but different in origin, meaning, or pronunciation (as the *bow* of a ship, a *bow* and arrow)

ho·mol·o·gy \hō-ˈmä-lə-jē, hə-\ *n, pl* **-gies 1** : structural likeness between corresponding parts of different plants or animals due to evolution from a common ancestor **2** : structural likeness between different parts of the same individual — **ho·mol·o·gous** \-lə-gəs\ *adj*

hom·onym \ˈhä-mə-ˌnim, ˈhō-\ *n* **1** : HOMOPHONE, HOMOGRAPH **2** : one of two or more words spelled and pronounced alike but different in meaning (as *pool* of water and *pool* the game)

ho·mo·pho·bia \ˈhō-mə-ˈfō-bē-ə\ *n* : irrational fear of, aversion to, or discrimination against homosexuality or gay people — **ho·mo·phobe** \ˈhō-mə-ˌfōb\ *n* — **ho·mo·pho·bic** \-ˈfō-bik\ *adj*

ho·mo·phone \ˈhä-mə-ˌfōn, ˈhō-\ *n* : one of two or more words (as *to, too, two*) pronounced alike but different in meaning or derivation or spelling

Ho·mo sa·pi·ens \ˌhō-mō-ˈsā-pē-ənz, -ˈsa-\ *n* ♦ : the human race : HUMANKIND

♦ humanity, humankind, man, mankind

ho·mo·sex·u·al \ˌhō-mō-ˈsek-shə-wəl\ *adj, now sometimes disparaging and offensive* : of, relating to, or marked by sexual or romantic attraction to people of the same sex as oneself : GAY; *also* : of, relating to, or involving sexual activity between people of the same sex — **homosexual** *n, now often disparaging and offensive* — **ho·mo·sex·u·al·i·ty** \-ˌsek-shə-ˈwa-lə-tē\ *n, now sometimes offensive*

hon *abbr* honor; honorable; honorary

Hon·du·ran \hän-ˈdu̇r-ən\ *or* **Hon·du·ra·ne·an** *or* **Hon·du·ra·ni·an** \ˌhan-du̇-ˈrä-nē-ən, -ˈdyü-\ *n* : a native or inhabitant of Honduras — **Honduran** *or* **Honduranean** *or* **Honduranian** *adj*

¹**hone** \ˈhōn\ *n* : WHETSTONE

²**hone** *vb* **1** ♦ : to sharpen or smooth with a whetstone **2** : to make more acute, intense, or effective — **hon·er** *n*

♦ edge, grind, sharpen, strop, whet

hone in *vb* : to move toward or direct attention to an objective

¹**hon·est** \ˈä-nəst\ *adj* **1** ♦ : free from deception : TRUTHFUL; *also* : GENUINE, REAL **2** : REPUTABLE **3** : CREDITABLE **4** ♦ : marked by integrity **5** ♦ : marked by free, forthright, and sincere expression : FRANK

♦ [1] artless, genuine, ingenuous, innocent, naive, natural, real, simple, sincere, true, unaffected, unpretentious ♦ [4] decent, ethical, good, honorable (*or* honourable), just, moral, principled, right, righteous, straight, upright, virtuous ♦ [4] conscientious, honorable (*or* honourable), just, moral, principled, scrupulous ♦ [5] candid, direct, forthright, foursquare, frank, open, outspoken, plain, straight, straightforward, unguarded, unreserved

²**honest** *adv* : HONESTLY; *also* : with all sincerity ⟨I didn't do it, ~⟩

hon·est·ly \ˈä-nəst-lē\ *adv* **1** : in an honest manner **2** ♦ : to be honest ⟨~, I don't know⟩

♦ actually, frankly, really, truly, truthfully, verily

hon·es·ty \ˈä-nə-stē\ *n* **1** ♦ : fairness and straightforwardness of conduct **2** ♦ : adherence to the facts

♦ [1] character, decency, goodness, honor (*or* honour), integrity, morality, probity, rectitude, righteousness, uprightness, virtue ♦ [2] integrity, probity, truthfulness, veracity, verity *Ant* deceit, deceitfulness, dishonesty, lying, mendacity

hon·ey \ˈhə-nē\ *n, pl* **honeys 1** : a sweet sticky substance made by honeybees from the nectar of flowers **2** ♦ : a loved one

♦ beloved, darling, dear, flame, love, sweet, sweetheart

hon·ey·bee \ˈhə-nē-ˌbē\ *n* : a social and colonial 4-winged insect often kept in hives for the honey it produces

¹**hon·ey·comb** \-ˌkōm\ *n* : a mass of 6-sided wax cells built by honeybees; *also* : something of similar structure or appearance

²**honeycomb** *vb* : to make or become full of cavities like a honeycomb

hon·ey·dew \-ˌdü, -ˌdyü\ *n* : a sweetish deposit secreted on plants by aphids, scale insects, or fungi

honeydew melon *n* : a smooth-skinned muskmelon with sweet green flesh

honey locust *n* : a tall usu. spiny No. American leguminous tree with hard durable wood and long twisted pods

hon·ey·moon \ˈhə-nē-ˌmün\ *n* **1** : a period of harmony esp. just after marriage **2** : a holiday taken by a newly married couple — **honeymoon** *vb*

hon·ey·suck·le \ˈhə-nē-ˌsə-kəl\ *n* : any of a genus of shrubs with fragrant tube-shaped flowers rich in nectar

honk \ˈhäŋk, ˈhȯŋk\ *n* : the cry of a goose; *also* : a similar sound (as of a horn) — **honk** *vb* — **honk·er** *n*

hon·ky-tonk \ˈhäŋ-kē-ˌtäŋk, ˈhȯŋ-kē-ˌtȯŋk\ *n* : a tawdry nightclub or dance hall — **honky-tonk** *adj*

¹**hon·or** \ˈä-nər\ *or Can and Brit* **hon·our** *n* **1** ♦ : good name : REPUTATION; *also* : outward respect **2** ♦ : an exclusive or special right, power, or privilege **3** : a person of superior standing — used esp. as a title **4** : one that brings respect or fame **5** ♦ : an evidence or symbol of distinction **6** : CHASTITY, PURITY **7** ♦ : a keen sense of ethical conduct : INTEGRITY

♦ [1] boast, credit, glory, jewel, pride, treasure ♦ [2] boon, concession, privilege ♦ [5] acclaim, accolade, credit, distinction, glory, homage, laurels ♦ [5] award, decoration, distinction, plume, prize ♦ [7] honesty, integrity, probity, rectitude, righteousness, uprightness *Ant* baseness, lowness

²**honor** *or Can and Brit* **honour** *vb* **1** : to regard or treat with honor **2** : to confer honor on **3** : to fulfill the terms of; *also* : to accept as payment — **hon·or·ee** \ˌä-nə-ˈrē\ *n* — **hon·or·er** *n*

hon·or·able \ˈä-nə-rə-bəl\ *or Can and Brit* **hon·our·able** *adj* **1** : deserving of honor **2** : of great renown **3** : accompanied with marks of honor **4** : doing credit to the possessor **5** ♦ : characterized by integrity — **hon·or·able·ness** *n*

♦ decent, ethical, good, honest, just, moral, right, righteous, straight, upright, virtuous ♦ decent, ethical, honest, just, noble, principled, respectable, righteous, upright, upstanding *Ant* base, dishonest, ignoble, low, unethical, unjust, unprincipled, unrighteous ♦ conscientious, honest, just, moral, principled, scrupulous

hon·or·ably \ˈä-nə-rə-blē\ *or Can and Brit* **hon·our·ably** *adv* ♦ : in an honorable manner

♦ gallantly, grandly, greatly, heroically, magnanimously, nobly

hon·o·rar·i·um \ˌä-nə-ˈrer-ē-əm\ *n, pl* **-ia** \-ē-ə\ *also* **-iums** : a reward usu. for services on which custom or propriety forbids a price to be set

hon·or·ary \ˈä-nə-ˌrer-ē\ *adj* **1** : having or conferring distinction **2** : conferred in recognition of achievement without the usual prerequisites ⟨~ degree⟩ **3** : UNPAID, VOLUNTARY — **hon·or·ari·ly** \ˌä-nə-ˈrer-ə-lē\ *adv*

hon·or·if·ic \ˌä-nə-ˈri-fik\ *adj* : conferring or conveying honor ⟨~ titles⟩

hon·our, hon·our·able *Can and Brit var of* HONOR, HONORABLE

¹**hood** \ˈhu̇d\ *n* **1** : a covering for the head and neck and sometimes the face **2** : an ornamental fold (as at the back of an ecclesiastical vestment) **3 a** ♦ : something resembling a hood in form or use **b** : a cover for parts of mechanisms; *esp* : the covering over an automobile engine — **hood·ed** \ˈhu̇-dəd\ *adj*

♦ cloak, curtain, mantle, mask, shroud, veil

²**hood** \ˈhu̇d, ˈhüd\ *n* : a brutal ruffian : HOODLUM

³**hood** \ˈhu̇d\ *n* : an inner-city neighborhood

-hood \ˌhu̇d\ *n suffix* **1** : state : condition : quality : character ⟨boy*hood*⟩ ⟨hardi*hood*⟩ **2** : instance of a (specified) state or quality ⟨false*hood*⟩ **3** : individuals sharing a (specified) state or character ⟨brother*hood*⟩

hood·ie \ˈhu̇-dē\ *n* : a hooded sweatshirt

hood·lum \ˈhüd-ləm, ˈhu̇d-\ *n* **1** ♦ : a brutal ruffian : THUG **2** : a young ruffian or loafer

♦ bully, gangster, goon, hood, mobster, mug, punk, rowdy, ruffian, thug, tough

hoo·doo \ˈhü-dü\ *n, pl* **hoodoos 1** : a body of magical practices traditional esp. among African Americans in the southern U.S. **2** : something that brings bad luck — **hoodoo** *vb*

hood·wink \ˈhu̇d-ˌwiŋk\ *vb* : to deceive by false appearance

♦ beguile, bluff, cozen, deceive, delude, dupe, fool, gull, have, hoax, humbug, misinform, mislead, string along, take in, trick

hoo·ey \ˈhü-ē\ *n* : NONSENSE

hoof \'hu̇f, 'hüf\ *n, pl* **hooves** \'hu̇vz, 'hüvz\ *or* **hoofs** : a horny covering that protects the ends of the toes of ungulate mammals (as horses or cattle); *also* : a hoofed foot — **hoofed** \'hu̇ft, 'hüft\ *adj*

¹hook \'hu̇k\ *n* **1** : a curved or bent device for catching, holding, or pulling **2** : something curved or bent like a hook **3** : a flight of a ball (as in golf) that curves in a direction opposite to the dominant hand of the player propelling it **4** : a short punch delivered with a circular motion and with the elbow bent and rigid

²hook *vb* **1** ♦ : to form into a hook : CURVE, CROOK **2 a** : to seize or make fast with a hook **b** ♦ : to connect by or as if by a hook — often used with *up* **3** ♦ : to take the property of another wrongfully : STEAL **4** : to work as a prostitute

♦ [1] arc, arch, bend, bow, crook, curve, round, sweep, swerve, wheel ♦ [2b] chain, compound, connect, couple, hitch, join, link, yoke ♦ [3] appropriate, filch, misappropriate, nip, pilfer, pocket, purloin, snitch, steal, swipe, thieve

hoo·kah \'hu̇-kə, 'hü-\ *n* : WATER PIPE

hook·er \'hu̇-kər\ *n* **1** : one that hooks **2** : PROSTITUTE

hook·up \'hu̇-ˌkəp\ *n* **1** ♦ : a state of cooperation or alliance **2** : an assemblage (as of apparatus or circuits) used for a specific purpose (as in radio)

♦ affiliation, alliance, association, collaboration, confederation, connection, cooperation, liaison, partnership, relation, relationship, union

hook up *vb* : to become involved in a working, social, or sexual relationship

hook·worm \'hu̇k-ˌwərm\ *n* : any of several parasitic intestinal nematode worms having hooks or plates around the mouth; *also* : infestation with or disease caused by hookworms

hoo·li·gan \'hü-li-gən\ *n* ♦ : a brutal person : RUFFIAN, HOODLUM

♦ bully, gangster, goon, homeboy, hood, hoodlum, mobster, mug, punk, rowdy, ruffian, thug, tough

hoop \'hu̇p, 'hüp\ *n* **1** : a circular strip used esp. for holding together the staves of a barrel **2** ♦ : a circular figure or object : RING **3** : a circle of flexible material for expanding a woman's skirt **4** : BASKETBALL — usu. used in pl.

♦ band, circle, ring, round

hoop·la \'hüp-ˌlä, 'hu̇p-\ *n* : TO-DO; *also* : BALLYHOO

hoop·ster \'hüp-stər\ *n* : a basketball player

hoo·ray \hu̇-'rā\ *interj* — used to express joy, approval, or encouragement

hoose·gow \'hüs-ˌgau̇\ *n* : JAIL

¹hoot \'hüt\ *vb* **1** : to shout or laugh usu. in contempt **2** : to make the natural throat noise of an owl — **hoot·er** *n*

²hoot *n* **1** ♦ : a sound of hooting **2** ♦ : the least bit ⟨don't give a ~⟩ **3** : something or someone amusing ⟨the play is a real ~⟩

♦ [1] cry, holler, howl, shout, whoop, yell, yowl ♦ [1] boo, catcall, hiss, jeer, raspberry, snort ♦ [2] jot, lick, modicum, rap, tittle, whit

hoot·e·nan·ny \'hü-tə-ˌna-nē\ *n, pl* **-nies** : a gathering at which folksingers entertain often with the audience joining in

¹hop \'häp\ *vb* **hopped; hop·ping** **1** ♦ : to move by a quick springy leap or in a series of leaps **2** : to make a quick trip **3** : to ride on esp. surreptitiously and without authorization

♦ bound, jump, leap, spring, vault

²hop *n* **1** ♦ : a short brisk leap esp. on one leg **2** : a social gathering for dancing : DANCE **3** : a short trip by air

♦ bound, jump, leap, spring, vault

³hop *n* : a vine related to the mulberry whose ripe dried pistillate catkins are used esp. in flavoring malt liquors; *also, pl* : its pistillate catkins

¹hope \'hōp\ *vb* **hoped; hop·ing** ♦ : to desire with expectation of fulfillment ⟨*hopes* for a promotion⟩

♦ *usu* **hope for** anticipate, await, expect, watch

²hope *n* **1** : TRUST, RELIANCE **2** : desire accompanied by expectation of fulfillment; *also* : something hoped for **3** : one that gives promise for the future

HOPE *abbr* Health Opportunity for People Everywhere

hope·ful \'hōp-fəl\ *adj* **1** ♦ : having qualities which inspire hope **2** : full of hope — **hope·ful·ness** *n*

♦ auspicious, bright, encouraging, fair, golden, heartening, likely, promising, propitious, rosy, upbeat *Ant* bleak, dark, desperate, discouraging, disheartening, dismal, dreary, gloomy, hopeless, inauspicious, pessimistic, unlikely, unpromising

hope·ful·ly \'hōp-fə-lē\ *adv* **1** : in a hopeful manner **2** : it is hoped

hope·less \'hō-pləs\ *adj* **1** ♦ : having no expectation of good or success **2 a** ♦ : incapable of solution, management, or accomplishment : IMPOSSIBLE **b** ♦ : not susceptible to remedy or cure; *also* : incapable of redemption or improvement — **hope·less·ly** *adv*

♦ [1] defeatist, despairing, pessimistic ♦ [2a] impossible, unattainable, unsolvable, unworkable ♦ [2b] incorrigible, incurable, irredeemable, irremediable, unrecoverable, unredeemable *Ant* curable, correctable, reclaimable, recoverable, redeemable, reformable, remediable, retrievable

hope·less·ness \-nəs\ *n* ♦ : the quality or state of being hopeless

♦ despair, desperation, despondency, forlornness

Ho·pi \'hō-pē\ *n, pl* **Hopi** *or* **Hopis** : a member of an Indigenous people of Arizona; *also* : the language of the Hopi people

hopped–up \'häpt-ˌəp\ *adj* **1** : being under the influence of a narcotic; *also* : full of enthusiasm or excitement **2** : having more power than usual ⟨a ~ engine⟩

hop·per \'hä-pər\ *n* **1** : a usu. immature hopping insect (as a grasshopper) **2** : a usu. funnel-shaped container for delivering material (as grain) **3** : a freight car with hinged doors in a sloping bottom **4** : a box into which a bill to be considered by a legislative body is dropped **5** : a tank holding a liquid and having a device for releasing its contents through a pipe

hop·scotch \'häp-ˌskäch\ *n* : a child's game in which a player tosses an object (as a stone) into areas of a figure drawn on the ground and hops through the figure to pick up the object

hor *abbr* horizontal

horde \'hōrd\ *n* ♦ : a teeming crowd or throng : SWARM

♦ army, crowd, crush, drove, flock, host, legion, mob, multitude, press, swarm, throng

ho·ri·zon \hə-'rī-zᵊn\ *n* **1** : the apparent junction of earth and sky **2** : range of outlook or experience

hor·i·zon·tal \ˌhȯr-ə-'zänt-ᵊl\ *adj* : parallel to the horizon : LEVEL — **horizontal** *n* — **hor·i·zon·tal·ly** *adv*

hor·mon·al \hȯr-'mōn-ᵊl\ *adj* : of, relating to, or effected by hormones

hor·mone \'hȯr-ˌmōn\ *n* : a product of living cells that circulates in body fluids and has a specific effect on the activity of cells remote from its point of origin

horn \'hȯrn\ *n* **1** : one of the hard projections of bone or keratin on the head of many hoofed mammals **2** : something resembling or suggesting a horn **3** : a brass wind instrument **4** : a usu. electrical device that makes a noise ⟨automobile ~⟩ — **horned** \'hȯrnd\ *adj* — **horn·less** *adj*

horn·book \'hȯrn-ˌbu̇k\ *n* **1** : a child's primer consisting of a sheet of parchment or paper protected by a sheet of transparent horn **2** : a rudimentary treatise

horned toad *n* : any of several small harmless insect-eating lizards with spines on the head resembling horns and spiny scales on the body

hor·net \'hȯr-nət\ *n* : any of the larger social wasps

horn in *vb* : to participate without invitation : INTRUDE

horn·pipe \'hȯrn-ˌpīp\ *n* : a lively folk dance of the British Isles

horny \'hȯr-nē\ *adj* **horn·i·er; -est** **1** : of or made of horn; *also* : HARD, CALLOUS **2** : having horns **3** : desiring sexual gratification; *also* : excited sexually

ho·rol·o·gy \hə-'rä-lə-jē\ *n* : the science of measuring time or constructing time-indicating instruments — **hor·o·log·ic** \ˌhȯr-ə-'lä-jik\ *adj* — **ho·rol·o·gist** \hə-'rä-lə-jist\ *n*

horo·scope \'hȯr-ə-ˌskōp\ *n* **1** : a diagram of the relative positions of planets and signs of the zodiac at a particular time for use by astrologers to foretell events of a person's life **2** : an astrological forecast

hor·ren·dous \hȯ-'ren-dəs\ *adj* : inspiring horror : DREADFUL, HORRIBLE

hor·ri·ble \'hȯr-ə-bəl\ *adj* **1** ♦ : marked by or arousing horror **2** ♦ : highly disagreeable ⟨a ~ mistake⟩ — **hor·ri·ble·ness** *n* — **hor·ri·bly** \-blē\ *adv*

♦ [1] dreadful, fearful, fearsome, hair-raising, scary, terrifying ♦ [2] abhorrent, abominable, distasteful, horrid, obnoxious, odious, offensive, repellent, repugnant, repulsive, revolting, scandalous, ugly ♦ [2] appalling, atrocious, awful, dreadful, frightful, ghastly, grisly, gruesome, hideous, horrid, lurid, macabre, monstrous, nightmarish, shocking, terrible

hor·rid \'hȯr-əd\ *adj* **1** : inspiring horror : HIDEOUS **2** ♦ : highly disagreeable — **hor·rid·ly** *adv*

♦ abhorrent, abominable, appalling, awful, distasteful, dreadful, horrible, obnoxious, offensive, repugnant, repulsive, revolting, scandalous, shocking, ugly

hor·rif·ic \hò-'ri-fik\ *adj* : having the power to horrify ⟨a ∼ crime⟩ — **hor·rif·i·cal·ly** \-fi-k(ə-)lē\ *adv*

hor·ri·fy \'hòr-ə-ˌfī\ *vb* **-fied; -fy·ing** ♦ : to cause to feel horror

♦ alarm, frighten, panic, scare, shock, spook, startle, terrify, terrorize

hor·ror \'hòr-ər\ *n* **1** ♦ : painful and intense fear, dread, or dismay **2** : intense repugnance **3 a** ♦ : something that horrifies **b** : a repulsive or dismal quality or character **4** ♦ : the quality of inspiring horror

♦ [1] alarm, anxiety, apprehension, dread, fear, fright, panic, terror, trepidation ♦ [3a] agony, hell, misery, murder, nightmare, torment, torture ♦ [4] atrociousness, atrocity, frightfulness, hideousness, monstrosity, repulsiveness

horror story *n* : an account of an unsettling or unfortunate occurrence

hors de com·bat \ˌòr-də-kōⁿ-'bä\ *adv or adj* : in a disabled condition

hors d'oeuvre \òr-'dərv\ *n, pl* **hors d'oeuvres** *same or* -'dərvz\ *also* **hors d'oeuvre** : any of various savory foods usu. served as appetizers

horse \'hòrs\ *n, pl* **hors·es** *also* **horse** **1** : a large solid-hoofed herbivorous mammal domesticated as a draft and saddle animal **2** : a supporting framework usu. with legs — **horse·less** *adj*

¹**horse·back** \'hòrs-ˌbak\ *n* : the back of a horse

²**horseback** *adv* : on horseback

horse chestnut *n* : a large tree with palmate leaves, erect conical clusters of showy flowers, and large glossy brown seeds enclosed in a prickly bur; *also* : its seed

horse·flesh \'hòrs-ˌflesh\ *n* : horses for riding, driving, or racing

horse·fly \-ˌflī\ *n* : any of a family of large dipteran flies with bloodsucking females

horse·hair \-ˌhar\ *n* **1** : the hair of a horse esp. from the mane or tail **2** : cloth made from horsehair

horse·hide \-ˌhīd\ *n* **1** : the dressed or raw hide of a horse **2** : the ball used in baseball

horse latitudes *n pl* : either of two calm regions near 30°N and 30°S latitude

horse·laugh \'hòrs-ˌlaf, -ˌlåf\ *n* : a loud boisterous laugh

horse·man \-mən\ *n* **1** : one who rides horseback; *also* : one skilled in managing horses **2** : a breeder or raiser of horses — **horse·man·ship** *n*

horse·play \-ˌplā\ *n* ♦ : rough boisterous play

♦ foolery, high jinks, monkeyshines, roughhouse, shenanigans, tomfoolery

horse·play·er \-ər\ *n* : a bettor on horse races

horse·pow·er \'hòrs-ˌpau̇(-ə)r\ *n* : a unit of power equal in the U.S. to 746 watts

horse·rad·ish \-ˌra-dish\ *n* : a tall white-flowered herb related to the mustards whose pungent root is used as a condiment; *also* : the pungent condiment

horse sense *n* ♦ : sound and prudent judgment based on a simple perception of the situation or facts

♦ common sense, prudence, sense, wisdom, wit

horse·shoe \'hòrs-ˌshü\ *n* **1** : a usu. U-shaped protective metal plate fitted to the rim of a horse's hoof **2** *pl* : a game in which horseshoes are pitched at a fixed object — **horse·shoe** *vb* — **horse·sho·er** *n*

horseshoe crab *n* : any of several marine arthropods with a broad crescent-shaped combined head and thorax

horse·tail \'hòrs-ˌtāl\ *n* : any of a genus of primitive spore-producing plants with hollow jointed stems and leaves reduced to sheaths about the joints

horse·whip \-ˌhwip\ *vb* : to flog with a whip made to be used on a horse

horse·wom·an \-ˌwu̇-mən\ *n* : a woman skilled in riding horseback or in caring for or managing horses; *also* : a woman who breeds or raises horses

hors·ey *also* **horsy** \'hòr-sē\ *adj* **hors·i·er; -est** **1** : of, relating to, or suggesting a horse **2** : having to do with horses or horse racing

hort *abbr* horticultural; horticulture

hor·ta·tive \'hòr-tə-tiv\ *adj* : giving exhortation

hor·ta·to·ry \'hòr-tə-ˌtōr-ē\ *adj* : HORTATIVE

hor·ti·cul·ture \'hòr-tə-ˌkəl-chər\ *n* : the science and art of growing fruits, vegetables, flowers, and ornamental plants — **hor·ti·cul·tur·al** \ˌhòr-tə-'kəl-chə-rəl\ *adj* — **hor·ti·cul·tur·ist** \-rist\ *n*

Hos *abbr* Hosea

ho·san·na \hō-'za-nə, -'zä-\ *interj* — used as a cry of acclamation and adoration — **hosanna** *n*

¹**hose** \'hōz\ *n, pl* **hose** *or* **hos·es** **1** *pl* **hose** : STOCKING, SOCK; *also* : a close-fitting garment covering the legs and waist **2** : a flexible tube for conveying fluids (as from a faucet)

²**hose** *vb* **hosed; hos·ing** : to spray, water, or wash with a hose ⟨*hosed* off the car⟩

Ho·sea \hō-'zā-ə, -'zē-\ *n* : a book of the canonical Jewish and Christian Scriptures

ho·siery \'hō-zhə-rē, -zə-\ *n* : STOCKINGS, SOCKS

hosp *abbr* hospital

hos·pice \'häs-pəs\ *n* **1** ♦ : a lodging for travelers or for young persons or the underprivileged **2** : a facility or program for caring for dying persons

♦ hotel, inn, lodge, public house, tavern

hos·pi·ta·ble \hä-'spi-tə-bəl, 'häs-(ˌ)pi-\ *adj* **1** ♦ : given to generous and cordial reception of guests **2** : readily receptive — **hos·pi·ta·bly** \-blē\ *adv*

♦ affable, cordial, genial, gracious, sociable

hos·pi·tal \'häs-ˌpit-ᵊl\ *n* : an institution where the sick or injured receive medical or surgical care

hos·pi·tal·ise *chiefly Brit var of* HOSPITALIZE

hos·pi·tal·ist \'häs-ˌpit-ᵊl-ist\ *n* : a physician who specializes in providing and managing the care and treatment of hospitalized patients

hos·pi·tal·i·ty \ˌhäs-pə-'ta-lə-tē\ *n, pl* **-ties** : hospitable treatment, reception, or disposition

hos·pi·tal·ize \'häs-ˌpit-ᵊl-ˌīz\ *vb* **-ized; -iz·ing** : to place in a hospital as a patient — **hos·pi·tal·i·za·tion** \ˌhäs-ˌpit-ᵊl-ə-'zā-shən\ *n*

¹**host** \'hōst\ *n* **1** : a large organized body of armed personnel trained for war esp. on land : ARMY **2** ♦ : a very large number : MULTITUDE ⟨a ∼ of options⟩

♦ army, crowd, crush, drove, flock, horde, legion, mob, multitude, press, swarm, throng

²**host** *n* **1** : one who receives or entertains guests **2** : one who talks to guests on a show **3** : an animal or plant on or in which a parasite lives **4** : one into which something (as an organ) is transplanted **5** : SERVER 2 — **host** *vb*

³**host** *n, often cap* : the eucharistic bread

hos·tage \'häs-tij\ *n* **1** : a person kept as a pledge pending the fulfillment of an agreement **2** : a person taken by force to secure the taker's demands

hos·tel \'häst-ᵊl\ *n* **1** : an establishment for the lodging and entertaining of travelers : INN **2** : a supervised lodging for youth — **hos·tel·er** *n*

hos·tel·ry \-rē\ *n, pl* **-ries** : an establishment for the lodging and entertaining of travelers : INN, HOTEL

host·ess \'hō-stəs\ *n* **1** : a woman who receives or entertains guests **2** : a woman who talks to guests on a show

hos·tile \'häst-ᵊl, 'häs-ˌtīl\ *adj* ♦ : marked by usu. overt antagonism : UNFRIENDLY — **hostile** *n* — **hos·tile·ly** *adv*

♦ antagonistic, inhospitable, inimical, jaundiced, negative, unfriendly, unsympathetic *Ant* friendly, hospitable, sympathetic

hos·til·i·ty \hä-'sti-lə-tē\ *n, pl* **-ties** **1** ♦ : an unfriendly state or action **2** *pl* : overt acts of war

♦ animosity, antagonism, antipathy, bitterness, enmity, gall, grudge, rancor

hos·tler \'häs-lər, 'äs-\ *n* : one who takes care of horses or mules

hot \'hät\ *adj* **hot·ter; hot·test** **1** ♦ : marked by a high temperature or an uncomfortable degree of body heat **2** : giving a sensation of heat or of burning **3** : ARDENT, FIERY **4** : sexually excited **5** ♦ : marked by enthusiastic or impatient desire or interest : EAGER **6** ♦ : newly made or received **7** : PUNGENT **8** : unusually lucky or favorable ⟨∼ dice⟩ **9** : recently and illegally obtained ⟨∼ jewels⟩ **10** ♦ : currently popular or in demand **11** ♦ : marked by extreme force or sudden intense activity : VIOLENT — **hot** *adv* — **hot·ly** *adv*

♦ [1] broiling, burning, fiery, red-hot, scorching, sultry, torrid *Ant* arctic, chill, chilled, cold, freezing, frigid, frozen, glacial, iced, icy ♦ [5] agog, anxious, ardent, athirst, avid, crazy, eager, enthusiastic, gung ho, hungry, keen, nuts, raring, solicitous, thirsty, voracious ♦ [6] contemporary, current, mod, modern, new, newfangled, red-hot, space-age, ultramodern, up-to-date ♦ [10] fashionable, in, modish, popular, vogue ♦ [11] explosive, ferocious, fierce, furious, rabid, rough, stormy, tempestuous, turbulent, violent, volcanic

hot air *n* ♦ : empty talk

♦ bombast, gas, grandiloquence, rhetoric, wind

hot·bed \-,bed\ *n* **1** : a glass-covered bed of soil heated (as by fermenting manure) and used esp. for raising seedlings **2** : an environment that favors rapid growth or development

hot–blood·ed \-'blə-dəd\ *adj* ♦ : easily roused or excited

♦ ardent, burning, charged, emotional, fervent, fiery, impassioned, passionate, red-hot, vehement

hot·box \-,bäks\ *n* : a bearing (as of a railroad car) overheated by friction

hot button *n* : an emotional issue or concern that triggers immediate intense reaction

hot·cake \-,kāk\ *n* : a flat cake made of thin batter and cooked (as on a griddle) on both sides : PANCAKE

hot dog *n* : a cooked frankfurter usu. served in a long split roll

ho·tel \hō-'tel\ *n* ♦ : a building where lodging and usu. meals, entertainment, and various personal services are provided for the public

♦ hospice, inn, lodge, public house, tavern

hot flash *n* : a sudden brief flushing and sensation of heat usu. associated with menopausal endocrine imbalance

hot·head·ed \'hät-'he-dəd\ *adj* : FIERY, IMPETUOUS ⟨a ~ troublemaker⟩ — **hot·head** \-,hed\ *n* — **hot·head·ed·ly** *adv* — **hot·head·ed·ness** *n*

hot·house \-,hau̇s\ *n* : a heated greenhouse esp. for raising tropical plants

hot·line \'hät-,līn\ *n* : a telephone line for emergency use (as between governments or to a counseling service)

hot·ness \-nəs\ *n* : the quality or state of being hot

hot pants *n pl* : very short shorts

hot pepper *n* : a small usu. thin-walled pepper with a pungent taste; *also* : a plant bearing hot peppers

hot plate *n* : a simple portable appliance for heating or for cooking

hot potato *n* : an embarrassing or controversial issue

hot rod *n* : an automobile modified for high speed and fast acceleration — **hot–rod·der** \-'rä-dər\ *n*

hots \'häts\ *n pl* : strong sexual desire — usu. used with *the*

hot seat *n* : a position of anxiety or embarrassment

hot·shot \'hät-,shät\ *n* ♦ : a showily skillful person

♦ ace, adept, artist, authority, crackerjack, expert, guru, hand, maestro, master, scholar, shark, virtuoso, whiz, wizard

hot tub *n* : a large tub of hot water for one or more bathers

hot water *n* : TROUBLE, DIFFICULTY

hot–wire \'hät-,wī(-ə)r\ *vb* : to start (an automobile) by short-circuiting the ignition system

¹hound \'hau̇nd\ *n* **1** : a domestic mammal closely related to the gray wolf; *esp* : any of various hunting dogs that track prey by scent or sight **2** : FAN, ADDICT

²hound *vb* ♦ : to pursue relentlessly

♦ chase, dog, follow, pursue, shadow, tag, tail, trace, track, trail ♦ henpeck, nag, needle

hour \'au̇(-ə)r\ *n* **1** : the 24th part of a day : 60 minutes **2** : the time of day **3** : a particular or customary time **4** : a class session — **hour·ly** *adv or adj*

hour·glass \'au̇(-ə)r-,glas\ *n* : a glass vessel for measuring time in which sand runs from an upper compartment to a lower compartment in an hour

hou·ri \'hu̇r-ē\ *n* : one of the beautiful maidens of the Muslim paradise

¹house \'hau̇s\ *n, pl* **hous·es** \'hau̇-zəz\ **1** ♦ : a building for human habitation **2** : an animal shelter (as a den or nest) **3** : a building in which something is stored **4 a** : those who dwell under the same roof and compose a family : HOUSEHOLD **b** ♦ : a family including ancestors, descendants, and kindred : FAMILY **5** : a residence for a religious community or for students; *also* : those in residence **6** : a legislative body **7** : a place of business or entertainment **8** ♦ : a business organization **9** : the audience in a theater or concert hall — **house·ful** *n*

♦ [1] abode, domicile, dwelling, home, lodging, quarters, residence ♦ [4b] blood, clan, family, folks, kin, kindred, kinfolk, line, lineage, people, race, stock, tribe ♦ [8] business, company, concern, enterprise, establishment, firm, outfit

²house \'hau̇z\ *vb* **housed; hous·ing** **1** ♦ : to provide with or take shelter : LODGE **2** ♦ : to encase, enclose, or shelter as if by putting in a house

♦ [1] accommodate, billet, chamber, domicile, harbor (*or* harbour), lodge, put up, quarter, roof, shelter, take in ♦ [2] cage, closet, coop up, corral, encase, enclose, envelop, fence, hedge, hem, immure, pen, wall

house·boat \'hau̇s-,bōt\ *n* : a pleasure boat fitted for use as a dwelling or for leisurely cruising

house·boy \-,bȯi\ *n* : a boy or man hired to act as a household servant

house·break \-,brāk\ *vb* **-broke; -bro·ken; -break·ing** : to train (a pet) in excretory habits acceptable in indoor living

house·break·ing \-,brā-kiŋ\ *n* : the act of breaking into a dwelling with the intent of committing a felony

house·clean \-,klēn\ *vb* : to clean a house and its furniture — **house·clean·ing** *n*

house·coat \-,kōt\ *n* : a woman's often long-skirted informal garment for wear around the house

house·fly \-,flī\ *n* : a dipteran fly that is common about human habitations

¹house·hold \-,hōld\ *n* ♦ : those who dwell as a family under the same roof — **house·hold·er** *n*

♦ house

²household *adj* **1** : DOMESTIC **2** ♦ : frequently seen or experienced : FAMILIAR, COMMON ⟨a ~ name⟩

♦ common, commonplace, customary, everyday, familiar, frequent, ordinary, routine, usual

house·keep·er \-,kē-pər\ *n* : a person employed to take care of a house

house·keep·ing \-,kē-piŋ\ *n* : the care and management of a house or institutional property

house·lights \-,līts\ *n pl* : the lights that illuminate the auditorium of a theater

house·maid \-,mād\ *n* ♦ : a girl or woman who is a servant employed to do housework

♦ domestic, girl, maid, maidservant

house·moth·er \-,mə-thər\ *n* : a woman acting as hostess, chaperone, and often housekeeper in a group residence

House of Commons : the lower house of the British or Canadian parliaments

house·plant \-,plant\ *n* : a plant grown or kept indoors

house sparrow *n* : a Eurasian sparrow widely introduced in urban and agricultural areas

house·top \'hau̇s-,täp\ *n* : ROOF

house·wares \-,warz\ *n pl* : small articles of household equipment

house·warm·ing \-,wȯr-miŋ\ *n* : a party to celebrate the taking possession of a house or premises

house·wife \-,wīf\ *n* : a married woman in charge of a household — **house·wife·ly** *adj* — **house·wif·ery** \-,wī-fə-rē\ *n*

house·work \-,wərk\ *n* : the work of housekeeping

¹hous·ing \'hau̇-ziŋ\ *n* **1** : SHELTER; *also* : dwellings provided for people **2** ♦ : something that covers or protects

♦ armor, capsule, case, casing, cocoon, cover, husk, jacket, pod, sheath, shell

²housing *n* : CAPARISON 1

HOV *abbr* high-occupancy vehicle

hove *past and past part of* HEAVE

hov·el \'hə-vəl, 'hä-\ *n* : a small, wretched, and often dirty house : HUT

hov·er \'hə-vər, 'hä-\ *vb* **hov·ered; hov·er·ing** **1 a** : FLUTTER **b** ♦ : to remain suspended over a place or object **2** : to move to and fro **3** ♦ : to be in an uncertain state of uncertainty, irresolution, or suspense

♦ [1b] drift, float, glide, hang, poise, ride, sail, waft ♦ [3] hang, menace, overhang, threaten

hov·er·craft \-,kraft\ *n* : a vehicle that rides on a cushion of air over a surface

¹how \'hau̇\ *adv* **1** : in what way or manner ⟨~ was it done⟩ **2** : with what meaning ⟨~ do we interpret such behavior⟩ **3** : for what reason ⟨~ could you have done such a thing⟩ **4** : to what extent or degree ⟨~ deep is it⟩ **5** : in what state or condition ⟨~ are you⟩ — **how about** : what do you say to or think of ⟨*how about* coming with me⟩ — **how come** : why is it that

²how *conj* **1** : the way or manner in which ⟨remember ~ they fought⟩ **2** : HOWEVER ⟨do it ~ you like⟩

¹how·be·it \hau̇-'bē-ət\ *conj* ♦ : even though : ALTHOUGH

♦ albeit, although, though, when, while

²howbeit *adv* ♦ : on the other hand : NEVERTHELESS

♦ but, however, nevertheless, nonetheless, notwithstanding, still, though, withal, yet

how·dah \'hau̇-də\ *n* : a seat or covered pavilion on the back of an elephant or camel

¹how·ev·er \hau̇-'e-vər\ *conj* : in whatever manner that

²**however** *adv* **1 :** to whatever degree; *also* **:** in whatever manner **2 ♦ :** on the other hand

♦ but, howbeit, nevertheless, nonetheless, notwithstanding, still, though, withal, yet

how·it·zer \'hau̇-ət-sər\ *n* **:** a short cannon that shoots shells at a high angle

¹**howl** \'hau̇(-ə)l\ *vb* **1 ♦ :** to emit a loud long doleful sound characteristic of dogs **2 ♦ :** to cry loudly

♦ [1] bay, keen, wail, yowl ♦ [2] scream, shriek, shrill, squeal, yell, yelp

²**howl** *n* **1 :** a loud protracted mournful cry characteristic of dogs **2 a ♦ :** a prolonged cry of distress **b ♦ :** a yell or outcry of disappointment, rage, or protest

♦ [2a] groan, keen, lament, moan, plaint, wail ♦ [2b] cry, holler, hoot, shout, whoop, yell, yowl ♦ [2b] clamor (*or* clamour), hubbub, hue and cry, hullabaloo, noise, outcry, roar, tumult, uproar

howl·er \'hau̇-lər\ *n* **1 :** one that howls **2 :** a humorous and ridiculous blunder

howl·ing *adj* **1 :** DESOLATE, WILD **2 :** very great ⟨a ∼ success⟩

how·so·ev·er \ˌhau̇-sə-'we-vər\ *adv* **:** HOWEVER 1

hoy·den \'hȯid-ᵊn\ *n* **:** a girl or woman of saucy, boisterous, or carefree behavior

hp *abbr* horsepower

HP *abbr* high pressure

HPF *abbr* highest possible frequency

HQ *abbr* headquarters

hr *abbr* **1** here **2** hour

HR *abbr* House of Representatives

HRH *abbr* **1** Her Royal Highness **2** His Royal Highness

hrzn *abbr* horizon

Hs *symbol* hassium

HS *abbr* high school

HST *abbr* Hawaiian standard time

ht *abbr* height

HT *abbr* **1** Hawaii time **2** high-tension

HTML \ˌāch-ˌtē-ˌem-'el\ *n* **:** a computer language used to create World Wide Web documents

http *abbr* hypertext transfer protocol

hua·ra·che \wə-'rä-chē\ *n* **:** a sandal with an upper made of interwoven leather strips

hub \'həb\ *n* **1 :** the central part of a circular object (as a wheel) **2 a ♦ :** a center of activity **b :** an airport or city through which an airline routes most of its traffic

♦ base, center (*or* centre), core, cynosure, eye, focus, heart, mecca, nucleus, seat

hub·bub \'hə-bəb\ *n* **1 ♦ :** a noisy confusion of sound **:** UPROAR **2 ♦ :** a state of tumultuous confusion or excitement **:** TURMOIL

♦ [1] clamor (*or* clamour), howl, hue and cry, hullabaloo, noise, outcry, roar, tumult, uproar ♦ [2] commotion, disturbance, furor, fuss, pandemonium, tumult, turmoil

hub·cap \'həb-ˌkap\ *n* **:** a removable metal cap over the end of an axle

hu·bris \'hyü-brəs\ *n* **:** exaggerated pride or self-confidence

huck·le·ber·ry \'hə-kəl-ˌber-ē\ *n* **1 :** any of a genus of American shrubs of the heath family; *also* **:** its edible dark blue berry **2 :** BLUEBERRY

huck·ster \'hək-stər\ *n* **:** PEDDLER, HAWKER — **huckster** *vb*

HUD *abbr* Department of Housing and Urban Development

¹**hud·dle** \'həd-ᵊl\ *vb* **hud·dled; hud·dling 1 ♦ :** to crowd together **2 :** CONFER **3 ♦ :** to curl up **:** CROUCH

♦ [1] bunch, cluster, crowd, press ♦ [3] crouch, hunch, squat

²**huddle** *n* **1 ♦ :** a closely packed group **2 ♦ :** an assembly for a common purpose **:** MEETING, CONFERENCE

♦ [1] array, assemblage, bank, batch, block, bunch, clump, cluster, collection, group, knot, lot, package, parcel, set, suite ♦ [2] assembly, conference, congress, convention, convocation, council, gathering, get-together, meeting, seminar

hue \'hyü\ *n* **1 ♦ :** a phenomenon of light or visual perception that enables one to differentiate otherwise identical objects **:** COLOR; *also* **:** gradation of color **2 :** the attribute of colors that permits them to be classed as red, yellow, green, blue, or an intermediate color — **hued** \'hyüd\ *adj*

♦ cast, color (*or* colour), shade, tinge, tint, tone

hue and cry *n* **♦ :** a clamor of pursuit or protest

♦ clamor (*or* clamour), howl, hubbub, hullabaloo, noise, outcry, roar, tumult, uproar

huff \'həf\ *n* **♦ :** a fit of anger or pique — **huff** *vb* — **huffy** *adj*

♦ dither, fluster, fret, fuss, lather, pother, stew, tizzy, twitter ♦ dudgeon, offense, peeve, pique, resentment, umbrage

hug \'həg\ *vb* **hugged; hug·ging 1 ♦ :** to press tightly esp. in the arms **:** EMBRACE **2 :** to stay close to — **hug** *n*

♦ caress, clasp, embrace, enfold, grasp

huge \'hyüj\ *adj* **hug·er; hug·est ♦ :** very large or extensive

♦ astronomical, colossal, enormous, giant, gigantic, grand, jumbo, mammoth, massive, prodigious, titanic, tremendous, vast, whopping *Ant* diminutive, microscopic, minute, teeny, tiny, wee

huge·ly *adv* **♦ :** to a great extent or degree

♦ broadly, considerably, greatly, largely, massively, monstrously, much, sizably, stupendously, tremendously, utterly, vastly

huge·ness \-nəs\ *n* **♦ :** the quality or state of being huge

♦ enormity, immensity, magnitude, massiveness, vastness

¹**hug·ger–mug·ger** \'hə-gər-ˌmə-gər\ *n* **1 :** SECRECY **2 :** CONFUSION, MUDDLE

²**hugger–mugger** *adj* **1 ♦ :** kept from knowledge or view **2 ♦ :** of a confused or disorderly nature

♦ [1] clandestine, covert, furtive, private, secret, sneak, sneaky, stealthy, surreptitious, undercover, underground, underhanded ♦ [2] chaotic, disheveled, disordered, disorderly, higgledy-piggledy, messy, pell-mell, topsy-turvy, unkempt, untidy

Hu·gue·not \'hyü-gə-ˌnät\ *n* **:** a French Protestant of the 16th and 17th centuries

hu·la \'hü-lə\ *n* **:** a sinuous Polynesian dance usu. accompanied by chants

hulk \'həlk\ *n* **1 :** a heavy clumsy ship **2 :** an old ship unfit for service **3 ♦ :** a bulky or unwieldy person or thing

♦ clod, lout, lubber, lug, oaf

hulk·ing \'həl-kiŋ\ *adj* **:** BURLY, MASSIVE

¹**hull** \'həl\ *n* **1 :** the outer covering of a fruit or seed **2 :** the frame or body esp. of a ship or boat

²**hull** *vb* **♦ :** to remove the hulls of — **hull·er** *n*

♦ bark, flay, husk, peel, shell, skin

hul·la·ba·loo \'hə-lə-bə-ˌlü\ *n, pl* **-loos ♦ :** a confused noise **:** UPROAR

♦ clamor (*or* clamour), howl, hubbub, hue and cry, noise, outcry, roar, tumult, uproar

hul·lo \ˌhə-'lō\ *chiefly Brit var of* HELLO

¹**hum** \'həm\ *vb* **hummed; hum·ming 1 :** to utter a sound like that of the speech sound m prolonged **2 ♦ :** to make the natural noise of an insect in motion or a similar sound **:** DRONE **3 :** to be busily active **4 :** to run smoothly **5 :** to sing with closed lips

♦ buzz, drone, whir, whish, whiz, zip, zoom

²**hum** *n* **♦ :** the act of humming or the sound made by humming

♦ buzz, drone, purr, whir, whiz, zoom

¹**hu·man** \'hyü-mən, 'yü-\ *adj* **1 :** of, relating to, being, or characteristic of humans **2 :** having human form or attributes — **hu·man·ly** *adv* — **hu·man·ness** *n*

²**human** *n* **♦ :** any of a species of bipedal primate mammals comprising all living persons and their recent ancestors; *also* **:** HOMINID

♦ being, body, creature, individual, man, mortal, person, stiff

hu·mane \hyü-'mān, yü-\ *adj* **1 ♦ :** marked by compassion, sympathy, or consideration for others **2 :** HUMANISTIC — **hu·mane·ly** *adv* — **hu·mane·ness** *n*

♦ beneficent, benevolent, compassionate, good-hearted, kind, kindly, sympathetic, tender, tenderhearted, warmhearted *Ant* barbarous, bestial, brutal, brutish, callous, cold-blooded, cruel, heartless, inhuman, inhumane, insensate, savage, unfeeling, unkind, unkindly, unsympathetic

human immunodeficiency virus *n* **:** HIV

hu·man·ism \'hyü-mə-ˌni-zəm, 'yü-\ *n* **1 :** devotion to the humanities; *also* **:** the revival of classical letters characteristic of the Renaissance **2 :** a doctrine or way of life centered on human interests or values — **hu·man·ist** \-nist\ *n or adj* — **hu·man·is·tic** \ˌhyü-mə-'nis-tik, ˌyü-\ *adj*

¹**hu·man·i·tar·i·an** \hyü-ˌma-nə-'ter-ē-ən, yü-\ *n* **:** one who practices philanthropy — **hu·man·i·tar·i·an·ism** *n*

²**humanitarian** *adj* ♦ : concerned for or active in the promotion of human welfare
  ♦ altruistic, beneficent, benevolent, charitable, philanthropic

hu·man·i·ty \hyü-'ma-nə-tē, yü-\ *n, pl* **-ties** **1** ♦ : the quality or state of being human or humane **2** *pl* : the branches of learning dealing with human concerns (as philosophy) as opposed to natural processes (as physics) **3** ♦ : the human race
  ♦ [1] charity, commiseration, compassion, feeling, heart, kindliness, kindness, mercy, pity, sympathy ♦ [3] folks, humankind, people, persons, public, society, world

hu·man·ize \'hyü-mə-ˌnīz, 'yü-\ *vb* **-ized; -iz·ing** : to make human or humane — **hu·man·iza·tion** \ˌhyü-mə-nə-'zā-shən, ˌyü-\ *n* — **hu·man·iz·er** *n*

hu·man·kind \'hyü-mən-ˌkīnd, 'yü-\ *n* ♦ : the human race
  ♦ Homo sapiens, humanity, man, mankind

hu·man·oid \'hyü-mə-ˌnȯid, 'yü-\ *adj* : having human form or characteristics — **humanoid** *n*

human pap·il·lo·ma·virus \-ˌpa-pə-'lō-mə-ˌvī-rəs\ *n* : any of numerous DNA-containing viruses that cause various human warts

¹**hum·ble** \'həm-bəl\ *adj* **hum·bler** \-bə-lər\; **hum·blest** \-bə-ləst\ **1** : not proud or haughty **2** : not pretentious : UNASSUMING **3** ♦ : ranking low in a hierarchy or scale
  ♦ [2] demure, lowly, meek, modest, retiring, unassuming, unpretentious *Ant* arrogant, conceited, presumptuous, proud, self-important ♦ [3] common, ignoble, inferior, low, lowly, mean, plebeian, vulgar

²**humble** *vb* **hum·bled; hum·bling** **1** : to make humble **2** ♦ : to destroy the power or prestige of — **hum·bler** *n*
  ♦ abase, debase, degrade, demean, discredit, disgrace, dishonor (*or* dishonour), humiliate, lower, shame, smirch, take down *Ant* aggrandize, elevate, exalt

hum·ble·ness \-nəs\ *n* ♦ : the quality or state of being humble
  ♦ humility, lowliness, meekness, modesty

hum·bly \'həm-blē\ *adv* ♦ : in a humble manner
  ♦ lowly, meekly, modestly, sheepishly

¹**hum·bug** \'həm-ˌbəg\ *n* **1** ♦ : something designed to deceive and mislead : HOAX **2** ♦ : language, conduct, or an idea that is absurd or contrary to good sense : NONSENSE **3** ♦ : a willfully false, deceptive, or insincere person
  ♦ [1] counterfeit, fake, forgery, hoax, phony, sham ♦ [2] bunk, claptrap, drivel, fiddlesticks, folly, foolishness, fudge, hogwash, nonsense, piffle, rot, silliness, slush, stupidity, trash ♦ [3] charlatan, fake, fraud, hoaxer, mountebank, phony, pretender, quack

²**humbug** *vb* **hum·bugged; hum·bug·ging** ♦ : to cause to accept as true or valid what is false or invalid : DECEIVE
  ♦ beguile, bluff, cozen, deceive, delude, dupe, fool, gull, have, hoax, hoodwink, misinform, mislead, string along, take in, trick

hum·ding·er \'həm-'diŋ-ər\ *n* : a person or thing of striking excellence

hum·drum \'həm-ˌdrəm\ *adj* ♦ : tediously uniform or unvarying : MONOTONOUS, DULL — **humdrum** *n*
  ♦ drab, dull, flat, monotonous, ponderous, stuffy, uninteresting

hu·mer·us \'hyü-mə-rəs\ *n, pl* **hu·meri** \'hyü-mə-ˌrī, -ˌrē\ : the long bone extending from shoulder to elbow

hu·mid \'hyü-məd, 'yü-\ *adj* ♦ : containing or characterized by perceptible moisture — **hu·mid·ly** *adv*
  ♦ muggy, sticky, sultry *Ant* dry

hu·mid·i·fy \hyü-'mi-də-ˌfī\ *vb* **-fied; -fy·ing** : to make humid — **hu·mid·i·fi·ca·tion** \-ˌmi-də-fə-'kā-shən\ *n* — **hu·mid·i·fi·er** \-'mi-də-ˌfī-ər\ *n*

hu·mid·i·ty \hyü-'mi-də-tē, yü-\ *n, pl* **-ties** : the amount of atmospheric moisture

hu·mi·dor \'hyü-mə-ˌdȯr, 'yü-\ *n* : a case (as for storing cigars) in which the air is kept properly humidified

hu·mil·i·ate \hyü-'mi-lē-ˌāt, yü-\ *vb* **-at·ed; -at·ing** ♦ : to injure the self-respect of — **hu·mil·i·at·ing·ly** *adv* — **hu·mil·i·a·tion** \-ˌmi-lē-'ā-shən\ *n*
  ♦ abase, debase, degrade, demean, discredit, disgrace, dishonor (*or* dishonour), humble, lower, shame, smirch, take down

hu·mil·i·ty \hyü-'mi-lə-tē, yü-\ *n* ♦ : the quality or state of being humble
  ♦ humbleness, lowliness, meekness, modesty *Ant* arrogance,

conceit, egoism, egotism, haughtiness, pretense, pretension, pretentiousness, pride, superiority

hum·mer \'hə-mər\ *n* : one that hums

hum·ming·bird \'hə-miŋ-ˌbərd\ *n* : any of a family of tiny brightly colored American birds related to the swifts

hum·mock \'hə-mək\ *n* : a rounded mound : KNOLL — **hum·mocky** \-mə-kē\ *adj*

hum·mus \'hə-məs, 'hu̇-\ *n* : a paste of pureed chickpeas usu. mixed with sesame oil or paste

hu·mon·gous \hyü-'məŋ-gəs, -'mäŋ-\ *adj* : extremely large ⟨a ~ stadium⟩

¹**hu·mor** *or Can and Brit* **hu·mour** \'hyü-mər, 'yü-\ *n* **1** : TEMPERAMENT **2** ♦ : a conscious state of mind or predominant emotion : MOOD **3** : WHIM **4** : a quality that appeals to a sense of the ludicrous or incongruous; *also* : a keen perception of the ludicrous or incongruous **5** ♦ : comical or amusing entertainment
  ♦ [2] cheer, frame, mode, mood, spirit, temper ♦ [5] comedy, farce, slapstick

²**humor** *or Can and Brit* **humour** *vb* ♦ : to comply with the wishes or mood of ⟨~ed their boss⟩
  ♦ cater to, gratify, indulge

hu·mor·ist \'hyü-mə-rist, 'yü-\ *n* ♦ : a person specializing in or noted for humor
  ♦ card, comedian, comic, jester, joker, wag, wit

hu·mor·less *or Can and Brit* **hu·mour·less** \'hyü-mər-ləs, 'yü-\ *adj* **1** ♦ : lacking a sense of humor **2** : lacking humorous characteristics — **hu·mor·less·ly** *adv* — **hu·mor·less·ness** *n*
  ♦ earnest, grave, serious, severe, sober, solemn, staid, unsmiling, weighty

hu·mor·ous \'hyü-mə-rəs, 'yü-\ *adj* **1** ♦ : full of or characterized by humor **2** ♦ : indicating or expressive of a sense of humor — **hu·mor·ous·ly** *adv*
  ♦ [1] antic, comic, comical, droll, farcical, funny, hilarious, hysterical, laughable, ludicrous, ridiculous, riotous, risible, screaming, uproarious ♦ [2] clever, facetious, jocular, smart, witty

hu·mor·ous·ness *n* : the quality or state of being humorous

hu·mour *Can and Brit var of* HUMOR

hump \'həmp\ *n* **1** : a rounded protuberance (as on the back of a camel) **2** : a difficult phase or obstacle ⟨over the ~⟩ — **humped** *adj*

hump·back \'həmp-ˌbak; *1 also* -'bak\ *n* **1** : HUNCHBACK **2** : HUMPBACK WHALE — **hump·backed** *adj*

humpback whale *n* : a large baleen whale having very long flippers

hu·mus \'hyü-məs, 'yü-\ *n* : the dark organic part of soil formed from decaying matter

Hun \'hən\ *n* : a member of an Asian people that gained control of a large part of Europe about A.D. 450

¹**hunch** \'hənch\ *vb* **1** : to thrust oneself forward **2** ♦ : to assume or cause to assume a bent or crooked posture
  ♦ crouch, huddle, squat

²**hunch** *n* **1** : PUSH **2** : a strong intuitive feeling about what will happen

hunch·back \'hənch-ˌbak\ *n* : a person with a crooked back; *also* : a back with a hump — **hunch·backed** *adj*

hun·dred \'hən-drəd\ *n, pl* **hundreds** *or* **hundred** : 10 times 10 — **hundred** *adj* — **hun·dredth** \-drədth\ *adj or n*

hun·dred·weight \-ˌwāt\ *n, pl* **hundredweight** *or* **hundredweights** : a unit of measurement typically equal to 100 pounds

¹**hung** *past and past part of* HANG

²**hung** *adj* : unable to reach a decision or verdict ⟨a ~ jury⟩

Hung *abbr* Hungarian; Hungary

Hun·gar·i·an \ˌhəŋ-'ger-ē-ən\ *n* **1** : a native or inhabitant of Hungary **2** : the language of the Hungarians — **Hungarian** *adj*

¹**hun·ger** \'həŋ-gər\ *n* **1** : a craving or urgent need for food **2** ♦ : a strong desire
  ♦ appetite, craving, desire, drive, hankering, itch, longing, lust, passion, thirst, urge, yearning, yen ♦ appetite, ardor, avidity, eagerness, enthusiasm, excitement, impatience, keenness, thirst

²**hunger** *vb* **1** : to feel or suffer hunger **2** ♦ : to have an eager desire
  ♦ ache, die, hanker, itch, long, pant, pine, sigh, thirst, yearn ♦ *usu* **hunger for** ache for, covet, crave, desire, die for, hanker for, long for, lust (for *or* after), pine for, repine for, thirst for, want, wish for, yearn for

hung·over \'həŋ-'ō-vər\ *adj* : having a hangover

hun·gry \'həŋ-grē\ adj **1 ♦** : feeling hunger **2 ♦** : marked by enthusiastic or impatient desire or interest — **hun·gri·ly** adv

  ♦ [1] empty, famished **Ant** full, satisfied ♦ [2] agog, anxious, ardent, athirst, avid, crazy, eager, enthusiastic, gung ho, hot, keen, nuts, raring, solicitous, thirsty, voracious

hung up adj **1** : DELAYED **2** : ENTHUSIASTIC; also : PREOCCU-PIED **3** : anxiously nervous

hunk \'həŋk\ n **1 ♦** : a large piece **2** : an attractive well-built man — **hunky** adj

  ♦ blob, chunk, clod, clump, glob, gob, lump, nub, wad

hun·ker \'həŋ-kər\ vb **1** : CROUCH, SQUAT — usu. used with *down* **2** : to settle in for a sustained period — used with *down*

hun·ky–do·ry \,həŋ-kē-'dōr-ē\ adj : quite satisfactory : FINE

¹hunt \'hənt\ vb **1** : to pursue for food or in sport; also : to take part in a hunt **2 ♦** : to try to find : SEEK **3** : to drive or chase esp. by harrying **4** : to traverse or go over in search of prey or quar-ry **5 ♦** : to find, uncover, or obtain after diligent search — used with *through*, *up*, or *down* — **hunt·er** n

  ♦ [2] cast about, forage, pursue, quest, search (for or out), seek ♦ usu **hunt through** [5] dig, dredge, rake, ransack, rifle, rum-mage, scour, search ♦ usu **hunt down** or **hunt up** [5] detect, determine, dig up, discover, ferret out, find, hit on, locate, track down

²hunt n : an act, practice, or instance of hunting

Hun·ting·ton's disease \'hən-tiŋ-tənz-\ n : a chorea that usu. begins in middle age and leads to dementia

hunt·ress \'hən-trəs\ n : a woman who hunts game

hunts·man \'hənts-mən\ n **1** : HUNTER **2** : a person who man-ages a hunt and looks after the hounds

hur·dle \'hərd-ᵊl\ n **1** : a barrier to leap over in a race **2** : some-thing that impedes progress or achievement : OBSTACLE — **hur·dle** vb — **hur·dler** n

hur·dy–gur·dy \,hər-dē-'gər-dē, 'hər-dē-,gər-dē\ n, pl -**gur·dies** : a musical instrument in which the sound is produced by turning a crank

hurl \'hərl\ vb **1** : to move or cause to move vigorously **2** : to throw down with violence **3 a ♦** : to throw forcefully : FLING **b** : to throw (a baseball) to a batter : PITCH — **hurl** n — **hurl·er** n

  ♦ cast, catapult, chuck, dash, fire, fling, heave, hurtle, launch, peg, pelt, pitch, sling, throw, toss

hur·ly–bur·ly \,hər-lē-'bər-lē\ n : a state of commotion, excite-ment, or violent disturbance : UPROAR

Hu·ron \'hyùr-ən, 'hyùr-,än\ n, pl **Hurons** or **Huron** : a mem-ber of a confederacy of Indigenous peoples formerly living be-tween Georgian Bay and Lake Ontario; also : the language of the Huron people

hur·rah \hù-'rò, -'rä\ also **hur·ray** \hù-'rā\ interj — used to ex-press joy, approval, or encouragement

hur·ri·cane \'hər-ə-,kān\ n : a tropical cyclone with winds of 74 miles (118 kilometers) per hour or greater that is usu. accompa-nied by rain, thunder, and lightning

hur·ried·ly \'hər-əd-lē\ adv **♦** : in a hurried manner

  ♦ cursorily, hastily, headlong, pell-mell, precipitately, rashly

¹hur·ry \'hər-ē\ vb **hur·ried**; **hur·ry·ing** **1 ♦** : to carry or cause to go with haste **2** : to impel to a greater speed **3 ♦** : to move or act with haste — **hur·ried·ness** n

  ♦ [1, 3] accelerate, hasten, quicken, rush, speed (up), step up, whisk **Ant** decelerate, retard, slow (down) ♦ [3] course, dash, fly, hasten, hurtle, hustle, pelt, race, rocket, run, rush, shoot, speed, step, tear, zip, zoom **Ant** crawl, creep, poke

²hurry n **♦** : extreme haste or eagerness

  ♦ celerity, fastness, fleetness, haste, quickness, rapidity, speed, swiftness, velocity ♦ haste, hustle, precipitation, rush **Ant** delib-erateness, deliberation

¹hurt \'hərt\ vb **hurt**; **hurt·ing** **1 ♦** : to feel or cause to feel phys-ical or emotional pain **2 ♦** : to do harm to : DAMAGE **3** : OF-FEND **4** : HAMPER **5** : to be in need — usu. used with *for* — **hurt** adj

  ♦ [1] agonize, bleed, feel, grieve, mourn, sorrow, suffer ♦ [1] ache, pain, smart ♦ [2] damage, harm, injure, wound ♦ [2] blemish, break, cripple, damage, deface, disfigure, flaw, harm, injure, mar, spoil, vitiate

²hurt n **1** : a bodily injury or wound **2** : SUFFERING **3 ♦** : physi-cal or mental damage : HARM

  ♦ damage, detriment, harm, injury

hurt·ful \'hərt-fəl\ adj **♦** : causing injury, detriment, or suffering — **hurt·ful·ness** n

  ♦ adverse, bad, baleful, baneful, damaging, deleterious, detri-mental, evil, harmful, ill, injurious, mischievous, noxious, perni-cious, prejudicial

hur·tle \'hərt-ᵊl\ vb **hur·tled**; **hur·tling** **1 ♦** : to move rapidly or forcefully **2** : to throw forcefully : HURL, FLING

  ♦ dash, fly, hasten, hurry, rocket, run, rush, speed, tear, zip, zoom

¹hus·band \'həz-bənd\ n : a male partner in a marriage

²husband vb : to manage prudently

hus·band·man \'həz-bənd-mən\ n : FARMER

hus·band·ry \'həz-bən-drē\ n **1 ♦** : the control or judicious use of resources **2** : AGRICULTURE **3** : the production and care of domestic animals

  ♦ economy, frugality, providence, thrift

¹hush \'həsh\ vb **1 ♦** : to make or become quiet or calm **2** : SUP-PRESS

  ♦ calm (down), cool (off or down), quiet, settle (down) ♦ mute, quell, settle, silence, still

²hush n **♦** : a silence or calm esp. following noise

  ♦ calm, calmness, peace, placidity, quiet, quietness, repose, se-renity, still, stillness, tranquility

hushed \'həsht\ adj **1 ♦** : free of noise or agitation **2 ♦** : marked by secrecy or caution

  ♦ [1] calm, halcyon, peaceful, placid, quiet, serene, still, tran-quil, untroubled ♦ [1] muted, noiseless, quiet, silent, soundless, still ♦ [2] confidential, inside, intimate, private, secret

hush–hush \'həsh-,həsh\ adj : SECRET, CONFIDENTIAL

¹husk \'həsk\ n **1** : a usu. thin dry outer covering of a seed or fruit **2 ♦** : an outer layer : SHELL

  ♦ armor, capsule, case, casing, cocoon, cover, housing, jacket, pod, sheath, shell

²husk vb **♦** : to strip the husk from — **husk·er** n

  ♦ bark, flay, hull, peel, shell, skin

¹hus·ky \'həs-kē\ adj **hus·ki·er**; **-est ♦** : hoarse with or as if with emotion — **hus·ki·ly** \-kə-lē\ adv — **hus·ki·ness** \-kē-nəs\ n

  ♦ coarse, gravelly, gruff, hoarse, scratchy, throaty

²husky adj **1 ♦** : strongly formed or constructed : BURLY **2** : LARGE

  ♦ beefy, brawny, burly

³husky n, pl **huskies** : a heavy-coated working dog of the New World arctic region

hus·sar \(,)hə-'zär\ n : a member of any of various European cavalry units

hus·sy \'hə-zē, -sē\ n, pl **hussies** **1** : a lewd or brazen wom-an **2** : a pert or mischievous girl

hus·tings \'həs-tiŋz\ n pl : a place where political campaign speeches are made; also : the proceedings in an election campaign

¹hus·tle \'hə-səl\ vb **hus·tled**; **hus·tling** **1** : JOSTLE, SHOVE **2** : to move or act quickly : HASTEN, HURRY **3** : to work energeti-cally **4 ♦** : to sell something to or obtain something from by energetic and esp. underhanded activity

  ♦ bleed, cheat, chisel, cozen, defraud, fleece, mulct, rook, short-change, skin, squeeze, stick, sting, swindle, victimize

²hustle n **1 ♦** : energetic activity **2 ♦** : an act or instance of fraud

  ♦ [1] haste, hurry, precipitation, rush ♦ [2] racket, swindle

hus·tler \'həs-lər\ n **♦** : one that hustles

  ♦ go-getter, live wire, powerhouse, self-starter

hut \'hət\ n **♦** : an often small and temporary dwelling of simple construction : SHACK

  ♦ cabin, camp, hutch, shack, shanty

hutch \'həch\ n **1** : a chest or compartment for storage **2 ♦** : a cupboard usu. surmounted with open shelves **3** : a pen or coop for an animal **4** : a small and often temporary dwelling : HUT

  ♦ buffet, cabinet, closet, cupboard, locker, sideboard

huz·zah or **huz·za** \(,)hə-'zä\ n : a shout of acclaim — often used interjectionally to express joy or approbation

HV abbr **1** high velocity **2** high voltage

HVAC abbr heating, ventilating and air-conditioning

hvy abbr heavy

HW *abbr* hot water

hwy *abbr* highway

hy·a·cinth \'hī-ə-(ˌ)sinth\ *n* : a bulbous Mediterranean herb related to the lilies that is widely grown for its spikes of fragrant bell-shaped flowers

¹**hy·brid** \'hī-brəd\ *n* **1** ♦ : an offspring of genetically differing parents (as members of different breeds or species) **2** : one of mixed origin or composition — **hy·brid·i·za·tion** \ˌhī-brə-də-'zā-shən\ *n* — **hy·brid·ize** \'hī-brə-ˌdīz\ *vb* — **hy·brid·iz·er** *n*

♦ cross, mongrel

²**hybrid** *adj* ♦ : of, relating to, or being a hybrid

♦ mixed, mongrel

hy·dra \'hī-drə\ *n* : any of numerous small tubular freshwater coelenterates that are polyps having at one end a mouth surrounded by tentacles

hy·dran·gea \hī-'drān-jə\ *n* : any of a genus of shrubs related to the currants and grown for their showy clusters of white or tinted flowers

hy·drant \'hī-drənt\ *n* : a pipe with a valve and spout at which water may be drawn from a main pipe

hy·drate \'hī-ˌdrāt\ *n* : a compound formed by union of water with some other substance — **hydrate** *vb*

hy·drau·lic \hī-'drȯ-lik\ *adj* **1** : operated, moved, or effected by means of water **2** : of or relating to hydraulics **3** : operated by the resistance offered or the pressure transmitted when a quantity of liquid is forced through a small orifice or through a tube **4** : hardening or setting under water

hy·drau·lics \-liks\ *n* : a science that deals with practical applications of liquid (as water) in motion

hydro \'hī-drō\ *n* : HYDROPOWER

hy·dro·car·bon \ˌhī-drō-'kär-bən\ *n* : an organic compound containing only carbon and hydrogen

hy·dro·ceph·a·lus \ˌhī-drō-'se-fə-ləs\ *n* : abnormal increase in the amount of fluid in the cranial cavity accompanied by enlargement of the skull and atrophy of the brain

hy·dro·chlo·ric acid \ˌhī-drə-'klȯr-ik-\ *n* : a sharp-smelling corrosive acid used in the laboratory and in industry and present in dilute form in gastric juice

hy·dro·dy·nam·ics \ˌhī-drō-dī-'na-miks\ *n* : a science that deals with the motion of fluids and the forces acting on moving bodies immersed in fluids — **hy·dro·dy·nam·ic** *adj*

hy·dro·elec·tric \ˌhī-drō-i-'lek-trik\ *adj* : of or relating to production of electricity by waterpower — **hy·dro·elec·tric·i·ty** \-ˌlek-'tri-sə-tē\ *n*

hy·dro·foil \'hī-drə-ˌfȯi(-ə)l\ *n* : a boat that has fins attached to the bottom by struts for lifting the hull clear of the water to allow faster speeds

hy·dro·gen \'hī-drə-jən\ *n* : a gaseous colorless odorless highly flammable chemical element that is the lightest of the elements — **hy·drog·e·nous** \hī-'drä-jə-nəs\ *adj*

hy·dro·ge·nate \hī-'drä-jə-ˌnāt, 'hī-drə-\ *vb* **-nat·ed; -nat·ing** : to combine or treat with hydrogen; *esp* : to add hydrogen to the molecule of — **hy·dro·ge·na·tion** \hī-ˌdrä-jə-'nā-shən, ˌhī-drə-\ *n*

hydrogen bomb *n* : a bomb whose violent explosive power is due to the sudden release of atomic energy resulting from the fusion of light nuclei (as of hydrogen atoms)

hydrogen peroxide *n* : an unstable compound of hydrogen and oxygen used esp. as an oxidizing and bleaching agent, an antiseptic, and a propellant

hy·dro·graph·ic \ˌhī-drə-'gra-fik\ *adj* : of or relating to the description and study of bodies of water — **hy·drog·ra·pher** *n* — **hy·drog·ra·phy** \hī-'drä-grə-fē\ *n*

hy·drol·o·gy \hī-'drä-lə-jē\ *n* : a science dealing with the properties, distribution, and circulation of water — **hy·dro·log·ic** \ˌhī-drə-'lä-jik\ *or* **hy·dro·log·i·cal** \-ji-kəl\ *adj* — **hy·drol·o·gist** \hī-'drä-lə-jist\ *n*

hy·dro·ly·sis \hī-'drä-lə-səs\ *n* : a chemical decomposition involving the addition of the elements of water

hy·drom·e·ter \hī-'drä-mə-tər\ *n* : a floating instrument for determining specific gravities of liquids and hence the strength (as of alcoholic liquors)

hy·dro·pho·bia \ˌhī-drə-'fō-bē-ə\ *n* : RABIES

hy·dro·phone \'hī-drə-ˌfōn\ *n* : an underwater listening device

¹**hy·dro·plane** \'hī-drə-ˌplān\ *n* **1** : a powerboat designed for racing that skims the surface of the water **2** : SEAPLANE

²**hydroplane** *vb* : to skid on a wet road due to loss of contact between the tires and road

hy·dro·pon·ics \ˌhī-drə-'pä-niks\ *n* : the growing of plants in nutrient solutions — **hy·dro·pon·ic** *adj*

hy·dro·pow·er \'hī-drə-ˌpau̇(-ə)r\ *n* : hydroelectric power

hy·dro·sphere \'hī-drə-ˌsfir\ *n* : the water (as vapor or lakes) of the earth

hy·dro·stat·ic \ˌhī-drə-'sta-tik\ *adj* : of or relating to fluids at rest or to the pressures they exert or transmit

hy·dro·ther·a·py \ˌhī-drə-'ther-ə-pē\ *n* : the use of water esp. externally in the treatment of disease or disability

hy·dro·ther·mal \ˌhī-drə-'thər-məl\ *adj* : of or relating to hot water

hy·drous \'hī-drəs\ *adj* : containing water

hy·drox·ide \hī-'dräk-ˌsīd\ *n* **1** : a negatively charged ion consisting of one atom of oxygen and one atom of hydrogen **2** : a compound of hydroxide with an element or group

hy·e·na \hī-'ē-nə\ *n* : any of several large doglike carnivorous mammals of Asia and Africa

hy·giene \'hī-ˌjēn\ *n* **1** : a science concerned with establishing and maintaining good health **2** : conditions or practices conducive to health — **hy·gien·i·cal·ly** \-ni-k(ə-)lē\ *adv* — **hy·gien·ist** \hī-'jē-nist, 'hī-ˌjē-, hī-'je-\ *n*

hy·gien·ic \hī-'je-nik, -'jē-\ *adj* ♦ : having or showing good hygiene

♦ aseptic, sanitary, sterile

hy·grom·e·ter \hī-'grä-mə-tər\ *n* : any of several instruments for measuring the humidity of the atmosphere

hy·gro·scop·ic \ˌhī-grə-'skä-pik\ *adj* : readily taking up and retaining moisture

hying *pres part of* HIE

hy·men \'hī-mən\ *n* : a fold of mucous membrane partly closing the opening of the vagina

hy·me·ne·al \ˌhī-mə-'nē-əl\ *adj* : NUPTIAL

hymn \'him\ *n* ♦ : a song of praise esp. to God — **hymn** *vb*

♦ anthem, canticle, carol, chorale, psalm, spiritual

hym·nal \'him-nəl\ *n* : a book of hymns

hyp *abbr* hypothesis; hypothetical

¹**hype** \'hīp\ *vb* **hyped; hyp·ing** **1** : STIMULATE — usu. used with *up* **2** : INCREASE — **hyped—up** *adj*

²**hype** *vb* **hyped; hyping** **1** : DECEIVE **2** : PUBLICIZE

³**hype** *n* **1** : DECEPTION, PUT-ON **2** : PUBLICITY

hy·per \'hī-pər\ *adj* **1** : HIGH-STRUNG, EXCITABLE **2** : extremely active

hy·per·acid·i·ty \ˌhī-pər-ə-'si-də-tē\ *n* : the condition of containing excessive acid esp. in the stomach — **hy·per·ac·id** \-'a-səd\ *adj*

hy·per·ac·tive \-'ak-tiv\ *adj* ♦ : excessively or pathologically active — **hy·per·ac·tiv·i·ty** \-ˌak-'ti-və-tē\ *n*

♦ agitated, feverish, frenzied, heated, hectic, overactive, overwrought

hy·per·bar·ic \ˌhī-pər-'bar-ik\ *adj* : of, relating to, or utilizing greater than normal pressure (as of oxygen)

hy·per·bo·la \hī-'pər-bə-lə\ *n, pl* **-las** *or* **-lae** \-(ˌ)lē\ : a curve formed by the intersection of a double right circular cone with a plane that cuts both halves of the cone — **hy·per·bol·ic** \ˌhī-pər-'bä-lik\ *adj*

hy·per·bo·le \hī-'pər-bə-(ˌ)lē\ *n* ♦ : extravagant exaggeration used as a figure of speech

♦ caricature, elaboration, embellishment, exaggeration, magnification, overstatement, padding

hy·per·crit·i·cal \ˌhī-pər-'kri-ti-kəl\ *adj* ♦ : excessively critical — **hy·per·crit·i·cal·ly** \-k(ə-)lē\ *adv*

♦ captious, carping, critical, overcritical

hy·per·drive \'hī-pər-ˌdrīv\ *n* : a state of extremely heightened activity

hy·per·ex·tend \ˌhī-pər-ik-'stend\ *vb* : to extend beyond the normal range of motion — **hy·per·ex·ten·sion** \-'sten-shən\ *n*

hy·per·gly·ce·mia \ˌhī-pər-glī-'sē-mē-ə\ *n* : excess of sugar in the blood — **hy·per·gly·ce·mic** \-mik\ *adj*

hy·per·ki·net·ic \-kə-'ne-tik\ *adj* : characterized by fast-paced or frenetic activity

hy·per·link \'hī-pər-ˌliŋk\ *n* : a connecting element (as highlighted text) between one place in a hypertext or hypermedia document and another

hy·per·me·dia \'hī-pər-ˌmē-dē-ə\ *n* : a database format offering direct access to text, sound, or images related to that on display

hy·per·opia \ˌhī-pə-'rō-pē-ə\ *n* : a condition in which visual images come to focus behind the retina resulting esp. in defective vision for near objects — **hy·per·opic** \-'rō-pik, -'rä-\ *adj*

hy·per·sen·si·tive \-'sen-sə-tiv\ *adj* **1** : excessively or abnormally sensitive **2** : abnormally susceptible physiologically to a specific agent (as a drug) — **hy·per·sen·si·tive·ness** *n* — **hy·per·sen·si·tiv·i·ty** \-ˌsen-sə-'ti-və-tē\ *n*

hy·per·ten·sion \\'hī-pər-ˌten-chən\ *n* : high blood pressure — **hy·per·ten·sive** \ˌhī-pər-'ten-siv\ *adj or n*

hy·per·text \'hī-pər-ˌtekst\ *n* : a database format in which information related to that on display can be accessed directly from the display

hy·per·thy·roid·ism \ˌhī-pər-'thī-ˌrȯi-ˌdi-zəm\ *n* : excessive activity of the thyroid gland; *also* : the resulting bodily condition — **hy·per·thy·roid** \-'thī-ˌrȯid\ *adj*

hy·per·tro·phy \hī-'pər-trə-fē\ *n, pl* **-phies** : excessive development of a body part — **hy·per·tro·phic** \ˌhī-pər-'trō-fik\ *adj* — **hypertrophy** *vb*

hy·per·ven·ti·late \ˌhī-pər-'ven-tə-ˌlāt\ *vb* : to breathe rapidly and deeply esp. to the point of losing an abnormal amount of carbon dioxide from the blood — **hy·per·ven·ti·la·tion** \-ˌven-tə-'lā-shən\ *n*

hy·phen \'hī-fən\ *n* : a punctuation mark - used esp. to divide or to compound words or word parts — **hyphen** *vb*

hy·phen·ate \'hī-fə-ˌnāt\ *vb* **-at·ed; -at·ing** : to connect or divide with a hyphen — **hy·phen·ation** \ˌhī-fə-'nā-shən\ *n*

hyp·no·sis \hip-'nō-səs\ *n, pl* **-no·ses** \-ˌsēz\ : an induced state that resembles sleep and in which the subject is responsive to suggestions of the inducer (**hyp·no·tist** \'hip-nə-tist\) — **hyp·no·tism** \'hip-nə-ˌti-zəm\ *n*

¹**hyp·not·ic** \hip-'nä-tik\ *adj* **1** ♦ : inducing sleep **2** : of or relating to hypnosis or hypnotism **3** : readily holding the attention — **hyp·not·i·cal·ly** \-ti-k(ə-)lē\ *adv*

♦ drowsy, narcotic, opiate, slumberous *Ant* stimulant

²**hypnotic** *n* : a sleep-inducing drug

hyp·no·tise *chiefly Brit var of* HYPNOTIZE

hyp·no·tize \'hip-nə-ˌtīz\ *vb* **1** : to induce hypnosis in **2** ♦ : to dazzle or overcome by or as if by suggestion — **hyp·no·tiz·able** \'hip-nə-ˌtī-zə-bəl\ *adj*

♦ arrest, enchant, enthrall, fascinate, grip, mesmerize

hy·po \'hī-pō\ *n, pl* **hypos** : SODIUM THIOSULFATE

hy·po·al·ler·gen·ic \ˌhī-pō-ˌa-lər-'je-nik\ *adj* : having little likelihood of causing an allergic response

hy·po·cen·ter \'hī-pə-ˌsen-tər\ *n* : the point of origin of an earthquake

hy·po·chon·dria \ˌhī-pə-'kän-drē-ə\ *n* : depression of mind often centered on imaginary physical ailments — **hy·po·chon·dri·ac** \-drē-ˌak\ *adj or n*

hy·poc·ri·sy \hi-'pä-krə-sē\ *n, pl* **-sies** ♦ : a feigning to be what one is not or to believe what one does not; *esp* : the false assumption of an appearance of virtue or religion

♦ cant, dissimulation, insincerity, piety *Ant* genuineness, sincerity

hyp·o·crit·i·cal \ˌhi-pə-'kri-ti-kəl\ *adj* ♦ : characterized by hypocrisy; *also* : being a hypocrite — **hyp·o·crite** \'hi-pə-ˌkrit\ *n* — **hyp·o·crit·i·cal·ly** \-k(ə-)lē\ *adv*

♦ artificial, double-dealing, feigned, insincere, left-handed, mealy, mealymouthed, two-faced, unctuous

¹**hy·po·der·mic** \ˌhī-pə-'dər-mik\ *adj* : administered by or used in making an injection beneath the skin

²**hypodermic** *n* : a small syringe with a hollow needle for injecting material into or through the skin : HYPODERMIC SYRINGE; *also* : an injection made with this

hypodermic needle *n* **1** : NEEDLE 3 **2** : a small syringe with a hollow needle for injecting material into or through the skin : HYPODERMIC SYRINGE

hypodermic syringe *n* ♦ : a small syringe with a hollow needle for injecting material into or through the skin

♦ needle, syringe

hy·po·gly·ce·mia \ˌhī-pō-glī-'sē-mē-ə\ *n* : abnormal decrease of sugar in the blood — **hy·po·gly·ce·mic** \-mik\ *adj*

hy·pot·e·nuse \hī-'pät-ᵊn-ˌüs, -ˌyüs, -ˌüz, -ˌyüz\ *n* : the side of a triangle having a right angle that is opposite the right angle; *also* : its length

hy·po·thal·a·mus \ˌhī-pō-'tha-lə-məs\ *n* : a part of the brain that lies beneath the thalamus and is a control center for the autonomic nervous system

hy·poth·e·sis \hī-'pä-thə-səs\ *n, pl* **-e·ses** \-ˌsēz\ ♦ : an assumption made esp. in order to test its logical or empirical consequences

♦ conjecture, proposition, supposition, theory

hy·poth·e·size \-ˌsīz\ *vb* **-sized; -siz·ing** : to adopt as a hypothesis

hy·po·thet·i·cal \ˌhī-pə-'the-ti-kəl\ *adj* ♦ : being or involving a hypothesis — **hy·po·thet·i·cal·ly** \-k(ə-)lē\ *adv*

♦ conjectural, speculative, theoretical

hy·po·thy·roid·ism \ˌhī-pō-'thī-ˌrȯi-ˌdi-zəm\ *n* : deficient activity of the thyroid gland; *also* : a resultant lowered metabolic rate and general loss of vigor — **hy·po·thy·roid** *adj*

hys·sop \'hi-səp\ *n* : a European mint sometimes used as a potherb

hys·ter·ec·to·my \ˌhis-tə-'rek-tə-mē\ *n, pl* **-mies** : surgical removal of the uterus

hys·te·ria \hi-'ster-ē-ə, -'stir-\ *n* **1** : a nervous disorder marked esp. by defective emotional control **2** ♦ : unmanageable fear or outburst of emotion — **hys·ter·ic** \-'ster-ik\ *n* — **hys·ter·i·cal·ly** \-k(ə-)lē\ *adv*

♦ agitation, delirium, distraction, frenzy, furor, fury, rage, rampage, uproar

hys·ter·i·cal \-'ster-i-kəl\ *also* **hysteric** *adj* **1** : of, relating to, or marked by hysteria **2** ♦ : exhibiting unrestrained emotionalism

♦ agitated, delirious, distraught, frantic, frenzied

hys·ter·ics \-'ster-iks\ *n pl* : a fit of uncontrollable laughter or crying

Hz *abbr* hertz

¹**i** \'ī\ *n, pl* **i's** *or* **is** \'īz\ *often cap* : the 9th letter of the English alphabet

²**i** *abbr, often cap* island; isle

³**i** *symbol* imaginary unit

¹**I** \'ī, ə\ *pron* : the one speaking or writing

²**I** *abbr* interstate

³**I** *symbol* iodine

Ia *or* **IA** *abbr* Iowa

-ial *adj suffix* : ¹-AL ⟨manor*ial*⟩

iamb \'ī-ˌam\ *or* **iam·bus** \ī-'am-bəs\ *n, pl* **iambs** \'ī-ˌamz\ *or* **iam·bus·es** : a metrical foot of one unaccented syllable followed by one accented syllable — **iam·bic** \ī-'am-bik\ *adj or n*

-i·at·ric \ē-'a-trik\ *also* **-i·at·ri·cal** \-tri-kəl\ *adj comb form* : of or relating to (such) medical treatment or healing ⟨ped*iatric*⟩

-i·at·rics \ē-'a-triks\ *n pl comb form* : medical treatment ⟨ped*iatrics*⟩

ib *or* **ibid** *abbr* ibidem

ibex \'ī-ˌbeks\ *n, pl* **ibex** *or* **ibex·es** : any of several Old World wild goats with large curved horns

ibi·dem \'i-bə-ˌdem, i-'bī-dəm\ *adv* : in the same place

ibis \'ī-bəs\ *n, pl* **ibis** *or* **ibis·es** : any of various wading birds related to the herons but having a downwardly curved bill

ibu·pro·fen \ˌī-byü-'prō-fən\ *n* : a nonsteroidal anti-inflammatory drug used to relieve pain and fever

IC \ˌī-'sē\ *n* : INTEGRATED CIRCUIT

¹**-ic** \ik\ *adj suffix* **1** : of, relating to, or having the form of : being ⟨panoram*ic*⟩ **2** : related to, derived from, or containing ⟨alcohol*ic*⟩ **3** : in the manner of : like that of : characteristic of **4** : associated or dealing with : utilizing ⟨electron*ic*⟩ **5** : characterized by : exhibiting ⟨nostalg*ic*⟩ : affected with ⟨allerg*ic*⟩ **6** : caused by **7** : tending to produce ⟨analges*ic*⟩

²**-ic** *n suffix* : one having the character or nature of : one belonging to or associated with : one exhibiting or affected by : one that produces

-i·cal \i-kəl\ *adj suffix* : -IC ⟨symmetri*cal*⟩ ⟨geologi*cal*⟩ — **-i·cal·ly** \i-kə-lē, -klē\ *adv suffix*

ICBM \ˌī-ˌsē-(ˌ)bē-'em\ *n, pl* **ICBM's** *or* **ICBMs** \-'emz\ : an intercontinental ballistic missile

ICC *abbr* Interstate Commerce Commission

¹**ice** \'īs\ *n* **1** : frozen water **2** : a substance resembling ice **3** : a state of coldness (as from formality or reserve) **4** : a flavored frozen dessert; *esp* : one containing no milk or cream

²**ice** *vb* **iced; ic·ing 1** : FREEZE **2** : CHILL **3** : to cover with or as if with icing

ice age *n* : a time of widespread glaciation

ice bag *n* : a waterproof bag to hold ice for local application of cold to the body

ice·berg \'īs-ˌbərg\ *n* : a large floating mass of ice broken off from a glacier

iceberg lettuce *n* : any of various crisp light green lettuces that form a compact head like a cabbage

ice·boat \'īs-ˌbōt\ *n* : a boatlike frame on runners propelled on ice by sails

ice·bound \-ˌbaùnd\ *adj* : surrounded, obstructed, or covered by ice

ice·box \-ˌbäks\ *n* : REFRIGERATOR

ice·break·er \-ˌbrā-kər\ *n* : a ship equipped to make a channel through ice

ice cap *n* : a glacier forming on relatively level land and flowing outward from its center

ice cream *n* : a frozen food containing sweetened or flavored cream or butterfat

ice hockey *n* : a game in which two teams of ice-skating players try to shoot a puck into the opponent's goal

ice·house \'īs-ˌhaùs\ *n* : a building in which ice is made or stored

Ice·land·er \-ˌlan-dər, -lən-\ *n* : a native or inhabitant of Iceland

¹**Ice·lan·dic** \īs-'lan-dik\ *adj* : of, relating to, or characteristic of Iceland, the Icelanders, or their language

²**Icelandic** *n* : the language of Iceland

ice·man \'īs-ˌman\ *n* : one who sells or delivers ice

ice milk *n* : a sweetened frozen food made of skim milk

ice pick *n* : a hand tool ending in a spike for chipping ice

ice–skate \'īs-ˌskāt\ *vb* : to skate on ice — **ice–skater** *n*

ice storm *n* : a storm in which falling rain freezes on contact

ice water *n* : chilled or iced water esp. for drinking

ich·thy·ol·o·gy \ˌik-thē-'ä-lə-jē\ *n* : a branch of zoology dealing with fishes — **ich·thy·ol·o·gist** \-jist\ *n*

ici·cle \'ī-si-kəl\ *n* : a hanging mass of ice formed by the freezing of dripping water

ic·ing \'ī-siŋ\ *n* : a sweet usu. creamy mixture used to coat baked goods

ICJ *abbr* International Court of Justice

icky \'i-kē\ *adj* **ick·i·er; -est** : OFFENSIVE, DISTASTEFUL — **ick·i·ness** *n*

icon \'ī-ˌkän\ *n* **1** : IMAGE; *esp* : a religious image painted on a wood panel **2** ♦ : a sign (as a word or graphic symbol) whose form suggests its meaning **3** : a small picture on a computer display that suggests the purpose of an available function

♦ character, sign, symbol

icon·o·clasm \ī-'kä-nə-ˌkla-zəm\ *n* : the doctrine, practice, or attitude of an iconoclast

icon·o·clast \-ˌklast\ *n* **1** : one who destroys religious images or opposes their veneration **2** : one who attacks cherished beliefs or institutions

-ics \iks\ *n sing or pl suffix* **1** : study : knowledge : skill : practice ⟨linguist*ics*⟩ ⟨electron*ics*⟩ **2** : characteristic actions or activities ⟨acrobat*ics*⟩ **3** : characteristic qualities, operations, or phenomena ⟨mechan*ics*⟩

ic·tus \'ik-təs\ *n* : the recurring stress or beat in a rhythmic or metrical series of sounds

ICU *abbr* intensive care unit

icy \'ī-sē\ *adj* **ic·i·er; -est 1** : covered with, abounding in, or consisting of ice **2** ♦ : intensely cold **3** ♦ : being cold and unfriendly — **ic·i·ly** \'ī-sə-lē\ *adv* — **ic·i·ness** \-sē-nəs\ *n*

♦ [2] arctic, bitter, chill, cold, freezing, frigid, frosty, glacial, polar, raw, wintry ♦ [3] chill, chilly, cold, cold-blooded, cool, frigid, frosty, glacial, unfriendly, unsympathetic, wintry

¹**id** \'id\ *n* : the part of the psyche in psychoanalytic theory that is completely unconscious and concerned with instinctual needs and drives

²**id** *abbr* idem

¹**ID** \'ī-'dē\ *n* : a document with identifying information about an individual whose name appears on it

²**ID** *vb* **ID'd** *or* **IDed; ID'ing** *or* **IDing** : IDENTIFY

³**ID** *abbr* **1** Idaho **2** identification

idea \ī-'dē-ə\ *n* **1** : a plan for action : DESIGN **2** ♦ : something (as a thought, concept, sensation, or image) present in the mind **3** : a central meaning or purpose

♦ concept, image, impression, notion, picture, thought

¹**ide·al** \ī-'dēl\ *adj* **1** : existing only in the mind : IMAGINARY; *also* : lacking practicality **2** ♦ : of or relating to an ideal or to perfection : PERFECT

♦ absolute, faultless, flawless, impeccable, letter-perfect, perfect, unblemished

²**ideal** *n* **1** ♦ : a standard of excellence **2** ♦ : one regarded as a model worthy of imitation **3** : GOAL

♦ [1] classic, epitome, exemplar, perfection, quintessence ♦ [2] beau ideal, classic, exemplar, model, nonpareil, paragon

ide·al·ise *chiefly Brit var of* IDEALIZE

ide·al·ism \ī-'dē-ə-ˌli-zəm\ *n* : the practice of forming ideals or living under their influence; *also* : an idealized representation — **ide·al·is·tic** \ī-ˌdē-ə-'lis-tik\ *adj* — **ide·al·is·ti·cal·ly** \-ti-k(ə-)lē\ *adv*

ide·al·ist \-list\ *n* ♦ : one guided by ideals; *also* : one that places ideals before practical considerations

♦ dreamer, romantic, utopian, visionary *Ant* realist

ide·al·ize \ī-'dē-ə-ˌlīz\ *vb* **-ized; -iz·ing** : to think of or represent as ideal — **ide·al·i·za·tion** \-ˌdē-ə-lə-'zā-shən\ *n*

♦ dream, glamorize, glorify

ide·al·ly \ī-'dē-lē, -'dē-ə-lē\ *adv* **1** : in idea or imagination : MENTALLY **2** ♦ : in agreement with an ideal : PERFECTLY

♦ faultlessly, flawlessly, impeccably, perfectly

ide·a·tion \ˌī-dē-'ā-shən\ *n* : the forming of ideas — **ide·ate** \'ī-dē-ˌāt\ *vb* — **ide·a·tion·al** \ˌī-dē-'ā-shə-nəl\ *adj*

idem \'ī-ˌdem, 'ē-, 'i-\ *pron* : the same as something previously mentioned

iden·ti·cal \ī-'den-ti-kəl\ *adj* **1** ♦ : being the same **2** ♦ : essentially alike

♦ duplicate, equal, even, indistinguishable, same

iden·ti·fi·ca·tion \ī-ˌden-tə-fə-'kā-shən\ *n* **1** : an act of identifying : the state of being identified **2** : evidence of identity **3** : an unconscious psychological process by which an individual models thoughts, feelings, and actions after another person or an object

iden·ti·fy \ī-'den-tə-ˌfī\ *vb* **-fied; -fy·ing 1** : to regard as identical **2** ♦ : to think of as united (as in spirit, outlook, or principle) : ASSOCIATE **3** ♦ : to establish the identity of **4** : to practice psychological identification — **iden·ti·fi·able** \-ˌden-tə-'fī-ə-bəl\ *adj* — **iden·ti·fi·ably** \-blē\ *adv* — **iden·ti·fi·er** \-ˌfī-(ə-)r\ *n*

♦ [2] associate, connect, correlate, link, relate ♦ [3] distinguish, pinpoint, single

iden·ti·ty \ī-'den-tə-tē\ *n, pl* **-ties 1** : sameness of essential character **2** ♦ : the distinguishing character or personality of an individual : INDIVIDUALITY **3** : the fact of being the same person or thing as claimed

♦ character, individuality, personality, self-identity

identity crisis *n* : psychological conflict esp. in adolescence involving confusion about one's social role and one's personality

identity theft *n* : the illegal use of someone else's personal information to obtain money or credit

ideo·gram \'ī-dē-ə-ˌgram, 'i-\ *n* **1** : a picture or symbol used in a system of writing to represent a thing or an idea **2** : a character or symbol used in a system of writing to represent an entire word

ideo·logue *also* **idea·logue** \'ī-dē-ə-ˌlòg\ *n* : a partisan advocate or adherent of a particular ideology

ide·ol·o·gy \ˌī-dē-'ä-lə-jē, ˌi-\ *also* **ide·al·o·gy** \-'ä-lə-jē, -'a-\ *n, pl* **-gies 1** : the body of ideas characteristic of a particular individual, group, or culture **2** : the assertions, theories, and aims that constitute a political, social, and economic program — **ide·o·log·i·cal** \ˌī-dē-ə-'lä-ji-kəl, ˌi-\ *adj* — **ide·ol·o·gist** \-dē-'ä-lə-jist\ *n*

♦ creed, doctrine, gospel, philosophy

ides \'īdz\ *n sing or pl* : the 15th day of March, May, July, or October or the 13th day of any other month in the ancient Roman calendar

id·i·o·cy \'i-dē-ə-sē\ *n, pl* **-cies 1** ♦ : something notably stupid or foolish **2** *dated, now offensive* : extreme intellectual disability

♦ absurdity, fatuity, folly, foolery, foolishness, inanity, madness, stupidity

id·i·om \'i-dē-əm\ *n* **1** : the language peculiar to a person or group **2 :** the characteristic form or structure of a language **3 :** an expression that cannot be understood from the meanings of its separate words (as *give way*) — **id·i·o·mat·ic** \ˌi-dē-ə-ˈma-tik\ *adj* — **id·i·o·mat·i·cal·ly** \-ti-k(ə-)lē\ *adv*

id·i·o·path·ic \ˌi-dē-ə-ˈpa-thik\ *adj* : arising spontaneously or from an obscure or unknown cause ⟨an ∼ disease⟩

id·i·o·syn·cra·sy \ˌi-dē-ə-ˈsiɲ-krə-sē\ *n, pl* **-sies** ♦ : personal peculiarity — **id·i·o·syn·crat·ic** \ˌi-dē-ō-sin-ˈkra-tik\ *adj* — **id·i·o·syn·crat·i·cal·ly** \-ˈkra-ti-k(ə-)lē\ *adv*

♦ crotchet, eccentricity, mannerism, oddity, peculiarity, quirk, singularity, trick

id·i·ot \ˈi-dē-ət\ *n* **1** ♦ : a foolish or stupid person **2** *dated, now offensive* : a person affected with extreme intellectual disability — **id·i·ot·ic** \ˌi-dē-ˈä-tik\ *adj* — **id·i·ot·i·cal·ly** \-ti-k(ə-)lē\ *adv*

♦ blockhead, cretin, dodo, dolt, dope, dummy, imbecile, jackass, moron, nitwit, numskull, simpleton *Ant* brain, genius

id·i·ot-proof \ˈi-dē-ət-ˌprüf\ *adj* : extremely easy to operate or maintain

¹**idle** \ˈīd-ᵊl\ *adj* **idler** \ˈī-də-lər\; **idlest** \ˈī-də-ləst\ **1 :** GROUNDLESS, WORTHLESS, USELESS ⟨∼ talk⟩ **2** ♦ : not occupied or employed : INACTIVE **3** ♦ : lacking in ambition or incentive : LAZY — **idly** \ˈīd-lē\ *adv*

♦ [2] dead, dormant, fallow, free, inactive, inert, inoperative, latent, off, vacant ♦ [3] indolent, lazy, shiftless, slothful

²**idle** *vb* **idled; idling 1** ♦ : to spend time doing nothing **2 :** to make idle **3 :** to run without being connected so that power is not used for useful work

♦ dally, dawdle, dillydally, hang around, hang out, loaf, loll, lounge

idle·ness *n* ♦ : the quality or state of being idle (as through lack of worth, occupation, employment, industry)

♦ indolence, inertia, laziness, sloth ♦ dormancy, inaction, inactivity, inertness, quiescence

idler *n* ♦ : one that idles or is unoccupied : a lazy person

♦ lazybones, loafer, slouch, slug, sluggard

idol \ˈīd-ᵊl\ *n* **1 :** an image worshipped as a god; *also* : a false god **2 :** an object of passionate devotion ⟨a sports ∼⟩

idol·a·ter *or* **idol·a·tor** \ī-ˈdä-lə-tər\ *n* : a worshiper of idols

idol·a·try \-trē\ *n, pl* **-tries 1 :** the worship of a physical object as a god **2** ♦ : excessive devotion — **idol·a·trous** \-trəs\ *adj*

♦ adulation, deification, worship

idol·i·za·tion \ˌīd-ᵊl-ə-ˈzā-shən\ *n* : the act of idolizing or state of being idolized

idol·ize \ˈīd-ᵊl-ˌīz\ *vb* **-ized; -iz·ing** ♦ : to make an idol of

♦ adore, canonize, deify, dote on, worship

idyll \ˈīd-ᵊl\ *n* **1 :** a simple work of writing or poetry that describes country life or suggests a peaceful setting **2** ♦ : a light-hearted carefree episode that is a fit subject for an idyll — **idyl·lic** \ī-ˈdi-lik\ *adj*

♦ binge, fling, frolic, gambol, lark, revel, rollick, romp

i.e. \ˈī-ˈē\ *abbr* that is

IE *abbr* industrial engineer

IED *abbr* improvised explosive device

if \ˈif\ *conj* **1 :** in the event that ⟨∼ he stays, I leave⟩ **2 :** WHETHER ⟨ask ∼ he left⟩ **3** — used as a function word to introduce an exclamation expressing a wish ⟨∼ it would only rain⟩ **4 :** even though ⟨an interesting ∼ untenable argument⟩

IF *abbr* intermediate frequency

if·fy \ˈi-fē\ *adj* : full of contingencies or unknown conditions

-i·fy \ə-ˌfī\ *vb suffix* : -FY

IG *abbr* inspector general

ig·loo \ˈi-glü\ *n, pl* **igloos** : a house or hut that is often made of blocks of snow in the shape of a dome and that is associated esp. with Indigenous peoples of arctic regions

ig·ne·ous \ˈig-nē-əs\ *adj* **1 :** FIERY **2 :** formed by solidification of molten rock

ig·nit·able \-ˈnī-tə-bəl\ *adj* ♦ : capable of being ignited

♦ combustible, flammable, inflammable

ig·nite \ig-ˈnīt\ *vb* **ig·nit·ed; ig·nit·ing** ♦ : to set afire or catch fire

♦ burn, fire, inflame, kindle, light

ig·ni·tion \ig-ˈni-shən\ *n* **1 :** a setting on fire **2 :** the process or means (as an electric spark) of igniting the fuel mixture in an engine

ig·no·ble \ig-ˈnō-bəl\ *adj* **1** ♦ : of common birth **2** ♦ : not honorable : BASE, MEAN — **ig·no·bly** *adv*

♦ [1] common, humble, inferior, low, lowly, mean, plebeian, vulgar *Ant* aristocratic, high, highborn, lofty, noble, wellborn
♦ [2] base, contemptible, despicable, detestable, dirty, dishonorable (*or* dishonourable), low, mean, snide, sordid, vile, wretched *Ant* high, high-minded, honorable, lofty, noble, straight, upright, venerable, virtuous

ig·no·min·i·ous \ˌig-nə-ˈmi-nē-əs\ *adj* **1** ♦ : marked with or characterized by disgrace or shame : DISHONORABLE **2 :** DESPICABLE **3 :** HUMILIATING, DEGRADING — **ig·no·min·i·ous·ly** *adv*

♦ discreditable, disgraceful, dishonorable (*or* dishonourable), disreputable, infamous, notorious, shameful

ig·no·min·y \ˈig-nə-ˌmi-nē, ig-ˈnä-mə-nē\ *n* **1** ♦ : deep personal humiliation and disgrace **2 :** disgraceful or dishonorable conduct, quality, or action

♦ discredit, disgrace, dishonor (*or* dishonour), disrepute, infamy, odium, opprobrium, reproach, shame

ig·no·ra·mus \ˌig-nə-ˈrā-məs\ *n* : an utterly ignorant person

ig·no·rance \ˈig-nə-rəns\ *n* ♦ : the state of being ignorant

♦ obliviousness, unawareness *Ant* acquaintance, awareness, familiarity

ig·no·rant \ˈig-nə-rənt\ *adj* **1** ♦ : lacking knowledge **2 :** resulting from or showing lack of knowledge or intelligence **3** ♦ : not aware : UNAWARE, UNINFORMED — **ig·no·rant·ly** *adv*

♦ [1] dark, illiterate, simple, uneducated, unlearned, untaught *Ant* educated, knowledgeable, literate, schooled ♦ [3] oblivious, unaware, unconscious, uninformed, unknowing, unwitting *Ant* acquainted, aware, cognizant, conscious, conversant, grounded, informed, knowing, mindful, witting

ig·nore \ig-ˈnōr\ *vb* **ig·nored; ig·nor·ing** ♦ : to refuse to take notice of

♦ disregard, forget, neglect, overlook, pass over, slight, slur
♦ condone, disregard, excuse, gloss over, pardon, pass over, shrug off, wink at

igua·na \i-ˈgwä-nə\ *n* : any of various large tropical American lizards

ihp *abbr* indicated horsepower

IHS \ˌi-ˌāch-ˈes\ — used as a Christian symbol and monogram for *Jesus*

ikon *var of* ICON

IL *abbr* Illinois

il·e·itis \ˌi-lē-ˈī-təs\ *n* : inflammation of the ileum

il·e·um \ˈi-lē-əm\ *n, pl* **il·ea** \-lē-ə\ : the part of the small intestine between the jejunum and the large intestine

il·i·ac \ˈi-lē-ˌak\ *adj* : of, relating to, or located near the ilium

il·i·um \ˈi-lē-əm\ *n* : the uppermost and largest of the three bones making up either side of the pelvis

ilk \ˈilk\ *n* ♦ : a group set up on the basis of any characteristic in common : SORT, KIND

♦ breed, class, description, feather, kind, like, manner, nature, order, sort, species, type

¹**ill** \ˈil\ *adj* **worse** \ˈwərs\; **worst** \ˈwərst\ **1** ♦ : attended or caused by an evil intent ⟨∼ deeds⟩ **2 a :** not normal or sound ⟨∼ health⟩ **b** ♦ : not in good health : SICK; *also* : feeling nauseated **3 :** BAD, UNLUCKY ⟨∼ omen⟩ **4 :** not right or proper ⟨∼ manners⟩ **5 :** UNFRIENDLY, HOSTILE ⟨∼ feeling⟩

♦ [1] adverse, baleful, baneful, damaging, deleterious, detrimental, evil, harmful, hurtful, injurious, mischievous, noxious, pernicious, prejudicial ♦ [2b] nauseous, queasy, sick, squeamish ♦ [2b] bad, down, indisposed, peaked, punk, sick, unhealthy, unsound, unwell

²**ill** *adv* **worse; worst 1 :** with displeasure **2** ♦ : in a harsh manner **3 :** probably not : HARDLY ⟨can ∼ afford it⟩ **4 :** BADLY, UNLUCKILY **5 :** in a faulty way

♦ hard, hardly, harshly, oppressively, roughly, severely, sternly, stiffly

³**ill** *n* **1** ♦ : the reverse of good : EVIL **2 :** MISFORTUNE, DISTRESS **3 :** AILMENT, SICKNESS; *also* : TROUBLE

♦ bad, evil, immorality, iniquity, sin, villainy, wrong

⁴**ill** *abbr* illustrated; illustration; illustrator

Ill *abbr* Illinois

ill-ad·vised \ˌil-əd-ˈvīzd\ *adj* ♦ : not well counseled ⟨∼ efforts⟩ — **ill-ad·vis·ed·ly** \-ˈvī-zəd-lē\ *adv*

♦ imprudent, indiscreet, tactless, unwise

ill–bred \-'bred\ *adj* ♦ : showing bad upbringing : IMPOLITE

♦ discourteous, ill-mannered, impertinent, impolite, inconsiderate, rude, thoughtless, uncivil, ungracious, unmannerly

il·le·gal \il-'lē-gəl\ *adj* ♦ : not lawful; *also* : not sanctioned by official rules — **il·le·gal·i·ty** \ˌi-li-'ga-lə-tē\ *n* — **il·le·gal·ly** *adv*

♦ criminal, illegitimate, illicit, unlawful, wrongful *Ant* lawful, legal, legitimate ♦ dirty, foul, unfair, unsportsmanlike

il·leg·i·ble \il-'le-jə-bəl\ *adj* : not legible — **il·leg·i·bil·i·ty** \il-ˌle-jə-'bi-lə-tē\ *n* — **il·leg·i·bly** \il-'le-jə-blē\ *adv*

il·le·git·i·mate \ˌi-li-'ji-tə-mət\ *adj* **1** : born of parents not married to each other **2** : ILLOGICAL **3** ♦ : not sanctioned by law : ILLEGAL — **il·le·git·i·ma·cy** \-'ji-tə-mə-sē\ *n* — **il·le·git·i·mate·ly** *adv*

♦ criminal, illegal, illicit, unlawful, wrongful

ill–fat·ed \'il-'fā-təd\ *adj* ♦ : having or destined to a hapless fate : UNFORTUNATE

♦ hapless, ill-starred, luckless, unfortunate, unhappy, unlucky

ill–fa·vored \-'fā-vərd\ *adj* : unattractive in physical appearance : UGLY

ill–got·ten \-'gät-ᵊn\ *adj* : acquired by improper means ⟨~ gains⟩

ill–hu·mored \-'hyü-mərd, -'yü-\ *adj* ♦ : irritably sullen and churlish in mood or manner : SURLY

♦ bearish, bilious, cantankerous, disagreeable, dyspeptic, ill-tempered, ornery, splenetic, surly

il·lib·er·al \il-'li-bə-rəl\ *adj* : not liberal : NARROW, BIGOTED

il·lic·it \il-'li-sət\ *adj* ♦ : not permitted : UNLAWFUL — **il·lic·it·ly** *adv*

♦ criminal, illegal, illegitimate, unlawful, wrongful

il·lim·it·able \il-'li-mə-tə-bəl\ *adj* ♦ : incapable of being limited or bounded : BOUNDLESS, MEASURELESS — **il·lim·it·ably** \-blē\ *adv*

♦ boundless, endless, immeasurable, indefinite, infinite, limitless, measureless, unbounded, unfathomable, unlimited

Il·li·nois \ˌi-lə-'nȯi *also* -'nȯiz\ *n, pl* **Illinois** : a member of an Algonquian-speaking confederation of Indigenous peoples of Illinois, Iowa, and Wisconsin

il·lit·er·ate \il-'li-tə-rət\ *adj* **1** ♦ : having little or no education; *esp* : unable to read or write **2** : showing a lack of familiarity with the fundamentals of a particular field of knowledge — **il·lit·er·a·cy** \-'li-tə-rə-sē\ *n* — **illiterate** *n*

♦ dark, ignorant, simple, uneducated, unlearned, untaught

ill–man·nered \'il-'ma-nərd\ *adj* ♦ : marked by bad manners : RUDE

♦ discourteous, ill-bred, impertinent, impolite, inconsiderate, rude, thoughtless, uncivil, ungracious, unmannerly

ill–na·tured \-'nā-chərd\ *adj* : having a bad disposition : CROSS, SURLY — **ill–na·tured·ly** *adv*

ill·ness \'il-nəs\ *n* ♦ : an unhealthy condition of body or mind : SICKNESS; *also* : a specific disease

♦ ailment, bug, complaint, complication, condition, disease, disorder, fever, infirmity, malady, sickness, trouble

il·log·i·cal \il-'lä-ji-kəl\ *adj* ♦ : lacking sound reasoning; *also* : SENSELESS — **il·log·i·cal·ly** \-ji-k(ə-)lē\ *adv*

♦ fallacious, invalid, irrational, senseless, unreasonable, unsound, weak

ill–starred \'il-'stärd\ *adj* ♦ : having or meeting with misfortune : UNLUCKY

♦ hapless, ill-fated, luckless, unfortunate, unhappy, unlucky

ill–tem·pered \-'tem-pərd\ *adj* ♦ : having a bad disposition : CROSS

♦ bearish, bilious, cantankerous, cross, disagreeable, dyspeptic, ill-humored, ornery, splenetic, surly *Ant* amiable, good-natured, good-tempered

ill–treat \-'trēt\ *vb* ♦ : to treat cruelly or improperly : MALTREAT — **ill–treat·ment** *n*

♦ abuse, maltreat, manhandle, mishandle, mistreat, misuse

il·lu·mi·nate \i-'lü-mə-ˌnāt\ *vb* **-nat·ed; -nat·ing** **1** ♦ : to supply or brighten with light : light up **2** ♦ : to make clear : ELUCIDATE **3** : to decorate (as a manuscript) with designs or pictures in gold or colors — **il·lu·mi·nat·ing·ly** *adv* — **il·lu·mi·na·tor** \-'lü-mə-ˌnā-tər\ *n*

♦ [1] light *Ant* blacken, darken ♦ [2] clarify, clear (up), construe, demonstrate, elucidate, explain, explicate, expound, illustrate, interpret, spell out

il·lu·mi·na·tion \-ˌlü-mə-'nā-shən\ *n* **1** ♦ : the action of illuminating **2** ♦ : the state of being illuminated

♦ [1] blaze, flare, fluorescence, glare, gleam, glow, incandescence, light, luminescence, radiance, shine ♦ [2] brilliance, dazzle, effulgence, lightness, lucidity, luminosity, radiance, refulgence, splendor

il·lu·mine \i-'lü-mən\ *vb* **-mined; -min·ing** : to make clear or bright : ILLUMINATE

ill–us·age \'il-'yü-sij\ *n* : harsh, unkind, or abusive treatment

ill–use \-'yüz\ *vb* : to use badly : MALTREAT, ABUSE

il·lu·sion \i-'lü-zhən\ *n* **1** ♦ : a mistaken idea : MISCONCEPTION **2** ♦ : a misleading visual image; *also* : HALLUCINATION

♦ [1] error, fallacy, falsehood, falsity, misconception, myth, untruth ♦ [2] chimera, conceit, daydream, delusion, dream, fancy, fantasy, figment, hallucination, phantasm, pipe dream, unreality, vision

il·lu·sion·ist \i-'lü-zhə-nist\ *n* ♦ : one that produces illusions; *esp* : a sleight-of-hand performer

♦ conjurer, magician, trickster

il·lu·sive \i-'lü-siv\ *adj* : DECEPTIVE

il·lu·so·ry \i-'lü-sə-rē, -zə-\ *adj* : DECEPTIVE

illust *or* **illus** *abbr* illustrated; illustration

il·lus·trate \'i-ləs-ˌtrāt\ *vb* **-trat·ed; -trat·ing** **1** ♦ : to explain by use of examples; *also* : DEMONSTRATE **2** : to provide with pictures or figures that explain or decorate **3** : to serve to explain or decorate — **il·lus·tra·tor** \'i-lə-ˌstrā-tər\ *n*

♦ exemplify, instance

il·lus·tra·tion \ˌi-lə-'strā-shən\ *n* **1** : the act of illustrating : the condition of being illustrated **2** ♦ : an example or instance that helps make something clear **3** ♦ : a picture or diagram that explains or decorates

♦ [2] clarification, construction, elucidation, explanation, explication, exposition, illumination, interpretation ♦ [3] diagram, figure, graphic, plate

il·lus·tra·tive \i-'ləs-trə-tiv, 'i-lə-ˌstrā-\ *adj* : serving, tending, or designed to illustrate — **il·lus·tra·tive·ly** *adv*

il·lus·tri·ous \i-'ləs-trē-əs\ *adj* ♦ : notably outstanding because of rank or achievement — **il·lus·tri·ous·ness** *n*

♦ distinguished, eminent, noble, notable, noteworthy, outstanding, preeminent, prestigious, signal, star, superior

ill will *n* : unfriendly feeling

ILS *abbr* instrument landing system

¹**IM** \'ī-'em\ *vb* **IM'd; IM'ing** **1** : to send an instant message to **2** : to communicate by instant message

²**IM** *abbr* instant message

¹**im·age** \'i-mij\ *n* **1** : a likeness or imitation of a person or thing; *esp* : STATUE **2** : a picture of an object formed by a device (as a mirror or lens) **3** ♦ : a person strikingly like another person ⟨he is the ~ of his father⟩ **4** ♦ : a mental picture or conception : IMPRESSION, IDEA, CONCEPT **5** : a vivid representation or description

♦ [3] carbon copy, counterpart, double, duplicate, duplication, facsimile, likeness, match, picture, replica, ringer, spit ♦ [4] concept, idea, impression, notion, picture, thought

²**image** *vb* **im·aged; im·ag·ing** **1** : to call up a mental picture of **2** ♦ : to describe or portray in words **3** ♦ : to create a representation of **4** : REFLECT, MIRROR **5** : to make appear : PROJECT

♦ [2] delineate, depict, describe, draw, paint, picture, portray, sketch ♦ [3] depict, depict, picture, portray, represent

im·ag·ery \'i-mij-rē\ *n, pl* **-er·ies** **1** : IMAGES; *also* : the art of making images **2** : figurative language **3** : mental images; *esp* : the products of imagination

imag·in·able \i-'ma-jə-nə-bəl\ *adj* : capable of being imagined : CONCEIVABLE — **imag·in·ably** *adv*

imag·i·nary \i-'ma-jə-ˌner-ē\ *adj* **1** ♦ : existing only in the imagination **2** : containing or relating to a quantity (**imaginary unit**) that is the positive square root of minus 1 ($\sqrt{-1}$)

♦ chimerical, fabulous, fanciful, fantastic, fictitious, made-up, mythical, phantom, pretend, unreal *Ant* actual, existent, existing, real

imaginary number *n* : a complex number (as $2 + 3i$) with a nonzero term (**imaginary part**) containing the imaginary unit as a factor

imag·i·na·tion \i-ˌma-jə-'nā-shən\ n **1 ♦** : the act or power of forming a mental image of something not present to the senses or not previously known or experienced **2** : creative ability **3** : RESOURCEFULNESS **4** : a mental image : a creation of the mind

♦ creativity, fancy, fantasy, invention, inventiveness

imag·i·na·tive \i-'ma-jə-nə-tiv, -ˌnā-\ adj ♦ : of, relating to, or characterized by imagination — **imag·i·na·tive·ly** adv

♦ creative, ingenious, innovative, inventive, original

imag·ine \i-'ma-jən\ vb **imag·ined; imag·in·ing** **1 ♦** : to form a mental picture of something not present **2 ♦** : to hold as an opinion : THINK, GUESS ⟨I ~ it will rain⟩

♦ [1] conceive, dream, envisage, fancy, picture, vision, visualize ♦ [2] believe, consider, deem, feel, figure, guess, hold, suppose, think

imag·in·ings \-'maj-niŋz, -'ma-jə-\ n pl : products of the imagination

im·ag·ism \'i-mi-ˌji-zəm\ n, often cap : a movement in poetry advocating free verse and the expression of ideas and emotions through clear precise images — **im·ag·ist** \-jist\ n

ima·go \i-'mā-gō, -'mä-\ n, pl **imagoes** or **ima·gi·nes** \-'mā-gə-ˌnēz, -'mä-\ : an insect in its final adult stage — **ima·gi·nal** \i-'mā-gən-ᵊl, -'mä-\ adj

im·bal·ance \im-'ba-ləns\ n : lack of balance : the state of being out of equilibrium or out of proportion

im·be·cile \'im-bə-səl, -ˌsil\ n **1 ♦** : a person lacking in judgment or prudence : IDIOT **2** dated, now offensive : a person affected with moderate intellectual disability — **imbecile** or **im·be·cil·ic** \ˌim-bə-'si-lik\ adj

♦ blockhead, dope, dummy, idiot, jackass, nitwit, numskull, simpleton

im·be·cil·i·ty \ˌim-bə-'si-lə-tē\ n **1** : the quality or state of being imbecile or an imbecile **2** : something that is foolish or nonsensical

imbed var of EMBED

im·bibe \im-'bīb\ vb **im·bibed; im·bib·ing** **1** : to receive and retain in the mind **2 ♦** : to take through the mouth and esophagus into the stomach : DRINK **3 ♦** : to take in or up : ABSORB — **im·bib·er** n

♦ [2] drink, guzzle, quaff, sup, swig, toss ♦ [3] absorb, drink, soak, sponge, suck

im·bri·ca·tion \ˌim-brə-'kā-shən\ n **1** : an overlapping of edges (as of tiles) **2** : a pattern showing imbrication — **im·bri·cate** \'im-bri-kət\ adj

im·bro·glio \im-'brōl-yō\ n, pl **-glios** **1** : a confused mass **2** : a complicated situation; also : a serious or embarrassing misunderstanding

im·brue \im-'brü\ vb **im·brued; im·bru·ing** : STAIN ⟨hands imbrued with blood⟩

im·bue \-'byü\ vb **im·bued; im·bu·ing** **1 ♦** : to permeate or influence as if by dyeing **2** : to tinge or dye deeply

♦ inculcate, infuse, ingrain, invest, steep, suffuse

IMF abbr International Monetary Fund

imit abbr imitative

im·i·ta·ble \'i-mə-tə-bəl\ adj : capable or worthy of being imitated or copied

im·i·tate \'i-mə-ˌtāt\ vb **-tat·ed; -tat·ing** **1 ♦** : to follow as a model **2** : RESEMBLE **3 ♦** : to produce a copy of : REPRODUCE **4 ♦** : to copy or feign esp. with intent to deceive : MIMIC

♦ [1] ape, copy, emulate, mime, mimic ♦ [3] copy, duplicate, replicate, reproduce ♦ [4] burlesque, caricature, mimic, mock, parody, take off, travesty

¹im·i·ta·tion \ˌi-mə-'tā-shən\ n **1** : an act of imitating **2 ♦** : something produced as a copy **3** : a literary work that reproduces the style of another author

♦ carbon copy, copy, duplicate, duplication, facsimile, replica, replication, reproduction

²imitation adj ♦ : resembling something else that is usu. genuine and of better quality : not real

♦ artificial, bogus, factitious, fake, false, mimic, mock, sham, substitute, synthetic Ant genuine, natural, real

im·i·ta·tive \'i-mə-ˌtā-tiv\ adj **1 ♦** : marked by imitation **2** : inclined to imitate **3** : COUNTERFEIT

♦ mimic, unoriginal Ant original

im·i·ta·tor \-ˌtā-tər\ n ♦ : one that imitates

♦ impersonator, impressionist, mimic

im·mac·u·late \i-'ma-kyə-lət\ adj **1 ♦** : being without stain or blemish : PURE **2 ♦** : spotlessly clean ⟨~ linen⟩ — **im·mac·u·late·ly** adv

♦ [1] chaste, clean, decent, modest, pure ♦ [2] clean, spick-and-span, spotless, stainless, unsoiled, unsullied

im·ma·nent \'i-mə-nənt\ adj **1** : INHERENT **2** : being within the limits of experience or knowledge — **im·ma·nence** \-nəns\ n — **im·ma·nen·cy** \-nən-sē\ n

im·ma·te·ri·al \ˌi-mə-'tir-ē-əl\ adj **1 ♦** : not consisting of matter : SPIRITUAL **2** : of no substantial consequence : UNIMPORTANT, TRIFLING **3 ♦** : not material or essential — **im·ma·te·ri·al·i·ty** \-ˌtir-ē-ˌa-lə-tē\ n

♦ [1] bodiless, incorporeal, insubstantial, nonmaterial, nonphysical, spiritual, unsubstantial Ant bodily, corporeal, material, physical, substantial ♦ [3] extraneous, irrelevant

im·ma·ture \ˌi-mə-'tur, -'tyur\ adj ♦ : lacking complete development : not yet mature ⟨~ behavior⟩ — **im·ma·tu·ri·ty** \-'tur-ə-tē, -'tyur-\ n

♦ adolescent, babyish, childish, infantile, juvenile, kiddish
♦ adolescent, callow, green, inexperienced, juvenile, raw

im·mea·sur·able \(ˌ)i-'me-zhə-rə-bəl\ adj ♦ : not capable of being measured : indefinitely extensive — **im·mea·sur·ably** \-blē\ adv

♦ boundless, endless, illimitable, indefinite, infinite, limitless, measureless, unbounded, unfathomable, unlimited

im·me·di·a·cy \i-'mē-dē-ə-sē\ n, pl **-cies** **1 ♦** : the quality or state of being immediate **2** : something that is of immediate importance

♦ closeness, contiguity, nearness, proximity

im·me·di·ate \i-'mē-dē-ət\ adj **1 ♦** : acting directly and alone : DIRECT ⟨the ~ cause of death⟩ **2** : being next in line or relation ⟨members of the ~ family⟩ **3 ♦** : not distant : CLOSE **4 ♦** : made or done at once ⟨an ~ response⟩ **5 ♦** : near to or related to the present time ⟨the ~ future⟩

♦ [1] direct, firsthand, primary ♦ [3, 5] close, near, nearby, nigh ♦ [4] prompt, punctual, timely ♦ [4] instant, instantaneous, straightaway

im·me·di·ate·ly adv **1 ♦** : in direct connection or relation **2 ♦** : without interval of time

♦ directly, forthwith, instantly, now, promptly, pronto, right away, right now

im·me·mo·ri·al \ˌi-mə-'mōr-ē-əl\ adj ♦ : extending beyond the reach of memory, record, or tradition ⟨from time ~⟩

♦ age-old, ancient, antediluvian, antique, dateless, hoary, old, venerable

im·mense \i-'mens\ adj **1** : very great in size or degree : VAST **2** : EXCELLENT — **im·mense·ly** adv

im·men·si·ty \-'men-sə-tē\ n **1 ♦** : the quality or state of being immense **2** : something immense

♦ enormity, hugeness, magnitude, massiveness, vastness Ant minuteness

im·merse \i-'mərs\ vb **im·mersed; im·mers·ing** **1 ♦** : to plunge or dip esp. into a fluid **2 ♦** : to take or engage the whole attention of : ENGROSS, ABSORB **3** : to baptize by immersing

♦ [1] dip, douse, duck, dunk, souse, submerge ♦ [2] absorb, busy, engage, engross, enthrall, fascinate, grip, interest, intrigue, involve, occupy

im·mer·sion \-'mər-zhən\ n : the act of immersing or the state of being immersed; esp : absorbing involvement

im·mer·sive \-'mər-siv\ adj : providing, involving, or characterized by deep absorption or immersion in something

im·mi·grant \'i-mi-grənt\ n **1 ♦** : a person who immigrates **2** : a plant or animal that becomes established where it did not previously occur

♦ emigrant, émigré, migrant, settler

im·mi·grate \'i-mə-ˌgrāt\ vb **-grat·ed; -grat·ing** : to come into a foreign country and take up residence — **im·mi·gra·tion** \ˌi-mə-'grā-shən\ n

im·mi·nent \'i-mə-nənt\ adj ♦ : ready to take place; esp : hanging threateningly over one's head ⟨~ danger⟩ — **im·mi·nence** \-nəns\ n — **im·mi·nent·ly** adv

♦ coming, forthcoming, impending, oncoming, pending ♦ impending, pending

im·mis·ci·ble \(ˌ)i-'mi-sə-bəl\ adj : incapable of mixing

im·mis·er·a·tion \(ˌ)i-ˌmi-zə-ˈrā-shən\ *n* : IMPOVERISHMENT

im·mo·bile \(ˌ)i-ˈmō-bəl\ *adj* ♦ : incapable of moving or being moved : IMMOVABLE — **im·mo·bil·i·ty** \ˌi-mō-ˈbi-lə-tē\ *n*

♦ immovable, standing, static, stationary, unmovable

im·mo·bi·lize \i-ˈmō-bə-ˌlīz\ *vb* ♦ : to make immobile — **im·mo·bi·li·za·tion** \i-ˌmō-bə-lə-ˈzā-shən\ *n*

♦ cripple, disable, hamstring, incapacitate, paralyze, prostrate

im·mod·er·ate \(ˌ)i-ˈmä-də-rət\ *adj* ♦ : lacking in moderation : EXCESSIVE ⟨∼ drinking⟩ — **im·mod·er·a·cy** \-rə-sē\ *n* — **im·mod·er·ate·ly** *adv*

♦ devilish, excessive, exorbitant, extravagant, extreme, inordinate, lavish, overmuch, overweening, steep, stiff, towering, unconscionable

im·mod·est \(ˌ)i-ˈmä-dəst\ *adj* ♦ : not modest ⟨∼ conduct⟩; *specif* : not conforming to the sexual mores of a particular time or place ⟨an ∼ dress⟩ — **im·mod·est·ly** *adv* — **im·mod·es·ty** \-də-stē\ *n*

♦ bold, familiar, forward, free, presumptuous

im·mo·late \ˈi-mə-ˌlāt\ *vb* **-lat·ed; -lat·ing 1** : to offer in sacrifice; *esp* : to kill as a sacrificial victim **2** : to kill or destroy esp. by fire

im·mo·la·tion \ˌi-mə-ˈlā-shən\ *n* **1** : the act of immolating : the state of being immolated **2** : something that is immolated

im·mor·al \(ˌ)i-ˈmȯr-əl\ *adj* ♦ : not moral — **im·mor·al·ly** *adv*

♦ bad, evil, iniquitous, nefarious, rotten, sinful, unethical, unsavory, vicious, vile, villainous, wicked, wrong ♦ cutthroat, Machiavellian, unconscionable, unethical, unprincipled, unscrupulous

im·mo·ral·i·ty \ˌi-mȯ-ˈra-lə-tē, ˌi-mə-\ *n* **1** ♦ : the quality or state of being immoral; *esp* : UNCHASTITY **2** ♦ : an immoral act or practice

♦ [1] bad, evil, ill, iniquity, sin, villainy, wrong ♦ [2] corruption, debauchery, depravity, iniquity, licentiousness, sin, vice

¹im·mor·tal \(ˌ)i-ˈmȯrt-ᵊl\ *adj* **1** ♦ : not mortal : exempt from death ⟨∼ gods⟩ **2** ♦ : destined to be remembered forever ⟨those ∼ words⟩ — **im·mor·tal·ly** *adv*

♦ [1, 2] ceaseless, dateless, deathless, endless, eternal, everlasting, permanent, perpetual, undying, unending

²immortal *n* **1** : one exempt from death **2** *pl, often cap* : the gods in Greek and Roman mythology **3** : a person whose fame is lasting ⟨an ∼ of baseball⟩

im·mor·tal·ise *chiefly Brit var of* IMMORTALIZE

im·mor·tal·i·ty \ˌi-mȯr-ˈta-lə-tē\ *n* ♦ : the quality or state of being immortal; *esp* : unending existence

♦ afterlife, eternity, hereafter

im·mor·tal·ize \i-ˈmȯrt-ᵊl-ˌīz\ *vb* **-ized; -iz·ing** : to make immortal

im·mov·able \(ˌ)i-ˈmü-və-bəl\ *adj* **1** ♦ : firmly fixed, settled, or fastened ⟨∼ mountains⟩ **2** : firm in belief, determination, or adherence : UNYIELDING **3** : IMPASSIVE — **im·mov·abil·i·ty** \-ˌmü-və-ˈbi-lə-tē\ *n* — **im·mov·ably** \-blē\ *adv*

♦ immobile, nonmotile, unbudging, unmovable *Ant* mobile, motile, movable, moving

im·mune \i-ˈmyün\ *adj* **1** : EXEMPT **2** : having a special capacity for resistance (as to a disease) **3** : containing or producing antibodies — **im·mu·ni·ty** \i-ˈmyü-nə-tē\ *n*

immune response *n* : a response of the body to an antigen resulting in the formation of antibodies and cells designed to react with the antigen and render it harmless

immune system *n* : the bodily system that protects the body from foreign substances, cells, and tissues by producing the immune response and that includes esp. the thymus, spleen, lymph nodes, and lymphocytes

im·mu·nize \ˈi-myə-ˌnīz\ *vb* **-nized; -niz·ing** : to make immune — **im·mu·ni·za·tion** \ˌi-myə-nə-ˈzā-shən\ *n*

im·mu·no·de·fi·cien·cy \ˌi-myə-nō-di-ˈfi-shən-sē\ *n* : inability to produce the normal number of antibodies or immunologically sensitized cells esp. in response to specific antigens — **im·mu·no·de·fi·cient** \-ˈfi-shənt\ *adj*

im·mu·no·glob·u·lin \ˌi-myə-nō-ˈglä-byə-lən\ *n* : ANTIBODY

im·mu·nol·o·gy \ˌi-myə-ˈnä-lə-jē\ *n* : a science that deals with the immune system, immunity, and the immune response — **im·mu·no·log·ic** \-nə-ˈlä-jik\ *or* **im·mu·no·log·i·cal** \-ji-kəl\ *adj* — **im·mu·no·log·i·cal·ly** \-ji-k(ə-)lē\ *adv* — **im·mu·nol·o·gist** \-ˈnä-lə-jist\ *n*

im·mu·no·sup·pres·sion \ˌi-myə-nō-sə-ˈpre-shən\ *n* : sup-pression (as by drugs) of natural immune responses — **im·mu·no·sup·press** \-ˈpres\ *vb* — **im·mu·no·sup·pres·sive** \-ˈpre-siv\ *adj*

im·mu·no·ther·a·py \-ˈther-ə-pē\ *n* : treatment or prevention of disease by attempting to induce immunity

im·mure \i-ˈmyu̇r\ *vb* **im·mured; im·mur·ing 1** ♦ : to enclose within or as if within walls; *also* : IMPRISON **2** : to build into a wall; *esp* : to entomb in a wall

♦ cage, closet, coop up, corral, encase, enclose, envelop, fence, hedge, hem, house, pen, wall ♦ commit, confine, imprison, jail

im·mu·ta·bil·i·ty \ˌi-ˌmyü-tə-ˈbi-lə-tē\ *n* ♦ : the quality or state of being immutable

♦ constancy, fixedness, stability, steadiness

im·mu·ta·ble \(ˌ)i-ˈmyü-tə-bəl\ *adj* ♦ : not capable of or susceptible to change : UNCHANGEABLE, UNCHANGING — **im·mu·ta·bly** \-ˈmyü-tə-blē\

♦ fast, fixed, hard-and-fast, inflexible, unalterable, unchangeable, unchanging

¹imp \ˈimp\ *n* **1** ♦ : a small demon : FIEND **2** ♦ : a mischievous child

♦ [1] demon, devil, fiend, ghoul ♦ [2] devil, hellion, mischief, monkey, rapscallion, rascal, rogue, scamp, urchin

²imp *abbr* **1** imperative **2** imperfect **3** imperial **4** import; imported

¹im·pact \im-ˈpakt\ *vb* **1** : to press together **2** ♦ : to have an impact on **3** ♦ : to strike forcefully

♦ [2] affect, impress, influence, move, strike, sway, tell, touch
♦ [3] bang, bash, bump, collide, crash, hit, knock, ram, slam, smash, strike, swipe, thud

²im·pact \ˈim-ˌpakt\ *n* **1** ♦ : a forceful contact, collision, or on-set; *also* : the impetus communicated in or as if in a collision **2** ♦ : the force of impression of one thing on another : EFFECT

♦ [1] bump, collision, concussion, crash, jar, jolt, shock, smash, strike, wallop ♦ [2] effect, influence, mark, repercussion, sway

im·pact·ed \im-ˈpak-təd\ *adj* **1** : packed or wedged in **2** : wedged between the jawbone and another tooth

im·pair \im-ˈpar\ *vb* : to diminish in quantity, value, excellence, or strength : DAMAGE, LESSEN — **im·pair·ment** *n*

im·paired \-ˈpard\ *adj* : being in a less than perfect or whole condition; *esp* : disabled or functionally defective — often used in combination ⟨hearing-*impaired*⟩

im·pa·la \im-ˈpa-lə\ *n, pl* **impalas** *or* **impala** : a large brownish African antelope that in the male has slender curved horns with ridges

im·pale \im-ˈpāl\ *vb* **im·paled; im·pal·ing** ♦ : to pierce with or as if with something pointed — **im·pale·ment** *n*

♦ gore, harpoon, lance, pierce, puncture, skewer, spear, spike, stab, stick, transfix

im·pal·pa·ble \(ˌ)im-ˈpal-pə-bəl\ *adj* **1** : unable to be felt by touch : INTANGIBLE **2** ♦ : not easily seen or understood — **im·pal·pa·bly** \-blē\ *adv*

♦ imperceptible, inappreciable, indistinguishable

im·pan·el \im-ˈpan-ᵊl\ *vb* : to enter in or on a panel : ENROLL ⟨∼ a jury⟩

im·part \im-ˈpärt\ *vb* **1** ♦ : to give from one's store or abundance ⟨the sun ∼s warmth⟩ **2** ♦ : to make known

♦ [1, 2] communicate, convey, spread, transfer, transfuse, transmit

im·par·tial \(ˌ)im-ˈpär-shəl\ *adj* ♦ : not partial : UNBIASED, JUST — **im·par·tial·ly** *adv*

♦ disinterested, dispassionate, equal, equitable, fair, just, nonpartisan, objective, square, unbiased, unprejudiced

im·par·tial·i·ty \-ˌpär-shē-ˈa-lə-tē\ *n* ♦ : the quality or state of being impartial : freedom from bias or favoritism

♦ detachment, disinterestedness, neutrality, objectivity

im·pass·able \(ˌ)im-ˈpa-sə-bəl\ *adj* ♦ : incapable of being passed, traversed, or crossed ⟨∼ roads⟩ — **im·pass·ably** \-blē\ *adv*

♦ impenetrable, impervious

im·passe \ˈim-ˌpas\ *n* **1** : an impassable road or way **2** ♦ : a predicament from which there is no obvious escape

♦ deadlock, halt, stalemate, standstill

im·pas·si·ble \(ˌ)im-ˈpa-sə-bəl\ *adj* : incapable of feeling : IMPASSIVE

im·pas·sioned \im-'pa-shənd\ *adj* ♦ **:** filled with passion or zeal **:** showing great warmth or intensity of feeling

♦ ardent, burning, charged, emotional, fervent, fiery, hot-blooded, passionate, red-hot, vehement

im·pas·sive \(ˌ)im-'pa-siv\ *adj* ♦ **:** showing no signs of feeling, emotion, or interest **:** EXPRESSIONLESS; *also* **:** lacking or not feeling emotion — **im·pas·sive·ly** *adv*

♦ blank, deadpan, expressionless, inexpressive, stolid, vacant ♦ apathetic, cold-blooded, phlegmatic, stoic, stolid, unemotional *Ant* demonstrative, emotional, fervent, fervid, hot-blooded, impassioned, passionate

im·pas·siv·i·ty \ˌim-pa-'si-və-tē\ *n* ♦ **:** the quality or state of being impassive **:** lack or absence of feeling or expression

♦ apathy, numbness, phlegm, stupor

im·pas·to \im-'pas-tō, -'päs-\ *n* **:** the thick application of a pigment to a canvas or panel in painting; *also* **:** the body of pigment so applied

im·pa·tience \-shəns\ *n* ♦ **:** the quality or state of being impatient

♦ appetite, ardor, avidity, eagerness, enthusiasm, excitement, hunger, keenness, thirst

im·pa·tiens \im-'pā-shənz, -shəns\ *n* **:** any of a genus of herbs with usu. spurred flowers and seed capsules that readily split open

im·pa·tient \(ˌ)im-'pā-shənt\ *adj* **1 :** not patient **:** restless or short of temper esp. under irritation, delay, or opposition **2 :** IN-TOLERANT 〈~ of poverty〉 **3 :** prompted or marked by impatience **4 :** eagerly desirous **:** ANXIOUS — **im·pa·tient·ly** *adv*

im·peach \im-'pēch\ *vb* **1 :** to charge (a public official) before an authorized tribunal with misconduct in office **2 :** to challenge the credibility or validity of **3 :** to remove from public office for misconduct — **im·peach·ment** *n*

im·pec·ca·bil·i·ty \(ˌ)im-ˌpe-kə-'bi-lə-tē\ *n* **:** the quality or state of being impeccable

im·pec·ca·ble \(ˌ)im-'pe-kə-bəl\ *adj* **1 :** not capable of sinning or wrongdoing **2** ♦ **:** free from fault or blame **:** FAULTLESS 〈a man of ~ character〉

♦ faultless, flawless, irreproachable *Ant* censurable, defective, faulty, reproachable ♦ absolute, ideal, letter-perfect, perfect, unblemished

im·pec·ca·bly \(ˌ)im-'pe-kə-blē\ *adv* ♦ **:** in an impeccable manner

♦ faultlessly, flawlessly, ideally, perfectly

im·pe·cu·nious \ˌim-pi-'kyü-nyəs, -nē-əs\ *adj* ♦ **:** having little or no money

♦ broke, destitute, indigent, needy, penniless, penurious, poor, poverty-stricken

im·pe·cu·nious·ness *n* ♦ **:** the quality or state of being impecunious

♦ beggary, destitution, impoverishment, indigence, need, pauperism, penury, poverty, want

im·ped·ance \im-'pēd-ᵊns\ *n* **:** the opposition in an electrical circuit to the flow of an alternating current

im·pede \im-'pēd\ *vb* **im·ped·ed; im·ped·ing** ♦ **:** to interfere with the progress of

♦ encumber, fetter, hamper, hinder, hold back, hold up, inhibit, interfere with, obstruct

im·ped·i·ment \im-'pe-də-mənt\ *n* **1 :** something that impedes, hinders, or obstructs **2 :** a speech defect

im·ped·i·men·ta \im-ˌpe-də-'men-tə\ *n pl* **:** things that impede

im·pel \im-'pel\ *vb* **im·pelled; im·pel·ling** ♦ **:** to urge or drive forward or on; *also* **:** PROPEL

♦ actuate, drive, move, propel, work

im·pel·ler *also* **im·pel·lor** \im-'pe-lər\ *n* **:** a rotor esp. in a pump

im·pend \im-'pend\ *vb* **1 :** to hover or hang over threateningly **:** MENACE **2 :** to be about to occur

impending *adj* ♦ **:** that is about to occur

♦ coming, forthcoming, imminent, oncoming, pending

im·pen·e·tra·ble \(ˌ)im-'pe-nə-trə-bəl\ *adj* **1** ♦ **:** incapable of being penetrated or pierced 〈an ~ jungle〉 **2** ♦ **:** incapable of being comprehended **:** INSCRUTABLE 〈an ~ mystery〉 — **im·pen·e·tra·bil·i·ty** \-ˌpe-nə-trə-'bi-lə-tē\ *n* — **im·pen·e·tra·bly** \-'pe-nə-trə-blē\ *adv*

♦ [1] impervious, tight ♦ [2] cryptic, darkling, deep, enigmatic, inscrutable, mysterious, mystic, occult, uncanny ♦ [2] incomprehensible, unfathomable

im·pen·i·tent \(ˌ)im-'pe-nə-tənt\ *adj* **:** not penitent **:** not repenting of sin — **im·pen·i·tence** \-təns\ *n*

im·per·a·tive \im-'per-ə-tiv\ *adj* **1 :** expressing a command, request, or encouragement 〈~ sentence〉 **2** ♦ **:** having power to restrain, control, or direct **3** ♦ **:** not to be avoided or evaded — **imperative** *n* — **im·per·a·tive·ly** *adv*

♦ [2] compulsory, incumbent, involuntary, mandatory, necessary, nonelective, obligatory, peremptory ♦ [3] acute, critical, dire, imperious, instant, pressing, urgent

im·per·cep·ti·ble \ˌim-pər-'sep-tə-bəl\ *adj* ♦ **:** not perceptible; *esp* **:** too slight to be perceived 〈~ changes〉 — **im·per·cep·ti·bly** \-blē\ *adv*

♦ impalpable, inappreciable, indistinguishable *Ant* appreciable, discernible, palpable, perceptible, sensible

im·per·cep·tive \ˌim-pər-'sep-tiv\ *adj* **:** not perceptive

imperf *abbr* imperfect

¹im·per·fect \(ˌ)im-'pər-fikt\ *adj* **1** ♦ **:** not perfect esp. by having a fault or a lack **2 :** of, relating to, or being a verb tense used to designate a continuing state or an incomplete action esp. in the past — **im·per·fect·ly** *adv*

♦ bad, defective, faulty

²imperfect *n* **:** the imperfect tense; *also* **:** a verb form in it

im·per·fec·tion \ˌim-pər-'fek-shən\ *n* **1 :** the quality or state of being imperfect **2** ♦ **:** the quality or aspect which makes something incomplete or defective **:** FAULT, BLEMISH

♦ blemish, defect, deformity, disfigurement, fault, flaw, mark, pockmark, scar

im·pe·ri·al \im-'pir-ē-əl\ *adj* **1 :** of, relating to, or befitting an empire or an emperor; *also* **:** of or relating to the United Kingdom or to the Commonwealth or British Empire **2 :** ROYAL, SOVEREIGN; *also* **:** REGAL, IMPERIOUS **3** ♦ **:** of unusual size or excellence

♦ august, baronial, gallant, glorious, grand, grandiose, heroic, imposing, magnificent, majestic, monumental, noble, proud, regal, royal, splendid, stately

im·pe·ri·al·ism \im-'pir-ē-ə-ˌli-zəm\ *n* **:** the policy of seeking to extend the power, dominion, or territories of a nation — **im·pe·ri·al·ist** \-list\ *n or adj* — **im·pe·ri·al·is·tic** \-ˌpir-ē-ə-'lis-tik\ *adj* — **im·pe·ri·al·is·ti·cal·ly** \-ti-k(ə-)lē\ *adv*

im·per·il \im-'per-əl\ *vb* **-iled** *or* **-illed; -il·ing** *or* **-il·ling** ♦ **:** to bring into peril **:** ENDANGER

♦ adventure, compromise, gamble with, hazard, jeopardize, menace, risk, venture

im·pe·ri·ous \im-'pir-ē-əs\ *adj* **1 :** befitting or characteristic of one of eminent rank or attainments **:** COMMANDING, LORDLY **2** ♦ **:** marked by arrogant assurance **:** DOMINEERING **3** ♦ **:** intensely compelling **:** IMPERATIVE, URGENT — **im·pe·ri·ous·ly** *adv*

♦ [2] authoritarian, autocratic, bossy, despotic, dictatorial, domineering, overbearing, peremptory, tyrannical, tyrannous ♦ [2] arbitrary, dictatorial, high-handed, peremptory, willful ♦ [3] acute, critical, dire, imperative, instant, pressing, urgent

im·per·ish·able \(ˌ)im-'per-i-shə-bəl\ *adj* **:** not perishable or subject to decay

im·per·ma·nent \(ˌ)im-'pər-mə-nənt\ *adj* ♦ **:** not permanent — **im·per·ma·nent·ly** *adv*

♦ interim, provisional, short-term, temporary ♦ ephemeral, evanescent, flash, fleeting, momentary, short-lived, transient

im·per·me·able \(ˌ)im-'pər-mē-ə-bəl\ *adj* **:** not permitting passage (as of a fluid) through its substance

im·per·mis·si·ble \ˌim-pər-'mi-sə-bəl\ *adj* ♦ **:** not permissible 〈~ by law〉

♦ forbidden, taboo *Ant* allowable, permissible, permissive, sufferable

im·per·son·al \(ˌ)im-'pər-sə-nəl\ *adj* **1 :** not referring to any particular person or thing **2 :** not involving human emotions — **im·per·son·al·i·ty** \-ˌpər-sə-'na-lə-tē\ *n* — **im·per·son·al·ly** *adv*

im·per·son·ate \im-'pər-sə-ˌnāt\ *vb* **-at·ed; -at·ing** ♦ **:** to assume or act the character of — **im·per·son·a·tion** \-ˌpər-sə-'nā-shən\ *n*

♦ act, perform, play, portray ♦ masquerade, play, pose

im·per·son·a·tor \-'pər-sə-ˌnā-tər\ *n* ♦ **:** one that impersonates; *esp* **:** an entertainer who impersonates an individual, a type of person, an animal, or an inanimate object

♦ imitator, impressionist, mimic

im·per·ti·nence \(ˌ)im-ˈpərt-ᵊn-əns\ *n* ♦ : the quality or state of being impertinent; *also* : an instance of impertinence

♦ brazenness, discourtesy, disrespect, impudence, incivility, insolence, rudeness

im·per·ti·nent \(ˌ)im-ˈpərt-ᵊn-ənt\ *adj* **1** : IRRELEVANT **2** ♦ : not restrained within due or proper bounds ⟨an ∼ reply⟩ — **im·per·ti·nent·ly** *adv*

♦ arch, bold, brash, brazen, cheeky, cocky, fresh, impudent, insolent, nervy, sassy, saucy ♦ discourteous, ill-bred, ill-mannered, impolite, inconsiderate, rude, thoughtless, uncivil, ungracious, unmannerly

im·per·turb·able \ˌim-pər-ˈtər-bə-bəl\ *adj* ♦ : marked by extreme calm, impassivity, and steadiness

♦ nerveless, unflappable, unshakable

im·per·vi·ous \(ˌ)im-ˈpər-vē-əs\ *adj* **1** ♦ : incapable of being penetrated (as by moisture) **2** : not capable of being affected or disturbed ⟨∼ to criticism⟩

♦ impenetrable, tight

im·pe·ti·go \ˌim-pə-ˈtē-gō, -ˈtī-\ *n* : a contagious skin disease characterized by vesicles, pustules, and yellowish crusts
im·pet·u·ous \im-ˈpe-chə-wəs\ *adj* **1** : marked by impulsive vehemence ⟨∼ temper⟩ **2** : marked by force and violence ⟨with ∼ speed⟩ — **im·pet·u·os·i·ty** \(ˌ)im-ˌpe-chə-ˈwä-sə-tē\ *n* — **im·pet·u·ous·ly** *adv*
im·pe·tus \ˈim-pə-təs\ *n* **1** ♦ : a driving force : IMPULSE; *also* : INCENTIVE **2** : MOMENTUM

♦ boost, encouragement, goad, impulse, incentive, incitement, instigation, momentum, motivation, provocation, spur, stimulus, yeast

im·pi·e·ty \(ˌ)im-ˈpī-ə-tē\ *n, pl* **-ties** **1** : the quality or state of being impious **2** ♦ : an impious act

♦ blasphemy, defilement, desecration, irreverence, sacrilege

im·pinge \im-ˈpinj\ *vb* **im·pinged; im·ping·ing** **1** : to strike or dash esp. with a sharp collision **2** : ENCROACH, INFRINGE — **im·pinge·ment** *n*
im·pi·ous \ˈim-pē-əs, (ˌ)im-ˈpī-\ *adj* : not pious : IRREVERENT, PROFANE
imp·ish \ˈim-pish\ *adj* ♦ : of, relating to, or befitting an imp; *esp* : MISCHIEVOUS — **imp·ish·ly** *adv*

♦ devilish, knavish, mischievous, rascally, roguish, sly, waggish, wicked

imp·ish·ness *n* ♦ : the quality or state of being impish

♦ friskiness, mischief, mischievousness, playfulness

im·pla·ca·ble \(ˌ)im-ˈpla-kə-bəl, -ˈplā-\ *adj* ♦ : not capable of being appeased, pacified, mitigated, or changed ⟨an ∼ enemy⟩ — **im·pla·ca·bil·i·ty** \-ˌpla-kə-ˈbi-lə-tē, -ˌplā-\ *n* — **im·pla·ca·bly** \-ˈpla-kə-blē\ *adv*

♦ adamant, hard, immovable, inflexible, pat, rigid, unbending, uncompromising, unrelenting, unyielding

im·plant \im-ˈplant\ *vb* **1** ♦ : to set firmly or deeply **2** : to fix in the mind or spirit **3** : to insert in living tissue (as for growth or absorption) — **im·plant** \ˈim-ˌplant\ *n* — **im·plan·ta·tion** \ˌim-ˌplan-ˈtā-shən\ *n*

♦ embed, entrench, fix, ingrain, lodge, root

im·plau·si·ble \(ˌ)im-ˈplȯ-zə-bəl\ *adj* ♦ : not plausible — **im·plau·si·bil·i·ty** \-ˌplȯ-zə-ˈbi-lə-tē\ *n* — **im·plau·si·bly** \-ˈplȯ-zə-blē\ *adv*

♦ fantastic, inconceivable, incredible, unbelievable, unconvincing, unimaginable, unthinkable

¹**im·ple·ment** \ˈim-plə-mənt\ *n* ♦ : a device used in the performance of a task : TOOL, UTENSIL

♦ device, instrument, tool, utensil

²**im·ple·ment** \-ˌment\ *vb* **1** ♦ : to put into execution or bring to completion **2** : to provide implements for

♦ administer, apply, enforce, execute

im·ple·men·ta·tion \ˌim-plə-mən-ˈtā-shən\ *n* ♦ : the act of implementing or the state of being implemented

♦ accomplishment, achievement, commission, discharge, enactment, execution, fulfillment, performance, perpetration

im·pli·cate \ˈim-plə-ˌkāt\ *vb* **-cat·ed; -cat·ing** **1** : IMPLY **2** : INVOLVE — **im·pli·ca·tion** \ˌim-plə-ˈkā-shən\ *n*
im·plic·it \im-ˈpli-sət\ *adj* **1** ♦ : understood though not directly

stated or expressed : IMPLIED; *also* : POTENTIAL **2** : COMPLETE, UNQUESTIONING, ABSOLUTE ⟨∼ faith⟩ — **im·plic·it·ly** *adv*

♦ potential, tacit, unexpressed, unspoken, unvoiced, wordless *Ant* explicit, express, expressed, spoken, stated

im·plode \im-ˈplōd\ *vb* **im·plod·ed; im·plod·ing** **1** ♦ : to burst or collapse inward **2** : SELF-DESTRUCT — **im·plo·sion** \-ˈplō-zhən\ *n* — **im·plo·sive** \-siv\ *adj*

♦ buckle, cave in, collapse, crumple, give, go, yield

im·plore \im-ˈplȯr\ *vb* **im·plored; im·plor·ing** ♦ : to call upon in supplication : BESEECH, ENTREAT

♦ appeal, beg, beseech, entreat, importune, petition, plead, pray, solicit, supplicate

im·ply \im-ˈplī\ *vb* **im·plied; im·ply·ing** **1** : to involve or indicate by inference, association, or necessary consequence rather than by direct statement ⟨war *implies* fighting⟩ **2** ♦ : to express indirectly : hint at

♦ allude, hint, indicate, infer, insinuate, intimate, suggest

im·po·lite \ˌim-pə-ˈlīt\ *adj* ♦ : not polite : RUDE, DISCOURTEOUS

♦ discourteous, ill-bred, ill-mannered, impertinent, inconsiderate, rude, thoughtless, uncivil, ungracious, unmannerly *Ant* civil, considerate, courteous, genteel, gracious, mannerly, polite, thoughtful, well-bred

im·pol·i·tic \(ˌ)im-ˈpä-lə-ˌtik\ *adj* : not politic : UNWISE
im·pon·der·a·ble \(ˌ)im-ˈpän-də-rə-bəl\ *adj* : incapable of being weighed or evaluated with exactness — **imponderable** *n*
¹**im·port** \im-ˈpȯrt\ *vb* **1** : to bear or convey as meaning or portent : MEAN **2** : to bring (as merchandise) into a place or country from a foreign or external source — **im·port·er** *n*
²**im·port** \ˈim-ˌpȯrt\ *n* **1** : IMPORTANCE, SIGNIFICANCE **2** ♦ : meaning conveyed, professed, or implied : SIGNIFICATION **3** : something (as merchandise) brought in from another country

♦ denotation, drift, intent, meaning, purport, sense, significance, signification

im·por·tance \im-ˈpȯrt-ᵊns\ *n* : the quality or state of being important : MOMENT, SIGNIFICANCE
im·por·tant \im-ˈpȯrt-ᵊnt\ *adj* **1** ♦ : marked by importance : SIGNIFICANT **2** ♦ : giving an impression of self-importance — **im·por·tant·ly** *adv*

♦ [1] big, consequential, eventful, major, material, meaningful, momentous, significant, substantial, weighty *Ant* insignificant, little, minor, slight, small, trivial, unimportant ♦ [1] influential, mighty, potent, powerful, significant, strong *Ant* impotent, insignificant, little, powerless, unimportant, weak ♦ [2] complacent, conceited, egotistic, overweening, pompous, prideful, proud, self-important, self-satisfied, smug, stuck-up, vain

im·por·ta·tion \ˌim-ˌpȯr-ˈtā-shən, -pər-\ *n* **1** : the act or practice of importing **2** : something imported
im·por·tu·nate \im-ˈpȯr-chə-nət\ *adj* **1** : troublesomely urgent or persistent **2** : BURDENSOME, TROUBLESOME
im·por·tune \ˌim-pər-ˈtün, -ˈtyün; im-ˈpȯr-chən\ *vb* **-tuned; -tun·ing** ♦ : to urge or beg with troublesome persistence — **im·por·tu·ni·ty** \-pər-ˈtü-nə-tē, -ˈtyü-\ *n*

♦ appeal, beg, beseech, entreat, implore, petition, plead, pray, solicit, supplicate

im·pose \im-ˈpōz\ *vb* **im·posed; im·pos·ing** **1** ♦ : to establish or apply by authority ⟨∼ a tax⟩; *also* : to establish by force ⟨*imposed* a government⟩ **2** : OBTRUDE ⟨*imposed* herself on others⟩ **3** : to take unwarranted advantage of something ⟨∼ on her good nature⟩

♦ assess, charge, exact, fine, lay, levy, put *Ant* remit

im·pos·ing *adj* ♦ : impressive because of size, bearing, dignity, or grandeur — **im·pos·ing·ly** *adv*

♦ august, baronial, gallant, glorious, grand, grandiose, heroic, magnificent, majestic, monumental, noble, proud, regal, royal, splendid, stately

im·po·si·tion \ˌim-pə-ˈzi-shən\ *n* : something imposed: as **a** : an amount levied **b** : an excessive or uncalled-for requirement or burden
im·pos·si·ble \(ˌ)im-ˈpä-sə-bəl\ *adj* **1** : incapable of being or of occurring **2** ♦ : enormously difficult : felt to be incapable of being done, attained, or fulfilled **3** : extremely undesirable : UNACCEPTABLE — **im·pos·si·bil·i·ty** \-ˌpä-sə-ˈbi-lə-tē\ *n* — **im·pos·si·bly** \-ˈpä-sə-blē\ *adv*

♦ hopeless, unattainable, unsolvable, unworkable *Ant* achievable, attainable, doable, feasible, possible, realizable, workable

¹**im·post** \'im-ˌpōst\ *n* ♦ : something imposed or levied : TAX, DUTY

♦ assessment, duty, levy, tax

²**impost** *n* : a block, capital, or molding from which an arch springs
im·pos·tor *or* **im·pos·ter** \im-'päs-tər\ *n* : one that assumes an identity or title not one's own in order to deceive
im·pos·ture \im-'päs-chər\ *n* : DECEPTION; *esp* : fraudulent impersonation
im·po·tence \-təns\ *n* ♦ : the quality or state of being impotent

♦ inability, inadequacy, incapability, incompetence, ineptitude

im·po·tent \'im-pə-tənt\ *adj* **1** ♦ : lacking in power or strength : deficient in capacity **2 a** : unable to copulate **b** ♦ : failing to produce or incapable of producing offspring : STERILE — **im·po·ten·cy** \-tən-sē\ *n* — **im·po·tent·ly** *adv*

♦ [1] helpless, powerless, weak ♦ [2b] barren, infertile, sterile

im·pound \im-'paůnd\ *vb* **1** : CONFINE, ENCLOSE ⟨∼ stray dogs⟩ **2** : to seize and hold in legal custody **3** : to collect in a reservoir ⟨∼ water⟩ — **im·pound·ment** *n*
im·pov·er·ish \im-'pä-və-rish\ *vb* : to make poor; *also* : to deprive of strength, richness, or fertility
impoverished *adj* **1** : represented by few species or individuals ⟨∼ flora and fauna⟩ **2** : deprived of strength, richness, or fertility
im·pov·er·ish·ment *n* ♦ : the act of impoverishing or the state of being impoverished

♦ beggary, destitution, impecuniousness, indigence, need, pauperism, penury, poverty, want

im·prac·ti·ca·ble \(ˌ)im-'prak-ti-kə-bəl\ *adj* : not practicable : incapable of being put into practice or use ⟨an ∼ plan⟩
im·prac·ti·cal \(ˌ)im-'prak-ti-kəl\ *adj* **1** : not practical **2** ♦ : incapable of being done by the means available : IMPRACTICABLE

♦ inoperable, unusable, unworkable, useless *Ant* practicable, practical, usable, useful, workable

im·pre·cate \'im-pri-ˌkāt\ *vb* **-cat·ed; -cat·ing** : CURSE
im·pre·ca·tion \ˌim-pri-'kā-shən\ *n* ♦ : a prayer or invocation for harm or injury to come upon one; *also* : the act of imprecating

♦ anathema, curse, execration, malediction

im·pre·cise \ˌim-pri-'sīs\ *adj* ♦ : not precise — **im·pre·cise·ly** *adv* — **im·pre·cise·ness** *n* — **im·pre·ci·sion** \-'si-zhən\ *n*

♦ inaccurate, inexact, loose

im·preg·na·ble \im-'preg-nə-bəl\ *adj* **1** ♦ : incapable of being taken by assault : UNCONQUERABLE **2** : not liable to doubt, attack, or question — **im·preg·na·bil·i·ty** \(ˌ)im-ˌpreg-nə-'bi-lə-tē\ *n*

♦ indomitable, insurmountable, invincible, invulnerable, unbeatable, unconquerable

im·preg·nate \im-'preg-ˌnāt\ *vb* **-nat·ed; -nat·ing** **1** : to fertilize or make pregnant **2** ♦ : to cause to be filled, permeated, or saturated — **im·preg·na·tion** \ˌim-ˌpreg-'nā-shən\ *n*

♦ drench, drown, saturate, soak, sop, souse, steep

im·pre·sa·rio \ˌim-prə-'sär-ē-ˌō\ *n, pl* **-ri·os** **1** : the manager or conductor of an opera or concert company **2** : one who puts on an entertainment **3** : MANAGER, PRODUCER
¹**im·press** \im-'pres\ *vb* **1** : to apply with or produce (as a mark) by pressure : IMPRINT **2** : to press, stamp, or print in or upon **3** ♦ : to imprint a vivid impression of (as on the memory) **4** ♦ : to affect esp. forcibly or deeply — **im·press·ible** *adj*

♦ [3] engrave, etch, imprint, ingrain, inscribe ♦ [4] affect, impact, influence, move, strike, sway, tell, touch

²**im·press** \'im-ˌpres\ *n* **1** : a characteristic or distinctive mark **2** : IMPRESSION, EFFECT **3** : IMPRESSION 2 **4** : an image of something formed by or as if by pressure; *esp* : SEAL **5** : a product of pressure or influence
³**im·press** \im-'pres\ *vb* **1** : to force into naval service **2** : to get the aid or services of by forcible argument or persuasion — **im·press·ment** *n*
im·pres·sion \im-'pre-shən\ *n* **1** : a characteristic trait or feature resulting from influence : IMPRESS **2** : a stamp, form, or figure made by impressing : IMPRINT **3** : an esp. marked influence or effect on feeling, sense, or mind **4** : a single print or copy (as from type or from an engraved plate or book) **5** : all the copies of a publication (as a book) printed for one issue : PRINTING **6** ♦ : a usu. vague notion or remembrance **7** : an imitation in caricature of a noted personality as a form of entertainment

♦ [2] impress, imprint, print, stamp ♦ [6] concept, idea, image, notion, picture, thought

im·pres·sion·able \im-'pre-shə-nə-bəl\ *adj* : capable of being easily impressed : easily molded or influenced
im·pres·sion·ism \im-'pre-shə-ˌni-zəm\ *n, often cap* : a theory or practice in modern art of depicting the natural appearances of objects by dabs or strokes of primary unmixed colors in order to simulate actual reflected light — **im·pres·sion·is·tic** \-ˌpre-shə-'nis-tik\ *adj*
im·pres·sion·ist \im-'pre-shə-nist\ *n* **1** *often cap* : a painter who practices impressionism **2** ♦ : an entertainer who does impressions

♦ imitator, impersonator, mimic

im·pres·sive \im-'pre-siv\ *adj* ♦ : making or tending to make a marked impression ⟨an ∼ speech⟩ — **im·pres·sive·ly** *adv* — **im·pres·sive·ness** *n*

♦ affecting, emotional, moving, poignant, stirring, touching

im·pri·ma·tur \ˌim-prə-'mä-ˌtůr\ *n* **1** : a license to print or publish; *also* : official approval of a publication by a censor **2** ♦ : explicit or official approval, permission, or ratification

♦ approbation, approval, blessing, favor (*or* favour), OK

¹**im·print** \im-'print, 'im-ˌprint\ *vb* **1** : to stamp or mark by or as if by pressure : IMPRESS **2** ♦ : to fix firmly (as on the memory)

♦ engrave, etch, impress, ingrain, inscribe

²**im·print** \'im-ˌprint\ *n* **1** ♦ : something imprinted or printed; *also* : a mark or depression made by pressure **2** : a publisher's name printed at the foot of a title page **3** : an indelible distinguishing effect or influence

♦ trace, track, trail ♦ impress, impression, print, stamp

im·pris·on \im-'priz-ᵊn\ *vb* ♦ : to put in or as if in prison : CONFINE

♦ commit, confine, immure, jail *Ant* discharge, free, liberate, release

im·pris·on·ment *n* ♦ : the act of imprisoning or the state of being imprisoned

♦ captivity, confinement, incarceration, internment

im·prob·a·ble \(ˌ)im-'prä-bə-bəl\ *adj* ♦ : unlikely to be true or to occur — **im·prob·a·bil·i·ty** \-ˌprä-bə-'bi-lə-tē\ *n* — **im·prob·a·bly** \-'prä-bə-blē\ *adv*

♦ doubtful, dubious, flimsy, questionable, unlikely *Ant* likely, probable

im·promp·tu \im-'prämp-tü, -tyü\ *adj* **1** : made or done on or as if on the spur of the moment **2** : composed or uttered without previous preparation : EXTEMPORANEOUS, UNREHEARSED — **impromptu** *adv or n*

♦ ad-lib, extemporaneous, offhand, snap, unplanned, unpremeditated, unprepared, unrehearsed

im·prop·er \(ˌ)im-'prä-pər\ *adj* **1** ♦ : not proper, fit, or suitable **2** : INCORRECT, INACCURATE **3** : not in accord with propriety, modesty, or good manners

♦ inappropriate, inapt, infelicitous, unbecoming, unfit, unseemly, unsuitable, wrong

improper fraction *n* : a fraction whose numerator is equal to or larger than the denominator
im·prop·er·ly *adv* ♦ : in an improper manner

♦ amiss, erroneously, faultily, inaptly, incorrectly, mistakenly, wrongly

im·pro·pri·e·ty \ˌim-prə-'prī-ə-tē\ *n, pl* **-ties** **1** ♦ : an improper act or remark; *esp* : an unacceptable use of a word or of language **2** ♦ : the quality or state of being improper

♦ [1] familiarity, gaffe, indiscretion *Ant* amenity, civility, courtesy, formality, gesture ♦ [2] incorrectness, indecency *Ant* appropriateness, correctness, decency, fitness, propriety, rightness, suitability

im·prov \'im-ˌpräv\ *adj* : of, relating to, or being an improvised comedy routine — **improv** *n*
im·prove \im-'prüv\ *vb* **im·proved; im·prov·ing** **1** ♦ : to enhance or increase in value or quality **2** : to grow or become better ⟨your work is *improving*⟩ **3** : to make good use of ⟨∼ the time by reading⟩ — **im·prov·able** \-'prü-və-bəl\ *adj*

♦ ameliorate, amend, better, enhance, enrich, perfect, refine *Ant* worsen

im·prove·ment \im-'prüv-mənt\ *n* **1** : the act or process of improving **2** : increased value or excellence of something **3** ♦ : something that adds to the value or appearance of a thing

♦ advance, advancement, breakthrough, enhancement, refinement

im·prov·i·dent \(ₙ)im-'prä-və-dənt\ *adj* : not providing for the future — **im·prov·i·dence** \-dəns\ *n*

im·pro·vise \'im-prə-ₙvīz\ *vb* **-vised; -vis·ing** **1** : to compose, recite, play, or sing on the spur of the moment : EXTEMPORIZE ⟨∼ on the piano⟩ **2** : to make, invent, or arrange offhand ⟨∼ a sail out of shirts⟩ — **im·pro·vi·sa·tion** \im-ₙprä-və-'zā-shən, ₙim-prə-və-\ *n* — **im·pro·vis·er** *or* **im·pro·vi·sor** \ₙim-prə-'vī-zər, 'im-prə-ₙvī-\ *n*

im·pru·dent \(ₙ)im-'prüd-ᵊnt\ *adj* ♦ : not prudent : lacking discretion, wisdom, or good judgment — **im·pru·dence** \-ᵊns\ *n*

♦ ill-advised, indiscreet, tactless, unwise

im·pu·dence \'im-pyü-dəns\ *n* ♦ : the quality or state of being impudent; *also* : an impudent remark or act

♦ brazenness, discourtesy, disrespect, impertinence, incivility, insolence, rudeness

im·pu·dent \-dənt\ *adj* ♦ : marked by contemptuous boldness or disregard of others — **im·pu·dent·ly** *adv*

♦ arch, bold, brash, brazen, cheeky, cocky, fresh, impertinent, insolent, nervy, sassy, saucy

im·pugn \im-'pyün\ *vb* : to attack by words or arguments : oppose or attack as false or as lacking integrity ⟨∼ed his rival's character⟩

im·pulse \'im-ₙpəls\ *n* **1** : a force that starts a body into motion; *also* : the motion produced by such a force **2** ♦ : an arousing of the mind and spirit to some usu. unpremeditated action **3** : NERVE IMPULSE

♦ boost, encouragement, goad, impetus, incentive, incitement, instigation, momentum, motivation, provocation, spur, stimulus, yeast

im·pul·sion \im-'pəl-shən\ *n* **1** : the act of impelling : the state of being impelled **2** : a force that impels **3** : IMPULSE 2; *also* : COMPULSION 3

im·pul·sive \im-'pəl-siv\ *adj* **1** : having the power of or actually driving or impelling **2** ♦ : acting or prone to act on impulse ⟨∼ buying⟩ — **im·pul·sive·ly** *adv* — **im·pul·sive·ness** *n*

♦ capricious, whimsical

im·pu·ni·ty \im-'pyü-nə-tē\ *n* : exemption from punishment, harm, or loss

im·pure \(ₙ)im-'pyùr\ *adj* **1** : not pure : UNCHASTE, OBSCENE **2** : DIRTY, FOUL **3** ♦ : mixed or impregnated with an extraneous and usu. unwanted substance : ADULTERATED

♦ dilute, polluted *Ant* pure, unadulterated, unalloyed, uncontaminated, undiluted, unpolluted, untainted

im·pu·ri·ty \-'pyùr-ə-tē\ *n* ♦ : something that is impure or makes something else impure; *also* : the quality or state of being impure

♦ adulterant, contaminant, defilement, pollutant

im·pute \im-'pyüt\ *vb* **im·put·ed; im·put·ing** **1** : to lay the responsibility or blame for often falsely or unjustly **2** ♦ : to credit to a person or a cause : ATTRIBUTE — **im·put·able** \-'pyü-tə-bəl\ *adj* — **im·pu·ta·tion** \ₙim-pyù-'tä-shən\ *n*

♦ accredit, ascribe, attribute, credit

¹in \'in\ *prep* **1** — used to indicate physical surroundings ⟨swim ∼ the lake⟩ **2** : INTO 1 ⟨ran ∼ the house⟩ **3** : DURING ⟨∼ the summer⟩ **4** : WITH ⟨written ∼ pencil⟩ **5** — used to indicate one's situation or state of being ⟨∼ luck⟩ ⟨∼ love⟩ **6** — used to indicate manner or purpose ⟨∼ a hurry⟩ ⟨said ∼ reply⟩ **7** : INTO 2 ⟨broke ∼ pieces⟩

²in *adv* **1** : to or toward the inside ⟨come ∼⟩; *also* : to or toward some destination or place ⟨flew ∼ from the South⟩ **2** ♦ : at close quarters : NEAR ⟨the enemy closed ∼⟩ **3** : into the midst of something ⟨mix ∼ the flour⟩ **4** : to or at its proper place ⟨fit a piece ∼⟩ **5** : WITHIN ⟨locked ∼⟩ **6** : in vogue or season **7** : in one's presence, possession, or control ⟨the results are ∼⟩

♦ around, by, close, hard, near, nearby, nigh

³in *adj* **1** : located inside or within **2** : that is in position, operation, or power ⟨the ∼ party⟩ **3** : directed inward : INCOMING ⟨the ∼ train⟩ **4** ♦ : keenly aware of and responsive to what is new and fashionable ⟨the ∼ crowd⟩; *also* : extremely fashionable ⟨the ∼ thing to do⟩

♦ à la mode, chic, fashionable, modish, popular, sharp, smart, snappy, stylish

⁴in *n* **1** : one who is in office or power or on the inside **2** : INFLUENCE, PULL ⟨he has an ∼ with the owner⟩

⁵in *abbr* **1** inch **2** inlet

In *symbol* indium

IN *abbr* Indiana

in- \(ₙ)in\ *prefix* : not : absence of : NON-, UN-

inadmissibility	indiscernible
inadmissibleinadvisability	inedible
inadvisable	ineducable
inapparent	ineffaceable
inapplicable	inefficacious
inapposite	inefficacy
inapproachable	inelastic
inaptitude	inelasticity
inarguable	inequitable
inartistic	inequity
inaudible	ineradicable
inaudibly	inerrant
incautious	inexpedient
incombustible	inextinguishable
incomprehension	infeasible
inconclusive	injudicious
incongruent	inoffensive
inconsistency	insanitary
incoordination	insensitive
indecipherable	insensitivity
indemonstrable	insignificance
indestructible	insolvable
indeterminable	insusceptible

in·abil·i·ty \ₙi-nə-'bi-lə-tē\ *n* ♦ : the quality or state of being unable

♦ impotence, inadequacy, incapability, incompetence, ineptitude *Ant* ability, adequacy, capability, capacity, competence, potency

in ab·sen·tia \ₙin-ab-'sen-chə, -chē-ə\ *adv* : in one's absence

in·ac·ces·si·ble \ₙi-nik-'se-sə-bəl, (ₙ)i-ₙnak-\ *adj* ♦ : not accessible — **in·ac·ces·si·bil·i·ty** \-ₙse-sə-'bi-lə-tē\ *n*

♦ inconvenient, unapproachable, unattainable, unavailable, unobtainable, unreachable, untouchable *Ant* accessible, approachable, attainable, convenient, obtainable, reachable

in·ac·cu·ra·cy \(ₙ)i-'na-kyə-rə-sē, -k(ə-)rə-sē\ *n, pl* **-cies** **1** : the quality or state of being inaccurate **2** : something (as a statement or act) that is inaccurate

in·ac·cu·rate \-'a-kyə-rət, -k(ə-)rət\ *adj* ♦ : not accurate

♦ erroneous, false, incorrect, inexact, invalid, off, unsound, untrue, wrong

in·ac·tion \(ₙ)i-'nak-shən\ *n* ♦ : not occupied or employed

♦ dormancy, idleness, inactivity, inertness, quiescence *Ant* action, activeness, activity

in·ac·ti·vate \(ₙ)i-'nak-tə-ₙvāt\ *vb* : to make inactive — **in·ac·ti·va·tion** \(ₙ)i-ₙnak-tə-'vā-shən\ *n*

in·ac·tive \(ₙ)i-'nak-tiv\ *adj* ♦ : not active, energetic, or in use

♦ dull, inert, lethargic, quiescent, sleepy, sluggish, torpid *Ant* active ♦ dead, dormant, fallow, free, idle, inert, inoperative, latent, off, vacant *Ant* active, alive, busy, employed, functioning, on, operating, operative, running, working

in·ac·tiv·i·ty \-ₙnak-'ti-və-tē\ *n* ♦ : the quality or state of being inactive

♦ dormancy, idleness, inaction, inertness, quiescence

in·ad·e·qua·cy \(ₙ)i-'na-di-kwə-sē\ *n* ♦ : the quality or state of being inadequate or insufficient

♦ dearth, deficiency, deficit, failure, famine, insufficiency, lack, paucity, poverty, scantiness, scarcity, shortage, want ♦ impotence, inability, incapability, incompetence, ineptitude

in·ad·e·quate \-kwət\ *adj* ♦ : not adequate : INSUFFICIENT — **in·ad·e·quate·ly** *adv* — **in·ad·e·quate·ness** *n*

♦ deficient, insufficient, scarce, short, shy, wanting

in·ad·ver·tent \ₙi-nəd-'vərt-ᵊnt\ *adj* **1** : HEEDLESS, INATTENTIVE **2** : not intentional : UNINTENTIONAL — **in·ad·ver·tence** \-ᵊns\ *n* — **in·ad·ver·ten·cy** \-ᵊn-sē\ *n* — **in·ad·ver·tent·ly** *adv*

in·alien·able \(ₙ)i-'nāl-yə-nə-bəl, -'nā-lē-ə-\ *adj* : incapable of being alienated, surrendered, or transferred ⟨∼ rights⟩ — **in·alien·abil·i·ty** \(ₙ)i-ₙnāl-yə-nə-'bi-lə-tē, -ₙnā-lē-ə-\ *n* — **in·alien·ably** *adv*

in·amo·ra·ta \i-ₙnä-mə-'rä-tə\ *n* : a woman with whom one is in love

inane \i-'nān\ *adj* **inan·er; -est** **1** : EMPTY, INSUBSTANTIAL **2** : lacking significance, meaning, or point

in·an·i·mate \(ˌ)i-'na-nə-mət\ *adj* : not animate or animated : lacking the qualities of living things — **in·an·i·mate·ly** *adv* — **in·an·i·mate·ness** *n*

inan·i·ty \i-'na-nə-tē\ *n* **1** ♦ : the quality or state of being inane **2** ♦ : something that is inane

♦ [1, 2] absurdity, asininity, balminess, daftness, fatuity, folly, foolishness, silliness, simplicity, zaniness ♦ [2] absurdity, fatuity, folly, foolery, foolishness, idiocy, madness, stupidity

in·ap·pre·cia·ble \ˌi-nə-'prē-shə-bəl\ *adj* ♦ : too small to be perceived — **in·ap·pre·cia·bly** \-blē\ *adv*

♦ impalpable, imperceptible, indistinguishable

in·ap·pro·pri·ate \ˌi-nə-'prō-prē-ˌət\ *adj* : not in good taste or suitable for a particular occasion or situation

♦ amiss, graceless, improper, inapt, incongruous, incorrect, indecorous, inept, infelicitous, unapt, unbecoming, unfit, unhappy, unseemly, unsuitable, wrong *Ant* appropriate, becoming, befitting, correct, fit, fitting, proper, right, seemly, suitable

in·apt \(ˌ)i-'napt\ *adj* **1** : not suitable ⟨an ~ analogy⟩ **2** ♦ : inappropriate or incompetent often to an absurd degree : INEPT — **in·apt·ness** *n*

♦ [1, 2] improper, inappropriate, infelicitous, unbecoming, unfit, unseemly, unsuitable, wrong

in·apt·ly *adv* ♦ : in an inapt manner

♦ amiss, erroneously, faultily, improperly, incorrectly, mistakenly, wrongly

in·ar·tic·u·late \ˌi-när-'ti-kyə-lət\ *adj* **1** : not understandable as spoken words **2** ♦ : incapable of speech esp. under stress of emotion : MUTE **3** : incapable of being expressed by speech; *also* : UNSPOKEN **4** : not having the power of distinct utterance or effective expression — **in·ar·tic·u·late·ly** *adv*

♦ dumb, mute, speechless, voiceless

in·as·much as \ˌi-nəz-'məch-\ *conj* : seeing that : SINCE
in·at·ten·tion \ˌi-nə-'ten-chən\ *n* : failure to pay attention : DISREGARD
in·at·ten·tive \-'ten-tiv\ *adj* : not paying attention : not attentive
¹**in·au·gu·ral** \i-'no-gyə-rəl, -gə-\ *adj* **1** : of or relating to an inauguration **2** ♦ : marking a beginning

♦ first, initial, maiden, original, pioneer, premier

²**inaugural** *n* **1** : an inaugural address **2** : an act of inaugurating : INAUGURATION; *esp* : a ceremonial induction into office
in·au·gu·rate \i-'no-gyə-ˌrāt, -gə-\ *vb* **-rat·ed; -rat·ing** **1** ♦ : to introduce into an office with suitable ceremonies : INSTALL **2** ♦ : to dedicate ceremoniously **3** ♦ : to bring about the beginning of : INITIATE

♦ [1] baptize, induct, initiate, install, invest ♦ [3] constitute, establish, found, initiate, innovate, institute, introduce, launch, pioneer, set up, start

in·au·gu·ra·tion \-ˌno-gyə-'rā-shən, -gə-\ *n* ♦ : an act of inaugurating; *also* : a ceremonial induction into office

♦ inaugural, induction, installation, investiture

in·aus·pi·cious \ˌi-ˌno-'spi-shəs\ *adj* ♦ : not auspicious

♦ foreboding, ominous, portentous, prophetic

in·au·then·tic \ˌi-no-'then-tik\ *adj* ♦ : not authentic

♦ bogus, counterfeit, fake, false, phony, sham, spurious, unauthentic

in·board \'in-ˌbōrd\ *adv* **1** : inside the hull of a ship **2** : close or closest to the center line of a vehicle or craft — **inboard** *adj*
in·born \'in-'bȯrn\ *adj* **1** ♦ : present from or as if from birth **2** ♦ : genetically transmitted or transmittable from parent to offspring : HEREDITARY, INHERITED

♦ [1] essential, ingrained, inherent, innate, integral, intrinsic, natural ♦ [2] genetic, hereditary, heritable, inherited

in·bound \'in-ˌbau̇nd\ *adj* : inward bound ⟨~ traffic⟩
in–box \-ˌbäks\ *n* : a receptacle for incoming interoffice letters; *also* : a computer folder for incoming e-mail
in·bred \'in-'bred\ *adj* **1** : ingrained in one's nature as deeply as if by heredity **2** : subjected to or produced by inbreeding
in·breed·ing \'in-ˌbrē-diŋ\ *n* **1** : the interbreeding of closely related individuals esp. to preserve and fix desirable characters of and to eliminate unfavorable characters from a stock **2** : confinement to a narrow range or a local or limited field of choice — **in·breed** \-'brēd\ *vb*

inc *abbr* **1** incomplete **2** incorporated **3** increase
In·ca \'iŋ-kə\ *n* **1** : a noble or a member of the Quechua-speaking peoples of Peru until the Spanish conquest **2** : a member of any people under Inca influence
in·cal·cu·la·ble \(ˌ)in-'kal-kyə-lə-bəl\ *adj* : not capable of being calculated; *esp* : too large or numerous to be calculated ⟨~ consequences⟩ — **in·cal·cu·la·bly** \-blē\ *adv*
in·can·des·cence \ˌin-kən-'des-ᵊns\ *n* ♦ : the quality or state of being incandescent; *esp* : emission by a hot body of radiation that makes it visible

♦ blaze, flare, fluorescence, glare, gleam, glow, illumination, light, luminescence, radiance, shine

in·can·des·cent \ˌin-kən-'des-ᵊnt\ *adj* **1** : glowing with heat **2** ♦ : strikingly bright, radiant, or clear : SHINING, BRILLIANT

♦ beaming, bright, brilliant, effulgent, glowing, lambent, lucent, luminous, lustrous, radiant, refulgent, shiny

incandescent lamp *n* : a lamp in which an electrically heated filament emits light
in·can·ta·tion \ˌin-ˌkan-'tā-shən\ *n* ♦ : a use of spells or verbal charms spoken or sung as a part of a ritual of magic; *also* : a formula of words used in or as if in such a ritual

♦ bewitchment, charm, conjuration, enchantment, spell

in·ca·pa·bil·i·ty \(ˌ)in-ˌkā-pə-'bi-lə-tē\ *n* ♦ : the quality or state of being incapable

♦ impotence, inability, inadequacy, incompetence, ineptitude

in·ca·pa·ble \(ˌ)in-'kā-pə-bəl\ *adj* ♦ : lacking ability or qualification for a particular purpose; *also* : UNQUALIFIED

♦ incompetent, inept, inexpert, unfit, unqualified, unskilled, unskillful

in·ca·pac·i·tate \ˌin-kə-'pa-sə-ˌtāt\ *vb* **-tat·ed; -tat·ing** ♦ : to make incapable or unfit : DISABLE

♦ cripple, disable, hamstring, immobilize, paralyze, prostrate

in·ca·pac·i·ty \ˌin-kə-'pa-sə-tē\ *n, pl* **-ties** : the quality or state of being incapable
in·car·cer·ate \in-'kär-sə-ˌrāt\ *vb* **-at·ed; -at·ing** : to put in prison : IMPRISON, CONFINE
in·car·cer·a·tion \(ˌ)in-ˌkär-sə-'rā-shən\ *n* ♦ : a confining or state of being confined

♦ captivity, confinement, imprisonment, internment

in·car·na·dine \in-'kär-nə-ˌdīn, -ˌdēn\ *vb* **-dined; -din·ing** : REDDEN
¹**in·car·nate** \in-'kär-nət, -ˌnāt\ *adj* **1** : having bodily and esp. human form and substance **2** : PERSONIFIED
²**in·car·nate** \-ˌnāt\ *vb* : to make incarnate: as **a** : to give bodily form and substance to **b** : to give a concrete or actual form to
in·car·na·tion \ˌin-ˌkär-'nā-shən\ *n* **1 a** : the embodiment of a deity or spirit in an earthly form **b** ♦ : a concrete or actual form of a quality or concept **2** *cap* : the union of divine and human natures in Jesus Christ **3** : a person showing a trait or typical character to a marked degree **4** : the act of incarnating : the state of being incarnate

♦ embodiment, epitome, manifestation, personification

¹**in·cen·di·ary** \in-'sen-dē-ˌer-ē\ *adj* **1** : of or relating to a deliberate burning of property **2** : tending to excite or inflame **3** : designed to start fires ⟨an ~ bomb⟩
²**incendiary** *n* **1 a** : a person who commits arson **b** : an incendiary agent (as a bomb) **2** ♦ : a person who excites factions, quarrels, or sedition

♦ agitator, demagogue, firebrand, inciter, rabble-rouser

¹**in·cense** \'in-ˌsens\ *n* **1** : material used to produce a fragrant odor when burned **2** ♦ : the perfume or smoke from some spices and gums when burned

♦ aroma, bouquet, fragrance, perfume, redolence, scent, spice

²**in·cense** \in-'sens\ *vb* **in·censed; in·cens·ing** ♦ : to make extremely angry

♦ anger, antagonize, enrage, inflame, infuriate, madden, outrage, rankle, rile, roil

in·cen·tive \in-'sen-tiv\ *n* ♦ : something that incites or is likely to incite to determination or action

♦ boost, encouragement, goad, impetus, impulse, incitement, instigation, momentum, motivation, provocation, spur, stimulus, yeast

in·cep·tion \in-'sep-shən\ *n* : an act, process, or instance of beginning : COMMENCEMENT

in·cer·ti·tude \(ˌ)in-'sər-tə-ˌtüd, -ˌtyüd\ *n* **1** ♦ : absence of assurance or confidence : UNCERTAINTY, DOUBT **2** : INSECURITY, INSTABILITY

♦ distrust, doubt, misgiving, mistrust, skepticism, suspicion, uncertainty

in·ces·sant \(ˌ)in-'ses-ᵊnt\ *adj* ♦ : continuing or flowing without interruption ⟨~ rains⟩

♦ ceaseless, continual, continuous, unbroken, unceasing, uninterrupted

in·ces·sant·ly *adv* ♦ : in an unceasing manner or course : without intermission or relief

♦ always, constantly, continually, ever, forever, invariably, perpetually, unfailingly

in·cest \'in-ˌsest\ *n* : sexual intercourse between persons so closely related that marriage is illegal — **in·ces·tu·ous** \in-'ses-chü-wəs\ *adj*

¹**inch** \'inch\ *n* **1** : a unit of length equal to ¹/₃₆ yard **2** ♦ : a small amount, distance, or degree

♦ ace, hair, step, stone's throw

²**inch** *vb* ♦ : to move by small degrees

♦ crawl, creep, drag, plod, poke

in·cho·ate \in-'kō-ət, 'in-kə-ˌwāt\ *adj* : being only partly in existence or operation : INCOMPLETE ⟨~ yearnings⟩
inch·worm \'inch-ˌwərm\ *n* : LOOPER
in·ci·dence \'in-sə-dəns\ *n* : rate of occurrence or effect
¹**in·ci·dent** \-dənt\ *n* **1** ♦ : an occurrence of an action or situation that is a separate unit of experience : HAPPENING **2** : an action likely to lead to grave consequences esp. in diplomatic matters

♦ affair, circumstance, episode, event, happening, occasion, occurrence, thing

²**incident** *adj* **1** : occurring or likely to occur esp. in connection with some other happening **2** : falling or striking on something ⟨~ light rays⟩
¹**in·ci·den·tal** \ˌin-sə-'dent-ᵊl\ *adj* **1** : subordinate, nonessential, or attendant in position or significance ⟨~ expenses⟩ **2** ♦ : occurring merely by chance or without intention or planning : CASUAL, CHANCE

♦ accidental, casual, chance, fluky, fortuitous, unintended, unintentional, unplanned, unpremeditated, unwitting

²**incidental** *n* **1** *pl* : minor items (as of expense) that are not individually accounted for **2** : something incidental
in·ci·den·tal·ly \ˌin-sə-'den-tə-lē, -'dent-lē\ *adv* **1** : in an incidental manner **2** : by the way
in·cin·er·ate \in-'si-nə-ˌrāt\ *vb* **-at·ed; -at·ing** : to burn to ashes
in·cin·er·a·tor \in-'si-nə-ˌrā-tər\ *n* : a furnace for burning waste
in·cip·i·ent \in-'si-pē-ənt\ *adj* : beginning to be or become apparent
in·cise \in-'sīz\ *vb* **in·cised; in·cis·ing** **1** : to cut into **2** : to carve figures, letters, or devices into : ENGRAVE
in·ci·sion \in-'si-zhən\ *n* : a wound made by something sharp : GASH; *esp* : a surgical cut
in·ci·sive \in-'sī-siv\ *adj* : impressively direct and decisive — **in·ci·sive·ly** *adv*
in·ci·sor \in-'sī-zər\ *n* : a front tooth typically adapted for cutting
in·cite \in-'sīt\ *vb* **in·cit·ed; in·cit·ing** ♦ : to arouse to action

♦ abet, ferment, foment, instigate, provoke, raise, stir, whip
♦ arouse, encourage, excite, fire, instigate, move, pique, provoke, stimulate, stir

in·cite·ment *n* ♦ : the act of inciting or the state of being incited

♦ excitement, instigation, provocation, stimulus

in·cit·er *n* ♦ : one that incites

♦ agitator, demagogue, firebrand, incendiary, rabble-rouser

in·ci·vil·i·ty \ˌin-sə-'vi-lə-tē\ *n* **1** ♦ : the quality or state of being uncivil : RUDENESS, DISCOURTESY **2** : a rude or discourteous act

♦ brazenness, discourtesy, disrespect, impertinence, impudence, insolence, rudeness

incl *abbr* include; included; including; inclusive
in·clem·ent \(ˌ)in-'kle-mənt\ *adj* ♦ : lacking mildness; *esp* : physically severe : STORMY ⟨~ weather⟩ — **in·clem·en·cy** \-mən-sē\ *n*

♦ bleak, dirty, foul, nasty, raw, rough, squally, stormy, tempestuous, turbulent

in·cli·na·tion \ˌin-klə-'nā-shən\ *n* **1** ♦ : a particular disposition of mind or character : PROPENSITY; *esp* : LIKING **2** : BOW, NOD ⟨an

~ of the head⟩ **3** : a tilting of something **4** ♦ : the degree of deviation from the true vertical or horizontal : SLANT, SLOPE

♦ [1] affinity, bent, devices, disposition, genius, leaning, partiality, penchant, predilection, predisposition, proclivity, propensity, talent, tendency, turn ♦ [4] cant, diagonal, grade, incline, lean, pitch, slant, slope, tilt, upgrade

¹**in·cline** \in-'klīn\ *vb* **in·clined; in·clin·ing** **1** : BOW, BEND **2** ♦ : to be drawn toward an opinion or course of action **3** ♦ : to deviate from the vertical or horizontal : SLOPE **4** : INFLUENCE, PERSUADE — **in·clin·er** *n*

♦ [2] lean, run, tend, trend ♦ [3] angle, cant, cock, heel, lean, list, slant, slope, tilt, tip

²**in·cline** \'in-ˌklīn\ *n* : an inclined plane : SLOPE
in·clined *adj* **1** ♦ : having inclination, disposition, or tendency **2 a** ♦ : having a leaning or slope **b** ♦ : making an angle with a line or plane

♦ [1] amenable, disposed, game, glad, ready, willing ♦ [1] apt, given, prone ♦ [2a, b] canted, diagonal, listing, oblique, slantwise

inclose, inclosure *var of* ENCLOSE, ENCLOSURE
in·clude \in-'klüd\ *vb* **in·clud·ed; in·clud·ing** ♦ : to take in or comprise as a part of a whole ⟨the price ~s tax⟩ — **in·clu·sion** \in-'klü-zhən\ *n*

♦ carry, comprehend, contain, embrace, encompass, entail, involve, number, take in *Ant* exclude, omit

in·clu·sive \-'klü-siv\ *adj* **1** : comprehending stated limits or extremes **2** ♦ : broad in orientation or scope; *also* : covering or intended to cover all items, costs, or services

♦ compendious, complete, comprehensive, encyclopedic, full, global, omnibus, panoramic, universal

incog *abbr* incognito
¹**in·cog·ni·to** \ˌin-käg-'nē-tō, in-'käg-nə-ˌtō\ *n, pl* **-tos** **1** : one appearing or living incognito **2** : the state or disguise of an incognito
²**incognito** *adv or adj* : with one's identity concealed
in·co·her·ent \ˌin-kō-'hir-ənt, -'her-\ *adj* **1** : not sticking closely or compactly together : LOOSE **2** ♦ : not clearly or logically connected : RAMBLING — **in·co·her·ence** \-əns\ *n* — **in·co·her·ent·ly** *adv*

♦ disconnected, disjointed, rambling, unconnected *Ant* coherent, connected

in·come \'in-ˌkəm\ *n* ♦ : a gain usu. measured in money that derives from labor, business, or property

♦ earnings, proceeds, profit, return, revenue, yield

income tax *n* : a tax on the net income of an individual or business concern
in·com·ing \'in-ˌkə-miŋ\ *adj* : coming in ⟨the ~ tide⟩ ⟨~ freshmen⟩
in·com·men·su·rate \ˌin-kə-'men-sə-rət, -'men-chə-\ *adj* : not commensurate; *esp* : INADEQUATE
in·com·mode \ˌin-kə-'mōd\ *vb* **-mod·ed; -mod·ing** : to give inconvenience or distress to : DISTURB
in·com·mu·ni·ca·ble \ˌin-kə-'myü-ni-kə-bəl\ *adj* : not capable of being communicated or imparted; *also* : UNCOMMUNICATIVE
in·com·mu·ni·ca·do \ˌin-kə-ˌmyü-nə-'kä-dō\ *adv or adj* : without means of communication; *also* : in solitary confinement ⟨a prisoner held ~⟩
in·com·pa·ra·ble \(ˌ)in-'käm-pə-rə-bəl, -prə-\ *adj* **1** ♦ : eminent beyond comparison : MATCHLESS **2** : not suitable for comparison — **in·com·pa·ra·bly** \-blē\ *adv*

♦ inimitable, matchless, nonpareil, only, peerless, unequaled, unmatched, unparalleled, unrivaled, unsurpassed

in·com·pat·i·ble \ˌin-kəm-'pa-tə-bəl\ *adj* ♦ : incapable of or unsuitable for association or use together ⟨~ colors⟩ ⟨temperamentally ~⟩ — **in·com·pat·i·bil·i·ty** \ˌin-kəm-ˌpa-tə-'bi-lə-tē\ *n*

♦ discordant, discrepant, incongruous, inharmonious

in·com·pe·tence \-təns\ *n* ♦ : the state or fact of being incompetent

♦ impotence, inability, inadequacy, incapability, ineptitude

in·com·pe·tent \(ˌ)in-'käm-pə-tənt\ *adj* **1** : not legally qualified **2** ♦ : not competent : lacking sufficient knowledge, skill, or ability — **in·com·pe·ten·cy** \-tən-sē\ *n* — **incompetent** *n*

♦ incapable, inept, inexpert, unfit, unqualified, unskilled, unskillful *Ant* able, capable, competent, expert, fit, qualified, skilled, skillful

in·com·plete \ˌin-kəm-ˈplēt\ *adj* ♦ : lacking a part or parts : UN-FINISHED, IMPERFECT — **in·com·plete·ness** *n*

♦ deficient, fragmentary, halfway, imperfect, partial *Ant* complete, entire, full, intact, whole

in·com·plete·ly *adv* : in an incomplete manner or to an incomplete degree : not wholly, perfectly, or fully

in·com·pre·hen·si·ble \ˌin-ˌkäm-prē-ˈhen-sə-bəl\ *adj* ♦ : impossible to comprehend : UNINTELLIGIBLE ⟨~ muttering⟩

♦ impenetrable, unfathomable *Ant* fathomable, intelligible, understandable

in·con·ceiv·able \ˌin-kən-ˈsē-və-bəl\ *adj* 1 : impossible to comprehend 2 ♦ : impossible to believe : UNBELIEVABLE

♦ fantastic, implausible, incredible, unbelievable, unconvincing, unimaginable, unthinkable

in·con·gru·ous \(ˌ)in-ˈkäŋ-grü-wəs\ *adj* 1 : not consistent with or suitable to the surroundings or associations 2 ♦ : lacking harmony — **in·con·gru·i·ty** \ˌin-kən-ˈgrü-ə-tē, -ˌkän-\ *n* — **in·con·gru·ous·ly** *adv*

♦ discordant, discrepant, incompatible, inharmonious

in·con·se·quen·tial \ˌin-ˌkän-sə-ˈkwen-chəl\ *adj* 1 : ILLOGICAL; *also* : IRRELEVANT 2 ♦ : of no significance : UNIMPORTANT — **in·con·se·quence** \(ˌ)in-ˈkän-sə-ˌkwens\ *n* — **in·con·se·quen·tial·ly** *adv*

♦ frivolous, inconsiderable, insignificant, little, minor, minute, negligible, slight, small, trifling, trivial, unimportant

in·con·sid·er·able \ˌin-kən-ˈsi-də-rə-bəl\ *adj* ♦ : not considerable : SLIGHT, TRIVIAL

♦ inconsequential, insignificant, measly, minute, negligible, nominal, paltry, petty, slight, trifling, trivial

in·con·sid·er·ate \ˌin-kən-ˈsi-də-rət\ *adj* ♦ : not taking heed : THOUGHTLESS; *esp* : not respecting the rights or feelings of others — **in·con·sid·er·ate·ly** *adv* — **in·con·sid·er·ate·ness** *n*

♦ discourteous, ill-bred, ill-mannered, impertinent, impolite, rude, thoughtless, uncivil, ungracious, unmannerly

in·con·sis·tent \ˌin-kən-ˈsis-tənt\ *adj* : lacking consistency : not compatible with facts or claims

in·con·sol·able \ˌin-kən-ˈsō-lə-bəl\ *adj* : incapable of being consoled — **in·con·sol·ably** \-blē\ *adv*

in·con·spic·u·ous \ˌin-kən-ˈspi-kyə-wəs\ *adj* : not readily noticeable — **in·con·spic·u·ous·ly** *adv*

in·con·stan·cy \-stən-sē\ *n* ♦ : the quality or state of being inconstant

♦ disloyalty, faithlessness, falseness, falsity, infidelity, perfidy, unfaithfulness

in·con·stant \(ˌ)in-ˈkän-stənt\ *adj* ♦ : not constant : CHANGEABLE — **in·con·stant·ly** *adv*

♦ capricious, changeable, fickle, fluid, mercurial, mutable, temperamental, uncertain, unpredictable, unsettled, unstable, unsteady, variable, volatile

in·con·test·able \ˌin-kən-ˈtes-tə-bəl\ *adj* ♦ : not contestable : INDISPUTABLE

♦ indisputable, indubitable, irrefutable, unanswerable, undeniable, unquestionable

in·con·test·ably \-ˈtes-tə-blē\ *adv* ♦ : in an incontestable manner or to an incontestable degree or level : with certainty

♦ certainly, definitely, doubtless, indeed, indisputably, really, surely, truly, undeniably, undoubtedly, unquestionably

in·con·ti·nent \(ˌ)in-ˈkänt-ᵊn-ənt\ *adj* 1 : lacking self-restraint 2 : unable to retain urine or feces voluntarily — **in·con·ti·nence** \-əns\ *n*

in·con·tro·vert·ible \ˌin-ˌkän-trə-ˈvər-tə-bəl\ *adj* : not open to question : INDISPUTABLE ⟨~ evidence⟩

in·con·tro·vert·ibly \-blē\ *adv* : not open to question

¹**in·con·ve·nience** \ˌin-kən-ˈvē-nyəns\ *n* 1 ♦ : something that is inconvenient 2 : the quality or state of being inconvenient

♦ aggravation, annoyance, bother, exasperation, frustration, hassle, headache, irritant, nuisance, peeve, pest, problem, thorn

²**inconvenience** *vb* **-nienced; -niencing** ♦ : to subject to inconvenience

♦ discommode, disoblige, disturb, trouble *Ant* accommodate, oblige

in·con·ve·nient \ˌin-kən-ˈvē-nyənt\ *adj* 1 ♦ : not convenient 2 ♦ : causing trouble or annoyance — **in·con·ve·nient·ly** *adv*

♦ [1] inaccessible, unapproachable, unattainable, unavailable, unobtainable, unreachable, untouchable ♦ [2] awkward *Ant* convenient

in·cor·po·rate \in-ˈkȯr-pə-ˌrāt\ *vb* **-rat·ed; -rat·ing** 1 ♦ : to unite closely or so as to form one body 2 : to form, form into, or become a corporation 3 : to give material form to : EMBODY — **in·cor·po·ra·tion** \-ˌkȯr-pə-ˈrā-shən\ *n*

♦ assimilate, commingle, integrate, intermingle, merge

in·cor·po·re·al \ˌin-kȯr-ˈpōr-ē-əl\ *adj* ♦ : having no material body or form

♦ bodiless, immaterial, insubstantial, nonmaterial, nonphysical, spiritual, unsubstantial

in·cor·rect \ˌin-kə-ˈrekt\ *adj* 1 : marked by fault or defect : IN-ACCURATE 2 ♦ : not true : WRONG 3 ♦ : not according with appropriate standards : UNBECOMING, IMPROPER

♦ [2] erroneous, false, inaccurate, inexact, invalid, off, unsound, untrue, wrong ♦ [3] improper, inappropriate, inapt, infelicitous, unbecoming, unfit, unseemly, unsuitable, wrong

in·cor·rect·ly *adv* ♦ : in an incorrect manner

♦ amiss, erroneously, faultily, improperly, inaptly, mistakenly, wrongly

in·cor·rect·ness *n* ♦ : the quality or state of being incorrect

♦ impropriety, indecency

in·cor·ri·gi·ble \(ˌ)in-ˈkȯr-ə-jə-bəl\ *adj* ♦ : incapable of being corrected, amended, or reformed — **in·cor·ri·gi·bil·i·ty** \(ˌ)in-ˌkȯr-ə-jə-ˈbi-lə-tē\ *n* — **in·cor·ri·gi·bly** \-ˈkȯr-ə-jə-blē\ *adv*

♦ hopeless, incurable, irredeemable, irremediable, unrecoverable, unredeemable

in·cor·rupt·ible \ˌin-kə-ˈrəp-tə-bəl\ *adj* 1 : not subject to decay or dissolution 2 : incapable of being bribed or morally corrupted — **in·cor·rupt·ibil·i·ty** \-ˌrəp-tə-ˈbi-lə-tē\ *n* — **in·cor·rupt·ibly** \-ˈrəp-tə-blē\ *adv*

incr *abbr* increase; increased

¹**in·crease** \in-ˈkrēs, ˈin-ˌkrēs\ *vb* **in·creased; in·creas·ing** 1 ♦ : to become greater : GROW 2 : to multiply by the production of young ⟨rabbits ~ rapidly⟩ 3 ♦ : to make greater — **in·creas·ing·ly** \-ˈkrē-siŋ-lē\ *adv*

♦ [1] accumulate, appreciate, balloon, build, burgeon, enlarge, escalate, expand, grow, mount, multiply, mushroom, proliferate, rise, snowball, swell, wax *Ant* contract, decrease, diminish, lessen, wane ♦ [3] add, aggrandize, amplify, augment, boost, compound, enlarge, escalate, expand, extend, multiply, raise, swell, up *Ant* abate, contract, decrease, diminish, lessen, lower, reduce, subtract (from)

²**in·crease** \ˈin-ˌkrēs, in-ˈkrēs\ *n* 1 ♦ : addition or enlargement in size, extent, or quantity : GROWTH 2 ♦ : something that is added to an original stock or amount (as by growth)

♦ accretion, addition, augmentation, boost, expansion, gain, growth, increment, plus, proliferation, raise, rise, supplement *Ant* abatement, decrease, lessening, lowering, reduction

in·cred·i·ble \(ˌ)in-ˈkre-də-bəl\ *adj* ♦ : too extraordinary and improbable to be believed; *also* : hard to believe — **in·cred·i·bil·i·ty** \(ˌ)in-ˌkre-də-ˈbi-lə-tē\ *n*

♦ fantastic, implausible, inconceivable, unbelievable, unconvincing, unimaginable, unthinkable *Ant* believable, conceivable, convincing, credible, imaginable, plausible

in·cred·i·bly \(ˌ)in-ˈkre-də-blē\ *adv* ♦ : in an incredible manner : to an incredible extent : EXTREMELY

♦ extremely, greatly, highly, hugely, mightily, mighty, mortally, most, much, real, right, so, very

in·cred·u·lous \-ˈkre-jə-ləs\ *adj* 1 ♦ : unwilling to admit or accept what is offered as true : SKEPTICAL 2 : expressing disbelief — **in·cre·du·li·ty** \ˌin-kri-ˈdü-lə-tē, -ˈdyü-\ *n* — **in·cred·u·lous·ly** *adv*

♦ distrustful, leery, mistrustful, skeptical, suspicious

in·cre·ment \ˈiŋ-krə-mənt, ˈin-\ *n* 1 : the action or process of increasing esp. in quantity or value : ENLARGEMENT; *also* : QUAN-TITY 2 ♦ : something gained or added; *esp* : one of a series of regular consecutive additions

♦ accretion, addition, augmentation, boost, expansion, gain, increase, plus, proliferation, raise, rise, supplement

in·cre·men·tal \ˌiŋ-krə-ˈment-ᵊl, ˌin-\ *adj* : of, relating to, being, or occurring in esp. small increments — **in·cre·men·tal·ly** *adv*

in·crim·i·nate \in-ˈkri-mə-ˌnāt\ *vb* **-nat·ed; -nat·ing** ♦ : to charge with or prove involvement in a crime or fault : ACCUSE — **in·crim·i·na·tion** \-ˌkri-mə-ˈnā-shən\ *n* — **in·crim·i·na·to·ry** \-ˈkri-mə-nə-ˌtōr-ē\ *adj*

  ♦ accuse, charge, indict

incrust *var of* ENCRUST
in·crus·ta·tion \ˌin-ˌkrəs-ˈtā-shən\ *also* **en·crus·ta·tion** \ˌin-, ˌen-\ **1** : CRUST; *also* : an accumulation (as of habits, opinions, or customs) resembling a crust **2** : the act of encrusting : the state of being encrusted

in·cu·bate \ˈiŋ-kyū-ˌbāt, ˈin-\ *vb* **-bat·ed; -bat·ing** ♦ : to sit on (eggs) to hatch by the warmth of the body; *also* : to keep (as an embryo) under conditions favorable for development — **in·cu·ba·tion** \ˌiŋ-kyū-ˈbā-shən, ˌin-\ *n*

  ♦ brood, hatch, set, sit

in·cu·ba·tor \ˈiŋ-kyū-ˌbāt-ər, ˈin-\ *n* : one that incubates; *esp* : an apparatus providing suitable conditions (as of warmth and moisture) for incubating something (as a premature baby)
in·cu·bus \ˈiŋ-kyə-bəs, ˈin-\ *n, pl* **-bi** \-ˌbī, -ˌbē\ *also* **-bus·es** **1** : a spirit supposed to work evil on persons in their sleep **2** : NIGHTMARE 1 **3** : one that oppresses like a nightmare
in·cul·cate \in-ˈkəl-ˌkāt, ˈin-(ˌ)kəl-\ *vb* **-cat·ed; -cat·ing** ♦ : to teach and impress by frequent repetitions or admonitions — **in·cul·ca·tion** \ˌin-(ˌ)kəl-ˈkā-shən\ *n*

  ♦ imbue, infuse, ingrain, invest, steep, suffuse

in·cul·pa·ble \(ˌ)in-ˈkəl-pə-bəl\ *adj* : free from guilt : INNOCENT
in·cul·pate \in-ˈkəl-ˌpāt, ˈin-(ˌ)kəl-\ *vb* **-pat·ed; -pat·ing** : IN-CRIMINATE
in·cum·ben·cy \in-ˈkəm-bən-sē\ *n, pl* **-cies** **1** : something that is incumbent **2** : the quality or state of being incumbent **3** : the office or period of office of an incumbent
¹**in·cum·bent** \in-ˈkəm-bənt\ *n* : the holder of an office or position
²**incumbent** *adj* **1** ♦ : imposed as a duty **2** : occupying a specified office **3** : lying or resting on something else

  ♦ compulsory, imperative, involuntary, mandatory, necessary, nonelective, obligatory, peremptory

in·cu·nab·u·lum \ˌin-kyə-ˈna-byə-ləm, ˌiŋ-\ *n, pl* **-la** \-lə\ : a book printed before 1501
in·cur \in-ˈkər\ *vb* **in·curred; in·cur·ring** : to become liable or subject to : bring down upon oneself
in·cur·able \(ˌ)in-ˈkyur-ə-bəl\ *adj* **1** ♦ : not curable **2** ♦ : not likely to be changed — **incurable** *n* — **in·cur·ably** \(ˌ)in-ˈkyur-ə-blē\ *adv*

  ♦ [1, 2] hopeless, incorrigible, irredeemable, irremediable, unrecoverable, unredeemable

in·cu·ri·ous \(ˌ)in-ˈkyur-ē-əs\ *adj* : lacking a normal or usual curiosity
in·cur·sion \in-ˈkər-zhən\ *n* **1** ♦ : a sudden hostile invasion : RAID **2** : an entering in or into (as an activity)

  ♦ descent, foray, invasion, irruption, raid

in·cus \ˈiŋ-kəs\ *n, pl* **in·cu·des** \iŋ-ˈkyü-(ˌ)dēz\ : the middle bone of a chain of three small bones in the middle ear of a mammal
ind *abbr* **1** independent **2** index **3** industrial; industry
Ind *abbr* **1** Indian **2** Indiana
in·debt·ed \in-ˈde-təd\ *adj* **1** ♦ : owing gratitude or recognition to another **2** ♦ : owing money — **in·debt·ed·ness** *n*

  ♦ [1, 2] beholden, obligated, obliged

in·de·cen·cy \(ˌ)in-ˈdēs-ᵊn-sē\ *n* ♦ : the quality or state of being indecent

  ♦ impropriety, incorrectness

in·de·cent \(ˌ)in-ˈdēs-ᵊnt\ *adj* ♦ : not decent; *esp* : morally offensive — **in·de·cent·ly** *adv*

  ♦ bawdy, coarse, crude, dirty, filthy, foul, gross, lascivious, lewd, nasty, obscene, pornographic, ribald, smutty, unprintable, vulgar, wanton

in·de·ci·sion \ˌin-di-ˈsi-zhən\ *n* ♦ : a wavering between two or more possible courses of action : IRRESOLUTION

  ♦ hesitancy, hesitation, irresolution, vacillation

in·de·ci·sive \ˌin-di-ˈsī-siv\ *adj* **1** : leading to no conclusion or definite result **2** : marked by or prone to indecision **3** : INDEFINITE — **in·de·ci·sive·ly** *adv* — **in·de·ci·sive·ness** *n*

in·de·co·rous \(ˌ)in-ˈde-kə-rəs; ˌin-di-ˈkōr-əs\ *adj* ♦ : not decorous — **in·de·co·rous·ly** *adv* — **in·de·co·rous·ness** *n*

  ♦ improper, inappropriate, inapt, infelicitous, unbecoming, unfit, unseemly, wrong

in·deed \in-ˈdēd\ *adv* **1** ♦ : without any question — often used interjectionally to express irony, disbelief, or surprise **2** ♦ : in reality **3** : all things considered

  ♦ [1] certainly, definitely, doubtless, incontestably, indisputably, really, surely, truly, undeniably, undoubtedly, unquestionably ♦ [2] even, nay, truly, verily, yea

indef *abbr* indefinite
in·de·fat·i·ga·ble \ˌin-di-ˈfa-ti-gə-bəl\ *adj* ♦ : incapable of being fatigued : UNTIRING

  ♦ inexhaustible, tireless, unflagging, untiring

in·de·fat·i·ga·bly \-blē\ *adv* : in an indefatigable manner
in·de·fea·si·ble \-ˈfē-zə-bəl\ *adj* : not capable of being annulled or voided — **in·de·fea·si·bly** \-blē\ *adv*
in·de·fen·si·ble \-ˈfen-sə-bəl\ *adj* **1** : incapable of being maintained as right or valid **2** ♦ : incapable of being justified or excused : INEXCUSABLE **3** : incapable of being protected against physical attack

  ♦ inexcusable, unforgivable, unjustifiable, unpardonable, unwarrantable

in·de·fin·able \-ˈfī-nə-bəl\ *adj* : incapable of being precisely described or analyzed — **in·de·fin·ably** \-blē\ *adv*
in·def·i·nite \(ˌ)in-ˈde-fə-nət\ *adj* **1** : not defining or identifying ⟨*an* is an ∼ article⟩ **2** ♦ : not precise : VAGUE **3** ♦ : having no fixed limit — **in·def·i·nite·ly** *adv* — **in·def·i·nite·ness** *n*

  ♦ [2] bleary, dim, faint, foggy, fuzzy, hazy, indistinct, indistinguishable, murky, nebulous, obscure, opaque, shadowy, unclear, undefined, undetermined, vague ♦ [3] boundless, endless, illimitable, immeasurable, infinite, limitless, measureless, unbounded, unfathomable, unlimited

in·del·i·ble \in-ˈde-lə-bəl\ *adj* **1** : not capable of being removed or erased **2** : making marks that cannot be erased **3** : LASTING, UNFORGETTABLE ⟨an ∼ performance⟩ — **in·del·i·bly** \in-ˈde-lə-blē\ *adv*
in·del·i·ca·cy \in-ˈde-lə-kə-sē\ *n* **1** ♦ : the quality or state of being indelicate **2** : something that is indelicate

  ♦ coarseness, grossness, lowness, rudeness, vulgarity

in·del·i·cate \(ˌ)in-ˈde-li-kət\ *adj* : not delicate; *esp* : IMPROPER, COARSE, TACTLESS
in·dem·ni·fi·ca·tion \-ˌdem-nə-fə-ˈkā-shən\ *n* **1** : the action of indemnifying; *also* : the condition of being indemnified **2** : something that indemnifies
in·dem·ni·fy \in-ˈdem-nə-ˌfī\ *vb* **-fied; -fy·ing** **1** : to secure against hurt, loss, or damage **2** ♦ : to make compensation to for hurt, loss, or damage

  ♦ compensate, recompense, recoup, remunerate, requite

in·dem·ni·ty \in-ˈdem-nə-tē\ *n, pl* **-ties** **1** : security against hurt, loss, or damage; *also* : exemption from incurred penalties or liabilities **2** ♦ : something that indemnifies

  ♦ compensation, damages, quittance, recompense, redress, remuneration, reparation, requital, restitution, satisfaction

¹**in·dent** \in-ˈdent\ *vb* **1** : to notch the edge of **2** : INDENTURE **3** : to set (as a line of a paragraph) in from the margin
²**indent** *vb* **1** : to force inward so as to form a depression **2** : to form a dent in
in·den·ta·tion \ˌin-ˌden-ˈtā-shən\ *n* **1** ♦ : a V-shaped cut usu. on an edge or a surface : NOTCH; *also* : a usu. deep recess (as in a coastline) **2** : the action of indenting : the condition of being indented **3** ♦ : a depression or hollow made by a blow or by pressure : DENT **4** : INDENTION 2

  ♦ [1] chip, hack, nick, notch ♦ [3] cavity, concavity, dent, depression, hole, hollow, pit, recess

in·den·tion \in-ˈden-chən\ *n* **1** : INDENTATION 2 **2** : the blank space produced by indenting
¹**in·den·ture** \in-ˈden-chər\ *n* **1** : a written certificate or agreement; *esp* : a contract binding one person (as an apprentice) to work for another for a given period of time — usu. used in pl. **2** : INDENTATION 1 **3** : DENT
²**indenture** *vb* **in·den·tured; in·den·tur·ing** : to bind (as an apprentice) by indentures
in·de·pen·dence \ˌin-də-ˈpen-dəns\ *n* ♦ : the quality or state of being independent : FREEDOM

  ♦ autonomy, freedom, liberty, self-government, sovereignty

Independence Day *n* : July 4 observed as a legal holiday in commemoration of the adoption of the Declaration of Independence in 1776

in·de·pen·dent \ˌin-də-ˈpen-dənt\ *adj* **1** ♦ : not subject to control by others : SELF-GOVERNING; *also* : not affiliated with a larger controlling unit **2** ♦ : not requiring or relying on something else or somebody else ⟨an ∼ conclusion⟩ ⟨∼ of her parents⟩ **3** : not easily influenced : showing self-reliance and personal freedom ⟨an ∼ mind⟩ **4** : not committed to a political party ⟨an ∼ voter⟩ **5** : MAIN ⟨an ∼ clause⟩ — **independent** *n*

   ♦ [1] autonomous, free, self-governing, separate, sovereign
   ♦ [2] self-reliant, self-sufficient, self-supporting

in·de·pen·dent·ly *adv* ♦ : in an independent manner : without dependence on another

   ♦ alone, singly, solely, unaided, unassisted

independent variable *n* : a variable whose value is not determined by that of any other variable in a function
in·de·scrib·able \ˌin-di-ˈskrī-bə-bəl\ *adj* **1** ♦ : that cannot be described **2** : being too intense or great for description — **in·de·scrib·ably** \-blē\ *adv*

   ♦ ineffable, inexpressible, nameless, unspeakable, unutterable *Ant* communicable, definable

in·de·ter·mi·nate \ˌin-di-ˈtər-mə-nət\ *adj* **1** : VAGUE; *also* : not known in advance **2** : not limited in advance; *also* : not leading to a definite end or result — **in·de·ter·mi·na·cy** \-nə-sē\ *n* — **in·de·ter·mi·nate·ly** *adv*
¹in·dex \ˈin-ˌdeks\ *n, pl* **in·dex·es** *or* **in·di·ces** \-də-ˌsēz\ **1** ♦ : a device (as the pointer on a scale) that serves to indicate a value or quantity **2** : SIGN, INDICATION ⟨an ∼ of character⟩ **3** : a guide for facilitating references; *esp* : an alphabetical list of items treated in a printed work with the page number where each item may be found **4** : a list of restricted or prohibited material **5** *pl usu* **indices** : a number or symbol or expression (as an exponent) associated with another to indicate a mathematical operation or use or position in an arrangement or expansion **6** : a character ☞ used to direct attention (as to a note) **7** : INDEX NUMBER

   ♦ indicator, needle, pointer

²index *vb* **1** ♦ : to provide with or put into an index **2** : to serve as an index of **3** : to regulate by indexation

   ♦ catalog, enroll, enter, inscribe, list, put down, record, register, schedule, slate

in·dex·ation \ˌin-ˌdek-ˈsā-shən\ *n* : a system of economic control in which a body of variables (as wages and interest) rise or fall at the same rate as an index of the cost of living
index finger *n* : the finger next to the thumb
in·dex·ing *n* : INDEXATION
index number *n* : a number used to indicate change in magnitude (as of cost) as compared with the magnitude at some specified time usu. taken as 100
index of refraction : REFRACTIVE INDEX
in·dia ink \ˈin-dē-ə-\ *n, often cap 1st I* **1** : a solid black pigment used in drawing **2** : a fluid made from india ink
In·di·an \ˈin-dē-ən\ *n* **1** : a native or inhabitant of India or of the East Indies **2** : a person of Indian descent **3** : AMERICAN INDIAN — **Indian** *adj*
Indian corn *n* **1** : CORN 2 **2** : corn having hard kernels of various colors (as reddish-brown or purple) used esp. for ornament
Indian meal *n* : CORNMEAL
Indian paintbrush *n* : any of a genus of herbaceous plants related to the snapdragon that have brightly colored bracts
Indian pipe *n* : a waxy white leafless saprophytic herb of Asia and the U.S.
Indian summer *n* : a period of mild weather in late autumn or early winter
In·dia paper \ˈin-dē-ə-\ *n* **1** : a thin absorbent paper used esp. for taking impressions (as of steel engravings) **2** : a thin tough opaque printing paper
indic *abbr* indicative
in·di·cate \ˈin-də-ˌkāt\ *vb* **-cat·ed; -cat·ing** **1** : to point out or to **2** ♦ : to show indirectly **3** : to state briefly

   ♦ allude, hint, imply, infer, insinuate, intimate, suggest

in·di·ca·tion \ˌin-də-ˈkā-shən\ *n* **1** ♦ : something that serves to indicate; *also* : something that is indicated as advisable or necessary **2** : the action of indicating

   ♦ clue, cue, hint, inkling, intimation, lead, suggestion

¹in·dic·a·tive \in-ˈdi-kə-tiv\ *adj* **1** : of, relating to, or being a verb form that represents an act or state as a fact ⟨∼ mood⟩ **2** ♦ : serving to indicate ⟨actions ∼ of fear⟩

   ♦ denotative, significant, telltale

²indicative *n* **1** : the indicative mood of a language **2** : a form in the indicative mood
in·di·ca·tor \ˈin-də-ˌkā-tər\ *n* ♦ : one that indicates; *esp* : an index hand (as on a dial)

   ♦ hand, index, needle, pointer

in·di·cia \in-ˈdi-shə, -shē-ə\ *n pl* **1** : distinctive marks **2** : postal markings often imprinted on mail or mailing labels
in·dict \in-ˈdīt\ *vb* **1** ♦ : to charge with a fault or offense **2** : to charge with a crime by the finding of a jury — **in·dict·able** *adj*

   ♦ accuse, charge, incriminate

in·dict·ment \-mənt\ *n* ♦ : the action or the legal process of indicting

   ♦ charge, complaint, count, rap

in·die \ˈin-dē\ *n* **1** : one that is independent; *esp* : an unaffiliated record or motion-picture production company **2** : something produced by an indie — **indie** *adj*
in·dif·fer·ence \-frəns, -fə-rəns\ *n* ♦ : the quality, state, or fact of being indifferent; *also* : absence of compulsion to or toward one thing or another

   ♦ apathy, disinterestedness, disregard, insouciance, nonchalance *Ant* concern, interest, regard

in·dif·fer·ent \in-ˈdi-frənt, -fə-rənt\ *adj* **1** : UNBIASED, UNPREJUDICED **2** : of no importance one way or the other **3** ♦ : marked by no special liking for or dislike of something **4** : being neither excessive nor inadequate **5** ♦ : being neither good nor bad : PASSABLE, MEDIOCRE **6** : being neither right nor wrong — **in·dif·fer·ent·ly** *adv*

   ♦ [3] apathetic, casual, disinterested, insouciant, nonchalant, perfunctory, unconcerned, uncurious, uninterested *Ant* concerned, interested ♦ [5] common, fair, mediocre, medium, middling, ordinary, passable, run-of-the-mill, second-rate, so-so

in·di·gence \-jəns\ *n* ♦ : a level of poverty in which real hardship and deprivation are suffered and comforts of life are wholly lacking

   ♦ beggary, destitution, impecuniousness, impoverishment, need, pauperism, penury, poverty, want

in·dig·e·nous \in-ˈdi-jə-nəs\ *adj* **1** ♦ : produced, growing, or living naturally in a particular region **2** *usu cap* : of or relating to the earliest known inhabitants of a place and esp. of a place that was colonized

   ♦ aboriginal, born, endemic, native

in·di·gent \ˈin-di-jənt\ *adj* ♦ : suffering from indigence : NEEDY

   ♦ broke, destitute, impecunious, needy, penniless, penurious, poor, poverty-stricken

in·di·gest·ible \ˌin-dī-ˈjes-tə-bəl, -də-\ *adj* : not readily digested
in·di·ges·tion \-ˈjes-chən\ *n* : inadequate or difficult digestion : DYSPEPSIA
in·dig·nant \in-ˈdig-nənt\ *adj* : filled with or marked by indignation — **in·dig·nant·ly** *adv*
in·dig·na·tion \ˌin-dig-ˈnā-shən\ *n* ♦ : anger aroused by something unjust, unworthy, or mean

   ♦ anger, furor, fury, ire, outrage, rage, spleen, wrath, wrathfulness

in·dig·ni·ty \in-ˈdig-nə-tē\ *n, pl* **-ties** ♦ : an offense against personal dignity or self-respect; *also* : humiliating treatment

   ♦ affront, barb, dart, dig, insult, name, offense, outrage, put-down, sarcasm, slight, slur, wound

in·di·go \ˈin-di-ˌgō\ *n, pl* **-gos** *or* **-goes** **1** : a blue dye obtained from plants or synthesized **2** : a deep reddish blue color
in·di·rect \ˌin-də-ˈrekt, -dī-\ *adj* **1** : not straight ⟨an ∼ route⟩ **2** ♦ : not straightforward and open ⟨∼ methods⟩ **3** : not having a plainly seen connection ⟨an ∼ cause⟩ **4** : not directly to the point ⟨an ∼ answer⟩ — **in·di·rec·tion** \-ˈrek-shən\ *n* — **in·di·rect·ly** *adv* — **in·di·rect·ness** *n*

   ♦ circuitous, circular, roundabout *Ant* direct, straight, straightforward

in·dis·creet \ˌin-di-ˈskrēt\ *adj* ♦ : not discreet : IMPRUDENT — **in·dis·creet·ly** *adv*

   ♦ ill-advised, imprudent, tactless, unwise *Ant* advisable, discreet, judicious, prudent, tactful, wise

in·dis·cre·tion \,in-di-'skre-shən\ *n* **1** : IMPRUDENCE **2** ♦ : something marked by lack of discretion; *esp* : an act deviating from accepted morality

♦ familiarity, gaffe, impropriety

in·dis·crim·i·nate \,in-di-'skri-mə-nət\ *adj* **1** : not careful in making choices **2** : HAPHAZARD, RANDOM ⟨an ∼ application of a law⟩ **3** : UNRESTRAINED **4** : MOTLEY — **in·dis·crim·i·nate·ly** *adv*

in·dis·pens·able \,in-di-'spen-sə-bəl\ *adj* ♦ : absolutely essential : REQUISITE — **in·dis·pens·abil·i·ty** \-,spen-sə-'bi-lə-tē\ *n* — **indispensable** *n* — **in·dis·pens·ably** \-'spen-sə-blē\ *adv*

♦ essential, imperative, integral, necessary, needful, requisite, vital

in·dis·posed \-'spōzd\ *adj* **1** ♦ : slightly ill **2** ♦ : having an active feeling of reluctance or dislike : AVERSE

♦ [1] bad, down, ill, peaked, punk, sick, unhealthy, unsound, unwell ♦ [2] afraid, dubious, hesitant, reluctant

in·dis·po·si·tion \(,)in-,dis-pə-'zi-shən\ *n* : the condition of being indisposed: as **a** : slight aversion **b** : a usu. slight illness

in·dis·put·able \,in-di-'spyü-tə-bəl, (,)in-'dis-pyə-\ *adj* ♦ : not disputable : UNQUESTIONABLE ⟨∼ proof⟩

♦ incontestable, indubitable, irrefutable, unanswerable, undeniable, unquestionable

in·dis·put·ably \-blē\ *adv* ♦ : not open to question

♦ certainly, definitely, doubtless, incontestably, indeed, really, surely, truly, undeniably, undoubtedly, unquestionably

in·dis·sol·u·ble \,in-di-'säl-yə-bəl\ *adj* : not capable of being dissolved, undone, or broken : PERMANENT

in·dis·tinct \,in-di-'stiŋkt\ *adj* **1** : not sharply outlined or separable : BLURRED, FAINT, DIM **2** ♦ : not readily distinguishable — **in·dis·tinct·ly** *adv* — **in·dis·tinct·ness** *n*

♦ bleary, dim, faint, foggy, fuzzy, hazy, indefinite, indistinguishable, murky, nebulous, obscure, opaque, shadowy, unclear, undefined, undetermined, vague

in·dis·tin·guish·able \,in-di-'stiŋ-gwi-shə-bəl, -'stiŋ-wi-\ *adj* : not distinguishable: as **a** : indeterminate in shape or structure **b** ♦ : not clearly recognizable or understandable **c** ♦ : lacking identifying or individualizing qualities

♦ [b] impalpable, imperceptible, inappreciable ♦ [c] duplicate, equal, even, identical, same

in·dite \in-'dīt\ *vb* **in·dit·ed**; **in·dit·ing** : COMPOSE ⟨∼ a poem⟩; *also* : to put in writing ⟨∼ a letter⟩

in·di·um \'in-dē-əm\ *n* : a malleable silvery metallic chemical element

indiv *abbr* individual

¹in·di·vid·u·al \,in-də-'vi-jə-wəl\ *adj* **1** ♦ : of, relating to, or associated with an individual ⟨∼ traits⟩ **2** : being an individual : existing as an indivisible whole **3** : intended for one person **4** : SEPARATE ⟨∼ copies⟩ **5** ♦ : having marked individuality ⟨an ∼ style⟩ — **in·di·vid·u·al·ly** *adv*

♦ [1] particular, peculiar, personal, private, separate, singular, unique *Ant* general, generic, public, popular, shared, universal ♦ [5] different, respective, separate

²individual *n* **1** ♦ : a single member of a category : a particular person, animal, or thing **2** ♦ : a single human being ⟨a disagreeable ∼⟩

♦ [1] being, entity, object, substance, thing ♦ [2] being, body, creature, human, man, mortal, person

in·di·vid·u·al·ise *chiefly Brit var of* INDIVIDUALIZE

in·di·vid·u·al·ism \,in-də-'vi-jə-wə-,li-zəm\ *n* **1** : a doctrine that the interests of the individual are primary **2** : a doctrine holding that the individual has political or economic rights with which the state must not interfere **3** : INDIVIDUALITY

in·di·vid·u·al·ist \-list\ *n* **1** ♦ : one that pursues a markedly independent course in thought or action **2** : one that advocates or practices individualism — **individualist** *or* **in·di·vid·u·al·is·tic** \-,vi-jə-wə-'lis-tik\ *adj*

♦ bohemian, deviant, loner, maverick, nonconformist

in·di·vid·u·al·i·ty \-,vi-jə-'wa-lə-tē\ *n, pl* **-ties** **1** ♦ : the sum of qualities that characterize and distinguish an individual from all others; *also* : PERSONALITY **2** : separate or distinct existence **3** : INDIVIDUAL, PERSON

♦ character, identity, personality, self-identity

in·di·vid·u·al·ize \-'vi-jə-wə-,līz\ *vb* **-ized**; **-iz·ing** **1** : to make

individual in character **2** : to treat or notice individually : PARTICULARIZE **3** : to adapt to the needs of an individual

individual retirement account *n* : IRA

in·di·vid·u·ate \,in-də-'vi-jə-,wāt\ *vb* **-at·ed**; **-at·ing** : to give individuality to : form into an individual — **in·di·vid·u·a·tion** \-,vi-jə-'wā-shən\ *n*

in·di·vis·i·ble \,in-də-'vi-zə-bəl\ *adj* : impossible to divide or separate — **in·di·vis·i·bil·i·ty** \-,vi-zə-'bi-lə-tē\ *n* — **in·di·vis·i·bly** *adv*

In·do-Ar·y·an \,in-dō-'er-ē-ən\ *n* : a branch of the Indo-European language family that includes Hindi and other languages of south Asia

in·doc·tri·nate \in-'däk-trə-,nāt\ *vb* **-nat·ed**; **-nat·ing** **1** ♦ : to instruct esp. in fundamentals or rudiments : TEACH **2** : to teach the beliefs and doctrines of a particular group — **in·doc·tri·na·tion** \(,)in-,däk-trə-'nā-shən\ *n* — **in·doc·tri·na·tor** *n*

♦ educate, instruct, school, teach, train, tutor

In·do-Eu·ro·pe·an \,in-dō-,yu̇r-ə-'pē-ən\ *adj* : of, relating to, or constituting a family of languages comprising those spoken in most of Europe and in the parts of the world colonized by Europeans since 1500 and also in Persia, the subcontinent of India, and some other parts of Asia

in·do·lence \-ləns\ *n* ♦ : inclination to laziness

♦ idleness, inertia, laziness, sloth

in·do·lent \'in-də-lənt\ *adj* **1** : slow to develop or heal ⟨∼ ulcers⟩ **2** ♦ : averse to activity, effort, or movement : LAZY — **in·do·lent·ly** *adv*

♦ idle, lazy, shiftless, slothful

in·dom·i·ta·ble \in-'dä-mə-tə-bəl\ *adj* ♦ : incapable of being subdued : UNCONQUERABLE ⟨∼ courage⟩ — **in·dom·i·ta·bly** \-blē\ *adv*

♦ impregnable, insurmountable, invincible, invulnerable, unbeatable, unconquerable

In·do·ne·sian \,in-do-'nē-zhən\ *n* : a native or inhabitant of the Republic of Indonesia — **Indonesian** *adj*

in·door \'in-,dōr\ *adj* **1** : of or relating to the inside of a building **2** : living, located, or carried on within a building

in·doors \in-'dōrz\ *adv* : in or into a building

indorse, indorsement *var of* ENDORSE, ENDORSEMENT

in·du·bi·ta·ble \(,)in-'dü-bə-tə-bəl, -'dyü-\ *adj* ♦ : too evident to be doubted : UNQUESTIONABLE ⟨∼ truths⟩ — **in·du·bi·ta·bly** \-blē\ *adv*

♦ incontestable, indisputable, irrefutable, unanswerable, undeniable, unquestionable

in·duce \in-'düs, -'dyüs\ *vb* **in·duced**; **in·duc·ing** **1** ♦ : to move by persuasion or influence : PERSUADE **2** : to serve as the cause of : BRING ABOUT **3** : to produce (as an electric current) by induction **4** : to determine by induction; *esp* : to infer from particulars — **in·duc·er** *n*

♦ argue, convince, get, move, persuade, prevail, satisfy, talk, win

in·duce·ment \-mənt\ *n* **1** : something that induces : MOTIVE **2** ♦ : the act or process of inducing

♦ convincing, persuasion

in·duct \in-'dəkt\ *vb* **1** ♦ : to place in office **2** ♦ : to admit as a member **3** : to enroll for military training or service — **in·duct·ee** \-,dək-'tē\ *n*

♦ [1, 2] baptize, inaugurate, initiate, install, invest

in·duc·tance \in-'dək-təns\ *n* : a property of an electric circuit by which a varying current produces an electromotive force in that circuit or in a nearby circuit; *also* : the measure of this property

in·duc·tion \in-'dək-shən\ *n* **1** ♦ : the act or process of inducting; *also* : INITIATION **2** : the formality by which a civilian is inducted into military service **3** : inference of a generalized conclusion from particular instances; *also* : a conclusion so reached **4** : the act of causing or bringing on or about **5** : the process by which an electric current, an electric charge, or magnetism is produced in a body by the proximity of an electric or magnetic field

♦ inaugural, inauguration, installation, investiture

in·duc·tive \in-'dək-tiv\ *adj* : of, relating to, or employing induction

in·duc·tor \in-'dək-tər\ *n* : an electrical component that acts upon another or is itself acted upon by induction

in·dulge \in-'dəlj\ *vb* **in·dulged**; **in·dulg·ing** **1** ♦ : to give free rein to : GRATIFY   **2** : HUMOR   **3** : to gratify one's taste or desire for ⟨∼ in alcohol⟩

♦ cater to, gratify, humor (*or* humour)

in·dul·gence \in-'dəl-jəns\ *n*   **1** : remission of temporal punishment due in Roman Catholic doctrine for sins whose eternal punishment has been remitted by reception of the sacrament of penance   **2** : the act of indulging : the state of being indulgent   **3** : an indulgent act   **4** ♦ : the thing indulged in   **5** : SELF-INDULGENCE

♦ amenity, comfort, extra, frill, luxury, superfluity

in·dul·gent \in-'dəl-jənt\ *adj*   ♦ : indulging or characterized by indulgence — **in·dul·gent·ly** *adv*

♦ accommodating, friendly, obliging

in·du·rat·ed \'in-dyù-ˌrā-təd, -dù-\ *adj* : physically or emotionally hardened — **in·du·ra·tion** \ˌin-dyù-'rā-shən, -dù-\ *n*
in·dus·tri·al \in-'dəs-trē-əl\ *adj*   **1** : of or relating to industry; *also* : HEAVY-DUTY   **2** : characterized by highly developed industries — **in·dus·tri·al·ly** *adv*
in·dus·tri·al·ise *chiefly Brit var of* INDUSTRIALIZE
in·dus·tri·al·ist \-ə-list\ *n* : a person owning or engaged in the management of an industry
in·dus·tri·al·ize \in-'dəs-trē-ə-ˌlīz\ *vb* **-ized; -iz·ing** : to make or become industrial — **in·dus·tri·al·i·za·tion** \-ˌdəs-trē-ə-lə-'zā-shən\ *n*
in·dus·tri·ous \in-'dəs-trē-əs\ *adj* : constantly, regularly, or habitually active or occupied : DILIGENT, BUSY
in·dus·tri·ous·ly *adv* : in an industrious manner
in·dus·tri·ous·ness *n* : the quality or state of being industrious
in·dus·try \'in-(ˌ)dəs-trē\ *n, pl* **-tries**   **1** ♦ : steady or habitual effort : DILIGENCE   **2** : a department or branch of a craft, art, business, or manufacture; *esp* : one that employs a large personnel and capital   **3** : a distinct group of productive enterprises   **4** : manufacturing activity as a whole

♦ assiduity, diligence

in·dwell \(ˌ)in-'dwel\ *vb* : to exist within as an activating spirit or force
In·dy car \'in-dē-\ *n* : a single-seat, open-cockpit racing car with the engine in the rear
¹in·e·bri·ate \i-'nē-brē-ˌāt\ *vb* **-at·ed; -at·ing** : to make drunk : INTOXICATE — **in·e·bri·a·tion** \-ˌnē-brē-'ā-shən\ *n*
²in·e·bri·ate \-ət\ *n* ♦ : one that is drunk; *esp* : DRUNKARD

♦ drunk, drunkard, soak, sot, souse, tippler

in·ef·fa·ble \(ˌ)in-'e-fə-bəl\ *adj*   **1** ♦ : incapable of being expressed in words : INDESCRIBABLE ⟨∼ joy⟩   **2** : UNSPEAKABLE ⟨∼ disgust⟩   **3** : not to be uttered : TABOO — **in·ef·fa·bly** \-blē\ *adv*

♦ indescribable, inexpressible, nameless, unspeakable, unutterable

in·ef·fec·tive \ˌi-nə-'fek-tiv\ *adj*   **1** : not producing an intended effect : INEFFECTUAL   **2** : incapable of performing efficiently — **in·ef·fec·tive·ly** *adv* — **in·ef·fec·tive·ness** *n*
in·ef·fec·tu·al \-'fek-chə-wəl\ *adj* : INEFFECTIVE — **in·ef·fec·tu·al·ly** *adv*
in·ef·fi·cient \ˌi-nə-'fi-shənt\ *adj*   **1** : not producing the desired effect   **2** : wasteful of time or energy   **3** : INCAPABLE, INCOMPETENT — **in·ef·fi·cien·cy** \-'fi-shən-sē\ *n* — **in·ef·fi·cient·ly** *adv*
in·el·e·gant \(ˌ)i-'ne-li-gənt\ *adj*   ♦ : lacking in refinement, grace, or good taste — **in·el·e·gance** \-gəns\ *n* — **in·el·e·gant·ly** *adv*

♦ awkward, clumsy, gauche, graceless, stiff, stilted, uncomfortable, uneasy, ungraceful, wooden ♦ dowdy, tacky, tasteless, trashy, unfashionable, unstylish

in·el·i·gi·ble \(ˌ)i-'ne-lə-jə-bəl\ *adj* : not qualified for an office or position — **in·el·i·gi·bil·i·ty** \(ˌ)i-ˌne-lə-jə-'bi-lə-tē\ *n*
in·eluc·ta·ble \ˌi-ni-'lək-tə-bəl\ *adj* : not to be avoided, changed, or resisted — **in·eluc·ta·bly** \-blē\ *adv*
in·ept \i-'nept\ *adj*   **1** ♦ : lacking in fitness or aptitude : UNFIT   **2** : FOOLISH   **3** ♦ : inappropriate to the time or circumstances   **4** ♦ : generally incompetent : BUNGLING — **in·ept·ly** *adv* — **in·ept·ness** *n*

♦ [1, 4] incapable, incompetent, inexpert, unfit, unqualified, unskilled, unskillful ♦ [3] improper, inappropriate, inapt, infelicitous, unbecoming, unfit, unseemly, unsuitable, wrong

in·ep·ti·tude \(ˌ)i-'nep-ti-ˌtüd, -ˌtyüd\ *n* ♦ : the quality or state of being inept; *esp* : INCOMPETENCE

♦ impotence, inability, inadequacy, incapability, incompetence

in·equal·i·ty \ˌi-ni-'kwä-lə-tē\ *n*   **1** : the quality or state of being un-

equal or uneven; *esp* : UNEVENNESS, DISPARITY   **2** : an instance of being unequal
in·ert \i-'nərt\ *adj*   **1** ♦ : powerless to move   **2** ♦ : averse to activity or exertion : SLUGGISH   **3** : lacking in active properties ⟨chemically ∼⟩ — **in·ert·ly** *adv*

♦ [1] dead, dormant, fallow, free, idle, inactive, inoperative, latent, off, vacant ♦ [2] dull, inactive, lethargic, quiescent, sleepy, sluggish, torpid

in·er·tia \i-'nər-shə, -shē-ə\ *n*   **1** : a property of matter whereby it remains at rest or continues in uniform motion unless acted upon by some outside force   **2** ♦ : indisposition to motion, exertion, or change — **in·er·tial** \-shəl\ *adj*

♦ idleness, indolence, laziness, sloth

in·ert·ness *n* ♦ : the quality or state of being inert : lack of activity

♦ dormancy, idleness, inaction, inactivity, quiescence

in·es·cap·able \ˌi-nə-'skā-pə-bəl\ *adj* : incapable of being escaped : INEVITABLE
in·es·cap·ably \-blē\ *adv* : in an inevitable way
in·es·ti·ma·ble \(ˌ)i-'nes-tə-mə-bəl\ *adj*   **1** : incapable of being estimated or computed ⟨∼ errors⟩   **2** : too valuable or excellent to be fully appreciated — **in·es·ti·ma·bly** \-blē\ *adv*
in·ev·i·ta·ble \i-'ne-və-tə-bəl\ *adj* ♦ : incapable of being avoided or evaded : bound to happen ⟨the ∼ result⟩ — **in·ev·i·ta·bil·i·ty** \(ˌ)i-ˌne-və-tə-'bi-lə-tē\ *n*

♦ certain, necessary, sure, unavoidable *Ant* avoidable, uncertain, unsure

in·ev·i·ta·bly \-blē\ *adv*   **1** : in an inevitable way   **2** ♦ : as is to be expected

♦ necessarily, needs, perforce, unavoidably

in·ex·act \ˌi-nig-'zakt\ *adj*   **1** ♦ : not precisely correct or true : INACCURATE   **2** : not rigorous and careful — **in·ex·act·ly** *adv* — **in·ex·act·ness** *n*

♦ erroneous, false, inaccurate, incorrect, invalid, off, unsound, untrue, wrong ♦ imprecise, inaccurate, loose *Ant* accurate, dead, exact, precise

in·ex·cus·able \ˌi-nik-'skyü-zə-bəl\ *adj* ♦ : being without excuse or justification — **in·ex·cus·ably** \-blē\ *adv*

♦ indefensible, unforgivable, unjustifiable, unpardonable, unwarrantable *Ant* defensible, excusable, forgivable, justifiable, pardonable

in·ex·haust·ible \ˌi-nig-'zȯ-stə-bəl\ *adj*   **1** : incapable of being used up ⟨an ∼ supply⟩   **2** ♦ : incapable of being wearied or worn out : UNTIRING — **in·ex·haust·ibly** \-blē\ *adv*

♦ indefatigable, tireless, unflagging, untiring

in·ex·o·ra·ble \(ˌ)i-'nek-sə-rə-bəl\ *adj* ♦ : not to be moved by entreaty : RELENTLESS — **in·ex·o·ra·bly** *adv*
in·ex·pen·sive \ˌi-nik-'spen(t)-siv\ *adj* : reasonable in price
in·ex·pe·ri·ence \ˌi-nik-'spir-ē-əns\ *n* : lack of experience or of knowledge gained by experience
in·ex·pe·ri·enced \-ənst\ *adj* ♦ : lacking practical experience

♦ amateur, amateurish, inexpert, nonprofessional, unprofessional, unskilled, unskillful

in·ex·pert \(ˌ)i-'nek-ˌspərt\ *adj* ♦ : not expert : UNSKILLED — **in·ex·pert·ly** *adv*

♦ amateur, amateurish, inexperienced, nonprofessional, unprofessional, unskilled, unskillful

in·ex·pi·a·ble \(ˌ)i-'nek-spē-ə-bəl\ *adj* : not capable of being atoned for
in·ex·pli·ca·ble \ˌi-nik-'spli-kə-bəl, (ˌ)i-'nek-(ˌ)spli-\ *adj* : incapable of being explained or accounted for ⟨an ∼ mistake⟩ — **in·ex·pli·ca·bly** \-blē\ *adv*
in·ex·press·ible \-'spre-sə-bəl\ *adj* ♦ : not capable of being expressed ⟨∼ joy⟩ — **in·ex·press·ibly** \-blē\ *adv*

♦ indescribable, ineffable, nameless, unspeakable, unutterable

in·ex·pres·sive \-'spre-siv\ *adj* ♦ : lacking expression or meaning

♦ blank, deadpan, expressionless, impassive, stolid, vacant

in ex·tre·mis \ˌin-ik-'strā-məs, -'strē-\ *adv* : in extreme circumstances; *esp* : at the point of death
in·ex·tri·ca·ble \ˌi-nik-'stri-kə-bəl, (ˌ)i-'nek-(ˌ)stri-\ *adj*   **1** : forming a maze or tangle from which it is impossible to get free   **2** : incapable of being disentangled or untied — **in·ex·tri·ca·bly** \-blē\ *adv*

inf *abbr* **1** infantry **2** infinitive

in·fal·li·ble \(ˌ)in-ˈfa-lə-bəl\ *adj* **1 :** incapable of error : UNERR-ING **2 ♦ :** not liable to mislead, deceive, or disappoint : SURE, CERTAIN ⟨an ∼ remedy⟩ — **in·fal·li·bil·i·ty** \(ˌ)in-ˌfa-lə-ˈbi-lə-tē\ *n* — **in·fal·li·bly** \(ˌ)in-ˈfa-lə-blē\ *adv*

♦ certain, sure, unfailing *Ant* fallible

in·fa·mous \ˈin-fə-məs\ *adj* **1 ♦ :** having a reputation of the worst kind **2 ♦ :** causing or bringing infamy : DISGRACEFUL — **in·fa·mous·ly** *adv*

♦ [1, 2] discreditable, disgraceful, dishonorable (*or* dishonourable), disreputable, ignominious, notorious, shameful

in·fa·my \-mē\ *n, pl* **-mies 1 :** evil reputation brought about by something grossly criminal, shocking, or brutal **2 :** an extreme and publicly known criminal or evil act **3 ♦ :** the state of being infamous

♦ discredit, disgrace, dishonor (*or* dishonour), disrepute, ignominy, odium, opprobrium, reproach, shame

in·fan·cy \ˈin-fən-sē\ *n, pl* **-cies 1 :** early childhood **2 :** a beginning or early period of existence

in·fant \ˈin-fənt\ *n* **♦ :** a child in the first period of life : BABY; *also* **:** a person who is a legal minor

♦ baby, child, newborn

in·fan·ti·cide \in-ˈfan-tə-ˌsīd\ *n* **:** the killing of an infant

in·fan·tile \ˈin-fən-ˌtīl, -tᵊl, -ˌtēl\ *adj* **♦ :** of or relating to infants; *also* **:** CHILDISH

♦ adolescent, babyish, childish, immature, juvenile, kiddish

infantile paralysis *n* **:** POLIOMYELITIS

in·fan·try \ˈin-fən-trē\ *n, pl* **-tries :** soldiers trained, armed, and equipped to fight on foot — **in·fan·try·man** \-mən\ *n*

in·farct \ˈin-ˌfärkt\ *n* **:** an area of dead tissue (as of the heart wall) caused by blocking of local blood circulation — **in·farc·tion** \in-ˈfärk-shən\ *n*

in·fat·u·ate \in-ˈfa-chə-ˌwāt\ *vb* **-at·ed; -at·ing :** to inspire with a foolish or extravagant love or admiration — **in·fat·u·a·tion** \-ˌfa-chə-ˈwā-shən\ *n*

in·fect \in-ˈfekt\ *vb* **1 :** to contaminate with disease-producing matter **2 :** to communicate a pathogen or disease to **3 :** to cause to share one's feelings

in·fec·tion \in-ˈfek-shən\ *n* **1 :** a disease or condition caused by a germ or parasite; *also* **:** such a germ or parasite **2 :** an act or process of infecting — **in·fec·tive** \-ˈfek-tiv\ *adj*

in·fec·tious \-shəs\ *adj* **1 :** capable of causing infection; *also* **:** communicable by infection **2 ♦ :** spreading or capable of spreading rapidly to others

♦ catching, contagious

infectious mononucleosis *n* **:** an acute infectious disease characterized by fever, swelling of lymph glands, and increased numbers of lymph cells in the blood

in·fe·lic·i·tous \ˌin-fi-ˈli-sə-təs\ *adj* **♦ :** not appropriate in application or expression — **in·fe·lic·i·ty** \-sə-tē\ *n*

♦ improper, inappropriate, inapt, unbecoming, unfit, unseemly, unsuitable, wrong

in·fer \in-ˈfər\ *vb* **in·ferred; in·fer·ring 1 ♦ :** to derive as a conclusion from facts or premises **2 :** GUESS, SURMISE **3 :** to lead to as a conclusion or consequence **4 ♦ :** to convey indirectly and by allusion rather than explicitly : HINT, SUGGEST

♦ [1] conclude, deduce, extrapolate, gather, judge, reason, understand ♦ [4] allude, hint, imply, indicate, insinuate, intimate, suggest

¹in·fe·ri·or \in-ˈfir-ē-ər\ *adj* **1 :** situated lower down **2 ♦ :** of low or lower degree or rank **3 ♦ :** of lesser quality **4 ♦ :** of little or less importance, value, or merit ⟨an ∼ opponent⟩ — **in·fe·ri·or·i·ty** \(ˌ)in-ˌfir-ē-ˈȯr-ə-tē\ *n*

♦ [2] common, humble, ignoble, low, lowly, mean, plebeian, vulgar ♦ [3] cheap, cut-rate, junky, lousy, mediocre, shoddy, sleazy, trashy ♦ [4] junior, less, lesser, lower, minor, subordinate, under ♦ [4] mean, minor, secondary, second-rate *Ant* superior

²inferior *n* **♦ :** a person or thing inferior to another (as in worth, status, or importance)

♦ junior, subordinate, underling

in·fer·nal \in-ˈfər-nᵊl\ *adj* **1 :** of or relating to hell **2 :** HELLISH, FIENDISH ⟨∼ schemes⟩ **3 :** DAMNABLE ⟨an ∼ pest⟩ — **in·fer·nal·ly** *adv*

in·fer·no \in-ˈfər-nō\ *n, pl* **-nos ♦ :** a place or a state that resembles or suggests hell; *also* **:** intense heat

♦ conflagration, fire, holocaust

in·fer·tile \(ˌ)in-ˈfərt-ᵊl\ *adj* **♦ :** not fertile or productive : BARREN — **in·fer·til·i·ty** \ˌin-fər-ˈti-lə-tē\ *n*

♦ barren, impotent, sterile, unproductive

in·fest \in-ˈfest\ *vb* **:** to trouble by spreading or swarming in or over; *also* **:** to live in or on as a parasite — **in·fes·ta·tion** \ˌin-ˌfes-ˈtā-shən\ *n*

in·fi·del \ˈin-fə-dᵊl, -fə-ˌdel\ *n* **1 :** one who is not a Christian or opposes Christianity **2 :** an unbeliever esp. with respect to a particular religion

in·fi·del·i·ty \ˌin-fə-ˈde-lə-tē, -fī-\ *n, pl* **-ties 1 :** lack of belief in a religion **2 ♦ :** unfaithfulness to a moral obligation : DISLOYALTY **3 ♦ :** marital unfaithfulness or an instance of it

♦ [2, 3] betrayal, disloyalty, double cross, treachery, treason ♦ [3] disloyalty, faithlessness, falseness, falsity, inconstancy, perfidy, unfaithfulness *Ant* allegiance, constancy, devotion, faith, faithfulness, fealty, fidelity, loyalty

in·field \ˈin-ˌfēld\ *n* **:** the part of a baseball field inside the baselines — **in·field·er** *n*

in·fight·ing \ˈin-ˌfī-tiŋ\ *n* **1 :** fighting at close quarters **2 :** dissension or rivalry among members of a group

in·fil·trate \in-ˈfil-ˌtrāt, ˈin-(ˌ)fil-\ *vb* **-trat·ed; -trat·ing 1 :** to enter or filter into or through something **2 ♦ :** to pass into or through by or as if by filtering or permeating — **in·fil·tra·tion** \ˌin-(ˌ)fil-ˈtrā-shən\ *n* — **in·fil·tra·tor** *n*

♦ insinuate, slip, sneak, work, worm

in·fi·nite \ˈin-fə-nət\ *adj* **1 ♦ :** extending indefinitely : LIMITLESS, ENDLESS ⟨∼ space⟩ ⟨∼ patience⟩ **2 :** VAST, IMMENSE; *also* **:** INEXHAUSTIBLE ⟨∼ wealth⟩ **3 :** greater than any preassigned finite value however large ⟨∼ number of positive integers⟩; *also* **:** extending to infinity ⟨∼ plane surface⟩ — **infinite** *n* — **in·fi·nite·ly** *adv*

♦ boundless, endless, illimitable, immeasurable, indefinite, limitless, measureless, unbounded, unfathomable, unlimited *Ant* bounded, circumscribed, confined, definite, finite, limited, restricted

in·fin·i·tes·i·mal \(ˌ)in-ˌfi-nə-ˈte-sə-məl\ *adj* **♦ :** immeasurably or incalculably small — **in·fin·i·tes·i·mal·ly** *adv*

♦ atomic, microscopic, miniature, minute, teeny, tiny, wee

in·fin·i·tive \in-ˈfi-nə-tiv\ *n* **:** a verb form having the characteristics of both verb and noun and in English usu. being used with *to*

in·fin·i·tude \in-ˈfi-nə-ˌtüd, -ˌtyüd\ *n* **1 :** the quality or state of being infinite **2 :** something that is infinite esp. in extent

in·fin·i·ty \in-ˈfi-nə-tē\ *n, pl* **-ties 1 :** the quality of being infinite **2 :** unlimited extent of time, space, or quantity **3 :** an indefinitely great number or amount

in·firm \in-ˈfərm\ *adj* **1 ♦ :** deficient in vitality; *esp* **:** feeble from age **2 :** weak of mind, will, or character : IRRESOLUTE **3 :** not solid or stable : INSECURE

♦ delicate, faint, feeble, frail, wasted, weak

in·fir·ma·ry \in-ˈfər-mə-rē\ *n, pl* **-ries :** a place for the care of the infirm or sick

in·fir·mi·ty \in-ˈfər-mə-tē\ *n, pl* **-ties 1 ♦ :** the condition of being feeble : FEEBLENESS **2 ♦ :** a disease or disorder of the animal body : AILMENT **3 :** a personal failing : FOIBLE

♦ [1] debility, delicacy, enfeeblement, faintness, feebleness, frailty, languor, lowness, weakness ♦ [2] ailment, bug, complaint, complication, condition, disease, disorder, fever, illness, malady, sickness, trouble

infl *abbr* influenced

in fla·gran·te de·lic·to \ˌin-flə-ˈgrän-tē-di-ˈlik-tō, -ˈgran-\ *adv* **1 :** in the very act of committing a misdeed **2 :** in the midst of sexual activity

in·flame \in-ˈflām\ *vb* **in·flamed; in·flam·ing 1 ♦ :** to set on fire : KINDLE **2 ♦ :** to excite to excessive or uncontrollable action or feeling; *also* **:** INTENSIFY **3 :** to affect or become affected with inflammation

♦ [1] burn, fire, ignite, kindle, light ♦ [2] anger, antagonize, enrage, incense, infuriate, intensify, madden, outrage, rankle, rile, roil

in·flam·ma·ble \in-ˈfla-mə-bəl\ *adj* **1 ♦ :** capable of being easily ignited and of burning quickly : FLAMMABLE **2 :** easily inflamed, excited, or angered : IRASCIBLE

♦ combustible, flammable, ignitable

in·flam·ma·tion \ˌin-flə-ˈmā-shən\ *n* **:** a bodily response to injury in which an affected area becomes red, hot, and painful and congested with blood

in·flam·ma·to·ry \in-'fla-mə-ˌtōr-ē\ *adj* **1 :** tending to excite the senses or to arouse anger, disorder, or tumult : SEDITIOUS **2 :** causing or accompanied by inflammation ⟨an ~ disease⟩

in·flate \in-'flāt\ *vb* **in·flat·ed; in·flat·ing 1 :** to swell with air or gas ⟨~ a balloon⟩ **2 :** to puff up : ELATE **3 :** to expand or increase abnormally ⟨~ prices⟩ — **in·flat·able** *adj*

in·fla·tion \in-'flā-shən\ *n* **1 :** an act of inflating : the state of being inflated **2 :** empty pretentiousness : POMPOSITY **3 :** a continuing rise in the general price level usu. attributed to an increase in the volume of money and credit

in·fla·tion·ary \-shə-ˌner-ē\ *adj* **:** of, characterized by, or productive of inflation

in·flect \in-'flekt\ *vb* **1 :** to turn from a direct line or course : CURVE **2 :** to vary a word by inflection **3 :** to change or vary the pitch of the voice

in·flec·tion \in-'flek-shən\ *n* **1 :** the act or result of curving or bending **2 :** a change in pitch or loudness of the voice **3 :** the change of form that words undergo to mark case, gender, number, tense, person, mood, or voice — **in·flec·tion·al** \-shə-nəl\ *adj*

in·flex·i·bil·i·ty \-ˌflek-sə-'bi-lə-tē\ *n* ♦ **:** the quality or state of being inflexible

  ♦ hardness, harshness, rigidity, severity, sternness, strictness

in·flex·i·ble \(ˌ)in-'flek-sə-bəl\ *adj* **1 :** ♦ rigidly firm in will or purpose : UNYIELDING **2 :** ♦ not readily bent : RIGID **3 :** ♦ incapable of change — **in·flex·i·bly** \-'flek-sə-blē\ *adv*

  ♦ [1, 2] adamant, hard, immovable, implacable, pat, rigid, steadfast, unbending, uncompromising, unflinching, unrelenting, unyielding *Ant* acquiescent, agreeable, amenable, compliant, flexible, pliant, pliable ♦ [3] fast, fixed, hard-and-fast, immutable, unalterable, unchangeable *Ant* changeable, flexible, mutable, variable

in·flex·ion \in-'flek-shən\ *chiefly Brit var of* INFLECTION

in·flict \in-'flikt\ *vb* **:** AFFLICT; *also* **:** to give by or as if by striking ⟨~ pain⟩ — **in·flic·tion** \-'flik-shən\ *n*

in·flo·res·cence \ˌin-flə-'res-ᵊns\ *n* **:** the manner of development and arrangement of flowers on a stem; *also* **:** a flowering stem with its appendages **:** a flower cluster

in·flow \'in-ˌflō\ *n* **:** a flowing in

¹**in·flu·ence** \'in-ˌflü-əns\ *n* **1** ♦ **:** the act or power of producing an effect without apparent force or direct authority **2** ♦ **:** the power or capacity of causing an effect in indirect or intangible ways ⟨under the ~ of liquor⟩ **3 :** a person or thing that exerts influence — **in·flu·enc·er** *n*

  ♦ [1] authority, clout, pull, sway, weight ♦ [2] effect, impact, mark, repercussion, sway

²**influence** *vb* **-enced; -enc·ing 1** ♦ **:** to affect or alter by influence : SWAY **2 :** to have an effect on the condition or development of : MODIFY

  ♦ affect, impact, impress, move, strike, sway, tell, touch

in·flu·en·tial \ˌin-flü-'en-chəl\ *adj* ♦ **:** exerting or possessing influence; *also* **:** having authority or ascendancy

  ♦ important, mighty, potent, powerful, significant, strong ♦ authoritative, forceful, weighty

in·flu·en·za \ˌin-flü-'en-zə\ *n* **:** an acute and highly contagious virus disease marked by fever, prostration, aches and pains, and respiratory inflammation; *also* **:** any of various feverish usu. virus diseases typically with respiratory symptoms

in·flux \'in-ˌfləks\ *n* **:** a coming in

in·fo \'in-(ˌ)fō\ *n* **:** INFORMATION

in·fold \in-'fōld\ *vb* **1 :** ENFOLD **2 :** to fold inward or toward one another

in·fo·mer·cial \'in-fō-ˌmər-shəl\ *n* **:** a television program that is an extended advertisement often including a discussion or demonstration

in·form \in-'fȯrm\ *vb* **1** ♦ **:** to communicate knowledge to : TELL **2 :** to give information or knowledge **3** ♦ **:** to act as an informer

  ♦ [1] acquaint, advise, apprise, brief, clue, enlighten, familiarize, fill in, instruct, tell, wise ♦ [3] snitch, squeal, talk, tell

in·for·mal \(ˌ)in-'fȯr-məl\ *adj* **1** ♦ **:** conducted or carried out without formality or ceremony ⟨an ~ party⟩ **2** ♦ **:** characteristic of or appropriate to ordinary, casual, or familiar use ⟨~ clothes⟩ — **in·for·mal·i·ty** \ˌin-fȯr-'ma-lə-tē, -fər-\ *n* — **in·for·mal·ly** \(ˌ)in-'fȯr-mə-lē\ *adv*

  ♦ [1] irregular, unceremonious, unconventional, unorthodox

Ant ceremonial, ceremonious, conventional, formal, orthodox, regular, routine ♦ [2] casual, everyday, workaday

in·for·mant \in-'fȯr-mənt\ *n* **:** a person who gives information : INFORMER

in·for·ma·tion \ˌin-fər-'mā-shən\ *n* **1 :** the communication or reception of knowledge or intelligence **2 :** knowledge obtained from investigation, study, or instruction : FACTS, DATA

in·for·ma·tion·al \-shə-nəl\ *adj* **:** relating to or giving information

information superhighway *n* **:** INTERNET

information technology *n* **:** technology involving computer systems and networks for the processing and distribution of data

in·for·ma·tive \in-'fȯr-mə-tiv\ *adj* ♦ **:** imparting knowledge : INSTRUCTIVE

  ♦ educational, instructive *Ant* uninstructive

in·formed \in-'fȯrmd\ *adj* **1** ♦ **:** having or based on information **2** ♦ **:** having an education : KNOWLEDGEABLE

  ♦ [1] good, hard, just, levelheaded, logical, rational, reasonable, reasoned, sensible, sober, solid, valid, well-founded ♦ [2] abreast, conversant, familiar, knowledgeable, up, up-to-date, versed

informed consent *n* **:** consent to a medical procedure by someone who understands what is involved

in·form·er \-'for-mər\ *n* ♦ **:** one that informs; *esp* **:** a person who informs against others for illegalities esp. for financial gain

  ♦ betrayer, blabbermouth, rat, snitch, stool pigeon, tattler, tattletale

in·fo·tain·ment \ˌin-fō-'tān-mənt\ *n* **:** a television program that presents information (as news) in a manner intended to be entertaining

in·frac·tion \in-'frak-shən\ *n* ♦ **:** the act of infringing : VIOLATION

  ♦ breach, infringement, offense, transgression, trespass, violation

in·fra dig \ˌin-frə-'dig\ *adj* **:** being beneath one's dignity

in·fra·red \ˌin-frə-'red\ *adj* **:** being, relating to, or using radiation having wavelengths longer than those of red light — **infrared** *n*

in·fra·struc·ture \'in-frə-ˌstrək-chər\ *n* **1 :** the underlying foundation or basic framework (as of a system or organization) **2 :** the system of public works of a country, state, or region; *also* **:** the resources (as buildings or equipment) required for an activity

in·fre·quent \(ˌ)in-'frē-kwənt\ *adj* **1** ♦ **:** seldom happening : RARE **2 :** placed or occurring at wide intervals in space or time

  ♦ occasional, rare, sporadic *Ant* frequent

in·fre·quent·ly \-lē\ *adv* ♦ **:** in an infrequent manner

  ♦ little, rarely, seldom

in·fringe \in-'frinj\ *vb* **in·fringed; in·fring·ing 1 :** to encroach upon in a way that violates law or the rights of another : VIOLATE, TRANSGRESS ⟨~ a patent⟩ **2 :** ENCROACH, TRESPASS

in·fringe·ment *n* ♦ **:** the act of infringing; *also* **:** an encroachment or trespass on a right or privilege

  ♦ breach, infraction, offense, transgression, trespass, violation

in·fu·ri·ate \in-'fyůr-ē-ˌāt\ *vb* **-at·ed; -at·ing** ♦ **:** to make furious : ENRAGE — **in·fu·ri·at·ing·ly** *adv*

  ♦ anger, antagonize, enrage, incense, inflame, madden, outrage, rankle, rile, roil

in·fuse \in-'fyüz\ *vb* **in·fused; in·fus·ing 1** ♦ **:** to instill a principle or quality in **2 :** INSPIRE, ANIMATE **3 :** to steep (as tea) without boiling — **in·fu·sion** \-'fyü-zhən\ *n*

  ♦ imbue, inculcate, ingrain, invest, steep, suffuse

¹**-ing** \iŋ\ *n suffix* **1 :** action or process ⟨sleep*ing*⟩ **:** instance of an action or process ⟨a meet*ing*⟩ **2 :** product or result of an action or process ⟨an engrav*ing*⟩ ⟨earn*ings*⟩ **3 :** something used in an action or process ⟨a bed cover*ing*⟩ **4 :** something connected with, consisting of, or used in making (a specified thing) ⟨scaffold*ing*⟩ **5 :** something related to (a specified concept) ⟨off*ing*⟩

²**-ing** *n suffix* **:** one of a (specified) kind

³**-ing** *vb suffix or adj suffix* — used to form the present participle ⟨sail*ing*⟩ and sometimes to form an adjective resembling a present participle but not derived from a verb ⟨swashbuckl*ing*⟩

in·ga·ther \'in-ˌga-thər\ *vb* **:** to gather in : ASSEMBLE

in·ge·nious \in-'jēn-yəs\ *adj* **1** ♦ **:** marked by special aptitude at discovering, inventing, or contriving **2** ♦ **:** marked by originality, resourcefulness, and cleverness in conception or execution — **in·ge·nious·ly** *adv*

♦ [1, 2] creative, imaginative, innovative, inventive, original

♦ [2] artful, clever, creative, imaginative

in·ge·nious·ness *n* : the power or quality of ready invention

in·ge·nue *or* **in·gé·nue** \'än-jə-ˌnü, 'än-; 'aⁿ-zhə-, 'äⁿ-\ *n* : a naive girl or young woman; *esp* : an actress portraying such a person

in·ge·nu·i·ty \ˌin-jə-'nü-ə-tē, -'nyü-\ *n, pl* **-ties** ♦ : skill or cleverness in planning or inventing : INVENTIVENESS

♦ creativity, invention, inventiveness, originality

in·gen·u·ous \in-'jen-yə-wəs\ *adj* **1** : STRAIGHTFORWARD, FRANK **2** ♦ : showing innocent or childlike simplicity and candidness : NAIVE

♦ green, innocent, naive, simple, unknowing, unsophisticated, unwary, unworldly

in·gen·u·ous·ly *adv* ♦ : in an ingenuous manner

♦ artlessly, naively, naturally, unaffectedly

in·gen·u·ous·ness *n* ♦ : the quality of being ingenuous : absence of guile, reserve, or disguise

♦ artlessness, greenness, innocence, naïveté, naturalness, simplicity, unworldliness

in·gest \in-'jest\ *vb* : to take in for or as if for digestion — **in·ges·tion** \-'jes-chən\ *n*

in·gle·nook \'iŋ-gəl-ˌnùk\ *n* : a nook by a large open fireplace; *also* : a bench occupying this nook

in·glo·ri·ous \(ˌ)in-'glōr-ē-əs\ *adj* **1** : SHAMEFUL **2** : not glorious : lacking fame or honor — **in·glo·ri·ous·ly** *adv*

in·got \'iŋ-gət\ *n* : a mass of metal cast in a form convenient for storage or transportation

¹**in·grain** \(ˌ)in-'grān\ *vb* ♦ : to work indelibly into the natural texture or mental or moral constitution

♦ imbue, inculcate, infuse, invest, steep, suffuse

²**in·grain** \'in-ˌgrān\ *adj* **1** : made of fiber that is dyed before being spun into yarn **2** : made of yarn that is dyed before being woven or knitted **3** : INNATE — **in·grain** *n*

in·grained *adj* **1** : worked into the grain or fiber **2** ♦ : forming a part of the essence or inmost being

♦ essential, inborn, inherent, innate, integral, intrinsic, natural

in·grate \'in-ˌgrāt\ *n* : an ungrateful person

in·gra·ti·ate \in-'grā-shē-ˌāt\ *vb* **-at·ed; -at·ing** : to gain favor by deliberate effort

in·gra·ti·at·ing *adj* **1** ♦ : capable of winning favor ⟨an ∼ smile⟩ **2** : FLATTERING ⟨an ∼ manner⟩

♦ endearing, winning, winsome

in·grat·i·tude \(ˌ)in-'gra-tə-ˌtüd, -ˌtyüd\ *n* : lack of gratitude : UNGRATEFULNESS

in·gre·di·ent \in-'grē-dē-ənt\ *n* ♦ : one of the substances that make up a mixture or compound : CONSTITUENT

♦ component, constituent, element, factor, member

in·gress \'in-ˌgres\ *n* ♦ : a means or place of entry : ENTRANCE, ACCESS — **in·gres·sion** \in-'gre-shən\ *n*

♦ access, admission, doorway, entrance, entrée, entry, gateway

in·grow·ing \'in-ˌgrō-iŋ\ *adj* : growing or tending inward

in·grown \-ˌgrōn\ *adj* : grown in; *esp* : having the free tip or edge embedded in the flesh ⟨∼ toenail⟩

in·gui·nal \'iŋ-gwən-ᵊl\ *adj* : of, relating to, or situated in or near the region of the groin

in·hab·it \in-'ha-bət\ *vb* : to live or dwell in — **in·hab·it·able** *adj*

in·hab·i·tant \in-'ha-bə-tənt\ *n* ♦ : a permanent resident in a place

♦ denizen, dweller, occupant, resident *Ant* transient

in·hal·ant \in-'hā-lənt\ *n* : something (as a medicine) that is inhaled

in·ha·la·tor \'in-hə-ˌlā-tər\ *n* : a device that provides a mixture of carbon dioxide and oxygen for breathing

in·hale \in-'hāl\ *vb* **in·haled; in·hal·ing** : to breathe in — **in·ha·la·tion** \ˌin-hə-'lā-shən\ *n*

in·hal·er \in-'hā-lər\ *n* : a device by means of which medicinal material is inhaled

in·har·mo·ni·ous \-'mō-nē-əs\ *adj* **1** ♦ : not harmonious **2** ♦ : not fitting or congenial

♦ discordant, discrepant, incompatible, incongruous

in·here \in-'hir\ *vb* **in·hered; in·her·ing** : to be inherent

in·her·ent \in-'hir-ənt, -'her-\ *adj* ♦ : established as an essential part of something : INTRINSIC

♦ essential, inborn, ingrained, innate, integral, intrinsic, natural *Ant* adventitious, extraneous, extrinsic

in·her·ent·ly \-lē\ *adv* ♦ : in an inherent manner

♦ constitutionally, innately, intrinsically, naturally

in·her·it \in-'her-ət\ *vb* **1** : to receive esp. from one's ancestors **2** : to receive by genetic transmission — **in·her·i·tor** \-ə-tər\ *n*

in·her·it·able \-ə-tə-bəl\ *adj* **1** : capable of being inherited **2** : capable of taking by inheritance

in·her·i·tance \-ə-təns\ *n* **1** : the act of inheriting **2** ♦ : something that is or may be passed on to another generation

♦ bequest, birthright, heritage, legacy

inherited *adj* ♦ : being something received by inheritance

♦ genetic, hereditary, heritable, inborn

in·hib·it \in-'hi-bət\ *vb* **1** : PROHIBIT, FORBID **2** ♦ : to hold in check ⟨∼ed by fear⟩

♦ bridle, check, constrain, contain, control, curb, govern, regulate, rein, restrain, tame

in·hi·bi·tion \ˌin-hə-'bi-shən\ *n* **1** : something that forbids or restricts **2** ♦ : a usu. inner check on free activity, expression, or functioning

♦ repression, restraint, self-control, self-restraint, suppression

in·hos·pi·ta·ble \ˌin-(ˌ)hä-'spi-tə-bəl, (ˌ)in-'häs-(ˌ)pi-\ *adj* **1** ♦ : not showing hospitality : not friendly or receptive **2** : providing no shelter or sustenance

♦ antagonistic, hostile, inimical, jaundiced, negative, unfriendly, unsympathetic

in–house \'in-ˌhaus, -'haus\ *adj* : existing, originating, or carried on within a group or organization

in·hu·man \(ˌ)in-'hyü-mən, -'yü-\ *adj* **1** ♦ : lacking pity, kindness, or mercy **2** : not engaging the human personality or emotions **3** ♦ : not worthy of or conforming to the needs of human beings ⟨∼ conditions⟩ **4** : of or suggesting a nonhuman class of beings — **in·hu·man·ly** *adv* — **in·hu·man·ness** *n*

♦ [1] callous, hard, heartless, inhumane, pitiless, soulless, unfeeling, unsympathetic ♦ [3] bitter, brutal, burdensome, cruel, excruciating, grievous, grim, hard, harsh, heavy, murderous, onerous, oppressive, rough, rugged, severe, stiff, tough, trying

in·hu·mane \ˌin-hyü-'mān, -yü-\ *adj* ♦ : not humane : not devoted or sympathetic to humans or human needs

♦ barbarous, brutal, cruel, heartless, sadistic, savage, vicious, wanton

in·hu·man·i·ty \-'ma-nə-tē\ *n, pl* **-ties** **1** ♦ : the quality or state of being cruel or barbarous **2** : a cruel or barbarous act

♦ barbarity, brutality, cruelty, sadism, savagery, viciousness, wantonness

in·im·i·cal \i-'ni-mi-kəl\ *adj* **1** : being adverse often by reason of hostility **2** ♦ : having the disposition of an enemy : HOSTILE, UNFRIENDLY — **in·im·i·cal·ly** *adv*

♦ antagonistic, hostile, inhospitable, jaundiced, negative, unfriendly, unsympathetic

in·im·i·ta·ble \(ˌ)i-'ni-mə-tə-bəl\ *adj* ♦ : not capable of being imitated

♦ incomparable, matchless, nonpareil, only, peerless, unequaled, unmatched, unparalleled, unrivaled, unsurpassed

in·iq·ui·tous \i-'ni-kwə-təs\ *adj* ♦ : characterized by iniquity

♦ bad, evil, immoral, nefarious, rotten, sinful, unethical, unsavory, vicious, vile, villainous, wicked, wrong

in·iq·ui·ty \i-'ni-kwə-tē\ *n, pl* **-ties** **1** : gross injustice : WICKEDNESS **2** ♦ : a wicked act

♦ corruption, debauchery, depravity, immorality, licentiousness, sin, vice

¹**ini·tial** \i-'ni-shəl\ *adj* **1** : of or relating to the beginning : INCIPIENT **2** ♦ : placed at the beginning : FIRST

♦ first, inaugural, maiden, original, pioneer, premier

²**initial** *n* : the first letter of a word or name

³**initial** *vb* **-tialed** *or* **-tialled; -tial·ing** *or* **-tial·ling** : to affix an initial to

ini·tial·ly *adv* ♦ : in the first place : at the beginning

♦ firstly, originally, primarily

¹**ini·ti·ate** \i-'ni-shē-ˌāt\ *vb* **-at·ed; -at·ing** **1** ♦ : set going : START, BEGIN **2** ♦ : to induct into membership by or as if by

special ceremonies **3** ♦ : to instruct in the rudiments or principles of something

  ♦ [1] begin, constitute, establish, found, inaugurate, innovate, institute, introduce, launch, pioneer, set up, start ♦ [2] baptize, inaugurate, induct, install, invest ♦ [3] acquaint, familiarize, introduce, orient

²**ini•ti•ate** \i-ˈni-shē-ət\ *n* **1** : a person who is undergoing or has passed an initiation **2** : a person who is instructed or adept in some special field

ini•ti•a•tion \-ˌni-shē-ˈā-shən\ *n* **1** : the act or an instance of initiating **2** : the process of being initiated; *specif* : the rites, ceremonies, ordeals, or instructions with which one is made a member of a sect or society or is invested with a particular function or status

ini•tia•tive \i-ˈni-shə-tiv\ *n* **1** : an introductory step **2** ♦ : self-reliant enterprise ⟨showed great ∼⟩ **3** : a process by which laws may be introduced or enacted directly by vote of the people

  ♦ aggressiveness, ambition, drive, enterprise, go, hustle

ini•tia•to•ry \i-ˈni-shē-ə-ˌtōr-ē\ *adj* **1** : INTRODUCTORY **2** : tending or serving to initiate ⟨∼ rites⟩

in•ject \in-ˈjekt\ *vb* **1** : to force into something ⟨∼ serum with a needle⟩ **2** ♦ : to introduce as an element into some situation or subject ⟨∼ a note of suspicion⟩ — **in•jec•tion** \-ˈjek-shən\ *n*

  ♦ fit, insert, insinuate, interject, interpose, introduce

in•junc•tion \in-ˈjəŋk-shən\ *n* **1** : ORDER, ADMONITION **2** : a court writ whereby one is required to do or to refrain from doing a specified act

in•jure \ˈin-jər\ *vb* **in•jured; in•jur•ing** **1** : to do an injustice to : WRONG **2** ♦ : to inflict bodily hurt on : HURT; *also* : to impair the soundness of

  ♦ damage, harm, hurt, wound

in•ju•ri•ous \in-ˈjùr-ē-əs\ *adj* ♦ : inflicting or tending to inflict injury

  ♦ adverse, bad, baleful, baneful, damaging, deleterious, detrimental, evil, harmful, hurtful, ill, mischievous, noxious, pernicious, prejudicial

in•ju•ry \ˈin-jə-rē\ *n, pl* **-ries** **1** ♦ : an act that damages or hurts **2** : hurt, damage, or loss sustained

  ♦ damage, detriment, harm, hurt

in•jus•tice \(ˌ)in-ˈjəs-təs\ *n* **1** ♦ : violation of a person's rights : UNFAIRNESS **2** ♦ : an unjust act or deed : WRONG

  ♦ [1, 2] disservice, injury, raw deal, wrong

¹**ink** \ˈiŋk\ *n* : a usu. liquid and colored material for writing and printing — **inky** *adj*

²**ink** *vb* : to put ink on; *esp* : SIGN

ink•blot test \ˈiŋk-ˌblät-\ *n* : any of several psychological tests based on the interpretation of irregular figures

ink•horn \-ˌhȯrn\ *n* : a small bottle (as of horn) for holding ink

in–kind \ˈin-ˈkīnd\ *adj* : consisting of something (as goods) other than money

ink–jet *n* : a computer printer that sprays electrically charged droplets of ink onto paper — **inkjet** *adj*

in•kling \ˈiŋ-kliŋ\ *n* **1** ♦ : a slight indication or suggestion : HINT, INTIMATION **2** : a vague idea

  ♦ clue, cue, hint, indication, intimation, lead, suggestion

ink•stand \ˈiŋk-ˌstand\ *n* : INKWELL; *also* : a pen and ink stand

ink•well \-ˌwel\ *n* : a container for ink

in•laid \ˈin-ˈlād\ *adj* : decorated with material set into a surface

¹**in•land** \ˈin-ˌland, -lənd\ *adj* **1** *chiefly Brit* : not foreign : DOMESTIC ⟨∼ revenue⟩ **2** : of or relating to the interior of a country

²**inland** *n* : the interior of a country

³**inland** *adv* : into or toward the interior

in–law \ˈin-ˌlȯ\ *n* : a relative by marriage

¹**in•lay** \(ˌ)in-ˈlā, ˈin-ˌlā\ *vb* **in•laid** \-ˈlād\; **in•lay•ing** : to set (a material) into a surface or ground material esp. for decoration

²**in•lay** \ˈin-ˌlā\ *n* **1** : inlaid work **2** : a shaped filling cemented into a tooth

in•let \ˈin-ˌlet, -lət\ *n* **1** ♦ : a small or narrow bay **2** : an opening for intake esp. of a fluid

  ♦ bay, bight, cove, estuary, fjord, gulf

in–line skate *n* : a roller skate whose four wheels are set in a straight line

in•mate \ˈin-ˌmāt\ *n* : any of a group occupying a single place of residence; *esp* : a person confined (as in a hospital or prison)

in me•di•as res \in-ˌmā-dē-əs-ˈrās\ *adv* : in or into the middle of a narrative or plot

in me•mo•ri•am \ˌin-mə-ˈmōr-ē-əm\ *prep* : in memory of

in•most \ˈin-ˌmōst\ *adj* : deepest within : INNERMOST

inn \ˈin\ *n* ♦ : an establishment for the lodging and entertaining of travelers : HOTEL, TAVERN

  ♦ hospice, hotel, lodge, public house, tavern

in•nards \ˈi-nərdz\ *n pl* **1** : the internal organs of a human being or animal; *esp* : VISCERA **2** : the internal parts of a structure or mechanism

in•nate \i-ˈnāt\ *adj* **1** : existing in, belonging to, or determined by factors present in an individual from birth : NATIVE **2** ♦ : belonging to the essential nature of something : INHERENT, INTRINSIC ⟨the ∼ defects of the plan⟩

  ♦ essential, inborn, ingrained, inherent, integral, intrinsic, natural

in•nate•ly *adv* ♦ : in an innate manner

  ♦ constitutionally, inherently, intrinsically, naturally

in•ner \ˈi-nər\ *adj* **1** ♦ : located farther in ⟨the ∼ bark⟩ **2** : near a center esp. of influence ⟨the ∼ circle⟩ **3** ♦ : of or relating to the mind or spirit

  ♦ [1] inside, interior, internal, inward *Ant* exterior, external, outer, outside, outward ♦ [3] cerebral, intellectual, mental, psychological

inner city *n* : the usu. older, poorer, and more densely populated section of a city — **inner–city** *adj*

in•ner–di•rect•ed \ˌi-nər-də-ˈrek-təd, -(ˌ)dī-\ *adj* : directed in thought and action by one's own scale of values as opposed to external norms

inner ear *n* : the part of the ear that is most important for hearing, is located in a cavity in the temporal bone, and contains sense organs of hearing and of awareness of position in space

in•ner•most \ˈi-nər-ˌmōst\ *adj* : farthest inward : INMOST

in•ner•sole \ˈi-nər-ˈsōl\ *n* : INSOLE

in•ner•spring \ˈi-nər-ˈspriŋ\ *adj* : having coil springs inside a padded casing

inner tube *n* : an airtight rubber tube inside a tire to hold air under pressure

in•ning \ˈi-niŋ\ *n* **1** *sing or pl* : a division of a cricket match **2** : a baseball team's turn at bat; *also* : a division of a baseball game consisting of a turn at bat for each team

inn•keep•er \ˈin-ˌkē-pər\ *n* **1** : a proprietor of an inn **2** : a hotel manager

in•no•cence \ˈi-nə-səns\ *n* **1** ♦ : freedom from guilt or sin through being unacquainted with evil : BLAMELESSNESS; *also* : freedom from legal guilt **2** ♦ : freedom from guile or cunning : SIMPLICITY; *also* : IGNORANCE

  ♦ [1] decency, goodness, honesty, integrity, righteousness *Ant* blameworthiness, culpability, guilt, guiltiness ♦ [2] artlessness, greenness, ignorance, ingenuousness, naïveté, naturalness, simplicity, unworldliness

¹**in•no•cent** \-sənt\ *adj* **1** ♦ : free from guilt or sin : BLAMELESS **2** ♦ : harmless in effect or intention; *also* : CANDID **3** : free from legal guilt or fault : LAWFUL **4** ♦ : lacking or reflecting a lack of sophistication, guile, or self-consciousness : INGENUOUS **5** : UNAWARE

  ♦ [1] blameless, clear, faultless, guiltless, impeccable, irreproachable *Ant* guilty ♦ [2] candid, harmless, innocuous, safe ♦ [4] green, ingenuous, naive, simple, unknowing, unsophisticated, unwary, unworldly

²**innocent** *n* ♦ : an innocent one

  ♦ angel, dove, lamb, sheep

in•no•cent•ly \-lē\ *adv* : in an innocent manner

in•noc•u•ous \i-ˈnä-kyə-wəs\ *adj* **1** ♦ : producing no injury : HARMLESS **2** : not offensive; *also* : INSIPID

  ♦ harmless, innocent, safe

in•nom•i•nate \i-ˈnä-mə-nət\ *adj* : having no name; *also* : ANONYMOUS

in•no•vate \ˈi-nə-ˌvāt\ *vb* **-vat•ed; -vat•ing** ♦ : to introduce as or as if new; *also* : to make changes

  ♦ constitute, establish, found, inaugurate, initiate, institute, introduce, launch, pioneer, set up, start

in•no•va•tion \ˌi-nə-ˈvā-shən\ *n* **1** : the introduction of something new **2** ♦ : a new idea, method, or device

  ♦ coinage, concoction, contrivance, creation, invention, wrinkle

in•no•va•tive \-ˌvā-tiv\ *adj* ♦ : characterized by, tending to, or introducing innovations

  ♦ creative, imaginative, ingenious, inventive, original

in·no·va·tor \-ˌvā-tər\ *n* ♦ : one that innovates

♦ designer, developer, inventor, originator

in·nu·en·do \ˌin-yə-ˈwen-dō\ *n, pl* **-dos** *or* **-does** : HINT, INSINU-ATION; *esp* : a veiled reflection on character or reputation

in·nu·mer·a·ble \i-ˈnü-mə-rə-bəl, -ˈnyü-\ *adj* ♦ : too many to be numbered

♦ countless, numberless, uncountable, unnumbered, untold

in·oc·u·late \i-ˈnä-kyə-lāt\ *vb* **-lat·ed; -lat·ing** : to introduce something into: as **a** : to introduce a serum or antibody into (an organism) to treat or prevent a disease **b** : to introduce informa-tion to — **in·oc·u·la·tion** \-ˌnä-kyə-ˈlā-shən\ *n*

in·op·er·a·ble \(ˌ)i-ˈnä-pə-rə-bəl\ *adj* **1** : not suitable for sur-gery **2** ♦ : not operable

♦ inoperative, nonfunctional *Ant* functional, functioning, oper-able, operating, operational, operative, running, working ♦ im-practical, unusable, unworkable, useless

in·op·er·a·tive \-ˈnä-pə-rə-tiv, -ˈnä-pə-ˌrā-\ *adj* ♦ : not func-tioning

♦ dead, dormant, fallow, free, idle, inactive, inert, latent, off, vacant

in·op·por·tune \(ˌ)i-ˌnä-pər-ˈtün, -ˈtyün\ *adj* : not opportune : INCONVENIENT

in·op·por·tune·ly \-lē\ *adv* : in an inopportune manner

in·or·di·nate \i-ˈnòrd-ᵊn-ət\ *adj* ♦ : exceeding reasonable limits : IMMODERATE ⟨an ∼ curiosity⟩

♦ devilish, excessive, exorbitant, extravagant, extreme, immod-erate, lavish, overmuch, overweening, steep, stiff, towering, un-conscionable

in·or·di·nate·ly *adv* ♦ : to an excessive or unreasonable degree

♦ devilishly, excessively, monstrously, overly, overmuch, too

in·or·gan·ic \ˌi-nòr-ˈga-nik\ *adj* : being or composed of matter of other than plant or animal origin : MINERAL

in·pa·tient \ˈin-ˌpā-shənt\ *n* : a hospital patient who receives lodging and food as well as treatment

in·put \ˈin-ˌpút\ *n* **1** : something put in **2** : power or energy put into a machine or system **3** : information fed into a computer or data processing system **4** ♦ : recommendation with regard to a course of action : ADVICE — **input** *vb*

♦ advice, counsel, guidance

in·quest \ˈin-ˌkwest\ *n* **1** : an official inquiry or examination esp. before a jury **2** : a systematic investigation : INQUIRY, INVES-TIGATION

in·qui·etude \(ˌ)in-ˈkwī-ə-ˌtüd, -ˌtyüd\ *n* : UNEASINESS, REST-LESSNESS

in·quire \in-ˈkwīr\ *vb* **in·quired; in·quir·ing** **1** ♦ : to ask or ask about **2** ♦ : to make investigation or inquiry : INVESTIGATE — often used with *into* — **in·quir·er** *n* — **in·quir·ing·ly** *adv*

♦ *usu* **inquire of** [1] ask, query, question, quiz ♦ *usu* **inquire into** [2] delve, dig, explore, go, investigate, look, probe, re-search

in·qui·ry \ˈin-ˌkwīr-ē, in-ˈkwīr-ē; ˈin-kwə-rē, ˈiŋ-\ *n, pl* **-ries** ♦ : a request for information; *also* : RESEARCH **2** ♦ : a systematic investigation of a matter of public interest

♦ [1] query, question, request ♦ [2] examination, exploration, investigation, probe, research, study

in·qui·si·tion \ˌin-kwə-ˈzi-shən, ˌiŋ-\ *n* **1** : a judicial or official inquiry usu. before a jury **2** *cap* : a former Roman Catholic tri-bunal for the discovery and punishment of heresy **3** : a severe questioning **4** : the act of inquiring — **in·quis·i·tor** \in-ˈkwi-zə-tər\ *n* — **in·quis·i·to·ri·al** \-ˌkwi-zə-ˈtòr-ē-əl\ *adj*

in·quis·i·tive \in-ˈkwi-zə-tiv\ *adj* **1** : given to examination or investigation ⟨an ∼ mind⟩ **2** ♦ : unduly curious — **in·quis·i·tive·ly** *adv*

♦ curious, nosy, prying

in·quis·i·tive·ness *n* : the quality or state of being inquisitive

in re \in-ˈrā, -ˈrē\ *prep* : in the matter of

INRI *abbr* Jesus of Nazareth, King of the Jews

in·road \ˈin-ˌrōd\ *n* **1** : a sudden hostile incursion : INVASION, RAID **2** : an advance made usu. at the expense of another

in·rush \ˈin-ˌrəsh\ *n* : a crowding or flooding in

ins *abbr* **1** inches **2** insurance

INS *abbr* Immigration and Naturalization Service

in·sa·lu·bri·ous \ˌin-sə-ˈlü-brē-əs\ *adj* : UNWHOLESOME, NOX-IOUS ⟨∼ air⟩

ins and outs *n pl* **1** : characteristic peculiarities **2** : RAMIFICA-TIONS

in·sane \(ˌ)in-ˈsān\ *adj* **1** : exhibiting a severely disordered state of mind; *also* : used by or for people having a severely disordered state of mind **2** ♦ : ridiculously unreasonable, unsound, or in-congruous : ABSURD — **in·sane·ly** *adv*

♦ absurd, bizarre, fanciful, fantastic, foolish, nonsensical, pre-posterous, unreal, wild

in·san·i·ty \in-ˈsa-nə-tē\ *n* **1** *dated* : a severely disordered state of mind usu. occurring as a specific disorder (as schizophre-nia) **2** ♦ : extreme folly or unreasonableness; *also* : something utterly foolish or unreasonable

♦ absurdity, asininity, balminess, daftness, fatuity, folly, foolish-ness, inanity, silliness, simplicity, zaniness

in·sa·tia·ble \(ˌ)in-ˈsā-shə-bəl\ *adj* : incapable of being satisfied — **in·sa·tia·bil·i·ty** \(ˌ)in-ˌsā-shə-ˈbi-lə-tē\ *n* — **in·sa·tia·bly** *adv*

in·sa·tiate \(ˌ)in-ˈsā-shē-ət, -shət\ *adj* : INSATIABLE — **in·sa·tiate·ly** *adv*

in·scribe \in-ˈskrīb\ *vb* **1** : to write, engrave, or print as a lasting record **2** ♦ : to enter on a list : ENROLL **3** ♦ : to write, engrave, or print characters upon **4** : to dedicate to someone **5** : to draw within a figure so as to touch in as many places as possible — **in·scrip·tion** \-ˈskrip-shən\ *n*

♦ [2] catalog, enroll, enter, index, list, put down, record, regis-ter, schedule, slate ♦ [3] engrave, etch, grave

in·scru·ta·ble \in-ˈskrü-tə-bəl\ *adj* ♦ : not readily comprehen-sible : MYSTERIOUS — **in·scru·ta·bly** \-blē\ *adv*

♦ cryptic, darkling, deep, enigmatic, impenetrable, mysterious, mystic, occult, uncanny

in·seam \ˈin-ˌsēm\ *n* : the seam on the inside of the leg of a pair of pants; *also* : the length of this seam

in·sect \ˈin-ˌsekt\ *n* : any of a class of small usu. winged arthro-pod animals (as flies, bees, beetles, and moths) with usu. three pairs of legs as adults

in·sec·ti·cide \in-ˈsek-tə-ˌsīd\ *n* : an agent for destroying insects — **in·sec·ti·cid·al** \-ˌsek-tə-ˈsīd-ᵊl\ *adj*

in·sec·tiv·o·rous \ˌin-ˌsek-ˈti-və-rəs\ *adj* : feeding on insects

in·se·cure \ˌin-si-ˈkyúr\ *adj* **1** : UNCERTAIN **2** : not protected : UNSAFE **3** ♦ : not firmly fastened or fixed : LOOSE **4** : not highly stable; *also* : lacking assurance : ANXIOUS, FEARFUL — **in·se·cure·ly** *adv*

♦ lax, loose, relaxed, slack

in·se·cu·ri·ty \-ˈkyúr-ə-tē\ *n* ♦ : the quality or state of being in-secure

♦ instability, precariousness, shakiness, unsteadiness

in·sem·i·nate \in-ˈse-mə-ˌnāt\ *vb* **-nat·ed; -nat·ing** : to intro-duce semen into the genital tract of (a female) — **in·sem·i·na·tion** \-ˌse-mə-ˈnā-shən\ *n*

in·sen·sate \(ˌ)in-ˈsen-ˌsāt, -sət\ *adj* **1** : lacking sense or un-derstanding; *also* : FOOLISH **2** : INANIMATE **3** : lacking humane feeling : INHUMAN ⟨∼ rage⟩

in·sen·si·bil·i·ty \-ˌsen-sə-ˈbi-lə-tē\ *n* : the quality or state of be-ing insensible: as **a** : lack of mental or emotional feeling or re-sponse **b** : an unconscious or comatose state

in·sen·si·ble \(ˌ)in-ˈsen-sə-bəl\ *adj* **1** : not perceptible by a sense or by the mind : IMPERCEPTIBLE; *also* : SLIGHT, GRADU-AL **2** : INANIMATE **3** : not knowing or perceiving : UNCON-SCIOUS **4** : lacking sensory perception or ability to react ⟨∼ to pain⟩ **5** : APATHETIC, INDIFFERENT; *also* : UNAWARE ⟨∼ of their danger⟩ **6** : MEANINGLESS **7** : lacking delicacy or refinement — **in·sen·si·bly** \-ˈsen-sə-blē\ *adv*

in·sen·tient \(ˌ)in-ˈsen-chē-ənt\ *adj* : lacking perception, con-sciousness, or animation — **in·sen·tience** \-chē-əns\ *n*

in·sep·a·ra·bil·i·ty \-ˌse-prə-ˈbi-lə-tē, -pə-rə-\ *n* : the quality or state of being inseparable

in·sep·a·ra·ble \(ˌ)in-ˈse-prə-bəl, -pə-rə-\ *adj* **1** : incapable of being separated or disjoined **2** : very close or intimate — **in·separable** *n* — **in·sep·a·ra·bly** \-ˈse-prə-blē, -pə-rə-\ *adv*

¹**in·sert** \in-ˈsərt\ *vb* **1** : to put or thrust in ⟨∼ a key in a lock⟩ ⟨∼ a comma⟩ **2** ♦ : to put or introduce into the body of some-thing : INTERPOLATE **3** : to set in (as a piece of fabric) and make fast

♦ fit, inject, insinuate, interject, interpose, introduce

²**in·sert** \ˈin-ˌsərt\ *n* : something that is inserted or is for insertion; *esp* : written or printed material inserted (as between the leaves of a book)

in·ser·tion \in-ˈsər-shən\ *n* **1** : something that is inserted **2** : the act or process of inserting

in·set \'in-,set\ *vb* **inset** *or* **in·set·ted; in·set·ting** : to set in : IN-SERT — **inset** *n*

¹**in·shore** \'in-'shōr\ *adj* **1** : situated, living, or carried on near shore **2** : moving toward shore

²**inshore** *adv* : to or toward shore

¹**in·side** \in-'sīd, 'in-,sīd\ *n* **1** : an inner side or surface : INTERIOR **2** : inward nature, thoughts, or feeling **3** *pl* : VISCERA, ENTRAILS **4** : a position of power, trust, or familiarity

²**inside** *adv* **1** : on the inner side **2** : in or into the interior

³**inside** *prep* **1** : in or into the inside of **2** : WITHIN ⟨~ an hour⟩

⁴**inside** *adj* **1** ♦ : of, relating to, or being on or near the inside **2** ♦ : relating or known to a select group

    ♦ [1] inner, interior, internal, inward ♦ [2] confidential, hushed, intimate, private, secret

inside of *prep* : INSIDE

inside out *adv* **1** : in such a manner that the inner surface becomes the outer ⟨turned the shirt *inside out*⟩ **2** : in a state of disarray or reorganization ⟨turned her life *inside out*⟩

in·sid·er \in-'sī-dər\ *n* : a person who is in a position of power or has access to confidential information

in·sid·i·ous \in-'si-dē-əs\ *adj* **1** : SLY, TREACHEROUS **2** : SEDUCTIVE **3** : having a gradual and cumulative effect : SUBTLE — **in·sid·i·ous·ly** *adv* — **in·sid·i·ous·ness** *n*

in·sight \'in-,sīt\ *n* ♦ : the power, act, or result of seeing into a situation

    ♦ discernment, perception, sagacity, sapience, wisdom

in·sight·ful \'in-,sīt-fəl, in-'sīt-\ *adj* ♦ : exhibiting or characterized by insight

    ♦ discerning, perceptive, sagacious, sage, sapient, wise

in·sig·nia \in-'sig-nē-ə\ *also* **in·sig·ne** \-(,)nē\ *n, pl* **-nia** *or* **-ni·as** : a distinguishing mark esp. of authority or honor : BADGE

in·sig·nif·i·cant \-kənt\ *adj* : not significant: as **a** ♦ : lacking meaning or import **b** ♦ : not worth considering

    ♦ frivolous, inconsequential, inconsiderable, little, minor, minute, negligible, slight, small, trifling, trivial, unimportant

in·sin·cere \,in-sin-'sir\ *adj* ♦ : not sincere : HYPOCRITICAL — **in·sin·cere·ly** *adv*

    ♦ artificial, double-dealing, feigned, hypocritical, left-handed, mealy, mealymouthed, two-faced, unctuous *Ant* genuine, heartfelt, honest, sincere, unfeigned

in·sin·cer·i·ty \-'ser-ə-tē\ *n* ♦ : the quality or state of being insincere

    ♦ cant, dissimulation, hypocrisy, piety

in·sin·u·ate \in-'sin-yə-,wāt\ *vb* **-at·ed; -at·ing** **1** ♦ : to introduce gradually or in a subtle, indirect, or artful way **2** ♦ : to imply in a subtle or devious way — **in·sin·u·a·tion** \(,)in-,sin-yə-'wā-shən\ *n*

    ♦ [1] infiltrate, insert, interpose, introduce, slip, sneak, work, worm ♦ [2] allude, hint, imply, indicate, infer, intimate, suggest

in·sin·u·at·ing *adj* **1** : winning favor and confidence by imperceptible degrees **2** : tending gradually to cause doubt, distrust, or change of outlook

in·sip·id \in-'si-pəd\ *adj* **1** ♦ : lacking taste or savor **2** ♦ : lacking in qualities that interest, stimulate, or challenge : FLAT — **in·si·pid·i·ty** \,in-sə-'pi-də-tē\ *n*

    ♦ [1] flat, flavorless (*or* flavourless), tasteless *Ant* flavorful, savory, tasty ♦ [2] banal, flat, wishy-washy

in·sist \in-'sist\ *vb* ♦ : to take a resolute stand

    ♦ affirm, allege, assert, aver, avouch, avow, claim, contend, declare, maintain, profess, protest, warrant ♦ *usu* **insist on** call, claim, clamor (*or* clamour), command, demand, enjoin, exact, press, quest, stipulate (for)

in·sis·tence \in-'sis-təns\ *n* : the act of insisting; *also* : an insistent attitude or quality : URGENCY

in·sis·tent \in-'sis-tənt\ *adj* ♦ : disposed to insist — **in·sis·tent·ly** *adv*

    ♦ dogged, patient, persevering, persistent, pertinacious, tenacious

in si·tu \in-'sī-tü, -'sē-\ *adv or adj* : in the natural or original position

in·so·far as \,in-sə-'fär-\ *conj* : to the extent or degree that

insol *abbr* insoluble

in·so·la·tion \,in-(,)sō-'lā-shən\ *n* : solar radiation that has been received

in·sole \'in-,sōl\ *n* **1** : an inside sole of a shoe **2** : a loose thin strip placed inside a shoe for warmth or comfort

in·so·lence \-ləns\ *n* **1** : the quality or state of being insolent **2** ♦ : an instance of insolent conduct or treatment

    ♦ back talk, cheek, impertinence, impudence, sauce ♦ brazenness, discourtesy, disrespect, impertinence, impudence, incivility, rudeness

in·so·lent \'in-sə-lənt\ *adj* ♦ : contemptuous, rude, disrespectful, or bold in behavior or language

    ♦ bold, brash, fresh, impertinent, impudent, nervy, sassy, saucy

in·sol·u·ble \(,)in-'säl-yə-bəl\ *adj* **1** ♦ : having or admitting of no solution or explanation **2** : difficult or impossible to dissolve — **in·sol·u·bil·i·ty** \-,säl-yə-'bi-lə-tē\ *n*

    ♦ hopeless, impossible, unattainable, unsolvable

in·sol·vent \(,)in-'säl-vənt\ *adj* **1** : unable or insufficient to pay all debts ⟨an ~ estate⟩ **2** : IMPOVERISHED, DEFICIENT — **in·sol·ven·cy** \-'vən-sē\ *n*

in·som·nia \in-'säm-nē-ə\ *n* : prolonged and usu. abnormal sleeplessness — **in·som·ni·ac** \-nē-,ak\ *n*

in·so·much as \,in-sə-'məch-\ *conj* : INASMUCH AS

insomuch that *conj* : to such a degree that : SO

in·sou·ci·ance \in-'sü-sē-əns, aⁿ-süs-'yäⁿs\ *n* ♦ : lighthearted unconcern ⟨youthful ~⟩

    ♦ apathy, disinterestedness, disregard, indifference, nonchalance

in·sou·ci·ant \in-'sü-sē-ənt, aⁿ-süs-'yäⁿ\ *adj* ♦ : exhibiting or characterized by insouciance

    ♦ carefree, careless, cavalier, easygoing, happy-go-lucky, lighthearted, nonchalant, unconcerned

insp *abbr* inspector

in·spect \in-'spekt\ *vb* ♦ : to view closely and critically : EXAMINE — **in·spec·tor** \-tər\ *n*

    ♦ audit, check, examine, review, scan, scrutinize, survey

in·spec·tion \-'spek-shən\ *n* **1** : the act of inspecting **2** ♦ : a checking or testing of an individual against established standards

    ♦ audit, check, checkup, examination, review, scan, scrutiny, survey

inspector general *n* : the head of a system of inspection (as of an army)

in·spi·ra·tion \,in-spə-'rā-shən\ *n* **1** : the act or power of moving the intellect or emotions **2** : INHALATION **3** : the quality or state of being inspired; *also* : something that is inspired **4** : an inspiring agent or influence — **in·spi·ra·tion·al** \-shə-nəl\ *adj*

in·spire \in-'spīr\ *vb* **in·spired; in·spir·ing** **1** : to influence, move, or guide by divine or supernatural inspiration **2** ♦ : to exert an animating, enlivening, or exalting influence upon; *also* : AFFECT **3** : to communicate to an agent supernaturally; *also* : to bring out or about **4** : INHALE **5** : INCITE **6** : to spread by indirect means — **in·spir·er** *n*

    ♦ buoy (up), cheer, comfort, embolden, encourage, hearten, steel

in·spir·it \in-'spir-ət\ *vb* : ENCOURAGE, HEARTEN

inst *abbr* **1** instant **2** institute; institution; institutional

in·sta·bil·i·ty \,in-stə-'bi-lə-tē\ *n* ♦ : lack of steadiness; *esp* : lack of emotional or mental stability

    ♦ insecurity, precariousness, shakiness, unsteadiness *Ant* fixedness, security, stability, steadiness

in·stall *or* **in·stal** \in-'stol\ *vb* **in·stalled; in·stall·ing** **1** ♦ : to place formally in office : induct into an office, rank, or order **2** ♦ : to establish in an indicated place, condition, or status **3** : to set up for use or service

    ♦ [1] baptize, inaugurate, induct, initiate, invest ♦ [2] ensconce, lodge, perch, roost, settle

in·stal·la·tion \,in-stə-'lā-shən\ *n* **1** ♦ : the act of installing : the state of being installed **2** ♦ : a military camp, fort, or base

    ♦ [1] inaugural, inauguration, induction, investiture ♦ [2] complex, establishment, facility

¹**in·stall·ment** *also* **in·stal·ment** \in-'stol-mənt\ *n* : INSTALLATION

²**installment** *also* **instalment** *n* **1** : one of the parts into which a debt or sum is divided for payment **2** : one of several parts presented at intervals

¹**in·stance** \'in-stəns\ *n* **1** : INSTIGATION, REQUEST **2** ♦ : an individual illustrative of a category or brought forward in support or disproof of a generalization : EXAMPLE ⟨for ~⟩ **3** : an event or step that is part of a process or series

♦ case, example, exemplar, illustration, representative, sample, specimen

²instance vb **in·stanced; in·stanc·ing** **1** ♦ : to mention as a case or example **2** ♦ : to explain by reference to examples

♦ [1] advert (to), cite, mention, name, note, notice, quote, refer (to), specify, touch (on or upon) ♦ [2] demonstrate, exemplify, illustrate

¹in·stant \'in-stənt\ n **1** ♦ : an immeasurably small space of time : MOMENT ⟨the ~ we met⟩ **2** : the present or current month

♦ flash, jiffy, minute, moment, second, shake, trice, twinkle, twinkling, wink

²instant adj **1** : calling for immediate attention : URGENT **2** : PRESENT, CURRENT **3** : occurring, acting, or accomplished without loss or interval of time : IMMEDIATE ⟨~ relief⟩ **4** : premixed or precooked for easy final preparation ⟨~ cake mix⟩; also : immediately soluble in water ⟨~ coffee⟩

in·stan·ta·neous \,in-stən-'tā-nē-əs\ adj ♦ : done or occurring in an instant or without delay — **in·stan·ta·neous·ly** adv

♦ immediate, instant, straightaway

in·stan·ter \in-'stan-tər\ adv : at once
in·stan·ti·ate \in-'stan-chē-,āt\ vb **-at·ed; -at·ing** : to represent (an abstraction) by a concrete example — **in·stan·ti·a·tion** \-,stan-chē-'ā-shən\ n
in·stant·ly \'in-stənt-lē\ adv ♦ : at once : IMMEDIATELY

♦ directly, forthwith, immediately, now, promptly, pronto, right away, right now

instant messaging n : a means or system for transmitting electronic messages instantly — **instant message** n or vb
in·state \in-'stāt\ vb : to establish in a rank or office : INSTALL
in·stead \in-'sted\ adv **1** : as a substitute or equivalent **2** : as an alternative : RATHER
instead of prep : as a substitute for or alternative to
in·step \'in-,step\ n : the arched part of the human foot in front of the ankle joint; esp : its upper surface
in·sti·gate \'in-stə-,gāt\ vb **-gat·ed; -gat·ing** ♦ : to goad or urge forward : PROVOKE, INCITE ⟨~ a revolt⟩

♦ abet, ferment, foment, incite, provoke, raise, stir, whip

in·sti·ga·tion \,in-stə-'gā-shən\ n **1** : an act of instigating or the state of being instigated **2** ♦ : something that instigates

♦ boost, encouragement, goad, impetus, impulse, incentive, incitement, momentum, motivation, provocation, spur, stimulus, yeast

in·sti·ga·tor \'in-stə-,gā-tər\ n : one that instigates
in·stil chiefly Brit var of INSTILL
in·still \in-'stil\ vb **in·stilled; in·still·ing** **1** : to cause to enter drop by drop **2** : to impart gradually
¹in·stinct \'in-,stiŋkt\ n **1** : a natural aptitude **2** : a largely inheritable and unalterable tendency of an organism to make a complex and specific response to environmental stimuli without involving reason; also : behavior originating below the conscious level
²in·stinct \in-'stiŋkt, 'in-,stiŋkt\ adj : IMBUED, INFUSED
in·stinc·tive \in-'stiŋk-tiv\ adj **1** : of, relating to, or being instinct **2** : prompted by natural instinct or propensity : arising spontaneously — **in·stinc·tive·ly** adv
in·stinc·tu·al \in-'stiŋk-chə-wəl\ adj : of, relating to, or based on instinct
¹in·sti·tute \'in-stə-,tüt, -,tyüt\ vb **-tut·ed; -tut·ing** **1** : to establish in a position or office **2** : ORGANIZE **3** ♦ : to bring about the beginning of : INAUGURATE, INITIATE

♦ constitute, establish, found, inaugurate, initiate, innovate, introduce, launch, pioneer, set up, start

²institute n **1** : an elementary principle recognized as authoritative; also, pl : a collection of such principles and precepts **2** ♦ : an organization for the promotion of a cause : ASSOCIATION **3** : an educational institution **4** : a brief course of instruction on a particular field

♦ association, brotherhood, club, college, congress, council, fellowship, fraternity, guild, institution, league, order, organization, society

in·sti·tu·tion \,in-stə-'tü-shən, -'tyü-\ n **1** : an act of originating, setting up, or founding **2** : an established practice, law, or custom **3** ♦ : a society or corporation esp. of a public character ⟨a charitable ~⟩ **4** : ASYLUM 3 — **in·sti·tu·tion·al** \-'tü-shə-nəl, -'tyü-\ adj — **in·sti·tu·tion·al·ize** \-nə-,līz\ vb — **in·sti·tu·tion·al·ly** adv

♦ establishment, foundation, institute

instr abbr **1** instructor **2** instrument; instrumental
in·struct \in-'strəkt\ vb **1** ♦ : to give knowledge to : TEACH **2** ♦ : to provide with authoritative information or advice : INFORM **3** ♦ : to give an order or a command to

♦ [1] educate, indoctrinate, school, teach, train, tutor ♦ [2] acquaint, advise, apprise, brief, clue, enlighten, familiarize, fill in, inform, tell, wise ♦ [3] bid, boss, charge, command, direct, enjoin, order, tell

in·struc·tion \in-'strək-shən\ n **1** : LESSON, PRECEPT **2** ♦ : a direction calling for compliance : COMMAND, ORDER **3** pl : DIRECTIONS **4** ♦ : the action, practice, or profession of a teacher

♦ [2] behest, charge, command, commandment, decree, dictate, direction, directive, edict, order, word ♦ [4] education, teaching, training, tutelage

in·struc·tion·al \-shə-nəl\ adj **1** : relating to, serving for, or promoting instruction **2** : containing or conveying instruction or information
in·struc·tive \in-'strək-tiv\ adj ♦ : carrying a lesson

♦ educational, informative

in·struc·tor \in-'strək-tər\ n ♦ : one that instructs; esp : a college teacher below professorial rank — **in·struc·tor·ship** n

♦ educator, pedagogue, schoolteacher, teacher

in·stru·ment \'in-strə-mənt\ n **1** : a device used to produce music **2** ♦ : a means by which something is done **3** ♦ : a device for doing work and esp. precision work **4** : a legal document (as a deed) **5** : a device used in navigating an airplane — **in·stru·ment** \-,ment\ vb

♦ [2] agency, agent, instrumentality, machinery, means, medium, organ, vehicle ♦ [3] device, implement, tool, utensil

in·stru·men·tal \,in-strə-'men-t³l\ adj **1** : acting as a crucial agent or means **2** : of, relating to, or done with an instrument **3** : relating to, composed for, or performed on a musical instrument
in·stru·men·tal·ist \-'men-tə-list\ n : a player on a musical instrument
in·stru·men·tal·i·ty \,in-strə-mən-'ta-lə-tē, -,men-\ n, pl **-ties** **1** : the quality or state of being instrumental **2** ♦ : something useful or helpful to a desired end : MEANS, AGENCY

♦ agency, agent, instrument, machinery, means, medium, organ, vehicle

in·stru·men·ta·tion \,in-strə-mən-'tā-shən, -,men-\ n **1** : ORCHESTRATION **2** : instruments for a particular purpose
instrument panel n : DASHBOARD
in·sub·or·di·nate \,in-sə-'bord-³n-ət\ adj : disobedient to authority
in·sub·or·di·na·tion \-,bord-³n-'ā-shən\ n ♦ : the quality or state of being insubordinate : defiance of authority

♦ defiance, disobedience, rebelliousness, recalcitrance, refractoriness, unruliness

in·sub·stan·tial \,in-səb-'stan-chəl\ adj **1** : lacking substance or reality **2** : lacking firmness or solidity

♦ flimsy, gauzy, unsubstantial

in·suf·fer·able \(,)in-'sə-fə-rə-bəl\ adj ♦ : not to be endured : INTOLERABLE ⟨an ~ bore⟩ — **in·suf·fer·ably** \-blē\ adv

♦ insupportable, intolerable, unbearable, unendurable, unsupportable

in·suf·fi·cien·cy \-shən-sē\ n : the quality or state of being insufficient: as **a** : lack of mental or moral fitness **b** ♦ : lack of adequate supply

♦ dearth, deficiency, deficit, failure, famine, inadequacy, lack, paucity, poverty, scantiness, scarcity, shortage, want

in·suf·fi·cient \,in-sə-'fi-shənt\ adj ♦ : not sufficient — **in·suf·fi·cient·ly** adv

♦ deficient, inadequate, scarce, short, shy, wanting

in·su·lar \'in-sə-lər, -syə-\ adj **1** : of, relating to, or forming an island **2** : dwelling or situated on an island **3** ♦ : being, having, or reflecting a narrow provincial viewpoint : NARROW-MINDED — **in·su·lar·i·ty** \,in-sə-'lar-ə-tē, -syə-\ n

♦ little, narrow, narrow-minded, parochial, petty, provincial, sectarian, small

in·su·late \'in-sə-,lāt\ vb **-lat·ed; -lat·ing** **1** ♦ : to place in a detached situation : ISOLATE **2** : to separate a conductor of electricity, heat, or sound from other conducting bodies by means of a nonconductor — **in·su·la·tor** \'in-sə-,lā-tər\ n

♦ cut off, isolate, seclude, segregate, separate, sequester

in·su·la·tion \ˌin-sə-ˈlā-shən\ *n* **1 a** : the action of insulating **b** ♦ : the state of being insulated **2** : material used in insulating
♦ isolation, seclusion, segregation, sequestration, solitude

in·su·lin \ˈin-sə-lən\ *n* : a pancreatic hormone essential esp. for the metabolism of carbohydrates and the regulation of glucose in the blood

¹in·sult \in-ˈsəlt\ *vb* ♦ : to treat with insolence or contempt : AFFRONT — **in·sult·ing·ly** *adv*
♦ affront, offend, outrage, slight, wound

²in·sult \ˈin-ˌsəlt\ *n* ♦ : a gross indignity
♦ affront, barb, dart, dig, indignity, name, offense, outrage, put-down, sarcasm, slight, slur, wound

in·su·per·a·ble \(ˌ)in-ˈsü-pə-rə-bəl\ *adj* ♦ : incapable of being surmounted, overcome, passed over, or solved — **in·su·per·a·bly** \-blē\ *adv*
♦ impregnable, indomitable, insurmountable, invincible, invulnerable, unbeatable, unconquerable

in·sup·port·able \ˌin-sə-ˈpōr-tə-bəl\ *adj* **1** ♦ : more than can be endured : UNENDURABLE **2** : UNJUSTIFIABLE
♦ insufferable, intolerable, unbearable, unendurable, unsupportable

in·sur·able \in-ˈshu̇r-ə-bəl\ *adj* : capable of being or proper to be insured

in·sur·ance \in-ˈshu̇r-əns\ *n* **1** : the business of insuring persons or property **2** : coverage by contract whereby one party agrees to guarantee another against a specified loss **3** : the sum for which something is insured **4** : a means of guaranteeing protection or safety

in·sure \in-ˈshu̇r\ *vb* **in·sured; in·sur·ing** **1** : to provide or obtain insurance on or for : UNDERWRITE **2** ♦ : to make certain : ENSURE
♦ assure, cinch, ensure, guarantee, guaranty, secure

in·sured \in-ˈshu̇rd\ *n* : a person whose life or property is insured

in·sur·er \in-ˈshu̇r-ər\ *n* : one that insures; *esp* : an insurance company

in·sur·gen·cy \-jən-sē\ *n* : the quality or state of being insurgent; *specif* : a condition of revolt against a government that is less than an organized revolution and that is not recognized as belligerency

¹in·sur·gent \in-ˈsər-jənt\ *n* **1** : a person who revolts against civil authority or an established government : REBEL **2** : a member of a political party who rebels against it — **in·sur·gence** \-jəns\ *n*

²in·sur·gent *adj* ♦ : rising in opposition to civil authority or established leadership
♦ mutinous, rebellious, revolutionary

in·sur·mount·able \ˌin-sər-ˈmau̇n-tə-bəl\ *adj* ♦ : incapable of being surmounted, overcome, passed over, or solved — **in·sur·mount·ably** \-blē\ *adv*
♦ impregnable, indomitable, invincible, invulnerable, unbeatable, unconquerable

in·sur·rec·tion \ˌin-sə-ˈrek-shən\ *n* ♦ : an act or instance of revolting against civil authority or an established government
♦ mutiny, rebellion, revolt, revolution, uprising

in·sur·rec·tion·ist \-shə-nist\ *n* ♦ : a favorer of or participant in insurrection
♦ insurgent, mutineer, rebel, red, revolter, revolutionary

int *abbr* **1** interest **2** interior **3** intermediate **4** internal **5** international **6** intransitive

in·tact \in-ˈtakt\ *adj* **1** : untouched esp. by anything that harms or diminishes **2** ♦ : being complete or entire
♦ complete, comprehensive, entire, full, grand, integral, perfect, plenary, total, whole

in·ta·glio \in-ˈtal-yō\ *n, pl* **-glios** : an engraving cut deeply into the surface of a hard material (as stone)

in·take \ˈin-ˌtāk\ *n* **1** : an opening through which fluid enters **2** : the act of taking in **3** : something taken in

in·tan·gi·ble \(ˌ)in-ˈtan-jə-bəl\ *adj* : incapable of being touched : IMPALPABLE ⟨~ benefits⟩ — **intangible** *n* — **in·tan·gi·bly** \-blē\ *adv*

in·te·ger \ˈin-ti-jər\ *n* ♦ : a number (as 1, 2, 3, 12, 432) that is not a fraction and does not include a fraction, is the negative of such a number, or is 0
♦ digit, figure, number, numeral, whole number

in·te·gral \ˈin-ti-grəl\ *adj* **1** ♦ : essential to completeness **2** : formed as a unit with another part **3** : composed of parts that make up a whole **4** ♦ : lacking nothing essential : ENTIRE **5** ♦ : being or involved in the essential nature of a thing
♦ [1] essential, imperative, indispensable, necessary, needful, requisite, vital ♦ [4] complete, comprehensive, entire, full, grand, intact, perfect, plenary, total, whole ♦ [5] essential, inborn, ingrained, inherent, innate, intrinsic, natural

integral calculus *n* : calculus concerned esp. with advanced methods of finding lengths, areas, and volumes

in·te·grate \ˈin-tə-ˌgrāt\ *vb* **-grat·ed; -grat·ing** **1** ♦ : to form, coordinate, or blend into a functioning whole **2** ♦ : to incorporate into a larger unit **3** : to end the segregation of and bring into equal membership in society or an organization; *also* : DESEGREGATE — **in·te·gra·tion** \ˌin-tə-ˈgrā-shən\ *n*
♦ [1] assimilate, embody, incorporate ♦ [2] amalgamate, blend, combine, commingle, fuse, incorporate, intermingle, merge, mingle, mix

integrated circuit *n* : a group of tiny electronic components and their connections that is produced in or on a small slice of material (as silicon)

in·teg·ri·ty \in-ˈte-grə-tē\ *n* **1** ♦ : adherence to a code of values **2** : SOUNDNESS **3** : COMPLETENESS
♦ character, decency, goodness, honesty, honor (*or* honour), morality, probity, rectitude, righteousness, uprightness, virtue

in·teg·u·ment \in-ˈte-gyə-mənt\ *n* : a covering layer (as a skin or cuticle) of an organism or one of its parts

in·tel·lect \ˈin-tə-ˌlekt\ *n* **1** : the power of knowing : the capacity for knowledge **2** : the capacity for rational or intelligent thought esp. when highly developed **3** ♦ : a person with great intellectual powers
♦ brain, genius, thinker, whiz, wizard

¹in·tel·lec·tu·al \ˌin-tə-ˈlek-chə-wəl\ *adj* **1** ♦ : of, relating to, or performed by the intellect **2** ♦ : given to study, reflection, and speculation **3** : engaged in activity requiring the creative use of the intellect — **in·tel·lec·tu·al·ly** *adv*
♦ [1] cerebral, inner, mental, psychological ♦ [2] cerebral, erudite, learned, literate, scholarly *Ant* lowbrow, nonintellectual

²intellectual *n* ♦ : an intellectual person
♦ highbrow, nerd *Ant* lowbrow, philistine

intellectual disability *n* : significant impairment in intellectual ability accompanied by deficits in skills necessary for independent daily functioning

in·tel·lec·tu·al·ism \-chə-wə-ˌli-zəm\ *n* : devotion to the exercise of intellect or to intellectual pursuits

in·tel·lec·tu·al·i·ty \ˌin-tə-ˌlek-chə-ˈwa-lə-tē\ *n* : the quality or state of being intellectual

in·tel·li·gence \in-ˈte-lə-jəns\ *n* **1** ♦ : ability to learn and understand or to deal with new or trying situations **2** : mental acuteness **3** : INFORMATION, NEWS **4** : an agency engaged in obtaining information esp. concerning an enemy or possible enemy; *also* : the information so gained
♦ brains, gray matter (*or* grey matter), intellect, reason, sense

intelligence quotient *n* : IQ

in·tel·li·gent \in-ˈte-lə-jənt\ *adj* ♦ : having or showing intelligence or intellect ⟨a ~ decision⟩ — **in·tel·li·gent·ly** *adv*
♦ alert, brainy, bright, brilliant, clever, keen, nimble, quick, quick-witted, sharp, smart *Ant* brainless, dumb, mindless, stupid, thick, unintelligent ♦ rational, reasonable, reasoning

in·tel·li·gen·tsia \in-ˌte-lə-ˈjent-sē-ə, -ˈgent-\ *n* : intellectuals forming a vanguard or elite

in·tel·li·gi·ble \in-ˈte-lə-jə-bəl\ *adj* : capable of being understood or comprehended — **in·tel·li·gi·bil·i·ty** \-ˌte-lə-jə-ˈbi-lə-tē\ *n* — **in·tel·li·gi·bly** \-ˈte-lə-jə-blē\ *adv*

in·tem·per·ance \(ˌ)in-ˈtem-pə-rəns\ *n* : lack of moderation; *esp* : habitual or excessive drinking of intoxicants — **in·tem·per·ate·ness** *n*

in·tem·per·ate \-pə-rət\ *adj* ♦ : not temperate; *also* : given to excessive use of intoxicating liquors
♦ rampant, unbridled, unchecked, uncontrolled, ungoverned, unhampered, unhindered, unrestrained

in·tend \in-ˈtend\ *vb* **1** ♦ : to have in mind as a purpose or aim **2** : to design for a specified use or future
♦ aim, aspire, contemplate, design, mean, meditate, plan, propose

in·ten·dant \in-'ten-dənt\ *n* : an official (as a governor) esp. under the French, Spanish, or Portuguese monarchies

¹**in·tend·ed** *adj* **1** : expected to be such in the future; *esp* : BETROTHED **2** : INTENTIONAL

²**intended** *n* ♦ : an engaged person

  ♦ betrothed

in·tense \in-'tens\ *adj* **1** ♦ : existing in an extreme degree **2** : marked by great zeal, energy, or eagerness **3** : showing strong feeling; *also* : deeply felt

  ♦ deep, explosive, exquisite, fearful, ferocious, fierce, furious, hard, heavy, profound, terrible, vehement, vicious, violent *Ant* light, moderate, soft

in·tense·ly \-lē\ *adv* : in an intense manner

in·ten·si·fy \in-'ten-sə-ˌfī\ *vb* **-fied; -fy·ing** **1** ♦ : to make or become intense or more intensive **2** : to make more acute : SHARPEN — **in·ten·si·fi·ca·tion** \-ˌten-sə-fə-'kā-shən\ *n*

  ♦ amplify, beef, boost, consolidate, deepen, enhance, heighten, magnify, redouble, step up, strengthen *Ant* abate, moderate

in·ten·si·ty \in-'ten-sə-tē\ *n, pl* **-ties** ♦ : the quality or state of being intense; *esp* : degree of strength, energy, or force

  ♦ ardor, emotion, fervency, fervor, heat, passion, vehemence, warmth

¹**in·ten·sive** \in-'ten-siv\ *adj* **1** : marked by intensity : highly concentrated **2** : serving to give emphasis

²**intensive** *n* : an intensive word, particle, or prefix ⟨the word "very" is an ∼⟩

intensive care *n* : continuous monitoring and treatment of seriously ill patients; *also* : an area of a hospital providing this treatment

in·ten·sive·ly \-lē\ *adv* : in an intensive manner

¹**in·tent** \in-'tent\ *n* **1** : the state of mind with which an act is done : VOLITION **2** ♦ : a usu. clearly formulated or planned intention : PURPOSE, AIM **3** ♦ : the thing that is conveyed or intended to be conveyed esp. by language : MEANING, SIGNIFICANCE

  ♦ [2] aim, ambition, aspiration, design, dream, end, goal, mark, meaning, object, objective, plan, pretension, purpose, thing ♦ [3] denotation, drift, import, meaning, purport, sense, significance, signification

²**intent** *adj* **1** : directed with keen attention ⟨an ∼ gaze⟩ **2** ♦ : having the mind, attention, or will concentrated on something or some end or purpose

  ♦ bound, decisive, determined, firm, purposeful, resolute, set, single-minded ♦ absorbed, attentive, engrossed, observant, rapt

in·ten·tion \in-'ten-chən\ *n* **1** : a determination to act in a certain way **2** : what one intends to do or bring about : PURPOSE, AIM

in·ten·tion·al \in-'ten-chə-nəl\ *adj* ♦ : done by intention or design : INTENDED

  ♦ deliberate, freewill, purposeful, voluntary, willful, willing

in·ten·tion·al·ly *adv* ♦ : in an intentional manner : with intention

  ♦ consciously, deliberately, knowingly, purposely, willfully *Ant* inadvertently, unconsciously, unintentionally, unknowingly, unwittingly

in·tent·ly *adv* : in an intent manner

in·tent·ness *n* ♦ : the quality or state of being intent

  ♦ earnest, earnestness, gravity, seriousness, sobriety, solemnity

in·ter \in-'tər\ *vb* **in·terred; in·ter·ring** : BURY

in·ter·ac·tion \ˌin-tər-'ak-shən\ *n* : mutual or reciprocal action or influence — **in·ter·act** \-'akt\ *vb*

in·ter·ac·tive \-'ak-tiv\ *adj* **1** : mutually or reciprocally active **2** : allowing two-way electronic communications (as between a person and a computer) — **in·ter·ac·tive·ly** *adv*

inter alia \ˌin-tər-'ā-lē-ə, -'ä-\ *adv* : among other things

in·ter·atom·ic \ˌin-tər-ə-'tä-mik\ *adj* : existing or acting between atoms

in·ter·breed \-'brēd\ *vb* **-bred** \-'bred\; **-breed·ing** : to breed together

in·ter·ca·la·ry \in-'tər-kə-ˌler-ē\ *adj* **1** : INTERCALATED ⟨February 29 is an ∼ day⟩ **2** : INTERPOLATED

in·ter·ca·late \-ˌlāt\ *vb* **-lat·ed; -lat·ing** **1** : to insert (as a day) in a calendar **2** : to insert between or among existing elements or layers — **in·ter·ca·la·tion** \-ˌtər-kə-'lā-shən\ *n*

in·ter·cede \ˌin-tər-'sēd\ *vb* **-ced·ed; -ced·ing** ♦ : to act between parties with a view to reconciling differences

  ♦ interpose, intervene, mediate

¹**in·ter·cept** \ˌin-tər-'sept\ *vb* **1** : to stop or interrupt the progress or course of **2** : to include (as part of a curve or solid) between two points, curves, or surfaces **3** : to gain possession of (an opponent's pass in football) — **in·ter·cep·tion** \-'sep-shən\ *n*

²**in·ter·cept** \'in-tər-ˌsept\ *n* : INTERCEPTION; *esp* : the interception of a target by an interceptor or missile

in·ter·cep·tor \ˌin-tər-'sep-tər\ *n* : a fighter plane designed for defense against attacking bombers

in·ter·ces·sion \ˌin-tər-'se-shən\ *n* **1** : MEDIATION **2** : prayer or petition in favor of another — **in·ter·ces·so·ry** \-'se-sə-rē\ *adj*

in·ter·ces·sor \-'se-sər\ *n* ♦ : one who intercedes

  ♦ arbiter, arbitrator, broker, go-between, intermediary, mediator, middleman, peacemaker

¹**in·ter·change** \ˌin-tər-'chānj\ *vb* **1** : to put each in the place of the other **2** : EXCHANGE **3** : to change places mutually — **in·ter·change·able** \-'chān-jə-bəl\ *adj* — **in·ter·change·ably** \-blē\ *adv*

²**in·ter·change** \'in-tər-ˌchānj\ *n* **1** : EXCHANGE **2** : a highway junction that by separated levels permits passage between highways without crossing traffic streams

in·ter·col·le·giate \ˌin-tər-kə-'lē-jət\ *adj* : existing or carried on between colleges

in·ter·com \'in-tər-ˌkäm\ *n* : a two-way system for localized communication

in·ter·con·nect \ˌin-tər-kə-'nekt\ *vb* ♦ : to connect with one another — **in·ter·con·nec·tion** \-'nek-shən\ *n*

  ♦ chain, compound, connect, couple, hitch, hook, join, link, yoke

in·ter·con·ti·nen·tal \-ˌkänt-ᵊn-'ent-ᵊl\ *adj* **1** : extending among or carried on between continents ⟨∼ trade⟩ **2** : capable of traveling between continents ⟨∼ ballistic missiles⟩

in·ter·course \'in-tər-ˌkōrs\ *n* **1** ♦ : connection or dealings between persons or nations **2** ♦ : physical sexual contact between individuals that involves the genitalia of at least one person ⟨anal ∼⟩; *esp* : SEXUAL INTERCOURSE

  ♦ [1] dealings, relations ♦ [2] copulation, sexual intercourse

in·ter·de·nom·i·na·tion·al \ˌin-tər-di-ˌnä-mə-'nā-shə-nəl\ *adj* : involving different denominations

in·ter·de·part·men·tal \ˌin-tər-di-ˌpärt-'ment-ᵊl, -ˌdē-\ *adj* : carried on between or involving different departments (as of a college)

in·ter·de·pen·dent \ˌin-tər-di-'pen-dənt\ *adj* : dependent upon one another — **in·ter·de·pen·dence** \-dəns\ *n*

in·ter·dict \ˌin-tər-'dikt\ *vb* **1** ♦ : to prohibit by decree **2** : to destroy, cut off, or damage (as an enemy line of supply) **3** : INTERCEPT

  ♦ ban, bar, enjoin, forbid, outlaw, prohibit, proscribe

in·ter·dic·tion \-'dik-shən\ *n* ♦ : the act of interdicting or state of being interdicted; *also* : a prohibitory decree

  ♦ barring, forbidding, prohibition, proscription

in·ter·dis·ci·plin·ary \-'di-sə-plə-ˌner-ē\ *adj* : involving two or more academic, scientific, or artistic disciplines

¹**in·ter·est** \'in-trəst; 'in-tə-rəst, -ˌrest\ *n* **1** ♦ : right, title, or legal share in something **2** : a charge for borrowed money that is generally a percentage of the amount borrowed; *also* : the return received by capital on its investment **3 a** ♦ : a benefit resulting from some course of action : WELFARE **b** : SELF-INTEREST **4** : CURIOSITY, CONCERN **5** : readiness to be concerned with or moved by an object or class of objects **6** : a quality in a thing that arouses interest

  ♦ [1] claim, share, stake ♦ [3a] good, weal, welfare, well-being

²**interest** *vb* **1** : to persuade to participate or engage **2** ♦ : to engage the attention of

  ♦ absorb, busy, engage, engross, enthrall, fascinate, grip, immerse, intrigue, involve, occupy

in·ter·est·ing *adj* ♦ : holding the attention — **in·ter·est·ing·ly** *adv*

  ♦ absorbing, engaging, engrossing, enthralling, fascinating, intriguing *Ant* boring, drab, dry, dull, heavy, monotonous, tedious, uninteresting

¹**in·ter·face** \'in-tər-ˌfās\ *n* **1** : a surface forming a common boundary of two bodies, spaces, or phases ⟨an oil-water ∼⟩ **2** : the place at which two independent systems meet and act on or communicate with each other ⟨the man-machine ∼⟩ **3** : the means by which interaction or communication is achieved at an interface — **in·ter·fa·cial** \ˌin-tər-'fā-shəl\ *adj*

²**in·ter·face** *vb* **-faced; -fac·ing 1 :** to connect by means of an interface **2 :** to serve as an interface

in·ter·faith \ˌin-tər-ˈfāth\ *adj* : involving persons of different religious faiths

in·ter·fere \ˌin-tər-ˈfir\ *vb* **-fered; -fer·ing 1 ♦ :** to come in collision or be in opposition : to interpose in a way that hinders or impedes **2 ♦ :** to take an unwarranted active part in the affairs of others **3 :** to affect one another

♦ *usu* **interfere with** [1] encumber, hamper, hinder, hold up, impede, inhibit, obstruct, tie up ♦ [2] butt in, intrude, meddle, mess, nose, obtrude, poke, pry, snoop

in·ter·fer·ence \-ˈfir-əns\ *n* **1 :** the act or process of interfering **2 ♦ :** something that interferes : OBSTRUCTION **3 :** the mutual effect on meeting of two waves resulting in areas of increased and decreased amplitude **4 :** the blocking of an opponent in football to make way for the ballcarrier **5 :** the illegal hindering of an opponent in sports

♦ bar, block, encumbrance, hindrance, inhibition, obstacle

in·ter·fer·om·e·ter \ˌin-tər-fə-ˈrä-mə-tər\ *n* : an apparatus that uses the interference of waves (as of light) for making precise measurements — **in·ter·fer·om·e·try** \-fə-ˈrä-mə-trē\ *n*

in·ter·fer·on \ˌin-tər-ˈfir-ˌän\ *n* : any of a group of antiviral proteins of low molecular weight produced usu. by animal cells in response to a virus, a parasite in the cell, or a chemical

in·ter·ga·lac·tic \ˌin-tər-gə-ˈlak-tik\ *adj* : relating to or situated in the spaces between galaxies

in·ter·gen·er·a·tion·al \-ˌje-nə-ˈrā-shə-nəl\ *adj* : existing or occurring between generations ⟨∼ conflicts⟩

in·ter·gla·cial \-ˈglā-shəl\ *n* : a warm period between successive glaciations

in·ter·gov·ern·men·tal \-ˌgə-vərn-ˈment-ᵊl\ *adj* : existing or occurring between two governments or levels of government

¹**in·ter·im** \ˈin-tə-rəm\ *n* ♦ : a time intervening : INTERVAL

♦ discontinuity, gap, hiatus, interlude, intermission, interruption, interval

²**interim** *adj* : done, made, appointed, or occurring for an interim

♦ impermanent, provisional, short-term, temporary

¹**in·te·ri·or** \in-ˈtir-ē-ər\ *adj* **1 ♦ :** lying, occurring, or functioning within the limiting boundaries : INSIDE **2 :** remote from the surface, border, or shore : INLAND

♦ inner, inside, internal, inward

²**interior** *n* **1 :** the inland part (as of a country) **2 :** INSIDE **3 :** the internal affairs of a state or nation **4 :** a scene or view of the interior of a building

interior decoration *n* : INTERIOR DESIGN — **interior decorator** *n*

interior design *n* : the art or practice of planning and supervising the design and execution of architectural interiors and their furnishings — **interior designer** *n*

interj *abbr* interjection

in·ter·ject \ˌin-tər-ˈjekt\ *vb* ♦ : to throw in between or among other things

♦ fit, inject, insert, insinuate, interpose, introduce

in·ter·jec·tion \ˌin-tər-ˈjek-shən\ *n* ♦ : an exclamatory word or phrase (as *ouch*) — **in·ter·jec·tion·al·ly** \-shə-nə-lē\ *adv*

♦ cry, ejaculation, exclamation

in·ter·lace \ˌin-tər-ˈlās\ *vb* ♦ : to unite by or as if by lacing together : INTERWEAVE

♦ intersperse, intertwine, interweave, lace, thread, weave, wreathe

in·ter·lard \ˌin-tər-ˈlärd\ *vb* : to vary by inserting or interjecting something ⟨a speech ∼*ed* with anecdotes⟩

in·ter·leave \ˌin-tər-ˈlēv\ *vb* **-leaved; -leav·ing** : to arrange in alternate layers

in·ter·leu·kin \ˌin-tər-ˈlü-kən\ *n* : any of several proteins of low molecular weight that are produced by cells of the body and regulate the immune system and immune responses

¹**in·ter·line** \ˌin-tər-ˈlīn\ *vb* : to insert between lines already written or printed

²**interline** *vb* : to provide (as a coat) with an interlining

in·ter·lin·ear \ˌin-tər-ˈli-nē-ər\ *adj* : inserted between lines already written or printed ⟨an ∼ translation of a text⟩

in·ter·lin·gual \ˌin-tər-ˈliŋ-gwəl\ *adj* : of, relating to, or existing between two or more languages

in·ter·lin·ing \ˌin-tər-ˌlī-niŋ\ *n* : a lining (as of a coat) between the ordinary lining and the outside fabric

in·ter·link \ˌin-tər-ˈliŋk\ *vb* : to link together

in·ter·lock \ˌin-tər-ˈläk\ *vb* **1 :** to engage or interlace together

: lock together : UNITE **2 :** to connect so that action of one part affects action of another part — **in·ter·lock** \ˈin-tər-ˌläk\ *n*

in·ter·loc·u·tor \ˌin-tər-ˈlä-kyə-tər\ *n* : one who takes part in dialogue or conversation

in·ter·loc·u·to·ry \-ˌtōr-ē\ *adj* : made during the progress of a legal action and not final or definite ⟨an ∼ decree⟩

in·ter·lope \ˌin-tər-ˈlōp\ *vb* **-loped; -lop·ing 1 :** to encroach on the rights (as in trade) of others **2 :** INTRUDE, INTERFERE

in·ter·lop·er *n* ♦ : one who interlopes; *esp* : one that intrudes in a place or sphere of activity

♦ busybody, intruder, kibitzer, meddler

in·ter·lude \ˈin-tər-ˌlüd\ *n* **1 :** a usu. short simple play or dramatic entertainment **2 ♦ :** an intervening period, space, or event **3 :** a piece of music inserted between the parts of a longer composition or a religious service

♦ discontinuity, gap, hiatus, interim, intermission, interruption, interval

in·ter·mar·riage \ˌin-tər-ˈmar-ij\ *n* **1 :** marriage within one's own group as required by custom **2 :** marriage between members of different groups

in·ter·mar·ry \-ˈmar-ē\ *vb* **1 :** to marry each other **2 :** to marry within a group **3 :** to become connected by intermarriage

¹**in·ter·me·di·ary** \ˌin-tər-ˈmē-dē-ˌer-ē\ *adj* **1 :** being or occurring at the middle place, stage, or degree or between extremes : INTERMEDIATE **2 :** acting as a mediator

²**intermediary** *n, pl* **-ar·ies** ♦ : one that mediates : MEDIATOR, GO-BETWEEN

♦ arbiter, arbitrator, broker, go-between, intercessor, mediator, middleman, peacemaker

¹**in·ter·me·di·ate** \ˌin-tər-ˈmē-dē-ət\ *adj* ♦ : being or occurring at the middle place or degree or between extremes

♦ halfway, intermediary, median, medium, middle, midmost

²**intermediate** *n* **1 :** one that is intermediate **2 :** INTERMEDIARY

intermediate school *n* **1 :** JUNIOR HIGH SCHOOL **2 :** a school usu. comprising grades 4–6

in·ter·ment \in-ˈtər-mənt\ *n* ♦ : the act or ceremony of interring : BURIAL

♦ burial, entombment, sepulture

in·ter·mez·zo \ˌin-tər-ˈmet-sō, -ˈmed-zō\ *n, pl* **-zi** \-sē, -zē\ *or* **-zos** : a short movement connecting major sections of an extended musical work (as a symphony); *also* : a short independent instrumental composition

in·ter·mi·na·ble \(ˌ)in-ˈtər-mə-nə-bəl\ *adj* : ENDLESS; *esp* : wearisomely protracted — **in·ter·mi·na·bly** \-blē\ *adv*

in·ter·min·gle \ˌin-tər-ˈmiŋ-gəl\ *vb* ♦ : to mingle or mix together

♦ amalgamate, blend, combine, commingle, fuse, incorporate, integrate, merge, mingle, mix

in·ter·mis·sion \ˌin-tər-ˈmi-shən\ *n* **1 ♦ :** the act of intermitting : the state of being intermitted : INTERRUPTION **2 :** a temporary halt esp. in a public performance

♦ discontinuity, gap, hiatus, interim, interlude, interruption, interval

in·ter·mit \-ˈmit\ *vb* **-mit·ted; -mit·ting** : DISCONTINUE; *also* : to be intermittent

in·ter·mit·tent \-ˈmit-ᵊnt\ *adj* ♦ : coming and going at intervals ⟨∼ rain⟩ — **in·ter·mit·tent·ly** *adv*

♦ casual, choppy, discontinuous, erratic, fitful, irregular, occasional, spasmodic, sporadic, spotty, unsteady

in·ter·mix \ˌin-tər-ˈmiks\ *vb* : to mix together : INTERMINGLE

in·ter·mix·ture \-ˈmiks-chər\ *n* ♦ : a mass formed by mixture : a mass of ingredients mixed

♦ admixture, amalgam, blend, combination, composite, compound, fusion, mix, mixture

in·ter·mo·lec·u·lar \-mə-ˈle-kyə-lər\ *adj* : existing or acting between molecules

¹**in·tern** \ˈin-ˌtərn, in-ˈtərn\ *vb* : to confine or impound esp. during a war

²**in·tern** *also* **in·terne** \ˈin-ˌtərn\ *n* : an advanced student or recent graduate (as in medicine) gaining supervised practical experience — **in·tern·ship** *n*

³**in·tern** \ˈin-ˌtərn\ *vb* : to work as an intern

in·ter·nal \in-ˈtərn-ᵊl\ *adj* **1 ♦ :** existing or situated within the limits or surface of something **2 :** relating to or located in the inside of the body ⟨∼ pain⟩ **3 :** of, relating to, or occurring within the confines of an organized structure ⟨∼ affairs⟩ **4 :** of, relating to, or existing within the mind **5** : INTRINSIC, INHERENT — **in·ter·nal·ly** *adv*

♦ inner, inside, interior, inward

internal combustion engine *n* : an engine in which the fuel is ignited within the engine cylinder

in·ter·nal·ise *chiefly Brit var of* INTERNALIZE

in·ter·nal·ize \in-'tər-nə-₁līz\ *vb* **-ized; -iz·ing** : to incorporate (as values) within the self through learning or socialization — **in·ter·nal·i·za·tion** \-₁tər-nə-lə-'zā-shən\ *n*

internal medicine *n* : a branch of medicine that deals with the diagnosis and treatment of diseases not requiring surgery

¹**in·ter·na·tion·al** \₁in-tər-'na-shə-nəl\ *adj* **1** : common to or affecting two or more nations 〈~ trade〉 **2** : of, relating to, or constituting a group having members in two or more nations — **in·ter·na·tion·al·ly** *adv*

²**international** *n* : one that is international; *esp* : an organization of international scope

in·ter·na·tion·al·ise *chiefly Brit var of* INTERNATIONALIZE

in·ter·na·tion·al·ism \-'na-shə-nə-₁li-zəm\ *n* : a policy of cooperation among nations; *also* : an attitude favoring such a policy

in·ter·na·tion·al·ize \-'na-shə-nə-₁līz\ *vb* : to make international; *esp* : to place under international control

International System of Units *n* : a system of units based on the metric system and used by international convention esp. for scientific work

in·ter·ne·cine \₁in-tər-'ne-₁sēn, -'nē-₁sīn\ *adj* **1** : DEADLY; *esp* : mutually destructive **2** : of, relating to, or involving conflict within a group 〈~ feuds〉

in·tern·ee \(₁)in-₁tər-'nē\ *n* ♦ : a person interned

♦ captive, capture, prisoner

In·ter·net \'in-tər-₁net\ *n, often not cap* : an electronic communications network that connects computer networks worldwide

Internet service provider *n* : a company that provides its customers with Internet access and related services

in·ter·nist \'in-₁tər-nist\ *n* : a physician who specializes in internal medicine

in·tern·ment \in-'tərn-mənt\ *n* ♦ : the act of interning or the state of being interned

♦ captivity, confinement, imprisonment, incarceration

in·ter·nun·cio \₁in-tər-'nən-sē-₁ō, -'nün-\ *n* : a papal legate of lower rank than a nuncio

in·ter·of·fice \-'ò-fəs\ *adj* : functioning or communicating between the offices of an organization

in·ter·per·son·al \-'pərs-³n-əl\ *adj* : being, relating to, or involving relations between persons 〈~ communication〉 — **in·ter·per·son·al·ly** *adv*

in·ter·plan·e·tary \₁in-tər-'pla-nə-₁ter-ē\ *adj* : existing, carried on, or operating between planets 〈~ space〉

in·ter·play \'in-tər-₁plā\ *n* : INTERACTION

in·ter·po·late \in-'tər-pə-₁lāt\ *vb* **-lat·ed; -lat·ing** **1** : to change (as a text) by inserting new or foreign matter **2** : to insert (as words) into a text or into a conversation **3** : to estimate values of (data or a function) between two known values **4** : to insert between other things or parts — **in·ter·po·la·tion** \-₁tər-pə-'lā-shən\ *n*

in·ter·pose \₁in-tər-'pōz\ *vb* **-posed; -pos·ing** **1** ♦ : to place between **2** ♦ : to thrust in : INTRUDE, INTERRUPT **3** : to inject between parts of a conversation or argument **4** : to come or be between — **in·ter·po·si·tion** \-pə-'zi-shən\ *n*

♦ [1] fit, inject, insert, insinuate, interject, introduce ♦ [2] break, chime in, cut in, interrupt, intrude

in·ter·pret \in-'tər-prət\ *vb* **1** ♦ : to explain the meaning of; *also* : to act as an interpreter **2** : to understand according to individual belief, judgment, or interest **3** : to represent artistically — **in·ter·pret·er** *n* — **in·ter·pre·tive** \-'tər-prə-tiv\ *adj*

♦ clarify, clear (up), construe, demonstrate, elucidate, explain, explicate, expound, illuminate, illustrate, spell out

in·ter·pre·ta·tion \in-₁tər-prə-'tā-shən\ *n* **1** ♦ : the act or the result of interpreting : EXPLANATION **2** : an instance of artistic interpretation in performance or adaptation

♦ clarification, construction, elucidation, explanation, explication, exposition, illumination, illustration

in·ter·pre·ta·tive \in-'tər-prə-₁tā-tiv\ *adj* : designed or fitted to interpret : EXPLANATORY

in·ter·ra·cial \-'rā-shəl\ *adj* : of, involving, or designed for members of different races

in·ter·reg·num \₁in-tə-'reg-nəm\ *n, pl* **-nums** *or* **-na** \-nə\ **1**

: the time during which a throne is vacant between two successive reigns or regimes **2** : a pause in a continuous series

in·ter·re·late \₁in-tər-ri-'lāt\ *vb* : to bring into or have a mutual relationship — **in·ter·re·lat·ed·ness** \-lā-təd-nəs\ *n* — **in·ter·re·la·tion** \-'lā-shən\ *n* — **in·ter·re·la·tion·ship** *n*

interrog *abbr* interrogative

in·ter·ro·gate \in-'ter-ə-₁gāt\ *vb* **-gat·ed; -gat·ing** ♦ : to question esp. formally and systematically — **in·ter·ro·ga·tion** \-₁ter-ə-'gā-shən\ *n* — **in·ter·ro·ga·tor** \-'ter-ə-₁gā-tər\ *n*

♦ ask, examine, grill, pump, query, question, quiz

in·ter·rog·a·tive \₁in-tə-'rä-gə-tiv\ *adj* : asking a question 〈~ sentence〉 — **interrogative** *n* — **in·ter·rog·a·tive·ly** *adv*

in·ter·rog·a·to·ry \₁in-tə-'rä-gə-₁tōr-ē\ *adj* : INTERROGATIVE

in·ter·rupt \₁in-tə-'rəpt\ *vb* **1** : to stop or hinder by breaking in **2** : to break the uniformity or continuity of **3** ♦ : to break in by speaking while another is speaking — **in·ter·rupt·er** *n* — **in·ter·rup·tive** \-'rəp-tiv\ *adv*

♦ break, chime in, cut in, interpose, intrude

in·ter·rup·tion \-'rəp-shən\ *n* ♦ : an act of interrupting or state of being interrupted; *also* : temporary cessation

♦ discontinuity, gap, hiatus, interim, interlude, intermission, interval ♦ break, breather, lull, pause

in·ter·scho·las·tic \₁in-tər-skə-'las-tik\ *adj* : existing or carried on between schools 〈~ sports〉

in·ter·sect \₁in-tər-'sekt\ *vb* **1** : to divide by passing through or across **2** : to meet and cross (as at a point); *also* : OVERLAP

in·ter·sec·tion \-'sek-shən\ *n* ♦ : a place or area where two or more things (as streets) intersect

♦ corner, crossing, crossroad

in·ter·sperse \₁in-tər-'spərs\ *vb* **-spersed; -spers·ing** **1** : to place something at intervals in or among **2** ♦ : to insert at intervals among other things — **in·ter·sper·sion** \-'spər-zhən\ *n*

♦ interlace, intertwine, interweave, lace, thread, weave, wreathe

¹**in·ter·state** \₁in-tər-'stāt\ *adj* : relating to, including, or connecting two or more states esp. of the U.S.

²**in·ter·state** \'in-tər-₁stāt\ *n* : an interstate highway

in·ter·stel·lar \₁in-tər-'ste-lər\ *adj* : located or taking place among the stars

in·ter·stice \in-'tər-stəs\ *n, pl* **-stic·es** \-stə-₁sēz, -stə-səz\ ♦ : a space that intervenes between things — **in·ter·sti·tial** \₁in-tər-'sti-shəl\ *adj*

♦ breach, break, discontinuity, gap, gulf, hiatus, hole, interval, opening, rent, rift, separation

in·ter·tid·al \₁in-tər-'tīd-³l\ *adj* : of, relating to, or being the area that is above low-tide mark but exposed to tidal flooding 〈life in the ~ mud〉

in·ter·twine \-'twīn\ *vb* ♦ : to twine or cause to twine about one another : INTERLACE — **in·ter·twine·ment** *n*

♦ interlace, interweave, lace

in·ter·twist \-'twist\ *vb* : INTERTWINE

in·ter·ur·ban \-'ər-bən\ *adj* : connecting cities or towns

in·ter·val \'in-tər-vəl\ *n* **1** ♦ : a space of time between events or states : PAUSE **2** ♦ : a space between objects, units, or states **3** : the difference in pitch between two tones

♦ [1] discontinuity, gap, hiatus, interim, interlude, intermission, interruption ♦ [2] breach, break, discontinuity, gap, gulf, hole, opening, rent, rift, separation

in·ter·vene \₁in-tər-'vēn\ *vb* **-vened; -ven·ing** **1** : to occur, fall, or come between points of time or between events **2** : to enter or appear as an unrelated feature or circumstance 〈rain *intervened* and we postponed the trip〉 **3** ♦ : to come in or between in order to stop, settle, or modify 〈~ in a quarrel〉 **4** : to occur or lie between two things — **in·ter·ven·tion** \-'ven-chən\ *n*

♦ intercede, interpose, mediate

in·ter·ven·tion·ism \-'ven-chə-₁ni-zəm\ *n* : interference by one country in the political affairs of another — **in·ter·ven·tion·ist** \-'ven-chə-nist\ *n or adj*

in·ter·view \'in-tər-₁vyü\ *n* **1** : a formal consultation usu. to evaluate qualifications **2** : a meeting at which a writer or reporter obtains information from a person; *also* : the recorded or written account of such a meeting — **interview** *vb* — **in·ter·view·ee** \₁in-tər-(₁)vyü-'ē\ *n* — **in·ter·view·er** *n*

in·ter·vo·cal·ic \₁in-tər-vō-'ka-lik\ *adj* : immediately preceded and immediately followed by a vowel 〈~ consonants〉

in·ter·weave \₁in-tər-'wēv\ *vb* **-wove** \-'wōv\ *also* **-weaved;**

-wo·ven \-'wō-vən\ *also* **-weaved; -weav·ing ♦** : to weave or blend together — **interwoven** *adj*

♦ interlace, intersperse, intertwine, lace, thread, weave, wreathe

in·tes·tate \in-'tes-ˌtāt, -tət\ *adj* **1** : having made no valid will ⟨died ∼⟩ **2** : not disposed of by will ⟨∼ estate⟩

in·tes·tine \in-'tes-tən\ *n* : the tubular part of the alimentary canal that extends from stomach to anus and consists of a long narrow upper part (**small intestine**) followed by a broader shorter lower part (**large intestine**) — **in·tes·ti·nal** \-tən-ᵊl\ *adj*

in·ti·fa·da \ˌin-tə-'fä-də\ *n* : an armed uprising of Palestinians against Israeli occupation of the West Bank and Gaza Strip

in·ti·ma·cy \'in-tə-mə-sē\ *n* **1 ♦** : the state of being intimate **2** : something of a personal or private nature

♦ closeness, familiarity, nearness

¹**in·ti·mate** \'in-tə-ˌmāt\ *vb* **-mat·ed; -mat·ing 1** : ANNOUNCE, NOTIFY **2 ♦** : to communicate indirectly : HINT

♦ allude, hint, imply, indicate, infer, insinuate, suggest

²**in·ti·mate** \'in-tə-mət\ *adj* **1** : INTRINSIC; *also* : INNERMOST **2 ♦** : marked by very close association, contact, or familiarity **3** : marked by a warm friendship ⟨∼ friends⟩ **4** : suggesting informal warmth or privacy **5 ♦** : of a very personal or private nature ⟨∼ feelings⟩ — **in·ti·mate·ly** *adv*

♦ [2] bosom, chummy, close, familiar, friendly, thick ♦ [5] confidential, hushed, inside, private, secret

³**in·ti·mate** \'in-tə-mət\ *n* **♦** : an intimate friend, associate, or confidant

♦ buddy, chum, comrade, crony, familiar, friend, pal

in·ti·ma·tion \ˌin-tə-mā-shən\ *n* **♦** : an indirect usu. hinted suggestion or notice; *also* : something intimated

♦ clue, cue, hint, indication, inkling, lead, suggestion

in·tim·i·date \in-'ti-mə-ˌdāt\ *vb* **-dat·ed; -dat·ing ♦** : to make timid or fearful; *esp* : to compel or deter by or as if by threats — **in·tim·i·dat·ing·ly** *adv* — **in·tim·i·da·tion** \-ˌti-mə-'dā-shən\ *n*

♦ browbeat, bully, cow, hector

intl *or* **intnl** *abbr* international

in·to \'in-tü\ *prep* **1** : to the inside of ⟨ran ∼ the house⟩ **2** : to the state, condition, or form of ⟨got ∼ trouble⟩ **3** : AGAINST ⟨ran ∼ a wall⟩

in·tol·er·a·ble \(ˌ)in-'tä-lə-rə-bəl\ *adj* **1 ♦** : not tolerable : UNBEARABLE **2** : EXCESSIVE — **in·tol·er·a·bly** \-blē\ *adv*

♦ insufferable, insupportable, unbearable, unendurable, unsupportable

in·tol·er·ant \(ˌ)in-'tä-lə-rənt\ *adj* **1** : unable or unwilling to tolerate **2 ♦** : unwilling to grant equality, freedom, or other social rights : BIGOTED — **in·tol·er·ance** \-rəns\ *n*

♦ bigoted, narrow, narrow-minded, prejudiced *Ant* liberal, broad-minded, open-minded, tolerant, unprejudiced

in·to·na·tion \ˌin-tō-'nā-shən\ *n* **1** : the act of intoning and esp. of chanting **2** : something that is intoned **3** : the manner of singing, playing, or uttering tones **4** : the rise and fall in pitch of the voice in speech

in·tone \in-'tōn\ *vb* **in·toned; in·ton·ing** : to utter in musical or prolonged tones : CHANT ⟨∼ a prayer⟩

in to·to \in-'tō-tō\ *adv* : TOTALLY, ENTIRELY

in·tox·i·cant \in-'täk-si-kənt\ *n* **♦** : something that intoxicates; *esp* : an alcoholic drink — **intoxicant** *adj*

♦ alcohol, booze, drink, liquor, moonshine, spirits

in·tox·i·cate \-sə-ˌkāt\ *vb* **-cat·ed; -cat·ing 1** : to affect by a drug (as alcohol or cocaine) esp. to the point of physical or mental impairment **2 ♦** : to excite to enthusiasm or frenzy

♦ electrify, excite, exhilarate, galvanize, thrill, titillate, turn on

in·tox·i·cat·ed \-sə-ˌkā-təd\ *adj* **♦** : affected by or as if by alcohol ⟨*intoxicated* by power⟩

♦ drunk, high, inebriate, tipsy ♦ ecstatic, elated, euphoric, rapturous, rhapsodic

in·tox·i·ca·tion \-ˌtäk-sə-'kā-shən\ *n* **♦** : the condition of being drunk; *also* : a strong excitement or elation

♦ ecstasy, elation, euphoria, exhilaration, heaven, paradise, rapture, rhapsody, transport

in·trac·ta·ble \(ˌ)in-'trak-tə-bəl\ *adj* **♦** : not easily controlled — **in·trac·ta·bil·i·ty** \(ˌ)in-ˌtrak-tə-'bi-lə-tē\ *n* — **in·trac·ta·bly** \(ˌ)in-'trak-tə-blē\ *adv*

♦ froward, headstrong, recalcitrant, refractory, uncontrollable, unmanageable, unruly, untoward, wayward, willful

in·tra·mu·ral \-'myùr-əl\ *adj* : being or occurring within the walls or limits (as of a city or college) ⟨∼ sports⟩

in·tra·mus·cu·lar \ˌin-trə-'məs-kyə-lər\ *adj* : situated within, occurring in, or administered by entering a muscle — **in·tra·mus·cu·lar·ly** *adv*

in·tra·net \'in-trə-ˌnet\ *n* : a network similar to the World Wide Web but having access limited to certain authorized users

intrans *abbr* intransitive

in·tran·si·gent \-jənt\ *adj* : UNCOMPROMISING; *also* : IRRECONCILABLE — **in·tran·si·gence** \-jəns\ *n* — **intransigent** *n*

in·tran·si·tive \(ˌ)in-'tran-sə-tiv, -zə-\ *adj* : not transitive; *esp* : not having or containing an object ⟨an ∼ verb⟩ — **in·tran·si·tive·ly** *adv* — **in·tran·si·tive·ness** *n*

in·tra·state \ˌin-trə-'stāt\ *adj* : existing or occurring within a state ⟨∼ rivals⟩

in·tra·uter·ine device \-'yü-tə-rən-, -ˌrīn-\ *n* : a device inserted into and left in the uterus to prevent pregnancy

in·tra·ve·nous \ˌin-trə-'vē-nəs\ *adj* : being within or entering by way of the veins; *also* : used in or using intravenous procedures — **in·tra·ve·nous·ly** *adv*

intrench *var of* ENTRENCH

in·trep·id \in-'tre-pəd\ *adj* **♦** : characterized by resolute fearlessness, fortitude, and endurance ⟨∼ explorers⟩

♦ brave, courageous, dauntless, doughty, fearless, gallant, greathearted, heroic, lionhearted, manful, stalwart, stout, undaunted, valiant, valorous

in·tre·pid·i·ty \ˌin-trə-'pi-də-tē\ *n* : the quality or state of being intrepid : resolute bravery

in·tri·ca·cy \-tri-kə-sē\ *n* **♦** : the quality or state of being intricate; *also* : something intricate

♦ complexity, complication, difficulty ♦ complexity, elaborateness, sophistication

in·tri·cate \'in-tri-kət\ *adj* **1 ♦** : having many complexly interrelated parts : COMPLICATED **2 ♦** : involving or done with precision; *also* : difficult to follow, understand, or solve — **in·tri·cate·ly** *adv*

♦ complex, complicated, convoluted, detailed, elaborate, involved, knotty, sophisticated

¹**in·trigue** \in-'trēg\ *vb* **in·trigued; in·trigu·ing 1** : to accomplish by intrigue **2 ♦** : to carry on an intrigue; *esp* : PLOT, SCHEME **3 ♦** : to arouse the interest, desire, or curiosity of

♦ [2] conspire, contrive, machinate, plot, scheme ♦ [3] absorb, busy, engage, engross, enthrall, fascinate, grip, immerse, interest, involve, occupy

²**in·trigue** \'in-ˌtrēg, in-'trēg\ *n* **1 ♦** : a secret scheme : PLOT **2** : a clandestine love affair

♦ conspiracy, design, machination, plot, scheme

intriguing *adj* **♦** : engaging the interest to a marked degree

♦ absorbing, engaging, engrossing, enthralling, fascinating, interesting

in·trin·sic \in-'trin-zik, -sik\ *adj* **♦** : belonging to the essential nature or constitution of a thing

♦ essential, inborn, ingrained, inherent, innate, integral, natural

in·trin·si·cal·ly \in-'trin-zi-k(ə-)lē, -si-\ *adv* **♦** : in an intrinsic manner : having an intrinsic quality

♦ constitutionally, inherently, innately, naturally

introd *abbr* introduction

in·tro·duce \ˌin-trə-'düs, -'dyüs\ *vb* **-duced; -duc·ing 1** : to lead or bring in esp. for the first time **2 ♦** : to bring into practice or use **3 ♦** : to cause to be acquainted **4 ♦** : to present for discussion **5 ♦** : to put in : INSERT — **in·tro·duc·to·ry** \-'dək-tə-rē\ *adj*

♦ [2] constitute, establish, found, inaugurate, initiate, innovate, institute, launch, pioneer, set up, start ♦ [3] acquaint, familiarize, initiate, orient [4] bring up, broach, moot, raise ♦ [5] fit, inject, insert, insinuate, interject, interpose

in·tro·duc·tion \-'dək-shən\ *n* **1 ♦** : something that introduces **2** : the act or process of introducing : the state of being introduced; *also* : something introduced

♦ foreword, preamble, preface, prologue *Ant* epilogue

in·troit \'in-ˌtròit, -trō-ət\ *n* **1** *often cap* : the first part of the traditional proper of the Mass **2** : a piece of music sung or played at the beginning of a worship service

in·tro·spec·tion \-'spek-shən\ *n* : a reflective looking inward : an examination of one's own thoughts or feelings — **in·tro·spect** \ˌin-trə-'spekt\ *vb* — **in·tro·spec·tive** \-'spek-tiv\ *adj* — **in·tro·spec·tive·ly** *adv*

in·tro·vert \'in-trə-ˌvərt\ *n* : a reserved or shy person — **in·tro·ver·sion** \ˌin-trə-'vər-zhən\ *n* — **introvert** *adj*

in·tro·vert·ed \ˌin-trə-ˌvər-təd\ *adj* ♦ : having the characteristics of an introvert : possessing a reserved or quiet nature typically with an inclination to solitude

♦ bashful, coy, demure, diffident, modest, retiring, sheepish, shy

in·trude \in-'trüd\ *vb* **in·trud·ed; in·trud·ing** 1 ♦ : to thrust, enter, or force in or upon 2 : ENCROACH, TRESPASS — **in·tru·sion** \-'trü-zhən\ *n*

♦ break, chime in, cut in, interpose, interrupt ♦ butt in, interfere, meddle, mess, nose, obtrude, poke, pry, snoop ♦ *usu* **intrude upon** bother, bug, disturb, pester

in·trud·er *n* ♦ : one that intrudes

♦ busybody, interloper, kibitzer, meddler

in·tru·sive \-'trü-siv\ *adj* ♦ : characterized by intrusion : intruding where one is not welcome or invited — **in·tru·sive·ness** *n*

♦ meddlesome, nosy, obtrusive, officious, presumptuous, prying *Ant* unobtrusive

intrust *var of* ENTRUST

in·tu·it \in-'tü-ət, -'tyü-\ *vb* : to know, sense, or understand by intuition

in·tu·ition \ˌin-tü-'wi-shən, -tyù-\ *n* 1 : quick and ready insight 2 : the power or faculty of knowing things without conscious reasoning — **in·tu·i·tive** \in-'tü-ə-tiv, -'tyü-\ *adj* — **in·tu·i·tive·ly** *adv*

In·u·it \'i-nü-wət, 'in-yü-\ *n* 1 *pl* **Inuit** *or* **Inuits** : a member of an Indigenous people of northern Alaska, arctic Canada, and Greenland 2 : the language of the Inuit people

in·un·date \'i-nən-ˌdāt\ *vb* **-dat·ed; -dat·ing** ♦ : to cover with or as if with a flood : OVERFLOW

♦ deluge, drown, engulf, flood, overflow, overwhelm, submerge, swamp

in·un·da·tion \ˌi-nən-'dā-shən\ *n* ♦ : an overflowing of the land by water; *also* : an overwhelming amount or number

♦ cataclysm, cataract, deluge, flood, overflow, spate, torrent

in·ure \i-'nùr, -'nyùr\ *vb* **in·ured; in·ur·ing** 1 : to accustom to accept something undesirable ⟨*inured* to violence⟩ 2 : to become of advantage

in utero \in-'yü-tə-ˌrō\ *adv or adj* : in the uterus : before birth

inv *abbr* 1 inventor 2 invoice

in vac·uo \in-'va-kyü-ˌwō\ *adv* : in a vacuum

in·vade \in-'vād\ *vb* **in·vad·ed; in·vad·ing** 1 ♦ : to enter in a hostile manner 2 : to encroach upon 3 : to spread through and usu. harm ⟨germs ∼ the tissues⟩ — **in·vad·er** *n*

♦ foray, overrun, raid

¹**in·val·id** \(ˌ)in-'va-ləd\ *adj* ♦ : being without foundation or force in fact, reason, or law — **in·va·lid·i·ty** \ˌin-və-'li-də-tē\ *n* — **in·val·id·ly** *adv*

♦ baseless, groundless, unfounded, unreasonable, unsubstantiated, unsupported, unwarranted ♦ null, void ♦ erroneous, false, inaccurate, incorrect, inexact, off, unsound, untrue, wrong

²**in·va·lid** \'in-və-ləd\ *adj* : being in ill health : SICKLY

³**invalid** \'in-və-ləd\ *n* : a person in usu. chronic ill health — **in·va·lid·ism** \-lə-ˌdi-zəm\ *n*

⁴**in·va·lid** \'in-və-ləd, -ˌlid\ *vb* 1 : to remove from active duty by reason of sickness or disability 2 : to make sickly or disabled

in·val·i·date \(ˌ)in-'va-lə-ˌdāt\ *vb* ♦ : to make invalid ⟨*invalidated* a contract⟩; *esp* : to weaken or make valueless — **in·val·i·da·tion** \in-ˌva-lə-'dā-shən\ *n*

♦ abolish, abrogate, annul, cancel, dissolve, negate, nullify, quash, repeal, rescind, void

in·valu·able \-'val-yə-bəl, -yə-wə-bəl\ *adj* : valuable beyond estimation

in·vari·able \-'ver-ē-ə-bəl\ *adj* : not changing or capable of change : CONSTANT

in·vari·ably \-blē\ *adv* ♦ : on every occasion

♦ always, constantly, continually, ever, forever, incessantly, perpetually, unfailingly

in·va·sion \in-'vā-zhən\ *n* ♦ : an act or instance of invading; *esp* : entry of an army into a country for conquest

♦ descent, foray, incursion, irruption, raid

in·va·sive \in-'vā-siv, -ziv\ *adj* 1 : tending to spread ⟨∼ cancer cells⟩ 2 : involving entry into the living body (as by surgery) ⟨∼ therapy⟩

in·vec·tive \in-'vek-tiv\ *n* 1 : an abusive expression or speech 2 ♦ : abusive language — **invective** *adj*

♦ abuse, fulmination, vitriol, vituperation

in·veigh \in-'vā\ *vb* : to protest or complain bitterly or vehemently : RAIL

in·vei·gle \in-'vā-gəl, -'vē-\ *vb* **in·vei·gled; in·vei·gling** 1 : to win over by flattery : ENTICE 2 : to acquire by ingenuity or flattery

in·vent \in-'vent\ *vb* 1 ♦ : to think up 2 ♦ : to create or produce for the first time

♦ [1, 2] concoct, contrive, cook up, devise, fabricate, make up, manufacture, think up

in·ven·tion \in-'ven-chən\ *n* 1 ♦ : productive imagination : INVENTIVENESS 2 ♦ : a creation of the imagination; *esp* : a false conception 3 ♦ : a device, contrivance, or process originated after study and experiment 4 : the act or process of inventing

♦ [1] creativity, fancy, fantasy, imagination, inventiveness ♦ [2] fabrication, fantasy, fiction, figment ♦ [3] coinage, concoction, contrivance, creation, innovation, wrinkle

in·ven·tive \in-'ven-tiv\ *adj* 1 ♦ : adept or prolific at producing inventions : CREATIVE, INGENIOUS ⟨an ∼ composer⟩ 2 : characterized by invention ⟨an ∼ turn of mind⟩

♦ creative, imaginative, ingenious, innovative, original

in·ven·tive·ness *n* ♦ : the quality or state of being inventive

♦ creativity, ingenuity, invention, originality

in·ven·tor \-'ven-tər\ *n* ♦ : one that invents: as **a** : one that conceives by creative imagination **b** : one that creates a new device or process

♦ designer, developer, innovator, originator

¹**in·ven·to·ry** \'in-vən-ˌtōr-ē\ *n, pl* **-ries** 1 : an itemized list of current goods or assets 2 : SURVEY, SUMMARY 3 : STOCK, SUPPLY 4 : the act or process of taking an inventory

²**inventory** *vb* **-ried; -ry·ing** ♦ : to make an inventory of

♦ enumerate, itemize, list, numerate

¹**in·verse** \(ˌ)in-'vərs, 'in-ˌvərs\ *adj* : opposite in order, nature, or effect : REVERSED — **in·verse·ly** *adv*

²**inverse** *n* : something inverse or resulting in or from inversion : OPPOSITE

in·ver·sion \in-'vər-zhən\ *n* 1 : a reversal of position, order, or relationship; *esp* : an increase of temperature with altitude through a layer of air 2 : the act or process of inverting

in·vert \in-'vərt\ *vb* 1 : to reverse in position, order, or relationship 2 : to turn upside down or inside out 3 : to turn inward

in·ver·te·brate \(ˌ)in-'vər-tə-brət, -ˌbrāt\ *adj* 1 : lacking a backbone; *also* : of or relating to invertebrate animals 2 : lacking in strength or vitality — **invertebrate** *n*

¹**in·vest** \in-'vest\ *vb* 1 ♦ : to install formally in an office or honor 2 ♦ : to furnish with power or authority 3 : to cover completely : ENVELOP 4 : to cover with or as if with cloth or clothing : CLOTHE, ADORN 5 : to surround with troops or ships so as to prevent escape or entry : BESIEGE 6 ♦ : to endow with a quality or characteristic

♦ [1] baptize, inaugurate, induct, initiate, install ♦ [2] accredit, authorize, certify, commission, empower, enable, license, qualify ♦ [6] imbue, inculcate, infuse, ingrain, steep, suffuse

²**invest** *vb* 1 : to commit (money) in order to earn a financial return 2 : to expend for future benefits or advantages 3 : to make an investment — **in·ves·tor** \-'ves-tər\ *n*

in·ves·ti·gate \in-'ves-tə-ˌgāt\ *vb* **-gat·ed; -gat·ing** ♦ : to study by close examination and systematic inquiry — **in·ves·ti·ga·tive** \-'ves-tə-ˌgā-tiv\ *adj*

♦ delve, dig, explore, go, inquire into, look, probe, research

in·ves·ti·ga·tion \-ˌves-tə-'gā-shən\ *n* ♦ : the action or process of investigating; *esp* : detailed examination or a searching inquiry

♦ examination, exploration, inquiry, probe, research, study

in·ves·ti·ga·tor \-ˌgā-tər\ *n* ♦ : one that investigates; *esp* : one employed or engaged in detecting lawbreakers or in getting information that is not readily or publicly accessible

♦ detective, operative, shadow, sleuth, tail

in·ves·ti·ture \in-'ves-tə-ˌchùr, -chər\ *n* 1 ♦ : the act of ratifying or establishing in office 2 : something that covers or adorns

♦ inaugural, inauguration, induction, installation

¹**in·vest·ment** \in-'vest-mənt\ *n* **1** : an outer layer : ENVELOPE **2** : INVESTITURE 1 **3** : BLOCKADE, SIEGE

²**investment** *n* : the outlay of money for income or profit; *also* : the sum invested or the property purchased

in·vet·er·ate \in-'ve-tə-rət\ *adj* **1** ♦ : firmly established by age or long persistence **2** ♦ : confirmed in a habit

♦ [1] confirmed, deep-rooted, deep-seated, settled ♦ [2] chronic, confirmed, habitual

in·vi·a·ble \(,)in-'vī-ə-bəl\ *adj* : incapable of surviving

in·vid·i·ous \in-'vi-dē-əs\ *adj* **1** : tending to cause discontent, animosity, or envy ⟨an ∼ comparison⟩ **2** : feeling or showing envy : ENVIOUS **3** : OBNOXIOUS — **in·vid·i·ous·ly** *adv*

in·vig·o·rate \in-'vi-gə-ˌrāt\ *vb* **-rat·ed; -rat·ing** ♦ : to give life and energy to : ANIMATE ⟨∼ the economy⟩ — **in·vig·o·ra·tion** \-ˌvi-gə-'rā-shən\ *n*

♦ animate, brace, energize, enliven, fire, jazz up, liven up, pep up, quicken, stimulate, vitalize, vivify, zip (up)

invigorating *adj* ♦ : having an enlivening effect

♦ bracing, refreshing, restorative, stimulative, tonic

in·vin·ci·ble \(,)in-'vin-sə-bəl\ *adj* ♦ : incapable of being conquered, overcome, or subdued — **in·vin·ci·bil·i·ty** \-ˌvin-sə-'bi-lə-tē\ *n* — **in·vin·ci·bly** \-'vin-sə-blē\ *adv*

♦ impregnable, indomitable, insurmountable, invulnerable, unbeatable, unconquerable *Ant* vulnerable

in·vi·o·la·ble \-'vī-ə-lə-bəl\ *adj* ♦ : safe from violation or profanation **2** : secure from assault or trespass : UNASSAILABLE — **in·vi·o·la·bil·i·ty** \-ˌvī-ə-lə-'bi-lə-tē\ *n*

♦ holy, sacred, sacrosanct

in·vi·o·late \-'vī-ə-lət\ *adj* : not violated or profaned : PURE

in·vis·i·ble \-'vi-zə-bəl\ *adj* **1** : incapable of being seen ⟨∼ to the naked eye⟩ **2** : HIDDEN **3** : IMPERCEPTIBLE, INCONSPICUOUS — **in·vis·i·bil·i·ty** \-ˌvi-zə-'bi-lə-tē\ *n* — **in·vis·i·bly** \-'vi-zə-blē\ *adv*

invisible hand *n* : a hypothetical economic force that works for the benefit of all

in·vi·ta·tion·al \ˌin-və-'tā-shə-nəl\ *adj* : limited to invited participants ⟨a ∼ tournament⟩ — **invitational** *n*

in·vite \in-'vīt\ *vb* **in·vit·ed; in·vit·ing** **1** : ENTICE, TEMPT **2** : to increase the likelihood of **3** : to request the presence or participation of : ASK **4** : to request formally **5** : ENCOURAGE — **in·vi·ta·tion** \ˌin-və-'tā-shən\ *n*

in·vit·ing *adj* : ATTRACTIVE, TEMPTING

in vi·tro \in-'vē-trō, -'vi-, -'vi-\ *adv or adj* : outside the living body and in an artificial environment ⟨*in vitro* fertilization⟩

in·vo·ca·tion \ˌin-və-'kā-shən\ *n* **1** : SUPPLICATION; *esp* : a prayer at the beginning of a service **2** : a formula for conjuring : INCANTATION

¹**in·voice** \'in-ˌvȯis\ *n* ♦ : an itemized list of goods shipped usu. specifying the price and the terms of sale : BILL

♦ account, bill, check, statement, tab

²**invoice** *vb* **in·voiced; in·voic·ing** : to send an invoice to or for : BILL

in·voke \in-'vōk\ *vb* **in·voked; in·vok·ing** **1** : to petition for help or support **2** : to appeal to or cite as authority ⟨∼ a law⟩ **3** : to call forth by incantation : CONJURE ⟨∼ spirits⟩ **4** : to make an earnest request for : SOLICIT **5** : to put into effect or operation **6** : to bring about : CAUSE

in·vol·un·tary \(,)in-'vä-lən-ˌter-ē\ *adj* **1** ♦ : done contrary to or without choice **2** ♦ : dictated by authority or circumstance : COMPULSORY **3** ♦ : not controlled by the will ⟨∼ contractions⟩ — **in·vol·un·tari·ly** \-ˌvä-lən-'ter-ə-lē\ *adv*

♦ [1] unintended, unintentional *Ant* deliberate, intentional, unforced, voluntary, willful, willing ♦ [2] compulsory, imperative, incumbent, mandatory, necessary, nonelective, obligatory, peremptory ♦ [3] automatic, mechanical, spontaneous

in·vo·lute \'in-və-ˌlüt\ *adj* : INVOLVED, INTRICATE

in·vo·lu·tion \ˌin-və-'lü-shən\ *n* **1** : the act or an instance of enfolding or entangling **2** : the quality or state of being complex : COMPLEXITY, INTRICACY

in·volve \in-'välv\ *vb* **in·volved; in·volv·ing** **1** ♦ : to draw in as a participant **2** : ENVELOP **3** ♦ : to occupy (as oneself) absorbingly; *esp* : to commit oneself emotionally **4** : to relate closely : CONNECT **5** ♦ : to have as part of itself : INCLUDE **6** : ENTAIL, IMPLY ⟨the job ∼s traveling⟩ **7** : to have an effect on — **in·volve·ment** *n*

♦ [1] affect, concern, interest, touch ♦ [3] absorb, busy, engage, engross, enthrall, fascinate, grip, immerse, interest, in-

trigue, occupy ♦ [5] carry, comprehend, contain, embrace, encompass, entail, include, number, take in

in·volved \-'välvd\ *adj* ♦ : marked by extreme and often needless or excessive complexity : INTRICATE, COMPLEX ⟨an ∼ plot⟩

♦ complex, complicated, convoluted, detailed, elaborate, intricate, knotty, sophisticated

in·vul·ner·a·ble \(,)in-'vəl-nə-rə-bəl\ *adj* **1** : incapable of being wounded, injured, or damaged **2** ♦ : immune to or proof against attack — **in·vul·ner·a·bil·i·ty** \-ˌvəl-nə-rə-'bi-lə-tē\ *n* — **in·vul·ner·a·bly** \-'vəl-nə-rə-blē\ *adv*

♦ impregnable, indomitable, insurmountable, invincible, unbeatable, unconquerable

¹**in·ward** \'in-wərd\ *adj* **1** ♦ : situated on the inside **2** : MENTAL; *also* : SPIRITUAL **3** : directed toward the interior

♦ inner, inside, interior, internal

²**inward** *or* **in·wards** \-wərdz\ *adv* **1** : toward the inside, center, or interior **2** : toward the inner being

in·ward·ly \'in-wərd-lē\ *adv* **1** : MENTALLY, SPIRITUALLY **2** : INTERNALLY ⟨bled ∼⟩ **3** : to oneself ⟨cursed ∼⟩

IOC *abbr* International Olympic Committee

io·dide \'ī-ə-ˌdīd\ *n* : a compound of iodine with another element or group

io·dine \'ī-ə-ˌdīn, -əd-ᵊn\ *n* **1** : a nonmetallic chemical element used esp. in medicine and photography **2** : a solution of iodine used as a local antiseptic

io·dise *chiefly Brit var of* IODIZE

io·dize \'ī-ə-ˌdīz\ *vb* **io·dized; io·diz·ing** : to treat with iodine or an iodide

ion \'ī-ən, 'ī-ˌän\ *n* : an electrically charged particle, atom, or group of atoms — **ion·ic** \ī-'ä-nik\ *adj*

-ion *n suffix* : act, process, state, or condition ⟨validat*ion*⟩

ion·ise *chiefly Brit var of* IONIZE

ion·ize \'ī-ə-ˌnīz\ *vb* **ion·ized; ion·iz·ing** **1** : to convert wholly or partly into ions **2** : to become ionized — **ion·iz·able** \ˌī-ə-'nī-zə-bəl\ *adj* — **ion·iza·tion** \ˌī-ə-nə-'zā-shən\ *n* — **ion·iz·er** \'ī-ə-ˌnī-zər\ *n*

ion·o·sphere \ī-'ä-nə-ˌsfir\ *n* : the part of the earth's atmosphere extending from about 30 miles (50 kilometers) to the exosphere that contains ionized atmospheric gases — **ion·o·spher·ic** \ī-ˌä-nə-'sfir-ik, -'sfer-\ *adj*

IOOF *abbr* Independent Order of Odd Fellows

io·ta \ī-'ō-tə\ *n* **1** : the 9th letter of the Greek alphabet — I or ι **2** : a very small quantity : JOT

IOU \ˌī-(ˌ)ō-'yü\ *n* : an acknowledgment of a debt

IP *abbr* innings pitched

IP address \'ī-ˌpē-\ *n* : the numeric address of a computer on the Internet

ip·e·cac \'i-pi-ˌkak\ *n* : an emetic and expectorant drug used esp. as a syrup in treating accidental poisoning; *also* : either of two tropical American plants or their rhizomes and roots used to make ipecac

IPO \ˌī-ˌpē-'ō\ *n, pl* **IPOs** : an initial public offering of a company's stock

ip·so fac·to \ˌip-sō-'fak-tō\ *adv* : by the very nature of the case

iq *abbr* the same as

IQ \'ī-ˌkyü\ *n* : a number used to express a person's relative intelligence as determined by a standardized test

¹**Ir** *abbr* Irish

²**Ir** *symbol* iridium

IR *abbr* infrared

¹**IRA** \ˌī-(ˌ)är-'ā; 'ī-rə\ *n* : a retirement savings account in which income taxes are deferred until withdrawals are made

²**IRA** *abbr* Irish Republican Army

Ira·ni·an \i-'rä-nē-ən *also* -'rä-\ *n* : a native or inhabitant of Iran — **Iranian** *adj*

Iraqi \i-'rä-kē, -'ra-\ *n* : a native or inhabitant of Iraq — **Iraqi** *adj*

iras·ci·bil·i·ty \i-ˌra-sə-'bi-lə-tē\ *n* : the quality or state of being irascible : proneness to anger

iras·ci·ble \i-'ra-sə-bəl\ *adj* ♦ : marked by hot temper and easily provoked anger

♦ choleric, crabby, cranky, cross, irritable, short-tempered, snappish, snappy, snippy, testy, waspish

irate \ī-'rāt\ *adj* **1** ♦ : roused to ire ⟨an ∼ customer⟩ **2** : arising from anger — **irate·ly** *adv*

♦ angry, boiling, enraged, furious, rabid, sore

¹**ire** \'īr\ *n* ♦ : intense and usu. openly displayed anger : ANGER, WRATH

♦ anger, furor, fury, indignation, outrage, rage, spleen, wrath, wrathfulness

²**ire** *vb* **ired; iring ♦** : to provoke to anger
  ♦ anger, antagonize, enrage, incense, inflame, infuriate, madden, outrage, rankle, rile, roil

Ire *abbr* Ireland
ire·ful *adj* : full of ire : marked by ire; *also* : easily angered
ire·nic \ī-'re-nik\ *adj* : favoring, conducive to, or operating toward peace or conciliation ⟨~ measures⟩
ir·i·des·cence \ir-ə-'des-³ns\ *n* : a rainbowlike play of colors — **ir·i·des·cent** \-³nt\ *adj*
irid·i·um \ir-'i-dē-əm\ *n* : a hard brittle heavy metallic chemical element
iris \'ī-rəs\ *n, pl* **iris·es** *also* **iri·des** \'ī-rə-,dēz, 'ir-ə-\ **1** : the colored part around the pupil of the eye **2** : any of a large genus of plants with linear basal leaves and large showy flowers
Irish \'ī-rish\ *n* **1** Irish *pl* : the people of Ireland **2** : the Celtic language of Ireland — **Irish** *adj* — **Irish·man** \-mən\ *n* — **Irish·wom·an** \-,wu̇-mən\ *n*
Irish bull *n* : an incongruous statement (as "it was hereditary in his family to have no children")
Irish coffee *n* : hot sugared coffee with Irish whiskey and whipped cream
Irish moss *n* : the dried and bleached plants of a red alga that is a source of carrageenan; *also* : this red alga
Irish setter *n* : any of a breed of hunting dogs with a mahogany-red coat
irk \'ərk\ *vb* ♦ : to make weary, irritated, or bored : ANNOY
  ♦ aggravate, annoy, bother, bug, chafe, exasperate, gall, get, grate, irritate, nettle, peeve, persecute, pique, put out, rasp, rile, vex
irk·some \'ərk-səm\ *adj* ♦ : tending to irk : ANNOYING — **irk·some·ly** *adv*
  ♦ aggravating, annoying, bothersome, frustrating, galling, irritating, pesty, vexatious
¹**iron** \'īrn, 'ī-ərn\ *n* **1** : a heavy malleable magnetic metallic chemical element that rusts easily and is vital to biological processes **2 a** : something made of metal and esp. iron **b** *pl* ♦ : something (as handcuffs) used to bind or restrain ⟨put them in ~s⟩ **3** : a household device with a flat base that is heated and used for pressing cloth **4** : STRENGTH, HARDNESS
  ♦ *usu* irons band, bond, chain, fetter, ligature, manacle, shackle
²**iron** *vb* **1** : to press or smooth with or as if with a heated iron **2** : to remove (as wrinkles) by ironing — **iron·er** *n*
¹**iron-clad** \-'klad\ *adj* **1** : sheathed in iron armor **2** : so firm or secure as to be unbreakable
²**iron-clad** \-,klad\ *n* : an armored naval vessel esp. of the 19th century
iron curtain *n* : a political, military, and ideological barrier that isolates an area; *esp, often cap* : one formerly isolating an area under Soviet control
iron·ic \ī-'rä-nik\ *also* **iron·i·cal** \-ni-kəl\ *adj* **1** : of, relating to, or marked by irony **2** : given to irony
iron·i·cal·ly \-ni-k(ə-)lē\ *adv* **1** : in an ironic manner **2** : it is ironic
iron·ing *n* : clothes ironed or to be ironed
iron lung *n* : a device for artificial respiration that encloses the chest in a chamber in which changes of pressure force air into and out of the lungs
iron out *vb* : to remove or lessen difficulties in or extremes of
iron oxide *n* : FERRIC OXIDE
iron·stone \'ī-(ə)rn-,stōn, 'ī-ərn-\ *n* **1** : a hard iron-rich sedimentary rock **2** : a hard heavy durable pottery developed in England in the 19th century
iron·ware \-,war\ *n* : articles made of iron
iron·weed \-,wēd\ *n* : any of a genus of mostly weedy plants related to the asters that have terminal heads of red, purple, or white flowers
iron·wood \-,wu̇d\ *n* : any of numerous trees or shrubs with exceptionally hard wood; *also* : the wood
iron·work \-,wərk\ *n* **1** : work in iron **2** *pl* : a mill or building where iron or steel is smelted or heavy iron or steel products are made — **iron·work·er** *n*
iro·ny \'ī-rə-nē\ *n, pl* **-nies 1** : the use of words to express the opposite of what one really means **2** : incongruity between the actual result of a sequence of events and the expected result
Ir·o·quois \'ir-ə-,kwȯi, *pl* **Iroquois** *same or* -,kwȯiz\ **1** *pl* : a confederacy of Indigenous peoples orig. of New York that consisted of the Cayuga, Mohawk, Oneida, Onondaga, and Seneca and later included the Tuscarora **2** : a member of any of the Iroquois peoples

ir·ra·di·ate \i-'rā-dē-,āt\ *vb* **-at·ed; -at·ing 1** : to supply or brighten with light : ILLUMINATE **2** : ENLIGHTEN **3** : to treat by exposure to radiation **4** : RADIATE — **ir·ra·di·a·tion** \-,rā-dē-'ā-shən\ *n*
¹**ir·ra·tio·nal** \(,)i-'ra-shə-nəl\ *adj* **1** : incapable of reasoning ⟨~ beasts⟩; *also* : lacking usual or normal mental clarity or coherence ⟨~ with fever⟩ **2** ♦ : not based on reason ⟨~ fears⟩ **3** : being or numerically equal to an irrational number — **ir·ra·tio·nal·i·ty** \(,)i-,ra-shə-'na-lə-tē\ *n* — **ir·ra·tio·nal·ly** *adv*
  ♦ fallacious, illogical, invalid, unreasonable, unsound, weak
²**irrational** *n* : IRRATIONAL NUMBER
irrational number *n* : a real number that cannot be expressed as the quotient of two integers
ir·rec·on·cil·able \(,)i-,re-kən-'sī-lə-bəl, -'re-kən-,sī-\ *adj* : impossible to reconcile or harmonize — **ir·rec·on·cil·abil·i·ty** \(,)i-,re-kən-,sī-lə-'bi-lə-tē\ *n*
ir·re·cov·er·able \,ir-i-'kə-və-rə-bəl\ *adj* : not capable of being recovered or rectified : IRREPARABLE — **ir·re·cov·er·ably** \-blē\ *adv*
ir·re·deem·able \,ir-i-'dē-mə-bəl\ *adj* **1** : not redeemable; *esp* : not terminable by payment of the principal ⟨an ~ bond⟩ **2** : not convertible into gold or silver at the will of the holder **3** ♦ : being beyond remedy ⟨~ villains⟩
  ♦ hopeless, incorrigible, incurable, irremediable, irreparable, unrecoverable, unredeemable
ir·re·den·tism \-'den-,ti-zəm\ *n* : a principle or policy directed toward the incorporation of a territory historically or ethnically part of another into that other — **ir·re·den·tist** \-tist\ *n or adj*
ir·re·duc·ible \,ir-i-'dü-sə-bəl, -'dyü-\ *adj* : not reducible ⟨an ~ fraction⟩ — **ir·re·duc·ibly** \-blē\ *adv*
ir·re·fut·able \,ir-i-'fyü-tə-bəl, (,)i-'re-fyət-\ *adj* ♦ : impossible to refute
  ♦ incontestable, indisputable, indubitable, unanswerable, undeniable, unquestionable *Ant* answerable, debatable, disputable, questionable
irreg *abbr* irregular
ir·reg·u·lar \(,)i-'re-gyə-lər\ *adj* **1** ♦ : not regular : not natural or uniform **2** : not conforming to the normal or usual manner of inflection ⟨~ verbs⟩ **3** : not belonging to a regular or organized army ⟨~ troops⟩ — **irregular** *n* — **ir·reg·u·lar·ly** *adv*
  ♦ aberrant, abnormal, anomalous, atypical, deviant, unnatural
  ♦ informal, unceremonious, unconventional, unorthodox
ir·reg·u·lar·i·ty \i-,re-gyə-'lar-ə-tē\ *n, pl* **-ties 1** : something that is irregular **2** : the quality or state of being irregular **3** : occasional constipation
ir·rel·e·vant \(,)i-'re-lə-vənt\ *adj* ♦ : not relevant — **ir·rel·e·vance** \-vəns\ *n*
  ♦ extraneous, immaterial
ir·re·li·gious \,ir-i-'li-jəs\ *adj* ♦ : lacking religious emotions, doctrines, or practices
  ♦ blasphemous, nonreligious, sacrilegious *Ant* religious
ir·re·me·di·a·ble \,ir-i-'mē-dē-ə-bəl\ *adj* ♦ : impossible to remedy or correct
  ♦ hopeless, incorrigible, incurable, irredeemable, unrecoverable, unredeemable
ir·re·mov·able \-'mü-və-bəl\ *adj* : not removable
ir·rep·a·ra·ble \(,)i-'re-pə-rə-bəl\ *adj* ♦ : impossible to make good, undo, repair, or remedy ⟨~ damage⟩
  ♦ irredeemable, irremediable, unrecoverable, unredeemable *Ant* redeemable, remediable, retrievable
ir·re·place·able \,ir-i-'plā-sə-bəl\ *adj* : not replaceable
ir·re·press·ible \-'pre-sə-bəl\ *adj* : impossible to repress or control ⟨~ curiosity⟩
ir·re·proach·able \-'prō-chə-bəl\ *adj* ♦ : not reproachable
  ♦ blameless, clear, faultless, guiltless, impeccable, innocent
ir·re·sist·ible \,ir-i-'zis-tə-bəl\ *adj* : impossible to successfully resist ⟨an ~ craving⟩ — **ir·re·sist·ibly** \-blē\ *adv*
ir·res·o·lute \(,)i-'re-zə-,lüt\ *adj* : uncertain how to act or proceed : VACILLATING — **ir·res·o·lute·ly** \-,lüt-lē; (,)i-,re-zə-'lüt-\ *adv*
ir·res·o·lu·tion \(,)i-,re-zə-'lü-shən\ *n* ♦ : lack of resolution : a fluctuation of mind (as in doubt or between hope and fear)
  ♦ hesitancy, hesitation, indecision, vacillation
ir·re·spec·tive of \,ir-i-'spek-tiv-\ *prep* : without regard to
ir·re·spon·si·ble \-'spän-sə-bəl\ *adj* ♦ : not responsible ⟨an ~

choice⟩ — **ir·re·spon·si·bil·i·ty** \-ˌspän-sə-ˈbi-lə-tē\ *n* — **ir·re·spon·si·bly** \-ˈspän-sə-blē\ *adv*

♦ foolhardy, reckless

ir·re·triev·able \ˌi-ri-ˈtrē-və-bəl\ *adj* : not retrievable : IRRECOVERABLE

ir·rev·er·ence \(ˌ)i-ˈre-və-rəns\ *n* **1** : lack of reverence **2**

♦ an irreverent act or utterance

♦ blasphemy, defilement, desecration, impiety, sacrilege

ir·rev·er·ent \-rənt\ *adj* : lacking proper respect or seriousness; *also* — SATIRIC — **ir·rev·er·ent·ly** *adv*

ir·re·vers·ible \ˌir-i-ˈvər-sə-bəl\ *adj* : incapable of being reversed ⟨an ∼ loss⟩

ir·rev·o·ca·ble \(ˌ)i-ˈre-və-kə-bəl\ *adj* : incapable of being revoked or recalled ⟨∼ change⟩ — **ir·rev·o·ca·bly** \-blē\ *adv*

ir·ri·gate \ˈir-ə-ˌgāt\ *vb* **-gat·ed; -gat·ing** ♦ : to supply (as land) with water by artificial means; *also* : to flush with liquid — **ir·ri·ga·tion** \ˌir-ə-ˈgā-shən\ *n*

♦ flush, rinse, sluice, wash

ir·ri·ta·bil·i·ty \ˌir-ə-tə-ˈbi-lə-tē\ *n* **1** : the property of living things and of protoplasm that enables reaction to stimuli **2** ♦ : the quality or state of being irritable; *esp* : readiness to become annoyed or angry

♦ grumpiness, peevishness

ir·ri·ta·ble \ˈir-ə-tə-bəl\ *adj* ♦ : capable of being irritated; *esp* : readily or easily irritated — **ir·ri·ta·bly** \-blē\ *adv*

♦ choleric, crabby, cranky, cross, crotchety, grouchy, grumpy, irascible, peevish, perverse, petulant, short-tempered, snappish, snappy, snippy, testy, waspish

ir·ri·tant \ˈir-ə-tənt\ *n* ♦ : something that irritates or excites — **irritant** *adj*

♦ aggravation, annoyance, bother, exasperation, frustration, hassle, headache, inconvenience, nuisance, peeve, pest, problem, thorn

ir·ri·tate \ˈir-ə-ˌtāt\ *vb* **-tat·ed; -tat·ing** **1** ♦ : to excite to anger : EXASPERATE **2** ♦ : to make sore or inflamed — **ir·ri·tat·ing·ly** *adv*

♦ [1] aggravate, annoy, bother, bug, chafe, exasperate, gall, get, grate, irk, nettle, peeve, persecute, pique, put out, rasp, rile, vex ♦ [2] abrade, chafe, gall

irritating *adj* ♦ : causing displeasure or annoyance

♦ aggravating, annoying, bothersome, frustrating, galling, irksome, pesty, vexatious

ir·ri·ta·tion \ˌir-ə-ˈtā-shən\ *n* : the act of irritating : the state of being irritated; *also* : something that irritates

ir·rupt \(ˌ)i-ˈrəpt\ *vb* **1** : to rush in forcibly or violently **2** : to increase suddenly in numbers ⟨rabbits ∼ in cycles⟩

ir·rup·tion \-ˈrəp-shən\ *n* ♦ : an act or instance of irrupting; *esp* : a sudden violent or forcible entry

♦ descent, foray, incursion, invasion, raid

IRS *abbr* Internal Revenue Service

is *pres 3d sing of* BE

Isa *or* **Is** *abbr* Isaiah

Isa·iah \ī-ˈzā-ə\ *n* **1** : a major Hebrew prophet in Judah about 740 to 701 B.C. **2** : a book of Jewish and Christian Scripture

Isa·ias \ī-ˈzā-əs\ *n* : ISAIAH

ISBN *abbr* International Standard Book Number

is·che·mia \is-ˈkē-mē-ə\ *n* : deficient supply of blood to a body part (as the brain) — **is·che·mic** \-mik\ *adj*

-ish \ish\ *adj suffix* **1** : of, relating to, or being ⟨Finn*ish*⟩ **2** : characteristic of ⟨boy*ish*⟩ ⟨mul*ish*⟩ **3** : inclined or liable to ⟨book*ish*⟩ **4** : having a touch or trace of : somewhat ⟨pur*plish*⟩ **5** : having the approximate age of ⟨forty*ish*⟩

isin·glass \ˈīz-ᵊn-ˌglas, ˈī-ziŋ-\ *n* **1** : a gelatin obtained from various fish **2** : mica esp. in thin sheets

isl *abbr* island

Is·lam \is-ˈläm, iz-, -ˈlam, ˈis-ˌ, ˈiz-ˌ\ *n* : the religious faith of Muslims including belief in Allah as the sole deity and in Muhammad as his prophet; *also* : the civilization built on this faith — **Is·lam·ic** \is-ˈlä-mik, iz-, -ˈla-\ *adj*

is·land \ˈī-lənd\ *n* **1** ♦ : a body of land smaller than a continent surrounded by water **2** : something resembling an island in its isolation

♦ cay, isle, key

is·land·er \ˈī-lən-dər\ *n* : a native or inhabitant of an island

isle \ˈī(-ə)l\ *n* ♦ : a small island

♦ cay, island, key

is·let \ˈī-lət\ *n* : a small island

ism \ˈi-zəm\ *n* : a distinctive doctrine, cause, or theory

-ism \ˌi-zəm\ *n suffix* **1** : act : practice : process ⟨critic*ism*⟩ **2** : manner of action or behavior characteristic of a (specified) person or thing ⟨fanatic*ism*⟩ **3** : state : condition : property ⟨dual*ism*⟩ **4** : abnormal state or condition ⟨alcohol*ism*⟩ **5** : doctrine : theory : cult ⟨Buddh*ism*⟩ **6** : adherence to a set of principles ⟨stoic*ism*⟩ **7** : prejudice or discrimination on the basis of a (specified) attribute ⟨rac*ism*⟩ ⟨sex*ism*⟩ **8** : characteristic or peculiar feature or trait ⟨colloquial*ism*⟩

iso·bar \ˈī-sə-ˌbär\ *n* : a line on a map connecting places of equal barometric pressure — **iso·bar·ic** \ˌī-sə-ˈbär-ik, -ˈbar-\ *adj*

iso·late \ˈī-sə-ˌlāt\ *vb* **-lat·ed; -lat·ing** ♦ : to place or keep by itself : separate from others

♦ cut off, insulate, seclude, segregate, separate, sequester *Ant* desegregate, integrate

iso·lat·ed *adj* **1** : occurring alone or once : UNIQUE **2** : SPORADIC ⟨∼ outbreaks⟩ **3** ♦ : placed alone or apart

♦ cloistered, covert, quiet, remote, secluded, secret

iso·la·tion \ˌī-sə-ˈlā-shən\ *n* ♦ : the action of isolating : the condition of being isolated

♦ insulation, seclusion, segregation, sequestration, solitude

iso·la·tion·ism \ˌī-sə-ˈlā-shə-ˌni-zəm\ *n* : a policy of national isolation by abstention from international political and economic relations — **iso·la·tion·ist** \-shə-nist\ *n or adj*

iso·mer \ˈī-sə-mər\ *n* : any of two or more chemical compounds that contain the same numbers of atoms of the same elements but differ in structural arrangement and properties — **iso·mer·ic** \ˌī-sə-ˈmer-ik\ *adj* — **isom·er·ism** \ī-ˈsä-mə-ˌri-zəm\ *n*

iso·met·rics \ˌī-sə-ˈme-triks\ *n sing or pl* : exercise involving a series of brief and intense contractions of muscles against each other or against an immovable resistance — **iso·met·ric** *adj*

iso·prene \ˈī-sə-ˌprēn\ *n* : a hydrocarbon used esp. in making synthetic rubber

isos·ce·les \ī-ˈsä-sə-ˌlēz\ *adj* : having two equal sides ⟨an ∼ triangle⟩

iso·therm \ˈī-sə-ˌthərm\ *n* : a line on a map connecting points having the same temperature

iso·ther·mal \ˌī-sə-ˈthər-məl\ *adj* : of, relating to, or marked by equality of temperature

iso·tope \ˈī-sə-ˌtōp\ *n* : any of the forms of a chemical element that differ chiefly in the number of neutrons in an atom — **iso·to·pic** \ˌī-sə-ˈtä-pik, -ˈtō-\ *adj* — **iso·to·pi·cal·ly** \-ˈtä-pi-k(ə-)lē, -ˈtō-\ *adv*

ISP *abbr* Internet service provider

Isr *abbr* Israel; Israeli

Is·rae·li \iz-ˈrā-lē\ *n, pl* **Israelis** *also* **Israeli** : a native or inhabitant of Israel — **Israeli** *adj*

Is·ra·el·ite \ˈiz-rē-ə-ˌlīt\ *n* : a member of the Hebrew people descended from Jacob

is·su·ance \ˈi-shü-wəns\ *n* ♦ : the act of issuing or giving out esp. officially

♦ allocation, dispensation, distribution, division

¹is·sue \ˈi-shü\ *n* **1** : the action of going, coming, or flowing out : EGRESS, EMERGENCE **2** : a means or place of going out : EXIT, OUTLET **3** ♦ : the product of the reproductive processes of an animal or plant : OFFSPRING, PROGENY **4** : OUTCOME, RESULT **5** : a point of debate or controversy; *also* : the point at which an unsettled matter is ready for a decision **6** : a discharge (as of blood) from the body **7** : something coming forth from a specified source **8** : the act of officially giving out or printing : PUBLICATION; *also* : the quantity of things given out at one time

♦ offspring, posterity, progeny, seed, spawn

²issue *vb* **is·sued; is·su·ing** **1** : to go, come, or flow out **2** ♦ : to come forth or cause to come forth : EMIT **3** : ACCRUE **4** : to descend from a specified parent or ancestor **5** : to result in **6** : to put forth or distribute officially **7** ♦ : to send out for sale or circulation : PUBLISH **8** : EMANATE, RESULT — **is·su·er** *n*

♦ [2] cast, discharge, emit, exhale, expel, release, shoot, vent ♦ [7] get out, print, publish

¹-ist \ist\ *n suffix* **1** : one that performs a (specified) action ⟨cyc*list*⟩ : one that makes or produces ⟨novel*ist*⟩ **2** : one that plays a (specified) musical instrument ⟨harp*ist*⟩ **3** : one that operates a (specified) mechanical instrument or contrivance ⟨machin*ist*⟩ **4** : one that specializes in a (specified) art or science or skill ⟨geolog*ist*⟩ **5** : one that adheres to or advocates a (specified) doctrine or system or code of behavior ⟨social*ist*⟩ or that of a (specified) individual ⟨Darwin*ist*⟩

²-ist *adj suffix* : -ISTIC

isth·mus \'is-məs\ *n* : a narrow strip of land connecting two larger land areas

-is·tic \'is-tik\ *or* **-is·ti·cal** \'is-ti-kəl\ *adj suffix* : of, relating to, or characteristic of ⟨altru*istic*⟩

¹it \'it\ *pron* **1** : that one — used of a lifeless thing, a plant, a person or animal, or an abstract entity ⟨∼'s a big building⟩ ⟨∼'s a shade tree⟩ ⟨who is ∼⟩ ⟨beauty is everywhere and ∼ is a source of joy⟩ **2** — used as a subject of an impersonal verb that expresses a condition or action without reference to an agent ⟨∼ is raining⟩ **3** — used as an anticipatory subject or object ⟨∼'s good to see you⟩

²it \'it\ *n* : the player in a game who performs the principal action of the game (as trying to find others in hide-and-seek)

It *abbr* Italian; Italy

ital *abbr* italic; italicized

Ital *abbr* Italian

Ital·ian \i-'tal-yən\ *n* **1** : a native or inhabitant of Italy **2** : the language of Italy — **Italian** *adj*

ital·ic \i-'ta-lik, ī-\ *adj* : relating to type in which the letters slope up toward the right (as in *"italic"*) — **italic** *n*

ital·i·cise *Brit var of* ITALICIZE

ital·i·cize \i-'ta-lə-ˌsīz, ī-\ *vb* **-cized; -ciz·ing** : to print in italics — **ital·i·ci·za·tion** \-ˌta-lə-sə-'zā-shən\ *n*

¹itch \'ich\ *n* **1** : an uneasy irritating skin sensation that evokes a desire to scratch the affected area **2** : a skin disorder accompanied by an itch **3** ♦ : a persistent desire — **itchy** *adj*

♦ appetite, craving, desire, drive, hankering, hunger, longing, lust, passion, thirst, urge, yearning, yen

²itch *vb* **1** : to have an itch; *also* : to produce an itchy sensation **2** ♦ : to have a restless desire or hankering for something — usu. used with *for*

♦ *usu* **itch for** ache for, crave, desire, die for, hanker for, hunger for, long for, lust (for *or* after), pine for, repine for, thirst for, want, wish for, yearn for

-ite \ˌīt\ *n suffix* **1** : native : resident ⟨suburban*ite*⟩ **2** : adherent : follower ⟨Lenin*ite*⟩ **3** : product ⟨metabol*ite*⟩ **4** : mineral : rock ⟨quartz*ite*⟩

item \'ī-təm\ *n* **1** ♦ : a separate particular in a list, account, or series : ARTICLE **2** ♦ : a separate piece of news (as in a newspaper)

♦ [1] article, constituent, detail, element, feature, ingredient, particular, point ♦ [2] intelligence, news, story, tidings, word

item·ise *chiefly Brit var of* ITEMIZE

item·ize \'ī-tə-ˌmīz\ *vb* **-ized; -iz·ing** ♦ : to set down in detail — **item·i·za·tion** \ˌī-tə-mə-'zā-shən\ *n*

♦ detail, enumerate, inventory, list, numerate

it·er·ate \'i-tə-ˌrāt\ *vb* **-at·ed; -at·ing** : REITERATE, REPEAT

it·er·a·tion \ˌi-tə-'rā-shən\ *n* **1** : REPETITION; *esp* : a computational process in which a series of operations is repeated until a condition is met **2** : one repetition of the series of operations in iteration

itin·er·ant \ī-'ti-nə-rənt, ə-\ *adj* ♦ : traveling from place to place; *esp* : covering a circuit ⟨an ∼ preacher⟩

♦ errant, nomad, nomadic, peripatetic, roaming, vagabond, vagrant

itin·er·ary \ī-'ti-nə-ˌrer-ē, ə-\ *n, pl* **-ar·ies** **1** : the route of a journey or the proposed outline of one **2** : a travel diary **3** : GUIDEBOOK

its \'its\ *adj* : of or relating to it or itself

it·self \it-'self\ *pron* : that identical one — used reflexively, for emphasis, or in absolute constructions

-ity \ə-tē\ *n suffix* : quality : state : degree ⟨alkalin*ity*⟩

IUD \ˌī-(ˌ)yü-'dē\ *n* : INTRAUTERINE DEVICE

IV \ˌī-'vē\ *n* : an apparatus used to administer a fluid (as of nutrients) intravenously; *also* : a fluid administered by IV

-ive \iv\ *adj suffix* : that performs or tends toward an (indicated) action ⟨correct*ive*⟩

ivo·ry \'ī-vrē, -və-rē\ *n, pl* **-ries** **1** : the hard creamy-white material composing the tusks of an elephant or walrus **2** : a pale yellow color **3** : something made of ivory or of a similar substance

ivory tower *n* **1** : an impractical lack of concern with urgent problems **2** : a place of learning

ivy \'ī-vē\ *n, pl* **ivies** : a trailing woody evergreen vine with small black berries that is related to ginseng

IWW *abbr* Industrial Workers of the World

-ize \ˌīz\ *vb suffix* **1** : cause to be or conform to or resemble ⟨American*ize*⟩ : cause to be formed into ⟨union*ize*⟩ **2** : subject to a (specified) action ⟨satir*ize*⟩ **3** : saturate, treat, or combine with ⟨macadam*ize*⟩ **4** : treat like ⟨idol*ize*⟩ **5** : become : become like ⟨crystall*ize*⟩ **6** : be productive in or of : engage in a (specified) activity ⟨philosoph*ize*⟩ **7** : adopt or spread the manner of activity or the teaching of ⟨Christian*ize*⟩

¹j \'jā\ *n, pl* **j's** *or* **js** \jāz\ *often cap* : the 10th letter of the English alphabet

²j *abbr, often cap* **1** jack **2** journal **3** judge **4** justice

¹jab \'jab\ *vb* **jabbed; jab·bing** : to thrust quickly or abruptly : POKE

²jab *n* ♦ : a usu. short straight punch

♦ dab, dig, poke

¹jab·ber \'ja-bər\ *vb* ♦ : to talk rapidly, indistinctly, or unintelligibly : CHATTER

♦ babble, chatter, drivel, gabble, gibber, prattle, sputter

²jabber *n* : unintelligible or meaningless language

jab·ber·er *n* ♦ : one that jabbers

♦ chatterbox, magpie, talker

jab·ber·wocky \'ja-bər-ˌwä-kē\ *n* ♦ : meaningless speech or writing

♦ babble, gabble, gibberish, gobbledygook, hogwash, jabber, nonsense, piffle, prattle

ja·bot \zha-'bō, 'ja-ˌbō\ *n* : a ruffle worn down the front of a dress or shirt

jac·a·ran·da \ˌja-kə-'ran-də\ *n* : any of a genus of pinnate-leaved tropical American trees with clusters of showy blue flowers

¹jack \'jak\ *n* **1** : a mechanical device; *esp* : one used to raise a heavy body a short distance **2** : a male donkey **3** : a small target ball in lawn bowling **4** ♦ : a small national flag flown by a ship **5** : a small 6-pointed metal object used in a game (**jacks**) **6**

: a playing card bearing the figure of a soldier or servant **7** : a socket into which a plug is inserted for connecting electric circuits **8 a** : an adult male human **b** : a member of a ship's crew

♦ banner, colors (*or* colours), ensign, flag, pennant, standard, streamer

²jack *vb* **1** : to raise by means of a jack **2** ♦ : to raise the level of ⟨∼ up prices⟩

♦ boost, crane, elevate, heave, heft, heighten, hike, hoist, lift, pick up, raise, up, uphold

jack·al \'ja-kəl\ *n* : any of several mammals of Asia and Africa related to the wolves

jack·a·napes \'ja-kə-ˌnāps\ *n* **1** : MONKEY, APE **2** : an impudent or conceited person

jack·ass \'jak-ˌas\ *n* **1** ♦ : the domestic ass : DONKEY; *esp* : a male donkey **2** ♦ : a stupid, annoying, or detestable person

♦ [1] ass, donkey ♦ [2] blockhead, dolt, donkey, dope, dummy, idiot, imbecile, nitwit, numskull, simpleton

jack·boot \-ˌbüt\ *n* **1** : a heavy military boot of glossy black leather extending above the knee **2** : a laceless military boot reaching to the calf

jack·daw \'jak-ˌdo\ *n* : a black and gray Old World crowlike bird

jack·et \'ja-kət\ *n* **1** : a garment for the upper body usu. having a front opening, collar, and sleeves **2** ♦ : an outer covering or casing ⟨a book ∼⟩

♦ armor, capsule, case, casing, cocoon, cover, housing, husk, pod, sheath, shell

Jack Frost *n* : frost or frosty weather personified

jack·ham·mer \'jak-ˌha-mər\ *n* : a pneumatic percussion tool for drilling rock or breaking pavement

jack–in–the–box *n, pl* **jack–in–the–boxes** *or* **jacks–in–the–box** : a toy consisting of a small box out of which a figure springs when the lid is raised

jack–in–the–pulpit *n, pl* **jack–in–the–pulpits** *also* **jacks–in–the–pulpit** : a No. American spring-flowering woodland herb having an upright club-shaped spadix arched over by a green and purple spathe

¹**jack·knife** \'jak-ˌnīf\ *n* **1** : a large pocketknife **2** : a dive in which the diver bends from the waist and touches the ankles before straightening out

²**jackknife** *vb* : to fold like a jackknife ⟨the trailer truck *jackknifed*⟩

jack·leg \'jak-ˌleg\ *adj* **1** : lacking skill or training **2** : MAKE-SHIFT

jack–of–all–trades *n, pl* **jacks–of–all–trades** : one who is able to do passable work at various tasks

jack–o'–lan·tern \'ja-kə-ˌlan-tərn\ *n* : a lantern made of a pumpkin cut to look like a human face

jack·pot \'jak-ˌpät\ *n* **1** : a large sum of money formed by the accumulation of stakes from previous play (as in poker) **2** : an impressive and often unexpected success or reward

jack·rab·bit \-ˌra-bət\ *n* : any of several large hares of western No. America with very long ears and hind legs

Jack Russell terrier \'jak-'rə-səl-\ *n* : any of a breed of small terriers having a white coat with dark markings

jack·straw \-ˌstrȯ\ *n* **1** *pl* : a game in which straws or thin sticks are let fall in a heap and each player in turn tries to remove them one at a time without disturbing the rest **2** : one of the straws or sticks in jackstraws

jack–tar \-'tär\ *n, often cap* ♦ : a member of a ship's crew : SAIL-OR

♦ gob, jack, mariner, sailor, seaman, swab, tar

Ja·cob's ladder \'jā-kəbz-\ *n* : any of several perennial herbs related to phlox that have pinnate leaves and blue or white bell-shaped flowers

jac·quard \'ja-ˌkärd\ *n, often cap* : a fabric of intricate variegated weave or pattern

¹**jade** \'jād\ *n* **1** : a broken-down, vicious, or worthless horse **2** : a disreputable woman

²**jade** *vb* **jad·ed; jad·ing** **1** : to wear out by overwork or abuse **2** ♦ : to become weary esp. through repetition or excess

♦ bore, tire, weary

³**jade** *n* : a usu. green gemstone that takes a high polish

jad·ed *adj* ♦ : fatigued by overwork; *also* : made dull, apathetic, or cynical by experience or by surfeit

♦ beat, bushed, dead, drained, limp, prostrate, spent, tired, weary, worn-out

¹**jag** \'jag\ *n* : a sharp projecting part

²**jag** *n* : SPREE

jag·ged \'ja-gəd\ *adj* ♦ : sharply notched

♦ broken, craggy, ragged, scraggly

jag·uar \'ja-ˌgwär\ *n* : a black-spotted tropical American cat that is larger and stockier than the Old World leopard

jai alai \'hī-ˌlī\ *n* : a court game played by usu. two or four players with a ball and a curved wicker basket strapped to the wrist

¹**jail** \'jāl\ *n* ♦ : a place of confinement for persons held in lawful custody : PRISON; *esp* : such a place for the confinement of persons awaiting trial or those convicted of minor crimes

♦ brig, hoosegow, jug, lockup, pen, penitentiary, prison, stockade

²**jail** *vb* ♦ : to confine in or as if in a jail

♦ commit, confine, immure, imprison

jail·bird \-ˌbərd\ *n* : an habitual criminal

jail·break \-ˌbrāk\ *n* : a forcible escape from jail

jail·er *also* **jail·or** \'jā-lər\ *n* : a keeper of a jail

jal·ap \'ja-ləp, 'jä-\ *n* : a powdered purgative drug from the root of a Mexican plant related to the morning glory; *also* : this root or plant

ja·la·pe·ño \ˌhä-lə-'pān-(ˌ)yō\ *n* : a small plump dark green chili pepper

ja·lopy \jə-'lä-pē\ *n, pl* **ja·lop·ies** : a dilapidated vehicle (as an automobile)

jal·ou·sie \'ja-lə-sē\ *n* : a blind, window, or door with adjustable horizontal slats or louvers

¹**jam** \'jam\ *vb* **jammed; jam·ming** **1** ♦ : to press into a close or tight position; *also* : to become blocked or wedged **2** : to cause to become wedged so as to be unworkable; *also* : to make or become unworkable through the jamming of a movable part **3** : to push forcibly ⟨∼ on the brakes⟩ **4** : CRUSH, BRUISE **5** : to make unintelligible by sending out interfering signals or messages **6** : to take part in a jam session **7** : to fill often to excess — **jam·mer** *n*

♦ cram, crowd, ram, sandwich, squeeze, stuff, wedge ♦ block, choke, clog, close (off), congest, dam, obstruct, plug (up), stop (up), stuff

²**jam** *n* **1** ♦ : a crowded mass that impedes or blocks ⟨traffic ∼⟩ **2** : a difficult state of affairs

♦ backup, bottleneck, snarl

³**jam** *n* : a food made by boiling fruit and sugar to a thick consistency

Jam *abbr* Jamaica

Ja·mai·can \jə-'mā-kən\ *n* : a native or inhabitant of Jamaica — **Jamaican** *adj*

jamb \'jam\ *n* : an upright piece forming the side of an opening (as of a door)

jam·ba·laya \ˌjəm-bə-'lī-ə\ *n* : rice cooked with ham, sausage, chicken, shrimp, or oysters and seasoned with herbs

jam·bo·ree \ˌjam-bə-'rē\ *n* : a large festive gathering

James \'jāmz\ *n* : a moral lecture addressed to early Christians and included as a book in the New Testament

jam–pack \'jam-'pak\ *vb* ♦ : to pack tightly or to excess

♦ charge, cram, fill, heap, jam, load, pack, stuff

jam session *n* : an impromptu performance esp. by jazz musicians

Jan *abbr* January

jan·gle \'jaŋ-gəl\ *vb* **jan·gled; jan·gling** : to make a harsh or discordant sound — **jangle** *n*

jan·i·tor \'ja-nə-tər\ *n* **1** ♦ : a person who has the care of a building **2** : a person who tends a door — **jan·i·to·ri·al** \ˌja-nə-'tōr-ē-əl\ *adj*

♦ caretaker, custodian, guardian, keeper, warden, watchman

Jan·u·ary \'ja-nyə-ˌwer-ē\ *n* : the 1st month of the year

¹**ja·pan** \jə-'pan\ *n* : a varnish giving a hard brilliant finish

²**japan** *vb* **ja·panned; ja·pan·ning** : to cover with a coat of japan

Jap·a·nese \ˌja-pə-'nēz, -'nēs\ *n, pl* **Japanese** **1** : a native or inhabitant of Japan **2** : the language of Japan — **Japanese** *adj*

Japanese beetle *n* : a small metallic green and brown scarab beetle introduced from Japan that is a pest on the roots of grasses as a grub and on foliage and fruits as an adult

¹**jape** \'jāp\ *vb* **japed; jap·ing** **1** : JOKE **2** : MOCK

²**jape** *n* : JEST, GIBE

¹**jar** \'jär\ *vb* **jarred; jar·ring** **1** : to make a harsh or discordant sound **2** : to have a harsh or disagreeable effect **3** : VIBRATE, SHAKE ⟨tremors *jarred* the house⟩

♦ clash, collide, conflict

²**jar** *n* **1** : a state of conflict **2** : a harsh discordant sound **3** ♦ : a sudden or unexpected shake : JOLT **4** : a painful effect : SHOCK

♦ bump, collision, concussion, crash, impact, jolt, shock, smash, strike, wallop

³**jar** *n* : a widemouthed container usu. of glass or earthenware

jar·di·niere \ˌjärd-ᵊn-'ir\ *n* : an ornamental stand for plants or flowers

jar·gon \'jär-gən\ *n* **1** : confused unintelligible language **2** ♦ : the special vocabulary of a particular group or activity **3** : obscure and often pretentious language

♦ argot, cant, language, lingo, slang, terminology, vocabulary

Jas *abbr* James

jas·mine \'jaz-mən\ *n* : any of various climbing shrubs with fragrant flowers

jas·per \'jas-pər\ *n* : a usu. red, yellow, or brown opaque quartz

jaun·dice \'jȯn-dəs\ *n* **1** : yellowish discoloration of skin, tissues, and body fluids by bile pigments; *also* : an abnormal condition marked by jaundice **2** : a state or attitude characterized by satiety, distaste, or hostility

jaun·diced \-dəst\ *adj* **1** : affected with or as if with jaundice **2** ♦ : exhibiting envy, distaste, or hostility

♦ covetous, envious, jealous, resentful ♦ antagonistic, hostile, inhospitable, inimical, negative, unfriendly, unsympathetic

jaunt \'jȯnt\ *n* ♦ : a short trip usu. for pleasure

♦ excursion, junket, outing, sally

jaun·ti·ly \ˈjȯn-tə-lē\ *adv* ♦ : in a light or carefree manner
 ♦ exuberantly, gaily, sprightly

jaun·ty \ˈjȯn-tē\ *adj* **jaun·ti·er; -est** ♦ : sprightly in manner or appearance — LIVELY — **jaun·ti·ness** \-tē-nəs\ *n*
 ♦ active, animate, animated, brisk, energetic, lively, snappy, spirited, sprightly, springy

ja·va \ˈja-və, ˈjä-\ *n* : COFFEE

Ja·va·nese \ˌja-və-ˈnēz, ˌjä-, -ˈnēs\ *n* : a native or inhabitant of the Indonesian island of Java

jav·e·lin \ˈja-və-lən\ *n* **1** : a light spear **2** : a slender shaft thrown for distance in a track-and-field contest

¹jaw \ˈjȯ\ *n* **1** : either of the bony or cartilaginous structures that support the soft tissues enclosing the mouth and that usu. bear teeth **2** : the parts forming the walls of the mouth and serving to open and close it — usu. used in pl. **3** : one of a pair of movable parts for holding or crushing something — **jawed** \ˈjȯd\ *adj*

²jaw *vb* ♦ : to talk abusively, indignantly, or at length
 ♦ admonish, chide, lecture, rail (at *or* against), rate, rebuke, reprimand, scold ♦ chat, converse, gab, palaver, patter, prattle, rattle, talk, visit

¹jaw·bone \-ˌbōn\ *n* : JAW 1

²jawbone *vb* : to talk forcefully and persuasively

jaw·break·er \-ˌbrā-kər\ *n* **1** : a word difficult to pronounce **2** : a round hard candy

jaw–drop·ping \ˈjȯ-ˌdra-piŋ\ *adj* : causing great surprise or astonishment

jaw·less fish \ˈjȯ-ləs-\ *n* : any of a group of primitive vertebrates (as lampreys) without jaws

jay \ˈjā\ *n* : any of various noisy brightly colored often largely blue birds smaller than the related crows

jay·bird \ˈjā-ˌbərd\ *n* : JAY

jay·vee \ˌjā-ˈvē\ *n* **1** : JUNIOR VARSITY **2** : a member of a junior varsity team

jay·walk \ˈjā-ˌwȯk\ *vb* : to cross a street carelessly without regard for traffic regulations — **jay·walk·er** *n*

¹jazz \ˈjaz\ *n* **1** : American music characterized by improvisation, syncopated rhythms, and contrapuntal ensemble playing **2** ♦ : empty talk **3** : similar but unspecified things : STUFF
 ♦ bunk, claptrap, drivel, gibberish, hogwash, nonsense, piffle, prattle, rot

²jazz *vb* ♦ : to increase the appeal or excitement of : ENLIVEN ⟨~ things up⟩
 ♦ *usu* **jazz up** animate, brace, energize, enliven, fire, invigorate, liven up, pep up, quicken, stimulate, vitalize, vivify, zip (up)

jazzy \ˈja-zē\ *adj* **jazz·i·er; -est** **1** : having the characteristics of jazz **2** ♦ : marked by unrestraint, animation, or flashiness
 ♦ active, animate, animated, flashy, jaunty, lively, racy, sharp, smart, snappy, spirited, sprightly

JCS *abbr* joint chiefs of staff

jct *abbr* junction

JD *abbr* **1** doctor of jurisprudence; doctor of law **2** doctor of laws **3** justice department **4** juvenile delinquent

jeal·ous \ˈje-ləs\ *adj* **1** : demanding complete devotion **2** ♦ : hostile toward a rival or one believed to enjoy an advantage **3** : VIGILANT — **jeal·ous·ly** *adv*
 ♦ covetous, envious, jaundiced, resentful

jeal·ou·sy \-lə-sē\ *n* **1** ♦ : a jealous disposition, attitude, or feeling **2** : zealous vigilance
 ♦ covetousness, enviousness, envy, resentment

jeans \ˈjēnz\ *n pl* : pants made of durable twilled cotton cloth

jeep \ˈjēp\ *n* : a small four-wheel drive general-purpose motor vehicle used in World War II

¹jeer \ˈjir\ *vb* ♦ : to speak or cry out in derision : MOCK
 ♦ deride, gibe, laugh, mock, ridicule, scout

²jeer *n* ♦ : a jeering remark or sound : TAUNT
 ♦ boo, catcall, hiss, hoot, raspberry, snort, taunt

Je·ho·vah \ji-ˈhō-və\ *n* ♦ : the supreme or ultimate reality
 ♦ Almighty, deity, Supreme Being

je·hu \ˈjē-hü, -hyü\ *n* : a driver of a coach or cab

je·june \ji-ˈjün\ *adj* : lacking interest or significance : DULL

je·ju·num \ji-ˈjü-nəm\ *n* : the section of the small intestine between the duodenum and the ileum — **je·ju·nal** \-ˈjün-ᵊl\ *adj*

jell \ˈjel\ *vb* **1** ♦ : to come to the consistency of jelly **2** ♦ : to take shape

 ♦ [1] clot, coagulate, congeal, gel, set ♦ [2] crystallize, form, shape, solidify

¹jel·ly \ˈje-lē\ *n, pl* **jellies** **1** : a food with a soft elastic consistency due usu. to the presence of gelatin or pectin; *esp* : a fruit product made by boiling sugar and the juice of a fruit **2** : a substance resembling jelly

²jelly *vb* : to bring to or come to the consistency of jelly

jelly bean *n* : a bean-shaped candy

jel·ly·fish \ˈje-lē-ˌfish\ *n* : a marine coelenterate with a nearly transparent jellylike body and stinging tentacles

jen·net \ˈje-nət\ *n* **1** : a small Spanish horse **2** : a female donkey

jen·ny \ˈje-nē\ *n, pl* **jennies** : a female bird or donkey

jeop·ar·dize \-ˌdīz\ *vb* ♦ : to expose to danger or risk
 ♦ adventure, compromise, gamble with, hazard, imperil, menace, risk, venture

jeop·ar·dy \ˈje-pər-dē\ *n* ♦ : exposure to death, loss, or injury
 ♦ danger, distress, peril, risk, trouble

Jer *abbr* Jeremiah; Jeremias

jer·e·mi·ad \ˌjer-ə-ˈmī-əd, -ˌad\ *n* : a prolonged lamentation or complaint; *also* : a cautionary or angry harangue

Jer·e·mi·ah \ˌjer-ə-ˈmī-ə\ *n* : a book of Jewish and Christian Scripture

Jer·e·mi·as \ˌjer-ə-ˈmī-əs\ *n* : JEREMIAH

¹jerk \ˈjərk\ *n* **1** ♦ : a short quick pull or twist : TWITCH **2** ♦ : an annoyingly stupid or foolish person — **jerk·i·ly** \ˈjər-kə-lē\ *adv*
 ♦ [1] draw, haul, pluck, pull, tug, twitch, wrench ♦ [2] beast, boor, churl, clown, creep, cretin, cur, heel, joker, louse, lout, skunk, slob, snake

²jerk *vb* **1** ♦ : to give a sharp quick push, pull, or twist **2** ♦ : to move in short abrupt motions
 ♦ [1] buck, hitch, jolt, twitch ♦ [2] fiddle, fidget, squirm, twitch, wiggle

jer·kin \ˈjər-kən\ *n* : a close-fitting usu. sleeveless jacket

jerk·wa·ter \ˈjərk-ˌwȯ-tər, -ˌwä-\ *adj* : of minor importance : INSIGNIFICANT ⟨~ towns⟩

jerky \ˈjər-kē\ *adj* **1** : moving along with or marked by fits and starts **2** : lacking in sense, judgment, or discretion

jer·ry–built \ˈjer-ē-ˌbilt\ *adj* : built cheaply and flimsily

jer·ry–rigged \-ˌrigd\ *adj* ♦ : organized or constructed in a crude or improvised manner
 ♦ artless, clumsy, crude, rough, rude, unrefined

jer·sey \ˈjər-zē\ *n, pl* **jerseys** **1** : a plain weft-knitted fabric **2** : a close-fitting knitted shirt **3** *often cap* : any of a breed of small usu. fawn-colored dairy cattle

Jersey barrier *n* : a concrete slab that is used with others to block or reroute traffic or to divide a highway

Je·ru·sa·lem artichoke \jə-ˈrü-sə-ləm-\ *n* : a No. American sunflower widely grown for its edible tubers that are used as a vegetable; *also* : its tubers

jess \ˈjes\ *n* : a leg strap by which a captive bird of prey may be controlled

jessamine *var of* JASMINE

¹jest \ˈjest\ *n* **1** ♦ : an act intended to provoke laughter **2** ♦ : a witty remark **3** ♦ : a frivolous mood ⟨said in ~⟩
 ♦ [1, 2] crack, gag, joke, laugh, pleasantry, quip, sally, waggery, wisecrack, witticism ♦ [3] fun, game, play, sport

²jest *vb* ♦ : to speak or act without seriousness or in a frivolous manner; *also* : to make a witty remark
 ♦ banter, fool, fun, jive, joke, josh, kid, quip, wisecrack

jest·er \ˈjes-tər\ *n* ♦ : a retainer formerly kept to provide casual entertainment; *broadly* : one given to jests
 ♦ card, comedian, comic, humorist, joker, wag, wit

¹jet \ˈjet\ *n* : a velvet-black coal that takes a good polish and is often used for jewelry

²jet *vb* **jet·ted; jet·ting** ♦ : to spout or emit in a stream
 ♦ gush, pour, rush, spew, spout, spurt, squirt

³jet *n* **1** : a forceful rush (as of liquid or gas) through a narrow opening; *also* : a nozzle for a jet of fluid **2** : a jet-propelled airplane

⁴jet *vb* **jet·ted; jet·ting** : to travel by jet

jet lag *n* : a condition that is marked esp. by fatigue and irritability and occurs following a long flight through several time zones — **jet–lagged** *adj*

jet·lin·er \ˈjet-ˌlī-nər\ *n* : a jet-propelled airliner

jet·port \-ˌpȯrt\ *n* : an airport designed to handle jets

jet–pro·pelled \ˌjet-prə-ˈpeld\ *adj* **:** driven by an engine (**jet en·gine**) that produces propulsion (**jet propulsion**) by the rearward discharge of a jet of fluid (as heated air and exhaust gases)

jet·sam \ˈjet-səm\ *n* **:** jettisoned goods; *esp* **:** such goods washed ashore

jet set *n* **:** an international group of wealthy people who frequent fashionable resorts

jet stream *n* **:** a long narrow high-altitude current of high-speed winds blowing generally from the west

¹**jet·ti·son** \ˈje-tə-sən\ *vb* **1 :** to throw (goods) overboard to lighten a ship or aircraft in distress **2 ♦ :** to get rid of as superfluous or encumbering : DISCARD ⟨~ed an old computer⟩

   ♦ cast, discard, ditch, dump, fling, junk, lose, reject, scrap, shed, shuck, slough, throw away, throw out, unload

²**jettison** *n* **:** a voluntary sacrifice of cargo to lighten a ship's load in time of distress

jet·ty \ˈje-tē\ *n, pl* **jetties 1 :** a pier built to influence the current or to protect a harbor **2 ♦ :** a landing wharf

   ♦ dock, float, landing, levee, pier, quay, wharf

jeu d'es·prit \zhœ-des-ˈprē\ *n, pl* **jeux d'esprit** *same*\ **:** a witty comment or composition

Jew \ˈjü\ *n* **1 :** one whose religion is Judaism **2 :** ISRAELITE — **Jew·ish** *adj*

¹**jew·el** \ˈjü-əl\ *n* **1 :** an ornament of precious metal **2 ♦ :** a precious stone : GEMSTONE **3 ♦ :** one that is highly esteemed

   ♦ [2] brilliant, gem, gemstone ♦ [3] boast, credit, glory, honor (*or* honour), pride, treasure ♦ [3] catch, gem, pearl, plum, prize, treasure

²**jewel** *vb* **-eled** *or* **-elled; -el·ing** *or* **-el·ling :** to adorn or equip with jewels

jewel box *n* **:** a thin plastic case for a CD or DVD

jew·el·er *or* **jew·el·ler** \ˈjü-ə-lər\ *n* **:** a person who makes or deals in jewelry and related articles

jew·el·ry *or Can and Brit* **jew·el·lery** \ˈjü-əl-rē\ *n* **:** JEWELS; *esp* **:** objects of precious metal set with gems and worn for personal adornment

Jew·ry \ˈju̇r-ē, ˈju̇-ər-ē, ˈjü-rē\ *n* **:** the Jewish people

jg *abbr* junior grade

¹**jib** \ˈjib\ *n* **:** a triangular sail set on a line running from the bow to the mast

²**jib** *vb* **jibbed; jib·bing :** to refuse to proceed further

¹**jibe** *var of* GIBE

²**jibe** \ˈjīb\ *vb* **jibed; jib·ing ♦ :** to be in accord : AGREE

   ♦ accord, agree, answer, check, coincide, comport, conform, correspond, dovetail, fit, go, harmonize, square, tally

ji·ca·ma \ˈhē-kə-mə\ *n* **:** an edible starchy tuber of a tropical American vine of the legume family

jif·fy \ˈji-fē\ *n, pl* **jiffies :** a small portion or point of time : MOMENT, INSTANT ⟨I'll be ready in a ~⟩

   ♦ flash, instant, minute, moment, second, shake, trice, twinkle, twinkling, wink

¹**jig** \ˈjig\ *n* **1 :** a lively dance in triple rhythm **2 ♦ :** a crafty procedure or practice meant to deceive or defraud ⟨the ~ is up⟩ **3 :** a device used to hold work during manufacture or assembly

   ♦ artifice, device, dodge, gimmick, ploy, scheme, sleight, stratagem, trick, wile

²**jig** *vb* **jigged; jig·ging :** to dance a jig

jig·ger \ˈji-gər\ *n* **1 :** a measure usu. holding 1 to 2 ounces (30 to 60 milliliters) used in mixing drinks **2 ♦ :** an often small mechanical or electronic device with a practical use but often thought of as a novelty

   ♦ contraption, contrivance, gadget, gimmick, gizmo

jig·gle \ˈji-gəl\ *vb* **jig·gled; jig·gling ♦ :** to move with quick little jerks — **jiggle** *n*

   ♦ fiddle, fidget, jerk, squirm, twitch, wiggle

jig·saw \ˈjig-ˌsȯ\ *n* **:** a machine saw with a narrow vertically reciprocating blade for cutting curved lines

jigsaw puzzle *n* **:** a puzzle consisting of small irregularly cut pieces to be fitted together to form a picture

ji·had \ji-ˈhäd, -ˈhad\ *n* **1 :** a Muslim holy war **2 :** a reforming enterprise undertaken with zeal

ji·had·ist \-ˈhä-dist, -ˈha-\ *n* **:** a Muslim who advocates or participates in a jihad

¹**jilt** \ˈjilt\ *vb* **:** to drop (a lover) capriciously or unfeelingly

²**jilt** *n* **:** one who jilts a lover

jim crow \ˈjim-ˈkrō\ *n, often cap J&C* **:** discrimination against Black people esp. by legal enforcement or traditional sanctions

— **jim crow** *adj, often cap J&C* — **jim crow·ism** \-ˈkrō-ˌi-zəm\ *n, often cap J&C*

¹**jim–dan·dy** \ˈjim-ˈdan-dē\ *n ♦ :* something excellent of its kind

   ♦ beauty, crackerjack, dandy, knockout, pip

²**jim–dandy** *adj* **:** fine or wonderful of its kind

jim·mies \ˈji-mēz\ *n pl* **:** tiny rod-shaped bits of usu. chocolate⸗flavored candy often sprinkled on ice cream

¹**jim·my** \ˈji-mē\ *n, pl* **jimmies :** a small crowbar

²**jimmy** *vb* **jim·mied; jim·my·ing ♦ :** to force open with a jimmy

   ♦ prize, pry

jim·son·weed \ˈjim-sən-ˌwēd\ *n, often cap* **:** a coarse poisonous weed related to the tomato that has large trumpet-shaped white or violet flowers

¹**jin·gle** \ˈjiŋ-gəl\ *vb* **jin·gled; jin·gling ♦ :** to make a light clinking or tinkling sound

   ♦ chink, tinkle

²**jingle** *n* **1 :** a light clinking or tinkling sound **2 ♦ :** a short verse or song with catchy repetition

   ♦ lay, lyric, song, vocal

jin·go·ism \ˈjiŋ-gō-ˌi-zəm\ *n* **:** extreme chauvinism or nationalism marked esp. by a belligerent foreign policy — **jin·go·ist** \-ist\ *n* — **jin·go·is·tic** \ˌjiŋ-gō-ˈis-tik\ *adj*

jin·rik·sha \jin-ˈrik-ˌshȯ\ *n* **:** RICKSHA

¹**jinx** \ˈjiŋks\ *n* **:** one that brings bad luck

²**jinx** *vb* **:** to foredoom to failure or misfortune

jit·ney \ˈjit-nē\ *n, pl* **jitneys :** a small bus that serves a regular route on a flexible schedule

jit·ter·bug \ˈji-tər-ˌbəg\ *n* **:** a dance in which couples two-step, balance, and twirl vigorously in standardized patterns — **jitterbug** *vb*

jit·ters \ˈji-tərz\ *n pl* **♦ :** extreme nervousness

   ♦ shakes, shivers, willies

jit·tery \-tə-rē\ *adj* **1 ♦ :** suffering from the jitters **2 :** marked by jittering movements

   ♦ excitable, flighty, fluttery, high-strung, jumpy, nervous, skittish, spooky ♦ aflutter, anxious, edgy, jumpy, nervous, nervy, perturbed, tense, troubled, uneasy, upset, worried

¹**jive** \ˈjīv\ *n* **1 :** swing music or dancing performed to it **2 :** glib, deceptive, or foolish talk **3 :** the jargon of jazz enthusiasts **4 ♦ :** a special jargon of difficult or slang terms

   ♦ argot, cant, dialect, jargon, language, lingo, patois, patter, slang, terminology, vocabulary

²**jive** *vb* **jived; jiv·ing 1 ♦ :** to persuade with flattery or gentle urging esp. in the face of reluctance : TEASE; *also* **:** kid around **2 :** to dance to or play jive

   ♦ chaff, josh, kid, rally, razz, rib, ride, roast, tease

Jn *or* **Jno** *abbr* John

Jo *abbr* Joel

¹**job** \ˈjäb\ *n* **1 :** a piece of work **2 ♦ :** something that has to be done : TASK; *also* **:** a specific duty, role, or function **3 ♦ :** a regular remunerative position — **job·less** *adj*

   ♦ [2] assignment, chore, duty, stint, task ♦ [2] assignment, charge, mission, operation, post ♦ [3] appointment, billet, capacity, function, place, position, post, situation

²**job** *vb* **jobbed; job·bing 1 :** to do occasional pieces of work for hire **2 :** to hire or let by the job

Job \ˈjōb\ *n* **:** a book of Jewish and Christian Scripture

job action *n* **:** a protest action by workers to force compliance with demands

job·ber \ˈjä-bər\ *n* **1 :** a person who buys goods and then sells them to other dealers : MIDDLEMAN **2 :** a person who does work by the job

job·hold·er \ˈjäb-ˌhōl-dər\ *n ♦ :* one having a regular job

   ♦ employee, hand, hireling, worker

jock \ˈjäk\ *n* **:** ATHLETE; *esp* **:** a college athlete

¹**jock·ey** \ˈjä-kē\ *n, pl* **jockeys :** one who rides a horse esp. as a professional in a race

²**jockey** *vb* **jock·eyed; jock·ey·ing :** to maneuver or manipulate by adroit or devious means ⟨rivals ~ed for power⟩

jock·strap \ˈjäk-ˌstrap\ *n* **:** ATHLETIC SUPPORTER

jo·cose \jō-ˈkōs\ *adj* **:** given to joking : MERRY ⟨~ partygoers⟩; *also* **:** characterized by joking

joc·u·lar \ˈjä-kyə-lər\ *adj* **♦ :** marked by jesting : PLAYFUL — **joc·u·lar·i·ty** \ˌjäk-yə-ˈlar-ə-tē\ *n* — **joc·u·lar·ly** *adv*

   ♦ clever, facetious, humorous, playful, smart, witty

jo·cund \'jä-kənd\ adj ♦ : marked by mirth or cheerfulness
♦ blithe, boon, festive, gleeful, jolly, jovial, merry, mirthful, sunny

jodh·pur \'jäd-pər\ n 1 pl : riding breeches loose above the knee and tight-fitting below 2 : an ankle-high boot fastened with a strap

Joe Blow \'jō-\ n : an average or ordinary man

Jo·el \'jō-əl\ n : a book of Jewish and Christian Scripture

Joe Six–Pack \'jō-\ n : a blue-collar worker

¹**jog** \'jäg\ vb **jogged; jog·ging** 1 : to give a slight shake or push to 2 : to go at a slow monotonous pace 3 : to run or ride at a slow trot 4 ♦ : to move up and down or along with a short heavy motion — **jog·ger** n
♦ bob, bobble, jounce, nod, pump, seesaw

²**jog** n 1 : a slight shake 2 : a jogging movement or pace

³**jog** n 1 : a projecting or retreating part of a line or surface 2 : a brief abrupt change in direction

jog·gle \'jä-gəl\ vb **jog·gled; jog·gling** : to shake slightly — **joggle** n

john \'jän\ n 1 : TOILET 2 : a prostitute's client

John \'jän\ n 1 : the fourth Gospel in the New Testament 2 : any of three short didactic letters addressed to early Christians and included in the New Testament

john·ny \'jä-nē\ n, pl **johnnies** : a short-sleeved gown opening in the back that is worn by hospital patients

John·ny–jump–up \₁jä-nē-'jəmp-₁əp\ n : any of various small-flowered cultivated pansies

joie de vi·vre \₁zhwä-də-'vēvrᵊ\ n : keen enjoyment of life

join \'jȯin\ vb 1 ♦ : to come or bring together so as to form a unit 2 : to come or bring into close association 3 ♦ : to become a member of 4 ♦ : to lie next to or in contact with : ADJOIN 5 ♦ : to take part in a collective activity
♦ [1] associate, coalesce, combine, conjoin, connect, couple, fuse, link, marry, unify, unite ♦ [3] enlist, enroll, enter, sign on, sign up ♦ [4] abut, adjoin, border (on), flank, fringe, skirt, touch, verge (on) ♦ [5] collaborate, concert, cooperate, team

join·er \'jȯi-nər\ n 1 : a worker who constructs articles by joining pieces of wood 2 : a gregarious person who joins many organizations

¹**joint** \'jȯint\ n 1 : the point of contact between bones of an animal skeleton with the parts that surround and support it 2 : a cut of meat suitable for roasting 3 ♦ : a place where two things or parts are connected 4 : a place of business or residence with its furnishings and staff : ESTABLISHMENT; esp : a shabby or disreputable establishment 5 : a marijuana cigarette — **joint·ed** adj
♦ connection, coupling, junction, juncture

²**joint** adj 1 ♦ : acting in concert : UNITED 2 : common to two or more — **joint·ly** adv
♦ collective, common, communal, concerted, conjoint, mutual, public, united

³**joint** vb 1 : to unite by or provide with a joint 2 : to separate the joints of

joist \'jȯist\ n : any of the small beams ranged parallel from wall to wall in a building to support a floor or ceiling

¹**joke** \'jōk\ n 1 ♦ : something said or done to provoke laughter; esp : a brief narrative with a humorous climax
♦ crack, gag, jest, laugh, pleasantry, quip, sally, waggery, wisecrack, witticism

²**joke** vb **joked; jok·ing** ♦ : to make jokes — **jok·ing·ly** adv
♦ banter, fool, fun, jest, jive, josh, kid, quip, wisecrack

jok·er \'jō-kər\ n 1 ♦ : a person who jokes 2 : an extra card used in some card games 3 : a misleading part of an agreement that works to one party's disadvantage 4 a : an adult male human b ♦ : an insignificant, obnoxious, or incompetent person
♦ [1] card, comedian, comic, humorist, jester, wag, wit ♦ [4b] beast, boor, churl, clown, creep, cretin, cur, heel, jerk, louse, lout, skunk, slob, snake

jol·li·fi·ca·tion \₁jä-li-fə-'kā-shən\ n ♦ : a festive celebration
♦ conviviality, festivity, gaiety, merriment, merrymaking, revelry

jol·li·ty \'jä-lə-tē\ n, pl **-ties** : the quality or state of being jolly : GAIETY, MERRIMENT

jol·ly \'jä-lē\ adj **jol·li·er; -est** ♦ : full of high spirits : MERRY
♦ blithe, boon, festive, gleeful, jocund, jovial, merry, mirthful, sunny

¹**jolt** \'jōlt\ vb 1 : to give a quick hard knock or blow to 2 ♦ : to move with a sudden jerky motion 3 ♦ : to disturb the composure of — **jolt·er** n
♦ [2] agitate, convulse, jounce, quake, quiver, shake, shudder, vibrate, wobble ♦ [3] buck, hitch, jerk, twitch ♦ [3] appall, bowl, floor, shake up, shock

²**jolt** n 1 ♦ : an abrupt jerky blow or movement 2 ♦ : a sudden shock
♦ [1] bump, collision, concussion, crash, impact, jar, shock, smash, strike, wallop ♦ [2] bolt, bombshell, jar, surprise

Jon abbr Jonah; Jonas

Jo·nah \'jō-nə\ n : a book of Jewish and Christian Scripture

Jo·nas \'jō-nəs\ n : JONAH

¹**jones** \'jōnz\ n 1 slang : addiction to heroin 2 slang : HEROIN 3 slang : a craving for something

²**jones** vb, slang : to have a craving for something

jon·gleur \zhōⁿ-'glər\ n : an itinerant medieval minstrel

jon·quil \'jän-kwəl\ n : a narcissus with fragrant clustered white or yellow flowers

Jor·da·ni·an \jȯr-'dā-nē-ən\ n : a native or inhabitant of Jordan — **Jordanian** adj

josh \'jäsh\ vb ♦ : to tease good-naturedly; also : JOKE
♦ chaff, jive, kid, rally, razz, rib, ride, roast, tease ♦ banter, fool, fun, jest, jive, joke, kid, quip, wisecrack

Josh abbr Joshua

Josh·ua \'jä-shú-ə\ n : a book of Jewish and Christian Scripture

Joshua tree n : a tall branched yucca of the southwestern U.S.

jos·tle \'jä-səl\ vb **jos·tled; jos·tling** 1 : to come in contact or into collision 2 : to make one's way by pushing and shoving ⟨jostled his way onto the bus⟩

Jos·ue \'jä-shú-ē\ n : JOSHUA

¹**jot** \'jät\ n ♦ : the least bit : IOTA
♦ hoot, iota, lick, modicum, rap, tittle, whit

²**jot** vb **jot·ted; jot·ting** ♦ : to write briefly and hurriedly
♦ usu jot down log, mark, note, put down, record, register, set down

jot·ting \'jä-tiŋ\ n : a brief note

joule \'jül\ n : a unit of work or energy equal to the work done by a force of one newton acting through a distance of one meter

jounce \'jaúns\ vb **jounced; jounc·ing** ♦ : to move or cause to move in an up-and-down manner : JOLT — **jounce** n
♦ agitate, convulse, jolt, quake, quiver, shake, shudder, vibrate, wobble

jour abbr 1 journal 2 journeyman

¹**jour·nal** \'jərn-ᵊl\ n 1 : a brief account of daily events 2 : a record of proceedings (as of a legislative body) 3 ♦ : a periodical (as a newspaper) dealing esp. with current events 4 : the part of a rotating axle or spindle that turns in a bearing
♦ magazine, organ, paper, review

²**journal** vb : to keep a personal journal : to enter or record daily thoughts, experiences, etc., in a journal

jour·nal·ese \₁jər-nə-'lēz, -'lēs\ n : a style of writing held to be characteristic of newspapers

jour·nal·ism \'jər-nə-₁li-zəm\ n 1 : the business of writing for, editing, or publishing periodicals (as newspapers) 2 : writing designed for or characteristic of newspapers — **jour·nal·ist** \-list\ n — **jour·nal·is·tic** \₁jər-nə-'lis-tik\ adj

jour·nal·ist \'jər-nə-₁list\ n 1 ♦ : a person engaged in journalism 2 : one who keeps a journal
♦ correspondent, newsman, reporter

¹**jour·ney** \'jər-nē\ n, pl **journeys** ♦ : a traveling from one place to another
♦ expedition, passage, peregrination, trek, trip

²**journey** vb **jour·neyed; jour·ney·ing** ♦ : to go on a journey : TRAVEL
♦ tour, travel, trek, voyage

jour·ney·man \-mən\ n 1 : a worker who has learned a trade and works for another person 2 : an experienced reliable worker

¹**joust** \'jaúst\ vb : to engage in a joust

²**joust** n : a combat on horseback between two knights with lances esp. as part of a tournament

jo·vial \'jō-vē-əl\ adj ♦ : marked by good humor ⟨a ∼ mood⟩
♦ blithe, boon, festive, gleeful, jocund, jolly, merry, mirthful, sunny

jo·vi·al·i·ty \₁jō-vē-'a-lə-tē\ n ♦ : the quality or state of being jovial

♦ cheer, cheerfulness, cheeriness, glee, hilarity, merriment, mirth

jo·vi·al·ly *adv* ♦ : in a jovial manner

♦ cheerfully, gaily, happily, heartily, merrily, mirthfully

¹jowl \ˈjaủ-(ə)l\ *n* : loose flesh about the lower jaw or throat
²jowl *n* **1** : the lower jaw **2** : CHEEK
¹joy \ˈjȯi\ *n* **1** ♦ : a feeling of happiness that comes from success, good fortune, or a sense of well-being **2** ♦ : a source of happiness

♦ [1] blessedness, bliss, felicity, gladness, happiness ♦ [2] delectation, delight, kick, manna, pleasure, treat

²joy *vb* : to experience great pleasure or delight : REJOICE
joy·ful \-fəl\ *adj* ♦ : experiencing, causing, or showing joy ⟨∼ news⟩ — **joy·ful·ly** *adv*

♦ blissful, delighted, glad, happy, pleased

joy·less *adj* **1** : not experiencing joy **2** : not inspiring or causing joy
joy·ous \ˈjȯi-əs\ *adj* : experiencing, causing, or showing joy : JOYFUL — **joy·ous·ly** *adv* — **joy·ous·ness** *n*
joy·ride \ˈjȯi-ˌrīd\ *n* : a ride for pleasure often marked by reckless driving — **joyride** *vb* — **joy·rid·er** *n* — **joy·rid·ing** *n*
joy·stick \-ˌstik\ *n* : a control device (as for a computer display) consisting of a lever capable of motion in two or more directions
JP *abbr* **1** jet propulsion **2** justice of the peace
JPEG \ˈjā-ˌpeg\ *n* : a computer file format for usu. high-quality digital images
Jr *abbr* junior
jt *or* **jnt** *abbr* joint
ju·bi·lant \ˈjü-bə-lənt\ *adj* ♦ : filled with or expressing great joy or triumph : EXULTANT ⟨∼ winners⟩ — **ju·bi·lant·ly** *adv*

♦ exultant, rejoicing, triumphant

ju·bi·la·tion \ˌjü-bə-ˈlā-shən\ *n* : EXULTATION
ju·bi·lee \ˈjü-bə-ˌlē, ˌjü-bə-ˈlē\ *n* **1** : a 50th anniversary **2** ♦ : a season or occasion of celebration

♦ carnival, celebration, festival, festivity, fete, fiesta, gala

ju·co \ˈjü-ˌkō\ *n, pl* **jucos** : JUNIOR COLLEGE; *also* : an athlete at a junior college
Jud *abbr* Judith
Ju·da·ic \jü-ˈdā-ik\ *also* **Ju·da·ical** \-ˈdā-ə-kəl\ *adj* : of, relating to, or characteristic of Jews or Judaism
Ju·da·ism \ˈjü-də-ˌi-zəm, -dā-, -dē-\ *n* : a religion developed among the ancient Hebrews and marked by belief in one God and by the moral and ceremonial laws of the Old Testament and the rabbinic tradition
Jude \ˈjüd\ *n* : a short hortatory epistle addressed to early Christians and included as a book in the New Testament
Judg *abbr* Judges
¹judge \ˈjəj\ *vb* **judged; judg·ing** **1** : to form an authoritative opinion **2** ♦ : to decide as a judge **3** ♦ : to form an estimate or evaluation about something

♦ [2] adjudicate, arbitrate, decide, determine, referee, rule, settle, umpire ♦ [3] calculate, call, conjecture, estimate, figure, gauge, guess, make, place, put, reckon, suppose ♦ [3] conclude, deduce, extrapolate, gather, infer, reason, understand

²judge *n* **1** ♦ : a public official authorized to decide questions brought before a court **2** ♦ : one appointed to decide in a contest or competition **3** : one who gives an authoritative opinion : CRITIC — **judge·ship** *n*

♦ [1] bench, court, justice, magistrate ♦ [2] arbiter, arbitrator, referee, umpire

Judges *n* : a book of Jewish and Christian Scripture
judg·ment *or* **judge·ment** \ˈjəj-mənt\ *n* **1** ♦ : a decision or opinion given after judging; *esp* : a formal decision given by a court **2** *cap* : the final judging of humankind by God **3** ♦ : the process of forming an opinion by discerning and comparing **4** : the capacity for judging : DISCERNMENT

♦ [1] appraisal, assessment, estimate, estimation, evaluation ♦ [1] doom, finding, holding, ruling, sentence ♦ [3] belief, conviction, eye, feeling, mind, notion, opinion, persuasion, sentiment, verdict, view ♦ [3] conclusion, decision, determination, diagnosis, resolution

judg·men·tal \ˌjəj-ˈmen-təl\ *adj* **1** : of, relating to, or involving judgment **2** : characterized by a tendency to judge harshly — **judg·men·tal·ly** *adv*
judgment call *n* : a subjective decision, ruling, or opinion
Judgment Day *n* : the day of the final judging of all human beings by God

ju·di·ca·ture \ˈjü-di-kə-ˌchủr\ *n* **1** : the administration of justice **2** : JUDICIARY 1
ju·di·cial \jü-ˈdi-shəl\ *adj* **1** : of or relating to the administration of justice or the judiciary **2** : ordered or enforced by a court **3** : CRITICAL — **ju·di·cial·ly** *adv*
ju·di·cia·ry \jü-ˈdi-shē-ˌer-ē, -shə-rē\ *n* **1** : a system of courts of law; *also* : the judges of these courts **2** : a branch of government in which judicial power is vested — **judiciary** *adj*
ju·di·cious \jü-ˈdi-shəs\ *adj* ♦ : having, exercising, or characterized by sound judgment — **ju·di·cious·ly** *adv*

♦ advisable, desirable, expedient, politic, prudent, tactical, wise

Ju·dith \ˈjü-dəth\ *n* : a book of Scripture in the Roman Catholic canon of the Old Testament and in the Protestant Apocrypha
ju·do \ˈjü-dō\ *n* : a sport derived from jujitsu that emphasizes the use of quick movement and leverage to throw an opponent — **ju·do·ist** \-ist\ *n*
ju·do·ka \ˈjü-dō-ˌkä\ *n, pl* **judoka** *or* **judokas** : one who participates in judo
¹jug \ˈjəg\ *n* **1** ♦ : a large deep container with a narrow mouth and a handle **2** : a place of confinement for persons held in lawful custody : JAIL, PRISON

♦ ewer, flagon, pitcher

²jug *vb* **jugged; jug·ging** : to confine in or as if in a jail : JAIL, IMPRISON
jug–eared \ˈjəg-ˌird\ *adj* : having protuberant ears
jug·ger·naut \ˈjə-gər-ˌnȯt\ *n* : a massive inexorable force or object that crushes everything in its path
jug·gle \ˈjə-gəl\ *vb* **jug·gled; jug·gling** **1** : to keep several objects in motion in the air at the same time **2** : to manipulate esp. in order to achieve a desired end — **jug·gler** \ˈjə-glər\ *n*
jug·u·lar \ˈjə-gyə-lər\ *adj* : of, relating to, or situated in or on the throat or neck ⟨the ∼ veins⟩
juice \ˈjüs\ *n* **1** : the extractable fluid contents of cells or tissues **2** *pl* : the natural fluids of an animal body **3** : something that supplies power; *esp* : ELECTRICITY 2
juic·er \ˈjü-sər\ *n* : an appliance for extracting juice (as from fruit)
juice up *vb* : to give life, energy, or spirit to
juicy \ˈjü-sē\ *adj* **juic·i·er; -est** **1** ♦ : full of juice : SUCCULENT **2** : rich in interest; *also* : RACY ⟨∼ gossip⟩ — **juic·i·ly** \-sə-lē\ *adv* — **juic·i·ness** \-sē-nəs\ *n*

♦ fleshy, pulpy, succulent

ju·jit·su *also* **ju·jut·su** \jü-ˈjit-sü\ *n* : an art of fighting employing holds, throws, and paralyzing blows
ju·ju \ˈjü-jü\ *n* : a style of African music characterized by a rapid beat, use of percussion instruments, and vocal harmonies
ju·jube \ˈjü-ˌjüb, ˈjü-jə-ˌbē\ *n* : a fruit-flavored gumdrop or lozenge
juke·box \ˈjük-ˌbäks\ *n* : a coin-operated machine that automatically plays selected recordings
Jul *abbr* July
ju·lep \ˈjü-ləp\ *n* : a drink made of bourbon, sugar, and mint served over crushed ice
Ju·ly \jủ-ˈlī\ *n* : the 7th month of the year
¹jum·ble \ˈjəm-bəl\ *vb* **jum·bled; jum·bling** : to mix in a confused mass
²jumble *n* ♦ : a mass of things mingled together without order or plan; *also* : a state of confusion

♦ chaos, confusion, disarray, disorder, disorganization, havoc, hell, mess, muddle, shambles ♦ assortment, clutter, medley, mélange, miscellany, motley, muddle, variety, welter

¹jum·bo \ˈjəm-bō\ *n, pl* **jumbos** ♦ : a very large specimen of its kind

♦ behemoth, blockbuster, colossus, giant, leviathan, mammoth, monster, titan, whale, whopper

²jumbo *adj* : very large ⟨a ∼ TV screen⟩
¹jump \ˈjəmp\ *vb* **1** ♦ : to spring into the air : leap over **2** ♦ : to give a start **3** : to rise or increase suddenly or sharply **4** ♦ : to make a sudden attack **5** : ANTICIPATE ⟨∼ the gun⟩ **6** : to leave hurriedly and often furtively ⟨∼ town⟩ **7** : to act or move before (as a signal) — **jump bail** : to abscond after being released from custody on bail — **jump ship** **1** : to leave the company of a ship without authority **2** : to desert a cause

♦ [1] bound, hop, leap, spring, vault ♦ [2] bolt, start, startle ♦ *usu* **jump on** [4] abuse, castigate, excoriate, lambaste, slam, vituperate ♦ *usu* **jump on** [4] assail, assault, attack, beset, charge, descend, pounce (on *or* upon), raid, rush, storm, strike

²jump *n* **1** ♦ : a spring into the air; *esp* : one made for height or distance in a track meet **2** : a sharp sudden increase **3** ♦ : an initial advantage ⟨got the ∼ on a rival⟩

♦ [1] bound, hop, leap, spring, vault ♦ [3] advantage, better, drop, edge, upper hand, vantage

¹jump·er \'jəm-pər\ *n* : one that jumps
²jumper *n* **1** : a loose blouse **2** : a sleeveless one-piece dress worn usu. with a blouse **3** *pl* : a child's sleeveless coverall
jumping bean *n* : a seed of any of several Mexican shrubs that tumbles about because of the movements of a small moth larva inside it
jumping–off place *n* **1** : a remote or isolated place **2** : a place from which an enterprise is launched
jump·mas·ter \'jəmp-ˌmas-tər\ *n* : a person who supervises parachutists
jump–start \'jəmp-ˌstärt\ *vb* : to start (an engine or vehicle) by connection to an external power source
jump·suit \'jəmp-ˌsüt\ *n* **1** : a coverall worn by parachutists in jumping **2** : a one-piece garment consisting of a blouse or shirt with attached pants or shorts
jumpy \'jəm-pē\ *adj* **jump·i·er; -est** ♦ : easily excited or irritated : NERVOUS, JITTERY

♦ edgy, excitable, high-strung, jittery, nervous, skittish, spooky

jun *abbr* junior
Jun *abbr* June
junc *abbr* junction
jun·co \'jəŋ-kō\ *n, pl* **juncos** *or* **juncoes** : any of a genus of small common pink-billed No. American finches that are largely gray with conspicuous white tail feathers
junc·tion \'jəŋk-shən\ *n* **1** ♦ : an act of joining **2** ♦ : a place or point of meeting

♦ [1] combination, connection, consolidation, coupling, unification, union ♦ [2] connection, coupling, joint, juncture

junc·ture \'jəŋk-chər\ *n* **1** : a place where two things or parts are joined : JOINT, CONNECTION **2** : UNION **3** ♦ : a critical time or state of affairs

♦ clutch, crisis, crunch, emergency, head

June \'jün\ *n* : the 6th month of the year
jun·gle \'jəŋ-gəl\ *n* **1** : a thick tangled mass of tropical vegetation; *also* : a tract overgrown with vegetation **2** : a place of ruthless struggle for survival
¹ju·nior \'jü-nyər\ *adj* **1** : YOUNGER **2** ♦ : lower in rank **3** : of or relating to juniors

♦ inferior, less, lesser, lower, minor, subordinate, under

²junior *n* **1** : a person who is younger or of lower rank than another **2** : a student in the next-to-last year before graduating
junior college *n* : a school that offers studies corresponding to those of the 1st two years of college
junior high school *n* : a school usu. including grades 7–9
junior varsity *n* : a team whose members lack the experience or qualifications required for the varsity
ju·ni·per \'jü-nə-pər\ *n* : any of numerous coniferous shrubs or trees with leaves like needles or scales and female cones like berries
¹junk \'jəŋk\ *n* **1** ♦ : old iron, glass, paper, or waste; *also* : discarded articles **2** : a shoddy product **3** *slang* : NARCOTICS; *esp* : HEROIN

♦ chaff, deadwood, dust, garbage, litter, refuse, riffraff, rubbish, scrap, trash, waste

²junk *vb* : to get rid of as worthless : DISCARD, SCRAP

♦ cast, discard, ditch, dump, fling, jettison, lose, reject, scrap, shed, shuck, slough, throw away, throw out, unload

³junk *n* : a ship of eastern Asia with a high stern and 4-cornered sails
junk·er \'jəŋ-kər\ *n* : something (as an old automobile) ready for scrapping
Jun·ker \'yu̇ŋ-kər\ *n* : a member of the Prussian landed aristocracy
jun·ket \'jəŋ-kət\ *n* **1** : a pudding of sweetened flavored milk set by rennet **2** ♦ : a pleasure trip or outing; *esp* : a trip made by an official at public expense ostensibly for public business

♦ excursion, jaunt, outing, sally

junk food *n* : food that is high in calories but low in nutritional content
junk·ie *also* **junky** \'jəŋ-kē\ *n, pl* **junkies** **1** *slang* : a narcotics peddler or addict **2** : one that derives inordinate pleasure from or is dependent on something ⟨sugar ∼⟩

junky *adj* ♦ : having the character of junk : constituting junk

♦ chaffy, empty, no-good, null, valueless, worthless

jun·ta \'hu̇n-tə, 'jən-, 'hən-\ *n* : a group of persons controlling a government esp. after a revolutionary seizure of power
Ju·pi·ter \'jü-pə-tər\ *n* : the largest of the planets and the one 5th in order of distance from the sun
Ju·ras·sic \ju̇-'ra-sik\ *adj* : of, relating to, or being the period of the Mesozoic era between the Triassic and the Cretaceous that is marked esp. by the presence of dinosaurs — **Jurassic** *n*
ju·rid·i·cal \ju̇-'ri-di-kəl\ *also* **ju·rid·ic** \-dik\ *adj* **1** : of or relating to the administration of justice **2** : LEGAL — **ju·rid·i·cal·ly** \-di-k(ə-)lē\ *adv*
ju·ris·dic·tion \ˌju̇r-əs-'dik-shən\ *n* **1** : the power, right, or authority to interpret and apply the law **2** ♦ : the authority of a sovereign power **3** : the limits or territory within which authority may be exercised — **ju·ris·dic·tion·al** \-shə-nəl\ *adj*

♦ administration, authority, government, regime, rule

ju·ris·pru·dence \-'prüd-ᵊns\ *n* **1** : a system of laws **2** : the science or philosophy of law
ju·rist \'ju̇r-ist\ *n* ♦ : one having a thorough knowledge of law; *esp* : JUDGE

♦ arbiter, arbitrator, judge, referee

ju·ris·tic \ju̇-'ris-tik\ *adj* **1** : of or relating to a jurist or jurisprudence **2** : of, relating to, or recognized in law
ju·ror \'ju̇r-ər, -ˌȯr\ *n* : a member of a jury
¹ju·ry \'ju̇r-ē\ *n, pl* **juries** **1** : a body of persons sworn to inquire into a matter submitted to them and to give their verdict **2** : a committee for judging and awarding prizes
²jury *adj* : improvised for temporary use esp. in an emergency ⟨a ∼ mast⟩
jury nullification *n* : the acquitting of a defendant by a jury in disregard of the judge's instructions and contrary to the jury's findings of fact
jury–rig \'ju̇r-ē-ˌrig\ *vb* : to construct or arrange in a makeshift fashion
¹just \'jəst\ *adj* **1** ♦ : having a basis in or conforming to fact or reason : REASONABLE ⟨∼ comment⟩ **2** ♦ : conforming to a standard of correctness ⟨∼ proportions⟩ **3** ♦ : morally or legally right ⟨a ∼ title⟩ **4** : being what is merited ⟨∼ punishment⟩ — **just·ly** *adv* — **just·ness** *n*

♦ [1] good, hard, informed, levelheaded, logical, rational, reasonable, reasoned, sensible, sober, solid, valid, well-founded ♦ [2] due, right **Ant** undeserved, undue, unjust, unwarranted ♦ [2] disinterested, dispassionate, equal, equitable, fair, impartial, nonpartisan, objective, square, unbiased, unprejudiced ♦ [3] decent, ethical, good, honest, honorable (*or* honourable), moral, principled, right, righteous, straight, upright, upstanding, virtuous

²just \'jəst, 'jist\ *adv* **1** ♦ : in a manner or measure or to a degree or number that strictly conforms to a fact or condition : EXACTLY ⟨∼ right⟩ **2** ♦ : very recently ⟨has ∼ left⟩ **3** ♦ : by a very small margin : BARELY ⟨∼ too late⟩ **4** : DIRECTLY ⟨∼ west of here⟩ **5** ♦ : to the exclusion of all else : ONLY ⟨∼ last year⟩ **6** : QUITE ⟨∼ wonderful⟩ **7** : POSSIBLY ⟨it ∼ might work⟩

♦ [1] accurately, exactly, precisely, right, sharp, squarely ♦ [2] freshly, late, lately, new, newly, now, only, recently ♦ [3] barely, hardly, marginally, scarcely, slightly **Ant** considerably, significantly, substantially, well ♦ [5] but, merely, only, simply

jus·tice \'jəs-təs\ *n* **1** : the administration of what is just (as by assigning merited rewards or punishments) **2** ♦ : a public official authorized to decide questions brought before a court : JUDGE **3** : the administration of law **4** : FAIRNESS; *also* : RIGHTEOUSNESS

♦ bench, court, judge, magistrate

justice of the peace : a local magistrate empowered chiefly to try minor cases, to administer oaths, and to perform marriages
jus·ti·fi·able *adj* ♦ : capable of being justified

♦ defensible, maintainable, supportable, sustainable, tenable

jus·ti·fi·ca·tion \ˌjəs-tə-fə-'kā-shən\ *n* ♦ : the act or an instance of justifying

♦ alibi, defense (*or* defence), excuse, plea, reason

jus·ti·fy \'jəs-tə-ˌfī\ *vb* **-fied; -fy·ing** **1** ♦ : to prove or show to be just, right, or reasonable **2** : to pronounce free from guilt or blame **3** : to adjust spaces in a line of printed text so the margins are even

♦ defend, maintain, support, uphold ♦ account, condone, excuse, explain, rationalize

jut \ˈjət\ *vb* **jut·ted; jut·ting** : to shoot out or forward : PROJECT, PROTRUDE

jute \ˈjüt\ *n* : a strong glossy fiber from either of two tropical plants used esp. for making sacks and twine

juv *abbr* juvenile

¹**ju·ve·nile** \ˈjü-və-ˌnīl, -nəl\ *adj* **1 ♦** : showing incomplete development **2 ♦** : of, relating to, or characteristic of children or young people

♦ [1] adolescent, immature, young, youthful ♦ [2] adolescent, babyish, childish, immature, infantile, kiddish

²**juvenile** *n* **1 ♦** : a young person; *esp* : one below the legally established age of adulthood **2** : a young animal (as a fish or a bird) or plant **3** : an actor or actress who plays youthful parts

♦ child, cub, kid, youngster, youth

juvenile delinquency *n* : violation of the law or antisocial behavior by a juvenile — **juvenile delinquent** *n*

jux·ta·pose \ˈjək-stə-ˌpōz\ *vb* **-posed; -pos·ing** : to place side by side — **jux·ta·po·si·tion** \ˌjək-stə-pə-ˈzi-shən\ *n*

JV *abbr* junior varsity

¹**k** \ˈkā\ *n, pl* **k's** *or* **ks** \ˈkāz\ **1** *often cap* : the 11th letter of the English alphabet **2** *cap* : STRIKEOUT

²**k** *abbr* **1** karat **2** kitchen **3** knit **4** kosher — often enclosed in a circle

¹**K** *abbr* Kelvin

²**K** *symbol* potassium

kab·ba·lah *also* **kab·ba·la** *or* **ka·ba·la** *or* **ca·ba·la** \kə-ˈbä-lə, ˈka-bə-lə\ *n, often cap* **1** : a medieval Jewish mysticism marked by belief in creation through emanation and a cipher method of interpreting Scripture **2** : esoteric or mysterious doctrine

kabob *var of* KEBAB

Ka·bu·ki \kə-ˈbü-kē\ *n* : traditional Japanese popular drama with highly stylized singing and dancing

kad·dish \ˈkä-dish\ *n, often cap* : a Jewish prayer recited in the daily synagogue ritual and by mourners at public services after the death of a close relative

kaf·fee·klatsch \ˈkȯ-fē-ˌklach, ˈkä-\ *n, often cap* : an informal social gathering for coffee and conversation

kai·ser \ˈkī-zər\ *n* : EMPEROR; *esp* : the ruler of Germany from 1871 to 1918

Ka·lash·ni·kov \kə-ˈlash-nə-ˌkȯf\ *n* : a Soviet-designed assault rifle

kale \ˈkāl\ *n* : a hardy cabbage with curled leaves that do not form a head

ka·lei·do·scope \kə-ˈlī-də-ˌskōp\ *n* : a tube containing loose bits of colored material (as glass) and two mirrors at one end that shows many different patterns as it is turned — **ka·lei·do·scop·ic** \-ˌlī-də-ˈskä-pik\ *adj* — **ka·lei·do·scop·i·cal·ly** \-pi-k(ə-)lē\ *adv*

ka·ma·ai·na \ˌkä-mə-ˈī-nə\ *n* : one who has lived in Hawaii for a long time

kame \ˈkām\ *n* : a short ridge or mound of material deposited by water from a melting glacier

ka·mi·ka·ze \ˌkä-mi-ˈkä-zē\ *n* : a member of a corps of Japanese pilots assigned to make a suicidal crash on a target; *also* : an airplane flown in such an attack

Kan *or* **Kans** *abbr* Kansas

kan·ga·roo \ˌkaŋ-gə-ˈrü\ *n, pl* **-roos** : any of various large leaping marsupial mammals of Australia and adjacent islands with powerful hind legs and a long thick tail

kangaroo court *n* : a court or an illegal self-appointed tribunal characterized by irresponsible, perverted, or irregular procedures

ka·o·lin \ˈkā-ə-lən\ *n* : a fine usu. white clay used in ceramics and refractories and for the treatment of diarrhea

ka·pok \ˈkā-ˌpäk\ *n* : silky fiber from the seeds of a tropical tree used esp. as a filling (as for life preservers)

Kap·o·si's sar·co·ma \ˈka-pə-sēz-sär-ˈkō-mə\ *n* : a neoplastic disease associated esp. with AIDS that affects esp. the skin and mucous membranes and is characterized usu. by the formation of pink to reddish-brown or bluish plaques

kap·pa \ˈka-pə\ *n* : the 10th letter of the Greek alphabet — K or κ

ka·put *also* **ka·putt** \kä-ˈpu̇t, kə-, -ˈpüt\ *adj* **1** : utterly defeated or destroyed **2** : unable to function : USELESS

kar·a·kul \ˈkar-ə-kəl\ *n* : the usu. curly glossy black coat of a very young lamb of a hardy Asian breed of sheep

kar·a·o·ke \ˌkar-ē-ˈō-kē\ *n* : a device that plays instrumental accompaniments for songs to which the user sings along

kar·at \ˈkar-ət\ *n* : a unit for expressing proportion of gold in an alloy equal to ¹/₂₄ part of pure gold

ka·ra·te \kə-ˈrä-tē\ *n* : an art of self-defense in which an attacker is disabled by crippling kicks and punches

kar·ma \ˈkär-mə\ *n* : the force generated by a person's actions held in Hinduism and Buddhism to perpetuate reincarnation and to determine the nature of the person's next existence — **kar·mic** \-mik\ *adj*

karst \ˈkärst\ *n* : an irregular limestone region with sinks, underground streams, and caverns

ka·ty·did \ˈkā-tē-ˌdid\ *n* : any of several large green tree-dwelling American grasshoppers with long antennae

kay·ak \ˈkī-ˌak\ *n* : a canoe that is made of a skin-covered frame with a small opening and propelled by a double-bladed paddle and that is associated esp. with Indigenous peoples of arctic regions; *also* : a similar portable boat — **kay·ak·er** *n*

kayo \(ˌ)kā-ˈō, ˈkā-ō\ *n* : KNOCKOUT — **kayo** *vb*

ka·zoo \kə-ˈzü\ *n, pl* **kazoos** : a toy musical instrument consisting of a tube with a membrane sealing one end and a side hole to sing or hum into

KB *abbr* kilobyte

kc *abbr* kilocycle

KC *abbr* **1** Kansas City **2** King's Counsel **3** Knights of Columbus

kc/s *abbr* kilocycles per second

KD *abbr* knocked down

ke·bab, ke·bob \kə-ˈbäb, ˈkā-ˌbäb\ *n* : cubes of meat cooked with vegetables usu. on a skewer

kedge \ˈkej\ *n* : a small anchor

¹**keel** \ˈkēl\ *n* **1** : the chief structural member of a ship running lengthwise along the center of its bottom **2** : something (as a bird's breastbone) like a ship's keel in form or use — **keeled** \ˈkēld\ *adj*

²**keel** *vb* : FAINT, SWOON — usu. used with *over*

keel·boat \ˈkēl-ˌbōt\ *n* : a shallow covered keeled riverboat for freight that is usu. rowed, poled, or towed

keel·haul \-ˌhȯl\ *vb* **1** : to haul under the keel of a ship as punishment **2 ♦** : to rebuke severely

♦ admonish, chide, lecture, rail (at *or* against), rate, rebuke, reprimand, scold

¹**keen** \ˈkēn\ *adj* **1 ♦** : having a fine edge or point : SHARP ⟨a ∼ knife⟩ **2 ♦** : affecting one as if by cutting ⟨a ∼ wind⟩ **3 ♦** : showing a quick and ardent responsiveness : ENTHUSIASTIC ⟨∼ about swimming⟩ **4 ♦** : mentally alert ⟨a ∼ mind⟩ **5 ♦** : extremely sensitive in perception : STRONG, ACUTE ⟨∼ eyesight⟩ **6** : unusually good : WONDERFUL, EXCELLENT — **keen·ly** *adv*

♦ [1] cutting, edgy, ground, sharp ♦ [2] biting, bitter, cutting, penetrating, piercing, raw, sharp ♦ [3] agog, anxious, ardent, athirst, avid, crazy, eager, enthusiastic, gung ho, hot, hungry, nuts, raring, solicitous, thirsty, voracious ♦ [4] alert, brainy, bright, brilliant, clever, intelligent, nimble, quick, quick-witted, sharp, smart ♦ [5] acute, delicate, perceptive, sensitive, sharp

²**keen** *n* **♦** : a lamentation for the dead uttered in a loud wailing voice or in a wordless cry

♦ groan, howl, lament, moan, plaint, wail

³**keen** *vb* **1** : to lament with a keen **2 ♦** : to make a sound suggestive of a keen

♦ bay, howl, wail, yowl

keen·ness *n* **♦** : the quality or state of being keen

♦ appetite, ardor, avidity, eagerness, enthusiasm, excitement, hunger, impatience, thirst ♦ acuity, acuteness, delicacy, sensitiveness, sensitivity

¹**keep** \'kēp\ *vb* **kept** \'kept\; **keep·ing** **1** ♦ : to be faithful to esp. by appropriate conduct : FULFILL, OBSERVE ⟨~ a promise⟩ ⟨~ a holiday⟩ **2** : GUARD ⟨~ us from harm⟩; *also* : to take care of ⟨~ a neighbor's children⟩ **3** : MAINTAIN ⟨~ silence⟩ **4** : to have in one's service or at one's disposal ⟨~ a horse⟩ **5** : to preserve a record in ⟨~ a diary⟩ **6** : to have in stock for sale **7** ♦ : to retain in one's possession ⟨~ what you find⟩ **8** : to carry on (as a business) : CONDUCT **9** : HOLD, DETAIN ⟨~ him in jail⟩ **10** : to refrain from revealing ⟨~ a secret⟩ **11** : to continue in good condition ⟨meat will ~ in a freezer⟩ **12** ♦ : to resist an impulse or desire : ABSTAIN, REFRAIN

♦ [1] answer, comply, fill, fulfill, meet, redeem, satisfy ♦ [1] celebrate, commemorate, observe *Ant* break, transgress, violate ♦ [7] hang on, hold, reserve, retain, withhold *Ant* hand over, relinquish, surrender ♦ *usu* **keep from** [12] abstain (from), forbear, forgo, refrain

²**keep** *n* **1** : FORTRESS **2** : the means or provisions by which one is kept — **for keeps** **1** : with the provision that one keep what one has won ⟨play marbles *for keeps*⟩ **2** : PERMANENTLY
keep–away \'kēp-ə-,wā\ *n* : a game in which players try to keep an object from one or more other players
keep·er *n* ♦ : one that keeps; *esp* : one who cares for another or another's property

♦ custodian, guard, guardian, lookout, picket, sentry, warden, warder, watch, watchman ♦ caretaker, custodian, janitor, warden, watchman

keep·ing *n* **1** : CONFORMITY ⟨in ~ with good taste⟩ **2** ♦ : the act of one that keeps : the care, possession, or observance of something

♦ care, custody, guardianship, safekeeping, trust, ward ♦ control, hands, possession

keeping room *n* : a common room used for multiple purposes
keep·sake \'kēp-,sāk\ *n* ♦ : something kept or given to be kept as a memento

♦ memento, memorial, monument, remembrance, souvenir, token

keep up *vb* **1** ♦ : to persist or persevere in **2** ♦ : to keep in an existing state : MAINTAIN **3** : to keep informed **4** ♦ : to continue without interruption

♦ [1, 4] abide, continue, endure, hold, last, persist, run on ♦ [2] conserve, maintain, preserve, save

keg \'keg\ *n* ♦ : a small cask or barrel

♦ barrel, cask, hogshead, pipe, puncheon

keg·ger \'ke-gər\ *n* : a party featuring one or more kegs of beer
keg·ler \'ke-glər\ *n* : ¹BOWLER
kelp \'kelp\ *n* : any of various coarse brown seaweeds; *also* : a mass of these or their ashes often used as fertilizer
kel·vin \'kel-vən\ *n* : a unit of temperature equal to ¹/₂₇₃.₁₆ of the Kelvin scale temperature of the triple point of water and equal to the Celsius degree
Kelvin *adj* : relating to, conforming to, or being a temperature scale according to which absolute zero is 0 K, the equivalent of −273.15°C
ken \'ken\ *n* **1** : range of vision : SIGHT **2** : range of understanding
ken·nel \'ken-ᵊl\ *n* : a shelter for a dog or cat; *also* : an establishment for the breeding or boarding of dogs or cats — **kennel** *vb*
ke·no \'kē-nō\ *n* : a game resembling bingo
ke·no·sis \kə-'nō-səs\ *n* : the relinquishment of divine attributes by Jesus Christ in becoming human — **ke·not·ic** \-'nä-tik\ *adj*
ken·te cloth \'ken-,tā-\ *n* : colorfully patterned cloth traditionally woven by hand in Ghana
Ken·tucky bluegrass \kən-'tə-kē-\ *n* : a valuable pasture and meadow grass of both Europe and America
Ken·yan \'ke-nyən, 'kē-\ *n* : a native or inhabitant of Kenya — **Kenyan** *adj*
Ke·ogh plan \'kē-(,)ō-\ *n* : an individual retirement account for the self-employed
ke·pi \'kā-pē, 'ke-\ *n* : a military cap with a round flat top and a visor
ker·a·tin \'ker-ət-ᵊn\ *n* : any of various sulfur-containing proteins that make up hair and horny tissues
kerb \'kərb\ *n, Brit* : CURB 3
ker·chief \'kər-chəf, -,chēf\ *n, pl* **kerchiefs** \-chəfs, -,chēfs\

also **kerchieves** \-,chēvz\ **1** ♦ : a square of cloth worn by women esp. as a head covering **2** : HANDKERCHIEF

♦ babushka, bandanna, do-rag, mantilla

kerf \'kərf\ *n* : a slit or notch made by a saw or cutting torch
ker·nel \'kərn-ᵊl\ *n* **1** : the inner softer part of a seed, fruit stone, or nut **2** : a whole seed of a cereal ⟨a ~ of corn⟩ **3** : a central or essential part : CORE
ker·o·sene *or* **ker·o·sine** \'ker-ə-,sēn, ,ker-ə-'sēn\ *n* : a flammable oil produced from petroleum and used for a fuel and as a solvent
kes·trel \'kes-trəl\ *n* : any of various small falcons that usu. hover in the air while searching for prey
ketch \'kech\ *n* : a large fore-and-aft rigged boat with two masts
ketch·up, catch·up \'ke-chəp, 'ka-\ *n* : a seasoned tomato puree
ket·tle \'ket-ᵊl\ *n* : a metallic vessel for boiling liquids
ket·tle·drum \-,drəm\ *n* : a brass, copper, or fiberglass drum with calfskin or plastic stretched across the top
¹**key** \'kē\ *n* **1** : a usu. metal instrument by which the bolt of a lock is turned; *also* : a device having the form or function of a key **2** : a means of gaining or preventing entrance, possession, or control **3** : EXPLANATION, SOLUTION **4** : one of the levers pressed by a finger in operating or playing an instrument **5** : a leading individual or principle **6** : a system of seven tones based on their relationship to a tonic; *also* : the tone or pitch of a voice **7** : a small switch for opening or closing an electric circuit ⟨a telegraph ~⟩
²**key** *vb* **1** : SECURE, FASTEN **2** : to regulate the musical pitch of **3** ♦ : to bring into harmony or conformity **4** : to make nervous — usu. used with *up*

♦ accommodate, conciliate, conform, coordinate, harmonize, reconcile

³**key** *adj* ♦ : marked by or indicative of significant worth or consequence ⟨~ issues⟩

♦ arch, cardinal, central, chief, dominant, first, foremost, grand, main, paramount, predominant, preeminent, premier, primary, principal, sovereign, supreme ♦ critical, crucial, pivotal, vital

⁴**key** *n* ♦ : a low island or reef (as off the southern coast of Florida)

♦ cay, island, isle

⁵**key** *n, slang* : a kilogram esp. of marijuana or heroin
key·board \-,bōrd\ *n* **1** : a row of keys (as on a piano) **2** : an assemblage of keys for operating a machine
key chain *n* : a device used to hold keys that usu. consists of a metal ring, a short chain, and sometimes a small decoration
key club *n* : a private club serving liquor and providing entertainment
key·hole \'kē-,hōl\ *n* : a hole for receiving a key
¹**key·note** \-,nōt\ *n* **1** : the first and harmonically fundamental tone of a scale **2** : the central fact, idea, or mood
²**keynote** *vb* **1** : to set the keynote of **2** : to deliver the major address (as at a convention) — **key·not·er** *n*
key·punch \'kē-,pənch\ *n* : a machine with a keyboard used to cut holes or notches in punch cards — **keypunch** *vb* — **key·punch·er** *n*
key ring *n* : a usu. metal ring used to hold keys; *also* : KEY CHAIN
key·stone \-,stōn\ *n* **1** : the wedge-shaped piece at the crown of an arch that locks the other pieces in place **2** ♦ : something on which associated things depend for support

♦ base, basis, bedrock, cornerstone, footing, foundation, ground, groundwork, underpinning

key·stroke \-,strōk\ *n* : an act or instance of depressing a key on a keyboard
key word *n* : a word that is a key; *esp, usu* **key·word** : a significant word from a title or document used esp. as an indication of the content
kg *abbr* kilogram
KGB *abbr* (Soviet) State Security Committee
kha·ki \'ka-kē, 'kä-\ *n* **1** : a light yellowish brown color **2** : a khaki-colored cloth; *also* : a military uniform of this cloth
khan \'kän, 'kan\ *n* : a Mongol leader; *esp* : a successor of Genghis Khan
khe·dive \kə-'dēv\ *n* : a ruler of Egypt from 1867 to 1914 governing as a viceroy of the sultan of Turkey
kHz *abbr* kilohertz
KIA *abbr* killed in action
kib·ble \'ki-bəl\ *vb* **kib·bled; kib·bling** : to grind coarsely — **kibble** *n*
kib·butz \ki-'bùts, -'büts\ *n, pl* **kib·but·zim** \-,bùt-'sēm, -,büt-\ : a communal farm or settlement in Israel
ki·bitz·er \'ki-bət-sər, kə-'bit-\ *n* ♦ : one who looks on and usu.

offers unwanted advice esp. at a card game — **kib·itz** \'ki-bəts\ *vb*

♦ busybody, interloper, intruder, meddler

ki·bosh \'kī-ˌbäsh\ *n* : something that serves as a check or stop ⟨put the ∼ on his plan⟩

¹**kick** \'kik\ *vb* **1** : to strike out or hit with the foot; *also* : to score by kicking a ball **2** ♦ : to object strongly **3** : to recoil when fired — **kick·er** *n*

♦ beef, bellyache, complain, fuss, gripe, grouse, growl, grumble, moan, object, squawk, wail, whine

²**kick** *n* **1** : a blow or thrust with the foot; *esp* : a propelling of a ball with the foot **2** : the recoil of a gun **3** ♦ : a feeling or expression of objection **4** ♦ : stimulating effect esp. of pleasure

♦ [3] challenge, complaint, demur, expostulation, fuss, objection, protest, question, remonstrance ♦ [4] bang, exhilaration, thrill, titillation

kick·back \'kik-ˌbak\ *n* **1** : a sharp violent reaction **2** : a secret return of a part of a sum received

kick back *vb* ♦ : to assume a relaxed position or attitude

♦ bask, loll, lounge, relax, repose, rest

kick·box·ing \'kik-ˌbäk-siŋ\ *n* : boxing in which boxers are permitted to kick with bare feet — **kick·box·er** \-sər\ *n*

kick in *vb* **1** ♦ : to give or supply in common with others : CONTRIBUTE **2** *slang* : DIE **3** : to begin operating or having an effect ⟨the caffeine started to *kick in*⟩

♦ chip in, contribute, pitch in

kick·off \'kik-ˌȯf\ *n* **1** : a kick that puts the ball in play (as in football) **2** : COMMENCEMENT

kick off *vb* **1** : to start or resume play with a placekick **2** : to begin proceedings ⟨*kick off* a campaign⟩ **3** *slang* : DIE

kick over *vb* : to begin or cause to begin to fire — used of an internal combustion engine

kick·shaw \'kik-ˌshȯ\ *n* **1** : DELICACY **2** : TRINKET

kick·stand \'kik-ˌstand\ *n* : a swiveling metal bar attached to a 2-wheeled vehicle for holding it up when not in use

kick–start \'kik-ˌstärt\ *vb* : JUMP-START

kicky \'ki-kē\ *adj* : providing a kick or thrill : EXCITING; *also* : excitingly fashionable

¹**kid** \'kid\ *n* **1** : a young goat **2** : the flesh, fur, or skin of a young goat; *also* : something made of kid **3** ♦ : a young person : CHILD, YOUNGSTER

♦ child, cub, juvenile, youngster, youth

²**kid** *vb* **kid·ded; kid·ding 1** ♦ : to deceive as a joke : FOOL **2** ♦ : to make fun of : TEASE — **kid·der** *n* — **kid·ding·ly** *adv*

♦ [1] banter, fool, fun, jest, jive, josh, joke, josh, quip, wisecrack ♦ [2] chaff, jive, josh, rally, razz, rib, ride, roast, tease

kid·dish *adj* ♦ : marked by or suggestive of immaturity and lack of poise

♦ adolescent, babyish, childish, immature, infantile, juvenile

kid·do \'ki-dō\ *n, pl* **kiddos 1** — used as a familiar form of address ⟨you're okay, ∼⟩ **2** ♦ : a young person who is between infancy and adulthood : CHILD, KID

♦ child, cub, juvenile, kid, moppet, whelp, youngster, youth

kid·nap \'kid-ˌnap\ *vb* **kid·napped** *also* **kid·naped** \-ˌnapt\; **kid·nap·ping** *also* **kid·nap·ing** \-ˌna-piŋ\ : to hold or carry a person away by unlawful force or by fraud and against one's will — **kid·nap·per** *also* **kid·nap·er** \-ˌna-pər\ *n*

kid·ney \'kid-nē\ *n, pl* **kidneys** : either of a pair of organs lying near the backbone that excrete waste products of the body in the form of urine

kidney bean *n* **1** : an edible seed of the common cultivated bean; *esp* : one that is large and dark red **2** : a plant bearing kidney beans

kid·skin \'kid-ˌskin\ *n* : the skin of a young goat used for leather

kiel·ba·sa \kēl-'bä-sə, kil-\ *n, pl* **-basas** *also* **-ba·sy** \-'bä-sē\ : a smoked sausage of Polish origin

¹**kill** \'kil\ *vb* **1** ♦ : to deprive of life **2** : to put an end to ⟨∼ competition⟩; *also* : DEFEAT ⟨∼ a proposed amendment⟩ **3** : USE UP ⟨∼ time⟩ **4** : to mark for omission — **kill·er** *n*

♦ destroy, dispatch, do in, fell, slay *Ant* animate

²**kill** *n* **1** : an act of killing **2** : an animal or animals killed (as in a hunt); *also* : an aircraft, ship, or vehicle destroyed by military action

kill·deer \'kil-ˌdir\ *n, pl* **killdeers** *or* **killdeer** : an American plover with a plaintive penetrating cry

killer app \-'ap\ *n* : a component (as a computer application) that in itself makes something worth having or using

killer bee *n* : AFRICANIZED BEE

killer whale *n* : a small gregarious black and white flesh-eating whale with a white oval patch behind each eye

kill·ing *n* : a sudden notable gain or profit

killing field *n* : a scene of mass killing

kill·joy \'kil-ˌjȯi\ *n* : one who spoils the pleasures of others

kiln \'kil, 'kiln\ *n* : a heated enclosure (as an oven) for processing a substance by burning, firing, or drying — **kiln** *vb*

ki·lo \'kē-lō\ *n, pl* **kilos** : KILOGRAM

ki·lo·byte \'ki-lə-ˌbīt, 'kē-\ *n* : 1024 bytes

kilo·cy·cle \'ki-lə-ˌsī-kəl\ *n* : KILOHERTZ

ki·lo·gram \'kē-lə-ˌgram, 'ki-\ *n* **1** : the basic metric unit of mass that is nearly equal to the mass of 1000 cubic centimeters of water at its maximum density **2** : the weight of a kilogram mass under earth's gravity

ki·lo·hertz \'ki-lə-ˌhərts, 'kē-, -ˌherts\ *n* : 1000 hertz

kilo·li·ter \'ki-lə-ˌlē-tər\ *n* : a metric unit of capacity equal to 1000 liters

ki·lo·me·ter \ki-'lä-mə-tər, 'ki-lə-ˌmē-\ *or Can and Brit* **ki·lo·me·tre** *n* : a metric unit of length equal to 1000 meters

ki·lo·ton \'ki-lə-ˌtən, 'kē-lō-\ *n* **1** : 1000 tons **2** : an explosive force equivalent to that of 1000 tons of TNT

ki·lo·volt \-ˌvōlt\ *n* : 1000 volts

kilo·watt \'ki-lə-ˌwät\ *n* : 1000 watts

kilowatt–hour *n* : a unit of energy equal to that expended by one kilowatt in one hour

kilt \'kilt\ *n* : a knee-length pleated skirt usu. of tartan worn by men in Scotland

kil·ter \'kil-tər\ *n* ♦ : proper condition ⟨out of ∼⟩

♦ condition, fettle, form, order, repair, shape, trim

ki·mo·no \kə-'mō-nə\ *n, pl* **-nos 1** : a loose robe with wide sleeves traditionally worn with a wide sash as an outer garment by the Japanese **2** : a loose dressing gown or jacket

kin \'kin\ *n* **1** ♦ : an individual's relatives **2** ♦ : a person connected with another by blood or marriage : KINSMAN

♦ [1] blood, clan, family, folks, house, kindred, kinfolk, line, lineage, people, race, stock, tribe ♦ [2] kinsman, relation, relative

ki·na·ra \kē-'nä-rə\ *n* : a candelabra with seven candlesticks used during Kwanzaa

¹**kind** \'kīnd\ *n* **1** : essential quality or character **2** ♦ : a group united by common traits or interests; *also* : VARIETY **3** : goods or commodities as distinguished from money

♦ breed, class, description, feather, ilk, like, manner, nature, order, sort, species, type, variety ♦ bracket, category, class, division, family, grade, group, set

²**kind** *adj* **1** ♦ : of a sympathetic, forbearing, or pleasant nature **2** ♦ : arising from sympathy or forbearance ⟨∼ deeds⟩

♦ [1] beneficent, benevolent, compassionate, good-hearted, humane, kindly, sympathetic, tender, tenderhearted, warmhearted ♦ [2] attentive, considerate, solicitous, thoughtful

kin·der·gar·ten \'kin-dər-ˌgärt-ᵊn\ *n* : a school or class for children usu. from four to six years old

kin·der·gart·ner \-ˌgärt-nər\ *n* **1** : a kindergarten pupil **2** : a kindergarten teacher

kind·heart·ed \ˌkīnd-'här-təd\ *adj* : marked by a sympathetic nature

kin·dle \'kind-ᵊl\ *vb* **kin·dled; kin·dling 1** ♦ : to set on fire : start burning **2** : to stir up : AROUSE **3** : ILLUMINATE, GLOW

♦ burn, fire, ignite, inflame, light

kind·li·ness *n* **1** ♦ : the quality or state of being kindly **2** : a kindly deed

♦ amity, benevolence, cordiality, fellowship, friendliness, friendship, goodwill ♦ charity, commiseration, compassion, feeling, heart, humanity, kindness, mercy, pity, sympathy

kin·dling \'kind-liŋ, 'kin-lən\ *n* : easily combustible material for starting a fire

¹**kind·ly** \'kīnd-lē\ *adj* **kind·li·er; -est 1** : of an agreeable or beneficial nature **2** ♦ : of a sympathetic or generous nature

♦ beneficent, benevolent, compassionate, good-hearted, humane, kind, sympathetic, tender, tenderhearted, warmhearted

²**kindly** *adv* **1** : READILY ⟨does not take ∼ to criticism⟩ **2** : SYMPATHETICALLY **3** ♦ : in a gracious manner : COURTEOUSLY

♦ courteously, nicely, thoughtfully, well

kind·ness *n* **1** ♦ : a kind deed **2** ♦ : the quality or state of being kind

♦ [1] boon, courtesy, favor (*or* favour), grace, indulgence, mercy, service, turn ♦ [2] charity, commiseration, compassion, feeling, heart, humanity, kindliness, mercy, pity, sympathy

kind of *adv* ♦ : to a moderate degree ⟨it's *kind of* late to begin⟩

♦ enough, fairly, moderately, pretty, quite, rather, somewhat, sort of, so-so

¹kin·dred \'kin-drəd\ *n* **1** ♦ : a group of related individuals **2** : one's relatives

♦ blood, clan, family, folks, house, kin, kinfolk, line, lineage, people, race, stock, tribe

²kindred *adj* ♦ : of a like nature or character

♦ akin, related

kine \'kīn\ *archaic pl of* COW

ki·ne·mat·ics \ˌki-nə-'ma-tiks\ *n* : a science that deals with motion apart from considerations of mass and force — **ki·ne·mat·ic** \-tik\ *or* **ki·ne·mat·i·cal** \-ti-kəl\ *adj*

kin·es·the·sia \ˌki-nəs-'thē-zhə, -zhē-ə\ *or* **kin·es·the·sis** \-'thē-səs\ *n, pl* **-the·sias** *or* **-the·ses** \-ˌsēz\ : a sense that perceives bodily movement, position, and weight and is mediated by nervous receptors in tendons, muscles, and joints; *also* : sensory experience derived from this sense — **kin·es·thet·ic** \-'the-tik\ *adj*

ki·net·ic \kə-'ne-tik\ *adj* : of or relating to the motion of material bodies and the forces and energy (**kinetic energy**) associated with them

ki·net·ics \-tiks\ *n sing or pl* : a science that deals with the effects of forces upon the motions of material bodies or with changes in a physical or chemical system

kin·folk \'kin-ˌfōk\ *or* **kinfolks** *n pl* ♦ : persons connected with each other by blood or affinity : RELATIVES

♦ blood, clan, family, folks, house, kin, kindred, line, lineage, people, race, stock, tribe

king \'kiŋ\ *n* **1** : a male monarch **2** ♦ : a chief among competitors ⟨home-run ∼⟩ **3** : the principal piece in the game of chess **4** : a playing card bearing the figure of a king **5** : a checker that has been crowned — **king·less** *adj* — **king·ship** *n*

♦ baron, czar, magnate, mogul, prince, tycoon

king crab **1** : HORSESHOE CRAB **2** : a large crab of the No. Pacific caught commercially for food

king·dom \'kiŋ-dəm\ *n* **1** : a country whose head is a king or queen **2** : a realm or region in which something or someone is dominant ⟨a cattle ∼⟩ **3** : one of the three primary divisions of lifeless material, plants, and animals into which natural objects are grouped; *also* : a biological category that ranks above the phylum

king·fish·er \-ˌfi-shər\ *n* : any of numerous usu. bright-colored crested birds that feed chiefly on fish

king·ly *adj* **1** : of, relating to, or befitting a king **2** ♦ : of, relating to, suggestive of a monarch or monarchy

♦ monarchical, princely, queenly, regal, royal

king·pin \'kiŋ-ˌpin\ *n* **1** : HEADPIN **2** ♦ : the leader in a group or undertaking

♦ boss, captain, chief, foreman, head, headman, helmsman, leader, taskmaster

Kings *n* : either of two books of Jewish and Christian Scripture

king–size \'kiŋ-ˌsīz\ *or* **king–sized** \-ˌsīzd\ *adj* **1** : longer than the regular or standard size **2** : unusually large **3** : having dimensions of about 76 by 80 inches (1.9 by 2.0 meters) ⟨a ∼ bed⟩; *also* : of a size that fits a king-size bed

kink \'kiŋk\ *n* **1** : a short tight twist or curl **2** : a mental peculiarity : QUIRK **3** : CRAMP ⟨a ∼ in the back⟩ **4** : an imperfection likely to cause difficulties in operation

kinky *adj* ♦ : strikingly out of the ordinary

♦ bizarre, curious, far-out, funny, odd, outlandish, outré, peculiar, quaint, quirky, remarkable, screwy, strange, wacky, weird, wild

kin·ship \'kin-ˌship\ *n* ♦ : the quality or state of being kin : RELATIONSHIP

♦ association, bearing, connection, liaison, linkage, relation, relationship

kins·man \'kinz-mən\ *n* ♦ : a person connected with another by blood or marriage : RELATIVE; *esp* : a male relative

♦ kin, relation, relative

kins·wom·an \-ˌwu̇-mən\ *n* : a female relative

ki·osk \'kē-ˌäsk\ *n* **1** : a small structure with one or more open sides **2** : a stand-alone device providing information and services on a computer screen

Ki·o·wa \'kī-ə-ˌwȯ, -ˌwä, -ˌwā\ *n, pl* **Kiowa** *or* **Kiowas** : a member of an Indigenous people of the southern Great Plains; *also* : the language of the Kiowa

kip·per \'ki-pər\ *n* : a fish (as a herring) preserved by salting and drying or smoking — **kipper** *vb*

kirk \'kərk, 'kirk\ *n, chiefly Scot* : CHURCH

kir·tle \'kərt-ᵊl\ *n* : a long gown or dress worn by women

kis·met \'kiz-ˌmet, -mət\ *n, often cap* : FATE

¹kiss \'kis\ *vb* **1** : to touch or caress with the lips as a mark of affection or greeting **2** ♦ : to touch gently or lightly

♦ brush, graze, nick, shave, skim

²kiss *n* **1** : a caress with the lips **2** : a gentle touch or contact **3** : a bite-size candy

kiss·er \'ki-sər\ *n* **1** : one that kisses **2** *slang* : MOUTH **3** *slang* : FACE

kit \'kit\ *n* **1** : a set of articles for personal use; *also* : a set of tools or implements or of parts to be assembled **2** : a container (as a case) for a kit

kitch·en \'ki-chən\ *n* **1** : a room with cooking facilities **2** : the staff that prepares, cooks, and serves food

kitch·en·ette \ˌki-chə-'net\ *n* : a small kitchen or an alcove containing cooking facilities

kitchen police *n* **1** : KP **2** : the work of KPs

kitch·en·ware \'ki-chən-ˌwar\ *n* : utensils and appliances for kitchen use

kite \'kīt\ *n* **1** : any of various long-winged hawks often with deeply forked tails **2** : a light frame covered with paper or cloth and designed to be flown in the air at the end of a long string

kith \'kith\ *n* : familiar friends, neighbors, or relatives ⟨∼ and kin⟩

kitsch \'kich\ *n* : something often of poor quality that appeals to popular or lowbrow taste — **kitschy** *adj*

kit·ten \'kit-ᵊn\ *n* : a young cat

kit·ten·ish *adj* ♦ : resembling or suggestive of a kitten; *esp* : coyly playful

♦ coquettish, coy, demure

¹kit·ty \'ki-tē\ *n, pl* **kitties** ♦ : a carnivorous mammal long domesticated as a pet and for catching rats and mice : CAT; *esp* : KITTEN

♦ cat, feline, puss

²kitty *n, pl* **kitties** ♦ : a fund in a poker game made up of contributions from each pot; *also* : POOL

♦ account, budget, deposit, fund, nest egg, pool

kit·ty–cor·ner *also* **cat·ty–cor·ner** *or* **cat·er·cor·ner** \'ki-tē-ˌkȯr-nər, 'ka-tə-\ *or* **kit·ty–cor·nered** *or* **cat·ty–cor·nered** *or* **cat·er·cornered** \-nərd\ *adv or adj* : in a diagonal or oblique position

ki·wi \'kē-(ˌ)wē\ *n* **1** : any of a small genus of flightless New Zealand birds **2** : KIWIFRUIT

ki·wi·fruit \-ˌfrüt\ *n* : a brownish hairy egg-shaped fruit of a subtropical vine that has sweet bright green flesh and small edible black seeds

KJV *abbr* King James Version

KKK *abbr* Ku Klux Klan

kl *abbr* kiloliter

klatch *or* **klatsch** \'klach\ *n* : a gathering marked by informal conversation

klep·toc·ra·cy \klep-'tä-krə-sē\ *n, pl* **-cies** : government by those who seek chiefly status and personal gain at the expense of the governed

klep·to·ma·nia \ˌklep-tə-'mā-nē-ə\ *n* : a persistent neurotic impulse to steal esp. without economic motive — **klep·to·ma·ni·ac** \-nē-ˌak\ *n*

klieg light *or* **kleig light** \'klēg-\ *n* : a very bright lamp used in making motion pictures

klutz \'kləts\ *n* : a clumsy person — **klutzy** *adj*

km *abbr* kilometer

kn *abbr* knot

knack \'nak\ *n* **1** : a clever way of doing something **2** ♦ : natural aptitude

♦ aptitude, endowment, faculty, flair, genius, gift, talent

knap·sack \'nap-ˌsak\ *n* : a bag (as of canvas) strapped on the back and used esp. for carrying supplies

knave \'nāv\ *n* **1** ♦ : a tricky deceitful fellow : ROGUE **2** : JACK 6

♦ beast, devil, evildoer, fiend, no-good, reprobate, rogue, varlet, villain, wretch

knav·ery \'nā-və-rē\ *n* ♦ : the character or actions of a rascal; *also* : a roguish or mischievous act

♦ devilishness, impishness, mischief, mischievousness, rascality, shenanigans, waggery, wickedness

knav·ish \'nā-vish\ *adj* ♦ : of, relating to, or characteristic of a knave

♦ devilish, impish, mischievous, rascally, roguish, sly, waggish, wicked

knead \'nēd\ *vb* : to work and press into a mass with the hands; *also* : MASSAGE — **knead·er** *n*

knee \'nē\ *n* : the joint in the middle part of the leg — **kneed** \'nēd\ *adj*

knee·cap \'nē-ˌkap\ *n* : a thick flat triangular movable bone forming the front of the knee

knee·hole \-ˌhōl\ *n* : a space (as under a desk) for the knees

knee–jerk \'nē-ˌjərk\ *adj* : readily predictable ⟨a ∼ reaction⟩

kneel \'nēl\ *vb* **knelt** \'nelt\ *or* **kneeled; kneel·ing** : to bend the knee : fall or rest on the knees

¹**knell** \'nel\ *vb* **1** ♦ : to ring esp. for a death or disaster **2** : to summon, announce, or proclaim by a knell

♦ chime, peal, ring, toll

²**knell** *n* **1** : a stroke of a bell esp. when tolled (as for a funeral) **2** : an indication of the end or failure of something

knew *past of* KNOW

knick·ers \'ni-kərz\ *n pl* : loose-fitting short pants gathered at the knee

knick·knack \'nik-ˌnak\ *n* ♦ : a small trivial article intended for ornament

♦ bauble, curiosity, gewgaw, novelty, tchotchke, trinket

¹**knife** \'nīf\ *n, pl* **knives** \'nīvz\ **1** : a cutting instrument consisting of a sharp blade fastened to a handle **2** : a sharp cutting tool in a machine

²**knife** *vb* **knifed; knif·ing** : to stab, slash, or wound with a knife

¹**knight** \'nīt\ *n* **1** : a mounted warrior of feudal times serving a king **2** : a man honored by a sovereign for merit and in Great Britain ranking below a baronet **3** : a man devoted to the service of a lady **4** : a member of an order or society **5** : a chess piece having an L-shaped move — **knight·ly** *adj*

²**knight** *vb* : to make a knight of

knight·hood \'nīt-ˌhud\ *n* **1** : the rank, dignity, or profession of a knight **2** : CHIVALRY **3** : knights as a class or body

knish \kə-'nish\ *n* : a small round or square of dough stuffed with a filling (as of meat or fruit) and baked or fried

¹**knit** \'nit\ *vb* **knit** *or* **knit·ted; knit·ting** **1** : to link firmly or closely **2** : WRINKLE ⟨∼ her brows⟩ **3** : to form a fabric by interlacing yarn or thread in connected loops with needles **4** : to grow together — **knit·ter** *n*

²**knit** *n* **1** : a basic knitting stitch **2** : a knitted garment or fabric

knit·wear \-ˌwar\ *n* : knitted clothing

knob \'näb\ *n* **1** : a rounded protuberance; *also* : a small rounded ornament or handle **2** : a rounded usu. isolated hill — **knobbed** \'näbd\ *adj* — **knob·by** \'nä-bē\ *adj*

¹**knock** \'näk\ *vb* **1** : to strike with a sharp blow **2** ♦ : to collide with something : BUMP **3** : to make a pounding noise; *esp* : to have engine knock **4** ♦ : to find fault with **5** ♦ : to move about without a fixed course, aim, or goal

♦ [2] bang, bash, bump, collide, crash, hit, impact, ram, slam, smash, strike, swipe, thud ♦ [4] blame, censure, condemn, criticize, denounce, fault, pan, reprehend ♦ [5] gad, gallivant, maunder, meander, mope, ramble, range, roam, rove, traipse, wander

²**knock** *n* **1** : a sharp blow **2** : a pounding noise; *esp* : one caused by abnormal ignition in an automobile engine **3** ♦ : a severe misfortune or hardship

♦ adversity, misadventure, mischance, misfortune, mishap

knock·down \'näk-ˌdaun\ *n* **1** : the action of knocking down **2** : something (as a blow) that knocks down **3** : something that can be easily assembled or disassembled

knock down *vb* **1** ♦ : to strike to the ground with or as if with a sharp blow **2** ♦ : to take apart : DISASSEMBLE **3** : to receive as income or salary : EARN **4** : to make a reduction in

♦ [1] bowl, down, drop, fell, floor, level ♦ [2] disassemble, dismantle, strike, take down

knock·er \'nä-kər\ *n* : one that knocks; *esp* : a device hinged to a door for use in knocking

knock–knee \'näk-ˌnē\ *n* : a condition in which the legs curve inward at the knees — **knock–kneed** \-ˌnēd\ *adj*

knock·off \'näk-ˌof\ *n* : a copy or imitation of someone or something popular

knock off *vb* **1** ♦ : to stop doing something **2** : to do quickly, carelessly, or routinely **3** : to deduct from a price **4** : KILL **5** : ROB **6** : COPY, IMITATE

♦ break, break off, cease, cut, desist, discontinue, drop, end, halt, layoff, leave off, quit, shut off, stop

knock·out \'näk-ˌaut\ *n* **1** : a blow that fells and immobilizes an opponent (as in boxing) **2** ♦ : something sensationally striking or attractive **3** ♦ : the act of knocking out; *also* : the condition of being knocked out

♦ [2] beauty, dream, enchantress, fox, goddess, queen ♦ [2] beauty, crackerjack, dandy, jim-dandy, pip ♦ [3] blackout, faint, swoon

knock out *vb* **1** : to defeat by a knockout **2** : to make unconscious or inoperative **3** : to tire out : EXHAUST

knock·wurst *also* **knack·wurst** \'näk-ˌwərst, -ˌvurst\ *n* : a short thick heavily seasoned sausage

knoll \'nōl\ *n* : a small round hill

¹**knot** \'nät\ *n* **1** : an interlacing (as of string) forming a lump or knob and often used for fastening or tying together **2** ♦ : something hard to solve : PROBLEM **3** ♦ : a bond of union; *esp* : the marriage bond **4** ♦ : a protuberant lump or swelling in tissue **5** : a rounded cross-grained area in lumber that is a section through the junction of a tree branch with the trunk; *also* : the woody tissue forming this junction in a tree **6** : a cluster of persons or things : GROUP **7** : an ornamental bow of ribbon **8** : one nautical mile per hour; *also* : one nautical mile

♦ [2] case, matter, problem, trouble ♦ [3] bond, cement, ligature, link, tie ♦ [4] bump, lump, nodule, swelling

²**knot** *vb* **knot·ted; knot·ting** **1** : to tie in or with a knot **2** ♦ : to unite closely or intricately : ENTANGLE

♦ entangle, interlace, intertwine, interweave, snarl, tangle

knot·hole \-ˌhōl\ *n* : a hole in a board or tree trunk where a knot has come out

knot·ty *adj* ♦ : marked by or full of knots; *esp* : so full of difficulties and complications as to be likely to defy solution

♦ complex, complicated, convoluted, elaborate, intricate, involved, sophisticated ♦ catchy, delicate, difficult, problematic, spiny, thorny, ticklish, touchy, tough, tricky

knout \'naut, 'nüt\ *n* : a whip used for flogging

know \'nō\ *vb* **knew** \'nü, 'nyü\; **known** \'nōn\; **know·ing** **1** ♦ : to perceive directly : have understanding or direct cognition of; *also* : to recognize the nature of **2** : to be acquainted or familiar with **3** ♦ : to be aware of the truth of **4** : to have a practical understanding of — **know·able** *adj* — **know·er** *n* — **in the know** : possessing confidential information

♦ [1] endure, experience, feel, have, see, suffer, sustain, taste, undergo ♦ [4] comprehend, grasp, understand

know–how \'nō-ˌhau\ *n* ♦ : knowledge of how to do something smoothly and efficiently

♦ experience, expertise, proficiency, savvy

knowing *adj* **1** : having or reflecting knowledge, intelligence, or information **2** ♦ : shrewdly and keenly alert **3** : DELIBERATE, INTENTIONAL

♦ astute, canny, hardheaded, sharp, shrewd, smart

know·ing·ly *adv* ♦ : in a knowing manner; *esp* : with awareness, deliberateness, or intention

♦ consciously, deliberately, intentionally, purposely, willfully

knowl·edge \'nä-lij\ *n* **1** : understanding gained by actual experience ⟨a ∼ of carpentry⟩ **2** : range of information ⟨to the best of my ∼⟩ **3** : clear perception of truth **4** ♦ : something learned and kept in the mind **5** ♦ : acquaintance with or understanding of a science, art, or technique

♦ [4] intelligence, lore, science, wisdom ♦ [5] education, erudition, learning, scholarship, science

knowl·edge·able \'nä-li-jə-bəl\ *adj* ♦ : having or showing knowledge or intelligence

♦ abreast, conversant, familiar, informed, up, up-to-date, versed ♦ educated, erudite, learned, literate, scholarly, well-read

know–noth·ing \'nō-ˌnə-thiŋ\ *n* ♦ : an utterly ignorant person : IGNORAMUS

♦ blockhead, dope, dummy, idiot, imbecile, jackass, moron, numskull

knuck·le \'nə-kəl\ *n* : the rounded knob at a joint and esp. at a finger joint

knuckle down *vb* : to apply oneself earnestly

knuckle under *vb* ♦ : to yield under insistence or entreaty : SUBMIT, SURRENDER

♦ blink, bow, budge, capitulate, concede, give in, quit, submit, succumb, surrender, yield

knurl \'nərl\ *n* **1** : KNOB **2** : one of a series of small ridges on a metal surface to aid in gripping — **knurled** \'nərld\ *adj* — **knurly** *adj*

¹KO \(ˌ)kā-'ō, 'kā-ō\ *n* : KNOCKOUT

²KO *vb* **KO'd; KO'·ing** : to knock out in boxing

ko·a·la \kō-'ä-lə\ *n* : a gray furry Australian marsupial that has large hairy ears and feeds on eucalyptus leaves

K of C *abbr* Knights of Columbus

kohl·ra·bi \kōl-'rä-bē\ *n, pl* **-bies** : a cabbage that forms no head but has a swollen fleshy edible stem

koi \'kȯi\ *n, pl* **koi** : a carp bred for large size and a variety of colors and often stocked in ornamental ponds

ko·lin·sky \kə-'lin-skē\ *n, pl* **-skies** : the fur of various Asian minks

Ko·mo·do dragon \kə-'mō-dō-\ *n* : a carnivorous lizard of Indonesia that is the largest of all known lizards

kook \'kük\ *n* ♦ : one whose ideas or actions are eccentric, fantastic, or crazy : SCREWBALL

♦ character, crank, eccentric, nut, oddball, screwball, weirdo

kooky *also* **kook·ie** \'kü-kē\ *adj* **kook·i·er; -est** ♦ : having the characteristics of a kook — **kook·i·ness** *n*

♦ absurd, cuckoo, fatuous, foolish, nonsensical, nutty, senseless, silly, stupid

Koo·te·nai *or* **Ku·te·nai** \'kü-tə-ˌnā\ *n, pl* **-nai** *or* **-nais** : a member of an Indigenous people of the Rocky Mountains in both the U.S. and Canada; *also* : their language

ko·ra \'kȯr-ə\ *n* : a 21-stringed African musical instrument

Ko·ran *or* **Qur·an** *also* **Qur·'an** \kə-'ran, -'rän\ *n* : a sacred book of Islam that contains revelations made to Muhammad by Allah

Ko·re·an \kə-'rē-ən\ *n* : a native or inhabitant of Korea — **Korean** *adj*

ko·sher \'kō-shər\ *adj* **1** : ritually fit for use according to Jewish law **2** : selling or serving kosher food

kow·tow \kaü-'taü, 'kaü-ˌtaü\ *vb* **1** ♦ : to show obsequious deference **2** : to kneel and touch the forehead to the ground as a sign of homage or deep respect

♦ fawn, fuss, toady

KP \ˌkā-'pē\ *n* **1** : an enlisted person detailed to help the cooks in a military mess **2** : the work of KPs

kph *abbr* kilometers per hour

Kr *symbol* krypton

kraal \'kräl, 'krȯl\ *n* **1** : a native village in southern Africa **2** : an enclosure for domestic animals in southern Africa

kraut \'kraüt\ *n* : SAUERKRAUT

Krem·lin \'krem-lən\ *n* : the Russian government

Krem·lin·ol·o·gist \ˌkrem-lə-'nä-lə-jist\ *n* : a specialist in the policies and practices of the former Soviet government

Kru·ger·rand \'krü-gər-ˌrand, -ˌränd\ *n* : a 1-ounce gold coin of the Republic of South Africa

kryp·ton \'krip-ˌtän\ *n* : a gaseous chemical element used esp. in electric lamps

KS *abbr* Kansas

kt *abbr* **1** karat **2** knight

ku·do \'kü-dō, 'kyü-\ *n, pl* **kudos 1** : AWARD, HONOR **2** : COMPLIMENT, PRAISE

ku·dos \'kü-ˌdäs, 'kyü-\ *n* : fame and renown resulting from achievement

kud·zu \'kud-zü, 'kəd-\ *n* : a fast-growing weedy leguminous vine used for forage and erosion control

ku·lak \kü-'lak, kyü-, -'läk\ *n* **1** : a wealthy peasant farmer in 19th century Russia **2** : a farmer characterized by Communists as too wealthy

kum·quat \'kəm-ˌkwät\ *n* : any of several small citrus fruits with sweet spongy rind and acid pulp

kung fu \ˌkəŋ-'fü, ˌkuŋ-\ *n* : a Chinese art of self-defense resembling karate

kung pao \ˌkəŋ-'paü, 'kuŋ-, 'kuŋ-\ *adj* : being stir-fried or deep-fried and served in a spicy hot sauce usu. with peanuts

kur·ta \'kər-tə\ *n* : a long loose-fitting collarless shirt

ku·rus \kə-'rüsh\ *n, pl* **kurus** : a Turkish piaster equal to ¹/₁₀₀ lira

Ku·waiti \kü-'wā-tē\ *n* : a native or inhabitant of Kuwait — **Kuwaiti** *adj*

kV *abbr* kilovolt

kvell \'kvel\ *vb* : to be extraordinarily proud

kvetch \'kvech, 'kfech\ *vb* : to complain habitually — **kvetch** *n*

kW *abbr* kilowatt

Kwan·zaa, Kwan·za \'kwän-zə\ *n* : an African American cultural festival held from December 26 to January 1

kwash·i·or·kor \ˌkwä-shē-'ȯr-kȯr, -ȯr-'kȯr\ *n* : a disease of young children caused by deficient intake of protein

kWh *abbr* kilowatt-hour

Ky *or* **KY** *abbr* Kentucky

¹l \'el\ *n, pl* **l's** *or* **ls** \'elz\ *often cap* : the 12th letter of the English alphabet

²l *abbr, often cap* **1** lake **2** large **3** left **4** pound **5** line **6** liter

¹La *abbr* Louisiana

²La *symbol* lanthanum

LA *abbr* **1** law agent **2** Los Angeles **3** Louisiana

lab \'lab\ *n* : LABORATORY

Lab *n* : LABRADOR RETRIEVER

¹la·bel \'lā-bəl\ *n* **1** ♦ : a slip attached to something for identification or description **2** : a descriptive or identifying word or phrase **3** : BRAND 3

♦ marker, tag, ticket

²label *vb* **-beled** *or* **-belled; -bel·ing** *or* **-bel·ling 1** ♦ : to affix a label to **2** ♦ : to describe or name with a label

♦ [1] mark, tag, ticket ♦ [2] baptize, call, christen, denominate, designate, dub, entitle, name, style, term, title

la·bi·al \'lā-bē-əl\ *adj* : of, relating to, or situated near the lips or labia

la·bia ma·jo·ra \'lā-bē-ə-mə-'jȯr-ə\ *n pl* : the outer fatty folds of the vulva

labia mi·no·ra \-mə-'nȯr-ə\ *n pl* : the inner highly vascular folds of the vulva

la·bile \'lā-ˌbī(-ə)l, -bəl\ *adj* **1** : UNSTABLE **2** : ADAPTABLE

la·bi·um \'lā-bē-əm\ *n, pl* **la·bia** \-ə\ : any of the folds at the margin of the vulva

¹la·bor *or Can and Brit* **la·bour** \'lā-bər\ *n* **1** ♦ : physical or mental effort; *also* : human activity that provides the goods or services in an economy **2** ♦ : the physical efforts of giving birth; *also* : the period of such labor **3** ♦ : an act or process requiring labor **4** : those who do manual labor or work for wages; *also* : labor unions or their officials

♦ [1] effort, exertion, expenditure, pains, sweat, trouble, while, work ♦ [2] childbirth, delivery ♦ [3] drudgery, grind, sweat, toil, travail

²labor *or Can and Brit* **labour** *vb* **1** ♦ : to exert oneself physically or mentally esp. with painful or strenuous effort : WORK **2** : to move with great effort **3** : to be in the labor of giving birth **4** : to suffer from some disadvantage or distress ⟨~ under a delusion⟩ **5** : to treat or work out laboriously

♦ drudge, endeavor (*or* endeavour), fag, grub, hustle, peg, plod, plug, slog, strain, strive, struggle, sweat, toil, work *Ant* dabble, fiddle (around), fool (around), mess (around), putter (around)

lab·o·ra·to·ry \'la-brə-ˌtȯr-ē, -bə-rə-\ *n, pl* **-ries** : a place equipped for making scientific experiments or tests

Labor Day *or Can* **Labour Day** *n* : the 1st Monday in September observed as a legal holiday in recognition of the working people

la·bored *or Can and Brit* **la·boured** \'lā-bərd\ *adj* : not freely or easily done ⟨∼ breathing⟩

la·bor·er *or Can and Brit* **la·bour·er** *n* : one that labors; *specif* : a person who does unskilled physical work for wages

la·bo·ri·ous \lə-'bȯr-ē-əs\ *adj* **1** ♦ : devoted to labor : INDUSTRIOUS **2** ♦ : requiring great effort

    ♦ [1] active, assiduous, busy, diligent, engaged, industrious, occupied, sedulous, working ♦ [2] arduous, challenging, demanding, difficult, exacting, formidable, grueling, hard, onerous, rough, stiff, strenuous, tall, taxing, toilsome, tough

la·bo·ri·ous·ly *adv* ♦ : in a laborious manner

    ♦ determinedly, diligently, hard, hardly, mightily, strenuously, tirelessly

la·bor-sav·ing *or Can and Brit* **labour–saving** \'lā-bər-,sā-viŋ\ *adj* ♦ : designed to replace or decrease labor

    ♦ automatic, robotic, self-acting

labor union *n* : an organization of workers formed to advance its members' interest in respect to wages and working conditions

la·bour *Can and Brit var of* LABOR

lab·ra·dor·ite \'la-brə-,dȯr-,īt\ *n* : an iridescent feldspar used in jewelry

Lab·ra·dor retriever \'la-brə-,dȯr-\ *n* : any of a breed of strongly built retrievers having a short dense black, yellow, or chocolate coat

la·bur·num \lə-'bər-nəm\ *n* : any of a genus of leguminous shrubs or trees with hanging clusters of yellow flowers

lab·y·rinth \'la-bə-,rinth\ *n* : a place constructed of or filled with confusing intricate passageways : MAZE

lab·y·rin·thine \,la-bə-'rin-thən, -,thin, -,thēn\ *adj* : INTRICATE, INVOLVED ⟨a ∼ plot⟩ ⟨∼ hallways⟩

lac \'lak\ *n* : a resinous substance secreted by a scale insect and used chiefly in the form of shellac

¹**lace** \'lās\ *vb* **laced; lac·ing** **1** : TIE **2** ♦ : to adorn with or as if with lace ⟨countryside *laced* with small villages⟩ **3** ♦ : to unite by twining one with another : INTERTWINE **4** : to hit repeatedly : BEAT **5** : to add something to impart zest or savor to **6** : to criticize sharply — used with *into* ⟨*laced* into her opponents⟩

    ♦ interlace, intersperse, intertwine, interweave, thread, weave, wreathe

²**lace** *n* **1** ♦ : a cord or string used for drawing together two edges **2** ♦ : an ornamental braid **3** : a fine openwork usu. figured fabric made of thread — **lacy** \'lā-sē\ *adj*

    ♦ [1] cable, cord, line, rope, string, wire ♦ [2] braid, plait

lac·er·ate \'la-sə-,rāt\ *vb* **-at·ed; -at·ing** : to tear roughly **lac·er·a·tion** \,la-sə-'rā-shən\ *n* ♦ : a torn and ragged wound

    ♦ gash, rent, rip, slash, slit, tear

lace·wing \'lās-,wiŋ\ *n* : any of various insects with delicate wing veins, long antennae, and often brilliant eyes

lach·ry·mal *or* **lac·ri·mal** \'la-krə-məl\ *adj* **1** *usu* lacrimal : of, relating to, or being glands that produce tears **2** : of, relating to, or marked by tears

lach·ry·mose \'la-krə-,mōs\ *adj* **1** : TEARFUL **2** : MOURNFUL

¹**lack** \'lak\ *vb* **1** : to be wanting or missing **2** : to be deficient in ⟨∼s experience⟩

²**lack** *n* ♦ : the fact or state of being wanting or deficient

    ♦ dearth, deficiency, deficit, failure, famine, inadequacy, insufficiency, paucity, poverty, scantiness, scarcity, shortage, want ♦ absence, need, want

lack·a·dai·si·cal \,la-kə-'dā-zi-kəl\ *adj* ♦ : lacking life, spirit, or zest — **lack·a·dai·si·cal·ly** \-k(ə-)lē\ *adv*

    ♦ enervated, languid, languorous, limp, listless, spiritless

lack·ey \'la-kē\ *n, pl* **lackeys** **1** ♦ : someone who does tasks or errands for another : FOOTMAN, SERVANT **2** : TOADY

    ♦ domestic, flunky, menial, retainer, servant, steward

lack·lus·ter *or Can and Brit* **lack·lus·tre** \'lak-,ləs-tər\ *adj* : DULL

la·con·ic \lə-'kä-nik\ *adj* ♦ : sparing of words : TERSE

    ♦ brief, compact, compendious, concise, crisp, epigrammatic, pithy, succinct, summary, terse

la·con·i·cal·ly \-ni-k(ə-)lē\ *adv* ♦ : in a laconic manner

    ♦ compactly, concisely, crisply, shortly, succinctly, summarily, tersely

lac·quer \'la-kər\ *n* : a clear or colored usu. glossy and quick-drying surface coating — **lacquer** *vb*

lac·ri·ma·tion \,la-krə-'mā-shən\ *n* : secretion of tears

la·crosse \lə-'krȯs\ *n* : a goal game in which players use a long-handled triangular-headed stick having a mesh pouch for catching, carrying, and throwing the ball

lac·tate \'lak-,tāt\ *vb* **lac·tat·ed; lac·tat·ing** : to secrete milk — **lac·ta·tion** \lak-'tā-shən\ *n*

lac·tic \'lak-tik\ *adj* **1** : of or relating to milk **2** : obtained from sour milk or whey

lactic acid *n* : a syrupy acid present in blood and muscle tissue and used esp. in food and medicine

lac·tose \'lak-,tōs\ *n* : a sugar present in milk

la·cu·na \lə-'kü-nə, -'kyü-\ *n, pl* **la·cu·nae** \-nē\ *also* **la·cu·nas** : a blank space or missing part : GAP

lad \'lad\ *n* ♦ : a male person of any age between early boyhood and maturity : YOUTH; *also* : FELLOW

    ♦ boy, nipper, shaver, stripling, youth ♦ buck, chap, dude, fellow, gent, gentleman, guy, hombre, jack, joker, male, man

lad·der \'la-dər\ *n* **1** : a structure for climbing that consists of two parallel sidepieces joined at intervals by crosspieces **2** ♦ : a series of usu. ascending steps or stages

    ♦ graduation, scale

lad·die \'la-dē\ *n* : a young lad

lad·en \'lād-ᵊn\ *adj* : LOADED, BURDENED

lad·ing \'lā-diŋ\ *n* ♦ : the goods or merchandise conveyed in a ship, airplane, or vehicle : CARGO, FREIGHT

    ♦ burden, cargo, freight, haul, load, payload, weight

¹**la·dle** \'lād-ᵊl\ *n* : a deep-bowled long-handled spoon used in taking up and conveying liquids

²**ladle** *vb* ♦ : to take up and convey in or as if in a ladle

    ♦ dip, scoop, spoon

la·dy \'lā-dē\ *n, pl* **ladies** **1** ♦ : a woman of property, rank, or authority; *also* : a woman of superior social position or of refinement **2** : WOMAN **3** ♦ : a female partner in a marriage : WIFE

    ♦ [1] dame, gentlewoman, noblewoman ♦ [3] helpmate, wife

lady beetle *n* : LADYBUG

la·dy·bird \'lā-dē-,bərd\ *n* : LADYBUG

la·dy·bug \-,bəg\ *n* : any of various small nearly hemispherical and usu. brightly colored beetles that feed mostly on other insects

la·dy·fin·ger \-,fiŋ-gər\ *n* : a small finger-shaped sponge cake

lady–in–waiting *n, pl* **ladies–in–waiting** : a lady appointed to attend or wait on a queen or princess

la·dy·like \'lā-dē-,līk\ *adj* : WELL-BRED

la·dy·ship \-,ship\ *n* : the condition of being a lady : rank of lady

lady's slipper *n* : any of several No. American orchids with slipper-shaped flowers

¹**lag** \'lag\ *n* **1** : a slowing up or falling behind; *also* : the amount by which one lags **2** : INTERVAL

²**lag** *vb* **lagged; lag·ging** **1** ♦ : to fail to keep up : stay behind **2** ♦ : to slacken gradually

    ♦ [1] crawl, creep, dally, dawdle, delay, dillydally, drag, linger, loiter, poke, tarry ♦ [2] decay, droop, fail, flag, go, languish, sag, waste, weaken, wilt

la·ger \'lä-gər\ *n* : a beer brewed by slow fermentation and matured under refrigeration

lag·gard \'la-gərd\ *adj* ♦ : tending to lag — **laggard** *n* — **lag·gard·ly** *adj* — **lag·gard·ness** *n*

    ♦ creeping, dilatory, languid, poky, slow, sluggish, tardy

lag·gard·ly *adv* ♦ : in a laggard manner

    ♦ slow, slowly, sluggishly, tardily

la·gniappe \'lan-,yap\ *n* ♦ : something given free esp. with a purchase

    ♦ bonus, dividend, extra, perquisite, tip ♦ bestowal, donation, freebie, gift, largesse, present

la·goon \lə-'gün\ *n* : a shallow sound, channel, or pond near or connected to a larger body of water

laid *past and past part of* LAY

laid–back \'lād-'bak\ *adj* ♦ : having a relaxed style or character ⟨∼ music⟩

    ♦ affable, breezy, easygoing, happy-go-lucky

lain *past part of* ¹LIE

lair \'lar\ *n* **1** ♦ : the resting or living place of a wild animal : DEN **2** ♦ : a refuge or place for hiding

♦ [1] burrow, den, hole, lodge ♦ [2] concealment, covert, den, hideout, nest

laird \'lärd\ *n, chiefly Scot* : a landed proprietor

lais·ser–faire *chiefly Brit var of* LAISSEZ-FAIRE

lais·sez–faire \ˌle-ˌsā-'far, ˌlā-, -ˌzā-\ *n* : a doctrine opposing governmental control of economic affairs beyond that necessary to maintain peace and property rights

la·ity \'lā-ə-tē\ *n* **1** : the people of a religious faith as distinct from its clergy **2** : the mass of people as distinct from those of a particular field

lake \'lāk\ *n* : an inland body of standing water of considerable size; *also* : a pool of liquid (as lava or pitch)

La·ko·ta \lə-'kō-tə\ *n, pl* **Lakota** *also* **Lakotas** : a member of a western division of the Dakota peoples; *also* : their language

¹**lam** \'lam\ *vb* **lammed; lam·ming** ♦ : to flee hastily

♦ abscond, clear out, escape, flee, fly, get out, run away, run off

²**lam** *abbr* laminated

³**lam** *n* ♦ : sudden or hurried flight esp. from the law

♦ escape, flight, getaway, slip

Lam *abbr* Lamentations

la·ma \'lä-mə\ *n* : a Buddhist monk of Tibet or Mongolia

la·ma·sery \'lä-mə-ˌser-ē\ *n, pl* **-ser·ies** : a monastery for lamas

¹**lamb** \'lam\ *n* **1** : a young sheep; *also* : its flesh used as food **2** ♦ : an innocent or gentle person

♦ angel, dove, innocent, sheep *Ant* wolf

²**lamb** *vb* : to bring forth a lamb

lam·baste *or* **lam·bast** \lam-'bāst, -'bast\ *vb* **1** : to assault violently : BEAT **2** ♦ : to attack verbally : EXCORIATE

♦ abuse, assail, attack, belabor, blast, castigate, excoriate, jump, slam, vituperate ♦ admonish, chide, lecture, rail (at *or* against), rate, rebuke, reprimand, scold

lamb·da \'lam-də\ *n* : the 11th letter of the Greek alphabet — Λ or λ

lam·bent \'lam-bənt\ *adj* **1** : FLICKERING **2** ♦ : softly radiant 〈~ eyes〉 **3** : marked by lightness or brilliance 〈~ humor〉 — **lam·ben·cy** \-bən-sē\ *n* — **lam·bent·ly** *adv*

♦ beaming, bright, brilliant, effulgent, glowing, incandescent, lucent, lucid, luminous, lustrous, radiant, refulgent, shiny

lamb·skin \'lam-ˌskin\ *n* : a lamb's skin or a small fine-grade sheepskin or the leather made from either

¹**lame** \'lām\ *adj* **lam·er; lam·est** **1** : having a body part and esp. a limb so disabled as to impair freedom of movement; *also* : marked by stiffness and soreness **2** : lacking substance : WEAK **3** : INFERIOR, PITIFUL — **lame·ly** *adv* — **lame·ness** *n*

²**lame** *vb* **lamed; lam·ing** ♦ : to make lame : CRIPPLE, DISABLE

♦ cripple, disable, maim, mutilate

la·mé \lä-'mā, la-\ *n* : a brocaded clothing fabric with tinsel filling threads (as of gold or silver)

lame·brain \'lām-ˌbrān\ *n* : DOLT

lame duck *n* : an elected official continuing to hold office between an election and the inauguration of a successor — **lame-duck** *adj*

¹**la·ment** \lə-'ment\ *vb* **1** : to mourn aloud : WAIL **2** ♦ : to express sorrow or regret for

♦ bemoan, bewail, deplore, grieve, mourn, wail *Ant* exult (in), glory (in), rejoice (in) ♦ bemoan, deplore, regret, repent, rue

²**lament** *n* **1** ♦ : a crying out in grief : WAIL **2** ♦ : a slow, solemn, and mournful piece of music : DIRGE, ELEGY **3** : COMPLAINT

♦ [1] groan, howl, keen, moan, plaint, wail *Ant* exultation, rejoicing ♦ [2] dirge, elegy, requiem, threnody

lam·en·ta·ble \'la-mən-tə-bəl, lə-'men-tə-\ *adj* **1** ♦ : that is to be regretted or lamented **2** ♦ : expressing grief — **lam·en·ta·bly** \-blē\ *adv*

♦ [1] deplorable, distressful, grievous, heartbreaking, regrettable, unfortunate, woeful ♦ [2] anguished, dolorous, mournful, plaintive, sorrowful, sorry, woeful

lam·en·ta·tion \ˌla-mən-'tā-shən\ *n* : an act or instance of lamenting

Lamentations *n* : a book of Jewish and Christian Scripture

la·mia \'lā-mē-ə\ *n* : a female demon

lam·i·na \'la-mə-nə\ *n, pl* **-nae** \-ˌnē\ *or* **-nas** : a thin plate or scale

¹**lam·i·nate** \'la-mə-ˌnāt\ *vb* **-nat·ed; -nat·ing** : to make by uniting layers of one or more materials — **lam·i·na·tion** \ˌla-mə-'nā-shən\ *n*

²**lam·i·nate** \-nət\ *n* : a product manufactured by laminating

lamp \'lamp\ *n* **1** : a vessel with a wick for burning a flammable liquid (as oil) to produce light **2** : a device for producing light or heat

lamp·black \-ˌblak\ *n* : black soot used esp. as a pigment

lamp·light·er \-ˌlī-tər\ *n* : one that lights a lamp

lam·poon \lam-'pün\ *n* : SATIRE; *esp* : a harsh satire directed against an individual — **lampoon** *vb*

lam·prey \'lam-prē\ *n, pl* **lampreys** : any of a family of eel-shaped jawless fishes that have well-developed eyes and a large disk-shaped sucking mouth armed with horny teeth

LAN \'lan, ˌel-ˌa-'en\ *n* : LOCAL AREA NETWORK

la·nai \lə-'nī\ *n* : PORCH, VERANDA

¹**lance** \'lans\ *n* **1** ♦ : a spear carried by mounted soldiers **2** : any of various sharp-pointed implements; *esp* : LANCET

♦ pike, spear

²**lance** *vb* **lanced; lanc·ing** ♦ : to pierce or open with a lance 〈~ a boil〉

♦ gore, harpoon, impale, pierce, puncture, skewer, spear, spike, stab, stick, transfix

lance corporal *n* : an enlisted person in the marine corps ranking above a private first class and below a corporal

lanc·er \'lan-sər\ *n* : a cavalryman of a unit formerly armed with lances

lan·cet \'lan-sət\ *n* : a sharp-pointed and usu. 2-edged surgical instrument

¹**land** \'land\ *n* **1** ♦ : the solid part of the surface of the earth; *also* : a part of the earth's surface 〈fenced ~〉 〈marshy ~〉 **2** ♦ : the people of a country : NATION **3** : REALM, DOMAIN 〈the ~ of the living〉 — **land·less** *adj*

♦ [1] belt, region, tract, zone ♦ [1] dirt, dust, earth, ground, soil ♦ [2] commonwealth, country, nation, sovereignty, state

²**land** *vb* **1** ♦ : to set or put on shore from a ship : DISEMBARK; *also* : to touch at a place on shore **2** ♦ : to alight or cause to alight on a surface **3** ♦ : to bring to or arrive at a destination **4** ♦ : to catch and bring in 〈~ a fish〉; *also* : GAIN, SECURE 〈~ a job〉

♦ [1] disembark, dock, moor, tie up ♦ [2] alight, light, perch, roost, settle ♦ [3] arrive, come, show up, turn up ♦ [4] acquire, attain, capture, carry, draw, earn, garner, get, make, obtain, procure, realize, secure, win

lan·dau \'lan-ˌdau\ *n* : a 4-wheeled carriage with a top divided into two sections that can be lowered, thrown back, or removed

land·ed *adj* : having an estate in land 〈~ gentry〉

land·er \'lan-dər\ *n* : a space vehicle designed to land on a celestial body

land·fall \'land-ˌfol\ *n* : a sighting or making of land (as after a voyage); *also* : the land first sighted

land·fill \-ˌfil\ *n* : a low-lying area on which refuse is buried between layers of earth

land·form \-ˌform\ *n* : a natural feature of a land surface

land·hold·er \-ˌhōl-dər\ *n* : a holder or owner of land — **land·hold·ing** \-diŋ\ *adj or n*

land·ing \'lan-diŋ\ *n* **1** : the action of one that lands **2** ♦ : a place for discharging or taking on passengers and cargo **3** : a level part of a staircase

♦ dock, float, jetty, levee, pier, quay, wharf

landing gear *n* : the part that supports the weight of an aircraft when it is on the ground

land·la·dy \'land-ˌlā-dē\ *n* : a woman who is a landlord

land·locked \-ˌläkt\ *adj* **1** : enclosed or nearly enclosed by land 〈a ~ country〉 **2** : confined to fresh water by some barrier 〈~ salmon〉

land·lord \-ˌlord\ *n* **1** : the owner of property leased or rented to another **2** : a person who rents lodgings : INNKEEPER

land·lub·ber \-ˌlə-bər\ *n* : one who knows little of the sea or seamanship

land·mark \-ˌmärk\ *n* **1** : an object that marks a course or boundary or serves as a guide **2** : an event that marks a turning point **3** : a structure of unusual historical and usu. aesthetic interest

land·mass \-ˌmas\ *n* : a large area of land

land mine *n* **1** : a mine placed on or just below the surface of the ground and designed to be exploded by the weight of someone or something passing over it **2** : a trap for the unwary

land·own·er \-ˌō-nər\ *n* : an owner of land

¹**land·scape** \-ˌskāp\ *n* **1** : a picture of natural inland scenery **2** : a portion of land that can be seen in one glance

²**landscape** *vb* **land·scaped; land·scap·ing** : to modify (a natural landscape) by grading, clearing, or decorative planting

land·slide \-ˌslīd\ *n* **1** : the slipping down of a mass of rocks or earth on a steep slope; *also* : the mass of material that slides **2** : an overwhelming victory

lands·man \'landz-mən\ *n* : a person who lives on land; *esp* : LANDLUBBER

land·ward \'land-wərd\ *adv or adj* : to or toward the land

lane \'lān\ *n* **1** : a narrow passageway (as between fences) **2** : a relatively narrow way or track ⟨traffic ∼⟩

lang *abbr* language

lan·guage \'laŋ-gwij\ *n* **1** ♦ : the words, their pronunciation, and the methods of combining them used and understood by a community **2** ♦ : form or style of verbal expression **3** ♦ : a system of signs and symbols and rules for using them that is used to carry information

♦ [1] argot, cant, jargon, lingo, slang, terminology, vocabulary ♦ [2] diction, phraseology, phrasing, wording ♦ [3] lingo, speech, tongue, vocabulary

lan·guid \'laŋ-gwəd\ *adj* **1** ♦ : drooping or flagging from or as if from exhaustion : WEAK **2** ♦ : sluggish in character or disposition : LISTLESS **3** ♦ : lacking force or quickness of movement : SLOW — **lan·guid·ly** *adv* — **lan·guid·ness** *n*

♦ [1] delicate, effete, enervated, faint, feeble, frail, infirm, low, prostrate, slight, soft, tender, torpid, unsubstantial, wasted, weak, wimpy ♦ [2] enervated, lackadaisical, languorous, limp, listless, spiritless ♦ [3] creeping, dilatory, laggard, poky, slow, sluggish, tardy

lan·guish \'laŋ-gwish\ *vb* **1** ♦ : to become languid **2** : to become dispirited : PINE **3** : to appeal for sympathy by assuming an expression of grief

♦ decay, droop, fail, flag, go, lag, sag, waste, weaken, wilt

lan·guor \'laŋ-gər\ *n* **1** ♦ : a languid feeling **2** ♦ : listless indolence or inertia

♦ [1, 2] debility, delicacy, enfeeblement, faintness, feebleness, frailty, infirmity, lowness, weakness

lan·guor·ous *adj* ♦ : full of or characterized by languor — **lan·guor·ous·ly** *adv*

♦ enervated, lackadaisical, languid, limp, listless, spiritless

La Ni·ña \lä-'nē-nyə\ *n* : an upwelling of unusually cold ocean water along the west coast of So. America that often follows an El Niño

lank \'laŋk\ *adj* **1** : not well filled out **2** ♦ : hanging straight and limp ⟨∼ hair⟩

♦ droopy, flaccid, floppy, limp, slack, yielding

lanky \'laŋ-kē\ *adj* **lank·i·er; -est** ♦ : ungracefully tall and thin

♦ gangling, rangy, spindly

lan·o·lin \'lan-ᵊl-ən\ *n* : the fatty coating of sheep's wool esp. when refined for use in ointments and cosmetics

lan·ta·na \lan-'tä-nə\ *n* : any of a genus of tropical shrubs related to the vervains with showy heads of small bright flowers

lan·tern \'lan-tərn\ *n* **1** : a usu. portable light with a protective covering **2** : the chamber in a lighthouse containing the light **3** : a projector for slides

lan·tha·num \'lan-thə-nəm\ *n* : a soft malleable metallic chemical element

lan·yard \'lan-yərd\ *n* : a piece of rope for fastening something in ships; *also* : any of various cords

Lao·tian \lā-'ō-shən, 'lau̇-shən\ *n* : a native or inhabitant of Laos — **Laotian** *adj*

¹**lap** \'lap\ *n* **1** : a loose panel of a garment **2** : the clothing that lies on the knees, thighs, and lower part of the trunk when one sits; *also* : the front part of the lower trunk and thighs of a seated person **3** : an environment of nurture ⟨the ∼ of luxury⟩ **4** : CHARGE, CONTROL ⟨in the ∼ of the gods⟩

²**lap** *vb* **lapped; lap·ping** **1** : FOLD **2** ♦ : to envelop entirely : WRAP **3** ♦ : to lay over or near so as to partly cover

♦ [2] embrace, enclose, encompass, enfold, enshroud, envelop, invest, mantle, shroud, swathe, veil, wrap ♦ [3] overlap, overlay, overlie, overspread

³**lap** *n* **1** : the amount by which an object overlaps another; *also* : the part of an object that overlaps another **2** ♦ : an act or instance of going over a course (as a track or swimming pool)

♦ leg, stage, step

⁴**lap** *vb* **lapped; lap·ping** **1** : to scoop up food or drink with the tip of the tongue; *also* : DEVOUR — usu. used with *up* **2** ♦ : to splash gently ⟨*lapping* waves⟩

♦ plash, slosh, splash, swash

⁵**lap** *n* **1** : an act or instance of lapping **2** : a gentle splashing sound

lap·a·ros·co·py \ˌla-pə-'räs-kə-pē\ *n, pl* **-pies** **1** : visual examination of the abdomen by means of an endoscope; *also* : surgery using laparoscopy — **lap·a·ro·scope** \'la-pə-rə-ˌskōp\ *n* — **lap·a·ro·scop·ic** \ˌla-pə-rə-'skä-pik\ *adj*

lap·dog \'lap-ˌdȯg\ *n* : a small dog that may be held in the lap

la·pel \lə-'pel\ *n* : the fold of the front of a coat that is usu. a continuation of the collar

¹**lap·i·dary** \'la-pə-ˌder-ē\ *n, pl* **-dar·ies** : a person who cuts, polishes, or engraves precious stones

²**lapidary** *adj* **1** : of, relating to, or suitable for engraved inscriptions **2** : of or relating to precious stones or the art of cutting them

lap·in \'la-pən\ *n* : rabbit fur usu. sheared and dyed

la·pis la·zu·li \ˌla-pəs-'la-zə-lē, -zhə-\ *n* : a usu. blue semiprecious stone often having sparkling bits of pyrite

lap·pet \'la-pət\ *n* : a fold or flap on a garment

¹**lapse** \'laps\ *n* **1** ♦ : a slight error **2** ♦ : a fall from a higher to a lower state **3** : the termination of a right or privilege through failure to meet requirements **4** : a gap in the continuity of something : INTERRUPTION **5** : APOSTASY **6** : a passage of time; *also* : INTERVAL

♦ [1] blunder, error, fault, flub, fumble, goof, miscue, misstep, mistake, oversight, slip, stumble ♦ [2] reversal, reverse, setback

²**lapse** *vb* **lapsed; laps·ing** **1** : to commit apostasy **2** : to sink or slip gradually : SUBSIDE ⟨*lapsed* into a coma⟩ **3** ♦ : to go out of existence : CEASE

♦ break off, break up, cease, close, conclude, die, discontinue, elapse, end, expire, finish, halt, leave off, let up, pass, quit, stop, terminate, wind up

lap·top \'lap-ˌtäp\ *adj* : of a size that can be used conveniently on one's lap ⟨a ∼ computer⟩ — **laptop** *n*

lap·wing \'lap-ˌwiŋ\ *n* : an Old World crested plover

lar·board \'lär-bərd\ *n* : ³PORT

lar·ce·ny \'lär-sə-nē\ *n, pl* **-nies** ♦ : the unlawful taking of personal property with intent to deprive the rightful owner of it permanently : THEFT — **lar·ce·nous** \-nəs\ *adj*

♦ robbery, theft, thievery

larch \'lärch\ *n* : any of a genus of trees related to the pines that shed their needles in the fall

¹**lard** \'lärd\ *vb* **1** : to insert strips of usu. pork fat into (meat) before cooking; *also* : GREASE **2** *obs* : ENRICH

²**lard** *n* : a soft white fat obtained by rendering fatty tissue of the hog

lar·der \'lär-dər\ *n* : a place where foods (as meat) are kept

lar·es and pe·na·tes \'lar-ēz . . . pə-'nä-tēz\ *n pl* **1** : household gods **2** : personal or household effects

large \'lärj\ *adj* **larg·er; larg·est** **1** : having more than usual power, capacity, or scope **2** ♦ : exceeding most other things of like kind in quantity or size — **at large** **1** : UNCONFINED **2** : as a whole

♦ big, bumper, considerable, goodly, grand, great, handsome, hefty, sizable, substantial, voluminous *Ant* little, puny, small, undersized

large·ly \'lärj-lē\ *adv* ♦ : to a large extent : for the greatest part

♦ altogether, basically, chiefly, generally, mainly, mostly, overall, predominantly, primarily, principally

large·ness *n* ♦ : the quality or state of being large

♦ bigness, grandness, greatness *Ant* fineness, littleness, smallness

lar·gesse \lär-'zhes, -'jes\ *n* **1** : liberal giving **2** ♦ : a generous gift **3** ♦ : the quality or fact of being generous

♦ [2] bestowal, donation, freebie, gift, lagniappe, present ♦ [3] bounty, generosity, liberality, philanthropy, unselfishness

¹**lar·go** \'lär-gō\ *adv or adj* : at a very slow tempo — used as a direction in music

²**largo** *n, pl* **largos** : a largo movement

lar·i·at \'lar-ē-ət\ *n* : a long rope used to catch or tether livestock : LASSO

¹**lark** \'lärk\ *n* : any of a family of small songbirds; *esp* : SKYLARK

²**lark** *n* ♦ : something done solely for fun or adventure

♦ binge, fling, frolic, gambol, revel, rollick, romp

³**lark** *vb* ♦ : to engage in harmless fun or mischief — often used with *about*

♦ caper, cavort, disport, frisk, frolic, gambol, rollick, romp, sport

lark·spur \'lärk-ˌspər\ *n* : DELPHINIUM; *esp* : any of the widely cultivated annual delphiniums

lar·va \'lär-və\ *n, pl* **lar·vae** \-(ˌ)vē\ *also* **larvas** : the wingless often wormlike form in which insects hatch from the egg; *also* : any young animal (as a tadpole) that is fundamentally unlike its parent — **lar·val** \-vəl\ *adj*

lar·yn·gi·tis \ˌlar-ən-ˈjī-təs\ *n* : inflammation of the larynx

lar·ynx \'lar-iŋks\ *n, pl* **la·ryn·ges** \lə-ˈrin-ˌjēz\ *or* **lar·ynx·es** : the upper part of the trachea containing the vocal cords — **la·ryn·ge·al** \lə-ˈrin-jəl\ *adj*

la·sa·gna \lə-ˈzän-yə\ *n* : boiled broad flat noodles baked with a sauce usu. of tomatoes, cheese, and meat

las·car \'las-kər\ *n* : an Indian sailor

las·civ·i·ous \lə-ˈsi-vē-əs\ *adj* ♦ : sexually unchaste or licentious : LEWD

♦ lewd, lustful, passionate, wanton

las·civ·i·ous·ness *n* : the quality or state of being lascivious

la·ser \'lā-zər\ *n* **1** : a device that produces an intense monochromatic beam of light **2** : something thrown or directed straight with high speed or intensity ⟨threw a ∼ into the end zone⟩

laser disc *n* : OPTICAL DISK; *esp* : one containing a video recording

¹**lash** \'lash\ *vb* **1** : to move violently or suddenly **2** ♦ : to thrash or beat violently : WHIP **3** : to attack verbally

♦ flail, flog, hide, scourge, slash, switch, thrash, whale, whip

²**lash** *n* **1 a** : a stroke esp. with a whip **b** ♦ : the flexible part of a whip; *also* : WHIP **2** : a stinging rebuke **3** : EYELASH

♦ scourge, switch, whip

³**lash** *vb* : to bind with or as if with a line

lass \'las\ *n* ♦ : a young woman : GIRL

♦ doll, girl, maid, maiden, miss

lass·ie \'la-sē\ *n* : a young woman : LASS

las·si·tude \'la-sə-ˌtüd, -ˌtyüd\ *n* **1** ♦ : weakness or weariness of body or mind : FATIGUE **2** : LANGUOR

♦ burnout, collapse, exhaustion, fatigue, prostration, tiredness, weariness

las·so \'la-sō, la-ˈsü\ *n, pl* **lassos** *or* **lassoes** : a rope or long leather thong with a noose used for catching livestock — **lasso** *vb*

¹**last** \'last\ *vb* **1** ♦ : to continue in existence or operation **2** : to remain fresh or unimpaired : ENDURE **3** : to manage to continue **4** ♦ : to be enough for the needs of

♦ [1] abide, continue, endure, hold, keep up, persist, run on ♦ [1, 4] hold, hold out, keep up, prevail, survive

²**last** *n* : a foot-shaped form on which a shoe is shaped or repaired

³**last** *vb* : to shape with a last

⁴**last** *adv* **1** : at the end **2** : most recently **3** : in conclusion

⁵**last** *adj* **1** ♦ : following all the rest : FINAL **2** : next before the present **3** : most up-to-date **4** : farthest from a specified quality, attitude, or likelihood ⟨the ∼ thing we want⟩ **5** : CONCLUSIVE; *also* : SUPREME — **last·ly** *adv*

♦ final, hindmost, latter, terminal, ultimate *Ant* beginning, earliest, first, inaugural, initial, maiden, opening, original, primary, starting

⁶**last** *n* : something that is last — **at last** : FINALLY

last–ditch \'last-ˌdich\ *adj* : made as a final effort esp. to avert disaster

last·ing \'las-tiŋ\ *adj* ♦ : existing or continuing a long while : ENDURING

♦ abiding, ageless, continuing, dateless, enduring, eternal, everlasting, immortal, imperishable, perennial, perpetual, timeless, undying

last laugh *n* : an ultimate satisfaction or triumph despite previous doubt or criticism

Last Supper *n* : the supper eaten by Jesus and his disciples on the night of his betrayal

lat *abbr* latitude

Lat *abbr* Latin

¹**latch** \'lach\ *vb* : to catch or get hold

²**latch** *n* : a catch that holds a door or gate closed

³**latch** *vb* : to make fast with a latch

latch·et \'la-chət\ *n* : a strap, thong, or lace for fastening a shoe or sandal

latch·key \'lach-ˌkē\ *n* : a key for opening a door latch esp. from the outside

latch·string \-ˌstriŋ\ *n* : a string on a latch that may be left hanging outside the door for raising the latch

¹**late** \'lāt\ *adj* **later; lat·est 1** ♦ : coming or remaining after the due, usual, or proper time **2** : far advanced toward the close or end **3** ♦ : recently deceased **4** : made, appearing, or happening just previous to the present : RECENT **5** ♦ : being something or holding some position or relationship recently but not now — **late·ness** *n*

♦ [1] behind, belated, delinquent, overdue, tardy *Ant* early, premature ♦ [3] breathless, dead, deceased, defunct, gone, lifeless ♦ [5] erstwhile, former, old, onetime, past, sometime, whilom

²**late** *adv* **later; lat·est 1** : after the usual or proper time; *also* : at or to an advanced point in time **2** : not long before the current time : RECENTLY

late·com·er \'lāt-ˌkə-mər\ *n* : one who arrives late

la·teen \lə-ˈtēn\ *adj* : relating to or being a triangular sail extended by a long spar slung to a low mast

late·ly *adv* ♦ : of late

♦ freshly, just, late, new, newly, now, only, recently

la·ten·cy \-ᵊn-sē\ *n* ♦ : the quality or state of being latent

♦ abeyance, doldrums, dormancy, quiescence, suspension

la·tent \'lāt-ᵊnt\ *adj* ♦ : present but not visible or active

♦ dead, dormant, fallow, free, idle, inactive, inert, inoperative, off, vacant

later *adv* ♦ : at some time subsequent to a given time

♦ after, afterward, subsequently, thereafter

¹**lat·er·al** \'la-tə-rəl\ *adj* : situated on, directed toward, or coming from the side ⟨a ∼ view⟩ — **lat·er·al·ly** *adv*

²**lateral** *n* **1** : a branch from the main part **2** : a football pass thrown parallel to the line of scrimmage or away from the opponent's goal

la·tex \'lā-ˌteks\ *n, pl* **la·ti·ces** \'lā-tə-ˌsēz, 'la-\ *or* **la·tex·es 1** : a milky juice produced by various plant cells (as of milkweeds, poppies, and the rubber tree) **2** : a water emulsion of a synthetic rubber or plastic used esp. in paint

lath \'lath, 'lath\ *n, pl* **laths** *or* **lath** : a thin narrow strip of wood used esp. as a base for plaster; *also* : a building material in sheets used for the same purpose — **lath** *vb*

lathe \'lāth\ *n* : a machine in which a piece of material is held and turned while being shaped by a tool

¹**lath·er** \'la-thər\ *n* **1** : a foam or froth formed when a detergent is agitated in water; *also* : foam from profuse sweating (as by a horse) **2** ♦ : an agitated or overwrought state : DITHER

♦ [1] foam, froth, head, spume ♦ [2] dither, fluster, fret, fuss, huff, pother, stew, tizzy, twitter

²**lather** *vb* : to spread lather over; *also* : to form a lather

Lat·in \'lat-ᵊn\ *n* **1** : the language of ancient Rome **2** : a member of any of the peoples whose languages derive from Latin — **Latin** *adj*

La·ti·na \lə-ˈtē-nə\ *n* : a woman or girl who is a native or inhabitant of Latin America; *also* : a woman or girl of Latin-American origin living in the U.S.

Latin American *n* : a native or inhabitant of any of the countries of No., Central, or So. America whose official language is Spanish or Portuguese — **Latin–American** *adj*

La·ti·no \lə-ˈtē-nō\ *n, pl* **-nos** : a native or inhabitant of Latin America; *also* : a person of Latin-American origin living in the U.S. — **Latino** *adj*

lat·i·tude \'la-tə-ˌtüd, -ˌtyüd\ *n* **1** : angular distance north or south from the earth's equator measured in degrees **2** : a region marked by its latitude **3** ♦ : freedom of action or choice

♦ authorization, freedom, license (*or* licence), run

lat·i·tu·di·nar·i·an \ˌla-tə-ˌtü-də-ˈner-ē-ən, -ˌtyü-\ *n* : a person who is liberal in religious belief and conduct

la·trine \lə-ˈtrēn\ *n* : a room with conveniences for washing and usu. with one or more toilets : TOILET

lat·ter \'la-tər\ *adj* **1** : more recent; *also* : FINAL **2** : of, relating to, or being the second of two things referred to

♦ final, hindmost, last, terminal, ultimate

lat·ter–day *adj* **1** : of present or recent times **2** : of a later or subsequent time

Latter–day Saint *n* : a member of a religious body founded by Joseph Smith in 1830 and accepting the Book of Mormon as divine revelation : MORMON

lat·ter·ly \'la-tər-lē\ *adv* **1** : LATER **2** : of late : RECENTLY

lat·tice \'la-təs\ *n* **1** : a framework of crossed wood or metal strips; *also* : a window, door, or gate having a lattice **2** : a regular geometrical arrangement

lat·tice·work \-ˌwərk\ *n* : LATTICE; *also* : work made of lattices

Lat·vi·an \'lat-vē-ən\ *n* **1 :** a native or inhabitant of Latvia **2** : the language of the Latvians — **Latvian** *adj*

¹**laud** \'lȯd\ *n* **:** PRAISE, ACCLAIM

²**laud** *vb* ♦ **:** to express a favorable judgment of **:** PRAISE — **laud·ably** *adv*

    ♦ acclaim, applaud, cheer, crack up, hail, praise, salute, tout ♦ bless, extol, glorify, magnify, praise

laud·able *adj* ♦ **:** worthy of praise

    ♦ admirable, commendable, creditable, meritorious, praiseworthy

lau·da·num \'lȯd-ᵊn-əm\ *n* **:** a tincture of opium

lau·da·to·ry \'lȯ-də-ˌtȯr-ē\ *adj* **:** of, relating to, or expressive of praise

¹**laugh** \'laf, 'låf\ *vb* ♦ **:** to show mirth, joy, or scorn with a smile and chuckle or explosive sound; *also* **:** to become amused or derisive — **laugh·ing·ly** *adv*

    ♦ *usu* laugh at deride, gibe, jeer, mock, ridicule, scout

²**laugh** *n* **1** ♦ **:** the act of laughing **2** ♦ **:** a cause for derision or merriment **:** JOKE; *also* **:** an expression of scorn or mockery **:** JEER **3** *pl* **:** SPORT 1

    ♦ [1] cackle, chortle, laughter, snicker, titter ♦ [2] crack, gag, jeer, jest, joke, pleasantry, quip, sally, waggery, wisecrack, witticism

laugh·able *adj* ♦ **:** of a kind to provoke laughter or sometimes derision **:** amusingly ridiculous

    ♦ antic, comic, comical, droll, farcical, funny, hilarious, humorous, hysterical, ludicrous, ridiculous, riotous, risible, screaming, uproarious ♦ absurd, comical, derisive, farcical, ludicrous, preposterous, ridiculous, risible, silly

laughing gas *n* **:** NITROUS OXIDE

laugh·ing·stock \'la-fiŋ-ˌstäk, 'lå-\ *n* ♦ **:** an object of ridicule

    ♦ butt, mark, mock, mockery, target

laugh·ter \'laf-tər, 'låf-\ *n* ♦ **:** the action or sound of laughing

    ♦ cackle, chortle, laugh, snicker, titter

¹**launch** \'lȯnch\ *vb* **1** ♦ **:** to throw forward **:** HURL; *also* **:** to send off ⟨∼ a rocket⟩ **2 :** to set afloat **3** ♦ **:** to set in operation **:** START ⟨∼ a business⟩ — **launch·er** *n*

    ♦ [1] cast, catapult, chuck, dash, fire, fling, heave, hurl, hurtle, peg, pelt, pitch, sling, throw, toss ♦ [3] constitute, establish, found, inaugurate, initiate, innovate, institute, introduce, pioneer, set up, start ♦ [3] begin, commence, embark (on *or* upon), enter, get off, open, start, strike

²**launch** *n* ♦ **:** an act or instance of launching

    ♦ beginning, birth, commencement, dawn, genesis, morning, onset, outset, start, threshold

³**launch** *n* **:** a small open or half-decked motorboat

launch·pad \'lȯnch-ˌpad\ *n* **:** a platform from which a rocket is launched

laun·der \'lȯn-dər\ *vb* **1 :** to wash or wash and iron clothing and household linens **2 :** to transfer (as money of an illegal origin) through an outside party to conceal the true source — **laun·der·er** *n*

laun·dress \'lȯn-drəs\ *n* **:** a woman who is a laundry worker

laun·dry \'lȯn-drē\ *n, pl* **laundries 1 :** a place where laundering is done **2 :** clothes or linens that have been or are to be laundered — **laun·dry·man** \-mən\ *n*

lau·re·ate \'lȯr-ē-ət\ *n* **:** the recipient of honor for achievement in an art or science — **lau·re·ate·ship** *n*

lau·rel \'lȯr-əl\ *n* **1 :** an evergreen tree or shrub of southern Europe that is related to the sassafras and cinnamon and has glossy aromatic leaves; *esp* **:** a small tree of southern Europe **2 :** MOUNTAIN LAUREL **3 a :** a crown of laurel **b** ♦ **:** a recognition of achievement **:** HONOR — usu. used in pl.

    ♦ *usu* laurels acclaim, accolade, credit, distinction, glory, homage, honor (*or* honour)

lav *abbr* lavatory

la·va \'lä-və, 'la-\ *n* **:** melted rock coming from a volcano; *also* **:** such rock that has cooled and hardened

la·vage \lə-'väzh\ *n* **:** WASHING; *esp* **:** the washing out (as of an organ) esp. for medicinal reasons

lav·a·to·ry \'la-və-ˌtȯr-ē\ *n, pl* **-ries 1 :** a fixed washbowl with running water and drainpipe **2** ♦ **:** a room with conveniences for washing and usu. with one or more toilets **:** BATHROOM

    ♦ bathroom, toilet

lave \'lāv\ *vb* **laved; lav·ing** ♦ **:** to wash or flow along or against **:** WASH

    ♦ lap, splash, wash

lav·en·der \'la-vən-dər\ *n* **1 :** a Mediterranean mint or its dried leaves and flowers used to perfume clothing and bed linen **2 :** a pale purple color

¹**lav·ish** \'la-vish\ *adj* **1** ♦ **:** expending or bestowing profusely **2** ♦ **:** expended or produced in abundance **3** ♦ **:** marked by excess

    ♦ [1] deluxe, luxuriant, luxurious, opulent, palatial, plush, sumptuous ♦ [2] copious, profuse, riotous ♦ [3] excessive, extravagant, extreme, immoderate, inordinate, overmuch

²**lavish** *vb* ♦ **:** to expend or give with profusion

    ♦ heap, pour, rain, shower ♦ blow, dissipate, fritter, misspend, run through, spend, squander, throw away, waste

lav·ish·ly *adv* ♦ **:** in a lavish manner

    ♦ expensively, extravagantly, grandly, high, luxuriously, opulently, richly

lav·ish·ness *n* ♦ **:** a lavish quality; *also* **:** a lavish manner or propensity

    ♦ extravagance, prodigality, wastefulness

law \'lȯ\ *n* **1** ♦ **:** a rule of conduct or action established by custom or laid down and enforced by a governing authority; *also* **:** the whole body of such rules **2 :** the control brought about by enforcing rules **3** *cap* **:** the revelation of the divine will set forth in the Old Testament of Christian Scripture; *also* **:** the first part of the Jewish Scripture **4 :** a rule or principle of construction or procedure **5 :** the science that deals with laws and their interpretation and application **6 :** the profession of a lawyer **7 :** a rule or principle stating something that always works in the same way under the same conditions

    ♦ act, enactment, ordinance, statute

law·break·er \'lȯ-ˌbrā-kər\ *n* ♦ **:** one who violates the law

    ♦ criminal, crook, culprit, felon, malefactor, offender

law·ful \'lȯ-fəl\ *adj* **1 :** permitted by law **2 :** RIGHTFUL — **law·ful·ly** *adv*

law·giv·er \-ˌgi-vər\ *n* **:** one that makes laws **:** LEGISLATOR

law·less \'lȯ-ləs\ *adj* **1 :** having no laws **2** ♦ **:** not restrained or controlled by law **:** UNRULY, DISORDERLY ⟨a ∼ mob⟩ — **law·less·ly** *adv* — **law·less·ness** *n*

    ♦ anarchic, disorderly, unruly *Ant* orderly

law·mak·er \-ˌmā-kər\ *n* ♦ **:** one that makes laws **:** LEGISLATOR

    ♦ legislator, solon

law·man \'lȯ-mən\ *n* **:** a law enforcement official (as a sheriff or marshal)

¹**lawn** \'lȯn\ *n* **:** ground (as around a house) covered with mowed grass

²**lawn** *n* **:** a fine sheer linen or cotton fabric

lawn bowling *n* **:** a bowling game played on a green with wooden balls which are rolled at a jack

law·ren·ci·um \lȯ-'ren-sē-əm\ *n* **:** a short-lived radioactive element

law·suit \'lȯ-ˌsüt\ *n* ♦ **:** a suit in law

    ♦ action, proceeding, suit

law·yer \'lȯ-yər\ *n* ♦ **:** one who conducts lawsuits for clients or advises as to legal rights and obligations in other matters — **law·yer·ly** *adj*

    ♦ advocate, attorney, counsel

lax \'laks\ *adj* **1** ♦ **:** not strict ⟨∼ discipline⟩ **2** ♦ **:** not tense, firm, or rigid — **lax·ly** *adv*

    ♦ [1] careless, derelict, negligent, remiss, slack ♦ [1] easygoing, flexible, relaxed, unrestrained, unrestricted ♦ [2] insecure, loose, slack

¹**lax·a·tive** \'lak-sə-tiv\ *adj* **:** relieving constipation

²**laxative** *n* **:** a usu. mild laxative drug

lax·i·ty \'lak-sə-tē\ *n* ♦ **:** the quality or state of being lax

    ♦ delinquency, dereliction, laxness, neglect, negligence, omission, remissness, slackness

lax·ness *n* ♦ **:** the quality or state of being lax

    ♦ carelessness, dereliction, heedlessness, negligence, remissness, slackness

¹**lay** \'lā\ *vb* **laid** \'lād\; **lay·ing 1 :** to beat or strike down **2** ♦ **:** to put on or set down **:** PLACE **3 :** to produce and deposit eggs **4 :** SETTLE; *also* **:** ALLAY **5 :** SPREAD **6** ♦ **:** to make ready

beforehand for some purpose, use, or activity : PREPARE, CONTRIVE **7** ♦ : to stake on the outcome of an issue or the performance of a contestant : WAGER **8** ♦ : to impose esp. as a duty or burden **9** ♦ : to set in order or position **10** : to bring to a specified condition ⟨*laid* waste to the land⟩ **11** : to put forward : SUBMIT

♦ [2, 9] deposit, dispose, fix, place, position, put, set, set up, stick ♦ [6] contrive, fit, fix, get, prepare, ready ♦ [7] bet, gamble, go, stake, wager ♦ [8] assess, charge, exact, fine, impose, levy, put

²lay *n* : the way in which something lies or is laid in relation to something else

³lay *past of* ¹LIE

⁴lay *n* **1** : a simple narrative poem **2** ♦ : a short musical composition of words and music : SONG

♦ air, melody, song, strain, tune, warble

⁵lay *adj* **1** : of or relating to the laity **2** : not of a particular profession; *also* : lacking extensive knowledge of a particular subject

lay•away \'lā-ə-ˌwā\ *n* : a purchasing agreement by which a retailer agrees to hold merchandise secured by a deposit until the price is paid in full

lay away *vb* ♦ : to put aside for future use or delivery

♦ cache, hoard, lay up, put by, salt away, stash, stockpile, store

lay down *vb* ♦ : to institute (as a law) by enactment or agreement; *also* : to assert or command dogmatically

♦ define, prescribe, specify ♦ enact, legislate, make, pass

lay•er \'lā-ər\ *n* **1** : one that lays **2** : one thickness, course, or fold laid or lying over or under another

lay•ette \lā-'et\ *n* : an outfit of clothing and equipment for a newborn infant

lay•man \'lā-mən\ *n* : a person who is a member of the laity

lay•off \'lā-ˌof\ *n* **1** : a period of inactivity **2** ♦ : the act of dismissing an employee usu. temporarily

♦ discharge, dismissal

lay off *vb* ♦ : to desist from

♦ *usu* **lay off of** discontinue, drop, give up, knock off, quit

lay on *vb* : to make an attack

lay•out \'lā-ˌaut\ *n* ♦ : the final arrangement, plan, or design of something

♦ arrangement, composition, configuration, design, form, format, makeup, pattern

lay out *vb* **1** ♦ : to use up or pay out **2** ♦ : to plan in detail

♦ [1] disburse, expend, give, pay, spend ♦ [2] arrange, blueprint, calculate, chart, design, frame, map, plan, project, scheme

lay•over \-ˌō-vər\ *n* : STOPOVER

lay•per•son \-ˌpər-sən\ *n* : a member of the laity

lay up *vb* ♦ : to store up

♦ cache, hoard, lay away, put by, salt away, stash, stockpile, store

lay•wom•an \'lā-ˌwu̇-mən\ *n* : a woman who is a member of the laity

la•zar \'la-zər, 'lā-\ *n* : LEPER

laze \'lāz\ *vb* **lazed; laz•ing** : to pass time in idleness or relaxation

la•zi•ness \-zē-nəs\ *n* ♦ : the quality or state of being lazy

♦ idleness, indolence, inertia, sloth *Ant* drive, industriousness, industry

la•zy \'lā-zē\ *adj* **la•zi•er; -est 1** ♦ : disliking activity or exertion **2** : encouraging idleness **3** : SLUGGISH **4** : DROOPY, LAX **5** : not rigorous or strict — **la•zi•ly** \-zə-lē\ *adv*

♦ idle, indolent, shiftless, slothful *Ant* industrious

la•zy•bones \-ˌbōnz\ *n sing or pl* ♦ : a lazy individual

♦ idler, loafer, slouch, slug, sluggard *Ant* doer, go-getter, hummer, hustler, rustler, self-starter

lazy Su•san \ˌlā-zē-'süz-ᵊn\ *n* : a revolving tray used for serving food

lb *abbr* pound

lc *abbr* lowercase

LC *abbr* Library of Congress

¹LCD \ˌel-(ˌ)sē-'dē\ *n* : a display (as of the time in a digital watch) that consists of segments of a liquid crystal whose reflectivity varies with the voltage applied to them

²LCD *abbr* least common denominator; lowest common denominator

LCDR *abbr* lieutenant commander

LCM *abbr* least common multiple; lowest common multiple

LCpl *abbr* lance corporal

LCS *abbr* League Championship Series

ld *abbr* **1** load **2** lord

LD *abbr* learning disabled; learning disability

LDC *abbr* less developed country

ldg *abbr* **1** landing **2** loading

LDL \ˌel-(ˌ)dē-'el\ *n* : a cholesterol-rich protein-poor lipoprotein of blood plasma correlated with increased probability of developing atherosclerosis

L–do•pa \'el-'dō-pə\ *n* : an isomer of dopa used esp. in the treatment of Parkinson's disease

LDS *abbr* Latter-day Saints

lea \'lē, 'lā\ *n* : farmland having chiefly forage plants and esp. grasses : PASTURE

leach \'lēch\ *vb* : to pass a liquid (as water) through to carry off the soluble components; *also* : to dissolve out by such means ⟨∼ alkali from ashes⟩

¹lead \'lēd\ *vb* **led** \'led\; **lead•ing 1** ♦ : to guide on a way **2** : LIVE ⟨∼ a quiet life⟩ **3** ♦ : to direct the operations, activity, or performance of ⟨∼ an orchestra⟩ **4** : to go at the head of : be first ⟨∼ a parade⟩ **5** : to begin play with; *also* : BEGIN, OPEN **6** : to tend toward a definite result ⟨study ∼*ing* to a degree⟩ **7** ♦ : to lie, run, or open in a specified place or direction

♦ [1] conduct, direct, guide, marshal, pilot, route, show, steer, usher *Ant* follow, trail ♦ [3] boss, captain, command, dominate, head, spearhead ♦ [7] extend, go, head, lie, run

²lead \'lēd\ *n* **1 a** : a position at the front **b** ♦ : a margin by which one leads **2** : the privilege of leading in cards; *also* : the card or suit led **3** : EXAMPLE **4** : one that leads **5** : a principal role (as in a play); *also* : one who plays such a role **6** ♦ : something serving as an indication, tip, or clue **7** : an insulated electrical conductor

♦ [1b] distance, length, remove, spread, stretch, way ♦ [6] clue, cue, hint, indication, inkling, intimation, suggestion, tip

³lead \'led\ *n* **1** : a heavy malleable bluish white chemical element **2** : an article made of lead; *esp* : a weight for sounding at sea **3** : a thin strip of metal used to separate lines of type in printing **4** : a thin stick of marking substance in or for a pencil

⁴lead \'led\ *vb* **1** : to cover, line, or weight with lead **2** : to fix (glass) in position with lead **3** : to treat or mix with lead or a lead compound

lead•en \'led-ᵊn\ *adj* **1 a** : made of lead **b** ♦ : of the color of lead **2 a** : SLUGGISH **b** ♦ : lacking spirit or animation : DULL ⟨a ∼ lecture⟩

♦ [1b] gray (*or* grey), pewter, silver, silvery, slate, steely ♦ [2b] drab, dreary, dry, dull, flat, heavy, humdrum, monotonous, ponderous

lead•er *n* **1** ♦ : something that leads; *also* : a conduit for leading fluid from one place to another **2** ♦ : a person who leads — **lead•er•less** *adj* — **lead•er•ship** *n*

♦ [1] channel, conduit, duct, line, penstock, pipe, tube ♦ [2] boss, captain, chief, foreman, head, headman, helmsman, kingpin, taskmaster

lead•off \'lēd-ˌof\ *adj* ♦ : of, relating to, or being one that leads off — **leadoff** *n*

♦ first, foremost, inaugural, initial, maiden, original, pioneer, premier

lead off *vb* : OPEN, BEGIN; *esp* : to bat first in an inning

lead on *vb* ♦ : to entice or induce to adopt or continue in a course or belief esp. when unwise or mistaken

♦ allure, beguile, decoy, entice, lure, seduce, tempt

¹leaf \'lēf\ *n, pl* **leaves** \'lēvz\ **1** : a usu. flat and green outgrowth of a plant stem that is a unit of foliage and functions esp. in photosynthesis; *also* : FOLIAGE **2** : something that is suggestive of a leaf — **leaf•less** *adj*

²leaf *vb* **1** : to produce leaves **2** : to turn the pages of a book

leaf•age \'lē-fij\ *n* ♦ : all the leaves of one or more plants : FOLIAGE

♦ flora, foliage, green, greenery, herbage, vegetation, verdure

leafed \'lēft\ *adj* : LEAVED

leaf•hop•per \'lēf-ˌhä-pər\ *n* : any of a family of small leaping insects related to the cicadas that suck the juices of plants

leaf•let \'lē-flət\ *n* **1** : a division of a compound leaf **2** ♦ : a usu. folded printed sheet intended for free distribution : PAMPHLET, FOLDER

♦ booklet, brochure, circular, folder, pamphlet

leaf mold *n* : a compost or layer composed chiefly of decayed leaves

leaf·stalk \'lēf-ˌstȯk\ *n* : PETIOLE

leafy *adj* **leaf·i·er; -est** ♦ : furnished with or abounding in leaves

♦ green, lush, luxuriant, verdant

¹league \'lēg\ *n* : a unit of distance equal to about three miles (five kilometers)

²league *n* **1** ♦ : an association or alliance for a common purpose **2** : CLASS, CATEGORY — **leagu·er** \'lē-gər\ *n*

♦ association, brotherhood, club, college, congress, council, fellowship, fraternity, guild, institute, institution, order, organization, society ♦ alliance, bloc, coalition, combination, combine, confederacy, confederation, federation, union

³league *vb* **leagued; leagu·ing** ♦ : to form a league

♦ ally, associate, band, club, confederate, conjoin, cooperate, federate, unite

¹leak \'lēk\ *vb* **1** : to enter or escape through a leak **2** : to let a substance in or out through an opening **3** ♦ : to become or make known

♦ *usu* **leak out** come out, get out, out, spread

²leak *n* **1** : a crack or hole that accidentally admits a fluid or light or lets it escape; *also* : something that secretly or accidentally permits the admission or escape of something else **2** : LEAKAGE — **leaky** *adj*

leak·age \'lē-kij\ *n* **1** : the act of leaking **2** : the thing or amount that leaks

¹lean \'lēn\ *vb* **1** ♦ : to bend from a vertical position : INCLINE **2** : to cast one's weight to one side for support **3** ♦ : to rely for support **4** ♦ : to incline in opinion, taste, or desire

♦ [1] angle, cant, cock, heel, incline, list, slant, slope, tilt, tip ♦ [3] count, depend, reckon, rely ♦ [4] incline, run, tend, trend ♦ *usu* **lean toward** [4] favor (*or* favour), like, prefer

²lean *adj* **1** ♦ : lacking or deficient in flesh and esp. in fat **2** : lacking richness or productiveness **3** : low in fuel content — **lean·ness** *n*

♦ skinny, slender, slim, spare, thin

³lean *n* ♦ : the act or an instance of leaning

♦ cant, diagonal, grade, inclination, incline, pitch, slant, slope, tilt, upgrade

leaning *n* ♦ : a definite but not decisive attraction or tendency — often used in pl.

♦ affinity, bent, devices, disposition, genius, inclination, partiality, penchant, predilection, predisposition, proclivity, propensity, talent, tendency, turn ♦ current, drift, run, tendency, tide, trend, wind

leant \'lent\ *chiefly Brit past of* LEAN

lean-to \'lēn-ˌtü\ *n, pl* **lean-tos** \-ˌtüz\ : a wing or extension of a building having a roof of only one slope; *also* : a rough shed or shelter with a similar roof

¹leap \'lēp\ *vb* **leapt** \'lēpt, 'lept\ *or* **leaped; leap·ing** ♦ : to spring free from a surface or over an obstacle : JUMP

♦ bound, hop, jump, spring, vault

²leap *n* ♦ : an act of leaping : JUMP

♦ bound, hop, jump, spring, vault

leap·frog \'lēp-ˌfrȯg, -ˌfräg\ *n* : a game in which a player bends down and is vaulted over by another — **leapfrog** *vb*

leap year *n* : a year containing 366 days with February 29 as the extra day

learn \'lərn\ *vb* **learned** \'lərnd, 'lərnt\ *or Can and Brit* **learnt** \'lərnt\; **learn·ing 1 a** ♦ : to gain knowledge, understanding, or skill by study or experience **b** : to commit to memory : MEMORIZE ⟨∼ the poem⟩ **2** ♦ : to find out : ASCERTAIN ⟨∼ the truth⟩ — **learn·er** *n*

♦ [1a] get, master, pick up *Ant* unlearn ♦ [2] detect, determine, dig up, discover, ferret out, find, hit on, locate, track down

learn·ed \'lər-nəd\ *adj* ♦ : characterized by or associated with learning : ERUDITE — **learn·ed·ly** *adv*

♦ educated, erudite, knowledgeable, literate, scholarly, well-read

learn·ing \'lər-niŋ\ *n* ♦ : knowledge or skill acquired by instruction or study : ERUDITION

♦ education, erudition, knowledge, scholarship, science

learning disability *n* : any of various conditions (as dyslexia) that interfere with a person's ability to learn and so result in impaired functioning (as in language) — **learning disabled** *adj*

learnt \'lərnt\ *chiefly Can and Brit past and past part of* LEARN

¹lease \'lēs\ *n* : a contract transferring real estate for a term of years or at will usu. for a specified rent

²lease *vb* **leased; leas·ing 1** : to grant by lease **2** ♦ : to hold under a lease

♦ engage, hire, let, rent

lease·hold \'lēs-ˌhōld\ *n* **1** : a tenure by lease **2** : land held by lease — **lease·hold·er** *n*

leash \'lēsh\ *n* : a line for leading or restraining an animal — **leash** *vb*

¹least \'lēst\ *adj* **1** : lowest in importance or position **2** ♦ : smallest in size or degree **3** : SLIGHTEST

♦ minimal, minimum

²least *n* : one that is least

³least *adv* : in the smallest or lowest degree

least common denominator *n* : the least common multiple of two or more denominators

least common multiple *n* : the smallest common multiple of two or more numbers

least·wise \'lēst-ˌwīz\ *adv* : at least

leath·er \'le-thər\ *n* : animal skin dressed for use — **leath·ern** \-thərn\ *adj* — **leath·ery** *adj*

leath·er·back \-ˌbak\ *n* : the largest existing sea turtle with a flexible leathery carapace

leath·er·neck \-ˌnek\ *n* : MARINE

¹leave \'lēv\ *vb* **left** \'left\; **leav·ing 1** ♦ : to allow or cause to remain behind **2** : to have as a remainder **3** ♦ : to give or leave by will : BEQUEATH **4** : to let stay without interference **5** : to go away : depart from **6** ♦ : to give up esp. with the intent of never again claiming a right or interest in

♦ [1] abandon, desert, forsake, quit ♦ [3] commend, commit, consign, delegate, deliver, entrust, give, hand over, pass, transfer, transmit, trust, turn over, vest ♦ [6] quit, resign, retire, step down

²leave *n* **1** ♦ : permission to do something; *also* : authorized absence from duty **2** : DEPARTURE

♦ break, recess, vacation ♦ allowance, authorization, clearance, concurrence, consent, license (*or* licence), permission, sanction, sufferance

³leave *vb* **leaved; leav·ing** : LEAF

leaved \'lēvd\ *adj* : having leaves

¹leav·en \'le-vən\ *n* **1** : a substance (as yeast) used to produce fermentation (as in dough) **2** : something that modifies or lightens

²leaven *vb* : to raise (dough) with a leaven; *also* : to permeate with a modifying or vivifying element

leav·en·ing *n* : LEAVEN

leave off *vb* ♦ : to cause to cease; *also* : to cease activity or operation

♦ break, break off, cease, cut, desist, discontinue, drop, end, halt, knock off, layoff, quit, shut off, stop

leaves *pl of* LEAF

leave–tak·ing \'lēv-ˌtā-kiŋ\ *n* ♦ : the act or an instance of departing : FAREWELL

♦ departure, exit, farewell, parting

leav·ings \'lē-viŋz\ *n pl* ♦ : a usu. small part, member, or trace remaining : REMNANT, RESIDUE

♦ balance, leftovers, odds and ends, remainder, remains, remnant, residue, rest

Leb·a·nese \ˌle-bə-'nēz, -'nēs\ *n* : a native or inhabitant of Lebanon — **Lebanese** *adj*

lech·ery \'le-chə-rē\ *n* : inordinate indulgence in sexual activity — **lech·er** \'le-chər\ *n* — **lech·er·ous** \'le-chə-rəs\ *adj* — **lech·er·ous·ly** *adv* — **lech·er·ous·ness** *n*

lec·i·thin \'le-sə-thən\ *n* : any of several waxy phosphorus-containing substances that are common in animals and plants, form colloidal solutions in water, and have emulsifying and wetting properties

lect *abbr* lecture; lecturer

lec·tern \'lek-tərn\ *n* : a stand to support a book for a standing reader

lec·tor \-tər\ *n* : one whose chief duty is to read the lessons in a church service

¹lec·ture \'lek-chər\ *n* **1** : a discourse given before an audience esp. for instruction **2** : REPRIMAND — **lec·tur·er** *n* — **lec·ture·ship** *n*

²lec·ture *vb* **lec·tured; lec·tur·ing 1 ♦ :** to deliver a lecture or a course of lectures **2 ♦ :** to reprove formally

♦ [1] declaim, descant, discourse, harangue, orate, speak, talk ♦ [2] rebuke, reprimand, reproach, scold

led *past and past part of* LEAD

LED \ˌel-(ˌ)ē-ˈdē\ *n* **:** a semiconductor diode that emits light when a voltage is applied to it and is used esp. for electronic displays

le·der·ho·sen \ˈlā-dər-ˌhōz-ᵊn\ *n pl* **:** leather shorts often with suspenders worn esp. in Bavaria

ledge \ˈlej\ *n* **1 :** a shelflike projection from a top or an edge **2 :** REEF

led·ger \ˈle-jər\ *n* **:** a book containing accounts to which debits and credits are transferred in final form

lee \ˈlē\ *n* **1 :** a protecting shelter **2 :** the side (as of a ship) that is sheltered from the wind — **lee** *adj*

leech \ˈlēch\ *n* **1 :** any of various bloodsucking segmented usu. freshwater worms that are related to the earthworms and have a sucker at each end **2 ♦ :** a hanger-on who seeks gain

♦ hanger-on, parasite, sponge

leek \ˈlēk\ *n* **:** an onionlike herb grown for its mildly pungent leaves and stalk

leer \ˈlir\ *n* **:** a suggestive, knowing, or malicious look — **leer** *vb*

leery \ˈlir-ē\ *adj* **♦ :** disposed to suspect **:** SUSPICIOUS

♦ distrustful, incredulous, mistrustful, skeptical, suspicious

lees \ˈlēz\ *n pl* **♦ :** the sediment of a liquor (as wine) during fermentation and aging **:** DREGS

♦ dregs, grounds, sediment

¹lee·ward \ˈlē-wərd, ˈlü-ərd\ *n* **:** the lee side

²leeward *adj* **:** situated away from the wind

lee·way \ˈlē-ˌwā\ *n* **1 :** lateral movement of a ship when under way **2 :** an allowable margin of freedom or variation

¹left \ˈleft\ *adj* **1 :** of, relating to, or being the side of the body in which the heart is mostly located; *also* **:** located nearer to this side than to the right **2** *often cap* **:** of, adhering to, or constituted by the political left — **left** *adv*

²left *n* **1 :** the left hand; *also* **:** the side or part that is on or toward the left side **2** *often cap* **:** those professing political views marked by desire to reform the established order and usu. to give greater freedom to the common people — **left·most** \-ˌmōst\ *adj*

³left *past and past part of* LEAVE

left–click \ˈleft-ˈklik\ *vb* **:** to press the leftmost button on a computer mouse or similar input device

left–hand *adj* **1 :** situated on the left **2 :** LEFT-HANDED

left–hand·ed \ˈleft-ˈhan-dəd\ *adj* **1 :** using the left hand habitually or more easily than the right **2 :** designed for or done with the left hand **3 ♦ :** not sincere **:** INSINCERE, BACKHANDED ⟨a ∼ compliment⟩ **4 :** COUNTERCLOCKWISE — **left–handed** *adv*

♦ artificial, double-dealing, feigned, hypocritical, insincere, mealy, mealymouthed, two-faced, unctuous

left·ism \ˈlef-ˌti-zəm\ *n* **1 :** the principles and views of the Left **2 :** advocacy of the doctrines of the Left — **left·ist** \-tist\ *n or adj*

left·over \ˈleft-ˌō-vər\ *n* **♦ :** something that remains unused or unconsumed; *esp* **:** leftover food served at a later meal — usu. used in pl.

♦ end, fag end, remainder, remnant, scrap ♦ *usu* **leftovers** balance, leavings, odds and ends, remainder, remains, residue, rest

lefty \ˈlef-tē\ *n, pl* **left·ies 1 :** a left-handed person **2 :** an advocate of leftism

¹leg \ˈleg\ *n* **1 :** a limb of an animal used esp. for supporting the body and in walking; *also* **:** the part of the vertebrate leg between knee and foot **2 :** something resembling or analogous to an animal leg ⟨table ∼⟩ **3 :** the part of an article of clothing that covers the leg **4 :** a portion of a trip **5** *pl* **:** long-term appeal or interest — **leg·ged** \ˈle-gəd\ *adj* — **leg·less** *adj*

♦ lap, stage, step

²leg *vb* **legged; leg·ging ♦ :** to use the legs in walking or esp. in running

♦ *usu* **leg it** foot, pad, step, traipse, tread, walk

³leg *abbr* **1** legal **2** legislative; legislature

leg·a·cy \ˈle-gə-sē\ *n, pl* **-cies :** something that is or may be inherited **:** INHERITANCE; *also* **:** something that has come from a predecessor or the past

le·gal \ˈlē-gəl\ *adj* **1 :** of or relating to law or lawyers **2 a ♦ :** conforming to or permitted by law or established rules **:** LAW-

FUL **b :** STATUTORY **3 :** enforced in courts of law — **le·gal·i·ty** \li-ˈga-lə-tē\ *n* — **le·gal·ize** \ˈlē-gə-ˌlīz\ *vb* — **le·gal·ly** *adv*

♦ clean, fair, sportsmanlike ♦ allowable, good, innocent, justifiable, permissible, proper, regulation, right **Ant** illegal, illegitimate, illicit, unlawful, wrongful

le·gal·ese \ˌlē-gə-ˈlēz\ *n* **:** the specialized language of the legal profession

le·gal·ism \ˈlē-gə-ˌli-zəm\ *n* **1 :** strict, literal, or excessive conformity to the law or to a religious or moral code **2 :** a legal term — **le·gal·is·tic** \ˌlē-gə-ˈlis-tik\ *adj*

leg·ate \ˈle-gət\ *n* **♦ :** an official representative

♦ ambassador, delegate, emissary, envoy, minister, representative

leg·a·tee \ˌle-gə-ˈtē\ *n* **:** a person to whom a legacy is bequeathed

le·ga·tion \li-ˈgā-shən\ *n* **1 :** a diplomatic mission headed by a minister **2 :** the official residence and office of a minister in a foreign country

le·ga·to \li-ˈgä-tō\ *adv or adj* **:** in a smooth and connected manner (as of music)

leg·end \ˈle-jənd\ *n* **1 a :** a story coming down from the past; *esp* **:** one popularly accepted as historical though not verifiable **b ♦ :** a body of popular stories **2 :** an inscription on an object; *also* **:** CAPTION **3 :** an explanatory list of the symbols on a map or chart

♦ folklore, lore, myth, mythology, tradition

leg·end·ary \ˈle-jən-ˌder-ē\ *adj* **1 ♦ :** of, relating to, or characteristic of a legend **2 :** FAMOUS ⟨∼ actors⟩ — **leg·en·dari·ly** \-ˌder-ə-lē\ *adv*

♦ fabled, fabulous, mythical

leg·er·de·main \ˌle-jər-də-ˈmān\ *n* **1 :** SLEIGHT OF HAND **2 a ♦ :** skill and dexterity in conjuring tricks **b ♦ :** adroitness in deception

♦ [2a] magic, prestidigitation ♦ [2b] artifice, chicanery, hanky-panky, subterfuge, trickery

leg·ging *or* **leg·gin** \ˈle-gən, -gin\ *n* **:** a covering for the leg; *also* **:** TIGHTS

leg·gy \ˈle-gē\ *adj* **leg·gi·er; -est 1 :** having unusually long legs **2 :** having long and attractive legs **3 :** SPINDLY — used of a plant

leg·horn \ˈleg-ˌhȯrn, ˈle-gərn\ *n* **1 :** a fine plaited straw; *also* **:** a hat made of this straw **2 :** any of a Mediterranean breed of small hardy chickens

leg·i·ble \ˈle-jə-bəl\ *adj* **:** capable of being read **:** CLEAR — **leg·i·bil·i·ty** \ˌle-jə-ˈbi-lə-tē\ *n* — **leg·i·bly** \ˈle-jə-blē\ *adv*

¹le·gion \ˈlē-jən\ *n* **1 :** a unit of the Roman army comprising 3000 to 6000 soldiers **2 :** a very large number **:** MULTITUDE ⟨∼s of fans⟩ **3 :** an association of ex-servicemen **4 ♦ :** a large military force

♦ [2] army, crowd, crush, drove, flock, horde, host, mob, multitude, press, swarm, throng ♦ [4] army, battalion, host

²legion *adj* **:** MANY, NUMEROUS

le·gion·ary \-jə-ˌner-ē\ *n* **:** LEGIONNAIRE

le·gion·naire \ˌlē-jə-ˈnar\ *n* **♦ :** a member of a legion

♦ fighter, man-at-arms, regular, serviceman, soldier, warrior

Legionnaires' disease *also* **Legionnaire's disease** \-ˈnerz-\ **:** a lobar pneumonia caused by a bacterium

legis *abbr* legislation; legislative; legislature

leg·is·late \ˈle-jəs-ˌlāt\ *vb* **-lat·ed; -lat·ing ♦ :** to make or enact laws; *also* **:** to bring about by legislation

♦ enact, lay down, make, pass

leg·is·la·tion \ˌle-jəs-ˈlā-shən\ *n* **1 :** the action of legislating **2 :** laws made by a legislative body

leg·is·la·tive \ˈle-jəs-ˌlā-tiv\ *adj* **1 :** having the power of legislating **2 :** of or relating to a legislature or legislation

leg·is·la·tor \-ˌlā-tər\ *n* **♦ :** one that makes laws esp. for a political unit; *esp* **:** a member of a legislative body

♦ lawmaker, solon

leg·is·la·ture \ˈle-jəs-ˌlā-chər\ *n* **:** an organized body of persons having the authority to make laws

le·git \li-ˈjit\ *adj, slang* **:** LEGITIMATE

¹le·git·i·mate \li-ˈji-tə-mət\ *adj* **1 :** lawfully begotten **2 :** GENUINE **3 :** LAWFUL **4 :** conforming to recognized principles or accepted rules or standards — **le·git·i·ma·cy** \-mə-sē\ *n* — **le·git·i·mate·ly** *adv*

²le·git·i·mate \-ˌmāt\ *vb* **-mat·ed; -mat·ing :** to make legitimate

le·git·i·mise *chiefly Brit var of* LEGITIMIZE

le·git·i·mize \li-'ji-tə-ˌmīz\ *vb* **-mized; -miz·ing** : LEGITIMATE

leg·man \'leg-ˌman\ *n* **1** : a reporter assigned usu. to gather information **2** : an assistant who gathers information and runs errands

le·gume \'le-ˌgyüm, li-'gyüm\ *n* **1** : any of a large family of plants having fruits that are dry pods and split when ripe and including important food and forage plants (as beans and clover); *also* : the part (as seeds or pods) of a legume used as food **2** : the pod of a legume — **le·gu·mi·nous** \li-'gyü-mə-nəs\ *adj*

lei \'lā, 'lā-ˌē\ *n* : a wreath or necklace usu. of flowers

lei·sure \'lē-zhər, 'le-, 'lā-\ *n* **1** ♦ : freedom provided by the cessation of activities; *also* : time free from work or duties **2** : EASE; *also* : CONVENIENCE ⟨read it at your ∼⟩

  ♦ ease, relaxation, repose, rest

¹**lei·sure·ly** *adj* : characterized by slowness

²**leisurely** *adv* : without haste

leit·mo·tif *also* **leit·mo·tiv** \'līt-mō-ˌtēf\ *n* : a dominant recurring theme

lem·ming \'le-miŋ\ *n* : any of various short-tailed rodents found mostly in northern regions and noted for recurrent mass migrations

lem·on \'le-mən\ *n* **1** : an acid yellow usu. nearly oblong citrus fruit; *also* : a citrus tree that bears lemons **2** ♦ : something (as an automobile) unsatisfactory or defective — **lem·ony** *adj*

  ♦ bummer, dud, failure, fizzle, flop, loser, turkey, washout

lem·on·ade \ˌle-mə-'nād\ *n* : a beverage of lemon juice, sugar, and water

lemon curd *n* : a custard made with lemon juice, butter, sugar, and eggs

lem·on·grass \'le-mən-ˌgras\ *n* : a tropical Asian grass grown for its lemon-scented foliage used as a seasoning

le·mur \'lē-mər\ *n* : any of various arboreal primates largely of Madagascar that have large eyes, very soft woolly fur, and a long furry tail

Len·a·pe \'le-nə-pē, lə-'nä-pē\ *n, pl* **Lenape** *or* **Lenapes** : DELAWARE

lend \'lend\ *vb* **lent** \'lent\; **lend·ing** **1** : to give for temporary use on condition that the same or its equivalent be returned **2** : AFFORD, FURNISH **3** : ACCOMMODATE — **lend·er** *n*

lend–lease \-'lēs\ *n* : the transfer of goods and services to an ally to aid in a common cause with payment made by a return of the items or their use in the cause or by a similar transfer of other goods and services

length \'leŋth\ *n* **1 a** : the longer or longest dimension of an object **b** ♦ : a measured distance **2** : duration or extent in time or space **3** : the length of something taken as a unit of measure **4** : a single piece of a series of pieces that may be joined together ⟨a ∼ of pipe⟩ — **at length** **1** : in full **2** : FINALLY

  ♦ distance, lead, remove, spread, stretch, way

length·en \'leŋ-thən\ *vb* ♦ : to make or become longer

  ♦ draw out, elongate, extend, prolong, protract, stretch

length·wise \'leŋth-ˌwīz\ *adv* : in the direction of the length — **lengthwise** *adj*

lengthy \'leŋ-thē\ *adj* **length·i·er; -est** **1** : protracted excessively **2** ♦ : drawn out in length esp. of time : EXTENDED, LONG

  ♦ extended, far, great, long

le·ni·en·cy \'lē-nē-ən-sē, -nyən-sē\ *n* ♦ : the quality or state of being lenient; *also* : a lenient disposition or practice

  ♦ charity, clemency, mercy, quarter

le·nient \'lē-nē-ənt, -nyənt\ *adj* : of mild and tolerant disposition or effect — **le·ni·ent·ly** *adv*

len·i·ty \'le-nə-tē\ *n* : the quality or state of being lenient : LENIENCY

lens \'lenz\ *n* **1** : a curved piece of glass or plastic used singly or combined in an optical instrument for forming an image; *also* : a device for focusing radiation other than light **2** : a transparent body in the eye that focuses light rays on receptors at the back of the eye

Lent \'lent\ *n* : a 40-day period of penitence and fasting observed from Ash Wednesday to Easter by many churches — **Lent·en** \-ᵊn\ *adj*

len·til \'lent-ᵊl\ *n* : a Eurasian annual legume grown for its flat edible seeds and for fodder; *also* : its seed

Leo \'lē-ō\ *n* **1** : a zodiacal constellation between Cancer and Virgo usu. pictured as a lion **2** : the 5th sign of the zodiac in astrology; *also* : one born under this sign

le·o·nine \'lē-ə-ˌnīn\ *adj* : of, relating to, or resembling a lion

leop·ard \'le-pərd\ *n* : a large usu. tawny and black-spotted cat of southern Asia and Africa

le·o·tard \'lē-ə-ˌtärd\ *n* : a close-fitting garment worn esp. by dancers and for exercise

lep·er \'le-pər\ *n* **1** : a person affected with leprosy **2** : OUTCAST

lep·re·chaun \'le-prə-ˌkän\ *n* ♦ : a mischievous elf of Irish folklore

  ♦ brownie, dwarf, elf, fairy, fay, gnome, hobgoblin, pixie, puck, troll

lep·ro·sy \'le-prə-sē\ *n* : a chronic bacterial disease marked esp. if not treated by slow-growing swellings with deformity and loss of sensation of affected parts — **lep·rous** \-prəs\ *adj*

lep·tin \'lep-tən\ *n* : a hormone that is produced by fat-containing cells and plays a role in body weight regulation

les·bi·an \'lez-bē-ən\ *n* : a gay woman — **lesbian** *adj* — **les·bi·an·ism** \-ə-ˌni-zəm\ *n*

lèse ma·jes·té *or* **lese maj·es·ty** \'läz-'ma-jə-stē, 'lez-, 'lēz-\ *n* : an offense violating the dignity of a sovereign

le·sion \'lē-zhən\ *n* : an abnormal structural change in the body due to injury or disease; *esp* : one clearly marked off from healthy tissue around it

¹**less** \'les\ *adj, comparative of* ¹LITTLE **1** : FEWER ⟨∼ than six⟩ **2** ♦ : of lower rank, degree, or importance **3** : SMALLER; *also* : more limited in quantity

  ♦ inferior, junior, lesser, lower, minor, subordinate, under

²**less** *adv, comparative of* ²LITTLE : to a lesser extent or degree

³**less** *n, pl* **less** **1** : a smaller portion **2** : something of less importance

⁴**less** *prep* : diminished by : MINUS

-less \ləs\ *adj suffix* **1** : destitute of : not having ⟨child*less*⟩ **2** : unable to be acted on or to act (in a specified way) ⟨daunt*less*⟩

les·see \le-'sē\ *n* : a tenant under a lease

less·en \'les-ᵊn\ *vb* ♦ : to make or become less

  ♦ abate, decline, decrease, de-escalate, die, diminish, dwindle, ebb, fall, let up, lower, moderate, recede, reduce, relent, shrink, subside, taper, wane

less·er \'le-sər\ *adj, comparative of* ¹LITTLE ♦ : of less size, quality, or significance

  ♦ inferior, junior, less, lower, minor, subordinate, under *Ant* major, more, primary, prime, senior, superior

les·son \'les-ᵊn\ *n* **1** : a passage from sacred writings read in a service of worship **2** : a reading or exercise to be studied by a pupil; *also* : something learned **3** : a period of instruction **4** : an instructive example

les·sor \'le-ˌsȯr, le-'sȯr\ *n* : one who conveys property by a lease

lest \ˌlest\ *conj* : for fear that

¹**let** \'let\ *n* **1** : something that impedes : HINDRANCE, OBSTACLE **2** : a shot or point in racket games that does not count

²**let** *vb* **let; let·ting** **1** : to cause to : MAKE ⟨∼ it be known⟩ **2** : to offer or grant for rent or lease; *also* : to assign esp. after bids **3** ♦ : to give opportunity or permission to : ALLOW ⟨∼ me go⟩

  ♦ allow, enable, permit, suffer

-let \lət\ *n suffix* **1** : small one ⟨book*let*⟩ **2** : article worn on ⟨wrist*let*⟩

let·down \'let-ˌdau̇n\ *n* **1** ♦ : the state or emotion of being disappointed **2** : a slackening of effort

  ♦ disappointment, dismay, dissatisfaction, frustration

let down *vb* ♦ : to fail to meet the expectation or hope of; *also* : to cause disappointment

  ♦ cheat, disappoint, dissatisfy, fail

le·thal \'lē-thəl\ *adj* ♦ : of, relating to, or causing death : DEADLY, FATAL ⟨∼ weapons⟩ — **le·thal·ly** *adv*

  ♦ baleful, deadly, deathly, fatal, fell, mortal, murderous, pestilent, vital

le·thar·gic \li-'thär-jik\ *adj* ♦ : of, relating to, or characterized by lethargy

  ♦ dull, inactive, inert, quiescent, sleepy, sluggish, torpid

leth·ar·gy \'le-thər-jē\ *n* **1** : abnormal drowsiness **2** : the quality or state of being lazy or indifferent

let on *vb* **1** : REVEAL 1 **2** : PRETEND

¹**let·ter** \'le-tər\ *n* **1** : a symbol that stands for a speech sound and constitutes a unit of an alphabet **2** ♦ : a written or printed communication **3** *pl* : LITERATURE; *also* : LEARNING **4** : the literal meaning ⟨the ∼ of the law⟩ **5** : a single piece of type

  ♦ dispatch, memorandum, missive, note

²letter *vb* : to mark with letters : INSCRIBE — **let·ter·er** *n*

letter bomb *n* : an explosive device concealed in an envelope and mailed to the intended victim

let·ter·boxed \'le-tər-ˌbäkst\ *adj* : being a video recording formatted to display a frame size proportional to a standard theater screen

letter carrier *n* ♦ : an individual who delivers mail

♦ mailman, postman

let·ter·head \'le-tər-ˌhed\ *n* : stationery with a printed or engraved heading; *also* : the heading itself

let·ter–per·fect \ˌle-tər-'pər-fikt\ *adj* ♦ : correct to the smallest detail

♦ absolute, faultless, flawless, ideal, impeccable, perfect, unblemished

let·ter·press \'le-tər-ˌpres\ *n* : printing done directly by impressing the paper on an inked raised surface

letters of marque \-'märk\ : a license granted to a private person by a government to fit out an armed ship to capture enemy shipping

letters patent *n pl* : a written grant from a government to a person in a form readily open for inspection by all

let·tuce \'le-təs\ *n* : a garden composite plant with crisp leaves used esp. in salads

let·up \'let-ˌəp\ *n* : a lessening of effort

let up *vb* ♦ : to diminish or slow down; *also* : to come to a stop

♦ cease, end, halt, quit, stop ♦ abate, decrease, die, diminish, dwindle, ebb, fall, lessen, subside, taper, wane

leu·kae·mia *chiefly Brit var of* LEUKEMIA

leu·ke·mia \lü-'kē-mē-ə\ *n* : a malignant disease characterized by an abnormal increase in the number of white blood cells in the blood-forming tissues — **leu·ke·mic** \-mik\ *adj or n*

leu·ko·cyte \'lü-kə-ˌsīt\ *n* : WHITE BLOOD CELL

Lev *or* **Levit** *abbr* Leviticus

¹le·vee \'le-vē; lə-'vē, -'vā\ *n* : a reception held by or for a person of distinction

²lev·ee \'le-vē\ *n* ♦ : an embankment to prevent or confine flooding; *also* : a river landing place

♦ dam, dike, embankment ♦ dock, landing, pier

¹lev·el \'le-vəl\ *n* **1** : a device for establishing a horizontal line or plane **2** : horizontal condition **3** : a horizontal position, line, or surface often taken as an index of altitude; *also* : a flat area of ground **4** ♦ : height, position, rank, or size in a scale

♦ degree, footing, place, position, rank, situation, standing, station, status

²level *vb* **-eled** *or* **-elled; -el·ing** *or* **-el·ling** **1** ♦ : to make flat or level; *also* : to come to a level **2** : to direct to or toward a specified object or goal : AIM **3** ♦ : to bring to a common level or plane : EQUALIZE **4** : RAZE **5** ♦ : to knock down — **lev·el·er** *n*

♦ [1] even, plane, smooth ♦ [3] balance, equalize, equate, even ♦ [5] bowl, down, drop, fell, floor, knock

³level *adj* **1** ♦ : having a flat even surface **2** : HORIZONTAL **3** : of the same height or rank; *also* : UNIFORM **4** : steady and cool in judgment — **lev·el·ly** *adv* — **lev·el·ness** *n*

♦ even, flat, flush, plane, smooth *Ant* bumpy, coarse, lumpy, rough, uneven

lev·el·head·ed \ˌle-vəl-'he-dəd\ *adj* ♦ : having sound judgment : SENSIBLE ⟨a ∼ decision⟩

♦ good, hard, informed, just, logical, rational, reasonable, reasoned, sensible, sober, solid, valid, well-founded

le·ver \'le-vər, 'lē-\ *n* **1** : a bar used for prying or dislodging something; *also* : a means for achieving one's purpose **2** : a rigid piece turning about an axis and used for transmitting and changing force and motion

le·ver·age \'le-vrij, 'lē-, -və-rij\ *n* : the action or mechanical effect of a lever

le·vi·a·than \li-'vī-ə-thən\ *n* **1** : a large sea animal **2** ♦ : something large or formidable

♦ behemoth, blockbuster, colossus, giant, jumbo, mammoth, monster, titan, whale, whopper

lev·i·tate \'le-və-ˌtāt\ *vb* **-tat·ed; -tat·ing** : to rise or cause to rise in the air in seeming defiance of gravitation — **lev·i·ta·tion** \ˌle-və-'tā-shən\ *n*

Le·vit·i·cus \li-'vi-tə-kəs\ *n* : a book of Jewish and Christian Scripture

lev·i·ty \'le-və-tē\ *n* ♦ : lack of seriousness

♦ facetiousness, flightiness, flippancy, frivolity, lightness

levo·do·pa \ˌle-və-'dō-pə\ *n* : L-DOPA

¹levy \'le-vē\ *n, pl* **lev·ies** **1** ♦ : the imposition or collection of an assessment; *also* : an amount levied **2** : the enlistment or conscription of men for military service; *also* : troops raised by levy

♦ assessment, duty, impost, tax

²levy *vb* **lev·ied; levy·ing** **1** ♦ : to impose or collect by legal authority ⟨∼ taxes⟩ **2** : to enlist for military service **3** : WAGE ⟨∼ war⟩ **4** : to seize property

♦ assess, charge, exact, fine, impose, lay, put

lewd \'lüd\ *adj* **1** ♦ : sexually unchaste **2** ♦ : abhorrent to morality or virtue : OBSCENE, VULGAR — **lewd·ly** *adv*

♦ [1] lascivious, lustful, passionate, wanton ♦ [2] bawdy, coarse, crude, indecent, lascivious, obscene, pornographic, ribald, smutty, unprintable, vulgar, wanton

lewd·ness *n* ♦ : the quality or state of being lewd

♦ bawdiness, coarseness, grossness, indecency, nastiness, obscenity, ribaldry, smut, vulgarity

lex·i·cog·ra·phy \ˌlek-sə-'kä-grə-fē\ *n* **1** : the editing or making of a dictionary **2** : the principles and practices of dictionary making — **lex·i·cog·ra·pher** \-fər\ *n* — **lex·i·co·graph·i·cal** \-kō-'gra-fi-kəl\ *or* **lex·i·co·graph·ic** \-fik\ *adj*

lex·i·con \'lek-sə-ˌkän\ *n, pl* **lex·i·ca** \-si-kə\ *or* **lexicons** **1** : DICTIONARY **2** : the vocabulary of a language, speaker, or subject

lg *abbr* **1** large **2** long

LGBT *abbr* lesbian, gay, bisexual, and transgender

LH *abbr* **1** left hand **2** lower half

li *abbr* link

Li *symbol* lithium

LI *abbr* Long Island

li·a·bil·i·ty \ˌlī-ə-'bi-lə-tē\ *n, pl* **-ties** **1** ♦ : the quality or state of being liable **2** *pl* : DEBTS **3** ♦ : one that acts as a disadvantage : DISADVANTAGE

♦ [1] blame, fault, responsibility ♦ [3] disadvantage, drawback, handicap, minus, penalty, strike

li·a·ble \'lī-ə-bəl\ *adj* **1** ♦ : legally obligated : RESPONSIBLE **2** : LIKELY, APT ⟨∼ to fall⟩ **3** ♦ : exposed or subject to something usu. adverse : SUSCEPTIBLE

♦ [1] accountable, answerable, responsible ♦ [3] exposed, open, sensitive, subject, susceptible, vulnerable *Ant* invulnerable, unexposed

li·ai·son \'lē-ə-ˌzän, lē-'ā-\ *n* **1** ♦ : a close bond or connection **2** : an illicit sexual relationship **3** : communication for mutual understanding (as between parts of an armed force); *also* : one that carries on a liaison

♦ affiliation, alliance, association, collaboration, confederation, connection, cooperation, hookup, partnership, relation, relationship, union

li·ar \'lī-ər\ *n* ♦ : a person who lies

♦ fibber, prevaricator

¹lib \'lib\ *n* : LIBERATION

²lib *abbr* **1** liberal **2** librarian; library

li·ba·tion \lī-'bā-shən\ *n* **1** : an act of pouring a liquid as a sacrifice (as to a god); *also* : the liquid poured **2** ♦ : a drinkable liquid : DRINK

♦ beverage, drink, quencher

¹li·bel \'lī-bəl\ *n* **1** : a spoken or written statement or a representation that gives an unjustly unfavorable impression of a person or thing **2** ♦ : the action or crime of publishing a libel

♦ defamation, slander, vilification

²libel *vb* **-beled** *or* **-belled; -bel·ing** *or* **-bel·ling** ♦ : to make or publish a libel — **li·bel·er** *n* — **li·bel·ist** *n*

♦ blacken, defame, malign, slander, smear, traduce, vilify

li·bel·ous *or* **li·bel·lous** \-bə-ləs\ *adj* ♦ : constituting or including a libel

♦ defamatory, scandalous, slanderous

¹lib·er·al \'li-brəl, -bə-rəl\ *adj* **1** : of, relating to, or based on the liberal arts **2** ♦ : given or provided in a generous and openhanded way : GENEROUS, BOUNTIFUL; *also* : generous or more than adequate in size, scope, or capacity **3** : not literal **4 a** : not narrow in opinion or judgment : TOLERANT **b** ♦ : not orthodox **5** : not conservative — **lib·er·al·ize** \'li-brə-ˌlīz, -bə-rə-\ *vb*

♦ [2] abundant, ample, comfortable, generous, plentiful ♦ [2] bountiful, charitable, free, generous, munificent, openhanded, unselfish, unsparing ♦ [4b] broad-minded, nonortho-dox, nontraditional, open-minded, progressive, radical, uncon-ventional, unorthodox *Ant* conservative, conventional, old-fashioned, orthodox, traditional

²lib·er·al *n* : a person who holds liberal views
lib·er·al arts *n pl* : the studies (as language, philosophy, history, literature, or abstract science) in a college or university intended to provide chiefly general knowledge and to develop the general intellectual capacities
lib·er·al·ism \'li-brə-,li-zəm, -bə-rə-\ *n* : liberal principles and theories
lib·er·al·i·ty \,li-bə-'ra-lə-tē\ *n* ♦ : the quality or state of being liberal; *also* : an instance of this

♦ bounty, generosity, largesse, philanthropy, unselfishness *Ant* cheapness, closeness, meanness, miserliness, parsimony, pinch-ing, stinginess, tightness

lib·er·al·ly *adv* ♦ : in a liberal manner

♦ bountifully, generously, handsomely, well

lib·er·ate \'li-bə-,rāt\ *vb* **-at·ed; -at·ing 1** ♦ : to free from bondage or restraint; *also* : to raise to equal rights and status **2** : to free (as a gas) from combination — **lib·er·a·tor** \'li-bə-,rā-tər\ *n*

♦ discharge, emancipate, enfranchise, free, loose, loosen, manu-mit, release, spring, unbind, unchain, unfetter

lib·er·at·ed *adj* : freed from or opposed to traditional social and sexual attitudes or roles ⟨a ～ marriage⟩
lib·er·a·tion \,li-bə-'rā-shən\ *n* ♦ : the act of liberating : the state of being liberated

♦ emancipation, enfranchisement, manumission *Ant* enslave-ment

Li·be·ri·an \lī-'bir-ē-ən\ *n* : a native or inhabitant of Liberia — **Liberian** *adj*
lib·er·tar·i·an \,li-bər-'ter-ē-ən\ *n* **1** : an advocate of the doc-trine of free will **2** : one who upholds the principles of unre-stricted liberty
lib·er·tine \'li-bər-,tēn\ *n* ♦ : a person who leads a dissolute life

♦ decadent, degenerate, pervert, profligate

lib·er·ty \'li-bər-tē\ *n, pl* **-ties 1** ♦ : the quality or state of being free : FREEDOM **2** : an action going beyond normal limits; *esp* : FAMILIARITY **3** : a short leave from naval duty

♦ autonomy, freedom, independence, self-government, sover-eignty

li·bid·i·nous \lə-'bid-ªn-əs\ *adj* **1** : LASCIVIOUS **2** : LIBIDINAL
li·bi·do \lə-'bē-dō, -'bī-\ *n, pl* **-dos 1** : psychic energy derived from basic biological urges **2** : sexual drive — **li·bid·i·nal** \lə-'bid-ªn-əl\ *adj*
Li·bra \'lē-brə\ *n* **1** : a zodiacal constellation between Virgo and Scorpio usu. pictured as a balance scale **2** : the 7th sign of the zodiac in astrology; *also* : one born under this sign
li·brar·i·an \lī-'brer-ē-ən\ *n* : a specialist in the management of a library
li·brary \'lī-,brer-ē\ *n, pl* **-brar·ies 1** : a place in which books and related materials are kept for use but not for sale **2** : a col-lection of books
li·bret·to \lə-'bre-tō\ *n, pl* **-tos** *or* **-ti** \-tē\ : the text esp. of an opera — **li·bret·tist** \-tist\ *n*
Lib·y·an \'li-bē-ən\ *n* : a native or inhabitant of Libya — **Libyan** *adj*
lice *pl of* LOUSE
¹li·cense *or* **li·cence** \'līs-ªns\ *n* **1** ♦ : permission to act **2** ♦ : a permission granted by authority to engage in an activity **3** : a document, plate, or tag providing proof of a license **4** : freedom used irresponsibly

♦ [1] authorization, freedom, latitude, run ♦ [2] allowance, authorization, clearance, concurrence, consent, leave, permis-sion, sanction, sufferance

²license *or chiefly Brit* **licence** *vb* ♦ : to issue a license to

♦ accredit, authorize, certify, commission, empower, enable, in-vest, qualify

licensed practical nurse *n* : a specially trained person who is licensed (as by a state) to provide routine care for the sick
li·cens·ee \,līs-ªn-'sē\ *n* : a licensed person
li·cen·ti·ate \lī-'sen-chē-ət\ *n* : one licensed to practice a profes-sion
li·cen·tious \lī-'sen-chəs\ *adj* : lacking legal or moral restraints; *also* : disregarding sexual restraints : LEWD, LASCIVIOUS — **li·cen·tious·ly** *adv*

li·cen·tious·ness *n* ♦ : the quality or state of being licentious

♦ corruption, debauchery, depravity, immorality, iniquity, sin, vice

lichee *var of* LITCHI
li·chen \'lī-kən\ *n* : any of various complex plantlike organisms made up of an alga and a fungus growing as a unit on a solid surface — **li·chen·ous** *adj*
lic·it \'li-sət\ *adj* : LAWFUL
¹lick \'lik\ *vb* **1** : to draw the tongue over; *also* : to flicker over like a tongue **2** : to beat soundly : THRASH; *also* : DEFEAT
²lick *n* **1** : a stroke of the tongue **2** ♦ : a small amount **3** : a hasty careless effort **4** : a sharp hit : BLOW **5** : a natural deposit of salt that animals lick

♦ bit, dab, little, particle, shred, touch, trace

lick·e·ty–split \,li-kə-tē-'split\ *adv* : at great speed
lick·spit·tle \'lik-,spit-ªl\ *n* : a fawning subordinate : TOADY
lic·o·rice \'li-kə-rish, -rəs\ *n* **1** : the dried root of a European leguminous plant; *also* : an extract from it used esp. as a flavoring and in medicine **2** : a candy flavored with licorice **3** : a plant yielding licorice
lid \'lid\ *n* **1** ♦ : a movable cover **2** : EYELID **3** : something that confines or suppresses — **lid·ded** \'li-dəd\ *adj*

♦ cap, cover, top

li·do \'lē-dō\ *n, pl* **lidos** : a fashionable beach resort
¹lie \'lī\ *vb* **lay** \'lā\; **lain** \'lān\; **ly·ing** \'lī-iŋ\ **1** : to be in, stay at rest in, or assume a horizontal position; *also* : to be in a helpless or defenseless state **2** ♦ : to have direction : EXTEND **3** ♦ : to occupy a certain relative position **4** : to have an effect esp. through mere presence

♦ [2] extend, go, head, lead, run ♦ [3] be, sit, stand

²lie *n* : the position in which something lies
³lie *vb* **lied; ly·ing** \'lī-iŋ\ ♦ : to tell a lie

♦ fabricate, fib, prevaricate

⁴lie *n* ♦ : an untrue statement made with intent to deceive

♦ fabrication, fairy tale, falsehood, falsity, fib, mendacity, pre-varication, story, tale, untruth, whopper *Ant* truth

lied \'lēt\ *n, pl* **lie·der** \'lē-dər\ : a German song esp. of the 19th century
lie detector *n* : a polygraph for detecting physiological evidence of the tension that accompanies lying
lief \'lēv, 'lēf\ *adv* : GLADLY, WILLINGLY
¹liege \'lēj\ *adj* : LOYAL, FAITHFUL
²liege *n* **1** : VASSAL **2** : a feudal superior
lien \'lēn, 'lē-ən\ *n* : a legal claim on the property of another for the satisfaction of a debt or duty
lieu \'lü\ *n, archaic* : PLACE, STEAD — **in lieu of** : in the place of
lieut *abbr* lieutenant
lieu·ten·ant \lü-'te-nənt\ *n* **1** : a representative of another in the performance of duty **2** : FIRST LIEUTENANT; *also* : SECOND LIEU-TENANT **3** : a commissioned officer in the navy ranking next be-low a lieutenant commander — **lieu·ten·an·cy** \-nən-sē\ *n*
lieutenant colonel *n* : a commissioned officer (as in the army) ranking next below a colonel
lieutenant commander *n* : a commissioned officer in the navy ranking next below a commander
lieutenant general *n* : a commissioned officer (as in the army) ranking next below a general
lieutenant governor *n* : a deputy or subordinate governor
lieutenant junior grade *n, pl* **lieutenants junior grade** : a com-missioned officer in the navy ranking next below a lieutenant
life \'līf\ *n, pl* **lives** \'līvz\ **1** : the quality that distinguishes a vital and functional being from a dead body or inanimate matter; *also* : a state of an organism characterized esp. by capacity for metabolism, growth, reaction to stimuli, and reproduction **2** : the physical and mental experiences of an individual **3** : a writ-ten history of a person's life : BIOGRAPHY **4** ♦ : a specific phase or period ⟨adult ～⟩ **5** : the period from birth to death; *also* : a sentence of imprisonment for the remainder of a person's life **6** ♦ : a way of living **7** : a vital or living being; *specif* : PERSON **8** ♦ : a lively or brisk quality in a person or a person's actions **9** : living beings ⟨forest ～⟩ **10** : animate activity ⟨signs of ～⟩ **11** : one providing interest and vigor ⟨～ of the party⟩

♦ [4] date, duration, lifetime, run, standing, time ♦ [6] civili-zation, culture, lifestyle, society ♦ [8] dash, energy, pep, vigor (*or* vigour), vim, vitality

life·blood \'līf-,bləd\ *n* : a basic source of strength and vitality
life·boat \-,bōt\ *n* : a sturdy boat designed for use in saving lives at sea

life·guard \\-₁gärd\\ *n* : a usu. expert swimmer employed to safeguard bathers

life·less *adj* ♦ : having no life

♦ breathless, dead, deceased, defunct, gone, late

life·like *adj* ♦ : accurately representing or imitating real life

♦ natural, near, realistic

life·line \\-₁līn\\ *n* **1** : a line to which persons may cling for safety **2** : something considered vital for survival

life·long \\-₁lȯŋ\\ *adj* : continuing through life

life preserver *n* : a buoyant device designed to save a person from drowning

lif·er \\'lī-fər\\ *n* **1** : a person sentenced to life imprisonment **2** : a person who makes a career in the armed forces

life raft *n* : a raft for use by people forced into the water

life·sav·ing \\'līf-₁sā-viŋ\\ *n* : the skill or practice of saving or protecting lives esp. of drowning persons — **life·sav·er** \\-₁sā-vər\\ *n*

life science *n* : a branch of science (as biology, medicine, and sometimes anthropology or sociology) that deals with living organisms and life processes — usu. used in pl. — **life scientist** *n*

life span *n* : the duration of existence of an individual

life·style \\'līf-stīl\\ *n* ♦ : a way of living

♦ civilization, culture, life, society

life·time \\-₁tīm\\ *n* ♦ : the duration of an individual's existence

♦ date, duration, life, run, standing, time

life·work \\-'wərk\\ *n* : the entire or principal work of one's lifetime; *also* : a work extending over a lifetime

life·world \\-₁wər-(ə)ld\\ *n* : the total of an individual's physical surroundings and everyday experiences

LIFO *abbr* last in, first out

¹lift \\'lift\\ *vb* **1** ♦ : to raise from a lower to a higher position : ELEVATE; *also* : RISE, ASCEND **2** : to put an end to : STOP ⟨~ a ban⟩ **3** : to pay off ⟨~ a mortgage⟩ — **lift·er** *n*

♦ boost, crane, elevate, heave, heft, heighten, hike, hoist, jack, pick up, raise, up, uphold ♦ arise, ascend, climb, mount, rise, soar, up

²lift *n* **1** : LOAD **2** : the action or an instance of lifting **3** ♦ : the act of assisting or the help supplied; *also* : a ride along one's way **4** : RISE, ADVANCE **5** *chiefly Brit* : ELEVATOR **6** : an elevation of the spirits **7** : the upward force that is developed by a moving airfoil and that opposes the pull of gravity

♦ aid, assist, assistance, backing, boost, help, support

lift·off \\'lif-₁tȯf\\ *n* : a vertical takeoff (as by a rocket)

lift truck *n* : a small truck for lifting and transporting loads

lig·a·ment \\'li-gə-mənt\\ *n* : a band of tough fibrous tissue that holds bones together or supports an organ in place

li·gate \\'lī-₁gāt\\ *vb* **li·gat·ed; li·gat·ing** : to tie with a ligature — **li·ga·tion** \\lī-'gā-shən\\ *n*

lig·a·ture \\'li-gə-₁chu̇r, -chər\\ *n* **1** ♦ : something that binds or ties; *also* : a thread used in surgery esp. for tying blood vessels **2** : a printed or written character consisting of two or more letters or characters (as æ) united

♦ bond, cement, knot, link, tie

¹light \\'līt\\ *n* **1** ♦ : something that makes vision possible : electromagnetic radiation visible to the human eye; *also* : the sensation aroused by stimulation of the visual sense organs **2** : DAYLIGHT **3** ♦ : a source of light (as a candle) **4** : ENLIGHTENMENT; *also* : TRUTH **5** : public knowledge ⟨facts brought to ~⟩ **6** : a particular aspect presented to view ⟨saw the matter in a different ~⟩ **7** : WINDOW **8** *pl* : STANDARDS ⟨according to his ~s⟩ **9** ♦ : a noteworthy person in a particular place or field : CELEBRITY **10** : LIGHTHOUSE, BEACON; *also* : TRAFFIC LIGHT **11** : a flame for lighting something

♦ [1] blaze, flare, fluorescence, glare, gleam, glow, illumination, incandescence, luminescence, radiance, shine ♦ [3] flare ♦ [9] celebrity, figure, luminary, notable, personage, personality, somebody, standout, star, superstar, VIP

²light *adj* **1** ♦ : having light : BRIGHT **2** : not dark, intense, or swarthy in color or coloring : PALE ⟨~ blue⟩

♦ ablaze, alight, bright

³light *vb* **lit** \\'lit\\ *or* **light·ed; light·ing 1** : to make or become light **2** ♦ : to cause to burn : BURN **3** : to conduct with a light **4** ♦ : to supply or brighten with light : ILLUMINATE

♦ [2] burn, fire, ignite, inflame, kindle ♦ [4] illuminate

⁴light *adj* **1** ♦ : not heavy **2** : not serious ⟨~ reading⟩ **3** : not abundant : SCANTY ⟨~ rain⟩ **4** : easily disturbed ⟨a ~ sleeper⟩ **5 a** : exerting a minimum of force or pressure : GENTLE ⟨a

~ blow⟩ **b** ♦ : requiring minimal effort or energy **6** ♦ : easily endurable ⟨a ~ cold⟩; *also* : requiring little effort ⟨~ exercise⟩ **7** ♦ : capable of moving swiftly or nimbly **8** : FRIVOLOUS **9** : DIZZY **10** : made with lower calorie content or less of some ingredient than usual ⟨~ salad dressing⟩ **11** : producing goods for direct consumption by the consumer ⟨~ industry⟩

♦ [1] airy, ethereal, feathery, fluffy, weightless **Ant** heavy, hefty, leaden, overweight, ponderous, weighty ♦ [5b] easy, effortless, facile, fluent, fluid, painless, ready, simple, smooth, snap, soft ♦ [6] balmy, benign, bland, delicate, gentle, mellow, mild, soft, soothing, tender ♦ [7] agile, graceful, lissome, lithe, nimble, spry

⁵light *adv* **1** : LIGHTLY **2** : with little baggage ⟨travel ~⟩

⁶light *vb* **lit** \\'lit\\ *or* **light·ed; light·ing 1** ♦ : to descend from or as if from the air and come to rest : SETTLE, ALIGHT **2** : to fall unexpectedly **3** : HAPPEN ⟨~ed on a solution⟩

♦ alight, land, perch, roost, settle

light bulb *n* **1** : a lamp in which an electrically heated filament emits light **2** : FLUORESCENT LAMP

light–emitting diode *n* : LED

¹light·en \\'līt-ᵊn\\ *vb* **1** : to make light or clear : ILLUMINATE **2** : to give out flashes of lightning

²lighten *vb* **1** : to relieve of a burden **2** : GLADDEN **3** : to become lighter

lighten up *vb* : to take things less seriously

¹ligh·ter \\'lī-tər\\ *n* : a barge used esp. in loading or unloading ships

²light·er \\'lī-tər\\ *n* : one that lights; *esp* : a device for lighting

light·face \\'līt-₁fās\\ *n* : a type having light thin lines — **light-faced** \\-₁fāst\\ *adj*

light–head·ed \\'līt-₁he-dəd\\ *adj* **1** ♦ : feeling confused or dizzy **2** ♦ : lacking maturity or seriousness

♦ [1] dizzy, giddy ♦ [2] flighty, frivolous, giddy, goofy, harebrained, scatterbrained, silly

light·heart·ed \\-₁här-təd\\ *adj* ♦ : free from worry — **light·heart·ed·ly** *adv*

♦ carefree, careless, cavalier, easygoing, happy-go-lucky, insouciant, unconcerned

light·heart·ed·ness *n* ♦ : the quality or state of being lighthearted

♦ abandon, abandonment, ease, naturalness, spontaneity, unrestraint

light·house \\-₁hau̇s\\ *n* : a structure with a powerful light for guiding sailors

light·ly *adv* ♦ : in a light manner

♦ easily, effortlessly, fluently, freely, handily, painlessly, readily, smoothly

light meter *n* : a usu. handheld device for indicating correct photographic exposure

¹light·ness *n* ♦ : the quality or state of being illuminated

♦ brilliance, dazzle, effulgence, illumination, lucidity, luminosity, radiance, refulgence, splendor

²light·ness *n* **1** ♦ : lack of seriousness and stability of character often accompanied by casual heedlessness **2** : the quality or state of being light esp. in weight

♦ facetiousness, flightiness, flippancy, frivolity, levity

¹light·ning \\'līt-niŋ\\ *n* : the flashing of light produced by a discharge of atmospheric electricity; *also* : the discharge itself

²lightning *adj* ♦ : extremely fast

♦ breakneck, breathless, brisk, dizzy, fast, fleet, hasty, nippy, quick, rapid, rattling, snappy, speedy, swift

lightning bug *n* : FIREFLY

lightning rod *n* : a grounded metallic rod set up on a structure to protect it from lightning

light out *vb* : to leave in a hurry

light·proof \\'līt-₁prüf\\ *adj* : impenetrable by light

lights \\'līts\\ *n pl* : the lungs esp. of a slaughtered animal

light·ship \\'līt-₁ship\\ *n* : a ship with a powerful light moored at a place dangerous to navigation

light show *n* : a kaleidoscopic display (as of colored lights)

light·some \\'līt-səm\\ *adj* **1** ♦ : free from care **2** : NIMBLE

♦ blithe, bright, buoyant, cheerful, cheery, chipper, sunny, upbeat

¹light·weight \\'līt-₁wāt\\ *n* **1** : one of less than average weight; *esp* : a boxer weighing not over 135 pounds **2** : one of little consequence or ability

²**lightweight** *adj* **1 :** INCONSEQUENTIAL **2 :** of less than average weight

light·year \'līt-,yir\ *n* **1 :** an astronomical unit of distance equal to the distance that light travels in one year in a vacuum or about 5.88 trillion miles (9.46 trillion kilometers) **2 :** an extremely large measure of comparison ⟨saw it ∼s ago⟩

lig·nin \'lig-nən\ *n* **:** a substance related to cellulose that occurs in the woody cell walls of plants and in the cementing material between them

lig·nite \'lig-,nīt\ *n* **:** brownish black soft coal

¹**like** \'līk\ *vb* **liked; lik·ing 1 ♦ :** to feel attraction toward or take pleasure in **:** ENJOY ⟨∼s baseball⟩ **2 ♦ :** to wish to have **:** WANT **3 ♦ :** to feel inclined **:** CHOOSE ⟨does as she ∼s⟩ — **lik·able** *or* **like·able** \'lī-kə-bəl\ *adj*

♦ [1] favor (*or* favour), lean, prefer ♦ [1] adore, delight, dig, enjoy, fancy, groove, love, relish, revel ♦ [2, 3] choose, want, will, wish

²**like** *n* ♦ **:** favorable regard **:** PREFERENCE

♦ appetite, fancy, favor (*or* favour), fondness, liking, love, partiality, preference, relish, shine, taste, use

³**like** *adj* ♦ **:** the same or nearly the same (as in appearance, character, or quantity) **:** SIMILAR

♦ akin, alike, analogous, comparable, correspondent, parallel, similar, such

⁴**like** *prep* **1 :** similar or similarly to ⟨it's ∼ when we were kids⟩ **2 :** typical of **3 :** comparable to **4 :** as though there would be ⟨looks ∼ rain⟩ **5 :** such as ⟨a subject ∼ physics⟩

⁵**like** *n* **1 a :** one that is similar **b ♦ :** a group having common traits **2 ♦ :** one that is similar to another ⟨we may never see his ∼ again⟩ — **and the like :** ET CETERA

♦ [1b] breed, class, description, feather, ilk, kind, manner, nature, order, sort, species, type ♦ [2] coordinate, counterpart, equal, equivalent, fellow, match, parallel, peer, rival

⁶**like** *conj* **:** in the same way that

-like \,līk\ *adj comb form* **:** resembling or characteristic of ⟨ladylike⟩ ⟨lifelike⟩

like·li·hood \'lī-klē-,hùd\ *n* **:** PROBABILITY

¹**like·ly** \'lī-klē\ *adj* **like·li·er; -est 1 ♦ :** very probable **2 ♦ :** offering reasonable grounds for being believed **:** BELIEVABLE **3 ♦ :** likely to succeed or to yield good results **:** PROMISING ⟨a ∼ place to fish⟩

♦ [1] apt, bound, probable *Ant* doubtful, dubious, improbable, questionable, unlikely ♦ [2] believable, credible, plausible, probable ♦ [3] auspicious, bright, encouraging, fair, golden, heartening, hopeful, promising, propitious, rosy, upbeat

²**likely** *adv* ♦ **:** in all probability

♦ doubtless, presumably, probably

lik·en \'lī-kən\ *vb* ♦ **:** to represent as similar **:** COMPARE

♦ bracket, compare, equate

like·ness \'līk-nəs\ *n* **1 ♦ :** a pictorial representation (as a painting) of a person esp. showing the face; *also* **:** one that resembles or corresponds to another **2 :** SEMBLANCE **3 ♦ :** the quality or state of being like **:** RESEMBLANCE

♦ [1] illustration, image, picture ♦ [3] community, correspondence, parallelism, resemblance, similarity, similitude

like·wise \,wīz\ *adv* **1 ♦ :** in the same manner **2 ♦ :** in addition **:** ALSO

♦ [1] alike, also, correspondingly, similarly, so ♦ [2] additionally, again, also, besides, further, furthermore, more, moreover, then, too, withal, yet

lik·ing \'lī-kiŋ\ *n* ♦ **:** favorable regard; *also* **:** TASTE

♦ appetite, fancy, favor (*or* favour), fondness, like, love, partiality, preference, relish, shine, taste, use *Ant* aversion, dislike, disfavor, distaste, hatred, loathing

li·lac \'lī-lək, -,lak, -,läk\ *n* **1 :** a shrub related to the olive that produces large clusters of fragrant grayish pink, purple, or white flowers **2 :** a moderate purple color

lil·li·pu·tian \,li-lə-'pyü-shən\ *adj, often cap* **1 :** SMALL, MINIATURE **2 :** PETTY

lilt \'lilt\ *n* **1 :** a cheerful lively song or tune **2 :** a rhythmical swing or flow

lily \'li-lē\ *n, pl* **lil·ies :** any of a genus of tall bulbous herbs with leafy stems and usu. funnel-shaped flowers; *also* **:** any of various related plants

lily of the valley : a low perennial herb related to the lilies that produces a raceme of fragrant nodding bell-shaped white flowers

li·ma bean \'lī-mə-\ *n* **:** a bushy or tall-growing bean widely cultivated for its flat edible usu. pale green or whitish seeds; *also* **:** the seed

limb \'lim\ *n* **1 :** one of the projecting paired appendages (as legs, arms, or wings) used by an animal esp. in moving or grasping **2 :** a large branch of a tree **:** BOUGH — **limb·less** *adj*

¹**lim·ber** \'lim-bər\ *adj* **1 ♦ :** capable of being shaped **:** FLEXIBLE, SUPPLE **2 :** LITHE, NIMBLE

♦ flexible, lissome, lithe, pliable, supple, willowy

²**limber** *vb* **:** to make or become limber

lim·bic \'lim-bik\ *adj* **:** of, relating to, or being a group of structures of the brain (**limbic system**) concerned esp. with emotion and motivation

¹**lim·bo** \'lim-bō\ *n, pl* **limbos 1** *often cap* **:** an abode of souls barred from heaven through no fault of their own **2 :** a place or state of confinement, oblivion, or uncertainty

²**limbo** *n, pl* **limbos :** an acrobatic dance or contest that involves passing under a horizontal pole

Lim·burg·er \'lim-,bər-gər\ *n* **:** a pungent semisoft surface-ripened cheese

¹**lime** \'līm\ *n* **:** a caustic powdery white solid that consists of calcium and oxygen, is obtained from limestone or shells, and is used in making cement and in fertilizer — **lime** *vb* — **limy** \'lī-mē\ *adj*

²**lime** *n* **:** a small yellowish green citrus fruit with juicy acid pulp

lime·ade \,līm-'ād, 'lī-,mād\ *n* **:** a beverage of lime juice, sugar, and water

lime·light \'līm-,līt\ *n* **1 :** a device in which flame is directed against a cylinder of lime formerly used in the theater to cast a strong white light on the stage **2 :** the center of public attention

lim·er·ick \'li-mə-rik\ *n* **:** a light or humorous poem of 5 lines

lime·stone \'līm-,stōn\ *n* **:** a rock that is formed by accumulation of organic remains (as shells), is used in building, and yields lime when burned

¹**lim·it** \'li-mət\ *n* **1 ♦ :** something that restrains or confines; *also* **:** the utmost extent **2 :** BOUNDARY; *also, pl* **:** BOUNDS **3 :** a prescribed maximum or minimum — **lim·it·less·ness** *n*

♦ bound, boundary, ceiling, confines, end, extent, limitation, line, termination

²**limit** *vb* **1 a ♦ :** to set limits to **b ♦ :** to confine within set limits **2 :** to reduce in quantity or extent

♦ [1a] bound, circumscribe, define, delimit, demarcate, mark, terminate ♦ [1b] check, circumscribe, confine, control, curb, inhibit, restrain, restrict *Ant* exceed

lim·i·ta·tion \,li-mə-'tā-shən\ *n* **1 :** an act or instance of limiting **2 ♦ :** something that limits

♦ check, condition, constraint, curb, fetter, restraint, restriction

lim·it·ed *adj* **1 ♦ :** confined within limits **2 :** offering faster service esp. by making fewer stops ⟨a ∼ train⟩

♦ definite, determinate, finite, measured, narrow, restricted *Ant* boundless, endless, illimitable, immeasurable, indefinite, infinite, limitless, measureless, unbounded, undefined, unlimited, unmeasured

lim·it·less *adj* ♦ **:** having no limits

♦ boundless, endless, illimitable, immeasurable, indefinite, infinite, measureless, unbounded, unfathomable, unlimited

limn \'lim\ *vb* **limned; limn·ing** \'li-miŋ, 'lim-niŋ\ **1 :** DRAW; *also* **:** PAINT **2 :** DELINEATE **3 :** DESCRIBE

limo \'li-(,)mō\ *n, pl* **limos :** LIMOUSINE

li·mo·nite \'lī-mə-,nīt\ *n* **:** a ferric oxide that is a major ore of iron — **li·mo·nit·ic** \,lī-mə-'ni-tik\ *adj*

lim·ou·sine \'li-mə-,zēn, ,li-mə-'zēn\ *n* **1 :** a large luxurious often chauffeur-driven sedan **2 :** a large vehicle for transporting passengers to and from an airport

¹**limp** \'limp\ *vb* ♦ **:** to walk lamely; *also* **:** to proceed with difficulty

♦ flounder, lumber, plod, stumble

²**limp** *n* **:** a limping movement or gait

³**limp** *adj* **1 ♦ :** having no defined shape; *also* **:** not stiff or rigid **2 ♦ :** lacking in strength or firmness ⟨∼ from fatigue⟩ — **limp·ly** *adv* — **limp·ness** *n*

♦ [1] droopy, flaccid, floppy, lank, slack, yielding *Ant* inflexible, resilient, rigid, stiff, sturdy, tense; firm, hard, indurated, solid, sound, strong ♦ [2] enervated, lackadaisical, languid, languorous, listless, spiritless, weary

lim·pet \'lim-pət\ *n* **:** any of numerous gastropod sea mollusks with a conical shell that clings to rocks or timbers

lim·pid \'lim-pəd\ *adj* ♦ : marked by transparency : CLEAR
♦ clear, liquid, lucent, pellucid, transparent

lin *abbr* **1** lineal **2** linear

lin·age \'lī-nij\ *n* : the number of lines of written or printed matter

linch·pin \'linch-,pin\ *n* : a locking pin inserted crosswise (as through the end of an axle)

lin·den \'lin-dən\ *n* : any of a genus of trees with large heart=shaped leaves and clustered yellowish flowers rich in nectar

¹**line** \'līn\ *n* **1** ♦ : a length of cord or cord-like material : ROPE, WIRE; *also* : a length of material used in measuring and leveling **2** ♦ : pipes for conveying a fluid ⟨a gas ∼⟩ **3** : a horizontal row of written or printed characters; *also* : VERSE **4** : NOTE **5** : the words making up a part in a drama — usu. used in pl. **6 a** : something distinct, long, and narrow **b** ♦ : the course or direction of something in motion : ROUTE **7** : a state of agreement **8** ♦ : a course of conduct, action, or thought; *also* : a field of activity or interest : OCCUPATION **9** : something that bounds, restrains, or confines : LIMIT **10** ♦ : an arrangement of persons or objects of one kind in an orderly series ⟨waiting in ∼⟩ **11** : a transportation system **12** : the football players who are stationed on the line of scrimmage **13** : a long narrow mark; *also* : EQUATOR **14** : a geometric element that is the path of a moving point **15** : CONTOUR **16** : a general plan **17** : an indication based on insight or investigation **18** ♦ : a group of persons of common ancestry

♦ [1] cable, cord, lace, rope, string, wire ♦ [2] channel, conduit, duct, leader, penstock, pipe, tube ♦ [6b] course, path, route, track, way ♦ [8] area, arena, discipline, domain, field, province, realm, specialty, sphere ♦ [8] course, policy, procedure, program ♦ [8] calling, employment, occupation, profession, trade, vocation, work ♦ [10] column, cue, file, queue, range, string, train ♦ [18] ancestry, birth, blood, bloodline, breeding, descent, extraction, family tree, genealogy, lineage, origin, parentage, pedigree, stock, strain

²**line** *vb* **lined; lin·ing 1** : to mark with a line **2** : to place or form a line along **3** : ALIGN

³**line** *vb* **lined; lin·ing** : to cover the inner surface of

lin·eage \'li-nē-ij\ *n* ♦ : lineal descent from a common progenitor; *also* : FAMILY

♦ blood, clan, family, folks, house, kin, kindred, kinfolk, line, people, race, stock, tribe ♦ ancestry, birth, bloodline, breeding, descent, extraction, family tree, genealogy, origin, parentage

lin·eal \'li-nē-əl\ *adj* **1** : LINEAR **2** : consisting of or being in a direct line of ancestry; *also* : HEREDITARY

lin·ea·ment \'li-nē-ə-mənt\ *n* : an outline, feature, or contour of a body and esp. of a face — usu. used in pl.

lin·ear \'li-nē-ər\ *adj* **1** : of, relating to, resembling, or having a graph that is a line and esp. a straight line : STRAIGHT **2** : composed of simply drawn lines with little attempt at pictorial representation ⟨∼ script⟩ **3** : being long and uniformly narrow

line·back·er \'līn-,ba-kər\ *n* : a defensive football player who lines up just behind the line of scrimmage

line drive *n* : a batted baseball hit in a flatter path than a fly ball

line·man \'līn-mən\ *n* **1** : a person who sets up or repairs communication or power lines **2** : a player in the line in football

lin·en \'li-nən\ *n* **1** : cloth made of flax; *also* : thread or yarn spun from flax **2** : clothing or household articles made of linen cloth or similar fabric

line of scrimmage : an imaginary line in football parallel to the goal lines and tangent to the nose of the ball laid on the ground before a play

¹**lin·er** \'lī-nər\ *n* : a ship or airplane of a regular transportation line

²**liner** *n* : one that lines or is used as a lining — **lin·er·less** *adj*

line score *n* : a score of a baseball game giving the runs, hits, and errors made by each team

lines·man \'līnz-mən\ *n* **1** : LINEMAN 1 **2** : an official who assists a referee

line·up \'lī-,nəp\ *n* **1** : a list of players taking part in a game (as of baseball) **2** : a line of persons arranged esp. for identification by police

ling \'liŋ\ *n* : any of various fishes related to the cod

-ling \liŋ\ *n suffix* **1** : one associated with ⟨nestling⟩ **2** : young, small, or minor one ⟨duckling⟩

lin·ger \'liŋ-gər\ *vb* ♦ : to be slow in parting or in quitting something : TARRY; *also* : to be slow to act — **lin·ger·er** *n*

♦ crawl, creep, dally, dawdle, delay, dillydally, drag, lag, loiter, poke, tarry

lin·ge·rie \,län-jə-'rā, ,laⁿ-zhə-, -'rē\ *n* : women's intimate apparel

lin·go \'liŋ-gō\ *n, pl* **lingoes** ♦ : a usu. strange or incomprehensible language

♦ argot, cant, jargon, language, slang, terminology, vocabulary

lin·gua fran·ca \,liŋ-gwə-'fraŋ-kə\ *n, pl* **lingua francas** *or* **lin·guae fran·cae** \-gwē-'fraŋ-,kē\ **1** *often cap* : a common language consisting of Italian mixed with French, Spanish, Greek, and Arabic that was formerly spoken in Mediterranean ports **2** : a common or commercial tongue among speakers of different languages

lin·gual \'liŋ-gwəl\ *adj* : of, relating to, or produced by the tongue

lin·gui·ca \liŋ-'gwē-sə\ *n* : a spicy Portuguese sausage

lin·guist \'liŋ-gwist\ *n* **1** : a person skilled in languages **2** : a person who specializes in linguistics

lin·guis·tics \liŋ-'gwis-tiks\ *n* : the study of human speech including the units, nature, structure, and modification of language — **lin·guis·tic** \-tik\ *adj*

lin·i·ment \'li-nə-mənt\ *n* : a liquid preparation rubbed on the skin esp. to relieve pain

lin·ing \'lī-niŋ\ *n* : material used to line esp. an inner surface

¹**link** \'liŋk\ *n* **1** : a connecting structure; *esp* : a single ring of a chain **2** ♦ : a connecting element or factor : BOND, TIE

♦ bond, cement, knot, ligature, tie

²**link** *vb* ♦ : to couple or connect by or as if by a link; *also* : to become connected by or as if by a link — often used with *up* — **link·er** *n*

♦ chain, compound, connect, couple, hitch, hook, join, yoke ♦ associate, connect, correlate, identify, relate ♦ *usu* **link up** coalesce, combine, conjoin, marry, unify, unite

link·age \'liŋ-kij\ *n* **1** : the manner or style of being united **2** ♦ : the quality or state of being linked **3** : a system of links

♦ association, bearing, connection, kinship, liaison, relation, relationship

linking verb *n* : a word or expression (as a form of *be, become, feel,* or *seem*) that links a subject with its predicate

links \'liŋks\ *n pl* : a golf course

link·up \'liŋ-,kəp\ *n* **1** : MEETING **2** : something that serves as a linking device or factor

lin·net \'li-nət\ *n* : an Old World finch

li·no·leum \lə-'nō-lē-əm\ *n* : a floor covering with a canvas back and a surface of hardened linseed oil and a filler

lin·seed \'lin-,sēd\ *n* : the seeds of flax yielding a yellowish oil (**linseed oil**) used esp. in paints and linoleum

lin·sey–wool·sey \,lin-zē-'wul-zē\ *n* : a coarse sturdy fabric of wool and linen or cotton

lint \'lint\ *n* **1** : linen made into a soft fleecy substance **2** ♦ : fine ravels and short fibers of yarn or fabric **3** : the fibers that surround cotton seeds and form the cotton staple

♦ down, floss, fluff, fur, fuzz, nap, pile

lin·tel \'lint-ᵊl\ *n* : a horizontal piece across the top of an opening (as of a door) that carries the weight of the structure above it

linz·er torte \'lin-sər-, -zər-\ *n, often cap L* : a baked buttery torte made with chopped almonds, sugar, and spices and filled with jam or preserves

li·on \'lī-ən\ *n, pl* **lions** : a large heavily-built cat of Africa and southern Asia with a shaggy mane in the male

li·on·ess \'lī-ə-nəs\ *n* : a female lion

li·on·heart·ed \,lī-ən-'här-təd\ *adj* ♦ : having or characterized by courage : BRAVE

♦ brave, courageous, dauntless, doughty, fearless, gallant, greathearted, heroic, intrepid, manful, stalwart, stout, undaunted, valiant, valorous

li·on·ise *chiefly Brit var of* LIONIZE

li·on·ize \'lī-ə-,nīz\ *vb* **-ized; -iz·ing** : to treat as an object of great interest or importance — **li·on·i·za·tion** \,lī-ə-nə-'zā-shən\ *n*

lion's den *n* : a place or state of extreme disadvantage, antagonism, or hostility

lip \'lip\ *n* **1** : either of the two fleshy folds that surround the mouth; *also* : the margin of the human lip **2** : a part or projection suggesting a lip **3** : the edge of a hollow vessel or cavity — **lipped** \'lipt\ *adj*

lip·id \'li-pəd\ *n* : any of various substances (as fats and waxes) that with proteins and carbohydrates make up the principal structural parts of living cells

lip–lock \'lip-,läk\ *n* : a long amorous kiss

li·po·pro·tein \,lī-pō-'prō-,tēn, ,li-\ *n* : a protein that is a complex of protein and lipid

li·po·suc·tion \'li-pə-ˌsək-shən, 'lī-\ *n* : surgical removal of local fat deposits (as in the thighs) esp. for cosmetic purposes

lip·read·ing \'lip-ˌrē-diŋ\ *n* : the interpreting of a speaker's words by watching lip and facial movements without hearing the voice

lip service *n* : an avowal of allegiance that is not matched by action

lip·stick \'lip-ˌstik\ *n* : a waxy solid colored cosmetic in stick form for the lips — **lip·sticked** \-ˌstikt\ *adj*

liq *abbr* **1** liquid **2** liquor

liq·ue·fy *also* **liq·ui·fy** \'li-kwə-ˌfī\ *vb* **-fied; -fy·ing** ♦ : to make or become liquid — **liq·ue·fi·er** \-ˌfī-ər\ *n*

♦ deliquesce, flux, fuse, melt, run, thaw *Ant* harden, set, solidify

li·queur \li-'kər\ *n* : a distilled alcoholic liquor flavored with aromatic substances and usu. sweetened

¹**liq·uid** \'li-kwəd\ *adj* **1** ♦ : flowing freely like water **2** : neither solid nor gaseous **3** ♦ : shining and clear ⟨large ∼ eyes⟩ **4** : smooth and musical in tone; *also* : smooth and unconstrained in movement **5** : consisting of or capable of ready conversion into cash ⟨∼ assets⟩ — **li·quid·i·ty** \li-'kwi-də-tē\ *n*

♦ [1] fluent, fluid, runny ♦ [3] clear, limpid, lucent, pellucid, transparent

²**liquid** *n* : a liquid substance

liq·ui·date \'li-kwə-ˌdāt\ *vb* **-dat·ed; -dat·ing 1** : to settle the accounts and distribute the assets of (as a business) **2** ♦ : to pay off ⟨∼ a debt⟩ **3** ♦ : to get rid of; *esp* : to get rid of by force or violence and esp. by killing — **liq·ui·da·tion** \ˌli-kwə-'dā-shən\ *n*

♦ [2] clear, discharge, foot, pay, pay off, quit, recompense, settle, spring, stand ♦ [3] annihilate, blot out, demolish, eradicate, exterminate, obliterate, root, rub out, snuff, stamp, wipe out
♦ [3] dispatch, do in, execute, murder, slay

liquid crystal *n* : an organic liquid that resembles a crystal in having ordered molecular arrays

liquid crystal display *n* : LCD

liquid measure *n* : a unit or series of units for measuring liquid capacity

li·quor \'li-kər\ *n* **1** : a liquid substance **2** ♦ : a distilled alcoholic beverage

♦ alcohol, booze, drink, intoxicant, moonshine, spirits

li·quo·rice *chiefly Brit var of* LICORICE

li·ra \'lir-ə, 'lē-rə\ *n* **1** *pl* **li·ras** : a basic monetary unit of Turkey **2** *pl* **li·re** \'lē-rā\ *also* **liras** : the former basic monetary unit of Italy

lisle \'līl\ *n* : a smooth tightly twisted thread usu. made of long‑staple cotton

lisp \'lisp\ *vb* : to pronounce s and z imperfectly esp. by turning them into th and th; *also* : to speak childishly — **lisp** *n* — **lisp·er** *n*

lis·some *also* **lis·som** \'li-səm\ *adj* **1** ♦ : easily flexed **2** : LITHE 2 ⟨a ∼ dancer⟩ **3** ♦ : quick and light in motion : NIMBLE — **lis·some·ly** *adv*

♦ [1] flexible, limber, lithe, pliable, supple, willowy ♦ [3] agile, graceful, light, lithe, nimble, spry

¹**list** \'list\ *vb, archaic* : PLEASE; *also* : WISH

²**list** *vb, archaic* : LISTEN

³**list** *n* **1** : a simple series of words or numerals; *also* : an official roster **2** ♦ : a written record containing regular entries of items or details : CATALOG, CHECKLIST

♦ catalog, checklist, listing, menu, register, roll, roster, schedule, table

⁴**list** *vb* ♦ : to make a list of; *also* : to include on a list — **list·ee** \li-'stē\ *n*

♦ enumerate, inventory, itemize, numerate ♦ catalog, enroll, enter, index, inscribe, put down, record, register, schedule, slate

⁵**list** *vb* ♦ : to tilt to one side; *also* : to cause to list

♦ angle, cant, cock, heel, incline, lean, slant, slope, tilt, tip

⁶**list** *n* : a leaning to one side : TILT

⁷**list** *n* : a band or strip of material

lis·ten \'lis-ᵊn\ *vb* **1** ♦ : to pay attention in order to hear **2** ♦ : give consideration : HEED — **lis·ten·er** *n*

♦ [1] attend, hark, hear, heed, mind *Ant* ignore, tune out
♦ [2] follow, heed, mind, note, observe, regard, watch

lis·ten·er·ship \'lis-ᵊn-ər-ˌship\ *n* : the audience for a radio program or recording

list·ing \'lis-tiŋ\ *n* **1** : an act or instance of making or including

in a list **2** : something that is listed **3** ♦ : a simple series of words or numerals (as the names of persons or objects)

♦ catalog, checklist, list, menu, register, registry, roll, roster, schedule, table

list·less \'list-ləs\ *adj* ♦ : characterized by lack of interest, energy, or spirit : SPIRITLESS, LANGUID — **list·less·ly** *adv*

♦ enervated, lackadaisical, languid, languorous, limp, spiritless *Ant* ambitious, animated, energetic, enterprising, motivated

list·less·ness *n* ♦ : the quality or state of being listless

♦ boredom, doldrums, ennui, restlessness, tedium, tiredness, weariness

list price *n* : the price of an item as published in a catalog, price list, or advertisement before being discounted

lists \'lists\ *n pl* : an arena for combat (as jousting)

¹**lit** \'lit\ *past and past part of* LIGHT

²**lit** *abbr* **1** liter **2** literal; literally **3** literary **4** literature

lit·a·ny \'lit-ᵊn-ē\ *n, pl* **-nies 1** : a prayer consisting of a series of supplications and responses said alternately by a leader and a group **2** : a lengthy list or series ⟨a ∼ of complaints⟩

li·tchi *var of* LYCHEE

lite \'līt\ *adj* **1** : ¹LIGHT 10 **2** : lacking in substance or seriousness

li·ter *or chiefly Can and Brit* **li·tre** \'lē-tər\ *n* : the basic metric unit of volume measure

lit·er·al \'li-tə-rəl\ *adj* **1** ♦ : adhering to fact or to the ordinary or usual meaning (as of a word) **2** : UNADORNED; *also* : PROSAIC **3** : VERBATIM

♦ documentary, factual, hard, historical, matter-of-fact, nonfictional, objective, true

lit·er·al·ism \-rə-ˌli-zəm\ *n* **1** : adherence to the explicit substance (as of an idea) **2** : fidelity to observable fact — **lit·er·al·ist** \-list\ *n* — **lit·er·al·is·tic** \ˌli-tə-rə-'lis-tik\ *adj*

lit·er·al·ly \'li-tə-rə-lē, 'li-trə-\ *adv* **1** : ACTUALLY ⟨was ∼ soaked⟩ **2** : VIRTUALLY ⟨∼ poured out new ideas⟩

lit·er·ary \'li-tə-ˌrer-ē\ *adj* **1 a** : of or relating to literature **b** ♦ : having a formal style characteristic of the language of literature **2** : WELL-READ

♦ bookish, erudite, learned

lit·er·ate \'li-tə-rət, -tə-rət\ *adj* **1** ♦ : having an education : EDUCATED; *also* : able to read and write **2** : LITERARY; *also* : POLISHED, LUCID — **lit·er·a·cy** \'li-trə-sē, -tə-rə-\ *n* — **literate** *n*

♦ educated, erudite, knowledgeable, learned, scholarly, well‑read

lit·te·ra·ti \ˌli-tə-'rä-tē\ *n pl* **1** : the educated class **2** : persons interested in literature or the arts

lit·er·a·ture \'li-trə-ˌchur, -tə-rə-, -chər\ *n* **1** : the production of written works having excellence of form or expression and dealing with ideas of permanent interest **2** : the written works produced in a particular language, country, or age

lithe \'līth, 'līth\ *adj* **1** ♦ : easily bent or flexed : SUPPLE **2 a** ♦ : characterized by effortless grace **b** : athletically slim

♦ [1] flexible, limber, lissome, pliable, supple, willowy ♦ [2a] agile, graceful, light, lissome, nimble, spry

lithe·some \'līth-səm, 'līth-\ *adj* : quick and light in motion : LISSOME

lith·i·um \'li-thē-əm\ *n* : a light silver-white metallic chemical element

li·thog·ra·phy \li-'thä-grə-fē\ *n* : the process of printing from a plane surface (as a smooth stone or metal plate) on which the image to be printed is ink-receptive and the blank area ink-repellent — **lith·o·graph** \'li-thə-ˌgraf\ *vb* — **li·thog·ra·pher** \li-'thä-grə-fər, 'li-thə-ˌgra-fər\ *n* — **lith·o·graph·ic** \ˌli-thə-'gra-fik\ *adj* — **lith·o·graph·i·cal·ly** \-fi-k(ə-)lē\ *adv*

li·thol·o·gy \li-'thä-lə-jē\ *n, pl* **-gies** : the study of rocks — **lith·o·log·ic** \ˌli-thə-'lä-jik\ *or* **lith·o·log·i·cal** \-ji-kəl\ *adj*

lith·o·sphere \'li-thə-ˌsfir\ *n* : the outer part of the solid earth

Lith·u·a·nian \ˌli-thə-'wā-nē-ən, -thyü-\ *n* **1** : a native or inhabitant of Lithuania **2** : the language of the Lithuanians — **Lithuanian** *adj*

lit·i·gant \'li-tə-gənt\ *n* : a party to a lawsuit — **litigant** *adj*

lit·i·gate \-ˌgāt\ *vb* **-gat·ed; -gat·ing** : to carry on a legal contest by judicial process; *also* : to contest at law — **lit·i·ga·tion** \ˌli-tə-'gā-shən\ *n*

li·ti·gious \lə-'ti-jəs\ *adj* **1** : CONTENTIOUS **2** : prone to engage in lawsuits **3** : of or relating to litigation — **li·ti·gious·ly** *adv* — **li·ti·gious·ness** *n*

lit·mus \'lit-məs\ *n* : a coloring matter from lichens that turns red in acid solutions and blue in alkaline

litmus test *n* : a test in which a single factor (as an attitude) is decisive

Litt D *or* **Lit D** *abbr* : doctor of letters; doctor of literature

¹**lit·ter** \'li-tər\ *n* **1** : a covered and curtained couch with shafts that is used to carry a single passenger; *also* : a device (as a stretcher) for carrying a sick or injured person **2** : material used as bedding for animals; *also* : material used to absorb the urine and feces of animals **3** : the offspring of an animal at one birth **4** ♦ : trash, wastepaper, or garbage lying scattered about : RUBBISH; *also* : an untidy accumulation of objects

♦ chaff, deadwood, dust, garbage, junk, refuse, riffraff, rubbish, scrap, trash, waste ♦ assortment, clutter, jumble, medley, mélange, miscellany, motley, muddle, variety, welter

²**litter** *vb* **1** : to give birth to young **2** : to strew or mark with scattered objects

lit·ter·bug \'li-tər-ˌbəg\ *n* : one who litters a public area

¹**lit·tle** \'lit-ᵊl\ *adj* **lit·tler** \'lit-ᵊl-ər\ *or* **less** \'les\ *or* **less·er** \'le-sər\; **lit·tlest** \'lit-ᵊl-əst\ *or* **least** \'lēst\ **1 a** ♦ : not big **b** : YOUNG **2** ♦ : not important **3** ♦ : illiberal in views or disposition : PETTY **3 4** : not much **5** ♦ : short in duration — **lit·tle·ness** *n*

♦ [1a] dwarf, dwarfish, fine, pocket, pygmy, slight, small, undersized ♦ [2] frivolous, inconsequential, inconsiderable, insignificant, minor, minute, negligible, slight, small, trifling, trivial, unimportant ♦ [3] insular, narrow, parochial, petty, provincial, sectarian, small ♦ [5] brief, short, short-lived

²**little** *adv* **less** \'les\; **least** \'lēst\ **1** : in only a small quantity or degree : SLIGHTLY; *also* : not at all **2** ♦ : in few instances : INFREQUENTLY

♦ infrequently, rarely, seldom

³**little** *n* **1** : a small amount or quantity **2** : a short time or distance

Little Dipper *n* : the seven bright stars of Ursa Minor arranged in a form resembling a dipper

little finger *n* : PINKIE

little theater *n* : a small theater for low-cost dramatic productions designed for a limited audience

lit·to·ral \'li-tə-rəl, ˌli-tə-'ral\ *adj* : of, relating to, or growing on or near a shore esp. of the sea — **littoral** *n*

lit·ur·gy \'li-tər-jē\ *n, pl* **-gies** : a rite or body of rites prescribed for public worship — **li·tur·gi·cal** \lə-'tər-ji-kəl\ *adj* — **li·tur·gi·cal·ly** \-k(ə-)lē\ *adv* — **lit·ur·gist** \'li-tər-jist\ *n*

liv·able *also* **live·able** \'li-və-bəl\ *adj* **1** : suitable for living in or with **2** : ENDURABLE — **liv·a·bil·i·ty** \ˌli-və-'bi-lə-tē\ *n*

¹**live** \'liv\ *vb* **lived; liv·ing 1** ♦ : to be or continue alive **2** : SUBSIST **3** ♦ : to occupy a home : RESIDE **4** : to conduct one's life **5** : to remain in human memory or record

♦ [1] be, breathe, exist, subsist ♦ [3] abide, dwell, reside

²**live** \'līv\ *adj* **1** ♦ : having life **2** : BURNING, GLOWING ⟨a ~ cigar⟩ **3** : connected to electric power ⟨a ~ wire⟩ **4** : charged with explosive but not yet exploded ⟨a ~ bomb⟩ **5** : of continuing interest ⟨a ~ issue⟩ **6** : of or involving the actual presence of real people ⟨~ audience⟩; *also* : broadcast directly at the time of production ⟨a ~ radio program⟩ **7** : being in play ⟨a ~ ball⟩

♦ alive, animate, living

lived–in \'livd-ˌin\ *adj* : of or suggesting long-term human habitation or use

live down *vb* : to live so as to wipe out the memory or effects of

live in *vb* : to live in one's place of employment — used of a servant — **live–in** \'liv-ˌin\ *adj*

live·li·hood \'līv-lē-ˌhud\ *n* : means of support or subsistence

live·li·ness *n* ♦ : the quality or state of being lively

♦ animation, briskness, exuberance, lustiness, robustness, sprightliness, vibrancy, vitality

live·long \'liv-ˌlȯn\ *adj* : WHOLE, ENTIRE ⟨the ~ day⟩

live·ly \'līv-lē\ *adj* **live·li·er; -est 1** ♦ : briskly alert and energetic : ANIMATED ⟨~ debate⟩ **2** : KEEN, VIVID ⟨~ interest⟩ **3** : showing activity or vigor ⟨a ~ manner⟩ **4** : quick to rebound ⟨a ~ ball⟩ **5** ♦ : full of life — **live·ly** *adv*

♦ [1] active, animate, animated, brisk, energetic, frisky, peppy, perky, pert, spirited, sprightly, springy, vital, vivacious *Ant* inactive, inanimate, languid, languorous, limp, listless, spiritless ♦ [5] alive, animated, astir, busy, vibrant

liv·en \'lī-vən\ *vb* ♦ : to give life, action, or spirit to : ENLIVEN — often used with *up*; *also* : to become lively

♦ *usu* **liven up** animate, brace, energize, enliven, fire, invigorate, jazz up, pep up, quicken, stimulate, vitalize, vivify, zip (up)

live oak *n* : any of several American evergreen oaks; *esp* : one of the southeastern U.S. that is often planted as a shade tree

¹**liv·er** \'li-vər\ *n* **1** : a large glandular organ of vertebrates that secretes bile and is a center of metabolic activity **2** : the liver of an animal (as a calf or chicken) eaten as food

²**liver** *n* : one that lives esp. in a specified way ⟨a fast ~⟩

liv·er·ish \'li-və-rish\ *adj* **1** : resembling liver esp. in color **2** : BILIOUS **3** : PEEVISH — **liv·er·ish·ness** *adj*

liv·er·mo·ri·um \ˌli-vər-'mȯr-ē-əm\ *n* : a short-lived artificially produced radioactive chemical element

liv·er·wort \'li-vər-ˌwərt\ *n* : any of a class of flowerless plants resembling the related mosses

liv·er·wurst \-ˌwərst, -ˌwu̇rst\ *n* : a sausage consisting chiefly of liver

liv·ery \'li-və-rē\ *n, pl* **-er·ies 1** : a servant's uniform; *also* : distinctive dress **2** : the feeding, care, and stabling of horses for pay; *also* : an establishment (as a stable or business) keeping horses or vehicles for hire — **liv·er·ied** \-rēd\ *adj*

liv·ery·man \-mən\ *n* : the keeper of a livery

lives *pl of* LIFE

live·stock \'līv-ˌstäk\ *n* : farm animals kept for use and profit

live wire *n* ♦ : an alert, active, or aggressive person

♦ go-getter, hustler, powerhouse, self-starter

liv·id \'li-vəd\ *adj* **1** : discolored by bruising **2** ♦ : deadly pale : ASHEN, PALLID **3** : REDDISH **4** : ENRAGED — **li·vid·i·ty** \li-'vi-də-tē\ *n*

♦ ashen, cadaverous, lurid, pale, pasty, peaked

¹**liv·ing** \'li-viŋ\ *adj* **1** ♦ : having life or existence **2** : NATURAL **3** : full of life and vigor; *also* : VIVID **4** ♦ : marked by present operation, transaction, movement, or use

♦ [1] alive, animate, existent, extant, live ♦ [4] active, alive, functional, on, operational, operative, running, working

²**living** *n* **1** : the condition of being alive **2** : LIVELIHOOD **3** : manner of life

living room *n* : a room in a residence used for the common social activities of the occupants

living wage *n* : a wage sufficient to provide an acceptable standard of living

living will *n* : a document requesting that the signer not be kept alive by artificial means unless there is a reasonable expectation of recovery

livre \'lēvrᵊ\ *n* : the pound of Lebanon

liz·ard \'li-zərd\ *n* : any of a group of 4-legged reptiles with long tapering tails

Lk *abbr* Luke

ll *abbr* lines

lla·ma \'lä-mə\ *n* : any of a genus of wild or domesticated So. American mammals related to the camels but smaller and without a hump

lla·no \'lä-nō\ *n, pl* **llanos** : an open grassy plain esp. of Latin America

LLD *abbr* doctor of laws

LNG *abbr* liquefied natural gas

¹**load** \'lōd\ *n* **1 a** : PACK **b** ♦ : whatever is put in a ship or vehicle or airplane for conveyance : CARGO **2** : a mass of weight supported by something **3** : something that burdens the mind or spirits **4** ♦ : a large quantity — usu. used in pl. **5** : a standard, expected, or authorized burden

♦ [1b] burden, cargo, freight, haul, lading, payload, weight ♦ *usu* **loads** [4] abundance, deal, gobs, heap, lot, pile, plenty, quantity, scads

²**load** *vb* **1 a** ♦ : to put a load in or on; *also* : to receive a load **b** ♦ : to fill with a load **2** : to encumber with an obligation or something heavy or disheartening **3** : to increase the weight of by adding something **4** : to supply abundantly **5** : to put a charge in (as a firearm)

♦ [1a] burden, encumber, lumber, saddle, weight *Ant* disencumber, unburden, unload ♦ [1b] charge, cram, fill, heap, jam, jam-pack, pack, stuff

load·ed *adj* **1** *slang* : HIGH **12 2** ♦ : having a large amount of money **3** : equipped with an abundance of options

♦ affluent, flush, moneyed, opulent, rich, wealthy, well-fixed, well-heeled, well-off, well-to-do

load·stone *var of* LODESTONE

¹**loaf** \'lōf\ *n, pl* **loaves** \'lōvz\ : a shaped or molded mass esp. of bread

²**loaf** *vb* ♦ : to spend time in idleness : LOUNGE

♦ dally, dawdle, dillydally, hang around, hang out, idle, loll, lounge

loaf·er *n* **1** ♦ : one that loafs **2** : a low step-in shoe

♦ idler, lazybones, slouch, slug, sluggard

loam \\'lōm, 'lüm\\ *n* : SOIL; *esp* : a loose soil of mixed clay, sand, and silt — **loamy** *adj*

¹**loan** \\'lōn\\ *n* **1** : money lent at interest; *also* : something lent for the borrower's temporary use **2** : the grant of temporary use

²**loan** *vb* : LEND

loan shark *n* : a person who lends money at excessive rates of interest — **loan·shark·ing** \\'lōn-ˌshär-kiŋ\\ *n*

loan·word \\'lōn-ˌwərd\\ *n* : a word taken from another language and at least partly naturalized

loath \\'lōth, 'lōth\\ *also* **loathe** \\lōth, lōth\\ *adj* : RELUCTANT

loathe \\'lōth\\ *vb* **loathed; loath·ing** ♦ : to dislike greatly

♦ abhor, abominate, despise, detest, execrate, hate

loath·ing \\'lō-thiŋ\\ *n* ♦ : extreme disgust

♦ disgust, distaste, nausea, repugnance, repulsion, revulsion ♦ abhorrence, abomination, execration, hate, hatred

loath·some \\'lōth-səm, 'lōth-\\ *adj* : exciting loathing : REPULSIVE

lob \\'läb\\ *vb* **lobbed; lob·bing** : to throw, hit, or propel something in a high arc — **lob** *n*

¹**lob·by** \\'lä-bē\\ *n, pl* **lobbies** **1** ♦ : a corridor used esp. as a passageway or waiting room **2** : a group of persons engaged in lobbying

♦ entry, foyer, hall, vestibule

²**lobby** *vb* **lob·bied; lob·by·ing** : to try to influence public officials and esp. legislators — **lob·by·ist** *n*

lobe \\'lōb\\ *n* : a curved or rounded part esp. of a bodily organ — **lo·bar** \\'lō-bər\\ *adj* — **lobed** \\'lōbd\\ *adj*

lo·be·lia \\lō-'bēl-yə\\ *n* : any of a genus of plants often grown for their clusters of showy flowers

lo·bot·o·my \\lō-'bä-tə-mē\\ *n, pl* **-mies** : surgical severance of certain nerve fibers in the brain performed esp. formerly to relieve some mental disorders

lob·ster \\'läb-stər\\ *n* : any of a family of edible marine crustaceans with two large pincerlike claws and four other pairs of legs; *also* : SPINY LOBSTER

¹**lo·cal** \\'lō-kəl\\ *adj* **1** : of, relating to, or occupying a particular place **2** : serving a particular limited district; *also* : making all stops ⟨a ~ train⟩ **3** : affecting a small part of the body ⟨~ infection⟩ — **lo·cal·ly** *adv*

²**local** *n* ♦ : one that is local; *esp* : a local or particular branch, lodge, or chapter of an organization (as a labor union)

♦ affiliate, branch, chapter

local area network *n* : a network of personal computers in a small area (as an office)

lo·cale \\lō-'kal\\ *n* ♦ : a place that is the setting for a particular event

♦ location, place, point, position, site, spot

lo·cal·ise *chiefly Brit var of* LOCALIZE

lo·cal·i·ty \\lō-'ka-lə-tē\\ *n, pl* **-ties** : a particular spot, situation, or location

lo·cal·ize \\'lō-kə-ˌlīz\\ *vb* **-ized; -iz·ing** : to fix in or confine to a definite place or locality — **lo·cal·i·za·tion** \\ˌlō-kə-lə-'zā-shən\\ *n*

lo·cate \\'lō-ˌkāt, lō-'kāt\\ *vb* **lo·cat·ed; lo·cat·ing** **1** : STATION, SETTLE **2** ♦ : to determine the site of **3** : to find or fix the place of in a sequence

♦ detect, determine, dig up, discover, ferret out, find, hit on, track down

lo·ca·tion \\lō-'kā-shən\\ *n* **1** ♦ : a position or site occupied or available for occupancy or marked by some distinguishing feature : PLACE **2** : the process of locating **3** : a place outside a studio where a motion picture is filmed

♦ locale, place, point, position, site, spot

lo·ca·vore \\'lō-kə-ˌvȯr\\ *n* : one who eats food grown locally whenever possible

loc cit *abbr* in the place cited

loch \\'läk, 'läk\\ *n, Scot* : LAKE; *also* : a bay or arm of the sea esp. when nearly landlocked

¹**lock** \\'läk\\ *n* : a tuft, strand, or ringlet of hair; *also* : a cohering bunch (as of wool or flax)

²**lock** *n* **1** : a fastening in which a bolt is operated **2** : the mechanism of a firearm by which the charge is exploded **3** : an enclo-

sure (as in a canal) used in raising or lowering boats from level to level **4** : AIR LOCK **5** : a wrestling hold

³**lock** *vb* **1** : to fasten the lock of; *also* : to make fast with a lock **2** ♦ : to confine or exclude by means of a lock — often used with *in* or *up* **3** : INTERLOCK **4** : to make or become motionless by the interlocking of parts

♦ commit, confine, immure, imprison, jail

lock·er \\'lä-kər\\ *n* **1** ♦ : a drawer, cupboard, or compartment for individual storage use **2** : an insulated compartment for storing frozen food

♦ box, caddy, case, casket, chest, trunk ♦ buffet, cabinet, closet, cupboard, hutch, sideboard

lock·et \\'lä-kət\\ *n* : a small usu. metal case for a memento worn suspended from a chain or necklace

lock·jaw \\'läk-ˌjȯ\\ *n* : a symptom of tetanus marked by spasms of the jaw muscles and inability to open the jaws; *also* : TETANUS

lock·nut \\-ˌnət\\ *n* **1** : a nut screwed tight on another to prevent it from slacking back **2** : a nut designed to lock itself when screwed tight

lock·out \\-ˌaut\\ *n* : the suspension of work by an employer during a labor dispute in order to make employees accept the terms being offered

lock·smith \\-ˌsmith\\ *n* : one who makes or repairs locks

lock·step \\-ˌstep\\ *n* : a mode of marching in step by a body of persons moving in a very close single file

lock·up \\-ˌəp\\ *n* : JAIL; *esp* : a local jail where persons are detained prior to court hearing

lo·co \\'lō-kō\\ *adj, slang* : mentally disordered : CRAZY, FRENZIED

lo·co·mo·tion \\ˌlō-kə-'mō-shən\\ *n* **1** : the act or power of moving from place to place **2** : TRAVEL

¹**lo·co·mo·tive** \\ˌlō-kə-'mō-tiv\\ *adj* : of or relating to locomotion or a locomotive

²**locomotive** *n* : a self-propelled vehicle used to move railroad cars

lo·co·mo·tor \\ˌlō-kə-'mō-tər\\ *adj* : of or relating to locomotion or organs used in locomotion

lo·co·weed \\'lō-kō-ˌwēd\\ *n* : any of several leguminous plants of western No. America that are poisonous to livestock

lo·cus \\'lō-kəs\\ *n, pl* **lo·ci** \\'lō-ˌsī\\ **1** : the place where something is situated or occurs : LOCALITY **2** : the set of all points whose location is determined by stated conditions

lo·cust \\'lō-kəst\\ *n* **1** : a usu. destructive migratory grasshopper **2** : CICADA **3** : any of various leguminous trees; *also* : the wood of a locust

lo·cu·tion \\lō-'kyü-shən\\ *n* ♦ : a particular form of expression; *also* : PHRASEOLOGY

♦ manner, mode, phraseology, style, tone, vein

lode \\'lōd\\ *n* : an ore deposit

lode·stone \\-ˌstōn\\ *n* **1** : an iron-containing rock with magnetic properties **2** ♦ : something that strongly attracts

♦ attraction, draw, magnet

¹**lodge** \\'läj\\ *vb* **lodged; lodg·ing** **1** ♦ : to provide quarters for; *also* : to settle in a place **2** : CONTAIN **3** : to come to a rest and remain **4** : to deposit for safekeeping **5** : to vest (as authority) in an agent **6** : FILE ⟨~ a complaint⟩

♦ ensconce, install, perch, roost, settle ♦ accommodate, billet, domicile, harbor (*or* harbour), house, put up, quarter, roof, shelter, take in

²**lodge** *n* **1** ♦ : a house set apart for residence in a special season or by an employee on an estate; *also* : INN **2** ♦ : a den or lair esp. of gregarious animals **3** : the meeting place of a branch of a fraternal organization; *also* : the members of such a branch

♦ [1] cabin, camp, chalet, cottage ♦ [1] hospice, hotel, inn, public house, tavern ♦ [2] burrow, den, hole, lair

lodg·er \\'lä-jər\\ *n* ♦ : a person who occupies a rented room in another's house

♦ boarder, renter, roomer, tenant

lodg·ing \\'lä-jiŋ\\ *n* **1** : a place to live : DWELLING **2** ♦ : a room or suite of rooms in another's house rented as a dwelling place — usu. used in pl.

♦ flat, suite

lodg·ment *or* **lodge·ment** \\'läj-mənt\\ *n* **1** ♦ : a lodging place **2** : the act or manner of lodging **3** : DEPOSIT

♦ accommodation, lodging

loess \\'les, 'ləs\\ *n* : a usu. yellowish brown loamy deposit believed to be chiefly deposited by the wind

lo–fi \\'lō-ˌfī\\ *n* : audio production of rough or unpolished sound quality — **lo-fi** *adj*

¹**loft** \\'lȯft\\ *n* **1** : ATTIC **2** : GALLERY ⟨organ ∼⟩ **3** : an upper floor (as in a warehouse or barn) esp. when not partitioned **4** : the thickness of a fabric or insulated material (as of a sleeping bag)

²**loft** *vb* : to strike or throw (a ball) so that it rises high in the air
loft·i·ness \\-tē-nəs\\ *n* ♦ : the quality or state of being lofty

♦ arrogance, haughtiness, pretense, pretension, pretentiousness, self-importance, superiority

lofty \\'lȯf-tē\\ *adj* **loft·i·er; -est** **1** ♦ : elevated in character and spirit : NOBLE; *also* : SUPERIOR **2** ♦ : extremely proud; *also* : haughty and overbearingly arrogant **3** : rising to a great height : HIGH, TALL — **loft·i·ly** \\'lȯf-tə-lē\\ *adv*

♦ [1] chivalrous, gallant, great, greathearted, high, high-minded, lordly, magnanimous, noble, sublime ♦ [1] eloquent, formal, high-flown, majestic, stately, superior, towering ♦ [2] arrogant, haughty, highfalutin, imperious, peremptory, pompous, presumptuous, pretentious, supercilious

¹**log** \\'lȯg, 'läg\\ *n* **1** : a bulky piece of a cut or fallen tree **2** : an apparatus for measuring a ship's speed **3** : the daily record of a ship's progress; *also* : a regularly kept record of performance or events

²**log** *vb* **logged; log·ging** **1** : to cut (trees) for lumber; *also* : to clear (land) of trees in lumbering **2** ♦ : to enter in a log; *broadly* : to make a note or record of **3** : to sail a ship or fly an airplane for (an indicated distance or period of time) **4** : to have (an indicated record) to one's credit : ACHIEVE — **log·ger** \\'lȯ-gər, 'lä-\\ *n*

♦ jot, mark, note, put down, record, register, set down

³**log** *n* : LOGARITHM

lo·gan·ber·ry \\'lō-gən-ˌber-ē\\ *n* : a red-fruited upright-growing dewberry; *also* : its berry

log·a·rithm \\'lȯg-ə-ˌri-t͟həm, 'lä-\\ *n* : the exponent that indicates the power to which a base is raised to produce a given number ⟨the ∼ of 100 to base 10 is 2 since $10^2 = 100$⟩ — **log·a·rith·mic** \\ˌlȯg-ə-'rith-mik, ˌlä-\\ *adj*

loge \\'lōzh\\ *n* **1** : a small compartment; *also* : a box in a theater **2** : a small partitioned area; *also* : the forward section of a theater mezzanine

log·ger·head \\'lȯ-gər-ˌhed, 'lä-\\ *n* : a large sea turtle of subtropical and temperate waters — **at loggerheads** : in a state of quarrelsome disagreement

log·gia \\'lō-jē-ə, 'lȯ-jä\\ *n, pl* **loggias** \\'lō-jē-əz, 'lȯ-jäz\\ : a roofed open gallery

log·ic \\'lä-jik\\ *n* **1** : a science that deals with the rules and tests of sound thinking and proof by reasoning **2** ♦ : sound reasoning **3** : the arrangement of circuit elements for arithmetical computation in a computer — **log·i·cal·ly** \\-jik(ə-)lē\\ *adv* — **lo·gi·cian** \\lō-'ji-shən\\ *n*

♦ reason, reasoning, sense

log·i·cal \\-ji-kəl\\ *adj* ♦ : of, relating to, involving, or being in accordance with logic

♦ analytic, coherent, good, rational, reasonable, sensible, sober, sound, valid *Ant* incoherent, illogical, invalid, irrational, unreasonable, unsound

lo·gis·tics \\lō-'jis-tiks\\ *n sing or pl* : the procurement, maintenance, and transportation of matériel, facilities, and personnel — **lo·gis·tic** \\-tik\\ *or* **lo·gis·ti·cal** \\-ti-kəl\\ *adj*

log·jam \\'lȯg-ˌjam, 'läg-\\ *n* **1** : a deadlocked jumble of logs in a watercourse **2** : DEADLOCK

logo \\'lō-gō\\ *n, pl* **log·os** \\-gōz\\ ♦ : an identifying symbol (as for advertising)

♦ emblem, hallmark, symbol, trademark

log off *vb* : to end the connection of a computer to a network or system

log on *vb* : to start the connection of a computer to a network or system

logo·type \\'lȯ-gə-ˌtīp, 'lä-\\ *n* : LOGO

log out *vb* : LOG OFF

log·roll·ing \\-ˌrō-liŋ\\ *n* : the trading of votes by legislators to secure favorable action on projects of individual interest

lo·gy \\'lō-gē\\ *also* **log·gy** \\'lȯ-gē, 'lä-\\ *adj* **lo·gi·er; -est** : deficient in vitality : SLUGGISH

loin \\'lȯin\\ *n* **1** : the part of the body on each side of the spinal column and between the hip and the lower ribs; *also* : a cut of meat from this part of an animal **2** *pl* : the pubic region; *also* : the organs of reproduction

loin·cloth \\-ˌklȯth\\ *n* : a cloth worn about the loins often as the sole article of clothing in warm climates

loi·ter \\'lȯi-tər\\ *vb* **1** ♦ : to delay an activity with idle stops and pauses : LINGER **2** : to hang around idly — **loi·ter·er** *n*

♦ crawl, creep, dally, dawdle, delay, dillydally, drag, lag, linger, poke, tarry

loll \\'läl\\ *vb* **1** ♦ : to hang loosely or laxly : DROOP, DANGLE **2** ♦ : to act or move in a lax, lazy, or indolent manner : LOUNGE ⟨∼ing by the pool⟩

♦ [1] dangle, droop, flag, hang, sag, wilt ♦ [2] bask, lounge, relax, repose, rest

lol·la·pa·loo·za \\ˌlä-lə-pə-'lü-zə\\ *n* : something extraordinarily impressive or outstanding

lol·li·pop *or* **lol·ly·pop** \\'lä-li-ˌpäp\\ *n* : a lump of hard candy on a stick

lol·ly·gag \\'lä-lē-ˌgag\\ *vb* **-gagged; -gag·ging** : DAWDLE

Lond *abbr* London

lone \\'lōn\\ *adj* **1** ♦ : having no company : SOLITARY ⟨a ∼ sentinel⟩ **2** ♦ : alone in a class or category : SOLE, ONLY ⟨the ∼ theater in town⟩ **3** : ISOLATED ⟨a ∼ tree⟩

♦ alone, only, singular, sole, solitary, special, unique

lone·ly \\'lōn-lē\\ *adj* **lone·li·er; -est** **1** ♦ : being without company **2** : UNFREQUENTED ⟨a ∼ spot⟩ **3** : sad from being alone : LONESOME — **lone·li·ness** *n*

♦ alone, lone, lonesome, solitary, unaccompanied

lon·er \\'lō-nər\\ *n* ♦ : one that avoids others; *also* : one who pursues an independent course of thought or action

♦ bohemian, deviant, individualist, maverick, nonconformist

lone·some \\'lōn-səm\\ *adj* **1** ♦ : sad from lack of companionship **2 a** : REMOTE **b** : having no company : SOLITARY — **lone·some·ly** *adv* — **lone·some·ness** *n*

♦ desolate, forlorn, lonely

¹**long** \\'lȯŋ\\ *adj* **long·er** \\'lȯŋ-gər\\; **long·est** \\'lȯŋ-gəst\\ **1** ♦ : extending for a considerable distance; *also* : having greater height than usual : ELONGATED **2** : having a specified length **3** ♦ : extending over a considerable time; *also* : TEDIOUS **4** : containing many items in a series **5** : being a syllable or speech sound of relatively great duration **6** : extending far into the future **7** : well furnished with something — used with *on* ⟨∼ on talent⟩

♦ [1] extended, lengthy *Ant* brief, short ♦ [3] extended, far, great, lengthy, marathon *Ant* brief, short, short-lived, short-term

²**long** *adv* : for or during a long time

³**long** *n* : a long period of time

⁴**long** *vb* **longed; long·ing** \\'lȯŋ-iŋ\\ ♦ : to feel a strong desire or wish

♦ *usu* **long for** ache for, covet, crave, desire, die for, hanker for, hunger for, lust (for *or* after), pine for, repine for, thirst for, want, wish for, yearn for

⁵**long** *abbr* longitude

long·boat \\'lȯŋ-ˌbōt\\ *n* : a large boat usu. carried by a merchant sailing ship

long·bow \\-ˌbō\\ *n* : a wooden bow drawn by hand and used esp. by medieval English archers

long COVID *also* **long COVID–19** *or* **long–haul COVID** *or* **long–haul COVID–19** *n* : a condition marked by the presence of symptoms (such as fatigue, cough, shortness of breath, or headache) which persist for an extended time following a person's initial recovery from COVID-19 infection

lon·gev·i·ty \\län-'je-və-tē\\ *n* : a long duration of individual life; *also* : length of life

long·hair \\'lȯŋ-ˌher\\ *n* **1** : a lover of classical music **2** : HIPPIE **3** : a domestic cat having long outer fur — **long·haired** \\-ˌherd\\ *or* **long·hair** *adj*

long·hand \\-ˌhand\\ *n* : writing done by hand : HANDWRITING; *also* : cursive writing

long·horn \\-ˌhȯrn\\ *n* : any of the cattle with long horns formerly common in the southwestern U.S.

long hundredweight *n, Brit* : a unit of weight equal to 112 pounds

long·ing \\'lȯŋ-iŋ\\ *n* ♦ : a strong desire esp. for something unattainable — **long·ing·ly** *adv*

♦ appetite, craving, desire, drive, hankering, hunger, itch, lust, passion, thirst, urge, yearning, yen

lon·gi·tude \\'län-jə-ˌtüd, -ˌtyüd\\ *n* : angular distance expressed usu. in degrees east or west from the prime meridian through Greenwich, England

lon·gi·tu·di·nal \ˌlän-jə-'tüd-ᵊn-əl, -'tyüd-\ *adj* **1 :** extending lengthwise **2 :** of or relating to length — **lon·gi·tu·di·nal·ly** *adv*

long–range \'lȯŋ-'rānj\ *adj* **1 :** relating to or fit for long distances **2 :** involving a long period of time

long·shore·man \'lȯŋ-ˌshȯr-mən\ *n* : a laborer at a wharf who loads and unloads cargo

long–suf·fer·ing \-'sə-friŋ, -fə-riŋ\ *adj* ♦ : patiently enduring lasting offense or hardship

♦ forbearing, patient, stoic, tolerant, uncomplaining

long–term \'lȯŋ-'tərm\ *adj* **1 :** extending over or involving a long period of time **2 :** constituting a financial obligation based on a term usu. of more than 10 years ⟨∼ bonds⟩

long·time \'lȯŋ-'tīm\ *adj* : of long duration ⟨∼ friends⟩

long ton *n* : a British unit of weight equal to 20 long hundred-weight

lon·gueur \lōⁿ-'gœr\ *n, pl* **longueurs** \same or -'gœrz\ : a dull tedious portion (as of a book)

long–wind·ed \ˌlȯŋ-'win-dəd\ *adj* ♦ : tediously long in speaking or writing

♦ circuitous, diffuse, prolix, rambling, verbose, windy, wordy

loo·fah \'lü-fə\ *n* : a sponge consisting of the fibrous skeleton of a gourd

¹look \'lu̇k\ *vb* **1 :** to exercise the power of vision : SEE **2 :** EXPECT **3 :** to have an appearance that befits ⟨∼s the part⟩ **4** ♦ : to have the appearance or likelihood of being : SEEM ⟨∼s thin⟩ **5 :** to direct one's attention : HEED **6** ♦ : to have a specified direction : POINT, FACE **7 :** to show a tendency **8** ♦ : to express by the eyes or facial expression — **look after :** to take care of — **look for :** EXPECT

♦ [4] act, appear, make, seem, sound ♦ *usu* **look toward** [6] face, front, point ♦ [8] air, express, give, sound, state, vent, voice

²look *n* **1** ♦ : the action of looking : GLANCE **2** ♦ : the expression of the countenance; *also* : physical appearance — usu. used in pl. **3** ♦ : the state or form in which something appears : ASPECT

♦ [1] cast, eye, gander, glance, glimpse, peek, peep, regard, sight, view ♦ [2] cast, countenance, expression, face, visage ♦ *usu* **looks** [2] attractiveness, beauty, comeliness, handsomeness, loveliness, prettiness ♦ [3] appearance, aspect, mien, presence

look down *vb* : to regard with contempt — used with *on* or *upon*

looking glass *n* : MIRROR

look into *vb* ♦ : to investigate, study, or analyze

♦ delve, dig, explore, go, inquire into, investigate, probe, research

look·out \'lu̇k-ˌau̇t\ *n* **1** ♦ : a person assigned to watch (as on a ship) **2** ♦ : a careful watch **3** ♦ : a view from a particular place : VIEW **4 :** a matter of concern **5 :** an elevated place or structure affording a wide view for observation

♦ [1] custodian, guard, guardian, keeper, picket, sentry, warden, warder, watch, watchman ♦ [2] alertness, attentiveness, vigilance, watch ♦ [3] outlook, panorama, prospect, view, vista

look up *vb* **1 :** IMPROVE ⟨business is *looking up*⟩ **2 :** to search for in or as if in a reference work **3 :** to seek out esp. for a brief visit

¹loom \'lüm\ *n* : a frame or machine for weaving together threads or yarns into cloth

²loom *vb* **1 :** to come into sight in an unnaturally large, indistinct, or distorted form **2 :** to appear in an impressively exaggerated form **3 :** to take shape as an impending occurrence

loon \'lün\ *n* : any of several web-footed black-and-white fish-eating diving birds

loon·ie \'lü-nē\ *n, Can* : a coin worth one Canadian dollar

loo·ny *also* **loo·ney** \'lü-nē\ *adj* **loo·ni·er; -est** : CRAZY, FOOLISH

loony bin *n, informal and often offensive* : a psychiatric hospital

¹loop \'lüp\ *n* **1 a :** a fold or doubling of a line through which another line or hook can be passed **b :** a loop-shaped figure or course ⟨a ∼ in a river⟩ **2 :** a circular airplane maneuver executed in the vertical plane **3 :** a continuously repeated segment of film, music, or sound

²loop *vb* ♦ : to make a loop in, on, or about

♦ circle, circumnavigate, coil, compass, girdle, orbit, ring, round

loop·er \'lü-pər\ *n* : any of numerous rather small hairless moth caterpillars that move with a looping motion

loop·hole \'lüp-ˌhōl\ *n* **1 :** a small opening in a wall through which firearms may be discharged **2 :** a means of escape; *esp*

: an ambiguity or omission that allows one to evade the intent of a law or contract

¹loose \'lüs\ *adj* **loos·er; loos·est** ♦ : not rigidly fastened **2** ♦ : free from restraint or obligation **3 :** not dense or compact in structure **4 :** not chaste : LEWD **5** ♦ : not tightly drawn or stretched : SLACK **6** ♦ : not precise or exact — **loose·ly** *adv* — **loose·ness** *n*

♦ [1, 5] insecure, lax, relaxed, slack *Ant* taut, tense, tight ♦ [2] footloose, free, unbound, unconfined, unrestrained ♦ [6] imprecise, inaccurate, inexact

²loose *vb* **loosed; loos·ing** **1** ♦ : to let loose : RELEASE; *also* : to free from restraint **2 :** UNTIE **3 :** DETACH **4** ♦ : to let fly : DISCHARGE **5 :** RELAX, SLACKEN

♦ [1] discharge, emancipate, enfranchise, free, liberate, loosen, manumit, release, spring, unbind, unchain, unfetter ♦ [4] blast, discharge, fire, shoot

³loose *adv* : LOOSELY

loos·en \'lüs-ᵊn\ *vb* **1** ♦ : to release from restraint : FREE **2** ♦ : to make or become loose **3 :** to relax the severity of

♦ [1] free, loose, release, uncork, unleash, unlock, unloosen ♦ [2] ease, relax, slack, slacken

loosen up *vb* : to become less tense

¹loot \'lüt\ *n* ♦ : goods taken in war or by robbery : PLUNDER — **loot·er** *n*

♦ booty, plunder, spoil, swag

²loot *vb* ♦ : to plunder or sack in war

♦ despoil, maraud, pillage, plunder, ransack, sack, strip

¹lop \'läp\ *vb* **lopped; lop·ping** **1 :** to cut branches or twigs from **2** ♦ : to eliminate as unnecessary or undesirable — usu. used with *off*

♦ *usu* **lop off** bob, clip, crop, curtail, cut, cut back, dock, nip, prune, shave, shear, trim

²lop *vb* **lopped; lop·ping** : to hang downward; *also* : to flop or sway loosely

¹lope \'lōp\ *n* : an easy bounding gait

²lope *vb* : to move or ride at a lope

lop·sid·ed \'läp-'sī-dəd\ *adj* **1** ♦ : leaning to one side **2 :** not symmetrical — **lop·sid·ed·ly** *adv* — **lop·sid·ed·ness** *n*

♦ askew, awry, cockeyed, crooked, listing, slantwise, uneven

lo·qua·cious \lō-'kwā-shəs\ *adj* ♦ : excessively talkative — **lo·quac·i·ty** \-'kwa-sə-tē\ *n*

♦ chatty, conversational, gabby, garrulous, talkative

¹lord \'lȯrd\ *n* **1 :** one having power and authority over others; *esp* : a person from whom a feudal fee or estate is held **2 :** a man of rank or high position; *esp* : a British nobleman **3** *pl, cap* : the upper house of the British parliament **4 :** a person of great power in some field **5** *cap* : GOD 1

²lord *vb* : to act like a lord; *esp* : to put on airs — usu. used with *it*

lord chancellor *n, pl* **lords chancellor** : a British officer of state who presides over the House of Lords, serves as head of the British judiciary, and is usu. a leading member of the cabinet

lord·ly \-lē\ *adj* **lord·li·er; -est** **1** ♦ : of, relating to, or having the characteristics of a lord : DIGNIFIED; *also* : possessing or arising from a sense of high moral character **2** ♦ : exhibiting the pride and assurance associated with one of the highest birth or rank : HAUGHTY

♦ [1] chivalrous, dignified, gallant, great, greathearted, high, high-minded, lofty, magnanimous, noble, sublime ♦ [2] disdainful, haughty, highfalutin, lofty, prideful, proud, superior

lord·ship \-ˌship\ *n* **1 :** the rank or dignity of a lord — used as a title **2 :** the authority or territory of a lord

Lord's Supper *n* : COMMUNION

lore \'lȯr\ *n* **1** ♦ : something that has been learned : KNOWLEDGE; *esp* : traditional knowledge or belief **2** ♦ : a particular body of knowledge or tradition

♦ [1] intelligence, knowledge, science, wisdom ♦ [2] folklore, legend, myth, mythology, tradition

lor·gnette \lȯrn-'yet\ *n* : a pair of eyeglasses or opera glasses with a handle

lorn \'lȯrn\ *adj* : miserable and forlorn as if deserted : DESOLATE

lor·ry \'lȯr-ē\ *n, pl* **lorries** *chiefly Brit* : MOTORTRUCK

lose \'lüz\ *vb* **lost** \'lȯst\; **los·ing** \'lü-ziŋ\ **1 :** DESTROY **2 :** to miss from a customary place : MISLAY **3 :** to suffer deprivation of **4 :** to fail to use : WASTE **5 :** to fail to win or obtain ⟨∼ the game⟩ **6 :** to fail to keep or maintain ⟨∼ his balance⟩ **7 :** to wander from ⟨∼ her way⟩ **8** ♦ : to get rid of

♦ cast, discard, ditch, dump, fling, jettison, junk, reject, scrap, shed, shuck, slough, throw away, throw out, unload

los·er *n* **1** : a person or thing that loses esp. consistently **2 a** : a person who is incompetent or unable to succeed **b** ♦ : something doomed to fail or disappoint

♦ bummer, bust, catastrophe, debacle, dud, failure, fiasco, fizzle, flop, lemon, turkey, washout

loss \'lȯs\ *n* **1** ♦ : the state or fact of being destroyed : RUIN **2** : the harm resulting from losing **3** ♦ : something that is lost **4** *pl* : killed, wounded, or captured soldiers **5** ♦ : failure to win **6** : an amount by which the cost exceeds the selling price **7** ♦ : decrease in amount or degree **8** : the act of losing possession

♦ [1] annihilation, demolition, desolation, destruction, devastation, havoc, obliteration, ruin, wastage, wreckage ♦ [3] casualty, fatality, victim ♦ [5] defeat, rout, shellacking ♦ [7] abatement, decline, decrease, decrement, diminution, drop, fall, reduction, shrinkage

loss leader *n* : an article sold at a loss in order to draw customers

lost \'lȯst\ *adj* **1** : not used, won, or claimed **2** ♦ : no longer possessed or known **3** : ruined or destroyed physically or morally **4** : DENIED; *also* : HARDENED **5** : unable to find the way; *also* : HELPLESS **6** : ABSORBED, RAPT **7** : not appreciated or understood ⟨his jokes were ～ on me⟩

♦ gone, missing *Ant* owned, possessed, retained

lot \'lät\ *n* **1** : an object used in deciding something by chance; *also* : the use of lots to decide something **2 a** : SHARE, PORTION **b** ♦ : one's way of life or worldly fate : FORTUNE **3** ♦ : a plot of land **4** ♦ : a group of individuals **5** ♦ : a considerable quantity ⟨a ～ of trouble⟩

♦ [2b] circumstance, destiny, doom, fate, fortune, portion ♦ [3] parcel, plat, plot, property, tract ♦ [4] array, batch, body, bunch, cluster, crop, group, huddle, knot, parcel, party ♦ [5] abundance, barrel, bucket, bushel, chunk, deal, gobs, heap, loads, mass, mess, mountain, much, oodles, pile, plenty, profusion, quantity, reams, scads, stack, wad, wealth *Ant* bit, hint, little, pinch, smidgen, speck, spot, touch, trace

loth *var of* LOATH

lo·tion \'lō-shən\ *n* : a liquid preparation for cosmetic and external medicinal use

lot·tery \'lä-tə-rē\ *n, pl* **-ter·ies** **1** : a drawing of lots in which prizes are given to the winning names or numbers **2** : a matter determined by chance

lo·tus \'lō-təs\ *n* **1** : a fruit held in Greek legend to cause dreamy contentment and forgetfulness **2** : any of various water lilies represented esp. in ancient Egyptian and Hindu art **3** : any of several leguminous forage plants

loud \'laud\ *adj* **1** ♦ : marked by intensity or volume of sound **2** : CLAMOROUS, NOISY **3** ♦ : obtrusive or offensive in color or pattern ⟨a ～ suit⟩ — **loud** *adv* — **loud·ly** *adv* — **loud·ness** *n*

♦ [1] booming, clamorous (*or* clamourous), deafening, earsplitting, piercing, resounding, ringing, roaring, sonorous, stentorian, thunderous *Ant* gentle, low, soft ♦ [3] flamboyant, flashy, garish, gaudy, glitzy, ostentatious, swank, tawdry

loud-mouthed \-ˌmautht, -ˌmauthd\ *adj* : given to loud offensive talk

loud·speak·er \-ˌspē-kər\ *n* : a device that changes electrical signals into sound

¹lounge \'launj\ *vb* **lounged**; **loung·ing** ♦ : to act or move lazily or listlessly

♦ bask, loll, relax, repose, rest ♦ dally, dawdle, dillydally, hang around, hang out, idle, loaf, loll

²lounge *n* **1** : a room with comfortable furniture; *also* : a room (as in a theater) with lounging, smoking, and toilet facilities **2** ♦ : a long couch

♦ couch, davenport, divan, settee, sofa

lour, loury *var of* LOWER, LOWERY

louse \'laus\ *n, pl* **lice** \'līs\ **1** : any of various small wingless usu. flattened insects parasitic on warm-blooded animals **2** : a plant pest (as an aphid) **3** *pl* **lous·es** ♦ : a contemptible person

♦ beast, boor, churl, clown, creep, cretin, cur, heel, jerk, joker, lout, skunk, slob, snake

lousy \'lau-zē\ *adj* **lous·i·er; -est** **1** : infested with lice **2** ♦ : miserably poor or inferior **3** : amply supplied ⟨～ with money⟩ **4** ♦ : totally repulsive — **lous·i·ly** \-zə-lē\ *adv* — **lous·i·ness** \-zē-nəs\ *n*

♦ [2] atrocious, awful, bad, deficient, inferior, off, poor, punk, rotten, substandard, terrible, unacceptable, unsatisfactory, wanting, wretched, wrong ♦ [4] contemptible, despicable, nasty, pitiful, scabby, scurvy, sorry, wretched

lout \'laut\ *n* ♦ : a stupid awkward fellow

♦ clod, hulk, lubber, lug, oaf

lout·ish *adj* ♦ : resembling or befitting a lout — **lout·ish·ly** *adv*

♦ boorish, churlish, clownish, uncouth

lou·ver *or* **lou·vre** \'lü-vər\ *n* **1** : an opening having parallel slanted slats to allow flow of air but to exclude rain or sun or to provide privacy; *also* : a slat in such an opening **2** : a device with movable slats for controlling the flow of air or light

lov·able \'lə-və-bəl\ *adj* ♦ : having qualities that attract affection

♦ adorable, darling, dear, endearing, precious, sweet, winning *Ant* abhorrent, abominable, detestable, hateful, odious, unlovable

¹love \'ləv\ *n* **1** ♦ : strong affection **2** ♦ : warm attachment ⟨～ of the sea⟩ **3** : attraction based on sexual desire **4** ♦ : a beloved person **5** : unselfish loyal and benevolent concern for others **6** : a score of zero in tennis — **love·less** *adj*

♦ [1] appetite, fancy, favor (*or* favour), fondness, like, liking, partiality, preference, relish, shine, taste, use ♦ [2] affection, attachment, devotion, fondness, passion *Ant* abomination, hate, hatred, loathing, rancor ♦ [4] beloved, darling, dear, flame, honey, sweet, sweetheart

²love *vb* **loved; lov·ing** **1** ♦ : to value highly : CHERISH **2** ♦ : to feel a lover's passion, devotion, or tenderness for **3** ♦ : to touch or stroke lightly in a loving or endearing manner : CARESS **4** ♦ : to like or desire actively ⟨～s to play bridge⟩

♦ [1] appreciate, cherish, prize, treasure, value ♦ [2] adore, cherish, worship *Ant* abhor, abominate, despise, detest, execrate, hate, loathe ♦ [3] caress, fondle, pat, pet, stroke ♦ [4] adore, delight, dig, enjoy, fancy, groove, like, relish, revel

love affair *n* ♦ : a romantic attachment or episode between lovers

♦ affair, amour, romance

love·bird \'ləv-ˌbərd\ *n* : any of various small usu. gray or green parrots that seem to show caring behavior for their mates

loved *adj* ♦ : held dear

♦ beloved, darling, dear, favorite (*or* favourite), pet, precious, special, sweet

love·li·ness *n* ♦ : the quality or state of being lovely

♦ attractiveness, beauty, comeliness, handsomeness, looks, prettiness

love·lorn \-ˌlȯrn\ *adj* : deprived of love or of a lover

love·ly \'ləv-lē\ *adj* **love·li·er; -est** ♦ : delightful for beauty, harmony, or grace : BEAUTIFUL — **love·li·ly** \'ləv-lə-lē\ *adv* — **lovely** *adv*

♦ attractive, beautiful, cute, fair, gorgeous, handsome, knockout, pretty, ravishing, stunning

love·mak·ing \-ˌmā-kiŋ\ *n* **1** : COURTSHIP **2** : sexual activity; *esp* : COPULATION

lov·er *n* ♦ : a person in love; *also* : an ardent follower, supporter, or enthusiast (as of a religion, art form, or sport)

♦ addict, aficionado, buff, bug, devotee, enthusiast, fan, fanatic, fancier, fiend, freak, maniac, nut

love seat *n* : a seat or sofa for two people

love·sick \-ˌsik\ *adj* **1** : YEARNING ⟨a ～ suitor⟩ **2** : expressing a lover's longing — **love·sick·ness** *n*

lov·ing \'lə-viŋ\ *adj* **1** ♦ : having affection or warm regard : AFFECTIONATE **2** : PAINSTAKING — **lov·ing·ly** *adv*

♦ affectionate, devoted, fond, tender, tenderhearted *Ant* unloving

¹low \'lō\ *vb* : MOO

²low *n* : MOO

³low *adj* **low·er** \'lō-ər\; **low·est** \'lō-əst\ **1** : not high or tall ⟨～ wall⟩; *also* : DÉCOLLETÉ **2** : situated or passing below the normal level or surface ⟨～ ground⟩; *also* : marking a nadir **3** : not loud ⟨～ voice⟩ **4** : being near the equator **5 a** ♦ : humble in status **b** ♦ : lacking in cultural advancement **c** ♦ : lacking in dignity **6** ♦ : lacking strength, health, or vitality : WEAK; *also* : DEPRESSED **7** : STRICKEN, PROSTRATE **8** ♦ : less than usual in number, amount, or value; *also* : of lesser degree than average **9** : falling short of a standard **10** : UNFAVORABLE — **low** *adv*

♦ [3] dull, quiet, soft ♦ [5a] common, humble, ignoble, inferior, lowly, mean, plebeian, vulgar ♦ [5b] crude, primitive, rude, rudimentary ♦ [5b] coarse, common, crass, crude, gross, ill-bred, rough, rude, tasteless, uncouth, uncultivated, uncultured, unpolished, unrefined, vulgar ♦ [5c] base, contemptible, despicable, detestable, dirty, dishonorable (*or* dishonourable), ignoble, mean, snide, sordid, vile, wretched ♦ [6] blue, dejected, depressed, down, downcast, glum, melancholy, sad, sorrowful, sorry, unhappy, woeful, wretched ♦ [6] faint, feeble, frail, infirm, unsubstantial, weak ♦ [8] cheap, cut-rate, reasonable

⁴low *n* **1 :** something that is low **2 :** a region of low barometric pressure **3 :** the arrangement of gears in an automobile transmission that gives the slowest speed and greatest power
low-ball \'lō-ˌbȯl\ *vb* : to give a deceptively low price, cost estimate, or offer to
low beam *n* : a vehicle headlight beam with short-range focus
low blow *n* : an unprincipled attack
low-brow \'lō-ˌbraů\ *adj* : having little taste or intellectual interest — **lowbrow** *n*
low–density lipoprotein *n* : LDL
low-down \-ˌdaůn\ *n* ♦ : pertinent and esp. guarded information

♦ dope, scoop, tip

low–down \-ˌdaůn\ *adj* **1 :** MEAN, CONTEMPTIBLE **2 :** deeply emotional
low–end \-ˌend\ *adj* : of, relating to, or being the lowest-priced merchandise in a manufacturer's line
¹low-er \'laů-ər\ *vb* **1 ♦ :** to look sullen : FROWN **2 :** to become dark, gloomy, and threatening

♦ frown, glare, gloom, glower, scowl

²low-er \'lō-ər\ *adj* **1 ♦ :** relatively low (as in rank) **2 :** situated beneath the earth's surface **3 :** constituting the popular and more representative branch of a bicameral legislative body **4 :** less advanced in the scale of evolutionary development

♦ inferior, junior, less, lesser, minor, subordinate, under

³low-er \'lō-ər\ *vb* **1 ♦ :** to move down : DROP; *also* : DIMINISH **2** : to let descend by its own weight; *also* : to reduce the height of **3** ♦ : to reduce or decline in value, number, or amount **4 ♦ :** to bring down in quality or character : DEGRADE; *also* : HUMBLE

♦ [1] decline, descend, diminish, dip, drop, fall, plummet, plunge, sink, tumble ♦ [3] abate, decrease, de-escalate, diminish, downsize, dwindle, lessen, reduce ♦ [4] abase, debase, degrade, demean, discredit, disgrace, dishonor (*or* dishonour), humble, humiliate, shame, smirch, take down

low•er•case \ˌlō-ər-ˈkās\ *adj* : being a letter that belongs to or conforms to the series a, b, c, etc., rather than A, B, C, etc. — **lowercase** *n*
lower class *n* : a social class occupying a position below the middle class and having the lowest status in a society — **lower–class** \-ˈklas\ *adj*
low•er•most \'lō-ər-ˌmōst\ *adj* : LOWEST
low•ery \'laů-ə-rē\ *adj* : GLOOMY, LOWERING ⟨a ∼ sky⟩
lowest common denominator *n* **1 :** LEAST COMMON DENOMINATOR **2 :** something designed to appeal to a lowbrow audience; *also* : such an audience
lowest common multiple *n* : LEAST COMMON MULTIPLE
low–key \'lō-ˈkē\ *also* **low–keyed** \-ˈkēd\ *adj* : of low intensity : RESTRAINED
low•land \'lō-lənd, -ˌland\ *n* : low and usu. level country
low•lev•el \'lō-ˈle-vəl\ *adj* **1 :** being of low importance or rank **2 :** being or relating to nuclear waste of low concentration
low•life \'lō-ˌlīf\ *n, pl* **low•lifes** \-ˌlīfs\ *also* **low•lives** \-ˌlīvz\ : a person of low social status or moral character
low•li•ness *n* ♦ : the quality or state of being lowly

♦ humbleness, humility, meekness, modesty

low•ly \'lō-lē\ *adj* **low•li•er; -est** **1 ♦ :** humble in manner or spirit : MEEK **2 ♦ :** ranking low in some hierarchy

♦ [1] demure, humble, meek, modest, retiring, unassuming, unpretentious ♦ [2] common, humble, ignoble, inferior, low, mean, plebeian, vulgar

low•ness *n* ♦ : the quality or state of being low

♦ debility, delicacy, enfeeblement, faintness, feebleness, frailty, infirmity, languor, weakness ♦ coarseness, grossness, indelicacy, rudeness, vulgarity

low–rise \'lō-ˈrīz\ *adj* **1 :** having few stories and not equipped with elevators ⟨a ∼ building⟩ **2 :** of, relating to, or characterized by low-rise buildings
low–slung \'lō-ˈsləŋ\ *adj* : relatively low to the ground or floor ⟨a ∼ building⟩ ⟨∼ pants⟩

low–tech \'lō-ˈtek\ *adj* : technologically simple or unsophisticated
¹lox \'läks\ *n* : liquid oxygen
²lox *n, pl* **lox** *or* **lox•es** : salmon cured in brine and sometimes smoked
loy•al \'lȯi-əl\ *adj* **1 :** faithful in allegiance to one's government **2 ♦ :** faithful esp. to a cause or ideal : CONSTANT — **loy•al•ly** \'lȯi-ə-lē\ *adv*

♦ constant, devoted, faithful, fast, good, pious, staunch, steadfast, steady, true, true-blue

loy•al•ist \'lȯi-ə-list\ *n* : one who is or remains loyal to a political party, government, or sovereign
loy•al•ty \'lȯi-əl-tē\ *n* ♦ : the quality or state or an instance of being loyal

♦ allegiance, constancy, dedication, devotion, faith, faithfulness, fastness, fealty, fidelity, steadfastness

loz•enge \'lä-zənj\ *n* **1 :** a diamond-shaped figure **2 :** a small flat often medicated candy
LP *abbr* low pressure
LPG *abbr* liquefied petroleum gas
LPGA *abbr* Ladies Professional Golf Association
LPN \'el-ˈpē-ˈen\ *n* : LICENSED PRACTICAL NURSE
Lr *symbol* Lawrencium
LSD \ˌel-(ˌ)es-ˈdē\ *n* : an illicit and highly potent hallucinogenic drug derived from ergot or produced synthetically
lt *abbr* light
Lt *abbr* lieutenant
LT *abbr* long ton
LTC *or* **Lt Col** *abbr* lieutenant colonel
Lt Comdr *abbr* lieutenant commander
ltd *abbr* limited
LTG *or* **Lt Gen** *abbr* lieutenant general
LTJG *abbr* lieutenant, junior grade
ltr *abbr* letter
Lu *symbol* lutetium
lu•au \'lü-ˌaů\ *n* : a Hawaiian feast
lub *abbr* lubricant; lubricating
lub•ber \'lə-bər\ *n* **1 ♦ :** a big clumsy fellow : LOUT **2 :** an unskilled seaman

♦ clod, hulk, lout, lug, oaf

lub•ber•ly *adj* ♦ : resembling or having the characteristics of a lubber

♦ awkward, clumsy, gawky, graceless, heavy-handed, lumpish, ungainly, unhandy

lube \'lüb\ *n* : LUBRICANT; *also* : an application of a lubricant
lu•bri•cant \'lü-bri-kənt\ *n* : a material capable of reducing friction when applied between moving parts
lu•bri•cate \'lü-brə-ˌkāt\ *vb* **-cat•ed; -cat•ing** ♦ : to apply a lubricant to — **lu•bri•ca•tion** \ˌlü-brə-ˈkā-shən\ *n* — **lu•bri•ca•tor** \'lü-brə-ˌkā-tər\ *n*

♦ grease, oil, slick, wax

lu•bri•cious \lü-ˈbri-shəs\ *or* **lu•bri•cous** \'lü-bri-kəs\ *adj* **1** : SMOOTH, SLIPPERY **2** : LECHEROUS; *also* : SALACIOUS — **lu•bric•i•ty** \lü-ˈbri-sə-tē\ *n*
lu•cent \'lüs-ᵊnt\ *adj* **1 ♦ :** glowing with light : LUMINOUS **2** ♦ : marked by clarity or translucence — **lu•cent•ly** *adv*

♦ [1] beaming, bright, brilliant, effulgent, glowing, incandescent, lambent, lucid, luminous, lustrous, radiant, refulgent, shiny ♦ [2] clear, limpid, liquid, pellucid, transparent

lu•cerne \lü-ˈsərn\ *n, chiefly Brit* : ALFALFA
lu•cid \'lü-səd\ *adj* **1 :** suffused with light : SHINING **2 ♦ :** mentally sound **3 ♦ :** easily understood ⟨a ∼ explanation⟩ — **lu•cid•ly** *adv*

♦ [2] balanced, clearheaded, normal, right, sane, stable ♦ [3] apparent, broad, clear, clear-cut, distinct, evident, manifest, obvious, palpable, patent, perspicuous, plain, transparent, unambiguous, unequivocal, unmistakable

lu•cid•i•ty \lü-ˈsi-də-tē\ *n* ♦ : clearness of thought or style

♦ clarity, explicitness, perspicuity, simplicity

lu•cid•ness *n* : the quality or state of being lucid esp. in thought or style
Lu•ci•fer \'lü-sə-fər\ *n* : DEVIL, SATAN
¹luck \'lək\ *n* **1 ♦ :** a force that brings good fortune or adversity : CHANCE **2 ♦ :** good fortune

♦ [1] accident, chance, circumstance, hazard ♦ [2] chance, fortune *Ant* mischance, misfortune

²luck *vb* **1 :** to prosper or succeed esp. through chance or good fortune — usu. used with *out* **2 :** to come upon something desirable by chance — usu. used with *out*, *on*, *onto*, or *into*

luck·i·ly \'lə-kə-lē\ *adv* **1 :** in a lucky manner **2 :** FORTUNATELY 2

luck·less *adj* ♦ **:** being without luck

♦ hapless, ill-fated, ill-starred, unfortunate, unhappy, unlucky

lucky \'lə-kē\ *adj* **luck·i·er; -est 1** ♦ **:** favored by luck **:** FORTUNATE **2** ♦ **:** happening by chance **:** FORTUITOUS **3 :** seeming to bring good luck — **luck·i·ness** *n*

♦ [1] blessed, fortunate, happy *Ant* hapless, ill-fated, ill-starred, luckless, unfortunate, unlucky ♦ [2] fluky, fortuitous, fortunate, happy, providential

lu·cra·tive \'lü-krə-tiv\ *adj* ♦ **:** producing wealth **:** PROFITABLE — **lu·cra·tive·ly** *adv* — **lu·cra·tive·ness** *n*

♦ fat, gainful, profitable, remunerative

lu·cre \'lü-kər\ *n* ♦ **:** monetary gain **:** PROFIT; *also* **:** MONEY

♦ earnings, gain, net, payoff, proceeds, profit, return ♦ cash, currency, dough, money, pelf, tender

lu·cu·bra·tion \,lü-kyə-'brā-shən, -kə-\ *n* **:** laborious study **:** MEDITATION

Lud·dite \'lə-,dīt\ *n* **:** one who is opposed to technological change

lu·di·crous \'lü-də-krəs\ *adj* ♦ **:** amusing or laughable through obvious absurdity, incongruity, exaggeration, or eccentricity **:** RIDICULOUS ⟨a ∼ idea⟩; *also* **:** meriting derisive laughter or scorn as absurdly inept, false, or foolish — **lu·di·crous·ly** *adv* — **lu·di·crous·ness** *n*

♦ antic, comic, droll, funny, hilarious, humorous, hysterical, laughable, riotous, screaming, uproarious ♦ absurd, comical, derisive, farcical, laughable, preposterous, ridiculous, risible, silly

luff \'ləf\ *vb* **:** to turn the head of a ship toward the wind

¹lug \'ləg\ *vb* **lugged; lug·ging 1** ♦ **:** to draw slowly or heavily **:** DRAG, PULL **2** ♦ **:** to carry laboriously

♦ [1] drag, draw, hale, haul, pull, tow, tug ♦ [2] bear, carry, cart, convey, ferry, haul, pack, tote, transport

²lug *n* **1 :** a projecting piece (as for fastening, support, or traction) **2 :** a nut securing a wheel on an automobile **3** ♦ **:** a big clumsy fellow

♦ clod, hulk, lout, lubber, oaf

lug·gage \'lə-gij\ *n* **:** containers (as suitcases) for carrying personal belongings **:** BAGGAGE

lu·gu·bri·ous \lú-'gü-brē-əs\ *adj* ♦ **:** mournful often to an exaggerated degree ⟨∼ music⟩ — **lu·gu·bri·ous·ly** *adv* — **lu·gu·bri·ous·ness** *n*

♦ dolorous, funeral, mournful, plaintive, regretful, rueful, sorrowful, weeping, woeful

Luke \'lük\ *n* **:** a book of the New Testament of Christian Scripture

luke·warm \'lük-'wôrm\ *adj* **1 :** moderately warm **:** TEPID **2 :** not enthusiastic — **luke·warm·ly** *adv*

¹lull \'ləl\ *vb* **1** ♦ **:** to make peaceful **:** SOOTHE, CALM **2 :** to cause to relax vigilance

♦ allay, calm, compose, quiet, settle, soothe, still, tranquilize

²lull *n* **1 :** a temporary calm (as during a storm) **2** ♦ **:** a temporary drop in activity

♦ break, breath, breather, interruption, pause

lul·la·by \'lə-lə-,bī\ *n, pl* **-bies :** a song to lull children to sleep

lum·ba·go \,ləm-'bā-gō\ *n* **:** acute or chronic pain in the lower back

lum·bar \'ləm-bər, -,bär\ *adj* **:** of, relating to, or constituting the loins or the vertebrae between the thoracic vertebrae and sacrum ⟨∼ region⟩

¹lum·ber \'ləm-bər\ *vb* **1** ♦ **:** to move heavily or clumsily **2** ♦ **:** to make a low heavy rolling sound

♦ [1] clump, flounder, lump, plod, scuff, scuffle, shamble, shuffle, stamp, stomp, stumble, tramp, tromp *Ant* breeze, coast, glide, slide, waltz, whisk ♦ [2] growl, grumble, roll, rumble

²lumber *n* **1 :** surplus or disused articles that are stored away **2 :** timber or logs esp. when dressed for use

³lumber *vb* **1 :** to cut logs; *also* **:** to saw logs into lumber **2** ♦ **:** to clutter with or as if with lumber — **lum·ber·man** \-mən\ *n*

♦ burden, encumber, load, saddle, weight

lum·ber·jack \-,jak\ *n* **:** LOGGER

lum·ber·yard \-,yärd\ *n* **:** a place where lumber is kept for sale

lu·mi·nary \'lü-mə-,ner-ē\ *n, pl* **-nar·ies 1** ♦ **:** a very famous person **2 :** a source of light; *esp* **:** a celestial body

♦ celebrity, figure, light, notable, personage, personality, somebody, standout, star, superstar, VIP

lu·mi·nes·cence \,lü-mə-'nes-ᵊns\ *n* ♦ **:** the low-temperature emission of light (as by a chemical or physiological process); *also* **:** such light — **lu·mi·nes·cent** \-ᵊnt\ *adj*

♦ blaze, flare, fluorescence, glare, gleam, glow, illumination, incandescence, light, radiance, shine

lu·mi·nos·i·ty \,lü-mə-'nä-sə-tē\ *n* ♦ **:** the quality or state of being luminous

♦ brilliance, dazzle, effulgence, illumination, lightness, lucidity, radiance, refulgence, splendor

lu·mi·nous \'lü-mə-nəs\ *adj* **1** ♦ **:** emitting light; *also* **:** LIGHTED **2 :** CLEAR, INTELLIGIBLE **3 :** ILLUSTRIOUS — **lu·mi·nance** \-nəns\ *n* — **lu·mi·nous·ly** *adv*

♦ beaming, bright, brilliant, effulgent, glowing, incandescent, lambent, lucent, lucid, lustrous, radiant, refulgent, shiny

lum·mox \'lə-məks\ *n* **:** a clumsy person

¹lump \'ləmp\ *n* **1** ♦ **:** a piece or mass of indefinite size and shape **2 :** AGGREGATE, TOTALITY **3** ♦ **:** a usu. abnormal swelling

♦ [1] blob, chunk, clod, clump, glob, gob, hunk, nub, wad ♦ [3] excrescence, growth, neoplasm, tumor ♦ [3] bump, knot, nodule, swelling

²lump *vb* **1** ♦ **:** to heap together in a lump **2 :** to form into lumps **3 :** to move noisily and clumsily

♦ accumulate, amass, assemble, collect, concentrate, garner, gather, group, pick up, round up, scrape

³lump *adj* **:** not divided into parts ⟨a ∼ sum⟩

lump·ec·to·my \,ləm-'pek-tə-mē\ *n, pl* **-mies :** excision of a breast tumor

lump·ish *adj* ♦ **:** lacking ease or grace (as of movement or expression)

♦ awkward, clumsy, gawky, graceless, heavy-handed, lubberly, ungainly, unhandy

lumpy *adj* ♦ **:** filled or covered with lumps

♦ broken, bumpy, coarse, irregular, jagged, pebbly, ragged, rough, rugged, uneven

lu·na·cy \'lü-nə-sē\ *n, pl* **-cies 1** *dated* **:** a severely disordered state of the mind **:** INSANITY **2** ♦ **:** extreme folly; *also* **:** a foolish act

♦ absurdity, fatuity, folly, foolery, foolishness, idiocy, inanity, stupidity

lu·nar \'lü-nər\ *adj* **:** of or relating to the moon

¹lu·na·tic \'lü-nə-,tik\ *adj* **1 a** *dated* **:** affected with a severely disordered state of mind **:** INSANE **b** *dated* **:** designed for the care of mentally ill people **2** ♦ **:** extremely foolish

♦ absurd, cuckoo, fatuous, foolish, nonsensical, nutty, senseless, silly, stupid

²lunatic *n* **1** *dated* **:** a person affected with lunacy **2 :** an extremely foolish person

¹lunch \'lənch\ *n* **1 :** a light meal usu. eaten in the middle of the day **2 :** the food prepared for a lunch

²lunch *vb* **:** to eat lunch

lun·cheon \'lən-chən\ *n* **:** a usu. formal lunch

lun·cheon·ette \,lən-chə-'net\ *n* **:** a small restaurant serving light lunches

lunch·room \'lənch-,rüm, -,rúm\ *n* **1 :** LUNCHEONETTE **2 :** a room (as in a school) where lunches are sold and eaten or lunches brought from home may be eaten

lu·nette \lü-'net\ *n* **:** something shaped like a crescent

lung \'ləŋ\ *n* **1 :** one of the usu. paired baglike breathing organs in the chest of an air-breathing vertebrate **2 :** a mechanical device to promote breathing and make it easier — **lunged** \'ləŋd\ *adj*

lunge \'lənj\ *n* **1 :** a sudden thrust or pass (as with a sword) **2 :** a sudden forward stride or leap — **lunge** *vb*

lu·pine \'lü-pən\ *n* **:** any of a genus of leguminous plants with long upright clusters of pealike flowers

lu·pus \'lü-pəs\ *n* **:** any of several diseases characterized by skin lesions; *esp* **:** SYSTEMIC LUPUS ERYTHEMATOSUS

¹lurch \'lərch\ *n* **:** a sudden swaying or tipping movement

²lurch *vb* ♦ **:** to roll or tip abruptly; *also* **:** to move with a lurch

♦ careen, pitch, rock, roll, seesaw, sway, toss, wobble ♦ careen, dodder, reel, stagger, teeter, totter

¹lure \'lúr\ *n* **1** ♦ **:** an inducement to pleasure or gain **:** ENTICEMENT; *also* **:** APPEAL ⟨the ∼ of easy money⟩ **2 :** an artificial bait for catching fish

♦ appeal, attraction, bait, call, decoy, enticement, incentive, inducement, persuasion, seduction, snare, spur, temptation, trap

²**lure** *vb* **lured; lur·ing** ♦ : to draw on with a promise of pleasure or gain

♦ allure, beguile, decoy, entice, lead on, seduce, tempt

lu·rid \'lür-əd\ *adj* **1** ♦ : wan and ghostly pale in appearance **2** : shining with the red glow of fire seen through smoke or cloud **3 a** ♦ : causing horror or revulsion : GRUESOME **b** : SENSATIONAL — **lu·rid·ly** *adv*

♦ [1] ashen, cadaverous, livid, pale, pasty, peaked ♦ [3a] appalling, atrocious, awful, dreadful, frightful, ghastly, grisly, gruesome, hideous, horrible, horrid, macabre, monstrous, nightmarish, shocking, terrible

lurk \'lərk\ *vb* **1** ♦ : to move furtively : SNEAK **2** : to lie concealed

♦ pussyfoot, skulk, slide, slink, slip, snake, sneak, steal

lus·cious \'lə-shəs\ *adj* **1** ♦ : having a pleasingly sweet taste or smell **2** ♦ : sensually appealing ⟨a ∼ voice⟩ — **lus·cious·ly** *adv*

♦ [1] agreeable, ambrosial, appetizing, delectable, delicious, delightful, enjoyable, flavorful (*or* flavourful), palatable, savory, scrumptious, tasty, toothsome, yummy ♦ [2] carnal, fleshly, sensual, sensuous, voluptuous

lus·cious·ness *n* ♦ : the quality or state of being luscious

♦ savor, tastiness

¹**lush** \'ləsh\ *adj* ♦ : having or covered with abundant growth ⟨∼ pastures⟩

♦ green, leafy, luxuriant, verdant *Ant* barren, leafless

²**lush** *n* : an habitual heavy drinker

¹**lust** \'ləst\ *n* **1** : usu. intense or unbridled sexual desire : LASCIVIOUSNESS **2** ♦ : an intense longing

♦ appetite, craving, desire, drive, hankering, hunger, itch, longing, passion, thirst, urge, yearning, yen

²**lust** *vb* ♦ : to have an intense desire or need

♦ *usu* **lust for** *or* **lust after** ache for, covet, crave, desire, die for, hanker for, hunger for, long for, pine for, repine for, thirst for, want, wish for, yearn for

lus·ter *or* **lus·tre** \'ləs-tər\ *n* **1** ♦ : a shine or sheen esp. from reflected light **2** : BRIGHTNESS, GLITTER **3** : GLORY, SPLENDOR

♦ gloss, polish, sheen, shine

lus·ter·less *adj* ♦ : lacking luster

♦ dim, dull, flat

lust·ful *adj* ♦ : excited by lust

♦ lascivious, lewd, passionate, wanton

lust·i·ness \-tē-nəs\ *n* ♦ : the quality or state of being lusty

♦ animation, briskness, exuberance, liveliness, robustness, sprightliness, vibrancy, vitality

lus·tral \'ləs-trəl\ *adj* : serving or intended to purify
lus·trous \-trəs\ *adj* ♦ : reflecting light evenly and efficiently without glitter or sparkle

♦ beaming, bright, brilliant, effulgent, glowing, incandescent, lambent, lucent, lucid, luminous, radiant, refulgent, shiny ♦ glossy, polished, satiny, sleek

lusty \'ləs-tē\ *adj* **lust·i·er; -est 1** ♦ : full of vitality : ROBUST **2** ♦ : full of energy or activity — **lust·i·ly** \'ləs-tə-lē\ *adv*

♦ [1] dynamic, energetic, flush, peppy, robust, strenuous, vigorous, vital ♦ [2] firm, forceful, hearty, robust, solid, stout, strong, sturdy, vigorous

lute \'lüt\ *n* : a stringed musical instrument with a large pear-shaped body and a fretted fingerboard — **lu·te·nist** *or* **lu·ta·nist** \'lüt-ᵊn-ist\ *n*
lu·te·tium *also* **lu·te·cium** \lü-'tē-shē-əm, -shəm\ *n* : a metallic chemical element
Lu·ther·an \'lü-thə-rən\ *n* : a member of a Protestant denomination adhering to the doctrines of Martin Luther — **Lu·ther·an·ism** \-rə-,ni-zəm\ *n*
lux·u·ri·ant \,ləg-'zhur-ē-ənt, ,lək-'shur-\ *adj* **1** ♦ : yielding or growing abundantly : LUSH, PRODUCTIVE **2** ♦ : abundantly rich and varied; *also* : FLORID **3** : characterized by luxury — **lux·u·ri·ance** \-ē-əns\ *n* — **lux·u·ri·ant·ly** *adv*

♦ green, leafy, lush, verdant ♦ fat, fecund, fertile, fruitful, productive, prolific, rich

lux·u·ri·ate \-ē-,āt\ *vb* **-at·ed; -at·ing 1** : to grow profusely **2** : REVEL
lux·u·ri·ous \,ləg-'zhur-ē-əs, ,lək-'shur-\ *adj* ♦ : of, relating to, or marked by luxury

♦ deluxe, lavish, luxuriant, opulent, palatial, plush, sumptuous *Ant* ascetic, austere, humble

lux·u·ri·ous·ly *adv* ♦ : in a luxurious manner

♦ expensively, extravagantly, grandly, high, lavishly, opulently, richly

¹**lux·u·ry** \'lək-shə-rē, 'ləg-zhə-\ *n, pl* **-ries 1** : great ease and comfort **2** ♦ : something adding to pleasure or comfort but not absolutely necessary

♦ amenity, comfort, extra, frill, indulgence, superfluity *Ant* basic, essential, fundamental, necessity, requirement

²**luxury** *adj* ♦ : of or relating to luxury or luxuries or catering to luxurious tastes

♦ deluxe, lavish, luxuriant, luxurious, opulent, palatial, plush, sumptuous

lv *abbr* leave
Lv *symbol* livermorium
LWV *abbr* League of Women Voters
¹**-ly** \lē\ *adj suffix* **1** : like in appearance, manner, or nature ⟨queen*ly*⟩ **2** : characterized by regular recurrence in (specified) units of time : every ⟨hour*ly*⟩
²**-ly** *adv suffix* **1** : in a (specified) manner ⟨slow*ly*⟩ **2** : from a (specified) point of view ⟨grammatical*ly*⟩
ly·ce·um \lī-'sē-əm, 'lī-sē-\ *n* **1** : a hall for public lectures **2** : an association providing public lectures, concerts, and entertainments
ly·chee *or* **li·tchi** \'lē-chē\ *n* **1** : an oval fruit with a hard scaly outer covering, a small hard seed, and edible flesh **2** : an Asian tree bearing lychees
lye \'lī\ *n* : a corrosive alkaline substance used esp. in making soap
ly·ing \'lī-iŋ\ *adj* ♦ : marked by or containing falsehoods : UNTRUTHFUL

♦ dishonest, mendacious

ly·ing–in \,lī-iŋ-'in\ *n, pl* **lyings–in** *or* **lying–ins** : the state during and consequent to childbirth : CONFINEMENT
Lyme disease \'līm-\ *n* : an acute inflammatory disease that is caused by a spirochete transmitted by ticks, is characterized usu. by chills and fever, and if left untreated may result in joint pain, arthritis, and cardiac and neurological disorders
lymph \'limf\ *n* : a usu. clear fluid consisting chiefly of blood plasma and white blood cells, circulating in thin-walled tubes (**lymphatic vessels**), and bathing the body tissues — **lym·phat·ic** \lim-'fa-tik\ *adj*
lymph·ade·nop·a·thy \,lim-,fad-ᵊn-'ä-pə-thē\ *n, pl* **-thies** : abnormal enlargement of the lymph nodes
lymph node *n* : any of the rounded masses of lymphoid tissue surrounded by a capsule
lym·pho·cyte \'lim-fə-,sīt\ *n* : any of the white blood cells arising from lymphoid tissue that are typically found in lymph and blood and that include the cellular mediators (as a B cell or a T cell) of immunity — **lym·pho·cyt·ic** \,lim-fə-'si-tik\ *adj*
lym·phoid \'lim-,fȯid\ *adj* **1** : of, relating to, or being tissue (as of the lymph nodes) containing lymphocytes **2** : of, relating to, or resembling lymph
lym·pho·ma \lim-'fō-mə\ *n, pl* **-mas** *or* **-ma·ta** \-mə-tə\ : a usu. malignant tumor of lymphoid tissue
lynch \'linch\ *vb* : to put to death by mob action without legal sanction or due process of law — **lynch·er** *n*
lynx \'liŋks\ *n, pl* **lynx** *or* **lynx·es** : any of several wildcats with a short tail, long legs, and usu. tufted ears
lyre \'līr\ *n* : a stringed musical instrument of the harp class having a U-shaped frame and used by the ancient Greeks
¹**lyr·ic** \'lir-ik\ *n* **1** ♦ : a lyric poem **2** : the words of a popular song — usu. used in pl.

♦ poem, song, verse

²**lyric** *adj* **1** ♦ : suitable for singing : MELODIC **2** ♦ : expressing direct and usu. intense personal emotion ⟨∼ poetry⟩

♦ [1] euphonious, mellifluous, mellow, melodic, melodious, musical ♦ [2] bardic, lyrical, poetic

lyr·i·cal \-i-kəl\ *adj* ♦ : having qualities suggestive of music or poetry : LYRIC

♦ bardic, lyric, poetic

ly·ser·gic acid di·eth·yl·am·ide \lə-'sər-jik . . . ,dī-,e-thə-'la-,mīd, lī-, -'la-məd\ *n* : LSD
LZ *abbr* landing zone

¹m \\'em\\ *n, pl* **m's** *or* **ms** \\'emz\\ *often cap* : the 13th letter of the English alphabet

²m *abbr, often cap* **1** Mach **2** male **3** married **4** masculine **5** medium **6** noon **7** meter **8** mile **9** thousand **10** minute **11** month **12** moon

ma \\'mä, 'mȯ\\ *n* ♦ : a female parent : MOTHER

♦ mom, mommy, mother

MA *abbr* **1** master of arts **2** Massachusetts **3** mental age

ma'am \\'mam, *after "yes" often* əm\\ *n* : MADAM

¹Mac *abbr* Machabees

²Mac *or* **Macc** *abbr* Maccabees

ma·ca·bre \\mə-'käb; -'kä-brə, -bər\\ *adj* **1** : having death as a subject **2** : dwelling on the gruesome **3** ♦ : tending to produce horror in a beholder

♦ appalling, atrocious, awful, dreadful, frightful, ghastly, grisly, gruesome, hideous, horrible, horrid, lurid, monstrous, nightmarish, shocking, terrible

mac·ad·am \\mə-'ka-dəm\\ *n* : a roadway or pavement of small closely packed broken stone — **mac·ad·am·ize** \\-də-,mīz\\ *vb*

mac·a·da·mia nut \\,ma-kə-'dā-mē-ə\\ *n* : a hard-shelled richly-flavored nut of any of several Australian trees

ma·caque \\mə-'kak, -'käk\\ *n* : any of a genus of short-tailed chiefly Asian monkeys; *esp* : RHESUS MONKEY

mac·a·ro·ni \\,ma-kə-'rō-nē\\ *n* **1** : pasta made chiefly of wheat flour and shaped in the form of slender tubes **2** *pl* **-nís** *or* **-nies** : FOP, DANDY

mac·a·roon \\,ma-kə-'rün\\ *n* : a small cookie made chiefly of egg whites, sugar, and ground almonds or coconut

ma·caw \\mə-'kȯ\\ *n* : any of numerous parrots of Central and So. America

Mac·ca·bees \\'ma-kə-,bēz\\ *n* : either of two books of Scripture in the Roman Catholic canon and the Protestant Apocrypha

¹mace \\'mās\\ *n* : a spice made from the fibrous coating of the nutmeg

²mace *n* **1** : a heavy often spiked club used as a weapon esp. in the Middle Ages **2** : an ornamental staff carried as a symbol of authority

Mac·e·do·nian \\,ma-sə-'dō-nyən, -nē-ən\\ *n* : a native or inhabitant of Macedonia — **Macedonian** *adj*

mac·er·ate \\'ma-sə-,rāt\\ *vb* **-at·ed; -at·ing** **1** : to cause to waste away **2** : to soften by steeping or soaking so as to separate the parts — **mac·er·a·tion** \\,ma-sə-'rā-shən\\ *n*

Mac·Guf·fin *or* **Mc·Guf·fin** \\mə-'gə-fən\\ *n* : an object, event, or character whose main purpose is to advance the plot of a motion picture

mach *abbr* machine; machinery; machinist

Mach \\'mäk\\ *n* : a speed expressed by a Mach number

Mach·a·bees \\'ma-kə-,bēz\\ *n* : MACCABEES

ma·chete \\mə-'she-tē\\ *n* : a large heavy knife used for cutting sugarcane and underbrush and as a weapon

Ma·chi·a·vel·lian \\,ma-kē-ə-'ve-lē-ən\\ *adj* ♦ : characterized by cunning, duplicity, and bad faith — **Ma·chi·a·vel·lian·ism** *n*

♦ cutthroat, immoral, unconscionable, unethical, unprincipled, unscrupulous

mach·i·nate \\'ma-kə-,nāt, 'ma-shə-\\ *vb* ♦ : to plan or plot esp. to do harm

♦ conspire, contrive, intrigue, plot, scheme ♦ contrive, finagle, finesse, frame, maneuver (*or* manoeuvre), mastermind, negotiate, wangle

mach·i·na·tion \\,ma-kə-'nā-shən, ,ma-shə-\\ *n* ♦ : an act of planning esp. to do harm; *esp* : PLOT

♦ conspiracy, design, intrigue, plot, scheme

¹ma·chine \\mə-'shēn\\ *n* **1** ♦ : an automotive vehicle not operated on rails; *esp* : AUTOMOBILE **2** : a combination of mechanical parts that transmit forces, motion, and energy one to another **3** : an instrument (as a lever) for transmitting or modifying force or motion **4** : an electrical, electronic, or mechanical device for performing a task ⟨a sewing ∼⟩ **5** : a highly organized political group under the leadership of a boss or small clique

♦ automobile, car, motor vehicle

²machine *vb* **ma·chined; ma·chin·ing** : to shape or finish by machine-operated tools — **ma·chin·able** \\-'shē-nə-bəl\\ *adj*

machine gun *n* : an automatic gun capable of rapid continuous firing — **machine–gun** *vb* — **machine gunner** *n*

machine language *n* : the set of symbolic instruction codes used to represent operations and data in a machine (as a computer)

machine–readable *adj* : directly usable by a computer

ma·chin·ery \\mə-'shē-nə-rē\\ *n, pl* **-er·ies** **1** : MACHINES; *also* : the working parts of a machine **2** ♦ : the means by which something is done

♦ agency, agent, instrument, instrumentality, means, medium, organ, vehicle

ma·chin·ist \\mə-'shē-nist\\ *n* : a person who makes or works on machines

ma·chis·mo \\mä-'chēz-(,)mō, -'chiz-\\ *n* : a strong or exaggerated pride in one's masculinity

Mach number \\'mäk-\\ *n* : a number representing the ratio of the speed of a body (as an aircraft) to the speed of sound in the surrounding atmosphere

ma·cho \\'mä-chō\\ *adj* : characterized by machismo

mack·er·el \\'ma-kə-rəl\\ *n, pl* **mackerel** *or* **mackerels** : a No. Atlantic food fish greenish above and silvery below

mack·i·naw \\'ma-kə-,nȯ\\ *n* : a short heavy plaid coat

mack·in·tosh *also* **mac·in·tosh** \\'ma-kən-,täsh\\ *n* **1** *chiefly Brit* : RAINCOAT **2** : a lightweight waterproof fabric

mac·ra·mé *also* **mac·ra·me** \\'ma-krə-,mā\\ *n* : a coarse lace or fringe made by knotting threads or cords in a geometrical pattern

¹mac·ro \\'ma-(,)krō\\ *adj* : very large; *also* : involving large quantities or being on a large scale

²macro *n, pl* **macros** : a single computer instruction that stands for a sequence of operations

mac·ro·bi·ot·ic \\,ma-krō-bī-'ä-tik, -bē-\\ *adj* : relating to or being a very restricted diet (as one containing chiefly whole cereals or grains)

mac·ro·cosm \\'ma-krə-,kä-zəm\\ *n* ♦ : the great world : UNIVERSE

♦ cosmos, creation, nature, universe, world

ma·cron \\'mā-,krän, 'ma-\\ *n* : a mark {macr} placed over a vowel (as in māk) to show that the vowel is long

mac·ro·scop·ic \\,ma-krə-'skä-pik\\ *adj* : visible to the naked eye — **mac·ro·scop·i·cal·ly** \\-pi-k(ə-)lē\\ *adv*

mac·u·la \\'ma-kyə-lə\\ *n, pl* **-lae** \\-,lē, -,lī\\ *also* **-las** : an anatomical spot distinguishable from surrounding tissues — **mac·u·lar** \\-lər\\ *adj*

mad \\'mad\\ *adj* **mad·der; mad·dest** **1** : marked by mental disorder — not used technically **2** ♦ : being rash and foolish **3** ♦ : carried away by intense anger : FURIOUS, ENRAGED ⟨∼ at myself⟩ ⟨∼ about the delay⟩ **4** ♦ : carried away by enthusiasm or desire ⟨∼ about horses⟩ ⟨∼ for the boy next door⟩ **5** : RABID **6** : marked by wild gaiety and merriment **7** ♦ : intensely excited : FRANTIC **8** ♦ : marked by intense and often chaotic activity : WILD ⟨a ∼ rush⟩

♦ [2] absurd, cuckoo, fatuous, foolish, nonsensical, nutty, senseless, silly, stupid ♦ [3] angry, boiling, enraged, furious, irate, rabid, sore, wrathful ♦ *usu* **mad about** [4] crazy, nuts ♦ [7, 8] delirious, feverish, fierce, frantic, frenetic, frenzied, furious, rabid, violent, wild

Mad·a·gas·can \\,ma-də-'gas-kən\\ *n* : a native or inhabitant of Madagascar

mad·am \\'ma-dəm\\ *n* **1** *pl* **mes·dames** \\mā-'däm\\ — used as a form of polite address to a woman **2** *pl* **madams** : the female head of a house of prostitution

ma·dame \\mə-'dam, *before a surname also* 'ma-dəm\\ *n, pl* **mes·dames** \\mā-'däm\\ : MISTRESS — used as a title equivalent to *Mrs.* for a married woman not of English-speaking nationality

¹mad·cap \\'mad-,kap\\ *adj* ♦ : marked by capriciousness, recklessness, or foolishness — **madcap** *n*

♦ brash, foolhardy, overbold, overconfident, reckless

²madcap *n* ♦ : one who is madcap

♦ daredevil, devil

mad cow disease *n* : a fatal disease of the brain of cattle affecting the nervous system and probably caused by infected tissue in food
mad·den \'mad-ᵊn\ *vb* ♦ : to make mad

♦ craze, derange, unhinge ♦ anger, antagonize, enrage, incense, inflame, infuriate, outrage, rankle, rile, roil

mad·den·ing *adj* ♦ : tending to infuriate or irritate — **mad·den·ing·ly** *adv*

♦ aggravating, annoying, galling, irritating

mad·der \'ma-dər\ *n* : a Eurasian herb with yellow flowers and fleshy red roots; *also* : its root or a dye prepared from it
made *past and past part of* MAKE
Ma·dei·ra \mə-'dir-ə\ *n* : an amber-colored dessert wine
ma·de·moi·selle \,ma-də-mə-'zel, -mwə-, mam-'zel\ *n, pl* **ma·de·moi·selles** \-'zelz\ *or* **mes·de·moi·selles** \,mā-də-me-'zel, -mwe-\ : an unmarried girl or woman — used as a title for an unmarried woman not of English-speaking nationality
made–to–measure *adj* : CUSTOM-MADE
made–up \'mā-'dəp\ *adj* ♦ **1** : fancifully or falsely devised **2** : marked by the use of makeup

♦ chimerical, fabulous, fanciful, fantastic, fictitious, imaginary, mythical, phantom, pretend, unreal

mad·house \'mad-,haus\ *n* **1** *often offensive* : an institution providing care to mentally ill individuals **2** ♦ : a place of great uproar

♦ bedlam, circus, hell

mad·ly \'mad-lē\ *adv* **1** ♦ : in a mad manner **2** : to an extreme or excessive degree

♦ amok, berserk, frantically, harum-scarum, hectically, helter-skelter, pell-mell, wild, wildly

mad·man \'mad-,man, -mən\ *n* : a man who is or acts as if insane
mad·ness \'mad-nəs\ *n* **1** : the quality or state of being mad **2** ♦ : lack of good sense or judgment

♦ absurdity, asininity, balminess, daftness, fatuity, folly, foolishness, inanity, silliness, simplicity, zaniness

Ma·don·na \mə-'dä-nə\ *n* : a representation (as a picture or statue) of the Virgin Mary
ma·dras \'ma-drəs; ,mə-'dras, -'dräs\ *n* : a fine usu. cotton fabric with various designs (as plaid)
ma·dra·sa *or* **ma·dra·sa** \mə-'dra-sə, -'drä-\ *n* : a Muslim school, college, or university that is often part of a mosque
mad·ri·gal \'ma-dri-gəl\ *n* **1** : a short lyrical poem in a strict poetic form **2** : an elaborate part-song esp. of the 16th and 17th centuries
mad·wom·an \'mad-,wu-mən\ *n* : a woman who is or acts as if insane
mael·strom \'māl-strəm\ *n* **1** : a violent whirlpool **2** : TUMULT
mae·stro \'mī-strō\ *n, pl* **maestros** *or* **mae·stri** \-,strē\ **1** ♦ : a master in an art **2** : an eminent composer, conductor, or teacher of music

♦ ace, adept, artist, authority, crackerjack, expert, master, scholar, shark, virtuoso, whiz, wizard

Ma·fia \'mä-fē-ə\ *n* : a secret criminal society of Sicily or Italy; *also* : a similar organization elsewhere
ma·fi·o·so \,mä-fē-'ō-(,)sō\ *n, pl* **-si** \-(,)sē\ : a member of the Mafia
¹mag \'mag\ *n* : MAGAZINE
²mag *abbr* **1** magnetism **2** magneto **3** magnitude
mag·a·zine \'ma-gə-,zēn\ *n* **1** ♦ : a storehouse esp. for military supplies **2** : a place for keeping gunpowder in a fort or ship **3** : a publication usu. containing stories, articles, or poems and issued periodically **4** : a container in a gun for holding cartridges; *also* : a chamber (as on a camera) for film

♦ armory, arsenal, depot, dump

ma·gen·ta \mə-'jen-tə\ *n* : a deep purplish red color
mag·got \'ma-gət\ *n* : the legless wormlike larva of a dipteran fly — **mag·goty** *adj*
ma·gi \'mā-jī\ *n pl, often cap* : the three wise men from the East who paid homage to the infant Jesus
¹mag·ic \'ma-jik\ *n* **1** : the use of means (as charms or spells) believed to have supernatural power over natural forces **2 a** ♦ : an extraordinary power or influence seemingly from a supernatural force **b** ♦ : something that seems to cast a spell **3** ♦ : the art of producing illusions by sleight of hand

♦ [2a] bewitchment, enchantment, necromancy, sorcery, witchcraft, wizardry ♦ [2b] allure, appeal, attractiveness, captivation,

charisma, charm, enchantment, fascination, glamour, magnetism ♦ [3] legerdemain, prestidigitation

²magic *adj* **1** : of or relating to magic **2** ♦ : having unusually distinctive qualities resembling the supernatural

♦ magical, mystic, occult, weird

mag·i·cal \'ma-ji-kəl\ *adj* **1** : of or relating to magic **2** ♦ : resembling magic; *also* : giving a feeling of enchantment — **mag·i·cal·ly** \-ji-k(ə-)lē\ *adv*

♦ miraculous, phenomenal, superhuman, supernatural, uncanny, unearthly

ma·gi·cian \mə-'ji-shən\ *n* ♦ : a person skilled in magic

♦ conjurer, enchanter, necromancer, sorcerer, voodoo, witch, wizard ♦ conjurer, illusionist, trickster

mag·is·te·ri·al \,ma-jə-'stir-ē-əl\ *adj* **1** : AUTHORITATIVE ⟨a ∼ attitude⟩ **2** : of or relating to a magistrate or a magistrate's office or duties
ma·gis·tral \'ma-jə-strəl\ *adj* : AUTHORITATIVE
mag·is·trate \'ma-jə-,strāt\ *n* ♦ : an official entrusted with administration of the laws — **mag·is·tra·cy** \-strə-sē\ *n*

♦ bench, court, judge, justice

mag·lev \'mag-lev\ *n* **1** : the use of magnetic fields to float an object above a solid surface **2** : a train using maglev technology
mag·ma \'mag-mə\ *n* : molten rock material within the earth — **mag·mat·ic** \mag-'ma-tik\ *adj*
mag·nan·i·mous \mag-'na-nə-məs\ *adj* **1** : showing or suggesting a lofty and courageous spirit **2** ♦ : showing or suggesting nobility of feeling and generosity of mind — **mag·na·nim·i·ty** \,mag-nə-'ni-mə-tē\ *n* — **mag·nan·i·mous·ness** *n*

♦ chivalrous, gallant, great, greathearted, high, high-minded, lofty, lordly, noble, sublime

mag·nan·i·mous·ly \-lē\ *adv* ♦ : in a magnanimous manner

♦ gallantly, grandly, greatly, heroically, honorably (*or* honourably), nobly

mag·nate \'mag-,nāt\ *n* ♦ : a person of rank, influence, or distinction

♦ baron, czar, king, mogul, prince, tycoon

mag·ne·sia \mag-'nē-shə, -zhə\ *n* : a light white oxide of magnesium used as a laxative
mag·ne·sium \mag-'nē-zē-əm, -zhəm\ *n* : a silver-white light malleable metallic chemical element
mag·net \'mag-nət\ *n* **1** : LODESTONE **2** : a body that is able to attract iron **3** ♦ : something that attracts

♦ attraction, draw, lodestone

mag·net·ic \mag-'ne-tik\ *adj* **1** ♦ : having an unusual ability to attract ⟨a ∼ leader⟩ **2** : of or relating to a magnet or magnetism **3** : magnetized or capable of being magnetized — **mag·net·i·cal·ly** \-ti-k(ə-)lē\ *adv*

♦ alluring, attractive, captivating, charming, elfin, engaging, fascinating, fetching, glamorous, seductive

magnetic disk *n* : DISK 3
magnetic levitation *n* : MAGLEV 1
magnetic north *n* : the northerly direction in the earth's magnetic field indicated by the north-seeking pole of a compass needle
magnetic resonance imaging *n* : a noninvasive diagnostic technique that produces computerized images of internal body tissues based on electromagnetically induced activity of atoms within the body
magnetic tape *n* : a ribbon coated with a magnetic material on which information (as sound) may be stored
mag·ne·tise *chiefly Brit var of* MAGNETIZE
mag·ne·tism \'mag-nə-,ti-zəm\ *n* **1** : the power (as of a magnet) to attract iron **2** : the science that deals with magnetic phenomena **3** ♦ : an ability to attract or charm

♦ allure, appeal, attractiveness, captivation, charisma, charm, enchantment, fascination, glamour, magic

mag·ne·tite \'mag-nə-,tīt\ *n* : a black mineral that is an important iron ore
mag·ne·tize \'mag-nə-,tīz\ *vb* **-tized; -tiz·ing** **1** : to induce magnetic properties in **2** : to attract like a magnet : CHARM — **mag·ne·tiz·able** *adj* — **mag·ne·ti·za·tion** \,mag-nə-tə-'zā-shən\ *n* — **mag·ne·tiz·er** *n*
mag·ne·to \mag-'nē-tō\ *n, pl* **-tos** : a generator used to produce sparks in an internal combustion engine
mag·ne·tom·e·ter \,mag-nə-'tä-mə-tər\ *n* : an instrument for measuring the strength of a magnetic field

mag·ne·to·sphere \mag-'nē-tə-ˌsfir, -'ne-\ n : a region around a celestial object (as the earth) in which charged particles are trapped by its magnetic field — **mag·ne·to·spher·ic** \-ˌnē-tə-'sfir-ik, -'sfer-\ adj

mag·ni·fi·ca·tion \ˌmag-nə-fə-'kā-shən\ n **1 ♦** : the act of magnifying **2** : the amount by which an optical lens or instrument magnifies

   ♦ caricature, elaboration, embellishment, exaggeration, hyperbole, overstatement, padding

mag·nif·i·cence \mag-'ni-fə-səns\ n **1 ♦** : the quality or state of being magnificent **2** : splendor of surroundings

   ♦ augustness, brilliance, glory, grandeur, grandness, majesty, nobility, nobleness, resplendence, splendor, stateliness

mag·nif·i·cent \mag-'ni-fə-sənt\ adj **1 ♦** : characterized by grandeur or beauty : SPLENDID **2** : EXALTED, NOBLE — **mag·nif·i·cent·ly** adv

   ♦ august, baronial, gallant, glorious, grand, grandiose, heroic, imposing, majestic, monumental, noble, proud, regal, royal, splendid, stately

mag·nif·i·co \mag-'ni-fi-ˌkō\ n, pl **-coes** or **-cos** **1** : a nobleman of Venice **2** : a person of high position

mag·ni·fy \'mag-nə-ˌfī\ vb **-fied; -fy·ing** **1 a** : to praise highly : EXTOL, LAUD **b ♦** : to cause to be held in greater esteem **2 a ♦** : to increase in significance : INTENSIFY **b ♦** : to enlarge beyond bounds or the truth : EXAGGERATE **3** : to enlarge in fact or in appearance ⟨a microscope magnifies an object⟩ — **mag·ni·fi·er** \'mag-nə-ˌfī-ər\ n

   ♦ [1b] aggrandize, dignify, ennoble, exalt, glorify ♦ [2a] amplify, beef, boost, consolidate, deepen, enhance, heighten, intensify, redouble, step up, strengthen ♦ [2b] color (or colour), elaborate, embellish, embroider, exaggerate, pad, stretch

mag·nil·o·quent \mag-'ni-lə-kwənt\ adj : characterized by an exalted and often bombastic style or manner — **mag·nil·o·quence** \-kwəns\ n

mag·ni·tude \'mag-nə-ˌtüd, -ˌtyüd\ n **1 ♦** : greatness of size or extent **2 ♦** : spatial quality : SIZE **3** : QUANTITY **4** : a number representing the brightness of a celestial body **5 ♦** : the importance, quality, or caliber of something **6** : a number representing the intensity of an earthquake

   ♦ [1] enormity, hugeness, immensity, massiveness, vastness ♦ [2] dimension, extent, measure, measurement, proportion, size ♦ [5] consequence, import, moment, significance, weight

mag·no·lia \mag-'nōl-yə\ n : any of a genus of usu. spring-flowering shrubs and trees with large often fragrant flowers

mag·num opus \'mag-nəm-'ō-pəs\ n : the greatest achievement of an artist or writer

mag·pie \'mag-ˌpī\ n **1** : any of various long-tailed often black-and-white birds related to the jays **2 ♦** : a person who chatters noisily

   ♦ chatterbox, jabberer, talker

Mag·yar \'mag-ˌyär, 'mäg-; 'mä-ˌjär\ n : a member of the dominant people of Hungary — **Magyar** adj

ma·ha·ra·ja or **ma·ha·ra·jah** \ˌmä-hə-'rä-jə\ n : a Hindu prince ranking above a raja

ma·ha·ra·ni or **ma·ha·ra·nee** \-'rä-nē\ n **1** : the wife of a maharaja **2** : a Hindu princess ranking above a rani

ma·ha·ri·shi \ˌmä-hə-'rē-shē\ n : a Hindu teacher of mystical knowledge

ma·hat·ma \mə-'hät-mə, -'hat-\ n : a person revered for high-mindedness, wisdom, and selflessness

Mahican var of MOHICAN

ma·hog·a·ny \mə-'hä-gə-nē\ n, pl **-nies** : the reddish wood of any of various chiefly tropical trees that is used in furniture; also : a tree yielding this wood

ma·hout \mə-'haůt\ n : a keeper and driver of an elephant

maid \'mād\ n **1** : an unmarried girl or young woman **2 ♦** : a female servant : MAIDSERVANT

   ♦ domestic, girl, housemaid, maidservant

¹maid·en \'mād-ᵊn\ n **1 ♦** : an unmarried girl or young woman : MAID — **maid·en·ly** adj

   ♦ doll, girl, lass, maid, miss

²maiden adj **1** : UNMARRIED; also : VIRGIN **2** : of, relating to, or befitting a maiden **3 ♦** : preceding all others in time or order : FIRST ⟨~ voyage⟩

   ♦ first, inaugural, initial, original, pioneer, premier

maid·en·hair fern \-ˌhar-\ n : any of a genus of ferns with delicate feathery fronds

maid·en·head \'mād-ᵊn-ˌhed\ n **1** : VIRGINITY **2** : HYMEN

maid·en·hood \-ˌhůd\ n : the condition or time of being a maiden

maid–in–waiting n, pl **maids–in–waiting** : a young woman appointed to attend a queen or princess

maid of honor : a bride's principal unmarried wedding attendant

maid·ser·vant \'mād-ˌsər-vənt\ n **♦** : a girl or woman who is a servant

   ♦ domestic, girl, housemaid, maid

¹mail \'māl\ n **1 ♦** : something sent or carried in the postal system **2** : a nation's postal system — often used in pl.

   ♦ matter, parcel post, post, snail mail

²mail vb : to send by mail

³mail n : armor made of metal links or plates

mail·box \'māl-ˌbäks\ n **1** : a public box for the collection of mail **2** : a private box for the delivery of mail

mail carrier n : LETTER CARRIER

mail·man \-ˌman\ n **♦** : a man who delivers mail

   ♦ letter carrier, postman

maim \'mām\ vb **♦** : to mutilate, disfigure, or wound seriously : CRIPPLE

   ♦ cripple, disable, lame, mutilate

¹main \'mān\ n **1 ♦** : physical strength : FORCE ⟨with might and ~⟩ **2** : MAINLAND; also : HIGH SEA **3 ♦** : the chief part **4** : a principal pipe, duct, or circuit of a utility system

   ♦ [1] energy, force, might, muscle, potency, power, sinew, strength, vigor (or vigour) ♦ [3] body, bulk, core, generality, mass, staple, weight

²main adj **1 ♦** : of greatest importance or influence : CHIEF, PRINCIPAL **2** : fully exerted ⟨~ force⟩ **3** : expressing the chief predication in a complex sentence ⟨the ~ clause⟩

   ♦ arch, cardinal, central, chief, dominant, first, foremost, grand, key, paramount, predominant, preeminent, premier, primary, principal, sovereign, supreme

main·frame \'mān-ˌfrām\ n : a large fast computer

main·land \-ˌland, -lənd\ n : a continuous body of land constituting the chief part of a country or continent

main·line \-ˌlīn\ vb, slang : to inject a narcotic drug into a vein

main line n : a principal highway or railroad line

main·ly \'mān-lē\ adv **♦** : for the most part : CHIEFLY

   ♦ altogether, basically, chiefly, generally, largely, mostly, overall, predominantly, primarily, principally

main·mast \'mān-ˌmast, -məst\ n : the principal mast on a sailing ship

main·sail \-ˌsāl, -səl\ n : the largest sail on the mainmast

main·spring \-ˌspriŋ\ n **1** : the chief spring in a mechanism (as of a watch) **2** : the chief motive, agent, or cause

main·stay \-ˌstā\ n **1** : a stay running from the head of the mainmast to the foot of the foremast **2 ♦** : a chief support

   ♦ buttress, dependence, pillar, reliance, standby, support

main·stream \-ˌstrēm\ n : a prevailing current or direction of activity or influence — **mainstream** adj

main·tain \mān-'tān\ vb **1 ♦** : to keep in an existing state (as of repair) **2 ♦** : to sustain against opposition or danger **3** : to continue in : CARRY ON **4** : to provide for : SUPPORT **5 ♦** : to affirm in or as if in argument : ASSERT

   ♦ [1] conserve, keep up, preserve, save ♦ [2] defend, justify, support, uphold ♦ [5] affirm, allege, argue, assert, aver, avouch, avow, claim, contend, declare, insist, profess, protest, warrant

main·tain·able \mān-'tā-nə-bəl\ adj **♦** : capable of being maintained — **main·tain·abil·i·ty** \-ˌtā-nə-'bi-lə-tē\ n

   ♦ defensible, justifiable, supportable, sustainable, tenable

main·te·nance \'mānt-ᵊn-əns\ n **♦** : the act of maintaining : the state of being maintained

   ♦ conservation, preservation, upkeep

main·top \'mān-ˌtäp\ n : a platform at the head of the mainmast of a square-rigged ship

mai·son·ette \ˌmāz-ᵊn-'et\ n **1** : a small house **2** : an apartment often on two floors

mai tai \'mī-ˌtī\ n : a cocktail made with liquors and fruit juices

maî·tre d' or **mai·tre d'** \ˌmā-trə-'dē, ˌme-\ n, pl **maître d's** or **maitre d's** \-'dēz\ : MAÎTRE D'HÔTEL

maî·tre d'hô·tel \ˌmā-trə-dō-'tel, ˌme-\ n, pl **maîtres d'hôtel** \same\ **1** : MAJORDOMO **2** : HEADWAITER

maize \'māz\ *n* : CORN 2

Maj *abbr* major

ma·jes·tic \mə-'jes-tik\ *adj* ♦ : having or exhibiting majesty — **ma·jes·ti·cal·ly** \-ti-k(ə-)lē\ *adv*

  ♦ august, baronial, gallant, glorious, grand, grandiose, heroic, imposing, magnificent, monumental, noble, proud, regal, royal, splendid, stately

maj·es·ty \'ma-jə-stē\ *n, pl* **-ties** 1 : sovereign power, authority, or dignity; *also* : the person of a sovereign — used as a title 2 ♦ : greatness or splendor of quality or character

  ♦ augustness, brilliance, glory, grandeur, grandness, magnificence, nobility, nobleness, resplendence, splendor, stateliness

Maj Gen *abbr* Major General

ma·jol·i·ca \mə-'jä-li-kə\ *also* **ma·iol·i·ca** \-'yä-\ *n* : any of several faiences; *esp* : an Italian tin-glazed pottery

¹**major** \'mā-jər\ *adj* 1 ♦ : greater in number, extent, or importance ⟨a ∼ poet⟩ 2 : notable or conspicuous in effect or scope ⟨a ∼ improvement⟩ 3 : SERIOUS ⟨a ∼ illness⟩ 4 : having half steps between the 3d and 4th and the 7th and 8th degrees ⟨∼ scale⟩; *also* : based on a major scale ⟨∼ key⟩ ⟨∼ chord⟩

  ♦ big, consequential, eventful, important, material, meaningful, momentous, significant, substantial, weighty

²**major** *n* 1 : a commissioned officer (as in the army) ranking next below a lieutenant colonel 2 : an academic subject chosen as a field of specialization; *also* : a student specializing in such a field

³**major** *vb* : to pursue an academic major

ma·jor·do·mo \,mā-jər-'dō-mō\ *n, pl* **-mos** 1 : a head steward 2 : BUTLER

ma·jor·ette \,mā-jə-'ret\ *n* : DRUM MAJORETTE

major general *n* : a commissioned officer (as in the army) ranking next below a lieutenant general

ma·jor·i·ty \mə-'jȯr-ə-tē\ *n, pl* **-ties** 1 : the age at which full civil rights are accorded; *also* : the status of one who has attained this age 2 : a number greater than half of a total; *also* : the excess of this greater number over the remainder 3 : the rank of a major

ma·jus·cule \'ma-jəs-,kyül, mə-'jəs-\ *n* : a large letter (as a capital)

Ma·kah \'mä-kä\ *n, pl* Makah *or* Makahs : a member of an Indigenous people of the northwest coast of No. America; *also* : their language

¹**make** \'māk\ *vb* **made** \'mād\; **mak·ing** 1 a ♦ : to cause to exist, occur, or appear b : DESTINE ⟨was *made* to be an actor⟩ 2 a ♦ : to bring into being by forming, shaping, or altering material ⟨∼ a dress⟩ b : COMPOSE 3 : to formulate in the mind ⟨∼ plans⟩ 4 ♦ : to put together from components ⟨house *made* of stone⟩ 5 ♦ : to compute or estimate to be 6 : to set in order : PREPARE ⟨∼ a bed⟩ 7 : to cause to be or become; *also* : APPOINT 8 a : to establish by legal and authoritative act : ENACT b : EXECUTE ⟨∼ a will⟩ 9 : CONCLUDE ⟨didn't know what to ∼ of it⟩ 10 a ♦ : to carry out (an action indicated or implied by the object) ⟨∼ war⟩ b : to perform with a bodily movement ⟨∼ a gesture⟩ 11 ♦ : to cause to act in a certain way : COMPEL 12 : to assure the success of ⟨will ∼ us or break us⟩ 13 : to amount to in significance ⟨∼s no difference⟩ 14 : to be capable of developing or being fashioned into 15 : to reach as an end : ATTAIN; *also* : GAIN 16 : to start out : GO 17 : to have weight or effect ⟨courtesy ∼s for safer driving⟩ 18 : to act so as to be or to seem to be ⟨∼ merry⟩ 19 ♦ : to gain (as money) by working, trading, or dealing — **mak·er** *n* — **make believe** : PRETEND — **make do** : to manage with the means at hand — **make fun of** : RIDICULE, MOCK — **make good** 1 : INDEMNIFY ⟨*make good* the loss⟩; *also* : to carry out successfully ⟨*make good* his promise⟩ 2 : SUCCEED — **make way** 1 : to give room for passing, entering, or occupying 2 : to make progress

  ♦ [1a] bring about, cause, create, effect, effectuate, generate, induce, produce, prompt, result, work, yield ♦ [2a] fabricate, fashion, form, frame, manufacture, produce ♦ [4] assemble, build, construct, erect, fabricate, make up, piece, put up, raise, rear, set up ♦ [5] calculate, call, conjecture, estimate, figure, gauge, guess, judge, place, put, reckon, suppose ♦ [10a] accomplish, achieve, carry out, commit, compass, do, execute, follow through, fulfill, perform ♦ [11] coerce, compel, constrain, drive, force, muscle, obligate, oblige, press, pressure ♦ [19] acquire, attain, capture, carry, draw, earn, gain, garner, get, land, obtain, procure, realize, secure, win

²**make** *n* 1 : the manner or style of construction; *also* : BRAND 3 2 : MAKEUP 3 : the action of manufacturing — **on the make** : in search of wealth, social status, or sexual adventure

¹**make–be·lieve** \'māk-bə-,lēv\ *n* : a pretending that what is not real is real

²**make–believe** *adj* : existing only in the imagination

make–do \-,dü\ *adj* : MAKESHIFT

make out *vb* 1 : to draw up in writing ⟨*make out* a list⟩ 2 ♦ : to find or grasp the meaning of ⟨can you *make* that *out*⟩ 3 : to represent as being 4 : to pretend to be true 5 : DISCERN ⟨*make out* a ship in the fog⟩ 6 ♦ : to meet one's needs : GET ALONG, FARE ⟨*make out* well in life⟩ 7 ♦ : to engage in amorous kissing and caressing

  ♦ [2] appreciate, apprehend, catch, catch on (to), comprehend, get, grasp, make, perceive, see, seize, understand ♦ [6] cope, do, fare, get along, manage, shift ♦ [7] kiss, pet

make over *vb* 1 ♦ : to transfer the title of (property) 2 ♦ : to make anew or in a different form — **make-over** \'mā-,kō-vər\ *n*

  ♦ [1] alienate, assign, cede, deed, transfer ♦ [2] alter, change, convert, modify, recast, redo, refashion, remake, remodel, revamp, revise, rework, vary

¹**make·shift** \'māk-,shift\ *n* : a temporary expedient

²**makeshift** *adj* : serving as a temporary expedient

make·up \'mā-,kəp\ *n* 1 ♦ : the way in which something is put together; *also* : physical, mental, and moral constitution 2 : cosmetics esp. for the face; *also* : materials (as wigs and cosmetics) used in making up

  ♦ arrangement, composition, configuration, design, form, format, layout, pattern

make up *vb* 1 a : to form by fitting together or assembling b ♦ : to form the substance of : COMPOSE 2 ♦ : to compensate for (as a deficiency or omission) ⟨*make up* for lost time⟩ 3 : SETTLE ⟨*made up* my mind⟩ 4 ♦ : to devise by thinking : INVENT, IMPROVISE 5 : to become reconciled 6 : to put on makeup (as for a play)

  ♦ [1b] compose, comprise, constitute, form ♦ *usu* **make up for** [2] annul, cancel, compensate, correct, counteract, counterbalance, neutralize, offset ♦ [4] concoct, contrive, cook up, devise, fabricate, invent, manufacture, think up

make–work \'māk-,wərk\ *n* : BUSYWORK

mak·ings \'mā-kiŋz\ *n pl* : the material from which something is made

Mal *abbr* Malachi

Mal·a·chi \'ma-lə-,kī\ *n* : a book of Jewish and Christian Scripture

Mal·a·chi·as \,ma-lə-'kī-əs\ *n* : MALACHI

mal·a·chite \'ma-lə-,kīt\ *n* : a mineral that is a green carbonate of copper used for making ornamental objects

mal·adapt·ed \,ma-lə-'dap-təd\ *adj* : poorly suited to a particular use, purpose, or situation

mal·ad·just·ed \,ma-lə-'jəs-təd\ *adj* : poorly or inadequately adjusted (as to one's environment) — **mal·ad·just·ment** \-'jəst-mənt\ *n*

mal·adroit \,ma-lə-'drȯit\ *adj* ♦ : not adroit : INEPT

  ♦ awkward, clumsy, inept, inexpert

mal·a·dy \'ma-lə-dē\ *n, pl* **-dies** ♦ : a disease or disorder of body or mind

  ♦ ailment, bug, complaint, condition, disease, disorder, fever, ill, illness, infirmity, sickness, trouble

mal·aise \mə-'lāz, ma-\ *n* : a hazy feeling of not being well

mal·a·mute \'ma-lə-,myüt\ *n* : a dog often used to draw sleds esp. in northern No. America

mal·a·prop·ism \'ma-lə-,prä-,pi-zəm\ *n* : a usu. humorous misuse of a word

mal·ap·ro·pos \,ma-la-prə-'pō, ma-'la-prə-,pō\ *adv* : in an inappropriate or inopportune way — **malapropos** *adj*

ma·lar·ia \mə-'ler-ē-ə\ *n* : a disease marked by recurring chills and fever and caused by a protozoan parasite of the blood that is transmitted by anopheles mosquitoes — **ma·lar·i·al** \-əl\ *adj*

ma·lar·key \mə-'lär-kē\ *n* : insincere or foolish talk

mal·a·thi·on \,ma-lə-'thī-ən, -,än\ *n* : an insecticide with a relatively low toxicity for mammals

Ma·la·wi·an \mə-'lä-wē-ən\ *n* : a native or inhabitant of Malawi — **Malawian** *adj*

Ma·lay \mə-'lā, 'mā-,lā\ *n* 1 : a member of a people of the Malay Peninsula and Archipelago 2 : the language of the Malays — **Malay** *adj* — **Ma·lay·an** \mə-'lā-ən, 'mā-,lā-\ *n or adj*

Ma·lay·sian \mə-'lā-zhən, -shən\ *n* : a native or inhabitant of Malaysia — **Malaysian** *adj*

mal·con·tent \,mal-kən-'tent\ *adj* ♦ : marked by a dissatisfaction with the existing state of affairs : DISCONTENTED — **malcontent** *n*

  ♦ aggrieved, discontent, discontented, dissatisfied

mal de mer \ˌmal-də-ˈmer\ *n* : SEASICKNESS
¹**male** \ˈmāl\ *adj* **1** : of, relating to, or being the sex that typically produces germ cells which fertilize the eggs of a female; *also* : STAMINATE **2** ♦ : of, relating to, or characteristic of boys or men — **male•ness** *n*

♦ manly, mannish, man size, masculine, virile

²**male** *n* ♦ : a male individual

♦ buck, chap, dude, fellow, gent, gentleman, guy, hombre, jack, joker, lad, man

male•dic•tion \ˌma-lə-ˈdik-shən\ *n* ♦ : a prayer or invocation for harm or injury to come upon one : CURSE, EXECRATION

♦ anathema, curse, execration, imprecation

mal•e•fac•tion \ˌma-lə-ˈfak-shən\ *n* ♦ : an evil deed

♦ breach, crime, error, misdeed, misdoing, offense, sin, transgression, trespass, violation, wrongdoing

male•fac•tor \ˈma-lə-ˌfak-tər\ *n* ♦ : one who does ill toward another; *esp* : one who commits an offense against the law

♦ criminal, crook, culprit, felon, lawbreaker, offender

ma•lef•ic \mə-ˈle-fik\ *adj* **1** : BALEFUL **2** : MALICIOUS
ma•lef•i•cent \-fə-sənt\ *adj* : working or productive of harm or evil
ma•lev•o•lence \mə-ˈle-və-ləns\ *n* : the quality or state of being malevolent
ma•lev•o•lent \mə-ˈle-və-lənt\ *adj* ♦ : having, showing, or arising from ill will, spite, or hatred

♦ catty, cruel, hateful, malicious, malign, malignant, mean, nasty, spiteful, virulent

mal•fea•sance \mal-ˈfēz-ᵊns\ *n* ♦ : wrongful conduct esp. by a public official

♦ misbehavior, misconduct, misdoing, wrongdoing

mal•for•ma•tion \ˌmal-fȯr-ˈmā-shən\ *n* : irregular or faulty formation or structure; *also* : an instance of this
mal•formed \mal-ˈfȯrmd\ *adj* ♦ : characterized by malformation

♦ deformed, distorted, misshapen, monstrous, shapeless *Ant* shapely

mal•func•tion \mal-ˈfəŋk-shən\ *vb* : to fail to operate normally — **malfunction** *n*
Ma•li•an \ˈmä-lē-ən\ *n* : a native or inhabitant of Mali — **Malian** *adj*
mal•ice \ˈma-ləs\ *n* ♦ : desire to cause injury or distress to another

♦ cattiness, despite, hatefulness, malignity, meanness, nastiness, spite, spleen, venom, viciousness

ma•li•cious \mə-ˈli-shəs\ *adj* ♦ : given to, marked by, or arising from malice

♦ catty, cruel, hateful, malevolent, malign, malignant, mean, nasty, spiteful, virulent

ma•li•cious•ly \-lē\ *adv* ♦ : in a malicious manner

♦ hatefully, meanly, nastily, spitefully, viciously, wickedly

¹**ma•lign** \mə-ˈlīn\ *adj* **1** ♦ : evil in nature, influence, or effect; *also* : MALIGNANT **2** ♦ : moved by ill will

♦ [1, 2] catty, cruel, hateful, malevolent, malicious, malignant, mean, nasty, spiteful, virulent

²**malign** *vb* ♦ : to speak evil of : DEFAME

♦ blacken, defame, libel, slander, smear, traduce, vilify

ma•lig•nan•cy \mə-ˈlig-nən-sē\ *n* : the quality or state of being malignant
ma•lig•nant \mə-ˈlig-nənt\ *adj* **1** ♦ : passionately and relentlessly malevolent : MALIGN **2** : tending to produce death or deterioration ⟨a ∼ tumor⟩

♦ catty, cruel, hateful, malevolent, malicious, malign, mean, nasty, spiteful, virulent

ma•lig•nant•ly \-lē\ *adv* : in a malignant manner
ma•lig•ni•ty \mə-ˈlig-nə-tē\ *n* ♦ : the quality or state of being malignant

♦ cattiness, despite, hatefulness, malice, meanness, nastiness, spite, spleen, venom, viciousness

ma•lin•ger \mə-ˈliŋ-gər\ *vb* : to pretend illness so as to avoid duty — **ma•lin•ger•er** *n*
mal•i•son \ˈma-lə-sən, -zən\ *n* : CURSE
mall \ˈmȯl, ˈmal\ *n* **1** : a shaded walk : PROMENADE **2** : an ur-

ban shopping area featuring a variety of shops surrounding a concourse **3** : a usu. large enclosed suburban shopping area containing various shops
mal•lard \ˈma-lərd\ *n, pl* **mallard** *or* **mallards** : a common wild duck that is the source of domestic ducks
mal•lea•ble \ˈma-lē-ə-bəl\ *adj* **1** : capable of being extended or shaped by beating with a hammer or by the pressure of rollers **2 a** ♦ : capable of being altered or controlled by outside forces or influences **b** : having a capacity for adaptive change — **mal•le•a•bil•i•ty** \ˌma-lē-ə-ˈbi-lə-tē\ *n*

♦ adaptable, adjustable, changeable, elastic, flexible, fluid, variable

mal•let \ˈma-lət\ *n* **1** : a tool with a large head for driving another tool or for striking a surface without marring it **2** : a long-handled hammerlike implement for striking a ball (as in croquet)
mal•le•us \ˈma-lē-əs\ *n, pl* **mal•lei** \-lē-ˌī, -lē-ˌē\ : the outermost of the three small bones of the mammalian middle ear
mal•low \ˈma-lō\ *n* : any of a genus of herbs with lobed leaves, usu. showy flowers, and a disk-shaped fruit
malm•sey \ˈmälm-zē\ *n, often cap* : the sweetest variety of Madeira
mal•nour•ished \mal-ˈnər-isht\ *adj* : UNDERNOURISHED
mal•nu•tri•tion \ˌmal-nü-ˈtri-shən, -nyü-\ *n* : faulty and esp. inadequate nutrition
mal•oc•clu•sion \ˌma-lə-ˈklü-zhən\ *n* : faulty coming together of teeth in biting
mal•odor•ous \ma-ˈlō-də-rəs\ *adj* ♦ : ill-smelling — **mal•odor•ous•ly** *adv* — **mal•odor•ous•ness** *n*

♦ fetid, foul, fusty, musty, noisome, rank, reeky, smelly, strong *Ant* ambrosial, aromatic, fragrant, perfumed, redolent, savory, scented, sweet

mal•prac•tice \mal-ˈprak-təs\ *n* : a dereliction of professional duty or a failure of professional skill that results in injury, loss, or damage
malt \ˈmȯlt\ *n* **1** : grain and esp. barley steeped in water until it has sprouted and used in brewing and distilling **2** : liquor made with malt — **malty** *adj*
malted milk \ˈmȯl-təd-\ *n* : a powder prepared from dried milk and an extract from malt; *also* : a beverage of this powder in milk or other liquid
Mal•thu•sian \mal-ˈthü-zhən, -ˈthyü-\ *adj* : of or relating to a theory that population unless checked (as by war) tends to increase faster than its means of subsistence — **Malthusian** *n* — **Mal•thu•sian•ism** \-zhə-ˌni-zəm\ *n*
malt•ose \ˈmȯl-ˌtōs\ *n* : a sugar formed esp. from starch by the action of enzymes
mal•treat \mal-ˈtrēt\ *vb* ♦ : to treat cruelly or roughly — **mal•treat•ment** *n*

♦ abuse, ill-treat, manhandle, mishandle, mistreat, misuse

mal•ware \ˈmal-ˌwer\ *n* : software designed to interfere with a computer's normal functioning
ma•ma *also* **mam•ma** \ˈmä-mə\ *n* : a female parent : MOTHER
mam•bo \ˈmäm-bō\ *n, pl* **mambos** : a dance of Cuban origin related to the rumba — **mambo** *vb*
mam•mal \ˈma-məl\ *n* : any of a class of warm-blooded vertebrates that includes humans and all other animals which nourish their young with milk and have the skin more or less covered with hair — **mam•ma•li•an** \mə-ˈmā-lē-ən, ma-\ *adj or n*
mam•ma•ry \ˈma-mə-rē\ *adj* : of, relating to, or being the glands (**mammary glands**) that in female mammals secrete milk
mam•mo•gram \ˈma-mə-ˌgram\ *n* : an X-ray photograph of the breasts
mam•mog•ra•phy \ma-ˈmä-grə-fē\ *n* : X-ray examination of the breasts (as for early detection of cancer)
mam•mon \ˈma-mən\ *n, often cap* : material wealth having a debasing influence
¹**mam•moth** \ˈma-məth\ *n* **1** : any of a genus of large hairy extinct elephants **2** ♦ : something immense of its kind

♦ behemoth, blockbuster, colossus, giant, jumbo, leviathan, monster, titan, whale, whopper

²**mammoth** *adj* : of very great size : GIGANTIC
¹**man** \ˈman\ *n, pl* **men** \ˈmen\ **1 a** ♦ : a human being **b** ♦ : an adult male person **2** ♦ : the human race : HUMANKIND **3** : one possessing in high degree the qualities considered distinctive of manhood **4** : an adult male servant or employee **5** : the individual who can fulfill one's requirements ⟨he's your ∼⟩ **6** : one of the pieces with which various games (as chess) are played; *also* : one of the players on a team **7** *often cap* : white society or people ⟨having difficulty coping with the *Man*⟩ **8** ♦ : a male lover

♦ [1a] being, body, creature, human, individual, mortal, person ♦ [1b] buck, chap, dude, fellow, gent, gentleman, guy, hombre, jack, joker, lad, male ♦ [2] Homo sapiens, humanity, humankind, mankind ♦ [8] beau, boyfriend, fellow, swain

²**man** *vb* **manned; man•ning** **1 :** to supply with people ⟨~ a fleet⟩ **2 :** FORTIFY, BRACE

³**man** *abbr* manual

Man *abbr* Manitoba

man–about–town *n, pl* **men–about–town :** a worldly and socially active man

man•a•cle \'ma-ni-kəl\ *n* **1 :** a shackle for the hand or wrist **2** ♦ **:** something used as a restraint

♦ band, bond, chain, fetter, irons, ligature, shackle

man•age \'ma-nij\ *vb* **man•aged; man•ag•ing** **1** ♦ **:** to handle or direct with a degree of skill **2 :** to make and keep compliant **3 :** to treat with care **4** ♦ **:** to achieve one's purpose; *also* **:** to get on or along **5 :** to direct the career of ⟨the agent who ~s the actor⟩ — **man•age•abil•i•ty** \ˌma-ni-jə-'bi-lə-tē\ *n* — **man•age•able** \'ma-ni-jə-bəl\ *adj* — **man•age•able•ness** *n* — **man•age•ably** \-blē\ *adv*

♦ [1] contend with, cope with, grapple with, handle, maneuver (*or* manoeuvre), negotiate, swing, treat ♦ [1] administer, carry on, conduct, control, direct, govern, guide, handle, operate, oversee, regulate, run, superintend, supervise ♦ [4] cope, do, fare, get along, make out, shift

managed care *n* **:** a health-care system that controls costs by limiting doctor's fees and by restricting the patient's choice of doctors

man•age•ment \'ma-nij-mənt\ *n* **1** ♦ **:** the act or art of managing **:** CONTROL **2 :** judicious use of means to accomplish an end **3 :** the group of those who manage or direct an enterprise

♦ administration, conduct, control, direction, government, guidance, operation, oversight, regulation, running, superintendence, supervision

man•ag•er \'ma-ni-jər\ *n* ♦ **:** one that manages

♦ administrator, director, executive, superintendent, supervisor

man•a•ge•ri•al \ˌma-nə-'jir-ē-əl\ *adj* ♦ **:** of, relating to, or characteristic of a manager

♦ directorial, executive, supervisory

ma•ña•na \mən-'yä-nə\ *n* **:** an indefinite time in the future

man–at–arms *n, pl* **men–at–arms** **:** one engaged in military service **:** SOLDIER; *esp* **:** one who is heavily armed and mounted

♦ fighter, legionnaire, regular, serviceman, soldier, warrior

man•a•tee \'ma-nə-ˌtē\ *n* **:** any of a genus of chiefly tropical plant-eating aquatic mammals having a rounded body, paddle-shaped flippers, and a broad, rounded tail

Man•chu•ri•an \man-'chur-ē-ən\ *n* **:** a native or inhabitant of Manchuria, China — **Manchurian** *adj*

man•ci•ple \'man-sə-pəl\ *n* **:** a steward or purveyor esp. for a college or monastery

man•da•mus \man-'dā-məs\ *n* **:** a writ issued by a superior court commanding that an official act or duty be performed

man•da•rin \'man-də-rən\ *n* **1 :** a public official of high rank under the Chinese Empire **2** *cap* **:** the chief dialect group of China **3 :** a yellow to reddish orange loose-skinned citrus fruit; *also* **:** a tree that bears mandarins

man•date \'man-ˌdāt\ *n* **1 :** an authoritative command **2** ♦ **:** an authorization to act given to a representative **3 :** a commission granted by the League of Nations to a member nation for governing conquered territory; *also* **:** a territory so governed

♦ authorization, commission, delegation, license (*or* licence)

man•da•to•ry \'man-də-ˌtōr-ē\ *adj* **1** ♦ **:** containing or constituting a command **:** OBLIGATORY **2 :** of or relating to a League of Nations mandate

♦ compulsory, imperative, incumbent, involuntary, necessary, nonelective, obligatory, peremptory *Ant* elective, optional, voluntary

man•di•ble \'man-də-bəl\ *n* **1 :** JAW; *esp* **:** a lower jaw **2 :** either segment of a bird's bill — **man•dib•u•lar** \man-'di-byə-lər\ *adj*

man•do•lin \ˌman-də-'lin, 'mand-ᵊl-ən\ *n* **:** a stringed musical instrument with a pear-shaped body and a fretted neck

man•drake \'man-ˌdrāk\ *n* **1 :** an Old World herb related to the nightshades or its large forked root formerly credited with magical properties **2 :** MAYAPPLE

man•drel *also* **man•dril** \'man-drəl\ *n* **1 :** an axle or spindle inserted into a hole in a piece of work to support it during machin-

ing **2 :** a metal bar used as a core around which material may be cast, shaped, or molded

man•drill \'man-drəl\ *n* **:** a large baboon of western central Africa

mane \'mān\ *n* **:** long heavy hair growing about the neck of some mammals (as a horse) — **maned** \'mānd\ *adj*

man–eat•er \'man-ˌē-tər\ *n* **:** one (as a shark or cannibal) that has or is thought to have an appetite for human flesh — **man–eat•ing** *adj*

ma•nège \ma-'nezh, mə-\ *n* **:** the art of horsemanship or of training horses

ma•nes \'mä-ˌnās, 'mā-ˌnēz\ *n pl, often cap* **:** the spirits of the dead and gods of the lower world in ancient Roman belief

¹**ma•neu•ver** *or Can and Brit* **ma•noeu•vre** \mə-'nü-vər, -'nyü-\ *n* **1 :** a military or naval movement; *also* **:** an armed forces training exercise — often used in pl. **2 :** a procedure involving expert physical movement **3 :** an evasive movement or shift of tactics; *also* **:** an action taken to gain a tactical end — **maneuver** *vb* — **ma•neu•ver•abil•i•ty** \-ˌnü-və-rə-'bi-lə-tē, -ˌnyü-\ *n* — **ma•neu•ver•able** \-'nü-və-rə-bəl, -'nyü-\ *adj*

²**maneuver** *or Can and Brit* **manoeuvre** *vb* **maneuvered** *or* **manoeuvred; maneuvering** *or* **manoeuvring** ♦ **:** to guide with adroitness and design; *also* **:** to use stratagems

♦ contend with, cope with, grapple with, handle, manage, negotiate, swing, treat ♦ contrive, finagle, finesse, frame, machinate, mastermind, negotiate, wangle

man Friday *n* **:** an efficient and devoted aide or employee

man•ful \'man-fəl\ *adj* ♦ **:** having or showing courage and resolution — **man•ful•ly** *adv*

♦ brave, courageous, dauntless, doughty, fearless, gallant, greathearted, heroic, intrepid, lionhearted, stalwart, stout, undaunted, valiant, valorous

man•ga \'män-gə\ *n* **:** a Japanese comic book or graphic novel

man•ga•nese \'maŋ-gə-ˌnēz, -ˌnēs\ *n* **:** a metallic chemical element resembling iron but not magnetic

mange \'mānj\ *n* **:** any of several contagious itchy skin diseases esp. of domestic animals

man•ger \'mān-jər\ *n* **:** a trough or open box for livestock feed or fodder

¹**man•gle** \'maŋ-gəl\ *vb* **man•gled; man•gling** **1 :** to cut, bruise, or hack with repeated blows **2** ♦ **:** to spoil, injure or make incoherent esp. through ineptitude ⟨a story *mangled* beyond recognition⟩ — **man•gler** *n*

♦ bobble, botch, bungle, butcher, flub, foul up, fumble, mess up, screw up

²**mangle** *n* **:** a machine with heated rollers for ironing laundry

man•go \'maŋ-gō\ *n, pl* **mangoes** *also* **mangos :** an edible juicy yellowish-red fruit borne by a tropical evergreen tree related to the sumacs; *also* **:** this tree

man•grove \'man-ˌgrōv\ *n* **:** any of a genus of tropical maritime trees that send out many prop roots and form dense thickets important in coastal land building

mangy \'mān-jē\ *adj* **1 :** affected with or resulting from mange **2** ♦ **:** decayed, deteriorated, or fallen into partial ruin esp. through neglect or misuse

♦ dilapidated, grungy, mean, neglected, ratty, seedy, shabby

man•han•dle \'man-ˌhand-ᵊl\ *vb* ♦ **:** to handle roughly

♦ maltreat, maul, mishandle, rough

man•hat•tan \man-'hat-ᵊn\ *n, often cap* **:** a cocktail made of whiskey and vermouth

man•hole \'man-ˌhōl\ *n* **:** a hole through which a person may go esp. to gain access to an underground or enclosed structure

man•hood \-ˌhud\ *n* **1 :** the state of being a man **2** ♦ **:** qualities associated with men **:** MANLINESS **3 :** MEN ⟨the nation's ~⟩

♦ manliness, masculinity, virility

man–hour \-'aur\ *n* **:** a unit of one hour's work by one person

man•hunt \-ˌhənt\ *n* **:** an organized hunt for a person and esp. for one charged with a crime

ma•nia \'mā-nē-ə, -nyə\ *n* **1 :** excitement manifested by mental and physical hyperactivity, disorganized behavior, and elevated mood **2 a :** excessive enthusiasm **b** ♦ **:** the object of enthusiasm

♦ fetish, fixation, obsession, preoccupation, prepossession

ma•ni•ac \'mā-nē-ˌak\ *n* **1 :** LUNATIC, MADMAN **2** ♦ **:** a person characterized by an inordinate or ungovernable enthusiasm for something

♦ addict, aficionado, buff, bug, devotee, enthusiast, fan, fanatic, fancier, fiend, freak, lover, nut

ma·ni·a·cal \mə-'nī-ə-kəl\ *also* **ma·ni·ac** \'mā-nē-ak\ *adj* **1** : affected with or suggestive of madness **2** : FRANTIC

man·ic \'ma-nik\ *adj* : affected with, relating to, characterized by, or resulting from mania — **manic** *n* — **man·i·cal·ly** \-ni-k(ə-)lē\ *adv*

manic depression *n* : BIPOLAR DISORDER

man·ic–de·pres·sive \ˌma-nik-di-'pre-siv\ *adj* : characterized by or affected with either mania or depression or alternating episodes of mania and depression (as in bipolar disorder) — **man·ic–depressive** *n*

¹**man·i·cure** \'ma-nə-ˌkyùr\ *n* **1** : MANICURIST **2** : a treatment for the care of the hands and nails

²**manicure** *vb* **-cured; -cur·ing** **1** : to do manicure work on **2** : to trim closely and evenly

man·i·cur·ist \-ˌkyùr-ist\ *n* : a person who gives manicure treatments

¹**man·i·fest** \'ma-nə-ˌfest\ *adj* **1** : readily perceived by the senses and esp. by the sight **2** ♦ : easily understood : OBVIOUS — **man·i·fest·ly** *adv*

♦ apparent, broad, clear, clear-cut, distinct, evident, lucid, obvious, palpable, patent, perspicuous, plain, transparent, unambiguous, unequivocal, unmistakable

²**manifest** *vb* ♦ : to make evident or certain by showing or displaying

♦ bespeak, betray, demonstrate, display, evince, expose, give away, reveal, show

³**manifest** *n* : a list of passengers or an invoice of cargo for a ship or plane

man·i·fes·ta·tion \ˌma-nə-fə-'stā-shən\ *n* **1** : the act, process, or an instance of manifesting **2** ♦ : a perceptible, outward, or visible expression

♦ embodiment, epitome, incarnation, personification

man·i·fes·to \ˌma-nə-'fes-tō\ *n, pl* **-tos** *or* **-toes** : a public declaration of intentions, motives, or views

¹**man·i·fold** \'ma-nə-ˌfōld\ *adj* **1** ♦ : marked by diversity or variety **2** : consisting of or operating many of one kind combined

♦ multifarious, myriad

²**manifold** *n* : a pipe fitting with several lateral outlets for connecting it with other pipes

³**manifold** *vb* **1** : MULTIPLY **2** : to make a number of copies of (as a letter)

man·i·kin *also* **man·ni·kin** \'ma-ni-kən\ *n* **1** ♦ : a form representing the human figure used esp. for displaying clothes : MANNEQUIN **2** *dated, usu disparaging* : a little man : DWARF

♦ dummy, figure, form, mannequin

Ma·nila hemp \mə-'ni-lə-\ *n* : a tough fiber from a Philippine plant related to the banana that is used for cordage

manila paper *n, often cap M* : a tough brownish paper made orig. from Manila hemp

man·i·oc \'ma-nē-ˌäk\ *n* : CASSAVA

ma·nip·u·late \mə-'ni-pyə-ˌlāt\ *vb* **-lat·ed; -lat·ing** **1** : to treat or operate manually or mechanically esp. with skill **2** : to manage or use skillfully **3** : to influence esp. with intent to deceive — **ma·nip·u·la·tion** \mə-ni-pyə-'lā-shən\ *n* — **ma·nip·u·la·tive** \-'ni-pyə-ˌlā-tiv\ *adj* — **ma·nip·u·la·tor** \-ˌlā-tər\ *n*

ma·nip·u·la·tives \mə-'ni-pyə-ˌlā-tivz\ *n pl* : objects that a student is instructed to use in a way that teaches or reinforces a lesson

man·kind *n* **1** \'man-'kīnd\ ♦ : the totality of human beings **2** \-ˌkīnd\ : men as distinguished from women

♦ Homo sapiens, humanity, humankind, man

man·li·ness \'man-lē-nəs\ *n* ♦ : the quality or state of being manly

♦ manhood, masculinity, virility

¹**man·ly** \'man-lē\ *adj* **man·li·er; -est** **1** ♦ : having qualities generally associated with a man **2** : appropriate in character to a man

♦ male, mannish, man-size, masculine, virile

²**manly** *adv* : in a manly manner

man–made \'man-'mād\ *adj* : made by humans rather than nature ⟨~ systems⟩; *esp* : SYNTHETIC ⟨~ fibers⟩

man·na \'ma-nə\ *n* **1** : food miraculously supplied to the Israelites in the wilderness **2** ♦ : a usu. sudden and unexpected source of gratification, pleasure, or gain

♦ benefit, blessing, boon, felicity, godsend, good, windfall

manned \'mand\ *adj* : carrying or performed by one or more people ⟨~ spaceflight⟩

man·ne·quin \'ma-ni-kən\ *n* **1** ♦ : a form representing the human figure used esp. for displaying clothes **2** : a person employed to model clothing

♦ dummy, figure, form, manikin

man·ner \'ma-nər\ *n* **1** ♦ : a group united by common traits or interests : KIND, SORT **2 a** ♦ : a way of acting or proceeding ⟨worked in a brisk ~⟩ **b** ♦ : a characteristic or customary mode of acting ⟨spoke bluntly as was his ~⟩ **3** : a method of artistic execution **4** *pl* : social conduct; *also* : BEARING **5** *pl* ♦ : social conduct or rules of conduct as shown in the prevalent customs ⟨taught the child good ~s⟩

♦ [1] breed, class, description, feather, ilk, kind, like, nature, order, sort, species, type ♦ [2a] approach, fashion, form, method, strategy, style, system, tack, tactics, technique, way ♦ [2b] locution, mode, phraseology, style, tone, vein ♦ **manners** *pl* [5] etiquette, mores

man·nered \'ma-nərd\ *adj* **1** : having manners of a specified kind ⟨well-*mannered*⟩ **2** : having an artificial character ⟨a highly ~ style⟩

man·ner·ism \'ma-nə-ˌri-zəm\ *n* **1** : ARTIFICIALITY, PRECIOSITY **2** ♦ : a peculiarity of action, bearing, or treatment

♦ crotchet, eccentricity, idiosyncrasy, oddity, peculiarity, quirk, singularity, trick

man·ner·li·ness \'ma-nər-lē-nəs\ *n* ♦ : the quality or state of being mannerly

♦ civility, courtesy, gentility, graciousness, politeness

man·ner·ly \'ma-nər-lē\ *adj* ♦ : showing good manners : POLITE — **mannerly** *adv*

♦ civil, courteous, genteel, gracious, polite, well-bred

man·nish \'ma-nish\ *adj* **1** ♦ : resembling or suggesting a man rather than a woman **2** ♦ : generally associated with or characteristic of a man ⟨a ~ voice⟩ — **man·nish·ly** *adv* — **man·nish·ness** *n*

♦ male, manly, man-size, masculine, virile

ma·no a ma·no \ˌmä-nō-ä-'mä-nō\ *adv or adj* : in direct competition or conflict

ma·noeu·vre \mə-'nü-vər, -'nyü-\ *chiefly Can and Brit var of* MANEUVER

man–of–war \ˌman-əv-'wòr\ *n, pl* **men–of–war** \ˌmen-\ : WARSHIP

ma·nom·e·ter \mə-'nä-mə-tər\ *n* : an instrument for measuring the pressure of gases and vapors — **mano·met·ric** \ˌma-nə-'me-trik\ *adj*

man·or \'ma-nər\ *n* **1 a** ♦ : the house or hall of an estate **b** : a landed estate **2** : an English estate of a feudal lord — **ma·no·ri·al** \mə-'nòr-ē-əl\ *adj* — **ma·no·ri·al·ism** \-ə-ˌli-zəm\ *n*

♦ castle, estate, hall, mansion, palace, villa

man power *n* **1** : power available from or supplied by the physical effort of human beings **2** *usu* **man·pow·er** : the total supply of persons available and fitted for service

man·qué \mäⁿ-'kā\ *adj* : short of or frustrated in the fulfillment of one's aspirations or talents ⟨a poet ~⟩

man·sard \'man-ˌsärd, -sərd\ *n* : a roof having two slopes on all sides with the lower slope steeper than the upper one

manse \'mans\ *n* : the residence esp. of a Presbyterian minister

man·ser·vant \'man-ˌsər-vənt\ *n, pl* **men·ser·vants** \'men-ˌsər-vənts\ : a male servant

man·sion \'man-chən\ *n* **1** ♦ : a large imposing residence **2** : a separate apartment in a large structure

♦ castle, estate, hall, manor, palace, villa

man–size \'man-ˌsīz\ *or* **man–sized** \-ˌsīzd\ *adj* ♦ : suitable for or requiring a man ⟨a ~ job⟩

♦ male, manly, mannish, masculine, virile

man·slaugh·ter \-ˌslò-tər\ *n* : the unlawful killing of a human being without express or implied malice

man·ta \'man-tə\ *n* **1** : a square piece of cloth or blanket used in southwestern U.S. and Latin America as a cloak or shawl **2** : MANTA RAY

manta ray *n* : any of several extremely large rays

man·teau \man-'tō\ *n* : a loose cloak, coat, or robe

man·tel \'mant-ᵊl\ *n* : a beam, stone, or arch serving as a lintel to support the masonry above a fireplace; *also* : a shelf above a fireplace

man·tel·piece \'mant-ᵊl-ˌpēs\ *n* : the shelf of a mantel

man·til·la \man-'tē-yə, -'ti-lə\ *n* : a light scarf worn over the head and shoulders esp. by Spanish and Latin-American women

♦ babushka, bandanna, do-rag, kerchief

man·tis \'man-təs\ *n, pl* **man·tis·es** *also* **man·tes** \-ˌtēz\ : any of a group of large usu. green insect-eating insects that hold their prey in forelimbs folded as if in prayer

man·tis·sa \man-'ti-sə\ *n* : the part of a logarithm to the right of the decimal point

¹**man·tle** \'mant-ᵊl\ *n* **1** : a loose sleeveless garment worn over other clothes **2** ♦ : something that covers, enfolds, or envelops **3** : a lacy sheath that gives light by incandescence when placed over a flame **4** : the portion of the earth lying between the crust and the core **5** : MANTEL

♦ cloak, curtain, hood, mask, shroud, veil

²**mantle** *vb* **man·tled; man·tling** **1** ♦ : to cover with or as if with a mantle **2** : BLUSH

♦ embrace, enclose, encompass, enfold, enshroud, envelop, invest, lap, shroud, swathe, veil, wrap

man·tra \'man-trə\ *n* : a mystical formula of invocation or incantation (as in Hinduism)

¹**man·u·al** \'man-yə-wəl\ *adj* **1** : of, relating to, or involving the hands; *also* : worked by hand ⟨a ∼ pump⟩ **2** : requiring or using physical skill and energy ⟨∼ labor⟩ — **man·u·al·ly** *adv*

²**manual** *n* **1** ♦ : a small book; *esp* : a concise reference book covering a particular subject : HANDBOOK **2** : the prescribed movements in the handling of a military item and esp. a weapon during a drill or ceremony ⟨the ∼ of arms⟩ **3** : a keyboard esp. of an organ **4** : an automobile with a manual transmission

♦ handbook, primer, textbook

man·u·fac·to·ry \ˌman-yə-'fak-tə-rē\ *n* : a building or set of buildings with facilities for manufacturing : FACTORY

¹**man·u·fac·ture** \ˌman-yə-'fak-chər\ *n* **1** : something made from raw materials **2** : the process of making wares by hand or by machinery; *also* : a productive industry using machinery

²**manufacture** *vb* **-tured; -tur·ing** **1** ♦ : to make from raw materials by hand or by machinery; *also* : to engage in manufacture **2** ♦ : to devise by thinking : INVENT, FABRICATE — **man·u·fac·tur·er** *n*

♦ [1] fabricate, fashion, form, frame, make, produce ♦ [2] concoct, contrive, cook up, devise, fabricate, invent, make up, think up

man·u·mis·sion \-'mi-shən\ *n* ♦ : the act or process of manumitting

♦ emancipation, enfranchisement, liberation

man·u·mit \ˌman-yə-'mit\ *vb* **-mit·ted; -mit·ting** ♦ : to free from slavery

♦ discharge, emancipate, enfranchise, free, liberate, loose, loosen, release, spring, unbind, unchain, unfetter

¹**ma·nure** \mə-'nùr, -'nyùr\ *vb* **ma·nured; ma·nur·ing** : to fertilize land with manure

²**manure** *n* : FERTILIZER; *esp* : refuse from stables and barnyards — **ma·nu·ri·al** \-'nùr-ē-əl, -'nyùr-\ *adj*

man·u·script \'man-yə-ˌskript\ *n* **1** : a written or typed composition or document; *also* : a document submitted for publication **2** ♦ : writing as opposed to print

♦ handwriting, penmanship, script

Manx \'maŋks\ *n pl* : the people of the Isle of Man — **Manx** *adj*

¹**many** \'me-nē\ *adj* **more** \'mòr\; **most** \'mōst\ ♦ : consisting of or amounting to a large but indefinite number ⟨∼ years ago⟩

♦ multiple, multitudinous, numerous *Ant* few

²**many** *pron* : a large number ⟨∼ are called⟩

³**many** *n* : a large but indefinite number ⟨a good ∼ of them⟩

many·fold \ˌme-nē-'fōld\ *adv* : by many times

many–sid·ed \-'sī-dəd\ *adj* **1** : having many sides or aspects **2** : VERSATILE

Mao·ism \'maù-ˌi-zəm\ *n* : the theory and practice of Communism developed in China chiefly by Mao Zedong — **Mao·ist** \'maù-ist\ *n or adj*

Mao·ri \'maù(-ə)r-ē\ *n, pl* **Maori** *or* **Maoris** : a member of a Polynesian people native to New Zealand

¹**map** \'map\ *n* **1** : a representation usu. on a flat surface of the whole or part of an area **2** : a representation of the celestial sphere or part of it

²**map** *vb* **mapped; map·ping** **1** : to make a map of **2** ♦ : to plan in detail — often used with *out* ⟨∼ out a program⟩ — **map·pa·ble** \'ma-pə-bəl\ *adj* — **map·per** *n*

♦ *usu* **map out** arrange, blueprint, calculate, chart, design, frame, lay out, plan, project, scheme

MAP *abbr* modified American plan

ma·ple \'mā-pəl\ *n* : any of a genus of trees or shrubs with 2-winged dry fruit and opposite leaves; *also* : the hard light-colored wood of a maple used esp. for floors and furniture

maple sugar *n* : sugar made by boiling maple syrup

maple syrup *n* : syrup made by concentrating the sap of maple trees and esp. the sugar maple

mar \'mär\ *vb* **marred; mar·ring** ♦ : to detract from the wholeness or perfection of : SPOIL

♦ blemish, poison, spoil, stain, taint, tarnish, touch, vitiate

Mar *abbr* March

ma·ra·ca \mə-'rä-kə, -'ra-\ *n* : a rattle usu. made from a gourd and used as a percussion instrument

mar·a·schi·no \ˌmar-ə-'skē-nō, -'shē-\ *n, often cap* : a cherry preserved in a sweet liqueur made from the juice of a bitter wild cherry

¹**mar·a·thon** \'mar-ə-ˌthän\ *n* **1** : a long-distance race esp. on foot **2** : an endurance contest

²**marathon** *adj* ♦ : belonging to, suggestive of, or suited for a marathon race or competition (as in being marked by unusual length of time)

♦ extended, far, great, lengthy, long

mar·a·thon·er \'mar-ə-ˌthä-nər\ *n* : a person who takes part in a marathon — **mar·a·thon·ing** *n*

ma·raud \mə-'ròd\ *vb* ♦ : to roam about and raid in search of plunder : PILLAGE — **ma·raud·er** *n*

♦ despoil, loot, pillage, plunder, ransack, sack, strip

mar·ble \'mär-bəl\ *n* **1** : a limestone that can be polished and used in fine building work **2** : something resembling marble (as in coldness) **3** : a small ball (as of glass) used in various games; *also, pl* : a children's game played with these small balls — **marble** *adj*

mar·bling \-bə-liŋ, -bliŋ\ *n* : an intermixture of fat through the lean of a cut of meat

mar·cel \mär-'sel\ *n* : a deep soft wave made in the hair by the use of a heated curling iron — **marcel** *vb*

¹**march** \'märch\ *n* : a border region : FRONTIER

²**march** *vb* **1** ♦ : to move along in or as if in military formation **2 a** : to walk in a direct purposeful manner **b** ♦ : to make steady progress : ADVANCE **3** : TRAVERSE ⟨∼ed 10 miles⟩ — **march·er** *n*

♦ [1] file, pace, parade, stride ♦ [2b] advance, fare, forge, get along, go, proceed, progress

³**march** *n* **1** : the action of marching; *also* : the distance covered (as by a military unit) in a march **2** : a regular measured stride or rhythmic step used in marching **3** ♦ : forward movement **4** : a piece of music with marked rhythm suitable for marching to

♦ advance, advancement, furtherance, headway, onrush, passage, process, procession, progress, progression

March *n* : the 3d month of the year

mar·chio·ness \'mär-shə-nəs\ *n* **1** : the wife or widow of a marquess **2** : a woman holding the rank of a marquess in her own right

Mar·di Gras \'mär-dē-ˌgrä\ *n* : the Tuesday before Ash Wednesday often observed with parades and merrymaking

¹**mare** \'mar\ *n* : an adult female of the horse or a related mammal

²**ma·re** \'mär-(ˌ)ā\ *n, pl* **ma·ria** \'mär-ē-ə\ : any of several large dark areas on the surface of the moon or Mars

mar·ga·rine \'mär-jə-rən\ *n* : a food product made usu. from vegetable oils churned with skimmed milk and used as a substitute for butter

mar·ga·ri·ta \ˌmär-gə-'rē-tə\ *n* : a cocktail consisting of tequila, lime or lemon juice, and an orange-flavored liqueur

mar·gin \'mär-jən\ *n* **1** : the part of a page outside the main body of printed or written matter **2** ♦ : the outside limit and adjoining surface of something : EDGE **3** : a spare amount, measure, or degree allowed for use if needed **4** : measure or degree of difference ⟨a one-vote ∼⟩

♦ border, bound, boundary, circumference, compass, confines, edge, end, fringe, perimeter, periphery, rim, skirt, verge

mar·gin·al \-jə-nəl\ *adj* **1** : written or printed in the margin **2** : of, relating to, or situated at a margin or border **3** : close to the lower limit of quality or acceptability **4** : excluded from or existing outside the mainstream of society or a group

mar·gi·na·lia \ˌmär-jə-'nā-lē-ə\ *n pl* : marginal notes or embellishments

mar·gin·al·ize \ˈmär-jə-nᵊl-ˌīz\ *vb* **-ized; -iz·ing** : to relegate to an unimportant position within a society or group

mar·gin·al·ly \ˌmärj-nə-lē, ˈmär-jə-nᵊl-ē\ *adv* ♦ : in a marginal manner

♦ barely, hardly, just, scarcely, slightly

mar·grave \ˈmär-ˌgrāv\ *n* : the military governor esp. of a medieval German border province

ma·ri·a·chi \ˌmär-ē-ˈä-chē, ˌmar-\ *n* : a Mexican street band; *also* : a member of or the music of such a band

mari·gold \ˈmar-ə-ˌgōld, ˈmer-\ *n* : any of a genus of tropical American herbs related to the daisies that are grown for their showy usu. yellow, orange, or maroon flower heads

mar·i·jua·na *also* **mar·i·hua·na** \ˌmar-ə-ˈwä-nə, -ˈhwä-\ *n* : the dried leaves and flowering tops of the female hemp plant smoked usu. illegally for their intoxicating effect; *also* : HEMP

ma·rim·ba \mə-ˈrim-bə\ *n* : a xylophone of southern Africa and Central America; *also* : a modern version of it

ma·ri·na \mə-ˈrē-nə\ *n* : a dock or basin providing secure moorings for pleasure boats

mar·i·nade \ˌmer-ə-ˈnäd\ *n* : a savory usu. acidic sauce in which meat, fish, or a vegetable is soaked to enrich its flavor or to tenderize it

mar·i·na·ra \ˌmar-ə-ˈnar-ə\ *adj* : made with tomatoes, onions, garlic, and spices; *also* : served with marinara sauce

mar·i·nate \ˈmar-ə-ˌnāt\ *vb* **-nat·ed; -nat·ing** : to steep (as meat or fish) in a brine or pickle

¹**ma·rine** \mə-ˈrēn\ *adj* **1** ♦ : of or relating to the sea or its navigation or commerce **2** : of or relating to marines

♦ maritime, oceanic, pelagic

²**marine** *n* **1** : the mercantile and naval shipping of a country **2** : any of a class of soldiers serving on shipboard or with a naval force

mar·i·ner \ˈmar-ə-nər\ *n* ♦ : a person who navigates or assists in navigating a ship : SAILOR

♦ gob, jack, jack-tar, sailor, seaman, swab, tar

mar·i·o·nette \ˌmar-ē-ə-ˈnet, ˌmer-\ *n* : a puppet moved by strings or by hand

mar·i·tal \ˈmar-ət-ᵊl\ *adj* ♦ : of or relating to marriage : CONJUGAL

♦ conjugal, connubial, matrimonial, nuptial

mar·i·time \ˈmar-ə-ˌtīm\ *adj* **1** ♦ : of, relating to, or bordering on the sea **2** ♦ : of or relating to navigation or commerce of the sea

♦ [1] marine, oceanic, pelagic ♦ [2] marine

mar·jo·ram \ˈmär-jə-rəm\ *n* : any of various fragrant mints often used as seasoning

¹**mark** \ˈmärk\ *n* **1** : something (as a line or fixed object) designed to record position; *also* : the starting line or position in a track event **2 a** : TARGET **b** : the end toward which effort is directed : GOAL, OBJECT **3** ♦ : an object of abuse or ridicule **4** : the question under discussion **5** ♦ : a standard of performance, quality, or condition ⟨not up to the ∼⟩ **6 a** : a visible sign : INDICATION **b** ♦ : a distinguishing trait or quality : CHARACTERISTIC **7** : a written or printed symbol **8** : GRADE ⟨a ∼ of B+⟩ **9** : IMPORTANCE, DISTINCTION **10 a** ♦ : a lasting impression : an enduring effect ⟨made his ∼ in the world⟩ **b** : a damaging impression (as a scratch, scar, or stain) left on a surface

♦ [3] butt, laughingstock, mock, mockery, target ♦ [5] criterion, grade, measure, par, standard, touchstone, yardstick ♦ [6b] attribute, character, characteristic, feature, peculiarity, point, property, quality, trait ♦ [10a] effect, impact, influence, repercussion, sway

²**mark** *vb* **1** ♦ : to set apart by a line or boundary **2** : to designate by a mark or make a mark on **3** : CHARACTERIZE ⟨the vehemence that ∼s his speeches⟩; *also* : SIGNALIZE ⟨this year ∼s our 50th anniversary⟩ **4** : to take notice of : OBSERVE ⟨∼ my words⟩ **5** ♦ : to label so as to indicate price or quality **6** ♦ : to make note of in writing

♦ [1] bound, circumscribe, define, delimit, demarcate, limit, terminate ♦ [5] label, tag, ticket ♦ [6] jot, log, note, put down, record, register, set down

³**mark** *n* : a former monetary unit of Germany

Mark \ˈmärk\ *n* : a book of the New Testament of Christian Scripture

mark·down \ˈmärk-ˌdau̇n\ *n* **1** : a lowering of price **2** : the amount by which an original price is reduced

mark down *vb* ♦ : to put a lower price on

♦ cheapen, depreciate, depress, write off

marked \ˈmärkt\ *adj* ♦ : having a distinctive or emphasized character : NOTICEABLE — **mark·ed·ly** \ˈmär-kəd-lē\ *adv*

♦ bold, catchy, conspicuous, emphatic, noticeable, prominent, pronounced, remarkable, striking

mark·er \ˈmär-kər\ *n* ♦ : one that marks

♦ label, tag, ticket

¹**mar·ket** \ˈmär-kət\ *n* **1** : a meeting together of people for trade by purchase and sale; *also* : a public place where such a meeting is held **2** : the rate or price offered for a commodity or security **3** : a geographic area of demand for commodities; *also* ♦ : extent of demand **4** : a retail establishment usu. of a specific kind

♦ call, demand, request

²**market** *vb* **1** : to go to a market to buy or sell **2** ♦ : to offer for sale : SELL — **mar·ket·able** *adj*

♦ deal, merchandise, put up, retail, sell, vend *Ant* buy, purchase

mar·ket·place \ˈmär-kət-ˌplās\ *n* **1** : an open square in a town where markets are held **2** ♦ : the world of trade or economic activity

♦ business, commerce, trade, traffic

mark·ka \ˈmär-ˌkä\ *n, pl* **mark·kaa** \ˈmär-ˌkä\ *or* **markkas** \-ˌkäz\ : the basic monetary unit of Finland from 1917 to 2001

marks·man \ˈmärks-mən\ *n* ♦ : a person skillful at hitting a target — **marks·man·ship** *n*

♦ sharpshooter, shooter, shot

mark·up \ˈmär-ˌkəp\ *n* **1** : a raising of price **2** : an amount added to the cost price of an article to determine the selling price

mark up *vb* : to put a higher price on

markup language *n* : a system for marking the components and layout of a computer document

marl \ˈmärl\ *n* : an earthy deposit rich in lime used esp. as fertilizer — **marly** \ˈmär-lē\ *adj*

mar·lin \ˈmär-lən\ *n* : any of several large oceanic sport fishes related to sailfishes

mar·line·spike *also* **mar·lin·spike** \ˈmär-lən-ˌspīk\ *n* : a pointed iron tool used to separate strands of rope or wire (as in splicing)

mar·ma·lade \ˈmär-mə-ˌlād\ *n* : a clear jelly holding in suspension pieces of fruit and fruit rind

mar·mo·re·al \mär-ˈmōr-ē-əl\ *adj* : of, relating to, or suggestive of marble

mar·mo·set \ˈmär-mə-ˌset\ *n* : any of numerous small bushy=tailed monkeys of Central and So. America

mar·mot \ˈmär-mət\ *n* : any of a genus of stout short-legged burrowing No. American rodents

¹**ma·roon** \mə-ˈrün\ *vb* **1** : to put ashore (as on a desolate island) and leave to one's fate **2** ♦ : to leave in isolation and without hope of escape

♦ abandon, desert, forsake, quit

²**maroon** *n* : a dark red color

¹**mar·quee** \mär-ˈkē\ *n* **1** : a large tent set up (as for an outdoor party) **2** : a usu. metal and glass canopy over an entrance (as of a theater) **3** : a sign over the entrance of a theater or arena advertising a performance

²**marquee** *adj* : having or being a great attraction : PREEMINENT ⟨∼ athletes⟩

mar·quess \ˈmär-kwəs\ *or* **mar·quis** \ˈmär-kwəs, mär-ˈkē\ *n* **1** : a nobleman of hereditary rank in Europe and Japan **2** : a member of the British peerage ranking below a duke and above an earl

mar·que·try \ˈmär-kə-trē\ *n* : inlaid work of wood, shell, or ivory (as on a table or cabinet)

mar·quis \ˈmär-kwəs, mär-ˈkē\ *n* : MARQUESS

mar·quise \mär-ˈkēz\ *n, pl* **mar·quises** *same or* -ˈkē-zəz\ : MARCHIONESS

mar·riage \ˈmar-ij\ *n* **1** ♦ : the state of being united as spouses in a consensual and contractual relationship recognized by law **2** ♦ : a wedding ceremony and attendant festivities **3** : a close union — **mar·riage·able** *adj*

♦ [1] match, matrimony ♦ [2] espousal, wedding

married name *n* : a woman's surname acquired through marriage

mar·row \ˈmar-ō\ *n* : a soft vascular tissue that fills the cavities of most bones

mar·row·bone \ˈmar-ə-ˌbōn, ˈmar-ō-\ *n* : a bone (as a shinbone) rich in marrow

mar·ry \ˈmar-ē\ *vb* **mar·ried; mar·ry·ing** **1 a** : to join in marriage **b** ♦ : to give in marriage ⟨trying to *marry* their children off⟩ **2 :** to take as a spouse **:** WED **3 ♦ :** to enter into a close union **4 :** ¹COMBINE, UNITE — **mar·ried** *adj or n*

♦ [1b] match ♦ [3] associate, coalesce, combine, conjoin, connect, couple, fuse, join, link, unify, unite

Mars \'märz\ *n* **:** the planet 4th from the sun and conspicuous for its red color

marsh \'märsh\ *n ♦* **:** a tract of soft wet land — **marshy** *adj*

♦ bog, fen, mire, morass, slough, swamp

¹**mar·shal** \'mär-shəl\ *n* **1 :** a high official in a medieval household; *also* **:** a person in charge of the ceremonial aspects of a gathering **2 :** a general officer of the highest military rank **3 :** an administrative officer (as of a U.S. judicial district) having duties similar to a sheriff's **4 :** the administrative head of a city police or fire department

²**marshal** *vb* **mar·shaled** *or* **mar·shalled; mar·shal·ing** *or* **mar·shal·ling 1 ♦ :** to arrange in order, rank, or position **2 ♦ :** to bring together and order in an appropriate or effective way **3 ♦ :** to lead with ceremony **:** USHER

♦ [1] arrange, array, classify, codify, dispose, draw up, order, organize, range, systematize ♦ [2] mobilize, muster, rally ♦ [3] conduct, direct, guide, lead, pilot, route, show, steer, usher

marsh gas *n* **:** METHANE

marsh·mal·low \'märsh-ˌme-lō, -ˌma-\ *n* **:** a light spongy confection made from corn syrup, sugar, albumen, and gelatin

marsh marigold *n* **:** a swamp herb related to the buttercups that has bright yellow flowers

mar·su·pi·al \mär-'sü-pē-əl\ *n* **:** any of an order of primitive mammals (as opossums, kangaroos, or wombats) that bear very immature young which are nourished in a pouch on the abdomen of the female — **marsupial** *adj*

mart \'märt\ *n* **:** MARKET

mar·ten \'märt-ᵊn\ *n, pl* **marten** *or* **martens :** a slender mammal that is larger than the related weasels and has soft gray or brown fur; *also* **:** this fur

mar·tial \'mär-shəl\ *adj* **1 :** of, relating to, or suited for war or a warrior ⟨∼ music⟩ **2 :** of or relating to an army or military life **3 :** WARLIKE

martial art *n* **:** any of several arts of combat (as karate and judo) practiced as sport

martial law *n* **1 :** the law applied in occupied territory by the occupying military forces **2 :** the established law of a country administered by military forces in an emergency when civilian law enforcement agencies are unable to maintain public order and safety

mar·tian \'mär-shən\ *adj, often cap* **:** of or relating to the planet Mars or its hypothetical inhabitants — **martian** *n, often cap*

mar·tin \'märt-ᵊn\ *n* **:** any of several swallows and esp. one of No. America with purplish blue plumage

mar·ti·net \ˌmärt-ᵊn-'et\ *n* **:** a strict disciplinarian

mar·tin·gale \'märt-ᵊn-ˌgāl\ *n* **:** a strap connecting a horse's girth to the bit or reins so as to hold down its head

mar·ti·ni \mär-'tē-nē\ *n* **:** a cocktail made of gin or vodka and dry vermouth

¹**mar·tyr** \'mär-tər\ *n* **1 :** a person who dies rather than renounce a religion; *also* **:** a person who makes a great sacrifice for the sake of principle **2 :** a great or constant sufferer

²**martyr** *vb* **1 :** to put to death for adhering to a belief **2 ♦ :** to inflict agonizing pain on **:** TORTURE

♦ afflict, agonize, bedevil, curse, harrow, persecute, plague, rack, torment, torture

mar·tyr·dom \'mär-tər-dəm\ *n* **1 :** the suffering and death of a martyr **2 :** TORTURE

¹**mar·vel** \'mär-vəl\ *n* **1 ♦ :** one that causes wonder or astonishment **2 :** intense surprise or interest

♦ caution, flash, miracle, phenomenon, portent, prodigy, sensation, wonder

²**marvel** *vb* **mar·veled** *or* **mar·velled; mar·vel·ing** *or* **mar·vel·ling :** to feel surprise, wonder, or amazed curiosity

mar·vel·ous *or* **mar·vel·lous** \'mär-və-ləs\ *adj* **1 ♦ :** causing wonder **2 ♦ :** of the highest kind or quality — **mar·vel·ous·ly** *adv* — **mar·vel·ous·ness** *n*

♦ [1] amazing, astonishing, astounding, awesome, eye-opening, fabulous, marvelous, portentous, prodigious, stunning, stupendous, sublime, surprising, wonderful ♦ [2] excellent, fabulous, fine, grand, great, sensational, splendid, superb, superior, swell, terrific, wonderful

Marx·ism \'märk-ˌsi-zəm\ *n* **:** the political, economic, and social principles and policies advocated by Karl Marx — **Marx·ist** \-sist\ *n or adj*

mar·zi·pan \'märt-sə-ˌpän, -ˌpan; 'mär-zə-ˌpan\ *n* **:** a confection of almond paste, sugar, and egg whites

masc *abbr* masculine

mas·cara \mas-'kar-ə\ *n* **:** a cosmetic esp. for darkening the eyelashes

mas·car·po·ne \ˌmas-kär-'pō-nä\ *n* **:** an Italian cream cheese

mas·cot \'mas-ˌkät, -kət\ *n ♦* **:** a person, animal, or object adopted usu. by a group to bring good luck

♦ amulet, charm, fetish, talisman

¹**mas·cu·line** \'mas-kyə-lən\ *adj* **1 a :** MALE **b ♦ :** having qualities appropriate to or usu. associated with a man **:** MANLY **2 :** of, relating to, or constituting the gender that includes most words or grammatical forms referring to males

♦ male, manly, mannish, man-size, virile *Ant* effeminate, unmanly, unmasculine

²**masculine** *n* **:** a noun, pronoun, adjective, or inflectional form or class of the masculine gender; *also* **:** the masculine gender

mas·cu·lin·i·ty \ˌmas-kyə-'li-nə-tē\ *n ♦* **:** the quality, state, or degree of being masculine

♦ manhood, manliness, virility

¹**mash** \'mash\ *n* **1 :** a mixture of ground feeds for livestock **2 :** crushed malt or grain steeped in hot water to make wort **3 :** a soft pulpy mass

²**mash** *vb* **1 ♦ :** to reduce to a soft pulpy state **2 :** CRUSH, SMASH ⟨∼ a finger⟩ — **mash·er** *n*

♦ crush, squash

MASH *abbr* mobile army surgical hospital

mash–up \'mash-ˌəp\ *n* **:** something created by combining elements from two or more sources

¹**mask** \'mask\ *n* **1 :** a cover for the face usu. for disguise or protection **2 :** MASQUE **3 :** a figure of a head worn on the stage in antiquity **4 :** a copy of a face made by means of a mold ⟨death ∼⟩ **5 ♦ :** something that conceals or disguises **6 :** the face of an animal **7 :** a cosmetic preparation for the skin of the face that is applied moist and removed after it dries

♦ cloak, curtain, hood, mantle, shroud, veil

²**mask** *vb* **1 ♦ :** to conceal from view or perception **2 :** to cover for protection

♦ camouflage, cloak, disguise, dress up ♦ blanket, blot out, cloak, conceal, cover, curtain, enshroud, hide, obscure, occult, screen, shroud, veil

mask·er \'mas-kər\ *n* **:** a participant in a masquerade

mas·och·ism \'ma-sə-ˌki-zəm, 'ma-zə-\ *n* **1 :** a sexual perversion characterized by pleasure in being subjected to pain or humiliation **2 :** pleasure in being abused or dominated — **mas·och·ist** \-kist\ *n* — **mas·och·is·tic** \ˌma-sə-'kis-tik, ˌma-zə-\ *adj*

ma·son \'mās-ᵊn\ *n* **1 :** a skilled worker who builds with stone, brick, or concrete **2** *cap* **:** FREEMASON

Ma·son·ic \mə-'sä-nik\ *adj* **:** of or relating to Freemasons or Freemasonry

ma·son·ry \'mās-ᵊn-rē\ *n, pl* **-ries 1 :** something constructed of materials used by masons **2 :** the art, trade, or work of a mason **3** *cap* **:** FREEMASONRY

masque \'mask\ *n* **1 :** MASQUERADE **2 :** a short allegorical dramatic performance (as of the 17th century)

¹**mas·quer·ade** \ˌmas-kə-'rād\ *n* **1 :** a social gathering of persons wearing masks; *also* **:** a costume for wear at such a gathering **2 :** DISGUISE **3 ♦ :** an action or appearance that is mere disguise or show

♦ act, airs, facade, front, guise, pose, pretense, put-on, semblance, show

²**masquerade** *vb* **-ad·ed; -ad·ing 1 ♦ :** to disguise oneself **2 :** to take part in a masquerade — **mas·quer·ad·er** *n*

♦ impersonate, play, pose

¹**mass** \'mas\ *n* **1** *cap* **:** a sequence of prayers and ceremonies forming the eucharistic service of the Roman Catholic Church **2** *often cap* **:** a celebration of the Eucharist **3 :** a musical setting for parts of the Mass

²**mass** *n* **1 :** a quantity or aggregate of matter usu. of considerable size **2 :** EXPANSE, BULK; *also* **:** MASSIVENESS **3 :** the principal part **4 :** AGGREGATE, WHOLE **5 :** the quantity of matter that a body possesses as measured by its inertia **6 :** a large quantity, amount, or number **7 ♦ :** the great body of people — usu. used in pl. — **massy** *adj*

♦ [3] body, bulk, core, generality, main, staple, weight ♦ *usu*
masses *pl* [7] commoners, herd, mob, people, plebeians, populace, rank and file *Ant* elite

³**mass** *vb* ♦ : to form or collect into a mass

♦ accumulate, amass, collect, conglomerate, gather, heap, pile up

Mass *abbr* Massachusetts

¹**mas·sa·cre** \'ma-si-kər\ *n* 1 ♦ : the killing of many persons under cruel or atrocious circumstances 2 : a wholesale slaughter

♦ butchery, carnage, slaughter

²**massacre** *vb* ♦ : to kill by massacre

♦ butcher, slaughter

¹**mas·sage** \mə-'säzh, -'säj\ *n* : manipulation of tissues (as by rubbing and kneading) esp. for therapeutic purposes
²**massage** *vb* **mas·saged; mas·sag·ing** 1 : to subject to massage 2 : to treat flatteringly; *also* : MANIPULATE, DOCTOR ⟨~ data⟩
mas·seur \ma-'sər\ *n* : a man who practices massage
mas·seuse \-'sərz, -'süz\ *n* : a woman who practices massage
mas·sif \ma-'sēf\ *n* : a principal mountain mass
mas·sive \'ma-siv\ *adj* 1 ♦ : forming or consisting of a large mass 2 ♦ : large in structure, scope, or degree

♦ [1] heavy, hefty, ponderous, weighty ♦ [2] colossal, enormous, giant, gigantic, grand, huge, mammoth, monumental, prodigious, titanic, tremendous

mas·sive·ly \-lē\ *adv* ♦ : in a massive manner

♦ broadly, considerably, greatly, hugely, largely, monstrously, much, sizably, stupendously, tremendously, utterly, vastly

mas·sive·ness \-nəs\ *n* ♦ : the quality or state of being massive

♦ enormity, hugeness, immensity, magnitude, vastness

mass·less \'mas-ləs\ *adj* : having no mass ⟨~ particles⟩
mass medium *n, pl* **mass media** : a medium of communication (as the newspapers or television) that is designed to reach the mass of the people
mass–pro·duce \,mas-prə-'düs, -'dyüs\ *vb* : to produce in quantity usu. by machinery — **mass production** *n*
¹**mast** \'mast\ *n* 1 : a long pole or spar rising from the keel or deck of a ship and supporting the yards, booms, and rigging 2 : a slender vertical structure — **mast·ed** \'mas-təd\ *adj*
²**mast** *n* : nuts (as acorns) accumulated on the forest floor and often serving as food for animals (as hogs)
mas·tec·to·my \ma-'stek-tə-mē\ *n, pl* **-mies** : surgical removal of the breast
¹**mas·ter** \'mas-tər\ *n* 1 : a male teacher; *also* : a person holding an academic degree higher than a bachelor's but lower than a doctor's 2 ♦ : one highly skilled (as in an art or profession) 3 : one having authority or control 4 : one that conquers or masters : VICTOR 5 : the commander of a merchant ship 6 ♦ : a youth or boy too young to be called *mister* — used as a title 7 : an original from which copies are made — **master** *adj*

♦ ace, adept, artist, authority, crackerjack, expert, maestro, scholar, shark, virtuoso, whiz, wizard

²**master** *vb* 1 : to become master of : OVERCOME 2 : to become skilled or proficient in 3 : to produce a master recording of (as a musical performance)
master chief petty officer *n* : a petty officer of the highest rank in the navy
mas·ter·ful \'mas-tər-fəl\ *adj* 1 : inclined and usu. competent to act as a master 2 ♦ : having or reflecting the skill of a master 3 : suggestive of a domineering nature

♦ [2] adroit, artful, dexterous, practiced, skillful, virtuoso
♦ [2] accomplished, adept, consummate, crack, crackerjack, good, great, proficient, skilled

mas·ter·ful·ly \-fə-lē\ *adv* ♦ : in a masterful manner

♦ ably, adeptly, capably, expertly, proficiently, skillfully, well

mas·ter·ful·ness \-nəs\ *n* ♦ : the quality or state of being masterful

♦ adeptness, adroitness, art, artfulness, artifice, artistry, cleverness, craft, cunning, deftness, skill

master gunnery sergeant *n* : a noncommissioned officer in the marine corps ranking above a master sergeant
master key *n* : a key designed to open several different locks
mas·ter·ly \'mas-tər-lē\ *adj* 1 ♦ : indicating thorough knowledge or superior skill ⟨~ performance⟩ 2 ♦ : having the power and skill of a master — **mas·ter·ly** *adv*

♦ accomplished, adept, consummate, crack, crackerjack, expert, good, great, master, masterful, proficient, skilled, skillful, virtuoso

¹**mas·ter·mind** \-,mīnd\ *n* : a person who provides the directing or creative intelligence for a project
²**mastermind** *vb* ♦ : to be the mastermind of

♦ contrive, finagle, finesse, frame, machinate, maneuver (*or* manoeuvre), negotiate, wangle

master of ceremonies : a person who acts as host for a special event or a program of entertainment (as on television)
mas·ter·piece \'mas-tər-,pēs\ *n* : a work done with extraordinary skill
master plan *n* : an overall plan
mas·ter's \'mas-tərz\ *n* : a master's degree
master sergeant *n* 1 : a noncommissioned officer in the army ranking next below a sergeant major 2 : a noncommissioned officer in the air force ranking next below a senior master sergeant 3 : a noncommissioned officer in the marine corps ranking next below a master gunnery sergeant
mas·ter·stroke \'mas-tər-,strōk\ *n* : a masterly performance or move
mas·ter·work \-,wərk\ *n* : MASTERPIECE
mas·tery \'mas-tə-rē\ *n* 1 : the authority of a master : DOMINION; *also* : SUPERIORITY 2 : possession or display of great skill or knowledge
mast·head \'mast-,hed\ *n* 1 : the top of a mast 2 : the printed matter in a newspaper or periodical giving the title and details of ownership and rates of subscription or advertising
mas·tic \'mas-tik\ *n* : a pasty material used as a coating or cement
mas·ti·cate \'mas-tə-,kāt\ *vb* **-cat·ed; -cat·ing** : to grind or crush (food) with or as if with the teeth : CHEW — **mas·ti·ca·tion** \,mas-tə-'kā-shən\ *n*
mas·tiff \'mas-təf\ *n* : any of a breed of large smooth-coated dogs used esp. as guard dogs
mast·odon \'mas-tə-,dän\ *n* : any of numerous huge extinct mammals related to the mammoths
mas·toid \'mas-,tóid\ *n* : a bony prominence behind the ear — **mastoid** *adj*
mas·tur·ba·tion \,mas-tər-'bā-shən\ *n* : stimulation of the genital organs apart from sexual intercourse, usu. to orgasm, and esp. by use of one's own hand — **mas·tur·bate** \'mas-tər-,bāt\ *vb* — **mas·tur·ba·to·ry** \'mas-tər-bə-,tōr-ē\ *adj*
¹**mat** \'mat\ *n* 1 : a piece of coarse woven or plaited fabric 2 : something made up of many intertwined strands 3 : a large thick pad used as a surface for wrestling and gymnastics
²**mat** *vb* **mat·ted; mat·ting** 1 : to provide with a mat 2 : to form into a tangled mass
³**mat** *vb* **mat·ted; mat·ting** 1 : to make (as a color) matte 2 : to provide (a picture) with a mat
⁴**mat** *var of* MATTE
⁵**mat** *or* **matt** *or* **matte** *n* : a border going around a picture between picture and frame or serving as the frame
mat·a·dor \'ma-tə-,dór\ *n* : a bullfighter whose role is to kill the bull in a bullfight
¹**match** \'mach\ *n* 1 ♦ : a person or thing equal or similar to another; *also* : one able to cope with another : RIVAL 2 : a suitable pairing of persons or objects 3 ♦ : a contest or game between two or more individuals 4 : a marriage union; *also* : a prospective marriage partner

♦ [1] coordinate, counterpart, equal, equivalent, fellow, like, parallel, peer, rival ♦ [2] carbon copy, counterpart, double, duplicate, duplication, facsimile, image, likeness, picture, replica, ringer, spit ♦ [3] bout, competition, contest, event, game, meet, tournament

²**match** *vb* 1 : to meet as an antagonist; *also* : PIT 2 : to provide with a worthy competitor; *also* : to set in comparison with 3 : to join or give in marriage : MARRY 4 : to combine suitably or congenially; *also* : ADAPT, SUIT 5 ♦ : to provide with a counterpart 6 ♦ : to be the counterpart of

♦ [5] equal, meet, tie ♦ [6] correspond, equal, parallel

³**match** *n* : a short slender piece of flammable material (as wood) tipped with a combustible mixture that ignites through friction
match·book \'mach-,bùk\ *n* : a small folder containing rows of paper matches
match·less \-ləs\ *adj* ♦ : having no equal

♦ incomparable, inimitable, nonpareil, only, peerless, unequaled, unmatched, unparalleled, unrivaled, unsurpassed

match·lock \-,läk\ *n* : a musket with a slow-burning cord lowered over a hole in the breech to ignite the charge

match·mak·er \-ˌmā-kər\ *n* : one who arranges a match and esp. a marriage

match·wood \-ˌwu̇d\ *n* : small pieces of wood

¹mate \ˈmāt\ *vb* **mat·ed; mat·ing** : CHECKMATE — **mate** *n*

²mate *n* **1 a ♦** : one that customarily associates with another : ASSOCIATE, COMPANION **b ♦** : an assistant to a more skilled worker : HELPER **2** : a deck officer on a merchant ship ranking below the captain **3 a ♦** : one of a pair **b ♦** : either member of a married couple or a breeding pair of animals

♦ [1a] associate, cohort, companion, comrade, crony, fellow ♦ [1b] aid, apprentice, assistant, deputy, helper, helpmate, sidekick ♦ [3a] companion, half, match, twin ♦ [3b] consort, partner, spouse

³mate *vb* **mat·ed; mat·ing** **1** : to join or fit together **2** : to come or bring together as mates **3** : COPULATE

¹ma·te·ri·al \mə-ˈtir-ē-əl\ *adj* **1 ♦** : having material existence : PHYSICAL ⟨~ world⟩; *also* : of or relating to the body : BODILY ⟨~ needs⟩ **2** : of or relating to matter rather than form ⟨~ cause⟩; *also* : EMPIRICAL ⟨~ knowledge⟩ **3 ♦** : highly important : SIGNIFICANT **4 ♦** : of a physical or worldly nature ⟨~ progress⟩ — **ma·te·ri·al·ly** *adv*

♦ [1] bodily, concrete, physical, substantial *Ant* immaterial, nonmaterial, nonphysical ♦ [3] big, consequential, eventful, important, major, meaningful, momentous, significant, substantial, weighty ♦ [3] applicable, apposite, apropos, germane, pertinent, pointed, relative, relevant ♦ [4] carnal, earthly, fleshly, mundane, temporal, terrestrial, worldly

²material *n* **1 ♦** : the elements or substance of which something is composed or made **2** : apparatus necessary for doing or making something

♦ raw material, stuff, substance

ma·te·ri·al·ise *chiefly Brit var of* MATERIALIZE

ma·te·ri·al·ism \mə-ˈtir-ē-ə-ˌli-zəm\ *n* **1** : a theory that everything can be explained as being or coming from matter **2** : a preoccupation with material rather than intellectual or spiritual things — **ma·te·ri·al·ist** \-list\ *n or adj* — **ma·te·ri·al·is·tic** \-ˌtir-ē-ə-ˈlis-tik\ *adj* — **ma·te·ri·al·is·ti·cal·ly** \-ti-k(ə-)lē\ *adv*

ma·te·ri·al·ize \mə-ˈtir-ē-ə-ˌlīz\ *vb* **-ized; -iz·ing** **1 ♦** : to give material form to; *also* : to assume bodily form **2 ♦** : to make an often unexpected appearance **3 ♦** : to come into existence — **ma·te·ri·al·i·za·tion** \mə-ˌtir-ē-ə-lə-ˈzā-shən\ *n*

♦ [1] embody, epitomize, manifest, personify, substantiate ♦ [2] appear, come out, show up, turn up ♦ [2, 3] arise, begin, commence, dawn, form, originate, spring, start

ma·té·ri·el *or* **ma·te·ri·el** \mə-ˌtir-ē-ˈel\ *n* ♦ : equipment, apparatus, and supplies used by an organization

♦ accoutrements (*or* accouterments), apparatus, equipment, gear, outfit, paraphernalia, tackle

ma·ter·nal \mə-ˈtərn-əl\ *adj* **1** : MOTHERLY **2** : related through or inherited or derived from a female parent ⟨our ~ grandparents⟩ — **ma·ter·nal·ly** *adv*

¹ma·ter·ni·ty \mə-ˈtər-nə-tē\ *n, pl* **-ties** **1** : the quality or state of being a mother; *also* : MOTHERLINESS **2** : a hospital facility for the care of women before and during childbirth and for newborn babies

²maternity *adj* **1** : designed for wear during pregnancy ⟨a ~ dress⟩ **2** : effective for the period close to and including childbirth ⟨~ leave⟩

¹math \ˈmath\ *n* : MATHEMATICS

²math *abbr* mathematical; mathematician

math·e·mat·i·cal \ˌma-thə-ˈma-ti-kəl\ *adj* **1** : of, relating to, or according with mathematics **2 ♦** : rigorously exact

♦ accurate, close, delicate, exact, fine, pinpoint, precise, rigorous

math·e·mat·ics \ˌma-thə-ˈma-tiks\ *n* : the science of numbers and their properties, operations, and relations and with shapes in space and their structure and measurement — **math·e·mat·i·cal·ly** \-ti-k(ə-)lē\ *adv* — **math·e·ma·ti·cian** \ˌma-thə-mə-ˈti-shən\ *n*

mat·i·nee *or* **mat·i·née** \ˌmat-ᵊn-ˈā\ *n* : a musical or dramatic performance in the daytime and esp. the afternoon

mat·ins \ˈmat-ᵊnz\ *n pl, often cap* **1** : special prayers said between midnight and 4 a.m. **2** : a morning service of liturgical prayer in Anglican churches

ma·tri·arch \ˈmā-trē-ˌärk\ *n* ♦ : a woman who rules or dominates a family, group, or state — **ma·tri·ar·chal** \ˌmā-trē-ˈär-kəl\ *adj* — **ma·tri·ar·chy** \ˈmā-trē-ˌär-kē\ *n*

♦ dame, dowager, matron

ma·tri·cide \ˈma-trə-ˌsīd, ˈmā-\ *n* : the murder of a mother by her child — **ma·tri·cid·al** \ˌma-trə-ˈsīd-ᵊl, ˌmā-\ *adj*

ma·tric·u·late \mə-ˈtri-kyə-ˌlāt\ *vb* **-lat·ed; -lat·ing** ♦ : to enroll as a member of a body and esp. of a college or university — **ma·tric·u·la·tion** \-ˌtri-kyə-ˈlā-shən\ *n*

♦ enroll, inscribe, list, register

mat·ri·mo·ni·al \ˌma-trə-ˈmō-nē-əl\ *adj* ♦ : of or relating to matrimony — **mat·ri·mo·ni·al·ly** *adv*

♦ conjugal, connubial, marital, nuptial

mat·ri·mo·ny \ˈma-trə-ˌmō-nē\ *n* ♦ : the state of being married : MARRIAGE

♦ marriage, match

ma·trix \ˈmā-triks\ *n, pl* **ma·tri·ces** \ˈmā-trə-ˌsēz, ˈma-\ *or* **ma·trix·es** \ˈmā-trik-səz\ **1** : something within or from which something else originates, develops, or takes form **2** : a mold from which a relief surface (as a piece of type) is made

ma·tron \ˈmā-trən\ *n* **1** : a married woman usu. of dignified maturity or social distinction **2** : a woman supervisor (as in a school or police station) — **ma·tron·ly** *adj*

♦ dame, dowager, matriarch

Matt *abbr* Matthew

¹matte *or* **matt** *var of* ³MAT

²matte *also* **mat** *or* **matt** \ˈmat\ *adj* : not shiny : DULL

¹mat·ter \ˈma-tər\ *n* **1 ♦** : a subject of interest or concern **2** *pl* : events or circumstances of a particular situation **3** : the subject of a discourse or writing **4 ♦** : a source of perplexity, distress, or vexation : TROUBLE ⟨what's the ~⟩ **5** : the substance of which a physical object is composed **6** : PUS **7** : an indefinite amount or quantity ⟨a ~ of a few days⟩ **8** : something written or printed **9 ♦** : something sent through the mail

♦ [1] content, motif, question, subject, theme, topic ♦ [1] affair, business, thing ♦ [4] case, knot, problem, trouble ♦ [9] mail, parcel post, post, snail mail

²matter *vb* ♦ : to have significance

♦ count, import, mean, signify, weigh

mat·ter-of-fact \ˌma-tə-rəv-ˈfakt\ *adj* **1 ♦** : adhering to fact **2 ♦** : being plain, straightforward, or unemotional — **mat·ter-of-fact·ly** *adv* — **mat·ter-of-fact·ness** *n*

♦ [1] documentary, factual, hard, historical, literal, nonfictional, objective, true ♦ [2] down-to-earth, earthy, hardheaded, practical, pragmatic, realistic

Mat·thew \ˈma-thyü\ *n* : a book of the New Testament of Christian Scripture

mat·tins *often cap, chiefly Brit var of* MATINS

mat·tock \ˈma-tək\ *n* : a digging and grubbing tool with features of an adze and an ax or pick

mat·tress \ˈma-trəs\ *n* **1** : a fabric case filled with resilient material used as or for a bed **2** : an inflatable airtight sack for use as a mattress

mat·u·rate \ˈma-chə-ˌrāt\ *vb* **-rat·ed; -rat·ing** : MATURE

mat·u·ra·tion \ˌma-chə-ˈrā-shən\ *n* **1 ♦** : the process of maturing **2** : the emergence of personal and behavioral characteristics through growth processes — **mat·u·ra·tion·al** \-shə-nəl\ *adj*

♦ development, growth

¹ma·ture \mə-ˈtu̇r, -ˈtyu̇r\ *adj* **ma·tur·er; -est** **1** : based on slow careful consideration **2 ♦** : having attained a final or desired state **3** : of or relating to a condition of full development **4** : due for payment **5** : suitable only for adults — **ma·ture·ly** *adv*

♦ adult, full-blown, full-fledged, ripe *Ant* green, immature, juvenile, unripened, young, youthful

²mature *vb* **ma·tured; ma·tur·ing** ♦ : to reach or bring to maturity or completion

♦ age, develop, grow, grow up, progress, ripen

ma·tu·ri·ty \mə-ˈtu̇r-ə-tē, -ˈtyu̇r-\ *n* **1** : the quality or state of being mature; *esp* : full development **2** : the date when a note becomes due for payment

ma·tu·ti·nal \ˌma-chü-ˈtīn-əl; mə-ˈtüt-ᵊn-əl, -ˈtyüt-\ *adj* : of, relating to, or occurring in the morning : EARLY

mat·zo *or* **mat·zoh** \ˈmät-sə\ *n, pl* **mat·zoth** \-ˌsōt, -ˌsōth, -sōs\ *or* **mat·zos** *or* **mat·zohs** : unleavened bread eaten esp. at Passover

maud·lin \ˈmȯd-lən\ *adj* **1** : drunk enough to be silly **2 ♦** : weakly and effusively sentimental

♦ corny, mawkish, mushy, saccharine, sappy, schmaltzy, sentimental

¹maul \\'mȯl\\ *n* : a heavy hammer often with a wooden head used esp. for driving wedges

²maul *vb* **1 a :** to strike repeatedly : BEAT **b :** MANGLE **2 ♦ :** to handle roughly

♦ maltreat, manhandle, mishandle, rough

maun·der \\'mȯn-dər\\ *vb* **1 ♦ :** to wander slowly and idly **2 ♦ :** to speak indistinctly or disconnectedly

♦ [1] gad, gallivant, knock, meander, mope, ramble, range, roam, rove, traipse, wander ♦ [2] ramble, rattle, run on

mau·so·le·um \\ˌmȯ-sə-'lē-əm, ˌmȯ-zə-\\ *n, pl* **-leums** *or* **-lea** \\-'lē-ə\\ : a large tomb; *esp* : a usu. stone building for entombment of the dead above ground

mauve \\'mōv, 'mȯv\\ *n* : a moderate purple, violet, or lilac color

ma·ven *also* **ma·vin** \\'mā-vən\\ *n* : EXPERT

mav·er·ick \\'ma-vrik, -və-rik\\ *n* **1 :** an unbranded range animal **2 ♦ :** a person who does not conform to a generally accepted pattern of thought or action : NONCONFORMIST

♦ bohemian, deviant, individualist, loner, nonconformist

maw \\'mȯ\\ *n* **1 :** STOMACH; *also* : the crop of a bird **2 :** the throat, gullet, or jaws esp. of a voracious animal

mawk·ish \\'mȯ-kish\\ *adj* ♦ **:** sickly sentimental ⟨~ poetry⟩ — **mawk·ish·ly** *adv*

♦ corny, maudlin, mushy, saccharine, sappy, schmaltzy, sentimental

mawk·ish·ness \\-nəs\\ *n* ♦ **:** the quality or state of being mawkish

♦ mush, sentimentality

max *abbr* maximum

maxi \\'mak-sē\\ *n, pl* **max·is** : a long skirt, dress, or coat

maxi- *comb form* **1 :** extra long ⟨*maxi*-kilt⟩ **2 :** extra large ⟨*maxi*-problems⟩

max·il·la \\mak-'si-lə\\ *n, pl* **max·il·lae** \\-'si-(ˌ)lē\\ *or* **maxillas** : JAW 1; *esp* : an upper jaw — **max·il·lary** \\'mak-sə-ˌler-ē\\ *adj*

max·im \\'mak-səm\\ *n* ♦ **:** a proverbial saying

♦ adage, aphorism, byword, epigram, proverb, saying

max·i·mal \\'mak-sə-məl\\ *adj* : MAXIMUM — **max·i·mal·ly** *adv*

max·i·mise *chiefly Brit var of* MAXIMIZE

max·i·mize \\'mak-sə-ˌmīz\\ *vb* **-mized; -miz·ing** **1 :** to increase to a maximum **2 :** to make the most of **3 :** to increase the size of a computer program's window to fill an entire screen — **max·i·mi·za·tion** \\ˌmak-sə-mə-'zā-shən\\ *n*

¹max·i·mum \\'mak-sə-məm\\ *n, pl* **-ma** \\-mə\\ *or* **-mums** **1 :** the greatest quantity, value, or degree **2 :** an upper limit allowed by authority **3 :** the largest of a set of numbers

²maximum *adj* ♦ **:** greatest in quantity or highest in degree attainable or attained

♦ consummate, full, most, nth, paramount, supreme, top, ultimate, utmost

max out *vb* **1 :** to push to or reach a limit or an extreme **2 :** to use up all available credit on (a credit card)

may \\'mā\\ *verbal auxiliary, past* **might** \\'mīt\\ *pres sing & pl* **may** **1 :** have permission or liberty to ⟨you ~ go now⟩ **2 :** be in some degree likely to ⟨you ~ be right⟩ **3** — used as an auxiliary to express a wish, purpose, contingency, or concession

May \\'mā\\ *n* : the 5th month of the year

Ma·ya \\'mī-ə\\ *n, pl* **Maya** *or* **Mayas** : a member of a group of Indigenous peoples of Yucatán, Guatemala, and adjacent areas — **Ma·yan** \\'mī-ən\\ *n or adj*

may·ap·ple \\'mā-ˌa-pəl\\ *n* : a No. American woodland herb related to the barberry that has a poisonous root, one or two large leaves, and an edible egg-shaped yellow fruit

may·be \\'mā-bē, 'me-\\ *adv* ♦ **:** possibly but not certainly : PERHAPS

♦ conceivably, perchance, perhaps, possibly

May Day \\'mā-ˌdā\\ *n* : May 1 celebrated as a springtime festival and in some countries as Labor Day

may·flow·er \\'mā-ˌflau̇-ər\\ *n* : any of several spring blooming herbs (as the trailing arbutus or an anemone)

may·fly \\'mā-flī\\ *n* : any of an order of insects with an aquatic nymph and a short-lived fragile adult having membranous wings

may·hem \\'mā-ˌhem, 'mā-əm\\ *n* **1 :** willful and permanent crippling, mutilation, or disfigurement of a person **2 :** needless or willful damage

may·on·naise \\'mā-ə-ˌnāz\\ *n* : a dressing made of egg yolks, vegetable oil, and vinegar or lemon juice

may·or \\'mā-ər\\ *n* : an official elected to act as chief executive or nominal head of a city or borough — **may·or·al** \\-əl\\ *adj* — **may·or·al·ty** \\-əl-tē\\ *n*

may·pole \\'mā-ˌpōl\\ *n, often cap* : a tall flower-wreathed pole forming a center for May Day sports and dances

maze \\'māz\\ *n* : a confusing intricate network of passages — **mazy** *adj*

ma·zur·ka \\mə-'zər-kə\\ *n* : a Polish dance in moderate triple measure

MB *abbr* Manitoba

MBA *abbr* master of business administration

mc *abbr* megacycle

Mc *symbol* moscovium

¹MC *n* : MASTER OF CEREMONIES

²MC *abbr* member of Congress

Mc- \\mək; mə *before forms beginning with* k *or* g\\ *prefix* : used to indicate a convenient, low-quality version of a specified thing ⟨*Mc*Book⟩

Mc·Coy \\mə-'kȯi\\ *n* : something that is neither imitation nor substitute ⟨the real ~⟩

McGuffin *var of* MACGUFFIN

MCPO *abbr* master chief petty officer

¹Md *abbr* Maryland

²Md *symbol* mendelevium

MD *abbr* **1** doctor of medicine **2** Maryland **3** muscular dystrophy

MDMA \\ˌem-ˌdē-ˌem-'ā\\ *n* : ECSTASY 2

mdnt *abbr* midnight

mdse *abbr* merchandise

MDT *abbr* mountain daylight (saving) time

me \\'mē\\ *pron, objective case of* I

Me *abbr* Maine

ME *abbr* **1** Maine **2** mechanical engineer **3** medical examiner

¹mead \\'mēd\\ *n* : an alcoholic beverage brewed from water and honey, malt, and yeast

²mead *n, archaic* : MEADOW

mead·ow \\'me-dō\\ *n* : land in or mainly in grass; *esp* : a tract of moist low-lying usu. level grassland — **mead·ow·land** \\-ˌland\\ *n* — **mead·owy** \\'me-də-wē\\ *adj*

mead·ow·lark \\'me-dō-ˌlärk\\ *n* : any of several American songbirds related to the orioles that are streaked brown above and in northernmost forms have a yellow breast marked with a black crescent

mead·ow·sweet \\-ˌswēt\\ *n* : a No. American native or naturalized spirea

mea·ger *or* **mea·gre** \\'mē-gər\\ *adj* **1 :** THIN **2 a :** lacking richness, fertility, or strength **b ♦ :** deficient in quality or quantity : POOR — **mea·ger·ly** *adv* — **mea·ger·ness** *n*

♦ light, niggardly, poor, scant, scanty, scarce, skimpy, slender, slim, spare, sparse, stingy **Ant** abundant, ample, bountiful, copious, generous, liberal, plenteous, plentiful

¹meal \\'mēl\\ *n* **1 :** an act or the time of eating a portion of food **2 ♦ :** the portion of food eaten at a meal

♦ board, chow, feed, mess, repast, table

²meal *n* **1 :** usu. coarsely ground seeds of a cereal **2 :** a product resembling seed meal

meal·time \\'mēl-ˌtīm\\ *n* : the usual time at which a meal is served

mealy \\'mē-lē\\ *adj* ♦ **:** not plain and straightforward

♦ artificial, double-dealing, feigned, hypocritical, insincere, left-handed, mealymouthed, two-faced, unctuous

mealy·bug \\'mē-lē-ˌbəg\\ *n* : any of a family of scale insects with a white cottony or waxy covering that are destructive pests esp. of fruit trees

mealy·mouthed \\'mē-lē-ˌmau̇thd, -ˌmau̇tht\\ *adj* ♦ **:** not plain and straightforward ⟨a ~ politician⟩

♦ artificial, double-dealing, feigned, hypocritical, insincere, left-handed, mealy, two-faced, unctuous

¹mean \\'mēn\\ *vb* **meant** \\'ment\\; **mean·ing** **1 ♦ :** to have in the mind as a purpose **2 ♦ :** to serve to convey, show, or indicate : SIGNIFY **3 ♦ :** to have importance to the degree of **4 :** to direct to a particular individual

♦ [1] aim, aspire, contemplate, design, intend, meditate, plan, propose ♦ [2] denote, express, import, signify, spell ♦ [3] count, import, matter, signify, weigh

²mean *adj* **1 ♦ :** lacking distinction or eminence : HUMBLE **2 :** lacking acumen : DULL **3 a ♦ :** of poor shabby inferior quality or status **b ♦ :** worthy of little regard **4 ♦ :** lacking dignity or honor : IGNOBLE, BASE **5 :** sparing or scant in using, giving, or spending : STINGY **6 ♦ :** pettily selfish or malicious **7 :** VEXATIOUS **8 :** very good of its kind : EXCELLENT

♦ [1] common, humble, ignoble, inferior, low, lowly, plebeian, vulgar ♦ [3a] dilapidated, grungy, neglected, ratty, seedy, shabby ♦ [3b] inferior, minor, secondary, second-rate ♦ [4] base, contemptible, despicable, detestable, dirty, dishonorable (*or* dishonourable), ignoble, low, snide, sordid, vile, wretched ♦ [6] catty, cruel, hateful, malevolent, malicious, malign, malignant, nasty, spiteful, virulent

³**mean** *adj* **1** : occupying a middle position (as in space, order, or time) **2** : being a mean : AVERAGE ⟨a ∼ value⟩
⁴**mean** *n* **1** ♦ : a middle point between extremes **2** *pl* ♦ : something helpful in achieving a desired end **3** *pl* ♦ : material resources affording a secure life **4** : ARITHMETIC MEAN

♦ [1] medium, middle, midpoint ♦ **means** *pl* [2] agency, agent, instrument, instrumentality, machinery, medium, organ, vehicle ♦ **means** *pl* [3] assets, capital, fortune, opulence, riches, substance, wealth, wherewithal

¹**me·an·der** \mē-'an-dər\ *n* **1** : a winding course **2** : a winding of a stream
²**meander** *vb* **1** : to follow a winding course **2** ♦ : to wander aimlessly or casually

♦ gad, gallivant, knock, maunder, mope, ramble, range, roam, rove, traipse, wander

mean·ing *n* **1** ♦ : the thing one intends to convey esp. by language; *also* : the thing that is thus conveyed **2** ♦ : something meant or intended : AIM **3** : SIGNIFICANCE; *esp* : implication of a hidden significance **4** ♦ : the logical connotation of a word or phrase; *esp* : DENOTATION

♦ [1, 4] denotation, drift, import, intent, purport, sense, significance, signification ♦ [2] aim, ambition, aspiration, design, dream, end, goal, intent, mark, object, objective, plan, pretension, purpose, thing

mean·ing·ful \-fəl\ *adj* ♦ : full of meaning : SIGNIFICANT — **mean·ing·ful·ly** *adv*

♦ eloquent, expressive, meaning, pregnant, significant, suggestive ♦ big, consequential, eventful, important, major, material, momentous, significant, substantial, weighty

mean·ing·less \-ləs\ *adj* ♦ : having no meaning

♦ empty, pointless, senseless *Ant* meaningful

mean·ly \'mēn-lē\ *adv* ♦ : in a mean manner

♦ hatefully, maliciously, nastily, spitefully, viciously, wickedly

mean·ness \'mēn-nəs\ *n* ♦ : the quality or state of being mean

♦ cattiness, despite, hatefulness, malice, malignity, nastiness, spite, spleen, venom, viciousness

¹**mean·time** \'mēn-,tīm\ *n* : the intervening time
²**meantime** *adv* : MEANWHILE
¹**mean·while** \-,hwīl(-ə)l\ *n* : MEANTIME
²**meanwhile** *adv* **1** : during the intervening time **2** : at the same time

meas *abbr* measure
mea·sles \'mē-zəlz\ *n sing or pl* : an acute virus disease marked by fever and an eruption of distinct circular red spots
mea·sly \'mēz-lē, -zə-lē\ *adj* **mea·sli·er; -est** ♦ : contemptibly small or insignificant

♦ inconsequential, inconsiderable, insignificant, minute, negligible, nominal, paltry, petty, slight, trifling, trivial

¹**mea·sure** \'me-zhər, 'mā-\ *n* **1** : an adequate or moderate portion; *also* : a suitable limit **2** ♦ : the dimensions, capacity, or amount of something ascertained by measuring; *also* : an instrument for measuring **3** : a unit of measurement; *also* : a system of such units **4** : the act or process of measuring **5** ♦ : rhythmic structure or movement **6** : the part of a musical staff between two bars **7** ♦ : a basis or standard of comparison : CRITERION **8** ♦ : a means to an end **9** : a legislative bill **10** ♦ : the total number or quantity

♦ [2] dimension, extent, magnitude, measurement, proportion, size ♦ [5] beat, cadence, meter (*or* metre), rhythm ♦ [7] criterion, grade, mark, par, standard, touchstone, yardstick ♦ [8] expedient, move, shift, step ♦ [10] amount, quantity

²**measure** *vb* **mea·sured; mea·sur·ing** **1** : to mark or fix in multiples of a specific unit ⟨∼ off five centimeters⟩ **2** ♦ : to ascertain the measurements of **3** : to bring into comparison or competition **4** : to serve as a means of measuring **5** : to have a specified measurement — **mea·sur·able** \'me-zhə-rə-bəl, 'mā-\ *adj* — **mea·sur·ably** \-blē\ *adv* — **mea·sur·er** *n*

♦ gauge, scale, span

measured *adj* **1** ♦ : marked by rhythm **2** ♦ : confined within limits **3** ♦ : characterized by or resulting from careful and thorough consideration : DELIBERATE, CALCULATED

♦ [1] cadenced, metrical, rhythmic ♦ [2] definite, determinate, finite, limited, narrow, restricted ♦ [3] advised, calculated, deliberate, reasoned, studied, thoughtful, thought-out

mea·sure·less \-ləs\ *adj* **1** ♦ : having no observable limit **2** ♦ : very great ⟨had ∼ energy⟩

♦ [1, 2] boundless, endless, illimitable, immeasurable, indefinite, infinite, unbounded, unfathomable, unlimited

mea·sure·ment \'me-zhər-mənt, 'mā-\ *n* **1** : the act or process of measuring **2** ♦ : a figure, extent, or amount obtained by measuring

♦ dimension, extent, magnitude, measure, proportion, size

measure up *vb* **1** : to have necessary or fitting qualifications — often used with *to* **2** ♦ : to equal esp. in ability — used with *to*

♦ *usu* **measure up to** approach, approximate, compare, stack up

meat \'mēt\ *n* **1** ♦ : material taken into an organism and used for growth, repair, and vital processes and as a source of energy : FOOD; *esp* : solid food as distinguished from drink **2** : animal and esp. mammal flesh considered as food **3** : the edible part inside a covering (as a shell or rind) — **meaty** *adj*

♦ chow, fare, food, grub, provender, provisions, viands, victuals

meat·ball \-,bȯl\ *n* : a small ball of chopped or ground meat
meat loaf *n* : a dish of ground meat seasoned and baked in the form of a loaf
mec·ca \'me-kə\ *n, often cap* ♦ : a center of a specified activity or interest

♦ base, center (*or* centre), core, cynosure, eye, focus, heart, hub, nucleus, seat

mech *abbr* mechanical; mechanics
¹**me·chan·ic** \mi-'ka-nik\ *adj* : of or relating to manual work or skill
²**mechanic** *n* **1** : a manual worker **2** : MACHINIST; *esp* : one who repairs cars
me·chan·i·cal \mi-'ka-ni-kəl\ *adj* **1** : of or relating to machinery, manual operations, or mechanics **2** ♦ : done as if by a machine — **me·chan·i·cal·ly** \-k(ə-)lē\ *adv*

♦ automatic, involuntary, spontaneous

mechanical drawing *n* : drawing done with the aid of instruments
me·chan·ics \mi-'ka-niks\ *n sing or pl* **1** : a branch of physics that deals with energy and forces and their effect on bodies **2** : the practical application of mechanics (as to the operation of machines) **3** : mechanical or functional details
mech·a·nism \'me-kə-,ni-zəm\ *n* **1** : a piece of machinery; *also* : a process or technique for achieving a result **2** : mechanical operation or action **3** : the fundamental processes involved in or responsible for a natural phenomenon ⟨the visual ∼⟩
mech·a·nis·tic \,me-kə-'nis-tik\ *adj* **1** : mechanically determined ⟨∼ universe⟩ **2** : MECHANICAL — **mech·a·nis·ti·cal·ly** \-ti-k(ə-)lē\ *adv*
mech·a·nize \'me-kə-,nīz\ *vb* **-nized; -niz·ing** **1** : to make mechanical **2** : to equip with machinery esp. in order to replace human or animal labor **3** : to equip with armed and armored motor vehicles — **mech·a·ni·za·tion** \,me-kə-nə-'zā-shən\ *n* — **mech·a·niz·er** *n*
med *abbr* **1** medical; medicine **2** medieval **3** medium
MEd *abbr* master of education
med·al \'me-dᵊl\ *n* **1** : a small usu. metal object bearing a religious emblem or picture **2** : a piece of metal issued to commemorate a person or event or to award excellence or achievement
med·al·ist *or* **med·al·list** \'med-ᵊl-ist\ *n* **1** : a designer or maker of medals **2** : a recipient of a medal as an award
me·dal·lion \mə-'dal-yən\ *n* **1** : a large medal **2** : a tablet or panel bearing a portrait or an ornament
med·dle \'med-ᵊl\ *vb* **med·dled; med·dling** ♦ : to interfere without right or propriety

♦ butt in, interfere, intrude, mess, nose, obtrude, poke, pry, snoop

med·dler \'med-ᵊl-ər\ *n* ♦ : one that meddles

♦ busybody, interloper, intruder, kibitzer

med·dle·some \'med-ᵊl-səm\ *adj* ♦ : inclined to meddle

♦ intrusive, nosy, obtrusive, officious, presumptuous, prying

med·e·vac *also* **med·i·vac** \'me-də-ˌvak\ *n* **1** : emergency evacuation of the sick or wounded **2** : a helicopter used for medevac

me·dia \'mē-dē-ə\ *n, pl* **me·di·as 1** : MEDIUM 4 **2** *sing or pl in constr* : MASS MEDIA

me·di·al \'mē-dē-əl\ *adj* : occurring in or extending toward the middle

¹**me·di·an** \'mē-dē-ən\ *n* **1** : a value in an ordered set of values below and above which there are an equal number of values **2** : MEDIAN STRIP

²**median** *adj* **1** ♦ : being in the middle or in an intermediate position **2** ♦ : relating to or constituting a statistical median

♦ [1] halfway, intermediary, intermediate, medium, middle, midmost ♦ [2] average, middle, moderate, modest

median strip *n* : a strip dividing a highway into lanes according to the direction of travel

me·di·ate \'mē-dē-ˌāt\ *vb* **-at·ed; -at·ing 1** ♦ : to act as an intermediary; *esp* : to work with opposing sides in order to resolve (as a dispute) or bring about (as a settlement) **2** : to bring about, influence, or transmit (as a physical process or effect) by acting as an intermediate or controlling agent or mechanism — **me·di·a·tion** \ˌmē-dē-'ā-shən\ *n*

♦ intercede, interpose, intervene

me·di·a·tor \'mē-dē-ˌā-tər\ *n* ♦ : one that mediates

♦ arbiter, arbitrator, broker, go-between, intercessor, intermediary, middleman, peacemaker

med·ic \'me-dik\ *n* : one engaged in medical work; *esp* : CORPSMAN

med·i·ca·ble \'me-di-kə-bəl\ *adj* : CURABLE

Med·ic·aid \'me-di-ˌkād\ *n* : a program of financial assistance for medical care designed for those unable to afford regular medical service and financed jointly by the state and federal governments

med·i·cal \'me-di-kəl\ *adj* : of or relating to the science or practice of medicine or the treatment of disease — **med·i·cal·ly** \-k(ə-)lē\ *adv*

medical examiner *n* : a public officer who performs autopsies on bodies to find the cause of death

me·di·ca·ment \mi-'di-kə-mənt, 'me-di-kə-\ *n* : a substance used in therapy

Medi·care \'me-di-ˌker\ *n* : a government program of financial assistance for medical care esp. for the aged

med·i·cate \'me-də-ˌkāt\ *vb* **-cat·ed; -cat·ing** : to treat with medicine

med·i·ca·tion \ˌme-də-'kā-shən\ *n* **1** : the act or process of medicating **2** : a substance or preparation used in treating disease : MEDICINE

me·dic·i·nal \mə-'dis-ᵊn-əl\ *adj* : tending or used to cure disease or relieve pain — **me·dic·i·nal·ly** *adv*

med·i·cine \'me-də-sən\ *n* **1** ♦ : a substance or preparation used in treating disease **2** : a science and art dealing with the prevention, alleviation, and cure of disease

♦ cure, drug, pharmaceutical, remedy, specific

medicine ball *n* : a heavy stuffed leather ball used for conditioning exercises

medicine man *n* : a person esp. among Indigenous Americans believed to possess supernatural powers that can heal illnesses and keep away evil spirits

med·i·co \'me-di-ˌkō\ *n, pl* **-cos** : a medical practitioner or student

me·di·e·val *or* **me·di·ae·val** \ˌmē-dē-'ē-vəl, ˌme-, ˌmē-'dē-vəl\ *adj* **1** : of, relating to, or characteristic of the Middle Ages **2** : extremely outmoded or antiquated — **me·di·e·val·ism** \-və-ˌli-zəm\ *n* — **me·di·e·val·ist** \-list\ *n*

me·di·o·cre \ˌmē-dē-'ō-kər\ *adj* ♦ : of moderate or low quality — **me·di·oc·ri·ty** \-'ä-krə-tē\ *n*

♦ common, fair, indifferent, medium, middling, ordinary, passable, run-of-the-mill, second-rate, so-so

med·i·tate \'me-də-ˌtāt\ *vb* **-tat·ed; -tat·ing 1** ♦ : to muse over : CONTEMPLATE, PONDER **2** : to plan or project in the mind : INTEND — **med·i·ta·tion** \ˌme-də-'tā-shən\ *n*

♦ chew over, cogitate, consider, contemplate, debate, deliberate, entertain, mull, ponder, question, ruminate, study, think, weigh

med·i·ta·tive \'me-də-ˌtā-tiv\ *adj* **1** ♦ : marked by or conducive to meditation **2** ♦ : disposed or given to meditation — **med·i·ta·tive·ly** *adv*

♦ [1, 2] contemplative, melancholy, pensive, reflective, ruminant, thoughtful

Med·i·ter·ra·nean \ˌme-də-tə-'rā-nē-ən, -'rā-nyən\ *adj* : of or relating to the Mediterranean Sea or to the lands or people around it

¹**me·di·um** \'mē-dē-əm\ *n, pl* **mediums** *or* **me·dia** \-dē-ə\ **1 a** : something in a middle position **b** ♦ : a middle position or degree **2** ♦ : a means of effecting or conveying something **3** : a surrounding or enveloping substance **4** : a channel or system of communication, information, or entertainment **5** : a mode of artistic expression **6** : an individual held to be a channel of communication between the earthly world and a world of spirits **7** ♦ : a condition or environment in which something may function or flourish

♦ [1b] mean, middle, midpoint ♦ [2] agency, agent, instrument, instrumentality, machinery, means, organ, vehicle ♦ [7] atmosphere, climate, environment, environs, milieu, setting, surroundings

²**medium** *adj* ♦ : intermediate in amount, quality, position, or degree

♦ average, intermediate, median, middle, moderate, modest ♦ halfway, middle, midmost ♦ common, fair, indifferent, mediocre, middling, ordinary, passable, run-of-the-mill, second-rate, so-so

me·di·um·is·tic \ˌmē-dē-ə-'mis-tik\ *adj* : of, relating to, or being a spiritualistic medium

medivac *var of* MEDEVAC

med·ley \'med-lē\ *n, pl* **medleys 1** ♦ : a diverse assortment or mixture : HODGEPODGE **2** : a musical composition made up esp. of a series of songs

♦ assortment, clutter, jumble, mélange, miscellany, motley, muddle, variety, welter

me·dul·la \mə-'də-lə\ *n, pl* **-las** *or* **-lae** \-(ˌ)lē, -ˌlī\ : an inner or deep anatomical part; *also* : the posterior part (**medulla ob·lon·ga·ta** \-ˌä-ˌblȯŋ-'gä-tə\) of the vertebrate brain that is continuous with the spinal cord

meed \'mēd\ *n* : a fitting return

meek \'mēk\ *adj* **1** ♦ : characterized by patience and longsuffering **2** : deficient in spirit and courage **3** : MODERATE

♦ demure, humble, lowly, modest, retiring, unassuming, unpretentious

meek·ly \-lē\ *adv* ♦ : in a meek manner

♦ humbly, lowly, modestly, sheepishly

meek·ness \-nəs\ *n* ♦ : the quality or state of being meek

♦ humbleness, humility, lowliness, modesty

meer·schaum \'mir-shəm, -ˌshȯm\ *n* : a tobacco pipe made of a light white clayey mineral

¹**meet** \'mēt\ *vb* **met** \'met\; **meet·ing 1** ♦ : to come upon **2** : JOIN, INTERSECT **3** : to appear to the perception of **4** : OPPOSE, FIGHT **5 a** : to join in conversation or discussion **b** ♦ : to come together : ASSEMBLE **6** : to conform to ⟨∼s requirements⟩ **7** ♦ : to pay fully or fulfill the obligations of **8 a** : to contend successfully with : cope with **b** ♦ : to produce or provide a counterpart or equal to : MATCH **9** : to provide for **10** : to be introduced to

♦ [1] chance, encounter, happen, stumble ♦ [5b] assemble, cluster, collect, concentrate, conglomerate, congregate, convene, forgather, gather, rendezvous ♦ [7] answer, comply, fill, fulfill, keep, redeem, satisfy ♦ [8b] equal, match, tie

²**meet** *n* ♦ : an assembling esp. for a hunt or for competitive sports

♦ bout, competition, contest, event, game, match, tournament

³**meet** *adj* ♦ : precisely adapted to a particular situation, need, or circumstance : SUITABLE, PROPER

♦ applicable, appropriate, apt, felicitous, fit, fitting, good, happy, proper, right, suitable

meet·ing \'mē-tiŋ\ *n* **1** ♦ : the act or process of coming together : ASSEMBLY **2** ♦ : a point where things come together

♦ [1] assembly, conference, congress, convention, convocation, council, gathering, get-together, huddle, seminar ♦ [2] confluence, conjunction, convergence

meet·ing·house \-ˌhaús\ *n* : a building for public assembly and esp. for Protestant worship

meg \'meg\ *n* : MEGABYTE

mega- *or* **meg-** *comb form* **1** : great : large ⟨*mega*hit⟩ **2** : million ⟨*mega*hertz⟩

mega·byte \'me-gə-ˌbīt\ *n* : 1024 kilobytes or 1,048,576 bytes; *also* : one million bytes

mega·cy·cle \-ˌsī-kəl\ *n* : MEGAHERTZ

mega·death \-ˌdeth\ *n* : one million deaths — used as a unit in reference to nuclear warfare

mega·hertz \ˈme-gə-ˌhərts, -ˌherts\ *n* : a unit of frequency equal to one million hertz

mega·lith \ˈme-gə-ˌlith\ *n* : a large stone used in prehistoric monuments — **mega·lith·ic** \ˌme-gə-ˈli-thik\ *adj*

meg·a·lo·ma·nia \ˌme-gə-lō-ˈmā-nē-ə, -nyə\ *n* : a mental disorder marked by feelings of personal omnipotence and grandeur — **meg·a·lo·ma·ni·ac** \-ˈmā-nē-ˌak\ *adj or n*

meg·a·lop·o·lis \ˌme-gə-ˈlä-pə-ləs\ *n* : a very large urban unit

mega·phone \ˈme-gə-ˌfōn\ *n* : a cone-shaped device used to intensify or direct the voice — **megaphone** *vb*

mega·pix·el \-ˌpik-səl\ *n* : one million pixels

mega·plex \-ˌpleks\ *n* : a cineplex having usu. at least 16 movie theaters

mega·ton \-ˌtən\ *n* : an explosive force equivalent to that of one million tons of TNT

mega·vi·ta·min \-ˌvī-tə-mən\ *adj* : relating to or consisting of very large doses of vitamins — **mega·vi·ta·mins** *n pl*

meh \ˈme\ *interj* — used to express indifference or mild disappointment

mei·o·sis \mī-ˈō-səs\ *n* : a process of cell division in gametes producing cells in which the number of chromosomes is reduced to one half — **mei·ot·ic** \mī-ˈä-tik\ *adj*

meit·ner·i·um \mīt-ˈnir-ē-əm, -ˈner-\ *n* : an artificially produced radioactive chemical element

mel·an·cho·lia \ˌme-lən-ˈkō-lē-ə\ *n* : severe depression characterized esp. by profound sadness and despair

mel·an·chol·ic \ˌme-lən-ˈkä-lik\ *adj* **1** : DEPRESSED **2** : of or relating to melancholia

¹mel·an·choly \ˈme-lən-ˌkä-lē\ *n, pl* **-chol·ies** ♦ : depression of spirits : DEJECTION — **melancholy** *adj*

　　♦ blues, dejection, depression, desolation, despondency, doldrums, dumps, forlornness, gloom, heartsickness, sadness

²melancholy *adj* **1 a** : suggestive or expressive of melancholy **b** ♦ : causing or tending to cause sadness or depression of mind or spirit **2 a** ♦ : depressed in spirits **b** : musingly or dreamily thoughtful

　　♦ [1b] depressing, dismal, dreary, heartbreaking, pathetic, sad, sorry, tearful ♦ [2a] blue, depressed, down, downcast, glum, low, sad, unhappy

Mel·a·ne·sian \ˌme-lə-ˈnē-zhən\ *n* : a member of the dominant Indigenous group of the Pacific island grouping of Melanesia — **Melanesian** *adj*

mé·lange \mā-ˈläⁿzh, -ˈlänj\ *n* ♦ : a mixture esp. of incongruous elements

　　♦ assortment, clutter, jumble, medley, miscellany, motley, muddle, variety, welter

mel·a·nin \ˈme-lə-nən\ *n* : any of various dark brown pigments of animal or plant structures (as skin or hair)

mel·a·nism \ˈme-lə-ˌni-zəm\ *n* : an increased amount of black or nearly black pigmentation

mel·a·no·ma \ˌme-lə-ˈnō-mə\ *n, pl* **-mas** *also* **-ma·ta** \-mə-tə\ : a usu. malignant tumor containing dark pigment

¹meld \ˈmeld\ *vb* : to show or announce for a score in a card game

²meld *n* : a card or combination of cards that is or can be melded

³meld *n* : a product of blending : BLEND, MIXTURE

me·lee \ˈmā-ˌlā, mā-ˈlā\ *n* ♦ : a confused struggle

　　♦ brawl, fracas, fray, free-for-all, row

me·lio·rate \ˈmēl-yə-ˌrāt, ˈmē-lē-ə-\ *vb* **-rat·ed; -rat·ing** : to make or grow better : AMELIORATE — **me·lio·ra·tion** \ˌmēl-yə-ˈrā-shən, ˌmē-lē-ə-\ *n* — **me·lio·ra·tive** \ˈmēl-yə-ˌrā-tiv, ˈmē-lē-ə-\ *adj*

mel·lif·lu·ous \me-ˈli-flə-wəs, mə-\ *adj* ♦ : sweetly flowing — **mel·lif·lu·ous·ly** *adv* — **mel·lif·lu·ous·ness** *n*

　　♦ euphonious, lyric, mellow, melodic, melodious, musical

¹mel·low \ˈme-lō\ *adj* **1** : soft and sweet because of ripeness; *also* : well aged and pleasingly mild ⟨~ wine⟩ **2** : made gentle by age or experience **3** ♦ : being rich and full but not garish or strident ⟨~ colors⟩ **4** : of soft loamy consistency ⟨~ soil⟩ — **mel·low·ness** *n*

　　♦ balmy, benign, bland, delicate, gentle, light, mild, soft, soothing, tender

²mellow *vb* : to make or become mellow

me·lod·ic \mə-ˈlä-dik\ *adj* ♦ : relating to, containing, constituting, or made up of melody — **me·lod·i·cal·ly** \-di-k(ə-)lē\ *adv*

　　♦ euphonious, lyric, mellifluous, mellow, melodious, musical

me·lo·di·ous \mə-ˈlō-dē-əs\ *adj* ♦ : pleasing to the ear ⟨a ~ sound⟩ — **me·lo·di·ous·ly** *adv* — **me·lo·di·ous·ness** *n*

　　♦ lyric, mellifluous, mellow, melodic, musical ♦ euphonious, harmonious, musical, symphonic, tuneful

melo·dra·ma \ˈme-lə-ˌdrä-mə, -ˌdra-\ *n* **1** : an extravagantly theatrical play in which action and plot predominate over characterization **2** : something having a sensational or theatrical quality — **melo·dra·ma·tist** \ˌme-lə-ˈdra-mə-tist, -ˈdrä-\ *n*

melo·dra·mat·ic \ˌme-lə-drə-ˈma-tik\ *adj* **1** ♦ : of, relating to, or characteristic of melodrama **2** : appealing to the emotions — **melo·dra·mat·i·cal·ly** \-ti-k(ə-)lē\ *adv*

　　♦ dramatic, histrionic, theatrical

mel·o·dy \ˈme-lə-dē\ *n, pl* **-dies** **1** : sweet or agreeable sound **2** ♦ : a particular succession of notes : TUNE, AIR

　　♦ air, lay, song, strain, tune, warble

mel·on \ˈme-lən\ *n* : any of various typically sweet fruits (as a muskmelon or watermelon) of the gourd family usu. eaten raw

¹melt \ˈmelt\ *vb* **1** ♦ : to change from a solid to a liquid state usu. by heat **2 a** : DISSOLVE, DISINTEGRATE **b** ♦ : to disperse or disappear or cause to disperse or disappear as if melting **3** : to make or become tender or gentle

　　♦ [1] deliquesce, flux, fuse, liquefy, run, thaw ♦ [2b] disappear, dissolve, evaporate, fade, flee, go, vanish

²melt *n* : a melted substance

melt·down \ˈmelt-ˌdaún\ *n* **1** : the melting of the core of a nuclear reactor **2** : a rapid or disastrous decline or disaster

melting pot *n* : a place where different peoples, cultures, or individuals assimilate into a cohesive whole

melt·wa·ter \-ˌwȯ-tər, -ˌwä-\ *n* : water derived from the melting of ice and snow

mem *abbr* **1** member **2** memoir **3** memorial

mem·ber \ˈmem-bər\ *n* **1** : a part (as an arm, leg, leaf, or branch) of an animal or plant **2** : one of the individuals composing a group **3** ♦ : a constituent part of a whole

　　♦ component, constituent, element, factor, ingredient ♦ part, partition, portion, section, segment

mem·ber·ship \-ˌship\ *n* **1** : the state or status of being a member **2** : the body of members

mem·brane \ˈmem-ˌbrān\ *n* : a thin pliable layer esp. of animal or plant origin — **mem·bra·nous** \-brə-nəs\ *adj*

me·men·to \mə-ˈmen-tō\ *n, pl* **-tos** *or* **-toes** ♦ : something that serves to warn or remind; *also* : SOUVENIR

　　♦ keepsake, memorial, monument, remembrance, souvenir, token

memo \ˈme-mō\ *n, pl* **mem·os** : MEMORANDUM

mem·oir \ˈmem-ˌwär\ *n* **1** : MEMORANDUM **2** : AUTOBIOGRAPHY — usu. used in pl. **3** : an account of something noteworthy; *also, pl* : the record of the proceedings of a learned society

mem·o·ra·bil·ia \ˌme-mə-rə-ˈbi-lē-ə, -ˈbil-yə\ *n pl* : things worthy of remembrance; *also* : MEMENTOS

mem·o·ra·ble \ˈme-mə-rə-bəl\ *adj* : worth remembering : NOTABLE — **mem·o·ra·bil·i·ty** \ˌme-mə-rə-ˈbi-lə-tē\ *n* — **mem·o·ra·ble·ness** *n* — **mem·o·ra·bly** \-blē\ *adv*

mem·o·ran·dum \ˌme-mə-ˈran-dəm\ *n, pl* **-dums** *or* **-da** \-də\ **1** : an informal record or written reminder **2** ♦ : an informal written note

　　♦ directive, letter, missive, note, notice

¹me·mo·ri·al \mə-ˈmȯr-ē-əl\ *adj* : serving to preserve remembrance

²memorial *n* **1** ♦ : something designed to keep remembrance alive; *esp* : MONUMENT **2** : a statement of facts often accompanied with a petition — **me·mo·ri·al·ize** *vb*

　　♦ keepsake, memento, monument, remembrance, souvenir, token

Memorial Day *n* : the last Monday in May or formerly May 30 observed as a legal holiday in honor of those who died in war

mem·o·rise *chiefly Brit var of* MEMORIZE

mem·o·rize \ˈme-mə-ˌrīz\ *vb* **-rized; -riz·ing** ♦ : to learn by heart — **mem·o·ri·za·tion** \ˌme-mə-rə-ˈzā-shən\ *n* — **mem·o·riz·er** *n*

　　♦ learn, study *Ant* unlearn

mem·o·ry \ˈme-mə-rē\ *n, pl* **-ries** **1** ♦ : the power or process of remembering **2** : the store of things remembered **3** : COMMEMORATION **4** ♦ : something remembered **5** : the time within which past events are remembered **6** : a device (as in a computer) in which information can be stored

　　♦ [1, 4] recall, recollection, remembrance, reminiscence

men *pl of* MAN

¹**men·ace** \'me-nəs\ *n* **1** : THREAT **2 a** ♦ : one that represents a threat : DANGER **b** : NUISANCE

♦ danger, hazard, peril, pitfall, risk, threat, trouble

²**menace** *vb* **men·aced; men·ac·ing** **1** ♦ : to make a show of intention to harm : THREATEN **2** ♦ : to represent or pose a threat to : ENDANGER

♦ [1] hang, hover, overhang, threaten ♦ [2] adventure, compromise, endanger, gamble with, hazard, imperil, jeopardize, risk, venture

men·ac·ing *adj* ♦ : presenting, suggesting, or constituting a menace — **men·ac·ing·ly** *adv*

♦ baleful, dire, foreboding, ominous, portentous, sinister ♦ dangerous, grave, grievous, hazardous, parlous, perilous, risky, serious, unhealthy, unsafe, venturesome

mé·nage \mā-'näzh\ *n* : a domestic establishment : HOUSEHOLD

ménage à trois \-ä-'trwä\ *n* : an arrangement in which three persons share sexual relations esp. while living together

me·nag·er·ie \mə-'na-jə-rē\ *n* : a collection of wild animals esp. for exhibition

¹**mend** \'mend\ *vb* **1** : to improve in manners or morals **2** ♦ : to put into good shape : REPAIR **3** ♦ : to improve in or restore to health : HEAL — **mend·er** *n*

♦ [2] doctor, fix, patch, recondition, renovate, repair, revamp ♦ [3] convalesce, gain, heal, rally, recover, recuperate, snap back

²**mend** *n* **1** : an act of mending **2** : a mended place

men·da·cious \men-'dā-shəs\ *adj* ♦ : given to deception or falsehood : UNTRUTHFUL — **men·da·cious·ly** *adv*

♦ dishonest, lying

men·dac·i·ty \-'da-sə-tē\ *n* **1** : the quality or state of being mendacious **2** ♦ : an untrue statement made with intent to deceive : LIE

♦ fabrication, fairy tale, falsehood, falsity, fib, lie, prevarication, story, tale, untruth, whopper

men·de·le·vi·um \,men-də-'lē-vē-əm, -'lā-\ *n* : a radioactive chemical element artificially produced

men·di·cant \'men-di-kənt\ *n* **1** : BEGGAR **2** *often cap* : FRIAR — **men·di·can·cy** \-kən-sē\ *n* — **mendicant** *adj*

men·folk \'men-,fōk\ *or* **men·folks** \-,fōks\ *n pl* **1** : men in general **2** : the men of a family or community

men·ha·den \men-'hād-ᵊn, mən-\ *n, pl* **-den** *also* **-dens** : a marine fish related to the herring that is abundant along the Atlantic coast of the U.S.

¹**me·nial** \'mē-nē-əl, -nyəl\ *adj* **1** : of or relating to servants **2** : HUMBLE; *also* : SERVILE — **me·ni·al·ly** *adv*

²**menial** *n* ♦ : a domestic servant

♦ domestic, flunky, lackey, retainer, servant, steward

men·in·gi·tis \,me-nən-'jī-təs\ *n, pl* **-git·i·des** \-'ji-tə-,dēz\ : inflammation of the membranes enclosing the brain and spinal cord; *also* : a usu. bacterial disease marked by this

me·ninx \'mē-niŋks, 'me-\ *n, pl* **me·nin·ges** \mə-'nin-(,)jēz\ : any of the three membranes that envelop the brain and spinal cord — **men·in·ge·al** \,me-nən-'jē-əl\ *adj*

me·nis·cus \mə-'nis-kəs\ *n, pl* **me·nis·ci** \-'nis-,kī, -,kē\ *also* **me·nis·cus·es** **1** : CRESCENT **2** : the curved upper surface of a column of liquid

men·o·pause \'me-nə-,pöz\ *n* : the period of life when menstruation stops naturally — **men·o·paus·al** \,me-nə-'pö-zəl\ *adj*

me·no·rah \mə-'nōr-ə\ *n* : a candelabrum that is used in Jewish worship

men·ses \'men-,sēz\ *n sing or pl* : the menstrual flow

menstrual cycle *n* : the complete cycle of physiological changes from the beginning of one menstrual period to the beginning of the next

men·stru·a·tion \,men-strə-'wā-shən, men-'strā-\ *n* : a discharging of bloody matter at approximately monthly intervals from the uterus of breeding-age nonpregnant primate females; *also* : PERIOD 6 — **men·stru·al** \'men-strə-wəl\ *adj* — **men·stru·ate** \'men-strə-,wāt, -,strāt\ *vb*

men·su·ra·ble \'men-sə-rə-bəl, 'mench-ə-\ *adj* : MEASURABLE

men·su·ra·tion \,men-sə-'rā-shən, ,mench-ə-\ *n* : MEASUREMENT

-ment \mənt\ *n suffix* **1** : concrete result, object, or agent of a (specified) action ⟨embank*ment*⟩ ⟨entangle*ment*⟩ **2** : concrete means or instrument of a (specified) action ⟨entertain*ment*⟩ **3** : action : process ⟨encircle*ment*⟩ ⟨develop*ment*⟩ **4** : place of a

(specified) action ⟨encamp*ment*⟩ **5** : state : condition ⟨amaze*ment*⟩

men·tal \'ment-ᵊl\ *adj* **1** ♦ : of or relating to the mind **2** : of, relating to, or affected with a disorder of the mind ⟨∼ illness⟩ — **men·tal·ly** *adv*

♦ cerebral, inner, intellectual, psychological

mental age *n* : a measure of a child's mental development in terms of the number of years it takes an average child to reach the same level

mental deficiency *n* : INTELLECTUAL DISABILITY

men·tal·i·ty \men-'ta-lə-tē\ *n, pl* **-ties** **1** ♦ : mental power or capacity **2** : mode or way of thought

♦ brains, gray matter (*or* grey matter), intellect, intelligence, reason, sense

mental retardation *n, now often offensive* : INTELLECTUAL DISABILITY — **mentally retarded** *adj, now often offensive*

men·tee \men-'tē\ *n* : PROTÉGÉ

men·thol \'men-,thöl, -,thōl\ *n* : an alcohol occurring esp. in mint oils that has the odor and cooling properties of peppermint — **men·tho·lat·ed** \-thə-,lā-təd\ *adj*

¹**men·tion** \'men-chən\ *n* **1** : a brief or casual reference **2** : a formal citation for outstanding achievement

²**mention** *vb* **1** ♦ : to refer to : CITE **2** : to cite for superior achievement — **not to mention** : to say nothing of

♦ advert (to), cite, instance, name, note, notice, quote, refer (to), specify, touch (*on* or *upon*)

¹**men·tor** \'men-,tòr, -tər\ *n* : a trusted counselor or guide; *also* : TUTOR, COACH

²**mentor** *vb* ♦ : to serve as a mentor for

♦ coach, counsel, guide, lead, pilot, shepherd, show, tutor

menu \'men-yü, 'mān-\ *n, pl* **menus** **1** : a list of the dishes available (as in a restaurant) for a meal; *also* : the dishes served **2** ♦ : a list of offerings or options

♦ catalog, checklist, list, listing, register, registry, roll, roster, schedule, table

me·ow \mē-'aù\ *vb* : to make the characteristic cry of a cat — **meow** *n*

mer *abbr* meridian

mer·can·tile \'mər-kən-,tēl, -,tīl\ *adj* : of or relating to merchants or trading

¹**mer·ce·nary** \'mərs-ᵊn-,er-ē\ *n, pl* **-nar·ies** : a person who serves merely for wages; *esp* : a soldier hired into foreign service

²**mercenary** *adj* **1** ♦ : serving merely for pay or gain **2** : hired for service in a foreign army

♦ acquisitive, avaricious, avid, covetous, grasping, greedy, rapacious

mer·cer \'mər-sər\ *n, Brit* : a dealer in usu. expensive fabrics

mer·cer·ise *chiefly Brit var of* MERCERIZE

mer·cer·ize \'mər-sə-,rīz\ *vb* **-ized; -iz·ing** : to treat cotton yarn or cloth with alkali so that it looks silky or takes a better dye

¹**mer·chan·dise** \'mər-chən-,dīz, -,dīs\ *n* ♦ : the commodities or goods that are bought and sold in business

♦ commodities, wares

²**mer·chan·dise** \-,dīz\ *vb* **-dised; -dis·ing** ♦ : to buy and sell in business

♦ deal, market, put up, retail, sell, vend

mer·chan·dis·er *n* : one that buys and sells in business

mer·chant \'mər-chənt\ *n* **1** ♦ : a buyer and seller of commodities for profit **2** : STOREKEEPER

♦ dealer, trader, trafficker

mer·chant·able \'mər-chən-tə-bəl\ *adj* : acceptable to buyers : MARKETABLE

mer·chant·man \'mər-chənt-mən\ *n* : a ship used in commerce

merchant marine *n* : the commercial ships of a nation

merchant ship *n* : MERCHANTMAN

mer·ci·ful·ly \'mər-si-fə-lē\ *adv* **1** : in a merciful manner **2** : FORTUNATELY 2

mer·ci·less \'mər-si-ləs\ *adj* ♦ : having or showing no mercy — **mer·ci·less·ly** *adv*

♦ callous, hard, heartless, inhuman, inhumane, pitiless, soulless, unfeeling, unsympathetic

mer·cu·ri·al \,mər-'kyùr-ē-əl\ *adj* **1** ♦ : unpredictably changeable ⟨a ∼ personality⟩ **2** : MERCURIC — **mer·cu·ri·al·ly** *adv* — **mer·cu·ri·al·ness** *n*

♦ capricious, changeable, fickle, inconstant, unpredictable

mer·cu·ric \mər-'kyur-ik\ *adj* : of, relating to, or containing mercury

mercuric chloride *n* : a poisonous compound of mercury and chlorine used as an antiseptic and fungicide

mer·cu·ry \'mər-kyə-rē\ *n, pl* **-ries** **1** : a heavy silver-white liquid metallic chemical element used esp. in scientific instruments **2** *cap* : the planet nearest the sun

mer·cy \'mər-sē\ *n, pl* **mercies** **1** ♦ : compassion shown to an offender; *also* : imprisonment rather than death for first-degree murder **2** : a blessing resulting from divine favor or compassion; *also* : a fortunate circumstance **3** ♦ : compassionate treatment of those in distress — **mer·ci·ful** \-si-fəl\ *adj* — **mercy** *adj*

♦ [1] charity, clemency, leniency, quarter ♦ [3] boon, courtesy, favor (*or* favour), grace, indulgence, kindness, service, turn

mercy killing *n* : EUTHANASIA

¹mere \'mir\ *n* : LAKE, POOL

²mere *adj, superlative* **mer·est** **1** : being nothing more than ⟨a ∼ child⟩ **2** : not diluted : PURE

mere·ly \-lē\ *adv* ♦ : no more than

♦ but, just, only, simply

mer·e·tri·cious \mer-ə-'tri-shəs\ *adj* : tawdrily attractive; *also* : SPECIOUS — **mer·e·tri·cious·ly** *adv* — **mer·e·tri·cious·ness** *n*

mer·gan·ser \(,)mər-'gan-sər\ *n* : any of various fish-eating wild ducks with a usu. crested head and a slender bill hooked at the end and serrated along the margins

merge \'mərj\ *vb* **merged; merg·ing** **1** : to blend gradually **2** ♦ : to combine, unite, or coalesce into one

♦ amalgamate, blend, commingle, fuse, incorporate, integrate, intermingle, mingle, mix

merg·er \'mər-jər\ *n* **1** : the act or process of merging **2** : absorption by a corporation of one or more others

me·rid·i·an \mə-'ri-dē-ən\ *n* **1** ♦ : the highest point : CULMINATION **2** : any of the imaginary circles on the earth's surface passing through the north and south poles — **meridian** *adj*

♦ acme, apex, climax, crown, culmination, head, height, peak, pinnacle, summit, tip-top, top, zenith

me·ringue \mə-'raŋ\ *n* : a baked dessert topping of stiffly beaten egg whites and powdered sugar

me·ri·no \mə-'rē-nō\ *n, pl* **-nos** **1** : any of a breed of sheep noted for fine soft wool **2** : a fine soft fabric or yarn of wool or wool and cotton

¹mer·it \'mer-ət\ *n* **1** : laudable or blameworthy traits or actions **2** ♦ : a praiseworthy quality; *also* : character or conduct deserving reward or honor **3** *pl* : the intrinsic nature of a legal case; *also* : legal significance

♦ distinction, excellence, value, virtue ♦ account, valuation, value, worth

²merit *vb* ♦ : to be worthy of or entitled to or liable to : EARN, DESERVE

♦ deserve, earn, rate

mer·i·toc·ra·cy \mer-ə-'tä-krə-sē\ *n, pl* **-cies** : a system in which the talented are chosen and moved ahead based on their achievement; *also* : leadership by the talented

mer·i·to·ri·ous \mer-ə-'tōr-ē-əs\ *adj* ♦ : deserving honor or esteem — **mer·i·to·ri·ous·ly** *adv* — **mer·i·to·ri·ous·ness** *n*

♦ admirable, commendable, creditable, laudable, praiseworthy
♦ deserving, good, worthy

mer·lin \'mər-lən\ *n* : a small compact falcon of the northern hemisphere

mer·lot \mer-'lō, mər-\ *n* : a dry red wine made from a widely grown grape; *also* : the grape itself

mer·maid \'mər-,mād\ *n* : a legendary sea creature with a woman's upper body and a fish's tail

mer·man \-,man, -mən\ *n* : a legendary sea creature with a man's upper body and a fish's tail

mer·ri·ly \'mer-ə-lē\ *adv* ♦ : in a merry manner

♦ cheerfully, gaily, happily, heartily, jovially, mirthfully

mer·ri·ment \'mer-i-mənt\ *n* **1** ♦ : lighthearted gaiety or fun-making : HILARITY **2** ♦ : a lively celebration or party : FESTIVITY

♦ [1] cheer, cheerfulness, cheeriness, glee, hilarity, joviality, mirth ♦ [2] conviviality, festivity, gaiety, jollification, merry-making, revelry

mer·ry \'mer-ē\ *adj* **mer·ri·er; -est** **1** ♦ : full of gaiety or high spirits **2** : marked by festivity **3** : BRISK ⟨a ∼ pace⟩

♦ blithe, boon, festive, gleeful, jocund, jolly, jovial, mirthful, sunny

merry–go–round \'mer-ē-gō-,raund\ *n* **1** : a circular revolv-

ing platform with benches and figures of animals on which people sit for a ride **2** : a busy round of activities

mer·ry·mak·er \'mer-ē-,mā-kər\ *n* ♦ : one who engages in merrymaking

♦ celebrant, reveler, roisterer

mer·ry·mak·ing \'mer-ē-,mā-kiŋ\ *n* **1** ♦ : jovial or festive activity **2** : a festive occasion

♦ conviviality, festivity, gaiety, jollification, merriment, revelry

me·sa \'mā-sə\ *n* ♦ : a flat-topped hill with steep sides

♦ plateau, table, tableland

mes·cal \me-'skal, mə-\ *n* **1** : PEYOTE **2** : a usu. colorless liquor distilled from the leaves of an agave; *also* : this agave

mes·ca·line \'mes-kə-lən, -,lēn\ *n* : a hallucinatory alkaloid from the peyote cactus

mes·clun \'mes-klən\ *n* : a mixture of young tender greens; *also* : a salad made with mesclun

mesdames *pl of* MADAM *or of* MADAME *or of* MRS.

mesdemoiselles *pl of* MADEMOISELLE

¹mesh \'mesh\ *n* **1** : one of the openings between the threads or cords of a net; *also* : one of the similar spaces in a network **2** : the fabric of a net **3** : NETWORK **4** : working contact (as of the teeth of gears) ⟨in ∼⟩ **5** ♦ : a woven, knit, or knotted material of open texture with evenly spaced holes — **meshed** \'mesht\ *adj*

♦ net, network

²mesh *vb* **1** ♦ : to catch in or as if in a mesh **2** : to be in or come into mesh : ENGAGE **3** : to fit together properly

♦ enmesh, ensnare, entangle, entrap, snare, tangle, trap

mesh·work \'mesh-,wərk\ *n* : NETWORK

me·si·al \'mē-zē-əl, -sē-\ *adj* : of, relating to, or being the surface of a tooth that is closest to the middle of the front of the jaw

mes·mer·ise *chiefly Brit var of* MESMERIZE

mes·mer·ize \'mez-mə-,rīz\ *vb* **-ized; -iz·ing** ♦ : to dazzle or overcome by or as if by suggestion : HYPNOTIZE — **mes·mer·ic** \mez-'mer-ik\ *adj* — **mes·mer·ism** \'mez-mə-,ri-zəm\ *n*

♦ arrest, enchant, enthrall, fascinate, grip, hypnotize

Me·so·lith·ic \me-zə-'li-thik\ *adj* : of, relating to, or being a transitional period of the Stone Age between the Paleolithic and the Neolithic periods

me·so·sphere \'me-zə-,sfir\ *n* : a layer of the atmosphere between the stratosphere and the thermosphere

Me·so·zo·ic \me-zə-'zō-ik, ,mē-\ *adj* : of, relating to, or being the era of geologic history between the Paleozoic and the Cenozoic and extending from about 245 million years ago to about 65 million years ago — **Mesozoic** *n*

mes·quite \mə-'skēt, me-\ *n* : any of several spiny leguminous trees and shrubs chiefly of the southwestern U.S. with sugar-rich pods important as fodder; *also* : mesquite wood used esp. in grilling food

¹mess \'mes\ *n* **1 a** ♦ : a quantity of food **b** : enough food of a specified kind for a dish or meal ⟨a ∼ of beans⟩ **2** ♦ : a group of persons who regularly eat together; *also* : a meal eaten by such a group **3** : a place where meals are regularly served to a group **4** ♦ : a confused, dirty, or offensive state

♦ [1a, 2] board, chow, feed, meal, repast, table ♦ [4] chaos, confusion, disarray, disorder, disorganization, eyesore, havoc, hell, jumble, muddle, shambles

²mess *vb* **1** : to supply with meals; *also* : to take meals with a mess **2 a** ♦ : to make dirty or untidy — often used with *up* **b** ♦ : to become confused or in error — usu. used with *up* **3** ♦ : to interest oneself in what is not one's concern : INTERFERE, MEDDLE **4** : PUTTER, TRIFLE **5** ♦ : to handle or play with something esp. carelessly

♦ *often* **mess up** [2a] confuse, disorder, jumble, mix, muddle, rumple ♦ *usu* **mess up** [2b] bobble, botch, bungle, butcher, flub, foul up, fumble, mangle, screw up ♦ [3] butt in, interfere, intrude, meddle, nose, obtrude, poke, pry, snoop ♦ *usu* **mess with** [5] fiddle, fool, monkey, play, tamper, tinker

mes·sage \'me-sij\ *n* : a communication sent by one person to another — **message** *vb*

message board *n* : BULLETIN BOARD 2

mess around *vb* ♦ : to waste time

♦ fiddle, fool, monkey, play, potter, putter, trifle

messeigneurs *pl of* MONSEIGNEUR

mes·sen·ger \'mes-ᵊn-jər\ *n* ♦ : one who carries a message or does an errand

♦ courier, go-between, page, runner

messenger RNA *n* : an RNA that carries the code for a particular protein from DNA in the nucleus to a ribosome in the cytoplasm and acts as a template for the formation of that protein

Mes·si·ah \mə-'sī-ə\ *n* **1** : the expected king and deliverer of the Jews **2** : Jesus **3** *not cap* : a professed or accepted leader of a cause — **mes·si·an·ic** \,me-sē-'a-nik\ *adj*

messieurs *pl of* MONSIEUR

mess·i·ness \'me-sē-nəs\ *n* ♦ : the quality or state of being messy

♦ chaos, confusion, disarray, disorder, disorganization, havoc, hell, jumble, mess, muddle, muss, shambles, tumble, welter

mess·mate \'mes-,māt\ *n* : a member of a group who eat regularly together

Messrs. \'me-sərz\ *pl of* MR.

messy \'me-sē\ *adj* ♦ : marked by confusion, disorder, or dirt

♦ chaotic, confused, disheveled, disordered, muddled, sloppy, unkempt, untidy *Ant* neat, ordered, orderly, tidy

mes·ti·zo \me-'stē-zō\ *n, pl* **-zos** : a person of mixed blood

¹met *past and past part of* MEET

²met *abbr* metropolitan

me·tab·o·lism \mə-'ta-bə-,li-zəm\ *n* : the processes by which the substance of plants and animals incidental to life is built up and broken down; *also* : the processes by which a substance is handled in the living body ⟨~ of sugar⟩ — **met·a·bol·ic** \,me-tə-'bä-lik\ *adj* — **me·tab·o·lize** \mə-'ta-bə-,līz\ *vb*

me·tab·o·lite \-,līt\ *n* **1** : a product of metabolism **2** : a substance essential to the metabolism of a particular organism or to a metabolic process

meta·car·pal \,me-tə-'kär-pəl\ *n* : any of usu. five more or less elongated bones of the part of the hand or forefoot between the wrist and the bones of the digits — **metacarpal** *adj*

meta·car·pus \-'kär-pəs\ *n* : the part of the hand or forefoot that contains the metacarpals

met·al \'met-°l\ *n* **1** : any of various opaque, fusible, ductile, and typically lustrous substances that are good conductors of electricity and heat **2** : METTLE; *also* : the material out of which a person or thing is made — **me·tal·lic** \mə-'ta-lik\ *adj*

met·al·lur·gy \'met-°l-,ər-jē\ *n* : the science and technology of metals — **met·al·lur·gi·cal** \,met-°l-'ər-ji-kəl\ *adj* — **met·al·lur·gist** \'met-°l-,ər-jist\ *n*

met·al·ware \'met-°l-,war\ *n* : metal utensils for household use

met·al·work \-,wərk\ *n* : work and esp. artistic work made of metal — **met·al·work·er** \-,wər-kər\ *n* — **met·al·work·ing** *n*

meta·mor·phism \,me-tə-'mor-,fi-zəm\ *n* : a change in the structure of rock; *esp* : a change to a more compact and more highly crystalline form produced by pressure, heat, and water — **meta·mor·phic** \-'mor-fik\ *adj*

meta·mor·phose \,me-tə-'mor-,fōz, -,fōs\ *vb* **1** : to change into a different physical form esp. by supernatural means **2** ♦ : to change strikingly the appearance or character of

♦ convert, make over, transfigure, transform

meta·mor·pho·sis \,me-tə-'mor-fə-səs\ *n, pl* **-pho·ses** \-,sēz\ **1 a** : a change of physical form, structure, or substance esp. by supernatural means **b** ♦ : a striking alteration (as in appearance or character) **2** : a fundamental change in form and often habits of an animal accompanying the transformation of a larva into an adult

♦ changeover, conversion, transfiguration, transformation

met·a·phor \'me-tə-,fȯr\ *n* : a figure of speech in which a word for one idea or thing is used in place of another to suggest a likeness between them (as in "the ship plows the sea") — **met·a·phor·ic** \,me-tə-'fȯr-ik\ *or* **met·a·phor·i·cal** \,me-tə-'fȯr-i-kəl\ *adj* — **met·a·phor·i·cal·ly** \-i-k(ə-)lē\ *adv*

meta·phys·i·cal \,me-tə-'fi-zi-kəl\ *adj* **1** : of or relating to metaphysics **2** ♦ : of or relating to the transcendent or to a reality beyond what is perceptible to the senses

♦ preternatural, superhuman, supernatural, unearthly

meta·phys·ics \,me-tə-'fi-ziks\ *n pl* : the philosophical study of the ultimate causes and underlying nature of things — **meta·phy·si·cian** \-fə-'zi-shən\ *n*

me·tas·ta·sis \mə-'tas-tə-səs\ *n, pl* **-ta·ses** \-,sēz\ : the spread of a health-impairing agency (as cancer cells) from the initial or primary site of disease to another part of the body; *also* : a secondary growth of a malignant tumor — **me·tas·ta·size** \-tə-,sīz\ *vb* — **met·a·stat·ic** \,me-tə-'sta-tik\ *adj*

meta·tar·sal \,me-tə-'tär-səl\ *n* : any of the bones of the foot between the tarsus and the bones of the digits that in humans include five elongated bones — **metatarsal** *adj*

meta·tar·sus \-'tär-səs\ *n* : the part of the human foot or the hind foot in quadrupeds that contains the metatarsals

¹mete \'mēt\ *vb* **met·ed; met·ing** **1** *archaic* : MEASURE **2** ♦ : to give out by measure — usu. used with *out*

♦ *usu* mete out administer, allocate, apportion, deal, dispense, distribute, parcel, portion, prorate

²mete *n* : BOUNDARY ⟨~s and bounds⟩

me·te·or \'mē-tē-ər, -,ȯr\ *n* **1** : a small particle of matter in the solar system directly observable only by its glow from frictional heating on falling into the earth's atmosphere **2** : the streak of light produced by a meteor

me·te·or·ic \,mē-tē-'ȯr-ik\ *adj* **1** : of, relating to, or resembling a meteor **2** : transiently brilliant ⟨a ~ career⟩ — **me·te·or·i·cal·ly** \-i-k(ə-)lē\ *adv*

me·te·or·ite \'mē-tē-ə-,rīt\ *n* : a meteor that reaches the surface of the earth

me·te·or·oid \'mē-tē-ə-,rȯid\ *n* : a small particle of matter in the solar system

me·te·o·rol·o·gy \,mē-tē-ə-'rä-lə-jē\ *n* : a science that deals with the atmosphere and its phenomena and esp. with weather forecasting — **me·te·o·ro·log·ic** \,mē-tē-,ȯr-ə-'lä-jik\ *or* **me·te·o·ro·log·i·cal** \-'lä-ji-kəl\ *adj* — **me·te·o·rol·o·gist** \,mē-tē-ə-'rä-lə-jist\ *n*

¹me·ter *or Can and Brit* **metre** \'mē-tər\ *n* ♦ : rhythm in verse or music

♦ beat, cadence, measure, rhythm

²meter *or Can and Brit* **metre** *n* : the basic metric unit of length

³meter *n* : a measuring and sometimes recording instrument

⁴meter *vb* **1** : to measure by means of a meter **2** : to print postal indicia on by means of a postage meter ⟨~ed mail⟩

meter–kilogram–second *or Can and Brit* **metre–kilogram–second** *adj* : of, relating to, or being a system of units based on the meter, the kilogram, and the second

meter maid *n* : a woman assigned to write tickets for parking violations

meth·a·done \'me-thə-,dōn\ *also* **meth·a·don** \-,dän\ *n* : a synthetic addictive narcotic drug used esp. as a substitute narcotic in the treatment of heroin addiction

meth·am·phet·amine \,me-tham-'fe-tə-,mēn, -thəm-, -mən\ *n* : a drug used medically in the form of its hydrochloride in the treatment of obesity and often illicitly as a stimulant

meth·ane \'me-,thān\ *n* : a colorless odorless flammable gas produced by decomposition of organic matter or from coal and used esp. as a fuel

meth·a·nol \'me-thə-,nȯl, -,nōl\ *n* : a volatile flammable poisonous liquid alcohol used esp. as a solvent and as an antifreeze

meth·aqua·lone \me-'tha-kwə-,lōn\ *n* : a sedative and hypnotic habit-forming drug that is not a barbiturate

meth·od \'me-thəd\ *n* ♦ : a procedure or process for achieving an end **2** : orderly arrangement : PLAN

♦ approach, fashion, form, manner, strategy, style, system, tack, tactics, technique, way

meth·od·i·cal \mə-'thä-di-kəl\ *adj* **1** ♦ : arranged, characterized by, or performed with method or order ⟨a ~ treatment of the subject⟩ **2** : habitually proceeding according to method ⟨~ in his daily routine⟩ — **meth·od·i·cal·ly** \-k(ə-)lē\ *adv* — **meth·od·i·cal·ness** *n*

♦ orderly, regular, systematic *Ant* disorganized, haphazard, irregular, unsystematic

meth·od·ise *chiefly Brit var of* METHODIZE

Meth·od·ist \'me-thə-dist\ *n* : a member of a Protestant denomination adhering to the doctrines of John Wesley — **Meth·od·ism** \-,di-zəm\ *n*

meth·od·ize \'me-thə-,dīz\ *vb* **-ized; -iz·ing** : SYSTEMATIZE

meth·od·ol·o·gy \,me-thə-'dä-lə-jē\ *n, pl* **-gies** **1** : a body of methods and rules followed in a science or discipline **2** : the study of the principles or procedures of inquiry in a particular field

meth·yl \'me-thəl\ *n* : a chemical radical consisting of carbon and hydrogen

methyl alcohol *n* : METHANOL

meth·yl·mer·cu·ry \,me-thəl-'mər-kyə-rē\ *n* : any of various toxic compounds of mercury that often occur as pollutants which accumulate in animals esp. at the top of a food chain

me·tic·u·lous \mə-'ti-kyə-ləs\ *adj* ♦ : extremely careful in attending to details — **me·tic·u·lous·ly** *adv* — **me·tic·u·lous·ness** *n*

♦ careful, conscientious, fussy, painstaking

me·tic·u·lous·ness \mə-'ti-kyə-ləs-nəs\ *n* ♦ : the quality or state of being meticulous

♦ care, carefulness, heed, heedfulness, pains, scrupulousness

mé·tier \'me-ˌtyā, me-'tyā\ *n* : an area of activity in which one is expert or successful

me·tre \'mē-tər\ *Can and Brit var of* ¹METER, ²METER

met·ric \'me-trik\ *adj* **1** : of or relating to measurement; *esp* : of or relating to the metric system **2** : METRICAL 1

met·ri·cal \'me-tri-kəl\ *adj* **1** ♦ : of, relating to, or composed in meter **2** : of or relating to measure and esp. the metric system — **met·ri·cal·ly** \-k(ə-)lē\ *adv*

♦ cadenced, measured, rhythmic

met·ri·ca·tion \ˌme-tri-'kā-shən\ *n* : the act or process of converting into or expressing in the metric system

met·ri·cize \'me-trə-ˌsīz\ *vb* **-cized; -ciz·ing** : to change into or express in the metric system

metric system *n* : a decimal system of weights and measures based on the meter and on the kilogram

metric ton *n* : a metric unit of weight equal to 1,000 kilograms

¹**met·ro** \'me-trō\ *n, pl* **metros** : SUBWAY

²**metro** *adj* : of, relating to, or characteristic of a metropolis and sometimes including its suburbs

met·ro·nome \'me-trə-ˌnōm\ *n* : an instrument for marking exact time by a regularly repeated tick

me·trop·o·lis \mə-'trä-pə-ləs\ *n* ♦ : the chief or capital city of a country, state, or region; *also* : a large important city — **met·ro·pol·i·tan** \ˌme-trə-'pä-lət-ᵊn\ *adj*

♦ city, municipality

met·tle \'met-ᵊl\ *n* **1** : SPIRIT, COURAGE **2** : quality of temperament

met·tle·some \'met-ᵊl-səm\ *adj* ♦ : full of mettle

♦ fiery, high-spirited, peppery, spirited, spunky

MeV *abbr* million electron volts

¹**mew** \'myü\ *vb* : MEOW — **mew** *n*

²**mew** *vb* : CONFINE

mews \'myüz\ *n sing or pl, chiefly Brit* : stables usu. with living quarters built around a court; *also* : a narrow street with dwellings converted from stables

Mex *abbr* Mexican; Mexico

Mex·i·can \'mek-si-kən\ *n* : a native or inhabitant of Mexico — **Mexican** *adj*

mez·za·nine \'mez-ᵊn-ˌēn, ˌmez-ᵊn-'ēn\ *n* **1** : a low-ceilinged story between two main stories of a building **2** : the lowest balcony in a theater; *also* : the first few rows of such a balcony

mez·zo for·te \ˌmet-(ˌ)sō-'fȯr-ˌtā, ˌmed-(ˌ)zō-, -tē\ *adj or adv* : moderately loud — used as a direction in music

mez·zo pia·no \-pē-'ä-(ˌ)nō\ *adj or adv* : moderately soft — used as a direction in music

mez·zo–so·pra·no \-sə-'pra-nō, -'prä-\ *n* : a woman's voice having a range between that of the soprano and contralto; *also* : a singer having such a voice

MFA *abbr* master of fine arts

mfr *abbr* manufacture; manufacturer

mg *abbr* milligram

Mg *symbol* magnesium

MG *abbr* **1** machine gun **2** major general **3** military government

mgr *abbr* **1** manager **2** monseigneur **3** monsignor

mgt *or* **mgmt** *abbr* management

MGy Sgt *abbr* master gunnery sergeant

MHz *abbr* megahertz

mi *abbr* **1** mile; mileage **2** mill

MI *abbr* **1** Michigan **2** military intelligence

MIA \ˌem-(ˌ)ī-'ā\ *n* : a member of the armed forces whose whereabouts following a combat mission are unknown

Mi·ami \mī-'a-mē, -mə\ *n, pl* **Mi·ami** *or* **Mi·am·is** : a member of an Indigenous people orig. of Wisconsin, Illinois, and Indiana

mi·as·ma \mī-'az-mə, mē-\ *n, pl* **-mas** *also* **-ma·ta** \-mə-tə\ **1** : a vapor from a swamp formerly believed to cause disease **2** : a harmful influence or atmosphere ⟨a ~ of smog⟩ — **mi·as·mal** \-məl\ *adj* — **mi·as·mic** \-mik\ *adj*

mic \'mik\ *n* : MICROPHONE

Mic *abbr* Micah

mi·ca \'mī-kə\ *n* : any of various mineral silicates readily separable into thin transparent sheets

Mi·cah \'mī-kə\ *n* : a book of Jewish and Christian Scripture

mice *pl of* MOUSE

Mich *abbr* Michigan

Mi·che·as \'mī-kē-əs, mī-'kē-əs\ *n* : MICAH

Micmac *var of* MI'KMAQ

micr- *or* **micro-** *comb form* **1** : small : minute ⟨*micro*capsule⟩ **2** : one millionth part of a specified unit ⟨*micro*second⟩

¹**mi·cro** \'mī-krō\ *adj* **1** : very small; *esp* : MICROSCOPIC **2** : involving minute quantities or variations

²**micro** *n, pl* **mi·cros** : MICROCOMPUTER

mi·crobe \'mī-ˌkrōb\ *n* : MICROORGANISM; *esp* : one causing disease — **mi·cro·bi·al** \mī-'krō-bē-əl\ *adj*

mi·cro·bi·ol·o·gy \ˌmī-krō-bī-'ä-lə-jē\ *n* : a branch of biology dealing esp. with microscopic forms of life — **mi·cro·bi·o·log·i·cal** \-ˌbī-ə-'lä-ji-kəl\ *adj* — **mi·cro·bi·ol·o·gist** \-bī-'ä-lə-jist\ *n*

mi·cro·brew·ery \'mī-krō-ˌbrü-ə-rē\ *n* : a small brewery making specialty beer in limited quantities

mi·cro·burst \-ˌbərst\ *n* : a violent short-lived localized downdraft that creates extreme wind shears at low altitudes

mi·cro·cap·sule \'mī-krō-ˌkap-səl, -ˌsül\ *n* : a tiny capsule containing material (as a medicine) released when the capsule is broken, melted, or dissolved

mi·cro·chip \-ˌchip\ *n* : INTEGRATED CIRCUIT

mi·cro·cir·cuit \-ˌsər-kət\ *n* : a compact electronic circuit

mi·cro·com·put·er \-kəm-ˌpyü-tər\ *n* : a small computer that uses a microprocessor; *esp* : PERSONAL COMPUTER

mi·cro·cosm \'mī-krə-ˌkä-zəm\ *n* : an individual or community thought of as a miniature world or universe

mi·cro·elec·tron·ics \ˌmī-krō-i-ˌlek-'trä-niks\ *n* : a branch of electronics that deals with the miniaturization of electronic circuits and components — **mi·cro·elec·tron·ic** \-nik\ *adj*

mi·cro·en·cap·su·late \ˌmī-krō-in-'kap-sə-ˌlāt\ *vb* : to enclose (as a drug) in a microcapsule — **mi·cro·en·cap·su·la·tion** \-in-ˌkap-sə-'lā-shən\ *n*

mi·cro·fiber \'mī-krō-ˌfī-bər\ *n* : a fine usu. soft polyester fiber; *also* : a fabric made from such fibers

mi·cro·fiche \'mī-krō-ˌfēsh, -ˌfish\ *n, pl* **-fiche** *or* **-fiches** *same or* -ˌfē-shəz, -ˌfi-\ : a sheet of microfilm containing rows of images of pages of printed matter

mi·cro·film \-ˌfilm\ *n* : a film bearing a photographic record (as of print) on a reduced scale — **microfilm** *vb*

mi·cro·graph \'mī-krə-ˌgraf\ *n* : a graphic reproduction of the image of an object formed by a microscope

mi·cro·man·age \ˌmī-krō-'ma-nij\ *vb* : to manage esp. with excessive control or attention to details — **mi·cro·man·age·ment** \-mənt\ *n* — **mi·cro·man·ag·er** \-ni-jər\ *n*

mi·cro·me·te·or·ite \ˌmī-krō-'mē-tē-ə-ˌrīt\ *n* : a very small particle in interplanetary space

mi·crom·e·ter \mī-'krä-mə-tər\ *n* : an instrument used with a telescope or microscope for measuring minute distances

mi·cro·min·ia·tur·iza·tion \ˌmī-krō-ˌmi-nē-ə-ˌchúr-ə-'zā-shən, -ˌmi-ni-ˌchúr-, -ˌchər-\ *n* : the process of producing things in a very small size and esp. in a size smaller than one considered miniature — **mi·cro·min·ia·tur·ized** \-'mi-nē-ə-chə-ˌrīzd, -'mi-ni-chə-\ *adj*

mi·cron \'mī-ˌkrän\ *n* : one millionth of a meter

mi·cro·or·gan·ism \ˌmī-krō-'ȯr-gə-ˌni-zəm\ *n* : an organism (as a bacterium) too tiny to be seen by the unaided eye

mi·cro·phone \'mī-krə-ˌfōn\ *n* : an instrument for converting sound waves into variations of an electric current for transmitting or recording sound

mi·cro·pho·to·graph \ˌmī-krə-'fō-tə-ˌgraf\ *n* : PHOTOMICROGRAPH

mi·cro·pro·ces·sor \ˌmī-krō-'prä-ˌse-sər\ *n* : a computer processor contained on a microchip

mi·cro·scope \'mī-krə-ˌskōp\ *n* : an instrument for making magnified images of minute objects usu. using light — **mi·cros·co·py** \mī-'kräs-kə-pē\ *n*

mi·cro·scop·ic \ˌmī-krə-'skä-pik\ *also* **mi·cro·scop·i·cal** \-pi-kəl\ *adj* **1** : of, relating to, or involving the use of the microscope **2 a** : too tiny to be seen without the use of a microscope **b** ♦ : very small — **mi·cro·scop·i·cal·ly** \-pi-k(ə-)lē\ *adv*

♦ atomic, infinitesimal, miniature, minute, teeny, tiny, wee

mi·cro·sec·ond \'mī-krō-ˌse-kənd\ *n* : one millionth of a second

mi·cro·sur·gery \ˌmī-krō-'sər-jə-rē\ *n* : minute dissection or manipulation (as by a laser beam) of living structures or tissue — **mi·cro·sur·gi·cal** \-'sər-ji-kəl\ *adj*

mi·cro·tech·nol·o·gy \-tek-'nä-lə-jē\ *n* : technology on a small or microscopic scale

¹**mi·cro·wave** \'mī-krə-ˌwāv\ *n* **1** : a radio wave between one millimeter and one meter in wavelength **2** : MICROWAVE OVEN

²**microwave** *vb* : to heat or cook in a microwave oven — **mi·cro·wav·able** *or* **mi·cro·wave·able** \ˌmī-krə-'wā-və-bəl\ *adj*

microwave oven *n* : an oven in which food is cooked by the absorption of microwave energy by water molecules in the food

¹**mid** \'mid\ *adj* : occupying a middle position : MIDDLE

²**mid** *abbr* middle

mid·air \'mid-'ar\ *n* : a point or region in the air well above the ground

mid·day \'mid-,dā, -'dā\ *n* ♦ : the middle part of the day

♦ noon, noontime

mid·den \'mid-ᵊn\ *n* : a refuse heap

¹**mid·dle** \'mid-ᵊl\ *adj* **1** ♦ : equally distant from the extremes **2** ♦ : being at neither extreme : INTERMEDIATE **3** *cap* : constituting an intermediate period

♦ [1, 2] central, halfway, intermediary, intermediate, median, medium, midmost *Ant* extreme, farthest, furthest, outermost
♦ [1, 2] average, intermediate, moderate, modest

²**middle** *n* **1** ♦ : a middle part, point, or position **2** ♦ : the central portion of the human body : WAIST **3** ♦ : the position of being among or in the midst of something ⟨caught in the ∼ of their conflict⟩

♦ [1] mean, medium, midpoint ♦ [2] midriff, waist ♦ [3] deep, depth, height, midst, thick

middle age *n* : the period of life from about 45 to about 64 — **mid·dle–aged** \,mid-ᵊl-'ājd\ *adj*

Middle Ages *n pl* : the period of European history from about A.D. 500 to about 1500

mid·dle·brow \'mid-ᵊl-,braù\ *n* : a person who is moderately but not highly cultivated — **middlebrow** *adj*

middle class *n* : a social class holding a position between the upper class and the lower class — **middle–class** *adj*

middle ear *n* : a small membrane-lined cavity of the ear through which sound waves are transmitted by a chain of tiny bones

middle finger *n* : the midmost of the five digits of the hand

mid·dle·man \'mid-ᵊl-,man\ *n* **1** ♦ : an intermediary or agent between two parties **2** : one who is intermediate between the producer of goods and the retailer or consumer

♦ arbiter, arbitrator, go-between, intercessor, intermediary, mediator, peacemaker

middle–of–the–road *adj* : standing for or following a course of action midway between extremes; *esp* : being neither liberal nor conservative in politics — **mid·dle–of–the–road·er** \-'rō-dər\ *n* — **mid·dle–of–the–road·ism** \-'rō-,di-zəm\ *n*

middle school *n* : a school usu. including grades 5 to 8 or 6 to 8

mid·dle·weight \'mid-ᵊl-,wāt\ *n* : one of average weight; *esp* : a boxer weighing not over 160 pounds

mid·dling \'mid-liŋ, -lən\ *adj* **1** ♦ : of middle, medium, or moderate size, degree, or quality **2** ♦ : of moderate or low quality, value, ability, or performance : MEDIOCRE

♦ common, fair, indifferent, mediocre, medium, ordinary, passable, run-of-the-mill, second-rate, so-so

mid·dy \'mi-dē\ *n, pl* **middies** : MIDSHIPMAN

midge \'mij\ *n* : a very small fly : GNAT

midg·et \'mi-jət\ *n* **1** ♦ : something (as an animal) very small for its kind **2** *sometimes offensive* : a very small person

♦ dwarf, mite, peewee, pygmy, runt

midi \'mi-dē\ *n* : a calf-length dress, coat, or skirt

MIDI \'mi-dē\ *n* : a protocol for the transmission of digitally encoded music

mid·land \'mid-lənd, -,land\ *n* : the interior or central region of a country

mid·life \'mid-'līf\ *n* : MIDDLE AGE

midlife crisis *n* : a period of emotional turmoil in middle age characterized esp. by a strong desire for change

mid·most \-,mōst\ *adj* ♦ : being in or near the exact middle — **midmost** *adv*

♦ halfway, intermediary, intermediate, median, medium, middle

mid·night \-,nīt\ *n* : 12 o'clock at night

mid–ocean ridge \'mid-'ō-shən-\ *n* : an elevation on an ocean floor at the boundary of diverging tectonic plates

mid·point \'mid-,point, -'point\ *n* ♦ : a point at or near the center or middle

♦ mean, medium, middle ♦ center (*or* centre), core, midst

mid·riff \'mi-,drif\ *n* **1** : DIAPHRAGM 1 **2** ♦ : the mid-region of the human torso

♦ middle, waist

mid·sec·tion \-,sek-shən\ *n* : a section midway between the extremes; *esp* : MIDRIFF 2

mid·ship·man \'mid-,ship-mən, (,)mid-'ship-\ *n* : a student in a naval academy

mid·ships \-,ships\ *adv* : AMIDSHIPS

¹**midst** \'midst\ *n* **1** ♦ : the interior or central part or point **2** : a

position of proximity to the members of a group ⟨in our ∼⟩ **3** ♦ : the condition of being surrounded or beset

♦ [1] center (*or* centre), core, midpoint ♦ [3] deep, depth, height, middle, thick

²**midst** *prep* ♦ : in the midst of

♦ amid, among, through

mid·stream \'mid-'strēm, -,strēm\ *n* : the middle of a stream

mid·sum·mer \-'sə-mər, -,sə-\ *n* **1** : the middle of summer **2** : the summer solstice

mid·town \'mid-,taùn, -'taùn\ *n* : a central section of a city; *esp* : one situated between sections called *downtown* and *uptown* — **midtown** *adj*

¹**mid·way** \'mid-,wā, -'wā\ *adv* : in the middle of the way or distance

²**mid·way** \-,wā\ *n* : an avenue (as at a carnival) for concessions and amusements

mid·week \-,wēk\ *n* : the middle of the week — **mid·week·ly** \-,wē-klē, -'wē-\ *adj or adv*

mid·wife \'mid-,wīf\ *n* : a person who helps women in childbirth — **mid·wife·ry** \-,wī-fə-rē\ *n*

mid·win·ter \'mid-'win-tər, -,win-\ *n* **1** : the winter solstice **2** : the middle of winter

mid·year \-,yir\ *n* **1** : the middle of a year **2** : a midyear examination — **midyear** *adj*

mien \'mēn\ *n* **1** : air or bearing esp. as expressive of mood or personality : DEMEANOR **2** ♦ : outward aspect : APPEARANCE

♦ appearance, aspect, look, presence

miff \'mif\ *vb* : to put into an ill humor

¹**might** \'mīt\ *verbal auxiliary, past of* MAY — used as an auxiliary to express permission or possibility in the past, a present condition contrary to fact, less probability or possibility than *may*, or as a polite alternative to *may, ought*, or *should*

²**might** *n* ♦ : the power, authority, or resources of an individual or a group

♦ energy, force, main, muscle, potency, power, sinew, strength, vigor (*or* vigour)

might·i·ly \'mī-tə-lē\ *adv* **1** ♦ : in a mighty manner ⟨applauded ∼⟩ **2** ♦ : very much ⟨depressed me ∼⟩

♦ [1] energetically, firmly, forcefully, forcibly, hard, powerfully, stiffly, stoutly, strenuously, strongly, sturdily, vigorously
♦ [2] especially, extremely, greatly, highly, hugely, mighty, mortally, most, much, real, right, so, very

¹**mighty** \'mī-tē\ *adj* **might·i·er; -est 1** ♦ : very strong : POWERFUL **2** : GREAT, NOTABLE — **might·i·ness** \-tē-nəs\ *n*

♦ important, influential, potent, powerful, significant, strong

²**mighty** *adv* : to a high degree

mi·gnon·ette \,min-yə-'net\ *n* : an annual garden herb with spikes of tiny fragrant flowers

mi·graine \'mī-,grān\ *n* : a condition marked by recurrent severe headache and often nausea; *also* : an attack of migraine

mi·grant \'mī-grənt\ *n* ♦ : one that migrates; *esp* : a person who moves in order to find work (as picking crops) — **migrant** *adj*

♦ emigrant, émigré, immigrant, settler

mi·grate \'mī-,grāt\ *vb* **mi·grat·ed; mi·grat·ing 1** : to move from one country or place to another **2** : to pass usu. periodically from one region or climate to another for feeding or breeding — **mi·gra·tion** \mī-'grā-shən\ *n* — **mi·gra·to·ry** \'mī-grə-,tōr-ē\ *adj*

mi·ka·do \mə-'kä-dō\ *n, pl* **-dos** : an emperor of Japan

mike \'mīk\ *n* : MICROPHONE

Mi'k·maq *or* **Mic·mac** \'mik-mak\ *n pl* **Mi'kmaq** *or* **Mi'k·maqs** *or* **Micmac** *or* **Mic·macs** : a member of a First Nations people of eastern Canada; *also* : their language

¹**mil** \'mil\ *n* : a unit of length equal to ¹/₁₀₀₀ inch

²**mil** *abbr* military

milch \'milk, 'milch\ *adj* : giving milk ⟨∼ cow⟩

mild \'mī(-ə)ld\ *adj* **1** ♦ : gentle in nature or behavior **2** : moderate in action or effect **3** ♦ : not severe : TEMPERATE — **mild·ly** *adv* — **mild·ness** *n*

♦ [1] balmy, benign, bland, delicate, gentle, light, mellow, soft, soothing, tender ♦ [3] balmy, clement, equable, gentle, moderate, temperate

mil·dew \'mil-,dü, -,dyü\ *n* : a superficial usu. whitish growth produced on organic matter and on plants by a fungus; *also* : a fungus producing this growth — **mildew** *vb*

mile \'mī(-ə)l\ *n* **1** : a unit of length equal to 5280 ft. **2** : NAUTICAL MILE

mile·age \'mī-lij\ *n* **1** : an allowance for traveling expenses at a certain rate per mile **2 :** distance in miles traveled (as in a day) **3 :** the amount of service yielded (as by a tire) expressed in terms of miles of travel **4 :** the average number of miles a motor vehicle will travel on a gallon of gasoline

mile·post \'mī(-ə)l-ˌpōst\ *n* : a post indicating the distance in miles from a given point

mile·stone \-ˌstōn\ *n* **1 :** a stone serving as a milepost **2 :** a significant point in development

mi·lieu \mēl-'yər, -'yü, -'yœ\ *n, pl* **mi·lieus** *or* **mi·lieux** *same or* -'yərz, -'yüz, -'yœz\ ♦ : the physical or social setting in which something occurs or develops : ENVIRONMENT, SETTING

♦ atmosphere, climate, environment, environs, medium, setting, surroundings

mil·i·tan·cy \'mi-lə-tən-sē\ *n* ♦ : the quality or state of being militant

♦ aggression, aggressiveness, belligerence, fight, pugnacity, truculence

¹**mil·i·tant** \'mi-lə-tənt\ *adj* **1 a :** engaged in warfare **b :** prone to fighting **2** ♦ : aggressively active esp. in a cause — **mil·i·tance** \-təns\ *n* — **mil·i·tant·ly** *adv*

♦ [1b] aggressive, argumentative, bellicose, belligerent, combative, contentious, discordant, disputatious, pugnacious, quarrelsome, scrappy, truculent, warlike ♦ [2] aggressive, ambitious, assertive, enterprising, fierce, go-getting, high-pressure, self-assertive

²**militant** *n* ♦ : one who is militant

♦ crusader, fanatic, partisan, zealot

mil·i·ta·rise *chiefly Brit var of* MILITARIZE

mil·i·ta·rism \'mi-lə-tə-ˌri-zəm\ *n* **1 :** predominance of the military class or its ideals **2 :** a policy of aggressive military preparedness — **mil·i·ta·rist** \-rist\ *n* — **mil·i·ta·ris·tic** \ˌmi-lə-tə-'ris-tik\ *adj*

mil·i·ta·rize \'mi-lə-tə-ˌrīz\ *vb* **-rized; -riz·ing** **1 :** to equip with military forces and defenses 〈∼ a region〉 **2 :** to give a military character to

¹**mil·i·tary** \'mi-lə-ˌter-ē\ *adj* **1 :** of or relating to soldiers, arms, war, or the army **2 :** performed by armed forces; *also :* supported by armed force — **mil·i·tar·i·ly** \ˌmi-lə-'ter-ə-lē\ *adv*

²**military** *n, pl* **military** *also* **mil·i·tar·ies** **1** ♦ : the military, naval, and air forces of a nation **2 :** military persons

♦ armed forces, services, troops

military police *n* : a branch of an army that exercises guard and police functions

mil·i·tate \'mi-lə-ˌtāt\ *vb* **-tat·ed; -tat·ing** : to have weight or effect

mi·li·tia \mə-'li-shə\ *n* : a part of the organized armed forces of a country liable to call only in an emergency — **mi·li·tia·man** \-mən\ *n*

¹**milk** \'milk\ *n* **1 :** a nutritive usu. whitish fluid secreted by female mammals for feeding their young **2 :** a milklike liquid (as a plant juice) — **milk·i·ness** \'mil-kē-nəs\ *n* — **milky** *adj*

²**milk** *vb* **1 :** to draw off the milk of 〈∼ a cow〉 **2 :** to draw something from as if by milking

milk·maid \'milk-ˌmād\ *n* : DAIRYMAID

milk·man \-ˌman, -mən\ *n* : a person who sells or delivers milk

milk of magnesia *n* : a milk-white mixture of hydroxide of magnesium and water used as an antacid and laxative

milk shake *n* : a thoroughly blended drink made of milk, a flavoring syrup, and often ice cream

milk·sop \'milk-ˌsäp\ *n* : an unmanly man

milk·weed \-ˌwēd\ *n* : any of a genus of herbs with milky juice and clustered flowers

Milky Way *n* **1 :** a broad irregular band of light that stretches across the sky and is caused by the light of a very great number of faint stars **2 :** MILKY WAY GALAXY

Milky Way galaxy *n* : the galaxy of which the sun is a member and which includes the stars that create the light of the Milky Way

¹**mill** \'mil\ *n* **1 :** a building with machinery for grinding grain into flour **2 :** a machine used in processing (as by grinding, stamping, cutting, or finishing) raw material **3** ♦ : a building or collection of buildings with machinery for manufacturing : FACTORY

♦ factory, plant, shop, works, workshop

²**mill** *vb* **1 :** to process in a mill **2 :** to move in a circle or in an eddying mass

³**mill** *n* : one tenth of a cent

mill·age \'mi-lij\ *n* : a rate (as of taxation) expressed in mills

¹**mil·len·ni·al** \mə-'le-nē-əl\ *adj* : of or relating to a millennium

²**millennial** *n* : a person born in the 1980s or 1990s — usu. used in pl.

mil·len·ni·um \mə-'le-nē-əm\ *n, pl* **-nia** \-nē-ə\ *or* **-niums** **1 :** a period of 1000 years; *also :* a 1000th anniversary or its celebration **2 :** the 1000 years mentioned in Revelation 20 when holiness is to prevail and Christ is to reign on earth **3 :** a period of great happiness or human perfection

mill·er \'mi-lər\ *n* **1 :** one that operates a mill and esp. a flour mill **2 :** any of various moths having powdery wings

mil·let \'mi-lət\ *n* : any of several small-seeded cereal and forage grasses cultivated for grain or hay; *also :* the grain of a millet

milli— *comb form* : one thousandth part of

mil·li·am·pere \ˌmi-lē-'am-ˌpir\ *n* : one thousandth of an ampere

mil·liard \'mil-ˌyärd, 'mi-lē-ˌärd\ *n, Brit* : a thousand millions

mil·li·bar \'mi-lə-ˌbär\ *n* : a unit of atmospheric pressure

mil·li·gram \-ˌgram\ *n* : a metric unit of weight equal to ¹/₁₀₀₀ gram

mil·li·li·ter \-ˌlē-tər\ *or Can and Brit* **mil·li·li·tre** *n* : a metric unit of volume equal to ¹/₁₀₀₀ liter

mil·li·me·ter \'mi-lə-ˌmē-tər\ *or Can and Brit* **mil·li·me·tre** *n* : a metric unit of length equal to ¹/₁₀₀₀ meter

mil·li·ner \'mi-lə-nər\ *n* : a person who designs, makes, trims, or sells women's hats

mil·li·nery \'mi-lə-ˌner-ē\ *n* **1 :** women's apparel for the head **2 :** the business or work of a milliner

mill·ing \'mi-liŋ\ *n* : a corrugated edge on a coin

mil·lion \'mil-yən\ *n, pl* **millions** *or* **million** : a thousand thousands — **million** *adj* — **mil·lionth** \-yənth\ *adj or n*

mil·lion·aire \ˌmil-yə-'ner, 'mil-yə-ˌner\ *n* : one whose wealth is estimated at a million or more (as of dollars or pounds)

mil·li·pede \'mi-lə-ˌpēd\ *n* : any of a class of arthropods related to the centipedes and having a long segmented body with a hard covering, two pairs of legs on most segments, and no poison fangs

mil·li·sec·ond \-ˌse-kənd\ *n* : one thousandth of a second

mil·li·volt \-ˌvōlt\ *n* : one thousandth of a volt

mill·pond \'mil-ˌpänd\ *n* : a pond made by damming a stream to produce a fall of water for operating a mill

mill·race \-ˌrās\ *n* : a canal in which water flows to and from a mill wheel

mill·stone \-ˌstōn\ *n* : either of two round flat stones used for grinding grain

mill·stream \-ˌstrēm\ *n* : a stream whose flow is used to run a mill; *also :* the stream in a millrace

mill wheel *n* : a waterwheel that drives a mill

mill·wright \'mil-ˌrīt\ *n* : a person who builds mills or sets up or maintains their machinery

milt \'milt\ *n* : the sperm-containing fluid of a male fish

¹**mime** \'mīm\ *n* **1 :** MIMIC **2 :** a story performed silently and entirely by body movements : PANTOMIME **3** ♦ : an actor in a mime

♦ mimic, mummer, pantomime

²**mime** *vb* ♦ : to imitate closely

♦ ape, copy, emulate, imitate, mimic

mim·eo·graph \'mi-mē-ə-ˌgraf\ *n* : a machine for making many copies by means of a stencil through which ink is pressed — **mimeograph** *vb*

mi·me·sis \mə-'mē-səs, mī-\ *n* : IMITATION, MIMICRY

mi·met·ic \-'me-tik\ *adj* **1 :** marked by imitation : IMITATIVE **2 :** relating to, characterized by, or exhibiting biological mimicry

¹**mim·ic** \'mi-mik\ *n* **1** ♦ : an actor in a mime **2** ♦ : one that mimics

♦ [1] mime, mummer, pantomime ♦ [2] imitator, impersonator, impressionist

²**mimic** *vb* **mim·icked** \-mikt\; **mim·ick·ing** **1** ♦ : to imitate closely **2** ♦ : to ridicule by imitation **3 :** to resemble by biological mimicry

♦ [1] ape, copy, emulate, imitate, mime ♦ [2] burlesque, caricature, imitate, mock, parody, take off, travesty

mim·ic·ry \'mi-mi-krē\ *n, pl* **-ries** **1 :** an instance of mimicking **2 :** a superficial resemblance of one organism to another or to natural objects among which it lives that gives it an advantage (as protection from predation)

mi·mo·sa \mə-'mō-sə, mī-, -zə\ *n* : any of a genus of trees, shrubs, and herbs of the legume family that occur in warm regions and have ball-shaped heads of small white or pink flowers

min *abbr* **1** minim **2** minimum **3** mining **4** minister **5** minor **6** minute

min·a·ret \ˌmi-nə-'ret\ *n* : a tall slender tower of a mosque from which a muezzin calls the faithful to prayer

mi·na·to·ry \'mi-nə-ˌtōr-ē, 'mī-\ *adj* : THREATENING, MENACING
mince \'mins\ *vb* **minced; minc·ing** **1** ♦ : to cut into very small pieces **2** : to restrain (words) within the bounds of decorum **3** : to walk in a prim affected manner

♦ chop, hash

mince·meat \'mins-ˌmēt\ *n* : a finely chopped mixture esp. of raisins, apples, spices, and often meat used as a filling for a pie
¹mind \'mīnd\ *n* **1** ♦ : the power or process of reproducing or recalling what has been learned and retained : MEMORY **2** : the part of an individual that feels, perceives, thinks, wills, and esp. reasons **3** : INTENTION, DESIRE **4** ♦ : normal mental condition **5** ♦ : a belief stronger than impression and less strong than positive knowledge : OPINION, VIEW **6** : MOOD **7** : mental qualities of a person or group **8** : intellectual ability **9** : ATTENTION ⟨pay them no ∼⟩

♦ [1] memory, recollection, remembrance, reminiscence ♦ [4] head, reason, sanity, wit *Ant* insanity, mania ♦ [5] belief, conviction, eye, feeling, judgment (*or* judgement), notion, opinion, persuasion, sentiment, verdict, view

²mind *vb* **1** *chiefly dial* : REMEMBER **2** ♦ : to attend to closely **3** ♦ : to follow the orders or instructions of : OBEY **4** : to be concerned about; *also* : DISLIKE **5** ♦ : to be careful or cautious about ⟨∼ the step⟩ **6** ♦ : to take charge of **7** : to regard with attention

♦ [2] attend, hark, hear, heed, listen ♦ [2, 3] comply, follow, heed, listen, note, obey, observe, regard, watch ♦ [5] beware (of), guard (against), watch out (for) ♦ [6] attend, care, oversee, superintend, supervise, tend

mind–bend·ing \'mīnd-ˌben-diŋ\ *adj* : MIND-BLOWING
mind–blow·ing \-ˌblō-iŋ\ *adj* : PSYCHEDELIC 1; *also* : MIND-BOGGLING ⟨∼ special effects⟩
mind–bog·gling \-ˌbä-gə-liŋ\ *adj* : mentally or emotionally exciting or overwhelming
mind·ed \'mīn-dəd\ *adj* **1** ♦ : having inclination, disposition, or tendency : INCLINED, DISPOSED **2** : having a mind of a specified kind or concerned with a specific thing — usu. used in combination ⟨narrow-*minded*⟩

♦ amenable, disposed, game, glad, inclined, ready, willing

mind·ful \'mīnd-fəl\ *adj* ♦ : bearing in mind : AWARE ⟨∼ of their needs⟩ — **mind·ful·ly** *adv* — **mind·ful·ness** *n*

♦ alive, aware, cognizant, conscious, sensible, sentient, witting

mind·less \-ləs\ *adj* **1 a** : marked by a lack of mind or consciousness **b** ♦ : marked by no use of the intellect **2** ♦ : not mindful : HEEDLESS — **mind·less·ly** *adv*

♦ [1b] dumb, senseless, stupid, witless ♦ [2] careless, heedless, unguarded, unsafe, unwary

mind·less·ness \-nəs\ *n* ♦ : the quality or state of being mindless

♦ dopiness, foolishness, imbecility, stupidity

¹mine \'mīn\ *pron* : that which belongs to me
²mine *n* **1** : an excavation in the earth from which minerals are taken; *also* : an ore deposit **2** : an underground passage beneath an enemy position **3** : an explosive device for destroying enemy personnel, vehicles, or ships **4** : a rich source of supply
³mine *vb* **mined; min·ing** **1** : to dig a mine **2** : UNDERMINE **3** : to get ore from the earth **4** : to place military mines in — **min·er** *n*
mine·field \'mīn-ˌfēld\ *n* **1** : an area set with mines **2** : something resembling a minefield esp. in having many dangers
mine·lay·er \-ˌlā-ər\ *n* : a naval vessel for laying underwater mines
min·er·al \'mi-nə-rəl\ *n* **1** : a crystalline substance (as diamond or quartz) of inorganic origin **2** : a naturally occurring substance (as coal, salt, or water) obtained usu. from the ground — **mineral** *adj*
min·er·al·ise *chiefly Brit var of* MINERALIZE
min·er·al·ize \'mi-nə-rə-ˌlīz\ *vb* **-ized; -iz·ing** **1** : to impregnate or supply with minerals **2** : to change into mineral form — **min·er·al·i·za·tion** \-rə-lə-'zā-shən\ *n*
min·er·al·o·gy \ˌmi-nə-'rä-lə-jē, -'ra-\ *n* : a science dealing with minerals — **min·er·al·og·i·cal** \ˌmi-nə-rə-'lä-ji-kəl\ *adj* — **min·er·al·o·gist** \ˌmi-nə-'rä-lə-jist, -'ra-\ *n*
mineral oil *n* : an oil of mineral origin; *esp* : a refined petroleum oil used as a laxative
mineral water *n* : water infused with mineral salts or gases
min·e·stro·ne \ˌmi-nə-'strō-nē, -'strōn\ *n* : a rich thick vegetable soup

mine·sweep·er \'mīn-ˌswē-pər\ *n* : a warship designed for removing or neutralizing underwater mines
min·gle \'miŋ-gəl\ *vb* **min·gled; min·gling** **1** ♦ : to bring or combine together **2** ♦ : to come into contact : ASSOCIATE; *also* : to move about (as in a group)

♦ [1] amalgamate, blend, combine, commingle, fuse, incorporate, integrate, intermingle, merge, mix ♦ [2] associate, fraternize, hobnob, mix, socialize

ming tree \'miŋ-\ *n* : a dwarfed usu. evergreen tree grown as bonsai; *also* : an artificial plant resembling this
mini \'mi-nē\ *n, pl* **min·is** : something small of its kind — **mini** *adj*
mini- *comb form* : smaller or briefer than usual, normal, or standard
¹min·ia·ture \'mi-nē-ə-ˌchùr, 'mi-ni-ˌchùr, -chər\ *n* **1** : a copy on a much reduced scale; *also* : something small of its kind **2** : a small painting (as on ivory or metal) — **min·ia·tur·ist** \-ˌchùr-ist, -chər-\ *n*
²miniature *adj* ♦ : being or represented on a small scale

♦ atomic, infinitesimal, microscopic, minute, teeny, tiny, wee

min·ia·tur·ize \'mi-nē-ə-chə-ˌrīz, 'mi-ni-\ *vb* **-ized; -iz·ing** : to design or construct in small size — **min·ia·tur·i·za·tion** \ˌmi-nē-ə-ˌchùr-ə-'zā-shən, 'mi-ni-\ *n*
mini·bar \'mi-nē-ˌbär\ *n* : a small refrigerator in a hotel room that is stocked with beverages and snacks
mini·bike \'mi-nē-ˌbīk\ *n* : a small one-passenger motorcycle
mini·bus \-ˌbəs\ *n* : a small bus or van
mini·com·put·er \-kəm-ˌpyü-tər\ *n* : a computer between a mainframe and a microcomputer in size and speed
mini·disc \'mi-nē-ˌdisk\ *n* : a miniature optical disk
min·im \'mi-nəm\ *n* : a unit of liquid measure equal to ¹/₆₀ fluid dram
min·i·mal \'mi-nə-məl\ *adj* **1** ♦ : relating to or being a minimum : LEAST **2** : of or relating to minimalism or minimal art — **min·i·mal·ly** *adv*

♦ least, minimum *Ant* full, largest, maximum, top, topmost, utmost

minimal art *n* : abstract art consisting primarily of simple geometric forms executed in an impersonal style — **minimal artist** *n*
min·i·mal·ism \'mi-nə-mə-ˌli-zəm\ *n* : MINIMAL ART; *also* : a style (as in music or literature) marked by extreme spareness or simplicity — **min·i·mal·ist** \-list\ *n*
mini·mart \'mi-nē-ˌmärt\ *n* : CONVENIENCE STORE
min·i·mise *chiefly Brit var of* MINIMIZE
min·i·mize \'mi-nə-ˌmīz\ *vb* **-mized; -miz·ing** **1** : to reduce or keep to a minimum **2 a** : to underestimate intentionally **b** ♦ : to speak slightingly of : BELITTLE **3** : to replace (a window) on a computer display with a small button or icon which will restore the window when selected

♦ belittle, cry down, decry, deprecate, depreciate, diminish, discount, disparage, put down, write off

¹min·i·mum \'mi-nə-məm\ *n, pl* **-ma** \-mə\ *or* **-mums** **1** : the least quantity assignable, admissible, or possible **2** : the least of a set of numbers **3** : the lowest degree or amount of variation (as of temperature) reached or recorded
²minimum *adj* ♦ : of, relating to, or constituting a minimum

♦ least, minimal

min·ion \'min-yən\ *n* **1** : a servile dependent, follower, or underling **2** ♦ : one highly favored **3** : a subordinate official

♦ darling, favorite (*or* favourite), pet, preference

min·is·cule \'mi-nəs-ˌkyül\ *var of* MINUSCULE
mini·se·ries \'mi-nē-ˌsir-ēz\ *n* : a television story presented in sequential episodes
mini·skirt \-ˌskərt\ *n* : a skirt with the hemline several inches above the knee
¹min·is·ter \'mi-nə-stər\ *n* **1** : AGENT **2** ♦ : a member of the clergy esp. of a Protestant communion **3** : a high officer of state who heads a division of governmental activities **4** ♦ : a diplomatic representative to a foreign state

♦ [2] clergyman, divine, ecclesiastic, father, preacher, priest, reverend ♦ [4] ambassador, delegate, emissary, envoy, legate, representative

²minister *vb* **1** : to perform the functions of a minister of religion **2** ♦ : to give aid or service ⟨∼ to the sick⟩ — **min·is·tra·tion** \ˌmi-nə-'strā-shən\ *n*

♦ *usu* minister to aid, care, mother, nurse

min·is·te·ri·al \ˌmi-nə-ˈstir-ē-əl\ *adj* ♦ : of, relating to, or characteristic of a minister or the ministry
♦ clerical, pastoral, priestly, sacerdotal

¹**min·is·trant** \ˈmi-nə-strənt\ *adj, archaic* : performing service as a minister
²**ministrant** *n* : one that ministers
min·is·try \ˈmi-nə-strē\ *n, pl* **-tries** **1** : MINISTRATION **2** : the office, duties, or functions of a minister; *also* : the period of service or office **3** : CLERGY **4** : AGENCY **5** *often cap* : the body of ministers governing a nation or state; *also* : a government department headed by a minister
mini·tower \ˈmi-nē-ˌtaů(-ə)r\ *n* : a computer tower of intermediate size
mini·van \ˈmi-nē-ˌvan\ *n* : a small van
mink \ˈmiŋk\ *n, pl* **mink** *or* **minks** : either of two slender flesh-eating mammals resembling the related weasels; *also* : the soft lustrous typically dark brown fur of a mink
min·ke whale \ˈmiŋ-kə-\ *n* : a small grayish baleen whale with a whitish underside
Minn *abbr* Minnesota
min·ne·sing·er \ˈmi-ni-ˌsiŋ-ər, -ˌziŋ-\ *n* : any of a class of German lyric poets and musicians of the 12th to the 14th centuries
min·now \ˈmi-nō\ *n, pl* **minnows** *also* **minnow** : any of numerous small freshwater fishes
¹**mi·nor** \ˈmī-nər\ *adj* **1** ♦ : inferior in importance, size, or degree **2** : not having reached majority **3** : having the third, sixth, and sometimes the seventh degrees lowered by a half step ⟨∼ scale⟩; *also* : based on a minor scale ⟨∼ key⟩ **4** : not serious ⟨∼ illness⟩
♦ inferior, junior, less, lesser, lower, subordinate, under ♦ frivolous, inconsequential, inconsiderable, insignificant, little, minute, negligible, slight, small, trifling, trivial, unimportant

²**minor** *n* **1** : a person who has not attained majority **2** : a subject of academic study chosen as a secondary field of specialization
³**minor** *vb* : to pursue an academic minor
mi·nor·i·ty \mə-ˈnȯr-ə-tē, mī-\ *n, pl* **-ties** **1** : the period or state of being a minor **2** : the smaller in number of two groups; *esp* : a group having less than the number of votes necessary for control **3** : a part of a population differing from others in some characteristics; *also* : a member of a minority
mi·nox·i·dil \mə-ˈnäk-sə-ˌdil\ *n* : a drug used orally to treat hypertension and topically in solution to promote hair regrowth in some forms of baldness
min·ster \ˈmin-stər\ *n* : a large or important church
min·strel \ˈmin-strəl\ *n* **1** : a medieval singer of verses **2 a** : MUSICIAN **b** ♦ : one who writes poetry : POET **2** : any of a group of performers caricaturing Black performers that originated in the U.S. in the early 19th century ⟨a ∼ show⟩
♦ bard, poet, versifier

min·strel·sy \-sē\ *n* : the singing and playing of a minstrel; *also* : a body of minstrels
¹**mint** \ˈmint\ *n* **1** : any of a large family of aromatic square-stemmed herbs and shrubs; *esp* : one (as spearmint) that is fragrant and is the source of a flavoring oil **2** : a mint-flavored piece of candy — **minty** *adj*
²**mint** *n* **1** : a place where coins are made **2** ♦ : a vast sum — **mint** *vb* — **mint·age** \-ij\ *n* — **mint·er** *n*
♦ fortune, wad

³**mint** *vb* **1** : to make (as coins) out of metal **2** : CREATE; *also* : to give a certain status to ⟨newly ∼ed lawyers⟩ — **mint·age** \-ij\ *n* — **mint·er** *n*
⁴**mint** *adj* : unmarred as if fresh from a mint ⟨in ∼ condition⟩
min·u·end \ˈmin-yə-ˌwend\ *n* : a number from which another is to be subtracted
min·u·et \ˌmin-yə-ˈwet\ *n* : a slow graceful dance
¹**mi·nus** \ˈmī-nəs\ *prep* **1** : diminished by : LESS ⟨7 ∼ 3 equals 4⟩ **2** ♦ : deprived of : WITHOUT ⟨∼ his hat⟩
♦ sans, wanting, without

²**minus** *n* ♦ : a negative quantity or quality
♦ disadvantage, drawback, handicap, liability, penalty, strike

³**minus** *adj* **1** : algebraically negative ⟨∼ quantity⟩ **2** : having negative qualities
¹**mi·nus·cule** \ˈmi-nəs-ˌkyül\ *n* : a lowercase letter
²**minuscule** *adj* ♦ : very small
♦ atomic, infinitesimal, microscopic, miniature, minute, tiny, wee

minus sign *n* : a sign – used in mathematics to indicate subtraction or a negative quantity

¹**min·ute** \ˈmi-nət\ *n* **1** : a 60th part of an hour or of a degree : 60 seconds **2** ♦ : a short space of time **3** *pl* : the official record of the proceedings of a meeting
♦ flash, instant, jiffy, moment, second, shake, trice, twinkle, twinkling, wink

²**mi·nute** \mī-ˈnüt, mə-, -ˈnyüt\ *adj* **mi·nut·er; -est** **1** ♦ : very small **2** ♦ : of little importance : TRIFLING **3** ♦ : marked by close attention to details — **mi·nute·ness** *n*
♦ [1] atomic, infinitesimal, microscopic, miniature, tiny, wee ♦ [2] frivolous, inconsequential, inconsiderable, insignificant, little, minor, negligible, slight, small, trifling, trivial, unimportant ♦ [3] circumstantial, detailed, elaborate, full, thorough

mi·nute·ly \mī-ˈnüt-lē, mə-, -ˈnyüt-\ *adv* ♦ : in a minute manner or degree
♦ completely, exhaustively, fully, roundly, thoroughly, totally

min·ute·man \ˈmi-nət-ˌman\ *n* : a member of a group of armed men pledged to take the field at a minute's notice during and immediately before the American Revolution
mi·nu·tia \mə-ˈnü-shə, -ˈnyü-, -shē-ə\ *n, pl* **-ti·ae** \-shē-ˌē\ : a minute or minor detail — usu. used in pl.
minx \ˈmiŋks\ *n* : a pert girl
Mio·cene \ˈmī-ə-ˌsēn\ *adj* : of, relating to, or being the epoch of the Tertiary between the Oligocene and the Pliocene — **Miocene** *n*
mir·a·cle \ˈmir-i-kəl\ *n* **1** : an extraordinary event manifesting divine intervention in human affairs **2** ♦ : an unusual event, thing, or accomplishment : WONDER, MARVEL
♦ caution, flash, marvel, phenomenon, portent, prodigy, sensation, wonder

miracle drug *n* : a usu. newly discovered drug that elicits a dramatic response in a patient's condition
mi·rac·u·lous \mə-ˈra-kyə-ləs\ *adj* **1** ♦ : of the nature of a miracle **2** ♦ : suggesting a miracle : MARVELOUS **3** : working or able to work miracles — **mi·rac·u·lous·ly** *adv*
♦ [1] magical, phenomenal, superhuman, supernatural, uncanny, unearthly ♦ [2] amazing, astonishing, astounding, awesome, fabulous, marvelous (*or* marvellous), stunning, stupendous, sublime, surprising, wonderful

mi·rage \mə-ˈräzh\ *n* **1** : an illusion that often appears as a pool of water or a mirror in which distant objects are seen inverted, is sometimes seen at sea, in the desert, or over a hot pavement, and results from atmospheric conditions **2** : something illusory and unattainable
¹**mire** \ˈmīr\ *n* ♦ : heavy and often deep mud or slush
♦ muck, mud, ooze, slime, slop, sludge, slush ♦ bog, fen, marsh, morass, slough, swamp

²**mire** *vb* **mired; mir·ing** **1** : to stick or sink in or as if in mire **2** ♦ : to cover or soil with mire
♦ befoul, begrime, besmirch, blacken, dirty, foul, grime, muddy, smirch, soil, stain

mire·poix \mir-ˈpwä\ *n, pl* **mirepoix** : a mixture of diced vegetables and sometimes meats used in soups, stews, and sauces
¹**mir·ror** \ˈmir-ər\ *n* **1** : a polished or smooth surface (as of glass) that forms images by reflection **2** : a true representation
²**mirror** *vb* **1** : to reflect in or as if in a mirror **2** : RESEMBLE
mirth \ˈmərth\ *n* ♦ : gladness or gaiety accompanied with laughter — **mirth·less** *adj*
♦ cheer, cheerfulness, cheeriness, glee, hilarity, joviality, merriment

mirth·ful \-fəl\ *adj* ♦ : full of mirth or merriment
♦ blithe, boon, festive, gleeful, jocund, jolly, jovial, merry, sunny

mirth·ful·ly \-fə-lē\ *adv* ♦ : in a mirthful manner
♦ cheerfully, gaily, happily, heartily, jovially, merrily

mirth·ful·ness \-nəs\ *n* ♦ : the quality or state of being mirthful
♦ cheer, cheerfulness, glee, hilarity, joviality, merriment, mirth

MIRV \ˈmərv\ *n* : an ICBM with multiple warheads that have different targets — **MIRV** *vb*
miry \ˈmīr-ē\ *adj* ♦ : resembling a mire : characterized by swampy ground
♦ mucky, muddy, oozy, slimy, slushy

mis·ad·ven·ture \ˌmi-səd-ˈven-chər\ *n* **1** ♦ : bad luck **2** ♦ : a piece of bad luck
♦ [1, 2] adversity, knock, mischance, misfortune, mishap

mis·aligned \ˌmi-sə-ˈlīnd\ *adj* : not properly aligned — **mis·align·ment** \-ˈlīn-mənt\ *n*

mis·al·li·ance \ˌmi-sə-ˈlī-əns\ *n* : an improper or unsuitable marriage

mis·al·lo·ca·tion \ˌmi-ˌsa-lə-ˈkā-shən\ *n* : faulty or improper allocation

mis·an·dry \ˈmi-ˌsan-drē\ *n* : a hatred of men — **mis·an·drist** \-drist\ *n or adj*

mis·an·thrope \ˈmis-ⁿn-ˌthrōp\ *n* : one who hates humankind — **mis·an·throp·ic** \ˌmis-ⁿn-ˈthrä-pik\ *adj* — **mis·an·throp·i·cal·ly** \-pi-k(ə-)lē\ *adv* — **mis·an·thro·py** \mi-ˈsan-thrə-pē\ *n*

mis·ap·pli·ca·tion \ˌmi-ˌsa-plə-ˈkā-shən\ *n* : the action of misapplying

mis·ap·ply \ˌmi-sə-ˈplī\ *vb* ♦ : to apply wrongly

  ♦ abuse, misuse, pervert

mis·ap·pre·hend \ˌmi-ˌsa-pri-ˈhend\ *vb* ♦ : to fail to understand : MISUNDERSTAND

  ♦ misconstrue, misinterpret, misread, miss, mistake, misunderstand

mis·ap·pre·hen·sion \-ˈhen-chən\ *n* ♦ : the act or instance of misapprehending

  ♦ misjudgment, mistake, misunderstanding ♦ misconstruction, misinterpretation, misunderstanding

mis·ap·pro·pri·ate \ˌmi-sə-ˈprō-prē-ˌāt\ *vb* ♦ : to appropriate wrongly (as by embezzlement) — **mis·ap·pro·pri·a·tion** \-ˌprō-prē-ˈā-shən\ *n*

  ♦ appropriate, filch, hook, nip, pilfer, pocket, purloin, snitch, steal, swipe, thieve

mis·be·got·ten \-bi-ˈgät-ⁿn\ *adj* **1** *dated* : born to parents not married to each other **2** : badly planned

mis·be·have \ˌmis-bi-ˈhāv\ *vb* : to behave improperly — **mis·be·hav·er** *n*

  ♦ act out, act up, carry on

mis·be·hav·ior \-ˈhā-vyər\ *n* ♦ : bad, improper, or rude behavior

  ♦ malfeasance, misconduct, misdoing, wrongdoing

mis·be·lief \ˌmis-bə-ˈlēf\ *n* ♦ : erroneous or false belief

  ♦ error, fallacy, falsehood, falsity, illusion, misconception, myth, untruth

mis·be·liev·er \-bə-ˈlē-vər\ *n* : one who holds a false or unorthodox belief

mis·brand \mis-ˈbrand\ *vb* : to brand falsely or in a misleading manner

misc *abbr* miscellaneous

mis·cal·cu·late \mis-ˈkal-kyə-ˌlāt\ *vb* ♦ : to calculate wrongly — **mis·cal·cu·la·tion** \ˌmis-ˌkal-kyə-ˈlā-shən\ *n*

  ♦ misconceive, misjudge, mistake

mis·call \mis-ˈkȯl\ *vb* : MISNAME

mis·car·riage \-ˈkar-ij\ *n* **1** : failure in the administration of justice **2** : spontaneous expulsion of a fetus before it is capable of independent life

mis·car·ry \-ˈkar-ē\ *vb* **1** : to have a miscarriage of a fetus **2** : to go wrong; *also* : to be unsuccessful

mis·ce·ge·na·tion \mi-se-jə-ˈnā-shən, ˌmi-si-jə-ˈnā-\ *n* : marriage, cohabitation, or sexual intercourse between a white person and a person of a different race

mis·cel·la·neous \ˌmi-sə-ˈlā-nē-əs\ *adj* **1** ♦ : consisting of diverse things or members **2** : having various traits; *also* : dealing with or interested in diverse subjects — **mis·cel·la·neous·ly** *adv* — **mis·cel·la·neous·ness** *n*

  ♦ assorted, heterogeneous, mixed, motley, varied *Ant* homogeneous

mis·cel·la·ny \ˈmi-sə-ˌlā-nē\ *n, pl* **-nies** **1** ♦ : a collection of writings on various subjects **2** ♦ : a mixture of various things : HODGEPODGE

  ♦ [1] album, anthology, compilation ♦ [2] assortment, clutter, hash, hodgepodge, jumble, litter, medley, mélange, motley, muddle, potpourri, rummage, scramble, shuffle, tumble, variety, welter

mis·chance \mis-ˈchans\ *n* **1** ♦ : bad luck **2** ♦ : a piece of bad luck; *also* : an unfortunate accident

  ♦ adversity, knock, misadventure, misfortune, mishap

mis·chief \ˈmis-chəf\ *n* **1** : injury caused by a particular agent **2** ♦ : a source of harm or irritation; *esp* : a person who

causes mischief **3 a** ♦ : action that annoys **b** ♦ : the quality or state of being mischievous : MISCHIEVOUSNESS

  ♦ [2] devil, hellion, imp, monkey, rapscallion, rascal, rogue, scamp, urchin ♦ [3a, b] devilishness, impishness, knavery, mischievousness, rascality, shenanigans, waggery, wickedness

mis·chie·vous \ˈmis-chə-vəs\ *adj* **1** ♦ : of a kind likely to be damaging : HARMFUL, INJURIOUS **2** : causing annoyance or minor injury **3** ♦ : irresponsibly playful ⟨~ children⟩ — **mis·chie·vous·ly** *adv*

  ♦ [1] adverse, damaging, detrimental, harmful, hurtful, injurious, prejudicial ♦ [3] devilish, impish, knavish, naughty, rascally, roguish, sly, waggish, wicked

mis·chie·vous·ness *n* ♦ : the quality or state of being mischievous

  ♦ devilishness, impishness, knavery, mischief, rascality, shenanigans, waggery, wickedness

mis·ci·ble \ˈmi-sə-bəl\ *adj* : capable of being mixed

mis·com·mu·ni·ca·tion \ˌmis-kə-ˌmyü-nə-ˈkā-shən\ *n* : failure to communicate clearly

mis·con·ceive \ˌmis-kən-ˈsēv\ *vb* ♦ : to interpret incorrectly

  ♦ miscalculate, misjudge, mistake

mis·con·cep·tion \-ˈsep-shən\ *n* ♦ : the act or result of misconceiving

  ♦ error, fallacy, falsehood, falsity, illusion, myth, untruth

mis·con·duct \mis-ˈkän-(ˌ)dəkt\ *n* **1** : MISMANAGEMENT **2** ♦ : intentional wrongdoing **3** ♦ : improper behavior

  ♦ [2, 3] malfeasance, misbehavior, misdoing, wrongdoing

mis·con·struc·tion \-ˈstrək-shən\ *n* ♦ : the action of misconstruing

  ♦ misapprehension, misinterpretation, misunderstanding

mis·con·strue \ˌmis-kən-ˈstrü\ *vb* ♦ : to interpret wrongly : MISINTERPRET

  ♦ misapprehend, misinterpret, misread, miss, mistake, misunderstand

mis·count \mis-ˈkaunt\ *vb* : to count incorrectly : MISCALCULATE

mis·cre·ant \ˈmis-krē-ənt\ *n* : one who behaves criminally or viciously — **miscreant** *adj*

mis·cue \mis-ˈkyü\ *n* ♦ : a wrong action or statement : MISTAKE, ERROR — **miscue** *vb*

  ♦ blunder, error, fault, flub, fumble, goof, lapse, misstep, mistake, oversight, slip, stumble

mis·deed \mis-ˈdēd\ *n* ♦ : a wrong deed

  ♦ breach, crime, error, malefaction, misdoing, offense, sin, transgression, violation, wrongdoing

mis·de·mean·or *or Can and Brit* **mis·de·mean·our** \ˌmis-di-ˈmē-nər\ *n* **1** : a crime less serious than a felony **2** : MISDEED

mis·di·rect \ˌmis-də-ˈrekt, -dī-\ *vb* : to give a wrong direction to — **mis·di·rec·tion** \-ˈrek-shən\ *n*

mis·do·ing \mis-ˈdü-iŋ\ *n* ♦ : the act or an instance of misbehaving : WRONGDOING — **mis·do** \-ˈdü\ *vb* — **mis·do·er** \-ˈdü-ər\ *n*

  ♦ malfeasance, misbehavior, misconduct, wrongdoing

mise–en–scène \ˌmē-ˌzäⁿ-ˈsen, -ˈsäⁿ\ *n, pl* **mise–en–scènes** *same or* -ˈsenz, -ˈsänz\ **1** : the arrangement of the scenery, property, and actors on a stage **2** : SETTING; *also* : ENVIRONMENT

mi·ser \ˈmī-zər\ *n* ♦ : a person who hoards and is stingy with money — **mi·ser·ly** *adj*

  ♦ cheapskate, niggard, skinflint, tightwad

mis·er·a·ble \ˈmi-zə-rə-bəl, ˈmiz-rə-\ *adj* **1 a** ♦ : wretchedly deficient, meager, or of poor quality **b** ♦ : causing extreme discomfort or unhappiness **2** ♦ : being in a state of poverty or distress **3** : being likely to discredit or shame — **mis·er·a·ble·ness** *n* — **mis·er·a·bly** \-blē\ *adv*

  ♦ [1a] bad, cheap, inferior, mediocre, poor, rotten, second-rate, shabby, shoddy, sleazy, tacky, terrible, threadbare, wretched ♦ [1b] bleak, dark, dismal, dreary, gloomy, gray (*or* grey), somber (*or* sombre), wretched ♦ [2] heartbreaking, pathetic, piteous, pitiful, poor, rueful, sorry, unhappy, wretched

mi·ser·li·ness \ˈmī-zər-lē-nəs\ *n* ♦ : the quality or state of being a miser or like a miser

  ♦ cheapness, closeness, parsimony, stinginess, tightness

mis·ery \ˈmi-zə-rē\ *n, pl* **-er·ies** **1** ♦ : suffering and want caused by poverty or affliction **2 :** a cause of suffering or discomfort **3 :** emotional distress

♦ affliction, agony, anguish, distress, pain, torment, torture, tribulation, woe

mis·fea·sance \mis-'fēz-ᵊns\ *n* : the performance of a lawful action in an illegal or improper manner
mis·file \-'fī(-ə)l\ *vb* : to file in the wrong place
mis·fire \-'fī(-ə)r\ *vb* **1 :** to fail to fire **2 :** to miss an intended effect — **misfire** *n*
mis·fit \'mis-ˌfit, *sense 1 also* mis-'fit\ *n* **1 :** something that fits badly **2 :** a person who is poorly adjusted to a situation or environment
mis·for·tune \mis-'fȯr-chən\ *n* **1** ♦ **:** bad luck **2** ♦ **:** an unfortunate condition or event

♦ [1, 2] adversity, knock, misadventure, mischance, mishap *Ant* fortune, luck

mis·giv·ing \-'gi-viŋ\ *n* ♦ **:** a feeling of doubt or suspicion esp. concerning an action or future event

♦ distrust, doubt, incertitude, mistrust, skepticism, suspicion, uncertainty ♦ compunction, qualm, scruple ♦ alarm, apprehension, dread, foreboding

mis·gov·ern \-'gə-vərn\ *vb* ♦ **:** to govern badly — **mis·gov·ern·ment** *n*

♦ misconduct, mishandle, mismanage, misrule

mis·guid·ance \mis-'gīd-ᵊns\ *n* : faulty guidance
mis·guide \mis-'gīd\ *vb* : to lead astray
mis·guid·ed \-'gī-dəd\ *adj* : led or prompted by wrong or inappropriate motives or ideals — **mis·guid·ed·ly** *adv*
mis·han·dle \-'hand-ᵊl\ *vb* **1** ♦ **:** to treat roughly : MALTREAT **2** ♦ **:** to manage wrongly

♦ [1] abuse, ill-treat, maltreat, manhandle, mistreat, misuse
♦ [2] misconduct, misgovern, mismanage, misrule

mis·hap \'mis-ˌhap\ *n* ♦ **:** an unfortunate accident

♦ accident, casualty ♦ adversity, knock, misadventure, mischance, misfortune

mish·mash \'mish-ˌmash, -ˌmäsh\ *n* : a mass of things mingled together : HODGEPODGE, JUMBLE
mis·in·form \ˌmis-ᵊn-'fȯrm\ *vb* ♦ **:** to give false or misleading information to — **mis·in·for·ma·tion** \ˌmi-sin-fər-'mā-shən\ *n*

♦ beguile, bluff, cozen, deceive, delude, dupe, fool, gull, have, hoax, hoodwink, humbug, mislead, string along, take in, trick

mis·in·ter·pret \ˌmis-ᵊn-'tər-prət\ *vb* ♦ **:** to understand or explain wrongly

♦ color (*or* colour), distort, falsify, garble, misrepresent, misstate, pervert, twist, warp ♦ misapprehend, misconstrue, misread, miss, mistake, misunderstand

mis·in·ter·pre·ta·tion \ˌmis-ᵊn-ˌtər-prə-'tā-shən\ *n* ♦ **:** incorrect interpretation

♦ misapprehension, misconstruction, misunderstanding

mis·judge \mis-'jəj\ *vb* **1 :** to estimate wrongly **2 :** to have an unjust opinion of

♦ miscalculate, misconceive, mistake

mis·judg·ment \mis-'jəj-mənt\ *n* ♦ **:** incorrect or distorted judgment

♦ misapprehension, mistake, misunderstanding

mis·la·bel \-'lā-bəl\ *vb* : to label incorrectly or falsely
mis·lay \mis-'lā\ *vb* **-laid** \-'lād\; **-lay·ing** : MISPLACE, LOSE
mis·lead \mis-'lēd\ *vb* **-led** \-'led\; **-lead·ing** ♦ **:** to lead in a wrong direction or into a mistaken action or belief — **mis·lead·ing·ly** *adv*

♦ beguile, bluff, cozen, deceive, delude, dupe, fool, gull, have, hoax, hoodwink, humbug, misinform, string along, take in, trick

misleading *adj* ♦ **:** tending to mislead

♦ deceitful, deceptive, delusive, fallacious, false, specious

mis·like \-'līk\ *vb* : DISLIKE — **mis·like** *n*
mis·man·age \-'ma-nij\ *vb* ♦ **:** to manage wrongly or incompetently — **mis·man·age·ment** *n*

♦ misconduct, misgovern, mishandle, misrule

mis·match \-'mach\ *vb* : to match unsuitably or badly — **mis·match** \-'mach, 'mis-ˌmach\ *n*
mis·name \-'nām\ *vb* : to name incorrectly : MISCALL
mis·no·mer \mis-'nō-mər\ *n* : a wrong or inappropriate name or designation

mi·so \'mē-sō\ *n* : a high-protein fermented food paste consisting chiefly of soybeans, salt, and usu. grain
mi·sog·y·ny \mə-'sä-jə-nē\ *n* : a hatred of women — **mi·sog·y·nist** \-nist\ *n or adj* — **mi·sog·y·nis·tic** \mə-ˌsä-jə-'nis-tik\ *adj*
mis·ori·ent \mi-'sȯr-ē-ˌent\ *vb* : to orient improperly or incorrectly — **mis·ori·en·ta·tion** \mi-ˌsȯr-ē-ən-'tā-shən\ *n*
mis·place \mis-'plās\ *vb* **1 :** to put in a wrong or unremembered place **2 :** to set on a wrong object ⟨∼ trust⟩
mis·play \-'plā\ *n* : a wrong or unskillful play — **mis·play** \mis-'plā, 'mis-ˌplā\ *vb*
mis·print \'mis-ˌprint\ *n* : a mistake in printed matter — **mis·print** \mis-'print\ *vb*
mis·pro·nounce \ˌmis-prə-'naůns\ *vb* : to pronounce incorrectly — **mis·pro·nun·ci·a·tion** \-prə-ˌnən-sē-'ā-shən\ *n*
mis·quote \mis-'kwōt\ *vb* : to quote incorrectly — **mis·quo·ta·tion** \ˌmis-kwō-'tā-shən\ *n*
mis·read \-'rēd\ *vb* **-read** \-'red\; **-read·ing** \-'rē-diŋ\ ♦ **:** to read or interpret incorrectly

♦ misapprehend, misconstrue, misinterpret, miss, mistake, misunderstand

mis·rep·re·sent \ˌmis-ˌre-pri-'zent\ *vb* ♦ **:** to represent falsely or unfairly ⟨∼ the facts⟩ — **mis·rep·re·sen·ta·tion** \-ˌzen-'tā-shən\ *n*

♦ color (*or* colour), distort, falsify, garble, misinterpret, misstate, pervert, twist, warp

¹**mis·rule** \mis-'rül\ *vb* ♦ **:** to rule incompetently : MISGOVERN

♦ misconduct, misgovern, mishandle, mismanage

²**misrule** *n* **1 :** MISGOVERNMENT **2 :** DISORDER
¹**miss** \'mis\ *vb* **1 :** to fail to hit, reach, or contact **2 :** to feel the absence of **3 :** to fail to obtain **4 :** AVOID ⟨just ∼ed hitting the other car⟩ **5 :** OMIT **6** ♦ **:** to fail to understand **7 :** to fail to perform or attend; *also* : MISFIRE

♦ misapprehend, misconstrue, misinterpret, misread, mistake, misunderstand

²**miss** *n* **1** ♦ **:** a failure to hit or to attain a result **2 :** MISFIRE

♦ default, delinquency, dereliction, failure, neglect, negligence, oversight

³**miss** *n* **1** *cap* — used as a title prefixed to the name of an unmarried woman or girl **2** ♦ **:** a young unmarried woman or girl

♦ doll, girl, lass, maid, maiden

Miss *abbr* Mississippi
mis·sal \'mi-səl\ *n* : a book containing all that is said or sung at mass during the entire year
mis·send \mis-'send\ *vb* : to send incorrectly ⟨*missent* mail⟩
mis·shap·en \-'shā-pən\ *adj* ♦ **:** badly shaped : having an ugly shape

♦ deformed, distorted, malformed, monstrous, shapeless

mis·sile \'mi-səl\ *n* : an object (as a stone, bullet, or rocket) thrown or projected usu. so as to strike a target
miss·ing \'mi-siŋ\ *adj* ♦ **:** not present or available; *also* : in an unknown location

♦ absent, away, out ♦ absent, nonexistent, wanting ♦ gone, lost

mis·sion \'mi-shən\ *n* **1 :** a group of missionaries; *also* : a place where missionaries work **2 :** a group of envoys to a foreign country; *also* : a team of specialists or cultural leaders sent to a foreign country **3** ♦ **:** a specific task with which a person or a group is charged

♦ assignment, charge, job, operation, post

¹**mis·sion·ary** \'mi-shə-ˌner-ē\ *adj* : of, relating to, or engaged in missions
²**missionary** *n, pl* **-ar·ies** : a person commissioned by a church to spread its faith or carry on humanitarian work
mis·sion·er \'mi-shə-nər\ *n* : MISSIONARY
Mis·sis·sip·pi·an \ˌmi-sə-'si-pē-ən\ *adj* : of, relating to, or being the period of the Paleozoic era between the Devonian and the Pennsylvanian — **Mississippian** *n*
mis·sive \'mi-siv\ *n* ♦ **:** a written communication : LETTER

♦ dispatch, letter, memorandum, note

mis·speak \mis-'spēk\ *vb* : to say imperfectly or incorrectly
mis·spell \-'spel\ *vb* : to spell incorrectly — **mis·spell·ing** *n*
mis·spend \-'spend\ *vb* **-spent** \-'spent\; **-spend·ing** ♦ **:** to spend wrongly : WASTE, SQUANDER ⟨my *misspent* youth⟩

♦ blow, dissipate, fritter, lavish, run through, spend, squander, throw away, waste

mis·state \mis-'stāt\ *vb* ♦ : to state incorrectly — **mis·state·ment** *n*

♦ color (*or* colour), distort, falsify, garble, misinterpret, misrepresent, pervert, twist, warp

mis·step \-'step\ *n* **1** ♦ : a wrong step **2** ♦ : a mistake in judgment or action : BLUNDER

♦ blunder, error, fault, flub, fumble, goof, lapse, miscue, mistake, oversight, slip, stumble

¹**mist** \'mist\ *n* **1** : water in the form of particles suspended or falling in the air **2** : something that obscures understanding
²**mist** *vb* **1** : to be or become misty **2** : to become moist or blurred **3** ♦ : to cover with or as if with a mist

♦ becloud, befog, blur, cloud, darken, dim, fog, haze, obscure, overshadow, shroud

mis·tak·able \mə-'stā-kə-bəl\ *adj* : capable of being misunderstood or mistaken
¹**mis·take** \mi-'stāk\ *vb* **-took** \-'tùk\; **-tak·en** \-'stā-kən\; **-tak·ing** **1** : to blunder in the choice of **2** ♦ : to misunderstand the meaning or intention of : MISINTERPRET **3** ♦ : to make a wrong judgment of the character or ability of **4** : to confuse with another — **mis·tak·er** *n*

♦ [2] misapprehend, misconstrue, misinterpret, misread, miss, misunderstand ♦ [3] miscalculate, misconceive, misjudge

²**mistake** *n* **1** ♦ : a wrong judgment : MISUNDERSTANDING **2** ♦ : a wrong action or statement : ERROR

♦ [1] misapprehension, misconstruction, misinterpretation, misjudgment, misunderstanding ♦ [2] blunder, error, fault, flub, fumble, goof, lapse, miscue, misstep, oversight, slip, stumble

mis·tak·en·ly \mi-'stā-kən-lē\ *adv* ♦ : in a way that is wrong in action or thought

♦ amiss, erroneously, faultily, improperly, inaptly, incorrectly, wrongly

¹**mis·ter** \'mis-tər\ *n* **1** *cap* — used sometimes instead of *Mr.* **2** : SIR — used without a name in addressing a man
²**mis·ter** \'mis-tər\ *n* : a device for spraying mist
mis·tle·toe \'mi-səl-ˌtō\ *n* : a European parasitic green shrub that grows on trees and has yellowish flowers and waxy white berries
mis·tral \'mis-trəl, mi-'sträl\ *n* : a strong cold dry northerly wind of southern France
mis·treat \mis-'trēt\ *vb* ♦ : to treat badly : ABUSE — **mis·treat·ment** *n*

♦ abuse, ill-treat, maltreat, manhandle, mishandle, misuse

mis·tress \'mis-trəs\ *n* **1** : a woman who has power, authority, or ownership ⟨~ of the house⟩ **2** : something personified as female that rules or dominates ⟨when Rome was ~ of the world⟩ **3** : a woman other than his wife with whom a married man has sexual relations; *also, archaic* : SWEETHEART **4** — used archaically as a title prefixed to the name of a married or unmarried woman
mis·tri·al \'mis-ˌtrī(-ə)l\ *n* : a trial that has no legal effect
¹**mis·trust** \mis-'trəst\ *n* ♦ : a lack of confidence : DISTRUST

♦ distrust, doubt, incertitude, misgiving, skepticism, suspicion, uncertainty

²**mistrust** *vb* ♦ : to have no trust or confidence in : SUSPECT

♦ distrust, doubt, question, suspect

mis·trust·ful \-fəl\ *adj* ♦ : marked by mistrust

♦ distrustful, incredulous, leery, skeptical, suspicious

mis·trust·ful·ly \-fə-lē\ *adv* ♦ : in a mistrustful manner

♦ askance, distrustfully, dubiously, suspiciously

mis·trust·ful·ness \-nəs\ *n* : the quality or state of being mistrustful
misty \'mis-tē\ *adj* **mist·i·er; -est** **1** ♦ : obscured by or as if by mist ⟨a ~ memory⟩ **2** : TEARFUL — **mist·i·ly** \-tə-lē\ *adv* — **mist·i·ness** \-tē-nəs\ *n*

♦ cloudy, foggy, hazy, murky, smoggy, soupy

mis·un·der·stand \ˌmi-ˌsən-dər-'stand\ *vb* **-stood** \-'stùd\; **-stand·ing** **1** ♦ : to fail to understand **2** ♦ : to interpret incorrectly

♦ [1, 2] misapprehend, misconstrue, misinterpret, misread, miss, mistake *Ant* apprehend, catch, comprehend, conceive, fathom, grasp, know, make out, penetrate, perceive, savvy, see, seize, take in, understand

mis·un·der·stand·ing \-'stan-diŋ\ *n* **1** ♦ : a failure to understand : MISINTERPRETATION **2** ♦ : a usu. verbal conflict between antagonists : DISAGREEMENT, QUARREL

♦ [1] misapprehension, misconstruction, misinterpretation
♦ [2] altercation, argument, bicker, brawl, disagreement, dispute, fight, hassle, quarrel, row, scrap, spat, squabble, wrangle

mis·us·age \mis-'yü-sij\ *n* **1** : bad treatment : ABUSE **2** : wrong or improper use
¹**mis·use** \mis-'yüz\ *vb* **1** ♦ : to use incorrectly **2** ♦ : to treat badly : ABUSE, MISTREAT

♦ [1] abuse, misapply, pervert, profane ♦ [2] abuse, ill-treat, maltreat, manhandle, mishandle, mistreat

²**misuse** \-'yüs\ *n* ♦ : wrong, careless, or improper use

♦ abuse, perversion

¹**mite** \'mīt\ *n* : any of numerous tiny arthropod animals related to the spiders that often live and feed on animals or plants
²**mite** *n* **1** ♦ : a small coin or sum of money **2** ♦ : a small amount : BIT **3** ♦ : a small object or creature

♦ [1] peanuts, pittance, shoestring, song *Ant* fortune, mint, wad
♦ [2] bit, dab, little, particle, speck, touch, trace ♦ [3] dwarf, midget, peewee, pygmy, runt

¹**mi·ter** *or* **mi·tre** \'mī-tər\ *n* **1** : a headdress worn by bishops and abbots **2** : MITER JOINT
²**miter** *or* **mitre** *vb* **mi·tered** *or* **mi·tred; mi·ter·ing** *or* **mi·tring** \'mī-tə-riŋ\ **1** : to match or fit together in a miter joint **2** : to bevel the ends of for making a miter joint
miter joint *n* : a usu. perpendicular joint made by fitting together two parts with the ends cut at an angle
mit·i·gate \'mi-tə-ˌgāt\ *vb* **-gat·ed; -gat·ing** **1** : to make less harsh or hostile **2** ♦ : to make less severe or painful — **mit·i·ga·tion** \ˌmi-tə-'gā-shən\ *n* — **mit·i·ga·tive** \'mi-tə-ˌgā-tiv\ *adj*

♦ allay, alleviate, assuage, ease, help, mollify, palliate, relieve, soothe

mi·to·chon·dri·on \ˌmī-tə-'kän-drē-ən\ *n, pl* **-dria** \-drē-ə\ : any of various round or long cellular organelles that produce energy for the cell — **mi·to·chon·dri·al** \-drē-əl\ *adj*
mi·to·sis \mī-'tō-səs\ *n, pl* **-to·ses** \-ˌsēz\ : a process that takes place in the nucleus of a dividing cell and results in the formation of two new nuclei each of which has the same number of chromosomes as the parent nucleus; *also* : cell division in which mitosis occurs — **mi·tot·ic** \-'tä-tik\ *adj*
mitt \'mit\ *n* **1** : a baseball catcher's or first baseman's glove **2** *slang* : HAND
mit·ten \'mit-ᵊn\ *n* : a covering for the hand having a separate section for the thumb only
¹**mix** \'miks\ *vb* **1** ♦ : to combine into one mass **2** ♦ : to enter into relations : ASSOCIATE **3** ♦ : to form by mingling components **4** : to produce (a recording) by electronically combining sounds from different sources **5** : HYBRIDIZE **6** ♦ : to put in disorder : CONFUSE — often used with *up* ⟨~es up the facts⟩ **7** : to become involved — **mix·able** *adj* — **mix·er** *n*

♦ [1] amalgamate, blend, combine, commingle, fuse, incorporate, integrate, intermingle, merge, mingle *Ant* segregate, separate, sort (out) ♦ [2] associate, fraternize, hobnob, mingle, socialize ♦ *usu* **mix up** [6] confuse, disorder, jumble, mess, muddle, scramble, shuffle

²**mix** *n* ♦ : a product of mixing; *esp* : a commercially prepared mixture of food ingredients

♦ admixture, amalgam, blend, combination, composite, compound, fusion, intermixture, mixture

mixed \'mikst\ *adj* **1** ♦ : made up of or involving individuals or items of more than one kind **2** : deriving from two or more races ⟨people of ~ race⟩ **3** ♦ : deriving from two or more breeds

♦ [1] assorted, heterogeneous, miscellaneous, motley, varied
♦ [3] hybrid, mongrel *Ant* full-blooded, purebred, thoroughbred

mixed number *n* : a number (as $5^2/_3$) composed of an integer and a fraction
mixed-up \'mikst-'əp\ *adj* : CONFUSED
mix·er \'mik-sər\ *n* **1** : one that mixes; *esp* : a machine or device for mixing **2** : an event (as a dance) that encourages meeting and socializing **3** : a nonalcoholic beverage used in a cocktail
mixt *abbr* mixture
mix·ture \'miks-chər\ *n* **1** : the act or process of mixing; *also* : the state of being mixed **2** ♦ : a product of mixing

♦ admixture, amalgam, blend, combination, composite, compound, fusion, intermixture, mix

mix–up \'miks-ˌəp\ n **1 :** an instance of confusion **2 :** CONFLICT, FIGHT

miz·zen also **miz·en** \'miz-ᵊn\ n **1 :** a fore-and-aft sail set on the mizzenmast **2 :** MIZZENMAST — **mizzen** also **mizen** adj

miz·zen·mast \-ˌmast, -məst\ n : the mast aft or next aft of the mainmast

mk abbr **1** mark **2** markka

Mk abbr Mark

mks abbr meter-kilogram-second

mkt abbr market

mktg abbr marketing

ml abbr milliliter

Mlle abbr mademoiselle

Mlles abbr mesdemoiselles

mm abbr millimeter

MM abbr messieurs

Mme abbr madame

Mmes abbr mesdames

Mn symbol manganese

MN abbr Minnesota

mne·mon·ic \nə-'mä-nik\ adj : assisting or designed to assist memory; also : of or relating to memory

mo abbr month

¹Mo abbr **1** Missouri **2** Monday

²Mo symbol molybdenum

MO abbr **1** mail order **2** medical officer **3** Missouri **4** modus operandi **5** money order

¹moan \'mōn\ n ♦ : a low prolonged sound indicative of pain or grief

♦ groan, howl, keen, lament, plaint, wail

²moan vb **1** ♦ : to express grief, pain, or discontent **2 :** to make a moan

♦ beef, bellyache, carp, complain, crab, croak, fuss, gripe, grouse, growl, grumble, kick, squawk, wail, whine

moat \'mōt\ n : a deep wide usu. water-filled trench around a castle

¹mob \'mäb\ n **1** ♦ : the lower classes of a community : MASSES **2** ♦ : a disorderly crowd **3** ♦ : a criminal gang

♦ [1] commoners, herd, masses, people, plebeians, populace, rank and file ♦ [2] army, crowd, crush, drove, flock, horde, host, legion, multitude, press, swarm, throng ♦ [3] cabal, conspiracy, gang, ring, syndicate

²mob vb **mobbed; mob·bing 1 :** to crowd about and attack or annoy **2** ♦ : to crowd into or around ⟨shoppers mobbed the stores⟩

♦ crowd, flock, swarm, throng

¹mo·bile \'mō-bəl, -ˌbīl, -ˌbēl\ adj **1 :** capable of moving or being moved **2 :** changeable in appearance, mood, or purpose; also : ADAPTABLE **3 :** having the opportunity for or undergoing a shift in social status **4 :** using vehicles for transportation ⟨∼ warfare⟩ — **mo·bil·i·ty** \mō-'bi-lə-tē\ n

²mo·bile \'mō-ˌbēl\ n : a construction or sculpture (as of wire and sheet metal) with parts that can be set in motion by air currents; also : a similar structure suspended so that it is moved by a current of air

mobile home n : a trailer used as a permanent dwelling

mobile phone n : CELL PHONE

mo·bi·lise chiefly Brit var of MOBILIZE

mo·bi·li·za·tion \ˌmō-bə-lə-'zā-shən\ n **1** ♦ : the act of mobilizing **2 :** the state of being mobilized

♦ muster, rally

mo·bi·lize \'mō-bə-ˌlīz\ vb **-lized; -liz·ing 1 :** to put into movement or circulation **2** ♦ : to assemble and make ready for use or action ⟨∼ army reserves⟩ — **mo·bi·liz·er** \'mō-bə-ˌlī-zər\ n

♦ marshal, muster, rally Ant demobilize

mob·ster \'mäb-stər\ n ♦ : a member of a criminal gang

♦ bully, gangster, goon, hood, hoodlum, mug, punk, rowdy, ruffian, thug, tough

moc·ca·sin \'mä-kə-sən\ n **1 :** a soft leather heelless shoe **2 :** WATER MOCCASIN

mo·cha \'mō-kə\ n **1 :** choice coffee grown in Arabia **2 :** a mixture of coffee and chocolate or cocoa **3 :** a dark chocolate-brown color

¹mock \'mäk, 'mȯk\ vb **1** ♦ : to treat with contempt or ridi-

cule **2 :** DELUDE **3 :** DEFY **4** ♦ : to mimic in sport or derision — **mock** n — **mock·ing·ly** adv

♦ [1] deride, gibe, jeer, laugh, ridicule, scout ♦ [4] burlesque, caricature, imitate, mimic, parody, take off, travesty

²mock adj **1** ♦ : of, relating to, or having the character of an imitation **2** ♦ : not real or genuine

♦ [1] artificial, fake, faux, imitation, sham, synthetic ♦ [2] affected, artificial, assumed, contrived, feigned, mechanical, phony, put-on, spurious, unnatural

mock·er n ♦ : one that mocks

♦ heckler, quiz, scoffer, taunter, tease

mock·ery \'mä-kə-rē, 'mȯ-\ n **1 :** insulting or contemptuous action or speech **2** ♦ : a subject of laughter, derision, or sport **3** ♦ : an insincere, contemptible, or impertinent imitation

♦ [2] butt, laughingstock, mark, mock, target ♦ [3] caricature, farce, joke, parody, sham, travesty

mock–he·ro·ic \ˌmäk-hi-'rō-ik, ˌmȯk-\ adj : ridiculing or burlesquing heroic style, character, or action ⟨a ∼ poem⟩

mock·ing·bird \'mä-kiŋ-ˌbərd, 'mȯ-\ n : a grayish No. American songbird related to the catbirds and thrashers that mimics the calls of other birds

mock–up \'mä-ˌkəp, 'mȯ-\ n : a full-sized structural model built for study, testing, or display ⟨a ∼ of a car⟩

¹mod \'mäd\ adj **1 :** of, relating to, or being the style of the 1960s British youth culture **2** ♦ : very fashionable

♦ contemporary, current, hot, modern, new, newfangled, red-hot, space-age, ultramodern, up-to-date

²mod abbr **1** moderate **2** modern **3** modification; modified

¹mode \'mōd\ n **1 a :** a particular form or variety of something **b** ♦ : a form or manner of expression : STYLE **2 :** a manner of doing something **3 :** the most frequent value of a set of data **4** ♦ : a conscious state of mind or predominant emotion — **mod·al** \'mōd-ᵊl\ adj

♦ [1b] locution, manner, phraseology, style, tone, vein

♦ [4] cheer, frame, humor (or humour), mood, spirit, temper

²mode n ♦ : a prevailing fashion or style (as of dress or behavior)

♦ craze, fad, rage, style, trend, vogue

¹mod·el \'mäd-ᵊl\ n **1 :** structural design **2 :** a miniature representation; also : a pattern of something to be made **3** ♦ : an example for imitation or emulation **4 :** one who poses (as for an artist or to display clothes); also : MANNEQUIN **5 :** TYPE, DESIGN

♦ beau ideal, classic, exemplar, ideal, nonpareil, paragon

²model vb **mod·eled** or **mod·elled; mod·el·ing** or **mod·el·ling 1 :** SHAPE, FASHION, CONSTRUCT **2 :** to work as a fashion model

³model adj **1** ♦ : serving as or worthy of being a pattern ⟨a ∼ student⟩ **2 :** being a miniature representation of something ⟨a ∼ airplane⟩

♦ classic, paradigmatic, quintessential

mo·dem \'mō-dəm, -ˌdem\ n : a device that converts signals produced by one type of device (as a computer) to a form compatible with another (as a telephone)

¹mod·er·ate \'mä-də-rət\ adj **1 a :** avoiding extremes **b** ♦ : having a climate that esp. lacks extremes in temperature **2** ♦ : tending toward the mean or average amount or dimension **3 :** limited in scope or effect **4 :** not expensive — **moderate** n — **mod·er·ate·ness** n

♦ [1b] balmy, clement, equable, gentle, mild, temperate

♦ [2] average, intermediate, median, medium, middle, modest

²mod·er·ate \'mä-də-ˌrāt\ vb **-at·ed; -at·ing 1 :** to lessen the intensity of : TEMPER **2 :** to act as a moderator **3** ♦ : to become less violent, severe, or intense — **mod·er·a·tion** \ˌma-də-'rā-shən\ n

♦ abate, decline, decrease, de-escalate, die, diminish, dwindle, ebb, fall, lessen, let up, lower, recede, relent, shrink, subside, taper, wane

mod·er·ate·ly \-lē\ adv ♦ : in a moderate manner or to a moderate extent

♦ enough, fairly, kind of, pretty, quite, rather, somewhat, sort of, so-so

mod·er·a·tor \'mä-də-ˌrā-tər\ n **1 :** MEDIATOR **2** ♦ : one who presides over an assembly, meeting, or discussion

♦ chair, chairman, president, speaker

mod·ern \'mä-dərn\ adj ♦ : of, relating to, or characteristic of the present or the immediate past : CONTEMPORARY ⟨∼ history⟩ — **modern** *n* — **mo·der·ni·ty** \mə-'dər-nə-tē\ *n* — **mod·ern·ly** *adv* — **mod·ern·ness** *n*

♦ contemporary, current, hot, mod, new, newfangled, red-hot, space-age, ultramodern, up-to-date *Ant* antiquated, archaic, dated, fusty, musty, old-fashioned, old-time, out-of-date, passé

mod·ern·ise, mod·ern·i·sa·tion *chiefly Brit var of* MODERNIZE, MODERNIZATION

mod·ern·ism \'mä-dər-ˌni-zəm\ *n* : a practice, movement, or belief peculiar to modern times

mod·ern·ize \'mä-dər-ˌnīz\ *vb* **-ized; -iz·ing** : to make or become modern — **mod·ern·i·za·tion** \ˌmä-dər-nə-'zā-shən\ *n* — **mod·ern·iz·er** *n*

mod·est \'mä-dəst\ *adj* **1 a** ♦ : having a moderate estimate of oneself **b** ♦ : neither bold nor self-assertive : DIFFIDENT **2** ♦ : observing the proprieties of dress and behavior **3** ♦ : limited in size, amount, or scope

♦ [1a] demure, humble, lowly, meek, retiring, unassuming, unpretentious ♦ [1b] bashful, coy, demure, diffident, introverted, retiring, sheepish, shy ♦ [2] chaste, clean, decent, immaculate, pure ♦ [3] average, intermediate, median, medium, middle, moderate

mod·est·ly \-lē\ *adv* ♦ : in a modest manner or to a modest extent

♦ humbly, lowly, meekly, sheepishly ♦ chastely, purely, righteously, virtuously

mod·es·ty \'mä-də-stē\ *n* **1** ♦ : freedom from conceit or vanity **2** ♦ : propriety in dress, speech, or conduct

♦ [1] humbleness, humility, lowliness, meekness ♦ [2] chastity, purity

mod·i·cum \'mä-di-kəm\ *n* ♦ : a small amount

♦ hoot, jot, lick, rap, tittle, whit

modif *abbr* modification

mod·i·fi·ca·tion \ˌmä-də-fə-'kā-shən\ *n* ♦ : the act, process, or result of modifying

♦ alteration, change, difference, revise, revision, variation

mod·i·fy \'mä-də-ˌfī\ *vb* **-fied; -fy·ing 1** : MODERATE **2** : to limit the meaning of esp. in a grammatical construction **3** ♦ : to make changes in — **mod·i·fi·er** \'mä-də-ˌfī-ər\ *n*

♦ alter, change, make over, recast, redo, refashion, remake, remodel, revamp, revise, rework, vary

mod·ish \'mō-dish\ *adj* ♦ : conforming to the custom, fashion, or established mode : FASHIONABLE ⟨∼ decor⟩ — **mod·ish·ly** *adv*

♦ à la mode, chic, fashionable, in, popular, sharp, smart, snappy, stylish

mod·ish·ness \-nəs\ *n* ♦ : the quality or state of being modish

♦ favor, popularity, vogue

mo·diste \mō-'dēst\ *n* : a maker of fashionable dresses and hats

mod·u·lar \'mä-jə-lər\ *adj* : constructed with standardized units ⟨∼ homes⟩

mod·u·lar·ized \'mä-jə-lə-ˌrīzd\ *adj* : containing or consisting of modules

mod·u·late \'mä-jə-ˌlāt\ *vb* **-lat·ed; -lat·ing 1** : to tune to a key or pitch **2** : to keep in proper measure or proportion : TEMPER **3** : to vary the amplitude or frequency of a carrier wave for the transmission of information (as in radio or television) — **mod·u·la·tion** \ˌmä-jə-'lā-shən\ *n* — **mod·u·la·tor** \'mä-jə-ˌlā-tər\ *n* — **mod·u·la·to·ry** \-lə-ˌtōr-ē\ *adj*

mod·ule \'mä-jül\ *n* **1** : any in a series of standardized units for use together **2** : an assembly of wired electronic parts for use with other such assemblies **3** : an independent unit that constitutes a part of the total structure of a space vehicle ⟨a propulsion ∼⟩

mo·dus ope·ran·di \ˌmō-dəs-ˌä-pə-'ran-dē, -ˌdī\ *n, pl* **mo·di operandi** \'mō-ˌdē-ˌä-, 'mō-ˌdī-\ : a method of procedure ⟨a criminal's *modus operandi*⟩

¹**mo·gul** \'mō-gəl, mō-'gəl\ *n* ♦ : an important person : MAGNATE

♦ baron, czar, king, magnate, prince, tycoon

²**mogul** \'mō-gəl\ *n* : a bump in a ski run

mo·hair \'mō-ˌhar\ *n* : a fabric or yarn made wholly or in part from the long silky hair of the Angora goat; *also* : this goat hair

Mo·ham·med·an *also* **Mu·ham·mad·an** \mō-'ha-mə-dən, -'hä-, mü-\ *n* : MUSLIM

Mo·hawk \'mō-ˌhȯk\ *n, pl* **Mohawk** *or* **Mohawks 1** : a member of an Indigenous people of the Mohawk River valley, New York;

also : the language of the Mohawk people **2** : a hairstyle with a narrow strip of upright hair down the center and the sides shaved

Mo·he·gan \mō-'hē-gən, mə-\ *or* **Mo·hi·can** \-'hē-kən\ *n, pl* **Mohegan** *or* **Mohegans** *or* **Mohican** *or* **Mohicans** : a member of an Indigenous people of southeastern Connecticut

mo·hel \'mō-(h)el, 'mȯi(-ə)l\ *n, pl* **mohels** *also* **mo·hal·im** \ˌmō-hä-'lēm\ *or* **mo·hel·im** \-(h)e-'lēm\ : a person who performs Jewish circumcisions

Mo·hi·can \mō-'hē-kən, mə-\ *or* **Ma·hi·can** \mə-\ *n, pl* **-can** *or* **-cans** : a member of an Indigenous people orig. of the upper Hudson River valley

moi·e·ty \'mȯi-ə-tē\ *n, pl* **-ties** : one of two equal or approximately equal parts

moil \'mȯi(-ə)l\ *vb* : to work hard : DRUDGE — **moil** *n* — **moil·er** *n*

moi·ré \mȯ-'rā, mwä-\ *or* **moire** *same or* 'mȯir, 'mwär\ *n* : a fabric (as silk) having a watered appearance

moist \'mȯist\ *adj* : slightly or moderately wet — **moist·ly** *adv* — **moist·ness** *n*

moist·en \'mȯis-ᵊn\ *vb* : to make or become moist — **moist·en·er** *n*

mois·ture \'mȯis-chər\ *n* : the small amount of liquid that causes dampness

mois·tur·ise *chiefly Brit var of* MOISTURIZE

mois·tur·ize \'mȯis-chə-ˌrīz\ *vb* **-ized; -iz·ing** : to add moisture to — **mois·tur·iz·er** *n*

mo·ji·to \mō-'hē-tō\ *n, pl* **-tos** : a cocktail made of rum, sugar, mint, lime juice, and soda water

mol *abbr* molecular; molecule

mo·lar \'mō-lər\ *n* : any of the broad teeth adapted to grinding food and located in the back of the jaw — **molar** *adj*

mo·las·ses \mə-'la-səz\ *n* : the thick brown syrup that is separated from raw sugar in sugar manufacture

¹**mold** *or Can and Brit* **mould** \'mōld\ *n* : crumbly soil rich in organic matter

²**mold** *or Can and Brit* **mould** *n* **1** : distinctive nature or character **2** : the frame on or around which something is constructed **3** : a cavity in which something is shaped; *also* : an object so shaped **4** : MOLDING

³**mold** *or Can and Brit* **mould** *vb* **1** : to shape in or as if in a mold **2** : to ornament with molding — **mold·er** *n*

⁴**mold** *or Can and Brit* **mould** *n* **1** : a surface growth of fungus esp. on damp or decaying matter; *also* : a fungus that produces molds — **mold·i·ness** \'mōl-dē-nəs\ *n* — **moldy** *adj*

⁵**mold** *or Can and Brit* **mould** *vb* : to become moldy

mold·board *or Can and Brit* **mould·board** \'mōld-ˌbōrd\ *n* : a curved iron plate attached above the plowshare to lift and turn the soil

mold·er *or Can and Brit* **mould·er** \'mōl-dər\ *vb* ♦ : to crumble into small pieces

♦ break down, corrupt, decay, decompose, disintegrate, putrefy, rot, spoil

mold·ing *or Can and Brit* **mould·ing** \'mōl-diŋ\ *n* **1** : an act or process of shaping in a mold; *also* : an object so shaped **2** : a decorative surface, plane, or curved strip

¹**mole** \'mōl\ *n* : a small often pigmented spot or protuberance on the skin

²**mole** *n* : any of numerous small burrowing insect-eating mammals related to the shrews and hedgehogs

³**mole** *n* : a massive breakwater or jetty

mo·lec·u·lar \mə-'le-kyə-lər\ *adj* : of, relating to, or being a molecule

molecular biology *n* : a branch of biology dealing with the ultimate physical and chemical organization of living matter and esp. with the molecular basis of inheritance and protein synthesis — **molecular biologist** *n*

molecular weight *n* : the mass of a molecule that is equal to the sum of the masses of all atoms contained in the molecule's formula

mol·e·cule \'mä-li-ˌkyül\ *n* **1** : the smallest particle of matter that is the same chemically as the whole mass **2** ♦ : a tiny bit

♦ atom, bit, crumb, fleck, flyspeck, grain, granule, morsel, mote, particle, patch, scrap, scruple, speck, tittle

mole·hill \'mōl-ˌhil\ *n* : a little ridge of earth thrown up by a mole

mole·skin \-ˌskin\ *n* **1** : the skin of the mole used as fur **2** : a heavy durable cotton fabric

mo·lest \mə-'lest\ *vb* **1** : ANNOY, DISTURB **2** : to make annoying sexual advances to; *esp* : to force physical and usu. sexual contact on — **mo·les·ta·tion** \ˌmō-ˌles-'tā-shən\ *n* — **mo·lest·er** *n*

moll \'mäl\ *n* : a gangster's girlfriend

mol·li·fy \'mä-lə-ˌfī\ *vb* **-fied; -fy·ing 1** ♦ : to soothe in temper

: APPEASE   **2** : SOFTEN   **3** ♦ : to reduce in intensity : ASSUAGE — **mol·li·fi·ca·tion** \ˌmä-lə-fə-ˈkā-shən\ *n*

  ♦ [1] appease, conciliate, disarm, pacify, placate, propitiate
  ♦ [3] allay, alleviate, assuage, ease, help, mitigate, palliate, relieve, soothe

mol·lusk *or* **mol·lusc** \ˈmä-ləsk\ *n* : any of a large phylum of usu. shelled and aquatic invertebrate animals (as snails, clams, and squids) — **mol·lus·can** *also* **mol·lus·kan** \mə-ˈləs-kən\ *adj*

¹**mol·ly·cod·dle** \ˈmä-lē-ˌkäd-ᵊl\ *n* : a pampered man or boy
²**mollycoddle** *vb* **mol·ly·cod·dled; mol·ly·cod·dling** ♦ : to treat with an excessive or absurd degree of indulgence and attention : PAMPER

  ♦ baby, coddle, nurse, pamper, spoil

Mo·lo·tov cocktail \ˈmä-lə-ˌtȯf-, ˈmȯ-\ *n* : a crude bomb made of a bottle filled usu. with gasoline and fitted with a wick (as a saturated rag) that is ignited just prior to hurling

¹**molt** *or Can and Brit* **moult** \ˈmōlt\ *vb* : to shed hair, feathers, outer skin, or horns periodically with the cast-off parts being replaced by new growth — **molt·er** *n*
²**molt** *or Can and Brit* **moult** *n* : the act or process of molting
mol·ten \ˈmōlt-ᵊn\ *adj*   **1** : fused or liquefied by heat   **2** : GLOWING

mo·ly \ˈmō-lē\ *n* : a mythical herb with black root, white flowers, and magic powers
mo·lyb·de·num \mə-ˈlib-də-nəm\ *n* : a metallic chemical element used in strengthening and hardening steel
mom \ˈmäm, ˈməm\ *n* ♦ : a female parent : MOTHER

  ♦ ma, mommy, mother

mom–and–pop *adj* : being a small owner-operated business
mo·ment \ˈmō-mənt\ *n*   **1** ♦ : a minute portion of time : INSTANT   **2** : a time of excellence ⟨he has his ∼*s*⟩   **3** : IMPORTANCE ⟨an event of great ∼⟩   **4** ♦ : present time

  ♦ [1] flash, instant, jiffy, minute, second, shake, trice, twinkle, twinkling, wink   ♦ [4] now, present, today

mo·men·tari·ly \ˌmō-mən-ˈter-ə-lē\ *adv*   **1** : for a moment   **2** *archaic* : INSTANTLY   **3** ♦ : at any moment : SOON

  ♦ anon, presently, shortly, soon

mo·men·tary \ˈmō-mən-ˌter-ē\ *adj*   **1** ♦ : continuing only a moment ⟨a ∼ pause⟩   **2** : recurring at every moment — **mo·men·tar·i·ness** \-ˌter-ē-nəs\ *n*

  ♦ ephemeral, evanescent, flash, fleeting, fugitive, impermanent, short-lived, transient *Ant* enduring, eternal, everlasting, lasting, permanent, perpetual

mo·men·tous \mō-ˈmen-təs\ *adj* ♦ : very important ⟨a ∼ decision⟩ — **mo·men·tous·ly** *adv* — **mo·men·tous·ness** *n*

  ♦ big, consequential, eventful, important, major, material, meaningful, significant, substantial, weighty

mo·men·tum \mō-ˈmen-təm\ *n, pl* **mo·men·ta** \-ˈmen-tə\ *or* **momentums**   **1** : a property that a moving body has due to its mass and motion   **2** ♦ : something that rouses or incites to activity : IMPETUS

  ♦ boost, encouragement, goad, impetus, impulse, incentive, incitement, instigation, motivation, provocation, spur, stimulus, yeast

mom·my \ˈmä-mē, ˈmə-\ *n, pl* **mom·mies** ♦ : MOTHER

  ♦ ma, mom, mother

Mon *abbr* Monday
mon·arch \ˈmä-nərk, -ˌnärk\ *n*   **1** ♦ : a person who reigns over a kingdom or an empire   **2** : one holding preeminent position or power   **3** : MONARCH BUTTERFLY

  ♦ autocrat, ruler, sovereign

monarch butterfly *n* : a large orange and black migratory American butterfly whose larva feeds on milkweed
mo·nar·chi·cal \mə-ˈnär-ki-kəl, mä-\ *also* **mon·ar·chic** *adj* ♦ : of, relating to, suggestive of, or characteristic of a monarch or monarchy

  ♦ kingly, princely, queenly, regal, royal

mon·ar·chist \ˈmä-nər-kist\ *n* : a believer in monarchical government — **mon·ar·chism** \-ˌki-zəm\ *n*
mon·ar·chy \ˈmä-nər-kē\ *n, pl* **-chies** : a nation or state governed by a monarch
mon·as·tery \ˈmä-nə-ˌster-ē\ *n, pl* **-ter·ies** ♦ : a house for persons under religious vows (as monks)

  ♦ abbey, cloister, friary, priory

mo·nas·tic \mə-ˈnas-tik\ *adj* : of or relating to monasteries or to monks or nuns — **monastic** *n* — **mo·nas·ti·cal·ly** \-ti-k(ə-)lē\ *adv* — **mo·nas·ti·cism** \-tə-ˌsi-zəm\ *n*
mon·au·ral \mä-ˈnȯr-əl\ *adj* : MONOPHONIC — **mon·au·ral·ly** *adv*
Mon·day \ˈmən-dē, -ˌdā\ *n* : the second day of the week
mon·e·tary \ˈmä-nə-ˌter-ē, ˈmə-\ *adj* ♦ : of or relating to money or to the mechanisms by which it is supplied and circulated in the economy

  ♦ financial, fiscal, pecuniary

mon·ey \ˈmə-nē\ *n, pl* **moneys** *or* **mon·ies** \ˈmə-nēz\   **1** ♦ : something (as metal currency) accepted as a medium of exchange   **2** : wealth reckoned in monetary terms   **3** : the 1st, 2d, and 3d places in a horse or dog race

  ♦ cash, currency, dough, lucre, pelf, tender

mon·eyed \ˈmə-nēd\ *adj*   **1** ♦ : having money : WEALTHY   **2** : consisting in or derived from money

  ♦ affluent, flush, loaded, opulent, rich, wealthy, well-fixed, well-heeled, well-off, well-to-do

mon·ey·lend·er \ˈmə-nē-ˌlen-dər\ *n* : one (as a bank or pawnbroker) whose business is lending money
money market *n* : the trade in short-term negotiable financial instruments
money of account : a denominator of value or basis of exchange used in keeping accounts
money order *n* : an order purchased at a post office, bank, or telegraph office directing another office to pay a sum of money to a party named on it
mon·ger \ˈməŋ-gər, ˈmäŋ-\ *n*   **1** : DEALER   **2** : one who tries to stir up or spread something
Mon·gol \ˈmäŋ-gəl, ˈmän-ˌgōl\ *n* : a member of any of several traditionally pastoral peoples of Mongolia — **Mongol** *adj*
Mon·go·lian \män-ˈgōl-yən, mäŋ-, -ˈgō-lē-ən\ *n*   **1** : a native or inhabitant of Mongolia   **2** : a member of a group of people formerly considered to constitute a race of humans having Asian ancestry — **Mongolian** *adj*
Mon·gol·oid \ˈmäŋ-gə-ˌlȯid\ *adj* : of or relating to a group of people formerly considered to constitute a race of humans having Asian ancestry and classified according to physical features — **Mongoloid** *n*
mon·goose \ˈmän-ˌgüs, ˈmäŋ-\ *n, pl* **mon·goos·es** *also* **mon·geese** \-ˌgēs\ : any of a group of small, agile Old World mammals that are related to the civet cats and feed chiefly on small animals and fruits
mon·grel \ˈmäŋ-grəl, ˈmən-\ *n* : an offspring of parents of different breeds; *esp* : one of uncertain ancestry

  ♦ cross, hybrid

mon·i·ker \ˈmä-ni-kər\ *n* : NAME, NICKNAME
mo·nism \ˈmō-ˌni-zəm, ˈmä-\ *n* : a view that reality is basically one unitary organic whole — **mo·nist** \ˈmō-nist, ˈmä-\ *n*
mo·ni·tion \mō-ˈni-shən, mə-\ *n* : WARNING, CAUTION
¹**mon·i·tor** \ˈmä-nə-tər\ *n*   **1** : a student appointed to assist a teacher   **2** : one that monitors; *esp* : a video display screen (as for a computer)
²**monitor** *vb* : to watch, check, or observe for a special purpose
mon·i·to·ry \ˈmä-nə-ˌtōr-ē\ *adj* : giving counsel or warning
¹**monk** \ˈməŋk\ *n* : a man belonging to a religious order and living in a monastery — **monk·ish** *adj*
²**monk** *n* : MONKEY
¹**mon·key** \ˈməŋ-kē\ *n, pl* **monkeys**   **1** : a nonhuman primate mammal; *esp* : one of the smaller, longer-tailed, and usu. more arboreal primates as contrasted with the apes   **2** ♦ : a person resembling a monkey in appearance or behavior

  ♦ devil, hellion, imp, mischief, rapscallion, rascal, rogue, scamp, urchin

²**monkey** *vb* **mon·keyed; mon·key·ing**   **1** ♦ : to behave foolishly : FOOL — often used with *around*   **2** ♦ : to try foolish or dangerous experiments : TAMPER — usu. used with *with*

  ♦ *usu* **monkey around** [1] act up, clown, cut up, fool, show off, skylark   ♦ *usu* **monkey around** [1] fiddle, fool, mess, play, potter, putter, trifle   ♦ *usu* **monkey with** [2] fiddle, fool, mess, play, tamper, tinker

monkey bars *n pl* : a framework of bars on which children can play
mon·key·shine \ˈmən-kē-ˌshīn\ *n* ♦ : a mischievous act; *also* : mischievous behavior — usu. used in pl.

  ♦ *usu* **monkeyshines** *pl* antic, caper, escapade, frolic, practical joke, prank, trick ♦ usu **monkeyshines** pl foolery, high jinks, horseplay, roughhouse, shenanigans, tomfoolery

monkey wrench n : a wrench with one fixed and one adjustable jaw at right angles to a handle

monk·fish \'mǝŋk-ˌfish\ n : either of two marine bony fishes that have a large flattened head and are used for food

monks·hood \'mǝŋks-ˌhùd\ n : any of a genus of poisonous plants related to the buttercups; esp : a tall Eurasian herb with white or purplish flowers

¹**mono** \'mä-nō\ adj : MONOPHONIC

²**mono** n : INFECTIOUS MONONUCLEOSIS

mono·chro·mat·ic \ˌmä-nǝ-krō-'ma-tik\ adj 1 : having or consisting of one color 2 : consisting of radiation (as light) of a single wavelength

mono·chrome \'mä-nǝ-ˌkrōm\ adj : involving or producing visual images in a single color or in varying tones of a single color ⟨∼ television⟩

mon·o·cle \'mä-ni-kǝl\ n : an eyeglass for one eye

mono·clo·nal \ˌmä-nǝ-'klō-nǝl\ adj : produced by, being, or composed of cells derived from a single cell ⟨∼ antibodies⟩

mono·cot·y·le·don \ˌmä-nǝ-ˌkät-ᵊl-'ēd-ᵊn\ n : any of a class or subclass of chiefly herbaceous seed plants having an embryo with a single cotyledon and usu. parallel-veined leaves

mon·o·dy \'mä-nǝ-dē\ n, pl **-dies** : ELEGY, DIRGE — **mo·nod·ic** \mǝ-'nä-dik\ or **mo·nod·i·cal** \-di-kǝl\ adj — **mon·o·dist** \'mä-nǝ-dist\ n

mo·nog·a·my \mǝ-'nä-gǝ-mē\ n 1 : marriage with but one person at a time 2 : the practice of having a single mate during a period of time — **mo·nog·a·mist** \-mist\ n — **mo·nog·a·mous** \-mǝs\ adj

mono·gram \'mä-nǝ-ˌgram\ n : a sign of identity composed of the combined initials of a name — **monogram** vb

mono·graph \'mä-nǝ-ˌgraf\ n : a learned treatise on a small area of learning

mono·lin·gual \ˌmä-nǝ-'liŋ-gwǝl\ adj : knowing or using only one language

mono·lith \'mä-nᵊl-ˌith\ n 1 : a single great stone often in the form of a monument or column 2 : something large and powerful that acts as a single unified force ⟨a bureaucratic ∼⟩ — **mono·lith·ic** \ˌmä-nᵊl-'i-thik\ adj

mono·logue also **mono·log** \'mä-nᵊl-ˌòg\ n 1 : a dramatic soliloquy; also : a long speech monopolizing conversation 2 : the routine of a stand-up comic — **mono·logu·ist** \-ˌòg-ist\ or **mo·nol·o·gist** \mǝ-'nä-lǝ-jist, 'mä-nᵊl-ˌò-gist\ n

mono·ma·nia \ˌmä-nǝ-'mā-nē-ǝ, -nyǝ\ n 1 : mental disorder limited in expression to one area of thought 2 : excessive concentration on a single object or idea — **mono·ma·ni·ac** \-nē-ˌak\ n or adj

mono·mer \'mä-nǝ-mǝr\ n : a simple chemical compound that can be polymerized

mono·nu·cle·o·sis \ˌmä-nō-ˌnü-klē-'ō-sǝs, -ˌnyü-\ n : INFECTIOUS MONONUCLEOSIS

mono·phon·ic \ˌmä-nǝ-'fä-nik\ adj : of or relating to sound recording or reproduction involving a single transmission path

mono·plane \'mä-nǝ-ˌplān\ n : an airplane with only one set of wings

mo·nop·o·ly \mǝ-'nä-pǝ-lē\ n, pl **-lies** 1 : exclusive ownership (as through command of supply) 2 : a commodity controlled by one party 3 : one that has a monopoly — **mo·nop·o·list** \-list\ n — **mo·nop·o·lis·tic** \mǝ-ˌnä-pǝ-'lis-tik\ adj — **mo·nop·o·li·za·tion** \-lǝ-'zā-shǝn\ n — **mo·nop·o·lize** \mǝ-'nä-pǝ-ˌlīz\ vb

mono·rail \'mä-nǝ-ˌrāl\ n : a single rail serving as a track for a vehicle; also : a vehicle traveling on such a track

mono·so·di·um glu·ta·mate \ˌmä-nǝ-ˌsō-dē-ǝm-'glü-tǝ-ˌmāt\ n : a crystalline salt used to enhance the flavor of food

mono·syl·la·ble \'mä-nǝ-ˌsi-lǝ-bǝl\ n : a word of one syllable — **mono·syl·lab·ic** \ˌmä-nǝ-sǝ-'la-bik\ adj — **mono·syl·lab·i·cal·ly** \-bi-k(ǝ-)lē\ adv

mono·the·ism \'mä-nǝ-(ˌ)thē-ˌi-zǝm\ n : a doctrine or belief that there is only one deity — **mono·the·ist** \-ˌthē-ist\ n — **mono·the·is·tic** \-thē-'is-tik\ adj

mono·tone \'mä-nǝ-ˌtōn\ n : a succession of syllables, words, or sentences in one unvaried key or pitch

mo·not·o·nous \mǝ-'nät-ᵊn-ǝs\ adj 1 : uttered or sounded in one unvarying tone 2 ♦ : tediously uniform — **mo·not·o·nous·ly** adv — **mo·not·o·nous·ness** n

♦ drab, dreary, dry, dull, flat, uninteresting, weary

mo·not·o·ny \mǝ-'nät-ᵊn-ē\ n : tedious sameness or uniformity

mono·un·sat·u·rat·ed \ˌmä-nō-ˌǝn-'sa-chǝ-ˌrā-tǝd\ adj : containing one double or triple bond per molecule — used esp. of an oil or fatty acid

mon·ox·ide \mǝ-'näk-ˌsīd\ n : an oxide containing one atom of oxygen in a molecule

mon·sei·gneur \ˌmōⁿ-ˌsän-'yǝr\ n, pl **mes·sei·gneurs** \ˌmā-ˌsän-'yǝr, -'yǝrz\ : a French dignitary — used as a title

mon·sieur \mǝs-'yǝr, mǝ-'shǝr, Fr mǝ-'syœ̄\ n, pl **mes·sieurs** \same or -'yǝrz, -'shǝrz\ : a Frenchman of high rank or station — used as a title equivalent to Mister

mon·si·gnor \män-'sē-nyǝr\ n, pl **monsignors** or **mon·si·gno·ri** \ˌmän-ˌsēn-'yòr-ē\ : a Roman Catholic prelate — used as a title

mon·soon \män-'sün\ n 1 : a periodic wind esp. in the Indian Ocean and southern Asia 2 : the season of the southwest monsoon esp. in India 3 : rainfall associated with the monsoon

¹**mon·ster** \'män-stǝr\ n 1 : an abnormally developed plant or animal 2 a : an animal of strange or terrifying shape b ♦ : one unusually large of its kind 3 ♦ : an extremely ugly, wicked, or cruel person 4 : something monstrous

♦ [2b] behemoth, blockbuster, colossus, giant, jumbo, leviathan, mammoth, titan, whale, whopper ♦ [3] beast, brute, devil, fiend, savage, villain

²**monster** adj : very large : ENORMOUS

mon·strance \'män-strǝns\ n : a vessel in which the consecrated Host is exposed for the adoration of the faithful

mon·stros·i·ty \män-'strä-sǝ-tē\ n 1 a : a malformation of a plant or animal b ♦ : something deviating from the normal : FREAK 2 ♦ : the quality or state of being monstrous 3 a : an object of great and often frightening size, force, or complexity b ♦ : an excessively bad or shocking example

♦ [1b] abnormality, freak, monster ♦ [2] atrociousness, atrocity, frightfulness, hideousness, horror, repulsiveness ♦ [2] atrociousness, atrocity, depravity, enormity, heinousness, vileness, wickedness ♦ [3b] eyesore, fright, horror, mess, sight

mon·strous \'män-strǝs\ adj 1 ♦ : having extraordinary often overwhelming size 2 ♦ : extraordinarily ugly or vicious 3 ♦ : deviating greatly from the natural form or character

♦ [1] enormous, giant, gigantic, huge, mammoth, massive, monster, monumental, prodigious, tremendous, whopping ♦ [2] appalling, atrocious, awful, dreadful, frightful, ghastly, grisly, gruesome, hideous, horrible, horrid, lurid, macabre, nightmarish, shocking, terrible ♦ [3] deformed, distorted, malformed, misshapen, shapeless

mon·strous·ly \-lē\ adv ♦ : in a monstrous manner

♦ devilishly, excessively, inordinately, overly, overmuch, too ♦ broadly, considerably, greatly, hugely, largely, massively, much, sizably, stupendously, tremendously, utterly, vastly

Mont abbr Montana

mon·tage \män-'täzh\ n 1 : a composite photograph made by combining several separate pictures 2 : an artistic composition made up of several different kinds of elements 3 : a varied mixture : JUMBLE

month \'mǝnth\ n, pl **months** \'mǝns, 'mǝnths\ : one of the 12 parts into which the year is divided — **month·ly** adv or adj or n

month·long \'mǝnth-ˌlòŋ\ adj : lasting a month

mon·u·ment \'män-yǝ-mǝnt\ n 1 ♦ : a lasting reminder; esp : a structure erected in remembrance of a person or event 2 : NATIONAL MONUMENT

♦ gravestone, headstone, tombstone ♦ keepsake, memento, memorial, remembrance, souvenir, token

mon·u·men·tal \ˌmän-yǝ-'men-ᵊl\ adj 1 : of or relating to a monument 2 a ♦ : having impressive bulk or size b : highly significant : OUTSTANDING 3 ♦ : very great ⟨a ∼ task⟩ — **mon·u·men·tal·ly** adv

♦ colossal, enormous, giant, gigantic, grand, heroic, huge, mammoth, massive, outsize, oversize, prodigious, titanic, tremendous, vast

moo \'mü\ vb : to make the natural throat noise of a cow — **moo** n

mooch·er \'mü-chǝr\ n ♦ : one that begs or lives off another's expense

♦ hanger-on, leech, parasite, sponge

¹**mood** \'müd\ n 1 ♦ : a conscious state of mind or predominant emotion 2 : a prevailing attitude : DISPOSITION 3 ♦ : a distinctive atmosphere

♦ [1] cheer, frame, humor (or humour), mode, spirit, temper ♦ [3] air, atmosphere, aura, climate, flavor (or flavour), note, temper

²**mood** n : distinction of form of a verb to express whether its ac-

tion or state is conceived as fact or in some other manner (as wish)

moody \'mü-dē\ *adj* **mood·i·er; -est** **1** : GLOOMY **2** ♦ : subject to moods : TEMPERAMENTAL — **mood·i·ly** \-də-lē\ *adv* — **mood·i·ness** \-dē-nəs\ *n*

  ♦ glum, morose, sulky, sullen, surly

¹**moon** \'mün\ *n* **1** : the earth's natural satellite **2** : SATELLITE 2 **3** ♦ : an indefinite usu. extended period of time — often used in pl.

  ♦ aeon (*or* eon), age, cycle, eternity

²**moon** *vb* : to engage in idle reverie

moon·beam \'mün-ˌbēm\ *n* : a ray of light from the moon

¹**moon·light** \-ˌlīt\ *n* : the light of the moon — **moon·lit** \-ˌlit\ *adj*

²**moonlight** *vb* **moon·light·ed; moon·light·ing** : to hold a second job in addition to a regular one — **moon·light·er** *n*

moon·roof \-ˌrüf, -ˌrüf\ *n* : a glass sunroof

moon·scape \-ˌskāp\ *n* : the surface of the moon as seen or as pictured

moon·shine \-ˌshīn\ *n* **1** : MOONLIGHT **2** : empty talk **3** ♦ : intoxicating liquor usu. illegally distilled

  ♦ alcohol, booze, drink, intoxicant, liquor, spirits

moon·stone \-ˌstōn\ *n* : a transparent or translucent feldspar of pearly luster used as a gem

moon·struck \-ˌstrək\ *adj* **1** : mentally unbalanced **2** : romantically sentimental **3** : lost in fantasy

¹**moor** \'mür\ *n* **1** *chiefly Brit* : an expanse of open rolling infertile land **2** : a boggy area; *esp* : one that is peaty and dominated by grasses and sedges

²**moor** *vb* ♦ : to make fast with or as if with cables, lines, or anchors

  ♦ anchor, catch, clamp, fasten, fix, hitch, secure, set ♦ disembark, dock, land, tie up

Moor \'mür\ *n* : one of the Arab and Berber conquerors of Spain — **Moor·ish** *adj*

moor·ing \'mür-iŋ\ *n* **1** : a place where or an object to which a craft can be made fast **2** : an established practice or stabilizing influence — usu. used in pl.

moor·land \-lənd, -ˌland\ *n* : land consisting of moors

moose \'müs\ *n, pl* **moose** : a large heavy-antlered ruminant mammal related to the deer that has humped shoulders and long legs and inhabits northern forested areas

¹**moot** \'müt\ *vb* **1** ♦ : to bring up for discussion **2** ♦ : to argue about : DEBATE

  ♦ [1] bring up, broach, introduce, raise ♦ [2] argue, chew over, debate, discuss, dispute, hash, talk over

²**moot** *adj* **1** ♦ : open to question; *also* : DISPUTED **2** : having no practical significance ⟨the issue is now ~⟩

  ♦ arguable, debatable, disputable, doubtful, questionable

¹**mop** \'mäp\ *n* : an implement made of absorbent material fastened to a handle and used esp. for cleaning floors

²**mop** *vb* **mopped; mop·ping** : to use a mop on : clean with a mop

mope \'mōp\ *vb* **moped; mop·ing** **1** : to become dull, dejected, or listless **2** ♦ : to move slowly or aimlessly

  ♦ gad, gallivant, knock, maunder, meander, ramble, range, roam, rove, traipse, wander

mo·ped \'mō-ˌped\ *n* : a light low-powered motorbike that can be pedaled

mop·pet \'mä-pət\ *n* ♦ : a young person who is between infancy and adulthood : CHILD

  ♦ child, cub, juvenile, kid, kiddo, whelp, youngster, youth

mo·raine \mə-ˈrān\ *n* : an accumulation of earth and stones left by a glacier

¹**mor·al** \'mör-əl\ *adj* **1** : of or relating to principles of right and wrong ⟨a ~ lesson⟩ **2** ♦ : conforming to a standard of right behavior; *also* : capable of right and wrong action **3** : probable but not proved ⟨a ~ certainty⟩ **4** : perceptual or psychological rather than tangible or practical in nature or effect ⟨a ~ victory⟩

  ♦ decent, ethical, good, honest, honorable (*or* honourable), just, right, righteous, straight, upright, virtuous

²**moral** *n* **1** : the practical meaning (as of a story) **2** *pl* ♦ : moral practices or teachings

  ♦ **morals** *pl* ethics, morality, principles, standards

mo·rale \mə-ˈral\ *n* **1** : MORALITY **2** : the mental and emotional attitudes of an individual toward the tasks at hand; *also* : ESPRIT DE CORPS

mor·al·ise *chiefly Brit var of* MORALIZE

mor·al·ist \'mör-ə-list\ *n* **1** : one who leads a moral life **2** : a thinker or writer concerned with morals **3** : one concerned with regulating the morals of others — **mor·al·is·tic** \ˌmör-ə-ˈlis-tik\ *adj* — **mor·al·is·ti·cal·ly** \-ti-k(ə-)lē\ *adv*

mo·ral·i·ty \mə-ˈra-lə-tē\ *n, pl* **-ties** **1** ♦ : a doctrine or system of moral conduct **2** ♦ : moral conduct : VIRTUE

  ♦ [1] ethics, morals, principles, standards ♦ [2] character, decency, goodness, honesty, honor (*or* honour), integrity, probity, rectitude, righteousness, uprightness, virtue *Ant* badness, evil, immorality, wickedness

mor·al·ize \'mör-ə-ˌlīz\ *vb* **-ized; -iz·ing** : to make moral reflections — **mor·al·i·za·tion** \ˌmör-ə-lə-ˈzā-shən\ *n* — **mor·al·iz·er** \'mör-ə-ˌlī-zər\ *n*

mor·al·ly \'mör-ə-lē\ *adv* : in accordance with morals : in a moral manner

mo·rass \mə-ˈras\ *n* ♦ : a tract of soft wet land : SWAMP; *also* : something that entangles, impedes, or confuses

  ♦ bog, fen, marsh, mire, slough, swamp

mor·a·to·ri·um \ˌmör-ə-ˈtȯr-ē-əm\ *n, pl* **-ri·ums** *or* **-ria** \-ē-ə\ ♦ : a suspension of activity

  ♦ abeyance, doldrums, dormancy, holding pattern, latency, quiescence, suspension

mo·ray eel \mə-ˈrā-, ˈmȯr-ˌā-\ *n* : any of numerous often brightly colored biting eels of warm seas

mor·bid \'mȯr-bəd\ *adj* **1** : of, relating to, or typical of disease; *also* : DISEASED, SICKLY **2** : characterized by gloomy or unwholesome ideas or feelings **3** : GRISLY, GRUESOME ⟨~ details⟩ — **mor·bid·i·ty** \mȯr-ˈbi-də-tē\ *n* — **mor·bid·ly** *adv* — **mor·bid·ness** *n*

mor·dant \'mȯrd-ᵊnt\ *adj* **1** ♦ : biting or caustic in manner or style **2** : BURNING, PUNGENT — **mor·dant·ly** *adv*

  ♦ acrid, biting, caustic, cutting, pungent, sarcastic, satiric, scathing, sharp, tart

¹**more** \'mȯr\ *adj* **1** : GREATER **2** ♦ : existing by way of addition : ADDITIONAL ⟨wanted ~ coffee⟩

  ♦ additional, another, else, farther, further, other

²**more** *adv* **1** : in addition **2** : to a greater or higher degree

³**more** *n* **1** : a greater quantity, number, or amount ⟨the ~ the merrier⟩ **2** : an additional amount ⟨costs a little ~⟩

⁴**more** *pron* : additional persons or things or a greater amount

mo·rel \mə-ˈrel\ *n* : any of several pitted edible fungi

more·over \mȯr-ˈō-vər\ *adv* ♦ : in addition : FURTHER

  ♦ additionally, again, also, besides, further, furthermore, likewise, more, then, too, withal, yet

mo·res \'mȯr-ˌāz\ *n pl* **1** ♦ : the fixed morally binding customs of a group **2** : HABITS, MANNERS

  ♦ etiquette, manners

Mor·gan \'mȯr-gən\ *n* : any of an American breed of lightly built horses

morgue \'mȯrg\ *n* : a place where the bodies of dead persons are kept until released for burial or autopsy

mor·i·bund \'mȯr-ə-ˌbənd\ *adj* : being in a dying condition

Mor·mon \'mȯr-mən\ *n* : a member of the Church of Jesus Christ of Latter-day Saints — **Mor·mon·ism** \-mə-ˌni-zəm\ *n*

morn \'mȯrn\ *n* **1** : the first appearance of light in the morning followed by sunrise **2** : MORNING

morn·ing \'mȯr-niŋ\ *n* **1 a** ♦ : the first appearance of light in the morning followed by sunrise **b** : the time from the sunrise to noon **2** ♦ : a period of first development : BEGINNING

  ♦ [1a] aurora, cockcrow, dawn, sunrise ♦ [2] beginning, birth, commencement, dawn, genesis, launch, onset, outset, start, threshold

morn·ing–after pill \ˌmȯr-niŋ-ˈaf-tər-\ *n* : a contraceptive drug taken up to usu. three days after sexual intercourse

morning glory *n* : any of various twining plants related to the sweet potato that have often showy bell-shaped or funnel-shaped flowers

morning sickness *n* : nausea and vomiting that typically occur in the morning esp. during early pregnancy

morning star *n* : a bright planet (as Venus) seen in the eastern sky before or at sunrise

Mo·roc·can \mə-ˈrä-kən\ *n* : a native or inhabitant of Morocco

mo·roc·co \mə-ˈrä-kō\ *n* : a fine leather made of goatskins tanned with sumac

mo·ron \'mȯr-ˌän\ *n* **1** ♦ : a very stupid person **2** *dated, now offensive* : a person affected with mild intellectual disability —

mo·ron·ic \mə-'rä-nik\ *adj* — **mo·ron·i·cal·ly** \-ni-k(ə-)lē\ *adv*

♦ blockhead, dolt, dope, dummy, idiot, imbecile, jackass, nitwit, numskull, simpleton

mo·rose \mə-'rōs\ *adj* **1** ♦ : having a sullen disposition **2** : marked by or expressive of gloom : GLOOMY — **mo·rose·ly** *adv* — **mo·rose·ness** *n*

♦ glum, moody, sulky, sullen, surly

morph \'mȯrf\ *vb* : to change the form or character of : TRANSFORM

mor·pheme \'mȯr-ˌfēm\ *n* : a meaningful linguistic unit that contains no smaller meaningful parts — **mor·phe·mic** \mȯr-'fē-mik\ *adj*

mor·phia \'mȯr-fē-ə\ *n* : MORPHINE

mor·phine \'mȯr-ˌfēn\ *n* : an addictive drug obtained from opium and used to ease pain or induce sleep

mor·phol·o·gy \mȯr-'fä-lə-jē\ *n* **1** : a branch of biology dealing with the form and structure of organisms **2** : a study and description of word formation in a language — **mor·pho·log·i·cal** \ˌmȯr-fə-'lä-ji-kəl\ *adj* — **mor·phol·o·gist** \mȯr-'fä-lə-jist\ *n*

mor·ris \'mȯr-əs\ *n* : a vigorous English dance traditionally performed by men wearing costumes and bells

mor·row \'mär-ō\ *n* : the next day

Morse code \'mȯrs-\ *n* : either of two codes consisting of dots and dashes or long and short sounds used for transmitting messages

mor·sel \'mȯr-səl\ *n* **1** ♦ : a small piece or quantity **2** : a tasty dish **3** ♦ : a small piece of food

♦ [1] bit, crumb, grain, granule, particle, scrap ♦ [3] bite, mouthful, nibble, taste, tidbit

¹mor·tal \'mȯrt-ᵊl\ *adj* **1 a** ♦ : causing death : FATAL **b** : leading to eternal punishment ⟨~ sin⟩ **2** : subject to death ⟨~ man⟩ **3** : implacably hostile ⟨~ foe⟩ **4** : very great : EXTREME ⟨~ fear⟩ **5** : HUMAN ⟨~ limitations⟩ **6** ♦ : of, relating to, or connected with death — **mor·tal·i·ty** \mȯr-'ta-lə-tē\ *n*

♦ baleful, deadly, deathly, fatal, fell, lethal, murderous, pestilent, vital

²mortal *n* ♦ : a human being

♦ being, body, creature, human, individual, man, person

mor·tal·ly \'mȯrt-ᵊl-ē\ *adv* **1** : in a deadly or fatal manner ⟨~ wounded⟩ **2** ♦ : to an extreme degree ⟨~ afraid⟩

♦ especially, extremely, greatly, highly, hugely, mightily, mighty, most, much, real, right, so, very

¹mor·tar \'mȯr-tər\ *n* **1** : a strong bowl in which substances are pounded or crushed with a pestle **2** : a short-barreled cannon used to fire shells at high angles

²mortar *n* : a building material (as a mixture of lime and cement with sand and water) that is spread between bricks or stones to bind them together as it hardens — **mortar** *vb*

mor·tar·board \'mȯr-tər-ˌbȯrd\ *n* **1** : a square board for holding mortar **2** : an academic cap with a flat square top

mort·gage \'mȯr-gij\ *n* : a transfer of rights to a piece of property usu. as security for the payment of a loan or debt that becomes void when the debt is paid — **mortgage** *vb* — **mort·gag·ee** \ˌmȯr-gi-'jē\ *n* — **mort·gag·or** \ˌmȯr-gi-'jȯr\ *n*

mor·ti·cian \mȯr-'ti-shən\ *n* : UNDERTAKER

mor·ti·fi·ca·tion \ˌmȯr-tə-fə-'kā-shən\ *n* ♦ : a sense of humiliation and shame caused by something that wounds one's pride or self-respect

♦ abashment, confusion, discomfiture, embarrassment, fluster

mor·ti·fy \'mȯr-tə-ˌfī\ *vb* **-fied; -fy·ing 1** : to subdue (as the body) esp. by abstinence or self-inflicted pain **2** ♦ : to subject to severe and vexing embarrassment **3** : to become necrotic or gangrenous

♦ abash, confound, confuse, discomfit, disconcert, discountenance, embarrass, faze, fluster, rattle

mor·tise *also* **mor·tice** \'mȯr-təs\ *n* : a hole cut in a piece of wood into which another piece fits to form a joint

mor·tu·ary \'mȯr-chə-ˌwer-ē\ *n, pl* **-ar·ies** : a place in which dead bodies are kept until burial

mos *abbr* months

mo·sa·ic \mō-'zā-ik\ *n* : a surface decoration made by inlaying small pieces (as of colored glass or stone) to form figures or patterns; *also* : a design made in mosaic — **mosaic** *adj*

mos·co·vi·um \mä-'skō-vē-əm\ *n* : a short-lived artificially produced radioactive element

mo·sey \'mō-zē\ *vb* **mo·seyed; mo·sey·ing** : SAUNTER

mosh \'mäsh\ *vb* : to engage in rough uninhibited dancing near the stage at a rock concert

mosh pit *n* : an area in front of a stage where rough dancing takes place at a rock concert

Mos·lem \'mäz-ləm\ *var of* MUSLIM

mosque \'mäsk\ *n* : a building used for public worship by Muslims

mos·qui·to \mə-'skē-tō\ *n, pl* **-toes** *also* **-tos** : any of a family of dipteran flies the female of which sucks the blood of animals

mosquito net *n* : a net or screen for keeping out mosquitoes

moss \'mȯs\ *n* : any of a class of green plants that lack flowers but have small leafy stems and often grow in clumps — **mossy** *adj*

moss·back \'mȯs-ˌbak\ *n* : an extremely conservative person : FOGY

¹most \'mōst\ *adj* **1** ♦ : greatest in quantity, extent, or degree ⟨the ~ ability⟩ **2** : the majority of ⟨~ people⟩

♦ consummate, maximum, nth, paramount, supreme, top, ultimate, utmost

²most *adv* **1** : to the greatest or highest degree ⟨~ beautiful⟩ **2** : to a very great degree ⟨a ~ careful driver⟩

³most *n* : the greatest amount ⟨the ~ I can do⟩

⁴most *pron* : the greatest number or part ⟨~ became discouraged⟩

⁵most *adv* ♦ : very nearly but not exactly or entirely : ALMOST

♦ about, almost, much, near, nearly, next to, nigh, practically, some, virtually, well-nigh

-most \ˌmōst\ *adj suffix* : most ⟨inner*most*⟩ : most toward ⟨end*most*⟩

most·ly \'mōst-lē\ *adv* ♦ : for the greatest part : MAINLY

♦ altogether, basically, chiefly, generally, largely, mainly, overall, predominantly, primarily, principally

mot \'mō\ *n, pl* **mots** *same or* 'mōz\ : a witty saying

mote \'mōt\ *n* ♦ : a small particle

♦ bit, fleck, flyspeck, molecule, particle, speck

mo·tel \mō-'tel\ *n* : a hotel in which the rooms are accessible from the parking area

mo·tet \mō-'tet\ *n* : a choral work on a sacred text for several voices usu. without instrumental accompaniment

moth \'mȯth\ *n, pl* **moths** \'mȯthz, 'mȯths\ : any of various insects belonging to the same order as the butterflies but usu. night-flying and with a stouter body and smaller wings

moth·ball \'mȯth-ˌbȯl\ *n* **1** : a ball (as of naphthalene) used to keep moths out of clothing **2** *pl* : protective storage

¹moth·er \'mə-t͟hər\ *n* **1** ♦ : a female parent **2** : the superior of a religious community of women **3** : SOURCE, ORIGIN — **moth·er·hood** \-ˌhüd\ *n* — **moth·er·less** *adj* — **moth·er·li·ness** \-lē-nəs\ *n* — **moth·er·ly** *adj*

♦ ma, mom, mommy

²mother *vb* **1** : to give birth to; *also* : PRODUCE **2** ♦ : to care for or protect like a mother

♦ aid, care, minister, nurse

moth·er·board \'mə-t͟hər-ˌbȯrd\ *n* : the main circuit board esp. of a microcomputer

moth·er–in–law \'mə-t͟hər-ən-ˌlȯ\ *n, pl* **mothers–in–law** \'mə-t͟hərz-\ : the mother of one's spouse

moth·er·land \'mə-t͟hər-ˌland\ *n* **1** : the land of origin of something **2** ♦ : the native land of one's ancestors

♦ country, fatherland, home, homeland, sod

moth·er–of–pearl \ˌmə-t͟hər-əv-'pərl\ *n* : the hard pearly matter forming the inner layer of a mollusk shell

mother ship *n* : a ship serving smaller craft

mo·tif \mō-'tēf\ *n* **1** ♦ : a dominant idea or central theme (as in a work of art) **2** ♦ : a single or repeated design or color

♦ [1] content, matter, question, subject, theme, topic ♦ [2] design, figure, motive, pattern

mo·tile \'mōt-ᵊl, 'mō-ˌtīl\ *adj* : capable of spontaneous movement ⟨~ cells⟩ — **mo·til·i·ty** \mō-'ti-lə-tē\ *n*

¹mo·tion \'mō-shən\ *n* **1** ♦ : an act, process, or instance of moving **2** : a proposal for action (as by a deliberative body) **3** *pl* : ACTIVITIES, MOVEMENTS — **mo·tion·less** *adj* — **mo·tion·less·ly** *adv* — **mo·tion·less·ness** *n*

♦ move, movement, moving, shift, stir, stirring

²motion *vb* ♦ : to direct or signal by a movement

♦ flag, gesture, signal, wave

motion picture *n* **1** : a series of pictures projected on a screen so rapidly that they produce a continuous picture in which persons and objects seem to move   **2** ♦ : a representation (as of a story) by means of motion pictures

♦ film, movie, picture

motion sickness *n* : sickness induced by motion and characterized by nausea

mo·ti·vate \ˈmō-tə-ˌvāt\ *vb* **-vat·ed; -vat·ing** : to provide with a motive : IMPEL — **mo·ti·va·tor** \ˈmō-tə-ˌvā-tər\ *n*

mo·ti·va·tion \ˌmō-tə-ˈvā-shən\ *n* **1 a** : the act or process of motivating   **b** : the condition of being motivated   **2** ♦ : a motivating force, stimulus, or influence — **mo·ti·va·tion·al** \-shə-nəl\ *adj*

♦ boost, encouragement, goad, impetus, impulse, incentive, incitement, instigation, momentum, provocation, spur, stimulus, yeast

¹**mo·tive** \ˈmō-tiv, 2 also mō-ˈtēv\ *n* **1** ♦ : something (as a need or desire) that causes a person to act   **2** : a recurrent theme in a musical composition   **3** : a dominant idea or central theme (as in a work of art) : MOTIF   **4** : a single or repeated design or color : MOTIF — **mo·tive·less** *adj*

♦ grounds, reason, wherefore, why

²**mo·tive** \ˈmō-tiv\ *adj* **1** : moving to action   **2** : of or relating to motion

¹**mot·ley** \ˈmät-lē\ *adj* **1** ♦ : variegated in color   **2** ♦ : made up of diverse often incongruous elements

♦ [1] multicolored, variegated ♦ [2] assorted, heterogeneous, miscellaneous, mixed, varied

²**motley** *n* : a mixture of incongruous elements

¹**mo·tor** \ˈmō-tər\ *n* **1** : one that imparts motion   **2** : a machine that produces motion or power for doing work   **3** : a usu. 4-wheeled automotive vehicle designed for passenger transportation : AUTOMOBILE

²**motor** *vb* : to travel or transport by automobile : DRIVE — **mo·tor·ist** *n*

mo·tor·bike \ˈmō-tər-ˌbīk\ *n* : a small lightweight motorcycle

mo·tor·boat \-ˌbōt\ *n* : a boat propelled by a motor

mo·tor·cade \-ˌkād\ *n* ♦ : a procession of motor vehicles

♦ armada, caravan, cavalcade, fleet, train

mo·tor·car \-ˌkär\ *n* : a usu. 4-wheeled automotive vehicle designed for passenger transportation : AUTOMOBILE

mo·tor·cy·cle \ˈmō-tər-ˌsī-kəl\ *n* : a 2-wheeled automotive vehicle — **mo·tor·cy·clist** \-k(ə-)list\ *n*

motor home *n* ♦ : a large motor vehicle equipped as living quarters

♦ camper, caravan, trailer

motor inn *n* : MOTEL

mo·tor·ise *chiefly Brit var of* MOTORIZE

mo·tor·ize \ˈmō-tə-ˌrīz\ *vb* **-ized; -iz·ing** **1** : to equip with a motor   **2** : to equip with automobiles

mo·tor·man \ˈmō-tər-mən\ *n* : an operator of a motor-driven vehicle (as a streetcar or subway train)

motor scooter *n* : a low 2- or 3-wheeled automotive vehicle resembling a child's scooter but having a seat

mo·tor·truck \ˈmō-tər-ˌtrək\ *n* : an automotive truck

motor vehicle *n* ♦ : an automotive vehicle (as an automobile) not operated on rails

♦ automobile, car, machine

mot·tle \ˈmät-əl\ *vb* **mot·tled; mot·tling** ♦ : to mark with spots of different color : BLOTCH

♦ blotch, dapple, dot, fleck, freckle, pepper, speck, spot, sprinkle, stipple

mot·tled \ˈmä-t°ld\ *adj* ♦ : marked with spots of different colors

♦ dappled, piebald, pied, spotted ♦ dappled, spotted, spotty, variegated

mot·to \ˈmä-tō\ *n, pl* **mottoes** *also* **mottos** **1** : a sentence, phrase, or word inscribed on something to indicate its character or use   **2** : a short expression of a guiding rule of conduct

moue \ˈmü\ *n* : a little grimace

mould *chiefly Can and Brit var of* MOLD

moult *chiefly Can and Brit var of* MOLT

¹**mound** \ˈmaund\ *vb* ♦ : to form into a mound

♦ heap, hill, pile, stack

²**mound** *n* **1** ♦ : an artificial bank or hill of earth or stones   **2** ♦ : a rounded hill or natural formation   **3** ♦ : a collection of things thrown one on another : HEAP, PILE; *also* : a great number or large quantity ⟨∼s of work⟩   **4** : a small rounded mass

♦ [1] bank, bar, drift ♦ [2] elevation, eminence, height, highland, hill, prominence, rise ♦ [3] cock, heap, hill, mountain, pile, rick, stack

¹**mount** \ˈmaunt\ *n* ♦ : a high hill

♦ mountain, peak

²**mount** *vb* **1 a** ♦ : to increase in amount or extent   **b** ♦ : to move upward : RISE, ASCEND   **2** : to get up on something; *esp* : to seat oneself on (as a horse) for riding   **3** : to put in position ⟨∼ artillery⟩   **4** : to set on something that elevates   **5** : to attach to a support   **6** ♦ : to prepare esp. for examination or display — **mount·able** *adj* — **mount·er** *n*

♦ [1a] accumulate, appreciate, balloon, build, burgeon, enlarge, escalate, expand, increase, multiply, mushroom, proliferate, rise, snowball, swell, wax ♦ [1b] arise, ascend, climb, lift, rise, soar, up ♦ [6] carry, give, offer, present, stage

³**mount** *n* **1** ♦ : an arrangement of structural parts that gives form or support : SUPPORT   **2** : a means of conveyance; *esp* : SADDLE HORSE

♦ brace, bulwark, buttress, shore, stay, support, underpinning

moun·tain \ˈmaunt-ⁿn\ *n* **1** ♦ : a landmass higher than a hill   **2 a** ♦ : a great mass   **b** ♦ : a vast number or quantity — **moun·tainy** \-ⁿn-ē\ *adj*

♦ [1] mount, peak ♦ [2a] cock, heap, hill, mound, pile, rick, stack ♦ [2b] abundance, deal, gobs, heap, loads, lot, pile, plenty, quantity, scads

mountain ash *n* : any of various trees related to the roses that have pinnate leaves and red or orange-red fruits

mountain bike *n* : a bicycle with wide knobby tires, straight handlebars, and 18 or 21 gears that is designed to operate esp. over unpaved terrain

moun·tain·eer \ˌmaunt-ⁿn-ˈir\ *n* **1** : a native or inhabitant of a mountainous region   **2** : one who climbs mountains for sport

mountain goat *n* : a ruminant mammal of mountainous northwestern No. America that resembles a goat

mountain laurel *n* : a No. American evergreen shrub or small tree of the heath family with glossy leaves and clusters of rose-colored or white flowers

mountain lion *n* ♦ : a large powerful tawny brown wild American cat : COUGAR

♦ cougar, panther

moun·tain·ous \ˈmaun-tə-nəs, ˈmaunt-nəs\ *adj* **1** : containing many mountains   **2** : resembling a mountain : HUGE

moun·tain·side \ˈmaunt-ⁿn-ˌsīd\ *n* : the side of a mountain

moun·tain·top \-ˌtäp\ *n* : the summit of a mountain

moun·te·bank \ˈmaunt-i-ˌbaŋk\ *n* ♦ : a boastful unscrupulous pretender : QUACK, CHARLATAN

♦ charlatan, fake, fraud, hoaxer, humbug, phony, pretender, quack

Mount·ie \ˈmaun-tē\ *n* : a member of the Royal Canadian Mounted Police

mount·ing \ˈmaun-tiŋ\ *n* : something that serves as a frame or support

mourn \ˈmōrn\ *vb* ♦ : to feel or express grief or sorrow — **mourn·er** *n*

♦ agonize, bleed, feel, grieve, hurt, sorrow, suffer ♦ *usu* **mourn for** bemoan, bewail, deplore, grieve, lament, wail

mourn·ful \-fəl\ *adj* ♦ : expressing, feeling, or causing sorrow ⟨a ∼ song⟩ — **mourn·ful·ness** *n*

♦ dolorous, funeral, lugubrious, plaintive, regretful, rueful, sorrowful, weeping, woeful ♦ blue, depressed, despondent, disconsolate, down, downcast, forlorn, gloomy, glum, low, melancholy, miserable, sad, sorrowful, sorry, unhappy

mourn·ful·ly \-fə-lē\ *adv* : in a mournful manner

mourn·ing \ˈmōr-niŋ\ *n* **1** : an outward sign (as black clothes) of grief for a person's death   **2** : a period of time during which signs of grief are shown

mouse \ˈmaus\ *n, pl* **mice** \ˈmīs\ **1** : any of numerous small rodents with pointed snout, long body, and slender tail   **2** : a small manual device that controls cursor movement on a computer display

mouse pad *n* : a thin flat pad on which a computer mouse is used

mous·er \ˈmau-sər\ *n* : a cat proficient at catching mice

mouse·trap \ˈmaus-ˌtrap\ *n* **1** : a trap for catching mice   **2** : a stratagem that lures one to defeat or destruction — **mousetrap** *vb*

mousse \ˈmüs\ *n* **1** : a molded chilled dessert made with sweetened and flavored whipped cream or egg whites and gelatin **2** : a foamy preparation used in styling hair — **mousse** *vb*

moustache *chiefly Can and Brit var of* MUSTACHE

mousy *or* **mous·ey** \'maù-sē, -zē\ *adj* **mous·i·er; -est** **1** : QUIET, STEALTHY **2** ♦ : lacking in boldness or determination : TIMID **3** : grayish brown — **mous·i·ness** \'maù-sē-nəs, -zē-\ *n*

♦ fainthearted, fearful, scary, shy, skittish, timid

¹**mouth** \'maùth\ *n, pl* **mouths** \'maùthz, 'maùths\ **1** : the opening through which an animal takes in food; *also* : the cavity that encloses the tongue, lips, and teeth in the typical vertebrate **2** : something resembling a mouth (as in affording entrance) **3** : a facial expression usu. of disgust, disapproval, or pain : GRIMACE — **mouthed** \'maùthd, 'maùtht\ *adj*

²**mouth** \'maùth\ *vb* **1** : SPEAK; *also* : DECLAIM **2** : to repeat without comprehension or sincerity ⟨∼*ed* platitudes⟩ **3** : to form soundlessly with the lips **4** ♦ : to utter indistinctly **5** ♦ : to talk pompously — often used with *off*

♦ [4] mumble, murmur, mutter ♦ *usu* **mouth off** [5] declaim, discourse, harangue, orate

mouth·ful \'maùth-fəl\ *n* **1** : as much as a mouth will hold **2** ♦ : the quantity usu. taken into the mouth at one time

♦ bite, morsel, nibble, taste, tidbit

mouth harp *n* : HARMONICA

mouth·part \'maùth-ˌpärt\ *n* : a structure or appendage near the mouth (as of an insect) esp. when adapted for eating

mouth·piece \-ˌpēs\ *n* **1** : a part (as of a musical instrument) that goes in the mouth or to which the mouth is applied **2** ♦ : one that expresses or interprets another's views : SPOKESMAN

♦ speaker, spokesman, spokesperson, spokeswoman

mouth–to–mouth *adj* : of, relating to, or being a method of artificial respiration in which air from a rescuer's mouth is forced into a victim's lungs

mouth·wash \-ˌwȯsh, -ˌwäsh\ *n* : a usu. antiseptic liquid preparation for cleaning the mouth and teeth

mou·ton \'mü-ˌtän\ *n* : processed sheepskin that has been sheared or dyed to resemble beaver or seal

¹**move** \'müv\ *vb* **moved; mov·ing** **1** ♦ : to change or cause to change position or posture **2** ♦ : to go or cause to go from one point to another; *also* : DEPART **3** ♦ : to take or cause to take action **4** : to show marked activity **5** ♦ : to stir the emotions **6** : to make a formal request, application, or appeal **7** : to change one's residence **8** : EVACUATE 2 **9** ♦ : to cause to operate or function — **mov·able** *or* **move·able** \'mü-və-bəl\ *adj*

♦ [1] budge, dislocate, displace, disturb, remove, shift, transfer ♦ [2] clear out, depart, exit, get off, go, pull, quit, sally, shove, take off ♦ [3] affect, impact, impress, influence, strike, sway, tell, touch ♦ [3] argue, convince, get, induce, persuade, prevail, satisfy, talk, win ♦ [5] arouse, encourage, excite, fire, incite, instigate, pique, provoke, stimulate, stir ♦ [9] activate, actuate, crank, drive, propel, run, set off, spark, start, touch off, trigger, turn on

²**move** *n* **1** : an act of moving **2** ♦ : a calculated step taken to gain an objective **3** : a change of location **4** : an agile action esp. in sports

♦ expedient, measure, shift, step

move·ment \'müv-mənt\ *n* **1** ♦ : the act or process of moving : MOVE **2** ♦ : a series of organized activities working toward an objective **3** : the moving parts of a mechanism (as of a watch) **4** : RHYTHM **5** : a section of an extended musical composition **6** : BOWEL MOVEMENT; *also* : STOOL 4

♦ [1] motion, move, moving, shift, stir, stirring *Ant* motionlessness ♦ [2] bandwagon, campaign, cause, crusade, drive

mov·er \'mü-vər\ *n* : one that moves; *esp* : one that moves the belongings of others from one location to another

mov·ie \'mü-vē\ *n* **1** ♦ : a representation (as of a story) by means of motion pictures **2** *pl* : a showing of a motion picture **3** *pl* ♦ : the motion-picture industry

♦ [1] film, motion picture, picture ♦ **movies** *pl* [3] film, screen

moving *adj* ♦ : stirring deeply in a way that evokes a strong emotional response

♦ affecting, emotional, impressive, poignant, stirring, touching *Ant* unemotional, unimpressive

¹**mow** \'maù\ *n* : the part of a barn where hay or straw is stored

²**mow** \'mō\ *vb* **mowed; mowed** *or* **mown** \'mōn\; **mow·ing** **1** : to cut (as grass) with a scythe or machine **2** : to cut the standing herbage of ⟨∼ the lawn⟩ — **mow·er** *n*

mox·ie \'mäk-sē\ *n* **1** : ENERGY, PEP **2** : COURAGE, DETERMINATION

Mo·zam·bi·can \ˌmō-zəm-'bē-kən\ *n* : a native or inhabitant of Mozambique

moz·za·rel·la \ˌmät-sə-'re-lə\ *n* : a moist white unsalted unripened mild cheese of a smooth rubbery texture

¹**MP** \'em-pē\ *n* **1** : a member of the military police **2** : an elected member of a parliament

²**MP** *abbr* **1** melting point **2** metropolitan police

MPEG \'em-ˌpeg\ *n* : any of a group of computer file formats for the compression and storage of digital video and audio data; *also* : a computer file (as of a movie) in an MPEG format

mpg *abbr* miles per gallon

mph *abbr* miles per hour

MP3 \'em-(ˌ)pē-'thrē\ *n* : a computer file format for the compression and storage of digital audio data; *also* : a computer file (as of a song) in the MP3 format

Mr. \'mis-tər\ *n, pl* **Messrs.** \'me-sərz\ — used as a conventional title of courtesy before a man's surname or his title of office

MRI \ˌem-ˌär-'ī\ *n* : MAGNETIC RESONANCE IMAGING

Mr. Right *n* : a man who would make the perfect husband

Mrs. \'mi-səz, -səs, *esp Southern* 'mi-zəz, -zəs\ *n, pl* **Mes·dames** \mā-'däm, -'dam\ — used as a conventional title of courtesy before a married woman's surname

Ms. \'miz\ *n, pl* **Mss.** *or* **Mses.** \'mi-zez\ — used as a conventional title of courtesy before a woman's surname

MS *abbr* **1** manuscript **2** master of science **3** military science **4** Mississippi **5** motor ship **6** multiple sclerosis

msec *abbr* millisecond

msg *abbr* message

MSG *abbr* **1** master sergeant **2** monosodium glutamate

msgr *abbr* **1** monseigneur **2** monsignor

MSgt *abbr* master sergeant

MSS *abbr* manuscripts

MST *abbr* mountain standard time

mt *abbr* mount; mountain

¹**Mt** *abbr* Matthew

²**Mt** *symbol* meitnerium

MT *abbr* **1** metric ton **2** Montana **3** mountain time

mtg *abbr* **1** meeting **2** mortgage

mtge *abbr* mortgage

mu \'myü, 'mü\ *n* : the 12th letter of the Greek alphabet — M or μ

¹**much** \'məch\ *adj* **more** \'mȯr\; **most** \'mōst\ : great in quantity, amount, extent, or degree ⟨∼ money⟩

²**much** *adv* **more; most** **1** ♦ : to a great degree or extent ⟨∼ happier⟩ **2** ♦ : almost but not quite : NEARLY ⟨looks ∼ as he did before⟩

♦ [1] broadly, considerably, greatly, hugely, largely, massively, monstrously, sizably, stupendously, tremendously, utterly, vastly ♦ [2] about, almost, most, near, nearly, next to, nigh, practically, some, virtually, well-nigh

³**much** *n* **1** ♦ : a great quantity, amount, extent, or degree **2** : something considerable or impressive

♦ abundance, deal, gobs, heap, loads, lot, pile, plenty, quantity, scads

mu·ci·lage \'myü-sə-lij\ *n* : a watery sticky solution (as of a gum) used esp. as an adhesive — **mu·ci·lag·i·nous** \ˌmyü-sə-'la-jə-nəs\ *adj*

muck \'mək\ *n* **1** : soft moist barnyard manure **2** ♦ : slimy dirt or filth **3 a** : a dark richly organic soil **b** : heavy often deep mud or slush : MUD, MIRE

♦ dirt, filth, grime, smut, soil

muck·rake \-ˌrāk\ *vb* : to expose publicly real or apparent misconduct of a prominent individual or business — **muck·rak·er** *n*

mucky \'mə-kē\ *adj* **1** ♦ : not clean **2** ♦ : consisting of, marked by, or full of muck

♦ [1] dirty, filthy, grubby, grungy, muddy, unclean ♦ [2] miry, muddy, oozy, slimy, slushy

mu·cus \'myü-kəs\ *n* : a slimy slippery protective secretion of membranes (**mucous membranes**) lining some body cavities — **mu·cous** \-kəs\ *adj*

mud \'məd\ *n* ♦ : soft wet earth : MIRE

♦ mire, muck, ooze, slime, slop, sludge, slush

¹**mud·dle** \'məd-ᵊl\ *vb* **mud·dled; mud·dling** **1** : to make muddy **2** ♦ : to confuse esp. with liquor **3** ♦ : to mix up or make a mess of **4** : to think or act in a confused way

♦ [2] addle, baffle, befog, befuddle, bemuse, bewilder, confound, confuse, disorient, muddy, mystify, perplex, puzzle

♦ [3] disarray, dishevel, dislocate, disorder, disrupt, disturb, mess, mix

²**muddle** n **1** ♦ : a state of esp. mental confusion **2** ♦ : a confused mess

♦ [1] daze, fog, haze, spin ♦ [1] bafflement, bewilderment, confusion, distraction, mystification, perplexity, puzzlement, whirl ♦ [2] chaos, confusion, disarray, disorder, jumble, mess, shambles ♦ [2] assortment, clutter, jumble, medley, mélange, miscellany, motley, variety, welter

muddled adj ♦ : characterized by a confused state

♦ chaotic, confused, disordered, messy

mud·dle·head·ed \ˌməd-ᵊl-ˈhe-dəd\ adj **1** : mentally confused **2** : INEPT

¹**mud·dy** \ˈmə-dē\ adj **mud·di·er; -est 1** ♦ : full of or covered with mud **2** ♦ : turbid with sediment — **mud·di·ness** \-dē-nəs\ n

♦ [1] miry, mucky, oozy, slimy, slushy ♦ [2] cloudy, turbid

²**muddy** vb **1** ♦ : to soil or stain with or as if with mud **2 a** ♦ : to make indistinct ⟨don't ∼ the issue⟩ **b** : to disturb in mind or purpose : CONFUSE — **mud·di·ly** \ˈmə-də-lē\ adv

♦ [1] befoul, begrime, besmirch, blacken, dirty, foul, grime, mire, smirch, soil, stain ♦ [2a] becloud, befog, blur, cloud, confuse, fog

mud·flat \ˈməd-ˌflat\ n : a level tract alternately covered and left bare by the tide

mud·guard \ˈməd-ˌgärd\ n : a guard over or a flap behind a wheel of a vehicle to catch or deflect mud

mud·room \-ˌrüm, -ˌru̇m\ n : a room in a house for removing dirty or wet footwear and clothing

mud·sling·er \-ˌsliŋ-ər\ n : one who uses invective esp. against a political opponent — **mud·sling·ing** \-ˌsliŋ-iŋ\ n

Muen·ster \ˈmən-stər, ˈmün-, ˈmu̇n-\ n : a semisoft bland cheese

mu·ez·zin \mü-ˈez-ᵊn, myü-\ n : a Muslim crier who calls the hour of daily prayer

¹**muff** \ˈməf\ n : a warm tubular covering for the hands

²**muff** vb ♦ : to act or do (something) stupidly or clumsily

♦ bobble, botch, bungle, butcher, flub, foul up, fumble, mangle, mess up, screw up

³**muff** n : a bungling performance; esp : a failure to hold a ball in attempting a catch — **muff** vb

muf·fin \ˈmə-fən\ n : a small soft cake baked in a pan having cuplike molds

muf·fle \ˈmə-fəl\ vb **muf·fled; muf·fling 1** : to wrap up so as to conceal or protect **2** : to wrap or pad with something to dull the sound of **3** : to keep down : SUPPRESS

muf·fler \ˈmə-flər\ n **1** : a scarf worn around the neck **2** : a device (as on a car's exhaust) to deaden noise

muf·ti \ˈməf-tē\ n : civilian clothes

¹**mug** \ˈməg\ n **1** : a usu. metal or earthenware cylindrical drinking cup **2** ♦ : the face or mouth of a person **3** ♦ : a usu. petty gangster, hoodlum, or ruffian

♦ [2] countenance, face, visage ♦ [3] bully, gangster, goon, hood, hoodlum, mobster, punk, rowdy, ruffian, thug, tough

²**mug** vb **mugged; mug·ging 1** : to pose or make faces esp. to attract attention or for a camera **2** : to take a photograph of : PHOTOGRAPH

³**mug** vb **mugged; mug·ging** : to assault usu. with intent to rob — **mug·ger** n

mug·gy \ˈmə-gē\ adj **mug·gi·er; -est** ♦ : being warm and humid — **mug·gi·ness** \-gē-nəs\ n

♦ humid, sticky, sultry

mug·wump \ˈməg-ˌwəmp\ n : an independent in politics

Mu·ham·mad·an \mō-ˈha-mə-dən, -ˈhä-; mü-\ n : MUSLIM

mu·ja·hid·een or **mu·ja·hed·in** \mü-ˌja-hi-ˈdēn, -ˌjä-\ n pl : Islamic guerrilla fighters esp. in the Middle East

muk·luk \ˈmək-ˌlək\ n **1** : a boot of sealskin or reindeer skin typically worn by Indigenous people of usu. arctic regions **2** : a boot with a soft leather sole worn over several pairs of socks

mu·lat·to \mu̇-ˈla-tō, myü-, -ˈlä-\ n, pl **-toes** or **-tos 1** usually offensive : the first-generation offspring of a Black person and a white person **2** usually offensive : a person of mixed white and Black ancestry

mul·ber·ry \ˈməl-ˌber-ē\ n : any of a genus of trees with edible berrylike fruit and leaves used as food for silkworms; also : the fruit

mulch \ˈməlch\ n : a protective covering (as of straw or leaves)

spread on the ground esp. to reduce evaporation or control weeds — **mulch** vb

¹**mulct** \ˈməlkt\ n : a sum imposed as punishment for an offense : FINE, PENALTY

²**mulct** vb **1** : FINE **2** ♦ : to defraud esp. of money : CHEAT

♦ bleed, cheat, chisel, cozen, defraud, fleece, hustle, rook, shortchange, skin, squeeze, stick, sting, swindle, victimize

¹**mule** \ˈmyül\ n **1** : a hybrid offspring of a male donkey and a female horse **2** : a very stubborn person

²**mule** n : a slipper whose upper does not extend around the heel of the foot

mule deer n : a long-eared deer of western No. America

mu·le·teer \ˌmyü-lə-ˈtir\ n : one who drives mules

mul·ish \ˈmyü-lish\ adj ♦ : unreasonably and inflexibly obstinate — **mul·ish·ly** adv

♦ dogged, hardheaded, headstrong, obdurate, obstinate, opinionated, peevish, pertinacious, perverse, pigheaded, stubborn, unyielding, willful

mu·lish·ness \-nəs\ n ♦ : the quality or state of being mulish

♦ hardheadedness, obduracy, obstinacy, peevishness, pertinacity, self-will, stubbornness, tenacity

¹**mull** \ˈməl\ vb ♦ : to consider at length : PONDER, MEDITATE — often used with over

♦ usu **mull over** chew over, cogitate, consider, contemplate, debate, deliberate, entertain, meditate, ponder, question, ruminate, study, think, weigh

²**mull** vb : to heat, sweeten, and flavor (as wine) with spices

mul·lein \ˈmə-lən\ n : a tall herb related to the snapdragons that has coarse woolly leaves and flowers in spikes

mul·let \ˈmə-lət\ n, pl **mullet** or **mullets** : any of a family of largely gray chiefly marine bony fishes including valuable food fishes

mul·li·gan stew \ˈmə-li-gən-\ n : a stew made from whatever ingredients are available

mul·li·ga·taw·ny \ˌmə-li-gə-ˈtȯ-nē\ n : a soup usu. of chicken stock seasoned with curry

mul·lion \ˈməl-yən\ n : a vertical strip separating windowpanes

multi- comb form **1** : many : multiple ⟨multiunit⟩ **2** : many times over ⟨multimillionaire⟩

mul·ti·col·ored \ˌməl-ti-ˈkə-lərd\ adj ♦ : having many colors

♦ colorful (or colourful), variegated

mul·ti·cul·tur·al \ˌməl-tē-ˈkəl-chə-rəl, -ˌtī-\ adj : of, relating to, reflecting, or adapted to diverse cultures ⟨a ∼ society⟩

mul·ti·di·men·sion·al \-ti-də-ˈmen-chə-nəl, -ˌtī-, -dī-\ adj : of, relating to, or having many facets or dimensions ⟨a ∼ problem⟩ ⟨∼ space⟩

mul·ti·eth·nic \-ˈeth-nik\ adj : including, involving, or made up of people of various ethnic groups

mul·ti·fac·et·ed \-ˈfa-sə-təd\ adj : having several distinct facets or aspects ⟨a ∼ career⟩

mul·ti·fam·i·ly \-ˈfam-lē, -ˈfa-mə-\ adj : designed for use by several families

mul·ti·far·i·ous \ˌməl-tə-ˈfar-ē-əs\ adj ♦ : having great variety ⟨∼ activities⟩ — **mul·ti·far·i·ous·ness** n

♦ manifold, myriad

mul·ti·form \ˈməl-ti-ˌfȯrm\ adj : having many forms or appearances — **mul·ti·for·mi·ty** \ˌməl-ti-ˈfȯr-mə-tē\ n

mul·ti·lat·er·al \ˌməl-ti-ˈla-tə-rəl, -ˌtī-\ adj : having many sides or participants ⟨∼ treaty⟩ — **mul·ti·lat·er·al·ism** \-ˈla-tə-rə-ˌli-zəm\ n

mul·ti·lay·ered \-ˈlā-ərd, -ˈlerd\ or **mul·ti·lay·er** \-ˈlā-ər, -ˈler\ adj : having or involving several distinct layers or levels

mul·ti·lev·el \-ˈle-vəl\ adj : having several levels

mul·ti·lin·gual \-ˈliŋ-gwəl\ adj : knowing or using several languages — **mul·ti·lin·gual·ism** \-gwə-ˌli-zəm\ n

¹**mul·ti·me·dia** \-ˈmē-dē-ə\ adj : using, involving, or encompassing several media ⟨a ∼ advertising campaign⟩

²**multimedia** n sing or pl : the technique of using several media (as in art); also : something (as software) that uses or facilitates it

mul·ti·mil·lion·aire \ˌməl-ti-ˌmil-yə-ˈnar, -ˌtī-, -ˈmil-yə-ˌnar\ n : a person worth several million dollars

mul·ti·na·tion·al \-ˈna-shə-nəl\ adj **1** : of or relating to several nationalities **2** : relating to or involving several nations **3** : having divisions in several countries ⟨a ∼ corporation⟩ — **multinational** n

mul·ti·pack \ˈməl-tē-ˌpak\ n : a package of several individually packed items sold as a unit

¹**mul·ti·ple** \ˈməl-tə-pəl\ adj **1 a** : more than one **b** ♦ : consist-

ing of or amounting to a large but indefinite number : MANY **2** : VARIOUS

♦ many, multitudinous, numerous

²**multiple** *n* : the product of a quantity by an integer ⟨35 is a ∼ of 7⟩

multiple–choice *adj* : having several answers given from which the correct one is to be chosen ⟨a ∼ question⟩

multiple personality disorder *n* : a neurosis in which the personality becomes separated into two or more parts each of which controls behavior part of the time

multiple sclerosis *n* : a disease marked by patches of hardened tissue in the brain or spinal cord and associated esp. with partial or complete paralysis and muscular tremor

mul•ti•plex \'məl-tə-ˌpleks\ *n* : CINEPLEX

mul•ti•pli•cand \ˌməl-tə-pli-'kand\ *n* : the number that is to be multiplied by another

mul•ti•pli•ca•tion \ˌməl-tə-plə-'kā-shən\ *n* **1** ♦ : the act or process of multiplying : the state of being multiplied **2** : a short method of finding the result of adding a figure the number of times indicated by another figure

♦ accumulation, addition, increase, proliferation *Ant* decrease

multiplication sign *n* **1** : TIMES SIGN **2** : a centered dot indicating multiplication

mul•ti•plic•i•ty \ˌməl-tə-'pli-sə-tē\ *n, pl* **-ties** : a great number or variety

mul•ti•pli•er \'məl-tə-ˌplī-ər\ *n* : one that multiplies; *esp* : a number by which another number is multiplied

mul•ti•ply \'məl-tə-ˌplī\ *vb* **-plied; -ply•ing** **1** ♦ : to increase in number (as by breeding) **2** : to find the product of by multiplication; *also* : to perform multiplication

♦ accumulate, appreciate, balloon, build, burgeon, enlarge, escalate, expand, increase, mount, mushroom, proliferate, rise, snowball, swell, wax ♦ add, aggrandize, amplify, augment, boost, compound, enlarge, escalate, expand, extend, increase, raise, swell, up ♦ breed, procreate, propagate, reproduce

mul•ti•pur•pose \ˌməl-ti-'pər-pəs, -ˌtī-\ *adj* : having or serving several purposes

mul•ti•ra•cial \-'rā-shəl\ *adj* **1** : composed of, involving, or representing various races **2** : having parents or ancestors of different races

mul•ti•sense \-ˌsens\ *adj* : having several meanings ⟨∼ words⟩

mul•ti•sto•ry \-ˌstōr-ē\ *adj* : having several stories ⟨∼ buildings⟩

mul•ti•task•ing \'məl-tē-ˌtas-kiŋ, -ˌtī-\ *n* **1** : the concurrent performance of several jobs by a computer **2** : the performance of multiple tasks at one time — **mul•ti•task** \-ˌtask\ *vb* — **mul•ti•task•er** \-ˌtaskər\ *n*

mul•ti•tude \'məl-tə-ˌtüd, -ˌtyüd\ *n* ♦ : a great number

♦ army, crowd, crush, drove, flock, horde, host, legion, mob, press, swarm, throng

mul•ti•tu•di•nous \ˌməl-tə-'tüd-ᵉn-əs, -'tyüd-\ *adj* ♦ : existing in a great multitude

♦ many, multiple, numerous

mul•ti•unit \ˌməl-ti-'yü-nət, -ˌtī-\ *adj* : having several units

mul•ti•vi•ta•min \-'vī-tə-mən\ *adj* : containing several vitamins and esp. all known to be essential to health — **multivitamin** *n*

¹**mum** \'məm\ *adj* ♦ : making no utterance : SILENT

♦ dumb, mute, silent, speechless, uncommunicative

²**mum** *n* : CHRYSANTHEMUM

³**mum** *chiefly Can and Brit var of* MOM

¹**mum•ble** \'məm-bəl\ *vb* **mum•bled; mum•bling** ♦ : to speak in a low indistinct manner — **mum•bler** *n* — **mum•bly** *adj*

♦ mouth, murmur, mutter *Ant* speak out, speak up

²**mumble** *n* ♦ : a low confused indistinct utterance

♦ murmur, mutter

mum•ble•ty–peg \'məm-bəl-tē-ˌpeg\ *also* **mum•ble–the–peg** \'məm-bəl-thə-\ *n* : a game in which the players try to flip a knife from various positions so that the blade will stick into the ground

mum•bo jum•bo \ˌməm-bō-'jəm-bō\ *n* **1** : a complicated ritual with elaborate trappings **2** : unnecessarily involved and incomprehensible language : GIBBERISH, NONSENSE

mum•mer \'mə-mər\ *n* **1 a** ♦ : a performer in a pantomime **b** : ACTOR **2** : a person who goes merrymaking in disguise during festivals — **mum•mery** *n*

♦ mime, mimic, pantomime

¹**mum•my** \'mə-mē\ *n, pl* **mummies** : a body embalmed for buri-

al in the manner of the ancient Egyptians — **mum•mi•fi•ca•tion** \ˌmə-mi-fə-'kā-shən\ *n* — **mum•mi•fy** \'mə-mi-ˌfī\ *vb*

²**mummy** *chiefly Can and Brit var of* MOMMY

mumps \'məmps\ *n sing or pl* : a virus disease marked by fever and swelling esp. of the salivary glands

mun *or* **munic** *abbr* municipal

munch \'mənch\ *vb* : to eat with a chewing action; *also* : to snack on

munch•ies \'mən-chēz\ *n pl* **1** : hunger pangs **2** : light snack foods

mun•dane \ˌmən-'dān, 'mən-ˌdān\ *adj* **1** ♦ : of or relating to the world **2** ♦ : concerned with the practical details of everyday life — **mun•dane•ly** *adv*

♦ [1] earthly, temporal, terrestrial, worldly ♦ [2] everyday, prosaic, workaday

mung bean \'məŋ-\ *n* : an erect bushy bean widely grown in warm regions for its edible seeds and as the chief source of bean sprouts; *also* : its seed

mu•nic•i•pal \myu̇-'ni-sə-pəl\ *adj* **1** : of, relating to, or characteristic of a municipality **2** : restricted to one locality — **mu•nic•i•pal•ly** *adv*

mu•nic•i•pal•i•ty \myu̇-ˌni-sə-'pa-lə-tē\ *n, pl* **-ties** ♦ : an urban political unit with corporate status and usu. powers of self-government

♦ city, metropolis

mu•nif•i•cent \myu̇-'ni-fə-sənt\ *adj* ♦ : liberal in giving : GENEROUS — **mu•nif•i•cence** \-səns\ *n*

♦ bountiful, charitable, free, generous, liberal, openhanded, unselfish, unsparing

mu•ni•tion \myu̇-'ni-shən\ *n* : ARMAMENT, AMMUNITION

¹**mu•ral** \'myu̇r-əl\ *adj* **1** : of or relating to a wall **2** : applied to and made part of a wall or ceiling surface

²**mural** *n* : a mural painting — **mu•ral•ist** *n*

¹**mur•der** \'mər-dər\ *n* **1** ♦ : the crime of unlawfully killing a person esp. with premeditated malice **2** ♦ : something unusually difficult or dangerous

♦ [1] homicide ♦ [2] agony, hell, horror, misery, nightmare, torment, torture

²**murder** *vb* **1 a** : to commit a murder **b** ♦ : to kill (a human being) unlawfully and with premeditated malice; *also* : to kill brutally **2** : to put an end to **3** ♦ : to spoil by performing poorly ⟨∼ a song⟩ — **mur•der•er** *n*

♦ [1b] dispatch, do in, execute, liquidate, slay ♦ [3] bobble, botch, bungle, butcher, flub, foul up, fumble, mangle, mess up, screw up

mur•der•ess \'mər-də-rəs\ *n* : a woman who murders

mur•der•ous \'mər-də-rəs\ *adj* **1** ♦ : having or appearing to have the purpose of murder ⟨∼ impulses⟩ **2** ♦ : marked by or causing murder or bloodshed ⟨∼ gunfire⟩ **3** ♦ : having the ability or power to overwhelm ⟨∼ heat⟩ **4** ♦ : characterized by extreme difficulty ⟨the exam was ∼⟩ — **mur•der•ous•ly** *adv*

♦ [1] bloodthirsty, bloody, homicidal, sanguinary, sanguine ♦ [2] baleful, deadly, deathly, fatal, fell, lethal, mortal, pestilent, vital ♦ [3] bitter, brutal, burdensome, cruel, excruciating, grievous, grim, hard, harsh, heavy, inhuman, onerous, oppressive, rough, rugged, severe, stiff, tough, trying ♦ [4] arduous, demanding, difficult, exacting, formidable, grueling, hard, herculean, laborious, rough, stiff, strenuous, tall, toilsome, tough

murk \'mərk\ *n* **1** ♦ : partial or total darkness : GLOOM **2** ♦ : a murky condition of the atmosphere or a substance causing it : FOG — **murk•i•ly** \'mər-kə-lē\ *adv*

♦ [1] dark, darkness, dusk, gloaming, gloom, night, semidarkness, shade, shadows, twilight ♦ [2] fog, haze, smog, soup

murk•i•ness \'mər-kē-nəs\ *n* ♦ : the quality or state of being murky

♦ ambiguity, darkness, obscurity, opacity

murky \'mər-kē\ *adj* **1** ♦ : characterized by a heavy dimness or obscurity caused by or like that caused by overhanging fog or smoke **2** ♦ : characterized by thickness and heaviness of air : FOGGY, MISTY **3** ♦ : darkly vague or obscure ⟨∼ writings⟩

♦ [1] dark, darkling, dim, dusky, gloomy, obscure, somber (*or* sombre) ♦ [2] cloudy, foggy, hazy, misty, smoggy, soupy ♦ [3] ambiguous, cryptic, dark, darkling, deep, enigmatic, equivocal, inscrutable, mysterious, mystic, nebulous, obscure, occult

¹**mur•mur** \'mər-mər\ *n* **1** ♦ : a muttered complaint **2 a** : a low

indistinct often continuous sound **b ♦ :** a soft or gentle utterance — **mur·mur·ous** *adj*

  ♦ [1] beef, complaint, fuss, grievance, gripe, grumble, plaint, squawk ♦ [2b] mumble, mutter

²**murmur** *vb* **1 :** to make a murmur ⟨traffic ~ed in the distance⟩ **2 :** to express grief, pain, or discontent
mur·mur·er *n* : one that murmurs
mus *abbr* **1** museum **2** music; musical; musician
mus·ca·tel \ˌməs-kə-ˈtel\ *n* : a sweet fortified wine
¹**mus·cle** \ˈmə-səl\ *n* **1 :** a body tissue consisting of long cells that contract when stimulated and produce motion; *also* : an organ consisting of this tissue and functioning in moving a body part **2 ♦ :** effective strength : BRAWN — **mus·cled** \ˈmə-səld\ *adj*

  ♦ energy, force, main, might, potency, power, sinew, strength, vigor (*or* vigour)

²**muscle** *vb* **mus·cled; mus·cling 1 ♦ :** to move or force by or as if by muscular effort **2 ♦ :** to make one's way by brute strength or by force

  ♦ [1] coerce, compel, constrain, drive, force, make, obligate, oblige, press, pressure ♦ [2] bulldoze, elbow, press, push

mus·cle–bound \ˈmə-səl-ˌbaůnd\ *adj* : having some of the muscles abnormally enlarged and lacking in elasticity (as from excessive exercise)
mus·cle·man \-ˌman\ *n* : a man with a muscular physique
mus·cu·lar \ˈməs-kyə-lər\ *adj* **1 a :** of, relating to, or constituting muscle **b :** of, relating to, or performed by the muscles **2 ♦ :** having well-developed musculature **3 :** of or relating to physical strength — **mus·cu·lar·i·ty** \ˌməs-kyə-ˈlar-ə-tē\ *n*

  ♦ brawny, rugged, sinewy, stalwart, stout, strong

muscular dystrophy *n* : any of a group of diseases characterized by progressive wasting of muscles
mus·cu·la·ture \ˈməs-kyə-lə-ˌchůr\ *n* : the muscles of the body or its parts
mus·cu·lo·skel·e·tal \ˌməs-kyə-lō-ˈske-lə-t°l\ *adj* : of, relating to, or involving both musculature and skeleton
¹**muse** \ˈmyüz\ *vb* **mused; mus·ing :** to become absorbed in thought — **mus·ing·ly** *adv*
²**muse** *n* : a source of inspiration
mu·se·um \myů-ˈzē-əm\ *n* : an institution devoted to the procurement, care, and display of objects of lasting interest or value
¹**mush** \ˈməsh\ *n* **1 :** cornmeal boiled in water **2 :** sentimental drivel **3 ♦ :** mawkish amorousness

  ♦ mawkishness, sentimentality

²**mush** *vb* : to travel esp. over snow with a sled drawn by dogs
¹**mush·room** \ˈməsh-ˌrüm, -ˌrům\ *n* : the fleshy usu. caplike spore-bearing organ of various fungi esp. when edible; *also* : such a fungus
²**mushroom** *vb* **1 :** to collect wild mushrooms **2 ♦ :** to spread out : EXPAND **3 :** to grow rapidly

  ♦ accumulate, appreciate, balloon, build, burgeon, enlarge, escalate, expand, increase, mount, multiply, proliferate, rise, snowball, swell, wax

mushy \ˈmə-shē\ *adj* **mush·i·er; -est 1 ♦ :** soft like mush **2 ♦ :** excessively sentimental ⟨a ~ movie⟩

  ♦ [1] flabby, pulpy, soft, spongy ♦ [2] corny, maudlin, mawkish, saccharine, sappy, schmaltzy, sentimental

mu·sic \ˈmyü-zik\ *n* **1 :** the science or art of combining tones into a composition having structure and continuity; *also* : vocal or instrumental sounds having rhythm, melody, or harmony **2 :** an agreeable sound
¹**mu·si·cal** \ˈmyü-zi-kəl\ *adj* **1 :** of or relating to music or musicians **2 ♦ :** having the pleasing tonal qualities of music **3 :** fond of or gifted in music ⟨a ~ family⟩ — **mu·si·cal·ly** \-k(ə-)lē\ *adv*

  ♦ euphonious, lyric, mellifluous, mellow, melodic, melodious ♦ harmonious, symphonic, tuneful

²**musical** *n* : a film or theatrical production consisting of musical numbers and dialogue based on a unifying plot
mu·si·cale \ˌmyü-zi-ˈkal\ *n* : a usu. private social gathering featuring music
mu·si·cian \myů-ˈzi-shən\ *n* : a composer, conductor, or performer of music — **mu·si·cian·ly** *adj* — **mu·si·cian·ship** *n*
mu·si·col·o·gy \ˌmyü-zi-ˈkä-lə-jē\ *n* : the study of music as a field of knowledge or research — **mu·si·co·log·i·cal** \-kə-ˈlä-ji-kəl\ *adj* — **mu·si·col·o·gist** \-ˈkä-lə-jist\ *n*
musk \ˈməsk\ *n* : a substance obtained esp. from a small Asian

deer (**musk deer**) and used as a perfume fixative — **musk·i·ness** \ˈməs-kē-nəs\ *n* — **musky** *adj*
mus·keg \ˈməs-ˌkeg\ *n* : wet spongy ground : BOG; *esp* : a mossy bog in northern No. America
mus·kel·lunge \ˈməs-kə-ˌlənj\ *n, pl* **muskellunge** : a large No. American pike that is a valuable sport fish
mus·ket \ˈməs-kət\ *n* : a heavy large-caliber muzzle-loading shoulder firearm — **mus·ke·teer** \ˌməs-kə-ˈtir\ *n*
mus·ket·ry \ˈməs-kə-trē\ *n* **1 :** MUSKETS **2 :** MUSKETEERS **3 :** musket fire
musk·mel·on \ˈməsk-ˌme-lən\ *n* : a small round to oval melon that has usu. a sweet edible green or orange flesh and a musky odor
musk ox *n* : a heavyset shaggy-coated wild ox of Greenland and the arctic tundra of northern No. America
musk·rat \ˈməs-ˌkrat\ *n, pl* **muskrat** *or* **muskrats** : a large No. American aquatic rodent with webbed feet and dark brown fur; *also* : its fur
Mus·lim \ˈməz-ləm\ *n* : an adherent of Islam — **Muslim** *adj*
mus·lin \ˈməz-lən\ *n* : a plain-woven sheer to coarse cotton fabric
¹**muss** \ˈməs\ *n* **♦ :** a state of disorder

  ♦ chaos, confusion, disarray, disorder, disorganization, havoc, hell, jumble, mess, messiness, muddle, shambles, tumble, welter

²**muss** *vb* : to make untidy : DISARRANGE
mus·sel \ˈmə-səl\ *n* **1 :** a dark edible saltwater bivalve mollusk **2 :** any of various freshwater bivalve mollusks of the central U.S. having shells with a pearly lining
mussy \ˈmə-sē\ *adj* : characterized by clutter or muss — **muss·i·ly** \ˈmə-sə-lē\ *adv* — **muss·i·ness** \-sē-nəs\ *n*
¹**must** \ˈməst\ *vb* **♦ :** — used as an auxiliary esp. to express a command, requirement, obligation, or necessity

  ♦ have, need, ought, shall, should

²**must** *n* **1 ♦ :** an imperative duty **2 ♦ :** an indispensable item

  ♦ [1, 2] condition, demand, essential, necessity, need, requirement, requisite

mus·tache *or chiefly Can and Brit* **mous·tache** \ˈməs-ˌtash, (ˌ)məs-ˈtash\ *n* : the hair growing on the human upper lip — **mus·tached** \-ˌtasht, -ˈtasht\ *adj*
mus·tang \ˈməs-ˌtaŋ\ *n* : a small hardy naturalized horse of the western plains of America; *also* : BRONC
mus·tard \ˈməs-tərd\ *n* **1 :** a pungent yellow powder of the seeds of an herb related to the cabbage and used as a condiment or in medicine **2 :** a plant that yields mustard; *also* : a closely related plant — **mus·tardy** *adj*
mustard gas *n* : a poison gas used in warfare that has violent irritating and blistering effects
¹**mus·ter** \ˈməs-tər\ *n* **1 a ♦ :** an act of assembling (as for military inspection) **b :** critical examination **2 ♦ :** an assembled group

  ♦ [1a] mobilization, rally ♦ [2] assemblage, assembly, conference, congregation, convocation, gathering, meeting

²**muster** *vb* **1 a ♦ :** to gather or cause to gather ⟨~ an army⟩ **b :** to call the roll of **2 :** ACCUMULATE **3 :** to call forth : ROUSE ⟨~ed support⟩ **4 :** to amount to : COMPRISE

  ♦ marshal, mobilize, rally ♦ assemble, call, convene, convoke, summon

muster out *vb* : to discharge from military service
musty \ˈməs-tē\ *adj* **mus·ti·er; -est 1 :** impaired by damp or mildew : MOLDY **2 ♦ :** tasting or smelling of damp or decay **3 ♦ :** tedious from familiarity : STALE — **must·i·ly** \-tə-lē\ *adv* — **must·i·ness** \-tē-nəs\ *n*

  ♦ [2] fetid, foul, fusty, malodorous, noisome, rank, reeky, smelly, strong ♦ [3] banal, commonplace, hackneyed, stale, stereotyped, threadbare, tired, trite

mu·ta·ble \ˈmyü-tə-bəl\ *adj* **1 ♦ :** prone to change : FICKLE **2 :** capable of or liable to mutation : VARIABLE — **mu·ta·bil·i·ty** \ˌmyü-tə-ˈbi-lə-tē\ *n*

  ♦ capricious, changeable, fickle, fluid, inconstant, mercurial, temperamental, uncertain, unpredictable, unsettled, unstable, unsteady, variable, volatile

mu·tant \ˈmyüt-°nt\ *adj* : of, relating to, or produced by mutation — **mutant** *n*
mu·tate \ˈmyü-ˌtāt\ *vb* **mu·tat·ed; mu·tat·ing ♦ :** to undergo or cause to undergo mutation — **mu·ta·tive** \ˈmyü-ˌtā-tiv, -tə-tiv\ *adj*

  ♦ change, fluctuate, shift, vary

mu·ta·tion \myü-'tā-shən\ *n* **1** : CHANGE **2** : an inherited physical or biochemical change in genetic material; *also* : the process of producing a mutation **3** : an individual, strain, or trait resulting from mutation — **mu·ta·tion·al** *adj*

¹**mute** \'myüt\ *adj* **mut·er; mut·est** **1** ♦ : unable to speak : DUMB **2** ♦ : characterized by absence of speech : SILENT — **mute·ly** *adv* — **mute·ness** *n*

♦ [1] dumb, inarticulate, speechless, voiceless ♦ [2] dumb, mum, silent, speechless, uncommunicative

²**mute** *n* **1** *sometimes offensive* : a person who cannot speak **2** : a device on a musical instrument that reduces, softens, or muffles the tone

³**mute** *vb* **mut·ed; mut·ing** ♦ : to muffle, reduce, or eliminate the sound of

♦ hush, quell, settle, silence, still

muted *adj* **1** ♦ : being mute : SILENT **2** ♦ : toned down : SUBDUED

♦ [1] hushed, noiseless, quiet, silent, soundless, still ♦ [2] conservative, quiet, restrained, subdued, unpretentious

mu·ti·late \'myüt-ᵊl-ˌāt\ *vb* **-lat·ed; -lat·ing** **1** : to cut up or alter radically so as to make imperfect **2** ♦ : to cut off or permanently destroy a limb or essential part of : MAIM, CRIPPLE — **mu·ti·la·tion** \ˌmyüt-ᵊl-'ā-shən\ *n* — **mu·ti·la·tor** \'myüt-ᵊl-ˌā-tər\ *n*

♦ cripple, disable, lame, maim

mu·ti·neer \ˌmyüt-ᵊn-'ir\ *n* ♦ : one that mutinies

♦ insurgent, insurrectionist, rebel, red, revolter, revolutionary

mu·ti·nous \'myüt-ᵊn-əs\ *adj* **1** ♦ : disposed to or being in a state of mutiny **2** : of, relating to, or constituting mutiny — **mu·ti·nous·ly** *adv*

♦ insurgent, rebellious, revolutionary

mu·ti·ny \'myü-tə-nē\ *n, pl* **-nies** ♦ : willful refusal to obey constituted authority; *esp* : revolt against a superior officer — **muti·ny** *vb*

♦ insurrection, rebellion, revolt, revolution, uprising

mutt \'mət\ *n* : MONGREL, CUR

¹**mut·ter** \'mə-tər\ *vb* **1** ♦ : to speak indistinctly or with a low voice and lips partly closed **2** ♦ : to murmur complainingly or angrily : GRUMBLE

♦ [1] mouth, mumble, murmur ♦ [2] beef, bellyache, carp, complain, crab, croak, fuss, gripe, grouse, growl, grumble, kick, moan, murmur, repine, squawk, wail, whine

²**mutter** *n* ♦ : a subdued scarcely audible utterance

♦ mumble, murmur

mut·ton \'mət-ᵊn\ *n* : the flesh of a mature sheep used for food — **mut·tony** *adj*

mut·ton·chops \'mət-ᵊn-ˌchäps\ *n pl* : whiskers on the side of the face that are narrow at the temple and broad and round by the lower jaws

mu·tu·al \'myü-chə-wəl\ *adj* **1** : given and received in equal amount ⟨∼ trust⟩ **2** : having the same feelings one for the other ⟨∼ enemies⟩ **3** ♦ : shared in common : COMMON, JOINT ⟨a ∼ friend⟩ — **mu·tu·al·ly** *adv*

♦ collective, common, communal, concerted, conjoint, joint, public, united

mutual fund *n* : an investment company that invests money of its shareholders in a usu. diversified group of securities of other corporations

muu·muu \'mü-ˌmü\ *n* : a loose dress of Hawaiian origin

¹**muz·zle** \'mə-zəl\ *n* **1** : the nose and jaws of an animal; *also* : a covering for the muzzle to prevent biting or eating **2** : the mouth of a gun

²**muzzle** *vb* **muz·zled; muz·zling** **1** : to put a muzzle on **2** : to restrain from expression : GAG ⟨tried to ∼ the press⟩

mV *abbr* millivolt

MV *abbr* motor vessel

MVP *abbr* most valuable player

MW *abbr* megawatt

my \'mī\ *adj* **1** : of or relating to me or myself **2** — used interjectionally esp. to express surprise

my·col·o·gy \mī-'kä-lə-jē\ *n* : a branch of biology dealing with fungi — **my·co·log·i·cal** \ˌmī-kə-'lä-ji-kəl\ *adj* — **my·col·o·gist** \mī-'kä-lə-jist\ *n*

my·elo·ma \ˌmī-ə-'lō-mə\ *n, pl* **-mas** *or* **-ma·ta** \-mə-tə\ : a primary tumor of the bone marrow

my·nah *or* **my·na** \'mī-nə\ *n* : any of several Asian starlings; *esp*

: a dark brown slightly crested bird sometimes taught to mimic speech

my·o·pia \mī-'ō-pē-ə\ *n* : a condition in which visual images come to a focus in front of the retina resulting esp. in defective vision of distant objects — **my·o·pic** \-'ō-pik, -'ä-\ *adj* — **my·o·pi·cal·ly** \-pi-k(ə-)lē\ *adv*

¹**myr·i·ad** \'mir-ē-əd\ *n* : an indefinitely large number

²**myriad** *adj* ♦ : consisting of a very great but indefinite number; *also* : both numerous and varied

♦ manifold, multifarious

myr·mi·don \'mər-mə-ˌdän\ *n* : a loyal follower; *esp* : one who executes orders without protest or pity

myrrh \'mər\ *n* : a fragrant aromatic plant gum used in perfumes and formerly for incense

myr·tle \'mərt-ᵊl\ *n* : an evergreen shrub of southern Europe with shiny leaves, fragrant flowers, and black berries; *also* : PERIWINKLE

my·self \mī-'self, mə-\ *pron* : I, ME — used reflexively, for emphasis, or in absolute constructions ⟨I hurt ∼⟩ ⟨I ∼ did it⟩ ⟨∼ busy, I sent him instead⟩

mys·te·ri·ous \mis-'tir-ē-əs\ *adj* **1** ♦ : of, relating to, or constituting mystery **2** ♦ : exciting wonder, curiosity, or surprise while baffling efforts to comprehend or identify — **mys·te·ri·ous·ly** *adv* — **mys·te·ri·ous·ness** *n*

♦ [1] ambiguous, equivocal, murky, nebulous, obscure ♦ [2] cryptic, darkling, deep, enigmatic, impenetrable, inscrutable, mystic, occult, uncanny

mys·tery \'mis-tə-rē\ *n, pl* **-ter·ies** **1** : a religious truth known by revelation alone **2** ♦ : something not understood or beyond understanding **3** : enigmatic quality or character **4** : a work of fiction dealing with the solution of a mysterious crime

♦ conundrum, enigma, mystification, puzzle, puzzlement, riddle, secret

¹**mys·tic** \'mis-tik\ *adj* **1** : of or relating to mystics or mysticism **2 a** : exciting wonder, curiosity, or surprise while baffling efforts to comprehend or identify : MYSTERIOUS **b** : MYSTIFYING **3** ♦ : having magical properties

♦ magic, magical, occult, weird

²**mystic** *n* : a person who follows, advocates, or experiences mysticism

mys·ti·cal \'mis-ti-kəl\ *adj* **1** : SPIRITUAL, SYMBOLIC **2** : of or relating to an intimate knowledge of or direct communion with God (as through contemplation or visions)

mys·ti·cism \'mis-tə-ˌsi-zəm\ *n* : the belief that direct knowledge of God or ultimate reality is attainable through immediate intuition or insight

mys·ti·fi·ca·tion \ˌmis-tə-fə-'kā-shən\ *n* **1** ♦ : the quality or state of being mystified **2** ♦ : something designed to mystify

♦ [1] bafflement, bewilderment, confusion, distraction, muddle, perplexity, puzzlement, whirl ♦ [2] conundrum, enigma, mystery, puzzle, puzzlement, riddle, secret

mys·ti·fy \'mis-tə-ˌfī\ *vb* **-fied; -fy·ing** **1** ♦ : to perplex the mind of **2** : to make mysterious

♦ addle, baffle, befog, befuddle, bemuse, bewilder, confound, confuse, disorient, muddle, muddy, perplex, puzzle

mys·tique \mi-'stēk\ *n* **1** : an air or attitude of mystery and reverence developing around something or someone **2** : the special esoteric skill essential in a calling or activity

myth \'mith\ *n* **1** : a usu. legendary narrative that presents part of the beliefs of a people or explains a practice or natural phenomenon **2** : an imaginary or unverifiable person or thing **3** ♦ : an unfounded or false notion **4** ♦ : the whole body of myths

♦ [3] error, fallacy, falsehood, falsity, illusion, misconception, untruth ♦ [4] folklore, legend, lore, mythology, tradition

myth·i·cal \'mi-thi-kəl\ *or* **myth·ic** *adj* **1** ♦ : based on or described in a myth esp. as contrasted with history **2** *usu mythical* ♦ : existing only in the imagination

♦ [1] fabled, fabulous, legendary ♦ [2] chimerical, fabulous, fanciful, fantastic, fictitious, imaginary, made-up, phantom, pretend, unreal

my·thol·o·gy \mi-'thä-lə-jē\ *n, pl* **-gies** ♦ : a body of myths and esp. of those dealing with the gods and heroes of a people — **myth·o·log·i·cal** \ˌmi-thə-'lä-ji-kəl\ *adj* — **my·thol·o·gist** \mi-'thä-lə-jist\ *n* — **my·thol·o·gize** \-ˌjīz\ *vb*

♦ folklore, legend, lore, myth, tradition

¹n \'en\ *n, pl* **n's** *or* **ns** \'enz\ *often cap* **1** : the 14th letter of the English alphabet **2** : an unspecified quantity

²n *abbr, often cap* **1** net **2** neuter **3** noon **4** normal **5** north; northern **6** note **7** noun **8** number

N *symbol* nitrogen

-n — see -EN

Na *symbol* sodium

NA *abbr* **1** no account **2** North America **3** not applicable **4** not available

NAACP \,en-,də-bəl-,ā-,sē-'pē, ,en-,ā-,ā-,sē-\ *abbr* National Association for the Advancement of Colored People

nab \'nab\ *vb* **nabbed**; **nab·bing** **1** ♦ : to seize suddenly : SEIZE **2** ♦ : to catch or seize in arrest : ARREST

♦ [1] bag, capture, catch, collar, corral, get, grab, grapple, hook, land, seize, snare, trap ♦ [2] apprehend, arrest, pick up, restrain, seize

NAB *abbr* New American Bible

na·bob \'nā-,bäb\ *n* ♦ : a person of great wealth or prominence

♦ big shot, celebrity, eminence, figure, immortal, light, luminary, notable, personage, personality, somebody, standout, star, superstar, VIP

na·celle \nə-'sel\ *n* : an enclosure (as for an engine) on an aircraft

na·cho \'nä-chō\ *n, pl* **nachos** : a tortilla chip topped with melted cheese and often additional savory toppings

na·cre \'nā-kər\ *n* : MOTHER-OF-PEARL

na·dir \'nā-,dir, -dər\ *n* **1** : the point of the celestial sphere that is directly opposite the zenith and directly beneath the observer **2** : the lowest point

¹nag \'nag\ *n* : a horse and esp. an old or decrepit horse

²nag *vb* **nagged**; **nag·ging** **1** : to find fault incessantly : COMPLAIN **2** ♦ : to irritate by constant scolding or urging **3** : to be a continuing source of annoyance ⟨a *nagging* backache⟩

♦ henpeck, hound, needle

³nag *n* : one who nags habitually

Nah *abbr* Nahum

Na·huatl \'nä-,wät-ᵊl\ *n* : a group of languages that includes the speech of several peoples (as the Aztecs) of central and southern Mexico

Na·hum \'nā-həm, -əm\ *n* : a book of Jewish and Christian Scripture

NAIA *abbr* National Association of Intercollegiate Athletes

na·iad \'nā-əd, 'nī-, -,ad\ *n, pl* **naiads** *or* **na·ia·des** \-ə-,dēz\ **1** : one of the nymphs in ancient mythology living in lakes, rivers, springs, and fountains **2** : an aquatic young of some insects (as a dragonfly)

¹na·if *or* **na·ïf** \nä-'ēf\ *adj* : NAIVE

²naïf *or* **naif** *n* : a naive person

¹nail \'nāl\ *n* **1** : a horny sheath protecting the end of each finger and toe in humans and related primates **2** : a slender pointed fastener with a head designed to be pounded in

²nail *vb* : to fasten with or as if with a nail — **nail·er** *n*

nail down *vb* : to settle or establish clearly and unmistakably ⟨*nailed down* the victory⟩

nain·sook \'nān-,sůk\ *n* : a soft lightweight muslin

na·ive *or* **na·ïve** \nä-'ēv\ *adj* **na·iv·er**; **-est** **1** ♦ : marked by unaffected simplicity : ARTLESS, INGENUOUS **2** ♦ : lacking in worldly wisdom or informed judgment — **na·ive·ness** *n*

♦ [1] artless, genuine, honest, ingenuous, innocent, natural, real, simple, sincere, true, unaffected, unpretentious ♦ [2] green, ingenuous, innocent, simple, unknowing, unsophisticated, unwary, unworldly *Ant* cynical, experienced, knowing, sophisticated, worldly, worldly-wise

na·ive·ly *adv* ♦ : in a naive manner : with naivete

♦ artlessly, ingenuously, naturally, unaffectedly

na·ive·te *or* **na·ïve·té** *also* **na·ive·té** \,nä-,ē-və-'tā, nä-'ē-və-,tā\ **1** : a naive remark or action **2** ♦ : the quality or state of being naive

♦ artlessness, greenness, ingenuousness, innocence, naturalness, simplicity, unworldliness *Ant* artfulness, cynicism, sophistication, worldliness

na·ked \'nā-kəd\ *adj* **1** ♦ : having no clothes on : NUDE **2** : UNSHEATHED ⟨a ~ sword⟩ **3** ♦ : lacking a usual or natural covering (as of foliage or feathers) **4** ♦ : lacking embellishment : PLAIN, UNADORNED ⟨the ~ truth⟩ **5** : not aided by artificial means ⟨seen by the ~ eye⟩ — **na·ked·ly** *adv* — **na·ked·ness** *n*

♦ [1] bare, nude, unclad, unclothed, undressed *Ant* appareled, attired, clad, clothed, invested, robed, suited ♦ [3] bald, bare, exposed, open, uncovered *Ant* covered ♦ [4] bald, bare, plain, simple, unadorned, undecorated, unvarnished

nam·by–pam·by \,nam-bē-'pam-bē\ *adj* **1** ♦ : lacking in character or substance **2** : WEAK, INDECISIVE

♦ bland, flat, wishy-washy

¹name \'nām\ *n* **1** ♦ : a word or words by which a person or thing is known **2** ♦ : a disparaging epithet ⟨call him ~s⟩ **3** ♦ : overall quality or character as seen or judged by people in general : REPUTATION; *esp* : distinguished reputation ⟨made a ~ for herself⟩ **4** : FAMILY, CLAN ⟨was a disgrace to their ~⟩ **5** ♦ : appearance as opposed to reality ⟨a friend in ~ only⟩

♦ [1] appellation, cognomen, denotation, designation, handle, title ♦ [2] affront, barb, dart, dig, indignity, insult, offense, outrage, put-down, sarcasm, slight, slur, wound ♦ [3] character, mark, note, report, reputation ♦ [5] appearance, face, guise, semblance, show

²name *vb* **named**; **nam·ing** **1** ♦ : to give a name to : CALL **2** : to mention or identify by name **3** ♦ : to assign to some purpose : APPOINT **4** ♦ : to decide on : CHOOSE **5** ♦ : to mention explicitly : SPECIFY ⟨~ a price⟩ — **name·able** *adj*

♦ [1] baptize, call, christen, denominate, designate, dub, entitle, label, style, term, title ♦ [3] appoint, assign, attach, commission, constitute, designate, detail ♦ [4] choose, cull, elect, handpick, opt, pick, prefer, select, single, take ♦ [5] advert (to), cite, instance, mention, note, notice, quote, refer (to), specify, touch (on or *upon*)

³name *adj* **1** : of, relating to, or bearing a name ⟨~ tag⟩ **2** ♦ : having an established reputation ⟨~ brands⟩

♦ prestigious, reputable, reputed, respectable

name day *n* : the church feast day of the saint after whom one is named

name·less \'nām-ləs\ *adj* **1** ♦ : having no name **2** : not marked with a name ⟨a ~ grave⟩ **3 a** ♦ : not known by name ⟨a ~ hero⟩ **b** : relatively unknown **4 a** ♦ : impossible to identify precisely or by name **b** : too distressing to be described ⟨~ fears⟩ — **name·less·ly** *adv*

♦ [1, 3a] anonymous, unbaptized, unchristened, unidentified, unnamed, untitled *Ant* baptized, christened, dubbed, named, termed ♦ [3b] anonymous, obscure, unknown, unsung ♦ [4a] indescribable, ineffable, inexpressible, unspeakable, unutterable

name·ly \-lē\ *adv* : that is to say : AS ⟨the cat family, ~, lions, tigers, and similar animals⟩

name·plate \-,plāt\ *n* : a plate or plaque bearing a name (as of a resident)

name·sake \-,sāk\ *n* : one that has the same name as another; *esp* : one named after another

Na·mib·ian \nə-'mi-bē-ən, -byən\ *n* : a native or inhabitant of Namibia — **Namibian** *adj*

nana \'na-nə\ *n* : GRANDMOTHER

nan·keen \nan-'kēn\ *n* : a durable brownish yellow cotton fabric orig. woven by hand in China

nan·ny \'na-nē\ *also* **nan·nie** *n, pl* **nan·nies** ♦ : a child's nurse or caregiver

♦ nurse, nursemaid

nan·ny goat \'na-nē-\ *n* : a female domestic goat

nano·me·ter \'na-nə-,mē-tər\ *n* : one billionth of a meter

nano·scale \-,skāl\ *adj* : having dimensions measured in nanometers

nano·sec·ond \-,se-kənd\ *n* : one billionth of a second

nano·tech \'na-nō-,tek\ *n* : NANOTECHNOLOGY

nano·tech·nol·o·gy \,na-nō-tek-'nä-lə-jē\ *n* : the science of manipulating materials on an atomic or molecular scale esp. to build microscopic objects or devices

¹nap \'nap\ *vb* **napped; nap•ping** **1** ♦ : to sleep briefly esp. during the day : DOZE **2** : to be off guard ⟨was caught *napping*⟩

♦ catnap, doze, drowse, slumber, snooze

²nap *n* ♦ : a short sleep esp. during the day

♦ catnap, doze, drowse, forty winks, siesta, snooze, wink

³nap *n* ♦ : a soft downy fibrous surface (as on yarn and cloth) — **nap•less** *adj* — **napped** \'napt\ *adj*

♦ down, floss, fluff, fur, fuzz, lint, pile

na•palm \'nā-,pälm, -,päm\ *n* **1** : a thickener used in jelling gasoline (as for incendiary bombs) **2** : fuel jelled with napalm

nape \'nāp, 'nap\ *n* : the back of the neck

na•pery \'nā-pə-rē\ *n* : household linen esp. for the table

naph•tha \'naf-thə, 'nap-\ *n* : any of various liquid hydrocarbon mixtures used chiefly as solvents

naph•tha•lene \-,lēn\ *n* : a crystalline substance used esp. in organic synthesis and as a moth repellent

nap•kin \'nap-kən\ *n* **1** : a piece of material (as cloth) used at table to wipe the lips or fingers and protect the clothes **2** : a small cloth or towel

na•po•leon \nə-'pōl-yən, -'pō-lē-ən\ *n* : an oblong pastry with a filling of cream, custard, or jelly

Na•po•le•on•ic \nə-,pō-lē-'ä-nik\ *adj* : of, relating to, or characteristic of Napoleon I or his family

narc *also* **nark** \'närk\ *n, slang* : a person (as a government agent) who investigates narcotics violations

nar•cis•sism \'när-sə-,si-zəm\ *n* **1** : undue dwelling on one's own self or attainments **2** : love of or sexual desire for one's own body — **nar•cis•sist** \-sist\ *n or adj* — **nar•cis•sis•tic** \,när-sə-'sis-tik\ *adj*

nar•cis•sus \när-'si-səs\ *n, pl* **nar•cis•si** \-,sī, -,sē\ *or* **nar•cis•sus•es** *or* **narcissus** : DAFFODIL; *esp* : one with short-tubed flowers usu. borne separately

nar•co•lep•sy \'när-kə-,lep-sē\ *n, pl* **-sies** : a condition characterized by brief attacks of deep sleep — **nar•co•lep•tic** \,när-kə-'lep-tik\ *adj or n*

nar•co•sis \när-'kō-səs\ *n, pl* **-co•ses** \-,sēz\ : a state of stupor, unconsciousness, or arrested activity produced by the influence of chemicals (as narcotics)

nar•co•ter•ror•ism \'när-kō-'ter-ər-,i-zəm\ *n* : terrorism financed by profits from illegal drug trafficking

¹nar•cot•ic \när-'kä-tik\ *n* **1** : a drug (as opium) that dulls the senses, relieves pain, and induces sleep **2** : an illegal drug (as marijuana or LSD)

²narcotic *adj* **1** ♦ : tending to calm the emotions and relieve stress ⟨the music's ~ effect⟩ **2** : of or relating to narcotics, to their use, or to addicts ⟨~ addiction⟩

♦ comforting, dreamy, sedative, soothing

nar•co•tize \'när-kə-,tīz\ *vb* **-tized; -tiz•ing** **1** : to treat with or subject to a narcotic; *also* : to put into a state of narcosis **2** : to soothe to unconsciousness or unawareness

nard \'närd\ *n* : a fragrant ointment of the ancients

na•res \'nar-(,)ēz\ *n pl* : the pair of openings of the nose

Nar•ra•gan•sett \,nar-ə-'gan-sət\ *n, pl* **-sett** *or* **-setts** **1** : a member of an Algonquian-speaking Indigenous people of Rhode Island **2** : the Algonquian language of the Narragansett people

nar•rate \'nar-,āt\ *vb* **nar•rat•ed; nar•rat•ing** ♦ : to recite the details of (as a story) : TELL — **nar•ra•tor** \'nar-,ā-tər\ *n*

♦ describe, recite, recount, rehearse, relate, report, tell

nar•ra•tion \na-'rā-shən\ *n* ♦ : an account of incidents or events : STORY

♦ account, chronicle, commentary, history, narrative, record, report, story

nar•ra•tive \'nar-ə-tiv\ *n* **1 a** : something that is narrated **b** ♦ : a fictional narrative shorter than a novel **2** ♦ : the art or practice of narrating

♦ [1b] novella, short story, story, tale ♦ [2] account, chronicle, history, record, report, story

¹nar•row \'nar-ō\ *adj* **1** ♦ : of slender or less than standard width **2** ♦ : limited in size or scope : RESTRICTED **3** ♦ : not liberal in views **4** : interpreted or interpreting strictly **5** ♦ : barely sufficient : CLOSE ⟨won by a ~ margin⟩; *also* : barely successful ⟨a ~ escape⟩ — **nar•row•ly** *adv* — **nar•row•ness** *n*

♦ [1] fine, skinny, slender, slim, thin *Ant* broad, fat, wide ♦ [2] definite, determinate, finite, limited, measured, restricted ♦ [3] bigoted, intolerant, narrow-minded, prejudiced ♦ [3] insular,

little, parochial, petty, provincial, sectarian, small *Ant* broadminded, catholic, cosmopolitan, liberal, open, open-minded, receptive, tolerant ♦ [5] close, neck and neck, nip and tuck, tight

²narrow *n* ♦ : a narrow passage : STRAIT — usu. used in pl.

♦ channel, sound, strait

³narrow *vb* : to lessen in width or extent

nar•row—mind•ed \,nar-ō-'mīn-dəd\ *adj* ♦ : not liberal or broad-minded

♦ bigoted, intolerant, narrow, prejudiced

nar•whal \'när-,hwäl, 'när-wəl\ *n* : an arctic sea mammal about 20 feet (6 meters) long that is related to the dolphins and in the male has a long twisted ivory tusk

NAS *abbr* naval air station

NASA \'na-sə\ *abbr* National Aeronautics and Space Administration

¹na•sal \'nā-zəl\ *n* **1** : a nasal part **2** : a nasal consonant or vowel

²nasal *adj* **1** : of or relating to the nose **2** : uttered through the nose — **na•sal•ly** *adv*

na•sal•ize \'nā-zə-,līz\ *vb* **-ized; -iz•ing** : to make nasal or pronounce as a nasal sound — **na•sal•i•za•tion** \,nā-zə-lə-'zā-shən\ *n*

na•scent \'nas-ᵊnt, 'nās-\ *adj* : coming into existence : beginning to grow or develop — **na•scence** \-ᵊns\ *n*

nas•ti•ly \'nas-tē-lē\ *adv* ♦ : in a nasty manner or condition

♦ hatefully, maliciously, meanly, spitefully, viciously, wickedly *Ant* benevolently, kindly

nas•ti•ness \'nas-tē-nəs\ *n* ♦ : the quality or state of being nasty

♦ cattiness, despite, hatefulness, malice, malignity, meanness, spite, spleen, venom, viciousness ♦ bawdiness, coarseness, dirt, dirtiness, filth, filthiness, foulness, grossness, indecency, lewdness, obscenity, ribaldry, smut, vulgarity ♦ dinginess, dirtiness, filthiness, foulness, grubbiness, uncleanliness

nas•tur•tium \nə-'stər-shəm, na-\ *n* : either of two widely cultivated watery-stemmed herbs with showy spurred flowers and pungent seeds

nas•ty \'nas-tē\ *adj* **nas•ti•er; -est** **1** : FILTHY **2** ♦ : abhorrent to morality or virtue : INDECENT, OBSCENE **3 a** : HARMFUL, DANGEROUS ⟨took a ~ fall⟩ **b** ♦ : causing severe pain or suffering **4** ♦ : sharply unpleasant ⟨~ weather⟩ **5** ♦ : characterized by petty selfishness or malice : MEAN, ILL-NATURED ⟨a ~ temper⟩ **6** : DIFFICULT, VEXATIOUS ⟨a ~ problem⟩ **7** : UNFAIR, DIRTY ⟨a ~ trick⟩

♦ [2] bawdy, coarse, crude, dirty, filthy, foul, gross, indecent, lascivious, lewd, obscene, pornographic, ribald, smutty, unprintable, vulgar, wanton ♦ [3b] achy, painful, sore ♦ [4] bad, bleak, dirty, disagreeable, foul, inclement, raw, rough, squally, stormy, tempestuous, turbulent, unpleasant ♦ [5] catty, cruel, hateful, malevolent, malicious, malign, malignant, mean, spiteful, virulent

nat *abbr* **1** national **2** native **3** natural

na•tal \'nāt-ᵊl\ *adj* **1** : NATIVE **2** : of, relating to, or present at birth

na•ta•to•ri•um \,nā-tə-'tōr-ē-əm, ,na-\ *n* : a swimming pool esp. indoors

na•tion \'nā-shən\ *n* **1** : NATIONALITY 5; *also* : a politically organized nationality **2** ♦ : a community of people composed of one or more nationalities with its own territory and government **3** : the territory of a nation **4** : a tribe or federation of tribes (as of Indigenous peoples) — **na•tion•hood** *n*

♦ commonwealth, country, land, sovereignty, state

¹na•tion•al \'na-shə-nəl\ *adj* **1** ♦ : of or relating to a nation **2** : comprising or characteristic of a nationality **3** : FEDERAL 3 — **na•tion•al•ly** *adv*

♦ civil, public, state

²national *n* **1** : one who owes allegiance to a nation **2** : a competition that is national in scope — usu. used in pl.

National Guard *n* **1** : a militia force recruited by each state of the U.S., equipped by the federal government, and jointly maintained subject to the call of either **2** *often not cap* : a military force serving as a national constabulary and defense force

na•tion•al•ise *chiefly Brit var of* NATIONALIZE

na•tion•al•ism \'na-shə-nə-,li-zəm\ *n* : devotion to national interests, unity, and independence

na•tion•al•ist \-list\ *n* **1** : an advocate of or believer in nationalism **2** *cap* : a member of a political party or group advocating national independence or strong national government — **nation•alist** *adj, often cap* — **na•tion•al•is•tic** \,na-shə-nə-'lis-tik\ *adj*

na·tion·al·i·ty \ˌna-shə-ˈna-lə-tē\ *n, pl* **-ties** **1 :** national character **2 :** a legal relationship involving allegiance of an individual and protection on the part of the state **3 :** membership in a particular nation **4 :** political independence or existence as a separate nation **5 :** a people having a common origin, tradition, and language and capable of forming a state **6 :** an ethnic group within a larger unit (as a nation)

na·tion·al·ize \ˈna-shə-nə-ˌlīz\ *vb* **-ized; -iz·ing** **1 :** to make national **:** make a nation of **2 :** to remove from private ownership and place under government control — **na·tion·al·i·za·tion** \ˌna-shə-nə-lə-ˈzā-shən\ *n*

national monument *n* **:** a place of historic, scenic, or scientific interest set aside for preservation usu. by presidential proclamation

national park *n* **:** an area of special scenic, historical, or scientific importance set aside and maintained by a national government esp. for recreation or study

national seashore *n* **:** a recreational area adjacent to a seacoast and maintained by the federal government

na·tion·wide \ˌnā-shən-ˈwīd\ *adj* **:** extending throughout a nation

¹**na·tive** \ˈnā-tiv\ *adj* **1 :** INBORN, NATURAL **2 ♦ :** born in a particular place or country **3 :** belonging to a person because of the place or circumstances of birth ⟨her ∼ language⟩ **4 ♦ :** grown, produced, or originating in a particular place **:** INDIGENOUS **5 ♦ :** left or remaining in a natural state **:** being without embellishment or artificial change **6** *cap* **:** of, relating to, or being a member of an Indigenous people of No. or So. America

♦ [2, 4] aboriginal, born, endemic, indigenous ♦ [5] crude, natural, raw, undressed, unprocessed, unrefined, untreated

²**native** *n* **:** one that is native; *esp* **:** a person who belongs to a particular country by birth

Native American *n* **:** a member of any of the Indigenous peoples of the western hemisphere; *esp* **:** a Native American of No. America and esp. the U.S.

na·tiv·ism \ˈnā-ti-ˌvi-zəm\ *n* **1 :** a policy of favoring native inhabitants over immigrants **2 :** the revival or perpetuation of a native culture esp. in opposition to acculturation

na·tiv·i·ty \nə-ˈti-və-tē, nā-\ *n, pl* **-ties** **1 :** the process or circumstances of being born **:** BIRTH **2** *cap* **:** the birth of Christ

natl *abbr* national

NATO \ˈnā-(ˌ)tō\ *abbr* North Atlantic Treaty Organization

nat·ty \ˈna-tē\ *adj* **nat·ti·er; -est ♦ :** trimly neat and tidy **:** SMART — **nat·ti·ly** \-tə-lē\ *adv* — **nat·ti·ness** \-tē-nəs\ *n*

♦ dapper, sharp, smart, spruce

¹**nat·u·ral** \ˈna-chə-rəl\ *adj* **1 ♦ :** determined by nature **:** INBORN, INNATE ⟨∼ ability⟩ **2 :** having a specified character by nature **:** BORN ⟨a ∼ fool⟩ **3 :** not recognized as lawful offspring; *specif* **:** born of parents not married to each other **4 :** HUMAN **5 ♦ :** of or relating to nature **6 ♦ :** not artificial **7 ♦ :** being simple and sincere **:** not affected **8 ♦ :** closely resembling an original **:** true to nature **9 :** being neither sharp nor flat

♦ [1] essential, inborn, ingrained, inherent, innate, integral, intrinsic ♦ [5] uncultivated, untamed, wild ♦ [6] crude, native, raw, undressed, unprocessed, unrefined, untreated ♦ [7] artless, genuine, honest, ingenuous, innocent, naive, real, simple, sincere, true, unaffected, unpretentious ♦ [8] lifelike, near, realistic *Ant* unrealistic

²**natural** *n* **1 :** one born without the usual powers of reason and understanding **2 :** a character ♮ placed on a line or space of the musical staff to nullify the effect of a preceding sharp or flat **3 :** one obviously suitable for a purpose **4 :** AFRO

natural childbirth *n* **:** a system of managing childbirth in which the mother prepares to remain conscious and assist in delivery with little or no use of drugs

natural gas *n* **:** a combustible gaseous mixture of hydrocarbons coming from the earth's crust and used chiefly as a fuel and raw material

natural history *n* **1 :** a treatise on some aspect of nature **2 :** the study of natural objects esp. from an amateur or popular point of view

nat·u·ral·ise *chiefly Brit var of* NATURALIZE

nat·u·ral·ism \ˈna-chə-rə-ˌli-zəm\ *n* **1 :** action or thought based only on natural desires and instincts **2 :** a doctrine that denies a supernatural explanation of the origin or development of the universe and holds that scientific laws account for all of nature **3 :** realism in art and literature — **nat·u·ral·is·tic** \ˌna-chə-rə-ˈlis-tik\ *adj*

nat·u·ral·ist \-list\ *n* **1 :** one that advocates or practices naturalism **2 :** a student of animals or plants esp. in the field

nat·u·ral·ize \-ˌlīz\ *vb* **-ized; -iz·ing** **1 :** to become or cause to become established as if native ⟨∼ new forage crops⟩ **2 :** to confer the rights of a citizen on — **nat·u·ral·i·za·tion** \ˌna-chə-rə-lə-ˈzā-shən\ *n*

nat·u·ral·ly \ˈna-chə-rə-lē, ˈnach-rə-\ *adv* **1 ♦ :** by nature **:** by natural character or ability **2 ♦ :** as might be expected **3 ♦ :** without artificial aid; *also* **:** without affectation **4 :** REALISTICALLY

♦ [1] constitutionally, inherently, innately, intrinsically ♦ [2] commonly, generally, normally, ordinarily, typically, usually *Ant* abnormally, atypically, extraordinarily, uncommonly, unusually ♦ [3] artlessly, ingenuously, naively, unaffectedly *Ant* affectedly, artificially, hypocritically, insincerely, pretentiously, unnaturally

nat·u·ral·ness *n* ♦ **:** the quality or state of being natural

♦ artlessness, greenness, ingenuousness, innocence, naïveté, simplicity, unworldliness

natural science *n* **:** a science (as physics, chemistry, or biology) that deals with matter, energy, and their interrelations and transformations or with objectively measurable phenomena — **natural scientist** *n*

natural selection *n* **:** the natural process that results in the survival of individuals or groups best adjusted to their environment

na·ture \ˈnā-chər\ *n* **1 ♦ :** the inherent quality or basic constitution of a person or thing **2 ♦ :** a kind or class usu. distinguished by fundamental or essential characteristics **3 ♦ :** the fundamental character, disposition, or temperament of a living being usu. innate and unchangeable **:** TEMPERAMENT, DISPOSITION **4 ♦ :** the physical universe **5 :** one's natural instincts or way of life ⟨quirks of human ∼⟩; *also* **:** primitive state ⟨a return to ∼⟩ **6 ♦ :** natural scenery or environment ⟨beauties of ∼⟩

♦ [1] essence, quintessence, soul, stuff, substance ♦ [1] character, complexion, constitution, genius, personality, tone ♦ [2] breed, class, description, feather, ilk, kind, like, manner, order, sort, species, type ♦ [3] disposition, grain, temper, temperament ♦ [4] cosmos, creation, macrocosm, universe, world ♦ [6] open, outdoors, wild, wilderness

naught \ˈnȯt, ˈnät\ *n* **1 :** NOTHING **2 ♦ :** the arithmetical symbol 0 **:** ZERO

♦ aught, cipher, nil, nothing, zero, zip

naugh·ty \ˈnȯ-tē, ˈnä-\ *adj* **naugh·ti·er; -est** **1 ♦ :** guilty of disobedience or misbehavior **2 :** lacking in taste or propriety ⟨∼ jokes⟩ — **naugh·ti·ly** \-tə-lē\ *adv* — **naugh·ti·ness** \-tē-nəs\ *n*

♦ bad, contrary, errant, froward, mischievous *Ant* behaved, behaving, nice, orderly

nau·sea \ˈnȯ-zē-ə, -sē-; ˈnȯ-zhə, -shə\ *n* **1 ♦ :** sickness of the stomach with a desire to vomit **2 ♦ :** extreme disgust

♦ [1] queasiness, sickness, squeamishness ♦ [2] aversion, disgust, distaste, loathing, repugnance, repulsion, revulsion

nau·se·ate \ˈnȯ-zē-ˌāt, -sē-, -zhē-, -shē-\ *vb* **-at·ed; -at·ing** ♦ **:** to affect or become affected with nausea — **nau·se·at·ing·ly** *adv*

♦ disgust, repel, repulse, revolt, sicken, turn off

nauseating *adj* ♦ **:** causing nausea or esp. disgust

♦ distasteful, noisome, offensive, repellent, repugnant, repulsive, revolting, ugly

nau·seous \ˈnȯ-shəs, -zē-əs\ *adj* **1 :** causing nausea or disgust **2 ♦ :** affected with nausea or disgust

♦ ill, queasy, sick, squeamish

naut *abbr* nautical

nau·ti·cal \ˈnȯ-ti-kəl\ *adj* **:** of or relating to sailors, navigation, or ships ⟨∼ terms⟩ — **nau·ti·cal·ly** \-k(ə-)lē\ *adv*

nautical mile *n* **:** a unit of distance equal to about 6080 feet (1852 meters)

nau·ti·lus \ˈnȯt-ᵊl-əs\ *n, pl* **-lus·es** *or* **-li** \-ᵊl-ˌī, -ˌē\ **:** any of a genus of sea mollusks related to the octopuses but having a spiral chambered shell

nav *abbr* **1** naval **2** navigable; navigation

Na·va·jo *also* **Na·va·ho** \ˈna-və-ˌhō, ˈnä-\ *n, pl* **-jo** *or* **-jos** *also* **-ho** *or* **-hos :** a member of an Indigenous people of northern New Mexico, Arizona, and south Utah; *also* **:** their language

na·val \ˈnā-vəl\ *adj* **:** of, relating to, or possessing a navy

naval stores *n pl* **:** products (as pitch, turpentine, or rosin) obtained from resinous conifers (as pines)

nave \ˈnāv\ *n* **:** the central part of a church running lengthwise

na·vel \'nā-vəl\ *n* : a depression in the middle of the abdomen that marks the point of attachment of fetus and mother

navel–gaz·ing \'nā-vəl-'gā-ziŋ\ *n* : useless or excessive self=contemplation

navel orange *n* : a seedless orange having a pit at the blossom end where the fruit encloses a small secondary fruit

nav·i·ga·ble \'na-vi-gə-bəl\ *adj* **1** : capable of being navigated ⟨a ∼ river⟩ **2** : capable of being steered — **nav·i·ga·bil·i·ty** \,na-vi-gə-'bi-lə-tē\ *n*

nav·i·gate \'na-və-,gāt\ *vb* **-gat·ed; -gat·ing** **1** : to sail on or through ⟨∼ the Atlantic Ocean⟩ **2** : to steer or direct the course of a ship or aircraft **3** : MOVE; *esp* : WALK ⟨could hardly ∼⟩ **4** ♦ : to travel by water : SAIL — **nav·i·ga·tion** \,na-və-'gā-shən\ *n*

  ♦ boat, cruise, sail, voyage

nav·i·ga·tor \'na-və-,gā-tər\ *n* : one that navigates or is qualified to navigate

na·vy \'nā-vē\ *n, pl* **navies** **1** : FLEET; *also* : the warships belonging to a nation **2** *often cap* : a nation's organization for naval warfare

navy yard *n* : a yard where naval vessels are built or repaired

na·wab \nə-'wäb\ *n* ♦ : a person of great wealth or prominence : NABOB

  ♦ big leaguer, big shot, bigwig, kingpin, nabob, wheel

¹nay \'nā\ *adv* : NO

²nay *n* **1** : a negative vote; *also* : a person casting such a vote **2** : refusal to satisfy a request or desire

³nay *conj* ♦ : not merely this but also : not only so but ⟨he was happy, ∼, ecstatic⟩

  ♦ even, indeed, truly, verily, yea

nay·say·er \'nā-,sā-ər\ *n* : one who denies, refuses, or opposes something

Na·zi \'nät-sē, 'nat-\ *n* : a member of a German fascist party controlling Germany from 1933 to 1945 under Adolf Hitler — **Nazi** *adj* — **Na·zism** \'nät-,si-zəm, 'nat-\ *also* **Na·zi·ism** \-sē-,i-zəm\ *n*

Nb *symbol* niobium

NB *abbr* **1** New Brunswick **2** nota bene

NBA *abbr* **1** National Basketball Association **2** National Boxing Association

NBC *abbr* National Broadcasting Company

NBS *abbr* National Bureau of Standards

NC *abbr* **1** no charge **2** North Carolina

NCAA *abbr* National Collegiate Athletic Association

NCO \,en-,sē-'ō\ *n* : NONCOMMISSIONED OFFICER

nd *abbr* no date

Nd *symbol* neodymium

ND *abbr* North Dakota

N Dak *abbr* North Dakota

Ne *symbol* neon

NE *abbr* **1** Nebraska **2** New England **3** northeast

¹Ne·an·der·thal \nē-'an-dər-,thȯl, nä-'än-dər-,täl\ *adj* **1** *or* **Ne·an·der·tal** \-,täl\ : of, relating to, or being an extinct Old World hominid that lived from about 200,000 to 30,000 years ago **2** ♦ : suggestive of a caveman

  ♦ barbarous, heathen, heathenish, rude, savage, uncivil, uncivilized, uncultivated, wild

²Neanderthal *or* **Neandertal** *n* ♦ : one who suggests a caveman in appearance, mentality, or behavior

  ♦ clod, gawk, hulk, lout, lubber, lug, oaf

neap tide \'nēp-\ *n* : a tide of minimum range occurring at the first and third quarters of the moon

¹near \'nir\ *adv* **1** ♦ : at, within, or to a short distance or time **2** : very nearly but not exactly or entirely : ALMOST

  ♦ around, by, close, hard, in, nearby, nigh *Ant* far

²near *prep* ♦ : close to

  ♦ about, around, by, next to

³near *adj* **1** : closely related or associated; *also* : INTIMATE **2** ♦ : not far away; *also* : being the closer or left-hand member of a pair **3** : barely avoided ⟨a ∼ accident⟩ **4** : DIRECT, SHORT ⟨by the ∼est route⟩ **5** : STINGY **6** ♦ : not real but very like ⟨∼ silk⟩ **7** : being the closer of two

  ♦ [2] close, immediate, nearby, nigh ♦ [6] lifelike, natural, realistic

⁴near *vb* **1** ♦ : to come closer in space or time : APPROACH **2** : to draw near to

  ♦ advance, approach, close

near beer *n* : any of various malt liquors low in alcohol

¹near·by \nir-'bī, 'nir-,bī\ *adj* ♦ : close at hand

  ♦ close, immediate, near, nigh

²near·by \nir-'bī, 'nir-,bī\ *adv* ♦ : close at hand

  ♦ around, by, close, hard, in, near, nigh

near·ly *adv* **1** : in a close manner or relationship **2** ♦ : almost but not quite

  ♦ about, almost, most, much, near, next to, nigh, practically, some, virtually, well-nigh

near·ness *n* **1** ♦ : the quality or state of being near **2** ♦ : the state of being in a close personal relationship esp. marked by affection or love

  ♦ [1] closeness, contiguity, immediacy, proximity ♦ [2] closeness, familiarity, intimacy

near·sight·ed \'nir-'sī-təd\ *adj* : able to see near things more clearly than distant ones : MYOPIC — **near·sight·ed·ly** *adv* — **near·sight·ed·ness** *n*

neat \'nēt\ *adj* **1** ♦ : being orderly and clean **2** ♦ : not mixed or diluted ⟨∼ brandy⟩ **3** : marked by tasteful simplicity **4** : PRECISE, SYSTEMATIC **5** : SKILLFUL, ADROIT **6** : superior in character, nature, ability, or prospects : FINE — **neat** *adv* — **neat·ly** *adv* — **neat·ness** *n*

  ♦ [1] crisp, orderly, shipshape, snug, tidy, trim, uncluttered *Ant* disheveled, disordered, disorderly, messy, mussed, mussy, slovenly, unkempt, untidy ♦ [2] absolute, fine, plain, pure, refined, straight, unadulterated, undiluted, unmixed

neath \'nēth\ *prep, dial* : BENEATH

neat·nik \'nēt-nik\ *n* : a person who is compulsively neat

neb \'neb\ *n* **1** : the beak of a bird or tortoise; *also* : NOSE, SNOUT **2** : NIB

Neb *or* **Nebr** *abbr* Nebraska

NEB *abbr* New English Bible

neb·u·la \'ne-byə-lə\ *n, pl* **-lae** \-,lē, -,lī\ *also* **-las** **1** : any of numerous clouds of gas or dust in interstellar space **2** : GALAXY — **neb·u·lar** \-lər\ *adj*

neb·u·liz·er \'ne-byə-,lī-zər\ *n* : ATOMIZER

neb·u·lous \'ne-byə-ləs\ *adj* **1** : of or relating to a nebula **2 a** ♦ : lacking clarity of feature or sharpness of outline : HAZY, INDISTINCT **b** ♦ : vaguely defined : dimly realized

  ♦ bleary, dim, faint, foggy, fuzzy, hazy, indefinite, indistinct, indistinguishable, murky, obscure, opaque, shadowy, unclear, undefined, undetermined, vague

nec·es·sar·i·ly \,ne-sə-'ser-ə-lē\ *adv* ♦ : of necessity

  ♦ inevitably, needs, perforce, unavoidably

¹nec·es·sary \'ne-sə-,ser-ē\ *n, pl* **-sar·ies** : an indispensable item

²necessary *adj* **1** ♦ : of an inevitable nature : INEVITABLE, INESCAPABLE; *also* : CERTAIN **2** : PREDETERMINED **3** ♦ : containing or constituting a command : COMPULSORY **4** ♦ : positively needed : INDISPENSABLE ⟨∼ supplies⟩

  ♦ [1] certain, inescapable, inevitable, sure, unavoidable ♦ [3] compulsory, imperative, incumbent, involuntary, mandatory, nonelective, obligatory, peremptory ♦ [4] essential, imperative, indispensable, integral, needful, requisite, vital

ne·ces·si·tate \ni-'se-sə-,tāt\ *vb* **-tat·ed; -tat·ing** ♦ : to make necessary

  ♦ demand, need, require, take, want, warrant

ne·ces·si·tous \ni-'se-sə-təs\ *adj* **1** : NEEDY, IMPOVERISHED **2** : URGENT **3** : NECESSARY

ne·ces·si·ty \ni-'se-sə-tē\ *n, pl* **-ties** **1** : conditions that cannot be changed **2** : WANT, POVERTY **3** ♦ : something that is necessary ⟨water is a ∼⟩ **4** : very great need

  ♦ condition, demand, essential, must, need, requirement, requisite

¹neck \'nek\ *n* **1** : the part of the body connecting the head and the trunk **2** : the part of a garment covering or near to the neck **3** : a relatively narrow part suggestive of a neck ⟨∼ of a bottle⟩ ⟨∼ of land⟩ **4** : a narrow margin esp. of victory ⟨won by a ∼⟩ — **necked** \'nekt\ *adj*

²neck *vb* : to kiss and caress amorously

¹neck and neck *adj* ♦ : being very close (as in margin or standing)

  ♦ close, narrow, nip and tuck, tight

²neck and neck *adv* : very close (as in a race)

neck·er·chief \'ne-kər-chəf, -,chēf\ *n, pl* **-chiefs** \-chəfs, -,chēfs\ *also* **-chieves** \-,chēvz\ : a square of cloth worn folded about the neck like a scarf

neck·lace \'ne-kləs\ *n* : an ornament worn around the neck

neck·line \'nek-ˌlīn\ *n* : the outline of the neck opening of a garment

neck·tie \-ˌtī\ *n* : a strip of cloth worn around the neck and tied in front

ne·crol·o·gy \nə-'krä-lə-jē\ *n, pl* **-gies** **1** : OBITUARY **2** : a list of the recently dead

nec·ro·man·cer \'ne-krə-ˌman-sər\ *n* ♦ : one that practices necromancy

♦ conjurer, enchanter, magician, sorcerer, voodoo, witch, wizard

nec·ro·man·cy \'ne-krə-ˌman-sē\ *n* **1** : the art or practice of conjuring up the spirits of the dead for purposes of magically revealing the future **2** : the use of means (as charms or spells) believed to have supernatural power over natural forces : MAGIC, SORCERY

♦ bewitchment, enchantment, magic, sorcery, witchcraft, wizardry

ne·crop·o·lis \nə-'krä-pə-ləs, ne-\ *n, pl* **-lis·es** *or* **-les** \-ˌlēz\ *or* **-leis** \-ˌlās\ *or* **-li** \-ˌlī, -ˌlē\ : CEMETERY; *esp* : a large elaborate cemetery of an ancient city

ne·cro·sis \nə-'krō-səs, ne-\ *n, pl* **ne·cro·ses** \-ˌsēz\ : usu. local death of body tissue — **ne·crot·ic** \-'krä-tik\ *adj*

nec·tar \'nek-tər\ *n* **1** : the drink of the Greek and Roman gods; *also* : any delicious drink **2** : a sweet plant secretion that is the raw material of honey

nec·tar·ine \ˌnek-tə-'rēn\ *n* : a smooth-skinned peach

née *or* **nee** \'nā\ *adj* — used to identify a woman by her maiden family name

¹need \'nēd\ *n* **1** ♦ : necessary duty : OBLIGATION ⟨no ∼ to hurry⟩ **2** ♦ : a lack of something requisite, desirable, or useful **3** ♦ : a condition requiring supply or relief ⟨when the ∼ arises⟩ **4** ♦ : lack of the means of subsistence : POVERTY **5** ♦ : a requirement for the well-being of an organism

♦ [1] burden, charge, commitment, duty, obligation, responsibility ♦ [2] absence, lack, want ♦ beggary, destitution, impecuniousness, impoverishment, indigence, pauperism, penury, poverty, want ♦ [5] condition, demand, essential, must, necessity, requirement, requisite

²need *vb* **1** : to be in want **2** ♦ : to have cause or occasion for : REQUIRE ⟨he ∼s advice⟩ **3** ♦ : to be under obligation or necessity ⟨we ∼ to know the truth⟩

♦ [2] demand, necessitate, require, take, want, warrant *Ant* have, hold ♦ [3] have, must, ought, shall, should

need·ful \'nēd-fəl\ *adj* ♦ : absolutely needed : NECESSARY, REQUISITE ⟨bought only what was ∼⟩

♦ essential, imperative, indispensable, integral, necessary, requisite, vital

¹nee·dle \'nēd-ᵊl\ *n* **1** : a slender pointed usu. steel implement used in sewing **2** : a slender rod (as for knitting, controlling a small opening, or transmitting vibrations to or from a recording) ⟨a phonograph ∼⟩ **3** ♦ : a slender hollow instrument by which material is introduced into or withdrawn from the body **4** ♦ : a slender indicator on a dial **5** : a needle-shaped leaf (as of a pine)

♦ [3] hypodermic syringe, syringe ♦ [4] hand, index, indicator, pointer

²needle *vb* **nee·dled; nee·dling** **1** ♦ : to vex by repeated sharp prods or gibes; *esp* : to incite to action by repeated gibes **2** ♦ : to disturb or annoy by persistent irritating or provoking esp. in a petty or mischievous way

♦ [1] henpeck, hound, nag ♦ [2] bait, bug, hassle, heckle, ride, taunt, tease

nee·dle-nose pliers \'nē-dᵊl-ˌnōz\ *n pl* : pliers with long slender jaws for grasping small or thin objects

nee·dle·point \'nē-dᵊl-ˌpoint\ *n* **1** : lace worked with a needle over a paper pattern **2** : embroidery done on canvas across counted threads — **needlepoint** *adj*

need·less \'nēd-ləs\ *adj* : not necessary — **need·less·ly** *adv* — **need·less·ness** *n*

nee·dle·wom·an \'nēd-ᵊl-ˌwu̇-mən\ *n* : a woman who does needlework; *esp* : SEAMSTRESS

nee·dle·work \-ˌwərk\ *n* : work done with a needle; *esp* : work (as embroidery) other than plain sewing

needs \'nēdz\ *adv* ♦ : of necessity : NECESSARILY ⟨must ∼ be recognized⟩

♦ inevitably, necessarily, perforce, unavoidably *Ant* unnecessarily

needy \'nē-dē\ *adj* **need·i·er; -est** ♦ : being in want : POVERTY-STRICKEN

♦ broke, destitute, impecunious, indigent, penniless, penurious, poor, poverty-stricken

ne'er \'ner\ *adv* : NEVER

ne'er-do-well \'ner-du̇-ˌwel\ *n* : an idle worthless person — **ne'er-do-well** *adj*

ne·far·i·ous \ni-'far-ē-əs\ *adj* ♦ : very wicked : EVIL — **ne·far·i·ous·ly** *adv*

♦ bad, evil, immoral, iniquitous, rotten, sinful, unethical, unsavory, vicious, vile, villainous, wicked, wrong

neg *abbr* negative

ne·gate \ni-'gāt\ *vb* **ne·gat·ed; ne·gat·ing** **1** ♦ : to deny the existence or truth of **2** ♦ : to cause to be ineffective or invalid : NULLIFY ⟨∼ a contract⟩

♦ [1] contradict, deny, disallow, disavow, disclaim, gainsay, negative, reject, repudiate ♦ [2] abolish, abrogate, annul, cancel, dissolve, invalidate, nullify, quash, repeal, rescind, void

ne·ga·tion \ni-'gā-shən\ *n* **1** ♦ : the action or operation of negating or making negative **2** : a negative doctrine or statement

♦ contradiction, denial, disallowance, disavowal, disclaimer, rejection, repudiation

¹neg·a·tive \'ne-gə-tiv\ *adj* **1** ♦ : marked by denial, prohibition, or refusal ⟨a ∼ reply⟩ **2** : not positive or constructive; *esp* : not affirming the presence of what is sought or suspected to be present ⟨test results were ∼⟩ **3** : less than zero ⟨a ∼ number⟩ **4** : being, relating to, or charged with electricity of which the electron is the elementary unit **5** : having the light and dark parts opposite to what they were in the original photographic subject — **neg·a·tive·ly** *adv* — **neg·a·tive·ness** *n* — **neg·a·tiv·i·ty** \ˌne-gə-'ti-və-tē\ *n*

♦ adverse, counter, disadvantageous, hostile, inimical, prejudicial, unfavorable (*or* unfavourable), unfriendly, unsympathetic

²negative *n* **1** : a negative word or statement **2** : a negative vote or reply; *also* : REFUSAL **3** ♦ : something that is the opposite or negation of something else **4** : the side that votes or argues for the opposition (as in a debate) **5** : a negative number **6** : a negative photographic image on transparent material

♦ antipode, antithesis, contrary, opposite, reverse

³negative *vb* **-tived; -tiv·ing** **1** : to refuse to accept or approve **2** ♦ : to vote against **3** : DISPROVE **4** : to imply the opposite or a denial of **5** ♦ : to deny the truth, reality, or validity of

♦ [2] blackball, kill, veto *Ant* confirm, ratify ♦ [5] contradict, deny, disallow, disavow, disclaim, gainsay, negate, reject, repudiate

negative income tax *n* : a system of federal subsidy payments to families with incomes below a stipulated level

neg·a·tiv·ism \'ne-gə-ti-ˌvi-zəm\ *n* : an attitude of skepticism and denial of nearly everything affirmed or suggested by others

¹ne·glect \ni-'glekt\ *vb* **1** ♦ : to give little attention or respect to : DISREGARD **2** ♦ : to leave undone or unattended to esp. through carelessness

♦ [1] disregard, forget, ignore, overlook, pass over, slight, slur *Ant* attend (to), heed, mind, regard, tend (to) ♦ [2] fail, forget, omit

²neglect *n* **1** ♦ : an act or instance of neglecting something **2** ♦ : the condition of being neglected

♦ [1] default, delinquency, dereliction, failure, negligence, oversight ♦ [2] desolation, dilapidation, disrepair *Ant* repair

ne·glect·ed \ni-'glek-təd\ *adj* ♦ : that evidences improper or insufficient attention or care

♦ dilapidated, grungy, mean, ratty, seedy, shabby

ne·glect·ful *adj* : given to neglecting

neg·li·gee *also* **neg·li·gé** \ˌne-glə-'zhā\ *n* : a woman's long flowing dressing gown

neg·li·gence \'ne-gli-jəns\ *n* **1** ♦ : the quality or state of being negligent **2** ♦ : an act or instance of being negligent

♦ [1] carelessness, dereliction, heedlessness, laxness, remissness, slackness *Ant* care, carefulness, caution, cautiousness, heedfulness ♦ [2] default, delinquency, dereliction, failure, neglect, oversight

neg·li·gent \'ne-gli-jənt\ *adj* ♦ : marked by neglect — **neg·li·gent·ly** *adv*

♦ careless, derelict, lax, remiss, slack *Ant* attentive, careful, conscientious

neg·li·gi·ble \'ne-gli-jə-bəl\ adj ♦ : so small or unimportant or of so little consequence as to warrant little or no attention

♦ inconsequential, inconsiderable, insignificant, measly, minute, nominal, paltry, petty, slight, trifling, trivial, unimportant *Ant* big, consequential, considerable, important, material, significant

ne·go·tiant \ni-'gō-shē-ənt\ n : NEGOTIATOR
ne·go·ti·ate \ni-'gō-shē-ˌāt\ vb **-at·ed; -at·ing 1 ♦** : to confer with another so as to arrive at the settlement of some matter; *also* : to arrange for or bring about by such conferences ⟨~ a treaty⟩ **2** : to transfer to another by delivery or endorsement in return for equivalent value ⟨~ a check⟩ **3** : to get through, around, or over successfully ⟨~ a turn⟩ **4 ♦** : to deal with (some matter or affair that requires ability for its successful handling) — **ne·go·tia·ble** \-shə-bəl, -shē-ə-\ adj — **ne·go·ti·a·tor** \-'gō-shē-ˌā-tər\ n

♦ [1] arrange, concert, conclude ♦ [4] contend with, cope with, grapple with, handle, manage, maneuver (or manoeuvre), swing, treat

ne·go·ti·a·tion \ni-ˌgō-sē-'ā-shən, -shē-\ n ♦ : the action or process of negotiating or being negotiated

♦ accommodation, compromise, concession, give-and-take

ne·gri·tude \'ne-grə-ˌtüd, -ˌtyüd, 'nē-\ n : a consciousness of and pride in one's African heritage
Ne·gro \'nē-grō\ n, pl **Ne·groes** dated, often offensive : a member of a group of people formerly considered to constitute a race of humans having African ancestry and classified according to physical traits (as dark skin pigmentation) — **Negro** adj, dated, often offensive — **ne·groid** \'nē-ˌgroid\ n or adj, often cap, dated, often offensive
Neh abbr Nehemiah
Ne·he·mi·ah \ˌnē-ə-'mī-ə\ n : a book of Jewish and Christian Scripture
neigh \'nā\ n : a loud prolonged cry of a horse — **neigh** vb
¹neigh·bor or Can and Brit **neigh·bour** \'nā-bər\ n **1** : one living or located near another **2** : FELLOW MAN
²neighbor or Can and Brit **neigh·bour** vb ♦ : to be next to or near to : border on

♦ abut, adjoin, border (on), flank, fringe, join, skirt, touch, verge (on)

neigh·bor·hood \'nā-bər-ˌhud\ or Can and Brit **neigh·bour·hood** \'nā-bər-ˌhud\ n **1** : NEARNESS **2** : a place or region near : VICINITY; *also* : a number or amount near ⟨costs in the ~ of $10⟩ **3** : the people living near one another **4 ♦** : a section lived in by neighbors and usu. having distinguishing characteristics

♦ district, quarter, section

neigh·bor·li·ness or Can and Brit **neigh·bour·li·ness** \'nā-bər-lē-nəs\ n ♦ : the quality or state of being neighborly

♦ amity, benevolence, cordiality, fellowship, friendliness, friendship, goodwill, kindliness

neigh·bor·ly or Can and Brit **neigh·bour·ly** \'nā-bər-lē\ adj ♦ : befitting congenial neighbors; *esp* : FRIENDLY

♦ amicable, companionable, comradely, cordial, friendly, genial, hearty, warm, warmhearted

neigh·bour Can and Brit var of NEIGHBOUR
¹nei·ther \'nē-thər, 'nī-\ pron : neither one : not the one and not the other ⟨~ of the two⟩
²neither conj **1** : not either ⟨~ good nor bad⟩ **2** : NOR ⟨~ did I⟩
³neither adj : not either ⟨~ hand⟩
nel·son \'nel-sən\ n : a wrestling hold in which one applies leverage against an opponent's arm, neck, and head
nem·a·tode \'ne-mə-ˌtōd\ n : any of a phylum of elongated cylindrical worms parasitic in animals or plants or free-living in soil or water
nem·e·sis \'ne-mə-səs\ n, pl **-e·ses** \-ˌsēz\ **1 ♦** : one that inflicts retribution or vengeance **2** : a formidable and usu. victorious rival **3 ♦** : an act or effect of retribution; *also* : CURSE

♦ [1] avenger, castigator, scourge ♦ [3] castigation, chastisement, correction, curse, desert, discipline, penalty, punishment, wrath

neo·clas·sic \ˌnē-ō-'kla-sik\ or **neo·clas·si·cal** \-si-kəl\ adj : of or relating to a revival or adaptation of the classical style esp. in literature, art, or music
neo·co·lo·nial·ism \ˌnē-ō-kə-'lō-nē-ə-ˌli-zəm\ n : the economic and political policies by which a nation indirectly maintains or

extends its influence over other areas or peoples — **neo·co·lo·nial** adj — **neo·co·lo·nial·ist** \-list\ n or adj
neo·con \'nē-ō-ˌkän\ n : NEOCONSERVATIVE
neo·con·ser·va·tive \-kən-'sər-və-tiv\ n : a former liberal espousing political conservatism — **neo·con·ser·va·tism** \-və-ˌti-zəm\ n — **neoconservative** adj
neo·dym·i·um \ˌnē-ō-'di-mē-əm\ n : a silver-white to yellow metallic chemical element
neo·im·pres·sion·ism \ˌnē-ō-im-'pre-shə-ˌni-zəm\ n, often cap N&I : a late 19th century French art movement that attempted to make impressionism more precise and to use a pointillist painting technique
Neo·lith·ic \ˌnē-ə-'li-thik\ adj : of or relating to the latest period of the Stone Age characterized by polished stone implements
ne·ol·o·gism \nē-'ä-lə-ˌji-zəm\ n : a new word or expression
ne·on \'nē-ˌän\ n **1** : a gaseous colorless chemical element used in electric lamps **2** : a lamp in which a discharge through neon gives a reddish glow — **neon** adj
neo·na·tal \ˌnē-ō-'nāt- əl\ adj : of, relating to, or affecting the newborn — **neo·na·tal·ly** adv
ne·o·nate \'nē-ə-ˌnāt\ n : a newborn child
neo·pa·gan \ˌnē-ō-'pā-gən\ n : a person who practices a contemporary form of paganism — **neo–pagan** adj
neo·phyte \'nē-ə-ˌfīt\ n **1** : a new convert : PROSELYTE **2** : NOVICE **3 ♦** : one that begins something; *esp* : an inexperienced person : BEGINNER

♦ beginner, fledgling, freshman, greenhorn, newcomer, novice, recruit, rookie, tenderfoot, tyro

neo·plasm \'nē-ə-ˌpla-zəm\ n ♦ : a new growth of tissue serving no useful purpose in the body : TUMOR — **neo·plas·tic** \ˌnē-ə-'plas-tik\ adj

♦ excrescence, growth, lump, tumor

neo·prene \'nē-ə-ˌprēn\ n : a synthetic rubber used esp. for special-purpose clothing (as wet suits)
neo·trop·i·cal \ˌnē-ō-'trä-pi-kəl\ adj, often cap : of or relating to a zoogeographic region of America that extends south from the central plateau of Mexico
Ne·pali \nə-'pȯ-lē, -'pä-\ n, pl **Nepali** : a native or inhabitant of Nepal — **Nepali** adj
ne·pen·the \nə-'pen-thē\ n **1** : a potion used by the ancients to dull pain and sorrow **2** : something capable of making one forget grief or suffering
neph·ew \'ne-fyü, chiefly Brit -vyü\ n : a son of one's brother, sister, brother-in-law, or sister-in-law
ne·phrit·ic \ni-'fri-tik\ adj **1** : RENAL **2** : of, relating to, or affected with nephritis
ne·phri·tis \ni-'frī-təs\ n, pl **ne·phrit·i·des** \-'fri-tə-ˌdēz\ : kidney inflammation
ne plus ul·tra \ˌnē-ˌpləs-'əl-trə\ n : the highest point capable of being attained
nep·o·tism \'ne-pə-ˌti-zəm\ n : favoritism shown to a relative (as in the granting of jobs)
Nep·tune \'nep-ˌtün, -ˌtyün\ n : the planet 8th in order from the sun — **Nep·tu·ni·an** \nep-'tü-nē-ən, -'tyü-\ adj
nep·tu·ni·um \nep-'tü-nē-əm, -'tyü-\ n : a short-lived radioactive element
nerd \'nərd\ n **1 ♦** : a person devoted to intellectual or technical pursuits **2** : an unstylish or socially inept person — **nerdy** adj

♦ highbrow, intellectual

Ne·re·id \'nir-ē-əd\ n : a sea nymph in Greek mythology
¹nerve \'nərv\ n **1** : SINEW, TENDON ⟨strain every ~⟩ **2** : any of the strands of nervous tissue that carry nerve impulses between the brain and spinal cord and every part of the body **3 a ♦** : power of endurance or control : FORTITUDE **b ♦** : the quality or state of being bold : BOLDNESS, DARING **4** pl : NERVOUSNESS **5** : a vein of a leaf or insect wing — **nerved** \'nərvd\ adj

♦ [3a] bravery, courage, daring, fearlessness, fortitude, gallantry, guts, hardihood, heart, heroism, stoutness, valor ♦ [3b] audacity, brass, brazenness, cheek, chutzpah, daring, effrontery, gall, presumption, sauce, sauciness, temerity

²nerve vb **nerved; nerv·ing** ♦ : to give strength or courage to

♦ brace, forearm, fortify, psych (up), ready, steel, strengthen

nerve cell n : NEURON; *also* : CELL BODY
nerve gas n : a chemical weapon damaging esp. to the nervous and respiratory systems
nerve impulse n : a physical and chemical change that moves along a process of a neuron after stimulation and carries a record of sensation or an instruction to act

nerve·less adj 1 ♦ : destitute of strength or courage 2 ♦ : exhibiting control or balance

♦ [1] effete, frail, soft, spineless, weak, wimpy, wishy-washy ♦ [2] imperturbable, unflappable, unshakable

nerve–rack·ing or **nerve–wrack·ing** \'nərv-ˌra-kiŋ\ adj : extremely trying on the nerves ⟨∼ noise⟩

ner·vous \'nər-vəs\ adj 1 : FORCIBLE, SPIRITED 2 : of, relating to, or made up of neurons or nerves 3 ♦ : easily excited or annoyed : JUMPY ⟨a ∼ horse⟩ 4 ♦ : viewing the future with anxiety or alarm ⟨a ∼ smile⟩ 5 ♦ : causing physical or mental discomfort — **ner·vous·ly** adv

♦ [3] excitable, flighty, fluttery, high-strung, jittery, jumpy, skittish, spooky ♦ [4] aflutter, anxious, edgy, jittery, jumpy, nervy, perturbed, tense, troubled, uneasy, upset, worried Ant calm, easy, collected, cool, nerveless, relaxed ♦ [5] anxious, distressful, restless, tense, unsettling, upsetting, worrisome Ant calming, comfortable, easy, peaceful, quiet, quieting, tranquil

nervous breakdown n : an attack of mental or emotional disorder esp. when of sufficient severity to require hospitalization
ner·vous·ness n ♦ : the quality or state of being nervous

♦ agitation, anxiety, apprehension, care, concern, disquiet, perturbation, uneasiness, worry

nervous system n : a bodily system that in vertebrates is made up of the brain and spinal cord, nerves, ganglia, and parts of the sense organs and that receives and interprets stimuli and transmits nerve impulses
ner·vy \'nər-vē\ adj **nerv·i·er; -est** 1 ♦ : showing calm courage 2 ♦ : marked by impudence or presumption ⟨a ∼ salesperson⟩ 3 : marked by nervousness : NERVOUS

♦ [1] adventurous, audacious, bold, daring, enterprising, gutsy, hardy, venturesome ♦ [2] arch, bold, brash, brazen, cheeky, cocky, fresh, impertinent, impudent, insolent, sassy, saucy Ant meek, mousy, retiring, shy, timid

-ness \nəs\ n suffix : state : condition : quality : degree ⟨goodness⟩
¹nest \'nest\ n 1 : the shelter prepared by a bird for its eggs and young 2 : a place where eggs (as of insects or fish) are laid and hatched 3 ♦ : a place of rest, retreat, or lodging 4 : DEN, HANGOUT ⟨a ∼ of thieves⟩ 5 : the occupants of a nest 6 : a series of objects (as bowls or tables) fitting inside or under one another

♦ concealment, covert, den, hideout, lair

²nest vb 1 : to build or occupy a nest 2 : to fit compactly together or within one another
nest egg n ♦ : a fund of money accumulated as a reserve

♦ account, budget, deposit, fund, kitty, pool

nes·tle \'ne-səl\ vb **nes·tled; nes·tling** 1 ♦ : to settle snugly or comfortably 2 ♦ : to press closely and affectionately : CUDDLE 3 : to settle, shelter, or house as if in a nest

♦ cuddle, curl up, snug, snuggle

nest·ling \'nest-liŋ\ n : a bird too young to leave its nest
¹net \'net\ n 1 ♦ : a meshed fabric twisted, knotted, or woven together at regular intervals 2 ♦ : a device made all or partly of net and used esp. to catch birds, fish, or insects 3 ♦ : something made of net used esp. for protecting, confining, carrying, or dividing ⟨a tennis ∼⟩ 4 : an entrapping device or situation : SNARE, TRAP 5 often cap : INTERNET

♦ [1] mesh, network ♦ [2, 3] entanglement, snare, web

²net vb **net·ted; net·ting** 1 : to cover or enclose with or as if with a net 2 : to catch in or as if in a net
³net adj : free from all charges or deductions ⟨∼ profit⟩ ⟨∼ weight⟩
⁴net vb **net·ted; net·ting** : to gain or produce as profit : CLEAR, YIELD ⟨his business netted $50,000 a year⟩
⁵net n ♦ : a net amount, profit, weight, or price

♦ earnings, gain, lucre, payoff, proceeds, profit, return

Neth abbr Netherlands
neth·er \'ne-thər\ adj : situated down or below ⟨the ∼ regions of the earth⟩
Neth·er·land·er \'ne-thər-ˌlan-dər\ n : a native or inhabitant of the Netherlands
neth·er·most \-ˌmōst\ adj : LOWEST
neth·er·world \-ˌwərld\ n 1 : the world of the dead 2 : UNDERWORLD
net·i·quette \'ne-ti-kət, -ˌket\ n : etiquette governing communication on the Internet
net·roots \'net-ˌrüts, -ˌrúts\ n pl : the grassroots political activists who communicate via the Internet

net·ting n 1 : a fabric or structure of cords or wires that cross at regular intervals and are knotted or secured at the crossings : NETWORK 2 : the act or process of making a net or network
¹net·tle \'net-ᵊl\ n : any of a genus of coarse herbs with stinging hairs
²nettle vb **net·tled; net·tling** ♦ : to arouse to sharp but transitory annoyance or anger : VEX, IRRITATE

♦ aggravate, annoy, bother, bug, chafe, exasperate, gall, get, grate, irk, irritate, peeve, persecute, pique, put out, rasp, rile, vex

net·tle·some \'net-ᵊl-səm\ adj : causing vexation : IRRITATING
net·work \'net-ˌwərk\ n 1 ♦ : a fabric or structure of cords or wires that cross at regular intervals and are knotted or secured at the crossings : NET 2 : a system of elements (as lines or channels) that cross in the manner of the threads in a net 3 : a group or system of related or connected parts; esp : a chain of radio or television stations 4 : a system of computers that are connected (as by telephone wires)

♦ mesh, net

net·work·ing \'net-ˌwər-kiŋ\ n : the exchange of information or services among individuals, groups, or institutions
neu·ral \'nûr-əl, 'nyûr-\ adj : of, relating to, or involving a nerve or the nervous system
neu·ral·gia \nü-'ral-jə, nyü-\ n : acute pain that follows the course of a nerve — **neu·ral·gic** \-jik\ adj
neur·as·the·nia \ˌnûr-əs-'thē-nē-ə\ n : a psychological disorder marked esp. by fatiguing easily, lack of motivation, feelings of inadequacy, and psychosomatic symptoms — **neur·as·then·ic** \-the-nik, -'thē-\ adj or n
neu·ri·tis \-'rī-təs\ n, pl **-rit·i·des** \-'ri-tə-ˌdēz\ or **-ri·tis·es** : inflammation of a nerve — **neu·rit·ic** \-'ri-tik\ adj or n
neu·ro·bi·ol·o·gy \ˌnûr-ō-bī-'ä-lə-jē\ n : a branch of biology that deals with the nervous system — **neu·ro·bi·o·log·i·cal** \-ˌbī-ə-'lä-ji-kəl\ adj — **neu·ro·bi·ol·o·gist** \-bī-'ä-lə-jist\ n
neu·rol·o·gy \nü-'rä-lə-jē, nyü-\ n : the scientific study of the nervous system — **neu·ro·log·i·cal** \ˌnûr-ə-'lä-ji-kəl, ˌnyûr-\ or **neu·ro·log·ic** \-jik\ adj — **neu·ro·log·i·cal·ly** \-ji-k(ə-)lē\ adv — **neu·rol·o·gist** \nü-'rä-lə-jist, nyü-\ n
neu·ro·mus·cu·lar \ˌnûr-ō-'məs-kyə-lər, ˌnyûr-\ adj : of, relating to, or affecting nerves and muscles ⟨a ∼ disease⟩
neu·ron \'nü-ˌrän, 'nyü-\ n : a cell with specialized processes that is the fundamental functional unit of nervous tissue — **neu·ro·nal** \'nûr-ə-nᵊl, 'nyûr-\ adj
neu·rone \-ˌrōn\ chiefly Brit var of NEURON
neu·ro·sci·ence \ˌnûr-ō-'sī-əns, ˌnyûr-\ n : a branch of the life sciences that deals with the anatomy, physiology, biochemistry, or molecular biology of nerves and nervous tissue and esp. with their relation to behavior and learning — **neu·ro·sci·en·tist** \-ən-tist\ n
neu·ro·sis \nü-'rō-səs, nyü-\ n, pl **-ro·ses** \-ˌsēz\ : a mental and emotional disorder that is less serious than a psychosis, is not characterized by disturbance of the use of language, and is accompanied by various bodily and mental disturbances (as visceral symptoms, anxieties, or phobias)
neu·ro·sur·gery \ˌnûr-ō-'sər-jə-rē, ˌnyûr-\ n : surgery of nervous structures (as nerves, the brain, or the spinal cord) — **neu·ro·sur·geon** \-'sər-jən\ n
¹neu·rot·ic \nü-'rä-tik, nyü-\ adj : of, relating to, being, or affected with a neurosis; also : NERVOUS — **neu·rot·i·cal·ly** \-ti-k(ə-)lē\ adv
²neurotic n : an emotionally unstable or neurotic person
neu·ro·trans·mit·ter \ˌnûr-ō-trans-'mi-tər, ˌnyûr-, -tranz-\ n : a substance (as acetylcholine) that transmits nerve impulses across a synapse
neut abbr neuter
¹neu·ter \'nü-tər, 'nyü-\ adj 1 : of, relating to, or constituting the gender that includes most words or grammatical forms referring to things classed as neither masculine nor feminine 2 : lacking or having imperfectly developed sex organs
²neuter n 1 : a noun, pronoun, adjective, or inflectional form or class of the neuter gender; also : the neuter gender 2 : WORKER 2; also : a spayed or castrated animal
³neuter vb : to remove the sex organs of : CASTRATE, SPAY
¹neu·tral \'nü-trəl, 'nyü-\ n 1 : one that is neutral 2 : a neutral color 3 : a position of disengagement (as of gears)
²neutral adj 1 ♦ : not favoring either side in a quarrel, contest, or war 2 : of or relating to a neutral state or power 3 : MIDDLING, INDIFFERENT 4 : having no hue : GRAY; also : not decided in color 5 : neither acid nor basic ⟨a ∼ solution⟩ 6 : not electrically charged

♦ disinterested, impartial, nonpartisan, unbiased Ant allied, confederate

neu·tral·ise *chiefly Brit var of* NEUTRALIZE

neu·tral·ism \'nü-trə-ˌli-zəm, 'nyü-\ *n* : a policy or the advocacy of neutrality esp. in international affairs

neu·tral·i·ty \nü-'tra-lə-tē, nyü-\ *n* ♦ : the quality or state of being neutral; *esp* : refusal to take part in a war between other powers

♦ detachment, disinterestedness, impartiality, objectivity

neu·tral·ize \'nü-trə-ˌlīz, 'nyü-\ *vb* **-ized; -iz·ing** ♦ : to make neutral; *esp* : to counteract the activity or effect of : COUNTERACT — **neu·tral·i·za·tion** \ˌnü-trə-lə-'zā-shən, ˌnyü-\ *n*

♦ annul, cancel, compensate, correct, counteract, counterbalance, make up, offset

neu·tri·no \nü-'trē-nō, nyü-\ *n, pl* **-nos** : an uncharged elementary particle held to be massless or very light

neu·tron \'nü-ˌträn, 'nyü-\ *n* : an uncharged atomic particle that is nearly equal in mass to the proton

neutron bomb *n* : a nuclear bomb designed to produce lethal neutrons but less blast and fire damage than other nuclear bombs

neutron star *n* : a dense celestial object that results from the collapse of a large star

Nev *abbr* Nevada

nev·er \'ne-vər\ *adv* **1** : not ever **2** ♦ : not in any degree, way, or condition

♦ no, none, nothing, nowise *Ant* anyhow, anyway, anywise, at all, ever, half, however

nev·er·more \ˌne-vər-'mōr\ *adv* : never again

nev·er–nev·er land \ˌne-vər-'ne-vər-\ *n* : an ideal or imaginary place

nev·er·the·less \ˌne-vər-thə-'les\ *adv* ♦ : in spite of that : HOWEVER

♦ but, howbeit, however, nonetheless, notwithstanding, still, though, withal, yet

ne·vus \'nē-vəs\ *n, pl* **ne·vi** \-ˌvī\ : a usu. pigmented area on the skin : MOLE

¹**new** \'nü, 'nyü\ *adj* **1** ♦ : having recently come into existence or occurred; *also* : of or characteristic of the present time : MODERN **2** ♦ : recently discovered, recognized, or learned about ⟨∼ drugs⟩ **3** : not familiar : UNFAMILIAR **4** ♦ : different from the former **5** : not accustomed ⟨∼ to the work⟩ **6** : beginning as a repetition of a previous act or thing ⟨a ∼ year⟩ **7** : made or become fresh : REFRESHED, REGENERATED ⟨awoke a ∼ person⟩ **8** : being in a position or place for the first time ⟨a ∼ member⟩ **9** *cap* : having been in use after medieval times : MODERN ⟨*New* Latin⟩ — **new·ish** *adj*

♦ [1] contemporary, current, hot, mod, modern, newfangled, red-hot, space-age, ultramodern, up-to-date ♦ [1] brand-new, spick-and-span, unused *Ant* hand-me-down, second hand, used ♦ [2] fresh, novel, original, strange, unfamiliar, unknown *Ant* familiar, old, time-honored, tired ♦ [4] backup, substitute *Ant* original

²**new** *adv* ♦ : not long ago : NEWLY ⟨*new*-mown hay⟩

♦ freshly, just, late, lately, newly, now, only, recently

new age *adj, often cap N&A* **1** : of, relating to, or being New Age **2** : CONTEMPORARY, MODERN

New Age *n* **1** : a group of late 20th century social attitudes adapted from a variety of ancient and modern beliefs relating to spirituality, right living, and health **2** : a soft soothing form of instrumental music

new·bie \'nü-bē, 'nyü-\ *n* ♦ : one that begins something without prior experience : NEWCOMER; *esp* : a newcomer to cyberspace

♦ beginner, fledgling, freshman, greenhorn, neophyte, newcomer, novice, recruit, rookie, tenderfoot, tyro

¹**new·born** \-ˌbȯrn\ *adj* **1** : recently born **2** : born anew ⟨∼ hope⟩

²**newborn** *n, pl* **newborn** *or* **newborns** ♦ : a newborn individual

♦ baby, child, infant

new·com·er \-ˌkə-mər\ *n* **1** : one recently arrived **2** ♦ : one that begins something without prior experience : BEGINNER

♦ beginner, fledgling, freshman, greenhorn, neophyte, novice, recruit, rookie, tenderfoot, tyro

New Deal *n* : the legislative and administrative program of President F. D. Roosevelt to promote economic recovery and social reform during the 1930s — **New Dealer** *n*

new·el \'nü-əl, 'nyü-\ *n* : a post about which the steps of a circular staircase wind; *also* : a post at the foot of a stairway or one at a landing

new·fan·gled \'nü-'faŋ-gəld, 'nyü-\ *adj* **1** : attracted to novelty **2** ♦ : of the newest style : NOVEL ⟨∼ gadgets⟩

♦ contemporary, current, hot, mod, modern, new, novel, red-hot, space-age, ultramodern, up-to-date

new–fash·ioned \-'fa-shənd\ *adj* **1** : made in a new fashion or form **2** : abreast of the times : UP-TO-DATE

new·found \-'faúnd\ *adj* : newly found

New Left *n* : a radical political movement originating in the 1960s

new·ly \'nü-lē, 'nyü-\ *adv* **1** ♦ : not long ago : LATELY, RECENTLY **2** : ANEW, AFRESH

♦ freshly, just, late, lately, new, now, only, recently

new·ly·wed \-ˌwed\ *n* : a person recently married

new moon *n* : the phase of the moon with its dark side toward the earth; *also* : the thin crescent moon seen for a few days after the new moon phase

new·ness *n* ♦ : the quality or state of being new

♦ freshness, novelty, originality

news \'nüz, 'nyüz\ *n* **1** ♦ : a report of recent events : TIDINGS **2** : material reported in a newspaper or news periodical or on a newscast

♦ intelligence, item, story, tidings, word

news·boy \'nüz-ˌbȯi, 'nyüz-\ *n* : one who delivers or sells newspapers

news·cast \-ˌkast\ *n* : a radio or television broadcast of news — **news·cast·er** \-ˌkas-tər\ *n*

news·group \-ˌgrüp\ *n* : an Internet bulletin devoted to a certain topic

news·let·ter \-ˌle-tər\ *n* : a small newspaper containing news or information of interest chiefly to a special group

news·mag·a·zine \-ˌma-gə-ˌzēn\ *n* : a usu. weekly magazine devoted chiefly to summarizing and analyzing news

news·man \-mən, -ˌman\ *n* ♦ : a person who gathers, reports, or comments on the news : REPORTER

♦ correspondent, journalist, reporter

news·pa·per \-ˌpā-pər\ *n* : a paper that is published at regular intervals and contains news, articles of opinion, features, and advertising

news·pa·per·man \-ˌpā-pər-ˌman\ *n* : a person who owns or is employed by a newspaper

news·print \-ˌprint\ *n* : paper made chiefly from wood pulp and used mostly for newspapers

news·reel \-ˌrēl\ *n* : a short motion picture portraying current events

news·stand \-ˌstand\ *n* : a place where newspapers and periodicals are sold

news·week·ly \-ˌwēk-lē\ *n* : a weekly newspaper or newsmagazine

news·wire \-ˌwī(-ə)r\ *n* : WIRE SERVICE

news·wom·an \-ˌwu̇-mən\ *n* : a woman who is a reporter

news·wor·thy \-ˌwər-thē\ *adj* : sufficiently interesting to the general public to warrant reporting (as in a newspaper)

newsy \'nü-zē, 'nyü-\ *adj* **news·i·er; -est** **1** : filled with news; *esp* : TALKATIVE **2** ♦ : given to gossip

♦ chatty, colloquial, conversational

newt \'nüt, 'nyüt\ *n* : any of various small chiefly aquatic salamanders

New Testament *n* : the second of the two chief divisions of the Christian Scripture

new·ton \'nüt-ᵊn, 'nyüt-\ *n* : the unit of force in the metric system equal to the force required to impart an acceleration of one meter per second per second to a mass of one kilogram

new wave *n, often cap N&W* : the latest and esp. the most outrageous style — **new–wave** *adj*

New World *n* : the western hemisphere; *esp* : the continental landmass of No. and So. America

New Year *n* **1** : NEW YEAR'S DAY; *also* : the first days of the year **2** : ROSH HASHANAH

New Year's Day *n* : January 1 observed as a legal holiday

New Zea·land·er \nü-'zē-lən-dər, nyü-\ *n* : a native or inhabitant of New Zealand

¹**next** \'nekst\ *adj* **1** : immediately preceding or following **2** ♦ : following that approaching or in progress

♦ coming, following, succeeding *Ant* antecedent, foregoing, precedent, preceding, previous, prior

²**next** *prep* : nearest or adjacent to

³**next** *adv* **1** : in the time, place, or order nearest or immediately succeeding **2** : on the first occasion to come

¹**next to** *prep* **1** ♦ : immediately following or adjacent to **2** : in comparison to ⟨*next to* you I'm wealthy⟩

♦ about, around, by, near

²**next to** *adv* ♦ : very nearly ⟨*next to* impossible to win⟩

♦ about, almost, most, much, near, nearly, nigh, practically, some, virtually, well-nigh

Nez Percé \'nez-'pərs, *F* nā-per-sā\ *n* : a member of an Indigenous people orig. of Idaho, Washington, and Oregon; *also* : the language of the Nez Percé

NF *abbr* Newfoundland

NFC *abbr* National Football Conference

NFL *abbr* National Football League

Nfld *abbr* Newfoundland

NG *abbr* **1** National Guard **2** no good

Nh *symbol* nihonium

NH *abbr* New Hampshire

NHL *abbr* National Hockey League

Ni *symbol* nickel

ni·a·cin \'nī-ə-sən\ *n* : an organic acid of the vitamin B complex found widely in plants and animals and used esp. against pellagra

nib \'nib\ *n* **1** : POINT; *esp* : a pen point **2** : the jaws of a bird together with their horny covering

¹**nib·ble** \'ni-bəl\ *vb* **nib·bled; nib·bling** : to bite gently or bit by bit; *also* : eat in small pieces

²**nibble** *n* ♦ : a small or cautious bite; *also* : an amount of food taken with a small bite

♦ bite, morsel, mouthful, taste, tidbit

ni·cad \'nī-ˌkad\ *n* : a rechargeable dry cell that has a nickel cathode and a cadmium anode

Nic·a·ra·guan \ˌni-kə-'rä-gwən\ *n* : a native or inhabitant of Nicaragua — **Nicaraguan** *adj*

nice \'nīs\ *adj* **nic·er; nic·est** **1** ♦ : showing fastidious or finicky tastes : FASTIDIOUS **2** ♦ : marked by delicate discrimination or treatment **3 a** ♦ : giving pleasure : PLEASING, AGREEABLE **b** : well-executed **4** : WELL-BRED ⟨~ people⟩ **5** ♦ : decent or correct in character or behavior : RESPECTABLE **6** ♦ : of a sympathetic or helpful nature

♦ [1] choosy, dainty, delicate, demanding, exacting, fastidious, finicky, fussy, old-maidish, particular, picky ♦ [2] delicate, exact, fine, minute, refined, subtle ♦ [3a] agreeable, congenial, delectable, delicious, delightful, dreamy, felicitous, good, grateful, gratifying, palatable, pleasant, pleasurable, satisfying ♦ [5] correct, decent, decorous, genteel, polite, proper, respectable, seemly ♦ [6] affable, agreeable, amiable, genial, good-natured, gracious, sweet, well-disposed

nice·ly *adv* ♦ : in a pleasing, satisfactory, courteous, or reasonable manner

♦ agreeably, favorably (*or* favourably), pleasantly, pleasingly, satisfyingly, well ♦ courteously, kindly, thoughtfully, well

nice–nel·ly \'nīs-'ne-lē\ *adj, often cap 2d N* **1** : marked by euphemism **2** : PRUDISH — **nice nelly** *n, often cap 2d N* — **nice–nel·ly·ism** \-ˌi-zəm\ *n, often cap 2d N*

nice·ness *n* ♦ : the quality or state of being nice

♦ agreeableness, amenity, amiability, geniality, graciousness, pleasantness, sweetness

nice·ty \'nī-sə-tē\ *n, pl* **-ties** **1** : a dainty, delicate, or elegant thing ⟨enjoy the *niceties* of life⟩ **2** : a fine point or distinction ⟨*niceties* of workmanship⟩ **3** : EXACTNESS, PRECISION, ACCURACY

niche \'nich\ *n* **1** ♦ : a recess in a wall esp. for a statue **2** : a place, employment, or activity for which a person or thing is best fitted **3** ♦ : the living space or role of an organism in an ecological community esp. with regard to food consumption

♦ [1] alcove, nook, recess ♦ [3] habitat, home, range, territory

¹**nick** \'nik\ *n* **1** ♦ : a small notch, groove, or chip **2** : the final critical moment ⟨in the ~ of time⟩

♦ chip, hack, indentation, notch

²**nick** *vb* : NOTCH, CHIP

nick·el \'ni-kəl\ *n* **1** : a hard silver-white metallic chemical element capable of a high polish and used in alloys **2** : the U.S. 5-cent piece made of copper and nickel; *also* : the Canadian 5-cent piece

nick·el·ode·on \ˌni-kə-'lō-dē-ən\ *n* **1** : an early movie theater to which admission cost five cents **2** : JUKEBOX

nick·er \'ni-kər\ *vb* : to neigh gently : NEIGH, WHINNY — **nicker** *n*

nick·name \'nik-ˌnām\ *n* **1** ♦ : a usu. descriptive name given instead of or in addition to the one belonging to a person, place, or thing **2** : a familiar form of a proper name — **nickname** *vb*

♦ alias, cognomen

nic·o·tine \'ni-kə-ˌtēn\ *n* : a poisonous and addictive substance in tobacco that is used as an insecticide

nic·o·tin·ic acid \ˌni-kə-'tē-nik-, -'ti-\ *n* : an organic acid of the vitamin B complex found in plants and animals and used against pellagra

niece \'nēs\ *n* : a daughter of one's brother, sister, brother-in-law, or sister-in-law

nif·ty \'nif-tē\ *adj* **nif·ti·er; -est** : very good : very attractive

Ni·ge·ri·an \nī-'jir-ē-ən\ *n* : a native or inhabitant of Nigeria — **Nigerian** *adj*

nig·gard \'ni-gərd\ *n* ♦ : a stingy person : MISER

♦ cheapskate, miser, skinflint, tightwad

nig·gard·ly *adj* **1** ♦ : grudgingly mean about spending or granting **2** ♦ : provided in meanly limited supply — **nig·gard·li·ness** \-lē-nəs\ *n* — **nig·gard·ly** *adv*

♦ [1] cheap, close, mean, parsimonious, penurious, spare, sparing, stingy, tight, tightfisted, uncharitable ♦ [2] light, meager (*or* meagre), poor, scant, scanty, scarce, skimpy, slender, slim, spare, sparse, stingy

nig·gling \'ni-gə-liŋ\ *adj* **1** : PETTY ⟨~ details⟩ **2** : bothersome in a petty way

¹**nigh** \'nī\ *adv* **1** ♦ : near in place, time, or relationship **2** ♦ : almost but not quite : NEARLY, ALMOST

♦ [1] around, by, close, hard, in, near, nearby ♦ [2] about, almost, most, much, near, nearly, next to, practically, some, virtually, well-nigh

²**nigh** *adj* : being near in time, space, effect, or degree : CLOSE, NEAR

³**nigh** *prep* : NEAR

¹**night** \'nīt\ *n* **1** ♦ : the period between dusk and dawn **2** ♦ : the darkness of night **3** : a period of misery or unhappiness **4** : NIGHTFALL

♦ [1] dark, darkness, nighttime *Ant* day, daytime ♦ [2] dark, darkness, dusk, gloaming, gloom, murk, semidarkness, shade, shadows, twilight

²**night** *adj* ♦ : of, relating to, or associated with the night

♦ nighttime, nocturnal

night blindness *n* : reduced visual capacity in faint light (as at night)

night·cap \'nīt-ˌkap\ *n* **1** : a cloth cap worn with nightclothes **2** : a usu. alcoholic drink taken at bedtime

night·clothes \-ˌklōthz, -ˌklōz\ *n pl* : garments worn in bed

night·club \-ˌkləb\ *n* ♦ : a place of entertainment open at night usu. serving food and liquor and providing music for dancing

♦ café, disco, discotheque

night crawl·er \-ˌkrȯ-lər\ *n* : EARTHWORM; *esp* : a large earthworm found on the soil surface at night

night·dress \'nīt-ˌdres\ *n* : a loose garment for wear in bed : NIGHTGOWN

night·fall \-ˌfȯl\ *n* ♦ : the coming of night

♦ dusk, evening, gloaming, sundown, sunset, twilight

night·gown \-ˌgaůn\ *n* : a loose garment for wear in bed

night·hawk \-ˌhȯk\ *n* : any of a genus of American birds related to and resembling the whip-poor-will

night·in·gale \'nīt-ᵊn-ˌgāl, 'nī-tiŋ-\ *n* : any of several Old World thrushes noted for the sweet usu. nocturnal song of the male

night·life \'nīt-ˌlīf\ *n* : the activity of pleasure-seekers at night

night·ly \'nīt-lē\ *adj* **1** : happening, done, or produced by night or every night **2** : of or relating to the night or every night — **nightly** *adv*

night·mare \'nīt-ˌmar\ *n* **1** : a frightening dream **2** ♦ : a frightening or horrible experience — **nightmare** *adj*

♦ agony, hell, horror, misery, murder, torment, torture

night·mar·ish *adj* ♦ : resembling or suggestive of a nightmare

♦ appalling, atrocious, awful, dreadful, frightful, ghastly, grisly, gruesome, hideous, horrible, horrid, lurid, macabre, monstrous, shocking, terrible

night rider *n* : a member of a secret band who ride masked at night doing violence to punish or terrorize

night·shade \'nīt-ˌshād\ *n* : any of a large genus of herbs, shrubs, and trees that includes poisonous forms (as the belladonna), ornamentals (as the petunias), and important food plants (as the potato and eggplant)

night·shirt \-ˌshərt\ *n* : a nightgown resembling a shirt

night soil *n* : human feces used esp. for fertilizing the soil

night·stick \'nīt-ˌstik\ *n* ♦ : a police officer's club

♦ bat, billy club, bludgeon, cudgel, truncheon

night·time \-,tīm\ *n* ♦ : the time from dusk to dawn

♦ dark, darkness, night

night·walk·er \-,wȯ-kər\ *n* : a person who roves about at night esp. with criminal or immoral intent

ni·hil·ism \'nī-ə-,li-zəm, 'nē-hə-\ *n* **1** : a viewpoint that traditional values and beliefs are unfounded and that existence is senseless and useless **2** : ANARCHISM — **ni·hil·ist** \-list\ *n or adj* — **ni·hil·is·tic** \,nī-ə-'lis-tik, ,nē-hə-\ *adj*

ni·ho·ni·um \ni-'hō-nē-əm\ *n* : a short-lived artificially produced radioactive chemical element

nil \'nil\ *n* ♦ : the arithmetical symbol 0 denoting the absence of all magnitude or quantity : ZERO, NOTHING

♦ aught, cipher, naught, nothing, zero, zip

nim·ble \'nim-bəl\ *adj* **nim·bler; nim·blest** **1** ♦ : quick and light in motion : AGILE ⟨a ~ dancer⟩ **2** ♦ : quick in understanding and learning : CLEVER ⟨a ~ mind⟩ — **nim·bly** \-blē\ *adv*

♦ [1] agile, graceful, light, lissome, lithe, spry ♦ [2] alert, brainy, bright, brilliant, clever, intelligent, keen, quick, quick= witted, sharp, smart

nim·ble·ness *n* ♦ : the quality or state of being nimble

♦ agility, deftness, dexterity, sleight

nim·bus \'nim-bəs\ *n, pl* **nim·bi** \-,bī, -bē\ *or* **nim·bus·es** **1** : a figure (as a disk) in an art work suggesting radiant light about the head of a divinity, saint, or sovereign **2** : a rain cloud; *also* : THUNDERHEAD

NIMBY \'nim-bē\ *n* : opposition to the placement of something undesirable (as a prison) in one's neighborhood

nim·rod \'nim-,räd\ *n* **1** : HUNTER **2** : IDIOT, JERK

nin·com·poop \'nin-kəm-,püp\ *n* **1** : a person lacking in judgment or prudence : FOOL, SIMPLETON **2** : an unsophisticated person

nine \'nīn\ *n* **1** : one more than eight **2** : the 9th in a set or series **3** : something having nine units; *esp* : a baseball team — **nine** *adj or pron* — **ninth** \'nīnth\ *adj or adv or n*

nine days' wonder *n* : something that creates a short-lived sensation

nine·pins \'nīn-,pinz\ *n* : a bowling game using nine pins arranged usu. in a diamond-shaped configuration

nine·teen \'nīn-'tēn\ *n* : one more than 18 — **nineteen** *adj or pron* — **nine·teenth** \-'tēnth\ *adj or n*

nine·ty \'nīn-tē\ *n, pl* **nineties** : nine times 10 — **nine·ti·eth** \-tē-əth\ *adj or n* — **ninety** *adj or pron*

nin·ja \'nin-jə, -(,)jä\ *n, pl* **ninja** *or* **ninjas** : a person trained in ancient Japanese martial arts and employed esp. for espionage and assassinations

nin·ny \'ni-nē\ *n, pl* **ninnies** **1** : a person lacking in judgment or prudence : FOOL **2** : an unsophisticated person

ni·o·bi·um \nī-'ō-bē-əm\ *n* : a gray metallic chemical element used in alloys

¹nip \'nip\ *vb* **nipped; nip·ping** **1** : to catch hold of and squeeze tightly between two surfaces, edges, or points **2** : to sever by or as if by pinching sharply; *also* : to remove by cutting or pinching **3** : to destroy the growth, progress, or fulfillment of ⟨nipped in the bud⟩ **4** : to injure or make numb with cold : CHILL **5** : to take or appropriate without right or leave and with intent to keep or make use of wrongfully : STEAL

²nip *n* **1** ♦ : a sharp stinging cold **2** : a biting or pungent flavor **3** : PINCH, BITE **4** : a small portion : BIT

♦ bite, bitterness, bleakness, chill, rawness, sharpness

³nip *n* : a small quantity of liquor : SIP

⁴nip *vb* **nipped; nip·ping** : to take liquor in nips : TIPPLE

nip and tuck *adj or adv* ♦ : so close that the lead shifts rapidly from one contestant to another

♦ close, narrow, neck and neck, tight

nip·per \'ni-pər\ *n* **1** : one that nips **2** *pl* : a gripping instrument with two handles and two jaws : PINCERS **3** ♦ : a young person esp. between infancy and youth : CHILD; *esp* : a small boy

♦ boy, child, lad, shaver, stripling, youth

nip·ple \'ni-pəl\ *n* : the protuberance of a mammary gland through which milk is drawn off : TEAT; *also* : something resembling a nipple

nip·py \'ni-pē\ *adj* **nip·pi·er; -est** **1** : having an intense flavor or odor : PUNGENT, SHARP **2** ♦ : noticeably cold : CHILLY **3** : brisk, quick, or nimble in movement

♦ bitter, chill, chilly, cold, cool, frosty, raw, sharp, snappy, wintry

nir·va·na \nir-'vä-nə\ *n, often cap* **1** : the final state of bliss; *esp* : the supreme happiness that according to Buddhism comes through the extinction of desire and individual consciousness **2** : OBLIVION; *also* : PARADISE

ni·sei \nē-'sā, ,nē-,sā\ *n, pl* **nisei** *often cap* : a son or daughter of immigrant Japanese parents who is born and educated in America

ni·si \'nī-,sī\ *adj* : taking effect at a specified time unless previously modified or voided ⟨a divorce decree ~⟩

nit \'nit\ *n* **1** : the egg of a parasitic insect (as a louse); *also* : the young insect **2** : a minor shortcoming

nite *var of* NIGHT

ni·ter *or Can and Brit* **ni·tre** \'nī-tər\ *n* : POTASSIUM NITRATE

nit·pick·er *n* ♦ : one who engages in nitpicking

♦ carper, castigator, caviler, censurer, critic, faultfinder, railer, scold

nit–pick·ing \'nit-,pi-kiŋ\ *n* : minute and usu. unjustified criticism

¹ni·trate \'nī-,trāt, -trət\ *n* **1** : a salt or ester of nitric acid **2** : sodium nitrate or potassium nitrate used as a fertilizer

²ni·trate \-,trāt\ *vb* **ni·trat·ed; ni·trat·ing** : to treat or combine with nitric acid or a nitrate — **ni·tra·tion** \nī-'trā-shən\ *n*

ni·tre *Can and Brit var of* NITER

ni·tric acid \'nī-trik-\ *n* : a corrosive liquid acid used esp. in making dyes, explosives, and fertilizers

ni·tri·fi·ca·tion \,nī-trə-fə-'kā-shən\ *n* : the oxidation (as by bacteria) of ammonium salts to nitrites and then to nitrates — **ni·tri·fy·ing** \'nī-trə-fī-iŋ\ *adj*

ni·trite \'nī-,trīt\ *n* : a salt of nitrous acid

ni·tro \'nī-trō\ *n, pl* **nitros** : any of various nitrated products; *esp* : NITROGLYCERIN

ni·tro·gen \'nī-trə-jən\ *n* : a tasteless odorless gaseous chemical element constituting 78 percent of the atmosphere by volume — **ni·trog·e·nous** \nī-'träj-ə-nəs\ *adj*

nitrogen narcosis *n* : a state of euphoria and confusion caused by nitrogen forced into a diver's bloodstream from atmospheric air under pressure

ni·tro·glyc·er·in *or* **ni·tro·glyc·er·ine** \,nī-trə-'gli-sə-rən\ *n* : an oily explosive liquid used to make dynamite and in medicine to dilate blood vessels

ni·trous acid \'nī-trəs-\ *n* : an unstable nitrogen-containing acid known only in solution or in the form of its salts

nitrous oxide *n* : a colorless gas used esp. as an anesthetic in dentistry

nit·ty–grit·ty \'ni-tē-,gri-tē, ,ni-tē-'gri-tē\ *n* : what is essential and basic : specific practical details

nit·wit \'nit-,wit\ *n* ♦ : a scatterbrained or stupid person

♦ booby, fool, goose, half-wit, jackass, nut, simpleton, turkey ♦ blockhead, dope, dummy, idiot, imbecile, jackass, moron, numskull

¹nix \'niks\ *n* : NOTHING

²nix *vb* : VETO, REJECT

³nix *adv* : NO

NJ *abbr* New Jersey

NL *abbr* National League

NLRB *abbr* National Labor Relations Board

NM *abbr* **1** nautical mile **2** New Mexico

N Mex *abbr* New Mexico

NMI *abbr* no middle initial

NNE *abbr* north-northeast

NNW *abbr* north-northwest

¹no \'nō\ *adv* **1** — used to express the negative of an alternative ⟨shall we continue or ~⟩ **2** ♦ : in no respect or degree ⟨he is ~ better than the others⟩ **3** : not so ⟨~, I'm not ready⟩ **4** — used with an adjective to imply a meaning opposite to the positive statement ⟨in ~ uncertain terms⟩ **5** — used to introduce a more emphatic or explicit statement ⟨has the right, ~, the duty to continue⟩ **6** ♦ — used as an interjection to express surprise or doubt ⟨~—you don't say⟩ **7** — used in combination with a verb to form a compound adjective ⟨no-bake pie⟩

♦ [2] never, none, nothing, nowise ♦ [6] indeed, well, why

²no *adj* **1** : not any; *also* : hardly any **2** : not a ⟨she's ~ expert⟩

³no \'nō\ *n, pl* **noes** *or* **nos** \'nōz\ **1** ♦ : an act or instance of refusing or denying by the use of the word no : REFUSAL, DENIAL **2** ♦ : a negative vote or decision; *also, pl* : persons voting in the negative

♦ blackball, denial, nay, negation, negative, refusal, veto *Ant* positive, yea, yes

⁴no *abbr* **1** north; northern **2** number

¹No *var of* NOH

²No *symbol* nobelium

No•bel•ist \\'nō-'be-list\\ *n* : a winner of a Nobel prize

no•bel•i•um \\nō-'be-lē-əm\\ *n* : a radioactive metallic chemical element produced artificially

No•bel prize \\nō-'bel-, 'nō-ˌbel-\\ *n* : any of various annual prizes (as in peace, literature, or medicine) established by the will of Alfred Nobel for the encouragement of persons who work for the interests of humanity

no•bil•i•ty \\nō-'bi-lə-tē\\ *n* **1** ♦ : the quality or state of being noble in character, quality, or rank **2** : nobles considered as forming a class

♦ augustness, brilliance, glory, grandeur, grandness, magnificence, majesty, nobleness, resplendence, splendor, stateliness

¹**no•ble** \\'nō-bəl\\ *adj* **no•bler; no•blest 1** ♦ : possessing outstanding qualities : ILLUSTRIOUS; *also* : FAMOUS, NOTABLE **2** ♦ : of high birth, rank, or station : ARISTOCRATIC **3** : possessing very high or excellent qualities or properties : EXCELLENT **4** ♦ : grand or impressive esp. in appearance : STATELY, IMPOSING ⟨a ∼ edifice⟩ **5** ♦ : of a superior nature esp. in character

♦ [1] distinguished, eminent, famous, illustrious, notable, noteworthy, outstanding, preeminent, prestigious, signal, star, superior ♦ [2] aristocratic, genteel, gentle, grand, highborn, patrician, wellborn *Ant* baseborn, common, humble, ignoble, low, lowly, mean, plebeian ♦ [4] august, baronial, gallant, glorious, grand, grandiose, heroic, imposing, magnificent, majestic, monumental, proud, regal, royal, splendid, stately ♦ [5] decent, ethical, honest, honorable, just, principled, respectable, righteous, upright, upstanding ♦ [5] chivalrous, gallant, great, greathearted, high, high-minded, lofty, lordly, magnanimous, sublime *Ant* base, debased, degenerate, degraded, ignoble, low

²**no•ble** *n* ♦ : a person of noble rank or birth

♦ aristocrat, gentleman, grandee, patrician

no•ble•man \\'nō-bəl-mən\\ *n* : a member of the nobility

no•ble•ness *n* ♦ : the quality or state of being noble

♦ augustness, brilliance, glory, grandeur, grandness, magnificence, majesty, nobility, resplendence, splendor, stateliness

no•blesse oblige \\nō-ˌbles-ə-'blēzh\\ *n* : the obligation of honorable, generous, and responsible behavior associated with high rank or birth

no•ble•wom•an \\'nō-bəl-ˌwu̇-mən\\ *n* ♦ : a woman of noble rank

♦ dame, gentlewoman, lady

no•bly \\-blē\\ *adv* ♦ : with greatness of soul

♦ gallantly, grandly, greatly, heroically, honorably (*or* honourably), magnanimously

¹**no•body** \\'nō-ˌbä-dē, -bə-\\ *pron* : no person

²**nobody** *n, pl* **no•bod•ies** ♦ : a person of no influence or importance

♦ nonentity, nothing, whippersnapper, zero *Ant* big shot, bigwig, eminence, figure, magnate, nabob, personage, somebody, VIP

no–brain•er \\'nō-ˌbrā-nər\\ *n* : something that requires a minimum of thought

noc•tur•nal \\näk-'tərn-ᵊl\\ *adj* **1** ♦ : of, relating to, or occurring in the night **2** : active at night ⟨a ∼ bird⟩

♦ night, nighttime *Ant* daily, diurnal

noc•turne \\'näk-ˌtərn\\ *n* : a work of art dealing with night; *esp* : a dreamy pensive composition for the piano

noc•u•ous \\'nä-kyə-wəs\\ *adj* : HARMFUL — **noc•u•ous•ly** *adv*

nod \\'näd\\ *vb* **nod•ded; nod•ding 1** : to bend the head downward or forward (as in bowing, going to sleep, or giving assent) **2** ♦ : to move up and down ⟨tulips *nodding* in the breeze⟩ **3** : to show by a nod of the head ⟨∼ agreement⟩ **4** : to make a slip or error in a moment of abstraction — **nod** *n*

♦ bob, bobble, jog, jounce, pump, seesaw

nod•dle \\'näd-ᵊl\\ *n* : a person's head esp. as the seat of intellect : HEAD

nod•dy \\'nä-dē\\ *n, pl* **noddies 1** : FOOL **2** : a stout-bodied tropical tern

node \\'nōd\\ *n* : a thickened, swollen, or differentiated area (as of tissue); *esp* : the part of a stem from which a leaf arises — **nod•al** \\-ᵊl\\ *adj*

nod•ule \\'nä-jül\\ *n* ♦ : a small lump or swelling — **nod•u•lar** \\'nä-jə-lər\\ *adj*

♦ bump, knot, lump, swelling

no•el \\nō-'el\\ *n* **1** : a Christmas carol **2** *cap* ♦ : the Christmas season

♦ Christmastide, Christmastime, yuletide

noes *pl of* NO

no–fault \\'nō-'fȯlt\\ *adj* **1** : of, relating to, or being a motor vehicle insurance plan under which someone involved in an accident is compensated usu. up to a stipulated limit for actual losses by that person's own insurance company regardless of who is responsible **2** : of, relating to, or being a divorce law under which neither party is held responsible for the breakup of the marriage

nog•gin \\'nä-gən\\ *n* **1** : a small mug or cup; *also* : a small quantity of drink **2** ♦ : a person's head

♦ head, pate, poll

no–good \\'nō-'gu̇d\\ *adj* ♦ : having no worth, virtue, use, or chance of success — **no–good** \\'nō-ˌgu̇d\\ *n*

♦ chaffy, empty, junky, null, valueless, worthless

Noh *also* **No** \\'nō\\ *n, pl* **Noh** *also* **No** : classic Japanese dance drama having a heroic theme, a chorus, and highly stylized action, costuming, and scenery

no–hit•ter \\(ˌ)nō-'hi-tər\\ *n* : a baseball game or part of a game in which a pitcher allows no base hits

no•how \\'nō-ˌhau̇\\ *adv* : in no manner

¹**noise** \\'nȯiz\\ *n* **1** ♦ : loud, confused, or senseless shouting or outcry **2** ♦ : sound or a sound that lacks agreeable musical quality or is noticeably loud, harsh, or discordant **3** : unwanted electronic signal or disturbance — **noise•less•ly** *adv*

♦ [1] clamor (*or* clamour), howl, hubbub, hue and cry, hullabaloo, outcry, roar, tumult, uproar ♦ [2] bluster, cacophony, clamor, din, racket, sound *Ant* quiet, silence, still, stillness

²**noise** *vb* **noised; nois•ing** ♦ : to spread by rumor or report ⟨the story was *noised* about⟩

♦ *usu* **noise about** circulate, rumor, whisper

noise•less *adj* ♦ : making or causing no noise or stir : free from noise

♦ hushed, muted, quiet, silent, soundless, still

noise•mak•er \\'nȯiz-ˌmā-kər\\ *n* : one that makes noise; *esp* : a device used to make noise at parties

noise pollution *n* : annoying or harmful noise in an environment

noi•some \\'nȯi-səm\\ *adj* **1** ♦ : physically harmful or destructive to living beings : UNWHOLESOME **2** ♦ : offensive to the senses (as smell); *also* : highly objectionable

♦ [1] noxious, unhealthy, unwholesome ♦ [2] fetid, foul, fusty, malodorous, musty, rank, reeky, smelly, strong

noisy \\'nȯi-zē\\ *adj* **nois•i•er; -est 1** : making loud noises **2** ♦ : full of noises : LOUD — **nois•i•ly** \\-zə-lē\\ *adv* — **nois•i•ness** \\-zē-nəs\\ *n*

♦ boisterous, clamorous, loud, raucous, resounding, uproarious *Ant* hushed, noiseless, quiet, silent, soundless, stilled

nol•le pro•se•qui \\ˌnä-lē-'prä-sə-ˌkwī\\ *n* : an entry on the record of a legal action that the prosecutor or plaintiff will proceed no further in an action or suit or in some aspect of it

no•lo con•ten•de•re \\ˌnō-lō-kən-'ten-də-rē\\ *n* : a plea in a criminal prosecution that subjects the defendant to conviction but does not admit guilt or preclude denying the charges in another proceeding

nol–pros \\'näl-'präs\\ *vb* **nol–prossed; nol–pros•sing** : to discontinue by entering a nolle prosequi

nom *abbr* nominative

¹**no•mad** \\'nō-ˌmad\\ *n* **1** : a member of a people who have no fixed residence but move from place to place **2** ♦ : an individual who roams about aimlessly

♦ drifter, rambler, rover, vagabond, wanderer

²**nomad** *adj* ♦ : traversing a random course

♦ errant, itinerant, nomadic, peripatetic, roaming, vagabond, vagrant

no•mad•ic \\nō-'ma-dik\\ *adj* **1** : of, relating to, or characteristic of nomads **2** ♦ : roaming from place to place aimlessly, frequently, or without a fixed pattern of movement

♦ errant, itinerant, nomad, peripatetic, roaming, vagabond, vagrant

no–man's–land \\'nō-ˌmanz-ˌland\\ *n* **1** : an area of unowned, unclaimed, or uninhabited land **2** : an unoccupied area between opposing troops

nom de guerre \\ˌnäm-di-'ger\\ *n, pl* **noms de guerre** *same or* ˌnämz-\\ : PSEUDONYM

nom de plume \\-'plüm\\ *n, pl* **noms de plume** *same or* ˌnämz-\\ : PEN NAME

no•men•cla•ture \\'nō-mən-ˌklā-chər\\ *n* **1** : NAME, DESIGNATION **2** : a system of terms used in a science or art

nom·i·nal \'nä-mən-ᵊl\ *adj* **1** ♦ : being something in name or form only ⟨~ head of a party⟩ **2** ♦ : lacking in significance or solid worth : TRIFLING ⟨a ~ price⟩ — **nom·i·nal·ly** *adv*

♦ [1] formal, paper, titular ♦ [2] inconsequential, inconsiderable, insignificant, measly, minute, negligible, paltry, petty, slight, trifling, trivial

nom·i·nate \'nä-mə-ˌnāt\ *vb* **-nat·ed; -nat·ing** : to choose as a candidate for election, appointment, or honor — **nom·i·na·tion** \ˌnä-mə-'nā-shən\ *n*

nom·i·na·tive \'nä-mə-nə-tiv\ *adj* : of, relating to, or constituting a grammatical case marking typically the subject of a verb — **nominative** *n*

nom·i·nee \ˌnä-mə-'nē\ *n* : a person nominated for an office, duty, or position

non- \(')nän *or* ˌnän *before stressed syllables*; ˌnän *elsewhere*\ *prefix* **1** : not : reverse of : absence of **2** : having no importance

nonabrasive	nonelectric
nonabsorbent	nonelectrical
nonacademic	nonemotional
nonacceptance	nonenforcement
nonaccredited	nonethical
nonacid	non–euclidean
nonactivated	nonexclusive
nonadaptive	nonexempt
nonaddictive	nonexistence
nonadhesive	nonexplosive
nonadjacent	nonfarm
nonadjustable	nonfatal
nonaggression	nonfattening
nonalcoholic	nonfederated
nonappearance	nonferrous
nonaromatic	nonfiction
nonathletic	nonfilamentous
nonattendance	nonfilterable
nonbeliever	nonflowering
nonbelligerent	nonfood
nonbiodegradable	nonfreezing
nonbreakable	nonfulfillment
noncaloric	nonglare
noncancerous	nongraded
noncandidate	nonhazardous
noncellular	nonhereditary
noncitizen	nonhomogeneous
nonclerical	nonhomologous
noncoital	nonhuman
noncombat	nonidentical
noncombative	nonimportation
noncommercial	nonindustrial
noncommunist	noninfectious
noncompeting	nonintellectual
noncompetitive	nonintercourse
noncompliance	noninterference
noncomplying	nonintoxicant
nonconducting	nonintoxicating
nonconfidence	noninvasive
nonconflicting	nonionizing
nonconformance	nonirritating
nonconsensual	nonlegal
nonconstructive	nonlethal
noncontagious	nonlife
noncontinuous	nonlinear
noncorroding	nonliterate
noncorrosive	nonliving
noncriminal	nonlogical
noncritical	nonmagnetic
noncrystalline	nonmalignant
nondeductible	nonmember
nondelivery	nonmembership
nondemocratic	nonmigratory
nondenominational	nonmilitary
nondepartmental	nonmoral
nondestructive	nonmoving
nondevelopment	nonnegotiable
nondiscrimination	nonobservance
nondiscriminatory	nonoccurrence
nondistinctive	nonofficial
nondurable	nonoily
noneconomic	nonparallel
noneducational	nonparasitic
nonelastic	nonparticipant
nonelection	nonparticipating

nonpathogenic	nonsexist
nonpaying	nonsexual
nonpayment	nonshrinkable
nonperformance	nonsinkable
nonperishable	nonsmoker
nonpoisonous	nonsmoking
nonpolar	nonsocial
nonpolitical	nonspeaking
nonporous	nonspecialist
nonpregnant	nonsteroidal
nonproductive	nonstudent
nonprotein	nonsurgical
nonradioactive	nontaxable
nonrandom	nonteaching
nonrated	nontechnical
nonreactive	nontemporal
nonreciprocal	nontenured
nonrecognition	nontheistic
nonrecurrent	nontoxic
nonrecurring	nontransferable
nonrefillable	nontypical
nonrenewable	nonuniform
nonresidential	nonvascular
nonrestricted	nonvenomous
nonreturnable	nonverbal
nonreusable	nonveteran
nonreversible	nonviable
nonruminant	nonvisual
nonsalable	nonvocal
nonscientific	nonvolatile
nonscientist	nonvoter
nonseasonal	nonvoting
nonsectarian	nonworker
nonsegregated	nonworking
nonselective	nonzero
non–self–governing	

non·age \'nä-nij, 'nō-\ *n* **1** : legal minority **2** : a period of youth **3** : IMMATURITY

no·na·ge·nar·i·an \ˌnō-nə-jə-'ner-ē-ən, ˌnä-\ *n* : a person whose age is in the nineties

non·aligned \ˌnän-ə-'līnd\ *adj* : not allied with other nations

no–name \'nō-ˌnām\ *adj* : not having a readily recognizable name ⟨~ brands⟩

non·bi·na·ry \ˌnän-'bī-nər-ē, -ˌner-ē\ *adj* **1** : not binary **2** : relating to or being a person who identifies with or expresses a gender identity that is neither entirely male nor entirely female

non·book \'nän-ˌbuk\ *n* : a book of little literary merit that is often a compilation (as of pictures or speeches)

¹**nonce** \'näns\ *n* : the one, particular, or present occasion or purpose ⟨for the ~⟩

²**nonce** *adj* : occurring, used, or made only once or for a special occasion ⟨a ~ word⟩

non·cha·lance \ˌnän-shə-'läns\ *n* ♦ : the quality or state of being nonchalant

♦ disinterestedness, disregard, indifference, insouciance

non·cha·lant \ˌnän-shə-'länt\ *adj* ♦ : giving an effect of unconcern or indifference — **non·cha·lant·ly** *adv*

♦ casual, disinterested, indifferent, insouciant, unconcerned

non·com \'nän-ˌkäm\ *n* : NONCOMMISSIONED OFFICER

non·com·ba·tant \ˌnän-kəm-'bat-ᵊnt, nän-'käm-bə-tənt\ *n* : a member (as a chaplain) of the armed forces whose duties do not include fighting; *also* : CIVILIAN — **noncombatant** *adj*

non·com·bus·ti·ble \ˌnän-kəm-'bəs-tə-bəl\ *adj* ♦ : not combustible : incapable of catching fire and burning when subjected to fire

♦ fireproof, nonflammable, noninflammable

non·com·mis·sioned officer \ˌnän-kə-'mi-shənd-\ *n* : a subordinate officer in the armed forces appointed from enlisted personnel

non·com·mit·tal \ˌnän-kə-'mit-ᵊl\ *adj* : indicating neither consent nor dissent

non com·pos men·tis \ˌnän-ˌkäm-pəs-'men-təs\ *adj* : not of sound mind

non·con·duc·tor \ˌnän-kən-'dək-tər\ *n* : a substance that is a very poor conductor of heat, electricity, or sound

non·con·form·ing \ˌnän-kən-'fȯr-miŋ\ *adj* ♦ : not conforming : declining conformity

♦ dissident, heretical, heterodox, nonconformist, nonorthodox, unconventional, unorthodox

non·con·form·ist \-kən-'fȯr-mist\ *n* **1** *often cap* : a person who does not conform to an established church and esp. the Church of England **2** ♦ : a person who does not conform to a generally accepted pattern of thought or action — **nonconformist** *adj*

♦ dissenter, dissident, heretic ♦ bohemian, deviant, individualist, loner, maverick

non·con·for·mi·ty \-'fȯr-mə-tē\ *n* ♦ : refusal to conform to an established or conventional creed, rule, or practice

♦ dissent, heresy, heterodoxy

non·co·op·er·a·tion \ˌnän-kō-ˌä-pə-'rā-shən\ *n* : failure or refusal to cooperate; *esp* : refusal through civil disobedience of a people to cooperate with the government of a country

non·cred·it \(ˌ)nän-'kre-dət\ *adj* : not offering credit toward a degree

non·cus·to·di·al \ˌnän-kə-'stō-dē-əl\ *adj* : of or being a parent who does not have legal custody of a child

non·dairy \'nän-ˌder-ē\ *adj* : containing no milk or milk products ⟨∼ whipped topping⟩

non·de·script \ˌnän-di-'skript\ *adj* **1** : not belonging to any particular class or kind **2** : lacking distinctive qualities

non·drink·er \-'driŋ-kər\ *n* : a person who abstains from alcohol

¹none \'nən\ *pron* **1** : not any ⟨∼ of them went⟩ **2** : not one ⟨∼ of the family⟩ **3 a** : not any such thing ⟨half a loaf is better than ∼⟩ **b** : not any such person

²none *adj, archaic* : not any : NO

³none *adv* **1** : by no means : not at all ⟨he got there ∼ too soon⟩ **2** ♦ : in no way : to no extent ⟨∼ the worse for wear⟩

♦ hardly, no, scarcely ♦ never, no, nothing, nowise

non·elec·tive \nän-ˌi-'lek-tiv\ *adj* ♦ : not permitting a choice

♦ compulsory, imperative, incumbent, involuntary, mandatory, necessary, obligatory, peremptory

non·en·ti·ty \nän-'en-tə-tē\ *n* **1** : something that does not exist or exists only in the imagination **2** ♦ : one of no consequence or significance

♦ nobody, nothing, shrimp, whippersnapper, zero

nones \'nōnz\ *n sing or pl* : the 7th day of March, May, July, or October or the 5th day of any other month in the ancient Roman calendar

non·es·sen·tial \ˌnän-i-'sen-shəl\ *adj* **1** : not essential **2** : being a substance synthesized by the body in sufficient quantity to satisfy dietary needs

none·such \'nən-ˌsəch\ *n* : one without an equal — **nonesuch** *adj*

none·the·less \ˌnən-t͟hə-'les\ *adv* ♦ : in spite of that : NEVERTHELESS

♦ but, howbeit, however, nevertheless, notwithstanding, still, though, withal, yet

non·event \'nän-i-ˌvent\ *n* **1** : an event that fails to take place or to satisfy expectations **2** : a highly promoted event of little intrinsic interest

non·ex·is·tent \ˌnän-ig-'zis-tənt\ *adj* ♦ : not having existence

♦ absent, missing, wanting

non·fat \-'fat\ *adj* : lacking fat solids : having fat solids removed ⟨∼ milk⟩

non·fic·tion·al \-'fik-shə-nəl\ *adj* ♦ : not fictional

♦ documentary, factual, hard, historical, literal, matter-of-fact, objective, true

non·fig·u·ra·tive \'nän-'fi-gyə-rə-tiv, -'fi-gə-\ *adj* ♦ : representing or intended to represent no natural or actual object, figure, or scene

♦ abstract, metaphysical, theoretical

non·flam·ma·ble \-'fla-mə-bəl\ *adj* ♦ : not flammable

♦ fireproof, noncombustible, noninflammable

non·func·tion·al \-'fəŋk-shə-nəl\ *adj* : not performing or able to perform its regular function

♦ inoperable, inoperative

non·gono·coc·cal \ˌnän-ˌgä-nə-'kä-kəl\ *adj* : not caused by a gonococcus

non·he·ro \'nän-'hē-rō\ *n* : ANTIHERO

non–Hodg·kin's lymphoma \'nän-'häj-kənz-\ *n* : any of numerous malignant lymphomas not classified as Hodgkin's disease

non·in·flam·ma·ble \ˌnän-in-'fla-mə-bəl\ *adj* ♦ : incapable of being easily ignited and of burning very quickly

♦ fireproof, noncombustible, nonflammable

non·in·ter·ven·tion \ˌnän-ˌin-tər-'ven-chən\ *n* : refusal or failure to intervene (as in the affairs of other countries)

non·is·sue \'nän-ˌi-shü\ *n* : an issue of little importance or concern

non·lit·er·ary \ˌnän-'li-tə-ˌrer-ē\ *adj* ♦ : colloquial and informal as opposed to literary and formal

♦ colloquial, conversational, informal, vernacular, vulgar

non·ma·te·ri·al \ˌnän-mə-'tir-ē-əl\ *adj* ♦ : not consisting of matter

♦ bodiless, immaterial, incorporeal, insubstantial, nonphysical, spiritual, unsubstantial

non·met·al \'nän-'met-ᵊl\ *n* : a chemical element (as carbon) that lacks the characteristics of a metal — **non·me·tal·lic** \ˌnän-mə-'ta-lik\ *adj*

non·mo·tile \ˌnän-'mō-ˌtī(-ə)l\ *adj* ♦ : not exhibiting or capable of movement

♦ immobile, immovable, unbudging, unmovable

non·neg·a·tive \-'ne-gə-tiv\ *adj* : not negative : being either positive or zero

non·nu·cle·ar \'nän-'nü-klē-ər\ *adj* **1** : not nuclear **2** : not having, using, or involving nuclear weapons

non·ob·jec·tive \ˌnän-əb-'jek-tiv\ *adj* **1** : not objective **2** : representing no natural or actual object, figure, or scene ⟨∼ art⟩

non·or·tho·dox \ˌnän-'ȯr-thə-ˌdäks\ *adj* **1** ♦ : not conforming to established doctrine esp. in religion **2** ♦ : not according with, sanctioned by, or based on convention

♦ [1] dissident, heretical, heterodox, nonconforming, nonconformist, unconventional, unorthodox ♦ [2] broad-minded, liberal, nontraditional, open-minded, progressive, radical, unconventional, unorthodox

¹non·pa·reil \ˌnän-pə-'rel\ *adj* ♦ : having no equal : PEERLESS

♦ incomparable, inimitable, matchless, only, peerless, unequaled, unmatched, unparalleled, unrivaled, unsurpassed

²nonpareil *n* **1** ♦ : an individual of unequaled excellence : PARAGON **2** : a small flat disk of chocolate covered with white sugar pellets

♦ beau ideal, classic, exemplar, ideal, model, paragon

non·par·ti·san \ˌnän-'pär-tə-zən\ *adj* ♦ : not partisan; *esp* : not influenced by political party spirit or interests

♦ disinterested, dispassionate, equal, equitable, fair, impartial, just, objective, square, unbiased, unprejudiced

non·per·son \-'pərs-ᵊn\ *n* **1** : UNPERSON **2** : a person having no social or legal status

non·phys·i·cal \ˌnän-'fi-zi-kəl\ *adj* ♦ : not physical : incapable of being touched or perceived by touch

♦ bodiless, immaterial, incorporeal, insubstantial, nonmaterial, spiritual, unsubstantial

non·plus \'nän-'pləs\ *vb* **-plussed** *also* **-plused** \-'pləst\; **-plus·sing** *also* **-plus·ing** : to cause to be at a loss as to what to say, think, or do : PUZZLE, PERPLEX

non·pre·scrip·tion \ˌnän-pri-'skrip-shən\ *adj* : available for sale legally without a doctor's prescription

non·pro·fes·sion·al \ˌnän-prə-'fe-shə-nəl\ *adj* ♦ : not characterized by or conforming to the technical or ethical standards of a profession; *also* : not having the training or experience of a professional

♦ amateur, amateurish, inexperienced, inexpert, unprofessional, unskilled, unskillful

non·prof·it \'nän-'prä-fət\ *adj* : not conducted or maintained for the purpose of making a profit ⟨a ∼ organization⟩

non·pro·lif·er·a·tion \ˌnän-prə-ˌli-fə-'rā-shən\ *adj* : providing for the stoppage of proliferation (as of nuclear arms) ⟨a ∼ treaty⟩

non·read·er \'nän-'rē-dər\ *n* : one who does not read or has difficulty reading

non·re·li·gious \ˌnän-ri-'li-jəs\ *adj* **1** ♦ : not religious : not having a religious character **2** : having no religion

♦ profane, secular, temporal

non·rep·re·sen·ta·tion·al \ˌnän-ˌre-pri-ˌzen-'tā-shə-nəl\ *adj* : NONOBJECTIVE 2

non·res·i·dent \'nän-'re-zə-dənt\ *adj* : not living in a particular place — **non·res·i·dence** \-dəns\ *n* — **nonresident** *n*

non·re·sis·tance \ˌnän-ri-'zis-təns\ *n* : the principles or practice of passive submission to authority even when unjust or oppressive

non·re·stric·tive \-ri-'strik-tiv\ *adj* **1** : not serving or tending to restrict **2** : not limiting the reference of the word or phrase modified ⟨a ~ clause⟩

non·rig·id \nän-'ri-jəd\ *adj* : maintaining form by pressure of contained gas ⟨a ~ airship⟩

non·sched·uled \nän-'ske-jüld\ *adj* : licensed to carry passengers or freight by air without a regular schedule

non·sense \'nän-,sens, -səns\ *n* **1** ♦ : foolish or meaningless words or actions **2** : things of no importance or value

  ♦ bunk, claptrap, drivel, fiddlesticks, folly, foolishness, fudge, hogwash, humbug, piffle, rot, silliness, slush, stupidity, trash

non·sen·si·cal \nän-'sen-si-kəl\ *adj* ♦ : being nonsense or full of nonsense — **non·sen·si·cal·ly** \-k(ə-)lē\ *adv*

  ♦ absurd, cuckoo, fatuous, foolish, nutty, senseless, silly, stupid

non se·qui·tur \nän-'se-kwə-tər\ *n* : an inference that does not follow from the premises

non·skid \'nän-'skid\ *adj* : designed to prevent skidding

non·slip \-'slip\ *adj* : designed to prevent slipping

non·spe·cif·ic \-spi-'si-fik\ *adj* ♦ : not specific

  ♦ all-around, bird's-eye, broad, general, overall

non·stan·dard \,nän-'stan-dərd\ *adj* **1** : not standard **2** : not conforming to the usage characteristic of educated native speakers of a language

non·start·er \'nän-'stär-tər\ *n* **1** : one that does not start **2** : one that is not productive or effective

non·stick \-'stik\ *adj* : allowing easy removal of cooked food particles

non·stop \-'stäp\ *adj* : done or made without a stop ⟨~ action⟩ — **nonstop** *adv*

non·suc·cess \-sək-'ses\ *n* ♦ : the failure to attain wealth, favor, or eminence

  ♦ collapse, crash, cropper, defeat, failure, fizzle

non·sup·port \,nän-sə-'pōrt\ *n* : failure to support; *esp* : failure on the part of one under obligation to provide maintenance

non·threat·en·ing \-'thret-niŋ, -'thre-t°n-iŋ\ *adj* : not likely to cause danger or anxiety ⟨a ~ illness⟩ ⟨a ~ environment⟩

non·tra·di·tion·al \-trə-'di-shə-nəl\ *adj* ♦ : not traditional : not conforming to tradition

  ♦ broad-minded, liberal, nonorthodox, open-minded, progressive, radical, unconventional, unorthodox

non–U \'nän-'yü\ *adj* : not characteristic of the upper classes

non·union \-'yü-nyən\ *adj* **1** : not belonging to a trade union ⟨~ carpenters⟩ **2** : not recognizing or favoring trade unions or their members ⟨~ employers⟩

non·us·er \-'yü-zər\ *n* : one who does not make use of something (as drugs)

non·vi·o·lence \'nän-'vī-ə-ləns\ *n* **1** : abstention from violence as a matter of principle **2** : avoidance of violence **3** : nonviolent political demonstrations — **non·vi·o·lent** \-lənt\ *adj*

non–white \,nän-'hwīt, -'wīt\ *n* : a person who is not of a white race — **non–white** *adj*

non·wo·ven \'nän-'wō-vən\ *adj* : made of fibers held together by interlocking or bonding (as by chemical or thermal means) — **nonwoven** *n*

noo·dle \'nüd-°l\ *n* : a food paste made usu. with egg and shaped typically in ribbon form

nook \'nuk\ *n* **1** : an interior angle or corner formed usu. by two walls ⟨a chimney ~⟩ **2** : a sheltered or hidden place ⟨searched every ~ and cranny⟩ **3** ♦ : a small often recessed section of a larger room ⟨a breakfast ~⟩

  ♦ alcove, niche, recess

noon \'nün\ *n* ♦ : the middle of the day : 12 o'clock in the daytime — **noon** *adj*

  ♦ midday, noontime

noon·day \'nün-,dā\ *n* : the middle of the day : NOON, MIDDAY

no one *pron* : no person : NOBODY

noon·tide \'nün-,tīd\ *n* : the middle of the day : NOON

noon·time \-,tīm\ *n* ♦ : the middle of the day : NOON

  ♦ midday, noon

noose \'nüs\ *n* : a loop with a slipknot that binds closer the more it is drawn

nope \'nōp\ *adv* : NO

nor \'nór\ *conj* : and not ⟨not for you ~ for me⟩ — used esp. to introduce and negate the second member and each later member of a series of items preceded by *neither* ⟨neither here ~ there⟩

Nor·dic \'nór-dik\ *adj* **1** : of or relating to the Germanic peoples of northern Europe and esp. of Scandinavia **2** : of or relating to

competitive ski events involving cross-country racing, ski jumping, or biathlon — **Nordic** *n*

nor·epi·neph·rine \'nór-,e-pə-'ne-frən\ *n* : a nitrogen-containing neurotransmitter in parts of the sympathetic and central nervous systems

norm \'nórm\ *n* **1** ♦ : an authoritative standard or model; *esp* : a set standard of development or achievement usu. derived from the average or median achievement of a large group **2** : a typical or widespread practice, procedure, or custom

  ♦ average, normal, par, standard

¹**nor·mal** \'nór-məl\ *adj* **1** ♦ : conforming to a type, standard, or regular pattern : STANDARD **2 a** : of average intelligence **b** ♦ : sound in mind and body

  ♦ [1] average, common, commonplace, everyday, ordinary, prosaic, regular, routine, run-of-the-mill, standard, typical, unexceptional, unremarkable, usual, workaday ♦ [2b] balanced, clearheaded, lucid, right, sane, stable

²**normal** *n* **1** : one that is normal **2** : the usual condition, level, or quantity — **nor·mal·cy** \-sē\ *n* — **nor·mal·i·ty** \nór-'ma-lə-tē\ *n*

nor·mal·ise *chiefly Brit var of* NORMALIZE

nor·mal·ize \'nór-mə-,līz\ *vb* **-ized; -iz·ing** ♦ : to make or restore to normal — **nor·mal·i·za·tion** \,nór-mə-lə-'zā-shən\ *n*

  ♦ formalize, homogenize, regularize, standardize

nor·mal·ly *adv* ♦ : as a general thing : often in the usual course of events

  ♦ commonly, generally, naturally, ordinarily, typically, usually

Nor·man \'nór-mən\ *n* **1** : a native or inhabitant of Normandy **2** : one of the 10th century Scandinavian conquerors of Normandy **3** : one of the Norman-French conquerors of England in 1066 — **Norman** *adj*

nor·ma·tive \'nór-mə-tiv\ *adj* : of, relating to, or determining norms — **nor·ma·tive·ly** *adv* — **nor·ma·tive·ness** *n*

Norse \'nórs\ *n, pl* **Norse** **1** : NORWEGIAN; *also* : any of the western Scandinavian dialects or languages **2** *pl* : SCANDINAVIANS; *also* : NORWEGIANS

Norse·man \-mən\ *n* : any of the ancient Scandinavians

¹**north** \'nórth\ *adv* : to, toward, or in the north

²**north** *adj* **1** : situated toward or at the north **2** : coming from the north

³**north** *n* **1** : the direction to the left of one facing east **2** : the compass point directly opposite to south **3** *cap* : regions or countries north of a specified or implied point — **north·er·ly** \'nór-thər-lē\ *adv or adj* — **north·ern** \-thərn\ *adj* — **North·ern·er** \-thər-nər\ *n* — **north·ern·most** \-thərn-,mōst\ *adj* — **north·ward** \'nórth-wərd\ *adv or adj* — **north·wards** \-wərdz\ *adv*

north·east \nór-'thēst\ *n* **1** : the general direction between north and east **2** : the compass point midway between north and east **3** *cap* : regions or countries northeast of a specified or implied point — **northeast** *adj or adv* — **north·east·er·ly** \-'thē-stər-lē\ *adv or adj* — **north·east·ern** \-stərn\ *adj*

north·east·er \-'thēs-tər\ *n* **1** : a strong northeast wind **2** : a storm with northeast winds

north·er \'nór-thər\ *n* **1** : a strong north wind **2** : a storm with north winds

northern lights *n pl* : AURORA BOREALIS

north pole *n, often cap N&P* : the northernmost point of the earth

North Star *n* : the star toward which the northern end of the earth's axis points

north·west \nórth-'west\ *n* **1** : the general direction between north and west **2** : the compass point midway between north and west **3** *cap* : regions or countries northwest of a specified or implied point — **northwest** *adj or adv* — **north·west·er·ly** \-'we-stər-lē\ *adv or adj* — **north·west·ern** \-'we-stərn\ *adj*

Norw *abbr* Norway; Norwegian

Nor·we·gian \nór-'wē-jən\ *n* **1** : a native or inhabitant of Norway **2** : the language of Norway — **Norwegian** *adj*

nos *abbr* numbers

¹**nose** \'nōz\ *n* **1** : the part of the face or head containing the nostrils and covering the front of the nasal cavity **2** : the sense of smell **3** : something (as a point, edge, or projecting front part) that resembles a nose ⟨the ~ of a plane⟩ — **nosed** \'nōzd\ *adj*

²**nose** *vb* **nosed; nos·ing** **1** ♦ : to detect by or as if by smell : SCENT **2** : to push or move with the nose **3** : to touch or rub with the nose : NUZZLE **4** ♦ : to search impertinently : PRY **5** : to move ahead slowly ⟨the ship *nosed* into her berth⟩

  ♦ [1] scent, smell, whiff ♦ [4] butt in, interfere, intrude, meddle, mess, obtrude, poke, pry, snoop

nose•bleed \'nōz-‚blēd\ *n* : a bleeding from the nose

nose cone *n* : a protective cone constituting the forward end of an aerospace vehicle

nose-dive \'nōz-‚dīv\ *n* **1** : a downward nose-first plunge (as of an airplane) **2** : a sudden extreme drop (as in prices)

nose•gay \'nōz-‚gā\ *n* : a small bunch of flowers : POSY

nose out *vb* **1** : to discover often by prying **2** : to defeat by a narrow margin

nose•piece \-‚pēs\ *n* **1** : a fitting at the lower end of a microscope tube to which the objectives are attached **2** : the bridge of a pair of eyeglasses

no—show \'nō-‚shō\ *n* : a person who does not show up for an event as expected

nos•tal•gia \nä-'stal-jə\ *n* **1** : HOMESICKNESS **2** : a wistful yearning for something past or irrecoverable — **nos•tal•gic** \-jik\ *adj*

nos•tril \'näs-trəl\ *n* **1** : either of the nares usu. with the adjoining nasal wall and passage **2** : either fleshy lateral wall of the nose

nos•trum \'näs-trəm\ *n* : a questionable medicine or remedy

nosy *or* **nos•ey** \'nō-zē\ *adj* **nos•i•er; -est** ♦ : of prying or inquisitive disposition or quality : PRYING ⟨∼ neighbors⟩

  ♦ inquisitive, intrusive, meddlesome, obtrusive, officious, presumptuous, prying

not \'nät\ *adv* **1** — used to make negative a group of words or a word ⟨the boys are ∼ here⟩ **2** — used to stand for the negative of a preceding group of words ⟨sometimes hard to see and sometimes ∼⟩

no•ta be•ne \‚nō-tə-'bē-nē, -'be-\ — used to call attention to something important

no•ta•bil•i•ty \‚nō-tə-ə-'bi-lə-tē\ *n, pl* **-ties** **1** : the quality or state of being notable **2** : NOTABLE

¹**no•ta•ble** \'nō-tə-bəl\ *adj* **1** : NOTEWORTHY, REMARKABLE ⟨a ∼ achievement⟩ **2** ♦ : marked by eminence, distinction, or excellence : DISTINGUISHED ⟨two ∼ politicians made speeches⟩

  ♦ distinguished, eminent, illustrious, noble, noteworthy, outstanding, preeminent, prestigious, signal, star, superior

²**notable** *n* ♦ : a person of note

  ♦ celebrity, eminence, figure, light, luminary, personage, personality, somebody, standout, star, superstar, VIP

no•ta•bly \'nō-tə-blē\ *adv* **1** : in a notable manner **2** : ESPECIALLY, PARTICULARLY

no•tar•i•al \nō-'ter-ē-əl\ *adj* : of, relating to, or done by a notary public

no•ta•rize \'nō-tə-‚rīz\ *vb* **-rized; -riz•ing** : to acknowledge or make legally authentic as a notary public

no•ta•ry public \'nō-tə-rē-\ *n, pl* **notaries public** *or* **notary publics** : a public official who attests or certifies writings (as deeds) to make them legally authentic

no•ta•tion \nō-'tā-shən\ *n* **1** : a written reminder : NOTE **2** : the act, process, or method of representing data by marks, signs, figures, or characters; *also* : a system of symbols (as letters, numerals, or musical notes) used in such notation

¹**notch** \'näch\ *n* **1** ♦ : a V-shaped hollow in an edge or surface **2** ♦ : a narrow pass between two mountains **3** ♦ : a step or stage in a process, course, or order of classification

  ♦ [1] chip, hack, indentation, nick ♦ [2] canyon, defile, flume, gap, gorge, gulch, gulf, pass, ravine ♦ [3] cut, degree, grade, inch, peg, phase, point, stage, step

²**notch** *vb* **1** : to cut or make notches in **2** ♦ : to score or record by or as if by cutting a series of notches ⟨∼ed 20 points for the team⟩

  ♦ achieve, attain, gain, hit, make, score, win

notch•back \'näch-‚bak\ *n* : an automobile with a trunk whose lid forms a distinct deck

¹**note** \'nōt\ *vb* **not•ed; not•ing** **1** ♦ : to notice or observe with care ⟨*noted* her reaction⟩; *also* : to record or preserve in writing **2** ♦ : to make special mention of

  ♦ [1] jot, log, mark, put down, record, register, set down ♦ [1] behold, descry, discern, distinguish, espy, eye, look, notice, observe, perceive, regard, remark, see, sight, spy, view, witness
  ♦ [2] advert (to), cite, instance, mention, name, notice, quote, refer (to), remark, specify, touch (*on* or *upon*)

²**note** *n* **1** : a musical sound **2** : a cry, call, or sound esp. of a bird **3** : a special tone in a person's words or voice ⟨a ∼ of fear⟩ **4** : a character in music used to indicate duration of a tone by its shape and pitch by its position on the staff **5** ♦ : a characteristic feature : MOOD ⟨a ∼ of optimism⟩ **6** ♦ : a written re-

minder : MEMORANDUM **7** : a brief and informal record; *also* : a written or printed comment or explanation **8** : a written promise to pay a debt **9** : a piece of paper money **10** ♦ : a short informal letter **11** : a formal diplomatic or official communication **12** ♦ : overall quality or character as seen or judged by people in general : REPUTATION ⟨an artist of ∼⟩ **13** : OBSERVATION, NOTICE, HEED ⟨take ∼ of the time⟩

  ♦ [5] air, atmosphere, aura, climate, flavor (*or* flavour), mood, temper ♦ [6, 10] dispatch, letter, memorandum, missive ♦ [12] character, mark, name, report, reputation

note•book \'nōt-‚bùk\ *n* : a book for notes or memoranda

not•ed \'nō-təd\ *adj* ♦ : well known by reputation : EMINENT, CELEBRATED ⟨a ∼ violinist⟩

  ♦ celebrated, eminent, famed, famous, notorious, prominent, renowned, star, well-known

note•wor•thy \'nōt-‚wər-thē\ *adj* ♦ : worthy of note

  ♦ distinguished, eminent, illustrious, noble, notable, outstanding, preeminent, prestigious, signal, star, superior

¹**noth•ing** \'nə-thiŋ\ *pron* **1** : no thing ⟨leaves ∼ to the imagination⟩ **2** : no part **3** : one of no interest, value, or importance ⟨she's ∼ to me⟩

²**nothing** *adv* ♦ : not at all : in no degree

  ♦ never, no, none, nowise

³**nothing** *n* **1** : something that does not exist **2** ♦ : the arithmetical symbol 0 denoting the absence of all magnitude or quantity : ZERO **3** ♦ : a person or thing of little or no value or importance

  ♦ [2] aught, cipher, naught, nil, zero, zip ♦ [3] nobody, nonentity, whippersnapper, zero

⁴**nothing** *adj* : of no account : WORTHLESS

noth•ing•ness \'nə-thiŋ-nəs\ *n* **1** : the quality or state of being nothing **2 a** : the state or fact of having no existence **b** : utter insignificance **3** : something insignificant or valueless

¹**no•tice** \'nō-təs\ *n* **1** ♦ : warning or intimation of something : WARNING **2** : notification of the termination of an agreement or contract at a specified time **3** ♦ : consideration with a view to action : ATTENTION, HEED ⟨bring the matter to my ∼⟩ **4** ♦ : a written or printed announcement **5** : a short critical account or examination (as of a play) : REVIEW

  ♦ [1] admonition, alarm, alert, caution, warning ♦ [3] attention, awareness, cognizance, ear, eye, heed, observance, observation
  ♦ [4] announcement, directive, memorandum, notification

²**notice** *vb* **no•ticed; no•tic•ing** **1** ♦ : to make mention of : remark on **2** ♦ : to take notice of : OBSERVE

  ♦ [1] advert (to), cite, instance, mention, name, note, quote, refer (to), specify, touch (*on* or *upon*) ♦ [2] behold, descry, discern, distinguish, espy, eye, look, note, observe, perceive, regard, remark, see, sight, spy, view, witness

no•tice•able \'nō-tə-sə-bəl\ *adj* **1** : worthy of notice **2** ♦ : capable of being or likely to be noticed ⟨a ∼ scar⟩ — **no•tice•ably** \-blē\ *adv*

  ♦ bold, catchy, conspicuous, emphatic, marked, prominent, pronounced, remarkable, striking *Ant* inconspicuous, unemphatic, unnoticeable, unobtrusive, unremarkable

no•ti•fi•ca•tion \‚nō-tə-fə-'kā-shən\ *n* ♦ : the act or an instance of notifying

  ♦ advertisement, announcement, bulletin, notice, release

no•ti•fy \'nō-tə-‚fī\ *vb* **-fied; -fy•ing** **1** : to give notice of : report the occurrence of **2** : to give notice to

no•tion \'nō-shən\ *n* **1** ♦ : an individual's conception or impression of something known, experienced, or imagined : IDEA, CONCEPTION ⟨have a ∼ of what he means⟩ **2** ♦ : a belief held : OPINION, VIEW **3** ♦ : a personal inclination : WHIM, FANCY ⟨a sudden ∼ to go⟩ **4** *pl* ♦ : small useful articles (as pins, needles, or thread)

  ♦ [1] concept, idea, image, impression, picture, thought ♦ [2] belief, conviction, eye, feeling, judgment (*or* judgement), mind, opinion, persuasion, sentiment, verdict, view ♦ [3] caprice, fancy, freak, vagary, whim ♦ **notions** [4] novelties, odds and ends, sundries

no•tion•al \'nō-shə-nəl\ *adj* **1** : existing in the mind only : IMAGINARY, UNREAL **2** : given to foolish or fanciful moods or ideas : WHIMSICAL

no•to•ri•ety \‚nō-tə-'rī-ə-tē\ *n* ♦ : the quality or state of being notorious

  ♦ celebrity, fame, renown

no•to•ri•ous \nō-'tōr-ē-əs\ *adj* ♦ : generally known and talked of; *esp* : widely and unfavorably known — **no•to•ri•ous•ly** \nō-'tōr-ē-əs-lē\ *adv*

♦ celebrated, famed, famous, noted, prominent, renowned, star, well-known ♦ discreditable, disgraceful, dishonorable (*or* dishonourable), disreputable, ignominious, infamous, shameful

¹**not•with•stand•ing** \ˌnät-with-'stan-diŋ, -with-\ *prep* ♦ : in spite of

♦ despite, regardless of, with

²**notwithstanding** *adv* ♦ : in spite of that : NEVERTHELESS

♦ but, howbeit, however, nevertheless, nonetheless, still, though, withal, yet

³**notwithstanding** *conj* : ALTHOUGH

nou•gat \'nü-gət\ *n* : a confection of nuts or fruit pieces in a sugar paste

nought *var of* NAUGHT

noun \'naủn\ *n* : a word that is the name of a subject of discourse (as a person or place)

nour•ish \'nər-ish\ *vb* ♦ : to promote the growth or development of

♦ advance, cultivate, encourage, forward, foster, further, nurture, promote

nour•ish•ing *adj* ♦ : giving nourishment

♦ nutritious

nour•ish•ment \'nər-ish-mənt\ *n* **1** : FOOD, NUTRIENT **2** : the action or process of nourishing

nou•veau riche \ˌnü-ˌvō-'rēsh\ *n, pl* **nou•veaux riches** *same*\ : a person newly rich : PARVENU

Nov *abbr* November

no•va \'nō-və\ *n, pl* **novas** *or* **no•vae** \-(ˌ)vē, -ˌvī\ : a star that suddenly increases greatly in brightness and then within a few months or years grows dim again

¹**nov•el** \'nä-vəl\ *adj* **1** ♦ : having no precedent : NEW **2** : STRANGE, UNUSUAL

♦ fresh, new, original, strange, unfamiliar, unknown

²**novel** *n* : a long invented prose narrative dealing with human experience through a connected sequence of events — **nov•el•ist** \-və-list\ *n*

nov•el•ette \ˌnä-və-'let\ *n* : a brief novel or long short story

nov•el•ize \'nä-və-ˌlīz\ *vb* **-ized; -iz•ing** : to convert into the form of a novel — **nov•el•i•za•tion** \ˌnä-və-lə-'zā-shən\ *n*

no•vel•la \nō-'ve-lə\ *n, pl* **novellas** *or* **no•vel•le** \-'ve-lē\ ♦ : a work of fiction between a short story and a novel in length and complexity : NOVELETTE

♦ narrative, short story, story, tale

nov•el•ty \'nä-vəl-tē\ *n, pl* **-ties** **1** : something new or unusual **2** ♦ : the quality or state of being new : NEWNESS **3** ♦ : a small manufactured article intended mainly for personal or household adornment — usu. used in pl.

♦ [2] freshness, newness, originality ♦ [3] bauble, curiosity, gewgaw, knickknack, tchotchke, trinket ♦ *usu* **novelties** [3] notions, odds and ends, sundries

No•vem•ber \nō-'vem-bər\ *n* : the 11th month of the year

no•ve•na \nō-'vē-nə\ *n* : a Roman Catholic nine-day period of prayer

nov•ice \'nä-vəs\ *n* **1** : a new member of a religious order who is preparing to take the vows of religion **2** ♦ : one who is inexperienced or untrained

♦ beginner, fledgling, freshman, greenhorn, neophyte, newcomer, recruit, rookie, tenderfoot, tyro

no•vi•tiate \nō-'vi-shət\ *n* **1** : the period or state of being a novice **2** : a house where novices are trained **3** : NOVICE

¹**now** \'naủ\ *adv* **1** ♦ : at the present time or moment **2** ♦ : in the time immediately before the present **3** ♦ : in the time immediately to follow : IMMEDIATELY, FORTHWITH **4** — used with the sense of present time weakened or lost (as to express command, introduce an important point, or indicate a transition) ⟨~ hear this⟩ **5** : at times : SOMETIMES ⟨~ one and ~ another⟩ **6** : under the present circumstances **7** : at the time referred to

♦ [1] anymore, nowadays, presently, right now, today *Ant* before, formerly, long, once, then ♦ [2] freshly, just, late, lately, new, newly, only, recently ♦ [3] directly, forthwith, immediately, instantly, promptly, pronto, right away, right now

²**now** *conj* ♦ : in view of the fact ⟨~ that you're here, we'll start⟩

♦ because, for, since, whereas

³**now** *n* ♦ : the present time or moment : PRESENT

♦ moment, present, today

⁴**now** *adj* **1** : of or relating to the present time ⟨the ~ president⟩ **2** : excitingly new ⟨~ clothes⟩; *also* : constantly aware of what is new ⟨~ people⟩

NOW *abbr* **1** National Organization for Women **2** negotiable order of withdrawal

now•a•days \'naủ-ə-ˌdāz\ *adv* ♦ : at the present time

♦ anymore, now, presently, right now, today

no•way \'nō-ˌwā\ *or* **no•ways** \-ˌwāz\ *adv* : NOWISE

no•where \-ˌhwer\ *adv* : not anywhere — **nowhere** *n*

nowhere near *adv* : not nearly

no•wise \'nō-ˌwīz\ *adv* ♦ : in no way

♦ never, no, none, nothing

nox•ious \'näk-shəs\ *adj* ♦ : harmful esp. to health or morals

♦ noisome, unhealthy, unwholesome ♦ adverse, bad, baleful, baneful, damaging, deleterious, detrimental, evil, harmful, hurtful, ill, injurious, mischievous, pernicious, prejudicial

noz•zle \'nä-zəl\ *n* : a short tube constricted in the middle or at one end and used (as on a hose) to speed up or direct a flow of fluid

np *abbr* **1** no pagination **2** no place (of publication)

Np *symbol* neptunium

NP *abbr* notary public

NR *abbr* not rated

NRA *abbr* National Rifle Association

NS *abbr* **1** not specified **2** Nova Scotia

NSA *abbr* National Security Agency

NSC *abbr* National Security Council

NSF *abbr* **1** National Science Foundation **2** not sufficient funds

NSW *abbr* New South Wales

NT *abbr* **1** New Testament **2** Northern Territory **3** Northwest Territories

nth \'enth\ *adj* **1** : numbered with an unspecified or indefinitely large ordinal number ⟨for the ~ time⟩ **2** ♦ : of the greatest or highest degree, quantity, number, or amount : UTMOST ⟨to the ~ degree⟩

♦ consummate, maximum, most, paramount, supreme, top, ultimate, utmost

NTP *abbr* normal temperature and pressure

nt wt *or* **n wt** *abbr* net weight

nu \'nü, 'nyü\ *n* : the 13th letter of the Greek alphabet — N *or* ν

NU *abbr* name unknown

nu•ance \'nü-ˌäns; 'nyü-, nü-'äns, nyủ-\ *n* : a shade of difference : a delicate variation (as in tone or meaning)

nub \'nəb\ *n* **1** : a piece or mass of indefinite size and shape : KNOB, LUMP **2** ♦ : the main point or part : GIST ⟨the ~ of the story⟩

♦ core, crux, gist, heart, pith, pivot

nub•bin \'nə-bən\ *n* **1** : something (as an ear of corn) that is small for its kind, stunted, undeveloped, or imperfect **2** : a small usu. projecting part or bit

nu•bile \'nü-ˌbīl, 'nyü-, -bəl\ *adj* **1** : of marriageable condition or age : sexually mature **2** : sexually attractive — used of a young woman

nu•cle•ar \'nü-klē-ər, 'nyü-\ *adj* **1** : of, relating to, or constituting a nucleus **2** : of, relating to, or using the atomic nucleus or energy derived from it **3** : of, relating to, or being a weapon whose destructive power results from an uncontrolled nuclear reaction

nuclear family *n* : a family group that consists only of parents and children

nu•cle•ate \'nü-klē-ˌāt, 'nyü-\ *vb* **-at•ed; -at•ing** : to form, act as, or have a nucleus — **nu•cle•ation** \ˌnü-klē-'ā-shən, ˌnyü-\ *n*

nu•cle•ic acid \nủ-'klē-ik-, nyủ-, -'klā-\ *n* : any of various complex organic acids (as DNA or RNA) found esp. in cell nuclei

nu•cle•o•tide \'nü-klē-ə-ˌtīd, 'nyü-\ *n* : any of several compounds that are the basic structural units of nucleic acids

nu•cle•us \'nü-klē-əs, 'nyü-\ *n, pl* **nu•clei** \-klē-ˌī\ *also* **nu•cle•us•es** **1** : a central mass or part about which matter gathers or is collected : CORE **2** : a cell part that is characteristic of all living things except viruses, bacteria, and certain algae, that is necessary for heredity and for making proteins, that contains the chromosomes with their genes, and that is enclosed in a membrane **3** : a mass of gray matter or group of cell bodies of neurons in the central nervous system **4** : the central part of an atom that comprises nearly all of its atomic mass **5** ♦ : a basic or essential part

♦ base, center (*or* centre), core, cynosure, eye, focus, heart, hub, mecca, seat

¹nude \'nüd, 'nyüd\ *adj* **nud•er; nud•est** **1** ♦ : devoid of a natural or conventional covering : BARE, NAKED **2** : featuring or catering to naked people — **nu•di•ty** \'nü-də-tē, 'nyü-\ *n*

♦ bare, naked, unclad, unclothed, undressed

²nude *n* **1** : a nude human figure esp. as depicted in art **2** : the condition of being nude ⟨in the ∼⟩

nudge \'nəj\ *vb* **nudged; nudg•ing** : to touch or push gently (as with the elbow) usu. in order to seek attention — **nudge** *n*

nud•ism \'nü-ˌdi-zəm, 'nyü-\ *n* : the practice of going nude esp. in mixed groups at specially secluded places — **nud•ist** \-dist\ *n*

nu•ga•to•ry \-gə-ˌtōr-ē\ *adj* **1** : INCONSEQUENTIAL, WORTHLESS **2** : having no force : INEFFECTUAL

nug•get \'nə-gət\ *n* **1** : a solid lump; *esp* : a lump of precious metal (as gold) **2** : TIDBIT

nui•sance \'nüs-³ns, 'nyüs-\ *n* ♦ : an annoying or troublesome person or thing

♦ annoyance, bother, gadfly, persecutor, pest, tease ♦ aggravation, annoyance, bother, exasperation, frustration, hassle, headache, inconvenience, irritant, peeve, pest, problem, thorn

nuisance tax *n* : an excise tax collected in small amounts directly from the consumer

¹nuke \'nük, 'nyük\ *n* **1** : a nuclear weapon **2** : a nuclear power plant

²nuke *vb* **nuked; nuk•ing** **1** : to attack with nuclear weapons **2** : MICROWAVE

null \'nəl\ *adj* **1** ♦ : having no legal or binding force : INVALID, VOID **2** ♦ : amounting to nothing **3** : INSIGNIFICANT — **nul•li•ty** \'nə-lə-tē\ *n*

♦ [1] invalid, void *Ant* binding, good, valid ♦ [2] chaffy, empty, junky, no-good, valueless, worthless

null and void *adj* : having no force, binding power, or validity

nul•li•fy \'nə-lə-ˌfī\ *vb* **-fied; -fy•ing** ♦ : to make null or valueless; *also* : to declare or make legally invalid or void — **nul•li•fi•ca•tion** \ˌnə-lə-fə-'kā-shən\ *n*

♦ abolish, abrogate, annul, cancel, dissolve, invalidate, negate, quash, repeal, rescind, void

num *abbr* numeral
Num *or* **Numb** *abbr* Numbers

¹numb \'nəm\ *adj* ♦ : lacking sensation or emotion — **numb•ly** *adv*

♦ asleep, dead, unfeeling *Ant* feeling, sensitive

²numb *vb* ♦ : to make as if dead : impair in vigor, force, activity, or sensation

♦ blunt, dampen, deaden, dull

¹num•ber \'nəm-bər\ *n* **1** : the total of individuals or units taken together **2** : an indefinite total ⟨a small ∼ of tickets remain unsold⟩ **3** : an ascertainable total ⟨the sands of the desert are without ∼⟩ **4** : a distinction of word form to denote reference to one or more than one **5** : a unit belonging to a mathematical system and subject to its laws; *also, pl* : ARITHMETIC **6** ♦ : a symbol used to represent a mathematical number; *also* : such a number used to identify or designate ⟨a phone ∼⟩ **7** : one in a series of musical or theatrical performances ⟨the best ∼ on the program⟩

♦ digit, figure, integer, numeral, whole number

²number *vb* **1** : to indicate or name by units or groups so as to find the total number of units involved : COUNT, ENUMERATE **2** ♦ : to include with or be one of a group **3** : to restrict to a small or definite number **4** : to assign a number to **5** ♦ : to comprise in number : TOTAL

♦ [2] carry, comprehend, contain, embrace, encompass, entail, include, involve, take in ♦ [5] add up, amount, come, sum, total

number crunching *n* ♦ : the performance of long complex often repetitive mathematical calculations; *also* : statistical analysis

♦ arithmetic, calculation, computation, reckoning

num•ber•less \-ləs\ *adj* ♦ : too many to be numbered : INNUMERABLE, COUNTLESS ⟨∼ stars in the sky⟩

♦ countless, innumerable, uncountable, unnumbered, untold

Numbers *n* : a book of Jewish and Christian Scripture
numb•ing \'nə-miŋ\ *adj* : tending to make numb ⟨a ∼ lecture⟩ ⟨a ∼ realization⟩
numb•ness *n* ♦ : reduced sensitivity to perception or emotion

♦ apathy, impassivity, phlegm, stupor

numbskull *var of* NUMSKULL

nu•mer•a•cy \'nü-mə-rə-sē, 'nyü-\ *n* : the capacity for quantitative thought or expression

nu•mer•al \'nü-mə-rəl, 'nyü-\ *n* ♦ : a conventional symbol representing a number — **numeral** *adj*

♦ digit, figure, integer, number, whole number

nu•mer•ate \'nü-mə-ˌrāt, 'nyü-\ *vb* **-at•ed; -at•ing** **1** : to ascertain the number of **2** ♦ : to specify one after another

♦ detail, enumerate, itemize, list, rehearse, tick (off)

nu•mer•a•tor \-ˌrā-tər\ *n* : the part of a fraction above the line

nu•mer•ic \nú-'mer-ik, nyü-\ *adj* : NUMERICAL; *esp* : denoting a number or a system of numbers

nu•mer•i•cal \-'mer-i-kəl\ *adj* **1** : of or relating to numbers ⟨in ∼ order⟩ **2** : expressed in or involving numbers — **nu•mer•i•cal•ly** \-k(ə-)lē\ *adv*

nu•mer•ol•o•gy \ˌnü-mə-'rä-lə-jē, ˌnyü-\ *n* : the study of the occult significance of numbers — **nu•mer•ol•o•gist** \-jist\ *n*

nu•mer•ous \'nü-mə-rəs, 'nyü-\ *adj* ♦ : consisting of, including, or relating to a great number : MANY

♦ many, multiple, multitudinous

nu•mis•mat•ics \ˌnü-məz-'ma-tiks, ˌnyü-\ *n* : the study or collection of monetary objects — **nu•mis•mat•ic** \-tik\ *adj* — **nu•mis•ma•tist** \nü-'miz-mə-tist, nyü-\ *n*

num•skull \'nəm-ˌskəl\ *n* ♦ : a stupid person : DUNCE

♦ blockhead, dope, dummy, idiot, imbecile, jackass, moron

nun \'nən\ *n* : a woman belonging to a religious order; *esp* : one under solemn vows of poverty, chastity, and obedience

nun•cio \'nən-sē-ˌō, 'nün-\ *n, pl* **-ci•os** : a permanent high-ranking papal representative to a civil government

nun•nery \'nə-nə-rē\ *n, pl* **-ner•ies** : a convent of nuns

¹nup•tial \'nəp-shəl\ *adj* ♦ : of or relating to marriage or a wedding ⟨∼ vows⟩

♦ conjugal, connubial, marital, matrimonial

²nuptial *n* : MARRIAGE, WEDDING — usu. used in pl.

¹nurse \'nərs\ *n* **1** ♦ : a girl or woman employed to take care of children **2** : a person trained to care for sick people

♦ nanny, nursemaid

²nurse *vb* **nursed; nurs•ing** **1** : SUCKLE **2** ♦ : to take charge of and watch over **3** : TEND ⟨∼ an invalid⟩ **4** ♦ : to treat with special care ⟨∼ a headache⟩ **5** ♦ : to hold in one's mind or consideration ⟨∼ a grudge⟩ **6** : to act or serve as a nurse

♦ [2] aid, care, minister, mother ♦ [4] baby, coddle, mollycoddle, pamper, spoil ♦ [5] bear, cherish, entertain, harbor (*or* harbour), have, hold

nurse•maid \'nərs-ˌmād\ *n* ♦ : a girl or woman who is regularly employed to look after children : NURSE 1

♦ nanny, nurse

nurse–prac•ti•tion•er \-prak-'ti-shə-nər\ *n* : a registered nurse who is qualified to assume some of the duties formerly assumed only by a physician

nurs•ery \'nər-sə-rē\ *n, pl* **-er•ies** **1** : a room for children **2** : a place where children are temporarily cared for in their parents' absence **3** : a place where young plants are grown usu. for transplanting

nurs•ery•man \-mən\ *n* : a man who keeps or works in a plant nursery

nursery school *n* : a school for children under kindergarten age

nursing home *n* : a private establishment providing care for persons (as the aged or the chronically ill) who are unable to care for themselves

nurs•ling \'nərs-liŋ\ *n* **1** : one that is solicitously cared for **2** : a nursing child

¹nur•ture \'nər-chər\ *n* **1** : TRAINING, UPBRINGING; *also* : the influences that modify the expression of an individual's heredity **2** : FOOD, NOURISHMENT

²nurture *vb* **nur•tured; nur•tur•ing** **1** : to care for : FEED, NOURISH **2** ♦ : to develop mentally, morally, or aesthetically esp. by instruction : EDUCATE ⟨∼ students⟩ **3** ♦ : to further the development of : FOSTER ⟨∼ creativity⟩

♦ [2] edify, educate, enlighten ♦ [3] advance, cultivate, encourage, forward, foster, further, nourish, promote

nut \'nət\ *n* **1** : a dry fruit or seed with a hard shell and a firm inner kernel; *also* : its kernel **2** : a metal block with a hole through it that is fastened to a bolt or screw by means of a screw thread within the hole **3** : the ridge on the upper end of the fingerboard in a stringed musical instrument over which the strings pass **4 ♦** : a foolish, eccentric, or crazy person **5 ♦** : one who is ardently attached to a cause, object, or pursuit : ENTHUSIAST

   ♦ [4] character, crackpot, crank, eccentric, kook, oddball, screwball, weirdo ♦ [4] booby, fool, goose, half-wit, jackass, nitwit, simpleton, turkey ♦ [5] addict, aficionado, buff, bug, devotee, enthusiast, fan, fanatic, fancier, fiend, freak, lover, maniac

nut·crack·er \'nət-ˌkra-kər\ n : an instrument for cracking nuts
nut·hatch \-ˌhach\ n : any of various small tree-climbing chiefly insect-eating birds
nut·meg \-ˌmeg, -ˌmāg\ n : a spice made by grinding the nutlike aromatic seed of a tropical tree; also : the seed or tree
nu·tria \'nü-trē-ə, 'nyü-\ n 1 : the durable usu. light brown fur of a nutria 2 : a large So. American aquatic rodent with webbed hind feet
¹nu·tri·ent \'nü-trē-ənt, 'nyü-\ adj : furnishing nourishment : NOURISHING
²nutrient n : a nutritive substance or ingredient
nu·tri·ment \-trə-mənt\ n : NUTRIENT
nu·tri·tion \nú-'tri-shən, nyú-\ n : the act or process of nourishing; esp : the processes by which an individual takes in and utilizes food material
nu·tri·tion·al \-shə-nəl\ adj : of, relating to, or functioning in nutrition
nu·tri·tious \-shəs\ adj ♦ : giving nourishment

   ♦ nourishing

nu·tri·tive \'nü-trə-tiv, 'nyü-\ adj : of or relating to nutrition
nuts \'nəts\ adj 1 ♦ : filled with or marked by enthusiasm 2 : mentally disordered : DEMENTED — not used technically

   ♦ ardent, eager, enthusiastic, gung ho, keen ♦ usu nuts about crazy, mad

nut·shell \'nət-ˌshel\ n : the shell of a nut — **in a nutshell** : in a few words ⟨that's the story in a nutshell⟩
nut·ty \'nə-tē\ adj **nut·ti·er; -est** 1 : containing or suggesting nuts ⟨a ∼ flavor⟩ 2 : mentally unbalanced — not used technically 3 ♦ : lacking in seriousness : SILLY

   ♦ absurd, cuckoo, fatuous, foolish, nonsensical, senseless, silly, stupid

nuz·zle \'nə-zəl\ vb **nuz·zled; nuz·zling** 1 : to root around, push, or touch with or as if with the nose 2 ♦ : to press closely and affectionately : SNUGGLE

   ♦ cuddle, nestle, snug, snuggle

NV abbr Nevada
NW abbr northwest
NWT abbr Northwest Territories
NY abbr New York
NYC abbr New York City
ny·lon \'nī-ˌlän\ n 1 : any of numerous strong tough elastic synthetic materials used esp. in textiles and plastics 2 pl : stockings made of nylon
nymph \'nimf\ n 1 : any of the lesser goddesses in ancient mythology represented as maidens living in the mountains, forests, meadows, and waters 2 : GIRL 3 : an immature insect resembling the adult but smaller, less differentiated, and usu. lacking wings
nym·pho·ma·nia \ˌnim-fə-'mā-nē-ə, -nyə\ n : excessive sexual desire by a female — **nym·pho·ma·ni·ac** \-nē-ˌak\ n or adj
NZ abbr New Zealand

¹o \'ō\ n, pl **o's** or **os** \'ōz\ often cap 1 : the 15th letter of the English alphabet 2 : ZERO
²o abbr, often cap 1 ocean 2 Ohio 3 ohm
¹O var of OH
²O abbr Ohio
³O symbol oxygen
o/a abbr on or about
oaf \'ōf\ n ♦ : a stupid or awkward person

   ♦ clod, gawk, hulk, lout, lubber, lug

oaf·ish adj : having the qualities typical of an oaf
oak \'ōk\ n, pl **oaks** or **oak** : any of a genus of trees or shrubs related to the beech and chestnut and bearing a rounded thin-shelled nut surrounded at the base by a hardened cup; also : the usu. tough hard durable wood of an oak — **oak·en** \'ō-kən\ adj
oa·kum \'ō-kəm\ n : loosely twisted hemp or jute fiber impregnated with tar and used esp. in caulking ships
oar \'ōr\ n : a long pole with a broad blade at one end used for propelling or steering a boat
oar·lock \'ōr-ˌläk\ n : a U-shaped device for holding an oar in place
oars·man \'ōrz-mən\ n : one who rows esp. in a racing crew
OAS abbr Organization of American States
oa·sis \ō-'ā-səs\ n, pl **oa·ses** \-ˌsēz\ : a fertile or green area in an arid region
oat \'ōt\ n : a cereal grass widely grown for its edible seed; also : this seed — **oat·en** \-ᵊn\ adj
oat·cake \'ōt-ˌkāk\ n : a thin flat oatmeal cake
oath \'ōth\ n, pl **oaths** \'ōthz, 'ōths\ 1 ♦ : a solemn appeal to God to witness to the truth of a statement or the sacredness of a promise 2 : an irreverent or careless use of a sacred name

   ♦ pledge, promise, troth, vow, word

oat·meal \'ōt-ˌmēl\ n 1 : ground or rolled oats 2 : porridge made from ground or rolled oats
Ob or **Obad** abbr Obadiah
Oba·di·ah \ˌō-bə-'dī-ə\ n : a book of canonical Jewish and Christian Scripture
ob·bli·ga·to \ˌä-blə-'gä-tō\ n, pl **-tos** also **-ti** \-'gä-tē\ : an accompanying part usu. played by a solo instrument

ob·du·ra·cy \'äb-də-rə-sē, -dyə-\ n ♦ : the quality or state of being obdurate

   ♦ hardheadedness, mulishness, obstinacy, peevishness, pertinacity, self-will, stubbornness, tenacity

ob·du·rate \'äb-də-rət, -dyə-\ adj 1 ♦ : stubbornly resistant : UNYIELDING ⟨an ∼ denial⟩ 2 ♦ : hardened in feelings

   ♦ [1] dogged, hardheaded, headstrong, mulish, obstinate, opinionated, peevish, pertinacious, perverse, pigheaded, stubborn, unyielding, willful ♦ [2] callous, hard, heartless, inhuman, inhumane, pitiless, soulless, unfeeling, unsympathetic

obe·di·ence \ō-'bē-dē-əns\ n ♦ : an act or instance of obeying

   ♦ compliance, conformity, observance, submission, subordination Ant disobedience, insubordination, noncompliance, rebelling, rebellion

obe·di·ent \ō-'bē-dē-ənt\ adj ♦ : submissive to the restraint or command of authority — **obe·di·ent·ly** adv

   ♦ amenable, compliant, conformable, docile, submissive, tractable Ant contrary, disobedient, froward, insubordinate, intractable, rebellious, recalcitrant, refractory, unruly

obei·sance \ō-'bē-səns, -'bā-\ n : a bow made to show respect or submission; also : DEFERENCE, HOMAGE
obe·lisk \'ä-bə-ˌlisk\ n : a 4-sided pillar that tapers toward the top and ends in a pyramid
obese \ō-'bēs\ adj ♦ : excessively fat

   ♦ chubby, corpulent, fat, fleshy, full, gross, overweight, plump, portly, rotund, round

obe·si·ty \ō-'bē-sə-tē\ n ♦ : a condition characterized by the excessive accumulation and storage of fat in the body

   ♦ corpulence, fatness, grossness, plumpness

obey \ō-'bā\ vb **obeyed; obey·ing** 1 : to follow the commands or guidance of : behave obediently 2 ♦ : to comply with ⟨∼ orders⟩

   ♦ comply, conform, follow, mind, observe Ant disobey

ob·fus·cate \'äb-fə-ˌskāt\ vb **-cat·ed; -cat·ing** 1 : to make dark or obscure 2 : to make difficult to understand ⟨obfuscating the issue⟩ — **ob·fus·ca·tion** \ˌäb-fəs-'kā-shən\ n

OB–GYN *abbr* obstetrician gynecologist; obstetrics gynecology

obi \'ō-bē\ *n* : a broad sash worn esp. with a Japanese kimono

obit \ō-'bit, 'ō-bət\ *n* : OBITUARY

obi·ter dic·tum \,ō-bə-tər-'dik-təm\ *n, pl* **obiter dic·ta** \-tə\ : an incidental remark or observation

obit·u·ary \ə-'bi-chə-,wer-ē\ *n, pl* **-ar·ies** : a notice of a person's death usu. with a short biographical account

obj *abbr* object; objective

¹**ob·ject** \'äb-jikt\ *n* **1** ♦ : something that may be seen or felt; *also* : something that may be perceived or examined mentally **2** : something that arouses an emotional response (as of affection or pity) **3** ♦ : the goal or end of an effort or activity : AIM, PURPOSE **4** : a word or word group denoting that which the action of the verb is directed on or toward; *also* : a noun or noun equivalent in a prepositional phrase

♦ [1] being, entity, individual, substance, thing ♦ [3] aim, ambition, aspiration, design, dream, end, goal, intent, mark, meaning, objective, plan, pretension, purpose, thing

²**ob·ject** \əb-'jekt\ *vb* **1** ♦ : to offer in opposition **2** ♦ : to oppose something; *also* : DISAPPROVE — **ob·jec·tor** \-'jek-tər\ *n*

♦ [1, 2] challenge, complain, criticize, demur, disapprove, dispute, kick, protest, quarrel, remonstrate

object code *n* : a computer program after translation from source code

ob·jec·ti·fy \əb-'jek-tə-,fī\ *vb* **-fied; -fy·ing** : to make objective

ob·jec·tion \əb-'jek-shən\ *n* **1** ♦ : the act of objecting **2** : a reason for or a feeling of disapproval

♦ challenge, complaint, demur, expostulation, fuss, kick, protest, question, remonstrance

ob·jec·tion·able \əb-'jek-shə-nə-bəl\ *adj* ♦ : arousing objection : UNDESIRABLE, OFFENSIVE — **ob·jec·tion·ably** \-blē\ *adv*

♦ censurable, obnoxious, offensive, reprehensible *Ant* inoffensive, unobjectionable

¹**ob·jec·tive** \əb-'jek-tiv\ *adj* **1** : of or relating to an object or end **2** : existing outside and independent of the mind **3** : of, relating to, or constituting a grammatical case marking typically the object of a verb or preposition **4** ♦ : treating or dealing with facts without distortion by personal feelings or prejudices — **ob·jec·tive·ly** *adv* — **ob·jec·tive·ness** *n*

♦ disinterested, dispassionate, equal, equitable, fair, impartial, just, nonpartisan, square, unbiased, unprejudiced

²**objective** *n* **1** : the lens (as in a microscope) nearest the object and forming an image of it **2** ♦ : an aim, goal, or end of action

♦ aim, ambition, aspiration, design, dream, end, goal, intent, mark, meaning, object, plan, pretension, purpose, thing

ob·jec·tiv·i·ty \,äb-jek-'ti-və-tē\ *n* ♦ : the quality, state, or relation of being objective

♦ detachment, disinterestedness, impartiality, neutrality

ob·jet d'art \,ób-,zhä-'där\ *n, pl* **ob·jets d'art** *same*\ : an article of artistic worth; *also* : CURIO

ob·jet trou·vé \'ób-,zhā-trü-'vā\ *n, pl* **objets trouvés** *same*\ : a found natural or discarded object (as a piece of driftwood) held to have aesthetic value

ob·jur·ga·tion \,äb-jər-'gā-shən\ *n* : a harsh rebuke — **ob·jur·gate** \'äb-jər-,gāt\ *vb*

obl *abbr* **1** oblique **2** oblong

ob·late \ä-'blāt\ *adj* : flattened or depressed at the poles ⟨an ∼ spheroid⟩

ob·la·tion \ə-'blā-shən\ *n* : a religious offering

ob·li·gate \'ä-blə-,gāt\ *vb* **-gat·ed; -gat·ing** ♦ : to bind legally or morally

♦ coerce, compel, constrain, drive, force, make, muscle, oblige, press, pressure

ob·li·gat·ed \'ä-blə-,gā-təd\ *adj* ♦ : bound legally or morally

♦ beholden, indebted, obliged

ob·li·ga·tion \,ä-blə-'gā-shən\ *n* **1** : an act of obligating oneself to a course of action **2** ♦ : something (as a promise or a contract) that binds one to a course of action **3** : INDEBTEDNESS; *also* : LIABILITY **4** : DUTY

♦ burden, charge, commitment, duty, need, responsibility

oblig·a·to·ry \ə-'bli-gə-,tōr-ē\ *adj* ♦ : binding in law or conscience

♦ compulsory, imperative, incumbent, involuntary, mandatory, necessary, nonelective, peremptory

oblige \ə-'blīj\ *vb* **obliged; oblig·ing** **1** ♦ : to constrain by physical, moral, or legal force or by the requirements of circumstance : FORCE, COMPEL **2** : to bind by a favor; *also* : to do a favor for or do something as a favor

♦ coerce, compel, constrain, drive, force, make, muscle, obligate, press, pressure

obliged \ə-'blījd\ *adj* **1** ♦ : full of appreciation **2** ♦ : in someone's debt by a favor or service

♦ [1] appreciative, grateful, thankful ♦ [2] beholden, indebted, obligated

oblig·ing *adj* ♦ : willing to do favors — **oblig·ing·ly** *adv*

♦ accommodating, friendly, indulgent

oblique \ō-'blēk\ *adj* **1** ♦ : neither perpendicular nor parallel : having a slant **2** : not straightforward : INDIRECT — **oblique·ness** *n* — **obliq·ui·ty** \-'bli-kwə-tē\ *n*

♦ canted, diagonal, inclined, leaning, listing, slantwise

oblique case *n* : a grammatical case other than the nominative or vocative

oblique·ly *adv* ♦ : in an oblique way or direction

♦ athwart, crosswise, transversely

oblit·er·ate \ə-'bli-tə-,rāt\ *vb* **-at·ed; -at·ing** **1** : to make undecipherable by wiping out or covering over **2** : to remove from recognition or memory **3** : CANCEL **4** ♦ : to remove from existence

♦ annihilate, blot out, demolish, eradicate, exterminate, liquidate, root, rub out, snuff, stamp, wipe out

oblit·er·a·tion \ə-,bli-tə-'rā-shən\ *n* ♦ : the state of being obliterated

♦ annihilation, demolition, desolation, destruction, devastation, havoc, loss, ruin, wastage, wreckage

obliv·i·on \ə-'bli-vē-ən\ *n* **1** : the condition of being oblivious **2** : the condition or state of being forgotten

obliv·i·ous \ə-'bli-ve-əs\ *adj* **1** : lacking memory or mindful attention **2** ♦ : lacking active conscious knowledge or awareness : UNAWARE — **obliv·i·ous·ly** *adv*

♦ ignorant, unaware, unconscious, uninformed, unknowing, unwitting

obliv·i·ous·ness *n* ♦ : the quality or state of being oblivious

♦ ignorance, unawareness

ob·long \'ä-,blòn\ *adj* : deviating from a square, circular, or spherical form by elongation in one dimension — **oblong** *n*

ob·lo·quy \'ä-blə-kwē\ *n, pl* **-quies** **1** : strongly condemnatory utterance or language : DISGRACE **2** : bad repute : DISGRACE

ob·nox·ious \äb-'näk-shəs\ *adj* **1** ♦ : odiously or disgustingly objectionable : highly offensive : REPUGNANT, OFFENSIVE **2** *archaic* : deserving of censure — **ob·nox·ious·ly** *adv* — **ob·nox·ious·ness** *n*

♦ abhorrent, abominable, appalling, awful, distasteful, dreadful, foul, nauseating, noisome, odious, offensive, repellent, repugnant, repulsive, revolting

oboe \'ō-bō\ *n* : a woodwind instrument with a slender conical tube and a double reed mouthpiece — **obo·ist** \'ō-,bō-ist\ *n*

ob·scene \äb-'sēn\ *adj* **1** : disgusting to the senses : REPULSIVE **2** ♦ : deeply offensive to morality or decency; *esp* : designed to incite to lust or depravity — **ob·scene·ly** *adv*

♦ bawdy, coarse, crude, dirty, filthy, foul, gross, indecent, lascivious, lewd, nasty, pornographic, ribald, smutty, unprintable, vulgar, wanton *Ant* clean, decent

ob·scen·i·ty \-'se-nə-tē\ *n* ♦ : the quality or state of being obscene

♦ bawdiness, coarseness, dirt, dirtiness, filth, filthiness, foulness, grossness, indecency, lewdness, nastiness, ribaldry, smut, vulgarity

ob·scu·ran·tism \äb-'skyür-ən-,ti-zəm, ,äb-skyü-'ran-\ *n* **1** : opposition to the spread of knowledge **2** : deliberate vagueness or abstruseness — **ob·scu·ran·tist** \-tist\ *n or adj*

¹**ob·scure** \äb-'skyür\ *adj* **1** ♦ : emitting or having a limited or insufficient amount of light : DIM, GLOOMY **2** ♦ : not readily understood **3** ♦ : relatively unknown; *also* : HUMBLE — **ob·scure·ly** *adv*

♦ [1] dark, darkling, dim, dusky, gloomy, murky, somber (*or* sombre) ♦ [2] ambiguous, cryptic, dark, darkling, deep, enigmatic, equivocal, inscrutable, murky, mysterious, mystic, nebulous, occult, unclear, vague *Ant* clear, obvious, plain, unambiguous, unequivocal ♦ [3] anonymous, humble, nameless, unknown, unsung *Ant* celebrated, famed, famous, noted, notorious, prominent, renowned, well-known

²**ob·scure** *vb* **ob·scured; ob·scur·ing 1** ♦ : to make dark, dim, or indistinct **2** ♦ : to conceal or hide by or as if by covering
♦ [1] becloud, befog, blur, cloud, darken, dim, fog, haze, mist, overcast, overshadow, shroud ♦ [2] blanket, blot out, cloak, conceal, cover, curtain, enshroud, hide, mask, occult, screen, shroud, veil

ob·scu·ri·ty \-'skyùr-ə-tē\ *n* ♦ : the quality or state of being obscure
♦ ambiguity, darkness, murkiness, opacity *Ant* clarity, clearness, obviousness, plainness

ob·se·qui·ous \əb-'sē-kwē-əs\ *adj* : humbly or excessively attentive (as to a person in authority) : FAWNING, SYCOPHANTIC — **ob·se·qui·ous·ly** *adv* — **ob·se·qui·ous·ness** *n*
ob·se·quy \'äb-sə-kwē\ *n, pl* **-quies** : a funeral or burial rite — usu. used in pl.
ob·serv·able \əb-'zər-və-bəl\ *adj* **1** : NOTEWORTHY **2** ♦ : capable of being observed — **ob·serv·abil·ity** \-'bi-lə-tē\ *n*
♦ apparent, visible, visual

ob·ser·vance \əb-'zər-vəns\ *n* **1** ♦ : a customary practice or ceremony **2** ♦ : an act or instance of following a custom, rule, or law **3** ♦ : an act or instance of watching : OBSERVATION
♦ [1] ceremonial, ceremony, form, formality, rite, ritual, solemnity ♦ [2] compliance, conformity, obedience, submission, subordination ♦ [3] attention, awareness, cognizance, ear, eye, heed, notice, observation

ob·ser·vant \-vənt\ *adj* **1** ♦ : paying strict attention ⟨~ spectators⟩ **2** : KEEN, PERCEPTIVE **3** : MINDFUL ⟨~ of the amenities⟩
♦ absorbed, attentive, engrossed, intent, rapt

ob·ser·va·tion \,äb-sər-'vā-shən, -zər-\ *n* **1** ♦ : an act or instance of observing **2** : the gathering of information (as for scientific studies) by noting facts or occurrences **3** ♦ : a conclusion drawn from observing; *also* : REMARK **4** : the fact of being observed — **ob·ser·va·tion·al** \-shə-nəl\ *adj*
♦ [1] attention, awareness, cognizance, ear, eye, heed, notice, observance ♦ [3] comment, note, reflection, remark

ob·ser·va·to·ry \əb-'zər-və-,tōr-ē\ *n, pl* **-ries** : a place or institution equipped for observation of natural phenomena (as in astronomy)
ob·serve \əb-'zərv\ *vb* **ob·served; ob·serv·ing 1** ♦ : to conform one's action or practice to **2** ♦ : to celebrate or solemnize (as a ceremony or festival) in a customary or accepted way : CELEBRATE **3** : to make a scientific observation of **4** ♦ : to see or sense esp. through careful attention **5** : to come to realize esp. through consideration of noted facts **6** ♦ : to utter as a remark : REMARK — **ob·serv·er** *n*
♦ [1] comply, conform, follow, mind, obey ♦ [2] celebrate, commemorate, keep ♦ [4] behold, descry, discern, distinguish, espy, eye, look, note, notice, perceive, regard, remark, see, sight, spy, view, witness ♦ [6] comment, note, opine, remark

ob·sess \əb-'ses\ *vb* : to preoccupy intensely or abnormally
ob·ses·sion \äb-'se-shən\ *n* ♦ : a persistent disturbing preoccupation with an idea or feeling; *also* : an emotion or idea causing such a preoccupation — **ob·ses·sive** \-'se-siv\ *adj or n* — **ob·ses·sive·ly** *adv*
♦ fetish, fixation, mania, preoccupation, prepossession

obsessive–compulsive *adj* : relating to, characterized by, or affected with recurring obsessions and compulsions esp. as symptoms of a neurotic state
ob·sid·i·an \əb-'si-dē-ən\ *n* : a dark natural glass formed by the cooling of molten lava
ob·so·les·cent \,äb-sə-'les-ᵊnt\ *adj* : going out of use : becoming obsolete — **ob·so·les·cence** \-ᵊns\ *n*
ob·so·lete \,äb-sə-'lēt, 'äb-sə-,lēt\ *adj* ♦ : no longer in use; *also* : OLD-FASHIONED
♦ antiquated, archaic, dated, old-fashioned, outdated, outmoded, outworn, passé

ob·sta·cle \'äb-sti-kəl\ *n* ♦ : something that stands in the way or opposes
♦ bar, block, clog, crimp, drag, embarrassment, encumbrance, fetter, handicap, hindrance, let, stop, stumbling block

ob·stet·rics \əb-'ste-triks\ *n sing or pl* : a branch of medicine that deals with birth and with its antecedents and sequels — **ob·stet·ric**

\-trik\ *or* **ob·stet·ri·cal** \-tri-kəl\ *adj* — **ob·ste·tri·cian** \,äb-stə-'tri-shən\ *n*
ob·sti·na·cy \'äb-stə-nə-sē\ *n* ♦ : the quality or state of being obstinate
♦ hardheadedness, mulishness, obduracy, peevishness, pertinacity, self-will, stubbornness, tenacity

ob·sti·nate \'äb-stə-nət\ *adj* ♦ : fixed and unyielding (as in an opinion or course) despite reason or persuasion : STUBBORN ⟨~ opposition⟩ — **ob·sti·nate·ly** *adv*
♦ dogged, hardheaded, headstrong, mulish, obdurate, opinionated, peevish, pertinacious, perverse, pigheaded, stubborn, unyielding, willful

ob·strep·er·ous \əb-'stre-pə-rəs\ *adj* **1** ♦ : uncontrollably noisy **2** : stubbornly resistant to control : UNRULY — **ob·strep·er·ous·ness** *n*
♦ blatant, clamorous, vociferous

ob·struct \əb-'strəkt\ *vb* **1** ♦ : to block by an obstacle **2** ♦ : to impede the passage, action, or operation of **3** : to cut off from sight — **ob·struc·tive** \-'strək-tiv\ *adj* — **ob·struc·tor** \-tər\ *n*
♦ [1] block, choke, clog, close (off), congest, dam, jam, plug (up), stop (up), stuff ♦ [2] delay, hamper, hinder, hold back, hold up, impede, inhibit, interfere with

ob·struc·tion \əb-'strək-shən\ *n* **1** : an act of obstructing : the state of being obstructed **2** : something that obstructs : HINDRANCE
ob·struc·tion·ist \-shə-nist\ *n* : a person who hinders progress or business esp. in a legislative body — **ob·struc·tion·ism** \-shə-,ni-zəm\ *n*
ob·tain \əb-'tān\ *vb* **1** ♦ : to gain or attain usu. by planning or effort **2** : to be generally recognized or established
♦ acquire, attain, capture, carry, draw, earn, gain, garner, get, land, make, procure, realize, secure, win

ob·tain·able *adj* ♦ : capable of being obtained
♦ accessible, acquirable, attainable, available, procurable

ob·trude \əb-'trüd\ *vb* **ob·trud·ed; ob·trud·ing 1** : to thrust out **2** : to thrust forward without warrant or request **3** ♦ : to become unduly prominent or interfering : INTRUDE — **ob·tru·sion** \-'trü-zhən\ *n* — **ob·tru·sive·ly** *adv* — **ob·tru·sive·ness** *n*
♦ butt in, interfere, intrude, meddle, mess, nose, poke, pry, snoop

ob·tru·sive \-'trü-siv\ *adj* ♦ : forward in manner or conduct
♦ intrusive, meddlesome, nosy, officious, presumptuous, prying

ob·tuse \äb-'tüs, -'tyüs\ *adj* **ob·tus·er; -est 1** : exceeding 90 degrees but less than 180 degrees ⟨~ angle⟩ **2** : not pointed or acute : BLUNT **3** ♦ : not sharp or quick of wit ⟨too ~ to take a hint⟩ — **ob·tuse·ly** *adv*
♦ [2] blunt, dull ♦ [3] dense, dull, dumb, slow, stupid, thick, unintelligent

ob·tuse·ness *n* ♦ : the quality or state of being obtuse
♦ denseness, stupidity

obv *abbr* obverse
¹**ob·verse** \äb-'vərs, 'äb-,vərs\ *adj* **1** : facing the observer or opponent **2** : being a counterpart or complement — **ob·verse·ly** *adv*
²**ob·verse** \'äb-,vərs, äb-'vərs\ *n* **1** : the side (as of a coin) bearing the principal design and lettering **2** : a front or principal surface **3** : a counterpart having the opposite orientation or force
ob·vi·ate \'äb-vē-,āt\ *vb* **-at·ed; -at·ing** ♦ : to anticipate and prevent (as a situation) or make unnecessary (as an action) — **ob·vi·a·tion** \,äb-vē-'ā-shən\ *n*
♦ avert, forestall, help, preclude, prevent

ob·vi·ous \'äb-vē-əs\ *adj* ♦ : easily found, seen, or understood — **ob·vi·ous·ly** *adv* — **ob·vi·ous·ness** *n*
♦ apparent, broad, clear, clear-cut, distinct, evident, lucid, manifest, palpable, patent, perspicuous, plain, transparent, unambiguous, unequivocal, unmistakable ♦ blatant, conspicuous, egregious, flagrant, glaring, gross, patent, prominent, pronounced, rank, striking

OC *abbr* officer candidate
oc·a·ri·na \,ä-kə-'rē-nə\ *n* : a wind instrument typically having an oval body with finger holes and a projecting mouthpiece
occas *abbr* occasionally
¹**oc·ca·sion** \ə-'kā-zhən\ *n* **1** ♦ : a favorable opportunity **2** ♦ : a direct or indirect cause **3** : the time of an event **4** : EXI-

GENCY **5** *pl* : AFFAIRS, BUSINESS **6** : a special event : CELEBRATION **7** ♦ : something that happens

♦ [1] chance, opening, opportunity, room ♦ [2] antecedent, cause, reason ♦ [7] affair, circumstance, episode, event, happening, incident, occurrence, thing

²**occasion** *vb* : BRING ABOUT, CAUSE
oc·ca·sion·al \ə-'kā-zhə-nəl\ *adj* **1** ♦ : happening or met with now and then \an ~ visits\ **2** : used or designed for a special occasion \an ~ verse\ — **oc·ca·sion·al·ly** *adv*

♦ casual, choppy, discontinuous, erratic, fitful, intermittent, irregular, spasmodic, sporadic, spotty, unsteady ♦ infrequent, rare, sporadic

oc·ci·den·tal \ˌäk-sə-'dent-ᵊl\ *adj, often cap* : WESTERN — **Occidental** *n*
Oc·ci·tan \'äk-sə-ˌtan\ *n* : a Romance language spoken in southern France
oc·clude \ə-'klüd\ *vb* **oc·clud·ed; oc·clud·ing 1** ♦ : to block by an obstacle : OBSTRUCT \an *occluded* artery\ **2** : to come together with opposing surfaces in contact — used of teeth — **oc·clu·sion** \-'klü-zhən\ *n* — **oc·clu·sive** \-'klü-siv\ *adj*

♦ block, choke, clog, close (off), congest, dam, jam, obstruct, plug (up), stop (up), stuff

¹**oc·cult** \ə-'kəlt\ *adj* **1** : not revealed : SECRET **2** ♦ : not easily apprehended or understood : MYSTERIOUS **3** ♦ : of or relating to supernatural agencies, their effects, or knowledge of them \the ~ arts\ — **oc·cult·ism** \-'kəl-ˌti-zəm\ *n* — **oc·cult·ist** \-'tist\ *n*

♦ [2] cryptic, darkling, deep, enigmatic, impenetrable, inscrutable, mysterious, mystic, uncanny ♦ [3] magic, magical, mystic, weird

²**occult** *n* : occult matters — used with *the*
oc·cu·pan·cy \'ä-kyə-pən-sē\ *n, pl* **-cies 1** : the act of occupying : the state of being occupied **2** : an occupied building or part of a building
oc·cu·pant \-pənt\ *n* ♦ : one who occupies something; *esp* : RESIDENT

♦ denizen, dweller, inhabitant, resident

oc·cu·pa·tion \ˌä-kyə-'pā-shən\ *n* **1** ♦ : an activity in which one engages; *esp* : VOCATION **2** : the taking possession of property; *also* : the taking possession of an area by a foreign military force — **oc·cu·pa·tion·al** \-shə-nəl\ *adj* — **oc·cu·pa·tion·al·ly** *adv*

♦ calling, employment, line, profession, trade, vocation, work

occupational therapy *n* : therapy by means of activity; *esp* : creative activity prescribed for its effect in promoting recovery or rehabilitation — **occupational therapist** *n*
oc·cu·pied \'ä-kyə-ˌpīd\ *adj* ♦ : engaged in activity

♦ active, assiduous, busy, diligent, engaged, laborious, sedulous, working

oc·cu·py \'ä-kyə-ˌpī\ *vb* **-py·ing 1** ♦ : to engage the attention or energies of **2** : to fill up (an extent in space or time) **3** ♦ : to take or hold possession of **4** : to reside in as owner or tenant — **oc·cu·pi·er** *n*

♦ [1] absorb, busy, engage, engross, enthrall, fascinate, grip, immerse, interest, intrigue, involve ♦ [3] command, enjoy, have, hold, own, possess, retain

oc·cur \ə-'kər\ *vb* **oc·curred; oc·cur·ring 1** : to be found or met with : APPEAR **2** ♦ : to come into existence : HAPPEN **3** : to come to mind \it *occurred* to her\

♦ be, befall, betide, chance, come, go, happen, pass, transpire

oc·cur·rence \ə-'kər-əns\ *n* **1** ♦ : something that takes place **2** : the action or process of occurring

♦ affair, circumstance, episode, event, happening, incident, occasion, thing

ocean \'ō-shən\ *n* **1** ♦ : the whole body of salt water that covers nearly three fourths of the surface of the earth **2** : any of the large bodies of water into which the great ocean is divided

♦ blue, brine, deep, sea

ocean·ar·i·um \ˌō-shə-'nar-ē-əm\ *n, pl* **-iums** *or* **-ia** \-ē-ə\ : a large marine aquarium
ocean·front \'ō-shən-ˌfrənt\ *n* : a shore area on the ocean
ocean·go·ing \-ˌgō-iŋ\ *adj* : of, relating to, or suitable for travel on the ocean
oce·an·ic \ˌō-shē-'a-nik\ *adj* ♦ : of or relating to the ocean

♦ marine, maritime, pelagic

ocean·og·ra·phy \ˌō-shə-'nä-grə-fē\ *n* : a science dealing with the ocean and its phenomena — **ocean·og·ra·pher** \-fər\ *n* — **ocean·o·graph·ic** \-nə-'gra-fik\ *adj*
oce·lot \'ä-sə-ˌlät, 'ō-\ *n* : a medium-sized American wildcat ranging southward from Texas to northern Argentina and having a tawny yellow or gray coat with black markings
ocher *or* **ochre** \'ō-kər\ *n* : an earthy usu. red or yellow iron ore used as a pigment; *also* : the color esp. of yellow ocher
o'·clock \ə-'kläk\ *adv* : according to the clock
OCR *abbr* optical character reader; optical character recognition
OCS *abbr* officer candidate school
oct *abbr* octavo
Oct *abbr* October
oc·ta·gon \'äk-tə-ˌgän\ *n* : a polygon of eight angles and eight sides — **oc·tag·o·nal** \äk-'ta-gən-ᵊl\ *adj*
oc·tane \'äk-ˌtān\ *n* : OCTANE NUMBER
octane number *n* : a number used to measure the antiknock properties of gasoline that increases as the likelihood of knocking decreases
oc·tave \'äk-tiv\ *n* **1** : a musical interval embracing eight degrees; *also* : a tone or note at this interval or the whole series of notes, tones, or keys within this interval **2** : a group of eight
oc·ta·vo \äk-'tā-vō, -'tä-\ *n, pl* **-vos 1** : the size of a piece of paper cut eight from a sheet **2** : a book printed on octavo pages
oc·tet \äk-'tet\ *n* **1** : a musical composition for eight voices or eight instruments; *also* : the performers of such a composition **2** : a group or set of eight
Oc·to·ber \äk-'tō-bər\ *n* : the 10th month of the year
oc·to·ge·nar·i·an \ˌäk-tə-jə-'ner-ē-ən\ *n* : a person whose age is in the eighties
oc·to·pus \'äk-tə-pəs\ *n, pl* **-pus·es** *or* **-pi** \-ˌpī\ : any of various sea mollusks with eight long muscular arms furnished with suckers
oc·to·syl·lab·ic \ˌäk-tə-sə-'la-bik\ *adj* : composed of verses having eight syllables — **octosyllabic** *n*
¹**oc·u·lar** \'ä-kyə-lər\ *adj* **1** ♦ : based on what has been seen : VISUAL **2** : of or relating to the eye or the eyesight

♦ optical, visual

²**ocular** *n* : EYEPIECE
oc·u·list \'ä-kyə-list\ *n* **1** : OPHTHALMOLOGIST **2** : OPTOMETRIST
¹**OD** \ˌō-'dē\ *n* : an overdose of a drug *esp.* a narcotic
²**OD** *vb* **OD'd** *or* **ODed; OD'·ing; OD's** : to become ill or die from an OD
³**OD** *abbr* **1** doctor of optometry **2** right eye **3** officer of the day **4** olive drab **5** overdraft **6** overdrawn
odd \'äd\ *adj* **1** : being only one of a pair or set \an ~ shoe\ **2** : somewhat more than the number mentioned \forty ~ years ago\ **3** : being an integer (as 1, 3, or 5) not divisible by two without leaving a remainder **4** : additional to what is usual \~ jobs\ **5** ♦ : differing markedly from the usual or ordinary or accepted : STRANGE \an ~ way of behaving\ — **odd·ness** *n*

♦ bizarre, curious, far-out, funny, kinky, outlandish, outré, peculiar, quaint, quirky, remarkable, screwy, strange, wacky, weird, wild ♦ aberrant, abnormal, atypical, exceptional, extraordinary, freak, peculiar, phenomenal, rare, singular, uncommon, uncustomary, unique, unusual, unwonted

odd·ball \'äd-ˌbȯl\ *n* ♦ : one that is eccentric — **oddball** *adj*

♦ character, crackpot, crank, eccentric, kook, nut, screwball, weirdo

odd·i·ty \'ä-də-tē\ *n, pl* **-ties 1** ♦ : one that is odd **2** ♦ : the quality or state of being odd

♦ [1] crotchet, eccentricity, idiosyncrasy, mannerism, peculiarity, quirk, singularity, trick ♦ [1, 2] curiosity, exotic, rarity

odd·ly \'äd-lē\ *adv* **1** : in an odd manner \an ~ shaped roof\ **2** : as is odd \~ enough, I agree\
odd·ment \'äd-mənt\ *n* : something left over : REMNANT
odds \'ädz\ *n pl* **1** ♦ : a difference by which one thing is favored over another **2** : DISAGREEMENT — usu. used with *at* **3** : the ratio between the amount to be paid for a winning bet and the amount of the bet \the horse went off at ~ 6–1\

♦ chance, percentage, probability

odds and ends *n pl* **1** ♦ : miscellaneous things or matters **2** ♦ : miscellaneous remnants or leftovers

♦ [1] notions, novelties, sundries ♦ [2] balance, leavings, leftovers, remainder, remains, remnant, residue, rest

odds–on \'ädz-'ȯn, -'än\ *adj* : having a better than even chance to win

ode \'ōd\ *n* : a lyric poem that expresses a noble feeling with dignity

odi•ous \'ō-dē-əs\ *adj* ♦ : causing or deserving hatred or repugnance — **odi•ous•ly** *adv* — **odi•ous•ness** *n*

♦ abhorrent, abominable, appalling, awful, distasteful, nauseating, noisome, obnoxious, offensive, repellent, repugnant, repulsive, revolting

odi•um \'ō-dē-əm\ *n* **1** : merited loathing : HATRED **2** ♦ : disrepute or infamy attached to something : DISGRACE ⟨the ∼ of defeat⟩

♦ discredit, disgrace, dishonor (*or* dishonour), disrepute, ignominy, infamy, opprobrium, reproach, shame

odom•e•ter \ō-'dä-mə-tər\ *n* : an instrument for measuring distance traveled (as by a vehicle)

odor *or Can and Brit* **odour** \'ō-dər\ *n* **1** ♦ : the quality of something that stimulates the sense of smell; *also* : a sensation resulting from such stimulation **2** : REPUTE, ESTIMATION — **odored** \'ō-dərd\ *adj* — **odor•less** *adj* — **odor•ous** *adj*

♦ redolence, scent, smell

odor•if•er•ous \ˌō-də-'ri-fə-rəs\ *adj* : having or yielding an odor

odour *Can and Brit var of* ODOR

od•ys•sey \'ä-də-sē\ *n, pl* **-seys** : a long wandering marked usu. by many changes of fortune

oe•cu•men•i•cal \ˌē-\ *chiefly Brit var of* ECUMENICAL

OED *abbr* Oxford English Dictionary

oe•de•ma *chiefly Brit var of* EDEMA

oe•di•pal \'e-də-pəl, 'ē-\ *adj, often cap* : of, relating to, or resulting from the Oedipus complex

Oe•di•pus complex \-pəs-\ *n* : the positive sexual feelings of a child toward the parent of the opposite sex and hostile or jealous feelings toward the parent of the same sex that may be a source of adult personality disorder when unresolved

OEO *abbr* Office of Economic Opportunity

o'er \'ōr\ *adv or prep* **1** : across a barrier or intervening space : OVER **2** : once more **3** : in or to a higher place

OES *abbr* Order of the Eastern Star

oe•soph•a•gus *chiefly Brit var of* ESOPHAGUS

oeu•vre \'ər-vrə\ *n, pl* **oeuvres** *same*\ : a substantial body of work constituting the lifework of a writer, an artist, or a composer

of \'əv, 'äv\ *prep* **1** : FROM ⟨a man ∼ the West⟩ **2** : having as a significant background or character element ⟨a man ∼ noble birth⟩ ⟨a woman ∼ ability⟩ **3** : owing to ⟨died ∼ flu⟩ **4** : BY ⟨the plays ∼ Shakespeare⟩ **5** : having as component parts or material, contents, or members ⟨a house ∼ brick⟩ ⟨a glass ∼ water⟩ ⟨a pack ∼ wolves⟩ **6** : belonging to or included by ⟨the front ∼ the house⟩ ⟨a time ∼ life⟩ ⟨one ∼ you⟩ ⟨the best ∼ its kind⟩ ⟨the son ∼ a doctor⟩ **7** ♦ : relating to : ABOUT ⟨tales ∼ the West⟩ **8** : connected with : OVER ⟨the queen ∼ England⟩ **9** : that is : signified as ⟨the city ∼ Rome⟩ **10** — used to indicate apposition of the words it joins ⟨a huge barn ∼ a house⟩ **11** : as concerns : FOR ⟨love ∼ nature⟩ **12** — used to indicate the application of an adjective ⟨fond ∼ candy⟩ **13** ♦ : preceding in time : BEFORE ⟨quarter ∼ ten⟩

♦ [7] about, apropos of, concerning, on, regarding, respecting, toward ♦ [13] ahead of, before, ere, previous to, prior to, to

OF *abbr* outfield

¹off \'òf\ *adv* **1** : from a place or position ⟨drove ∼ in a new car⟩; *also* : ASIDE ⟨turned ∼ into a side road⟩ **2** : at a distance in time or space ⟨stood ∼ a few yards⟩ ⟨several years ∼⟩ **3** : so as to be unattached or removed ⟨the lid blew ∼⟩ **4** : to a state of discontinuance, exhaustion, or completion ⟨shut the radio ∼⟩ **5** : away from regular work ⟨took time ∼ for lunch⟩

²off *prep* **1** : away from ⟨just ∼ the highway⟩ ⟨take it ∼ the table⟩ **2** : to seaward of ⟨two miles ∼ the coast⟩ **3** : FROM ⟨borrowed a dollar ∼ me⟩ **4** : at the expense of ⟨lives ∼ his parents⟩ **5** : not now engaged in ⟨∼ duty⟩ **6** : abstaining from ⟨∼ liquor⟩ **7** : below the usual level of ⟨∼ his game⟩

³off *adj* **1** : more removed or distant **2** : started on the way **3** ♦ : not operating **4** ♦ : not correct **5** : small in degree : REMOTE, SLIGHT **6** : of poor quality : INFERIOR **7** : provided for ⟨well ∼⟩

♦ [3] dead, dormant, fallow, free, idle, inactive, inert, inoperative, latent, vacant ♦ [4] erroneous, false, inaccurate, incorrect, inexact, invalid, unsound, untrue, wrong

⁴off *abbr* office; officer; official

of•fal \'ò-fəl\ *n* : the waste or by-product of a process; *esp* : the viscera and trimmings of a butchered animal removed in dressing

off and on *adv* : INTERMITTENTLY

¹off•beat \'òf-ˌbēt\ *n* : the unaccented part of a musical measure

²offbeat *adj* ♦ : deviating from conventional or accepted usage or conduct esp. in odd or whimsical ways

♦ curious, extraordinary, funny, odd, peculiar, rare, strange, unaccustomed, uncommon, unique, unusual, weird

off–col•or \'òf-'kə-lər\ *or* **off–col•ored** \-lərd\ *adj* **1** : not having the right or standard color **2** : of doubtful propriety : verging on indecency ⟨∼ stories⟩

of•fend \ə-'fend\ *vb* **1** ♦ : to violate a law or rule : SIN, TRANSGRESS **2** : to cause discomfort or pain : HURT **3** ♦ : to cause dislike or vexation

♦ [1] err, sin, transgress, trespass ♦ [3] affront, insult, outrage, slight, wound

of•fend•er *n* ♦ : one that offends

♦ criminal, crook, culprit, felon, lawbreaker, malefactor

of•fense *or* **of•fence** \ə-'fens, *esp for 2 & 3* 'ä-ˌfens\ *n* **1** : something that outrages the senses **2** ♦ : the act of attacking : ATTACK, ASSAULT **3** : the offensive team or members of a team playing offensive positions **4 a** ♦ : the act of displeasing or affronting **b** ♦ : the state of being insulted or morally outraged **5** ♦ : a breach of a moral or social code : SIN, MISDEED **6** ♦ : an infraction of law : CRIME

♦ [2] aggression, assault, attack, charge, descent, offensive, onset, onslaught, raid, rush, strike ♦ [4a] affront, barb, dart, dig, indignity, insult, name, outrage, put-down, sarcasm, slight, slur, wound ♦ [4b] dudgeon, huff, peeve, pique, resentment, umbrage ♦ [5, 6] breach, crime, error, malefaction, misdeed, misdoing, sin, transgression, trespass, violation, wrongdoing

¹of•fen•sive \ə-'fen-siv, *esp for 1 & 2* 'ä-ˌfen-\ *adj* **1** : AGGRESSIVE **2** : of or relating to an attempt to score in a game; *also* : of or relating to a team in possession of the ball or puck **3** ♦ : giving painful or unpleasant sensations : OBNOXIOUS **4** : INSULTING — **of•fen•sive•ly** *adv* — **of•fen•sive•ness** *n*

♦ awful, distasteful, foul, horrible, horrid, nauseating, noisome, objectionable, obnoxious, odious, repellent, repugnant, repulsive, shocking, ugly *Ant* inoffensive

²offensive *n* : the act of attacking with physical force or unfriendly words : ATTACK

¹of•fer \'ò-fər\ *vb* **of•fered**; **of•fer•ing 1** : SACRIFICE **2** ♦ : to present for acceptance : TENDER; *also* : to propose as payment **3** ♦ : to set before the mind (as for discussion, imitation, or action) : PROPOSE, SUGGEST; *also* : to declare one's readiness **4** : to try or begin to exert ⟨∼ resistance⟩ **5** : to place on sale **6** ♦ : to present in performance or exhibition

♦ [2] extend, give, proffer, tender ♦ [3] advance, pose, proffer, propose, propound, suggest, vote ♦ [6] carry, give, mount, present, stage

²offer *n* **1** ♦ : a presenting of something for acceptance : PROPOSAL **2** : BID **3** : TRY

♦ proffer, proposal, proposition, suggestion

of•fer•ing *n* : a sacrifice ceremonially offered as a part of worship

of•fer•to•ry \'ò-fər-ˌtōr-ē\ *n, pl* **-ries** : the presentation of offerings at a church service; *also* : the musical accompaniment during it

off–gas•sing \'òf-ˌga-siŋ\ *n* : the emission of esp. noxious gases (as from a building material)

off•hand \'òf-'hand\ *adj* ♦ : done or made without previous thought or preparation — **offhand** *adv*

♦ ad-lib, extemporaneous, impromptu, snap, unplanned, unpremeditated, unprepared, unrehearsed

off–hour \-ˌaů(-ə)r\ *n* : a period of time other than a rush hour; *also* : a period of time other than business hours

of•fice \'ò-fəs\ *n* **1** : a special duty or position; *esp* : a position of authority in government ⟨run for ∼⟩ **2** : a prescribed form or service of worship; *also* : RITE **3** : an assigned or assumed duty or role **4** : a place where a business is transacted or a service is supplied **5** ♦ : a major administrative unit in some governments

♦ bureau, department, desk, division

of•fice•hold•er \'ò-fəs-ˌhōl-dər\ *n* ♦ : one holding a public office

♦ functionary, officer, official, public servant

of•fi•cer \'ò-fə-sər\ *n* **1** ♦ : one charged with the enforcement of law **2** : one who holds an office of trust or authority **3** : a person who holds a position of authority or command in the armed forces; *esp* : COMMISSIONED OFFICER

♦ constable, cop, police officer

¹**of·fi·cial** \ə-'fi-shəl\ *n* ♦ : one who holds or is invested with an office : OFFICER

♦ functionary, officeholder, officer, public servant

²**official** *adj* **1** : of or relating to an office or to officers **2** : AUTHORIZED, AUTHORITATIVE **3** : befitting or characteristic of a person in office — **of·fi·cial·ly** *adv*

of·fi·cial·dom \ə-'fi-shəl-dəm\ *n* : officials as a class

of·fi·cial·ism \ə-'fi-shə-ˌli-zəm\ *n* \ : lack of flexibility and initiative combined with excessive adherence to regulations

of·fi·ci·ant \ə-'fi-shē-ənt\ *n* : one (as a priest) who officiates at a religious rite

of·fi·ci·ate \ə-'fi-shē-ˌāt\ *vb* **-at·ed; -at·ing 1** : to perform a ceremony, function, or duty **2** : to act in an official capacity

of·fi·cious \ə-'fi-shəs\ *adj* ♦ : volunteering one's services where they are neither asked for nor needed 〈an ∼ busybody〉 — **of·fi·cious·ly** *adv* — **of·fi·cious·ness** *n*

♦ intrusive, meddlesome, nosy, obtrusive, presumptuous, prying

off·ing \'ȯ-fiŋ\ *n* : the near or foreseeable future

off–line \'ȯf-ˌlīn\ *adj or adv* : not connected to or controlled directly by a computer

off of *prep* : OFF

off·print \'ȯf-ˌprint\ *n* : a separately printed excerpt (as from a magazine)

off–road \-'rōd\ *adj* : of, relating to, or being a vehicle designed for use away from public roads

off–sea·son \-ˌsēz-ᵊn\ *n* : a time of suspended or reduced activity

¹**off·set** \-ˌset\ *n* **1** : a sharp bend (as in a pipe) by which one part is turned aside out of line **2** : a printing process in which an inked impression is first made on a rubber-blanketed cylinder and then transferred to the paper **3** ♦ : something that serves to counterbalance or to compensate for something else

♦ balance, canceler, counterbalance, counterweight, equipoise

²**off·set** *vb* **off·set; off·set·ting 1** : to place over against : BALANCE **2** ♦ : to compensate for **3** : to form an offset in (as a wall)

♦ annul, cancel, compensate, correct, counteract, counterbalance, make up, neutralize

off·shoot \'ȯf-ˌshüt\ *n* **1** ♦ : a collateral or derived branch, descendant, or member **2** : a branch of a main stem (as of a plant)

♦ derivative, outgrowth, spin-off

¹**off·shore** \'ȯf-'shȯr\ *adv* **1** : at a distance from the shore **2** : outside the country : ABROAD

²**off·shore** \'ȯf-'shȯr\ *adj* **1** : moving away from the shore **2** : situated off the shore but within waters under a country's control

off·side \-'sīd\ *adv or adj* : illegally in advance of the ball or puck

off·spring \-ˌspriŋ\ *n, pl* **offspring** *also* **offsprings** ♦ : the product of the reproductive processes of an animal or plant : PROGENY

♦ issue, posterity, progeny, seed, spawn

off·stage \'ȯf-ˌstāj, -ˌstāj\ *adv or adj* **1** : off or away from the stage **2** : out of the public view 〈deals made ∼〉

off–the–record *adj* : given or made in confidence and not for publication

off–the–shelf *adj* : available as a stock item : not specially designed or made

off–the–wall *adj* : highly unusual : BIZARRE 〈∼ humor〉

off·track \'ȯf-ˌtrak\ *adv or adj* : away from a racetrack

off–white \'ȯf-'hwīt\ *n* : a yellowish or grayish white color

off year *n* **1** : a year in which no major election is held **2** : a year of diminished activity or production

oft \'ȯft\ *adv* : OFTEN

of·ten \'ȯ-fən\ *adv* ♦ : many times : FREQUENTLY

♦ constantly, continually, frequently, repeatedly *Ant* infrequently, rarely, seldom

of·ten·times \-ˌtīmz\ *or* **oft·times** \'ȯf-ˌtīmz, 'ȯft-\ *adv* : OFTEN

Og *symbol* oganesson

oga·nes·son \ˌō-gə-'ne-ˌsän, ä-\ *n* : a short-lived artificially produced radioactive chemical element

ogle \'ō-gəl\ *vb* **ogled; ogling** : to look at in a flirtatious way — **ogle** *n* — **ogler** *n*

ogre \'ō-gər\ *n* **1** : a monster of fairy tales and folklore that eats people **2** ♦ : a dreaded person or object

♦ bête noire, bogey, bugbear, hobgoblin

ogress \'ō-grəs\ *n* : a female ogre

oh \'ō\ *interj* **1** — used to express an emotion or in response to physical stimuli **2** — used in direct address

OH *abbr* Ohio

ohm \'ōm\ *n* : a unit of electrical resistance equal to the resistance of a circuit in which a potential difference of one volt produces a current of one ampere — **ohm·ic** \'ō-mik\ *adj*

ohm·me·ter \'ōm-ˌmē-tər\ *n* : an instrument for indicating resistance in ohms directly

¹**oil** \'ȯil\ *n* **1** : any of numerous fatty or greasy liquid substances obtained from plants, animals, or minerals and used for fuel, food, medicines, and manufacturing **2** : PETROLEUM **3 a** : artists' colors made with oil **b** : a painting in oil artist's colors — **oil·i·ness** \'ȯi-lē-nəs\ *n* — **oily** \'ȯi-lē\ *adj*

²**oil** *vb* ♦ : to put oil in or on — **oil·er** *n*

♦ grease, lubricate, slick, wax

oil·cloth \'ȯil(-ə)l-ˌklȯth\ *n* : cloth treated with oil or paint and used for table and shelf coverings

oil pan *n* : the lower section of a crankcase used as an oil reservoir

oil shale *n* : a rock (as shale) from which oil can be recovered

oil·skin \'ȯil(-ə)l-ˌskin\ *n* **1** : an oiled waterproof cloth **2** : an oilskin raincoat **3** *pl* : an oilskin coat and pants

oink \'ȯiŋk\ *n* : the natural noise of a hog — **oink** *vb*

oint·ment \'ȯint-mənt\ *n* : a salve for use on the skin

OJ *abbr* orange juice

Ojib·wa *or* **Ojib·way** \ō-'jib-ˌwä\ *n, pl* **Ojibwa** *or* **Ojibwas** *or* **Ojibway** *or* **Ojibways 1** : a member of a First Nations people of the region around Lake Superior and westward **2** : the Algonquian language of the Ojibwa people

OJT *abbr* on-the-job training

¹**OK** *or* **okay** \ō-'kā\ *adv* ♦ : ALL RIGHT

♦ all right, alright, yea, yes ♦ adequately, all right, fine, good, nicely, passably, satisfactorily, so-so, tolerably, well

²**OK** *or* **okay** *adj* ♦ : ALL RIGHT

♦ acceptable, adequate, all right, decent, fine, passable, respectable, satisfactory, tolerable ♦ agreeable, all right, alright, fine, good, palatable, satisfactory

³**OK** *or* **okay** *vb* **OK'd** *or* **okayed; OK'·ing** *or* **okay·ing 1** ♦ : to give formal or official sanction to : APPROVE, AUTHORIZE **2** ♦ : to have or express a favorable opinion of

♦ [1] approve, authorize, clear, ratify, sanction, warrant ♦ [2] accept, approve, care, countenance, favor (*or* favour), subscribe

⁴**OK** *or* **okay** *n* ♦ : an act or instance of approving

♦ approbation, approval, blessing, favor (*or* favour), imprimatur

⁵**OK** *abbr* Oklahoma

Okla *abbr* Oklahoma

okra \'ō-krə\ *n* : a tall annual plant related to the mallows that has edible green pods; *also* : these pods

¹**old** \'ōld\ *adj* **1** : ANCIENT; *also* : of long standing **2** *cap* : belonging to an early period 〈*Old* Irish〉 **3** : having existed for a specified period of time **4** ♦ : of or relating to a past era **5** ♦ : advanced in years **6** : showing the effects of age or use **7** : no longer in use **8** ♦ : having been previously — **old·ish** \'ōl-dish\ *adj*

♦ [4] age-old, ancient, antediluvian, antique, dateless, hoary, venerable ♦ [5] ancient, elderly, geriatric, senior ♦ [8] erstwhile, former, late, onetime, past, sometime, whilom

²**old** *n* : old or earlier time 〈days of ∼〉

old·en \'ōl-dən\ *adj* : of or relating to a bygone era

¹**old–fash·ioned** \'ōld-'fa-shənd\ *adj* **1** ♦ : of, relating to, or characteristic of a past era **2** ♦ : adhering to customs of a past era : CONSERVATIVE

♦ [1] antique, old-time, quaint *Ant* contemporary, hot, mod, modern, newfangled, new-fashioned, ultramodern ♦ [2] conservative, orthodox, reactionary, traditional

²**old–fashioned** *n* : a cocktail usu. made with whiskey, bitters, sugar, a twist of lemon peel, and water or soda water

old–growth \'ōld-'grōth\ *adj* : of, relating to, or being a forest with large old trees, numerous snags and woody debris, and a multilayered canopy

old guard *n, often cap O&G* : the conservative members of an organization

old hat *adj* **1** : OLD-FASHIONED **2** : STALE, TRITE

old·ie \'ōl-dē\ *n* : something old; *esp* : a popular song from the past

old lady *n* ♦ : a female partner in a marriage

♦ helpmate, lady, wife

old–line \'ōld-'līn\ *adj* **1** : ORIGINAL, ESTABLISHED 〈an ∼ business〉 **2** : adhering to old policies or practices

old maid *n* **1** : SPINSTER **2** : a prim fussy person

old–maid·ish \'ōld-'mā-dish\ *adj* ♦ : characteristic of an old maid

♦ choosy, dainty, delicate, demanding, exacting, fastidious, finicky, fussy, nice, particular, picky

old man *n* 1 : HUSBAND 2 : a male parent : FATHER

old–school *adj* : adhering to traditional policies or practices ⟨an ~ politician⟩

old•ster \'ōld-stər\ *n* ♦ : an old or elderly person

♦ ancient, elder, golden-ager, senior citizen

Old Testament *n* : the first of the two chief divisions of the Christian Scripture

old–time \'ōld-'tīm\ *adj* 1 ♦ : of, relating to, or characteristic of an earlier period 2 : of long standing

♦ antique, old-fashioned, quaint

old–tim•er \-'tī-mər\ *n* 1 : veteran 2 : an aging or elderly person : OLDSTER

old wives' tale *n* ♦ : an often traditional belief that is not based on fact

♦ error, fallacy, falsehood, falsity, illusion, misconception, myth, untruth

old–world \-'wərld\ *adj* : having old-fashioned charm

Old World *n* : the eastern hemisphere exclusive of Australia; *esp* : continental Europe

ole•ag•i•nous \ˌō-lē-'a-jə-nəs\ *adj* : OILY

ole•an•der \'ō-lē-ˌan-dər\ *n* : a poisonous evergreen shrub often grown for its fragrant white to red flowers

oleo \'ō-lē-ˌō\ *n, pl* **ole•os** : MARGARINE

oleo•mar•ga•rine \ˌō-lē-ō-'mär-jə-rən\ *n* : MARGARINE

ol•fac•to•ry \äl-'fak-tə-rē, ōl-\ *adj* : of or relating to the sense of smell

oli•gar•chy \'ä-lə-ˌgär-kē, 'ō-\ *n, pl* **-chies** 1 : a government in which power is in the hands of a few 2 : a state having an oligarchy; *also* : the group holding power in such a state — **oli•garch** \-ˌgärk\ *n* — **oli•gar•chic** \ˌä-lə-'gär-kik, ˌō-\ *or* **oli•gar•chi•cal** \-ki-kəl\ *adj*

Oli•go•cene \'ä-li-gō-ˌsēn, ə-'li-gə-ˌsēn\ *adj* : of, relating to, or being the epoch of the Tertiary between the Eocene and the Miocene — **Oligocene** *n*

olio \'ō-lē-ˌō\ *n, pl* **oli•os** : HODGEPODGE, MEDLEY

ol•ive \'ä-liv\ *n* 1 : an Old World evergreen tree grown in warm regions for its fruit that is a food and the source of an edible oil (**olive oil**); *also* : the fruit 2 : a dull yellowish green color

olive drab *n* 1 : a grayish olive color 2 : an olive drab wool or cotton fabric; *also* : a uniform of this fabric

ol•iv•ine \'ä-lə-ˌvēn\ *n* : a usu. greenish mineral that is a complex silicate of magnesium and iron

Olym•pic Games \ō-'lim-pik-\ *n pl* : a modified revival of an ancient Greek festival consisting of international athletic contests that are held at separate winter and summer gatherings at four-year intervals

om \'ōm\ *n* : a mantra consisting of the sound "om" used in contemplating ultimate reality

Oma•ha \'ō-mə-ˌhä, -ˌhó\ *n, pl* **Omaha** *or* **Omahas** : a member of an Indigenous people of northeastern Nebraska; *also* : the language of the Omaha people

om•buds•man \'äm-ˌbudz-mən, äm-'budz-\ *n, pl* **-men** \-mən\ 1 : a government official appointed to investigate complaints made by individuals against abuses or capricious acts of public officials 2 : one that investigates reported complaints (as from students or consumers)

ome•ga \ō-'mā-gə\ *n* : the 24th and last letter of the Greek alphabet — Ω or ω

om•elet *or* **om•elette** \'äm-lət, 'ä-mə-\ *n* : eggs beaten with milk or water, cooked without stirring until set, and folded over

omen \'ō-mən\ *n* ♦ : an event or phenomenon believed to be a sign or warning of a future occurrence

♦ augury, auspice, foreboding, portent, presage

om•i•cron \'ä-mə-ˌkrän, 'ō-\ *n* : the 15th letter of the Greek alphabet — O or o

om•i•nous \'ä-mə-nəs\ *adj* 1 ♦ : foretelling evil : THREATENING 2 : being or exhibiting an omen — **om•i•nous•ly** *adv* — **om•i•nous•ness** *n*

♦ baleful, dire, foreboding, menacing, portentous, sinister

omis•si•ble \ō-'mi-sə-bəl\ *adj* : that may be omitted

omis•sion \ō-'mi-shən\ *n* 1 : something neglected or left undone 2 : the act of omitting : the state of being omitted 3 ♦ : apathy toward or neglect of duty : lack of action

♦ delinquency, dereliction, laxity, laxness, neglect, negligence, remissness, slackness

omit \ō-'mit\ *vb* **omit•ted; omit•ting** 1 : to leave out or leave unmentioned 2 ♦ : to fail to perform : NEGLECT

♦ fail, forget, neglect

¹**om•ni•bus** \'äm-ni-(ˌ)bəs\ *n* : BUS

²**omnibus** *adj* ♦ : of, relating to, or providing for many things at once ⟨an ~ bill⟩

♦ compendious, complete, comprehensive, encyclopedic, full, global, inclusive, panoramic, universal

om•nip•o•tent \äm-'ni-pə-tənt\ *adj* : having unlimited authority or influence : ALMIGHTY ⟨an ~ ruler⟩ — **om•nip•o•tence** \-tən(t)s\ *n* — **om•nip•o•tent•ly** *adv*

om•ni•pres•ent \ˌäm-ni-'prez-ᵊnt\ *adj* : present in all places at all times ⟨an ~ problem⟩ — **om•ni•pres•ence** \-ᵊns\ *n*

om•ni•scient \äm-'ni-shənt\ *adj* : having infinite awareness, understanding, and insight — **om•ni•science** \-shəns\ *n* — **om•ni•scient•ly** *adv*

om•ni•um–gath•er•um \ˌäm-nē-əm-'ga-thə-rəm\ *n, pl* **omnium–gatherums** : a miscellaneous collection

om•niv•o•rous \äm-'ni-və-rəs\ *adj* 1 : feeding on both animal and vegetable substances 2 : AVID ⟨an ~ reader⟩ — **om•niv•o•rous•ly** *adv*

¹**on** \'ón, 'än\ *prep* 1 : in or to a position over and in contact with ⟨jumped ~ his horse⟩ 2 : touching the surface of ⟨shadows ~ the wall⟩ 3 : AT, TO ⟨~ the right were the mountains⟩ 4 : IN, ABOARD ⟨went ~ the train⟩ 5 : during or at the time of ⟨came ~ Monday⟩ ⟨every hour ~ the hour⟩ 6 : through the agency of ⟨was cut ~ a tin can⟩ 7 : in a state or process of ⟨~ fire⟩ ⟨~ the wane⟩ 8 : connected with as a member or participant ⟨~ a committee⟩ ⟨~ tour⟩ 9 — used to indicate a basis, source, or standard of computation ⟨has it ~ good authority⟩ ⟨10 cents ~ the dollar⟩ 10 : with regard to ⟨a monopoly ~ wheat⟩ 11 : at or toward as an object ⟨crept up ~ her⟩ 12 : used as a function word to indicate the subject of study, discussion, or consideration : ABOUT, CONCERNING ⟨a book ~ minerals⟩

²**on** *adv* 1 : in or into a position of contact with or attachment to a surface 2 ♦ : forward or at a more advanced point in space or time : FORWARD 3 : into operation

♦ ahead, along, forth, forward, onward

³**on** *adj* ♦ : being in operation or in progress

♦ active, alive, functional, living, operational, operative, running, working

ON *abbr* Ontario

¹**once** \'wəns\ *adv* 1 : one time only 2 : at any one time 3 : FORMERLY 4 : by one degree of relationship

²**once** *n* : one single time — **at once** 1 : at the same time 2 : IMMEDIATELY

³**once** *adj* : FORMER

⁴**once** *conj* : AS SOON AS

once–over \'wəns-ˌō-vər\ *n* : a swift examination or survey

on•co•gene \'äŋ-kō-ˌjēn\ *n* : a gene having the potential to cause a normal cell to become cancerous

on•col•o•gy \än-'kä-lə-jē\ *n* : the study of tumors — **on•co•log•i•cal** \ˌäŋ-kə-'lä-ji-kəl\ *also* **on•co•log•ic** \-jik\ *adj* — **on•col•o•gist** \än-'kä-lə-jist\ *n*

on•com•ing \'ón-ˌkə-miŋ, 'än-\ *adj* ♦ : coming nearer in time or space ⟨~ traffic⟩

♦ coming, forthcoming, imminent, impending, pending

¹**one** \'wən\ *adj* 1 : being a single unit or thing ⟨~ person went⟩ 2 : being one in particular ⟨early ~ morning⟩ 3 : being the same in kind or quality ⟨both of ~ species⟩; *also* : UNITED 4 ♦ : being not specified or fixed ⟨~ day soon⟩

♦ anonymous, certain, some, unidentified, unnamed, unspecified

²**one** *n* 1 : the number denoting unity 2 : the 1st in a set or series 3 : a single person or thing — **one•ness** \'wən-nəs\ *n*

³**one** *pron* 1 : a certain indefinitely indicated person or thing ⟨saw ~ of his friends⟩ 2 : a person in general ⟨~ never knows⟩ 3 — used in place of a first-person pronoun

Onei•da \ō-'nī-də\ *n, pl* **Oneida** *or* **Oneidas** : a member of an Indigenous people orig. of New York; *also* : the language of the Oneida people

one–man band *n* 1 : a musician who plays several instruments during a solo performance 2 : a person who alone undertakes or is responsible for several tasks

oner•ous \'ä-nə-rəs, 'ō-\ *adj* ♦ : imposing or constituting a burden ⟨an ~ task⟩

♦ arduous, burdensome, challenging, demanding, exacting, grueling, laborious, taxing, toilsome

one·self \(ˌ)wən-'self\ *also* **one's self** *pron* : one's own self — usu. used reflexively or for emphasis

one–sid·ed \'wən-'sī-dəd\ *adj* **1** : having or occurring on one side only; *also* : having one side prominent or more developed **2** ♦ : of, relating to, or affecting one side of a subject : PARTIAL ⟨a ~ interpretation⟩

♦ biased, partial, partisan, prejudiced

one·time \-ˌtīm\ *adj* ♦ : of, relating to, or occurring in the past : FORMER

♦ erstwhile, former, late, old, past, sometime, whilom

one–to–one \ˌwən-tə-'wən\ *adj* : pairing each element of a set uniquely with an element of another set

one up *adj* : being in a position of advantage ⟨was *one up* on the others⟩

one–way *adj* : moving, allowing movement, or functioning in only one direction ⟨~ streets⟩

on·go·ing \'ȯn-ˌgō-iŋ, 'än-\ *adj* **1** ♦ : continuously moving forward **2** ♦ : being actually in process

♦ [1] afoot, proceeding *Ant* arrested, halted, stalled, stopped ♦ [2] current, extant, present

on·ion \'ən-yən\ *n* : the pungent edible bulb of a widely cultivated plant related to the lilies; *also* : this plant

on·ion·skin \-ˌskin\ *n* : a thin strong translucent paper of very light weight

on·line \'ȯn-'līn, 'än-\ *adj or adv* : connected to, served by, or available through a computer network (as the Internet); *also* : done while online

on·look·er \'ȯn-ˌlu̇-kər, 'än-\ *n* : SPECTATOR

¹on·ly \'ōn-lē\ *adj* **1** ♦ : unquestionably the best **2** ♦ : alone in a class or category : SOLE

♦ [1] incomparable, inimitable, matchless, nonpareil, peerless, unequaled, unmatched, unparalleled, unrivaled, unsurpassed ♦ [2] alone, lone, singular, sole, solitary, special, unique

²only *adv* **1** : as a single fact or instance and nothing more or different : MERELY, JUST ⟨~ $2⟩ **2** ♦ : to the exclusion of all else : SOLELY ⟨known ~ to me⟩ **3** : at the very least ⟨was ~ too true⟩ **4** : as a final result ⟨will ~ make you sick⟩ **5** ♦ : in the immediate past

♦ [2] alone, exclusively, just, simply, solely ♦ [5] freshly, just, late, lately, new, newly, now, recently

³only *conj* ♦ : except that

♦ but, except, yet

on·o·mato·poe·ia \ˌä-nə-ˌmä-tə-'pē-ə\ *n* **1** : formation of words in imitation of natural sounds (as *buzz* or *hiss*) **2** : the use of words whose sound suggests the sense — **on·o·mato·poe·ic** \-'pē-ik\ *or* **on·o·mato·po·et·ic** \-pō-'e-tik\ *adj* — **on·o·mato·poe·i·cal·ly** \-'pē-ə-k(ə-)lē\ *or* **on·o·mato·po·et·i·cal·ly** \-pō-'e-ti-k(ə-)lē\ *adv*

On·on·da·ga \ˌä-nən-'dȯ-gə, -'dä-, -'dä-\ *n, pl* **-ga** *or* **-gas** : a member of an Indigenous people of New York and Canada; *also* : the language of the Onondaga people

on·rush \'ȯn-ˌrəsh, 'än-\ *n* ♦ : a rushing onward — **on·rush·ing** *adj*

♦ advance, advancement, furtherance, headway, march, passage, process, procession, progress, progression

on–screen \'ȯn-ˌskrēn, 'än-\ *adv or adj* : on a screen (as of a computer or television)

on·set \-ˌset\ *n* **1** : the act of attacking with physical force or unfriendly words : ATTACK **2** ♦ : the point at which something begins : BEGINNING

♦ beginning, birth, commencement, dawn, genesis, launch, morning, outset, start, threshold

on·shore \-ˌshȯr\ *adj* **1** : moving toward the shore **2** : situated on or near the shore — **on·shore** \-'shȯr\ *adv*

on·slaught \'ȯn-ˌslȯt, 'än-\ *n* ♦ : a fierce attack; *also* : something resembling such an attack ⟨an ~ of questions⟩

♦ aggression, assault, attack, charge, descent, offense (*or* offence), offensive, onset, raid, rush, strike

Ont *abbr* Ontario

on·to \'ȯn-tü, 'än-\ *prep* : to a position or point on

onus \'ō-nəs\ *n* **1** : BURDEN **2** : OBLIGATION **3** : BLAME

¹on·ward \'ȯn-wərd, 'än-\ *also* **on·wards** \-wərdz\ *adv* ♦ : toward or at a point lying ahead in space or time : FORWARD

♦ ahead, along, forth, forward, on

²onward *adj* : directed or moving onward : FORWARD

on·yx \'ä-niks\ *n* : a translucent chalcedony in parallel layers of different colors

oo·dles \'üd-ᵊlz\ *n pl* ♦ : a great quantity : LOT

♦ abundance, deal, gobs, heap, loads, lot, pile, plenty, quantity, scads

oo·lite \'ō-ə-ˌlīt\ *n* : a rock consisting of small round grains cemented together — **oo·lit·ic** \ˌō-ə-'li-tik\ *adj*

¹ooze \'üz\ *n* **1** : a soft deposit (as of mud) on the bottom of a body of water **2** ♦ : soft wet ground : MUD

♦ mire, muck, mud, slime, slop, sludge, slush

²ooze *vb* **oozed; ooz·ing** **1** ♦ : to flow or leak out slowly or imperceptibly **2** ♦ : EXUDE

♦ [1, 2] bleed, exude, percolate, seep, strain, sweat, weep

³ooze *n* : something that oozes

oozy \'ü-zē\ *adj* ♦ : containing or composed of ooze

♦ miry, mucky, muddy, slimy, slushy

op *abbr* **1** operation; operative; operator **2** opportunity **3** opus

OP *abbr* **1** observation post **2** out of print

opac·i·ty \ō-'pa-sə-tē\ *n, pl* **-ties** **1** : the quality or state of being opaque **2** ♦ : obscurity of meaning **3** : mental dullness **4** : an opaque spot in a normally transparent structure

♦ ambiguity, darkness, murkiness, obscurity

opal \'ō-pəl\ *n* : a mineral with iridescent colors that is used as a gem

opal·es·cent \ˌō-pə-'les-ᵊnt\ *adj* : IRIDESCENT — **opal·es·cence** \-ᵊns\ *n*

opaque \ō-'pāk\ *adj* **1** : blocking the passage of radiant energy and esp. light **2** ♦ : not easily understood **3** : OBTUSE — **opaque·ly** *adv* — **opaque·ness** *n*

♦ bleary, dim, faint, foggy, fuzzy, hazy, indefinite, indistinct, indistinguishable, murky, nebulous, obscure, shadowy, unclear, undefined, undetermined, vague

op art \'äp-\ *n* : OPTICAL ART — **op artist** *n*

op cit *abbr* in the work cited

ope \'ōp\ *vb* **oped; op·ing** *archaic* : OPEN

OPEC *abbr* Organization of Petroleum Exporting Countries

op–ed \'äp-'ed\ *n, often cap O&E* : a page of special features usu. opposite the editorial page of a newspaper

¹open \'ō-pən\ *adj* **open·er; open·est** **1** : not shut or shut up ⟨an ~ door⟩ **2 a** : not secret or hidden **b** ♦ : free from reserve or pretense : FRANK **3 a** : not enclosed or covered ⟨an ~ fire⟩ **b** ♦ : not protected or covered **4** ♦ : free to be entered or used ⟨an ~ tournament⟩ **5** ♦ : easy to get through or see ⟨~ country⟩ **6** : spread out : EXTENDED **7** : not decided ⟨an ~ question⟩ **8 a** : readily accessible and cooperative; *also* : GENEROUS **b** : willing to hear and consider or to accept and deal with **9** : having components separated by a space in writing and printing ⟨the name *Spanish moss* is an ~ compound⟩ **10** : having openings, interruptions, or spaces ⟨an ~ mesh⟩ **11** : ready to operate ⟨stores are ~⟩ **12** : free from restraints or controls ⟨~ season⟩ — **open·ly** *adv*

♦ [2b] candid, direct, forthright, foursquare, frank, honest, outspoken, plain, straight, straightforward, unguarded, unreserved ♦ [3b] bald, bare, exposed, naked, uncovered ♦ [4] free-for-all, public, unrestricted *Ant* closed, exclusive, private, restricted ♦ [5] clear, free, unobstructed *Ant* blocked, closed, obstructed, uncleared ♦ [7] pending, undecided, undetermined, unresolved, unsettled

²open \'ō-pən\ *vb* **opened; open·ing** **1 a** : to change or move from a shut position **b** ♦ : to make open by clearing away obstacles **2** : to make accessible **3** : to make openings in **4** : to make or become functional ⟨~ a store⟩ **5** : REVEAL; *also* : ENLIGHTEN **6** ♦ : to enter upon : BEGIN — **open·er** *n*

♦ [1b] clear, free, unblock ♦ [6] begin, commence, embark (on *or* upon), enter, get off, launch, start, strike

³open *n* **1** ♦ : open and unobstructed space : OUTDOORS **2** : a contest or tournament open to all

♦ nature, outdoors, wild, wilderness

open–air *adj* : of or relating to the outdoors : OUTDOOR ⟨~ theaters⟩

open arms *n pl* : an eager or warm welcome

open–hand·ed \ˌō-pən-'han-dəd\ *adj* ♦ : liberal in giving : GENEROUS — **open–hand·ed·ly** *adv*

♦ bountiful, charitable, free, generous, liberal, munificent, unselfish, unsparing

open–heart *adj* : of, relating to, or performed on a heart temporarily relieved of circulatory function and laid open for repair of defects or damage

open–hearth *adj* : of, relating to, or being a process of making steel in a furnace that reflects the heat from the roof onto the material

open·ing *n* **1** : an act or instance of making or becoming open **2** : BEGINNING **3 ♦** : something that is open **4 ♦** : a favorable opportunity or circumstance : OCCASION; *also* : an opportunity for employment

♦ [3] breach, break, discontinuity, gap, gulf, hole, interval, rent, rift, separation ♦ [4] chance, occasion, opportunity, room

open mike *n* : an event in which amateurs may perform

open–mind·ed \ˌō-pən-ˈmīn-dəd\ *adj* **♦** : free from rigidly fixed preconceptions — **open–mind·ed·ness** *n*

♦ broad-minded, liberal, nonorthodox, nontraditional, progressive, radical, unconventional, unorthodox ♦ broad-minded, open, receptive *Ant* narrow-minded

open·ness *n* **♦** : the quality or state of being open

♦ candor (*or* candour), directness, forthrightness, frankness, plainness

open sentence *n* : a statement (as in mathematics) containing at least one blank or unknown so that when the blank is filled or a quantity substituted for the unknown the statement becomes a complete statement that is either true or false

open shop *n* : an establishment having members and nonmembers of a labor union on the payroll

open·work \ˈō-pən-ˌwərk\ *n* : work so made as to show openings through its substance ⟨a railing of wrought-iron ∼⟩ — **open–worked** \-ˌwərkt\ *adj*

¹**opera** *pl of* OPUS

²**op·era** \ˈä-prə, -pə-rə\ *n* : a drama set to music — **op·er·at·ic** \ˌä-pə-ˈra-tik\ *adj*

op·er·a·ble \ˈä-pə-rə-bəl\ *adj* **1 ♦** : fit, possible, or desirable to use **2** : likely to result in a favorable outcome upon surgical treatment

♦ available, fit, functional, practicable, serviceable, usable, useful

opera glasses *n pl* : small binoculars for use in a theater

op·er·ate \ˈä-pə-ˌrāt\ *vb* **-at·ed; -at·ing 1 ♦** : to perform work : FUNCTION **2 ♦** : to produce an effect **3 ♦** : to put or keep in operation; *also* : to manage the operation of **4** : to perform or subject to an operation — **op·er·a·tor** \-ˌrā-tər\ *n*

♦ [1, 2] act, function, perform, take, work ♦ [3] command, control, direct, drive, guide, handle, maneuver, pilot, run, steer, use, wield, work ♦ [3] administer, carry on, conduct, govern, guide, handle, manage, oversee, regulate, run, superintend, supervise

operating system *n* : software that controls the operation of a computer

op·er·a·tion \ˌä-pə-ˈrā-shən\ *n* **1** : a doing or performing of practical work **2 a ♦** : an exertion of power or influence **b ♦** : method or manner of functioning **3** : a surgical procedure **4 a** : a process of deriving one mathematical expression from others according to a rule **b** : a function or correlation when conceived as a process of proceeding from one or more entities to another according to a definite rule **5** : a usu. military action or mission **6** : a usu. small business

♦ [2a] administration, conduct, control, direction, government, guidance, management, oversight, regulation, running, superintendence, supervision ♦ [2b] course, procedure, proceeding, process ♦ [2b] application, employment, exercise, play, use

op·er·a·tion·al \-shə-nəl\ *adj* **♦** : of or relating to operation or an operation

♦ active, alive, functional, living, on, operative, running, working

¹**op·er·a·tive** \ˈä-pə-rə-tiv, -ˌrā-\ *adj* **1** : producing an appropriate effect **2** : engaged in some form of operation : OPERATING ⟨an ∼ force⟩ **3** : having to do with physical operations; *also* : WORKING ⟨an ∼ craftsman⟩ **4** : based on or consisting of an operation ⟨∼ dentistry⟩

²**operative** *n* **1** : OPERATOR **2 a** : a secret agent **b ♦** : a person not a member of a police force who is licensed to do detective work

♦ detective, investigator, shadow, sleuth, tail

op·er·et·ta \ˌä-pə-ˈre-tə\ *n* : a light musical-dramatic work with a romantic plot, spoken dialogue, and dancing scenes

oph·thal·mic \äf-ˈthal-mik, äp-\ *adj* : of, relating to, or located near the eye

oph·thal·mol·o·gy \ˌäf-ˌthal-ˈmä-lə-jē, ˌäp-\ *n* : a branch of medicine dealing with the structure, functions, and diseases of the eye — **oph·thal·mol·o·gist** \-jist\ *n*

oph·thal·mo·scope \äf-ˈthal-mə-ˌskōp, äp-\ *n* : an instrument for use in viewing the interior of the eye and esp. the retina

¹**opi·ate** \ˈō-pē-ət, -pē-ˌāt\ *n* **1** : a preparation or derivative of opium **2** : a narcotic or a substance with similar activity

²**opiate** *adj* : inducing sleep : NARCOTIC

♦ drowsy, hypnotic, narcotic, slumberous

opine \ō-ˈpīn\ *vb* **opined; opin·ing ♦** : to express an opinion

♦ comment, note, observe, remark

opin·ion \ə-ˈpin-yən\ *n* **1 ♦** : a belief stronger than impression and less strong than positive knowledge **2** : JUDGMENT **3 ♦** : a formal statement by an expert after careful study

♦ [1] belief, conviction, eye, feeling, judgment (*or* judgement), mind, notion, persuasion, sentiment, verdict, view ♦ [3] conclusion, decision, deliverance, determination, diagnosis, judgment (*or* judgement), resolution, verdict

opin·ion·at·ed \ə-ˈpin-yə-ˌnā-təd\ *adj* **♦** : obstinately adhering to personal opinions

♦ dogged, hardheaded, headstrong, mulish, obdurate, obstinate, peevish, pertinacious, perverse, pigheaded, stubborn, unyielding, willful

opi·um \ˈō-pē-əm\ *n* : an addictive narcotic drug that is the dried latex of a Eurasian poppy

opos·sum \ə-ˈpä-səm\ *n, pl* **opossums** *also* **opossum** : an omnivorous tree-dwelling No. American marsupial that is active chiefly at night and has a pointed snout and a prehensile tail

opp *abbr* opposite

op·po·nent \ə-ˈpō-nənt\ *n* **♦** : one that opposes : ADVERSARY

♦ adversary, antagonist, rival

op·por·tune \ˌä-pər-ˈtün, -ˈtyün\ *adj* : SUITABLE — **op·por·tune·ly** *adv*

op·por·tun·ism \ˌä-pər-ˈtü-ˌni-zəm, -ˈtyü-\ *n* : a taking advantage of opportunities or circumstances esp. with little regard for principles or ultimate consequences — **op·por·tun·ist** \-nist\ *n* — **op·por·tu·nis·tic** \-ˌtü-ˈnis-tik, -tyü-\ *adj*

op·por·tu·ni·ty \ˌä-pər-ˈtü-nə-tē, -ˈtyü-\ *n, pl* **-ties 1 ♦** : a favorable combination of circumstances, time, and place **2** : a chance for advancement

♦ chance, occasion, opening, room

op·pose \ə-ˈpōz\ *vb* **op·posed; op·pos·ing 1** : to place opposite or against something (as to provide resistance or contrast) **2 ♦** : to strive against : offer resistance to — **op·po·si·tion** \ˌä-pə-ˈzi-shən\ *n*

♦ buck, defy, fight, repel, resist, withstand ♦ battle, combat, contend, counter, fight

¹**op·po·site** \ˈä-pə-zət\ *adj* **1** : set over against something that is at the other end or side **2** : OPPOSED, HOSTILE; *also* : CONTRARY **3** : contrarily turned or moving **4 ♦** : diametrically different **5** : being the other of a matching or contrasting pair — **op·po·site·ly** *adv* — **op·po·site·ness** *n*

♦ antipodal, antithetical, contradictory, contrary, diametric, polar

²**opposite** *n* **♦** : one that is opposed or contrary

♦ antipode, antithesis, contrary, negative, reverse

³**opposite** *adv* : on or to an opposite side

⁴**opposite** *prep* : across from and usu. facing ⟨the house ∼ ours⟩

op·press \ə-ˈpres\ *vb* **1** : to crush by abuse of power or authority **2 ♦** : to be a burden to mentally or spiritually

♦ burden, depress, sadden ♦ carry away, crush, devastate, floor, overcome, overpower, overwhelm, prostrate, snow under, swamp

op·pres·sion \ə-ˈpre-shən\ *n* **1** : unjust or cruel exercise of power or authority **2** : a sense of being affected as if with a heavy weight in body or mind : DEPRESSION

op·pres·sive \-ˈpre-siv\ *adj* **♦** : unreasonably burdensome or severe

♦ burdensome, grim, hard, harsh, heavy, onerous, rough, rugged, severe, stiff, tough, trying

op·pres·sive·ly *adv* **♦** : in an oppressive manner

♦ hard, hardly, harshly, ill, roughly, severely, sternly, stiffly

op·pres·sor \-ˈpre-sər\ *n* **♦** : one that oppresses esp. when in a position of public authority

♦ autocrat, despot, dictator, tyrant

op·pro·bri·ous \ə-'prō-brē-əs\ *adj* ♦ : expressing or deserving opprobrium — **op·pro·bri·ous·ly** *adv*

♦ abusive, scurrilous

op·pro·bri·um \-brē-əm\ *n* **1** : something that brings disgrace **2** ♦ : public disgrace or ill fame that follows from conduct considered grossly wrong or vicious : INFAMY

♦ discredit, disgrace, dishonor (*or* dishonour), disrepute, ignominy, infamy, odium, reproach, shame

[1]**opt** \'äpt\ *vb* **1** ♦ : to make a choice **2** ♦ : to decide in favor of something — usu. used with *for*

♦ [1] choose, conclude, decide, determine, figure, resolve ♦ *usu* **opt for** [2] choose, cull, elect, handpick, name, pick, prefer, select, single, take

[2]**opt** *abbr* **1** optical; optician; optics **2** option; optional
op·tic \'äp-tik\ *adj* : of or relating to vision or the eye
op·ti·cal \'äp-ti-kəl\ *adj* **1** : relating to optics **2** ♦ : of or relating to vision : OPTIC **3** : of, relating to, or using light

♦ ocular, visual

optical art *n* : nonobjective art characterized by the use of geometric patterns often for an illusory effect
optical disk *n* : a disk on which information has been recorded digitally and which is read using a laser
optical fiber *n* : a single fiber-optic strand
op·ti·cian \äp-'ti-shən\ *n* **1** : a maker of or dealer in optical items and instruments **2** : a person who makes or orders eyeglass and contact lenses to prescription and sells glasses
op·tics \'äp-tiks\ *n pl* **1** : a science that deals with the nature and properties of light **2** : the aspects of an action, policy, or decision that relate to public perceptions
op·ti·mal \'äp-tə-məl\ *adj* : most desirable or satisfactory — **op·ti·mal·ly** *adv*
op·ti·mism \'äp-tə-ˌmi-zəm\ *n* **1** : a doctrine that this world is the best possible world **2** : an inclination to anticipate the best possible outcome of actions — **op·ti·mist** \-ˌmist\ *n* — **op·ti·mis·tic** \-ˌmis-tik\ *adj*
op·ti·mize \'äp-tə-ˌmīz\ *vb* **-mized; -miz·ing** : to make as perfect, effective, or functional as possible — **op·ti·mi·za·tion** \ˌäp-tə-mə-'zā-shən\ *n*
op·ti·mum \'äp-tə-məm\ *n, pl* **-ma** \-mə\ *also* **-mums** : the amount or degree of something most favorable to an end; *also* : greatest degree attained under implied or specified conditions
op·tion \'äp-shən\ *n* **1** ♦ : the power or right to choose **2** : a right to buy or sell something at a specified price during a specified period **3** : something offered for choice **4** ♦ : an act of choosing

♦ [1] accord, choice, free will, self-determination, volition, will ♦ [4] alternative, choice, discretion, pick, preference, way

op·tion·al \-shə-nəl\ *adj* ♦ : involving an option : not compulsory

♦ discretionary, elective, voluntary *Ant* compulsory, mandatory, nonelective, obligatory, required

op·tom·e·try \äp-'tä-mə-trē\ *n* : the health-care profession concerned esp. with examining the eyes for defects of vision and with prescribing corrective lenses or eye exercises — **op·tom·e·trist** \-trist\ *n*
opt out *vb* : to choose not to participate
op·u·lence \'ä-pyə-ləns\ *n* **1** ♦ : abundance of valuable material possessions or resources : WEALTH **2** : ABUNDANCE

♦ assets, capital, fortune, means, riches, substance, wealth, wherewithal

op·u·lent \'ä-pyə-lənt\ *adj* **1** ♦ : exhibiting or characterized by opulence **2** : richly abundant

♦ deluxe, lavish, luxuriant, luxurious, palatial, plush, sumptuous ♦ affluent, flush, loaded, moneyed, rich, wealthy, well-fixed, well-heeled, well-off, well-to-do

op·u·lent·ly *adv* ♦ : with opulence : in an opulent manner

♦ expensively, extravagantly, grandly, high, lavishly, luxuriously, richly

opus \'ō-pəs\ *n, pl* **opera** \'ō-pə-rə, 'ä-\ *also* **opus·es** \'ō-pə-səz\ ♦ : something produced by the exercise of creative talent or expenditure of creative effort; *esp* : a musical composition

♦ composition, piece, work

or \'ȯr\ *conj* — used as a function word to indicate an alternative ⟨sink ~ swim⟩
OR *abbr* **1** operating room **2** Oregon
-or \ər\ *n suffix* : one that does a (specified) thing ⟨calculat*or*⟩
or·a·cle \'ȯr-ə-kəl\ *n* **1** : one held to give divinely inspired answers or revelations **2** : an authoritative or wise utterance; *also* : a person of great authority or wisdom — **orac·u·lar** \ȯ-'ra-kyə-lər\ *adj*

[1]**oral** \'ȯr-əl\ *adj* **1** ♦ : uttered by the mouth or in words **2** : of, given through, or involving the mouth **3** : of, relating to, or characterized by the first stage of psychosexual development in psychoanalytic theory in which libidinal gratification is derived from intake (as of food), by sucking, and later by biting **4** : relating to or characterized by personality traits of passive dependency and aggressiveness — **oral·ly** *adv*

♦ vocal, voiced ♦ spoken, unwritten, verbal

[2]**oral** *n* : an oral examination — usu. used in pl.
oral sex *n* : oral stimulation of the genitals : CUNNILINGUS, FELLATIO
orang \ə-'raŋ\ *n* : ORANGUTAN
or·ange \'ȯr-inj\ *n* **1** : a juicy citrus fruit with reddish yellow rind; *also* : an evergreen tree with fragrant white flowers that bears this fruit **2** : a color between red and yellow
or·ange·ade \ˌȯr-in-'jād\ *n* : a beverage of orange juice, sugar, and water
orange hawkweed *n* : a weedy herb related to the daisies with bright orange-red flower heads
or·ange·ry \'ȯr-inj-rē\ *n, pl* **-ries** : a protected place (as a greenhouse) for raising oranges in cool climates
orang·utan \ə-'raŋ-ə-ˌtaŋ, -ˌtan\ *n* : a large reddish brown tree-living anthropoid ape of Borneo and Sumatra
orate \ȯ-'rāt\ *vb* **orat·ed; orat·ing** ♦ : to speak in a declamatory manner

♦ declaim, discourse, harangue, lecture, mouth, speak, talk

ora·tion \ə-'rā-shən\ *n* ♦ : an elaborate discourse delivered in a formal and dignified manner

♦ address, declamation, harangue, speech, talk

or·a·tor \'ȯr-ə-tər\ *n* : one noted for skill and power as a public speaker
or·a·tor·i·cal \ˌȯr-ə-'tȯr-i-kəl\ *adj* ♦ : of, relating to, or characteristic of an orator or oratory; *also* : of or relating to an inflated style of speech or writing — **or·a·tor·i·cal·ly** \-'tȯr-i-k(ə-)lē\ *adv*

♦ bombastic, gaseous, grandiloquent, rhetorical, windy

or·a·to·rio \ˌȯr-ə-'tȯr-ē-ˌō\ *n, pl* **-rios** : a lengthy choral work usu. on a scriptural subject
[1]**or·a·to·ry** \'ȯr-ə-ˌtȯr-ē\ *n, pl* **-ries** : a private or institutional chapel
[2]**oratory** *n* **1** : the art of speaking eloquently and effectively in public **2** : the substance of oratorical speech
orb \'ȯrb\ *n* ♦ : a spherical body; *also* : EYE

♦ ball, sphere

[1]**or·bit** \'ȯr-bət\ *n* **1** : a path described by one body in its revolution about another **2** : range or sphere of activity — **or·bit·al** \-ᵊl\ *adj*
[2]**orbit** *vb* **1** ♦ : to revolve in an orbit around : CIRCLE **2** : to send up and make revolve in an orbit ⟨~ a satellite⟩ — **or·bit·er** *n*

♦ circle, circumnavigate, coil, compass, encircle, girdle, loop, ring, round

or·ca \'ȯr-kə\ *n* : KILLER WHALE
orch *abbr* orchestra
or·chard \'ȯr-chərd\ *n* : a place where fruit trees, sugar maples, or nut trees are grown; *also* : the trees of such a place — **or·chard·ist** \-chər-dist\ *n*
or·ches·tra \'ȯr-kə-strə\ *n* **1** : the front section of seats on the main floor of a theater **2** : a group of instrumentalists organized to perform ensemble music — **or·ches·tral** \ȯr-'kes-trəl\ *adj* — **or·ches·tral·ly** *adv*
or·ches·trate \'ȯr-kə-ˌstrāt\ *vb* **-trat·ed; -trat·ing** **1** : to compose or arrange for an orchestra **2** : to arrange so as to achieve a desired effect ⟨~ a campaign⟩ — **or·ches·tra·tion** \ˌȯr-kə-'strā-shən\ *n*
or·chid \'ȯr-kəd\ *n* : any of a large family of plants having often showy flowers with three petals of which the middle one is enlarged into a lip; *also* : a flower of an orchid
ord *abbr* **1** order **2** ordnance
or·dain \ȯr-'dān\ *vb* **1** : to admit to the ministry or priesthood by the ritual of a church **2 a** ♦ : to order by fiat or by virtue of great or supreme authority : DECREE **b** ♦ : to predestine or destine : DESTINE — **or·dain·ment** *n*

♦ [2a] command, decree, dictate, direct, order ♦ [2b] destine, doom, fate, foredoom, foreordain, predestine

or·deal \ȯr-'dēl, 'ȯr-ˌdēl\ *n* ♦ : a severe trial or experience

♦ cross, gauntlet, trial

¹**or•der** \\'ȯr-dər\\ *vb* **1 ♦** : to arrange according to a particular plan **2 ♦** : to give an order to : COMMAND **3 ♦** : to place an order **4 ♦** : to issue orders

♦ [1] arrange, array, classify, codify, dispose, draw up, marshal, organize, range, systematize *Ant* derange, disarrange, disarray, disorder, mess (up), muss (up), rumple, upset ♦ [2] command, decree, dictate, direct, ordain ♦ [3] ask, request, requisition ♦ [4] bid, boss, charge, command, direct, enjoin, instruct, tell

²**order** *n* **1 a** : a group of people formally united **b** : a badge or medal of such a group **2** : any of the several grades of the Christian ministry; *also, pl* : ORDINATION **3 a ♦** : a rank, class, or special group of persons or things **b ♦** : a division within a system of classification **4** : a category of biological classification ranking above the family and below the class **5 ♦** : the arrangement or sequence of objects or of events in time : ARRANGEMENT, SEQUENCE; *also* : the prevailing state of things **6** : a customary mode of procedure; *also* : the rule of law or proper authority **7 ♦** : a specific rule, regulation, or authoritative direction **8** : a style of building; *also* : an architectural column forming the unit of a style **9 ♦** : condition esp. with regard to repair **10** : a written direction to pay money or to buy or sell goods; *also* : goods bought or sold **11 ♦** : a particular sphere or aspect of a sociopolitical system

♦ [3a, 11] caste, class, estate, folk, stratum ♦ [3b] bracket, category, class, division, family, grade, group, kind, set, species, type ♦ [5] arrangement, array, disposal, disposition, distribution, sequence, setup ♦ [7] behest, charge, command, commandment, decree, dictate, direction, directive, edict, instruction, word ♦ [9] condition, estate, fettle, form, repair, shape, trim

¹**or•der•ly** \\'ȯr-dər-lē\\ *adj* **1 a ♦** : arranged according to some order **b ♦** : marked by order : NEAT, TIDY **2** : well behaved ⟨an ∼ crowd⟩ — **or•der•li•ness** *n*

♦ [1a] methodical, regular, systematic ♦ [1b] crisp, neat, shipshape, snug, tidy, trim, uncluttered

²**orderly** *n, pl* **-lies** **1** : a soldier who attends a superior officer **2** : a hospital attendant who does general work

or•di•nal \\'ȯrd-ᵊn-əl\\ *adj* : indicating order or rank (as sixth) in a series

ordinal number *n* : a number (as first, second, or third) that designates the place of an item in an ordered sequence — compare CARDINAL NUMBER

or•di•nance \\'ȯrd-ᵊn-əns\\ *n ♦* : an authoritative decree or law; *esp* : a municipal regulation

♦ act, enactment, law, statute

or•di•nar•i•ly \\ˌȯrd-ᵊn-'er-ə-lē\\ *adv ♦* : in an ordinary manner

♦ commonly, generally, naturally, normally, typically, usually

or•di•nary \\'ȯrd-ᵊn-ˌer-ē\\ *adj* **1 ♦** : to be expected : USUAL **2 ♦** : of common quality, rank, or ability; *also* : POOR, INFERIOR — **or•di•nar•i•ness** \\'ȯrd-ᵊn-ˌer-ē-nəs\\ *n*

♦ [1] average, common, commonplace, everyday, normal, prosaic, routine, run-of-the-mill, standard, unexceptional, unremarkable, usual, workaday *Ant* abnormal, exceptional, extraordinary, odd, out-of-the-way, strange, unusual ♦ [2] common, fair, indifferent, inferior, mediocre, medium, middling, passable, poor, run-of-the-mill, second-rate, so-so

or•di•nate \\'ȯrd-ᵊn-ət, -ˌāt\\ *n* : the vertical coordinate of a point in a plane coordinate system obtained by measuring parallel to the y-axis

or•di•na•tion \\ˌȯrd-ᵊn-'ā-shən\\ *n* : the act or ceremony by which a person is ordained

ord•nance \\'ȯrd-nəns\\ *n* **1** : military supplies **2** : CANNON, ARTILLERY

Or•do•vi•cian \\ˌȯr-də-'vi-shən\\ *adj* : of, relating to, or being the period of the Paleozoic era between the Cambrian and the Silurian — **Ordovician** *n*

or•dure \\'ȯr-jər\\ *n* : EXCREMENT

ore \\'ȯr\\ *n* : a naturally occurring mineral mined to obtain a substance that it contains

Ore *or* **Oreg** *abbr* Oregon

oreg•a•no \\ə-'re-gə-ˌnō\\ *n* : a bushy perennial mint used as a seasoning and a source of oil

org *abbr* organization; organized

or•gan \\'ȯr-gən\\ *n* **1** : a musical instrument having sets of pipes sounded by compressed air and controlled by keyboards; *also* : an electronic keyboard instrument that approximates the sounds of the pipe organ by electronic devices **2** : a differentiated animal or plant structure (as a heart or a leaf) made up of cells and tissues and performing some bodily function **3** : a group that performs a specialized function ⟨the various ∼s of government⟩ **4** : PERIODICAL **5 ♦** : a means exercising some function or accomplishing some end

♦ agency, agent, instrument, instrumentality, machinery, means, medium, vehicle

or•gan•dy *also* **or•gan•die** \\'ȯr-gən-dē\\ *n, pl* **-dies** : a fine transparent muslin with a stiff finish

or•gan•elle \\ˌȯr-gə-'nel\\ *n* : a specialized cell part that resembles an organ in having a special function

or•gan•ic \\ȯr-'ga-nik\\ *adj* **1** : of, relating to, or arising in a bodily organ **2** : of, relating to, or derived from living things **3** : of, relating to, or containing carbon compounds **4** : of or relating to a branch of chemistry dealing with carbon compounds **5** : involving, producing, or dealing in foods produced without the use of laboratory-made fertilizers, growth substances, antibiotics, or pesticides **6** : ORGANIZED ⟨an ∼ whole⟩ — **or•gan•i•cal•ly** \\-ni-k(ə-)lē\\ *adv*

or•ga•ni•sa•tion, or•ga•nise *chiefly Brit var of* ORGANIZATION, ORGANIZE

or•gan•ism \\'ȯr-gə-ˌni-zəm\\ *n* : an individual living thing (as a person, animal, or plant) — **or•gan•is•mic** \\ˌȯr-gə-'niz-mik\\ *adj*

or•gan•ist \\'ȯr-gə-nist\\ *n* : a person who plays an organ

or•ga•ni•za•tion \\ˌȯr-gə-nə-'zā-shən\\ *n* **1** : the act or process of organizing or of being organized; *also* : the condition or manner of being organized **2 ♦** : an association of persons having a common interest : SOCIETY **3** : an administrative structure (as a business or a political party); *also* : the personnel of such a structure — **or•ga•ni•za•tion•al** \\-shə-nəl\\ *adj*

♦ association, brotherhood, club, college, congress, council, fellowship, fraternity, guild, institute, institution, league, order, society

or•ga•nize \\'ȯr-gə-ˌnīz\\ *vb* **-nized; -niz•ing** **1** : to develop an organic structure **2** : to form into a complete and functioning whole **3** : to set up an administrative structure for **4 ♦** : to arrange by systematic planning and united effort **5** : to join in a union; *also* : UNIONIZE — **or•ga•niz•er** *n*

♦ arrange, array, classify, codify, dispose, draw up, marshal, order, range, systematize

or•gano•chlo•rine \\ˌȯr-ga-nə-'klȯr-ˌēn\\ *adj* : of, relating to, or being a chlorinated hydrocarbon pesticide (as DDT) — **organochlorine** *n*

or•gano•phos•phate \\-'fäs-ˌfāt\\ *n* : an organophosphorus pesticide — **organophosphate** *adj*

or•gano•phos•pho•rus \\-'fäs-fə-rəs\\ *also* **or•gano•phos•pho•rous** \\-ˌfäs-'fōr-əs\\ *adj* : of, relating to, or being a phosphorus-containing organic pesticide (as malathion)

or•gan•za \\ȯr-'gan-zə\\ *n* : a sheer dress fabric resembling organdy and usu. made of silk, rayon, or nylon

or•gasm \\'ȯr-ˌga-zəm\\ *n* : the climax of sexual excitement — **or•gas•mic** \\ȯr-'gaz-mik\\ *adj*

or•gi•as•tic \\ˌȯr-jē-'as-tik\\ *adj* : of, relating to, or marked by orgies

or•gu•lous \\'ȯr-gyə-ləs, -gə-\\ *adj* : PROUD

or•gy \\'ȯr-jē\\ *n, pl* **orgies** : a gathering marked by unrestrained indulgence (as in sexual activity, alcohol, or drugs)

ori•el \\'ȯr-ē-əl\\ *n* : a window built out from a wall and usu. supported by a bracket

ori•ent \\'ȯr-ē-ˌent\\ *vb* **1** : to set in a definite position esp. in relation to the points of the compass **2 ♦** : to acquaint with an existing situation or environment **3** : to direct toward the interests of a particular group

♦ acquaint, familiarize, initiate, introduce

Orient *n* : EAST 3; *esp* : the countries of eastern Asia

ori•en•tal \\ˌȯr-ē-'ent-ᵊl\\ *adj, often cap* : of or situated in the Orient — **Oriental** *n*

ori•en•tate \\'ȯr-ē-ən-ˌtāt\\ *vb* **-tat•ed; -tat•ing** **1** : to acquaint with the existing situation or environment : ORIENT **2** : to face east

ori•en•ta•tion \\ˌȯr-ē-ən-tā-shən\\ *n* **1** : the act or state of being oriented **2** : a person's sexual identity as bisexual, straight, gay, pansexual, etc.

or•i•fice \\'ȯr-ə-fəs\\ *n ♦* : an opening (as a vent, mouth, or hole) through which something may pass : OPENING

♦ aperture, hole, opening, perforation

ori•flamme \\'ȯr-ə-ˌflam\\ *n* : a brightly colored banner used as a standard or ensign in battle

orig *abbr* original; originally

ori·ga·mi \ˌȯr-ə-ˈgä-mē\ *n* : the art or process of Japanese paper folding

or·i·gin \ˈȯr-ə-jən\ *n* **1 ♦** : line of descent : ANCESTRY **2** : rise, beginning, or derivation from a source; *also* : CAUSE **3** : the intersection of coordinate axes

♦ ancestry, birth, blood, bloodline, breeding, descent, extraction, family tree, genealogy, line, lineage, parentage, pedigree, stock, strain

¹**orig·i·nal** \ə-ˈri-jə-nəl\ *n* : something from which a copy, reproduction, or translation is made : PROTOTYPE

²**original** *adj* **1 ♦** : existing from the start : FIRST, INITIAL **2 ♦** : not copied from something else : FRESH **3 ♦** : gifted with powers of independent thought, direct insight, or constructive imagination : INVENTIVE

♦ [1] first, inaugural, initial, maiden, pioneer, premier ♦ [2] fresh, new, novel, strange, unfamiliar, unknown ♦ [3] creative, imaginative, ingenious, innovative, inventive

orig·i·nal·i·ty \-ˌri-jə-ˈna-lə-tē\ *n* **1 ♦** : freshness of aspect, design, or style **2 ♦** : the power of independent thought or constructive imagination

♦ [1] freshness, newness, novelty ♦ [2] creativity, ingenuity, invention, inventiveness

orig·i·nal·ly \-ˈri-jən-ᵊl-ē\ *adv* **♦** : in the beginning : in the first place

♦ firstly, initially, primarily

orig·i·nate \ə-ˈri-jə-ˌnāt\ *vb* **-nat·ed; -nat·ing** **1** : to give rise to : INITIATE **2 ♦** : to come into existence : BEGIN

♦ arise, begin, commence, dawn, form, materialize, spring, start

orig·i·na·tor \-ˌnā-tər\ *n* **♦** : one that originates

♦ author, creator, father, founder ♦ designer, developer, innovator, inventor

ori·ole \ˈȯr-ē-ˌōl\ *n* : any of various New World birds of which the males are usu. black and yellow or black and orange

ori·son \ˈȯr-ə-sən\ *n* : PRAYER

or·mo·lu \ˈȯr-mə-ˌlü\ *n* : a golden or gilded brass used for decorative purposes

¹**or·na·ment** \ˈȯr-nə-mənt\ *n* **♦** : something that lends grace or beauty — **or·na·men·ta·tion** \ˌȯr-nə-mən-ˈtā-shən\ *n*

♦ adornment, caparison, decoration, embellishment, frill, garnish, trim

²**or·na·ment** \-ˌment\ *vb* **♦** : to provide with ornament : ADORN

♦ adorn, array, beautify, bedeck, deck, decorate, do, dress, embellish, enrich, garnish, grace, trim

or·na·men·tal \ˌȯr-nə-ˈment-ᵊl\ *adj* : DECORATIVE : of, relating to, or serving as ornament

or·nate \ȯr-ˈnāt\ *adj* **♦** : elaborately decorated — **or·nate·ly** *adv* — **or·nate·ness** *n*

♦ florid, overwrought *Ant* austere, plain, severe, stark, unadorned

or·nery \ˈȯr-nə-rē, ˈä-nə-\ *adj* **♦** : having an irritable disposition

♦ bearish, bilious, cantankerous, disagreeable, dyspeptic, ill-humored, ill-tempered, splenetic, surly

or·ni·thol·o·gy \ˌȯr-nə-ˈthä-lə-jē\ *n, pl* **-gies** : a branch of zoology dealing with birds — **or·ni·tho·log·i·cal** \-thə-ˈlä-ji-kəl\ *adj* — **or·ni·thol·o·gist** \-ˈthä-lə-jist\ *n*

oro·tund \ˈȯr-ə-ˌtənd\ *adj* **1** : SONOROUS **2** : POMPOUS — **oro·tun·di·ty** \ˌȯr-ə-ˈtən-di-tē\ *n*

or·phan \ˈȯr-fən\ *n* : a child deprived by death of one or usu. both parents — **orphan** *vb*

or·phan·age \ˈȯr-fə-nij\ *n* : an institution for the care of orphans

or·tho·don·tia \ˌȯr-thə-ˈdän-chə, -chē-ə\ *n* : ORTHODONTICS

or·tho·don·tics \ˌȯr-thə-ˈdän-tiks\ *n* : a branch of dentistry concerned with the correction of faults in the arrangement and placing of the teeth — **or·tho·don·tist** \-ˈdän-tist\ *n*

or·tho·dox \ˈȯr-thə-ˌdäks\ *adj* **1 ♦** : conforming to established doctrine esp. in religion **2 ♦** : according with, sanctioned by, or based on convention : CONVENTIONAL **3** *cap* : of or relating to a Christian church originating in the church of the Eastern Roman Empire — **or·tho·doxy** \-ˌdäk-sē\ *n*

♦ [1] conservative, old-fashioned, reactionary, traditional ♦ [2] ceremonial, ceremonious, conventional, formal, regular, routine

or·thog·ra·phy \ȯr-ˈthä-grə-fē\ *n* : SPELLING — **or·tho·graph·ic** \ˌȯr-thə-ˈgra-fik\ *adj*

or·tho·pe·dics \ˌȯr-thə-ˈpē-diks\ *n sing or pl* : a branch of medicine concerned with the correction or prevention of skeletal injuries or disorders — **or·tho·pe·dic** \-dik\ *adj* — **or·tho·pe·dist** \-dist\ *n*

-ory \ˌȯr-ē, ə-rē\ *adj suffix* **1** : of, relating to, or characterized by ⟨anticipat*ory*⟩ **2** : serving for, producing, or maintaining ⟨illus*ory*⟩

Os *symbol* osmium

OS *abbr* **1** left eye **2** ordinary seaman **3** out of stock

Osage \ō-ˈsāj\ *n, pl* **Osag·es** *or* **Osage** : a member of an Indigenous people orig. of southwestern Missouri and adjacent parts of Kansas, Oklahoma, and Arkansas; *also* : the language of the Osage people

os·cil·late \ˈä-sə-ˌlāt\ *vb* **-lat·ed; -lat·ing** **1** : to swing backward and forward like a pendulum **2** : to move or travel back and forth between two points **3** : VARY, FLUCTUATE — **os·cil·la·tor** \ˈä-sə-ˌlā-tər\ *n* — **os·cil·la·to·ry** \ˈä-sə-lə-ˌtȯr-ē\ *adj*

os·cil·la·tion \ˌä-sə-ˈlā-shən\ *n* : the action or state of oscillating

♦ quivering, vibration

os·cil·lo·scope \ä-ˈsi-lə-ˌskōp\ *n* : an instrument in which variations in current or voltage appear as a visible wave form on a fluorescent screen

os·cu·late \ˈäs-kyə-ˌlāt\ *vb* **-lat·ed; -lat·ing** : KISS — **os·cu·la·tion** \ˌäs-kyə-ˈlā-shən\ *n* — **os·cu·la·to·ry** \ˈäs-kyə-lə-ˌtōr-ē\ *adj*

Osee \ˈō-ˌzē, ō-ˈzä-ə\ *n* : HOSEA

OSHA \ˈō-shə\ *abbr* Occupational Safety and Health Administration

osier \ˈō-zhər\ *n* : any of various willows with pliable twigs used esp. in making baskets and furniture; *also* : a twig from an osier

os·mi·um \ˈäz-mē-əm\ *n* : a heavy hard brittle metallic chemical element used esp. as a catalyst and in alloys

os·mo·sis \äz-ˈmō-səs, äs-\ *n* : movement of a solvent through a semipermeable membrane into a solution of higher concentration that tends to equalize the concentrations of the solutions on either side of the membrane — **os·mot·ic** \-ˈmä-tik\ *adj*

os·prey \ˈäs-prē, -ˌprā\ *n, pl* **ospreys** : a large dark brown and white fish-eating hawk

os·si·fy \ˈä-sə-ˌfī\ *vb* **-fied; -fy·ing** : to make or become hardened or set in one's ways ⟨an *ossified* regime⟩ — **os·si·fi·ca·tion** \ˌä-sə-fə-ˈkā-shən\ *n*

os·su·ary \ˈä-shə-ˌwer-ē, -syə-\ *n, pl* **-ar·ies** : a depository for the bones of the dead

os·ten·si·ble \ä-ˈsten-sə-bəl\ *adj* **♦** : shown outwardly : APPARENT

♦ apparent, assumed, evident, reputed, seeming, supposed

os·ten·si·bly \-blē\ *adv* **1** : in an ostensible manner **2 ♦** : to all outward appearances

♦ apparently, evidently, presumably, seemingly, supposedly

os·ten·ta·tion \ˌäs-tən-ˈtā-shən\ *n* **♦** : pretentious or excessive display — **os·ten·ta·tious·ly** *adv*

♦ flamboyance, flashiness, gaudiness, glitz, pretentiousness, showiness, swank *Ant* austerity, plainness, severity

os·ten·ta·tious \-shəs\ *adj* **♦** : marked by or fond of conspicuous or sometimes pretentious display

♦ flamboyant, flashy, garish, gaudy, glitzy, loud, swank, tawdry ♦ affected, grandiose, highfalutin, pompous, pretentious

os·teo·path \ˈäs-tē-ə-ˌpath\ *n* : a practitioner of osteopathy

os·te·op·a·thy \ˌäs-tē-ˈä-pə-thē\ *n* : a system of treating diseases emphasizing manipulation (as of joints) but not excluding other agencies (as the use of medicine and surgery) — **os·teo·path·ic** \ˌäs-tē-ə-ˈpa-thik\ *adj*

os·teo·po·ro·sis \ˌäs-tē-ō-pə-ˈrō-səs\ *n, pl* **-ro·ses** \-ˌsēz\ : a condition affecting esp. older women and characterized by fragile and porous bones

os·tra·cise *chiefly Brit var of* OSTRACIZE

os·tra·cize \ˈäs-trə-ˌsīz\ *vb* **-cized; -ciz·ing** : to exclude from a group by common consent — **os·tra·cism** \-ˌsi-zəm\ *n*

os·trich \ˈäs-trich, ˈȯs-\ *n* : a very large swift-footed flightless bird of Africa and Arabia

Os·we·go tea \ä-ˈswē-gō-\ *n* : a No. American mint with showy scarlet flowers

OT *abbr* **1** occupational therapy **2** Old Testament **3** overtime

¹**oth·er** \ˈə-thər\ *adj* **1** : being the one left; *also* : being the ones distinct from those first mentioned **2** : ALTERNATE ⟨every ∼ day⟩ **3 ♦** : not the same : DIFFERENT **4 ♦** : existing by way of addition : ADDITIONAL **5** : recently past ⟨the ∼ night⟩

♦ [3] different, disparate, dissimilar, distinct, distinctive, distinguishable, diverse, unlike, unalike ♦ [4] additional, another, else, farther, further, more

²**other** *pron* **1** : remaining one or ones **2** : a different or additional one ⟨something or ∼⟩
other than *prep* ♦ : with the exception of : BESIDES

♦ aside from, bar, barring, besides, but, except, except for, exclusive of, outside (of), save

oth·er·wise \'ə-thər-ˌwīz\ *adv* **1** ♦ : in a different way **2** : in different circumstances **3** : in other respects **4** : if not **5** : NOT — **otherwise** *adj*

♦ differently, else, other *Ant* likewise

oth·er·world \-ˌwərld\ *n* : a world beyond death or beyond present reality
oth·er·world·ly \ˌə-thər-'wərld-lē\ *adj* : not worldly : concerned with spiritual, intellectual, or imaginative matters
oti·ose \'ō-shē-ˌōs, 'ō-tē-\ *adj* **1** : FUTILE **2** : IDLE **3** : USELESS
oto·lar·yn·gol·o·gy \ˌō-tō-ˌlar-ən-'gä-lə-jē\ *n* : a medical specialty concerned esp. with the ear, nose, and throat — **oto·lar·yn·gol·o·gist** \-jist\ *n*
oto·rhi·no·lar·yn·gol·o·gy \ˌō-tō-ˌrī-nō-ˌlar-ən-'gä-lə-jē\ *n* : OTOLARYNGOLOGY — **oto·rhi·no·lar·yn·gol·o·gist** \-jist\ *n*
OTS *abbr* officers' training school
Ot·ta·wa \'ä-tə-wə, -ˌwä, -ˌwȯ\ *n, pl* **Ottawas** *or* **Ottawa** : a member of an Indigenous people of Michigan and southern Ontario
ot·ter \'ä-tər\ *n, pl* **otters** *also* **otter** : any of various web-footed fish-eating mammals with dark brown fur that are related to the weasels; *also* : the fur
ot·to·man \'ä-tə-mən\ *n* : an upholstered seat or couch usu. without a back; *also* : an overstuffed footstool
ou·bli·ette \ˌü-blē-'et\ *n* : a dungeon with an opening at the top
ought \'ȯt\ *verbal auxiliary* ♦ — used to express moral obligation, advisability, natural expectation, or logical consequence ⟨you ∼ to apologize⟩

♦ *usu* **ought to** have, must, need, shall, should

ounce \'aůns\ *n* **1 a** : a unit of avoirdupois, troy, and apothecaries' weight; *specif* : a unit of weight equal to ¹/₁₆ pound **b** ♦ : a small amount **2** : FLUID OUNCE

♦ bit, little, particle, shred, speck, touch, trace

our \är, 'aůr\ *adj* : of or relating to us or ourselves
ours \'aůrz, 'ärz\ *pron* : that which belongs to us
our·selves \är-'selvz, aůr-\ *pron* : our own selves — used reflexively, for emphasis, or in absolute constructions ⟨we pleased ∼⟩ ⟨we'll do it ∼⟩ ⟨we were tourists ∼⟩
-ous \əs\ *adj suffix* : full of : abounding in : having : possessing the qualities of ⟨clamor*ous*⟩ ⟨poison*ous*⟩
oust \'aůst\ *vb* ♦ : to eject from or deprive of property or position

♦ banish, boot (out), bounce, cast, chase, dismiss, drum, eject, expel, rout, run off, throw out ♦ depose

oust·er \'aůs-tər\ *n* : EXPULSION
¹**out** \'aůt\ *adv* **1** : in a direction away from the inside or center **2** : beyond control **3** : to extinction, exhaustion, or completion **4** : in or into the open **5** : so as to retire a batter or base runner; *also* : so as to be retired
²**out** *vb* ♦ : to become known ⟨the truth will ∼⟩

♦ come out, get out, leak out, spread

³**out** *prep* **1** : out through ⟨looked ∼ the window⟩ **2** : outward on or along ⟨drive ∼ the river road⟩
⁴**out** *adj* **1** : situated outside or at a distance **2** ♦ : not in : ABSENT; *also* : not being in power **3** : removed from play as a batter or base runner **4** : not being in vogue or fashion : not up-to-date

♦ absent, away, missing

⁵**out** *n* **1** : one who is out of office **2** : the retiring of a batter or base runner **3** ♦ : a way of escaping from an embarrassing or difficult situation

♦ avoidance, cop-out, escape, evasion

out·age \'aů-tij\ *n* : a period or instance of interruption esp. of electricity
out–and–out *adj* ♦ : being such completely at all times, in every way, or from every point of view : COMPLETE, THOROUGHGOING ⟨an ∼ fraud⟩

♦ absolute, all-out, complete, consummate, outright, thorough, thoroughgoing, total, unqualified, utter

out·bid \ˌaůt-'bid\ *vb* : to make a higher bid than
¹**out·board** \'aůt-ˌbōrd\ *adj* **1** : situated outboard **2** : having or using an outboard motor
²**outboard** *adv* **1** : outside a ship's hull : away from the long axis of a ship **2** : in a position closer to the wing tip of an airplane

outboard motor *n* : a small internal combustion engine with propeller attached for mounting at the stern of a small boat
out·bound \'aůt-ˌbaůnd\ *adj* : outward bound ⟨∼ traffic⟩
out·break \-ˌbrāk\ *n* **1** ♦ : a sudden increase in activity, incidence, or numbers **2** : INSURRECTION, REVOLT

♦ burst, flare, flare-up, flash, flurry, flutter, outburst, spurt

out·build·ing \-ˌbil-diŋ\ *n* : a building separate from but accessory to a main house
out·burst \-ˌbərst\ *n* **1 a** : ERUPTION **b** ♦ : a violent expression of feeling **2** : a surge of activity or growth

♦ agony, burst, eruption, explosion, fit, flare, flare-up, flash, flush, gale, gush, gust, paroxysm, spasm, storm

out·cast \-ˌkast\ *n* ♦ : one that is cast out by society

♦ castaway, reject

out·class \aůt-'klas\ *vb* ♦ : to be superior to in quality, degree, or performance : SURPASS

♦ beat, better, eclipse, excel, outdistance, outdo, outshine, outstrip, surpass, top, transcend

out·come \'aůt-ˌkəm\ *n* ♦ : a final consequence : RESULT

♦ aftermath, conclusion, consequence, corollary, development, effect, issue, outgrowth, product, result, resultant, sequence, upshot

out·crop \-ˌkräp\ *n* : a coming out of bedrock to the surface of the ground; *also* : the part of a rock formation that thus appears — **outcrop** *vb*
out·cry \-ˌkrī\ *n* ♦ : a loud cry : CLAMOR

♦ clamor (*or* clamour), howl, hubbub, hue and cry, hullabaloo, noise, roar, tumult, uproar

out·dat·ed \aůt-'dā-təd\ *adj* ♦ : no longer current : OUTMODED

♦ antiquated, archaic, dated, obsolete, outmoded, outworn, passé

out·dis·tance \-'dis-təns\ *vb* ♦ : to leave behind : go ahead of

♦ beat, better, eclipse, excel, outdo, outshine, outstrip, surpass, top, transcend

out·do \-'dü\ *vb* **-did** \-'did\; **-done** \-'dən\; **-do·ing; -does** \-'dəz\ ♦ : to go beyond in action or performance

♦ beat, better, eclipse, excel, outdistance, outshine, outstrip, surpass, top, transcend

out·door \'aůt-ˌdōr, -'dōr\ *also* **out·doors** \-ˌdōrz, -'dōrz\ *adj* **1** : of or relating to the outdoors **2** : performed outdoors **3** : not enclosed (as by a roof)
¹**out·doors** \'aůt-ˌdōrz, -'dōrz\ *adv* : in or into the open air
²**outdoors** *n* **1** : the open air **2** ♦ : the world away from human habitation — **out·doorsy** \ˌaůt-'dȯr-zē\ *adj*

♦ nature, open, wild, wilderness

out·draw \aůt-'drȯ\ *vb* **-drew** \-'drü\; **-drawn** \-'drȯn\; **-draw·ing 1** : to attract a larger audience than **2** : to draw a handgun more quickly than
out·er \'aů-tər\ *adj* ♦ : of, relating to, or connected with the outside or an outer part : EXTERNAL **2** ♦ : situated farther out; *also* : being away from a center

♦ [1, 2] exterior, external, outside, outward *Ant* inner, inside, interior, internal, inward

outer ear *n* : the outer visible portion of the ear that collects and directs sound waves toward the eardrum
out·er·most \-ˌmōst\ *adj* ♦ : farthest out

♦ extreme, farthest, furthest, ultimate, utmost

outer space *n* : SPACE 5
out·er·wear \'aů-tər-ˌwer\ *n* **1** : clothing for outdoor wear **2** : outer clothing as opposed to underwear
out·face \aůt-'fās\ *vb* **1** : to cause to waver or submit **2** : DEFY
out·field \'aůt-ˌfēld\ *n* : the part of a baseball field beyond the infield and within the foul lines; *also* : players in the outfield — **out·field·er** \-ˌfēl-dər\ *n*
out·fight \aůt-'fīt\ *vb* : to surpass in fighting : DEFEAT
¹**out·fit** \'aůt-ˌfit\ *n* **1** ♦ : the equipment or apparel for a special purpose or occasion **2** ♦ : a group that works as a team **3** ♦ : an organization engaged in a particular industry or activity

♦ [1] dress, garb, getup, guise ♦ [1] accoutrements (*or* accouterments), apparatus, equipment, gear, matériel, paraphernalia, tackle ♦ [2] band, company, crew, gang, party, squad, team ♦ [3] business, company, concern, enterprise, establishment, firm, house

²**outfit** *vb* **out·fit·ted; out·fit·ting** ♦ : to provide or supply with what is needed, useful, or desirable : EQUIP — **out·fit·ter** *n*

♦ accoutre, equip, fit, furnish, rig, supply

out·flank \aut-'flaŋk\ *vb* : to get around the flank of (an opposing force)
out·flow \'aut-ˌflō\ *n* **1** ♦ : a flowing out **2** : something that flows out

♦ gush, outpouring *Ant* flux, inflow, influx, inrush

out·fox \aut-'fäks\ *vb* ♦ : to outdo in trickery : OUTWIT

♦ fox, outmaneuver, outsmart, outwit, overreach

out·go \'aut-ˌgō\ *n, pl* **outgoes** ♦ : something that goes out : OUTLAY

♦ cost, disbursement, expenditure, expense, outlay

out·go·ing \-ˌgō-iŋ\ *adj* **1** : going out ⟨∼ tide⟩ **2** : retiring from a place or position **3** ♦ : openly friendly and responsive

♦ boon, companionable, convivial, extroverted, gregarious, sociable, social

out·grow \aut-'grō\ *vb* **-grew** \-'grü\; **-grown** \-'grōn\; **-growing** **1** : to grow faster than **2** : to grow too large for
out·growth \'aut-ˌgrōth\ *n* **1** ♦ : a product of growing out : OFFSHOOT **2** : something produced by a cause or necessarily following from a set of conditions : CONSEQUENCE, RESULT

♦ derivative, offshoot, spin-off

out·guess \aut-'ges\ *vb* : OUTWIT
out·gun \-'gən\ *vb* : to surpass in firepower
out·house \'aut-ˌhaus\ *n* : OUTBUILDING; *esp* : an outdoor toilet
out·ing \'au-tiŋ\ *n* ♦ : a brief stay or trip in the open

♦ excursion, jaunt, junket, sally

out·land·ish \aut-'lan-dish\ *adj* **1 a** ♦ : of foreign appearance or manner **b** ♦ : strikingly out of the ordinary **2** : remote from civilization — **out·land·ish·ly** *adv*

♦ bizarre, curious, exotic, far-out, funny, kinky, odd, outré, peculiar, quaint, quirky, remarkable, screwy, strange, wacky, weird, wild

out·last \-'last\ *vb* : to last longer than
¹**out·law** \'aut-ˌlo\ *n* **1** : a person excluded from the protection of the law **2** : a lawless person
²**outlaw** *vb* **1** : to deprive of the protection of the law **2** : to make illegal **3** ♦ : to place under a ban or restriction — **out·law·ry** \'aut-ˌlor-ē\ *n*

♦ ban, bar, enjoin, forbid, interdict, prohibit, proscribe

out·lay \'aut-ˌlā\ *n* **1** : the act of spending **2** ♦ : something expended : EXPENDITURE

♦ cost, disbursement, expenditure, expense, outgo

out·let \'aut-ˌlet, -lət\ *n* **1** ♦ : a place or opening through which something is let out : EXIT **2** : a means of release (as for an emotion) **3** : a market for a commodity **4** : a receptacle for the plug of an electrical device

♦ egress, exit, issue

¹**out·line** \'aut-ˌlīn\ *n* **1** ♦ : a line marking the outer limits of an object or figure **2** : a drawing in which only contours are marked **3** ♦ : a condensed treatment of a particular subject : a summary of a written work : SUMMARY, SYNOPSIS **4** : PLAN

♦ [1] contour, figure, silhouette ♦ [3] abstract, digest, encapsulation, epitome, précis, recapitulation, roundup, résumé (*or* resume), sum, summary, synopsis, wrap-up

²**outline** *vb* **1** ♦ : to draw the outline of **2** : to indicate the chief features or parts of

♦ define, delineate, silhouette, sketch, trace

out·live \aut-'liv\ *vb* : to live longer than
out·look \'aut-ˌluk\ *n* **1 a** : a place offering a view **b** ♦ : a view from a particular place : VIEW **2** ♦ : a position from which something is considered or evaluated : STANDPOINT **3** : the prospect for the future

♦ [1b] lookout, panorama, prospect, view, vista ♦ [2] angle, perspective, point of view, slant, standpoint, viewpoint

out·ly·ing \-ˌlī-iŋ\ *adj* : distant from a center or main body
out·ma·neu·ver \ˌaut-mə-'nü-vər, -'nyü-\ *vb* ♦ : to defeat by more skillful maneuvering

♦ fox, outfox, outsmart, outwit, overreach

out·mod·ed \aut-'mō-dəd\ *adj* **1** ♦ : no longer in style **2** ♦ : no longer acceptable, current, or usable

♦ [1, 2] antiquated, archaic, dated, obsolete, outdated, outworn, passé

out·num·ber \-'nəm-bər\ *vb* : to exceed in number

out of *prep* **1** : out from within or behind ⟨walk *out of* the room⟩ ⟨look *out of* the window⟩ **2** : from a state of ⟨wake up *out of* a deep sleep⟩ **3** : beyond the limits of ⟨*out of* sight⟩ **4** : BECAUSE OF ⟨asked *out of* curiosity⟩ **5** : FROM, WITH ⟨built it *out of* scrap⟩ **6** : in or into a state of loss or not having ⟨cheated him *out of* $5000⟩ ⟨we're *out of* matches⟩ **7** : from among ⟨one *out of* four⟩ — **out of it** : SQUARE, OLD-FASHIONED
out-of-bounds *adv or adj* : outside the prescribed boundaries or limits
out-of-date *adj* : no longer in fashion or in use : OUTMODED
out-of-door *or* **out-of-doors** *adj* : of or relating to the outdoors : OUTDOOR
out-of-the-way *adj* **1** : UNUSUAL **2** : being off the beaten track
out·pa·tient \'aut-ˌpā-shənt\ *n* : a patient who visits a hospital or clinic for diagnosis or treatment without staying overnight
out·per·form \ˌaut-pər-'form\ *vb* : to perform better than
out·play \aut-'plā\ *vb* : to play more skillfully than
out·point \-'point\ *vb* : to win more points than
out·post \'aut-ˌpōst\ *n* **1** : a security detachment dispatched by a main body of troops to protect it from enemy surprise; *also* : a military base established (as by treaty) in a foreign country **2** : an outlying or frontier settlement
out·pour·ing \-ˌpōr-iŋ\ *n* ♦ : something that pours out or is poured out

♦ gush, outflow

out·pull \aut-'pul\ *vb* : OUTDRAW 1
¹**out·put** \'aut-ˌput\ *n* **1 a** ♦ : the amount produced (as by a machine or factory) : PRODUCTION **b** ♦ : mental or artistic production **2** : the information produced by a computer

♦ [1a, b] affair, handiwork, produce, product, thing, work, yield

²**output** *vb* **out·put·ted** *or* **output; out·put·ting** : to produce as output
¹**out·rage** \'aut-ˌrāj\ *n* **1** : a violent or shameful act **2** ♦ : a gross indignity : INSULT **3** ♦ : the anger or resentment aroused by an outrage

♦ [2] affront, barb, dart, dig, indignity, insult, name, offense, put-down, sarcasm, slight, slur, wound ♦ [3] anger, furor, fury, indignation, ire, rage, spleen, wrath, wrathfulness

²**outrage** *vb* **out·raged; out·rag·ing** **1** : RAPE **2** ♦ : to subject to violent injury or gross insult **3** ♦ : to arouse to extreme resentment

♦ [2] affront, insult, offend, slight, wound ♦ [3] anger, antagonize, enrage, incense, inflame, infuriate, madden, rankle, rile, roil

out·ra·geous \aut-'rā-jəs\ *adj* : extremely offensive, insulting, or shameful : SHOCKING — **out·ra·geous·ly** *adv*
out·rank \-'raŋk\ *vb* : to rank higher than
ou·tré \ü-'trā\ *adj* ♦ : violating convention or propriety : BIZARRE ⟨∼ creations⟩

♦ bizarre, curious, far-out, funny, kinky, odd, outlandish, peculiar, quaint, quirky, remarkable, screwy, strange, wacky, weird, wild

¹**out·reach** \aut-'rēch\ *vb* **1** : to surpass in reach **2** : to get the better of by trickery
²**out·reach** \'aut-ˌrēch\ *n* **1** : the act of reaching out **2** : the extent of reach **3** : the extending of services beyond usual limits
out·rid·er \-ˌrī-dər\ *n* : a mounted attendant
out·rig·ger \-ˌri-gər\ *n* **1** : a frame attached to the side of a boat to prevent capsizing **2** : a craft equipped with an outrigger
¹**out·right** \aut-'rīt\ *adv* **1** : COMPLETELY **2** : INSTANTANEOUSLY
²**out·right** \'aut-ˌrīt\ *adj* **1** : being exactly what is stated ⟨an ∼ lie⟩ **2** ♦ : given or made without reservation or encumbrance ⟨an ∼ sale⟩

♦ absolute, all-out, complete, consummate, out-and-out, perfect, pure, sheer, thorough, thoroughgoing, total, utter

out·run \aut-'rən\ *vb* **-ran** \-'ran\; **-run; -run·ning** **1** : to run faster than **2** ♦ : to go or be beyond the limit of : EXCEED

♦ exceed, overreach, overrun, overshoot, overstep, surpass, transcend

out·sell \-'sel\ *vb* **-sold** \-'sōld\; **-sell·ing** : to exceed in sales
out·set \'aut-ˌset\ *n* ♦ : a setting out : BEGINNING, START

♦ beginning, birth, commencement, dawn, genesis, launch, morning, onset, start, threshold

out·shine \aut-'shīn\ *vb* **-shone** \-'shōn\ *or* **-shined; -shin·ing** **1** : to shine brighter than **2** ♦ : to go beyond in action or performance : SURPASS

♦ beat, better, eclipse, excel, outdistance, outdo, outstrip, surpass, top, transcend

¹out·side \aút-'sīd, 'aút-ˌsīd\ *n* **1** : a place or region beyond an enclosure or boundary **2** ♦ : an outer side or surface : EXTERIOR **3** : the utmost limit or extent

♦ exterior, face, skin, surface, veneer

²outside *adj* **1** ♦ : of, relating to, or being on or toward the outer side or surface : OUTER **2** : coming from without ⟨∼ influences⟩ **3** : being apart from one's regular duties ⟨∼ activities⟩ **4** ♦ : barely possible : REMOTE ⟨an ∼ chance⟩

♦ [1] exterior, external, outer, outward ♦ [4] negligible, off, remote, slight, slim, small

³outside *adv* : on or to the outside
⁴outside *prep* **1** : on or to the outside of **2** ♦ : beyond the limits of **3** ♦ : with the exclusion or exception of : EXCEPT

♦ [2] beyond, without ♦ *usu* **outside of** [3] aside from, bar, barring, besides, but, except, save

outside of *prep* **1** : with the exclusion or exception of : OUTSIDE **2** : BESIDES **3** : beyond the limits or compass of
out·sid·er \aút-'sī-dər\ *n* : a person who does not belong to a group
out·size \'aút-ˌsīz\ *also* **out·sized** \-ˌsīzd\ *adj* ♦ : unusually large : extravagant in size or degree

♦ astronomical, enormous, giant, gigantic, grand, huge, jumbo, mammoth, massive, monumental, oversize, prodigious, titanic, tremendous, vast

out·skirts \-ˌskərts\ *n pl* ♦ : the outlying parts (as of a city)

♦ environs, exurbia, suburbia

out·smart \aút-'smärt\ *vb* ♦ : to get the better of : OUTWIT

♦ fox, outfox, outmaneuver, outwit, overreach

out·source \'aút-ˌsórs\ *vb* **-sourced; -sourc·ing** : to obtain (goods or services) from an outside supplier
out·spend \-'spend\ *vb* **1** : to exceed the limits of in spending ⟨∼s his income⟩ **2** : to spend more than
out·spo·ken \aút-'spō-kən\ *adj* ♦ : direct and open in speech or expression — **out·spo·ken·ly** *adv*

♦ candid, direct, forthright, foursquare, frank, honest, open, plain, straight, straightforward, unguarded, unreserved

out·spo·ken·ness \aút-'spō-kən-nəs\ *n* ♦ : the quality or state of being outspoken

♦ candidness, candor, directness, forthrightness, frankness, openness, plainness

out·spread \-'spred\ *vb* **-spread; -spread·ing** : to spread out
out·stand·ing \-'stan-diŋ\ *adj* **1** : PROJECTING **2 a** ♦ : not paid : UNPAID **b** : UNRESOLVED **3** : publicly issued and sold **4 a** : CONSPICUOUS **b** ♦ : marked by eminence and distinction : DISTINGUISHED — **out·stand·ing·ly** *adv*

♦ [2a] overdue, payable, unpaid, unsettled *Ant* cleared, liquidated, paid (off *or* up), repaid, settled ♦ [4b] distinguished, eminent, illustrious, noble, notable, noteworthy, preeminent, prestigious, signal, star, superior

out·stay \-'stā\ *vb* **1** : OVERSTAY **2** : to surpass in endurance
out·stretch \ˌaút-'strech\ *vb* : to stretch out : EXTEND
out·strip \-'strip\ *vb* **1** : to go faster than **2** ♦ : to get ahead of : EXCEL, SURPASS

♦ beat, better, eclipse, excel, outdistance, outdo, outshine, surpass, top, transcend

out·take \'aút-ˌtāk\ *n* : something taken out; *esp* : a take that is not used in an edited version of a film or videotape
out·vote \-'vōt\ *vb* : to defeat by a majority of votes
¹out·ward \'aút-wərd\ *adj* **1** : moving or directed toward the outside **2** : showing outwardly **3** ♦ : situated or lying on the outside of an enclosure or surface

♦ exterior, external, outer, outside

²outward *or* **out·wards** \-wərdz\ *adv* : toward the outside
out·ward·ly \-wərd-lē\ *adv* : on the outside : EXTERNALLY
out·wear \aút-'war\ *vb* **-wore** \-'wōr\; **-worn** \-'wōrn\; **-wear·ing** : to wear longer than : OUTLAST
out·weigh \-'wā\ *vb* ♦ : to exceed in weight, value, or importance

♦ overshadow

out·wit \-'wit\ *vb* ♦ : to get the better of by superior cleverness

♦ fox, outfox, outmaneuver, outsmart, overreach

¹out·work \-'wərk\ *vb* : to outdo in working

²out·work \'aút-ˌwərk\ *n* : a minor defensive position outside a fortified area
out·worn \aút-'wōrn\ *adj* ♦ : no longer useful or accepted : OUTMODED

♦ antiquated, archaic, dated, obsolete, outdated, outmoded, passé

ou·zo \'ü-(ˌ)zō\ *n* : a colorless anise-flavored unsweetened Greek liqueur
ova *pl of* OVUM
oval \'ō-vəl\ *adj* : egg-shaped; *also* : broadly elliptical — **oval** *n*
ova·ry \'ō-və-rē\ *n, pl* **-ries** **1** : one of the usu. paired female reproductive organs producing eggs and in vertebrates sex hormones **2** : the part of a flower in which seeds are produced — **ovar·i·an** \ō-'var-ē-ən, -'ver-\ *adj*
ovate \'ō-ˌvāt\ *adj* : egg-shaped
ova·tion \ō-'vā-shən\ *n* ♦ : an enthusiastic popular tribute

♦ acclamation, applause

ov·en \'ə-vən\ *n* : a chamber (as in a stove) for baking, heating, or drying
oven·bird \-ˌbərd\ *n* : a large olive-green American warbler that builds its dome-shaped nest on the ground
¹over \'ō-vər\ *adv* **1** : across a barrier or intervening space **2** : across the brim ⟨boil ∼⟩ **3** ♦ : so as to bring the underside up or the upside down **4** : out of a vertical position **5** : beyond some quantity, limit, or norm **6** ♦ : in or to a higher place : ABOVE **7** : at an end **8** ♦ : from beginning to end : THROUGH; *also* : THOROUGHLY ⟨think it ∼⟩ **9** ♦ : for a second or successive time : AGAIN ⟨do it ∼⟩

♦ [3] below, down, downward ♦ [6] above, aloft, overhead, skyward ♦ [8] around, round, thoroughly, through, throughout ♦ [9] again, anew

²over *prep* **1** : above in position, authority, or scope ⟨towered ∼ her⟩ ⟨obeyed those ∼ him⟩ **2** : more than ⟨cost ∼ $100⟩ **3** : ON, UPON ⟨a cape ∼ her shoulders⟩ **4** : along the length of ⟨∼ the road⟩ **5** : through the medium of : ON ⟨spoke ∼ TV⟩ **6** ♦ : all through ⟨showed me ∼ the house⟩ **7** ♦ : on or to the other side or beyond ⟨jump ∼ a ditch⟩ **8** : throughout the duration of : DURING ⟨∼ the past 25 years⟩ **9** : on account of ⟨trouble ∼ money⟩

♦ [6] about, around, round, through, throughout ♦ [7] across, athwart, through

³over *adj* **1** : being higher or in a superior position **2** : REMAINING **3** ♦ : being at an end : ENDED

♦ complete, done, down, through, up

over- *prefix* **1** : so as to exceed or surpass **2** : excessive; excessively

overabundant	overextend
overachiever	overfatigued
overaggressive	overfeed
overambitious	overgeneralization
overanxious	overgeneralize
overbid	overgenerous
overbuild	overgraze
overbuy	overhasty
overcapacity	overheat
overcapitalize	overhype
overcareful	overindulge
overcautious	overindulgence
overcompensation	overindulgent
overconfidence	overinflate
overconscientious	overlarge
overcook	overlearn
overcrowd	overlong
overdecorated	overmodest
overdependence	overnice
overdetermined	overoptimism
overdevelop	overoptimistic
overdress	overpay
overeager	overproduce
overeat	overproduction
overeducated	overprotect
overemphasis	overprotective
overemphasize	overrate
overenthusiastic	overreact
overestimate	overreaction
overexcite	overrefinement
overexcited	overregulate
overexert	overreliance
overexertion	overrepresented

oversensitive
oversensitiveness
oversimple
oversimplification
oversimplify
overspecialization
overspecialize
overspend
overstimulation

overstock
oversubtle
oversupply
overtax
overtired
overtrain
overuse
overvalue
overzealous

over·abun·dance \ō-vər-ə-'bən-dən(t)s\ *n* ♦ : an excessive abundance

   ♦ excess, fat, overflow, overkill, overmuch, superabundance, superfluity, surfeit, surplus

over·act \ō-vər-'akt\ *vb* : to exaggerate in acting
over·ac·tive \-'ak-tiv\ *adj* ♦ : excessively or abnormally active ⟨∼ glands⟩ ⟨an ∼ imagination⟩ — **over·ac·tiv·i·ty** \-ak-'ti-və-tē\ *n*

   ♦ agitated, feverish, frenzied, heated, hectic, overwrought

¹**over·age** \ō-vər-'āj\ *adj* **1** : too old to be useful **2** : older than is normal for one's position, function, or grade
²**over·age** \'ō-və-rij\ *n* : SURPLUS
¹**over·all** \ō-vər-'ol\ *adj* **1** ♦ : including everything ⟨∼ expenses⟩ **2** : viewed as a whole

   ♦ [1] blanket, common, general, generic, global, universal ♦ [1] all around, altogether, collectively, together ♦ [1, 2] all-around, bird's-eye, broad, general, nonspecific

²**over·all** \ō-vər-'ol\ *adv* ♦ : as a whole

   ♦ altogether, basically, chiefly, generally, largely, mainly, mostly, predominantly, primarily, principally

over·alls \'ō-vər-olz\ *n pl* : pants of strong material usu. with a piece extending up to cover the chest
over·arm \-arm\ *adj* : done with the arm raised above the shoulder
over·awe \ō-vər-'o\ *vb* : to restrain or subdue by awe
over·bal·ance \-'ba-ləns\ *vb* **1** : to exceed in weight, value, or importance : OUTWEIGH **2** : to cause to lose balance
over·bear·ing \-'bar-iŋ\ *adj* ♦ : decisively important : DOMINEERING

   ♦ authoritarian, autocratic, bossy, despotic, dictatorial, domineering, imperious, peremptory, tyrannical, tyrannous

over·bite \'ō-vər-bīt\ *n* : the projection of the upper front teeth over the lower
over·blown \-'blōn\ *adj* **1** : PORTLY **2** : INFLATED, PRETENTIOUS
over·board \'ō-vər-bōrd\ *adv* **1** : over the side of a ship into the water **2** : to extremes of enthusiasm
over·bold \-'bōld\ *adj* ♦ : excessively bold or forward

   ♦ brash, foolhardy, madcap, overconfident, reckless

over·bur·den \-'bər-d²n\ *vb* ♦ : to place an excessive burden on

   ♦ overcharge, overload

¹**over·cast** \'ō-vər-kast\ *adj* ♦ : clouded over : GLOOMY

   ♦ cloudy, dull, gloomy, hazy, heavy *Ant* clear, cloudless

²**overcast** *n* : COVERING; *esp* : a covering of clouds
over·charge \ō-vər-'chärj\ *vb* **1** ♦ : to charge too much **2** : to fill or load too full — **over·charge** \'ō-vər-chärj\ *n*

   ♦ gouge, soak, sting *Ant* undercharge

over·coat \'ō-vər-kōt\ *n* : a warm coat worn over indoor clothing
over·come \ō-vər-'kəm\ *vb* **-came** \-'kām\; **-come; -coming 1** ♦ : to get the better of : CONQUER **2** ♦ : to make helpless or exhausted

   ♦ [1] beat, best, clobber, conquer, crush, defeat, drub, lick, master, prevail, rout, skunk, subdue, surmount, thrash, trim, triumph, trounce, wallop, whip, win ♦ [2] carry away, crush, devastate, floor, oppress, overpower, overwhelm, prostrate, snow under, swamp

over·con·fi·dent \-'kän-fə-dənt, -dent\ *adj* ♦ : marked by or reflecting overconfidence

   ♦ brash, foolhardy, madcap, overbold, reckless

over·crit·i·cal \-'kri-ti-kəl\ *adj* ♦ : meticulously or excessively critical

   ♦ captious, carping, critical, hypercritical

over·do \ō-vər-'dü\ *vb* **-did** \-'did\; **-done** \-'dən\; **-do·ing;**

does \-'dəz\ **1** : to do too much; *also* : to tire oneself **2** ♦ : to do in excess : EXAGGERATE **3** : to cook too long

   ♦ exaggerate, overstate, put on

over·dose \'ō-vər-dōs\ *n* : too great a dose (as of medicine); *also* : a lethal or toxic amount (as of a drug) — **over·dose** \ō-vər-'dōs\ *vb*
over·draft \'ō-vər-draft, -dräft\ *n* : an overdrawing of a bank account; *also* : the sum overdrawn
over·draw \ō-vər-'dro\ *vb* **-drew** \-'drü\; **-drawn** \-'drón\; **-draw·ing 1** : to draw checks on a bank account for more than the balance **2** : to do in excess : EXAGGERATE
over·drive \'ō-vər-drīv\ *n* : an automotive transmission gear that transmits to the driveshaft a speed greater than the engine speed
over·dub \ō-vər-'dəb\ *vb* : to transfer (recorded sound) onto an earlier recording for a combined effect — **over·dub** \'ō-vər-dəb\ *n*
over·due \-'dü, -'dyü\ *adj* **1 a** ♦ : unpaid when due **b** ♦ : not appearing or presented on time **2** : more than ready

   ♦ [1a] outstanding, payable, unpaid, unsettled ♦ [1b] behind, belated, delinquent, late, tardy

over·ex·pose \ō-vər-ik-'spōz\ *vb* : to expose (as film) for more time than is needed — **over·ex·po·sure** \-'spō-zhər\ *n*
¹**over·flow** \-'flō\ *vb* **1** ♦ : to cover with or as if with water : INUNDATE; *also* : to pour forth in a flood **2** : to flow over the brim or top of

   ♦ deluge, drown, engulf, flood, inundate, overwhelm, submerge, swamp

²**over·flow** \'ō-vər-flō\ *n* **1 a** ♦ : a flowing over : FLOOD **b** ♦ : a flowing over : SURPLUS **2** : an outlet for surplus liquid

   ♦ [1a] cataclysm, cataract, deluge, flood, inundation, spate, torrent ♦ [1b] excess, fat, overabundance, overkill, overmuch, superabundance, superfluity, surfeit, surplus

over·fly \ō-vər-'flī\ *vb* **-flew** \-'flü\; **-flown** \-'flōn\; **-fly·ing** : to fly over in an aircraft or spacecraft — **over·flight** \'ō-vər-flīt\ *n*
over·grow \ō-vər-'grō\ *vb* **-grew** \-'grü\; **-grow·ing 1** : to grow over so as to cover **2** : OUTGROW **3** : to grow excessively
over·grown \-'grōn\ *adj* : covered with overgrowth
over·hand \'ō-vər-hand\ *adj* : made with the hand brought down from above — **overhand** *adv* — **over·hand·ed** \-han-dəd\ *adv or adj*
¹**over·hang** \'ō-vər-haŋ, ō-vər-'haŋ\ *vb* **-hung** \-həŋ, -'həŋ\; **-hang·ing 1** : to project over : jut out **2** ♦ : to hang over threateningly

   ♦ hang, hover, menace, threaten

²**over·hang** \'ō-vər-haŋ\ *n* : a part (as of a roof) that overhangs

   ♦ bulge, projection, protrusion

over·haul \ō-vər-'hol\ *vb* **1** : to examine thoroughly and make necessary repairs and adjustments **2** : OVERTAKE
¹**over·head** \ō-vər-'hed\ *adv* ♦ : above one's head : ALOFT

   ♦ above, aloft, over, skyward

²**over·head** \'ō-vər-hed\ *adj* : operating or lying above ⟨∼ storage bins⟩
³**over·head** \'ō-vər-hed\ *n* : business expenses not chargeable to a particular part of the work
over·hear \ō-vər-'hir\ *vb* **-heard** \-'hərd\; **-hear·ing** : to hear without the speaker's knowledge or intention
over·joyed \ō-vər-'joid\ *adj* : filled with great joy
over·kill \'ō-vər-kil\ *n* **1** : destructive capacity greatly exceeding that required for a target **2** ♦ : a large excess

   ♦ excess, fat, overabundance, overflow, overmuch, superabundance, superfluity, surfeit, surplus

over·land \'ō-vər-land, -lənd\ *adv or adj* : by, on, or across land
¹**over·lap** \ō-vər-'lap\ *vb* **1** ♦ : to lap over **2** : to have something in common

   ♦ lap, overlay, overlie, overspread

²**over·lap** \'ō-vər-lap\ *n* : the condition or relationship of things that overlap
over·lay \ō-vər-'lā\ *vb* **-laid** \-'lād\; **-lay·ing** ♦ : to lay or spread over or across — **over·lay** \'ō-vər-lā\ *n*

   ♦ blanket, carpet, coat, cover, overlie, overspread

over·leap \ō-vər-'lēp\ *vb* **-leaped** *or* **-leapt** \-'lēpt, -'lept\; **-leap·ing 1** : to leap over or across **2** : to defeat (oneself) by going too far

over•lie \ˌō-vər-ˈlī\ vb **-lay** \-ˈlā\; **-lain** \-ˈlān\; **-ly•ing** ♦ : to lie over or upon

♦ lap, overlap, overlay, overspread

over•load \-ˈlōd\ vb ♦ : to load to excess

♦ overburden, overcharge

¹**over•look** \ˌō-vər-ˈlůk\ vb **1** : INSPECT **2** : to look down on from above **3** : to fail to see **4** ♦ : to refuse to take notice of : IGNORE ⟨∼ed his faults⟩; also : EXCUSE **5** : SUPERINTEND

♦ disregard, excuse, forget, ignore, neglect, pass over, slight, slur

²**over•look** \ˈō-vər-ˌlůk\ n : a place from which to look upon a scene below

over•lord \-ˌlȯrd\ n : a lord who has supremacy over other lords

over•ly \ˈō-vər-lē\ adv ♦ : to an excessive degree : EXCESSIVELY

♦ devilishly, excessively, inordinately, monstrously, overmuch, too

over•match \ˌō-vər-ˈmach\ vb : to be more than a match for : DEFEAT

¹**over•much** \-ˈməch\ adj ♦ : too much

♦ devilish, excessive, exorbitant, extravagant, extreme, immoderate, inordinate, lavish, overweening, steep, stiff, towering, unconscionable

²**overmuch** adv ♦ : in too great a degree

♦ devilishly, excessively, inordinately, monstrously, overly, too

¹**over•night** \-ˈnīt\ adv **1** : on or during the night **2** : SUDDENLY ⟨became famous ∼⟩

²**overnight** adj : of, lasting, or staying the night ⟨∼ guests⟩

over•pass \ˈō-vər-ˌpas\ n **1** : a crossing (as of two highways) at different levels by means of a bridge **2** : the upper level of an overpass

over•play \ˌō-vər-ˈplā\ vb **1** : EXAGGERATE; also : to put undue emphasis on **2** : to rely too much on the strength of

over•pop•u•la•tion \ˌō-vər-ˌpä-pyə-ˈlā-shən\ n : the condition of having a population so dense as to cause a decline in population or in living conditions — **over•pop•u•lat•ed** \-ˈpä-pyə-ˌlā-təd\ adj

over•pow•er \-ˈpaů-ər\ vb **1** ♦ : to overcome by superior force **2** ♦ : to affect with overwhelming intensity

♦ [1] conquer, dominate, subdue, subject, vanquish ♦ [2] carry away, crush, devastate, floor, oppress, overcome, overwhelm, prostrate, snow under, swamp

over•praise \-ˈprāz\ vb ♦ : to praise excessively

♦ blarney, flatter

over•price \ˌō-vər-ˈprīs\ vb : to price too high

over•print \-ˈprint\ vb : to print over with something additional — **over•print** \ˈō-vər-ˌprint\ n

over•qual•i•fied \-ˈkwä-lə-ˌfīd\ adj : having more education, training, or experience than a job calls for

over•reach \ˌō-vər-ˈrēch\ vb **1** : to defeat (oneself) by too great an effort **2** ♦ : to get the better of esp. in dealing and bargaining and typically by unscrupulous or crafty methods **3** ♦ : to reach above or beyond

♦ [2] fox, outfox, outmaneuver, outsmart, outwit ♦ [3] exceed, overrun, overshoot, overstep, surpass

over•ride \-ˈrīd\ vb **-rode** \-ˈrōd\; **-rid•den** \-ˈrid-ᵊn\; **-rid•ing** **1** : to ride over or across **2** : to prevail over; also : to set aside ⟨∼ a veto⟩

over•ripe \ˌō-və(r)-ˈrīp\ adj ♦ : marked by decay or decline : DECADENT — **over•ripe•ness** \-nəs\ n

♦ decadent, degenerate, effete

over•rule \-ˈrül\ vb **1** : to prevail over **2** : to rule against **3** : to set aside

¹**over•run** \-ˈrən\ vb **-ran** \-ˈran\; **-run•ning** **1** ♦ : to defeat and occupy the positions of **2** : OVERSPREAD; also : INFEST **3** : to go beyond **4** : to flow over

♦ foray, invade, raid

²**over•run** \ˈō-vər-ˌrən\ n **1** : an act or instance of overrunning; esp : an exceeding of estimated costs **2** : the amount by which something overruns

over•sea \ˌō-vər-ˈsē, ˈō-vər-ˌsē\ adj or adv : OVERSEAS

over•seas \ˌō-vər-ˈsēz, -ˌsēz\ adv or adj : beyond or across the sea : ABROAD

over•see \ˌō-vər-ˈsē\ vb **-saw** \-ˈsȯ\; **-seen** \-ˈsēn\; **-see•ing** **1** : OVERLOOK **2 a** : INSPECT **b** ♦ : to have or exercise the charge and oversight of : SUPERVISE — **over•seer** \ˈō-vər-ˌsir\ n

♦ administer, carry on, conduct, control, direct, govern, guide, handle, manage, operate, regulate, run, superintend, supervise

over•sell \ˌō-vər-ˈsel\ vb **-sold**; **-sel•ling** : to sell too much to or too much of

over•sexed \ˌō-vər-ˈsekst\ adj : exhibiting excessive sexual drive or interest

over•shad•ow \-ˈsha-dō\ vb **1** ♦ : to cast a shadow over **2** ♦ : to exceed in importance

♦ [1] becloud, befog, blur, cloud, darken, dim, fog, haze, mist, obscure, overcast, shroud ♦ [2] outweigh

over•shoe \ˈō-vər-ˌshü\ n : a protective outer shoe; esp : GALOSH

over•shoot \ˌō-vər-ˈshüt\ vb **-shot** \-ˈshät\; **-shoot•ing** **1** : to pass swiftly beyond **2** ♦ : to shoot over or beyond **3** ♦ : to overreach (oneself) or cause (oneself) to go astray

♦ [2, 3] exceed, overreach, overrun, overstep, surpass

over•sight \ˈō-vər-ˌsīt\ n **1** ♦ : watchful and responsible care : SUPERVISION **2** ♦ : an inadvertent omission or error

♦ [1] administration, care, charge, conduct, control, direction, government, guidance, management, operation, regulation, running, superintendence, supervision ♦ [2] blunder, error, fault, flub, fumble, goof, lapse, miscue, misstep, mistake, slip, stumble

over•size \ˌō-vər-ˈsīz\ or **over•sized** \-ˈsīzd\ adj ♦ : of more than ordinary size

♦ big, considerable, goodly, grand, great, hefty, large, outsize, sizable, substantial

over•sleep \ˌō-vər-ˈslēp\ vb **-slept** \-ˈslept\; **-sleep•ing** : to sleep beyond the time for waking

over•spread \-ˈspred\ vb **-spread**; **-spread•ing** ♦ : to spread over or above

♦ blanket, carpet, coat, cover, overlay, overlie

over•state \-ˈstāt\ vb ♦ : to state in too strong terms : EXAGGERATE

♦ exaggerate, overdo, put on **Ant** understate

over•state•ment n ♦ : the act of overstating

♦ caricature, elaboration, embellishment, exaggeration, hyperbole, magnification, padding

over•stay \-ˈstā\ vb : to stay beyond the time or limits of

over•step \-ˈstep\ vb ♦ : to step over or beyond : EXCEED

♦ exceed, overreach, overrun, overshoot, surpass

over•sub•scribe \-səb-ˈskrīb\ vb : to subscribe for more of than is available, asked for, or offered for sale

overt \ō-ˈvərt, ˈō-ˌvərt\ adj : not secret — **overt•ly** adv

over•take \ˌō-vər-ˈtāk\ vb **-took** \-ˈtůk\; **-tak•en** \-ˈtā-kən\; **-tak•ing** : to catch up with; also : to catch up with and pass by

over–the–counter adj : sold lawfully without a prescription ⟨∼ drugs⟩

over–the–hill adj **1** : past one's prime **2** : advanced in age

over–the–top adj : extremely flamboyant or outrageous

¹**over•throw** \ˌō-vər-ˈthrō\ vb **-threw** \-ˈthrü\; **-thrown** \-ˈthrōn\; **-throw•ing** **1** : UPSET **2** : to bring down : DEFEAT ⟨∼ a government⟩ **3** : to throw over or past

²**over•throw** \ˈō-vər-ˌthrō\ n : an act of overthrowing or the state of being overthrown

over•time \ˈō-vər-ˌtīm\ n : time beyond a set limit; esp : working time in excess of a standard day or week — **overtime** adv

over•tone \-ˌtōn\ n **1** : one of the higher tones in a complex musical tone **2** : IMPLICATION, SUGGESTION ⟨political ∼s⟩

over•trick \ˈō-vər-ˌtrik\ n : a card trick won in excess of the number bid

over•ture \ˈō-vər-ˌchůr, -chər\ n **1** : an opening offer **2** : an orchestral introduction to a musical dramatic work

over•turn \ˌō-vər-ˈtərn\ vb **1** : to turn over : UPSET **2** : INVALIDATE

over•view \ˈō-vər-ˌvyü\ n : a general survey : SUMMARY

over•ween•ing \ˌō-vər-ˈwē-niŋ\ adj **1** ♦ : unduly confident ⟨∼ pride⟩ **2** ♦ : exceeding what is usual, proper, necessary, or normal : IMMODERATE

♦ [1] complacent, conceited, egotistic, important, pompous, prideful, proud, self-important, self-satisfied, smug, stuck-up, vain ♦ [2] devilish, excessive, exorbitant, extravagant, extreme, immoderate, inordinate, lavish, overmuch, steep, stiff, towering, unconscionable

over•weight \ˈō-vər-ˌwāt\ adj **1** : having weight above what is required or allowed **2** ♦ : having bodily weight greater than normal — **overweight** n

♦ chubby, corpulent, fat, fleshy, full, gross, obese, plump, portly, rotund, round

over·whelm \ˌō-vər-ˈhwelm\ *vb* **1** : OVERTHROW **2** ♦ : to cover over completely (as by a great wave) : SUBMERGE **3** ♦ : to overcome completely (as in thought or feeling)

♦ [2] deluge, drown, engulf, flood, inundate, overflow, submerge, swamp ♦ [3] carry away, crush, devastate, floor, oppress, overcome, overpower, prostrate, snow under, swamp

over·whelm·ing *adj* : EXTREME, GREAT ⟨∼ joy⟩ — **over·whelm·ing·ly** *adv*

over·win·ter \-ˈwin-tər\ *vb* : to survive or pass the winter

over·work \-ˈwərk\ *vb* **1** : to work or cause to work too hard or long **2** : to use too much — **overwork** *n*

over·wrought \ˌō-vər-ˈrȯt\ *adj* **1** ♦ : extremely excited **2** ♦ : elaborated to excess

♦ [1] agitated, feverish, frenzied, heated, hectic, overactive ♦ [2] florid, ornate

ovi·duct \ˈō-və-ˌdəkt\ *n* : a tube that serves for the passage of eggs from an ovary

ovip·a·rous \ō-ˈvi-pə-rəs\ *adj* : reproducing by eggs that hatch outside the parent's body

ovoid \ˈō-ˌvȯid\ *or* **ovoi·dal** \ō-ˈvȯid-ᵊl\ *adj* : egg-shaped : OVAL

ovu·la·tion \ˌäv-yə-ˈlā-shən, ˌōv-\ *n* : the discharge of a mature egg from the ovary — **ovu·late** \ˈäv-yə-ˌlāt, ˈōv-\ *vb*

ovule \ˈäv-yül, ˈōv-\ *n* : any of the bodies in a plant ovary that after fertilization become seeds

ovum \ˈō-vəm\ *n, pl* **ova** \-və\ : EGG 2

ow \ˈaù\ *interj* — used esp. to express sudden pain

owe \ˈō\ *vb* **owed; ow·ing** **1** : to be under obligation to pay or render **2** : to be indebted to or for; *also* : to be in debt

owing to *prep* ♦ : because of

♦ because of, due to, through, with

owl \ˈaù-(ə)l\ *n* : any of an order of chiefly nocturnal birds of prey with a large head and eyes and strong talons — **owl·ish** *adj* — **owl·ish·ly** *adv*

owl·et \ˈaù-lət\ *n* : a young or small owl

¹**own** \ˈōn\ *adj* : belonging to oneself — used as an intensive after a possessive adjective ⟨her ∼ car⟩

²**own** *vb* **1** ♦ : to have or hold as property **2** ♦ : to admit or confess frankly and fully : ACKNOWLEDGE; *also* : CONFESS — **own·er·ship** *n*

♦ [1] command, enjoy, have, hold, occupy, possess, retain ♦ *usu* **own up** [2] acknowledge, admit, agree, allow, concede, confess, grant

³**own** *pron* : one or ones belonging to oneself

own·er *n* ♦ : one that owns : one that has the legal or rightful title whether the possessor or not

♦ holder, possessor, proprietor

ox \ˈäks\ *n, pl* **ox·en** \ˈäk-sən\ *also* **ox** : any of the large domestic bovine mammals kept for milk, draft, and meat; *esp* : an adult castrated male ox

ox·blood \ˈäks-ˌbləd\ *n* : a moderate reddish brown

ox·bow \-ˌbō\ *n* **1** : a U-shaped collar worn by a draft ox **2** : a U-shaped bend in a river — **oxbow** *adj*

ox·ford \ˈäks-fərd\ *n* : a low shoe laced or tied over the instep

ox·i·dant \ˈäk-sə-dənt\ *n* : OXIDIZING AGENT — **oxidant** *adj*

ox·i·da·tion \ˌäk-sə-ˈdā-shən\ *n* : the act or process of oxidizing; *also* : the condition of being oxidized — **ox·i·da·tive** \ˈäk-sə-ˌdā-tiv\ *adj*

ox·ide \ˈäk-ˌsīd\ *n* : a compound of oxygen with another element or group

ox·i·dize \ˈäk-sə-ˌdīz\ *vb* **-dized; -diz·ing** : to combine with oxygen ⟨iron rusts because it is *oxidized* by exposure to the air⟩ — **ox·i·diz·er** *n*

oxidizing agent *n* : a substance (as oxygen or nitric acid) that oxidizes by taking up electrons

ox·y·gen \ˈäk-si-jən\ *n* : a colorless odorless gaseous chemical element that is found in the air, is essential to life, and is involved in combustion

ox·y·gen·ate \ˈäk-si-jə-ˌnāt\ *vb* **-at·ed; -at·ing** : to impregnate, combine, or supply with oxygen — **ox·y·gen·a·tion** \ˌäk-si-jə-ˈnā-shən\ *n*

oxygen mask *n* : a device worn over the nose and mouth through which oxygen is supplied

oxygen tent *n* : a canopy which can be placed over a bedridden person and within which a flow of oxygen can be maintained

ox·y·mo·ron \ˌäk-sē-ˈmȯr-ˌän\ *n* : a combination of contradictory words (as *cruel kindness*)

oys·ter \ˈȯi-stər\ *n* : any of various marine mollusks with an irregular 2-valved shell that include commercially important edible shellfish and pearl producers — **oys·ter·ing** *n* — **oys·ter·man** \ˈȯi-stər-mən\ *n*

oz *abbr* ounce; ounces

ozone \ˈō-ˌzōn\ *n* **1** : a bluish gaseous reactive form of oxygen that is formed naturally in the atmosphere and is used for disinfecting, deodorizing, and bleaching **2** : pure and refreshing air

ozone layer *n* : an atmospheric layer at heights of about 25 miles (40 kilometers) with high ozone content which blocks most solar ultraviolet radiation

¹**p** \ˈpē\ *n, pl* **p's** *or* **ps** \ˈpēz\ *often cap* : the 16th letter of the English alphabet

²**p** *abbr, often cap* **1** page **2** participle **3** past **4** pawn **5** pence; penny **6** per **7** petite **8** pint **9** pressure **10** purl

P *symbol* phosphorus

pa \ˈpä, ˈpȯ\ *n* : a man who has begotten a child : FATHER

¹**Pa** *abbr* **1** pascal **2** Pennsylvania

²**Pa** *symbol* protactinium

¹**PA** \ˌ(ˌ)pē-ˈā\ *n* : PHYSICIAN'S ASSISTANT

²**PA** *abbr* **1** Pennsylvania **2** per annum **3** power of attorney **4** press agent **5** private account **6** professional association **7** public address **8** purchasing agent

pab·u·lum \ˈpa-byə-ləm\ *n* : usu. soft digestible food

Pac *abbr* Pacific

PAC *abbr* political action committee

¹**pace** \ˈpās\ *n* **1** : rate of movement or progress (as in walking or working) **2** : a step in walking; *also* : a measure of length based on such a step **3** : GAIT; *esp* : a horse's gait in which the legs on the same side move together

²**pace** *vb* **paced; pac·ing** **1** ♦ : to go or cover at a pace or with slow steps **2** : to measure off by paces ⟨∼ off a 15-yard penalty⟩ **3** : to set or regulate the pace of

♦ file, march, parade, stride

³**pace** \ˈpā-sē; ˈpä-ˌkā, -ˌchä\ *prep* : contrary to the opinion of

pace·mak·er \ˈpās-ˌmā-kər\ *n* **1** : one that sets the pace for another **2** : a body part (as of the heart) that serves to establish and maintain a rhythmic activity **3** : an electrical device for stimulating or steadying the heartbeat

pac·er \ˈpā-sər\ *n* **1** : a horse that paces **2** : PACEMAKER

pachy·derm \ˈpa-ki-ˌdərm\ *n* : any of various thick-skinned hoofed mammals (as an elephant)

pach·ys·an·dra \ˌpa-ki-ˈsan-drə\ *n* : any of a genus of low perennial evergreen plants used as a ground cover

pa·cif·ic \pə-ˈsi-fik\ *adj* **1** ♦ : tending to lessen conflict **2** : CALM, PEACEFUL

♦ conciliatory, propitiatory *Ant* antagonizing

pac·i·fi·er \ˈpa-sə-ˌfī-ər\ *n* : one that pacifies; *esp* : a device for a baby to chew or suck on

pac·i·fism \ˈpa-sə-ˌfi-zəm\ *n* : opposition to war or violence as a means of settling disputes — **pac·i·fist** \-fist\ *n or adj* — **pac·i·fis·tic** \ˌpa-sə-ˈfis-tik\ *adj*

pac·i·fy \ˈpa-sə-ˌfī\ *vb* **-fied; -fy·ing** **1** ♦ : to allay anger or agitation in **2** : SETTLE; *also* : SUBDUE — **pac·i·fi·ca·tion** \ˌpa-sə-fə-ˈkā-shən\ *n*

♦ appease, conciliate, disarm, mollify, placate, propitiate *Ant* anger, enrage, incense, infuriate, madden, outrage

¹**pack** \ˈpak\ *n* **1** : a compact bundle; *also* : a flexible container

for carrying a bundle esp. on the back **2** : a large amount : HEAP **3** : a set of playing cards **4** : a group or band of people or animals **5** : wet absorbent material for application to the body

²pack *vb* **1** : to stow goods in for transportation **2 ♦** : to fill in or surround so as to prevent passage of air, steam, or water **3** : to put into a protective container **4** : to load with a pack ⟨~ a mule⟩ **5** : to crowd in **6** : to make into a pack **7** : to cause to go without ceremony ⟨~ them off to school⟩ **8 ♦** : to wear or carry as equipment ⟨~ a gun⟩

♦ [2] charge, cram, fill, heap, jam, jam-pack, load ♦ [8] bear, carry, cart, convey, ferry, haul, lug, tote, transport

³pack *vb* : to make up fraudulently so as to secure a desired result ⟨~ a jury⟩

¹pack•age \'pa-kij\ *n* **1 ♦** : a wrapped bundle : PARCEL **2 ♦** : a group of related things offered as a whole

♦ [1] bundle, pack, parcel ♦ [2] array, assemblage, bank, batch, block, bunch, clump, cluster, collection, group, huddle, knot, lot, parcel, set, suite

²package *vb* **pack•aged; pack•ag•ing** : to make into or enclose in a package

package deal *n* : an offer containing several items all or none of which must be accepted

package store *n* : a store that sells alcoholic beverages in sealed containers for consumption off the premises

packed \'pakt\ *adj* **1 a** : COMPRESSED **b ♦** : having elements crowded or stuffed **2 ♦** : filled to capacity

♦ [1b] close, compact, crowded, dense, serried, thick, tight ♦ [2] brimful, chock-full, crowded, fat, fraught, full, loaded, replete

pack•er \'pa-kər\ *n* : one that packs; *esp* : a wholesale food dealer

pack•et \'pa-kət\ *n* **1** : a small bundle or package **2** : a passenger boat carrying mail and cargo on a regular schedule

pack•horse \'pak-ˌhȯrs\ *n* : a horse used to carry goods or supplies

pack•ing \'pa-kiŋ\ *n* : material used to pack something

pack•ing•house \-ˌhau̇s\ *n* : an establishment for processing and packing food and esp. meat and its by-products

pack rat *n* **1** : a bushy-tailed rodent of western No. America that hoards food and miscellaneous objects **2** : a person who collects or saves many esp. unneeded items

pack•sad•dle \'pak-ˌsad-ᵊl\ *n* : a saddle for supporting loads on the back of an animal

pack•thread \-ˌthred\ *n* : strong thread for tying

pact \'pakt\ *n* **♦** : an agreement or covenant between two or more parties

♦ accord, agreement, bargain, compact, contract, convention, covenant, deal, settlement, understanding

¹pad \'pad\ *vb* **♦** : to traverse or go on foot

♦ foot, leg, step, traipse, tread, walk

²pad *n* **1 ♦** : a cushioning part or thing : CUSHION **2** : the cushioned underside of the foot or toes of some mammals **3** : the floating leaf of a water plant **4** : a writing tablet **5** : LAUNCH-PAD **6 a** : living quarters **b** : a piece of furniture on or in which to lie and sleep : BED

♦ buffer, bumper, cushion, fender

³pad *vb* **pad•ded; pad•ding** **1** : to furnish with a pad or padding **2 ♦** : to expand with needless or fraudulent matter

♦ color (*or* colour), elaborate, embellish, embroider, exaggerate, magnify, stretch

pad•ding *n* **♦** : the material with which something is padded

♦ fill, filler, filling, stuffing ♦ caricature, elaboration, embellishment, exaggeration, hyperbole, magnification, overstatement

¹pad•dle \'pad-ᵊl\ *vb* **pad•dled; pad•dling** : to move the hands and feet about in shallow water

²paddle *n* **1** : an implement with a flat blade used in propelling and steering a small craft (as a canoe) **2** : an implement used for stirring, mixing, or beating **3** : a broad board on the outer rim of a waterwheel or a paddle wheel

³paddle *vb* **pad•dled; pad•dling** **1** : to move on or through water by or as if by using a paddle **2** : to beat or stir with a paddle

paddle wheel *n* : a wheel with paddles around its outer edge used to move a boat

paddle wheeler *n* : a steam-driven vessel propelled by a paddle wheel

pad•dock \'pa-dək\ *n* **1** : a usu. enclosed area for pasturing or exercising animals; *esp* : one where racehorses are saddled and paraded before a race **2** : an area at a racecourse where racing cars are parked

pad•dy \'pa-dē\ *n, pl* **paddies** : wet land where rice is grown

paddy wagon *n* : an enclosed motortruck for carrying prisoners

pad•lock \'pad-ˌläk\ *n* : a removable lock with a curved piece that snaps into a catch — **padlock** *vb*

pa•dre \'pä-drā\ *n* **1** : a Christian clergyman; *esp* : PRIEST **2** : a military chaplain

pad thai \'päd-ˈtī\ *n, often cap T* : a Thai dish of rice noodles stir-fried with additional ingredients

pae•an \'pē-ən\ *n* **♦** : an exultant song of praise or thanksgiving

♦ accolade, citation, commendation, encomium, eulogy, homage, panegyric, salutation, tribute

pae•di•at•ric, pae•di•a•tri•cian, pae•di•at•rics *chiefly Brit var of* PEDIATRIC, PEDIATRICIAN, PEDIATRICS

pa•el•la \pä-ˈe-lə; -ˈäl-yə, -ˈä-yə\ *n* : a saffron-flavored dish of rice, meat, seafood, and vegetables

pa•gan \'pā-gən\ *n* : an unconverted member of a people or nation that does not acknowledge the God of the Bible : HEATHEN — **pagan** *adj* — **pa•gan•ism** \-gə-ˌni-zəm\ *n*

¹page \'pāj\ *n* **♦** : one employed to deliver messages, assist patrons, serve as a guide, or attend to similar duties

♦ courier, go-between, messenger, runner

²page *vb* **paged; pag•ing** **1** : to summon by repeatedly calling out the name of **2** : to send a message to via a pager

³page *n* **1** : a single leaf (as of a book); *also* : a single side of such a leaf **2** : the information at a single World Wide Web address

⁴page *vb* **paged; pag•ing** : to mark or number the pages of

pag•eant \'pa-jənt\ *n* : an elaborate spectacle, show, or procession esp. with tableaux or floats — **pag•eant•ry** \-jən-trē\ *n*

page•boy \'pāj-ˌbȯi\ *n* : an often shoulder-length hairdo with the ends of the hair turned smoothly under

pag•er \'pā-jər\ *n* : one that pages; *esp* : a small radio receiver that alerts its user to incoming messages

pag•i•nate \'pa-jə-ˌnāt\ *vb* **-nat•ed; -nat•ing** : ⁴PAGE

pag•i•na•tion \ˌpa-jə-ˈnā-shən\ *n* **1** : the paging of written or printed matter **2** : the number and arrangement of pages (as of a book)

pa•go•da \pə-ˈgō-də\ *n* : a tower with roofs curving upward at the division of each of several stories

paid *past and past part of* PAY

pail \'pāl\ *n* : a usu. cylindrical vessel with a handle — **pail•ful** \-ˌfu̇l\ *n*

¹pain \'pān\ *n* **1** : PUNISHMENT, PENALTY **2 a ♦** : suffering or distress of body or mind **b ♦** : a basic bodily sensation marked by discomfort (as throbbing or aching) **3** *pl* **♦** : great care **4** : one that irks or annoys

♦ [2a] affliction, agony, anguish, distress, misery, torment, torture, tribulation, woe ♦ [2b] ache, pang, prick, smart, sting, stitch, tingle, twinge ♦ **pains** [3] care, carefulness, heed, heedfulness, scrupulousness ♦ **pains** [3] effort, exertion, expenditure, labor (*or* labour), sweat, trouble, while, work

²pain *vb* **♦** : to cause or experience pain

♦ ache, hurt, smart

pain•ful \-fəl\ *adj* **♦** : feeling or giving pain

♦ achy, nasty, sore *Ant* painless

pain•ful•ly \-f(ə-)lē\ *adv* : in a painful manner

pain•kill•er \'pān-ˌki-lər\ *n* : something (as a drug) that relieves pain — **pain•kill•ing** *adj*

pain•less \-ləs\ *adj* **♦** : not causing pain

♦ easy, effortless, facile, fluent, fluid, light, ready, simple, smooth, snap, soft

pain•less•ly \-ləs-lē\ *adv* **♦** : in a painless manner

♦ easily, effortlessly, fluently, freely, handily, lightly, readily, smoothly

pains•tak•ing \'pānz-ˌstā-kiŋ\ *adj* **♦** : taking pains : showing care — **painstaking** *n* — **pains•tak•ing•ly** *adv*

♦ careful, conscientious, fussy, meticulous *Ant* careless

¹paint \'pānt\ *vb* **1 ♦** : to apply color, pigment, or paint to **2** : to produce or portray in lines or colors on a surface; *also* : to practice the art of painting **3** : to decorate with colors **4** : to use cosmetics **5 ♦** : to describe vividly **6** : SWAB — **paint•er** *n*

♦ [1] color (*or* colour), dye, stain, tinge, tint ♦ [5] delineate, depict, describe, draw, image, picture, portray, sketch

²paint *n* **1** : something produced by painting **2** : MAKEUP **3** : a mixture of a pigment and a liquid that forms a thin adherent coating when spread on a surface; *also* : the dry pigment used in making this mixture **4** : an applied coating of paint

paint·ball \'pānt-ˌbȯl\ *n* : a game in which two teams try to capture each other's flag using guns that shoot paint-filled pellets
paint·brush \'pānt-ˌbrəsh\ *n* : a brush for applying paint
painted lady *n* : a migratory butterfly with wings mottled in brown, orange, black, and white
paint·ing \'pān-tiŋ\ *n* **1** ♦ : a work (as a picture) produced by painting **2** : the art or occupation of painting

♦ oil

¹pair \'par\ *n, pl* **pairs** *also* **pair** **1** ♦ : two things of a kind designed for use together **2** : something made up of two corresponding pieces ⟨a ~ of pants⟩ **3** : a set of two people or animals

♦ brace, couple, duo, twain, twosome

²pair *vb* **1** : to arrange in pairs **2** : to form a pair : MATCH **3** : to become associated with another
pais·ley \'pāz-lē\ *adj, often cap* : decorated with colorful curved abstract figures ⟨a ~ fabric⟩
Pai·ute \'pī-ˌüt, -ˌyüt\ *n* : a member of an Indigenous people orig. of the U.S. Great Basin*; also* : either of the two languages of the Paiute people
pa·ja·mas *chiefly Can and Brit* **py·ja·mas** \pə-'jä-məz, -'ja-\ *n pl* : a loose suit for sleeping or lounging
Pak·i·stani \ˌpa-ki-'sta-nē, ˌpä-ki-'stä-nē\ *n* : a native or inhabitant of Pakistan — **Pakistani** *adj*
pal \'pal\ *n* ♦ : a close friend

♦ buddy, chum, comrade, crony, familiar, friend, intimate

pal·ace \'pa-ləs\ *n* **1** : the official residence of a chief of state **2** ♦ : a large stately house : MANSION

♦ castle, estate, hall, manor, mansion, villa

pal·a·din \'pa-lə-dən\ *n* **1** : a trusted military leader (as for a medieval prince) **2** ♦ : a leading champion of a cause

♦ advocate, apostle, backer, booster, champion, exponent, friend, promoter, proponent, supporter

pa·laes·tra \pə-'les-trə\ *n, pl* **-trae** \-(ˌ)trē\ : a school in ancient Greece or Rome for sports (as wrestling)
pa·lan·quin \ˌpa-lən-'kēn\ *n* : an enclosed couch for one person borne on the shoulders of men by means of poles
pal·at·abil·i·ty \ˌpa-lə-tə-'bi-lə-tē\ *n* ♦ : the quality or state of being palatable

♦ deliciousness, lusciousness, savor, tastiness

pal·at·able \'pa-lə-tə-bəl\ *adj* **1** ♦ : agreeable to the taste **2** ♦ : agreeable or acceptable to the mind

♦ [1, 2] agreeable, all right, alright, fine, good, OK, satisfactory ♦ [2] agreeable, congenial, felicitous, good, grateful, gratifying, nice, pleasant, pleasurable, satisfying

pal·a·tal \'pa-lət-ᵊl\ *adj* **1** : of or relating to the palate **2** : pronounced with some part of the tongue near or touching the hard palate ⟨the y in *yeast* and the sh in *she* are ~ sounds⟩
pal·a·tal·ize \'pa-lət-ᵊl-ˌīz\ *vb* **-ized; -iz·ing** : to pronounce as or change into a palatal sound — **pal·a·tal·i·za·tion** \ˌpa-lət-ᵊl-ə-'zā-shən\ *n*
pal·ate \'pa-lət\ *n* **1** : the roof of the mouth separating the mouth from the nasal cavity **2** : TASTE
pa·la·tial \pə-'lā-shəl\ *adj* **1** : of, relating to, or being a palace **2** ♦ : suitable to a palace

♦ deluxe, lavish, luxuriant, luxurious, opulent, plush, sumptuous

pa·lat·i·nate \pə-'lat-ᵊn-ət\ *n* : the territory of a palatine
¹pal·a·tine \'pa-lə-ˌtīn\ *adj* **1** : possessing royal privileges; *also* : of or relating to a palatine or a palatinate **2** : of or relating to a palace : PALATIAL
²palatine *n* **1** : a feudal lord having sovereign power within his domains **2** : a high officer of an imperial palace
¹pa·la·ver \pə-'la-vər, -'lä-\ *n* **1** : a long parley **2** ♦ : idle talk — **palaver** *vb*

♦ chat, chatter, chitchat, gabfest, gossip, rap, talk

²palaver *vb* : to talk profusely or idly
¹pale \'pāl\ *n* **1** : a stake or picket of a fence **2** : an enclosed place; *also* : a district or territory within certain bounds or under a particular jurisdiction **3** : LIMITS, BOUNDS ⟨conduct beyond the ~⟩
²pale *vb* **paled; pal·ing** : to enclose with or as if with pales : FENCE
³pale *adj* **pal·er; pal·est** **1** ♦ : deficient in color or intensity : WAN ⟨a ~ face⟩ **2** : lacking in brightness : DIM ⟨a ~ star⟩ **3** ♦ : not dark or intense in hue ⟨a ~ blue⟩ — **pale·ness** *n*

♦ [1] ashen, cadaverous, livid, lurid, pasty, peaked *Ant* florid,

flush, rubicund, ruddy, sanguine ♦ [3] dull, light, pastel, washed-out *Ant* dark, deep, rich

⁴pale *vb* **paled; pal·ing** ♦ : to make or become pale

♦ blanch, bleach, blench, dull, fade, wash out, whiten *Ant* darken, deepen

pale ale *n* : a medium-colored very dry ale
pale·face \'pāl-ˌfās\ *n, disparaging* : a white person
Pa·leo·cene \'pā-lē-ə-ˌsēn\ *adj* : of, relating to, or being the earliest epoch of the Tertiary — **Paleocene** *n*
pa·leo·con·ser·va·tive \ˌpā-lē-ō-kən-'sər-və-tiv\ *n* : a conservative espousing traditional principles and policies
pa·le·og·ra·phy \ˌpā-lē-'ä-grə-fē\ *n* : the study of ancient writings and inscriptions — **pa·le·og·ra·pher** *n*
Pa·leo·lith·ic \ˌpā-lē-ə-'li-thik\ *adj* : of or relating to the earliest period of the Stone Age characterized by rough or chipped stone implements
pa·le·on·tol·o·gy \ˌpā-lē-ˌän-'tä-lə-jē\ *n* : a science dealing with the life of past geologic periods as known from fossil remains — **pa·le·on·tol·o·gist** \-ˌän-'tä-lə-jist, -ən-\ *n*
Pa·leo·zo·ic \ˌpā-lē-ə-'zō-ik\ *adj* : of, relating to, or being the era of geologic history extending from about 570 million years ago to about 245 million years ago — **Paleozoic** *n*
pal·ette \'pa-lət\ *n* : a thin often oval board that a painter holds and mixes colors on; *also* : the colors on a palette
pal·frey \'pȯl-frē\ *n, pl* **palfreys** *archaic* : a saddle horse that is not a warhorse; *esp* : one suitable for a woman
pa·limp·sest \'pa-ləmp-ˌsest\ *n* : writing material (as a parchment) used after the erasure of earlier writing
pal·in·drome \'pa-lən-ˌdrōm\ *n* : a word, verse, or sentence (as "Able was I ere I saw Elba") or a number (as 1881) that reads the same backward or forward
pal·ing \'pā-liŋ\ *n* **1** : a fence of pales **2** : material for pales **3** : PALE, PICKET
pal·i·sade \ˌpa-lə-'sād\ *n* **1** : a high fence of stakes esp. for defense **2** : a line of steep cliffs

♦ bluff, cliff, crag, escarpment, precipice, scarp

¹pall \'pȯl\ *vb* **1** : to lose in interest or attraction **2** : SATIATE, CLOY
²pall *n* **1** : a heavy cloth draped over a coffin **2** : something that produces a gloomy atmosphere
pal·la·di·um \pə-'lā-dē-əm\ *n* : a silver-white metallic chemical element used esp. as a catalyst and in alloys
pall·bear·er \'pȯl-ˌbar-ər\ *n* : a person who attends the coffin at a funeral
¹pal·let \'pa-lət\ *n* : a small, hard, or makeshift bed
²pallet *n* : a portable platform for transporting and storing materials
pal·li·ate \'pa-lē-ˌāt\ *vb* **-at·ed; -at·ing** **1** ♦ : to ease (as a disease) without curing **2** ♦ : to cover by excuses and apologies ⟨~ faults⟩ — **pal·li·a·tion** \ˌpa-lē-'ā-shən\ *n* — **pal·li·a·tive** \'pa-lē-ˌā-tiv\ *adj or n*

♦ [1] allay, alleviate, assuage, ease, help, mitigate, mollify, relieve, soothe ♦ [2] excuse, gloss, whitewash

pal·lid \'pa-ləd\ *adj* : deficient in color : PALE, WAN
pal·lor \'pa-lər\ *n* ♦ : PALENESS
¹palm \'päm, 'pälm\ *n* **1** : any of a family of mostly tropical trees, shrubs, or vines usu. with a tall unbranched stem topped by a crown of large leaves **2** : a symbol of victory; *also* : VICTORY
²palm *n* : the underpart of the hand between the fingers and the wrist
³palm *vb* **1** : to conceal in or with the hand ⟨~ a card⟩ **2** : to impose by fraud
pal·mate \'pal-ˌmāt, 'päl-\ *also* **pal·mat·ed** \-ˌmā-təd\ *adj* : resembling a hand with the fingers spread
pal·met·to \pal-'me-tō\ *n, pl* **-tos** *or* **-toes** : any of several usu. small palms with fan-shaped leaves
palm·is·try \'pä-mə-strē, 'päl-\ *n* : the practice of reading a person's character or future from the markings on the palms — **palm·ist** \'pä-mist, 'päl-\ *n*
Palm Sunday *n* : the Sunday preceding Easter and commemorating Christ's triumphal entry into Jerusalem
palm·top \'päm-ˌtäp, 'pälm-\ *n* : a portable computer small enough to hold in the hand
palmy \'pä-mē, 'päl-\ *adj* **palm·i·er; -est** **1** : abounding in or bearing palms **2** ♦ : marked by prosperity : PROSPEROUS

♦ booming, golden, prosperous, roaring, successful

pal·o·mi·no \ˌpa-lə-'mē-nō\ *n, pl* **-nos** : a horse with a pale cream to golden coat and cream or white mane and tail
pal·pa·ble \'pal-pə-bəl\ *adj* **1** ♦ : capable of being touched or felt **2** ♦ : easily perceptible by the mind ⟨a ~ sense of relief⟩ — **pal·pa·bly** \-blē\ *adv*

♦ [1, 2] appreciable, detectable, discernible, distinguishable, perceptible, sensible ♦ [2] apparent, broad, clear, clear-cut, distinct, evident, lucid, manifest, obvious, patent, perspicuous, plain, transparent, unambiguous, unequivocal, unmistakable

pal·pate \'pal-ˌpāt\ vb **pal·pat·ed; pal·pat·ing** : to examine by touch esp. medically — **pal·pa·tion** \pal-'pā-shən\ n

pal·pi·tate \'pal-pə-ˌtāt\ vb **-tat·ed; -tat·ing** ♦ : to beat rapidly and strongly : THROB

♦ beat, pitter-patter, pulsate, pulse, throb

pal·pi·ta·tion \ˌpal-pə-'tā-shən\ n ♦ : a rapid pulsation

♦ beat, pulsation, pulse, throb

pal·sy \'pȯl-zē\ n, pl **palsies 1** : PARALYSIS **2** : a condition marked by tremor — **pal·sied** \-zēd\ adj
pal·ter \'pȯl-tər\ vb **pal·tered; pal·ter·ing 1** : to act insincerely : EQUIVOCATE **2** ♦ : to negotiate over the terms of a purchase, agreement, or contract : HAGGLE

♦ bargain, chaffer, deal, dicker, haggle, negotiate

pal·try \'pȯl-trē\ adj **pal·tri·er; -est 1** : TRASHY ⟨a ~ pamphlet⟩ **2** : MEAN, DESPICABLE ⟨a ~ trick⟩ **3** ♦ : of little worth or importance : TRIVIAL ⟨~ excuses⟩ **4** : MEAGER, MEASLY ⟨a ~ sum⟩

♦ inconsequential, inconsiderable, insignificant, measly, minute, negligible, nominal, petty, slight, trifling, trivial

pam abbr pamphlet
pam·pas \'pam-pəz, 'päm-, -pəs\ n pl : wide grassy So. American plains
pam·per \'pam-pər\ vb ♦ : to treat with excessive attention

♦ baby, coddle, mollycoddle, nurse, spoil

pam·phlet \'pam-flət\ n ♦ : an unbound printed publication

♦ booklet, brochure, circular, folder, leaflet

pam·phle·teer \ˌpam-flə-'tir\ n : a writer of pamphlets attacking something or urging a cause
¹**pan** \'pan\ n **1** : a usu. broad, shallow, and open container for domestic use; also : something resembling such a container **2** : a basin or depression in land **3** : HARDPAN
²**pan** vb **panned; pan·ning 1** : to wash earth or gravel in a pan in searching for gold **2** ♦ : to criticize severely

♦ blame, censure, condemn, criticize, denounce, fault, knock, reprehend

Pan abbr Panama
pan·a·cea \ˌpa-nə-'sē-ə\ n : a remedy for all ills or difficulties : CURE-ALL
pa·nache \pə-'nash, -'näsh\ n **1** : an ornamental tuft (as of feathers) esp. on a helmet **2** : dash or flamboyance in style and action
pan·a·ma \'pa-nə-ˌmä, -ˌmȯ\ n, often cap : a handmade hat braided from strips of the leaves from a tropical American tree
Pan·a·ma·ni·an \ˌpa-nə-'mā-nē-ən\ n : a native or inhabitant of Panama — **Panamanian** adj
pan·cake \'pan-ˌkāk\ n ♦ : a flat cake made of thin batter and fried on both sides

♦ flapjack, griddle cake

pan·chro·mat·ic \ˌpan-krō-'ma-tik\ adj : sensitive to all colors of visible light ⟨~ film⟩
pan·cre·as \'paŋ-krē-əs, 'pan-\ n : a large compound gland of vertebrates that produces insulin and discharges enzymes into the intestine — **pan·cre·at·ic** \ˌpaŋ-krē-'a-tik, ˌpan-\ adj
pan·da \'pan-də\ n **1** : a long-tailed reddish brown Himalayan mammal related to and resembling the raccoon **2** : a large black-and-white mammal of China usu. classified with the bears
pan·dem·ic \pan-'de-mik\ n : a widespread outbreak of disease — **pandemic** adj
pan·de·mo·ni·um \ˌpan-də-'mō-nē-əm\ n ♦ : a wild uproar : TUMULT

♦ commotion, disturbance, furor, hubbub, hullabaloo, row, tumult, turmoil, uproar

¹**pan·der** \'pan-dər\ n **1** : a go-between in love intrigues **2** : PIMP **3** : a person who caters to or exploits others' desires or weaknesses
²**pander** vb : to act as a pander ⟨~ing to popular taste⟩
P & I abbr principal and interest
P & L abbr profit and loss
Pan·do·ra's box \pan-'dȯr-əz-\ n : a prolific source of troubles
pan·dow·dy \pan-'daú-dē\ n, pl **-dies** : a deep-dish apple dessert spiced, sweetened, and covered with a crust
pane \'pān\ n : a sheet of glass (as in a door or window)

pan·e·gy·ric \ˌpa-nə-'jir-ik\ n ♦ : a eulogistic oration or writing — **pan·e·gyr·ist** \-'jir-ist\ n

♦ accolade, citation, commendation, encomium, eulogy, homage, paean, salutation, tribute

¹**pan·el** \'pan-ᵊl\ n **1 a** : a list of persons appointed for special duty ⟨a jury ~⟩ **b** : a group of people taking part in a discussion or quiz program **c** ♦ : a formal discussion by a panel **2** : a section of something (as a wall or door) often sunk below the level of the frame; also : a flat piece of construction material **3** : a flat piece of wood on which a picture is painted **4** : a mount for controls or dials

♦ colloquy, conference, council, forum, parley, seminar, symposium

²**panel** vb **-eled** or **-elled; -el·ing** or **-el·ling** : to decorate with panels
paneling n : decorative panels
pan·el·ist \'pan-ᵊl-ist\ n : a member of a discussion or quiz panel
panel truck n : a small motortruck with a fully enclosed body
pang \'paŋ\ n ♦ : a sudden sharp spasm (as of pain) or attack (as of remorse)

♦ ache, pain, prick, smart, sting, stitch, tingle, twinge

¹**pan·han·dle** \'pan-ˌhand-ᵊl\ n : a narrow projection of a larger territory (as a state) ⟨the Texas ~⟩
²**panhandle** vb **-dled; -dling** : to ask for money on the street — **pan·han·dler** n
¹**pan·ic** \'pa-nik\ n ♦ : a sudden overpowering fright — **pan·icky** \-ni-kē\ adj

♦ alarm, anxiety, apprehension, dread, fear, fright, horror, terror, trepidation

²**panic** vb **pan·icked** \-nikt\; **pan·ick·ing** ♦ : to affect or be affected with panic

♦ alarm, frighten, horrify, scare, shock, spook, startle, terrify, terrorize

pan·i·cle \'pa-ni-kəl\ n : a branched flower cluster (as of a lilac) in which each branch from the main stem has one or more flowers
pa·ni·ni \pə-'nē-nē\ also **pa·ni·no** \-'nē-nō\ n, pl **-nini** or **-ninis** : a usu. grilled sandwich made with Italian bread
pan·jan·drum \pan-'jan-drəm\ n, pl **-drums** also **-dra** \-drə\ : a powerful personage or pretentious official
pan·nier also **pan·ier** \'pan-yər\ n : a large basket esp. for bearing on the back
pan·o·ply \'pa-nə-plē\ n, pl **-plies 1** : a full suit of armor **2** : a protective covering **3** : an impressive array
pan·o·ra·ma \ˌpa-nə-'ra-mə, -'rä-\ n **1** : a picture unrolled before one's eyes **2** ♦ : a complete view in every direction

♦ lookout, outlook, prospect, view, vista

pan·oram·ic \ˌpa-nə-'ra-mik\ adj ♦ : of, relating to, or resembling a panorama

♦ compendious, complete, comprehensive, encyclopedic, full, global, inclusive, omnibus, universal

pan out vb **1** ♦ : to become in maturity : TURN OUT **2** ♦ : to turn out well : SUCCEED

♦ [1] come out, prove, turn out ♦ [2] click, deliver, go over, succeed, work out

pan·sex·u·al \ˌpan-'sek-shə-wəl\ adj : of, relating to, or characterized by sexual or romantic attraction that is not limited to people of a particular gender identity or sexual orientation; also : not solely straight or gay
pan·sy \'pan-zē\ n, pl **pansies** : a low-growing garden herb related to the violet; also : its showy flower
¹**pant** \'pant\ vb **1** : to breathe in a labored manner **2** : to long eagerly : YEARN **3** : THROB

♦ blow, gasp, puff, wheeze

²**pant** n : a panting breath or sound
³**pant** n **1** ♦ : an outer garment covering each leg separately and usu. extending from the waist to the ankle — usu. used in pl. **2** pl : PANTIE

♦ **pants** britches, pantaloons, slacks, trousers

pan·ta·loons \ˌpan-tə-'lünz\ n pl **1** : close-fitting pants of the 19th century usu. having straps passing under the instep **2** ♦ : loose-fitting usu. shorter than ankle-length trousers

♦ britches, pants, slacks, trousers

pan·the·ism \'pan-thē-ˌi-zəm\ n : a doctrine that equates God with the forces and laws of the universe — **pan·the·ist** \-ist\ n — **pan·the·is·tic** \ˌpan-thē-'is-tik\ adj

pan·the·on \'pan-thē-,än, -ən\ *n* **1** : a temple dedicated to all the gods; *also* : the gods of a people **2** : a group of illustrious people ⟨a ∼ of great writers⟩
pan·ther \'pan-thər\ *n* **panthers** *also* **panther** **1** : LEOPARD; *esp* : a black one **2** ♦ : a large powerful tawny brown wild American cat : COUGAR **3** : JAGUAR

♦ cougar, mountain lion

pant·ie *or* **panty** \'pan-tē\ *n, pl* **pant·ies** : a woman's or child's short underpants — usu. used in pl.
pan·to·mime \'pan-tə-,mīm\ *n* **1** : a play in which the actors use no words **2** : expression of something by bodily or facial movements only **3** ♦ : an actor or dancer in pantomimes — **pantomime** *vb* — **pan·to·mim·ic** \,pan-tə-'mi-mik\ *adj*

♦ mime, mimic, mummer

pan·try \'pan-trē\ *n, pl* **pantries** : a storage room for food or dishes
pant·suit \'pant-,süt\ *n* : a woman's outfit consisting usu. of a long jacket and pants of the same material
panty hose *n pl* : a one-piece undergarment for women consisting of hosiery combined with a pantie
panty·waist \'pan-tē-,wāst\ *n* : SISSY
pap \'pap\ *n* : soft food for infants or invalids
pa·pa \'pä-pə\ *n* ♦ : a man who has begotten a child : FATHER

♦ daddy, father, pop

pa·pa·cy \'pā-pə-sē\ *n, pl* **-cies** **1** : the office of pope **2** : a succession of popes **3** : the term of a pope's reign **4** *cap* : the system of government of the Roman Catholic Church
pa·pa·in \pə-'pā-ən, -'pī-ən\ *n* : an enzyme in papaya juice used esp. as a meat tenderizer and in medicine
pa·pal \'pā-pəl\ *adj* : of or relating to the pope or to the Roman Catholic Church
pa·pa·raz·zo \,pä-pə-'rät-(,)sō\ *n, pl* **-raz·zi** \-'rät-(,)sē\ : a freelance photographer who aggressively pursues celebrities for the purpose of taking candid photographs
papaw *var of* PAWPAW
pa·pa·ya \pə-'pī-ə\ *n* : a tropical American tree with large yellow black-seeded edible fruit; *also* : its fruit
¹pa·per \'pā-pər\ *n* **1** : a pliable substance made usu. of vegetable matter and used to write or print on, to wrap things in, or to cover walls; *also* : a single sheet of this substance **2** ♦ : a printed or written document **3** : NEWSPAPER **4** : WALLPAPER 1 **5** ♦ : a formal written composition often designed for publication and often intended to be read aloud — **paper** *vb* — **pa·pery** \'pā-pə-rē\ *adj*

♦ [2] blank, document, form ♦ [5] article, composition, essay, theme

²paper *adj* **1** : made of paper, cardboard, or papier-mâché **2** : of or relating to clerical work or written communication **3** : existing only in theory : NOMINAL
pa·per·back \-,bak\ *n* : a paper-covered book
pa·per·board \-,bōrd\ *n* : CARDBOARD
pa·per·hang·er \'pā-pər-,haŋ-ər\ *n* : one that applies wallpaper — **pa·per·hang·ing** *n*
pa·per·weight \-,wāt\ *n* : an object used to hold down loose papers by its weight
pa·pier–mâ·ché \,pā-pər-mə-'shā, ,pa-,pyā-mə-, -ma-\ *n* : a molding material of wastepaper and additives (as glue) — **papier–mâché** *adj*
pa·pil·la \pə-'pi-lə\ *n, pl* **-lae** \-(,)lē, -,lī\ : a small projecting bodily part (as one of the nubs on the surface of the tongue) that resembles a tiny nipple in form — **pap·il·lary** \'pa-pə-,ler-ē, pə-'pi-lə-rē\ *adj*
pa·poose \pa-'püs, pə-\ *n, dated, offensive* : an Indigenous baby or young child of No. America
pa·pri·ka \pə-'prē-kə, pa-\ *n* : a mild red spice made from the fruit of various cultivated sweet peppers
Pap smear \'pap-\ *n* : a method for the early detection of cancer esp. of the uterine cervix
Pap test *n* : PAP SMEAR
pap·ule \'pa-pyül\ *n* : a small solid usu. conical elevation of the skin — **pap·u·lar** \-pyə-lər\ *adj*
pa·py·rus \pə-'pī-rəs\ *n, pl* **-rus·es** *or* **-ri** \-(,)rē, -,rī\ **1** : a tall grassy sedge of the Nile valley **2** : paper made from papyrus pith
¹par \'pär\ *n* **1** : a stated value (as of a security) **2** ♦ : a common level : EQUALITY **3** ♦ : an accepted standard or normal condition **4** : the score standard set for each hole of a golf course — **par** *adj*

♦ [2] equality, equivalence, parity, sameness ♦ [3] criterion, grade, mark, measure, standard, touchstone, yardstick ♦ [3] average, norm, normal, standard

²par *abbr* **1** paragraph **2** parallel **3** parish
par·a·ble \'par-ə-bəl\ *n* : a simple story told to illustrate a moral truth
pa·rab·o·la \pə-'ra-bə-lə\ *n* : a plane curve formed by a point moving so that its distance from a fixed point is equal to its distance from a fixed line — **par·a·bol·ic** \,par-ə-'bä-lik\ *adj*
para·chute \'par-ə-,shüt\ *n* : a device for slowing the descent of a person or object through the air that consists of a usu. hemispherical canopy beneath which the person or object is suspended — **parachute** *vb* — **para·chut·ist** \-'shü-tist\ *n*
parachute pants *n pl* : baggy casual pants of lightweight fabric
¹pa·rade \pə-'rād\ *n* **1** : a pompous display : EXHIBITION **2** : MARCH, PROCESSION; *esp* : a ceremonial formation and march **3** : a place for strolling
²parade *vb* **pa·rad·ed; pa·rad·ing** **1** ♦ : to march in a parade **2** : PROMENADE **3** ♦ : to exhibit ostentatiously : SHOW OFF **4** : MASQUERADE

♦ [1] file, march, pace, stride ♦ [3] display, disport, exhibit, expose, flash, flaunt, show, show off, sport, strut, unveil

par·a·digm \'par-ə-,dīm, -,dim\ *n* **1** : MODEL, PATTERN **2** : a systematic inflection of a verb or noun showing a complete conjugation or declension
par·a·dig·mat·ic \,par-ə-dig-'ma-tik\ *adj* ♦ : serving as a pattern; *also* : deserving imitation

♦ classic, model, quintessential

par·a·dise \'par-ə-,dīs, -,dīz\ *n* **1** : HEAVEN **2** ♦ : a place or state of bliss

♦ Eden, Elysium, heaven, utopia *Ant* hell ♦ ecstasy, elation, euphoria, exhilaration, heaven, intoxication, rapture, rhapsody, transport

par·a·di·si·a·cal \,par-ə-də-'sī-ə-kəl\ *or* **par·a·dis·i·ac** \-'di-zē-,ak, -sē-\ *adj* : of, relating to, or resembling paradise
par·a·dox \'par-ə-,däks\ *n* : a statement that seems contrary to common sense and yet is perhaps true — **par·a·dox·i·cal** \,par-ə-'däk-si-kəl\ *adj* — **par·a·dox·i·cal·ly** \-k(ə-)lē\ *adv*
par·af·fin \'par-ə-fən\ *n* : a waxy substance used esp. for making candles and sealing foods
para·glid·ing \'pa-rə-,glī-diŋ\ *n* : the sport of soaring from a slope or cliff using a modified parachute
par·a·gon \'par-ə-,gän, -gən\ *n* ♦ : a model of perfection

♦ beau ideal, classic, exemplar, ideal, model, nonpareil

¹para·graph \'par-ə-,graf\ *n* : a subdivision of a written composition that deals with one point or gives the words of one speaker; *also* : a character (as ¶) marking the beginning of a paragraph
²paragraph *vb* : to divide into paragraphs
Par·a·guay·an \,par-ə-'gwī-ən, -'gwä-\ *n* : a native or inhabitant of Paraguay — **Paraguayan** *adj*
par·a·keet \'par-ə-,kēt\ *n* : any of numerous usu. small slender parrots with a long graduated tail
para·le·gal \,par-ə-'lē-gəl\ *adj* : of, relating to, or being a paraprofessional who assists a lawyer — **paralegal** *n*
Par·a·li·pom·e·non \,par-ə-lə-'pä-mə-,nän\ *n* : CHRONICLES
par·al·lax \'par-ə-,laks\ *n* : the difference in apparent direction of an object as seen from two different points
¹par·al·lel \'par-ə-,lel\ *adj* **1** : lying or moving in the same direction but always the same distance apart **2** ♦ : similar in essential parts

♦ akin, alike, analogous, comparable, correspondent, like, similar, such

²parallel *n* **1** : a parallel line, curve, or surface **2** : one of the imaginary circles on the earth's surface that parallel the equator and mark the latitude **3** ♦ : something essentially similar to another **4** ♦ : a comparable aspect : SIMILARITY

♦ [3] coordinate, counterpart, equal, equivalent, fellow, like, match, peer, rival ♦ [4] correspondence, resemblance, similarity, similitude

³parallel *vb* **1** : COMPARE **2** ♦ : to correspond to **3** : to extend in a parallel direction with

♦ correspond, equal, match

par·al·lel·ism \'par-ə-,le-,li-zəm\ *n* **1** : the quality or state of being parallel **2** ♦ : the quality or state of being similar in essential parts

♦ community, correspondence, likeness, resemblance, similarity, similitude

par·al·lel·o·gram \,par-ə-'le-lə-,gram\ *n* : a 4-sided geometric figure with opposite sides equal and parallel
par·a·lyse *chiefly Brit var of* PARALYZE

pa·ral·y·sis \pə-'ra-lə-səs\ *n, pl* **-y·ses** \-ˌsēz\ : complete or partial loss of function esp. when involving the motion or sensation in a part of the body — **par·a·lyt·ic** \ˌpar-ə-'li-tik\ *adj or n*

par·a·lyze \'par-ə-ˌlīz\ *vb* **-lyzed; -lyz·ing** **1** : to affect with paralysis **2 ♦** : to make powerless or inactive ⟨*paralyzed* by fear⟩ — **par·a·lyz·ing·ly** *adv*

  ♦ cripple, disable, hamstring, immobilize, incapacitate, prostrate

par·a·me·cium \ˌpar-ə-'mē-shəm, -shē-əm, -sē-əm\ *n, pl* **-cia** \-shə, -shē-ə, -sē-ə\ *also* **-ciums** : any of a genus of slipper-shaped protozoans that move by cilia

para·med·ic \ˌpar-ə-'me-dik\ *also* **para·med·i·cal** \-di-kəl\ *n* **1** : a person who assists a physician in a paramedical capacity **2** : a specially trained medical technician licensed to provide a wide range of emergency services before or during transportation to a hospital

para·med·i·cal \ˌpar-ə-'me-di-kəl\ *also* **para·med·ic** \-'me-dik\ *adj* : concerned with supplementing the work of trained medical professionals

pa·ram·e·ter \pə-'ra-mə-tər\ *n* **1** : a quantity whose value characterizes a statistical population or a member of a system (as a family of curves) **2** : a physical property whose value determines the characteristics or behavior of a system **3** : a characteristic element : FACTOR

para·mil·i·tary \ˌpar-ə-'mi-lə-ˌter-ē\ *adj* : formed on a military pattern esp. as an auxiliary military force

par·a·mount \'par-ə-ˌmau̇nt\ *adj* **♦** : superior to all others : SUPREME

  ♦ arch, cardinal, central, chief, dominant, first, foremost, grand, key, main, predominant, preeminent, premier, primary, principal, sovereign, supreme **♦** consummate, maximum, most, nth, supreme, top, ultimate, utmost

par·amour \'par-ə-ˌmu̇r\ *n* : an illicit lover

para·noia \ˌpar-ə-'noi̇-ə\ *n* : a psychosis marked by delusions and irrational suspicion usu. without hallucinations — **par·a·noid** \'par-ə-ˌnoi̇d\ *adj or n*

para·nor·mal \ˌpa-rə-'nȯr-məl\ *adj* : not scientifically explainable : SUPERNATURAL ⟨~ phenomena⟩

par·a·pet \'par-ə-pət, -ˌpet\ *n* **1** : a protecting rampart **2** : a low wall or railing (as at the edge of a bridge)

par·a·pher·na·lia \ˌpar-ə-fə-'nāl-yə, -fər-\ *n sing or pl* **1** **♦** : personal belongings **2 ♦** : articles of equipment : APPARATUS

  ♦ [1] belongings, chattels, effects, holdings, possessions, things **♦** [2] accoutrements (*or* accouterments), apparatus, equipment, gear, matériel, outfit, tackle

¹para·phrase \'par-ə-ˌfrāz\ *n* **♦** : a restatement of a text giving the meaning in different words

  ♦ translation *Ant* quotation, quote

²paraphrase *vb* **♦** : to make a paraphrase

  ♦ rephrase, restate, translate *Ant* quote

para·ple·gia \ˌpar-ə-'plē-jə, -jē-ə\ *n* : paralysis of the lower trunk and legs — **para·ple·gic** \-jik\ *adj or n*

para·pro·fes·sion·al \-prə-'fe-shə-nəl\ *n* : a trained aide who assists a professional — **paraprofessional** *adj*

para·psy·chol·o·gy \ˌpar-ə-sī-'kä-lə-jē\ *n* : a field of study concerned with investigating paranormal psychological phenomena (as extrasensory perception) — **para·psy·chol·o·gist** \-jist\ *n*

par·a·site \'par-ə-ˌsīt\ *n* **1** : a plant or animal living in, with, or on another organism usu. to its harm **2 ♦** : one depending on another and not making adequate return — **par·a·sit·ic** \ˌpar-ə-'si-tik\ *adj* — **par·a·sit·ism** \'par-ə-sə-ˌti-zəm, -ˌsī-ti-\ *n* — **par·a·sit·ize** \-sə-ˌtīz\ *vb*

  ♦ hanger-on, leech, sponge

par·a·si·tol·o·gy \ˌpar-ə-sə-'tä-lə-jē\ *n* : a branch of biology dealing with parasites and parasitism esp. among animals — **par·a·si·tol·o·gist** \-jist\ *n*

para·sol \'par-ə-ˌsȯl\ *n* : a lightweight umbrella used as a shield against the sun

para·sym·pa·thet·ic nervous system \ˌpar-ə-ˌsim-pə-'the-tik-\ *n* : the part of the autonomic nervous system that tends to induce secretion, to increase the tone and contractility of smooth muscle, and to slow heart rate

para·thi·on \ˌpar-ə-'thī-ən, -ˌän\ *n* : an extremely toxic insecticide

para·thy·roid \-'thī-ˌroi̇d\ *n* : PARATHYROID GLAND — **parathyroid** *adj*

parathyroid gland *n* : any of usu. four small endocrine glands adjacent to or embedded in the thyroid gland that produce a hormone (**parathyroid hormone**) concerned with calcium and phosphorus metabolism

para·tran·sit \ˌpa-rə-'tran-sət, -zət\ *n* : transportation service that provides individualized rules without fixed routes or timetables

para·troop·er \'par-ə-ˌtrü-pər\ *n* : a member of the paratroops

para·troops \-ˌtrüps\ *n pl* : troops trained to parachute from an airplane

para·ty·phoid \ˌpar-ə-'tī-ˌfoi̇d\ *n* : a bacterial food poisoning resembling typhoid fever

par·boil \'pär-ˌboi̇l\ *vb* : to boil briefly

¹par·cel \'pär-səl\ *n* **1 ♦** : a tract or plot of land **2 ♦** : a company, collection, or group of persons, animals, or things : LOT **3** : a wrapped bundle : PACKAGE

  ♦ [1] field, ground, lot, plat, plot, tract **♦** [2] array, assemblage, bank, batch, block, bunch, clump, cluster, collection, group, huddle, knot, lot, package, set, suite

²parcel *vb* **-celed** *or* **-celled; -cel·ing** *or* **-cel·ling** **♦** : to divide into portions — often used with *out*

  ♦ *usu* **parcel out** administer, allocate, apportion, deal, dispense, distribute, mete, portion, prorate

parcel post *n* **1 ♦** : a mail service handling parcels **2 ♦** : packages handled by parcel post

  ♦ mail, matter, post, snail mail

parch \'pärch\ *vb* **1** : to toast under dry heat **2 ♦** : to shrivel with heat

  ♦ dehydrate, dry, sear

parch·ment \'pärch-mənt\ *n* : the skin of an animal prepared for writing on; *also* : a writing on such material

pard \'pärd\ *n* : LEOPARD

¹par·don \'pärd-ᵊn\ *n* **♦** : excuse of an offense without penalty; *esp* : an official release from legal punishment

  ♦ absolution, amnesty, forgiveness, remission *Ant* penalty, punishment, retribution

²pardon *vb* **♦** : to free from penalty : EXCUSE, FORGIVE

  ♦ condone, disregard, excuse, forgive, gloss over, ignore, pass over, shrug off, wink at

par·don·able \'pärd-ᵊn-ə-bəl\ *adj* **♦** : worthy of or subject to being pardoned : EXCUSABLE

  ♦ excusable, forgivable, venial

par·don·er \'pärd-ᵊn-ər\ *n* **1** : a medieval preacher delegated to raise money for religious works by soliciting offerings and granting indulgences **2** : one that pardons

pare \'par\ *vb* **pared; par·ing** **1** : to trim off an outside, excess, or irregular part of **2** : to reduce as if by paring ⟨~ expenses⟩ — **par·er** *n*

par·e·gor·ic \ˌpar-ə-'gȯr-ik\ *n* : an alcoholic preparation of opium and camphor used esp. to relieve pain

par·ent \'par-ənt\ *n* **1** : one that begets or brings forth offspring : FATHER, MOTHER **2** : one who brings up and cares for another **3** : SOURCE, ORIGIN — **pa·ren·tal** \pə-'rent-ᵊl\ *adj* — **par·ent·hood** *n*

par·ent·age \-ən-tij\ *n* **♦** : descent from parents or ancestors

  ♦ ancestry, birth, blood, bloodline, breeding, descent, extraction, family tree, genealogy, line, lineage, origin, pedigree, stock, strain

pa·ren·the·sis \pə-'ren-thə-səs\ *n, pl* **-the·ses** \-ˌsēz\ **1** : a word, phrase, or sentence inserted in a passage to explain or modify the thought **2** : one of a pair of punctuation marks ( ) used esp. to enclose parenthetic matter — **par·en·thet·ic** \ˌpar-ən-'the-tik\ *or* **par·en·thet·i·cal** \-ti-kəl\ *adj* — **par·en·thet·i·cal·ly** \-k(ə-)lē\ *adv*

pa·ren·the·size \pə-'ren-thə-ˌsīz\ *vb* **-sized; -siz·ing** : to make a parenthesis of

par·ent·ing \'par-ən-tiŋ, 'per-\ *n* : the raising of a child by its parents

pa·re·sis \pə-'rē-səs, 'par-ə-\ *n, pl* **pa·re·ses** \-ˌsēz\ : a usu. incomplete paralysis; *also* : insanity caused by syphilitic alteration of the brain that leads to dementia and paralysis

par ex·cel·lence \ˌpär-ek-sə-'läⁿs\ *adj* : being the best of a kind : PREEMINENT

par·fait \pär-'fā\ *n* : a cold dessert made of layers of fruit, syrup, ice cream, and whipped cream

pa·ri·ah \pə-'rī-ə\ *n* : one that is despised or rejected : OUTCAST

pa·ri·etal \pə-'rī-ət-ᵊl\ *adj* **1** : of, relating to, or forming the walls of an anatomical structure **2** : of or relating to college living or its regulation

pari–mu•tu•el \ˌpar-i-ˈmyü-chə-wəl\ *n* : a betting system in which winners share the total stakes minus a percentage for the management

par•ing \ˈpar-iŋ\ *n* : a pared-off piece

pa•ri pas•su \ˌpar-i-ˈpa-sü\ *adv or adj* : at an equal rate or pace

par•ish \ˈpar-ish\ *n* 1 : a church district in the care of one pastor; *also* : the residents of such an area 2 : a local church community 3 : a civil division of the state of Louisiana : COUNTY

pa•rish•io•ner \pə-ˈri-shə-nər\ *n* : a member or resident of a parish

par•i•ty \ˈpar-ə-tē\ *n, pl* **-ties** ♦ : the quality or state of being equal or equivalent

♦ equality, equivalence, par, sameness

¹**park** \ˈpärk\ *n* 1 : a tract of ground kept as a game preserve or recreation area 2 : a place where vehicles (as automobiles) are parked 3 : an enclosed stadium used esp. for ball games 4 ♦ : a tract of land attached to a country house

♦ demesne, grounds, premises, yard

²**park** *vb* 1 : to leave a vehicle temporarily (as in a parking lot or garage) 2 : to set and leave temporarily

par•ka \ˈpär-kə\ *n* : a very warm jacket with a hood

Par•kin•son's disease \ˈpär-kən-sənz-\ *n* : a chronic progressive neurological disease chiefly of later life marked esp. by tremor and weakness of resting muscles and by a shuffling gait

Parkinson's Law *n* : an observation in office organization: work expands so as to fill the time available for its completion

par•kour \pär-ˈkur, ˈpär-ˌkur\ *n* : the sport of traversing environmental obstacles by running, climbing, or leaping rapidly

park•way \ˈpärk-ˌwā\ *n* : a broad landscaped thoroughfare

par•lance \ˈpär-ləns\ *n* 1 : SPEECH 2 : manner of speaking ⟨military ∼⟩

¹**par•lay** \ˈpär-ˌlā, -lē\ *vb* : to increase or change into something of much greater value

²**parlay** *n* : a series of bets in which the original stake plus its winnings are risked on successive wagers

¹**par•ley** \ˈpär-lē\ *vb* : to speak with another : CONFER

²**parley** *n, pl* **parleys** ♦ : a conference usu. over matters in dispute

♦ argument, colloquy, conference, deliberation, discourse, discussion, give-and-take, talk

par•lia•ment \ˈpär-lə-mənt\ *n* 1 : a formal governmental conference 2 *cap* : an assembly that constitutes the supreme legislative body of a country (as the United Kingdom) — **par•lia•men•ta•ry** \ˌpär-lə-ˈmen-tə-rē\ *adj*

par•lia•men•tar•i•an \ˌpär-lə-ˌmen-ˈter-ē-ən\ *n* 1 *often cap* : an adherent of the parliament during the English Civil War 2 : an expert in parliamentary procedure

par•lor *or Can and Brit* **par•lour** \ˈpär-lər\ *n* 1 : a room for conversation or the reception of guests 2 : a place of business ⟨beauty ∼⟩

par•lous \ˈpär-ləs\ *adj* ♦ : full of danger or risk — **par•lous•ly** *adv*

♦ dangerous, grave, grievous, hazardous, menacing, perilous, risky, serious, unhealthy, unsafe, venturesome

Par•me•san \ˈpär-mə-ˌzän, -ˌzhän, -ˌzan\ *n* : a hard dry cheese with a sharp flavor

par•mi•gia•na \ˌpär-mi-ˈjä-nə, ˌpär-mi-ˈzhän\ *or* **par•mi•gia•no** \-ˈjä-(ˌ)nō\ *adj* : made or covered with Parmesan cheese ⟨veal ∼⟩

pa•ro•chi•al \pə-ˈrō-kē-əl\ *adj* 1 : of or relating to a church parish 2 ♦ : limited in scope : NARROW, PROVINCIAL — **pa•ro•chi•al•ism** \-ə-ˌli-zəm\ *n*

♦ insular, little, narrow, petty, provincial, sectarian, small

parochial school \ˈpär-ə-dē\ *n* : a school maintained by a religious body

¹**par•o•dy** \ˈpär-ə-dē\ *n, pl* **-dies** 1 ♦ : a humorous or satirical imitation 2 ♦ : a feeble or inferior imitation — **parody** *vb*

♦ [1] burlesque, caricature, spoof, takeoff ♦ [2] caricature, farce, joke, mockery, sham, travesty

²**parody** *vb* 1 : to compose a parody on 2 ♦ : to imitate in the manner of a parody

♦ burlesque, caricature, imitate, mimic, mock, take off, travesty

pa•role \pə-ˈrōl\ *n* : a conditional release of a prisoner whose sentence has not expired — **parole** *vb* — **pa•rol•ee** \-ˌrō-ˈlē, -ˈrō-ˌlē\ *n*

par•ox•ysm \ˈpar-ək-ˌsi-zəm, pə-ˈräk-\ *n* 1 : a sudden sharp attack (as of pain or coughing) : CONVULSION 2 ♦ : a sudden violent emotion or action — **par•ox•ys•mal** \ˌpar-ək-ˈsiz-məl, pə-ˌräk-\ *adj*

♦ agony, burst, eruption, explosion, fit, flare, flare-up, flash, flush, gale, gush, gust, outburst, spasm, storm

par•quet \ˈpär-ˌkā, pär-ˈkā\ *n* 1 : a flooring of parquetry 2 : the lower floor of a theater; *esp* : the forward part of the orchestra

par•que•try \ˈpär-kə-trē\ *n, pl* **-tries** : fine woodwork inlaid in patterns

par•ri•cide \ˈpar-ə-ˌsīd\ *n* 1 : one that murders a parent or a close relative 2 : the act of a parricide

par•rot \ˈpar-ət\ *n* : any of numerous bright-colored tropical birds that have a stout hooked bill

parrot fever *n* : PSITTACOSIS

par•ry \ˈpar-ē\ *vb* **par•ried; par•ry•ing** 1 : to ward off a weapon or blow 2 : to evade esp. by an adroit answer — **parry** *n*

parse \ˈpärs *also* ˈpärz\ *vb* **parsed; pars•ing** : to give a grammatical description of a word or a group of words

par•sec \ˈpär-ˌsek\ *n* : a unit of measure for interstellar space equal to 3.26 light-years

par•si•mo•ni•ous \ˌpär-sə-ˈmō-nē-əs\ *adj* ♦ : exhibiting or marked by parsimony — **par•si•mo•ni•ous•ly** *adv*

♦ cheap, close, mean, niggardly, penurious, spare, sparing, stingy, tight, tightfisted, uncharitable

par•si•mo•ny \ˈpär-sə-ˌmō-nē\ *n* ♦ : extreme or excessive frugality

♦ cheapness, closeness, miserliness, stinginess, tightness *Ant* generosity, liberality, philanthropy

pars•ley \ˈpär-slē\ *n* : a garden plant related to the carrot that has finely divided leaves used as a seasoning or garnish; *also* : the leaves

pars•nip \ˈpär-snəp\ *n* : a garden plant related to the carrot that has a long edible usu. whitish root which is cooked as a vegetable; *also* : the root

par•son \ˈpärs-ᵊn\ *n* : a member of the clergy : MINISTER

par•son•age \ˈpärs-ᵊn-ij\ *n* : a house provided by a church for its pastor

¹**part** \ˈpärt\ *n* 1 ♦ : a division or portion of a whole 2 : the melody or score for a particular voice or instrument 3 : a spare piece for a machine 4 : DUTY, FUNCTION 5 : one of the sides in a dispute 6 : ROLE; *also* : an actor's lines in a play 7 *pl* : TALENTS, ABILITY 8 : the line where one's hair divides (as in combing) 9 ♦ : something falling to one in a division or apportionment 10 ♦ : a function or course of action performed

♦ [1] member, partition, portion, section, segment ♦ [9] allotment, allowance, cut, portion, proportion, quota, share ♦ [10] capacity, function, job, place, position, purpose, role, task, work

²**part** *vb* 1 : to take leave of someone 2 ♦ : to divide or break into parts 3 : to go away : DEPART; *also* : DIE 4 : to give up possession ⟨∼ed with her jewels⟩ 5 : APPORTION, SHARE

♦ break up, disconnect, disjoint, dissever, dissociate, disunite, divide, divorce, resolve, separate, sever, split, sunder, unyoke

³**part** *abbr* 1 participial; participle 2 particular

par•take \pär-ˈtāk\ *vb* **-took** \-ˈtuk\; **-tak•en** \-ˈtā-kən\; **-tak•ing** 1 : to have a share or part 2 : to take a portion (as of food)

par•tak•er \-ˈtā-kər\ *n* ♦ : one that partakes

♦ participant, party, sharer

par•terre \pär-ˈter\ *n* 1 : an ornamental garden with paths between the flower beds 2 : the part of a theater floor behind the orchestra

par•the•no•gen•e•sis \ˌpär-thə-nō-ˈje-nə-səs\ *n* : development of a new individual from an unfertilized usu. female sex cell — **par•the•no•ge•net•ic** \-jə-ˈne-tik\ *adj*

par•tial \ˈpär-shəl\ *adj* 1 ♦ : of or relating to a part rather than the whole 2 ♦ : favoring one party over the other : BIASED 3 ♦ : markedly fond — used with *to*

♦ [1] deficient, fragmentary, halfway, incomplete ♦ [2] biased, one-sided, partisan, prejudiced *Ant* evenhanded, impartial, neutral, nonpartisan, unbiased, unprejudiced ♦ [3] fond, inclined

par•tial•i•ty \ˌpär-shē-ˈa-lə-tē\ *n* 1 ♦ : the quality or state of being partial 2 ♦ : a special taste or liking

♦ [1] bias, favor (*or* favour), partisanship, prejudice ♦ [2] bent, devices, disposition, genius, inclination, leaning, penchant, predilection, proclivity, propensity, tendency, turn ♦ [2] appetite, fancy, favor (*or* favour), fondness, like, liking, love, preference, relish, shine, taste, use

par•tial•ly \ˈpär-sh(ə-)lē\ *adv* ♦ : to some extent : in some degree

♦ part, partly

par·tic·i·pant \pär-'ti-sə-pənt\ *n* ♦ : one that participates — **participant** *adj*

  ♦ partaker, party, sharer *Ant* nonparticipant

par·tic·i·pate \pär-'ti-sə-ˌpāt\ *vb* **-pat·ed; -pat·ing** **1** : to take part in something ⟨∼ in a game⟩ **2** : SHARE — **par·tic·i·pa·tion** \-ˌti-sə-'pā-shən\ *n* — **par·tic·i·pa·to·ry** \-'ti-sə-pə-ˌtōr-ē\ *adj*
par·tic·i·pa·tor \pär-'ti-sə-ˌpā-tər\ *n* : one that participates
par·ti·ci·ple \'pär-tə-ˌsi-pəl\ *n* : a word having the characteristics of both verb and adjective — **par·ti·cip·i·al** \ˌpär-tə-'si-pē-əl\ *adj*
par·ti·cle \'pär-ti-kəl\ *n* **1** ♦ : a very small quantity or fragment **2** : a unit of speech (as an article, preposition, or conjunction) expressing some general aspect of meaning or some connective or limiting relation

  ♦ atom, fleck, grain, granule, molecule, morsel, scrap ♦ bit, crumb, dab, glimmer, hint, lick, little, mite, nip, ounce, shred, speck, spot, suspicion, touch, trace

par·ti·cle·board \-ˌbōrd\ *n* : a board made of very small pieces of wood bonded together
par·ti–col·or \ˌpär-tē-'kə-lər\ *or* **par·ti–col·ored** \-lərd\ *adj* : showing different colors or tints; *esp* : having one main color broken by patches of one or more other colors
¹**par·tic·u·lar** \pər-'ti-kyə-lər\ *adj* **1** ♦ : of or relating to a specific person or thing ⟨the laws of a ∼ state⟩ **2** : DISTINCTIVE, SPECIAL ⟨the ∼ point of his talk⟩ **3** : SEPARATE, INDIVIDUAL ⟨each ∼ hair⟩ **4** : attentive to details **5** ♦ : hard to please ⟨∼ about her clothes⟩

  ♦ [1] individual, peculiar, personal, private, separate, singular, unique ♦ [5] choosy, dainty, delicate, demanding, exacting, fastidious, finicky, fussy, nice, old-maidish, picky

²**particular** *n* ♦ : an individual fact or detail

  ♦ detail, fact, item, point

par·tic·u·lar·ise *chiefly Brit var of* PARTICULARIZE
par·tic·u·lar·i·ty \pər-ˌti-kyə-'lar-ə-tē\ *n* : a minute detail
par·tic·u·lar·ize \pər-'ti-kyə-lə-ˌrīz\ *vb* **-ized; -iz·ing** **1** : to state in detail : SPECIFY **2** : to go into details
par·tic·u·lar·ly \-lē\ *adv* **1** : to an unusual degree **2** : in particular : SPECIFICALLY
par·tic·u·late \pər-'ti-kyə-lət, pär-, -ˌlāt\ *adj* : relating to or existing as minute separate particles — **particulate** *n*
¹**part·ing** *n* **1** : a place or point of separation or divergence **2** ♦ : a mutual separation of two or more persons

  ♦ farewell, leave-taking, separation

²**parting** *adj* : given, taken, or done at parting ⟨a ∼ kiss⟩
¹**par·ti·san** *also* **par·ti·zan** \'pär-tə-zən, -sən\ *n* **1** ♦ : one that takes the part of another : ADHERENT **2** : GUERRILLA **3** ♦ : a strong or devoted supporter

  ♦ [1] adherent, convert, disciple, follower, pupil, votary ♦ [3] crusader, fanatic, militant, zealot

²**partisan** *adj* ♦ : exhibiting, characterized by, or resulting from partisanship

  ♦ biased, one-sided, partial, prejudiced

par·ti·san·ship \-ˌship\ *n* ♦ : the quality or state of being a partisan

  ♦ bias, favor (*or* favour), partiality, prejudice

par·tite \'pär-ˌtīt\ *adj* : divided into a usu. specified number of parts
par·ti·tion \pär-'ti-shən\ *n* **1** ♦ : the action of parting : the state of being parted **2** : something that divides or separates; *esp* : an interior dividing wall **3** ♦ : one of the parts or sections of a whole — **partition** *vb*

  ♦ [1] breakup, dissolution, division, schism, separation, split ♦ [3] member, part, portion, section, segment

par·ti·tive \'pär-tə-tiv\ *adj* : of, relating to, or denoting a part
part·ly \'pärt-lē\ *adv* ♦ : in part : in some measure or degree

  ♦ part, partially *Ant* completely, entirely, totally, wholly

part·ner \'pärt-nər\ *n* **1** : ASSOCIATE, COLLEAGUE **2** : either of two persons who dance together **3** : one who plays on the same team with another **4** ♦ : married person : SPOUSE **5** : one of two or more persons contractually associated as joint principals in a business

  ♦ consort, mate, spouse

part·ner·ship \-ˌship\ *n* ♦ : a relationship usu. involving close cooperation between parties having specified and joint rights and responsibilities

  ♦ affiliation, alliance, association, collaboration, confederation, connection, cooperation, hookup, liaison, relation, relationship, union

part of speech : a class of words (as nouns or verbs) distinguished according to the kind of idea denoted and the function performed in a sentence
par·tridge \'pär-trij\ *n, pl* **partridge** *or* **par·tridg·es** : any of various stout-bodied Old World game birds
part–song \'pärt-ˌsȯn\ *n* : a song with two or more voice parts
part–time \-'tīm\ *adj or adv* : involving or working less than a full or regular schedule — **part–tim·er** \-ˌtī-mər\ *n*
par·tu·ri·tion \ˌpär-tə-'ri-shən, ˌpär-chə-, ˌpär-tyü-\ *n* : the action or process of giving birth to offspring : CHILDBIRTH
part·way \'pärt-'wā\ *adv* : to some extent : PARTLY
par·ty \'pär-tē\ *n, pl* **parties** **1** : a person or group taking one side of a question; *esp* : a group of persons organized for the purpose of directing the policies of a government **2** ♦ : a person or group concerned in an action or affair : PARTICIPANT **3** ♦ : a group of persons detailed for a common task **4** ♦ : a social gathering **5** : a particular individual

  ♦ [2] partaker, participant, sharer ♦ [3] band, company, crew, gang, group, outfit, squad, team ♦ [4] affair, blowout, event, fete, function, get-together

party animal *n* : a person known for frequent attendance at parties
par·ty·go·er \'pär-tē-ˌgō-ər\ *n* : a person who attends a party or who attends parties frequently
par·ve·nu \'pär-və-ˌnü, -ˌnyü\ *n* : one who has recently or suddenly risen to wealth or power but has not yet secured the social position associated with it
pas \'pä\ *n, pl* **pas** *same or* 'päz\ : a dance step or combination of steps
pas·cal \pas-'kal\ *n* : a unit of pressure in the metric system equal to one newton per square meter
pas·chal \'pas-kəl\ *adj* : of, relating to, appropriate for, or used during Passover or Easter ceremonies
pa·sha \'pä-shə, 'pa-; pə-'shä\ *n* : a man (as formerly a governor in Turkey) of high rank
pash·mi·na \ˌpəsh-'mē-nə\ *n* : a fine wool from the undercoat of domestic Himalayan goats; *also* : a shawl made from this wool
¹**pass** \'pas\ *vb* **1** : MOVE, PROCEED **2 a** : to go away **b** ♦ : to stop existing or functioning : DIE — often used with *on* **3** : to move past, beyond, or over **4** : to allow to elapse : SPEND **5** ♦ : to go or make way through **6** : to go or allow to go unchallenged **7 a** : to undergo transfer **b** ♦ : to transfer or transmit from one to another **8** : to render a legal judgment **9** ♦ : to come into existence : OCCUR **10** ♦ : to become approved by a legislature or body empowered to sanction or reject **11** : to go or cause to go through an inspection, test, or course of study successfully **12** : to be regarded **13** : CIRCULATE **14** : VOID 2 **15** : to transfer the ball or puck to another player **16** : to decline to bid or bet on one's hand in a card game **17** : to give a base on balls to — **pass·er** *n*

  ♦ *usu* **pass on** [2b] decease, depart, die, expire, pass away, perish, succumb ♦ *usu* **pass over** [5] cover, crisscross, cross, cut, follow, go, proceed, travel, traverse ♦ [7b] hand, hand over, reach, transfer ♦ [9] be, befall, betide, chance, come, go, happen, occur, transpire ♦ [10] enact, lay down, legislate, make

²**pass** *n* ♦ : a gap in a mountain range

  ♦ canyon, defile, flume, gap, gorge, gulch, gulf, notch, ravine

³**pass** *n* **1** : the act or an instance of passing **2** ♦ : the state of being realized or accomplished : REALIZATION, ACCOMPLISHMENT **3** : a state of affairs **4** ♦ : a written authorization to leave, enter, or move about freely **5** : a transfer of a ball or puck from one player to another **6** : BASE ON BALLS **7** ♦ : a serious attempt : TRY **8** : a sexually inviting gesture or approach

  ♦ [2] accomplishment, achievement, actuality, attainment, consummation, fruition, fulfillment, realization ♦ [4] check, ticket ♦ [7] attempt, bid, crack, endeavor (*or* endeavour), essay, fling, go, shot, stab, trial, try, whack

⁴**pass** *abbr* **1** passenger **2** passive
pass·able \'pa-sə-bəl\ *adj* **1** ♦ : capable of being passed or traveled on **2** ♦ : just good enough ⟨did a ∼ job⟩

  ♦ [1, 2] acceptable, adequate, all right, decent, fine, OK, respectable, satisfactory, tolerable ♦ [2] common, fair, indifferent, mediocre, medium, middling, ordinary, run-of-the-mill, second-rate, so-so

pass·ably \-blē\ *adv* ♦ : in a passable manner or to a passable extent

♦ adequately, all right, fine, good, nicely, OK, satisfactorily, so–so, tolerably, well

pas•sage \'pa-sij\ n **1** ♦ : a means (as a road or corridor) of passing **2** ♦ : the action or process of passing **3** ♦ : a voyage esp. by sea or air **4** : a right or permission to pass **5** : ENACT-MENT **6** : a usu. brief portion or section (as of a book) **7** : a continuous movement or flow

♦ [1] approach, avenue, path, route, way ♦ [2] expedition, journey, peregrination, trek, trip ♦ [3] crossing, cruise, sail, voyage

pas•sage•way \-,wā\ n : a way that allows passage
pass away vb **1** : to go out of existence **2** ♦ : to pass from physical life

♦ decease, depart, die, expire, pass, perish, succumb

pass•book \'pas-,bùk\ n : BANKBOOK
pas•sé \pa-'sā\ adj **1** : past one's prime **2** ♦ : not up-to-date : OUTMODED

♦ antiquated, archaic, dated, obsolete, outdated, outmoded, outworn

pas•sel \'pa-səl\ n : a large number ⟨a ∼ of children⟩
pas•sen•ger \'pas-ᵊn-jər\ n : a traveler in a public or private conveyance
pass•er•by \'pa-sər-,bī\ n, pl **pass•ers•by** : one who passes by
pas•ser•ine \'pa-sə-,rīn\ adj : of or relating to the large order of birds comprising singing birds that perch
pas•sim \'pa-səm\ adv : here and there : THROUGHOUT
pass•ing \'pa-siŋ\ n ♦ : the act of one that passes or causes to pass; esp : DEATH

♦ death, decease, demise, doom, end, quietus

pas•sion \'pa-shən\ n **1** often cap : the sufferings of Christ between the night of the Last Supper and his death **2** ♦ : strong feeling; also, pl : the emotions as distinguished from reason **3** : RAGE, ANGER **4** ♦ : ardent affection : LOVE; also : an object of affection or enthusiasm **5** : sexual desire **6** ♦ : a strong liking or desire for or devotion to some activity, object, or concept — **pas•sion•less** adj

♦ [2] ardor, emotion, fervency, fervor, heat, intensity, vehemence, warmth ♦ [4] affection, attachment, devotion, fondness, love ♦ [6] appetite, craving, desire, drive, hankering, hunger, itch, longing, lust, thirst, urge, yearning, yen

pas•sion•ate \'pa-shə-nət\ adj **1 a** ♦ : capable of, affected by, or expressing intense feeling **b** : ENTHUSIASTIC **2** ♦ : swayed by or affected with sexual desire — **pas•sion•ate•ly** adv

♦ [1a] ardent, burning, charged, emotional, fervent, fiery, hot-blooded, impassioned, red-hot, vehement ♦ [2] lascivious, lewd, lustful, wanton

pas•sion•flow•er \'pa-shən-,flaù-ər\ n : any of a genus of chiefly tropical woody climbing vines or erect herbs with showy flowers and pulpy often edible berries (**passion fruit**)
pas•sive \'pa-siv\ adj **1** : not active : acted upon **2** : asserting that the grammatical subject is subjected to or affected by the action represented by the verb ⟨∼ voice⟩ **3** : making use of the sun's heat usu. without the aid of mechanical devices **4** ♦ : receiving or enduring without resistance — **passive** n — **pas•sive•ly** adv — **pas•siv•i•ty** \pa-'si-və-tē\ n

♦ acquiescent, resigned, tolerant, unresistant, unresisting, yielding Ant protesting, resistant, resisting, unyielding

pas•sive–ma•trix \-'mā-triks\ adj : of, relating to, or being on LCD in which pixels are controlled in groups
pass•key \'pas-,kē\ n : a key for opening two or more locks
pass out vb ♦ : to lose consciousness

♦ black out, faint, swoon

Pass•over \'pas-,ō-vər\ n : a Jewish holiday celebrated in March or April in commemoration of the Hebrews' liberation from slavery in Egypt
pass over vb **1** ♦ : to ignore in passing **2** ♦ : to pay no attention to the claims of

♦ [1] disregard, forget, ignore, neglect, overlook, slight, slur ♦ [1, 2] condone, disregard, excuse, gloss over, ignore, pardon, shrug off, wink at

pass•port \'pas-,pōrt\ n **1** ♦ : an official document issued by a country upon request to a citizen requesting protection during travel abroad **2** ♦ : something that secures admission, acceptance, or attainment

♦ gateway, key

pass up vb : DECLINE, REJECT

pass•word \'pas-,wərd\ n **1** ♦ : a word or phrase that must be spoken by a person before being allowed to pass a guard **2** : a sequence of characters required for access to a computer system
¹past \'past\ adj **1** : AGO ⟨10 years ∼⟩ **2** : just gone or elapsed ⟨the ∼ month⟩ **3** ♦ : having existed or taken place in a period before the present **4** : of, relating to, or constituting a verb tense that expresses time gone by

♦ erstwhile, former, late, old, onetime, sometime, whilom

²past prep or adv : BEYOND
³past n **1** : time gone by **2** ♦ : something that happened or was done in a former time **3** : the past tense; also : a verb form in it **4** : a secret past life

♦ history, yesteryear, yore

pas•ta \'päs-tə\ n **1** : a paste in processed form (as macaroni) or in the form of fresh dough (as ravioli) **2** : a dish of cooked pasta
¹paste \'pāst\ n **1** : DOUGH **2** : a smooth food product made by evaporation or grinding ⟨tomato ∼⟩ **3** : a shaped dough (as spaghetti or ravioli) **4** : a preparation (as of flour and water) for sticking things together **5** : a brilliant glass used for artificial gems
²paste vb **past•ed; past•ing** **1** : to cause to adhere by paste : STICK **2** : to put (something copied or cut from a computer document) into another place
³paste vb **past•ed; past•ing** : to strike hard at
paste•board \'pāst-,bōrd\ n : CARDBOARD
¹pas•tel \pas-'tel\ n **1** : a paste made of powdered pigment; also : a crayon of such paste **2** : a drawing in pastel **3** : a pale or light color
²pastel adj **1** : of or relating to a pastel **2** ♦ : pale in color

♦ dull, light, pale, washed-out

pas•tern \'pas-tərn\ n : the part of a horse's foot extending from the fetlock to the top of the hoof
pas•teur•iza•tion \,pas-chə-rə-'zā-shən, ,pas-tə-\ n : partial sterilization of a substance (as milk) by heat or radiation — **pas•teur•ize** \'pas-chə-,rīz, 'pas-tə-\ vb — **pas•teur•iz•er** n
pas•tiche \pas-'tēsh\ n : a composition (as in literature or music) made up of selections from different works
pas•tille \pas-'tēl\ n : LOZENGE 2
pas•time \'pas-,tīm\ n : DIVERSION; esp : something that serves to make time pass agreeably
pas•tor \'pas-tər\ n : a minister or priest serving a local church or parish — **pas•tor•ate** \-tə-rət\ n
¹pas•to•ral \'pas-tə-rəl\ adj **1** ♦ : of or relating to shepherds or to rural life **2** : of or relating to spiritual guidance esp. of a congregation **3** ♦ : of or relating to the pastor of a church

♦ [1] bucolic, country, rural, rustic ♦ [3] clerical, ministerial, priestly, sacerdotal

²pastoral n : a literary work dealing with shepherds or rural life
pas•to•rale \,pas-tə-'räl, -'ral\ n : a musical composition having a pastoral theme
past participle n : a participle that typically expresses completed action, that is one of the principal parts of the verb, and that is used in the formation of perfect tenses in the active voice and of all tenses in the passive voice
pas•tra•mi \pə-'strä-mē\ n : a highly seasoned smoked beef prepared esp. from shoulder cuts
pas•try \'pā-strē\ n, pl **pastries** : sweet baked goods made of dough or with a crust made of enriched dough
pas•tur•age \'pas-chə-rij\ n : PASTURE
¹pas•ture \'pas-chər\ n **1** : plants (as grass) for the feeding esp. of grazing livestock **2** ♦ : land or a plot of land used for grazing

♦ range

²pasture vb **pas•tured; pas•tur•ing** **1** ♦ : to feed on growing herbage : GRAZE **2** : to use as pasture

♦ browse, forage, graze

pasty \'pā-stē\ adj **past•i•er; -est** **1** : resembling paste **2** ♦ : pallid and unhealthy in appearance

♦ ashen, cadaverous, livid, lurid, pale, peaked, sallow

¹pat \'pat\ n **1** : a light tap esp. with the hand or a flat instrument; also : the sound made by it **2** : something (as butter) shaped into a small flat usu. square individual portion
²pat adv : in a pat manner : PERFECTLY
³pat vb **pat•ted; pat•ting** **1** : to strike lightly with a flat instrument **2** : to flatten, smooth, or put into place or shape with a pat **3** : to tap gently or lovingly with the hand
⁴pat adj **1** : exactly suited to the occasion : APT **2** : memorized exactly **3** ♦ : characterized by firmness or obduracy : UNYIELD-ING

♦ adamant, hard, immovable, implacable, inflexible, rigid, unbending, uncompromising, unrelenting, unyielding

PAT *abbr* point after touchdown

¹**patch** \'pach\ *n* **1 :** a piece used to cover a torn or worn place; *also* **:** one worn on a garment as an ornament or insignia **2 :** a small area distinct from that about it **3 :** a shield worn over the socket of an injured or missing eye **4 :** a small piece : SCRAP

²**patch** *vb* **1 :** to mend or cover with a patch **2 :** to make of fragments **3 ♦ :** to repair usu. in hasty fashion

♦ doctor, fix, mend, recondition, renovate, repair, revamp

patch·ou·li \'pa-chə-lē, pə-'chü-lē\ *n* **:** a heavy perfume made from the fragrant essential oil of an Asian mint; *also* **:** the plant itself

patch test *n* **:** a test for allergic sensitivity made by applying to the unbroken skin small pads soaked with the allergen to be tested

patch·work \'pach-,wərk\ *n* **:** something made of pieces of different materials, shapes, or colors

patchy \'pa-chē\ *adj* **patch·i·er; -est :** marked by or consisting of patches; *also* **:** irregular in appearance or quality — **patch·i·ness** \-chē-nəs\ *n*

pate \'pāt\ *n* ♦ **:** a person's head; *esp* **:** the crown of the head

♦ head, noggin, poll

pâ·té *also* **pate** \pä-'tā\ *n* **1 :** a meat or fish pie or patty **2 :** a spread of finely chopped or pureed seasoned meat

pa·tel·la \pə-'te-lə\ *n, pl* **-lae** \-'te-(,)lē, -,lī\ *or* **-las :** KNEECAP

pat·en \'pat-ᵊn\ *n* **1 :** PLATE; *esp* **:** one of precious metal for the eucharistic bread **2 :** a thin disk

¹**pa·tent** *I & 4 are* 'pat-ᵊnt, *Brit also* 'pāt-, *2 & 3 are* 'pat-ᵊnt, 'pāt-\ *adj* **1 :** open to public inspection — used chiefly in the phrase *letters patent* **2 :** free from obstruction **3 ♦ :** readily visible or intelligible : OBVIOUS **4 :** protected by a patent — **pat·ent·ly** *adv*

♦ apparent, broad, clear, clear-cut, distinct, evident, lucid, manifest, obvious, palpable, perspicuous, plain, transparent, unambiguous, unequivocal, unmistakable

²**pat·ent** \'pat-ᵊnt, *Brit also* 'pāt-\ *n* **1 :** an official document conferring a right or privilege **2 :** a document securing to an inventor for a term of years exclusive right to his or her invention **3 :** something patented

³**pat·ent** *vb* **:** to secure by patent

pat·en·tee \,pat-ᵊn-'tē, *Brit also* ,pāt-\ *n* **:** one to whom a grant is made or a privilege secured by patent

pat·ent medicine \'pat-ᵊnt-\ *n* **:** a packaged nonprescription drug protected by a trademark; *also* **:** any proprietary drug

pa·ter·fa·mil·i·as \,pā-tər-fə-'mi-lē-əs\ *n, pl* **pa·tres·fa·mil·i·as** \,pā-,trēz-\ **:** the father of a family : the male head of a household

pa·ter·nal \pə-'tərn-ᵊl\ *adj* **1 :** FATHERLY **2 :** related through or inherited or derived from a father — **pa·ter·nal·ly** *adv*

pa·ter·nal·ism \-,i-zəm\ *n* **:** a system under which an authority treats those under its control paternally (as by regulating their conduct and supplying their needs)

pa·ter·ni·ty \pə-'tər-nə-tē\ *n* **1 :** FATHERHOOD **2 :** descent from a father

¹**path** \'path, 'pàth\ *n, pl* **paths** \'pathz, 'paths, 'pàthz, 'pàths\ **1 ♦ :** a trodden way **2 ♦ :** a line of travel : ROUTE — **path·less** *adj*

♦ [1] footpath, trace, track, trail ♦ [2] course, line, route, track, way

²**path** *or* **pathol** *abbr* pathology

path·break·ing \'path-,brā-kiŋ\ *adj* **:** TRAILBLAZING

pa·thet·ic \pə-'the-tik\ *adj* **1 ♦ :** evoking tenderness, pity, or sorrow **2 :** pitifully inadequate — **pa·thet·i·cal·ly** \-ti-k(ə-)lē\ *adv*

♦ depressing, dismal, dreary, heartbreaking, melancholy, sad, sorry, tearful

path·find·er \'path-,fīn-dər, 'pàth-\ *n* **:** one that discovers a way; *esp* **:** one that explores untraveled regions to mark out a new route

patho·gen \'pa-thə-jən\ *n* **:** a specific agent (as a bacterium) causing disease — **patho·gen·ic** \,pa-thə-'je-nik\ *adj* — **patho·ge·nic·i·ty** \-jə-'ni-sə-tē\ *n*

pa·thog·ra·phy \pə-'thä-grə-fē\ *n* **:** biography focusing on a person's flaws and misfortunes

pa·thol·o·gy \pə-'thä-lə-jē\ *n, pl* **-gies** **1 :** the study of the essential nature of disease **2 :** the abnormality of structure and function characteristic of a disease — **path·o·log·i·cal** \,pa-thə-'lä-ji-kəl\ *adj* — **pa·thol·o·gist** \pə-'thä-lə-jist\ *n*

pa·thos \'pā-,thäs, -,thȯs\ *n* **:** an element in experience or artistic representation evoking pity or compassion

path·way \'path-,wā, 'pàth-\ *n* **:** PATH

pa·tience \'pā-shəns\ *n* **1 ♦ :** the capacity, habit, or fact of being patient **2** *chiefly Brit* **:** SOLITAIRE 2

♦ forbearance, long-suffering, sufferance, tolerance *Ant* impatience

¹**pa·tient** \'pā-shənt\ *adj* **1 ♦ :** bearing pain or trials without complaint **2 :** showing self-control : CALM **3 ♦ :** steadfast despite opposition, difficulty, or adversity : PERSEVERING — **pa·tient·ly** *adv*

♦ [1] forbearing, long-suffering, stoic, tolerant, uncomplaining *Ant* complaining, fed up, impatient, protesting ♦ [3] dogged, insistent, persevering, persistent, pertinacious, tenacious

²**patient** *n* **:** one under medical care

pa·ti·na \'pa-tə-nə, pə-'tē-\ *n, pl* **pa·ti·nas** \-nəz\ *or* **pa·ti·nae** \'pa-tə-,nē, -,nī\ **1 :** a green film formed on copper and bronze by exposure to moist air **2 :** a superficial covering or exterior

pa·tio \'pa-tē-,ō, 'pä-\ *n, pl* **pa·ti·os** **1 :** a court or enclosure adjacent to a building : COURTYARD **2 :** an often paved area near a dwelling used esp. for outdoor dining

pa·tois \'pa-,twä, *pl* **pa·tois** \-,twäz\ **1 :** a dialect other than the standard dialect; *esp* **:** uneducated or provincial speech **2 ♦ :** the characteristic special language of an occupational or social group : JARGON

♦ argot, cant, dialect, jargon, language, lingo, patter, slang, vocabulary

pa·tri·arch \'pā-trē-,ärk\ *n* **1 :** a man who is father or founder **2 :** a venerable old man **3 :** an ecclesiastical dignitary (as the bishop of an Eastern Orthodox see) — **pa·tri·ar·chal** \,pā-trē-'är-kəl\ *adj* — **pa·tri·arch·ate** \'pā-trē-,är-kət, -,kät\ *n* — **pa·tri·ar·chy** \-,är-kē\ *n*

¹**pa·tri·cian** \pə-'tri-shən\ *n* **:** a person of high birth : ARISTOCRAT

²**patrician** *adj* ♦ **:** of, relating to, or characteristic of patricians

♦ aristocratic, genteel, gentle, grand, highborn, noble, wellborn

pat·ri·cide \'pa-trə-,sīd\ *n* **1 :** one who murders his or her own father **2 :** the murder of one's own father

pat·ri·mo·ny \'pa-trə-,mō-nē\ *n* **:** something (as an estate) inherited or derived esp. from one's father : HERITAGE — **pat·ri·mo·ni·al** \,pa-trə-'mō-nē-əl\ *adj*

pa·tri·ot \'pā-trē-ət, -,ät\ *n* **:** one who loves his or her country — **pa·tri·ot·ic** \,pā-trē-'ä-tik\ *adj* — **pa·tri·ot·i·cal·ly** \-ti-k(ə-)lē\ *adv* — **pa·tri·o·tism** \'pā-trē-ə-,ti-zəm\ *n*

pa·tris·tic \pə-'tris-tik\ *adj* **:** of or relating to the church fathers or their writings

¹**pa·trol** \pə-'trōl\ *n* **:** the action of going the rounds (as of an area) for observation or the maintenance of security; *also* **:** a person or group performing such an action

²**patrol** *vb* **pa·trolled; pa·trol·ling :** to carry out a patrol

pa·trol·man \pə-'trōl-mən\ *n* **:** a police officer assigned to a beat

patrol wagon *n* **:** PADDY WAGON

pa·tron \'pā-trən\ *n* **1 :** a person chosen or named as special protector **2 ♦ :** a wealthy or influential supporter ⟨~ of poets⟩; *also* **:** BENEFACTOR **3 ♦ :** a regular client or customer

♦ [2] backer, guarantor, sponsor, surety ♦ [3] customer, guest

pa·tron·age \'pa-trə-nij, 'pā-\ *n* **1 :** the support or influence of a patron **2 :** the trade of customers **3 :** control of appointment to government jobs

pa·tron·ess \'pā-trə-nəs\ *n* **:** a woman who is a patron

pa·tron·ise *chiefly Brit var of* PATRONIZE

pa·tron·ize \'pā-trə-,nīz, 'pa-\ *vb* **-ized; -iz·ing** **1 :** to be a customer of **2 :** to treat condescendingly, haughtily, or coolly **3 ♦ :** to act as patron of : provide aid or support for

♦ advocate, back, champion, endorse, support

pat·ro·nym·ic \,pa-trə-'ni-mik\ *n* **:** a name derived from the name of one's father or a paternal ancestor usu. by the addition of an affix

pa·troon \pə-'trün\ *n* **:** the proprietor of a manorial estate esp. in New York under Dutch rule

pat·sy \'pat-sē\ *n, pl* **pat·sies :** a person who is easily duped or victimized

¹**pat·ter** \'pa-tər\ *vb* **:** to talk glibly or mechanically

²**patter** *n* **1 ♦ :** a specialized lingo **2 :** extremely rapid talk ⟨a comedian's ~⟩

♦ argot, cant, dialect, jargon, language, lingo, patois, slang, vocabulary

³**patter** *vb* **:** to strike, pat, or tap rapidly

⁴**patter** *n* **:** a quick succession of taps or pats ⟨the ~ of rain⟩

¹**pat·tern** \'pa-tərn\ *n* **1 :** an ideal model **2 :** something used as

a model for making things ⟨a dressmaker's ∼⟩ **3** : SAMPLE **4**
♦ : an artistic design **5** : CONFIGURATION **6** ♦ : an established
mode of behavior or set of beliefs or attitudes

♦ [4] design, figure, motif, motive ♦ [6] custom, fashion,
groove, habit, practice, routine, rut, treadmill, way, wont

²**pattern** *vb* : to form according to a pattern
pat·ty *also* **pat·tie** \'pa-tē\ *n, pl* **patties** **1** : a little pie **2** ♦ : a
small flat cake esp. of chopped food

♦ cutlet, fritter

pau·ci·ty \'pȯ-sə-tē\ *n* ♦ : smallness of number or quantity

♦ dearth, deficiency, deficit, failure, famine, inadequacy, insufficiency, lack, poverty, scantiness, scarcity, shortage, want

paunch \'pȯnch\ *n* : a usu. large belly : POTBELLY — **paunchy**
adj
pau·per \'pȯ-pər\ *n* : a person without means of support except
from charity — **pau·per·ize** \-pə-ˌrīz\ *vb*
pau·per·ism \'pȯ-pə-ˌri-zəm\ *n* ♦ : the quality or state of being
a pauper

♦ beggary, destitution, impecuniousness, impoverishment, indigence, need, penury, poverty, want

¹**pause** \'pȯz\ *n* **1** ♦ : a temporary stop; *also* : a period of inaction **2** : a brief suspension of the voice **3** : a sign (⌒) above
or below a musical note or rest to show it is to be prolonged **4** : a
reason for pausing **5** : a function of an electronic device that
pauses a recording

♦ break, breath, breathe, interruption, lull

²**pause** *vb* **paused; paus·ing** : to stop, rest, or linger for a time
pave \'pāv\ *vb* **paved; pav·ing** : to cover (as a road) with hard
material in order to smooth or firm the surface
pave·ment \'pāv-mənt\ *n* **1** : a paved surface **2** : the material
with which something is paved
pa·vil·ion \pə-'vil-yən\ *n* **1** : a large tent **2** : a light structure (as
in a park) used for entertainment or shelter
pav·ing \'pā-viŋ\ *n* : PAVEMENT
¹**paw** \'pȯ\ *n* : the foot of a quadruped (as a dog or lion) having
claws
²**paw** *vb* **1** : to touch or strike with a paw; *also* : to scrape with a
hoof **2** : to feel or handle clumsily or rudely **3** : to flail about or
grab for with the hands
pawl \'pȯl\ *n* : a pivoted tongue or sliding bolt designed to fall
into notches on another machine part to permit motion in one direction only
¹**pawn** \'pȯn\ *n* : a chess piece of the least value
²**pawn** *n* **1** ♦ : something deposited as security for a loan; *also*
: HOSTAGE **2** : the state of being pledged

♦ gage, guarantee, guaranty, pledge, security

³**pawn** *vb* : to deposit as a pledge
pawn·bro·ker \'pȯn-ˌbrō-kər\ *n* : one who lends money on
goods pledged
Paw·nee \pȯ-'nē\ *n, pl* **Pawnee** *or* **Pawnees** : a member of an
Indigenous people who lived in Nebraska and are now located in
Oklahoma
pawn·shop \'pȯn-ˌshäp\ *n* : a pawnbroker's place of business
paw·paw *also* **pa·paw** \¹'pȯ\: PAPAYA **2** \'pä-ˌpȯ, 'pȯ-\ : a
No. American tree with green-skinned edible fruit; *also* : its fruit
¹**pay** \'pā\ *vb* **paid** \'pād\ *also in sense 7* **payed; pay·ing** **1**
♦ : to make due return to for goods or services ⟨∼ the gro-
cer⟩ **2** ♦ : to discharge indebtedness for : SETTLE ⟨∼ a bill⟩ **3**
: to give in forfeit ⟨∼ the penalty⟩ **4** : REQUITE **5** : to give, offer, or make freely or as fitting ⟨∼ attention⟩ **6** ♦ : to be profitable to : RETURN **7** : to make slack and allow to run out ⟨∼ out
a rope⟩ **8** ♦ : to give in return for goods or service ⟨∼ good
money⟩ — **pay·ee** \pā-'ē\ *n* — **pay·er** *n*

♦ [1] compensate, recompense, remunerate ♦ [2] clear, discharge, foot, liquidate, pay off, quit, recompense, settle, spring,
stand *Ant* repudiate ♦ [6] give, return, yield ♦ [8] disburse, expend, give, lay out, spend

²**pay** *n* **1** : something paid for a purpose and esp. as a salary or
wage **2** : the status of being paid by an employer : EMPLOY

♦ compensation, consideration, payment, recompense, remittance, remuneration, requital ♦ emolument, hire, payment, salary, stipend, wage

³**pay** *adj* **1** : containing something valuable (as gold) ⟨∼ dirt⟩ **2**
: equipped to receive a fee for use ⟨∼ telephone⟩ **3** : requiring
payment
pay·able \'pā-ə-bəl\ *adj* ♦ : that may, can, or must be paid

♦ outstanding, overdue, unpaid, unsettled

pay·back \'pā-ˌbak\ *n* **1** : a return on an investment equal to the
original capital outlay **2** : something given in return, compensation, or retaliation
pay·check \'pā-ˌchek\ *n* **1** : a check in payment of wages or
salary **2** : WAGES, SALARY
pay·load \-ˌlōd\ *n* ♦ : the load carried by a vehicle in addition to
what is necessary for its operation; *also* : the weight of such a load

♦ burden, cargo, draft, freight, haul, lading, load, weight

pay·mas·ter \-ˌmas-tər\ *n* : one who distributes the payroll
pay·ment \'pā-mənt\ *n* **1** ♦ : the act of paying **2** ♦ : something paid

♦ [1] compensation, disbursement, remittance, remuneration
Ant nonpayment, repudiation ♦ [2] compensation, consideration, deposit, disbursement, expenditure, indemnity, outlay,
pay, recompense, redress, remittance, remuneration, rent, reparation, requital, restitution, salary, settlement, stipend, wage

pay·off \-ˌȯf\ *n* **1** ♦ : a valuable return : PROFIT; *also* : RETRIBU-
TION **2** : the climax of an incident or enterprise ⟨the ∼ of a
story⟩

♦ earnings, gain, lucre, net, proceeds, profit, return

pay off *vb* ♦ : to pay (a debt or a creditor) in full

♦ clear, discharge, foot, liquidate, pay, quit, recompense, settle,
spring, stand

pay–per–view *n* : a cable television service by which customers
can order access to a single airing of a TV feature
pay·roll \-ˌrōl\ *n* : a list of persons entitled to receive pay; *also*
: the money to pay those on such a list
payt *abbr* payment
pay up *vb* : to pay what is due; *also* : to pay in full
pay·wall \'pā-ˌwȯl\ *n* : a system that prevents Internet users from
accessing certain Web content without a paid subscription
Pb *symbol* lead
PBS *abbr* Public Broadcasting Service
PBX \ˌpē-(ˌ)bē-'eks\ *n* : a private telephone switchboard
¹**PC** \ˌpē-'sē\ *n, pl* **PCs** *or* **PC's** : MICROCOMPUTER
²**PC** *abbr* **1** Peace Corps **2** percent; percentage **3** politically
correct **4** postcard **5** after meals **6** professional corporation
PCB \ˌpē-ˌsē-'bē\ *n* : POLYCHLORINATED BIPHENYL
PCP \ˌpē-ˌsē-'pē\ *n* : PHENCYCLIDINE
pct *abbr* percent; percentage
pd *abbr* paid
Pd *symbol* palladium
PD *abbr* **1** per diem **2** police department **3** potential difference
PDA \ˌpē-ˌdē-'ā\ *n* : a small microprocessor device for storing
and organizing personal information
PDQ \ˌpē-ˌdē-'kyü\ *adv, often not cap* : IMMEDIATELY
PDT *abbr* Pacific daylight (saving) time
PE *abbr* **1** physical education **2** printer's error **3** professional
engineer
pea \'pē\ *n, pl* **peas** *also* **pease** \'pēz\ **1** : the round edible
protein-rich seed borne in the pod of a widely grown leguminous
vine; *also* : this vine **2** : any of various plants resembling or related to the pea
peace \'pēs\ *n* **1** ♦ : a state of calm and quiet; *esp* : public security under law **2** : freedom from disturbing thoughts or emotions **3** ♦ : a state of concord (as between persons or governments); *also* : an agreement to end hostilities — **peace·able**
\'pē-sə-bəl\ *adj* — **peace·ably** \-blē\ *adv*

♦ [1] calm, calmness, hush, placidity, quiet, quietness, repose,
serenity, still, stillness, tranquility ♦ [3] compatibility, concord,
harmony

peace·ful \'pēs-fəl\ *adj* ♦ : untroubled by conflict, agitation, or
commotion — **peace·ful·ly** *adv*

♦ calm, halcyon, hushed, placid, quiet, serene, still, tranquil, untroubled

peace·keep·ing \'pēs-ˌkē-piŋ\ *n* : the preserving of peace; *esp*
: international enforcement and supervision of a truce —
peace·keep·er *n*
peace·mak·er \-ˌmā-kər\ *n* ♦ : one who settles an argument or
stops a fight

♦ arbiter, arbitrator, go-between, intercessor, intermediary, mediator, middleman

peace·time \-ˌtīm\ *n* : a time when a nation is not at war
peach \'pēch\ *n* : a sweet juicy fuzzy-skinned fruit of a small usu.
pink-flowered tree related to the cherry and plums; *also* : this tree
— **peachy** *adj*
pea·cock \'pē-ˌkäk\ *n* : the male peafowl that can spread its long
tail feathers to make a colorful display

pea·fowl \-ˌfau̇(-ə)l\ *n* : any of three very large pheasants often raised as ornamental birds

pea·hen \-ˌhen\ *n* : the female peafowl

¹**peak** \ˈpēk\ *n* **1** : a pointed or projecting part **2 a** : the top of a hill or mountain **b** ♦ : a prominent mountain usu. having a well-defined summit : MOUNTAIN **3** ♦ : the front projecting part of a cap **4** : the narrow part of a ship's bow or stern **5** ♦ : the highest level or greatest degree — **peak** *adj*

♦ [2b] mount, mountain ♦ [3] bill, visor ♦ [5] acme, apex, climax, crown, culmination, head, height, meridian, pinnacle, summit, tip-top, top, zenith

²**peak** *vb* : to bring to or reach a maximum

¹**peak·ed** \ˈpēkt\ *adj* : having a peak : POINTED

²**peaked** \ˈpē-kəd\ *adj* ♦ : being pale and wan or emaciated; *also* : somewhat unwell

♦ ashen, cadaverous, livid, lurid, pale, pasty ♦ bad, down, ill, indisposed, punk, sick, unhealthy, unsound, unwell

¹**peal** \ˈpēl\ *n* **1** : the loud ringing of bells **2** : a set of tuned bells **3** : a loud sound or succession of sounds

²**peal** *vb* ♦ : to give out peals : RESOUND

♦ chime, knell, ring, toll

pea·nut \ˈpē-(ˌ)nət\ *n* **1** : an annual herb related to the pea but having pods that ripen underground; *also* : this pod or one of its edible seeds **2** *pl* ♦ : a very small amount

♦ mite, pittance, shoestring, song

pear \ˈpar\ *n* : the fleshy fruit of a tree related to the apple; *also* : this tree

pearl \ˈpərl\ *n* **1** : a small hard often lustrous body formed within the shell of some mollusks and used as a gem **2** ♦ : one that is choice or precious ⟨∼s of wisdom⟩ **3** : a slightly bluish medium gray color — **pearly** \ˈpər-lē\ *adj*

♦ catch, gem, jewel, plum, prize, treasure

peas·ant \ˈpez-ᵊnt\ *n* **1** : any of a class of small landowners or laborers tilling the soil **2** : a usu. uneducated person of low social status — **peas·ant·ry** \-ᵊn-trē\ *n*

pea·shoot·er \ˈpē-ˌshü-tər\ *n* : a toy blowgun for shooting peas

peat \ˈpēt\ *n* : a dark substance formed by partial decay of plants (as mosses) in water — **peaty** *adj*

peat moss *n* : SPHAGNUM

¹**peb·ble** \ˈpe-bəl\ *n* : a small usu. round stone

²**pebble** *vb* **peb·bled; peb·bling** : to produce a rough surface texture in ⟨∼ leather⟩

peb·bly \ˈpe-b(ə-)lē\ *adj* ♦ : containing or resembling pebbles

♦ broken, bumpy, coarse, irregular, jagged, lumpy, ragged, rough, rugged, uneven

pec \ˈpek\ *n* : PECTORAL MUSCLE

pe·can \pi-ˈkän, -ˈkan; ˈpē-ˌkan\ *n* : the smooth thin-shelled edible nut of a large American hickory; *also* : this tree

pec·ca·dil·lo \ˌpe-kə-ˈdi-lō\ *n, pl* **-loes** *or* **-los** : a slight offense

pec·ca·ry \ˈpe-kə-rē\ *n, pl* **-ries** : any of several American chiefly tropical mammals resembling but smaller than the related pigs

pec·ca·vi \pe-ˈkä-ˌvē\ *n* : an acknowledgment of sin

¹**peck** \ˈpek\ *n* **1** : a unit of dry capacity equal to ¼ bushel : a large amount

²**peck** *vb* **1** : to strike or pierce with or as if with the bill **2** : to make (as a hole) by pecking **3** : to pick up with or as if with the bill

³**peck** *n* **1** : an impression made by pecking **2** : a quick sharp stroke

pecking order *also* **peck order** *n* : a basic pattern of social organization within a flock of poultry in which each bird pecks another lower in the scale without being pecked in return and submits to pecking by one of higher rank; *also* : a social hierarchy

pec·tin \ˈpek-tən\ *n* : any of various water-soluble plant substances that cause fruit jellies to set — **pec·tic** \-tik\ *adj*

pec·to·ral \ˈpek-tə-rəl\ *adj* : of or relating to the breast or chest

pectoral muscle *n* : either of two muscles on each side of the body which connect the front walls of the chest with the bones of the upper arm and shoulder

pe·cu·liar \pi-ˈkyül-yər\ *adj* **1** ♦ : belonging exclusively to one person or group **2** ♦ : characteristic of only one person, group, or thing : DISTINCTIVE **3** ♦ : differing markedly from the usual or ordinary or accepted : ODD — **pe·cu·liar·ly** *adv*

♦ [1] individual, particular, personal, private, separate, singular, unique ♦ [2] characteristic, classic, distinct, distinctive, individual, proper, symptomatic, typical ♦ [3] curious, extraordinary, funny, odd, rare, strange, unaccustomed, uncommon, unique, unusual, weird

pe·cu·liar·i·ty \pi-ˌkyül-ˈyar-ə-tē, -ˌkyü-lē-ˈar-\ *n* **1** : the quality or state of being peculiar **2** ♦ : a distinguishing characteristic **3** ♦ : an odd person, thing, event, or trait

♦ [2] attribute, character, characteristic, feature, mark, point, property, quality, trait ♦ [3] crotchet, eccentricity, idiosyncrasy, mannerism, oddity, quirk, singularity, trick

pe·cu·ni·ary \pi-ˈkyü-nē-ˌer-ē\ *adj* ♦ : of or relating to money : MONETARY

♦ financial, fiscal, monetary

ped·a·gogue *also* **ped·a·gog** \ˈpe-də-ˌgäg\ *n* ♦ : one that teaches : TEACHER

♦ educator, instructor, schoolteacher, teacher

ped·a·go·gy \ˈpe-də-ˌgō-jē, -ˌgä-\ *n* : the art or profession of teaching; *esp* : EDUCATION **2** — **ped·a·gog·ic** \ˌpe-də-ˈgä-jik, -ˈgō-\ *or* **ped·a·gog·i·cal** \-ji-kəl\ *adj*

¹**ped·al** \ˈped-ᵊl\ *n* : a lever worked by the foot

²**pedal** *adj* : of or relating to the foot

³**ped·al** \ˈped-ᵊl\ *vb* **ped·aled** *also* **ped·alled; ped·al·ing** *also* **ped·al·ling** **1** : to use or work a pedal (as of a piano or bicycle) **2** : to ride a bicycle

ped·ant \ˈped-ᵊnt\ *n* **1** : a person who makes a show of knowledge **2** : a formal uninspired teacher — **pe·dan·tic** \pi-ˈdan-tik\ *adj* — **ped·ant·ry** \ˈped-ᵊn-trē\ *n*

ped·dle \ˈped-ᵊl\ *vb* **ped·dled; ped·dling** : to sell or offer for sale from place to place — **ped·dler** *also* **ped·lar** \ˈped-lər\ *n*

ped·er·ast \ˈpe-də-ˌrast\ *n* : a man who desires or engages in sexual activity with a boy — **ped·er·as·ty** \ˈpe-də-ˌras-tē\ *n*

ped·es·tal \ˈpe-dəst-ᵊl\ *n* **1** : the support or foot of something (as a column, statue, or vase) that is upright **2** : a position of high regard

¹**pe·des·tri·an** \pə-ˈdes-trē-ən\ *adj* **1** : marked by dullness or ordinariness : ORDINARY **2** : going on foot

²**pedestrian** *n* : WALKER

pe·di·at·rics \ˌpē-dē-ˈa-triks\ *n* : a branch of medicine dealing with the development, care, and diseases of children — **pe·di·at·ric** \-trik\ *adj* — **pe·di·a·tri·cian** \ˌpē-dē-ə-ˈtri-shən\ *n*

pedi·cab \ˈpe-di-ˌkab\ *n* : a pedal-driven tricycle with seats for a driver and two passengers

ped·i·cure \ˈpe-di-ˌkyu̇r\ *n* : care of the feet, toes, and nails; *also* : a single treatment of these parts — **ped·i·cur·ist** \-ˌkyu̇r-ist\ *n*

ped·i·gree \ˈpe-də-ˌgrē\ *n* **1** : a record of a line of ancestors **2** ♦ : an ancestral line — **ped·i·greed** \-ˌgrēd\ *adj*

♦ ancestry, birth, blood, bloodline, breeding, descent, extraction, family tree, genealogy, line, lineage, origin, parentage, stock, strain

ped·i·ment \ˈpe-də-mənt\ *n* : a low triangular gablelike decoration (as over a door or window) on a building

pe·dom·e·ter \pi-ˈdä-mə-tər\ *n* : an instrument that measures the distance one walks

pe·do·phile \ˈpe-də-ˌfī(-ə)l, ˈpē-\ *n* : one affected with pedophilia

pe·do·phil·ia \ˌpe-də-ˈfi-lē-ə, ˌpē-\ *n* : sexual perversion in which children are the preferred sexual object

pe·dun·cle \ˈpē-ˌdəŋ-kəl\ *n* : a narrow supporting stalk

¹**peek** \ˈpēk\ *vb* **1** : to look furtively **2** : to peer from a place of concealment **3** : to take a brief look : GLANCE

²**peek** *n* **1** : a furtive look **2** ♦ : a brief look : GLANCE

♦ cast, eye, gander, glance, glimpse, look, peep, regard, sight, view

¹**peel** \ˈpēl\ *vb* **1** ♦ : to strip the skin, bark, or rind from **2 a** ♦ : to strip off (as a coat) — often used with *off* **b** : to come off **3** : to lose the skin, bark, or rind

♦ [1] bark, flay, hull, husk, shell, skin ♦ *usu* **peel off** [2a] doff, put off, remove, take off

²**peel** *n* : a skin or rind esp. of a fruit

peel·ing \ˈpē-liŋ\ *n* : a peeled-off piece or strip (as of skin or rind)

peen \ˈpēn\ *n* : the usu. hemispherical or wedge-shaped end of the head of a hammer opposite the face

¹**peep** \ˈpēp\ *vb* ♦ : to utter a feeble shrill sound or the slightest sound

♦ cheep, chirp, pipe, tweet, twitter

²**peep** *n* : a feeble shrill sound

³**peep** *vb* **1** : to look slyly esp. through an aperture : PEEK **2** : to begin to emerge **3** : to look at : WATCH — **peep·er** *n*

⁴**peep** *n* **1** : a first faint appearance **2** ♦ : a brief or furtive look

♦ cast, eye, gander, glance, glimpse, look, peek, regard, sight, view

peep·hole \ˈpēp-ˌhōl\ *n* : a hole to peep through

¹peer \'pir\ *n* **1** ♦ : one of equal standing with another : EQUAL **2** : NOBLE — **peer·age** \-ij\ *n*

♦ coordinate, counterpart, equal, equivalent, fellow, like, match, parallel, rival

²peer *vb* **1** : to look intently or curiously **2** : to come slightly into view

peer·ess \'pir-əs\ *n* : a woman who is a peer
peer·less \'pir-ləs\ *adj* ♦ : having no equal : MATCHLESS

♦ incomparable, inimitable, matchless, unequaled, unmatched, unparalleled, unrivaled, unsurpassed

¹peeve \'pēv\ *vb* **peeved; peev·ing** ♦ : to make resentful : ANNOY

♦ aggravate, annoy, bother, bug, chafe, exasperate, gall, get, grate, irk, irritate, nettle, persecute, pique, put out, rasp, rile, vex

²peeve *n* **1** ♦ : a feeling or mood of resentment **2** ♦ : a particular grievance

♦ [1] dudgeon, huff, offense, pique, resentment, umbrage ♦ [2] aggravation, annoyance, bother, exasperation, frustration, hassle, headache, inconvenience, irritant, nuisance, pest, problem, thorn

pee·vish \'pē-vish\ *adj* **1** : querulous in temperament : FRETFUL **2** ♦ : perversely obstinate **3** ♦ : marked by ill temper — **pee·vish·ly** *adv*

♦ [2] dogged, hardheaded, headstrong, mulish, obdurate, obstinate, opinionated, pertinacious, perverse, pigheaded, stubborn, unyielding, willful ♦ [3] crabby, cranky, cross, crotchety, grouchy, grumpy, irritable, short-tempered, snappish, snappy, snippy, testy, waspish

pee·vish·ness \-nəs\ *n* ♦ : the quality or state of being peevish

♦ hardheadedness, mulishness, obduracy, obstinacy, pertinacity, self-will, stubbornness, tenacity ♦ biliousness, grumpiness, irritability, perverseness, perversity

pee·wee \'pē-(ˌ)wē\ *n* ♦ : one that is diminutive or tiny

♦ dwarf, midget, mite, pygmy, runt

¹peg \'peg\ *n* **1** ♦ : a small pointed piece (as of wood) used to pin down or fasten things or to fit into holes **2** : a projecting piece used as a support or boundary marker **3** : SUPPORT, PRETEXT **4** ♦ : a step or degree esp. in estimation ⟨set him down a ∼⟩ **5** : THROW

♦ cut, degree, grade, inch, notch, phase, point, stage, step

²peg *vb* **pegged; peg·ging** **1** : to put a peg into : fasten, pin down, or attach with or as if with pegs **2** : to work hard and steadily : PLUG **3** : HUSTLE **4** : to mark by pegs **5** : to hold (as prices) at a set level or rate **6** ♦ : to place in a definite category **7** : to propel through the air by a forward motion of the hand and arm : THROW **8** ♦ : to work steadily and diligently — often used with *away*

♦ [6] assort, break down, categorize, class, classify, grade, group, place, range, rank, separate, sort ♦ *usu* **peg away** [8] drudge, endeavor (*or* endeavour), fag, grub, hustle, labor (*or* labour), plod, plug, slog, strain, strive, struggle, sweat, toil, work

PEI *abbr* Prince Edward Island
pei·gnoir \pān-'wär, pen-\ *n* : NEGLIGEE
¹pe·jo·ra·tive \pi-'jòr-ə-tiv\ *n* : a pejorative word or phrase
²pejorative *adj* : having negative connotations : DISPARAGING — **pe·jo·ra·tive·ly** *adv*
peke \'pēk\ *n, often cap* : PEKINGESE
Pe·king·ese *or* **Pe·kin·ese** \ˌpē-kə-'nēz, -'nēs; -kiŋ-'ēz, -'ēs\ *n, pl* **Pekingese** *or* **Pekinese** : any of a breed of Chinese origin of small short-legged long-haired dogs
pe·koe \'pē-(ˌ)kō\ *n* : a black tea made from young tea leaves
pel·age \'pe-lij\ *n* ♦ : the hairy covering of a mammal

♦ coat, fleece, fur, hair, pile, wool

pe·lag·ic \pə-'la-jik\ *adj* ♦ : of, relating to, or living or occurring in the open sea : OCEANIC

♦ marine, maritime, oceanic

pelf \'pelf\ *n* ♦ : something generally accepted as a medium of exchange : MONEY

♦ cash, currency, dough, lucre, money, tender

pel·i·can \'pe-li-kən\ *n* : any of a genus of large web-footed birds having a pouched lower bill used to scoop in fish
pel·la·gra \pə-'la-grə, -'lā-\ *n* : a disease caused by a diet with too little niacin and protein and marked by a skin rash, disease of the digestive system, and mental disturbances

pel·let \'pe-lət\ *n* **1** : a little ball (as of medicine) **2** : BULLET — **pel·let·al** \-lə-təl\ *adj* — **pel·let·ize** \-ˌtīz\ *vb*
pell-mell \ˌpel-'mel\ *adv* **1** ♦ : in mingled confusion **2** ♦ : in confused haste : HEADLONG

♦ [1] amok, berserk, frantically, harum-scarum, hectically, helter-skelter, madly, wild, wildly ♦ [2] cursorily, hastily, headlong, hurriedly, precipitately, rashly

pel·lu·cid \pə-'lü-səd\ *adj* ♦ : extremely clear : LIMPID, TRANSPARENT

♦ clear, limpid, liquid, lucent, transparent

pe·lo·ton \ˌpe-lə-'tän\ *n* : the main body of riders in a bicycle race
¹pelt \'pelt\ *n* ♦ : a skin esp. of a fur-bearing animal

♦ fur, hide, skin

²pelt *vb* **1** ♦ : to strike with a succession of blows or missiles **2** : to propel through the air by a forward motion of the hand and arm : THROW **3** ♦ : to move rapidly and vigorously

♦ [1] bash, bat, batter, beat, hammer, pound, thrash, thump ♦ [3] dash, fly, hasten, hurry, hustle, race, rocket, run, rush, shoot, speed, tear, zip, zoom

pel·vis \'pel-vəs\ *n, pl* **pel·vis·es** \-və-səz\ *or* **pel·ves** \-ˌvēz\ : a basin-shaped part of the vertebrate skeleton consisting of the large bone of each hip and the nearby bones of the spine — **pel·vic** \-vik\ *adj*
pem·mi·can *also* **pem·i·can** \'pe-mi-kən\ *n* : dried meat pounded fine and mixed with melted fat
¹pen \'pen\ *vb* **penned; pen·ning** ♦ : to shut in or as if in a pen

♦ cage, closet, coop up, corral, encase, enclose, envelop, fence, hedge, hem, house, immure, wall

²pen *n* **1** ♦ : a small enclosure for animals **2** : a small place of confinement or storage

♦ cage, coop, corral, pound

³pen *n* **1** : an implement for writing or drawing with ink or a similar fluid **2** : a writing instrument regarded as a means of expression **3** : STYLUS 3
⁴pen *vb* **penned; pen·ning** ♦ : to set down in writing as the author of : WRITE

♦ author, scribble, write

⁵pen *n* ♦ : a state or federal prison : PENITENTIARY

♦ brig, hoosegow, jail, jug, lockup, penitentiary, prison, stockade

⁶pen *abbr* peninsula
PEN *abbr* International Association of Poets, Playwrights, Editors, Essayists and Novelists
pe·nal \'pēn-ᵊl\ *adj* ♦ : of or relating to punishment

♦ corrective, disciplinary, punitive

pe·nal·ise *chiefly Brit var of* PENALIZE
pe·nal·ize \'pēn-ᵊl-ˌīz, 'pen-\ *vb* **-ized; -iz·ing** ♦ : to put a penalty on

♦ castigate, chasten, chastise, correct, discipline, punish

pen·al·ty \'pen-ᵊl-tē\ *n, pl* **-ties** **1** ♦ : punishment for crime or offense **2** ♦ : something forfeited when a person fails to do something agreed to **3** : disadvantage, loss, or hardship due to some action

♦ [1] castigation, chastisement, correction, desert, discipline, nemesis, punishment, wrath ♦ [2] damages, fine, forfeit, mulct

pen·ance \'pe-nəns\ *n* **1** : an act performed to show sorrow or repentance for sin **2** : a sacrament (as in the Roman Catholic Church) consisting of confession, absolution, and a penance directed by the confessor
pence \'pens\ *pl of* PENNY
pen·chant \'pen-chənt\ *n* ♦ : a strong inclination ⟨a ∼ for mathematics⟩

♦ bent, devices, disposition, genius, inclination, leaning, partiality, predilection, proclivity, propensity, tendency, turn

¹pen·cil \'pen-səl\ *n* : a writing or drawing tool consisting of or containing a slender cylinder of a solid marking substance
²pencil *vb* **-ciled** *or* **-cilled; -cil·ing** *or* **-cil·ling** : to draw or write with a pencil
pen·dant *also* **pen·dent** \'pen-dənt\ *n* ♦ : a hanging ornament

♦ charm

pen·dent *or* **pen·dant** \'pen-dənt\ *adj* : supported from above : SUSPENDED, OVERHANGING

¹pend·ing \'pen-diŋ\ *prep* **1** : DURING **2** : while awaiting
²pending *adj* **1** ♦ : not yet decided **2** ♦ : ready to take place : IMMINENT

♦ [1] open, undecided, undetermined, unresolved, unsettled *Ant* decided, determined, resolved, settled ♦ [2] coming, forthcoming, imminent, impending, oncoming

pen·du·lous \'pen-jə-ləs, -də-\ *adj* ♦ : hanging loosely

♦ droopy ♦ dependent

pen·du·lum \-ləm\ *n* : a body that swings freely from a fixed point
pe·ne·plain *also* **pe·ne·plane** \'pē-ni-ˌplān\ *n* : a large almost flat land surface shaped by erosion
pen·e·tra·ble \'pe-nə-trə-bəl\ *adj* ♦ : capable of being penetrated

♦ passable, permeable, porous *Ant* impassable, impenetrable, impermeable, impervious, nonporous

pen·e·trate \'pe-nə-ˌtrāt\ *vb* **-trat·ed; -trat·ing** **1** ♦ : to enter into : PIERCE **2** : PERMEATE **3** : to see into : UNDERSTAND **4** : to affect deeply — **pen·e·tra·tion** \ˌpe-nə-'trā-shən\ *n* — **pen·e·tra·tive** \'pe-nə-ˌtrā-tiv\ *adj*

♦ access, enter, pierce, probe

pen·e·trat·ing *adj* **1** ♦ : having the power of entering, piercing, or pervading 〈a ~ shriek〉 〈a ~ wind〉 **2** : ACUTE, DISCERNING 〈a ~ look〉

♦ biting, bitter, cutting, keen, piercing, raw, sharp

pen·guin \'pen-gwən, 'peŋ-\ *n* : any of various erect short-legged flightless seabirds of the southern hemisphere
pen·i·cil·lin \ˌpe-nə-'si-lən\ *n* : any of several antibiotics produced by molds or synthetically and used against various bacteria
pen·in·su·la \pə-'nin-sə-lə\ *n* ♦ : a long narrow portion of land extending out into the water — **pen·in·su·lar** \-lər\ *adj*

♦ arm, cape, headland, point, promontory, spit

pe·nis \'pē-nəs\ *n, pl* **pe·nis·es** *also* **pe·nes** \-ˌnēz\ : a male organ of copulation that in the human male also functions as the channel by which urine leaves the body
pen·i·tence \'pe-nə-təns\ *n* ♦ : the quality or state of being penitent

♦ contrition, guilt, remorse, repentance, self-reproach, shame

¹pen·i·tent \'pe-nə-tənt\ *adj* ♦ : feeling sorrow for sins or offenses : REPENTANT — **pen·i·ten·tial** \ˌpe-nə-'ten-chəl\ *adj*

♦ apologetic, contrite, regretful, remorseful, repentant, rueful, sorry

²penitent *n* : a penitent person
¹pen·i·ten·tia·ry \ˌpe-nə-'ten-chə-rē\ *n, pl* **-ries** ♦ : a state or federal prison

♦ brig, hoosegow, jail, jug, lockup, pen, prison

²penitentiary *adj* : of, relating to, or incurring confinement in a penitentiary
pen·knife \'pen-ˌnīf\ *n* : a small pocketknife
pen·light *also* **pen·lite** \-ˌlīt\ *n* : a small flashlight resembling a fountain pen in size or shape
pen·man \'pen-mən\ *n* **1** : COPYIST **2** : one skilled in penmanship **3** : AUTHOR
pen·man·ship \-ˌship\ *n* **1** ♦ : the art or practice of writing with the pen **2** ♦ : quality or style of handwriting

♦ handwriting, manuscript, script

Penn *or* **Penna** *abbr* Pennsylvania
pen name *n* : an author's pseudonym
pen·nant \'pe-nənt\ *n* **1** ♦ : a tapering flag used esp. for signaling **2** : a flag symbolic of championship

♦ banner, colors (*or* colours), ensign, flag, jack, standard, streamer

pen·ne \'pe-nā\ *n* : short diagonally cut tubular pasta
pen·ni·less \'pe-ni-ləs\ *adj* ♦ : destitute of money

♦ broke, destitute, impecunious, indigent, needy, penurious, poor, poverty-stricken

pen·non \'pe-nən\ *n* **1** : a long narrow ribbonlike flag borne on a lance **2** : WING
Penn·syl·va·nian \ˌpen-səl-'vā-nyən\ *adj* **1** : of or relating to Pennsylvania or its people **2** : of, relating to, or being the period of the Paleozoic era between the Mississippian and the Permian — **Pennsylvanian** *n*
pen·ny \'pe-nē\ *n, pl* **pennies** \-nēz\ *or* **pence** \'pens\ **1** : a British monetary unit formerly equal to ¹/₁₂ shilling but now

equal to ¹/₁₀₀ pound; *also* : a coin of this value **2** *pl* **pennies** : a cent of the U.S. or Canada
pen·ny–pinch·ing \'pe-nē-ˌpin-chin\ *n* : PARSIMONY — **pen·ny–pinch·er** *n* — **penny–pinching** *adj*
pen·ny·weight \-ˌwāt\ *n* : a unit of troy weight equal to ¹/₂₀ troy ounce
pen·ny–wise \-ˌwīz\ *adj* : wise or prudent only in small matters
pe·nol·o·gy \pi-'nä-lə-jē\ *n* : a branch of criminology dealing with prisons and the treatment of offenders
¹pen·sion \'pen-chən\ *n* : a fixed sum paid regularly esp. to a person retired from service
²pension *vb* : to pay a pension to — **pen·sion·er** *n*
pen·sive \'pen-siv\ *adj* ♦ : musingly, dreamily, or sadly thoughtful — **pen·sive·ly** *adv*

♦ contemplative, meditative, melancholy, reflective, ruminant, thoughtful

pen·stock \'pen-ˌstäk\ *n* **1** : a sluice or gate for regulating a flow **2** ♦ : a pipe for carrying water

♦ channel, conduit, duct, leader, line, pipe, tube

pent \'pent\ *adj* : shut up : CONFINED
pen·ta·gon \'pen-tə-ˌgän\ *n* : a polygon of five angles and five sides — **pen·tag·o·nal** \pen-'ta-gən-ᵊl\ *adj*
pen·tam·e·ter \pen-'ta-mə-tər\ *n* : a line of verse containing five metrical feet
pen·tath·lon \pen-'tath-lən\ *n* : a composite athletic contest consisting of five events
Pen·te·cost \'pen-ti-ˌkóst\ *n* : the 7th Sunday after Easter observed as a church festival commemorating the descent of the Holy Spirit on the apostles — **Pen·te·cos·tal** \ˌpen-ti-'käst-ᵊl\ *adj*
Pentecostal *n* : a member of a Christian religious body that stresses expressive worship, evangelism, and spiritual gifts — **Pen·te·cos·tal·ism** \ˌpen-ti-'käst-ᵊl-ˌi-zəm\ *n*
pent·house \'pent-ˌhaus\ *n* **1** : a shed or sloping roof attached to a wall or building **2** : an apartment built on the top floor or roof of a building **3** ♦ : a smaller structure joined to a building

♦ addition, annex, extension

pen·ul·ti·mate \pi-'nəl-tə-mət\ *adj* : next to the last 〈~ syllable〉
pen·um·bra \pə-'nəm-brə\ *n, pl* **-brae** \-(ˌ)brē\ *or* **-bras** : the partial shadow surrounding a complete shadow (as in an eclipse)
pe·nu·ri·ous \pə-'nur-ē-əs, -'nyur-\ *adj* **1** ♦ : marked by or suffering from penury **2** ♦ : given to or marked by extreme stinting frugality

♦ [1] broke, destitute, impecunious, indigent, needy, penniless, poor, poverty-stricken ♦ [2] cheap, close, mean, niggardly, parsimonious, spare, sparing, stingy, tight, tightfisted, uncharitable

pen·u·ry \'pe-nyə-rē\ *n* **1** ♦ : extreme poverty **2** : extreme frugality

♦ beggary, destitution, impecuniousness, impoverishment, indigence, need, pauperism, poverty, want

pe·on \'pē-ˌän, -ən\ *n, pl* **peons** *or* **pe·o·nes** \pā-'ō-nēz\ **1** : a member of the landless laboring class in Spanish America **2** : one bound to service for payment of a debt **3** ♦ : one who does menial or tedious labor — **pe·on·age** \-ə-nij\ *n*

♦ drudge, toiler, worker

pe·o·ny \'pē-ə-nē\ *n, pl* **-nies** : any of a genus of chiefly Eurasian plants with large often double red, pink, or white flowers; *also* : the flower
¹peo·ple \'pē-pəl\ *n, pl* **people** **1** *pl* : human beings making up a group or linked by a common characteristic or interest **2** *pl* ♦ : human beings — often used in compounds instead of *persons* 〈sales*people*〉 **3** *pl* ♦ : the mass of persons in a community : POPULACE; *also* : ELECTORATE 〈the ~'s choice〉 **4** *pl* **peoples** ♦ : a body of persons united by a common culture, sense of kinship, or political organization

♦ [2] folks, humanity, humankind, persons, public, society, world ♦ [3] commoners, herd, masses, mob, plebeians, populace, rank and file ♦ [4] blood, clan, family, folks, house, kin, kindred, kinfolk, line, lineage, race, stock, tribe

²people *vb* **peo·pled; peo·pling** : to supply or fill with or as if with people
¹pep \'pep\ *n* ♦ : brisk energy or initiative

♦ dash, energy, life, vigor (*or* vigour), vim, vitality

²pep *vb* **pepped; pep·ping** ♦ : to put pep into : STIMULATE

♦ *usu* **pep up** animate, brace, energize, enliven, fire, invigorate, jazz up, liven up, quicken, stimulate, vitalize, vivify, zip (up)

¹pep·per \'pe-pər\ *n* **1 :** either of two pungent condiments from the berry (**pep·per·corn** \-ˌkȯrn\) of an Indian climbing plant; *also* : this plant **2 :** a plant related to the tomato and widely grown for its hot or mild sweet fruit; *also* : this fruit

²pepper *vb* **pep·pered; pep·per·ing 1** ♦ **:** to sprinkle or season with or as if with pepper **2 :** to shower with missiles or rapid blows

♦ dot, scatter, sow, spray, sprinkle, strew

pep·per·mint \-ˌmint, -mənt\ *n* : a pungent aromatic mint; *also* : candy flavored with its oil

pep·per·o·ni \ˌpe-pə-'rō-nē\ *n* : a highly seasoned beef and pork sausage

pepper spray *n* : a temporarily disabling aerosol that causes irritation and blinding of the eyes and inflammation of the nose, throat, and skin

pep·pery \'pe-pə-rē\ *adj* **1** ♦ **:** having the qualities of pepper : PUNGENT, HOT **2 :** having a hot temper **3** ♦ **:** full of or exuding emotion or spirit : FIERY

♦ fiery, high-spirited, mettlesome, spirited, spunky

pep·py \'pe-pē\ *adj* ♦ **:** full of pep

♦ active, animate, animated, brisk, energetic, frisky, jaunty, jazzy, lively, perky, pert, racy, snappy, spirited, sprightly, springy, vital, vivacious

pep·sin \'pep-sən\ *n* : an enzyme of the stomach that promotes digestion by breaking down proteins; *also* : a preparation of this used medicinally

pep·tic \'pep-tik\ *adj* **1 :** relating to or promoting digestion **2** : caused by digestive juices ⟨a ∼ ulcer⟩

Pe·quot \'pē-ˌkwät\ *n* : a member of an Indigenous people of eastern Connecticut

¹per \'pər\ *prep* **1** ♦ **:** by means of **2 :** to or for each **3 :** ACCORDING TO

♦ by, through, with

²per *adv* **:** for each : APIECE

³per *abbr* **1** period **2** person

¹per·ad·ven·ture \'pər-əd-ˌven-chər\ *adv, archaic* : PERHAPS

²peradventure *n* **1 :** DOUBT **2 :** CHANCE 4

per·am·bu·late \pə-'ram-byə-ˌlāt\ *vb* **-lat·ed; -lat·ing :** to travel over esp. on foot

per·am·bu·la·tion \pə-ˌram-byə-'lā-shən\ *n* ♦ **:** an act of walking about : STROLL

♦ ramble, stroll, turn, walk

per·am·bu·la·tor \pə-'ram-byə-ˌlā-tər\ *n, chiefly Brit* : a baby carriage

per an·num \(ˌ)pər-'a-nəm\ *adv* **:** in or for each year : ANNUALLY

per·cale \(ˌ)pər-'kāl, 'pər-ˌ; (ˌ)pər-'kal\ *n* : a fine woven cotton cloth

per cap·i·ta \(ˌ)pər-'ka-pə-tə\ *adv or adj* **:** by or for each person

per·ceive \pər-'sēv\ *vb* **per·ceived; per·ceiv·ing 1** ♦ **:** to attain awareness or understanding of **2** ♦ **:** to become aware of through the senses — **per·ceiv·able** *adj*

♦ [1] appreciate, apprehend, catch, catch on (to), comprehend, get, grasp, make, make out, notice, see, seize, understand ♦ [2] feel, scent, see, sense, smell, taste

¹per·cent \pər-'sent\ *adv* **:** in each hundred

²percent *n, pl* **percent** *or* **percents 1** : one part in a hundred : HUNDREDTH **2 :** PERCENTAGE

per·cent·age \pər-'sen-tij\ *n* **1 :** a part of a whole expressed in hundredths **2 :** the result obtained by multiplying a number by a percent **3 :** ADVANTAGE, PROFIT **4** ♦ **:** a likelihood based on cumulative statistics : PROBABILITY; *also* : favorable odds

♦ chance, odds, probability

percentage point *n* : one hundredth of a whole ⟨rates rose one *percentage point* from 6.5 to 7.5 percent⟩

per·cen·tile \pər-'sen-ˌtīl\ *n* : a value on a scale of one hundred indicating the standing of a score or grade in terms of the percentage of scores or grades falling with or below it

per·cept \'pər-ˌsept\ *n* : an impression of an object obtained by use of the senses

per·cep·ti·ble \pər-'sep-tə-bəl\ *adj* ♦ **:** capable of being perceived — **per·cep·ti·bly** \-blē\ *adv*

♦ appreciable, detectable, discernible, distinguishable, palpable, sensible *Ant* impalpable, imperceptible, inappreciable, indistinguishable, insensible

per·cep·tion \pər-'sep-shən\ *n* **1** ♦ **:** an act or result of perceiv-

ing **2** ♦ **:** awareness of one's environment through physical sensation **3** ♦ **:** ability to understand

♦ [1] appreciation, apprehension, comprehension, grasp, grip, understanding ♦ [3] discernment, insight, sagacity, sapience, wisdom

per·cep·tive \pər-'sep-tiv\ *adj* ♦ **:** capable of or exhibiting keen perception — **per·cep·tive·ly** *adv*

♦ acute, delicate, keen, sensitive, sharp ♦ discerning, insightful, sagacious, sage, sapient, wise

per·cep·tu·al \pər-'sep-chə-wəl\ *adj* : of, relating to, or involving sensory stimulus as opposed to abstract concept ⟨∼ stimulation⟩ — **per·cep·tu·al·ly** *adv*

¹perch \'pərch\ *n* **1 :** a roost for a bird **2 :** a resting place or vantage point

²perch *vb* **1** ♦ **:** to alight, settle, or rest on a perch, a height, or a precarious spot **2** ♦ **:** to place on a perch, a height, or a precarious spot

♦ [1, 2] alight, land, light, roost, settle

³perch *n, pl* **perch** *or* **perch·es :** either of two small freshwater bony fishes used for food; *also* : any of various fishes resembling or related to these

per·chance \pər-'chans\ *adv* ♦ **:** possibly but not certainly : PERHAPS

♦ conceivably, maybe, perhaps, possibly

per·cip·i·ent \pər-'si-pē-ənt\ *adj* : capable of or characterized by perception — **per·cip·i·ence** \-əns\ *n*

per·co·late \'pər-kə-ˌlāt\ *vb* **-lat·ed; -lat·ing 1** ♦ **:** to trickle or filter through a permeable substance **2 :** to filter hot water through to extract the essence ⟨∼ coffee⟩ **3** ♦ **:** to spread gradually — **per·co·la·tor** \-ˌlā-tər\ *n*

♦ [1] bleed, exude, ooze, seep, strain, sweat, weep ♦ *usu* **percolate into** [3] permeate, suffuse, transfuse

per con·tra \(ˌ)pər-'kän-trə\ *adv* **1 :** on the contrary **2 :** by way of contrast

per·cus·sion \pər-'kə-shən\ *n* **1 :** a sharp blow : IMPACT; *esp* : a blow upon a cap (**percussion cap**) designed to explode the charge in a firearm **2 :** the beating or striking of a musical instrument; *also* : instruments sounded by striking, shaking, or scraping

per di·em \pər-'dē-əm, -'dī-\ *adv* **:** by the day — **per diem** *adj or n*

per·di·tion \pər-'di-shən\ *n* **1 :** eternal damnation **2 :** HELL

per·du·ra·ble \(ˌ)pər-'dur-ə-bəl, -'dyur-\ *adj* : very durable — **per·du·ra·bil·i·ty** \-ˌdur-ə-'bi-lə-tē, -ˌdyur-\ *n*

per·e·gri·na·tion \ˌper-ə-grə-'nā-shən\ *n* ♦ **:** a traveling about esp. on foot

♦ expedition, journey, passage, trek, trip

per·e·grine falcon \'per-ə-grən, -ˌgrēn\ *n* : a swift nearly cosmopolitan falcon that often nests in cities and is often used in falconry

pe·remp·to·ry \pə-'remp-tə-rē\ *adj* **1 :** barring a right of action or delay **2** ♦ **:** expressive of urgency or command : IMPERATIVE **3** ♦ **:** marked by arrogant self-assurance — **pe·remp·to·ri·ly** \-tə-rə-lē\ *adv*

♦ [2] compulsory, imperative, incumbent, involuntary, mandatory, necessary, nonelective, obligatory ♦ [3] arrogant, cavalier, domineering, haughty, high-handed, high-hat, imperious, important, lofty, lordly, overbearing, overweening, pompous, presumptuous, pretentious, supercilious, superior

¹pe·ren·ni·al \pə-'re-nē-əl\ *adj* **1 :** present at all seasons of the year ⟨∼ streams⟩ **2 :** continuing to live from year to year ⟨∼ plants⟩ **3** ♦ **:** existing or continuing a long while : ENDURING **4** : recurring regularly : PERMANENT ⟨∼ problems⟩ — **pe·ren·ni·al·ly** *adv*

♦ abiding, ageless, continuing, dateless, enduring, eternal, everlasting, immortal, imperishable, perpetual, timeless, undying

²perennial *n* : a perennial plant

perf *abbr* **1** perfect **2** perforated

¹per·fect \'pər-fikt\ *adj* **1** ♦ **:** being without fault or defect **2** : EXACT, PRECISE **3** ♦ **:** lacking in no essential detail : COMPLETE **4 :** relating to or being a verb tense that expresses an action or state completed at the time of speaking or at a time spoken of **5 :** being completely or exactly what is stated — **per·fect·ness** *n*

♦ [1] absolute, faultless, flawless, ideal, impeccable, letter-perfect, unblemished *Ant* bad, defective, faulty, imperfect ♦ [3] complete, comprehensive, entire, full, grand, intact, integral, plenary, total, whole

²**per·fect** \pər-'fekt\ vb **1** ♦ : to bring to final form **2** ♦ : to make perfect : IMPROVE

♦ [1] complete, consummate, finalize, finish ♦ [2] ameliorate, amend, better, enhance, enrich, improve, refine

³**per·fect** \'pər-fikt\ n : the perfect tense; also : a verb form in it
per·fect·ible \pər-'fek-tə-bəl, 'pər-fik-\ adj : capable of improvement or perfection — **per·fect·ibil·i·ty** \pər-ˌfek-tə-'bi-lə-tē, ˌpər-fik-\ n
per·fec·tion \pər-'fek-shən\ n **1** : the quality or state of being perfect **2** : the highest degree of excellence **3** : the act or process of perfecting **4** ♦ : an exemplification of supreme excellence

♦ beau ideal, classic, epitome, exemplar, ideal, quintessence

per·fec·tion·ist \-sha-nist\ n : a person who will not accept or be content with anything less than perfection
per·fect·ly \'pər-fik(t)-lē\ adv **1** ♦ : in a perfect manner **2** ♦ : to a complete or adequate extent

♦ [1] faultlessly, flawlessly, ideally, impeccably Ant badly, faultily, imperfectly ♦ [2] altogether, completely, dead, entirely, fast, flat, full, fully, quite, thoroughly, well, wholly

per·fec·to \pər-'fek-tō\ n, pl **-tos** : a cigar that is thick in the middle and tapers almost to a point at each end
per·fid·i·ous \pər-'fi-dē-əs\ adj ♦ : of, relating to, or characterized by perfidy — **per·fid·i·ous·ly** adv

♦ disloyal, faithless, false, fickle, inconstant, loose, recreant, traitorous, treacherous, unfaithful, untrue

per·fi·dy \'pər-fə-dē\ n, pl **-dies** ♦ : violation of faith or loyalty

♦ betrayal, disloyalty, faithlessness, falseness, falsity, inconstancy, infidelity, treachery, unfaithfulness

per·fo·rate \'pər-fə-ˌrāt\ vb **-rat·ed; -rat·ing** ♦ : to bore through : PIERCE; esp : to make a line of holes in to facilitate separation

♦ bore, drill, hole, pierce, punch, puncture

per·fo·ra·tion \ˌpər-fə-'rā-shən\ n **1** : the act or process of perforating **2 a** ♦ : a hole or pattern made by or as if by piercing or boring **b** : one of the series of holes (as between rows of postage stamps) in a sheet that serve as an aid in separation

♦ hole, pinhole, prick, punch, puncture, stab

per·force \pər-'fōrs\ adv ♦ : of necessity

♦ inevitably, necessarily, needs, unavoidably

per·form \pər-'fȯrm\ vb **1** : to adhere to the terms of : FULFILL **2** ♦ : to bring to a successful issue : CARRY OUT **3** ♦ : to carry out an action or pattern of behavior : FUNCTION **4** : to do in a set manner **5** ♦ : to give a performance (of) — **per·form·er** n

♦ [2] accomplish, achieve, carry out, commit, compass, do, execute, follow through, fulfill, make ♦ [3] act, function, operate, take, work ♦ [5] act, impersonate, play, portray

per·for·mance \pər-'fȯr-məns\ n **1** ♦ : the act or process of performing **2** : DEED, FEAT **3** : a public presentation

♦ accomplishment, achievement, commission, discharge, enactment, execution, fulfillment, implementation, perpetration

¹**per·fume** \pər-'fyüm, 'pər-ˌfyüm\ n **1** ♦ : a usu. pleasant odor : FRAGRANCE **2** : a preparation used for scenting

♦ aroma, bouquet, fragrance, incense, redolence, scent, spice

²**perfume** vb **per·fumed; per·fum·ing** : SCENT
per·fum·ery \ˌpər-'fyü-mə-rē\ n, pl **-er·ies** **1** : the art or process of making perfume **2** : PERFUMES **3** : an establishment where perfumes are made
per·func·to·ry \pər-'fəŋk-tə-rē\ adj **1** : done merely as a duty **2** ♦ : lacking in interest or enthusiasm — **per·func·to·ri·ly** adv

♦ apathetic, casual, disinterested, indifferent, insouciant, nonchalant, unconcerned, uncurious, uninterested

per·go·la \'pər-gə-lə\ n : a structure consisting of posts supporting an open roof in the form of a trellis
perh abbr perhaps
per·haps \pər-'haps\ adv ♦ : possibly but not certainly

♦ conceivably, maybe, perchance, possibly

per·i·gee \'per-ə-ˌjē\ n : the point at which an orbiting object is nearest the body (as the earth) being orbited
per·i·he·lion \ˌper-ə-'hēl-yən\ n, pl **-he·lia** \-'hēl-yə\ : the point in the path of a celestial body (as a planet) that is nearest to the sun
per·il \'per-əl\ n **1** ♦ : exposure to the risk of being injured, destroyed, or lost **2** ♦ : something that imperils

♦ danger, hazard, menace, pitfall, risk, threat, trouble

per·il·ous \'per-ə-ləs\ adj ♦ : full of or involving peril — **per·il·ous·ly** adv

♦ dangerous, grave, grievous, hazardous, menacing, parlous, risky, serious, unhealthy, unsafe, venturesome

pe·rim·e·ter \pə-'ri-mə-tər\ n **1** : the boundary of a closed plane figure; also : its length **2** ♦ : a line bounding or protecting an area

♦ border, bound, boundary, confines, edge, periphery

peri·na·tal \ˌper-ə-'nā-tᵊl\ adj : occurring in, concerned with, or being in the period around the time of birth ⟨∼ care⟩
¹**pe·ri·od** \'pir-ē-əd\ n **1** : SENTENCE; also : the full pause closing the utterance of a sentence **2** : END, STOP **3** : a punctuation mark . used esp. to mark the end of a declarative sentence or an abbreviation **4** ♦ : an extent of time; esp : one regarded as a stage or division in a process or development **5** : a portion of time in which a recurring phenomenon completes one cycle and is ready to begin again **6** : a single cyclic occurrence of menstruation

♦ age, epoch, era, time

²**period** adj : of or relating to a particular historical period ⟨∼ furniture⟩
pe·ri·od·ic \ˌpir-ē-'ä-dik\ adj **1** ♦ : occurring at regular intervals of time **2** ♦ : happening repeatedly from time to time **3** : of or relating to a sentence that has no trailing elements following full grammatical statement of the essential idea

♦ [1] constant, frequent, habitual, regular, repeated, steady ♦ [2] continual, intermittent, recurrent

¹**pe·ri·od·i·cal** \ˌpir-ē-'ä-di-kəl\ adj **1** : occurring or recurring at regular intervals or from time to time : PERIODIC **2** : published with a fixed interval between the issues or numbers **3** : of or relating to a periodical — **pe·ri·od·i·cal·ly** \-k(ə-)lē\ adv
²**periodical** n : a periodical publication
periodic table n : an arrangement of chemical elements based on their atomic structure and on their properties
peri·odon·tal \ˌper-ē-ō-'dänt-ᵊl\ adj **1** : surrounding a tooth **2** : of or affecting periodontal tissues or regions
per·i·pa·tet·ic \ˌper-ə-pə-'te-tik\ adj ♦ : performed or performing while moving about : ITINERANT

♦ errant, itinerant, nomad, nomadic, roaming, vagabond, vagrant

¹**pe·riph·er·al** \pə-'ri-fə-rəl\ adj **1** : of, relating to, involving, or forming a periphery or surface part **2** ♦ : added or serving as a supplement

♦ accessory, auxiliary, supplementary

²**pe·riph·er·al** n : a device connected to a computer to provide communication or auxiliary functions
peripheral nervous system n : the part of the nervous system that is outside the central nervous system and comprises the spinal nerves, the cranial nerves except the one supplying the retina, and the autonomic nervous system
pe·riph·ery \pə-'ri-fə-rē\ n, pl **-er·ies** **1** : the boundary of a rounded figure **2** ♦ : outward bounds : border area

♦ border, bound, boundary, circumference, compass, confines, edge, end, fringe, margin, perimeter, rim, skirt, verge

pe·riph·ra·sis \pə-'ri-frə-səs\ n, pl **-ra·ses** \-ˌsēz\ : CIRCUMLOCUTION
peri·scope \'per-ə-ˌskōp\ n : a tubular optical instrument enabling an observer to see an otherwise blocked field of view
per·ish \'per-ish\ vb ♦ : to become destroyed or ruined; esp : to have one's life come to an end

♦ decease, depart, die, expire, pass, pass away, succumb

per·ish·able \'per-i-shə-bəl\ adj : easily spoiled ⟨∼ foods⟩ — **perishable** n
peri·stal·sis \ˌper-ə-'stȯl-səs, -'stal-\ n, pl **-stal·ses** \-ˌsēz\ : waves of contraction passing along the walls of a hollow muscular organ (as the intestine) and forcing its contents onward — **per·i·stal·tic** \-'stȯl-tik, -'stal-\ adj
peri·style \'per-ə-ˌstīl\ n : a row of columns surrounding a building or court
peri·to·ne·um \ˌper-ə-tə-'nē-əm\ n, pl **-ne·ums** or **-nea** : the smooth transparent serous membrane that lines the cavity of the abdomen — **peri·to·ne·al** \-'nē-əl\ adj
peri·to·ni·tis \ˌper-ə-tə-'nī-təs\ n : inflammation of the peritoneum
peri·wig \'per-i-ˌwig\ n : WIG
¹**per·i·win·kle** \'per-i-ˌwiŋ-kəl\ n : a usu. blue-flowered creeping plant cultivated as a ground cover
²**periwinkle** n : any of various small edible seashore snails

per·ju·ry \'pər-jə-rē\ *n* : the voluntary violation of an oath to tell the truth : lying under oath — **per·jure** \'pər-jər\ *vb* — **per·jur·er** *n*

¹**perk** \'pərk\ *vb* **1** : to thrust (as the head) up impudently or jauntily **2** : to regain vigor or spirit **3** : to make trim or brisk : FRESHEN

²**perk** *vb* : PERCOLATE

³**perk** *n* : PERQUISITE — usu. used in pl.

perky \'pər-kē\ *adj* ♦ : sprightly in manner or appearance

♦ active, animate, animated, brisk, energetic, frisky, jaunty, lively, peppy, spirited, sprightly, springy

per·lite \'pər-ˌlīt\ *n* : volcanic glass that when expanded by heat forms a lightweight material used esp. in concrete and plaster and for potting plants

¹**perm** \'pərm\ *n* : PERMANENT

²**perm** *vb* : to give (hair) a permanent

³**perm** *abbr* permanent

per·ma·frost \'pər-mə-ˌfrȯst\ *n* : a permanently frozen layer below the surface in frigid regions of a planet

¹**per·ma·nent** \'pər-mə-nənt\ *adj* ♦ : continuing or enduring without fundamental or marked change — **per·ma·nence** \-nəns\ *n* — **per·ma·nen·cy** \-nən-sē\ *n*

♦ ceaseless, dateless, deathless, endless, eternal, everlasting, immortal, perpetual, undying, unending

²**permanent** *n* : a long-lasting hair wave or straightening

per·ma·nent·ly \-lē\ *adv* ♦ : in a permanent manner

♦ always, eternally, ever, everlastingly, forever, perpetually

permanent press *n* : the process of treating fabrics with chemicals (as resin) and heat for setting the shape and for aiding wrinkle resistance

per·me·able \'pər-mē-ə-bəl\ *adj* ♦ : having small openings that permit liquids or gases to seep through — **per·me·a·bil·i·ty** \ˌpər-mē-ə-'bi-lə-tē\ *n*

♦ passable, penetrable, porous

per·me·ate \'pər-mē-ˌāt\ *vb* **-at·ed; -at·ing 1** ♦ : to spread or diffuse through : PERVADE **2** : to seep through the pores of : PENETRATE — **per·me·ation** \ˌpər-mē-'ā-shən\ *n*

♦ percolate, suffuse, transfuse

Perm·ian \'pər-mē-ən\ *adj* : of, relating to, or being the latest period of the Paleozoic era — **Permian** *n*

per·mis·si·ble \pər-'mi-sə-bəl\ *adj* ♦ : that may be permitted : ALLOWABLE

♦ admissible, allowable, sufferable *Ant* banned, barred, forbidden, impermissible, interdicted, prohibited, proscribed

per·mis·sion \pər-'mi-shən\ *n* ♦ : formal consent : AUTHORIZATION

♦ allowance, authorization, clearance, concurrence, consent, leave, license (*or* licence), sanction, sufferance *Ant* interdiction, prohibition, proscription

per·mis·sive \pər-'mi-siv\ *adj* : granting permission; *esp* : INDULGENT — **per·mis·sive·ly** *adv* — **per·mis·sive·ness** *n*

¹**per·mit** \pər-'mit\ *vb* **per·mit·ted; per·mit·ting 1** ♦ : to consent to : ALLOW ⟨~ access⟩ **2** ♦ : to make possible **3** ♦ : to give leave ⟨~ him to go⟩

♦ allow, have, let, suffer

²**per·mit** \'pər-ˌmit, pər-'mit\ *n* : a written permission : LICENSE ⟨a fishing ~⟩

per·mu·ta·tion \ˌpər-myü-'tā-shən\ *n* **1** : a major or fundamental change **2** : the act or process of changing the order of an ordered set of objects

per·ni·cious \pər-'ni-shəs\ *adj* ♦ : very destructive or injurious ⟨a ~ influence⟩ — **per·ni·cious·ly** *adv*

♦ adverse, bad, baleful, baneful, damaging, deleterious, detrimental, evil, harmful, hurtful, ill, injurious, mischievous, noxious, prejudicial

per·ora·tion \'per-ə-ˌrā-shən, 'pər-\ *n* : the concluding part of a speech

¹**per·ox·ide** \pə-'räk-ˌsīd\ *n* : an oxide containing a large proportion of oxygen; *esp* : HYDROGEN PEROXIDE

²**peroxide** *vb* **-id·ed; -id·ing** : to bleach with hydrogen peroxide

perp *abbr* **1** perpendicular **2** perpetrator

per·pen·dic·u·lar \ˌpər-pən-'di-kyə-lər\ *adj* **1** ♦ : standing at right angles to the plane of the horizon **2** : forming a right angle with each other or with a given line or plane — **perpendicular** *n* — **per·pen·dic·u·lar·i·ty** \-ˌdi-kyə-'lar-ə-tē\ *n* — **per·pen·dic·u·lar·ly** *adv*

♦ erect, standing, upright, upstanding, vertical

per·pe·trate \'pər-pə-ˌtrāt\ *vb* **-trat·ed; -trat·ing** : to carry out (as a crime) : COMMIT — **per·pe·tra·tor** \'pər-pə-ˌtrā-tər\ *n*

per·pe·tra·tion \ˌpər-pə-'trā-shən\ *n* ♦ : the act or process of perpetrating

♦ accomplishment, achievement, commission, discharge, enactment, execution, fulfillment, implementation, performance

per·pet·u·al \pər-'pe-chə-wəl\ *adj* **1** ♦ : continuing forever : EVERLASTING **2** : occurring continually : CONSTANT ⟨~ annoyance⟩

♦ ceaseless, dateless, deathless, endless, eternal, everlasting, immortal, permanent, undying, unending

per·pet·u·al·ly \pər-'pe-chə-wə-lē\ *adv* **1** ♦ : for a limitless time **2** ♦ : at all times : CONTINUALLY

♦ [1] always, eternally, ever, everlastingly, forever, permanently
♦ [2] always, constantly, continually, ever, forever, incessantly, invariably, unfailingly

per·pet·u·ate \pər-'pe-chə-ˌwāt\ *vb* **-at·ed; -at·ing** : to make perpetual : cause to last indefinitely ⟨~ a belief⟩ — **per·pet·u·a·tion** \-ˌpe-chə-'wā-shən\ *n*

per·pe·tu·ity \ˌpər-pə-'tü-ə-tē, -'tyü-\ *n, pl* **-ties 1** : ETERNITY 1 **2** : the quality or state of being perpetual

per·plex \pər-'pleks\ *vb* ♦ : to disturb mentally; *esp* : CONFUSE

♦ addle, baffle, befog, befuddle, bemuse, bewilder, confound, confuse, disorient, muddle, muddy, mystify, puzzle

per·plexed \-'plekst\ *adj* **1** : filled with uncertainty : PUZZLED ⟨a ~ look⟩ **2** : full of difficulty : COMPLICATED — **per·plexed·ly** \-'plek-səd-lē\ *adv*

per·plex·i·ty \pər-'plek-sə-tē\ *n* ♦ : the state of being perplexed

♦ bafflement, bewilderment, confusion, distraction, muddle, mystification, puzzlement, whirl

per·qui·site \'pər-kwə-zət\ *n* ♦ : a privilege or profit beyond regular pay

♦ bonus, dividend, extra, lagniappe, tip

pers *abbr* person; personal

¹**per se** \(ˌ)pər-'sā\ *adv* : by, of, or in itself : as such

²**per se** *adj* : being such inherently, clearly, or as a matter of law

per·se·cute \'pər-si-ˌkyüt\ *vb* **-cut·ed; -cut·ing** : to pursue in such a way as to injure or afflict : HARASS; *esp* : to cause to suffer because of belief — **per·se·cu·tion** \ˌpər-si-'kyü-shən\ *n*

♦ afflict, agonize, bedevil, curse, harrow, martyr, plague, rack, torment, torture ♦ aggravate, annoy, bother, bug, chafe, exasperate, gall, get, grate, irk, irritate, nettle, peeve, pique, put out, rasp, rile, vex

per·se·cu·tor \'pər-si-ˌkyü-tər\ *n* ♦ : one that persecutes

♦ heckler, oppressor, taunter, tormentor, torturer ♦ annoyance, bother, gadfly, nuisance, pest, tease

per·se·vere \ˌpər-sə-'vir\ *vb* **-vered; -ver·ing** : to persist (as in an undertaking) in spite of difficulties — **per·se·ver·ance** \-'vir-əns\ *n*

persevering *adj* ♦ : of or characterized by perseverance

♦ dogged, insistent, patient, persistent, pertinacious, tenacious

Per·sian \'pər-zhən\ *n* **1** : a native or inhabitant of ancient Persia **2** : a member of one of the peoples of modern Iran **3** : the language of the Persians

Persian cat *n* : any of a breed of stocky round-headed domestic cats that have a long silky coat

Persian lamb *n* : a pelt with very silky tightly curled fur that is obtained from newborn lambs which are older than those yielding broadtail

per·si·flage \'pər-si-ˌfläzh, 'per-\ *n* ♦ : lightly jesting or mocking talk

♦ banter, chaff, raillery, repartee

per·sim·mon \pər-'si-mən\ *n* : either of two trees related to the ebony; *also* : the edible usu. orange or red plumlike fruit of a persimmon

per·sist \pər-'sist, -'zist\ *vb* **1** : to go on resolutely or stubbornly in spite of difficulties **2** ♦ : to continue to exist

♦ abide, continue, endure, hold, keep up, last, run on

per·sis·tence \pər-'sis-təns, -'zis-\ *n* **1** ♦ : the action or fact of persisting **2** : the quality or state of being persistent — **per·sis·ten·cy** \-tən-sē\ *n*

♦ continuance, continuation, duration, endurance, subsistence

per·sis·tent \pər-'sis-tənt\ *adj* **1** ♦ : continuing or inclined to persist in a course   **2** : continuing to exist in spite of interference or treatment ⟨a ∼ cough⟩ — **per·sis·tent·ly** *adv*

  ♦ dogged, insistent, patient, persevering, pertinacious, tenacious

per·snick·e·ty \pər-'sni-kə-tē\ *adj* : fussy about small details

per·son \'pər-sən\ *n*   **1** ♦ : a human being : INDIVIDUAL — used in combination esp. by those who prefer to avoid *man* in compounds applicable to both sexes ⟨chair*person*⟩   **2** : one of the three modes of being in the Godhead as understood by Trinitarians   **3** : the body of a human being   **4** : the individual personality of a human being : SELF   **5** : reference of a segment of discourse to the speaker, to one spoken to, or to one spoken of esp. as indicated by certain pronouns

  ♦ being, body, creature, human, individual, man, mortal ♦ **persons** folks, humanity, humankind, people, public, society, world

per·so·na \pər-'sō-nə\ *n, pl* **-nae** \-nē\ *or* **-nas** : the personality that a person projects in public

per·son·able \'pər-sə-nə-bəl\ *adj* : pleasant in person : ATTRACTIVE

per·son·age \'pər-sə-nij\ *n* ♦ : a person of rank, note, or distinction

  ♦ celebrity, figure, light, luminary, notable, personality, somebody, standout, star, superstar, VIP

¹**per·son·al** \'pər-sə-nəl\ *adj*   **1** ♦ : of, relating to, or affecting a person : PRIVATE ⟨∼ correspondence⟩   **2** : done in person ⟨a ∼ inquiry⟩   **3** : relating to the person or body ⟨∼ injuries⟩   **4** : relating to an individual esp. in an offensive way ⟨resented such ∼ remarks⟩   **5** : of or relating to temporary or movable property as distinguished from real estate   **6** : denoting grammatical person   **7** : intended for use by one person

  ♦ individual, particular, peculiar, private, separate, singular, unique

²**personal** *n*   **1** : a short newspaper paragraph relating to a person or group or to personal matters   **2** : a short personal or private communication in the classified ads section of a newspaper

personal computer *n* : a computer with a microprocessor designed for an individual user to run esp. commercial software

personal digital assistant *n* : PDA

per·son·al·ise *chiefly Brit var of* PERSONALIZE

per·son·al·i·ty \ˌpər-sə-'na-lə-tē\ *n, pl* **-ties**   **1** : an offensively personal remark ⟨indulges in *personalities*⟩   **2** ♦ : the collection of emotional and behavioral traits that characterize a person   **3** : distinction of personal and social traits   **4** ♦ : a well-known person ⟨a TV ∼⟩

  ♦ [2] character, identity, individuality, self-identity ♦ [4] celebrity, figure, light, luminary, notable, personage, somebody, standout, star, superstar, VIP

per·son·al·ize \'pər-sə-nə-ˌlīz\ *vb* **-ized; -iz·ing**   **1** : to conceive of or represent as a person or as having human qualities or powers   **2** : to make personal or individual; *esp* : to mark as belonging to a particular person

per·son·al·ly \-nə-lē\ *adv*   **1** : in person   **2** : as a person   **3** : as far as oneself is concerned

per·son·al·ty \'pər-sə-nəl-tē\ *n, pl* **-ties** ♦ : personal property

  ♦ belongings, chattels, effects, holdings, paraphernalia, possessions, things

per·so·na non gra·ta \pər-'sō-nə-ˌnän-'grä-tə, -ˌgrä-\ *adj* : being personally unacceptable or unwelcome

per·son·ate \'pər-sə-ˌnāt\ *vb* **-at·ed; -at·ing** : IMPERSONATE, REPRESENT

per·son·i·fi·ca·tion \pər-ˌsä-nə-fə-'kā-shən\ *n* ♦ : a visible representation of something abstract (as a quality)

  ♦ embodiment, epitome, incarnation, manifestation

per·son·i·fy \pər-'sä-nə-ˌfī\ *vb* **-fied; -fy·ing**   **1** ♦ : to think of or represent as a person   **2** ♦ : to be the embodiment of : INCARNATE ⟨∼ the law⟩

  ♦ [1, 2] embody, epitomize, manifest, materialize, substantiate

per·son·nel \ˌpər-sə-'nel\ *n* ♦ : a body of persons employed

  ♦ force, help, pool, staff

per·spec·tive \pər-'spek-tiv\ *n*   **1** : the science of painting and drawing so that objects represented have apparent depth and distance   **2** ♦ : the aspect in which a subject or its parts are mentally viewed; *esp* : a view of things (as objects or events) in their true relationship or relative importance

  ♦ angle, outlook, point of view, slant, standpoint, viewpoint

per·spi·ca·cious \ˌpər-spə-'kā-shəs\ *adj* : having or showing keen understanding or discernment ⟨a ∼ observation⟩ — **per·spi·cac·i·ty** \-'ka-sə-tē\ *n*

per·spi·cu·i·ty \ˌpər-spə-'kyü-ə-tē\ *n* ♦ : the quality or state of being clear to the understanding

  ♦ clarity, explicitness, lucidity, simplicity

per·spic·u·ous \pər-'spi-kyə-wəs\ *adj* ♦ : plain to the understanding ⟨a ∼ argument⟩

  ♦ apparent, broad, clear, clear-cut, distinct, evident, lucid, manifest, obvious, palpable, patent, plain, transparent, unambiguous, unequivocal, unmistakable

per·spire \pər-'spīr\ *vb* **per·spired; per·spir·ing** : SWEAT — **per·spi·ra·tion** \ˌpər-spə-'rā-shən\ *n*

per·suade \pər-'swād\ *vb* **per·suad·ed; per·suad·ing** ♦ : to win over to a belief or course of action by argument or entreaty

  ♦ argue, convince, get, induce, move, prevail, satisfy, talk, win

per·sua·sion \pər-'swā-zhən\ *n*   **1** ♦ : the act or process of persuading   **2** ♦ : a system of religious beliefs; *also* : a group holding such beliefs   **3** ♦ : an opinion held with complete assurance

  ♦ [1] convincing, inducement ♦ [2] creed, cult, faith, religion ♦ [3] belief, conviction, eye, feeling, judgment (*or* judgement), mind, notion, opinion, sentiment, verdict, view

per·sua·sive \pər-'swā-siv, -ziv\ *adj* ♦ : tending to persuade — **per·sua·sive·ly** *adv*

  ♦ cogent, compelling, conclusive, convincing, decisive, effective, forceful, satisfying, strong, telling

per·sua·sive·ness \-nəs\ *n* ♦ : the quality or state of being persuasive

  ♦ cogency, effectiveness, force

pert \'pərt\ *adj*   **1** ♦ : saucily free and forward   **2** : stylishly trim : JAUNTY   **3** : briskly alert and energetic : LIVELY

  ♦ facetious, flip, flippant, smart

per·tain \pər-'tān\ *vb*   **1** : to belong to as a part, quality, or function ⟨duties ∼*ing* to the office⟩   **2** ♦ : to have reference : RELATE ⟨books ∼*ing* to birds⟩

  ♦ appertain, apply, bear, refer, relate ♦ *usu* **pertain to** concern, cover, deal, treat

per·ti·na·cious \ˌpər-tə-'nā-shəs\ *adj*   **1** ♦ : holding resolutely to an opinion or purpose   **2** ♦ : obstinately persistent ⟨a ∼ bill collector⟩

  ♦ [1] dogged, hardheaded, headstrong, mulish, obdurate, obstinate, opinionated, peevish, perverse, pigheaded, stubborn, unyielding, willful ♦ [2] dogged, insistent, patient, persevering, persistent, tenacious

per·ti·nac·i·ty \ˌpər-tə-'na-sə-tē\ *n* ♦ : the quality or state of being pertinacious

  ♦ hardheadedness, mulishness, obduracy, obstinacy, peevishness, self-will, stubbornness, tenacity

per·ti·nence \'pərt-ᵊn-əns\ *n* ♦ : the quality or state of being pertinent

  ♦ applicability, bearing, connection, relevance *Ant* irrelevance

per·ti·nent \'pərt-ᵊn-ənt\ *adj* ♦ : relating to the matter under consideration

  ♦ applicable, apposite, apropos, germane, material, pointed, relative, relevant *Ant* extraneous, immaterial, inapplicable, irrelevant, pointless

per·turb \pər-'tərb\ *vb* ♦ : to cause to be worried or upset

  ♦ agitate, bother, concern, discompose, disquiet, distress, disturb, exercise, freak out, undo, unhinge, unsettle, upset, worry

per·tur·ba·tion \ˌpər-tər-'bā-shən\ *n* ♦ : the action of perturbing : the state of being perturbed

  ♦ agitation, anxiety, apprehension, care, concern, disquiet, nervousness, uneasiness, worry

perturbed \pər-'tərbd\ *adj* ♦ : emotionally disturbed or agitated

  ♦ aflutter, anxious, edgy, jittery, jumpy, nervous, nervy, tense, troubled, uneasy, upset, worried

per·tus·sis \pər-'tə-səs\ *n* : WHOOPING COUGH

pe·ruke \pə-'rük\ *n* : WIG

pe·ruse \pə-'rüz\ *vb* **pe·rused; pe·rus·ing** : READ; *esp* : to read over attentively or leisurely — **pe·rus·al** \-'rü-zəl\ *n*

Pe·ru·vi·an \pə-'rü-vē-ən\ *n* : a native or inhabitant of Peru

perv \'pərv\ *n, slang* : PERVERT

per·vade \pər-'vād\ *vb* **per·vad·ed; per·vad·ing** : to spread through every part of **:** PERMEATE ⟨excitement *pervaded* the room⟩ — **per·va·sive** \-'vā-siv, -ziv\ *adj*

per·verse \pər-'vərs\ *adj* **1 ♦ :** turned away from what is right or good **:** CORRUPT **2 ♦ :** obstinate in opposing what is reasonable or accepted **3 ♦ :** marked by peevishness or petulance — **per·verse·ly** *adv*

♦ [1] corrupt, debauched, decadent, degenerate, dissolute, perverted, reprobate ♦ [2] dogged, hardheaded, headstrong, mulish, obdurate, obstinate, opinionated, peevish, pertinacious, pigheaded, stubborn, unyielding, willful ♦ [3] choleric, crabby, cranky, cross, crotchety, grouchy, grumpy, irascible, irritable, peevish, petulant, short-tempered, snappish, snappy, snippy, testy, waspish

per·verse·ness \-nəs\ *n* **♦ :** the quality or state of being perverse

♦ biliousness, grumpiness, irritability, peevishness, perversity

per·ver·sion \pər-'vər-zhən\ *n* **1 ♦ :** the action of perverting **:** the condition of being perverted **2 ♦ :** a perverted form of something; *esp* **:** aberrant sexual behavior

♦ corruption, debasement, debauchery, decadence, degeneracy, degeneration, degradation, demoralization, depravity, dissipation, dissoluteness

per·ver·si·ty \pər-'vər-sə-tē\ *n* **♦ :** the quality or state of being perverse

♦ biliousness, grumpiness, irritability, peevishness, perverseness

¹per·vert \pər-'vərt\ *vb* **1 ♦ :** to lead astray **:** CORRUPT ⟨~ the young⟩ **2 ♦ :** to divert to a wrong purpose **:** MISAPPLY ⟨~ evidence⟩ **3 ♦ :** to twist the meaning or sense of — **per·ver·ter** *n*

♦ [1] debase, degrade, demean, demoralize, humble, subvert, warp ♦ [2] abuse, misapply, misuse, profane ♦ [3] color (*or* colour), distort, falsify, garble, misinterpret, misrepresent, misstate, twist, warp

²per·vert \'pər-ˌvərt\ *n* **:** one that is perverted; *esp* **:** one given to sexual perversion

♦ decadent, degenerate, libertine, profligate

per·vert·ed \pər-'vər-təd\ *adj* **♦ :** morally degenerate **:** DEPRAVED

♦ corrupt, debauched, decadent, degenerate, dissolute, perverse, reprobate

pes·ky \'pes-kē\ *adj* **pes·ki·er; -est :** causing annoyance **:** TROUBLESOME

pe·so \'pā-sō\ *n, pl* **pesos :** the basic monetary unit in many Latin American countries (as Mexico or Chile)

pes·si·mism \'pe-sə-ˌmi-zəm\ *n* **:** an inclination to take the least favorable view (as of events) or to expect the worst — **pes·si·mist** \-mist\ *n*

pes·si·mis·tic \ˌpe-sə-'mis-tik\ *adj* **♦ :** of, relating to, or characterized by pessimism

♦ defeatist, despairing, hopeless *Ant* hopeful, rosy, upbeat

pest \'pest\ *n* **1 :** a destructive epidemic disease **:** PLAGUE **2 :** a plant or animal detrimental to humans **3 ♦ :** one that pesters **:** NUISANCE

♦ aggravation, annoyance, bother, exasperation, frustration, hassle, headache, inconvenience, irritant, nuisance, peeve, problem, thorn

pes·ter \'pes-tər\ *vb* **♦ :** to harass with petty irritations

♦ bother, bug, disturb, intrude

pes·ti·cide \'pes-tə-ˌsīd\ *n* **:** an agent used to destroy pests
pes·tif·er·ous \pes-'ti-fə-rəs\ *adj* **1 :** PESTILENT **2 ♦ :** causing vexation **:** ANNOYING ⟨~ vermin⟩

♦ aggravating, annoying, frustrating, galling, irksome, irritating, pesty, vexatious

pes·ti·lence \'pes-tə-ləns\ *n* **:** a destructive infectious swiftly spreading disease; *esp* **:** BUBONIC PLAGUE
pes·ti·lent \-lənt\ *adj* **1 ♦ :** dangerous to life **:** DEADLY **2 :** PERNICIOUS, HARMFUL **3 :** TROUBLESOME **4 :** INFECTIOUS, CONTAGIOUS ⟨a ~ disease⟩

♦ baleful, deadly, deathly, fatal, fell, lethal, mortal, murderous, vital

pes·ti·len·tial \ˌpes-tə-'len-chəl\ *adj* **1 :** causing or tending to cause pestilence **:** DEADLY **2 :** morally harmful
pes·tle \'pes-əl, 'pest-ᵊl\ *n* **:** an implement for grinding substances in a mortar — **pestle** *vb*
pesty \'pes-tē\ *adj* **♦ :** causing trouble or annoyance

♦ aggravating, annoying, bothersome, frustrating, galling, irksome, irritating, vexatious

¹pet \'pet\ *n* **1 ♦ :** a person who is treated with unusual kindness or consideration **:** FAVORITE, DARLING **2 :** a domesticated animal kept for pleasure rather than utility

♦ darling, favorite (*or* favourite), minion, preference

²pet *adj* **1 :** kept or treated as a pet ⟨~ dog⟩ **2 :** expressing fondness ⟨~ name⟩ **3 ♦ :** particularly liked or favored

♦ beloved, darling, dear, favorite (*or* favourite), loved, precious, special, sweet

³pet *vb* **pet·ted; pet·ting** **1 ♦ :** to stroke gently or lovingly **2 :** to make a pet of **:** PAMPER **3 ♦ :** to engage in amorous kissing and caressing

♦ [1] caress, fondle, love, pat, stroke ♦ [3] kiss, make out

⁴pet *n* **♦ :** a fit of peevishness, sulkiness, or anger

♦ pout, sulk, sullenness

Pet *abbr* Peter
pet·al \'pet-ᵊl\ *n* **:** one of the modified leaves of a flower's corolla
pe·tard \pə-'tärd, -'tär\ *n* **:** a case containing an explosive to break down a door or gate or breach a wall
pe·ter \'pē-tər\ *vb* **:** to diminish gradually and come to an end ⟨his energy ~ed out⟩
Pe·ter \'pē-tər\ *n* **:** either of two books of the New Testament of the Christian Scripture
pet·i·ole \'pe-tē-ˌōl\ *n* **:** a slender stem that supports a leaf
pe·tite \pə-'tēt\ *adj* **:** having a small trim figure — usu. used of a woman — **petite** *n*
pe·tit four \ˌpe-tē-'fōr\ *n, pl* **petits fours** *or* **petit fours** \-'fōrz\ **:** a small cake cut from pound or sponge cake and frosted
¹pe·ti·tion \pə-'ti-shən\ *n* **♦ :** an earnest request **:** ENTREATY; *esp* **:** a formal written request made to an authority

♦ appeal, cry, entreaty, plea, prayer, solicitation, suit, supplication

²petition *vb* **:** to make a request to or for
pe·ti·tion·er \-sh(ə-)nər\ *n* **:** one that petitions
pet·rel \'pe-trəl\ *n* **:** any of numerous seabirds that fly far from land
pe·tri dish \'pē-trē-\ *n* **1 :** a small shallow dish used esp. for growing bacteria **2 :** something fostering development or innovation
pet·ri·fy \'pe-trə-ˌfī\ *vb* **-fied; -fy·ing** **1 :** to convert (organic matter) into stone or stony material **2 :** to make rigid or inactive (as from fear or awe) — **pet·ri·fac·tion** \ˌpe-trə-'fak-shən\ *n*
pet·ro·chem·i·cal \ˌpe-trō-'ke-mi-kəl\ *n* **:** a chemical isolated or derived from petroleum or natural gas — **pet·ro·chem·is·try** \-'ke-mə-strē\ *n*
pet·rol \'pe-trəl\ *n, chiefly Brit* **:** GASOLINE
pet·ro·la·tum \ˌpe-trə-'lā-təm\ *n* **:** PETROLEUM JELLY
pe·tro·leum \pə-'trō-lē-əm\ *n* **:** an oily flammable liquid obtained from wells drilled in the ground and refined into gasoline, fuel oils, and other products
petroleum jelly *n* **:** a tasteless, odorless, and oily or greasy substance from petroleum that is used esp. in ointments and dressings
¹pet·ti·coat \'pe-tē-ˌkōt\ *n* **1 :** a skirt worn under a dress **2 :** an outer skirt
²petticoat *adj* **:** of, relating to, or exercised by women **:** FEMALE
pet·ti·fog \'pe-tē-ˌfóg, -ˌfäg\ *vb* **-fogged; -fog·ging** **1 :** to engage in legal trickery **2 :** to quibble over insignificant details — **pet·ti·fog·ger** *n*
pet·ti·fog·ger \'pe-tē-ˌfó-gər, -ˌfä-\ *n* **1 :** a lawyer whose methods are petty, underhanded, or disreputable **2 :** one given to quibbling over trifles — **pet·ti·fog·ging** \-giŋ\ *adj or n*
pet·tish \'pe-tish\ *adj* **:** querulous in temperament or mood **:** PEEVISH
pet·ty \'pe-tē\ *adj* **pet·ti·er; -est** **1 :** having secondary rank **:** MINOR ⟨~ prince⟩ **2 ♦ :** of little importance **:** TRIFLING ⟨~ faults⟩ **3 ♦ :** marked by or reflective of narrow interests and sympathies — **pet·ti·ly** \'pe-tə-lē\ *adv* — **pet·ti·ness** \-tē-nəs\ *n*

♦ [2] inconsequential, inconsiderable, insignificant, measly, minute, negligible, nominal, paltry, slight, trifling, trivial ♦ [3] insular, little, narrow, parochial, provincial, sectarian, small

petty cash *n* **:** cash kept on hand for payment of minor items
petty officer *n* **:** a subordinate officer in the navy or coast guard appointed from among the enlisted personnel
petty officer first class *n* **:** a petty officer ranking below a chief petty officer

petty officer second class *n* : a petty officer ranking below a petty officer first class

petty officer third class *n* : a petty officer ranking below a petty officer second class

pet·u·lance \'pe-chə-ləns\ *n* : the quality or state of being petulant

pet·u·lant \'pe-chə-lənt\ *adj* ♦ : marked by capricious ill humor — **pet·u·lant·ly** *adv*

♦ choleric, crabby, cranky, cross, crotchety, grouchy, grumpy, irascible, irritable, peevish, perverse, short-tempered, snappish, snappy, snippy, testy, waspish

pe·tu·nia \pi-'tün-yə, -'tyün-\ *n* : any of a genus of tropical American herbs related to the potato and having bright funnel-shaped flowers

pew \'pyü\ *n* : any of the benches with backs fixed in rows in a church

pe·wee \'pē-(₁)wē\ *n* : any of various small American flycatchers

pew·ter \'pyü-tər\ *n* **1** : an alloy of tin used esp. for household utensils **2** ♦ : a bluish gray color — **pewter** *adj* — **pew·ter·er** *n*

♦ gray (*or* grey), leaden, silver, silvery, slate, steely

pey·o·te \pā-'ō-tē\ *also* **pey·otl** \-'ōt-°l\ *n* **1** : a hallucinogenic drug derived from the peyote cactus and containing mescaline **2** : a small cactus of the southwestern U.S. and Mexico

pf *abbr* **1** pfennig **2** preferred

PFC *or* **Pfc** *abbr* private first class

pfd *abbr* preferred

pg *abbr* page

PG *abbr* postgraduate

PGA *abbr* Professional Golfers' Association

pH \(₁)pē-'āch\ *n* : a value used to express acidity and alkalinity; *also* : the condition represented by such a value

PH *abbr* **1** pinch hit **2** public health

pha·eton \'fā-ət-°n\ *n* **1** : a light 4-wheeled horse-drawn vehicle **2** : an open automobile with two cross seats

phage \'fāj\ *n* : BACTERIOPHAGE

pha·lanx \'fā-₁laŋks\ *n, pl* **pha·lanx·es** *or* **pha·lan·ges** \fə-'lan-jēz\ **1** : a group or body (as of troops) in compact formation **2** *pl phalanges* : one of the digital bones of the hand or foot of a vertebrate

phal·a·rope \'fa-lə-₁rōp\ *n, pl* **-ropes** *also* **-rope** : any of a genus of small shorebirds related to sandpipers

phal·lic \'fa-lik\ *adj* **1** : of, relating to, or resembling a phallus **2** : relating to or being the stage of psychosexual development in psychoanalytic theory during which children become interested in their own sexual organs

phal·lus \'fa-ləs\ *n, pl* **phal·li** \'fa-₁lī\ *or* **phal·lus·es** : PENIS; *also* : a symbolic representation of the penis

Phan·er·o·zo·ic \₁fa-nə-rə-'zō-ik\ *adj* : of, relating to, or being an eon of geologic history comprising the Paleozoic, Mesozoic, and Cenozoic

phan·tasm \'fan-₁ta-zəm\ *n* **1** ♦ : a product of the imagination : ILLUSION **2** ♦ : a visible disembodied spirit : GHOST

♦ [1] chimera, conceit, daydream, delusion, dream, fancy, fantasy, figment, hallucination, illusion, pipe dream, unreality, vision ♦ [2] apparition, bogey, ghost, phantom, poltergeist, shade, shadow, specter, spirit, spook, vision, wraith

phan·tas·ma·go·ria \fan-₁taz-mə-'gōr-ē-ə\ *n* : a constantly shifting complex succession of things seen or imagined; *also* : a scene that constantly changes or fluctuates

phan·tas·mal \₁fan-'taz-məl\ *adj* : of, relating to, or like a phantasm

phantasy *var of* FANTASY

¹**phan·tom** \'fan-təm\ *n* **1** ♦ : something (as a specter) that is apparent to sense but has no substantial existence **2** : one that is something in appearance but not in reality : a mere show

♦ apparition, bogey, ghost, phantasm, poltergeist, shade, shadow, specter, spirit, spook, vision, wraith

²**phantom** *adj* ♦ : of the nature of, suggesting, or being a phantom

♦ chimerical, fabulous, fanciful, fantastic, fictitious, imaginary, made-up, mythical, pretend, unreal

pha·raoh \'fer-ō, 'fā-rō\ *n, often cap* : a ruler of ancient Egypt

phar·i·sa·ical \₁far-ə-'sā-ə-kəl\ *adj* : hypocritically self-righteous

phar·i·see \'far-ə-₁sē\ *n* **1** *cap* : a member of an ancient Jewish sect noted for strict observance of rites and ceremonies of the traditional law **2** : a self-righteous or hypocritical person — **phar·i·sa·ic** \₁far-ə-'sā-ik\ *adj*

pharm *abbr* pharmaceutical; pharmacist; pharmacy

¹**phar·ma·ceu·ti·cal** \₁fär-mə-'sü-ti-kəl\ *adj* : of, relating to, or engaged in pharmacy or the manufacture and sale of medicinal drugs

²**pharmaceutical** *n* ♦ : a medicinal drug

♦ cure, drug, medicine, remedy, specific

phar·ma·col·o·gy \₁fär-mə-'kä-lə-jē\ *n* **1** : the science of drugs esp. as related to medicinal uses **2** : the reactions and properties of one or more drugs — **phar·ma·co·log·i·cal** \-kə-'lä-ji-kəl\ *also* **phar·ma·co·log·ic** \-kə-'lä-jik\ *adj* — **phar·ma·col·o·gist** \-'kä-lə-jist\ *n*

phar·ma·co·poe·ia *also* **phar·ma·co·pe·ia** \-kə-'pē-ə\ *n* **1** : a book describing drugs and medicinal preparations **2** : a stock of drugs

phar·ma·cy \'fär-mə-sē\ *n, pl* **-cies** **1** : the art, practice, or profession of preparing and dispensing medical drugs **2** : DRUG-STORE — **phar·ma·cist** \-sist\ *n*

phar·ynx \'far-iŋks\ *n, pl* **pha·ryn·ges** \fə-'rin-jēz\ *also* **phar·ynx·es** : the muscular tubular passage extending from the back of the nasal cavity and mouth to the esophagus — **pha·ryn·ge·al** \fə-'rin-jəl, ₁far-ən-'jē-əl\ *adj*

phase \'fāz\ *n* **1** : a particular appearance in a recurring series of changes ⟨~s of the moon⟩ **2** : a stage or interval in a process or cycle ⟨first ~ of an experiment⟩ **3** ♦ : an aspect or part under consideration — **pha·sic** \'fā-zik\ *adj*

♦ [2] cut, degree, grade, inch, notch, peg, point, stage, step ♦ [3] angle, aspect, facet, hand, side

phase down *vb* : to reduce the size or amount of by phases

phase in *vb* : to introduce in stages

phase·out \'fā-₁zaút\ *n* : a gradual stopping of operations or production

phase out *vb* : to stop production or use of in stages

PhD *abbr* doctor of philosophy

pheas·ant \'fez-°nt\ *n, pl* **pheasant** *or* **pheasants** : any of numerous long-tailed brilliantly colored game birds related to the domestic chicken

phen·cy·cli·dine \₁fen-'sī-klə-₁dēn\ *n* : a drug used esp. as a veterinary anesthetic and sometimes illicitly as a hallucinogenic drug

phe·no·bar·bi·tal \₁fē-nō-'bär-bə-₁tól\ *n* : a crystalline drug used as a hypnotic and sedative

phe·nol \'fē-₁nól\ *n* : a corrosive poisonous acidic compound present in coal and wood tars and used in solution as a disinfectant

phe·nom·e·nal \fi-'nä-mən-°l\ *adj* ♦ : relating to or being a phenomenon; *also* : so unusual as to be remarkable — **phe·nom·e·nal·ly** *adv*

♦ aberrant, abnormal, atypical, exceptional, extraordinary, freak, odd, peculiar, rare, singular, uncommon, uncustomary, unique, unusual, unwonted ♦ magical, miraculous, superhuman, supernatural, uncanny, unearthly

phe·nom·e·non \fi-'nä-mə-₁nän, -nən\ *n, pl* **-na** \-nə\ *or* **-nons** **1** *pl -na* : an observable fact or event **2** : an outward sign of the working of a law of nature **3** *pl -nons* ♦ : an extraordinary person or thing : PRODIGY

♦ caution, flash, marvel, miracle, portent, prodigy, sensation, wonder

pher·o·mone \'fer-ə-₁mōn\ *n* : a chemical substance that is produced by an animal and serves to stimulate a behavioral response in other individuals of the same species — **pher·o·mon·al** \₁fer-ə-'mōn-°l\ *adj*

phi \'fī\ *n* : the 21st letter of the Greek alphabet — Φ *or* φ

phi·al \'fī-əl\ *n* : VIAL

Phil *abbr* Philippians

phi·lan·der \fə-'lan-dər\ *vb* : to have casual or illicit sexual relations with many women — **phi·lan·der·er** *n*

phil·an·throp·ic \₁fi-lən-'thrä-pik\ *adj* ♦ : of, relating to, or characterized by philanthropy — **phil·an·throp·i·cal·ly** \-pi-k(ə-)lē\ *adv*

♦ altruistic, beneficent, benevolent, charitable, humanitarian

phi·lan·thro·py \fə-'lan-thrə-pē\ *n, pl* **-pies** **1** : goodwill toward all people; *esp* : effort to promote human welfare **2** ♦ : a charitable act or gift; *also* : an organization that distributes or is supported by donated funds — **phi·lan·thro·pist** \fə-'lan-thrə-pist\ *n*

♦ alms, benefaction, beneficence, charity, contribution, donation

phi·lat·e·ly \fə-'lat-°l-ē\ *n* : the collection and study of postage and imprinted stamps — **phil·a·tel·ic** \₁fi-lə-'te-lik\ *adj* — **phil·at·e·list** \fə-'lat-°l-ist\ *n*

Phi·le·mon \fə-'lē-mən, fī-\ *n* : a book of the New Testament of the Christian Scripture

Phi·lip·pi·ans \fə-'li-pē-ənz\ *n* : a book of the New Testament of the Christian Scripture

phi·lip·pic \fə-'li-pik\ *n* : TIRADE

phi·lis·tine \'fi-lə-ˌstēn; fə-'lis-tən\ *n, often cap* : a person who is smugly insensitive or indifferent to intellectual or artistic values — **philistine** *adj, often cap*

Phil·lips \'fi-ləps\ *adj* : of, relating to, or being a screw having a head with a cross slot or its corresponding screwdriver

philo·den·dron \ˌfi-lə-'den-drən\ *n, pl* **-drons** *also* **-dra** \-drə\ : any of various plants of the arum family grown for their showy foliage

phi·lol·o·gy \fə-'lä-lə-jē\ *n* **1** : the study of literature and relevant fields **2** : LINGUISTICS; *esp* : historical and comparative linguistics — **phil·o·log·i·cal** \ˌfi-lə-'lä-ji-kəl\ *adj* — **phi·lol·o·gist** \fə-'lä-lə-jist\ *n*

philos *abbr* philosopher; philosophy

phi·los·o·pher \fə-'lä-sə-fər\ *n* **1** : a reflective thinker : SCHOLAR **2** : a student of or specialist in philosophy **3** : a person whose philosophical perspective makes it possible to meet trouble calmly

phi·los·o·phise *chiefly Brit var of* PHILOSOPHIZE

phi·los·o·phize \fə-'lä-sə-ˌfīz\ *vb* **-phized; -phiz·ing** **1** : to reason like a philosopher : THEORIZE **2** : to expound a philosophy esp. superficially

phi·los·o·phy \fə-'lä-sə-fē\ *n, pl* **-phies** **1** : sciences and liberal arts exclusive of medicine, law, and theology ⟨doctor of ∼⟩ **2** : a critical study of fundamental beliefs and the grounds for them **3** : a system of philosophical concepts ⟨Aristotelian ∼⟩ **4** : a basic theory concerning a particular subject or sphere of activity **5** ♦ : the sum of the ideas and convictions of an individual or group ⟨her ∼ of life⟩ **6** : calmness of temper and judgment — **phil·o·soph·i·cal** \ˌfi-lə-'sä-fi-kəl\ *also* **phil·o·soph·ic** \-fik\ *adj* — **phil·o·soph·i·cal·ly** \-k(ə-)lē\ *adv*

     ♦ creed, doctrine, gospel, ideology

phil·ter *or Can and Brit* **phil·tre** \'fil-tər\ *n* **1** : a potion, drug, or charm held to arouse sexual passion **2** : a magic potion

phish·ing \'fi-shiŋ\ *n* : a scam by which an e-mail user is fooled into revealing personal or confidential information which can be used illegally — **phish·er** \-shər\ *n*

phle·bi·tis \fli-'bī-təs\ *n* : inflammation of a vein

phle·bot·o·my \fli-'bä-tə-mē\ *n, pl* **-mies** : the opening of a vein esp. for removing or releasing blood

phlegm \'flem\ *n* **1** : thick mucus secreted in abnormal quantity esp. in the nose and throat **2** ♦ : dull or apathetic coldness or indifference

     ♦ apathy, impassivity, numbness, stupor

phleg·mat·ic \fleg-'ma-tik\ *adj* ♦ : having or showing a slow and stolid temperament

     ♦ apathetic, cold-blooded, impassive, stoic, stolid, unemotional

phlo·em \'flō-ˌem\ *n* : a vascular plant tissue external to the xylem that carries dissolved food material and functions in support and storage

phlox \'fläks\ *n, pl* **phlox** *or* **phlox·es** : any of a genus of American herbs that have tall stalks with showy spreading terminal clusters of flowers

pho·bia \'fō-bē-ə\ *n* : an irrational persistent fear or dread — **pho·bic** \'fō-bik\ *adj*

phoe·be \'fē-(ˌ)bē\ *n* : a flycatcher of the eastern U.S. that has a slight crest and is grayish brown above and yellowish white below

phoe·nix \'fē-niks\ *n* : a legendary bird held to live for centuries and then to burn itself to death and rise fresh and young from its ashes

¹**phone** \'fōn\ *n* **1** : TELEPHONE **2** : EARPHONE

²**phone** *vb* **phoned; phon·ing** : to speak to or attempt to reach by telephone : TELEPHONE

phone card *n* : a prepaid card used in paying for telephone calls

pho·neme \'fō-ˌnēm\ *n* : one of the elementary units of speech that distinguish one utterance from another — **pho·ne·mic** \fō-'nē-mik\ *adj*

pho·net·ics \fə-'ne-tiks\ *n* : the study and systematic classification of the sounds made in spoken utterance — **pho·net·ic** \-tik\ *adj* — **pho·ne·ti·cian** \ˌfō-nə-'ti-shən\ *n*

pho·nic \'fä-nik\ *adj* **1** : of, relating to, or producing sound **2** : of or relating to the sounds of speech or to phonics — **pho·ni·cal·ly** \-ni-k(ə-)lē\ *adv*

pho·nics \'fä-niks\ *n* : a method of teaching people to read and

pronounce words by learning the phonetic value of letters, letter groups, and esp. syllables

pho·no·graph \'fō-nə-ˌgraf\ *n* : an instrument for reproducing sounds by means of the vibration of a needle following a spiral groove on a revolving disc

pho·nol·o·gy \fə-'nä-lə-jē\ *n* : a study and description of the sound changes in a language — **pho·no·log·i·cal** \ˌfō-nə-'lä-ji-kəl\ *adj* — **pho·nol·o·gist** \fə-'nä-lə-jist\ *n*

¹**pho·ny** *also* **pho·ney** \'fō-nē\ *adj* **pho·ni·er; -est** ♦ : not genuine or real : claiming or claimed to be what one is not

     ♦ bogus, counterfeit, fake, false, inauthentic, sham, spurious, unauthentic ♦ affected, artificial, assumed, contrived, feigned, put-on, unnatural

²**phony** *n* ♦ : one that is phony

     ♦ counterfeit, fake, forgery, hoax, humbug, sham ♦ charlatan, fake, fraud, hoaxer, humbug, mountebank, pretender, quack

phos·phate \'fäs-ˌfāt\ *n* : a salt of a phosphoric acid — **phos·phat·ic** \fäs-'fa-tik\ *adj*

phos·phor \'fäs-fər\ *n* : a phosphorescent substance

phos·pho·res·cence \ˌfäs-fə-'res-ᵊns\ *n* **1** : luminescence caused by the absorption of radiations (as light or electrons) and continuing after these radiations stop **2** : an enduring luminescence without sensible heat — **phos·pho·res·cent** \-ᵊnt\ *adj* — **phos·pho·res·cent·ly** *adv*

phosphoric acid \ˌfäs-'fòr-ik-, -'fär-\ *n* : any of several oxygen=containing acids of phosphorus

phos·pho·rus \'fäs-fə-rəs\ *n* : a nonmetallic chemical element that has characteristics similar to nitrogen and occurs widely esp. as phosphates — **phos·phor·ic** \fäs-'fòr-ik, -'fär-\ *adj* — **phos·pho·rous** \'fäs-fə-rəs; fäs-'fòr-əs, -'fòr-\ *adj*

phot- *or* **photo-** *comb form* **1** : light ⟨*photo*graphy⟩ **2** : photograph : photographic ⟨*photo*engraving⟩ **3** : photoelectric ⟨*photo*cell⟩

¹**pho·to** \'fō-tō\ *n, pl* **photos** : a picture or likeness obtained by photography : PHOTOGRAPH — **photo** *adj*

²**photo** *vb* : to take a photograph of

pho·to·cell \'fō-tə-ˌsel\ *n* : PHOTOELECTRIC CELL

pho·to·chem·i·cal \ˌfō-tō-'ke-mi-kəl\ *adj* : of, relating to, or resulting from the chemical action of radiant energy

pho·to·com·pose \-kəm-'pōz\ *vb* : to compose reading matter for reproduction by means of characters photographed on film — **pho·to·com·po·si·tion** \-ˌkäm-pə-'zi-shən\ *n*

pho·to·copy \'fō-tə-ˌkä-pē\ *n* : a photographic reproduction of graphic matter — **photocopy** *vb*

pho·to·elec·tric \ˌfō-tō-i-'lek-trik\ *adj* : relating to an electrical effect due to the interaction of light with matter — **pho·to·elec·tri·cal·ly** \-tri-k(ə-)lē\ *adv*

photoelectric cell *n* : a device whose electrical properties are modified by the action of light

pho·to·en·grave \ˌfō-tō-in-'grāv\ *vb* : to make a photoengraving of

pho·to·en·grav·ing *n* : a process by which an etched printing plate is made from a photograph or drawing; *also* : a print made from such a plate

photo finish *n* : a race finish so close that a photograph of the finish is used to determine the winner

pho·tog \fə-'täg\ *n* : PHOTOGRAPHER

pho·to·gen·ic \ˌfō-tə-'je-nik\ *adj* : eminently suitable esp. aesthetically for being photographed

¹**pho·to·graph** \'fō-tə-ˌgraf\ *n* ♦ : a picture taken by photography — **pho·tog·ra·pher** \fə-'tä-grə-fər\ *n*

     ♦ print, shot, snap, snapshot

²**photograph** *vb* ♦ : to take a photograph of

     ♦ mug, shoot, snap

pho·tog·ra·phy \fə-'tä-grə-fē\ *n* : the art or process of producing images on a sensitive surface (as film or a CCD chip) by the action of radiant energy — **pho·to·graph·ic** \ˌfō-tə-'gra-fik\ *adj* — **pho·to·graph·i·cal·ly** \-fi-k(ə-)lē\ *adv*

pho·to·gra·vure \ˌfō-tə-grə-'vyùr\ *n* : a process for making prints from an intaglio plate prepared by photographic methods

pho·to·li·thog·ra·phy \ˌfō-tō-li-'thä-grə-fē\ *n* : the process of photographically transferring a pattern to a surface for etching (as in making an integrated circuit)

pho·tom·e·ter \fō-'tä-mə-tər\ *n* : an instrument for measuring the intensity of light — **pho·to·met·ric** \ˌfō-tə-'me-trik\ *adj* — **pho·tom·e·try** \fō-'tä-mə-trē\ *n*

pho·to·mi·cro·graph \ˌfō-tə-'mī-krə-ˌgraf\ *n* : a photograph of a microscope image — **pho·to·mi·crog·ra·phy** \-mī-'krä-grə-fē\ *n*

pho·ton \'fō-ˌtän\ *n* : a quantum of electromagnetic radiation

photo op *n* : a situation or event that lends itself to the taking of pictures which favor the individuals photographed

pho·to·play \'fō-tō-ˌplā\ *n* : MOTION PICTURE

pho·to·sen·si·tive \ˌfō-tə-'sen-sə-tiv\ *adj* : sensitive or sensitized to the action of radiant energy

pho·to·shop \'fō-tō-ˌshäp\ *vb, often cap* : to alter a digital image with image-editing software

pho·to·sphere \'fō-tə-ˌsfir\ *n* : the luminous surface of a star — **pho·to·spher·ic** \ˌfō-tə-'sfir-ik, -'sfer-\ *adj*

pho·to·syn·the·sis \ˌfō-tō-'sin-thə-səs\ *n* : the process by which chlorophyll-containing plants make carbohydrates from water and from carbon dioxide in the air in the presence of light — **pho·to·syn·the·size** \-ˌsīz\ *vb* — **pho·to·syn·thet·ic** \-sin-'the-tik\ *adj*

phr *abbr* phrase

¹**phrase** \'frāz\ *n* **1** : a brief expression **2** : a group of two or more grammatically related words that form a sense unit expressing a thought

²**phrase** *vb* **phrased; phras·ing** ♦ : to express in words

♦ articulate, clothe, couch, express, formulate, put, say, state, word

phrase·ol·o·gy \ˌfrā-zē-'ä-lə-jē\ *n, pl* **-gies** ♦ : a manner of phrasing : STYLE

♦ fashion, locution, manner, mode, style, tone, vein

phras·ing *n* ♦ : style of expression

♦ diction, language, phraseology, wording

phren·ic \'fre-nik\ *adj* : of or relating to the diaphragm ⟨∼ nerves⟩

phre·nol·o·gy \fri-'nä-lə-jē\ *n* : the study of the conformation of the skull based on the belief that it indicates mental faculties and character traits

phy·lac·tery \fə-'lak-tə-rē\ *n, pl* **-ter·ies** **1** : one of two small square leather boxes inscribed with scripture passages and traditionally worn on the left arm and forehead by Jewish men during morning weekday prayers **2** : an ornament worn as a charm against evil : AMULET

phy·lum \'fī-ləm\ *n, pl* **phy·la** \-lə\ : a major category in biological classification esp. of animals that ranks above the class and below the kingdom; *also* : a group (as of people) apparently of common origin

phys *abbr* **1** physical **2** physics

¹**phys·ic** \'fi-zik\ *n* **1** : the profession of medicine **2** : a substance or preparation used in treating disease : MEDICINE; *esp* : PURGATIVE

²**physic** *vb* **phys·icked; phys·ick·ing** : PURGE 2

¹**phys·i·cal** \'fi-zi-kəl\ *adj* **1** : of or relating to nature or the laws of nature **2** ♦ : material as opposed to mental or spiritual **3** : of, relating to, or produced by the forces and operations of physics **4** ♦ : of or relating to the body — **phys·i·cal·ly** \-k(ə-)lē\ *adv*

♦ [2] concrete, material, substantial ♦ [4] animal, bodily, carnal, corporal, fleshly, material, somatic *Ant* nonmaterial, nonphysical

²**physical** *n* : PHYSICAL EXAMINATION

physical education *n* : instruction in the development and care of the body ranging from simple calisthenics to training in hygiene, gymnastics, and the performance and management of athletic games

physical examination *n* : an examination of the bodily functions and condition of an individual

phys·i·cal·ize \'fi-zə-kə-ˌlīz\ *vb* **-ized; -iz·ing** : to give physical form or expression to

physical science *n* : any of the sciences (as physics and astronomy) that deal primarily with nonliving materials — **physical scientist** *n*

physical therapy *n* : the treatment of disease by physical and mechanical means (as massage, exercise, water, or heat) — **physical therapist** *n*

phy·si·cian \fə-'zi-shən\ *n* : a doctor of medicine

physician's assistant *n* : a person certified to provide basic medical care usu. under a licensed physician's supervision

phys·i·cist \'fi-zə-sist\ *n* : a scientist who specializes in physics

phys·ics \'fi-ziks\ *n* **1** : the science of matter and energy and their interactions **2** : the physical properties and composition of something

phys·iog·no·my \ˌfi-zē-'äg-nə-mē\ *n, pl* **-mies** : facial appearance esp. as a reflection of inner character

phys·iog·ra·phy \ˌfi-zē-'ä-grə-fē\ *n* : geography dealing with physical features of the earth — **phys·io·graph·ic** \ˌfi-zē-ō-'gra-fik\ *adj*

phys·i·ol·o·gy \ˌfi-zē-'ä-lə-jē\ *n* **1** : a branch of biology dealing with the functions and functioning of living matter and organisms **2** : functional processes in an organism or any of its parts — **phys·i·o·log·i·cal** \-zē-ə-'lä-ji-kəl\ *or* **phys·i·o·log·ic** \-jik\ *adj* — **phys·i·o·log·i·cal·ly** \-ji-k(ə-)lē\ *adv* — **phys·i·ol·o·gist** \-zē-'ä-lə-jist\ *n*

phys·io·ther·a·py \ˌfi-zē-ō-'ther-ə-pē\ *n* : PHYSICAL THERAPY — **phys·io·ther·a·pist** \-pist\ *n*

phy·sique \fə-'zēk\ *n* ♦ : the build of a person's body : bodily constitution

♦ build, constitution, figure, form, frame, shape

phy·to·chem·i·cal \ˌfī-tō-'ke-mi-kəl\ *n* : a chemical compound occurring naturally in plants

phy·to·plank·ton \'fī-tō-ˌplaŋk-tən\ *n* : plant life of the plankton

pi \'pī\ *n, pl* **pis** \'pīz\ **1** : the 16th letter of the Greek alphabet — Π *or* π **2** : the symbol π denoting the ratio of the circumference of a circle to its diameter; *also* : the ratio itself equal to approximately 3.1416

PI *abbr* private investigator

pi·a·nis·si·mo \ˌpē-ə-'ni-sə-ˌmō\ *adv or adj* : very softly — used as a direction in music

pi·a·nist \pē-'a-nist, 'pē-ə-\ *n* : a person who plays the piano

¹**pi·a·no** \pē-'ä-nō\ *adv or adj* : SOFTLY — used as a direction in music

²**piano** \pē-'a-nō\ *n, pl* **pianos** : a musical instrument having steel strings sounded by felt-covered hammers operated from a keyboard

pi·ano·forte \pē-ˌa-nō-'fȯr-ˌtā, -tē; pē-'a-nə-ˌfȯrt\ *n* : PIANO

pi·az·za \pē-'a-zə, *esp for 1* -'at-sə\ *n, pl* **piazzas** *or* **pi·az·ze** \-'at-(ˌ)sā, -'ät-\ **1** : an open square esp. in an Italian town **2** : a long hall with an arched roof **3** *dial* : VERANDA, PORCH

pi·broch \'pē-ˌbräk\ *n* : a set of variations for the bagpipe

pic \'pik\ *n, pl* **pics** *or* **pix** \'piks\ **1** : PHOTOGRAPH **2** : MOTION PICTURE

pi·ca \'pī-kə\ *n* : a typewriter type with 10 characters to the inch

pic·a·resque \ˌpi-kə-'resk, ˌpē-\ *adj* : of or relating to rogues ⟨∼ fiction⟩

pic·a·yune \ˌpi-kē-'yün\ *adj* : of little value : TRIVIAL; *also* : PETTY

pic·ca·lil·li \ˌpi-kə-'li-lē\ *n* : a relish of chopped vegetables and spices

pic·co·lo \'pi-kə-ˌlō\ *n, pl* **-los** : a small shrill flute pitched an octave higher than the ordinary flute

¹**pick** \'pik\ *vb* **1** : to pierce or break up with a pointed instrument **2** : to remove bit by bit; *also* : to remove covering matter from **3** ♦ : to gather by plucking ⟨∼ apples⟩ **4** ♦ : to select from a group : CULL, SELECT **5** : ROB ⟨∼ a pocket⟩ **6** : PROVOKE ⟨∼ a quarrel⟩ **7** : to dig into or pull lightly at **8** : to pluck with fingers or a pick **9** : to loosen or pull apart with a sharp point ⟨∼ wool⟩ **10** : to unlock with a wire **11** : to eat sparingly — **pick·er** *n*

♦ [3] gather, harvest, reap ♦ [4] choose, cull, elect, handpick, name, opt, prefer, select, single, take

²**pick** *n* **1** ♦ : the act or privilege of choosing **2** ♦ : the best or choicest one **3** : the part of a crop gathered at one time

♦ [1] alternative, choice, discretion, option, preference, way
♦ [2] best, choice, cream, elect, elite, fat, flower, prime

³**pick** *n* **1** : a heavy wooden-handled tool pointed at one or both ends **2** : a pointed implement used for picking **3** : a small thin piece (as of plastic) used to pluck the strings of a stringed instrument

pick·a·back \'pi-gē-ˌbak, 'pi-kə-\ *var of* PIGGYBACK

pick·ax \'pik-ˌaks\ *n* : ³PICK 1

pick·er·el \'pi-kə-rəl\ *n, pl* **pickerel** *or* **pickerels** : either of two bony fishes related to the pikes; *also* : WALLEYE 1

pick·er·el·weed \-ˌwēd\ *n* : a No. American shallow-water herb that bears spikes of purplish blue flowers

¹**pick·et** \'pi-kət\ *n* **1** : a pointed stake (as for a fence) **2 a** : a detached body of soldiers on outpost duty **b** ♦ : one that watches or guards : SENTINEL **3** : a person posted by a labor union where workers are on strike; *also* : a person posted for a protest

♦ [2b] custodian, guard, guardian, keeper, lookout, sentinel, sentry, warden, warder, watch, watchman

²**picket** *vb* **1** : to guard with pickets **2** : TETHER **3** : to post pickets at ⟨∼ a factory⟩ **4** : to serve as a picket

pick·ings \'pi-kiŋz, -kənz\ *n pl* **1** : gleanable or eatable fragments : SCRAPS **2** : yield for effort expended : RETURN

pick·le \'pi-kəl\ *n* **1** : a brine or vinegar solution for preserving foods; *also* : a food (as a cucumber) preserved in a pickle **2** ♦ : a difficult situation — **pickle** *vb*

♦ corner, fix, hole, jam, predicament, spot

pick·lock \'pik-,läk\ n **1** : BURGLAR, THIEF **2** : a tool for picking locks

pick·pock·et \'pik-,pä-kət\ n : one who steals from pockets

pick·up \'pik-,əp\ n **1** : a hitchhiker who is given a ride **2** : a temporary chance acquaintance **3** : a picking up **4** : revival of business activity **5** : ACCELERATION **6** : the conversion of mechanical movements into electrical impulses in the reproduction of sound; *also* : a device for making such conversion **7** : a light truck having an enclosed cab and an open body with low sides and a tailgate

pick up vb **1 ♦** : to take hold of and lift **2** : IMPROVE **3** : to put in order **4** : to gather together : COLLECT **5 ♦** : to acquire by study or experience : LEARN **6 ♦** : to obtain esp. by payment **7 ♦** : to become progressively greater (as in size, amount, number, or intensity) **8 ♦** : to take into custody

♦ [1] boost, crane, elevate, heave, heft, heighten, hike, hoist, jack, lift, raise, up, uphold ♦ [5] get, learn, master ♦ [6] buy, purchase, take ♦ [7] build, gain, gather, grow ♦ [8] apprehend, arrest, nab, restrain, seize

picky \'pi-kē\ adj **pick·i·er; -est ♦** : fastidiously selective

♦ choosy, dainty, delicate, demanding, exacting, fastidious, finicky, fussy, nice, old-maidish, particular, selective

¹pic·nic \'pik-,nik\ n **1** : an outing with food usu. provided by members of the group and eaten in the open **2 ♦** : an easy task or feat

♦ breeze, child's play, cinch, pushover, snap

²picnic vb **pic·nicked; pic·nick·ing** : to go on a picnic : eat in picnic fashion

pi·cot \'pē-,kō\ n : one of a series of small loops forming an edging on ribbon or lace

pic·to·ri·al \pik-'tōr-ē-əl\ adj **1** : of, relating to, or consisting of pictures **2** : suggesting or conveying visual images ⟨a ~ poetry⟩

¹pic·ture \'pik-chər\ n **1 ♦** : a representation made by painting, drawing, or photography **2 ♦** : a vivid description in words **3** : something that by its likeness vividly suggests some other thing : IMAGE **4** : a transitory visual image (as on a TV screen) **5** : a representation (as of a story) by means of motion pictures : MOVIE **6** : position with respect to conditions and circumstances : SITUATION **7 ♦** : a mental image

♦ [1] illustration, image, likeness ♦ [2] delineation, depiction, description, portrait, portrayal, sketch ♦ [7] concept, idea, image, impression, notion, thought

²picture vb **pic·tured; pic·tur·ing 1 ♦** : to paint or draw a picture of **2 ♦** : to describe vividly in words **3 ♦** : to form a mental image of

♦ [1] depict, image, portray, represent ♦ [2] delineate, depict, describe, draw, image, paint, portray, sketch ♦ [3] conceive, dream, envisage, fancy, imagine, vision, visualize

picture–perfect adj **♦** : completely flawless : PERFECT

♦ absolute, faultless, flawless, ideal, immaculate, impeccable, irreproachable, letter-perfect, perfect, unblemished

pic·tur·esque \,pik-chə-'resk\ adj **1** : resembling a picture ⟨a ~ landscape⟩ **2** : CHARMING, QUAINT ⟨a ~ character⟩ **3** : evoking mental images : GRAPHIC, VIVID ⟨a ~ account⟩ — **pic·tur·esque·ness** n

picture tube n : a cathode-ray tube on which the picture in a television set appears

pid·dle \'pid-ᵊl\ vb **pid·dled; pid·dling** : to act or work idly : DAWDLE

pid·dling \'pid-ᵊl-ən, -iŋ\ adj : of little worth or importance : TRIVIAL, PALTRY

pid·dly \'pid-lē\ adj : TRIVIAL, PIDDLING

pid·gin \'pi-jən\ n : a simplified speech used for communication between people with different languages

pie \'pī\ n : a dish consisting of a pastry crust and a filling (as of fruit or meat)

¹pie·bald \'pī-,bȯld\ adj **♦** : of different colors; *esp* : blotched with white and black ⟨a ~ horse⟩

♦ dappled, mottled, pied, spotted

²piebald n : a piebald animal

¹piece \'pēs\ n **1 ♦** : a part of a whole : FRAGMENT **2** : one of a group, set, or mass; *also* : a single item ⟨a ~ of news⟩ **3** : a length, weight, or size in which something is made or sold **4** : a product (as an essay) of creative work **5** : a weapon from which a shot is discharged by gunpowder : FIREARM **6** : COIN **7 ♦** : a literary, journalistic, artistic, dramatic, or musical composition

♦ [1] bit, fragment, scrap ♦ [7] composition, opus, work

²piece vb **pieced; piec·ing 1** : to repair or complete by adding pieces : PATCH **2 ♦** : to join into a whole

♦ assemble, build, construct, erect, fabricate, make, make up, put up, raise, rear, set up

pièce de ré·sis·tance \pē-,es-də-rā-,zē-'stäns\ n, pl **pièces de ré·sis·tance** \same\ **1** : the chief dish of a meal **2** : an outstanding item

piece·meal \'pēs-,mēl\ adv or adj : one piece at a time : GRADUALLY

piece·work \-,wərk\ n : work done and paid for by the piece — **piece·work·er** n

pie chart n : a circular chart that shows quantities or frequencies by parts of a circle shaped like pieces of pie

pied \'pīd\ adj **♦** : of two or more colors in blotches

♦ dappled, mottled, piebald, spotted

pied–à–terre \pē-,ā-də-'ter\ n, pl **pieds–à–terre** \same\ : a temporary or second lodging

pier \'pir\ n **1** : a support for a bridge span **2 ♦** : a structure built out into the water for use as a landing place or a promenade or to protect or form a harbor **3 ♦** : an upright supporting part (as a pillar) of a building or structure

♦ [2] dock, float, jetty, landing, levee, quay, wharf ♦ [3] column, pillar, post, stanchion

pierce \'pirs\ vb **pierced; pierc·ing 1 ♦** : to enter or thrust into sharply or painfully : STAB **2 ♦** : to make a hole in or through : PERFORATE **3 ♦** : to force or make a way into or through : PENETRATE **4** : to see through : DISCERN

♦ [1] gore, harpoon, impale, lance, puncture, skewer, spear, spike, stab, stick, transfix ♦ [2] bore, drill, hole, perforate, punch, puncture ♦ [3] access, enter, penetrate, probe

piercing adj **1 ♦** : marked by intensity or volume of sound **2** : PERCEPTIVE ⟨~ eyes⟩ **3 ♦** : penetratingly cold **4** : CUTTING, INCISIVE ⟨~ sarcasm⟩

♦ [1] booming, clamorous (or clamourous), deafening, earsplitting, loud, resounding, ringing, roaring, sonorous, stentorian, thunderous ♦ [3] biting, bitter, cutting, keen, penetrating, raw, sharp

pies pl of PIE

pi·ety \'pī-ə-tē\ n, pl **pi·et·ies 1** : fidelity to natural obligations (as to parents) **2 ♦** : dutifulness in religion **3** : a pious act

♦ devotion, faith, religion ♦ blessedness, devoutness, godliness, holiness, sainthood, sanctity

pif·fle \'pi-fəl\ n **♦** : trivial nonsense

♦ bunk, claptrap, drivel, foolishness, hogwash, nonsense

pig \'pig\ n **1** : SWINE; *esp* : a young domesticated swine **2** : PORK **3** : a dirty, gluttonous, or repulsive person **4** : a crude casting of metal (as iron)

pi·geon \'pi-jən\ n **1** : any of numerous stout-bodied short-legged birds with smooth thick plumage **2 ♦** : an easy mark : DUPE

♦ dupe, gull, sap, sucker, tool

¹pi·geon·hole \'pi-jən-,hōl\ n : a small open compartment (as in a desk) for keeping letters or documents

²pigeonhole vb **1** : to place in or as if in a pigeonhole : FILE **2** : to lay aside **3** : to assign to a usu. restrictive category

pi·geon–toed \-,tōd\ adj : having the toes turned in

pig·gish \'pi-gish\ adj **♦** : having a strong desire for food or drink : GREEDY **2** : STUBBORN

♦ gluttonous, greedy, hoggish, rapacious, ravenous, voracious

pig·gy·back \'pi-gē-,bak\ adv or adj **1** : up on the back and shoulders **2** : on a railroad flatcar

pig·head·ed \'pig-'he-dəd\ adj **♦** : willfully or perversely unyielding : OBSTINATE, STUBBORN

♦ dogged, hardheaded, headstrong, mulish, obdurate, obstinate, opinionated, peevish, pertinacious, perverse, stubborn, unyielding, willful

pig latin n, often cap L : a jargon that is made by systematic alteration of English

pig·let \'pig-lət\ n : a small usu. young swine

pig·ment \'pig-mənt\ n **1 ♦** : coloring matter **2** : a powder mixed with a liquid to give color (as in paints) — **pig·ment·ed** \-mən-təd\ adj

♦ color (or colour), dye, stain

pig·men·ta·tion \,pig-mən-'tā-shən\ n : coloration with or deposition of pigment; *esp* : an excessive deposition of bodily pigment

pigmy *var of* PYGMY

pig·nut \'pig-ˌnət\ *n* : the bitter nut of any of several hickory trees; *also* : any of these trees

pig·pen \-ˌpen\ *n*　**1** : a pen for pigs　**2** ♦ : a dirty place
　♦ hole, pigsty, shambles

pig·skin \-ˌskin\　**1** : the skin of a swine or leather made of it　**2** : FOOTBALL 2

pig·sty \-ˌstī\ *n*　**1** : a pen for pigs　**2** ♦ : a dirty place
　♦ hole, pigpen, shambles

pig·tail \-ˌtāl\ *n* : a tight braid of hair

pi·ka \'pī-kə\ *n* : any of various small short-eared mammals related to the rabbits and occurring in rocky uplands of Asia and western No. America

¹pike \'pīk\ *n* : a sharp point or spike

²pike *n, pl* **pike** *or* **pikes** : a large slender long-snouted freshwater bony fish valued for food; *also* : any of various related fishes

³pike *n* ♦ : a long wooden shaft with a pointed steel head formerly used as a foot soldier's weapon
　♦ lance, spear

⁴pike *n* : a main road; *esp* : a paved highway with a rounded surface : TURNPIKE

pik·er \'pī-kər\ *n*　**1** : one who does things in a small way or on a small scale　**2** : a close or miserly person : TIGHTWAD, CHEAPSKATE

pike·staff \'pīk-ˌstaf\ *n* : the staff of a foot soldier's pike

pi·laf *also* **pi·laff** \pi-'läf, 'pē-ˌläf\ *or* **pi·lau** \pi-'lȯ, -'lȯ, 'pē-lō, -lȯ\ *n* : a dish made of seasoned rice often with meat

pi·las·ter \pi-'las-tər, 'pī-ˌlas-tər\ *n* : an architectural support that looks like a rectangular column and projects slightly from a wall

pil·chard \'pil-chərd\ *n* : a small European marine fish related to the herrings and often packed as a sardine

¹pile \'pīl\ *n* : a long slender column (as of wood or steel) driven into the ground to support a vertical load

²pile *n*　**1** ♦ : a quantity of things heaped together　**2** : PYRE　**3** ♦ : a great number or quantity : LOT ⟨~s of money⟩
　♦ [1] cock, heap, hill, mound, mountain, rick, stack ♦ [3] abundance, deal, gobs, heap, loads, lot, plenty, quantity

³pile *vb* **piled; pil·ing**　**1** ♦ : to lay in a pile : STACK　**2** ♦ : to heap up : ACCUMULATE — usu. used with *up*　**3** : to press forward in a mass : CROWD
　♦ [1] heap, hill, mound, stack *Ant* unpile ♦ *usu* **pile up** [2] accumulate, collect, conglomerate, gather, heap

⁴pile *n*　**1** ♦ : a coat or surface of usu. short close fine furry hairs　**2** ♦ : a velvety surface produced by an extra set of filling yarns that form raised loops which are cut and sheared — **piled** \'pīld\ *adj* — **pile·less** *adj*
　♦ [1] coat, fleece, fur, hair, pelage, wool ♦ [2] down, floss, fluff, fur, fuzz, lint, nap

piles \'pīlz\ *n pl* : HEMORRHOIDS

pil·fer \'pil-fər\ *vb* ♦ : to steal in small quantities
　♦ appropriate, filch, hook, misappropriate, nip, pocket, purloin, snitch, steal, swipe, thieve

pil·grim \'pil-grəm\ *n*　**1** : one who journeys in foreign lands : WAYFARER　**2** : one who travels to a shrine or holy place as an act of devotion　**3** *cap* : one of the English settlers founding Plymouth colony in 1620

pil·grim·age \-grə-mij\ *n* : a journey of a pilgrim esp. to a shrine or holy place

pil·ing \'pī-liŋ\ *n* : a structure of piles

pill \'pil\ *n*　**1** ♦ : a medicine in a small rounded mass to be swallowed whole　**2** : a disagreeable or tiresome person　**3** *often cap* : an oral contraceptive — usu. used with *the*
　♦ capsule, tablet

pil·lage \'pi-lij\ *vb* **pil·laged; pil·lag·ing** ♦ : to take booty : LOOT — **pillage** *n* — **pil·lag·er** *n*
　♦ despoil, loot, maraud, plunder, ransack, sack, strip

pil·lar \'pi-lər\ *n*　**1** ♦ : a strong upright support (as for a roof)　**2** : a column or shaft standing alone esp. as a monument　**3** ♦ : a supporting, integral, or upstanding member or part — **pil·lared** \-lərd\ *adj*
　♦ [1] column, pier, post, stanchion ♦ [3] buttress, dependence, mainstay, reliance, standby, support

pill·box \'pil-ˌbäks\ *n*　**1** : a shallow round box for pills　**2** : a low concrete emplacement esp. for machine guns

pil·lion \'pil-yən\ *n*　**1** : a pad or cushion placed behind a saddle for an extra rider　**2** *chiefly Brit* : a motorcycle or bicycle saddle for a passenger

¹pil·lo·ry \'pi-lə-rē\ *n, pl* **-ries** : a wooden frame for public punishment having holes in which the head and hands can be locked

²pillory *vb* **-ried; -ry·ing**　**1** : to set in a pillory　**2** : to expose to public scorn

¹pil·low \'pi-lō\ *n* : a case filled with springy material (as feathers) and used to support the head of a resting person

²pillow *vb* : to rest or place on or as if on a pillow; *also* : to serve as a pillow for

pil·low·case \-ˌkās\ *n* : a removable covering for a pillow

¹pi·lot \'pī-lət\ *n*　**1** : HELMSMAN, STEERSMAN　**2** : a person qualified and licensed to take ships into and out of a port　**3** : GUIDE, LEADER　**4** ♦ : one that flies an aircraft or spacecraft　**5** : a television show filmed or taped as a sample of a proposed series — **pi·lot·less** *adj*
　♦ airman, aviator, flier

²pilot *vb* ♦ : to act as a guide to : lead or conduct over a usu. difficult course
　♦ coach, counsel, guide, lead, mentor, shepherd, show, tutor
　♦ conduct, direct, guide, lead, marshal, route, show, steer, usher

³pilot *adj* : serving as a guiding or activating device or as a testing or trial unit ⟨a ~ light⟩ ⟨a ~ factory⟩

pi·lot·house \'pī-lət-ˌhaús\ *n* : a shelter on the upper deck of a ship for the steering gear and the helmsman

pilot whale *n* : either of two mostly black medium-sized whales

pil·sner *also* **pil·sen·er** \'pilz-nər, 'pil-zə-\ *n*　**1** : a light beer with a strong flavor of hops　**2** : a tall slender footed glass for beer

pi·men·to \pə-'men-tō\ *n, pl* **pimentos** *or* **pimento**　**1** : ALLSPICE　**2** : PIMIENTO

pi·mien·to \pə-'men-tō\ *n, pl* **-tos** : any of various mild red sweet pepper fruits used esp. to stuff olives and to make paprika

pimp \'pimp\ *n* : a criminal who lives off the earnings of and usu. exerts control over one or more prostitutes — **pimp** *vb*

pim·per·nel \'pim-pər-ˌnel, -nəl\ *n* : any of a genus of herbs related to the primroses

pim·ple \'pim-pəl\ *n* : a small inflamed swelling on the skin often containing pus — **pim·ply** \-p(ə-)lē\ *adj*

¹pin \'pin\ *n*　**1** : a piece of wood or metal used esp. for fastening things together or as a support by which one thing may be suspended from another; *esp* : a small pointed piece of wire with a head used for fastening clothes or attaching papers　**2** : an ornament or emblem fastened to clothing with a pin　**3** : one of the wooden pieces constituting the target (as in bowling); *also* : the staff of the flag marking a hole on a golf course　**4** : LEG

²pin *vb* **pinned; pin·ning**　**1** : to fasten, join, or secure with a pin　**2** : to hold fast or immobile　**3** : ATTACH, HANG ⟨*pinned* their hopes on a miracle⟩　**4** : to assign the blame for ⟨~ a crime on someone⟩　**5** : to define clearly : ESTABLISH ⟨~ down an idea⟩

PIN *abbr* personal identification number

pi·ña co·la·da \ˌpēn-yə-kō-'lä-də, ˌpē-nə-\ *n* : a tall drink made of rum, cream of coconut, and pineapple juice mixed with ice

pin·afore \'pi-nə-ˌfȯr\ *n* : a sleeveless dress or apron fastened at the back

pin·ball machine \'pin-ˌbȯl-\ *n* : an amusement device in which a ball is maneuvered along a slanted surface among a series of targets for points

pince-nez \paⁿs-'nā\ *n, pl* **pince-nez** *same or* -'nāz\ : eyeglasses clipped to the nose by a spring

pin·cer \'pin-sər\ *n*　**1** *pl* : a gripping instrument with two handles and two grasping jaws　**2** : a claw (as of a lobster) resembling pincers

¹pinch \'pinch\ *vb*　**1** : to squeeze between the finger and thumb or between the jaws of an instrument　**2** : to compress painfully　**3** : CONTRACT, SHRIVEL　**4** : to be miserly; *also* : to subject to strict economy　**5** : to confine or limit narrowly　**6** : to take (the property of another) wrongfully : STEAL　**7** : to take or keep in custody by authority of law : ARREST

²pinch *n*　**1** : a critical point　**2** : EMERGENCY　**3** : painful effect　**3** : an act of pinching　**4** : a very small quantity　**5** : ARREST

³pinch *adj* : SUBSTITUTE ⟨a ~ runner⟩

pinch-hit \ˌpinch-'hit\ *vb*　**1** : to bat in the place of another player esp. when a hit is particularly needed　**2** ♦ : to act or serve in place of another — **pinch hit** *n*
　♦ cover, fill in, stand in, sub, substitute, take over

pinch hitter *n* ♦ : one that pinch-hits
　♦ backup, relief, replacement, reserve, stand-in, sub, substitute

pin curl *n* : a curl made usu. by dampening a strand of hair, coiling it, and securing it by a hairpin or clip

pin·cush·ion \'pin-ˌku̇-shən\ *n* : a cushion for pins not in use

¹**pine** \'pīn\ *n* : any of a genus of evergreen cone-bearing trees; *also* : the light durable resinous wood of a pine

²**pine** *vb* **pined; pin·ing** **1** : to lose vigor or health through distress **2** ♦ : to long for something intensely

   ♦ *usu* **pine for** ache for, covet, crave, desire, die (to *or* for), hanker for, hunger for, long for, lust (for *or* after), repine for, thirst for, want, wish for, yearn for

pi·ne·al \'pī-nē-əl, pī-ˈnē-əl\ *n* : PINEAL GLAND — **pineal** *adj*

pineal gland *n* : a small usu. conical appendage of the brain of all vertebrates with a cranium that functions primarily as an endocrine organ

pine·ap·ple \'pīn-ˌa-pəl\ *n* : a tropical plant bearing a large edible juicy fruit; *also* : its fruit

pin·feath·er \'pin-ˌfe-<u>th</u>ər\ *n* : a new feather just coming through the skin

ping \'piŋ\ *n* **1** : a sharp sound like that of a bullet striking **2** : engine knock

pin·hole \'pin-ˌhōl\ *n* ♦ : a small hole made by, for, or as if by a pin

   ♦ perforation, prick, punch, puncture, stab

¹**pin·ion** \'pin-yən\ *n* : the end section of a bird's wing; *also* : WING

²**pinion** *vb* : to restrain by binding the arms; *also* : SHACKLE

³**pinion** *n* : a gear with a small number of teeth designed to mesh with a larger wheel or rack

¹**pink** \'piŋk\ *n* **1** : any of a genus of plants with narrow leaves often grown for their showy flowers **2** : the highest degree : HEIGHT ⟨the ∼ of condition⟩

²**pink** *n* : a light tint of red

³**pink** *adj* **1** : of the color pink **2** : holding socialistic views — **pink·ish** *adj*

⁴**pink** *vb* **1** : to perforate in an ornamental pattern **2** : PIERCE, STAB **3** : to cut a saw-toothed edge on

pink·eye \'piŋk-ˌī\ *n* : an acute contagious eye inflammation

pin·kie *or* **pin·ky** \'piŋ-kē\ *n, pl* **pinkies** : the smallest finger of the hand

pin·nace \'pi-nəs\ *n* **1** : a light sailing ship **2** : a ship's boat

pin·na·cle \'pi-ni-kəl\ *n* **1** : a turret ending in a small spire **2** : a lofty peak **3** ♦ : the highest point of development or achievement : ACME

   ♦ acme, apex, climax, crown, culmination, head, height, meridian, peak, summit, tip-top, top, zenith

pin·nate \'pi-ˌnāt\ *adj* : resembling a feather esp. in having similar parts arranged on each side of an axis ⟨a ∼ leaf⟩

pi·noch·le \'pē-ˌnə-kəl\ *n* : a card game played with a 48-card deck

pi·ñon *or* **pin·yon** \'pin-ˌyōn, -ˌyän\ *n, pl* **pi·ñons** *or* **pi·ño·nes** \pin-ˈyō-nēz\ *or* **pin·yons** : any of various small pines of western No. America with edible seeds; *also* : the edible seed of a piñon

pin·point \'pin-ˌpȯint\ *vb* ♦ : to locate, hit, or aim with great precision

   ♦ distinguish, identify, single

pin·prick \-ˌprik\ *n* **1** : a small puncture made by or as if by a pin **2** : a petty irritation or annoyance

pins and needles *n pl* : a pricking tingling sensation in a limb growing numb or recovering from numbness — **on pins and needles** : in a nervous or jumpy state of anticipation

pin·stripe \'pin-ˌstrīp\ *n* : a narrow stripe on a fabric; *also* : a suit with such stripes — **pin–striped** \-ˌstrīpt\ *adj*

pint \'pīnt\ *n* : a unit of capacity equal to ¹⁄₂ quart

pin·to \'pin-ˌtō\ *n, pl* **pintos** *also* **pintoes** : a spotted horse or pony

pinto bean *n* : a spotted seed produced by a kind of kidney bean and used for food

pint–size \'pīnt-ˌsīz\ *or* **pint–sized** \-ˌsīzd\ *adj* : having comparatively little size or slight dimensions : SMALL

pin·up \'pin-ˌəp\ *adj* : suitable or designed for hanging on a wall; *also* : suited (as by beauty) to be the subject of a pinup photograph

pin·wheel \-ˌhwēl, -ˌwēl\ *n* **1** : a fireworks device in the form of a revolving wheel of colored fire **2** : a toy consisting of lightweight vanes that revolve at the end of a stick

pin·worm \-ˌwərm\ *n* : a nematode worm parasitic in the human intestine

pin·yin \'pin-ˈyin\ *n, often cap* : a system for writing Chinese ideograms by using Roman letters to represent the sounds

¹**pi·o·neer** \ˌpī-ə-ˈnir\ *n* **1** : one that originates or helps open up a new line of thought or activity **2** ♦ : an early settler in a territory

   ♦ colonist, frontiersman, homesteader, settler

²**pioneer** *vb* **1** : to act as a pioneer **2** : to open or prepare for others to follow; *also* : SETTLE **3** ♦ : to originate or take part in the development of

   ♦ constitute, establish, found, inaugurate, initiate, innovate, institute, introduce, launch, set up, start

pi·ous \'pī-əs\ *adj* **1** ♦ : marked by reverence for deity : DEVOUT **2** : excessively or affectedly religious **3** : SACRED, DEVOTIONAL **4** ♦ : showing loyal reverence for a person or thing **5** : marked by sham or hypocrisy — **pi·ous·ly** *adv*

   ♦ [1] devout, faithful, godly, holy, religious, sainted, saintly ♦ [4] constant, devoted, faithful, fast, good, loyal, staunch, steadfast, steady, true, true-blue

¹**pip** \'pip\ *n* : one of the dots used on dice and dominoes to indicate numerical value

²**pip** *n* **1** : a small fruit seed (as of an apple) **2** ♦ : one extraordinary of its kind

   ♦ beauty, crackerjack, dandy, jim-dandy, knockout

¹**pipe** \'pīp\ *n* **1** : a tubular musical instrument played by forcing air through it **2** : BAGPIPE **3** ♦ : a tube designed to conduct something (as water, steam, or oil) **4** : a device for smoking having a tube with a bowl at one end and a mouthpiece at the other **5** : a large cask of varying capacity used esp. for wine and oil

   ♦ channel, conduit, duct, leader, line, penstock, tube

²**pipe** *vb* **piped; pip·ing** **1** : to play on a pipe **2 a** : to speak in a high or shrill voice **b** : to emit a shrill sound **3** ♦ : to convey by or as if by pipes — **pip·er** *n*

   ♦ channel, conduct, direct, funnel, siphon

pipe down *vb* ♦ : to stop talking or making noise

   ♦ calm (down), cool (off *or* down), hush, quiet, settle (down) ♦ clam up, hush, quiet (down), shut up

pipe dream *n* ♦ : an illusory or fantastic hope

   ♦ chimera, conceit, daydream, delusion, dream, fancy, fantasy, figment, hallucination, illusion, phantasm, unreality, vision

pipe·line \'pīp-ˌlīn\ *n* **1** : a line of pipe with pumps, valves, and control devices for conveying fluids **2** : a channel for information

pi·pette *or* **pi·pet** \pī-ˈpet\ *n* : a device for measuring and transferring small volumes of liquid

pipe up *vb* : to speak loudly and distinctly; *also* : to express an opinion freely

pip·ing \'pī-piŋ\ *n* **1** : the music of pipes **2** : a narrow fold of material used to decorate edges or seams

piping hot *adj* : very hot

pip·pin \'pi-pən\ *n* : a crisp tart usu. yellowish apple

pip–squeak \'pip-ˌskwēk\ *n* ♦ : one that is small or insignificant

   ♦ nobody, nonentity, nothing, whippersnapper, zero

pi·quant \'pē-kənt\ *adj* **1** : pleasantly savory : PUNGENT ⟨a ∼ sauce⟩ **2** : engagingly provocative; *also* : having a lively charm — **pi·quan·cy** \-kən-sē\ *n*

¹**pique** \'pēk\ *n* ♦ : a passing feeling of wounded vanity : RESENTMENT

   ♦ dudgeon, huff, offense, peeve, resentment, umbrage

²**pique** *vb* **piqued; piqu·ing** **1** ♦ : to arouse anger or resentment in : IRRITATE **2** ♦ : to arouse by a provocation or challenge

   ♦ [1] aggravate, annoy, bother, bug, chafe, exasperate, gall, get, grate, irk, irritate, nettle, peeve, persecute, put out, rasp, rile, vex ♦ [2] arouse, encourage, excite, fire, incite, instigate, move, provoke, stimulate, stir

pi·qué *or* **pi·que** \pi-ˈkā\ *n* : a durable ribbed clothing fabric

pi·quet \pi-ˈkā\ *n* : a 2-handed card game played with 32 cards

pi·ra·cy \'pī-rə-sē\ *n, pl* **-cies** **1** : robbery on the high seas; *also* : an act resembling such robbery **2** : the unauthorized use of another's production or invention

pi·ra·nha \pə-ˈrä-nə, -ˈrän-yə\ *n* : any of various usu. small So. American fishes with sharp teeth that include some known to attack humans and large animals

pi·rate \'pī-rət\ *n* ♦ : one who commits piracy — **pirate** *vb* — **pi·rat·i·cal** \pə-ˈra-ti-kəl, pī-\ *adj*

   ♦ buccaneer, corsair, freebooter, rover

¹**pir·ou·ette** \ˌpir-ə-ˈwet\ *n* : a rapid whirling about of the body; *esp* : a full turn on the toe or ball of one foot in ballet

²**pirouette** *vb* ♦ : to turn in or as if in a pirouette

   ♦ gyrate, revolve, roll, rotate, spin, turn, twirl, wheel, whirl

pis *pl of* PI
pis·ca·to·ri·al \ˌpis-kə-'tōr-ē-əl\ *adj* : of or relating to fishing
Pi·sces \'pī-sēz\ *n* **1** : a zodiacal constellation between Aquarius and Aries usu. pictured as a fish **2** : the 12th sign of the zodiac in astrology; *also* : one born under this sign
pis·mire \'pis-ˌmīr\ *n* : ANT
pis·ta·chio \pə-'sta-shē-ˌō, -'stä-\ *n, pl* **-chios** : the greenish edible seed of a small Asian tree related to the sumacs; *also* : the tree
pis·til \'pist-ᵊl\ *n* : the female reproductive organ in a flower —
   pis·til·late \'pis-tə-ˌlāt\ *adj*
pis·tol \'pist-ᵊl\ *n* : a handgun whose chamber is integral with the barrel
pis·tol–whip \-ˌhwip\ *vb* : to beat with a pistol
pis·ton \'pis-tən\ *n* : a sliding piece that receives and transmits motion and that usu. consists of a short cylinder inside a large cylinder
¹**pit** \'pit\ *n* **1** ♦ : a hole, shaft, or cavity in the ground **2** : an often sunken area designed for a particular use; *also* : an enclosed place (as for cockfights) **3** : HELL; *also, pl* : WORST ⟨it's the ∼s⟩ **4** ♦ : a natural hollow or indentation in a surface **5** : a small indented mark or scar (as from disease or corrosion) **6** : an area beside a racecourse where cars are fueled and repaired during a race

   ♦ [1, 4] cavity, concavity, dent, depression, hole, hollow, indentation, recess

²**pit** *vb* **pit·ted; pit·ting 1** : to form pits in or become marred with pits **2** : to match for fighting
³**pit** *n* : the stony seed of some fruits (as the cherry, peach, and date)
⁴**pit** *vb* **pit·ted; pit·ting** : to remove the pit from
pi·ta \'pē-tə\ *n* : a thin flat bread
pit–a–pat \ˌpi-ti-'pat\ *n* : PITTER-PATTER — **pit–a–pat** *adv or adj*
pit bull *n* : a powerful compact short-haired dog developed for fighting
¹**pitch** \'pich\ *n* **1** : a dark sticky substance left over esp. from distilling tar or petroleum **2** : resin from various conifers
²**pitch** *vb* **1** ♦ : to erect and fix firmly in place ⟨∼ a tent⟩ **2** ♦ : to throw usu. with a particular objective or toward a particular point **3** : to deliver a baseball to a batter **4** : to toss (as coins) toward a mark **5** : to set at a particular level ⟨∼ the voice low⟩ **6** : to fall headlong **7** : to have the front end (as of a ship) alternately plunge and rise **8** : to incline downward : SLOPE

   ♦ [1] erect, put up, raise, rear, set up ♦ [2] cast, catapult, chuck, dash, fire, fling, heave, hurl, hurtle, launch, peg, pelt, sling, throw, toss

³**pitch** *n* **1** : the action or a manner of pitching **2** ♦ : degree of slope ⟨∼ of a roof⟩ **3** : the relative level of some quality or state ⟨a high ∼ of excitement⟩ **4** : highness or lowness of sound; *also* : a standard frequency for tuning instruments **5** : a presentation delivered to sell or promote something **6** : the delivery of a baseball to a batter; *also* : the baseball delivered

   ♦ cant, diagonal, grade, inclination, incline, lean, slant, slope, tilt, upgrade

pitch·blende \'pich-ˌblend\ *n* : a dark mineral that is the chief source of uranium
¹**pitch·er** \'pi-chər\ *n* ♦ : a container for liquids that usu. has a lip and a handle

   ♦ ewer, flagon, jug

²**pitcher** *n* : one that pitches esp. in a baseball game
pitcher plant *n* : any of various plants with leaves modified to resemble pitchers in which insects are trapped and digested
pitch·fork \'pich-ˌfȯrk\ *n* : a long-handled fork used esp. in pitching hay
pitch in *vb* **1** : to begin to work **2** ♦ : to contribute to a common effort

   ♦ chip in, contribute, kick in

pitch·man \'pich-mən\ *n* **1** : SALESMAN; *esp* : one who sells merchandise on the streets or from a concession **2** : one who does radio or TV commercials
pitch–per·fect \'pich-'pər-fikt\ *adj* : having just the right tone or style ⟨a ∼ translation⟩
pitchy \'pi-chē\ *adj* **1 a** : full of pitch **b** : of, relating to, or having the qualities of pitch **2** : extremely dark or black
pit·e·ous \'pi-tē-əs\ *adj* ♦ : arousing pity : PITIFUL — **pit·e·ous·ly** *adv*

   ♦ heartbreaking, miserable, pathetic, pitiful, poor, rueful, sorry, wretched

pit·fall \'pit-ˌfȯl\ *n* **1** : TRAP, SNARE; *esp* : a covered pit used for capturing animals **2** ♦ : a hidden danger or difficulty

   ♦ booby trap, catch, snag ♦ danger, hazard, menace, peril, risk, threat, trouble

pith \'pith\ *n* **1** : loose spongy tissue esp. in the center of the stem of vascular plants **2** ♦ : the essential part : CORE

   ♦ core, crux, gist, heart, nub, pivot

pithy \'pi-thē\ *adj* **pith·i·er; -est 1** : consisting of or filled with pith **2** ♦ : having substance and point : CONCISE

   ♦ brief, compact, compendious, concise, crisp, epigrammatic, laconic, succinct, summary, terse

piti·able \'pi-tē-ə-bəl\ *adj* **1** : arousing or deserving pity : PITIFUL **2** : of a kind to evoke mingled pity and contempt esp. because of inadequacy
piti·ful \'pi-ti-fəl\ *adj* **1** ♦ : arousing or deserving pity ⟨a ∼ sight⟩ **2** ♦ : arousing pitying contempt (as by meanness or inadequacy) — **piti·ful·ly** *adv*

   ♦ [1] heartbreaking, miserable, pathetic, piteous, poor, rueful, sorry, wretched ♦ [2] contemptible, despicable, lousy, nasty, scabby, scurvy, sorry, wretched

piti·less \'pi-ti-ləs\ *adj* ♦ : devoid of pity : MERCILESS — **piti·less·ly** *adv*

   ♦ callous, hard, heartless, inhuman, inhumane, soulless, unfeeling, unsympathetic

pi·ton \'pē-ˌtän\ *n* : a spike, wedge, or peg that can be driven into a rock or ice surface as a support
pit·tance \'pit-ᵊns\ *n* ♦ : a small portion, amount, or allowance

   ♦ mite, peanuts, shoestring, song

pit·ted \'pi-təd\ *adj* : marked with pits
¹**pit·ter–pat·ter** \'pi-tər-ˌpa-tər, 'pi-tē-\ *n* : a rapid succession of light taps or sounds ⟨the ∼ of rain⟩ — **pitter–patter** \ˌpi-tər-'pa-tər, ˌpi-tē-\ *adv or adj*
²**pitter–patter** \ˌpi-tər-'pa-tər, ˌpi-tē-\ *vb* ♦ : to go pitter-patter

   ♦ beat, palpitate, pulsate, pulse, throb

pi·tu·i·tary \pə-'tü-ə-ˌter-ē, -'tyü-\ *n, pl* **-i·tar·ies** : PITUITARY GLAND — **pituitary** *adj*
pituitary gland *n* : a small oval endocrine gland located at the base of the brain that produces various hormones that affect most basic bodily functions (as growth and reproduction)
pit viper *n* : any of various mostly New World venomous snakes with a sensory pit on each side of the head and hollow perforated fangs
¹**pity** \'pi-tē\ *n, pl* **pit·ies 1** ♦ : sympathetic sorrow : COMPASSION **2** : something to be regretted

   ♦ charity, commiseration, compassion, feeling, heart, humanity, kindliness, kindness, mercy, sympathy

²**pity** *vb* **pit·ied; pity·ing** ♦ : to feel pity for

   ♦ bleed, commiserate, feel, sympathize

¹**piv·ot** \'pi-vət\ *n* **1** : a fixed pin on which something turns **2** ♦ : a person, thing, or factor having a major or central role, function, or effect — **pivot** *adj*

   ♦ core, crux, gist, heart, nub, pith

²**pivot** *vb* ♦ : to turn on or as if on a pivot

   ♦ revolve, roll, rotate, spin, swing, swirl, turn, twirl, twist, wheel, whirl

piv·ot·al \'pi-vət-ᵊl\ *adj* ♦ : vitally important : CRITICAL

   ♦ critical, crucial, key, vital

pix *pl of* PIC
pix·el \'pik-səl, -ˌsel\ *n* : any of the small elements that together make up an image (as on a television screen)
pix·ie *also* **pixy** \'pik-sē\ *n, pl* **pix·ies** : FAIRY; *esp* ♦ : a mischievous sprite

   ♦ brownie, dwarf, elf, fairy, fay, gnome, hobgoblin, leprechaun, puck, troll

piz·za \'pēt-sə\ *n* : an open pie made of rolled bread dough spread with a spiced mixture (as of tomatoes, cheese, and ground meat) and baked
piz·zazz *or* **pi·zazz** \pə-'zaz\ *n* **1** : GLAMOUR **2** : VITALITY
piz·ze·ria \ˌpēt-sə-'rē-ə\ *n* : an establishment where pizzas are made and sold
piz·zi·ca·to \ˌpit-si-'kä-tō\ *adv or adj* : by means of plucking instead of bowing — used as a direction in music
pj's \'pē-ˌjāz\ *n pl* : PAJAMAS
pk *abbr* **1** park **2** peak **3** peck **4** pike
pkg *abbr* package
pkt *abbr* **1** packet **2** pocket

pkwy *abbr* parkway
pl *abbr* **1** place **2** plate **3** plural
¹**plac·ard** \'pla-kərd, -ˌkärd\ *n* ♦ : a notice posted in a public place : POSTER

  ♦ bill, poster

²**plac·ard** \-ˌkärd, -kərd\ *vb* **1** : to cover with or as if with plac-ards **2** ♦ : to announce by or as if by posting

  ♦ advertise, announce, blaze, broadcast, declare, enunciate, post, proclaim, promulgate, publicize, publish, sound

pla·cate \'plā-ˌkāt, 'pla-\ *vb* **pla·cat·ed; pla·cat·ing** ♦ : to soothe esp. by concessions : APPEASE — **pla·ca·ble** \'pla-kə-bəl, 'plā-\ *adj*

  ♦ appease, conciliate, disarm, mollify, pacify, propitiate

¹**place** \'plās\ *n* **1** : physical environment : SPACE **2** : an indefinite region : AREA **3** ♦ : a building or locality used for a special purpose **4** : a center of population **5** : a particular part of a surface : SPOT **6** ♦ : relative position in a scale or sequence; *also* : position at the end of a competition ⟨last ∼⟩ **7** : ACCOMMODATION; *esp* : SEAT **8** : the position of a figure within a numeral ⟨12 is a two ∼ number⟩ **9** ♦ : paid employment : JOB; *esp* : public office **10** : a public square **11** : 2d place at the finish (as of a horse race) **12** ♦ : a proper or designated niche **13** ♦ : a building, part of a building, or area occupied as a home

  ♦ [3] establishment, joint, salon ♦ [3, 12] locale, location, point, position, site, spot *Ant* scene, region, section, sector ♦ [6] degree, footing, level, position, rank, situation, standing, station, status ♦ [9] appointment, billet, capacity, function, job, position, post, situation ♦ [12] part, purpose, role, task, work ♦ [13] abode, domicile, dwelling, home, house, lodging, quarters, residence

²**place** *vb* **placed; plac·ing** **1** ♦ : to put in a particular place : SET **2** ♦ : to distribute in an orderly manner **3** : IDENTIFY **4** : to give an order for ⟨∼ a bet⟩ **5** : to earn a given spot in a competition; *esp* : to come in 2d **6** ♦ : to judge tentatively or approximately the value, worth, or significance of : ESTIMATE

  ♦ [1] deposit, dispose, fix, lay, position, put, set, set up, stick ♦ [2] assort, break down, categorize, class, classify, grade, group, peg, range, rank, separate, sort ♦ [5] be, grade, rank, rate ♦ [6] calculate, call, conjecture, estimate, figure, gauge, guess, judge, make, put, reckon, suppose

pla·ce·bo \plə-'sē-bō\ *n, pl* **-bos** : an inert medication used for its psychological effect or for purposes of comparison in an experiment
place·hold·er \'plās-ˌhōl-dər\ *n* : a symbol in a mathematical or logical expression that may be replaced by the name of any element of a set
place·kick \-ˌkik\ *n* : the kicking of a ball placed or held on the ground — **placekick** *vb* — **place·kick·er** *n*
place·ment \'plās-mənt\ *n* : an act or instance of placing
place–name \-ˌnām\ *n* : the name of a geographic locality
pla·cen·ta \plə-'sen-tə\ *n, pl* **-tas** *or* **-tae** \-ˌtē\ : the organ in most mammals by which the fetus is joined to the maternal uterus and is nourished — **pla·cen·tal** \-'sent-ᵊl\ *adj*
plac·er \'pla-sər\ *n* : a deposit of sand or gravel containing particles of valuable mineral (as gold)
plac·id \'pla-səd\ *adj* ♦ : serenely free of interruption or disturbance — **plac·id·ly** *adv*

  ♦ calm, collected, composed, cool, self-possessed, serene, tranquil, undisturbed, unperturbed, unshaken, untroubled, unworried ♦ calm, halcyon, hushed, peaceful, quiet, still

pla·cid·i·ty \pla-'si-də-tē\ *n* ♦ : the quality or state of being placid

  ♦ calm, calmness, hush, peace, quiet, quietness, repose, serenity, still, stillness, tranquility

plack·et \'pla-kət\ *n* : a slit in a garment
pla·gia·rise *chiefly Brit var of* PLAGIARIZE
pla·gia·rize \'plā-jə-ˌrīz\ *vb* **-rized; -riz·ing** : to present the ideas or words of another as one's own — **pla·gia·rism** \-ˌri-zəm\ *n* — **pla·gia·rist** \-rist\ *n*
¹**plague** \'plāg\ *n* **1** ♦ : a disastrous evil or influx; *also* : NUISANCE **2** : PESTILENCE; *esp* : a destructive contagious bacterial disease (as bubonic plague)
²**plague** *vb* **plagued; plagu·ing** **1** ♦ : to afflict with or as if with disease or disaster **2 a** : to cause worry or distress to **b** ♦ : to disturb or annoy persistently

  ♦ [1, 2b] afflict, agonize, bedevil, curse, harrow, martyr, persecute, rack, torment, torture

plaid \'plad\ *n* **1** : a rectangular length of tartan worn esp. over the left shoulder as part of the Scottish national costume **2** : a twilled woolen fabric with a tartan pattern **3** : a pattern of unevenly spaced repeated stripes crossing at right angles — **plaid** *adj*
¹**plain** \'plān\ *n* ♦ : an extensive area of level or rolling treeless country

  ♦ down, grassland, prairie, savanna, steppe, veld

²**plain** *adj* **1** ♦ : lacking ornament ⟨a ∼ dress⟩ **2** ♦ : free of extraneous matter **3** : OPEN, UNOBSTRUCTED ⟨∼ view⟩ **4** : EVIDENT, OBVIOUS **5 a** ♦ : easily understood : CLEAR **b** ♦ : expressing oneself free of any attempt at deception or subterfuge **6** ♦ : marked by outspoken candor : CANDID, BLUNT **7** : SIMPLE ⟨∼ cooking⟩ **8** : lacking beauty or ugliness

  ♦ [1] bald, bare, naked, simple, unadorned, undecorated, unvarnished *Ant* adorned, decorated, embellished, fancy, ornamented ♦ [2] absolute, fine, neat, pure, refined, straight, unadulterated, undiluted, unmixed ♦ [5a] apparent, broad, clear, clear-cut, distinct, evident, lucid, manifest, obvious, palpable, patent, perspicuous, transparent, unambiguous, unequivocal, unmistakable ♦ [5b, 6] blunt, candid, direct, forthright, foursquare, frank, honest, open, outspoken, straight, straightforward, unguarded, unreserved

plain·clothes \'plān-ˌklō(th)z\ *adj* : dressed in civilian clothes while on duty — used esp. of a police officer ⟨∼ officers⟩
plain·ly \'plān-lē\ *adv* ♦ : in a plain manner

  ♦ directly, forthrightly, foursquare, plain, straight, straightforward

plain·ness \'plān-nəs\ *n* ♦ : the quality or state of being plain

  ♦ candor (*or* candour), directness, forthrightness, frankness, openness

plain·spo·ken \-'spō-kən\ *adj* : marked by honest sincere expression : FRANK
plaint \'plānt\ *n* **1** ♦ : an act or instance of lamenting : LAMENTATION, WAIL **2** ♦ : a critical protest : COMPLAINT

  ♦ [1] groan, howl, keen, lament, lamentation, moan, wail ♦ [2] beef, complaint, fuss, grievance, gripe, grumble, murmur, squawk

plain·tiff \'plān-təf\ *n* : the complaining party in a lawsuit
plain·tive \'plān-tiv\ *adj* ♦ : expressive of suffering or woe — **plain·tive·ly** *adv*

  ♦ dolorous, funeral, lugubrious, mournful, regretful, rueful, sorrowful, weeping, woeful

plait \'plāt, 'plat\ *n* **1** : PLEAT **2** ♦ : a braid esp. of hair or straw — **plait** *vb*

  ♦ braid, lace

¹**plan** \'plan\ *n* **1** : a drawing or diagram showing the parts or details of something **2 a** ♦ : a method for accomplishing an objective **b** ♦ : the end toward which effort is directed : GOAL, AIM

  ♦ [2a] arrangement, blueprint, design, game, project, scheme, strategy, system ♦ [2b] aim, ambition, aspiration, design, dream, end, goal, intent, mark, meaning, object, objective, pretension, purpose, thing

²**plan** *vb* **planned; plan·ning** **1** ♦ : to form a plan of ⟨∼ a new city⟩ **2** ♦ : to have in mind : INTEND ⟨*planned* to go⟩ — **plan·ner** *n*

  ♦ [1] arrange, blueprint, calculate, chart, design, frame, lay out, map, project, scheme ♦ [2] aim, aspire, contemplate, design, intend, mean, meditate, propose

¹**plane** \'plān\ *vb* **planed; plan·ing** ♦ : to smooth or level off with or as if with a plane — **plan·er** *n*

  ♦ even, level, smooth

²**plane** *n* : PLANE TREE
³**plane** *n* : a tool for smoothing or shaping a wood surface
⁴**plane** *n* **1** : a level or flat surface **2** : a level of existence, consciousness, or development **3** : AIRPLANE
⁵**plane** *adj* **1** ♦ : having no elevations or depressions : FLAT, LEVEL **2** : dealing with flat surfaces or figures ⟨∼ geometry⟩

  ♦ even, flat, flush, level, smooth

⁶**plane** *vb* ♦ : to fly while keeping the wings motionless

  ♦ fly, glide, soar, wing

plane·load \'plān-ˌlōd\ *n* : a load that fills an airplane
plan·et \'pla-nət\ *n* **1** : any of the large bodies in the solar system that revolve around the sun **2** ♦ : the celestial body on

which we live that is third in order from the sun — **plan·e·tary** \-nə-ˌter-ē\ *adj*

♦ earth, world

plan·e·tar·i·um \ˌpla-nə-ˈter-ē-əm\ *n, pl* **-i·ums** *or* **-ia** \-ē-ə\ : a building or room housing a device to project images of celestial bodies

plan·e·tes·i·mal \ˌpla-nə-ˈtes-ə-məl\ *n* : any of numerous small solid celestial bodies which may have existed during the formation of the solar system

plan·e·toid \ˈpla-nə-ˌtȯid\ *n* : a body resembling a planet; *esp* : ASTEROID

plane tree *n* : any of a genus of trees (as a sycamore) with large lobed leaves and globe-shaped fruit

plan·gent \ˈplan-jənt\ *adj* **1** : having a loud reverberating sound **2** : having an expressive esp. plaintive quality — **plan·gen·cy** \-jən-sē\ *n*

¹**plank** \ˈplaŋk\ *n* **1** : a heavy thick board **2** : an article in the platform of a political party

²**plank** *vb* **1** : to cover with planks **2** : to set or lay down forcibly **3** : to cook and serve on a board

plank·ing \ˈplaŋ-kiŋ\ *n* : a quantity or covering of planks

plank·ton \ˈplaŋk-tən\ *n* : the passively floating or weakly swimming animal and plant life of a body of water — **plank·ton·ic** \plaŋk-ˈtä-nik\ *adj*

¹**plant** \ˈplant\ *vb* **1** ♦ : to set in the ground to grow **2** : ESTABLISH, SETTLE **3** : to stock or provide with something **4** : to place firmly or forcibly **5** : to hide or arrange with intent to deceive

♦ drill, seed, sow

²**plant** *n* **1** : any of a kingdom of living things that usu. have no locomotor ability or obvious sense organs and have cellulose cell walls and usu. capacity for indefinite growth **2 a** : the land, buildings, and machinery used in carrying on a trade or business **b** ♦ : a factory or workshop for the manufacture of a particular product

♦ factory, mill, shop, works, workshop

¹**plan·tain** \ˈplant-ᵊn\ *n* : any of a genus of weedy herbs with spikes of tiny greenish flowers

²**plan·tain** \ˈplan-ˌtän, ˈplan-tən, ˈplant-ᵊn\ *n* : a banana plant with starchy greenish fruit that is eaten cooked; *also* : its fruit

plan·tar \ˈplan-tər, -ˌtär\ *adj* : of or relating to the sole of the foot

plan·ta·tion \plan-ˈtā-shən\ *n* **1** : a large group of plants and esp. trees under cultivation **2** : an agricultural estate usu. worked by resident laborers

plant·er \ˈplan-tər\ *n* **1** ♦ : one that plants or sows; *esp* : an owner or operator of a plantation **2** : a container for plants

♦ agriculturist, cultivator, farmer, grower, tiller

plant louse *n* : APHID

plaque \ˈplak\ *n* **1** : an ornamental brooch **2** : a flat thin piece (as of metal) used for decoration; *also* : a commemorative tablet **3** : a bacteria-containing film on a tooth

¹**plash** \ˈplash\ *n* : SPLASH

²**plash** *vb* **1** ♦ : to cause a splashing or spattering effect **2** ♦ : to splash with a liquid or with any wet substance

♦ [1] lap, slosh, splash, swash ♦ [2] dash, spatter, splash

plas·ma \ˈplaz-mə\ *n* **1** : the fluid part of blood, lymph, or milk **2** : a gas composed of ionized particles — **plas·mat·ic** \plaz-ˈma-tik\ *adj*

¹**plas·ter** \ˈplas-tər\ *n* **1** : a dressing consisting of a backing spread with an often medicated substance that clings to the skin ⟨adhesive ∼⟩ **2** : a paste that hardens as it dries and is used for coating walls and ceilings

²**plaster** *vb* : to cover with or as if with plaster — **plas·ter·er** *n*

plas·ter·board \ˈplas-tər-ˌbȯrd\ *n* : DRYWALL

plaster of par·is \-ˈpa-rəs\ *often cap 2d P* : a white powder made from gypsum and used as a quick-setting paste with water for casts and molds

¹**plas·tic** \ˈplas-tik\ *adj* **1** : capable of being molded ⟨∼ clay⟩ **2** : characterized by or using modeling ⟨∼ arts⟩ **3** : made or consisting of a plastic — **plas·tic·i·ty** \plas-ˈti-sə-tē\ *n*

²**plastic** *n* : a plastic substance; *esp* : a synthetic or processed material that can be formed into rigid objects or into films or filaments

plastic surgery *n* : surgery to repair, restore, or improve lost, injured, defective, or misshapen body parts — **plastic surgeon** *n*

¹**plat** \ˈplat\ *n* **1** ♦ : a small plot of ground **2** ♦ : a plan of a piece of land with actual or proposed features (as lots)

♦ [1, 2] lot, parcel, plot, property, tract

²**plat** *vb* **plat·ted; plat·ting** : to make a plat of

¹**plate** \ˈplāt\ *n* **1** : a flat thin piece of material **2** : domestic hollowware made of or plated with gold, silver, or base metals **3** : DISH **4** : HOME PLATE **5** : the molded metal or plastic cast of a page of type to be printed from **6** : a sheet of glass or plastic coated with a chemical sensitive to light and used in photography **7** : the part of a denture that fits to the mouth; *also* : DENTURE **8** : something printed from an engraving **9** : a huge mobile segment of the earth's crust **10** ♦ : a full-page illustration often on different paper from the text pages

♦ diagram, figure, graphic, illustration

²**plate** *vb* **plat·ed; plat·ing** **1** : to overlay with metal (as gold or silver) **2** : to make a printing plate of

pla·teau \pla-ˈtō\ *n, pl* **plateaus** *or* **pla·teaux** \-ˈtōz\ ♦ : a large level area of high land

♦ mesa, table, tableland

plate glass *n* : rolled, ground, and polished sheet glass

plate·let \ˈplāt-lət\ *n* : a minute flattened body; *esp* : a minute colorless disklike body of mammalian blood that assists in blood clotting

plat·en \ˈplat-ᵊn\ *n* **1** : a flat plate; *esp* : one that exerts or receives pressure (as in a printing press) **2** : the roller of a typewriter or printer

plate tectonics *n* **1** : a theory in geology that the lithosphere is divided into plates at the boundaries of which much of earth's seismic activity occurs **2** : the process and dynamics of tectonic plate movement

plat·form \ˈplat-ˌfȯrm\ *n* **1** ♦ : a raised flooring or stage for speakers, performers, or workers **2** : a declaration of the principles on which a group of persons (as a political party) stands

♦ dais, podium, rostrum, stage, stand

plat·ing \ˈplā-tiŋ\ *n* : a coating of metal plates or plate ⟨the ∼ of a ship⟩

plat·i·num \ˈplat-ᵊn-əm\ *n* : a heavy grayish white metallic chemical element

plat·i·tude \ˈpla-tə-ˌtüd, -ˌtyüd\ *n* ♦ : a flat or trite remark — **plat·i·tu·di·nous** \-ˈtüd-ᵊn-əs, -ˈtyüd-\ *adj*

♦ banality, cliché, commonplace, shibboleth

pla·ton·ic love \plə-ˈtä-nik-, plā-\ *n, often cap P* : a close relationship between two persons without sexual desire

pla·toon \plə-ˈtün\ *n* **1** : a subdivision of a company-size military unit usu. consisting of two or more squads or sections **2** : a group of football players trained either for offense or for defense and sent into the game as a body

platoon sergeant *n* : a noncommissioned officer in the army ranking below a first sergeant

plat·ter \ˈpla-tər\ *n* **1** : a large serving plate **2** : a phonograph record

platy \ˈpla-tē\ *n, pl* **platy** *or* **plat·ys** *or* **plat·ies** : either of two small stocky usu. brilliantly colored bony fishes often kept in tropical aquariums

platy·pus \ˈpla-ti-pəs\ *n, pl* **platy·pus·es** *also* **platy·pi** \-ˌpī\ : a small aquatic egg-laying marsupial mammal of Australia with webbed feet and a fleshy bill like a duck's

plau·dit \ˈplȯ-dət\ *n* : an act of applause

plau·si·ble \ˈplȯ-zə-bəl\ *adj* ♦ : seemingly worthy of belief — **plau·si·bil·i·ty** \ˌplȯ-zə-ˈbi-lə-tē\ *n* — **plau·si·bly** \ˈplȯ-zə-blē\ *adv*

♦ believable, credible, likely, probable

¹**play** \ˈplā\ *n* **1** : brisk handling of something (as a weapon) **2** : the course of a game; *also* : a particular act or maneuver in a game **3** ♦ : recreational activity; *esp* : the spontaneous activity of children **4** : absence of serious or harmful intent : JEST ⟨said in ∼⟩ **5** : the act or an instance of punning **6** : GAMBLING **7** ♦ : the state of being active, operative, or relevant : OPERATION ⟨bring extra force into ∼⟩ **8** : a brisk or light movement **9** : free motion (as of part of a machine) **10** : scope for action **11** : PUBLICITY **12** : an effort to arouse liking ⟨made a ∼ for her⟩ **13** : a stage representation of a drama; *also* : a dramatic composition **14** : a function of an electronic device that causes a recording to play — **in play** : in condition or position to be played

♦ [3] dalliance, frolic, fun, relaxation, sport ♦ [7] application, employment, exercise, operation, use

²**play** *vb* **1** : to engage in recreation : FROLIC **2** ♦ : to handle or behave lightly or absentmindedly **3** : to make a pun ⟨∼ on words⟩ **4** ♦ : to take advantage ⟨∼ on fears⟩ **5** : to move or operate in a brisk or irregular manner ⟨a flashlight ∼ed over the

wall⟩ **6 :** to perform music ⟨~ on a violin⟩; *also* **:** to perform (music) on an instrument ⟨~ a waltz⟩ **7 :** to perform music upon ⟨~ the piano⟩; *also* **:** to sound in performance ⟨the organ is ~*ing*⟩ **8 :** to cause to emit sounds ⟨~ a radio⟩; *also* **:** to cause to reproduce recorded material ⟨~ a DVD⟩ **9 a :** to act in a dramatic medium **b ♦ :** to act in the character of ⟨~ the hero⟩ **10 :** GAMBLE **11 a :** to behave in a specified way ⟨~ safe⟩ **b ♦ :** to feign a specified state or quality **c :** COOPERATE ⟨~ along with him⟩ **12 :** to deal with; *also* **:** EMPHASIZE ⟨~ up her good qualities⟩ **13 :** to perform for amusement ⟨~ a trick⟩ **14 :** WREAK **15 :** to contend with in a game; *also* **:** to fill (a certain position) on a team **16 :** to make wagers on ⟨~ the races⟩ **17 :** WIELD, PLY **18 :** to keep in action

♦ [1] dally, disport, frolic, recreate, rollick, sport ♦ [2] fiddle, fool, mess, monkey, potter, putter, trifle ♦ *usu* **play with** [2] fiddle, fool, mess, monkey, tamper, tinker ♦ *usu* **play on** *or* **play upon** [4] abuse, capitalize, cash in, exploit, impose, use ♦ [9b] act, impersonate, perform, portray ♦ [11b] impersonate, masquerade, pose

play•act•ing \'plā-ˌak-tiŋ\ *n* **1 :** performance in theatrical productions **2 :** insincere or artificial behavior
play•back \-ˌbak\ *n* **:** an act of reproducing recorded sound or pictures — **play back** *vb*
play•bill \-ˌbil\ *n* **:** a poster advertising the performance of a play
play•book \-ˌbûk\ *n* **:** a notebook containing diagrammed football plays
play•boy \-ˌbȯi\ *n* **:** a man whose chief interest is the pursuit of pleasure
play•date \-ˌdāt\ *n* **:** a usu. prearranged play session for small children
play•er \'plā-ər\ *n* ♦ **:** one that plays

♦ actor, impersonator, mummer, trouper

play•ful \-fəl\ *adj* ♦ **:** full of play **:** FROLICSOME — **play•ful•ly** *adv*

♦ antic, coltish, elfish, fay, frisky, frolicsome, sportive *Ant* earnest, sober

play•ful•ness \-nəs\ *n* ♦ **:** the quality or state of being playful

♦ friskiness, impishness, mischief, mischievousness *Ant* earnestness, soberness

play•go•er \-ˌgō-ər\ *n* **:** a person who frequently attends plays
play•ground \-ˌgrau̇nd\ *n* **:** an area used for games and play esp. by children
play•house \-ˌhau̇s\ *n* **1 :** THEATER **2 :** a small house for children to play in
playing card *n* **:** any of a set of 24 to 78 cards marked to show its rank and suit and used to play a game of cards
play•let \'plā-lət\ *n* **:** a short play
play•mate \-ˌmāt\ *n* **:** a companion in play
play•off \-ˌȯf\ *n* **:** a contest or series of contests to break a tie or determine a championship
play out *vb* **:** DEVELOP, UNFOLD ⟨see how things *play out*⟩
play•pen \-ˌpen\ *n* **:** a portable enclosure in which a young child may play
play•suit \-ˌsüt\ *n* **:** a sports and play outfit for women and children
play•thing \-ˌthiŋ\ *n* **:** TOY
play up *vb* ♦ **:** to place emphasis on

♦ accent, accentuate, emphasize, feature, highlight, point, stress, underline, underscore

play•wright \-ˌrīt\ *n* **:** a writer of plays
pla•za \'pla-zə, 'plä-\ *n* **1 :** a public square in a city or town **2 :** a shopping center
PLC *abbr, Brit* public limited company
plea \'plē\ *n* **1 :** a defendant's answer in law to a charge or indictment **2 :** something alleged as an excuse **3 ♦ :** an earnest entreaty **:** APPEAL

♦ [2] alibi, defense (*or* defence), excuse, justification, reason ♦ [3] appeal, cry, entreaty, petition, prayer, solicitation, suit, supplication

plead \'plēd\ *vb* **plead•ed** *or* **pled** \'pled\; **plead•ing** **1 :** to argue before a court or authority ⟨~ a case⟩ **2 :** to answer to a charge or indictment ⟨~ guilty⟩ **3 ♦ :** to argue for or against something ⟨~ for acquittal⟩ **4 ♦ :** to appeal earnestly ⟨~s for help⟩ ⟨~s to the judge⟩ **5 :** to offer as a plea (as in defense) ⟨~ed illness⟩

♦ [3] argue, assert, contend, maintain, reason ♦ *usu* **plead for** [4] ask, call, quest, request, seek, solicit, sue ♦ *usu* **plead to** [4] appeal, beg, beseech, entreat, implore, importune, petition, pray, solicit, supplicate

plead•er \'plē-dər\ *n* ♦ **:** one who pleads

♦ solicitor, suitor

pleas•ant \'plez-ᵊnt\ *adj* **1 ♦ :** giving pleasure **:** AGREEABLE ⟨a ~ experience⟩ **2 :** marked by pleasing behavior or appearance ⟨a ~ person⟩

♦ agreeable, congenial, delicious, delightful, felicitous, good, grateful, gratifying, nice, palatable, pleasurable, satisfying *Ant* disagreeable, unpalatable, unpleasant, unwelcome

pleas•ant•ly \-lē\ *adv* ♦ **:** in a pleasant manner

♦ agreeably, delightfully, favorably (*or* favourably), felicitously, nicely, pleasingly, satisfyingly, splendidly, well

pleas•ant•ness \-nəs\ *n* ♦ **:** the quality or state of being pleasant

♦ agreeableness, amenity, amiability, geniality, graciousness, niceness, sweetness

pleas•ant•ry \-ᵊn-trē\ *n, pl* **-ries** ♦ **:** a pleasant and casual act or speech

♦ crack, gag, jest, joke, laugh, quip, sally, waggery, wisecrack, witticism

¹please \'plēz\ *vb* **pleased; pleas•ing** **1 ♦ :** to give pleasure or satisfaction to **2 :** LIKE ⟨do as you ~⟩ **3 :** to be the will or pleasure of ⟨may it ~ his Majesty⟩

♦ content, delight, gladden, gratify, rejoice, satisfy, suit, warm *Ant* displease

²please *adv* — used as a function word to express politeness or emphasis in a request ⟨~ come in⟩
pleased \'plēzd\ *adj* ♦ **:** affected with or manifesting pleasure

♦ content, contented, glad, happy

pleas•ing *adj* **:** giving pleasure ⟨aesthetically ~ decor⟩
pleas•ing•ly \-lē\ *adv* ♦ **:** in a pleasing manner

♦ agreeably, delightfully, favorably (*or* favourably), felicitously, gloriously, nicely, pleasantly, satisfyingly, splendidly, well

plea•sur•able \'ple-zhə-rə-bəl\ *adj* ♦ **:** giving pleasure **:** PLEASANT ⟨a ~ activity⟩ — **plea•sur•ably** \-blē\ *adv*

♦ amusing, delightful, diverting, enjoyable, entertaining, fun, pleasant

plea•sure \'ple-zhər\ *n* **1 :** DESIRE, INCLINATION ⟨await your ~⟩ **2 ♦ :** a state of gratification **3 ♦ :** a source of delight or joy

♦ [2] contentment, delectation, delight, enjoyment, gladness, gratification, relish, satisfaction *Ant* discontent, displeasure, dissatisfaction ♦ [3] delight, diversion, entertainment, fun

¹pleat \'plēt\ *vb* **1 :** FOLD; *esp* **:** to arrange in pleats **2 :** BRAID
²pleat *n* **:** a fold (as in cloth) made by doubling material over on itself
plebe \'plēb\ *n* **:** a freshman at a military or naval academy
¹ple•be•ian \pli-'bē-ən\ *n* **1 :** a member of the Roman plebs **2 ♦ :** one of the common people

♦ *usu* **plebians** commoners, herd, masses, mob, people, populace, rank and file

²plebeian *adj* **1 :** of or relating to plebeians **2 ♦ :** crude or coarse in manner or style **:** COMMON, VULGAR ⟨~ tastes⟩

♦ common, humble, ignoble, inferior, low, lowly, mean, vulgar

pleb•i•scite \'ple-bə-ˌsīt, -sət\ *n* **:** a vote of the people (as of a country) on a proposal submitted to them
plebs \'plebz\ *n, pl* **ple•bes** \'ple-ˌbēz\ **1 :** the general populace **2 :** the common people of ancient Rome
plec•trum \'plek-trəm\ *n, pl* **plec•tra** \-trə\ *or* **plec•trums** **:** ³PICK 3
¹pledge \'plej\ *n* **1 ♦ :** something given as security for the performance of an act **2 :** the state of being held as a security or guaranty **3 :** TOAST 3 **4 ♦ :** a binding promise or agreement to do or forbear **:** VOW

♦ [1] gage, guarantee, guaranty, pawn, security ♦ [4] oath, promise, troth, vow, word

²pledge *vb* **pledged; pledg•ing** **1 :** to deposit as a pledge **2 :** TOAST **3 ♦ :** to bind by a pledge **4 ♦ :** to promise the performance of by a pledge **:** PROMISE

♦ [3] commit, engage, troth ♦ [4] covenant, promise, swear, vow

Pleis•to•cene \'plī-stə-ˌsēn\ *adj* **:** of, relating to, or being the earlier epoch of the Quaternary — **Pleistocene** *n*
ple•na•ry \'plē-nə-rē, 'ple-\ *adj* **1 ♦ :** complete in every respect **:** FULL ⟨~ power⟩ **2 :** including all entitled to attend ⟨~ session⟩

♦ complete, comprehensive, entire, full, grand, intact, integral, perfect, total, whole

pleni·po·ten·tia·ry \ˌple-nə-pə-'ten-chə-rē, -'ten-chē-ˌer-ē\ n, pl **-ries** : a diplomatic agent having full authority — **plenipotentiary** adj

plen·i·tude \'ple-nə-ˌtüd, -ˌtyüd\ n 1 : COMPLETENESS 2 : a great sufficiency : ABUNDANCE

plen·te·ous \'plen-tē-əs\ adj 1 : FRUITFUL 2 : existing in plenty

plen·ti·ful \'plen-ti-fəl\ adj 1 : containing or yielding plenty 2 ♦ : characterized by, constituting, or existing in plenty : ABUNDANT ⟨a ∼ harvest⟩ — **plen·ti·ful·ly** adv

♦ abundant, ample, bountiful, comfortable, generous, liberal Ant bare, minimal, scant

plen·ty \'plen-tē\ n ♦ : a more than adequate number or amount

♦ abundance, superabundance, wealth Ant deficiency, inadequacy, insufficiency ♦ abundance, deal, gobs, heap, loads, lot, pile, quantity

ple·num \'ple-nəm, 'plē-\ n, pl **-nums** or **-na** \-nə\ : a general assembly of all members esp. of a legislative body

pleth·o·ra \'ple-thə-rə\ n : an excessive quantity or fullness; also : PROFUSION

pleu·ri·sy \'plu̇r-ə-sē\ n : inflammation of the membrane that lines the chest and covers the lungs

plex·i·glass \'plek-si-ˌglas\ n : a transparent acrylic plastic often used in place of glass

plex·us \'plek-səs\ n, pl **plex·us·es** \-sə-səz\ : an interlacing network esp. of blood vessels or nerves

pli·able \'plī-ə-bəl\ adj 1 ♦ : supple enough to bend freely or repeatedly without breaking : FLEXIBLE 2 : yielding easily to others ⟨a ∼ child⟩ — **pli·abil·i·ty** \ˌplī-ə-'bi-lə-tē\ n

♦ flexible, limber, lissome, lithe, supple, willowy

pli·ant \'plī-ənt\ adj 1 : supple enough to bend freely or repeatedly without breaking : FLEXIBLE 2 : easily influenced ⟨a ∼ senator⟩ — **pli·an·cy** \-ən-sē\ n

pli·ers \'plī-ərz\ n pl : small pincers for bending or cutting wire or handling small objects

¹**plight** \'plīt\ vb : to put or give in pledge : ENGAGE

²**plight** n : an unfortunate, difficult, or precarious situation

plinth \'plinth\ n : the lowest part of the base of an architectural column

Plio·cene \'plī-ə-ˌsēn\ adj : of, relating to, or being the latest epoch of the Tertiary — **Pliocene** n

PLO abbr Palestine Liberation Organization

plod \'pläd\ vb **plod·ded; plod·ding** 1 ♦ : to walk heavily or slowly 2 ♦ : to work laboriously and monotonously : DRUDGE — **plod·der** n — **plod·ding·ly** adv

♦ [1] flounder, limp, lumber, stumble ♦ [2] drudge, endeavor (or endeavour), fag, grub, hustle, labor (or labour), peg, plug, slog, strain, strive, struggle, sweat, toil, work

plonk var of PLUNK

plop \'pläp\ vb **plopped; plop·ping** 1 : to fall or move with a sound like that of something dropping into water 2 ♦ : to set, drop, or throw heavily — **plop** n

♦ flop, plump, plunk

¹**plot** \'plät\ n 1 ♦ : a small area of ground 2 : a detailed diagram of the ground floor of a building 3 : the main story (as of a book or movie) 4 ♦ : a secret scheme : INTRIGUE

♦ [1] lot, parcel, plat, property, tract ♦ [4] conspiracy, design, intrigue, machination, scheme

²**plot** vb **plot·ted; plot·ting** 1 : to make a plot or plan of 2 : to mark on or as if on a chart 3 ♦ : to plan or contrive esp. secretly — **plot·ter** n

♦ conspire, contrive, intrigue, machinate, scheme

plo·ver \'plə-vər, 'plō-\ n, pl **plover** or **plovers** : any of a family of shorebirds that differ from the sandpipers in having shorter stouter bills

¹**plow** or chiefly Can and Brit **plough** \'plau̇\ n 1 : an implement used to cut, lift, turn over, and partly break up soil 2 : a device (as a snowplow) operating like a plow

²**plow** or chiefly Can and Brit **plough** vb 1 : to open, break up, or work with a plow 2 : to move through like a plow ⟨a ship ∼ing the waves⟩ 3 : to proceed laboriously ⟨∼ed through the work⟩ — **plow·able** adj — **plow·er** n

plow·boy or chiefly Can and Brit **plough·boy** \'plau̇-ˌbȯi\ n : a boy who leads the horse drawing a plow

plow·man or chiefly Can and Brit **plough·man** \-mən, -ˌman\ n 1 : a man who guides a plow 2 : a farm laborer

plow·share or chiefly Can and Brit **plough·share** \-ˌsher\ n : a part of a plow that cuts the earth

ploy \'plȯi\ n ♦ : a tactic intended to embarrass or frustrate an opponent

♦ artifice, device, dodge, gimmick, jig, scheme, sleight, stratagem, trick, wile

¹**pluck** \'plək\ vb 1 : to pull off or out : PICK; also : to pull something from 2 : to play (an instrument) by pulling the strings 3 : TUG, TWITCH

²**pluck** n 1 ♦ : an act or instance of plucking 2 ♦ : courageous readiness to fight or continue against odds : SPIRIT, COURAGE

♦ [1] draw, haul, jerk, pull, tug, wrench ♦ [2] backbone, courage, fiber (or fibre), fortitude, grit, guts, spirit, spunk

plucky \'plə-kē\ adj **pluck·i·er; -est** : COURAGEOUS, SPIRITED

¹**plug** \'pləg\ n 1 : STOPPER; also : an obstructing mass 2 : a cake of tobacco 3 : a poor or worn-out horse 4 : SPARK PLUG 5 : a lure with several hooks used in fishing 6 : a device on the end of a cord for making an electrical connection 7 : a piece of favorable publicity

²**plug** vb **plugged; plug·ging** 1 ♦ : to stop, make tight, or secure by inserting a plug 2 : to hit with a bullet : HIT, SHOOT 3 ♦ : to publicize insistently 4 ♦ : to work doggedly and persistently : PLOD, DRUDGE — often used with away

♦ [1] block, dam, fill, pack, stop, stuff ♦ usu **plug up** [1] block, choke, clog, close (off), congest, dam, jam, obstruct, stop (up), stuff ♦ [3] ballyhoo, boast, promote, publicize, tout ♦ often **plug away** [4] drudge, endeavor (or endeavour), fag, grub, hustle, labor (or labour), peg, plod, slog, strain, strive, struggle, sweat, toil, work

plug and play n : a computer feature enabling the operating system to automatically detect and configure peripherals — **plug–and–play** adj

plugged–in \'pləgd-'in\ adj : technologically or socially informed and connected

plug–in \'pləg-ˌin\ n : a small piece of software that supplements a larger program

plum \'pləm\ n 1 : a smooth-skinned juicy fruit borne by trees related to the peach and cherry; also : a tree bearing plums 2 : a raisin when used in desserts (as puddings) 3 ♦ : something excellent; esp : something desirable given in return for a favor

♦ catch, gem, jewel, pearl, prize, treasure

plum·age \'plü-mij\ n : the feathers of a bird — **plum·aged** \-mijd\ adj

¹**plumb** \'pləm\ n : a weight on the end of a line (**plumb line**) used esp. by builders to show vertical direction

²**plumb** adv 1 : straight down or up : VERTICALLY 2 : COMPLETELY ⟨∼ tired out⟩ 3 : EXACTLY; also : IMMEDIATELY

³**plumb** vb : to sound, adjust, or test with a plumb ⟨∼ the depth of a well⟩

⁴**plumb** adj 1 : exactly vertical or true : VERTICAL 2 : COMPLETE

plumb·er \'plə-mər\ n : a worker who fits or repairs pipes and fixtures

plumb·ing \'plə-min\ n : a system of pipes in a building for supplying and carrying off water

¹**plume** \'plüm\ n 1 : FEATHER; esp : a large, conspicuous, or showy feather 2 : a token of honor or prowess — **plumed** \'plümd\ adj — **plumy** \'plü-mē\ adj

♦ award, decoration, distinction, honor (or honour), prize

²**plume** vb **plumed; plum·ing** 1 : to provide or deck with feathers 2 ♦ : to indulge (oneself) in pride

♦ boast, brag, crow, swagger

¹**plum·met** \'plə-mət\ n : PLUMB; also : PLUMB LINE

²**plummet** vb ♦ : to drop or plunge straight down

♦ decline, descend, dip, drop, fall, lower, plunge, sink, tumble

¹**plump** \'pləmp\ vb 1 ♦ : to drop or fall suddenly or heavily 2 : to favor something strongly ⟨∼ing for change⟩

♦ flop, plop, plunk

²**plump** n : a sudden heavy fall or blow; also : the sound made by it

³**plump** adv 1 : straight down; also : straight ahead 2 : UNQUALIFIEDLY

⁴**plump** adj ♦ : having a full rounded usu. pleasing form

♦ chubby, fat, fleshy, full, overweight, portly, rotund, round

plump·ness \-nəs\ n ♦ : the quality or state of being plump

♦ corpulence, fatness, obesity

¹plun·der \'plən-dər\ vb ♦ : to take the goods of by force or wrongfully : PILLAGE — **plun·der·er** n

♦ despoil, loot, maraud, pillage, ransack, sack, strip

²plunder n ♦ : something taken by force or theft : LOOT

♦ booty, loot, spoil, swag

¹plunge \'plənj\ vb **plunged; plung·ing** 1 : IMMERSE, SUBMERGE 2 : to enter or cause to enter a state or course of action suddenly or violently ⟨~ into war⟩ 3 ♦ : to cast oneself into or as if into water 4 : to gamble heavily and recklessly 5 ♦ : to descend suddenly

♦ [3] dive, pitch, sound ♦ [5] decline, descend, dip, drop, fall, lower, plummet, sink, tumble

²plunge n ♦ : a sudden dive, leap, or rush

♦ descent, dip, dive, down, drop, fall

plung·er \'plən-jər\ n 1 : one that plunges 2 : a sliding piece driven by or against fluid pressure : PISTON 3 : a rubber cup on a handle pushed against an opening to free a waste outlet of an obstruction

plunk \'pləŋk\ vb 1 : to make or cause to make a hollow metallic sound 2 ♦ : to drop heavily or suddenly — **plunk** n

♦ flop, plop, plump

plu·per·fect \(ˌ)plü-'pər-fikt\ adj : of, relating to, or constituting a verb tense that denotes an action or state as completed at or before a past time spoken of — **pluperfect** n

plu·ral \'plu̇r-əl\ adj : of, relating to, or constituting a word form used to denote more than one — **pl.** n

plu·ral·i·ty \plu̇-'ra-lə-tē\ n, pl **-ties** 1 : the state of being plural 2 : an excess of votes over those cast for an opposing candidate 3 : the greatest number of votes cast when not a majority

plu·ral·ize \'plu̇r-ə-ˌlīz\ vb **-ized; -iz·ing** : to make plural or express in the plural form — **plu·ral·i·za·tion** \ˌplu̇r-ə-lə-'zā-shən\ n

¹plus \'pləs\ adj 1 : mathematically positive 2 : having or being in addition to what is anticipated 3 : falling high in a specified range ⟨a grade of B ~⟩

²plus n, pl **plus·es** \'plə-səz\ also **plus·ses** 1 : a sign + (**plus sign**) used in mathematics to indicate addition or a positive quantity 2 ♦ : an added quantity; also : a positive quality 3 : SURPLUS

♦ accretion, addition, augmentation, boost, expansion, gain, increase, increment, proliferation, raise, rise, supplement

³plus prep 1 : increased by : with the addition of ⟨3 ~ 4⟩ 2 : BESIDES

⁴plus conj : AND ⟨soup ~ salad and bread⟩

¹plush \'pləsh\ n : a fabric with a pile longer and less dense than velvet pile — **plushy** adj

²plush adj ♦ : notably luxurious ⟨a ~ hotel suite⟩ — **plush·ly** adv — **plush·ness** n

♦ deluxe, lavish, luxuriant, luxurious, opulent, palatial, sumptuous

plus/minus sign n : the sign ± used to indicate a quantity taking on both a positive value and its negative or to indicate a plus or minus quantity

plus or minus adj : indicating a quantity whose positive and negative values bracket a range of values ⟨plus or minus 3 inches⟩

plus–size \'pləs-ˌsīz\ also **plus–sized** \-ˌsīzd\ adj : extra large ⟨~ clothing⟩ ⟨~ shoppers⟩

Plu·to \'plü-tō\ n : a dwarf planet whose orbit crosses the orbit of Neptune

plu·toc·ra·cy \plü-'tä-krə-sē\ n, pl **-cies** 1 : government by the wealthy 2 : a controlling class of the wealthy — **plu·to·crat** \'plü-tə-ˌkrat\ n — **plu·to·crat·ic** \ˌplü-tə-'kra-tik\ adj

plu·to·ni·um \plü-'tō-nē-əm\ n : a radioactive chemical element formed by the decay of neptunium

plu·vi·al \'plü-vē-əl\ adj 1 : of or relating to rain 2 : characterized by abundant rain

¹ply \'plī\ vb **plied; ply·ing** 1 : to use, practice, or work diligently ⟨~ a trade⟩ 2 : to keep supplying something to ⟨plied them with liquor⟩ 3 : to go or travel regularly esp. by sea

²ply n, pl **plies** : one of the folds, thicknesses, or strands of which something (as plywood or yarn) is made

³ply vb **plied; ply·ing** : to twist together ⟨~ yarns⟩

ply·wood \'plī-ˌwu̇d\ n : material made of thin sheets of wood glued and pressed together

pm abbr premium

Pm symbol promethium

PM abbr 1 paymaster 2 police magistrate 3 postmaster 4 post

meridiem — often not cap. and often punctuated 5 postmortem 6 prime minister 7 provost marshal

pmk abbr postmark

PMS \ˌpē-ˌem-'es\ n : PREMENSTRUAL SYNDROME

pmt abbr payment

pneu·mat·ic \nu̇-'ma-tik, nyu̇-\ adj 1 : of, relating to, or using air or wind 2 : moved by air pressure 3 : filled with compressed air — **pneu·mat·i·cal·ly** \-ti-k(ə-)lē\ adv

pneu·mo·coc·cus \ˌnü-mə-'kä-kəs, ˌnyü-\ n, pl **-coc·ci** \-'käk-ˌsī, -ˌsē; -'kä-ˌkī, -ˌkē\ : a bacterium that causes pneumonia — **pneu·mo·coc·cal** \-'kä-kəl\ adj

pneu·mo·co·ni·o·sis \ˌnü-mō-ˌkō-nē-'ō-səs, ˌnyü-\ n : a disease of the lungs caused by habitual inhalation of irritant mineral or metallic particles

pneu·mo·nia \nu̇-'mō-nyə, nyu̇-\ n : an inflammatory disease of the lungs

Po symbol polonium

PO abbr 1 petty officer 2 post office

¹poach \'pōch\ vb : to cook (as an egg or fish) in simmering liquid

²poach vb : to hunt or fish unlawfully — **poach·er** n

POB abbr post office box

po·bla·no \pō-'blä-nō\ n, pl **-nos** : a heart-shaped usu. mild chili pepper esp. when fresh and dark green

po'boy var of POOR BOY

pock \'päk\ n : a small swelling on the skin (as in smallpox); also : a spot suggesting this

¹pock·et \'pä-kət\ n 1 : a small bag open at the top or side inserted in a garment 2 ♦ : supply of money 3 : RECEPTACLE, CONTAINER 4 : a small isolated area or group 5 : a small body of ore — **pock·et·ful** n

♦ finances, funds, resources, wherewithal

²pocket vb 1 : to put in or as if in a pocket 2 ♦ : to take or appropriate without right or leave and with intent to keep or make use of wrongfully : STEAL 3 ♦ : to set aside : SUPPRESS

♦ [2] appropriate, filch, hook, misappropriate, nip, pilfer, purloin, snitch, steal, swipe, thieve ♦ [3] choke, repress, smother, stifle, strangle, suppress, swallow

³pocket adj 1 a : small enough to fit in a pocket b ♦ : having comparatively little size or slight dimensions : SMALL 2 : carried in or paid from one's own pocket

♦ dwarf, dwarfish, fine, little, pygmy, slight, small, undersized

¹pock·et·book \-ˌbu̇k\ n 1 ♦ : a receptacle for carrying money and often other small objects 2 : financial resources

♦ bag, handbag, purse

²pocketbook adj : relating to money

pocket gopher n : GOPHER 2

pock·et·knife \'pä-kət-ˌnīf\ n : a knife with a folding blade to be carried in the pocket

pocket veto n : an indirect veto of a legislative bill by an executive through retention of the bill unsigned until after adjournment of the legislature

pock·mark \'päk-ˌmärk\ n ♦ : a pit or scar caused by smallpox or acne; also : an imperfection or depression like a pockmark — **pock·marked** \-ˌmärkt\ adj

♦ blemish, defect, deformity, disfigurement, fault, flaw, imperfection, mark, scar

po·co \'pō-kō, 'pȯ-\ adv : SOMEWHAT — used to qualify a direction in music ⟨~ allegro⟩

po·co a po·co \ˌpō-kō-ä-'pō-kō, ˌpȯ-kō-ä-'pȯ-\ adv : little by little : GRADUALLY — used as a direction in music

pod \'päd\ n 1 ♦ : a dry fruit (as of a pea) that splits open when ripe 2 ♦ : an external streamlined compartment (as for a jet engine) on an airplane 3 ♦ : a compartment (as for personnel, a power unit, or an instrument) on a ship or craft

♦ [1, 2, 3] armor, capsule, case, casing, cocoon, cover, housing, husk, jacket, sheath, shell

POD abbr pay on delivery

pod·cast \'päd-ˌkast\ n : a program made available in digital format for download over the Internet — **podcast** vb — **pod·cast·er** n

po·di·a·try \pə-'dī-ə-trē, pō-\ n : the medical care and treatment of the human foot — **po·di·a·trist** \pə-'dī-ə-trist, pō-\ n

po·di·um \'pō-dē-əm\ n, pl **podiums** or **po·dia** \-dē-ə\ 1 ♦ : a dais esp. for an orchestral conductor 2 : LECTERN

♦ dais, platform, rostrum, stage, stand

POE abbr port of entry

po·em \'pō-əm\ n ♦ : a composition in verse

♦ lyric, song, verse

po·esy \'pō-ə-zē\ *n* : POETRY
po·et \'pō-ət\ *n* ♦ : a writer of poetry; *also* : a creative artist of great sensitivity

♦ bard, minstrel, versifier

po·et·as·ter \'pō-ə-ˌtas-tər\ *n* : an inferior poet
po·et·ess \'pō-ə-təs\ *n* : a girl or woman who is a poet
po·et·ic \pō-'e-tik\ *or* **po·et·i·cal** \-ti-kəl\ *adj* ♦ : having or expressing the qualities of poetry

♦ bardic, lyric, lyrical *Ant* prosaic, prose, unpoetic

poetic justice *n* : an outcome in which vice is punished and virtue rewarded usu. in a manner peculiarly or ironically appropriate
po·et·ry \'pō-ə-trē\ *n* **1** : metrical writing **2** : POEMS **3** ♦ : writing that formulates a concentrated imaginative awareness of experience in language chosen and arranged to create a specific emotional response through meaning, sound, and rhythm

♦ song, verse *Ant* prose

po·grom \'pō-grəm, pō-'gräm\ *n* : an organized massacre of helpless people and esp. of Jews
poi \'pȯi\ *n, pl* **poi** *or* **pois** : food prepared from the cooked corms of taro that are mashed with water to the consistency of a paste or thick liquid
poi·gnan·cy \'pȯi-nyən-sē\ *n* : the quality or state of being poignant
poi·gnant \'pȯi-nyənt\ *adj* **1** ♦ : painfully affecting the feelings ⟨∼ grief⟩ **2** ♦ : deeply moving ⟨∼ scene⟩

♦ [1, 2] affecting, emotional, impressive, moving, stirring, touching

poin·ci·ana \ˌpȯin-sē-'a-nə\ *n* : any of several ornamental tropical leguminous trees or shrubs with bright orange or red flowers
poin·set·tia \pȯin-'se-tē-ə\ *n* : a showy tropical American spurge with usu. scarlet bracts that suggest petals and surround small yellow flowers
¹point \'pȯint\ *n* **1** ♦ : an individual detail : ITEM; *also* : the most important essential **2** : PURPOSE **3** : a geometric element that has position but no size **4** ♦ : a particular place : LOCALITY **5** ♦ : a particular stage or degree **6** ♦ : a sharp end : TIP **7** ♦ : a projecting piece of land **8** : a punctuation mark; *esp* : PERIOD **9** : DECIMAL POINT **10** : one of the divisions of the compass **11** : a unit of counting (as in a game score) **12** : a very small mark **13** ♦ : a distinguishing detail **14** : the quality of something spoken or written of being able to arouse interest and of being generally effective — **pointy** \'pȯin-tē\ *adj* — **beside the point** : IRRELEVANT — **to the point** : RELEVANT, PERTINENT

♦ [1] detail, fact, item, particular ♦ [4] locale, location, place, position, site, spot ♦ [5] cut, degree, grade, inch, notch, peg, phase, stage, step ♦ [6] apex, cusp, end, pike, tip ♦ [7] arm, cape, headland, peninsula, promontory, spit ♦ [13] attribute, character, characteristic, feature, mark, peculiarity, property, quality, trait

²point *vb* **1** : to furnish with a point : SHARPEN **2** : PUNCTUATE **3** : to separate (a decimal fraction) from an integer by a decimal point — usu. used with *off* **4** : to indicate the position of esp. by extending a finger **5** ♦ : to direct attention to ⟨∼ out an error⟩ — usu. used with *out* or *up* **6** : AIM, DIRECT **7** ♦ : to lie extended, aimed, or turned in a particular direction : FACE, LOOK

♦ *usu* **point up** [5] accent, accentuate, emphasize, feature, highlight, play, stress, underline, underscore ♦ *usu* **point toward** [7] face, front, look

point–and–click *adj* : relating to or being a computer interface that allows the activation of a file by selection with a pointing device (as a mouse)
point–and–shoot *adj* : having or using preset or automatically adjusted controls ⟨a ∼ camera⟩
point–blank \'pȯint-'blaŋk\ *adj* **1** : so close to the target that a missile fired will travel in a straight line to the mark **2** : DIRECT, BLUNT — **point–blank** *adv*
point·ed \'pȯin-təd\ *adj* **1** ♦ : having a point **2** ♦ : being to the point : PERTINENT **3** : aimed at a particular person or group; *also* : CONSPICUOUS, MARKED — **point·ed·ly** *adv*

♦ [1] peaked, sharp *Ant* blunt ♦ [2] applicable, apposite, apropos, germane, material, pertinent, relative, relevant

point·er \'pȯin-tər\ *n* **1** ♦ : one that points out : INDICATOR **2** : a large short-haired hunting dog **3** ♦ : a useful suggestion or hint : TIP

♦ [1] hand, index, indicator, needle ♦ [3] hint, lead, tip

poin·til·lism \'pwan-tē-ˌyi-zəm, 'pȯint-ᵊl-ˌi-zəm\ *n* : the theory or practice in painting of applying small strokes or dots of color

to a surface so that from a distance they blend together — **poin·til·list** \ˌpwan-tē-'yēst, 'pȯint-ᵊl-ist\ *n or adj*
point·less \-ləs\ *adj* ♦ : devoid of meaning

♦ empty, meaningless, senseless

point man *n* : a principal spokesman or advocate
point of no return : a critical point at which turning back or reversal is not possible
point of view *n* ♦ : a position or perspective from which something is considered or evaluated

♦ angle, outlook, perspective, slant, standpoint, viewpoint

point spread *n* : the number of points by which a favorite is expected to defeat an underdog
¹poise \'pȯiz\ *n* **1** ♦ : a stably balanced state **2** : self-possessed calmness; *also* : a particular way of carrying oneself

♦ balance, equilibrium, equipoise

²poise *vb* **poised; pois·ing 1** : BALANCE **2** ♦ : to remain suspended over a place or object

♦ drift, float, glide, hang, hover, ride, sail, waft

poi·sha \'pȯi-shə\ *n, pl* **poisha** : the paisa of Bangladesh
¹poi·son \'pȯiz-ᵊn\ *n* ♦ : a substance that through its chemical action can injure or kill — **poison** *adj*

♦ bane, toxin, venom

²poison *vb* **1** : to injure or kill with poison **2** ♦ : to treat or taint with poison **3** ♦ : to affect destructively ⟨∼ed her mind⟩ — **poi·son·er** *n*

♦ [2] befoul, contaminate, defile, foul, pollute, taint ♦ [3] blemish, mar, spoil, stain, taint, tarnish, touch, vitiate

poison hemlock *n* : a large branching poisonous herb with finely divided leaves and white flowers that is related to the carrot
poison ivy *n* **1** : a usu. climbing plant related to the sumacs that has leaves composed of three shiny leaflets and produces an irritating oil causing a usu. intensely itching skin rash; *also* : any of several related plants **2** : a skin rash caused by poison ivy
poison oak *n* : any of several shrubby plants closely related to poison ivy and having similar properties
poi·son·ous \'pȯiz-ᵊn-əs\ *adj* ♦ : having the properties or effects of poison

♦ poison, venomous *Ant* nonpoisonous, nontoxic, nonvenomous

poison sumac *n* : a No. American swamp shrub with pinnate leaves, greenish flowers, greenish white berries, and irritating properties
¹poke \'pōk\ *n, chiefly Southern & Midland* : BAG, SACK
²poke *vb* **poked; pok·ing 1** : PROD; *also* : to stir up by prodding **2** : to make a prodding or jabbing movement esp. repeatedly **3** : HIT, PUNCH **4** ♦ : to thrust forward obtrusively **5** : RUMMAGE **6** ♦ : to interest oneself in what is not one's concern : MEDDLE, PRY **7** ♦ : to move or act slowly or aimlessly : DAWDLE ⟨*poking* along toward home⟩ — **poke fun at** : RIDICULE, MOCK

♦ [4] bag, balloon, beetle, belly, billow, bulge, overhang, project, protrude, start, stick out ♦ [6] butt in, interfere, intrude, meddle, mess, nose, obtrude, pry, snoop ♦ [7] crawl, creep, dally, dawdle, delay, dillydally, drag, lag, linger, loiter, tarry

³poke *n* ♦ : a quick thrust; *also* : PUNCH

♦ dab, dig, jab

¹pok·er \'pō-kər\ *n* : a metal rod for stirring a fire
²po·ker \'pō-kər\ *n* : any of several card games in which the player with the highest hand at the end of the betting wins
poker face *n* : a face that does not reveal a person's thoughts or feelings
poke·weed \'pōk-ˌwēd\ *n* : a coarse American perennial herb with clusters of white flowers and dark purple juicy berries
poky *or* **pok·ey** \'pō-kē\ *adj* **pok·i·er; -est 1** : small and cramped **2** : SHABBY, DULL **3** ♦ : annoyingly slow

♦ creeping, dilatory, laggard, languid, slow, sluggish, tardy

pol \'päl\ *n* : POLITICIAN
po·lar \'pō-lər\ *adj* **1 a** : of or relating to a geographic pole **b** ♦ : coming from or having the characteristics (as cold) of such a region **2** : of or relating to a pole (as of a magnet) **3** ♦ : diametrically opposite

♦ [1b] arctic, bitter, chill, chilly, cold, cool, freezing, frigid, frosty, glacial, icy, nippy, raw, snappy, wintry ♦ [3] antipodal, antithetical, contradictory, contrary, diametric, opposite

polar bear *n* : a large creamy-white bear that inhabits arctic regions

Po·lar·is \pə-'lar-əs\ n : NORTH STAR

po·lar·ise chiefly Brit var of POLARIZE

po·lar·i·ty \pō-'lar-ə-tē\ n, pl **-ties** : the condition of having poles and esp. magnetic or electrical poles

po·lar·i·za·tion \ˌpō-lə-rə-'zā-shən\ n **1** : the action of polarizing : the state of being polarized **2** : concentration about opposing extremes

po·lar·ize \'pō-lə-ˌrīz\ vb **-ized; -iz·ing 1** : to cause (light waves) to vibrate in a definite way **2** : to give physical polarity to **3** : to break up into opposing groups

pol·der \'pōl-dər, 'päl-\ n : a tract of low land reclaimed from the sea

¹**pole** \'pōl\ n : a long slender piece of wood or metal ⟨telephone ∼⟩

²**pole** vb **poled; pol·ing** : to impel or push with a pole

³**pole** n **1** : either end of an axis esp. of the earth **2** : either of the terminals of an electric device (as a battery or generator) **3** : one of two or more regions in a magnetized body at which the magnetism is concentrated — **pole·ward** \'pōl-wərd\ adj or adv

Pole \'pōl\ n : a native or inhabitant of Poland

¹**pole·ax** \'pō-ˌlaks\ n : a battle-ax with a short handle

²**poleax** vb : to attack or fell with or as if with a poleax

pole·cat \'pōl-ˌkat\ n, pl **polecats** or **polecat 1** : a European carnivorous mammal of which the ferret is considered a domesticated variety **2** : SKUNK

po·lem·ic \pə-'le-mik\ n : the art or practice of disputation — usu. used in pl. — **po·lem·i·cal** \-mi-kəl\ also **po·lem·ic** \-mik\ adj — **po·lem·i·cist** \-sist\ n

pole·star \'pōl-ˌstär\ n **1** : NORTH STAR **2** : a directing principle : GUIDE

pole vault n : a field contest in which each contestant uses a pole to vault for height over a crossbar — **pole–vault** vb — **pole–vault·er** n

¹**po·lice** \pə-'lēs\ vb **po·liced; po·lic·ing 1** : to control, regulate, or keep in order esp. by use of police ⟨∼ a highway⟩ **2** : to make clean and put in order

²**police** n, pl **police 1** : the department of government that keeps public order and safety and enforces the laws; also : the members of this department **2** : a private organization resembling a police force; also : its members **3** : military personnel detailed to clean and put in order

po·lice·man \-mən\ n : a member of a police force : POLICE OFFICER

police officer n ♦ : a member of a police force

♦ constable, cop, officer

police state n : a state characterized by repressive, arbitrary, totalitarian rule by means of secret police

po·lice·wom·an \pə-'lēs-ˌwu̇-mən\ n : a woman who is a police officer

¹**pol·i·cy** \'pä-lə-sē\ n, pl **-cies** ♦ : a definite course or method of action selected to guide and determine present and future decisions

♦ course, line, procedure, program

²**policy** n, pl **-cies** : a writing whereby a contract of insurance is made

pol·i·cy·hold·er \'pä-lə-sē-ˌhōl-dər\ n : one granted an insurance policy

po·lio \'pō-lē-ˌō\ n : POLIOMYELITIS — **polio** adj

po·lio·my·eli·tis \-ˌmī-ə-'lī-təs\ n : an acute virus disease marked by inflammation of the gray matter of the spinal cord leading usu. to paralysis

¹**pol·ish** \'pä-lish\ vb **1** ♦ : to make smooth and glossy usu. by rubbing **2** : to refine or improve in manners, condition, or style

♦ buff, burnish, dress, gloss, grind, rub, shine, smooth

²**polish** n **1** ♦ : a smooth glossy surface appearance or finish **2** ♦ : enlightenment and excellence of taste acquired by intellectual and aesthetic training : CULTURE **3** : the action or process of polishing **4** : a preparation used to produce a gloss

♦ [1] gloss, luster (or lustre), sheen, shine ♦ [2] civilization, cultivation, culture, refinement

Pol·ish \'pō-lish\ n : the Slavic language of the Poles — **Polish** adj

polished \'pä-lisht\ adj **1** ♦ : having a smooth and glossy surface produced by or as if by polishing **2** ♦ : characterized by elegance and refinement

♦ [1] glossy, lustrous, satiny, sleek ♦ [2] civilized, cultivated, cultured, genteel, refined

polit abbr political; politician

po·lit·bu·ro \'pä-lət-ˌbyu̇r-ō, 'pō-, pə-'lit-\ n : the principal policy-making committee of a Communist party

po·lite \pə-'līt\ adj **po·lit·er; -est 1** ♦ : of, relating to, or having the characteristics of advanced culture ⟨∼ society⟩ **2** ♦ : marked by correct social conduct : COURTEOUS; also : CONSIDERATE, TACTFUL — **po·lite·ly** adv

♦ [1] correct, decent, decorous, genteel, nice, proper, respectable, seemly ♦ [2] civil, considerate, courteous, genteel, gracious, mannerly, well-bred **Ant** discourteous, impolite, inconsiderate, rude, ungracious, unmannerly

po·lite·ness \-nəs\ n ♦ : the quality or state of being polite

♦ civility, courtesy, gentility, graciousness, mannerliness **Ant** discourtesy, incivility, rudeness

po·li·tesse \ˌpä-li-'tes\ n : formal politeness

pol·i·tic \'pä-lə-ˌtik\ adj **1** : wise in promoting a policy ⟨a ∼ statesman⟩ **2** : shrewdly tactful ⟨a ∼ move⟩ **3** ♦ : suitable to the situation or circumstances

♦ advisable, desirable, expedient, judicious, prudent, tactical, wise

po·lit·i·cal \pə-'li-ti-kəl\ adj **1** : of or relating to government or politics **2** : involving or charged or concerned with acts against a government or a political system ⟨∼ prisoners⟩ — **po·lit·i·cal·ly** \-k(ə-)lē\ adv

politically correct adj : conforming to a belief that language and practices which could offend sensibilities (as in matters of sex or race) should be eliminated

pol·i·ti·cian \ˌpä-lə-'ti-shən\ n : a person actively engaged in government or politics

pol·i·tick \'pä-lə-ˌtik\ vb : to engage in political discussion or activity

po·lit·i·co \pə-'li-ti-ˌkō\ n, pl **-cos** also **-coes** : POLITICIAN

pol·i·tics \'pä-lə-ˌtiks\ n sing or pl **1** : the art or science of government, of guiding or influencing governmental policy, or of winning and holding control over a government **2** : political affairs or business; esp : competition between groups or individuals for power and leadership **3** : political opinions

pol·i·ty \'pä-lə-tē\ n, pl **-ties** : a politically organized unit; also : the form or constitution of such a unit

pol·ka \'pōl-kə, 'pō-kə\ n : a lively couple dance of Bohemian origin; also : music for this dance — **polka** vb

pol·ka dot \'pō-kə-ˌdät\ n : a dot in a pattern of regularly distributed dots — **polka–dot** or **polka–dot·ted** \-ˌdä-təd\ adj

¹**poll** \'pōl\ n **1** ♦ : a person's head; also : the total vote cast **3** : the place where votes are cast — usu. used in pl. **4** : a questioning of persons to obtain information or opinions to be analyzed

♦ head, noggin, pate

²**poll** vb **1** : to cut off or shorten a growth or part of : CLIP, SHEAR **2** : to receive and record the votes of **3** : to receive (as votes) in an election **4** ♦ : to question in a poll

♦ canvass, solicit, survey

pol·lack or **pol·lock** \'pä-lək\ n, pl **pollack** or **pollock** : an important No. Atlantic food fish that is related to the cods; also : a related food fish of the No. Pacific

pol·len \'pä-lən\ n : a mass of male spores of a seed plant usu. appearing as a yellow dust

pol·li·na·tion \ˌpä-lə-'nā-shən\ n : the carrying of pollen to the female part of a plant to fertilize the seed — **pol·li·nate** \'pä-lə-ˌnāt\ vb — **pol·li·na·tor** \-ˌnā-tər\ n

poll·ster \'pōl-stər\ n : one that conducts a poll or compiles data obtained by a poll

poll tax n : a tax of a fixed amount per person levied on adults and often linked to the right to vote

pol·lut·ant \pə-'lüt-ᵊnt\ n ♦ : something that pollutes

♦ adulterant, contaminant, defilement, impurity

pol·lute \pə-'lüt\ vb **pol·lut·ed; pol·lut·ing** ♦ : to make impure; esp : to contaminate (an environment) esp. with man-made waste — **pol·lut·er** n — **pol·lu·tion** \-'lü-shən\ n

♦ befoul, contaminate, defile, foul, poison, taint

polluted adj ♦ : made unclean or impure

♦ dilute, impure

pol·ly·wog or **pol·li·wog** \'pä-lē-ˌwäg\ n : TADPOLE

po·lo \'pō-lō\ n : a game played by two teams on horseback using long-handled mallets to drive a wooden ball

po·lo·ni·um \pə-'lō-nē-əm\ n : a radioactive metallic chemical element

pol·ter·geist \'pōl-tər-ˌgīst\ *n* ♦ : a noisy usu. mischievous ghost held to be responsible for unexplained noises

♦ apparition, bogey, ghost, phantasm, phantom, shade, shadow, specter, spirit, spook, vision, wraith

pol·troon \päl-'trün\ *n* ♦ : a spiritless coward

♦ chicken, coward, craven, dastard, recreant, sissy

poly- *comb form* **1** : many : several ⟨*poly*syllabic⟩ **2** : polymeric ⟨*poly*ester⟩

poly·chlo·ri·nat·ed bi·phe·nyl \ˌpä-li-'klōr-ə-ˌnā-təd-ˌbī-'fen-ᵊl, -'fēn-\ *n* : any of several industrial compounds that are toxic environmental pollutants

poly·clin·ic \ˌpä-li-'kli-nik\ *n* : a clinic or hospital treating diseases of many sorts

poly·es·ter \'pä-lē-ˌes-tər\ *n* : a polymer composed of ester groups used esp. in making fibers or plastics

poly·eth·yl·ene \ˌpä-lē-'e-thə-ˌlēn\ *n* : a lightweight plastic resistant to chemicals and moisture and used chiefly in packaging

po·lyg·a·my \pə-'li-gə-mē\ *n* : marriage in which a spouse of either sex may have more than one mate at the same time — **po·lyg·a·mist** \-mist\ *n* — **po·lyg·a·mous** \-məs\ *adj*

poly·glot \'pä-li-ˌglät\ *adj* **1** : speaking or writing several languages **2** : containing or made up of several languages — **polyglot** *n*

poly·gon \'pä-li-ˌgän\ *n* : a closed plane figure bounded by straight lines — **po·lyg·o·nal** \pə-'li-gən-ᵊl\ *adj*

poly·graph \'pä-li-ˌgraf\ *n* : an instrument (as a lie detector) for recording variations of several bodily functions (as blood pressure) simultaneously — **po·lyg·ra·pher** \pə-'li-grə-fər, 'pä-li-ˌgra-fər\ *n*

poly·he·dron \ˌpä-li-'hē-drən\ *n* : a solid formed by plane faces that are polygons — **poly·he·dral** \-drəl\ *adj*

poly·math \'pä-li-ˌmath\ *n* : a person of encyclopedic learning

poly·mer \'pä-lə-mər\ *n* : a chemical compound formed by union of small molecules and usu. consisting of repeating structural units — **poly·mer·ic** \ˌpä-lə-'mer-ik\ *adj*

po·lym·er·i·za·tion \pə-ˌli-mə-rə-'zā-shən\ *n* : a chemical reaction in which two or more small molecules combine to form polymers — **po·lym·er·ize** \pə-'li-mə-ˌrīz\ *vb*

Poly·ne·sian \ˌpä-lə-'nē-zhən\ *n* **1** : a member of any of the Indigenous peoples of Polynesia **2** : a group of Austronesian languages spoken in Polynesia — **Polynesian** *adj*

poly·no·mi·al \ˌpä-lə-'nō-mē-əl\ *n* : an algebraic expression having one or more terms each of which consists of a constant multiplied by one or more variables raised to a nonnegative integral power — **polynomial** *adj*

pol·yp \'pä-ləp\ *n* **1** : an invertebrate animal (as a coral) that is a coelenterate having a hollow cylindrical body closed at one end **2** : a growth projecting from a mucous membrane (as of the colon or vocal cords)

po·lyph·o·ny \pə-'li-fə-nē\ *n* : music consisting of two or more melodically independent but harmonizing voice parts — **poly·phon·ic** \ˌpä-li-'fä-nik\ *adj*

poly·pro·pyl·ene \ˌpä-lē-'prō-pə-ˌlēn\ *n* : any of various polymer plastics or fibers

poly·sty·rene \ˌpä-li-'stīr-ˌēn\ *n* : a rigid transparent nonconducting thermoplastic used esp. in molded products and foams

poly·syl·lab·ic \-sə-'la-bik\ *adj* **1** : having more than three syllables **2** : characterized by polysyllabic words

poly·syl·la·ble \'pä-li-ˌsi-lə-bəl\ *n* : a polysyllabic word

poly·tech·nic \ˌpä-li-'tek-nik\ *adj* : of, relating to, or instructing in many technical arts or applied sciences

poly·the·ism \'pä-li-thē-ˌi-zəm\ *n* : belief in or worship of many gods — **poly·the·ist** \-ˌthē-ist\ *adj or n* — **poly·the·is·tic** \ˌpä-li-thē-'is-tik\ *adj*

poly·un·sat·u·rat·ed \ˌpä-lē-ˌən-'sa-chə-ˌrā-təd\ *adj* : having many double or triple bonds in a molecule — used esp. of an oil or fatty acid

poly·ure·thane \ˌpä-lē-'yur-ə-ˌthān\ *n* : any of various polymers used esp. in foams and in resins (as for coatings)

poly·vi·nyl \ˌpä-li-'vīn-ᵊl\ *adj* : of, relating to, or being a polymerized vinyl compound, resin, or plastic — often used in combination

pome·gran·ate \'pä-mə-ˌgra-nət\ *n* : a many-seeded reddish fruit that has an edible crimson pulp and is borne by a tropical Asian tree; *also* : the tree

¹pom·mel \'pə-məl, 'pä-\ *n* **1** : the knob on the hilt of a sword **2** : the knoblike bulge at the front and top of a saddlebow

²pom·mel \'pə-məl\ *vb* **-meled** *or* **-melled; -mel·ing** *or* **-mel·ling** : to strike repeatedly : PUMMEL

pomp \'pämp\ *n* **1** : brilliant display : SPLENDOR **2** : OSTENTATION

pom·pa·dour \'päm-pə-ˌdōr\ *n* : a style of dressing the hair high over the forehead

pom·pa·no \'päm-pə-ˌnō, 'päm-\ *n, pl* **-no** *or* **-nos** : a narrow silvery fish of coastal waters of the western Atlantic

pom–pom \'päm-ˌpäm\ *n* **1** : an ornamental ball or tuft used on a cap or costume **2** : a fluffy ball flourished by cheerleaders

pom·pon \'päm-ˌpän\ *n* **1** : POM-POM **2** : a chrysanthemum or dahlia with small rounded flower heads

pomp·ous \'päm-pəs\ *adj* ♦ : suggestive of pomp; *esp* : OSTENTATIOUS **2** ♦ : having or exhibiting self-importance ⟨~ politicians⟩ **3** : excessively elevated or ornate — **pom·pos·i·ty** \päm-'pä-sə-tē\ *n* — **pomp·ous·ly** *adv*

♦ [1] affected, grandiose, highfalutin, ostentatious, pretentious ♦ [2] arrogant, complacent, conceited, egotistic, important, overweening, prideful, proud, self-important, self-satisfied, smug, stuck-up, vain

pon·cho \'pän-chō\ *n, pl* **ponchos** **1** : a blanket with a slit in the middle for the head so that it can be worn as a garment **2** : a waterproof garment resembling a poncho

pond \'pänd\ *n* : a small body of water

pon·der \'pän-dər\ *vb* **pon·dered; pon·der·ing** **1** ♦ : to weigh in the mind **2** ♦ : to consider carefully

♦ [1, 2] chew over, cogitate, consider, contemplate, debate, deliberate, entertain, meditate, mull, question, ruminate, study, think, weigh

pon·der·o·sa pine \ˌpän-də-ˌrō-sə-, -zə-\ *n* : a tall pine of western No. America with long needles; *also* : its strong reddish wood

pon·der·ous \'pän-də-rəs\ *adj* **1** ♦ : of very great weight **2** : UNWIELDY, CLUMSY ⟨a ~ weapon⟩ **3** ♦ : oppressively dull ⟨a ~ speech⟩

♦ [1] heavy, hefty, massive, weighty ♦ [3] dull, flat, heavy, leaden, weary

pone \'pōn\ *n, Southern & Midland* : an oval-shaped cornmeal cake; *also* : corn bread in the form of pones

pon·iard \'pän-yərd\ *n* : DAGGER

pon·tiff \'pän-təf\ *n* : POPE — **pon·tif·i·cal** \pän-'ti-fi-kəl\ *adj*

¹pon·tif·i·cate \pän-'ti-fi-kət, -fə-ˌkāt\ *n* : the state, office, or term of office of a pontiff

²pon·tif·i·cate \pän-'ti-fə-ˌkāt\ *vb* **-cat·ed; -cat·ing** : to deliver dogmatic opinions

pon·toon \pän-'tün\ *n* **1** : a flat-bottomed boat **2** : a boat or float used in building a floating temporary bridge **3** : a float of a seaplane

po·ny \'pō-nē\ *n, pl* **ponies** : a small horse

po·ny·tail \-ˌtāl\ *n* : a style of arranging hair to resemble the tail of a pony

pooch \'püch\ *n* : a flesh-eating domestic mammal related to the wolves : DOG

poo·dle \'püd-ᵊl\ *n* : any of a breed of active intelligent dogs with a dense curly solid-colored coat

pooh–pooh \'pü-'pü\ *also* **pooh** \'pü\ *vb* **1** : to express contempt or impatience **2** : DERIDE, SCORN

¹pool \'pül\ *n* **1** : a small deep body of usu. fresh water **2** : a small body of standing liquid **3** : SWIMMING POOL

²pool *vb* : to form a pool

³pool *n* **1** : all the money bet on the result of a particular event **2** : any of several games of billiards played on a table having six pockets **3** : the amount contributed by the participants in a joint venture **4** : a combination between competing firms for mutual profit **5** ♦ : a readily available supply (as of resources or workers)

♦ force, help, personnel, staff ♦ budget, fund, supply

⁴pool *vb* : to combine (as resources) in a common fund or effort

¹poop \'püp\ *n* : an enclosed superstructure at the stern of a ship

²poop *n, slang* : INFORMATION

poop deck *n* : a partial deck above a ship's main afterdeck

poor \'pur\ *adj* **1** ♦ : lacking material possessions ⟨~ people⟩ **2** : less than adequate : MEAGER ⟨a ~ crop⟩ **3** : arousing pity ⟨you ~ thing⟩ **4** ♦ : inferior in quality or value **5** : producing inferior or little vegetation : UNPRODUCTIVE, BARREN ⟨~ soil⟩ **6** : fairly unsatisfactory ⟨~ prospects⟩; *also* : UNFAVORABLE ⟨a ~ opinion⟩ — **poor·ly** *adv*

♦ [1] broke, destitute, impecunious, indigent, needy, penniless, penurious, poverty-stricken *Ant* affluent, flush, moneyed, opulent, rich, wealthy, well-heeled, well-off, well-to-do ♦ [4] cheap, inferior, junky, lousy, mediocre, second-rate, shoddy, sleazy

poor boy \'pō-ˌbói, 'pōr-\ *n* ♦ : a large sandwich on a long split roll : SUBMARINE

♦ grinder, hoagie, sub, submarine

poor·house \'pu̇r-ˌhau̇s\ *n* : a publicly supported home for needy or dependent persons

poor–mouth \-ˌmau̇th, -ˌmau̇th\ *vb* : to plead poverty as a defense or excuse

¹**pop** \'päp\ *vb* **popped; pop·ping** **1** ♦ : to go, come, enter, or issue forth suddenly, quickly, or unexpectedly ⟨~ into bed⟩ ⟨~ in for a visit⟩ **2** : to put or thrust suddenly ⟨~ questions⟩ **3** ♦ : to burst or cause to burst with a sharp sound; *also* : to make a sharp sound **4** : to protrude from the sockets **5** : to fire at : SHOOT **6** : to hit a pop-up

♦ *usu* **pop in** [1] call, drop (by *or* in), stop (by *or* in), visit ♦ [3] blow up, burst, detonate, explode, go off

²**pop** *n* **1** ♦ : a sharp explosive sound **2** : SHOT **3** : SODA POP

♦ bang, blast, boom, clap, crack, crash, report, slam, smash, snap, thwack, whack

³**pop** *n* ♦ : a male parent : FATHER

♦ daddy, father, papa

⁴**pop** *adj* **1** : POPULAR ⟨~ music⟩ **2** : of or relating to pop music ⟨a ~ singer⟩ **3** : of or relating to the popular culture disseminated through the mass media ⟨~ psychology⟩ **4** : of, relating to, or imitating pop art ⟨a ~ painter⟩

⁵**pop** *n* : pop music or culture; *also* : POP ART

⁶**pop** *abbr* population

pop art *n, often cap P & A* : art in which commonplace objects (as comic strips or soup cans) are used as subject matter — **pop art·ist** *n*

pop·corn \'päp-ˌkȯrn\ *n* : corn whose kernels burst open into a white starchy mass when heated; *also* : the burst kernels

pope \'pōp\ *n, often cap* : the head of the Roman Catholic Church

pop–eyed \'päp-ˌīd\ *adj* : having eyes that bulge (as from disease)

pop fly *n* : POP-UP

pop·gun \'päp-ˌgən\ *n* : a toy gun for shooting pellets with compressed air

pop·in·jay \'pä-pən-ˌjā\ *n* : a strutting supercilious person

pop·lar \'pä-plər\ *n* **1** : any of a genus of slender quick-growing trees (as a cottonwood) related to the willows **2** : the wood of a poplar

pop·lin \'pä-plən\ *n* : a strong plain-woven fabric with crosswise ribs

pop·over \'päp-ˌō-vər\ *n* : a hollow muffin made from a thin batter rich in egg

pop·per \'pä-pər\ *n* : a utensil for popping corn

pop·py \'pä-pē\ *n, pl* **poppies** : any of a genus of herbs with showy flowers including one that yields opium

pop·py·cock \-ˌkäk\ *n* : empty talk or writing : NONSENSE

pop·u·lace \'pä-pyə-ləs\ *n* **1** ♦ : the common people **2** : POPULATION

♦ commoners, herd, masses, mob, people, plebeians, rank and file

pop·u·lar \'pä-pyə-lər\ *adj* **1 a** ♦ : of or relating to the general public **b** ♦ : involving participation of all the people ⟨~ government⟩ **2** ♦ : suited to the tastes of the general public ⟨~ style⟩ **3** : INEXPENSIVE ⟨~ rates⟩ **4** ♦ : frequently encountered or widely accepted ⟨~ notion⟩ **5** ♦ : commonly liked or approved ⟨a ~ teacher⟩ — **pop·u·lar·ize** \'pä-pyə-lə-ˌrīz\ *vb* — **pop·u·lar·ly** *adv*

♦ [1a] common, general, public, vulgar ♦ [1b] democratic, republican, self-governing ♦ [2, 5] fashionable, in, modish, vogue *Ant* out, unpopular ♦ [4] conventional, current, customary, standard, stock, usual

pop·u·lar·i·ty \ˌpä-pyə-ˈlar-ə-tē\ *n* ♦ : the quality or state of being popular

♦ favor, modishness, vogue *Ant* disfavor, unpopularity

pop·u·late \'pä-pyə-ˌlāt\ *vb* **-lat·ed; -lat·ing** **1** : to have a place in : INHABIT **2** : PEOPLE

pop·u·la·tion \ˌpä-pyə-ˈlā-shən\ *n* **1** : the people or number of people in an area **2** : the organisms inhabiting a particular locality **3** : a group of individuals or items from which samples are taken for statistical measurement

population explosion *n* : a pyramiding of numbers of a biological population; *esp* : the recent great increase in human numbers resulting from increased survival and exponential population growth

pop·u·list \'pä-pyə-list\ *n* : a believer in or advocate of the rights, wisdom, or virtues of the common people — **pop·u·lism** \-ˌli-zəm\ *n*

pop·u·lous \'pä-pyə-ləs\ *adj* **1** : densely populated; *also* : having a large population **2** : CROWDED — **pop·u·lous·ness** *n*

¹**pop–up** \'päp-ˌəp\ *n* : a short high fly in baseball

²**pop–up** *adj* : of, relating to, or having a component or device that pops up

por·ce·lain \'pȯr-sə-lən\ *n* : a fine-grained translucent ceramic ware

porch \'pȯrch\ *n* : a covered entrance usu. with a separate roof

por·cine \'pȯr-ˌsīn\ *adj* : of, relating to, or suggesting swine

por·ci·ni \pȯr-ˈchē-nē\ *n, pl* **porcini** : a large edible brownish mushroom

por·ci·no \pȯr-ˈchē-nō\ *n, pl* **-ni** : PORCINI

por·cu·pine \'pȯr-kyə-ˌpīn\ *n* : any of various mammals having stiff sharp spines mingled with their hair

¹**pore** \'pȯr\ *vb* **pored; por·ing** **1** : to read studiously or attentively ⟨~ over a book⟩ **2** : PONDER, REFLECT

²**pore** *n* : a tiny hole or space (as in the skin or soil) — **pored** \'pȯrd\ *adj*

pork \'pȯrk\ *n* **1** : the flesh of swine dressed for use as food **2** : government funds, jobs, or favors distributed by politicians to gain political advantage

pork barrel *n* **1** : government projects or appropriations yielding rich patronage benefits **2** : PORK 2

pork·er \'pȯr-kər\ *n* : HOG; *esp* : a young pig suitable for use as fresh pork

por·no·graph·ic \ˌpȯr-nə-ˈgra-fik\ *adj* ♦ : of or relating to pornography

♦ bawdy, coarse, crude, dirty, filthy, foul, gross, indecent, lascivious, lewd, nasty, obscene, ribald, smutty, unprintable, vulgar, wanton

por·nog·ra·phy \pȯr-ˈnä-grə-fē\ *n* : the depiction of erotic behavior intended to cause sexual excitement

po·rous \'pȯr-əs\ *adj* **1** : full of pores **2** ♦ : permeable to fluids — **po·ros·i·ty** \pə-ˈrä-sə-tē\ *n*

♦ passable, penetrable, permeable

por·phy·ry \'pȯr-fə-rē\ *n, pl* **-ries** : a rock consisting of feldspar crystals embedded in a compact fine-grained base material — **por·phy·rit·ic** \ˌpȯr-fə-ˈri-tik\ *adj*

por·poise \'pȯr-pəs\ *n* : any of a family of small gregarious blunt-snouted whales with spadelike teeth; *also* : DOLPHIN 1

por·ridge \'pȯr-ij\ *n* : a soft food made by boiling meal of grains or legumes in milk or water

por·rin·ger \'pȯr-ən-jər\ *n* : a low one-handled metal bowl

¹**port** \'pȯrt\ *n* **1** ♦ : a place where ships may ride secure from storms : HARBOR **2** : a city with a harbor **3** : AIRPORT

♦ anchorage, harbor (*or* harbour), haven

²**port** *n* **1** : an inlet or outlet (as in an engine) for a fluid **2** : PORTHOLE

³**port** *vb* : to turn or put a helm to the left

⁴**port** *n* : the left side of a ship or airplane looking forward — **port** *adj*

⁵**port** *n* : a sweet fortified wine

portabella *or* **portabello** *var of* PORTOBELLO

por·ta·bil·i·ty \ˌpȯr-tə-ˈbil-ə-tē\ *n, pl* **-ties** **1** : the quality or state of being portable **2** : the ability to transfer benefits from one pension fund to another when a worker changes jobs

por·ta·ble \'pȯr-tə-bəl\ *adj* : capable of being carried — **porta·ble** *n*

¹**por·tage** \'pȯr-tij, pȯr-ˈtäzh\ *n* : the carrying of boats and goods overland between navigable bodies of water; *also* : a route for such carrying

²**portage** *vb* **por·taged; por·tag·ing** : to carry gear over a portage

por·tal \'pȯrt-ᵊl\ *n* **1** ♦ : the means or place of entry : DOOR; *esp* : a grand or imposing one **2** : a website serving as a guide or point of entry to the Internet

♦ door, gate, hatch

portal–to–portal *adj* : of or relating to the time spent by a worker in traveling from the entrance to an employer's property to the worker's actual job site (as in a mine)

port·cul·lis \pȯrt-ˈkə-ləs\ *n* : a grating at the gateway of a castle or fortress that can be let down to stop entrance

porte co·chere \ˌpȯrt-kō-ˈsher\ *n* : a roofed structure extending from the entrance of a building over an adjacent driveway and sheltering those getting in or out of vehicles

por·tend \pȯr-ˈtend\ *vb* **1** : to give a sign or warning of beforehand **2** : INDICATE, SIGNIFY

por·tent \'pȯr-ˌtent\ *n* **1** ♦ : something that foreshadows a coming event : OMEN **2** : one that causes wonder or astonishment : MARVEL, PRODIGY

♦ augury, auspice, foreboding, omen, presage

por·ten·tous \pȯr-'ten-təs\ *adj* **1** ♦ : of, relating to, or constituting a portent **2** ♦ : eliciting amazement or wonder : PRODIGIOUS **3** : self-consciously solemn : POMPOUS

♦ [1] baleful, dire, foreboding, menacing, ominous, sinister ♦ [2] amazing, astonishing, astounding, awesome, fabulous, marvelous (*or* marvellous), prodigious, stunning, surprising, wonderful

¹**por·ter** \'pōr-tər\ *n, chiefly Brit* : DOORKEEPER

²**porter** *n* **1** : a person who carries burdens; *esp* : one employed (as at a terminal) to carry baggage **2** : an attendant in a railroad car **3** : a dark heavy ale

por·ter·house \'pȯr-tər-ˌhau̇s\ *n* : a choice beefsteak with a large tenderloin

port·fo·lio \pȯrt-'fō-lē-ˌō\ *n, pl* **-li·os 1** : a portable case for papers or drawings **2** : the office and functions of a minister of state **3** : the securities held by an investor **4** : a set of drawings, paintings, or photographs usu. bound in a book or loose in a folder

port·hole \'pōrt-ˌhōl\ *n* : an opening (as a window) in the side of a ship or aircraft

por·ti·co \'pȯr-ti-ˌkō\ *n, pl* **-coes** *or* **-cos** : a row of columns supporting a roof around or at the entrance of a building

¹**por·tion** \'pōr-shən\ *n* **1** ♦ : one's part or share ⟨a ∼ of food⟩ **2** : DOWRY **3** ♦ : an individual's lot, fate, or fortune **4** ♦ : a part of a whole ⟨a ∼ of the sky⟩

♦ [1] allotment, allowance, cut, part, proportion, quota, share ♦ [3] circumstance, destiny, doom, fate, fortune, lot ♦ [4] member, part, partition, section, segment

²**portion** *vb* **1** : to divide into portions **2** ♦ : to allot to as a portion

♦ administer, allocate, apportion, deal, dispense, distribute, mete, parcel, prorate

port·land cement \'pōrt-lənd-\ *n* : a cement made by calcining and grinding a mixture of clay and limestone

port·ly \'pōrt-lē\ *adj* **port·li·er; -est** ♦ : somewhat stout

♦ chubby, fat, fleshy, full, plump, rotund, round

port·man·teau \pōrt-'man-ˌtō\ *n, pl* **-teaus** *or* **-teaux** \-ˌtōz\ ♦ : a large traveling bag

♦ carryall, grip, handbag, suitcase, traveling bag

por·to·bel·lo \pȯr-tə-'be-lō\ *also* **por·ta·bel·la** \-lə\ *or* **por·ta·bel·lo** \-lō\, *n, pl* **-los** *also* **-las** : a large dark mature mushroom noted for its meaty texture

port of call : an intermediate port where ships customarily stop for supplies, repairs, or transshipment of cargo

port of entry 1 : a place where foreign goods may be cleared through a customhouse **2** : a place where an alien may enter a country

por·trait \'pōr-trət, -ˌträt\ *n* **1** : a picture (as a painting or photograph) of a person usu. showing the face **2** ♦ : a graphic portrayal in words

♦ delineation, depiction, description, picture, portrayal, sketch

por·trait·ist \-trə-tist\ *n* : a maker of portraits

por·trai·ture \'pōr-trə-ˌchu̇r\ *n* : the practice or art of making portraits

por·tray \pȯr-'trā\ *vb* **1** ♦ : to make a picture of : DEPICT **2** ♦ : to describe in words **3** ♦ : to play the role of

♦ [1] depict, image, picture, represent ♦ [2] characterize, delineate, depict, describe, draw, image, paint, picture, sketch ♦ [3] act, impersonate, perform, play

por·tray·al \pȯr-'trā(-ə)l\ *n* ♦ : the act or process or an instance of portraying

♦ delineation, depiction, description, picture, portrait, sketch

Por·tu·guese \'pōr-chə-ˌgēz, -ˌgēs; ˌpōr-chə-'gēz, -'gēs\ *n, pl* **Portuguese 1** : a native or inhabitant of Portugal **2** : the language of Portugal and Brazil — **Portuguese** *adj*

Portuguese man–of–war *n* : any of several large colonial marine invertebrate animals related to the jellyfishes and having a large sac by which the colony floats at the surface

por·tu·laca \ˌpōr-chə-'la-kə\ *n* : any of a genus of succulent herbs cultivated for their showy flowers

pos *abbr* **1** position **2** positive

¹**pose** \'pōz\ *vb* **posed; pos·ing 1** : to assume or cause to assume a posture usu. for artistic purposes **2** ♦ : to set forth : PROPOSE ⟨∼ a question⟩ **3** ♦ : to affect an attitude or character

♦ [2] advance, offer, proffer, propose, propound, suggest, vote ♦ *usu* **pose as** [3] impersonate, masquerade, play

²**pose** *n* **1** : a sustained posture; *esp* : one assumed by a model **2** ♦ : an attitude assumed for effect : PRETENSE

♦ act, airs, facade, front, guise, masquerade, pretense, put-on, semblance, show

¹**pos·er** \'pō-zər\ *n* : a puzzling question

²**poser** *n* : a person who poses

po·seur \pō-'zər\ *n* : an affected or insincere person

posh \'päsh\ *adj* : FASHIONABLE

pos·it \'pä-zət\ *vb* : to assume the existence of : POSTULATE

¹**po·si·tion** \pə-'zi-shən\ *n* **1** : an arranging in order **2** : the stand taken on a question **3** ♦ : the point or area occupied by something or someone **4** : a certain arrangement of bodily parts ⟨exercise in a sitting ∼⟩ **5** ♦ : social or official rank or status **6** ♦ : an employment for which one has been hired : JOB

♦ [3] locale, location, place, point, site, spot ♦ [5] degree, footing, level, place, rank, situation, standing, station, status ♦ [6] appointment, billet, capacity, function, job, place, post, situation

²**position** *vb* ♦ : to put in a certain position

♦ deposit, dispose, fix, lay, place, put, set, set up, stick

¹**pos·i·tive** \'pä-zə-tiv\ *adj* **1** : expressed definitely ⟨her answer was a ∼ *no*⟩ **2** ♦ : fully assured : CONFIDENT, CERTAIN **3** : of, relating to, or constituting the degree of grammatical comparison that denotes no increase in quality, quantity, or relation **4** : not fictitious : REAL **5** : active and effective in function ⟨∼ leadership⟩ **6** : having the light and shade as existing in the original subject ⟨a ∼ photograph⟩ **7** : numerically greater than zero ⟨a ∼ number⟩ **8** : being, relating to, or charged with electricity of which the proton is the elementary unit **9** ♦ : marked by or indicating acceptance, approval, or affirmation ⟨a ∼ response⟩ — **pos·i·tive·ly** *adv*

♦ [2] assured, certain, clear, cocksure, confident, doubtless, sanguine, sure ♦ [9] appreciative, complimentary, favorable (*or* favourable), friendly, good

²**positive** *n* **1** : the positive degree or a positive form in a language **2** : a positive photograph

pos·i·tive·ness \-nəs\ *n* ♦ : the quality or state of being positive

♦ assurance, certainty, certitude, confidence, conviction, sureness

pos·i·tron \'pä-zə-ˌträn\ *n* : a positively charged particle having the same mass and magnitude of charge as the electron

po·zo·le *or* **po·zo·le** \pə-'sō-lä\ *n* : a thick Mexican soup made with pork, hominy, garlic, and chili

poss *abbr* possessive

pos·se \'pä-sē\ *n* : a body of persons organized to assist a sheriff in an emergency

pos·sess \pə-'zes\ *vb* **1** ♦ : to have as property : OWN **2** : to have as an attribute, knowledge, or skill **3** : to enter into and control firmly ⟨∼ed by a devil⟩

♦ command, enjoy, have, hold, occupy, own, retain

pos·ses·sion \-'ze-shən\ *n* **1** ♦ : control or occupancy of property without regard to ownership **2** : OWNERSHIP **3** ♦ : something owned : PROPERTY **4** : domination by something (as an evil spirit, a passion, or an idea) **5** : SELF-CONTROL

♦ [1] control, hands, keeping ♦ **possessions** [3] belongings, chattels, effects, holdings, paraphernalia, property, things

pos·ses·sive \pə-'ze-siv\ *adj* **1** : of, relating to, or constituting a grammatical case denoting ownership **2** : showing the desire to possess ⟨a ∼ nature⟩ — **possessive** *n* — **pos·ses·sive·ness** *n*

pos·ses·sor \-'ze-sər\ *n* ♦ : one that possesses

♦ holder, owner, proprietor

pos·si·bil·i·ty \ˌpä-sə-'bi-lə-tē\ *n* ♦ : something that is possible

♦ case, contingency, event, eventuality

pos·si·ble \'pä-sə-bəl\ *adj* **1** ♦ : being within the limits of ability, capacity, or realization **2** : being something that may or may not occur ⟨∼ dangers⟩ **3** : able or fitted to become ⟨a ∼ site for a bridge⟩

♦ achievable, attainable, doable, feasible, practicable, realizable, viable, workable *Ant* hopeless, impossible, impracticable, unattainable, unworkable

pos·si·bly \'pä-sə-blē\ *adv* **1** : in a possible manner : by any possibility ⟨it's all I can ∼ do⟩ **2** ♦ : it is possible or imaginable

♦ conceivably, maybe, perchance, perhaps

pos·sum \\'pä-səm\ *n* : OPOSSUM

¹post \\'pōst\ *n* **1** ♦ : an upright piece of timber or metal serving esp. as a support : PILLAR **2** : a pole or stake set up as a mark or indicator

♦ column, pier, pillar, stanchion

²post *vb* **1** : to affix to a usual place (as a wall) for public notices **2** ♦ : to publish or announce by or as if by a public notice ⟨∼ grades⟩ **3** : to forbid (property) to trespassers by putting up a notice **4** : SCORE 4 ⟨∼ed a 70 in the final round⟩ **5** : to publish in an online forum

♦ advertise, announce, blaze, broadcast, declare, enunciate, placard, proclaim, promulgate, publicize, publish, sound

³post *n* **1** *obs* : COURIER **2** *chiefly Brit* ♦ : something sent through the mail; *also* : POST OFFICE

♦ mail, matter, parcel post, snail mail

⁴post *vb* **1** : to ride or travel with haste : HURRY **2** : MAIL ⟨∼ a letter⟩ **3** : to enter in a ledger **4** : INFORM ⟨kept him ∼ed on new developments⟩

⁵post *n* **1** ♦ : the place at which a soldier is stationed; *esp* : a sentry's beat or station **2** ♦ : a station or task to which a person is assigned **3** : the place at which a body of troops is stationed : CAMP **4** ♦ : an office or position to which a person is appointed **5** : a trading settlement or station

♦ [1] position, quarter, station ♦ [2] assignment, charge, job, mission, operation ♦ [4] appointment, billet, capacity, function, job, place, position, situation

⁶post *vb* **1** : to station in a given place **2** : to put up (as bond)

post·age \\'pō-stij\ *n* : the fee for postal service; *also* : stamps representing this fee

post·al \\'pōst-ʰl\ *adj* : of or relating to the mails or the post office

postal card *n* : POSTCARD

postal service *n* : a government agency or department handling the transmission of mail

post·card \\'pōst-ˌkärd\ *n* : a card on which a message may be written for mailing without an envelope

post chaise *n* : a 4-wheeled closed carriage for two to four persons

post·con·sum·er \\ˌpōst-kən-'sü-mər\ *adj* **1** : discarded by a consumer **2** : having been used and recycled for reuse in another product

post·date \\ˌpōst-'dāt\ *vb* **1** : to date with a date later than that of execution ⟨∼ a check⟩ **2** : to follow in time

post·doc·tor·al \-'däk-tə-rəl\ *also* **post·doc·tor·ate** \-tə-rət\ *adj* : of, relating to, or engaged in advanced academic or professional work beyond a doctor's degree

post·er \\'pō-stər\ *n* ♦ : a bill or placard for posting often in a public place

♦ bill, placard

¹pos·te·ri·or \pō-'stir-ē-ər, pä-\ *adj* **1** ♦ : later in time **2** ♦ : situated behind

♦ [1] after, later, subsequent ♦ [2] back, hind, hindmost, rear

²pos·te·ri·or \pä-'stir-ē-ər, pō-\ *n* ♦ : the hinder bodily parts; *esp* : BUTTOCKS

♦ backside, bottom, butt, buttocks, rear, rump, seat

pos·ter·i·ty \pä-'ster-ə-tē\ *n* **1** ♦ : the descendants from one ancestor **2** : all future generations

♦ issue, offspring, progeny, seed, spawn

pos·tern \\'pōs-tərn, 'päs-\ *n* **1** : a back door or gate **2** : a private or side entrance

post exchange *n* : a store at a military post that sells to military personnel and authorized civilians

post·grad \\'pōst-ˌgrad\ *adj* : POSTGRADUATE

post·grad·u·ate \\(ˌ)pōst-'gra-jə-wət\ *adj* : of or relating to studies beyond the bachelor's degree — **postgraduate** *n*

post·haste \\'pōst-'hāst\ *adv* ♦ : with all possible speed

♦ apace, briskly, fast, full tilt, hastily, presto, pronto, quick, quickly, rapidly, soon, speedily, swift, swiftly

post·hole \-ˌhōl\ *n* : a hole for a post and esp. a fence post

post·hu·mous \\'päs-chə-məs\ *adj* **1** : born after the death of the father **2** : published after the death of the author — **post·hu·mous·ly** *adv*

post·hyp·not·ic \\ˌpōst-hip-'nä-tik\ *adj* : of, relating to, or characteristic of the period following a hypnotic trance

pos·til·ion *or* **pos·til·lion** \pō-'stil-yən\ *n* : a rider on the left-hand horse of a pair drawing a coach

Post·im·pres·sion·ism \ˌpōst-im-'pre-shə-ˌni-zəm\ *n* : a late 19th century French theory or practice of art that stresses variously volume, picture structure, or expressionism

post·lude \\'pōst-ˌlüd\ *n* : an organ solo played at the end of a church service

post·man \-mən, -ˌman\ *n* ♦ : a man who delivers mail : MAILMAN

♦ letter carrier, mailman

post·mark \-ˌmärk\ *n* : an official postal marking on a piece of mail; *esp* : the mark canceling the postage stamp — **postmark** *vb*

post·mas·ter \-ˌmas-tər\ *n* : a person who has charge of a post office

postmaster general *n, pl* **postmasters general** : an official in charge of a national postal service

post·men·o·paus·al \ˌpōst-ˌme-nə-'pȯ-zəl\ *adj* **1** : having undergone menopause **2** : occurring or administered after menopause

post me·ri·di·em \ˌpōst-mə-'ri-dē-əm\ *adj* : being after noon

post·mis·tress \\'pōst-ˌmis-trəs\ *n* : a woman who is a postmaster

post·mod·ern \ˌpōst-'mä-dərn\ *adj* : of, relating to, or being any of various movements in reaction to modernism

¹post·mor·tem \ˌpōst-'mȯr-təm\ *adj* **1** : done, occurring, or collected after death ⟨a ∼ examination⟩ **2** : following the event

²postmortem *n* **1** : an analysis or discussion of an event after it is over ⟨a ∼ of the election⟩ **2** : AUTOPSY

post·na·sal drip \ˌpōst-ˌnā-zəl-\ *n* : flow of mucous secretion from the posterior part of the nasal cavity onto the wall of the pharynx

post·na·tal \(ˌ)pōst-'nāt-ʰl\ *adj* : occurring or being after birth; *esp* : of or relating to a newborn infant

post office *n* **1** : POSTAL SERVICE **2** : a local branch of a post office department

post·op·er·a·tive \(ˌ)pōst-'ä-prə-tiv, -pə-ˌrā-\ *adj* : following or having undergone a surgical operation ⟨∼ care⟩

post·paid \\'pōst-'pād\ *adj* : having the postage paid by the sender and not chargeable to the receiver

post·par·tum \(ˌ)pōst-'pär-təm\ *adj* : following parturition — **postpartum** *adv*

post·pone \pōst-'pōn\ *vb* **post·poned; post·pon·ing** ♦ : to put off to a later time — **post·pone·ment** *n*

♦ defer, delay, hold up, put off, shelve

post road *n* : a road over which mail is carried

post·script \\'pōst-ˌskript\ *n* : a note added esp. to a completed letter

post time *n* : the designated time for the start of a horse race

post–traumatic *adj* : occurring after or as a result of trauma ⟨∼ stress⟩

pos·tu·lant \\'päs-chə-lənt\ *n* : a probationary candidate for membership in a religious order

¹pos·tu·late \\'päs-chə-ˌlāt\ *vb* **-lat·ed; -lat·ing** ♦ : to assume as true

♦ assume, premise, presume, presuppose, suppose

²pos·tu·late \\'päs-chə-lət, -ˌlāt\ *n* ♦ : a proposition taken for granted as true esp. as a basis for a chain of reasoning

♦ assumption, premise, presumption, supposition

¹pos·ture \\'päs-chər\ *n* **1** : the position or bearing of the body or one of its parts **2** ♦ : state or condition at a given time esp. with respect to capability in particular circumstances **3** : ATTITUDE

♦ footing, picture, scene, situation, status

²posture *vb* **pos·tured; pos·tur·ing** : to strike a pose esp. for effect

post·war \\'pōst-'wȯr\ *adj* : occurring or existing after a war

po·sy \\'pō-zē\ *n, pl* **posies** **1** : a brief sentiment : MOTTO **2** : a bunch of flowers; *also* : FLOWER

¹pot \\'pät\ *n* **1** : a rounded container used chiefly for domestic purposes **2** : the total of the bets at stake at one time **3** : RUIN ⟨go to ∼⟩ **4** : a large amount (as of money) — **pot·ful** *n*

²pot *vb* **pot·ted; pot·ting** **1** : to preserve or place in a pot **2** : SHOOT

³pot *n* : MARIJUANA

po·ta·ble \\'pō-tə-bəl\ *adj* : suitable for drinking — **po·ta·bil·i·ty** \ˌpō-tə-'bi-lə-tē\ *n*

po·tage \pō-'täzh\ *n* : a thick soup

pot·ash \\'pät-ˌash\ *n* : potassium or any of its various compounds esp. as used in agriculture

po·tas·si·um \pə-'ta-sē-əm\ *n* : a silver-white soft metallic chemical element that occurs abundantly in nature

potassium bromide *n* : a crystalline salt used as a sedative and in photography

potassium carbonate *n* : a white salt used in making glass and soap

potassium nitrate *n* : a soluble salt used in making gunpowder, as a fertilizer, and in medicine

po·ta·tion \pō-'tā-shən\ *n* : a usu. alcoholic drink; *also* : the act of drinking

po·ta·to \pə-'tā-tō\ *n, pl* **-toes** : the edible starchy tuber of a plant related to the tomato; *also* : this plant

potato beetle *n* : COLORADO POTATO BEETLE

potato bug *n* : COLORADO POTATO BEETLE

potbellied pig *n* : any of an Asian breed of small pigs having a straight tail, potbelly, and black, white, or black and white coat

pot·bel·ly \'pät-ˌbe-lē\ *n* : a protruding abdomen — **pot·bel·lied** \-ˌlēd\ *adj*

pot·boil·er \-ˌbȯi-lər\ *n* : a usu. inferior work of art or literature produced chiefly for profit

po·ten·cy \'pōt-ᵊn-sē\ *n* **1** ♦ : ability to act or produce an effect : POWER **2** ♦ : the quality or state of being potent

   ♦ [1, 2] energy, force, main, might, muscle, power, sinew, strength, vigor (*or* vigour)

po·tent \'pōt-ᵊnt\ *adj* **1** ♦ : having authority or influence : POWERFUL **2** : chemically or medicinally effective **3** : able to copulate — used esp. of the male **4** ♦ : rich in a characteristic constituent **5** ♦ : achieving or bringing about a particular result : EFFECTIVE

   ♦ [1] important, influential, mighty, powerful, significant, strong ♦ [4] concentrated, full, full-bodied, rich, robust, strong ♦ [5] effective, effectual, efficacious, efficient, fruitful, productive

po·ten·tate \'pōt-ᵊn-ˌtāt\ *n* : one who wields controlling power : RULER

¹**po·ten·tial** \pə-'ten-chəl\ *adj* : existing in possibility : capable of becoming actual ⟨a ∼ champion⟩ — **po·ten·tial·ly** \-'ten-chə-lē\ *adv*

²**potential** *n* **1** ♦ : something that can develop or become actual ⟨a ∼ for violence⟩ **2** : the work required to move a unit positive charge from infinity to a point in question; *also* : POTENTIAL DIFFERENCE

   ♦ eventuality, possibility

potential difference *n* : the difference in potential between two points that represents the work involved in the transfer of a unit quantity of electricity from one point to the other

potential energy *n* : the energy an object has because of its position or nature or the arrangement of its parts

po·ten·ti·al·i·ty \pə-ˌten-chē-'a-lə-tē\ *n* **1** : the ability to develop or come into existence **2** : something that can develop or become actual

po·ten·ti·ate \pə-'ten-chē-ˌāt\ *vb* **-at·ed; -at·ing** : to make potent; *esp* : to augment the activity of (as a drug) synergistically — **po·ten·ti·a·tion** \-ˌten-chē-'ā-shən\ *n*

pot·head \'pät-ˌhed\ *n* : a person who frequently smokes marijuana

poth·er \'pä-thər\ *n* **1** ♦ : a noisy disturbance **2** ♦ : mental turmoil

   ♦ [1] commotion, disturbance, furor, hubbub, turmoil ♦ [2] dither, fluster, fret, fuss, huff, lather, stew, tizzy, twitter

pot·herb \'pät-ˌərb, -ˌhərb\ *n* : an herb whose leaves or stems are boiled for greens or used to season food

pot·hole \'pät-ˌhōl\ *n* : a large pit or hole (as in a road surface)

pot·hook \-ˌhu̇k\ *n* : an S-shaped hook for hanging pots and kettles over an open fire

po·tion \'pō-shən\ *n* : a mixture of liquids (as liquor or medicine)

pot·luck \'pät-'lək\ *n* : the regular meal available to a guest for whom no special preparations have been made

pot·pie \-'pī\ *n* : pastry-covered meat and vegetables cooked in a deep dish

pot·pour·ri \ˌpō-pu̇-'rē\ *n* **1** : a mixture of flowers, herbs, and spices used for scent **2** ♦ : a miscellaneous collection

   ♦ assortment, clutter, jumble, medley, mélange, miscellany, motley, muddle, variety, welter

pot·sherd \'pät-ˌshərd\ *n* : a pottery fragment

pot·shot \-ˌshät\ *n* **1** : a shot taken from ambush or at a random or easy target **2** : a critical remark made in a random or sporadic manner

pot sticker *n* : a crescent-shaped dumpling that is steamed and fried

pot·tage \'pä-tij\ *n* : a thick soup of vegetables and often meat

¹**pot·ter** \'pä-tər\ *n* : one that makes pottery

²**potter** *vb* ♦ : to move or act aimlessly or idly : PUTTER

   ♦ usu **potter around** fiddle, fool, mess, monkey, play, putter, trifle

pot·tery \'pä-tə-rē\ *n, pl* **-ter·ies** **1** : a place where earthen pots and dishes are made **2** : the art of the potter **3** : dishes, pots, and vases made from clay

pot·ty–mouthed \'pä-tē-ˌmau̇thd, -ˌmau̇tht\ *adj* : given to the use of vulgar language

¹**pouch** \'pau̇ch\ *n* **1** : a small bag (as for tobacco) carried on the person **2** : a bag for storing or transporting goods ⟨mail ∼⟩ ⟨diplomatic ∼⟩ **3** : an anatomical sac; *esp* : one for carrying the young on the abdomen of a female marsupial (as a kangaroo)

²**pouch** *vb* : to put or form into or as if into a pouch

poult \'pōlt\ *n* : a young fowl; *esp* : a young turkey

poul·ter·er \'pōl-tər-ər\ *n* : one that deals in poultry

poul·tice \'pōl-təs\ *n* : a soft usu. heated and medicated mass spread on cloth and applied to a sore or injury — **poultice** *vb*

poul·try \'pōl-trē\ *n* : domesticated birds kept for eggs or meat — **poul·try·man** \-mən\ *n*

pounce \'pau̇ns\ *vb* **pounced; pounc·ing** **1** : to spring or swoop upon and seize something **2** ♦ : to make a sudden assault or approach

   ♦ usu **pounce on** or **pounce upon** assail, assault, attack, beset, charge, descend, jump, raid, rush, storm, strike

¹**pound** \'pau̇nd\ *n, pl* **pounds** *also* **pound** **1** : a unit of avoirdupois, troy, and apothecaries' weight **2** : a unit of weight equal to 16 ounces **3** : the basic monetary unit of any of several countries including Egypt and the United Kingdom

²**pound** *n* ♦ : a public enclosure where stray animals are kept

   ♦ cage, coop, corral, pen

³**pound** *vb* **1** : to crush to a powder or pulp by beating **2 a** ♦ : to strike or beat heavily or repeatedly **b** ♦ : to produce by repeated blows **3** : DRILL **4** : to move or move along heavily

   ♦ [2a] bash, bat, batter, beat, belt, bludgeon, club, hammer, hit, thrash, thump, wallop ♦ [2b] beat, forge, hammer

⁴**pound** *n* : an act or sound of pounding

pound·age \'pau̇n-dij\ *n* : POUNDS; *also* : weight in pounds

pound cake *n* : a rich cake made with a large proportion of eggs and shortening

pound–fool·ish \'pau̇nd-'fü-lish\ *adj* : imprudent in dealing with large sums or large matters

pour \'pōr\ *vb* **1** ♦ : to flow or cause to flow in a stream or flood **2** ♦ : to rain hard **3** ♦ : to supply freely and copiously

   ♦ [1] gush, jet, rush, spew, spout, spurt, squirt ♦ [1] flow, roll, run, stream ♦ [2] precipitate, rain, storm ♦ [3] heap, lavish, rain, shower

¹**pout** \'pau̇t\ *vb* : to show displeasure by thrusting out the lips; *also* : to look sullen

²**pout** *n* **1** ♦ : a protrusion of the lips expressive of displeasure **2** ♦ : a fit of pique

   ♦ [1] face, frown, grimace, lower, mouth, scowl ♦ [2] pet, sulk, sullenness

pov·er·ty \'pä-vər-tē\ *n* **1** ♦ : lack of money or material possessions : WANT **2** : poor quality (as of soil) **3** ♦ : meagerness of supply

   ♦ [1] beggary, destitution, impecuniousness, impoverishment, indigence, need, pauperism, penury, want *Ant* affluence, opulence, richness ♦ [3] dearth, deficiency, deficit, failure, famine, inadequacy, insufficiency, lack, paucity, scantiness, scarcity, shortage, want

poverty line *n* : a level of personal or family income below which one is classified as poor according to government standards

pov·er·ty–strick·en \'pä-vər-tē-ˌstri-kən\ *adj* ♦ : very poor : DESTITUTE

   ♦ broke, destitute, impecunious, indigent, needy, penniless, penurious, poor

POW \ˌpē-(ˌ)ō-'də-bəl-(ˌ)yü\ *n* : PRISONER OF WAR

¹**pow·der** \'pau̇-dər\ *n* **1** : dry material made up of fine particles; *also* : a usu. medicinal or cosmetic preparation in this form **2** : a solid explosive (as gunpowder)

²**powder** *vb* **1** : to sprinkle or cover with or as if with powder **2** ♦ : to reduce to powder

   ♦ atomize, crush, grind, pulverize

powder room *n* : a rest room for women

pow·dery \'pau̇-də-rē\ *adj* ♦ : resembling or consisting of powder

♦ dusty, fine, floury

¹**pow·er** \'pau̇-ər\ *n* **1** ♦ : the ability to act or produce an effect **2** ♦ : a position of ascendancy over others : AUTHORITY **3** : one that has control or authority; *esp* : a sovereign state **4** : physical might; *also* : mental or moral vigor **5** : the number of times as indicated by an exponent that a number occurs as a factor in a product ⟨5 to the third ∼ is 125⟩; *also* : the resulting product **6** : force or energy used to do work; *also* : the rate at which work is done or energy transferred **7** : MAGNIFICATION 2

♦ [1] energy, force, main, might, muscle, potency, sinew, strength, vigor (*or* vigour) *Ant* impotence, weakness ♦ [2] arm, authority, clutch, command, control, dominion, grip, hold, sway *Ant* impotence

²**power** *vb* : to supply with power and esp. motive power

³**power** *adj* : operated mechanically or electrically rather than manually

pow·er·boat \-ˌbōt\ *n* : MOTORBOAT

pow·er·ful \'pau̇-ər-fəl\ *adj* ♦ : having great power, prestige, or influence

♦ important, influential, mighty, potent, significant, strong

pow·er·ful·ly \-fə-lē\ *adv* ♦ : in a powerful manner

♦ energetically, firmly, forcefully, forcibly, hard, mightily, stiffly, stoutly, strenuously, strongly, sturdily, vigorously

pow·er·house \'pau̇-ər-ˌhau̇s\ *n* **1** : POWER PLANT 1 **2** ♦ : one having great drive, energy, or ability

♦ go-getter, hustler, live wire, self-starter

pow·er·less \-ləs\ *adj* **1** ♦ : devoid of strength or resources **2** ♦ : lacking the authority or capacity to act

♦ [1, 2] helpless, impotent, weak *Ant* mighty, potent, powerful, puissant, strong

power plant *n* **1** : a building in which electric power is generated **2** : an engine and related parts supplying the motive power of a self-propelled vehicle

pow·wow \'pau̇-ˌwau̇\ *n* **1** : a ceremony (as for victory in war) of No. American Indigenous people **2** *offensive* : a meeting for discussion : CONFERENCE

pox \'päks\ *n, pl* **pox** *or* **pox·es** : any of various diseases (as smallpox or syphilis) marked by a rash on the skin

pozole *var of* POSOLE

pp *abbr* **1** pages **2** pianissimo

PP *abbr* **1** parcel post **2** past participle **3** postpaid **4** prepaid

ppd *abbr* **1** postpaid **2** prepaid

PPO \ˌpē-ˌpē-'ō\ *n, pl* **PPOs** : a health-care organization that gives economic incentives to enrolled individuals who use certain health-care providers

PPS *abbr* an additional postscript

ppt *abbr* precipitate

PQ *abbr* Province of Quebec

pr *abbr* **1** pair **2** price

Pr *symbol* praseodymium

¹**PR** *or* **p.r.** \'pē-'är\ *n* : PUBLIC RELATIONS

²**PR** *abbr* **1** payroll **2** public relations **3** Puerto Rico

prac·ti·ca·ble \'prak-ti-kə-bəl\ *adj* **1** ♦ : capable of being put into practice, done, or accomplished **2** ♦ : capable of being used — **prac·ti·ca·bil·i·ty** \ˌprak-ti-kə-'bi-lə-tē\ *n*

♦ [1] achievable, attainable, doable, feasible, possible, realizable, viable, workable ♦ [2] available, fit, functional, operable, serviceable, usable, useful

prac·ti·cal \'prak-ti-kəl\ *adj* **1** : of, relating to, or shown in practice ⟨∼ questions⟩ **2** : VIRTUAL ⟨∼ control⟩ **3** ♦ : capable of being put to use ⟨a ∼ knowledge of French⟩ **4** ♦ : inclined to action as opposed to speculation or abstraction ⟨a ∼ person⟩ **5** : qualified by practice ⟨a good ∼ mechanic⟩ — **prac·ti·cal·i·ty** \ˌprak-ti-'ka-lə-tē\ *n*

♦ [3] applicable, functional, practicable, serviceable, usable, useful, workable, working *Ant* impracticable, impractical, unusable, unworkable, useless ♦ [4] down-to-earth, earthy, hardheaded, matter-of-fact, pragmatic, realistic

practical joke *n* ♦ : a prank intended to trick or embarrass someone or cause physical discomfort

♦ antic, caper, escapade, frolic, monkeyshine, prank, trick

prac·ti·cal·ly \'prak-ti-k(ə-)lē\ *adv* **1** : in a practical manner **2** ♦ : very nearly but not exactly or entirely : ALMOST

♦ about, almost, most, much, near, nearly, next to, nigh, some, virtually, well-nigh

practical nurse *n* : a professional nurse without all of the qualifications of a registered nurse; *esp* : LICENSED PRACTICAL NURSE

¹**prac·tice** *chiefly Can and Brit* **prac·tise** \'prak-təs\ *vb* **prac·ticed** *also* **prac·tised**; **prac·tic·ing** *also* **prac·tis·ing** **1** ♦ : CARRY OUT, APPLY ⟨∼ what you preach⟩ **2** : to perform or work at repeatedly so as to become proficient ⟨∼ tennis strokes⟩ **3** : to do or perform customarily ⟨∼ politeness⟩ **4** : to be professionally engaged in ⟨∼ law⟩

²**practice** *n* **1** : actual performance or application **2** ♦ : customary action : HABIT **3** ♦ : systematic exercise for proficiency **4** : the exercise of a profession; *also* : a professional business

♦ [2] custom, fashion, habit, pattern, way, wont ♦ [3] dry run, rehearsal, trial ♦ [3] drill, exercise, routine, training, workout

practiced *chiefly Can and Brit* **practised** *adj* **1** ♦ : made skillful or wise through experience **2** : learned by practice

♦ adroit, artful, delicate, dexterous, expert, masterful, masterly, skillful, virtuoso

prac·ti·tion·er \prak-'ti-shə-nər\ *n* : one who practices a profession

prae·tor \'prē-tər\ *n* : an ancient Roman magistrate ranking below a consul — **prae·to·ri·an** \prē-'tōr-ē-ən, -'tȯr-\ *adj*

prag·mat·ic \prag-'ma-tik\ *also* **prag·mat·i·cal** \-ti-kəl\ *adj* **1** ♦ : of or relating to practical affairs **2** : concerned with the practical consequences of actions or beliefs ⟨a ∼ leader⟩ — **pragmatic** *n* — **prag·mat·i·cal·ly** \-ti-k(ə-)lē\ *adv*

♦ down-to-earth, earthy, hardheaded, matter-of-fact, practical, realistic

prag·ma·tism \'prag-mə-ˌti-zəm\ *n* : a practical approach to problems and affairs

prai·rie \'prer-ē\ *n* ♦ : a broad tract of level or rolling grassland

♦ down, grassland, plain, savanna, steppe, veld

prairie dog *n* : an American burrowing black-tailed rodent related to the squirrels and living in colonies

prairie schooner *n* : a covered wagon used by pioneers in cross-country travel

praise \'prāz\ *vb* **praised**; **prais·ing** **1** ♦ : to express approval of **2** ♦ : to glorify (a divinity or a saint) esp. in song — **praise** *n*

♦ [1] acclaim, applaud, cheer, crack up, hail, laud, salute, tout ♦ [2] bless, extol, glorify, laud, magnify

praise·wor·thy \-ˌwər-ˌthē\ *adj* ♦ : worthy of praise : LAUDABLE

♦ admirable, commendable, creditable, laudable, meritorious

pra·line \'prä-ˌlēn, 'prā-\ *n* : a confection of nuts and sugar

pram \'pram\ *n, chiefly Brit* : PERAMBULATOR

prance \'prans\ *vb* **pranced**; **pranc·ing** **1** : to spring from the hind legs ⟨a *prancing* horse⟩ **2** : to walk or move in a spirited manner : SWAGGER; *also* : CAPER — **prance** *n* — **pranc·er** *n*

prank \'praŋk\ *n* ♦ : a playful or mildly mischievous act : TRICK

♦ antic, caper, escapade, frolic, monkeyshine, practical joke, trick

prank·ster \'praŋk-stər\ *n* : a person who plays pranks

pra·seo·dym·i·um \ˌprā-zē-ō-'di-mē-əm\ *n* : a yellowish white metallic chemical element

prate \'prāt\ *vb* **prat·ed**; **prat·ing** : to talk long and idly : chatter foolishly : PRATTLE

prat·fall \'prat-ˌfȯl\ *n* **1** : a fall on the buttocks **2** : a humiliating blunder

¹**prat·tle** \'prat-ᵊl\ *vb* **prat·tled**; **prat·tling** **1** : to talk long and idly : BABBLE **2** ♦ : to utter or make meaningless sounds suggestive of the chatter of children — **prat·tler** *n*

♦ babble, chatter, drivel, gabble, gibber, jabber, sputter

²**prattle** *n* ♦ : trifling or childish talk

♦ babble, gabble, gibberish, gobbledygook, nonsense, piffle, rot

prawn \'prȯn\ *n* : any of various edible shrimplike crustaceans; *also* : SHRIMP 1

pray \'prā\ *vb* **1** ♦ : to make a request to (someone) in an earnest manner : ENTREAT, IMPLORE **2** : to ask earnestly for something **3** : to address God or a god esp. with supplication

♦ appeal, beg, beseech, entreat, implore, importune, petition, plead, solicit, supplicate

prayer \'prar\ *n* **1** : a supplication or expression addressed to God or a god; *also* : a set order of words used in praying **2** ♦ : an earnest request or wish **3** : the act or practice of praying to God or a god **4** : a religious service consisting chiefly of prayers — often used in pl. **5** : something prayed for **6** : a slight chance

♦ appeal, cry, entreaty, petition, plea, solicitation, suit, supplication

prayer book *n* : a book containing prayers and often directions for worship

prayer·ful \'prar-fəl\ *adj* **1** : DEVOUT **2** : characterized by or proceeding from an intense and serious state of mind : EARNEST — **prayer·ful·ly** *adv*

praying mantis *n* : MANTIS

PRC *abbr* People's Republic of China

preach \'prēch\ *vb* **1** : to deliver a sermon **2** : to set forth in a sermon **3** : to advocate earnestly — **preach·ment** *n*

preach·er \'prē-chər\ *n* ♦ : one that preaches

♦ clergyman, divine, ecclesiastic, father, minister, priest, reverend

pre·ad·o·les·cence \'prē-,ad-ᵊl-'es-ᵊns\ *n* : the period of human development just preceding adolescence — **pre·ad·o·les·cent** \-ᵊnt\ *adj or n*

pre·am·ble \'prē-,am-bəl\ *n* ♦ : an introductory part ⟨the ∼ to a constitution⟩

♦ foreword, introduction, preface, prologue

pre·ap·prove \,prē-ə-'prüv\ *vb* : to approve in advance — **pre·ap·prov·al** \-'prü-vəl\ *n*

pre·ar·range \,prē-ə-'rānj\ *vb* : to arrange beforehand — **pre·ar·range·ment** *n*

pre·as·sign \,prē-ə-'sīn\ *vb* : to assign beforehand

pre·bake \,prē-'bāk\ *vb* : to bake in advance

prec *abbr* preceding

Pre·cam·bri·an \'prē-'kam-brē-ən, -'kām-\ *adj* : of, relating to, or being the era that is earliest in geologic history and is characterized esp. by the appearance of single-celled organisms — **Precambrian** *n*

pre·can·cel \(,)prē-'kan-səl\ *vb* : to cancel (a postage stamp) in advance of use — **precancel** *n* — **pre·can·cel·la·tion** \,prē-,kan-sə-'lā-shən\ *n*

pre·can·cer·ous \(,)prē-'kan-sə-rəs\ *adj* : likely to become cancerous

pre·car·i·ous \pri-'kar-ē-əs\ *adj* : dependent on uncertain conditions : dangerously insecure : UNSTABLE ⟨a ∼ foothold⟩ ⟨∼ prosperity⟩ — **pre·car·i·ous·ly** *adv*

pre·car·i·ous·ness \-nəs\ *n* ♦ : the quality or state of being precarious

♦ insecurity, instability, shakiness, unsteadiness

pre·cau·tion \pri-'kȯ-shən\ *n* : a measure taken beforehand to prevent harm or secure good — **pre·cau·tion·ary** \-shə-,ner-ē\ *adj*

pre·cede \pri-'sēd\ *vb* **pre·ced·ed; pre·ced·ing** ♦ : to be, go, or come ahead or in front of (as in rank or time)

♦ antedate, forego *Ant* follow, succeed

pre·ce·dence \'pre-sə-dəns, pri-'sēd-ᵊns\ *n* **1** : the act or fact of preceding **2** : consideration based on order of importance : PRIORITY

¹pre·ce·dent \pri-'sēd-ᵊnt, 'pre-sə-dənt\ *adj* : prior in time, order, or significance

²prec·e·dent \'pre-sə-dənt\ *n* : something said or done that may serve to authorize or justify further words or acts of the same or a similar kind

pre·ced·ing \pri-'sē-diŋ\ *adj* ♦ : that precedes

♦ antecedent, anterior, foregoing, previous, prior

pre·cen·tor \pri-'sen-tər\ *n* : a leader of the singing of a choir or congregation

pre·cept \'prē-,sept\ *n* : a command or principle intended as a general rule of action or conduct

pre·cep·tor \pri-'sep-tər, 'prē-,sep-\ *n* : a person charged with the instruction and guidance of another : TUTOR

pre·ces·sion \prē-'se-shən\ *n* : a slow gyration of the rotation axis of a spinning body (as the earth) — **pre·cess** \prē-'ses\ *vb* — **pre·ces·sion·al** \-'sə-shə-nəl\ *adj*

pre·cinct \'prē-,siŋkt\ *n* **1** : an administrative subdivision (as of a city) : DISTRICT ⟨police ∼⟩ ⟨electoral ∼⟩ **2** : an enclosure bounded by the limits of a building or place — often used in pl. **3** *pl* : ENVIRONS

pre·ci·os·i·ty \,pre-shē-'ä-sə-tē\ *n, pl* **-ties** : fastidious refinement

pre·cious \'pre-shəs\ *adj* **1** ♦ : of great value ⟨∼ jewels⟩ **2** ♦ : greatly cherished : DEAR ⟨∼ memories⟩ **3** : AFFECTED ⟨∼ language⟩

♦ [1] costly, dear, expensive, high, valuable ♦ [2] beloved, dar-

ling, dear, favorite (*or* favourite), loved, pet, special, sweet ♦ [2] adorable, darling, dear, endearing, lovable, sweet, winning

prec·i·pice \'pre-sə-pəs\ *n* ♦ : a steep cliff

♦ bluff, cliff, crag, escarpment, palisade, scarp

pre·cip·i·tan·cy \pri-'si-pə-tən-sē\ *n* : undue hastiness or suddenness

¹pre·cip·i·tate \pri-'si-pə-,tāt\ *vb* **-tat·ed; -tat·ing** **1** : to throw violently **2** : to throw down **3** : to cause to happen quickly or abruptly ⟨∼ a quarrel⟩ **4** : to cause to separate from solution or suspension **5** : to fall as rain, snow, or hail

²pre·cip·i·tate \pri-'si-pə-tət, -,tāt\ *n* ♦ : the solid matter that separates from a solution or suspension

♦ deposit, dregs, grounds, sediment

³pre·cip·i·tate \pri-'si-pə-tət\ *adj* **1** ♦ : showing extreme or unwise haste : RASH **2** : falling with steep descent; *also* : PRECIPITOUS — **pre·cip·i·tate·ness** *n*

♦ cursory, hasty, headlong, pell-mell, precipitous, rash

pre·cip·i·tate·ly \-lē\ *adv* ♦ : in a precipitate manner

♦ cursorily, hastily, headlong, hurriedly, pell-mell, rashly

pre·cip·i·ta·tion \pri-,si-pə-'tā-shən\ *n* **1** ♦ : rash haste **2** : the process of precipitating or forming a precipitate **3** : water that falls to earth esp. as rain or snow; *also* : the quantity of this water

♦ haste, hurry, hustle, rush

pre·cip·i·tous \pri-'si-pə-təs\ *adj* **1** : showing extreme or unwise haste : PRECIPITATE **2** ♦ : having the character of a precipice : very steep ⟨a ∼ slope⟩; *also* : containing precipices ⟨∼ trails⟩

♦ abrupt, bold, sheer, steep

pre·cip·i·tous·ly \-lē\ *adv* : in a precipitous manner

pré·cis \prā-'sē\ *n, pl* **pré·cis** \-'sēz\ ♦ : a concise summary of essentials

♦ abstract, digest, encapsulation, epitome, outline, recapitulation, résumé (*or* resume), roundup, sum, summary, synopsis, wrap-up

pre·cise \pri-'sīs\ *adj* **1** ♦ : exactly defined or stated **2** ♦ : highly accurate : EXACT **3** ♦ : conforming strictly to a standard : SCRUPULOUS ⟨a ∼ teacher⟩

♦ [1] distinct, especial, express, set, special, specific ♦ [2] accurate, correct, exact, proper, right, so, true ♦ [2, 3] accurate, close, delicate, exact, fine, mathematical, pinpoint, rigorous, scrupulous *Ant* coarse, imprecise, inaccurate, inexact, rough

pre·cise·ly \-lē\ *adv* ♦ : in a precise manner

♦ accurately, exactly, just, right, sharp, squarely, strictly

pre·cise·ness \-nəs\ *n* : the quality or state of being precise

pre·ci·sion \pri-'si-zhən\ *n* ♦ : the quality or state of being precise

♦ accuracy, closeness, delicacy, exactness, fineness, veracity *Ant* coarseness, impreciseness, imprecision, inaccuracy, inexactness, roughness

pre·clude \pri-'klüd\ *vb* **pre·clud·ed; pre·clud·ing** ♦ : to make impossible : PREVENT

♦ avert, forestall, help, obviate, prevent

pre·co·cious \pri-'kō-shəs\ *adj* **1** ♦ : exceptionally early in development or occurrence **2** : exhibiting mature qualities at an unusually early age — **pre·coc·i·ty** \pri-'kä-sə-tē\ *n*

♦ early, premature, unseasonable, untimely

pre·co·cious·ly \-lē\ *adv* ♦ : in a precocious manner

♦ beforehand, early, prematurely, unseasonably

pre·con·ceive \,prē-kən-'sēv\ *vb* : to form an opinion of beforehand — **pre·con·cep·tion** \-'sep-shən\ *n*

pre·con·di·tion \-'di-shən\ *vb* : to put in proper or desired condition or frame of mind in advance

pre·cook \,prē-'kuk\ *vb* : to cook partially or entirely before final cooking or reheating

pre·cur·sor \pri-'kər-sər\ *n* **1** ♦ : one that precedes and indicates the approach of another : FORERUNNER **2** ♦ : one that precedes another in an office or process

♦ [1] angel, forerunner, harbinger, herald ♦ [2] ancestor, antecedent, forerunner

pred *abbr* predicate

pre·da·ceous *or* **pre·da·cious** \pri-'dā-shəs\ *adj* : living by preying on others : PREDATORY

pre·date \'prē-'dāt\ *vb* : to precede in time : ANTEDATE

pre·da·tion \pri-'dā-shən\ *n* **1** : the act of preying or plundering **2** : a mode of life in which food is primarily obtained by killing and consuming animals

pred·a·tor \'pre-də-tər\ *n* : an animal that lives by predation

pred·a·to·ry \'pre-də-ˌtōr-ē\ *adj* **1** : of or relating to plunder ⟨∼ warfare⟩ **2** : disposed to exploit others **3** : preying upon other animals

pre·dawn \(')prē-'dȯn\ *adj* : of or relating to the time just before dawn

pre·de·cease \ˌprē-di-'sēs\ *vb* **-ceased; -ceas·ing** : to die before another person

pre·de·ces·sor \'pre-də-ˌse-sər, 'prē-\ *n* **1** : a previous holder of a position to which another has succeeded **2** : something that has been followed or displaced by another

pre·des·ig·nate \(ˌ)prē-'de-zig-ˌnāt\ *vb* : to designate beforehand

pre·des·ti·na·tion \ˌprē-ˌdes-tə-'nā-shən\ *n* : the act of foreordaining to an earthly lot or eternal destiny by divine decree; *also* : the state of being so foreordained — **pre·des·ti·nate** \prē-'des-tə-ˌnāt\ *vb*

pre·des·tine \prē-'des-tən\ *vb* ♦ : to settle beforehand : FOREORDAIN

♦ destine, doom, fate, foredoom, foreordain, ordain

pre·de·ter·mine \ˌprē-di-'tər-mən\ *vb* : to determine beforehand

pred·i·ca·ble \'pre-di-kə-bəl\ *adj* : capable of being predicated or affirmed

pre·dic·a·ment \pri-'di-kə-mənt\ *n* ♦ : a difficult or trying situation

♦ corner, fix, hole, jam, pickle, spot

¹pred·i·cate \'pre-di-kət\ *n* : the part of a sentence or clause that expresses what is said of the subject

²pred·i·cate \'pre-də-ˌkāt\ *vb* **-cat·ed; -cat·ing 1** : AFFIRM **2** : to assert to be a quality or attribute **3** : to set or ground on something : BASE — **pred·i·ca·tion** \ˌpre-də-'kā-shən\ *n*

pre·dict \pri-'dikt\ *vb* ♦ : to declare in advance — **pre·dict·abil·i·ty** \-ˌdik-tə-'bi-lə-tē\ *n* — **pre·dict·able** \-'dik-tə-bəl\ *adj* — **pre·dict·ably** \-blē\ *adv*

♦ augur, forecast, foretell, presage, prognosticate, prophesy

pre·dic·tion \pri-'dik-shən\ *n* **1** ♦ : an act of predicting **2** : something that is predicted

♦ cast, forecast, prognostication, prophecy, soothsaying

pre·di·gest \ˌprē-dī-'jest\ *vb* : to simplify for easy use; *also* : to subject to artificial or natural partial digestion

pre·di·lec·tion \ˌpre-də-'lek-shən, ˌprē-\ *n* ♦ : an established preference for something

♦ bent, devices, disposition, genius, inclination, leaning, partiality, penchant, proclivity, propensity, tendency, turn

pre·dis·pose \ˌprē-di-'spōz\ *vb* : to incline in advance : make susceptible ⟨*predisposed* to infection⟩

pre·dis·po·si·tion \ˌprē-ˌdis-pə-'zi-shən\ *n* ♦ : a condition of being predisposed

♦ affinity, bent, devices, disposition, genius, inclination, leaning, partiality, penchant, predilection, proclivity, propensity, talent, tendency, turn

pre·dom·i·nance \pri-'dä-mə-nəns\ *n* ♦ : the quality or state of being predominant

♦ ascendancy, dominance, dominion, preeminence, supremacy

pre·dom·i·nant \pri-'dä-mə-nənt\ *adj* ♦ : greater in importance, strength, influence, or authority

♦ arch, cardinal, central, chief, dominant, first, foremost, grand, key, main, paramount, preeminent, premier, primary, principal, sovereign, supreme

pre·dom·i·nant·ly \-nənt-lē\ *adv* ♦ : for the most part : MAINLY

♦ altogether, basically, chiefly, generally, largely, mainly, mostly, overall, primarily, principally

pre·dom·i·nate \pri-'dä-mə-ˌnāt\ *vb* : to be superior esp. in power or numbers : PREVAIL

pre·dom·i·nate·ly \pri-'dä-mə-nət-lē\ *adv* : PREDOMINANTLY

pree·mie \'prē-mē\ *n* : a premature baby

pre·em·i·nence \prē-'e-mə-nəns\ *n* ♦ : the quality or state of being preeminent

♦ distinction, dominance, excellence, greatness, superiority, supremacy

pre·em·i·nent \prē-'e-mə-nənt\ *adj* ♦ : having highest rank — **pre·em·i·nent·ly** *adv*

♦ arch, cardinal, central, chief, dominant, first, foremost, grand, key, main, paramount, predominant, premier, primary, principal, sovereign, supreme ♦ distinguished, eminent, illustrious, noble, notable, noteworthy, outstanding, prestigious, signal, star, superior

pre·empt \prē-'empt\ *vb* **1** : to settle upon (public land) with the right to purchase before others; *also* : to take by such right **2** ♦ : to seize upon before someone else can **3** : to take the place of — **pre·emp·tion** \-'emp-shən\ *n*

♦ appropriate, arrogate, commandeer, usurp

pre·emp·tive \prē-'emp-tiv\ *adj* : marked by the seizing of the initiative : initiated by oneself ⟨∼ attack⟩

preen \'prēn\ *vb* **1** : to dress or smooth up : PRIMP **2** : to groom with the bill — used of a bird **3** : to pride (oneself) for achievement

pre·ex·ist \ˌprē-ig-'zist\ *vb* : to exist before — **pre·ex·is·tence** \-'zis-təns\ *n* — **pre·ex·is·tent** \-tənt\ *adj*

pref *abbr* **1** preface **2** preference **3** preferred **4** prefix

¹pre·fab \(ˌ)prē-'fab, 'prē-ˌfab\ *n* : a prefabricated structure

²pre·fab *adj* : produced by prefabrication ⟨a ∼ house⟩

pre·fab·ri·cate \prē-'fa-brə-ˌkāt\ *vb* : to manufacture the parts of (a structure) beforehand for later assembly — **pre·fab·ri·ca·tion** \ˌprē-ˌfa-bri-'kā-shən\ *n*

¹pref·ace \'pre-fəs\ *n* ♦ : the introductory remarks of a speaker or writer — **pref·a·to·ry** \'pre-fə-ˌtōr-ē\ *adj*

♦ foreword, introduction, preamble, prologue

²preface *vb* **pref·aced; pref·ac·ing** : to introduce with a preface

pre·fect \'prē-ˌfekt\ *n* **1** : a high official; *esp* : a chief officer or magistrate **2** : a student monitor

pre·fec·ture \'prē-ˌfek-chər\ *n* : the office, term, or residence of a prefect

pre·fer \pri-'fər\ *vb* **pre·ferred; pre·fer·ring 1** : PROMOTE **2** ♦ : to like better **3** : to bring (as a charge) against a person — **pref·er·a·ble** \'pre-fə-rə-bəl\ *adj*

♦ choose, cull, elect, handpick, name, opt, pick, select, single, take ♦ favor (*or* favour), lean, like

pref·er·a·bly \'pre-fə-rə-blē\ *adv* ♦ : it is preferred

♦ first, rather, readily, soon

pref·er·ence \'pre-frəns, -fə-rəns\ *n* **1** ♦ : a special liking for one thing over another **2** ♦ : the power or opportunity of choosing : CHOICE **3** ♦ : one that is preferred — **pref·er·en·tial** \ˌpre-fə-'ren-chəl\ *adj*

♦ [1] appetite, fancy, favor (*or* favour), fondness, like, liking, love, partiality, relish, shine, taste, use ♦ [2] alternative, choice, discretion, option, pick, way ♦ [3] darling, favorite (*or* favourite), pet, prize, treasure

pref·er·ment \pri-'fər-mənt\ *n* : advancement or promotion in dignity, office, or station : PROMOTION, ADVANCEMENT

preferred provider organization *n* : PPO

pre·fig·ure \prē-'fi-gyər\ *vb* **1** ♦ : to show, suggest, or announce beforehand : FORESHADOW **2** ♦ : to imagine beforehand

♦ foreshadow, harbinger

¹pre·fix \'prē-ˌfiks, prē-'fiks\ *vb* : to place before ⟨∼ a title to a name⟩

²pre·fix \'prē-ˌfiks\ *n* : an affix occurring at the beginning of a word

pre·flight \ˌprē-'flīt\ *adj* : preparing for or preliminary to flight

pre·form \(ˌ)prē-'fȯrm, 'prē-ˌfȯrm\ *vb* : to form or shape beforehand

preg·na·ble \'preg-nə-bəl\ *adj* : vulnerable to capture ⟨a ∼ fort⟩

preg·nant \'preg-nənt\ *adj* **1** : containing unborn offspring within the body **2** ♦ : rich in significance : MEANINGFUL — **preg·nan·cy** \-nən-sē\ *n*

♦ eloquent, expressive, meaning, meaningful, significant, suggestive

pre·heat \ˌprē-'hēt\ *vb* : to heat beforehand; *esp* : to heat (an oven) to a designated temperature before using

pre·hen·sile \prē-'hen-səl, -ˌsīl\ *adj* : adapted for grasping esp. by wrapping around ⟨a monkey with a ∼ tail⟩

pre·his·tor·ic \ˌprē-his-'tȯr-ik\ *also* **pre·his·tor·i·cal** \-i-kəl\ *adj* : of, relating to, or existing in the period before written history began

pre·judge \(ˌ)prē-'jəj\ *vb* : to judge before full hearing or examination

¹prej·u·dice \'pre-jə-dəs\ *n* **1** : DAMAGE; *esp* : detriment to one's rights or claims **2** ♦ : an opinion made without adequate basis ⟨racial ∼⟩

♦ bias, favor (or favour), partiality, partisanship

²prejudice vb **-diced; -dic·ing 1** : to damage by a judgment or action esp. at law **2** : to cause to have prejudice
prejudiced adj ♦ : resulting from or having a prejudice or bias for or esp. against

♦ biased, one-sided, partial, partisan ♦ bigoted, intolerant, narrow, narrow-minded

prej·u·di·cial \ˌpre-jə-ˈdi-shəl\ adj **1** ♦ : tending to injure or impair **2** : leading to premature judgment or unwarranted opinion

♦ adverse, counter, disadvantageous, harmful, hostile, inimical, negative, unfavorable (or unfavourable), unfriendly, unsympathetic

pre·kin·der·gar·ten \(ˈ)prē-ˈkin-dər-ˌgär-tᵊn\ n **1** : NURSERY SCHOOL **2** : a class or program preceding kindergarten
prel·ate \ˈpre-lət\ n : an ecclesiastic (as a bishop) of high rank — **prel·a·cy** \-lə-sē\ n
pre·launch \ˈprē-ˈlónch\ adj : preparing for or preliminary to launch
pre·lim \ˈprē-ˌlim, pri-ˈlim\ n or adj : PRELIMINARY
¹pre·lim·i·nary \pri-ˈli-mə-ˌner-ē\ n, pl **-naries** : something that precedes or introduces the main business or event
²preliminary adj : preceding the main discourse or business
pre·lude \ˈprel-ˌyüd; ˈprē-ˌlüd, ˈprā-\ n **1** : an introductory performance or event **2** : a musical section or movement introducing the main theme; also : an organ solo played at the beginning of a church service
prem abbr premium
pre·mar·i·tal \(ˌ)prē-ˈmar-ət-ᵊl\ adj : existing or occurring before marriage
pre·ma·ture \ˌprē-mə-ˈtùr, -ˈtyùr, -ˈchùr\ adj ♦ : happening, coming, born, or done before the usual or proper time

♦ early, precocious, unseasonable, untimely

pre·ma·ture·ly \-lē\ adv ♦ : in a premature manner : too soon

♦ beforehand, early, precociously, unseasonably

¹pre·med \ˌprē-ˈmed\ n : a premedical student or course of study
²premed adj : PREMEDICAL
pre·med·i·cal \(ˌ)prē-ˈme-di-kəl\ adj : preceding and preparing for the professional study of medicine
pre·med·i·tate \pri-ˈme-də-ˌtāt\ vb : to consider and plan beforehand — **pre·med·i·ta·tion** \-ˌme-də-ˈtā-shən\ n
pre·men·o·paus·al \(ˌ)prē-ˌme-nə-ˈpò-zəl\ adj : of, relating to, or being in the period preceding menopause
pre·men·stru·al \(ˌ)prē-ˈmen-strə-wəl\ adj : of, relating to, or occurring in the period just before menstruation
premenstrual syndrome n : a varying group of symptoms manifested by some women prior to menstruation
premie var of PREEMIE
¹pre·mier \pri-ˈmir, -ˈmyir, ˈprē-mē-ər\ adj **1** : first in rank or importance : CHIEF **2** ♦ : earliest in time

♦ [1] chief, first, foremost, head, high, lead, preeminent, primary, prime, principal, supreme ♦ [2] first, inaugural, initial, maiden, original, pioneer

²premier n : PRIME MINISTER — **pre·mier·ship** n
¹pre·miere \pri-ˈmyer, -ˈmir\ n : a first performance
²premiere also **pre·mier** \same as ¹PREMIERE\ vb **pre·miered; pre·mier·ing** : to give or receive a first public performance
prem·ise \ˈpre-məs\ n **1** ♦ : a statement of fact or a supposition made or implied as a basis of argument **2** pl ♦ : a piece of land with the structures on it; also : the place of business of an enterprise

♦ [1] assumption, postulate, presumption, supposition **premises** ♦ [2] demesne, grounds, park, yard

pre·mi·um \ˈprē-mē-əm\ n **1** : a reward or recompense for a particular act : REWARD, PRIZE **2** : a sum over and above the stated value **3** : something paid over and above a fixed wage or price **4** : something given with a purchase **5** : the sum paid for a contract of insurance **6** : an unusually high value
pre·mix \ˌprē-ˈmiks\ vb : to mix before use
pre·mo·lar \(ˌ)prē-ˈmō-lər\ adj : situated in front of or preceding the molar teeth; esp : being or relating to those teeth of a mammal in front of the true molars and behind the canines — **premolar** n
pre·mo·ni·tion \ˌprē-mə-ˈni-shən, ˌpre-\ n **1** : previous warning **2** ♦ : anticipation of an event without conscious reason : PRESENTIMENT — **pre·mon·i·to·ry** \pri-ˈmä-nə-ˌtōr-ē\ adj

♦ foreboding, presage, presentiment

pre·na·tal \ˈprē-ˈnāt-ᵊl\ adj : occurring, existing, or taking place before birth
pre·nup·tial \prē-ˈnəp-shəl\ adj : made or occurring before marriage
prenuptial agreement n : an agreement between a couple before marrying in which they give up future rights to each other's property in the event of divorce or death
pre·oc·cu·pa·tion \prē-ˌä-kyə-ˈpā-shən\ n **1** : complete absorption of the mind or interests **2** ♦ : something that causes complete absorption of the mind or interests

♦ fetish, fixation, mania, obsession, prepossession

pre·oc·cu·pied \prē-ˈä-kyə-ˌpīd\ adj **1** ♦ : lost in thought; also : absorbed in some preoccupation **2** : already occupied

♦ absent, absentminded, abstracted

pre·oc·cu·py \-ˌpī\ vb **1** : to occupy the attention of beforehand **2** : to take possession of before another
pre·op·er·a·tive \(ˌ)prē-ˈä-prə-tiv, -pə-ˌrā-\ adj : occurring before a surgical operation
pre·or·dain \ˌprē-òr-ˈdān\ vb : FOREORDAIN
pre—owned \(ˌ)prē-ˈōnd\ adj : SECONDHAND
prep abbr **1** preparatory **2** preposition
pre·pack·age \(ˌ)prē-ˈpa-kij\ vb : to package (as food) before offering for sale to the customer
preparatory school n **1** : a usu. private school preparing students primarily for college **2** Brit : a private elementary school preparing students primarily for British public schools
pre·pare \pri-ˈpar\ vb **pre·pared; pre·par·ing 1** ♦ : to make or get ready ⟨∼ dinner⟩ ⟨∼ a student for college⟩ **2** ♦ : to get ready beforehand **3** : to put together : COMPOUND ⟨∼ a prescription⟩ **4** ♦ : to put into written form — **prep·a·ra·tion** \ˌpre-pə-ˈrā-shən\ n — **pre·pa·ra·to·ry** \pri-ˈpar-ə-ˌtōr-ē\ adj

♦ [1] equip, fit, qualify, ready, season ♦ [2] fit, fix, get, lay, ready ♦ [4] cast, compose, craft, draft, draw, formulate, frame

prepared adj **1** : made ready, fit, or suitable beforehand **2** : subjected to a special process or treatment
pre·pared·ness \pri-ˈpar-əd-nəs\ n : a state of adequate preparation
pre·pay \(ˌ)prē-ˈpā\ vb **-paid** \-ˈpād\; **-pay·ing** : to pay or pay the charge on in advance
pre·pon·der·ant \pri-ˈpän-də-rənt\ adj : having greater weight, force, influence, or frequency — **pre·pon·der·ance** \-rəns\ n — **pre·pon·der·ant·ly** adv
pre·pon·der·ate \pri-ˈpän-də-ˌrāt\ vb **-at·ed; -at·ing** : to exceed in weight, force, influence, or frequency : PREDOMINATE
prep·o·si·tion \ˌpre-pə-ˈzi-shən\ n : a word that combines with a noun or pronoun to form a phrase — **prep·o·si·tion·al** \-ˈzi-shə-nəl\ adj
pre·pos·sess \ˌprē-pə-ˈzes\ vb **1** : to cause to be preoccupied **2** : to influence beforehand esp. favorably
pre·pos·sess·ing adj : tending to create a favorable impression ⟨a ∼ manner⟩
pre·pos·ses·sion \-ˈze-shən\ n **1** : PREJUDICE **2** ♦ : an exclusive concern with one idea or object

♦ fetish, fixation, mania, obsession, preoccupation

pre·pos·ter·ous \pri-ˈpäs-tə-rəs\ adj ♦ : contrary to nature or reason : ABSURD

♦ absurd, bizarre, fanciful, fantastic, foolish, nonsensical, unreal, wild ♦ absurd, comical, derisive, farcical, laughable, ludicrous, ridiculous, risible, silly

prep·py or **prep·pie** \ˈpre-pē\ n, pl **preppies 1** : a student at or a graduate of a preparatory school **2** : a person deemed to dress or behave like a preppy
pre·puce \ˈprē-ˌpyüs\ n : FORESKIN
pre·quel \ˈprē-kwəl\ n : a literary or dramatic work whose story precedes that of an earlier work
pre·re·cord·ed \(ˌ)prē-ri-ˈkór-dəd\ adj : recorded for later broadcast or play
pre·req·ui·site \prē-ˈre-kwə-zət\ n : something required beforehand or for the end in view — **prerequisite** adj
pre·rog·a·tive \pri-ˈrä-gə-tiv\ n ♦ : an exclusive or special right, power, or privilege

♦ birthright, right

pres abbr **1** present **2** president
¹pres·age \ˈpre-sij\ n **1** ♦ : something that foreshadows a future event : OMEN **2** ♦ : an intuition or feeling of what is going to happen in the future : FOREBODING

♦ [1] augury, auspice, foreboding, omen, portent ♦ [2] foreboding, premonition, presentiment

²pre·sage \'pre-sij, pri-'sāj\ *vb* **pre·saged; pre·sag·ing 1 :** to give an omen or warning of : FORESHADOW **2** ♦ **:** to tell beforehand : FORETELL, PREDICT

♦ augur, forecast, foretell, predict, prognosticate, prophesy

pres·by·o·pia \ˌprez-bē-'ō-pē-ə\ *n* **:** a visual condition in which loss of elasticity of the lens of the eye causes defective accommodation and inability to focus sharply for near vision — **pres·by·o·pic** \-'ō-pik, -'ä-\ *adj or n*

pres·by·ter \'prez-bə-tər\ *n* **1 :** PRIEST, MINISTER **2 :** an elder in a Presbyterian church

¹Pres·by·te·ri·an \ˌprez-bə-'tir-ē-ən\ *n* **:** a member of a Presbyterian church

²Presbyterian *adj* **1** *often not cap* **:** characterized by a graded system of representative ecclesiastical bodies (as presbyteries) exercising legislative and judicial powers **2 :** of or relating to a group of Protestant Christian bodies that are presbyterian in government — **Pres·by·te·ri·an·ism** \-ə-ˌni-zəm\ *n*

pres·by·tery \'prez-bə-ˌter-ē\ *n, pl* **-ter·ies 1 :** the part of a church reserved for the officiating clergy **2 :** a ruling body in Presbyterian churches consisting of the ministers and representative elders of a district

¹pre·school \'prē-ˌskül\ *adj* **:** of or relating to the period in a child's life from infancy to the age of five or six — **pre·school·er** \-ˌskü-lər\ *n*

²preschool *n* **:** NURSERY SCHOOL

pre·science \'pre-shəns, 'prē-\ *n* **1 :** foreknowledge of events **2** ♦ **:** the act or fact of being concerned for and making preparations for the future

♦ foresight, forethought, providence

pre·scient \-shənt, -shē-ənt\ *adj* ♦ **:** having or marked by prescience **:** characterized by foresight

♦ farsighted, foresighted, provident

pre·scribe \pri-'skrīb\ *vb* **pre·scribed; pre·scrib·ing 1** ♦ **:** to lay down as a guide or rule of action **2 :** to direct the use of (as a medicine) as a remedy

♦ define, lay down, specify

pre·scrip·tion \pri-'skrip-shən\ *n* **1 :** the action of prescribing rules or directions **2 :** a written direction for the preparation and use of a medicine; *also* **:** a medicine prescribed

pre·scrip·tive \pri-'skrip-tiv\ *adj* **1 :** serving to prescribe ⟨∼ rules⟩ **2 :** acquired by, based on, or determined by prescription or by custom

pres·ence \'prez-ᵊns\ *n* **1 :** the fact or condition of being present **2 :** the space immediately around a person **3 :** one that is present **4** ♦ **:** the bearing, carriage, or air of a person; *esp* **:** stately bearing

♦ appearance, aspect, look, mien

¹pres·ent \'prez-ᵊnt\ *n* ♦ **:** something presented : GIFT

♦ bestowal, donation, freebie, gift, lagniappe, largesse

²pre·sent \pri-'zent\ *vb* **1 :** to bring into the presence or acquaintance of : INTRODUCE **2** ♦ **:** to bring before the public ⟨∼ a play⟩ **3 :** to make a gift to **4** ♦ **:** to give formally **5 :** to lay (a charge) before a court for inquiry **6 :** to aim or direct (as a weapon) so as to face in a particular direction — **pre·sent·able** *adj* — **pre·sent·ment** \pri-'zent-mənt\ *n*

♦ [2] carry, give, mount, offer, stage ♦ [4] bestow, contribute, donate, give

³pres·ent \'prez-ᵊnt\ *adj* **1** ♦ **:** now existing or in progress ⟨∼ conditions⟩ **2 :** being in view or at hand ⟨∼ at the meeting⟩ **3 :** under consideration ⟨the ∼ problem⟩ **4 :** of, relating to, or constituting a verb tense that expresses present time or the time of speaking

♦ current, extant, ongoing *Ant* ago, past; future

⁴pres·ent \'prez-ᵊnt\ *n* **1** *pl* **:** the present legal document **2 :** the present tense; *also* **:** a verb form in it **3** ♦ **:** the present time

♦ moment, now, today *Ant* past; future

pre·sen·ta·tion \ˌprē-ˌzen-'tā-shən, ˌprez-ᵊn-\ *n* **1 :** the act of presenting **2 :** something presented

pres·ent–day \'prez-ᵊnt-ˌdā\ *adj* **:** now existing or occurring : CURRENT

pre·sen·ti·ment \pri-'zen-tə-mənt\ *n* ♦ **:** a feeling that something is about to happen : PREMONITION ⟨a ∼ of danger⟩

♦ foreboding, premonition, presage

pres·ent·ly \'prez-ᵊnt-lē\ *adv* **1** ♦ **:** in the near future : SOON **2** ♦ **:** at the present time : NOW

♦ [1] anon, momentarily, shortly, soon ♦ [2] anymore, now, nowadays, right now, today

present participle *n* **:** a participle that typically expresses present action and that in English is formed with the suffix *-ing* and is used in the formation of the progressive tenses

pres·er·va·tion \ˌpre-zər-'vā-shən\ *n* ♦ **:** the act of preserving or the state of being preserved

♦ conservation, maintenance, upkeep

¹pre·serve \pri-'zərv\ *vb* **pre·served; pre·serv·ing 1 :** to keep safe : GUARD, PROTECT **2 :** to keep from decaying; *esp* **:** to process food (as by canning or pickling) to prevent spoilage **3** **:** MAINTAIN ⟨∼ silence⟩ **4** ♦ **:** to keep alive, intact, in existence, or from decay — **pre·ser·va·tive** \pri-'zər-və-tiv\ *adj or n* — **pre·serv·er** *n*

♦ conserve, keep up, maintain, save

²preserve *n* **1 :** preserved fruit — often used in pl. **2 :** an area for the protection of natural resources (as animals)

pre·set \(ˌ)prē-'set\ *vb* **-set; -set·ting :** to set beforehand

pre·shrink \prē-'shriŋk\ *vb* **-shrank** \-'shraŋk\; **-shrunk** \-'shrəŋk\; **-shrink·ing :** to shrink (as a fabric) before making into a garment

pre·side \pri-'zīd\ *vb* **pre·sid·ed; pre·sid·ing 1** ♦ **:** to exercise guidance or control **2 :** to occupy the place of authority; *esp* **:** to act as chairman

♦ *usu* **preside over** boss, captain, command, control, govern, rule

pres·i·dent \'pre-zə-dənt\ *n* **1** ♦ **:** one chosen to preside ⟨∼ of the assembly⟩ **2 :** the chief officer of an organization (as a corporation or society) **3 :** an elected official serving as both chief of state and chief political executive; *also* **:** a chief of state often with only minimal political powers — **pres·i·den·cy** \-dən-sē\ *n* — **pres·i·den·tial** \ˌpre-zə-'den-chəl\ *adj*

♦ chair, chairman, moderator, speaker

pre·si·dio \pri-'sē-dē-ˌō, -'si-\ *n, pl* **-di·os :** a military post or fortified settlement in an area currently or orig. under Spanish control

pre·sid·i·um \pri-'si-dē-əm\ *n, pl* **-ia** \-dē-ə\ *or* **-iums :** a permanent executive committee that acts for a larger body in a Communist country

¹pre·soak \(ˌ)prē-'sōk\ *vb* **:** to soak beforehand

²pre·soak \'prē-ˌsōk\ *n* **1 :** an instance of presoaking **2 :** a preparation used in presoaking clothes

pre·sort \(ˌ)prē-'sȯrt\ *vb* **:** to sort (mail) by zip code usu. before delivery to a post office

¹press \'pres\ *n* **1** ♦ **:** a crowd or crowded condition : THRONG **2** **:** a machine for exerting pressure **3 :** CLOSET, CUPBOARD **4** **:** PRESSURE **5 :** the properly creased condition of a freshly pressed garment **6 :** PRINTING PRESS; *also* **:** the act or the process of printing **7 :** a printing or publishing establishment **8 :** the media (as newspapers and magazines) of public news and comment; *also* **:** persons (as reporters) employed in these media **9** **:** comment in newspapers and periodicals

♦ army, crowd, crush, drove, flock, horde, host, legion, mob, multitude, swarm, throng

²press *vb* **1** ♦ **:** to bear down upon : push steadily against **2 :** ASSAIL, COMPEL **3** ♦ **:** to squeeze out the juice or contents of ⟨∼ grapes⟩ **4 :** to squeeze to a desired density, shape, or smoothness; *esp* **:** IRON **5 a :** to try hard to persuade : URGE **b** ♦ **:** to move to action or reaction through pressure **6 :** to follow through **:** PROSECUTE **7** ♦ **:** to crowd closely **8** ♦ **:** to force one's way **9** **:** to require haste or speed in action **10** ♦ **:** to insist on or request urgently — **press·er** *n*

♦ [1] bear, depress, shove, weigh ♦ [3] crush, express, mash, squeeze ♦ [5b] coerce, compel, constrain, drive, force, make, muscle, obligate, oblige, pressure, urge ♦ [7] bunch, cluster, crowd, huddle ♦ [8] bulldoze, elbow, muscle, push ♦ *often* **press for** [10] call, claim, clamor (*or* clamour), command, demand, enjoin, exact, insist, quest, stipulate (for)

press agent *n* **:** an agent employed to establish and maintain good public relations through publicity

press·ing *adj* ♦ **:** urgently important

♦ acute, critical, dire, imperative, imperious, instant, urgent

press·man \'pres-mən, -ˌman\ *n* **:** the operator of a press and esp. a printing press

press·room \-rüm, -ˌrum\ *n* **1** : a room in a printing plant containing the printing presses **2** : a room for the use of reporters

¹pres·sure \'pre-shər\ *n* **1** : the burden of physical or mental distress **2** : the action of pressing; *esp* : the application of force to something by something else in direct contact with it **3** : the force exerted over a surface divided by its area **4 ♦** : the stress or urgency of matters demanding attention

♦ strain, stress, tension ♦ coercion, compulsion, constraint, duress, force

²pressure *vb* **pres·sured; pres·sur·ing 1** : to apply pressure to **2 ♦** : to cause an action or reaction as a result of applied pressure

♦ coerce, compel, constrain, drive, force, make, muscle, obligate, oblige, press

pressure group *n* : a group that seeks to influence governmental policy but not to elect candidates to office
pressure suit *n* : an inflatable suit for high-altitude flight or spaceflight to protect the body from low pressure
pres·sur·ise *chiefly Brit var of* PRESSURIZE
pres·sur·ize \'pre-shə-ˌrīz\ *vb* **-ized; -iz·ing 1** : to maintain higher pressure within than without; *esp* : to maintain normal atmospheric pressure within (as an airplane cabin) during high-altitude flight or spaceflight **2** : to apply pressure to **3** : to design to withstand pressure — **pres·sur·i·za·tion** \ˌpre-shə-rə-'zā-shən\ *n*

pres·ti·dig·i·ta·tion \ˌpres-tə-ˌdi-jə-'tā-shən\ *n* **♦** : skill and dexterity in executing tricks or deception : SLEIGHT OF HAND

♦ legerdemain, magic

pres·tige \pres-'tēzh, -'tēj\ *n* : standing or estimation in the eyes of people : REPUTATION
pres·ti·gious \pres-'ti-jəs, -'tē-\ *adj* **♦** : having prestige

♦ name, reputable, reputed, respectable ♦ distinguished, eminent, illustrious, noble, notable, noteworthy, outstanding, preeminent, signal, star, superior

pres·to \'pres-tō\ *adv or adj* **1 ♦** : suddenly as if by magic : IMMEDIATELY **2** : at a rapid tempo — used as a direction in music

♦ apace, briskly, fast, full tilt, hastily, immediately, posthaste, pronto, quick, quickly, rapidly, soon, speedily, swift, swiftly

pre·stress \(ˌ)prē-'stres\ *vb* : to introduce internal stresses into (as a structural beam) to counteract later load stresses
pre·sum·ably \pri-'zü-mə-blē\ *adv* **♦** : by reasonable assumption

♦ apparently, evidently, ostensibly, seemingly, supposedly ♦ doubtless, likely, probably

pre·sume \pri-'züm\ *vb* **pre·sumed; pre·sum·ing 1** : to take upon oneself without leave or warrant : DARE **2 ♦** : to take for granted : ASSUME **3** : to act or behave with undue boldness — **pre·sum·able** \-'zü-mə-bəl\ *adj*

♦ assume, postulate, premise, presuppose, suppose

pre·sump·tion \pri-'zəmp-shən\ *n* **1 ♦** : presumptuous attitude or conduct : AUDACITY **2 ♦** : an attitude or belief dictated by probability; *also* : the grounds lending probability to a belief — **pre·sump·tive** \-tiv\ *adj*

♦ [1] audacity, brass, brazenness, cheek, chutzpah, effrontery, gall, nerve, sauce, sauciness, temerity ♦ [2] assumption, postulate, premise, supposition

pre·sump·tu·ous \pri-'zəmp-chə-wəs\ *adj* **♦** : overstepping due bounds (as of propriety or courtesy) : taking liberties — **pre·sump·tu·ous·ly** *adv*

♦ arrogant, cavalier, haughty, high-handed, imperious, important, overweening, pompous, pretentious, supercilious, superior ♦ bold, familiar, forward, free, immodest *Ant* modest, unassuming ♦ intrusive, meddlesome, nosy, obtrusive, officious, prying

pre·sup·pose \ˌprē-sə-'pōz\ *vb* **1 ♦** : to suppose beforehand **2** : to require beforehand as a necessary condition

♦ assume, postulate, premise, presume, suppose

pre·sup·po·si·tion \(ˌ)prē-ˌsə-pə-'zi-shən\ *n* : an act of presupposing or an assumption made in advance
pre·teen \'prē-'tēn\ *n* : a boy or girl not yet 13 years old — **pre·teen** *adj*
pre·tend \pri-'tend\ *vb* **1** : PROFESS \doesn't ~ to be scientific\ **2** : to make believe : FEIGN \~ to be angry\ **3** : to lay claim \~ to a throne\

♦ affect, assume, counterfeit, fake, feign, profess, put on, sham, simulate ♦ dissemble, dissimulate, let on

pre·tend·er \pri-'ten-dər\ *n* **♦** : one that pretends

♦ charlatan, fake, fraud, hoaxer, humbug, mountebank, phony, quack

pre·tense *or* **pre·tence** \'prē-ˌtens, pri-'tens\ *n* **1** : a claim made or implied; *esp* : one not supported by fact **2 ♦** : an assumed display or attitude of superiority or dignity **3** : an inadequate or insincere attempt to attain a certain condition \made a ~ at discipline\ **4** : false show : PRETEXT **5 ♦** : excessive display : PRETENTIOUSNESS

♦ [2] act, airs, facade, front, guise, masquerade, pose, put-on, semblance, show ♦ [5] affectation, pretension, pretentiousness

pre·ten·sion \pri-'ten-chən\ *n* **1** : an allegation of doubtful value : PRETEXT **2 ♦** : claim or an effort to establish a claim **3** : a claim or right to attention or honor because of merit **4 ♦** : an aspiration or intention that may or may not reach fulfillment **5** : the quality or act of making usu. unjustified claims (as to excellence) **6** : an exaggerated sense of self-importance

♦ [2] call, claim, pretense, right ♦ [4] aim, ambition, aspiration, design, dream, end, goal, intent, mark, meaning, object, objective, plan, purpose, thing

pre·ten·tious \pri-'ten-chəs\ *adj* **1 ♦** : making or possessing usu. unjustified claims (as to excellence) \a ~ literary style\ **2** : making demands on one's ability or means : AMBITIOUS \too ~ an undertaking\ — **pre·ten·tious·ly** *adv*

♦ affected, grandiose, highfalutin, ostentatious, pompous *Ant* modest, unpretentious

pre·ten·tious·ness \-nəs\ *n* **♦** : the quality or state of being pretentious

♦ affectation, arrogance, haughtiness, loftiness, pretense, pretension, self-importance, superiority

pret·er·it *or* **pret·er·ite** \'pre-tə-rət\ *n* : a verb form expressing action in the past
pre·term \(ˌ)prē-'tərm, 'prē-ˌ\ *adj* : of, relating to, being, or brought forth by premature birth \a ~ infant\
pre·ter·nat·u·ral \ˌprē-tər-'na-chə-rəl\ *adj* **1** : exceeding what is natural \his ~ calm\ **2 ♦** : inexplicable by ordinary means — **pre·ter·nat·u·ral·ly** *adv*

♦ metaphysical, superhuman, supernatural, unearthly

pre·text \'prē-ˌtekst\ *n* : a purpose stated or assumed to cloak the real intention or state of affairs
pret·ti·fy \'pri-ti-ˌfī\ *vb* **-fied; -fy·ing** : to make pretty — **pret·ti·fi·ca·tion** \ˌpri-ti-fə-'kā-shən\ *n*
pret·ti·ness \'pri-tē-nəs\ *n* **♦** : the quality or state of being pretty

♦ attractiveness, beauty, comeliness, handsomeness, looks, loveliness

¹pret·ty \'pri-tē\ *adj* **pret·ti·er; -est 1 ♦** : pleasing by delicacy or grace : having conventionally accepted elements of beauty \~ flowers\ **2** : MISERABLE, TERRIBLE \a ~ state of affairs\ **3** : moderately large \a ~ profit\ **4** : PLEASANT — **pret·ti·ly** \-tə-lē\ *adv*

♦ attractive, beautiful, cute, fair, handsome, lovely

²pretty *adv* **♦** : in some degree : MODERATELY

♦ enough, fairly, kind of, moderately, quite, rather, somewhat, sort of, so-so

³pretty *vb* **pret·tied; pret·ty·ing** : to make pretty
pretty boy *n, usu disparaging* : a man who is notably good-looking
pret·zel \'pret-səl\ *n* : a brittle or chewy glazed usu. salted slender bread often shaped like a loose knot
prev *abbr* previous; previously
pre·vail \pri-'vāl\ *vb* **1 ♦** : to gain ascendency through strength or superiority : TRIUMPH **2** : to be or become effective : SUCCEED **3 ♦** : to urge successfully \~ed upon her to sing\ **4** : to be frequent : PREDOMINATE **5** : to be or continue in use or fashion — **pre·vail·ing·ly** *adv*

♦ [1] conquer, triumph, win ♦ *usu* **prevail over** [1] beat, defeat, master, triumph, win ♦ *usu* **prevail on** *or* **prevail upon** [3] argue, convince, get, induce, move, persuade, satisfy, talk, win ♦ [5] hold, hold out, keep up, last, survive

prev·a·lent \'pre-və-lənt\ *adj* : generally or widely existent : WIDESPREAD — **prev·a·lence** \-ləns\ *n*
pre·var·i·cate \pri-'var-ə-ˌkāt\ *vb* **-cat·ed; -cat·ing ♦** : to deviate from the truth

♦ fabricate, fib, lie

pre·var·i·ca·tion \pri-ˌvar-ə-'kā-shən\ *n* **1** : the act or an instance of prevaricating **2** ♦ : a statement that deviates from or perverts the truth

♦ fabrication, fairy tale, falsehood, falsity, fib, lie, mendacity, story, tale, untruth, whopper

pre•var•i•ca•tor \pri-'var-ə-ˌkā-tər\ n ♦ : one who evades or perverts the truth

♦ fibber, liar

pre•vent \pri-'vent\ vb **1** ♦ : to keep from happening or existing ⟨steps to ~ war⟩ **2** : to hold back : HINDER, STOP ⟨~ us from going⟩ — **pre•vent•able** also **pre•vent•ible** \-'ven-tə-bəl\ adj — **pre•ven•ta•tive** \-'ven-tə-tiv\ adj or n — **pre•ven•tive** \-'ven-tiv\ adj or n

♦ avert, forestall, help, obviate, preclude

pre•ven•tion \pri-'ven-chən\ n : the act of preventing or hindering
pre•ver•bal \ˌprē-'vər-bəl\ adj : having not yet acquired the faculty of speech
¹**pre•view** \'prē-ˌvyü\ vb : to see or discuss beforehand; esp : to view or show in advance of public presentation
²**preview** n **1** : an advance showing or viewing **2** also **pre•vue** \-ˌvyü\ : a showing of snatches from a motion picture advertised for future appearance **3** : FORETASTE
pre•vi•ous \'prē-vē-əs\ adj ♦ : going before

♦ antecedent, anterior, foregoing, preceding, prior *Ant* after, ensuing, following, subsequent, succeeding

pre•vi•ous•ly \-lē\ adv ♦ : in time past

♦ ahead, before, beforehand

previous to prep ♦ : in advance of : BEFORE

♦ ahead of, before, ere, of, prior to, to

pre•vi•sion \prē-'vi-zhən\ n **1** : FORESIGHT, PRESCIENCE **2** : FORECAST, PREDICTION ⟨a ~ of success⟩
pre•war \'prē-'wȯr\ adj : occurring or existing before a war
¹**prey** \'prā\ n, pl **prey** also **preys 1** : an animal taken for food by a predator; also : VICTIM **2** : the act or habit of preying
²**prey** vb **1** : to raid for booty **2** : to seize and devour prey **3** : to have a harmful or wearing effect
prf abbr proof
¹**price** \'prīs\ n **1** archaic : VALUE **2** ♦ : the amount of money paid or asked for the sale of a specified thing; also : the cost at which something is obtained

♦ charge, cost, fee, figure

²**price** vb **priced; pric•ing 1** : to set a price on **2** : to ask the price of **3** : to drive by raising prices ⟨priced themselves out of the market⟩
price–fix•ing \'prīs-ˌfik-siŋ\ n : the setting of prices artificially (as by producers or government)
price•less \-ləs\ adj : having a value beyond any price : INVALUABLE
price support n : artificial maintenance of prices of a commodity at a level usu. fixed through government action
price war n : a period of commercial competition in which prices are repeatedly cut by the competitors
pric•ey also **pricy** \'prī-sē\ adj **pric•i•er; -est** : EXPENSIVE
¹**prick** \'prik\ n **1** ♦ : a mark or small wound made by a pointed instrument **2** : something sharp or pointed **3 a** : an instance of pricking **b** ♦ : a sensation of being pricked

♦ [1] perforation, pinhole, punch, puncture, stab ♦ [3b] ache, pain, pang, smart, sting, stitch, tingle, twinge

²**prick** vb **1** : to pierce slightly with a sharp point; also : to have or cause a pricking sensation **2** : to affect with anguish or remorse ⟨~s his conscience⟩ **3** : to outline with punctures ⟨~ out a pattern⟩ **4** : to stand or cause to stand erect ⟨the dog's ears ~ed up at the sound⟩
prick•er \'pri-kər\ n : BRIAR; also : THORN
¹**prick•le** \'pri-kəl\ n **1** : a small sharp process (as on a plant) **2** : a slight stinging pain
²**prickle** vb **prick•led; prick•ling 1** : to prick lightly **2** : TINGLE
prick•ly \'pri-klē\ adj ♦ : full of or covered with prickles

♦ brambly, scratchy, thorny

prickly heat n : a red cutaneous eruption with intense itching and tingling caused by inflammation around the ducts of the sweat glands
prickly pear n : any of numerous cacti with usu. yellow flowers and prickly flat or rounded joints; also : the sweet pulpy pear-shaped edible fruit of various prickly pears
¹**pride** \'prīd\ n **1** ♦ : inordinate self-esteem : CONCEIT **2**

♦ : justifiable self-respect **3** : elation over an act or possession **4** : haughty behavior : DISDAIN **5** : ostentatious display **6** ♦ : a source of pride

♦ [1] complacence, conceit, ego, egotism, self-conceit, self-esteem, self-importance, self-satisfaction, smugness, vainglory, vanity ♦ [2] ego, self-esteem, self-regard, self-respect ♦ [6] boast, credit, glory, honor (or honour), jewel, treasure

²**pride** vb **prid•ed; prid•ing** : to indulge (as oneself) in pride
pride•ful \'prīd-fəl\ adj ♦ : full of pride

♦ disdainful, haughty, highfalutin, lofty, lordly, proud, superior

priest \'prēst\ n : a person having authority to perform the sacred rites of a religion; esp ♦ : a member of the Anglican, Eastern, or Roman Catholic clergy ranking below a bishop and above a deacon — **priest•hood** n — **priest•li•ness** n

♦ clergyman, divine, ecclesiastic, father, minister, preacher, reverend

priest•ess \'prēs-təs\ n : a woman authorized to perform the sacred rites of a religion
priest•ly \'prēst-lē\ adj ♦ : of, relating to, or characteristic of a priest or the priesthood

♦ clerical, ministerial, pastoral, sacerdotal

prig \'prig\ n : one who irritates by rigid or pointed observance of proprieties — **prig•gish** \'pri-gish\ adj — **prig•gish•ly** adv
¹**prim** \'prim\ adj **prim•mer; prim•mest** ♦ : stiffly formal and precise — **prim•ly** adv — **prim•ness** n

♦ prudish, puritanical, straitlaced

²**prim** abbr **1** primary **2** primitive
pri•ma•cy \'prī-mə-sē\ n **1** ♦ : the state of being first (as in rank) **2** : the office, rank, or character of an ecclesiastical primate

♦ distinction, dominance, eminence, preeminence, superiority, supremacy, transcendence

pri•ma don•na \ˌpri-mə-'dä-nə\ n, pl **prima donnas 1** : a principal female singer (as in an opera company) **2** : a vain undisciplined usu. uncooperative person
pri•ma fa•cie \ˌprī-mə-'fā-shə, -sē, -shē\ adj or adv **1** : based on immediate impression : APPARENT **2** : SELF-EVIDENT
pri•mal \'prī-məl\ adj **1** ♦ : of or relating to the first period or state : PRIMITIVE **2** : first in importance

♦ ancient, early, primeval, primitive

pri•mar•i•ly \prī-'mer-ə-lē\ adv **1** ♦ : for the most part **2** ♦ : in the first place : ORIGINALLY

♦ [1] altogether, basically, chiefly, generally, largely, mainly, mostly, overall, predominantly, principally ♦ [2] firstly, initially, originally

¹**pri•ma•ry** \'prī-ˌmer-ē, -mə-rē\ adj **1** : first in order of time or development; also : PREPARATORY **2** ♦ : of first rank or importance; also : FUNDAMENTAL **3** ♦ : not derived from or dependent on something else ⟨~ sources⟩

♦ [2] arch, cardinal, central, chief, dominant, first, foremost, fundamental, grand, key, main, paramount, predominant, preeminent, premier, principal, sovereign, supreme ♦ [3] direct, firsthand, immediate

²**primary** n, pl **-ries** : a preliminary election in which voters nominate or express a preference among candidates usu. of their own party
primary care n : health care provided by a medical professional with whom a patient has initial contact
primary color n : any of a set of colors from which all other colors may be derived
primary school n **1** : a school usu. including grades 1–3 and sometimes kindergarten **2** : ELEMENTARY SCHOOL
pri•mate \'prī-ˌmāt or esp for 1 -mət\ n **1** often cap : the highest-ranking bishop of a province or nation **2** : any of an order of mammals including humans, apes, and monkeys
¹**prime** \'prīm\ n **1** : the earliest stage of something; esp : SPRINGTIME **2** ♦ : the most active, thriving, or successful stage or period (as of one's life) **3** ♦ : the best individual or part **4** : any integer other than 0, +1, or –1 that is not divisible without remainder by any integer except +1, –1, and plus or minus itself; esp : any such integer that is positive

♦ [2] bloom, blossom, flower, flush, heyday ♦ [3] best, choice, cream, elect, elite, fat, flower, pick

²**prime** adj **1** ♦ : standing first (as in time, rank, significance, or quality) ⟨~ requisite⟩ **2** : of, relating to, or being a number that is prime

♦ chief, first, foremost, head, high, lead, preeminent, premier, primary, principal, supreme

³**prime** *vb* **primed; prim·ing** **1** : FILL, LOAD **2** : to lay a preparatory coating upon (as in painting) **3** : to put in working condition **4** : to instruct beforehand : COACH

prime meridian *n* : the meridian of 0° longitude which runs through Greenwich, England, and from which other longitudes are reckoned east and west

prime minister *n* **1** : the chief minister of a ruler or state **2** : the chief executive of a parliamentary government

¹**prim·er** \'pri-mər\ *n* **1** : a small book for teaching children to read **2** : a small introductory book on a subject ⟨a ~ on modern art⟩ **3** : a short informative piece of writing

♦ handbook, manual, textbook

²**prim·er** \'pri-mər\ *n* **1** : one that primes **2** : a device for igniting an explosive **3** : material for priming a surface

prime rate *n* : an interest rate announced by a bank to be the lowest available to its most credit-worthy customers

prime time *n* **1** : the time period when the television or radio audience is largest; *also* : television shows aired in prime time **2** : the choicest or busiest time

pri·me·val \prī-'mē-vəl\ *adj* ♦ : of or relating to the earliest ages : PRIMITIVE

♦ ancient, early, primal, primitive

¹**prim·i·tive** \'pri-mə-tiv\ *adj* **1** : ORIGINAL, PRIMARY **2** ♦ : of, relating to, or characteristic of an early stage of development **3** : ELEMENTAL, NATURAL **4** *sometimes offensive* : of, relating to, or produced by a people or culture that is nonindustrial and often nonliterate and tribal **5** : SELF-TAUGHT; *also* : produced by a self-taught artist — **prim·i·tive·ly** *adv* — **prim·i·tive·ness** *n* — **prim·i·tiv·i·ty** \,pri-mə-'ti-və-tē\ *n*

♦ crude, low, rude, rudimentary *Ant* advanced, developed, evolved

♦ ancient, early, primal, primeval

²**primitive** *n* **1** : something primitive **2** : a primitive artist **3** : a member of a primitive people

prim·i·tiv·ism \'pri-mə-ti-,vi-zəm\ *n* **1** : belief in the superiority of a simple way of life close to nature **2** : the style of art of primitive peoples or primitive artists

pri·mo·gen·i·tor \,prī-mō-'je-nə-tər\ *n* : ANCESTOR, FOREFATHER

pri·mo·gen·i·ture \-'je-nə-,chùr\ *n* **1** : the state of being the firstborn of a family **2** : an exclusive right of inheritance belonging to the eldest son

pri·mor·di·al \prī-'mòr-dē-əl\ *adj* : first created or developed : existing in its original state : PRIMEVAL

primp \'primp\ *vb* : to dress in a careful or finicky manner

prim·rose \'prim-,rōz\ *n* : any of a genus of perennial herbs with large leaves arranged at the base of the stem and clusters of showy flowers

prin *abbr* **1** principal **2** principle

prince \'prins\ *n* **1** : MONARCH, KING **2** : a male member of a royal family; *esp* : a son of the monarch **3** ♦ : a person of high standing (as in a class) ⟨a ~ of poets⟩ — **prince·dom** \-dəm\ *n*

♦ baron, czar, king, magnate, mogul, tycoon

prince·ling \-liŋ\ *n* : a petty prince

prince·ly \'prin(t)s-lē\ *adj* ♦ : of, relating to, or befitting a prince

♦ kingly, monarchical, queenly, regal, royal

prin·cess \'prin-səs, -,ses\ *n* **1** : a female member of a royal family **2** : the consort of a prince

¹**prin·ci·pal** \'prin-sə-pəl\ *adj* ♦ : most important

♦ arch, cardinal, central, chief, dominant, first, foremost, grand, key, main, paramount, predominant, preeminent, premier, primary, sovereign, supreme

²**principal** *n* **1** : a leading person (as in a play) **2** : the chief officer of an educational institution **3** : the person from whom an agent's authority derives **4** : a capital sum earning interest or used as a fund

prin·ci·pal·i·ty \,prin-sə-'pa-lə-tē\ *n, pl* **-ties** : the position, territory, or jurisdiction of a prince

prin·ci·pal·ly \'prin-sə-p(ə-)lē\ *adv* ♦ : in the chief place or degree : CHIEFLY

♦ altogether, basically, chiefly, generally, largely, mainly, mostly, overall, primarily

principal parts *n pl* : the inflected forms of a verb

prin·ci·ple \'prin-sə-pəl\ *n* **1** ♦ : a general or fundamental law, doctrine, or assumption **2** ♦ : a rule or code of conduct; *also* : devotion to such a code **3** : the laws or facts of nature underlying the working of an artificial device **4** : a primary source

: ORIGIN; *also* : an underlying faculty or endowment **5** : the active part (as of a drug)

♦ **principles** [1] elements, essentials, rudiments **principles** [2] ethics, morality, morals, standards

prin·ci·pled \-pəld\ *adj* ♦ : exhibiting, based on, or characterized by principle ⟨high-*principled*⟩

♦ decent, ethical, honest, honorable, just, moral, noble, respectable, righteous, upright, upstanding

prink \'priŋk\ *vb* : PRIMP

¹**print** \'print\ *n* **1** ♦ : a mark made by pressure **2** : something stamped with an impression **3** : printed state or form **4** : printed matter **5** ♦ : a copy made by printing **6** : cloth with a pattern applied by printing

♦ [1] impress, impression, imprint, stamp ♦ [5] photograph, shot, snap, snapshot

²**print** *vb* **1** : to stamp (as a mark) in or on something **2** : to produce impressions of (as from type) **3** : to write in letters like those of printer's type **4** : to make (a positive picture) from a photographic negative **5** ♦ : to publish in print

♦ get out, issue, publish

print·able \'prin-tə-bəl\ *adj* **1** : capable of being printed or of being printed from **2** : worthy or fit to be published

print·er \'prin-tər\ *n* : one that prints; *esp* : a device that produces printout

print·ing *n* **1** : reproduction in printed form **2** : the art, practice, or business of a printer **3** : IMPRESSION 5

printing press *n* : a machine that produces printed copies

print·out \'print-,aùt\ *n* : a printed output produced by a computer — **print out** *vb*

¹**pri·or** \'prī-ər\ *n* : the superior ranking next to the abbot or abbess of a religious house

²**prior** *adj* **1** ♦ : earlier in time or order **2** : taking precedence logically or in importance — **pri·or·i·ty** \prī-'òr-ə-tē\ *n*

♦ antecedent, anterior, foregoing, preceding, previous

pri·or·ess \'prī-ə-rəs\ *n* : a nun corresponding in rank to a prior

pri·or·i·tize \prī-'òr-ə-,tīz, 'prī-ə-rə-,tīz\ *vb* **-tized; -tiz·ing** : to list or rate in order of priority

prior to *prep* ♦ : in advance of : BEFORE

♦ ahead of, before, ere, of, previous to, to

pri·o·ry \'prī-ə-rē\ *n, pl* **-ries** ♦ : a religious house under a prior or prioress

♦ abbey, cloister, friary, monastery

prise *chiefly Brit var of* ⁵PRIZE

prism \'pri-zəm\ *n* **1** : a solid whose sides are parallelograms and whose ends are parallel and alike in shape and size **2** : a usu. 3-sided transparent object that refracts light so that it breaks up into rainbow colors — **pris·mat·ic** \priz-'ma-tik\ *adj*

pris·on \'priz-ᵊn\ *n* ♦ : a place or state of confinement esp. for criminals

♦ brig, jail, lockup, pen, penitentiary

pris·on·er \'priz-ᵊn-ər\ *n* ♦ : a person deprived of liberty; *esp* : one on trial or in prison

♦ captive, capture, internee

prisoner of war : a person and esp. a member of the armed forces of a nation captured in war

pris·sy \'pri-sē\ *adj* **pris·si·er; -est** : being overly prim and precise : PRIGGISH — **pris·si·ness** \-sē-nəs\ *n*

pris·tine \'pris-,tēn, pri-'stēn\ *adj* **1** : PRIMITIVE **2** ♦ : having the purity of its original state

♦ brand-new, fresh, virgin

prith·ee \'pri-thē\ *interj, archaic* — used to express a wish or request

pri·va·cy \'prī-və-sē\ *n, pl* **-cies** **1** : the quality or state of being apart from others **2** : SECRECY

¹**pri·vate** \'prī-vət\ *adj* **1** : belonging to or intended for a particular individual or group ⟨~ property⟩ **2** ♦ : restricted to the individual : PERSONAL ⟨~ opinion⟩ **3** : carried on by the individual independently ⟨~ study⟩ **4** : not holding public office ⟨a ~ citizen⟩ **5** : withdrawn from company or observation ⟨a ~ place⟩ **6** ♦ : not known publicly — **pri·vate·ly** *adv*

♦ [2] individual, particular, peculiar, personal, separate, singular, unique ♦ [6] confidential, hushed, inside, intimate, secret *Ant* common, open, public

²**private** *n* : an enlisted person of the lowest rank in the marine

corps or of one of the two lowest ranks in the army — **in private** : not openly or in public

pri·va·teer \ˌprī-və-'tir\ *n* : an armed private ship licensed to attack enemy shipping; *also* : a sailor on such a ship

private first class *n* : an enlisted person ranking next below a corporal in the army and next below a lance corporal in the marine corps

pri·va·tion \prī-'vā-shən\ *n* **1** : the act of depriving **2** : the state of being deprived; *esp* : lack of what is needed for existence

priv·et \'pri-vət\ *n* : a nearly evergreen shrub related to the olive and widely used for hedges

¹priv·i·lege \'priv-lij, 'pri-və-\ *n* ♦ : a right or immunity granted as an advantage or favor esp. to some and not others

♦ boon, concession, honor (*or* honour)

²privilege *vb* **-leged; -leg·ing** ♦ : to grant a privilege to

♦ authorize, entitle, qualify

priv·i·leged *adj* **1** : having or enjoying one or more privileges ⟨∼ classes⟩ **2** : not subject to disclosure in a court of law ⟨a ∼ communication⟩

¹privy \'pri-vē\ *adj* **1** : of, relating to, or affecting a particular person exclusively : PERSONAL, PRIVATE **2** : kept from knowledge or view : SECRET **3** : admitted as one sharing in a secret ⟨∼ to the conspiracy⟩ — **priv·i·ly** \'pri-və-lē\ *adv*

²privy *n, pl* **priv·ies** : TOILET; *esp* : OUTHOUSE

¹prize \'prīz\ *n* **1** ♦ : something offered or striven for in competition or in contests of chance **2** ♦ : something exceptionally desirable

♦ [1] award, decoration, distinction, honor (*or* honour), plume ♦ [2] catch, gem, jewel, pearl, plum, treasure

²prize *adj* **1** : awarded or worthy of a prize ⟨a ∼ essay⟩; *also* : awarded as a prize ⟨a ∼ medal⟩ **2** : OUTSTANDING

³prize *vb* **prized; priz·ing** ♦ : to value highly : ESTEEM

♦ appreciate, cherish, love, treasure, value

⁴prize *n* : property (as a ship) lawfully captured in time of war

⁵prize *or Can and Brit* **prise** *vb* **prized** *or* **prised; priz·ing** *or* **prising** ♦ : to press, force, or move with or as if with a lever : PRY

♦ jimmy, pry

prize·fight \'prīz-ˌfīt\ *n* : a professional boxing match — **prize·fight·ing** *n*

prize·fight·er \-ˌfī-tər\ *n* ♦ : one who participates in a prizefight

♦ boxer, fighter, pugilist

prize·win·ner \-ˌwi-nər\ *n* : a winner of a prize — **prize·win·ning** *adj*

¹pro \'prō\ *n, pl* **pros** : a favorable argument, person, or position

²pro *adv* : in favor of : FOR

³pro *n or adj* : PROFESSIONAL

PRO *abbr* public relations officer

pro·ac·tive \prō-'ak-tiv\ *adj* ♦ : acting in anticipation of future problems or needs — **pro·ac·tive·ly** *adv*

♦ farsighted, foresighted, prescient, provident, visionary

pro–am \'prō-'am\ *adj* : involving professionals competing alongside or against amateurs ⟨a ∼ tournament⟩ — **pro–am** *n*

prob *abbr* **1** probable; probably **2** problem

prob·a·bil·i·ty \ˌprä-bə-'bi-lə-tē\ *n, pl* **-ties** **1** : the quality or state of being probable **2** : something probable **3** ♦ : a measure of how often a particular event will occur if something (as tossing a coin) is done repeatedly which results in any of a number of possible events

♦ chance, odds, percentage

prob·a·ble \'prä-bə-bəl\ *adj* **1** ♦ : apparently or presumably true ⟨a ∼ hypothesis⟩ **2** : likely to be or become true or real ⟨a ∼ result⟩

♦ believable, credible, likely, plausible

prob·a·bly \'prä-bə-blē\ *adv* ♦ : without much doubt

♦ doubtless, likely, presumably *Ant* improbably

¹pro·bate \'prō-ˌbāt\ *n* : the judicial determination of the validity of a will

²pro·bate *vb* **pro·bat·ed; pro·bat·ing** : to establish (a will) by probate as genuine and valid

pro·ba·tion \prō-'bā-shən\ *n* **1** : subjection of an individual to a period of testing and trial to ascertain fitness (as for a job) **2** : the action of giving a convicted offender freedom during good behavior under the supervision of a probation officer — **pro·ba·tion·ary** \-shə-ˌner-ē\ *adj*

pro·ba·tion·er \-shə-nər\ *n* **1** : a person (as a newly admitted student nurse) whose fitness is being tested during a trial period **2** : a convicted offender on probation

pro·ba·tive \'prō-bə-tiv\ *adj* **1** : serving to test or try **2** : serving to prove

¹probe \'prōb\ *n* **1** : a slender instrument for examining a cavity (as a wound) **2** : an information-gathering device sent into outer space **3** ♦ : a penetrating investigation

♦ examination, exploration, inquiry, investigation, research, study

²probe *vb* **probed; prob·ing** **1** : to examine with a probe **2** ♦ : to search into and investigate thoroughly

♦ delve, dig, explore, go, inquire into, investigate, look, research

pro·bi·ty \'prō-bə-tē\ *n* ♦ : adherence to the highest principles and ideals : HONESTY

♦ character, decency, goodness, honesty, integrity, morality, rectitude, righteousness, uprightness, virtue

prob·lem \'prä-bləm\ *n* **1** : a question raised for consideration or solution **2** ♦ : an intricate unsettled question **3** ♦ : a source of perplexity or vexation — **problem** *adj*

♦ [2] case, knot, matter, trouble *Ant* answer, solution ♦ [3] aggravation, annoyance, bother, exasperation, frustration, hassle, headache, inconvenience, irritant, nuisance, peeve, pest, thorn

prob·lem·at·ic \ˌprä-blə-'ma-tik\ *also* **prob·lem·at·i·cal** \-ti-kəl\ *adj* **1** ♦ : difficult to solve or decide **2** ♦ : open to question or debate : QUESTIONABLE

♦ [1] catchy, delicate, difficult, knotty, spiny, thorny, ticklish, touchy, tough, tricky ♦ [2] debatable, disputable, doubtful, dubious, equivocal, fishy, questionable, shady, shaky, suspect, suspicious

pro·bos·cis \prə-'bä-səs, -'bäs-kəs\ *n, pl* **-bos·cis·es** *also* **-bos·ci·des** \-'bä-sə-ˌdēz\ : a long flexible snout (as the trunk of an elephant)

proc *abbr* proceedings

pro·caine \'prō-ˌkān\ *n* : a drug used esp. as a local anesthetic

pro·ce·dure \prə-'sē-jər\ *n* **1** ♦ : a particular way of doing something ⟨democratic ∼⟩ **2** ♦ : a series of steps followed in a regular order ⟨a surgical ∼⟩ — **pro·ce·dur·al** \-'sē-jə-rəl\ *adj*

♦ [1] course, line, policy, program ♦ [2] course, operation, proceeding, process

pro·ceed \prō-'sēd\ *vb* **1** : to come forth : ISSUE **2** : to go on in an orderly way; *also* : CONTINUE **3** : to begin and carry on an action **4** : to take legal action **5** ♦ : to move along a course

♦ advance, fare, forge, get along, go, march, progress ♦ *usu* **proceed along** cover, crisscross, cross, cut, follow, go, pass, travel, traverse

pro·ceed·ing *n* **1** : a series of steps followed in a regular definite order : PROCEDURE **2** *pl* : DOINGS **3** *pl* ♦ : legal action **4** : TRANSACTION **5** *pl* : an official record of things said or done

♦ action, lawsuit, suit

pro·ceeds \'prō-ˌsēdz\ *n pl* ♦ : the total amount or the profit arising from a business deal

♦ earnings, income, profit, return, revenue, yield

¹pro·cess \'prä-ˌses, 'prō-\ *n, pl* **pro·cess·es** \-ˌse-səz, -sə-səz, -sə-ˌsēz\ **1** : a forward or onward movement (as to an objective or to a goal) : ADVANCE **2** : something going on : PROCEEDING **3** : a natural phenomenon marked by gradual changes that lead toward a particular result ⟨the ∼ of growth⟩ **4** ♦ : a series of actions or operations directed toward a particular result ⟨a manufacturing ∼⟩ **5** : legal action **6** : a mandate issued by a court; *esp* : SUMMONS **7** : a projecting part of an organism or organic structure

♦ course, operation, procedure, proceeding

²process *vb* : to subject to a special process

pro·ces·sion \prə-'se-shən\ *n* **1** : a group of individuals moving along in an orderly often ceremonial way **2** ♦ : continuous forward movement

♦ advance, advancement, furtherance, headway, march, onrush, passage, process, progress, progression

pro·ces·sion·al \-'se-shə-nəl\ *n* **1** : music for a procession **2** : a ceremonial procession

pro·ces·sor \'prä-ˌse-sər, 'prō-\ *n* **1** : one that processes **2** : CPU

pro–choice \(ˌ)prō-'chȯis\ *adj* : favoring the legalization of abortion

pro·claim \prō-'klām\ *vb* ♦ : to make known publicly : DECLARE

♦ advertise, announce, blaze, broadcast, declare, enunciate, placard, post, promulgate, publicize, publish, sound

proc·la·ma·tion \ˌprä-klə-ˈmā-shən\ *n* : an official public announcement

pro·cliv·i·ty \prō-ˈkli-və-tē\ *n, pl* **-ties** ♦ : an inherent inclination esp. toward something objectionable

♦ bent, devices, disposition, genius, inclination, leaning, partiality, penchant, predilection, propensity, tendency, turn

pro·con·sul \-ˈkän-səl\ *n* **1** : a governor or military commander of an ancient Roman province **2** : an administrator in a modern colony or occupied area — **pro·con·su·lar** \-sə-lər\ *adj*

pro·cras·ti·nate \prə-ˈkras-tə-ˌnāt, prō-\ *vb* **-nat·ed; -nat·ing** : to put off usu. habitually doing something that should be done — **pro·cras·ti·na·tion** \-ˌkras-tə-ˈnā-shən\ *n* — **pro·cras·ti·na·tor** \-ˈkras-tə-ˌnā-tər\ *n*

pro·cre·ate \ˈprō-krē-ˌāt\ *vb* **-at·ed; -at·ing** ♦ : to beget or bring forth offspring — **pro·cre·ation** \ˌprō-krē-ˈā-shən\ *n* — **pro·cre·ative** \ˈprō-krē-ˌā-tiv\ *adj* — **pro·cre·ator** \-ˌā-tər\ *n*

♦ breed, multiply, propagate, reproduce

pro·crus·te·an \prō-ˈkrəs-tē-ən\ *adj, often cap* : marked by arbitrary often ruthless disregard of individual differences or special circumstances

proc·tor \ˈpräk-tər\ *n* : one appointed to supervise students (as at an examination) — **proctor** *vb* — **proc·to·ri·al** \präk-ˈtōr-ē-əl\ *adj*

pro·cur·able \prə-ˈkyu̇r-ə-bəl\ *adj* ♦ : capable of being procured

♦ accessible, acquirable, attainable, available, obtainable

proc·u·ra·tor \ˈprä-kyə-ˌrā-tər\ *n* **1** : one that manages another's affairs **2** : a Roman provincial administrator

pro·cure \-ˈkyu̇r\ *vb* **pro·cured; pro·cur·ing** **1** ♦ : to get possession of : obtain by particular care and effort **2** : to obtain (someone) to be employed for sexual intercourse **3** : ACHIEVE — **pro·cure·ment** *n* — **pro·cur·er** *n*

♦ acquire, attain, capture, carry, draw, earn, gain, garner, get, land, make, obtain, realize, secure, win

¹prod \ˈpräd\ *vb* **prod·ded; prod·ding** **1** : to thrust a pointed instrument into : GOAD **2** ♦ : to incite to action — **prod** *n*

♦ egg on, encourage, exhort, goad, press, prompt, urge

²prod *abbr* product; production

¹prod·i·gal \ˈprä-di-gəl\ *adj* **1** : recklessly extravagant; *also* : LUXURIANT **2** ♦ : recklessly spendthrift : WASTEFUL ⟨the ∼ prince⟩

♦ extravagant, profligate, spendthrift, thriftless, unthrifty, wasteful *Ant* conserving, economical, economizing, frugal, scrimping, skimping, thrifty

²prodigal *n* ♦ : one who spends or gives lavishly and foolishly

♦ profligate, spendthrift, wastrel *Ant* economizer

prod·i·gal·i·ty \ˌprä-də-ˈga-lə-tē\ *n* ♦ : reckless spending of resources

♦ extravagance, lavishness, wastefulness

pro·di·gious \prə-ˈdi-jəs\ *adj* **1** ♦ : exciting wonder **2** ♦ : extraordinary in size or degree : ENORMOUS — **pro·di·gious·ly** *adv*

♦ [1] amazing, astonishing, astounding, awesome, marvelous (*or* marvellous), stunning, stupendous, surprising, wonderful ♦ [2] colossal, enormous, giant, gigantic, huge, mammoth, massive, tremendous, vast

prod·i·gy \ˈprä-də-jē\ *n, pl* **-gies** **1** ♦ : something extraordinary : WONDER **2** : a highly talented child

♦ caution, flash, marvel, miracle, phenomenon, portent, sensation, wonder

¹pro·duce \prə-ˈdüs, -ˈdyüs\ *vb* **pro·duced; pro·duc·ing** **1** : to present to view : EXHIBIT **2a** ♦ : to give birth or rise to **b** ♦ : to become the father of **3** : EXTEND, PROLONG **4** ♦ : to give being or form to : MAKE; *esp* : MANUFACTURE **5** : to cause to accrue ⟨∼ a profit⟩ — **pro·duc·er** *n*

♦ [2a, 4] bear, bring about, cause, create, effect, effectuate, generate, induce, make, prompt, result, work, yield ♦ [2b] beget, father, get, sire ♦ [4] fabricate, fashion, form, frame, make, manufacture

²pro·duce \ˈprä-(ˌ)düs, ˈprō- *also* -(ˌ)dyüs\ *n* **1** : something produced : PRODUCT **2** : agricultural products and esp. fresh fruits and vegetables

prod·uct \ˈprä-(ˌ)dəkt\ *n* **1** : the number resulting from multi-

plication **2** ♦ : something produced **3** ♦ : something resulting from or necessarily following from a set of conditions

♦ [2] affair, fruit, handiwork, output, produce, thing, work, yield ♦ [3] aftermath, conclusion, consequence, corollary, development, effect, issue, outcome, outgrowth, result, resultant, sequence, upshot

pro·duc·tion \prə-ˈdək-shən\ *n* **1** : something produced : PRODUCT **2** : the act or process of producing

pro·duc·tive \prə-ˈdək-tiv\ *adj* **1** ♦ : having the quality or power of producing esp. in abundance **2** ♦ : effective in bringing about — **pro·duc·tiv·i·ty** \(ˌ)prō-ˌdək-ˈti-və-tē, ˌprä-(ˌ)dək-\ *n*

♦ [1] fat, fecund, fertile, fruitful, luxuriant, prolific, rich ♦ [2] effective, effectual, efficacious, efficient, fruitful, potent

pro·duc·tive·ness \-nəs\ *n* ♦ : the quality or state of being productive

♦ effectiveness, efficacy, efficiency

product placement *n* : the inclusion of a product in a television program or film as a means of advertising

pro·em \ˈprō-ˌem\ *n* **1** : preliminary comment : PREFACE **2** : PRELUDE

¹prof \ˈpräf\ *n* : PROFESSOR

²prof *abbr* professional

¹pro·fane \prō-ˈfān\ *vb* **pro·faned; pro·fan·ing** **1** ♦ : to treat (something sacred) with irreverence or contempt **2** ♦ : to debase by an unworthy use — **prof·a·na·tion** \ˌprä-fə-ˈnā-shən\ *n*

♦ [1] defile, desecrate, violate ♦ [2] debase, degrade, demean, demoralize, humble, subvert, warp

²profane *adj* **1** ♦ : not concerned with religion : SECULAR **2** : not holy because unconsecrated, impure, or defiled **3** ♦ : serving to debase what is holy : IRREVERENT **4** : OBSCENE, VULGAR — **pro·fane·ly** *adv* — **pro·fane·ness** *n*

♦ [1] nonreligious, secular, temporal *Ant* religious, sacred ♦ [3] blasphemous, irreverent, sacrilegious

pro·fan·i·ty \prō-ˈfa-nə-tē\ *n, pl* **-ties** **1** : the quality or state of being profane **2** : the use of profane language **3** : profane language

pro·fess \prə-ˈfes\ *vb* **1** ♦ : to declare or admit openly : AFFIRM **2** ♦ : to declare in words only : PRETEND **3** : to confess one's faith in **4** : to practice or claim to be versed in (a calling or occupation) — **pro·fess·ed·ly** \-ˈfe-səd-lē\ *adv*

♦ [1] affirm, allege, assert, aver, avouch, avow, claim, contend, declare, insist, maintain, protest, warrant ♦ [2] affect, assume, counterfeit, fake, feign, pretend, put on, sham, simulate

pro·fes·sion \prə-ˈfe-shən\ *n* **1** ♦ : an open declaration or avowal of a belief or opinion **2** ♦ : a calling requiring specialized knowledge and often long academic preparation **3** : the whole body of persons engaged in a calling

♦ [1] affirmation, assertion, avowal, claim, declaration, protestation ♦ [2] calling, employment, line, occupation, trade, vocation, work

¹pro·fes·sion·al \prə-ˈfe-shə-nəl\ *adj* **1** : of, relating to, or characteristic of a profession **2** : engaged in one of the professions **3** : participating for gain in an activity often engaged in by amateurs — **pro·fes·sion·al·ly** *adv*

²professional *n* : one that engages in an activity professionally

pro·fes·sion·al·ism \-nə-ˌli-zəm\ *n* **1** : the conduct, aims, or qualities that characterize or mark a profession or a professional person **2** : the following of a profession (as athletics) for gain or livelihood

pro·fes·sion·al·ize \-nə-ˌlīz\ *vb* **-ized; -iz·ing** : to give a professional nature to

pro·fes·sor \prə-ˈfe-sər\ *n* : a teacher at a university or college; *esp* : a faculty member of the highest academic rank — **pro·fes·so·ri·al** \ˌprō-fə-ˈsōr-ē-əl, ˌprä-\ *adj* — **pro·fes·sor·ship** *n*

¹prof·fer \ˈprä-fər\ *vb* **prof·fered; prof·fer·ing** ♦ : to present for acceptance : OFFER

♦ advance, offer, pose, propose, propound, suggest, vote

²proffer *n* ♦ : something proposed for acceptance

♦ offer, proposal, proposition, suggestion

pro·fi·cien·cy \prə-ˈfi-shən-sē\ *n* ♦ : the quality or state of being proficient

♦ experience, expertise, know-how, savvy

pro·fi·cient \prə-ˈfi-shənt\ *adj* ♦ : well advanced in an art, occupation, or branch of knowledge — **proficient** *n*

♦ accomplished, adept, consummate, crack, crackerjack, expert, good, great, master, masterful, masterly, skilled, skillful, virtuoso *Ant* amateur, amateurish, inexpert, unpolished, unprofessional, unskilled, unskillful

pro•fi•cient•ly \-lē\ *adv* ♦ : in a proficient manner

♦ ably, adeptly, capably, expertly, masterfully, skillfully, well

¹**pro•file** \'prō-ˌfīl\ *n* **1** : a representation of something in outline; *esp* : a human head seen in side view **2** : a concise biographical sketch **3** : degree or level of public exposure ⟨keep a low ∼⟩
²**profile** *vb* **pro•filed; pro•fil•ing** : to write or draw a profile of

profiling *n* : the act of suspecting or targeting a person solely on the basis of observed characteristics or behavior ⟨racial ∼⟩

¹**prof•it** \'prä-fət\ *n* **1** ♦ : a valuable return **2** ♦ : the excess of the selling price of goods over their cost

♦ [1] earnings, income, proceeds, return, revenue, yield ♦ [2] earnings, gain, lucre, net, payoff, proceeds, return

²**profit** *vb* **1** ♦ : to be of use : BENEFIT **2** : to derive benefit : GAIN ⟨∼ed from his mistakes⟩

♦ avail, benefit, serve

prof•it•able \'prä-fə-tə-bəl\ *adj* ♦ : affording profits : yielding advantageous returns or results — **prof•it•ably** \-blē\ *adv*

♦ advantageous, beneficial, favorable (*or* favourable), helpful, salutary ♦ fat, gainful, lucrative, remunerative *Ant* unprofitable

prof•i•teer \ˌprä-fə-'tir\ *n* : one who makes what is considered an unreasonable profit — **profiteer** *vb*
prof•it•less \'prä-fət-ləs\ *adj* ♦ : having no profit

♦ fruitless, futile, ineffective, unproductive, unsuccessful

prof•li•ga•cy \'prä-fli-gə-sē\ *n* ♦ : the quality or state of being profligate

♦ corruption, debauchery, depravity, immorality, iniquity, licentiousness, sin, vice

¹**prof•li•gate** \'prä-fli-gət, -flə-ˌgāt\ *adj* **1** : completely given up to dissipation and licentiousness **2** ♦ : wildly extravagant — **prof•li•gate•ly** *adv*

♦ extravagant, prodigal, spendthrift, thriftless, unthrifty, wasteful

²**profligate** *n* ♦ : a profligate person

♦ decadent, degenerate, libertine, pervert ♦ prodigal, spendthrift, wastrel

pro for•ma \(ˌ)prō-'fȯr-mə\ *adj* : done or existing as a matter of form
pro•found \prə-'faund, prō-\ *adj* **1** ♦ : marked by intellectual depth or insight ⟨a ∼ thought⟩ **2** : coming from or reaching to a depth ⟨a ∼ sigh⟩ **3** : deeply felt : INTENSE ⟨∼ sympathy⟩ **4** ♦ : all encompassing : THOROUGH — **pro•found•ly** *adv* — **pro•fun•di•ty** \-'fən-də-tē\ *n*

♦ [1] abstruse, deep, esoteric *Ant* shallow ♦ [4] absolute, complete, thorough, thoroughgoing, total, utter

pro•fuse \-'fyüs, prō-\ *adj* ♦ : pouring forth liberally — **pro•fuse•ly** *adv*

♦ copious, extravagant, lavish, luxuriant, riotous *Ant* dribbling, trickling

pro•fu•sion \prə-'fyü-zhən\ *n* ♦ : great quantity

♦ abundance, deal, gobs, heap, loads, lot, pile, plenty, quantity, scads

prog *abbr* program
pro•gen•i•tor \prō-'je-nə-tər\ *n* **1** : a direct ancestor : FOREFATHER **2** : ORIGINATOR, PRECURSOR
prog•e•ny \'prä-jə-nē\ *n, pl* **-nies** ♦ : offspring of a person, animal, or plant

♦ issue, offspring, posterity, seed, spawn

pro•ges•ter•one \prō-'jes-tə-ˌrōn\ *n* : a female hormone that causes the uterus to undergo changes so as to provide a suitable environment for a fertilized egg
prog•na•thous \'präg-nə-thəs\ *adj* : having the lower jaw projecting beyond the upper part of the face
prog•no•sis \präg-'nō-səs\ *n, pl* **-no•ses** \-ˌsēz\ **1** : the prospect of recovery from disease **2** : a prophecy, estimate, or prediction of a future happening or condition : FORECAST
¹**prog•nos•tic** \präg-'näs-tik\ *n* **1** : PORTENT **2** : PROPHECY
²**prognostic** *adj* : of, relating to, or serving as ground for prognostication or a prognosis
prog•nos•ti•cate \präg-'näs-tə-ˌkāt\ *vb* **-cat•ed; -cat•ing** ♦ : to foretell from signs or symptoms

♦ augur, forecast, foretell, predict, presage, prophesy

prog•nos•ti•ca•tion \präg-ˌnäs-tə-'kā-shən\ *n* ♦ : an act, the fact, or the power of prognosticating

♦ cast, forecast, prediction, prophecy, soothsaying

prog•nos•ti•ca•tor \präg-'näs-tə-ˌkā-tər\ *n* ♦ : one that prognosticates

♦ augur, diviner, forecaster, fortune-teller, futurist, prophet, seer, soothsayer

¹**pro•gram** *also* **programme** \'prō-ˌgram, -grəm\ *n* **1** ♦ : a brief outline of the order to be pursued or the subjects included (as in a public entertainment); *also* : PERFORMANCE **2** ♦ : a plan of procedure **3** : coded instructions for a computer — **pro•gram•mat•ic** \ˌprō-grə-'ma-tik\ *adj*

♦ [1] agenda, calendar, docket, schedule, timetable ♦ [2] course, line, policy, procedure ♦ [2] blueprint, scheme, strategy, system

²**program** *also* **programme** *vb* **-grammed** *or* **-gramed; -gram•ming** *or* **-gram•ing** **1** : to arrange or furnish a program of or for **2** : to enter in a program **3** : to provide (as a computer) with a program — **pro•gram•ma•bil•i•ty** \ˌprō-grə-mə-'bi-lə-tē\ *n* — **pro•gram•ma•ble** \'prō-ˌgra-mə-bəl\ *adj* — **pro•gram•mer** *also* **pro•gram•er** \'prō-ˌgra-mər, -grə-\ *n*
programmed instruction *n* : instruction through information given in small steps with each requiring a correct response by the learner before going on to the next step
pro•gram•ming *also* **pro•gram•ing** *n* **1** : the planning, scheduling, or performing of a program **2** : the process of instructing or learning by means of an instruction program **3** : the process of preparing an instruction program
¹**prog•ress** \'prä-grəs, -ˌgres\ *n* **1** ♦ : a forward movement : ADVANCE **2** ♦ : the action or process of advancing or improving by marked stages or degrees

♦ [1] advance, advancement, furtherance, headway, march, onrush, passage, process, procession, progression ♦ [2] development, elaboration, evolution, expansion, growth, progression

²**pro•gress** \prə-'gres\ *vb* **1** ♦ : to move forward : PROCEED **2** ♦ : to develop to a higher, better, or more advanced stage

♦ [1] advance, fare, forge, get along, go, march, proceed ♦ [2] age, develop, grow, grow up, mature, ripen

pro•gres•sion \prə-'gre-shən\ *n* **1** ♦ : an act of progressing **2** ♦ : a continuous and connected series

♦ [1] advance, advancement, furtherance, headway, march, onrush, passage, process, procession, progress ♦ [2] chain, sequence, string, train

¹**pro•gres•sive** \prə-'gre-siv\ *adj* **1** ♦ : of, relating to, or characterized by progress ⟨a ∼ city⟩ **2** : moving forward or onward : ADVANCING **3** : increasing in extent or severity ⟨a ∼ disease⟩ **4** *often cap* : of or relating to political Progressives **5** : of, relating to, or constituting a verb form that expresses action in progress at the time of speaking or a time spoken of **6** ♦ : making use of or interested in new ideas, findings, or opportunities — **pro•gres•sive•ly** *adv*

♦ [1] advanced, high, refined ♦ [6] broad-minded, liberal, nonorthodox, nontraditional, open-minded, radical, unconventional, unorthodox

²**progressive** *n* **1** : one that is progressive **2** : a person believing in moderate political change and social improvement by government action; *esp, cap* : a member of a Progressive Party in the U.S.
pro•hib•it \prō-'hi-bət\ *vb* **1** ♦ : to forbid by authority **2** : to prevent from doing something

♦ ban, bar, enjoin, forbid, interdict, outlaw, proscribe

pro•hi•bi•tion \ˌprō-ə-'bi-shən\ *n* **1** ♦ : the act of prohibiting **2** : the forbidding by law of the sale or manufacture of alcoholic beverages **3** ♦ : an order to restrain or stop — **pro•hi•bi•tion•ist** \-'bi-shə-nist\ *n* — **pro•hib•i•tive** \prō-'hi-bə-tiv\ *adj* — **pro•hib•i•tive•ly** *adv* — **pro•hib•i•to•ry** \-'hi-bə-ˌtōr-ē\ *adj*

♦ [1] barring, forbidding, interdiction, proscription ♦ [3] ban, embargo, interdict, interdiction, proscription, veto *Ant* prescription

¹**proj•ect** \'prä-ˌjekt, -jikt\ *n* **1** ♦ : a specific plan or design : SCHEME **2** : a planned undertaking ⟨a research ∼⟩

♦ arrangement, blueprint, design, game, plan, scheme, strategy, system

²**pro•ject** \prə-'jekt\ *vb* **1** ♦ : to devise in the mind : DESIGN **2** : to throw forward **3** : to jut out : PROTRUDE **4** : to cause (light

or shadow) to fall into space or (an image) to fall on a surface ⟨~ a beam of light⟩ **5** : to attribute (a thought, feeling, or personal characteristic) to a person, group, or object

♦ arrange, blueprint, calculate, chart, design, frame, lay out, map, plan, scheme

pro·jec·tile \prə-'jekt-ᵊl, -'jek-tīl\ n **1** : a body hurled or projected by external force; esp : a missile for a firearm **2** : a self-propelling weapon

pro·jec·tion \prə-'jek-shən\ n ♦ : a part that juts out

♦ bulge, overhang, protrusion

pro·jec·tion·ist \prə-'jek-shə-nist\ n : one that operates a motion-picture projector or television equipment

pro·jec·tor \-'jek-tər\ n : one that projects; esp : a device for projecting pictures on a screen

pro·lapse \prō-'laps, 'prō-\ n : the falling down or slipping of a body part from its usual position

pro·le·gom·e·non \ˌprō-li-'gä-mə-ˌnän, -nən\ n, pl **-e·na** \-nə\ : prefatory remarks

pro·le·tar·i·an \ˌprō-lə-'ter-ē-ən\ n : a member of the proletariat — **proletarian** adj

pro·le·tar·i·at \-ē-ət\ n : the laboring class; esp : industrial workers who sell their labor to live

pro-life \(ˌ)prō-'līf\ n : ANTIABORTION

pro·lif·er·ate \prə-'li-fə-ˌrāt\ vb **-at·ed; -at·ing** ♦ : to grow or increase by rapid production of new units (as cells or offspring)

♦ accumulate, appreciate, balloon, build, burgeon, enlarge, escalate, expand, increase, mount, multiply, mushroom, rise, snowball, swell, wax

pro·lif·er·a·tion \prə-ˌli-fə-'rā-shən\ n **1** : rapid and repeated production of new parts or of buds or offspring **2** ♦ : the act, process, or result of increasing by or as if by proliferation

♦ accretion, addition, augmentation, boost, expansion, gain, increase, increment, plus, raise, rise, supplement ♦ accumulation, multiplication

pro·lif·ic \prə-'li-fik\ adj **1** ♦ : producing young or fruit abundantly **2** ♦ : marked by abundant inventiveness or productivity ⟨a ~ writer⟩ — **pro·lif·i·cal·ly** \-fik(ə-)lē\ adv

♦ [1, 2] fecund, fertile, fruitful, luxuriant, productive, rich

pro·lix \prō-'liks, 'prō-ˌliks\ adj ♦ : marked by or using an excess of words : VERBOSE

♦ circuitous, diffuse, long-winded, rambling, verbose, windy, wordy

pro·lix·i·ty \prō-'lik-sə-tē\ n ♦ : the quality or state of being prolix

♦ circumlocution, redundancy, verbiage, wordiness

pro·logue also **pro·log** \'prō-ˌlóg, -ˌläg\ n ♦ : the preface or introduction to a literary or dramatic work : PREFACE

♦ foreword, introduction, preamble, preface

pro·long \prə-'lóŋ\ vb **1** ♦ : to lengthen in time ⟨~ a meeting⟩ **2** ♦ : to lengthen in extent or range

♦ [1, 2] draw out, elongate, extend, lengthen, protract, stretch

pro·lon·ga·tion \ˌprō-ˌlóŋ-'gā-shən\ n ♦ : an act or instance of prolonging

♦ elongation, extension

prom \'präm\ n ♦ : a formal dance given by a high school or college class

♦ ball, dance, formal

¹prom·e·nade \ˌprä-mə-'nād, -'näd\ vb **-nad·ed; -nad·ing** **1** : to take a promenade **2** : to walk about in or on

²promenade n **1** : a place for strolling **2** : a leisurely walk for pleasure or display **3** : an opening grand march at a formal ball

pro·me·thi·um \prə-'mē-thē-əm\ n : a metallic chemical element obtained from uranium or neodymium

prom·i·nence \'prä-mə-nəns\ n **1** ♦ : something prominent **2** : the quality, state, or fact of being prominent or conspicuous **3** : a mass of cloudlike gas that arises from the sun's chromosphere

♦ elevation, eminence, height, highland, hill, mound, rise

prom·i·nent \-nənt\ adj **1** : jutting out : PROJECTING **2** ♦ : readily noticeable : CONSPICUOUS **3** ♦ : widely and popularly known ⟨a ~ writer⟩ — **prom·i·nent·ly** adv

♦ [2] bold, catchy, conspicuous, emphatic, marked, noticeable, pronounced, remarkable, striking ♦ [3] celebrated, famed, famous, noted, notorious, renowned, star, well-known

pro·mis·cu·ous \prə-'mis-kyə-wəs\ adj **1** : consisting of various sorts and kinds : MIXED **2** : not restricted to one class or person **3** : having a number of sexual partners — **pro·mis·cu·i·ty** \ˌprä-mis-'kyü-ə-tē, ˌprō-ˌmis-\ n — **pro·mis·cu·ous·ly** adv — **pro·mis·cu·ous·ness** n

¹prom·ise \'prä-məs\ n **1** ♦ : a pledge to do or not to do something specified **2** : ground for expectation of success or improvement **3** : something promised

♦ oath, pledge, troth, vow, word

²promise vb **prom·ised; prom·is·ing** **1** ♦ : to engage to do, bring about, or provide ⟨~ help⟩ **2** : to suggest beforehand ⟨dark clouds ~ rain⟩ **3** ♦ : to give ground for expectation ⟨it ~s to be a good game⟩

♦ [1] covenant, pledge, swear, vow ♦ [3] augur, bode

promised land n ♦ : something and esp. a place or condition believed to promise final satisfaction or realization of hopes

♦ Eden, Elysium, heaven, paradise, utopia

promising adj ♦ : likely to succeed or yield good results — **prom·is·ing·ly** adv

♦ auspicious, bright, encouraging, fair, golden, heartening, hopeful, likely, propitious, rosy, upbeat ♦ auspicious, bright, encouraging, favorable (or favourable), hopeful, propitious

prom·is·so·ry \'prä-mə-ˌsōr-ē\ adj : containing a promise

prom·on·to·ry \'prä-mən-ˌtōr-ē\ n, pl **-ries** ♦ : a point of land jutting into the sea : HEADLAND

♦ arm, cape, headland, peninsula, point, spit

pro·mote \prə-'mōt\ vb **pro·mot·ed; pro·mot·ing** **1** ♦ : to advance in station, rank, or honor **2** ♦ : to contribute to the growth or prosperity of **3** : LAUNCH **4** ♦ : to present (merchandise) for buyer acceptance through advertising, publicity, or discounting — **pro·mo·tion·al** \-shə-nəl\ adj

♦ [1] advance, elevate, raise, upgrade Ant abase, degrade, demote, downgrade, lower, reduce ♦ [2] advance, cultivate, encourage, forward, foster, further, nourish, nurture ♦ [4] ballyhoo, boast, plug, publicize, tout

pro·mot·er \-'mō-tər\ n ♦ : one that promotes; esp : one that assumes the financial responsibilities of a sports event

♦ advocate, apostle, backer, booster, champion, exponent, friend, proponent, supporter

pro·mo·tion \prə-'mō-shən\ n ♦ : the act or fact of being raised in position or rank

♦ advancement, ascent, elevation, rise, upgrade

¹prompt \'prämpt\ vb **1** ♦ : to move to action **2** : to assist (one acting or reciting) by suggesting the next words **3** ♦ : to serve as the inciting cause of — **prompt·er** n

♦ [1] egg on, encourage, exhort, goad, press, prod, urge ♦ [3] bring about, cause, create, effect, effectuate, generate, induce, make, produce, result, work, yield

²prompt adj **1** ♦ : being ready and quick to act; also : being on time **2** ♦ : performed readily or immediately ⟨~ service⟩

♦ [1, 2] immediate, punctual, quick, ready, timely Ant belated, late, tardy

prompt·book \-ˌbùk\ n : a copy of a play with directions for performance used by a theater prompter

prompt·i·tude \'prämp-tə-ˌtüd, -ˌtyüd\ n ♦ : the quality or habit of being prompt : PROMPTNESS

♦ punctuality, timeliness Ant tardiness

prompt·ly \'präm(p)t-lē, 'präm-plē\ adv ♦ : in a prompt manner

♦ directly, forthwith, immediately, instantly, now, pronto, right away, right now

prompt·ness \-nəs\ n : the quality or habit of being prompt

pro·mul·gate \'prä-məl-ˌgāt; prō-'məl-\ vb **-gat·ed; -gat·ing** ♦ : to make known or put into force by open declaration — **prom·ul·ga·tion** \ˌprä-məl-'gā-shən, ˌprō-(ˌ)məl-\ n

♦ advertise, announce, blaze, broadcast, declare, enunciate, placard, post, proclaim, publicize, publish, sound

pron abbr **1** pronoun **2** pronounced **3** pronunciation

prone \'prōn\ adj **1** ♦ : having a tendency or inclination **2** : lying face downward; also : lying flat or prostrate

♦ apt, given, inclined

prone·ness \'prōn-nəs\ n ♦ : the condition or fact of being prone

♦ aptness, propensity, tendency, way

prong \'pròn\ *n* : one of the sharp points of a fork : TINE; *also* : a slender projecting part (as of an antler) — **pronged** \'pròŋd\ *adj*

prong·horn \'prŏŋ-ˌhòrn\ *n, pl* **pronghorn** *or* **pronghorns** : a swift horned ruminant mammal chiefly of grasslands of western No. America that resembles an antelope

pro·noun \'prō-ˌnaún\ *n* : a word used as a substitute for a noun

pro·nounce \prǝ-'naúns\ *vb* **pro·nounced; pro·nounc·ing** 1 : to utter officially or as an opinion ⟨~ sentence⟩ 2 : to employ the organs of speech in order to produce ⟨~ a word⟩; *esp* : to say or speak correctly ⟨she can't ~ his name⟩ — **pro·nounce·able** *adj* — **pro·nun·ci·a·tion** \-ˌnǝn-sē-'ā-shǝn\ *n*

pro·nounced *adj* ♦ : strongly marked : easily recognizable

♦ bold, catchy, conspicuous, emphatic, marked, noticeable, prominent, remarkable, striking

pro·nounce·ment \prǝ-'naúns-mǝnt\ *n* : a formal declaration of opinion; *also* : ANNOUNCEMENT

pron·to \'prän-ˌtō\ *adv* ♦ : without delay; *also* : very quickly

♦ directly, forthwith, immediately, instantly, now, promptly, right away, right now ♦ apace, briskly, fast, full tilt, hastily, posthaste, presto, quick, quickly, rapidly, soon, speedily, swift, swiftly

pro·nu·clear \'prō-'nü-klē-ǝr, -'nyü-\ *adj* : supporting the use of nuclear-powered electric generating stations

pro·nun·ci·a·men·to \prō-ˌnǝn-sē-ǝ-'men-tō\ *n, pl* **-tos** *or* **-toes** : PROCLAMATION, MANIFESTO

¹**proof** \'prüf\ *n* 1 ♦ : the evidence that compels acceptance by the mind of a truth or fact 2 : a process or operation that establishes validity or truth : TEST 3 : a trial impression (as from type) 4 : a trial print from a photographic negative 5 : alcoholic content (as of a beverage) indicated by a number that is twice the percent by volume of alcohol present ⟨whiskey of 90 ~ is 45% alcohol⟩

♦ attestation, confirmation, corroboration, documentation, evidence, substantiation, testament, testimony, validation, witness *Ant* disproof

²**proof** *adj* 1 : successful in resisting or repelling ⟨~ against tampering⟩ ⟨water*proof*⟩ 2 : of standard strength or quality or alcoholic content

proof·read \-ˌrēd\ *vb* : to read and mark corrections in — **proof·read·er** *n*

¹**prop** \'präp\ *n* : something that props

²**prop** *vb* **propped; prop·ping** 1 ♦ : to support by placing something under or against — often used with *up* 2 ♦ : to give support or relief to — often used with *up* 3 : to support by placing against something

♦ *usu* **prop up** [1] bear, bolster, brace, buttress, carry, shore, stay, support, uphold ♦ *usu* **prop up** [2] abet, aid, assist, back, help, support

³**prop** *n* : PROPERTY 4 ⟨stage ~s⟩

⁴**prop** *n* : PROPELLER

⁵**prop** *abbr* 1 property 2 proposition 3 proprietor

pro·pa·gan·da \ˌprä-pǝ-'gan-dǝ, ˌprō-\ *n* : the spreading of ideas or information to further or damage a cause; *also* : ideas or allegations spread for such a purpose — **pro·pa·gan·dist** \-dist\ *n*

pro·pa·gan·dize \-ˌdīz\ *vb* **-dized; -diz·ing** : to subject to or carry on propaganda

prop·a·gate \'prä-pǝ-ˌgāt\ *vb* **-gat·ed; -gat·ing** 1 ♦ : to reproduce or cause to reproduce biologically 2 ♦ : to cause to spread — **prop·a·ga·tion** \ˌprä-pǝ-'gā-shǝn\ *n*

♦ [1] breed, multiply, procreate, reproduce ♦ [2] broadcast, circulate, disseminate, spread, strew

pro·pane \'prō-ˌpān\ *n* : a heavy flammable gas found in petroleum and natural gas and used esp. as a fuel

pro·pel \prǝ-'pel\ *vb* **pro·pelled; pro·pel·ling** ♦ : to drive forward or onward

♦ actuate, drive, impel, move, work

pro·pel·lant *also* **pro·pel·lent** \-'pe-lǝnt\ *n* : something (as a fuel) that propels — **propellant** *also* **propellent** *adj*

pro·pel·ler \prǝ-'pe-lǝr\ *n* : a device consisting of a hub fitted with blades that is used to propel a vehicle (as a motorboat or an airplane)

pro·pen·si·ty \prǝ-'pen-sǝ-tē\ *n, pl* **-ties** ♦ : an often intense natural inclination or preference

♦ bent, devices, disposition, genius, inclination, leaning, partiality, penchant, predilection, proclivity, tendency, turn

¹**prop·er** \'prä-pǝr\ *adj* 1 : referring to one individual only ⟨~ noun⟩ 2 : belonging characteristically to a species or individual : PECULIAR 3 : very satisfactory : EXCELLENT 4 : strictly limited

to a specified thing ⟨the city ~⟩ 5 ♦ : strictly accurate : CORRECT ⟨the ~ way to proceed⟩ 6 ♦ : strictly decorous 7 ♦ : marked by suitability or rightness ⟨~ punishment⟩

♦ [5] accurate, correct, exact, precise, right, so, true ♦ [6] correct, decent, decorous, formal, genteel, nice, polite, respectable, seemly *Ant* improper, incorrect, indecent, indecorous, unbecoming, unseemly ♦ [7] applicable, appropriate, apt, felicitous, fit, fitting, good, happy, meet, right, suitable

²**proper** *n* : the parts of the Mass that vary according to the liturgical calendar

prop·er·ly \-lē\ *adv* ♦ : in a proper manner

♦ appropriately, correctly, fittingly, happily, rightly, suitably *Ant* improperly, incongruously, incorrectly, wrongly

prop·er·tied \'prä-pǝr-tēd\ *adj* : owning property and esp. much property

prop·er·ty \'prä-pǝr-tē\ *n, pl* **-ties** 1 ♦ : a quality peculiar to an individual or thing 2 ♦ : something owned; *esp* : a piece of real estate 3 : OWNERSHIP 4 : an article or object used in a play or motion picture other than painted scenery and actor's costumes

♦ [1] attribute, character, characteristic, feature, mark, peculiarity, point, quality, trait ♦ [2] lot, parcel, plat, plot, tract

proph·e·cy *also* **proph·e·sy** \'prä-fǝ-sē\ *n, pl* **-cies** *also* **-sies** 1 : an inspired utterance of a prophet 2 ♦ : a prediction of something to come

♦ cast, forecast, prediction, prognostication, soothsaying

proph·e·si·er \'prä-fǝ-ˌsī-(ǝ)r\ *n* : one that prophesies

proph·e·sy \-ˌsī\ *vb* **-sied; -sy·ing** 1 : to speak or utter by divine inspiration 2 ♦ : to predict with assurance

♦ augur, forecast, foretell, predict, presage, prognosticate

proph·et \'prä-fǝt\ *n* 1 : one who utters divinely inspired revelations 2 ♦ : one who foretells future events

♦ augur, diviner, forecaster, fortune-teller, futurist, prognosticator, seer, soothsayer

proph·et·ess \'prä-fǝ-tǝs\ *n* : a woman who is a prophet

pro·phet·ic \prǝ-'fe-tik\ *or* **pro·phet·i·cal** \-ti-kǝl\ *adj* ♦ : of, relating to, or characteristic of a prophet or prophecy — **pro·phet·i·cal·ly** \-ti-k(ǝ-)lē\ *adv*

♦ foreboding, inauspicious, ominous, portentous *Ant* auspicious, promising, propitious, rosy

Proph·ets \'prä-fǝts\ *n pl* : the second part of the canonical Jewish Scripture

¹**pro·phy·lac·tic** \ˌprō-fǝ-'lak-tik, ˌprä-\ *adj* 1 : preventing or guarding from the spread or occurrence of disease or infection 2 : PREVENTIVE

²**prophylactic** *n* : something prophylactic; *esp* : a device (as a condom) for preventing venereal infection or conception

pro·phy·lax·is \-'lak-sǝs\ *n, pl* **-lax·es** \-'lak-ˌsēz\ : measures designed to preserve health and prevent the spread of disease

pro·pin·qui·ty \prǝ-'piŋ-kwǝ-tē\ *n* 1 : KINSHIP 2 : nearness in place or time : PROXIMITY

pro·pi·ti·ate \prō-'pi-shē-ˌāt\ *vb* **-at·ed; -at·ing** ♦ : to gain or regain the favor of : APPEASE ⟨~ the angry gods⟩ — **pro·pi·ti·a·tion** \-ˌpi-shē-'ā-shǝn\ *n*

♦ appease, conciliate, disarm, mollify, pacify, placate

pro·pi·tia·to·ry \prō-'pi-shē-ǝ-ˌtòr-ē\ *adj* 1 ♦ : intended to propitiate 2 : of or relating to propitiation

♦ conciliatory, pacific

pro·pi·tious \prǝ-'pi-shǝs\ *adj* 1 : favorably disposed ⟨~ deities⟩ 2 ♦ : being of good omen ⟨~ circumstances⟩

♦ auspicious, bright, encouraging, fair, golden, heartening, hopeful, likely, promising, rosy, upbeat

prop·man \'präp-ˌman\ *n* : one who is in charge of stage properties

pro·po·nent \prǝ-'pō-nǝnt\ *n* ♦ : one who argues in favor of something

♦ advocate, apostle, backer, booster, champion, exponent, friend, promoter, supporter

¹**pro·por·tion** \prǝ-'pòr-shǝn\ *n* 1 ♦ : harmonious relation of parts to each other or to the whole : BALANCE, SYMMETRY 2 ♦ : proper or equal share 3 : the relation of one part to another or to the whole with respect to magnitude, quantity, or degree : RATIO 4 : physical magnitude, extent, or bulk : SIZE — **in proportion** : PROPORTIONAL

♦ [1] balance, coherence, consonance, harmony, symmetry,

symphony, unity ♦ [2] allotment, allowance, cut, part, portion, quota, share

²pro·por·tion *vb* **-tioned; -tion·ing** **1** : to adjust (a part or thing) in size relative to other parts or things **2** : to make the parts of harmonious
pro·por·tion·al \prə-'pȯr-shə-nəl\ *adj* : corresponding in size, degree, or intensity; *also* : having the same or a constant ratio — **pro·por·tion·al·ly** *adv*
pro·por·tion·ate \prə-'pȯr-shə-nət\ *adj* : PROPORTIONAL — **pro·por·tion·ate·ly** *adv*
pro·pos·al \prə-'pō-zəl\ *n* **1** : an act of putting forward or stating something for consideration **2** ♦ : something that is proposed

♦ offer, proffer, proposition, suggestion

pro·pose \prə-'pōz\ *vb* **pro·posed; pro·pos·ing** **1** ♦ : to form or put forward a plan or intention ⟨~s to buy a house⟩ **2** : to make an offer of marriage **3** ♦ : to offer for consideration : SUGGEST ⟨~ a policy⟩ — **pro·pos·er** *n*

♦ [1] aim, aspire, contemplate, design, intend, mean, meditate, plan ♦ [3] advance, offer, pose, proffer, propound, suggest, vote

¹prop·o·si·tion \ˌprä-pə-'zi-shən\ *n* **1** : something proposed for consideration : PROPOSAL **2** : a request for sexual intercourse **3** ♦ : a statement of something to be discussed, proved, or explained **4** : SITUATION, AFFAIR ⟨a tough ~⟩ — **prop·o·si·tion·al** \-'zi-shə-nəl\ *adj*

♦ conjecture, hypothesis, supposition, theory

²proposition *vb* **-tioned; -tion·ing** : to make a proposal to; *esp* : to suggest sexual intercourse to
pro·pound \prə-'pau̇nd\ *vb* ♦ : to set forth for consideration ⟨~ a doctrine⟩

♦ advance, offer, pose, proffer, propose, suggest, vote

pro·pri·e·tary \prə-'prī-ə-ˌter-ē\ *adj* **1** : of, relating to, or characteristic of a proprietor ⟨~ rights⟩ **2** : made and sold by one with the sole right to do so ⟨~ medicines⟩
pro·pri·e·tor \prə-'prī-ə-tər\ *n* ♦ : a person who has the legal right or exclusive title to something : OWNER — **pro·pri·e·tor·ship** *n*

♦ holder, owner, possessor

pro·pri·e·tress \-'prī-ə-trəs\ *n* : a woman who is a proprietor
pro·pri·e·ty \prə-'prī-ə-tē\ *n, pl* **-ties** **1** ♦ : conformity to what is socially acceptable in conduct or speech **2** *pl* : the customs of polite society

♦ decency, decorum, form

props \'präps\ *n sing or pl* **1** *slang* : DUE 1 ⟨gave him his ~⟩ **2** *slang* : RESPECT 2 ⟨earned the ~ of his peers⟩ **3** *slang* : ACKNOWLEDGMENT ⟨deserves ~ for the effort⟩
pro·pul·sion \prə-'pəl-shən\ *n* **1** : the action or process of propelling **2** : something that propels — **pro·pul·sive** \-siv\ *adj*
pro ra·ta \(ˌ)prō-'rā-tə, -'rä-\ *adv* : in proportion to the share of each : PROPORTIONALLY
pro·rate \(ˌ)prō-'rāt\ *vb* **pro·rat·ed; pro·rat·ing** ♦ : to divide, distribute, or assess proportionately

♦ administer, allocate, apportion, deal, dispense, distribute, mete, parcel, portion

pro·rogue \prə-'rōg\ *vb* **pro·rogued; pro·rogu·ing** : to suspend or end a session of (a legislative body) — **pro·ro·ga·tion** \ˌprō-rō-'gā-shən\ *n*
pros *pl of* PRO
pro·sa·ic \prō-'zā-ik\ *adj* **1** : lacking imagination or excitement : DULL **2** ♦ : of a kind to be expected in the normal order of events : EVERYDAY

♦ average, common, commonplace, everyday, normal, ordinary, routine, run-of-the-mill, standard, unexceptional, unremarkable, usual, workaday

pro·sce·ni·um \prō-'sē-nē-əm\ *n* **1** : the part of a stage in front of the curtain **2** : the wall containing the arch that frames the stage
pro·scribe \prō-'skrīb\ *vb* **pro·scribed; pro·scrib·ing** **1** : to publish the name of as condemned to death with the property of the condemned forfeited to the state **2** ♦ : to condemn or forbid as harmful or unlawful

♦ ban, bar, enjoin, forbid, interdict, outlaw, prohibit

pro·scrip·tion \prō-'skrip-shən\ *n* **1** ♦ : the act of proscribing : the state of being proscribed **2** ♦ : an imposed restraint or restriction

♦ [1, 2] ban, barring, embargo, forbidding, interdiction, prohibition

prose \'prōz\ *n* : the ordinary language people use in speaking or writing
pros·e·cute \'prä-si-ˌkyüt\ *vb* **-cut·ed; -cut·ing** **1** : to follow to the end ⟨~ an investigation⟩ **2** : to seek legal punishment of ⟨~ a forger⟩ — **pros·e·cu·tion** \ˌprä-si-'kyü-shən\ *n* — **pros·e·cu·tor** \'prä-si-ˌkyü-tər\ *n*
¹pros·e·lyte \'prä-sə-ˌlīt\ *n* : a new convert to a religion, belief, or party — **pros·e·ly·tism** \-ˌlī-ˌti-zəm\ *n*
²proselyte *vb* **-lyt·ed; -lyt·ing** : PROSELYTIZE
pros·e·ly·tise *chiefly Brit var of* PROSELYTIZE
pros·e·ly·tize \'prä-sə-lə-ˌtīz\ *vb* **-tized; -tiz·ing** **1** : to induce someone to convert to one's faith **2** : to recruit someone to join one's party, institution, or cause
pros·o·dy \'prä-sə-dē, -zə-\ *n, pl* **-dies** : the study of versification and esp. of metrical structure
¹pros·pect \'prä-ˌspekt\ *n* **1** ♦ : an extensive view; *also* : OUTLOOK **2** : the act of looking forward **3** : a mental vision of something to come **4** : something that is awaited or expected : POSSIBILITY **5 a** : a potential buyer or customer **b** ♦ : a likely candidate — **pro·spec·tive** \prə-'spek-tiv, 'prä-ˌspek-\ *adj* — **pro·spec·tive·ly** *adv*

♦ [1] lookout, outlook, panorama, view, vista ♦ [5b] applicant, aspirant, campaigner, candidate, contender, hopeful, seeker

²pros·pect \'prä-ˌspekt\ *vb* ♦ : to explore esp. for mineral deposits — **pros·pec·tor** \-ˌspek-tər, prä-'spek-\ *n*

♦ explore, hunt, probe, search

pro·spec·tus \prə-'spek-təs\ *n* : a preliminary statement that describes an enterprise and is distributed to prospective buyers or participants
pros·per \'präs-pər\ *vb* **pros·pered; pros·per·ing** **1** ♦ : to succeed in an enterprise or activity; *esp* : to achieve economic success **2** ♦ : to become strong and flourishing

♦ [1, 2] flourish, succeed, thrive

pros·per·i·ty \präs-'per-ə-tē\ *n* : thriving condition : SUCCESS; *esp* : economic well-being
pros·per·ous \'präs-pə-rəs\ *adj* **1** : FAVORABLE ⟨~ winds⟩ **2** ♦ : marked by success or economic well-being ⟨a ~ business⟩ **3** ♦ : enjoying vigorous and healthy growth

♦ [2] palmy, successful, triumphant ♦ [3] booming, golden, palmy, roaring, successful *Ant* unsuccessful

pros·ta·glan·din \ˌpräs-tə-'glan-dən\ *n* : any of various oxygenated unsaturated fatty acids of animals that perform a variety of hormonelike actions
pros·tate \'präs-ˌtāt\ *n* : PROSTATE GLAND — **pros·tat·ic** \prä-'sta-tik\ *adj*
prostate gland *n* : a glandular body about the base of the male urethra that produces a secretion which is a major part of the fluid ejaculated during an orgasm
pros·ta·ti·tis \ˌpräs-tə-'tī-təs\ *n* : inflammation of the prostate gland
pros·the·sis \präs-'thē-səs, 'präs-thə-\ *n, pl* **-the·ses** \-ˌsēz\ : an artificial replacement for a missing body part — **pros·thet·ic** \präs-'the-tik\ *adj*
pros·thet·ics \-'the-tiks\ *n pl* : the surgical or dental specialty concerned with the design, construction, and fitting of prostheses
¹pros·ti·tute \'präs-tə-ˌtüt, -ˌtyüt\ *vb* **-tut·ed; -tut·ing** **1** : to offer for sexual activity esp. for money **2** : to devote to corrupt or unworthy purposes — **pros·ti·tu·tion** \ˌpräs-tə-'tü-shən, -'tyü-\ *n*
²prostitute *n* : one who engages in sexual activities for money
¹pros·trate \'prä-ˌstrāt\ *adj* **1** : stretched out with face on the ground in adoration or submission **2** : lying flat **3** ♦ : completely overcome and lacking vitality ⟨~ with a cold⟩

♦ beat, bushed, dead, drained, effete, jaded, limp, spent, tired, weak, weary, worn-out

²prostrate *vb* **pros·trat·ed; pros·trat·ing** **1** : to throw or put into a prostrate position **2** ♦ : to reduce to a weak or powerless condition

♦ debilitate, enervate, enfeeble, sap, soften, tire, waste, weaken ♦ carry away, crush, devastate, floor, oppress, overcome, overpower, overwhelm, snow under, swamp

pros·tra·tion \prä-'strā-shən\ *n* ♦ : complete physical or mental exhaustion

♦ burnout, collapse, exhaustion, fatigue, lassitude, tiredness, weariness

prosy \'prō-zē\ adj **pros·i·er; -est 1 :** PROSAIC, ORDINARY **2** : TEDIOUS

Prot abbr Protestant

prot·ac·tin·i·um \ˌprō-tak-'ti-nē-əm\ n : a metallic radioactive chemical element of relatively short life

pro·tag·o·nist \prō-'ta-gə-nist\ n **1 :** the principal character in a drama or story **2 :** a leader or supporter of a cause

pro·te·an \'prō-tē-ən\ adj ♦ : able to assume different shapes or roles

♦ adaptable, all-around, universal, versatile

pro·tect \prə-'tekt\ vb ♦ : to shield from injury : GUARD

♦ cover, defend, guard, safeguard, screen, secure, shield, ward

pro·tec·tion \prə-'tek-shən\ n **1 :** the act of protecting : the state of being protected **2** ♦ : one that protects ⟨wear a helmet as a ⁓⟩ **3 :** the supervision or support of one that is smaller and weaker **4 :** the freeing of producers from foreign competition in their home market by high duties on foreign competitive goods — **pro·tec·tive** \-'tek-tiv\ adj

♦ aegis, armor, cover, defense (or defence), guard, safeguard, screen, security, shield, wall, ward

pro·tec·tion·ist \-shə-nist\ n : an advocate of government economic protection for domestic producers through restrictions on foreign competitors — **pro·tec·tion·ism** \-shə-ˌni-zəm\ n

pro·tec·tor \prə-'tek-tər\ n **1** ♦ : one that protects **2 :** a device used to prevent injury : GUARD **3 :** REGENT 1

♦ custodian, defender, defense (or defence), guard, protection

pro·tec·tor·ate \-tə-rət\ n **1 :** government by a protector **2** : the relationship of superior authority assumed by one state over a dependent one; also : the dependent political unit in such a relationship

pro·té·gé \'prō-tə-ˌzhā\ n : one who is protected, trained, or guided by an influential person

pro·tein \'prō-ˌtēn\ n : any of various complex nitrogen-containing substances that consist of chains of amino acids, are present in all living cells, and are an essential part of the human diet

pro tem \prō-'tem\ adv : PRO TEMPORE

pro tem·po·re \prō-'tem-pə-rē\ adv : for the time being

Pro·te·ro·zo·ic \ˌprä-tə-rə-'zō-ik, ˌprō-\ adj : of, relating to, or being the eon of geologic history between the Archean and the Phanerozoic — **Proterozoic** n

¹**pro·test** \'prō-ˌtest\ n **1 :** the act of protesting; esp : an organized public demonstration of disapproval **2** ♦ : a complaint or objection against an idea, an act, or a course of action

♦ challenge, complaint, demur, expostulation, fuss, kick, objection, question, remonstrance

²**pro·test** \prō-'test\ vb **1** ♦ : to assert positively : make solemn declaration of ⟨⁓s his innocence⟩ **2** ♦ : to object strongly : make a protest against ⟨⁓ a ruling⟩ — **pro·test·er** or **pro·tes·tor** \-tər\ n

♦ [1] affirm, allege, assert, aver, avouch, avow, claim, contend, declare, insist, maintain, profess, warrant ♦ [2] demur, kick, object, remonstrate

Prot·es·tant \'prä-təs-tənt, 3 also prə-'tes-\ n **1 :** a member or adherent of one of the Christian churches deriving from the Reformation **2 :** a Christian not of a Catholic or Orthodox church **3** not cap : one who makes a protest — **Prot·es·tant·ism** \'prä-təs-tən-ˌti-zəm\ n

pro·tes·ta·tion \ˌprä-təs-'tā-shən\ n **1 :** the act or fact of protesting **2** ♦ : a formal declaration of dissent to or support of something

♦ affirmation, assertion, avowal, claim, declaration, profession Ant disavowal

pro·tha·la·mi·on \ˌprō-thə-'lā-mē-ən\ or **pro·tha·la·mi·um** \-mē-əm\ n, pl **-mia** \-mē-ə\ : a song in celebration of a marriage

pro·to·col \'prō-tə-ˌköl\ n **1 :** an original draft or record **2 :** a preliminary memorandum of diplomatic negotiation **3 :** a code of diplomatic or military etiquette **4 :** a set of conventions for formatting data in an electronic communications system

pro·ton \'prō-ˌtän\ n : a positively charged atomic particle present in all atomic nuclei — **pro·ton·ic** \-'tä-nik\ adj

pro·to·plasm \'prō-tə-ˌpla-zəm\ n : the complex colloidal largely protein substance of living plant and animal cells — **pro·to·plas·mic** \ˌprō-tə-'plaz-mik\ adj

pro·to·type \'prō-tə-ˌtīp\ n : an original model : ARCHETYPE

pro·to·zo·an \ˌprō-tə-'zō-ən\ n : any of a phylum or subkingdom of unicellular lower invertebrate animals that include some pathogenic parasites of humans and domestic animals — **protozoan** adj

pro·tract \prō-'trakt\ vb ♦ : to prolong in time or space

♦ draw out, elongate, extend, lengthen, prolong, stretch

pro·trac·tor \-'trak-tər\ n : an instrument for drawing and measuring angles

pro·trude \prō-'trüd\ vb **pro·trud·ed; pro·trud·ing** ♦ : to stick out or cause to stick out : jut out

♦ bag, balloon, beetle, belly, billow, bulge, overhang, poke, project, start, stick out

pro·tru·sion \prō-'trü-zhən\ n **1 :** the act of protruding : the state of being protruded **2** ♦ : something that protrudes

♦ bulge, overhang, projection

pro·tu·ber·ance \prō-'tü-bə-rəns, -'tyü-\ n : something that protrudes

pro·tu·ber·ant \-rənt\ adj : extending beyond the surrounding surface in a bulge

proud \'praud\ adj **1** ♦ : having or showing excessive self-esteem : HAUGHTY **2 :** highly pleased : EXULTANT **3 :** having proper self-respect ⟨too ⁓ to beg⟩ **4** ♦ : giving reason for pride : GLORIOUS ⟨a ⁓ occasion⟩ **5 :** SPIRITED ⟨a ⁓ steed⟩ — **proud·ly** adv

♦ [1] arrogant, disdainful, haughty, highfalutin, lofty, lordly, prideful, superior Ant humble, lowly, modest ♦ [4] august, baronial, gallant, glorious, grand, grandiose, heroic, imposing, magnificent, majestic, monumental, noble, regal, royal, splendid, stately

prov abbr **1** province; provincial **2** provisional

Prov abbr Proverbs

prov·able \'prü-və-bəl\ adj ♦ : capable of being proved

♦ demonstrable, supportable, sustainable, verifiable

prove \'prüv\ vb **proved; proved** or **prov·en** \'prü-vən\; **prov·ing 1 :** to test by experiment or by a standard **2** ♦ : to establish the truth of by argument or evidence **3 :** to show to be correct, valid, or genuine **4** ♦ : to turn out esp. after trial or test ⟨the car proved to be a good choice⟩

♦ [2] demonstrate, document, establish, show, substantiate, validate Ant disprove, rebut, refute ♦ [4] come out, pan out, turn out

prov·e·nance \'prä-və-nəns\ n : ORIGIN, SOURCE

Pro·ven·çal \ˌprō-ˌvän-'säl, ˌprä-\ n **1 :** a native or inhabitant of Provence **2 :** OCCITAN — **Provençal** adj

prov·en·der \'prä-vən-dər\ n **1 :** dry food for domestic animals : FEED **2** ♦ : food usable by people : VICTUALS

♦ chow, fare, food, grub, meat, provisions, viands, victuals

pro·ve·nience \prə-'vē-nyəns\ n : ORIGIN, SOURCE

prov·erb \'prä-ˌvərb\ n ♦ : a pithy popular saying : ADAGE

♦ adage, aphorism, byword, epigram, maxim, saying

pro·ver·bi·al \prə-'vər-bē-əl\ adj **1 :** of, relating to, or resembling a proverb **2 :** commonly spoken of

Proverbs n : a book of moral sayings in the canonical Jewish and Christian Scripture

pro·vide \prə-'vīd\ vb **pro·vid·ed; pro·vid·ing 1 :** to take measures beforehand ⟨⁓ against inflation⟩ **2 :** to make a proviso or stipulation **3 :** to supply what is needed ⟨⁓ for a family⟩ **4** : EQUIP **5** ♦ : to supply for use — **pro·vid·er** n

♦ deliver, feed, furnish, give, hand, hand over, supply

pro·vid·ed conj : on condition that : IF

prov·i·dence \'prä-və-dəns\ n **1** often cap : divine guidance or care **2** cap : GOD 1 **3** ♦ : the quality or state of being provident

♦ foresight, forethought, prescience ♦ economy, frugality, husbandry, thrift

prov·i·dent \-dənt\ adj **1** ♦ : making provision for the future **2** ♦ : characterized by or reflecting economy in the use of resources : FRUGAL — **prov·i·dent·ly** adv

♦ [1] farsighted, forehanded, foresighted, prescient ♦ [2] economical, frugal, sparing, thrifty

prov·i·den·tial \ˌprä-və-'den-chəl\ adj **1 :** of, relating to, or determined by Providence **2** ♦ : occurring by or as if by an intervention of Providence : LUCKY

♦ fluky, fortuitous, fortunate, happy, lucky

pro·vid·ing conj : PROVIDED

prov·ince \'prä-vəns\ n **1 :** an administrative district or division of a country **2** pl : all of a country except the metropolises **3** ♦ : proper business or scope : SPHERE

♦ area, arena, demesne, department, discipline, domain, field, line, realm, specialty, sphere

pro·vin·cial \prə-'vin-chəl\ *adj* **1** : of or relating to a province **2** ♦ : limited in outlook : NARROW ⟨∼ ideas⟩ — **pro·vin·cial·ism** \-chə-ˌli-zəm\ *n*

♦ insular, little, narrow, parochial, petty, sectarian, small

proving ground *n* : a place for scientific experimentation or testing

¹pro·vi·sion \prə-'vi-zhən\ *n* **1** : the act or process of providing; *also* : a measure taken beforehand **2** ♦ : a stock of needed supplies; *esp* : a stock of food — usu. used in pl. **3** : a conditional stipulation : PROVISO

provisions ♦ chow, fare, food, grub, meat, provender, viands, victuals

²provision *vb* ♦ : to supply with provisions

♦ board, cater, feed

pro·vi·sion·al \-'vi-zhə-nəl\ *adj* ♦ : provided for a temporary need — **pro·vi·sion·al·ly** *adv*

♦ impermanent, interim, short-term, temporary

pro·vi·so \prə-'vī-zō\ *n, pl* **-sos** *also* **-soes** **1** : an article or clause that introduces a condition **2** ♦ : a conditional stipulation

♦ condition, provision, qualification, reservation, stipulation

pro·vo·ca·teur \prō-ˌvä-kə-'tər\ *n* : one who provokes
prov·o·ca·tion \ˌprä-və-'kā-shən\ *n* **1** : the act of provoking **2** ♦ : something that provokes

♦ boost, encouragement, goad, impetus, impulse, incentive, momentum, motivation, spur, yeast ♦ excitement, incitement, instigation, stimulus

pro·voc·a·tive \prə-'vä-kə-tiv\ *adj* ♦ : serving to provoke or excite

♦ exciting

pro·voke \prə-'vōk\ *vb* **pro·voked**; **pro·vok·ing** **1** : to incite to anger : INCENSE **2** : to call forth : EVOKE ⟨a remark that *provoked* laughter⟩ **3** ♦ : to stir up on purpose ⟨∼ an argument⟩ — **pro·vok·er** *n*

♦ abet, ferment, foment, incite, instigate, raise, stir, whip

pro·vo·lo·ne \ˌprō-və-'lō-nē\ *n* : a usu. firm pliant often smoked Italian cheese
pro·vost \'prō-ˌvōst, 'prä-vəst\ *n* : a high official; *esp* : a high-ranking university administrative officer
pro·vost mar·shal \'prō-ˌvō-'mär-shəl\ *n* : an officer who supervises the military police of a command
prow \'prau̇\ *n* : the bow of a ship
prow·ess \'prau̇-əs\ *n* **1** : military valor and skill **2** : extraordinary ability
prowl \'prau̇(-ə)l\ *vb* : to roam about stealthily — **prowl** *n* — **prowl·er** *n*
prox·i·mal \'präk-sə-məl\ *adj* **1** : next to or nearest the point of attachment or origin; *esp* : located toward the center of the body **2** : of, relating to, or being the mesial and distal surfaces of a tooth — **prox·i·mal·ly** *adv*
prox·i·mate \'präk-sə-mət\ *adj* **1** : DIRECT ⟨the ∼ cause⟩ **2** : very near
prox·im·i·ty \präk-'si-mə-tē\ *n* ♦ : the quality or state of being proximate : NEARNESS

♦ closeness, contiguity, immediacy, nearness **Ant** distance, remoteness

prox·i·mo \'präk-sə-ˌmō\ *adj* : of or occurring in the next month after the present
proxy \'präk-sē\ *n, pl* **prox·ies** **1** : the authority or power to act for another; *also* : a document giving such authorization **2** ♦ : a person authorized to act for another — **proxy** *adj*

♦ agent, attorney, commissary, delegate, deputy, envoy, factor, representative

prude \'prüd\ *n* : a person who shows or affects extreme modesty — **prud·ery** \'prü-də-rē\ *n*
pru·dence \'prüd-ᵊns\ *n* ♦ : sagacity or shrewdness in the management of affairs

♦ common sense, discretion, horse sense, sagacity **Ant** imprudence, indiscretion

pru·dent \'prüd-ᵊnt\ *adj* **1** : shrewd in the management of practical affairs **2** : CAUTIOUS, DISCREET **3** : PROVIDENT, FRUGAL **4** ♦ : marked by wisdom or judiciousness — **pru·den·tial** \prü-'den-chəl\ *adj* — **pru·dent·ly** *adv*

♦ advisable, desirable, expedient, judicious, politic, tactical, wise

prud·ish \'prü-dish\ *adj* ♦ : marked by prudery — **prud·ish·ly** *adv*

♦ prim, puritanical, straitlaced

¹prune \'prün\ *n* : a dried plum
²prune *vb* **pruned**; **prun·ing** ♦ : to cut off unwanted parts (as of a tree)

♦ bob, clip, crop, curtail, cut, cut back, dock, lop, nip, shave, shear, trim

pru·ri·ent \'prur-ē-ənt\ *adj* : LASCIVIOUS; *also* : exciting to lasciviousness — **pru·ri·ence** \-ē-əns\ *n*
¹pry \'prī\ *vb* **pried**; **pry·ing** **1** : to look closely or inquisitively **2** ♦ : to make a nosy or presumptuous inquiry

♦ butt in, interfere, intrude, meddle, mess, nose, obtrude, poke, snoop

²pry *vb* **pried**; **pry·ing** **1** ♦ : to raise, move, or pull apart with a pry or lever **2** ♦ : to extract, detach, or open with difficulty

♦ [1] jimmy, prize ♦ [2] extract, prize, pull, root, tear, uproot, wrest

³pry *n* : a tool for prying
pry·ing *adj* ♦ : inquisitive in an annoying, officious, or meddlesome way

♦ curious, inquisitive, nosy ♦ intrusive, meddlesome, nosy, obtrusive, officious, presumptuous

Ps *or* **Psa** *abbr* Psalms
PS *abbr* **1** postscript **2** public school
PSA *abbr* public service announcement
psalm \'säm, 'sälm\ *n, often cap* : a sacred song or poem; *esp* : one of the hymns collected in the Book of Psalms — **psalm·ist** *n*

♦ anthem, canticle, carol, chorale, hymn, spiritual

Psalms *n* : a book of sacred poems in canonical Jewish and Christian Scripture
Psal·ter \'sȯl-tər\ *n* : the Book of Psalms; *also* : a collection of the Psalms arranged for devotional use
pseud *abbr* pseudonym; pseudonymous
pseu·do \'sü-dō\ *adj* : being apparently rather than actually as stated : SPURIOUS, SHAM
pseu·do·nym \'sü-də-ˌnim\ *n* : a fictitious name — **pseu·don·y·mous** \sü-'dä-nə-məs\ *adj*
pseu·do·sci·ence \ˌsü-dō-'sī-əns\ *n* : a system of theories, assumptions, and methods erroneously regarded as scientific — **pseu·do·sci·en·tif·ic** \-ˌsī-ən-'ti-fik\ *adj*
PSG *abbr* platoon sergeant
¹psi \'sī, 'psī\ *n* : the 23d letter of the Greek alphabet — Ψ *or* ψ
²psi *abbr* pounds per square inch
psit·ta·co·sis \ˌsi-tə-'kō-səs\ *n* : an infectious disease of birds marked by diarrhea and wasting and transmissible to humans
pso·ri·a·sis \sə-'rī-ə-səs\ *n* : a chronic skin disease characterized by red patches covered with white scales
PST *abbr* Pacific standard time
¹psych *or* **psyche** \'sīk\ *vb* **psyched**; **psych·ing** **1** : OUTWIT, OUTGUESS; *also* : to analyze beforehand **2** : INTIMIDATE **3** ♦ : to prepare oneself psychologically ⟨get *psyched* up for the game⟩ — often used with *up*

♦ *sometimes* **psych up** brace, encourage, forearm, fortify, nerve, ready, steel, strengthen

²psych *abbr* psychology
psy·che \'sī-kē\ *n* : SOUL, PERSONALITY; *also* : MIND
psy·che·del·ic \ˌsī-kə-'de-lik\ *adj* **1** : of, relating to, or causing abnormal psychic effects ⟨∼ drugs⟩ **2** : relating to the taking of psychedelic drugs ⟨∼ experience⟩ **3** : imitating, suggestive of, or reproducing the effects of psychedelic drugs ⟨∼ art⟩ ⟨∼ colors⟩ — **psychedelic** *n* — **psy·che·del·i·cal·ly** \-li-k(ə-)lē\ *adv*
psy·chi·a·try \sə-'kī-ə-trē, sī-\ *n* : a branch of medicine dealing with mental, emotional, and behavioral disorders — **psy·chi·at·ric** \ˌsī-kē-'a-trik\ *adj* — **psy·chi·a·trist** \sə-'kī-ə-trist, sī-\ *n*
¹psy·chic \'sī-kik\ *also* **psy·chi·cal** \-ki-kəl\ *adj* **1** : of or relating to the psyche **2** : lying outside the sphere of physical science **3** : sensitive to nonphysical or supernatural forces — **psy·chi·cal·ly** \-k(ə-)lē\ *adv*
²psychic *n* : a person apparently sensitive to nonphysical forces; *also* : MEDIUM 6
psy·cho \'sī-kō\ *n, pl* **psychos** : a mentally disturbed person — not used technically — **psycho** *adj*
psy·cho·ac·tive \ˌsī-kō-'ak-tiv\ *adj* : affecting the mind or behavior
psy·cho·anal·y·sis \ˌsī-kō-ə-'na-lə-səs\ *n* : a method of dealing with psychic disorders by having the patient talk freely about personal experiences and esp. about early childhood and dreams —

psy·cho·an·a·lyst \-'an-ᵊl-ist\ *n* — **psy·cho·an·a·lyt·ic** \-ᵢan-ᵊl-i-tik\ *adj* — **psy·cho·an·a·lyze** \-'an-ᵊl-ᵢīz\ *vb*
psy·cho·bab·ble \'sī-kō-ᵢba-bəl\ *n* : psychological jargon esp. when used in a trite or simplistic manner
psy·cho·dra·ma \ᵢsī-kə-'drä-mə, -'dra-\ *n* **1** : an extemporized dramatization designed to afford catharsis for one or more of the participants from whose life the plot is taken **2** : a dramatic event or story with psychological overtones
psy·cho·gen·ic \-'je-nik\ *adj* : originating in the mind or in mental or emotional conflict
psy·cho·graph·ics \ᵢsī-kə-'gra-fiks\ *n sing or pl* : market research or statistics classifying population groups according to psychological variables
psychol *abbr* psychologist; psychology
psy·cho·log·i·cal \ᵢsī-kə-'lä-ji-kəl\ *adj* **1** : of or relating to psychology **2** ♦ : of or relating to the mind — **psy·cho·log·i·cal·ly** \-ji-k(ə-)lē\ *adv*

   ♦ cerebral, inner, intellectual, mental

psy·chol·o·gy \sī-'kä-lə-jē\ *n, pl* **-gies 1** : the science of mind and behavior **2** : the mental and behavioral characteristics of an individual or group — **psy·chol·o·gist** \sī-'kä-lə-jist\ *n*
psy·cho·path \'sī-kō-ᵢpath\ *n* : a mentally ill or unstable person; *esp* : a person who engages in antisocial behavior and exhibits a pervasive disregard for the rights, feelings, and safety of others — **psy·cho·path·ic** \ᵢsī-kə-'pa-thik\ *adj*
psy·cho·sex·u·al \ᵢsī-kō-'sek-shə-wəl\ *adj* **1** : of or relating to the mental, emotional, and behavioral aspects of sexual development **2** : of or relating to the physiological psychology of sex
psy·cho·sis \sī-'kō-səs\ *n, pl* **-cho·ses** \-ᵢsēz\ : a serious mental illness (as schizophrenia) marked by loss of or greatly lessened ability to test whether what one is thinking and feeling about the real world is really true
psy·cho·so·cial \ᵢsī-kō-'sō-shəl\ *adj* **1** : involving both psychological and social aspects **2** : relating social conditions to mental health
psy·cho·so·mat·ic \ᵢsī-kō-sə-'ma-tik\ *adj* : of or relating to, involving, or concerned with bodily symptoms caused by mental or emotional disturbance
psy·cho·ther·a·py \ᵢsī-kō-'ther-ə-pē\ *n* : treatment of mental or emotional disorder or of related bodily ills by psychological means — **psy·cho·ther·a·pist** \-'pist\ *n*
¹psy·chot·ic \sī-'kä-tik\ *adj* : of, relating to, marked by, or affected with psychosis ⟨~ behavior⟩
²psychotic *n* : an individual who is psychotic
psy·cho·tro·pic \ᵢsī-kə-'trō-pik\ *adj* : acting on the mind ⟨~ drugs⟩
pt *abbr* **1** part **2** payment **3** pint **4** point **5** port
Pt *symbol* platinum
PT *abbr* **1** Pacific time **2** part-time **3** physical therapy **4** physical training
PTA *abbr* Parent-Teacher Association
ptar·mi·gan \'tär-mi-gən\ *n, pl* **-gan** *or* **-gans** : any of various grouses of northern regions with completely feathered feet
PT boat \(ᵢ)pē-'tē-\ *n* : a small fast patrol craft usu. armed with torpedos
pte *abbr, Brit* private
ptg *abbr* printing
PTO *abbr* **1** Parent-Teacher Organization **2** please turn over
pto·maine \'tō-ᵢmān\ *n* : any of various chemical substances formed by bacteria in decaying matter (as meat) and including a few poisonous ones
PTV *abbr* public television
Pu *symbol* plutonium
¹pub \'pəb\ *n* ♦ : an establishment where alcoholic beverages are sold and consumed : TAVERN

   ♦ bar, barroom, café, saloon, tavern

²pub *abbr* **1** public **2** publication **3** published; publisher; publishing
pu·ber·ty \'pyü-bər-tē\ *n* : the condition of being or period of becoming first capable of reproducing sexually — **pu·ber·tal** \-bərt-ᵊl\ *adj*
pu·bes \'pyü-bēz\ *n, pl* **pubes 1** : the hair that appears upon the lower middle region of the abdomen at puberty **2** : the pubic region
pu·bes·cence \pyü-'bes-ᵊns\ *n* **1** : the quality or state of being pubescent **2** : a pubescent covering or surface
pu·bes·cent \-ᵊnt\ *adj* **1** : arriving at or having reached puberty **2** : covered with fine soft short hairs
pu·bic \'pyü-bik\ *adj* : of, relating to, or situated near the pubes or the pubis

pu·bis \'pyü-bəs\ *n, pl* **pu·bes** \-bēz\ : the ventral and anterior of the three principal bones composing either half of the pelvis
publ *abbr* **1** publication **2** published; publisher
¹pub·lic \'pə-blik\ *adj* **1** : exposed to general view ⟨the story became — ⟩ **2** : of, relating to, or affecting the people as a whole ⟨~ opinion⟩ **3** : CIVIC, GOVERNMENTAL ⟨~ expenditures⟩ **4** : of, relating to, or serving the community ⟨~ officials⟩ **5** : not private : SOCIAL ⟨~ morality⟩ **6** ♦ : accessible to or shared by all members of the community ⟨~ library⟩ **7** : well known : PROMINENT ⟨~ figures⟩ **8** ♦ : of, relating to, or affecting all the people or the whole area of a nation or state — **pub·lic·ly** *adv*

   ♦ [2] common, general, popular, vulgar ♦ [6] free-for-all, open, unrestricted ♦ [6] collective, common, communal, concerted, conjoint, joint, mutual, united ♦ [8] civil, national, state

²public *n* **1** ♦ : the people as a whole **2** : a group of people having common interests

   ♦ folks, humanity, humankind, people, persons, society, world

pub·li·can \'pə-bli-kən\ *n* **1** : a Jewish tax collector for the ancient Romans **2** *chiefly Brit* : the licensee of a pub
pub·li·ca·tion \ᵢpə-blə-'kā-shən\ *n* **1** : the act or process of publishing **2** : a published work
public house *n* **1** ♦ : an establishment for the lodging and entertaining of travelers : INN **2** *chiefly Brit* : a licensed saloon or bar

   ♦ hospice, hotel, inn, lodge, tavern

pub·li·cise *chiefly Brit var of* PUBLICIZE
pub·li·cist \'pə-blə-sist\ *n* : one that publicizes; *esp* : PRESS AGENT
pub·lic·i·ty \(ᵢ)pə-'bli-sə-tē\ *n* **1** : information with news value issued to gain public attention or support **2** : public attention or acclaim
pub·li·cize \'pə-blə-ᵢsīz\ *vb* **-cized; -ciz·ing** ♦ : to bring to public attention ⟨*publicizing* the book⟩

   ♦ advertise, announce, blaze, broadcast, declare, enunciate, placard, post, proclaim, promulgate, publish, sound ♦ ballyhoo, boast, plug, promote, tout

pub·lic–key \'pə-blik-ᵢkē\ *n* : the publicly shared element of a code usable only to encode messages
public relations *n sing or pl* : the business of fostering public goodwill toward a person, firm, or institution; *also* : the degree of goodwill and understanding achieved
public school *n* **1** : an endowed secondary boarding school in Great Britain offering a classical curriculum and preparation for the universities or public service **2** : a free tax-supported school controlled by a local governmental authority
public servant *n* ♦ : a government official or employee

   ♦ functionary, officeholder, officer, official

public–spirited *adj* : motivated by devotion to the general or national welfare
public television *n* : television supported by public funds and private contributions rather than by commercials
public works *n pl* : works (as schools or highways) constructed with public funds for public use
pub·lish \'pə-blish\ *vb* **1** ♦ : to make generally known : announce publicly **2** ♦ : to produce or release literature, information, musical scores or sometimes recordings, or art for sale to the public — **pub·lish·er** *n*

   ♦ [1] advertise, announce, blaze, broadcast, declare, enunciate, placard, post, proclaim, promulgate, publicize, sound ♦ [2] get out, issue, print

¹puck \'pək\ *n* ♦ : a mischievous sprite — **puck·ish** *adj* — **puck·ish·ly** *adv*

   ♦ brownie, dwarf, elf, fairy, fay, gnome, hobgoblin, leprechaun, pixie, troll

²puck *n* : a disk used in ice hockey
¹puck·er \'pə-kər\ *vb* : to contract into folds or wrinkles
²pucker *n* : FOLD, WRINKLE
pud·ding \'pu-diŋ\ *n* : a soft, spongy, or thick creamy dessert
pud·dle \'pəd-ᵊl\ *n* : a very small pool of usu. dirty or muddy water
pu·den·dum \pyü-'den-dəm\ *n, pl* **-da** \-də\ : the human external genital organs esp. of a woman
pudgy \'pə-jē\ *adj* **pudg·i·er; -est** : being short and plump : CHUBBY
pueb·lo \'pwe-blō, pü-'e-\ *n, pl* **-los 1** : a village of Indigenous people of Arizona or New Mexico that consists of flat-roofed stone or adobe houses joined in groups sometimes several stories high **2** *cap* : a member of a group of Indigenous peoples of the southwestern U.S.

pu·er·ile \'pyu̇-ə-rəl\ adj : marked by or suggestive of immaturity and lack of poise : CHILDISH, SILLY — **pu·er·il·i·ty** \,pyu̇-ə-'ri-lə-tē\ n

pu·er·per·al \pyu̇-'ər-pə-rəl\ adj : of, relating to, or occurring during childbirth or the period immediately following ⟨~ infection⟩ ⟨~ depression⟩

puerperal fever n : an abnormal condition that results from infection of the placental site following childbirth or abortion

Puer·to Ri·can \,pȯr-tə-'rē-kən, ,pwer-\ n : a native or inhabitant of Puerto Rico — **Puerto Rican** adj

¹**puff** \'pəf\ vb **1** : to blow in short gusts **2** ♦ : to breathe hard : PANT **3** : to emit small whiffs or clouds **4** : BLUSTER, BRAG **5** : INFLATE, SWELL **6** : to make proud or conceited **7** : to praise extravagantly

♦ blow, gasp, pant, wheeze

²**puff** n **1** ♦ : a short discharge (as of air or smoke); also : a slight explosive sound accompanying it **2** : a light fluffy pastry **3** : a slight swelling **4** : a fluffy mass; also : a small pad for applying cosmetic powder **5** : a laudatory notice or review — **puffy** adj

♦ air, breath, breeze, waft, zephyr

puff·ball \'pəf-,bȯl\ n : any of various globe-shaped and often edible fungi

puf·fin \'pə-fən\ n : any of several seabirds having a short neck and a deep grooved parti-colored bill

¹**pug** \'pəg\ n **1** : any of a breed of small stocky short-haired dogs with a wrinkled face **2** : a close coil of hair

²**pug** n : ¹BOXER

pu·gi·lism \'pyü-jə-,li-zəm\ n : BOXING

pu·gi·list \'pyü-jə-list\ n ♦ : one that fights; esp : a professional boxer — **pu·gi·lis·tic** \,pyü-jə-'lis-tik\ adj

♦ boxer, fighter, prizefighter

pug·na·cious \,pəg-'nā-shəs\ adj ♦ : having a quarrelsome or combative nature

♦ aggressive, argumentative, bellicose, belligerent, combative, contentious, discordant, disputatious, quarrelsome, scrappy, truculent

pug·nac·i·ty \,pəg-'na-sə-tē\ n ♦ : a readiness or inclination to fight

♦ aggression, aggressiveness, belligerence, fight, truculence

puis·sance \'pwi-səns, 'pyü-ə-\ n : capacity for exertion or endurance : POWER, STRENGTH ⟨the ~ of the king⟩

puis·sant \'pwi-sənt, 'pyü-ə-\ adj : having puissance : POWERFUL

puke \'pyük\ vb **puked; puk·ing** ♦ : to discharge the contents of the stomach through the mouth : VOMIT — **puke** n

♦ barf, gag, heave, hurl, retch, spit up, throw up, vomit

puk·ka \'pə-kə\ adj : GENUINE, AUTHENTIC; also : FIRST-CLASS, COMPLETE

pul·chri·tude \'pəl-krə-,tüd, -,tyüd\ n : BEAUTY — **pul·chri·tu·di·nous** \,pəl-krə-'tüd-ᵊn-əs, -'tyüd-\ adj

¹**pull** \'pu̇l\ vb **1** ♦ : to exert force so as to draw (something) toward the force; also : MOVE ⟨~ out of a driveway⟩ **2 a** : PLUCK **b** ♦ : to take out forcibly : EXTRACT ⟨~ a tooth⟩ **3** ♦ : to strain abnormally ⟨~ a tendon⟩ **4** : to draw apart : TEAR **5** : to make (as a proof) by printing **6** : REMOVE **7** : DRAW ⟨~ a gun⟩ **8** : to carry out esp. with daring ⟨~ a robbery⟩ **9** : PERPETRATE, COMMIT **10** : ATTRACT **11** : to express strong sympathy — **pull·er** n

♦ [1] drag, draw, hale, haul, lug, move, tow, tug Ant drive, propel, push ♦ [2b] extract, prize, pry, root, tear, uproot, wrest ♦ [3] rack, strain, stretch, wrench

²**pull** n **1** ♦ : the act or an instance of pulling **2** : the effort expended in moving **3 a** : ADVANTAGE **b** ♦ : special influence **4** : a device for pulling something or for operating by pulling **5** ♦ : a force that attracts or compels **6** : an injury from abnormal straining or stretching ⟨a muscle ~⟩

♦ [1] draw, haul, jerk, pluck, tug, wrench Ant push ♦ [3b, 5] authority, clout, influence, sway, weight

pull·back \'pu̇l-,bak\ n : an orderly withdrawal of troops

pull–down adj : appearing below a selected item (as a menu title) on a computer display ⟨a ~ menu⟩

pul·let \'pu̇-lət\ n : a young hen esp. of the domestic chicken when less than a year old

pul·ley \'pu̇-lē\ n, pl **pulleys** : a wheel used to transmit power by means of a belt, rope, or chain; esp : one with a grooved rim that forms part of a tackle for hoisting or for changing the direction of a force

Pull·man \'pu̇l-mən\ n : a railroad passenger car with comfortable furnishings esp. for night travel

pull off vb : to accomplish successfully

pull·out \'pu̇l-,au̇t\ n : PULLBACK

pull out vb **1** ♦ : to go away from : DEPART **2** : to take back or away : REMOVE

♦ clear out, depart, exit, get off, go, move, quit, sally, shove, take off

pull·over \'pu̇l-,ō-vər\ adj : put on by being pulled over the head ⟨~ sweater⟩ — **pull·over** n

pull–up \'pu̇l-,əp\ n : CHIN-UP

pull up vb : to bring or come to an often abrupt halt : STOP

pul·mo·nary \'pu̇l-mə-,ner-ē, 'pəl-\ adj : of, relating to, or carried on by the lungs ⟨the ~ circulation⟩

pulp \'pəlp\ n **1** : the soft juicy or fleshy part of a fruit or vegetable **2** : a soft moist mass **3** : the soft sensitive tissue that fills the central cavity of a tooth **4** : a material (as from wood) used in making paper **5** : a magazine using cheap paper and often dealing with sensational material

pul·pit \'pu̇l-,pit\ n : a raised platform or high reading desk used in preaching or conducting a worship service

pulp·wood \'pəlp-,wu̇d\ n : wood used in making pulp for paper

pulpy \'pəl-pē\ adj ♦ : resembling or consisting of pulp

♦ fleshy, juicy, succulent ♦ flabby, mushy, soft, spongy

pul·sar \'pəl-,sär\ n : a celestial source of pulsating electromagnetic radiation (as radio waves)

pul·sate \'pəl-,sāt\ vb **pul·sat·ed; pul·sat·ing** ♦ : to expand and contract rhythmically : BEAT

♦ beat, palpitate, pitter-patter, pulse, throb

pul·sa·tion \,pəl-'sā-shən\ n ♦ : rhythmical throbbing or vibrating

♦ beat, palpitation, pulse, throb

¹**pulse** \'pəls\ n **1** : the regular throbbing in the arteries caused by the contractions of the heart **2** : rhythmical beating, vibrating, or sounding **3** : a brief change in electrical current or voltage

²**pulse** vb ♦ : to exhibit a pulse or pulsation

♦ beat, palpitate, pitter-patter, pulsate, throb

pul·ver·ise chiefly Brit var of PULVERIZE

pul·ver·ize \'pəl-və-,rīz\ vb **-ized; -iz·ing 1** ♦ : to reduce (as by crushing or grinding) or be reduced to very small particles **2** ♦ : to destroy by or as if by smashing into fragments : DEMOLISH

♦ [1] atomize, crush, grind, powder ♦ [2] annihilate, blot out, demolish, desolate, destroy, devastate, do in, exterminate, extinguish, obliterate, ruin, shatter, smash, tear down, waste, wipe out, wreck

pu·ma \'pü-mə, 'pyü-\ n, pl **pumas** also **puma** : a large powerful tawny brown wild American cat : COUGAR

pum·ice \'pə-məs\ n : a light porous volcanic glass used esp. for smoothing and polishing

pum·mel \'pə-məl\ vb **-meled** also **-melled; -mel·ing** also **-mel·ling** : to strike repeatedly : BEAT

¹**pump** \'pəmp\ n : a device for raising, transferring, or compressing fluids esp. by suction or pressure

²**pump** vb **1** : to raise (as water) with a pump **2** : to draw fluid from with a pump; also : to fill by means of a pump ⟨~ up a tire⟩ **3** : to force or propel in the manner of a pump **4** ♦ : to move in a manner that resembles the action of a pump handle **5** ♦ : to question persistently — **pump·er** n

♦ [4] bob, bobble, jog, jounce, nod, seesaw ♦ [5] examine, grill, interrogate, query, question, quiz

³**pump** n : a low shoe that grips the foot chiefly at the toe and heel

pumped \'pəmpt\ adj : filled with energetic excitement and enthusiasm

pum·per·nick·el \'pəm-pər-,ni-kəl\ n : a dark rye bread

pump·kin \'pəmp-kən, 'pəŋ-kən\ n : the large usu. orange fruit of a vine of the gourd family that is widely used as food; also : this vine

pun \'pən\ n : the humorous use of a word in a way that suggests two or more interpretations — **pun** vb

¹**punch** \'pənch\ vb **1 a** : PROD, POKE **b** : to frighten or prod (as game or cattle) into moving in a desired direction : DRIVE, HERD ⟨~ing cattle⟩ **2** ♦ : to strike with the fist **3** ♦ : to emboss, perforate, or make with a punch **4** : to operate, produce, or enter (as data) by or as if by punching — **punch·er** n

♦ [2] bang, bash, belt, clout, hit, knock, slug, strike, thump, wallop, whack ♦ [3] bore, drill, hole, perforate, pierce, puncture

²punch *n* **1** ♦ : a quick blow with or as if with the fist **2** ♦ : effective energy or forcefulness

♦ [1] belt, blow, box, clout, hit, slug, smash, wallop, whack ♦ [2] bounce, dash, drive, esprit, pep, snap, spirit, verve, vim, zing, zip ♦ [2] cogency, effectiveness, force, impact, point

³punch *n* **1** : a tool for piercing, stamping, cutting, or forming **2** ♦ : a hole or notch from a perforating operation

♦ perforation, pinhole, prick, puncture, stab

⁴punch *n* : a drink usu. composed of wine or alcoholic liquor and nonalcoholic beverages; *also* : a drink composed of nonalcoholic beverages

punch card \\'pənch-\ *n* : a card with holes punched in particular positions to represent data

punch–drunk \\'pənch-ˌdrəŋk\ *adj* **1** : suffering from brain injury resulting from repeated head blows received in boxing **2** : DAZED, CONFUSED

pun•cheon \\'pən-chən\ *n* ♦ : a large cask

♦ barrel, cask, hogshead, keg, pipe

punch line *n* : the sentence or phrase in a joke that makes the point
punch list *n* : a list of tasks to be completed at the end of a project
punchy \\'pən-chē\ *adj* **punch•i•er; -est** **1** : having punch : FORCEFUL **2** : DAZED, CONFUSED **3** : VIVID, VIBRANT
punc•til•io \ˌpəŋk-'ti-lē-ˌō\ *n, pl* **-i•os** **1** : a nice detail of conduct in a ceremony or in observance of a code **2** : careful observance of forms (as in social conduct)
punc•til•i•ous \ˌpəŋk-'ti-lē-əs\ *adj* ♦ : marked by precise accordance with codes or conventions

♦ ceremonious, correct, decorous, formal, proper, starchy

punc•tu•al \\'pəŋk-chə-wəl\ *adj* ♦ : being on time : PROMPT — **punc•tu•al•ly** *adv*

♦ immediate, prompt, timely

punc•tu•al•i•ty \ˌpəŋk-chə-'wa-lə-tē\ *n* ♦ : the quality, state, or habit of being punctual

♦ promptitude, timeliness

punc•tu•ate \\'pəŋk-chə-ˌwāt\ *vb* **-at•ed; -at•ing** **1** : to mark or divide (written matter) with punctuation marks **2** : to break into at intervals **3** : EMPHASIZE
punc•tu•a•tion \ˌpəŋk-chə-'wā-shən\ *n* : the act, practice, or system of inserting standardized marks in written matter to clarify the meaning and separate structural units
¹punc•ture \\'pəŋk-chər\ *n* **1** : an act of puncturing **2** ♦ : a small hole or wound made by puncturing

♦ perforation, pinhole, prick, punch, stab

²puncture *vb* **punc•tured; punc•tur•ing** **1** ♦ : to pierce with or as if with a pointed instrument or object **2** : to make useless as if by a puncture

♦ bore, drill, hole, perforate, pierce, punch

pun•dit \\'pən-dət\ *n* **1** : a learned person : TEACHER **2** : AUTHORITY, CRITIC
pun•dit•oc•ra•cy \ˌpən-dət-'ä-krə-sē\ *n, pl* **-cies** : a group of powerful and influential political commentators
pun•gen•cy \\'pən-jən-sē\ *n* ♦ : the quality or state of being pungent

♦ acidity, acrimony, asperity, bite, bitterness, edge, harshness, keenness, sharpness, tartness

pun•gent \\'pən-jənt\ *adj* **1** ♦ : having a sharp incisive quality : CAUSTIC ⟨a ∼ editorial⟩ **2 a** : causing a sharp or irritating sensation; *esp* : ACRID ⟨∼ smell of burning leaves⟩ **b** ♦ : having an intense flavor or odor — **pun•gent•ly** *adv*

♦ [1] acrid, biting, caustic, cutting, mordant, sarcastic, satiric, scathing, sharp, tart ♦ [2b] nippy, sharp, strong

pun•ish \\'pə-nish\ *vb* **1** : to impose a penalty on for a fault or crime ⟨∼ an offender⟩ **2** ♦ : to inflict a penalty for ⟨∼ treason with death⟩ **3** : to inflict injury on : HURT — **pun•ish•able** *adj*

♦ castigate, chasten, chastise, correct, discipline, penalize *Ant* excuse, pardon, spare

pun•ish•ment *n* **1** ♦ : retributive suffering, pain, or loss : PENALTY **2** : rough treatment

♦ castigation, chastisement, correction, desert, discipline, nemesis, penalty, wrath

pu•ni•tive \\'pyü-nə-tiv\ *adj* ♦ : inflicting, involving, or aiming at punishment

♦ corrective, disciplinary, penal

¹punk \\'pəŋk\ *n* **1** : a young inexperienced person **2** ♦ : a petty hoodlum

♦ bully, gangster, goon, hood, hoodlum, mobster, mug, rowdy, ruffian, thug, tough

²punk *adj* **1** ♦ : very poor **2** ♦ : being in poor health

♦ [1] bad, deficient, inferior, lousy, off, poor, rotten, substandard, unacceptable, unsatisfactory, wanting, wretched, wrong ♦ [2] bad, down, ill, indisposed, peaked, sick, unhealthy, unsound, unwell

³punk *n* : dry crumbly wood useful for tinder; *also* : a substance made from fungi for use as tinder
pun•ster \\'pən-stər\ *n* : one who is given to punning
¹punt \\'pənt\ *n* : a long narrow flat-bottomed boat with square ends
²punt *vb* : to propel (as a punt) with a pole
³punt *vb* : to kick a football or soccer ball dropped from the hands before it touches the ground
⁴punt *n* : the act or an instance of punting a ball
pu•ny \\'pyü-nē\ *adj* **pu•ni•er; -est** : slight in power, size, or importance
pup \\'pəp\ *n* : a young dog; *also* : one of the young of some other animals
pu•pa \\'pyü-pə\ *n, pl* **pu•pae** \-(ˌ)pē\ *or* **pupas** : a form of some insects (as a bee, moth, or beetle) between the larva and the adult that usu. has a protective covering (as a cocoon) — **pu•pal** \-pəl\ *adj*
¹pu•pil \\'pyü-pəl\ *n* **1** : a child or young person in school or in the charge of a tutor **2** : one who has been taught or influenced by a famous or distinguished person : DISCIPLE

♦ adherent, convert, disciple, follower, partisan, votary

²pupil *n* : the dark central opening of the iris of the eye
pup•pet \\'pə-pət\ *n* **1** : a small figure of a person or animal moved by hand or by strings or wires **2** : DOLL **3** : one whose acts are controlled by an outside force or influence
pup•pe•teer \ˌpə-pə-'tir\ *n* : one who manipulates puppets
pup•py \\'pə-pē\ *n, pl* **puppies** : a young domestic dog
pu•pu \\'pü-ˌpü\ *n* : an Asian dish consisting of a variety of foods
pur•blind \\'pər-ˌblīnd\ *adj* **1** : partly blind **2** : lacking in insight : OBTUSE
pur•chas•able \\'pər-chə-sə-bəl\ *adj* **1** : capable of being purchased **2** ♦ : open to corrupt influence and esp. bribery

♦ bribable, corruptible, venal

¹pur•chase \\'pər-chəs\ *vb* **pur•chased; pur•chas•ing** ♦ : to obtain by paying money or its equivalent : BUY — **pur•chas•er** *n*

♦ buy, pick up, take

²purchase *n* **1** : an act or instance of purchasing **2** : something purchased **3** : a secure hold or grasp; *also* : advantageous leverage
pur•dah \\'pər-də\ *n* : seclusion of women from public observation among Muslims and some Hindus esp. in India; *also* : a state of seclusion
pure \\'pyur\ *adj* **pur•er; pur•est** **1** ♦ : unmixed with any other matter : free from taint ⟨∼ gold⟩ ⟨∼ water⟩ **2** : being thus and no other : ABSOLUTE ⟨∼ nonsense⟩ **3** : ABSTRACT, THEORETICAL ⟨∼ mathematics⟩ **4** : free from what vitiates, weakens, or pollutes ⟨speaks a ∼ French⟩ **5** : free from moral fault : INNOCENT **6** ♦ : marked by chastity : CHASTE

♦ [1] absolute, fine, neat, plain, refined, straight, unadulterated, undiluted, unmixed *Ant* adulterated, diluted, impure, mixed ♦ [6] chaste, clean, decent, immaculate, modest

pure–blood•ed \-ˌblə-dəd\ *or* **pure–blood** \-ˌbləd\ *adj* : FULL-BLOODED — **pure•blood** *n*
pure•bred \-'bred\ *adj* ♦ : bred from members of a recognized breed, strain, or kind without crossbreeding over many generations — **pure•bred** \-ˌbred\ *n*

♦ full-blooded, thoroughbred *Ant* hybrid, mixed, mongrel

¹pu•ree \pyu-'rā, -'rē\ *n* : a paste or thick liquid suspension usu. made from finely ground cooked food; *also* : a thick soup made of pureed vegetables
²puree *vb* **pu•reed; pu•ree•ing** : to make a puree of
pure•ly \\'pyur-lē\ *adv* **1 a** : to a full extent : TOTALLY ⟨∼ by accident⟩ **b** : WHOLLY, EXCLUSIVELY ⟨a selection based ∼ on merit⟩ **2** : without admixture of anything injurious or foreign **3** : SIMPLY, MERELY ⟨read ∼ for relaxation⟩ **4** ♦ : in a chaste or innocent manner

♦ chastely, modestly, righteously, virtuously *Ant* evilly, immorally, sinfully, wickedly

pur•ga•tion \ˌpər-'gā-shən\ *n* : the act or result of purging

¹pur·ga·tive \'pər-gə-tiv\ *adj* : purging or tending to purge

²purgative *n* : a strong laxative : CATHARTIC

pur·ga·to·ry \'pər-gə-ˌtōr-ē\ *n, pl* **-ries 1** : an intermediate state after death for expiatory purification **2** : a place or state of temporary punishment — **pur·ga·tor·i·al** \ˌpər-gə-'tōr-ē-əl\ *adj*

¹purge \'pərj\ *vb* **purged; purg·ing 1** : to cleanse or purify esp. from sin **2** : to have or cause strong and usu. repeated emptying of the bowels **3** : to get rid of ⟨the leaders had been *purged*⟩

²purge *n* **1** : something that purges; *esp* : PURGATIVE **2** : an act or result of purging; *esp* : a ridding of persons regarded as treacherous or disloyal

pu·ri·fy \'pyùr-ə-ˌfī\ *vb* **-fied; -fy·ing** ♦ : to make or become pure — **pu·ri·fi·ca·tion** \ˌpyùr-ə-fə-'kā-shən\ *n* — **pu·ri·fi·ca·to·ry** \pyù-'ri-fi-kə-ˌtōr-ē\ *adj* — **pu·ri·fi·er** *n*

　♦ sanctify ♦ clarify, clear, distill, filter

Pu·rim \'pùr-(ˌ)im\ *n* : a Jewish holiday celebrated in February or March in commemoration of the deliverance of the Jews from the massacre plotted by Haman

pu·rine \'pyùr-ˌēn\ *n* : any of a group of bases including several (as adenine or guanine) that are constituents of DNA or RNA

pur·ism \'pyùr-ˌi-zəm\ *n* : rigid adherence to or insistence on purity or nicety esp. in use of words — **pur·ist** \-ist\ *n* — **pu·ris·tic** \pyù-'ris-tik\ *adj*

pu·ri·tan \'pyùr-ət-ᵊn\ *n* **1** *cap* : a member of a 16th and 17th century Protestant group in England and New England opposing the ceremonies and government of the Church of England **2** : one who practices or preaches a stricter or professedly purer moral code than that which prevails

pu·ri·tan·i·cal \ˌpyùr-ə-'ta-ni-kəl\ *adj* **1** ♦ : of, relating to, or characterized by a rigid morality **2** : of or relating to puritans, the Puritans, or puritanism — **pu·ri·tan·i·cal·ly** *adv*

　♦ prim, prudish, straitlaced

pu·ri·ty \'pyùr-ə-tē\ *n* ♦ : the quality or state of being pure

　♦ chastity, modesty

¹purl \'pərl\ *vb* : to knit in purl stitch

²purl *n* : a stitch in knitting

³purl *n* : a gentle murmur or movement (as of purling water)

⁴purl *vb* **1** : EDDY, SWIRL **2** : to make a soft murmuring sound

pur·lieu \'pər-lü, 'pərl-yü\ *n* **1** : an outlying district : SUBURB **2** *pl* : the districts around a city : ENVIRONS

pur·loin \(ˌ)pər-'lòin, 'pər-ˌlòin\ *vb* ♦ : to take or make use of wrongfully and often by a breach of trust : STEAL

　♦ appropriate, filch, hook, misappropriate, nip, pilfer, pocket, snitch, steal, swipe, thieve

¹pur·ple \'pər-pəl\ *adj* **pur·pler; pur·plest 1** : of the color purple **2** : highly rhetorical ⟨a ~ passage⟩ **3** : PROFANE ⟨~ language⟩ — **pur·plish** *adj*

²purple *n* **1** : a bluish red color **2** : a purple robe emblematic esp. of regal rank or authority

¹pur·port \'pər-ˌpōrt\ *n* ♦ : meaning conveyed or implied; *also* : GIST ⟨the ~ of the letter⟩

　♦ denotation, drift, gist, import, intent, meaning, sense, significance, signification

²pur·port \(ˌ)pər-'pōrt\ *vb* : to convey or profess outwardly as the meaning or intention : CLAIM ⟨~s to be objective⟩ — **pur·port·ed·ly** \-'pōr-təd-lē\ *adv*

¹pur·pose \'pər-pəs\ *n* **1** ♦ : something set up as an object or end to be attained **2** : RESOLUTION, DETERMINATION — **pur·pose·less** *adj*

　♦ aim, ambition, aspiration, design, dream, end, goal, intent, mark, meaning, object, objective, plan, pretension, thing ♦ capacity, function, job, part, place, position, role, task, work

²purpose *vb* **pur·posed; pur·pos·ing** : to propose as an aim to oneself

pur·pose·ful \'pər-pəs-fəl\ *adj* **1** : having a purpose: as **a** : MEANINGFUL ⟨~ activities⟩ **b** ♦ : done by intention or design : INTENTIONAL ⟨~ ambiguity⟩ **2** ♦ : full of determination

　♦ [1b] deliberate, freewill, intentional, voluntary, willful, willing ♦ [2] bound, decisive, determined, firm, intent, resolute, set, single-minded

pur·pose·ful·ly \-fə-lē\ *adv* : in a purposeful manner

pur·pose·ly *adv* ♦ : with a deliberate or express purpose

　♦ consciously, deliberately, intentionally, knowingly, willfully

purr \'pər\ *n* ♦ : a low murmur typical of a contented cat — **purr** *vb*

　♦ buzz, drone, hum, whir, whiz, zoom

¹purse \'pərs\ *n* **1** ♦ : a receptacle (as a pouch) to carry money and often other small objects **2** : RESOURCES **3** : a sum of money offered as a prize or present

　♦ bag, handbag, pocketbook

²purse *vb* **pursed; purs·ing** : PUCKER

purs·er \'pər-sər\ *n* : an official on a ship who keeps accounts and attends to the comfort of passengers

purs·lane \'pər-slən, -ˌslān\ *n* : a fleshy-leaved weedy trailing plant with tiny yellow flowers that is sometimes used in salads

pur·su·ance \pər-'sü-əns\ *n* ♦ : the act of carrying out or into effect

　♦ accomplishment, achievement, commission, discharge, enactment, execution, fulfillment, implementation, performance, perpetration

pur·su·ant to \-'sü-ənt-\ *prep* : in carrying out : ACCORDING TO

pur·sue \pər-'sü\ *vb* **pur·sued; pur·su·ing 1** ♦ : to follow in order to overtake or overcome **2** : to seek to accomplish ⟨~ a goal⟩ **3** : to proceed along ⟨~ a course⟩ **4** : to engage in ⟨~ a career⟩ — **pur·su·er** *n*

　♦ chase, dog, follow, hound, shadow, tag, tail, trace, track, trail

pur·suit \pər-'süt\ *n* **1** ♦ : the act of pursuing **2** : OCCUPATION, BUSINESS

　♦ chase, following, tracing

pu·ru·lent \'pyùr-ə-lənt, -yə-\ *adj* : containing or accompanied by pus ⟨a ~ discharge⟩ — **pu·ru·lence** \-ləns\ *n*

pur·vey \(ˌ)pər-'vā\ *vb* **pur·veyed; pur·vey·ing** : to supply (as provisions) usu. as a business — **pur·vey·ance** \-əns\ *n* — **pur·vey·or** \-ər\ *n*

pur·view \'pər-ˌvyü\ *n* **1** : the range or limit esp. of authority, responsibility, or intention **2** : range of vision, understanding, or cognizance

pus \'pəs\ *n* : thick yellowish white fluid matter (as in a boil) formed at a place of inflammation and infection (as an abscess) and containing germs, white blood cells, and tissue debris

¹push \'pùsh\ *vb* **1** ♦ : to press against with force in order to drive or impel **2** ♦ : to thrust forward, downward, or outward **3** : to urge on : press forward **4** : to cause to increase ⟨~ prices to record levels⟩ **5** : to urge or press the advancement, adoption, or practice of; *esp* : to make aggressive efforts to sell **6** : to engage in the illicit sale of narcotics

　♦ [1, 2] drive, propel, shove, thrust ♦ [2] bulldoze, elbow, muscle, press

²push *n* **1** : a vigorous effort : DRIVE **2** : an act of pushing : SHOVE **3** : vigorous enterprise : ENERGY

push–button *adj* **1** : operated or done by means of push buttons **2** : using or dependent on complex and more or less automatic mechanisms ⟨~ warfare⟩

push button *n* : a small button or knob that when pushed operates something esp. by closing an electric circuit

push·cart \'pùsh-ˌkärt\ *n* : a cart or barrow pushed by hand

push·er \'pù-shər\ *n* : one that pushes; *esp* : one that pushes illegal drugs

push·over \-ˌō-vər\ *n* **1** : an opponent easy to defeat **2** : SUCKER **3** ♦ : something easily accomplished

　♦ breeze, child's play, cinch, picnic, snap

push–up \-ˌəp\ *n* : a conditioning exercise performed in a prone position by raising and lowering the body with the straightening and bending of the arms while keeping the back straight and supporting the body on the hands and toes

pushy \'pù-shē\ *adj* **push·i·er; -est** : aggressive often to an objectionable degree

pu·sil·lan·i·mous \ˌpyü-sə-'la-nə-məs\ *adj* ♦ : contemptibly timid : COWARDLY — **pu·sil·la·nim·i·ty** \ˌpyü-sə-lə-'ni-mə-tē\ *n*

　♦ chicken, cowardly, craven, dastardly, recreant, spineless, yellow

¹puss \'pùs\ *n* ♦ : a domestic cat

　♦ cat, feline, kitty

²puss *n, slang* : FACE

¹pussy \'pù-sē\ *n, pl* **puss·ies** : PUSS

²pus·sy \'pə-sē\ *adj* **pus·si·er; -est** : full of or resembling pus

pussy·cat \'pù-sē-ˌkat\ *n* : CAT

pussy·foot \-ˌfùt\ *vb* **1** ♦ : to tread or move warily or stealthily **2** ♦ : to refrain from committing oneself

　♦ [1] lurk, skulk, slide, slink, slip, snake, sneak, steal ♦ [2] equivocate, fudge, hedge

pussy willow \'pù-sē-\ *n* : a willow having large silky catkins

pus·tule \'pəs-chül\ *n* : a pus-filled pimple

put \'pu̇t\ *vb* **put; put·ting 1 ♦ :** to bring into a specified position : PLACE ⟨∼ the book on the table⟩ **2 :** SEND, THRUST **3 :** to throw with an upward pushing motion ⟨∼ the shot⟩ **4 :** to bring into a specified state ⟨∼ the plan into effect⟩ **5 :** SUBJECT ⟨∼ traitors to death⟩ **6 ♦ :** to establish or apply by authority : IMPOSE **7 :** to set before one for decision ⟨∼ the question⟩ **8 ♦ :** to represent in words : EXPRESS **9 :** TRANSLATE, ADAPT **10 :** APPLY, ASSIGN ⟨∼ them to work⟩ **11 ♦ :** to give as an estimate ⟨∼ the number at 20⟩ **12 :** ATTACH, ATTRIBUTE ⟨∼ a high value on it⟩ **13 :** to take a specified course ⟨the ship ∼ out to sea⟩

♦ [1] deposit, dispose, fix, lay, place, position, set, set up, stick ♦ [6] assess, charge, exact, fine, impose, lay, levy ♦ [8] articulate, clothe, couch, express, formulate, phrase, say, state, word ♦ [11] calculate, call, conjecture, estimate, figure, gauge, guess, judge, make, place, reckon, suppose

pu·ta·tive \'pyü-tə-tiv\ *adj* **1 :** commonly accepted ⟨a ∼ expert⟩ **2 :** assumed to exist or to have existed

put by *vb* ♦ **:** to lay aside

♦ cache, hoard, lay away, lay up, salt away, stash, stockpile, store

put–down \'pu̇t-ˌdȧu̇n\ *n* ♦ **:** an act or instance of putting down; *esp* **:** a humiliating remark

♦ affront, barb, dart, dig, indignity, insult, name, offense, outrage, sarcasm, slight, slur, wound ♦ deprecation, depreciation, detraction, disparagement

put down *vb* **1 ♦ :** to bring to an end **2 ♦ :** to speak slightingly of : DISPARAGE, BELITTLE **3 a ♦ :** to put in writing **b ♦ :** to enter in a list

♦ [1] clamp down, crack down, crush, quash, quell, repress, silence, snuff, squash, squelch, subdue, suppress ♦ [2] belittle, cry down, decry, deprecate, depreciate, diminish, discount, disparage, minimize, write off ♦ [3a] jot, log, mark, note, record, register, set down ♦ [3b] catalog, enroll, enter, index, inscribe, list, record, register, schedule, slate

put in *vb* **1 :** to come in with : INTERPOSE ⟨*put in* a good word for me⟩ **2 :** to spend time at some occupation or job ⟨*put in* eight hours at the office⟩ **3 :** to put or set in the ground for growth : PLANT

put off *vb* **1 ♦ :** to hold back to a later time : POSTPONE, DELAY **2 :** to rid oneself of : TAKE OFF

♦ defer, delay, hold up, postpone, shelve

¹put–on \'pu̇t-ˌȯn, -ˌän\ *adj* **:** professed or avowed but not genuine : ASSUMED ⟨a ∼ accent⟩

²put–on *n* **1 ♦ :** a deliberate act of misleading someone **2 :** PARODY, SPOOF

♦ act, airs, facade, front, guise, masquerade, pose, pretense, semblance, show

put on *vb* **1 a ♦ :** to dress oneself in **b ♦ :** to give a false appearance of : FEIGN **2 ♦ :** to enlarge beyond bounds or the truth

♦ [1a] don, slip, throw *Ant* doff, remove, take off ♦ [1b] affect, assume, counterfeit, fake, feign, pretend, profess, sham, simulate ♦ [2] exaggerate, overdo, overstate

put out *vb* **1 ♦ :** to cause to cease burning : EXTINGUISH **2 :** to disturb or irritate esp. by repeated acts : ANNOY; *also* **:** INCONVENIENCE **3 :** to cause to be out (as in baseball) **4 ♦ :** to bring to bear esp. with sustained effort or lasting effect : EXERT

♦ [1] douse, extinguish, quench, snuff ♦ [4] apply, exercise, exert, wield

pu·tre·fac·tion \ˌpyü-trə-'fak-shən\ *n* ♦ **:** the decomposition of organic matter — **pu·tre·fac·tive** \-tiv\ *adj*

♦ breakdown, corruption, decay, decomposition, rot, spoilage

pu·tre·fy \'pyü-trə-ˌfī\ *vb* **-fied; -fy·ing** ♦ **:** to make or become putrid : ROT ⟨*putrefied* meat⟩

♦ break down, corrupt, decay, decompose, disintegrate, molder, rot, spoil

pu·tres·cent \pyü-'tres-ᵊnt\ *adj* **:** becoming putrid : ROTTING ⟨∼ carcasses⟩ — **pu·tres·cence** \-ᵊns\ *n*

pu·trid \'pyü-trəd\ *adj* **1 ♦ :** being in a state of putrefaction : ROTTEN **2 :** VILE, CORRUPT — **pu·trid·i·ty** \pyü-'tri-də-tē\ *n*

♦ bad, rotten

putsch \'pu̇ch\ *n* **:** a secretly plotted and suddenly executed attempt to overthrow a government

putt \'pət\ *n* **:** a golf stroke made on the green to cause the ball to roll into the hole — **putt** *vb*

put·ta·nes·ca \ˌpü-tä-'nes-kä\ *adj* **:** served with or being a pungent tomato sauce

¹put·ter \'pu̇-tər\ *n* **:** one that puts

²putt·er \'pə-tər\ *n* **1 :** a golf club used in putting **2 :** one that putts

³put·ter \'pə-tər\ *vb* **1 ♦ :** to move or act aimlessly or idly **2 :** TINKER

♦ *usu* **putter around** fiddle, fool, mess, monkey, play, potter, trifle

put·ty \'pə-tē\ *n, pl* **putties 1 :** a doughlike cement used esp. to fasten glass in sashes **2 :** one who is easily manipulated — **putty** *vb*

put up *vb* **1 :** SHEATHE **2 :** to prepare so as to preserve for later use **3 ♦ :** to offer for public sale ⟨*put* the house *up* for auction⟩ **4 ♦ :** to give food and shelter to : ACCOMMODATE **5 ♦ :** to form by the fitting together of materials or parts : BUILD **6 :** to engage in ⟨*put up* a struggle⟩ **7 :** CONTRIBUTE, PAY — **put up with :** TOLERATE 2

♦ [3] deal, market, merchandise, retail, sell, vend ♦ [4] accommodate, billet, chamber, domicile, harbor (*or* harbour), house, lodge, quarter, roof, shelter, take in ♦ [5] assemble, build, construct, erect, fabricate, make, make up, piece, raise, rear, set up

¹puz·zle \'pə-zəl\ *vb* **puz·zled; puz·zling 1 ♦ :** to bewilder mentally : PERPLEX **2 :** to solve with difficulty or ingenuity ⟨∼ out a riddle⟩ **3 :** to be in a quandary ⟨∼ over what to do⟩ **4 :** to attempt a solution of a puzzle ⟨∼ over a person's words⟩ — **puz·zler** *n*

♦ [1] addle, baffle, befog, befuddle, bemuse, bewilder, confound, confuse, disorient, muddle, muddy, mystify, perplex ♦ *usu* **puzzle out** [2] answer, break, crack, dope, figure out, resolve, riddle, solve, unravel, work, work out

²puzzle *n* **1 ♦ :** something that puzzles **2 :** a question, problem, or contrivance designed for testing ingenuity

♦ conundrum, enigma, mystery, mystification, puzzlement, riddle, secret

puz·zle·ment \'pə-zəl-mənt\ *n* **1 ♦ :** the state of being puzzled **2 :** something that puzzles

♦ bafflement, bewilderment, confusion, distraction, muddle, mystification, perplexity, whirl

PVC *abbr* polyvinyl chloride

pvt *abbr* private

PW *abbr* prisoner of war

pwt *abbr* pennyweight

PX *abbr* post exchange

¹pyg·my *also* **pig·my** \'pig-mē\ *n, pl* **-mies 1** *cap* **:** any of a small people of equatorial Africa **2 :** an unusually small person; *also* **:** an insignificant or unimpressive person **3 ♦ :** something very small of its kind

♦ dwarf, midget, mite, peewee, runt

²pygmy *adj* **1 :** of or relating to the Pygmies or a pygmy **2 ♦ :** very small

♦ dwarf, dwarfish, fine, little, pocket, slight, small, undersized

py·ja·mas \pə-'jä-məz\ *chiefly Can and Brit var of* PAJAMAS

py·lon \'pī-ˌlän, -lən\ *n* **1 :** a usu. massive gateway; *esp* **:** an Egyptian one flanked by flat-topped pyramids **2 :** a tower that supports wires over a long span **3 :** a post or tower marking the course in an airplane race

py·or·rhea \ˌpī-ə-'rē-ə\ *n* **:** an inflammation with pus of the sockets of the teeth

¹pyr·a·mid \'pir-ə-ˌmid\ *n* **1 :** a massive structure with a square base and four triangular faces meeting at a point **2 :** a geometrical solid having a polygon for its base and three or more triangles for its sides that meet at a point to form the top — **py·ra·mi·dal** \pə-'ra-məd-ᵊl, ˌpir-ə-'mid-\ *adj*

²pyramid *vb* **1 :** to build up in the form of a pyramid : heap up **2 :** to increase rapidly on a broadening base

pyramid scheme *n* **:** a usu. illegal operation in which participants pay to join and profit from payments made by subsequent participants

pyre \'pī(-ə)r\ *n* **:** a combustible heap for burning a dead body as a funeral rite

py·re·thrum \pī-'rē-thrəm\ *n* **:** an insecticide made from the dried heads of any of several Old World chrysanthemums

py·rim·i·dine \pī-'ri-mə-ˌdēn\ *n* **:** any of a group of bases including several (as cytosine, thymine, or uracil) that are constituents of DNA or RNA

py·rite \'pī-ˌrīt\ *n* **:** a mineral containing sulfur and iron that is brass-yellow in color

py·rol·y·sis \pī-'rä-lə-səs\ *n* : chemical change caused by the action of heat

py·ro·ma·nia \ˌpī-rō-'mā-nē-ə\ *n* : an irresistible impulse to start fires — **py·ro·ma·ni·ac** \-nē-ˌak\ *n*

py·ro·tech·nics \ˌpī-rə-'tek-niks\ *n pl* **1** : a display of fireworks **2** : a spectacular display (as of extreme virtuosity) 〈musical ∼〉 — **py·ro·tech·nic** \-nik\ *also* **py·ro·tech·ni·cal** \-ni-kəl\ *adj*

Pyr·rhic \'pir-ik\ *adj* : achieved at excessive cost 〈a ∼ victory〉; *also* : costly to the point of outweighing expected benefits

Py·thag·o·re·an theorem \pī-ˌtha-gə-'rē-ən-\ *n* : a theorem in geometry: the square of the length of the hypotenuse of a right triangle equals the sum of the squares of the lengths of the other two sides

py·thon \'pī-ˌthän, -thən\ *n* : a large snake (as a boa) that squeezes and suffocates its prey; *esp* : any of the large Old World snakes that include the largest snakes living at the present time

pyx \'piks\ *n* : a small case used to carry the Eucharist to the sick

Q

¹q \'kyü\ *n, pl* **q's** *or* **qs** \'kyüz\ *often cap* : the 17th letter of the English alphabet

²q *abbr, often cap* **1** quart **2** quarto **3** queen **4** query **5** question

QB *abbr* quarterback

QED *abbr* which was to be demonstrated

qi·vi·ut \'kē-vē-ˌüt\ *n* : the wool of the undercoat of the musk ox

Qld *abbr* Queensland

QM *abbr* quartermaster

QMC *abbr* quartermaster corps

QMG *abbr* quartermaster general

qq v *abbr* which (*pl*) see

qr *abbr* quarter

Q rating *n* : a scale measuring popularity based on dividing an assessment of familiarity or recognition by an assessment of favorable opinion; *also* : position on such a scale

qt *abbr* **1** quantity **2** quart

q.t. \ˌkyü-'tē\ *n, often cap Q&T* : QUIET — usu. used in the phrase *on the q.t.*

qto *abbr* quarto

qty *abbr* quantity

qu *or* **ques** *abbr* question

¹quack \'kwak\ *vb* : to make the characteristic cry of a duck

²quack *n* : a sound made by quacking

³quack *n* **1** ♦ : one making usu. showy pretenses to knowledge or ability : CHARLATAN **2** : a pretender to medical skill — **quack** *adj* — **quack·ery** \'kwa-kə-rē\ *n* — **quack·ish** *adj*

♦ charlatan, fake, fraud, hoaxer, humbug, mountebank, phony, pretender

¹quad \'kwäd\ *n* : QUADRANGLE

²quad *n* : QUADRUPLET

³quad *n* : quadrant

quad·ran·gle \'kwä-ˌdraŋ-gəl\ *n* **1** : QUADRILATERAL **2** ♦ : a 4-sided courtyard or enclosure — **quad·ran·gu·lar** \kwä-'draŋ-gyə-lər\ *adj*

♦ close, court, courtyard, yard

quad·rant \'kwä-drənt\ *n* **1** : one quarter of a circle : an arc of 90° **2** : any of the four quarters into which something is divided by two lines intersecting each other at right angles

qua·drat·ic \kwä-'dra-tik\ *adj* : having or being a term in which the variable (as *x*) is squared but containing no term in which the variable is raised to a higher power than a square 〈a ∼ equation〉 — **quadratic** *n*

qua·dren·ni·al \kwä-'dre-nē-əl\ *adj* **1** : consisting of or lasting for four years **2** : occurring every four years

qua·dren·ni·um \-nē-əm\ *n, pl* **-ni·ums** *or* **-nia** \-nē-ə\ : a period of four years

quad·ri·ceps \'kwä-drə-ˌseps\ *n* : a muscle of the front of the thigh that is divided into four parts

¹quad·ri·lat·er·al \ˌkwä-drə-'la-tə-rəl\ *n* : a polygon of four sides

²quadrilateral *adj* : having four sides

qua·drille \kwä-'dril, kə-\ *n* : a square dance made up of five or six figures in various rhythms

quad·ri·par·tite \ˌkwä-drə-'pär-ˌtīt\ *adj* **1** : consisting of four parts **2** : shared by four parties or persons

quad·ri·ple·gia \ˌkwä-drə-'plē-jə, -jē-ə\ *n* : paralysis of both arms and both legs — **quad·ri·ple·gic** \-jik\ *adj or n*

qua·driv·i·um \kwä-'dri-vē-əm\ *n* : the four liberal arts of arithmetic, music, geometry, and astronomy in a medieval university

quad·ru·ped \'kwä-drə-ˌped\ *n* : an animal having four feet — **qua·dru·pe·dal** \kwä-'drü-pəd-ᵊl, ˌkwä-drə-'ped-\ *adj*

¹qua·dru·ple \kwä-'drü-pəl, -'drə-; 'kwä-drə-\ *vb* **qua·dru·pled; qua·dru·pling** : to make or become four times as great or as many

²quadruple *adj* : FOURFOLD

qua·dru·plet \kwä-'drə-plət, -'drü-; 'kwä-drə-\ *n* **1** : one of four offspring born at one birth **2** : a group of four of a kind

¹qua·dru·pli·cate \kwä-'drü-pli-kət\ *adj* **1** : repeated four times **2** : FOURTH

²qua·dru·pli·cate \-plə-ˌkāt\ *vb* **-cat·ed; -cat·ing** **1** : QUADRUPLE **2** : to prepare in quadruplicate — **qua·dru·pli·ca·tion** \-ˌdrü-plə-'kā-shən\ *n*

³qua·dru·pli·cate \-'drü-pli-kət\ *n* **1** : four copies all alike 〈typed in ∼〉 **2** : one of four like things

¹quaff \'kwäf, 'kwaf\ *vb* ♦ : to drink deeply or repeatedly

♦ drink, guzzle, imbibe, sup, swig, toss

²quaff *n* ♦ : a drink quaffed

♦ draft, drag, drink, nip, shot, slug, snort, swallow, swig

quag·mire \'kwag-ˌmī(-ə)r, 'kwäg-\ *n* **1** : soft miry land that yields under the foot **2** ♦ : a difficult or trying situation : PREDICAMENT

♦ corner, fix, hole, jam, morass, pickle, predicament, spot

qua·hog \'kō-ˌhȯg, 'kwȯ-, 'kwō-, -ˌhäg\ *n* : a round thick-shelled edible No. American clam

quai \'kā\ *n* : QUAY

¹quail \'kwāl\ *n, pl* **quail** *or* **quails** : any of numerous small short‐winged plump game birds (as a bobwhite) related to the domestic chicken

²quail *vb* **1** ♦ : to lose heart : COWER **2** ♦ : to recoil in dread or terror

♦ [1, 2] blench, cower, cringe, flinch, recoil, shrink, wince

quaint \'kwānt\ *adj* **1** ♦ : unusual or different in character or appearance **2** ♦ : pleasingly old-fashioned or unfamiliar — **quaint·ly** *adv* — **quaint·ness** *n*

♦ [1] bizarre, curious, odd, outré, peculiar, quirky, remarkable, screwy, strange ♦ [2] antique, old-fashioned, old-time

¹quake \'kwāk\ *vb* **quaked; quak·ing** **1** ♦ : to shake usu. from shock or instability **2** ♦ : to tremble usu. from cold or fear

♦ [1, 2] agitate, convulse, jolt, jounce, quiver, shake, shudder, vibrate, wobble

²quake *n* : a shaking or trembling; *esp* : EARTHQUAKE

Quak·er \'kwā-kər\ *n* : FRIEND 5

qual *abbr* quality

qual·i·fi·ca·tion \ˌkwä-lə-fə-'kā-shən\ *n* **1** : LIMITATION, MODIFICATION **2** ♦ : a special skill that fits a person for some work or position **3** ♦ : a condition or standard that must be complied with

♦ [2] capability, command, credentials, expertise, mastery, proficiency ♦ [3] condition, provision, proviso, reservation, stipulation

qual·i·fied \'kwä-lə-ˌfīd\ *adj* **1** ♦ : fitted for a given purpose or job **2** : limited in some way

♦ able, capable, competent, fit, good, suitable

qual·i·fi·er \'kwä-lə-ˌfī(-ə)r\ *n* **1** : one that satisfies requirements **2** : a word or word group that limits the meaning of another word or word group

qual·i·fy \'kwä-lə-ˌfī\ *vb* **-fied; -fy·ing** **1** : to reduce from a general to a particular form : MODIFY **2** : to make less harsh **3** : to limit the meaning of (as a noun) **4 ♦ :** to fit by skill or training for some purpose **5 ♦ :** to give or have a legal right to do something **6 :** to demonstrate the necessary ability ⟨∼ for the finals⟩

  ♦ [4] equip, fit, prepare, ready, season ♦ [5] accredit, authorize, certify, commission, empower, enable, invest, license

qual·i·ta·tive \ˈkwä-lə-ˌtā-tiv\ *adj* **:** of, relating to, or involving quality — **qual·i·ta·tive·ly** *adv*

¹**qual·i·ty** \ˈkwä-lə-tē\ *n, pl* **-ties** **1 :** peculiar and essential character **:** NATURE **2 ♦ :** degree of excellence **3 ♦ :** high social status **4 ♦ :** a distinguishing attribute

  ♦ [2] caliber (*or* calibre), class, grade, rate ♦ [3] class, rank, standing ♦ [4] attribute, character, characteristic, feature, mark, peculiarity, point, property, trait

²**quality** *adj* **:** being of high quality

qualm \ˈkwäm, ˈkwälm\ *n* **1 :** a sudden attack (as of nausea) **2 ♦ :** a sudden feeling of doubt, fear, or uneasiness esp. in not following one's conscience or better judgment

  ♦ compunction, doubt, misgiving, scruple, uneasiness

qualm·ish \ˈkwä-mish, ˈkwäl-\ *adj* **1 :** feeling qualms **:** NAUSEATED **2 :** overly scrupulous **:** SQUEAMISH **3 :** of, relating to, or producing qualms

quan·da·ry \ˈkwän-drē\ *n, pl* **-ries :** a state of perplexity or doubt

quan·ti·fy \ˈkwän-tə-ˌfī\ *vb* **-fied; -fy·ing :** to determine, express, or measure the quantity of — **quan·ti·fi·able** \ˌkwän-tə-ˈfī-ə-bəl\ *adj*

quan·ti·ta·tive \ˈkwän-tə-ˌtā-tiv\ *adj* **:** of, relating to, or involving quantity — **quan·ti·ta·tive·ly** *adv*

quan·ti·ty \ˈkwän-tə-tē\ *n, pl* **-ties** **1 :** a determinate or estimated amount **:** AMOUNT, NUMBER **2 ♦ :** a considerable amount ⟨buys food in ∼⟩

  ♦ abundance, deal, gobs, heap, loads, lot, pile, plenty, scads

quan·tize \ˈkwän-ˌtīz\ *vb* **quan·tized; quan·tiz·ing :** to subdivide (as energy) into small units

¹**quan·tum** \ˈkwän-təm\ *n, pl* **quan·ta** \-tə\ **1 :** QUANTITY, AMOUNT **2 :** an elemental unit of energy

²**quantum** *adj* **1 :** LARGE, SIGNIFICANT **2 :** relating to or employing the principles of quantum mechanics

quantum mechanics *n sing or pl* **:** a theory of matter based on the concept of possession of wave properties by elementary particles — **quantum mechanical** *adj* — **quantum mechanically** *adv*

quantum theory *n* **:** a theory in physics based on the idea that radiant energy (as light) is composed of small separate packets of energy

quar *abbr* quarterly

quar·an·tine \ˈkwȯr-ən-ˌtēn\ *n* **1 :** a period during which a ship suspected of carrying contagious disease is forbidden contact with the shore **2 :** a restraint on the movements of persons or goods to prevent the spread of pests or disease **3 :** a place or period of quarantine **4 :** a state of enforced isolation — **quarantine** *vb*

quark \ˈkwȯrk, ˈkwärk\ *n* **:** a hypothetical elementary particle that carries a fractional charge and is held to be a constituent of heavier particles (as protons and neutrons)

¹**quar·rel** \ˈkwȯr-əl\ *n* **1 :** a ground of dispute **2 ♦ :** a verbal clash

  ♦ altercation, argument, bicker, brawl, disagreement, dispute, fight, hassle, misunderstanding, row, scrap, spat, squabble, wrangle

²**quarrel** *vb* **-reled** *or* **-relled; -rel·ing** *or* **-rel·ling** **1 :** to find fault **2 ♦ :** to dispute angrily **:** WRANGLE

  ♦ argue, bicker, brawl, dispute, fall out, fight, hassle, row, scrap, spat, squabble, wrangle

quar·rel·some \-səm\ *adj* **♦ :** apt or disposed to quarrel in an often petty manner

  ♦ aggressive, argumentative, bellicose, belligerent, combative, contentious, discordant, disputatious, pugnacious, scrappy, truculent

¹**quar·ry** \ˈkwȯr-ē\ *n, pl* **quarries** **1 :** game hunted with hawks **2 :** PREY

²**quarry** *n, pl* **quarries :** an open excavation usu. for obtaining building stone or limestone — **quarry** *vb*

quart \ˈkwȯrt\ *n* **1 :** a unit of liquid capacity equal to ¼ gallon **2 :** a unit of dry capacity equal to ¹/₃₂ bushel

¹**quar·ter** \ˈkwȯr-tər\ *n* **1 :** one of four equal parts **2 :** a fourth of a dollar; *also* **:** a coin of this value **3 ♦ :** a district of a city **4** *pl* **♦ :** living accommodations ⟨moved into new ∼s⟩ **5 ♦ :** mer-

ciful consideration of an opponent **:** MERCY ⟨gave no ∼⟩ **6 :** a fourth part of the moon's period **7 ♦ :** an assigned station or post

  ♦ [3] district, neighborhood (*or* neighbourhood), section
  ♦ **quarters** [4] abode, domicile, dwelling, home, house, lodging, place, residence ♦ [5] charity, clemency, leniency, mercy
  ♦ [7] position, post, station

²**quarter** *vb* **1 :** to divide into four equal parts **2 ♦ :** to provide with shelter

  ♦ accommodate, billet, chamber, domicile, harbor (*or* harbour), house, lodge, put up, roof, shelter, take in

¹**quar·ter·back** \-ˌbak\ *n* **:** a football player who calls the signals and directs the offensive play for the team

²**quarterback** *vb* **1 :** to direct the offensive play of a football team **2 :** LEAD, BOSS

quar·ter·deck \-ˌdek\ *n* **:** the stern area of a ship's upper deck

quarter horse *n* **:** any of a breed of compact muscular saddle horses characterized by great endurance and by high speed for short distances

¹**quar·ter·ly** \ˈkwȯr-tər-lē\ *adv* **:** at 3-month intervals

²**quarterly** *adj* **:** occurring, issued, or payable at 3-month intervals

³**quarterly** *n, pl* **-lies :** a periodical published four times a year

quar·ter·mas·ter \-ˌmas-tər\ *n* **1 :** a petty officer who attends to a ship's helm, binnacle, and signals **2 :** an army officer who provides clothing and subsistence for troops

quar·ter·staff \-ˌstaf\ *n, pl* **-staves** \-ˌstavz, -ˌstāvz\ **:** a long stout staff formerly used as a weapon

quar·tet *also* **quar·tette** \kwȯr-ˈtet\ *n* **1 :** a musical composition for four instruments or voices **2 :** a group of four and esp. of four musicians

quar·to \ˈkwȯr-tō\ *n, pl* **quartos** **1 :** the size of a piece of paper cut four from a sheet **2 :** a book printed on quarto pages

quartz \ˈkwȯrts\ *n* **:** a common often transparent crystalline mineral that is a form of silica

quartz·ite \ˈkwȯrt-ˌsīt\ *n* **:** a compact granular rock composed of quartz and derived from sandstone

qua·sar \ˈkwā-ˌzär, -ˌsär\ *n* **:** any of a class of extremely distant starlike celestial objects

¹**quash** \ˈkwäsh, ˈkwȯsh\ *vb* **♦ :** to suppress or extinguish summarily and completely **:** QUELL

  ♦ clamp down, crack down, crush, put down, quell, repress, silence, snuff, squash, squelch, subdue, suppress

²**quash** *vb* **♦ :** to set aside by judicial action

  ♦ abolish, abrogate, annul, cancel, dissolve, invalidate, negate, nullify, repeal, rescind, void

qua·si \ˈkwā-ˌzī, -ˌsī; ˈkwä-zē, -sē\ *adj* **:** being in some sense or degree ⟨a ∼ corporation⟩

quasi- *comb form* **:** in some sense or degree ⟨*quasi*-historical⟩

qua·si–gov·ern·men·tal \-gə-vərn-ˈmen-t³l\ *adj* **:** supported by the government but managed privately

Qua·ter·na·ry \ˈkwä-tər-ˌner-ē, kwə-ˈtər-nə-rē\ *adj* **:** of, relating to, or being the geologic period from the end of the Tertiary to the present — **Quaternary** *n*

qua·train \ˈkwä-ˌtrān\ *n* **:** a unit of four lines of verse

qua·tre·foil \ˈka-tər-ˌfȯil, ˈka-trə-\ *n* **:** a stylized figure often of a flower with four petals

qua·ver \ˈkwā-vər\ *vb* **1 :** TREMBLE, SHAKE ⟨∼ed with fear⟩ **2 :** TRILL **3 :** to speak in tremulous tones — **quaver** *n*

quay \ˈkē, ˈkwā, ˈkā\ *n* **♦ :** a structure built parallel to the bank of a waterway for use as a landing place **:** WHARF

  ♦ dock, float, jetty, landing, levee, pier, wharf

Que *abbr* Quebec

quean \ˈkwēn\ *n* **:** PROSTITUTE

quea·si·ness \ˈkwē-zē-nəs\ *n* **♦ :** the quality or state of being queasy

  ♦ nausea, sickness, squeamishness

quea·sy \ˈkwē-zē\ *adj* **quea·si·er; -est ♦ :** suffering from nausea **:** NAUSEATED — **quea·si·ly** \-zə-lē\ *adv*

  ♦ ill, nauseous, sick, squeamish

Que·chua \ˈke-chə-wə, ˈkech-wə\ *n* **:** a family of languages spoken in Peru and adjacent countries of the So. American Andes

queen \ˈkwēn\ *n* **1 :** the wife or widow of a king **2 :** a female monarch **3 ♦ :** a woman notable in rank, power, or attractiveness **4 :** the most powerful piece in the game of chess **5 :** a playing card bearing the figure of a queen **6 :** a fertile female of a social insect (as a bee)

  ♦ beauty, enchantress, fox, goddess, knockout

Queen Anne's lace \-'anz-\ *n* : a widely naturalized Eurasian herb from which the cultivated carrot originated

queen consort *n, pl* **queens consort** : the wife of a reigning king

queen·ly *adj* ♦ : of, relating to, suggestive of, or characteristic of a monarch or monarchy

♦ monarchical, regal, royal

queen mother *n* : a dowager queen who is mother of the reigning sovereign

queen–size *adj* : having dimensions of approximately 60 inches by 80 inches ⟨~ bed⟩; *also* : of a size that fits a queen-size bed

¹**queer** \'kwir\ *adj* **1** ♦ : differing from the usual or normal : PECULIAR, STRANGE **2** : COUNTERFEIT **3** : not quite well **4** *sometimes disparaging and offensive* : of, relating to, or being a person who is not straight and/or who is not cisgender: as **a** : GAY **b** : of, relating to, or characterized by sexual or romantic attraction not limited to people of a particular gender identity or sexual orientation **c** : NONBINARY **d** : TRANSGENDER — **queer·ly** *adv* — **queer·ness** *n*

♦ curious, extraordinary, funny, odd, peculiar, rare, strange, unaccustomed, uncommon, unique, unusual, weird

²**queer** *vb* : to spoil the effect of : DISRUPT ⟨~ed our plans⟩

³**queer** *n* **1** *sometimes offensive* : a person who is gay, lesbian, bisexual, pansexual, or otherwise not heterosexual **2** *sometimes offensive* : a person who is not cisgender

queer theory *n* : an approach to literary and cultural study that rejects traditional categories of gender and sexuality

quell \'kwel\ *vb* **1** ♦ : to put an end to by force ⟨~ a riot⟩ **2** ♦ : to cause to be quiet

♦ [1] clamp down, crack down, crush, put down, quash, repress, silence, snuff, squash, squelch, subdue, suppress ♦ [2] hush, mute, settle, silence, still

quench \'kwench\ *vb* **1** ♦ : to put out the light or fire of : PUT OUT, EXTINGUISH **2** : SUBDUE **3** ♦ : to bring (something immaterial) to an end typically by satisfying, damping, cooling, or decreasing : SATISFY ⟨~ed his thirst⟩ — **quench·able** *adj* — **quench·less** *adj*

♦ [1] douse, extinguish, put out, snuff ♦ [3] assuage, sate, satiate, satisfy

quench·er *n* ♦ : a satisfying drink

♦ beverage, drink, libation

quer·u·lous \'kwer-ə-ləs, -yə-\ *adj* **1** ♦ : constantly complaining **2** : FRETFUL, WHINING — **quer·u·lous·ly** *adv* — **quer·u·lous·ness** *n*

♦ crabby, cranky, fussy, grouchy, grumpy, peevish, petulant

¹**que·ry** \'kwir-ē, 'kwer-\ *n, pl* **queries** ♦ : the action or an instance of asking : QUESTION

♦ call, inquiry, question, request

²**query** *vb* **1** ♦ : to ask questions about esp. in order to resolve a doubt **2** ♦ : to ask questions of esp. with a desire for authoritative information

♦ [1] challenge, contest, dispute, question ♦ [2] ask, examine, grill, inquire of, interrogate, pump, question, quiz

que·sa·dil·la \ˌkā-sə-'dē-ə\ *n* : a tortilla filled with a savory mixture, folded, and usu. fried

¹**quest** \'kwest\ *n* : SEARCH

²**quest** *vb* **1** ♦ : to search for **2** ♦ : to ask for

♦ [1] cast about, forage, hunt, pursue, search (for *or* out), seek ♦ [2] ask, call, plead, request, seek, solicit, sue

¹**ques·tion** \'kwes-chən\ *n* **1** : an interrogative expression : QUERY **2** : a subject for debate; *also* : a proposition to be voted on **3** ♦ : an act or instance of asking : INQUIRY **4** ♦ : a subject or aspect in dispute or open for discussion **5** ♦ : a reason or argument presented in opposition : a feeling or expression of disapproval

♦ [3] call, inquiry, query, request ♦ [4] content, matter, motif, motive, subject, theme, topic ♦ [5] challenge, complaint, demur, expostulation, fuss, kick, objection, protest, remonstrance

²**question** *vb* **1** ♦ : to ask questions **2** ♦ : to engage in argument : DISPUTE **3** ♦ : to subject to analysis **4** ♦ : to lack confidence in

♦ [1] ask, examine, grill, inquire of, interrogate, pump, query, quiz ♦ [2] challenge, contest, dispute, query ♦ [3] chew over, cogitate, consider, contemplate, debate, deliberate, entertain, meditate, mull, ponder, ruminate, study, think, weigh ♦ [4] distrust, doubt, mistrust, suspect

ques·tion·able \'kwes-chə-nə-bəl\ *adj* **1** ♦ : not certain or exact : DOUBTFUL **2** ♦ : not believed to be true, sound, or moral — **ques·tion·ably** \-blē\ *adv*

♦ [1] arguable, debatable, disputable, doubtful, dubious, equivocal, fishy, problematical, shady, shaky, suspect, suspicious ♦ [2] doubtful, dubious, flimsy, improbable, unlikely

ques·tion·er *n* ♦ : one that questions

♦ disbeliever, doubter, skeptic, unbeliever

question mark *n* : a punctuation mark ? used esp. at the end of a sentence to indicate a direct question

ques·tion·naire \ˌkwes-chə-'nar\ *n* : a set of questions for obtaining information

quet·zal \ket-'säl, -'sal\ *n, pl* **quetzals** *or* **quet·za·les** \-'sä-lās, -'sa-\ : a Central American bird with brilliant plumage

¹**queue** \'kyü\ *n* **1** : a braid of hair usu. worn hanging at the back of the head **2** ♦ : a waiting line (as of persons)

♦ column, cue, file, line, range, string, train

²**queue** *vb* **queued; queu·ing** *or* **queue·ing** : to line up in a queue

¹**quib·ble** \'kwi-bəl\ *n* **1** : an evasion of or shifting from the point at issue **2** : a minor objection or criticism — **quib·bler** *n*

²**quibble** *vb* ♦ : to criticize or object to something on trivial grounds

♦ carp, cavil, fuss

¹**quick** \'kwik\ *adj* **1** : LIVING **2** ♦ : acting or capable of acting with speed ⟨~ steps⟩ **3** ♦ : prompt to understand, think, or perceive : ALERT **4** : easily aroused ⟨a ~ temper⟩ **5** : turning or bending sharply ⟨a ~ turn in the road⟩

♦ [2] alert, expeditious, prompt, ready, willing ♦ [2] brisk, fast, fleet, hasty, rapid, snappy, speedy, swift ♦ [3] alert, brainy, bright, brilliant, clever, intelligent, keen, nimble, quick-witted, sharp, smart

²**quick** *adv* ♦ : in a quick manner

♦ apace, briskly, fast, full tilt, hastily, posthaste, presto, pronto, quickly, rapidly, soon, speedily, swift, swiftly

³**quick** *n* **1** : a sensitive area of living flesh **2** : a vital part : HEART **3** ♦ : the inmost sensibilities

♦ core, heart, soul

quick bread *n* : a bread made with a leavening agent that permits immediate baking of the dough or batter

quick·en \'kwi-kən\ *vb* **1** : to come to life : REVIVE **2** ♦ : to cause to be enlivened : STIMULATE **3** ♦ : to increase in speed : HASTEN **4** : to show vitality (as by growing or moving)

♦ [2] animate, brace, energize, enliven, fire, invigorate, jazz up, liven up, pep up, stimulate, vitalize, vivify, zip (up) ♦ [3] accelerate, hasten, hurry, rush, speed (up), step up, whisk

quick–freeze \'kwik-'frēz\ *vb* **-froze** \-'frōz\; **-fro·zen** \-'frōz-ᵊn\; **-freez·ing** : to freeze (food) for preservation so rapidly that the natural juices and flavor are not lost

quick·ie \'kwi-kē\ *n* : something hurriedly done or made

quick·lime \'kwik-ˌlīm\ *n* : ¹LIME

quick·ly *adv* ♦ : in a quick manner

♦ apace, briskly, fast, full tilt, hastily, posthaste, presto, pronto, quick, rapidly, soon, speedily, swift, swiftly

quick·ness *n* ♦ : the quality or state of being quick

♦ celerity, fastness, fleetness, haste, hurry, rapidity, speed, swiftness, velocity

quick·sand \-ˌsand\ *n* : a deep mass of loose sand mixed with water

quick·sil·ver \-ˌsil-vər\ *n* : MERCURY 1

quick·step \-ˌstep\ *n* : a spirited march tune or dance

quick–wit·ted \'kwik-'wi-təd\ *adj* ♦ : mentally alert

♦ alert, brainy, bright, brilliant, clever, intelligent, keen, nimble, quick, sharp, smart

quid \'kwid\ *n* : a lump of something chewable ⟨a ~ of tobacco⟩

quid pro quo \ˌkwid-ˌprō-'kwō\ *n* : something given or received for something else

qui·es·cence \kwī-'es-ᵊns\ *n* ♦ : the quality or state of being quiescent

♦ abeyance, doldrums, dormancy, latency, suspension ♦ dormancy, idleness, inaction, inactivity, inertness

qui·es·cent \kwī-'es-ᵊnt\ *adj* ♦ : being at rest : QUIET

♦ dull, inactive, inert, lethargic, quiet, sleepy, sluggish, torpid

¹**qui·et** \'kwī-ət\ *n* ♦ : the quality or state of being quiet : REPOSE

♦ calm, calmness, hush, peace, placidity, quietness, repose, serenity, silence, still, stillness, tranquility

²**quiet** *adj* **1** ♦ : marked by little motion or activity : CALM **2** : GENTLE, MILD ⟨a ∼ disposition⟩ **3** : enjoyed in peace and relaxation ⟨a ∼ cup of tea⟩ **4** ♦ : free from noise or uproar **5** ♦ : not showy : MODEST ⟨∼ clothes⟩ **6** ♦ : screened or hidden from view : SECLUDED ⟨a ∼ nook⟩

♦ [1, 4] calm, hushed, noiseless, peaceful, restful, serene, silent, soundless, still, tranquil *Ant* boisterous, clamorous, deafening, loud, noisy, raucous, roistering, romping, rowdy, tumultuous, uproarious, woolly ♦ [5] conservative, muted, restrained, subdued, unpretentious *Ant* flamboyant, flashy, garish, gaudy, glitzy, loud, ostentatious, swank, tawdry ♦ [6] cloistered, covert, isolated, remote, secluded, secret

³**quiet** *adv* : QUIETLY
⁴**quiet** *vb* **1** ♦ : to cause to be quiet : CALM **2** ♦ : to become quiet — often used with *down* ⟨∼ down⟩

♦ [1] allay, calm, compose, settle, soothe, still, tranquilize ♦ *often* **quite down** [2] calm (down), cool (off *or* down), hush, settle (down) *Ant* act up, carry on, cut up

qui·et·ly *adv* ♦ : in a quiet manner
♦ calmly, quiet, still

qui·et·ness *n* ♦ : the quality or state of being quiet
♦ calm, calmness, hush, peace, placidity, quiet, repose, serenity, silence, still, stillness, tranquility

qui·etude \ˈkwī-ə-ˌtüd, -ˌtyüd\ *n* : a quiet state : QUIETNESS, REPOSE
qui·etus \kwī-ˈē-təs\ *n* **1** ♦ : final settlement (as of a debt) **2** ♦ : removal from activity : DEATH

♦ [1] delivery, discharge, quittance, release ♦ [2] death, decease, demise, doom, end, passing

quill \ˈkwil\ *n* **1** : a large stiff feather; *also* : the hollow tubular part of a feather **2** : one of the hollow sharp spines of a hedgehog or porcupine **3** : a pen made from a feather
¹**quilt** \ˈkwilt\ *n* : a padded bed coverlet
²**quilt** *vb* **1** : to fill, pad, or line like a quilt **2** : to stitch or sew in layers with padding in between **3** : to make quilts
quince \ˈkwins\ *n* : a hard yellow applelike fruit; *also* : a tree related to the roses that bears this fruit
qui·nine \ˈkwī-ˌnīn\ *n* : a bitter white drug obtained from cinchona bark and used esp. in treating malaria
qui·noa \ˈkēn-ˌwä, kē-ˈnō-ə\ *n* : the starchy seeds of an annual herb related to spinach which are used as food and ground into flour; *also* : this herb
quint \ˈkwint\ *n* : QUINTUPLET
quin·tal \ˈkwint-ᵊl, ˈkant-\ *n* : HUNDREDWEIGHT
quin·tes·sence \kwin-ˈtes-ᵊns\ *n* **1** ♦ : the purest essence of something **2** ♦ : the most typical example ⟨the ∼ of self-control⟩ — **quin·tes·sen·tial·ly** *adv*

♦ [1] essence, nature, soul, stuff, substance ♦ [2] beau ideal, classic, epitome, exemplar, ideal, perfection

quint·es·sen·tial \ˌkwin-tə-ˈsen-chəl\ *adj* ♦ : being a quintessence
♦ classic, model, paradigmatic

quin·tet *also* **quin·tette** \kwin-ˈtet\ *n* **1** : a musical composition for five instruments or voices **2** : a group of five and esp. of five musicians
¹**quin·tu·ple** \kwin-ˈtü-pəl, -ˈtyü-, -ˈtə-\ *adj* **1** : having five units or members **2** : being five times as great or as many — **quintuple** *n*
²**quintuple** *vb* **quin·tu·pled; quin·tu·pling** : to make or become five times as great or as many
quin·tu·plet \kwin-ˈtə-plət, -ˈtü-, -ˈtyü-\ *n* **1** : a group of five of a kind **2** : one of five offspring born at one birth
¹**quin·tu·pli·cate** \kwin-ˈtü-pli-kət, -ˈtyü-\ *adj* **1** : repeated five times **2** : FIFTH
²**quintuplicate** *n* **1** : one of five like things **2** : five copies all alike ⟨typed in ∼⟩
³**quin·tu·pli·cate** \-plə-ˌkāt\ *vb* **-cat·ed; -cat·ing** **1** : QUINTUPLE **2** : to provide in quintuplicate
¹**quip** \ˈkwip\ *n* ♦ : a clever remark

♦ crack, gag, jest, joke, laugh, pleasantry, sally, waggery, wisecrack, witticism

²**quip** *vb* **quipped; quip·ping** **1** ♦ : to make quips : GIBE **2** ♦ : to jest or gibe at

♦ [1, 2] banter, fool, fun, gibe, jest, jive, joke, josh, kid, wisecrack

quire \ˈkwī(-ə)r\ *n* : a set of 24 or sometimes 25 sheets of paper of the same size and quality
quirk \ˈkwərk\ *n* ♦ : a peculiarity of action or behavior

♦ crotchet, eccentricity, idiosyncrasy, mannerism, oddity, peculiarity, singularity, trick

quirky *adj* ♦ : full of quirks

♦ bizarre, curious, far-out, funny, kinky, odd, outlandish, outré, peculiar, quaint, remarkable, screwy, strange, wacky, weird, wild

quirt \ˈkwərt\ *n* : a riding whip with a short handle and a rawhide lash
quis·ling \ˈkwiz-liŋ\ *n* : one who helps the invaders of one's own country : one who commits treason

♦ apostate, betrayer, double-crosser, recreant, traitor, turncoat

quit \ˈkwit\ *vb* **quit** *also* **quit·ted; quit·ting** **1** : to conduct (oneself) usu. satisfactorily esp. under stress ⟨CONDUCT, BEHAVE ∼ themselves well⟩ **2 a** : to depart from : LEAVE **b** ♦ : to bring to an end **3** ♦ : to give up for good ⟨∼ smoking⟩ ⟨∼ my job⟩ **4** : to leave the company of **5** ♦ : to admit defeat **6** : to make full payment of — **quit·ter** *n*

♦ [2b] break, break off, cease, cut, desist, discontinue, drop, end, halt, knock off, layoff, leave off, shut off, stop ♦ [3] leave, resign, retire, step down *Ant* stay (at) ♦ [3] discontinue, drop, give up, knock off, lay off *Ant* carry on, continue, keep, keep up, maintain ♦ [5] blink, bow, budge, capitulate, concede, give in, knuckle under, submit, succumb, surrender, yield

quite \ˈkwīt\ *adv* **1** ♦ : to a complete degree : COMPLETELY **2** : to an extreme : POSITIVELY **3** ♦ : to a considerable extent : RATHER ⟨∼ rich⟩

♦ [1] altogether, completely, dead, entirely, fast, flat, full, fully, perfectly, thoroughly, well, wholly ♦ [3] enough, fairly, kind of, moderately, pretty, rather, somewhat, sort of, so-so

quits \ˈkwits\ *adj* : even or equal with another ⟨call it ∼⟩
quit·tance \ˈkwit-ᵊns\ *n* **1** ♦ : something given in return, compensation, or retaliation : REQUITAL **2** ♦ : discharge from a debt or an obligation

♦ [1] compensation, damages, indemnity, recompense, redress, remuneration, reparation, requital, restitution, satisfaction ♦ [2] delivery, discharge, quietus, release

¹**quiv·er** \ˈkwi-vər\ *n* : a case for carrying arrows
²**quiver** *vb* **quiv·ered; quiv·er·ing** ♦ : to shake with a slight trembling motion ⟨∼ed with rage⟩ — **quiv·er·ing·ly** *adv*

♦ agitate, convulse, jolt, jounce, quake, shake, shudder, vibrate, wobble

³**quiver** *n* : the act or action of quivering : TREMOR
quiv·er·ing \ˈkwi-v(ə-)riŋ\ *n* ♦ : the action or condition of one that trembles

♦ oscillation, vibration

qui vive \kē-ˈvēv\ *n* : ALERT ⟨on the qui vive for prowlers⟩
quix·ot·ic \kwik-ˈsä-tik\ *adj* : foolishly impractical esp. in the pursuit of ideals — **quix·ot·i·cal·ly** \-ti-kə-lē\ *adv*
¹**quiz** \ˈkwiz\ *n, pl* **quiz·zes** **1** : an eccentric person **2** : PRACTICAL JOKE **3** ♦ : a short oral or written test **4** ♦ : a person who ridicules or mocks

♦ [3] examination, test ♦ [4] heckler, mocker, scoffer, taunter, tease

²**quiz** *vb* **quizzed; quiz·zing** **1** : MOCK **2** : to look at inquisitively **3** ♦ : to question closely

♦ ask, examine, grill, inquire of, interrogate, pump, query, question

quiz·zi·cal \ˈkwi-zi-kəl\ *adj* **1** : comically quaint **2** : mildly teasing or mocking **3** : expressive of puzzlement, curiosity, or disbelief ⟨gave me a ∼ look⟩
quoit \ˈkwāt, ˈkwȯit, ˈkȯit\ *n* **1** : a flattened ring of iron or circle of rope used in a throwing game **2** *pl* : a game in which quoits are thrown at an upright pin in an attempt to ring the pin
quon·dam \ˈkwän-dəm, -ˌdam\ *adj* : FORMER
quo·rum \ˈkwȯr-əm\ *n* : the number of members required to be present for business to be legally transacted
quot *abbr* quotation
quo·ta \ˈkwō-tə\ *n* ♦ : a proportional part esp. when assigned : SHARE

♦ allotment, allowance, cut, part, portion, proportion, share

quot·able \ˈkwō-tə-bəl\ *adj* : fit for or worth quoting — **quot·abil·i·ty** \-ˌbi-lə-tē\ *n*
quo·ta·tion \kwō-ˈtā-shən\ *n* **1** : the act or process of quoting **2**

: the price currently bid or offered for something **3** : something that is quoted

quotation mark *n* : one of a pair of punctuation marks " " or ' ' used esp. to indicate the beginning and end of a quotation in which exact phraseology is directly cited

quote \'kwōt\ *vb* **quot·ed; quot·ing** **1 a** ♦ : to speak or write a passage from another usu. with acknowledgment **b** ♦ : to repeat a passage in substantiation or illustration **2** : to state the market price of a commodity, stock, or bond **3** : to inform a hearer or reader that matter following is quoted — **quote** *n*

♦ [1a] advert (to), cite, instance, mention, name, note, notice,

refer (to), specify, touch (*on* or *upon*) ♦ [1b] adduce, cite, instance, mention

quoth \'kwōth\ *vb past, archaic* : SAID — usu. used in the 1st and 3d persons with the subject following

quo·tid·i·an \kwō-'ti-dē-ən\ *adj* **1** : DAILY **2** : COMMONPLACE, ORDINARY

quo·tient \'kwō-shənt\ *n* : the number obtained by dividing one number by another

Quran *also* **Qu'ran** *var of* KORAN

qv *abbr* which see

qy *abbr* query

¹**r** \'är\ *n, pl* **r's** *or* **rs** \'ärz\ *often cap* : the 18th letter of the English alphabet

²**r** *abbr, often cap* **1** rabbi **2** radius **3** rare **4** Republican **5** rerun **6** resistance **7** right **8** river **9** roentgen **10** rook **11** run

Ra *symbol* radium

RA *abbr* **1** regular army **2** research assistant **3** Royal Academy

¹**rab·bet** \'ra-bət\ *n* : a groove in the edge or face of a surface (as a board) esp. to receive another piece

²**rabbet** *vb* : to cut a rabbet in; *also* : to join by means of a rabbet

rab·bi \'ra-ˌbī\ *n* **1** : MASTER, TEACHER — used by Jews as a term of address **2** : a Jew trained and ordained for professional religious leadership — **rab·bin·ic** \rə-'bi-nik\ *or* **rab·bin·i·cal** \-ni-kəl\ *adj*

rab·bin·ate \'ra-bə-nət, -ˌnāt\ *n* **1** : the office of a rabbi **2** : the whole body of rabbis

rab·bit \'ra-bət\ *n, pl* **rabbit** *or* **rabbits** : any of various longeared short-tailed burrowing mammals distinguished from the related hares by being blind, furless, and helpless at birth; *also* : the pelt of a rabbit

rabbit ears *n pl* : an indoor V-shaped television antenna

rabble \'ra-bəl\ *n* **1** : MOB 2 **2** ♦ : the lowest class of people

♦ riffraff, scum, trash *Ant* aristocracy, elite, gentry, society, upper class, upper crust

rab·ble-rous·er \'ra-bəl-ˌrau̇-zər\ *n* ♦ : one that stirs up (as to hatred or violence) the masses of the people

♦ agitator, demagogue, firebrand, incendiary, inciter

ra·bid \'ra-bəd\ *adj* **1** ♦ : extremely violent : FURIOUS **2** ♦ : being fanatical or extreme ⟨~ supporters⟩ **3** : affected with rabies — **ra·bid·ly** *adv*

♦ [1] angry, boiling, enraged, fierce, frenzied, furious, irate, mad, sore, violent ♦ [2] extreme, extremist, fanatic, radical, revolutionary, ultra

ra·bies \'rā-bēz\ *n, pl* **rabies** : an acute deadly virus disease of the nervous system transmitted by the bite of an affected animal

rac·coon \ra-'kün\ *n, pl* **raccoon** *or* **raccoons** : a gray No. American chiefly tree-dwelling mammal with a black mask, a bushy ringed tail, and nocturnal habits; *also* : its pelt

¹**race** \'rās\ *n* **1** : a strong current of running water; *also* : its channel **2** : an onward course (as of time or life) **3** : a contest of speed **4** : a contest for a desired end (as election to office)

²**race** *vb* **raced; rac·ing** **1** : to run in a race **2** ♦ : to run swiftly : RUSH **3** ♦ : to engage in a race with **4** : to drive or ride at high speed — **rac·er** *n*

♦ [2] barrel, career, course, dash, fly, hasten, hurry, hurtle, hustle, pelt, rip, rocket, run, rush, shoot, speed, tear, whirl, whisk, zip, zoom ♦ [3] battle, compete, contend, fight, vie

³**race** *n* **1** *dated* : a group of people sharing a common cultural, geographic, linguistic, or religious origin or background **2** : a group of individuals within a biological species able to breed together **3** : any one of the groups that humans are often divided into based on physical traits regarded as common among people of shared ancestry; *also* : categorization into such groups **4** : a group of living things considered as a category ⟨the human ~⟩ — **ra·cial** \'rā-shəl\ *adj* — **ra·cial·ly** *adv*

race·course \'rās-ˌkȯrs\ *n* : a course for racing

race·horse \-ˌhȯrs\ *n* : a horse bred or kept for racing

ra·ceme \rā-'sēm\ *n* : a flower cluster with flowers borne along a

stem and blooming from the base toward the tip — **rac·e·mose** \'ra-sə-ˌmōs\ *adj*

race·track \'rās-ˌtrak\ *n* : a usu. oval course on which races are run

race·way \-ˌwā\ *n* **1** ♦ : a channel for a current of water **2** : RACECOURSE

♦ aqueduct, canal, channel, conduit, flume, watercourse

ra·cial \'rā-shəl\ *adj* **1** : of, relating to, or based on a race ⟨a ~ minority⟩ **2** : existing or occurring between races ⟨~ equality⟩ — **ra·cial·ly** \-shə-lē\ *adv*

ra·cial·ism \'rā-shə-ˌli-zəm\ *n* : a theory that race determines human traits and capacities; *also* : RACISM 1 — **ra·cial·ist** \-list\ *n* — **ra·cial·is·tic** \ˌrā-shə-'lis-tik\ *adj*

ra·cial·ize \'rā-shə-ˌlīz\ *vb* **-ized; -iz·ing** : to give a racial character to

racing form *n* : a paper giving data about racehorses for use by bettors

rac·ism \'rā-ˌsi-zəm\ *n* **1** : a belief that race is a fundamental determinant of human traits and capacities and that racial differences produce an inherent superiority of a particular race; *also* : racial discrimination or prejudice **2 a** : the systemic oppression of a racial group to the advantage of another; *specif* : WHITE SUPREMACY **b** : a political or social system founded on racism and designed to execute its principles — **rac·ist** \-sist\ *n*

¹**rack** \'rak\ *n* **1** : an instrument of torture on which a body is stretched **2** : a framework on or in which something may be placed (as for display or storage) **3** : a bar with teeth on one side to mesh with a pinion or worm gear

²**rack** *vb* **1** : to torture on or as if on a rack **2** ♦ : to stretch or strain by force **3** ♦ : to cause to suffer torture, pain, anguish, or ruin : TORMENT **4** : to place on or in a rack

♦ [2] pull, strain, stretch, wrench ♦ [3] afflict, agonize, bedevil, curse, harrow, martyr, persecute, plague, torment, torture

¹**rack·et** *or* **rac·quet** \'ra-kət\ *n* : a light bat made of netting stretched in an oval open frame having a handle and used for striking a ball or shuttlecock

²**racket** *n* **1** ♦ : confused noise : DIN **2** ♦ : a fraudulent or dishonest scheme or activity ⟨a criminal ~⟩

♦ [1] bluster, cacophony, clamor (*or* clamour), din, noise, roar ♦ [2] hustle, swindle

³**racket** *vb* : to make a racket

rack·e·teer \ˌra-kə-'tir\ *n* ♦ : a person who obtains money by an illegal enterprise usu. involving intimidation — **rack·e·teer·ing** *n*

♦ extortionist

rack up *vb* : ACCUMULATE, GAIN

ra·con·teur \ˌra-ˌkän-'tər\ *n* : one good at telling anecdotes

rac·quet·ball \'ra-kət-ˌbȯl\ *n* : a game similar to handball that is played on a 4-walled court with a short-handled racket

racy \'rā-sē\ *adj* **rac·i·er; -est** **1** ♦ : full of zest **2** : PUNGENT, SPICY **3** ♦ : verging on impropriety or indecency : RISQUÉ, SUGGESTIVE — **rac·i·ly** \'rā-sə-lē\ *adv* — **rac·i·ness** \-sē-nəs\ *n*

♦ [1] active, animate, animated, brisk, energetic, frisky, jaunty, jazzy, lively, peppy, perky, pert, snappy, spirited, sprightly, springy, vital, vivacious ♦ [3] bawdy, lewd, ribald, risqué, spicy, suggestive

rad *abbr* **1** radical **2** radio **3** radius

ra·dar \'rā-ˌdär\ *n* : a device that emits radio waves for detecting and locating an object by the reflection of the radio waves and that may use this reflection to determine the object's direction and speed

radar gun *n* : a handheld device that uses radar to measure the speed of a moving object

ra·dar·scope \'rā-ˌdär-ˌskōp\ *n* : a visual display for a radar receiver

¹**ra·di·al** \'rā-dē-əl\ *adj* : arranged or having parts arranged like rays around a common center ⟨the ∼ form of a starfish⟩ — **ra·di·al·ly** *adv*

²**radial** *n* : a pneumatic tire with cords laid perpendicular to the center line

radial engine *n* : an internal combustion engine with cylinders arranged radially like the spokes of a wheel

ra·di·an \'rā-dē-ən\ *n* : a unit of measure for angles that is equal to approximately 57.3 degrees

ra·di·ance \-əns\ *n* ♦ : the quality or state of being radiant

♦ brilliance, dazzle, effulgence, illumination, lightness, lucidity, luminosity, refulgence, splendor ♦ blaze, flare, fluorescence, glare, gleam, glow, illumination, incandescence, light, luminescence, shine

ra·di·ant \'rā-dē-ənt\ *adj* **1** ♦ : vividly bright and shining : GLOWING **2** ♦ : beaming with happiness ⟨a ∼ smile⟩ **3** : transmitted by radiation — **ra·di·ant·ly** *adv*

♦ [1] beaming, bright, brilliant, effulgent, glowing, incandescent, lambent, lucent, lucid, luminous, lustrous, refulgent, shiny ♦ [2] aglow, beaming, glowing, sunny

radiant energy *n* : energy traveling as electromagnetic waves
ra·di·ate \'rā-dē-ˌāt\ *vb* **-at·ed; -at·ing** **1** : to send out rays : SHINE, GLOW **2** : to issue in or as if in rays ⟨light ∼s⟩ **3** ♦ : to spread around as from a center

♦ branch, diverge, fan *Ant* concentrate, converge, focus, funnel, meet

ra·di·a·tion \ˌrā-dē-'ā-shən\ *n* **1** : the action or process of radiating **2** : the process of emitting radiant energy in the form of waves or particles; *also* : something (as an X-ray beam) that is radiated

radiation sickness *n* : sickness that results from exposure to radiation and is commonly marked by fatigue, nausea, vomiting, loss of teeth and hair, and in more severe cases by damage to blood-forming tissue

radiation therapy *n* : RADIOTHERAPY

ra·di·a·tor \'rā-dē-ˌā-tər\ *n* : any of various devices (as a set of pipes or tubes) for transferring heat from a fluid within to an area or object outside

¹**rad·i·cal** \'ra-di-kəl\ *adj* **1** : FUNDAMENTAL, EXTREME, THOROUGHGOING **2** : of or relating to radicals in politics **3** ♦ : marked by a considerable departure from the usual or traditional — **rad·i·cal·ism** \-kə-ˌli-zəm\ *n* — **rad·i·cal·ly** *adv*

♦ extreme, extremist, fanatic, rabid, revolutionary, ultra ♦ broad-minded, liberal, nonorthodox, nontraditional, open-minded, progressive, unconventional, unorthodox

²**radical** *n* **1** ♦ : a person who favors rapid and sweeping changes in laws and methods of government **2** : FREE RADICAL; *also* : a group of atoms considered as a unit in certain reactions or as a subunit of a larger molecule **3** : a mathematical expression indicating a root by means of a radical sign; *also* : RADICAL SIGN

♦ extremist, revolutionary *Ant* moderate

rad·i·cal·ise *chiefly Brit var of* RADICALIZE
rad·i·cal·ize \-kə-ˌlīz\ *vb* **-ized; -iz·ing** : to make radical esp. in politics — **rad·i·cal·i·za·tion** \ˌra-di-kə-lə-'zā-shən\ *n*

radical sign *n* : the sign √ placed before a mathematical expression to indicate that its root is to be taken

ra·dic·chio \ra-'di-kē-ō\ *n, pl* **–chios** : a chicory with reddish variegated leaves

radii *pl of* RADIUS

¹**ra·dio** \'rā-dē-ˌō\ *n, pl* **ra·di·os** **1** : the wireless transmission or reception of signals using electromagnetic waves **2** : a radio receiving set **3** : the radio broadcasting industry — **radio** *adj*

²**radio** *vb* : to communicate or send a message to by radio

ra·dio·ac·tiv·i·ty \ˌrā-dē-ō-ˌak-'ti-və-tē\ *n* : the property that some elements or isotopes have of spontaneously emitting energetic particles by the disintegration of their atomic nuclei — **ra·dio·ac·tive** \-'ak-tiv\ *adj*

radio astronomy *n* : astronomy dealing with radio waves received from outside the earth's atmosphere

ra·dio·car·bon \ˌrā-dē-ō-'kär-bən\ *n* : CARBON 14

radio frequency *n* : an electromagnetic wave frequency intermediate between audio frequencies and infrared frequencies used esp. for communication and radar signals

ra·dio·gram \'rā-dē-ō-ˌgram\ *n* : a message transmitted by radio
ra·dio·graph \-ˌgraf\ *n* : a photograph made by some form of radiation other than light; *esp* : an X-ray photograph — **radiograph** *vb* — **ra·dio·graph·ic** \ˌrā-dē-ō-'gra-fik\ *adj* — **ra·dio·graph·i·cal·ly** \-fi-k(ə-)lē\ *adv* — **ra·di·og·ra·phy** \ˌrā-dē-'ä-grə-fē\ *n*

ra·dio·iso·tope \ˌrā-dē-ō-'ī-sə-ˌtōp\ *n* : a radioactive isotope
ra·di·ol·o·gy \ˌrā-dē-'ä-lə-jē\ *n* : the use of radiant energy (as X-rays and radium radiations) in medicine — **ra·di·ol·o·gist** \-jist\ *n*

ra·dio·man \'rā-dē-ō-ˌman\ *n* : a radio operator or technician
ra·di·om·e·ter \ˌrā-dē-'ä-mə-tər\ *n* : an instrument for measuring the intensity of radiant energy — **ra·dio·met·ric** \ˌrā-dē-ō-'me-trik\ *adj* — **ra·di·om·e·try** \-'ä-mə-trē\ *n*

ra·dio·phone \'rā-dē-ō-ˌfōn\ *n* : RADIOTELEPHONE
ra·dio·sonde \'rā-dē-ō-ˌsänd\ *n* : a small radio transmitter carried aloft (as by balloon) and used to transmit meteorological data

ra·dio·tele·phone \ˌrā-dē-ō-'te-lə-ˌfōn\ *n* : a telephone that uses radio waves wholly or partly instead of connecting wires — **ra·dio·te·le·pho·ny** \-tə-'le-fə-nē, -'te-lə-ˌfō-nē\ *n*

radio telescope *n* : a radio receiver-antenna combination used for observation in radio astronomy

ra·dio·ther·a·py \ˌrā-dē-ō-'ther-ə-pē\ *n* : the treatment of disease by means of radiation (as X-rays) — **ra·dio·ther·a·pist** \-pist\ *n*

rad·ish \'ra-dish\ *n* : a pungent fleshy root usu. eaten raw; *also* : a plant related to the mustards that produces this root

ra·di·um \'rā-dē-əm\ *n* : a very radioactive metallic chemical element that is used in the treatment of cancer

ra·di·us \'rā-dē-əs\ *n, pl* **ra·dii** \-ē-ˌī\ *also* **ra·di·us·es** **1** : a straight line extending from the center of a circle or a sphere to the circumference or surface; *also* : the length of a radius **2** : the bone on the thumb side of the human forearm **3** : a circular area defined by the length of its radius

RADM *abbr* rear admiral
ra·don \'rā-ˌdän\ *n* : a heavy radioactive gaseous chemical element

RAF *abbr* Royal Air Force
raf·fia \'ra-fē-ə\ *n* : fiber used esp. for making baskets and hats that is obtained from the stalks of the leaves of a tropical African palm (**raffia palm**)

raff·ish \'ra-fish\ *adj* : jaunty or sporty esp. in a flashy or vulgar manner — **raff·ish·ly** *adv*

raff·ish·ness *n* : marked by or suggestive of flashy vulgarity or crudeness

¹**raf·fle** \'ra-fəl\ *vb* **raf·fled; raf·fling** : to dispose of by a raffle
²**raffle** *n* : a lottery in which the prize is won by one of a number of persons buying chances

¹**raft** \'raft\ *n* **1** : a number of logs or timbers fastened together to form a float **2** : a flat structure for support or transportation on water

²**raft** *vb* **1** : to travel or transport by raft **2** : to make into a raft
³**raft** *n* : a large amount or number : LOT
raf·ter \'raf-tər\ *n* : any of the parallel beams that support a roof
¹**rag** \'rag\ *n* **1 a** : a waste piece of cloth **b** *pl* : clothes usu. in poor or ragged condition **2** : a sleazy newspaper
²**rag** *n* : a composition in ragtime
ra·ga \'rä-gə\ *n* **1** : a traditional melodic pattern or mode in Indian music **2** : an improvisation based on a raga
rag·a·muf·fin \'ra-gə-ˌmə-fən\ *n* : a ragged dirty person
rag·bag \'rag-ˌbag\ *n* ♦ : a miscellaneous collection

♦ assortment, clutter, jumble, medley, mélange, miscellany, motley, muddle, variety, welter

¹**rage** \'rāj\ *n* **1** ♦ : violent and uncontrolled anger **2** ♦ : a fad pursued with intense enthusiasm : VOGUE, FASHION **3** : an intense feeling

♦ [1] anger, furor, fury, indignation, ire, outrage, spleen, wrath, wrathfulness ♦ [2] craze, enthusiasm, fad, fashion, go, mode, sensation, style, trend, vogue

²**rage** *vb* **raged; rag·ing** **1** ♦ : to be furiously angry **2** : to continue out of control ⟨the fire *raged*⟩ **3** ♦ : to go on a rampage

♦ [1] boil, burn, fume, seethe, steam ♦ [3] fume, storm

rag·ged \'ra-gəd\ *adj* **1** ♦ : torn or worn to tatters; *also* : wearing tattered clothes **2** : done in an uneven way ⟨a ∼ performance⟩ **3** ♦ : having an irregular edge or outline — **rag·ged·ly** *adv* — **rag·ged·ness** *n*

♦ [1] ratty, seedy, shabby, tattered, threadbare, worn-out ♦ [3] broken, craggy, jagged, scraggly *Ant* clean, even, smooth, unbroken

rag·lan \'ra-glən\ *n* : an overcoat with sleeves (**raglan sleeves**) sewn in with seams slanting from neck to underarm

ra·gout \ra-'gü\ *n* : a highly seasoned meat stew with vegetables

rag·pick·er \'rag-ˌpi-kər\ *n* : one who collects rags and refuse for a living

rag·time \-ˌtīm\ *n* : music in which there is more or less continuous syncopation in the melody

rag·top \'rag-ˌtäp\ *n* : CONVERTIBLE

rag·weed \-ˌwēd\ *n* : any of several chiefly No. American weedy composite herbs with allergenic pollen

¹raid \'rād\ *n* ♦ : a sudden usu. surprise attack or invasion

♦ descent, foray, incursion, invasion, irruption ♦ aggression, assault, attack, charge, descent, offense (*or* offence), offensive, onset, onslaught, rush, strike

²raid *vb* ♦ : to make a raid on — **raid·er** *n*

♦ foray, invade, overrun ♦ assail, assault, attack, beset, charge, descend, jump, pounce (on *or* upon), rush, storm, strike

¹rail \'rāl\ *n* **1** : a bar extending from one support to another as a guard or barrier **2** : a bar of steel forming a track for wheeled vehicles **3** : RAILROAD

²rail *vb* : to provide with a railing

³rail *n, pl* **rail** *or* **rails** : any of numerous small wading birds often hunted as game birds

⁴rail *vb* ♦ : to revile or scold in harsh, insolent, or abusive language : SCOLD

♦ *usu* **rail at** *or* **rail against** admonish, chide, lecture, rate, rebuke, reprimand, scold

rail·er *n* ♦ : one that rails

♦ carper, castigator, caviler, censurer, critic, faultfinder, nitpicker, scold

rail·ing \'rā-liŋ\ *n* ♦ : a barrier of rails

♦ rail

rail·lery \'rā-lə-rē\ *n, pl* **-ler·ies** ♦ : good-natured ridicule : BANTER

♦ banter, chaff, persiflage, repartee

¹rail·road \'rāl-ˌrōd\ *n* ♦ : a permanent road with rails fixed to ties providing a track for cars; *also* : such a road and its assets constituting a property

♦ rail, road

²railroad *vb* **1** : to put through (as a law) too hastily **2** : to convict hastily or with insufficient or improper evidence **3** : to send by rail **4** : to work on a railroad — **rail·road·er** *n* — **rail·road·ing** *n*

rail·way \-ˌwā\ *n* : a permanent road with rails fixed to ties providing a track for cars : RAILROAD

rai·ment \'rā-mənt\ *n* ♦ : garments in general : CLOTHING

♦ apparel, attire, clothing, dress, duds, wear

¹rain \'rān\ *n* **1** ♦ : water falling in drops from the clouds **2** ♦ : a shower of objects ⟨a ∼ of bullets⟩

♦ [1] cloudburst, deluge, downpour, rainstorm, storm, wet ♦ [2] hail, shower, storm

²rain *vb* **1** : to send down rain **2** ♦ : to fall as or like rain **3** ♦ : to pour down

♦ [2] heap, lavish, pour, shower ♦ [3] pour, precipitate, storm

rain·bow \-ˌbō\ *n* : an arc or circle of colors formed by the refraction and reflection of the sun's rays in rain, spray, or mist

rainbow trout *n* : a large stout-bodied fish of western No. America closely related to the salmons of the Pacific and usu. having red or pink stripes with black dots along its sides

rain check *n* **1** : a ticket stub good for a later performance when the scheduled one is rained out **2** : an assurance of a deferred extension of an offer

rain·coat \'rān-ˌkōt\ *n* : a waterproof or water-repellent coat

rain date *n* : an alternative date for an event postponed due to rain

rain·drop \-ˌdräp\ *n* : a drop of rain

rain·fall \-ˌfȯl\ *n* **1** : amount of precipitation measured by depth **2** : a fall of rain

rain forest *n* : a tropical woodland having an annual rainfall of at least 100 inches (254 centimeters) and marked by lofty broad-leaved evergreen trees forming a continuous canopy

rain·mak·ing \'rān-ˌmā-kiŋ\ *n* : the action or process of producing or attempting to produce rain by artificial means — **rain·mak·er** *n*

rain out *vb* : to interrupt or prevent by rain

rain·storm \'rān-ˌstȯrm\ *n* ♦ : a storm of or with rain

♦ cloudburst, deluge, downpour, rain, storm, wet

rain·wa·ter \-ˌwȯ-tər, -ˌwä-\ *n* : water fallen as rain

rainy *adj* ♦ : marked by, abounding with, or bringing rain

♦ stormy, wet

¹raise \'rāz\ *vb* **raised; rais·ing 1** ♦ : to cause or help to rise : LIFT ⟨∼ a window⟩ **2** : AWAKEN, AROUSE ⟨enough to ∼ the dead⟩ **3** ♦ : to set upright by lifting or building : ERECT ⟨∼ a monument⟩ **4** : to place higher in rank or dignity : PROMOTE ⟨was *raised* to captain⟩ **5** : END ⟨∼ a siege⟩ **6** : COLLECT ⟨∼ money⟩ **7 a** ♦ : to cause to grow : GROW ⟨∼ cattle⟩ ⟨∼ corn⟩ **b** ♦ : to bring to maturity : BRING UP ⟨∼ a family⟩ **8** ♦ : to cause to arise or appear : stimulate the appearance of ⟨∼ a laugh⟩ **9** ♦ : to bring to notice ⟨∼ an objection⟩ **10** ♦ : to cause to rise in level or amount : INCREASE ⟨∼ prices⟩; *also* : to bet more than **11** : to make light and spongy ⟨∼ dough⟩ **12** : to multiply a quantity by itself a specified number of times **13** : to cause to form ⟨∼ a blister⟩ — **rais·er** *n*

♦ [1] boost, crane, elevate, heave, heft, heighten, hike, hoist, jack, lift, pick up, up, uphold *Ant* drop, lower ♦ [3] assemble, build, construct, erect, fabricate, make, make up, piece, put up, rear, set up ♦ [7a] crop, cultivate, culture, grow, promote, rear, tend ♦ [7b] breed, bring up, foster, rear ♦ [8] elicit, evoke ♦ [9] bring up, broach, introduce, moot ♦ [10] add, aggrandize, amplify, augment, boost, compound, enlarge, escalate, expand, extend, increase, multiply, swell, up

²raise *n* ♦ : an increase in amount (as of a bid or bet or one's pay)

♦ accretion, addition, augmentation, boost, expansion, gain, increase, increment, plus, proliferation, rise, supplement

rai·sin \'rāz-ᵊn\ *n* : a grape dried for food

rai·son d'être \ˌrā-ˌzōⁿ-'detrᵊ\ *n, pl* **rai·sons d'être** \-ˌzōⁿz-\ : reason or justification for existence

ra·ja *or* **ra·jah** \'rä-jə\ *n* : an Indian or Malay prince or chief

¹rake \'rāk\ *n* : a long-handled garden tool having a crossbar with prongs

²rake *vb* **raked; rak·ing 1** : to gather, loosen, or smooth with or as if with a rake **2** : to sweep the length of (as a trench or ship) with gunfire **3** ♦ : to search through

♦ dig, dredge, hunt, ransack, rifle, rummage, scour, search

³rake *n* : inclination from either perpendicular or horizontal : SLANT

⁴rake *n* : a dissolute person : LIBERTINE

rake–off \'rāk-ˌȯf\ *n* : a percentage or cut taken

¹rak·ish \'rā-kish\ *adj* : DISSOLUTE — **rak·ish·ness** *n*

²rakish *adj* **1** : having a trim appearance indicative of speed ⟨a ∼ sloop⟩ **2** : JAUNTY, SPORTY ⟨∼ clothes⟩ — **rak·ish·ness** *n* **rak·ish·ly** *adv* ♦ : in a rakish manner

♦ flamboyantly, flashily, gaily, jauntily

¹ral·ly \'ra-lē\ *vb* **ral·lied; ral·ly·ing 1** ♦ : to bring together for a common purpose; *also* : to bring back to order ⟨a leader ∼ing his forces⟩ **2** : to arouse to activity or from depression or weakness **3** ♦ : to make a comeback

♦ [1] marshal, mobilize, muster ♦ [3] rebound, recover, snap back

²rally *n, pl* **rallies 1** ♦ : an act of rallying **2** ♦ : a mass meeting to arouse enthusiasm **3** : a competitive automobile event run over public roads

♦ [1] comeback, convalescence, recovery, recuperation, rehabilitation ♦ [2] mobilization, muster

³rally *vb* **ral·lied; ral·ly·ing** : BANTER

rallying cry *n* : WAR CRY 2

¹ram \'ram\ *n* **1** : a male sheep **2** : BATTERING RAM

²ram *vb* **rammed; ram·ming 1** : to force or drive in or through **2** ♦ : to make compact : CRAM, CROWD **3** ♦ : to strike against violently

♦ [2] cram, crowd, jam, sandwich, squeeze, stuff, wedge ♦ [3] bang, bash, bump, collide, crash, hit, impact, knock, slam, smash, strike, swipe, thud

RAM \'ram\ *n* : a computer memory that provides the main internal storage for programs and data

Ram·a·dan \'rä-mə-ˌdän\ *n* : the ninth month of the Islamic year observed as sacred with daily fasting from dawn to sunset

¹ram·ble \'ram-bəl\ *vb* **ram·bled; ram·bling 1** ♦ : to go about aimlessly : ROAM, WANDER **2** ♦ : to talk or write in a long-winded wandering fashion

♦ gad, gallivant, knock, maunder, meander, mope, range, roam, rove, traipse, wander ♦ maunder, rattle, run on

²ramble *n* ♦ : a leisurely excursion; *esp* : an aimless walk

  ♦ perambulation, stroll, turn, walk

ram·bler \\'ram-blər\\ *n* **1** ♦ : a person who rambles **2** : any of various climbing roses with large clusters of small often double flowers

  ♦ drifter, nomad, rover, stroller, vagabond, wanderer

ram·bling \\'ram-b(ə-)liŋ\\ *adj* ♦ : straying from subject to subject

  ♦ desultory, digressive, discursive ♦ circuitous, diffuse, long-winded, prolix, verbose, windy, wordy

ram·bunc·tious \\ram-'bəŋk-shəs\\ *adj* ♦ : marked by uncontrollable exuberance

  ♦ boisterous, raucous, rowdy

ra·mie \\'rā-mē, 'ra-\\ *n* : a strong lustrous bast fiber from an Asian nettle

ram·i·fi·ca·tion \\,ra-mə-fə-'kā-shən\\ *n* **1** : the act or process of branching **2** : CONSEQUENCE, OUTGROWTH

ram·i·fy \\'ra-mə-,fī\\ *vb* **-fied; -fy·ing 1** : to branch out **2** : to separate into divisions

ramp \\'ramp\\ *n* : a sloping passage or roadway connecting different levels

¹ram·page \\'ram-,pāj, (,)ram-'pāj\\ *vb* **ram·paged; ram·pag·ing** : to rush about wildly ⟨*rampaging* soccer fans⟩

²ram·page \\'ram-,pāj\\ *n* ♦ : a course of violent or riotous action or behavior — **ram·pa·geous** \\ram-'pā-jəs\\ *adj*

  ♦ agitation, delirium, distraction, frenzy, furor, fury, hysteria, rage, uproar

ram·pant \\'ram-pənt\\ *adj* ♦ : unchecked in growth or spread ⟨∼ weeds⟩ ⟨fear was ∼ in the town⟩ — **ram·pan·cy** \\-pən-sē\\ *n* — **ram·pant·ly** *adv*

  ♦ intemperate, unbridled, unchecked, uncontrolled, ungoverned, unhampered, unhindered, unrestrained *Ant* checked, controlled, curbed, hampered, hindered, restrained, temperate

ram·part \\'ram-,pärt\\ *n* **1** : a protective barrier **2** : a broad embankment raised as a fortification

¹ram·rod \\'ram-,räd\\ *n* **1** : a rod used to ram a charge into a muzzle-loading gun **2** : a cleaning rod for small arms **3** : BOSS, OVERSEER

²ramrod *adj* ♦ : marked by rigidity or severity

  ♦ austere, authoritarian, flinty, hard, harsh, heavy-handed, rigid, rigorous, severe, stern, strict

³ramrod *vb* : to direct, supervise, and control

ram·shack·le \\'ram-,sha-kəl\\ *adj* : RICKETY, TUMBLEDOWN

ran *past of* RUN

¹ranch \\'ranch\\ *n* **1** : an establishment for the raising and grazing of livestock (as cattle, sheep, or horses) **2** : a large farm devoted to a specialty **3** : RANCH HOUSE 2

²ranch *vb* : to live or work on a ranch — **ranch·er** *n*

ranch house *n* **1** : the main house on a ranch **2** : a one-story house typically with a low-pitched roof

ran·cho \\'ran-chō, 'rän-\\ *n, pl* **ranchos** : RANCH 1

ran·cid \\'ran-səd\\ *adj* **1** : having a rank smell or taste **2** : OBNOXIOUS — **ran·cid·i·ty** \\ran-'si-də-tē\\ *n*

ran·cor *or Can and Brit* **ran·cour** \\'raŋ-kər\\ *n* ♦ : bitter deep-seated ill will

  ♦ animosity, antagonism, antipathy, bitterness, enmity, gall, grudge, hostility

ran·cor·ous *adj* ♦ : deeply malevolent

  ♦ acrid, acrimonious, bitter, hard, resentful, sore

rand \\'rand, 'ränd, 'ränt\\ *n, pl* **rand** : the basic monetary unit of the Republic of South Africa

R & B *abbr* rhythm and blues

R & D *abbr* research and development

ran·dom \\'ran-dəm\\ *adj* ♦ : lacking a definite plan, purpose, or pattern : HAPHAZARD — **ran·dom·ly** *adv* — **ran·dom·ness** *n*

  ♦ aimless, arbitrary, desultory, erratic, haphazard, scattered, stray *Ant* methodical, nonrandom, orderly, systematic

random–access *adj* : allowing access to stored data in any order the user desires

random–access memory *n* : RAM

ran·dom·ize \\'ran-də-,mīz\\ *vb* **-ized; -iz·ing** : to select, assign, or arrange in a random way — **ran·dom·i·za·tion** \\,ran-də-mə-'zā-shən\\ *n*

R and R *abbr* rest and recreation; rest and recuperation

rang *past of* RING

¹range \\'rānj\\ *n* **1** ♦ : a series of things in a row **2** : a cooking stove having an oven and a flat top with burners **3 a** ♦ : open land where animals (as livestock) may roam and graze **b** ♦ : the region throughout which a kind of organism or ecological community naturally lives or occurs **4** : the act of ranging about : STROLL **5** : the distance a weapon will shoot or is to be shot **6** : a place where shooting is practiced **7** ♦ : the space or extent included, covered, or used : SCOPE **8** ♦ : a variation within limits

  ♦ [1] column, cue, file, line, queue, string, train ♦ [3a] pasture ♦ [3b] habitat, home, niche, territory ♦ [7] amplitude, breadth, compass, extent, reach, realm, scope, sweep, width ♦ [8] gamut, scale, spectrum, spread, stretch

²range *vb* **ranged; rang·ing 1** ♦ : to set in a row or in proper order **2** ♦ : to set in place among others of the same kind **3** : to roam over or through : EXPLORE **4** ♦ : to roam at large or freely **5** : to correspond in direction or line **6** ♦ : to vary within limits **7** : to find the range of an object by instrument (as radar)

  ♦ [1] arrange, array, classify, codify, dispose, draw up, marshal, order, organize, systematize ♦ [2] assort, break down, categorize, class, classify, grade, group, peg, place, rank, separate, sort ♦ [4] gad, gallivant, knock, maunder, meander, mope, ramble, roam, rove, traipse, wander ♦ [6] go, run, vary

rang·er \\'rān-jər\\ *n* **1** : FOREST RANGER **2** : a member of a body of troops who range over a region **3** : an expert in close-range fighting and raiding tactics

rangy \\'rān-jē\\ *adj* **rang·i·er; -est** ♦ : being long-limbed and slender ⟨a ∼ teenager⟩ — **rang·i·ness** \\'rān-jē-nəs\\ *n*

  ♦ gangling, lanky, spindly

ra·ni *or* **ra·nee** \\rä-'nē, 'rä-,nē\\ *n* : a Hindu queen : a raja's wife

¹rank \\'raŋk\\ *adj* **1** ♦ : strong and vigorous and usu. coarse in growth ⟨∼ weeds⟩ **2** ♦ : unpleasantly strong-smelling **3** ♦ : shockingly conspicuous — **rank·ly** *adv* — **rank·ness** *n*

  ♦ [1] lush, luxuriant, prosperous, rampant, weedy *Ant* sparse ♦ [2] fetid, foul, fusty, malodorous, musty, noisome, reeky, smelly, strong ♦ [3] blatant, conspicuous, egregious, flagrant, glaring, gross, obvious, patent, prominent, pronounced, striking

²rank *n* **1** : ROW **2** : a line of soldiers ranged side by side **3** *pl* : the body of enlisted personnel ⟨rose from the ∼s⟩ **4** : an orderly arrangement **5** : CLASS, DIVISION **6** ♦ : a grade of official standing (as in an army) **7** : position in a group **8** ♦ : superior position

  ♦ [6] degree, footing, level, place, position, situation, standing, station, status ♦ [8] class, quality, standing

³rank *vb* **1** : to arrange in lines or in regular formation **2** ♦ : to determine the relative position of **3** : to rate above (as in official standing) **4** ♦ : to take or have a relative position

  ♦ [2] assort, break down, categorize, class, classify, grade, group, peg, place, range, separate, sort ♦ [4] be, grade, place, rate

rank and file *n* ♦ : the general membership of a body as contrasted with its leaders

  ♦ commoners, herd, masses, mob, people, plebeians, populace

rank·ing \\'raŋ-kiŋ\\ *adj* **1** : having a high position : of the highest rank **2** : being next to the chairman in seniority

ran·kle \\'raŋ-kəl\\ *vb* **ran·kled; ran·kling** ♦ : to cause anger, irritation, or bitterness

  ♦ anger, antagonize, enrage, incense, inflame, infuriate, madden, outrage, rile, roil

ran·sack \\'ran-,sak\\ *vb* **1** ♦ : to search thoroughly **2** ♦ : to search through and rob

  ♦ [1] dig, dredge, hunt, rake, rifle, rummage, scour, search ♦ [2] despoil, loot, maraud, pillage, plunder, sack, strip

¹ran·som \\'ran-səm\\ *n* **1** : something paid or demanded for the freedom of a captive **2** : the act of ransoming

²ransom *vb* : to free from captivity or punishment by paying a price — **ran·som·er** *n*

ran·som·ware \\-,war\\ *n* : malware that requires the victim to pay a ransom to access encrypted files

¹rant \\'rant\\ *vb* **1** ♦ : to talk in a noisy, excited, or bombastic manner **2** : to scold violently ⟨∼ed against his opponent⟩ — **rant·er** — **rant·ing·ly** *adv*

  ♦ bluster, fulminate, rave, spout

²rant *n* ♦ : a bombastic extravagant speech; *also* : the act of ranting

  ♦ diatribe, harangue, tirade ♦ bluster, bombast, brag, gas, grandiloquence

¹rap \\'rap\\ *n* **1** : a sharp blow **2** : a sharp rebuke **3** : a negative often undeserved reputation ⟨a bum ∼⟩ **4** ♦ : responsibility for or consequences of an action ⟨take the ∼⟩ **5** ♦ : a criminal charge

♦ [4] blame, culpability, fault, guilt ♦ [5] charge, complaint, count, indictment

²**rap** *vb* **rapped; rap·ping** **1** : to strike sharply : KNOCK **2** : to utter sharply **3** : to criticize sharply

³**rap** *vb* **rapped; rap·ping** **1** : to talk freely and frankly **2** : to perform rap music — **rap·per** *n*

⁴**rap** *n* **1** : an instance or period of speech or conversation : TALK, CONVERSATION **2** : a rhythmic chanting of usu. rhymed couplets to a musical accompaniment; *also* : a piece so performed

⁵**rap** *n* ♦ : a minimum amount or degree

♦ hoot, jot, lick, modicum, tittle, whit

ra·pa·cious \rə-'pā-shəs\ *adj* **1** ♦ : excessively greedy or covetous **2** : living on prey **3** ♦ : having a huge appetite : RAVENOUS **2** — **ra·pa·cious·ly** *adv*

♦ [1] acquisitive, avaricious, avid, covetous, grasping, greedy, mercenary ♦ [3] gluttonous, greedy, hoggish, piggish, ravenous, voracious

ra·pa·cious·ness *n* ♦ : the quality or state of being rapacious

♦ acquisitiveness, avarice, avidity, covetousness, cupidity, greed

ra·pac·i·ty \-'pa-sə-tē\ *n* : RAPACIOUSNESS

¹**rape** \'rāp\ *n* : a European herb related to the mustards that is grown as a forage crop and for its seeds (**rapeseed** \-ˌsēd\)

²**rape** *vb* **raped; rap·ing** : to commit rape on — **rap·er** *n* — **rap·ist** \'rā-pist\ *n*

³**rape** *n* **1** : a carrying away by force **2** : unlawful sexual activity and usu. sexual intercourse carried out forcibly or under threat of injury or with a person under a certain age or incapable of valid consent

¹**rap·id** \'ra-pəd\ *adj* ♦ : very fast : SWIFT

♦ fast, fleet, quick, speedy, swift

²**rapid** *n* : a place in a stream where the current flows very fast usu. over obstructions — usu. used in pl.

rapid eye movement *n* : rapid conjugate movement of the eyes associated with REM sleep

ra·pid·i·ty \rə-'pi-də-tē, ra-\ *n* ♦ : the quality or state of being rapid

♦ celerity, fastness, fleetness, haste, hurry, quickness, speed, swiftness, velocity

rap·id·ly \'ra-pəd-lē\ *adv* ♦ : in a rapid manner : at a rapid rate

♦ apace, briskly, fast, full tilt, hastily, posthaste, presto, pronto, quick, quickly, soon, speedily, swift, swiftly

rapid transit *n* : fast passenger transportation (as by subway) in cities

¹**ra·pi·er** \'rā-pē-ər\ *n* : a straight 2-edged sword with a narrow pointed blade

²**rapier** *adj* : extremely sharp or keen ⟨∼ wit⟩

rap·ine \'ra-pən, -ˌpīn\ *n* : PILLAGE, PLUNDER

rap·pel \ra-'pel, ra-\ *vb* **-pelled; -pel·ling** : to descend (as from a cliff) by sliding down a rope

rap·port \ra-'pōr\ *n* **1** : RELATION **2** : relation characterized by harmony

rap·proche·ment \ˌra-ˌprōsh-'mäⁿ, ra-'prōsh-ˌmäⁿ\ *n* : the establishment of or a state of having cordial relations

rap·scal·lion \rap-'skal-yən\ *n* **1** : RASCAL **2** ♦ : a mischievous person or animal : SCAMP

♦ devil, hellion, imp, mischief, monkey, rascal, rogue, scamp, urchin

rapt \'rapt\ *adj* **1** : carried away with emotion **2** ♦ : wholly absorbed : ENGROSSED — **rapt·ly** \'rapt-lē\ *adv* — **rapt·ness** *n*

♦ absorbed, attentive, engrossed, intent, observant

rap·tor \'rap-tər, -ˌtòr\ *n* **1** : BIRD OF PREY **2** : a usu. small-to-medium-sized predatory dinosaur

rap·ture \'rap-chər\ *n* ♦ : spiritual or emotional ecstasy — **rap·tur·ous·ly** *adv*

♦ ecstasy, elation, euphoria, exhilaration, heaven, intoxication, paradise, rhapsody, transport

rapture of the deep *n* : NITROGEN NARCOSIS

rap·tur·ous \-chə-rəs\ *adj* ♦ : feeling, expressing, or marked by rapture

♦ ecstatic, elated, euphoric, intoxicated, rhapsodic

ra·ra avis \ˌrar-ə-'ā-vəs\ *n*, *pl* **ra·ra avis·es** \-'ā-və-səz\ *or* **ra·rae aves** \ˌrär-ˌī-'ä-ˌwās\ : a rare person or thing : RARITY

¹**rare** \'rar\ *adj* **rar·er; rar·est** **1** : not thick or dense : THIN ⟨∼

air⟩ **2** ♦ : unusually fine **3** ♦ : seldom seen, encountered, or experienced — **rare·ness** *n*

♦ [2] choice, dainty, delicate, elegant, exquisite, select ♦ [3] aberrant, abnormal, atypical, exceptional, extraordinary, freak, odd, peculiar, phenomenal, singular, uncommon, uncustomary, unique, unusual, unwonted ♦ [3] infrequent, occasional, sporadic

²**rare** *adj* **rar·er; rar·est** : cooked so that the inside is still red ⟨∼ beef⟩

rare·bit \'rar-bət\ *n* : WELSH RABBIT

rar·efac·tion \ˌrar-ə-'fak-shən\ *n* **1** : the action or process of rarefying **2** : the state of being rarefied

rar·e·fy *also* **rar·i·fy** \'rar-ə-ˌfī\ *vb* **-fied; -fy·ing** : to make or become rare, thin, or less dense

rare·ly *adv* ♦ : not often

♦ infrequently, little, seldom

rar·ing \'rar-ən, -iŋ\ *adj* ♦ : full of enthusiasm or eagerness ⟨∼ to go⟩

♦ agog, anxious, ardent, athirst, avid, crazy, eager, enthusiastic, gung ho, hot, hungry, keen, nuts, solicitous, thirsty, voracious

rar·i·ty \'rar-ə-tē\ *n* ♦ : something rare

♦ curiosity, exotic, oddity

ras·cal \'ras-kəl\ *n* **1** ♦ : a mean or dishonest person **2** ♦ : a mischievous person

♦ [1] beast, evildoer, fiend, no-good, reprobate, rogue, varlet, villain, wretch ♦ [2] devil, hellion, imp, mischief, monkey, rapscallion, rogue, scamp, urchin

ras·cal·i·ty \ras-'ka-lə-tē\ *n* ♦ : the character or actions of a rascal

♦ devilishness, impishness, knavery, mischief, mischievousness, shenanigans, waggery, wickedness

ras·cal·ly \'ras-kə-lē\ *adj* ♦ : of or characteristic of a rascal

♦ devilish, impish, knavish, mischievous, roguish, sly, waggish, wicked

¹**rash** \'rash\ *adj* ♦ : having or showing little regard for consequences : too hasty in decision, action, or speech — **rash·ness** *n*

♦ cursory, hasty, headlong, pell-mell, precipitate, precipitous

²**rash** *n* : an eruption on the body

rash·er \'ra-shər\ *n* : a thin slice of bacon or ham broiled or fried; *also* : a portion consisting of several such slices

rash·ly \'rash-lē\ *adv* ♦ : in a rash manner

♦ cursorily, hastily, headlong, hurriedly, pell-mell, precipitately

¹**rasp** \'rasp\ *vb* **1** ♦ : to rub with or as if with a rough file **2** ♦ : to grate harshly on (as one's nerves) **3** : to speak in a grating tone

♦ [1] grate, grind, scrape, scratch ♦ [2] aggravate, annoy, bother, bug, chafe, exasperate, gall, get, grate, irk, irritate, nettle, peeve, persecute, pique, put out, rile, vex

²**rasp** *n* **1** : a coarse file with cutting points instead of ridges **2** ♦ : a rasping sound, sensation, or effect

♦ grind, scrape, scratch

rasp·ber·ry \'raz-ˌber-ē, -bə-rē\ *n* **1** : any of various edible usu. black or red berries produced by some brambles; *also* : such a bramble **2** ♦ : a sound of contempt made by protruding the tongue through the lips and expelling air forcibly

♦ boo, catcall, hiss, hoot, jeer, snort

¹**rat** \'rat\ *n* **1** : any of numerous rodents larger than the related mice **2** : a contemptible person; *esp* ♦ : one that betrays friends or associates

♦ betrayer, blabbermouth, informer, snitch, stool pigeon, tattler, tattletale

²**rat** *vb* **rat·ted; rat·ting** **1** : to betray or inform on one's associates **2** : to hunt or catch rats

rat cheese *n* : CHEDDAR

ratch·et \'ra-chət\ *n* : a device that consists of a bar or wheel having slanted teeth into which a pawl drops so as to allow motion in only one direction

¹**rate** \'rāt\ *vb* **rat·ed; rat·ing** ♦ : to scold violently

♦ admonish, chide, lecture, rail (at *or* against), rebuke, reprimand, scold

²**rate** *n* **1** : quantity, amount, or degree measured by some standard **2** : an amount (as of payment) measured by its relation to some other amount (as of time) **3** : a charge, payment, or price

fixed according to a ratio, scale, or standard ⟨tax ~⟩ **4** ♦ : relative condition or quality : CLASS

♦ caliber (or calibre), class, grade, quality

³**rate** vb **rat·ed; rat·ing 1** ♦ : to set an estimate on **2** ♦ : to show respect or consideration for : CONSIDER, REGARD **3** : to settle the relative rank or class of **4** ♦ : to be classed : RANK **5** ♦ : to have a right to : DESERVE ⟨the museum ~s a visit⟩ **6** : to be of consequence — **rat·er** n

♦ [1] appraise, assess, estimate, evaluate, set, value ♦ [2] account, call, consider, count, esteem, hold, reckon, regard, take ♦ [4] be, grade, place, rank ♦ [5] deserve, earn, merit

rath·er \'ra-thər, 'rä-, -rə-\ adv **1** ♦ : more properly **2** ♦ : more readily or willingly : PREFERABLY **3** : more correctly speaking **4** : to the contrary : INSTEAD **5** ♦ : in some degree : SOMEWHAT

♦ [2] first, preferably, readily, soon **Ant** involuntarily, unwillingly ♦ [5] enough, fairly, kind of, moderately, pretty, quite, somewhat, sort of, so-so

rather than prep : INSTEAD OF
raths·kel·ler \'rät-ˌske-lər, 'rat-\ n : a usu. basement tavern or restaurant
rat·i·fy \'ra-tə-ˌfī\ vb **-fied; -fy·ing** ♦ : to approve and accept formally — **rat·i·fi·ca·tion** \ˌra-tə-fə-'kā-shən\ n

♦ approve, authorize, clear, OK, sanction, warrant

rat·ing \'rā-tiŋ\ n **1** ♦ : a classification according to grade : RANK **2** Brit : an enlisted person in the navy **3** : an estimate of the credit standing and business responsibility of a person or firm
ra·tio \'rā-shō, -shē-ō\ n, pl **ra·tios 1** : the indicated quotient of two numbers or mathematical expressions **2** : the relationship in number, quantity, or degree between two or more things
ra·ti·o·ci·na·tion \ˌra-tē-ˌōs-ᵊn-'ā-shən, -shē-, -ˌäs-\ n : exact thinking : REASONING — **ra·ti·o·ci·nate** \-'ōs-ᵊn-ˌāt, -'äs-\ vb — **ra·ti·o·ci·na·tive** \-'ōs-ᵊn-ˌā-tiv, -'äs-\ adj — **ra·ti·o·ci·na·tor** \-'ōs-ᵊn-ˌā-tər, -'äs-\ n
¹**ra·tion** \'ra-shən, 'rā-\ n **1** : a food allowance for one day **2** : FOOD, PROVISIONS, DIET — usu. used in pl. **3** : SHARE, ALLOTMENT
²**ration** vb **1** ♦ : to supply with or allot as rations **2** : to use or allot sparingly

♦ allocate, allot, allow, apportion, assign

¹**ra·tio·nal** \'ra-shə-nəl\ adj **1** ♦ : having reason or understanding **2** ♦ : of or relating to reason **3** : relating to, consisting of, or being one or more rational numbers **4** ♦ : of, relating to, or in accordance with the principles of rationalism — **ra·tio·nal·ly** adv

♦ [1] intelligent, reasonable, reasoning **Ant** irrational, unintelligent, unreasonable, unreasoning, unthinking ♦ [2, 4] good, hard, informed, just, levelheaded, logical, reasonable, reasoned, sensible, sober, solid, valid, well-founded

²**rational** n : RATIONAL NUMBER
ra·tio·nale \ˌra-shə-'nal\ n **1** ♦ : an explanation of principles controlling belief or practice **2** ♦ : an underlying reason

♦ argument, case, defense (or defence), explanation, reason

ra·tio·nal·ise chiefly Brit var of RATIONALIZE
ra·tio·nal·ism \'ra-shə-nə-ˌli-zəm\ n : the practice of guiding one's actions and thoughts by what seems reasonable — **ra·tio·nal·ist** \-list\ n — **rationalist** or **ra·tio·nal·is·tic** \ˌra-shə-nə-'lis-tik\ adj
ra·tio·nal·i·ty \ˌra-shə-'na-lə-tē\ n, pl **-ties** : the quality or state of being rational
ra·tio·nal·ize \'ra-shə-nə-ˌlīz\ vb **-ized; -iz·ing 1** ♦ : to make (something irrational) appear rational or reasonable **2** : to provide a natural explanation of (as a myth) **3** ♦ : to justify (as one's behavior or weaknesses) esp. to oneself **4** : to find plausible but untrue reasons for conduct — **ra·tio·nal·i·za·tion** \ˌra-shə-nə-lə-'zā-shən\ n

♦ [1, 3] account, explain

rational number n : a number that can be expressed as an integer or the quotient of an integer divided by a nonzero integer
rat race n : strenuous, tiresome, and usu. competitive activity or rush
rat·tan \ra-'tan, rə-\ n : a cane or switch made from one of the long stems of an Asian climbing palm; also : this palm
rat·ter \'ra-tər\ n : a rat-catching dog or cat
¹**rat·tle** \'rat-ᵊl\ vb **rat·tled; rat·tling 1** : to make or cause to make a series of clattering sounds **2** : to move with a clattering sound **3** : to say or do in a brisk lively fashion ⟨~ off the answers⟩ **4** ♦ : to upset esp. to the point of loss of poise and com-

posure : CONFUSE ⟨~ a witness⟩ **5** ♦ : to chatter incessantly and aimlessly

♦ [4] abash, confound, confuse, discomfit, disconcert, discountenance, embarrass, faze, fluster, mortify ♦ [5] maunder, ramble, run on

²**rattle** n **1** : a toy that produces a rattle when shaken **2** : a series of clattering and knocking sounds **3** : a rattling organ at the end of a rattlesnake's tail
rat·tler \'rat-lər\ n : RATTLESNAKE
rat·tle·snake \'rat-ᵊl-ˌsnāk\ n : any of various American pit vipers with a rattle at the end of the tail
rat·tle·trap \'rat-ᵊl-ˌtrap\ n : something (as an old car) rickety and full of rattles
rat·tling \'rat-liŋ\ adj **1** ♦ : acting or capable of acting with speed : BRISK **2** : FIRST-RATE, SPLENDID

♦ breakneck, breathless, brisk, dizzy, fast, fleet, hasty, lightning, nippy, quick, rapid, snappy, speedy, swift

rat·trap \'rat-ˌtrap\ n **1** : a trap for rats **2** : a dilapidated building
rat·ty \'ra-tē\ adj **rat·ti·er; -est 1** : infested with rats **2** : of, relating to, or suggestive of rats **3** ♦ : threadbare and faded from wear : SHABBY

♦ dilapidated, grungy, mean, neglected, seedy, shabby

rau·cous \'ro-kəs\ adj **1** : HARSH, HOARSE, STRIDENT **2** ♦ : boisterously disorderly — **rau·cous·ly** adv — **rau·cous·ness** n

♦ boisterous, rambunctious, rowdy

raun·chy \'ron-chē, 'rän-\ adj **raun·chi·er; -est 1** : SLOVENLY, DIRTY **2** : OBSCENE, SMUTTY — **raun·chi·ness** \-chē-nəs\ n
¹**rav·age** \'ra-vij\ n : an act or result of ravaging : DEVASTATION
²**ravage** vb **rav·aged; rav·ag·ing** ♦ : to lay waste : DEVASTATE — **rav·ag·er** n

♦ destroy, devastate, ruin, scourge

¹**rave** \'rāv\ vb **raved; rav·ing 1** : to talk wildly in or as if in delirium : STORM, RAGE **2** ♦ : to talk with extreme enthusiasm **3** ♦ : to speak out wildly

♦ [2] enthuse, fuss, gush, rhapsodize, slobber ♦ [3] bluster, fulminate, rant, spout

²**rave** n **1** : an act or instance of raving **2** : an extravagantly favorable criticism
¹**rav·el** \'ra-vəl\ vb **-eled** or **-elled; -el·ing** or **-el·ling 1** : to undo the intricacies of : UNRAVEL **2** : TANGLE, CONFUSE
²**ravel** n **1** : something tangled **2** : something raveled out; esp : a loose thread
¹**ra·ven** \'rā-vən\ n : a large black bird related to the crow
²**raven** adj ♦ : black and glossy like a raven's feathers

♦ black, ebony

³**rav·en** \'ra-vən\ vb **1** : to devour greedily **2** : DESPOIL, PLUNDER **3** : PREY
rav·en·ous \'ra-və-nəs\ adj **1** ♦ : having a huge appetite : VORACIOUS **2** : eager for food : very hungry — **rav·en·ous·ly** adv — **rav·en·ous·ness** n

♦ gluttonous, greedy, hoggish, piggish, rapacious, voracious

ra·vine \rə-'vēn\ n ♦ : a small narrow steep-sided valley larger than a gully

♦ canyon, defile, flume, gap, gorge, gulch, gulf, notch, pass

rav·i·o·li \ˌra-vē-'ō-lē\ n, pl **ravioli** also **raviolis** : small cases of dough with a savory filling (as of meat or cheese)
rav·ish \'ra-vish\ vb **1** : to seize and take away by violence **2** ♦ : to overcome with emotion and esp. with joy or delight **3** : RAPE — **rav·ish·er** n — **rav·ish·ment** n

♦ carry away, enrapture, enthrall, entrance, transport

rav·ish·ing \'ra-vi-shiŋ\ adj ♦ : unusually attractive, pleasing, or striking

♦ attractive, beautiful, fair, gorgeous, handsome, knockout, lovely, pretty, stunning

¹**raw** \'ro\ adj **raw·er** \'ro-ər\; **raw·est** \'ro-əst\ **1** : not cooked **2** ♦ : changed little from the original form : not processed ⟨~ materials⟩ **3** : having the surface abraded or irritated ⟨a ~ sore⟩ **4** ♦ : not trained or experienced ⟨~ recruits⟩ **5** : VULGAR, COARSE **6** ♦ : disagreeably cold and damp ⟨a ~ day⟩ **7** : UNFAIR ⟨~ deal⟩

♦ [2] crude, native, natural, undressed, unprocessed, unrefined, untreated ♦ [4] adolescent, callow, green, immature, inexperienced, juvenile ♦ [6] bitter, bleak, chill, chilly, nippy, sharp

²**raw** *n* : a raw place or state; *esp* : NUDITY

raw·boned \'rȯ-ˌbōnd\ *adj* **1** : LEAN, GAUNT **2** : having a heavy frame that seems to have little flesh

raw deal *n* ♦ : an instance of unfair treatment

♦ disservice, injury, injustice, wrong

raw·hide \'rȯ-ˌhīd\ *n* : the untanned skin of cattle; *also* : a whip made of this

raw material *n* ♦ : something with a potential for improvement, development, or elaboration

♦ material, stuff, substance

raw·ness *n* ♦ : the quality or state of being raw

♦ bite, bitterness, bleakness, chill, nip, sharpness

¹**ray** \'rā\ *n* : any of an order of large flat cartilaginous fishes that have the eyes on the upper surface and the hind end of the body slender and taillike

²**ray** *n* **1** : any of the lines of light that appear to radiate from a bright object **2** : a thin beam of radiant energy (as light) **3** : light from a beam **4** : a thin line like a beam of light **5** : an animal or plant structure resembling a ray **6** : a tiny bit : PARTICLE ⟨a ∼ of hope⟩

ray·on \'rā-ˌän\ *n* : a fiber made from cellulose; *also* : a yarn, thread, or fabric made from such fibers

raze \'rāz\ *vb* **razed; raz·ing** **1** : to scrape, cut, or shave off **2** : to destroy to the ground : DEMOLISH

ra·zor \'rā-zər\ *n* : a sharp cutting instrument used to shave off hair

ra·zor–backed \'rā-zər-ˌbakt\ *or* **ra·zor·back** \-ˌbak\ *adj* : having a sharp narrow back ⟨∼ horse⟩

razor clam *n* : any of a family of marine bivalve mollusks having a long narrow curved thin shell

razor wire *n* : coiled wire fitted with sharp edges and used as an obstacle or barrier

¹**razz** \'raz\ *n* : RASPBERRY 2

²**razz** *vb* ♦ : to harass and try to disconcert with questions, challenges, or gibes : TEASE

♦ chaff, jive, josh, kid, rally, rib, ride, roast, tease

Rb *symbol* rubidium

RBC *abbr* red blood cells

RBI \ˌär-(ˌ)bē-'ī, 'ri-bē-'ī\ *n, pl* **RBIs** *or* **RBI** : a run in baseball that is driven in by a batter

RC *abbr* **1** Red Cross **2** Roman Catholic

RCAF *abbr* Royal Canadian Air Force

RCMP *abbr* Royal Canadian Mounted Police

RCN *abbr* Royal Canadian Navy

rct *abbr* recruit

rd *abbr* **1** road **2** rod **3** round

RD *abbr* rural delivery

RDA *abbr* recommended daily allowance; recommended dietary allowance

re \'rā, 'rē\ *prep* : with regard to

Re *symbol* rhenium

re- \rē, ˌrē, 'rē\ *prefix* **1** : again : for a second time **2** : anew : in a new or different form **3** : back : backward

reabsorb	reappraise
reacquire	rearm
reactivate	rearmament
reactivation	rearouse
readjust	rearrange
readjustment	rearrangement
readmission	rearrest
readmit	reascend
reaffirm	reassemble
reaffirmation	reassembly
realign	reassert
realignment	reassess
reallocate	reassessment
reallocation	reassign
reanalysis	reassignment
reanimation	reassume
reannex	reattach
reannexation	reattachment
reappear	reattain
reappearance	reattempt
reapplication	reauthorization
reapply	reauthorize
reappoint	reawaken
reappointment	rebaptism
reapportion	rebaptize
reapportionment	rebid

rebind	reequip
reboil	reestablish
rebroadcast	reestablishment
reburial	reevaluation
rebury	reexport
recalculate	refight
recalculation	refigure
rechannel	refinish
recharge	refit
rechargeable	refix
recharter	refloat
recheck	refold
rechristen	reforge
reclassification	reformulate
reclassify	reformulation
recoin	refortify
recolonization	refound
recolonize	refreeze
recolor	refuel
recombine	refurnish
recommence	regather
recommission	regild
recommit	regive
recompile	regrade
recompose	regrind
recomputation	regrow
recompute	regrowth
reconcentrate	rehandle
reconception	rehear
recondensation	rehouse
recondense	reimpose
reconfirm	reimposition
reconfirmation	reincorporate
reconnect	reinsert
reconquer	reinsertion
reconquest	reintegrate
reconsecrate	reinterpret
reconsecration	reinterpretation
recontact	reintroduce
recontaminate	reintroduction
recontamination	reinvention
reconvene	reinvest
reconvert	reinvestment
recook	reinvigoration
recopy	reissue
recross	rejudge
recrystallize	reknit
recut	relaunch
redecorate	relearn
redecoration	relight
rededicate	reline
rededication	reload
redefine	remanufacture
redefinition	remap
redeposit	remarriage
redesign	remarry
redetermination	rematch
redetermine	remelt
redevelop	remigration
redevelopment	remix
redirect	remold
rediscount	rename
rediscover	renegotiate
rediscovery	renegotiation
redissolve	renominate
redistill	renomination
redistillation	renumber
redraw	reoccupy
reedit	reoccur
reelect	reorder
reelection	reorganization
reemerge	reorganize
reemergence	reorient
reemphasis	reorientation
reemphasize	repack
reemploy	repaint
reemployment	repass
reenact	repeople
reenactment	rephotograph
reenergize	replant
reenlist	repopulate
reenlistment	reprice
reenter	reprocess

reprogram
republication
republish
repurchase
reradiate
reread
rereading
rerecord
reroute
reschedule
rescore
rescreen
reseal
reseed
resell
reset
resettle
resettlement
resew
reshow
resocialization
resow
respell
restaff
restatement
restock
restrengthen
restructure
restudy
restuff
restyle

resubmit
resummon
resupply
resurface
resurvey
resynthesis
resynthesize
retaste
retell
retest
retrain
retransmission
retransmit
retrial
reunification
reunify
reunite
reusable
reuse
revaluate
revaluation
revalue
revisit
rewarm
rewash
reweave
rewed
reweigh
rewire
rezone

¹**reach** \'rēch\ *vb* **1 :** to stretch out **2 :** to touch or attempt to touch or seize **3 :** to extend to **4 :** to communicate with **5 :** to arrive at **6 ♦ :** to hand over — **reach•er** *n*

♦ hand, hand over, pass, transfer

²**reach** *n* **1 :** an unbroken stretch of a river **2 :** the act of reaching **3 :** a reachable distance; *also* **:** ability to reach **4 ♦ :** a range of knowledge or comprehension **5 ♦ :** a continuous stretch or expanse

♦ [4] amplitude, breadth, compass, extent, range, realm, scope, sweep, width ♦ [5] breadth, expanse, extent, spread, stretch

reach•able *adj* ♦ **:** capable of being reached

♦ accessible, convenient, handy

re•act \rē-'akt\ *vb* **1 :** to exert a return or counteracting influence **2 :** to have or show a reaction **3 :** to act in opposition to a force or influence **4 :** to move or tend in a reverse direction **5 :** to undergo chemical reaction

re•ac•tant \rē-'ak-tənt\ *n* **:** a chemically reacting substance

re•ac•tion \rē-'ak-shən\ *n* **1 :** the act or process of reacting **2 :** a counter tendency; *esp* **:** a tendency toward a former esp. outmoded political or social order or policy **3 ♦ :** bodily, mental, or emotional response to a stimulus **4 :** chemical change **5 :** a process involving change in atomic nuclei

♦ reply, response, take

¹**re•ac•tion•ary** \rē-'ak-shə-ˌner-ē\ *adj* **1 ♦ :** relating to, marked by, or favoring esp. political reaction **2 ♦ :** relating to, marked by, or favoring reaction

♦ conservative, old-fashioned, orthodox, traditional

²**reactionary** *n* **:** one that is reactionary; *esp* **:** one tending to favor established ideas, conditions, or institutions

♦ conservative, rightist, Tory

re•ac•tive \rē-'ak-tiv\ *adj* **:** reacting or tending to react

re•ac•tor \rē-'ak-tər\ *n* **1 :** one that reacts **2 :** a device for the controlled release of nuclear energy

¹**read** \'rēd\ *vb* **read** \'red\; **read•ing** **1 :** to understand language by interpreting written symbols for speech sounds **2 :** to utter aloud written or printed words **3 :** to learn by observing ⟨~ nature's signs⟩ **4 :** to study by a course of reading ⟨~s law⟩ **5 :** to discover the meaning of ⟨~ the clues⟩ **6 :** to recognize or interpret as if by reading **7 :** to attribute (a meaning) to something ⟨~ guilt in his manner⟩ **8 :** INDICATE ⟨thermometer ~s 10°⟩ **9 :** to consist in phrasing or meaning ⟨the two versions ~ differently⟩ — **read•abil•i•ty** \ˌrē-də-'bi-lə-tē\ *n* — **read•able** \'rē-də-bəl\ *adj* — **read•ably** \-blē\ *adv* — **read•er** *n*

²**read** \'red\ *adj* **:** informed by reading ⟨widely ~⟩

re•ad•dress \rē-ə-'dres\ *vb* ♦ **:** to deal with again

♦ reanalyze, reconceive, reconsider, reexamine, rethink, review

read•er•ship \'rē-dər-ˌship\ *n* **:** the mass or a particular group of readers

read•i•ly \'re-də-lē\ *adv* **1 :** in a ready manner **2 ♦ :** without much difficulty

♦ easily, effortlessly, fluently, freely, handily, lightly, painlessly, smoothly

read•ing \'rēd-iŋ\ *n* **1 :** something read or for reading **2 :** a particular version **3 :** data indicated by an instrument ⟨thermometer ~⟩ **4 :** a particular interpretation (as of a law) **5 :** a particular performance (as of a musical work) **6 :** an indication of a certain state of affairs

read–only memory *n* **:** ROM

read•out \'rēd-ˌaut\ *n* **1 :** the process of removing information from an automatic device (as a computer) and displaying it in an understandable form; *also* **:** the information removed from such a device **2 :** an electronic device that presents information in visual form

read out *vb* **1 :** to read aloud **2 :** to expel from an organization

¹**ready** \'re-dē\ *adj* **read•i•er; -est** **1 ♦ :** prepared for use or action **2 a :** likely to do something indicated **b ♦ :** willingly inclined toward **:** prepared to do **3 ♦ :** spontaneously prompt ⟨her ~ wit⟩ **4 :** immediately available ⟨~ cash⟩ — **read•i•ness** \-dē-nəs\ *n* — **at the ready** **:** ready for immediate use

♦ [1] fit, go, set *Ant* unprepared, unready ♦ [2b] amenable, disposed, game, glad, inclined, willing ♦ [3] alert, expeditious, prompt, quick, willing

²**ready** *vb* **read•ied; ready•ing** ♦ **:** to make ready

♦ equip, fit, prepare, qualify, season ♦ brace, forearm, fortify, nerve, psych (up), steel, strengthen

ready–made \ˌre-dē-'mād\ *adj* **:** already made up for general sale **:** not specially made — **ready–made** *n*

ready room *n* **:** a room in which pilots are briefed and await orders

re•agent \rē-'ā-jənt\ *n* **:** a substance that takes part in or brings about a particular chemical reaction

¹**re•al** \'rēl\ *adj* **1 :** of or relating to fixed or immovable things (as land) ⟨~ property⟩ **2 ♦ :** not artificial, fraudulent, or illusory **:** GENUINE **3 ♦ :** occurring or existing in actuality — **re•al•ness** *n* — **for real** **1 :** in earnest **2 :** GENUINE

♦ [2] artless, authentic, bona fide, genuine, honest, ingenuous, innocent, naive, natural, simple, sincere, true, unaffected, unpretentious ♦ [3] actual, concrete, existent, factual, true, very

²**real** *adv* **:** to a high degree **:** VERY

real estate *n* **:** property in buildings and land

re•al•ism \'rē-ə-ˌli-zəm\ *n* **1 :** the disposition to face facts and to deal with them practically **2 :** true and faithful portrayal of nature and of people in art or literature — **re•al•ist** \-list\ *adj or n* — **re•al•is•ti•cal•ly** \-ti-k(ə-)lē\ *adv*

re•al•is•tic \ˌrē-ə-'lis-tik\ *adj* **1 ♦ :** of, relating to, or marked by literary or artistic realism **2 ♦ :** facing reality squarely **:** not impractical or visionary

♦ [1] lifelike, natural, near ♦ [2] down-to-earth, earthy, hardheaded, matter-of-fact, practical, pragmatic *Ant* idealistic, impractical, unrealistic, utopian, visionary

re•al•i•ty \rē-'a-lə-tē\ *n, pl* **-ties** **1 ♦ :** the quality or state of being real **2 :** something real **3 :** the totality of real things and events

♦ actuality, existence, subsistence

re•al•iz•able \'rē-ə-ˌlī-zə-bəl\ *adj* ♦ **:** capable of being realized

♦ achievable, attainable, doable, feasible, possible, practicable, viable, workable

re•al•i•za•tion \ˌrē-ə-lə-'zā-shən\ *n* ♦ **:** the action of realizing **:** the state of being realized

♦ accomplishment, achievement, actuality, attainment, consummation, fruition, fulfillment

re•al•ize \'rē-ə-ˌlīz\ *vb* **-ized; -iz•ing** **1 :** to make actual **:** ACCOMPLISH **2 :** to convert into money ⟨~ assets⟩ **3 :** to bring or get by sale, investment, or effort **:** OBTAIN, GAIN ⟨~ a profit⟩ **4 ♦ :** to be aware of

♦ ascertain, catch on, discover, find out, hear, learn, see

re•al•ly \'rē-lē, 'ri-\ *adv* **1 ♦ :** in truth **:** in fact **2 ♦ :** without any question — used as an intensifier ⟨a ~ beautiful day⟩

♦ [1] actually, frankly, genuinely, honestly, truly, truthfully, verily ♦ [2] certainly, definitely, doubtless, incontestably, indeed, indisputably, surely, truly, undeniably, undoubtedly, unquestionably

realm \'relm\ *n* **1 :** KINGDOM **2 ♦ :** an area or range over or within which someone or something acts, exists, or has influence or significance : SPHERE, DOMAIN

♦ area, arena, demesne, department, discipline, domain, field, line, province, specialty, sphere

real number *n* : a number that has no imaginary part ⟨the set of all *real numbers* comprises the rationals and the irrationals⟩

re·al·po·li·tik \rā-ˈäl-ˌpō-li-ˌtēk\ *n, often cap* : politics based on practical and material factors rather than on theoretical or ethical objectives

real time *n* : the actual time during which something takes place — **real–time** *adj*

re·al·ty \ˈrēl-tē\ *n* : REAL ESTATE

¹ream \ˈrēm\ *n* **1** : a quantity of paper that is variously 480, 500, or 516 sheets **2** ♦ : a great amount — usu. used in the pl. ⟨∼s of information⟩

♦ **reams** abundance, deal, gobs, heap, loads, lot, pile, plenty, quantity, scads

²ream *vb* : to enlarge, shape, or clear with a reamer

ream·er \ˈrē-mər\ *n* : a tool with cutting edges that is used to enlarge or shape a hole

re·an·a·lyze \rē-ˈan-ᵊl-ˌīz\ *vb* ♦ : to analyze again

♦ readdress, reconceive, reconsider, reexamine, rethink, review

re·an·i·mate \rē-ˈa-nə-ˌmāt\ *vb* ♦ : to give renewed spirit and support to

♦ regenerate, reinvigorate, rejuvenate, renew, resuscitate, revitalize, revive

reap \ˈrēp\ *vb* **1** : to cut or clear with a scythe, sickle, or machine **2** ♦ : to gather by or as if by cutting : HARVEST ⟨∼ a reward⟩ — **reap·er** *n*

♦ gather, harvest, pick

re·ap·prais·al \rē-ə-ˈprā-zəl\ *n* ♦ : a second or fresh appraisal

♦ reexamination, retrospection, review

¹rear \ˈrir\ *vb* **1** ♦ : to erect by building **2** : to set or raise upright **3** : to breed and raise for use or market ⟨∼ livestock⟩ **4** ♦ : to bring to maturity or self-sufficiency usu. through nurturing care **5** : to lift or rise up; *esp* : to rise on the hind legs

♦ [1] assemble, build, construct, erect, fabricate, make, make up, piece, put up, raise, set up ♦ [3] crop, cultivate, culture, grow, promote, raise, tend ♦ [4] breed, bring up, foster, raise

²rear *n* **1** : the unit (as of an army) or area farthest from the enemy **2** : BACK; *also* : the position at the back of something **3** ♦ : the seat of the body

♦ backside, bottom, butt, buttocks, posterior, rump, seat

³rear *adj* ♦ : being at the back

♦ back, hind, hindmost, posterior

rear admiral *n* : a commissioned officer in the navy or coast guard ranking next below a vice admiral

¹rear·ward \ˈrir-wərd\ *adj* **1** : being at or toward the rear **2** : directed toward the rear

²rear·ward *also* **rear·wards** \-wərdz\ *adv* : at or toward the rear

reas *abbr* reasonable

¹rea·son \ˈrēz-ᵊn\ *n* **1** ♦ : a statement offered in explanation or justification **2** ♦ : a person or thing that is the occasion of an action or state : CAUSE **3** : the power to think : INTELLECT **4** ♦ : a sane or sound mind **5** ♦ : due exercise of the faculty of logical thought

♦ [1] alibi, argument, case, defense (*or* defence), excuse, explanation, justification, rationale ♦ [2] antecedent, cause, grounds, motive, occasion, wherefore, why ♦ [4] head, mind, sanity, wit ♦ [5] logic, reasoning, sense

²reason *vb* **1** : to talk with another to cause a change of mind **2** : to use the faculty of reason : THINK **3** ♦ : to discover or formulate by the use of reason **4** ♦ : to persuade or influence by the use of reason — **rea·son·er** *n*

♦ [3] conclude, deduce, extrapolate, gather, infer, judge, understand ♦ [4] argue, assert, contend, maintain, plead

rea·son·able \ˈrēz-ᵊn-ə-bəl\ *adj* **1** : being within the bounds of reason : not extreme **2** : reasonable in price : INEXPENSIVE **3** ♦ : able to reason : RATIONAL **4** ♦ : being in accordance with reason — **rea·son·able·ness** *n*

♦ [3] intelligent, rational, reasoning ♦ [4] good, hard, informed, just, levelheaded, logical, rational, reasoned, sensible, sober, solid, valid, well-founded

rea·son·ably \-blē\ *adv* : in a reasonable manner

rea·soned *adj* ♦ : based on or marked by reasoning

♦ advised, calculated, deliberate, measured, studied, thoughtful, thought-out

rea·son·ing *n* ♦ : the use of reason

♦ logic, reason, sense

re·as·sure \ˌrē-ə-ˈshu̇r\ *vb* **1** : to assure again **2** ♦ : to restore confidence to : free from fear — **re·as·sur·ance** \-ˈshu̇r-əns\ *n* — **re·as·sur·ing·ly** *adv*

♦ assure, cheer, comfort, console, solace, soothe

¹re·bate \ˈrē-ˌbāt\ *vb* **re·bat·ed; re·bat·ing** : to make or give a rebate

²rebate *n* : a return of part of a payment

¹reb·el \ˈre-bəl\ *adj* : of or relating to rebels

²rebel *n* ♦ : one that rebels against authority

♦ insurgent, insurrectionist, mutineer, red, revolter, revolutionary

³re·bel \ri-ˈbel\ *vb* **re·belled; re·bel·ling** **1** : to resist the authority of one's government **2** : to act in or show disobedience **3** : to feel or exhibit anger or revulsion

re·bel·lion \ri-ˈbel-yən\ *n* ♦ : resistance to authority; *esp* : defiance against a government through uprising or revolt

♦ insurrection, mutiny, revolt, revolution, uprising

re·bel·lious \-yəs\ *adj* **1** ♦ : given to or engaged in rebellion **2** ♦ : inclined to resist authority — **re·bel·lious·ly** *adv*

♦ [1] insurgent, mutinous, revolutionary ♦ [1, 2] contrary, defiant, disobedient, froward, intractable, recalcitrant, refractory, unruly, untoward, wayward, willful

re·bel·lious·ness *n* ♦ : the quality or state of being rebellious

♦ defiance, disobedience, insubordination, recalcitrance, refractoriness, unruliness

re·birth \ˌrē-ˈbərth\ *n* **1** : a new or second birth **2** ♦ : a return or renewal of vigor, freshness, or productivity : REVIVAL

♦ regeneration, rejuvenation, renewal, resurgence, resurrection, resuscitation, revival

re·born \-ˈbȯrn\ *adj* : born again : REGENERATED, REVIVED

¹re·bound \ˌrē-ˈbau̇nd, ˈrē-ˌbau̇nd\ *vb* **1** ♦ : to spring back on or as if on striking another body **2** ♦ : to recover from a setback or frustration ⟨∼ed quickly from the loss⟩

♦ [1] bounce, carom, glance, ricochet, skim, skip ♦ [2] rally, recover, snap back

²re·bound \ˈrē-ˌbau̇nd\ *n* **1** : the action of rebounding **2** : a rebounding ball **3** : a reaction to setback or frustration

¹re·buff \ri-ˈbəf\ *vb* : to reject or criticize sharply

²rebuff *n* ♦ : an abrupt rejection of an offer or advance

♦ brush-off, cold shoulder, repulse, snub

re·build \(ˌ)rē-ˈbild\ *vb* **-built** \-ˈbilt\; **-build·ing** **1** : REPAIR, RECONSTRUCT; *also* : REMODEL **2** : to build again

¹re·buke \ri-ˈbyük\ *vb* **re·buked; re·buk·ing** ♦ : to reprimand sharply

♦ censure, condemn, denounce, reprimand, reproach, reprove ♦ admonish, chide, lecture, rail (at *or* against), rate, reprimand, scold

²rebuke *n* ♦ : a sharp reprimand

♦ censure, denunciation, reprimand, reproach, reproof, stricture

re·bus \ˈrē-bəs\ *n* : a representation of syllables or words by means of pictures; *also* : a riddle composed of such pictures

re·but \ri-ˈbət\ *vb* **re·but·ted; re·but·ting** ♦ : to refute esp. formally (as in debate) by evidence and arguments — **re·but·ter** *n*

♦ belie, confute, disprove, refute

re·but·tal \ri-ˈbət-ᵊl\ *n* : the act of rebutting; *also* ♦ : argument or proof that rebuts

♦ confutation, refutation

rec *abbr* **1** receipt **2** record; recording **3** recreation

re·cal·ci·trance \ri-ˈkal-sə-trəns\ *n* ♦ : the state of being recalcitrant

♦ defiance, disobedience, insubordination, rebelliousness, refractoriness, unruliness

re·cal·ci·trant \ri-ˈkal-sə-trənt\ *adj* **1** ♦ : stubbornly resisting authority ⟨a ∼ prisoner⟩ **2** : resistant to handling or treatment

♦ contrary, defiant, disobedient, froward, intractable, rebellious, refractory, unruly, untoward, wayward, willful

¹**re·call** \ri-'kȯl\ *vb* **1 :** to call back **2 ♦ :** to bring back to mind **:** REMEMBER, RECOLLECT **3 ♦ :** to call off usu. without expectation of conducting or performing at a later time **:** REVOKE, CANCEL

    ♦ [2] recollect, remember, reminisce, think ♦ [3] abort, call, call off, cancel, drop, repeal, rescind, revoke

²**re·call** \ri-'kȯl, 'rē-ˌkȯl\ *n* **1 :** a summons to return **2 :** the procedure of removing an official by popular vote **3 ♦ :** remembrance of things learned or experienced **4 ♦ :** the act of revoking **5 :** a call by a manufacturer for the return of a product that may be defective or contaminated

    ♦ [3] memory, recollection, remembrance, reminiscence ♦ [4] abortion, calling, cancellation, repeal, rescission, revocation

re·cant \ri-'kant\ *vb* ♦ **:** to take back (something one has said) publicly **:** make an open confession of error — **re·can·ta·tion** \ˌrē-ˌkan-'tā-shən\ *n*

    ♦ abjure, renounce, retract, take back, unsay, withdraw

¹**re·cap** \'rē-ˌkap, rē-'kap\ *vb* **re·capped; re·cap·ping :** to repeat the principal stages or phases of **:** RECAPITULATE

²**recap** *vb* **re·capped; re·cap·ping :** RETREAD — **recap** \'rē-ˌkap\ *n*

³**re·cap** \'rē-ˌkap\ *n* **:** RECAPITULATION

re·ca·pit·u·late \ˌrē-kə-'pi-chə-ˌlāt\ *vb* **-lat·ed; -lat·ing** ♦ **:** to restate briefly **:** SUMMARIZE ⟨~ a news story⟩

    ♦ abstract, digest, encapsulate, epitomize, outline, sum up, summarize, wrap up

re·ca·pit·u·la·tion \-ˌpi-chə-'lā-shən\ *n* ♦ **:** a concise summary

    ♦ abstract, digest, encapsulation, epitome, outline, précis, résumé (*or* resume), roundup, sum, summary, synopsis, wrap-up

re·cap·ture \(ˌ)rē-'kap-chər\ *vb* **1 ♦ :** to capture again **2 :** to experience again ⟨~ happy times⟩

    ♦ reclaim, recoup, recover, regain, repossess, retake, retrieve

re·cast \(ˌ)rē-'kast\ *vb* **1 :** to cast again **2 ♦ :** to alter the structure of **:** REVISE, REMODEL ⟨~ a sentence⟩

    ♦ alter, change, make over, modify, redo, refashion, remake, remodel, revamp, revise, rework, vary

recd *abbr* received

re·cede \ri-'sēd\ *vb* **re·ced·ed; re·ced·ing 1 ♦ :** to move back or away **2 :** to slant backward **3 ♦ :** to grow less or smaller **:** DIMINISH

    ♦ [1] back, fall back, retire, retreat, withdraw ♦ [3] abate, decline, decrease, de-escalate, die, diminish, dwindle, ebb, fall, lessen, let up, lower, moderate, relent, shrink, subside, taper, wane

¹**re·ceipt** \ri-'sēt\ *n* **1 :** RECIPE **2 :** the act of receiving **3 :** something received — usu. used in pl. **4 :** a written acknowledgment of something received

²**receipt** *vb* **1 :** to give a receipt for **2 :** to mark as paid

re·ceiv·able \ri-'sē-və-bəl\ *adj* **1 :** capable of being received; *esp* **:** acceptable as legal ⟨~ certificates⟩ **2 :** subject to call for payment ⟨notes ~⟩

re·ceive \ri-'sēv\ *vb* **re·ceived; re·ceiv·ing 1 :** to take in or accept (as something sent or paid) **:** come into possession of **:** GET **2 :** CONTAIN, HOLD **3 :** to permit to enter **:** GREET, WELCOME **4 :** to be at home to visitors **5 :** to accept as true or authoritative **6 :** to be the subject of **:** UNDERGO, EXPERIENCE ⟨~ a shock⟩ **7 :** to change incoming radio waves into sounds or pictures ⟨~ a broadcast⟩

re·ceiv·er \ri-'sē-vər\ *n* **1 :** one that receives **2 :** a person legally appointed to receive and have charge of property or money involved in a lawsuit **3 :** a device for converting electromagnetic waves or signals into audio or visual form ⟨telephone ~⟩

re·ceiv·er·ship \-ˌship\ *n* **1 :** the office or function of a receiver **2 :** the condition of being in the hands of a receiver

re·cen·cy \'rēs-ᵊn-sē\ *n* **:** RECENTNESS

re·cent \'rēs-ᵊnt\ *adj* **1 :** of the present time or time just past ⟨~ history⟩ **2 :** having lately come into existence **:** NEW, FRESH ⟨~ buds⟩ **3** *cap* **:** HOLOCENE — **re·cent·ness** *n*

re·cent·ly *adv* ♦ **:** during a recent period of time

    ♦ freshly, just, late, lately, new, newly, now, only

re·cep·ta·cle \ri-'sep-ti-kəl\ *n* **1 ♦ :** something used to receive and hold something else **:** CONTAINER **2 :** the enlarged end of a flower stalk upon which the parts of the flower grow **3 :** an electrical fitting containing the live parts of a circuit

    ♦ container, holder, vessel

re·cep·tion \ri-'sep-shən\ *n* **1 :** the act of receiving **2 :** a social gathering at which guests are formally welcomed

re·cep·tion·ist \ri-'sep-shə-nist\ *n* **:** a person employed to greet callers

re·cep·tive \ri-'sep-tiv\ *adj* **1 :** able or inclined to receive **2 ♦ :** open and responsive to ideas, impressions, or suggestions ⟨a ~ audience⟩ — **re·cep·tive·ly** *adv* — **re·cep·tive·ness** *n* — **re·cep·tiv·i·ty** \ˌrē-ˌsep-'ti-və-tē\ *n*

    ♦ broad-minded, open, open-minded

re·cep·tor \ri-'sep-tər\ *n* **1 :** one that receives stimuli **:** SENSE ORGAN **2 :** a chemical group or molecule in the outer cell membrane or in the cell interior that has an affinity for a specific chemical group, molecule, or virus

¹**re·cess** \'rē-ˌses, ri-'ses\ *n* **1 :** a secret or secluded place **2 ♦ :** an indentation in a line or surface (as an alcove in a room) **3 ♦ :** a suspension of business or procedure for rest or relaxation

    ♦ [2] alcove, niche, nook ♦ [3] break, leave, vacation ♦ [3] break, breath, breather, respite

²**recess** *vb* **1 :** to put into a recess **2 :** to make a recess in **3 :** to interrupt for a recess **4 :** to take a recess

re·ces·sion \ri-'se-shən\ *n* **1 :** the act of receding **:** WITHDRAWAL **2 :** a departing procession (as at the end of a church service) **3 :** a period of reduced economic activity

re·ces·sion·al \ri-'se-shə-nəl\ *n* **1 :** a hymn or musical piece at the conclusion of a service or program **2 :** RECESSION 2

¹**re·ces·sive** \ri-'se-siv\ *adj* **1 :** tending to recede **2 :** producing or being a bodily characteristic that is masked or not expressed when a contrasting dominant gene or trait is present ⟨~ genes⟩ ⟨~ traits⟩

²**recessive** *n* **:** a recessive characteristic or gene; *also* **:** an individual that has one or more recessive characteristics

re·cher·ché \rə-ˌsher-'shā, -'sher-ˌshā\ *adj* **1 :** CHOICE, RARE **2 :** excessively refined ⟨~ poetry⟩

re·cid·i·vism \ri-'si-də-ˌvi-zəm\ *n* **:** a tendency to relapse into a previous condition; *esp* **:** relapse into criminal behavior — **re·cid·i·vist** \-vist\ *n*

rec·i·pe \'re-sə-(ˌ)pē\ *n* **1 :** a set of instructions for making something from various ingredients **2 :** a method of procedure **:** FORMULA

re·cip·i·ent \ri-'si-pē-ənt\ *n* **:** one that receives

¹**re·cip·ro·cal** \ri-'si-prə-kəl\ *adj* **1 :** inversely related **2 :** MUTUAL, SHARED **3 :** serving to reciprocate **4 :** mutually corresponding — **re·cip·ro·cal·ly** *adv*

²**reciprocal** *n* **1 :** something in a reciprocal relationship to another **2 :** one of a pair of numbers (as ²/₃ and ³/₂) whose product is one

re·cip·ro·cate \-ˌkāt\ *vb* **-cat·ed; -cat·ing 1 :** to move backward and forward alternately **2 :** to give and take mutually **3 :** to make a return for something done or given — **re·cip·ro·ca·tion** \-ˌsi-prə-'kā-shən\ *n*

rec·i·proc·i·ty \ˌre-sə-'prä-sə-tē\ *n, pl* **-ties 1 :** the quality or state of being reciprocal **2 :** mutual exchange of privileges (as trade advantages between countries)

re·cit·al \ri-'sīt-ᵊl\ *n* **1 :** an act or instance of reciting **:** ACCOUNT **2 :** a public reading or recitation ⟨a poetry ~⟩ **3 :** a concert given by a musician, dancer, or dance troupe **4 :** a public exhibition of skill given by music or dance pupils — **re·cit·al·ist** \-ᵊl-ist\ *n*

rec·i·ta·tion \ˌre-sə-'tā-shən\ *n* **1 :** RECITING, RECITAL **2 :** delivery before an audience usu. of something memorized ⟨~ of a speech⟩ **3 :** a classroom exercise in which pupils answer questions on a lesson they have studied

re·cite \ri-'sīt\ *vb* **re·cit·ed; re·cit·ing 1 :** to repeat verbatim (as something memorized) **2 ♦ :** to recount in some detail **:** RELATE **3 :** to reply to a teacher's questions on a lesson — **re·cit·er** *n*

    ♦ describe, narrate, recount, rehearse, relate, report, tell

reck·less \'re-kləs\ *adj* ♦ **:** lacking caution — **reck·less·ly** *adv* — **reck·less·ness** *n*

    ♦ brash, foolhardy, irresponsible **Ant** responsible

reck·on \'re-kən\ *vb* **1 ♦ :** to arrive at or estimate by calculation **:** CALCULATE **2 ♦ :** to regard or think of as **:** CONSIDER ⟨was ~ed as the leader⟩ **3** *chiefly dial* **:** THINK, SUPPOSE, GUESS **4 ♦ :** to accept something as certain **:** place reliance ⟨I ~ on your promise to help⟩

    ♦ [1] calculate, call, conjecture, estimate, figure, gauge, guess, judge, make, place, put, suppose ♦ [2] account, call, consider, count, esteem, hold, rate, regard, take ♦ [4] count, depend, lean, rely

reck·on·ing *n* **1 ♦ :** an act or instance of reckoning **2 :** a settling of accounts ⟨day of ~⟩

♦ appraisal, assessment, estimate, estimation, evaluation, valuation ♦ arithmetic, calculation, computation

re·claim \ri-ˈklām\ vb **1** ♦ : to correct or change from a pattern of wrong conduct : REFORM **2** : to change from an undesirable to a desired condition ⟨∼ marshy land⟩ **3** : to obtain from a waste product or by-product **4** ♦ : to demand or obtain the return of — **re·claim·able** adj

♦ [1] redeem, reform, rehabilitate ♦ [4] recapture, recoup, recover, regain, repossess, retake, retrieve

rec·la·ma·tion \ˌre-klə-ˈmā-shən\ n ♦ : the act or process of reclaiming

♦ recovery, repossession, retrieval

re·cline \ri-ˈklīn\ vb **re·clined; re·clin·ing 1** : to lean or incline backward **2** : to lie down : REST

re·clin·er \ri-ˈklī-nər\ n : a chair with an adjustable back and footrest

re·cluse \ˈre-ˌklüs, ri-ˈklüs\ n ♦ : a person who leads a secluded or solitary life : HERMIT — **re·clu·sive** \ri-ˈklü-siv\ adj

♦ anchorite, hermit, solitary

rec·og·nise chiefly Brit var of RECOGNIZE
rec·og·ni·tion \ˌre-kəg-ˈni-shən\ n **1** : the act of recognizing : the state of being recognized : ACKNOWLEDGMENT **2** : special notice or attention

re·cog·ni·zance \ri-ˈkä-nə-zəns\ n : a promise recorded before a court or magistrate to do something (as to appear in court or to keep the peace) usu. under penalty of a money forfeiture

rec·og·nize \ˈre-kəg-ˌnīz\ vb **-nized; -niz·ing 1** : to acknowledge (as a speaker in a meeting) as one entitled to be heard at the time **2** : to acknowledge the existence or the independence of (a country or government) **3** : to take notice of **4** : to acknowledge with appreciation **5** : to acknowledge acquaintance with **6** : to identify as previously known **7** : to perceive clearly : REALIZE — **rec·og·niz·able** \ˈre-kəg-ˌnī-zə-bəl\ adj — **rec·og·niz·ably** \-blē\ adv

¹**re·coil** \ri-ˈkȯi(-ə)l\ vb **1** ♦ : to draw back **2** : to spring back to or as if to a starting point

♦ blench, flinch, quail, shrink, wince

²**re·coil** \ˈrē-ˌkȯil, ri-ˈkȯil\ n : the action of recoiling (as by a gun or spring)

rec·ol·lect \ˌre-kə-ˈlekt\ vb ♦ : to recall to mind : REMEMBER

♦ recall, remember, reminisce, think

rec·ol·lec·tion \ˌre-kə-ˈlek-shən\ n **1** ♦ : the act or power of recollecting **2** : something recollected

♦ memory, recall, remembrance, reminiscence

re·com·bi·nant \(ˌ)rē-ˈkäm-bə-nənt\ adj **1** : relating to genetic recombination **2** : containing or produced by recombinant DNA ⟨∼ vaccines⟩

re·com·bi·nant DNA \(ˌ)rē-ˈkäm-bə-nənt-\ n : genetically engineered DNA prepared in vitro by joining together DNA usu. from more than one species of organism

re·com·bi·na·tion \ˌrē-ˌkäm-bə-ˈnā-shən\ n : the formation of new combinations of genes

rec·om·mend \ˌre-kə-ˈmend\ vb **1** : to present as deserving of acceptance or trial **2** : to give in charge : COMMIT **3** : to make acceptable **4** : to give advice to : ADVISE, COUNSEL — **rec·om·mend·able** \-ˈmen-də-bəl\ adj

rec·om·men·da·tion \ˌre-kə-mən-ˈdā-shən\ n **1** : the act of recommending **2** : something recommended **3** : something that recommends

¹**rec·om·pense** \ˈre-kəm-ˌpens\ vb **-pensed; -pens·ing 1** ♦ : to give compensation to : pay for ⟨were recompensed for their losses⟩ **2** ♦ : to return in kind : REQUITE

♦ [1] clear, discharge, foot, liquidate, pay, pay off, quit, settle, spring, stand ♦ [2] compensate, indemnify, recoup, remunerate, requite

²**recompense** n ♦ : an equivalent or a return for something done, suffered, or given : COMPENSATION

♦ compensation, damages, indemnity, payment, quittance, redress, remuneration, reparation, requital, restitution, satisfaction

re·con·ceive \ˌrē-kən-ˈsēv\ vb ♦ : to form again a conception of

♦ readdress, reanalyze, reconsider, reexamine, rethink, review

rec·on·cile \ˈre-kən-ˌsīl\ vb **-ciled; -cil·ing 1** ♦ : to cause to be friendly or harmonious again **2** : ADJUST, SETTLE ⟨∼ differences⟩ **3** : to bring to submission or acceptance — **rec·on·cil·able** adj — **rec·on·cile·ment** n — **rec·on·cil·er** n

♦ accommodate, conciliate, conform, coordinate, harmonize, key

rec·on·cil·i·a·tion \ˌre-kən-ˌsi-lē-ˈā-shən\ n **1** : the action of reconciling **2** : the Roman Catholic sacrament of penance

re·con·dite \ˈre-kən-ˌdīt\ adj **1** : hard to understand : PROFOUND, ABSTRUSE **2** : little known : OBSCURE

re·con·di·tion \ˌrē-kən-ˈdi-shən\ vb **1** ♦ : to restore to good condition (as by replacing parts) **2** : to condition anew

♦ doctor, fix, mend, patch, renovate, repair, revamp

re·con·nais·sance \ri-ˈkä-nə-zəns, -səns\ n : a preliminary survey of an area; esp : an exploratory military survey of enemy territory

re·con·noi·ter or **re·con·noi·tre** \ˌrē-kə-ˈnȯi-tər, ˌre-\ vb **-noitered** or **-noi·tred; -noi·ter·ing** or **-noi·tring** : to make a reconnaissance of : engage in reconnaissance

re·con·sid·er \ˌrē-kən-ˈsi-dər\ vb ♦ : to consider again with a view to changing or reversing ⟨∼ed the decision⟩

♦ readdress, reanalyze, reconceive, reexamine, rethink, review

re·con·sid·er·a·tion \-ˌsi-də-ˈrā-shən\ n : the action of reconsidering or state of being reconsidered

re·con·sti·tute \ˌrē-ˈkän-stə-ˌtüt, -ˌtyüt\ vb : to restore to a former condition by adding water ⟨∼ powdered milk⟩

re·con·struct \ˌrē-kən-ˈstrəkt\ vb : to construct again : REBUILD

re·con·struc·tion \ˌrē-kən-ˈstrək-shən\ n **1** : the action of reconstructing : the state of being reconstructed **2** often cap : the reorganization and reestablishment of the seceded states in the Union after the American Civil War **3** : something reconstructed

¹**re·cord** \ri-ˈkȯrd\ vb **1** ♦ : to set down in writing **2** : to register permanently **3** : INDICATE, READ **4** : to give evidence of **5** : to cause (as sound or visual images) to be registered (as on a disc or a magnetic tape) in a form that permits reproduction

♦ jot, log, mark, note, set down ♦ catalog, enroll, enter, index, inscribe, list, schedule, slate

²**rec·ord** \ˈre-kərd\ n **1** : the act of being recorded **2** ♦ : a written account of proceedings **3** : known facts about a person; also : a collection of items of information (as in a database) treated as a unit **4** : an attested top performance **5** : something on which sound or visual images have been recorded

♦ account, chronicle, history, narrative, report, story

³**re·cord** \ri-ˈkȯrd\ n : a function of an electronic device that causes it to record

re·cord·er \ri-ˈkȯr-dər\ n **1** : a judge in some city courts **2** : one who records transactions officially **3** : a recording device **4** : a wind instrument with a whistle mouthpiece and eight fingerholes

re·cord·ing n : RECORD 5
re·cord·ist \ri-ˈkȯr-dist\ n : one who records sound esp. on film
¹**re·count** \ri-ˈkau̇nt\ vb ♦ : to relate in detail : TELL

♦ describe, narrate, recite, rehearse, relate, report, tell

²**re·count** \ˈrē-ˌkau̇nt, (ˌ)rē-ˈkau̇nt\ vb : to count again
³**recount** n : a second or fresh count
re·coup \ri-ˈküp\ vb **1** ♦ : to get an equivalent or compensation for : make up for something lost ⟨∼ed their costs⟩ **2** ♦ : to gain anew : get again

♦ [1] compensate, indemnify, recompense, remunerate, requite
♦ [2] recapture, reclaim, recover, regain, repossess, retake, retrieve

re·course \ˈrē-ˌkȯrs, ri-ˈkȯrs\ n **1** : a turning to someone or something for assistance or protection **2** ♦ : a source of aid : RESORT

♦ expedient, resort, resource

re·cov·er \ri-ˈkə-vər\ vb **1** ♦ : to get back again : REGAIN **2** ♦ : to regain normal health, poise, or status **3** : to make up for : RECOUP ⟨∼ed all his losses⟩ **4** : RECLAIM ⟨∼ land from the sea⟩ **5** : to obtain a legal judgment in one's favor — **re·cov·er·able** adj

♦ [1] recapture, reclaim, recoup, regain, repossess, retake, retrieve ♦ [2] convalesce, gain, heal, mend, recuperate ♦ [2] rally, rebound, snap back

re–cov·er \ˌrē-ˈkə-vər\ vb : to cover again
recovering adj : being in the process of overcoming a shortcoming or problem ⟨a ∼ alcoholic⟩
re·cov·ery \ri-ˈkə-və-rē\ n **1** ♦ : the act, process, or an instance of recovering **2** ♦ : the process of combating a disorder (as alcoholism) or a real or perceived problem

♦ [1] reclamation, repossession, retrieval ♦ [2] comeback, convalescence, rally, recuperation, rehabilitation

¹rec·re·ant \'re-krē-ənt\ *adj* **1 ♦** : crying for mercy or yielding in a cowardly manner **2 ♦** : unfaithful to duty or allegiance

♦ [1] chicken, cowardly, craven, dastardly, pusillanimous, spineless, yellow ♦ [2] disloyal, faithless, false, fickle, inconstant, loose, perfidious, traitorous, treacherous, unfaithful, untrue

²recreant *n* **1** : a cowardly wretch : COWARD **2 ♦** : one who forsakes a duty, a cause, or anyone to whom he or she owes service : DESERTER **3 ♦** : one that is unfaithful

♦ [2] defector, deserter, renegade ♦ [3] apostate, betrayer, double-crosser, quisling, traitor, turncoat

rec·re·ate \'re-krē-,āt\ *vb* **-at·ed; -at·ing** **1 ♦** : to give new life or freshness to **2 ♦** : to take recreation ⟨*recreated* at the beach⟩ — **rec·re·ative** \-,ā-tiv\ *adj*

♦ [1] freshen, refresh, regenerate, rejuvenate, renew, restore, revitalize, revive ♦ [2] dally, disport, frolic, play, rollick, sport

re–cre·ate \,rē-krē-'āt\ *vb* : to create again — **re–cre·ation** \-'ā-shən\ *n* — **re–cre·ative** \-'ā-tiv\ *adj*

rec·re·ation \,re-krē-'ā-shən\ *n* : a refreshing of strength or spirits after work; *also* : a means of refreshment — **rec·re·ation·al** \-shə-nəl\ *adj*

recreational vehicle *n* ♦ : a vehicle designed for recreational use (as camping)

♦ camper, caravan, motor home, RV, trailer

re·crim·i·na·tion \ri-,kri-mə-'nā-shən\ *n* : a retaliatory accusation — **re·crim·i·nate** \-'kri-mə-,nāt\ *vb* — **re·crim·i·na·tory** \-'kri-mə-nə-,tōr-ē\ *adj*

re·cru·des·cence \,rē-krü-'des-⁰ns\ *n* : a renewal or breaking out again esp. of something unhealthful or dangerous

¹re·cruit \ri-'krüt\ *vb* **1** : to form or strengthen with new members ⟨~ an army⟩ **2** : to enlist as a member of an armed service **3** : to secure the services of **4** : to seek to enroll **5** : to restore or increase in health or vigor ⟨resting to ~ his strength⟩ — **re·cruit·er** *n* — **re·cruit·ment** *n*

²recruit *n* ♦ : a newcomer to an activity or field; *esp* : a newly enlisted member of the armed forces

♦ beginner, fledgling, freshman, greenhorn, neophyte, newcomer, novice, rookie, tenderfoot, tyro

rec·tal \'rekt-⁰l\ *adj* : of or relating to the rectum — **rec·tal·ly** *adv*

rect·an·gle \'rek-,taŋ-gəl\ *n* : a 4-sided figure with four right angles; *esp* : one with adjacent sides of unequal length — **rect·an·gu·lar** \rek-'taŋ-gyə-lər\ *adj*

rec·ti·fi·er \'rek-tə-,fī-ər\ *n* : one that rectifies; *esp* : a device for converting alternating current into direct current

rec·ti·fy \'rek-tə-,fī\ *vb* **-fied; -fy·ing** ♦ : to make or set right : CORRECT — **rec·ti·fi·ca·tion** \,rek-tə-fə-'kā-shən\ *n*

♦ amend, correct, debug, emend, reform, remedy

rec·ti·lin·ear \,rek-tə-'li-nē-ər\ *adj* **1** : moving in a straight line ⟨~ motion⟩ **2** : characterized by straight lines

rec·ti·tude \'rek-tə-,tüd, -,tyüd\ *n* **1 ♦** : moral integrity **2** : correctness of procedure

♦ character, decency, goodness, honesty, honor (*or* honour), integrity, morality, probity, righteousness, uprightness, virtue

rec·to \'rek-tō\ *n, pl* **rectos** : a right-hand page

rec·tor \'rek-tər\ *n* **1** : a priest or minister in charge of a parish **2** : the head of a university or school — **rec·to·ri·al** \rek-'tōr-ē-əl\ *adj*

rec·to·ry \'rek-tə-rē\ *n, pl* **-ries** : the residence of a rector or a parish priest

rec·tum \'rek-təm\ *n, pl* **rectums** *or* **rec·ta** \-tə\ : the last part of the intestine joining the colon and anus

re·cum·bent \ri-'kəm-bənt\ *adj* : lying down : RECLINING

re·cu·per·ate \ri-'kü-pə-,rāt-, -'kyü-\ *vb* **-at·ed; -at·ing** ♦ : to get back (as health or strength) : RECOVER — **re·cu·per·a·tive** \-'kü-pə-,rā-tiv, -'kyü-\ *adj*

♦ convalesce, gain, heal, mend, rally, recover, snap back

re·cu·per·a·tion \-,kü-pə-'rā-shən, -,kyü-\ *n* ♦ : restoration to health or strength

♦ comeback, convalescence, rally, recovery, rehabilitation

re·cur \ri-'kər\ *vb* **re·curred; re·cur·ring** **1** : to go or come back in thought or discussion **2** : to occur or appear again esp. after an interval : occur time after time — **re·cur·rence** \-'kər-əns\ *n*

re·cur·rent \-ənt\ *adj* ♦ : returning or happening time after time

♦ continual, intermittent, periodic

re·cur·ring \ri-'kə-riŋ\ *adj* : coming or happening again

re·cy·cle \rē-'sī-kəl\ *vb* **1** : to pass again through a cycle of changes or treatment **2** : to process (as liquid body waste, glass, or cans) in order to regain materials for human use — **re·cy·cla·ble** \-k(ə-)lə-bəl\ *adj or n* — **recycle** *n*

¹red \'red\ *adj* **red·der; red·dest** **1** : of the color red **2** : endorsing radical social or political change esp. by force **3** *often cap* : of or relating to the former U.S.S.R. or its allies **4** : tending to support Republican candidates ⟨~ states⟩ — **red·ly** *adv* — **red·ness** *n*

²red *n* **1** : the color of blood or of the ruby **2 ♦** : a revolutionary in politics **3** *cap* : COMMUNIST **4** : the condition of showing a loss ⟨in the ~⟩

♦ insurgent, insurrectionist, mutineer, rebel, revolter, revolutionary

re·dact \ri-'dakt\ *vb* **1** : to put in writing : FRAME ⟨~ed the proclamation⟩ **2** : EDIT **3** : to obscure or remove (text) from a document — **re·dac·tor** \-'dak-tər\ *n*

re·dac·tion \-'dak-shən\ *n* **1** : an act or instance of redacting **2** : EDITION

red alga *n* : any of a group of reddish usu. marine algae

red blood cell *n* : any of the hemoglobin-containing cells that carry oxygen from the lungs to the tissues and are responsible for the red color of vertebrate blood

red·breast \'red-,brest\ *n* : ROBIN

red–carpet *adj* : marked by ceremonial courtesy

red cedar *n* : an American juniper with scalelike leaves and fragrant close-grained red wood; *also* : its wood

red clover *n* : a European clover that has globe-shaped heads of reddish flowers and is widely cultivated for hay and forage

red·coat \'red-,kōt\ *n* : a British soldier esp. during the Revolutionary War

red·den \'red-⁰n\ *vb* ♦ : to make or become red or reddish

♦ bloom, blush, color (*or* colour), crimson, flush, glow

red·dish \'re-dish\ *adj* : tinged with red — **red·dish·ness** *n*

red dwarf *n* : a star with lower temperature and less mass than the sun

re·deem \ri-'dēm\ *vb* **1** : to recover (property) by discharging an obligation **2** : to ransom, free, or rescue by paying a price **3** : to free from the consequences of sin **4** : to remove the obligation of by payment ⟨the government ~s savings bonds⟩; *also* : to convert into something of value **5 ♦** : to make good (a promise) by performing : FULFILL **6 ♦** : to atone for **7 ♦** : to change for the better — **re·deem·able** *adj*

♦ [5] answer, comply, fill, fulfill, keep, meet, satisfy ♦ [7] reclaim, reform, rehabilitate

re·deem·er *n* ♦ : a person who redeems

♦ deliverer, rescuer, savior

re·demp·tion \ri-'demp-shən\ *n* : the act of redeeming : the state of being redeemed — **re·demp·tive** \-tiv\ *adj* — **re·demp·to·ry** \-tə-rē\ *adj*

re·de·ploy \,rē-di-'ploi\ *vb* **1** : to transfer from one area or activity to another **2** : to relocate personnel or equipment — **re·de·ploy·ment** *n*

red–eye \'red-,ī\ *n* **1** : cheap whiskey **2** : a late night or overnight flight

red·fish \'red-,fish\ *n* : any of various reddish marine fishes of the Atlantic including some used for food

red fox *n* : a fox with orange-red to reddish brown fur

red giant *n* : a very large star with a relatively low surface temperature

red–hand·ed \'red-'han-dəd\ *adv or adj* : in the act of committing a misdeed

red·head \-,hed\ *n* : a person having red hair — **red·head·ed** \-,he-dəd\ *adj*

red herring *n* : a diversion intended to distract attention from the real issue

red–hot \'red-'hät\ *adj* **1 ♦** : extremely hot; *esp* : glowing with heat **2 ♦** : exhibiting or marked by intense emotion, enthusiasm, or violence **3** : very new ⟨~ news⟩

♦ [1] broiling, burning, fiery, hot, scorching, sultry, torrid ♦ [2] ardent, burning, charged, emotional, fervent, fiery, hot-blooded, impassioned, passionate, vehement

re·dial \'rē-,dī-(-ə)l\ *n* : a telephone function that automatically repeats the dialing of the last number called — **redial** *vb*

re·dis·trib·ute \,rē-də-'stri-byüt\ *vb* **1** : to alter the distribution of **2** : to spread to other areas — **re·dis·tri·bu·tion** \(,)rē-,dis-trə-'byü-shən\ *n*

re·dis·trict \,rē-'dis-(,)trikt\ *vb* : to organize into new territorial and esp. political divisions

red–let·ter \'red-ˌle-tər\ adj : of special significance : MEMORA-BLE ⟨a ∼ day⟩

red–light district n : a district with many houses of prostitution

re·do \(ˌ)rē-'dü\ vb 1 ♦ : to do over or again 2 : to freshen or change a decorative scheme : REDECORATE

♦ alter, change, make over, modify, recast, refashion, remake, remodel, revamp, revise, rework, vary ♦ duplicate, reiterate, remake, repeat, replicate

red oak n : any of various No. American oaks with leaves usu. having spiny-tipped lobes and acorns that take two years to mature; also : the wood of a red oak

red·o·lence \'red-ᵊl- əns\ n 1 ♦ : the quality or state of being redolent 2 ♦ : an often pungent or agreeable odor

♦ [1] odor (or odour), scent, smell ♦ [2] aroma, bouquet, fragrance, incense, perfume, scent, spice

red·o·lent \'red-ᵊl-ənt\ adj 1 ♦ : exuding fragrance : FRA-GRANT 2 : having a specified fragrance ⟨a room ∼ of cooked cabbage⟩ 3 : REMINISCENT, SUGGESTIVE ⟨a tavern ∼ of colonial times⟩ — **red·o·lent·ly** adv

♦ ambrosial, aromatic, fragrant, savory, scented, sweet

re·dou·ble \(ˌ)rē-'də-bəl\ vb 1 ♦ : to make twice as great in size or amount 2 ♦ : to make intense or more intensive : INTENSIFY

♦ amplify, beef, boost, consolidate, deepen, enhance, heighten, intensify, magnify, step up, strengthen

re·doubt \ri-'daut\ n : a small usu. temporary fortification

re·doubt·able \ri-'dau-tə-bəl\ adj ♦ : arousing dread or fear : FORMIDABLE

♦ dire, dreadful, fearful, fearsome, forbidding, formidable, frightful, hair-raising, scary

re·dound \ri-'daund\ vb 1 : to have an effect 2 : to become added or transferred : ACCRUE

red pepper n 1 : CAYENNE PEPPER 2 : a mature red hot pepper or sweet pepper

re·draft \rē-'draft\ vb ♦ : to prepare a revised copy or a new version of

♦ edit, revamp, revise, rework

¹**re·dress** \ri-'dres\ vb 1 : to set right : REMEDY 2 : COMPEN-SATE 3 : to remove the cause of (a grievance) 4 : AVENGE

²**redress** n 1 : relief from distress 2 : means or possibility of seeking a remedy 3 ♦ : compensation for loss or injury 4 : an act or instance of redressing

♦ compensation, damages, indemnity, quittance, recompense, remuneration, reparation, requital, restitution, satisfaction

red·shift \'red-ˌshift\ n : displacement of the spectrum of a celestial body toward longer wavelengths; also : a measure of this displacement

red snapper n : any of various reddish fishes including several food fishes

red spider n : SPIDER MITE

red squirrel n : a common American squirrel with the upper parts chiefly red

red–tailed hawk \'red-ˌtāld-\ n : a rodent-eating No. American hawk with a rather short typically reddish tail

red tape n : official routine or procedure marked by excessive complexity which results in delay or inaction

red tide n : seawater discolored by the presence of large numbers of dinoflagellates which produce a toxin that renders infected shellfish poisonous

re·duce \ri-'düs, -'dyüs\ vb **re·duced; re·duc·ing** 1 ♦ : to diminish in size, amount, extent, or number : LESSEN 2 : to bring to a specified state or condition ⟨reduced them to tears⟩ 3 ♦ : to put in a lower rank or grade 4 : CONQUER ⟨∼ a fort⟩ 5 : to bring into a certain order or classification 6 : to correct (as a fracture) by restoration of displaced parts 7 : to lessen one's weight — **re·duc·er** n — **re·duc·ible** \-'dü-sə-bəl, -'dyü-\ adj

♦ [1] abate, decrease, de-escalate, diminish, downsize, lessen, lower ♦ [3] break, bust, degrade, demote, downgrade

re·duc·tion \ri-'dək-shən\ n 1 ♦ : the act of reducing : the state of being reduced 2 : something made by reducing 3 ♦ : the amount taken off in reducing something

♦ [1, 3] abatement, decline, decrease, decrement, diminution, drop, fall, loss, shrinkage ♦ [3] abatement, deduction, discount

re·dun·dan·cy \ri-'dən-dən-sē\ n, pl **-cies** 1 : the quality or state of being redundant : SUPERFLUITY 2 : something redundant or in excess 3 ♦ : the use of surplus words

♦ circumlocution, prolixity, verbiage, wordiness

re·dun·dant \-dənt\ adj ♦ : exceeding what is needed or normal : SUPERFLUOUS; esp : using more words than necessary — **re·dun·dant·ly** adv

♦ excess, extra, spare, superfluous, supernumerary, surplus

red–winged blackbird \'red-ˌwiŋd-\ n : a No. American blackbird of which the adult male is black with a patch of bright scarlet on the wings

red·wood \'red-ˌwud\ n : a tall coniferous timber tree esp. of coastal California; also : its durable wood

re·echo \rē-'e-kō\ vb ♦ : to continue to resound with echoes

♦ echo, resonate, resound, reverberate, sound

reed \'rēd\ n 1 : any of various tall slender grasses of wet areas; also : a stem or growth of reed 2 : a musical instrument made from the hollow stem of a reed 3 : an elastic tongue of cane, wood, or metal by which tones are produced in organ pipes and certain other wind instruments — **reedy** adj

re·ed·u·cate \(ˌ)rē-'e-jə-ˌkāt\ vb : to train again; esp : to rehabilitate through education — **re·ed·u·ca·tion** n

¹**reef** \'rēf\ n 1 : a part of a sail taken in or let out in regulating the sail's size 2 : reduction in sail area by reefing

²**reef** vb : to reduce the area of a sail by rolling or folding part of it

³**reef** n : a ridge of rocks, sand or coral at or near the surface of the water

reef·er \'rē-fər\ n : a marijuana cigarette

¹**reek** \'rēk\ n 1 : a strong or disagreeable fume or odor 2 : a murky condition of the atmosphere or a substance causing it

²**reek** vb 1 : to give off or become permeated with a strong or offensive odor 2 : to give a strong impression of some constituent quality ⟨an excuse that ∼ed of falsehood⟩ — **reek·er** n

reeky \'rē-kē\ adj ♦ : emitting or permeated with a reek

♦ fetid, foul, fusty, malodorous, musty, noisome, rank, smelly, strong

¹**reel** \'rēl\ n : a revolvable device on which something flexible (as film or tape) is wound; also : a quantity of something wound on such a device

²**reel** vb 1 : to wind on or as if on a reel 2 : to pull or draw (as a fish) by reeling a line — **reel·able** adj — **reel·er** n

³**reel** vb 1 ♦ : to be in a whirl : WHIRL; also : to be giddy 2 : to waver or fall back (as from a blow) 3 ♦ : to walk or move unsteadily

♦ [1] spin, swim, whirl ♦ [3] careen, dodder, lurch, stagger, teeter, totter

⁴**reel** n ♦ : a reeling motion

♦ gyration, pirouette, revolution, roll, rotation, spin, twirl, wheel, whirl

⁵**reel** n : a lively Scottish dance or its music

reel off vb ♦ : to tell or recite rapidly and easily ⟨reeled off the right answers⟩

♦ detail, enumerate, itemize, list, numerate, recite, rehearse, tick (off)

re·en·try \rē-'en-trē\ n 1 : a second or new entry 2 : the action of reentering the earth's atmosphere from space

re·eval·u·ate \rē-i-'val-yü-ˌwāt\ vb : to determine again the significance, worth, or condition of usu. by careful appraisal and study

reeve \'rēv\ vb **rove** \'rōv\ or **reeved; reev·ing** : to pass (as a rope) through a hole in a block or cleat

re·ex·am·i·na·tion \rē-ig-ˌza-mə-'nā-shən\ n ♦ : a second or new examination

♦ reappraisal, retrospection, review

re·ex·am·ine \-ig-'za-mən\ vb ♦ : to subject to reexamination

♦ readdress, reanalyze, reconceive, reconsider, rethink, review

¹**ref** \'ref\ n : REFEREE 2

²**ref** abbr 1 reference 2 referred 3 reformed 4 refunding

re·fash·ion \rē-'fa-shən\ vb ♦ : to make again : make over

♦ alter, change, make over, modify, recast, redo, remake, remodel, revamp, revise, rework, vary

re·fec·tion \ri-'fek-shən\ n 1 : refreshment esp. after hunger or fatigue 2 : food and drink together : REPAST

re·fec·to·ry \ri-'fek-tə-rē\ n, pl **-ries** : a dining hall (as in a monastery or college)

re·fer \ri-'fər\ vb **re·ferred; re·fer·ring** 1 : to assign to a certain source, cause, or relationship 2 : to direct or send to some person or place (as for information or help) 3 : to submit to someone else for consideration or action 4 ♦ : to have recourse (as for information or aid) 5 ♦ : to have connection : RELATE 6

♦ : to direct attention to or speak of : MENTION — **re·fer·able** \'re-fə-rə-bəl, ri-'fər-ə-\ *adj*

♦ *usu* **refer to** [4] go, resort, turn ♦ [5] appertain, apply, bear, pertain, relate ♦ *usu* **refer to** [6] advert (to), cite, instance, mention, name, note, notice, quote, specify, touch (*on* or *upon*)

[1]**ref·er·ee** \,re-fə-'rē\ *n* **1** ♦ : a person to whom an issue esp. in law is referred for investigation or settlement **2** : an umpire in certain games

♦ arbiter, arbitrator, judge, umpire

[2]**referee** *vb* **-eed; -ee·ing** ♦ : to act as referee

♦ adjudicate, arbitrate, decide, determine, judge, rule, settle, umpire

ref·er·ence \'re-frəns, -fə-rəns\ *n* **1** : the act of referring **2** : RELATION, RESPECT **3** : ALLUSION, MENTION **4** : something that refers a reader to another passage or book **5** : consultation esp. for obtaining information ⟨books for ∼⟩ **6** : a person of whom inquiries as to character or ability can be made **7** : a written recommendation of a person for employment

ref·er·en·dum \,re-fə-'ren-dəm\ *n, pl* **-da** \-də\ *or* **-dums** : the submitting of legislative measures to the voters for approval or rejection; *also* : a vote on a measure so submitted

ref·er·ent \'re-frənt, -fə-rənt\ *n* : one that refers or is referred to; *esp* : the thing a word stands for — **referent** *adj*

re·fer·ral \ri-'fər-əl\ *n* **1** : the act or an instance of referring **2** : one that is referred

[1]**re·fill** \,rē-'fil\ *vb* : to fill again : REPLENISH — **re·fill·able** *adj*

[2]**re·fill** \'rē-,fil\ *n* : a new or fresh supply of something

re·fi·nance \,rē-fə-'nans, (,)rē-'fī-nans\ *vb* : to renew or reorganize the financing of

re·fine \ri-'fīn\ *vb* **re·fined; re·fin·ing** **1** : to free from impurities or waste matter **2** ♦ : to improve or perfect by pruning or polishing : IMPROVE **3** : to free or become free of what is coarse or uncouth **4** : to make improvements by introducing subtle changes — **re·fin·er** *n*

♦ ameliorate, amend, better, enhance, enrich, improve, perfect

re·fined \ri-'fīnd\ *adj* **1** ♦ : freed from impurities **2** ♦ : reflecting a meticulous, sensitive, or demanding attitude **3** ♦ : marked by subtlety of discrimination or precision of method or technique : SUBTLE

♦ [1] absolute, fine, neat, plain, pure, straight, unadulterated, undiluted, unmixed ♦ [2] civilized, cultivated, cultured, genteel, polished ♦ [3] delicate, exact, fine, minute, nice, subtle

re·fine·ment \ri-'fīn-mənt\ *n* **1** : the action of refining **2** ♦ : the quality or state of being refined **3** : a refined feature or method **4** ♦ : something intended to improve or perfect

♦ [2] civilization, cultivation, culture, polish ♦ [4] advance, advancement, breakthrough, enhancement, improvement

re·fin·ery \ri-'fī-nə-rē\ *n, pl* **-er·ies** : a building and equipment for refining metals, oil, or sugar

re·flect \ri-'flekt\ *vb* **1** : to bend or cast back (as light, heat, or sound) **2** : to give back a likeness or image of as a mirror does **3** : to bring as a result ⟨∼ed credit on him⟩ **4** : to cast reproach or blame ⟨their bad conduct ∼ed on their training⟩ **5** : PONDER, MEDITATE — **re·flec·tiv·i·ty** \(,)rē-,flek-'ti-və-tē\ *n*

re·flec·tion \-'flek-shən\ *n* ♦ : a thought, idea, or opinion formed or a remark made as a result of meditation

♦ comment, note, observation, remark

re·flec·tive \-tiv\ *adj* ♦ : marked by reflection

♦ contemplative, meditative, melancholy, pensive, ruminant, thoughtful

re·flec·tor \ri-'flek-tər\ *n* : one that reflects; *esp* : a polished surface for reflecting radiation (as light)

[1]**re·flex** \'rē-,fleks\ *n* **1** : an automatic and usu. inborn response to a stimulus not involving higher mental centers **2** *pl* : the power of acting or responding with enough speed ⟨an athlete with great ∼es⟩

[2]**reflex** *adj* **1** : bent or directed back **2** : of, relating to, or produced by a reflex — **re·flex·ly** *adv*

[1]**re·flex·ive** \ri-'flek-siv\ *adj* : of or relating to an action directed back upon the doer or the grammatical subject ⟨a ∼ verb⟩ ⟨the ∼ pronoun *himself*⟩ — **re·flex·ive·ly** *adv* — **re·flex·ive·ness** *n*

[2]**reflexive** *n* : a reflexive verb or pronoun

re·flex·ol·o·gy \,rē-,flek-'sä-lə-jē\ *n* : massage in which pressure is applied to specific points on the hands and feet

re·flux \'rē-,fləks\ *n* : a flowing back

re·fo·cus \(,)rē-'fō-kəs\ *vb* **1** : to focus again **2** : to change the emphasis or direction of ⟨∼ed her life⟩

re·for·es·ta·tion \,rē-,fȯr-ə-'stā-shən\ *n* : the action of renewing forest cover by planting seeds or young trees — **re·for·est** \rē-'fȯr-əst\ *vb*

[1]**re·form** \ri-'fȯrm\ *vb* **1** ♦ : to make better or improve by removal of faults **2** ♦ : to correct or improve one's own character or habits — **re·form·able** *adj*

♦ [1] amend, correct, debug, emend, rectify, remedy ♦ [2] reclaim, redeem, rehabilitate

[2]**reform** *n* : improvement or correction of what is corrupt or defective

re–form \rē-'fȯrm\ *vb* : to form again

ref·or·ma·tion \,re-fər-'mā-shən\ *n* **1** : the act of reforming : the state of being reformed **2** *cap* : a 16th-century religious movement marked by the establishment of the Protestant churches

re·for·ma·tive \-'fȯr-mə-tiv\ *adj* ♦ : intended or tending to reform

♦ corrective, remedial

[1]**re·for·ma·to·ry** \ri-'fȯr-mə-,tōr-ē\ *adj* : aiming at or tending toward reformation : REFORMATIVE

[2]**reformatory** *n, pl* **-ries** : a penal institution for reforming esp. young or first offenders

re·form·er \ri-'fȯr-mər\ *n* **1** : one that works for or urges reform **2** *cap* : a leader of the Protestant Reformation

refr *abbr* refraction

re·fract \ri-'frakt\ *vb* : to subject to refraction

re·frac·tion \-'frak-shən\ *n* : the bending of a ray (as of light) when it passes obliquely from one medium into another in which its speed is different — **re·frac·tive** \-tiv\ *adj*

refractive index *n* : the ratio of the speed of radiation in one medium to that in another medium

re·frac·to·ri·ness \ri-'frak-tə-rē-nəs\ *n* ♦ : the quality or state of being refractory

♦ defiance, disobedience, insubordination, rebelliousness, recalcitrance, unruliness

re·frac·to·ry \ri-'frak-tə-rē\ *adj* **1** ♦ : resisting control or authority **2** : capable of enduring high temperature ⟨∼ bricks⟩ — **refractory** *n*

♦ contrary, defiant, disobedient, froward, headstrong, intractable, rebellious, recalcitrant, unruly, untoward, wayward, willful

[1]**re·frain** \ri-'frān\ *vb* ♦ : to hold oneself back : FORBEAR ⟨∼ from interfering⟩ — **re·frain·ment** *n*

♦ *usu* **refrain from** abstain (from), forbear, forgo, keep

[2]**refrain** *n* : a phrase or verse recurring regularly in a poem or song

re·fresh \ri-'fresh\ *vb* **1** ♦ : to make or become fresh or fresher **2** ♦ : to revive by or as if by renewal of supplies ⟨∼ one's memory⟩ **3** ♦ : to freshen up : restore to a state of newness or vitality **4** : to supply or take refreshment — **re·fresh·er** *n* — **re·fresh·ing·ly** *adv*

♦ [1, 2, 3] freshen, recreate, regenerate, rejuvenate, renew, restore, revitalize, revive

re·fresh·ing *adj* ♦ : serving to refresh

♦ bracing, invigorating, restorative, stimulative, tonic

re·fresh·ment \-mənt\ *n* **1** : the act of refreshing : the state of being refreshed **2** : something that refreshes **3** *pl* : a light meal; *also* : assorted light foods

re·fried beans \,rē-,frīd-\ *n pl* : beans cooked with seasonings, fried, then mashed and fried again

refrig *abbr* refrigerating; refrigeration

re·frig·er·ate \ri-'fri-jə-,rāt\ *vb* **-at·ed; -at·ing** : to make cool; *esp* : to chill or freeze (food) for preservation — **re·frig·er·ant** \-jə-rənt\ *adj or n* — **re·frig·er·a·tion** \-,fri-jə-'rā-shən\ *n* — **re·frig·er·a·tor** \-'fri-jə-,rā-tər\ *n*

ref·uge \'re-,fyüj\ *n* **1** ♦ : shelter or protection from danger or distress **2** ♦ : a place that provides protection

♦ [1, 2] asylum, haven, retreat, sanctuary, shelter

ref·u·gee \,re-fyu̇-'jē\ *n* ♦ : one who flees for safety esp. to a foreign country

♦ émigré, evacuee, exile, expatriate

re·ful·gence \ri-'fu̇l-jəns, -'fəl-\ *n* ♦ : a radiant or resplendent quality or state

♦ brilliance, dazzle, effulgence, illumination, lightness, lucidity, luminosity, radiance, splendor

re·ful·gent \-jənt\ *adj* ♦ : giving out a bright light : richly radiant

♦ beaming, bright, brilliant, effulgent, glowing, incandescent, lambent, lucent, lucid, luminous, lustrous, radiant, shiny

¹re•fund \ri-ˌfənd, ˈrē-ˌfənd\ vb : to give or put back (money) : REPAY — **re•fund•able** adj

²re•fund \ˈrē-ˌfənd\ n **1** : the act of refunding **2** : a sum refunded

re•fur•bish \ri-ˈfər-bish\ vb : to brighten or freshen up : RENOVATE

re•fus•al \ri-ˈfyü-zəl\ n ♦ : the act of refusing or denying

♦ denial, disallowance, nay, no, rejection

¹re•fuse \ri-ˈfyüz\ vb **re•fused; re•fus•ing 1** ♦ : to decline to accept : REJECT **2** ♦ : to decline to do, give, or grant

♦ [1] decline, disallow, disapprove, negative, reject, repudiate, spurn, turn down ♦ [2] decline, deny, disallow, reject, withhold

²ref•use \ˈre-ˌfyüs, -ˌfyüz\ n ♦ : rejected or worthless matter : RUBBISH, TRASH

♦ chaff, deadwood, dust, garbage, junk, litter, riffraff, rubbish, scrap, trash, waste

ref•u•ta•tion \ˌre-fyu̇-ˈtā-shən\ n ♦ : the act or process of refuting; also : proof of falsehood or error

♦ confutation, rebuttal

re•fute \ri-ˈfyüt\ vb **re•fut•ed; re•fut•ing** ♦ : to prove to be false by argument or evidence — **re•fut•er** n

♦ belie, confute, disprove, rebut

¹reg \ˈreg\ n : REGULATION

²reg abbr **1** region **2** register; registered; registration **3** regular

re•gain \rē-ˈgān\ vb ♦ : to acquire or get possession of again

♦ recapture, reclaim, recoup, recover, repossess, retake, retrieve

re•gal \ˈrē-gəl\ adj **1** ♦ : of, relating to, or befitting a king : ROYAL **2** ♦ : of notable excellence or magnificence : STATELY, SPLENDID — **re•gal•ly** adv

♦ [1] kingly, monarchical, royal ♦ [2] august, baronial, gallant, glorious, grand, grandiose, heroic, imposing, magnificent, majestic, monumental, noble, proud, royal, splendid, stately

re•gale \ri-ˈgāl\ vb **re•galed; re•gal•ing 1** ♦ : to entertain richly or agreeably esp. with fine food and drink **2** ♦ : to give pleasure or amusement to

♦ [1] banquet, dine, feast, junket ♦ [2] amuse, disport, divert, entertain

re•ga•lia \ri-ˈgāl-yə\ n pl **1** : the emblems, symbols, or paraphernalia of royalty (as the crown and scepter) **2** : the insignia of an office or order **3** ♦ : special costume : FINERY

♦ array, best, bravery, caparison, feather, finery, frippery, full dress, gaiety

¹re•gard \ri-ˈgärd\ n **1** : CONSIDERATION, HEED; also : CARE, CONCERN **2** ♦ : a quick or cursory look : GLANCE, LOOK **3** ♦ : a feeling of respect and affection : RESPECT, ESTEEM **4** pl ♦ : friendly greetings implying respect and esteem **5** : an aspect to be considered : PARTICULAR — **re•gard•less** adj

♦ [2] cast, eye, gander, glance, glimpse, look, peek, peep, sight, view ♦ [3] admiration, appreciation, esteem, estimation, favor (or favour), respect ♦ **regards** [4] compliments, greetings, respects

²regard vb **1** ♦ : to think of : CONSIDER **2** : to pay attention to **3** ♦ : to show respect for : HEED ⟨~ our elders⟩ **4** ♦ : to hold in high esteem : care for **5** : to look at : gaze upon **6** archaic : to relate to

♦ [1] account, call, consider, count, esteem, hold, rate, reckon, take ♦ [3] follow, heed, listen, mind, note, observe, watch ♦ [4] admire, appreciate, esteem, respect

re•gard•ful adj ♦ : full or expressive of regard or respect

♦ deferential, dutiful, respectful

re•gard•ing prep ♦ : with respect to : CONCERNING

♦ about, apropos of, concerning, of, on, respecting, toward

regardless of \ri-ˈgärd-ləs-\ prep ♦ : in spite of

♦ despite, notwithstanding, with

re•gat•ta \ri-ˈgä-tə, -ˈga-\ n : a boat race or a series of boat races

re•gen•cy \ˈrē-jən-sē\ n, pl **-cies 1** : the office or government of a regent or body of regents **2** : a body of regents **3** : the period during which a regent governs

re•gen•er•a•cy \ri-ˈje-nə-rə-sē\ n : the state of being regenerated

¹re•gen•er•ate \ri-ˈje-nə-rət\ adj **1** : formed or created again **2** : spiritually reborn or converted

²re•gen•er•ate \ri-ˈje-nə-ˌrāt\ vb **1** : to subject to spiritual renewal **2** : to reform completely **3** : to replace (a body part) by a new growth of tissue **4** ♦ : to give new life to : REVIVE **5** ♦ : to restore to original strength or properties — **re•gen•er•a•tive** \-ˈje-nə-ˌrā-tiv\ adj — **re•gen•er•a•tor** \-ˌrā-tər\ n

♦ [4] reanimate, reinvigorate, rejuvenate, renew, resuscitate, revitalize, revive ♦ [5] freshen, recreate, refresh, renew, restore

re•gen•er•a•tion \-ˌje-nə-ˈrā-shən\ n ♦ : an act or the process of regenerating

♦ rebirth, rejuvenation, renewal, resurgence, resurrection, resuscitation, revival

re•gent \ˈrē-jənt\ n **1** : a person who rules during the childhood, absence, or incapacity of the sovereign **2** : a member of a governing board (as of a state university) — **regent** adj

reg•gae \ˈre-ˌgā\ n : popular music of Jamaican origin that combines native styles with elements of rock and soul music

reg•i•cide \ˈre-jə-ˌsīd\ n **1** : one who murders a king **2** : murder of a king

re•gift \(ˌ)rē-ˈgift\ vb : to give a previously received gift to someone else

re•gime also **ré•gime** \rā-ˈzhēm, ri-\ n **1** : REGIMEN **2** : a form or system of government **3** ♦ : a government in power; also : a period of rule

♦ administration, authority, government, jurisdiction, rule

reg•i•men \ˈre-jə-mən\ n **1** : a systematic course of treatment or training ⟨a strict dietary ~⟩ **2** : the continuous exercise of authority over and the performance of functions for a political unit : GOVERNMENT

¹reg•i•ment \ˈre-jə-mənt\ n : a military unit consisting usu. of a number of battalions — **reg•i•men•tal** \ˌre-jə-ˈment-təl\ adj

²reg•i•ment \ˈre-jə-ˌment\ vb : to organize rigidly so as to regulate or control; also : to subject to order or uniformity — **reg•i•men•ta•tion** \ˌre-jə-mən-ˈtā-shən\ n

reg•i•men•tals \ˌre-jə-ˈmen-təlz\ n pl **1** : a regimental uniform **2** : military dress

re•gion \ˈrē-jən\ n ♦ : an often indefinitely defined part or area

♦ area, demesne, field, zone ♦ belt, land, tract, zone

re•gion•al \ˈrē-jə-nəl\ adj **1** : affecting a particular region : LOCALIZED **2** : of, relating to, characteristic of, or serving a region — **re•gion•al•ly** adv

¹reg•is•ter \ˈre-jə-stər\ n **1** ♦ : a record of items or details; also : a book or system for keeping such a record **2** : the range of a voice or instrument **3** : a device to regulate ventilation or heating **4** : an automatic device recording a number or quantity **5** : CASH REGISTER

♦ catalog, checklist, list, listing, menu, registry, roll, roster, schedule, table

²register vb **-tered; -ter•ing 1** ♦ : to enter in a register (as in a list of guests) **2** : to record automatically **3** : to secure special care for (mail matter) by paying additional postage **4** : to convey an impression of : EXPRESS **5** : to make or adjust so as to correspond exactly **6** ♦ : to make a record of

♦ [1] catalog, enroll, enter, index, inscribe, list, put down, record, schedule, slate ♦ [6] jot, log, mark, note, put down, record, set down

³register n : one who registers or records

registered nurse n : a graduate trained nurse who has been licensed to practice by a state authority after passing qualifying examinations

reg•is•trant \ˈre-jə-strənt\ n : one that registers or is registered

reg•is•trar \-ˌsträr\ n ♦ : an official recorder or keeper of records (as at an educational institution)

♦ clerk, register, scribe

reg•is•tra•tion \ˌre-jə-ˈstrā-shən\ n **1** : the act of registering **2** : an entry in a register **3** : the number of persons registered : ENROLLMENT **4** : a document certifying an act of registering

reg•is•try \ˈre-jə-strē\ n, pl **-tries 1** : ENROLLMENT, REGISTRATION **2** : a place of registration **3** ♦ : an official record book or an entry in one

♦ catalog, checklist, list, listing, menu, register, roll, roster, schedule, table

reg•nant \ˈreg-nənt\ adj **1** : REIGNING **2** : DOMINANT **3** : of common or widespread occurrence

¹re•gress \ˈrē-ˌgres\ n **1** : an act or the privilege of going or coming back **2** : RETROGRESSION

²re•gress \ri-ˈgres\ vb : to go or cause to go back or to a lower level — **re•gres•sive** adj — **re•gres•sor** \-ˈgre-sər\ n

re•gres•sion \ri-ˈgre-shən\ n : the act or an instance of regressing; esp : reversion to an earlier mental or behavioral level

¹re•gret \ri-ˈgret\ *vb* **re•gret•ted; re•gret•ting 1 :** to mourn the loss or death of **2 ♦ :** to be very sorry for **3 :** to experience regret — **re•gret•ter** *n*

♦ bemoan, deplore, lament, repent, rue

²regret *n* **1 ♦ :** sorrow caused by something beyond one's power to remedy **2 :** an expression of sorrow **3** *pl* **:** a note politely declining an invitation

♦ contrition, penitence, remorse, repentance, rue

re•gret•ful \-fəl\ *adj* **♦ :** full of regret

♦ apologetic, contrite, penitent, remorseful, repentant, rueful, sorry

re•gret•ful•ly *adv* **:** with regret

re•gret•ta•ble \-ˈgre-tə-bəl\ *adj* **♦ :** deserving regret

♦ deplorable, distressful, grievous, heartbreaking, lamentable, unfortunate, woeful

re•gret•ta•bly \-ˈgre-tə-blē\ *adv* **1 :** to a regrettable extent **2 :** it is to be regretted

re•group \(ˌ)rē-ˈgrüp\ *vb* **:** to form into a new grouping

regt *abbr* regiment

¹reg•u•lar \ˈre-gyə-lər\ *adj* **1 :** belonging to a religious order **2 ♦ :** made, built, or arranged according to a rule, standard, or type; *also* **:** even or symmetrical in form or structure **3 a :** ORDERLY, METHODICAL ⟨~ habits⟩ **b ♦ :** recurring, attending, or functioning at fixed, uniform, or normal intervals **:** not varying ⟨a ~ pace⟩ **4 :** made, selected, or conducted according to rule or custom **5 :** properly qualified ⟨not a ~ lawyer⟩ **6 :** conforming to the normal or usual manner of inflection **7 :** of, relating to, or constituting the permanent standing military force of a state **8 :** having no restriction, exception, or qualification **9 ♦ :** conforming to a type, standard, or regular pattern — **reg•u•lar•i•ty** \ˌre-gyə-ˈlar-ə-tē\ *n* — **reg•u•lar•ly** *adv*

♦ [2] methodical, orderly, systematic ♦ [3b] constant, frequent, habitual, periodic, repeated, steady *Ant* inconstant, infrequent, irregular ♦ [9] average, characteristic, normal, representative, standard, typical

²regular *n* **1 :** one that is regular (as in attendance) **2 :** a member of the regular clergy **3 :** a soldier in a regular army **4 :** a player on an athletic team who is usu. in the starting lineup

reg•u•lar•ize \ˈre-gyə-lə-ˌrīz\ *vb* **♦ :** to make regular by conformance to law, rules, or custom

♦ formalize, homogenize, normalize, standardize

reg•u•late \ˈre-gyə-ˌlāt\ *vb* **-lat•ed; -lat•ing 1 ♦ :** to govern or direct according to rule **:** CONTROL **2 :** to bring under the control of law or authority **3 :** to put in good order **4 :** to fix or adjust the time, amount, degree, or rate of — **reg•u•la•tive** \-ˌlā-tiv\ *adj* — **reg•u•la•tor** \-ˌlā-tər\ *n* — **reg•u•la•to•ry** \-lə-ˌtȯr-ē\ *adj*

♦ administer, carry on, conduct, control, direct, govern, guide, handle, manage, operate, oversee, run, superintend, supervise

reg•u•la•tion \ˌre-gyə-ˈlā-shən\ *n* **1 ♦ :** the act of regulating **:** the state of being regulated **2 :** a rule dealing with details of procedure **3 :** an order issued by an executive authority of a government and having the force of law

♦ administration, conduct, control, direction, government, guidance, management, operation, oversight, running, superintendence, supervision

re•gur•gi•tate \rē-ˈgər-jə-ˌtāt\ *vb* **-tat•ed; -tat•ing :** to throw or be thrown back, up, or out ⟨~ food⟩ — **re•gur•gi•ta•tion** \-ˌgər-jə-ˈtā-shən\ *n*

re•hab \ˈrē-ˌhab\ *n* **1 :** REHABILITATION **2 :** a rehabilitated building — **rehab** *vb*

re•ha•bil•i•tate \ˌrē-hə-ˈbi-lə-ˌtāt, ˌrē-ə-\ *vb* **-tat•ed; -tat•ing 1 :** to restore to a former capacity, rank, or right **:** REINSTATE **2 ♦ :** to restore to good condition or health — **re•ha•bil•i•ta•tive** \-ˌtā-tiv\ *adj*

♦ cure, heal, mend

re•ha•bil•i•ta•tion \-ˌbi-lə-ˈtā-shən\ *n* **♦ :** the action or process of rehabilitating or of being rehabilitated

♦ comeback, convalescence, rally, recovery, recuperation

re•hash \ˌrē-ˈhash\ *vb* **:** to present again in another form without real change or improvement — **rehash** *n*

re•hear•ing \ˌrē-ˈhir-iŋ\ *n* **:** a second or new hearing by the same tribunal

re•hears•al \ri-ˈhər-səl\ *n* **1 :** something told again **:** RECITAL **2 ♦ :** a private performance or practice session preparatory to a public appearance

♦ dry run, practice, trial

re•hearse \ri-ˈhərs\ *vb* **re•hearsed; re•hears•ing 1 :** to say again **:** REPEAT **2 a ♦ :** to recount in order **:** ENUMERATE **b ♦ :** to present an account of **:** RELATE **3 :** to give a rehearsal of **4 :** to train by rehearsal **5 :** to engage in a rehearsal — **re•hears•er** *n*

♦ [2a] detail, enumerate, itemize, list, numerate, tick (off) ♦ [2b] describe, narrate, recite, recount, relate, report, tell

re•heat \ˌrē-ˈhēt\ *vb* **:** to heat again

¹reign \ˈrān\ *n* **1 :** the authority or rule of a sovereign **2 :** the time during which a sovereign rules

²reign *vb* **1 :** to rule as a sovereign **2 :** to be predominant or prevalent

re•im•burse \ˌrē-əm-ˈbərs\ *vb* **-bursed; -burs•ing :** to pay back **:** make restitution — **re•im•burs•able** *adj* — **re•im•burse•ment** *n*

¹rein \ˈrān\ *n* **1 :** a strap fastened to a bit by which a rider or driver controls an animal **2 :** a restraining influence **:** CHECK **3 ♦ :** controlling or guiding power **4 :** complete freedom — usu. used in the phrase *give rein to*

♦ chair, head, headship, helm

²rein *vb* **♦ :** to check or direct by reins

♦ *usu* **rein in** bridle, check, constrain, contain, control, curb, govern, inhibit, regulate, restrain, tame

re•in•car•na•tion \ˌrē-(ˌ)in-(ˌ)kär-ˈnā-shən\ *n* **:** rebirth of the soul in a new body — **re•in•car•nate** \ˌrē-in-ˈkär-ˌnāt\ *vb*

rein•deer \ˈrān-ˌdir\ *n* **:** CARIBOU — used esp. for one of the Old World

reindeer moss *n* **:** a gray, erect, tufted, and much-branched edible lichen of northern regions that is an important food of reindeer

re•in•fec•tion \ˌrē-in-ˈfek-shən\ *n* **:** infection following another infection of the same type

re•in•force \ˌrē-ən-ˈfȯrs\ *vb* **1 :** to strengthen with additional forces ⟨~ our troops⟩ **2 :** to strengthen with new force, aid, material, or support — **re•in•force•ment** *n* — **re•in•forc•er** *n*

re•in•scribe \ˌrē-ən-ˈskrīb\ *vb* **:** to reestablish or rename in a new and esp. stronger form or context

re•in•state \ˌrē-in-ˈstāt\ *vb* **-stat•ed; -stat•ing :** to restore to a former position, condition, or capacity — **re•in•state•ment** *n*

re•in•vent \ˌrē-in-ˈvent\ *vb* **1 :** to make as if for the first time something already invented ⟨~ the wheel⟩ **2 :** to remake completely

re•in•vig•o•rate \ˌrē-in-ˈvi-gə-ˌrāt\ *vb* **♦ :** to give life and energy to again

♦ reanimate, regenerate, rejuvenate, renew, resuscitate, revitalize, revive

re•it•er•ate \rē-ˈi-tə-ˌrāt\ *vb* **-at•ed; -at•ing ♦ :** to state or do over again or repeatedly

♦ duplicate, redo, remake, repeat, replicate

re•it•er•a•tion \-ˌi-tə-ˈrā-shən\ *n* **♦ :** the action of reiterating

♦ duplication, repeat, repetition, replication

¹re•ject \ri-ˈjekt\ *vb* **1 ♦ :** to refuse to accept, consider, use, or submit to **2 ♦ :** to refuse to hear, receive, or admit **3 :** to rebuff or withhold love from **4 ♦ :** to throw out esp. as useless or unsatisfactory **5 :** to subject (a transplanted tissue) to an attack by immune system components of the recipient organism

♦ [1] decline, disallow, disapprove, negative, refuse, repudiate, spurn, turn down ♦ [2] contradict, deny, disallow, disavow, disclaim, gainsay, negate, negative, repudiate ♦ [4] cast, discard, ditch, dump, fling, jettison, junk, lose, scrap, shed, shuck, slough, throw away, throw out, unload

²re•ject \ˈrē-ˌjekt\ *n* **♦ :** a rejected person or thing

♦ castaway, outcast ♦ cull, discard, rejection

re•jec•tion \ri-ˈjek-shən\ *n* **1 ♦ :** the action of rejecting **:** the state of being rejected **2 :** something rejected

♦ contradiction, denial, disallowance, disavowal, disclaimer, negation, refusal, repudiation

re•joice \ri-ˈjȯis\ *vb* **re•joiced; re•joic•ing 1 ♦ :** to give joy to **:** GLADDEN **2 ♦ :** to feel joy or great delight — **re•joic•er** *n*

♦ [1] content, delight, gladden, gratify, please, satisfy, suit, warm ♦ [2] crow, delight, exult, glory, joy, triumph

re•joic•ing \ri-ˈjȯi-siŋ\ *adj* **♦ :** having or expressing feelings of joy or triumph

♦ exultant, jubilant, triumphant

re·join \(ˌ)rē-ˈjȯin *for 1*, ri- *for 2*\ *vb* **1** : to join again **2** ♦ : to say in answer (as to a plaintiff's plea in court) : REPLY

♦ answer, reply, respond, retort, return

re·join·der \ri-ˈjȯin-dər\ *n* : something said, written, or done in answer or response : REPLY; *esp* : an answer to a reply

re·ju·ve·nate \ri-ˈjü-və-ˌnāt\ *vb* **-nat·ed; -nat·ing** **1** ♦ : to make young or youthful again : give new vigor to **2** ♦ : to restore to an original or new state

♦ [1] reanimate, regenerate, reinvigorate, renew, resuscitate, revitalize, revive ♦ [2] freshen, recreate, refresh, renew, restore, revive

re·ju·ve·na·tion \-ˌjü-və-ˈnā-shən\ *n* ♦ : the action of rejuvenating or the state of being rejuvenated

♦ rebirth, regeneration, renewal, resurgence, resurrection, resuscitation, revival

re·kin·dle \rē-ˈkin-dᵊl\ *vb* : to kindle again : arouse again

rel *abbr* **1** relating; relative **2** religion; religious

¹re·lapse \ri-ˈlaps, ˈrē-ˌlaps\ *n* **1** : the act or process of backsliding or worsening **2** : a recurrence of illness after a period of improvement

²re·lapse \ri-ˈlaps\ *vb* **re·lapsed; re·laps·ing** : to slip or fall back into a former worse state (as of illness)

re·late \ri-ˈlāt\ *vb* **re·lat·ed; re·lat·ing** **1** ♦ : to give an account of : TELL **2** ♦ : to show or establish logical or causal connection between **3** ♦ : to have relationship or connection **4** : to have or establish relationship ⟨the way a child ∼s to a teacher⟩ **5** : to respond favorably — **re·lat·able** *adj* — **re·lat·er** *or* **re·la·tor** \-ˈlā-tər\ *n*

♦ [1] describe, narrate, recite, recount, rehearse, report, tell ♦ [2] associate, connect, correlate, identify, link ♦ [3] appertain, apply, bear, pertain, refer

re·lat·ed *adj* **1** ♦ : connected by some understood relationship **2** : connected through membership in the same family — **re·lat·ed·ness** *n*

♦ akin, kindred *Ant* unrelated

re·la·tion \ri-ˈlā-shən\ *n* **1** : NARRATION, ACCOUNT **2** ♦ : an aspect or quality (as resemblance) that connects two or more things or parts as being or belonging or working together or as being of the same kind : CONNECTION, RELATIONSHIP **3** : connection by blood or marriage : KINSHIP; *also* : RELATIVE **4** : REFERENCE, RESPECT ⟨in ∼ to⟩ **5** : the state of being mutually interested or involved (as in social or commercial matters) **6** *pl* ♦ : commercial, professional, public, or personal business : DEALINGS **7** *pl* : SEXUAL INTERCOURSE — **re·la·tion·al** \-shə-nəl\ *adj*

♦ [2] association, bearing, connection, kinship, liaison, linkage, relationship ♦ **relations** [6] dealings, intercourse

re·la·tion·ship \-ˌship\ *n* ♦ : the state of being related or interrelated

♦ association, bearing, connection, kinship, liaison, linkage, relation ♦ affiliation, alliance, association, collaboration, confederation, connection, cooperation, hookup, liaison, partnership, relation, union

¹rel·a·tive \ˈre-lə-tiv\ *n* **1** : a word referring grammatically to an antecedent **2** : a thing having a relation to or a dependence upon another thing **3** ♦ : a person connected with another by blood or marriage

♦ kin, kinsman, relation

²relative *adj* **1** : introducing a subordinate clause qualifying an expressed or implied antecedent ⟨∼ pronoun⟩; *also* : introduced by such a connective ⟨∼ clause⟩ **2** ♦ : having significant and demonstrable bearing on the matter at hand : PERTINENT **3** ♦ : not absolute or independent : COMPARATIVE **4** : expressed as the ratio of the specified quantity to the total magnitude or to the mean of all quantities involved — **rel·a·tive·ness** *n*

♦ [2] applicable, apposite, apropos, germane, material, pertinent, pointed, relevant ♦ [3] approximate, comparative, near

relative humidity *n* : the ratio of the amount of water vapor actually present in the air to the greatest amount possible at the same temperature

rel·a·tive·ly *adv* ♦ : to a relative degree or extent

♦ fairly, kind of, like, pretty, quite, rather, somewhat, sort of

rel·a·tiv·is·tic \ˌre-lə-ti-ˈvis-tik\ *adj* **1** : of, relating to, or characterized by relativity **2** : moving at a velocity that is a significant fraction of the speed of light so that effects predicted by the theory of relativity become evident ⟨a ∼ electron⟩ — **rel·a·tiv·is·ti·cal·ly** \-ti-k(ə-)lē\ *adv*

rel·a·tiv·i·ty \ˌre-lə-ˈti-və-tē\ *n, pl* **-ties** **1** : the quality or state of

being relative **2** : a theory in physics that considers mass and energy to be equivalent and that predicts changes in mass, dimension, and time which are related to speed but are noticeable esp. at speeds approaching that of light

re·lax \ri-ˈlaks\ *vb* **1** ♦ : to make or become less firm, tense, or rigid **2** : to make less severe or strict **3** ♦ : to seek rest or recreation — **re·lax·er** *n*

♦ [1] ease, loosen, slack, slacken ♦ [3] bask, loll, lounge, repose, rest ♦ [3] chill out, de-stress, unwind *Ant* tense (up)

¹re·lax·ant \ri-ˈlak-sənt\ *adj* : of, relating to, or producing relaxation

²relaxant *n* : a relaxing agent; *esp* : a drug that induces muscular relaxation

re·lax·ation \ˌrē-ˌlak-ˈsā-shən\ *n* **1** ♦ : the act of relaxing or state of being relaxed : a lessening of tension **2** ♦ : a relaxing or recreative state, activity, or pastime

♦ [1] ease, leisure, repose, rest ♦ [2] dalliance, frolic, fun, play, sport

re·laxed \ri-ˈlakst\ *adj* **1** ♦ : freed from or lacking in precision or stringency **2** ♦ : set or being at rest or at ease **3** : easy of manner

♦ [1] easygoing, flexible, lax, loose, slack, unrestrained, unrestricted ♦ [2] comfortable, snug

¹re·lay \ˈrē-ˌlā\ *n* **1** : a fresh supply (as of horses) arranged beforehand to relieve others **2** : a race between teams in which each team member covers a specified part of a course **3** : an electromagnetic device in which the opening or closing of one circuit activates another device (as a switch in another circuit) **4** : the act of passing along by stages

²re·lay \ˈrē-ˌlā, ri-ˈlā\ *vb* **re·layed; re·lay·ing** **1** : to place in or provide with relays **2** : to pass along by relays **3** : to control or operate by a relay

³re·lay \(ˌ)rē-ˈlā\ *vb* **-laid** \-ˈlād\; **-lay·ing** : to lay again

¹re·lease \ri-ˈlēs\ *vb* **re·leased; re·leas·ing** **1 a** ♦ : to set free from confinement or restraint **b** : DISMISS **2** : to relieve from something that oppresses, confines, or burdens **3** : RELINQUISH ⟨∼ a claim⟩ **4** : to permit publication, performance, exhibition, or sale of; *also* : to make available to the public

♦ discharge, emancipate, enfranchise, free, liberate, loose, loosen, manumit, spring, unbind, unchain, unfetter ♦ loose, loosen, uncork, unleash, unlock, unloosen *Ant* bridle, check, constrain, contain, control, curb, govern, hold in, inhibit, regulate, rein (in), restrain, tame

²release *n* **1** : relief or deliverance from sorrow, suffering, or trouble **2** ♦ : discharge from an obligation or responsibility **3** : an act of setting free : the state of being freed **4** : a document effecting a legal release **5** ♦ : a releasing for performance or publication; *also* : the matter released (as to the press) **6** : a device for holding or releasing a mechanism as required

♦ [2] delivery, discharge, quietus, quittance ♦ [5] advertisement, announcement, bulletin, notice, notification

rel·e·gate \ˈre-lə-ˌgāt\ *vb* **-gat·ed; -gat·ing** **1** : to send into exile : BANISH **2** : to remove or dismiss to some less prominent position **3** : to assign to a particular class or sphere **4** : to submit to someone or something for appropriate action : DELEGATE — **rel·e·ga·tion** \ˌre-lə-ˈgā-shən\ *n*

re·lent \ri-ˈlent\ *vb* **1** ♦ : to become less stern, severe, or harsh **2** : to make slack (as by lessening tension or firmness) : SLACKEN

♦ abate, decline, decrease, de-escalate, die, diminish, dwindle, ebb, fall, lessen, let up, lower, moderate, recede, shrink, subside, taper, wane

re·lent·less \-ləs\ *adj* ♦ : showing or promising no abatement of severity, intensity, or pace ⟨∼ pressure⟩ — **re·lent·less·ly** *adv* — **re·lent·less·ness** *n*

♦ determined, dogged, grim, implacable, unflinching, unrelenting, unyielding

rel·e·vance \ˈre-lə-vəns\ *n* ♦ : relation to the matter at hand; *also* : practical and esp. social applicability

♦ applicability, bearing, connection, pertinence

rel·e·van·cy \-vən-sē\ *n* : RELEVANCE

rel·e·vant \ˈre-lə-vənt\ *adj* ♦ : bearing on the matter at hand : PERTINENT — **rel·e·vant·ly** *adv*

♦ applicable, apposite, apropos, germane, material, pertinent, pointed, relative

re·li·abil·i·ty \ri-ˌlī-ə-ˈbi-lə-tē\ *n* ♦ : the quality or state of being reliable

♦ dependability, solidity, sureness, trustworthiness

re·li·able \ri-ˈlī-ə-bəl\ *adj* ♦ : fit to be trusted or relied on : DE-PENDABLE, TRUSTWORTHY — **re·li·ably** \-ˈlī-ə-blē\ *adv*

♦ dependable, good, responsible, safe, solid, steady, sure, tried, true, trustworthy

re·li·able·ness *n* : the quality or state of being reliable
re·li·ance \ri-ˈlī-əns\ *n* **1** : the act of relying **2** : the state of be-ing reliant **3** ♦ : one relied on

♦ buttress, dependence, mainstay, pillar, standby, support

re·li·ant \ri-ˈlī-ənt\ *adj* : having reliance on someone or some-thing : DEPENDENT
rel·ic \ˈre-lik\ *n* **1** : an object venerated because of its associa-tion with a saint or martyr **2** : SOUVENIR, MEMENTO **3** *pl* : RE-MAINS, RUINS **4** ♦ : a remaining trace : VESTIGE

♦ shadow, trace, vestige

rel·ict \ˈre-likt\ *n* : WIDOW
re·lief \ri-ˈlēf\ *n* **1** ♦ : removal or lightening of something op-pressive, painful, or distressing **2** : WELFARE **2** : military as-sistance to an endangered post or force **4 a** : release from a post or from performance of a duty **b** ♦ : one that takes the place of another on duty **5** : legal remedy or redress **6** : projection of figures or ornaments from the background (as in sculpture) **7** : the elevations of a land surface

♦ [1] alleviation, comfort, ease ♦ [4b] backup, pinch hitter, re-placement, reserve, stand-in, sub, substitute

relief pitcher *n* : a baseball pitcher who takes over for another during a game
re·lieve \ri-ˈlēv\ *vb* **re·lieved; re·liev·ing 1** ♦ : to free partly or wholly from a burden or from distress **2** ♦ : to bring about the removal or alleviation of : MITIGATE **3** : to release from a post or duty; *also* : to take the place of **4** : to break the monotony of **5** : to discharge the bladder or bowels of (oneself) — **re·liev·er** *n*

♦ [1] clear, disburden, disencumber, free, rid, unburden ♦ [2] al-lay, alleviate, assuage, ease, help, mitigate, mollify, palliate, soothe

relig *abbr* religion
re·li·gion \ri-ˈli-jən\ *n* **1** ♦ : the service and worship of God or the supernatural **2** : devotion to a religious faith **3** ♦ : a per-sonal set or institutionalized system of religious beliefs, attitudes, and practices **4** : a cause, principle, or belief held to with faith and ardor — **re·li·gion·ist** *n*

♦ [1] devotion, faith, piety ♦ [3] creed, cult, faith, persuasion

¹**re·li·gious** \ri-ˈli-jəs\ *adj* **1** : relating or devoted to an acknowl-edged ultimate reality or deity **2** ♦ : of or relating to religious beliefs or observances **3** ♦ : scrupulously and conscientiously faithful **4** : FERVENT, ZEALOUS ⟨~ about football⟩ — **re·li·gious·ly** *adv*

♦ [2] devotional, sacred, spiritual *Ant* nonreligious, profane, secular ♦ [3] devout, faithful, godly, holy, pious, sainted, saintly

²**religious** *n, pl* **religious** : a member of a religious order under monastic vows
re·lin·quish \ri-ˈliŋ-kwish, -ˈlin-\ *vb* **1** : to withdraw or retreat from : ABANDON, QUIT **2** ♦ : to yield control or possession of ⟨~ a title⟩ **3** : to let go of : RELEASE

♦ cede, deliver, give up, hand over, leave, render, surrender, turn over, yield ♦ abdicate, abnegate, cede, renounce, resign, step down, surrender

re·lin·quish·ment *n* ♦ : the act of relinquishing : a giving up

♦ capitulation, submission, surrender

rel·i·quary \ˈre-lə-ˌkwer-ē\ *n, pl* **-quar·ies** : a container for reli-gious relics
¹**rel·ish** \ˈre-lish\ *n* **1** : characteristic flavor : SAVOR **2** ♦ : keen enjoyment or delight in something **3** ♦ : a strong liking : APPE-TITE **4** : a highly seasoned sauce (as of pickles) eaten with other food to add flavor

♦ [2] contentment, delectation, delight, enjoyment, gladness, gratification, pleasure, satisfaction ♦ [3] appetite, fancy, favor (*or* favour), fondness, like, liking, love, partiality, preference, shine, taste, use

²**relish** *vb* **1** : to add relish to **2** ♦ : to be pleased or gratified by : ENJOY **3** : to eat with pleasure — **rel·ish·able** *adj*

♦ adore, delight, dig, enjoy, fancy, groove, like, love, revel

re·live \(ˌ)rē-ˈliv\ *vb* : to live again or over again; *esp* : to experi-ence again in the imagination
re·lo·cate \(ˌ)rē-ˈlō-ˌkāt, ˌrē-lō-ˈkāt\ *vb* **1** : to locate again **2** : to move to a new location — **re·lo·ca·tion** \ˌrē-lō-ˈkā-shən\ *n*
re·luc·tance \ri-ˈlək-tən(t)s\ *n* ♦ : the quality or state of being reluctant

♦ disinclination, hesitancy, reticence *Ant* inclination, willing-ness

re·luc·tant \ri-ˈlək-tənt\ *adj* ♦ : feeling or showing aversion, hesitation, or unwillingness ⟨~ to get involved⟩ — **re·luc·tant·ly** *adv*

♦ afraid, dubious, hesitant, indisposed

re·ly \ri-ˈlī\ *vb* **re·lied; re·ly·ing** ♦ : to place faith or confidence : DEPEND

♦ count, depend, lean, reckon

REM \ˈrem\ *n* : RAPID EYE MOVEMENT
re·main \ri-ˈmān\ *vb* **1** : to be left after others have been re-moved, subtracted, or destroyed **2** : to be something yet to be shown, done, or treated ⟨it ~s to be seen⟩ **3** : to stay after oth-ers have gone **4** : to continue unchanged **5** ♦ : to stay in the same place or with the same person or group

♦ abide, dwell, hang around, stay, stick around, tarry

re·main·der \ri-ˈmān-dər\ *n* **1** ♦ : that which is left over : a remaining group, part, or trace **2** : the number left after a sub-traction **3** : the number that is left over from the dividend after division and that is less than the divisor **4** : a book sold at a re-duced price by the publisher after sales have slowed

♦ end, fag end, leftover, remnant, scrap ♦ balance, leavings, leftovers, odds and ends, remains, remnant, residue, rest

re·mains \-ˈmānz\ *n pl* **1** ♦ : a remaining part or trace ⟨the ~ of a meal⟩ **2** : a dead body

♦ debris, rubble, ruins, wreck, wreckage

¹**re·make** \(ˌ)rē-ˈmāk\ *vb* **-made** \-ˈmād\; **-mak·ing** ♦ : to make anew or in a different form

♦ alter, change, make over, modify, recast, redo, refashion, re-model, revamp, revise, rework, vary ♦ duplicate, redo, reiterate, repeat, replicate

²**re·make** \ˈrē-ˌmāk\ *n* : one that is remade; *esp* : a new version of a motion picture
re·mand \ri-ˈmand\ *vb* : to order back; *esp* : to return to custody pending trial or for further detention
¹**re·mark** \ri-ˈmärk\ *n* **1** : the act of remarking : OBSERVATION, NOTICE **2** ♦ : a passing observation or comment

♦ comment, note, observation, reflection

²**remark** *vb* **1** ♦ : to take notice of : OBSERVE **2** ♦ : to express as an observation or comment

♦ [1] behold, descry, discern, distinguish, espy, eye, look, note, notice, observe, perceive, regard, see, sight, spy, view, witness ♦ [2] comment, note, observe, opine, say

re·mark·able \ri-ˈmär-kə-bəl\ *adj* ♦ : worthy of being or likely to be noticed esp. as being uncommon or extraordinary : NOTE-WORTHY — **re·mark·able·ness** *n*

♦ bold, catchy, conspicuous, emphatic, marked, noteworthy, no-ticeable, prominent, pronounced, striking

re·mark·ably \ri-ˈmär-kə-blē\ *adv* **1** : in a remarkable man-ner **2** : as is remarkable
re·me·di·a·ble \ri-ˈmē-dē-ə-bəl\ *adj* : capable of being remedied
re·me·di·al \ri-ˈmē-dē-əl\ *adj* ♦ : intended to remedy or improve ⟨a class in ~ reading⟩

♦ corrective, reformative

¹**rem·e·dy** \ˈre-mə-dē\ *n, pl* **-dies 1** ♦ : a medicine or treatment that cures or relieves a disease or condition **2** : something that corrects or counteracts an evil or compensates for a loss

♦ cure, drug, medicine, pharmaceutical, specific

²**remedy** *vb* **-died; -dy·ing** ♦ : to provide or serve as a remedy for

♦ amend, correct, debug, emend, rectify, reform

re·mem·ber \ri-ˈmem-bər\ *vb* **-bered; -ber·ing 1** ♦ : to bring to mind or think of again : RECOLLECT **2** : to keep from forgetting : keep in mind **3** : to convey greetings from **4** : COMMEMORATE

♦ recall, recollect, reminisce, think *Ant* forget, unlearn

re·mem·brance \-brəns\ *n* **1** ♦ : an act of remembering : RECOL-LECTION **2** ♦ : the ability to remember : MEMORY **3** : the period over which one's memory extends **4** : a memory of a person, thing, or event **5 ♦ :** something that serves to bring to mind : RE-MINDER **6 :** a greeting or gift recalling or expressing friendship or affection

♦ [1, 2] memory, recall, recollection, reminiscence ♦ [5] keep-sake, memento, memorial, monument, souvenir, token

Remembrance Day *n* : November 11 set aside in commemoration of the end of hostilities in 1918 and 1945 and observed as a legal holiday in Canada; *also* : REMEMBRANCE SUNDAY
Remembrance Sunday *n* : a Sunday that is usu. closest to November 11 and that in Great Britain is set aside in commemoration of the end of hostilities in 1918 and 1945
re·mind \ri-'mīnd\ *vb* : to put in mind of something : cause to remember
re·mind·er *n* : something that reminds by association
rem·i·nisce \,re-mə-'nis\ *vb* **-nisced; -nisc·ing ♦ :** to indulge in reminiscence

♦ *usu* **reminisce about** recall, recollect, remember, think

rem·i·nis·cence \-'nis-ᵊns\ *n* **1 ♦ :** a recalling or telling of a past experience **2 :** an account of a memorable experience

♦ memory, recall, recollection, remembrance

rem·i·nis·cent \-ᵊnt\ *adj* **1 :** of or relating to reminiscence **2** : marked by or given to reminiscence **3 :** serving to remind : SUGGESTIVE — **rem·i·nis·cent·ly** *adv*
re·miss \ri-'mis\ *adj* **1 :** negligent or careless in the performance of work or duty **2 ♦ :** showing neglect or inattention — **re·miss·ly** *adv*

♦ careless, derelict, lax, negligent, slack

re·mis·si·ble \ri-'mi-sə-bəl\ *adj* **♦ :** capable of being forgiven

♦ excusable, forgivable, pardonable, venial

re·mis·sion \ri-'mi-shən\ *n* **1 ♦ :** the act or process of remitting **2 :** a state or period during which something is remitted

♦ absolution, amnesty, forgiveness, pardon

re·miss·ness *n* ♦ : the quality or state of being remiss

♦ carelessness, dereliction, heedlessness, laxness, neglect, negligence, slackness

re·mit \ri-'mit\ *vb* **re·mit·ted; re·mit·ting 1 :** FORGIVE, PARDON **2 :** to give or gain relief from (as pain) **3 :** to refer for consideration, report, or decision **4 :** to refrain from exacting or enforcing (as a penalty) **5 :** to send (money) in payment of a bill **6 :** to abate in force or intensity **7 :** to place later in order of precedence, preference, or importance
re·mit·tal \ri-'mit-ᵊl\ *n* : the act or process of remitting : REMISSION
re·mit·tance \ri-'mit-ᵊns\ *n* **1 ♦ :** a sum of money remitted **2** ♦ : transmittal of money (as to a distant place)

♦ [1, 2] compensation, consideration, disbursement, pay, payment, recompense, remuneration, requital

rem·nant \'rem-nənt\ *n* **1 ♦ :** a usu. small part or trace remaining **2 :** an unsold or unused end of a fabric that is sold by the yard

♦ end, fag end, leftover, remainder, scrap

re·mod·el \,rē-'mäd-ᵊl\ *vb* **♦ :** to alter the structure of : MAKE OVER

♦ alter, change, make over, modify, recast, redo, refashion, remake, revamp, revise, rework, vary

re·mon·strance \ri-'män-strəns\ *n* **♦ :** an act or instance of remonstrating

♦ challenge, complaint, demur, expostulation, fuss, kick, objection, protest, question

re·mon·strant \-strənt\ *adj* : vigorously objecting or opposing — **remonstrant** *n* — **re·mon·strant·ly** *adv*
re·mon·strate \ri-'män-,strāt\ *vb* **-strat·ed; -strat·ing ♦ :** to plead in opposition to something : speak in protest or reproof — usu. used with *with* — **re·mon·stra·tion** \ri-,män-'strā-shən, ,re-mən-\ *n* — **re·mon·stra·tor** \ri-'män-,strā-tər\ *n*

♦ *usu* **remonstrate with** demur, kick, object, protest

rem·o·ra \'re-mə-rə\ *n* : any of a family of marine bony fishes with sucking organs on the head by which they cling esp. to other fishes
re·morse \ri-'mȯrs\ *n* **♦ :** a gnawing distress arising from a sense of guilt for past wrongs

♦ contrition, guilt, penitence, repentance, self-reproach, shame

re·morse·ful *adj* **♦ :** motivated or marked by remorse

♦ apologetic, contrite, guilty, penitent, regretful, repentant, rueful, sorry

re·morse·less \-ləs\ *adj* **1 :** MERCILESS **2 :** PERSISTENT, RELENTLESS
¹re·mote \ri-'mōt\ *adj* **re·mot·er; -est 1 ♦ :** far off in place or time : not near **2 :** not closely related : DISTANT **3 ♦ :** located out of the way : SECLUDED ⟨a ∼ village⟩ **4 :** acting, acted on, or controlled indirectly or from a distance **5 ♦ :** small in degree : SLIGHT ⟨a ∼ chance⟩ **6 ♦ :** distant or aloof in manner — **re·mote·ly** *adv* — **re·mote·ness** *n*

♦ [1] away, distant, far, far-off ♦ [3] cloistered, covert, isolated, quiet, secluded, secret ♦ [5] negligible, off, outside, slight, slim, small *Ant* good ♦ [6] aloof, antisocial, cold, cool, detached, distant, frosty, standoffish, unsociable

²remote *n* **1 :** a radio or television program or a portion of a program originating outside the studio **2 :** REMOTE CONTROL 2
remote control *n* **1 :** control (as by radio signal) of operation from a point at some distance removed **2 :** a device or mechanism for controlling something from a distance
¹re·mount \(,)rē-'maůnt\ *vb* **1 :** to mount again **2 :** to furnish remounts to
²re·mount \'rē-,maůnt\ *n* : a fresh horse to replace one no longer available
re·mov·al \ri-'mü-vəl\ *n* **♦ :** the act or process of removing

♦ disposal, disposition, dumping, jettison, riddance

¹re·move \ri-'müv\ *vb* **re·moved; re·mov·ing 1 ♦ :** to move from one place to another : TRANSFER **2 ♦ :** to move by lifting or taking off or away **3 ♦ :** to dismiss from office **4 :** to get rid of : ELIMINATE **5 :** to change one's residence or location **6 :** to go away : DEPART **7 :** to be capable of being removed — **re·mov·able** *adj* — **re·mov·er** *n*

♦ [1] budge, dislocate, displace, disturb, move, shift, transfer ♦ [2] doff, peel, put off, take off *Ant* don, put on, slip (into) ♦ [2] clear, draw, withdraw *Ant* place, put ♦ [3] cashier, dismiss, fire, retire, sack

²remove *n* **1 :** a transfer from one location to another : MOVE **2** ♦ : a degree or stage of separation

♦ distance, lead, length, spread, stretch, way

REM sleep *n* : a state of sleep that recurs cyclically several times during normal sleep and is associated with rapid eye movements and dreaming
re·mu·ner·ate \ri-'myü-nə-,rāt\ *vb* **-at·ed; -at·ing ♦ :** to pay an equivalent for or to : RECOMPENSE ⟨their services were *remunerated*⟩ — **re·mu·ner·a·tor** \-,rā-tər\ *n*

♦ compensate, indemnify, pay, recompense, recoup, requite

re·mu·ner·a·tion \ri-,myü-nə-'rā-shən\ *n* **1 ♦ :** something that remunerates : COMPENSATION, PAYMENT **2 ♦ :** an act or fact of remunerating

♦ [1] compensation, consideration, disbursement, pay, payment, recompense, remittance, requital ♦ [2] compensation, damages, indemnity, quittance, recompense, redress, reparation, requital, restitution, satisfaction

re·mu·ner·a·tive \ri-'myü-nə-rə-tiv, -,rā-\ *adj* **♦ :** serving to remunerate : GAINFUL

♦ fat, gainful, lucrative, profitable

re·nais·sance \,re-nə-'säns, -'zäns\ *n* **1** *cap* : the cultural revival and beginnings of modern science in Europe in the 14th–17th centuries; *also* : the period of the Renaissance **2** *often cap* : a movement or period of vigorous artistic and intellectual activity **3 :** REBIRTH, REVIVAL
re·nal \'rēn-ᵊl\ *adj* : of, relating to, or located in or near the kidneys
re·na·scence \ri-'nas-ᵊns, -'nās-\ *n, often cap* : RENAISSANCE
rend \'rend\ *vb* **rent** \'rent\; **rend·ing 1 :** to remove by violence : WREST **2 ♦ :** to tear forcibly apart

♦ rip, rive, shred, tatter, tear

ren·der \'ren-dər\ *vb* **1 :** to extract (as lard) by heating **2 ♦ :** to give to another; *also* : YIELD **3 :** to give in return **4 :** to do (a service) for another ⟨∼ aid⟩ **5 :** to cause to be or become : MAKE **6 :** to reproduce or represent by artistic or verbal means **7 :** TRANSLATE ⟨∼ into English⟩

♦ cede, deliver, give up, hand over, leave, relinquish, surrender, turn over, yield

¹ren·dez·vous \'rän-di-,vü, -dā-\ *n, pl* **ren·dez·vous** \-,vüz\ **1 a :** a place appointed for a meeting; *also* : a meeting at an appointed place **b ♦ :** an agreement to meet each other or with another person or thing **2 ♦** : a place of popular resort **3** : the process of bringing two spacecraft together

♦ [1b] appointment, date, engagement, tryst ♦ [2] hangout, haunt, resort

²ren·dez·vous *vb* **-voused** \-ˌvüd\; **-vous·ing** \-ˌvü-iŋ\; **-vouses** \-ˌvüz\ ♦ : to come or bring together at a rendezvous

♦ assemble, cluster, collect, concentrate, conglomerate, congregate, convene, forgather, gather, meet

ren·di·tion \ren-ˈdi-shən\ *n* : an act or a result of rendering ⟨first ∼ of the work into English⟩

ren·e·gade \ˈre-ni-ˌgād\ *n* ♦ : a deserter from one faith, cause, principle, or party for another

♦ defector, deserter, recreant *Ant* loyalist

re·nege \ri-ˈnig, -ˈneg, -ˈnäg\ *vb* **re·neged; re·neg·ing 1 ♦** : to go back on a promise or commitment **2** : to fail to follow suit when able in a card game in violation of the rules — **re·neg·er** *n*

♦ back down, cop out

re·new \ri-ˈnü, -ˈnyü\ *vb* **1 ♦** : to make or become new, fresh, or strong again **2 ♦** : to restore to existence : REVIVE **3** : to make or do again : REPEAT ⟨∼ a complaint⟩ **4 ♦** : to begin again : RESUME ⟨∼ed his efforts⟩ **5** : REPLACE ⟨∼ the lining of a coat⟩ **6** : to grant or obtain an extension of or on ⟨∼ a subscription⟩ — **re·new·er** *n*

♦ [1] freshen, recreate, refresh, regenerate, rejuvenate, restore, revitalize, revive ♦ [1, 2] reanimate, reinvigorate, resuscitate, revive ♦ [4] continue, reopen, restart, resume

re·new·able \ri-ˈnü-ə-bəl, -ˈnyü-\ *adj* **1** : capable of being renewed **2** : capable of being replaced by natural ecological cycles or sound management procedures ⟨∼ resources⟩

re·new·al \ri-ˈnü-əl, -ˈnyü-\ *n* **1 ♦** : the act of renewing : the state of being renewed **2** : something renewed

♦ rebirth, regeneration, rejuvenation, resurgence, resurrection, resuscitation, revival

ren·net \ˈre-nət\ *n* **1** : the contents of the stomach of an unweaned animal (as a calf) or the lining membrane of the stomach used for curdling milk **2** : rennin or a substitute used to curdle milk

ren·nin \ˈre-nən\ *n* : a stomach enzyme that coagulates casein and is used commercially to curdle milk in the making of cheese

re·nounce \ri-ˈnau̇ns\ *vb* **re·nounced; re·nounc·ing 1 ♦** : to give up, refuse, or resign usu. by formal declaration **2 ♦** : to refuse further to follow, obey, or recognize

♦ [1] abdicate, abnegate, cede, relinquish, resign, step down, surrender ♦ [2] abjure, recant, retract, take back, unsay, withdraw

re·nounce·ment *n* ♦ : the act or practice of renouncing

♦ abnegation, renunciation, repudiation, self-denial

ren·o·vate \ˈre-nə-ˌvāt\ *vb* **-vat·ed; -vat·ing 1 ♦** : to make like new again : put in good condition ⟨*renovated* the kitchen⟩ **2** : to restore to vigor or activity — **ren·o·va·tion** \ˌre-nə-ˈvā-shən\ *n* — **ren·o·va·tor** \ˈre-nə-ˌvā-tər\ *n*

♦ doctor, fix, mend, patch, recondition, repair, revamp

re·nown \ri-ˈnau̇n\ *n* ♦ : a state of being widely acclaimed and honored ⟨a writer of ∼⟩

♦ celebrity, fame, notoriety

re·nowned \-ˈnau̇nd\ *adj* ♦ : having renown

♦ celebrated, famed, famous, noted, notorious, prominent, star, well-known

¹rent \ˈrent\ *n* **1** : money or the amount of money paid or due at intervals for the use of another's property **2** : property rented or for rent

²rent *vb* **1** : to give possession and use of in return for rent **2 ♦** : to take and hold under an agreement to pay rent **3** : to be for rent ⟨∼s for $100 a month⟩

♦ engage, hire, lease, let

³rent *n* **1 ♦** : an act or instance of rending **2** : a split in a party or organized group : SCHISM **3 ♦** : an opening made by or as if by rending

♦ [1] gash, laceration, rip, slash, slit, tear ♦ [3] breach, break, discontinuity, gap, gulf, hole, interval, opening, rift, separation

¹rent·al \ˈren-təl\ *n* **1** : an amount paid or collected as rent **2** : something that is rented **3** : an act of renting

²rental *adj* : of or relating to rent

rent·er *n* ♦ : one that rents

♦ boarder, lodger, roomer, tenant

re·nun·ci·a·tion \ri-ˌnən-sē-ˈā-shən\ *n* ♦ : the act of renouncing : REPUDIATION

♦ abnegation, renouncement, repudiation, self-denial *Ant* indulgence, self-indulgence

re·open \ˌre-ˈō-pən\ *vb* ♦ : to enter upon again

♦ continue, renew, restart, resume

¹rep \ˈrep\ *n* ♦ : one that represents another : REPRESENTATIVE ⟨sales ∼s⟩

♦ agent, attorney, commissary, delegate, deputy, envoy, factor, proxy, representative

²rep *abbr* **1** repair **2** repeat **3** report; reporter **4** republic **Rep** *abbr* Republican

re·pack·age \(ˌ)rē-ˈpa-kij\ *vb* : to package again or anew; *esp* : to put into a more attractive form

¹re·pair \ri-ˈpar\ *vb* : to make one's way : GO ⟨∼ed to the drawing room⟩

²repair *vb* **1 ♦** : to restore to good condition : FIX **2** : to restore to a healthy state **3** : REMEDY ⟨∼ a wrong⟩ — **re·pair·er** *n* — **re·pair·man** \-ˌman\ *n*

♦ doctor, fix, mend, patch, recondition, renovate, revamp

³repair *n* **1** : a result of repairing **2** : an act of repairing **3** : condition with respect to need of repairing ⟨in bad ∼⟩ **4 ♦** : the state of being in good or sound condition

♦ condition, estate, fettle, form, order, shape, trim

rep·a·ra·tion \ˌre-pə-ˈrā-shən\ *n* **1** : the act of making amends for a wrong **2 ♦** : amends made for a wrong or injury; *esp* : money paid by a defeated nation in compensation for damages caused during hostilities — usu. used in pl.

♦ compensation, damages, indemnity, quittance, recompense, redress, remuneration, requital, restitution, satisfaction

re·par·a·tive \ri-ˈpar-ə-tiv\ *adj* **1** : of, relating to, or effecting repairs **2** : serving to make amends

rep·ar·tee \ˌre-pər-ˈtē\ *n* **1 ♦** : a witty reply **2 a ♦** : a succession of clever replies **b** : skill in making such replies

♦ [1] comeback, retort, riposte ♦ [2a] banter, chaff, persiflage, raillery

re·past \ri-ˈpast, ˈrē-ˌpast\ *n* ♦ : a supply of food and drink served as a meal

♦ board, chow, feed, meal, mess, table

re·pa·tri·ate \rē-ˈpā-trē-ˌāt\ *vb* **-at·ed; -at·ing** : to send or bring back to the country of origin or citizenship ⟨∼ prisoners of war⟩ — **re·pa·tri·ate** \-trē-ət, -trē-ˌāt\ *n* — **re·pa·tri·a·tion** \-ˌpā-trē-ˈā-shən\ *n*

re·pay \rē-ˈpā\ *vb* **-paid** \-ˈpād\; **-pay·ing 1** : to pay back : REFUND **2** : to give or do in return or requital **3** : to make a return payment to : RECOMPENSE, REQUITE — **re·pay·able** *adj* — **re·pay·ment** *n*

¹re·peal \ri-ˈpēl\ *vb* ♦ : to annul by authoritative and esp. legislative action — **re·peal·er** *n*

♦ abolish, abrogate, annul, cancel, dissolve, invalidate, negate, nullify, quash, rescind, void

²repeal *n* : the act or an instance of repealing

¹re·peat \ri-ˈpēt\ *vb* **1 ♦** : to say again **2 ♦** : to do again **3** : to say over from memory **4 ♦** : to say after another — **re·peat·able** *adj* — **re·peat·er** *n*

♦ [2] duplicate, redo, reiterate, remake, replicate ♦ [4] echo, quote

²re·peat \ri-ˈpēt, ˈrē-ˌpēt\ *n* **1 ♦** : the act of repeating **2** : something repeated or to be repeated (as a radio or television program)

³re·peat \ri-ˈpēt\ *adj* : of, relating to, or being one that repeats an offense, achievement, or action

♦ duplication, reiteration, repetition, replication

re·peat·ed \ri-ˈpē-təd\ *adj* ♦ : done or recurring again and again : FREQUENT ⟨∼ requests⟩

♦ constant, frequent, habitual, periodic, regular, steady

re·peat·ed·ly *adv* ♦ : renewed or recurring again and again

♦ constantly, continually, frequently, often

re·pel \ri-ˈpel\ *vb* **re·pelled; re·pel·ling 1 ♦** : to drive away : REPULSE **2 ♦** : to fight against : RESIST **3** : to turn away : REJECT **4 ♦** : to cause aversion in : DISGUST

♦ [1] fend, repulse, stave off ♦ [2] buck, defy, fight, oppose, resist, withstand ♦ [4] disgust, nauseate, repulse, revolt, sicken, turn off

¹**re·pel·lent** *also* **re·pel·lant** \ri-'pe-lənt\ *adj* **1** : tending to drive away ⟨bug-*repellent* spray⟩ **2** ♦ : causing disgust

♦ abhorrent, awful, distasteful, foul, nasty, nauseating, noisome, obnoxious, obscene, odious, offensive, repugnant, repulsive, revolting

²**repellent** *also* **repellant** *n* : something that repels; *esp* : a substance that repels insects

re·pent \ri-'pent\ *vb* **1** : to turn from sin and resolve to reform one's life **2** ♦ : to feel sorry for (something done) : REGRET ⟨∼ed their decision⟩

♦ bemoan, deplore, lament, regret, rue

re·pen·tance \ri-'pent-ᵊns\ *n* ♦ : the action or process of repenting esp. for misdeeds or moral shortcomings

♦ contrition, guilt, penitence, remorse, self-reproach, shame

re·pen·tant \-ᵊnt\ *adj* ♦ : experiencing repentance

♦ apologetic, contrite, guilty, penitent, regretful, remorseful, rueful, sorry

re·per·cus·sion \ˌrē-pər-'kə-shən, ˌre-\ *n* **1** : REVERBERATION **2** : a reciprocal action or effect **3** ♦ : a widespread, indirect, or unforeseen effect of something done or said

♦ effect, impact, influence, mark, sway

rep·er·toire \'re-pər-ˌtwär\ *n* **1** : a list of plays, operas, pieces, or parts which a company or performer is prepared to present **2** : a list of the skills or devices possessed by a person or needed in a person's occupation

rep·er·to·ry \'re-pər-ˌtōr-ē\ *n, pl* **-ries 1** : REPOSITORY **2** : REPERTOIRE **3** : a company that presents its repertoire in the course of one season at one theater

rep·e·ti·tion \ˌre-pə-'ti-shən\ *n* **1** ♦ : the act or an instance of repeating **2** : the fact of being repeated

♦ duplication, reiteration, repeat, replication

rep·e·ti·tious \-'ti-shəs\ *adj* : marked by repetition; *esp* : tediously repeating ⟨∼ work⟩ — **rep·e·ti·tious·ly** *adv* — **rep·e·ti·tious·ness** *n*

re·pet·i·tive \ri-'pe-ti-tiv\ *adj* : REPETITIOUS — **re·pet·i·tive·ly** *adv* — **re·pet·i·tive·ness** *n*

re·phrase \-'frāz\ *vb* ♦ : to express again in words or in appropriate or telling terms

♦ paraphrase, restate, translate

re·pine \ri-'pīn\ *vb* **re·pined; re·pin·ing 1** ♦ : to feel or express discontent or dejection **2** ♦ : to long for something

♦ [1] beef, bellyache, complain, fuss, gripe, grouse, grumble ♦ *usu* **repine for** [2] ache for, covet, crave, desire, die (to *or* for), hanker for, hunger for, long for, lust (for *or* after), pine for, thirst for, want, wish for, yearn for

repl *abbr* replace; replacement

re·place \ri-'plās\ *vb* **1** : to restore to a former place or position **2** ♦ : to take the place of : SUPPLANT **3** : to put something new in the place of — **re·place·able** *adj* — **re·plac·er** *n*

♦ displace, substitute, supersede, supplant

re·place·ment \ri-'plās-mənt\ *n* **1** : the act of replacing : the state of being replaced **2** ♦ : one that replaces another esp. in a job or function

♦ backup, pinch hitter, relief, reserve, stand-in, sub, substitute

¹**re·play** \ˌˌrē-'plā\ *vb* : to play again or over

²**re·play** \'rē-ˌplā\ *n* **1** : an act or instance of replaying **2** : the playing of a tape (as a videotape)

re·plen·ish \ri-'ple-nish\ *vb* : to fill or build up again : stock or supply anew — **re·plen·ish·ment** *n*

re·plete \ri-'plēt\ *adj* **1** : fully provided **2** ♦ : fully or abundantly provided or filled : FULL; *esp* : full of food — **re·plete·ness** *n*

♦ flush, fraught, full, rife, thick

re·ple·tion \ri-'plē-shən\ *n* : the state of being replete

rep·li·ca \'re-pli-kə\ *n* **1** : an exact reproduction (as of a painting) executed by the original artist **2** ♦ : a copy exact in all details : DUPLICATE

♦ carbon copy, counterpart, double, duplicate, duplication, facsimile, image, likeness, match, picture, ringer, spit

¹**rep·li·cate** \'re-plə-ˌkāt\ *vb* **-cat·ed; -cat·ing 1** ♦ : to make a copy of : DUPLICATE **2** ♦ : to do over or again : REPEAT

♦ [1] copy, duplicate, imitate, reproduce ♦ [2] duplicate, redo, reiterate, remake, repeat

²**rep·li·cate** \-pli-kət\ *n* : one of several identical experiments or procedures

rep·li·ca·tion \ˌre-plə-'kā-shən\ *n* **1** : ANSWER, REPLY **2** ♦ : precise copying or reproduction; *also* : an act or process of this **3** ♦ : an imitation, transcript, or reproduction of an original work

♦ [2] duplication, reiteration, repeat, repetition ♦ [3] carbon copy, copy, duplicate, duplication, facsimile, imitation, replica, reproduction

¹**re·ply** \ri-'plī\ *vb* **re·plied; re·ply·ing** ♦ : to say or do in answer : RESPOND

♦ answer, rejoin, respond, retort, return

²**reply** *n, pl* **replies** ♦ : something said, written, or done in answer or response : RESPONSE

♦ answer, comeback, response, retort, return

repo \'rē-ˌpō\ *adj* : of, relating to, or being in the business of repossessing property (as a car)

¹**re·port** \ri-'pōrt\ *n* **1** : common talk : RUMOR **2** ♦ : quality of reputation **3** ♦ : a usu. detailed account or statement **4** ♦ : an explosive noise

♦ [2] character, mark, name, note, reputation ♦ [3] account, chronicle, history, narrative, record, story ♦ [4] bang, blast, boom, clap, crack, crash, pop, slam, smash, snap, thwack, whack

²**report** *vb* **1** ♦ : to give an account of : RELATE, TELL **2** : to serve as carrier of (a message) **3** : to prepare or present (as an account of an event) for a newspaper or a broadcast **4** : to make a charge of misconduct against **5** : to present oneself (as for work) **6** : to make known to the authorities ⟨∼ a fire⟩ **7** : to return or present (as a matter referred to a committee) with conclusions and recommendations — **re·port·able** *adj*

♦ describe, narrate, recite, recount, rehearse, relate, tell

re·port·age \ri-'pōr-tij, *esp for 2* ˌre-pər-'täzh, ˌre-ˌpōr-'\ *n* **1** : the act or process of reporting news **2** : writing intended to give an account of observed or documented events

report card *n* : a periodic report on a student's grades

re·port·ed·ly \ri-'pōr-təd-lē\ *adv* : according to report

re·port·er \ri-'pōr-tər\ *n* : one that reports; *esp* : a person who gathers and reports news for a news medium — **re·por·to·ri·al** \ˌre-pər-'tōr-ē-əl\ *adj*

¹**re·pose** \ri-'pōz\ *vb* **re·posed; re·pos·ing 1** : to lay at rest **2** : to lie at rest **3** : to lie dead **4** ♦ : to take a rest **5** : to have as a basis or support — *usu.* used with *on*

♦ bask, loll, lounge, relax, rest

²**repose** *n* **1** ♦ : a state of resting (as after exertion); *esp* : SLEEP **2** : eternal or heavenly rest **3** ♦ : freedom from something that disturbs or excites : CALM, PEACE **4** ♦ : cessation or absence of activity, movement, or animation **5** : composure of manner : POISE — **re·pose·ful** *adj*

♦ [1] rest, sleep, slumber ♦ [3] calm, calmness, hush, peace, placidity, quiet, quietness, serenity, still, stillness, tranquility ♦ [4] ease, leisure, relaxation, rest

³**repose** *vb* **re·posed; re·pos·ing 1** : to place (as trust) in someone or something **2** : to place for control, management, or use

re·pos·i·to·ry \ri-'pä-zə-ˌtōr-ē\ *n, pl* **-ries 1** ♦ : a place where something is deposited or stored **2** : a person to whom something is entrusted

♦ depository, depot, magazine, storage, storehouse, warehouse

re·pos·sess \ˌrē-pə-'zes\ *vb* **1** ♦ : to regain possession of **2** : to take possession of in default of the payment of installments due

♦ recapture, reclaim, recoup, recover, regain, retake, retrieve

re·pos·ses·sion \-'ze-shən\ *n* ♦ : the act or state of possessing again

♦ reclamation, recovery, retrieval

re·post \ˌˌrē-'pōst\ *vb* : to post again ⟨∼ a message⟩

rep·re·hend \ˌre-pri-'hend\ *vb* ♦ : to express disapproval of : CENSURE — **rep·re·hen·sion** \-'hen-chən\ *n*

♦ blame, censure, condemn, criticize, denounce, fault, knock, pan

rep·re·hen·si·ble \-'hen-sə-bəl\ *adj* ♦ : deserving blame or censure : CULPABLE — **rep·re·hen·si·bly** \-blē\ *adv*

♦ blamable, blameworthy, censurable, culpable ♦ censurable, objectionable, obnoxious, offensive

rep·re·sent \‚re-pri-'zent\ *vb* **1** ♦ : to present a picture or a likeness of : DEPICT **2** : to serve as a sign or symbol of **3** : to act the role of **4** : to stand in the place of : act or speak for; *also* : to manage the legal or business affairs of **5** : to be a member or example of : TYPIFY **6** : to serve as an elected representative of **7** ♦ : to describe as having a specified quality or character **8** : to state with the purpose of affecting judgment or action

♦ [1] depict, image, picture, portray ♦ [7] characterize, define, depict, describe, portray

rep·re·sen·ta·tion \‚re-pri-‚zen-'tā-shən\ *n* **1** : the act of representing **2** : one (as a picture or image) that represents something else **3** : the state of being represented in a legislative body; *also* : the body of persons representing a constituency **4** : a usu. formal statement made to effect a change

¹**rep·re·sen·ta·tive** \‚re-pri-'zen-tə-tiv\ *adj* **1** ♦ : serving to represent **2** : standing or acting for another **3** : founded on the principle of representation : carried on by elected representatives ⟨~ government⟩ — **rep·re·sen·ta·tive·ly** *adv* — **rep·re·sen·ta·tive·ness** *n*

♦ average, characteristic, normal, regular, standard, typical

²**representative** *n* **1** ♦ : a typical example of a group, class, or quality **2** ♦ : one that represents another; *esp* : one representing a district in a legislative body usu. as a member of a lower house

♦ [1] case, example, exemplar, illustration, instance, sample, specimen ♦ [2] ambassador, delegate, emissary, envoy, legate, minister ♦ [2] agent, attorney, commissary, delegate, deputy, envoy, factor, proxy

re·press \ri-'pres\ *vb* **1 a** : to check by or as if by pressure : CURB **b** ♦ : to put down by force : SUBDUE **2** ♦ : to prevent the natural or normal expression, activity, or development of : SUPPRESS **3** : to exclude from consciousness ⟨~ a painful memory⟩ — **re·pres·sive** \-'pre-siv\ *adj*

♦ [1b] clamp down, crack down, crush, put down, quash, quell, silence, snuff, squash, squelch, subdue, suppress ♦ [2] choke, pocket, smother, stifle, strangle, suppress, swallow

re·pres·sion \-'pre-shən\ *n* ♦ : the action or process of repressing

♦ constraint, inhibition, restraint, self-control, self-restraint, suppression

¹**re·prieve** \ri-'prēv\ *vb* **re·prieved; re·priev·ing 1** : to delay the punishment or execution of **2** : to give temporary relief to
²**reprieve** *n* **1** : the act of reprieving : the state of being reprieved **2** : a formal temporary suspension of a sentence esp. of death **3** : a temporary respite

¹**rep·ri·mand** \'re-prə-‚mand\ *n* ♦ : a severe or formal reproof

♦ censure, denunciation, rebuke, reproach, reproof, stricture

²**reprimand** *vb* ♦ : to reprove severely or formally from a position of authority

♦ censure, condemn, denounce, rebuke, reproach, reprove ♦ admonish, chide, lecture, rail (at *or* against), rate, rebuke, scold

¹**re·print** \(‚)rē-'print\ *vb* : to print again
²**re·print** \'rē-‚print\ *n* : a reproduction of printed matter
re·pri·sal \ri-'prī-zəl\ *n* ♦ : an act in retaliation for something done by another

♦ requital, retaliation, retribution, revenge, vengeance

re·prise \ri-'prēz\ *n* : a recurrence, renewal, or resumption of an action; *also* : a musical repetition

¹**re·proach** \ri-'prōch\ *n* **1** ♦ : an expression of disapproval **2** : the condition of one fallen from grace or honor : DISGRACE **3** : the act of reproaching : REBUKE **4** : a cause or occasion of blame or disgrace — **re·proach·ful** \-fəl\ *adj* — **re·proach·ful·ly** *adv* — **re·proach·ful·ness** *n*

♦ censure, denunciation, rebuke, reprimand, reproof, stricture

²**reproach** *vb* **1** ♦ : to express disappointment in or displeasure with (a person) for conduct that is blameworthy or in need of amendment : REBUKE **2** : to cast discredit on — **re·proach·able** *adj*

♦ admonish, chide, lecture, rail (at *or* against), rate, rebuke, reprimand, scold ♦ censure, condemn, denounce, rebuke, reprimand, reprove

¹**rep·ro·bate** \'re-prə-‚bāt\ *n* **1** : a person foreordained to damnation **2** : a thoroughly bad person : SCOUNDREL

²**reprobate** *adj* ♦ : of, relating to, or having the characteristics of a reprobate

♦ corrupt, debauched, decadent, degenerate, dissolute, perverse, perverted

rep·ro·ba·tion \‚re-prə-'bā-shən\ *n* : strong disapproval : CONDEMNATION

re·pro·duce \‚rē-prə-'düs, -'dyüs\ *vb* **1** ♦ : to produce again or anew **2** ♦ : to produce offspring — **re·pro·duc·ible** \-'dü-sə-bəl, -'dyü-\ *adj* — **re·pro·duc·tive** \-'dək-tiv\ *adj*

♦ [1] copy, duplicate, imitate, replicate ♦ [2] breed, multiply, procreate, propagate

re·pro·duc·tion \-'dək-shən\ *n* ♦ : something reproduced

♦ carbon copy, copy, duplicate, duplication, facsimile, imitation, replica, replication

re·proof \ri-'prüf\ *n* ♦ : blame or censure for a fault

♦ censure, denunciation, rebuke, reprimand, reproach, stricture

re·prove \ri-'prüv\ *vb* **re·proved; re·prov·ing 1** ♦ : to administer a rebuke to **2** ♦ : to express disapproval of — **re·prov·er** *n*

♦ [1] admonish, chide, rebuke, reprimand, reproach ♦ [2] censure, condemn, denounce

rept *abbr* report
rep·tile \'rep-təl, -‚tīl\ *n* : any of a large class of air-breathing scaly vertebrates including snakes, lizards, alligators, turtles, and extinct related forms (as dinosaurs) — **rep·til·i·an** \rep-'ti-lē-ən\ *adj or n*

re·pub·lic \ri-'pə-blik\ *n* **1** : a government having a chief of state who is not a monarch and is usu. a president; *also* : a nation or other political unit having such a government **2** : a government in which supreme power is held by the citizens entitled to vote and is exercised by elected officers and representatives governing according to law; *also* : a nation or other political unit having such a form of government **3** : a constituent political and territorial unit of the former nations of Czechoslovakia, the U.S.S.R., or Yugoslavia

¹**re·pub·li·can** \-bli-kən\ *adj* **1** ♦ : of, relating to, or resembling a republic **2** : favoring or supporting a republic **3** *cap* : of, relating to, or constituting one of the two major political parties in the U.S. evolving in the mid-19th century — **re·pub·li·can·ism** *n, often cap*

♦ democratic, popular, self-governing

²**republican** *n* **1** : one that favors or supports a republican form of government **2** *cap* : a member of a republican party and esp. of the Republican party of the U.S.

re·pu·di·ate \ri-'pyü-dē-‚āt\ *vb* **-at·ed; -at·ing 1** ♦ : to give up or renounce as one's own : DISOWN **2** ♦ : to refuse to have anything to do with : refuse to acknowledge, accept, or pay ⟨~ a charge⟩ ⟨~ a debt⟩ **3** ♦ : to reject as untrue or unjust — **re·pu·di·a·tor** \-'pyü-dē-‚ā-tər\ *n*

♦ [1, 2] disavow, disclaim, disown ♦ [2, 3] decline, deny, disallow, disapprove, negative, refuse, reject, spurn, turn down

re·pu·di·a·tion \-‚pyü-dē-'ā-shən\ *n* ♦ : the act of repudiating : the state of being repudiated

♦ contradiction, denial, disallowance, disavowal, disclaimer, negation, rejection

re·pug·nance \ri-'pəg-nəns\ *n* **1** : the quality or fact of being contradictory or inconsistent **2** ♦ : strong dislike, distaste, or antagonism

♦ aversion, disgust, distaste, loathing, nausea, repulsion, revulsion

re·pug·nant \-nənt\ *adj* **1** : marked by repugnance **2** ♦ : contrary to a person's tastes or principles : exciting distaste or aversion — **re·pug·nant·ly** *adv*

♦ distasteful, foul, nasty, nauseating, noisome, obnoxious, obscene, odious, offensive, repellent, repulsive, revolting

¹**re·pulse** \ri-'pəls\ *vb* **re·pulsed; re·puls·ing 1** ♦ : to drive or beat back : REPEL **2** : to repel by discourtesy or denial : REBUFF **3** ♦ : to cause a feeling of repulsion in : DISGUST

♦ [1] fend, repel, stave off ♦ [3] disgust, nauseate, repel, revolt, sicken, turn off

²**repulse** *n* **1** ♦ : an abrupt rejection of an offer or advance : REBUFF **2** : the action of repelling an attacker : the fact of being repelled

♦ brush-off, cold shoulder, rebuff, snub

re·pul·sion \ri-'pəl-shən\ *n* **1** : the action of repulsing : the state of being repulsed **2** : the force with which bodies, particles, or like forces repel one another **3** ♦ : a feeling of aversion

♦ aversion, disgust, distaste, loathing, nausea, repugnance, revulsion

re·pul·sive \-siv\ adj **1** : serving or tending to repel or reject **2** ♦ : arousing aversion or disgust — **re·pul·sive·ly** adv

♦ abhorrent, distasteful, horrible, horrid, nasty, nauseating, noisome, obnoxious, offensive, repellent, repugnant, revolting

re·pul·sive·ness n ♦ : the quality or state of being repulsive

♦ atrociousness, atrocity, frightfulness, hideousness, horror, monstrosity

re·pur·pose \(ˌ)rē-ˈpər-pəs\ vb : to give a new purpose or use to
rep·u·ta·ble \ˈre-pyə-tə-bəl\ adj ♦ : having a good reputation ⟨a ∼ lawyer⟩ — **rep·u·ta·bly** \-blē\ adv

♦ name, prestigious, reputed, respectable

rep·u·ta·tion \ˌre-pyu̇-ˈtā-shən\ n **1** ♦ : overall quality or character as seen or judged by people in general **2** : place in public esteem or regard

♦ character, mark, name, note, report

¹**re·pute** \ri-ˈpyüt\ vb **re·put·ed; re·put·ing** : BELIEVE, CONSIDER
²**repute** n **1** : the character or status commonly ascribed to one : REPUTATION **2** : the state of being favorably known or spoken of

re·put·ed \ri-ˈpyü-təd\ adj **1** ♦ : having a good repute : REPUTABLE **2** ♦ : according to reputation : SUPPOSED — **re·put·ed·ly** adv

♦ [1] name, prestigious, reputable, respectable ♦ [2] apparent, assumed, evident, ostensible, seeming, supposed

req abbr **1** request **2** require; required **3** requisition
¹**re·quest** \ri-ˈkwest\ n **1** ♦ : an act or instance of asking for something **2** : a thing asked for **3** : the condition of being asked for ⟨available on ∼⟩

♦ call, inquiry, query, question

²**request** vb **1** : to make a request to or of **2** ♦ : to ask for — **re·quest·er** n

♦ ask, call, order, requisition

re·qui·em \ˈre-kwē-əm, ˈrā-\ n **1** : a mass for a dead person; also : a musical setting for this **2** ♦ : a musical service or hymn in honor of the dead **3** : something that resembles a solemn chant in honor of the dead

♦ dirge, elegy, lament, threnody

re·quire \ri-ˈkwīr\ vb **re·quired; re·quir·ing** **1** ♦ : to demand as necessary or essential **2** : COMMAND, ORDER

♦ demand, necessitate, need, take, want, warrant

re·quire·ment \-mənt\ n **1** : something (as a condition or quality) required ⟨entrance ∼s⟩ **2** ♦ : something wanted or needed : NECESSITY

♦ condition, demand, essential, must, necessity, need, requisite

¹**req·ui·site** \ˈre-kwə-zət\ adj ♦ : of the utmost importance : NECESSARY

♦ essential, imperative, indispensable, integral, necessary, needful, vital

²**requisite** n : something that is required or necessary
¹**req·ui·si·tion** \ˌre-kwə-ˈzi-shən\ n **1** : formal application or demand (as for supplies) **2** : the state of being in demand or use
²**requisition** vb ♦ : to make a requisition for

♦ ask, order, request

re·quit·al \ri-ˈkwīt-ᵊl\ n **1** ♦ : something given in return, compensation, or retaliation **2** ♦ : the act or action of requiting : the state of being requited

♦ [1] compensation, damages, indemnity, payment, quittance, recompense, redress, remuneration, reparation, restitution, satisfaction ♦ [2] reprisal, retaliation, retribution, revenge, vengeance

re·quite \ri-ˈkwīt\ vb **re·quit·ed; re·quit·ing** **1** : to make return for : REPAY **2** ♦ : to make retaliation for : AVENGE **3** ♦ : to make return to

♦ [2] avenge, retaliate, revenge ♦ [3] compensate, indemnify, recompense, recoup, remunerate

rere·dos \ˈrer-ə-ˌdäs\ n : a usu. ornamental wood or stone screen or partition wall behind an altar

re·run \ˈrē-ˌrən, (ˌ)rē-ˈrən\ n **1** : the act or an instance of running again or anew **2** : a show or program that is shown again — **re·run** \(ˌ)rē-ˈrən\ vb
res abbr **1** research **2** reservation; reserve **3** reservoir **4** residence; resident **5** resolution
re·sale \ˈrē-ˌsāl, (ˌ)rē-ˈsāl\ n : the act of selling again usu. to a new party — **re·sal·able** \(ˌ)rē-ˈsā-lə-bəl\ adj
re·scind \ri-ˈsind\ vb ♦ : to destroy the force, effectiveness, or validity of : REPEAL

♦ abolish, abrogate, annul, cancel, dissolve, invalidate, negate, nullify, quash, repeal, void

re·scis·sion \-ˈsi-zhən\ n ♦ : an act of rescinding

♦ abortion, calling, cancellation, recall, repeal, revocation

re·script \ˈrē-ˌskript\ n : an official or authoritative order or decree
¹**res·cue** \ˈres-kyü\ vb **res·cued; res·cu·ing** ♦ : to free from danger, harm, or confinement

♦ deliver, save

²**rescue** n ♦ : an act of rescuing

♦ deliverance, salvation

res·cu·er n ♦ : one that rescues

♦ deliverer, redeemer, savior

¹**re·search** \ri-ˈsərch, ˈrē-ˌsərch\ n **1** : careful or diligent search **2** ♦ : studious inquiry or examination aimed at the discovery and interpretation of new knowledge **3** : the collecting of information about a particular subject — **re·search·er** n

♦ examination, exploration, inquiry, investigation, probe, study

²**research** vb ♦ : to search or investigate exhaustively

♦ delve, dig, explore, go, inquire into, investigate, look, probe

re·sec·tion \ri-ˈsek-shən\ n : the surgical removal of part of an organ or structure
re·sem·blance \ri-ˈzem-bləns\ n ♦ : the quality or state of resembling; also : a point of likeness

♦ community, correspondence, likeness, parallelism, similarity, similitude

re·sem·ble \ri-ˈzem-bəl\ vb **-bled; -bling** : to be like or similar to
re·sent \ri-ˈzent\ vb : to feel or exhibit annoyance or indignation at ⟨∼ed his interference⟩
re·sent·ful \-fəl\ adj ♦ : full of resentment : inclined to resent — **re·sent·ful·ly** adv

♦ acrid, acrimonious, bitter, hard, rancorous, sore ♦ covetous, envious, jaundiced, jealous

re·sent·ment n ♦ : a feeling of indignant displeasure or ill will at something regarded as a wrong, insult, or injury

♦ dudgeon, huff, offense, peeve, pique, umbrage

re·ser·pine \ri-ˈsər-ˌpēn, -pən\ n : a drug used in treating high blood pressure and nervous tension
res·er·va·tion \ˌre-zər-ˈvā-shən\ n **1** : an act of reserving **2** : something (as a room in a hotel) arranged for in advance **3** : something reserved; esp : a tract of public land set aside for special use **4** ♦ : a limiting condition

♦ condition, provision, proviso, qualification, stipulation

¹**re·serve** \ri-ˈzərv\ vb **re·served; re·serv·ing** **1** ♦ : to store for future or special use **2** ♦ : to hold back for oneself **3** ♦ : to set aside or arrange to have set aside or held for special use

♦ [1] accumulate, cache, garner, hoard, lay up, stash, stockpile, store ♦ [2] hang on, hold, keep, retain, withhold ♦ [3] allocate, consecrate, dedicate, devote, earmark, save

²**reserve** n **1** ♦ : something reserved : STORE **2** : a military force withheld from action for later use — usu. used in pl. **3** : the military forces of a country not part of the regular services; also : RESERVIST **4** : a tract set apart : RESERVATION **5** : an act of reserving **6** ♦ : restraint or caution in one's words or bearing **7** : money or its equivalent kept in hand or set apart to meet liabilities **8** ♦ : a person or thing that takes the place or function of another

♦ [1] cache, deposit, hoard, store ♦ [6] constraint, restraint, self-control ♦ [8] backup, pinch hitter, relief, replacement, stand-in, sub, substitute

re·served \ri-ˈzərvd\ adj **1** ♦ : restrained in words and actions **2** : set aside for future or special use — **re·serv·ed·ly** \-ˈzər-vəd-lē\ adv — **re·serv·ed·ness** \-vəd-nəs\ n

♦ closemouthed, laconic, reticent, silent, taciturn, uncommunicative

re·serv·ist \ri-'zər-vist\ *n* : a member of a military reserve
res·er·voir \'re-zə-ˌvwär, -zər-, -ˌvwȯr\ *n* : a place where something is kept in store; *esp* : an artificial lake where water is collected and kept for use
re·shuf·fle \rē-'shə-fəl\ *vb* **1** : to shuffle again **2** : to reorganize usu. by redistribution of existing elements ⟨*reshuffled* our schedules⟩ — **reshuffle** *n*
re·side \ri-'zīd\ *vb* **re·sid·ed; re·sid·ing** **1** ♦ : to make one's home : DWELL **2** : to be present as a quality or vested as a right

♦ abide, dwell, live

res·i·dence \'re-zə-dəns\ *n* **1** : the act or fact of residing in a place as a dweller or in discharge of a duty or an obligation **2** ♦ : the place where one actually lives **3** : a building used as a home : DWELLING **4** : the period of living in a place

♦ abode, domicile, dwelling, home, house, lodging, quarters

res·i·den·cy \'re-zə-dən-sē\ *n, pl* **-cies** **1** : the residence of or the territory under a diplomatic resident **2** : a period of advanced training in a medical specialty
¹**res·i·dent** \-dənt\ *adj* **1** : RESIDING **2** : being in residence **3** : not migratory
²**resident** *n* **1** ♦ : one who resides in a place **2** : a diplomatic representative with governing powers (as in a protectorate) **3** : a physician serving a residency

♦ denizen, dweller, inhabitant, occupant

res·i·den·tial \ˌre-zə-'den-chəl\ *adj* **1** : used as a residence or by residents **2** : occupied by or restricted to residences — **res·i·den·tial·ly** *adv*
¹**re·sid·u·al** \ri-'zi-jə-wəl\ *adj* : being a residue or remainder
²**residual** *n* **1** : a residual product or substance **2** : a payment (as to an actor or writer) for each rerun after an initial showing (as of a taped TV show)
re·sid·u·ary \ri-'zi-jə-ˌwer-ē\ *adj* : of, relating to, or constituting a residue esp. of an estate
res·i·due \'re-zə-ˌdü, -ˌdyü\ *n* ♦ : a part remaining after another part has been taken away

♦ balance, leavings, leftovers, odds and ends, remainder, remains, remnant, rest

re·sid·u·um \ri-'zi-jə-wəm\ *n, pl* **re·sid·ua** \-jə-wə\ **1** : something remaining or residual after certain deductions are made **2** : a residual product
re·sign \ri-'zīn\ *vb* **1** ♦ : to give up deliberately (as one's position) esp. by a formal act **2** : to give (oneself) over (as to grief or despair) without resistance — **re·sign·ed·ly** \-'zī-nəd-lē\ *adv*

♦ abdicate, abnegate, cede, relinquish, renounce, step down, surrender ♦ *usu* **resign from** leave, quit, retire, step down

re–sign \ˌrē-'sīn\ *vb* : to sign again
res·ig·na·tion \ˌre-zig-'nā-shən\ *n* **1** : an act or instance of resigning; *also* : a formal notification of such an act **2** : the quality or state of being resigned
re·signed \ri-'zīnd\ *adj* ♦ : being resigned to something : characterized by resignation

♦ acquiescent, passive, tolerant, unresistant, unresisting, yielding

re·sil·ience \ri-'zil-yəns\ *n* **1** : the ability of a body to regain its original size and shape after being compressed, bent, or stretched **2** : an ability to recover from or adjust easily to change or misfortune
re·sil·ien·cy \-yən-sē\ *n* : RESILIENCE
re·sil·ient \-yənt\ *adj* ♦ : marked by resilience ⟨∼ athletes⟩

♦ elastic, flexible, rubbery, springy, stretch, supple

res·in \'rez-ᵊn\ *n* : any of various substances obtained from the gum or sap of some trees and used esp. in varnishes, plastics, and medicine; *also* : a comparable synthetic product — **res·in·ous** *adj*
¹**re·sist** \ri-'zist\ *vb* **1** ♦ : to fight against : OPPOSE ⟨∼ aggression⟩ **2** : to withstand the force or effect of ⟨∼ disease⟩ — **re·sist·ible** \-'zis-tə-bəl\ *adj* — **re·sist·less** *adj*

♦ buck, defy, fight, oppose, repel, withstand *Ant* bow (to), capitulate (to), give in (to), submit (to), succumb (to), surrender (to), yield (to)

²**resist** *n* : something (as a coating) that resists or prevents a particular action
re·sis·tance \ri-'zis-təns\ *n* **1** : the act or an instance of resisting : OPPOSITION **2** : the power or capacity to resist; *esp* : the inherent ability of an organism to resist harmful influences (as disease or infection) **3** : the opposition offered by a body to the passage through it of a steady electric current
re·sis·tant \-tənt\ *adj* : giving or capable of resistance
re·sis·tor \ri-'zis-tər\ *n* : a device used to provide resistance to the flow of an electric current in a circuit
res·o·lute \'re-zə-ˌlüt\ *adj* ♦ : firmly determined in purpose — **res·o·lute·ly** *adv*

♦ bound, decisive, determined, firm, intent, purposeful, set, single-minded

res·o·lute·ness *n* : the quality or state of being resolute
res·o·lu·tion \ˌre-zə-'lü-shən\ *n* **1** : the act or process of resolving **2** : the action of solving; *also* : SOLUTION **3** ♦ : the quality of being resolute : DETERMINATION **4** ♦ : a formal statement expressing the opinion, will, or intent of a body of persons **5** : a measure of the sharpness of an image or of the fineness with which a device can produce or record such an image

♦ [3] decision, decisiveness, determination, firmness, granite, resolve ♦ [4] conclusion, decision, judgment (*or* judgement), opinion, verdict

re·solv·able *adj* ♦ : capable of being resolved

♦ answerable, explicable, soluble, solvable

¹**re·solve** \ri-'zälv\ *vb* **re·solved; re·solv·ing** **1** : to break up into constituent parts **2** : to distinguish between or make visible adjacent parts of **3** ♦ : to find an answer to : SOLVE **4** ♦ : to reach a firm decision about : DECIDE **5** : to make or pass a formal resolution

♦ [3] answer, break, crack, dope, figure out, puzzle, riddle, solve, unravel, work, work out ♦ [4] choose, conclude, decide, determine, figure, opt

²**resolve** *n* **1** ♦ : fixity of purpose **2** : something resolved

♦ decision, decisiveness, determination, firmness, granite, resolution

res·o·nance \'re-zə-nəns\ *n* **1** : the quality or state of being resonant **2** : a reinforcement of sound in a vibrating body caused by waves from another body vibrating at nearly the same rate
res·o·nant \-nənt\ *adj* **1** : continuing to sound : RESOUNDING **2** : relating to or exhibiting resonance **3** ♦ : intensified and enriched by or as if by resonance — **res·o·nant·ly** *adv*

♦ golden, resounding, ringing, round, sonorous, vibrant

res·o·nate \-ˌnāt\ *vb* **-nat·ed; -nat·ing** **1** : to produce or exhibit resonance **2** ♦ : to produce or exhibit resonance : REVERBERATE

♦ echo, reecho, resound, reverberate, sound

res·o·na·tor \-ˌnā-tər\ *n* : something that resounds or exhibits resonance
re·sorp·tion \rē-'sȯrp-shən, -'zȯrp-\ *n* : the action or process of breaking down and assimilating something (as a tooth or an embryo)
¹**re·sort** \ri-'zȯrt\ *n* **1** : one looked to for help : REFUGE **2** ♦ : a turning to someone or something for help or protection : RECOURSE **3** : frequent or general visiting ⟨place of ∼⟩ **4** ♦ : a frequently visited place : HAUNT **5** : a place providing recreation esp. to vacationers

♦ [2] expedient, recourse, resource ♦ [4] hangout, haunt, rendezvous

²**resort** *vb* **1** ♦ : to go often or habitually **2** : to have recourse ⟨∼ed to violence⟩

♦ *usu* **resort to** [1] frequent, hang around, hang out, haunt, visit ♦ *usu* **resort to** [2] go, refer, turn

re·sound \ri-'zaund\ *vb* **1** ♦ : to become filled with sound : REVERBERATE **2** : to sound loudly

♦ echo, reecho, resonate, reverberate, sound

re·sound·ing *adj* **1** ♦ : producing or characterized by resonant sound : RESONANT **2** ♦ : impressively sonorous ⟨∼ name⟩ **3** ♦ : uttered with or marked by emphasis : EMPHATIC ⟨a ∼ success⟩ — **re·sound·ing·ly** *adv*

♦ [1, 2] golden, resonant, ringing, round, sonorous, vibrant ♦ [3] aggressive, assertive, dynamic, emphatic, energetic, forceful, strenuous, vehement, vigorous

re·source \'rē-ˌsȯrs, ri-'sȯrs\ *n* **1** : a source of supply or support — usu. used in pl. **2** *pl* ♦ : available funds **3** : a possibility of relief or recovery **4** : a means of spending leisure time **5** : ability to meet and handle situations **6** ♦ : something to which one has recourse in difficulty — **re·source·ful** \ri-'sȯrs-fəl\ *adj* — **re·source·ful·ness** *n*

♦ **resources** [2] finances, funds, pocket, wherewithal ♦ [6] expedient, recourse, resort

¹**re·spect** \ri-'spekt\ *n* **1** ♦ : relation to something usu. specified : REGARD ⟨in ~ to⟩ **2** ♦ : high or special regard : ESTEEM **3** *pl* ♦ : an expression of respect or deference **4** : DETAIL, PARTICULAR — **re·spect·ful·ly** *adv* — **re·spect·ful·ness** *n*

♦ [2] admiration, appreciation, esteem, estimation, favor (*or* favour), regard ♦ **respects** [3] compliments, greetings, regards

²**respect** *vb* **1** ♦ : to consider deserving of high regard : ESTEEM **2** : to refrain from interfering with ⟨~ her privacy⟩ **3** : to have reference to : CONCERN — **re·spect·er** *n*

♦ admire, appreciate, esteem, regard

re·spect·able \ri-'spek-tə-bəl\ *adj* **1** ♦ : worthy of respect **2** ♦ : decent or correct in conduct **3** ♦ : fair in size, quantity, or quality : TOLERABLE **4** : fit to be seen : PRESENTABLE — **re·spect·a·bil·i·ty** \-ˌspek-tə-'bi-lə-tē\ *n* — **re·spect·ably** \-'spek-tə-blē\ *adv*

♦ [1] name, prestigious, reputable, reputed *Ant* disreputable, loose ♦ [2] correct, decent, decorous, genteel, nice, polite, proper, seemly ♦ [3] acceptable, adequate, all right, decent, fine, OK, passable, satisfactory, tolerable

re·spect·ful \-fəl\ *adj* ♦ : marked by or showing respect or deference

♦ deferential, dutiful, regardful *Ant* disrespectful

re·spect·ing *prep* ♦ : with regard to

♦ about, apropos of, concerning, of, on, regarding, toward

re·spec·tive \-tiv\ *adj* ♦ : not shared with another : SEPARATE ⟨returned to their ~ homes⟩

♦ different, individual, separate

re·spec·tive·ly \-lē\ *adv* **1** : as relating to each **2** : each in the order given

res·pi·ra·tion \ˌres-pə-'rā-shən\ *n* **1** : an act or the process of breathing **2** : the physical and chemical processes (as breathing and oxidation) by which a living thing obtains oxygen and eliminates waste gases (as carbon dioxide) — **re·spi·ra·to·ry** \'res-pə-rə-ˌtōr-ē, ri-'spī-rə-\ *adj* — **re·spire** \ri-'spīr\ *vb*

res·pi·ra·tor \'res-pə-ˌrā-tər\ *n* **1** : a device covering the mouth and nose esp. to prevent inhaling harmful vapors **2** : a device for artificial respiration

re·spite \'res-pət\ *n* **1** : a temporary delay **2** ♦ : an interval of rest or relief

♦ break, breath, breather, recess

re·splen·dence \-dəns\ *n* ♦ : the quality or state of being resplendent

♦ augustness, brilliance, glory, grandeur, grandness, magnificence, majesty, nobility, nobleness, splendor, stateliness

re·splen·dent \ri-'splen-dənt\ *adj* : SPLENDID ⟨~ uniforms⟩ — **re·splen·dent·ly** *adv*

re·spond \ri-'spänd\ *vb* **1** ♦ : to say something in return : ANSWER, REPLY **2** : REACT ⟨~ed to a call for help⟩ **3** : to show favorable reaction ⟨~ to medication⟩ — **re·spond·er** *n*

♦ answer, rejoin, reply, retort, return

re·spon·dent \ri-'spän-dənt\ *n* : one who responds; *esp* : one who answers in various legal proceedings — **respondent** *adj*

re·sponse \ri-'späns\ *n* **1** ♦ : an act of responding **2** ♦ : something constituting a reply or a reaction

♦ [1] reaction, reply, take ♦ [2] answer, comeback, reply, retort, return

re·spon·si·bil·i·ty \ri-ˌspän-sə-'bi-lə-tē\ *n, pl* **-ties** **1** ♦ : the quality or state of being responsible **2** ♦ : something for which one is responsible

♦ [1] blame, fault, liability ♦ [2] burden, charge, commitment, duty, need, obligation

re·spon·si·ble \ri-'spän-sə-bəl\ *adj* **1** ♦ : liable to be called upon to answer for one's acts or decisions : ANSWERABLE **2** ♦ : able to fulfill one's obligations : TRUSTWORTHY **3** : able to choose for oneself between right and wrong **4** : involving accountability or important duties ⟨~ position⟩ — **re·spon·si·ble·ness** *n* — **re·spon·si·bly** \-blē\ *adv*

♦ [1] accountable, answerable, liable *Ant* irresponsible, unaccountable ♦ [2] dependable, good, reliable, safe, solid, steady, sure, tried, true, trustworthy

re·spon·sive \-siv\ *adj* **1** : RESPONDING **2** : quick to respond **3** : using responses ⟨~ readings⟩ — **re·spon·sive·ly** *adv* — **re·spon·sive·ness** *n*

¹**rest** \'rest\ *n* **1** ♦ : a bodily state characterized by minimal functional and metabolic activities : SLEEP **2** ♦ : freedom from work or activity **3** : a state of motionlessness or inactivity **4** : a place of shelter or lodging **5** : a silence in music equivalent in duration to a note of the same value; *also* : a character indicating this **6** : something used as a support — **rest·ful·ly** *adv*

♦ [1] repose, sleep, slumber ♦ [2] ease, leisure, relaxation, repose *Ant* exertion, labor, toil, work

²**rest** *vb* **1** ♦ : to get rest by lying down; *esp* : SLEEP **2** ♦ : to cease from action or motion **3** : to give rest to : set at rest **4** : to sit or lie fixed or supported **5** : to place on or against a support **6** : to remain based or founded **7** ♦ : to cause to be firmly fixed : GROUND **8** : to remain for action : DEPEND

♦ [1] catnap, doze, nap, sleep, slumber, snooze ♦ [2] bask, loll, lounge, relax, repose ♦ [7] base, ground

³**rest** *n* ♦ : something left over

♦ balance, leavings, leftovers, odds and ends, remainder, remains, remnant, residue

re·start \(ˈ)rē-'stärt\ *vb* ♦ : to begin again an activity or undertaking

♦ continue, renew, reopen, resume

re·state \(ˈ)rē-'stāt\ *vb* ♦ : to express again in words

♦ paraphrase, rephrase, translate

res·tau·rant \'res-trənt, -tə-ˌränt\ *n* ♦ : a public eating place

♦ café, diner, grill

res·tau·ra·teur \ˌres-tə-rə-'tər\ *also* **res·tau·ran·teur** \-ˌrän-\ *n* : the operator or proprietor of a restaurant

rest·ful \'rest-fəl\ *adj* ♦ : marked by, affording, or suggesting rest and repose

♦ calm, hushed, peaceful, quiet, serene, still, tranquil

rest home *n* : an establishment that gives care for the aged or convalescent

res·ti·tu·tion \ˌres-tə-'tü-shən, -'tyü-\ *n* **1** : the act of restoring : the state of being restored; *esp* : restoration of something to its rightful owner **2** ♦ : a compensating, repaying, or giving an equivalent for some injury

♦ compensation, damages, indemnity, quittance, recompense, redress, remuneration, reparation, requital, satisfaction

res·tive \'res-tiv\ *adj* **1** : stubbornly resisting control : BALKY **2** : marked by impatience or uneasiness : UNEASY — **res·tive·ly** *adv* — **res·tive·ness** *n* : the quality or state of being restive

rest·less \'rest-ləs\ *adj* **1** ♦ : lacking or denying rest ⟨a ~ night⟩ **2** : never resting or settled : always moving ⟨the ~ sea⟩ **3** ♦ : marked by or showing unrest esp. of mind ⟨~ pacing back and forth⟩ — **rest·less·ly** *adv*

♦ [1] uneasy *Ant* restful ♦ [3] anxious, distressful, nervous, tense, unsettling, upsetting, worrisome

rest·less·ness *n* ♦ : the quality or state of being restless

♦ disquiet, ferment, turmoil, uneasiness, unrest

re·stor·able \ri-'stōr-ə-bəl\ *adj* : fit for restoring or reclaiming

res·to·ra·tion \ˌres-tə-'rā-shən\ *n* **1** : an act of restoring : the state of being restored **2** : something (as a building) that has been restored

¹**re·stor·ative** \ri-'stōr-ə-tiv\ *n* : something that restores esp. to consciousness or health

²**restorative** *adj* ♦ : of or relating to restoration; *esp* : having power to restore

♦ healthful, healthy, salubrious, salutary, wholesome ♦ bracing, invigorating, refreshing, stimulative, tonic

re·store \ri-'stōr\ *vb* **re·stored; re·stor·ing** **1** : to give back : RETURN **2** : to put back into use or service **3** ♦ : to put or bring back into a former or original state **4** : to put again in possession of something — **re·stor·er** *n*

♦ freshen, recreate, refresh, regenerate, rejuvenate, renew, revitalize, revive

re·strain \ri-'strān\ *vb* **1** : to prevent from doing something **2** ♦ : to limit, restrict, or keep under control : CURB **3** ♦ : to place under restraint or arrest — **re·strain·able** *adj* — **re·strain·er** *n*

♦ [2] bridle, check, constrain, contain, control, curb, govern, inhibit, regulate, rein, tame ♦ [3] apprehend, arrest, nab, pick up, seize

re·strained \ri-'strānd\ *adj* ♦ : marked by restraint — **re·strain·ed·ly** \-'strā-nəd-lē\ *adv*

♦ conservative, muted, quiet, subdued, unpretentious

restraining order *n* : a legal order directing one person to stay away from another

re·straint \ri-'strānt\ *n* **1** : an act of restraining : the state of being restrained **2** ♦ : a restraining force, agency, or device **3** : deprivation or limitation of liberty : CONFINEMENT **4** ♦ : control over the expression of one's feelings

♦ [2] check, condition, constraint, curb, fetter, limitation, restriction ♦ [4] self-control, self-discipline, self-government, self-possession, self-restraint, will, willpower ♦ [4] constraint, inhibition, repression, suppression

re·strict \ri-'strikt\ *vb* **1** ♦ : to confine within bounds : LIMIT **2** : to place under restriction as to use — **re·stric·tive** *adj* — **re·stric·tive·ly** *adv*

♦ check, circumscribe, confine, control, curb, inhibit, limit, restrain

re·strict·ed \ri-'strik-təd\ *adj* ♦ : subject or subjected to restriction

♦ definite, determinate, finite, limited, measured, narrow

re·stric·tion \ri-'strik-shən\ *n* **1** ♦ : something (as a law or rule) that restricts **2** : an act of restricting : the state of being restricted

♦ check, condition, constraint, curb, fetter, limitation, restraint

rest room *n* : a room or suite of rooms that includes sinks and toilets

¹**re·sult** \ri-'zəlt\ *vb* **1** : to come about as an effect or consequence **2** ♦ : to have an issue or result ⟨the disease ∼ed in death⟩

♦ *usu* **result in** bring about, cause, create, effect, effectuate, generate, induce, make, produce, prompt, work, yield

²**result** *n* **1** ♦ : something that results : EFFECT **2** : beneficial or discernible effect **3** : something obtained by calculation or investigation

♦ aftermath, conclusion, consequence, corollary, development, effect, issue, outcome, outgrowth, product, resultant, sequence, upshot

¹**re·sul·tant** \-'zəlt-ᵊnt\ *adj* ♦ : derived from or resulting from something else

♦ attendant, consequent, consequential, due

²**resultant** *n* : something that results

re·sume \ri-'züm\ *vb* **re·sumed; re·sum·ing** **1** : to take or assume again **2** ♦ : to return to or begin again after interruption **3** : to take back to oneself — **re·sump·tion** \-'zəmp-shən\ *n*

♦ continue, renew, reopen, restart

ré·su·mé *or* **re·su·me** *also* **re·su·mé** \'re-zə-ˌmā, ˌre-zə-'mā\ *n* **1** ♦ : an abstract, abridgment, or compendium : SUMMARY **2** : a short account of one's career and qualifications usu. prepared by a job applicant

♦ abstract, digest, encapsulation, epitome, outline, précis, recapitulation, roundup, sum, summary, synopsis, wrap-up

re·sur·gence \ri-'sər-jəns\ *n* ♦ : a rising again into life, activity, or prominence — **re·sur·gent** \-jənt\ *adj*

♦ rebirth, regeneration, rejuvenation, renewal, resurrection, resuscitation, revival

res·ur·rect \ˌre-zə-'rekt\ *vb* **1** : to raise from the dead **2** : to bring to attention or use again

res·ur·rec·tion \ˌre-zə-'rek-shən\ *n* **1** *cap* : the rising of Christ from the dead **2** *often cap* : the rising to life of all human dead before the final judgment **3** ♦ : an act or instance of reviving : REVIVAL ⟨the ∼ of her career⟩

♦ rebirth, regeneration, rejuvenation, renewal, resurgence, resuscitation, revival

re·sus·ci·tate \ri-'sə-sə-ˌtāt\ *vb* **-tat·ed; -tat·ing** ♦ : to revive from apparent death or unconsciousness; *also* : REVITALIZE — **re·sus·ci·ta·tor** \-ˌtā-tər\ *n*

♦ reanimate, regenerate, reinvigorate, rejuvenate, renew, revitalize, revive

re·sus·ci·ta·tion \ri-ˌsə-sə-'tā-shən, ˌrē-\ *n* ♦ : an act of resuscitating or the state of being resuscitated

♦ rebirth, regeneration, rejuvenation, renewal, resurgence, resurrection, revival

ret *abbr* retired

¹**re·tail** \'rē-ˌtāl, *esp for 2 also* ri-'tāl\ *vb* **1** ♦ : to sell in small quantities directly to the ultimate consumer **2** : to tell in detail or to one person after another — **re·tail·er** *n*

♦ deal, market, merchandise, put up, sell, vend

²**re·tail** \'rē-ˌtāl\ *n* : the sale of goods in small amounts to ultimate consumers — **retail** *adj or adv*

re·tain \ri-'tān\ *vb* **1** ♦ : to hold in possession or use **2** ♦ : to engage (as a lawyer) by paying a fee in advance **3** : to keep in a fixed place or position

♦ [1] hang on, hold, keep, reserve, withhold ♦ [2] employ, engage, hire, take on

¹**re·tain·er** \ri-'tā-nər\ *n* **1** : one that retains **2** ♦ : a servant in a wealthy household **3** : EMPLOYEE **4** : a device that holds something (as teeth) in place

♦ domestic, flunky, lackey, menial, servant, steward

²**retainer** *n* : a fee paid to secure services (as of a lawyer)

¹**re·take** \(ˌ)rē-'tāk\ *vb* **-took** \-'tůk\; **-tak·en** \-'tā-kən\; **-tak·ing** **1** ♦ : to take or seize again **2** : to photograph again

♦ recapture, reclaim, recoup, recover, regain, repossess, retrieve

²**re·take** \'rē-ˌtāk\ *n* : a second photographing of a motion-picture scene

re·tal·i·ate \ri-'ta-lē-ˌāt\ *vb* **-at·ed; -at·ing** ♦ : to return like for like; *esp* : to get revenge — **re·tal·ia·to·ry** \-'tal-yə-ˌtōr-ē\ *adj*

♦ avenge, requite, revenge

re·tal·i·a·tion \-ˌta-lē-'ā-shən\ *n* ♦ : an act of retaliating

♦ reprisal, requital, retribution, revenge, vengeance

re·tard \ri-'tärd\ *vb* ♦ : to hold back : delay the progress of — **re·tar·da·tion** \ˌrē-ˌtär-'dā-shən, ri-\ *n* — **re·tard·er** *n*

♦ brake, decelerate, slow

re·tar·dant \ri-'tär-dᵊnt\ *adj* : serving or tending to retard — **retardant** *n*

re·tard·ed *adj, dated, offensive* : affected by intellectual disability

retch \'rech\ *vb* **1** : to try to vomit **2** : to throw up : VOMIT

re·ten·tion \ri-'ten-chən\ *n* **1** : the act of retaining : the state of being retained **2** : the power of retaining esp. in the mind : RETENTIVENESS

re·ten·tive \-'ten-tiv\ *adj* : having the power of retaining; *esp* : retaining knowledge easily — **re·ten·tive·ness** *n*

re·think \(ˌ)rē-'thiŋk\ *vb* **-thought** \-'thȯt\; **-think·ing** ♦ : to think about again : RECONSIDER

♦ readdress, reanalyze, reconceive, reconsider, reexamine, review

ret·i·cence \'re-tə-səns\ *n* ♦ : the quality or state or an instance of being reticent

♦ disinclination, hesitancy, reluctance

ret·i·cent \'re-tə-sənt\ *adj* **1** ♦ : tending not to talk or give out information **2** : RELUCTANT **3** : restrained in expression, presentation, or appearance — **ret·i·cent·ly** *adv*

♦ closemouthed, laconic, reserved, silent, taciturn, uncommunicative

ret·i·na \'ret-ᵊn-ə\ *n, pl* **retinas** *or* **ret·i·nae** \-ˌē\ : the sensory membrane lining the eye that receives the image formed by the lens — **ret·i·nal** \'ret-ᵊn-əl\ *adj*

ret·i·nue \'ret-ᵊn-ˌü, -ˌyü\ *n* ♦ : the body of attendants or followers of a distinguished person

♦ cortege, following, suite, train

re·tire \ri-'tīr\ *vb* **re·tired; re·tir·ing** **1** ♦ : to withdraw from action or danger : RETREAT **2** : to withdraw esp. for privacy **3** ♦ : to withdraw from one's occupation or position : conclude one's career **4** : to go to bed **5** : to cause to be out in baseball **6** ♦ : to cause to retire **7** : to withdraw from use or service

♦ [1] back, fall back, recede, retreat, withdraw ♦ *usu* **retire from** [3] leave, quit, resign, step down ♦ [6] cashier, dismiss, fire, remove, sack

re·tired \ri-'tīrd\ *adj* **1** : screened or hidden from view : SECLUDED, QUIET **2** : withdrawn from active duty or from one's career

re·tir·ee \ri-ˌtī-'rē\ *n* : a person who has retired from a career

re·tire·ment *n* : an act of retiring : the state of being retired

re·tir·ing *adj* ♦ : sensitively diffident : SHY

♦ bashful, coy, demure, diffident, introverted, modest, reserved, shy

re·tool \(ˌ)rē-'tül\ *vb* **1** : to reequip with tools **2** : to modify with usu. minor improvements ⟨∼ed the team for next year⟩

¹**re·tort** \ri-'tȯrt\ *vb* **1** ♦ : to say in reply : answer back usu. sharply **2** : to answer (an argument) by a counter argument **3** : RETALIATE

♦ answer, rejoin, reply, respond, return

²retort *n* ♦ : a quick, witty, or cutting reply; *esp* : one that turns back or counters the first speaker's words

♦ comeback, repartee, riposte ♦ answer, comeback, reply, response, return

³re·tort \ri-ˈtȯrt, ˈrē-ˌtȯrt\ *n* : a vessel in which substances are distilled or broken up by heat

re·touch \(ˌ)rē-ˈtəch\ *vb* : TOUCH UP; *esp* : to change (as a photographic negative) in order to produce a more desirable appearance

re·trace \(ˌ)rē-ˈtrās\ *vb* : to go over again or in a reverse direction ⟨*retraced* his steps⟩

re·tract \ri-ˈtrakt\ *vb* **1** : to draw back or in **2** ♦ : to withdraw (as a charge or promise) — **re·tract·able** *adj* — **re·trac·tion** \-ˈtrak-shən\ *n*

♦ abjure, recant, renounce, take back, unsay, withdraw

re·trac·tile \ri-ˈtrakt-ᵊl, -ˈtrak-ˌtīl\ *adj* : capable of being drawn back or in ⟨∼ claws⟩

¹re·tread \(ˌ)rē-ˈtred\ *vb* **re·tread·ed; re·tread·ing** : to put a new tread on (a worn tire)

²re·tread \ˈrē-ˌtred\ *n* **1** : a retreaded tire **2** : one pressed into service again; *also* : REMAKE

¹re·treat \ri-ˈtrēt\ *n* **1** ♦ : an act of withdrawing esp. from something dangerous, difficult, or disagreeable **2** : a military signal for withdrawal; *also* : a military flag-lowering ceremony **3** ♦ : a place of privacy or safety : REFUGE **4** : a period of group withdrawal for prayer, meditation, or study

♦ [1] revulsion, withdrawal *Ant* advancement ♦ [3] asylum, harbor (*or* harbour), haven, refuge, sanctuary, shelter

²retreat *vb* **1** ♦ : to make a retreat **2** : to slope backward

♦ back, fall back, recede, retire, withdraw *Ant* advance

re·trench \ri-ˈtrench\ *vb* **1** : to cut down or pare away : REDUCE, CURTAIL **2** : to cut down expenses : ECONOMIZE — **re·trench·ment** *n*

ret·ri·bu·tion \ˌre-trə-ˈbyü-shən\ *n* ♦ : something administered or exacted in recompense; *esp* : PUNISHMENT — **re·trib·u·tive** \ri-ˈtri-byə-tiv\ *adj* — **re·trib·u·to·ry** \-byə-ˌtȯr-ē\ *adj*

♦ punishment, reprisal, requital, retaliation, revenge, vengeance

re·triev·al \-ˈtrē-vəl\ *n* ♦ : an act or process of retrieving

♦ reclamation, recovery, repossession

re·trieve \ri-ˈtrēv\ *vb* **re·trieved; re·triev·ing** **1** : to search about for and bring in (killed or wounded game) **2** ♦ : to get back again : RECOVER — **re·triev·able** *adj*

♦ recapture, reclaim, recoup, recover, regain, repossess, retake

re·triev·er \ri-ˈtrē-vər\ *n* : one that retrieves; *esp* : a dog of any of several breeds used esp. for retrieving game

ret·ro \ˈre-trō\ *adj* : relating to or being the styles and fashions of the past ⟨∼ clothing⟩

ret·ro·ac·tive \ˌre-trō-ˈak-tiv\ *adj* : made effective as of a date prior to enactment ⟨a ∼ pay raise⟩ — **ret·ro·ac·tive·ly** *adv*

ret·ro·fit \ˈre-trō-ˌfit, ˌre-trō-ˈfit\ *vb* : to furnish (as an aircraft) with newly available equipment — **ret·ro·fit** \ˈre-trō-ˌfit\ *n*

¹ret·ro·grade \ˈre-trə-ˌgrād\ *adj* **1** : moving or tending backward **2** : tending toward or resulting in a worse condition

²retrograde *vb* **1** : RETREAT **2** : DETERIORATE, DEGENERATE

ret·ro·gres·sion \ˌre-trə-ˈgre-shən\ *n* : return to a former and less complex level of development or organization — **ret·ro·gress** \ˌre-trə-ˈgres\ *vb* — **ret·ro·gres·sive** \ˌre-trə-ˈgre-siv\ *adj*

ret·ro·rock·et \ˈre-trō-ˌrä-kət\ *n* : an auxiliary rocket engine (as on a spacecraft) used to slow forward motion

ret·ro·spect \ˈre-trə-ˌspekt\ *n* : a review of past events

ret·ro·spec·tion \ˌre-trə-ˈspek-shən\ *n* ♦ : the act or process or an instance of surveying the past

♦ reappraisal, reexamination, review

ret·ro·spec·tive \ˌre-trə-ˈspek-tiv\ *n* **1** : a comprehensive examination of an artist's work over many years **2** : REVIEW 4 ⟨a war ∼⟩ — **retrospective** *adj* — **ret·ro·spec·tive·ly** *adv*

ret·ro·vi·rus \ˈre-trō-ˌvī-rəs\ *n* : any of a group of RNA-containing viruses (as HIV) that make DNA using RNA instead of the reverse

¹re·turn \ri-ˈtərn\ *vb* **1** : to go or come back **2** : to pass, give, or send back to an earlier possessor **3** : to put back to or in a former place or state **4** : to respond in words or writing : REPLY, ANSWER **5** : to report esp. officially **6** : to elect to office **7** : to bring in (as profit) : YIELD **8** : to give or perform in return — **re·turn·er** *n*

²return *n* **1** : an act of coming or going back to or from a former place or state **2** : RECURRENCE **3** : a report of the results of bal-

loting **4** : a formal statement of taxable income **5** ♦ : the profit from labor, investment, or business **6** : the act of returning something **7** : something that returns or is returned; *also* : a means for conveying something (as water) back to its starting point **8 a** : something given in repayment or reciprocation **b** : something said, written, or done in answer or response : ANSWER, RETORT **9** : an answering play — **return** *adj*

♦ earnings, gain, income, net, payoff, proceeds, profit, revenue, yield

¹re·turn·able \ri-ˈtər-nə-bəl\ *adj* : capable of being returned (as for reuse or recycling); *also* : permitted to be returned

²returnable *n* : a returnable beverage container

re·turn·ee \ri-ˌtər-ˈnē\ *n* : one who returns

re·tweet \(ˌ)rē-ˈtwēt\ *vb* : to repost to the Twitter online messaging service ⟨fans ∼ed her tweet⟩

re·union \rē-ˈyü-nyən\ *n* **1** : an act of reuniting : the state of being reunited **2** : a meeting of persons after separation

¹rev \ˈrev\ *n* : a revolution of a motor

²rev *vb* **revved; rev·ving** : to increase the revolutions per minute of (a motor)

³rev *abbr* **1** revenue **2** reverse **3** review; reviewed **4** revised; revision **5** revolution

Rev *abbr* **1** Revelation **2** Reverend

re·vamp \(ˌ)rē-ˈvamp\ *vb* **1** ♦ : to make a new, amended, improved, or up-to-date version of : REVISE **2** ♦ : to restore to a former better state (as by cleaning, repairing, or rebuilding)

♦ [1] alter, change, make over, modify, recast, redo, refashion, remake, remodel, revise, rework, vary ♦ [2] doctor, fix, mend, patch, recondition, renovate, repair

re·vanche \rə-ˈvän⁽ʰ⁾sh\ *n* : REVENGE; *esp* : a usu. political policy designed to recover lost territory or status

re·veal \ri-ˈvēl\ *vb* **1** ♦ : to make known **2** : to show plainly : open up to view

♦ bare, disclose, discover, divulge, expose, show, spill, tell, unbosom, uncloak, uncover, unmask, unveil *Ant* cloak, conceal, cover (up), enshroud, hide, mask, shroud, veil

re·veil·le \ˈre-və-lē\ *n* : a military signal sounded at about sunrise

¹rev·el \ˈre-vəl\ *vb* **-eled** *or* **-elled; -el·ing** *or* **-el·ling** **1** : to take part in a revel **2** ♦ : to take great pleasure or satisfaction ⟨∼ed in the quiet after everyone had gone⟩

♦ *usu* revel in adore, delight, dig, enjoy, fancy, groove, like, love, relish

²revel *n* ♦ : a usu. wild party or celebration

♦ binge, fling, frolic, gambol, lark, rollick, romp

rev·e·la·tion \ˌre-və-ˈlā-shən\ *n* **1** : an act of revealing **2** : something revealed; *esp* : an enlightening or astonishing disclosure

Revelation *n* : a book of the New Testament of Christian Scripture

rev·e·la·to·ry \ˈre-və-lə-ˌtȯr-ē, ri-ˈve-lə-\ *adj* ♦ : of or relating to revelation : serving to reveal something

♦ eloquent, expressive, meaning, meaningful, pregnant, significant, suggestive

rev·el·er *or* **rev·el·ler** \ˈre-vəl-ər\ *n* ♦ : one who engages in revelry

♦ celebrant, merrymaker, roisterer

rev·el·ry \ˈre-vəl-rē\ *n* ♦ : noisy partying or merrymaking

♦ conviviality, festivity, gaiety, jollification, merriment, merrymaking

¹re·venge \ri-ˈvenj\ *vb* **re·venged; re·veng·ing** ♦ : to inflict harm or injury in return for (a wrong) : AVENGE — **re·veng·er** *n*

♦ avenge, requite, retaliate

²revenge *n* **1** : a desire for revenge **2** ♦ : an act or instance of retaliation to get even **3** : an opportunity for getting satisfaction — **re·venge·ful** *adj*

♦ reprisal, requital, retaliation, retribution, vengeance

rev·e·nue \ˈre-və-ˌnü, -ˌnyü\ *n* **1** : investment income **2** : money collected by a government (as through taxes) **3** ♦ : the total income produced by a given source

♦ earnings, income, proceeds, profit, return, yield

re·verb \ri-ˈvərb, ˈrē-ˌvərb\ *n* : an electronically produced echo effect in recorded music; *also* : a device for producing reverb

re·ver·ber·ate \ri-ˈvər-bə-ˌrāt\ *vb* **-at·ed; -at·ing** **1** : REFLECT

⟨~ light or heat⟩ **2 ♦ :** to resound in or as if in a series of echoes — **re•ver•ber•a•tion** \-ˌvər-bə-ˈrā-shən\ *n*

　♦ echo, reecho, resonate, resound, sound

re•vere \ri-ˈvir\ *vb* **re•vered; re•ver•ing ♦ :** to show honor and devotion to : VENERATE

　♦ adore, deify, glorify, venerate, worship

¹**rev•er•ence** \ˈre-vrəns, -və-rəns\ *n* **1 :** honor or respect felt or shown **2 :** a gesture (as a bow or curtsy) of respect
²**reverence** *vb* **-enced; -enc•ing :** to regard or treat with reverence
¹**rev•er•end** \ˈre-vrənd, -və-rənd\ *adj* **1 ♦ :** worthy of reverence : REVERED **2 :** being a member of the clergy — used as a title

　♦ hallowed, venerable

²**reverend** *n* **♦ :** a member of the clergy

　♦ clergyman, divine, ecclesiastic, father, minister, preacher, priest

rev•er•ent \ˈre-vrənt, -və-rənt\ *adj* **:** expressing reverence — **rev•er•ent•ly** *adv*
rev•er•en•tial \ˌre-və-ˈren-chəl\ *adj* **:** REVERENT
rev•er•ie *also* **rev•ery** \ˈre-və-rē\ *n, pl* **-er•ies 1 :** DAYDREAM **2 ♦ :** the condition of being lost in thought

　♦ study, trance, woolgathering

re•ver•sal \ri-ˈvər-səl\ *n* **1 :** an act or process of reversing **2 ♦ :** a change (as of fortune) often for the worse

　♦ lapse, reverse, setback

¹**re•verse** \ri-ˈvərs\ *adj* **1 :** opposite to a previous or normal condition ⟨in ~ order⟩ **2 :** acting or working in a manner opposite the usual **3 :** bringing about reverse movement ⟨~ gear⟩ — **re•verse•ly** *adv*
²**reverse** *vb* **re•versed; re•vers•ing 1 ♦ :** to turn upside down or completely about in position or direction **2 :** to set aside or change (as a legal decision) **3 :** to change to the contrary ⟨~ a policy⟩ **4 :** to go or cause to go in the opposite direction **5 :** to put (as a car) in reverse — **re•vers•ible** \-ˈvər-sə-bəl\ *adj*

　♦ flip, turn

³**reverse** *n* **1 ♦ :** something contrary to something else : OPPOSITE **2 ♦ :** an act or instance of reversing; *esp* **:** a change for the worse **3 :** the back side of something **4 :** a gear that reverses something

　♦ [1] antipode, antithesis, contrary, negative, opposite ♦ [2] lapse, reversal, setback

reverse engineer *vb* **:** to disassemble or analyze in detail in order to discover concepts involved in manufacture — **reverse engineering** *n*
re•ver•sion \ri-ˈvər-zhən\ *n* **1 :** the right of succession or future possession (as to a title or property) **2 :** return toward some former or ancestral condition; *also* **:** a product of this — **re•ver•sion•ary** \-zhə-ˌner-ē\ *adj*
re•vert \ri-ˈvərt\ *vb* **1 :** to come or go back ⟨~ed to savagery⟩ **2 :** to return to a proprietor or his or her heirs **3 :** to return to an ancestral type

¹**re•view** \ri-ˈvyü\ *n* **1 :** an act of revising **2 :** a formal military inspection **3 :** a general survey **4 ♦ :** an act or the process of reviewing : INSPECTION **5 :** a critical evaluation (as of a book) **6 :** a magazine devoted to reviews and essays **7 ♦ :** a renewed study of previously studied material **8 :** REVUE **9 ♦ :** a retrospective view or survey (as of one's life)

　♦ [4] audit, check, checkup, examination, inspection, scan, scrutiny, survey ♦ [9] reappraisal, reexamination, retrospection

²**re•view** \ri-ˈvyü, *1 also* ˈrē-\ *vb* **1 a ♦ :** to examine or study again **b :** to reexamine judicially **2 :** to hold a review of ⟨~ troops⟩ **3 :** to write a critical examination of ⟨~ a novel⟩ **4 :** to look back over ⟨~ed her accomplishments⟩

　♦ audit, check, examine, inspect, scan, scrutinize, survey ♦ re-address, reanalyze, reconceive, reconsider, reexamine, rethink

re•view•er \ri-ˈvyü-ər\ *n* **:** one that reviews; *esp* **:** a writer of critical reviews
re•vile \ri-ˈvī(-ə)l\ *vb* **re•viled; re•vil•ing :** to abuse verbally : rail at — **re•vile•ment** *n* — **re•vil•er** *n*
¹**re•vise** \ri-ˈvīz\ *vb* **re•vised; re•vis•ing 1 ♦ :** to look over something written in order to correct or improve **2 ♦ :** to make a new version of — **re•vis•able** *adj* — **re•vis•er** *or* **re•vi•sor** \-ˈvī-zər\ *n*

　♦ [1] edit, redraft, revamp, rework ♦ [2] alter, change, make over, modify, recast, redo, refashion, remake, remodel, revamp, rework, vary

²**revise** *n* **:** an act of revising
re•vi•sion \-ˈvi-zhən\ *n* **♦ :** an act of revising

　♦ alteration, change, difference, modification, revise, variation

re•vi•tal•ise *chiefly Brit var of* REVITALIZE
re•vi•tal•i•za•tion \(ˌ)rē-ˌvīt-ˀl-ə-ˈzā-shən\ *n* **:** an act or instance of revitalizing
re•vi•tal•ize \ˌrē-ˈvīt-ˀl-ˌīz\ *vb* **-ized; -iz•ing ♦ :** to give new life or vigor to

　♦ reanimate, regenerate, reinvigorate, rejuvenate, renew, resuscitate, revive

re•viv•al \ri-ˈvī-vəl\ *n* **1 ♦ :** an act of reviving : the state of being revived **2 :** a new publication or presentation (as of a book or play) **3 :** an evangelistic meeting or series of meetings

　♦ rebirth, regeneration, rejuvenation, renewal, resurgence, resurrection, resuscitation

re•vive \ri-ˈvīv\ *vb* **re•vived; re•viv•ing 1 ♦ :** to bring back or return to life, consciousness, or activity : make or become fresh or strong again **2 :** to bring back into use ⟨*reviving* an old custom⟩ — **re•viv•er** *n*

　♦ reanimate, regenerate, reinvigorate, rejuvenate, renew, resuscitate, revitalize ♦ come around, come round, come to

re•viv•i•fy \rē-ˈvi-və-ˌfī\ *vb* **:** REVIVE — **re•viv•i•fi•ca•tion** \-ˌvi-və-fə-ˈkā-shən\ *n*
re•vo•ca•ble \ˈre-və-kə-bəl *also* ri-ˈvō-kə-bəl\ *adj* **:** capable of being revoked
re•vo•ca•tion \ˌre-və-ˈkā-shən\ *n* **♦ :** an act or instance of revoking

　♦ abortion, calling, cancellation, recall, repeal, rescission

re•voke \ri-ˈvōk\ *vb* **re•voked; re•vok•ing 1 ♦ :** to annul by recalling or taking back : REPEAL, RESCIND **2 :** RENEGE 2 — **re•vok•er** *n*

　♦ abort, call, call off, cancel, drop, recall, repeal, rescind

¹**re•volt** \ri-ˈvōlt\ *vb* **1 :** to throw off allegiance to a ruler or government : REBEL **2 :** to experience disgust or shock **3 ♦ :** to turn or cause to turn away with disgust or abhorrence

　♦ disgust, nauseate, repel, repulse, sicken, turn off

²**revolt** *n* **♦ :** a renouncing of allegiance (as to a government or party); *esp* **:** a determined armed uprising : REBELLION

　♦ insurrection, mutiny, rebellion, revolution, uprising

re•volt•er *n* **♦ :** one that revolts

　♦ insurgent, insurrectionist, mutineer, rebel, red, revolutionary

re•volt•ing *adj* **♦ :** extremely offensive — **re•volt•ing•ly** *adv*

　♦ abhorrent, abominable, appalling, awful, distasteful, hideous, horrible, horrid, nasty, nauseating, noisome, offensive, repellent, repugnant, repulsive

rev•o•lu•tion \ˌre-və-ˈlü-shən\ *n* **1 :** the action by a celestial body of going round in an orbit **2 ♦ :** motion of any figure about a center or axis; *also* **:** one complete turn : ROTATION **3 a :** a sudden, radical, or complete change **b ♦ :** the overthrow or renunciation of one ruler or government and substitution of another by the governed

　♦ [2] gyration, pirouette, reel, roll, rotation, spin, twirl, wheel, whirl ♦ [3b] insurrection, mutiny, rebellion, revolt, uprising

¹**rev•o•lu•tion•ary** \-shə-ˌner-ē\ *adj* **1 ♦ :** of or relating to revolution **2 :** tending to or promoting revolution **3 :** constituting or bringing about a major change

　♦ insurgent, mutinous, rebellious

²**revolutionary** *n, pl* **-ar•ies ♦ :** one who takes part in a revolution or who advocates revolutionary doctrines

　♦ insurgent, insurrectionist, mutineer, rebel, red, revolter

rev•o•lu•tion•ise *chiefly Brit var of* REVOLUTIONIZE
¹**rev•o•lu•tion•ist** \ˌre-və-ˈlü-shə-nist\ *n* **:** REVOLUTIONARY
²**revolutionist** *adj* **:** of or relating to revolution or revolutionists
rev•o•lu•tion•ize \-ˌnīz\ *vb* **-ized; -iz•ing :** to change fundamentally or completely
rev•o•lu•tion•iz•er *n* **:** one that revolutionizes
re•volve \ri-ˈvälv\ *vb* **re•volved; re•volv•ing 1 :** to turn over in the mind : reflect upon : PONDER **2 ♦ :** to move in an orbit; *also* **:** ROTATE — **re•volv•able** *adj*

　♦ pivot, roll, rotate, spin, swing, swirl, turn, twirl, twist, wheel, whirl

re•volv•er \ri-ˈväl-vər\ *n* **:** a pistol with a revolving cylinder of several chambers

re•vue \ri-'vyü\ *n* : a theatrical production consisting typically of brief often satirical sketches and songs

re•vul•sion \ri-'vəl-shən\ *n* **1** : a strong sudden reaction or change of feeling **2** ♦ : a feeling of complete distaste or repugnance **3** ♦ : a strong pulling or drawing away

♦ [2] aversion, disgust, distaste, loathing, nausea, repugnance, repulsion ♦ [3] retreat, withdrawal

revved *past and past part of* REV
revving *pres part of* REV

¹**re•ward** \ri-'wȯrd\ *vb* **1** : to give a reward to or for **2** : RECOMPENSE

²**reward** *n* **1** : something given in return for good or evil done or received or for some service or attainment **2** : a stimulus that is administered to an organism after a response and that increases the probability of occurrence of the response

re•ward•ing *adj* **1** : yielding or likely to yield a reward **2** ♦ : serving as a reward : giving pleasure as if a reward

♦ comforting, encouraging, gratifying, heartening, heartwarming, satisfying

re•warm \(ˌ)rē-'wȯrm\ *vb* : to make warm again ⟨∼ food⟩ ⟨∼ed herself by the fire⟩

¹**re•wind** \(ˌ)rē-'wīnd\ *vb* **-wound; -wind•ing** **1** : to wind again **2** : to reverse the winding of (as film)

²**re•wind** \'rē-ˌwīnd\ *n* **1** : something that rewinds **2** : an act of rewinding **3** : a function of an electronic device that reverses a recording to a previous portion

re•work \(ˌ)rē-'wərk\ *vb* **1** ♦ : to work again or anew : REVISE **2** : to reprocess for further use

♦ alter, change, edit, make over, modify, recast, redo, refashion, remake, remodel, revamp, revise, vary

¹**re•write** \(ˌ)rē-'rīt\ *vb* **-wrote; -writ•ten; -writ•ing** : to make a revision of : REVISE

²**re•write** \'rē-ˌrīt\ *n* : an instance or a piece of rewriting

Rf *symbol* rutherfordium
RF *abbr* radio frequency
Rg *symbol* roentgenium
Rh *symbol* rhodium
RH *abbr* right hand

rhap•sod•ic \rap-'sä-dik\ *adj* ♦ : extravagantly emotional — **rhap•sod•i•cal•ly** \-di-k(ə-)lē\ *adv*

♦ ecstatic, elated, euphoric, intoxicated, rapturous

rhap•so•dize \'rap-sə-ˌdīz\ *vb* ♦ : to speak or write in a rhapsodic manner

♦ enthuse, fuss, gush, ráve, slobber

rhap•so•dy \'rap-sə-dē\ *n, pl* **-dies** **1** : an expression of extravagant praise or ecstasy **2** : a musical composition of irregular form **3** ♦ : a state or experience of being carried away by overwhelming emotion

♦ ecstasy, elation, euphoria, exhilaration, heaven, intoxication, paradise, rapture, transport

rhea \'rē-ə\ *n* : either of two large flightless 3-toed So. American birds that resemble but are smaller than the African ostrich

rhe•ni•um \'rē-nē-əm\ *n* : a rare heavy hard metallic chemical element

rheo•stat \'rē-ə-ˌstat\ *n* : a resistor for regulating an electric current by means of variable resistances — **rheo•stat•ic** \ˌrē-ə-'sta-tik\ *adj*

rhe•sus monkey \'rē-səs-\ *n* : a pale brown Asian monkey often used in medical research

rhet•o•ric \'re-tə-rik\ *n* **1** ♦ : the art of speaking or writing effectively **2** ♦ : insincere or grandiloquent language — **rhet•o•ri•cian** \ˌre-tə-'ri-shən\ *n*

♦ [1] articulateness, eloquence, poetry ♦ [2] bombast, gas, grandiloquence, hot air, wind

rhe•tor•i•cal \ri-'tȯr-i-kəl\ *adj* **1** : of, relating to, or concerned with rhetoric **2** ♦ : given to rhetoric **3** : asked merely for effect with no answer expected ⟨a ∼ question⟩

♦ bombastic, gaseous, grandiloquent, oratorical, windy

rheum \'rüm\ *n* : a watery discharge from the mucous membranes esp. of the eyes or nose — **rheumy** *adj*

rheu•mat•ic fever \rü-'ma-tik-\ *n* : an acute disease chiefly of children and young adults that is characterized by fever, by inflammation and pain in and around the joints, and by inflammation of the membranes surrounding the heart and the heart valves

rheu•ma•tism \'rü-mə-ˌti-zəm, 'rü-\ *n* : any of various conditions marked by stiffness, pain, or swelling in muscles or joints **2** : RHEUMATOID ARTHRITIS — **rheu•mat•ic** \rü-'ma-tik\ *adj*

rheu•ma•toid arthritis \-ˌtȯid-\ *n* : a usu. chronic progressive autoimmune disease characterized by inflammation and swelling of joint structures

rheu•ma•tol•o•gy \ˌrü-mə-'tä-lə-jē, ˌrü-\ *n* : a medical science dealing with rheumatic diseases — **rheu•ma•tol•o•gist** \-jist\ *n*

Rh factor \ˌär-'āch-\ *n* : any of one or more inherited substances in red blood cells that may cause dangerous reactions in some infants or in transfusions

rhine•stone \'rīn-ˌstōn\ *n* : a colorless imitation stone of high luster made of glass, paste, or gem quartz

rhi•no \'rī-nō\ *n, pl* **rhinos** *also* **rhino** : RHINOCEROS

rhi•noc•er•os \rī-'nä-sə-rəs\ *n, pl* **-noc•er•os•es** *also* **-noc•er•os** *or* **-noc•eri** \-'nä-sə-ˌrī\ : any of a family of large thick-skinned mammals of Africa and Asia with one or two upright horns of keratin on the snout and three toes on each foot

rhi•zome \'rī-ˌzōm\ *n* : a fleshy, rootlike, and usu. horizontal underground plant stem that forms shoots above and roots below — **rhi•zom•a•tous** \rī-'zä-mə-təs\ *adj*

Rh–neg•a•tive \ˌär-ˌāch-'ne-gə-tiv\ *adj* : lacking Rh factors in the red blood cells

rho \'rō\ *n* : the 17th letter of the Greek alphabet — **P** or ρ

rho•di•um \'rō-dē-əm\ *n* : a rare hard ductile metallic chemical element

rho•do•den•dron \ˌrō-də-'den-drən\ *n* : any of a genus of shrubs or trees of the heath family with clusters of large bright flowers

rhom•boid \'räm-ˌbȯid\ *n* : a parallelogram with unequal adjacent sides and angles that are not right angles — **rhomboid** *or* **rhom•boi•dal** \räm-'bȯid-ᵊl\ *adj*

rhom•bus \'räm-bəs\ *n, pl* **rhom•bus•es** *or* **rhom•bi** \-ˌbī\ : a parallelogram having all four sides equal

Rh–pos•i•tive \ˌär-ˌāch-'pä-zə-tiv\ *adj* : containing one or more Rh factors in the red blood cells

rhu•barb \'rü-ˌbärb\ *n* : a garden plant related to the buckwheat having leaves with thick juicy edible pink and red stems

¹**rhyme** \'rīm\ *n* **1** : a composition in verse that rhymes; *also* : POETRY **2** : correspondence in terminal sounds (as of two lines of verse)

²**rhyme** *vb* **rhymed; rhym•ing** **1** : to make rhymes; *also* : to write poetry **2** : to have rhymes : be in rhyme — **rhym•er** *n*

rhythm \'ri-thəm\ *n* **1** ♦ : regular rise and fall in the flow of sound in speech **2** : a movement or activity in which some action or element recurs regularly — **rhyth•mi•cal•ly** \-k(ə-)lē\ *adv*

♦ beat, cadence, measure, meter (*or* metre)

rhythm and blues *n* : popular music based on blues and African American folk music

rhyth•mic \'rith-mik\ *or* **rhyth•mi•cal** \-mi-kəl\ *adj* ♦ : marked by or moving in pronounced rhythm

♦ cadenced, measured, metrical *Ant* unmeasured, unrhythmic

rhythm method *n* : birth control by refraining from sexual intercourse during the time when ovulation is most likely to occur

RI *abbr* Rhode Island

¹**rib** \'rib\ *n* **1** : any of the series of curved bones of the chest of most vertebrates that are joined to the backbone in pairs and help to support the body wall and protect the organs inside **2** : something resembling a rib in shape or function **3** : an elongated ridge (as in fabric)

²**rib** *vb* **ribbed; rib•bing** **1** : to furnish or strengthen with ribs **2** : to knit so as to form ridges

³**rib** *vb* **ribbed; rib•bing** ♦ : to poke fun at : TEASE — **rib•ber** *n*

♦ chaff, jive, josh, kid, rally, razz, ride, roast, tease

rib•ald \'ri-bəld\ *adj* ♦ : coarse or indecent esp. in language ⟨∼ jokes⟩

♦ bawdy, coarse, crude, indecent, lewd, obscene, smutty, vulgar
♦ racy, risqué, spicy, suggestive

rib•ald•ry \-bəl-drē\ *n* ♦ : a ribald quality or element

♦ bawdiness, coarseness, indecency, lewdness, obscenity, smut, vulgarity

rib•and \'ri-bənd\ *n* : RIBBON

rib•bon \'ri-bən\ *n* **1** : a narrow fabric typically of silk or velvet used for trimming and for badges **2** : a strip of inked cloth (as in a typewriter) **3** : TATTER, SHRED ⟨torn to ∼s⟩

ri•bo•fla•vin \ˌrī-bə-'flā-vən, 'rī-bə-ˌflā-vən\ *n* : a growth-promoting vitamin of the vitamin B complex occurring esp. in milk and liver

ri•bo•nu•cle•ic acid \ˌrī-bō-nü-ˌklē-ik-, -nyü-, -ˌklā-\ *n* : RNA

ri•bose \'rī-ˌbōs\ *n* : a sugar with five carbon atoms and five oxygen atoms in each molecule that is part of RNA

ri•bo•some \'rī-bə-ˌsōm\ *n* : any of the RNA-rich cytoplasmic granules in a cell that are sites of protein synthesis — **ri·bo·som·al** \ˌrī-bə-ˈsō-məl\ adj

rice \ˈrīs\ n : the starchy seeds of an annual grass that are cooked and used for food; also : this widely cultivated grass of warm wet areas

rich \ˈrich\ adj 1 ♦ : possessing or controlling great wealth : WEALTHY 2 : COSTLY, VALUABLE 3 : deep and pleasing in color or tone 4 ♦ : having great plenty 5 : containing much sugar, fat, or seasoning; also : high in combustible content 6 : highly productive or remunerative : FRUITFUL, FERTILE — **rich·ness** n

♦ [1] affluent, flush, loaded, moneyed, opulent, wealthy, well-fixed, well-heeled, well-off, well-to-do **Ant** destitute, impecunious, impoverished, indigent, needy, penniless, penurious, poor, poverty-stricken ♦ [4] concentrated, full, full-bodied, potent, robust, strong

rich·es \ˈri-chəz\ n pl ♦ : things that make one rich : WEALTH

♦ assets, capital, fortune, means, opulence, substance, wealth, wherewithal

rich·ly \ˈrich-lē\ adv ♦ : in a rich manner

♦ expensively, extravagantly, grandly, high, lavishly, luxuriously, opulently

Rich·ter scale \ˈrik-tər-\ n : a scale for expressing the magnitude of a seismic disturbance (as an earthquake) in terms of the energy dissipated in it

rick \ˈrik\ n ♦ : a large stack (as of hay) in the open air

♦ cock, heap, hill, mound, mountain, pile, stack

rick·ets \ˈri-kəts\ n : a childhood deficiency disease marked esp. by soft deformed bones and caused by lack of vitamin D

rick·ett·sia \ri-ˈket-sē-ə\ n, pl **-si·as** or **-si·ae** \-sē-ˌē\ : any of a group of usu. rod-shaped bacteria that cause various diseases (as typhus)

rick·ety \ˈri-kə-tē\ adj 1 : affected with rickets 2 : SHAKY; also : in unsound physical condition

rick·shaw also **rick·sha** \ˈrik-ˌshȯ\ n : a small covered 2-wheeled carriage pulled by one person and used orig. in Japan

¹**ric·o·chet** \ˈri-kə-ˌshā, Brit also -ˌshet\ n : a bouncing off at an angle (as of a bullet off a wall); also : an object that ricochets

²**ricochet** vb **-cheted** \-ˌshād\ also **-chet·ted** \-ˌshe-təd\; **-chet·ing** \-ˌshā-iŋ\ also **-chet·ting** \-ˌshe-tiŋ\ ♦ : to skip with or as if with glancing rebounds

♦ bounce, carom, glance, rebound, skim, skip

ri·cot·ta \ri-ˈkä-tə, -ˈkȯ-\ n : a white unripened whey cheese of Italy that resembles cottage cheese

rid \ˈrid\ vb **rid** also **rid·ded**; **rid·ding** ♦ : to make free of something burdensome : CLEAR ⟨∼ the house of mice⟩

♦ clear, disburden, disencumber, free, relieve, unburden **Ant** burden, encumber, saddle

rid·dance \ˈrid-ᵊns\ n ♦ : an act of ridding

♦ disposal, disposition, dumping, jettison, removal

rid·den \ˈrid-ᵊn\ adj 1 : harassed, oppressed, or obsessed by ⟨debt-*ridden*⟩ 2 : excessively full of or supplied with ⟨slum-*ridden*⟩

¹**rid·dle** \ˈrid-ᵊl\ n 1 : a puzzling question to be solved or answered by guessing 2 ♦ : something or someone difficult to understand

♦ conundrum, enigma, mystery, mystification, puzzle, puzzlement, secret

²**riddle** vb **rid·dled**; **rid·dling** 1 ♦ : to find the solution of : SOLVE 2 : to speak in riddles

♦ answer, break, crack, dope, figure out, puzzle, resolve, solve, unravel, work, work out

³**riddle** n : a coarse sieve

⁴**riddle** vb **rid·dled**; **rid·dling** 1 : to sift with a riddle 2 : to pierce with many holes 3 : PERMEATE

¹**ride** \ˈrīd\ vb **rode** \ˈrōd\; **rid·den** \ˈrid-ᵊn\; **rid·ing** 1 : to go on an animal's back or in a conveyance (as a boat, car, or airplane); also : to sit on and control so as to be carried along ⟨∼ a bicycle⟩ 2 ♦ : to float or move on water ⟨∼ at anchor⟩; also : to move like a floating object 3 : to bear along : CARRY ⟨rode her on their shoulders⟩ 4 : to travel over a surface ⟨the car ∼s well⟩ 5 : to proceed over on horseback 6 ♦ : to torment by nagging or teasing; also : to poke fun at 7 : to last longer than — usu. used with *out*

♦ [2] drift, float, glide, hang, hover, poise, sail, waft ♦ [6] bait, bug, hassle, heckle, needle, taunt, tease ♦ [6] chaff, jive, josh, kid, rally, razz, rib, roast, tease

²**ride** n 1 : an act of riding; esp : a trip on horseback or by vehicle 2 : a way (as a road or path) suitable for riding 3 : a mechanical device (as a merry-go-round) for riding on 4 : a means of transportation

rid·er \ˈrī-dər\ n 1 : one that rides 2 : an addition to a document often attached on a separate piece of paper 3 : a clause dealing with an unrelated matter attached to a legislative bill during passage — **rid·er·less** adj

¹**ridge** \ˈrij\ n 1 : a range of hills 2 : a raised line or strip 3 : the line made where two sloping surfaces (as of a roof) meet — **ridgy** adj

²**ridge** vb **ridged**; **ridg·ing** 1 : to form into a ridge 2 : to extend in ridges

¹**rid·i·cule** \ˈri-də-ˌkyül\ n : the act of ridiculing : DERISION, MOCKERY

²**ridicule** vb **-culed**; **-cul·ing** ♦ : to laugh at or make fun of mockingly or contemptuously

♦ deride, gibe, jeer, laugh, mock, scout

ri·dic·u·lous \rə-ˈdi-kyə-ləs\ adj ♦ : arousing or deserving ridicule : ABSURD; also : provoking laughter — **ri·dic·u·lous·ly** adv — **ri·dic·u·lous·ness** n

♦ absurd, comical, derisive, farcical, laughable, ludicrous, preposterous, risible, silly ♦ antic, comic, comical, droll, farcical, funny, hilarious, humorous, hysterical, laughable, ludicrous, riotous, risible, screaming, uproarious

rid·ley \ˈrid-lē\ n : either of two relatively small sea turtles

Ries·ling \ˈrēz-liŋ, ˈrēs-\ n : a sweet to very dry white wine made from a single variety of grape orig. grown in Germany

RIF abbr reduction in force

rife \ˈrīf\ adj ♦ : occurring in abundance — **rife** adv — **rife·ly** adv

♦ flush, fraught, replete, thick

riff \ˈrif\ n : a repeated phrase in jazz typically supporting a solo improvisation; also : a piece based on such a phrase — **riff** vb

riff·raff \ˈrif-ˌraf\ n 1 ♦ : disreputable persons : RABBLE 2 : something worth little or nothing : REFUSE

♦ rabble, scum, trash

¹**ri·fle** \ˈrī-fəl\ vb **ri·fled**; **ri·fling** ♦ : to ransack esp. with the intent to steal — **ri·fler** n

♦ dig, dredge, hunt, rake, ransack, rummage, scour, search

²**rifle** vb **ri·fled**; **ri·fling** : to cut spiral grooves into the bore of ⟨*ri·fled* pipe⟩ — **rifling** n

³**rifle** n 1 : a shoulder weapon with a rifled bore 2 pl : soldiers armed with rifles — **ri·fle·man** \-fəl-mən\ n

rift \ˈrift\ n 1 ♦ : a narrow opening or crack of considerable length and depth usu. from some breaking or parting 2 : FAULT 6 3 : ESTRANGEMENT, SEPARATION 4 ♦ : a clear space or interval — **rift** vb

♦ [1] chink, cleft, crack, cranny, crevice, fissure, split ♦ [4] breach, break, discontinuity, gap, gulf, hole, interval, opening, rent, separation

¹**rig** \ˈrig\ vb **rigged**; **rig·ging** 1 : to fit out (as a ship) with rigging 2 ♦ : to provide with clothes : CLOTHE, DRESS — usu. used with *out* 3 ♦ : to furnish with special gear : EQUIP 4 : to set up esp. as a makeshift ⟨∼ up a shelter⟩

♦ usu **rig out** [2] apparel, array, attire, caparison, clothe, deck, dress, garb, invest, suit ♦ [3] accoutre, equip, fit, furnish, outfit, supply

²**rig** n 1 : the distinctive shape, number, and arrangement of sails and masts of a ship 2 : a carriage with its horse 3 : CLOTHING, DRESS 4 : EQUIPMENT

³**rig** vb **rigged**; **rig·ging** 1 : to manipulate or control esp. by deceptive or dishonest means 2 : to fix in advance for a desired result — **rig·ger** n

rig·ging \ˈri-giŋ, -gən\ n 1 : the ropes and chains that hold and move masts, sails, and spars of a ship 2 : a network (as in theater scenery) used for support and manipulation

¹**right** \ˈrīt\ adj 1 ♦ : morally right or justifiable : RIGHTEOUS 2 ♦ : being in accordance with what is just, good, or proper : JUST 3 ♦ : conforming to truth or fact : CORRECT 4 ♦ : adapted to a use or purpose : APPROPRIATE 5 : free from curves, bends, angles, or irregularities : STRAIGHT ⟨a ∼ line⟩ 6 : not artificial, fraudulent, or illusory : GENUINE 7 : of, relating to, or being the side of the body which is away from the side on which the heart is mostly located 8 : located nearer to the right hand; esp : being on the right when facing in the same direction as the observer 9 : made to be placed or worn outward ⟨∼ side of a rug⟩ 10 ♦ : being in good physical or mental order : NORMAL ⟨not in her ∼ mind⟩

♦ [1] decent, ethical, good, honest, honorable (*or* honourable), just, moral, straight, upright, virtuous ♦ [2] due, just ♦ [3] accurate, correct, exact, precise, proper, so, true ♦ [4] applicable, appropriate, apt, felicitous, fit, fitting, good, happy, meet, proper, suitable ♦ [10] balanced, clearheaded, lucid, normal, sane, stable

²right *n* **1** : qualities that constitute what is correct, just, proper, or honorable **2** ♦ : something (as a power or privilege) to which one has a just or lawful claim **3** : just action or decision : the cause of justice **4** : the side or part that is on or toward the right side **5** *cap* : political conservatives **6** *often cap* : a conservative position — **right·most** \-ˌmōst\ *adj* — **right·ward** \-wərd\ *adj or adv*

♦ birthright, due, perquisite, prerogative, privilege

³right *adv* **1** : according to what is right ⟨live ∼⟩ **2** ♦ : in an exact manner : EXACTLY, PRECISELY ⟨∼ here and now⟩ **3** ♦ : in a direct line, course, or manner : DIRECTLY ⟨went ∼ home⟩ **4** : according to fact or truth ⟨guess ∼⟩ **5** : all the way : COMPLETELY ⟨∼ to the end⟩ **6** : IMMEDIATELY ⟨∼ after lunch⟩ **7** : to a great degree : VERY ⟨∼ nice weather⟩ **8** : on or to the right ⟨looked ∼ and left⟩

♦ [2] accurately, exactly, just, precisely, sharp, squarely ♦ [3] dead, direct, directly, due, plump, straight

⁴right *vb* **1** : to relieve from wrong **2** : to adjust or restore to a proper state or position **3** : to bring or restore to an upright position **4** : to become upright — **right·er** *n*

right angle *n* : an angle whose measure is 90° : an angle whose sides are perpendicular to each other — **right–an·gled** \ˈrīt-ˈaŋ-gəld\ *or* **right–an·gle** \-gəl\ *adj*

right away *adv* ♦ : without delay or hesitation

♦ directly, forthwith, immediately, instantly, now, promptly, pronto, right now

right circular cone *n* : CONE 2

right–click \ˈrīt-ˈklik\ *vb* : to press the rightmost button on a computer mouse or a similar input device

righ·teous \ˈrī-chəs\ *adj* ♦ : acting or being in accordance with what is just, honorable, and free from guilt or wrong : UPRIGHT

♦ decent, ethical, good, honest, honorable (*or* honourable), just, moral, right, straight, upright, virtuous

righ·teous·ly *adv* ♦ : in a righteous manner

♦ chastely, modestly, purely, virtuously

righ·teous·ness *n* ♦ : the quality or state of being righteous

♦ character, decency, goodness, honesty, integrity, morality, probity, rectitude, uprightness, virtue

right·ful \ˈrīt-fəl\ *adj* **1 a** : acting or being in conformity with what is morally upright or good : JUST **b** : FITTING **2** : having or held by a legally just claim — **right·ful·ly** *adv* — **right·ful·ness** *n*

right–hand \ˈrīt-ˌhand\ *adj* **1** : situated on the right **2** : RIGHT-HANDED **3** : chiefly relied on ⟨his ∼ man⟩

right–hand·ed \-ˈhan-dəd\ *adj* **1** : using the right hand habitually or better than the left **2** : designed for or done with the right hand **3** : CLOCKWISE ⟨a ∼ twist⟩ — **right–handed** *adv* — **right–hand·ed·ly** *adv* — **right–hand·ed·ness** *n*

right·ist \ˈrī-tist\ *n, often cap* ♦ : an advocate of or adherent to the doctrines of the Right

♦ conservative, reactionary, Tory

right·ly \ˈrīt-lē\ *adv* **1** : FAIRLY, JUSTLY **2** ♦ : in the right or proper manner : PROPERLY **3** : CORRECTLY, EXACTLY

♦ appropriately, correctly, fittingly, happily, properly, suitably

right·ness *n* ♦ : the quality or state of being right

♦ appropriateness, aptness, fitness, suitability

right now *adv* **1** ♦ : without delay or hesitation **2** ♦ : at present

♦ [1] directly, forthwith, immediately, instantly, now, promptly, pronto, right away ♦ [2] anymore, now, nowadays, presently, today

right–of–way *n, pl* **rights–of–way** **1** : a legal right of passage over another person's ground **2** : the area over which a right-of-way exists **3** : the land on which a public road is built **4** : the land occupied by a railroad **5** : the land used by a public utility **6** : the right of traffic to take precedence over other traffic

right on *interj* — used to express agreement or give encouragement

right–to–life *adj* : ANTIABORTION — **right–to–lifer** *n*

right triangle *n* : a triangle having one right angle

right whale *n* : any of a family of large baleen whales having a very large head on a stocky body

rig·id \ˈri-jəd\ *adj* **1 a** ♦ : lacking flexibility **b** ♦ : inflexibly exact with respect to opinions or observances **2** ♦ : strictly observed

♦ [1a] inflexible, stiff, unyielding ♦ [1b] adamant, hard, immovable, implacable, pat, unbending, uncompromising, unrelenting, unyielding ♦ [2] exacting, inflexible, rigorous, strict, stringent, uncompromising *Ant* flexible, lax, loose, relaxed

ri·gid·i·ty \rə-ˈji-də-tē\ *n* ♦ : the quality or state of being rigid

♦ hardness, harshness, inflexibility, severity, sternness, strictness

rig·id·ly *adv* ♦ : in a rigid manner

♦ exactly, precisely, rigorously, strictly

rig·ma·role \ˈri-gə-mə-ˌrōl\ *n* **1** : confused or senseless talk **2** : a complex and ritualistic procedure

rig·or *or Can and Brit* **rig·our** \ˈri-gər\ *n* **1** : the quality of being inflexible or unyielding esp. in opinion or behavior **2** ♦ : a condition that makes life difficult, challenging, or uncomfortable **3** *Can usu* **rigor** : a tremor caused by a chill **4** : strict precision : EXACTNESS ⟨scientific ∼⟩ **5** *Can usu* **rigor** : unnatural rigidity of a body part

♦ adversity, asperity, difficulty, hardness, hardship

rig·or mor·tis \ˌri-gər-ˈmȯr-təs\ *n* : temporary rigidity of muscles occurring after death

rig·or·ous *adj* ♦ : manifesting, exercising, or favoring rigor

♦ accurate, close, delicate, exact, fine, mathematical, pinpoint, precise ♦ exacting, inflexible, rigid, strict, stringent, uncompromising

rig·or·ous·ly *adv* ♦ : in a rigorous manner

♦ exactly, precisely, rigidly, strictly

rig·our *Can and Brit var of* RIGOR

rile \ˈrī(-ə)l\ *vb* **riled**; **ril·ing** **1** ♦ : to make angry **2** : to stir or move from a state of calm or order

♦ aggravate, anger, annoy, bother, bug, chafe, exasperate, gall, get, grate, irk, irritate, nettle, peeve, persecute, pique, put out, rasp, vex

rill \ˈril\ *n* ♦ : a very small brook

♦ brook, creek, rivulet, streamlet

¹rim \ˈrim\ *n* **1** : the outer part of a wheel **2** ♦ : an outer edge esp. of something curved : MARGIN

♦ border, bound, boundary, circumference, compass, confines, edge, end, fringe, margin, perimeter, periphery, skirt, verge

²rim *vb* **rimmed**; **rim·ming** **1** : to serve as a rim for : BORDER **2** : to run around the rim of

¹rime \ˈrīm\ *n* : FROST 2 — **rimy** \ˈrī-mē\ *adj*

²rime *var of* RHYME

rind \ˈrīnd\ *n* : a usu. hard or tough outer layer ⟨lemon ∼⟩

¹ring \ˈriŋ\ *n* **1** : a circular band worn as an ornament or token or used for holding or fastening ⟨wedding ∼⟩ ⟨key ∼⟩ **2** ♦ : something circular in shape ⟨smoke ∼⟩ **3** : a place for contest or display ⟨boxing ∼⟩; *also* : PRIZEFIGHTING **4** : ANNUAL RING **5** ♦ : a group of people who work together for selfish or dishonest purposes ⟨a ∼ of smugglers⟩ **6** ♦ : a temporary group of persons working cooperatively — **ringed** *adj* — **ring·like** \ˈriŋ-ˌlīk\ *adj*

♦ [2] band, circle, eye, hoop, loop, round ♦ [5] cabal, conspiracy, gang, mob, syndicate ♦ [6] body, bunch, circle, clan, clique, community, coterie, crowd, fold, gang, lot, set

²ring *vb* **ringed**; **ring·ing** \ˈriŋ-iŋ\ **1** ♦ : to place or form a ring around : ENCIRCLE **2** : to throw a ring over (a mark) in a game (as quoits) **3** : to move in a ring or spirally

♦ circle, encircle, enclose, encompass, surround

³ring *vb* **rang** \ˈraŋ\; **rung** \ˈrəŋ\; **ring·ing** \ˈriŋ-iŋ\ **1** : to sound resonantly when struck; *also* : to feel as if filled with such sound **2** ♦ : to cause to make a clear metallic sound by striking **3** : to announce or call by or as if by striking a bell ⟨∼ an alarm⟩ **4** : to repeat loudly and persistently **5** : to summon esp. by a bell ⟨∼ for the butler⟩

♦ chime, knell, peal, toll

⁴ring *n* **1** : a set of bells **2** : the clear resonant sound of vibrating metal **3** : resonant tone : SONORITY **4** : a sound or character expressive of a particular quality **5** : an act or instance of ringing; *esp* : a telephone call

¹ring·er \ˈriŋ-ər\ *n* **1** : one that sounds by ringing **2** : one that enters a competition under false representations **3 ♦** : one that closely resembles another

♦ carbon copy, counterpart, double, duplicate, duplication, facsimile, image, likeness, match, picture, replica, spit

²**ring·er** n : one that encircles or puts a ring around

ring finger n : the third finger of the hand counting the index finger as the first

ring·ing adj ♦ : clear and full in tone

♦ golden, resonant, resounding, round, sonorous, vibrant

ring·lead·er \'riŋ-ˌlē-dər\ n : a leader esp. of a group of troublemakers

ring·let \-lət\ n : a long curl

ring·mas·ter \-ˌmas-tər\ n : one in charge of performances in a circus ring

ring·tone \-ˌtōn\ n : the sound made by a cell phone to signal an incoming call

ring up vb **1** : to total and record esp. by means of a cash register **2** : ACHIEVE ⟨*rang up* many triumphs⟩

ring·worm \'riŋ-ˌwərm\ n : any of several contagious skin diseases caused by fungi and marked by ring-shaped discolored patches

rink \'riŋk\ n : a level extent of ice marked off for skating or various games; *also* : a similar surface (as of wood) marked off or enclosed for a sport or game ⟨roller-skating ∼⟩

¹**rinse** \'rins\ vb **rinsed; rins·ing 1** : to wash lightly or in water only **2 ♦** : to cleanse (as of soap) with clear water **3** : to treat (hair) with a rinse — **rins·er** n

♦ flush, irrigate, sluice, wash

²**rinse** n **1** : an act of rinsing **2** : a liquid used for rinsing **3** : a solution that temporarily tints hair

ri·ot \'rī-ət\ n **1** *archaic* : disorderly behavior **2** : disturbance of the public peace; *esp* : a violent public disorder **3** : random or disorderly profusion ⟨a ∼ of color⟩ **4** : one that is wildly amusing ⟨the comedy is a ∼⟩ — **riot** vb — **ri·ot·er** n

ri·ot·ous adj ♦ : practicing or marked by license or excess; *also* : existing in abundance

♦ copious, lavish, profuse

¹**rip** \'rip\ vb **ripped; rip·ping 1 ♦** : to cut or tear open **2** : to saw or split (wood) with the grain **3 ♦** : to slash or slit with or as if with a sharp blade **4 ♦** : to rush headlong **5** : CRITICIZE, DISPARAGE ⟨*ripped* into the team⟩ — **rip·per** n

♦ [1] rend, rive, shred, tatter, tear ♦ [3] cut, gash, slash, slice, slit ♦ [4] barrel, dash, fly, hurry, hurtle, hustle, pelt, race, rocket, run, shoot, speed, tear, zip, zoom

²**rip** n ♦ : an opening made by ripping

♦ gash, laceration, rent, slash, slit, tear

RIP abbr may he rest in peace, may she rest in peace may they rest in peace

ri·par·i·an \rə-'per-ē-ən\ adj : of or relating to the bank of a stream, river, or lake

rip cord n : a cord that is pulled to release a parachute out of its container

¹**ripe** \'rīp\ adj **rip·er; rip·est 1 ♦** : fully grown and developed : MATURE ⟨∼ fruit⟩ **2** : fully prepared : READY — **ripe·ly** adv — **ripe·ness** n

♦ adult, full-blown, full-fledged, mature

rip·en \'rī-pən\ vb **rip·ened; rip·en·ing 1 ♦** : to make ripe : become ripe **2** : to bring to completeness or perfection; *also* : to age or cure (cheese) to develop characteristic flavor, odor, body, texture, and color

♦ age, develop, grow, grow up, mature, progress

rip–off \'rip-ˌof\ n **1 ♦** : an act of stealing : THEFT **2** : a cheap imitation

♦ grab, theft

rip off vb ♦ : to take something away from by force : steal from

♦ burglarize, rob, steal

ri·poste \ri-'pōst\ n **1** : a fencer's return thrust after a parry **2 ♦** : a retaliatory maneuver or response; *esp* : a quick retort — **ri·poste** vb

♦ comeback, repartee, retort

ripped \'ript\ adj : having high muscle definition

rip·ple \'ri-pəl\ vb **rip·pled; rip·pling 1** : to become lightly ruffled on the surface **2** : to make a sound like that of rippling water **3 ♦** : to flow in small waves — **ripple** n

♦ dribble, gurgle, lap, plash, slosh, splash, trickle, wash

rip·saw \'rip-ˌso\ n : a coarse-toothed saw used to cut wood in the direction of the grain

rip·stop \-ˌstäp\ adj : being a fabric woven in such a way that small tears do not spread ⟨∼ nylon⟩ — **ripstop** n

¹**rise** \'rīz\ vb **rose** \'rōz\; **ris·en** \'riz-ᵊn\; **ris·ing 1** : to get up from sitting, kneeling, or lying **2** : to get up from sleep or from one's bed **3** : to return from death **4** : to take up arms **5** : to end a session : ADJOURN **6** : to appear above the horizon **7 ♦** : to move upward : ASCEND **8** : to extend above other objects **9** : to attain a higher level or rank **10 ♦** : to increase in quantity, intensity, or pitch **11** : to come into being : HAPPEN, BEGIN, ORIGINATE

♦ [7] arise, ascend, climb, lift, mount, soar, up ♦ [10] accumulate, appreciate, balloon, build, burgeon, enlarge, escalate, expand, increase, mount, multiply, mushroom, proliferate, snowball, swell, wax

²**rise** n **1 ♦** : a spot higher than surrounding ground **2** : an upward slope **3 ♦** : an act of rising : a state of being risen **4** : BEGINNING, ORIGIN **5** : the elevation of one point above another **6 ♦** : an increase in amount, number, or volume **7** : an angry reaction

♦ [1] elevation, eminence, height, highland, hill, mound, prominence ♦ [3] advancement, ascent, elevation, promotion, upgrade ♦ [6] accretion, addition, augmentation, boost, expansion, gain, increase, increment, plus, proliferation, raise, supplement

ris·er \'rī-zər\ n **1** : one that rises **2** : the upright part between stair treads

ris·i·bil·i·ty \ˌri-zə-'bi-lə-tē\ n, pl **-ties** : the ability or inclination to laugh — often used in pl.

ris·i·ble \'ri-zə-bəl\ adj **1** : able or inclined to laugh **2 ♦** : arousing laughter; *esp* : amusingly ridiculous

♦ antic, comic, comical, droll, farcical, funny, hilarious, humorous, hysterical, laughable, ludicrous, ridiculous, riotous, screaming, uproarious

¹**risk** \'risk\ n **1 ♦** : exposure to possible loss or injury : DANGER ⟨health ∼s⟩ **2 ♦** : someone or something that creates or suggests a hazard — **risk·i·ness** \'ris-kē-nəs\ n

♦ [1, 2] danger, hazard, menace, peril, pitfall, threat, trouble

²**risk** vb **1 ♦** : to expose to danger ⟨∼ed his life⟩ **2 ♦** : to incur the danger of

♦ [1] adventure, compromise, gamble with, hazard, imperil, jeopardize, menace, venture ♦ [2] chance, gamble, hazard, venture

risky adj ♦ : attended with risk or danger

♦ dangerous, grave, grievous, hazardous, menacing, parlous, perilous, serious, unhealthy, unsafe, venturesome

ri·sot·to \ri-'so-tō, -'zo-\ n, pl **-tos** : rice cooked usu. in meat or seafood stock and seasoned

ris·qué \ris-'kā\ adj : verging on impropriety or indecency

♦ bawdy, lewd, ribald, spicy, suggestive

ri·tard \ri-'tärd\ adv or adj : with a gradual slackening in tempo — used as a direction in music

rite \'rīt\ n **1** : a set form for conducting a ceremony **2** : the liturgy of a church **3 ♦** : a ceremonial act or action

♦ ceremonial, ceremony, form, formality, observance, ritual, solemnity

¹**rit·u·al** \'ri-chə-wəl\ n **1** : the established form esp. for a religious ceremony **2** : a system of rites **3** : a ceremonial act or action **4** : an act or series of acts regularly repeated in a precise manner — **rit·u·al·ism** \-wə-ˌli-zəm\ n — **rit·u·al·is·tic** \ˌri-chə-wə-'lis-tik\ adj — **rit·u·al·is·ti·cal·ly** \-ti-k(ə-)lē\ adv — **rit·u·al·ly** adv

²**ritual** adj ♦ : of, relating to, or employed in rites or a ritual

♦ ceremonial, ceremonious, formal

ritzy \'rit-sē\ adj **ritz·i·er; -est** : showily elegant : POSH

riv abbr river

¹**ri·val** \'rī-vəl\ n **1 ♦** : one of two or more trying to get what only one can have **2 ♦** : one striving for competitive advantage **3 ♦** : one that equals another esp. in desired qualities : MATCH, PEER

♦ [1] challenger, competition, competitor, contender, contestant ♦ [2] adversary, antagonist, opponent ♦ [3] coordinate, counterpart, equal, equivalent, fellow, like, match, parallel, peer

²**rival** adj : COMPETING

³**rival** vb **-valed** or **-valled; -val·ing** or **-val·ling 1** : to be in competition with **2** : to try to equal or excel **3** : to have qualities that approach or equal another's

ri·val·ry \\'rī-vəl-rē\\ *n, pl* **-ries** ♦ : the act of competing : the state of being a rival

♦ battle, combat, conflict, confrontation, contest, duel, face-off, struggle, tug-of-war, warfare

rive \\'rīv\\ *vb* **rived** \\'rīvd\\; **riv·en** \\'ri-vən\\ *also* **rived; riv·ing** 1 ♦ : to wrench open or tear apart or to pieces : REND 2 : SHATTER

♦ rend, rip, shred, tatter, tear

riv·er \\'ri-vər\\ *n* 1 : a natural stream larger than a brook 2 : a large stream or flow
riv·er·bank \\-ˌbaŋk\\ *n* : the bank of a river
riv·er·bed \\-ˌbed\\ *n* : the channel occupied by a river
riv·er·boat \\-ˌbōt\\ *n* : a boat for use on a river
riv·er·front \\-ˌfrənt\\ *n* : the land or area along a river
riv·er·side \\-ˌsīd\\ *n* : the side or bank of a river
¹riv·et \\'ri-vət\\ *n* : a metal bolt with a head at one end used to join parts by being put through holes in them and then being flattened on the plain end to make another head
²rivet *vb* 1 : to fasten with or as if with a rivet 2 ♦ : to fix and hold (as the attention) — **riv·et·er** *n*

♦ concentrate, fasten, focus, train

riv·u·let \\'ri-vyə-lət, -və-\\ *n* ♦ : a small stream

♦ brook, creek, rill, streamlet

rm *abbr* room
Rn *symbol* radon
¹RN \\ˌär-'en\\ *n* : REGISTERED NURSE
²RN *abbr* Royal Navy
RNA \\ˌär-(ˌ)en-'ā\\ *n* : any of various nucleic acids (as messenger RNA) that are found esp. in the cytoplasm of cells, have ribose as the 5-carbon sugar, and are associated with the control of cellular chemical activities
rnd *abbr* round
¹roach \\'rōch\\ *n, pl* **roach** *also* **roach·es** : any of various bony fishes related to the carp; *also* : any of several sunfishes
²roach *n* 1 : COCKROACH 2 : the butt of a marijuana cigarette
road \\'rōd\\ *n* 1 : ROADSTEAD — often used in pl. 2 ♦ : an open way for vehicles, persons, and animals : HIGHWAY 3 : a way to a conclusion or end ⟨the ~ to success⟩ 4 : a series of scheduled visits (as games or performances) in several locations or the travel necessary to make these visits ⟨the team is on the ~⟩ 5 : RAILROAD

♦ artery, highway, pike, route, thoroughfare, trace, turnpike, way

road·bed \\'rōd-ˌbed\\ *n* 1 : the foundation of a road or railroad 2 : the part of the surface of a road on which vehicles travel
road·block \\-ˌbläk\\ *n* 1 : a barricade on the road ⟨a police ~⟩ 2 : an obstruction to progress
road·ie \\'rō-dē\\ *n* : a person who works for traveling entertainers
road·kill \\'rōd-ˌkil\\ *n* : the remains of an animal that has been killed on a road by a motor vehicle
road·run·ner \\-ˌrə-nər\\ *n* : a largely terrestrial bird of the southwestern U.S. and Mexico that is a speedy runner
road·side \\'rōd-ˌsīd\\ *n* : the strip of land along a road — **road·side** *adj*
road·stead \\-ˌsted\\ *n* : an anchorage for ships usu. less sheltered than a harbor
road·ster \\'rōd-stər\\ *n* 1 : a driving horse 2 : an open automobile that seats two
road·way \\-ˌwā\\ *n* 1 : an open way for vehicles, persons, and animals : ROAD 2 : ROADBED
road·work \\-ˌwərk\\ *n* 1 : work done in constructing or repairing roads 2 : conditioning for an athletic contest (as a boxing match) consisting mainly of long runs
roam \\'rōm\\ *vb* 1 ♦ : to go from place to place without purpose or direction : WANDER 2 : to range or wander over or about 3 : to use a cell phone outside one's local calling area

♦ gad, gallivant, knock, maunder, meander, mope, ramble, range, rove, traipse, wander

roaming *adj* ♦ : being one that roams; *also* : involving cell phone use beyond one's local calling area

♦ errant, itinerant, nomad, nomadic, peripatetic, vagabond, vagrant

¹roan \\'rōn\\ *adj* : of dark color (as black, red, or brown) sprinkled with white ⟨a ~ horse⟩
²roan *n* : an animal (as a horse) with a roan coat; *also* : its color
¹roar \\'rōr\\ *vb* 1 ♦ : to utter a full loud prolonged sound 2 : to make a loud confused sound (as of wind or waves) — **roar·er** *n*

♦ bellow, boom, growl, thunder

²roar *n* ♦ : a sound of roaring

♦ clamor (*or* clamour), howl, hubbub, hue and cry, noise, outcry, tumult, uproar ♦ bluster, cacophony, clamor, din, noise, racket

roar·ing \\'rō-riŋ\\ *adj* 1 ♦ : making or characterized by a noise like a roar 2 ♦ : marked by prosperity or bustle esp. of a temporary nature

♦ [1] booming, clamorous (*or* clamourous), deafening, earsplitting, loud, piercing, resounding, ringing, sonorous, stentorian, thunderous ♦ [2] booming, golden, palmy, prosperous, successful

¹roast \\'rōst\\ *vb* 1 : to cook by exposure to dry heat or an open flame 2 ♦ : to criticize severely or kiddingly

♦ chaff, jive, josh, kid, rally, razz, rib, ride, tease

²roast *n* 1 : a piece of meat suitable for roasting 2 : an outing at which food is roasted ⟨corn ~⟩ 3 : severe criticism or kidding
³roast *adj* : ROASTED
roast·er \\'rō-stər\\ *n* 1 : one that roasts 2 : a device for roasting 3 : something suitable for roasting
rob \\'räb\\ *vb* **robbed; rob·bing** 1 ♦ : to steal from 2 : to deprive of something due or expected 3 : to commit robbery — **rob·ber** *n*

♦ burglarize, rip off, steal

robber fly *n* : any of a family of predaceous flies resembling bumblebees
rob·bery \\'rä-bə-rē\\ *n, pl* **-ber·ies** ♦ : the act or practice of robbing; *esp* : theft of something from a person by use of violence or threat

♦ larceny, theft, thievery

¹robe \\'rōb\\ *n* 1 : a long flowing outer garment; *esp* : one used for ceremonial occasions 2 : a wrap or covering for the lower body (as for sitting outdoors)
²robe *vb* **robed; rob·ing** 1 ♦ : to clothe with or as if with a robe 2 : to dress or cover with clothing : DRESS
rob·in \\'rä-bən\\ *n* 1 : a small chiefly European thrush with a somewhat orange face and breast 2 : a large No. American thrush with a grayish back, a streaked throat, and a chiefly dull reddish breast
ro·bo·call \\'rō-bō-ˌkȯl\\ *n* : a telephone call from an automated source that delivers a message to a large number of people
ro·bot \\'rō-ˌbät, -bət\\ *n* 1 : a machine that looks and acts like a human being 2 : an efficient but insensitive person 3 : a device that automatically performs esp. repetitive tasks 4 : something guided by automatic controls
ro·bot·ic \\rō-'bä-tik\\ *adj* ♦ : of or relating to mechanical robots

♦ automatic, laborsaving (*or* laboursaving), self-acting

ro·bot·ics \\rō-'bä-tiks\\ *n* : technology dealing with the design, construction, and operation of robots
ro·bust \\rō-'bəst, 'rō-(ˌ)bəst\\ *adj* 1 ♦ : strong and vigorously healthy; *also* : having or showing vigor, strength, or firmness 2 : capable of performing without failure under a wide range of conditions 3 ♦ : imparting to the palate the general impression of substantial weight and rich texture — **ro·bust·ly** *adv*

♦ [1] able-bodied, chipper, fit, hale, healthy, hearty, sound, well, whole, wholesome ♦ [1] firm, forceful, hearty, lusty, solid, stout, strong, sturdy, vigorous ♦ [3] concentrated, full, full-bodied, potent, rich, strong

ro·bust·ness *n* ♦ : the quality or state of being robust

♦ fitness, health, heartiness, soundness, wellness, wholeness, wholesomeness

ROC *abbr* Republic of China (Taiwan)
¹rock \\'räk\\ *vb* 1 ♦ : to move back and forth in or as if in a cradle 2 ♦ : to sway or cause to sway back and forth 3 : to arouse to excitement (as with rock music) ⟨~ed the crowd⟩ 4 *slang* : to be extremely enjoyable or effective ⟨this car ~s⟩

♦ [1, 2] careen, lurch, pitch, roll, seesaw, sway, toss, wobble

²rock *n* 1 : a rocking movement 2 : popular music usu. played on electric instruments and characterized by a strong beat and much repetition
³rock *n* 1 : a mass of stony material; *also* : broken pieces of stone 2 : solid mineral deposits 3 : something like a rock in firmness 4 : GEM; *esp* : DIAMOND — **rock** *adj* — **rock·like** *adj* — **rocky** *adj*
rock and roll *n* : ²ROCK 2
rock·bound \\'räk-ˌbau̇nd\\ *adj* : fringed or covered with rocks

rock·er \'rä-kər\ n **1 :** one of the curved pieces on which something (as a chair or cradle) rocks **2 :** a chair that rocks on rockers **3 :** a device that works with a rocking motion **4 :** a rock performer, song, or enthusiast

¹rock·et \'rä-kət\ n **1 :** a firework that is propelled through the air by the discharge of gases produced by a burning substance **2 :** a jet engine that operates on the same principle as a firework rocket but carries the oxygen needed for burning its fuel **3 :** a rocket-propelled bomb or missile

²rocket vb **1 :** to convey by means of a rocket **2 ♦ :** to rise up swiftly, spectacularly, and with force **3 :** to travel rapidly in or as if in a rocket

  ♦ shoot, skyrocket, soar, zoom

rock·et·ry \'rä-kə-trē\ n **:** the study or use of rockets
rocket ship n **:** a rocket-propelled spacecraft
rock·fall \'räk-ˌfȯl\ n **:** a mass of falling or fallen rocks
rock·fish \-ˌfish\ n **:** any of various bony fishes that live among rocks or on rocky bottoms
rock salt n **:** common salt in rocklike masses or large crystals
Rocky Mountain sheep n **:** BIGHORN
ro·co·co \rə-'kō-kō\ adj **:** of or relating to an artistic style esp. of the 18th century marked by fanciful curved forms and elaborate ornamentation — **rococo** n
rod \'räd\ n **1 :** a straight slender stick **2 a :** a stick or bundle of twigs used in punishing a person **b :** PUNISHMENT **3 :** a staff borne to show rank **4 :** a unit of length equal to 5½ yards **5 :** any of the rod-shaped receptor cells of the retina that are sensitive to faint light **6** slang **:** HANDGUN
rode past of RIDE
ro·dent \'rōd-ᵊnt\ n **:** any of an order of relatively small mammals (as mice, squirrels, and beavers) with sharp front teeth used for gnawing
ro·deo \'rō-dē-ˌō, rə-'dā-ō\ n, pl **ro·de·os** **1 :** ROUNDUP 1 **2 :** a public performance featuring cowboy skills (as riding and roping)
¹roe \'rō\ n, pl **roe** or **roes :** DOE
²roe n **:** the eggs of a fish esp. while bound together in a mass
roe·buck \'rō-ˌbək\ n, pl **roebuck** or **roebucks :** a male roe deer
roe deer n **:** either of two small nimble European or Asian deers
roent·gen \'rent-gən, 'rənt-, -jən\ n **:** the international unit of measurement for X-rays and gamma rays
roent·gen·i·um \rent-'ge-nē-əm, rənt-, -'je-\ n **:** a short-lived radioactive chemical element
rog·er \'rä-jər\ interj — used esp. in radio and signaling to indicate that a message has been received and understood
rogue \'rōg\ n **1 :** a dishonest person **:** SCOUNDREL **2 ♦ :** a mischievous person **:** SCAMP — **rogu·ery** \'rō-gə-rē\ n

  ♦ devil, hellion, imp, mischief, monkey, rapscallion, rascal, scamp, urchin

rogu·ish adj ♦ **:** of, relating to, or having the characteristics of a rogue — **rogu·ish·ly** adv — **rogu·ish·ness** n

  ♦ devilish, impish, knavish, mischievous, rascally, sly, waggish, wicked

roil \'rȯil, for 2 also 'rīl\ vb **1 :** to make cloudy or muddy by stirring up **2 ♦ :** to provoke to anger **3 ♦ :** to move turbulently **:** be in a state of turbulence or agitation — **roily** \'rȯi-lē\ adj

  ♦ [2] anger, antagonize, enrage, incense, inflame, infuriate, madden, outrage, rankle, rile ♦ [3] boil, churn, seethe

rois·ter \'rȯi-stər\ vb **rois·tered; rois·ter·ing :** to engage in noisy revelry **:** CAROUSE — **rois·ter·ous** \-stə-rəs\ adj
rois·ter·er n **:** one that roisters

  ♦ celebrant, merrymaker, reveler

ROK abbr Republic of Korea (South Korea)
role also **rôle** \'rōl\ n **1 :** an assigned or assumed character; also **:** a part played (as by an actor) **2 ♦ :** a function or part performed esp. in a particular operation or process **:** FUNCTION

  ♦ capacity, function, job, part, place, position, purpose, task, work

role model n **:** a person whose behavior in a particular role is imitated by others
¹roll \'rōl\ n **1 :** a document containing an official record **2 ♦ :** an official list of names **3 :** bread baked in a small rounded mass **4 :** something that rolls **:** ROLLER

  ♦ catalog, checklist, list, listing, menu, register, registry, roster, schedule, table

²roll vb **1 ♦ :** to move by causing to tumble or swivel **2 :** to press with a roller **3 :** to move on wheels **4 ♦ :** to sound with a full reverberating tone **5 :** to make a continuous beating sound (as on

a drum) **6 :** to utter with a trill **7 :** to move onward as if by completing a revolution ⟨years *~ed* by⟩ **8 ♦ :** to flow or seem to flow in a continuous stream or with a rising and falling motion ⟨the river *~ed* on⟩ **9 ♦ :** to swing or sway from side to side **10 ♦ :** to shape or become shaped in rounded form **11 :** to move by or as if by turning a crank ⟨*~* down the window⟩

  ♦ [1] pivot, revolve, rotate, spin, swing, swirl, turn, twirl, twist, wheel, whirl ♦ [4] growl, grumble, lumber, rumble ♦ [8] bowl, breeze, coast, drift, flow, glide, run, sail, skim, slide, slip, stream, sweep, whisk ♦ [9] careen, lurch, pitch, rock, seesaw, sway, toss, wobble ♦ [10] agglomerate, ball, conglomerate, round, wad

³roll n **1 :** a sound produced by rapid strokes on a drum **2 :** a heavy reverberating sound **3 :** a rolling movement or action **4 :** a swaying movement (as of a ship) **5 :** a somersault made in contact with the ground
roll·back \'rōl-ˌbak\ n **:** the act or an instance of rolling back
roll back vb **1 :** to reduce (as a commodity price) on a national scale **2 :** to cause to withdraw **:** push back
roll bar n **:** an overhead metal bar on an automobile designed to protect riders in case the automobile overturns
roll call n **:** the act or an instance of calling off a list of names (as of soldiers); also **:** a time for a roll call
roll·er \'rō-lər\ n **1 :** a revolving cylinder used for moving, pressing, shaping, applying, or smoothing something **2 :** a rod on which something is rolled up **3 :** a long heavy ocean wave
roll·er coast·er \'rō-lər-ˌkō-stər\ n **:** an amusement ride consisting of an elevated railway having sharp curves and steep slopes
roller skate n **:** a skate with wheels instead of a runner — **roll·er–skate** vb — **roller skater** n
rol·lick \'rä-lik\ vb ♦ **:** to move or behave in a carefree joyous manner **:** FROLIC

  ♦ caper, cavort, disport, frisk, frolic, gambol, lark, romp, sport

rol·lick·ing adj **:** full of fun and good spirits
roly–poly \ˌrō-lē-'pō-lē\ adj **:** being short and pudgy **:** ROTUND
Rom abbr **1** Roman **2** Romance **3** Romania; Romanian **4** Romans
ROM \'räm\ n **:** a computer memory that contains special-purpose information (as a program) which cannot be altered
ro·maine \rō-'mān\ n **:** a garden lettuce with a tall loose head of long crisp leaves
¹Ro·man \'rō-mən\ n **1 :** a native or resident of Rome **2** not cap **:** roman letters or type
²Roman adj **1 :** of or relating to Rome or the Romans and esp. the ancient Romans **2** not cap **:** relating to type in which the letters are upright (as in this definition) **3 :** of or relating to the Roman Catholic Church
Roman candle n **:** a cylindrical firework that discharges balls of fire
Roman Catholic adj **:** of, relating to, or being a Christian church led by the pope and having a liturgy centered in the Mass — **Roman Catholicism** n
¹ro·mance \rō-'mans, 'rō-ˌmans\ n **1 :** a medieval tale of knightly adventure **2 :** a prose narrative dealing with heroic or mysterious events set in a remote time or place **3 :** a love story **4 ♦ :** a romantic attachment or episode between lovers — **ro·manc·er** n

  ♦ affair, amour, love affair

²romance vb **ro·manced; ro·manc·ing** **1 :** to exaggerate or invent detail or incident **2 :** to have romantic fancies **3 :** to carry on a romantic episode with
Ro·mance \rō-'mans, 'rō-ˌmans\ adj **:** of or relating to any of several languages developed from Latin
Ro·ma·ni or **Ro·ma·ny** \'rä-mə-nē, 'rō-\ n, pl **-ni** or **-nis** or **-nies :** a member of a traditionally traveling people coming orig. from India and living chiefly in Europe and in smaller numbers throughout the world; also **:** the language of the Romani
Ro·ma·nian \ru̇-'mā-nē-ən, rō-, -nyən\ also **Ru·ma·nian** \ru̇-\ n **1 :** a native or inhabitant of Romania **2 :** the language of the Romanians
Roman numeral n **:** a numeral in a system of notation that is based on the ancient Roman system
Ro·ma·no \rō-'mä-nō\ n **:** a hard Italian cheese that is sharper than Parmesan
Ro·mans \'rō-mənz\ n **:** a book of the New Testament of Christian Scripture
¹ro·man·tic \rō-'man-tik\ n ♦ **:** a romantic person; esp **:** a romantic writer, composer, or artist

  ♦ dreamer, idealist, utopian, visionary

²romantic adj **1 :** IMAGINARY **2 :** VISIONARY **3 :** having an imaginative or emotional appeal **4** : of, relating to, or having the characteristics of romanticism — **ro·man·ti·cal·ly** \-ti-k(ə-)lē\ *adv*

ro·man·ti·cism \rō-'man-tə-ˌsi-zəm\ *n, often cap* : a literary movement (as in early 19th-century England) marked esp. by emphasis on the imagination and the emotions and by the use of autobiographical material

ro·man·ti·cist \-sist\ *n* : a romantic person, trait, or component

ro·man·ti·cize \-'man-tə-ˌsīz\ *vb* **-cized; -ciz·ing** **1** : to make romantic **2** : to have romantic ideas

¹**romp** \'rämp\ *vb* **1** ♦ : to play actively and noisily **2** : to win a contest easily

> ♦ caper, cavort, disport, frisk, frolic, gambol, lark, rollick, sport

²**romp** *n* ♦ : high-spirited, carefree, and boisterous play

> ♦ binge, fling, frolic, gambol, lark, revel, rollick

romp·er \'räm-pər\ *n* **1** : one that romps **2** : a jumpsuit usu. for infants — usu. used in pl.

rood \'rüd\ *n* : CROSS, CRUCIFIX

¹**roof** \'rüf, 'ruf\ *n, pl* **roofs** \'rüfs, 'rufs; 'rüvz, 'ruvz\ **1** : the upper covering part of a building **2** ♦ : something suggesting a roof of a building **3** ♦ : the roof of a dwelling conventionally designating the home itself — **roofed** \'rüft, 'ruft\ *adj* — **roof·ing** *n* — **roof·less** *adj*

> ♦ [2] canopy, ceiling, tent ♦ [3] abode, domicile, dwelling, home, house, lodging, quarters, residence

²**roof** *vb* **1** : to cover with a roof **2** : to provide with shelter or a home

roof·top \-ˌtäp\ *n* : the roof esp. of a house

¹**rook** \'ruk\ *n* : a crow that nests in usu. treetop colonies

²**rook** *vb* ♦ : to defraud by cheating or swindling

> ♦ bleed, cheat, chisel, cozen, defraud, fleece, hustle, mulct, shortchange, skin, squeeze, stick, sting, swindle, victimize

³**rook** *n* : a chess piece that can move parallel to the sides of the board across any number of unoccupied squares

rook·ery \'ru-kə-rē\ *n, pl* **-er·ies** : a breeding ground or haunt of gregarious birds or mammals; *also* : a colony of such birds or mammals

rook·ie \'ru-kē\ *n* **1** ♦ : one that begins something : BEGINNER **2** : a first-year player in a professional sport

> ♦ beginner, fledgling, freshman, greenhorn, neophyte, newcomer, novice, recruit, tenderfoot, tyro

¹**room** \'rüm, 'rum\ *n* **1** ♦ : an extent of space occupied by or sufficient or available for something **2 a** ♦ : a partitioned part of a building : CHAMBER **b** : the people in a room **3** ♦ : a suitable or fit occasion or opportunity : OPPORTUNITY ⟨~ to develop his talents⟩ — **room·ful** *n*

> ♦ [1] place, space, way ♦ [2a] cell, chamber, closet ♦ [3] chance, occasion, opening, opportunity

²**room** *vb* : to occupy lodgings : LODGE

room·er *n* ♦ : one who occupies a rented room in another's house

> ♦ boarder, lodger, renter, tenant

room·ette \rü-'met, ru-\ *n* : a small private room on a railroad sleeping car

room·ie \'rü-mē, 'ru-\ *n* : ROOMMATE

room·mate \'rüm-ˌmāt, 'rum-\ *n* : one of two or more persons sharing the same room or dwelling

roomy *adj* ♦ : having ample room

> ♦ ample, capacious, commodious, spacious

¹**roost** \'rüst\ *n* : a support on which or a place where birds perch

²**roost** *vb* ♦ : to settle on or as if on a roost

> ♦ alight, land, light, perch, settle ♦ ensconce, install, lodge, perch, settle

roost·er \'rüs-tər, 'rus-\ *n* : an adult male domestic chicken : COCK

¹**root** \'rüt, 'rut\ *n* **1** : the leafless usu. underground part of a seed plant that functions in absorption, aeration, and storage or as a means of anchorage; *also* : an underground plant part esp. when fleshy and edible **2** : something (as the basal part of a tooth or hair) resembling a root **3** : SOURCE, ORIGIN **4** : the essential core : HEART ⟨get to the ~ of the matter⟩ **5** : a number that when taken as a factor an indicated number of times gives a specified number **6** : the lower part — **root·less** *adj* — **root·like** *adj*

²**root** *vb* **1** : to form roots **2** ♦ : to fix or become fixed by or as if by roots : ESTABLISH **3** ♦ : to remove altogether by or as if by pulling out by the roots — usu. used with *out*

> ♦ [2] embed, entrench, establish, fix, implant, ingrain, lodge
> ♦ *usu* **root out** [3] extract, prize, pry, pull, tear, uproot, wrest

³**root** *vb* **1** : to turn up or dig with the snout ⟨pigs ~ing⟩ **2** : to poke or dig around (as in search of something)

⁴**root** \'rut\ *vb* **1** : to applaud or encourage noisily : CHEER **2** : to wish success or lend support to — **root·er** *n*

root beer *n* : a sweetened carbonated beverage flavored with extracts of roots and herbs

root canal *n* : a dental operation to save a tooth by removing the pulp in the root of the tooth and filling the cavity with a protective substance

root·let \'rüt-lət, 'rut-\ *n* : a small root

root·stock \-ˌstäk\ *n* : an underground part of a plant that resembles a rhizome

¹**rope** \'rōp\ *n* **1** ♦ : a large strong cord made of strands of fiber **2** : a hangman's noose **3** : a thick string (as of pearls) made by twisting or braiding

> ♦ cable, cord, lace, line, string, wire

²**rope** *vb* **roped; rop·ing** **1** : to bind, tie, or fasten together with a rope **2** : to separate or divide by means of a rope **3** : LASSO

Ror·schach test \'rōr-ˌshäk-\ *n* : a psychological test in which a subject interprets ink-blot designs in terms that reveal intellectual and emotional factors

ro·sa·ry \'rō-zə-rē\ *n, pl* **-ries** **1** *often cap* : a Roman Catholic devotion consisting of meditation on sacred mysteries during recitation of Hail Marys **2** : a string of beads used in praying

¹**rose** *past of* RISE

²**rose** \'rōz\ *n* **1** : any of a genus of usu. prickly often climbing shrubs with divided leaves and bright often fragrant flowers; *also* : one of these flowers **2** : something resembling a rose in form **3** : a moderate purplish red color — **rose** *adj*

ro·sé \rō-'zā\ *n* : a light pink wine

ro·se·ate \'rō-zē-ət, -zē-ˌāt\ *adj* **1** : resembling a rose esp. in color **2** : overly optimistic ⟨a ~ view of the future⟩

rose·bud \'rōz-ˌbəd\ *n* : the flower of a rose when it is at most partly open

rose·bush \-ˌbush\ *n* : a shrubby rose

rose·mary \'rōz-ˌmer-ē\ *n, pl* **-mar·ies** : a fragrant shrubby Mediterranean mint; *also* : its leaves used as a seasoning

ro·sette \rō-'zet\ *n* **1** : a usu. small badge or ornament of ribbon gathered in the shape of a rose **2** : a circular ornament filled with representations of leaves

rose·wa·ter \'rōz-ˌwò-tər, -ˌwä-\ *n* : a watery solution of the fragrant constituents of the rose used as a perfume

rose·wood \-ˌwud\ *n* : any of various tropical trees with dark red wood streaked with black; *also* : this wood

Rosh Ha·sha·nah \ˌräsh-hə-'shä-nə, ˌrōsh-, -'shō-\ *n* : the Jewish New Year observed as a religious holiday in September or October

ros·in \'räz-ᵊn\ *n* : a brittle resin obtained esp. from pine trees and used esp. in varnishes and on violin bows

ros·ter \'räs-tər\ *n* **1** : a list of personnel; *also* : the persons listed on a roster **2** : an itemized list

> ♦ catalog, checklist, list, listing, menu, register, registry, roll, schedule, table

ros·trum \'räs-trəm\ *n, pl* **rostrums** *or* **ros·tra** \-trə\ ♦ : a stage or platform for public speaking

> ♦ dais, platform, podium, stage, stand

rosy \'rō-zē\ *adj* **ros·i·er; -est** **1** ♦ : of the color rose **2** ♦ : having or promoting optimism : HOPEFUL — **ros·i·ly** \'rō-zə-lē\ *adv* — **ros·i·ness** \-zē-nəs\ *n*

> ♦ [1] florid, flush, glowing, ruddy, sanguine ♦ [2] auspicious, bright, encouraging, fair, golden, heartening, hopeful, likely, promising, propitious, upbeat

¹**rot** \'rät\ *vb* **rot·ted; rot·ting** **1** ♦ : to undergo decomposition : DECAY **2** ♦ : to go to ruin

> ♦ [1] break down, corrupt, decay, decompose, disintegrate, molder, putrefy, spoil ♦ [2] decay, decline, degenerate, descend, deteriorate, ebb, sink, worsen

²**rot** *n* **1** ♦ : the process of rotting : DECAY **2** : any of various diseases of plants or animals in which tissue breaks down **3** ♦ : language, conduct, or an idea that is absurd or contrary to good sense : NONSENSE; *also* : words or language having no meaning or conveying no intelligible ideas

> ♦ [1] breakdown, corruption, decay, decomposition, putrefaction, spoilage ♦ [3] bunk, claptrap, drivel, fiddlesticks, folly, foolishness, fudge, hogwash, humbug, nonsense, piffle, silliness, slush, stupidity, trash

¹**ro·ta·ry** \'rō-tə-rē\ *adj* **1** : turning on an axis like a wheel **2** : having a rotating part

²rotary *n, pl* **-ries 1 :** a rotary machine **2 :** a one-way circular road junction

ro·tate \'rō-ˌtāt\ *vb* **ro·tat·ed; ro·tat·ing 1 ♦ :** to turn or cause to turn about an axis or a center **: REVOLVE 2 :** to alternate in a series — **ro·ta·tor** \'rō-ˌtā-tər\ *n* — **ro·ta·to·ry** \'rō-tə-ˌtōr-ē\ *adj*

♦ pivot, revolve, roll, spin, swing, swirl, turn, twirl, twist, wheel, whirl

ro·ta·tion \rō-'tā-shən\ *n* ♦ **:** the action or process of rotating on or as if on an axis or center

♦ gyration, pirouette, reel, revolution, roll, spin, twirl, wheel, whirl

ROTC *abbr* Reserve Officers' Training Corps

rote \'rōt\ *n* **1 :** repetition from memory often without attention to meaning **2 ♦ :** fixed routine or repetition — **rote** *adj*

♦ groove, pattern, routine, rut, treadmill

ro·tis·ser·ie \rō-'ti-sə-rē\ *n* **1 :** a restaurant specializing in broiled and barbecued meats **2 :** an appliance fitted with a spit on which food is rotated before or over a source of heat

ro·tor \'rō-tər\ *n* **1 :** a part that rotates; *esp* **:** the rotating part of an electrical machine **2 :** a system of rotating horizontal blades for supporting a helicopter

ro·to·till·er \'rō-tō-ˌti-lər\ *n* **:** an engine-powered machine with rotating blades used to lift and turn over soil

rot·ten \'rät-ᵊn\ *adj* **1 :** having rotted **2 ♦ :** morally corrupt **3 ♦ :** extremely unpleasant or inferior **4 ♦ :** of very poor quality — **rot·ten·ness** *n*

♦ [1] bad, putrid ♦ [2] bad, evil, immoral, iniquitous, nefarious, sinful, unethical, unsavory, vicious, vile, villainous, wicked, wrong ♦ [3] bad, disagreeable, distasteful, nasty, sour, uncongenial, unlovely, unpleasant, unwelcome ♦ [3, 4] bad, deficient, inferior, lousy, off, poor, punk, substandard, unacceptable, unsatisfactory, wanting, wretched, wrong ♦ [4] cheap, junky, lousy, mediocre, second-rate, shoddy, sleazy, trashy

rot·ten·stone \'rät-ᵊn-ˌstōn\ *n* **:** a decomposed siliceous limestone used for polishing

rott·wei·ler \'rät-ˌwī-lər\ *n, often cap* **:** any of a breed of tall powerful black-and-tan short-haired dogs

ro·tund \rō-'tənd\ *adj* **1 :** rounded out **2 ♦ :** notably plump

♦ chubby, fat, plump, portly, round

ro·tun·da \rō-'tən-də\ *n* **1 :** a round building; *esp* **:** one covered by a dome **2 :** a large round room

ro·tun·di·ty \-'tən-də-tē\ *n* **:** the quality or state of being rotund

roué \rù-'ā\ *n* **:** a man devoted to a life of sensual pleasure **: RAKE**

rouge \'rüzh, 'rüj\ *n* **:** a cosmetic used to give a red color to cheeks and lips — **rouge** *vb*

¹rough \'rəf\ *adj* **rough·er; rough·est 1 ♦ :** uneven in surface **:** not smooth **2 :** covered with or made up of coarse and often shaggy hair **: SHAGGY 3 :** not calm **: TURBULENT 4 ♦ :** marked by harshness or violence **5 :** presenting a challenge **: DIFFICULT 6 :** coarse or rugged in character or appearance **7 ♦ :** marked by lack of refinement **8 :** not brought to an end or to the desired final state **: CRUDE 9 :** done or made hastily or tentatively ⟨~ estimates⟩

♦ [1] broken, bumpy, coarse, irregular, jagged, lumpy, pebbly, ragged, rugged, uneven ♦ [4] bitter, brutal, burdensome, cruel, excruciating, grievous, grim, hard, harsh, heavy, inhuman, murderous, onerous, oppressive, rugged, severe, stiff, tough, trying ♦ [5] arduous, demanding, difficult, exacting, formidable, grueling, hard, herculean, laborious, strenuous, tall, toilsome, tough ♦ [7] coarse, common, crass, crude, gross, ill-bred, low, rude, tasteless, uncouth, uncultivated, uncultured, unpolished, unrefined, vulgar

²rough *n* **1 :** uneven ground covered with high grass esp. along a golf fairway **2 :** a crude, unfinished, or preliminary state; *also* **:** something in such a state **3 : ROWDY, TOUGH**

³rough *vb* **1 : ROUGHEN 2 ♦ :** to subject to abuse **: MANHANDLE** — usu. used with *up* **3 :** to make or shape roughly esp. in a preliminary way — **rough·er** *n*

♦ *usu* **rough up** maltreat, manhandle, maul, mishandle

rough·age \'rə-fij\ *n* **: FIBER 2;** *also* **:** food containing much indigestible material acting as fiber

rough–and–ready \ˌrə-fən-'re-dē\ *adj* **:** rude or unpolished in nature, method, or manner but effective in action or use ⟨a ~ solution⟩

rough–and–tum·ble \-'təm-bəl\ *n* **:** rough unrestrained fighting or struggling — **rough–and–tumble** *adj*

rough·en \'rə-fən\ *vb* **rough·ened; rough·en·ing :** to make or become rough

rough–hewn \'rəf-'hyün\ *adj* **1 :** being rough and unfinished ⟨~ beams⟩ **2 :** lacking smooth manners or social grace — **rough–hew** \-'hyü\ *vb*

¹rough·house \'rəf-ˌhaùs\ *vb* **rough·housed; rough·hous·ing :** to participate in rough noisy behavior

²roughhouse *n* ♦ **:** violence or rough boisterous play

♦ foolery, high jinks, horseplay, monkeyshines, shenanigans, tomfoolery

rough·ly *adv* ♦ **:** in a rough manner

♦ hard, hardly, harshly, ill, oppressively, severely, sternly, stiffly

rough·neck \'rəf-ˌnek\ *n* **1 :** a rough or uncouth person **: ROWDY 2 :** a worker on a crew drilling oil wells

rough·ness *n* **:** the quality or state of being rough

rough·shod \'rəf-ˌshäd\ *adv* **:** in a roughly forceful manner ⟨rode ~ over the opposition⟩

rou·lette \rü-'let\ *n* **1 :** a gambling game in which a whirling wheel is used **2 :** a wheel or disk with teeth around the outside

¹round \'raùnd\ *adj* **1 ♦ :** having every part of the surface or circumference the same distance from the center **2 : CYLINDRICAL 3 : COMPLETE, FULL 4 a :** approximately correct **b ♦ :** exact only to a specific decimal or place ⟨~ numbers⟩ **5 :** liberal or ample in size or amount **6 : BLUNT, OUTSPOKEN 7 :** moving in or forming a circle **8 :** having curves rather than angles **9 ♦ :** well filled out **10 ♦ :** having full or unimpeded resonance or tone — **round·ish** *adj* — **round·ness** *n*

♦ [1] circular, global ♦ [4b] even, exact, flat, precise ♦ [9] fat, full, plump, portly, rotund ♦ [10] golden, resonant, resounding, ringing, sonorous, vibrant

²round *adv* **1 :** from beginning to end **: AROUND 2 ♦ :** in the reverse or opposite direction **3 ♦ :** in all or various directions from a fixed point

♦ [2] about, around, back ♦ [3] about, around, over, through, throughout

³round *n* **1 ♦ :** something round (as a circle, globe, or ring) **2 :** a curved or rounded part (as a rung of a ladder) **3 :** an indirect path or course; *also* **:** a regularly covered route (as of a security guard) **4 :** a series or cycle of recurring actions or events **5 :** one shot fired by a soldier or a gun; *also* **:** ammunition for one shot **6 :** a period of time or a unit of play in a game or contest **7 :** a cut of meat (as beef) esp. between the rump and the lower leg — **in the round 1 : FREESTANDING 2 :** with a center stage surrounded by an audience ⟨theater *in the round*⟩

♦ band, circle, eye, hoop, loop, ring

⁴round *vb* **1 :** to make or become round **2 ♦ :** to go or pass around or part way around **3 ♦ :** to bring to completion or perfection **: FINISH** — often used with *out* or *off* **4 :** to become plump or shapely **5 :** to express as a round number — often used with *off* **6 ♦ :** to follow a winding course **: BEND**

♦ [1] agglomerate, ball, conglomerate, roll, wad ♦ [2] circle, circumnavigate, coil, compass, encircle, girdle, loop, orbit, ring ♦ *usu* **round off** *or* **round out** [3] close, conclude, end, finish, terminate, wind up, wrap up ♦ [6] arc, arch, bend, bow, crook, curve, hook, sweep, swerve, wheel

⁵round *prep* **: AROUND**

¹round·about \'raùn-də-ˌbaùt\ *adj* ♦ **:** having a circular or winding course **: INDIRECT** ⟨a ~ explanation⟩

♦ circuitous, circular, indirect

²roundabout *n* **1** *Brit* **: MERRY-GO-ROUND 2 : ROTARY 2**

roun·de·lay \'raùn-də-ˌlā\ *n* **1 :** a simple song with a refrain **2 :** a poem with a recurring refrain

round·house \'raùnd-ˌhaùs\ *n* **1 :** a circular building for housing and repairing locomotives **2 :** a blow with the hand made with a wide swing

round·ly \'raùnd-lē\ *adv* **1 a ♦ :** in a complete manner **b : WIDELY 2 :** in a blunt way **3 :** with vigor

♦ completely, exhaustively, fully, minutely, thoroughly, totally

round–rob·in \'raùnd-ˌrä-bən\ *n* **:** a tournament in which each contestant meets every other contestant in turn

round–shoul·dered \-ˌshōl-dərd\ *adj* **:** having the shoulders stooping or rounded

round–trip *n* **:** a trip to a place and back

round·up \'raùnd-ˌdəp\ *n* **1 :** the gathering together of cattle on the range by riding around them and driving them in; *also* **:** the ranch hands and horses engaged in a roundup **2 :** a gathering in of scattered persons or things **3 ♦ :** a summary of information **: SUMMARY** ⟨news ~⟩

♦ abstract, digest, encapsulation, epitome, outline, précis, recapitulation, résumé (*or* resume), sum, summary, synopsis, wrap=up

round up *vb* ♦ : to gather in or bring together from various quarters

♦ accumulate, amass, assemble, collect, concentrate, garner, gather, group, lump, pick up, scrape

round-worm \-,wərm\ *n* : NEMATODE

rouse \'raúz\ *vb* **roused; rous-ing 1** : to excite to activity : stir up **2** ♦ : to wake from sleep — **rous-er** *n*

♦ arouse, awake, wake

rous-ing \'raú-ziŋ\ *adj* ♦ : giving rise to excitement

♦ breathtaking, electric, exciting, exhilarating, stirring, thrilling

roust-about \'raús-tə-,baút\ *n* : one who does heavy unskilled labor (as on a dock or in an oil field)

¹rout \'raút\ *n* **1** : MOB 1, 2 **2** : DISTURBANCE **3** : a fashionable gathering

²rout *vb* **1** : RUMMAGE **2** : to gouge out **3** ♦ : to expel by force ⟨∼ed out of their homes⟩

♦ banish, boot (out), bounce, cast, chase, dismiss, drum, eject, expel, oust, run off, throw out

³rout *n* **1** : a state of wild confusion or disorderly retreat **2** ♦ : a disastrous defeat

♦ defeat, loss, shellacking

⁴rout *vb* **1** ♦ : to put to flight **2** ♦ : to defeat decisively

♦ [1] banish, boot (out), bounce, cast, chase, dismiss, drum, eject, expel, oust, run off, throw out ♦ [2] beat, best, clobber, conquer, crush, defeat, drub, lick, master, overcome, prevail, skunk, subdue, surmount, thrash, trim, triumph, trounce, wallop, whip, win

¹route \'rüt, 'raút\ *n* **1** ♦ : a traveled way **2** : CHANNEL **3** ♦ : a line of travel

♦ [1] artery, avenue, highway, road, thoroughfare, way ♦ [3] course, line, path, track, way

²route *vb* **rout-ed; rout-ing** : to send by a selected route : DIRECT

¹rout-er \'raú-tər\ *n* : a machine with a revolving spindle and cutter for shaping a surface (as of wood)

²rout-er \'rü-tər, 'raú-\ *n* : a device that sends data from one place to another within a computer network or between computer networks

¹rou-tine \rü-'tēn\ *n* **1** ♦ : a regular course of procedure **2** : an often repeated speech or formula **3** : a part fully worked out ⟨a comedy ∼⟩ **4** : a set of computer instructions that will perform a certain task — **rou-tin-ize** \-'tē-,nīz\ *vb*

♦ groove, pattern, rote, rut, treadmill ♦ drill, exercise, practice, training, workout

²routine *adj* **1** ♦ : of a commonplace or repetitious character **2** ♦ : of, relating to, or being in accordance with established procedure — **rou-tine-ly** *adv*

♦ [1] average, common, commonplace, everyday, normal, ordinary, prosaic, run-of-the-mill, standard, unexceptional, unremarkable, usual, workaday ♦ [2] ceremonial, ceremonious, conventional, formal, orthodox, regular

¹rove \'rōv\ *vb* **roved; rov-ing** ♦ : to wander over or through

♦ gad, gallivant, knock, maunder, meander, mope, ramble, range, roam, traipse, wander

²rove *past and past part of* REEVE

¹rov-er *n* ♦ : one that wanders

♦ drifter, nomad, rambler, stroller, vagabond, wanderer

²rov-er *n* ♦ : one who commits or practices piracy

♦ buccaneer, corsair, freebooter, pirate

¹row \'rō\ *vb* **1** ♦ : to propel a boat with oars **2** : to transport in a rowboat **3** : to pull an oar in a crew — **row-er** \'rō-ər\ *n*

♦ scull

²row *n* : an act or instance of rowing

³row *n* **1** : a number of objects in an orderly sequence **2** : a thoroughfare for travel or transportation from place to place : WAY

⁴row \'raú\ *n* **1** ♦ : a noisy quarrel **2** ♦ : a noisy disturbance

♦ [1] altercation, argument, bicker, brawl, disagreement, dispute, fight, quarrel, scrap, spat, squabble, wrangle ♦ [2] commotion, disturbance, furor, hullabaloo, pandemonium, tumult, turmoil, uproar

⁵row \'raú\ *vb* ♦ : to engage in a row

♦ argue, bicker, brawl, dispute, fall out, fight, hassle, quarrel, scrap, spat, squabble, wrangle

row-boat \'rō-,bōt\ *n* : a small boat designed to be rowed

¹row-dy \'raú-dē\ *adj* **row-di-er; -est** ♦ : coarse or boisterous in behavior — **row-di-ness** \'raú-dē-nəs\ *n* — **row-dy-ish** *adj* — **row-dy-ism** *n*

♦ boisterous, rambunctious, raucous

²rowdy *n* ♦ : a rowdy person

♦ bully, hoodlum, punk, ruffian, thug, tough

row-el \'raú-əl\ *n* : a small pointed wheel on a rider's spur — **rowel** *vb*

¹roy-al \'rói-əl\ *adj* **1** : of or relating to a sovereign : REGAL **2** ♦ : fit for a king or queen ⟨a ∼ welcome⟩ **3** ♦ : of superior size, magnitude, or quality — **roy-al-ly** *adv*

♦ [2] kingly, monarchical, princely, queenly, regal ♦ [3] august, baronial, gallant, glorious, grand, grandiose, heroic, imposing, magnificent, majestic, monumental, noble, proud, regal, splendid, stately

²royal *n* : a person of royal blood

royal flush *n* : a straight flush having an ace as the highest card

roy-al-ist \'rói-ə-list\ *n* : an adherent of a king or of monarchical government

roy-al-ty \'rói-əl-tē\ *n, pl* **-ties 1** : the state of being royal **2** : royal persons **3** : a share of a product or profit (as of a mine or oil well) claimed by the owner for allowing another person to use the property **4** : a payment made to an author or composer for each copy of a work sold or to an inventor for each article sold under a patent

RP *abbr* **1** relief pitcher **2** Republic of the Philippines

rpm *abbr* revolutions per minute

rps *abbr* revolutions per second

rpt *abbr* **1** repeat **2** report

RR *abbr* **1** railroad **2** rural route

RS *abbr* **1** recording secretary **2** revised statutes **3** Royal Society

RSV *abbr* Revised Standard Version

RSVP *abbr* please reply

rt *abbr* **1** right **2** route

RT *abbr* round-trip

rte *abbr* route

Ru *symbol* ruthenium

¹rub \'rəb\ *vb* **rubbed; rub-bing 1** : to use pressure and friction on a body or object **2** ♦ : to fret or chafe with friction **3** ♦ : to scour, polish, erase, or smear by pressure and friction

♦ [2] abrade, chafe, erode, fray, fret, gall, wear ♦ [3] buff, file, grind, hone, rasp, sand ♦ [3] buff, burnish, dress, gloss, grind, polish, shine, smooth

²rub *n* **1** : DIFFICULTY, OBSTRUCTION **2** ♦ : something grating to the feelings

♦ aggravation, annoyance, bother, bugbear, exasperation, frustration, hassle, headache, inconvenience, irritant, nuisance, peeve, pest, problem, ruffle, thorn, vexation

¹rub-ber \'rə-bər\ *n* **1** : one that rubs **2** : ERASER **3** : a flexible waterproof elastic substance made from the milky juice of various tropical plants or made synthetically; *also* : something made of this material **4** : CONDOM — **rubber** *adj* — **rub-ber-ize** \'rə-bə-,rīz\ *vb*

²rubber *n* **1** : a contest that consists of an odd number of games and is won by the side that takes a majority **2** : an extra game played to decide a tie

¹rub-ber-neck \-,nek\ *n* **1** : an idly or overly inquisitive person **2** : a person on a guided tour

²rubberneck *vb* ♦ : to look about, stare, or listen with excessive curiosity — **rub-ber-neck-er** *n*

♦ gape, gawk, gaze, goggle, peer, stare

rub-bery *adj* ♦ : resembling rubber (as in elasticity, consistency, or texture)

♦ elastic, flexible, resilient, springy, stretch, supple

rub-bish \'rə-bish\ *n* **1** ♦ : useless waste or rejected matter : TRASH **2** : something worthless or nonsensical

♦ chaff, deadwood, dust, garbage, junk, litter, refuse, riffraff, scrap, trash, waste

rub-ble \'rə-bəl\ *n* ♦ : broken fragments esp. of a destroyed building

♦ debris, remains, ruins, wreck, wreckage

ru·bel·la \rü-'be-lə\ *n* : GERMAN MEASLES

ru·bi·cund \'rü-bi-(,)kənd\ *adj* : having a healthy reddish color : RED, RUDDY ⟨∼ faces⟩

ru·bid·i·um \rü-'bi-dē-əm\ *n* : a soft silvery metallic chemical element

ru·ble \'rü-bəl\ *n* : the basic monetary unit of Russia

rub out *vb* ♦ : to destroy completely

　♦ annihilate, blot out, demolish, eradicate, exterminate, liquidate, obliterate, root, snuff, stamp, wipe out

ru·bric \'rü-brik\ *n* 1 : a heading of a part of a book or manuscript 2 : a rule esp. for the conduct of a religious service

ru·by \'rü-bē\ *n, pl* **rubies** : a clear red precious stone — **ruby** *adj*

ru·by–throat·ed hummingbird \'rü-bē-,thrō-təd-\ : a bright green and whitish hummingbird of eastern No. America with a red throat in the male

ruck·us \'rə-kəs\ *n* : a noisy disturbance or quarrel : ROW

rud·der \'rə-dər\ *n* : a movable flat piece attached at the rear of a ship or aircraft for steering

rud·dy \'rə-dē\ *adj* **rud·di·er; -est** 1 : REDDISH 2 ♦ : of a healthy reddish complexion ⟨the boy's ∼ cheeks⟩ — **rud·di·ness** \'rə-dē-nəs\ *n*

　♦ florid, flush, glowing, rosy, sanguine

rude \'rüd\ *adj* **rud·er; rud·est** 1 ♦ : roughly made : CRUDE 2 : not developed : PRIMITIVE 3 ♦ : lacking refinement or delicacy 4 : marked by or suggestive of lack of training or skill : UN-SKILLED 5 ♦ : not being in a cultural or civilized state — **rude·ly** *adv*

　♦ [1] artless, clumsy, crude, rough, unrefined ♦ [3] coarse, common, crass, crude, gross, ill-bred, low, rough, tasteless, uncouth, uncultivated, uncultured, unpolished, unrefined, vulgar ♦ [3] discourteous, ill-bred, ill-mannered, impertinent, impolite, inconsiderate, thoughtless, uncivil, ungracious, unmannerly ♦ [5] barbarous, heathen, heathenish, Neanderthal, savage, uncivilized, wild

rude·ness *n* 1 ♦ : the quality or state of being rude 2 ♦ : a rude action

　♦ [1] coarseness, grossness, indelicacy, lowness, vulgarity ♦ [2] brazenness, discourtesy, disrespect, impertinence, impudence, incivility, insolence

ru·di·ment \'rü-də-mənt\ *n* 1 ♦ : an elementary principle or basic skill — usu. used in pl. 2 : something not fully developed — usu. used in pl.

　♦ **rudiments** elements, essentials, principles

ru·di·men·ta·ry \,rü-də-'men-tə-rē\ *adj* 1 ♦ : consisting in basic principles 2 ♦ : of a primitive kind

　♦ [1] basic, elemental, elementary, essential, fundamental, underlying ♦ [2] crude, low, primitive, rude

¹**rue** \'rü\ *n* ♦ : deep distress, sadness, or regret — **rue·ful·ness** *n*

　♦ contrition, penitence, regret, remorse, repentance

²**rue** *vb* **rued; ru·ing** ♦ : to feel regret, remorse, or penitence for ⟨∼ing the decision⟩

　♦ bemoan, deplore, lament, regret, repent

³**rue** *n* : a European strong-scented woody herb with bitter-tasting leaves

rue·ful \-fəl\ *adj* 1 ♦ : expressing sorrow 2 ♦ : full of sorrow 3 ♦ : exciting pity or sympathy

　♦ [1] dolorous, funeral, lugubrious, mournful, plaintive, regretful, sorrowful, weeping, woeful ♦ [2] apologetic, contrite, penitent, regretful, remorseful, repentant, sorry ♦ [3] heartbreaking, miserable, pathetic, piteous, pitiful, poor, sorry, wretched

rue·ful·ly *adv* : in a rueful manner

ruff \'rəf\ *n* 1 : a large round pleated collar worn in the 16th and 17th centuries 2 : a fringe of long hair or feathers around the neck of an animal — **ruffed** \'rəft\ *adj*

ruf·fi·an \'rə-fē-ən\ *n* ♦ : a brutal person — **ruf·fi·an·ly** *adj*

　♦ bully, gangster, goon, hood, hoodlum, mobster, mug, punk, rowdy, thug, tough

¹**ruf·fle** \'rə-fəl\ *vb* **ruf·fled; ruf·fling** 1 : to roughen the surface of 2 ♦ : to excite to anger : IRRITATE, VEX 3 : to erect (as hair or feathers) in or like a ruff 4 : to flip through (as pages) 5 : to draw into or provide with plaits or folds

　♦ aggravate, annoy, bother, bug, chafe, exasperate, gall, get, grate, irk, irritate, nettle, peeve, persecute, pique, put out, rasp, rile, spite, vex

²**ruffle** *n* 1 ♦ : a strip of fabric gathered or pleated on one edge 2 : RUFF 2 3 : RIPPLE — **ruf·fly** \'rə-fə-lē, -flē\ *adj*

　♦ flounce, frill, furbelow

RU–486 \'är-,yü-,fōr-,ā-tē-'siks\ *n* : a drug taken orally to induce abortion esp. early in pregnancy

rug \'rəg\ *n* 1 : a covering for the legs, lap, and feet 2 : a piece of heavy fabric usu. with a nap or pile used as a floor covering

rug·by \'rəg-bē\ *n, often cap* : a football game in which play is continuous and interference and forward passing are not permitted

rug·ged \'rə-gəd\ *adj* 1 ♦ : having a rough uneven surface 2 : TURBULENT, STORMY 3 : austere or stern in aspect, conduct, or character : STERN 4 ♦ : strongly built or constituted : STURDY 5 ♦ : presenting a severe test of ability, stamina, or resolution — **rug·ged·ize** \'rə-gə-,dīz\ *vb* — **rug·ged·ly** *adv* — **rug·ged·ness** *n*

　♦ [1] broken, bumpy, coarse, irregular, jagged, lumpy, pebbly, ragged, rough, uneven ♦ [4] hard, hard-bitten, hardy, stout, strong, sturdy, tough, vigorous ♦ [5] bitter, brutal, burdensome, cruel, excruciating, grievous, grim, hard, harsh, heavy, inhuman, murderous, onerous, oppressive, rough, severe, stiff, tough, trying

¹**ru·in** \'rü-ən\ *n* 1 ♦ : complete collapse or destruction 2 ♦ : the remains of something destroyed — usu. used in pl. 3 : a cause of destruction 4 : the action of destroying

　♦ [1] annihilation, demolition, desolation, destruction, devastation, havoc, loss, obliteration, wastage, wreckage ♦ **ruins** [2] debris, remains, rubble, wreck, wreckage

²**ruin** *vb* 1 ♦ : to reduce to ruins : DESTROY 2 ♦ : to damage beyond repair 3 : BANKRUPT

　♦ [1] destroy, devastate, ravage, scourge ♦ [2] annihilate, blot out, demolish, desolate, destroy, devastate, do in, exterminate, extinguish, obliterate, pulverize, shatter, smash, tear down, waste, wipe out, wreck

ru·in·ation \,rü-ə-'nā-shən\ *n* : the state of being ruined : RUIN, DESTRUCTION

ru·in·ous \'rü-ə-nəs\ *adj* 1 : RUINED, DILAPIDATED 2 ♦ : causing ruin ⟨∼ conflicts⟩ — **ru·in·ous·ly** *adv*

　♦ calamitous, catastrophic, destructive, devastating, disastrous, fatal, fateful, unfortunate

¹**rule** \'rül\ *n* 1 ♦ : a guide or principle for governing action : REGULATION 2 : the usual way of doing something 3 ♦ : the exercise of authority or control : GOVERNMENT 4 : RULER 2

　♦ [1] regulation ♦ [3] administration, authority, government, jurisdiction, regime

²**rule** *vb* **ruled; rul·ing** 1 ♦ : to exert control, direction, or influence on; *also* : GOVERN 2 ♦ : to be supreme or outstanding in 3 ♦ : to give or state as a considered decision 4 : to mark on paper with or as if with a ruler

　♦ [1] boss, captain, command, control, govern, preside ♦ *usu* **rule on** [3] adjudicate, decide, determine, judge, referee, settle, umpire

rule out *vb* ♦ : to remove from consideration

　♦ ban, bar, debar, eliminate, except, exclude

rul·er \'rü-lər\ *n* 1 ♦ : one that rules 2 : a straight strip of material (as wood or metal) marked off in units and used for measuring or as a straightedge

　♦ autocrat, monarch, sovereign

ruling *n* ♦ : an official or authoritative decision, decree, statement, or interpretation (as by a judge on a point of law)

　♦ doom, finding, holding, judgment (*or* judgement), sentence ♦ decree, directive, edict, fiat

rum \'rəm\ *n* 1 : an alcoholic liquor made from sugarcane products (as molasses) 2 : alcoholic liquor

Ru·ma·nian *var of* ROMANIAN

rum·ba \'rəm-bə, 'rum-\ *n* : a dance of Cuban origin marked by strong rhythmic movements

¹**rum·ble** \'rəm-bəl\ *vb* **rum·bled; rum·bling** 1 ♦ : to make a low heavy rolling sound 2 : to move along with such a sound — **rum·bler** *n*

　♦ growl, grumble, lumber, roll

²**rumble** *n* 1 : a low heavy rolling sound 2 : a street fight esp. among gangs

rumble seat *n* : a folding seat in the back of an automobile that is not covered by the top

rum·bling \'rəm-bliŋ\ *n* **1** : RUMBLE **2** : widespread talk or complaints — usu. used in pl.

ru·men \'rü-mən\ *n, pl* **ru·mi·na** \-mə-nə\ *or* **rumens** : the large first compartment of the stomach of a ruminant (as a cow)

¹ru·mi·nant \'rü-mə-nənt\ *n* : a ruminant mammal

²ruminant *adj* **1** : chewing the cud; *also* : of or relating to a group of hoofed mammals (as cattle, deer, and camels) that chew the cud and have a complex 3- or 4-chambered stomach **2** ♦ : given to or engaged in contemplation : MEDITATIVE

   ♦ contemplative, meditative, pensive, reflective, thoughtful

ru·mi·nate \'rü-mə-ˌnāt\ *vb* **-nat·ed; -nat·ing** **1** ♦ : to engage in contemplation : to spend time in thought on **2** : to chew the cud — **ru·mi·na·tion** \ˌrü-mə-'nā-shən\ *n*

   ♦ chew over, cogitate, consider, contemplate, debate, deliberate, entertain, meditate, mull, ponder, question, study, think, weigh

¹rum·mage \'rə-mij\ *vb* **rum·maged; rum·mag·ing** ♦ : to search thoroughly — **rum·mag·er** *n*

   ♦ dig, dredge, hunt, rake, ransack, rifle, scour, search

²rummage *n* **1** ♦ : a miscellaneous collection **2** : an act of rummaging

   ♦ assortment, clutter, jumble, medley, mélange, miscellany, motley, muddle, variety, welter

rummage sale *n* : a usu. informal sale of miscellaneous goods

rum·my \'rə-mē\ *n* : any of several card games for two or more players

¹ru·mor *or Can and Brit* **ru·mour** \'rü-mər\ *n* **1** : common talk **2** : a statement or report current but not authenticated

²rumor *or Can and Brit* **rumour** *vb* ♦ : to tell or spread by rumor

   ♦ circulate, noise, whisper

rump \'rəmp\ *n* **1** : the rear part of an animal; *also* : a cut of meat (as beef) behind the upper sirloin **2** : a small or inferior remnant (as of a group) **3** ♦ : the upper rounded part of the hindquarters of a quadruped mammal

   ♦ backside, bottom, butt, buttocks, posterior, rear, seat

rum·ple \'rəm-pəl\ *vb* **rum·pled; rum·pling** **1** ♦ : to become or cause to become marked with or contracted into irregular folds : WRINKLE **2** ♦ : to make unkempt : MUSS — **rumple** *n* — **rum·ply** \'rəm-pə-lē\ *adj*

   ♦ [1] crease, crinkle, furrow, wrinkle ♦ [2] dishevel, disorder, muddle, muss, tumble, upset

rum·pus \'rəm-pəs\ *n* : a usu. noisy commotion : RUCKUS

rumpus room *n* : a room usu. in the basement of a home that is used for games, parties, and recreation

¹run \'rən\ *vb* **ran** \'ran\; **run; run·ning** **1** ♦ : to go faster than a walk **2** ♦ : to take to flight : FLEE **3** : to go without restraint ⟨let chickens ∼ loose⟩ **4** : to go rapidly or hurriedly : HASTEN, RUSH **5** : to make a quick or casual trip or visit **6** : to contend in a race; *esp* : to enter an election **7** : to put forward as a candidate for office **8** : to move on or as if on wheels : pass or slide freely **9** : to go back and forth : PLY **10 a** : to move in large numbers esp. to a spawning ground ⟨shad are *running*⟩ **b** : to drive (livestock) esp. to a grazing place **11** : FUNCTION, OPERATE ⟨left the motor *running*⟩ **12** : to continue in force ⟨two years to ∼⟩ **13 a** : to flow rapidly or under pressure : MELT **b** : DISCHARGE 7 ⟨my nose is *running*⟩ **14** : to tend to produce or to recur ⟨family ∼s to blonds⟩ **15** ♦ : to take a certain direction **16** : to be worded or written **17** : to be current ⟨rumors *running* wild⟩ **18** ♦ : to cause to produce a flow **19** : TRACE ⟨∼ down a rumor⟩ **20** : to perform or bring about by running **21** : to cause to pass ⟨∼ a wire from the antenna⟩ **22** : to cause to collide **23** : SMUGGLE **24** ♦ : to direct the business or activities of : MANAGE ⟨∼ a business⟩ **25** : INCUR ⟨∼ a risk⟩ **26** : to permit to accumulate before settling ⟨∼ up a bill⟩ **27** : PRINT, PUBLISH **28** ♦ : to exist or occur in a continuous range of variation

   ♦ [1] dash, gallop, jog, scamper, sprint, trip ♦ [2] bolt, break, flee, fly, retreat, run away, run off ♦ [13a] flow, liquefy, melt, pour, roll, stream, thaw ♦ [15] extend, go, head, lead, lie ♦ [18] activate, actuate, crank, drive, move, propel, set off, spark, start, touch off, trigger, turn on ♦ [24] administer, carry on, conduct, control, direct, govern, guide, handle, manage, operate, oversee, regulate, superintend, supervise ♦ [28] go, range, vary

²run *n* **1** : an act or the action of running **2** : a migration of fish; *also* : the migrating fish **3** : a score in baseball **4** : BROOK, CREEK **5** ♦ : a continuous series esp. of similar things : a period of existence ⟨the play's long ∼⟩ **6** : persistent heavy demands from depositors, creditors, or customers **7** : the quantity of work

turned out in a continuous operation; *also* : a period of operation (as of a machine) **8** : the usual or normal kind ⟨the ordinary ∼ of students⟩ **9** : the distance covered in continuous travel or sailing **10** : a regular course or trip **11** ♦ : freedom of movement in a place or area ⟨has the ∼ of the house⟩ **12** : an enclosure for animals **13** : an inclined course (as for skiing) **14** : a lengthwise ravel (as in a stocking) **15** : general tendency or direction — **run·less** *adj*

   ♦ [5] date, duration, life, lifetime, standing, time ♦ [11] authorization, freedom, latitude, license (*or* licence)

run·about \'rə-nə-ˌbaut\ *n* : a light wagon, automobile, or motorboat

run·around \'rə-nə-ˌraund\ *n* : evasive or delaying action esp. in response to a request

¹run·away \'rə-nə-ˌwā\ *n* **1** : one that runs away : FUGITIVE **2** : the act of running away out of control; *also* : something (as a horse) that is running out of control

²runaway *adj* **1** : FUGITIVE **2** : won by a long lead; *also* : extremely successful **3** : subject to uncontrolled changes ⟨∼ inflation⟩ **4** : operating out of control ⟨a ∼ locomotive⟩

run away *vb* ♦ : to leave quickly in order to avoid or escape something

   ♦ abscond, clear out, escape, flee, fly, get out, lam, run off

run·down \'rən-ˌdaun\ *n* : an item-by-item report or review : SUMMARY

run–down \'rən-'daun\ *adj* **1** : EXHAUSTED, WORN-OUT ⟨that ∼ feeling⟩ **2** : being in poor repair ⟨a ∼ farm⟩

run down *vb* **1** : to collide with and knock down **2** : to chase until exhausted or captured **3** ♦ : to find by search **4** : DISPARAGE **5** : to cease to operate for lack of motive power **6** : to decline in physical condition

   ♦ detect, determine, dig up, discover, ferret out, hit on, locate, track down

rune \'rün\ *n* **1** : any of the characters of any of several alphabets formerly used by the Germanic peoples **2** : MYSTERY, MAGIC **3** : a poem esp. in Finnish or Old Norse — **ru·nic** \'rü-nik\ *adj*

¹rung *past part of* RING

²rung \'rəŋ\ *n* **1** : a rounded crosspiece between the legs of a chair **2** : one of the crosspieces of a ladder

run–in \'rən-ˌin\ *n* **1** ♦ : a noisy heated angry dispute **2** : something run in

   ♦ brush, encounter, hassle, scrape, skirmish

run in *vb* **1** : to insert as additional matter **2** : to arrest esp. for a minor offense **3** : to pay a casual visit

run·nel \'rən-ᵊl\ *n* : BROOK, STREAMLET

run·ner \'rə-nər\ *n* **1** : one that runs **2** : BASE RUNNER **3** : BALLCARRIER **4** : a thin piece or part on which something (as a sled or an ice skate) slides **5** : the support of a drawer or a sliding door **6** : a horizontal branch from the base of a plant that produces new plants **7** : a plant producing runners **8** : a long narrow carpet **9** : a narrow decorative cloth cover for a table or dresser top **10** ♦ : one who bears a message or does an errand

   ♦ courier, go-between, messenger, page

run·ner–up \'rə-nər-ˌəp\ *n, pl* **runners–up** *also* **runner–ups** : the competitor in a contest who finishes second

¹run·ning *adj* **1** : FLOWING **2** : FLUID, RUNNY **3** : CONTINUOUS, INCESSANT **4** : measured in a straight line ⟨cost per ∼ foot⟩ **5** : of or relating to an act of running **6** : made or trained for running ⟨∼ horse⟩ ⟨∼ shoes⟩ **7** ♦ : carrying on a function or being in action

   ♦ active, alive, functional, living, on, operational, operative, working

²running *adv* : in succession

running light *n* : any of the lights carried by a vehicle (as a ship) at night

run·ny \'rə-nē\ *adj* ♦ : having a tendency to run ⟨a ∼ dough⟩ ⟨a ∼ nose⟩

   ♦ fluent, fluid, liquid

run·off \'rən-ˌof\ *n* : a final contest (as an election) to decide a previous indecisive contest

run off *vb* **1** ♦ : to drive off (as trespassers) **2** ♦ : to run away

   ♦ [1] banish, boot (out), bounce, cast, chase, dismiss, drum, eject, expel, oust, rout, throw out ♦ [2] bolt, break, flee, fly, retreat, run, run away

run–of–the–mill *adj* ♦ : not outstanding ⟨a ∼ performance⟩

   ♦ average, common, commonplace, everyday, normal, ordinary,

prosaic, routine, standard, unexceptional, unremarkable, usual, workaday

run on vb **1** ♦ : to talk at length **2** : to continue (matter in type) without a break or a new paragraph **3** : to place or add (as an entry in a dictionary) at the end of a paragraphed item **4** ♦ : to keep going — **run–on** \'rən-ˌón, -ˌän\ n

   ♦ [1] maunder, ramble, rattle ♦ [4] abide, continue, endure, hold, keep up, last, persist

run out vb : to use up or exhaust a supply ⟨ran out of gas⟩
runt \'rənt\ n **1** ♦ : an animal unusually small of its kind **2** usu disparaging : a person of small stature — **runty** adj

   ♦ dwarf, midget, mite, peewee, pygmy

run through vb ♦ : to spend or consume wastefully

   ♦ blow, dissipate, fritter, lavish, misspend, spend, squander, throw away, waste

run·way \'rən-ˌwā\ n **1** : a beaten path made by animals; also : a passage for animals **2** : a paved strip of ground for the landing and takeoff of aircraft **3** : a narrow platform from a stage into an auditorium **4** : a support (as a track) on which something runs
ru·pee \rü-'pē, 'rü-ˌpē\ n : the basic monetary unit of several countries on the Indian subcontinent (as India and Pakistan)
¹rup·ture \'rəp-chər\ n : a breaking or tearing apart; also : HERNIA
²rupture vb **rup·tured; rup·tur·ing** : to cause or undergo rupture
ru·ral \'rür-əl\ adj ♦ : of or relating to the country, country people, or agriculture

   ♦ bucolic, country, pastoral, rustic Ant urban

ruse \'rüs, 'rüz\ n : a wily subterfuge : TRICK, ARTIFICE
¹rush \'rəsh\ n : any of various often tufted and hollow-stemmed grasslike marsh plants — **rushy** adj
²rush vb **1** ♦ : to move forward or act with too great haste or eagerness or without preparation **2** : to perform in a short time or at high speed **3** ♦ : to run toward or against in attack : CHARGE **4** ♦ : to urge to an unnatural or extreme speed — **rush·er** n

   ♦ [1] dash, fly, hasten, hurry, pelt, race, rip, rocket, run, shoot, speed, whirl, whisk, zip, zoom ♦ [3] assail, assault, attack, beset, charge, descend, jump, pounce (on or upon), raid, storm, strike ♦ [4] accelerate, hasten, hurry, quicken, speed (up), step up, whisk

³rush n **1** ♦ : a violent forward motion **2** : unusual demand or activity **3** : a crowding of people to one place **4** : a running play in football **5** : a sudden feeling of pleasure **6** ♦ : a burst of activity, productivity, or speed

   ♦ [1] aggression, assault, attack, charge, descent, offense (or offence), offensive, onset, onslaught, raid, strike ♦ [6] haste, hurry, hustle, precipitation

⁴rush adj : requiring or marked by special speed or urgency ⟨~ orders⟩
rush hour n : a time when the amount of traffic or business is at a peak
rusk \'rəsk\ n : a sweet or plain bread baked, sliced, and baked again until dry and crisp

rus·set \'rə-sət\ n **1** : a coarse reddish brown cloth **2** : a reddish brown **3** : a baking potato — **russet** adj
Rus·sian \'rə-shən\ n **1** : a native or inhabitant of Russia **2** : a Slavic language of the Russian people — **Russian** adj
rust \'rəst\ n **1** : a reddish coating formed on iron when it is exposed to esp. moist air **2** : any of numerous plant diseases characterized by usu. reddish spots; also : a fungus causing rust **3** : a strong reddish brown — **rust** vb — **rusty** adj
¹rus·tic \'rəs-tik\ adj ♦ : of, relating to, or suitable for the country or country people ⟨~ inn⟩ — **rus·ti·cal·ly** \-ti-k(ə-)lē\ adv — **rus·tic·i·ty** \ˌrəs-'ti-sə-tē\ n

   ♦ bucolic, country, pastoral, rural

²rustic n ♦ : a rustic person

   ♦ bumpkin, clodhopper, hick, yokel

rus·ti·cate \'rəs-ti-ˌkāt\ vb **-cat·ed; -cat·ing** : to go into or reside in the country — **rus·ti·ca·tion** \ˌrəs-ti-'kā-shən\ n
¹rus·tle \'rə-səl\ vb **rus·tled; rus·tling** **1** : to make or cause a rustle **2** : to cause to rustle ⟨~ a newspaper⟩ **3 a** : to act or move with energy or speed **b** : to procure in this way **4** : to forage food **5** : to steal cattle from the range
²rustle n : a quick series of small sounds ⟨~ of leaves⟩
rus·tler n : one that rustles: as **a** : an alert energetic driving person **b** : a cattle thief
¹rut \'rət\ n : state or period of sexual excitement esp. in male deer — **rut** vb
²rut n **1** : a track worn by wheels or by habitual passage of something **2** ♦ : a usual or fixed routine

   ♦ groove, pattern, rote, routine, treadmill

ru·ta·ba·ga \ˌrü-tə-'bā-gə, ˌrü-\ n : a turnip with a large yellowish root
Ruth \'rüth\ n : a book of Jewish and Christian Scripture
ru·the·ni·um \rü-'thē-nē-əm\ n : a hard brittle metallic chemical element
ruth·er·ford·ium \ˌrə-thər-'fór-dē-əm\ n : an artificially produced radioactive chemical element
ruth·less \'rüth-ləs\ adj ♦ : having no pity : MERCILESS — **ruth·less·ly** adv — **ruth·less·ness** n

   ♦ callous, hard, heartless, inhuman, inhumane, pitiless, soulless, unfeeling, unsympathetic

¹RV \ˌär-'vē\ n ♦ : a vehicle designed for recreational use (as camping) : RECREATIONAL VEHICLE

   ♦ camper, caravan, motor home, recreational vehicle, trailer

²RV abbr Revised Version
R–value \'är-ˌval-yü\ n : a measure of resistance to the flow of heat through a substance (as insulation)
RW abbr **1** right worshipful **2** right worthy
rwy or **ry** abbr railway
Rx \ˌär-'eks\ n : PRESCRIPTION 2
-ry \rē\ n suffix : -ERY ⟨bigotry⟩
rye \'rī\ n **1** : a hardy annual grass grown for grain or as a cover crop; also : its seed **2** : a whiskey distilled from a rye mash

---

S

¹s \'es\ n, pl **s's** or **ss** \'e-səz\ often cap : the 19th letter of the English alphabet
²s abbr, often cap **1** saint **2** second **3** senate **4** series **5** shilling **6** singular **7** small **8** son **9** south; southern
¹-s \s after sounds f, k, k̲, p, t, th; əz after sounds ch, j, s, sh, z, zh; z after other sounds\ n pl suffix — used to form the pl. of most nouns that do not end in s, z, sh, ch or y following a consonant ⟨heads⟩ ⟨books⟩ ⟨boys⟩ ⟨beliefs⟩, to form the pl. of proper nouns that end in y following a consonant ⟨Marys⟩, and with or without a preceding apostrophe to form the pl. of abbreviations, numbers, letters, and symbols used as nouns ⟨MCs⟩ ⟨4s⟩ ⟨#s⟩ ⟨B's⟩
²-s adv suffix — used to form adverbs denoting usual or repeated action or state ⟨works nights⟩
³-s vb suffix — used to form the third person singular present of most verbs that do not end in s, z, sh, or ch or in y following a consonant ⟨falls⟩ ⟨takes⟩ ⟨plays⟩

S symbol sulfur
SA abbr **1** Salvation Army **2** seaman apprentice **3** sex appeal **4** without date **5** South Africa **6** South America **7** subject to approval
Sab·bath \'sa-bəth\ n **1** : the 7th day of the week observed as a day of worship by Jews and some Christians **2** : Sunday observed among Christians as a day of worship
sab·bat·i·cal \sə-'ba-ti-kəl\ n : a leave often with pay granted (as to a college professor) usu. every 7th year for rest, travel, or research
sa·ber or **sa·bre** \'sā-bər\ n : a cavalry sword with a curved blade and thick back
saber saw n : a portable electric saw with a pointed reciprocating blade; esp : JIGSAW
sa·ble \'sā-bəl\ n, pl **sables** **1** : the color black **2** pl : mourning garments **3** : a dark brown mammal chiefly of northern Asia related to the weasels; also : its fur or pelt

[1] blessed, hallowed, holy, sacred, sanctified ♦ **[2]** holy, inviolable, sacred

¹**sab·o·tage** \'sa-bə-ˌtäzh\ *n* **1** : deliberate destruction of an employer's property or hindering of production by workers **2** : destructive or hampering action by enemy agents or sympathizers in time of war

²**sabotage** *vb* **-taged; -tag·ing** : to practice sabotage on : WRECK

sab·o·teur \ˌsa-bə-ˈtər\ *n* : a person who practices sabotage

sac \'sak\ *n* : a pouch in an animal or plant often containing a fluid

SAC *abbr* Strategic Air Command

sac·cha·rin \'sa-kə-rən\ *n* : a white crystalline compound used as an artificial calorie-free sweetener

sac·cha·rine \'sa-kə-rən\ *adj* ♦ : nauseatingly sweet ⟨∼ poetry⟩

♦ corny, maudlin, mawkish, mushy, sappy, schmaltzy, sentimental

sac·er·do·tal \ˌsa-sər-ˈdōt-ᵊl, -kər-\ *adj* ♦ : of or relating to priests or a priesthood : PRIESTLY

♦ clerical, ministerial, pastoral, priestly

sac·er·do·tal·ism \-ᵊl-ˌi-zəm\ *n* : a religious belief emphasizing the powers of priests as essential mediators between God and humankind

sa·chem \'sā-chəm\ *n* : a No. American Indigenous chief

sa·chet \sa-ˈshā\ *n* : a small bag filled with perfumed powder for scenting clothes

¹**sack** \'sak\ *n* **1** : a usu. rectangular-shaped bag (as of paper or burlap) **2** : a loose jacket or short coat **3** ♦ : a place for sleeping ⟨hit the ∼⟩

♦ bed, bunk, pad

²**sack** *vb* ♦ : to dismiss esp. summarily : FIRE

♦ cashier, dismiss, fire, remove, retire

³**sack** *n* : a white wine popular in England in the 16th and 17th centuries

⁴**sack** *vb* ♦ : to plunder a captured town

♦ despoil, loot, maraud, pillage, plunder, ransack, strip

sack·cloth \-ˌklȯth\ *n* : a rough garment worn as a sign of penitence

sac·ra·ment \'sa-krə-mənt\ *n* **1** : a formal religious act or rite; *esp* : one (as baptism or the Eucharist) held to have been instituted by Christ **2** : the elements of the Eucharist — **sac·ra·men·tal** \ˌsa-krə-ˈment-ᵊl\ *adj*

sa·cred \'sā-krəd\ *adj* **1** ♦ : set apart for the service or worship of deity **2** : devoted exclusively to one service or use **3** ♦ : worthy of veneration or reverence **4** ♦ : of or relating to religion : RELIGIOUS — **sa·cred·ly** *adv* — **sa·cred·ness** *n*

♦ **[1]** blessed, hallowed, holy, sacrosanct, sanctified ♦ **[3]** holy, inviolable, sacrosanct ♦ **[4]** devotional, religious, spiritual

sacred cow *n* : one that is often unreasonably immune from criticism

¹**sac·ri·fice** \'sa-krə-ˌfīs\ *n* **1** : the offering of something precious to deity **2** ♦ : something offered in sacrifice **3** : LOSS, DEPRIVATION **4** : a bunt allowing a base runner to advance while the batter is put out; *also* : a fly ball allowing a runner to score after the catch — **sac·ri·fi·cial** \ˌsa-krə-ˈfi-shəl\ *adj* — **sac·ri·fi·cial·ly** *adv*

♦ victim

²**sac·ri·fice** *vb* **-ficed; -fic·ing** **1** ♦ : to offer up or kill as a sacrifice **2** : to accept the loss or destruction of for an end, cause, or ideal **3** : to make a sacrifice in baseball

♦ offer

sac·ri·lege \'sa-krə-lij\ *n* **1** ♦ : violation of something consecrated to God **2** ♦ : gross irreverence toward a hallowed person, place, or thing

♦ **[1, 2]** blasphemy, defilement, desecration, impiety, irreverence

sac·ri·le·gious \ˌsa-krə-ˈli-jəs, -ˈlē-\ *adj* ♦ : committing sacrilege : characterized by or involving sacrilege — **sac·ri·le·gious·ly** *adv*

♦ blasphemous, irreverent, profane

sac·ris·tan \'sa-krə-stən\ *n* **1** : a church officer in charge of the sacristy **2** : SEXTON

sac·ris·ty \'sa-krə-stē\ *n, pl* **-ties** : VESTRY

sac·ro·il·i·ac \ˌsa-krō-ˈi-lē-ˌak\ *n* : the joint between the upper part of the hipbone and the sacrum

sac·ro·sanct \'sa-krō-ˌsaŋkt\ *adj* **1** ♦ : most sacred or holy **2** ♦ : treated as if holy : immune from criticism

sa·crum \'sa-krəm, 'sā-\ *n, pl* **sa·cra** \'sa-krə, 'sā-\ : the part of the vertebral column that is directly connected with or forms a part of the pelvis and in humans consists of five fused vertebrae

sad \'sad\ *adj* **sad·der; sad·dest** **1** ♦ : affected with or expressive of grief or unhappiness : DOWNCAST **2** ♦ : causing sorrow **3** ♦ : DULL, SOMBER

♦ **[1]** bad, blue, dejected, depressed, disconsolate, down, downcast, droopy, forlorn, gloomy, glum, low, melancholy, miserable, mournful, sorrowful, sorry, unhappy, woeful, wretched *Ant* cheerful, chipper, glad, happy, joyful, joyous, sunny, upbeat ♦ **[2]** depressing, dismal, dreary, heartbreaking, melancholy, pathetic, sorry, tearful *Ant* cheering, cheery, glad, happy

sad·den \'sad-ᵊn\ *vb* ♦ : to make or become sad

♦ burden, depress, oppress

¹**sad·dle** \'sad-ᵊl\ *n* : a usu. padded leather-covered seat (as for a rider on horseback)

²**saddle** *vb* **sad·dled; sad·dling** **1** : to put a saddle on **2** ♦ : to place a burden or encumbrance upon : BURDEN

♦ burden, encumber, load, lumber, weight

sad·dle·bow \'sad-ᵊl-ˌbō\ *n* : the arch in the front of a saddle

saddle horse *n* : a horse suited for or trained for riding

Sad·du·cee \'sa-jə-ˌsē, 'sa-dyə-\ *n* : a member of an ancient Jewish sect consisting of a ruling class of priests and rejecting certain doctrines — **Sad·du·ce·an** \ˌsa-jə-ˈsē-ən, ˌsa-dyə-\ *adj*

sa·dism \'sā-ˌdi-zəm, 'sa-\ *n* **1** : the derivation of sexual gratification from the infliction of physical pain or humiliation on another person **2** ♦ : delight in physical or mental cruelty; *also* : excessive cruelty — **sa·dist** \'sā-dist, 'sa-\ *n*

♦ barbarity, brutality, cruelty, inhumanity, savagery, viciousness, wantonness

sa·dis·tic \sə-ˈdis-tik\ *adj* ♦ : of or characterized by sadism — **sa·dis·ti·cal·ly** \-ti-k(ə-)lē\ *adv*

♦ barbarous, brutal, cruel, heartless, inhumane, savage, vicious, wanton

sad·ly *adv* ♦ : in a sad manner or way

♦ agonizingly, bitterly, grievously, hard, hardly, sorrowfully, unhappily, woefully, wretchedly

sad·ness *n* ♦ : the quality or state of being sad : an instance (as a mood or an appearance) of being sad

♦ blues, dejection, depression, desolation, despondency, doldrums, dumps, forlornness, gloom, heartsickness, melancholy *Ant* elation, euphoria, exuberance, gladness, happiness, joy, joyousness, jubilation

SAE *abbr* **1** self-addressed envelope **2** Society of Automotive Engineers **3** stamped addressed envelope

sa·fa·ri \sə-ˈfär-ē, -ˈfar-\ *n* **1** : a hunting expedition esp. in eastern Africa **2** : JOURNEY, TRIP

¹**safe** \'sāf\ *adj* **saf·er; saf·est** **1** ♦ : free from harm or risk **2** ♦ : secure from danger or loss **3** : affording safety **4** ♦ : not likely to take risks; *also* : RELIABLE **5** ♦ : not threatening danger — **safe·ly** *adv*

♦ **[1, 2]** all right, alright, secure *Ant* endangered, imperiled, insecure, liable, threatened, unsafe, vulnerable ♦ **[4]** dependable, good, reliable, responsible, solid, steady, sure, tried, true, trustworthy ♦ **[5]** harmless, innocent, innocuous

²**safe** *n* : a container for keeping articles (as valuables) safe

safe–con·duct \-ˈkän-(ˌ)dəkt\ *n* : a pass permitting a person to go through enemy lines

¹**safe·guard** \-ˌgärd\ *n* ♦ : a measure or device for preventing accident

♦ aegis, armor (*or* armour), cover, defense (*or* defence), guard, protection, screen, security, shield, wall, ward

²**safeguard** *vb* ♦ : to provide a safeguard for : PROTECT

♦ cover, defend, guard, protect, screen, secure, shield, ward

safe·keep·ing \'sāf-ˈkē-piŋ\ *n* ♦ : a keeping or being kept in safety

♦ care, custody, guardianship, keeping, trust, ward

safe sex *n* : sexual activity and esp. sexual intercourse in which various measures (as the use of latex condoms) are taken to avoid disease (as AIDS) transmitted by sexual contact

safe·ty \'sāf-tē\ *n, pl* **safeties** **1** : freedom from danger : SECURITY **2** : a protective device **3** : a football play in which the ball is downed by the offensive team behind its own goal line **4** : a defensive football back in the deepest position — **safety** *adj*

safety glass *n* : shatter-resistant material formed of two sheets of glass with a sheet of clear plastic between them

safety match *n* : a match that ignites only when struck on a special surface

saf·flow·er \'sa-ˌflaù-ər\ *n* : a widely grown Old World herb related to the daisies that has large orange or red flower heads yielding a dyestuff and seeds rich in edible oil

saf·fron \'sa-frən\ *n* : a deep orange powder from the flower of a crocus used to color and flavor foods

¹**sag** \'sag\ *vb* **sagged; sag·ging** **1** : to droop or settle from or as if from pressure **2** ♦ : to lose firmness or vigor

♦ decay, droop, fail, flag, go, lag, languish, waste, weaken, wilt

²**sag** *n* **1** : a sagging part **2** ♦ : an instance or amount of sagging

♦ droop, slack, slackness

sa·ga \'sä-gə\ *n* : a narrative of heroic deeds; *esp* : one recorded in Iceland in the 12th and 13th centuries

sa·ga·cious \sə-'gā-shəs\ *adj* ♦ : of keen mind

♦ discerning, insightful, perceptive, sage, sapient, wise

sa·gac·i·ty \-'ga-sə-tē\ *n* ♦ : the quality of being sagacious

♦ discernment, insight, perception, sapience, wisdom

sag·a·more \'sa-gə-ˌmōr\ *n* : a subordinate No. American Indigenous chief

¹**sage** \'sāj\ *adj* ♦ : wise through reflection and experience; *also* : proceeding from or characterized by wisdom, prudence, and good judgment — **sage·ly** *adv*

♦ discerning, insightful, perceptive, sagacious, sapient, wise

²**sage** *n* : one who is distinguished for wisdom

³**sage** *n* **1** : a perennial mint with aromatic leaves used in flavoring; *also* : its leaves **2** : SAGEBRUSH

sage·brush \'sāj-ˌbrəsh\ *n* : any of several low shrubby No. American composite plants; *esp* : one of the western U.S. with a sagelike odor

Sag·it·tar·i·us \ˌsa-jə-'ter-ē-əs\ *n* **1** : a zodiacal constellation between Scorpio and Capricorn usu. pictured as a centaur archer **2** : the 9th sign of the zodiac in astrology; *also* : one born under this sign

sa·go \'sā-gō\ *n, pl* **sagos** : a dry granulated starch esp. from the pith of various tropical palms (**sago palm**)

sa·gua·ro \sə-'wär-ə, -'gwär-, -ō\ *n, pl* **-ros** : a tall columnar usu. sparsely-branched cactus of dry areas of the southwestern U.S. and Mexico that may attain a height of up to 50 feet (16 meters)

said *past and past part of* SAY

¹**sail** \'sāl\ *n* **1** : a piece of fabric by means of which the wind is used to propel a ship **2** : a sailing ship **3** : something resembling a sail **4** ♦ : a trip on a sailboat

♦ crossing, cruise, passage, voyage

²**sail** *vb* **1** ♦ : to travel on a sailing ship **2** : to pass over in a ship **3** : to manage or direct the course of a ship **4** ♦ : to move with ease, grace, nonchalance, or without resistance **5** ♦ : to travel on water; *also* : to move through the air

♦ [1] boat, cruise, navigate, voyage ♦ [4] bowl, breeze, coast, drift, flow, glide, roll, skim, slide, slip, stream, sweep, whisk ♦ [5] drift, float, glide, hang, hover, poise, ride, waft

sail·board \'sāl-ˌbōrd\ *n* : a modified surfboard having a mast and sailed by a standing person

sail·boat \-ˌbōt\ *n* : a boat propelled primarily by sail

sail·cloth \-ˌklóth\ *n* : a heavy canvas used for sails, tents, or upholstery

sail·fish \-ˌfish\ *n* : any of a genus of large marine bony fishes with a large dorsal fin that are related to marlins

sail·ing *n* : the sport of handling or riding in a sailboat

sail·or \'sā-lər\ *n* ♦ : one that sails; *esp* : a member of a ship's crew

♦ gob, jack, jack-tar, mariner, seaman, swab, tar

sail·plane \'sāl-ˌplān\ *n* : a glider designed to rise in an upward air current

saint \'sānt, *before a name* (ˌ)sānt *or* sənt\ *n* **1** : one officially recognized as preeminent for holiness **2** : one of the spirits of the departed in heaven **3** : a holy or godly person

Saint Ber·nard \-bər-'närd\ *n* : any of a Swiss alpine breed of tall powerful working dogs used esp. formerly in aiding lost travelers

saint·ed \-'sān-təd\ *adj* ♦ : relating to, resembling, or befitting a

saint; *esp* : marked by or showing reverence for deity and devotion to divine worship

♦ devout, faithful, godly, holy, pious, religious, saintly

saint·hood \-ˌhùd\ *n* ♦ : the quality or state of being a saint

♦ blessedness, devoutness, godliness, holiness, piety, sanctity

Saint–John's–wort \'sānt-'jänz-ˌwərt, -ˌwórt\ *n* **1** : any of a genus of herbs and shrubs with showy yellow flowers **2** : the dried aerial parts of a Saint-John's-wort used esp. in herbal remedies

saint·li·ness \-lē-nəs\ *n* : the quality or state of being saintly

saint·ly \'sānt-lē\ *adj* ♦ : relating to, resembling, or befitting a saint ⟨~ zeal⟩

♦ devout, faithful, godly, holy, pious, religious, sainted

Saint Val·en·tine's Day \-'va-lən-ˌtīnz-\ *n* : VALENTINE'S DAY

¹**sake** \'sāk\ *n* **1** : END, PURPOSE **2** : personal or social welfare, safety, or well-being

²**sa·ke** *or* **sa·ki** \'sä-kē\ *n* : a Japanese alcoholic beverage of fermented rice

sa·laam \sə-'läm\ *n* **1** : a salutation or ceremonial greeting in the East **2** : an obeisance performed by bowing very low and placing the right palm on the forehead — **salaam** *vb*

sa·la·cious \sə-'lā-shəs\ *adj* **1** : arousing sexual desire or imagination **2** : LUSTFUL — **sa·la·cious·ly** *adv* — **sa·la·cious·ness** *n*

sal·ad \'sa-ləd\ *n* : a cold dish (as of lettuce, vegetables, fish, eggs, or fruit) served with dressing

sal·a·man·der \'sa-lə-ˌman-dər\ *n* : any of numerous amphibians that look like lizards but have scaleless usu. smooth moist skin

sa·la·mi \sə-'lä-mē\ *n* : a highly seasoned sausage of pork and beef

sal·a·ry \'sa-lə-rē\ *n, pl* **-ries** ♦ : payment made at regular intervals for services

♦ emolument, hire, pay, payment, stipend, wage

sale \'sāl\ *n* **1** ♦ : transfer of ownership of property from one person to another in return for money **2** : ready market : DEMAND **3** : AUCTION **4** : a selling of goods at bargain prices — **sal·able** *or* **sale·able** \'sā-lə-bəl\ *adj*

♦ deal, trade, transaction

sales·girl \'sālz-ˌgərl\ *n* : SALESWOMAN

sales·man \-mən\ *n* : one who sells in a given territory, in a store, or by telephone — **sales·man·ship** *n*

sales·per·son \-ˌpər-sən\ *n* : a salesman or saleswoman

sales·wom·an \-ˌwù-mən\ *n* : a woman who sells in a given territory, in a store, or by telephone

sal·i·cyl·ic acid \ˌsa-lə-'si-lik-\ *n* : a crystalline organic acid used in making aspirin and other medicinal preparations (as skin lotions)

¹**sa·lient** \'sāl-yənt, 'sā-lē-ənt\ *adj* : jutting forward beyond a line; *also* : PROMINENT ⟨a ~ feature⟩

²**salient** *n* : a projecting part in a line of defense

¹**sa·line** \'sā-ˌlēn, -ˌlīn\ *adj* ♦ : consisting of or containing salt : SALTY — **sa·lin·i·ty** \sā-'li-nə-tē, sə-\ *n*

♦ briny, salty

²**saline** *n* **1** : a metallic salt esp. with a purgative action **2** : a saline solution

sa·li·va \sə-'lī-və\ *n* ♦ : a liquid secreted into the mouth that helps digestion — **sal·i·vary** \'sa-lə-ˌver-ē\ *adj*

♦ slobber, spit

sal·i·vate \'sa-lə-ˌvāt\ *vb* **-vat·ed; -vat·ing** ♦ : to produce saliva esp. in excess — **sal·i·va·tion** \ˌsa-lə-'vā-shən\ *n*

♦ dribble, drivel, drool, slaver, slobber

sal·low \'sa-lō\ *adj* ♦ : of a yellowish sickly color ⟨a ~ face⟩

♦ cadaverous, green, lurid, pale, pasty, peaked, sickly

¹**sal·ly** \'sa-lē\ *n, pl* **sallies** **1** : a rushing attack on besiegers by troops of a besieged place **2** ♦ : a witty remark or retort **3** ♦ : a brief excursion

♦ [2] crack, gag, jest, joke, laugh, pleasantry, quip, waggery, wisecrack, witticism ♦ [3] excursion, jaunt, junket, outing

²**sally** *vb* **sal·lied; sal·ly·ing** **1** : to leap out or burst forth suddenly **2** ♦ : to start out on a course or a journey — often used with *forth*

♦ *usu* **sally forth** clear out, depart, exit, get off, go, move, pull, quit, shove, take off

salm·on \'sa-mən\ *n, pl* **salmon** *also* **salmons** **1** : any of several bony fishes with pinkish flesh that are used for food and are related to the trouts **2** : a strong yellowish pink color

sal·mo·nel·la \ˌsal-mə-ˈne-lə\ *n, pl* **-nel·lae** \-ˈne-(ˌ)lē, -ˌlī\ *or* **-nellas** *or* **-nella** : any of a genus of rod-shaped bacteria that cause various illnesses (as food poisoning)

sa·lon \sə-ˈlän, ˈsa-ˌlän, sa-ˈlōⁿ\ *n* **1** : an elegant drawing room **2** ♦ : a fashionable shop ⟨beauty ∼⟩

♦ establishment, place

sa·loon \sə-ˈlün\ *n* **1** : a large public cabin on a ship **2** ♦ : a place where liquors are sold and drunk : BARROOM **3** *Brit* : SEDAN 2

♦ bar, barroom, café, pub, public house, tavern

sal·sa \ˈsȯl-sə, ˈsäl-\ *n* : a spicy sauce of tomatoes, onions, and hot peppers

¹salt \ˈsȯlt\ *n* **1** : a white crystalline substance that consists of sodium and chlorine and is used in seasoning foods **2** : a saltlike cathartic substance (as Epsom salts) **3** : a compound formed usu. by action of an acid on metal **4** : one that sails : SAILOR — **salt·i·ness** \ˈsȯl-tē-nəs\ *n*

²salt *vb* : to preserve, season, or feed with salt

³salt *adj* : preserved or treated with salt; *also* : SALTY

SALT *abbr* Strategic Arms Limitation Talks

salt away *vb* ♦ : to lay away safely

♦ cache, hoard, lay away, lay up, put by, stash, stockpile, store

salt·box \ˈsȯlt-ˌbäks\ *n* : a frame dwelling with two stories in front and one behind and a long sloping roof

salt·cel·lar \-ˌse-lər\ *n* : a small container for holding salt at the table

sal·tine \sȯl-ˈtēn\ *n* : a thin crisp cracker sprinkled with salt

salt lick *n* : LICK 5

salt·pe·ter \ˈsȯlt-ˈpē-tər\ *n* **1** : POTASSIUM NITRATE **2** : SODIUM NITRATE

salt·wa·ter \-ˌwȯ-tər, -ˌwä-\ *adj* : of, relating to, or living in salt water

salty \ˈsȯl-tē\ *adj* **salt·i·er; -est** **1** ♦ : of, seasoned with, or containing salt **2** : suggesting the sea or nautical life **3** ♦ : marked by uncultivated vulgarity

♦ [1] briny, saline ♦ [3] racy, spicy, suggestive

sa·lu·bri·ous \sə-ˈlü-brē-əs\ *adj* ♦ : favorable to health

♦ healthful, healthy, restorative, salutary, wholesome

sal·u·tary \ˈsal-yə-ˌter-ē\ *adj* ♦ : health-giving; *also* : BENEFICIAL

♦ advantageous, beneficial, favorable (*or* favourable), helpful, profitable ♦ healthful, healthy, restorative, salubrious, wholesome

sal·u·ta·tion \ˌsal-yə-ˈtā-shən\ *n* ♦ : an expression of greeting, goodwill, or courtesy usu. by word or gesture; *also* : a speech of honor or praise

♦ greeting, hello, salute ♦ accolade, citation, commendation, encomium, eulogy, homage, paean, panegyric, tribute

sa·lu·ta·to·ri·an \sə-ˌlü-tə-ˈtōr-ē-ən\ *n* : the student having the 2d highest rank in a graduating class who delivers the salutatory address

sa·lu·ta·to·ry \sə-ˈlü-tə-ˌtōr-ē\ *adj* : relating to or being the welcoming oration delivered at an academic commencement

¹sa·lute \sə-ˈlüt\ *vb* **sa·lut·ed; sa·lut·ing** **1** : GREET **2** : to honor by special ceremonies **3** : to show respect to (a superior officer) by a formal position of hand, rifle, or sword **4** ♦ : to express commendation of

♦ acclaim, applaud, cheer, crack up, hail, laud, praise, tout

²salute *n* **1** : an expression of greeting, goodwill, or courtesy by word, gesture, or ceremony : GREETING **2** : the formal position assumed in saluting a superior

¹sal·vage \ˈsal-vij\ *n* **1** : money paid for saving a ship, its cargo, or passengers when the ship is wrecked or in danger **2** : the saving of a ship **3** : the saving of possessions in danger of being lost **4** : things saved from loss or destruction (as by a wreck or fire)

²salvage *vb* **sal·vaged; sal·vag·ing** : to rescue from destruction

sal·va·tion \sal-ˈvā-shən\ *n* **1** : the saving of a person from sin or its consequences esp. in the life after death **2** ♦ : the saving from danger, difficulty, or evil **3** : something that saves ⟨tourism became the island's ∼⟩

♦ deliverance, rescue

¹salve \ˈsav, ˈsȧv\ *n* **1** : a medicinal substance applied to the skin **2** : a soothing influence

²salve *vb* **salved; salv·ing** : EASE, SOOTHE

sal·ver \ˈsal-vər\ *n* : a small serving tray

sal·vo \ˈsal-vō\ *n, pl* **salvos** *or* **salvoes** ♦ : a simultaneous discharge of guns; *also* : something suggestive of a salvo

♦ barrage, bombardment, cannonade, fusillade, hail, shower, storm, volley

Sam *or* **Saml** *abbr* Samuel

SAM \ˈsam, ˌes-ˌā-ˈem\ *n* : a guided missile for use against aircraft by ground units

Sa·mar·i·tan \sə-ˈmer-ə-tən\ *n* **1** : a native or inhabitant of Samaria **2** : a person who is generous in helping those in distress

sa·mar·i·um \sə-ˈmer-ē-əm\ *n* : a silvery-white lustrous rare metallic chemical element

¹same \ˈsām\ *adj* **1** ♦ : being the one referred to : not different **2** ♦ : resembling in every relevant respect

♦ [1] identical, selfsame, very *Ant* another, different, other ♦ [2] duplicate, equal, even, identical, indistinguishable *Ant* different, dissimilar, distinguishable, other, unalike, unlike

²same *pron* : the same one or ones

³same *adv* : in the same manner

same·ness *n* ♦ : the quality or state of being the same; *also* : tedious similarity

♦ equality, equivalence, par, parity

same–sex \ˈsām-ˈseks\ *adj* : of, relating to, or involving members of the same sex

Sa·mi *also* **Saa·mi** \ˈsä-mē\ *n, pl* **Sami** *or* **Samis** *also* **Saami** *or* **Saamis** : a member of a people of northern Scandinavia, Finland, and the Kola Peninsula of Russia

Sa·mo·an \sə-ˈmō-ən\ *n* : a native or inhabitant of Samoa — **Samoan** *adj*

sa·mo·sa \sə-ˈmō-sə\ *n* : a small triangular pastry filled with spiced meat or vegetables and fried

sam·o·var \ˈsa-mə-ˌvär\ *n* : an urn with a spigot at the base used esp. in Russia to boil water for tea

sam·pan \ˈsam-ˌpan\ *n* : a flat-bottomed skiff of eastern Asia usu. propelled by two short oars

¹sam·ple \ˈsam-pəl\ *n* ♦ : a representative piece, item, or set of individuals that shows the quality or nature of the whole from which it was taken : EXAMPLE

♦ case, example, exemplar, illustration, instance, representative, specimen

²sample *vb* **sam·pled; sam·pling** : to judge the quality of by a sample

sam·pler \ˈsam-plər\ *n* **1** : a piece of needlework; *esp* : one testing skill in embroidering **2** : a collection of various examples of something ⟨a chocolate ∼⟩

Sam·u·el \ˈsam-yə-wəl\ *n* : either of two books of Jewish and Christian Scripture

sam·u·rai \ˈsa-mə-ˌrī, ˈsam-yə-\ *n, pl* **samurai** : a military retainer of a Japanese feudal lord who adhered to strict principles of honor and duty

san·a·to·ri·um \ˌsa-nə-ˈtōr-ē-əm\ *n, pl* **-ri·ums** *or* **-ria** \-ē-ə\ **1** : a health resort **2** : an establishment for the care esp. of convalescents or the chronically ill

sanc·ti·fi·ca·tion \ˌsaŋk-tə-fə-ˈkā-shən\ *n* ♦ : an act of sanctifying; *also* : the state of being sanctified

♦ blessing, consecration

sanc·ti·fied *adj* : made holy : made free of sin; *also* : set apart to sacred duty or use

♦ blessed, hallowed, holy, sacred, sacrosanct

sanc·ti·fy \ˈsaŋk-tə-ˌfī\ *vb* **-fied; -fy·ing** **1** ♦ : to make holy : CONSECRATE **2** ♦ : to free from sin

♦ [1] bless, consecrate, hallow ♦ [2] purify

sanc·ti·mo·nious \ˌsaŋk-tə-ˈmō-nē-əs\ *adj* : hypocritically pious ⟨∼ politicians⟩ — **sanc·ti·mo·nious·ly** *adv*

¹sanc·tion \ˈsaŋk-shən\ *n* **1** ♦ : authoritative approval **2** : a measure (as a threat or fine) designed to enforce a law or standard ⟨economic ∼s⟩

♦ allowance, authorization, clearance, concurrence, consent, leave, license (*or* licence), permission, sufferance

²sanction *vb* ♦ : to give approval to : RATIFY

♦ approve, authorize, clear, OK, ratify, warrant

sanc·ti·ty \ˈsaŋk-tə-tē\ *n, pl* **-ties** **1** ♦ : holiness of life and character : GODLINESS **2** : SACREDNESS

♦ blessedness, devoutness, godliness, holiness, piety, sainthood

sanc·tu·ary \ˈsaŋk-chə-ˌwer-ē\ *n, pl* **-ar·ies** **1** : a consecrated place (as the part of a church in which the altar is placed) **2 ♦ :** a place of refuge ⟨bird ~⟩

   ♦ asylum, haven, refuge, retreat, shelter

sanc·tum \'saŋk-təm\ *n, pl* **sanctums** *also* **sanc·ta** \-tə\ : a private office or study : DEN ⟨an editor's ~⟩

¹sand \'sand\ *n* **1 :** loose particles of hard broken rock **2 :** a yellowish-gray color

²sand *vb* **1 :** to cover or fill with sand **2 ♦ :** to scour, smooth, or polish with an abrasive (as sandpaper) — **sand·er** *n*

   ♦ buff, file, grind, hone, rasp, rub

san·dal \'sand-ᵊl\ *n* **:** a shoe consisting of a sole strapped to the foot; *also* **:** a low or open slipper or rubber overshoe

san·dal·wood \-ˌwu̇d\ *n* **:** the fragrant yellowish heartwood of a parasitic tree of southern Asia that is much used in ornamental carving and cabinetwork; *also* **:** the tree

sand·bag \'sand-ˌbag\ *n* **:** a bag filled with sand and used in fortifications, as ballast, or as a weapon

sand·bank \-ˌbaŋk\ *n* **:** a deposit of sand (as in a bar or shoal)

sand·bar \-ˌbär\ *n* **:** a ridge of sand formed in water by tides or currents

sand·blast \-ˌblast\ *vb* **:** to treat with a stream of sand blown (as for cleaning stone) by compressed air — **sand·blast·er** *n*

sand dollar *n* **:** any of numerous flat circular sea urchins living chiefly on sandy bottoms in shallow water

S & H *abbr* shipping and handling

sand·hog \'sand-ˌhȯg, -ˌhäg\ *n* **:** a laborer who builds underwater tunnels

sand·lot \-ˌlät\ *n* **:** a vacant lot esp. when used for the unorganized sports of children — **sand·lot** *adj* — **sand·lot·ter** *n*

sand·man \-ˌman\ *n* **:** the genie of folklore who makes children sleepy

sand·pa·per \-ˌpā-pər\ *n* **:** paper with abrasive (as sand) glued on one side used in smoothing and polishing surfaces — **sandpaper** *vb*

sand·pip·er \-ˌpī-pər\ *n* **:** any of various shorebirds with a soft-tipped bill longer than that of the related plovers

sand·stone \-ˌstōn\ *n* **:** rock made of sand united by a natural cement

sand·storm \-ˌstȯrm\ *n* **:** a windstorm that drives clouds of sand

sand trap *n* **:** a hazard on a golf course consisting of a hollow containing sand

¹sand·wich \'sand-(ˌ)wich\ *n* **1 :** two or more slices of bread with a layer (as of meat or cheese) spread between them **2 :** something resembling a sandwich

²sandwich *vb* **♦ :** to squeeze or crowd in

   ♦ cram, crowd, jam, ram, squeeze, stuff, wedge

sandy *adj* **sand·i·er; -est** **1 :** consisting of or containing sand **2 ♦ :** of the color sand

   ♦ blond, fair, flaxen, golden, straw

sane \'sān\ *adj* **san·er; san·est** **1 ♦ :** mentally sound and healthy **2 :** proceeding from a sound mind : SENSIBLE, RATIONAL — **sane·ly** *adv*

   ♦ balanced, clearheaded, lucid, stable *Ant* insane, unsound

sang *past of* SING

sang·froid \sä�207-'frwä\ *n* **:** self-possession or an imperturbable state esp. under strain

san·gui·nary \'saŋ-gwə-ˌner-ē\ *adj* **♦ :** willing or anxious to shed blood; *also* **:** marked by bloodshed ⟨~ battle⟩

   ♦ bloodthirsty, bloody, homicidal, murderous, sanguine

san·guine \'saŋ-gwən\ *adj* **1 ♦ :** having a healthy reddish color : RUDDY **2 ♦ :** anticipating the best ⟨a ~ disposition⟩ **3 :** willing or anxious to shed blood

   ♦ [1] florid, flush, glowing, rosy, ruddy ♦ [2] assured, certain, clear, cocksure, confident, doubtless, positive, sure

sanit *abbr* sanitary; sanitation

san·i·tar·i·an \ˌsa-nə-'ter-ē-ən\ *n* **:** a specialist in sanitation and public health

san·i·tar·i·um \ˌsa-nə-'ter-ē-əm\ *n, pl* **-i·ums** *or* **-ia** \-ē-ə\ : SANATORIUM

san·i·tary \'sa-nə-ˌter-ē\ *adj* **1 :** of or relating to health : HYGIENIC **2 ♦ :** free from filth or infective matter

   ♦ aseptic, hygienic, sterile *Ant* unhygienic, unsanitary

sanitary napkin *n* **:** a disposable absorbent pad used to absorb uterine flow (as during menstruation)

san·i·ta·tion \ˌsa-nə-'tā-shən\ *n* **:** the act or process of making sanitary; *also* **:** protection of health by maintenance of sanitary conditions

san·i·tize \'sa-nə-ˌtīz\ *vb* **-tized; -tiz·ing** **1 :** to make sanitary **2 :** to make more acceptable by removing unpleasant features

san·i·ty \'sa-nə-tē\ *n* **♦ :** soundness of mind

   ♦ head, mind, reason, wit

sank *past of* SINK

sans \'sanz\ *prep* **♦ :** deprived or destitute of : WITHOUT

   ♦ minus, wanting, without

San·skrit \'san-ˌskrit\ *n* **:** an ancient language that is the classical language of India and of Hinduism — **Sanskrit** *adj*

San·ta Ana \ˌsan-tə-'a-nə\ *n* **:** a hot dry wind from the north, northeast, or east in southern California

¹sap \'sap\ *n* **1 a :** a vital fluid; *esp* **:** a watery fluid that circulates through a vascular plant **b ♦ :** bodily health and vigor **2 ♦ :** a foolish gullible person — **sap·less** *adj*

   ♦ [1b] dash, energy, life, pep, vigor (*or* vigour), vim, vitality ♦ [2] dupe, gull, pigeon, sucker, tool

²sap *vb* **sapped; sap·ping** **1 :** UNDERMINE **2 ♦ :** to weaken gradually

   ♦ debilitate, enervate, enfeeble, prostrate, soften, tire, waste, weaken

sa·pi·ence \ˌsā-pē-əns\ *n* **♦ :** keen and farsighted judgment : profound knowledge

   ♦ discernment, insight, perception, sagacity, wisdom

sa·pi·ent \'sā-pē-ənt, 'sa-\ *adj* **♦ :** possessing or expressing great intelligence : WISE

   ♦ discerning, insightful, perceptive, sagacious, sage, wise

sap·ling \'sa-pliŋ\ *n* **:** a young tree

sap·phire \'sa-ˌfīr\ *n* **:** a hard transparent usu. rich blue gem

sap·py \'sa-pē\ *adj* **sap·pi·er; -est** **1 :** full of sap **2 ♦ :** overly sentimental **3 :** lacking in good sense : SILLY, FOOLISH

   ♦ corny, maudlin, mawkish, mushy, saccharine, schmaltzy, sentimental

sap·ro·phyte \'sa-prə-ˌfīt\ *n* **:** a living thing and esp. a plant living on dead or decaying organic matter — **sap·ro·phyt·ic** \ˌsa-prə-'fi-tik\ *adj*

sap·suck·er \'sap-ˌse-kər\ *n* **:** any of a genus of No. American woodpeckers

sap·wood \-ˌwu̇d\ *n* **:** the younger active and usu. lighter and softer outer layer of wood (as of a tree trunk)

sar·casm \'sär-ˌka-zəm\ *n* **1 ♦ :** a cutting or contemptuous remark **2 :** ironic criticism or reproach

   ♦ affront, barb, dart, dig, indignity, insult, name, offense, outrage, put-down, slight, slur, wound

sar·cas·tic \sär-'kas-tik\ *adj* **♦ :** having the character of sarcasm; *also* **:** given to the use of sarcasm — **sar·cas·ti·cal·ly** \-ti-k(ə-)lē\ *adv*

   ♦ acrid, biting, caustic, cutting, mordant, pungent, satiric, scathing, sharp, tart

sar·co·ma \sär-'kō-mə\ *n, pl* **-mas** *also* **-ma·ta** \-mə-tə\ : a malignant tumor esp. of connective tissue, bone, cartilage, or striated muscle

sar·coph·a·gus \sär-'kä-fə-gəs\ *n, pl* **-gi** \-ˌgī, -ˌjī\ *also* **-gus·es** : a large stone coffin

sar·dine \sär-'dēn\ *n, pl* **sardines** *also* **sardine** : a young or small fish preserved for use as food

sar·don·ic \sär-'dä-nik\ *adj* **:** disdainfully or skeptically humorous : derisively mocking : SARCASTIC — **sar·don·i·cal·ly** \-ni-k(ə-)lē\ *adv*

sa·ri *also* **sa·ree** \'sär-ē\ *n* **:** a garment worn by women in southern Asia that consists of a long cloth draped around the body and head or shoulder

sa·rin \'sär-ən, zä-'rēn\ *n* **:** an extremely toxic chemical weapon used as a lethal nerve gas

sa·rong \sə-'rȯŋ, -'räŋ\ *n* **:** a loose garment wrapped around the body and worn by men and women of the Malay Archipelago and the Pacific islands

sar·sa·pa·ril·la \ˌsas-ə-pə-'ri-lə, ˌsärs-\ *n* **1 :** the dried roots of a tropical American smilax used esp. for flavoring; *also* **:** the plant **2 :** a sweetened carbonated beverage flavored with sassafras and an oil from a birch

sar·to·ri·al \sär-'tōr-ē-əl\ *adj* **:** of or relating to a tailor or tailored clothes — **sar·to·ri·al·ly** *adv*

SASE *abbr* self-addressed stamped envelope

¹sash \'sash\ *n* **♦ :** a broad band worn around the waist or over the shoulder

   ♦ belt, cincture, cummerbund, girdle

²sash *n, pl* **sash** *also* **sash·es** : a frame for panes of glass in a door or window; *also* : the movable part of a window

sa·shay \sa-'shā\ *vb* **1** ♦ : to strut or move about in an ostentatious manner **3** : to proceed in a diagonal or sideways manner

Sask *abbr* Saskatchewan

Sas·quatch \'sas-ˌkwach, -ˌkwäch\ *n* : a large hairy humanlike creature reported to exist in the northwestern U.S. and western Canada

sas·sa·fras \'sa-sə-ˌfras\ *n* : an aromatic No. American tree related to the laurel; *also* : its carcinogenic dried root bark

sassy \'sa-sē\ *adj* **sass·i·er; -est** ♦ : marked by contemptuous or cocky boldness or disregard of others : SAUCY

♦ arch, bold, brash, brazen, cheeky, cocky, fresh, impertinent, impudent, insolent, nervy, saucy

¹sat *past and past part of* SIT
²sat *abbr* **1** satellite **2** saturated
Sat *abbr* Saturday
Sa·tan \'sāt-ᵊn\ *n* : DEVIL

sa·tan·ic \sə-'ta-nik, sā-\ *adj* **1** : of or characteristic of Satan **2** ♦ : extremely malicious or wicked — **sa·tan·i·cal·ly** \-ni-k(ə-)lē\ *adv*

♦ [1, 2] demonic, devilish, diabolical, fiendish

satch·el \'sa-chəl\ *n* : SUITCASE

sate \'sāt\ *vb* **sat·ed; sat·ing** ♦ : to satisfy to the full; *also* : GLUT

♦ assuage, quench, satiate, satisfy ♦ glut, gorge, stuff, surfeit

sated *adj* ♦ : filled to the point of excess

♦ full, satiate, satiated

sa·teen \sa-'tēn, sə-\ *n* : a cotton cloth finished to resemble satin

sat·el·lite \'sat-ᵊl-ˌīt\ *n* **1** : an obsequious follower of a distinguished person : TOADY **2** : a celestial body that orbits a larger body **3** : a manufactured object that orbits a celestial body

satellite dish *n* : a microwave dish for receiving usu. television transmissions from an orbiting satellite

sa·ti·ate \'sā-shē-ˌāt\ *vb* **-at·ed; -at·ing** ♦ : to satisfy fully or to excess

♦ assuage, quench, sate, satisfy

satiated *adj* ♦ : filled to satiety

♦ full, sated, satiate

sa·ti·ety \sə-'tī-ə-tē\ *n* : fullness to the point of excess

sat·in \'sat-ᵊn\ *n* : a fabric (as of silk) with a glossy surface

sat·in·wood \'sat-ᵊn-ˌwùd\ *n* : a hard yellowish brown wood of satiny luster; *also* : a tree yielding this wood

sat·iny *adj* ♦ : having or resembling the soft texture or lustrous smoothness of satin

♦ glossy, lustrous, polished, sleek ♦ cottony, downy, silken, soft, velvety

sat·ire \'sa-ˌtīr\ *n* : biting wit, irony, or sarcasm used to expose vice or folly; *also* : a literary work having these qualities — **sat·i·rist** \'sa-tə-rist\ *n* — **sat·i·rize** \-tə-ˌrīz\ *vb*

sa·tir·ic \sə-'tir-ik\ *or* **sa·tir·i·cal** \-i-kəl\ *adj* ♦ : of, relating to, or constituting satire; *also* : manifesting or given to satire — **sa·tir·i·cal·ly** *adv*

♦ acrid, biting, caustic, cutting, mordant, pungent, sarcastic, scathing, sharp, tart

sat·is·fac·tion \ˌsa-təs-'fak-shən\ *n* **1** : payment through penance of punishment incurred by sin **2** ♦ : the quality or state of being satisfied : GRATIFICATION **3** : reparation for an insult **4** ♦ : settlement of a claim

♦ [2] contentment, delectation, delight, enjoyment, gladness, gratification, pleasure, relish ♦ [4] compensation, damages, indemnity, quittance, recompense, redress, remuneration, reparation, requital, restitution

sat·is·fac·to·ri·ly \-'fak-tə-rə-lē\ *adv* ♦ : in a satisfactory manner

♦ adequately, all right, fine, good, nicely, OK, passably, so-so, tolerably, well ♦ adequately, enough

sat·is·fac·to·ry \-'fak-tə-rē\ *adj* ♦ : giving satisfaction; *also* : ADEQUATE

♦ agreeable, all right, alright, fine, good, OK, palatable *Ant* disagreeable, unsatisfactory ♦ acceptable, adequate, all right, decent, fine, OK, passable, respectable, tolerable

sat·is·fy \'sa-təs-ˌfī\ *vb* **-fied; -fy·ing 1** : to answer or discharge (a claim) in full **2** ♦ : to make happy : GRATIFY **3** : to pay what

is due to **4** ♦ : to bring (as by argument) to belief, consent, or a course of action : CONVINCE **5** ♦ : to meet the requirements of

♦ [2] content, delight, gladden, gratify, please, rejoice, suit, warm ♦ [4] argue, convince, get, induce, move, persuade, prevail, talk, win ♦ [5] answer, comply, fill, fulfill, keep, meet, redeem

satisfying *adj* ♦ : giving satisfaction

♦ agreeable, congenial, delectable, delicious, delightful, dreamy, felicitous, good, grateful, gratifying, nice, palatable, pleasant, pleasurable ♦ cogent, compelling, conclusive, convincing, decisive, effective, forceful, persuasive, strong, telling

sat·is·fy·ing·ly *adv* ♦ : in a pleasant way

♦ agreeably, delightfully, favorably (*or* favourably), felicitously, gloriously, nicely, pleasantly, pleasingly, splendidly, well

sa·trap \'sā-ˌtrap, 'sa-\ *n* : a petty prince : a subordinate ruler

sat·u·rate \'sa-chə-ˌrāt\ *vb* **-rat·ed; -rat·ing 1** ♦ : to soak thoroughly **2** : to treat or charge with something to the point where no more can be absorbed, dissolved, or retained — **sat·u·ra·ble** \'sa-chə-rə-bəl\ *adj* — **sat·u·ra·tion** \ˌsa-chə-'rā-shən\ *n*

♦ drench, drown, impregnate, soak, sop, souse, steep

saturated *adj* **1** ♦ : full of moisture : made thoroughly wet **2** : being a solution that is unable to absorb or dissolve any more of a solute at a given temperature and pressure **3** *of a color* : having high saturation **4** : having no double or triple bonds between carbon atoms ⟨~ fats⟩

♦ sodden, soggy, waterlogged, watery, wet

Sat·ur·day \'sa-tər-dē, -ˌdā\ *n* : the 7th day of the week
Saturday night special *n* : a cheap easily concealed handgun
Sat·urn \'sa-tərn\ *n* : the planet 6th in order from the sun
sat·ur·nine \'sa-tər-ˌnīn\ *adj* : cold and steady in mood; *also* : of a gloomy or surly disposition : SULLEN
sa·tyr \'sā-tər\ *n* **1** *often cap* : a woodland deity in Greek mythology having certain characteristics of a horse or goat **2** : a lecherous man

¹sauce \'sȯs, 3 usu 'sas\ *n* **1** : a fluid dressing or topping for food **2** : stewed fruit **3** ♦ : pert or impudent language or actions

♦ back talk, cheek, impertinence, impudence, insolence

²sauce \'sȯs, 2 usu 'sas\ *vb* **sauced; sauc·ing 1** : to put sauce on; *also* : to add zest to **2** : to be impudent to
sauce·pan \'sȯs-ˌpan\ *n* : a small deep cooking pan with a handle
sau·cer \'sȯ-sər\ *n* : a rounded shallow dish for use under a cup
sauc·i·ness \-sē-nəs\ *n* ♦ : the quality or state of being saucy

♦ audacity, brass, brazenness, cheek, chutzpah, effrontery, gall, nerve, presumption, sauce, temerity

saucy \'sa-sē, 'sȯ-\ *adj* **sauc·i·er; -est** ♦ : impertinently bold and impudent — **sauc·i·ly** \-sə-lē\ *adv*

♦ arch, bold, brash, brazen, cheeky, cocky, fresh, impertinent, impudent, insolent, nervy, sassy

Sau·di \'saù-dē, 'sȯ-; sä-'ü-dē\ *n* : SAUDI ARABIAN — **Saudi** *adj*
Saudi Arabian *n* : a native or inhabitant of Saudi Arabia — **Saudi Arabian** *adj*
sau·er·kraut \'saù-ər-ˌkraut\ *n* : finely cut cabbage fermented in brine
Sauk \'sȯk\ *or* **Sac** \'sak, 'sȯk\ *n, pl* **Sauk** *or* **Sauks** *or* **Sac** *or* **Sacs** : a member of an Algonquian-speaking Indigenous people formerly living in what is now Wisconsin
sau·na \'sȯ-nə, 'saù-nə\ *n* **1** : a Finnish steam bath in which the steam is provided by water thrown on hot stones **2** : a dry heat bath; *also* : a room or cabinet used for such a bath
saun·ter \'sȯn-tər, 'sän-\ *vb* : STROLL
sau·ro·pod \'sȯr-ə-ˌpäd\ *n* : any of a suborder of plant-eating dinosaurs (as a brontosaurus) with a long neck and tail and a small head — **sauropod** *adj*
sau·sage \'sȯ-sij\ *n* : minced and highly seasoned meat (as pork) usu. enclosed in a tubular casing
S Aust *abbr* South Australia
sau·té \sȯ-'tā, sō-\ *vb* **sau·téed** *or* **sau·téd; sau·té·ing** : to fry lightly in a little fat — **sauté** *n*
sau·terne \sō-'tərn, sȯ-\ *n, often cap* : a usu. semisweet American white wine
¹sav·age \'sa-vij\ *adj* **1** ♦ : not domesticated or under human control : WILD, UNTAMED **2** ♦ : lacking complex or advanced culture : UNCIVILIZED **3** ♦ : lacking the restraints normal to civilized human beings : FIERCE — **sav·age·ly** *adv*

♦ [1] feral, unbroken, undomesticated, untamed, wild ♦ [2] barbarous, heathen, heathenish, Neanderthal, rude, uncivil, uncivilized, uncultivated, wild *Ant* civilized ♦ [3] barbarous, brutal, cruel, heartless, inhumane, sadistic, vicious, wanton ♦ [3] fell, ferocious, fierce, grim, vicious

²savage *n* **1** : a member of a primitive human society **2** ♦ : a rude, unmannerly, or brutal person

♦ beast, brute, devil, fiend, monster, villain

sav·age·ness *n* : the quality or state of being savage
sav·age·ry \-rē\ *n* **1 a** : the quality of being savage **b** ♦ : an act of cruelty or violence **2** : an uncivilized state

♦ barbarity, brutality, cruelty, inhumanity, sadism, viciousness, wantonness

sa·van·na *also* **sa·van·nah** \sə-'va-nə\ *n* ♦ : grassland containing scattered trees

♦ down, grassland, plain, prairie, steppe, veld

sa·vant \sa-'vänt, sə-, 'sa-vənt\ *n* **1** : a learned person : SCHOLAR **2** : a person affected with a developmental disorder who exhibits exceptional skill in some limited field

¹save \'sāv\ *vb* **saved; sav·ing** **1** : to redeem from sin **2** ♦ : to rescue from danger **3** ♦ : to preserve or guard from destruction or loss; *also* : to store (data) in a computer or on a storage device **4** ♦ : to put aside as a store or reserve

♦ [2] deliver, rescue *Ant* compromise, endanger, imperil, jeopardize ♦ [3] economize, scrimp, skimp ♦ [3] conserve, keep up, maintain, preserve ♦ [4] allocate, consecrate, dedicate, devote, earmark, reserve

²save *n* : a play that prevents an opponent from scoring or winning
³save *prep* ♦ : other than : EXCEPT

♦ aside from, bar, barring, besides, but, except, outside (of)

⁴save *conj* ♦ : BUT
sav·er *n* : one that saves
savings and loan association *n* : a cooperative association that holds savings of members in the form of dividend-bearing shares and that invests chiefly in mortgage loans
savings bank *n* : a bank that holds funds of individual depositors in interest-bearing accounts and makes long-term investments (as mortgage loans)
savings bond *n* : a registered U.S. bond issued in denominations of $50 to $10,000
sav·ior *or* **sav·iour** \'sāv-yər\ *n* **1** ♦ : one who saves **2** *cap* : Jesus Christ

♦ deliverer, redeemer, rescuer

sa·voir faire \,sav-,wär-'far\ *n* : sureness in social behavior
¹sa·vor *also* **sa·vour** \'sā-vər\ *n* **1** : the taste and odor of something **2** ♦ : a special flavor or quality affecting taste

♦ deliciousness, lusciousness, tastiness

²savor *also* **savour** *vb* **1** : to have a specified taste, smell, or quality **2** : to taste with pleasure **3** ♦ : to give flavor to

♦ flavor (*or* flavour), season, spice

¹sa·vory *or chiefly Can and Brit* **sa·voury** \'sā-və-rē\ *adj* ♦ : having savor: as **a** : pleasing to the sense of taste esp. by reason of effective seasoning **b** : pungently flavorful without sweetness

♦ ambrosial, appetizing, delectable, delicious, flavorful (*or* flavourful), luscious, palatable, scrumptious, tasty, toothsome, yummy

²sa·vo·ry *n, pl* **-ries** : either of two aromatic mints used in cooking
¹sav·vy \'sa-vē\ *vb* **sav·vied; sav·vy·ing** ♦ : to recognize the meaning of : UNDERSTAND, COMPREHEND

♦ appreciate, apprehend, catch, catch on (to), comprehend, dig, discern, get, grasp, make, make out, perceive, see, seize, understand

²savvy *n* ♦ : practical know-how ⟨political ∼⟩ — **savvy** *adj*

♦ experience, expertise, know-how, proficiency

¹saw *past of* SEE
²saw \'so\ *n* : a cutting tool with a blade having a line of teeth along its edge
³saw *vb* **sawed** \'sod\; **sawed** *or* **sawn** \'son\; **saw·ing** : to cut or shape with or as if with a saw
⁴saw *n* : a common saying : MAXIM
saw·dust \'so-(,)dəst\ *n* : fine particles made by a saw in cutting
saw·fly \-,flī\ *n* : any of numerous insects belonging to the same order as bees and wasps and including many whose larvae are plant-feeding pests
saw·horse \-,hors\ *n* : a rack on which wood is rested while being sawed by hand

saw·mill \-,mil\ *n* : a mill for sawing logs
saw palmetto *n* : any of several shrubby palms with spiny-toothed petioles
saw·yer \'so-yər\ *n* : a person who saws timber
sax \'saks\ *n* : SAXOPHONE
sax·i·frage \'sak-sə-frij, -,frāj\ *n* : any of a genus of plants with showy flowers and usu. with leaves growing in tufts close to the ground
sax·o·phone \'sak-sə-,fōn\ *n* : a musical instrument having a conical metal tube with a reed mouthpiece and finger keys — **sax·o·phon·ist** \-,fō-nist\ *n*
¹say \'sā\ *vb* **said** \'sed\; **say·ing; says** \'sez\ **1** ♦ : to express in words ⟨∼ what you mean⟩ **2** : to state as opinion or belief **3** : PRONOUNCE; *also* : RECITE, REPEAT ⟨∼ your prayers⟩ **4** : INDICATE ⟨the clock ∼s noon⟩

♦ articulate, clothe, couch, express, formulate, phrase, put, state, word ♦ articulate, speak, state, talk, tell, utter, verbalize, vocalize

²say *n, pl* **says** \'sāz\ **1** : an expression of opinion **2** : power of decision
say·ing *n* ♦ : a commonly repeated statement

♦ adage, aphorism, byword, epigram, maxim, proverb

say–so \'sā-(,)sō\ *n* : an esp. authoritative assertion or decision; *also* ♦ : the right to decide

♦ say, voice, vote

sb *abbr* substantive
Sb *symbol* antimony
SB *abbr* bachelor of science
SBA *abbr* Small Business Administration
sc *abbr* **1** scale **2** scene **3** science
Sc *symbol* scandium
SC *abbr* **1** South Carolina **2** supreme court
¹scab \'skab\ *n* **1** : scabies of domestic animals **2** : a crust of hardened blood forming over a wound **3** : a worker who replaces a striker or works under conditions not authorized by a union **4** : any of various bacterial or fungus plant diseases marked by crusted spots on stems or leaves
²scab *vb* **scabbed; scab·bing** **1** : to become covered with a scab **2** : to work as a scab
scab·bard \'ska-bərd\ *n* : a sheath for the blade of a weapon (as a sword)
scab·by *adj* **scab·bi·er; -est** **1** : covered with or full of scabs **2** ♦ : worthy of contempt

♦ contemptible, despicable, lousy, nasty, pitiful, scurvy, sorry, wretched

sca·bies \'skā-bēz\ *n* : contagious itch or mange caused by mites living as parasites under the skin
sca·brous \'ska-brəs, 'skā-\ *adj* **1** : DIFFICULT, KNOTTY **2** : rough to the touch : SCALY, SCURFY ⟨a ∼ leaf⟩ **3** : dealing with suggestive, indecent, or scandalous themes ⟨∼ lyrics⟩; *also* : SQUALID
scad \'skad\ *n* ♦ : a large number or quantity — usu. used in pl.

♦ abundance, deal, gobs, heap, loads, lot, pile, plenty, quantity

scaf·fold \'ska-fəld, -,fōld\ *n* **1** : a raised platform for workers to sit or stand on **2** : a platform on which a criminal is executed (as by hanging)
scaf·fold·ing *n* : a system of scaffolds; *also* : materials for scaffolds
scal·a·wag *or* **scal·ly·wag** \'ska-li-,wag\ *n* ♦ : a mean, unprincipled, or dishonest person : RASCAL

♦ beast, evildoer, fiend, no-good, reprobate, rogue, varlet, villain, wretch

¹scald \'skold\ *vb* **1** : to burn with or as if with hot liquid or steam **2** : to heat to just below the boiling point
²scald *n* : a burn caused by scalding
¹scale \'skāl\ *n* **1** : either pan of a balance **2** : BALANCE — usu. used in pl. **3** : a weighing instrument
²scale *vb* **scaled; scal·ing** ♦ : to weigh in scales

♦ gauge, measure, span

³scale *n* **1** : one of the small thin plates that cover the body esp. of a fish or reptile **2** : a thin plate or flake **3** : a thin coating, layer, or incrustation **4** : SCALE INSECT — **scaled** \'skāld\ *adj* — **scale·less** \'skāl-ləs\ *adj* — **scaly** *adj*
⁴scale *vb* **scaled; scal·ing** ♦ : to strip of scales
⁵scale *n* **1** : something divided into regular spaces as a help in drawing or measuring **2** ♦ : a graduated series **3** : the size of a sample (as a model) in proportion to the size of the actual thing **4** : a standard of estimation or judgment **5** : a

series of musical tones going up or down in pitch according to a specified scheme **6 ♦** : a distinctive relative size, extent, or degree

♦ [2] graduation, ladder ♦ [6] gamut, range, spectrum, spread, stretch

⁶scale *vb* **scaled; scal•ing 1** : to climb by or as if by a ladder **2** : to arrange in a graded series

scale insect *n* : any of numerous small insects with wingless scale-covered females that are related to aphids and feed on and are often pests of plants

scale•pan \'skāl-ˌpan\ *n* : ¹SCALE 1

scal•lion \'skal-yən\ *n* : an onion without an enlarged bulb; *also* : GREEN ONION

¹scal•lop \'skä-ləp, 'ska-\ *n* **1** : any of numerous marine bivalve mollusks with radially ridged shells; *also* : a large edible muscle of this mollusk **2** : one of a continuous series of rounded projections forming an edge

²scallop *vb* **1** : to bake in a casserole ⟨~ed potatoes⟩ **2** : to shape, cut, or finish in scallops ⟨~ed edges⟩

¹scalp \'skalp\ *n* : the part of the skin and flesh of the head usu. covered with hair

²scalp *vb* **1** : to remove the scalp from **2** : to resell at greatly increased prices ⟨~ tickets⟩ — **scalp•er** *n*

scal•pel \'skal-pəl\ *n* : a small straight knife with a thin blade used esp. in surgery

scam \'skam\ *n* ♦ : a fraudulent or deceptive act or operation

♦ hustle, racket, swindle

scamp \'skamp\ *n* ♦ : a dishonest person : RASCAL; *also* : an impish or playful young person

♦ beast, evildoer, fiend, no-good, reprobate, rogue, varlet, villain, wretch ♦ devil, hellion, imp, mischief, monkey, rapscallion, rascal, rogue, urchin

scam•per \'skam-pər\ *vb* ♦ : to run nimbly and playfully — **scamper** *n*

♦ dash, gallop, jog, run, sprint, trip

scam•pi \'skam-pē\ *n, pl* **scampi** : a usu. large shrimp; *also* : large shrimp prepared with a garlic-flavored sauce

¹scan \'skan\ *vb* **scanned; scan•ning 1** : to read (verses) so as to show metrical structure **2 ♦** : to examine closely **3** : to input or examine systematically in order to obtain data esp. for display or storage **4** : to make a scan of (as the human body)

♦ audit, check, examine, inspect, review, scrutinize, survey

²scan *n* **1 ♦** : the act or process of scanning **2** : a picture of the distribution of radioactive material in something; *also* : an image of a bodily part produced (as by computer) by combining radiographic data obtained from several angles or sections

♦ audit, check, checkup, examination, inspection, review, scrutiny, survey

Scand *abbr* Scandinavia

scan•dal \'skand-ᵊl\ *n* **1 ♦** : a circumstance or action that offends propriety or established moral conceptions or disgraces those associated with it : DISGRACE, DISHONOR **2** : malicious gossip : SLANDER — **scan•dal•ize** *vb*

♦ crime, disgrace, dishonor, reflection, reproach

scan•dal•mon•ger \-ˌmən-gər, -ˌmäŋ-\ *n* : a person who circulates scandal

scan•dal•ous *adj* ♦ : containing defamatory information; *also* : offensive to propriety or morality — **scan•dal•ous•ly** *adv*

♦ defamatory, libelous, slanderous ♦ appalling, awful, distasteful, dreadful, obnoxious, obscene, odious, offensive, repellent, repugnant, shocking

Scan•di•na•vian \ˌskan-də-'nā-vē-ən\ *n* : a native or inhabitant of Scandinavia — **Scandinavian** *adj*

scan•di•um \'skan-dē-əm\ *n* : a silvery white metallic chemical element

scan•ner \'ska-nər\ *n* **1** : a radio receiver that sequentially scans a range of frequencies for a signal **2** : a device that scans an image or document esp. for use or storage on a computer

¹scant \'skant\ *adj* **1 ♦** : barely sufficient ⟨food is in ~ supply⟩ **2** : having scarcely enough

♦ light, meager (or meagre), niggardly, poor, scanty, scarce, skimpy, slender, slim, spare, sparse, stingy

²scant *vb* **1** : SKIMP **2 ♦** : to provide with a meager or inadequate portion or supply : STINT

♦ skimp, spare, stint

scant•i•ness \-tē-nəs\ *n* ♦ : the quality or state of being scanty

♦ dearth, deficiency, deficit, failure, famine, inadequacy, insufficiency, lack, paucity, poverty, scarcity, shortage, want

scant•ling \'skant-liŋ\ *n* : a small piece of lumber (as an upright in a house)

scanty \'skan-tē\ *adj* **scant•i•er; -est** ♦ : barely sufficient : SCANT ⟨wore a ~ outfit⟩ — **scant•i•ly** \'skan-tə-lē\ *adv*

♦ light, meager (or meagre), niggardly, poor, scant, scarce, skimpy, slender, slim, spare, sparse, stingy

scape•goat \'skāp-ˌgōt\ *n* : one that bears the blame for others

scape•grace \-ˌgrās\ *n* : an incorrigible rascal

scap•u•la \'ska-pyə-lə\ *n, pl* **-lae** \-ˌlē\ *or* **-las** : SHOULDER BLADE

scap•u•lar \-lər\ *n* : a pair of small cloth squares worn on the breast and back under the clothing esp. for religious purposes

scar \'skär\ *n* ♦ : a mark left after injured tissue has healed — **scar** *vb*

♦ blemish, defect, deformity, disfigurement, fault, flaw, imperfection, mark, pockmark

scar•ab \'skar-əb\ *n* : any of a family of large stout beetles; *also* : an ornament (as a gem) representing such a beetle

scarce \'skers\ *adj* **scarc•er; scarc•est 1 ♦** : deficient in quantity or number : not plentiful **2** : intentionally absent ⟨made himself ~ at inspection time⟩

♦ deficient, inadequate, insufficient, short, shy, wanting

scarce•ly \-lē\ *adv* **1 ♦** : by a narrow margin : BARELY ⟨can ~ see them⟩ **2** : almost not **3** : very probably not

♦ barely, hardly, just, marginally, slightly

scar•ci•ty \'sker-sə-tē\ *n* ♦ : the quality or state of being scarce; *esp* : want of provisions for the support of life

♦ dearth, deficiency, deficit, failure, famine, inadequacy, insufficiency, lack, paucity, poverty, scantiness, shortage, want

¹scare \'sker\ *vb* **scared; scar•ing** ♦ : to frighten esp. suddenly : STARTLE

♦ alarm, frighten, horrify, panic, shock, spook, startle, terrify, terrorize

²scare *n* : FRIGHT

scare•crow \'sker-ˌkrō\ *n* : a crude figure set up to scare birds away from crops

scared *adj* ♦ : thrown into or being in a state of fear, fright, or panic

♦ afraid, aghast, fearful, terrified

¹scarf \'skärf\ *n, pl* **scarves** \'skärvz\ *or* **scarfs 1** : a broad band (as of cloth) worn about the shoulders, around the neck, over the head, or about the waist **2** : a long narrow cloth cover for a table or dresser top

²scarf *vb* ♦ : to eat greedily ⟨~ed down his lunch⟩

♦ bolt, devour, gobble, gorge, gormandize, gulp, scoff, wolf

scar•i•fy \'skar-ə-ˌfī\ *vb* **-fied; -fy•ing 1** : to make scratches or small cuts in ⟨~ skin for vaccination⟩ ⟨~ seeds to help them germinate⟩ **2** : to lacerate the feelings of **3** : to break up and loosen the surface of (as a road) — **scar•i•fi•ca•tion** \ˌskar-ə-fə-'kā-shən\ *n*

scar•let \'skär-lət\ *n* : a bright red color — **scarlet** *adj*

scarlet fever *n* : an acute contagious disease marked by fever, sore throat, and red rash and caused by certain streptococci

scarp \'skärp\ *n* ♦ : a line of cliffs produced by faulting or erosion

♦ bluff, cliff, crag, escarpment, palisade, precipice

scary \'sker-ē\ *adj* **scar•i•er; -est 1 ♦** : causing fright **2** ♦ : easily scared **3** : feeling alarm or fright

♦ [1] dire, dreadful, fearful, fearsome, forbidding, formidable, frightful, hair-raising, horrible, redoubtable, shocking, terrible, terrifying ♦ [2] fainthearted, fearful, mousy, shy, skittish, timid

scath•ing \'skā-thiŋ\ *adj* ♦ : bitterly severe ⟨a ~ condemnation⟩

♦ acrid, biting, caustic, cutting, mordant, pungent, sarcastic, satiric, sharp, tart

scat•o•log•i•cal \ˌska-tə-'lä-ji-kəl\ *adj* : concerned with obscene matters

scat•ter \'ska-tər\ *vb* **1 ♦** : to distribute or strew about irregularly **2 ♦** : to cause to separate widely : DISPERSE

♦ [1] dot, pepper, sow, spray, sprinkle, strew ♦ [2] clear out, disband, disperse, dissipate *Ant* assemble, cluster, collect, concentrate, congregate, gather

scat·ter·brain \'ska-tər-ˌbrān\ *n* : a silly careless person
scat·ter·brained \-ˌbrānd\ *adj* ♦ : having the characteristics of a scatterbrain
   ♦ flighty, frivolous, giddy, goofy, harebrained, light-headed, silly

scattered *adj* ♦ : marked by disorganized dispersion
   ♦ aimless, arbitrary, desultory, erratic, haphazard, random, stray

scav·enge \'ska-vənj\ *vb* **scav·enged; scav·eng·ing** : to work or function as a scavenger
scav·en·ger \'ska-vən-jər\ *n* : a person or animal that collects, eats, or disposes of refuse or waste
sce·nar·io \sə-'nar-ē-ˌō\ *n, pl* **-i·os** : the plot or outline of a dramatic work; *also* : an account of a possible action
scene \'sēn\ *n* **1** : a division of one act of a play **2** : a single situation or sequence in a play or motion picture **3** : a stage setting **4** : VIEW, PROSPECT **5** : the place of an occurrence or action **6** ♦ : a display of strong feeling and esp. anger **7** : a sphere of activity ⟨the fashion ∼⟩ **8** ♦ : a critical, trying, or unusual state of affairs — **sce·nic** \'sē-nik\ *adj*
   ♦ [6] blowup, dudgeon, explosion, fireworks, fit, huff, tantrum
   ♦ [8] footing, picture, posture, situation, status

scen·ery \'sē-nə-rē\ *n, pl* **-er·ies 1** : the painted scenes or hangings and accessories used on a theater stage **2** : a picturesque view or landscape
¹**scent** \'sent\ *n* **1** ♦ : effluvia from a substance that affect the sense of smell : ODOR, SMELL **2** : sense of smell **3** : course of pursuit : TRACK **4** : PERFUME 2 **5** ♦ : an agreeable odor — **scent·less** *adj*
   ♦ [1] odor (*or* odour), redolence, smell, sniff ♦ [5] aroma, bouquet, fragrance, incense, perfume, redolence, spice
²**scent** *vb* **1** ♦ : to perceive by the olfactory organs : SMELL **2** : to imbue or fill with odor **3** ♦ : to get or have an inkling of
   ♦ [1] nose, smell, sniff, whiff ♦ [3] feel, perceive, see, sense, smell, taste

scent·ed \'sen-təd\ *adj* ♦ : having scent
   ♦ ambrosial, aromatic, fragrant, redolent, savory, sweet

scep·ter *or Can and Brit* **scep·tre** \'sep-tər\ *n* : a staff borne by a sovereign as an emblem of authority
sceptic *chiefly Brit var of* SKEPTIC
sch *abbr* school
¹**sched·ule** \'ske-jül, *esp Brit* 'she-dyül\ *n* **1** ♦ : a list of items or details **2** ♦ : a brief usu. printed outline of the order to be followed, of the features to be presented, and the persons participating (as in a public performance) : TIMETABLE
   ♦ [1] catalog, checklist, list, listing, menu, register, registry, roll, roster, table ♦ [2] agenda, calendar, docket, program, timetable
²**schedule** *vb* **sched·uled; sched·ul·ing 1** ♦ : to make a schedule of; *also* : to enter on a schedule **2** : to appoint, assign, or designate for a fixed time
   ♦ catalog, enroll, enter, index, inscribe, list, put down, record, register, slate

sche·ma \'skē-mə\ *n, pl* **sche·ma·ta** \-mə-tə\ *also* **schemas** : a diagrammatic presentation or plan : OUTLINE
sche·mat·ic \ski-'ma-tik\ *adj* : of or relating to a scheme or diagram : DIAGRAMMATIC — **schematic** *n* — **sche·mat·i·cal·ly** \-ti-k(ə-)lē\ *adv*
¹**scheme** \'skēm\ *n* **1** ♦ : a plan for doing something; *esp* : a crafty plot **2** ♦ : a systematic design
   ♦ [1] artifice, device, dodge, gimmick, jig, ploy, sleight, stratagem, trick, wile ♦ [1] conspiracy, design, intrigue, machination, plot ♦ [2] blueprint, program, strategy, system
²**scheme** *vb* **schemed; schem·ing** ♦ : to form a plot : INTRIGUE — **schem·er** *n*
   ♦ conspire, contrive, intrigue, machinate, plot

schism \'si-zəm, 'ski-\ *n* **1** ♦ : the act or process of dividing : DIVISION; *also* : DISCORD **2** : a formal division in or separation from a religious body
   ♦ breakup, dissolution, division, partition, separation, split
   ♦ conflict, discord, dissension, dissent, disunity, friction, strife, variance, war, warfare

schis·mat·ic \siz-'ma-tik, ski-\ *n* : one who creates or takes part in schism — **schismatic** *adj*
schist \'shist\ *n* : a metamorphic crystalline rock
schizo·phre·nia \ˌskit-sə-'frē-nē-ə\ *n* : a psychotic mental illness that is characterized by a distorted view of the real world, by

a greatly reduced ability to carry out one's daily tasks, and by abnormal ways of thinking, feeling, perceiving, and behaving — **schiz·oid** \'skit-ˌsóid\ *adj or n* — **schizo·phren·ic** \ˌskit-sə-'fre-nik\ *adj or n*
schle·miel *also* **shle·miel** \shlə-'mēl\ *n* : an unlucky bungler : CHUMP
schlep *or* **schlepp** \'shlep\ *vb* **1** : DRAG, HAUL **2** : to move slowly or awkwardly
schlock \'shläk\ *or* **schlocky** \'shlä-kē\ *adj* : of low quality or value — **schlock** *n*
schlub *also* **shlub** \'shləb\ *n, slang* : a stupid, ineffectual, or unattractive person
schmaltz *also* **schmalz** \'shmólts, 'shmälts\ *n* : sentimental or florid music or art
schmaltzy *adj* ♦ : excessively sentimental
   ♦ corny, maudlin, mawkish, mushy, saccharine, sappy, sentimental

schmooze *or* **shmooze** \'shmüz\ *vb* ♦ : to chat informally esp. to gain favor — **schmooze** *n*
   ♦ chat, converse, gab, jaw, palaver, patter, prattle, rattle, talk, visit

schmuck \'shmək\ *n, slang* : a stupid, foolish, or unlikeable person : JERK
schnapps \'shnaps\ *n, pl* **schnapps** : a liquor (as gin) of high alcoholic content
schnau·zer \'shnaút-sər, 'shnaú-zər\ *n* : a dog of any of three breeds that are characterized by a wiry coat, long head, pointed ears, heavy eyebrows, and long hair on the muzzle
schol·ar \'skä-lər\ *n* **1** : STUDENT, PUPIL **2** : a learned person : SAVANT **3** ♦ : a person who has done advanced study in a special field
   ♦ ace, adept, artist, authority, crackerjack, expert, maestro, master, shark, virtuoso, whiz, wizard

schol·ar·ly *adj* ♦ : of, characteristic of, or suitable to learned persons
   ♦ educated, erudite, knowledgeable, learned, literate, well-read
   ♦ academic, educational, scholastic

schol·ar·ship \-ˌship\ *n* **1** ♦ : the qualities or learning of a scholar **2** : money awarded to a student to help pay for further education
   ♦ education, erudition, knowledge, learning, science

scho·las·tic \skə-'las-tik\ *adj* : of or relating to schools, scholars, or scholarship
   ♦ academic, educational, scholarly

¹**school** \'skül\ *n* **1** : an institution for teaching and learning; *also* : the pupils in attendance **2** : a body of persons of like opinions or beliefs ⟨the radical ∼⟩
²**school** *vb* ♦ : to teach or drill in a specific knowledge or skill : TRAIN
   ♦ educate, indoctrinate, instruct, teach, train, tutor

³**school** *n* : a large number of one kind of water animal swimming and feeding together
school·boy \-ˌbói\ *n* : a boy attending school
school·fel·low \-ˌfe-lō\ *n* : SCHOOLMATE
school·girl \-ˌgərl\ *n* : a girl attending school
school·house \-ˌhaús\ *n* : a building used as a school
school·marm \-ˌmärm\ *or* **school·ma'am** \-ˌmäm, -ˌmam\ *n* **1** : a woman who is a schoolteacher **2** : a person who exhibits characteristics popularly attributed to schoolteachers
school·mas·ter \-ˌmas-tər\ *n* : a man who is a schoolteacher
school·mate \-ˌmāt\ *n* : a school companion
school·mis·tress \-ˌmis-trəs\ *n* : a woman who is a schoolteacher
school·room \-ˌrüm, -ˌrúm\ *n* : CLASSROOM
school·teach·er \-ˌtē-chər\ *n* ♦ : one who teaches in a school
   ♦ educator, instructor, pedagogue, teacher

schoo·ner \'skü-nər\ *n* : a fore-and-aft rigged sailing ship
schtick *var of* SHTICK
schuss \'shús, 'shüs\ *vb* : to ski down a slope at high speed — **schuss** *n*
sci *abbr* science; scientific
sci·at·i·ca \sī-'a-ti-kə\ *n* : pain in the region of the hips or along the course of the nerve at the back of the thigh
sci·ence \'sī-əns\ *n* **1** : an area of knowledge that is an object of study; *esp* : NATURAL SCIENCE **2** ♦ : knowledge covering general truths or the operation of general laws esp. as obtained and tested through the scientific method **3** ♦ : knowledge as distinguished from ignorance or misunderstanding — **sci·en·tif·ic** \ˌsī-ən-'ti-fik\

adj — **sci·en·tif·i·cal·ly** \-fi-k(ə-)lē\ *adv* — **sci·en·tist** \'sī-ən-tist\ *n*

♦ [2] knowledge, lore, wisdom ♦ [3] education, erudition, knowledge, learning, scholarship

science fiction *n* : fiction dealing principally with the impact of actual or imagined science on society or individuals

scientific method *n* : the rules and methods for the pursuit of knowledge involving the finding and stating of a problem, the collection of facts through observation and experiment, and the making and testing of ideas that need to be proven right or wrong

scim·i·tar \'si-mə-tər\ *n* : a curved sword used chiefly by Arabs and Turks

scin·til·la \sin-'ti-lə\ *n* : SPARK, TRACE

scin·til·late \'sint-ᵊl-ˌāt\ *vb* **-lat·ed; -lat·ing** 1 ♦ : to throw off as a spark or as sparkling flashes : SPARKLE, GLEAM 2 : DAZZLE, IMPRESS — **scin·til·la·tion** \ˌsint-ᵊl-'ā-shən\ *n*

♦ flame, flash, glance, gleam, glimmer, glisten, glitter, shimmer, sparkle, twinkle, wink

sci·on \'sī-ən\ *n* 1 : a shoot of a plant joined to a stock in grafting 2 : DESCENDANT

scis·sors \'si-zərz\ *n pl* : a cutting instrument like shears but usu. smaller

scissors kick *n* : a swimming kick in which the legs move like scissors

sclero·der·ma \ˌskler-ə-'dər-mə\ *n* : a chronic disease characterized by the usu. progressive hardening and thickening of the skin

scle·ro·sis \sklə-'rō-səs\ *n* : abnormal hardening of tissue (as of an artery); *also* : a disease characterized by this — **scle·rot·ic** \-'rä-tik\ *adj*

¹**scoff** \'skäf\ *vb* : MOCK, JEER ⟨~ed at the idea⟩
²**scoff** *vb* ♦ : to eat greedily

♦ bolt, devour, gobble, gorge, gormandize, gulp, scarf, wolf

scoff·er *n* ♦ : one that scoffs

♦ heckler, mocker, quiz, taunter, tease

scoff·law \-ˌlo\ *n* : a contemptuous law violator

¹**scold** \'skōld\ *n* ♦ : a person who scolds

♦ carper, castigator, caviler, censurer, critic, faultfinder, nitpicker, railer

²**scold** *vb* ♦ : to censure severely or angrily

♦ berate, castigate, chew out, dress down, flay, jaw, keelhaul, lambaste, lecture, rail (at *or* against), rate, rebuke, reprimand, reproach, score, upbraid

sconce \'skäns\ *n* : a candlestick or an electric light fixture fastened to a wall

scone \'skōn, 'skän\ *n* : a biscuit (as of oatmeal) baked on a griddle

¹**scoop** \'sküp\ *n* 1 ♦ : a large shovel; *also* : a utensil with a shovel-like or rounded end 2 : an act of scooping 3 ♦ : information of immediate interest

♦ [1] ladle, spoon ♦ [3] dope, lowdown, tip

²**scoop** *vb* 1 ♦ : to take out or up or empty with or as if with a scoop 2 : to make hollow 3 : to report a news item in advance of ⟨~ed the other newspapers⟩

♦ dip, ladle, spoon

scoot \'sküt\ *vb* ♦ : to move swiftly

♦ course, dash, fly, hasten, hurry, hustle, run, rush, shoot, speed, zip, zoom

scoot·er \'skü-tər\ *n* 1 : a child's vehicle consisting of a narrow board mounted between two wheels tandem with an upright steering handle attached to the front wheel 2 : MOTOR SCOOTER

¹**scope** \'skōp\ *n* 1 : space or opportunity for action or thought 2 ♦ : extent covered : RANGE ⟨is beyond the ~ of the essay⟩

♦ amplitude, breadth, compass, extent, range, reach, realm, sweep, width

²**scope** *n* : an instrument (as a microscope or telescope) for viewing

scorch \'skorch\ *vb* 1 ♦ : to burn the surface of 2 : to dry or shrivel with heat ⟨~ed lawns⟩

♦ char, sear, singe

scorch·ing *adj* ♦ : that scorches

♦ broiling, burning, fiery, hot, red-hot, sultry, torrid

¹**score** \'skor\ *n, pl* **scores** 1 *or pl* **score** : TWENTY 2 : CUT,

SCRATCH, SLASH 3 : a record of points made (as in a game) 4 : DEBT 5 : REASON, GROUND 6 : the music of a composition or arrangement with different parts indicated 7 : success in obtaining something (as drugs) esp. illegally 8 ♦ : a feeling of deep-seated resentment or ill will

♦ grievance, grudge, resentment

²**score** *vb* **scored; scor·ing** 1 : RECORD 2 : to keep score in a game 3 ♦ : to mark with lines, grooves, scratches, or notches 4 : to gain or tally in or as if in a game ⟨scored a point⟩ 5 : to assign a grade or score to ⟨~ the tests⟩ 6 : to compose a score for 7 ♦ : to be successful 8 : to scold or condemn vehemently and at length — **score·less** *adj* — **scor·er** *n*

♦ [3] groove, scribe ♦ [7] achieve, attain, hit, make, win

¹**scorn** \'skorn\ *n* ♦ : an emotion involving both anger and disgust : CONTEMPT — **scorn·ful·ly** *adv*

♦ contempt, despite, disdain

²**scorn** *vb* ♦ : to hold in contempt : DISDAIN

♦ disdain, high-hat, slight, sniff at, snub *Ant* honor, respect
♦ despise, disregard, flout

scorn·er *n* : one that scorns
scorn·ful \-fəl\ *adj* ♦ : full of scorn

♦ contemptuous, degrading, derogatory, disdainful, uncomplimentary

Scor·pio \'skor-pē-ˌō\ *n* 1 : a zodiacal constellation between Libra and Sagittarius usu. pictured as a scorpion 2 : the 8th sign of the zodiac in astrology; *also* : one born under this sign

scor·pi·on \'skor-pē-ən\ *n* : any of an order of arthropods related to the spiders that have a poisonous stinger at the tip of a long jointed tail

¹**Scot** \'skät\ *n* : a native or inhabitant of Scotland
²**Scot** *abbr* Scotland; Scottish

Scotch \'skäch\ *n* 1 : SCOTS 2 **Scotch** *pl* : the people of Scotland 3 : a whiskey distilled in Scotland esp. from malted barley — **Scotch** *adj* — **Scotch·wom·an** \-ˌwu-mən\ *n*

Scotch bonnet *n* : a small roundish very hot chili pepper esp. of the Caribbean

Scotch·man \-mən\ *n* : a native or inhabitant of Scotland

Scotch pine *n* : a pine that is naturalized in the U.S. from northern Europe and Asia and is a valuable timber tree

Scotch terrier *n* : SCOTTISH TERRIER

scot–free \'skät-'frē\ *adj* : free from obligation, harm, or penalty

Scots \'skäts\ *n* : the English language of Scotland

Scots·man \'skäts-mən\ *n* : a native or inhabitant of Scotland : SCOT

Scots·wom·an \-ˌwu-mən\ *n* : a woman who is a Scot

Scot·tie \'skä-tē\ *n* 1 : SCOTTISH TERRIER 2 : a native or inhabitant of Scotland : SCOT

Scot·tish \'skä-tish\ *adj* : of, relating to, or characteristic of Scotland, Scots, or the Scots

Scottish terrier *n* : any of an old Scottish breed of terrier with short legs, a long head with small erect ears, a broad deep chest, and a thick rough coat

scoun·drel \'skaun-drəl\ *n* : a disreputable person : VILLAIN

¹**scour** \'skaur\ *vb* 1 : to rub (as with a gritty substance) in order to clean 2 : to cleanse by or as if by rubbing

²**scour** *vb* 1 : to move rapidly through : RUSH 2 ♦ : to examine thoroughly

♦ dig, dredge, hunt, rake, ransack, rifle, rummage, search

¹**scourge** \'skərj\ *n* 1 : an instrument consisting usu. of a handle and lash forming a flexible rod that is used for whipping : LASH, WHIP 2 **a** : PUNISHMENT **b** : a cause of affliction (as a plague)

²**scourge** *vb* **scourged; scourg·ing** 1 ♦ : to beat with or as if with a rod or whip : LASH 2 ♦ : to punish severely; *also* : to distress so severely as to cause persistent suffering or anguish

♦ [1] flog, lash, thrash, whale, whip ♦ [2] destroy, devastate, ravage, ruin

¹**scout** \'skaut\ *vb* 1 : to look around : RECONNOITER 2 : to inspect or observe to get information 3 ♦ : to find by making a search

♦ usu **scout up** detect, determine, dig up, discover, ferret out, hit on, locate, track down

²**scout** *n* 1 : a person sent out to get information; *also* : a soldier, airplane, or ship sent out to reconnoiter 2 : BOY SCOUT 3 : GIRL SCOUT 4 : a human being

³**scout** *vb* ♦ : to treat with contempt or ridicule; *also* : to reject scornfully

♦ deride, gibe, jeer, laugh, mock, ridicule

scout·mas·ter \-ˌmas-tər\ *n* : an adult leader of a Boy Scout troop

scow \ˈskau̇\ *n* : a large flat-bottomed boat with square ends

¹**scowl** \ˈskau̇l\ *vb* ♦ : to make a frowning expression of displeasure
- ♦ frown, glare, gloom, glower, lower

²**scowl** *n* ♦ : a facial expression of displeasure
- ♦ face, frown, grimace, lower, mouth, pout

SCPO *abbr* senior chief petty officer

¹**scrab·ble** \ˈskra-bəl\ *vb* **scrab·bled; scrab·bling** 1 : SCRAPE, SCRATCH 2 ♦ : to climb awkwardly : CLAMBER, SCRAMBLE 3 : to work hard and long 4 : SCRIBBLE — **scrab·bler** *n*
- ♦ clamber, climb, scramble

²**scrabble** *n* ♦ : the act or an instance of scrambling
- ♦ battle, fight, fray, struggle

scrag·gly \ˈskra-glē\ *adj* ♦ : irregular in form or growth; *also* : RAGGED
- ♦ broken, craggy, jagged, ragged

scram \ˈskram\ *vb* **scrammed; scram·ming** : to go away at once

¹**scram·ble** \ˈskram-bəl\ *vb* **scram·bled; scram·bling** 1 : to clamber clumsily around 2 : to struggle for or as if for possession of something 3 : to spread irregularly 4 ♦ : to mix together 5 : to cook (eggs) by stirring during frying
- ♦ confuse, disarray, disorder, jumble, mix, muddle

²**scramble** *n* 1 : the act or an instance of scrambling 2 ♦ : a disordered mass
- ♦ assortment, clutter, jumble, medley, mélange, miscellany, motley, muddle, variety, welter

¹**scrap** \ˈskrap\ *n* 1 ♦ : a small detached piece 2 ♦ : discarded material
- ♦ [1] bit, fragment, piece ♦ [2] chaff, deadwood, dust, garbage, junk, litter, refuse, riffraff, rubbish, trash, waste ♦ [2] end, fag end, leftover, remainder, remnant

²**scrap** *vb* **scrapped; scrap·ping** 1 : to make into scrap ⟨∼ a battleship⟩ 2 ♦ : to get rid of as useless
- ♦ cast, discard, ditch, dump, fling, jettison, junk, lose, reject, shed, shuck, slough, throw away, throw out, unload

³**scrap** *n* ♦ : a hostile encounter : FIGHT; *also* : a verbal disagreement
- ♦ argument, brawl, disagreement, dispute, fight, hassle, quarrel, row, spat, squabble

⁴**scrap** *vb* **scrapped; scrap·ping** ♦ : to contend against in or as if in battle or physical combat : FIGHT — **scrap·per** *n*
- ♦ argue, bicker, brawl, dispute, fall out, fight, hassle, quarrel, row, spat, squabble, wrangle

scrap·book \ˈskrap-ˌbu̇k\ *n* : a blank book in which mementos are kept

¹**scrape** \ˈskrāp\ *vb* **scraped; scrap·ing** 1 : to remove by drawing a knife over; *also* : to clean or smooth by rubbing off the covering 2 ♦ : to damage or injure the surface of by contact with something rough 3 ♦ : to draw across a surface with a grating sound 4 ♦ : to get together (as money) in small amounts by laborious effort — often used with *up* or *together* 5 : to get along with difficulty — **scrap·er** *n*
- ♦ [2] abrade, graze, scratch, scuff ♦ [3] grate, grind, rasp, scratch ♦ [4] eke out, squeeze, wrest, wring ♦ *usu* **scrape together** [4] accumulate, amass, assemble, collect, concentrate, garner, gather, group, lump, pick up, round up

²**scrape** *n* 1 ♦ : the act or the effect of scraping 2 : a bow accompanied by a drawing back of the foot 3 ♦ : an unpleasant predicament; *also* : a noisy heated angry dispute
- ♦ [1] grind, rasp, scratch ♦ [3] brush, encounter, hassle, run-in, skirmish

¹**scrap·py** \ˈskra-pē\ *adj* **scrap·pi·er; -est** : DISCONNECTED, FRAGMENTARY

²**scrappy** *adj* **scrap·pi·er; -est** 1 ♦ : apt or disposed to quarrel in an often petty manner : QUARRELSOME 2 : having an aggressive and determined spirit
- ♦ argumentative, contentious, disputatious, quarrelsome

¹**scratch** \ˈskrach\ *vb* 1 ♦ : to scrape, dig, or rub with or as if with claws or nails ⟨a dog ∼ing at the door⟩ ⟨∼ed my arm⟩ 2 ♦ : to draw across a surface with a grating sound ⟨∼ed his nails

across the blackboard⟩ 3 : SCRAPE 4 4 : to cancel or erase by or as if by drawing a line through 5 : to withdraw from a contest
- ♦ [1] abrade, graze, scrape, scuff ♦ [2] grate, grind, rasp, scrape

²**scratch** *n* 1 **a** : a mark or injury made by or as if by scratching **b** ♦ : a sound made by scratching 2 : the starting line in a race — **from scratch** : with no steps completed or ingredients prepared ahead of time ⟨built it *from scratch*⟩
- ♦ grind, rasp, scrape

³**scratch** *adj* 1 : made as or used for a trial attempt ⟨∼ paper⟩ 2 : made or done by chance ⟨a ∼ hit⟩

scratchy *adj* **scratch·i·er; -est** 1 ♦ : likely to scratch 2 ♦ : making a scratching noise
- ♦ [1] brambly, prickly, thorny ♦ [2] coarse, gravelly, gruff, hoarse, husky, throaty

scrawl \ˈskrȯl\ *vb* : to write hastily and carelessly — **scrawl** *n*

scraw·ny \ˈskrȯ-nē\ *adj* **scraw·ni·er; -est** : very thin : SKINNY

¹**scream** \ˈskrēm\ *vb* ♦ : to cry out loudly and shrilly
- ♦ howl, shriek, shrill, squeal, yell, yelp

²**scream** *n* : a loud shrill cry

scream·ing \ˈskrē-miŋ\ *adj* 1 : so striking as to attract notice as if by screaming ⟨∼ headlines⟩ 2 ♦ : so funny as to provoke screams of laughter
- ♦ antic, comic, comical, droll, farcical, funny, hilarious, humorous, hysterical, laughable, ludicrous, ridiculous, riotous, risible, uproarious

screech \ˈskrēch\ *vb* : to utter a high shrill piercing cry : SHRIEK — **screech** *n* — **screechy** \ˈskrē-chē\ *adj*

¹**screen** \ˈskrēn\ *n* 1 **a** : a device or partition used to hide, restrain, protect, or decorate ⟨a window ∼⟩ **b** ♦ : something that shelters, protects, or conceals 2 : a sieve or perforated material for separating finer from coarser parts (as of sand) 3 : a surface on which an image is made to appear (as in television); *also* : the information displayed on a computer screen at one time 4 : the motion-picture industry
- ♦ aegis, armor, cover, defense (*or* defence), guard, protection, safeguard, security, shield, wall, ward

²**screen** *vb* 1 ♦ : to shield with or as if with a screen 2 : to separate with or as if with a screen; *also* : to select or categorize methodically ⟨∼ contestants⟩ 3 : to present (as a motion picture) on the screen
- ♦ cover, defend, guard, protect, safeguard, secure, shield, ward
- ♦ blanket, blot out, cloak, conceal, cover, curtain, enshroud, hide, mask, obscure, occult, shroud, veil

screen·ing \ˈskrē-niŋ\ *n* 1 : metal or plastic mesh (as for window screens) 2 : a showing of a motion picture

screen saver *n* : a computer program that displays something (as images) on the screen of a computer that is on but not in use

¹**screw** \ˈskrü\ *n* 1 : a machine consisting of a solid cylinder with a spiral groove around it and a corresponding hollow cylinder into which it fits 2 : a naillike metal piece with a spiral groove and a head with a slot that is inserted into material by rotating and is used to fasten pieces of solid material together 3 : PROPELLER

²**screw** *vb* 1 : to fasten or close by means of a screw 2 : to operate or adjust by means of a screw 3 : to move or cause to move spirally; *also* : to close or set in position by such an action 4 ♦ : to twist into strained configurations : CONTORT ⟨∼ed up his face⟩
- ♦ contort, deform, distort, warp

screw·ball \ˈskrü-ˌbȯl\ *n* 1 : a baseball pitch breaking in a direction opposite to a curve 2 ♦ : a whimsical, eccentric, or crazy person
- ♦ character, crackpot, crank, eccentric, kook, nut, oddball, weirdo

screw·driv·er \-ˌdrī-vər\ *n* 1 : a tool for turning screws 2 : a drink made of vodka and orange juice

screw-up \ˈskrü-ˌəp\ *n* ♦ : an avoidable and usu. serious mistake
- ♦ blunder, error, fault, flub, fumble, gaffe, goof, lapse, miscue, misstep, mistake, oversight, slip, stumble, trip

screw up *vb* ♦ : to foul up hopelessly : BUNGLE
- ♦ blow, bobble, botch, bungle, butcher, flub, foul up, fumble, mangle, mess up

screw·worm \ˈskrü-ˌwərm\ *n* : an American blowfly of warm regions whose larva matures in wounds or sores of mammals and may cause disease or death; *esp* : its larva

screwy \ˈskrü-ē\ *adj* **screw·i·er; -est** 1 ♦ : crazily absurd,

eccentric, or unusual   **2** : disordered in mind : CRAZY — not used technically
  ♦ bizarre, curious, far-out, funny, kinky, odd, outlandish, outré, peculiar, quaint, quirky, remarkable, strange, wacky, weird, wild

scrib·ble \'skri-bəl\ vb **scrib·bled; scrib·bling** ♦ : to write hastily or carelessly — **scribble** n — **scrib·bler** n
  ♦ author, pen, write

scribe \'skrīb\ n   **1** : a scholar of Jewish law in New Testament times   **2** ♦ : a person whose business is the copying of writing   **3** : JOURNALIST
  ♦ clerk, register, registrar

scrim \'skrim\ n : a light loosely woven cotton or linen cloth
¹scrim·mage \'skri-mij\ n   **1** : the play between two football teams beginning with the snap of the ball; also : practice play between two teams   **2** ♦ : a confused fight
  ♦ battle, clash, combat, conflict, contest, fight, fracas, fray, hassle, scrap, scuffle, skirmish, struggle, tussle

²scrimmage vb **scrim·maged; scrim·mag·ing** ♦ : to take part in a scrimmage
  ♦ usu **scrimmage with** battle, clash, combat, fight, skirmish, war

scrimp \'skrimp\ vb ♦ : to economize greatly ⟨∼ and save⟩
  ♦ economize, save, skimp

scrim·shaw \'skrim-ˌshȯ\ n : carved or engraved articles made orig. by American whalers usu. from baleen or whale ivory — **scrimshaw** vb
scrip \'skrip\ n   **1** : a certificate showing its holder is entitled to something (as stock or land)   **2** : paper money issued for temporary use in an emergency
¹script \'skript\ n   **1** : written matter (as lines for a play or broadcast)   **2** ♦ : written characters : HANDWRITING
  ♦ handwriting, manuscript, penmanship

²script abbr scripture
scrip·ture \'skrip-chər\ n   **1** cap : the books of the Bible — often used in pl.   **2** : the sacred writings of a religion — **scrip·tur·al** \'skrip-chə-rəl\ adj — **scrip·tur·al·ly** adv
scriv·en·er \'skri-və-nər\ n : SCRIBE, COPYIST, WRITER
scrod \'skräd\ n : a young fish (as a cod or haddock); esp : one split and boned for cooking
scrof·u·la \'skrȯ-fyə-lə\ n : tuberculosis of lymph nodes esp. in the neck
¹scroll \'skrōl\ n : a roll of paper or parchment for writing a document; also : a spiral or coiled ornamental form suggesting a loosely or partly rolled scroll
²scroll vb : to move or cause to move text or graphics up, down, or across a display screen
scroll saw n   **1** : FRETSAW   **2** : a machine saw with a narrow vertically reciprocating blade for cutting curved lines or openwork
scro·tum \'skrō-təm\ n, pl **scro·ta** \-tə\ or **scrotums** : a pouch that in most male mammals contains the testes
scrounge \'skraunj\ vb **scrounged; scroung·ing** : to collect by or as if by foraging
¹scrub \'skrəb\ n   **1** : a thick growth of stunted trees or shrubs; also : an area of land covered with scrub   **2** : an inferior domestic animal   **3** : a person of insignificant size or standing   **4** : a player not on the first team — **scrub** adj — **scrub·by** adj
²scrub vb **scrubbed; scrub·bing**   **1** : to clean or wash by rubbing ⟨∼ clothes⟩ ⟨∼ out a spot⟩   **2** : CANCEL
³scrub n   **1** : an act or instance of scrubbing ⟨gave the clothes a good ∼⟩   **2** pl : loose-fitting clothing worn by hospital staff ⟨surgical ∼s⟩
scrub·ber \'skrə-bər\ n : one that scrubs; esp : an apparatus for removing impurities esp. from gases
scruff \'skrəf\ n : the loose skin of the back of the neck : NAPE
scruffy \'skrə-fē\ adj **scruff·i·er; -est** ♦ : not in order or neat ⟨a ∼ beard⟩
  ♦ dilapidated, grungy, mean, neglected, ratty, seedy, shabby

scrump·tious \'skrəmp-shəs\ adj ♦ : highly pleasing; esp : DELICIOUS ⟨a ∼ meal⟩ — **scrump·tious·ly** adv
  ♦ ambrosial, appetizing, delectable, delicious, flavorful (or flavourful), luscious, palatable, savory, tasty, toothsome, yummy

scrunch·ie or **scrunchy** \'skrən-chē, 'skrün-\ n : a fabric-covered elastic for the hair
¹scru·ple \'skrü-pəl\ n   **1** : a point of conscience or honor   **2** ♦ : hesitation due to ethical considerations
  ♦ compunction, misgiving, qualm

²scruple vb **scru·pled; scru·pling** : to be reluctant on grounds of conscience : HESITATE
³scruple n : a minute part or quantity
scru·pu·lous \'skrü-pyə-ləs\ adj   **1** ♦ : having moral integrity   **2** : PAINSTAKING — **scru·pu·lous·ly** adv
  ♦ conscientious, ethical, honest, honorable (or honourable), just, moral, principled

scru·pu·lous·ness n ♦ : conformity to high standards of ethics or excellence
  ♦ care, carefulness, heed, heedfulness, pains

scru·ti·nise chiefly Brit var of SCRUTINIZE
scru·ti·nize \'skrü-tə-ˌnīz\ vb **-nized; -niz·ing** ♦ : to examine closely
  ♦ audit, check, examine, inspect, review, scan, survey

scru·ti·ny \'skrüt-ᵊn-ē\ n, pl **-nies** ♦ : a careful looking over
  ♦ audit, check, checkup, examination, inspection, review, scan, survey

scu·ba \'skü-bə\ n : an apparatus for breathing while swimming underwater
scuba diver n : one who swims underwater with the aid of scuba gear
¹scud \'skəd\ vb **scud·ded; scud·ding** : to move speedily
²scud n : light clouds driven by the wind
¹scuff \'skəf\ vb   **1** : to scrape the feet while walking : SHUFFLE   **2** ♦ : to scratch or become scratched or worn away
  ♦ abrade, graze, scrape, scratch

²scuff n   **1** : a mark or injury caused by scuffing   **2** : a flat-soled slipper without heel strap
¹scuf·fle \'skə-fəl\ vb **scuf·fled; scuf·fling**   **1** ♦ : to struggle confusedly at close quarters   **2** : to shuffle one's feet
  ♦ grapple, tussle, wrestle

²scuffle n ♦ : a rough haphazard struggle with scrambling and confusion
  ♦ battle, clash, combat, conflict, contest, fight, fracas, fray, hassle, scrap, scrimmage, skirmish, struggle, tussle

¹scull \'skəl\ n   **1** : an oar for use in sculling; also : one of a pair of short oars for a single oarsman   **2** : a racing shell propelled by one or two persons using sculls
²scull vb ♦ : to propel (a boat) by an oar over the stern
  ♦ row

scul·lery \'skə-lə-rē\ n, pl **-ler·ies** : a small room near the kitchen used for cleaning dishes, cooking utensils, and vegetables
scul·lion \'skəl-yən\ n : a kitchen helper
sculpt \'skəlpt\ vb : to cut with care or precision : CARVE, SCULPTURE
sculp·tor \'skəlp-tər\ n : a person who produces works of sculpture
¹sculp·ture \'skəlp-chər\ n : the act, process, or art of carving or molding material (as stone, wood, or plastic); also : work produced this way — **sculp·tur·al** \'skəlp-chə-rəl\ adj
²sculpture vb **sculp·tured; sculp·tur·ing** : to form or alter as or as if a work of sculpture ⟨sculptured hedges⟩
scum \'skəm\ n   **1** : a slimy or filmy covering on the surface of a liquid   **2** : waste matter   **3** ♦ : a low, vile, or worthless person or group of people : RABBLE
  ♦ rabble, riffraff, trash

scup·per \'skə-pər\ n : an opening in the side of a ship through which water on deck is drained overboard
scurf \'skərf\ n : thin dry scales of skin (as dandruff); also : a scaly deposit or covering — **scurfy** \'skər-fē\ adj
scur·ri·lous \'skər-ə-ləs\ adj ♦ : using or marked by the use of coarse or abusive language
  ♦ abusive, opprobrious

scur·ry \'skər-ē\ vb **scur·ried; scur·ry·ing** ♦ : to move in or as if in a brisk pace : SCAMPER ⟨scurried for cover⟩
  ♦ dash, fly, hasten, hurry, run, rush, scamper, scoot, shoot, speed

¹scur·vy \'skər-vē\ n : a disease caused by a lack of vitamin C and characterized by spongy gums, loosened teeth, and bleeding under the skin
²scurvy adj ♦ : arousing disgust or scorn : CONTEMPTIBLE — **scur·vi·ly** \'skər-və-lē\ adv
  ♦ contemptible, despicable, lousy, nasty, pitiful, scabby, sorry, wretched

scutch·eon \'skə-chən\ n : ESCUTCHEON

[1]**scut·tle** \'skət-ᵊl\ n : a pail for carrying coal

[2]**scuttle** n : a small opening with a lid esp. in the deck, side, or bottom of a ship

[3]**scuttle** vb **scut·tled; scut·tling** : to cut a hole in the deck, side, or bottom of (a ship) in order to sink

[4]**scuttle** vb **scut·tled; scut·tling** : to move in or as if in a brisk pace : SCURRY, SCAMPER

scut·tle·butt \'skət-ᵊl-ˌbət\ n : GOSSIP

scythe \'sīth\ n : an implement for mowing (as grass or grain) by hand — **scythe** vb

SD abbr **1** South Dakota **2** special delivery

S Dak abbr South Dakota

SDI abbr Strategic Defense Initiative

Se symbol selenium

SE abbr southeast

sea \'sē\ n **1** : a large body of salt water **2** ♦ : the waters of the earth as distinguished from the land and air : OCEAN **3** : rough water; also : a large wave **4** : something likened to the sea esp. in vastness — **sea** adj — **at sea** : LOST, BEWILDERED

   ♦ blue, brine, deep, ocean

sea anemone n : any of numerous coelenterate polyps whose form, bright and varied colors, and cluster of tentacles superficially resemble a flower

sea·bird \'sē-ˌbərd\ n : a bird (as a gull) frequenting the open ocean

sea·board \-ˌbōrd\ n : SEACOAST; also : the land bordering a coast

sea·borg·i·um \sē-'bòr-gē-əm\ n : a short-lived radioactive chemical element produced artificially

sea·coast \-ˌkōst\ n : the shore of the sea

sea·far·er \-ˌfar-ər\ n : a person who navigates or assists in navigating a ship : SEAMAN 1

sea·far·ing \-ˌfar-iŋ\ n : the use of the sea for travel or transportation — **seafaring** adj

sea·food \-ˌfüd\ n : edible marine fish and shellfish

sea·go·ing \-ˌgō-iŋ\ adj : OCEANGOING

sea·gull \'sē-ˌgəl\ n : GULL

sea horse n : any of a genus of small marine fishes with the head and forepart of the body sharply flexed like the head and neck of a horse

[1]**seal** \'sēl\ n, pl **seals** also **seal** **1** : any of numerous large carnivorous sea mammals occurring chiefly in cold regions and having limbs adapted for swimming **2** : the pelt of a seal

[2]**seal** vb : to hunt seals

[3]**seal** n **1** : GUARANTEE, PLEDGE **2** : a device having a raised design that can be stamped on clay or wax; also : the impression made by stamping with such a device **3** : something that seals or closes up ⟨safety ~⟩

[4]**seal** vb **1** : to affix a seal to; also : AUTHENTICATE **2** : to fasten with or as if with a seal to prevent tampering **3** : to close or make secure against access, leakage, or passage **4** : to determine irrevocably ⟨~ed his fate⟩

sea·lane \'sē-ˌlān\ n : an established sea route

seal·ant \'sē-lənt\ n : a sealing agent

seal·er \'sē-lər\ n : a coat applied to prevent subsequent coats of paint or varnish from sinking in

sea level n : the level of the surface of the sea esp. at its mean midway between mean high and low water

sea lion n : any of several large Pacific seals with small external ears

seal·skin \'sēl-ˌskin\ n **1** : [1]SEAL 2 **2** : a garment of sealskin

[1]**seam** \'sēm\ n **1** : the line of junction of two edges and esp. of edges of fabric sewn together **2** : a layer of mineral matter **3** : WRINKLE

[2]**seam** vb **1** : to join by or as if by sewing **2** : to mark with lines suggesting seams

sea·man \'sē-mən\ n **1** ♦ : one who assists in the handling of ships : MARINER **2** : an enlisted person in the navy ranking next below a petty officer third class

   ♦ gob, jack, jack-tar, mariner, sailor, swab, tar

seaman apprentice n : an enlisted person in the navy ranking next below a seaman

seaman recruit n : an enlisted person of the lowest rank in the navy

sea·man·ship \'sē-mən-ˌship\ n : the art or skill of handling a ship

seam·less \'sēm-ləs\ adj : having no flaws or interruptions ⟨a ~ transition⟩ — **seam·less·ly** adv

sea·mount \'sē-ˌmaunt\ n : an underwater mountain

seam·stress \'sēm-strəs\ n : a woman whose occupation is sewing

seamy \'sē-mē\ adj **seam·i·er; -est** **1** : UNPLEASANT **2** : DEGRADED, SORDID

sé·ance \'sā-ˌäns\ n : a meeting to receive communications from spirits

sea·plane \'sē-ˌplān\ n : an airplane that can take off from and land on water

sea·port \-ˌpōrt\ n : a port for oceangoing ships

sear \'sir\ vb **1** ♦ : to make withered and dry **2 a** ♦ : to burn or scorch esp. on the surface **b** : BRAND — **sear** n

   ♦ [1] dehydrate, dry, parch ♦ [2a] char, scorch, singe

[1]**search** \'sərch\ vb **1** ♦ : to look through in trying to find something **2** ♦ : to uncover, find, or come to know by inquiry or scrutiny : SEEK **3** ♦ : subject to a penetrating investigation : PROBE — **search·er** n

   ♦ [1, 3] explore, hunt, probe, prospect ♦ usu **search for** or **search out** [2] cast about, forage, hunt, pursue, quest, seek
   ♦ [3] dig, dredge, hunt, rake, ransack, rifle, rummage, scour

[2]**search** n : the act of searching

search engine n : computer software or a website used to search data (as text or other websites) for specified information

search·light \-ˌlīt\ n : an apparatus for projecting a powerful beam of light; also : the light projected

sear·ing \'sir-iŋ\ adj : very sharp, harsh or intense ⟨~ pain⟩ ⟨a ~ review⟩

sea scallop n : a large scallop of the Atlantic coast of No. America that is harvested for food

sea·scape \'sē-ˌskāp\ n **1** : a view of the sea **2** : a picture representing a scene at or of the sea

sea·shell \'sē-ˌshel\ n : the shell of a marine animal and esp. a mollusk

sea·shore \-ˌshōr\ n : the shore of a sea

sea·sick \-ˌsik\ adj : nauseated by or as if by the motion of a ship — **sea·sick·ness** n

sea·side \'sē-ˌsīd\ n : SEASHORE

[1]**sea·son** \'sē-zən\ n **1** : one of the divisions of the year (as spring or summer) **2** : a period of the year associated with a particular activity, event, or holiday ⟨the Easter ~⟩ ⟨hunting ~⟩ — **sea·son·al** \-zə-nəl\ adj — **sea·son·al·ly** adv

[2]**season** vb **1** ♦ : to make pleasant to the taste by use of salt, pepper, or spices **2** : to make (as by aging or drying) suitable for use **3** ♦ : to accustom or habituate to something (as hardship) — **sea·son·er** n

   ♦ [1] flavor (or flavour), savor, spice ♦ [3] fortify, harden, steel, strengthen, toughen

sea·son·able \'sē-zə-nə-bəl\ adj : occurring at a good or proper time ⟨~ weather⟩ — **sea·son·ably** \-blē\ adv

seasonal affective disorder n : depression that recurs as the days grow shorter during the fall and winter

sea·soned adj **1** : made fit by use **2** ♦ : made skillful or wise through experience

   ♦ [2] accomplished, ace, adept, crack, experienced, expert, master, masterful, masterly, practiced, proficient, skilled, skillful, versed

sea·son·ing n ♦ : something that seasons

   ♦ flavor (or flavour), spice

[1]**seat** \'sēt\ n **1** : a chair, bench, or stool for sitting on **2** ♦ : a place which serves as a capital or center **3** ♦ : the part of the body that bears the weight in sitting

   ♦ [2] base, center (or centre), core, cynosure, eye, focus, heart, hub, mecca, nucleus ♦ [3] backside, bottom, butt, buttocks, posterior, rear, rump

[2]**seat** vb **1** ♦ : to place in or on a seat **2** : to provide seats for

   ♦ place, put, set down, sit

seat belt n : straps designed to hold a person in a seat

seat–of–the–pants adj : employing or based on personal experience, judgment, and effort rather than technological aids ⟨~ navigation⟩

sea turtle n : any of two families of marine turtles that have the feet modified into paddles

sea urchin n : any of numerous spiny marine echinoderms having thin brittle globular shells

sea·wall \'sē-ˌwòl\ n : an embankment to protect the shore from erosion

[1]**sea·ward** \'sē-wərd\ n : the direction or side away from land and toward the open sea

[2]**seaward** also **sea·wards** \-wərdz\ adv : toward the sea

³sea·ward *adj* **1 :** directed or situated toward the sea **2 :** coming from the sea

sea·wa·ter \'sē-ˌwȯ-tər, -ˌwä-\ *n* **:** water in or from the sea

sea·way \-ˌwā\ *n* **:** an inland waterway that admits ocean shipping

sea·weed \-ˌwēd\ *n* **:** a marine alga (as a kelp); *also* **:** a mass of marine algae

sea·wor·thy \-ˌwər-ṯẖē\ *adj* **:** fit for a sea voyage ⟨a ∼ ship⟩

se·ba·ceous \si-'bā-shəs\ *adj* **:** of, relating to, or secreting fatty material

sec *abbr* **1** second; secondary **2** secretary **3** section **4** according to

SEC *abbr* Securities and Exchange Commission

se·cede \si-'sēd\ *vb* **se·ced·ed; se·ced·ing :** to withdraw from an organized body and esp. from a political body

se·ces·sion \si-'se-shən\ *n* **:** the act of seceding — **se·ces·sion·ist** *n*

se·clude \si-'klüd\ *vb* **se·clud·ed; se·clud·ing ♦ :** to keep or shut away from others ⟨*secluded* herself in her room⟩

♦ cut off, insulate, isolate, segregate, separate, sequester

secluded *adj* **1 ♦ :** screened or hidden from view **2 :** living in seclusion

♦ cloistered, covert, isolated, quiet, remote, secret

se·clu·sion \si-'klü-zhən\ *n* **♦ :** the act of secluding **:** the state of being secluded — **se·clu·sive** \-siv\ *adj*

♦ insulation, isolation, segregation, sequestration, solitude

¹sec·ond \'se-kənd\ *adj* **1 :** being number two in a countable series **2 :** next after the first **3 :** ALTERNATE ⟨every ∼ year⟩ — **second** *or* **sec·ond·ly** *adv*

²second *n* **1 :** one that is second **2 :** one who assists another (as in a duel) **3 :** an inferior or flawed article (as of merchandise) **4 :** the second forward gear in a motor vehicle

³second *n* **1 :** the 60th part of a minute of time or angular measure **2 ♦ :** an instant of time

♦ flash, instant, jiffy, minute, moment, shake, trice, twinkle, twinkling, wink

⁴second *vb* **1 :** to encourage or give support to **2 :** to act as a second to **3 :** to support (a motion) by adding one's voice to that of a proposer

¹sec·ond·ary \'se-kən-ˌder-ē\ *adj* **1 ♦ :** second in rank, value, or occurrence **2 :** belonging to a second or later stage of development **3 :** coming after the primary or elementary ⟨∼ schools⟩

♦ inferior, mean, minor, second-rate

²secondary *n, pl* **-ar·ies :** the defensive backfield of a football team

secondary sex characteristic *n* **:** a physical characteristic that appears in members of one sex at puberty or in seasonal breeders at breeding season and is not directly concerned with reproduction

second fiddle *n* **:** one that plays a supporting or subservient role

sec·ond–guess \ˌse-kənd-'ges\ *vb* **1 :** to think out other strategies or explanations for after the event **2 :** to seek to anticipate or predict ⟨∼ the stock market⟩

sec·ond·hand \-'hand\ *adj* **1 :** not original **2 :** not new **:** USED ⟨∼ clothes⟩ **3 :** dealing in used goods

secondhand smoke *n* **:** tobacco smoke that is exhaled by smokers or is given off by burning tobacco and is inhaled by persons nearby

second lieutenant *n* **:** a commissioned officer (as in the army) ranking next below a first lieutenant

sec·ond–rate \ˌse-kənd-'rāt\ *adj* **♦ :** of second or inferior quality or value ⟨∼ hotels⟩

♦ common, fair, indifferent, mediocre, medium, middling, ordinary, passable, run-of-the-mill, so-so ♦ cheap, cut-rate, inferior, junky, lousy, mediocre, poor, sleazy

sec·ond–string \'se-kənd-'striŋ\ *adj* **:** being a substitute (as on a team)

se·cre·cy \'sē-krə-sē\ *n, pl* **-cies :** the habit or practice of being secretive **2 :** the condition of being hidden or concealed

¹se·cret \'sē-krət\ *adj* **1 :** kept from knowledge or view ⟨a ∼ staircase⟩ **2 ♦ :** working with hidden aims or methods ⟨COVERT, STEALTHY; *also* **:** engaged in detecting or spying ⟨a ∼ agent⟩ **3 ♦ :** kept from general knowledge — **se·cret·ly** *adv*

♦ [2] clandestine, covert, furtive, hugger-mugger, private, sneak, sneaky, stealthy, surreptitious, undercover, underground, underhanded *Ant* open, overt, public ♦ [3] confidential, hushed, inside, intimate, private

²secret *n* **1 ♦ :** something kept hidden or unexplained **:** MYSTERY **2 :** something kept from the knowledge of others

♦ conundrum, enigma, mystery, mystification, puzzle, puzzlement, riddle

sec·re·tar·i·at \ˌse-krə-'ter-ē-ət\ *n* **1 :** the office of a secretary **2 :** the secretarial staff in an office **3 :** the administrative department of a governmental organization ⟨the UN ∼⟩

sec·re·tary \'se-krə-ˌter-ē\ *n, pl* **-tar·ies 1 :** a person employed to handle records, correspondence, and routine work for another person **2 ♦ :** an officer of a corporation or business who is in charge of correspondence and records **3 :** an official at the head of a department of government **4 :** a writing desk — **sec·re·tar·i·al** \ˌse-krə-'ter-ē-əl\ *adj* — **sec·re·tary·ship** \'se-krə-ˌter-ē-ˌship\ *n*

♦ clerk, register, registrar, scribe

¹se·crete \si-'krēt\ *vb* **se·cret·ed; se·cret·ing :** to form and give off (a secretion)

²se·crete \si-'krēt, 'sē-krət\ *vb* **se·cret·ed; se·cret·ing ♦ :** to deposit or conceal in a hiding place **:** HIDE

♦ bury, cache, conceal, ensconce, hide

se·cre·tion \si-'krē-shən\ *n* **1 :** the process of secreting something **2 :** a product of glandular activity; *esp* **:** one (as a hormone) useful in the organism **3 ♦ :** the act of hiding something — **se·cre·to·ry** \'sē-krə-ˌtōr-ē\ *adj*

♦ concealment

se·cre·tive \'sē-krə-tiv, si-'krē-\ *adj* **♦ :** tending to keep secrets or to act secretly ⟨∼ about his past⟩ — **se·cre·tive·ly** *adv* — **se·cre·tive·ness** *n*

♦ close, closemouthed, dark, reticent, uncommunicative *Ant* communicative, open

¹sect \'sekt\ *n* **1 :** a dissenting religious body **2 :** a religious denomination **3 :** a group adhering to a distinctive doctrine or to a leader **4 ♦ :** an opinionated faction (as of a party)

♦ bloc, body, coalition, combination, combine, faction, party, set, side, wing

²sect *abbr* section; sectional

¹sec·tar·i·an \sek-'ter-ē-ən\ *adj* **1 :** of or relating to a sect or sectarian **2 ♦ :** limited in character or scope — **sec·tar·i·an·ism** *n*

♦ insular, little, narrow, parochial, petty, provincial, small

²sectarian *n* **1 :** an adherent of a sect **2 :** a narrow or bigoted person

¹sec·tion \'sek-shən\ *n* **1 ♦ :** a part cut off or separated **2 ♦ :** a distinct part (as of a territorial or political area, community, or group of people) **3 :** the appearance that a thing has or would have if cut straight through

♦ [1] member, part, partition, portion, segment ♦ [2] district, neighborhood (*or* neighbourhood), quarter

²section *vb* **1 :** to separate or become separated into sections ⟨∼ an orange⟩ **2 :** to represent in sections

sec·tion·al \'sek-shə-nəl\ *adj* **1 :** of, relating to, or characteristic of a section **2 :** local or regional rather than general in character **3 :** divided into sections — **sec·tion·al·ism** *n*

sec·tor \'sek-tər\ *n* **1 :** a part of a circle between two radii **2 :** an area assigned to a military leader to defend **3 :** a subdivision of society

sec·u·lar \'se-kyə-lər\ *adj* **1 ♦ :** not sacred or ecclesiastical **2 :** not bound by monastic vows ⟨a ∼ priest⟩

♦ nonreligious, profane, temporal

sec·u·lar·ise *chiefly Brit var of* SECULARIZE

sec·u·lar·ism \'se-kyə-lə-ˌri-zəm\ *n* **:** indifference to or exclusion of religion — **sec·u·lar·ist** \-rist\ *n* — **secularist** *also* **sec·u·lar·is·tic** \ˌse-kyə-lə-'ris-tik\ *adj*

sec·u·lar·ize \'se-kyə-lə-ˌrīz\ *vb* **-ized; -iz·ing 1 :** to make secular **2 :** to transfer from ecclesiastical to civil or lay use, possession, or control — **sec·u·lar·i·za·tion** \ˌse-kyə-lə-rə-'zā-shən\ *n* — **sec·u·lar·iz·er** \'se-kyə-lə-ˌrī-zər\ *n*

¹se·cure \si-'kyur\ *adj* **se·cur·er; -est 1 :** easy in mind **:** free from fear **2 ♦ :** free from danger or risk of loss **:** SAFE **3 ♦ :** characterized by certainty or security — **se·cure·ly** *adv*

♦ [2] all right, alright, safe ♦ [3] assured, confident, self-assured, self-confident

²secure *vb* **se·cured; se·cur·ing 1 ♦ :** to make safe **:** GUARD **2 :** to assure payment of by giving a pledge or collateral **3 ♦ :** to fasten safely ⟨∼ a door⟩ **4 ♦ :** to get secure usu. lasting possession or control of **:** ACQUIRE ⟨∼ permission⟩

♦ [1] cover, defend, guard, protect, safeguard, screen, shield, ward ♦ [1] assure, cinch, ensure, guarantee, guaranty, insure

♦ [3] anchor, catch, clamp, fasten, fix, hitch, moor, set ♦ [4] acquire, attain, capture, carry, draw, earn, gain, garner, get, land, make, obtain, procure, realize, win

se·cu·ri·ty \si-'kyùr-ə-tē\ *n, pl* **-ties** **1 :** SAFETY **2 :** freedom from worry **3** ♦ **:** something given as pledge of payment ⟨a ∼ deposit⟩ **4** *pl* ♦ **:** bond or stock certificates **5** ♦ **:** something that secures **:** PROTECTION

♦ [3] gage, guarantee, guaranty, pawn, pledge ♦ [5] aegis, armor (*or* armour), cover, defense (*or* defence), guard, protection, safeguard, screen, shield, wall, ward

secy *abbr* secretary

se·dan \si-'dan\ *n* **1 :** a covered chair borne on poles by two people **2 :** an automobile seating four or more people and usu. having a permanent top

1se·date \si-'dāt\ *adj* **:** quiet and dignified in behavior — **se·date·ly** *adv*

2sedate *vb* **se·dat·ed; se·dat·ing :** to dose with sedatives — **se·da·tion** \si-'dā-shən\ *n*

1sed·a·tive \'se-də-tiv\ *adj* ♦ **:** serving or tending to relieve tension

♦ comforting, dreamy, narcotic, soothing

2sedative *n* **:** a sedative drug

sed·en·tary \'sed-ᵊn-ˌter-ē\ *adj* **:** characterized by or requiring much sitting

sedge \'sej\ *n* **:** any of a family of plants esp. of marshy areas that differ from the related grasses esp. in having solid stems — **sedgy** \'se-jē\ *adj*

sed·i·ment \'se-də-mənt\ *n* **1** ♦ **:** the material that settles to the bottom of a liquid **2 :** material (as stones and sand) deposited by water, wind, or a glacier — **sed·i·men·ta·ry** \ˌse-də-'men-tə-rē\ *adj* — **sed·i·men·ta·tion** \-mən-'tā-shən, -ˌmen-\ *n*

♦ deposit, dregs, grounds, lees, precipitate

se·di·tion \si-'di-shən\ *n* **:** the causing of discontent, insurrection, or resistance against a government — **se·di·tious** \-shəs\ *adj*

se·duce \si-'düs, -'dyüs\ *vb* **se·duced; se·duc·ing** **1 :** to persuade to disobedience or disloyalty **2** ♦ **:** to lead astray **3 :** to entice to sexual intercourse — **se·duc·er** *n*

♦ allure, beguile, decoy, entice, lead on, lure, tempt

se·duc·tion \si-'dək-shən\ *n* **1 :** the act of seducing **2** ♦ **:** something that seduces **3 :** something that attracts or charms

♦ enticement, lure, solicitation, temptation

se·duc·tive \-tiv\ *adj* ♦ **:** tending to seduce **:** having alluring or tempting qualities

♦ alluring, attractive, captivating, charming, elfin, engaging, fascinating, fetching, glamorous, magnetic

sed·u·lous \'se-jə-ləs\ *adj* ♦ **:** diligent in application or pursuit

♦ active, assiduous, busy, diligent, engaged, laborious, occupied, working

1see \'sē\ *vb* **saw** \'sô\; **seen** \'sēn\; **see·ing** **1** ♦ **:** to perceive by the eye; *also* **:** to have the power of sight **2** ♦ **:** to have experience of **3** ♦ **:** to perceive the meaning or importance of; *also* **:** to be aware of **4 :** to make sure ⟨∼ that order is kept⟩ **5 :** to meet with **6 :** to keep company with esp. in dating **7 :** ACCOMPANY, ESCORT

♦ [1] behold, descry, discern, distinguish, espy, eye, look, note, notice, observe, perceive, regard, remark, sight, spy, view, witness ♦ [2] endure, experience, feel, have, know, suffer, sustain, taste, undergo ♦ [3] ascertain, catch on, discover, find out, hear, learn, realize ♦ [3] appreciate, apprehend, catch, catch on (to), comprehend, get, grasp, make, make out, perceive, seize, understand

2see *n* **:** the authority or jurisdiction of a bishop

1seed \'sēd\ *n, pl* **seed** *or* **seeds** **1 :** the grains of plants used for sowing **2 :** a ripened ovule of a flowering plant that may develop into a new plant; *also* **:** a plant structure (as a spore or small dry fruit) capable of producing a new plant **3** ♦ **:** offspring of animals or plants **4 :** SOURCE, ORIGIN — **seed·less** *adj* — **go to seed** *or* **run to seed** **1 :** to develop seed **2 :** DECAY

♦ issue, offspring, posterity, progeny, spawn

2seed *vb* **1** ♦ **:** to sprinkle with seed **:** PLANT ⟨∼ land to grass⟩ **2** **:** to bear or shed seeds **3 :** to remove seeds from — **seed·er** *n*

♦ drill, plant, sow

seed·bed \-ˌbed\ *n* **:** soil or a bed of soil prepared for planting seed

seed·ling \'sēd-liŋ\ *n* **1 :** a young plant grown from seed **2 :** a young tree before it becomes a sapling

seed·time \'sēd-ˌtīm\ *n* **:** the season for sowing

seedy \'sē-dē\ *adj* **seed·i·er; -est** **1 :** containing or full of seeds **2** ♦ **:** inferior in condition or quality **:** SHABBY

♦ ragged, ratty, shabby, tattered, threadbare, worn-out

seek \'sēk\ *vb* **sought** \'sôt\; **seek·ing** **1** ♦ **:** to search for **2** ♦ **:** to try to reach or obtain **3** ♦ **:** to make an attempt

♦ [1] cast about, forage, hunt, pursue, quest, search (for *or* out) ♦ [2] ask, call, plead, quest, request, solicit, sue ♦ [3] assay, attempt, endeavor (*or* endeavour), essay, strive, try

seek·er *n* ♦ **:** one that seeks or is used in seeking

♦ applicant, aspirant, campaigner, candidate, contender, hopeful, prospect

seem \'sēm\ *vb* **1 :** to appear to the observation or understanding **2** ♦ **:** to be so in appearance **:** APPEAR

♦ act, appear, look, make, sound

seem·ing *adj* ♦ **:** outwardly apparent ⟨∼ indifference⟩

♦ apparent, assumed, evident, ostensible, reputed, supposed

seem·ing·ly *adv* ♦ **:** so far as can be seen or judged

♦ apparently, evidently, ostensibly, presumably, supposedly

seem·ly \'sēm-lē\ *adj* **seem·li·er; -est** **1** ♦ **:** conventionally proper **2 :** FIT

♦ correct, decent, decorous, genteel, nice, polite, proper, respectable

seep \'sēp\ *vb* ♦ **:** to flow or pass slowly through fine pores or cracks — **seep·age** \'sē-pij\ *n*

♦ bleed, exude, ooze, percolate, strain, sweat, weep

seer \'sir\ *n* ♦ **:** a person who foresees or predicts events **:** PROPHET

♦ augur, diviner, forecaster, fortune-teller, futurist, prognosticator, prophet, soothsayer

seer·suck·er \'sir-ˌsə-kər\ *n* **:** a light fabric of linen, cotton, or rayon usu. striped and slightly puckered

1see·saw \'sē-ˌsô\ *n* **1 :** a contest in which each side assumes then relinquishes the lead **2 :** a children's sport of riding up and down on the ends of a plank supported in the middle; *also* **:** the plank so used

2seesaw *vb* ♦ **:** to move backward and forward or up and down

♦ careen, lurch, pitch, rock, roll, sway, toss, wobble ♦ bob, bobble, jog, jounce, nod, pump

seethe \'sēth\ *vb* **seethed; seeth·ing** ♦ **:** to become violently agitated

♦ boil, burn, fume, rage, steam ♦ boil, churn, roil

seg·ment \'seg-mənt\ *n* **1** ♦ **:** a division of a thing **:** SECTION **2** **:** a part cut off from a geometrical figure (as a circle) by one or more points, lines, or planes — **seg·ment·ed** \-ˌmen-təd\ *adj*

♦ member, part, partition, portion, section

seg·re·gate \'se-gri-ˌgāt\ *vb* **-gat·ed; -gat·ing** **1** ♦ **:** to cut off from others **2 :** to separate esp. by races or ethnic groups

♦ cut off, insulate, isolate, seclude, separate, sequester

seg·re·ga·tion \ˌse-gri-'gā-shən\ *n* ♦ **:** the act or process of segregating **:** the state of being segregated

♦ insulation, isolation, seclusion, sequestration, solitude

seg·re·ga·tion·ist \ˌse-gri-'gā-shə-nist\ *n* **:** one who believes in or practices segregation esp. of races

1se·gue \'se-(ˌ)gwā, 'sā-\ *vb* **se·gued; se·gue·ing** **1 :** to proceed without pause from one musical number to another **2 :** to make a transition without interruption from one activity, topic, scene, or part to another

2se·gue *n* **:** the act or an instance of segueing

sei·gneur \sān-'yər\ *n, often cap* **:** a feudal lord

1seine \'sān\ *n* **:** a large weighted fishing net

2seine *vb* **seined; sein·ing :** to fish or catch with a seine — **sein·er** *n*

seis·mic \'sīz-mik, 'sīs-\ *adj* **:** of, relating to, resembling, or caused by an earthquake — **seis·mi·cal·ly** \-mik(ə-)lē\ *adv* — **seis·mic·i·ty** \sīz-'mi-sə-tē, sīs-\ *n*

seis·mo·gram \'sīz-mə-ˌgram, 'sīs-\ *n* **:** the record of an earth tremor made by a seismograph

seis·mo·graph \-ˌgraf\ *n* **:** an apparatus to measure and record seismic vibrations — **seis·mo·graph·ic** \ˌsīz-mə-'gra-fik, ˌsīs-\ *adj* — **seis·mog·ra·phy** \sīz-'mä-grə-fē, sīs-\ *n*

seis·mol·o·gy \sīz-'mä-lə-jē, sīs-\ *n* : a science that deals with earthquakes — **seis·mo·log·i·cal** \ˌsīz-mə-'lä-ji-kəl, ˌsīs-\ *adj* — **seis·mol·o·gist** \sīz-'mä-lə-jist, sīs-\ *n*

seis·mom·e·ter \sīz-'mä-mə-tər, sīs-\ *n* : a seismograph measuring the actual movement of the ground

seize \'sēz\ *vb* **seized; seiz·ing** **1** ♦ : to lay hold of or take possession of by force **2** ♦ : to take prisoner : ARREST **3** ♦ : to understand fully and distinctly **4** : to attack or overwhelm physically : AFFLICT ⟨*seized* by panic⟩

  ♦ [1] bag, capture, catch, collar, corral, get, grab, grapple, hook, land, nab, snare, trap ♦ [2] apprehend, arrest, nab, pick up, restrain ♦ [3] appreciate, apprehend, catch, catch on (to), comprehend, get, grasp, make, make out, perceive, see, understand

sei·zure \'sē-zhər\ *n* **1** : the act of seizing : the state of being seized **2** ♦ : a sudden attack (as of disease)

  ♦ attack, bout, case, fit, siege, spell

sel *abbr* select; selected; selection

sel·dom \'sel-dəm\ *adv* ♦ : in few instances : RARELY

  ♦ infrequently, little, rarely *Ant* frequently, often

¹se·lect \sə-'lekt\ *adj* **1** ♦ : chosen from a number or group by fitness or preference; *also* : of special value or excellence : CHOICE **2** : judicious or restrictive in choice : DISCRIMINATING

  ♦ choice, dainty, delicate, elegant, exquisite, rare ♦ chosen, elect

²select *vb* ♦ : to choose from a number or group : pick out

  ♦ choose, cull, elect, handpick, name, opt, pick, prefer, single, take

se·lect·ed *adj* : chosen by fitness or preference : SELECT; *specif* : of a higher grade or quality than the ordinary

se·lec·tion \sə-'lek-shən\ *n* **1** ♦ : the act or process of selecting **2** : something selected : CHOICE **3** : a natural or artificial process that tends to favor the survival and reproduction of individuals with certain traits but not those with others

  ♦ choice, election

se·lec·tive \sə-'lek-tiv\ *adj* ♦ : of or relating to selection : selecting or tending to select ⟨~ shoppers⟩

  ♦ choosy, particular, picky *Ant* nonselective

selective service *n* : a system for calling men up for military service : DRAFT

se·lect·man \si-'lekt-ˌman, -mən\ *n* : one of a board of officials elected in towns of most New England states to administer town affairs

se·le·ni·um \sə-'lē-nē-əm\ *n* : a photosensitive chemical element

self \'self\ *n, pl* **selves** \'selvz\ **1** : the essential person distinct from all other persons in identity **2** : a particular side of a person's character **3** : personal interest : SELFISHNESS

self- *comb form* **1** : oneself : itself **2** : of oneself or itself **3** : by oneself or itself; *also* : automatic **4** : to, for, or toward oneself

self–abasement
self–absorbed
self–absorption
self–acceptance
self–accusation
self–addressed
self–adjusting
self–administer
self–advancement
self–aggrandizement
self–aggrandizing
self–analysis
self–anointed
self–appointed
self–appraisal
self–asserting
self–assertion
self–awareness
self–betrayal
self–cleaning
self–closing
self–complacent
self–concern
self–condemned
self–confessed
self–congratulation
self–congratulatory
self–constituted
self–contempt

self–contradiction
self–contradictory
self–correcting
self–created
self–criticism
self–cultivation
self–deceit
self–deception
self–defeating
self–definition
self–delusion
self–denying
self–deprecating
self–deprecation
self–depreciation
self–described
self–despair
self–destruction
self–destructive
self–directed
self–distrust
self–doubt
self–educated
self–employed
self–employment
self–enhancement
self–examination
self–explaining
self–explanatory

self–expression
self–forgetful
self–giving
self–harm
self–hate
self–hypnosis
self–image
self–improvement
self–incrimination
self–induced
self–indulgent
self–inflicted
self–knowledge
self–limiting
self–love
self–lubricating
self–luminous
self–operating
self–perception
self–perpetuating
self–pity
self–portrait
self–preservation
self–proclaimed

self–professed
self–promotion
self–propelled
self–propelling
self–protection
self–realization
self–referential
self–reliance
self–renewing
self–respecting
self–revelation
self–rule
self–sacrifice
self–sacrificing
self–service
self–serving
self–starting
self–styled
self–sustaining
self–taught
self–torment
self–winding
self–worth

self–act·ing \'self-'ak-tiŋ\ *adj* ♦ : acting or capable of acting of or by itself

  ♦ automatic, laborsaving (*or* laboursaving), robotic

self–as·ser·tive \-ə-'sər-tiv\ *adj* ♦ : given to or characterized by a forceful claim or demand to being recognized or listened to

  ♦ aggressive, ambitious, assertive, enterprising, fierce, go-getting, high-pressure, militant

self–as·sur·ance \-ə-'shùr-ən(t)s\ *n* ♦ : confidence in oneself and in one's powers and abilities

  ♦ aplomb, assurance, confidence, self-confidence, self-esteem

self–as·sured \-ə-'shùrd\ *adj* ♦ : sure of oneself

  ♦ assured, confident, secure, self-confident

self–cen·tered \'self-'sen-tərd\ *adj* : concerned only with one's own self

self–cen·tered·ness *n* ♦ : the quality or state of being self-centered

  ♦ egoism, egotism, self-interest, selfishness, self-regard

self–com·posed \ˌself-kəm-'pōzd\ *adj* : having control over one's emotions

self–con·ceit \'self-kən-'sēt\ *n* ♦ : an exaggerated opinion of one's own qualities or abilities

  ♦ complacence, conceit, ego, egotism, pride, self-esteem, self-importance, self-satisfaction, smugness, vainglory, vanity

self–con·fi·dence \-'kän-fə-dən(t)s, -ˌden(t)s\ *n* ♦ : confidence in oneself and in one's powers and abilities

  ♦ aplomb, assurance, confidence, self-assurance, self-esteem

self–con·fi·dent \-'kän-fə-dənt, -ˌdent\ *adj* ♦ : confident of one's own strength or ability

  ♦ assured, confident, secure, self-assured

self–con·scious \'self-'kän-chəs\ *adj* : uncomfortably conscious of oneself as an object of observation by others — **self–con·scious·ly** *adv* — **self–con·scious·ness** *n*

self–con·tained \ˌself-kən-'tānd\ *adj* **1** : complete in itself **2** : showing self-control; *also* : reserved in manner

self–con·trol \'self-kən-'trōl\ *n* ♦ : restraint exercised over one's own impulses, emotions, or desires

  ♦ constraint, inhibition, repression, restraint, self-restraint, suppression ♦ self-discipline, self-government, self-possession, will, willpower

self–de·fense \'self-di-'fens\ *n* **1** : a plea of justification for the use of force or for homicide **2** : the act of defending oneself, one's property, or a close relative

self–de·ni·al \-di-'nī(-ə)l\ *n* ♦ : a restraint or limitation of one's own desires or interests

  ♦ abnegation, renouncement, renunciation, repudiation

self–de·struct \-di-'strəkt\ *vb* : to bring about one's own ruin or destruction

self–de·ter·mi·na·tion \-di-ˌtər-mə-'nā-shən\ *n* **1** ♦ : free choice of one's own acts or states without external compulsion **2** : determination by the people of a territorial unit of their own future political status

  ♦ accord, choice, free will, option, volition, will

self–dis·ci·pline \-'di-sə-plən\ *n* ♦ : correction or regulation of oneself for the sake of improvement

♦ restraint, self-control, self-government, self-possession, self-restraint, will, willpower

self–ef·fac·ing \-ə-'fā-siŋ\ *adj* : RETIRING, SHY
self–es·teem \-ə-'stēm\ *n* ♦ : a confidence and satisfaction in oneself; *also* : SELF-CONCEIT

♦ aplomb, assurance, confidence, self-assurance, self-confidence, self-respect, self-regard ♦ complacence, conceit, ego, egotism, pride, self-conceit, self-importance, self-satisfaction, smugness, vainglory, vanity

self–ev·i·dent \ˌself-'e-və-dənt\ *adj* : evident without proof or reasoning
self–fer·til·iza·tion \ˌself-ˌfərt-ᵊl-ə-'zā-shən\ *n* : fertilization of a plant or animal by its own pollen or sperm
self–ful·fill·ing \ˌself-fül-'fi-liŋ\ *adj* : becoming real or true by virtue of having been predicted or expected ⟨a ∼ prophecy⟩
self–gov·ern·ing \-'gə-vər-niŋ\ *adj* ♦ : having control or rule over oneself; *specif* : having self-government

♦ autonomous, free, independent, separate, sovereign ♦ democratic, popular, republican

self–gov·ern·ment \-'gə-vər(n)-mənt, -'gə-vᵊm-ənt\ *n* **1** ♦ : restraint exercised over one's own impulses, emotions, or desires **2** ♦ : government under the control and direction of the inhabitants of a political unit rather than by an outside authority

♦ [1] restraint, self-control, self-discipline, self-possession, self-restraint, will, willpower ♦ [2] autonomy, freedom, independence, liberty, sovereignty

self–help \'self-'help\ *n* : the process of bettering oneself or coping with one's problems without the aid of others — **self–help** *adj*
self–iden·ti·ty \-ī-'den-tə-tē, -'de-nə-tē\ *n* **1** : sameness of a thing with itself **2** ♦ : total character peculiar to and distinguishing an individual from others

♦ character, identity, individuality, personality

self·ie \'sel-fē\ *n* : a digital image of oneself taken by oneself ⟨post a ∼⟩
self–im·por·tance \'self-im-'pȯr-tᵊn(t)s, -tən(t)s\ *n* ♦ : an exaggerated estimate of one's own importance; *also* : arrogant or pompous behavior

♦ arrogance, haughtiness, loftiness, pretense, pretension, pretentiousness, superiority ♦ complacence, conceit, ego, egotism, pride, self-conceit, self-esteem, self-satisfaction, smugness, vainglory, vanity

self–important \-tᵊnt, -tənt\ *adj* ♦ : having or showing self-importance

♦ complacent, conceited, egotistic, important, overweening, pompous, prideful, proud, self-satisfied, smug, stuck-up, vain

self–imposed *adj* : imposed by oneself or itself : voluntarily assumed
self–in·dul·gence \-in-'dəl-jəns\ *n* : excessive or unrestrained gratification of one's own appetites, desires, or whims
self–in·ter·est \-'in-t(ə-)rəst; -'in-tə-ˌrest, -ˌtrest; -'in-tərst\ *n* ♦ : a concern for one's own advantage and well-being

♦ egoism, egotism, self-centeredness, self-regard, selfishness

self·ish \'sel-fish\ *adj* ♦ : concerned with one's own welfare excessively or without regard for others — **self·ish·ly** *adv*

♦ egocentric, egotistic, self-seeking

self·ish·ness *n* ♦ : the quality or state of being selfish

♦ egoism, egotism, self-centeredness, self-interest, self-regard

self·less \'self-ləs\ *adj* : UNSELFISH — **self·less·ness** *n*
self–made \'self-'mād\ *adj* : having achieved success or prominence by one's own efforts ⟨a ∼ millionaire⟩
self–pol·li·na·tion \ˌself-ˌpä-lə-'nā-shən\ *n* : pollination of a flower by its own pollen or sometimes by pollen from another flower on the same plant
self–pos·sessed \'self-pə-'zest *also* -'sest\ *adj* ♦ : having or showing self-possession : composed in mind or manner

♦ calm, collected, composed, cool, placid, serene, tranquil, undisturbed, unperturbed, unshaken, untroubled, unworried

self–pos·ses·sion \-pə-'ze-shən *also* -'se-\ *n* ♦ : control of one's emotions or reactions esp. when under stress

♦ aplomb, calmness, composure, coolness, equanimity, placidi-

ty, serenity, tranquility ♦ restraint, self-control, self-discipline, self-government, self-restraint, will, willpower

self–re·gard \-ri-'gärd\ *n* ♦ : regard for or consideration of oneself or one's own interests

♦ ego, pride, self-esteem, self-respect ♦ egoism, egotism, self-centeredness, self-interest, selfishness

self–reg·u·lat·ing \'self-'re-gyə-ˌlā-tiŋ\ *adj* : AUTOMATIC
self–re·li·ant \-ri-'lī-ənt\ *adj* ♦ : having confidence in and exercising one's own powers or judgment

♦ independent, self-sufficient, self-supporting

self–re·proach \-ri-'prōch\ *n* ♦ : the act or an instance of reproaching oneself

♦ contrition, guilt, penitence, remorse, repentance, shame

self–re·spect \-ri-'spekt\ *n* **1** : a proper respect for oneself as a human being **2** ♦ : regard for one's own standing or position

♦ ego, pride, self-esteem, self-regard

self–re·straint \-ri-'strānt\ *n* ♦ : restraint imposed on oneself

♦ constraint, inhibition, repression, restraint, self-control, suppression ♦ self-discipline, self-government, self-possession, will, willpower

self–righ·teous \-'rī-chəs\ *adj* : strongly convinced of one's own righteousness — **self–righ·teous·ly** *adv*
self·same \'self-ˌsām\ *adj* : precisely the same : IDENTICAL

♦ identical, same, very

self–sat·is·fac·tion \ˌself-ˌsa-təs-'fak-shən\ *n* ♦ : a usu. smug satisfaction with oneself or one's position or achievements

♦ complacence, conceit, ego, egotism, pride, self-conceit, self-esteem, self-importance, smugness, vainglory, vanity

self–sat·is·fied \'self-'sa-təs-ˌfīd\ *adj* ♦ : feeling or showing self-satisfaction

♦ complacent, conceited, egotistic, important, overweening, pompous, prideful, proud, self-important, smug, stuck-up, vain

self–seal·ing \'self-'sē-liŋ\ *adj* : capable of sealing itself (as after puncture)
self–seek·ing \'self-'sē-kiŋ\ *adj* ♦ : seeking only to further one's own interests — **self–seeking** *n*

♦ ambitious, go-getting ♦ egocentric, egotistic, selfish

self–start·er \-'stär-tər\ *n* ♦ : a person who has initiative

♦ go-getter, hustler, live wire, powerhouse

self–suf·fi·cien·cy \-sə-'fi-shən(t)-sē\ *n* : the quality or state of being self-sufficient
self–suf·fi·cient \-'fi-shənt\ *adj* ♦ : able to maintain oneself or itself without outside aid : capable of providing for one's own needs

♦ independent, self-reliant, self-supporting *Ant* dependent, reliant

self–sup·port·ing \-sə-'pȯr-tiŋ\ *adj* ♦ : meeting one's needs by one's own efforts or output

♦ independent, self-reliant, self-sufficient

self–will \'self-'wil\ *n* ♦ : stubborn or willful adherence to one's own desires or ideas : OBSTINACY

♦ hardheadedness, mulishness, obduracy, obstinacy, peevishness, pertinacity, stubbornness, tenacity

sell \'sel\ *vb* **sold** \'sōld\; **sell·ing 1** : to transfer (property) in return for money or something else of value **2** ♦ : to deal in as a business **3** : to achieve satisfactory sales ⟨cars are ∼ing well⟩ **4** ♦ : to have a specified price — usu. used with *at* or *for*

♦ [2] deal, market, merchandise, put up, retail, vend ♦ *usu* **sell for** [4] bring, cost, fetch, go

sell·er *n* ♦ : one that offers for sale

♦ dealer, vendor

sell out *vb* **1** : to dispose of entirely by sale; *esp* : to sell one's business **2** : BETRAY — **sell·out** \'sel-ˌaút\ *n*
selt·zer \'selt-sər\ *n* : artificially carbonated water
sel·vage *or* **sel·vedge** \'sel-vij\ *n* : the edge of a woven fabric so formed as to prevent raveling
selves *pl of* SELF
sem *abbr* **1** semicolon **2** seminar **3** seminary
se·man·tic \si-'man-tik\ *also* **se·man·ti·cal** \-ti-kəl\ *adj* : of or relating to meaning in language ⟨∼ change⟩

se·man·tics \si-'man-tiks\ *n sing or pl* : the study of meanings in language

sema·phore \'se-mə-ˌfōr\ *n* **1** : a visual signaling apparatus with movable arms **2** : signaling by handheld flags

sem·blance \'sem-bləns\ *n* **1** ♦ : outward and often deceptive appearance or show **2** : IMAGE, LIKENESS

♦ appearance, face, guise, name, show

se·men \'sē-mən\ *n* : a sticky whitish fluid of the male reproductive tract that contains the sperm

se·mes·ter \sə-'mes-tər\ *n* **1** : half a year **2** : one of the two terms into which many colleges divide the school year

semi \'se-ˌmī\ *n, pl* **sem·is** : SEMITRAILER

semi- \'se-mi, -ˌmī\ *prefix* **1** : precisely half of **2** : half in quantity or value; *also* : half of or occurring halfway through a specified period **3** : partly : incompletely **4** : partial : incomplete **5** : having some of the characteristics of

semiannual	semiofficial
semiarid	semipermanent
semicentennial	semipolitical
semicircle	semiprecious
semicircular	semiprivate
semicivilized	semiprofessional
semiclassical	semireligious
semiconscious	semiretired
semidivine	semiskilled
semiformal	semisoft
semigloss	semisolid
semi–independent	semisweet
semiliquid	semitransparent
semiliterate	semiweekly
semimonthly	semiyearly

semi·au·to·mat·ic \ˌse-mē-ˌȯ-tə-'ma-tik\ *adj, of a firearm* : able to fire repeatedly but requiring release and another press of the trigger for each successive shot

semi·co·lon \'se-mi-ˌkō-lən\ *n* : a punctuation mark; used esp. to separate major sentence elements

semi·con·duc·tor \ˌse-mi-kən-'dək-tər\ *n* : a substance whose electrical conductivity is between that of a conductor and an insulator — **semi·con·duct·ing** *adj*

semi·dark·ness \-'därk-nəs\ *n* ♦ : partial darkness

♦ dusk, gloaming, gloom, murk, shade, shadows, twilight

¹**semi·fi·nal** \ˌse-mi-'fīn-ᵊl\ *adj* : being next to the last in an elimination tournament

²**semi·fi·nal** \'se-mi-ˌfīn-ᵊl\ *n* : a semifinal round or match — **semi·fi·nal·ist** \-ist\ *n*

sem·i·nal \'se-mən-ᵊl\ *adj* **1** : of, relating to, or consisting of seed or semen **2** : containing or contributing the seeds of later development : CREATIVE, ORIGINAL — **sem·i·nal·ly** *adv*

sem·i·nar \'se-mə-ˌnär\ *n* **1** : a course of study pursued by a group of advanced students doing original research under a professor **2** ♦ : a meeting for giving and discussing information : CONFERENCE

♦ assembly, conference, congress, convention, convocation, council, gathering, get-together, huddle, meeting ♦ colloquy, conference, council, forum, panel, parley, symposium

sem·i·nary \'se-mə-ˌner-ē\ *n, pl* **-nar·ies** : an educational institution; *esp* : one that gives theological training — **sem·i·nar·i·an** \ˌse-mə-'ner-ē-ən\ *n*

Sem·i·nole \'se-mə-ˌnōl\ *n, pl* **Seminoles** *or* **Seminole** : a member of an Indigenous people of Florida and Oklahoma

semi·per·me·able \ˌse-mi-'pər-mē-ə-bəl\ *adj* : partially but not freely or wholly permeable; *esp* : permeable to some usu. small molecules but not to other usu. larger particles ⟨a ∼ membrane⟩ — **semi·per·me·abil·i·ty** \-ˌpər-mē-ə-'bi-lə-tē\ *n*

Sem·ite \'se-ˌmīt\ *n* : a member of any of a group of peoples (as the Hebrews or Arabs) of southwestern Asia — **Se·mit·ic** \sə-'mi-tik\ *adj*

semi·trail·er \'se-mi-ˌtrā-lər, -ˌmī-\ *n* : a freight trailer that when attached is supported at its forward end by the truck tractor; *also* : a semitrailer with attached tractor

sem·o·li·na \ˌse-mə-'lē-nə\ *n* : the purified hard grains produced from the milling of wheat and used esp. for pasta

sen *abbr* **1** senate; senator **2** senior

sen·ate \'se-nət\ *n* : the second of two chambers of a legislature

sen·a·tor \'se-nə-tər\ *n* : a member of a senate — **sen·a·to·ri·al** \ˌse-nə-'tōr-ē-əl\ *adj*

send \'send\ *vb* **sent** \'sent\; **send·ing** **1** ♦ : to cause to go **2** : EMIT **3** : to propel or drive esp. with force **4** : to put or bring into a certain condition — **send·er** *n*

♦ consign, dispatch, pack, ship, transfer, transmit, transport *Ant* accept, receive

send–off \'send-ˌȯf\ *n* : a demonstration of goodwill and enthusiasm at the start of a new venture (as a trip)

send–up \'send-ˌəp\ *n* : PARODY, TAKEOFF

Sen·e·ca \'se-ni-kə\ *n, pl* **Seneca** *or* **Senecas** : a member of an Indigenous people of western New York; *also* : the language of the Seneca people

Sen·e·ga·lese \ˌse-ni-gə-'lēz, -'lēs\ *n, pl* **Senegalese** : a native or inhabitant of Senegal — **Senegalese** *adj*

se·nes·cence \si-'nes-ᵊns\ *n* : the state of being old; *also* : the process of becoming old — **se·nes·cent** \-ᵊnt\ *adj*

se·nile \'sē-ˌnīl, 'se-\ *adj* : OLD, AGED; *esp* : exhibiting a loss of cognitive abilities associated with old age — **se·nil·i·ty** \si-'ni-lə-tē\ *n*

¹**se·nior** \'sē-nyər\ *n* **1** ♦ : a person older or of higher rank than another **2** : a member of the graduating class of a high school or college

♦ better, elder, superior

²**senior** *adj* **1** ♦ : of earlier birth or greater age **2** : more advanced in dignity or rank **3** : belonging to the final year of a school or college course

♦ ancient, elderly, geriatric, old

senior airman *n* : an enlisted person in the airforce ranking next below a staff sergeant

senior chief petty officer *n* : a petty officer in the navy or coast guard ranking next below a master chief petty officer

senior citizen *n* ♦ : an elderly person; *esp* : one who has retired

♦ ancient, elder, golden-ager, oldster *Ant* youth, youngster

senior high school *n* : a school usu. including grades 10 to 12

se·nior·i·ty \sēn-'yȯr-ə-tē\ *n* **1** : the quality or state of being senior **2** : a privileged status owing to length of continuous service

senior master sergeant *n* : a noncommissioned officer in the air force ranking next below a chief master sergeant

sen·na \'se-nə\ *n* **1** : CASSIA 2; *esp* : one used medicinally **2** : the dried leaflets or pods of a cassia used as a purgative

sen·sa·tion \sen-'sā-shən\ *n* **1 a** : awareness (as of noise or heat) or a mental process (as seeing or hearing) due to stimulation of a sense organ **b** ♦ : an indefinite bodily feeling **2** ♦ : a condition of excitement; *also* : the thing that causes this condition

♦ [1b] feel, feeling, sense ♦ [2] craze, enthusiasm, fad, fashion, go, mode, rage, style, trend, vogue ♦ [2] caution, flash, marvel, miracle, phenomenon, portent, prodigy, wonder

sen·sa·tion·al \-shə-nəl\ *adj* **1** ♦ : of or relating to sensation or the senses **2** : arousing an intense and usu. superficial interest or emotional reaction **3** ♦ : exceedingly or unexpectedly excellent or great ⟨a ∼ talent⟩ — **sen·sa·tion·al·ly** *adv*

♦ [1] sensitive, sensory, sensuous ♦ [3] classic, excellent, fabulous, fine, grand, great, splendid, superb, superior, terrific, wonderful

sen·sa·tion·al·ise *chiefly Brit var of* SENSATIONALIZE

sen·sa·tion·al·ism \-nə-ˌli-zəm\ *n* : the use or effect of sensational subject matter or treatment — **sen·sa·tion·al·ist** \-nə-list\ *adj or n* — **sen·sa·tion·al·is·tic** \-ˌsā-shə-nə-'lis-tik\ *adj*

sen·sa·tion·al·ize \-nə-ˌlīz\ *vb* **-ized; -iz·ing** : to present in a sensational manner

¹**sense** \'sens\ *n* **1** ♦ : semantic content : MEANING **2** : the faculty of perceiving by means of sense organs; *also* : a bodily function or mechanism (as sight, hearing, or smell) involving the action and effect of a stimulus on a sense organ **3** ♦ : a particular sensation; *also* : a motivating or discerning awareness **4** ♦ : capacity for effective application of the powers of the mind as a basis for action or response **5** : OPINION ⟨the ∼ of the meeting⟩ — **sense·less·ly** *adv*

♦ [1] denotation, drift, import, intent, meaning, purport, significance, signification ♦ [3] feel, feeling, sensation ♦ [4] common sense, horse sense, wisdom, wit ♦ [4] logic, reason, reasoning

²**sense** *vb* **sensed; sens·ing** **1** ♦ : to be or become aware of ⟨∼ danger⟩; *also* : to perceive by the senses **2** : to detect (as radiation) automatically

♦ feel, perceive, scent, see, smell, taste

sense·less *adj* ♦ : destitute of, deficient in, or contrary to sense

♦ cold, unconscious ♦ empty, meaningless, pointless ♦ dumb, fatuous, foolish, mindless, silly, stupid, unintelligent, vacuous, witless

sense organ *n* : a bodily structure (as an eye or ear) that receives stimuli (as heat or light) which excite neurons to send information to the brain

sen·si·bil·i·ty \ˌsen-sə-'bi-lə-tē\ *n, pl* **-ties** : delicacy of feeling : SENSITIVITY

sen·si·ble \'sen-sə-bəl\ *adj* **1** ♦ : capable of being perceived by the senses or the mind; *also* : capable of receiving sense impressions **2** ♦ : emotionally aware and responsive : CONSCIOUS **3** ♦ : having, containing, or indicative of good sense or reason : REASONABLE ⟨a ∼ decision⟩ — **sen·si·bly** \-blē\ *adv*

  ♦ [1] appreciable, detectable, discernible, distinguishable, palpable, perceptible ♦ [2] alive, aware, cognizant, conscious, mindful, sentient, witting ♦ [3] good, hard, informed, just, levelheaded, logical, rational, reasonable, reasoned, sober, solid, valid, well-founded

sen·si·tive \'sen-sə-tiv\ *adj* **1** ♦ : subject to excitation by or responsive to stimuli **2** ♦ : having power of feeling **3** ♦ : of such a nature as to be easily affected; *also* : easily hurt or damaged **4** : TOUCHY ⟨a ∼ issue⟩

  ♦ [1] acute, delicate, keen, perceptive, sharp ♦ [3] delicate, fragile, frail, tender ♦ [3] demonstrative, emotional, feeling, intense, passionate, sentimental, soulful

sen·si·tive·ness \'sen-sə-tiv-nəs\ *n* ♦ : the quality or state of being sensitive

  ♦ acuity, acuteness, delicacy, keenness, sensitivity

sensitive plant *n* : any of several mimosas with leaves that fold or droop when touched

sen·si·tiv·i·ty \ˌsen-sə-'ti-və-tē\ *n* ♦ : the ability to sense and to respond to slight impressions or differences

  ♦ acuity, acuteness, delicacy, keenness, sensitiveness

sen·si·tize \'sen-sə-ˌtīz\ *vb* **-tized; -tiz·ing** : to make or become sensitive or hypersensitive — **sen·si·ti·za·tion** \ˌsen-sə-tə-'zā-shən\ *n*

sen·sor \'sen-ˌsȯr, -sər\ *n* : a device that responds to a physical stimulus

sen·so·ry \'sen-sə-rē\ *adj* **1** ♦ : of or relating to sensation or the senses ⟨∼ perceptions⟩ **2** : AFFERENT

  ♦ sensational, sensitive, sensuous

sen·su·al \'sen-shə-wəl\ *adj* **1** : relating to gratification of the senses **2** ♦ : devoted to the pleasures of the senses — **sen·su·al·ist** *n* — **sen·su·al·i·ty** \ˌsen-shə-'wa-lə-tē\ *n* — **sen·su·al·ly** *adv*

  ♦ carnal, fleshly, luscious, sensuous, voluptuous

sen·su·ous \'sen-shə-wəs\ *adj* **1** ♦ : relating to the senses or to things that can be perceived by the senses **2** : producing or characterized by gratification of the senses : VOLUPTUOUS — **sen·su·ous·ly** *adv* — **sen·su·ous·ness** *n*

  ♦ sensational, sensitive, sensory

sent *past and past part of* SEND

¹**sen·tence** \'sent-ᵊns, -ᵊnz\ *n* **1** ♦ : the punishment set by a court **2** : a grammatically self-contained speech unit that expresses an assertion, a question, a command, a wish, or an exclamation

  ♦ doom, finding, holding, judgment (*or* judgement), ruling

²**sentence** *vb* **sen·tenced; sen·tenc·ing** : to impose a sentence on

  ♦ condemn, damn, doom

sen·ten·tious \sen-'ten-chəs\ *adj* : using wise sayings or proverbs; *also* : using pompous language — **sen·ten·tious·ly** *adv* — **sen·ten·tious·ness** *n*

sen·tient \'sen-chənt, -chē-ənt\ *adj* ♦ : capable of feeling : having perception

  ♦ alive, aware, cognizant, conscious, mindful, sensible, witting

sen·ti·ment \'sen-tə-mənt\ *n* **1** ♦ : an emotional state or reaction : FEELING; *also* : thought and judgment influenced by feeling **2** ♦ : a specific view or notion

  ♦ [1] emotion, feeling, passion ♦ [2] belief, conviction, eye, feeling, judgment (*or* judgement), mind, notion, opinion, persuasion, verdict, view

sen·ti·men·tal \ˌsen-tə-'ment-ᵊl\ *adj* **1** ♦ : influenced by tender feelings **2** ♦ : affecting the emotions — **sen·ti·men·tal·ist** *n* — **sen·ti·men·tal·ly** *adv*

  ♦ [1] demonstrative, emotional, feeling, intense, passionate, sensitive, soulful ♦ [2] corny, maudlin, mawkish, mushy, saccharine, sappy, schmaltzy

sen·ti·men·tal·ise *chiefly Brit var of* SENTIMENTALIZE

sen·ti·men·tal·ism *n* : the disposition to favor or indulge in sentimentality; *also* : an excessively sentimental conception or statement

sen·ti·men·tal·i·ty \-ˌmen-'ta-lə-tē, -mən-\ *n* **1** ♦ : the quality or state of being sentimental esp. to excess or in affectation **2** : a sentimental idea or its expression

  ♦ mawkishness, mush

sen·ti·men·tal·ize \-'ment-ᵊl-ˌīz\ *vb* **-ized; -iz·ing** **1** : to indulge in sentiment **2** : to look upon or imbue with sentiment — **sen·ti·men·tal·i·za·tion** \-ˌment-ᵊl-ə-'zā-shən\ *n*

sen·ti·nel \'sent-ᵊn-əl\ *n* : one that watches or guards : SENTRY

sen·try \'sen-trē\ *n, pl* **sentries** ♦ : person who keeps watch : GUARD; *esp* : a soldier standing guard at a point of passage (as a gate)

  ♦ custodian, guard, guardian, keeper, lookout, picket, warden, warder, watch, watchman

SEO *abbr* search engine optimization

sep *abbr* separate, separated

Sep *abbr* September

SEP *abbr* simplified employee pension

se·pal \'sē-pəl, 'se-\ *n* : one of the modified leaves comprising a flower calyx

sep·a·ra·ble \'se-pə-rə-bəl\ *adj* : capable of being separated

¹**sep·a·rate** \'se-pə-ˌrāt\ *vb* **-rat·ed; -rat·ing** **1** ♦ : to set or keep apart : DISCONNECT **2** : to keep apart by something intervening **3** : to cease to be together : PART ⟨the couple decided to ∼⟩ **4** ♦ : to make a distinction between; *also* : to put in a certain place or rank according to kind, class, or nature **5** ♦ : to go in different directions

  ♦ [1] break up, disconnect, disjoint, dissever, dissociate, disunite, divide, divorce, part, resolve, sever, split, sunder, unyoke *Ant* join, link, unify, unite ♦ [1] cut off, insulate, isolate, seclude, segregate, sequester ♦ [4] differentiate, discern, discriminate, distinguish ♦ [4] assort, break down, categorize, class, classify, grade, group, peg, place, range, rank, sort ♦ [5] branch, diverge, divide, fork *Ant* converge, join

²**sep·a·rate** \'se-prət, -pə-rət\ *adj* **1** : not connected **2** : divided from each other **3** : SINGLE, PARTICULAR ⟨the ∼ pieces of the puzzle⟩ **4** ♦ : existing by itself **5** ♦ : not shared with another — **sep·a·rate·ly** *adv*

  ♦ [4] detached, disconnected, discrete, freestanding, single, unattached, unconnected *Ant* attached, connected, joined ♦ [5] different, individual, respective *Ant* same

³**sep·a·rate** *n* : an article of dress designed to be worn interchangeably with others to form various combinations

sep·a·ra·tion \ˌse-pə-'rā-shən\ *n* **1** ♦ : the act or process of separating : the state of being separated **2** ♦ : a point, line, means, or area of division **3** : a formal separating of a married couple by agreement but without divorce

  ♦ [1] breakup, dissolution, division, partition, schism, split *Ant* unification, union ♦ [1] demarcation, discrimination, distinction ♦ [2] breach, break, discontinuity, gap, gulf, hole, interval, opening, rent, rift

sep·a·rat·ist \'se-prə-tist, 'se-pə-ˌrā-\ *n* : an advocate of separation (as from a political body) — **sep·a·rat·ism** \'se-prə-ˌti-zəm\ *n*

sep·a·ra·tive \'se-pə-ˌrā-tiv, 'se-prə-tiv\ *adj* : tending toward, causing, or expressing separation ⟨∼ influences⟩

sep·a·ra·tor \'se-pə-ˌrā-tər\ *n* : one that separates; *esp* : a device for separating cream from milk

se·pia \'sē-pē-ə\ *n* : a brownish gray to dark brown color

sep·sis \'sep-səs\ *n, pl* **sep·ses** \'sep-ˌsēz\ : a toxic condition due to spread of bacteria or their toxic products in the body

Sept *abbr* September

Sep·tem·ber \sep-'tem-bər\ *n* : the 9th month of the year having 30 days

sep·tic \'sep-tik\ *adj* **1** : PUTREFACTIVE **2** : relating to or involving sepsis **3** : of, relating to, or used for sewage treatment and disposal

sep·ti·ce·mia \ˌsep-tə-'sē-mē-ə\ *n* : BLOOD POISONING

septic tank *n* : a tank in which sewage is disintegrated by bacteria

sep·tu·a·ge·nar·i·an \sep-ˌtü-ə-jə-'ner-ē-ən, -ˌtyü-\ *n* : a person whose age is in the seventies — **septuagenarian** *adj*

Sep·tu·a·gint \sep-'tü-ə-jənt, -'tyü-\ *n* : a Greek version of the Old Testament prepared in the 3d and 2d centuries B.C. by Jewish scholars

sep·tum \'sep-təm\ *n, pl* **sep·ta** \-tə\ : a dividing wall or membrane esp. between bodily spaces or masses of soft tissue

se·pul·chral \sə-'pəl-krəl\ *adj* **1** : relating to burial or the grave **2** ♦ : suited to or suggestive of a sepulchre : GLOOMY

♦ bleak, dark, dismal, dreary, gloomy, gray (*or* grey), somber (*or* sombre), wretched

¹**sep·ul·chre** *or* **sep·ul·cher** \'se-pəl-kər\ *n* : a burial vault : TOMB

²**sepulchre** *or* **sepulcher** *vb* **-chred** *or* **-chered; -chring** *or* **-cher·ing** : BURY, ENTOMB

sep·ul·ture \'se-pəl-ˌchùr\ *n* **1** ♦ : the act or process of burying : BURIAL **2** : SEPULCHRE

♦ burial, entombment, interment

se·quel \'sē-kwəl\ *n* **1** : logical consequence **2** : a literary or cinematic work continuing a story begun in a preceding one

se·quence \'sē-kwəns\ *n* **1** ♦ : a continuous or connected series **2** ♦ : chronological order of events **3** : something produced by a cause or necessarily following from a set of conditions : RESULT, SEQUEL — **se·quen·tial·ly** *adv*

♦ [1] chain, progression, string, train ♦ [2] arrangement, array, disposal, disposition, distribution, order, setup

se·quent \'sē-kwənt\ *adj* **1** : SUCCEEDING, CONSECUTIVE **2** : RESULTANT

se·quen·tial \si-'kwen-chəl\ *adj* ♦ : of, relating to, or arranged in a sequence

♦ consecutive, successive

se·ques·ter \si-'kwes-tər\ *vb* **1** ♦ : to set apart : SEGREGATE **2** : to place (property) in custody esp. in sequestration

♦ cut off, insulate, isolate, seclude, segregate, separate

se·ques·trate \'sē-kwəs-ˌtrāt, si-'kwes-\ *vb* **-trat·ed; -trat·ing** : SEQUESTER

se·ques·tra·tion \ˌsē-kwəs-'trā-shən, ˌse-\ *n* **1** ♦ : the act of sequestering : the state of being sequestered **2** : a deposit whereby a neutral depositary agrees to hold property in litigation and to restore it to the party to whom it is adjudged to belong

♦ insulation, isolation, seclusion, segregation, solitude

se·quin \'sē-kwən\ *n* **1** : an old gold coin of Turkey and Italy **2** : a small metal or plastic plate used for ornamentation esp. on clothing — **se·quined** *or* **se·quinned** \-kwənd\ *adj*

se·quoia \si-'kwòi-ə\ *n* : either of two huge California coniferous trees

ser *abbr* **1** serial **2** series **3** service

sera *pl of* SERUM

se·ra·glio \sə-'ral-yō\ *n, pl* **-glios** : HAREM

se·ra·pe \sə-'rä-pē\ *n* : a colorful woolen shawl worn over the shoulders esp. by Mexican men

ser·aph \'ser-əf\ *n, pl* **ser·a·phim** \-ə-ˌfim, -ˌfēm\ *or* **seraphs** : one of the 6-winged angels standing in the presence of God

ser·a·phim \'ser-ə-ˌfim, -ˌfēm\ *n pl* **1** : the highest order of angels **2** *sing, pl* **seraphim** : SERAPH — **se·raph·ic** \sə-'ra-fik\ *adj*

Serb \'sərb\ *n* : a native or inhabitant of Serbia

Ser·bi·an \'sər-bē-ən\ *n* **1** : SERB **2** : a south Slavic language spoken by the Serbian people — **Serbian** *adj*

Ser·bo–Cro·a·tian \ˌsər-(ˌ)bō-krō-'ā-shən\ *n* : the Serbian and Croatian languages together with the Slavic speech of Bosnia, Herzegovina, and Montenegro taken as a single language with regional variants

sere \'sir\ *adj* ♦ : being dried and withered : DRY

♦ arid, dry, thirsty

¹**ser·e·nade** \ˌser-ə-'nād\ *n* : music sung or played as a compliment esp. outdoors at night for a woman being courted

²**serenade** *vb* **-nad·ed; -nad·ing** : to entertain with or perform a serenade

ser·en·dip·i·ty \ˌser-ən-'di-pə-tē\ *n* : the gift of finding valuable or agreeable things not sought for — **ser·en·dip·i·tous** \-təs\ *adj*

se·rene \sə-'rēn\ *adj* **1** ♦ : clear and free of storms or unpleasant change ⟨~ skies⟩ **2** ♦ : marked by or suggestive of utter calm and unruffled repose or quiet — **se·rene·ly** *adv*

♦ [1, 2] calm, halcyon, hushed, peaceful, placid, quiet, still, tranquil, untroubled ♦ [2] calm, collected, composed, cool, self-possessed, undisturbed, unperturbed, unshaken, unworried

se·ren·i·ty \sə-'re-nə-tē\ *n* ♦ : the quality or state of being serene

♦ calm, calmness, hush, peace, placidity, quiet, quietness, repose, still, stillness, tranquility ♦ aplomb, composure, coolness, equanimity, self-possession

serf \'sərf\ *n* : a member of a servile class bound to the land and subject to the will of the landowner — **serf·dom** \-dəm\ *n*

serge \'sərj\ *n* : a twilled woolen cloth

ser·geant \'sär-jənt\ *n* **1** : a noncommissioned officer (as in the army) ranking next below a staff sergeant **2** : an officer in a police force

sergeant at arms : an officer of an organization who preserves order and executes commands

sergeant first class *n* : a noncommissioned officer in the army ranking next below a master sergeant

sergeant major *n, pl* **sergeants major** *or* **sergeant majors** **1** : a noncommissioned officer in the army or marine corps serving as chief administrative assistant in a headquarters **2** : a noncommissioned officer in the marine corps ranking above a first sergeant

¹**se·ri·al** \'sir-ē-əl\ *adj* **1** ♦ : appearing in successive parts or numbers ⟨a ~ story⟩ **2** : performing a series of similar acts over a period of time ⟨a ~ killer⟩; *also* : occurring in such a series — **se·ri·al·ly** *adv*

♦ episodic, periodic

²**serial** *n* : a serial story or other writing — **se·ri·al·ist** \-ə-list\ *n*

se·ries \'sir-ēz\ *n, pl* **series** : a number of things or events arranged in order and connected by being alike in some way

seri·graph \'ser-ə-ˌgraf\ *n* : an original silk-screen print — **se·rig·ra·pher** \sə-'ri-grə-fər\ *n* — **se·rig·ra·phy** \-fē\ *n*

se·ri·ous \'sir-ē-əs\ *adj* **1** ♦ : thoughtful or subdued in appearance or manner : SOBER **2** : requiring much thought or work **3** : EARNEST, DEVOTED **4** ♦ : having important or dangerous possible consequences **5** : excessive or impressive in quantity or degree ⟨making ~ money⟩ **6** ♦ : of or relating to a matter of importance — **se·ri·ous·ly** *adv*

♦ [1] earnest, grave, humorless (*or* humourless), severe, sober, solemn, staid, unsmiling, weighty *Ant* facetious, flip, flippant, humorous, jocular, joking, playful ♦ [4] dangerous, grave, grievous, hazardous, menacing, parlous, perilous, risky, unhealthy, unsafe, venturesome ♦ [6] grave, heavy, weighty *Ant* light

se·ri·ous·ness *n* ♦ : the quality or state of being serious

♦ earnestness, gravity, intentness, sobriety, solemnity

ser·mon \'sər-mən\ *n* **1** : a religious discourse esp. as part of a worship service **2** : a lecture on conduct or duty

ser·mon·ize \'sər-mə-ˌnīz\ *vb* **-ized; -iz·ing** **1** : to compose or deliver a sermon **2** : to preach to or on at length

se·rol·o·gy \sə-'rä-lə-jē\ *n* : a science dealing with serums and esp. their reactions and properties — **se·ro·log·i·cal** \ˌsir-ə-'lä-ji-kəl\ *or* **se·ro·log·ic** \-jik\ *adj*

se·ro·to·nin \ˌsir-ə-'tō-nən, ˌser-\ *n* : a neurotransmitter that is a powerful vasoconstrictor

se·rous \'sir-əs\ *adj* : of, relating to, resembling, or producing serum; *esp* : of thin watery constitution

ser·pent \'sər-pənt\ *n* : SNAKE

¹**ser·pen·tine** \'sər-pən-ˌtēn, -ˌtīn\ *adj* **1** : SLY, CRAFTY **2** ♦ : winding or turning one way and another

♦ crooked, devious, sinuous, tortuous, winding

²**ser·pen·tine** \-ˌtēn\ *n* : a dull-green mineral having a mottled appearance

ser·rate \'ser-ˌāt\ *adj* : having a saw-toothed edge ⟨a ~ leaf⟩

ser·ried \'ser-ēd\ *adj* ♦ : crowded or pressed together : DENSE

♦ close, compact, crowded, dense, packed, thick, tight

se·rum \'sir-əm\ *n, pl* **serums** *or* **se·ra** \-ə\ : the clear yellowish antibody-containing fluid that can be separated from blood when it clots; *also* : a preparation of animal serum containing specific antibodies and used to prevent or cure disease

serv *abbr* service

ser·vant \'sər-vənt\ *n* ♦ : one that serves others; *esp* : a person employed for domestic or personal work

♦ domestic, flunky, lackey, menial, retainer, steward

¹**serve** \'sərv\ *vb* **served; serv·ing** **1** : to work as a servant **2** : to render obedience and worship to (God) **3** : to comply with the commands or demands of **4** : to work through or perform a term of service (as in the army) **5** : PUT IN ⟨*served* five years in jail⟩ **6** ♦ : to be of use ⟨pine boughs *served* for a bed⟩ **7** ♦ : to provide services that benefit or help : BENEFIT **8** : to prove adequate or satisfactory for ⟨a pie that ~s eight people⟩ **9** : to make ready and pass out ⟨~ drinks⟩ **10** : to furnish or supply with something ⟨one power company *serving* the whole state⟩ **11** : to wait on ⟨~ a customer⟩ **12** ♦ : to treat or act

toward in a specified way ⟨~ed as her assistant⟩ **13** : to put the ball in play (as in tennis)

♦ [6] act, function, perform, work ♦ [7] avail, benefit, profit ♦ [12] act, be, deal, handle, treat, use

²serve *n* : the act of serving a ball (as in tennis)
serv•er *n* **1** ♦ : one that serves **2** : a computer in a network that is used to provide services (as access to files) to other computers in the network

♦ waiter, waitperson, waitress

¹ser•vice \'sər-vəs\ *n* **1** : the occupation of a servant **2** : HELP, BENEFIT **3** : a meeting for worship; *also* : a form followed in worship or in a ceremony ⟨burial ~⟩ **4** ♦ : the act, fact, or means of serving **5** ♦ : performance of official or professional duties **6** : SERVE **7** : a set of dishes or silverware **8 a** : a branch of public employment; *also* : the persons in it ⟨civil ~⟩ **b** ♦ : one of a nation's organized fighting forces (as the army, navy, or air force) — often used in pl. **9** : military or naval duty **10** ♦ : contribution to the welfare of others; *also* : disposal for use

♦ [4] boon, courtesy, favor (*or* favour), grace, indulgence, kindness, mercy, turn ♦ **services** [8b] armed forces, military, troops ♦ [10] account, avail, use, utility

²service *vb* **ser•viced; ser•vic•ing** : to do maintenance or repair work on or for
ser•vice•able \'sər-və-sə-bəl\ *adj* ♦ : prepared for service : USEFUL

♦ applicable, functional, practicable, practical, usable, useful, workable, working

ser•vice•man \'sər-vəs-ˌman, -mən\ *n* **1** ♦ : a man who is a member of the armed forces **2** : a man employed to repair or maintain equipment

♦ fighter, legionnaire, man-at-arms, regular, soldier, warrior

service mark *n* : a mark or device used to identify a service (as transportation or insurance) offered to customers
service station *n* : a retail station for servicing motor vehicles
ser•vice•wom•an \'sər-vəs-ˌwu̇-mən\ *n* : a woman who is a member of the armed forces
ser•vi•ette \ˌsər-vē-'et\ *n, chiefly Can and Brit* : a table napkin
ser•vile \'sər-vəl, -ˌvīl\ *adj* **1** : of or befitting a menial position **2** : lacking spirit or independence : SUBMISSIVE — **ser•vile•ly** *adv*
ser•vil•i•ty \ˌsər-'vi-lə-tē\ *n* : the quality or state of being submissive
serv•ing \'sər-viŋ\ *n* : HELPING
ser•vi•tor \'sər-və-tər\ *n* : a male servant
ser•vi•tude \'sər-və-ˌtüd, -ˌtyüd\ *n* ♦ : a condition in which one lacks liberty esp. to determine one's course of action or way of life and is forced to work for another person without pay

♦ bondage, enslavement, slavery, thrall, yoke

ser•vo \'sər-vō\ *n, pl* **servos** **1** : SERVOMOTOR **2** : SERVOMECHANISM
ser•vo•mech•a•nism \'sər-vō-ˌme-kə-ˌni-zəm\ *n* : a device for automatically correcting the performance of a mechanism
ser•vo•mo•tor \-ˌmō-tər\ *n* : a mechanism that supplements a primary control
ses•a•me \'se-sə-mē\ *n* : a widely cultivated annual herb of warm regions; *also* : its seeds that yield an edible oil (**sesame oil**) and are used in flavoring
ses•qui•cen•ten•ni•al \ˌses-kwi-sen-'te-nē-əl\ *n* : a 150th anniversary or its celebration — **sesquicentennial** *adj*
ses•qui•pe•da•lian \ˌses-kwə-pə-'dāl-yən\ *adj* **1** : having many syllables : LONG **2** : using long words
ses•sile \'se-ˌsīl, -səl\ *adj* : permanently attached and not free to move about
ses•sion \'se-shən\ *n* **1** : a meeting or series of meetings of a body (as a court or legislature) for the transaction of business **2** : a meeting or period devoted to a particular activity
¹set \'set\ *vb* **set; set•ting** **1** : to cause to sit **2** : PLACE **3** ♦ : to put into a desired position, adjustment, or condition **4** : to cause to be or do **5** ♦ : to fix or decide on as a time, limit, or regulation : SETTLE **6** : to fix in a frame **7** : to fix at a certain amount **8** : WAGER, STAKE **9** ♦ : to make or become fast or rigid **10** : to adapt (as words) to something (as music) **11** ♦ : to become fixed or firm or solid **12** : to be suitable : FIT **13** ♦ : to cover and warm eggs to hatch them : BROOD **14** ♦ : to have a certain direction **15** : to pass below the horizon **16** : to defeat in bridge — **set about** : to begin to do — **set forth** : to begin a trip — **set out** : to begin a trip or undertaking — **set sail** : to begin a voyage — **set upon** : to attack usu. with violence

♦ [3] deposit, dispose, fix, lay, place, position, put, set up, stick ♦ [3, 9] anchor, catch, clamp, fasten, fix, hitch, moor, secure ♦ [5] arrange, decide, fix, name, settle ♦ [11] concrete, congeal, firm, freeze, gel, harden, jell, solidify ♦ [13] brood, hatch, incubate, sit ♦ [14] aim, bend, cast, direct, head, level, train

²set *n* **1** : a setting or a being set **2** : DIRECTION, COURSE; *also* : TENDENCY **3** : FORM, BUILD **4** : the fit of something (as a coat) **5** : an artificial setting for the scene of a play or motion picture **6** : a group of tennis games in which one side wins at least six **7** ♦ : a group of persons or things of the same kind or having a common characteristic usu. classed together **8** : a collection of things and esp. of mathematical elements (as numbers or points) **9** : an electronic apparatus ⟨a television ~⟩

♦ bloc, body, coalition, combination, combine, faction, party, sect, side, wing ♦ circle, clan, clique, community, coterie, crowd ♦ array, assemblage, cluster, collection, group, package, parcel, suite

³set *adj* **1** ♦ : firmly resolved : INTENT **2** ♦ : fixed by authority or custom ⟨~ a price⟩ **3** ♦ : incapable of being moved **4** : PERSISTENT **5** ♦ : being in readiness

♦ [1] bound, decisive, determined, firm, intent, purposeful, resolute, single-minded ♦ [2] certain, determinate, final, firm, fixed, flat, frozen, hard, hard-and-fast, settled, stable ♦ [2] distinct, especial, express, precise, special, specific ♦ [3] fast, firm, frozen, secure, snug, tight ♦ [5] fit, go, ready

set•back \'set-ˌbak\ *n* ♦ : a temporary defeat : REVERSE

♦ lapse, reversal, reverse

set back *vb* **1** : HINDER, DELAY; *also* : REVERSE **2** : COST
set down *vb* **1** : to cause to sit down **2** ♦ : to put in writing

♦ jot, log, mark, note, put down, record, register

set off *vb* **1** : to start out on a course or trip **2** ♦ : to set in motion : cause to begin

♦ activate, actuate, crank, drive, move, propel, run, spark, start, touch off, trigger, turn on

set•screw \'set-ˌskrü\ *n* : a screw screwed through one part tightly upon or into another part to prevent relative movement
set•tee \se-'tē\ *n* ♦ : a bench or sofa with a back and arms

♦ couch, davenport, divan, lounge, sofa

set•ter \'se-tər\ *n* : a large long-coated hunting dog
set•ting \'se-tiŋ\ *n* **1** : the frame in which a gem is set **2** ♦ : the time, place, and circumstances in which something occurs or develops **3** : music written for a text (as of a poem) **4** : the eggs that a fowl sits on for hatching at one time

♦ atmosphere, climate, environment, environs, medium, milieu, surroundings

set•tle \'set-ᵊl\ *vb* **set•tled; set•tling** **1** ♦ : to place or become established in a place **2** : to establish in residence; *also* : COLONIZE **3** : to make compact **4** ♦ : to make or become quiet or orderly — often used with *down* **5** : to establish or secure permanently **6** : to direct one's efforts **7** ♦ : to fix by agreement : to reach an agreement on **8** : to conclude legally ⟨~ a lawsuit⟩ **9** ♦ : to fix or resolve conclusively ⟨~ the question⟩ **10** ♦ : to make a final disposition of ⟨~ an account⟩ **11** ♦ : to come to rest **12** : to sink gradually to a lower level **13** : to become clear by depositing sediment

♦ [1] ensconce, install, lodge, perch, roost ♦ [4] allay, calm, compose, quiet, soothe, still, tranquilize ♦ *usu* **settle down** [4] calm (down), cool (off *or* down), hush, quiet ♦ [7] arrange, decide, fix, set ♦ [9] adjudicate, arbitrate, decide, determine, judge, referee, rule, umpire ♦ [10] clear, discharge, foot, liquidate, pay, pay off, quit, recompense, spring, stand ♦ [11] alight, land, light, perch, roost

settled *adj* ♦ : unlikely to change or be changed : established or decided beyond dispute or doubt

♦ confirmed, deep-rooted, deep-seated, inveterate ♦ certain, determinate, final, firm, fixed, flat, frozen, hard, hard-and-fast, set, stable

set•tle•ment \'set-ᵊl-mənt\ *n* **1** : the act or process of settling **2** : BESTOWAL ⟨a marriage ~⟩ **3** : payment or adjustment of an account **4** : COLONY **5** : a small village **6** : an institution providing various community services esp. to large city populations **7** ♦ : adjustment of doubts and differences

♦ accord, agreement, bargain, compact, contract, convention, covenant, deal, pact, understanding

set•tler *n* ♦ : one that settles (as a new region)

♦ colonist, frontiersman, homesteader, pioneer ♦ emigrant, émigré, immigrant, migrant

set–to \'set-ˌtü\ *n, pl* **set–tos** : FIGHT

set–up \'set-ˌəp\ *n* **1** ♦ : the manner or act of arranging **2** : glass, ice, and nonalcoholic beverage for mixing served to patrons who supply their own liquor **3** : something (as a plot) that has been constructed or contrived; *also* : FRAME-UP

♦ arrangement, configuration, conformation, format, layout ♦ arrangement, array, disposal, disposition, distribution, order, sequence

set up *vb* **1** ♦ : to place in position; *also* : ASSEMBLE **2** : CAUSE **3** ♦ : to bring about the beginning of : FOUND ⟨*set up* a school⟩ **4** : FRAME **5** **5** ♦ : to place upright

♦ [1] assemble, deposit, dispose, fix, lay, place, position, put, set, stick ♦ [3] constitute, establish, found, inaugurate, initiate, innovate, institute, introduce, launch, pioneer, start ♦ [5] erect, pitch, put up, raise, rear

sev·en \'se-vən\ *n* **1** : one more than six **2** : the 7th in a set or series **3** : something having seven units — **seven** *adj or pron* — **sev·enth** \-vənth\ *adj or adv or n*

sev·en·teen \ˌse-vən-'tēn\ *n* : one more than 16 — **seventeen** *adj or pron* — **sev·en·teenth** \-'tēnth\ *adj or n*

seventeen–year locust *n* : a cicada of the U.S. that has in the North a life of 17 years and in the South of 13 years of which most is spent underground as a nymph and only a few weeks as a winged adult

sev·en·ty \'se-vən-tē\ *n, pl* **-ties** : seven times 10 — **sev·en·ti·eth** \-tē-əth\ *adj or n* — **seventy** *adj or pron*

sev·er \'se-vər\ *vb* **sev·ered; sev·er·ing** ♦ : to separate into individual parts : DIVIDE; *esp* : to separate by or as if by cutting — **sev·er·ance** \'sev-rəns, 'se-və-\ *n*

♦ break up, disconnect, disjoint, dissever, dissociate, disunite, divide, divorce, part, resolve, separate, split, sunder, unyoke

sev·er·al \'sev-rəl, 'se-və-\ *adj* **1** : INDIVIDUAL, DISTINCT ⟨federal union of the ~ states⟩ **2** : consisting of an indefinite number but yet not very many ⟨ate ~ cookies⟩ — **sev·er·al·ly** *adv*

severance pay *n* : extra pay given an employee upon termination of employment

se·vere \sə-'vir\ *adj* **se·ver·er; -est** **1** ♦ : marked by strictness or sternness : AUSTERE **2** ♦ : strict in discipline **3** : causing distress and esp. physical discomfort or pain ⟨~ weather⟩ ⟨a ~ wound⟩ **4** ♦ : hard to endure ⟨~ trials⟩ **5** : of a great degree : SERIOUS ⟨~ depression⟩

♦ [1, 2] austere, authoritarian, flinty, hard, harsh, heavy-handed, ramrod, rigid, rigorous, stern, strict *Ant* forbearing, indulgent, lax, lenient, tolerant ♦ [4] bitter, brutal, burdensome, cruel, excruciating, grievous, grim, hard, harsh, heavy, inhuman, murderous, onerous, oppressive, rough, rugged, stiff, tough, trying

se·vere·ly *adv* ♦ : in a severe manner : with severity

♦ hard, hardly, harshly, ill, oppressively, roughly, sternly, stiffly

se·ver·i·ty \sə-'ver-ə-tē\ *n* ♦ : quality or state of being severe

♦ hardness, harshness, inflexibility, rigidity, sternness, strictness *Ant* gentleness, flexibility, laxness, mildness

sew \'sō\ *vb* **sewed; sewn** \'sōn\ *or* **sewed; sew·ing** **1** : to unite or fasten by stitches **2** : to engage in sewing

sew·age \'sü-ij\ *n* : waste materials carried off by sewers

¹**sew·er** \'sō-ər\ *n* : one that sews

²**sew·er** \'sü-ər\ *n* : an artificial pipe or channel to carry off waste matter

sew·er·age \'sü-ə-rij\ *n* **1** : a system of sewers **2** : SEWAGE

sew·ing *n* **1** : the activity of one who sews **2** : material that has been or is to be sewed

sex \'seks\ *n* **1 a** : either of the two major forms of individuals that occur in many species and that are designated male or female esp. on the basis of their reproductive organs **b** : the sum of the structural, functional, and sometimes behavioral characteristics that distinguish males and females **c** : the state of being male or female **d** : males or females considered as a group ⟨the female ~⟩ **2 a** : sexual activity or behavior **b** : SEXUAL INTERCOURSE **3** : GENITALIA — **sexed** \'sekst\ *adj* — **sex·less** *adj*

sex·a·ge·nar·i·an \ˌsek-sə-jə-'ner-ē-ən\ *n* : a person whose age is in the sixties — **sexagenarian** *adj*

sex appeal *n* : personal appeal or physical attractiveness esp. for members of the opposite sex

sex cell *n* : an egg cell or sperm cell

sex chromosome *n* : one of usu. a pair of chromosomes that are usu. similar in one sex but different in the other sex and are concerned with the inheritance of sex

sex hormone *n* : a steroid hormone (as estrogen or testosterone)

that is produced esp. by the gonads or adrenal cortex and chiefly affects the growth or function of the reproductive organs

sex·ism \'sek-ˌsi-zəm\ *n* : prejudice or discrimination based on sex; *esp* : discrimination against women — **sex·ist** \'sek-sist\ *adj or n*

sex·ol·o·gy \sek-'sä-lə-jē\ *n* : the study of sex or of the interactions of the sexes — **sex·ol·o·gist** \-jist\ *n*

sex·pot \'seks-ˌpät\ *n* : a conspicuously sexy woman

sex symbol *n* : a usu. renowned person (as an entertainer) noted and admired for conspicuous attractiveness

sex·tant \'sek-stənt\ *n* : a navigational instrument for determining latitude

sex·tet \sek-'stet\ *n* **1** : a musical composition for six voices or instruments; *also* : the performers of such a composition **2** : a group or set of six

sext·ing \'sek-stiŋ\ *n* : the sending of sexually explicit messages or images by cell phone

sex·ton \'sek-stən\ *n* : one who takes care of church property

sex·u·al \'sek-shə-wəl\ *adj* : of, relating to, or involving sex or the sexes ⟨a ~ spore⟩ ⟨~ relations⟩ — **sex·u·al·i·ty** \ˌsek-shə-'wa-lə-tē\ *n* — **sex·u·al·ly** \'sek-shə-wə-lē\ *adv*

sexual intercourse *n* **1** ♦ : intercourse between a male and a female in which the penis is inserted into the vagina **2** : intercourse between individuals involving genital contact other than insertion of the penis into the vagina

♦ copulation, intercourse

sexually transmitted disease *n* : a disease (as syphilis, gonorrhea, AIDS, or the genital form of herpes simplex) that is caused by a microorganism or virus usu. or often transmitted by direct sexual contact

sexual relations *n pl* : physical sexual contact between individuals that involves the genitalia : SEXUAL INTERCOURSE

sexy \'sek-sē\ *adj* **sex·i·er; -est** ♦ : sexually suggestive or stimulating : EROTIC — **sex·i·ly** \-sə-lē\ *adv* — **sex·i·ness** \-sē-nəs\ *n*

♦ amatory, amorous, erotic

SF *abbr* **1** sacrifice fly **2** science fiction

SFC *abbr* sergeant first class

Sg *symbol* seaborgium

SG *abbr* **1** senior grade **2** sergeant **3** solicitor general **4** surgeon general

sgd *abbr* signed

Sgt *abbr* sergeant

Sgt Maj *abbr* sergeant major

sh *abbr* share

shab·by \'sha-bē\ *adj* **shab·bi·er; -est** **1** : dressed in worn clothes **2** ♦ : threadbare and faded from wear **3** : DESPICABLE, MEAN; *also* : UNFAIR ⟨~ treatment⟩ — **shab·bi·ly** \'sha-bə-lē\ *adv* — **shab·bi·ness** \-bē-nəs\ *n*

♦ dilapidated, grungy, mangy, mean, neglected, ragged, ratty, scruffy, seedy, tacky, tattered, threadbare

shack \'shak\ *n* ♦ : an often small and temporary dwelling of simple construction : HUT

♦ cabin, camp, hut, hutch, shanty

¹**shack·le** \'sha-kəl\ *n* **1** ♦ : something (as a manacle or fetter) that confines the legs or arms **2** ♦ : a check on free action made as if by fetters **3** : a device for making something fast or secure

♦ [1] band, bond, chain, fetter, irons, ligature, manacle ♦ [2] bar, block, encumbrance, hindrance, inhibition, obstacle

²**shackle** *vb* **shack·led; shack·ling** **1** ♦ : to bind or fasten with shackles **2** ♦ : to limit free movement or expression with restrictions or handicaps

♦ [1] bind, chain, enchain, fetter, handcuff, manacle, trammel ♦ [2] encumber, hamper, hinder, hold up, impede, inhibit, interfere with, obstruct, tie up

shad \'shad\ *n, pl* **shad** : any of several sea fishes related to the herrings that swim up rivers to spawn and include some important food fishes

¹**shade** \'shād\ *n* **1 a** : partial obscurity **b** *pl* ♦ : the shadows that gather as darkness comes on **2** : space sheltered from the light esp. of the sun **3** ♦ : a disembodied spirit : PHANTOM **4** : something that shelters from or intercepts light or heat; *also, pl* : SUNGLASSES **5** ♦ : a dark color or a variety of a color **6** : a small difference

♦ [1b] dark, darkness, dusk, gloaming, gloom, murk, night, semidarkness, shadows, twilight ♦ [3] apparition, bogey, ghost, phantasm, phantom, poltergeist, shadow, specter, spirit, spook, vision, wraith ◆ [5] cast, color (*or* colour), hue, tinge, tint, tone

²shade *vb* **shad·ed; shad·ing 1 :** to shelter from light and heat **2 :** DARKEN, OBSCURE **3 :** to mark with degrees of light or color **4 :** to show slight differences esp. in color or meaning
shaded *adj* ◆ **:** protected from heat or light (as with shade or shadow)

◆ shadowy, shady

shad·ing *n* **:** the color and lines representing darkness or shadow in a drawing or painting
¹shad·ow \'sha-dō\ *n* **1 a :** partial darkness in a space from which light rays are cut off **b** *pl* ◆ **:** a place or time of little or no light **2 :** SHELTER **3 :** shade cast upon a surface by something intercepting rays from a light ⟨the ∼ of a tree⟩ **4 :** something (as a specter) apparent to sense but with no substantial existence **:** PHANTOM **5 :** a shaded portion of a picture **6** ◆ **:** a small portion or degree **:** TRACE ⟨a ∼ of doubt⟩ **7 :** a source of gloom or unhappiness **8** ◆ **:** one (as a spy or detective) that shadows

◆ **shadows** [1b] dark, darkness, dusk, gloaming, gloom, murk, night, semidarkness, shade, twilight ◆ [6] relic, trace, vestige ◆ [8] detective, investigator, operative, sleuth, tail

²shadow *vb* **1** ◆ **:** to cast a shadow on **2 :** to represent faintly or vaguely **3** ◆ **:** to follow and watch closely

◆ [1] becloud, blacken, cloud, darken, dim, obscure, overcast, overshadow ◆ [3] chase, dog, follow, hound, pursue, tag, tail, trace, track, trail

shad·ow·box \'sha-dō-ˌbäks\ *vb* **:** to box with an imaginary opponent esp. for training
shad·owy *adj* **1** ◆ **:** faintly perceptible **2 :** being in or obscured by shadow; *also* **:** producing or providing shade

◆ bleary, dim, faint, foggy, fuzzy, hazy, indefinite, indistinct, indistinguishable, murky, nebulous, obscure, opaque, unclear, undefined, undetermined, vague

shady \'shā-dē\ *adj* **shad·i·er; -est 1** ◆ **:** affording shade **2** ◆ **:** of questionable honesty or reputation

◆ [1] shaded, shadowy *Ant* sunny ◆ [2] crooked, deceptive, dishonest, fast, fraudulent, sharp, shifty, underhanded ◆ [2] debatable, disputable, doubtful, dubious, equivocal, fishy, problematic, questionable, shaky, suspect, suspicious

¹shaft \'shaft\ *n, pl* **shafts 1 :** the long handle of a spear or lance **2 :** a thrusting or throwing weapon with long shaft and sharp head or blade **:** SPEAR, LANCE **3** *or pl* **shaves** \'shavz\ **:** POLE; *esp* **:** one of two poles between which a horse is hitched to pull a vehicle **4 :** something (as a column) long and slender **5 :** a bar to support a rotating piece or to transmit power by rotation **6 :** an inclined opening in the ground (as for finding or mining ore) **7 :** a vertical opening (as for an elevator) through the floors of a building **8 :** harsh or unfair treatment — usu. used with *the* **9 :** a sharply delineated beam of light shining through an opening
²shaft *vb* **1 :** to fit with a shaft **2 :** to treat unfairly or harshly
shag \'shag\ *n* **:** a shaggy tangled mass or covering (as of wool) **:** long coarse or matted fiber, nap, or pile
shag·gy \'sha-gē\ *adj* **shag·gi·er; -est 1** ◆ **:** rough with or as if with long hair or wool **2 :** tangled or rough in surface

◆ fleecy, furry, hairy, hirsute, rough, unshorn, woolly

shah \'shä, 'shò\ *n, often cap* **:** a sovereign of Iran
Shak *abbr* Shakespeare
¹shake \'shāk\ *vb* **shook** \'shùk\; **shak·en** \'shā-kən\; **shak·ing 1** ◆ **:** to move or cause to move jerkily or irregularly **2 :** BRANDISH, WAVE ⟨*shaking* his fist⟩ **3 :** to disturb emotionally ⟨*shaken* by her death⟩ **4 :** WEAKEN ⟨*shook* his faith⟩ **5 :** to bring or come into a certain position, condition, or arrangement by or as if by moving jerkily **6 :** to clasp (hands) in greeting or as a sign of goodwill or agreement **7** ◆ **:** to get away from **:** get rid of — **shak·able** *or* **shakeable** \'shā-kə-bəl\ *adj*

◆ [1] agitate, convulse, jolt, jounce, quake, quiver, shudder, vibrate, wobble ◆ [7] avoid, dodge, duck, elude, escape, eschew, evade, shirk, shun

²shake *n* **1 :** the act or a result of shaking **2 :** DEAL, TREATMENT ⟨a fair ∼⟩ **3** ◆ **:** a very brief period of time **4** *pl* ◆ **:** a condition of trembling or nervousness

◆ [3] flash, instant, jiffy, minute, moment, second, trice, twinkle, twinkling, wink ◆ **shakes** [4] jitters, shivers, willies

shake·down \'shāk-ˌdaùn\ *n* **1 :** an improvised bed **2 :** EXTORTION **3 :** a process or period of adjustment **4 :** a test (as of a new ship or airplane) under operating conditions

shake down *vb* **1 :** to take up temporary quarters **2 :** to occupy a makeshift bed **3 :** to become accustomed esp. to new surroundings or duties **4 :** to settle down **5 :** to give a shakedown test to **6 :** to obtain money from in a deceitful or illegal manner **7 :** to bring about a reduction of
shak·er \'shā-kər\ *n* **1 :** one that shakes ⟨pepper ∼⟩ **2** *cap* **:** a member of a religious sect founded in England in 1747
Shake·spear·ean *or* **Shake·spear·ian** \shāk-'spir-ē-ən\ *adj* **:** of, relating to, or having the characteristics of Shakespeare or his writings
shake·up \'shāk-ˌəp\ *n* **:** an extensive often drastic reorganization
shake up *vb* ◆ **:** to jar by or as if by a physical shock

◆ appall, bowl, floor, jolt, shock

shak·i·ness \'shā-kē-nəs\ *n* ◆ **:** the quality or state of being shaky

◆ insecurity, instability, precariousness, unsteadiness

shaky \'shā-kē\ *adj* **shak·i·er; -est 1** ◆ **:** lacking in authority or reliability **2** ◆ **:** characterized by shaking — **shak·i·ly** \'shā-kə-lē\ *adv*

◆ [1] debatable, disputable, doubtful, dubious, equivocal, fishy, problematic, questionable, shady, suspect, suspicious ◆ [2] tremulous, wobbly

shale \'shāl\ *n* **:** a finely layered rock formed from clay, mud, or silt
shall \shəl, 'shal\ *vb, past* **should** \shəd, 'shùd\ *pres sing & pl* **shall** ◆ — used as an auxiliary to express a command, what seems inevitable in the future, simple futurity, or determination

◆ have, must, need, ought, should

shal·lop \'sha-ləp\ *n* **:** a light open boat
shal·lot \shə-'lät, 'sha-lət\ *n* **1 :** a small clustered bulb that is used in seasoning and is produced by a perennial herb belonging to a subspecies of the onion; *also* **:** this herb **2 :** GREEN ONION
¹shal·low \'sha-lō\ *adj* **1 :** not deep **2 :** not intellectually profound
²shallow *n* **:** a shallow place in a body of water — usu. used in pl.
¹sham \'sham\ *n* **1 :** an ornamental covering for a pillow **2** ◆ **:** an imitation or counterfeit purporting to be genuine; *also* **:** cheap falseness **3 :** a person who shams

◆ counterfeit, fake, forgery, hoax, humbug, phony ◆ caricature, farce, joke, mockery, parody, travesty

²sham *vb* **shammed; sham·ming** ◆ **:** to act intentionally so as to give a false impression **:** PRETEND — **sham·mer** *n*

◆ affect, assume, counterfeit, fake, feign, pretend, profess, put on, simulate

³sham *adj* ◆ **:** not genuine **:** FALSE

◆ bogus, counterfeit, fake, false, inauthentic, phony, spurious, unauthentic ◆ affected, artificial, assumed, contrived, factitious, feigned, imitation, mechanical, mock, put-on, unnatural

sha·man \'shä-mən, 'shā-\ *n* **:** a priest or priestess who uses magic to cure the sick, to divine the hidden, and to control events
sham·ble \'sham-bəl\ *vb* **sham·bled; sham·bling** ◆ **:** to shuffle along — **sham·ble** *n*

◆ lumber, scuff, scuffle, shuffle, stumble, tramp, tromp

sham·bles \'sham-bəlz\ *n* **1 :** a scene of great slaughter **2** ◆ **:** a scene or state of great destruction or disorder; *also* **:** MESS

◆ chaos, confusion, disarray, disorder, disorganization, havoc, hell, jumble, mess, muddle

¹shame \'shām\ *n* **1** ◆ **:** a painful sense of having done something wrong, improper, or immodest **2** ◆ **:** condition of humiliating disgrace or disrepute **:** DISGRACE **3 :** a cause of feeling shame **4 :** something to be regretted ⟨it's a ∼ you'll miss the party⟩ — **shame·ful·ly** *adv*

◆ [1] contrition, guilt, penitence, remorse, repentance, self-reproach ◆ [2] discredit, disgrace, dishonor (*or* dishonour), disrepute, ignominy, infamy, odium, opprobrium, reproach

²shame *vb* **shamed; sham·ing 1** ◆ **:** to bring shame to **:** DISGRACE **2 :** to make ashamed

◆ abase, debase, degrade, demean, discredit, disgrace, dishonor (*or* dishonour), humble, humiliate, lower, smirch, take down

shame·faced \'shām-ˌfāst\ *adj* ◆ **:** showing shame **:** ASHAMED — **shame·faced·ly** \-ˌfā-səd-lē, -ˌfāst-lē\ *adv*

◆ ashamed, contrite, guilty, hangdog, penitent, remorseful, repentant

shame·ful \-fəl\ *adj* ♦ : bringing shame; *also* : arousing the feeling of shame

♦ discreditable, disgraceful, dishonorable (*or* dishonourable), disreputable, ignominious, infamous, notorious

shame·less *adj* ♦ : having no shame — **shame·less·ly** *adv*

♦ unabashed, unashamed, unblushing, unembarrassed

¹**sham·poo** \sham-'pü\ *vb* : to wash (as the hair) with soap and water or with a special preparation; *also* : to clean (as a rug) similarly

²**shampoo** *n, pl* **shampoos** **1** : the act or an instance of shampooing **2** : a preparation for use in shampooing

sham·rock \'sham-ˌräk\ *n* : a plant of folk legend with leaves composed of three leaflets that is associated with St. Patrick and Ireland

shang·hai \shaŋ-'hī\ *vb* **shang·haied; shang·hai·ing** : to force aboard a ship for service as a sailor; *also* : to trick or force into an undesirable position

Shan·gri–la \ˌshaŋ-gri-'lä\ *n* : a remote idyllic hideaway

shank \'shaŋk\ *n* **1** : the part of the leg between the knee and the human ankle or a corresponding part of a quadruped **2** : a cut of meat from the leg **3** : the narrow part of the sole of a shoe beneath the instep **4** : the part of a tool or instrument (as a key or anchor) connecting the functioning part with a part by which it is held or moved

shan·tung \ˌshan-'təŋ\ *n* : a fabric in plain weave having a slightly irregular surface

shan·ty \'shan-tē\ *n, pl* **shanties** ♦ : a small roughly built shelter or dwelling

♦ cabin, camp, hut, hutch, shack

¹**shape** \'shāp\ *vb* **shaped; shap·ing** **1** : to form esp. in a particular shape **2** : DESIGN **3** ♦ : to make fit for (as a particular use or purpose) : ADAPT, ADJUST **4** : REGULATE **5** ♦ : to come to pass; *also* : to take on or approach a mature or definite form — often used with *up*

♦ [3] acclimate, accommodate, adapt, adjust, condition, conform, fit ♦ *usu* **shape up** [5] crystallize, form, jell, solidify

²**shape** *n* **1** ♦ : spatial form or contour **2** : surface configuration : FORM **3** : bodily contour apart from the head and face : FIGURE **4** : PHANTOM **5** ♦ : the condition in which someone or something exists at a particular time **6** ♦ : the appearance of the body as distinguished from that of the face — **shaped** *adj*

♦ [1] cast, configuration, conformation, figure, form, geometry ♦ [5] condition, estate, fettle, form, order, repair, trim ♦ [6] build, constitution, figure, form, frame, physique

shape·less \'shā-pləs\ *adj* **1** ♦ : having no definite shape **2** ♦ : not shapely — **shape·less·ly** *adv* — **shape·less·ness** *n*

♦ [1] amorphous, formless, unformed, unshaped, unstructured ♦ [2] deformed, distorted, malformed, misshapen, monstrous

shape·ly \'shā-plē\ *adj* **shape·li·er; -est** : having a pleasing shape ⟨a ~ model⟩ — **shape·li·ness** *n*

shape–shift·er \'shāp-ˌshif-tər\ *n* : one that seems able to change form or identity at will

shard \'shärd\ *also* **sherd** \'shərd\ *n* : a broken piece : FRAGMENT

¹**share** \'shar\ *n* : PLOWSHARE

²**share** *n* **1** ♦ : a portion belonging to one person or group **2** ♦ : any of the equal interests into which the capital stock of a corporation is divided

♦ [1] allotment, allowance, cut, part, portion, proportion, quota ♦ [2] claim, interest, stake

³**share** *vb* **shared; shar·ing** **1** : APPORTION **2** : to use or enjoy with others **3** : PARTICIPATE

share·crop·per \-ˌkrä-pər\ *n* : a farmer who works another's land in return for a share of the crop — **share·crop** *vb*

share·hold·er \-ˌhōl-dər\ *n* : STOCKHOLDER

shar·er *n* ♦ : one that shares

♦ partaker, participant, party

share·ware \'sher-ˌwer\ *n* : software available for usu. limited trial use at little or no cost but that can be upgraded for a fee

¹**shark** \'shärk\ *n* : any of various active, usu. predatory, and mostly large marine cartilaginous fishes

²**shark** *n* **1** ♦ : a greedy crafty person **2** ♦ : one who excels greatly esp. in a particular field

♦ [1] cheat, dodger, hoaxer, sharper, swindler, trickster ♦ [2] ace, adept, artist, authority, crackerjack, expert, maestro, master, scholar, virtuoso, whiz, wizard

shark·skin \-ˌskin\ *n* **1** : the hide of a shark or leather made from it **2** : a fabric woven from strands of many fine threads and having a sleek appearance and silky feel

¹**sharp** \'shärp\ *adj* **1** ♦ : having a thin cutting edge or fine point : not dull or blunt **2** : briskly or bitingly cold : COLD ⟨a ~ wind⟩ **3** ♦ : keen in intellect, perception, or attention **4** : BRISK, ENERGETIC **5** : IRRITABLE ⟨a ~ temper⟩ **6** ♦ : causing intense distress ⟨a ~ pain⟩ **7** : cutting in language or import : HARSH ⟨a ~ rebuke⟩ **8** ♦ : affecting the senses as if cutting or piercing ⟨a ~ sound⟩ ⟨a ~ smell⟩ **9** : not smooth or rounded ⟨~ features⟩ **10** : involving an abrupt or extreme change ⟨a ~ turn⟩ **11** : CLEAR, DISTINCT ⟨mountains in ~ relief⟩; *also* : easy to perceive ⟨a ~ contrast⟩ **12 a** : higher than the true pitch **b** : raised by a half step **13** : being in the latest or current fashion : STYLISH ⟨a ~ dresser⟩ **14** : keen in attention to one's own interest sometimes to the point of being unethical — **sharp·ly** *adv*

♦ [1] cutting, edgy, ground, keen *Ant* blunt, blunted, dull, dulled, obtuse ♦ [1] peaked, pointed ♦ [3] acute, astute, canny, hardheaded, knowing, shrewd, smart ♦ [3] alert, brainy, bright, brilliant, clever, intelligent, keen, nimble, quick, quick-witted ♦ [6] acute, agonizing, biting, excruciating, smart *Ant* dull ♦ [8] nippy, pungent, strong *Ant* bland, smooth, mild

²**sharp** *adv* **1** : in a sharp manner **2** ♦ : in a manner or measure or to a degree or number that strictly conforms to a fact or condition : EXACTLY ⟨left at 8 ~⟩

♦ accurately, exactly, just, precisely, right, squarely

³**sharp** *n* **1** : a sharp edge or point **2** : a character ♯ which indicates that a specified note is to be raised by a half step; *also* : the resulting note **3** : SHARPER

⁴**sharp** *vb* : to raise in pitch by a half step

shar–pei \ˌshä-'pā, ˌshär-\ *n, pl* **shar–peis** *often cap S&P* : any of a Chinese breed of dogs that have loose wrinkled skin esp. when young

sharp·en \'shär-pən\ *vb* ♦ : to make or become sharp — **sharp·en·er** *n*

♦ edge, grind, hone, strop, whet *Ant* blunt, dull

sharp·er \'shär-pər\ *n* ♦ : an unduly sharp or canny person; *esp* : a cheating gambler

♦ cheat, dodger, hoaxer, shark, swindler, trickster

sharp·ie *or* **sharpy** \'shär-pē\ *n, pl* **sharp·ies** **1** : SHARPER **2** : a person who is exceptionally keen or alert

sharp·ness *n* ♦ : the quality or state of being sharp

♦ acidity, acrimony, acuteness, asperity, bite, bitterness, edge, harshness, keenness, pungency, tartness ♦ bite, bitterness, bleakness, chill, nip, rawness

sharp·shoot·er \'shärp-ˌshü-tər\ *n* ♦ : a good marksman — **sharp·shoot·ing** *n*

♦ marksman, shooter, shot

shat·ter \'sha-tər\ *vb* ♦ : to dash or burst into fragments; *also* : to cause the disruption or annihilation of — **shat·ter·proof** \'sha-tər-ˌprüf\ *adj*

♦ blast, blow up, burst, demolish, destroy, explode, pop, smash

¹**shave** \'shāv\ *vb* **shaved; shaved** *or* **shav·en** \'shā-vən\; **shav·ing** **1** : to slice in thin pieces **2** : to make bare or smooth by cutting the hair from **3** : to cut or pare off by the sliding movement of a razor **4** ♦ : to skim along or near the surface of

♦ brush, graze, kiss, nick, skim

²**shave** *n* **1** : any of various tools for cutting thin slices **2** : an act or process of shaving

shav·er \'shā-vər\ *n* **1** : an electric razor **2** ♦ : a male child from birth to adulthood : BOY

♦ boy, lad, nipper, stripling, youth

shav·ing *n* **1** : the act of one that shaves **2** : something shaved off

shawl \'shȯl\ *n* : a square or oblong piece of fabric used esp. by women as a loose covering for the head or shoulders

Shaw·nee \shȯ-'nē, shä-\ *n, pl* **Shawnee** *or* **Shawnees** : a member of an Indigenous people orig. of the central Ohio valley; *also* : their language

shd *abbr* should

she \'shē\ *pron* : that female one ⟨who is ~⟩; *also* : that one regarded as feminine ⟨~'s a fine ship⟩

sheaf \'shēf\ *n, pl* **sheaves** \'shēvz\ **1** : a bundle of stalks and ears of grain **2** : a group of things bound together

¹**shear** \'shir\ *vb* **sheared; sheared** *or* **shorn** \'shōrn\; **shear·ing** **1** ♦ : to cut the hair or wool from : CLIP **2** : to deprive by or as if by cutting **3** : to cut or break sharply

♦ bob, clip, crop, curtail, cut, cut back, dock, lop, nip, prune, shave, trim

²shear *n* **1** : any of various cutting tools that consist of two blades fastened together so that the edges slide one by the other — usu. used in pl. **2** *chiefly Brit* : the act, an instance, or the result of shearing **3** : an action or stress caused by applied forces that causes two parts of a body to slide on each other

sheath \'shēth\ *n, pl* **sheaths** \'shēthz, 'shēths\ **1** ♦ : a case for a blade (as of a knife); *also* : an anatomical covering suggesting such a case **2** : a close-fitting dress usu. worn without a belt

♦ armor, capsule, case, casing, cocoon, cover, housing, husk, jacket, pod, shell

sheathe \'shēth\ *also* **sheath** \'shēth\ *vb* **sheathed; sheathing 1** : to put into a sheath **2** : to cover with something that guards or protects

sheath·ing \'shē-thiŋ, -thiŋ\ *n* : material used to sheathe something; *esp* : the first covering of boards or of waterproof material on the outside wall of a frame house or on a timber roof

sheave \'shiv, 'shēv\ *n* : a grooved wheel or pulley (as on a pulley block)

she·bang \shi-'baŋ\ *n* : everything involved in what is under consideration ⟨sold the whole ∼⟩

¹shed \'shed\ *vb* **shed; shed·ding 1** : to cause to flow from a cut or wound ⟨∼ blood⟩ **2** : to pour down in drops ⟨∼ tears⟩ **3** : to give out (as light) : DIFFUSE **4** : to throw off (as a natural covering) **5** ♦ : to rid oneself of temporarily or permanently as superfluous or unwanted

♦ cast, discard, ditch, dump, fling, jettison, junk, lose, reject, scrap, shuck, slough, throw away, throw out, unload

²shed *n* : a slight structure built for shelter or storage

sheen \'shēn\ *n* ♦ : a subdued luster

♦ gloss, luster (*or* lustre), polish, shine

sheep \'shēp\ *n, pl* **sheep 1** : any of various cud-chewing mammals that are stockier than the related goats and lack a beard in the male; *esp* : one raised for meat or for its wool or skin **2** ♦ : a timid or defenseless person **3** : SHEEPSKIN

♦ angel, dove, innocent, lamb

sheep·dog \'shēp-ˌdȯg\ *n* : a dog used to tend, drive, or guard sheep

sheep·fold \'shēp-ˌfōld\ *n* : a pen or shelter for sheep

sheep·herd·er \-ˌhər-dər\ *n* : a worker in charge of sheep esp. on open range — **sheep·herd·ing** *n*

sheep·ish \'shē-pish\ *adj* ♦ : resembling a sheep in meekness, stupidity, or timidity : BASHFUL; *esp* : embarrassed by consciousness of a fault

♦ bashful, coy, demure, diffident, introverted, modest, retiring, shy

sheep·ish·ly *adv* ♦ : in a sheepish manner

♦ humbly, lowly, meekly, modestly

sheep·skin \'shēp-ˌskin\ *n* **1** : the hide of a sheep or leather prepared from it; *also* : PARCHMENT **2** : DIPLOMA

¹sheer \'shir\ *vb* ♦ : to turn from a course

♦ detour, deviate, swerve, swing, turn, turn off, veer

²sheer *adj* **1** ♦ : very thin or transparent **2** : carried to the utmost point or highest degree : UNQUALIFIED ⟨∼ folly⟩ **3** : very steep — **sheer** *adv*

♦ gauzy, transparent

¹sheet \'shēt\ *n* **1** : a broad piece of cloth (as for a bed); *also* : SAIL 1 **2** : a single piece of paper **3** : a broad flat surface ⟨a ∼ of ice⟩ **4** : something broad and long and relatively thin

²sheet *n* : a rope used to trim a sail

sheet·ing \'shē-tiŋ\ *n* : material in the form of sheets or suitable for forming into sheets

sheikh *or* **sheik** \'shēk, 'shāk\ *n* : an Arab chief — **sheikh·dom** *or* **sheik·dom** \-dəm\ *n*

shek·el \'she-kəl\ *or* **sheq·el** *n* : a basic monetary unit of Israel

shelf \'shelf\ *n, pl* **shelves** \'shelvz\ **1** : a thin flat usu. long and narrow structure fastened horizontally (as on a wall) above the floor to hold things **2** : something (as a sandbar) that suggests a shelf

shelf life *n* : the period of storage time during which a material will remain useful

¹shell \'shel\ *n* **1** ♦ : a hard or tough often thin outer covering of an animal (as a beetle, turtle, or mollusk) or of an egg or a seed or fruit (as a nut); *also* : something that resembles a shell ⟨a pastry ∼⟩ **2** : a light narrow racing boat propelled by oarsmen **3** : a case holding an explosive and designed to be fired from a cannon;

also : a case holding the charge of powder and shot or bullet for small arms **4** : a plain usu. sleeveless blouse or sweater **5** ♦ : a framework or exterior structure; *esp* : a building with an unfinished interior — **shelled** \'sheld\ *adj* — **shelly** \'she-lē\ *adj*

♦ [1] armor, capsule, case, casing, cocoon, cover, housing, husk, jacket, pod, sheath ♦ [5] configuration, frame, framework, skeleton, structure

²shell *vb* **1** ♦ : to remove from a shell or husk **2** ♦ : to throw shells at, upon, or into: BOMBARD — **shell·er** *n*

♦ [1] bark, flay, hull, husk, peel, shuck, skin ♦ [2] blitz, bombard

¹shel·lac \shə-'lak\ *n* **1** : a purified lac **2** : lac dissolved in alcohol and used as a wood filler or finish

²shellac *vb* **shel·lacked; shel·lack·ing 1** : to coat or treat with shellac **2** : to defeat decisively

shel·lack·ing *n* ♦ : a sound drubbing

♦ defeat, loss, rout

shell bean *n* : a bean grown esp. for its edible seeds; *also* : its edible seed

shell·fish \-ˌfish\ *n* : an invertebrate water animal (as an oyster or lobster) with a shell

shell out *vb* : PAY

shell shock *n* : COMBAT FATIGUE — **shell–shocked** \'shel-ˌshäkt\ *adj*

¹shel·ter \'shel-tər\ *n* ♦ : something that gives protection : REFUGE

♦ asylum, harbor (*or* harbour), haven, refuge, retreat, sanctuary

²shelter *vb* **shel·tered; shel·ter·ing** ♦ : to give protection or refuge to

♦ accommodate, billet, chamber, domicile, harbor (*or* harbour), house, lodge, put up, quarter, roof, take in

shelve \'shelv\ *vb* **shelved; shelv·ing 1** : to slope gradually **2** : to store on shelves **3** : to dismiss from service or use **4** ♦ : to put aside : DEFER ⟨∼ a proposal⟩

♦ defer, delay, hold up, postpone, put off

shelv·ing \'shel-viŋ\ *n* : material for shelves; *also* : SHELVES

she·nan·i·gan \shə-'na-ni-gən\ *n* **1** : an underhand trick **2** : questionable conduct — usu. used in pl. **3** ♦ : high-spirited or mischievous activity — usu. used in pl.

♦ **shenanigans** devilishness, impishness, knavery, mischief, mischievousness, rascality, waggery, wickedness ♦ **shenanigans** foolery, high jinks, horseplay, monkeyshines, roughhouse, tomfoolery

¹shep·herd \'she-pərd\ *n* **1** : one who tends sheep **2** : GERMAN SHEPHERD

²shepherd *vb* ♦ : to tend as or in the manner of a shepherd

♦ coach, counsel, guide, lead, mentor, pilot, show, tutor

shep·herd·ess \'she-pər-dəs\ *n* : a woman who tends sheep

shepherd's pie *n* : a meat pie with a mashed potato crust

sheqel *n, pl* **sheqalim** *var of* SHEKEL

sher·bet \'shər-bət\ *n* **1** : a drink of sweetened diluted fruit juice **2** *also* **sher·bert** \-bərt\ : a frozen dessert of fruit juices, sugar, milk or water, and egg whites or gelatin

sher·iff \'sher-əf\ *n* : a county officer charged with the execution of the law and the preservation of order

sher·ry \'sher-ē\ *n, pl* **sherries** : a fortified wine with a nutty flavor

Shet·land pony \'shet-lənd-\ *n* : any of a breed of small stocky hardy ponies

shew \'shō\ *Brit var of* SHOW

Shia \'shē-ˌä\ *n* **1** : one of the two main branches of Islam **2** : SHIITE

shi·at·su *also* **shi·at·zu** \shē-'ät-sü\ *n* : a form of acupressure originating in Japan

shib·bo·leth \'shi-bə-ləth\ *n* **1** ♦ : a word or saying used by adherents of a party, sect, or belief and usu. regarded by others as empty of real meaning; *also* : a banal, trite, or stale remark **2** : language that is a criterion for distinguishing members of a group

♦ cry, slogan, watchword ♦ banality, cliché, commonplace, platitude

¹shield \'shēld\ *n* **1** : a broad piece of defensive armor carried on the arm **2** ♦ : something that protects or hides **3** : a police officer's badge

♦ aegis, armor (*or* armour), cover, defense (*or* defence), guard, protection, safeguard, screen, security, wall, ward

²**shield** *vb* ♦ : to protect or hide with a shield

♦ cover, defend, guard, protect, safeguard, screen, secure, ward

¹**shift** \'shift\ *vb* **1** ♦ : to exchange for or replace by another **2** ♦ : to change place, position, or direction : MOVE; *also* : to change gears **3** ♦ : to assume responsibility : GET BY **4** ♦ : to go through a change

♦ [1] change, commute, exchange, substitute, swap, switch, trade ♦ [2] budge, dislocate, displace, disturb, move, remove, transfer ♦ [3] cope, do, fare, get along, get by, make out, manage ♦ [4] change, fluctuate, mutate, vary

²**shift** *n* **1** : SCHEME, TRICK **2** : a woman's slip or loose-fitting dress **3** ♦ : a change in direction, emphasis, or attitude **4** : a group working together alternating with other groups **5** : TRANSFER **6** : GEARSHIFT **7** ♦ : a means or device for effecting an end

♦ [3] motion, move, movement, moving, stir, stirring ♦ [7] expedient, measure, move, step

shift·less \'shift-ləs\ *adj* ♦ : lacking in ambition or incentive : LAZY

♦ idle, indolent, lazy, slothful

shift·less·ness *n* : the quality or state of being shiftless
shifty \'shif-tē\ *adj* **shift·i·er; -est 1 a** ♦ : given to deception, evasion, or fraud **b** : ELUSIVE **2** : indicative of a tricky nature ⟨~ eyes⟩

♦ furtive, shady, slippery, sly, sneaky, stealthy ♦ crooked, deceptive, dishonest, fast, fraudulent, shady, sharp, underhanded

shih tzu \'shēd-'zü, 'shēt-'sü\ *n, pl* **shih tzus** *also* **shih tzu** *often cap S&T* : any of a breed of small short-legged dogs of Chinese origin that have a short muzzle and a long dense coat
shii·ta·ke \shē-'tä-kē\ *n* : a dark Asian mushroom widely cultivated for its edible cap
Shi·ite \'shē-ˌīt\ *n* : a Muslim of the Shia branch of Islam
shill \'shil\ *n* : one who acts as a decoy (as for a pitchman) — **shill** *vb*
shil·le·lagh *also* **shil·la·lah** \shə-'lā-lē\ *n* : a short heavy club : CUDGEL
shil·ling \'shi-liŋ\ *n* : a former monetary unit of the United Kingdom equal to ¹/₂₀ pound
shilly–shally \'shi-lē-ˌsha-lē\ *vb* **shilly–shall·ied; shilly–shally·ing 1** ♦ : to show hesitation or lack of decisiveness **2** : to waste time

♦ falter, hang back, hesitate, stagger, teeter, vacillate, waver, wobble

shim \'shim\ *n* : a thin often tapered piece of wood, metal, or stone used (as in leveling) to fill in space
shim·mer \'shi-mər\ *vb* ♦ : to shine waveringly or tremulously : GLIMMER — **shimmer** *n* — **shim·mery** *adj*

♦ flame, flash, glance, gleam, glimmer, glisten, glitter, scintillate, sparkle, twinkle, wink

shim·my \'shi-mē\ *n, pl* **shimmies** : an abnormal vibration esp. in the front wheels of a motor vehicle — **shimmy** *vb*
¹**shin** \'shin\ *n* : the front part of the leg below the knee
²**shin** *vb* **shinned; shin·ning** : to climb (as a pole) by gripping alternately with arms or hands and legs
shin·bone \'shin-ˌbōn\ *n* : TIBIA
¹**shine** \'shīn\ *vb* **shone** \'shōn\ *or* **shined; shin·ing 1** ♦ : to give or cause to give light **2** : GLEAM, GLITTER **3** : to be eminent, conspicuous, or distinguished ⟨gave her a chance to ~⟩ **4** ♦ : to make bright by polishing ⟨~ your shoes⟩

♦ [1] blaze, burn, fire, flame, gleam, glimmer, glisten, glitter, glow, radiate, shimmer ♦ [4] buff, burnish, dress, gloss, grind, polish, rub, smooth

²**shine** *n* **1** ♦ : brightness caused by the emission of light : RADIANCE **2** ♦ : brightness caused by the reflection of light : LUSTER **3** : fair weather : SUNSHINE ⟨rain or ~⟩ **4** ♦ : positive regard for something : LIKING, FANCY ⟨took a ~ to them⟩ **5** : a polish given to shoes

♦ [1] blaze, flare, fluorescence, glare, gleam, glow, illumination, incandescence, light, luminescence, radiance ♦ [2] gloss, luster (*or* lustre), polish, sheen ♦ [4] appetite, fancy, favor (*or* favour), fondness, like, liking, love, partiality, preference, relish, taste, use

shin·er \'shī-nər\ *n* **1** : a silvery fish; *esp* : any of numerous small freshwater American fishes related to the carp **2** : BLACK EYE
¹**shin·gle** \'shiŋ-gəl\ *n* **1** : a small thin piece of building material

used in overlapping rows for covering a roof or outside wall **2** : a small sign
²**shingle** *vb* **shin·gled; shin·gling** : to cover with shingles
³**shingle** *n* : a beach strewn with gravel; *also* : coarse gravel (as on a beach)
shin·gles \'shiŋ-gəlz\ *n* : an acute inflammation of the spinal and cranial nerves caused by reactivation of the chicken pox virus and associated with eruptions and pain along the course of the affected nerves
shin·ny \'shi-nē\ *vb* **shin·nied; shin·ny·ing** : SHIN
shin splints *n sing or pl* : a condition marked by pain and sometimes tenderness and swelling in the shin caused by repeated small injuries to muscles and associated tissue esp. from running
Shin·to \'shin-ˌtō\ *n* : the indigenous religion of Japan consisting esp. in reverence of the spirits of natural forces and imperial ancestors — **Shin·to·ism** *n* — **Shin·to·ist** *n or adj*
shiny \'shī-nē\ *adj* **shin·i·er; -est 1** ♦ : filled with light : BRIGHT **2** : having a smooth, glossy surface

♦ beaming, bright, brilliant, effulgent, glowing, incandescent, lambent, lucent, lucid, luminous, lustrous, radiant, refulgent

¹**ship** \'ship\ *n* **1** : a large oceangoing boat **2** : a ship's officers and crew **3** : AIRSHIP, AIRCRAFT, SPACECRAFT
²**ship** *vb* **shipped; ship·ping 1** : to put or receive on board a ship for transportation **2** ♦ : to have transported by a carrier **3** : to take or draw into a boat ⟨~ oars⟩ ⟨~ water⟩ **4** : to engage to serve on a ship — **ship·per** *n*

♦ consign, dispatch, pack, send, transfer, transmit, transport

-ship \ˌship\ *n suffix* **1** : state : condition : quality ⟨friend*ship*⟩ **2** : office : dignity : profession ⟨lord*ship*⟩ ⟨clerk*ship*⟩ **3** : art : skill ⟨horseman*ship*⟩ **4** : something showing, exhibiting, or embodying a quality or state ⟨town*ship*⟩ **5** : one entitled to a (specified) rank, title, or appellation ⟨his Lord*ship*⟩ **6** : the body of persons engaged in a specified activity ⟨reader*ship*⟩
ship·board \'ship-ˌbōrd\ *n* : SHIP
ship·build·er \-ˌbil-dər\ *n* : one who designs or builds ships
ship·fit·ter \-ˌfi-tər\ *n* : one who constructs ships
ship·mate \-ˌmāt\ *n* : a fellow sailor
ship·ment \-mənt\ *n* **1** : the process of shipping **2** ♦ : the goods shipped

♦ cargo, freight, load, payload

ship·ping *n* **1** : SHIPS; *esp* : ships in one port or belonging to one country **2** : transportation of goods
ship·shape \'ship-ˌshāp\ *adj* ♦ : exhibiting neatness or good order : TIDY

♦ crisp, neat, orderly, snug, tidy, trim, uncluttered

ship·worm \-ˌwərm\ *n* : any of various wormlike marine clams that have a shell used for burrowing in wood and damaging wooden ships and wharves
¹**ship·wreck** \-ˌrek\ *n* **1** : a wrecked ship **2** ♦ : destruction or loss of a ship **3** : total loss or failure : RUIN

♦ wreck, wreckage

²**shipwreck** *vb* : to cause or meet disaster at sea through destruction or foundering
ship·wright \'ship-ˌrīt\ *n* : a carpenter skilled in ship construction and repair
ship·yard \-ˌyärd\ *n* : a place where ships are built or repaired
shire \'shīr, *in place-name compounds* ˌshir, shər\ *n* : a county in Great Britain
shirk \'shərk\ *vb* ♦ : to avoid performing (duty or work) — **shirk·er** *n*

♦ avoid, dodge, duck, elude, escape, eschew, evade, shake, shun

shirr \'shər\ *vb* **1** : to make shirring in **2** : to bake (eggs removed from the shell) until set
shirr·ing \'shər-iŋ\ *n* : a decorative gathering in cloth made by drawing up parallel lines of stitches
shirt \'shərt\ *n* **1** : a loose cloth garment usu. having a collar, sleeves, a front opening, and a tail long enough to be tucked inside pants or a skirt **2** : UNDERSHIRT — **shirt·less** *adj*
shirt·ing \'shir-tiŋ\ *n* : cloth suitable for making shirts
shish ke·bab \'shish-kə-ˌbäb\ *n* : kebab cooked on skewers
shiv \'shiv\ *n, slang* : KNIFE
¹**shiv·er** \'shi-vər\ *vb* : TREMBLE, QUIVER
²**shiver** *n* ♦ : an instance of shivering; *also* : an intense shivery sensation esp. of fear — often used in pl. with *the*

♦ quiver, shudder, tremble ♦ **shivers** jitters, shakes, willies

shiv·ery *adj* : causing shivers
shlemiel *var of* SCHLEMIEL
shlub *var of* SCHLUB

shmooze *var of* SCHMOOZE

Sho•ah \'shō-ə, -ˌä\ *n* : HOLOCAUST 2

¹shoal \'shōl\ *n*   **1** : SHALLOW   **2** : a sandbank or bar creating a shallow

²shoal *n* : a large group (as of fish)

shoat \'shōt\ *n* : a weaned young pig

¹shock \'shäk\ *n* : a pile of sheaves of grain or cornstalks set up in a field

²shock *n*   **1** ♦ : a sharp impact or violent shake or jar   **2** ♦ : a sudden violent mental or emotional disturbance   **3** : a state of bodily collapse that is often marked by a drop in blood pressure and volume and that is caused esp. by crushing wounds, blood loss, or burns   **4** : the effect of a charge of electricity passing through the body   **5** : SHOCK ABSORBER — **shock•proof** \-ˌprüf\ *adj*

    ♦ [1] bump, collision, concussion, crash, impact, jar, jolt, smash, strike, wallop ♦ [2] amazement, astonishment, surprise

³shock *vb*   **1** ♦ : to strike with surprise, horror, or disgust   **2** : to subject to the action of an electrical discharge

    ♦ appall, bowl, floor, jolt, shake up ♦ amaze, astonish, astound, dumbfound, flabbergast, startle, stun, stupefy, surprise

⁴shock *n* : a thick bushy mass (as of hair)

shock absorber *n* : any of several devices for absorbing the energy of sudden shocks in machinery

shock•er \'shä-kər\ *n* : one that shocks; *esp* : a sensational work of fiction or drama

shock•ing \'shä-kiŋ\ *adj* ♦ : extremely startling and offensive — **shock•ing•ly** *adv*

    ♦ amazing, astonishing, astounding, eye-opening, startling, stunning, surprising ♦ dire, dreadful, fearful, fearsome, forbidding, formidable, frightful, hair-raising, horrible, redoubtable, scary, terrible, terrifying ♦ abhorrent, abominable, appalling, awful, distasteful, foul, hideous, horrid, nasty, nauseating, noisome, obnoxious, obscene, odious, offensive, repellent, repugnant, repulsive, revolting, scandalous, ugly

shock therapy *n* : the treatment of mental disorder by induction of coma or convulsions by drugs or electricity

shock wave *n* : a wave formed by the sudden violent compression of the medium through which it travels

¹shod•dy \'shä-dē\ *n*   **1** : wool reclaimed from old rags; *also* : a fabric made from it   **2** : inferior or imitation material

²shoddy *adj* **shod•di•er; -est**   **1** : made of shoddy   **2** ♦ : poorly done or made — **shod•di•ly** \'shä-də-lē\ *adv* — **shod•di•ness** \-dē-nəs\ *n*

    ♦ bad, bum, cheap, inferior, junky, lousy, mediocre, poor, sleazy

¹shoe \'shü\ *n*   **1** : a covering for the human foot   **2** : HORSESHOE   **3** : the part of a brake that presses on the wheel

²shoe *vb* **shod** \'shäd\ *also* **shoed** \'shüd\; **shoe•ing** : to put a shoe or shoes on

shoe•box \-ˌbäks\ *n*   **1** : a box that shoes are sold in   **2** : a very small space ⟨a ∼ apartment⟩

shoe•horn \-ˌhorn\ *n* : a curved implement (as of horn or plastic) used in putting on a shoe

shoe•lace \'shü-ˌlās\ *n* : a lace or string for fastening a shoe

shoe•mak•er \-ˌmā-kər\ *n* : one who makes or repairs shoes

shoe•string \-ˌstriŋ\ *n*   **1** : SHOELACE   **2** ♦ : a small sum of money

    ♦ mite, peanuts, pittance, song

sho•gun \'shō-gən\ *n* : any of a line of military governors ruling Japan until the revolution of 1867–68

shone *past and past part of* SHINE

shook *past of* SHAKE

shook–up \(ˌ)shuk-'əp\ *adj* : nervously upset : AGITATED

¹shoot \'shüt\ *vb* **shot** \'shät\; **shoot•ing**   **1** ♦ : to drive (as an arrow or bullet) forward quickly or forcibly   **2** ♦ : to hit, kill, or wound with a missile   **3** ♦ : to cause a missile to be driven forth or forth from ⟨∼ a gun⟩   **4** ♦ : to send forth (as a ray of light)   **5** : to thrust forward or out   **6** : to pass rapidly along ⟨∼ the rapids⟩   **7** : to take a picture or series of pictures of : PHOTOGRAPH   **8** : to move swiftly : DART   **9** : to grow by or as if by sending out shoots; *also* : MATURE, DEVELOP   **10** ♦ : to grow or rise rapidly — often used with *up*

    ♦ [1] blast, discharge, fire, loose ♦ [2] drill, gun, plug, pop ♦ [3] blast, discharge, fire ♦ [4] cast, discharge, emit, exhale, expel, issue, release, vent ♦ *usu* **shoot up** [10] rocket, skyrocket, soar, zoom

²shoot *n*   **1** : a plant stem with its leaves and branches esp. when not yet mature   **2** : an act of shooting   **3** : a shooting match

shoot•er *n* : one that shoots: as   **a** ♦ : a person who fires a mis-

sile-discharging device (as a rifle or bow)   **b** : one who photographs

    ♦ marksman, sharpshooter, shot

shooting iron *n* : FIREARM

shooting star *n* : METEOR 2

shoot up *vb* : to inject a narcotic into a vein

¹shop \'shäp\ *n*   **1** ♦ : a place where things are made or worked on : FACTORY, MILL   **2** ♦ : a retail store ⟨dress ∼⟩

    ♦ [1] factory, mill, plant, works, workshop ♦ [2] emporium, store

²shop *vb* **shopped; shop•ping** : to visit stores for purchasing or examining goods — **shop•per** *n*

shop•keep•er \'shäp-ˌkē-pər\ *n* : a retail merchant

shop•lift \-ˌlift\ *vb* : to steal goods on display from a store — **shop•lift•er** *n*

shopping cart *n*   **1** : a cart used for holding merchandise when shopping in a store   **2** : a temporary record of items selected for purchase from a website

shop•talk \-ˌtok\ *n* ♦ : talk about one's business or special interests

    ♦ argot, cant, dialect, jargon, jive, language, lingo, patois, patter, shop, slang, terminology, vocabulary

shop•worn \-ˌworn\ *adj*   **1** : soiled or frayed from much handling in a store   **2** ♦ : stale from excessive use or familiarity

    ♦ banal, commonplace, hackneyed, musty, stale, stereotyped, threadbare, tired, trite

¹shore \'shor\ *n* : land along the edge of a body of water — **shoreless** *adj*

²shore *vb* **shored; shor•ing** ♦ : to give support to : BRACE — usu. used with *up*

    ♦ *usu* **shore up** bear, bolster, brace, buttress, carry, prop, stay, support, uphold

³shore *n* ♦ : a prop for preventing sinking or sagging

    ♦ brace, bulwark, buttress, mount, stay, support, underpinning

shore•bird \-ˌbərd\ *n* : any of a suborder of birds (as the plovers and sandpipers) mostly found along the seashore

shore patrol *n* : a branch of a navy that exercises guard and police functions

shor•ing \'shor-iŋ\ *n* : a group of things that shore something up

shorn *past part of* SHEAR

¹short \'short\ *adj*   **1** : not long or tall   **2** : not great in distance   **3** ♦ : brief in time   **4** ♦ : not coming up to standard or to an expected amount   **5** : CURT, ABRUPT   **6** ♦ : insufficiently supplied   **7** : made with shortening : FLAKY   **8** : consisting of or relating to a sale of securities or commodities that the seller does not possess or has not contracted for at the time of the sale ⟨∼ sale⟩

    ♦ [3] brief, little, short-lived *Ant* extended, great, lengthy, long, marathon ♦ [4, 6] deficient, inadequate, insufficient, scarce, shy, wanting *Ant* adequate, enough, sufficient

²short *adv*   **1** : in an abrupt manner : ABRUPTLY   **2** : at some point before a goal aimed at

³short *n*   **1** : something shorter than normal or standard   **2** *pl* : drawers or pants of less than knee length   **3** : SHORT CIRCUIT

⁴short *vb* : SHORT-CIRCUIT

short•age \'shor-tij\ *n* ♦ : the fact or state of being wanting or deficient : LACK

    ♦ dearth, deficiency, deficit, failure, famine, inadequacy, insufficiency, lack, paucity, poverty, scantiness, scarcity, want

short•cake \'short-ˌkāk\ *n* : a dessert consisting of short biscuit spread with sweetened fruit

short•change \-'chānj\ *vb* ♦ : to cheat esp. by giving less than the correct amount of change

    ♦ bleed, cheat, chisel, cozen, defraud, fleece, hustle, mulct, rook, skin, squeeze, stick, sting, swindle, victimize

short circuit *n* : a connection made between points in an electric circuit where current is not intended to flow — **short–circuit** *vb*

short•com•ing \'short-ˌkə-miŋ\ *n* ♦ : an imperfection or lack that detracts from the whole : FAILING

    ♦ demerit, failing, fault, foible, frailty, vice, weakness

¹short•cut \-ˌkət\ *n*   **1** : a route more direct than that usu. taken   **2** : a quicker way of doing something

²shortcut *vb* : to shorten (as a route or procedure) by use of a shortcut; *also* ♦ : to manage to get around esp. by ingenuity or stratagem : CIRCUMVENT

    ♦ circumvent, dodge, get around, sidestep, skirt

short•en \'shòrt-ᵊn\ *vb* ♦ : to make or become short

♦ abbreviate, abridge, curtail, cut back *Ant* elongate, extend, lengthen, prolong, protract

short•en•ing \'shòrt-ᵊn-iŋ\ *n* : a substance (as lard or butter) that makes pastry tender and flaky

short•hand \'shòrt-₋hand\ *n* : a method of writing rapidly by using symbols and abbreviations for letters, words, or phrases : STENOGRAPHY

short•hand•ed \₋shòrt-'han-dəd\ *adj* : short of the needed number of people

short•horn \'shòrt-₋hòrn\ *n, often cap* : any of a breed of red, roan, or white cattle of English origin

short hundredweight *n* : a unit of weight equal to 100 pounds in the U.S.

short–lived \'shòrt-₋livd, -'līvd\ *adj* ♦ : of short life or duration

♦ brief, ephemeral, evanescent, flash, fleeting, fugitive, impermanent, momentary, transient

short•ly \'shòrt-lē\ *adv* **1** ♦ : in a few words **2** ♦ : in a short time : SOON

♦ [1] compactly, concisely, crisply, laconically, succinctly, summarily, tersely ♦ [2] anon, momentarily, presently, soon

short•ness *n* ♦ : the quality or state of being short esp. in duration

♦ brevity, briefness, conciseness

short–or•der \'shòrt-₋òr-dər\ *adj* : preparing or serving food that can be quickly cooked ⟨a ∼ cook⟩

short shrift *n* **1** : a brief respite from death **2** : little consideration

short•sight•ed \'shòrt-₋sī-təd\ *adj* **1** : NEARSIGHTED **2** : lacking foresight — **short•sight•ed•ness** *n*

short•stop \-₋stäp\ *n* : a baseball player defending the area between second and third base

short story *n* ♦ : a short work of fiction usu. dealing with a few characters and a single event

♦ narrative, novella, story, tale

short–tem•pered \₋shòrt-'tem-pərd\ *adj* ♦ : having a quick temper

♦ choleric, crabby, cranky, cross, crotchety, grouchy, grumpy, irascible, irritable, peevish, perverse, petulant, snappish, snappy, snippy, testy, waspish

short–term \'shòrt-₋tərm\ *adj* **1** ♦ : occurring over or involving a relatively short period of time **2** : of or relating to a financial transaction based on a term usu. of less than a year

♦ impermanent, interim, provisional, temporary

short ton *n* : a unit of weight equal to 2000 pounds in the U.S.

short–wave \'shòrt-₋wāv\ *n* : a radio wave with a wavelength between 10 and 100 meters

Sho•sho•ne *or* **Sho•sho•ni** \shə-'shō-nē\ *n, pl* **Shoshones** *or* **Shoshoni** : a member of an Indigenous people orig. ranging through California, Idaho, Nevada, Utah, and Wyoming; *also* : their language

¹shot \'shät\ *n* **1** : an act of shooting **2** : a stroke or throw in some games **3** : something that is shot : MISSILE, PROJECTILE; *esp* : small pellets forming a charge for a shotgun **4** : a metal sphere that is thrown for distance in the shot put **5** : RANGE, REACH **6** ♦ : one that shoots; *esp* : MARKSMAN **7** ♦ : a single photographic exposure **8** : a single sequence of a motion picture or a television program made by one camera **9** : an injection (as of medicine) into the body **10** ♦ : a small serving of undiluted liquor **11** ♦ : the act or an instance of attempting ⟨I'll give it a ∼⟩

♦ [6] marksman, sharpshooter, shooter ♦ [7] photograph, print, snap, snapshot ♦ [10] draft, drag, drink, nip, quaff, slug, snort, swallow, swig ♦ [11] attempt, crack, endeavor (*or* endeavour), essay, fling, go, pass, stab, trial, try, whack

²shot *past and past part of* SHOOT

shot•gun \'shät-₋gən\ *n* : a gun with a smooth bore used to fire shot at short range

shot put *n* : a field event in which a shot is heaved for distance

should \'shùd, shəd\ *past of* SHALL ♦ — used as an auxiliary to express condition, obligation or propriety, probability, or futurity from a point of view in the past

♦ have, must, need, ought, shall

¹shoul•der \'shōl-dər\ *n* **1** : the part of the body of a person or animal where the arm or foreleg joins the body **2** : either edge of a roadway **3** : a rounded or sloping part (as of a bottle) where the neck joins the body

²shoulder *vb* **1** : to push or thrust with the shoulder **2** : to bear on the shoulder **3** ♦ : to take the responsibility of

♦ accept, assume, bear, take over, undertake

shoulder belt *n* : an automobile safety belt worn across the torso and over the shoulder

shoulder blade *n* : a flat triangular bone at the back of each shoulder

¹shout \'shaùt\ *vb* ♦ : to utter a sudden loud cry; *also* : to utter in a loud voice

♦ bawl, call, cry, holler, vociferate, yell

²shout *n* ♦ : a loud cry or call

♦ cry, holler, hoot, howl, whoop, yell, yowl

shove \'shəv\ *vb* **shoved; shov•ing** **1** ♦ : to push along, aside, or away **2** ♦ : to go away — usu. used with *off* — **shove** *n*

♦ [1] drive, propel, push, thrust ♦ *usu* **shove off** [2] clear out, depart, exit, get off, go, move, pull, quit, sally, take off

¹shov•el \'shə-vəl\ *n* **1** : a broad long-handled scoop used to lift and throw material **2** : the amount a shovel will hold

²shovel *vb* **-eled** *or* **-elled; -el•ing** *or* **-el•ling** **1** : to take up and throw with a shovel **2** : to dig or clean out with a shovel

¹show \'shō\ *vb* **showed** \'shōd\; **shown** \'shōn\ *or* **showed; show•ing** **1** ♦ : to cause or permit to be seen : EXHIBIT ⟨∼ anger⟩ **2** : CONFER, BESTOW ⟨∼ mercy⟩ **3** ♦ : to reveal by one's condition, nature, or behavior : DISCLOSE ⟨∼ed courage in battle⟩ **4** ♦ : to communicate knowledge to : INSTRUCT ⟨∼ me how⟩ **5** ♦ : to demonstrate or establish by argument or reasoning : PROVE ⟨∼s he was guilty⟩ **6** : APPEAR **7** : to be noticeable **8** : to be third in a horse race **9** ♦ : to bring by or as if by leading : USHER

♦ [1] display, disport, exhibit, expose, flash, flaunt, parade, show off, sport, strut, unveil ♦ [3] bespeak, betray, demonstrate, disclose, display, evince, expose, give away, manifest, reveal ♦ [4] coach, counsel, guide, instruct, lead, mentor, pilot, shepherd, tutor ♦ [5] demonstrate, establish, prove, substantiate ♦ [9] conduct, direct, guide, lead, marshal, pilot, route, steer, usher

²show *n* **1** ♦ : a demonstrative display **2** ♦ : outward appearance ⟨a ∼ of resistance⟩ **3** : SPECTACLE **4** ♦ : a theatrical presentation **5** : a radio or television program **6** : third place in a horse race **7** ♦ : a large display or exhibition arranged to arouse interest or stimulate sales

♦ [1] demonstration, display, exhibition ♦ [2] appearance, face, guise, name, pretense, semblance ♦ [7] display, exhibit, exhibition, exposition, fair

¹show•case \'shō-₋kās\ *n* : a cabinet for displaying items (as in a store)

²showcase *vb* **show•cased; show•cas•ing** : EXHIBIT

show•down \'shō-₋daùn\ *n* : a decisive confrontation or contest; *esp* : the showing of poker hands to determine the winner of a pot

¹show•er \'shaù-ər\ *n* **1** : a brief fall of rain **2** : a party given by friends who bring gifts **3** : a bath in which water is showered on the person; *also* : a facility (as a stall) for such a bath **4** ♦ : something resembling a rain shower — **show•ery** *adj*

♦ hail, rain, storm

²shower *vb* **1** : to rain or fall in a shower **2** : to bathe in a shower **3** ♦ : to give in abundance

♦ heap, lavish, pour, rain

show•i•ness \-ē-nəs\ *n* ♦ : the quality or state of being showy

♦ flamboyance, flashiness, gaudiness, glitz, ostentation, pretentiousness, swank

show•man \'shō-mən\ *n* : a notably spectacular, dramatic, or effective performer — **show•man•ship** *n*

show–off \'shō-₋òf\ *n* : one that seeks to attract attention by conspicuous behavior

show off *vb* **1** ♦ : to display proudly **2** ♦ : to act as a show-off

♦ [1] display, disport, exhibit, expose, flash, flaunt, parade, show, sport, strut, unveil ♦ [2] act up, clown, cut up, fool, monkey, skylark

show•piece \'shō-₋pēs\ *n* : an outstanding example used for exhibition

show•place \-₋plās\ *n* : an estate or building that is a showpiece

show up *vb* **1** ♦ : to make an appearance : ARRIVE **2** ♦ : to expose or discredit esp. by revealing faults **3** ♦ : to be plainly evident

◆ [1] arrive, come, land, turn up ◆ [2] debunk, expose, uncloak, uncover, unmask ◆ [3] appear, come out, materialize, turn up

show·y \'shō-ē\ *adj* **show·i·er; -est** ◆ : superficially impressive or striking — **show·i·ly** \'shō-ə-lē\ *adv*

◆ catchy, conspicuous, dramatic, flamboyant, striking *Ant* inconspicuous, unobtrusive

shpt *abbr* shipment

shrap·nel \'shrap-nəl\ *n, pl* **shrapnel** : bomb, mine, or shell fragments

¹**shred** \'shred\ *n* : a narrow strip cut or torn off : a small fragment
²**shred** *vb* **shred·ded; shred·ding** ◆ : to cut or tear into shreds

◆ rend, rip, rive, tatter, tear

shrew \'shrü\ *n* **1** : any of a family of very small mammals with short velvety fur that are related to the moles **2** ◆ : an unpleasant and bad-tempered woman

◆ fury, harpy, termagant, virago

shrewd \'shrüd\ *adj* ◆ : given to wily and artful ways or dealing : ASTUTE — **shrewd·ly** *adv*

◆ astute, canny, hardheaded, knowing, sharp, smart *Ant* unknowing

shrewd·ness *n* ◆ : the quality or state of being shrewd

◆ acumen, astuteness, caginess, canniness, hardheadedness, intelligence, keenness, sharpness, wit

shrew·ish \'shrü-ish\ *adj* : having an irritable disposition : ILL-TEMPERED — **shrew·ish·ly** *adv*
¹**shriek** \'shrēk\ *n* : a shrill cry : SCREAM, YELL
²**shriek** *vb* ◆ : to utter a sharp shrill sound; *also* : to utter with a shriek

◆ howl, scream, shrill, squeal, yell, yelp

shrift \'shrift\ *n, archaic* : the act of shriving
shrike \'shrīk\ *n* : any of numerous usu. largely grayish or brownish birds that often impale their usu. insect prey upon thorns before devouring it
¹**shrill** \'shril\ *vb* ◆ : to make a high-pitched piercing sound

◆ howl, scream, shriek, squeal, yell, yelp

²**shrill** *adj* ◆ : high-pitched ⟨∼ whistle⟩ — **shril·ly** *adv*

◆ acute, sharp, squeaky, treble *Ant* bass, deep, low, throaty

shrimp \'shrimp\ *n, pl* **shrimps** *or* **shrimp** **1** : any of various small marine crustaceans related to the lobsters **2** *usu disparaging* : a small or puny person or thing
shrine \'shrīn\ *n* **1** : the tomb of a saint; *also* : a place where devotion is paid to a saint or deity **2** : a place or object hallowed by its associations
¹**shrink** \'shriŋk\ *vb* **shrank** \'shraŋk\ *or* **shrunk** \'shrəŋk\; **shrunk** *or* **shrunk·en** \'shrəŋ-kən\; **shrink·ing** **1** ◆ : to draw back or away **2** ◆ : to become smaller or more compact **3** ◆ : to lessen in value — **shrink·able** *adj*

◆ [1] blench, flinch, quail, recoil, wince ◆ [2] compress, condense, constrict, contract ◆ [2, 3] abate, decline, decrease, deescalate, die, diminish, dwindle, ebb, fall, lessen, let up, lower, moderate, recede, relent, subside, taper, wane

²**shrink** *n* : a clinical psychiatrist or psychologist
shrink·age \'shriŋ-kij\ *n* **1** : the act of shrinking **2** ◆ : the amount lost by shrinkage

◆ abatement, decline, decrease, decrement, diminution, drop, fall, loss, reduction

shrive \'shrīv\ *vb* **shrived** *or* **shrove** \'shrōv\; **shriv·en** \'shri-vən\ *or* **shrived; shriv·ing** : to administer the sacrament of reconciliation to
shriv·el \'shri-vəl\ *vb* **-eled** *or* **-elled; -el·ing** *or* **-el·ling** : to shrink and draw into wrinkles : DWINDLE
¹**shroud** \'shraůd\ *n* **1** ◆ : something that covers or screens **2** : a cloth placed over a dead body **3** : any of the ropes leading from the masthead of a ship to the side to support the mast

◆ cloak, curtain, hood, mantle, mask, veil

²**shroud** *vb* **1** ◆ : to veil or screen from view; *also* : to veil under another appearance (as by obscuring or disguising) **2** : to cover with a shroud

◆ blanket, blot out, cloak, conceal, cover, curtain, hide, mask, obscure, occult, screen ◆ embrace, enclose, encompass, enfold, enshroud, envelop, invest, lap, mantle, swathe, veil, wrap

shrub \'shrəb\ *n* : a low usu. several-stemmed woody plant — **shrub·by** *adj*

shrub·bery \'shrə-bə-rē\ *n, pl* **-ber·ies** : a planting or growth of shrubs
shrug \'shrəg\ *vb* **shrugged; shrug·ging** : to hunch (the shoulders) up to express aloofness, indifference, or uncertainty — **shrug** *n*
shrug off *vb* **1** ◆ : to brush aside : MINIMIZE **2** : to shake off **3** : to remove (a garment) by wriggling out

◆ condone, disregard, excuse, ignore, minimize, pardon, pass over, wink at

shtick *also* **schtick** *or* **shtik** \'shtik\ *n* **1** : a usu. comic or repetitious performance or routine **2** : one's special trait, interest, or activity
¹**shuck** \'shək\ *n* : SHELL, HUSK
²**shuck** *vb* **1** : to strip of shucks **2** ◆ : to lay aside — often used with *off*

◆ *usu* **shuck off** cast, discard, ditch, dump, fling, jettison, junk, lose, reject, scrap, shed, slough, throw away, throw out, unload

¹**shud·der** \'shə-dər\ *vb* ◆ : to tremble convulsively : QUAKE

◆ agitate, convulse, jolt, jounce, quake, quiver, shake, vibrate, wobble

²**shudder** *n* ◆ : an act of shuddering

◆ quiver, shiver, tremble

¹**shuf·fle** \'shə-fəl\ *vb* **shuf·fled; shuf·fling** **1** ◆ : to mix in a disorderly mass **2** : to rearrange the order of (cards in a pack) by mixing two parts of the pack together **3** : to shift from place to place **4** ◆ : to move with a sliding or dragging gait **5** : to dance in a slow lagging manner

◆ [1] confuse, derange, disarray, disorder, jumble, mess, mix, muddle, scramble, upset ◆ [4] lumber, scuff, scuffle, shamble

²**shuffle** *n* **1** : an act of shuffling (as of cards) **2** ◆ : a confusing jumble (as of papers or events)

◆ assortment, clutter, jumble, medley, mélange, miscellany, motley, muddle, variety, welter

shuf·fle·board \'shə-fəl-ˌbōrd\ *n* : a game in which players use long-handled cues to shove disks into scoring areas marked on a smooth surface
shun \'shən\ *vb* **shunned; shun·ning** ◆ : to avoid deliberately or habitually

◆ avoid, dodge, duck, elude, escape, eschew, evade, shake, shirk

¹**shunt** \'shənt\ *vb* : to turn off to one side; *esp* : to switch (a train) from one track to another
²**shunt** *n* **1** : a method or device for turning or thrusting aside **2** : a conductor joining two points in an electrical circuit forming an alternate path through which a portion of the current may pass
shut \'shət\ *vb* **shut; shut·ting** **1** : CLOSE **2** : to forbid entrance into **3** : to lock up **4** : to fold together ⟨∼ a penknife⟩ **5** : to cease or suspend activity ⟨∼ down an assembly line⟩
shut·down \-ˌdaůn\ *n* ◆ : a temporary cessation of activity (as in a factory)

◆ cessation, close, closure, conclusion, end, ending, expiration, finish, halt, lapse, stop, stoppage, termination

shut–in \'shət-ˌin\ *n* : an invalid confined to home, a room, or bed
shut·out \'shət-ˌaůt\ *n* : a game or contest in which one side fails to score
shut out *vb* **1** ◆ : to prevent from using or participating : EXCLUDE **2** : to prevent (an opponent) from scoring in a game or contest

◆ ban, bar, count out, debar, eliminate, except, exclude, rule out

shut off *vb* ◆ : to stop the operation of (as a machine); *also* : to cease operating

◆ break, break off, cease, cut, desist, discontinue, drop, end, halt, knock off, layoff, leave off, quit, stop

shut·ter \'shə-tər\ *n* **1** : a movable cover for a door or window : BLIND **2** : the part of a camera that opens and closes to allow light to enter
shut·ter·bug \'shə-tər-ˌbəg\ *n* : a photography enthusiast
¹**shut·tle** \'shə-t²l\ *n* **1** : an instrument used in weaving for passing the horizontal threads between the vertical threads **2** : a vehicle traveling back and forth over a short route ⟨a ∼ bus⟩ **3** : SPACE SHUTTLE
²**shuttle** *vb* **shut·tled; shut·tling** : to move back and forth frequently
shut·tle·cock \'shət-²l-ˌkäk\ *n* : a light conical object (as of cork or plastic) used in badminton

shut up *vb* ♦ : to cease or cause to cease talking

♦ clam up, hush, pipe down, quiet (down) *Ant* speak, talk

¹**shy** \'shī\ *adj* **shi·er** *or* **shy·er** \'shī-ər\; **shi·est** *or* **shy·est** \'shī-əst\ **1** ♦ : easily frightened : TIMID **2** : WARY **3** ♦ : sensitively diffident or retiring : BASHFUL **4** ♦ : having less than the full or specified amount or number : LACKING — **shy·ly** *adv* — **shy·ness** *n*

♦ [1] fainthearted, fearful, mousy, scary, skittish, timid *Ant* adventuresome, adventurous, audacious, bold, daring, dashing, gutsy, hardy, venturous, venturesome ♦ [3] bashful, coy, demure, diffident, introverted, modest, retiring, sheepish *Ant* extroverted, immodest, outgoing ♦ [4] deficient, inadequate, insufficient, scarce, short, wanting

²**shy** *vb* **shied; shy·ing 1** : to show a dislike : RECOIL **2** : to start suddenly aside through fright ⟨the horse *shied*⟩

shy·ster \'shīs-tər\ *n* : an unscrupulous lawyer or politician

Si *symbol* silicon

SI *abbr* International System of Units

Si·a·mese \ˌsī-ə-'mēz, -'mēs\ *n, pl* **Sia·mese** : THAI — **Siamese** *adj*

Siamese cat *n* : any of a breed of slender blue-eyed short-haired domestic cats of Asian origin

Siamese twin *n* : one of a pair of twins with bodies joined together at birth

Siberian husky *n* : any of a breed of thick-coated compact dogs orig. developed in Siberia to pull sleds

¹**sib·i·lant** \'si-bə-lənt\ *adj* : having, containing, or producing the sound of or a sound resembling that of the *s* or the *sh* in *sash* — **sib·i·lant·ly** *adv*

²**sibilant** *n* : a sibilant speech sound as English \s\, \z\, \sh\, \zh\, \ch (=tsh)\, or \j (=dzh)\)

sib·ling \'si-bliŋ\ *n* : a brother or sister considered irrespective of sex; *also* : one of two or more offspring having one common parent

sib·yl \'si-bəl\ *n, often cap* : PROPHETESS — **sib·yl·line** \-bə-ˌlīn, -ˌlēn\ *adj*

sic \'sik, 'sēk\ *adv* : intentionally so written — used after a printed word or passage to indicate that it exactly reproduces an original ⟨said he seed [*sic*] it all⟩

sick \'sik\ *adj* **1** ♦ : not in good health : ILL; *also* : of, relating to, or intended for use in sickness ⟨~ pay⟩ **2** ♦ : suffering from nausea : NAUSEATED **3** ♦ : having a strong distaste from an overabundance; *also* : DISGUSTED **4** : PINING **5** : MACABRE, SADISTIC ⟨~ jokes⟩

♦ [1] bad, down, ill, indisposed, peaked, punk, unhealthy, unsound, unwell *Ant* chipper, hale, healthful, healthy, sound, well, whole, wholesome ♦ [2] ill, nauseous, queasy, squeamish ♦ [3] fed up, jaded, tired, weary ♦ [3] disgusted, squeamish

sick·bed \'sik-ˌbed\ *n* : a bed on which one lies sick

sick·en \'si-kən\ *vb* ♦ : to make or become sick — **sick·en·ing·ly** *adv*

♦ disgust, nauseate, repel, repulse, revolt, turn off ♦ *usu* **sicken with** catch, come down, contract, get, take

sickening *adj* : causing sickness or disgust

sick·le \'si-kəl\ *n* : a cutting tool consisting of a curved metal blade with a short handle

sickle–cell anemia *n* : an inherited anemia in which red blood cells tend to become crescent-shaped and clog small blood vessels and which occurs esp. in individuals of African, Mediterranean, or southwest Asian ancestry

sick·ly \'sik-lē\ *adj* **1 a** : somewhat unwell **b** ♦ : habitually ailing **2** ♦ : produced by or associated with sickness

♦ [1b] invalid, weakly *Ant* healthy, well ♦ [2] cadaverous, green, lurid, pale, pasty, peaked, sallow *Ant* florid, flush, healthy, rubicund, ruddy, sanguine

sick·ness \'sik-nəs\ *n* **1** ♦ : ill health; *also* : a specific disease **2** : a stomach distress with distaste for food and an urge to vomit : NAUSEA

♦ affection, ailment, bug, complaint, complication, condition, disease, disorder, fever, ill, illness, infirmity, malady, trouble ♦ illness, unsoundness *Ant* health, healthiness, soundness, wellness, wholeness, wholesomeness

side \'sīd\ *n* **1** : the right or left part of the trunk of a body **2** : a place away from a central point or line **3** : a border of an object; *esp* : one of the longer borders as contrasted with an end **4** : an outer surface of an object **5** ♦ : a position regarded as opposite to another **6** ♦ : a body of partisans or contestants — **side** *adj*

♦ [5] angle, aspect, facet, hand, phase ♦ [6] bloc, body, coalition, combination, combine, faction, party, sect, set, wing

side·arm \-ˌärm\ *adj* : made with a sideways sweep of the arm — **sidearm** *adv*

side arm *n* : a weapon worn at the side or in the belt

side·bar \'sīd-ˌbär\ *n* : a short news story accompanying a major story and presenting related information

side·board \-ˌbȯrd\ *n* ♦ : a piece of dining-room furniture for holding articles of table service

♦ buffet, cabinet, closet, cupboard, hutch, locker

side·burns \-ˌbərnz\ *n pl* : whiskers on the side of the face in front of the ears

side by side *adv* **1** : beside one another **2** : in the same place, time, or circumstance — **side–by–side** *adj*

side·car \-ˌkär\ *n* : a one-wheeled passenger car attached to the side of a motorcycle

side effect *n* : a secondary and usu. adverse effect (as of a drug)

side·kick \'sīd-ˌkik\ *n* ♦ : a person closely associated with another as a subordinate or partner

♦ aid, apprentice, assistant, deputy, helper, helpmate, mate

side·line \'sīd-ˌlīn\ *n* **1** : an activity pursued in addition to one's regular occupation **2** : the space immediately outside the lines of an athletic field or court **3** : a sphere of little or no participation — usu. used in pl.

¹**side·long** \'sīd-ˌlȯŋ\ *adv* : in the direction of or along the side : OBLIQUELY

²**sidelong** *adj* : directed to one side ⟨~ look⟩

side·man \'sīd-ˌman\ *n* : a member of a jazz or swing orchestra

side·piece \-ˌpēs\ *n* : a piece forming or contained in the side of something

si·de·re·al \sī-'dir-ē-əl, sə-\ *adj* **1** : of or relating to the stars **2** : measured by the apparent motion of the stars

side·sad·dle \'sīd-ˌsad-ᵊl\ *n* : a saddle for women in which the rider sits with both legs on the same side of the horse — **side·saddle** *adv*

side·show \'sīd-ˌshō\ *n* **1** : a minor show offered in addition to a main exhibition (as of a circus) **2** : an incidental diversion

side·step \-ˌstep\ *vb* **1** : to step aside **2** ♦ : to move out of the way of; *also* : to avoid an issue or decision

♦ circumvent, dodge, skirt ♦ dodge, duck

side·stroke \-ˌstrōk\ *n* : a swimming stroke which is executed on the side and in which the arms are swept backward and downward and the legs do a scissors kick

side·swipe \-ˌswīp\ *vb* : to strike with a glancing blow along the side — **sideswipe** *n*

¹**side·track** \-ˌtrak\ *n* : SIDING 1

²**sidetrack** *vb* **1** : to switch from a main railroad line to a siding **2** : to turn aside from a purpose

side·walk \'sīd-ˌwȯk\ *n* : a paved walk at the side of a road or street

side·wall \-ˌwȯl\ *n* **1** : a wall forming the side of something **2** : the side of an automobile tire

side·ways \-ˌwāz\ *adv or adj* **1** : from the side **2** : with one side to the front **3** : to, toward, or at one side

side·wind·er \-ˌwīn-dər\ *n* : a small pale-colored desert rattlesnake of the southwestern U.S.

sid·ing \'sī-diŋ\ *n* **1** : a short railroad track connected with the main track **2** : material (as boards) covering the outside of frame buildings

si·dle \'sīd-ᵊl\ *vb* **si·dled; si·dling** : to move sideways or with one side foremost

SIDS *abbr* sudden infant death syndrome

siege \'sēj\ *n* **1** : the placing of an army around or before a fortified place to force its surrender **2** ♦ : a persistent attack (as of illness)

♦ attack, bout, case, fit, seizure, spell

sie·mens \'sē-mənz, 'zē-\ *n* : a unit of conductance equivalent to one ampere per volt

si·er·ra \sē-'er-ə\ *n* : a range of mountains esp. with jagged peaks

si·es·ta \sē-'es-tə\ *n* ♦ : a midday rest or nap

♦ catnap, doze, drowse, forty winks, nap, snooze, wink

sieve \'siv\ *n* : a utensil with meshes or holes to separate finer particles from coarser or solids from liquids

sift \'sift\ *vb* **1** : to pass through a sieve **2** : to separate with or as if with a sieve **3** : to examine carefully **4** : to scatter by or as if by passing through a sieve — **sift·er** *n*

sig *abbr* signature

SIG *abbr* special interest group

sigh \'sī\ *vb* **1** : to let out a deep audible breath (as in weariness or sorrow) **2** ♦ : to long persistently, wistfully, or sadly : YEARN — often used with *for* — **sigh** *n*

♦ ache, die, hanker, hunger, itch, long, pant, pine, thirst, yearn

¹**sight** \'sīt\ *n* **1** : something seen or worth seeing **2** ♦ : the process or power of seeing; *esp* : the sense of which the eye is the receptor and by which qualities of appearance (as position, shape, and color) are perceived **3** : INSPECTION **4** : a device (as a small bead on a gun barrel) that aids the eye in aiming **5** : the act of looking at or beholding : VIEW, GLIMPSE **6** : the range of vision **7** ♦ : something ludicrous or disorderly in appearance — **sight·less** *adj*

♦ [2] eye, vision ♦ [7] eyesore, fright, horror, mess, monstrosity

²**sight** *vb* **1** ♦ : to get sight of **2** : to aim by means of a sight

♦ behold, descry, discern, distinguish, espy, eye, look, note, notice, observe, perceive, regard, remark, see, spy, view, witness

sight·ed \'sī-təd\ *adj* : having sight
sight·ly \-lē\ *adj* : pleasing to the sight
sight·see·ing \'sīt-ˌsē-iŋ\ *adj* : engaged in or used for seeing sights of interest
sight·seer \-ˌsē-ər\ *n* ♦ : one that visits places of interest

♦ excursionist, tourist, traveler

sig·ma \'sig-mə\ *n* : the 18th letter of the Greek alphabet — Σ or σ or ς
¹**sign** \'sīn\ *n* **1** ♦ : a gesture expressing a command, wish, or thought **2** : SYMBOL **3** : a notice publicly displayed for advertising purposes or for giving direction or warning **4** : OMEN, PORTENT **5** : TRACE, VESTIGE

♦ gesture, pantomime, signal

²**sign** *vb* **1** : to mark with a sign **2** : to represent by a sign **3** : to make a sign or signal **4** : to write one's name on in token of assent or obligation ⟨~ed the contract⟩ **5** : to assign legally **6** : to use sign language — **sign·er** *n*
¹**sig·nal** \'sig-nəl\ *n* **1** : a sign agreed on as the start of some joint action **2** ♦ : a sign giving warning or notice of something **3** : the message, sound, or image transmitted in electronic communication (as radio)

♦ gesture, pantomime, sign

²**signal** *vb* **-naled** *or* **-nalled; -nal·ing** *or* **-nal·ling** **1** ♦ : to notify by a signal **2** : to communicate by signals

♦ flag, gesture, motion, wave

³**signal** *adj* ♦ : distinguished from the ordinary ⟨a ~ honor⟩ — **sig·nal·ly** *adv*

♦ distinguished, eminent, illustrious, noble, notable, noteworthy, outstanding, preeminent, prestigious, star, superior

sig·nal·ize \'sig-nə-ˌlīz\ *vb* **-ized; -iz·ing** : to point out or make conspicuous — **sig·nal·i·za·tion** \ˌsig-nə-lə-'zā-shən\ *n*
sig·nal·man \'sig-nəl-mən, -ˌman\ *n* : a person who signals or works with signals
sig·na·to·ry \'sig-nə-ˌtōr-ē\ *n, pl* **-ries** : a person or government that signs jointly with others — **signatory** *adj*
¹**sig·na·ture** \'sig-nə-ˌchur\ *n* **1** : the name of a person written by himself or herself **2** : the sign placed after the clef to indicate the key or the meter of a piece of music
²**signature** *adj* : closely and distinctly associated and identified with someone or something ⟨her ~ style⟩
sign·board \'sīn-ˌbōrd\ *n* : a board bearing a sign or notice
sig·net \'sig-nət\ *n* : a small intaglio seal (as in a ring)
sig·nif·i·cance \sig-'ni-fi-kəns\ *n* **1** ♦ : something signified : MEANING **2** : SUGGESTIVENESS **3** ♦ : the quality of being important : IMPORTANCE

♦ [1] denotation, drift, import, intent, meaning, purport, sense, signification ♦ [3] consequence, import, magnitude, moment, weight

sig·nif·i·cant \-kənt\ *adj* **1** ♦ : having meaning; *esp* : having a hidden or special meaning **2** ♦ : having or likely to have influence or effect : IMPORTANT **3** ♦ : of a noticeably or measurably large amount — **sig·nif·i·cant·ly** *adv*

♦ [1] big, consequential, eventful, important, major, material, meaningful, momentous, substantial, weighty ♦ [1] denotative, indicative, telltale ♦ [2] important, influential, mighty, potent, powerful, strong ♦ [3] considerable, good, goodly, healthy, respectable, sizable, substantial, tidy

sig·ni·fi·ca·tion \ˌsig-nə-fə-'kā-shən\ *n* **1** : the act or process of signifying by signs or other symbolic means **2** ♦ : the meaning that a term, symbol, or character regularly conveys or is intended to convey

♦ denotation, drift, import, intent, meaning, purport, sense, signification

sig·ni·fy \'sig-nə-ˌfī\ *vb* **-fied; -fy·ing** **1** : to show by a sign **2** ♦ : to serve or intend to convey, show, or indicate : MEAN **3** ♦ : to have significance

♦ [2] denote, express, import, mean, spell ♦ [3] count, import, matter, mean, weigh

sign in *vb* : to make a record of arrival (as by signing a register)
sign language *n* : a formal system of hand gestures used for communication (as by the deaf)
sign off *vb* : to announce the end (as of a program or broadcast)
sign of the cross : a gesture of the hand forming a cross (as to invoke divine blessing)
sign on *vb* **1** ♦ : to engage oneself by or as if by a signature **2** : to announce the start of broadcasting for the day

♦ *usu* **sign on for** enlist, enroll, enter, join, sign up

sign out *vb* : to make a record of departure (as by signing a register)
sign·post \'sīn-ˌpōst\ *n* : a post bearing a sign
sign up *vb* ♦ : to sign one's name (as to a contract) in order to obtain, do, or join something

♦ *usu* **sign up for** enlist, enroll, enter, join, sign on

Sikh \'sēk\ *n* : an adherent of a religion of India marked by rejection of caste — **Sikh·ism** *n*
si·lage \'sī-lij\ *n* : fodder fermented (as in a silo) to produce a rich moist animal feed
¹**si·lence** \'sī-ləns\ *n* **1** : forbearance from speech or noise **2** ♦ : absence of sound or noise : STILLNESS **3** : SECRECY

♦ hush, quiet, quietness, still, stillness *Ant* noise, sound

²**silence** *vb* **si·lenced; si·lenc·ing** **1** ♦ : to reduce to silence : STILL **2** ♦ : to cause to cease hostile firing or criticism

♦ [1] hush, mute, quell, settle, still ♦ [2] clamp down, crack down, crush, put down, quash, quell, repress, snuff, squash, squelch, subdue, suppress

si·lenc·er \'sī-lən-sər\ *n* : a device for muffling the noise of a gunshot
si·lent \'sī-lənt\ *adj* **1** ♦ : not speaking : MUTE; *also* : not inclined to talk **2** ♦ : free from sound or noise : STILL, QUIET **3** : performed or borne without utterance ⟨a ~ prayer⟩ — **si·lent·ly** *adv*

♦ [1] dumb, mum, mute, speechless, uncommunicative *Ant* communicative, speaking, talking ♦ [1] closemouthed, laconic, reserved, reticent, taciturn, uncommunicative *Ant* chatty, communicative, conversational, gabby, garrulous, loquacious, talkative, unreserved ♦ [2] hushed, muted, noiseless, quiet, soundless, still *Ant* noisy, unquiet

silent treatment *n* ♦ : an act of completely ignoring a person or thing by resort to silence esp. as a means of expressing contempt or disapproval

♦ brush-off, cold shoulder, rebuff, repulse, snub

¹**sil·hou·ette** \ˌsi-lə-'wet\ *n* **1** : a representation of the outlines of an object filled in with black or some other uniform color **2** ♦ : the outline of a body viewed as circumscribing a mass : OUTLINE ⟨~ of a ship⟩

♦ contour, figure, outline

²**silhouette** *vb* **-ett·ed; -ett·ing** ♦ : to represent by a silhouette; *also* : to show against a light background

♦ define, delineate, outline, sketch, trace

sil·i·ca \'si-li-kə\ *n* : a mineral that consists of silicon and oxygen
sil·i·cate \'si-lə-ˌkāt, 'si-li-kət\ *n* : a chemical salt that consists of a metal combined with silicon and oxygen
si·li·ceous *also* **si·li·cious** \sə-'li-shəs\ *adj* : of, relating to, or containing silica or a silicate
sil·i·con \'si-li-kən, 'si-lə-ˌkän\ *n* : a nonmetallic chemical element that occurs in combination as the most abundant element next to oxygen in the earth's crust and is used esp. in alloys and semiconductors
sil·i·cone \'si-lə-ˌkōn\ *n* : an organic silicon compound used esp. for lubricants and varnishes
sil·i·co·sis \ˌsi-lə-'kō-səs\ *n* : a lung disease caused by prolonged inhaling of silica dusts
silk \'silk\ *n* **1** : a fine strong lustrous protein fiber produced by insect larvae usu. for their cocoons; *esp* : one from moth larvae (**silk·worms** \-ˌwərmz\) used for cloth **2** : thread or cloth made from silk

silk·en \'sil-kən\ *adj* ♦ : resembling silk (as in texture or appearance)

♦ cottony, downy, satiny, soft, velvety

silk screen *n* : a stencil process in which coloring matter is forced through the meshes of a prepared silk or organdy screen; *also* : a print made by this process — **silk–screen** *vb*

silky *adj* : resembling silk (as in texture or appearance)

sill \'sil\ *n* : a heavy crosspiece (as of wood or stone) that forms the bottom member of a window frame or a doorway; *also* : a horizontal supporting piece at the base of a structure

sil·li·ness *n* ♦ : the quality or state of being silly; *also* : a silly practice

♦ absurdity, asininity, balminess, daftness, fatuity, folly, foolishness, inanity, nonsense, simplicity, zaniness

sil·ly \'si-lē\ *adj* **sil·li·er; -est** ♦ : exhibiting or indicative of a lack of common sense or sound judgment; *also* : lacking in seriousness

♦ absurd, cuckoo, fatuous, foolish, nonsensical, nutty, senseless, stupid ♦ flighty, frivolous, giddy, goofy, harebrained, light-headed, scatterbrained

si·lo \'sī-lō\ *n, pl* **silos** 1 : a trench, pit, or esp. a tall cylinder for making and storing silage 2 : an underground structure for housing a guided missile

¹**silt** \'silt\ *n* 1 : fine earth; *esp* : particles of such soil floating in rivers, ponds, or lakes 2 : a deposit (as by a river) of silt — **silty** *adj*

²**silt** *vb* : to obstruct or cover with silt — **silt·ation** \sil-'tā-shən\ *n*

Si·lu·ri·an \sī-'lur-ē-ən\ *adj* : of, relating to, or being the period of the Paleozoic era between the Ordovician and the Devonian marked by the appearance of the first land plants — **Silurian** *n*

¹**sil·ver** \'sil-vər\ *n* 1 : a white ductile metallic chemical element that takes a high polish and is a better conductor of heat and electricity than any other substance 2 : coin made of silver 3 ♦ : articles (as hollowware or table flatware) made of or plated with silver 4 : a grayish white color

♦ flatware, tableware

²**silver** *adj* 1 : relating to, made of, or coated with silver 2 ♦ : resembling silver (as in sheen or color) : SILVERY

♦ gray (*or* grey), leaden, pewter, silvery, slate, steely

³**silver** *vb* **sil·vered; sil·ver·ing** : to coat with or as if with silver — **sil·ver·er** *n*

silver bromide *n* : a light-sensitive compound used esp. in photography

sil·ver·fish \'sil-vər-ˌfish\ *n* : any of various small wingless insects found in houses and sometimes injurious esp. to sized paper and starched clothes

silver iodide *n* : a light-sensitive compound used in photography, rainmaking, and medicine

silver maple *n* : a No. American maple with deeply cut leaves that are green above and silvery white below

silver nitrate *n* : a soluble compound used in photography and as an antiseptic

sil·ver·ware \'sil-vər-ˌwar\ *n* : eating and serving utensils (as knives, forks, and spoons) : FLATWARE

sil·very *adj* ♦ : resembling or having the luster of silver

♦ gray (*or* grey), leaden, pewter, silver, slate, steely

sim·i·an \'si-mē-ən\ *n* : MONKEY, APE — **simian** *adj*

sim·i·lar \'si-mə-lər\ *adj* ♦ : marked by correspondence or resemblance

♦ akin, alike, analogous, comparable, correspondent, like, parallel, such

sim·i·lar·i·ty \ˌsi-mə-'lar-ə-tē\ *n* ♦ : the quality or state of being similar; *also* : a comparable aspect

♦ community, correspondence, likeness, parallel, parallelism, resemblance, similitude *Ant* dissimilarity, unlikeness

sim·i·lar·ly *adv* ♦ : in the same or a comparable manner

♦ alike, also, correspondingly, likewise, so

sim·i·le \'si-mə-(ˌ)lē\ *n* : a figure of speech in which two dissimilar things are compared by the use of *like* or *as* (as in "cheeks like roses")

si·mil·i·tude \sə-'mi-lə-ˌtüd, -ˌtyüd\ *n* ♦ : correspondence in kind or quality : RESEMBLANCE; *also* : a point of comparison

♦ community, correspondence, likeness, parallelism, resemblance, similarity

sim·mer \'si-mər\ *vb* **sim·mered; sim·mer·ing** 1 : to stew at or

just below the boiling point 2 : to be on the point of bursting out with violence or emotional disturbance — **simmer** *n*

simmer down *vb* : to become calm or peaceful

si·mo·nize \'sī-mə-ˌnīz\ *vb* **-nized; -niz·ing** : to polish with or as if with wax

si·mo·ny \'sī-mə-nē, 'si-\ *n* : the buying or selling of a church office

sim·pa·ti·co \sim-'pä-ti-ˌkō, -'pa-\ *adj* : CONGENIAL, LIKABLE

sim·per \'sim-pər\ *vb* : to smile in a silly manner — **simper** *n*

sim·ple \'sim-pəl\ *adj* **sim·pler** \-pə-lər\; **sim·plest** \-pə-ləst\ 1 ♦ : free from dishonesty or vanity : INNOCENT 2 ♦ : free from ostentation 3 : of humble origin or modest position 4 : slow of mind : STUPID 5 ♦ : not complex : PLAIN ⟨a ∼ melody⟩ ⟨∼ directions⟩ 6 ♦ : lacking education, experience, or intelligence 7 : developing from a single ovary ⟨a ∼ fruit⟩ 8 : not limited or restricted — **sim·ple·ness** *n*

♦ [1, 2] artless, genuine, honest, ingenuous, innocent, naive, natural, real, sincere, true, unaffected, unpretentious ♦ [5] bald, bare, naked, plain, unadorned, undecorated, unvarnished ♦ [5] easy, effortless, facile, fluent, fluid, light, painless, ready, smooth, snap, soft ♦ [6] green, ignorant, ingenuous, innocent, naive, unknowing, unsophisticated, unwary, unworldly

simple interest *n* : interest paid or computed on the original principal only of a loan or on the amount of an account

sim·ple·ton \'sim-pəl-tən\ *n* ♦ : a person lacking in common sense : FOOL

♦ booby, fool, goose, half-wit, jackass, nitwit, nut, turkey

sim·plic·i·ty \sim-'pli-sə-tē\ *n, pl* **-ties** 1 : lack of complication : CLEARNESS 2 ♦ : freedom from pretense or guile 3 : plainness in manners or way of life 4 : lack of good sense or normal prudence and foresight : SILLINESS, FOLLY 5 ♦ : directness of expression

♦ [2] artlessness, greenness, ingenuousness, innocence, naïveté, naturalness, unworldliness ♦ [5] clarity, explicitness, lucidity, perspicuity *Ant* obscurity

sim·pli·fy \'sim-plə-ˌfī\ *vb* **-fied; -fy·ing** : to make simple or simpler — **sim·pli·fi·ca·tion** \ˌsim-plə-fə-'kā-shən\ *n*

sim·plis·tic \sim-'plis-tik\ *adj* : excessively simple : tending to overlook complexities ⟨a ∼ solution⟩

sim·ply *adv* 1 : without ambiguity; *also* : without embellishment 2 ♦ : to the exclusion of all else; *also* : no more than

♦ alone, exclusively, just, only, solely

sim·u·late \'sim-yə-ˌlāt\ *vb* **-lat·ed; -lat·ing** ♦ : to give or create the effect or appearance of often with the intent to deceive; *also* : to make a simulation of — **sim·u·la·tor** \'sim-yə-ˌlā-tər\ *n*

♦ affect, assume, counterfeit, fake, feign, pretend, profess, put on, sham

sim·u·la·tion \ˌsim-yə-'lā-shən\ *n* 1 : the act or process of simulating 2 : an object that is not genuine 3 : the imitation by one system or process of the way in which another system or process works

si·mul·ta·ne·ous \ˌsī-məl-'tā-nē-əs, ˌsi-\ *adj* ♦ : occurring or operating at the same time — **si·mul·ta·ne·ous·ly** *adv* — **si·mul·ta·ne·ous·ness** *n*

♦ coeval, concurrent, contemporary, synchronous

¹**sin** \'sin\ *n* 1 ♦ : an offense esp. against God 2 : FAULT 3 : a weakened state of human nature in which the self is estranged from God 4 ♦ : an action that is or is felt to be highly reprehensible — **sin·less** *adj*

♦ [1] breach, crime, error, malefaction, misdeed, misdoing, offense, transgression, trespass, violation, wrongdoing ♦ [4] crime, disgrace, pity, shame ♦ [4] evil, ill, immorality, iniquity, villainy, wrong

²**sin** *vb* **sinned; sin·ning** ♦ : to commit a sin

♦ err, offend, transgress, trespass

³**sin** *abbr* sine

¹**since** \'sins\ *adv* 1 : from a past time until now 2 : backward in time : AGO 3 : after a time in the past

²**since** *conj* 1 : from the time when 2 ♦ : seeing that : BECAUSE

♦ because, for, now, whereas

³**since** *prep* 1 : in the period after ⟨changes made ∼ the war⟩ 2 : continuously from ⟨has been here ∼ 1980⟩

sin·cere \sin-'sir\ *adj* **sin·cer·er; sin·cer·est** 1 ♦ : free from hypocrisy : HONEST 2 ♦ : marked by genuineness : GENUINE — **sin·cer·i·ty** \-'ser-ə-tē\ *n*

♦ [1, 2] artless, genuine, honest, ingenuous, innocent, naive, natural, real, simple, true, unaffected, unpretentious

sin·cere·ly *adv* : in a sincere manner

sine \'sīn\ *n* : the trigonometric function that is the ratio between the side opposite an acute angle in a right triangle and the hypotenuse

si·ne·cure \'sī-ni-ˌkyur, 'si-\ *n* : a paying job that requires little or no work

si·ne die \ˌsī-ni-'dī-ˌē, ˌsi-nā-'dē-ˌä\ *adv* : INDEFINITELY

si·ne qua non \ˌsi-ni-ˌkwä-'nän, -'nōn\ *n, pl* **sine qua nons** *also* **sine qui·bus non** \-ˌkwi-(ˌ)bus-\ : something indispensable or essential

sin·ew \'sin-yü\ *n* **1** : TENDON **2** ♦ : physical strength

♦ energy, force, main, might, muscle, potency, power, strength, vigor (*or* vigour)

sin·ewy *adj* ♦ : having or marked by great physical power

♦ brawny, muscular, rugged, stalwart, stout, strong

sin·ful \'sin-fəl\ *adj* ♦ : marked by or full of sin : WICKED — **sin·ful·ly** *adv*

♦ bad, evil, immoral, iniquitous, nefarious, rotten, unethical, unsavory, vicious, vile, villainous, wicked, wrong

sin·ful·ness *n* : the quality or state of being sinful

¹sing \'siŋ\ *vb* **sang** \'saŋ\ *or* **sung** \'səŋ\; **sung; sing·ing** **1** ♦ : to produce musical tones with the voice; *also* : to utter with musical tones **2** : to make a prolonged shrill sound ⟨locusts ∼ing⟩ **3** : to produce harmonious sustained sounds ⟨birds ∼ing⟩ **4** : CHANT, INTONE **5** : to write poetry; *also* : to celebrate in song or verse **6** : to give information or evidence

♦ carol, chant, descant, vocalize

²sing *abbr* singular

Sin·ga·por·ean \ˌsiŋ-ə-'pōr-ē-ən\ *n* : a native or inhabitant of Singapore — **Singaporean** *adj*

singe \'sinj\ *vb* **singed; singe·ing** ♦ : to scorch lightly the outside of; *esp* : to remove the hair or down from usu. by passing over a flame

♦ char, scorch, sear

sing·er \'siŋ-ər\ *n* ♦ : one that sings

♦ caroler, songster, vocalist, voice

¹sin·gle \'siŋ-gəl\ *adj* **1** ♦ : not married **2** ♦ : being alone : being the only one **3** : having only one feature or part **4** : made for one person — **sin·gle·ness** *n*

♦ [1] unattached, unmarried, unwed *Ant* attached, married, wed ♦ [2] detached, disconnected, discrete, freestanding, separate, unattached, unconnected

²single *vb* **sin·gled; sin·gling** **1** ♦ : to select or distinguish (one) from a group — usu. used with *out* **2** : to hit a single

♦ *usu* **single out** choose, cull, elect, handpick, name, opt, pick, prefer, select, take ♦ *usu* **single out** distinguish, identify, pinpoint

³single *n* **1** : a separate person or thing; *also* : an unmarried person **2** : a hit in baseball that enables the batter to reach first base **3** *pl* : a tennis match with one player on each side

single bond *n* : a chemical bond in which one pair of electrons is shared by two atoms in a molecule

single–lens reflex *n* : a camera having a single lens that forms an image which is reflected to the viewfinder or recorded on film

sin·gle–mind·ed \ˌsiŋ-gəl-'mīn-dəd\ *adj* ♦ : having one driving purpose or resolve ⟨∼ determination⟩ — **sin·gle–mind·ed·ly** *adv* — **sin·gle–mind·ed·ness** *n*

♦ bound, decisive, determined, firm, intent, purposeful, resolute, set

sin·gly *adv* ♦ : without the company of others

♦ alone, independently, solely, unaided, unassisted

sin·gu·lar \'siŋ-gyə-lər\ *adj* **1** : of, relating to, or constituting a word form denoting one person, thing, or instance **2** : OUTSTANDING, EXCEPTIONAL **3** : of unusual quality **4** ♦ : departing from general usage or expectation : ODD **5** : of or relating to a separate person or thing — **singular** *n* — **sin·gu·lar·ly** *adv*

♦ [4] curious, extraordinary, funny, odd, peculiar, rare, strange, unaccustomed, uncommon, unique, unusual, weird ♦ [5] individual, particular, peculiar, personal, private, separate, unique

sin·gu·lar·i·ty \ˌsiŋ-gyə-'lar-ə-tē\ *n* ♦ : something that is singular; *esp* : unusual or distinctive manner or behavior

♦ crotchet, eccentricity, idiosyncrasy, mannerism, oddity, peculiarity, quirk, trick

sin·is·ter \'si-nəs-tər\ *adj* **1** : singularly evil or productive of evil **2** ♦ : accompanied by or leading to disaster

♦ baleful, dire, foreboding, menacing, ominous, portentous

¹sink \'siŋk\ *vb* **sank** \'saŋk\ *or* **sunk** \'səŋk\; **sunk; sink·ing** **1** : SUBMERGE **2** ♦ : to descend lower and lower **3** : to grow less in volume or height **4** : to slope downward **5** : to penetrate downward **6** ♦ : to deteriorate in health, strength, or condition **7** : LAPSE, DEGENERATE **8** : to cause (a ship) to descend to the bottom **9** : to make (a hole or shaft) by digging, boring, or cutting **10** : INVEST — **sink·able** *adj*

♦ [2] decline, descend, dip, drop, fall, lower, plummet, plunge, tumble ♦ [6] decay, decline, degenerate, descend, deteriorate, ebb, rot, worsen

²sink *n* **1** : DRAIN, SEWER **2** : a basin connected with a drain **3** : an extensive depression in the land surface

sink·er \'siŋ-kər\ *n* : a weight for sinking a fishing line or net

sink·hole \'siŋk-ˌhōl\ *n* : a hollow place in which drainage collects

sin·ner *n* ♦ : one that sins

♦ evildoer, malefactor, wrongdoer

si·nol·o·gy \sī-'nä-lə-jē\ *n, often cap* : the study of the Chinese and esp. their language, history, and culture — **si·no·log·i·cal** \ˌsī-nə-'lä-ji-kəl\ *adj, often cap* — **si·nol·o·gist** \sī-'nä-lə-jist\ *n, often cap*

sin tax *n* : a tax on substances or activities considered sinful or harmful

sin·u·ous \'sin-yə-wəs\ *adj* ♦ : bending in and out : WINDING — **sin·u·os·i·ty** \ˌsin-yə-'wä-sə-tē\ *n* — **sin·u·ous·ly** *adv*

♦ crooked, devious, serpentine, tortuous, winding

si·nus \'sī-nəs\ *n* **1** : any of several cavities of the skull usu. connecting with the nostrils **2** : a space forming a channel (as for the passage of blood)

si·nus·itis \ˌsī-nə-'sī-təs\ *n* : inflammation of a sinus of the skull

Sioux \'sü\ *n, pl* **Sioux** *same or* 'süz\ : DAKOTA

¹sip \'sip\ *vb* **sipped; sip·ping** : to drink in small quantities

²sip *n* : a small draft taken with the lips

¹si·phon *also* **syphon** \'sī-fən\ *n* **1** : a bent tube through which a liquid can be transferred by means of air pressure up and over the edge of one container and into another container placed at a lower level **2** *usu* **sy·phon** : a bottle that ejects soda water through a tube when a valve is opened

²siphon *also* **syphon** *vb* **si·phoned** *also* **sy·phoned; si·phon·ing** *also* **sy·phon·ing** ♦ : to draw off by or as if by means of a siphon

♦ channel, conduct, direct, funnel, pipe

sip·py cup \'si-pē-\ *n* : a cup having a lid with a perforated spout for a young child

sir \'sər\ *n* **1** : a man of rank or position — used as a title before the given name of a knight or baronet **2** — used as a usu. respectful form of address

Si·rach \'sī-rak, sə-'räk\ *n* : a book of the Roman Catholic canon of the Old Testament

¹sire \'sīr\ *n* **1** : FATHER; *also, archaic* : FOREFATHER **2** *archaic* : LORD — used as a form of address and a title **3** : the male parent of an animal (as a horse or dog)

²sire *vb* **sired; sir·ing** ♦ : to procreate as the father : BEGET

♦ beget, father, get, produce

si·ren \'sī-rən\ *n* **1** : a seductive or alluring woman **2** : an electrically operated device for producing a loud shrill warning signal — **siren** *adj*

sir·loin \'sər-ˌlȯin\ *n* : a cut of beef taken from the part in front of the round

sirup *var of* SYRUP

si·sal \'sī-səl, -zəl\ *n* : a strong cordage fiber from an agave; *also* : this agave

sis·sy \'si-sē\ *n, pl* **sissies** **1** *disparaging* : an effeminate boy or man **2** ♦ : a timid or cowardly person

♦ chicken, coward, craven, dastard, poltroon, recreant

sis·ter \'sis-tər\ *n* **1** : a female having one or both parents in common with another individual **2** : a member of a religious order of women **3** *chiefly Brit* : NURSE **4** : a girl or woman regarded as a comrade — **sis·ter·ly** *adj*

sis·ter·hood \-ˌhud\ *n* **1** : the state of being a sister **2** : a community or society of sisters **3** : the solidarity of women based on shared conditions

sis·ter–in–law \'sis-tə-rən-ˌlȯ\ *n, pl* **sisters–in–law** : the sister of one's spouse; *also* : the wife of one's sibling or of one's spouse's sibling

sit \'sit\ *vb* **sat** \'sat\; **sit•ting** **1** : to rest upon the buttocks or haunches **2** : ROOST, PERCH **3** : to occupy a seat **4** : to hold a session **5** ♦ : to cover eggs for hatching : BROOD **6** : to pose for a portrait **7** : to remain quiet or inactive **8** ♦ : FIT **9** : to cause (oneself) to be seated **10** : to place in position **11** : to keep one's seat on ⟨∼ a horse⟩ **12** : BABYSIT **13** ♦ : to occupy a position ⟨the house ∼s on a hill⟩

♦ [5] brood, hatch, incubate, set ♦ [13] be, lie, stand

si•tar \si-'tär\ *n* : an Indian lute with a long neck and a varying number of strings

sit•com \'sit-ˌkäm\ *n* : SITUATION COMEDY

site \'sīt\ *n* **1** ♦ : the spatial location of an actual or planned structure (as a building, town, or monuments) : LOCATION **2** : WEBSITE

♦ locale, location, place, point, position, spot

sit–in \'sit-ˌin\ *n* : an act of sitting in the seats or on the floor of an establishment as a means of organized protest

sit•ter *n* **1** : one that sits **2** : a person who babysits

sit•u•at•ed \'si-chə-ˌwā-təd\ *adj* : LOCATED, PLACED

sit•u•a•tion \ˌsi-chə-'wā-shən\ *n* **1** : LOCATION, SITE **2** ♦ : position or place of employment : JOB **3** ♦ : position with respect to conditions and circumstances **4** : relative position or combination of circumstances at a certain moment

♦ [2] appointment, billet, capacity, function, job, place, position, post ♦ [3] footing, picture, posture, scene, status

situation comedy *n* : a radio or television comedy series that involves a continuing cast of characters in a succession of episodes

sit–up \'sit-ˌəp\ *n* : an exercise performed from a supine position by raising the torso to a sitting position and returning to the original position without lifting the feet

six \'siks\ *n* **1** : one more than five **2** : the 6th in a set or series **3** : something having six units — **six** *adj or pron* — **sixth** \'siksth\ *adj or adv or n*

six–gun \'siks-ˌgən\ *n* : a 6-chambered revolver

six–pack \-ˌpak\ *n* : six bottles or cans (as of beer) packaged and purchased together; *also* : the contents of a six-pack

six•pence \-pəns, *US also* -ˌpens\ *n* : the sum of six pence; *also* : an English silver coin of this value

six–shoot•er \'siks-ˌshü-tər\ *n* : SIX-GUN

six•teen \ˌsiks-'tēn\ *n* : one more than 15 — **sixteen** *adj or pron* — **six•teenth** \-'tēnth\ *adj or n*

six•ty \'siks-tē\ *n, pl* **sixties** : six times 10 — **six•ti•eth** \'siks-tē-əth\ *adj or n* — **sixty** *adj or pron*

siz•able *or* **size•able** \'sī-zə-bəl\ *adj* ♦ : quite large

♦ big, considerable, goodly, grand, great, handsome, large, significant, substantial, tidy

siz•ably \-blē\ *adv* ♦ : in a sizable manner : to a sizable degree

♦ broadly, considerably, greatly, largely, much

¹**size** \'sīz\ *n* ♦ : physical extent or bulk : DIMENSION; *also* : considerable proportions — **sized** \'sīzd\ *adj*

♦ dimension, extent, magnitude, measure, measurement, proportion

²**size** *vb* **sized; siz•ing** **1** : to grade or classify according to size **2** : to form a judgment of ⟨∼ up the situation⟩

³**size** *n* : a gluey material used for filling the pores in paper, plaster, or textiles — **siz•ing** *n*

⁴**size** *vb* **sized; siz•ing** : to cover, stiffen, or glaze with size

¹**siz•zle** \'si-zəl\ *vb* **siz•zled; siz•zling** **1** : to fry or shrivel up with a hissing sound **2** ♦ : to make a hissing sound in or as if in burning or frying

♦ fizz, hiss, swish, whish, whiz

²**sizzle** *n* : a hissing sound (as of something frying over a fire)

SJ *abbr* Society of Jesus

SK *abbr* Saskatchewan

ska \'skä\ *n* : popular music of Jamaican origin combining traditional Caribbean rhythms and jazz

¹**skate** \'skāt\ *n, pl* **skates** *also* **skate** : any of a family of rays with thick broad winglike fins

²**skate** *n* **1** : a metal frame and runner attached to a shoe and used for gliding over ice **2** : ROLLER SKATE; *esp* : IN-LINE SKATE — **skate** *vb* — **skat•er** *n*

skate•board \'skāt-ˌbōrd\ *n* : a short board mounted on small wheels — **skateboard** *vb* — **skate•board•er** *n*

skeet \'skēt\ *n* : trapshooting in which clay targets are thrown in such a way that their angle of flight simulates that of a flushed game bird

skein \'skān\ *n* : a loosely twisted quantity of yarn or thread wound on a reel

skel•e•tal \'ske-lət-əl\ *adj* **1** : of, relating to, forming, attached to, or resembling a skeleton **2** ♦ : extremely thin from lack of nourishment or from disease

♦ cadaverous, gaunt, haggard, wasted

skel•e•ton \'ske-lət-ən\ *n* **1** : a usu. bony supporting framework of an animal body **2** : a bare minimum **3** ♦ : something forming a structural framework

♦ configuration, frame, framework, shell, structure

skep•tic \'skep-tik\ *n* **1** : one who believes in skepticism **2** ♦ : a person disposed to skepticism esp. regarding religion

♦ disbeliever, doubter, questioner, unbeliever

skep•ti•cal \-ti-kəl\ *adj* ♦ : relating to, characteristic of, or marked by skepticism — **skep•ti•cal•ly** \-k(ə-)lē\ *adv*

♦ distrustful, incredulous, leery, mistrustful, suspicious, uncertain, unsure *Ant* credulous, gullible, trustful, trusting, uncritical, unquestioning

skep•ti•cism \'skep-tə-ˌsi-zəm\ *n* **1** ♦ : a doubting state of mind **2** : a doctrine that certainty of knowledge cannot be attained **3** : doubt concerning religion

♦ distrust, doubt, incertitude, misgiving, mistrust, suspicion, uncertainty

¹**sketch** \'skech\ *n* **1** ♦ : a rough drawing or outline **2** ♦ : a short or light literary composition (as a story or essay); *also* : a short comedy piece — **sketchy** *adj*

♦ [1] cartoon, delineation, drawing ♦ [2] delineation, depiction, description, picture, portrait, portrayal

²**sketch** *vb* ♦ : to make a sketch, rough draft, or outline of

♦ define, delineate, outline, silhouette, trace ♦ delineate, depict, describe, draw, image, paint, picture, portray

¹**skew** \'skyü\ *vb* : to distort esp. from a true value or symmetrical form : TWIST, SWERVE

²**skew** *n* : SLANT

¹**skew•er** \'skyü-ər\ *n* : a long pin for holding small pieces of meat and vegetables for broiling

²**skewer** *vb* ♦ : to fasten or pierce with or as if with a skewer

♦ gore, harpoon, impale, lance, pierce, puncture, spear, spike, stab, stick, transfix

¹**ski** \'skē\ *n, pl* **skis** : one of a pair of long strips (as of wood, metal or plastic) curving upward in front that are used for gliding over snow or water

²**ski** *vb* **skied** \'skēd\; **ski•ing** : to glide on skis — **ski•able** \'skē-ə-bəl\ *adj* — **ski•er** *n*

¹**skid** \'skid\ *n* **1** : a plank for supporting something above the ground **2** : a device placed under a wheel to prevent turning **3** : a timber or rail over or on which something is slid or rolled **4** : the act of skidding **5** : a runner on the landing gear of an aircraft **6** : ²PALLET

²**skid** *vb* **skid•ded; skid•ding** **1** : to slide without rotating ⟨a *skidding* wheel⟩ **2** : to slide sideways on the road ⟨the car *skidded* on ice⟩ **3** : SLIDE, SLIP

skid row *n* : a district of cheap saloons frequented by vagrants and alcoholics

skiff \'skif\ *n* : a small boat

ski jump *n* : a jump made by a person wearing skis; *also* : a course or track prepared for such jumping — **ski jump** *vb* — **ski jump•er** *n*

skil•ful *Can and Brit var of* SKILLFUL

ski lift *n* : a mechanical device (as a chairlift) for carrying skiers up a long slope

skill \'skil\ *n* **1** ♦ : ability to use one's knowledge effectively in doing something **2** : developed or acquired ability

♦ adeptness, adroitness, art, artfulness, artifice, artistry, cleverness, craft, cunning, deftness, masterfulness *Ant* artlessness, ineptitude, ineptness

skilled \'skild\ *adj* **1** ♦ : having acquired mastery of or skill in something (as a technique or a trade) **2** : of, relating to, or requiring workers or labor with skill and training in a particular occupation, craft, or trade

♦ accomplished, adept, consummate, crack, crackerjack, expert, good, great, master, masterful, masterly, proficient, skillful, virtuoso

skil•let \'ski-lət\ *n* : a frying pan

skill•ful *or Can and Brit* **skil•ful** \'skil-fəl\ *adj* **1** : having or displaying skill : EXPERT **2** ♦ : accomplished with skill

♦ adroit, artful, delicate, dexterous, expert, masterful, masterly, practiced, proficient, virtuoso *Ant* amateur, amateurish, artless, rude, unprofessional, unskillful

skill·ful·ly *or Can and Brit* **skil·ful·ly** *adv* ♦ : in a skillful manner
♦ ably, adeptly, capably, expertly, masterfully, proficiently, well

skill·ful·ness *or Can and Brit* **skil·ful·ness** *n* : the quality or state of being skillful

¹**skim** \'skim\ *vb* **skimmed; skim·ming** **1** : to take off from the top of a liquid; *also* : to remove (scum or cream) from ⟨∼ milk⟩ **2** ♦ : to read rapidly and superficially **3** ♦ : to pass swiftly over; *also* : to glide or skip along, above, or near a surface **4** : to throw in a gliding path; *also* : to throw so as to ricochet along the surface of water — **skim·mer** *n*
♦ [2] browse, dip, glance, glimpse, peek ♦ [3] bowl, breeze, coast, drift, flow, glide, roll, sail, skip, slide, slip, stream, sweep, whisk

²**skim** *adj* : having the cream removed
skimp \'skimp\ *vb* ♦ : to give insufficient attention, effort, or funds; *also* : to save by skimping
♦ economize, save, scrimp ♦ *usu* skimp on scant, spare, stint

skimpy \'skim-pē\ *adj* **skimp·i·er; -est** ♦ : deficient in supply or execution
♦ light, meager (*or* meagre), niggardly, poor, scant, scanty, scarce, slender, slim, spare, sparse, stingy

¹**skin** \'skin\ *n* **1** ♦ : the outer limiting layer of an animal body; *also* : the usu. thin tough tissue of which this is made **2** ♦ : an outer or surface layer (as a rind or peel) — **skin·less** *adj* — **skinned** *adj*
♦ [1] fur, hide, pelt ♦ [2] exterior, face, outside, surface, veneer

²**skin** *vb* **skinned; skin·ning** **1** ♦ : to free from skin : remove the skin of **2** ♦ : to strip of money or property
♦ [1] bark, flay, hull, husk, peel, shell ♦ [2] bleed, cheat, chisel, cozen, defraud, fleece, hustle, mulct, rook, shortchange, squeeze, stick, sting, swindle, victimize

³**skin** *adj* : devoted to showing nudes ⟨∼ magazines⟩
skin diving *n* : the sport of swimming under water with a face mask and flippers and esp. without a portable breathing device — **skin–dive** *vb* — **skin diver** *n*
skin·flint \'skin-ˌflint\ *n* ♦ : a very stingy person
♦ cheapskate, miser, niggard, tightwad

skin graft *n* : a piece of skin surgically removed from one area to replace skin in another area — **skin grafting** *n*
skin·head \'skin-ˌhed\ *n* : a person whose hair is cut very short
¹**skin·ny** \'ski-nē\ *adj* **skin·ni·er; -est** **1** : resembling skin **2** ♦ : very thin
♦ lean, narrow, slender, slim, spare, thin

²**skinny** *n* : inside information
skin·ny–dip \'ski-nē-ˌdip\ *vb* : to swim in the nude — **skin·ny–dip·per** \-ˌdi-pər\ *n*
skin·tight \'skin-ˈtīt\ *adj* : closely fitted to the figure
¹**skip** \'skip\ *vb* **skipped; skip·ping** **1** ♦ : to move with leaps and bounds; *also* : to bound off one point after another **2** : to leap lightly over **3** : to pass from point to point (as in reading) disregarding what is in between **4** : to pass over without notice or mention
♦ bound, hop, spring, trip ♦ bounce, carom, glance, rebound, ricochet, skim

²**skip** *n* : a light bouncing step; *also* : a gait of alternate hops and steps
skip·jack \'skip-ˌjak\ *n* : a small sailboat with vertical sides and a bottom similar to a flat V
skip·per \'ski-pər\ *n* : the master of a ship; *also* : the manager of a baseball team — **skipper** *vb*
¹**skir·mish** \'skər-mish\ *n* ♦ : a minor engagement in war; *also* : a minor dispute or contest
♦ brush, encounter, hassle, run-in, scrape ♦ battle, clash, combat, conflict, contest, fight, fracas, fray, hassle, scrap, scrimmage, scuffle, struggle, tussle

²**skirmish** *vb* : to engage in a skirmish
¹**skirt** \'skərt\ *n* **1** : a free-hanging garment or part of a garment extending from the waist down **2** ♦ : the rim, periphery, or environs of an area
♦ border, bound, boundary, circumference, compass, confines, edge, end, fringe, margin, perimeter, periphery, rim, verge

²**skirt** *vb* **1** ♦ : to pass around the outer edge of **2** ♦ : to form or

run along the border or edge of : BORDER **3** ♦ : to avoid esp. because of difficulty or fear of controversy
♦ [1] bypass, circumvent, detour ♦ [2] abut, adjoin, border (on), flank, fringe, join, touch, verge (on) ♦ [3] circumvent, dodge, sidestep

skit \'skit\ *n* : a brief dramatic sketch
ski tow *n* : SKI LIFT
skit·ter \'ski-tər\ *vb* : to glide or skip lightly or quickly : skim along a surface
skit·tish \'ski-tish\ *adj* **1** ♦ : lively or frisky in action **2** ♦ : easily frightened ⟨a ∼ horse⟩; *also* : WARY
♦ excitable, flighty, fluttery, high-strung, jittery, jumpy, nervous, spooky, wary

ski·wear \'skē-ˌwar\ *n* : clothing suitable for wear while skiing
skosh \'skōsh\ *n* : a small amount : BIT
skul·dug·gery *or* **skull·dug·gery** \ˌskəl-ˈdə-gə-rē\ *n, pl* **-ger·ies** ♦ : underhanded or unscrupulous behavior
♦ artifice, chicanery, hanky-panky, legerdemain, subterfuge, trickery, wile

skulk \'skəlk\ *vb* ♦ : to move furtively : SNEAK — **skulk·er** *n*
♦ lurk, pussyfoot, slide, slink, slip, snake, sneak, steal

skull \'skəl\ *n* : the skeleton of the head of a vertebrate that protects the brain and supports the jaws
skull and crossbones *n, pl* **skulls and crossbones** : a depiction of a human skull over crossbones usu. indicating a danger
skull·cap \'skəl-ˌkap\ *n* : a close-fitting brimless cap
¹**skunk** \'skəŋk\ *n, pl* **skunks** *also* **skunk** **1** : any of various black-and-white New World mammals related to the weasels that can forcibly eject an ill-smelling fluid when startled **2** ♦ : a contemptible person
♦ beast, boor, churl, clown, creep, cretin, cur, heel, jerk, joker, louse, lout, slob, snake

²**skunk** *vb* ♦ : to defeat decisively; *esp* : to prevent from scoring at all in a game
♦ beat, best, clobber, conquer, crush, defeat, drub, lick, master, overcome, prevail, rout, subdue, surmount, thrash, trim, triumph, trounce, wallop, whip, win

skunk cabbage *n* : either of two No. American perennial herbs related to the arums that occur in shaded wet to swampy areas and have a fetid odor suggestive of a skunk
sky \'skī\ *n, pl* **skies** **1** ♦ : the upper air **2** : HEAVEN — **sky·ey** \'skī-ē\ *adj*
♦ blue, high

sky·cap \-ˌkap\ *n* : a person employed to carry luggage at an airport
sky·div·ing \-ˌdī-viŋ\ *n* : the sport of jumping from an airplane and executing various body maneuvers before opening a parachute — **sky·div·er** *n*
sky·jack \-ˌjak\ *vb* : to commandeer an airplane in flight by threat of violence — **sky·jack·er** *n* — **sky·jack·ing** *n*
¹**sky·lark** \-ˌlärk\ *n* : a European lark noted for singing during flight
²**skylark** *vb* ♦ : to play and run about happily
♦ act up, clown, cut up, fool, monkey, show off

sky·light \'skī-ˌlīt\ *n* : a window in a roof or ceiling — **sky·light·ed** \-ˌlī-təd\ *adj*
sky·line \-ˌlīn\ *n* **1** : HORIZON **2** : an outline (as of buildings) against the sky
¹**sky·rock·et** \-ˌrä-kət\ *n* : ROCKET 1
²**skyrocket** *vb* ♦ : to rise or cause to rise or increase abruptly and rapidly
♦ rocket, shoot, soar, zoom *Ant* plummet, plunge, slump, tumble

sky·scrap·er \-ˌskrā-pər\ *n* : a very tall building
sky·surf·ing \-ˌsər-fiŋ\ *n* : skydiving with a short modified surfboard attached to the feet — **sky·surf·er** \-fər\ *n*
sky·walk \-ˌwȯk\ *n* : an aerial walkway connecting two buildings
sky·ward \-wərd\ *adv* ♦ : toward the sky
♦ above, aloft, over, overhead

sky·writ·ing \-ˌrī-tiŋ\ *n* : writing in the sky formed by smoke emitted from an airplane — **sky·writ·er** *n*
slab \'slab\ *n* : a thick flat piece or slice
¹**slack** \'slak\ *adj* **1** ♦ : not using due diligence, care, or dispatch : CARELESS **2** : SLUGGISH, LISTLESS **3** ♦ : not taut : LOOSE **4** : not busy or active — **slack·ly** *adv*

♦ [1] careless, derelict, lax, negligent, remiss ♦ [3] insecure, lax, loose, relaxed

²**slack** *vb* **1** ♦ : to make or become slack : LOOSEN **2** : SLAKE 2

♦ ease, loosen, relax, slacken

³**slack** *n* **1** : cessation of movement or flow : LETUP **2** ♦ : a part that hangs loose without strain ⟨∼ of a rope⟩ **3** ♦ : pants esp. for casual wear — usu. used in pl.

♦ [2] droop, sag, slackness ♦ **slacks** [3] britches, pantaloons, pants, trousers

slack·en \'sla-kən\ *vb* ♦ : to make or become slack

♦ ease, loosen, relax, slack *Ant* strain, stretch, tense, tighten

slack·er \'sla-kər\ *n* **1** : one that shirks work or evades military duty **2** : a young person perceived to be disaffected, apathetic, cynical, or lacking ambition

slack·ness *n* ♦ : the quality or state of being slack or behaving slackly; *also* : something that is slack

♦ carelessness, dereliction, heedlessness, laxness, negligence, remissness

slag \'slag\ *n* : the waste left after the melting of ores and the separation of metal from them

slain *past part of* SLAY

slake \'slāk, *for 2 also* 'slak\ *vb* **slaked; slak·ing 1** : to relieve or satisfy with or as if with refreshing drink ⟨∼ thirst⟩ **2** : to cause (lime) to crumble by mixture with water

sla·lom \'slä-ləm\ *n* : skiing in a zigzag course between obstacles

¹**slam** \'slam\ *n* : the winning of every trick or of all tricks but one in bridge

²**slam** *n* **1** ♦ : a heavy jarring impact : BANG **2** : harsh criticism **3** : a poetry competition

♦ bang, blast, boom, clap, crack, crash, pop, report, smash, snap, thwack, whack

³**slam** *vb* **slammed; slam·ming 1** : to shut violently and noisily **2** ♦ : to throw or strike with a loud impact **3** : to strike or beat hard **4** ♦ : to criticize harshly

♦ [2] bang, bash, bump, collide, crash, hit, impact, knock, ram, smash, strike, swipe, thud ♦ [4] abuse, assail, attack, belabor, blast, castigate, excoriate, jump, lambaste, vituperate

slam·mer \'sla-mər\ *n* : JAIL, PRISON

¹**slan·der** \'slan-dər\ *vb* ♦ : to utter slander against : DEFAME — **slan·der·er** *n*

♦ blacken, defame, libel, malign, smear, traduce, vilify

²**slander** *n* ♦ : a false report maliciously uttered and tending to injure the reputation of a person

♦ defamation, libel, vilification

slan·der·ous *adj* ♦ : containing or constituting slander

♦ defamatory, libelous, scandalous

slang \'slaŋ\ *n* ♦ : an informal nonstandard vocabulary composed typically of invented words, arbitrarily changed words, and extravagant figures of speech — **slangy** *adj*

♦ argot, cant, jargon, language, lingo, terminology, vocabulary

¹**slant** \'slant\ *n* **1** ♦ : a sloping direction, line, or plane **2** ♦ : a particular or personal viewpoint — **slant** *adj*

♦ [1] cant, diagonal, grade, inclination, incline, lean, pitch, slope, tilt, upgrade ♦ [2] angle, outlook, perspective, point of view, standpoint, viewpoint

²**slant** *vb* **1** ♦ : to turn or incline from a right line or a level : SLOPE **2** : to interpret or present in accordance with a special viewpoint or bias — **slant·ing·ly** *adv*

♦ angle, cant, cock, heel, incline, lean, list, slope, tilt, tip

slant·wise \-ˌwīz\ *adj* ♦ : being at a slant : moving or directed in a slanting position or direction — **slant·wise** *adv*

♦ askew, awry, cockeyed, crooked, listing, lopsided, oblique, uneven ♦ canted, diagonal, inclined, leaning

¹**slap** \'slap\ *vb* **slapped; slap·ping 1** : to strike sharply with the open hand **2** : REBUFF, INSULT

²**slap** *n* : a quick sharp blow; *also* : a blow with the open hand

slap·stick \-ˌstik\ *n* ♦ : comedy stressing horseplay

♦ comedy, farce, humor (*or* humour)

¹**slash** \'slash\ *vb* **1** ♦ : to cut with sweeping strokes **2** : to cut slits in (a garment) **3** : to reduce sharply ⟨∼ed prices⟩ **4** : to hit with a stroke like that used in slashing — **slash·er** \'sla-shər\ *n*

♦ cut, gash, rip, slice, slit

²**slash** *n* **1** ♦ : a long cut or stroke made by or as if by slashing : GASH **2** : an ornamental slit in a garment **3** : a mark / used to denote "or" (as in *and/or*), "and/or" (as in *straggler/deserter*), or "per" (as in *feet/second*)

♦ gash, laceration, rent, rip, slit, tear

slat \'slat\ *n* : a thin narrow flat strip

¹**slate** \'slāt\ *n* **1** : a dense fine-grained rock that splits into thin layers **2** : a roofing tile or a writing tablet made from this rock **3** : a written or unwritten record ⟨start with a clean ∼⟩ **4** : a list of candidates for election

²**slate** *vb* **slat·ed; slat·ing 1** : to cover with slate **2** ♦ : to designate for action or appointment ⟨*slated* to open soon⟩

♦ catalog, enroll, enter, index, inscribe, list, put down, record, register, schedule

³**slate** *adj* ♦ : being or having the dark purplish gray color of slate

♦ gray (*or* grey), leaden, pewter, silver, silvery, steely

slath·er \'sla-thər\ *vb* : to spread with or on thickly or lavishly

slat·tern \'sla-tərn\ *n* : a slovenly woman — **slat·tern·ly** *adj*

¹**slaugh·ter** \'slȯ-tər\ *n* **1** : the butchering of livestock for market **2** ♦ : great destruction of lives esp. in battle

♦ butchery, carnage, massacre

²**slaughter** *vb* **1** : to kill (animals) for food : BUTCHER **2** : to kill in large numbers or in a bloody way : MASSACRE

slaugh·ter·house \-ˌhau̇s\ *n* : an establishment where animals are butchered

Slav \'släv, 'slav\ *n* : a person speaking a Slavic language

¹**slave** \'slāv\ *n* **1** ♦ : a person held in forced servitude **2** : a device (as the printer of a computer) that is directly responsive to another **3** ♦ : a toiler at hard monotonous work — **slave** *adj*

♦ [1] bondman, chattel, thrall *Ant* freeman ♦ [3] drudge, fag, peon, toiler, worker

²**slave** *vb* **slaved; slav·ing** ♦ : to work very hard for long hours or under difficult conditions : DRUDGE

♦ drudge, labor (*or* labour), plod, plug, slog, strain, strive, struggle, sweat, toil, work

¹**sla·ver** \'sla-vər, 'slā-\ *vb* ♦ : to secrete saliva in anticipation of food : SLOBBER — **slaver** *vb*

♦ dribble, drivel, drool, salivate, slobber

²**slav·er** \'slā-vər\ *n* : a ship or a person engaged in the trafficking of enslaved people

slav·ery \'slāv-rē, 'slā-və-\ *n* **1** ♦ : wearisome drudgery **2** ♦ : the state of a person who is held in forced servitude **3** : the practice of owning enslaved people

♦ [1] drudgery, grind, labor (*or* labour), sweat, toil, travail ♦ [2] bondage, enslavement, servitude, thrall, yoke *Ant* freedom, liberty

¹**Slav·ic** \'sla-vik, 'slä-\ *n* : a branch of the Indo-European language family including various languages (as Russian or Polish) of eastern Europe

²**Slavic** *adj* : of or relating to the Slavs or their languages

slav·ish \'slā-vish\ *adj* **1** : SERVILE **2** ♦ : obeying or imitating with no freedom of judgment or choice

♦ imitative, mimic, unoriginal

slav·ish·ly *adv* ♦ : in a servile manner

♦ determinedly, diligently, hard, hardly, laboriously, mightily, strenuously, tirelessly

slaw \'slȯ\ *n* : COLESLAW

slay \'slā\ *vb* **slew** \'slü\; **slain** \'slān\; **slay·ing** ♦ : to kill violently, wantonly, or in great numbers; *broadly* : to strike down : KILL — **slay·er** *n*

♦ destroy, dispatch, do in, fell, kill, murder

sleaze \'slēz\ *n* : a sleazy quality, appearance, or behavior

slea·zy \'slē-zē\ *adj* **slea·zi·er; -est 1** : FLIMSY, SHODDY **2** ♦ : marked by low character or quality ⟨a ∼ lawyer⟩

♦ bad, bum, cheap, coarse, common, lousy, mediocre, rotten, second-rate, terrible, trashy

¹**sled** \'sled\ *n* : a vehicle usu. on runners adapted esp. for sliding on snow

²**sled** *vb* **sled·ded; sled·ding** : to ride or carry on a sled

¹**sledge** \'slej\ *n* : SLEDGEHAMMER

²**sledge** *n* : a strong heavy sled

sledge·ham·mer \'slej-ˌha-mər\ *n* : a large heavy hammer wielded with both hands — **sledgehammer** *adj or vb*

¹**sleek** \'slēk\ *vb* **1** : to make smooth or glossy **2** : to gloss over

²**sleek** *adj* **1** ♦ : having a smooth well-groomed look **2** : trim and graceful in design ⟨a ∼ car⟩

    ♦ glossy, lustrous, polished, satiny

¹**sleep** \'slēp\ *n* **1** ♦ : the natural periodic suspension of consciousness during which bodily powers are restored **2** : a state (as death or coma) suggesting sleep

    ♦ repose, rest, slumber *Ant* consciousness, wakefulness

²**sleep** *vb* **slept** \'slept\; **sleep·ing 1** ♦ : to rest or be in a state of sleep; *also* : to spend in sleep **2** : to have sexual intercourse — usu. used with *with* **3** : to provide sleeping space for

    ♦ catnap, doze, nap, rest, slumber, snooze

sleep·er \'slē-pər\ *n* **1** : one that sleeps **2** : a horizontal beam to support something on or near ground level **3** : SLEEPING CAR **4** : someone or something unpromising or unnoticed that suddenly attains prominence or value

sleep·i·ness \-pē-nəs\ *n* : the quality or state of being sleepy

sleeping bag *n* : a warmly lined bag for sleeping esp. outdoors

sleeping car *n* : a railroad car with berths for sleeping

sleeping pill *n* : a drug in tablet or capsule form taken to induce sleep

sleeping sickness *n* : a serious disease of tropical Africa that is marked by fever, lethargy, confusion, and sleep disturbances and is caused by protozoans transmitted by the tsetse fly

sleep·less *adj* ♦ : not able to sleep; *also* : affording no sleep — **sleep·less·ness** *n*

    ♦ awake, wakeful, wide-awake

sleep·over \'slēp-ₐō-vər\ *n* : an overnight stay (as at another's home)

sleep·walk·er \'slēp-ₐwȯ-kər\ *n* : one that walks while or as if while asleep — **sleep·walk** \-ₐwȯk\ *vb*

sleepy \'slē-pē\ *adj* **sleep·i·er; -est 1** ♦ : ready for sleep **2** ♦ : quietly inactive — **sleep·i·ly** \'slē-pə-lē\ *adv*

    ♦ [1] drowsy, slumberous *Ant* alert, awake, conscious, wakeful, wide-awake ♦ [2] dull, inactive, inert, lethargic, quiescent, sluggish, torpid

sleet \'slēt\ *n* : frozen or partly frozen rain — **sleet** *vb* — **sleety** *adj*

sleeve \'slēv\ *n* **1** : a part of a garment covering an arm **2** : a tubular part designed to fit over another part — **sleeved** *adj* — **sleeve·less** *adj*

¹**sleigh** \'slā\ *n* : an open usu. horse-drawn vehicle on runners for use on snow or ice

²**sleigh** *vb* : to drive or travel in a sleigh

sleight \'slīt\ *n* **1** ♦ : deceitful craftiness : TRICK **2** ♦ : mental or physical skill or quickness : DEXTERITY

    ♦ [1] artifice, device, dodge, gimmick, jig, ploy, scheme, stratagem, trick, wile ♦ [2] adroitness, agility, cleverness, craft, dexterity, finesse

sleight of hand 1 : a cleverly executed trick or deception esp. requiring manual dexterity **2** : skill in deception

slen·der \'slen-dər\ *adj* **1** ♦ : spare in frame or flesh : THIN; *also* : small or narrow in circumference or width in proportion to length or height **2** : WEAK, SLIGHT **3** ♦ : limited or inadequate in amount or scope : MEAGER, INADEQUATE

    ♦ [1] lean, narrow, skinny, slim, spare, thin ♦ [1] narrow, skinny, slim, thin ♦ [3] meager (*or* meagre), poor, scant, scanty, scarce, skimpy, sparse, stingy

slen·der·ize \-də-ₐrīz\ *vb* **-ized; -iz·ing** : to make slender

sleuth \'slüth\ *n* ♦ : one employed or engaged in detecting lawbreakers or in getting information that is not readily or publicly accessible : DETECTIVE

    ♦ detective, investigator, operative, shadow, tail

¹**slew** \'slü\ *past of* SLAY

²**slew** *vb* ♦ : TURN, VEER, SKID

¹**slice** \'slīs\ *vb* **sliced; slic·ing 1** ♦ : to cut a slice from; *also* : to cut into slices **2** : to hit (a ball) so that a slice results

    ♦ cut, gash, rip, slash, slit

²**slice** *n* **1** : a thin flat piece cut from something **2** : a flight of a ball (as in golf) that curves in the direction of the dominant hand of the player hitting it

¹**slick** \'slik\ *vb* ♦ : to make smooth or sleek

    ♦ grease, lubricate, oil, wax

²**slick** *adj* **1** ♦ : very smooth : SLIPPERY **2** ♦ : characterized by subtlety or nimble wit

    ♦ [1] greasy, slippery, slithery ♦ [2] artful, cagey, crafty, cunning, devious, foxy, guileful, sly, subtle, wily

³**slick** *n* **1** : a smooth patch of water covered with a film of oil **2** : a popular magazine printed on coated paper

slick·er \'sli-kər\ *n* **1** : a long loose raincoat **2** : a sly tricky person **3** : a city dweller esp. of natty appearance or sophisticated mannerisms

¹**slide** \'slīd\ *vb* **slid** \'slid\; **slid·ing** \'slī-diŋ\ **1** ♦ : to move smoothly along a surface **2** : to fall or dive toward a base in baseball **3** : to fall by a loss of support **4** ♦ : to pass unobtrusively **5** : to move or pass smoothly; *also* : to pass unnoticed ⟨let it ∼ by⟩ **6** : to become worse gradually

    ♦ [1] bowl, breeze, coast, drift, flow, glide, roll, sail, skim, slip, stream, sweep, whisk ♦ [4] lurk, pussyfoot, skulk, slink, slip, snake, sneak, steal

²**slide** *n* **1** : an act or instance of sliding **2** : something (as a cover or fastener) that operates by sliding **3** : a fall of a mass of earth or snow down a hillside **4** : a surface on which something slides **5** : a glass plate on which a specimen is mounted for examination under a microscope **6** : a small transparent photograph that can be projected on a screen

slid·er \'slī-dər\ *n* **1** : one that slides **2** : a baseball pitch that looks like a fastball but curves slightly **3** : a small hamburger

slide rule *n* : a manual device for calculation consisting of a ruler and a movable middle piece graduated with logarithmic scales

slier *comparative of* SLY

sliest *superlative of* SLY

¹**slight** \'slīt\ *adj* **1 a** : having a slim or delicate build : SLENDER **b** ♦ : lacking in strength or substance : FRAIL **2** ♦ : deficient in weight, solidity, or importance **3** ♦ : small of its kind; *also* : small in amount

    ♦ [1b] delicate, effete, enervated, faint, feeble, frail, infirm, languid, low, prostrate, soft, tender, torpid, unsubstantial, wasted, weak, wimpy ♦ [2] frivolous, inconsequential, inconsiderable, insignificant, little, minor, minute, negligible, small, trifling, trivial, unimportant ♦ [3] negligible, off, outside, remote, slim, small

²**slight** *vb* **1** ♦ : to treat as unimportant **2** ♦ : to ignore discourteously **3** : to perform or attend to carelessly

    ♦ [1] disregard, forget, ignore, neglect, overlook, pass over, slur ♦ [1, 2] disdain, high-hat, scorn, sniff at, snub ♦ [2] affront, insult, offend, outrage, wound

³**slight** *n* ♦ : a humiliating discourtesy

    ♦ affront, barb, dart, dig, indignity, insult, name, offense, outrage, put-down, sarcasm, slur, wound

slight·ly *adv* ♦ : in a slight manner or degree

    ♦ barely, hardly, just, marginally, scarcely

¹**slim** \'slim\ *adj* **slim·mer; slim·mest 1 a** ♦ : of small diameter or thickness in proportion to the height or length : THIN **b** ♦ : having a relatively small proportion of flesh : SLENDER **2** ♦ : limited or less than sufficient in degree, quantity, or extent : SCANTY, MEAGER

    ♦ [1a] fine, narrow, skinny, slender, thin ♦ [1b] lean, skinny, slender, spare, thin ♦ [2] meager (*or* meagre), poor, scant, scanty, scarce, skimpy, sparse, stingy ♦ [2] negligible, off, outside, remote, slight, small

²**slim** *vb* **slimmed; slim·ming** : to make or become slender

slime \'slīm\ *n* **1** ♦ : sticky mud **2** : a slippery substance (as on the skin of a slug or catfish)

    ♦ mire, muck, mud, ooze, slop, sludge, slush

slimy *adj* **slim·i·er; -est 1** : of, relating to, or resembling slime **2** ♦ : covered with or yielding slime

    ♦ miry, mucky, muddy, oozy, slushy

¹**sling** \'sliŋ\ *vb* **slung** \'sləŋ\; **sling·ing 1** ♦ : to throw forcibly : FLING **2** : to hurl with or as if with a sling

    ♦ cast, catapult, chuck, dash, fire, fling, heave, hurl, hurtle, launch, peg, pelt, pitch, throw, toss

²**sling** *n* **1** : a short strap with strings attached for hurling stones or shot **2** : something (as a rope or chain) used to hoist, lower, support, or carry; *esp* : a bandage hanging from the neck to support an arm or hand

³**sling** *vb* **slung** \'sləŋ\; **sling·ing 1** : to place in a sling for hoisting or lowering **2** ♦ : to suspend by or as if by a sling

    ♦ dangle, hang, suspend, swing

sling·shot \'sliŋ-ₐshät\ *n* : a forked stick with elastic bands for shooting small stones or shot

slink \'sliŋk\ *vb* **slunk** \'sləŋk\ *also* **slinked** \'sliŋkt\; **slink·ing 1**

♦ : to move stealthily or furtively   **2** : to move sinuously — **slinky** *adj*

♦ lurk, pussyfoot, skulk, slide, slip, snake, sneak, steal

¹**slip** \'slip\ *vb* **slipped; slip·ping   1** : to escape quietly or secretly   **2** ♦ : to slide along or cause to slide along smoothly   **3** : to make a mistake   **4** : to pass unnoticed or undone   **5** : to fall off from a standard or level   **6** ♦ : to get speedily into or out of clothing   **7** ♦ : to insert quietly or secretly   **8** ♦ : to slide out of place or away from a support or one's grasp

♦ [2] bowl, breeze, coast, drift, flow, glide, roll, sail, skim, slide, stream, sweep, whisk ♦ *usu* **slip on** *or* **slip into** [6] don, put on, throw ♦ [7] infiltrate, insinuate, sneak, work, worm ♦ [8] fall, stumble, topple, trip, tumble

²**slip** *n*   **1** : a ramp for repairing ships   **2** : a ship's berth between two piers   **3** ♦ : secret or hurried departure, escape, or evasion   **4** ♦ : an unintentional and trivial mistake or fault : BLUNDER   **5** ♦ : the act or an instance of slipping down or out of a place; *also* : a sudden mishap   **6** : a woman's one-piece garment worn under a dress   **7** : PILLOWCASE

♦ [3] escape, flight, getaway, lam ♦ [4] blunder, error, fault, flub, fumble, goof, lapse, miscue, misstep, mistake, oversight, stumble ♦ [5] fall, spill, stumble, tumble

³**slip** *n*   **1** : a shoot or twig from a plant for planting or grafting   **2** : a long narrow strip; *esp* : one of paper used for a record ⟨deposit ~⟩

⁴**slip** *vb* **slipped; slip·ping** : to take slips from (a plant)
slip·knot \'slip-ˌnät\ *n* : a knot that slips along the rope around which it is made
slipped disk *n* : a protrusion of one of the disks of cartilage between vertebrae with pressure on spinal nerves resulting esp. in low back pain
slip·per \'sli-pər\ *n* : a light low shoe that may be easily slipped on and off
slip·pery \'sli-pə-rē\ *adj* **slip·per·i·er; -est   1** ♦ : icy, wet, smooth, or greasy enough to cause one to fall or lose one's hold   **2** ♦ : not to be trusted : TRICKY ⟨a ~ politician⟩ — **slip·per·i·ness** *n*

♦ [1] greasy, slick, slithery ♦ [2] furtive, shady, shifty, sly, sneaky, stealthy, tricky

slip·shod \'slip-'shäd\ *adj* : SLOVENLY, CARELESS ⟨~ work⟩
slip·stream \'slip-ˌstrēm\ *n* : a stream (as of air) driven aft by a propeller
slip·up \'slip-ˌəp\ *n*   **1** : a wrong action or statement proceeding from faulty judgment, inadequate knowledge, or inattention : MISTAKE   **2** : ACCIDENT
¹**slit** \'slit\ *vb* **slit; slit·ting   1** ♦ : to make a slit in : SLASH   **2** : to cut off or away

♦ cut, gash, rip, slash, slice

²**slit** *n* ♦ : a long narrow cut or opening — **slit** *adj*

♦ gash, laceration, rent, rip, slash, tear

slith·er \'sli-t͟hər\ *vb* ♦ : to slip or glide along like a snake

♦ crawl, creep, grovel, snake, worm

slith·ery *adj* ♦ : having a slippery surface, texture, or quality

♦ greasy, slick, slippery

sliv·er \'sli-vər\ *n* : a long slender piece cut or torn off : SPLINTER
slob \'släb\ *n* ♦ : a slovenly or boorish person

♦ beast, boor, churl, clown, creep, cretin, cur, heel, jerk, joker, louse, lout, skunk, snake

¹**slob·ber** \'slä-bər\ *vb* **slob·bered; slob·ber·ing   1** ♦ : to dribble saliva   **2** ♦ : to be excessively or unrestrainedly enthusiastic or emotional

♦ [1] dribble, drivel, drool, salivate, slaver ♦ [2] enthuse, fuss, gush, rave, rhapsodize

²**slobber** *n* ♦ : saliva drooled from the mouth

♦ saliva, spit

sloe \'slō\ *n* : the fruit of the blackthorn
slog \'släg\ *vb* **slogged; slog·ging   1** : to hit hard : BEAT   **2** ♦ : to work hard and steadily

♦ drudge, labor (*or* labour), peg, plod, plug, strain, strive, struggle, sweat, toil, work

slo·gan \'slō-gən\ *n* ♦ : a word or phrase expressing the spirit or aim of a party, group, or cause

♦ cry, shibboleth, watchword

slo–mo \'slō-ˌmō\ *n* : SLOW MOTION — **slo–mo** *adj*
sloop \'slüp\ *n* : a single-masted sailboat with a jib and a fore-and-aft mainsail
¹**slop** \'släp\ *n*   **1** : thin tasteless drink or liquid food — usu. used in pl.   **2** : food waste for animal feed : SWILL   **3** ♦ : excreted body waste — usu. used in pl.   **4** ♦ : soft mud

♦ **slops** [3] droppings, dung, waste ♦ [4] mire, muck, mud, ooze, slime, sludge, slush

²**slop** *vb* **slopped; slop·ping   1** : SPILL   **2** : to feed with slop ⟨~ hogs⟩
¹**slope** \'slōp\ *vb* **sloped; slop·ing** ♦ : to lie or fall in a slant : INCLINE; *also* : to cause to incline or slant

♦ angle, cant, cock, heel, incline, lean, list, slant, tilt, tip

²**slope** *n*   **1** ♦ : upward or downward slant or degree of slant   **2** : ground that forms an incline   **3** : the part of a landmass draining into a particular ocean

♦ cant, diagonal, grade, inclination, incline, lean, pitch, slant, tilt, upgrade

slop·py \'slä-pē\ *adj* **slop·pi·er; -est   1** : wet so as to spatter easily : MUDDY, SLUSHY   **2** ♦ : untidy esp. in personal appearance : SLOVENLY, MESSY; *also* : lazily slipshod   **3** ♦ : excessive in emotional expression

♦ dowdy, frowsy, messy, slovenly, unkempt, untidy *Ant* dapper, dashing, dolled up, sharp, smart, spruce

sloppy joe \-'jō\ *n* : ground beef cooked in a thick spicy sauce and usu. served on a bun
slosh \'släsh\ *vb*   **1** : to flounder through or splash about in or with water, mud, or slush   **2** ♦ : to move with a splashing motion

♦ lap, plash, splash, swash

slot \'slät\ *n*   **1** ♦ : a long narrow opening or groove   **2** : a position in a sequence
slot car *n* : an electric toy racing car that runs on a grooved track
sloth \'slōth\ *n, pl* **sloths** \'slōths, 'slòt͟hz\   **1** ♦ : disinclination to action or labor : LAZINESS, INDOLENCE   **2** : any of several slow-moving plant-eating arboreal mammals of So. and Central America

♦ idleness, indolence, inertia, laziness

sloth·ful *adj* ♦ : inclined to sloth

♦ idle, indolent, lazy, shiftless

slot machine *n*   **1** : a machine whose operation is begun by dropping a coin into a slot   **2** : a coin-operated gambling machine that pays off according to the matching of symbols on wheels spun by a handle
¹**slouch** \'slau̇ch\ *n*   **1** ♦ : a lazy or incompetent person   **2** : a loose or drooping gait or posture

♦ drone, idler, lazybones, loafer, slug, sluggard

²**slouch** *vb* : to walk, stand, or sit with a slouch : SLUMP
¹**slough** \'slü, 2 *usu* 'slau̇\ *n*   **1** ♦ : a wet and marshy or muddy place (as a swamp)   **2** : a discouraged state of mind

♦ bog, fen, marsh, mire, morass, swamp

²**slough** \'sləf\ *also* **sluff** *n* : something that has been or may be shed or cast off
³**slough** \'sləf\ *also* **sluff** *vb* ♦ : to cast off

♦ cast, discard, ditch, dump, fling, jettison, junk, lose, reject, scrap, shed, shuck, throw away, throw out, unload

Slo·vak \'slō-ˌväk, -ˌvak\ *n*   **1** : a member of a Slavic people of Slovakia   **2** : the language of the Slovaks — **Slovak** *adj* — **Slo·va·ki·an** \slō-'vä-kē-ən, -'va-\ *adj or n*
slov·en \'slə-vən\ *n* : an untidy person
Slo·vene \'slō-ˌvēn\ *n*   **1** : a member of a Slavic people living largely in Slovenia   **2** : the language of the Slovenes — **Slovene** *adj* — **Slo·ve·nian** \slō-'vē-nē-ən\ *adj or n*
slov·en·ly \'slə-vən-lē\ *adj*   **1** ♦ : untidy in dress or person   **2** : lazily or carelessly done : SLIPSHOD ⟨~ thinking⟩

♦ dowdy, frowsy, sloppy, unkempt, untidy

¹**slow** \'slō\ *adj*   **1 a** : SLUGGISH   **b** : dull in mind : STUPID   **2** ♦ : moving, flowing, or proceeding at less than the usual speed   **3** : taking more than the usual time   **4** : registering behind the correct time   **5** : not lively : BORING

♦ creeping, dilatory, laggard, languid, poky, sluggish, tardy *Ant* barreling, bolting, breakneck, breathless, brisk, careering, dizzy, fast, fleet, flying, hasty, hurrying, lightning, quick, racing, rapid, rocketing, running, rushing, scudding, scurrying, snappy, speeding, speedy, swift, whirling, whirlwind, whisking, zipping

²slow *vb* **1** ♦ : to make slow : hold back **2** : to go slower

♦ brake, decelerate, hinder, retard *Ant* accelerate, hasten, hurry, quicken, rush, speed (up), step up

³slow *adv* ♦ : in a slow manner : not quickly, fast, early, rashly, or readily

♦ laggardly, slowly, sluggishly, tardily *Ant* apace, briskly, fast, full tilt, hastily, quick, quickly, rapidly, speedily, swift, swiftly

slow•ly *adv* ♦ : in a slow manner : not quickly, fast, early, rashly, or readily

♦ laggardly, slow, sluggishly, tardily

slow motion *n* : motion-picture action photographed so as to appear much slower than normal — **slow–motion** *adj*
slow•ness *n* : the quality or state of being slow
SLR *abbr* single-lens reflex
sludge \'sləj\ *n* ♦ : a slushy mass : OOZE; *esp* : solid matter produced by sewage treatment processes

♦ mire, muck, mud, ooze, slime, slop, slush

¹slug \'sləg\ *n* **1** : a small mass of metal; *esp* : BULLET **2** : a metal disk for use (as in a slot machine) in place of a coin **3** : any of numerous wormlike mollusks related to the snails **4** ♦ : a quantity of liquor drunk **5** : an habitually lazy person : SLUGGARD

♦ draft, drag, drink, nip, quaff, shot, snort, swallow, swig

²slug *vb* **slugged; slug•ging** ♦ : to strike forcibly and heavily — **slug•ger** *n*

♦ belt, clout, hit, punch, strike, wallop

³slug *n* : a heavy blow esp. with the fist
slug•gard \'slə-gərd\ *n* ♦ : an habitually lazy person

♦ drone, idler, lazybones, loafer, slouch, slug

slug•gish \'slə-gish\ *adj* **1** : SLOTHFUL, LAZY **2** ♦ : slow in movement, flow, or growth 〈a ~ economy〉 **3** : STAGNANT, DULL — **slug•gish•ness** *n*

♦ creeping, dilatory, laggard, languid, poky, slow, tardy

slug•gish•ly *adv* ♦ : in a sluggish manner

♦ laggardly, slow, slowly, tardily

¹sluice \'slüs\ *n* **1** : an artificial passage for water with a gate for controlling the flow; *also* : the gate so used **2** : a channel that carries off surplus water **3** : an inclined trough or flume for washing ore or floating logs
²sluice *vb* **sluiced; sluic•ing** **1** : to draw off through a sluice **2** ♦ : to wash with running water : FLUSH

♦ flush, irrigate, rinse, wash

¹slum \'sləm\ *n* : a thickly populated area marked by poverty and dirty or deteriorated houses — **slum•my** \'slə-mē\ *adj*
²slum *vb* **slummed; slum•ming** : to visit slums esp. out of curiosity; *also* : to go somewhere or do something that might be considered beneath one's station
¹slum•ber \'sləm-bər\ *vb* **slum•bered; slum•ber•ing** **1 a** ♦ : to sleep lightly : DOZE **b** ♦ : to rest in a state of sleep **2** : to be in a sluggish or torpid state

♦ catnap, doze, drowse, nap, sleep, snooze

²slumber *n* ♦ : the natural periodic suspension of consciousness during which bodily powers are restored : SLEEP; *also* : a light sleep

♦ repose, rest, sleep

slum•ber•ous \'sləm-bə-rəs\ *or* **slum•brous** \-brəs\ *adj* **1** ♦ : feeling a strong inclination toward sleep : SLEEPY **2** : PEACEFUL, INACTIVE **3** ♦ : inducing slumber

♦ [1] drowsy, sleepy ♦ [3] hypnotic, narcotic, opiate

slum•lord \'sləm-,lȯrd\ *n* : a landlord who receives unusually large profits from substandard properties
slump \'sləmp\ *vb* **1** : to sink down suddenly : COLLAPSE **2** : SLOUCH **3** : to decline sharply — **slump** *n*
slung *past and past part of* SLING
slunk *past and past part of* SLINK
¹slur \'slər\ *vb* **slurred; slur•ring** **1** ♦ : to slide or slip over without due mention or emphasis 〈*slurred* over certain facts〉 **2** : to perform two or more successive notes of different pitch in a smooth or connected way

♦ *usu* slur over disregard, forget, ignore, neglect, overlook, pass over, slight

²slur *n* : a curved line connecting notes to be slurred; *also* : a group of slurred notes

³slur *n* ♦ : a slighting remark

♦ affront, barb, dart, dig, indignity, insult, name, offense, outrage, put-down, sarcasm, slight, wound

slurp \'slərp\ *vb* : to eat or drink noisily — **slurp** *n*
slur•ry \'slər-ē\ *n, pl* **slur•ries** : a watery mixture of insoluble matter
slush \'sləsh\ *n* **1** : partly melted or watery snow **2** ♦ : soft mud **3** : silly, worthless, or cheaply sentimental material

♦ mire, muck, mud, ooze, slime, slop, sludge

slush fund *n* : an unregulated fund often for illicit purposes
slushy *adj* **slush•i•er; -est** ♦ : full of or covered with slush

♦ miry, mucky, muddy, oozy, slimy

slut \'slət\ *n* **1** *dated, chiefly Brit, disparaging* : a slovenly woman **2** *offensive* : a promiscuous woman — **slut•ty** *adj, offensive*
sly \'slī\ *adj* **sli•er** *or* **sly•er** \'slī-ər\; **sli•est** *or* **sly•est** \'slī-əst\ **1** ♦ : displaying cleverness : CRAFTY **2** ♦ : clever in concealing one's aims or ends **3** ♦ : lightly mischievous : ROGUISH — **sly•ly** *adv*

♦ [1] artful, cagey, crafty, cunning, devious, foxy, guileful, slick, subtle, wily ♦ [2] furtive, shady, shifty, slippery, sneaky, stealthy ♦ [3] devilish, impish, knavish, mischievous, rascally, roguish, waggish, wicked

sly•ness *n* ♦ : the quality or state of being sly

♦ artfulness, artifice, caginess, canniness, craft, craftiness, cunning, guile, wiliness

sm *abbr* small
Sm *symbol* samarium
SM *abbr* **1** master of science **2** sergeant major **3** service mark **4** stage manager
¹smack \'smak\ *n* : characteristic flavor; *also* : a slight trace
²smack *vb* **1** : to have a taste **2** : to have a trace or suggestion
³smack *vb* **1** : to move (the lips) so as to make a sharp noise **2** : to kiss or slap with a loud noise
⁴smack *n* **1** : a sharp noise made by the lips **2** : a noisy slap
⁵smack *adv* : squarely and sharply
⁶smack *n* : a sailing ship used in fishing
⁷smack *n, slang* : HEROIN
smack•down \'smak-,daün\ *n* **1** : the act of knocking down an opponent **2** : a wrestling match **3** : a decisive defeat **4** : a competition between rivals
SMaj *abbr* sergeant major
¹small \'smȯl\ *adj* **1** ♦ : little in size or amount **2** : operating on a limited scale **3** : little or close to zero (as in number or value) **4** : made up of little things **5** ♦ : of little consequence : UNIMPORTANT **6** : lacking in mental discrimination : PETTY

♦ [1] dwarf, dwarfish, fine, little, pocket, pygmy, slight, undersized *Ant* big, bumper, considerable, goodly, grand, great, handsome, king-size, large, outsize, oversize, sizable, substantial, super, whacking, whopping ♦ [5] frivolous, inconsequential, inconsiderable, insignificant, little, minor, minute, negligible, slight, trifling, trivial, unimportant

²small *n* : a small part or product 〈the ~ of the back〉
small•ish *adj* : somewhat small : slightly below normal size
small•ness *n* **1** : the quality or state of being small **2** : something that is small
small•pox \'smȯl-,päks\ *n* : a contagious virus disease of humans formerly common but now eradicated
small talk *n* : light or casual conversation
small–time \'smȯl-'tīm\ *adj* : insignificant in performance and standing : MINOR — **small–tim•er** *n*
smarmy \'smär-mē\ *adj* **smarm•i•er; -est** : marked by a smug, ingratiating, or false earnestness 〈~ politeness〉
¹smart \'smärt\ *vb* **1** ♦ : to cause or feel a stinging pain **2** : to feel or endure distress

♦ ache, hurt, pain

²smart *adj* **1** ♦ : making one smart 〈a ~ blow〉 **2** ♦ : mentally quick, perceptive, or clever **3** : marked by or full of wit : WITTY **4** : appealing to sophisticated tastes : STYLISH **5** : being a guided missile **6** : containing a microprocessor for limited computing capability 〈~ terminal〉 **7** ♦ : exhibiting neatness, good order, or compactness of line or structure 〈soldiers in ~ uniforms〉 **8** ♦ : impertinently bold, impudent, or facetious — **smart•ness** *n*

♦ [1] acute, agonizing, biting, excruciating, sharp ♦ [2] alert, brainy, bright, brilliant, clever, intelligent, keen, nimble, quick, quick-witted, sharp, shrewd ♦ [7] dapper, natty, neat, spruce *Ant* sloppy, slovenly ♦ [8] facetious, flip, flippant, pert

³**smart** *n* ♦ : a smarting pain; *esp* : a stinging local pain

♦ ache, pain, pang, prick, sting, stitch, tingle, twinge

smart al·eck \'smärt-ˌa-lik\ *n* : a person given to obnoxious cleverness

smart card *n* : a small plastic card that has a built-in microprocessor to store and handle data

smart·en \'smär-t³n\ *vb* : to make smart or smarter — usu. used with *up*

smart·ly *adv* : in a smart manner : so as to be or seem smart

smart·phone \'smärt-ˌfōn\ *n* : a cell phone that includes additional software functions (as e-mail or an Internet browser)

¹**smash** \'smash\ *n* 1 : a smashing blow 2 : a hard, overhand stroke in tennis 3 ♦ : the act or sound of smashing 4 ♦ : collision of vehicles : CRASH 5 : COLLAPSE, RUIN; *esp* : BANKRUPTCY 6 ♦ : a striking success : HIT — **smash** *adj*

♦ [3] bang, blast, boom, clap, crack, crash, pop, report, slam, snap, thwack, whack ♦ [4] collision, crack-up, crash, wreck ♦ [6] blockbuster, hit, success, winner

²**smash** *vb* 1 ♦ : to break or be broken into pieces 2 ♦ : to move forward with force and shattering effect 3 : to destroy utterly : WRECK

♦ [1] blast, blow up, burst, demolish, explode, pop, shatter ♦ [2] bang, bash, bump, collide, crash, hit, impact, knock, ram, slam, strike, swipe, thud

smat·ter·ing \'sma-tə-riŋ\ *n* 1 : superficial knowledge 2 ♦ : a small scattered number or amount

♦ few, handful, sprinkle, sprinkling

¹**smear** \'smir\ *n* 1 : a spot left by an oily or sticky substance 2 : material smeared on a surface (as of a microscope slide)

²**smear** *vb* 1 ♦ : to overspread esp. with something oily or sticky 2 : SMUDGE, SOIL 3 ♦ : to injure by slander or insults

♦ [1] daub ♦ [3] blacken, defame, libel, malign, slander, traduce, vilify

¹**smell** \'smel\ *vb* **smelled** \'smeld\ *or* **smelt** \'smelt\; **smell·ing** 1 a ♦ : to perceive the odor of by sense organs of the nose b ♦ : to detect as if with the nose ⟨I ∼ trouble⟩ 2 : to have or give off an odor

♦ [1a] nose, scent, sniff, whiff ♦ [1b] feel, perceive, scent, see, sense, taste

²**smell** *n* 1 ♦ : the property of a thing that affects the olfactory organs : ODOR, SCENT 2 : the process or power of perceiving odor; *also* : the special sense by which one perceives odor 3 : an act of smelling

♦ odor (*or* odour), redolence, scent, sniff

smelling salts *n pl* : an aromatic preparation used as a stimulant and restorative (as to relieve faintness)

smelly *adj* ♦ : having a usu. bad smell

♦ fetid, foul, fusty, malodorous, musty, noisome, rank, reeky, strong

¹**smelt** \'smelt\ *n, pl* **smelts** *or* **smelt** : any of a family of small food fishes of coastal or fresh waters that are related to the trouts and salmons

²**smelt** *vb* : to melt or fuse (ore) in order to separate the metal; *also* : REFINE

smelt·er \'smel-tər\ *n* 1 : one that smelts 2 : an establishment for smelting

smid·gen *also* **smid·geon** *or* **smid·gin** \'smi-jən\ *n* : a small amount : BIT

smi·lax \'smī-ˌlaks\ *n* 1 : any of various mostly climbing and prickly plants related to the lilies 2 : an ornamental plant related to the asparagus

¹**smile** \'smīl\ *vb* **smiled; smil·ing** 1 : to look with a smile 2 : to be favorable 3 : to express by a smile

²**smile** *n* : a change of facial expression to express amusement, pleasure, or affection

smil·ey \'smī-lē\ *adj* : exhibiting a smile : frequently smiling

smiley face *n* : a line drawing that symbolizes a smiling face

¹**smirch** \'smərch\ *vb* 1 ♦ : to make dirty or stained 2 ♦ : to bring disgrace on

♦ [1] befoul, begrime, besmirch, blacken, dirty, foul, grime, mire, muddy, soil, stain ♦ [2] abase, debase, degrade, demean, discredit, disgrace, dishonor (*or* dishonour), humble, humiliate, lower, shame, take down

²**smirch** *n* 1 : a dirty blurred mark or blot 2 ♦ : something that tarnishes a reputation

♦ blot, brand, spot, stain, stigma, taint

smirk \'smərk\ *vb* : to wear a self-conscious or conceited smile : SIMPER — **smirk** *n*

smite \'smīt\ *vb* **smote** \'smōt\; **smit·ten** \'smit-³n\ *or* **smote; smit·ing** \'smī-tiŋ\ 1 : to strike heavily; *also* : to kill by striking 2 : to affect as if by a heavy blow

smith \'smith\ *n* : a worker in metals; *esp* : BLACKSMITH

smith·er·eens \ˌsmi-thə-'rēnz\ *n pl* : FRAGMENTS, BITS

smithy \'smi-thē\ *n, pl* **smith·ies** 1 : a smith's workshop 2 : BLACKSMITH

¹**smock** \'smäk\ *n* : a loose garment worn over other clothes as a protection

²**smock** *vb* : to gather (cloth) in regularly spaced tucks — **smock·ing** *n*

smog \'smäg, 'smȯg\ *n* ♦ : a thick haze caused by the action of sunlight on air polluted by smoke and automobile exhaust fumes

♦ fog, haze, mist, murk, soup

smog·gy *adj* **smog·gi·er; -est** ♦ : characterized by or abounding in smog

♦ cloudy, foggy, hazy, misty, murky, soupy

¹**smoke** \'smōk\ *n* 1 : the gas from burning material (as coal, wood, or tobacco) in which are suspended particles of soot 2 : a mass or column of smoke 3 : something (as a cigarette) to smoke; *also* : the act of smoking — **smoke·less** *adj* — **smoky** *adj*

²**smoke** *vb* **smoked; smok·ing** 1 : to emit smoke 2 : to inhale and exhale the fumes of burning tobacco; *also* : to use in smoking ⟨∼ a pipe⟩ 3 : to stupefy or drive away by smoke 4 : to discolor with smoke 5 : to cure (as meat) with smoke — **smok·er** *n*

smoke detector *n* : an alarm that sounds automatically when it detects smoke

smoke jumper *n* : a forest firefighter who parachutes to locations otherwise difficult to reach

smoke screen *n* 1 : a screen of smoke to hinder enemy observation 2 : something designed to obscure, confuse, or mislead

smoke·stack \'smōk-ˌstak\ *n* : a pipe or funnel through which smoke and gases are discharged

smol·der *or* **smoul·der** \'smōl-dər\ *vb* **smol·dered** *or* **smoul·dered; smol·der·ing** *or* **smoul·der·ing** 1 : to burn and smoke without flame 2 : to burn inwardly — **smolder** *n*

smooch \'smüch\ *vb* : to touch or caress with the lips as a mark of affection : KISS — **smooch** *n*

¹**smooth** \'smüth\ *adj* 1 ♦ : not rough or uneven 2 : not jarring or jolting 3 : BLAND, MILD 4 ♦ : fluent in speech and agreeable in manner 5 ♦ : free from difficulties or impediments — **smooth·ness** *n*

♦ [1] even, flat, flush, level, plane ♦ [4] debonair, sophisticated, suave, urbane ♦ [5] easy, effortless, facile, fluent, fluid, light, painless, ready, simple, snap, soft

²**smooth** *vb* 1 ♦ : to make smooth 2 ♦ : to free from trouble or difficulty

♦ [1] even, level, plane ♦ [1] buff, burnish, dress, gloss, grind, polish, rub, shine ♦ [2] ease, facilitate, loosen, unclog

smooth·ly *adv* ♦ : in a smooth manner : without difficulties

♦ easily, effortlessly, fluently, freely, handily, lightly, painlessly, readily

smooth muscle *n* : muscle with no cross striations that is typical of visceral organs (as the stomach and bladder) and is not under voluntary control

smoothy *or* **smooth·ie** \'smü-thē\ *n, pl* **smooth·ies** 1 : an artfully suave person 2 *smoothie* : a creamy beverage of fruit blended with juice, milk, or yogurt

s'more \'smȯr\ *n* : a dessert of marshmallow and pieces of chocolate sandwiched between graham crackers

smor·gas·bord \'smȯr-gəs-ˌbȯrd\ *n* : a luncheon or supper buffet consisting of many foods

smote *past and past part of* SMITE

¹**smoth·er** \'smə-thər\ *n* 1 : thick stifling smoke 2 : a dense cloud (as of fog or dust) 3 : a confused multitude of things

²**smother** *vb* **smoth·ered; smoth·er·ing** 1 ♦ : to be overcome by or die from lack of air 2 ♦ : to kill by depriving of air 3 ♦ : to suppress expression or knowledge of 4 : to cover thickly

♦ [1, 2] choke, stifle, strangle, suffocate ♦ [3] choke, pocket, repress, stifle, strangle, suppress, swallow

SMSgt *abbr* senior master sergeant

¹**smudge** \'sməj\ *vb* **smudged; smudg·ing** : to soil or blur by rubbing or smearing

²**smudge** *n* : a dirty or blurred spot — **smudgy** *adj*

smug \\'sməg\\ *adj* **smug·ger; smug·gest** ♦ : conscious of one's virtue and importance : SELF-SATISFIED ⟨a ∼ smile⟩ — **smug·ly** *adv*

♦ complacent, conceited, egotistic, important, overweening, pompous, prideful, proud, self-important, self-satisfied, stuck-up, vain

smug·gle \\'smə-gəl\\ *vb* **smug·gled; smug·gling** **1** : to import or export secretly, illegally, or without paying the duties required by law **2** : to convey secretly — **smug·gler** \\'smə-glər\\ *n*

smug·ness *n* ♦ : the quality or state of being smug

♦ complacence, conceit, ego, egotism, pride, self-conceit, self-esteem, self-importance, self-satisfaction, vainglory, vanity

smut \\'smət\\ *n* **1** : something (as soot) that smudges; *also* : SMUDGE, SPOT **2** : any of various destructive diseases of plants caused by fungi; *also* : a fungus causing smut **3** ♦ : indecent language or matter

♦ bawdiness, coarseness, dirt, dirtiness, filth, filthiness, foulness, grossness, indecency, lewdness, nastiness, obscenity, ribaldry, vulgarity

smut·ty *adj* **smut·ti·er; -est** ♦ : soiled or tainted with smut : not decent

♦ bawdy, coarse, crude, dirty, filthy, foul, gross, indecent, lascivious, lewd, nasty, obscene, pornographic, ribald, unprintable, vulgar, wanton

Sn *symbol* tin
SN *abbr* seaman
snack \\'snak\\ *n* : a light meal : BITE
snaf·fle \\'sna-fəl\\ *n* : a jointed bit for a horse's bridle
¹snag \\'snag\\ *n* **1** : a stump or piece of a tree esp. when under water **2** ♦ : an unexpected difficulty

♦ booby trap, catch, pitfall

²snag *vb* **snagged; snag·ging** **1** : to become caught on or as if on a snag **2** : to seize quickly : SNATCH
snail \\'snāl\\ *n* : any of numerous small gastropod mollusks with a spiral shell into which they can withdraw
snail mail *n* ♦ : mail delivered by a postal system

♦ mail, matter, parcel post, post

snake \\'snāk\\ *n* **1** : any of numerous long-bodied limbless reptiles **2** ♦ : a treacherous person **3** : something that resembles a snake — **snaky** *adj*

♦ beast, boor, churl, clown, creep, cretin, cur, heel, jerk, joker, louse, lout, skunk, slob

snake·bite \\-,bīt\\ *n* : the bite of a snake and esp. a venomous snake
¹snap \\'snap\\ *vb* **snapped; snap·ping** **1** : to grasp or slash at something with the teeth **2** ♦ : to get or buy quickly — usu. used with *up* **3** : to utter sharp or angry words **4** : to break suddenly with a sharp sound **5** : to give a sharp cracking noise **6** : to throw with a quick motion **7** : FLASH ⟨her eyes *snapped*⟩ **8** : to put a football into play **9** ♦ : to take photographically — **snap·per** *n* — **snap·py** *adj*

♦ *usu* **snap up** [2] catch, collar, grab, nab, seize ♦ [9] mug, photograph, shoot

²snap *n* **1** ♦ : the act or sound of snapping **2** ♦ : something very easy to do : CINCH **3 a** : a short period of cold weather **b** : a small amount **4** : a catch or fastening that closes with a click **5** : a thin brittle cookie **6** ♦ : a pleasing vigorous quality : ENERGY; *also* : smartness of movement **7** : the putting of the ball into play in football **8** : a casual photograph : SNAPSHOT

♦ [1] bang, blast, boom, clap, crack, crash, pop, report, slam, smash, thwack, whack ♦ [2] breeze, child's play, cinch, picnic, pushover ♦ [6] dash, energy, life, pep, vigor (*or* vigour), vim, vitality

³snap *adj* **1** ♦ : done, made, or carried through suddenly or without deliberation **2** ♦ : unusually easy or simple

♦ [1] ad-lib, extemporaneous, impromptu, offhand, unplanned, unpremeditated, unprepared, unrehearsed ♦ [2] easy, effortless, facile, fluent, fluid, light, painless, ready, simple, smooth, soft

snap back *vb* ♦ : to make a quick or vigorous recovery

♦ convalesce, gain, heal, mend, rally, recover, recuperate

snap bean *n* : a bean grown primarily for its long pods that are cooked as a vegetable when young and tender
snap·drag·on \\'snap-,dra-gən\\ *n* : any of a genus of herbs with long spikes of showy flowers
snapping turtle *n* : either of two large American turtles with powerful jaws and a strong musky odor

snap·pish *adj* ♦ : given to curt irritable speech

♦ choleric, crabby, cranky, cross, crotchety, grouchy, grumpy, irascible, irritable, peevish, perverse, petulant, short-tempered, snappy, testy, waspish

snap·py *adj* **snap·pi·er; -est** **1** : given to curt irritable speech **2** ♦ : quickly made or done; *also* : marked by vigor or liveliness **3** : briskly cold **4** ♦ : having style

♦ [2] fast, hasty, quick, rapid, speedy, swift ♦ [2] active, brisk, energetic, lively, peppy, spirited, sprightly, springy, vital, vivacious ♦ [4] à la mode, chic, fashionable, in, modish, sharp, smart, stylish

snap·shot \\'snap-,shät\\ *n* ♦ : a photograph taken usu. with an inexpensive handheld camera

♦ photograph, print, shot, snap

¹snare \\'snar\\ *n* ♦ : a trap often consisting of a noose for catching birds or mammals; *also* : something by which one is entangled, involved in difficulties, or impeded

♦ ambush, entanglement, net, trap, web

²snare *vb* ♦ : to capture by or as if by use of a snare

♦ enmesh, ensnare, entangle, entrap, mesh, tangle, trap ♦ bag, capture, catch, collar, corral, get, grab, grapple, hook, land, nab, seize, trap

snark \\'snärk\\ *n* : SARCASM 2
¹snarl \\'snärl\\ *vb* ♦ : to cause to become knotted and intertwined

♦ entangle, interlace, intertwine, interweave, knot, tangle

²snarl *n* **1** : a tangled, twisted mass : TANGLE **2** ♦ : a tangled situation

♦ backup, bottleneck, jam

³snarl *vb* : to growl angrily or threateningly
⁴snarl *n* : an angry ill-tempered growl
¹snatch \\'snach\\ *vb* **1** : to try to grasp something suddenly **2** : to seize or take away suddenly
²snatch *n* **1** : a short period **2** : an act of snatching **3** : something brief or fragmentary ⟨∼*es* of song⟩
¹sneak \\'snēk\\ *vb* **sneaked** \\'snēkt\\ *or* **snuck** \\'snək\\; **sneak·ing** ♦ : to go or act in a furtive manner; *also* : to put, bring, or take in a furtive or artful manner ⟨*snuck* past the guard⟩ — **sneak·ing·ly** *adv*

♦ lurk, pussyfoot, skulk, slide, slink, slip, snake, steal

²sneak *n* **1** : one who acts in a furtive or shifty manner **2** : a stealthy or furtive move or escape — **sneak** *adj*
sneak·er \\'snē-kər\\ *n* : a sports shoe with a pliable rubber sole
sneaky *adj* **sneak·i·er; -est** ♦ : marked by stealth, furtiveness, or shiftiness — **sneak·i·ly** \\'snē-kə-lē\\ *adv*

♦ furtive, shady, shifty, slippery, sly, stealthy ♦ clandestine, covert, furtive, hugger-mugger, private, secret, sneak, stealthy, surreptitious, undercover, underground, underhanded

sneer \\'snir\\ *vb* ♦ : to show scorn or contempt by curling the lip or by a jeering tone — **sneer** *n*

♦ jeer, laugh, snicker, sniff, snort

sneeze \\'snēz\\ *vb* **sneezed; sneez·ing** : to force the breath out suddenly and violently as a reflex act — **sneeze** *n*
SNF *abbr* skilled nursing facility
snick·er \\'sni-kər\\ *n* ♦ : a partly suppressed laugh — **snicker** *vb*

♦ cackle, chortle, laugh, laughter, titter

snide \\'snīd\\ *adj* **1** : unworthy of esteem : LOW ⟨a ∼ trick⟩ **2** : slyly disparaging ⟨a ∼ remark⟩ — **snide·ly** *adv*

♦ base, contemptible, despicable, detestable, dirty, dishonorable (*or* dishonourable), ignoble, low, mean, sordid, vile, wretched

sniff \\'snif\\ *vb* **1** : to draw air audibly up the nose esp. for smelling **2** ♦ : to show disdain or scorn — usu. used with *at* **3** ♦ : to detect by or as if by smelling — **sniff** *n*

♦ *usu* **sniff at** [2] disdain, high-hat, scorn, slight, snub ♦ [3] nose, scent, smell, whiff

snif·fle \\'sni-fəl\\ *n* **1** *pl* : a head cold marked by nasal discharge **2** : SNUFFLE — **sniffle** *vb*
¹snip \\'snip\\ *n* **1** : a fragment snipped off **2** : a simple stroke of the scissors or shears
²snip *vb* **snipped; snip·ping** : to cut off by bits : CLIP; *also* : to remove by cutting off ⟨∼ a flower⟩
¹snipe \\'snīp\\ *n, pl* **snipes** *or* **snipe** : any of several long-billed game birds esp. of marshy areas that belong to the same family as the sandpipers

²**snipe** *vb* **sniped; snip·ing :** to shoot at an exposed enemy from a concealed position — **snip·er** *n*

snip·py \'sni-pē\ *adj* **snip·pi·er; -est** **1 :** having a quick temper **:** SNAPPISH **2 ♦ :** unduly brief or curt ⟨a ~ comment⟩

    ♦ abrupt, bluff, blunt, brusque, curt

snips \'snips\ *n pl* **:** hand shears used esp. for cutting sheet metal ⟨tin ~⟩

¹**snitch** \'snich\ *vb* **1 ♦ :** to give information (as of another's wrongdoing) to an authority **:** INFORM **2 ♦ :** to take by stealth **:** PILFER — **snitch** *n*

    ♦ [1] inform, squeal, talk, tell ♦ [2] appropriate, filch, hook, misappropriate, nip, pilfer, pocket, purloin, steal, swipe, thieve

²**snitch** *n* **♦ :** one that snitches **:** TATTLETALE

    ♦ betrayer, blabbermouth, informer, rat, stool pigeon, tattler, tattletale

sniv·el \'sni-vəl\ *vb* **-eled** *or* **-elled; -el·ing** *or* **-el·ling** **1 :** to have a running nose; *also* **:** SNUFFLE **2 :** to whine in a snuffling manner — **snivel** *n*

snob \'snäb\ *n* **:** one who seeks association with persons of higher social position and looks down on those considered inferior — **snob·bish** *adj* — **snob·bish·ly** *adv* — **snob·bish·ness** *n* — **snob·by** \'snä-bē\ *adj*

snob·bery \'snä-bə-rē\ *n, pl* **-ber·ies** **:** snobbish conduct

¹**snoop** \'snüp\ *vb* **♦ :** to pry in a furtive or meddlesome way

    ♦ butt in, interfere, intrude, meddle, mess, nose, obtrude, poke, pry

²**snoop** *n* **:** a prying meddlesome person

snooty \'snü-tē\ *adj* **snoot·i·er; -est :** DISDAINFUL, SNOBBISH

¹**snooze** \'snüz\ *vb* **snoozed; snooz·ing ♦ :** to take a nap **:** DOZE

    ♦ catnap, doze, drowse, nap, slumber

²**snooze** *n* **♦ :** a short sleep esp. during the day

    ♦ catnap, doze, drowse, forty winks, nap, siesta, wink

snore \'snōr\ *vb* **snored; snor·ing :** to breathe with a rough hoarse noise while sleeping — **snore** *n*

snor·kel \'snȯr-kəl\ *n* **:** a tube projecting above the water used by swimmers for breathing with the face under water — **snorkel** *vb*

¹**snort** \'snȯrt\ *vb* **1 :** to force air violently and noisily through the nose ⟨his horse ~ed⟩ **2 :** to inhale (a drug) through the nostrils **3 :** to express scorn, anger, indignation, or surprise by a snort

²**snort** *n* **1 ♦ :** the act or sound of snorting **2 ♦ :** a drink of usu. straight liquor taken in one draft

    ♦ [1] boo, catcall, hiss, hoot, jeer, raspberry ♦ [2] draft, drag, drink, nip, quaff, shot, slug, swallow, swig

snot \'snät\ *n* **1 :** nasal mucus **2 :** a snotty person

snot·ty \'snä-tē\ *adj* **snot·ti·er; -est** **1 :** soiled with snot **2 :** rudely or spitefully unpleasant ⟨a ~ remark⟩

snout \'snaut\ *n* **1 :** a long projecting muzzle (as of a pig) **2 :** a usu. large or grotesque nose

¹**snow** \'snō\ *n* **1 :** crystals of ice formed from water vapor in the air **2 :** a descent or shower of snow crystals

²**snow** *vb* **1 :** to fall or cause to fall in or as snow **2 :** to cover or shut in with or as if with snow **3 :** deceive, persuade, or charm glibly

¹**snow·ball** \'snō-ˌbȯl\ *n* **:** a round mass of snow pressed into shape in the hand for throwing

²**snowball** *vb* **1 :** to throw snowballs at **2 ♦ :** to increase or expand at a rapidly accelerating rate

    ♦ accumulate, appreciate, balloon, build, burgeon, enlarge, escalate, expand, increase, mount, multiply, mushroom, proliferate, rise, swell, wax

snow·bank \-ˌbaŋk\ *n* **:** a mound or slope of snow

snow·belt \-ˌbelt\ *n, often cap* **:** a region that receives an appreciable amount of annual snowfall

snow·blow·er \-ˌblō-ər\ *n* **:** a machine in which a rotating spiral blade picks up and propels snow aside

snow·board \-ˌbȯrd\ *n* **:** a board like a wide ski ridden in a surfing position downhill over snow

snow·drift \-ˌdrift\ *n* **:** a bank of drifted snow

snow·drop \-ˌdräp\ *n* **:** a plant with narrow leaves and a nodding white flower that blooms early in the spring

snow·fall \-ˌfȯl\ *n* **:** a fall of snow

snow fence *n* **:** a fence across the path of prevailing winds to protect something (as a road) from drifting snow

snow·field \'snō-ˌfēld\ *n* **:** a mass of perennial snow at the head of a glacier

snow·mo·bile \'snō-mō-ˌbēl\ *n* **:** any of various automotive ve-

hicles for travel on snow — **snow·mo·bil·er** \-ˌbē-lər\ *n* — **snow·mo·bil·ing** \-liŋ\ *n*

snow pea *n* **:** a cultivated pea with flat edible pods

snow·plow \'snō-ˌplau̇\ *n* **1 :** a device for clearing away snow **2 :** a skiing maneuver in which the heels of both skis are slid outward for slowing down or stopping

¹**snow·shoe** \-ˌshü\ *n* **:** a lightweight platform for the foot designed to enable a person to walk on soft snow without sinking

²**snowshoe** *vb* **snow·shoed; snow·shoe·ing :** to travel on snowshoes

snow·storm \-ˌstȯrm\ *n* **:** a storm of falling snow

snow thrower *n* **:** SNOWBLOWER

snow under *vb* **♦ :** to overwhelm esp. in excess of capacity to absorb or deal with something

    ♦ carry away, crush, devastate, floor, oppress, overcome, overpower, overwhelm, prostrate, swamp

snowy \'snō-ē\ *adj* **snow·i·er; -est** **1 :** marked by snow **2 :** white as snow

¹**snub** \'snəb\ *vb* **snubbed; snub·bing ♦ :** to treat with disdain **:** SLIGHT

    ♦ disdain, high-hat, scorn, slight, sniff

²**snub** *n* **♦ :** an act or an instance of snubbing

    ♦ brush-off, cold shoulder, rebuff, repulse

snub–nosed \'snəb-ˌnōzd\ *adj* **:** having a nose slightly turned up at the end

snuck *past and past part of* SNEAK

¹**snuff** \'snəf\ *vb* **1 :** to pinch off the charred end of (a candle) **2 ♦ :** to put out (a candle) — often used with *out* **3 ♦ :** to make extinct; *also* **:** put an end to — usu. used with *out* — **snuff·er** *n*

    ♦ *usu* **snuff out** [2] douse, extinguish, put out, quench ♦ *usu* **snuff out** [3] annihilate, blot out, demolish, eradicate, exterminate, liquidate, obliterate, root, rub out, stamp, wipe out ♦ *usu* **snuff out** [3] clamp down, crack down, crush, put down, quash, quell, repress, silence, squash, squelch, subdue, suppress

²**snuff** *vb* **1 :** to draw forcibly into or through the nose **2 :** SMELL

³**snuff** *n* **:** SNIFF

⁴**snuff** *n* **:** pulverized tobacco

snuf·fle \'snə-fəl\ *vb* **snuf·fled; snuf·fling** **1 :** to snuff or sniff audibly and repeatedly **2 :** to breathe with a sniffing sound — **snuf·fle** *n*

snug \'snəg\ *adj* **snug·ger; snug·gest** **1 ♦ :** fitting closely and comfortably **2 :** CONCEALED **3 ♦ :** exhibiting neatness, good order, or compactness of line or structure **4 ♦ :** enjoying or affording warm secure shelter or cover and opportunity for ease and contentment ⟨a ~ cottage⟩ — **snug·ly** *adv* — **snug·ness** *n*

    ♦ [1] fast, firm, frozen, secure, set, tight ♦ [3] crisp, neat, orderly, shipshape, tidy, trim, uncluttered ♦ [4] comfortable, easy, soft

snug·gle \'snə-gəl\ *vb* **snug·gled; snug·gling ♦ :** to curl up or draw close comfortably **:** NESTLE

    ♦ cuddle, curl up, nestle, snug

¹**so** \'sō\ *adv* **1 :** in the manner indicated **2 ♦ :** in the same way **3 :** THUS **4 :** FINALLY **5 :** to an indicated or great extent ⟨I'm ~ bored⟩ **6 ♦ :** for that reason **:** THEREFORE **7 :** to a great extent or degree **:** VERY

    ♦ [2] alike, also, correspondingly, likewise, similarly ♦ [6] accordingly, consequently, ergo, hence, therefore, thus, wherefore

²**so** *conj* **:** for that reason ⟨he wanted it, ~ he took it⟩

³**so** *pron* **1 :** the same ⟨became chairman and remained ~⟩ **2 :** approximately that ⟨a dozen or ~⟩

⁴**so** *abbr* south; southern

SO *abbr* strikeout

¹**soak** \'sōk\ *vb* **1 :** to remain in a liquid **2 ♦ :** to make or become saturated by or as if by immersion **:** WET **3 ♦ :** to draw in by or as if by absorption **4 ♦ :** to cause to pay an exorbitant amount

    ♦ [2] drench, drown, immerse, impregnate, saturate, sop, souse, steep, wet *Ant* wring (out) ♦ [3] absorb, drink, imbibe, sponge, suck ♦ [4] gouge, overcharge, sting

²**soak** *n* **1 :** the act of soaking **2 :** the liquid in which something is soaked **3 :** one who is habitually drunk **:** DRUNKARD

soap \'sōp\ *n* **♦ :** a cleansing substance made usu. by action of alkali on fat — **soap** *vb* — **soapy** *adj*

    ♦ cleaner, detergent

soap·box \'sōp-ˌbäks\ *n* **:** an improvised platform used for delivering informal speeches

soap opera *n* **:** a radio or television daytime serial drama

soap·stone \\'sōp-ˌstōn\ n : a soft talc-containing stone with a soapy feel

soar \\'sōr\ vb ♦ : to fly upward or at a height on or as if on wings; also : to rise or increase dramatically (as in position, value, or price)

♦ arise, ascend, climb, lift, mount, rise, up ♦ fly, glide, plane, wing ♦ rocket, shoot, skyrocket, zoom

sob \\'säb\ vb **sobbed; sob·bing** ♦ : to weep with convulsive heavings of the chest or contractions of the throat — **sob** n

♦ bawl, blubber, cry, weep

so·ba \\'sō-bə\ n : a Japanese noodle made from buckwheat flour

so·ber \\'sō-bər\ adj **so·ber·er** \-bər-ər\; **so·ber·est** \-bə-rəst\ **1** ♦ : temperate in the use of liquor **2** ♦ : not drunk **3** ♦ : serious or grave in mood or disposition **4** : having a quiet tone or color — **so·ber·ly** adv — **so·ber·ness** n

♦ [2] clearheaded, dry, straight, temperate *Ant* drunk, high, inebriated, intoxicated, soused, tipsy ♦ [3] earnest, grave, humorless (*or* humourless), serious, severe, solemn, staid, unsmiling, weighty

so·bri·ety \sō-'brī-ə-tē\ n ♦ : the quality or state of being sober

♦ earnestness, gravity, intentness, seriousness, solemnity

so·bri·quet \\'sō-bri-ˌkā, -ˌket\ n : NICKNAME

soc abbr **1** social; society **2** sociology

so–called \\'sō-'kȯld\ adj : commonly but often inaccurately so termed

soc·cer \\'sä-kər\ n : a game played on a field by two teams with a round inflated ball that is kicked or hit with any body part other than the hands or arms

so·cia·bil·i·ty \ˌsō-shə-'bi-lə-tē\ n : the quality or state of being sociable; also : the act or an instance of being sociable

¹**so·cia·ble** \\'sō-shə-bəl\ adj **1** : liking companionship : FRIENDLY **2** ♦ : characterized by pleasant social relations — **so·cia·bly** \\'sō-shə-blē\ adv

♦ affable, cordial, genial, gracious, hospitable

²**sociable** n : SOCIAL

¹**so·cial** \\'sō-shəl\ adj **1** ♦ : marked by pleasant companionship with one's friends **2** : naturally living and breeding in organized communities (~ insects) **3** : of or relating to human society (~ institutions) **4** : of, relating to, or based on rank in a particular society (~ circles); also : of or relating to fashionable society — **so·cial·ly** adv

♦ boon, companionable, convivial, extroverted, gregarious, outgoing, sociable

²**social** n : a social gathering

social distancing n : the practice of maintaining a greater than usual physical distance (as six feet) from other people or of avoiding direct contact with people or objects in public places during the outbreak of a contagious disease

so·cial·ise chiefly Brit var of SOCIALIZE

so·cial·ism \\'sō-shə-ˌli-zəm\ n : any of various social systems based on shared or government ownership and administration of the means of production and distribution of goods — **so·cial·ist** \\'sō-shə-list\ n or adj — **so·cial·is·tic** \ˌsō-shə-'lis-tik\ adj

so·cial·ite \\'sō-shə-ˌlīt\ n : a person prominent in fashionable society

so·cial·ize \\'sō-shə-ˌlīz\ vb **-ized; -iz·ing** **1** : to regulate according to the theory and practice of socialism **2** : to adapt to social needs or uses **3** ♦ : to participate actively in a social gathering — **so·cial·i·za·tion** \ˌsō-shə-lə-'zā-shən\ n

♦ associate, fraternize, hobnob, mingle, mix

social media n pl : forms of electronic communication (as websites) for sharing content (as messages, photos, or videos) with other users

social networking n : the creation and maintenance of personal and business relationships esp. online

social science n : a science (as economics or political science) dealing with a particular aspect of human society — **social scientist** n

social work n : services, activities, or methods providing social services esp. to the economically or socially disadvantaged — **social worker** n

so·ci·ety \sə-'sī-ə-tē\ n, pl **-ties** **1** ♦ : the fellowship existing among companions : COMPANY **2** ♦ : a voluntary association of persons for common ends **3** : a part of a community bound together by common interests and values; esp : the group or set of fashionable people **4** : people in general — **societal** adj

♦ [1] camaraderie, companionship, company, comradeship, fel-

lowship ♦ [2] association, brotherhood, club, college, congress, council, fellowship, fraternity, guild, institute, institution, league, order, organization

so·cio·eco·nom·ic \ˌsō-sē-ō-ˌe-kə-'nä-mik, ˌsō-shē-, -ˌē-kə-\ adj : of, relating to, or involving both social and economic factors

sociol abbr sociologist; sociology

so·ci·ol·o·gy \ˌsō-sē-'ä-lə-jē, ˌsō-shē-\ n : the science of society, social institutions, and social relationships — **so·cio·log·i·cal** \ˌsō-sē-ə-'lä-ji-kəl, ˌsō-shē-\ adj — **so·ci·ol·o·gist** \-'ä-lə-jist\ n

so·cio·path \\'sō-sē-ə-ˌpath, 'sō-sh(ē-)ə-\ n : a person exhibiting antisocial behavior : PSYCHOPATH — **so·cio·path·ic** \ˌsō-sē-ə-'pa-thik, ˌsō-sh(ē-)ə-\ adj

¹**sock** \\'säk\ n, pl **socks** or **sox** \\'säks\ : a stocking with a short leg

²**sock** vb : to hit, strike, or apply forcefully

³**sock** n ♦ : a vigorous blow : PUNCH

♦ bat, belt, blow, box, clout, hit, punch, slug, thump, wallop, whack

sock·et \\'sä-kət\ n : an opening or hollow that forms a holder for something

socket wrench n : a wrench usu. in the form of a bar and removable socket made to fit a bolt or nut

sock·eye salmon \\'säk-ˌī-\ n : a commercially important Pacific salmon

¹**sod** \\'säd\ n **1** : TURF 1 **2** ♦ : one's native land

♦ country, fatherland, home, homeland, motherland

²**sod** vb **sod·ded; sod·ding** : to cover with sod

so·da \\'sō-də\ n **1** : SODIUM CARBONATE **2** : SODIUM BICARBONATE **3** : SODIUM **4** : SODA WATER **5** : SODA POP **6** : a sweet drink of soda water, flavoring, and often ice cream

soda pop n : a carbonated, sweetened, and flavored soft drink

soda water n : a beverage of water charged with carbon dioxide

sod·den \\'säd-ᵊn\ adj **1** : lacking spirit : DULLED **2** ♦ : heavy with or as if with moisture or water : SOAKED **3** : heavy or doughy from being improperly cooked (~ biscuits)

♦ saturated, soggy, waterlogged, watery, wet

so·di·um \\'sō-dē-əm\ n : a soft waxy silver white metallic chemical element occurring in nature in combined form (as in salt)

sodium bicarbonate n : a white weakly alkaline salt used esp. in baking powders, fire extinguishers, and medicine

sodium carbonate n : a carbonate of sodium used esp. in washing and bleaching textiles

sodium chloride n : SALT 1

sodium fluoride n : a salt used chiefly in tiny amounts (as in fluoridation) to prevent tooth decay

sodium hydroxide n : a white brittle caustic substance used in making soap and rayon and in bleaching

sodium nitrate n : a crystalline salt used as a fertilizer and in curing meat

sodium thiosulfate n : a hygroscopic crystalline salt used as a photographic fixing agent

sod·omy \\'sä-də-mē\ n : anal or oral sexual intercourse with a member of the same or opposite sex; also : sexual intercourse with an animal — **sod·om·ize** \\'sä-də-ˌmīz\ vb

so·ev·er \sō-'e-vər\ adv **1** : in any degree or manner (how bad ~) **2** : at all : of any kind (any help ~)

so·fa \\'sō-fə\ n : a couch usu. with upholstered back and arms

♦ couch, davenport, divan, lounge, settee

soft \\'sȯft\ adj **1** : not hard or rough : NONVIOLENT **2** ♦ : marked by a gentleness, kindness, or tenderness **3** : emotionally susceptible **4** : not prepared to endure hardship **5** : not containing certain salts that prevent lathering (~ water) **6** : occurring at such a speed as to avoid destructive impact (~ landing of a spacecraft on the moon) **7** : BIODEGRADABLE (a ~ pesticide) **8** : not alcoholic (~ drinks) **9** : less detrimental than a hard narcotic (~ drugs) **10** ♦ : demanding little work or effort **11** : lacking robust strength, stamina, or endurance **12** ♦ : lacking firmness or strength of character **13** ♦ : bringing ease, comfort, or quiet **14** ♦ : quiet in pitch or volume **15** ♦ : smooth or delicate in texture, grain, or fiber **16** ♦ : yielding to physical pressure — **soft·ly** adv — **soft·ness** n

♦ [2] balmy, benign, bland, delicate, gentle, light, mellow, mild, soothing, tender ♦ [10] easy, effortless, facile, fluent, fluid, light, painless, ready, simple, smooth, snap ♦ [12] effete, frail, nerveless, spineless, weak, wimpy, wishy-washy ♦ [13] comfortable, easy, snug ♦ [14] dull, low, quiet *Ant* blaring, clamorous, deafening, earsplitting, loud ♦ [15] cottony, downy, satiny, silken, velvety *Ant* coarse, harsh, rough, scratchy ♦ [16] flabby, mushy, pulpy, spongy *Ant* firm, hard, solid

soft·ball \'sȯft-ˌbȯl\ *n* : a game similar to baseball played with a ball larger and softer than a baseball; *also* : the ball used in this game

soft·bound \-ˌbau̇nd\ *adj* : not bound in hard covers ⟨~ books⟩

soft coal *n* : BITUMINOUS COAL

soft·en \'sȯ-fən\ *vb* ♦ : to make or become soft — **soft·en·er** *n*

♦ debilitate, enervate, enfeeble, prostrate, sap, tire, waste, weaken ♦ buffer, cushion, gentle

soft palate *n* : the fold at the back of the hard palate that partially separates the mouth from the pharynx

soft·ware \'sȯft-ˌwar\ *n* : the entire set of programs, procedures, and related documentation associated with a system; *esp* : computer programs

soft·wood \-ˌwu̇d\ *n* **1** : the wood of a coniferous tree as compared to that of a broad-leaved deciduous tree **2** : a tree yielding softwood — **softwood** *adj*

sog·gy \'sä-gē\ *adj* **sog·gi·er; -est** ♦ : heavy with water or moisture — **sog·gi·ly** \'sä-gə-lē\ *adv* — **sog·gi·ness** \-gē-nəs\ *n*

♦ saturated, sodden, waterlogged, watery, wet

soi·gné *or* **soi·gnée** \swän-'yā\ *adj* : elegantly maintained; *esp* : WELL-GROOMED

¹soil \'sȯil\ *vb* **1** : CORRUPT, POLLUTE **2** ♦ : to make or become dirty **3** : STAIN, DISGRACE

♦ befoul, begrime, besmirch, blacken, dirty, foul, grime, mire, muddy, smirch, stain

²soil *n* **1** : STAIN, DEFILEMENT **2** ♦ : something that spoils or pollutes

♦ dirt, filth, grime, muck, smut

³soil *n* **1** ♦ : firm land : EARTH **2** ♦ : the upper layer of earth in which plants grow **3** : COUNTRY, REGION

♦ [1] dirt, dust, earth, ground, land ♦ [2] dirt, earth, ground

soi·ree *or* **soi·rée** \swä-'rā\ *n* : an evening party

¹so·journ \'sō-ˌjərn, sō-'jərn\ *vb* ♦ : to dwell in a place temporarily — **so·journ·er** *n*

♦ stay, tarry, visit

²so·journ *n* : a temporary stay

¹sol *n* : a fluid colloidal system

²sol *abbr* **1** solicitor **2** soluble **3** solution

Sol \'säl\ *n* : SUN

¹sol·ace \'sä-ləs\ *n* ♦ : alleviation of grief or anxiety; *also* : a source of relief or consolation

♦ cheer, comfort, consolation, relief ♦ comforting, consolation

²solace *vb* **so·laced; so·lac·ing** ♦ : to give solace to : CONSOLE

♦ assure, cheer, comfort, console, reassure, soothe

so·lar \'sō-lər\ *adj* **1** : of, derived from, or relating to the sun **2** : measured by the earth's course in relation to the sun ⟨the ~ year⟩ **3** : operated by or using the sun's light or heat ⟨~ energy⟩

solar cell *n* : a photoelectric cell used as a power source

solar collector *n* : a device for the absorption of solar radiation for the heating of water or buildings or the production of electricity

solar flare *n* : a sudden temporary outburst of energy from a small area of the sun's surface

so·lar·i·um \sō-'lar-ē-əm\ *n, pl* **-ia** \-ē-ə\ *also* **-i·ums** : a room exposed to the sun; *esp* : a room (as in a hospital) for exposure of the body to sunshine

solar plexus *n* ♦ : the general area of the stomach below the sternum

♦ abdomen, belly, gut, stomach, tummy

solar system *n* : the sun together with the group of celestial bodies that revolve around it

solar wind *n* : plasma continuously ejected from the sun's surface

sold past and past part of SELL

sol·der \'sä-dər, 'sȯ-\ *n* : a metallic alloy used when melted to mend or join metallic surfaces — **solder** *vb*

soldering iron *n* : a metal device for applying heat in soldering

¹sol·dier \'sōl-jər\ *n* ♦ : a person in military service; *esp* : an enlisted person — **sol·dier·ly** *adj or adv*

♦ fighter, legionnaire, man-at-arms, regular, serviceman, warrior *Ant* civilian

²soldier *vb* **sol·diered; sol·dier·ing** **1** : to serve as a soldier **2** : to pretend to work while actually doing nothing

sol·diery \'sōl-jə-rē\ *n* : a body of soldiers

¹sole \'sōl\ *n* : any of various flatfishes including some used for food

²sole *n* **1** : the undersurface of the foot **2** : the bottom of a shoe

³sole *vb* **soled; sol·ing** : to furnish (a shoe) with a sole

⁴sole *adj* ♦ : being the only one : ONLY; *also* : belonging exclusively or otherwise limited to one usu. specified individual, unit, or group

♦ alone, lone, only, singular, solitary, special, unique

so·le·cism \'sä-lə-ˌsi-zəm, 'sō-\ *n* **1** : a mistake in grammar **2** : a breach of etiquette

sole·ly \'sōl-lē\ *adv* **1** ♦ : without another **2** ♦ : to the exclusion of all else

♦ [1] alone, independently, singly, unaided, unassisted ♦ [2] alone, exclusively, just, only, simply

sol·emn \'sä-ləm\ *adj* **1** : marked by or observed with full religious ceremony **2** : FORMAL, CEREMONIOUS **3** ♦ : highly serious **4** : SOMBER, GLOOMY — **sol·emn·ly** \'sä-ləm-lē\ *adv*

♦ august, dignified, imposing, staid, stately ♦ earnest, grave, humorless (*or* humourless), serious, severe, sober, staid, unsmiling, weighty

so·lem·ni·ty \sə-'lem-nə-tē\ *n* **1** ♦ : formal or ceremonious observance of an occasion or event **2** ♦ : a solemn condition or quality

♦ [1] ceremonial, ceremony, form, formality, observance, rite, ritual ♦ [2] earnestness, gravity, intentness, seriousness, sobriety

sol·em·nize \'sä-ləm-ˌnīz\ *vb* **-nized; -niz·ing** **1** : to observe or honor with solemnity **2** : to celebrate (a marriage) with religious rites — **sol·em·ni·za·tion** \ˌsä-ləm-nə-'zā-shən\ *n*

so·le·noid \'sō-lə-ˌnȯid, 'sä-\ *n* : a coil of wire usu. in cylindrical form that when carrying a current acts like a magnet

so·lic·it \sə-'li-sət\ *vb* **1** ♦ : to make petition to : ENTREAT **2** ♦ : to approach with a request or plea **3** : TEMPT, LURE **4** ♦ : to try to obtain by usu. urgent requests or pleas

♦ [1] appeal, beg, beseech, entreat, implore, importune, petition, plead, pray, supplicate ♦ [2] canvass, poll, survey ♦ [4] ask, -call, plead, quest, request, seek, sue

so·lic·i·ta·tion \-ˌli-sə-'tā-shən\ *n* ♦ : the practice or act or an instance of soliciting; *also* : a moving or drawing force

♦ appeal, cry, entreaty, petition, plea, prayer, suit, supplication

so·lic·i·tor \sə-'li-sə-tər\ *n* **1** ♦ : one that solicits **2** : LAWYER; *esp* : a legal official of a city or state

♦ pleader, suitor

so·lic·i·tous \sə-'li-sə-təs\ *adj* **1** : full of concern or fears : WORRIED, CONCERNED **2** : full of desire : EAGER **3** ♦ : manifesting or expressing attentive care and protectiveness — **so·lic·i·tous·ly** *adv*

♦ attentive, considerate, kind, thoughtful

so·lic·i·tude \sə-'li-sə-ˌtüd, -ˌtyüd\ *n* : the state of being concerned and anxious : ANXIETY, CONCERN

¹sol·id \'sä-ləd\ *adj* **1** : not hollow; *also* : written as one word without a hyphen ⟨a ~ compound⟩ **2** : having, involving, or dealing with three dimensions or with solids ⟨~ geometry⟩ **3** ♦ : not loose or spongy : COMPACT ⟨a ~ mass of rock⟩; *also* : neither gaseous nor liquid : HARD, RIGID ⟨~ ice⟩ **4** : of good substantial quality or kind ⟨~ comfort⟩ **5** ♦ : thoroughly dependable : RELIABLE ⟨a ~ citizen⟩; *also* : serious in purpose or character ⟨~ reading⟩ **6** : UNANIMOUS, UNITED ⟨~ for pay increases⟩ **7** : of one substance or character **8** ♦ : free from error, fallacy, or misapprehension — **solid** *adv* — **sol·id·ly** *adv*

♦ [3] compact, firm, hard, rigid, stiff, unyielding ♦ [5] dependable, good, reliable, responsible, safe, steady, sure, tried, true, trustworthy ♦ [8] good, hard, informed, just, levelheaded, logical, rational, reasonable, reasoned, sensible, sober, valid, well=founded

²solid *n* **1** : a geometrical figure (as a cube or sphere) having three dimensions **2** : a solid substance

sol·i·dar·i·ty \ˌsä-lə-'dar-ə-tē\ *n* : unity based on shared interests, objectives, or standards

so·lid·i·fy \sə-'li-də-ˌfī\ *vb* **-fied; -fy·ing** ♦ : to make or become solid — **so·lid·i·fi·ca·tion** \-ˌli-də-fə-'kā-shən\ *n*

♦ concrete, congeal, firm, freeze, harden, set ♦ crystallize, form, jell, shape

so·lid·i·ty \sə-'li-də-tē\ *n* **1** ♦ : the quality or state of being solid **2** : something solid

♦ dependability, reliability, sureness, trustworthiness

sol·id·ness *n* : the quality or state of being solid

sol–id–state *adj* **1** : relating to the structure and properties of solid material **2** : using semiconductor devices rather than vacuum tubes

so·lil·o·quize \sə-'li-lə-ˌkwīz\ *vb* **-quized; -quiz·ing** : to talk to oneself : utter a soliloquy

so·lil·o·quy \sə-'li-lə-kwē\ *n, pl* **-quies** **1** : the act of talking to oneself **2** : a dramatic monologue that represents unspoken reflections of a character

sol·i·taire \'sä-lə-ˌtar\ *n* **1** : a single gem (as a diamond) set alone **2** : a card game for one person

sol·i·tary \'sä-lə-ˌter-ē\ *adj* **1** ♦ : being or living apart from others **2** ♦ : LONELY, SECLUDED **3** ♦ : being the only one : ONLY ⟨a ∼ example⟩
   ♦ [1] alone, lone, lonely, lonesome, unaccompanied ♦ [3] alone, lone, only, singular, sole, special, unique

sol·i·tude \'sä-lə-ˌtüd, -ˌtyüd\ *n* **1** ♦ : the state of being alone : SECLUSION ⟨worked in ∼⟩ **2** : a lonely place
   ♦ insulation, isolation, seclusion, segregation, sequestration

soln *abbr* solution

¹**so·lo** \'sō-lō\ *n, pl* **solos** **1** : a piece of music for a single voice or instrument with or without accompaniment **2** : an action in which there is only one performer — **solo** *adj or vb* — **so·lo·ist** *n*

²**solo** *adv* : without a companion : ALONE

so·lon \'sō-lən\ *n* **1** : a wise and skillful lawgiver **2** ♦ : a member of a legislative body
   ♦ lawmaker, legislator

sol·stice \'säl-stəs, 'sōl-\ *n* : the time of the year when the sun is farthest north of the equator (**summer solstice**) about June 22 or farthest south (**winter solstice**) about Dec. 22 — **sol·sti·tial** \säl-'sti-shəl, sōl-\ *adj*

sol·u·ble \'säl-yə-bəl\ *adj* **1** : capable of being dissolved in or as if in a liquid **2** ♦ : capable of being solved or explained — **sol·u·bil·i·ty** \ˌsäl-yə-'bi-lə-tē\ *n*
   ♦ answerable, explicable, resolvable, solvable

sol·ute \'säl-ˌyüt\ *n* : a dissolved substance

so·lu·tion \sə-'lü-shən\ *n* **1** : an action or process of solving a problem; *also* : an answer to a problem **2** : an act or the process by which one substance is homogenously mixed with another usu. liquid substance; *also* : a mixture thus formed

solv·able \'säl-və-bəl\ *adj* ♦ : susceptible of solution or of being solved, resolved, or explained
   ♦ answerable, explicable, resolvable, soluble *Ant* inexplicable, insoluble, unsolvable

solve \'sälv\ *vb* **solved; solv·ing** ♦ : to find the answer to or a solution for
   ♦ answer, break, crack, dope, figure out, puzzle, resolve, riddle, unravel, work, work out

sol·ven·cy \'säl-vən-sē\ *n* : the condition of being solvent

¹**sol·vent** \-vənt\ *adj* **1** : able or sufficient to pay all legal debts **2** : dissolving or able to dissolve

²**solvent** *n* : a usu. liquid substance capable of dissolving or dispersing one or more other substances

So·ma·lian \sō-'mäl-yən\ *n* : a native or inhabitant of Somalia — **Somalian** *adj*

so·mat·ic \sō-'ma-tik\ *adj* ♦ : of, relating to, or affecting the body in contrast to the mind or the sex cells and their precursors
   ♦ animal, bodily, carnal, corporal, fleshly, material, physical

som·ber *or chiefly Can and Brit* **som·bre** \'säm-bər\ *adj* **1** ♦ : so shaded as to be dark and gloomy **2** ♦ : of a serious or depressing character : GRAVE, MELANCHOLY ⟨a ∼ mood⟩ — **som·ber·ly** *adv*
   ♦ [1] dark, darkling, dim, dusky, gloomy, murky, obscure ♦ [2] bleak, dark, dismal, dreary, gloomy, gray (*or* grey), wretched

som·bre·ro \səm-'brer-ō\ *n, pl* **-ros** : a broad-brimmed felt hat worn esp. in the Southwest and in Mexico

¹**some** \'səm\ *adj* **1** ♦ : one unspecified ⟨∼ man called⟩ **2** : an unspecified or indefinite number of ⟨∼ berries are ripe⟩ **3** : at least a few or a little ⟨∼ years ago⟩
   ♦ anonymous, certain, one, unidentified, unnamed, unspecified

²**some** *pron* : a certain number or amount ⟨∼ of the berries are ripe⟩ ⟨∼ of it is missing⟩

¹**-some** \səm\ *adj suffix* : characterized by a (specified) thing, quality, state, or action ⟨awe*some*⟩ ⟨burden*some*⟩

²**-some** *n suffix* : a group of (so many) members and esp. persons ⟨four*some*⟩

¹**some·body** \'səm-ˌbä-dē, -bə-\ *pron* : some person

²**somebody** *n* ♦ : a person of importance
   ♦ celebrity, figure, light, luminary, notable, personage, personality, standout, star, superstar, VIP

some·day \'səm-ˌdā\ *adv* : at some future time
   ♦ eventually, sometime, ultimately, yet

some·how \-ˌhau̇\ *adv* : by some means

some·one \-(ˌ)wən\ *pron* : some person

som·er·sault *also* **sum·mer·sault** \'sə-mər-ˌsȯlt\ *n* : a leap or roll in which a person turns heels over head — **somersault** *vb*

som·er·set \-ˌset\ *n or vb* : SOMERSAULT

some·thing \'səm-thiŋ\ *pron* : some undetermined or unspecified thing

some·time \-ˌtīm\ *adv* **1** ♦ : at a future time **2** : at an unknown or unnamed time
   ♦ eventually, someday, ultimately, yet

some·times \-ˌtīmz\ *adv* : at times : OCCASIONALLY

¹**some·what** \-ˌhwät, -ˌhwət\ *pron* : SOMETHING

²**somewhat** *adv* ♦ : in some degree
   ♦ enough, fairly, kind of, moderately, pretty, quite, rather, sort of, so-so

some·where \-ˌhwer\ *adv* : in, at, or to an unknown or unnamed place

som·nam·bu·lism \säm-'nam-byə-ˌli-zəm\ *n* : performance of motor acts (as walking) during sleep; *also* : an abnormal condition of sleep characterized by this — **som·nam·bu·list** \-list\ *n*

som·no·lent \'säm-nə-lənt\ *adj* : inclined to or heavy with sleep : SLEEPY, DROWSY — **som·no·lence** \-ləns\ *n*

son \'sən\ *n* **1** : a male offspring or descendant **2** *cap* : Jesus Christ **3** : a person closely associated with or deriving from a particular formative agent (as a country, race, or school)

so·nar \'sō-ˌnär\ *n* : a method or device for detecting and locating submerged objects (as submarines) by sound waves

so·na·ta \sə-'nä-tə\ *n* : an instrumental composition with three or four movements differing in rhythm and mood but related in key

son·a·ti·na \ˌsä-nə-'tē-nə\ *n* : a short usu. simplified sonata

song \'sȯŋ\ *n* **1** ♦ : vocal music; *also* : a short composition of words and music **2** ♦ : poetic composition **3** : a distinctive or characteristic sound (as of a bird) **4** ♦ : a small amount ⟨sold for a ∼⟩
   ♦ [1] air, lay, melody, strain, tune, warble ♦ [1] jingle, lay, lyric, vocal ♦ [2] poem, poetry, verse ♦ [4] mite, peanuts, pittance, shoestring

song·bird \'sȯŋ-ˌbərd\ *n* : a bird that utters a series of musical tones

Song of Songs : a book in the Jewish Scriptures and in the Roman Catholic canon of the Old Testament and corresponding to the Song of Solomon in the Protestant canon of the Old Testament

song·ster \'sȯŋ-stər\ *n* ♦ : one that sings
   ♦ caroler, singer, vocalist, voice

song·stress \-strəs\ *n* : a girl or woman who is a singer

son·ic \'sä-nik\ *adj* : of or relating to sound waves or the speed of sound

sonic boom *n* : an explosive sound produced by an aircraft traveling at supersonic speed

son–in–law \'sən-ən-ˌlȯ\ *n, pl* **sons–in–law** : the husband of one's daughter or son

son·net \'sä-nət\ *n* : a poem of 14 lines usu. in iambic pentameter with a definite rhyme scheme

son of a gun *n, pl* **sons of guns** : an offensive or disagreeable person

so·no·rous \sə-'nȯr-əs, 'sä-nə-rəs\ *adj* **1** : giving out sound when struck **2** ♦ : loud, deep, or rich in sound **3** : high-sounding : IMPRESSIVE — **so·nor·i·ty** \sə-'nȯr-ə-tē\ *n*
   ♦ golden, loud, resonant, resounding, ringing, round, vibrant

soon \'sün\ *adv* **1** ♦ : before long **2** : in a prompt manner : QUICKLY **3** *archaic* : EARLY **4** ♦ : in agreement with one's choice or preference : WILLINGLY
   ♦ [1] anon, momentarily, presently, shortly ♦ [4] first, preferably, rather, readily

soot \'su̇t, 'sət, 'süt\ *n* : a fine black powder consisting chiefly of carbon that is formed when something burns and that colors smoke — **sooty** *adj*

sooth \'süth\ *n, archaic* : TRUTH

soothe \'süth\ *vb* **soothed; sooth·ing** **1** : to please by flattery or attention **2** ♦ : to calm down **3** : RELIEVE, ALLEVIATE ⟨∼ a burn⟩ — **sooth·er** *n* — **sooth·ing·ly** *adv*

♦ assure, cheer, comfort, console, reassure, solace ♦ allay, alleviate, assuage, calm, ease, help, mitigate, mollify, palliate, relieve

soothing *adj* ♦ : tending to soothe; *also* : having a sedative effect

♦ comforting, dreamy, narcotic, sedative

sooth·say·er \'süth-ˌsā-ər\ *n* ♦ : one who foretells events

♦ augur, diviner, forecaster, fortune-teller, futurist, prognosticator, prophet, seer

sooth·say·ing *n* ♦ : the act of foretelling events; *also* : something that is predicted

♦ cast, forecast, prediction, prognostication, prophecy

¹**sop** \'säp\ *n* : a conciliatory bribe, gift, or concession
²**sop** *vb* **sopped; sop·ping** **1** : to steep or dip in or as if in a liquid **2** ♦ : to wet thoroughly : SOAK; *also* : to mop up (a liquid)

♦ drench, drown, impregnate, saturate, soak, souse, steep

SOP *abbr* standard operating procedure; standing operating procedure
soph *abbr* sophomore
soph·ism \'sä-ˌfi-zəm\ *n* **1** : an argument correct in form but embodying a subtle fallacy **2** : SOPHISTRY
soph·ist \'sä-fist\ *n* : PHILOSOPHER; *esp* : a captious or fallacious reasoner
so·phis·tic \sä-'fis-tik, sə-\ *or* **so·phis·ti·cal** \-ti-kəl\ *adj* : of or characteristic of sophists or sophistry
so·phis·ti·cat·ed \sə-'fis-tə-ˌkā-təd\ *adj* **1** ♦ : highly complicated or developed : COMPLEX ⟨∼ instruments⟩ **2** ♦ : made worldly-wise by wide experience **3** : intellectually appealing ⟨∼ novel⟩

♦ [1] complex, complicated, convoluted, elaborate, intricate, involved, knotty ♦ [2] cosmopolitan, smart, worldly, worldly-wise ♦ [2] debonair, smooth, suave, urbane

so·phis·ti·ca·tion \-ˌfis-tə-'kā-shən\ *n* **1** : the process or result of becoming cultured, knowledgeable, or disillusioned **2** ♦ : the process or result of becoming more complex, developed, or subtle

♦ complexity, elaborateness, intricacy

soph·ist·ry \'sä-fə-strē\ *n* : subtly deceptive reasoning or argument
soph·o·more \'säf-ˌmȯr, 'sä-fə-\ *n* : a student in the second year of high school or college
soph·o·mor·ic \ˌsäf-'mȯr-ik, ˌsä-fə-\ *adj* **1** : being overconfident of knowledge but poorly informed and immature **2** : of, relating to, or characteristic of a sophomore ⟨a ∼ prank⟩
So·pho·ni·as \ˌsä-fə-'nī-əs, ˌsō-\ *n* : ZEPHANIAH
sop·o·rif·ic \ˌsä-pə-'ri-fik\ *adj* **1** : causing sleep or drowsiness **2** : LETHARGIC
sopping *adj* : wet through : SOAKING
so·pra·no \sə-'pra-nō, -'prä-\ *n, pl* **-nos** **1** : the highest singing voice; *also* : a singer with this voice **2** : the highest part in a 4-part chorus — **soprano** *adj*
sor·bet \sȯr-'bā\ *n* : a usu. fruit-flavored ice served for dessert or between courses as a palate refresher
sor·cer·er \-rər\ *n* ♦ : a person who practices sorcery

♦ conjurer, enchanter, magician, necromancer, voodoo, witch, wizard

sor·cer·ess \-rəs\ *n* : a woman who is a sorcerer
sor·cery \'sȯr-sə-rē\ *n* ♦ : the use of magic : WITCHCRAFT

♦ bewitchment, enchantment, magic, necromancy, witchcraft, wizardry

sor·did \'sȯr-dəd\ *adj* **1** ♦ : marked by baseness or grossness : VILE **2** : marked by filthiness and degradation : DIRTY — **sor·did·ly** *adv* — **sor·did·ness** *n*

♦ base, contemptible, despicable, detestable, dirty, dishonorable (*or* dishonourable), ignoble, low, mean, snide, vile, wretched

¹**sore** \'sȯr\ *adj* **sor·er; sor·est** **1** ♦ : causing pain or distress ⟨a ∼ bruise⟩ **2** : painfully sensitive ⟨∼ muscles⟩ **3** : SEVERE, INTENSE **4** : feeling or showing anger : ANGRY — **sore·ness** *n*

♦ nasty, painful

²**sore** *n* **1** : a sore spot on the body; *esp* : one (as an ulcer) with the tissues broken and usu. infected **2** : a source of pain or vexation
sore·head \'sȯr-ˌhed, 'sȯr-\ *n* : a person easily angered or discontented
sore·ly *adv* **1** : in a sore manner **2** : to a high degree

sore throat *n* : painful throat due to inflammation of the fauces and pharynx
sor·ghum \'sȯr-gəm\ *n* : a tall variable Old World tropical grass grown widely for its edible seed, for forage, or for its sweet juice which yields a syrup
so·ror·i·ty \sə-'rȯr-ə-tē\ *n, pl* **-ties** : a women's student organization formed chiefly for social purposes
¹**sor·rel** \'sȯr-əl\ *n* : a brownish orange to light brown color; *also* : a sorrel-colored animal (as a horse)
²**sorrel** *n* : any of various herbs having a sour juice
¹**sor·row** \'sär-ō\ *n* **1** ♦ : deep distress, sadness, or regret; *also* : resultant unhappy or unpleasant state **2** : a cause of grief or sadness **3** : a display of grief or sadness

♦ affliction, anguish, dolor, grief, heartache, woe *Ant* blessedness, bliss, cheer, cheerfulness, cheeriness, delight, ecstasy, elation, euphoria, exhilaration, exuberance, exultation, gladness, glee, happiness, joy, joyousness, jubilation, pleasure, rapture

²**sorrow** *vb* ♦ : to feel or express sorrow

♦ agonize, bleed, feel, grieve, hurt, mourn, suffer

sor·row·ful \-fəl\ *adj* **1** ♦ : full of or marked by sorrow **2** ♦ : expressive of or inducing sorrow

♦ [1] anguished, dolorous, lamentable, mournful, plaintive, sad, sorry, woeful ♦ [2] dolorous, funeral, lugubrious, mournful, plaintive, regretful, rueful, weeping, woeful

sor·row·ful·ly \-f(ə-)lē\ *adv* ♦ : in a sorrowful manner

♦ agonizingly, bitterly, grievously, hard, hardly, sadly, unhappily, woefully, wretchedly

sor·ry \'sär-ē\ *adj* **sor·ri·er; -est** **1** ♦ : feeling sorrow, regret, or penitence **2** : full of sorrow : MOURNFUL **3** ♦ : causing sorrow, pity, or scorn

♦ [1] apologetic, contrite, penitent, regretful, remorseful, repentant, rueful ♦ [3] depressing, dismal, dreary, heartbreaking, melancholy, pathetic, sad, tearful ♦ [3] contemptible, despicable, pitiful

¹**sort** \'sȯrt\ *n* **1** ♦ : a group of persons or things that have similar characteristics : CLASS **2** : WAY, MANNER **3** : QUALITY, NATURE **4** : an instance of sorting **5** : a single human being ⟨he's a good ∼⟩ — **out of sorts** **1** : somewhat ill **2** : GROUCHY, IRRITABLE

♦ breed, class, description, feather, ilk, kind, like, manner, nature, order, species, type

²**sort** *vb* **1** ♦ : to put in a certain place according to kind, class, or nature **2** : to be in accord — **sort·er** *n*

♦ assort, break down, categorize, class, classify, grade, group, peg, place, range, rank, separate

sor·tie \'sȯr-tē, sȯr-'tē\ *n* **1** : a sudden issuing of troops from a defensive position against the enemy **2** : one mission or attack by one airplane
sort of *adv* ♦ : to a moderate degree

♦ enough, fairly, kind of, moderately, pretty, quite, rather, somewhat, so-so

SOS \ˌes-(ˌ)ō-'es\ *n* : a call or request for help or rescue
¹**so-so** \'sō-'sō\ *adv* ♦ : moderately well

♦ adequately, all right, fine, good, nicely, OK, passably, satisfactorily, tolerably, well

²**so-so** *adj* ♦ : neither very good nor very bad

♦ common, fair, indifferent, mediocre, medium, middling, ordinary, passable, run-of-the-mill, second-rate

sot \'sät\ *n* ♦ : an habitual drunkard — **sot·tish** *adj* — **sot·tish·ly** *adv*

♦ drunk, drunkard, inebriate, soak, souse, tippler

souf·flé \sü-'flā\ *n* : a spongy dish made light in baking by stiffly beaten egg whites
sough \'sau̇, 'səf\ *vb* : to make a moaning or sighing sound — **sough** *n*
sought *past and past part of* SEEK
¹**soul** \'sōl\ *n* **1** : the immaterial essence of an individual life **2** : the spiritual principle embodied in human beings or the universe **3** ♦ : an active or essential part **4** ♦ : the moral and emotional nature of human beings **5** : spiritual or moral force **6** : an individual human : PERSON ⟨a kindly ∼⟩ **7** : a strong, positive feeling (as of intense sensitivity and emotional fervor) conveyed esp. by African American performers **8** : SOUL MUSIC — **souled** \'sōld\ *adj*

♦ [3] core, heart, quick ♦ [4] essence, nature, quintessence, stuff, substance

²soul *adj* **1** : of, relating to, or characteristic of Black Americans or their culture ⟨∼ food⟩ **2** : designed for or controlled by Black people ⟨∼ radio stations⟩
soul brother *n* : a Black man or boy
soul·ful \'sōl-fəl\ *adj* ♦ : full of or expressing deep feeling — **soul·ful·ly** *adv*
   ♦ demonstrative, emotional, feeling, intense, passionate, sensitive, sentimental

soul·less \'sōl-ləs\ *adj* ♦ : having no soul or no greatness or warmth of mind or feeling
   ♦ callous, hard, heartless, inhuman, inhumane, pitiless, unfeeling, unsympathetic

soul music *n* : music that is closely related to rhythm and blues and characterized by intensity of feeling
¹sound \'saund\ *adj* **1** : not diseased or sickly **2** : free from flaw or defect **3** ♦ : securely or solidly fixed in place : STRONG **4** ♦ : free from error or fallacy **5** : LEGAL, VALID **6** : THOROUGH **7** : UNDISTURBED ⟨∼ sleep⟩ **8** : showing good judgment ⟨∼ reasoning⟩ — **sound·ly** *adv*
   ♦ [1] able-bodied, chipper, fit, hale, healthy, hearty, robust, well, whole, wholesome ♦ [3] fast, firm, stable, stalwart, steady, strong, sturdy ♦ [4] analytic, coherent, good, logical, rational, reasonable, sensible, sober, valid

²sound *n* **1** : the sensation of hearing; *also* : mechanical energy transmitted by longitudinal pressure waves (**sound waves**) (as in air) that is the stimulus to hearing **2** : something heard : NOISE, TONE; *also* ♦ : hearing distance : EARSHOT **3** : a musical style ⟨the band's ∼⟩ — **sound·less·ly** *adv*
   ♦ earshot, hail, hearing

³sound *vb* **1** : to make or cause to make a sound **2** ♦ : to order or proclaim by a sound ⟨∼ the alarm⟩ **3** ♦ : to convey a certain impression : SEEM **4** : to examine the condition of by causing to give out sounds — **sound·able** \'saun-də-bəl\ *adj*
   ♦ [2] air, express, give, state, vent, voice ♦ [2] advertise, announce, blaze, broadcast, declare, enunciate, placard, post, proclaim, promulgate, publicize, publish ♦ [3] act, appear, look, make, seem

⁴sound *n* ♦ : a long passage of water wider than a strait often connecting two larger bodies of water
   ♦ channel, narrows, strait

⁵sound *vb* **1** : to measure the depth of (water) esp. by a weighted line dropped from the surface : FATHOM **2** : PROBE **3** ♦ : to dive down suddenly ⟨the hooked fish ∼ed⟩ — **sound·ing** *n*
   ♦ dive, pitch, plunge

sound bite *n* : a brief recorded statement broadcast esp. on a news program
sound card *n* : a circuit board in a computer system designed to produce or reproduce sound
sound·er \'saun-dər\ *n* : one that sounds; *esp* : a device for making soundings
sound·less *adj* ♦ : making no sound
   ♦ hushed, muted, noiseless, quiet, silent, still

sound·ness *n* ♦ : the quality or state of being sound
   ♦ firmness, stability, steadiness, strength, sturdiness ♦ fitness, health, heartiness, robustness, wellness, wholeness, wholesomeness

sound off *vb* ♦ : to voice one's opinions freely and vigorously
   ♦ speak out, speak up, spout

sound·proof \'saun(d)-ˌprüf\ *vb* : to insulate so as to obstruct the passage of sound — **soundproof** *adj*
sound·stage \'saund-ˌstāj\ *n* : the part of a motion-picture studio in which a production is filmed
sound·track \'saun(d)-ˌtrak\ *n* : music recorded to accompany a film, DVD, or videotape
soup \'süp\ *n* **1** : a liquid food with stock as its base and often containing pieces of solid food **2** ♦ : something (as a heavy fog) having or suggesting the consistency of soup **3** : an unfortunate predicament ⟨in the ∼⟩
   ♦ fog, haze, mist, murk, smog

soup·çon \süp-'sōⁿ\ *n* : a little bit : ¹TRACE 2 ⟨a ∼ of garlic⟩
soup up *vb* : to increase the power of — **souped–up** \'süpt-ˈəp\ *adj*
soupy \'sü-pē\ *adj* **soup·i·er; -est** **1** : having the consistency of soup **2** ♦ : densely foggy or cloudy
   ♦ cloudy, foggy, hazy, misty, murky, smoggy

¹sour \'saur\ *adj* **1** ♦ : having an acid or tart taste ⟨∼ as vinegar⟩ **2** : SPOILED, PUTRID ⟨a ∼ odor⟩ **3** ♦ : not pleasant : DISAGREEABLE ⟨∼ disposition⟩; *also* : marked by overt hostility — **sour·ish** *adj* — **sour·ly** *adv* — **sour·ness** *n*
   ♦ [1] acid, tart, vinegary ♦ [3] bad, disagreeable, distasteful, nasty, rotten, uncongenial, unlovely, unpleasant, unwelcome

²sour *vb* ♦ : to become or make sour
   ♦ alienate, disaffect, disgruntle, estrange

source \'sōrs\ *n* **1** : ORIGIN, BEGINNING **2** : a supplier of information **3** : the beginning of a stream of water
source code *n* : a computer program in its original programming language and before translation (as by a compiler)
¹souse \'saus\ *vb* **soused; sous·ing** **1** : PICKLE **2** ♦ : to plunge into a liquid **3** ♦ : to wet thoroughly : DRENCH **4** : to make drunk
   ♦ [2] dip, douse, duck, dunk, immerse, submerge ♦ [3] drench, drown, impregnate, saturate, soak, sop, steep

²souse *n* **1** : something (as pigs' feet) steeped in pickle **2** : a soaking in liquid **3** ♦ : an habitual drunkard
   ♦ drunk, inebriate, soak, sot, tippler

¹south \'sauth\ *adv* : to or toward the south; *also* : into a state of decline
²south *adj* **1** : situated toward or at the south **2** : coming from the south
³south *n* **1** : the direction to the right of one facing east **2** : the compass point directly opposite to north **3** *cap* : regions or countries south of a specified or implied point; *esp* : the southeastern part of the U.S. — **south·er·ly** \'sə-thər-lē\ *adj or adv* — **south·ern** \'sə-thərn\ *adj* — **South·ern·er** *n* — **south·ern·most** \-ˌmōst\ *adj* — **south·ward** \'sauth-wərd\ *adv or adj* — **southwards** \-wərdz\ *adv*
South African *n* : a native or inhabitant of the Republic of South Africa — **South African** *adj*
south·east \sau-'thēst, *naut* sau-'ēst\ *n* **1** : the general direction between south and east **2** : the compass point midway between south and east **3** *cap* : regions or countries southeast of a specified or implied point — **southeast** *adj or adv* — **south·east·er·ly** *adv or adj* — **south·east·ern** \-'ēs-tərn\ *adj*
south·paw \'sauth-ˌpo\ *n* : a left-handed person; *esp* : a left-handed baseball pitcher — **southpaw** *adj*
south pole *n, often cap S&P* : the southernmost point of the earth
south·west \sauth-'west, *naut* sau-'west\ *n* **1** : the general direction between south and west **2** : the compass point midway between south and west **3** *cap* : regions or countries southwest of a specified or implied point — **southwest** *adj or adv* — **south·west·er·ly** *adv or adj* — **south·west·ern** \-'wes-tərn\ *adj*
sou·ve·nir \ˌsü-və-'nir\ *n* ♦ : something serving as a reminder
   ♦ keepsake, memento, memorial, monument, remembrance, token

sou'·west·er \sau-'wes-tər\ *n* : a long waterproof coat worn in storms at sea; *also* : a waterproof hat
¹sov·er·eign \'sä-vrən, -və-rən\ *n* **1** ♦ : one possessing the supreme power and authority in a state **2** : a gold coin of the United Kingdom
   ♦ autocrat, monarch, ruler

²sovereign *adj* **1** : EXCELLENT, FINE **2** : supreme in power or authority **3** : having undisputed ascendancy : CHIEF **4** ♦ : having independent authority
   ♦ autonomous, free, independent, self-governing, separate

sov·er·eign·ty \-tē\ *n, pl* **-ties** **1** : supremacy in rule or power **2** : power to govern without external control **3** : the supreme political power in a state **4** ♦ : one that is sovereign; *also* : an autonomous state
   ♦ autonomy, freedom, independence, liberty, self-government ♦ commonwealth, country, land, nation, state

so·vi·et \'sō-vē-ˌet, 'sä-, -ət\ *n* **1** : an elected governmental council in a Communist country **2** *pl, cap* : the people and esp. the leaders of the U.S.S.R. — **soviet** *adj, often cap* — **so·vi·et·ize** *vb, often cap*
¹sow \'sau\ *n* : an adult female swine
²sow \'sō\ *vb* **sowed; sown** \'sōn\ *or* **sowed; sow·ing** **1** ♦ : to plant seed esp. by scattering **2** : to strew with seed **3** ♦ : to scatter abroad — **sow·er** \'sō-ər\ *n*
   ♦ [1] drill, plant, seed ♦ [3] dot, pepper, scatter, spray, sprinkle, strew

sow bug \ˈsau̇-\ *n* : WOOD LOUSE
sox *pl of* SOCK
soy \ˈsȯi\ *n* : a sauce made from soybeans fermented in brine
soy·bean \ˈsȯi-ˌbēn\ *n* : an Asian legume widely grown for forage and for its edible seeds that yield a valuable oil (**soybean oil**); *also* : its seed
sp *abbr* **1** special **2** species **3** specimen **4** spelling **5** spirit
Sp *abbr* Spain
SP *abbr* **1** shore patrol; shore patrolman **2** shore police **3** specialist
spa \ˈspä\ *n* **1** : a resort with mineral springs **2** : a health and fitness facility **3** : a hot tub with a whirlpool device
¹**space** \ˈspās\ *n* **1** ♦ : a period of time **2** ♦ : some small measurable distance, area, or volume **3** : the limitless area in which all things exist and move **4** : an empty place **5** : the region beyond the earth's atmosphere **6** : a definite place (as a seat on a train or ship)
   ♦ [1] bit, spell, stretch, while ♦ [2] place, room, way
²**space** *vb* **spaced; spac·ing** : to place at intervals — **spac·er** *n*
space-age \ˈspās-ˌāj\ *adj* ♦ : of or relating to the age of space exploration
   ♦ contemporary, current, hot, mod, modern, new, newfangled, red-hot, ultramodern, up-to-date
space·craft \-ˌkraft\ *n* : a vehicle for travel beyond the earth's atmosphere
space·flight \-ˌflīt\ *n* : flight beyond the earth's atmosphere
space heater *n* : a usu. portable device for heating a relatively small area
space·man \ˈspās-ˌman, -mən\ *n* : one who travels outside the earth's atmosphere
space out *vb* : to become distracted or inattentive
space·ship \-ˌship\ *n* : a vehicle used for space travel
space shuttle *n* : a reusable spacecraft designed to transport people and cargo between earth and space
space station *n* : a large artificial satellite serving as a base (as for scientific observation)
space suit *n* : a suit equipped to make life in space possible for its wearer
space walk *n* : a period of activity outside a spacecraft by an astronaut in space — **space·walk** \ˈspās-ˌwȯk\ *vb* — **space·walk·er** *n*
spa·cious \ˈspā-shəs\ *adj* ♦ : very large in extent : ROOMY — **spa·cious·ly** *adv* — **spa·cious·ness** *n*
   ♦ ample, capacious, commodious, roomy
¹**spade** \ˈspād\ *n* : a shovel with a blade for digging — **spade·ful** *n*
²**spade** *vb* **spad·ed; spad·ing** : to dig with a spade — **spad·er** *n*
³**spade** *n* : any of a suit of playing cards marked with a black figure resembling an inverted heart with a short stem at the bottom
spa·dix \ˈspā-diks\ *n, pl* **spa·di·ces** \ˈspā-də-ˌsēz\ : a floral spike with a fleshy or succulent axis usu. enclosed in a spathe
spa·ghet·ti \spə-ˈge-tē\ *n* : thin solid pasta strings
spam \ˈspam\ *n* : unsolicited usu. commercial e-mail sent to a large number of addresses — **spam** *vb*
¹**span** \ˈspan\ *n* **1** : an English unit of length equal to nine inches (about 23 centimeters) **2** : a limited portion of time **3** : the spread (as of an arch) from one support to another
²**span** *vb* **spanned; span·ning** **1** ♦ : to ascertain the measurements of : MEASURE **2** : to extend across
   ♦ gauge, measure, scale
³**span** *n* : a pair of animals (as mules) driven together
Span *abbr* Spanish
span·dex \ˈspan-ˌdeks\ *n* : any of various elastic synthetic textile fibers
span·gle \ˈspaŋ-gəl\ *n* : a small disk of shining metal or plastic used esp. on a dress for ornament — **spangle** *vb*
Span·glish \ˈspaŋ-glish\ *n* : a combination of Spanish and English
Span·iard \ˈspan-yərd\ *n* : a native or inhabitant of Spain
span·iel \ˈspan-yəl\ *n* : a dog of any of several breeds of mostly small and short-legged dogs usu. with long wavy hair and large drooping ears
Span·ish \ˈspa-nish\ *n* **1** : the chief language of Spain and of the countries colonized by the Spanish **2 Spanish** *pl* : the people of Spain — **Spanish** *adj*
Spanish American *n* : a resident of the U.S. whose native language is Spanish; *also* : a native or inhabitant of one of the countries of America in which Spanish is the national language — **Spanish–American** *adj*
Spanish fly *n* : a toxic preparation of dried green European bee-

tles that causes the skin to blister and is thought to be an aphrodisiac
Spanish moss *n* : a plant related to the pineapple that grows in pendent tufts of grayish green filaments on trees from the southern U.S. to Argentina
Spanish rice *n* : rice cooked with onions, green peppers, and tomatoes
¹**spank** \ˈspaŋk\ *vb* : to hit on the buttocks with the open hand — **spank** *n*
²**spank** *n* : a blow usu. with the palm of the hand
spank·ing \ˈspaŋ-kiŋ\ *adj* : being fresh and strong : BRISK ⟨a ~ breeze⟩ — **spanking** *adv*
span·ner \ˈspan-ər\ *n, chiefly Brit* : WRENCH
¹**spar** \ˈspär\ *n* **1** : a stout pole **2** : a rounded wood or metal piece (as a mast, yard, boom, or gaff) for supporting sail rigging
²**spar** *vb* **sparred; spar·ring** : to box for practice without serious hitting; *also* : SKIRMISH, WRANGLE
¹**spare** \ˈspar\ *vb* **spared; spar·ing** **1** : to refrain from punishing or injuring : show mercy to ⟨spared the prisoners⟩ **2** : to exempt from something ⟨~ me the trouble⟩ **3** : to get along without ⟨can't ~ a dime⟩ **4** ♦ : to use frugally or rarely ⟨don't ~ the syrup⟩
   ♦ scant, skimp, stint
²**spare** *adj* **spar·er; spar·est** **1** : held in reserve **2** ♦ : being over and above what is needed : SUPERFLUOUS **3** ♦ : not liberal or profuse **4** ♦ : healthily lean : THIN **5** : not abundant or plentiful : SCANTY — **spare·ness** *n*
   ♦ [2] excess, extra, superfluous, supernumerary, surplus ♦ [3] cheap, close, mean, niggardly, parsimonious, penurious, stingy, tight, tightfisted, uncharitable ♦ [4] lean, skinny, slender, slim, thin
³**spare** *n* **1** ♦ : a duplicate kept in reserve; *esp* : a spare tire **2** : the knocking down of all the bowling pins with the first two balls
   ♦ backup, duplicate, extra, reserve, substitute
spar·ing \ˈspar-iŋ\ *adj* ♦ : marked by or practicing careful restraint : FRUGAL — **spar·ing·ly** *adv*
   ♦ economical, frugal, provident, thrifty
¹**spark** \ˈspärk\ *n* **1** : a small particle of a burning substance or a hot glowing particle struck from a mass (as by steel on flint) **2** : a short bright flash of electricity between two points **3** : SPARKLE **4** : a particle capable of being kindled or developed : GERM
²**spark** *vb* **1** : to emit or produce sparks **2** ♦ : to stir to activity : INCITE
   ♦ activate, actuate, crank, drive, incite, move, propel, run, set off, start, touch off, trigger, turn on
³**spark** *vb* : WOO, COURT
¹**spar·kle** \ˈspär-kəl\ *vb* **spar·kled; spar·kling** **1 a** : to throw out sparks **b** ♦ : to give off or reflect bright moving points of light : FLASH **2** : to perform brilliantly **3** : EFFERVESCE ⟨sparkling wine⟩ — **spar·kler** *n*
   ♦ flame, flash, glance, gleam, glimmer, glisten, glitter, scintillate, shimmer, twinkle, wink
²**sparkle** *n* **1** : GLEAM **2** : ANIMATION
spark plug *n* **1** : a device that produces a spark to ignite the fuel mixture in an engine cylinder **2** : one that begins something or drives something forward
spar·row \ˈspar-ō\ *n* : any of several small dull-colored singing birds
sparse \ˈspärs\ *adj* **spars·er; spars·est** ♦ : thinly scattered : SCANTY — **sparse·ly** *adv* — **sparse·ness** *n*
   ♦ light, meager (*or* meagre), poor, scant, scanty, scarce, skimpy, slender, slim, spare
spasm \ˈspa-zəm\ *n* **1** : a sudden involuntary and abnormal muscular contraction **2** ♦ : a sudden, violent, and temporary effort, feeling, or outburst
   ♦ agony, burst, eruption, explosion, fit, flare, flare-up, flash, flush, gale, gush, gust, outburst, paroxysm, storm
spas·mod·ic \spaz-ˈmä-dik\ *adj* **1** : relating to or affected or characterized by spasm ⟨~ movements⟩; *also* : resembling a spasm **2** ♦ : acting or proceeding fitfully : INTERMITTENT — **spas·mod·i·cal·ly** \-di-k(ə-)lē\ *adv*
   ♦ casual, choppy, discontinuous, erratic, fitful, intermittent, irregular, occasional, sporadic, spotty, unsteady
spas·tic \ˈspas-tik\ *adj* : of, relating to, marked by, or affected with muscular spasm ⟨~ paralysis⟩ — **spastic** *n*

¹spat \'spat\ *past and past part of* SPIT

²spat *n, pl* **spat** *or* **spats** : a young bivalve mollusk (as an oyster)

³spat *n* : a gaiter covering instep and ankle

⁴spat *n* : a brief petty quarrel : DISPUTE

⁵spat *vb* **spat·ted; spat·ting** ♦ : to quarrel briefly

♦ argue, bicker, brawl, dispute, fall out, fight, hassle, quarrel, row, scrap, squabble, wrangle

spate \'spāt\ *n* ♦ : a great rise or overflowing of a stream; *also* : a sudden outburst

♦ cataclysm, cataract, deluge, flood, inundation, overflow, torrent

spathe \'spāth\ *n* : a sheathing bract or pair of bracts enclosing an inflorescence (as of the calla lily) and esp. a spadix on the same axis

spa·tial \'spā-shəl\ *adj* : of or relating to space or to the facility to perceive objects in space — **spa·tial·ly** *adv*

spat·ter \'spa-tər\ *vb* ♦ : to splash with drops of liquid **2** : to sprinkle around — **spatter** *n*

♦ dash, plash, splash

spat·u·la \'spa-chə-lə\ *n* : a flexible knifelike implement for scooping, spreading, or mixing soft substances

spav·in \'spa-vən\ *n* : a bony enlargement of the hock of a horse — **spav·ined** \-vənd\ *adj*

¹spawn \'spȯn\ *vb* **1** : to produce eggs or offspring esp. in large numbers **2** ♦ : to bring into existence : GENERATE — **spawn·er** *n*

♦ create, engender, generate, induce, make, produce

²spawn *n* **1** : the eggs of water animals (as fishes or oysters) that lay many small eggs **2** ♦ : offspring esp. when produced in great numbers

♦ issue, offspring, posterity, progeny, seed

spay \'spā\ *vb* **spayed; spay·ing** : to remove the ovaries of (a female animal)

SPCA *abbr* Society for the Prevention of Cruelty to Animals

SPCC *abbr* Society for the Prevention of Cruelty to Children

speak \'spēk\ *vb* **spoke** \'spōk\; **spo·ken** \'spō-kən\; **speak·ing 1** : to utter words **2** ♦ : to express orally **3** : to mention in speech or writing **4** ♦ : to address an audience **5** : to use or be able to use (a language) in talking

♦ [2] articulate, say, state, talk, tell, utter, verbalize, vocalize ♦ [4] declaim, descant, discourse, harangue, lecture, orate, talk

speak·easy \'spēk-ˌē-zē\ *n, pl* **-eas·ies** : an illicit drinking place

speak·er \'spē-kər\ *n* **1** ♦ : one that speaks **2** ♦ : the presiding officer of a deliberative assembly **3** : LOUDSPEAKER

♦ [1] mouthpiece, spokesman, spokesperson, spokeswoman ♦ [2] chair, chairman, moderator, president

speak out *vb* **1** : to speak loud enough to be heard **2** ♦ : to speak boldly : express an opinion frankly

♦ sound off, speak up, spout

speak up *vb* **1** : to speak loudly and distinctly **2** ♦ : to express an opinion freely

♦ sound off, speak out, spout

¹spear \'spir\ *n* **1** ♦ : a long-shafted weapon with a sharp point for thrusting or throwing **2** : a sharp-pointed instrument with barbs used in spearing fish — **spear·man** \-mən\ *n*

♦ lance, pike

²spear *vb* ♦ : to strike or pierce with or as if with a spear — **spear·er** *n*

♦ gore, harpoon, impale, lance, pierce, puncture, skewer, spike, stab, stick, transfix

³spear *n* : a usu. young blade, shoot, or sprout (as of asparagus)

spear·head \-ˌhed\ *vb* ♦ : to serve as a leading force, element, or influence — **spearhead** *n*

♦ boss, captain, command, dominate, head, lead

spear·mint \-ˌmint\ *n* : a common highly aromatic garden mint

¹spec *abbr* **1** special **2** specifically **3** specialist

²spec \'spek\ *n* : SPECIFICATION 2 — usu. used in pl.

spe·cial \'spe-shəl\ *adj* **1** : UNCOMMON, NOTEWORTHY **2** ♦ : particularly favored **3** ♦ : readily distinguishable from others of the same category : UNIQUE **4** : EXTRA, ADDITIONAL **5** ♦ : confined to or designed for a definite field of action, purpose, or occasion — **special** *n*

♦ [2] beloved, darling, dear, favorite (*or* favourite), loved, pet,

precious, sweet ♦ [3] alone, lone, only, singular, sole, solitary, unique ♦ [5] distinct, especial, express, precise, set, specific

special delivery *n* : delivery of mail by messenger for an extra fee

special effects *n pl* : visual or sound effects introduced into a motion picture, video recording, or taped television production

Special Forces *n pl* : a branch of the army composed of soldiers specially trained in guerrilla warfare

spe·cial·ise *chiefly Brit var of* SPECIALIZE

spe·cial·ist \'spe-shə-list\ *n* **1** : a person who specializes in a particular branch of learning or activity **2** : a rank in the U.S. Army corresponding to that of corporal

spe·cial·ize \'spe-shə-ˌlīz\ *vb* **-ized; -iz·ing** : to concentrate one's efforts in a special activity or field; *also* : to change in an adaptive manner — **spe·cial·i·za·tion** \ˌspe-shə-lə-'zā-shən\ *n*

spe·cial·ly \'spe-shə-lē\ *adv* **1** : in a special manner **2** : for a special purpose : in particular

spe·cial·ty \'spe-shəl-tē\ *n, pl* **-ties 1** : a particular quality or detail **2** : a product of a special kind or of special excellence **3** ♦ : something (as a discipline) in which one specializes ⟨the doctor's ~ is dermatology⟩

♦ area, arena, demesne, department, discipline, domain, field, line, province, realm, sphere

spe·cie \'spē-shē, -sē\ *n* : money in coin

spe·cies \'spē-shēz, -sēz\ *n, pl* **spe·cies 1** ♦ : a group united by common traits or interests : KIND **2** : a category of biological classification ranking just below the genus or subgenus and comprising closely related organisms potentially able to breed with one another

♦ breed, class, description, feather, ilk, kind, like, manner, nature, order, sort, type ♦ bracket, category, class, division, family, grade, group, set

specif *abbr* specific; specifically

¹spe·cif·ic \spi-'si-fik\ *adj* **1** : having a unique effect or influence or reacting in only one way or with only one thing ⟨~ antibodies⟩ ⟨~ enzymes⟩ **2** ♦ : free from ambiguity : DEFINITE **3** : of, relating to, or constituting a species **4** ♦ : constituting or falling into a specifiable category — **spe·cif·i·cal·ly** \-fi-k(ə-)lē\ *adv*

♦ [2] clear-cut, definite, definitive, explicit, express, unambiguous, unequivocal ♦ [4] distinct, especial, express, precise, set, special

²specific *n* **1** : something specific : DETAIL, PARTICULAR — usu. used in pl. **2** ♦ : a drug or remedy having a specific mitigating effect on a disease ⟨used as a ~ against malaria⟩

♦ cure, drug, medicine, pharmaceutical, remedy

spec·i·fi·ca·tion \ˌspe-sə-fə-'kā-shən\ *n* **1** : the act or process of specifying **2** : a description of work to be done and materials to be used (as in building) — usu. used in pl.

specific gravity *n* : the ratio of the density of a substance to the density of some substance (as water) taken as a standard when both densities are obtained by weighing in air

spec·i·fy \'spe-sə-ˌfī\ *vb* **-fied; -fy·ing** ♦ : to mention or name explicitly

♦ define, lay down, prescribe ♦ advert (to), cite, instance, mention, name, note, notice, quote, refer (to), touch (*on or upon*)

spec·i·men \'spe-sə-mən\ *n* ♦ : an item or part typical of a group or whole; *also* : a single human being

♦ case, example, exemplar, illustration, instance, representative, sample

spe·cious \'spē-shəs\ *adj* ♦ : seeming to be genuine, correct, or beautiful but not really so ⟨~ reasoning⟩

♦ deceitful, deceptive, delusive, fallacious, false, misleading

¹speck \'spek\ *n* **1** : a small spot or blemish **2** ♦ : a small particle

♦ [1] blotch, dapple, dot, fleck, mottle, patch, point, spot ♦ [2] atom, bit, crumb, fleck, flyspeck, grain, granule, molecule, morsel, mote, particle, patch, scrap, scruple, tittle

²speck *vb* ♦ : to produce specks on or in

♦ blotch, dapple, dot, fleck, freckle, mottle, pepper, spot, sprinkle, stipple

¹speck·le \'spe-kəl\ *n* : a little speck

²speckle *vb* **1** : to mark with speckles **2** : to be distributed in or on like speckles

specs \'speks\ *n pl* : a pair of lenses used to correct defects of vision : GLASSES

spec·ta·cle \'spek-ti-kəl\ *n* **1** : an unusual or impressive public display **2** *pl* ♦ : a pair of lenses used to correct defects of vision : GLASSES — **spec·ta·cled** \-kəld\ *adj*

♦ eyeglasses, glasses

spec·tac·u·lar \spek-'ta-kyə-lər\ *adj* : exciting to see : SENSATIONAL

spec·ta·tor \'spek-ˌtā-tər\ *n* : a person who looks on (as at a sports event)

spec·ter *or* **spec·tre** \'spek-tər\ *n* ♦ : a visible disembodied spirit : GHOST

♦ apparition, bogey, ghost, phantasm, phantom, poltergeist, shade, shadow, spirit, spook, vision, wraith

spec·tral \'spek-trəl\ *adj* **1** : of, relating to, or resembling a specter **2** : of, relating to, or made by a spectrum

spec·tro·gram \'spek-trə-ˌgram\ *n* : a photograph, image, or diagram of a spectrum

spec·tro·graph \-ˌgraf\ *n* : an instrument for dispersing radiation into a spectrum and recording or mapping the spectrum — **spec·tro·graph·ic** \ˌspek-trə-'gra-fik\ *adj* — **spec·tro·graph·i·cal·ly** \-fi-k(ə-)lē\ *adv*

spec·trom·e·ter \spek-'trä-mə-tər\ *n* : an instrument for measuring spectra — **spec·tro·met·ric** \ˌspek-trə-'me-trik\ *adj* — **spec·trom·e·try** \spek-'trä-mə-trē\ *n*

spec·tro·scope \'spek-trə-ˌskōp\ *n* : an instrument that produces spectra esp. of visible electromagnetic radiation — **spec·tro·scop·ic** \ˌspek-trə-'skä-pik\ *adj* — **spec·tro·scop·i·cal·ly** \-pi-k(ə-)lē\ *adv* — **spec·tros·co·pist** \spek-'träs-kə-pist\ *n* — **spec·tros·co·py** \-pē\ *n*

spec·trum \'spek-trəm\ *n, pl* **spec·tra** \-trə\ *or* **spectrums 1** : a series of colors formed when a beam of white light is dispersed (as by a prism) so that its parts are arranged in the order of their wavelengths **2** : a series of radiations arranged in regular order **3** ♦ : a continuous sequence or range ⟨a wide ∼ of political opinions⟩

♦ gamut, range, scale, spread, stretch

spec·u·late \'spe-kyə-ˌlāt\ *vb* **-lat·ed; -lat·ing 1** ♦ : to think or wonder about a subject **2** : to take a business risk in hope of gain — **spec·u·la·tive·ly** *adv* — **spec·u·la·tor** \-ˌlā-tər\ *n*

♦ assume, conjecture, guess, presume, suppose, surmise, suspect

spec·u·la·tion \ˌspe-kyə-'lā-shən\ *n* ♦ : an act or instance of speculating

♦ chance, enterprise, flier, gamble, venture

spec·u·la·tive \'spe-kyə-ˌlā-tiv\ *adj* ♦ : involving, based on, or constituting intellectual speculation; *also* : theoretical rather than demonstrable

♦ conjectural, hypothetical, theoretical

speech \'spēch\ *n* **1** : the act of speaking **2** : TALK, CONVERSATION **3** ♦ : a public talk or lecture **4** : a variety of language identified with a region or group : LANGUAGE **5** : an individual manner of speaking **6** : the power of speaking

♦ address, declamation, harangue, oration, talk

speech·less *adj* ♦ : unable to speak; *also* : not speaking

♦ dumb, mum, mute, silent, uncommunicative

¹**speed** \'spēd\ *n* **1** *archaic* : SUCCESS **2** ♦ : the act or state of moving swiftly : SWIFTNESS **3** : rate of motion or performance **4** : a transmission gear (as of a bicycle) **5** : METHAMPHETAMINE; *also* : a related drug

♦ celerity, fastness, fleetness, haste, hurry, quickness, rapidity, swiftness, velocity *Ant* slowness, sluggishness

²**speed** *vb* **sped** \'sped\ *or* **speed·ed; speed·ing 1** *archaic* : PROSPER; *also* : GET ALONG, FARE **2** ♦ : to go fast; *esp* : to go at an excessive or illegal speed **3** ♦ : to cause to go faster — **speed·er** *n*

♦ [2] barrel, dash, fly, hurry, hurtle, hustle, pelt, race, rip, rocket, shoot, tear, zip, zoom ♦ *usu* **speed up** [3] accelerate, hasten, hurry, quicken, rush, step up, whisk

speed·boat \-ˌbōt\ *n* : a fast motorboat

speed bump *n* : a low raised ridge across a roadway (as in a parking lot) to limit vehicle speed

speed·i·ly \'spē-də-lē\ *adv* ♦ : in a speedy manner

♦ apace, briskly, fast, full tilt, hastily, posthaste, presto, pronto, quick, quickly, rapidly, soon, swiftly

speed of light : a fundamental physical constant that is the speed of electromagnetic radiation propagation in a vacuum and has the value of 299,792,458 meters per second

speed·om·e·ter \spi-'dä-mə-tər\ *n* : an instrument for indicating speed

speed·up \'spēd-ˌəp\ *n* : ACCELERATION

speed·way \-ˌwā\ *n* : a racecourse for motor vehicles

speed·well \'spēd-ˌwel\ *n* : VERONICA

speedy *adj* ♦ : marked by swiftness of motion or action

♦ breakneck, breathless, brisk, dizzy, fast, fleet, hasty, lightning, nippy, quick, rapid, rattling, snappy, swift

¹**spell** \'spel\ *vb* **spelled** \'speld, 'spelt\ *or Can and Brit* **spelt** \'spelt\; **spell·ing 1** : to name, write, or print in order the letters of a word **2** ♦ : to add up to : MEAN

♦ denote, express, import, mean, signify

²**spell** *n* **1** ♦ : a magic formula : INCANTATION **2** : a compelling influence

♦ bewitchment, charm, conjuration, enchantment, incantation

³**spell** *n* **1** : one's turn at work or duty **2** : a stretch of a specified kind of weather **3** ♦ : a period of bodily or mental distress or disorder : ATTACK ⟨a dizzy ∼⟩ **4** ♦ : an indeterminate period of time

♦ [3] attack, bout, case, fit, seizure, siege ♦ [4] bit, space, stretch, while

⁴**spell** *vb* **spelled** \'speld\; **spell·ing** : to take the place of for a time in work or duty : RELIEVE

⁵**spell** *vb* **spelled** \'speld\; **spell·ing** : to put under a spell

spell·bind·er \-ˌbīn-dər\ *n* : a speaker of compelling eloquence

spell·bound \-ˌbaúnd\ *adj* : held by or as if by a spell

spell·check·er \'spel-ˌche-kər\ *n* : a computer program that identifies possible misspellings in a block of text — **spell–check** \-ˌchek\ *vb*

spell·er \'spe-lər\ *n* **1** : one who spells words **2** : a book with exercises for teaching spelling

spell out *vt* **1** ♦ : to make plain **2** : to write or print in letters and in full

♦ clarify, clear (up), construe, demonstrate, elucidate, explain, explicate, expound, illuminate, illustrate, interpret

spelt \'spelt\ *chiefly Can and Brit past and past part of* ¹SPELL

spe·lunk·er \spi-'lən-kər, 'spē-ˌlən-kər\ *n* : one who makes a hobby of exploring caves — **spe·lunk·ing** *n*

spend \'spend\ *vb* **spent** \'spent\; **spend·ing 1** ♦ : to pay out : EXPEND **2** : to consume entirely : WEAR OUT, EXHAUST; *also* : to consume wastefully **3** : to cause or permit to elapse : PASS

♦ disburse, expend, give, lay out, pay

spend·er *n* : one that spends money; *esp* : one that spends lavishly

spend·thrift \'spend-ˌthrift\ *n* ♦ : one who spends wastefully or recklessly

♦ prodigal, profligate, wastrel

spent \'spent\ *adj* ♦ : drained of energy

♦ beat, bushed, dead, drained, effete, jaded, limp, prostrate, tired, weary, worn-out

sperm \'spərm\ *n, pl* **sperm** *or* **sperms 1** : SEMEN **2** : a male gamete

sper·ma·to·zo·on \(ˌ)spər-ˌma-tə-'zō-ˌän, -'zō-ən\ *n, pl* **-zoa** \-'zō-ə\ : a motile male gamete of an animal usu. with a rounded or elongated head and a long posterior flagellum

sperm cell *n* : SPERM 2

sper·mi·cide \'spər-mə-ˌsīd\ *n* : a preparation or substance used to kill sperm — **sper·mi·cid·al** \ˌspər-mə-'sī-dəl\ *adj*

sperm whale *n* : a large whale with a massive square-shaped head containing a fluid-filled cavity

spew \'spyü\ *vb* **1** ♦ : VOMIT **2** ♦ : to come in a flood or gush; *also* : emit or eject with vigor or violence

♦ gush, jet, pour, rush, spout, spurt, squirt ♦ belch, disgorge, eject, erupt, expel

SPF *abbr* sun protection factor

sp gr *abbr* specific gravity

sphag·num \'sfag-nəm\ *n* : any of a genus of atypical mosses that grow in wet acid areas where their remains become compacted with other plant debris to form peat; *also* : a mass of these mosses

sphere \'sfir\ *n* **1** ♦ : a globe-shaped body : BALL **2** : a celestial body **3** : a solid figure so shaped that every point on its surface is an equal distance from the center **4** ♦ : range of action or influence — **spher·i·cal** \'sfir-i-kəl, 'sfer-\ *adj* — **spher·i·cal·ly** \-i-k(ə-)lē\ *adv*

♦ [1] ball, orb ♦ [4] area, arena, demesne, department, discipline, domain, field, line, province, realm, specialty

spher·oid \'sfir-ˌóid, 'sfer-\ *n* : a figure similar to a sphere but not perfectly round — **sphe·roi·dal** \sfir-'ói-dəl\ *adj*

sphinc·ter \'sfiŋk-tər\ *n* : a muscular ring that closes a bodily opening

sphinx \'sfiŋks\ *n, pl* **sphinx·es** *or* **sphin·ges** \'sfin-ˌjēz\ **1** : a winged monster in Greek mythology having a woman's head and a lion's body and noted for killing anyone unable to answer its riddle **2** : an enigmatic or mysterious person **3** : an ancient Egyptian image having the body of a lion and the head of a man, ram, or hawk

¹**spice** \'spīs\ *n* **1** ♦ : any of various aromatic plant products (as pepper or nutmeg) used to season or flavor foods **2** : something that adds interest and relish **3** ♦ : a pungent or fragrant odor

♦ [1] flavor (*or* flavour), seasoning ♦ [3] aroma, bouquet, fragrance, incense, perfume, redolence, scent

²**spice** *vb* **spiced; spic·ing** ♦ : to season with spices

♦ flavor (*or* flavour), savor, season

spick–and–span *or* **spic–and–span** \ˌspik-ənd-'span\ *adj* **1** ♦ : quite new **2** ♦ : spotlessly clean

♦ [1] brand-new, new, unused ♦ [2] clean, immaculate, spotless, stainless, unsoiled, unsullied

spic·ule \'spi-kyül\ *n* : a slender pointed body esp. of calcium or silica ⟨sponge ∼s⟩

spicy *adj* **1** : having the quality, flavor, or fragrance of spice **2** ♦ : verging on impropriety or indecency; *also* : somewhat scandalous or salacious

♦ bawdy, lewd, racy, ribald, suggestive

spi·der \'spī-dər\ *n* **1** : any of an order of arachnids that have a 2-part body, eight legs, and two or more pairs of abdominal organs for spinning threads of silk used esp. in making webs for catching prey **2** : a cast-iron frying pan — **spi·dery** *adj*

spider mite *n* : any of various small web-spinning mites that feed on and are pests of plants

spider plant *n* : a houseplant of the lily family having long green leaves usu. striped with white and producing tufts of small plants on long hanging stems

spi·der·web \'spī-dər-ˌweb\ *n* : the web spun by a spider

spiel \'spēl\ *vb* : to talk in a fast, smooth, and usu. colorful manner — **spiel** *n*

spig·ot \'spi-gət, -kət\ *n* ♦ : a fixture for drawing or regulating the flow of liquid esp. from a pipe : FAUCET

♦ cock, faucet, gate, tap, valve

¹**spike** \'spīk\ *n* **1** : a very large nail **2** : any of various pointed projections (as on the sole of a shoe to prevent slipping) — **spiky** *adj*

²**spike** *vb* **spiked; spik·ing** **1** : to fasten with spikes **2** : to put an end to : QUASH ⟨∼ a rumor⟩ **3** ♦ : to pierce with or impale on a spike **4** : to add alcoholic liquor to (a drink)

♦ gore, harpoon, impale, lance, pierce, puncture, skewer, spear, stab, stick, transfix

³**spike** *n* **1** : an ear of grain **2** : a long cluster of usu. stemless flowers

¹**spill** \'spil\ *vb* **spilled** \'spild, 'spilt\ *also* **spilt** \'spilt\; **spill·ing** **1** : to cause or allow to fall, flow, or run out esp. unintentionally **2** : to cause (blood) to be lost by wounding **3** : to run out or over with resulting loss or waste **4** ♦ : to let out : DIVULGE — **spill·able** *adj*

♦ bare, disclose, discover, divulge, expose, reveal, tell, unbosom, uncloak, uncover, unmask, unveil

²**spill** *n* **1** ♦ : an act of spilling; *also* : a fall from a horse or vehicle or an erect position **2** : something spilled

♦ fall, slip, stumble, tumble

spill·way \-ˌwā\ *n* : a passage for surplus water to run over or around an obstruction (as a dam)

¹**spin** \'spin\ *vb* **spun** \'spən\; **spin·ning** **1** : to draw out (fiber) and twist into thread; *also* : to form (thread) by such means **2** : to form thread by extruding a sticky quickly hardening fluid; *also* : to construct from such thread ⟨spiders ∼ their webs⟩ **3** : to produce slowly and by degrees ⟨∼ a story⟩ **4** ♦ : to revolve rapidly : TWIRL; *also* : to cause to whirl **5** : to feel as if in a whirl : WHIRL, REEL ⟨my head is *spinning*⟩ **6** : to move rapidly along **7** ♦ : to present (as information) with a particular spin — **spin·ner** *n*

♦ gyrate, pirouette, revolve, roll, rotate, turn, twirl, wheel, whirl

²**spin** *n* **1** ♦ : a rapid rotating motion **2** : an excursion in a

wheeled vehicle **3** : a particular point of view, emphasis, or interpretation **4** ♦ : a state of mental confusion

♦ [1] gyration, pirouette, reel, revolution, roll, rotation, twirl, wheel, whirl ♦ [4] daze, fog, haze, muddle

spi·na bi·fi·da \ˌspī-nə-'bi-fə-də\ *n* : a birth defect in which the spinal column has a fissure

spin·ach \'spi-nich\ *n* : a dark green herb grown for its edible leaves

spi·nal \'spīn-ᵊl\ *adj* : of or relating to the backbone or spinal cord — **spi·nal·ly** *adv*

spinal column *n* : the bony column in the back of a vertebrate that extends from the neck to the tail and protects the spinal cord : BACKBONE

spinal cord *n* : the thick cord of nervous tissue that extends from the brain along the back in the cavity of the backbone and carries nerve impulses to and from the brain

spinal nerve *n* : any of the paired nerves which arise from the spinal cord and pass to various parts of the body and of which there are normally 31 pairs in human beings

spin control *n* : the act or practice of attempting to manipulate the way an event is interpreted

spin·dle \'spind-ᵊl\ *n* **1** : a round tapering stick or rod by which fibers are twisted in spinning **2** : a turned part of a piece of furniture ⟨the ∼s of a chair⟩ **3** : a slender pin or rod which turns or on which something else turns

spin·dling \'spind-liŋ\ *adj* : of a disproportionately tall or long and thin appearance : SPINDLY

spin·dly \'spind-lē\ *adj* ♦ : being long or tall and thin and usu. weak

♦ gangling, lanky, rangy

spin·drift \'spin-ˌdrift\ *n* : spray blown from waves

spine \'spīn\ *n* **1** ♦ : the bony column in the back of a vertebrate that extends from the neck to the tail and protects the spinal cord : BACKBONE **2** : a stiff sharp process esp. on a plant or animal **3** : the part of a book where the pages are attached

♦ backbone, vertebral column

spi·nel \spə-'nel\ *n* : a hard crystalline mineral of variable color used as a gem

spine·less \'spīn-ləs\ *adj* **1** : having no spines, thorns, or prickles **2** : lacking a backbone **3** ♦ : lacking courage or determination ⟨a ∼ politician⟩

♦ chicken, cowardly, craven, dastardly, pusillanimous, recreant, yellow ♦ effete, frail, nerveless, soft, weak, wimpy, wishy-washy

spin·et \'spi-nət\ *n* **1** : an early harpsichord having a single keyboard and only one string for each note **2** : a small upright piano

spin·na·ker \'spi-ni-kər\ *n* : a large triangular sail set on a long light pole

spinning jen·ny \-'je-nē\ *n* : an early multiple-spindle machine for spinning wool or cotton

spinning wheel *n* : a small machine for spinning thread or yarn in which a large wheel drives a single spindle

spin–off \'spin-ˌóf\ *n* **1** : a usu. useful by-product **2** : something (as a TV show) derived from an earlier work — **spin off** *vb*

♦ derivative, offshoot, outgrowth

spin·ster \'spin-stər\ *n* : an unmarried woman past the common age for marrying — **spin·ster·hood** \-ˌhúd\ *n*

spiny *adj* **1** ♦ : full of difficulties, obstacles, or annoyances **2** : covered or armed with spines

♦ catchy, delicate, difficult, knotty, problematic, thorny, ticklish, touchy, tough, tricky

spiny lobster *n* : any of several edible crustaceans differing from the related lobsters in lacking the large front claws and in having a spiny carapace

¹**spi·ral** \'spī-rəl\ *adj* ♦ : winding or coiling around a center or axis and usu. getting closer to or farther away from it — **spi·ral·ly** *adv*

♦ helical, winding

²**spiral** *n* **1** : something that has a spiral form; *also* : a single turn in a spiral object **2** : a continuously spreading and accelerating increase or decrease

³**spiral** *vb* **-raled** *or* **-ralled; -ral·ing** *or* **-ral·ling** **1** ♦ : to move and esp. to rise or fall in a spiral course **2** : to form into a spiral

♦ coil, curl, entwine, twine, twist, wind

spi·rant \'spī-rənt\ *n* : a consonant (as \f\, \s\, \sh\) uttered with decided friction of the breath against some part of the oral passage — **spirant** *adj*

spire \ˈspīr\ *n* **1** : a slender tapering stalk (as of grass) **2** : a pointed tip (as of an antler) **3** : STEEPLE — **spiry** *adj*

spi·rea *or* **spi·raea** \spī-ˈrē-ə\ *n* : any of a genus of shrubs related to the roses with dense clusters of small usu. white or pink flowers

¹**spir·it** \ˈspir-ət\ *n* **1** : a life-giving force; *also* : the animating principle : SOUL **2** *cap* : HOLY SPIRIT **3** ♦ : an often malevolent being that is bodiless but can become visible : GHOST **4** : PERSON **5** ♦ : an inclination, impulse, or tendency of a specified kind : MOOD **6** ♦ : a lively or brisk quality in a person or a person's actions **7** : essential or real meaning : INTENT **8** ♦ : distilled alcoholic liquor — often used in pl. **9** : LOYALTY ⟨school ∼⟩

♦ [3] apparition, bogey, ghost, phantasm, phantom, poltergeist, shade, shadow, specter, spook, vision, wraith ♦ [5] cheer, frame, humor (*or* humour), mode, mood, temper ♦ [6] bounce, dash, drive, esprit, ginger, pep, punch, snap, verve, vim, zing, zip ♦ **spirits** [8] alcohol, booze, drink, intoxicant, liquor, moonshine

²**spirit** *vb* : to carry off secretly or mysteriously

spir·it·ed \ˈspir-ə-təd\ *adj* **1** ♦ : full of energy or animation : ANIMATED **2** : full of courage : COURAGEOUS

♦ active, animate, animated, brisk, energetic, frisky, lively, peppy, sprightly, springy, vital, vivacious ♦ fiery, high-spirited, mettlesome, peppery, spunky *Ant* spiritless

spir·it·less *adj* ♦ : lacking animation, cheerfulness, or courage

♦ enervated, lackadaisical, languid, languorous, limp, listless

¹**spir·i·tu·al** \ˈspir-i-chəl, -chə-wəl\ *adj* **1** ♦ : of, relating to, consisting of, or affecting the spirit : INCORPOREAL ⟨∼ needs⟩ **2** ♦ : of or relating to sacred matters **3** : ecclesiastical rather than lay or temporal — **spir·i·tu·al·i·ty** \ˌspir-i-chə-ˈwa-lə-tē\ *n* — **spir·i·tu·al·ize** \ˈspir-i-chə-ˌlīz, -chə-wə-\ *vb* — **spir·i·tu·al·ly** *adv*

♦ [1] bodiless, immaterial, incorporeal, insubstantial, nonmaterial, nonphysical, unsubstantial ♦ [2] devotional, religious, sacred

²**spiritual** *n* ♦ : a religious song originating among Black people of the southern U.S.

♦ anthem, canticle, carol, chorale, hymn, psalm

spir·i·tu·al·ism \ˈspir-i-chə-ˌli-zəm, -chə-wə-\ *n* : a belief that spirits of the dead communicate with the living usu. through a medium — **spir·i·tu·al·ist** \-list\ *n, often cap* — **spir·i·tu·al·is·tic** \ˌspir-i-chə-ˈlis-tik, -chə-wə-\ *adj*

spir·i·tu·ous \ˈspir-i-chəs, -chə-wəs; ˈspir-ə-təs\ *adj* : containing alcohol

spi·ro·chete *also* **spi·ro·chaete** \ˈspī-rə-ˌkēt\ *n* : any of an order of spirally undulating bacteria including those causing syphilis and Lyme disease

spirt *var of* SPURT

¹**spit** \ˈspit\ *n* **1** : a thin pointed rod for holding meat over a fire **2** ♦ : a point of land that runs out into the water

♦ arm, cape, headland, peninsula, point, promontory

²**spit** *vb* **spit·ted; spit·ting** : to pierce with or as if with a spit

³**spit** *vb* **spit** *or* **spat** \ˈspat\; **spit·ting** **1** : to eject (saliva) from the mouth **2** : to express by or as if by spitting **3** : to rain or snow lightly

⁴**spit** *n* **1** : a watery digestive secretion that is secreted into the mouth by salivary glands : SALIVA **2** ♦ : perfect likeness ⟨∼ and image of his father⟩

♦ carbon copy, counterpart, double, duplicate, duplication, facsimile, image, likeness, match, picture, replica, ringer

spit·ball \ˈspit-ˌbȯl\ *n* **1** : paper chewed and rolled into a ball to be thrown as a missile **2** : a baseball pitch delivered after the ball has been moistened with saliva or sweat

¹**spite** \ˈspīt\ *n* ♦ : ill will with a wish to annoy, anger, or frustrate : petty malice — **in spite of** : in defiance or contempt of : NOTWITHSTANDING

♦ cattiness, despite, hatefulness, malice, malignity, meanness, nastiness, spleen, venom, viciousness

²**spite** *vb* **spit·ed; spit·ing** ♦ : to treat maliciously : ANNOY, OFFEND

♦ aggravate, annoy, bother, bug, chafe, exasperate, gall, get, grate, irk, irritate, nettle, peeve, persecute, pique, put out, rasp, rile, ruffle, vex

spite·ful \-fəl\ *adj* ♦ : filled with or showing spite — **spite·ful·ness** *n*

♦ catty, cruel, hateful, malevolent, malicious, malign, malignant, mean, nasty, virulent

spite·ful·ly *adv* ♦ : filled with or showing spite

♦ hatefully, maliciously, meanly, nastily, viciously, wickedly

spit·tle \ˈspit-ᵊl\ *n* : a watery digestive secretion that is secreted into the mouth by salivary glands : SALIVA

spit·tle·bug \-ˌbəg\ *n* : any of a family of leaping insects with froth-secreting larvae that are related to aphids

spit·toon \spi-ˈtün\ *n* : a receptacle for spit

spit up *vb* ♦ : to disgorge (the contents of the stomach) through the mouth

♦ gag, heave, throw up, vomit

splash \ˈsplash\ *vb* **1** ♦ : to dash a liquid about **2** ♦ : to scatter a liquid on : SPATTER **3** : to fall, move, or strike with a splashing noise — **splash** *n*

♦ [1] lap, plash, slosh, swash ♦ [2] dash, plash, spatter

splash·down \ˈsplash-ˌdaun\ *n* : the landing of a crewed spacecraft in the ocean — **splash down** *vb*

splashy \ˈspla-shē\ *adj* **splash·i·er; -est** : conspicuously showy : OSTENTATIOUS

splat·ter \ˈspla-tər\ *vb* : to splash with or as if with a liquid : SPATTER — **splatter** *n*

¹**splay** \ˈsplā\ *vb* : to spread outward or apart — **splay** *n*

²**splay** *adj* **1** : spread out : turned outward **2** : AWKWARD, CLUMSY

spleen \ˈsplēn\ *n* **1** : a vascular organ located near the stomach in most vertebrates that is concerned esp. with the filtration and storage of blood, destruction of red blood cells, and production of lymphocytes **2** ♦ : feelings of anger or ill will often suppressed

♦ anger, cattiness, despite, hatefulness, malice, malignity, meanness, nastiness, spite, venom, viciousness

splen·did \ˈsplen-dəd\ *adj* **1** : SHINING, BRILLIANT **2** : SHOWY, GORGEOUS **3** ♦ : fine or imposing in appearance or impression **4** : very good of its kind : EXCELLENT

♦ august, baronial, gallant, glorious, grand, grandiose, heroic, imposing, magnificent, majestic, monumental, noble, proud, regal, royal, stately

splen·did·ly *adv* ♦ : in a splendid manner

♦ agreeably, delightfully, favorably (*or* favourably), felicitously, gloriously, nicely, pleasantly, pleasingly, satisfyingly, well

splen·dor *or Can and Brit* **splen·dour** \ˈsplen-dər\ *n* **1** ♦ : great brightness or luster : BRILLIANCE **2** ♦ : a display of magnificence

♦ [1] brilliance, dazzle, effulgence, illumination, lightness, lucidity, luminosity, radiance, refulgence ♦ [2] augustness, brilliance, glory, grandeur, grandness, magnificence, majesty, nobility, nobleness, resplendence, stateliness

sple·net·ic \spli-ˈne-tik\ *adj* ♦ : marked by bad temper or spite

♦ bearish, bilious, cantankerous, disagreeable, dyspeptic, ill-humored, ill-tempered, ornery, surly

splen·ic \ˈsple-nik\ *adj* : of, relating to, or located in the spleen

splice \ˈsplīs\ *vb* **spliced; splic·ing** **1** : to unite (as two ropes) by weaving the strands together **2** : to unite (as two lengths of film) by connecting the ends together — **splice** *n*

splint \ˈsplint\ *n* **1** : a thin strip of wood interwoven with others to make something (as a basket) **2** : material or a device used to protect and keep in place an injured body part (as a broken arm) **3** : a thin piece split or broken off lengthwise

¹**splin·ter** \ˈsplin-tər\ *n* ♦ : a thin piece of something split off lengthwise : SLIVER

♦ chip, flake

²**splinter** *vb* : to split into splinters

¹**split** \ˈsplit\ *vb* **split; split·ting** **1** : to divide lengthwise or along a grain or seam **2** : to burst or break in pieces **3** ♦ : to divide into parts or sections **4** : LEAVE

♦ break up, disconnect, disjoint, dissever, dissociate, disunite, divide, divorce, part, resolve, separate, sever, sunder, unyoke

²**split** *n* **1** ♦ : a narrow break made by or as if by splitting **2** ♦ : the act or process of splitting

♦ [1] chink, cleft, crack, cranny, crevice, fissure, rift ♦ [2] breakup, dissolution, division, partition, schism, separation

split–lev·el \ˈsplit-ˈle-vəl\ *n* : a house divided so that the floor in one part is about halfway between two floors in the other

split personality *n* : SCHIZOPHRENIA; *also* : MULTIPLE PERSONALITY DISORDER

split–second \ˈsplit-ˈse-kənd\ *adj* **1** ♦ : occurring in a very brief time **2** : extremely precise ⟨∼ timing⟩

♦ immediate, instant, instantaneous, straightaway

split·ting *adj* : causing a piercing sensation ⟨a ∼ headache⟩

splotch \'spläch\ *n* : a small area visibly different (as in color, finish, or material) from the surrounding area : BLOTCH

splurge \'splərj\ *vb* **splurged; splurg·ing** : to spend more than usual esp. on oneself — **splurge** *n*

splut·ter \'splə-tər\ *n* : SPUTTER — **splutter** *vb*

¹spoil \'spȯil\ *n* ♦ : plunder taken from an enemy in war or from a victim in robbery ⟨∼s of war⟩

    ♦ booty, loot, plunder, swag

²spoil *vb* **spoiled** \'spȯild, 'spȯilt\ *or* **spoilt** \'spȯilt\; **spoil·ing 1** : ROB, PILLAGE **2** : to damage seriously : RUIN **3** ♦ : to impair the quality or effect of **4** ♦ : to damage the disposition of by pampering; *also* : INDULGE, CODDLE **5** ♦ : to lose valuable or useful qualities usu. as a result of decay : DECAY, ROT **6** : to have an eager desire ⟨∼ing for a fight⟩

    ♦ [3] blemish, mar, poison, stain, taint, tarnish, touch, vitiate
    ♦ [4] baby, coddle, indulge, mollycoddle, nurse, pamper ♦ [5] break down, corrupt, decay, decompose, disintegrate, molder, putrefy, rot

spoil·age \'spȯi-lij\ *n* ♦ : the act or process of spoiling

    ♦ breakdown, corruption, decay, decomposition, putrefaction, rot

spoil·er \'spȯi-lər\ *n* **1** : one that spoils **2** : a device (as on an airplane or automobile) used to disrupt airflow and decrease lift **3** : information about a movie or TV plot that can spoil a viewer's sense of surprise or suspense

spoil·sport \'spȯil-ˌspȯrt\ *n* : one who spoils the fun of others

¹spoke \'spōk\ *past & archaic past part of* SPEAK

²spoke *n* : any of the rods extending from the hub of a wheel to the rim

spo·ken *adj* ♦ : delivered by word of mouth; *also* : characterized by speaking in (such) a manner

    ♦ oral, unwritten, verbal

spokes·man \'spōks-mən\ *n* ♦ : a person who speaks as the representative of another or others

    ♦ mouthpiece, speaker, spokesperson, spokeswoman

spokes·per·son \-ˌpər-sən\ *n* ♦ : a person who speaks as the representative of another or others : SPOKESMAN

    ♦ mouthpiece, speaker, spokesman, spokeswoman

spokes·wom·an \-ˌwu̇-mən\ *n* ♦ : a woman who speaks as the representative of another or others

    ♦ mouthpiece, speaker, spokesman, spokesperson

spo·li·a·tion \ˌspō-lē-'ā-shən\ *n* : the act of plundering : the state of being plundered

¹sponge \'spənj\ *n* **1** : an elastic porous water-absorbing mass of fibers that forms the skeleton of various primitive sea animals; *also* : any of a phylum of chiefly marine sea animals that are the source of natural sponges **2** : a spongelike or porous mass or material **3** ♦ : one who lives on others

    ♦ hanger-on, leech, parasite

²sponge *vb* **sponged; spong·ing 1** : to bathe or wipe with a sponge **2** : to live at another's expense **3** : to gather sponges **4** ♦ : to absorb with or as if with or in the manner of a sponge

    ♦ absorb, drink, imbibe, soak, suck

sponge cake *n* : a light cake made without shortening

spong·er *n* : one that sponges

sponge rubber *n* : a cellular rubber resembling natural sponge

spongy \'spən-jē\ *adj* **1** : resembling a sponge **2** ♦ : not firm or solid

    ♦ flabby, mushy, pulpy, soft

spongy moth *n* : an Old World moth that was introduced into the U.S. where its caterpillar is a destructive defoliator of many trees

spon·sor \'spän-sər\ *n* **1** ♦ : one who takes the responsibility for some other person or thing : SURETY **2** : GODPARENT **3** : a business firm that pays the cost of a radio or television program usu. in return for advertising time during its course — **sponsor** *vb* — **spon·sor·ship** *n*

    ♦ backer, guarantor, patron, surety

spon·ta·ne·ity \ˌspän-tə-'nē-ə-tē, -'nā-\ *n* ♦ : the quality or state of being spontaneous

    ♦ abandon, abandonment, ease, lightheartedness, naturalness, unrestraint

spon·ta·ne·ous \spän-'tā-nē-əs\ *adj* **1** ♦ : done or produced freely or naturally **2** : acting or taking place without external force or cause — **spon·ta·ne·ous·ly** *adv*

    ♦ automatic, involuntary, mechanical, natural

spontaneous combustion *n* : a bursting into flame of material through heat produced within itself by chemical action (as oxidation)

¹spoof \'spüf\ *vb* **1** : DECEIVE, HOAX **2** : to make good-natured fun of ⟨the movie ∼s horror films⟩ — **spoof** *n*

²spoof *n* ♦ : a light humorous parody

    ♦ burlesque, caricature, parody, takeoff

¹spook \'spük\ *n* **1** : a disembodied soul : GHOST **2** : SPY 2

²spook *vb* ♦ : to make frightened or frantic : FRIGHTEN

    ♦ alarm, frighten, horrify, panic, scare, shock, startle, terrify, terrorize

spooky *adj* **1** ♦ : relating to, resembling, or suggesting spooks **2** ♦ : easily frightened

    ♦ [1] creepy, eerie, haunting, uncanny, unearthly, weird ♦ [2] excitable, flighty, fluttery, high-strung, jittery, jumpy, nervous, skittish

spool \'spül\ *n* : a cylinder on which flexible material (as thread) is wound

¹spoon \'spün\ *n* **1** ♦ : an eating or cooking implement consisting of a small shallow bowl with a handle **2** : a metal piece used on a fishing line as a lure — **spoon·ful** *n*

    ♦ ladle, scoop

²spoon *vb* ♦ : to take up and usu. transfer in a spoon

    ♦ dip, ladle, scoop

spoon·bill \'spün-ˌbil\ *n* : any of several wading birds related to the ibises that have a bill with a broad flat tip

spoon–feed \-ˌfēd\ *vb* **-fed** \-ˌfed\; **-feed·ing** : to feed by means of a spoon

spoor \'spu̇r, 'spȯr\ *n, pl* **spoor** *or* **spoors** : a track, a trail, a scent, or droppings esp. of a wild animal

spo·rad·ic \spə-'ra-dik\ *adj* ♦ : occurring now and then — **spo·rad·i·cal·ly** \-di-k(ə-)lē\ *adv*

    ♦ casual, choppy, discontinuous, erratic, fitful, intermittent, irregular, occasional, spasmodic, spotty, unsteady

spore \'spȯr\ *n* : a primitive usu. one-celled often environmentally resistant dormant or reproductive body produced by plants, fungi, and some microorganisms

spork \'spȯrk\ *n* : an eating utensil that combines the bowl of a spoon with the tines of a fork

¹sport \'spȯrt\ *vb* **1** ♦ : to amuse oneself : FROLIC **2** ♦ : to display or wear usu. ostentatiously : SHOW OFF

    ♦ [1] caper, cavort, disport, frisk, frolic, gambol, lark, play, rollick, romp ♦ [2] display, disport, exhibit, expose, flash, flaunt, parade, show, show off, strut, unveil

²sport *n* **1** ♦ : a source of diversion **2** : physical activity engaged in for pleasure **3** : a frivolous mood or manner : JEST **4** : MOCKERY ⟨make ∼ of his efforts⟩ **5** : BUTT, LAUGHINGSTOCK **6** : one who accepts results cheerfully whether favorable or not **7** : an individual exhibiting marked deviation from its normal type esp. as a result of mutation — **sporty** *adj*

    ♦ dalliance, frolic, fun, play, relaxation

³sport *or* **sports** *adj* : of, relating to, or suitable for sport or casual wear ⟨∼ coats⟩

sport fish *n* : a fish noted for the sport it affords anglers

sport·ive \'spȯr-tiv\ *adj* ♦ : full of gaiety : full of play

    ♦ antic, coltish, elfish, fay, frisky, frolicsome, playful

sports car *n* : a small and low car that usu. seats two people and that is made for fast driving

sports·cast \'spȯrts-ˌkast\ *n* : a broadcast dealing with sports events — **sports·cast·er** \-ˌkas-tər\ *n*

sports·man \'spȯrts-mən\ *n* **1** : a person who engages in sports (as in hunting or fishing) **2** : one who plays fairly and wins or loses gracefully — **sports·man·ship** *n*

sports·man·like \-ˌlīk\ *adj* ♦ : consistent with the ideals of good sportsmanship

    ♦ clean, fair, legal

sports medicine *n* : a field of medicine dealing with the prevention and treatment of sports-related injuries

sports·wom·an \-ˌwu̇-mən\ *n* : a woman who engages in sports

sports·writ·er \-ˌrī-tər\ *n* : one who writes about sports esp. for a newspaper — **sports·writ·ing** *n*

sport–util·ity vehicle \'spȯrt-yü-'ti-lə-tē-\ *n* : SUV

¹spot \'spät\ *n* **1** : a taint on character or reputation : STAIN **2** ♦ : a small part different (as in color) from the main part **3** ♦ : a particular place, area, or part : LOCATION **4** ♦ : a position usu. of difficulty or embarrassment **5** : a small quantity or amount — **on the spot 1** : at the place of action **2** : in difficulty or danger

♦ [2] blotch, dapple, dot, fleck, mottle, patch, point, speck ♦ [3] locale, location, place, point, position, site ♦ [4] corner, fix, hole, jam, pickle, predicament

²spot *vb* **spot·ted; spot·ting 1** ♦ : to mark or disfigure with spots **2** : to pick out : RECOGNIZE, IDENTIFY

♦ blotch, dapple, dot, fleck, freckle, mottle, pepper, speck, sprinkle, stipple

³spot *adj* **1** : being, done, or originating on the spot ⟨a ~ broadcast⟩ **2** : paid upon delivery **3** : made at random or at a few key points ⟨a ~ check⟩
spot–check \'spät-ˌchek\ *vb* : to make a spot check of
spot·less *adj* ♦ : having no spot : free from impurity, fault, or stain — **spot·less·ly** *adv*

♦ clean, immaculate, spick-and-span, stainless, unsoiled, unsullied

spot·light \-ˌlīt\ *n* **1** : a circle of brilliant light projected upon a particular area, person, or object (as on a stage); *also* : the device that produces this light **2** : public notice — **spotlight** *vb*
spot–on \'spät-'än\ *adj* : exactly correct ⟨a ~ forecast⟩
spotted *adj* ♦ : having spots

♦ dappled, mottled, pied, spotty, variegated

spotted owl *n* : a rare large dark brown dark-eyed owl of humid old growth forests and thickly wooded canyons from British Columbia to southern California and central Mexico
spot·ter \'spä-tər\ *n* **1** : one that keeps watch : OBSERVER **2** : one that removes spots
spot·ty \'spä-tē\ *adj* **spot·ti·er; -est 1** ♦ : uneven in quality; *also* : sparsely distributed ⟨~ attendance⟩ **2** : marked with spots : SPOTTED

♦ casual, choppy, discontinuous, erratic, fitful, intermittent, irregular, occasional, spasmodic, sporadic, unsteady

spou·sal \'spau̇-zəl, -səl\ *n* : MARRIAGE 2, WEDDING — usu. used in pl.
spouse \'spau̇s\ *n* ♦ : one's partner in a marriage (as husband or wife) — **spou·sal** \'spau̇-zəl, -səl\ *adj*

♦ consort, mate, partner

¹spout \'spau̇t\ *vb* **1** ♦ : to eject or issue forth forcibly and freely ⟨wells ~ing oil⟩ **2** ♦ : to speak pompously **3** ♦ : to speak or utter readily, volubly, and at length

♦ [1] gush, jet, pour, rush, spew, spurt, squirt ♦ [1] belch, disgorge, eject, erupt, expel ♦ [2, 3] bluster, fulminate, rant, rave ♦ *usu* **spout off** [3] sound off, speak out, speak up

²spout *n* **1** : a pipe or hole through which liquid spouts **2** : a jet of liquid; *esp* : WATERSPOUT 2
spp *abbr* species (*pl*)
¹sprain \'sprān\ *n* : a sudden or severe twisting of a joint with stretching or tearing of ligaments; *also* : a sprained condition
²sprain *vb* : to subject to sprain
sprat \'sprat\ *n* : a small European fish related to the herring; *also* : SARDINE
sprawl \'sprȯl\ *vb* **1** : to lie or sit with limbs spread out awkwardly **2** : to spread out irregularly — **sprawl** *n*
¹spray \'sprā\ *n* : a usu. flowering branch; *also* : a decorative arrangement of flowers and foliage
²spray *n* **1** : liquid flying in small drops like water blown from a wave **2** : a jet of fine vapor (as from an atomizer) **3** : an instrument (as an atomizer) for scattering fine liquid
³spray *vb* **1** ♦ : to scatter or let fall in a spray **2** : to discharge spray on or into — **spray·er** *n*

♦ dot, pepper, scatter, sow, sprinkle, strew

spray can *n* : a pressurized container from which aerosols are sprayed
spray gun *n* : a device for spraying liquids (as paint or insecticide)
¹spread \'spred\ *vb* **spread; spread·ing 1** : to scatter over a surface **2** ♦ : to flatten out : open out **3** ♦ : to distribute over a period of time or among many persons **4** : to cover something with ⟨~ rugs on the floor⟩ **5** : to prepare for a meal ⟨~ a table⟩ **6** ♦ : to pass on from person to person **7** : to stretch, force, or push apart ⟨a bird ~ing its wings⟩ **8** ♦ : to make widely known — **spread·er** *n*

♦ *usu* **spread out** [2] expand, extend, fan, flare, open, stretch,

unfold ♦ [3] broadcast, circulate, disseminate, propagate, strew ♦ [6, 8] communicate, convey, impart, transfer, transfuse, transmit

²spread *n* **1** : the act or process of spreading **2** ♦ : a surface area : EXPANSE **3** : a prominent display in a periodical **4** : a food to be spread on bread or crackers **5** ♦ : a cloth cover for a bed **6** ♦ : distance between two points **7** ♦ : a sumptuous meal

♦ [2] breadth, expanse, extent, reach, stretch ♦ [5] bedspread, counterpane ♦ [6] distance, lead, length, remove, stretch, way ♦ [7] banquet, dinner, feast, feed

spread·sheet \'spred-ˌshēt\ *n* : an accounting program for a computer
spree \'sprē\ *n* : an unrestrained outburst ⟨buying ~⟩; *also* : a drinking bout
sprig \'sprig\ *n* : a small shoot or twig
spright·li·ness \'sprīt-lē-nes\ *n* ♦ : the quality or state of being sprightly

♦ animation, briskness, exuberance, liveliness, lustiness, robustness, vibrancy, vitality

spright·ly \'sprīt-lē\ *adj* **spright·li·er; -est** ♦ : marked by a high-spirited lightness and vivacity : LIVELY

♦ active, animate, animated, brisk, energetic, frisky, lively, peppy, spirited, springy, vital, vivacious

¹spring \'spriŋ\ *vb* **sprang** \'spraŋ\ *or* **sprung** \'sprəŋ\; **sprung; spring·ing 1** ♦ : to move suddenly upward or forward **2** ♦ : to grow quickly ⟨weeds *sprang* up overnight⟩ **3** : to come from by birth or descent **4** : to move quickly by elastic force **5** : WARP **6** : to develop (a leak) through the seams **7** : to cause to close suddenly ⟨~ a trap⟩ **8** : to make known suddenly ⟨~ a surprise⟩ **9** : to make lame : STRAIN **10** ♦ : to come into being **11** ♦ : to release or cause to be released from confinement or custody **12** ♦ : to discharge indebtedness for — used with *for*

♦ [1] bound, hop, jump, leap, vault ♦ [10] arise, begin, commence, dawn, form, materialize, originate, start ♦ *usu* **spring up** [10] crop, emerge, surface ♦ [11] discharge, emancipate, enfranchise, free, liberate, loose, loosen, manumit, release, unbind, unchain, unfetter ♦ *usu* **spring for** [12] clear, discharge, foot, liquidate, pay, pay off, quit, recompense, settle, stand

²spring *n* **1** : a source of supply; *esp* : an issuing of water from the ground **2** : SOURCE, ORIGIN; *also* : MOTIVE **3** : the season between winter and summer **4** : an elastic body or device that recovers its original shape when it is released after being distorted **5** ♦ : the act or an instance of leaping up or forward **6** : RESILIENCE

♦ bound, hop, jump, leap, vault

spring·board \'spriŋ-ˌbōrd\ *n* : a springy board used in jumping or vaulting or for diving
spring fever *n* : a lazy or restless feeling often associated with the onset of spring
spring tide *n* : a tide of greater-than-average range that occurs at each new moon and full moon
spring·time \'spriŋ-ˌtīm\ *n* : the season of spring
springy *adj* **1** ♦ : having an elastic quality **2** ♦ : having or showing a lively and energetic movement

♦ [1] elastic, flexible, resilient, rubbery, stretch, supple ♦ [2] active, animate, animated, brisk, energetic, lively, spirited, sprightly

¹sprin·kle \'spriŋ-kəl\ *vb* **sprin·kled; sprin·kling** ♦ : to scatter in small drops or particles — **sprin·kler** *n*

♦ dot, pepper, scatter, sow, spray, strew

²sprinkle *n* **1** : a light rainfall **2** ♦ : a small number esp. distributed at random

♦ few, handful, smattering, sprinkling

sprin·kling *n* ♦ : a limited quantity or amount : SMATTERING

♦ few, handful, smattering, sprinkle

¹sprint \'sprint\ *vb* ♦ : to run at top speed esp. for a short distance — **sprint·er** *n*

♦ dash, gallop, jog, run, scamper, trip

²sprint *n* **1** : a short run at top speed **2** : a short distance race
sprite \'sprīt\ *n* **1** : GHOST, SPIRIT **2** : a small often mischievous fairy : ELF
spritz \'sprits, 'shprits\ *vb* : SPRAY ⟨~ the plants⟩ — **spritz** *n*
sprock·et \'sprä-kət\ *n* : a toothed wheel whose teeth engage the links of a chain
¹sprout \'sprau̇t\ *vb* : to send out new growth ⟨~ing seeds⟩
²sprout *n* : a usu. young and growing plant shoot (as from a seed)

¹**spruce** \'sprüs\ *vb* **spruced; spruc•ing** : to make or become spruce

²**spruce** *adj* **spruc•er; spruc•est ♦** : neat and smart in appearance

♦ dapper, natty, sharp, smart

³**spruce** *n, pl* **spruc•es** *also* **spruce** : any of a genus of evergreen pyramid-shaped trees related to the pines and having soft light wood; *also* : the wood of a spruce

sprung *past and past part of* SPRING

spry \'sprī\ *adj* **spri•er** *or* **spry•er** \'sprī-ər\; **spri•est** *or* **spry•est** \'sprī-əst\ ♦ : quick and light in motion : NIMBLE

♦ agile, graceful, light, lissome, lithe, nimble

spud \'spəd\ *n* **1** : a sharp narrow spade **2** : POTATO

spume \'spyüm\ *n* ♦ : frothy matter on liquids : FOAM — **spumy** \'spyü-mē\ *adj*

♦ foam, froth, head, lather

spu•mo•ni *also* **spu•mo•ne** \spu̇-'mō-nē\ *n* : ice cream in layers of different colors, flavors, and textures often with candied fruits and nuts

spun *past and past part of* SPIN

spun glass *n* : FIBERGLASS

spunk \'spəŋk\ *n* ♦ : vigor and strength of spirit or temperament : PLUCK

♦ backbone, fiber (*or* fibre), fortitude, grit, guts, pluck

spunky *adj* ♦ : full of spunk

♦ fiery, high-spirited, mettlesome, peppery, spirited

¹**spur** \'spər\ *n* **1** : a pointed device fastened to a rider's boot and used to urge on a horse **2** ♦ : something that urges to action **3** : a stiff sharp spine (as on the leg of a cock); *also* : a hollow projecting appendage of a flower (as a columbine) **4** : a ridge extending sideways from a mountain **5** : a branch of railroad track extending from the main line — **spurred** \'spərd\ *adj* — **on the spur of the moment** : on hasty impulse

♦ boost, encouragement, goad, impetus, impulse, incentive, incitement, instigation, momentum, motivation, provocation, stimulus, yeast

²**spur** *vb* **spurred; spur•ring** **1** : to urge a horse on with spurs **2** : INCITE

spurge \'spərj\ *n* : any of a family of herbs and woody plants with a bitter milky juice

spu•ri•ous \'spyu̇r-ē-əs\ *adj* ♦ : not genuine : FALSE

♦ affected, artificial, assumed, bogus, contrived, factitious, fake, false, feigned, mechanical, mock, phony, put-on, sham, unnatural

spurn \'spərn\ *vb* **1** : to kick away or trample on **2** ♦ : to reject with disdain

♦ decline, disallow, disapprove, negative, refuse, reject, repudiate, turn down

¹**spurt** \'spərt\ *vb* ♦ : to gush out : SPOUT

♦ gush, jet, pour, rush, spew, spout, squirt

²**spurt** *n* : a sudden gushing or spouting

³**spurt** *n* **1** : a sudden brief burst of effort, speed, or development **2** ♦ : a sharp increase of activity ⟨~ in sales⟩

♦ burst, flare, flare-up, flash, flurry, flutter, outbreak, outburst

⁴**spurt** *vb* : to make a spurt

sput•ter \'spə-tər\ *vb* **1** : to spit small scattered particles : SPLUTTER **2** ♦ : to utter words hastily or explosively in excitement or confusion **3** : to make small popping sounds — **sputter** *n*

♦ babble, chatter, drivel, gabble, gibber, jabber, prattle

spu•tum \'spyü-təm\ *n, pl* **spu•ta** \-tə\ : material (as phlegm) that is spit out or coughed up esp. during illness

¹**spy** \'spī\ *vb* **spied; spy•ing** **1** : to watch or search for information secretly : act as a spy **2** ♦ : to get a momentary or quick glimpse of : SEE

♦ behold, descry, discern, distinguish, espy, eye, look, note, notice, observe, perceive, regard, remark, see, sight, view, witness

²**spy** *n, pl* **spies** **1** : one who secretly watches others **2** : a secret agent who tries to get information for one country in the territory of an enemy

spy•glass \'spī-ˌglas\ *n* : a small telescope

sq *abbr* **1** squadron **2** square

squab \'skwäb\ *n, pl* **squabs** *or* **squab** : a young bird and esp. pigeon

¹**squab•ble** \'skwä-bəl\ *n* ♦ : a noisy altercation : WRANGLE

♦ altercation, argument, bicker, brawl, disagreement, dispute, fight, hassle, misunderstanding, quarrel, row, scrap, spat, wrangle

²**squabble** *vb* ♦ : to quarrel noisily and usu. over petty matters

♦ argue, bicker, brawl, dispute, fall out, fight, hassle, quarrel, row, scrap, spat, wrangle

squad \'skwäd\ *n* **1** : a small organized group of military personnel **2** ♦ : a small group engaged in a common effort

♦ band, company, crew, gang, outfit, party, team

squad car *n* : a police car connected by two-way radio with headquarters

squad•ron \'skwä-drən\ *n* : any of several units of military organization

squal•id \'skwä-ləd\ *adj* **1** : filthy or degraded through neglect or poverty **2** : SORDID, DEBASED

squall \'skwȯl\ *n* **1** : a sudden violent gust of wind often with rain or snow **2** : a short-lived commotion

squally *adj* ♦ : marked by squalls

♦ bleak, dirty, foul, inclement, nasty, raw, rough, stormy, tempestuous, turbulent

squa•lor \'skwä-lər\ *n* : the quality or state of being squalid

squan•der \'skwän-dər\ *vb* ♦ : to spend wastefully or foolishly

♦ blow, dissipate, fritter, lavish, misspend, run through, spend, throw away, waste

¹**square** \'skwar\ *n* **1** : an instrument used to lay out or test right angles **2** : a rectangle with all four sides equal **3** : something square **4** : the product of a number multiplied by itself **5** : an area bounded by four streets **6** : an open area in a city where streets meet **7** : a highly conventional person

²**square** *adj* **squar•er; squar•est** **1** : having four equal sides and four right angles **2** : forming a right angle ⟨cut a ~ corner⟩ **3** : multiplied by itself : SQUARED ⟨x^2 is the symbol for x ~⟩ **4** : being a unit of square measure equal to a square each side of which measures one unit ⟨a ~ foot⟩ **5** : being of a specified length in each of two dimensions ⟨an area 10 feet ~⟩ **6** : exactly adjusted **7** ♦ : marked by impartiality and honesty : JUST ⟨a ~ deal⟩ **8** : leaving no balance ⟨make accounts ~⟩ **9** : SUBSTANTIAL ⟨a ~ meal⟩ **10** : highly conservative or conventional

♦ disinterested, dispassionate, equal, equitable, fair, impartial, just, nonpartisan, objective, unbiased, unprejudiced

³**square** *vb* **squared; squar•ing** **1** : to form with four equal sides and right angles or with flat surfaces ⟨~ a timber⟩ **2** : to multiply (a number) by itself **3** ♦ : to agree precisely : CONFORM **4** : BALANCE, SETTLE ⟨~ an account⟩

♦ accord, agree, answer, check, coincide, comport, conform, correspond, dovetail, fit, go, harmonize, jibe, tally

square dance *n* : a dance for four couples arranged to form a square

square•ly *adv* ♦ : in a manner or measure or to a degree or number that strictly conforms to a fact or condition

♦ accurately, exactly, just, precisely, right, sharp

square measure *n* : a unit or system of units for measuring area

square–rigged \'skwar-ˌrigd\ *adj* : having the chief sails extended on yards that are fastened to the masts horizontally and at their center

square–rig•ger \-ˌri-gər\ *n* : a square-rigged craft

square root *n* : either of the two numbers whose squares are equal to a given number ⟨the *square root* of 9 is +3 or –3⟩

¹**squash** \'skwäsh, 'skwȯsh\ *vb* **1** ♦ : to beat or press into a pulp or flat mass **2** ♦ : to bring to an end : QUASH

♦ [1] crush, mash ♦ [2] clamp down, crack down, crush, put down, quash, quell, repress, silence, snuff, squelch, subdue, suppress

²**squash** *n* **1** : the impact of something soft and heavy; *also* : the sound of such impact **2** : a crushed mass **3** : a game played on a 4-wall court with a racket and rubber ball

³**squash** *n, pl* **squash•es** *or* **squash** : any of various fruits of plants of the gourd family that are used esp. as vegetables; *also* : a plant and esp. a vine bearing squashes

squash racquets *n* : SQUASH 3

¹**squat** \'skwät\ *vb* **squat•ted; squat•ting** **1** ♦ : to sit down upon the hams or heels **2** : to settle on land without right or title; *also* : to settle on public land with a view to acquiring title — **squat•ter** *n*

♦ crouch, huddle, hunch

²**squat** *n* : the act or posture of squatting

³squat *adj* **squat·ter; squat·test** **1** : low to the ground **2** ♦ : short and thick in stature

♦ chunky, dumpy, heavyset, stocky, stout, stubby, stumpy, thickset

squawk \'skwȯk\ *n* ♦ : a harsh loud cry; *also* : a noisy protest — **squawk** *vb*

♦ beef, complaint, fuss, grievance, gripe, grumble, murmur, plaint

squeak \'skwēk\ *vb* **1** ♦ : to utter or speak in a weak shrill tone **2** : to make a thin high-pitched sound — **squeak** *n*

♦ cheep, peep, squeal

squeaky *adj* ♦ : of the nature of, emitting, or tending to emit squeaks

♦ acute, sharp, shrill, treble

¹squeal \'skwēl\ *vb* **1** ♦ : to make a shrill sound or cry **2** ♦ : to betray a secret or turn informer **3** : COMPLAIN, PROTEST

♦ [1] howl, scream, shriek, shrill, yell, yelp ♦ [2] inform, snitch, talk, tell

²squeal *n* : a shrill sharp cry or noise

squea·mish \'skwē-mish\ *adj* **1** ♦ : easily nauseated; *also* : NAUSEATED **2** ♦ : easily disgusted

♦ [1] ill, nauseous, queasy, sick ♦ [2] disgusted, sick

squea·mish·ness *n* ♦ : the quality or state of being squeamish

♦ nausea, queasiness, sickness

squee·gee \'skwē-jē\ *n* : a blade set crosswise on a handle and used for spreading or wiping liquid on, across, or off a surface — **squeegee** *vb*

¹squeeze \'skwēz\ *vb* **squeezed; squeez·ing** **1** ♦ : to exert pressure on the opposite sides or parts of : COMPRESS **2** ♦ : to obtain by pressure ⟨∼ juice from a lemon⟩ **3** ♦ : to force or move into a small space ⟨*squeezed* into her jeans⟩ **4** : to pass, win, or get by narrowly **5** : to get or deprive by extortion — **squeez·er** *n*

♦ [1] compact, compress, condense, constrict, contract ♦ [2] crush, express, mash, press ♦ [3] cram, crowd, jam, ram, sandwich, stuff, wedge

²squeeze *n* **1** : an act of squeezing **2** : a quantity squeezed out **3** *slang* ♦ : a romantic partner

♦ beloved, darling, dear, flame, honey, love, sweet, sweetheart

squeeze bottle *n* : a flexible plastic bottle that dispenses its contents when it is squeezed

squelch \'skwelch\ *vb* **1** ♦ : to suppress completely : CRUSH **2** : to move in soft mud — **squelch** *n*

♦ clamp down, crack down, crush, put down, quash, quell, repress, silence, snuff, squash, subdue, suppress

squib \'skwib\ *n* : a brief witty writing or speech

squid \'skwid\ *n, pl* **squid** *or* **squids** : any of an order of long-bodied sea mollusks having eight short arms and two longer tentacles and usu. a slender internal shell

squint \'skwint\ *vb* **1** : to look or aim obliquely **2** : to look or peer with the eyes partly closed ⟨∼*ing* into the sun⟩ **3** : to be cross-eyed — **squint** *n or adj*

¹squire \'skwīr\ *n* **1** : an armor-bearer of a knight **2** : a man who devotedly attends a lady **3** : a member of the British gentry ranking below a knight and above a gentleman; *also* : a prominent landowner **4** : a local magistrate

²squire *vb* **squired; squir·ing** ♦ : to attend as a squire or escort

♦ accompany, attend, convoy, escort

squirm \'skwərm\ *vb* ♦ : to twist about like a worm : WRIGGLE

♦ fiddle, fidget, jerk, twitch, wiggle

¹squir·rel \'skwər-əl\ *n, pl* **squirrels** *also* **squirrel** : any of various rodents usu. with a long bushy tail and strong hind legs; *also* : the fur of a squirrel

²squirrel *vb* **-reled** *or* **-relled; -rel·ing** *or* **-rel·ling** : to store up for future use

¹squirt \'skwərt\ *vb* ♦ : to eject liquid in a thin spurt

♦ gush, jet, pour, rush, spew, spout, spurt

²squirt *n* **1** : an instrument (as a syringe) for squirting **2** : a small forcible jet of liquid

¹Sr *abbr* **1** senior **2** sister

²Sr *symbol* strontium

SR *abbr* seaman recruit

¹SRO \ˌes-(ˌ)är-'ō\ *n* : a house or apartment building in which low-income tenants live in single rooms

²SRO *abbr* standing room only

SS *abbr* **1** saints **2** Social Security **3** steamship **4** sworn statement

SSA *abbr* Social Security Administration

SSE *abbr* south-southeast

SSG *or* **SSgt** *abbr* staff sergeant

SSI *abbr* supplemental security income

SSM *abbr* staff sergeant major

SSN *abbr* Social Security Number

ssp *abbr* subspecies

SSR *abbr* Soviet Socialist Republic

SSS *abbr* Selective Service System

SST \ˌes-(ˌ)es-'tē\ *n* : a supersonic passenger airplane

SSW *abbr* south-southwest

st *abbr* **1** stanza **2** state **3** stitch **4** stone **5** street

St *abbr* saint

ST *abbr* **1** short ton **2** standard time

sta *abbr* station; stationary

¹stab \'stab\ *n* **1** ♦ : a wound produced by a pointed weapon **2** : a quick thrust **3** ♦ : a brief attempt

♦ [1] perforation, pinhole, prick, punch, puncture ♦ [3] attempt, crack, endeavor (*or* endeavour), essay, fling, go, pass, shot, trial, try, whack

²stab *vb* **stabbed; stab·bing** **1** ♦ : to pierce or wound with or as if with a pointed weapon **2** : THRUST, DRIVE

♦ gore, harpoon, impale, lance, pierce, puncture, skewer, spear, spike, stick, transfix

sta·bile \'stā-ˌbēl\ *n* : an abstract sculpture or construction similar to a mobile but made to be stationary

sta·bil·i·ty \stə-'bi-lə-tē\ *n* ♦ : the quality, state, or degree of being stable : the strength to stand or endure

♦ firmness, soundness, steadiness, strength, sturdiness *Ant* instability, unsoundness, unsteadiness ♦ constancy, fixedness, immutability, steadiness

sta·bi·lize \'stā-bə-ˌlīz\ *vb* **-lized; -liz·ing** **1** : to make stable **2** : to hold steady ⟨∼ prices⟩ — **sta·bi·li·za·tion** \ˌstā-bə-lə-'zā-shən\ *n* — **sta·bi·liz·er** \'stā-bə-ˌlī-zər\ *n*

¹sta·ble \'stā-bəl\ *n* : a building in which domestic animals are sheltered and fed — **sta·ble·man** \-mən, -ˌman\ *n*

²stable *vb* **sta·bled; sta·bling** : to put or keep in a stable

³stable *adj* **sta·bler; sta·blest** **1 a** ♦ : firmly established **b** ♦ : mentally and emotionally healthy **2** ♦ : steady in purpose : CONSTANT **3** ♦ : continuing or enduring without fundamental or marked change **4** ♦ : resistant to chemical or physical change

♦ [1a] certain, determinate, final, firm, fixed, flat, frozen, hard, hard-and-fast, set, settled ♦ [1b] balanced, clearheaded, lucid, normal, right, sane *Ant* unsound, unstable, unsteady ♦ [2, 3] constant, stationary, steady, unchanging, unvarying ♦ [3, 4] fast, firm, sound, stalwart, steady, strong, sturdy

stac·ca·to \stə-'kä-tō\ *adj or adv* : cut short so as not to sound connected ⟨∼ notes⟩

¹stack \'stak\ *n* **1** ♦ : a large pile (as of hay or grain) **2** : an orderly pile (as of poker chips) **3** ♦ : a large quantity **4** : a vertical pipe : SMOKESTACK **5** : a rack with shelves for storing books ⟨library ∼s⟩

♦ [1] cock, heap, hill, mound, mountain, pile, rick ♦ [3] abundance, deal, gobs, heap, loads, lot, pile, plenty, quantity, scads

²stack *vb* **1** ♦ : to pile up **2** : to arrange (cards) secretly for cheating

♦ heap, hill, mound, pile

stack up *vb* ♦ : to be equal or alike : MEASURE UP — usu. used with *against*; *also* : to add up

♦ *usu* **stack up against** approach, approximate, compare, measure up

sta·di·um \'stā-dē-əm\ *n, pl* **-dia** \-dē-ə\ *or* **-di·ums** ♦ : a structure with tiers of seats for spectators built around a field for sports events

♦ bowl, circus, coliseum

¹staff \'staf\ *n, pl* **staffs** \'stafs, 'stavz\ *or* **staves** \'stavz, 'stāvz\ **1** : a pole, stick, rod, or bar used for supporting, for measuring, or as a symbol of authority; *also* : CLUB, CUDGEL **2** : something that sustains ⟨bread is the ∼ of life⟩ **3** : the five horizontal lines on which music is written **4** ♦ : a body of assistants to an executive **5** : a group of officers holding no command but having duties concerned with planning and managing

♦ force, help, personnel, pool

²staff *vb* : to supply with a staff or with workers

staff•er \'sta-fər\ *n* : a member of a staff (as of a newspaper)

staff sergeant *n* : a noncommissioned officer ranking in the army next below a sergeant first class, in the air force next below a technical sergeant, and in the marine corps next below a gunnery sergeant

¹stag \'stag\ *n, pl* **stags** *or* **stag** : an adult male of various large deer

²stag *adj* : restricted to or intended for men ⟨a ~ party⟩ ⟨~ movies⟩

³stag *adv* : unaccompanied by a date

¹stage \'stāj\ *n* **1 ♦** : a raised platform on which an orator may speak or a play may be presented **2 ♦** : the acting profession : THEATER **3** : the scene of a notable action or event **4 a** : a station or resting place on a traveled road **b ♦** : the distance between two stopping places on a road **5** : STAGECOACH **6 ♦** : a degree of advance in an undertaking, process, or development **7** : a propulsion unit in a rocket — **stagy** \'stā-jē\ *adj*

♦ [1] dais, platform, podium, rostrum, stand ♦ [2] theater (*or* theatre), theatricals ♦ [4b] lap, leg, step ♦ [6] cut, degree, grade, inch, notch, peg, phase, point, step

²stage *vb* **staged; stag•ing ♦** : to produce or perform on or as if on a stage ⟨~ a play⟩ — **stage•able** *adj*

♦ carry, give, mount, offer, present

stage•coach \'stāj-ˌkōch\ *n* : a horse-drawn coach that runs regularly between stations

stage manager *n* : one who supervises the physical aspects of a stage production

stag•fla•tion \ˌstag-'flā-shən\ *n* : inflation with stagnant economic activity and high unemployment

¹stag•ger \'sta-gər\ *vb* **1 ♦** : to reel from side to side : TOTTER **2** : to begin to doubt : WAVER **3** : to cause to reel or waver **4** : to arrange in overlapping or alternating positions or times ⟨~ working hours⟩ **5** : ASTONISH

♦ careen, dodder, lurch, reel, teeter, totter

²stagger *n sing or pl* : an abnormal condition of domestic animals associated with damage to the central nervous system and marked by lack of coordination and a reeling unsteady gait **2** : a reeling or unsteady gait or stance

stag•ger•ing•ly *adv* : in a staggering manner or to a staggering degree

stag•ing \'stā-jiŋ\ *n* **1** : SCAFFOLDING **2** : the assembling of troops and matériel in transit in a particular place

stag•nant \'stag-nənt\ *adj* **1** : not flowing : MOTIONLESS ⟨~ water in a pond⟩ **2** : DULL, INACTIVE ⟨~ business⟩

stag•nate \'stag-ˌnāt\ *vb* **stag•nat•ed; stag•nat•ing** : to be or become stagnant — **stag•na•tion** \stag-'nā-shən\ *n*

staid \'stād\ *adj ♦* : marked by settled sedateness and often prim self-restraint

♦ august, dignified, imposing, solemn, stately ♦ earnest, grave, humorless (*or* humourless), serious, severe, sober, solemn, unsmiling, weighty

¹stain \'stān\ *vb* **1 ♦** : to discolor esp. with dirt : SOIL **2 ♦** : to touch or affect slightly with something bad : TAINT **3** : DISGRACE **4 ♦** : to color (as wood, paper, or cloth) by processes affecting the material itself

♦ [1] befoul, begrime, besmirch, blacken, dirty, foul, grime, mire, muddy, smirch, soil ♦ [2] blemish, mar, poison, spoil, taint, tarnish, touch, vitiate ♦ [4] color (*or* colour), dye, paint, tinge, tint

²stain *n* **1** : a small soiled or discolored area **2 ♦** : a taint of guilt : STIGMA **3 ♦** : a preparation (as a dye or pigment) used in staining

♦ [2] blot, brand, smirch, spot, stigma, taint ♦ [3] color (*or* colour), dye, pigment

stain•less *adj ♦* : free from stain or stigma

♦ clean, immaculate, spick-and-span, spotless, unsoiled, unsullied

stainless steel *n* : steel alloyed with chromium that is highly resistant to stain, rust, and corrosion

stair \'star\ *n* **1** : a series of steps or flights of steps for passing from one level to another — often used in pl. **2** : one step of a stairway

stair•case \-ˌkās\ *n* : a flight of steps with their supporting framework, casing, and balusters

stair•way \-ˌwā\ *n* : one or more flights of stairs with connecting landings

stair•well \-ˌwel\ *n* : a vertical shaft in which stairs are located

¹stake \'stāk\ *n* **1** : a pointed piece of material (as of wood) driv-

en into the ground as a marker or a support **2** : a post to which a person is bound for death by burning; *also* : execution by burning at the stake **3** : something that is ventured for gain or loss **4** : the prize in a contest **5 ♦** : an interest or share in an undertaking or enterprise

♦ claim, interest, share

²stake *vb* **staked; stak•ing** **1** : to mark the limits of by or as if by stakes **2** : to tie to a stake **3** : to support or secure with stakes **4** : BET, WAGER **5 ♦** : to back financially

♦ capitalize, endow, finance, fund, subsidize, underwrite

stake•out \'stāk-ˌaut\ *n* : a surveillance by police (as of a suspected criminal)

sta•lac•tite \stə-'lak-ˌtīt\ *n* : an icicle-shaped deposit hanging from the roof or sides of a cavern

sta•lag•mite \stə-'lag-ˌmīt\ *n* : a deposit resembling an inverted stalactite rising from the floor of a cavern

stale \'stāl\ *adj* **stal•er; stal•est** **1** : having lost good taste and quality from age ⟨~ bread⟩ **2** : dull or heard so often as to be dull ⟨~ news⟩ **3** : not as strong or effective as before ⟨~ from lack of practice⟩ — **stale•ness** *n*

♦ banal, commonplace, hackneyed, musty, stereotyped, threadbare, tired, trite **Ant** fresh, new, original

stale•mate \'stāl-ˌmāt\ *n ♦* : a drawn contest : DEADLOCK — **stalemate** *vb*

♦ deadlock, draw, halt, impasse, standoff, standstill, tie

¹stalk \'stok\ *n* : a plant stem; *also* : any slender usu. upright supporting or connecting part — **stalked** \'stokt\ *adj*

²stalk *vb* **1** : to pursue (game) stealthily **2 ♦** : to walk stiffly or haughtily **3** : to follow (a person) obsessively — **stalk•er** *n*

♦ strut, swagger

¹stall \'stol\ *n* **1** : a compartment in a stable or barn for one animal **2** : a booth or counter where articles may be displayed for sale **3** : a seat in a church choir; *also* : a church pew **4** *chiefly Brit* : a front orchestra seat in a theater

²stall *vb ♦* : to bring or come to a standstill unintentionally ⟨~ an engine⟩

♦ arrest, catch, check, draw up, fetch up, halt, hold up, stay, still, stop ♦ break, break down, conk, crash, cut out, die, fail

³stall *n* : the condition of an airfoil or aircraft in which lift is lost and the airfoil or aircraft tends to drop

⁴stall *n* : a ruse to deceive or delay

⁵stall *vb* : to hold off, divert, or delay by evasion or deception

stal•lion \'stal-yən\ *n* : a male horse

stal•wart \'stol-wərt\ *adj ♦* : marked by outstanding strength and vigor of body, mind, or spirit : STRONG; *also* : VALIANT

♦ brave, courageous, dauntless, doughty, fearless, gallant, greathearted, heroic, intrepid, lionhearted, manful, stout, undaunted, valiant, valorous ♦ brawny, muscular, rugged, sinewy, stout, strong

sta•men \'stā-mən\ *n* : an organ of a flower that produces pollen

stam•i•na \'sta-mə-nə\ *n ♦* : VIGOR, ENDURANCE

sta•mi•nate \'stā-mə-nət, 'sta-mə-, -ˌnāt\ *adj* **1** : having or producing stamens **2** : having stamens but no pistils

stam•mer \'sta-mər\ *vb* : to hesitate or stumble in speaking — **stammer** *n* — **stam•mer•er** *n*

¹stamp \'stamp; *for 2 also* 'stämp *or* 'stomp\ *vb* **1** : to pound or crush with a heavy instrument **2 ♦** : to strike or beat with the bottom of the foot **3** : IMPRESS, IMPRINT **4** : to put an end to or indent with a stamp or die **5** : to attach a postage stamp to **6 ♦** : to extinguish or destroy by or as if by stamping with the foot — used with *out* **7** : to strike or thrust the foot forcibly or noisily downward

♦ [2] stomp, tramp, trample, tromp ♦ *usu* **stamp out** [6] annihilate, blot out, demolish, eradicate, exterminate, liquidate, obliterate, root, rub out, snuff, wipe out

²stamp *n* **1** : a device or instrument for stamping **2 ♦** : the mark made by stamping; *also* : a distinctive mark or quality **3** : the act of stamping **4** : a stamped or printed paper affixed to show that a charge has been paid ⟨postage ~⟩ ⟨tax ~⟩

♦ impress, impression, imprint, print

¹stam•pede \stam-'pēd\ *n* : a wild headlong rush or flight esp. of frightened animals

²stampede *vb* **stam•ped•ed; stam•ped•ing** **1** : to flee or cause to flee in panic **2** : to act or cause to act together suddenly and heedlessly

stance \'stans\ *n* : a way of standing

¹stanch \'stonch, 'stänch, 'stanch\ *or* **staunch** \'stonch, 'stänch\

vb : to check the flowing of (as blood); *also* : to cease flowing or bleeding

²**stanch** *var of* ²STAUNCH

stan·chion \'stan-chən\ *n* ♦ : an upright bar, post, or support

♦ column, pier, pillar, post

¹**stand** \'stand\ *vb* **stood** \'stůd\; **stand·ing** **1** : to take or be at rest in an upright or firm position **2** : to assume a specified position **3** : to remain stationary or unchanged **4** : to be steadfast **5** : to act in resistance ⟨~ against a foe⟩ **6** : to maintain a relative position or rank **7** : to gather slowly and remain ⟨tears *stood* in her eyes⟩ **8** : to set upright **9** ♦ : to tolerate without flinching : ENDURE ⟨I won't ~ for that⟩ **10** : to submit to ⟨~ trial⟩ **11** ♦ : to pay the cost of (a treat) : pay for — **stand pat** : to oppose or resist change

♦ [9] abide, bear, brook, countenance, endure, meet, stick out, stomach, support, sustain, take, tolerate ♦ [11] clear, discharge, foot, liquidate, pay, pay off, quit, recompense, settle, spring

²**stand** *n* **1** : an act of standing, staying, or resisting **2** : a stop made to give a performance **3** : POSITION, VIEWPOINT **4** : a place taken by a witness to testify in court **5** *pl* : tiered seats for spectators **6** ♦ : a raised platform (as for speakers) **7** : a structure for a small retail business **8** : a structure for supporting or holding something upright ⟨music ~⟩ **9** : a group of plants growing in a continuous area

♦ dais, platform, podium, rostrum, stage

stand–alone \'stan-də-,lōn\ *adj* : SELF-CONTAINED; *esp* : capable of operation independent of a computer system

¹**stan·dard** \'stan-dərd\ *n* **1** : a figure adopted as an emblem by a people **2** ♦ : the personal flag of a ruler; *also* : FLAG **3** ♦ : something set up as a rule for measuring or as a model to be followed; *also* : a model of behavior established by custom — often used in pl. **4** : an upright support ⟨lamp ~⟩

♦ [2] banner, colors (*or* colours), ensign, flag, jack, pennant, streamer ♦ [3] criterion, gauge, mark, measure, par, touchstone, yardstick ♦ **standards** [3] ethics, morality, morals, principles

²**standard** *adj* **1** ♦ : constituting or conforming to a standard esp. as established by law or custom **2** ♦ : regularly and widely used, available, or supplied

♦ [1] average, characteristic, normal, regular, representative, typical ♦ [2] conventional, current, customary, popular, stock, usual

stan·dard–bear·er \-,bar-ər\ *n* : the leader of a cause
standard deviation *n* : a measure of dispersion in a set of data
stan·dard·ise *chiefly Brit var of* STANDARDIZE
stan·dard–is·sue \'stan-dərd-'i-shü\ *adj* : STANDARD, TYPICAL ⟨a ~ blue suit⟩
stan·dard·ize \'stan-dər-,dīz\ *vb* **-ized; -iz·ing** ♦ : to make standard or uniform — **stan·dard·i·za·tion** \,stan-dər-də-'zā-shən\ *n*

♦ formalize, homogenize, normalize, regularize

standard of living : the necessities, comforts, and luxuries that a person or group is accustomed to
standard time *n* : the time established by law or by general usage over a region or country

¹**stand·by** \'stand-,bī\ *n, pl* **stand·bys** \-,bīz\ **1** ♦ : one that can be relied on **2** : a substitute in reserve — **on standby** : ready or available for immediate action or use

♦ buttress, dependence, mainstay, pillar, reliance, support

²**standby** *adj* **1** : ready for use **2** : relating to airline travel in which the passenger must wait for an available unreserved seat — **standby** *adv*
stand–in \'stan-,din\ *n* **1** : someone employed to occupy an actor's place while lights and camera are readied **2** ♦ : a person or thing that takes the place or function of another : SUBSTITUTE

♦ backup, pinch hitter, relief, replacement, reserve, sub, substitute

stand in *vb* ♦ : to act as a stand-in

♦ cover, fill in, pinch-hit, sub, substitute, take over

¹**stand·ing** \'stan-diŋ\ *adj* **1** : ERECT **2** : not flowing : STAGNANT **3** : remaining at the same level or amount for an indefinite period ⟨~ offer⟩ **4** : PERMANENT **5** : done from a standing position ⟨a ~ jump⟩
²**standing** *n* **1 a** ♦ : length of service **b** ♦ : relative position in society or in a profession : RANK **2** : maintenance of position or condition : DURATION

♦ [1a] date, duration, life, lifetime, run, time ♦ [1b] degree, footing, level, place, position, rank, situation, station, status

stand–off \'stan-,dȯf\ *n* ♦ : a state of inaction or neutralization resulting from the opposition of equally powerful uncompromising persons or factions : TIE

♦ dead heat, draw, stalemate, tie

stand–off·ish \stan-'dȯ-fish\ *adj* ♦ : somewhat cold and reserved

♦ aloof, antisocial, cold, cool, detached, distant, frosty, remote, unsociable

stand·out \'stan-,daůt\ *n* ♦ : something conspicuously excellent

♦ celebrity, figure, light, luminary, notable, personage, personality, somebody, star, superstar, VIP

stand·pipe \'stand-,pīp\ *n* : a high vertical pipe or reservoir for water used to produce a uniform pressure
stand·point \-,pȯint\ *n* ♦ : a position from which objects or principles are judged

♦ angle, outlook, perspective, point of view, slant, viewpoint

stand·still \-,stil\ *n* ♦ : a state of rest

♦ deadlock, halt, impasse, stalemate

stank *past of* STINK
stand–up \'stan-,dəp\ *adj* : done or performing in a standing position ⟨a ~ comic⟩ ⟨~ comedy⟩
stan·za \'stan-zə\ *n* : a group of lines forming a division of a poem
sta·pes \'stā-,pēz\ *n, pl* **stapes** *or* **sta·pe·des** \'stā-pə-,dēz\ : the small innermost bone of the ear of mammals
staph \'staf\ *n* : STAPHYLOCOCCUS
staph·y·lo·coc·cus \,sta-fə-lō-'kä-kəs\ *n, pl* **-coc·ci** \-'kä-,kī, -'käk-,sī\ : any of various spherical bacteria including some pathogens of skin and mucous membranes — **staph·y·lo·coc·cal** \-'kä-kəl\ *adj*
¹**sta·ple** \'stā-pəl\ *n* : a U-shaped piece of metal or wire with sharp points to be driven into a surface or through thin layers (as paper) for attaching or holding together — **staple** *vb* — **sta·pler** *n*
²**staple** *n* **1** : a chief commodity or product **2** ♦ : a chief part of something ⟨a ~ of their diet⟩ **3** : unmanufactured or raw material **4** : a textile fiber suitable for spinning into yarn

♦ body, bulk, core, generality, main, mass, weight

³**staple** *adj* **1** : regularly produced in large quantities **2** : PRINCIPAL, MAIN
¹**star** \'stär\ *n* **1** : a celestial body that appears as a fixed point of light; *esp* : such a body that is gaseous, self-luminous, and of great mass **2** : a planet or configuration of planets that is held in astrology to influence one's fortune — usu. used in pl. **3** *obs* : DESTINY, FORTUNE **4** : a conventional figure representing a star; *esp* : ASTERISK **5** : an actor or actress playing the leading role **6** ♦ : a brilliant performer **7** ♦ : a person who is preeminent in a particular field — **star** *adj* — **star·dom** \'stär-dəm\ *n* — **star·less** *adj* — **star·like** *adj*

♦ [6, 7] celebrity, figure, light, luminary, notable, personage, personality, somebody, standout, superstar, VIP

²**star** *vb* **starred; star·ring** **1** : to adorn with stars **2** : to mark with an asterisk **3** : to play the leading role
star·board \'stär-bərd\ *n* : the right side of a ship or airplane looking forward — **starboard** *adj*
¹**starch** \'stärch\ *vb* : to stiffen with or as if with starch
²**starch** *n* **1** : a complex carbohydrate that is stored in plants, is an important foodstuff, and is used in adhesives and sizes, in laundering, and in pharmacy **2** : a stiff formal manner **3** : resolute vigor
starchy *adj* **1** : containing, consisting of, or resembling starch **2** ♦ : characterized by punctilious respect for form

♦ ceremonious, correct, decorous, formal, proper

stare \'star\ *vb* **stared; star·ing** ♦ : to look fixedly with wide-open eyes — **stare** *n* — **star·er** *n*

♦ gape, gawk, gaze, goggle, peer, rubberneck

star·fish \'stär-,fish\ *n* : any of a class of echinoderms that have usu. five arms arranged around a central disk and feed largely on mollusks
star fruit *n* : CARAMBOLA 1
¹**stark** \'stärk\ *adj* **1** : rigid as if in death; *also* : STRICT **2** *archaic* : STRONG, ROBUST **3** : SHEER, UTTER **4** ♦ : not productive : BARREN ⟨~ landscape⟩; *also* : being without a usual, typical, or expected attribute or accompaniment : UNADORNED ⟨~ real-

ism⟩ **5** : sharply delineated **6** : rigidly conforming (as to a pattern or doctrine) — **stark·ly** *adv*

   ♦ barren, infertile, poor, unproductive, waste

²**stark** *adv* : WHOLLY, ABSOLUTELY ⟨∼ naked⟩
star·light \'stär-,līt\ *n* : the light given by the stars
star·ling \'stär-liŋ\ *n* : a dark brown or in summer glossy greenish black European bird that is naturalized nearly worldwide and often considered a pest
star·ry *adj* ♦ : of, relating to, or consisting of stars

   ♦ astral, star, stellar

¹**start** \'stärt\ *vb* **1** ♦ : to give an involuntary twitch or jerk (as from surprise) **2** ♦ : to begin an activity or undertaking : BEGIN **3** : to set going **4** : to enter or cause to enter a game or contest; *also* : to be in the starting lineup **5** : to protrude or seem to protrude — **start·er** *n*

   ♦ [1] bolt, jump, startle ♦ [2] arise, begin, commence, dawn, form, materialize, originate, spring ♦ [2] embark (on *or* upon), enter, get off, launch, open, strike ♦ [3] constitute, establish, found, inaugurate, initiate, innovate, institute, introduce, pioneer, set up ♦ [3] activate, actuate, crank, drive, move, propel, run, set off, spark, touch off, trigger, turn on

²**start** *n* **1** : a sudden involuntary motion : LEAP **2** : a spasmodic and brief effort or action **3** ♦ : BEGINNING; *also* : the place of beginning

   ♦ beginning, birth, commencement, dawn, genesis, launch, morning, onset, outset, threshold

star·tle \'stärt-ᵊl\ *vb* **star·tled; star·tling** **1** ♦ : to frighten or surprise suddenly : cause to start ⟨the noise *startled* us⟩ **2** ♦ : to move or jump suddenly (as in surprise or alarm)

   ♦ [1] amaze, astonish, astound, floor, shock, stun, surprise ♦ [1] alarm, frighten, scare, spook ♦ [2] bolt, jump, start

star·tling *adj* ♦ : causing sudden fear, surprise, or anxiety

   ♦ amazing, astonishing, astounding, eye-opening, shocking, stunning, surprising

starve \'stärv\ *vb* **starved; starv·ing** **1** : to die or cause to die from hunger **2** : to suffer extreme hunger or deprivation ⟨*starving* for affection⟩ **3** : to subdue by famine — **star·va·tion** \stär-'vā-shən\ *n*
starve·ling \'stärv-liŋ\ *n* : one that is thin from lack of nourishment

¹**stash** \'stash\ *vb* ♦ : to store in a secret place for future use

   ♦ cache, hoard, lay away, lay up, put by, salt away, stockpile, store

²**stash** *n* ♦ : something stored or hidden away

   ♦ cache, hoard, stockpile, store

sta·sis \'stā-səs, 'sta-\ *n, pl* **sta·ses** \'stā-,sēz, 'sta-\ **1** : a stoppage or slowing of the normal flow of a bodily fluid (as blood) **2** : a state of static balance : STAGNATION
¹**stat** \'stat\ *adv* : without delay : IMMEDIATELY
²**stat** *abbr* statute
¹**state** \'stāt\ *n* **1** : mode or condition of being ⟨the four ∼s of matter⟩ **2** : condition of mind **3** : social position **4** ♦ : a body of people occupying a territory and organized under one government; *also* : the government of such a body of people **5** : one of the constituent units of a nation having a federal government — **state·hood** \-,hu̇d\ *n*

   ♦ commonwealth, country, land, nation, sovereignty

²**state** *vb* **stat·ed; stat·ing** **1** : to set by regulation or authority **2** ♦ : to express in words

   ♦ clothe, couch, express, formulate, phrase, put, say, word ♦ articulate, say, speak, talk, tell, utter, verbalize, vocalize

state·craft \'stāt-,kraft\ *n* : the art of conducting state affairs
state·house \-,hau̇s\ *n* : the building in which a state legislature meets
state·li·ness *n* ♦ : impressiveness in scale or proportion; *also* : imposing or courtly formality

   ♦ class, elegance, grace, handsomeness, majesty, refinement
   ♦ augustness, brilliance, glory, grandeur, grandness, magnificence, majesty, nobility, nobleness, resplendence, splendor

state·ly \'stāt-lē\ *adj* **state·li·er; -est** **1** ♦ : having lofty dignity **2** ♦ : impressive in size or proportions : MAJESTIC

   ♦ [1] august, dignified, imposing, lofty, solemn, staid ♦ [2] august, baronial, gallant, glorious, grand, grandiose, heroic, imposing, magnificent, majestic, monumental, noble, proud, regal, royal, splendid

state·ment \'stāt-mənt\ *n* **1** ♦ : the act or result of presenting in words **2** ♦ : a summary of a financial account

   ♦ [1] articulation, expression, formulation, utterance, voice
   ♦ [2] account, bill, check, invoice, tab

state·room \'stāt-,rüm, -,ru̇m\ *n* : a private room on a ship or railroad car
state·side \'stāt-,sīd\ *adj* : of or relating to the U.S. as regarded from outside its continental limits — **stateside** *adv*
states·man \'stāts-mən\ *n* : a person engaged in fixing the policies and conducting the affairs of a government; *esp* : one wise and skilled in such matters — **states·man·like** *adj* — **states·man·ship** *n*
¹**stat·ic** \'sta-tik\ *adj* **1** : acting by mere weight without motion ⟨∼ pressure⟩ **2** : relating to bodies at rest or forces in equilibrium **3** ♦ : not moving : not active **4** : of or relating to stationary charges of electricity **5** : of, relating to, or caused by radio static

   ♦ immobile, immovable, standing, stationary, unmovable

²**static** *n* : noise produced in a radio or television receiver by atmospheric or other electrical disturbances
¹**sta·tion** \'stā-shən\ *n* **1** ♦ : the place where a person or thing stands or is assigned to remain **2** : a regular stopping place on a transportation route **3** : a place where a fleet is assigned for duty **4** : a stock farm or ranch esp. in Australia or New Zealand **5** ♦ : social standing **6** : a complete assemblage of radio or television equipment for sending or receiving

   ♦ [1] position, post, quarter ♦ [5] degree, footing, level, place, position, rank, situation, standing, status

²**station** *vb* : to assign to a station
sta·tion·ary \'stā-shə-,ner-ē\ *adj* **1** ♦ : fixed in a station, course, or mode **2** ♦ : unchanging in condition

   ♦ [1] immobile, immovable, standing, static, unmovable *Ant* mobile, movable, moving ♦ [2] constant, stable, steady, unchanging, unvarying

stationary front *n* : the boundary between two air masses neither of which is advancing
station break *n* : a pause in a radio or television broadcast to announce the identity of the network or station
sta·tio·ner \'stā-shə-nər\ *n* : one that sells stationery
sta·tio·nery \'stā-shə-,ner-ē\ *n* : materials (as paper, pens, or ink) for writing; *esp* : letter paper with envelopes
station wagon *n* : an automobile having a long interior, one or more folding or removable rear seats, and usu. a door at the rear
sta·tis·tic \stə-'tis-tik\ *n* **1** : a single term or datum in a collection of statistics **2** : a quantity (as the mean) that is computed from a sample
sta·tis·tics \-tiks\ *n sing or pl* : a branch of mathematics dealing with the collection, analysis, and interpretation of masses of numerical data; *also* : a collection of such numerical data — **sta·tis·ti·cal** \-ti-kəl\ *adj* — **sta·tis·ti·cal·ly** \-ti-k(ə-)lē\ *adv* — **stat·is·ti·cian** \,sta-tə-'sti-shən\ *n*
stat·u·ary \'sta-chə-,wer-ē\ *n, pl* **-ar·ies** **1** : the art of making statues **2** : STATUES
stat·ue \'sta-chü\ *n* : a likeness (as of a person or animal) sculptured, modeled, or cast in a solid substance
stat·u·esque \,sta-chə-'wesk\ *adj* : tall and shapely
stat·u·ette \,sta-chə-'wet\ *n* : a small statue
stat·ure \'sta-chər\ *n* **1** : natural height (as of a person) **2** : quality or status gained (as by achievement)
sta·tus \'stā-təs, 'sta-\ *n* **1** : the condition of a person in the eyes of others or of the law **2** ♦ : state of affairs **3** ♦ : position or rank in relation to others

   ♦ [2] footing, picture, posture, scene, situation ♦ [3] degree, footing, level, place, position, rank, situation, standing, station

sta·tus quo \-'kwō\ *n* : the existing state of affairs
stat·ute \'sta-chüt\ *n* ♦ : a law enacted by a legislative body

   ♦ act, enactment, law, ordinance

stat·u·to·ry \'sta-chə-,tōr-ē\ *adj* : imposed by statute : LAWFUL
statutory rape *n* : sexual intercourse with a person who is below the statutory age of consent
¹**staunch** \'stȯnch\ *var of* ¹STANCH
²**staunch** *adj* **1** : WATERTIGHT ⟨a ∼ ship⟩ **2 a** : FIRM, STRONG **b** ♦ : steadfast in loyalty or principle — **staunch·ly** *adv*

   ♦ constant, devoted, faithful, fast, good, loyal, pious, steadfast, steady, true, true-blue

¹**stave** \'stāv\ *n* **1** : CUDGEL, STAFF **2** : any of several narrow strips of wood placed edge to edge to make something (as a barrel) **3** : STANZA

²stave vb **staved** or **stove** \'stōv\; **stav·ing** **1** : to break in the staves of; also : to break a hole in **2** : to drive or thrust away ⟨∼ off hunger⟩

stave off vb ♦ : to fend or ward off

  ♦ fend, repel, repulse

staves pl of STAFF

¹stay \'stā\ n **1** : a strong rope or wire used to support a mast **2** : ¹GUY

²stay vb **stayed** \'stād\ also **staid** \'stād\; **stay·ing** **1** : PAUSE, WAIT **2** ♦ : to continue in a place or condition **3** : to stand firm **4** : to take up residence : LIVE, DWELL **5** : DELAY, POSTPONE **6** : to last out (as a race) **7** ♦ : to stop or delay the proceeding or advance of : CHECK **8** : to satisfy (as hunger) for a time

  ♦ [2] abide, dwell, hang around, remain, stick around, tarry, visit **Ant** go, leave, quit ♦ [7] arrest, catch, check, draw up, fetch up, halt, hold up, stall, still, stop

³stay n **1** : STOP, HALT **2** ♦ : a residence or sojourn in a place

  ♦ sojourn, visit

⁴stay n **1** ♦ : one that serves as a prop : SUPPORT **2** : CORSET — usu. used in pl.

  ♦ brace, bulwark, buttress, mount, shore, support, underpinning

⁵stay vb ♦ : to hold up : PROP

  ♦ bear, bolster, brace, buttress, carry, prop, shore, support, uphold

staying power n : STAMINA
stbd abbr starboard
std abbr standard
STD \ˌes-(ˌ)tē-'dē\ n : SEXUALLY TRANSMITTED DISEASE
Ste abbr saint (female)
stead \'sted\ n **1** ♦ : superiority of position : ADVANTAGE ⟨stood him in good ∼⟩ **2** : the place or function ordinarily occupied or carried out by another ⟨acted in her brother's ∼⟩

  ♦ advantage, better, drop, edge, jump, upper hand, vantage

stead·fast \'sted-ˌfast\ adj **1** : firmly fixed in place **2** : not subject to change **3** ♦ : firm in belief, determination, or adherence : LOYAL — **stead·fast·ly** adv

  ♦ constant, devoted, faithful, fast, good, loyal, pious, staunch, steady, true, true-blue

stead·fast·ness n ♦ : the quality or state of being steadfast

  ♦ allegiance, constancy, dedication, devotion, faith, faithfulness, fastness, fealty, fidelity, loyalty

steadi·ness \'ste-dē-nəs\ n ♦ : the quality or state of being steady

  ♦ firmness, soundness, stability, strength, sturdiness ♦ constancy, fixedness, immutability, stability

¹steady \'ste-dē\ adj **steadi·er; -est** **1** : direct or sure in movement; also : CALM **2** : firm in position : FIRM, FIXED **3** ♦ : showing little variation or fluctuation **4** ♦ : constant in feeling, principle, purpose, or attachment **5** ♦ : not changed, replaced, or interrupted : REGULAR **6** ♦ : capable of being depended on : RELIABLE — **steadi·ly** \-də-lē\ adv — **steady** adv

  ♦ [3] constant, stable, stationary, unchanging, unvarying ♦ [3] undeviating, uniform, unwavering ♦ [4] constant, devoted, faithful, fast, good, loyal, pious, staunch, steadfast, true, true-blue ♦ [5] constant, frequent, habitual, periodic, regular, repeated ♦ [6] dependable, good, reliable, responsible, safe, solid, sure, tried, true, trustworthy

²steady vb **stead·ied; steady·ing** : to make or become steady
steak \'stāk\ n : a slice of meat and esp. beef; also : a slice of a large fish ⟨a tuna ∼⟩

¹steal \'stēl\ vb **stole** \'stōl\; **sto·len** \'stō-lən\; **steal·ing** **1** ♦ : to take and carry away without right or permission **2** ♦ : to come or go secretly or gradually **3** : to get for oneself slyly or by skill and daring ⟨∼ a kiss⟩ ⟨∼ the ball in basketball⟩ **4** : to gain or attempt to gain a base in baseball by running without the aid of a hit or an error

  ♦ [1] appropriate, filch, hook, misappropriate, nip, pilfer, pocket, purloin, snitch, swipe, thieve ♦ usu **steal from** [1] burglarize, rip off, rob ♦ [2] lurk, pussyfoot, skulk, slide, slink, slip, snake, sneak

²steal n **1** : an act of stealing **2** ♦ : an advantageous purchase : BARGAIN

  ♦ bargain, buy, deal

stealth \'stelth\ n **1** : secret or unobtrusive procedure **2** : an aircraft design intended to produce a weak radar return
stealthy \'stel-thē\ adj **stealth·i·er; -est** ♦ : done by stealth : FURTIVE, SLY — **stealth·i·ly** \'stel-thə-lē\ adv

  ♦ furtive, shady, shifty, slippery, sly, sneaky ♦ clandestine, covert, furtive, hugger-mugger, private, secret, sneak, sneaky, surreptitious, undercover, underground, underhanded

¹steam \'stēm\ n **1** : the vapor into which water is changed when heated to the boiling point **2** : water vapor when compressed so that it supplies heat and power **3** ♦ : POWER, FORCE, ENERGY
²steam vb **1** : to pass off as vapor **2** : to emit vapor **3** : to move by or as if by the agency of steam **4** ♦ : to be angry — **steam·er** n

  ♦ boil, burn, fume, rage, seethe

steam·boat \'stēm-ˌbōt\ n : a boat driven by steam
steam engine n : a reciprocating engine having a piston driven by steam
steam·fit·ter \'stēm-ˌfi-tər\ n : a worker who puts in or repairs equipment (as steam pipes) for heating, ventilating, or refrigerating systems
steam·punk \-ˌpəŋk\ n : science fiction involving historical or imagined steam-powered technology
steam·roll·er \-ˌrō-lər\ n : a machine for compacting roads or pavements — **steam·roll·er** also **steam·roll** \-ˌrōl\ vb
steam·ship \-ˌship\ n : a ship driven by steam
steamy \'stē-mē\ adj **1** : consisting of, characterized by, or full of steam **2** : relating to or dealing with sexual love : EROTIC
steed \'stēd\ n : a large solid-hoofed herbivorous mammal domesticated since prehistoric times and used as a pack or draft animal, or for riding : HORSE
¹steel \'stēl\ n **1** : iron treated with intense heat and mixed with carbon to make it hard and tough **2** : an article made of steel **3** : a quality (as hardness of mind) that suggests steel — **steel** adj
²steel vb ♦ : to fill with courage or determination

  ♦ encourage, fortify, harden, nerve, ready, season, strengthen, toughen

steel wool n : long fine steel shavings used esp. for cleaning and polishing
steely adj ♦ : resembling or suggesting steel (as in hardness, color, strength, or coldness)

  ♦ austere, dour, fierce, flinty, forbidding, grim, gruff, rough, rugged, severe, stark, stern ♦ gray (or grey), leaden, pewter, silver, silvery, slate

¹steep \'stēp\ adj **1** ♦ : having a very sharp slope : PRECIPITOUS **2** ♦ : too great or too high ⟨∼ prices⟩ — **steep·ly** adv — **steep·ness** n

  ♦ [1] abrupt, bold, precipitous, sheer **Ant** easy ♦ [2] excessive, extreme, immoderate, inordinate, stiff

²steep n : a steep slope
³steep vb **1** ♦ : to soak in a liquid; esp : to extract the essence of by soaking ⟨∼ tea⟩ **2** ♦ : to saturate with or subject thoroughly to (some strong or pervading influence) ⟨∼ed in learning⟩

  ♦ [1] drench, drown, impregnate, saturate, soak, sop, souse ♦ [2] imbue, inculcate, infuse, ingrain, invest, suffuse

stee·ple \'stē-pəl\ n : a tall tapering structure built on top of a church tower; also : a church tower
stee·ple·chase \-ˌchās\ n : a horse race across country; also : a race over a course obstructed by hurdles
¹steer \'stir\ n : a male bovine animal castrated before sexual maturity and usu. raised for beef
²steer vb **1** ♦ : to direct the course of (as by a rudder or wheel) **2** : GUIDE, CONTROL **3** : to pursue a course of action **4** : to be subject to guidance or direction — **steers·man** \'stirz-mən\ n

  ♦ conduct, direct, guide, lead, marshal, pilot, route, show, usher

steer·age \'stir-ij\ n **1** : DIRECTION, GUIDANCE **2** : a section in a passenger ship for passengers paying the lowest fares
stego·sau·rus \ˌste-gə-'sȯr-əs\ n : any of a genus of plant-eating armored dinosaurs with a series of bony plates along the backbone
stein \'stīn\ n : an earthenware mug
stel·lar \'ste-lər\ adj **1** ♦ : of or relating to stars : resembling a star **2** : marked by eminence and distinction

  ♦ astral, star, starry

¹stem \'stem\ n **1** : the main stalk of a plant; also : a plant part that supports another part (as a leaf or fruit) **2** : the bow of a ship **3** : a line of ancestry : STOCK **4** : that part of an inflected word which remains unchanged throughout a given inflection **5**

: something resembling the stem of a plant — **stem·less** *adj* —
stemmed \'stemd\ *adj*

²stem *vb* **stemmed; stem·ming** : to have a specified source : DERIVE

³stem *vb* **stemmed; stem·ming** : to make headway against ⟨~ the tide⟩

⁴stem *vb* **stemmed; stem·ming** : to stop or check by or as if by damming

STEM \'stem\ *abbr* science, technology, engineering and math

stem cell *n* : an undifferentiated cell that may give rise to many different types of cell

stench \'stench\ *n* : STINK

sten·cil \'sten-səl\ *n* : an impervious material (as metal or paper) perforated with lettering or a design through which a substance (as ink or paint) is applied to a surface to be printed — **stencil** *vb*

ste·nog·ra·phy \stə-'nä-grə-fē\ *n* : the art or process of writing in shorthand — **ste·nog·ra·pher** \-fər\ *n* — **steno·graph·ic** \ˌste-nə-'gra-fik\ *adj*

ste·no·sis \stə-'nō-səs\ *n, pl* **-no·ses** \-ˌsēz\ : a narrowing of a bodily passage or orifice

stent \'stent\ *n* : a short narrow tube inserted into an anatomical vessel esp. to keep a passage open

sten·to·ri·an \sten-'tor-ē-ən\ *adj* ♦ : extremely loud and powerful

♦ booming, clamorous (*or* clamourous), deafening, earsplitting, loud, piercing, resounding, ringing, roaring, sonorous, thunderous

¹step \'step\ *n* **1** : a rest for the foot in ascending or descending : STAIR **2** : an advance made by raising one foot and putting it down elsewhere **3** : manner of walking **4** : a small space or distance **5** : a degree, rank, or plane in a series **6** ♦ : a sequential measure leading to a result

♦ expedient, measure, move, shift ♦ cut, degree, grade, inch, notch, peg, phase, point, stage

²step *vb* **stepped; step·ping 1** : to advance or recede by steps **2** ♦ : to go on foot : WALK **3** : to move along briskly **4** : to press down with the foot **5** : to measure by steps **6** : to construct or arrange in or as if in steps **7** : to engage in or perform a dance

♦ foot, leg, pad, traipse, tread, walk

step aerobics *n sing or pl* : aerobics that involves repeatedly stepping on and off a raised platform

step·broth·er \'step-ˌbrə-t͟hər\ *n* : the son of one's stepparent by a former marriage

step·child \-ˌchīld\ *n* : a child of one's husband or wife by a former marriage

step·daugh·ter \-ˌdȯ-tər\ *n* : a daughter of one's wife or husband by a former marriage

step down *vb* **1** ♦ : to give up deliberately : RETIRE, RESIGN **2** : to lower (a voltage) by means of a transformer

♦ *usu* **step down from** leave, quit, resign, retire ♦ *usu* **step down from** abdicate, abnegate, cede, relinquish, renounce, resign, surrender

step·fa·ther \-ˌfä-t͟hər\ *n* : the husband of one's parent when distinct from one's natural or legal father

step·lad·der \'step-ˌla-dər\ *n* : a light portable set of steps in a hinged frame

step·moth·er \-ˌmə-t͟hər\ *n* : the wife of one's parent when distinct from one's natural or legal mother

step·par·ent \-ˌpar-ənt\ *n* : a person who is a stepfather or stepmother

steppe \'step\ *n* ♦ : dry level grass-covered treeless land in regions of wide temperature range esp. in southeastern Europe and Asia

♦ down, grassland, plain, prairie, savanna, veld

step·sis·ter \'step-ˌsis-tər\ *n* : the daughter of one's stepparent by a former marriage

step·son \-ˌsən\ *n* : a son of one's wife or husband by a former marriage

step up *vb* **1** : to increase (a voltage) by means of a transformer **2** ♦ : to increase, augment, or advance esp. by one or more steps **3** : to come forward — **step–up** \'step-ˌəp\ *n*

♦ amplify, beef, boost, consolidate, deepen, enhance, heighten, intensify, magnify, redouble, strengthen ♦ accelerate, hasten, hurry, quicken, rush, speed (up), whisk

ster *abbr* sterling

ste·reo \'ster-ē-ˌō, 'stir-\ *n, pl* **ste·re·os 1** : stereophonic reproduction **2** : a stereophonic sound system — **stereo** *adj*

ste·reo·phon·ic \ˌster-ē-ə-'fä-nik, ˌstir-\ *adj* : of or relating to

sound reproduction designed to create the effect of listening to the original — **ste·reo·phon·i·cal·ly** \-'fä-ni-k(ə-)lē\ *adv*

ster·e·o·scope \'ster-ē-ə-ˌskōp, 'stir-\ *n* : an optical instrument that blends two slightly different pictures of the same subject to give the effect of depth

ste·reo·scop·ic \ˌster-ē-ə-'skä-pik, ˌstir-\ *adj* **1** : of or relating to the stereoscope **2** : characterized by the seeing of objects in three dimensions ⟨~ vision⟩ — **ste·reo·scop·i·cal·ly** \-'skä-pi-k(ə-)lē\ *adv* — **ste·re·os·co·py** \ˌster-ē-'äs-kə-pē, ˌstir-\ *n*

ste·reo·type \'ster-ē-ə-ˌtīp, 'stir-\ *n* **1** : a metal printing plate cast from a mold made from set type **2** : something agreeing with a pattern; *esp* : an idea that many people have about a thing or a group and that may often be untrue or only partly true — **stereotype** *vb* — **ste·reo·typ·i·cal** \ˌster-ē-ə-'ti-pi-kəl\ *adj* — **ste·reo·typ·i·cal·ly** \-pi-k(ə-)lē\ *adv*

ste·reo·typed \-ˌtīpt\ *adj* ♦ : lacking originality or individuality

♦ banal, commonplace, hackneyed, musty, stale, threadbare, tired, trite

ster·ile \'ster-əl\ *adj* **1** ♦ : unable to bear fruit, crops, or offspring **2** ♦ : free from living things and esp. germs — **ste·ril·i·ty** \stə-'ri-lə-tē\ *n*

♦ [1] barren, impotent, infertile *Ant* fat, fertile, fruitful ♦ [2] aseptic, hygienic, sanitary

ster·il·ize \'ster-ə-ˌlīz\ *vb* **-ized; -iz·ing** : to make sterile; *esp* : to free from germs — **ster·il·i·za·tion** \ˌster-ə-lə-'zā-shən\ *n* — **ster·il·iz·er** \'ster-ə-ˌlī-zər\ *n*

¹ster·ling \'stər-liŋ\ *n* **1** : British money **2** : sterling silver

²sterling *adj* **1** : of, relating to, or calculated in terms of British sterling **2** : having a fixed standard of purity represented by an alloy of 925 parts of silver with 75 parts of copper **3** : made of sterling silver **4** : eminently good : EXCELLENT

¹stern \'stərn\ *adj* **1** ♦ : having a definite hardness or severity of nature or manner : SEVERE **2** : STOUT, STURDY ⟨~ resolve⟩

♦ austere, authoritarian, flinty, hard, harsh, heavy-handed, ramrod, rigid, rigorous, severe, strict

²stern *n* : the rear end of a boat

stern·ly *adv* ♦ : in a stern manner

♦ hard, hardly, harshly, ill, oppressively, roughly, severely, stiffly

stern·ness *n* : the quality or state of being stern

♦ hardness, harshness, inflexibility, rigidity, severity, strictness

ster·num \'stər-nəm\ *n, pl* **sternums** *or* **ster·na** \-nə\ : a long flat bone or cartilage at the center front of the chest connecting the ribs of the two sides

ste·roid \'stir-ˌȯid\ *n* : any of various compounds including numerous hormones (as anabolic steroids) and sugar derivatives — **steroid** *or* **ste·roi·dal** \stə-'rȯid-ᵊl\ *adj*

stetho·scope \'ste-thə-ˌskōp\ *n* : an instrument used to detect and listen to sounds produced in the body

ste·ve·dore \'stē-və-ˌdȯr\ *n* : one who works at loading and unloading ships

ste·via \'stē-vē-ə, -vyə\ *n* : a plant-derived powder used as a noncaloric sweetener

¹stew \'stü, 'styü\ *n* **1** : a dish of stewed meat and vegetables served in gravy **2** ♦ : a state of agitation, worry, or resentment

♦ dither, fluster, fret, fuss, huff, lather, pother, tizzy, twitter

²stew *vb* **1** : to boil slowly : SIMMER **2** ♦ : to be in a state of agitation, worry, or resentment ⟨~ed over the problem⟩

♦ bother, fear, fret, sweat, trouble, worry

stew·ard \'stü-ərd, 'styü-\ *n* **1** ♦ : one employed on a large estate to manage domestic concerns **2** : one who supervises the provision and distribution of food (as on a ship); *also* : an employee on a ship or airplane who serves passengers **3** : one actively concerned with the direction of the affairs of an organization

♦ domestic, flunky, lackey, menial, retainer, servant

stew·ard·ess \'stü-ər-dəs, 'styü-\ *n* : a woman who is a steward esp. on an airplane

stew·ard·ship *n* ♦ : the conducting, supervising, or managing of something; *esp* : the careful and responsible management of something entrusted to one's care

♦ administration, charge, conduct, control, direction, governance, government, guidance, management, operation, oversight, regulation, running, superintendence, supervision

stg *abbr* sterling

¹stick \'stik\ *n* **1** : a cut or broken branch or twig; *also* : a long slender piece of wood **2** : ROD, STAFF **3** : something resembling a stick **4** : a dull uninteresting person **5** *pl* ♦ : remote usu. rural areas

♦ *usu* **sticks** backwoods, bush, frontier, hinterland, up-country

²**stick** *vb* **stuck** \'stək\; **stick·ing 1** : STAB, PRICK **2** ♦ : to pierce with or as if with something pointed **3** : ATTACH, FASTEN **4** : to thrust or project in some direction or manner **5** : to be unable to proceed or move freely **6** ♦ : to hold fast by or as if by gluing : ADHERE **7** : to hold to something firmly or closely : CLING **8** : to become jammed or blocked **9** ♦ : to put or set in a specified place or position

♦ [2] gore, harpoon, impale, lance, pierce, puncture, skewer, spear, spike, stab, transfix ♦ [6] adhere, cling, hew ♦ [9] deposit, dispose, fix, lay, place, position, put, set, set up

stick around *vb* ♦ : to stay or wait about

♦ abide, dwell, hang around, remain, stay, tarry

stick·er \'sti-kər\ *n* : one that sticks (as a bur) or causes sticking (as glue); *esp* : an adhesive label
sticker shock *n* : astonishment and dismay on being informed of a product's unexpectedly high price
stick insect *n* : any of various usu. wingless insects with a long round body resembling a stick
stick·ler \'sti-klər, -kə-lər\ *n* : one who insists on exactness or completeness
stick out *vb* **1** ♦ : to jut out **2** ♦ : to regard with acceptance or tolerance

♦ [1] bag, balloon, beetle, belly, billow, bulge, overhang, poke, project, protrude, start ♦ [2] abide, bear, brook, countenance, endure, meet, stand, stomach, support, sustain, take, tolerate

stick shift *n* : a manually operated automobile gearshift usu. mounted on the floor
stick–to–it·ive·ness \stik-'tü-ə-tiv-nəs\ *n* : dogged perseverance : TENACITY
stick up *vb* : to rob at gunpoint — **stick·up** \'stik-ˌəp\ *n*
sticky \'sti-kē\ *adj* **stick·i·er; -est 1** : having the quality of remaining attached or associated **2** ♦ : being thick or tacky like glue : VISCOUS **3** : tending to stick ⟨~ valve⟩ **4** : DIFFICULT ⟨a ~ problem⟩ **5** ♦ : containing or characterized by perceptible moisture : HUMID

♦ [2] adhesive, gelatinous, gluey, glutinous, gooey, gummy, viscid, viscous *Ant* nonadhesive ♦ [5] humid, muggy, sultry

¹**stiff** \'stif\ *adj* **1** ♦ : not pliant : RIGID **2** : not limber ⟨~ joints⟩; *also* : TENSE, TAUT **3** : not flowing or working easily ⟨~ paste⟩ **4 a** : not natural and easy : FORMAL **b** ♦ : lacking in ease or grace : STILTED **5** : STRONG, FORCEFUL ⟨~ breeze⟩ **6** ♦ : inflicting physical discomfort or hardship : SEVERE **7** : extremely or excessively high ⟨paid a ~ fine⟩ — **stiff·ness** *n*

♦ [1] hard, inflexible, rigid, solid, unyielding *Ant* flexible, floppy, pliable, pliant, supple, yielding ♦ [4b] awkward, clumsy, gauche, graceless, inelegant, stilted, uncomfortable, uneasy, ungraceful, wooden ♦ [6] bitter, brutal, burdensome, cruel, excruciating, grievous, grim, hard, harsh, heavy, inhuman, murderous, onerous, oppressive, rough, rugged, severe, tough, trying

²**stiff** *vb* : to refuse to pay or tip
³**stiff** *n* ♦ : a human being : INDIVIDUAL

♦ being, body, creature, human, individual, man, mortal, person

stiff·en \'sti-fən\ *vb* : to make or become stiff — **stiff·en·er** *n*
stiff·ly *adv* ♦ : in a stiff manner

♦ hard, hardly, harshly, ill, oppressively, roughly, severely, sternly

stiff–necked \'stif-'nekt\ *adj* : STUBBORN, HAUGHTY
sti·fle \'stī-fəl\ *vb* **sti·fled; sti·fling 1** ♦ : to kill by depriving of oxygen or air; *also* : to die from lack of oxygen **2** ♦ : to keep in check by effort : SUPPRESS ⟨~ a sneeze⟩ — **sti·fling·ly** *adv*

♦ [1] choke, smother, strangle, suffocate ♦ [2] choke, pocket, repress, smother, strangle, suppress, swallow

stig·ma \'stig-mə\ *n, pl* **stig·ma·ta** \stig-'mä-tə, 'stig-mə-tə\ *or* **stigmas 1** ♦ : a mark of disgrace or discredit **2** *stigmata pl* : bodily marks resembling the wounds of the crucified Jesus **3** : the upper part of the pistil of a flower that receives the pollen in fertilization — **stig·mat·ic** \stig-'ma-tik\ *adj*

♦ blot, brand, smirch, spot, stain, taint

stig·ma·tize \'stig-mə-ˌtīz\ *vb* **-tized; -tiz·ing 1** : to mark with a stigma **2** : to characterize as disgraceful
stile \'stīl\ *n* : steps used for crossing a fence or wall
sti·let·to \stə-'le-tō\ *n, pl* **-tos** *or* **-toes** : a slender dagger
¹**still** \'stil\ *adj* **1** : MOTIONLESS **2** ♦ : making no sound

♦ hushed, muted, noiseless, quiet, silent, soundless ♦ calm, peaceful, quiet, restful, serene, tranquil

²**still** *vb* ♦ : to make or become still

♦ allay, calm, compose, quiet, settle, soothe, tranquilize ♦ hush, mute, quell, settle, silence

³**still** *adv* **1** ♦ : without motion ⟨sit ~⟩ **2** : up to and during this or that time **3** ♦ : in spite of that : NEVERTHELESS **4** : EVEN ⟨ran ~ faster⟩ **5** : BESIDES, YET

♦ [1] calmly, quiet, quietly ♦ [3] but, howbeit, however, nevertheless, nonetheless, notwithstanding, though, withal, yet

⁴**still** *n* **1** : the quality or state of being quiet : STILLNESS **2** : a static photograph esp. from a motion picture
⁵**still** *n* **1** : DISTILLERY **2** : apparatus used in distillation
still·birth \'stil-ˌbərth\ *n* : the birth of a dead fetus
still·born \-'bȯrn\ *adj* : born dead
still life *n, pl* **still lifes** : a picture of inanimate objects
still·ness *n* **1** ♦ : freedom from agitation **2** ♦ : the quality or state of being soundless

♦ [1] calm, calmness, hush, peace, placidity, quiet, quietness, repose, serenity, still, tranquility ♦ [2] hush, quiet, quietness, silence, still

stilt \'stilt\ *n* : one of a pair of poles for walking with each having a step or loop for the foot to elevate the wearer above the ground; *also* : a polelike support of a structure above ground or water level
stilt·ed \'stil-təd\ *adj* ♦ : not easy and natural ⟨~ language⟩

♦ awkward, clumsy, gauche, graceless, inelegant, stiff, uncomfortable, uneasy, ungraceful, wooden

Stil·ton \'stil-ᵊn\ *n* : a blue cheese of English origin
stim·u·lant \'sti-myə-lənt\ *n* **1** : an agent (as a drug) that temporarily increases the activity of an organism or any of its parts **2** : something that rouses or incites to activity : STIMULUS **3** : an alcoholic beverage — **stimulant** *adj*
stim·u·late \-ˌlāt\ *vb* **-lat·ed; -lat·ing** ♦ : to make active or more active — **stim·u·la·tion** \ˌsti-myə-'lā-shən\ *n*

♦ animate, brace, energize, enliven, fire, invigorate, jazz up, liven up, pep up, quicken, vitalize, vivify, zip (up) ♦ arouse, encourage, excite, fire, incite, instigate, move, pique, provoke, stir

stim·u·la·tive \'sti-myə-ˌlā-tiv\ *adj* ♦ : having power or tending to stimulate

♦ bracing, invigorating, refreshing, restorative, tonic

stim·u·lus \'sti-myə-ləs\ *n, pl* **-li** \-ˌlī\ **1** ♦ : something that moves to activity **2** : an agent that directly influences the activity of a living organism or one of its parts

♦ boost, encouragement, goad, impetus, impulse, incentive, incitement, instigation, momentum, motivation, provocation, spur, yeast

¹**sting** \'stiŋ\ *vb* **stung** \'stəŋ\; **sting·ing 1** : to prick painfully esp. with a sharp or poisonous process **2** : to cause to suffer acutely
²**sting** *n* **1 a** : an act of stinging **b** ♦ : a wound, sore, or pain resulting from a sting **2** : a pointed often venom-bearing organ (as of a bee) : STINGER **3** : an elaborate confidence game; *esp* : one worked by undercover police to trap criminals

♦ ache, pain, pang, prick, smart, stitch, tingle, twinge

sting·er \'stiŋ-ər\ *n* : one that stings; *specif* : a sharp blow or remark
stin·gi·ness \'stin-jē-nəs\ *n* ♦ : the quality or state of being stingy

♦ cheapness, closeness, miserliness, parsimony, tightness

stin·gy \'stin-jē\ *adj* **stin·gi·er; -est 1** ♦ : not generous : giving or spending as little as possible **2** ♦ : meanly scanty or small

♦ [1] cheap, close, mean, niggardly, parsimonious, penurious, spare, sparing, tight, tightfisted, uncharitable *Ant* bounteous, bountiful, charitable, generous, liberal, munificent, openhanded, unsparing, unstinting ♦ [2] light, meager (*or* meagre), niggardly, poor, scant, scanty, scarce, skimpy, slender, slim, spare, sparse

¹**stink** \'stiŋk\ *vb* **stank** \'staŋk\ *or* **stunk** \'stəŋk\; **stunk; stink·ing 1** : to give forth a strong and offensive smell **2** : to be extremely bad in quality or repute
²**stink** *n* : a strong offensive odor
stink·bug \'stiŋk-ˌbəg\ *n* : any of various true bugs that emit a disagreeable odor
stink·er *n* : an offensive or contemptible person

¹**stint** \'stint\ vb **1** ♦ : to be sparing or frugal **2** : to cut short in amount

♦ usu **stint on** scant, skimp, spare

²**stint** n **1** ♦ : an assigned amount of work **2** : RESTRAINT, LIMITATION **3** ♦ : a period of time spent at a particular activity

♦ [1] assignment, chore, duty, job, task ♦ [3] hitch, tenure, term, tour

sti·pend \'stī-ˌpend, -pənd\ n ♦ : a fixed sum of money paid periodically for services or to defray expenses

♦ emolument, hire, pay, payment, salary, wage

stip·ple \'sti-pəl\ vb **stip·pled; stip·pling 1** : to engrave by means of dots and light strokes **2** : to apply (as paint or ink) with small short touches **3** ♦ : to mark with speckles — **stipple** n

♦ blotch, dapple, dot, fleck, freckle, mottle, pepper, speck, spot, sprinkle

stip·u·late \'sti-pyə-ˌlāt\ vb **-lat·ed; -lat·ing 1** : to make an agreement **2** ♦ : to make a special demand (for something) as a condition in an agreement

♦ call, claim, clamor (or clamour), command, demand, enjoin, exact, insist, press, quest

stip·u·la·tion \ˌsti-pyə-'lā-shən\ n **1** : something stipulated **2** ♦ : a condition, requirement, or item specified in a legal instrument

♦ condition, provision, proviso, qualification, reservation

¹**stir** \'stər\ vb **stirred; stir·ring 1** ♦ : to move slightly **2** : to disturb the quiet of **3** ♦ : to mix, dissolve, or make by continued circular movement ⟨~ eggs into cake batter⟩ **4** ♦ : to move to activity (as by pushing, beating, or prodding)

♦ [1] budge, move, shift ♦ [3] agitate, churn, swirl, whirl ♦ usu **stir up** [4] abet, ferment, foment, incite, instigate, provoke, raise, whip ♦ [4] arouse, encourage, excite, fire, incite, instigate, move, pique, provoke, stimulate

²**stir** n **1** ♦ : a state of agitation or activity **2** ♦ : an act of stirring

♦ [1] bustle, commotion, disturbance, turmoil, uproar, welter, whirl ♦ [2] motion, move, movement, moving, shift, stirring

stir–fry \'stər-ˌfrī\ vb : to fry quickly over high heat while stirring continuously — **stir–fry** n

stir·ring \'stər-iŋ\ adj **1** : ACTIVE, BUSTLING **2** ♦ : giving rise to excitement

♦ breathtaking, electric, exciting, exhilarating, rousing, thrilling
♦ affecting, emotional, impressive, moving, poignant, touching

stir·rup \'stər-əp\ n **1** : a light frame hung from a saddle to support the rider's foot **2** : STAPES

¹**stitch** \'stich\ n **1** ♦ : a sudden sharp pain esp. in the side **2** : one of the series of loops formed by or over a needle in sewing

♦ ache, pain, pang, prick, smart, sting, tingle, twinge

²**stitch** vb **1** : to fasten or join with stitches **2** : to make (as a design) with stitches **3** : SEW

stk abbr stock

stoat \'stōt\ n, pl **stoats** also **stoat** : the common Old and New World ermine esp. in its brown summer coat

¹**stock** \'stäk\ n **1** archaic : a block of wood **2** : a stupid person **3** : a wooden part of a thing serving as its support, frame, or handle **4** pl : a device for publicly punishing offenders consisting of a wooden frame with holes in which the feet and hands can be locked **5** ♦ : the original from which others derive; also : a group having a common origin : FAMILY **6** : LIVESTOCK **7** : a supply of goods **8** : the ownership element in a corporation divided to give the owners an interest and usu. voting power **9** : a company of actors playing at a particular theater and presenting a series of plays **10** : liquid in which meat, fish, or vegetables have been simmered that is used as a basis for soup, gravy, or sauce

♦ ancestry, blood, clan, family, folks, house, kin, kindred, kinfolk, line, lineage, people, race, tribe

²**stock** vb : to provide with stock

³**stock** adj **1** : kept regularly for sale or use **2** ♦ : commonly used : STANDARD

♦ conventional, current, customary, popular, standard, usual

stock·ade \stä-'kād\ n ♦ : an enclosure (as of posts and stakes) for defense or confinement

♦ brig, hoosegow, jail, lockup, pen, penitentiary, prison

stock·bro·ker \-ˌbrō-kər\ n : one who executes orders to buy and sell securities

stock car n : a racing car that is similar to a regular car

stock exchange n : a place where the buying and selling of securities is conducted

stock·hold·er \'stäk-ˌhōl-dər\ n : one who owns corporate stock

stock·i·nette or **stock·i·net** \ˌstä-kə-'net\ n : an elastic knitted fabric used esp. for infants' wear and bandages

stock·ing \'stä-kiŋ\ n : a close-fitting knitted covering for the foot and leg

stock market n **1** : STOCK EXCHANGE **2** : a market for stocks

¹**stock·pile** \'stäk-ˌpīl\ n ♦ : a reserve supply esp. of something essential

♦ cache, hoard, stash, store

²**stockpile** vb ♦ : to place or store in or on a stockpile; also : to accumulate a stockpile of

♦ cache, hoard, lay away, lay up, put by, salt away, stash, store

stocky \'stä-kē\ adj **stock·i·er; -est** ♦ : being short and relatively thick

♦ chunky, dumpy, heavyset, squat, stout, stubby, stumpy, thickset

stock·yard \'stäk-ˌyärd\ n : a yard for stock; esp : one for livestock about to be slaughtered or shipped

stodgy \'stä-jē\ adj **stodg·i·er; -est 1** : not interesting : DULL **2** : extremely old-fashioned

¹**sto·ic** \'stō-ik\ n : one who suffers without complaining

²**stoic** or **sto·i·cal** \-i-kəl\ adj ♦ : not affected by passion or feeling; esp : showing indifference to pain — **sto·i·cal·ly** \-i-k(ə-)lē\ adv — **sto·icism** \'stō-ə-ˌsi-zəm\ n

♦ forbearing, long-suffering, patient, tolerant, uncomplaining
♦ apathetic, cold-blooded, impassive, phlegmatic, stolid, unemotional

stoke \'stōk\ vb **stoked; stok·ing 1** : to stir up a fire **2** : to tend and supply fuel to a furnace — **stok·er** n

STOL abbr short takeoff and landing

¹**stole** past of STEAL

²**stole** n **1** : a long narrow band worn round the neck by some members of the clergy **2** : a long wide scarf or similar covering worn by women

stolen past part of STEAL

stol·id \'stä-ləd\ adj ♦ : not easily aroused or excited : showing little or no emotion ⟨a ~ face⟩ — **sto·lid·i·ty** \stä-'li-də-tē\ n — **stol·id·ly** adv

♦ apathetic, cold-blooded, impassive, phlegmatic, stoic, unemotional ♦ blank, deadpan, expressionless, impassive, inexpressive, vacant

sto·lon \'stō-lən, -ˌlän\ n : RUNNER 6

¹**stom·ach** \'stə-mək\ n **1** : a saclike digestive organ of a vertebrate into which food goes from the mouth by way of the throat and which opens below into the intestine **2** : a cavity in an invertebrate animal that is analogous to a stomach **3** ♦ : the part of the body that contains the stomach : ABDOMEN **4** : desire for food caused by hunger : APPETITE **5** : INCLINATION, DESIRE

♦ abdomen, belly, gut, solar plexus, tummy

²**stomach** vb ♦ : to bear without open resentment : put up with

♦ abide, bear, brook, countenance, endure, meet, stand, stick out, support, sustain, take, tolerate

stom·ach·ache \-ˌāk\ n : pain in or in the region of the stomach

stom·ach·er \'stə-mi-kər, -chər\ n : the front of a bodice often appearing between the laces of an outer garment (as in 16th-century costume)

stomp \'stämp, 'stómp\ vb **1** ♦ : to walk with a loud heavy step usu. in anger **2** : to strike or beat forcibly with the bottom of the foot : STAMP — **stomp** n

♦ clump, lumber, pound, stamp, tramp, tromp

¹**stone** \'stōn\ n **1** : hardened earth and mineral matter : ROCK **2** : a small piece of rock **3** : a precious stone : GEM **4** : CALCULUS 3 **5** : a hard stony seed (as of a date) or one (as of a plum) with a stony covering **6** pl usu **stone** : a British unit of weight equal to 14 pounds

²**stone** vb **stoned; ston·ing 1** : to pelt or kill with stones **2** : to remove the stones of (a fruit)

Stone Age n : the first known period of prehistoric human culture characterized by the use of stone tools

stoned \'stōnd\ adj **1** : DRUNK **2** : being under the influence of a drug

stone's throw n ♦ : a short distance

♦ ace, hair, inch, step

stone·wall \'stōn-ˌwȯl\ *vb* : to refuse to comply or cooperate with

stone·washed \'stōn-ˌwȯsht, -ˌwäsht\ *adj* : having been washed with stones during manufacture to create a softer fabric ⟨∼ jeans⟩

stony *also* **ston·ey** \'stō-nē\ *adj* ♦ : manifesting no movement or reaction

  ♦ callous, hard, heartless, inhuman, inhumane, pitiless, soulless, unfeeling, unsympathetic

stood *past and past part of* STAND

stooge \'stüj\ *n* **1** : a person who plays a subordinate or compliant role to a principal **2** : STRAIGHT MAN

stool \'stül\ *n* **1** : a seat usu. without back or arms **2** : FOOTSTOOL **3** : a seat used while urinating or defecating **4** : a discharge of fecal matter

stool pigeon *n* ♦ : a person acting as a decoy or informer; *esp* : a spy sent into a group to report (as to the police) on its activities

  ♦ betrayer, blabbermouth, informer, rat, snitch, tattler, tattletale

¹**stoop** \'stüp\ *vb* **1** : to bend forward and downward **2** : CONDESCEND **3** : to lower oneself morally ⟨∼ to lying⟩

²**stoop** *n* **1** : an act of bending forward **2** : a bent position of head and shoulders

³**stoop** *n* : a porch, platform, or entrance stairway at a house door

¹**stop** \'stäp\ *vb* **stopped; stop·ping 1** ♦ : to close (an opening) by filling or covering closely **2** ♦ : to cause to cease : HALT **3** ♦ : to cease to go on **4** ♦ : to bring activity or operation to an end **5 a** : STAY, TARRY **b** ♦ : to make a brief call — usu. used with *by* or *in*

  ♦ *usu* **stop up** [1] block, choke, clog, close (off), congest, dam, fill, jam, obstruct, plug (up), stuff ♦ [2] arrest, catch, check, draw up, fetch up, halt, hold up, stall, stay, still ♦ [3, 4] break, break off, cease, cut, desist, discontinue, drop, end, halt, knock off, lay off, leave off, quit, shut off ♦ *usu* **stop by** *or* **stop in** [5b] call, drop (by *or* in), pop (in), visit

²**stop** *n* **1** ♦ : a temporary or final ceasing : END, CESSATION **2** : a set of organ pipes of one tone quality; *also* : a control knob for such a set **3** ♦ : something that impedes, obstructs, or brings to a halt : OBSTRUCTION **4** : PLUG, STOPPER **5** : an act of stopping : CHECK **6** : a delay in a journey **7** : a place for stopping **8** *chiefly Brit* : any of several punctuation marks **9** : a function of an electronic device that stops a recording

  ♦ [1] cessation, close, closure, conclusion, end, ending, expiration, finish, halt, lapse, shutdown, stoppage, termination ♦ [3] bar, block, clog, crimp, drag, embarrassment, hindrance, let, obstacle, stumbling block

stop–ac·tion \'stäp-ˌak-shən\ *n* : STOP-MOTION

stop·gap \'stäp-ˌgap\ *n* : something that serves as a temporary expedient : MAKESHIFT

stop·light \-ˌlīt\ *n* : TRAFFIC LIGHT

stop–mo·tion \'stäp-ˌmō-shən\ *n* : a filming technique in which successive positions of objects are photographed to produce the appearance of movement

stop·over \'stäp-ˌō-vər\ *n* **1** : a stop at an intermediate point in one's journey **2** : a stopping place on a journey

stop·page \'stä-pij\ *n* ♦ : the act of stopping : the state of being stopped

  ♦ cessation, close, closure, conclusion, end, ending, expiration, finish, halt, stop, termination

stop·per \'stä-pər\ *n* : something (as a cork) for sealing an opening

stop·watch \'stäp-ˌwäch\ *n* : a watch that can be started or stopped at will for exact timing

stor·age \'stȯr-ij\ *n* **1 a** ♦ : space for storing **b** : cost of storing **2** : MEMORY 6 **3** : the act of storing; *esp* : the safekeeping of goods (as in a warehouse)

  ♦ depository, depot, magazine, repository, storehouse, warehouse

storage battery *n* : a group of connected rechargeable electrochemical cells used to provide electric current

¹**store** \'stȯr\ *vb* **stored; stor·ing 1** ♦ : to place or leave in a safe location for preservation or future use **2** ♦ : to provide esp. for a future need ⟨∼ information⟩

  ♦ [1, 2] cache, hoard, lay away, lay up, put by, salt away, stash, stockpile

²**store** *n* **1** ♦ : something accumulated and kept for future use **2** : a large or ample quantity **3** : STOREHOUSE **4** ♦ : a retail business establishment

  ♦ [1] cache, deposit, hoard, reserve, stash, stock, stockpile ♦ [4] emporium, shop

store·house \-ˌhau̇s\ *n* **1** ♦ : a building for storing goods or supplies **2** : an abundant source or supply

  ♦ depository, depot, magazine, repository, storage, warehouse

store·keep·er \-ˌkē-pər\ *n* : one who operates a retail store

store·room \-ˌrüm, -ˌru̇m\ *n* : a room for storing goods or supplies

sto·ried \'stȯr-ēd\ *adj* : celebrated in story or history

stork \'stȯrk\ *n* : any of various large stout-billed Old World wading birds related to the herons and ibises

¹**storm** \'stȯrm\ *n* **1** ♦ : a heavy fall of rain, snow, or hail with high wind **2** ♦ : a sudden or violent outbreak or disturbance **3** : a mass attack on a defended position **4** ♦ : a heavy discharge of objects **5** : a disturbed or agitated state — **storm·i·ly** \'stȯr-mə-lē\ *adv* — **storm·i·ness** \-mē-nəs\ *n*

  ♦ [1] cloudburst, deluge, downpour, rain, rainstorm, wet ♦ [2] cataclysm, convulsion, paroxysm, tempest, tumult, upheaval, uproar ♦ [2] agony, burst, eruption, explosion, fit, flare, flare-up, flash, flush, gale, gush, gust, outburst, paroxysm, spasm ♦ [4] barrage, bombardment, cannonade, fusillade, hail, salvo, shower, volley

²**storm** *vb* **1 a** : to blow with violence **b** ♦ : to rain, snow, or hail heavily **2** ♦ : to make a mass attack against **3** : to be violently angry : RAGE **4** : to rush along furiously

  ♦ [1b] pour, precipitate, rain ♦ [2] assail, assault, attack, beset, charge, descend, jump, pounce (on *or* upon), raid, rush, strike

stormy *adj* **1** ♦ : relating to, characterized by, or indicative of a storm **2** ♦ : marked by turmoil or fury

  ♦ [1] bleak, dirty, foul, inclement, nasty, raw, rough, squally, tempestuous, turbulent, wild ♦ [1] rainy, wet ♦ [2] explosive, ferocious, fierce, furious, hot, rabid, rough, tempestuous, turbulent, violent, volcanic

¹**sto·ry** \'stȯr-ē\ *n, pl* **stories 1** ♦ : an account of incidents or events : NARRATIVE **2** ♦ : a statement regarding the facts of a situation : REPORT **3** ♦ : usu. short narrative of an interesting, amusing, or biographical incident : ANECDOTE **4** ♦ : a fictional narrative shorter than a novel : SHORT STORY **5** : an untrue statement made with intent to deceive : LIE, FALSEHOOD **6** ♦ : a news article or broadcast

  ♦ [1, 2] account, chronicle, history, narrative, record, report ♦ [3] anecdote, tale ♦ [4] narrative, novella, short story ♦ [6] intelligence, item, news, tidings, word

²**story** *also* **sto·rey** \'stȯr-ē\ *n, pl* **stories** *also* **storeys** : a floor of a building or the space between two adjacent floor levels

sto·ry·tell·er \-ˌte-lər\ *n* : a teller of stories

¹**stout** \'stau̇t\ *adj* **1** ♦ : strong of character : BRAVE **2** ♦ : not weak or uncertain : FIRM **3** ♦ : physically or materially strong **4** : STAUNCH, ENDURING **5** : SOLID **6 a** : possessing or filled with force : FORCEFUL **b** : VIOLENT **7** ♦ : bulky in body : THICKSET

  ♦ [1, 3] brave, hard, hard-bitten, hardy, rugged, strong, sturdy, tough, vigorous ♦ [2] firm, forceful, hearty, lusty, robust, solid, strong, sturdy, vigorous ♦ [7] chunky, dumpy, heavyset, squat, stocky, stubby, stumpy, thickset

²**stout** *n* : a dark heavy ale

stout·ly *adv* ♦ : in a stout manner

  ♦ energetically, firmly, forcefully, forcibly, hard, mightily, powerfully, stiffly, strenuously, strongly, sturdily, vigorously

stout·ness *n* **1** ♦ : the quality or state of being strong physically or morally **2** : bulkiness of structure

  ♦ bravery, courage, daring, fearlessness, gallantry, guts, hardihood, heart, heroism, nerve, valor

¹**stove** \'stōv\ *n* : an apparatus that burns fuel or uses electricity to provide heat (as for cooking or heating)

²**stove** *past and past part of* STAVE

stow \'stō\ *vb* **1** ♦ : to put away : STORE ⟨∼ baggage⟩ **2** : to pack in a compact mass

stow·away \'stō-ə-ˌwā\ *n* : one who hides on a vehicle to ride free

STP *abbr* standard temperature and pressure

strad·dle \'strad-ᵊl\ *vb* **strad·dled; strad·dling 1** : to stand, sit, or walk with legs spread apart **2** : to favor or seem to favor two apparently opposite sides — **straddle** *n*

strafe \'strāf\ *vb* **strafed; straf·ing** : to fire upon with machine guns from a low-flying airplane

strag·gle \'stra-gəl\ *vb* **strag·gled; strag·gling 1** : to wander from the direct course : ROVE, STRAY **2** : to become separated from others of the same kind — **strag·gler** *n* — **strag·gly** \'strag(ə-)lē\ *adj*

¹**straight** \'strāt\ *adj* **1** ♦ : free from curves, bends, angles, or irregularities **2** ♦ : not wandering from the main point or proper course ⟨∼ thinking⟩ **3** ♦ : exhibiting honesty and fairness : UPRIGHT **4** : having the elements in correct order **5** : free from extraneous matter : UNMIXED ⟨∼ whiskey⟩ **6** : CONVENTIONAL, SQUARE **7** : of, relating to, or characterized by sexual or romantic attraction to people of the opposite sex : HETEROSEXUAL **8** : marked by honest sincere expression

♦ [1] right, straightforward *Ant* crooked ♦ [2] direct, forthright, foursquare, plain, straightforward ♦ [3] decent, ethical, good, honest, honorable (*or* honourable), just, moral, right, righteous, upright, virtuous

²**straight** *adv* ♦ : in a straight manner

♦ dead, direct, directly, due, plump, right ♦ directly, forthrightly, foursquare, plain, plainly, straightforward

³**straight** *n* **1** : a straight line, course, or arrangement **2** : the part of a racetrack between the last turn and the finish **3** : a sequence of five cards in a poker hand

straight–arm \'strāt-ˌärm\ *n* : an act of warding off a person with the arm fully extended — **straight–arm** *vb*

¹**straight·away** \'strā-tə-ˌwā\ *n* : a straight stretch (as at a racetrack)

²**straight·away** \ˌstrā-tə-'wā\ *adv* ♦ : without delay : IMMEDIATELY

♦ immediate, instant, instantaneous

straight·edge \'strāt-ˌej\ *n* : a piece of material with a straight edge for testing straight lines and surfaces or drawing straight lines

straight·en \'strāt-ᵊn\ *vb* : to make or become straight

straight flush *n* : a poker hand containing five cards of the same suit in sequence

straight·for·ward \strāt-'fòr-wərd\ *adj* **1** ♦ : free from evasiveness or obscurity : CANDID **2** ♦ : proceeding in a straight course or manner

♦ [1] candid, direct, forthright, foursquare, frank, honest, open, outspoken, plain, straight, unguarded, unreserved ♦ [2] right, direct, forthright, foursquare, plain, straight *Ant* circuitous, indirect, roundabout

straight man *n* : an entertainer who feeds lines to a comedian who replies with usu. humorous quips

straight·way \'strāt-'wā, -ˌwā\ *adv* : without delay or hesitation : IMMEDIATELY

¹**strain** \'strān\ *n* **1** : line of descent : ANCESTRY **2** : a group (as of people or plants) of presumed common ancestry **3** : an inherited or inherent character or quality ⟨the nation's ∼ of creativity⟩ **4** : a slight admixture : TRACE **5** ♦ : a pleasing succession of musical tones : MELODY **6** : the general style or tone

♦ air, lay, melody, song, tune, warble

²**strain** *vb* **1** : to draw taut **2** ♦ : to exert to the utmost **3** : to strive violently **4** ♦ : to injure by improper or excessive use **5** : to filter or remove by filtering **6** : to stretch beyond a proper limit **7** : to pass through or as if through a strainer — **strain·er** *n*

♦ [2] drudge, endeavor (*or* endeavour), fag, grub, hustle, labor (*or* labour), peg, plod, plug, slog, strive, struggle, sweat, toil, work ♦ [4] pull, rack, stretch, wrench

³**strain** *n* **1** ♦ : excessive tension or exertion (as of body or mind) **2** : bodily injury from excessive tension, effort, or use; *esp* : one in which muscles or ligaments are unduly stretched usu. from a wrench or twist **3** : deformation of a material body under the action of applied forces

♦ pressure, stress, tension

strained *adj* : done or produced with excessive effort

¹**strait** \'strāt\ *adj* **1** *archaic* : STRICT **2** *archaic* : NARROW **3** *archaic* : CONSTRICTED **4** : DIFFICULT, STRAITENED

²**strait** *n* **1** ♦ : a narrow channel connecting two bodies of water **2** *pl* : DISTRESS

♦ channel, narrows, sound

strait·en \'strāt-ᵊn\ *vb* **1** : to hem in : CONFINE **2** : to subject to distress or difficulty ⟨∼ed by misfortune⟩

strait·jack·et *also* **straight·jack·et** \'strāt-ja-kət\ *n* : a cover or garment of strong material (as canvas) used to bind the body and esp. the arms closely in restraining a violent prisoner or patient — **straitjacket** *vb*

strait·laced *or* **straight·laced** \-'lāst\ *adj* ♦ : strict in manners, morals, or opinion

♦ prim, prudish, puritanical

¹**strand** \'strand\ *n* : SHORE, BEACH

²**strand** *vb* **1** : to run, drift, or drive upon the shore ⟨a ∼ed ship⟩ **2** : to place or leave in a helpless position

³**strand** *n* **1** : one of the fibers twisted or plaited together into a cord, rope, or cable; *also* : a cord, rope, or cable made up of such fibers **2** : a twisted or plaited ropelike mass ⟨a ∼ of pearls⟩ — **strand·ed** \'stran-dəd\ *adj*

strange \'strānj\ *adj* **strang·er**; **strang·est** **1** : of external origin, kind, or character **2** ♦ : not before known, heard, or seen **3** : DISTANT **6** **4** ♦ : not habituated : UNACCUSTOMED — **strange·ly** *adv* — **strange·ness** *n*

♦ [2] fresh, new, novel, original, unfamiliar, unknown ♦ [2] bizarre, curious, far-out, funny, kinky, odd, outlandish, outré, peculiar, quaint, quirky, remarkable, screwy, wacky, weird, wild ♦ [4] curious, extraordinary, funny, odd, peculiar, rare, unaccustomed, uncommon, unique, unusual, weird

strang·er \'strān-jər\ *n* **1** : FOREIGNER **2** : INTRUDER **3** : a person with whom one is unacquainted

stran·gle \'straŋ-gəl\ *vb* **stran·gled**; **stran·gling** **1** ♦ : to choke to death **2** : to withhold from circulation or expression : SUPPRESS — **stran·gler** *n*

♦ choke, garrote, throttle

stran·gu·late \'straŋ-gyə-ˌlāt\ *vb* **-lat·ed**; **-lat·ing** **1** : STRANGLE, CONSTRICT **2** : to become so constricted as to stop circulation

stran·gu·la·tion \ˌstraŋ-gyə-'lā-shən\ *n* : the act or process of strangling or strangulating; *also* : the state of being strangled or strangulated

¹**strap** \'strap\ *n* : a narrow strip of flexible material used esp. for fastening, holding together, or wrapping

²**strap** *vb* **strapped**; **strap·ping** **1** : to secure with a strap **2** : BIND, CONSTRICT **3** : to flog with a strap **4** : STROP

strap·less \-ləs\ *adj* : having no straps; *esp* : having no shoulder straps

¹**strap·ping** *adj* : LARGE, STRONG, HUSKY

²**strap·ping** *n* : material for a strap

strat·a·gem \'stra-tə-jəm, -ˌjem\ *n* **1** ♦ : a trick to deceive or outwit the enemy; *also* : a deceptive scheme **2** : skill in deception

♦ artifice, device, dodge, gimmick, jig, ploy, scheme, sleight, trick, wile

strat·e·gy \'stra-tə-jē\ *n, pl* **-gies** **1** : the science and art of military command aimed at meeting the enemy under conditions advantageous to one's own force **2** ♦ : a careful plan or method esp. for achieving an end — **stra·te·gic** \strə-'tē-jik\ *adj* — **strat·e·gist** \'stra-tə-jist\ *n*

♦ approach, fashion, form, manner, method, style, system, tack, tactics, technique, way

strat·i·fy \'stra-tə-ˌfī\ *vb* **-fied**; **-fy·ing** : to form or arrange in layers — **strat·i·fi·ca·tion** \ˌstra-tə-fə-'kā-shən\ *n*

stra·tig·ra·phy \strə-'ti-grə-fē\ *n* : geology that deals with rock strata — **strati·graph·ic** \ˌstra-tə-'gra-fik\ *adj*

strato·sphere \'stra-tə-ˌsfir\ *n* : the part of the earth's atmosphere between about 7 miles (11 kilometers) and 31 miles (50 kilometers) above the earth — **strato·spher·ic** \ˌstra-tə-'sfir-ik, -'sfer-\ *adj*

stra·tum \'strā-təm, 'stra-\ *n, pl* **stra·ta** \'strā-tə, 'stra-\ **1** : a bed, layer, or sheetlike mass (as of one kind of rock lying between layers of other kinds of rock) **2** ♦ : a level of culture; *also* : a group of people representing one stage in cultural development

♦ caste, class, estate, folk, order

¹**straw** \'strò\ *n* **1** : stalks of grain after threshing; *also* : a single coarse dry stem (as of a grass) **2** : a thing of small worth : TRIFLE **3** : a tube (as of paper or plastic) for sucking up a beverage

²**straw** *adj* **1** : made of straw **2** : having no real force or validity ⟨a ∼ vote⟩ **3** ♦ : of the color of straw

♦ blond, fair, flaxen, golden, sandy

straw·ber·ry \'strò-ˌber-ē, -bə-rē\ *n* : an edible juicy usu. red pulpy fruit of any of several low herbs with white flowers and long slender runners; *also* : one of these herbs

straw boss *n* : a foreman of a small group of workers

straw·flow·er \'strò-ˌflaù-ər\ *n* : any of several plants whose flowers can be dried with little loss of form or color

¹**stray** \'strā\ *n* **1** : a domestic animal wandering at large or lost **2** : WAIF

²stray vb **1** : to wander or roam without purpose **2** : DEVIATE ⟨~ed from the topic⟩

³stray adj **1** : having strayed : separated from the group or the main body **2 ♦** : occurring at random ⟨~ remarks⟩

♦ aimless, arbitrary, desultory, erratic, haphazard, random, scattered

¹streak \'strēk\ n **1 ♦** : a line or mark of a different color or texture from its background **2** : a narrow band of light; also : a lightning bolt **3** : a slight admixture : TRACE **4** : a brief run (as of luck); also : an unbroken series

♦ band, bar, stripe

²streak vb **1** : to form streaks in or on **2** : to move very swiftly

¹stream \'strēm\ n **1** : a body of water (as a river) flowing on the earth; also : any body of flowing fluid (as water or gas) **2** : a continuous procession ⟨a ~ of traffic⟩

²stream vb **1 ♦** : to flow in or as if in a stream **2** : to pour out streams of liquid **3** : to trail out in length **4** : to move forward in a steady stream **5** : to transfer (digital data, as audio or visual material) in a continuous stream esp. for processing or playback

♦ flow, pour, roll, run ♦ bowl, breeze, coast, drift, flow, glide, roll, sail, skim, slide, slip, sweep, whisk

stream·bed \'strēm-ˌbed\ n : the channel occupied by a stream

stream·er \'strē-mər\ n **1 ♦** : a long narrow ribbonlike flag **2** : a long ribbon on a dress or hat **3** : a newspaper headline that runs across the entire sheet **4** pl : AURORA

♦ banner, colors (or colours), ensign, flag, jack, pennant, standard

stream·ing \'strē-miŋ\ adj : relating to or being the transfer of data (as music or videos) in a continuous stream esp. for immediate processing or playback

stream·let \'strēm-lət\ n ♦ : a small stream

♦ brook, creek, rill, rivulet

stream·lined \-ˌlīnd\ adj **1** : made with contours to reduce resistance to motion through water or air **2** : SIMPLIFIED **3** : MODERNIZED — **stream·line** vb

street \'strēt\ n **1 ♦** : a thoroughfare esp. in a city, town, or village **2** : the occupants of the houses on a street

♦ artery, avenue, drag, drive, pass, road, route, thoroughfare, way

street·car \-ˌkär\ n : a passenger vehicle running on rails on city streets

street hockey n : a game resembling ice hockey played on a hard surface with hockey sticks and a small ball

street railway n : a company operating streetcars or buses

street·walk·er \'strēt-ˌwò-kər\ n : PROSTITUTE

strength \'streŋth\ n **1 ♦** : the quality of being strong : ability to do or endure **2 ♦** : power to resist force **3** : power to resist attack **4** : INTENSITY **5** : force as measured in numbers ⟨the ~ of an army⟩

♦ [1] energy, force, main, might, muscle, potency, power, sinew, vigor (or vigour) ♦ [2] firmness, soundness, stability, steadiness, sturdiness

strength·en \'streŋ-thən\ vb ♦ : to make or become stronger — **strength·en·er** n

♦ beef, fortify, harden, toughen Ant debilitate, enervate, enfeeble, weaken ♦ amplify, beef, boost, consolidate, deepen, enhance, heighten, intensify, magnify, redouble, step up

stren·u·ous \'stren-yə-wəs\ adj **1** : vigorously active : ENERGETIC **2 ♦** : requiring energy or stamina

♦ arduous, demanding, difficult, exacting, formidable, grueling, hard, herculean, laborious, murderous, rough, stiff, tall, toilsome, tough

stren·u·ous·ly adv ♦ : in a strenuous manner

♦ energetically, firmly, forcefully, forcibly, hard, mightily, powerfully, stiffly, stoutly, sturdily, vigorously

strep \'strep\ n : STREPTOCOCCUS

strep throat n : an inflammatory sore throat caused by streptococci and marked by fever, prostration, and toxemia

strep·to·coc·cus \ˌstrep-tə-'kä-kəs\ n, pl **-coc·ci** \-'kä-ˌkī, -'käk-ˌsī, -'käk-ˌkē, -'käk-ˌsē\ : any of various spherical bacteria that usu. grow in chains and include some causing serious diseases — **strep·to·coc·cal** \-kəl\ adj

strep·to·my·cin \-'mīs-ᵊn\ n : an antibiotic produced by soil bacteria and used esp. in treating tuberculosis

¹stress \'stres\ n **1** : PRESSURE, STRAIN; esp : a force that tends to distort a body **2 ♦** : a factor that induces bodily or mental ten-

sion; also : a state induced by such a stress **3 ♦** : force or intensity that gives impressiveness or importance to something : EMPHASIS **4** : relative prominence of sound **5** : ACCENT; also : any syllable carrying the accent — **stress·ful** \'stres-fəl\ adj

♦ [2] pressure, strain, tension ♦ [3] accent, accentuation, emphasis, weight

²stress vb **1** : to put pressure or strain on **2 ♦** : to put emphasis on : ACCENT

♦ accent, accentuate, emphasize, feature, highlight, play, point, underline, underscore

¹stretch \'strech\ vb **1 ♦** : to spread or reach out : EXTEND **2 ♦** : to draw out in length or breadth : EXPAND — often used with out **3** : to make tense; also : to injure by improper or excessive use : STRAIN **4 ♦** : to amplify or enlarge beyond natural or proper limits : EXAGGERATE **5** : to become extended without breaking ⟨rubber ~es easily⟩

♦ [1] draw out, elongate, extend, lengthen, prolong, protract ♦ usu **stretch out** [2] expand, extend, fan, flare, open, spread, unfold ♦ [4] color (or colour), elaborate, embellish, embroider, exaggerate, magnify, pad

²stretch n **1** : an act of extending or drawing out beyond ordinary or normal limits **2 ♦** : a continuous extent in length, area, or time **3** : the extent to which something may be stretched **4** : either of the straight sides of a racecourse

♦ distance, lead, length ♦ breadth, expanse, extent, reach, spread ♦ bit, space, spell, while

³stretch adj : easily stretched ⟨~ pants⟩

stretch·er \'stre-chər\ n **1** : one that stretches **2** : a device for carrying a sick, injured, or dead person

stretch marks n pl : striae on the skin (as of the abdomen) due to excessive stretching and rupture of elastic fibers (as from pregnancy)

strew \'strü\ vb **strewed**; **strewed** or **strewn** \'strün\; **strew·ing 1** : to spread by scattering **2 ♦** : to cover by or as if by scattering something over or on **3** : DISSEMINATE

♦ dot, pepper, scatter, sow, spray, sprinkle

stria \'strī-ə\ n, pl **stri·ae** \'strī-ˌē\ **1** : STRIATION 3 **2** : a stripe or line (as in the skin)

stri·at·ed muscle \'strī-ˌā-təd-\ n : muscle tissue made up of long thin cells with many nuclei and alternate light and dark stripes that includes esp. the muscle of the heart and muscle that moves the vertebrate skeleton and is mostly under voluntary control

stri·a·tion \strī-'ā-shən\ n **1** : the state of being marked with stripes or lines **2** : arrangement of striations or striae **3** : a minute groove, scratch, or channel esp. when one of a parallel series

strick·en \'stri-kən\ adj **1** : afflicted by or as if by disease, misfortune, or sorrow **2** : WOUNDED ⟨was ~ by an arrow⟩

strict \'strikt\ adj **1 ♦** : allowing no evasion or escape : RIGOROUS ⟨~ discipline⟩ **2 ♦** : free from error : PRECISE

♦ [1] austere, authoritarian, flinty, hard, harsh, heavy-handed, ramrod, rigid, rigorous, severe, stern ♦ [2] accurate, authentic, exact, faithful, precise, right, true, veracious

strict·ly adv ♦ : in a strict manner

♦ exactly, precisely, rigidly, rigorously Ant imprecisely, inexactly, loosely

strict·ness n ♦ : the quality or state of being strict

♦ hardness, harshness, inflexibility, rigidity, severity, sternness

stric·ture \'strik-chər\ n **1** : an abnormal narrowing of a bodily passage; also : the narrowed part **2 ♦** : hostile criticism : a critical remark

♦ censure, denunciation, rebuke, reprimand, reproach, reproof

¹stride \'strīd\ vb **strode** \'strōd\; **strid·den** \'strid-ᵊn\; **strid·ing ♦** : to walk or run with long regular steps — **strid·er** n

♦ file, march, pace, parade

²stride n **1** : a long step **2** : a stage of progress **3** : manner of striding : GAIT

stri·dent \'strīd-ᵊnt\ adj : harsh sounding : GRATING, SHRILL

strife \'strīf\ n **1 ♦** : the state or condition of distrust or enmity : CONFLICT **2** : FIGHT, STRUGGLE

♦ conflict, discord, dissension, dissent, disunity, friction, schism, variance, war, warfare

¹strike \'strīk\ vb **struck** \'strək\; **struck** also **strick·en** \'stri-kən\; **strik·ing 1** : to take a course : GO ⟨struck off through the brush⟩ **2 ♦** : to touch or hit sharply; also : to deliver a blow **3** : to produce by or as if by a blow ⟨*struck* terror in the foe⟩ **4** : to lower (as a flag or sail) **5** ♦ : to collide with; *also* : to injure or destroy by collision **6** : DELETE, CANCEL **7** : to produce by impressing ⟨*struck* a medal⟩; *also* : COIN ⟨~ a new cent⟩ **8** : to cause to sound ⟨~ a bell⟩ **9** : to afflict suddenly : lay low ⟨*stricken* with a high fever⟩ **10** ♦ : to appear to; *also* : to appear to as remarkable **11** : IMPRESS **11** : to reach by reckoning ⟨~ an average⟩ **12** : to stop work in order to obtain a change in conditions of employment **13** : to cause (a match) to ignite by rubbing **14** : to come upon ⟨~ gold⟩ **15** : TAKE ON, ASSUME ⟨~ a pose⟩ **16** : to occur to **17** ♦ : to dismantle and take away — **strik·er** *n*

♦ [2] bash, bat, clout, crack, hit, slug, swat ♦ [2] assail, assault, attack, beset, charge, descend, jump, pounce (on *or* upon), raid, rush, storm ♦ [5] bang, bash, bump, collide, crash, hit, impact, knock, ram, slam, smash, swipe, thud ♦ [10] affect, impact, impress, influence, move, sway, tell, touch ♦ [17] disassemble, dismantle, knock down, take down

²**strike** *n* **1** ♦ : an act or instance of striking **2** : a sudden discovery of rich ore or oil deposits **3** : a pitched baseball that is swung at but not hit **4** : the knocking down of all the bowling pins with the 1st ball **5** ♦ : a military attack **6** ♦ : a quality or circumstance that makes achievement unusually difficult

♦ [1] bump, collision, concussion, crash, impact, jar, jolt, shock, smash, wallop ♦ [5] aggression, assault, attack, charge, descent, offense (*or* offence), offensive, onset, onslaught, raid, rush ♦ [6] disadvantage, drawback, handicap, liability, minus, penalty

strike·break·er \-₁brā-kər\ *n* : a person hired to replace a striking worker
strike·out \-₁au̇t\ *n* : an out in baseball as a result of a batter's being charged with three strikes
strike out *vb* **1** : to enter upon a course of action **2** : to start out vigorously **3** : to make an out in baseball by a strikeout
strike up *vb* **1** : to begin or cause to begin to sing or play ⟨*strike up* the band⟩ **2** : BEGIN ⟨*strike up* a conversation⟩
strike zone *n* : the area over home plate through which a pitched baseball must pass to be called a strike
striking *adj* ♦ : attracting attention : very noticeable — **strik·ing·ly** *adv*

♦ bold, catchy, conspicuous, emphatic, marked, noticeable, prominent, pronounced, remarkable

¹**string** \'striŋ\ *n* **1** ♦ : a line usu. composed of twisted threads **2** ♦ : a series of things arranged as if strung on a cord **3** : a plant fiber (as a leaf vein) **4** *pl* : the stringed instruments of an orchestra

♦ [1] cable, cord, lace, line, rope, wire ♦ [2] column, cue, file, line, queue, range, train ♦ [2] chain, progression, sequence, train

²**string** *vb* **strung** \'strəŋ\; **string·ing** **1** : to provide with strings ⟨~ a racket⟩ **2** : to make tense **3** : to thread on or as if on a string ⟨~ pearls⟩ **4** : to hang, tie, or fasten by a string **5** : to take the strings out of ⟨~ beans⟩ **6** : to extend like a string
string along *vb* ♦ : to cause to accept as true or valid what is false or invalid

♦ beguile, bluff, cozen, deceive, delude, dupe, fool, gull, have, hoax, hoodwink, humbug, misinform, mislead, take in, trick

string bean *n* : a bean of one of the older varieties of kidney bean that have stringy fibers on the lines of separation of the pods; *also* : SNAP BEAN
string bikini *n* : a scanty bikini
string cheese *n* : cheese that can be pulled apart in narrow strips
stringed \'striŋd\ *adj* **1** : having strings ⟨~ instruments⟩ **2** : produced by strings
strin·gen·cy \'strin-jən-sē\ *n* **1** : STRICTNESS, SEVERITY **2** : SCARCITY ⟨~ of money⟩
strin·gent \-jənt\ *adj* ♦ : marked by rigor, strictness, or severity esp. with regard to rule or standard

♦ exacting, inflexible, rigid, rigorous, strict, uncompromising

string·er \'striŋ-ər\ *n* **1** : a long horizontal member in a framed structure or a bridge **2** : a news correspondent paid by the amount of copy
stringy \'striŋ-ē\ *adj* **string·i·er; -est** **1** : resembling string esp. in tough, fibrous, or disordered quality ⟨~ meat⟩ ⟨~ hair⟩ **2** : lean and sinewy in build
¹**strip** \'strip\ *vb* **stripped** \'stript\ *also* **stript; strip·ping** **1** ♦ : to take the covering or clothing from **2** : to take off one's clothes **3** : to pull or tear off **4** : to make bare or clear (as by cutting or grazing) **5** : to deprive of possessions : PLUNDER — **strip·per** *n*

♦ unclothe, undress

²**strip** *n* **1** : a long narrow flat piece **2** : AIRSTRIP
¹**stripe** \'strīp\ *vb* **striped** \'strīpt\; **strip·ing** ♦ : to mark with stripes

♦ band, bar, streak

²**stripe** *n* **1** ♦ : a line or long narrow division having a different color from the background **2** : a strip of braid (as on a sleeve) indicating military rank or length of service **3** : TYPE, CHARACTER — **striped** \'strīpt, 'strī-pəd\ *adj*

♦ band, bar, streak

striped bass *n* : a large black-striped marine bony fish that occurs along the Atlantic and Pacific coasts of the U.S. and is an excellent food and sport fish
strip·ling \'stri-pliŋ\ *n* **1** : YOUTH **2** ♦ : an adolescent male : LAD

♦ boy, lad, nipper, shaver, youth

strip mall *n* : a long building or group of buildings housing several retail stores or service establishments
strip mine *n* : a mine that is worked from the earth's surface by the stripping of the topsoil — **strip·mine** *vb*
strip·tease \'strip-₁tēz\ *n* : a burlesque act in which a performer removes clothing piece by piece — **strip·teas·er** *n*
strive \'strīv\ *vb* **strove** \'strōv\ *also* **strived** \'strīvd\; **striv·en** \'stri-vən\ *or* **strived; striv·ing** **1** ♦ : to make an effort : labor hard **2** : to struggle in opposition : CONTEND

♦ assay, attempt, endeavor (*or* endeavour), essay, seek, try

strobe \'strōb\ *n* **1** : STROBOSCOPE **2** : a device for high-speed intermittent illumination (as in photography)
stro·bo·scope \'strō-bə-₁skōp\ *n* : an instrument for studying rapid motion by means of a rapidly flashing light
strode *past of* STRIDE
¹**stroke** \'strōk\ *vb* **stroked; strok·ing** **1 a** : to rub gently **b** ♦ : to touch or stroke lightly in a loving or endearing manner **2** : to flatter in a manner designed to persuade

♦ caress, fondle, love, pat, pet

²**stroke** *n* **1** : the act of striking : BLOW **2** : a sudden action or process producing an impact ⟨~ of lightning⟩; *also* : an unexpected result **3** : sudden weakening or loss of consciousness or the power to move or feel caused by rupture or obstruction (as by a clot) of a blood vessel of the brain **4** : one of a series of movements against air or water to get through or over it ⟨the ~ of a bird's wing⟩ **5** : a rower who sets the pace for a crew **6** : a vigorous effort **7** : the sound of striking (as of a clock) **8** : a single movement with or as if with a tool or implement (as a pen)
¹**stroll** \'strōl\ *vb* : to walk in a leisurely or idle manner
²**stroll** *n* ♦ : an idle and leisurely walk

♦ perambulation, ramble, turn, walk

stroll·er *n* ♦ : one who goes idly about

♦ drifter, nomad, rambler, rover, vagabond, wanderer

strong \'stroṅ\ *adj* **stron·ger** \'stroṅ-gər\; **stron·gest** \'stroṅ-gəst\ **1** ♦ : having or marked by power **2** : HEALTHY, ROBUST **3** : of a specified number ⟨an army 10 thousand ~⟩ **4** ♦ : not mild or weak **5** : VIOLENT ⟨~ wind⟩ **6** : ZEALOUS **7** ♦ : not easily broken **8** : well established **9** ♦ : having an offensive or intense odor or flavor

♦ [1] brawny, muscular, powerful, rugged, sinewy, stalwart, stout *Ant* delicate, feeble, frail, weak, wimpy ♦ [1] cogent, compelling, conclusive, convincing, decisive, effective, forceful, persuasive, satisfying, telling ♦ [4] firm, forceful, hearty, lusty, robust, solid, stout, sturdy, vigorous ♦ [7] fast, firm, sound, stable, stalwart, steady, sturdy ♦ [9] fetid, foul, fusty, malodorous, musty, noisome, rank, reeky, smelly ♦ [9] nippy, pungent, sharp

strong–arm \'stroṅ-'ärm\ *adj* : having or using undue force ⟨~ methods⟩
strong force *n* : the physical force responsible for binding together nucleons in the atomic nucleus
strong·hold \-₁hōld\ *n* ♦ : a fortified place : FORTRESS

♦ bastion, citadel, fastness, fort, fortification, fortress, hold

strong·ly *adv* ♦ : in a strong manner

♦ energetically, firmly, forcefully, forcibly, hard, mightily, powerfully, stiffly, stoutly, strenuously, sturdily, vigorously

strong·man \-₁man\ *n* : one who leads or controls by force of will and character or by military strength
stron·tium \'strän-chē-əm, 'strän-tē-əm\ *n* : a soft malleable metallic chemical element
¹**strop** \'sträp\ *n* : STRAP; *esp* : one for sharpening a razor
²**strop** *vb* **stropped; strop·ping** ♦ : to sharpen a razor on a strop

♦ edge, grind, hone, sharpen, whet

stro·phe \'strō-fē\ *n* : a division of a poem — **stroph·ic** \'strä-fik\ *adj*

strove *past of* STRIVE

struck *past and past part of* STRIKE

¹**struc·ture** \'strək-chər\ *n* **1** : the action of building : CONSTRUC-TION **2** : something built (as a house or a dam); *also* : something made up of interdependent parts in a definite pattern of organization **3** ♦ : arrangement or relationship of elements (as particles, parts, or organs) in a substance, body, or system — **struc·tur·al** *adj*

♦ configuration, frame, framework, shell, skeleton

²**structure** *vb* **struc·tured; struc·tur·ing** : to make into a structure

stru·del \'strüd-ᵊl, 'shtrüd-\ *n* : a pastry made of a thin sheet of dough rolled up with filling and baked ⟨apple ∼⟩

¹**strug·gle** \'strə-gəl\ *vb* **strug·gled; strug·gling 1** : to make strenuous efforts against opposition : STRIVE **2** ♦ : to proceed with difficulty or with great effort

♦ drudge, endeavor (*or* endeavour), fag, grub, hustle, labor (*or* labour), peg, plod, plug, slog, strain, strive, sweat, toil, work

²**struggle** *n* **1** ♦ : exertion or contention for superiority : CON-TEST **2** ♦ : a violent effort or exertion

♦ [1] battle, combat, conflict, confrontation, contest, duel, face-off, rivalry, tug-of-war, warfare ♦ [2] battle, effort, exertion, fight, fray, scrabble

strum \'strəm\ *vb* **strummed; strum·ming** : to play on a stringed instrument by brushing the strings with the fingers ⟨∼ a guitar⟩

strum·pet \'strəm-pət\ *n, dated, usu disparaging* : PROSTITUTE

strung \'strəŋ\ *past and past part of* STRING

¹**strut** \'strət\ *vb* **strut·ted; strut·ting 1** ♦ : to walk with an affectedly proud gait **2** ♦ : to parade (as clothes) with a show of pride

♦ [1] stalk, swagger ♦ [2] display, disport, exhibit, expose, flash, flaunt, parade, show, show off, sport, unveil

²**strut** *n* **1** : a bar or rod for resisting lengthwise pressure **2** : a haughty or pompous gait

strych·nine \'strik-ˌnīn, -nən, -ˌnēn\ *n* : a bitter poisonous plant alkaloid used as a poison (as for rats) and medicinally as a stimulant of the central nervous system

¹**stub** \'stəb\ *n* **1** : STUMP 2 **2** : a short blunt end **3** : a small part of each leaf (as of a checkbook) kept as a memorandum of the items on the detached part

²**stub** *vb* **stubbed; stub·bing** : to strike (as one's toe) against something

stub·ble \'stə-bəl\ *n* **1** : the cut stem ends of herbs and esp. grasses left in the soil after harvest **2** : a rough surface or growth resembling stubble — **stub·bly** \-b(ə-)lē\ *adj*

stub·born \'stə-bərn\ *adj* **1** : FIRM, DETERMINED **2** ♦ : done or continued in a willful, unreasonable, or persistent manner **3** : not easily controlled or remedied ⟨a ∼ cold⟩ — **stub·born·ly** *adv*

♦ dogged, hardheaded, headstrong, mulish, obdurate, obstinate, opinionated, peevish, pertinacious, perverse, pigheaded, unyielding, willful

stub·born·ness *n* ♦ : the quality or state of being stubborn

♦ hardheadedness, mulishness, obduracy, obstinacy, peevishness, pertinacity, self-will, tenacity

stub·by \'stə-bē\ *adj* ♦ : short, blunt, and thick like a stub

♦ chunky, dumpy, heavyset, squat, stocky, stout, stumpy, thickset

stuc·co \'stə-kō\ *n, pl* **stuccos** *or* **stuccoes** : plaster for coating exterior walls — **stuc·coed** \-kōd\ *adj*

stuck *past and past part of* STICK

stuck–up \'stək-'əp\ *adj* ♦ : having or showing an excessively high opinion of oneself : CONCEITED

♦ complacent, conceited, egotistic, important, overweening, pompous, prideful, proud, self-important, self-satisfied, smug, vain

¹**stud** \'stəd\ *n* : a male animal and esp. a horse (**stud·horse** \-ˌhȯrs\) kept for breeding

²**stud** *n* **1** : one of the smaller uprights in a building to which the wall materials are fastened **2** : a removable device like a button used as a fastener or ornament ⟨shirt ∼s⟩ **3** : a projecting nail, pin, or rod

³**stud** *vb* **stud·ded; stud·ding 1** : to supply with or adorn with studs **2** : DOT

⁴**stud** *abbr* student

stud·book \'stəd-ˌbùk\ *n* : an official record of the pedigree of purebred animals (as horses or dogs)

stud·ding \'stə-diŋ\ *n* : the studs in a building or wall

stu·dent \'stüd-ᵊnt, 'styüd-\ *n* : SCHOLAR, PUPIL; *esp* : one who attends a school

stud·ied \'stə-dēd\ *adj* ♦ : carefully considered or prepared ⟨a ∼ insult⟩

♦ advised, calculated, deliberate, measured, reasoned, thoughtful, thought-out

stu·dio \'stü-dē-ˌō, 'styü-\ *n, pl* **-dios 1** : a place where an artist works; *also* : a place for the study of an art **2** : a place where motion pictures are made **3** : a place equipped for the transmission of radio or television programs

stu·di·ous \'stü-dē-əs, 'styü-\ *adj* : devoted to study — **stu·di·ous·ly** *adv*

¹**study** \'stə-dē\ *n, pl* **stud·ies 1** : the use of the mind to gain knowledge **2** : the act or process of learning about something **3** ♦ : careful examination **4** : INTENT, PURPOSE **5** : a branch of learning **6** : a room esp. for reading and writing **7** ♦ : a state of contemplation

♦ [3] examination, exploration, inquiry, investigation, probe, research ♦ [7] reverie, trance, woolgathering

²**study** *vb* **stud·ied; study·ing 1** : to engage in study or the study of **2** ♦ : to consider attentively or in detail

♦ chew over, cogitate, consider, contemplate, debate, deliberate, entertain, meditate, mull, ponder, question, ruminate, think, weigh

¹**stuff** \'stəf\ *n* **1** : personal property **2** ♦ : raw material **3** : a finished textile fabric; *esp* : a worsted fabric **4** : writing, talk, or ideas of little or transitory worth **5** : an unspecified material substance or aggregate of matter **6** ♦ : fundamental material **7** ♦ : special knowledge or capability

♦ [2] material, raw material, substance ♦ [6] essence, nature, quintessence, soul, substance ♦ [7] capability, credentials, qualification

²**stuff** *vb* **1** ♦ : to fill by packing things in : CRAM **2** ♦ : to eat greedily : GORGE **3** : to prepare (as meat) by filling with a stuffing **4** : to fill (as a cushion) with a soft material **5** ♦ : to stop up : PLUG

♦ [1] charge, cram, fill, heap, jam, jam-pack, load, pack ♦ [2] glut, gorge, sate, surfeit ♦ [5] block, choke, clog, close (off), congest, dam, jam, obstruct, plug (up), stop (up)

stuffed shirt \'stəft-\ *n* : a smug, conceited, and usu. pompous and inflexibly conservative person

stuff·ing *n* ♦ : material used to fill tightly; *esp* : a mixture of bread crumbs and spices used to stuff food

♦ fill, filler, filling, padding

stuffy \'stə-fē\ *adj* **stuff·i·er; -est 1** ♦ : lacking in vitality or interest **2** ♦ : lacking fresh air : CLOSE; *also* : blocked up ⟨a ∼ nose⟩

♦ [1] drab, dreary, dry, dull, flat, heavy, humdrum, leaden, monotonous, ponderous, stupid, tame, uninteresting, weary ♦ [2] breathless, close *Ant* airy, breezy

stul·ti·fy \'stəl-tə-ˌfī\ *vb* **-fied; -fy·ing 1** : to cause to appear foolish or stupid **2** : to impair, invalidate, or make ineffective **3** : to have a dulling effect on — **stul·ti·fi·ca·tion** \ˌstəl-tə-fə-'kā-shən\ *n*

¹**stum·ble** \'stəm-bəl\ *vb* **stum·bled; stum·bling 1** : to blunder morally **2** ♦ : to trip in walking or running **3 a** ♦ : to walk unsteadily **b** : to speak or act in a blundering or clumsy manner **4** : to happen by chance **5** ♦ : to come unexpectedly or by chance

♦ [2] fall, slip, topple, trip, tumble ♦ [3a] clump, flounder, limp, lumber, scuff, scuffle, shamble, shuffle, tramp, tromp ♦ *usu* **stumble on** *or* **stumble onto** *or* **stumble upon** [5] chance, encounter, find, happen (on *or* upon), hit, meet (on *or* upon)

²**stumble** *n* ♦ : an act or instance of stumbling

♦ fall, slip, spill, tumble ♦ blunder, error, fault, flub, fumble, goof, lapse, miscue, misstep, mistake, oversight, slip

stumbling block *n* ♦ : an obstacle to belief, understanding, or progress

♦ bar, block, clog, crimp, drag, embarrassment, hindrance, let, obstacle, stop

¹**stump** \'stəmp\ *n* **1** : the base of a bodily part (as a leg) left after the rest is removed **2** : the part of a plant and esp. a tree remain-

ing with the root after the trunk is cut off **3** : a place or occasion for political public speaking

²stump *vb* **1** : BAFFLE, PERPLEX **2** : to clear (land) of stumps **3** : to tour (a region) making political speeches **4** : to walk clumsily and heavily **5** : to challenge to perform an action

stumpy *adj* ♦ : short and thick

♦ chunky, dumpy, heavyset, squat, stocky, stout, stubby, thickset

stun \'stən\ *vb* **stunned; stun·ning 1** : to make senseless or dizzy by or as if by a blow **2** ♦ : to overcome esp. with paralyzing astonishment or disbelief : STUPEFY

♦ amaze, astonish, astound, bowl, dumbfound, flabbergast, floor, shock, startle, stupefy, surprise

stung *past and past part of* STING

stunk *past and past part of* STINK

stunned *adj* ♦ : affected by stunning; *also* : caused by or as if by stunning

♦ amazed, awestruck, thunderstruck ♦ confused, dizzy

stun·ning *adj* **1** ♦ : causing astonishment or disbelief **2** ♦ : strikingly beautiful — **stun·ning·ly** *adv*

♦ [1] amazing, astonishing, astounding, eye-opening, shocking, startling, surprising ♦ [1] awesome, fabulous, marvelous (*or* marvellous), miraculous, portentous, prodigious, stupendous, sublime, surprising, wonderful ♦ [2] attractive, beautiful, fair, gorgeous, handsome, knockout, lovely, pretty, ravishing

¹stunt \'stənt\ *vb* : to hinder the normal growth or progress of

²stunt *n* ♦ : an unusual or spectacular feat

♦ deed, exploit, feat, trick

stu·pe·fy \'stü-pə-ˌfī, 'styü-\ *vb* **-fied; -fy·ing 1** : to make stupid, groggy, or insensible **2** ♦ : to strike with sudden and usu. great wonder or surprise : ASTONISH — **stu·pe·fac·tion** \ˌstü-pə-'fak-shən, ˌstyü-\ *n*

♦ amaze, astonish, astound, bowl, dumbfound, flabbergast, floor, shock, startle, stun, surprise

stu·pen·dous \stù-'pen-dəs, styù-\ *adj* ♦ : causing astonishment esp. because of great size or height

♦ amazing, astonishing, astounding, awesome, awful, eye-opening, fabulous, marvelous (*or* marvellous), miraculous, portentous, prodigious, stunning, sublime, surprising, wonderful

stu·pen·dous·ly *adv* ♦ : to a stupendous degree

♦ broadly, considerably, greatly, hugely, largely, massively, monstrously, much, sizably, tremendously, utterly, vastly

stu·pid \'stü-pəd, 'styü-\ *adj* **1** : very dull in mind **2** ♦ : showing or resulting from dullness of mind **3** ♦ : lacking interest or intellectual stimulation ⟨a ∼ book⟩ — **stu·pid·ly** *adv*

♦ [1] dense, dull, dumb, fatuous, mindless, obtuse, senseless, simple, slow, thick, unintelligent, vacuous, witless *Ant* brainy, brilliant, clever, intelligent, quick-witted, sharp, smart ♦ [2] absurd, cuckoo, fatuous, foolish, nonsensical, nutty, senseless, silly ♦ [3] drab, dreary, monotonous, ponderous, uninteresting, weary

stu·pid·i·ty \stù-'pi-də-tē, styù-\ *n* **1** ♦ : the quality or state of being stupid **2** ♦ : a stupid idea or act

♦ [1] denseness, dopiness, fatuity, foolishness, imbecility, mindlessness, obtuseness, vacuity *Ant* brightness, brilliance, cleverness, intelligence, keenness, quickness, sharpness, smartness ♦ [2] absurdity, asininity, fatuity, folly, foolery, idiocy, imbecility, inanity

stu·por \'stü-pər, 'styü-\ *n* **1** ♦ : a condition of greatly dulled or completely suspended sense or feeling **2** : a state of extreme apathy or torpor often following stress or shock — **stu·por·ous** *adj*

♦ apathy, impassivity, numbness, phlegm

stur·di·ly \'stər-də-lē\ *adv* ♦ : in a sturdy manner

♦ energetically, firmly, forcefully, forcibly, hard, mightily, powerfully, stiffly, stoutly, strenuously, strongly, vigorously

stur·di·ness \-dē-nəs\ *n* ♦ : the quality or state of being sturdy

♦ firmness, soundness, stability, steadiness, strength

stur·dy \'stər-dē\ *adj* **stur·di·er; -est 1** : RESOLUTE, UNYIELDING **2** ♦ : capable of withstanding adverse conditions : STRONG

♦ hard, hard-bitten, hardy, rugged, stout, strong, tough, vigorous ♦ fast, firm, sound, stable, stalwart, steady, strong

stur·geon \'stər-jən\ *n* : any of a family of large bony fishes including some whose roe are made into caviar

stut·ter \'stə-tər\ *vb* : to speak with involuntary disruption or blocking of sounds — **stutter** *n* — **stut·ter·er** *n*

stutter step *n* : a move made by a runner (as in football) done to fake a defender out of position

¹sty \'stī\ *n, pl* **sties 1** : a pen for pigs **2** ♦ : a dirty place

♦ dump, hole, pigsty, shambles

²sty *or* **stye** *n, pl* **sties** *or* **styes** : an inflamed swelling of a skin gland on the edge of an eyelid

¹style \'stīl\ *n* **1** : mode of address : TITLE **2** ♦ : a way of speaking or writing; *esp* : one characteristic of an individual, period, school, or nation ⟨ornate ∼⟩ **3** ♦ : manner or method of acting, making, or performing; *also* : a distinctive or characteristic manner **4** : a slender pointed instrument or process; *esp* : STYLUS **5** ♦ : a fashionable manner or mode **6** : overall excellence, skill, or grace in performance, manner, or appearance **7** : the custom followed in spelling, capitalization, punctuation, and typography — **sty·lis·tic** \stī-'lis-tik\ *adj*

♦ [2] fashion, locution, manner, mode, phraseology, tone, vein ♦ [3] approach, fashion, form, manner, method, strategy, system, tack, tactics, technique, way ♦ [5] craze, fad, mode, rage, trend, vogue

²style *vb* **styled; styl·ing 1** ♦ : to call or designate by an identifying term : NAME **2** : to make or design in accord with a prevailing mode ⟨∼ hair⟩

♦ baptize, call, christen, denominate, designate, dub, entitle, label, name, term, title

styl·ing \'stī-liŋ\ *n* : the way in which something is styled

styl·ise *chiefly Brit var of* STYLIZE

styl·ish \'stī-lish\ *adj* ♦ : conforming to current fashion — **styl·ish·ly** *adv* — **styl·ish·ness** *n*

♦ à la mode, chic, fashionable, in, modish, sharp, smart, snappy *Ant* dowdy, outmoded, unfashionable, unstylish

styl·ist \'stī-list\ *n* **1** : one (as a writer) noted for a distinctive style **2** : a developer or designer of styles

styl·ize \'stī-ˌlīz, 'stī-ə-\ *vb* **styl·ized; styl·iz·ing** : to conform to a style; *esp* : to represent or design according to a pattern or style rather than according to nature or tradition — **styl·i·za·tion** \ˌstī-lə-'zā-shən\ *n*

sty·lus \'stī-ləs\ *n, pl* **sty·li** \'stī-ˌlī\ *also* **sty·lus·es** \'stī-lə-səz\ **1** : a pointed implement used by the ancients for writing on wax **2** : a phonograph needle **3** : a pen-shaped pointing device for entering data into a computer

sty·mie \'stī-mē\ *vb* **sty·mied; sty·mie·ing** ♦ : to present an obstacle to : stand in the way of

♦ encumber, hamper, hinder, hold up, impede, inhibit, interfere with, obstruct, tie up

styp·tic \'stip-tik\ *adj* : tending to check bleeding — **styptic** *n*

suave \'swäv\ *adj* ♦ : persuasively pleasing : smoothly agreeable — **suave·ly** *adv* — **sua·vi·ty** \'swä-və-tē\ *n*

♦ debonair, smooth, sophisticated, urbane *Ant* boorish, churlish, clownish, loutish, uncouth

¹sub \'səb\ *n* : a person or thing that takes the place or function of another : SUBSTITUTE

²sub *n* **1** : a naval vessel designed to operate underwater : SUBMARINE **2** : a large sandwich on a long split roll with any of a variety of fillings : SUBMARINE

³sub *abbr* **1** subtract **2** suburb

⁴sub *vb* ♦ : to serve as a substitute

♦ cover, fill in, pinch-hit, stand in, substitute, take over

sub- \'səb\ *prefix* **1** : under : beneath **2** : subordinate : secondary **3** : subordinate portion of : subdivision of **4** : with repetition of a process described in a simple verb so as to form, stress, or deal with subordinate parts or relations **5** : somewhat **6** : falling nearly in the category of : bordering on

subacute	subclassify
subagency	subcommittee
subagent	subcontract
subaqueous	subcontractor
subarctic	subculture
subarea	subcutaneous
subatmospheric	subdiscipline
subaverage	subentry
subbasement	subfamily
subcategory	subfield
subcellular	subfreezing
subchapter	subgenre
subclass	subgenus

subgroup
subhead
subheading
subhuman
subkingdom
sublethal
subliterate
subminimal
subminimum
suboptimal
suborder
subparagraph
subparallel
subphylum
subplot
subpopulation
subproblem
subprofessional
subprogram

subregion
subroutine
subsection
subsense
subsoil
substage
substation
subsystem
subteen
subthreshold
subtopic
subtotal
subtreasury
subtype
subunit
subvariety
subvisible
subzero

sub•al•pine \ˌsəb-ˈal-ˌpīn\ *adj* **1** : of or relating to the region about the foot and lower slopes of the Alps **2** : of, relating to, or inhabiting high upland slopes esp. just below the timberline
sub•al•tern \sə-ˈbȯl-tərn\ *n* : SUBORDINATE; *esp* : a junior officer (as in the British army)
sub•as•sem•bly \ˌsəb-ə-ˈsem-blē\ *n* : an assembled unit to be incorporated with other units in a finished product
sub•atom•ic \ˌsəb-ə-ˈtä-mik\ *adj* : of or relating to the inside of the atom or to particles smaller than atoms
sub•clin•i•cal \ˌsəb-ˈkli-ni-kəl\ *adj* : not detectable by the usual clinical tests ⟨a ∼ infection⟩
sub•com•pact \ˈsəb-ˈkäm-ˌpakt\ *n* : an automobile smaller than a compact
¹sub•con•scious \ˌsəb-ˈkän-chəs, ˈsəb-\ *adj* : existing in the mind without entering conscious awareness — **sub•con•scious•ly** *adv* — **sub•con•scious•ness** *n*
²subconscious *n* : mental activities just below the threshold of consciousness
sub•con•ti•nent \ˌsəb-ˈkänt-ᵊn-ənt\ *n* : a major subdivision of a continent — **sub•con•ti•nen•tal** \ˌsəb-ˌkänt-ᵊn-ˈent-ᵊl\ *adj*
sub•di•vide \ˌsəb-də-ˈvīd, ˈsəb-də-ˌvīd\ *vb* : to divide the parts of into more parts; *esp* : to divide (a tract of land) into building lots — **sub•di•vi•sion** \-ˈvi-zhən, -ˌvi-zhən\ *n*
sub•duc•tion \səb-ˈdək-shən\ *n* : the descent of the edge of one crustal plate beneath the edge of an adjacent plate
sub•due \səb-ˈdü, -ˈdyü\ *vb* **sub•dued; sub•du•ing 1** ♦ : to conquer and bring into subjection **2** : to bring under control : CURB **3** : to reduce the intensity of

♦ conquer, dominate, overpower, subject, vanquish

subdued *adj* ♦ : lacking in vitality, intensity, or strength

♦ conservative, muted, quiet, restrained, unpretentious

subj *abbr* **1** subject **2** subjunctive
¹sub•ject \ˈsəb-jikt\ *n* **1** : a person under the authority of another **2** : a person subject to a sovereign **3** : an individual that is studied or experimented on **4** ♦ : the person or thing discussed or treated : TOPIC **5** : a word or word group denoting that of which something is predicated

♦ content, matter, motif, motive, question, theme, topic

²subject *adj* **1** : being under the power or rule of another **2** ♦ : suffering a particular liability or exposure : LIABLE ⟨∼ to floods⟩ **3** ♦ : dependent on some act or condition ⟨appointment ∼ to senate approval⟩

♦ *usu* **subject to** [2] exposed, liable, open, sensitive, susceptible, vulnerable ♦ *usu* **subject to** [3] conditional, contingent, dependent

³sub•ject \səb-ˈjekt\ *vb* **1** ♦ : to bring under control : CONQUER **2** : to make liable **3** : to cause to undergo or endure

♦ conquer, dominate, overpower, subdue, vanquish

sub•jec•tion \-ˈjek-shən\ *n* ♦ : the act of subduing or subjecting

♦ conquest, domination

sub•jec•tive \(ˌ)səb-ˈjek-tiv\ *adj* **1** : of, relating to, or constituting a subject **2** : of, relating to, or arising within one's self or mind in contrast to what is outside : PERSONAL — **sub•jec•tive•ly** *adv* — **sub•jec•tiv•i•ty** \-ˌjek-ˈti-və-tē\ *n*
subject matter *n* : matter presented for consideration, discussion, or study
sub•join \(ˌ)səb-ˈjȯin\ *vb* : APPEND
sub ju•di•ce \(ˌ)sub-ˈyü-di-ˌkā, ˈsəb-ˈjü-də-(ˌ)sē\ *adv* : before a judge or court : not yet legally decided

sub•ju•gate \ˈsəb-ji-ˌgāt\ *vb* **-gat•ed; -gat•ing 1** : to bring under control and governance as a subject : CONQUER **2** : SUBDUE
sub•ju•ga•tion \ˌsəb-ji-ˈgā-shən\ *n* **1** : an act of subjugating **2** : the state of being subjugated
sub•junc•tive \səb-ˈjəŋk-tiv\ *adj* : of, relating to, or constituting a verb form that represents an act or state as contingent or possible or viewed emotionally (as with desire) ⟨the ∼ mood⟩ — **subjunctive** *n*
sub•lease \ˈsəb-ˌlēs, -ˌlēs\ *n* : a lease by a lessee of part or all of leased premises to another person with the original lessee retaining some right under the original lease — **sublease** *vb*
¹sub•let \ˈsəb-ˈlet\ *vb* **-let; -let•ting** : to let all or a part of (a leased property) to another; *also* : to rent (a property) from a lessee
²sublet \-ˌlet\ *n* : property and esp. housing obtained by or available through a sublease
sub•li•mate \ˈsə-blə-ˌmāt\ *vb* **-mat•ed; -mat•ing 1** : SUBLIME **2** : to direct the expression of (as a desire or impulse) from a primitive to a more socially and culturally acceptable form — **sub•li•ma•tion** \ˌsə-blə-ˈmā-shən\ *n*
¹sub•lime \sə-ˈblīm\ *vb* **sub•limed; sub•lim•ing** : to pass or cause to pass directly from the solid to the vapor state
²sublime *adj* **1** ♦ : lofty, grand, or exalted in thought, expression, or manner : NOBLE **2** ♦ : having awe-inspiring beauty or grandeur — **sub•lime•ly** *adv* — **sub•lim•i•ty** \-ˈbli-mə-tē\ *n*

♦ [1] chivalrous, gallant, great, greathearted, high, high-minded, lofty, lordly, magnanimous, noble ♦ [2] amazing, astonishing, astounding, awesome, awful, eye-opening, fabulous, marvelous (*or* marvellous), miraculous, portentous, prodigious, stunning, stupendous, surprising, wonderful

sub•lim•i•nal \(ˌ)səb-ˈli-mən-ᵊl, ˈsəb-\ *adj* **1** : inadequate to produce a sensation or mental awareness ⟨∼ stimuli⟩ **2** : existing or functioning below the threshold of consciousness ⟨the ∼ mind⟩ ⟨∼ advertising⟩
sub•ma•chine gun \ˌsəb-mə-ˈshēn-ˌgən\ *n* : an automatic firearm fired from the shoulder or hip
¹sub•ma•rine \ˈsəb-mə-ˌrēn, ˌsəb-mə-ˈrēn\ *adj* ♦ : lying, growing, worn, or operating below the surface of the water : UNDERWATER; *esp* : UNDERSEA

♦ sunken, underwater

²submarine *n* **1** : a naval vessel designed to operate underwater **2** ♦ : a large sandwich made from a long split roll with any of a variety of fillings

♦ grinder, hoagie, poor boy, sub

sub•merge \səb-ˈmərj\ *vb* **sub•merged; sub•merg•ing 1** ♦ : to put or plunge under the surface of water **2** ♦ : to cover or overflow with water : INUNDATE — **sub•mer•gence** \-ˈmər-jəns\ *n*

♦ [1] dip, douse, duck, dunk, immerse, souse ♦ [2] deluge, drown, engulf, flood, inundate, overflow, overwhelm, swamp

sub•merse \səb-ˈmərs\ *vb* **sub•mersed; sub•mers•ing** : to put or go under water : SUBMERGE — **sub•mer•sion** \-ˈmər-zhən\ *n*
¹sub•mers•ible \səb-ˈmər-sə-bəl\ *adj* : capable of being submerged
²submersible *n* : something that is submersible; *esp* : a small underwater craft used for deep-sea research
sub•mi•cro•sco•pic \ˌsəb-ˌmī-krə-ˈskä-pik\ *adj* : too small to be seen in an ordinary light microscope
sub•min•ia•ture \ˌsəb-ˈmi-nē-ə-ˌchu̇r, ˈsəb-, -ˈmi-ni-ˌchu̇r, -chər\ *adj* : very small
sub•mis•sion \-ˈmi-shən\ *n* ♦ : an act of submitting to the authority or control of another

♦ compliance, conformity, obedience, observance, subordination ♦ capitulation, relinquishment, surrender

sub•mis•sive \-ˈmi-siv\ *adj* ♦ : submitting to others

♦ amenable, compliant, conformable, docile, obedient, tractable

sub•mit \səb-ˈmit\ *vb* **sub•mit•ted; sub•mit•ting 1** ♦ : to commit to the discretion or decision of another or of others **2** ♦ : to yield oneself to the authority or will of another : SURRENDER **3** : to put forward as an opinion

♦ blink, bow, budge, capitulate, concede, give in, knuckle under, quit, succumb, surrender, yield

sub•nor•mal \ˌsəb-ˈnȯr-məl\ *adj* : falling below what is normal; *also* : having less of something and esp. intelligence than is normal — **sub•nor•mal•i•ty** \ˌsəb-nȯr-ˈma-lə-tē\ *n*
sub•or•bit•al \ˌsəb-ˈȯr-bət-ᵊl, ˈsəb-\ *adj* : being or involving less than one orbit
¹sub•or•di•nate \sə-ˈbȯrd-ᵊn-ət\ *adj* **1** ♦ : of lower class or

rank **2** : INFERIOR **3** : submissive to authority **4** : subordinated to other elements in a sentence ⟨∼ clause⟩
♦ inferior, junior, less, lesser, lower, minor, under

²subordinate *n* ♦ : one that is subordinate
♦ inferior, junior, underling

³sub·or·di·nate \sə-'bȯrd-ᵊn-ˌāt\ *vb* **-nat·ed; -nat·ing** **1** : to place in a lower rank or class **2** : SUBDUE
sub·or·di·na·tion \-ˌbȯrd-ᵊn-'ā-shən\ *n* **1** : the act of subordinating (as by making secondary or subject) **2** ♦ : the quality or state of being subordinate to authority : obedient submission
♦ compliance, conformity, obedience, observance, submission

sub·orn \sə-'bȯrn\ *vb* **1** : to induce secretly to do an unlawful thing **2** : to induce to commit perjury — **sub·or·na·tion** \ˌsə-ˌbȯr-'nā-shən\ *n*
¹sub·poe·na \sə-'pē-nə\ *n* : a writ commanding the person named in it to attend court under penalty for failure to do so
²subpoena *vb* **-naed; -na·ing** : to summon with a subpoena
sub–Sa·ha·ran \ˌsəb-sə-'har-ən\ *adj* : of, relating to, or being the part of Africa south of the Sahara
sub·scribe \səb-'skrīb\ *vb* **sub·scribed; sub·scrib·ing** **1** : to sign one's name to a document **2** : to give consent by or as if by signing one's name **3** : to promise to contribute by signing one's name with the amount promised **4** : to place an order by signing **5** : to receive a periodical or service regularly on order **6** ♦ : to feel favorably disposed : FAVOR — usu. used with *to* — **sub·scrib·er** *n*
♦ *usu* **subscribe to** accept, approve, care, countenance, favor (*or* favour), OK ♦ *usu* **subscribe to** accede, assent, come round, consent

sub·script \'səb-ˌskript\ *n* : a symbol (as a letter or number) immediately below or below and to the right or left of another written character — **subscript** *adj*
sub·scrip·tion \səb-'skrip-shən\ *n* **1** : the act of subscribing : SIGNATURE **2** : a purchase by signed order
sub·se·quent \'səb-si-kwənt, -sə-ˌkwent\ *adj* ♦ : following after : SUCCEEDING
♦ after, later, posterior *Ant* antecedent, anterior, fore, precedent, preceding, previous, prior

sub·se·quent·ly *adv* ♦ : in a subsequent manner
♦ after, afterward, later, thereafter

sub·ser·vi·ence \səb-'sər-vē-əns\ *n* **1** : a subordinate place or condition **2** : SERVILITY — **sub·ser·vi·en·cy** \-ən-sē\ *n* — **sub·ser·vi·ent** \-ənt\ *adj*
sub·set \'səb-ˌset\ *n* : a set each of whose elements is an element of an inclusive set
sub·side \səb-'sīd\ *vb* **sub·sid·ed; sub·sid·ing** **1** : to settle to the bottom of a liquid **2** : to tend downward : DESCEND **3** : SINK, SUBMERGE **4** ♦ : to become quiet and tranquil — **sub·sid·ence** \səb-'sīd-ᵊns, 'səb-sə-dəns\ *n*
♦ abate, decline, decrease, de-escalate, die, diminish, dwindle, ebb, fall, lessen, let up, lower, moderate, recede, relent, shrink, taper, wane

¹sub·sid·iary \səb-'si-dē-ˌer-ē\ *adj* **1** : furnishing aid or support **2** : of secondary importance **3** : of or relating to a subsidy
²subsidiary *n, pl* **-iar·ies** : one that is subsidiary; *esp* : a company controlled by another
sub·si·dise *chiefly Brit var of* SUBSIDIZE
sub·si·dize \'səb-sə-ˌdīz\ *vb* **-dized; -diz·ing** ♦ : to aid or furnish with a subsidy
♦ capitalize, endow, finance, fund, stake, underwrite

sub·si·dy \'səb-sə-dē\ *n, pl* **-dies** ♦ : a gift of public money to a private person or company or to another government
♦ allocation, allotment, appropriation, grant

sub·sist \səb-'sist\ *vb* **1** ♦ : to have existence; *also* : to continue to exist **2** : to have the means (as food and clothing) of maintaining life; *esp* : to nourish oneself
♦ be, breathe, exist, live

sub·sis·tence \səb-'sis-təns\ *n* **1** ♦ : real being : EXISTENCE; *also* : the condition of remaining in existence : PERSISTENCE **2** : means of subsisting : the minimum (as of food and clothing) necessary to support life
♦ actuality, existence, reality ♦ continuance, continuation, duration, endurance, persistence

sub·son·ic \ˌsəb-'sä-nik, 'səb-\ *adj* : being or relating to a speed less than that of sound; *also* : moving at such a speed

sub·species \'səb-ˌspē-shēz, -sēz\ *n* : a subdivision of a species; *esp* : a category in biological classification ranking just below a species that designates a geographic population genetically distinct from other such populations and potentially able to breed with them where its range overlaps theirs
sub·stance \'səb-stəns\ *n* **1** ♦ : essential nature : ESSENCE ⟨divine ∼⟩; *also* : the fundamental or essential part or quality ⟨the ∼ of the speech⟩ **2** ♦ : physical material from which something is made or which has discrete existence; *also* : matter of particular or definite chemical constitution **3** ♦ : material possessions : WEALTH **4** : something (as drugs or alcohol) deemed harmful and usu. subject to legal restriction ⟨∼ abuse⟩
♦ [1] essence, nature, quintessence, soul, stuff ♦ [2] being, entity, individual, object, thing ♦ [2] material, raw material, stuff ♦ [3] assets, capital, fortune, means, opulence, riches, wealth, wherewithal

substance abuse *n* : excessive use of a drug (as alcohol or cocaine) : use of a drug without medical justification
sub·stan·dard \ˌsəb-'stan-dərd\ *adj* ♦ : falling short of a standard or norm
♦ bad, deficient, inferior, lousy, off, poor, punk, rotten, unacceptable, unsatisfactory, wanting, wretched, wrong

sub·stan·tial \səb-'stan-chəl\ *adj* **1** ♦ : existing as or in substance : MATERIAL; *also* : not illusory : REAL **2** ♦ : marked by or indicative of significant worth or consequence : IMPORTANT **3** : NOURISHING, SATISFYING ⟨∼ meal⟩ **4** : having means : WELL-TO-DO **5** ♦ : large in extent or degree : CONSIDERABLE ⟨∼ profit⟩ **6** : STRONG, FIRM — **sub·stan·tial·ly** *adv*
♦ [1] concrete, material, physical, real ♦ [2] big, consequential, eventful, important, major, material, meaningful, momentous, significant, weighty ♦ [5] considerable, good, goodly, healthy, respectable, significant, sizable, tidy

sub·stan·ti·ate \səb-'stan-chē-ˌāt\ *vb* **-at·ed; -at·ing** **1** ♦ : to give substance or body to **2** ♦ : to establish by proof or competent evidence
♦ [1] embody, epitomize, manifest, materialize, personify ♦ [2] bear out, confirm, corroborate, prove, support, validate, verify, vindicate

sub·stan·ti·a·tion \-ˌstan-chē-'ā-shən\ *n* ♦ : something offered as proof
♦ attestation, confirmation, corroboration, documentation, evidence, proof, testament, testimony, validation, witness

¹sub·stan·tive \'səb-stən-tiv\ *n* : NOUN; *also* : a word or phrase used as a noun
²substantive *adj* : having substance : REAL ⟨∼ changes⟩
¹sub·sti·tute \'səb-stə-ˌtüt, -ˌtyüt\ *n* ♦ : a person or thing replacing another
♦ backup, pinch hitter, relief, replacement, reserve, stand-in, sub

²substitute *vb* **-tut·ed; -tut·ing** **1** ♦ : to put or use in the place of another **2** ♦ : to serve as a substitute — **sub·sti·tu·tion** \ˌsəb-stə-'tü-shən, -'tyü-\ *n*
♦ [1] change, commute, exchange, shift, swap, switch, trade ♦ [2] cover, fill in, pinch-hit, stand in, sub, take over ♦ [2] displace, replace, supersede, supplant

³substitute *adj* ♦ : serving as or fitted for use as a substitute
♦ backup, new

sub·strate \'səb-ˌstrāt\ *n* **1** : the base on which a plant or animal lives **2** : a substance acted upon (as by an enzyme)
sub·stra·tum \'səb-ˌstrā-təm, -ˌstra-\ *n, pl* **-stra·ta** \-tə\ : the layer or structure (as subsoil) lying underneath
sub·struc·ture \'səb-ˌstrək-chər\ *n* : FOUNDATION, GROUNDWORK
sub·sume \səb-'süm\ *vb* **sub·sumed; sub·sum·ing** ♦ : to include or place within something larger or more comprehensive
♦ carry, comprehend, contain, embrace, encompass, entail, include, involve, number, take in

sub·sur·face \'səb-ˌsər-fəs\ *n* : earth material near the surface of the ground — **subsurface** *adj*
sub·ter·fuge \'səb-tər-ˌfyüj\ *n* ♦ : deception by artifice or stratagem in order to conceal, escape, or evade; *also* : a trick or device used to deceive
♦ artifice, chicanery, hanky-panky, trickery, wile

sub·ter·ra·nean \ˌsəb-tə-'rā-nē-ən\ *adj* **1** : lying or being underground **2** : SECRET, HIDDEN
sub·tile \'sət-ᵊl\ *adj* **sub·til·er** \'sət-lər, -ᵊl-ər\; **sub·til·est** \'sət-ləst, -ᵊl-əst\ : SUBTLE

sub·ti·tle \'səb-ˌtīt-ᵊl\ *n* **1** : a secondary or explanatory title (as of a book) **2** : printed matter projected on a motion-picture screen during or between the scenes

sub·tle \'sət-ᵊl\ *adj* **sub·tler** \'sət-ᵊl-ər\; **sub·tlest** \'sət-ᵊl-əst\ **1** : hardly noticeable ⟨∼ differences⟩ **2** : SHREWD, PERCEPTIVE **3** : adept in the use of subtlety and cunning : CLEVER, SLY **4** ♦ : cunningly made or contrived — **sub·tly** \'sət-ᵊl-ē\ *adv*

 ♦ delicate, exact, fine, minute, nice, refined

sub·tle·ty \-tē\ *n* : the quality or state of being subtle

sub·tract \səb-'trakt\ *vb* : to take away (as one part or number) from another; *also* : to perform the operation of deducting one number from another — **sub·trac·tion** \-'trak-shən\ *n*

sub·tra·hend \'səb-trə-ˌhend\ *n* : a number that is to be subtracted from another

sub·trop·i·cal \ˌsəb-'trä-pi-kəl, 'səb-\ *also* **sub·trop·ic** \-pik\ *adj* : of, relating to, or being regions bordering on the tropical zone — **sub·trop·ics** \-piks\ *n pl*

sub·urb \'sə-ˌbərb\ *n* **1** : an outlying part of a city; *also* : a small community adjacent to a city **2** *pl* : a residential area adjacent to a city — **sub·ur·ban** \sə-'bər-bən\ *adj or n* — **sub·ur·ban·ite** \sə-'bər-bə-ˌnīt\ *n*

sub·ur·bia \sə-'bər-bē-ə\ *n* **1** ♦ : the suburbs of a city **2** : suburban people or customs

 ♦ environs, exurbia, outskirts

sub·ven·tion \səb-'ven-chən\ *n* : SUBSIDY, ENDOWMENT

sub·vert \səb-'vərt\ *vb* **1** : OVERTHROW, RUIN **2** ♦ : to pervert or corrupt by an undermining of morals, allegiance, or faith ⟨∼ the rule of law⟩ — **sub·ver·sion** \-'vər-zhən\ *n* — **sub·ver·sive** \-'vər-siv\ *adj*

 ♦ debase, degrade, demean, demoralize, humble, warp

sub·way \'səb-ˌwā\ *n* : an underground way; *esp* : an underground electric railway

sub·woof·er \'səb-'wü-fər\ *n* : a loudspeaker responsive only to the lowest acoustic frequencies

suc·ceed \sək-'sēd\ *vb* **1** : to follow next in order or next after another; *esp* : to inherit sovereignty, rank, title, or property **2** ♦ : to attain a desired object or end : be successful

 ♦ click, deliver, go over, pan out, work out *Ant* collapse, fail, flop, flunk, fold, wash out ♦ flourish, prosper, thrive *Ant* fail

suc·ceed·ing *adj* ♦ : following next in order or next after another

 ♦ coming, following, next

suc·cess \sək-'ses\ *n* **1** ♦ : favorable or desired outcome **2** : the gaining of wealth and fame **3** ♦ : one that succeeds — **suc·cess·ful·ly** *adv*

 ♦ [1] accomplishment, achievement, attainment, coup, triumph
 ♦ [3] blockbuster, hit, smash, winner

suc·cess·ful \-fəl\ *adj* ♦ : resulting or terminating in success ⟨a ∼ outcome⟩; *also* : gaining or having gained success ⟨a ∼ writer⟩

 ♦ palmy, prosperous, triumphant *Ant* failed, unsuccessful

suc·ces·sion \sək-'se-shən\ *n* **1** : the order, act, or right of succeeding to a property, title, or throne **2** : the act or process of following in order **3** : a series of persons or things that follow one after another

suc·ces·sive \sək-'se-siv\ *adj* ♦ : following in order : CONSECUTIVE ⟨three ∼ days⟩ — **suc·ces·sive·ly** *adv*

 ♦ consecutive, sequential

suc·ces·sor \sək-'se-sər\ *n* : one that succeeds (as to a throne, title, estate, or office)

suc·cinct \(ˌ)sək-'siŋkt, sə-'siŋkt\ *adj* ♦ : marked by compact precise expression without wasted words : BRIEF

 ♦ brief, compact, compendious, concise, crisp, epigrammatic, laconic, pithy, summary, terse

suc·cinct·ly *adv* ♦ : in a succinct manner : with concise and precise brevity

 ♦ compactly, concisely, crisply, laconically, shortly, summarily, tersely

suc·cinct·ness *n* ♦ : the quality or state of being succinct

 ♦ brevity, briefness, compactness, conciseness, crispness, terseness *Ant* prolixity, verbosity, wordiness

suc·cor *or Can and Brit* **suc·cour** \'sə-kər\ *n* : AID, HELP, RELIEF — **succor** *vb*

suc·co·tash \'sə-kə-ˌtash\ *n* : beans and corn kernels cooked together

¹**suc·cu·lent** \'sə-kyə-lənt\ *adj* ♦ : full of juice : JUICY; *also* : having fleshy tissues that conserve moisture ⟨∼ plants⟩ — **suc·cu·lence** \-ləns\ *n*

 ♦ fleshy, juicy, pulpy

²**succulent** *n* : a succulent plant (as a cactus or an aloe)

suc·cumb \sə-'kəm\ *vb* **1** ♦ : to yield to superior strength or force or overpowering appeal or desire **2** ♦ : to pass from physical life : DIE

 ♦ [1] blink, bow, budge, capitulate, concede, fall, give in, knuckle under, quit, submit, surrender, yield ♦ [2] decease, depart, die, expire, pass, pass away, perish

¹**such** \'səch, 'sich\ *adj* **1** ♦ : of this or that kind **2** : having a quality just specified or to be specified

 ♦ akin, alike, analogous, comparable, correspondent, like, parallel, similar

²**such** *pron* **1** : such a one or ones ⟨he's a star, and acted as ∼⟩ **2** : that or those similar or related thereto ⟨boards and nails and ∼⟩

³**such** *adv* : to that degree : so

such·like \'səch-ˌlīk\ *adj* : of like kind : SIMILAR

¹**suck** \'sək\ *vb* **1** : to draw in liquid and esp. mother's milk with the mouth **2** : to draw liquid from by action of the mouth ⟨∼ an orange⟩ **3** ♦ : to take in or up or remove by or as if by suction **4** : to be objectionable

 ♦ *usu* **suck up** absorb, drink, imbibe, soak, sponge

²**suck** *n* **1** : a sucking movement or force **2** : the act of sucking

suck·er \'sə-kər\ *n* **1** : one that sucks **2** : a part of an animal's body used for sucking or for clinging **3** : any of numerous freshwater fishes with thick soft lips for sucking in food **4** : a shoot from the roots or lower part of a plant **5** ♦ : a person easily deceived **6** — used as a generalized term of reference

 ♦ dupe, gull, pigeon, sap, tool

suck·le \'sə-kəl\ *vb* **suck·led**; **suck·ling** : to give or draw milk from the breast or udder; *also* : NURTURE

suck·ling \'sə-kliŋ\ *n* : a young unweaned mammal

suck–up \'sək-ˌəp\ *n* : a person who seeks to gain favor by flattery ⟨a ∼ to the teacher⟩

su·crose \'sü-ˌkrōs, -ˌkrōz\ *n* : a sweet sugar obtained commercially esp. from sugarcane or sugar beets

suc·tion \'sək-shən\ *n* **1** : the act of sucking **2** : the act or process of drawing something (as liquid or dust) into a space (as in a vacuum cleaner or a pump) by partially exhausting the air in the space — **suc·tion·al** \-shə-nəl\ *adj*

suction cup *n* : a cup-shaped device in which a partial vacuum is produced when applied to a surface

Su·da·nese \ˌsüd-ᵊn-'ēz, -'ēs\ *n* : a native or inhabitant of Sudan — **Sudanese** *adj*

sud·den \'səd-ᵊn\ *adj* **1** ♦ : happening or coming unexpectedly ⟨∼ shower⟩; *also* : changing angle or character all at once ⟨∼ turn⟩ ⟨∼ descent⟩ **2** : HASTY, RASH ⟨∼ decision⟩ **3** : made or brought about in a short time : PROMPT ⟨∼ cure⟩ — **sud·den·ness** *n*

 ♦ unanticipated, unexpected, unforeseen

sudden infant death syndrome *n* : death due to unknown causes of an apparently healthy infant usu. before one year of age and esp. during sleep

sud·den·ly *adv* ♦ : in a sudden manner

 ♦ aback, unaware, unawares

su·do·ku \sü-'dō-kü\ *n* : a puzzle in which several numbers are to be filled into a 9x9 grid of squares so that every row, every column, and every 3x3 box contains the numbers 1 through 9

suds \'sədz\ *n pl* : soapy water esp. when frothy — **sudsy** \'səd-zē\ *adj*

sue \'sü\ *vb* **sued**; **su·ing** **1** ♦ : to make a request or application : PETITION, SOLICIT — usu. used with *for* or *to* **2** : to seek justice or right by bringing legal action ⟨sued the company⟩

 ♦ *usu* **sue for** ask, call, petition, plead, quest, request, seek, solicit

suede *also* **suède** \'swād\ *n* **1** : leather with a napped surface **2** : a fabric with a suedelike nap

su·et \'sü-ət\ *n* : the hard fat from beef and mutton that yields tallow

suff *abbr* **1** sufficient **2** suffix

suf·fer \'sə-fər\ *vb* **suf·fered**; **suf·fer·ing** **1** ♦ : to feel or endure pain **2** : to have experience of : UNDERGO **3** : to bear loss, damage, or injury **4** ♦ : to allow esp. by reason of indifference : PERMIT — **suf·fer·er** *n*

 ♦ [1] agonize, bleed, feel, grieve, hurt, mourn, sorrow ♦ [2] endure, experience, feel, have, know, see, sustain, taste, undergo ♦ [4] allow, have, permit

suf·fer·able \'sə-fə-rə-bəl\ *adj* **1 :** not forbidden **2 ♦ :** that can be suffered

♦ bearable, endurable, supportable, sustainable, tolerable

suf·fer·ance \'sə-frəns, -fə-rəns\ *n* **1 ♦ :** consent or approval implied by lack of interference or resistance **2 ♦ :** power or ability to withstand : PATIENCE

♦ [1] allowance, authorization, clearance, concurrence, consent, leave, license (*or* licence), permission, sanction ♦ [2] forbearance, long-suffering, patience, tolerance

suf·fer·ing \'sə-friŋ, -fə-riŋ\ *n* : PAIN, MISERY, HARDSHIP
suf·fice \sə-'fīs\ *vb* **suf·ficed; suf·fic·ing 1 :** to satisfy a need : be sufficient **2 :** to be capable or competent
suf·fi·cien·cy \sə-'fi-shən-sē\ *n* **1 :** a sufficient quantity to meet one's needs **2 :** the quality or state of being sufficient : ADEQUACY
suf·fi·cient \sə-'fi-shənt\ *adj* **:** adequate to accomplish a purpose or meet a need — **suf·fi·cient·ly** *adv*
¹**suf·fix** \'sə-,fiks\ *n* **:** an affix occurring at the end of a word
²**suf·fix** \'sə-fiks, (,)sə-'fiks\ *vb* **:** to attach as a suffix — **suf·fix·ation** \,sə-,fik-'sā-shən\ *n*
suf·fo·cate \'sə-fə-,kāt\ *vb* **-cat·ed; -cat·ing ♦ :** to deprive of oxygen : SMOTHER — **suf·fo·cat·ing·ly** *adv* — **suf·fo·ca·tion** \,sə-fə-'kā-shən\ *n*

♦ choke, smother, stifle, strangle

suf·fra·gan \'sə-fri-gən\ *n* **:** an assistant bishop; *esp* **:** one not having the right of succession — **suffragan** *adj*
suf·frage \'sə-frij\ *n* **1 :** VOTE **2 ♦ :** the right to vote : FRANCHISE

♦ enfranchisement, franchise, vote

suf·frag·ette \,sə-fri-'jet\ *n* **:** a woman who advocates suffrage for women
suf·frag·ist \'səf-ri-jist\ *n* **:** one who advocates extension of suffrage esp. to women
suf·fuse \sə-'fyüz\ *vb* **suf·fused; suf·fus·ing ♦ :** to spread over or through in the manner of a fluid or light — **suf·fu·sion** \-'fyü-zhən\ *n*

♦ percolate, permeate, transfuse ♦ imbue, inculcate, infuse, ingrain, invest, steep

¹**sug·ar** \'shu̇-gər\ *n* **1 :** a sweet substance that is colorless or white when pure and is chiefly sucrose from sugarcane or sugar beets **2 :** a water-soluble compound (as glucose) similar to sucrose
²**sugar** *vb* **sug·ared; sug·ar·ing 1 :** to mix, cover, or sprinkle with sugar **2 :** SWEETEN ⟨∼ advice with flattery⟩ **3 :** to form sugar ⟨a syrup that ∼s⟩ **4 :** GRANULATE
sugar beet *n* **:** a large beet with a white root from which sugar is made
sug·ar·cane \'shu̇-gər-,kān\ *n* **:** a tall grass widely grown in warm regions for the sugar in its stalks
sugar daddy *n* **1 :** a well-to-do usu. older man who supports or spends lavishly on a mistress, girlfriend, or boyfriend **2 :** a generous benefactor of a cause
sugar maple *n* **:** a maple with a sweet sap; *esp* **:** one of eastern No. America with sap that is the chief source of maple syrup and maple sugar
sugar pea *n* **:** SNOW PEA
sug·ar·plum \'shu̇-gər-,pləm\ *n* **:** a small ball of candy
sug·ary *adj* **:** cloyingly sweet
sug·gest \səg-'jest, sə-\ *vb* **1 ♦ :** to put (as a thought, plan, or desire) into a person's mind **2 ♦ :** to remind or evoke by association of ideas

♦ [1] advise, counsel ♦ [1] advance, offer, pose, proffer, propose, propound, vote ♦ [2] allude, hint, imply, indicate, infer, insinuate, intimate

sug·gest·ible \səg-'jes-tə-bəl, sə-\ *adj* **:** easily influenced by suggestion
sug·ges·tion \-'jes-chən\ *n* **1 a :** an act or instance of suggesting **b ♦ :** something suggested **2 ♦ :** a slight indication

♦ [1b] offer, proffer, proposal, proposition ♦ [2] clue, cue, hint, indication, inkling, intimation, lead

sug·ges·tive \-'jes-tiv\ *adj* **:** tending to suggest something; *esp* **:** suggesting something improper or indecent — **sug·ges·tive·ly** *adv* — **sug·ges·tive·ness** *n*

♦ eloquent, expressive, meaning, meaningful, pregnant, significant ♦ bawdy, lewd, racy, ribald, risqué, spicy

¹**sui·cide** \'sü-ə-,sīd\ *n* **1 :** the act of killing oneself purposely **2 :** one that commits or attempts suicide — **sui·cid·al** \,sü-ə-'sīd-ᵊl\ *adj*
²**suicide** *adj* **:** being or performing a deliberate act resulting in the voluntary death of the person who does it ⟨a ∼ mission⟩ ⟨a ∼ bomber⟩
sui ge·ner·is \,sü-,ī-'je-nə-rəs, ,sü-ē-\ *adj* **:** being in a class by itself : UNIQUE
¹**suit** \'süt\ *n* **1 ♦ :** an action in court to recover a right or claim **2 a ♦ :** an act of suing or entreating **b :** COURTSHIP **3 :** a number of things used together ⟨∼ of clothes⟩ **4 :** all the playing cards in a pack bearing the same symbol

♦ [1] action, lawsuit, proceeding ♦ [2a] appeal, cry, entreaty, petition, plea, prayer, solicitation, supplication

²**suit** *vb* **1 ♦ :** to be appropriate or fitting **2 :** to be becoming to **3 ♦ :** to meet the needs or desires of : PLEASE **4 ♦ :** to outfit with clothes : DRESS

♦ [1] befit, do, fit, go, serve ♦ [3] content, delight, gladden, gratify, please, rejoice, satisfy, warm ♦ [4] apparel, array, attire, caparison, clothe, deck, dress, garb, invest, rig

suit·abil·i·ty \,sü-tə-'bi-lə-tē\ *n* **♦ :** the quality or state of being suitable

♦ appropriateness, aptness, fitness, rightness

suit·able \'sü-tə-bəl\ *adj* **♦ :** adapted to a use or purpose

♦ able, capable, competent, fit, good, qualified ♦ applicable, appropriate, apt, felicitous, fit, fitting, good, happy, meet, proper, right

suit·able·ness \'sü-tə-bəl-nəs\ *n* **:** the quality or state of being suitable
suit·ably \-tə-blē\ *adv* **♦ :** in a suitable manner

♦ appropriately, correctly, fittingly, happily, properly, rightly

suit·case \'süt-,kās\ *n* **♦ :** a portable case designed to hold a traveler's clothing and personal articles

♦ carryall, grip, handbag, portmanteau, traveling bag

suite \'swēt, *for 4 also* 'süt\ *n* **1 ♦ :** a group of retainers or attendants : RETINUE **2 :** a group of rooms occupied as a unit **3 :** a modern instrumental composition in several movements of different character; *also* **:** a long orchestral concert arrangement in suite form of material drawn from a longer work **4 :** a set of matched furniture for a room **5 :** a group of things forming a unit or constituting a collection

♦ cortege, following, retinue, train

suit·ing \'sü-tiŋ\ *n* **:** fabric for suits of clothes
suit·or \'sü-tər\ *n* **1 :** one who sues or petitions **2 ♦ :** one who seeks to marry a woman

♦ [1] pleader, solicitor ♦ [2] gallant, swain, wooer

su·ki·ya·ki \skē-'yä-kē, ,su̇-kē-'yä-\ *n* **:** thin slices of meat, tofu, and vegetables cooked in soy sauce and sugar
sul·fa drug \'səl-fə-\ *n* **:** any of various synthetic organic bacteria-inhibiting drugs
sul·fate *or Can and Brit* **sul·phate** \'səl-,fāt\ *n* **:** a salt or ester of sulfuric acid
sul·fide *or Can and Brit* **sul·phide** \'səl-,fīd\ *n* **:** a compound of sulfur
sul·fur *or chiefly Can and Brit* **sul·phur** \'səl-fər\ *n* **:** a nonmetallic chemical element used esp. in the chemical and paper industries and in vulcanizing rubber
sulfur di·ox·ide \-dī-'äk-sīd\ *n* **:** a heavy pungent toxic gas that is used esp. in bleaching, as a preservative, and as a refrigerant, and is a major air pollutant
sul·fu·ric *or Can and Brit* **sul·phu·ric** \,səl-'fyu̇r-ik\ *adj* **:** of, relating to, or containing sulfur
sulfuric acid *or* **sul·phu·ric acid** \,səl-'fyu̇r-ik-\ *n* **:** a heavy corrosive oily strong acid
sul·fu·rous *or chiefly Can and Brit* **sul·phu·rous** \'səl-fə-rəs, -fyə-, *also esp for 1* ,səl-'fyu̇r-əs\ *adj* **1 :** of, relating to, or containing sulfur **2 :** of or relating to brimstone or the fire of hell : INFERNAL **3 :** FIERY, INFLAMED ⟨∼ sermons⟩
¹**sulk** \'səlk\ *vb* **:** to be or become moodily silent or irritable
²**sulk** *n* **♦ :** a sulky mood or spell

♦ pet, pout, sullenness

sulk·i·ness \-kē-nəs\ *n* **:** SULK
¹**sulky** \'səl-kē\ *adj* **sulk·i·er; -est ♦ :** inclined to sulk : MOROSE, MOODY ⟨a ∼ mood⟩ — **sulk·i·ly** \'səl-kə-lē\ *adv*

♦ glum, moody, morose, sullen, surly

²**sulky** *n, pl* **sulkies** : a light 2-wheeled horse-drawn vehicle with a seat for the driver and usu. no body

sul·len \'sə-lən\ *adj* **1 ♦** : gloomily silent **2** : showing or causing gloom or depression : GLOOMY ⟨a ∼ sky⟩ — **sul·len·ly** *adv*

  ♦ glum, moody, morose, sulky, surly

sul·len·ness *n* ♦ : the quality or state of being sullen

  ♦ pet, pout, sulk

sul·ly \'sə-lē\ *vb* **sul·lied; sul·ly·ing** : to make or become soiled, tarnished, or defiled : SOIL, SMIRCH ⟨∼ his name⟩

sulphate, sulphide, sulphur *chiefly Can and Brit var of* SULFATE, SULFIDE, SULFUR

sul·tan \'səlt-ᵊn\ *n* : a sovereign esp. of a Muslim state — **sul·tan·ate** \-,āt\ *n*

sul·ta·na \,səl-'ta-nə\ *n* **1** : a female member of a sultan's family **2** : a pale seedless grape; *also* : a raisin of this grape

sul·try \'səl-trē\ *adj* **sul·tri·er; -est** **1 ♦** : very hot and moist; *also* : burning hot **2** : exciting sexual desire ⟨a ∼ look⟩

  ♦ humid, muggy, sticky ♦ broiling, burning, fiery, hot, red-hot, scorching, torrid

¹**sum** \'səm\ *n* **1** : a quantity of money **2 ♦** : the whole amount **3** : GIST **4** : the result obtained by adding numbers **5** : a problem in arithmetic **6** : a summary of the chief points or thoughts

  ♦ aggregate, full, total, totality, whole

²**sum** *vb* **summed; sum·ming** ♦ : to find the sum of by adding or counting; *also* : to reach a sum

  ♦ add, foot, total ♦ *usu* **sum to** *or* **sum into** add up, amount, come, number, total

su·mac *also* **su·mach** \'sü-,mak, 'shü-\ *n* : any of a genus of trees, shrubs, and woody vines having spikes or loose clusters of red or whitish berries

sum·mar·i·ly \(,)sə-'mer-ə-lē, 'sə-mə-rə-lē\ *adv* ♦ : in a summary manner or form

  ♦ compactly, concisely, crisply, laconically, shortly, succinctly, tersely

sum·ma·rise *chiefly Brit var of* SUMMARIZE

sum·ma·rize \'sə-mə-,rīz\ *vb* **-rized; -riz·ing** : to tell in a summary — **sum·ma·ri·za·tion** \,sə-mə-rə-'zā-shən\ *n*

  ♦ abstract, digest, encapsulate, epitomize, outline, recapitulate, sum up, wrap up

¹**sum·ma·ry** \'sə-mə-rē\ *adj* **1 ♦** : covering the main points briefly : CONCISE **2** : done without delay or formality ⟨∼ punishment⟩

  ♦ brief, compact, compendious, concise, crisp, epigrammatic, laconic, pithy, succinct, terse

²**summary** *n, pl* **-ries** ♦ : a concise statement of the main points

  ♦ abstract, digest, encapsulation, epitome, outline, précis, recapitulation, résumé (*or* resume), roundup, sum, synopsis, wrap-up

sum·ma·tion \(,)sə-'mā-shən\ *n* **1** : a summing up **2** : a speech in court summing up the arguments in a case

sum·mer \'sə-mər\ *n* : the season of the year in a region in which the sun shines most directly : the warmest period of the year — **sum·mery** *adj*

sum·mer·house \'sə-mər-,hau̇s\ *n* : a covered structure in a garden or park to provide a shady retreat

summersault *var of* SOMERSAULT

summer squash *n* : any of various squashes (as zucchini) used as a vegetable while immature

¹**sum·mit** \'sə-mət\ *n* **1 ♦** : the highest point **2** : a conference of highest-level officials

  ♦ acme, apex, climax, crown, culmination, head, height, meridian, peak, pinnacle, tip-top, top, zenith

²**summit** *vb* **sum·mit·ted; sum·mit·ting** **1** : to participate in a summit conference **2** : to climb to the summit

sum·mon \'sə-mən\ *vb* **1 ♦** : to call to a meeting : CONVOKE **2** : to send for; *also* : to order to appear in court **3** : to evoke esp. by an act of the will ⟨∼ up courage⟩ — **sum·mon·er** *n*

  ♦ assemble, call, convene, convoke, muster

sum·mons \'sə-mənz\ *n, pl* **sum·mons·es** **1** : an authoritative call to appear at a designated place or to attend to a duty **2** : a warning or citation to appear in court at a specified time to answer charges

sump·tu·ous \'səmp-shə-wəs, -chə-\ *adj* ♦ : extremely costly, rich, luxurious, or magnificent : LUXURIOUS

  ♦ deluxe, lavish, luxuriant, luxurious, opulent, palatial, plush

sum up *vb* ♦ : to tell in or reduce to a summary : SUMMARIZE

  ♦ abstract, digest, encapsulate, epitomize, outline, recapitulate, summarize, wrap up

¹**sun** \'sən\ *n* **1** : the shining celestial body around which the earth and other planets revolve and from which they receive light and heat **2** : a celestial body like the sun **3** : SUNSHINE — **sun·less** *adj*

²**sun** *vb* **sunned; sun·ning** **1** : to expose to or as if to the rays of the sun **2** : to sun oneself

Sun *abbr* Sunday

sun·bath \'sən-,bath, -,bȧth\ *n* : an exposure to sunlight or a sunlamp — **sun·bathe** \-,bāth\ *vb*

sun·beam \-,bēm\ *n* : a ray of sunlight

sun·block \'sən-,bläk\ *n* : a preparation used on the skin to prevent sunburn (as by blocking ultraviolet radiation)

sun·bon·net \-,bä-nət\ *n* : a bonnet with a wide brim to shield the face and neck from the sun

¹**sun·burn** \-,bərn\ *vb* **-burned** \-,bərnd\ *or* **-burnt** \-,bərnt\; **-burn·ing** : to cause or become affected with sunburn

²**sunburn** *n* : a skin inflammation caused by overexposure to ultraviolet radiation esp. from sunshine

sun·dae \'sən-(,)dā, -dē\ *n* : ice cream served with topping

Sun·day \'sən-dē, -,dā\ *n* : the 1st day of the week : the Christian Sabbath

sun·der \'sən-dər\ *vb* ♦ : to force apart

  ♦ break up, disconnect, disjoint, dissever, dissociate, disunite, divide, divorce, part, resolve, separate, sever, split, unyoke

sun·di·al \-,dī-(-ə)l\ *n* : a device for showing the time of day from the shadow cast on a plate by an object with a straight edge

sun·down \-,dau̇n\ *n* ♦ : the time at which the sun disappears below the horizon : SUNSET 2

  ♦ dusk, evening, gloaming, nightfall, sunset, twilight

sun·dries \'sən-drēz\ *n pl* ♦ : various small articles or items

  ♦ novelties, notions, odds and ends

sun·dry \'sən-drē\ *adj* : SEVERAL, DIVERS, VARIOUS

sun·fish \'sən-,fish\ *n* **1** : a large marine fish with a deep flattened body **2** : any of numerous often brightly colored No. American freshwater fishes related to the perches and usu. having the body flattened from side to side

sun·flow·er \-,flau̇-ər\ *n* : any of a genus of tall New World plants related to the daisies and often grown for the oil-rich seeds of their yellow-petaled dark-centered flowers

sung *past and past part of* SING

sun·glasses \'sən-,gla-səz\ *n pl* : glasses to protect the eyes from the sun

sunk *past and past part of* SINK

sunk·en \'sən-kən\ *adj* **1 ♦** : covered with water : SUBMERGED **2 ♦** : fallen in : HOLLOW ⟨∼ cheeks⟩ **3** : lying in a depression ⟨a ∼ garden⟩; *also* : constructed below the general floor level ⟨a ∼ living room⟩

  ♦ [1] submarine, underwater ♦ [2] concave, depressed, hollow

sun·lamp \'sən-,lamp\ *n* : an electric lamp designed to emit radiation of wavelengths from ultraviolet to infrared

sun·light \-,līt\ *n* : SUNSHINE

sun·lit \-,lit\ *adj* : lighted by or as if by the sun

Sun·ni \'sü-nē\ *n* **1** : one of the two main branches of Islam **2** : a Muslim of the Sunni branch of Islam

sun·ny \'sə-nē\ *adj* ♦ : full of sunshine; *also* : full of good spirits

  ♦ clear, cloudless, fair, sunshiny, unclouded ♦ blithe, bright, buoyant, cheerful, cheery, chipper, lightsome, merry, upbeat

sun protection factor *n* : a number that is the factor by which the time required for unprotected skin to become sunburned is increased when a sunscreen is used

sun·rise \-,rīz\ *n* **1** : the apparent rising of the sun above the horizon **2** ♦ : the time at which the sun rises

  ♦ aurora, cockcrow, dawn, morning

sun·roof \-,rüf, -,ru̇f\ *n* : a panel in an automobile roof that can be opened

sun·screen \-,skrēn\ *n* : a preparation on the skin to prevent sunburn (as by absorbing ultraviolet radiation)

sun·set \-,set\ *n* **1** : the apparent descent of the sun below the horizon **2** ♦ : the time at which the sun sets

  ♦ dusk, evening, gloaming, nightfall, sundown, twilight

sun·shade \'sən-,shād\ *n* : something (as a parasol or awning) used as a protection from the sun's rays

sun·shine \-,shīn\ *n* : the direct light of the sun

sun·shiny *adj* ♦ : bright with or as if with the rays of the sun

  ♦ clear, cloudless, fair, sunny, unclouded

sun·spot \-ˌspät\ *n* : any of the dark spots that appear at times on the sun's surface
sun·stroke \-ˌstrōk\ *n* : heatstroke caused by direct exposure to the sun
sun·tan \-ˌtan\ *n* : a browning of the skin from exposure to the sun's rays
sun·up \-ˌəp\ *n* : the apparent rising of the sun above the horizon : SUNRISE
¹**sup** \'səp\ *vb* **supped; sup·ping** ♦ : to take or drink in swallows or gulps

  ♦ drink, guzzle, imbibe, quaff, swig, toss

²**sup** *n* ♦ : a mouthful esp. of liquor or broth; *also* : a small quantity of liquid

  ♦ draft, swallow

³**sup** *vb* **supped; sup·ping** **1** : to eat the evening meal **2** : to make one's supper ⟨*supped* on roast beef⟩
⁴**sup** *abbr* **1** superior **2** supplement; supplementary **3** supply **4** supra
¹**su·per** \'sü-pər\ *n* : SUPERINTENDENT
²**super** *adj* **1** : very fine : EXCELLENT **2** : EXTREME, EXCESSIVE **3** : very large or powerful : HUGE
super- \ˌsü-pər\ *prefix* **1** : over and above : higher in quantity, quality, or degree than : more than **2** : in addition : extra **3** : exceeding a norm **4** : in excessive degree or intensity **5** : surpassing all or most others of its kind **6** : situated above, on, or at the top of **7** : next above or higher **8** : more inclusive than **9** : superior in status or position

superabsorbent	superpatriotism
superachiever	superpremium
superagency	superrich
superblock	supersalesman
superbomb	supersecret
supercity	supersize
superclean	supersized
superexpensive	supersmart
superfast	supersophisticated
superfine	superspy
superheat	superstate
superheavy	superstore
superhero	superstratum
superhumanly	superstrength
superindividual	superstrong
superliner	supersubtle
superman	supersystem
supermom	supertanker
supernormal	superthin
superpatriot	superwoman
superpatriotic	

su·per·abun·dance \ˌsü-pər-ə-'bən-dəns\ *n* ♦ : great abundance; *also* : the state or an instance of surpassing usual, proper, or specified limits

  ♦ abundance, plenty, wealth ♦ excess, fat, overabundance, overflow, overkill, overmuch, superfluity, surfeit, surplus

su·per·abun·dant \ˌsü-pər-ə-'bən-dənt\ *adj* : more than ample
su·per·an·nu·ate \ˌsü-pər-'an-yə-ˌwāt\ *vb* **-at·ed; -at·ing** **1** : to make out-of-date **2** : to retire and pension because of age or infirmity — **su·per·an·nu·at·ed** *adj*
su·per·an·nu·at·ed *adj* ♦ : no longer current : OUTDATED

  ♦ antiquated, archaic, dated, obsolete, outdated, outmoded, outworn, passé

su·perb \sù-'pərb\ *adj* ♦ : marked to the highest degree by excellence, brilliance, or competence — **su·perb·ly** *adv*

  ♦ excellent, fabulous, fine, grand, great, sensational, splendid, superior, swell, terrific, unsurpassed, wonderful

su·per·charg·er \'sü-pər-ˌchär-jər\ *n* : a device for increasing the amount of air supplied to an internal combustion engine
su·per·cil·ious \ˌsü-pər-'si-lē-əs\ *adj* ♦ : haughtily contemptuous

  ♦ arrogant, cavalier, haughty, imperious, overweening, peremptory, pompous, presumptuous, pretentious, superior, uppity

su·per·com·pu·ter \'sü-pər-kəm-ˌpyü-tər\ *n* : a large very fast mainframe
su·per·con·duc·tiv·i·ty \ˌsü-pər-ˌkän-ˌdək-'ti-və-tē\ *n* : a complete disappearance of electrical resistance in a substance esp. at very low temperatures — **su·per·con·duc·tive** \-kən-'dək-tiv\ *adj* — **su·per·con·duc·tor** \-'dək-tər\ *n*

su·per·con·ti·nent \'sü-pər-ˌkänt-ᵊn-ənt\ *n* : a former large continent from which other continents are held to have broken off and drifted away
su·per·ego \ˌsü-pər-'ē-gō\ *n* : the one of the three divisions of the psyche in psychoanalytic theory that functions to reward and punish through a system of moral attitudes, conscience, and a sense of guilt
su·per·fi·cial \ˌsü-pər-'fi-shəl\ *adj* **1** : of or relating to the surface or appearance only **2** : not thorough : SHALLOW — **su·per·fi·ci·al·i·ty** \-ˌfi-shē-'a-lə-tē\ *n* — **su·per·fi·cial·ly** *adv*
su·per·flu·i·ty \ˌsü-pər-'flü-ə-tē\ *n* ♦ : the state or an instance of surpassing usual, proper, or specified limits

  ♦ amenity, comfort, extra, frill, indulgence, luxury ♦ excess, fat, overabundance, overflow, overkill, overmuch, superabundance, surfeit, surplus

su·per·flu·ous \sù-'pər-flə-wəs\ *adj* ♦ : exceeding what is sufficient or necessary : SURPLUS ⟨~ details⟩

  ♦ excess, extra, spare, supernumerary, surplus

su·per·high·way \ˌsü-pər-'hī-ˌwā\ *n* : a broad highway designed for high-speed traffic
su·per·hu·man \ˌsü-pər-'hyu-mən\ *adj* ♦ : being above the human; *also* : exceeding normal human power, size, or capability

  ♦ magical, miraculous, phenomenal, supernatural, uncanny, unearthly

su·per·im·pose \-im-'pōz\ *vb* : to lay (one thing) over or above something else
su·per·in·tend \ˌsü-pə-rin-'tend\ *vb* ♦ : to have or exercise the charge and oversight of

  ♦ administer, carry on, conduct, control, direct, govern, guide, handle, manage, operate, oversee, regulate, run, supervise

su·per·in·ten·dence \-'ten-dəns\ *n* ♦ : the act or function of superintending or directing

  ♦ administration, conduct, control, direction, government, guidance, management, operation, oversight, regulation, running, supervision ♦ care, charge, guidance, headship, oversight, regulation, supervision

su·per·in·ten·den·cy \-dən-sē\ *n* **1** : the office, post, or jurisdiction of a superintendent **2** : the act or function of superintending or directing
su·per·in·ten·dent \-dənt\ *n* ♦ : one who has executive oversight and charge

  ♦ administrator, director, executive, manager, supervisor

¹**su·pe·ri·or** \sù-'pir-ē-ər\ *adj* **1** : situated higher up, over, or near the top; *also* : higher in rank or numbers **2** : of greater value or importance **3** : courageously indifferent (as to pain or misfortune) **4** : better than most others of its kind **5** ♦ : affecting or assuming an air of superiority : HAUGHTY

  ♦ [2] distinguished, eminent, illustrious, noble, notable, noteworthy, outstanding, preeminent, prestigious, signal, star ♦ [5] disdainful, haughty, highfalutin, lofty, lordly, prideful, proud

²**superior** *n* **1** ♦ : one who is above another in rank, office, or station; *esp* : the head of a religious house or order **2** : one higher in quality or merit

  ♦ better, boss, chief, elder, head, leader, senior *Ant* inferior, subordinate, underling

su·pe·ri·or·i·ty \-ˌpir-ē-'ȯr-ə-tē\ *n* : the quality or state of being superior; *also* : a superior characteristic

  ♦ distinction, excellence, greatness, preeminence, supremacy ♦ arrogance, haughtiness, loftiness, pretense, pretension, pretentiousness, self-importance

¹**su·per·la·tive** \sù-'pər-lə-tiv\ *adj* **1** : of, relating to, or constituting the degree of grammatical comparison that denotes an extreme or unsurpassed level or extent **2** : surpassing others : SUPREME — **su·per·la·tive·ly** *adv*
²**superlative** *n* **1** : the superlative degree or a superlative form in a language **2** : the utmost degree : ACME
su·per·mar·ket \'sü-pər-ˌmär-kət\ *n* : a self-service retail market selling foods and household merchandise
su·per·mod·el \'sü-pər-ˌmäd-ᵊl\ *n* : a famous and successful fashion model
su·per·mom \-ˌmäm\ *n* : an exemplary mother; *also* : a woman who performs traditional work of housekeeping and parenting while also having a full-time job
su·per·nal \sù-'pər-nəl\ *adj* **1** : being or coming from on high **2** ♦ : of heavenly or spiritual character **3** : superlatively good

  ♦ celestial, Elysian, empyrean, heavenly

su•per•nat•u•ral \ˌsü-pər-ˈna-chə-rəl\ *adj* 1 ♦ : of or relating to phenomena beyond or outside of nature 2 : relating to or attributed to a divinity, ghost, or devil — **su•per•nat•u•ral•ly** *adv*

♦ metaphysical, preternatural, superhuman, unearthly *Ant* natural ♦ magical, miraculous, phenomenal, superhuman, uncanny, unearthly

su•per•no•va \ˌsü-pər-ˈnō-və\ *n* : the explosion of a very large star

¹**su•per•nu•mer•ary** \-ˈnü-mə-ˌrer-ē, -ˈnyü-\ *adj* ♦ : exceeding the usual or required number : EXTRA

♦ excess, extra, spare, superfluous, surplus

²**supernumerary** *n, pl* **-ar•ies** : an extra person or thing; *esp* : an actor hired for a nonspeaking part

su•per•pose \ˌsü-pər-ˈpōz\ *vb* **-posed; -pos•ing** : SUPERIMPOSE — **su•per•po•si•tion** \-pə-ˈzi-shən\ *n*

su•per•pow•er \ˈsü-pər-ˌpau̇-ər\ *n* 1 : excessive or superior power 2 : one of a few politically and militarily dominant nations

su•per•sat•u•rat•ed \-ˈsa-chə-ˌrā-təd\ *adj* : containing an amount of a substance greater than that required for saturation

su•per•script \ˈsü-pər-ˌskript\ *n* : a symbol (as a numeral or letter) written immediately above or above and to one side of another character

su•per•sede \ˌsü-pər-ˈsēd\ *vb* **-sed•ed; -sed•ing** ♦ : to take the place of : REPLACE

♦ displace, replace, substitute, supplant

su•per•son•ic \-ˈsä-nik\ *adj* 1 : ULTRASONIC 2 : being or relating to speeds from one to five times the speed of sound; *also* : capable of moving at such a speed ⟨a ∼ airplane⟩

su•per•star \ˈsü-pər-ˌstär\ *n* ♦ : one that is very prominent or is a prime attraction

♦ celebrity, figure, light, luminary, notable, personage, personality, somebody, standout, star, VIP

su•per•sti•tion \ˌsü-pər-ˈsti-shən\ *n* 1 : beliefs or practices resulting from ignorance, fear of the unknown, or trust in magic or chance 2 : an unreasoning fear of nature, the unknown, or God resulting from superstition — **su•per•sti•tious** \-shəs\ *adj*

su•per•struc•ture \ˈsü-pər-ˌstrək-chər\ *n* : something built on a base or as a vertical extension

su•per•ti•tle \ˈsü-pər-ˌtī-t³l\ *n* : a translation of foreign-language dialogue displayed above a screen or performance

su•per•vene \ˌsü-pər-ˈvēn\ *vb* **-vened; -ven•ing** : to occur as something additional or unexpected

su•per•vise \ˈsü-pər-ˌvīz\ *vb* **-vised; -vis•ing** ♦ : to have or exercise the charge and oversight of

♦ administer, boss, captain, carry on, conduct, control, direct, govern, guide, handle, manage, operate, oversee, regulate, run, superintend ♦ attend, care, mind, tend

su•per•vi•sion \ˌsü-pər-ˈvi-zhən\ *n* ♦ : the action, process, or occupation of supervising; *esp* : a critical watching and directing (as of activities or a course of action)

♦ administration, conduct, control, direction, government, management, operation, running ♦ care, charge, guidance, headship, oversight, regulation, superintendence

su•per•vi•sor \ˈsü-pər-ˌvī-zər\ *n* ♦ : one that supervises; *esp* : an administrative officer in charge of a business, government, or school unit or operation

♦ administrator, director, executive, manager, superintendent

su•per•vi•so•ry \ˌsü-pər-ˈvī-zə-rē\ *adj* ♦ : of or relating to supervision

♦ directorial, executive, managerial

su•pine \sü-ˈpīn\ *adj* 1 : lying on the back or with the face upward 2 : LETHARGIC, SLUGGISH; *also* : ABJECT

supp *or* **suppl** *abbr* supplement; supplementary

sup•per \ˈsə-pər\ *n* : the evening meal esp. when dinner is taken at midday — **sup•per•time** \-ˌtīm\ *n*

sup•plant \sə-ˈplant\ *vb* 1 : to take the place of (another) esp. by force or trickery 2 ♦ : to take the place of esp. by reason of superior excellence or power : REPLACE

♦ displace, replace, substitute, supersede

sup•ple \ˈsə-pəl\ *adj* **sup•pler; sup•plest** 1 : COMPLIANT, ADAPTABLE 2 ♦ : capable of bending without breaking or creasing : LIMBER

♦ flexible, limber, lissome, lithe, pliable, willowy

¹**sup•ple•ment** \ˈsə-plə-mənt\ *n* 1 ♦ : something that supplies a want or makes an addition 2 : a continuation (as of a book) containing corrections or additional material 3 : DIETARY SUPPLEMENT

♦ accretion, addition, augmentation, boost, expansion, gain, increase, increment, plus, proliferation, raise, rise

²**sup•ple•ment** \ˈsə-plə-ˌment\ *vb* : to fill up the deficiencies of : add to

sup•ple•men•tal \ˌsə-plə-ˈment-³l\ *adj* : serving to supplement

sup•ple•men•ta•ry \-ˈmen-tə-rē\ *adj* ♦ : added or serving as a supplement

♦ accessory, auxiliary, peripheral

sup•pli•ant \ˈsə-plē-ənt\ *n* : one who supplicates : PETITIONER

sup•pli•cant \ˈsə-pli-kənt\ *n* : one who supplicates : SUPPLIANT

sup•pli•cate \ˈsə-plə-ˌkāt\ *vb* **-cat•ed; -cat•ing** 1 : to make a humble entreaty; *esp* : to pray to God 2 ♦ : to ask earnestly and humbly : BESEECH

♦ appeal, beg, beseech, entreat, implore, importune, petition, plead, pray, solicit

sup•pli•ca•tion \ˌsə-plə-ˈkā-shən\ *n* ♦ : a humble and earnest petition

♦ appeal, cry, entreaty, petition, plea, prayer, solicitation, suit

¹**sup•ply** \sə-ˈplī\ *vb* **sup•plied; sup•ply•ing** 1 : to add as a supplement 2 ♦ : to satisfy the needs of 3 ♦ : to make available for use : FURNISH, PROVIDE — **sup•pli•er** *n*

♦ [2] accoutre, equip, fit, furnish, outfit, rig ♦ [3] deliver, feed, furnish, give, hand, hand over, provide

²**supply** *n, pl* **supplies** 1 a ♦ : the quantity or amount (as of a commodity) needed or available b : PROVISIONS, STORES — usu. used in pl. 2 : the act or process of filling a want or need : PROVISION 3 : the quantities of goods or services offered for sale at a particular time or at one price

♦ budget, fund, pool

sup•ply–side \sə-ˈplī-ˌsīd\ *adj* : of, relating to, or being an economic theory that recommends the reduction of tax rates to expand economic activity

¹**sup•port** \sə-ˈpȯrt\ *vb* 1 : to endure bravely or quietly : BEAR 2 ♦ : to take sides with : BACK 3 ♦ : to provide with food, clothing, and shelter 4 ♦ : to hold up or serve as a foundation for 5 : to uphold or defend as valid or right 6 ♦ : to provide with substantiation : CORROBORATE 7 ♦ : to give usu. supplementary help or aid to — **sup•port•ive** \-ˈpȯr-tiv\ *adj*

♦ [2] advocate, back, champion, endorse, patronize ♦ [3, 7] abet, aid, assist, back, help, prop ♦ [4] bear, bolster, brace, buttress, carry, prop, shore, stay, uphold ♦ [6] bear out, confirm, corroborate, substantiate, validate, verify, vindicate

²**support** *n* 1 ♦ : the act of supporting : the state of being supported 2 ♦ : one that supports 3 : help given in the form of money, information, or services

♦ [1] aid, assist, assistance, backing, boost, help, lift ♦ [2] brace, bulwark, buttress, mount, shore, stay, underpinning ♦ [2] dependence, mainstay, pillar, reliance, standby

sup•port•able *adj* ♦ : capable of being supported

♦ bearable, endurable, sufferable, sustainable, tolerable ♦ defensible, justifiable, maintainable, sustainable, tenable

sup•port•er *n* ♦ : one that supports or acts as a support

♦ advocate, apostle, backer, booster, champion, exponent, friend, promoter, proponent ♦ abettor, ally, backer, confederate, sympathizer

support group *n* : a group of people with common experiences and concerns who provide emotional and moral support for one another

sup•pose \sə-ˈpōz\ *vb* **sup•posed; sup•pos•ing** 1 ♦ : to assume to be true (as for the sake of argument) 2 : EXPECT ⟨I am *supposed* to go⟩ 3 ♦ : to think probable ⟨I ∼ so⟩ 4 ♦ : to hold as an opinion — **sup•pos•al** *n*

♦ [1] assume, postulate, premise, presume, presuppose ♦ [3] assume, conjecture, guess, presume, speculate, surmise, suspect ♦ [4] believe, consider, deem, feel, figure, guess, hold, imagine, think

sup•posed \sə-ˈpōzd, -ˈpō-zəd\ *adj* ♦ : held as an opinion; *also* : mistakenly believed ⟨a ∼ cure⟩

♦ apparent, assumed, evident, ostensible, reputed, seeming

sup•pos•ed•ly \-ˈpō-zəd-lē, -ˈpōzd-lē\ *adv* ♦ : as supposed

♦ apparently, evidently, ostensibly, presumably, seemingly

sup•pos•ing *conj* : if by way of hypothesis : on the assumption that

sup•po•si•tion \ˌsə-pə-ˈzi-shən\ *n* 1 ♦ : something that is supposed 2 : the act of supposing

♦ conjecture, hypothesis, proposition, theory ♦ assumption, postulate, premise, presumption ♦ conjecture, guess, surmise

sup•pos•i•to•ry \sə-'pä-zə-ˌtōr-ē\ *n, pl* **-ries** : a small easily melted mass of usu. medicated material for insertion (as into the rectum)

sup•press \sə-'pres\ *vb* **1** ♦ : to put down by authority or force : SUBDUE ⟨~ a revolt⟩ **2** : to keep from being known; *also* : to stop the publication or circulation of **3** ♦ : to hold back : REPRESS ⟨~ anger⟩ ⟨~ a cough⟩ — **sup•press•ible** \-'pre-sə-bəl\ *adj* — **sup•pres•sor** \-'pre-sər\ *n*

♦ [1] clamp down, crack down, crush, put down, quash, quell, repress, silence, snuff, squash, squelch, subdue ♦ [3] choke, pocket, repress, smother, stifle, strangle, swallow

sup•pres•sant \sə-'pres-ᵊnt\ *n* : an agent (as a drug) suppressing rather than eliminating something ⟨a cough ~⟩

sup•pres•sion \-'pre-shən\ *n* **1** : an act or instance of suppressing : the state of being suppressed **2** ♦ : the conscious intentional exclusion from consciousness of a thought or feeling

♦ constraint, inhibition, repression, restraint, self-control, self=restraint

sup•pu•rate \'sə-pyə-ˌrāt\ *vb* **-rat•ed; -rat•ing** : to form or give off pus — **sup•pu•ra•tion** \ˌsə-pyə-'rā-shən\ *n*

su•pra \'sü-prə, -ˌprä\ *adv* : earlier in this writing : ABOVE

su•pra•na•tion•al \ˌsü-prə-'na-shə-nəl, -ˌprä-\ *adj* : going beyond national boundaries, authority, or interests ⟨~ organizations⟩

su•prem•a•cist \sù-'pre-mə-sist\ *n* : an advocate of group supremacy

su•prem•a•cy \sù-'pre-mə-sē\ *n, pl* **-cies** **1** ♦ : the quality or state of being supreme **2** ♦ : supreme authority or power

♦ [1] distinction, excellence, greatness, preeminence, superiority ♦ [2] ascendancy, dominance, dominion, predominance, preeminence

su•preme \sù-'prēm\ *adj* **1** ♦ : highest in rank or authority **2** ♦ : highest in degree or quality ⟨~ among poets⟩ **3** ♦ : the best or most extreme of its kind : ULTIMATE ⟨the ~ sacrifice⟩ — **su•preme•ness** *n*

♦ [1, 2] arch, cardinal, central, chief, dominant, first, foremost, grand, key, main, paramount, predominant, preeminent, premier, primary, principal, sovereign ♦ [3] consummate, maximum, most, nth, paramount, top, ultimate, utmost

Supreme Being *n* ♦ : the Being perfect in power, wisdom, and goodness who is worshiped as creator and ruler of the universe

♦ Almighty, deity, Jehovah

su•preme•ly *adv* : in a supreme manner : so as to be supreme

supt *abbr* superintendent

sur•cease \'sər-ˌsēs\ *n* : a temporary or final ceasing : CESSATION ⟨a ~ from pain⟩

¹sur•charge \'sər-ˌchärj\ *vb* **1** : to fill to excess : OVERLOAD **2** : to apply a surcharge to (postage stamps) **3** : to charge too much or too fully

²surcharge *n* **1** : an extra fee or cost **2** : an excessive load or burden **3** : something officially printed on a postage stamp esp. to change its value

sur•cin•gle \'sər-ˌsiŋ-gəl\ *n* : a band put around a horse's body to make something (as a saddle) fast

¹sure \'shùr\ *adj* **sur•er; sur•est** **1** : firmly established **2** ♦ : suitable or fit to be relied on : TRUSTWORTHY, RELIABLE **3** ♦ : characterized by a lack of wavering or hesitation : CONFIDENT **4** : not to be disputed : UNDOUBTED **5** ♦ : bound to happen **6** : careful to remember or attend to something ⟨be ~ to lock the door⟩

♦ [2] dependable, good, reliable, responsible, safe, solid, steady, tried, true, trustworthy ♦ [3] assured, certain, clear, cocksure, confident, doubtless, positive, sanguine ♦ [5] certain, inevitable, necessary, unavoidable ♦ [5] infallible, surefire, unfailing

²sure *adv* : SURELY

sure•fire \'shùr-ˌfīr\ *adj* ♦ : certain to get results : DEPENDABLE

♦ infallible, sure, unfailing

sure•ly \'shùr-lē\ *adv* **1** : in a sure manner **2** ♦ : without doubt **3** : INDEED, REALLY

♦ certainly, definitely, doubtless, incontestably, indeed, indisputably, really, truly, undeniably, undoubtedly, unquestionably

sure•ness *n* ♦ : the quality or state of being sure

♦ assurance, certainty, certitude, confidence, conviction, positiveness ♦ dependability, reliability, solidity, trustworthiness

sure•ty \'shùr-ə-tē\ *n, pl* **-ties** **1** : SURENESS, CERTAINTY **2** ♦ : something that makes sure : GUARANTEE **3** ♦ : one who is a guarantor for another person

♦ [2] bond, contract, covenant, guarantee, guaranty, warranty ♦ [3] backer, guarantor, patron, sponsor

¹surf \'sərf\ *n* : waves that break upon the shore; *also* : the sound or foam of breaking waves

²surf *vb* **1** : to ride the surf (as on a surfboard) **2** : to scan the offerings of (as television or the Internet) for something of interest — **surf•er** *n* — **surf•ing** *n*

¹sur•face \'sər-fəs\ *n* **1** ♦ : the outside of an object or body **2** : outward aspect or appearance — **surface** *adj*

♦ exterior, face, outside, skin, veneer

²surface *vb* **sur•faced; sur•fac•ing** **1** : to give a surface to : make smooth **2** ♦ : to rise to the surface **3** ♦ : to come into public view

♦ arise, crop, emerge, materialize, spring

surf•board \'sərf-ˌbōrd\ *n* : a buoyant board used in surfing

¹sur•feit \'sər-fət\ *n* **1** ♦ : an overabundant supply : EXCESS **2** : excessive indulgence (as in food or drink) **3** : disgust caused by excess

♦ excess, fat, overabundance, overflow, overkill, overmuch, superabundance, superfluity, surplus

²surfeit *vb* ♦ : to feed, supply, or indulge to the point of surfeit

♦ glut, gorge, sate, stuff

surg *abbr* surgeon; surgery; surgical

¹surge \'sərj\ *vb* **surged; surg•ing** **1** : to rise and fall actively : TOSS **2** : to move in waves **3** : to rise suddenly to an excessive or abnormal value

²surge *n* **1** : a sweeping onward like a wave of the sea ⟨a ~ of emotion⟩ **2** ♦ : a large billow **3** : a transient sudden increase of current or voltage in an electrical circuit

♦ billow, swell, wave

sur•geon \'sər-jən\ *n* : a physician who specializes in surgery

sur•gery \'sər-jə-rē\ *n, pl* **-ger•ies** **1** : a branch of medicine concerned with the correction of physical defects, the repair of injuries, and the treatment of disease esp. by operations **2** : a room or area where surgery is performed **3** : the work done by a surgeon

sur•gi•cal \'sər-ji-kəl\ *adj* : of, relating to, or associated with surgeons or surgery — **sur•gi•cal•ly** \-k(ə-)lē\ *adv*

sur•ly \'sər-lē\ *adj* **sur•li•er; -est** ♦ : having a rude unfriendly disposition — **sur•li•ness** \-lē-nəs\ *n*

♦ glum, moody, morose, sulky, sullen ♦ bearish, bilious, cantankerous, disagreeable, dyspeptic, ill-humored, ill-tempered, ornery, splenetic

¹sur•mise \sər-'mīz\ *vb* **sur•mised; sur•mis•ing** ♦ : to form a notion of from scanty evidence : GUESS

♦ assume, conjecture, guess, presume, speculate, suppose, suspect

²surmise *n* ♦ : a thought or idea based on scanty evidence

♦ conjecture, guess, supposition

sur•mount \sər-'maùnt\ *vb* **1** ♦ : to prevail over : OVERCOME ⟨~ a problem⟩ **2** : to get to or lie at the top of

♦ beat, conquer, crush, defeat, master, overcome, prevail, subdue, triumph, win

sur•name \'sər-ˌnām\ *n* **1** : NICKNAME **2** : the name borne in common by members of a family

sur•pass \sər-'pas\ *vb* **1** ♦ : to be superior to in quality, degree, or performance : EXCEL **2** ♦ : to go beyond the range or powers of — **sur•pass•ing•ly** *adv*

♦ [1] beat, better, eclipse, excel, outdistance, outdo, outshine, outstrip, top, transcend ♦ [2] exceed, overreach, overrun, overshoot, overstep

sur•plice \'sər-pləs\ *n* : a loose white outer vestment usu. of knee length

sur•plus \'sər-(ˌ)pləs\ *n* **1** ♦ : quantity left over : EXCESS **2** : the excess of assets over liabilities

♦ excess, fat, overabundance, overflow, overkill, overmuch, superabundance, superfluity, surfeit

¹sur•prise \sər-'prīz\ *n* **1** ♦ : an attack made without warning **2** : a taking unawares **3** ♦ : something that surprises **4** ♦ : the state of being surprised : AMAZEMENT

♦ [1] ambush, trap ♦ [3] bolt, bombshell, jar, jolt ♦ [4] amazement, astonishment, shock, wonder

²surprise *vb* **sur•prised; sur•pris•ing** **1** ♦ : to come upon and attack unexpectedly **2** : to take unawares **3** ♦ : to strike with wonder or amazement esp. because unexpected : AMAZE **4** : to cause astonishment or surprise

♦ [1] ambush, waylay ♦ [3] amaze, astonish, astound, bowl, dumbfound, flabbergast, floor, shock, startle, stun, stupefy

sur·pris·ing *adj* ♦ : of a nature that excites surprise

♦ amazing, astonishing, astounding, eye-opening, shocking, startling, stunning ♦ awesome, eye-opening, fabulous, marvelous (*or* marvellous), miraculous, portentous, prodigious, stupendous, sublime, wonderful

sur·pris·ing·ly \-'prī-ziŋ-lē\ *adv* **1** : in a surprising manner or degree **2** : it is surprising that
sur·re·al \sə-'rē-əl, -'rēl\ *adj* **1** : having the intense irrational reality of a dream **2** : of or relating to surrealism ⟨∼ art⟩ — **sur·re·al·ly** *adv*
sur·re·al·ism \sə-'rē-ə-ˌli-zəm\ *n* : art, literature, or theater characterized by fantastic or incongruous imagery or effects produced by unnatural juxtapositions and combinations — **sur·re·al·ist** \-list\ *n or adj* — **sur·re·al·is·tic** \sə-ˌrē-ə-'lis-tik\ *adj* — **sur·re·al·is·ti·cal·ly** \-ti-k(ə-)lē\ *adv*
¹sur·ren·der \sə-'ren-dər\ *vb* **1** ♦ : to yield to the power of another ; give up under compulsion **2** ♦ : to give up completely or agree to forgo esp. in favor of another : RELINQUISH **3** ♦ : to give (oneself) over to something (as an influence)

♦ [1] blink, bow, budge, capitulate, concede, fall, give in, knuckle under, quit, submit, succumb, yield ♦ [2] cede, deliver, give up, hand over, leave, relinquish, render, turn over, yield ♦ [3] bow, give in, submit, succumb, yield

²surrender *n* ♦ : the act of giving up or yielding oneself or the possession of something to another

♦ capitulation, relinquishment, submission

sur·rep·ti·tious \ˌsər-əp-'ti-shəs\ *adj* ♦ : done, made, or acquired by stealth : CLANDESTINE — **sur·rep·ti·tious·ly** *adv*

♦ clandestine, covert, furtive, hugger-mugger, private, secret, sneak, sneaky, stealthy, undercover, underground, underhanded

sur·rey \'sər-ē\ *n, pl* **surreys** : a 2-seated horse-drawn carriage
sur·ro·ga·cy \'sər-ə-gə-sē\ *n* : SURROGATE MOTHERHOOD
sur·ro·gate \'sər-ə-ˌgāt, -gət\ *n* **1** : DEPUTY, SUBSTITUTE **2** : a law officer in some states with authority in the probate of wills, the settlement of estates, and the appointment of guardians **3** : SURROGATE MOTHER
surrogate mother *n* : a woman who becomes pregnant (as by surgical implantation of a fertilized egg) in order to carry the fetus for another woman — **surrogate motherhood** *n*
sur·round \sə-'raund\ *vb* **1** ♦ : to enclose on all sides : ENCIRCLE **2** : to enclose so as to cut off retreat or escape

♦ circle, encircle, enclose, encompass, ring

sur·round·ings \sə-'raun-diŋz\ *n pl* ♦ : conditions by which one is surrounded

♦ atmosphere, climate, environment, environs, medium, milieu, setting

surround sound *n* : sound reproduction that uses three or more transmission channels
sur·tax \'sər-ˌtaks\ *n* : an additional tax over and above a normal tax
sur·tout \(ˌ)sər-'tü\ *n* : a man's long close-fitting overcoat
surv *abbr* survey; surveying; surveyor
sur·veil·lance \sər-'vā-ləns\ *n* : close watch; *also* : SUPERVISION
¹sur·vey \sər-'vā\ *vb* **sur·veyed; sur·vey·ing** **1** ♦ : to look over and examine closely **2** : to find and represent the contours, measurements, and position of a part of the earth's surface (as a tract of land) **3** : to view or study something as a whole **4** ♦ : to query (someone) in order to collect data for the analysis of some aspect of a group or area — **sur·vey·or** \-ər\ *n*

♦ [1] audit, check, examine, inspect, review, scan, scrutinize ♦ [4] canvass, poll, solicit

²sur·vey \'sər-ˌvā\ *n, pl* **surveys** ♦ : the act or an instance of surveying; *also* : something that is surveyed

♦ audit, check, checkup, examination, inspection, review, scan, scrutiny

sur·vive \sər-'vīv\ *vb* **sur·vived; sur·viv·ing** **1** : to remain alive or existent **2** ♦ : to continue to exist or live after **3** ♦ : to continue to function or prosper — **sur·viv·al** *n* — **sur·vi·vor** \-'vī-vər\ *n*

♦ [2] ride ♦ [3] hold, hold out, keep up, last, prevail

sus·cep·ti·bil·i·ty \sə-ˌsep-tə-'bi-lə-tē\ *n* : the quality or state of being susceptible; *esp* : lack of ability to resist some extraneous agent (as a pathogen or drug)
sus·cep·ti·ble \-'sep-tə-bəl\ *adj* **1** : of such a nature as to permit ⟨words ∼ of being misunderstood⟩ **2** ♦ : having little re-

sistance to a stimulus or agency ⟨∼ to colds⟩ **3** ♦ : capable of being easily influenced

♦ [2] exposed, liable, open, sensitive, subject, vulnerable ♦ [3] easy, gullible, naive

su·shi \'sü-shē\ *n* : cold rice formed into various shapes and garnished esp. with bits of raw fish or seafood
¹sus·pect \'səs-ˌpekt, sə-'spekt\ *adj* ♦ : regarded with suspicion; *also* : QUESTIONABLE ⟨his claim is ∼⟩

♦ debatable, disputable, doubtful, dubious, equivocal, fishy, problematic, questionable, shady, shaky, suspicious

²sus·pect \'səs-ˌpekt\ *n* : one who is suspected (as of a crime)
³sus·pect \sə-'spekt\ *vb* **1** ♦ : to have doubts of : MISTRUST **2** : to imagine to be guilty without proof **3** ♦ : to imagine to exist or be true, likely, or probable : SURMISE

♦ [1] distrust, doubt, mistrust, question ♦ [3] assume, conjecture, guess, presume, speculate, suppose, surmise

sus·pend \sə-'spend\ *vb* **1** : to bar temporarily from a privilege, office, or function **2** : to stop temporarily : make inactive for a time **3** : to withhold (judgment) for a time **4** ♦ : to fasten to some elevated point without support from below; *esp* : to hang so as to be free except at one point **5** : to keep from falling or sinking by some invisible support

♦ dangle, hang, sling, swing

sus·pend·er \sə-'spen-dər\ *n* : one of two supporting straps which pass over the shoulders and to which the pants are fastened
sus·pense \sə-'spens\ *n* **1** : the state of being suspended : SUSPENSION **2** : mental uncertainty : ANXIETY **3** : excitement as to an outcome — **sus·pense·ful** *adj*
sus·pen·sion \sə-'spen-chən\ *n* **1** ♦ : the act of suspending : the state or period of being suspended **2** : the state of a substance when its particles are mixed with but undissolved in a fluid or solid; *also* : a substance in this state **3** : something suspended **4** : the system of devices supporting the upper part of a vehicle on the axles

♦ abeyance, doldrums, dormancy, latency, quiescence

sus·pi·cion \sə-'spi-shən\ *n* **1** ♦ : the act or an instance of suspecting something wrong without proof **2** : a barely detectable amount : TRACE

♦ distrust, doubt, incertitude, misgiving, mistrust, skepticism, uncertainty

sus·pi·cious \sə-'spi-shəs\ *adj* **1** ♦ : open to or arousing suspicion **2** ♦ : inclined to suspect **3** ♦ : showing suspicion ⟨is ∼ of strangers⟩

♦ [1] debatable, disputable, doubtful, dubious, equivocal, fishy, problematic, questionable, shady, shaky, suspect ♦ [2, 3] distrustful, doubtful, dubious, mistrustful, skeptical, uncertain, undecided, unsettled, unsure

sus·pi·cious·ly *adv* ♦ : with suspicion

♦ askance, distrustfully, dubiously, mistrustfully

sus·tain \sə-'stān\ *vb* **1** : to provide with nourishment **2** : to keep going : PROLONG ⟨∼ed effort⟩ **3** : to hold up : PROP **4** ♦ : to hold up under : ENDURE **5** ♦ : to go through : SUFFER ⟨∼ a broken arm⟩ **6** : to support as true, legal, or valid ⟨the objection was ∼ed⟩ **7** : PROVE, CORROBORATE

♦ [4] abide, bear, brook, countenance, endure, meet, stand, stick out, stomach, support, take, tolerate ♦ [5] endure, experience, feel, have, know, see, suffer, taste, undergo

sus·tain·able \səs-'tā-nə-bəl\ *adj* ♦ : capable of being sustained

♦ defensible, justifiable, maintainable, supportable, tenable ♦ bearable, endurable, sufferable, tolerable

sus·te·nance \'səs-tə-nəns\ *n* **1** : FOOD, NOURISHMENT **2** : a supplying with the necessities of life **3** : something that sustains or supports
su·ture \'sü-chər\ *n* **1** : material or a stitch for sewing a wound together **2** : a seam or line along which two things or parts are joined by or as if by sewing
SUV \ˌes-ˌyü-'vē\ *n* : a vehicle similar to a station wagon but built on a light-truck chassis
su·zer·ain \'sü-zə-rən, -ˌrān\ *n* **1** : a feudal lord **2** : a nation that has political control over the foreign relations of another nation — **su·zer·ain·ty** \-tē\ *n*
svc *or* **svce** *abbr* service
svelte \'sfelt\ *adj* **svelt·er; svelt·est** ♦ : spare in frame or flesh : SLENDER

♦ lean, skinny, slender, slim, spare

svgs *abbr* savings
SW *abbr* **1** shortwave **2** southwest
¹**swab** \'swäb\ *n* **1** : MOP **2** : a wad of absorbent material esp. for applying medicine or for cleaning; *also* : a sample taken with a swab **3** ♦ : a member of a ship's crew : SAILOR

♦ gob, jack, jack-tar, mariner, sailor, seaman, tar

²**swab** *vb* **swabbed; swab·bing** : to use a swab on : MOP
swad·dle \'swäd-ᵊl\ *vb* **swad·dled; swad·dling 1** : to bind (an infant) in bands of cloth **2** : to wrap up : SWATHE
swaddling clothes *n pl* : bands of cloth wrapped around an infant
swag \'swag\ *n* ♦ : stolen goods : LOOT

♦ booty, loot, plunder, spoil

swag·ger \'swa-gər\ *vb* **1** ♦ : to walk with a conceited swing or strut **2** ♦ : to puff oneself up in speech : BOAST — **swagger** *n*

♦ [1] stalk, strut ♦ [2] boast, brag, crow, plume

swag·man \'swag-mən\ *n* : a person who has no job and wanders from place to place : VAGRANT
Swa·hi·li \swä-'hē-lē\ *n* : a language that is a trade and governmental language over much of eastern Africa and the Congo region
swain \'swān\ *n* **1** : RUSTIC; *esp* : SHEPHERD **2** ♦ : a male admirer or suitor

♦ beau, boyfriend, fellow, man ♦ gallant, suitor, wooer

SWAK *abbr* sealed with a kiss
¹**swal·low** \'swä-lō\ *n* : any of numerous small long-winged migratory birds that often have a deeply forked tail
²**swallow** *vb* **1** : to take into the stomach through the throat **2** : to envelop or take in as if by swallowing **3** ♦ : to accept or believe without question, protest, or anger **4** ♦ : to keep from expressing or showing

♦ [3] accept, believe, credit, trust ♦ [4] choke, pocket, repress, smother, stifle, strangle, suppress

³**swallow** *n* **1** : an act of swallowing **2** ♦ : an amount that can be swallowed at one time

♦ draft, drag, drink, nip, quaff, shot, slug, snort, swig

swal·low·tail \'swä-lō-ˌtāl\ *n* **1** : a deeply forked and tapering tail like that of a swallow **2** : TAILCOAT **3** : any of various large butterflies with the border of each hind wing usu. drawn out into a process resembling a tail — **swal·low–tailed** \-ˌtāld\ *adj*
swam *past of* SWIM
swa·mi \'swä-mē\ *n* : a Hindu ascetic or religious teacher
¹**swamp** \'swämp\ *n* ♦ : a spongy wetland — **swamp** *adj* — **swampy** *adj*

♦ bog, fen, marsh, mire, morass, slough

²**swamp** *vb* **1** ♦ : to fill or become filled with or as if with water **2** ♦ : to overwhelm numerically or by an excess of something

♦ [1] deluge, drown, engulf, flood, inundate, overflow, overwhelm, submerge ♦ [2] carry away, crush, devastate, floor, oppress, overcome, overpower, overwhelm, prostrate, snow under

swamp·land \-ˌland\ *n* : a spongy wetland : SWAMP
swan \'swän\ *n, pl* **swans** *also* **swan** : any of various heavy-bodied long-necked mostly pure white swimming birds related to the geese
¹**swank** \'swaŋk\ *or* **swanky** \'swaŋ-kē\ *adj* **swank·er** *or* **swank·i·er; -est** : showily smart and dashing; *also* : fashionably elegant ⟨a ~ hotel⟩
²**swank** *n* **1** ♦ : arrogance or ostentation of dress or manner : PRETENTIOUSNESS **2** : ELEGANCE

♦ flamboyance, flashiness, gaudiness, glitz, ostentation, pretentiousness, showiness

swans·down \'swänz-ˌdau̇n\ *n* **1** : the very soft down of a swan used esp. for trimming **2** : a soft thick cotton flannel
swan song *n* : a farewell appearance, act, or pronouncement
¹**swap** \'swäp\ *vb* **swapped; swap·ping** ♦ : to give in trade : EXCHANGE

♦ change, commute, exchange, shift, substitute, switch, trade

²**swap** *n* ♦ : to give in trade

♦ barter, commutation, exchange, trade, truck

sward \'swȯrd\ *n* : the grassy surface of land
¹**swarm** \'swȯrm\ *n* **1** : a great number of honeybees leaving together from a hive with a queen to start a new colony; *also* : a hive of bees **2** ♦ : a large crowd

♦ army, crowd, crush, drove, flock, horde, host, legion, mob, multitude, press, throng

²**swarm** *vb* **1** : to form in a swarm and depart from a hive **2** : to throng together : gather in great numbers **3** ♦ : to beset or surround in a swarm

♦ crowd, flock, mob, throng

swart \'swȯrt\ *adj* : SWARTHY
swar·thy \'swȯr-thē, -thē\ *adj* **swar·thi·er; -est** : dark in color or complexion : dark-skinned
swash \'swäsh\ *vb* ♦ : to move about with a splashing sound — **swash** *n*

♦ lap, plash, slosh, splash

swash·buck·ler \-ˌbə-klər\ *n* : a swaggering or daring soldier or adventurer — **swash·buck·ling** *adj*
swas·ti·ka \'swäs-ti-kə\ *n* : a symbol or ornament in the form of a cross with the ends of the arms bent at right angles
¹**swat** \'swät\ *vb* **swat·ted; swat·ting** ♦ : to hit sharply ⟨~ a fly⟩ ⟨~ a ball⟩ — **swat·ter** *n*

♦ bat, clout, crack, hit, slam, strike

²**swat** *n* : a powerful or crushing blow
SWAT *abbr* Special Weapons and Tactics
swatch \'swäch\ *n* : a sample piece (as of fabric) or a collection of samples
swath \'swäth, 'swȯth\ *or* **swathe** \'swäth, 'swȯth, 'swäth\ *n* **1** : a row of cut grass or grain **2** : the sweep of a scythe or mowing machine or the path cut in mowing
swathe \'swäth, 'swȯth, 'swäth\ *vb* **swathed; swath·ing** ♦ : to bind or wrap with or as if with a bandage

♦ embrace, enclose, encompass, enfold, enshroud, envelop, invest, lap, mantle, shroud, veil, wrap

¹**sway** \'swā\ *n* **1** : a gentle swinging from side to side **2** ♦ : controlling influence or power

♦ authority, clout, influence, power, pull, weight

²**sway** *vb* **1** ♦ : to swing gently from side to side **2** : RULE, GOVERN **3** : to cause to swing from side to side **4 a** : BEND, SWERVE **b** : to exert a guiding or controlling influence on : INFLUENCE ⟨tried to ~ the jury⟩

♦ careen, lurch, pitch, rock, roll, seesaw, toss, wobble

sway·backed \'swā-ˌbakt\ *also* **sway·back** \-ˌbak\ *adj* : having an abnormally sagging back ⟨a ~ mare⟩ — **swayback** *n*
¹**swear** \'swar\ *vb* **swore** \'swōr\; **sworn** \'swōrn\; **swear·ing 1** ♦ : to make a solemn statement or promise under oath **2** ♦ : to assert or promise emphatically or earnestly **3** : to administer an oath to **4** : to bind by or as if by an oath **5** : to use profane or obscene language — **swear·er** *n*

♦ [1] attest, depose, testify, witness ♦ [2] covenant, pledge, promise, vow

²**swear** *n* : a profane or obscene word
swear in *vb* : to induct into office by administration of an oath
¹**sweat** \'swet\ *vb* **sweat** *or* **sweat·ed; sweat·ing 1** : to excrete salty moisture from glands of the skin : PERSPIRE **2 a** : to form drops of moisture on the surface **b** ♦ : to become exuded through pores or a porous surface **3** ♦ : to work so that one sweats : TOIL **4** : to cause to sweat **5** : to draw out or get rid of by or as if by sweating **6** : to make a person overwork **7** ♦ : to undergo anxiety or mental or emotional distress — **sweaty** *adj*

♦ [2b] bleed, exude, ooze, percolate, seep, strain, weep ♦ [3] drudge, fag, grub, labor (*or* labour), toil ♦ [7] bother, fear, fret, stew, trouble, worry

²**sweat** *n* ♦ : hard work

♦ drudgery, grind, labor (*or* labour), toil, travail

sweat·er \'swe-tər\ *n* **1** : one that sweats **2** : a knitted or crocheted jacket or pullover
sweat out *vb* ♦ : to endure or wait through the course of

♦ bear, deliver, drop, have, produce

sweat·shirt \'swet-ˌshərt\ *n* : a loose collarless pullover usu. of heavy cotton jersey
sweat·shop \'swet-ˌshäp\ *n* : a shop or factory in which workers are employed for long hours at low wages and under unhealthy conditions
Swed *abbr* Sweden
swede \'swēd\ *n* **1** *cap* : a native or inhabitant of Sweden **2** *chiefly Brit* : RUTABAGA
Swed·ish \'swē-dish\ *n* **1** : the language of Sweden **2 Swedish** *pl* : the people of Sweden — **Swedish** *adj*
¹**sweep** \'swēp\ *vb* **swept** \'swept\; **sweep·ing 1** : to remove or clean by or as if by brushing **2** : to destroy completely; *also* : to remove or take with a single swift movement **3** : to remove from sight or consideration **4** ♦ : to move over with speed and force

⟨the tide *swept* over the shore⟩ **5** : to win an overwhelming victory in; *also* : to win all the games or contests of **6** ♦ : to move or extend in a wide curve **7** ♦ : to move swiftly, forcefully, or devastatingly — **sweep•er** *n*

♦ [4] bowl, breeze, coast, drift, flow, glide, roll, sail, skim, slide, slip, stream, whisk ♦ [6] arc, arch, bend, bow, crook, curve, hook, round, swerve, wheel

²**sweep** *n* **1** : something (as a long oar) that operates with a sweeping motion **2** : a clearing off or away **3** : a winning of all the contests or prizes in a competition **4** : a sweeping movement **5** : CURVE, BEND **6** ♦ : extent of treatment, activity, or influence : SCOPE

♦ amplitude, breadth, compass, extent, range, reach, realm, scope, width

sweeping *adj* : EXTENSIVE ⟨∼ reforms⟩; *also* : indiscriminately inclusive ⟨∼ generalities⟩
sweep•ings \'swē-piŋz\ *n pl* : things collected by sweeping
sweep–sec•ond hand \'swēp-,se-kənd-\ *n* : a hand marking seconds on a timepiece
sweep•stakes \'swēp-,stāks\ *also* **sweep•stake** \-,stāk\ *n, pl* **sweepstakes 1** : a race or contest in which the entire prize may go to the winner **2** : any of various lotteries
¹**sweet** \'swēt\ *adj* **1** : being or causing the one of the four basic taste sensations that is caused esp. by table sugar and is identified esp. by the taste buds at the front of the tongue; *also* : pleasing to the taste **2** ♦ : marked by gentle good humor or kindliness : AGREEABLE **3** ♦ : pleasing to a sense other than taste ⟨a ∼ smell⟩ ⟨∼ music⟩ **4** : not stale or spoiled : WHOLESOME ⟨∼ milk⟩ **5** : not salted ⟨∼ butter⟩ **6** ♦ : much loved — **sweet•ish** *adj* — **sweet•ly** *adv*

♦ [2] affable, agreeable, amiable, genial, good-natured, gracious, nice, well-disposed ♦ [3] ambrosial, aromatic, fragrant, redolent, savory, scented ♦ [6] beloved, darling, dear, favorite (*or* favourite), loved, pet, precious, special ♦ [6] adorable, endearing, lovable, winning

²**sweet** *n* **1** : something sweet **2** : a dearly loved person : DARLING
sweet•bread \'swēt-,bred\ *n* : the pancreas or thymus of an animal (as a calf or lamb) used for food
sweet•bri•ar *or* **sweet•bri•er** \-,brī-ər\ *n* : a thorny Old World rose with fragrant white to deep pink flowers
sweet clover *n* : any of a genus of erect legumes widely grown for soil improvement or hay
sweet corn *n* : corn of a variety having soft kernels containing a high percentage of sugar
sweet•en \'swēt-ᵊn\ *vb* **sweet•ened; sweet•en•ing** : to make sweet — **sweet•en•er** *n* — **sweet•en•ing** *n*
sweet•heart \'swēt-,härt\ *n* ♦ : one who is loved

♦ beloved, darling, dear, flame, honey, love, sweet

sweet•meat \-,mēt\ *n* : CANDY 1
sweet•ness *n* ♦ : the quality or state of being sweet

♦ agreeableness, amenity, amiability, geniality, graciousness, niceness, pleasantness

sweet pea *n* : a garden plant of the legume family with climbing stems and fragrant flowers of many colors; *also* : its flower
sweet pepper *n* : any of various large mild thick-walled fruits of a pepper; *also* : a plant bearing sweet peppers
sweet potato *n* : a tropical vine related to the morning glory; *also* : its large sweet edible root
sweet–talk \'swēt-,tȯk\ *vb* : FLATTER, COAX — **sweet talk** *n*
sweet tooth *n* : a craving or fondness for sweet food
sweet wil•liam \,swēt-'wil-yəm\ *n, often cap W* : a widely cultivated Old World pink with small white to deep red or purple flowers often showily spotted, banded, or mottled
¹**swell** \'swel\ *vb* **swelled; swelled** *or* **swol•len** \'swō-lən\; **swell•ing 1** ♦ : to grow big or make bigger **2** : to expand or distend abnormally or excessively ⟨a *swollen* joint⟩; *also* : BULGE **3** : to fill or be filled with emotion (as pride)

♦ accumulate, appreciate, balloon, build, burgeon, enlarge, escalate, expand, increase, mount, multiply, mushroom, proliferate, rise, snowball, wax ♦ add, aggrandize, amplify, augment, boost, compound, extend, increase, raise, up

²**swell** *n* **1** ♦ : a long crestless wave or series of waves in the open sea **2** : the condition of being protuberant **3** : a person dressed in the height of fashion; *also* : a person of high social position

♦ billow, surge, wave

³**swell** *adj* **1** : STYLISH; *also* : socially prominent **2** : very good of its kind : EXCELLENT
swelled head *n* : an exaggerated opinion of oneself : SELF-CONCEIT

swell•ing *n* ♦ : something that is swollen; *specif* : an abnormal bodily protuberance or localized enlargement

♦ bump, knot, lump, nodule

swel•ter \'swel-tər\ *vb* **1** : to be faint or oppressed with the heat **2** : to become exceedingly hot — **swel•ter•ing** \-tə-riŋ\ *adj*
swept *past and past part of* SWEEP
swerve \'swərv\ *vb* **swerved; swerv•ing** ♦ : to move abruptly aside from a straight line or course — **swerve** *n*

♦ sheer, veer, yaw *Ant* straighten

¹**swift** \'swift\ *adj* **1** ♦ : moving or capable of moving with great speed **2** : occurring suddenly **3** : READY, ALERT

♦ breakneck, breathless, brisk, dizzy, fast, fleet, hasty, lightning, nippy, quick, rapid, rattling, snappy, speedy

²**swift** *n* : any of numerous small insect-eating birds with long narrow wings
swift•ly *adv* ♦ : in a swift manner : with speed

♦ apace, briskly, fast, full tilt, hastily, posthaste, presto, pronto, quick, quickly, rapidly, soon, speedily

swift•ness *n* ♦ : the quality or state of being swift; *also* : the fact of being swift

♦ celerity, fastness, fleetness, haste, hurry, quickness, rapidity, speed, velocity

¹**swig** \'swig\ *vb* **swigged; swig•ging** ♦ : to drink in long drafts

♦ drink, guzzle, imbibe, quaff, sup, toss

²**swig** *n* ♦ : a quantity drunk at one time

♦ draft, drag, drink, nip, quaff, shot, slug, snort, swallow

¹**swill** \'swil\ *vb* **1** : to swallow greedily : GUZZLE **2** : to feed (as hogs) on swill
²**swill** *n* **1** : food for animals composed of edible refuse mixed with liquid **2** : GARBAGE **3** : a draft of liquor
¹**swim** \'swim\ *vb* **swam** \'swam\; **swum** \'swəm\; **swim•ming 1** : to propel oneself along in water by natural means (as by hands and legs, by tail, or by fins) **2** : to glide smoothly along **3** : FLOAT **4** : to be covered with or as if with a liquid **5** ♦ : to be dizzy ⟨his head *swam*⟩ **6** : to cross or go over by swimming ⟨*swam* the river⟩ — **swim•mer** *n*

♦ reel, spin, whirl

²**swim** *n* **1** : an act of swimming **2** : the main current of activity ⟨in the ∼⟩
swim•ming *n* : the action, art, or sport of swimming and diving
swimming pool *n* : a tank (as of concrete or plastic) designed for swimming
swim•suit \'swim-,süt\ *n* : a suit for swimming or bathing
swim•wear \'swim-,wer\ *n* : clothing for wear while swimming or bathing
¹**swin•dle** \'swin-dᵊl\ *vb* **swin•dled; swin•dling** ♦ : to take money or property from by fraud or deceit : CHEAT

♦ bleed, cheat, chisel, cozen, defraud, fleece, hustle, mulct, rook, shortchange, skin, squeeze, stick, sting, victimize

²**swindle** *n* ♦ : an act or instance of swindling

♦ hustle, racket

swin•dler *n* ♦ : one that swindles

♦ cheat, dodger, hoaxer, shark, sharper, trickster

swine \'swīn\ *n, pl* **swine 1** : any of a family of stout short-legged hoofed mammals with bristly skin and a long flexible snout; *esp* : one widely raised as a meat animal **2** ♦ : a contemptible person

♦ beast, boor, churl, clown, creep, cretin, cur, heel, jerk, joker, louse, lout, scum, skunk, slob, snake

¹**swing** \'swiŋ\ *vb* **swung** \'swəŋ\; **swing•ing 1** : to move or cause to move rapidly in an arc **2** : to sway or cause to sway back and forth **3** ♦ : to hang so as to move freely back and forth or in a curve **4** : to be executed by hanging **5** : to move or turn on a hinge or pivot **6** ♦ : to manage or handle successfully **7** : to march or walk with free swaying movements **8** : to have a steady pulsing rhythm; *also* : to play swing music **9** : to be lively and up-to-date; *also* : to engage freely in sex **10** ♦ : to cause to face or move in another direction — **swing•er** *n* — **swing•ing** *adj*

♦ [3] dangle, hang, sling, suspend ♦ [6] contend with, cope with, grapple with, handle, manage, maneuver (*or* manoeuvre), negotiate, treat ♦ [10] divert, swerve, turn, veer, wheel, whip

²**swing** *n* **1** : the act of swinging **2** : a swinging blow, movement,

or rhythm **3 :** the distance through which something swings : FLUCTUATION **4 :** progression of an activity or process ⟨in full ∼⟩ **5 :** a seat suspended by a rope or chain for swinging back and forth for pleasure **6 :** jazz music played esp. by a large band and marked by a steady lively rhythm, simple harmony, and a basic melody often submerged in improvisation

³**swing** *adj* **1 :** of or relating to swing music **2 :** that may swing often decisively either way (as on an issue) ⟨∼ voters⟩

swin·ish \'swī-nish\ *adj* **:** of, suggesting, or characteristic of swine

¹**swipe** \'swīp\ *n* **:** a strong sweeping blow

²**swipe** *vb* **swiped; swip·ing 1 :** to strike or wipe with a sweeping motion **2 ♦ :** to take or appropriate without right and with intent to keep **:** PILFER **3 :** to slide (a card having a magnetic code) through a reading device

   ♦ appropriate, filch, hook, misappropriate, nip, pilfer, pocket, purloin, snitch, steal, thieve

swirl \'swərl\ *vb* ♦ **:** to move or cause to move with a whirling motion — **swirl** *n* — **swirly** \'swər-lē\ *adj*

   ♦ pivot, revolve, roll, rotate, spin, swing, turn, twirl, twist, wheel, whirl

¹**swish** \'swish\ *n* **1 ♦ :** a prolonged hissing sound **2 :** a light sweeping or brushing sound

   ♦ fizz, hiss, sizzle, whish, whiz

²**swish** *vb* **:** to move, pass, swing, or whirl with the sound of a swish

Swiss \'swis\ *n, pl* **Swiss :** a native or inhabitant of Switzerland **2 :** a hard cheese with large holes — **Swiss** *adj*

Swiss chard *n* **:** a beet having large leaves and succulent stalks often cooked as a vegetable

¹**switch** \'swich\ *n* **1 ♦ :** a slender flexible whip, rod, or twig **2 :** a blow with a switch **3 :** a shift from one thing to another; *also* **:** change from the usual **4 :** a device for adjusting the rails of a track so that a locomotive or train may be turned from one track to another; *also* **:** a railroad siding **5 :** a device for making, breaking, or changing the connections in an electrical circuit **6 :** a heavy strand of hair often used in addition to a person's own hair for some coiffures

   ♦ lash, scourge, whip

²**switch** *vb* **1 ♦ :** to punish or urge on with a switch **2 :** WHISK ⟨a cow ∼*ing* her tail⟩ **3 :** to shift or turn by operating a switch **4** ♦ **:** to make a shift in or exchange of **:** CHANGE

   ♦ [1] flail, flog, hide, lash, scourge, slash, thrash, whale, whip
   ♦ [4] change, commute, exchange, shift, substitute, swap, trade

switch·back \'swich-ˌbak\ *n* **:** a zigzag road, trail, or section of railroad tracks for climbing a steep hill

switch·blade \-ˌblād\ *n* **:** a pocket-knife with a spring-operated blade

switch·board \-ˌbōrd\ *n* **:** a panel for controlling the operation of a number of electric circuits; *esp* **:** one used to make and break telephone connections

switch–hit·ter \-'hi-tər\ *n* **:** a baseball player who bats either right-handed or left-handed — **switch–hit** \-'hit\ *vb*

switch·man \'swich-mən\ *n* **:** one who attends a railroad switch

Switz *abbr* Switzerland

¹**swiv·el** \'swi-vəl\ *n* **:** a device joining two parts so that one or both can turn freely

²**swivel** *vb* **-eled** *or* **-elled; -el·ing** *or* **-el·ling :** to swing or turn on or as if on a swivel

swiv·et \'swi-vət\ *n* **:** an agitated state

swiz·zle stick \'swi-zəl-\ *n* **:** a stick used to stir mixed drinks

swollen *past part of* SWELL

¹**swoon** \'swün\ *vb* ♦ **:** to undergo a temporary loss of consciousness **:** FAINT

   ♦ black out, faint, pass out

²**swoon** *n* ♦ **:** a partial or total loss of consciousness; *also* **:** a state of suspended animation

   ♦ blackout, faint, knockout

swoop \'swüp\ *vb* **:** to move with a sweep ⟨the eagle ∼*ed* down on its prey⟩ — **swoop** *n*

swoopy \'swü-pē\ *adj* **:** having lines that extend in a wide curve ⟨a ∼ silhouette⟩

swop *chiefly Brit var of* SWAP

sword \'sōrd\ *n* **1 :** a weapon with a long blade for cutting or thrusting **2 :** the use of force

sword·fish \-ˌfish\ *n* **:** a very large ocean fish used for food that has the upper jaw prolonged into a long swordlike beak

sword·play \-ˌplā\ *n* **:** the art or skill of wielding a sword

swords·man \'sōrdz-mən\ *n* **:** one skilled in swordplay; *esp* **:** FENCER

sword·tail \'sōrd-ˌtāl\ *n* **:** a small brightly marked Central American fish often kept in aquariums

swore *past of* SWEAR

sworn *past part of* SWEAR

swum *past part of* SWIM

swung *past and past part of* SWING

syb·a·rite \'si-bə-ˌrīt\ *n* **:** a lover of luxury **:** VOLUPTUARY — **syb·a·rit·ic** \ˌsi-bə-'ri-tik\ *adj*

syc·a·more \'si-kə-ˌmōr\ *n* **:** a large spreading tree chiefly of the eastern and central U.S. that has light brown flaky bark and small round fruits hanging on long stalks

sy·co·phant \'si-kə-fənt\ *n* **:** a servile flatterer — **sy·co·phan·tic** \ˌsi-kə-'fan-tik\ *adj*

syl *or* **syll** *abbr* syllable

syl·lab·i·ca·tion \sə-ˌla-bə-'kā-shən\ *n* **:** the division of words into syllables

syl·lab·i·fy \sə-'la-bə-ˌfī\ *vb* **-fied; -fy·ing :** to form or divide into syllables — **syl·lab·i·fi·ca·tion** \-ˌla-bə-fə-'kā-shən\ *n*

syl·la·ble \'si-lə-bəl\ *n* **:** a unit of spoken language consisting of an uninterrupted utterance and forming either a whole word (as *cat*) or a commonly recognized division of a word (as *syl* in *syl-la-ble*); *also* **:** one or more letters representing such a unit — **syl·lab·ic** \sə-'la-bik\ *adj*

syl·la·bus \'si-lə-bəs\ *n, pl* **-bi** \-ˌbī\ *or* **-bus·es :** a summary containing the heads or main topics of a speech, book, or course of study

syl·lo·gism \'si-lə-ˌji-zəm\ *n* **:** a logical scheme of a formal argument consisting of a major and a minor premise and a conclusion which must logically be true if the premises are true — **syl·lo·gis·tic** \ˌsi-lə-'jis-tik\ *adj*

sylph \'silf\ *n* **1 :** an imaginary being inhabiting the air **2 :** a slender graceful woman or girl

syl·van \'sil-vən\ *adj* **1 :** living or located in a wooded area; *also* **:** of, relating to, or characteristic of forest **2 :** abounding in woods or trees

sym *abbr* **1** symbol **2** symmetrical

sym·bi·o·sis \ˌsim-bī-'ō-səs, -bē-\ *n, pl* **-o·ses** \-ˌsēz\ **:** the living together in close association of two dissimilar organisms esp. when mutually beneficial — **sym·bi·ot·ic** \-'ä-tik\ *adj*

sym·bol \'sim-bəl\ *n* **1 ♦ :** something that stands for something else; *esp* **:** something concrete that represents or suggests another thing that cannot in itself be pictured ⟨the lion is a ∼ of bravery⟩ **2 :** a letter, character, or sign used in writing or printing to represent operations, quantities, elements, sounds, or other ideas — **sym·bol·ic** \sim-'bä-lik\ *also* **sym·bol·i·cal** \-li-kəl\ *adj* — **sym·bol·i·cal·ly** \-k(ə-)lē\ *adv*

   ♦ emblem, hallmark, logo, trademark

sym·bol·ise *chiefly Brit var of* SYMBOLIZE

sym·bol·ism \'sim-bə-ˌli-zəm\ *n* **:** representation of abstract or intangible things by means of symbols

sym·bol·ize \'sim-bə-ˌlīz\ *vb* **-ized; -iz·ing 1 :** to serve as a symbol of **2 :** to represent by symbols — **sym·bol·i·za·tion** \ˌsim-bə-lə-'zā-shən\ *n*

sym·me·try \'si-mə-trē\ *n, pl* **-tries 1 ♦ :** an arrangement marked by regularity and balanced proportions **2 :** correspondence in size, shape, and position of parts that are on opposite sides of a dividing line or center — **sym·met·ri·cal** \sə-'me-tri-kəl\ *or* **sym·met·ric** \sə-'me-trik\ *adj* — **sym·met·ri·cal·ly** \-k(ə-)lē\ *adv*

   ♦ balance, coherence, consonance, harmony, proportion, symphony, unity

sym·pa·thet·ic \ˌsim-pə-'the-tik\ *adj* ♦ **:** given to, marked by, or arising from sympathy, compassion, friendliness, and sensitivity to others' emotions — **sym·pa·thet·i·cal·ly** \ˌsim-pə-'the-ti-k(ə-)lē\ *adv*

   ♦ compassionate, humane, understanding *Ant* callous, cold-blooded, heartless, inhuman, inhumane, unfeeling, unsympathetic ♦ beneficent, benevolent, good-hearted, humane, kind, kindly, tender, tenderhearted, warmhearted

sympathetic nervous system *n* **:** the part of the autonomic nervous system that is concerned esp. with the body's response to stress and that tends to decrease the tone and contractility of smooth muscle and increase blood pressure and the activity of the heart

sym·pa·thise *chiefly Brit var of* SYMPATHIZE

sym·pa·thize \'sim-pə-ˌthīz\ *vb* **-thized; -thiz·ing** ♦ **:** to feel or show sympathy

   ♦ *usu* **sympathize with** bleed, commiserate, feel, pity

sym·pa·thiz·er *n* ♦ : one that sympathizes : one that acts or reacts in sympathy

♦ abettor, ally, backer, confederate, supporter

sym·pa·thy \'sim-pə-thē\ *n, pl* **-thies** **1** : a relationship between persons or things wherein whatever affects one similarly affects the other **2** : harmony of interests and aims **3** : FAVOR, SUPPORT **4** ♦ : the capacity for entering into and sharing the feelings or interests of another; *also* : COMPASSION **5** : an expression of sorrow for another's loss, grief, or misfortune

♦ commiseration, compassion, feeling *Ant* callousness ♦ charity, heart, humanity, kindliness, kindness, mercy, pity

sym·phon·ic \sim-'fä-nik\ *adj* ♦ : musically concordant

♦ euphonious, harmonious, melodious, musical, tuneful

sym·pho·ny \'sim-fə-nē\ *n, pl* **-nies** **1** ♦ : harmony of sounds **2** : a large and complex composition for a full orchestra **3** : a large orchestra of a kind that plays symphonies

♦ balance, coherence, consonance, harmony, proportion, symmetry, unity

sym·po·sium \sim-'pō-zē-əm\ *n, pl* **-sia** \-zē-ə\ *or* **-siums** ♦ : a conference at which a particular topic is discussed by various speakers; *also* : a collection of opinions about a subject

♦ colloquy, conference, council, forum, panel, parley, seminar

symp·tom \'simp-təm\ *n* **1** : something that indicates the presence of disease or abnormality; *esp* : something (as a headache) that can be sensed only by the individual affected **2** : SIGN, INDICATION

symp·tom·at·ic \,simp-tə-'ma-tik\ *adj* ♦ : serving to indicate

♦ characteristic, classic, distinct, distinctive, individual, peculiar, proper, typical

syn *abbr* synonym; synonymous; synonymy

syn·a·gogue *also* **syn·a·gog** \'si-nə-,gäg\ *n* **1** : a Jewish congregation **2** : the house of worship of a Jewish congregation

syn·apse \'si-,naps, sə-'naps\ *n* : the point at which a nervous impulse passes from one neuron to another — **syn·ap·tic** \sə-'nap-tik\ *adj*

¹sync *also* **synch** \'siŋk\ *vb* **synced** *also* **synched** \'siŋkt\; **sync·ing** *also* **synch·ing** \'siŋ-kiŋ\ : SYNCHRONIZE

²sync *also* **synch** *n* : SYNCHRONIZATION, SYNCHRONISM

syn·chro·ni·sa·tion, syn·chro·nise *chiefly Brit var of* SYNCHRONIZATION, SYNCHRONIZE

syn·chro·nize \'siŋ-krə-,nīz, 'sin-\ *vb* **-nized; -niz·ing** **1** : to occur or cause to occur at the same instant **2** : to represent, arrange, or tabulate according to dates or time **3** : to cause to agree in time **4** : to make synchronous in operation — **syn·chro·nism** \-,ni-zəm\ *n* — **syn·chro·ni·za·tion** \,siŋ-krə-nə-'zā-shən, ,sin-\ *n* — **syn·chro·niz·er** *n*

syn·chro·nous \'siŋ-krə-nəs, 'sin-\ *adj* **1** ♦ : happening at the same time **2** : working, moving, or occurring together at the same rate and at the proper time

♦ coeval, concurrent, contemporary, simultaneous

syn·co·pa·tion \,siŋ-kə-'pā-shən, ,sin-\ *n* : a shifting of the regular musical accent : occurrence of accented notes on the weak beat — **syn·co·pate** \'siŋ-kə-,pāt, 'sin-\ *vb*

syn·co·pe \'siŋ-kə-(,)pē, 'sin-\ *n* : the loss of one or more sounds or letters in the interior of a word (as in *fo'c'sle* for *forecastle*)

¹syn·di·cate \'sin-di-kət\ *n* **1** ♦ : a group of persons who combine to carry out a financial or industrial undertaking **2** ♦ : a loose association of racketeers **3** : a business concern that sells materials for publication in many newspapers and periodicals at the same time

♦ [1] cartel, combination, combine, trust ♦ [2] cabal, conspiracy, gang, mob, ring

²syn·di·cate \-də-,kāt\ *vb* **-cat·ed; -cat·ing** **1** : to combine into or manage as a syndicate **2** : to publish through a syndicate — **syn·di·ca·tion** \,sin-də-'kā-shən\ *n*

syn·drome \'sin-,drōm\ *n* : a group of signs and symptoms that occur together and characterize a particular abnormality or condition

syn·er·gism \'sin-ər-,ji-zəm\ *n* : interaction of discrete agencies (as industrial firms), agents (as drugs), or conditions such that the total effect is greater than the sum of the individual effects — **syn·er·gist** \-jist\ *n* — **syn·er·gis·tic** \,si-nər-'jis-tik\ *adj* — **syn·er·gis·ti·cal·ly** \-ti-k(ə-)lē\ *adv*

syn·er·gy \'si-nər-jē\ *n, pl* **-gies** : SYNERGISM

syn·fuel \'sin-,fyül\ *n* : a fuel derived esp. from a fossil fuel

syn·od \'si-nəd\ *n* : COUNCIL, ASSEMBLY; *esp* : a religious governing body — **syn·od·al** \-nəd-ᵊl, -,näd-ᵊl\ *adj* — **syn·od·ic** \-dik\ *or* **syn·od·i·cal** \sə-'nä-di-kəl\ *adj*

syn·o·nym \'si-nə-,nim\ *n* : one of two or more words in the same language which have the same or very nearly the same meaning — **syn·on·y·mous** \sə-'nä-nə-məs\ *adj* — **syn·on·y·my** \-mē\ *n*

syn·op·sis \sə-'näp-səs\ *n, pl* **-op·ses** \-,sēz\ ♦ : a condensed statement or outline (as of a treatise) : ABSTRACT

♦ abstract, digest, encapsulation, epitome, outline, précis, recapitulation, résumé (*or* resume), roundup, sum, summary, wrap-up

syn·op·tic \sə-'näp-tik\ *also* **syn·op·ti·cal** \-ti-kəl\ *adj* : characterized by or affording a comprehensive view

syn·tax \'sin-,taks\ *n* : the way in which words are put together to form phrases, clauses, or sentences — **syn·tac·tic** \sin-'tak-tik\ *or* **syn·tac·ti·cal** \-ti-kəl\ *adj*

syn·the·sis \'sin-thə-səs\ *n, pl* **-the·ses** \-,sēz\ : the combination of parts or elements into a whole; *esp* : the production of a substance by union of chemically simpler substances — **syn·the·size** \-,sīz\ *vb* — **syn·the·siz·er** *n*

syn·thet·ic \sin-'the-tik\ *adj* ♦ : produced artificially esp. by chemical means; *also* : not genuine — **synthetic** *n* — **syn·thet·i·cal·ly** \-ti-k(ə-)lē\ *adv*

♦ artificial, fake, faux, imitation, mock, sham

syph·i·lis \'si-fə-ləs\ *n* : an infectious usu. venereal disease caused by a spirochete — **syph·i·lit·ic** \,si-fə-'li-tik\ *adj or n*

syphon *var of* SIPHON

Sy·rah \sē-'rä\ *n* : a red wine

Syr·i·an \'sir-ē-ən\ *n* : a native or inhabitant of Syria — **Syrian** *adj*

¹sy·ringe \sə-'rinj\ *n* ♦ : a device used esp. for injecting liquids into or withdrawing them from the body

♦ hypodermic syringe, needle

²syringe *vb* **sy·ringed; sy·ring·ing** : to flush or cleanse with or as if with a syringe

syr·up *also* **sir·up** \'sər-əp, 'sir-əp\ *n* **1** : a thick sticky solution of sugar and water often flavored or medicated **2** : the concentrated juice of a fruit or plant

syr·upy *adj* ♦ : resembling syrup in appearance or quality

♦ thick, viscid, viscous

syst *abbr* system

sys·tem \'sis-təm\ *n* **1** : a group of units so combined as to form a whole and to operate in unison **2** : the body as a functioning whole; *also* : a group of bodily organs (as the nervous system) that together carry on some vital function **3** ♦ : a definite scheme or method of procedure or classification **4** ♦ : regular method or order

♦ [3, 4] approach, fashion, form, manner, method, plan, strategy, style, tack, tactics, technique, way

sys·tem·at·ic \,sis-tə-'ma-tik\ *adj* ♦ : methodical in procedure or plan — **sys·tem·at·i·cal·ly** \-k(ə-)lē\ *adv*

♦ methodical, orderly, regular

sys·tem·a·tise *chiefly Brit var of* SYSTEMATIZE

sys·tem·a·tize \'sis-tə-mə-,tīz\ *vb* **-a·tized; -a·tiz·ing** ♦ : to make into a system : arrange methodically

♦ arrange, array, classify, codify, dispose, draw up, marshal, order, organize, range

¹sys·tem·ic \sis-'te-mik\ *adj* **1** : of, relating to, or affecting the whole body ⟨~ disease⟩ **2** : of, relating to, or being a pesticide that when absorbed into the sap or bloodstream makes the entire plant or animal toxic to a pest (as an insect or fungus)

²systemic *n* : a systemic pesticide

systemic lupus erythematosus *n* : a systemic disease esp. of women characterized by fever, skin rash, and arthritis, often by anemia, by small hemorrhages of the skin and mucous membranes, and in serious cases by involvement of various internal organs

sys·tem·ize \'sis-tə-,mīz\ *vb* **-ized; -iz·ing** : SYSTEMATIZE

systems analyst *n* : a person who studies a procedure or business to determine its goals or purposes and to discover the best ways to accomplish them — **systems analysis** *n*

sys·to·le \'sis-tə-(,)lē\ *n* : a rhythmically recurrent contraction of the heart — **sys·tol·ic** \sis-'tä-lik\ *adj*

¹t \'tē\ *n, pl* **t's** *or* **ts** \'tēz\ *often cap* : the 20th letter of the English alphabet

²t *abbr, often cap* **1** metric ton **2** tablespoon **3** teaspoon **4** temperature **5** ton **6** transitive **7** troy **8** true

T *abbr* **1** toddler **2** T-shirt

Ta *symbol* tantalum

TA *abbr* teaching assistant

¹tab \'tab\ *n* **1** : a short projecting flap, loop, or tag; *also* : a small insert or addition **2** : close surveillance : WATCH ⟨keep ∼s on him⟩ **3** ♦ : a creditor's statement : BILL **4** : a key on a keyboard esp. for putting data in columns

♦ account, bill, check, invoice, statement

²tab *vb* **tabbed; tab·bing** : DESIGNATE

tab·by \'ta-bē\ *n, pl* **tabbies** : a usu. striped or mottled domestic cat; *also* : a female domestic cat

tab·er·na·cle \'ta-bər-ˌna-kəl\ *n* **1** *often cap* : a tent sanctuary used by the Israelites during the Exodus **2** : a receptacle for the consecrated elements of the Eucharist **3** : a house of worship

¹ta·ble \'tā-bəl\ *n* **1** : a flat slab or plaque : TABLET **2** : a piece of furniture consisting of a smooth flat top fixed on legs **3** ♦ : a supply of food **4** : a group of people assembled at or as if at a table **5** ♦ : an orderly arrangement of data usu. in rows and columns **6** : a short list ⟨∼ of contents⟩ **7** : something that resembles a table esp. in having a flat surface : TABLELAND — **ta·ble·top** \-ˌtäp\ *n*

♦ [3] board, chow, feed, meal, mess, repast ♦ [5] catalog, checklist, list, listing, menu, register, registry, roll, roster, schedule

²table *vb* **ta·bled; ta·bling** **1** *Brit* : to place on the agenda **2** : to remove (a parliamentary motion) from consideration indefinitely

tab·leau \'ta-ˌblō\ *n, pl* **tab·leaux** \-ˌblōz\ *also* **tableaus** : a scene or event usu. presented on a stage by silent and motionless costumed participants

ta·ble·cloth \'tā-bəl-ˌklȯth\ *n* : a covering spread over a dining table before the table is set

ta·ble·land \'tā-bəl-ˌland\ *n* ♦ : a broad level elevated area : PLATEAU

♦ mesa, plateau, table

ta·ble·spoon \-ˌspün\ *n* **1** : a large spoon used esp. for serving **2** : a unit of measure equal to ¹/₂ fluid ounce (15 milliliters)

ta·ble·spoon·ful \-ˌfu̇l\ *n, pl* **-spoonfuls** \-ˌfu̇lz\ *also* **-spoons·ful** \-ˌspünz-ˌfu̇l\ : TABLESPOON 2

tab·let \'ta-blət\ *n* **1** : a flat slab suited for or bearing an inscription **2** : a collection of sheets of paper glued together at one edge **3 a** ♦ : a compressed or molded block of material **b** ♦ : a small mass of medicated material **4** : GRAPHICS TABLET **5** *or* **tablet computer** : a mobile computing device that has a flat rectangular form, is usu. controlled by means of a touch screen, and is typically used for accessing the Internet, watching videos, and reading e-books

♦ capsule, pill

table tennis *n* : a game resembling tennis played on a tabletop with wooden paddles and a small hollow plastic ball

ta·ble·ware \'tā-bəl-ˌwar\ *n* ♦ : utensils (as of china or silver) for table use

♦ flatware, silver

¹tab·loid \'ta-ˌblȯid\ *adj* : condensed into small scope

²tabloid *n* : a newspaper marked by small pages, condensation of the news, and usu. many photographs

¹ta·boo *also* **ta·bu** \tə-'bü, ta-\ *adj* ♦ : prohibited by a taboo

♦ forbidden, impermissible

²taboo *also* **tabu** *n, pl* **taboos** *also* **tabus** **1** : a prohibition against touching, saying, or doing something for fear of immediate harm from a supernatural force **2** : a prohibition imposed by social custom

ta·bor *also* **ta·bour** \'tā-bər\ *n* : a small drum used to accompany a pipe or fife played by the same person

tab·u·lar \'ta-byə-lər\ *adj* **1** : having a flat surface **2** : arranged

in a table; *esp* : set up in rows and columns **3** : computed by means of a table

tab·u·late \-ˌlāt\ *vb* **-lat·ed; -lat·ing** : to put into tabular form — **tab·u·la·tion** \ˌta-byə-'lā-shən\ *n* — **tab·u·la·tor** \'ta-byə-ˌlā-tər\ *n*

TAC \'tak\ *abbr* Tactical Air Command

tach \'tak\ *n* : TACHOMETER

ta·chom·e·ter \ta-'kä-mə-tər, tə-\ *n* : a device to indicate speed of rotation

tachy·car·dia \ˌta-ki-'kär-dē-ə\ *n* : relatively rapid heart action

tachy·on \'ta-kē-ˌän\ *n* : a hypothetical particle held to travel faster than light

tac·it \'ta-sət\ *adj* **1** : expressed without words or speech **2** ♦ : implied or indicated but not actually expressed ⟨∼ consent⟩ — **tac·it·ly** *adv* — **tac·it·ness** *n*

♦ implicit, unexpressed, unspoken, unvoiced, wordless

tac·i·turn \'ta-sə-ˌtərn\ *adj* ♦ : disinclined to talk — **tac·i·tur·ni·ty** \ˌta-sə-'tər-nə-tē\ *n*

♦ closemouthed, laconic, reserved, reticent, silent, uncommunicative

¹tack \'tak\ *vb* **1 a** : to fasten with tacks **b** ♦ : to add on **2** : to change the direction of (a sailing ship) from one tack to another **3** : to follow a zigzag course

♦ add, adjoin, annex, append

²tack *n* **1** : a small sharp nail with a broad flat head **2** : the direction toward the wind that a ship is sailing ⟨starboard ∼⟩; *also* : the run of a ship on one tack **3** : a change of course from one tack to another **4** : a zigzag course **5** ♦ : a course of action

♦ approach, fashion, form, manner, method, strategy, style, system, tactics, technique, way

³tack *n* : gear for harnessing a horse

¹tack·le \'ta-kəl, *naut often* 'tā-\ *n* **1** ♦ : a set of the equipment used in a particular activity : GEAR **2** : the rigging of a ship **3** : an arrangement of ropes and pulleys for hoisting or pulling heavy objects **4** : the act or an instance of tackling; *also* : a football lineman playing between guard and end

♦ accoutrements (*or* accouterments), apparatus, equipment, gear, matériel, outfit, paraphernalia

²tackle *vb* **tack·led; tack·ling** **1** : to attach and secure with or as if with tackle **2** : to seize, grapple with, or throw down with the intention of subduing or stopping **3** : to set about dealing with ⟨∼ a problem⟩ — **tack·ler** *n*

¹tacky \'ta-kē\ *adj* **tack·i·er; -est** : sticky to the touch

²tacky *adj* **tack·i·er; -est** **1** ♦ : decayed, deteriorated, or fallen into partial ruin esp. through neglect or misuse : SHABBY **2** ♦ : marked by lack of style or good taste; *also* : cheaply showy

♦ [1] dilapidated, grungy, mean, neglected, ratty, seedy, shabby ♦ [2] dowdy, inelegant, tasteless, trashy, unfashionable, unstylish *Ant* elegant, fashionable, modish, smart, stylish, tasteful

ta·co \'tä-kō\ *n, pl* **tacos** \-kōz\ : a usu. fried tortilla rolled up with or folded over a filling

tact \'takt\ *n* : a keen sense of what to do or say to keep good relations with others — **tact·ful** \-fəl\ *adj* — **tact·ful·ly** *adv*

tac·tic \'tak-tik\ *n* : a planned action for accomplishing an end

tac·ti·cal \'tak-ti-kəl\ *adj* ♦ : of or relating to tactics; *esp* : intended for a particular purpose

♦ advisable, desirable, expedient, judicious, politic, prudent, wise

tac·tics \'tak-tiks\ *n sing or pl* **1** : the science of maneuvering forces in combat **2** : the skill of using available means to accomplish an end **3** ♦ : a system or mode of procedure — **tac·ti·cian** \tak-'ti-shən\ *n*

♦ approach, fashion, form, manner, method, strategy, style, system, tack, technique, way

tac·tile \'takt-ᵊl, 'tak-ˌtīl\ *adj* : of, relating to, or perceptible through the sense of touch

tact·less \'takt-ləs\ *adj* ♦ : marked by lack of tact — **tact·less·ly** *adv*

♦ ill-advised, imprudent, indiscreet, unwise

tad·pole \'tad-,pōl\ *n* : an aquatic larva of a frog or toad that has a tail and gills

tae kwon do \'tī-'kwän-'dō\ *n* : a Korean martial art of self=defense

taf·fe·ta \'ta-fə-tə\ *n* : a crisp lustrous fabric (as of silk or rayon)

taff·rail \'taf-,rāl, -rəl\ *n* : the rail around a ship's stern

taf·fy \'ta-fē\ *n, pl* **taffies** : a candy usu. of molasses or brown sugar stretched until porous and light-colored

¹**tag** \'tag\ *n* **1** : a metal or plastic binding on an end of a shoelace **2** ♦ : a piece of hanging or attached material **3** : a hackneyed quotation or saying **4** : a descriptive or identifying epithet

    ♦ label, marker, ticket

²**tag** *vb* **tagged; tag·ging 1** ♦ : to provide or mark with or as if with a tag; *esp* : IDENTIFY **2** : to attach as an addition **3** ♦ : to follow closely and persistently ⟨~s along everywhere we go⟩ **4** : to hold responsible for something

    ♦ [1] identify, label, mark, ticket ♦ [3] chase, dog, follow, hound, pursue, shadow, tail, trace, track, trail

³**tag** *n* : a game in which one player chases others and tries to touch one of them

⁴**tag** *vb* **tagged; tag·ging 1** : to touch in or as if in a game of tag **2** : SELECT

TAG *abbr* the adjutant general

tag·line \'tag-,līn\ *n* **1** : a final line (as in a play or joke) **2** : a phrase identified with an individual, group, or product

tag sale *n* : GARAGE SALE

Ta·hi·tian \tə-'hē-shən\ *n* **1** : a native or inhabitant of Tahiti **2** : the Polynesian language of the Tahitians — **Tahitian** *adj*

tai·ga \'tī-gə\ *n* : a moist coniferous subarctic forest extending south from the tundra

¹**tail** \'tāl\ *n* **1** : the rear end or a process extending from the rear end of an animal **2** : something resembling an animal's tail **3** *pl* : full evening dress for men **4** : the back, last, lower, or inferior part of something; *esp* : the reverse of a coin **5** ♦ : one who follows or keeps watch on someone — **tailed** \'tāld\ *adj* — **tail·less** \'tāl-ləs\ *adj*

    ♦ detective, investigator, operative, shadow, sleuth

²**tail** *vb* ♦ : to follow for the purpose of surveillance

    ♦ chase, dog, follow, hound, pursue, shadow, tag, trace, track, trail

tail·coat \-'kōt\ *n* : a coat with tails; *esp* : a man's full-dress coat with two long tapering skirts at the back

¹**tail·gate** \-,gāt\ *n* : a board or gate at the back end of a vehicle that can be let down (as for loading)

²**tailgate** *vb* **tail·gat·ed; tail·gat·ing 1** : to drive dangerously close behind another vehicle **2** : to hold a tailgate picnic

³**tailgate** *adj* : relating to or being a picnic set up on a tailgate ⟨a ~ party⟩

tail·light \-,līt\ *n* : a usu. red warning light mounted at the rear of a vehicle

¹**tai·lor** \'tā-lər\ *n* : a person whose occupation is making or altering garments

²**tailor** *vb* **1** : to make or fashion as the work of a tailor **2** ♦ : to make or adapt to suit a special purpose

    ♦ acclimate, accommodate, adapt, adjust, condition, conform, fit, shape, suit

tai·lored *adj* ♦ : made by a tailor; *also* : altered or fitted as if custom-made

    ♦ custom, custom-made

tail·pipe \'tāl-,pīp\ *n* : an outlet by which engine exhaust gases are expelled from a vehicle (as an automobile)

tail·spin \'tāl-,spin\ *n* : a rapid descent or downward spiral

tail·wind \'tāl-,wind\ *n* : a wind blowing in the same general direction as a course of movement (as of an aircraft)

¹**taint** \'tānt\ *vb* **1** ♦ : to contaminate morally **2** ♦ : to affect or become affected with something bad (as putrefaction)

    ♦ [1] blemish, mar, poison, spoil, stain, tarnish, touch, vitiate
    ♦ [2] befoul, contaminate, defile, foul, poison, pollute

²**taint** *n* ♦ : a contaminating mark or influence

    ♦ blot, brand, smirch, spot, stain, stigma

Tai·wan·ese \,tī-wə-'nēz, -'nēs\ *n* : a native or inhabitant of Taiwan — **Taiwanese** *adj*

¹**take** \'tāk\ *vb* **took** \'tůk\; **tak·en** \'tā-kən\; **tak·ing 1** ♦ : to get into one's hands or possession : GRASP **2** : CAPTURE; *also* : DEFEAT **3** : to obtain or secure for use **4** ♦ : to catch or attack through the effect of a sudden force or influence ⟨was *taken* with the flu⟩ **5** : CAPTIVATE, DELIGHT **6** : to bring into a relation ⟨~

a wife⟩ **7** : REMOVE, SUBTRACT **8** ♦ : to pick out : CHOOSE **9** : ASSUME, UNDERTAKE **10** : RECEIVE, ACCEPT **11** : to use for transportation ⟨~ a bus⟩ **12** : to become impregnated with : ABSORB ⟨~s a dye⟩ **13** : to receive into one's body (as by swallowing) ⟨~ a pill⟩ **14** ♦ : to submit to : ENDURE **15** : to lead, carry, or cause to go along to another place **16** : to be in need of : REQUIRE **17** : to obtain as the result of a special procedure ⟨~ a snapshot⟩ **18** : to undertake and do, make, or perform ⟨~ a walk⟩ **19** ♦ : to take effect : ACT **20** : to hold without crowding or inconvenience : ACCOMMODATE **21** ♦ : to understand or regard in a certain way ⟨I ~ this to be your final offer⟩ ⟨do you ~ me for a fool?⟩ — **tak·er** *n* — **take advantage of 1** : to profit by **2** : EXPLOIT — **take after** : RESEMBLE — **take care** : to be careful — **take care of** : to attend to — **take effect** : to become operative — **take exception** : OBJECT — **take place** : HAPPEN — **take to 1** : to go to **2** : to apply or devote oneself to **3** : to conceive a liking for

    ♦ [1] clasp, grasp, grip, hold ♦ [4] catch, come down, contract, get, sicken ♦ [8] choose, cull, elect, handpick, name, opt, pick, prefer, select, single ♦ [14] abide, bear, brook, countenance, endure, meet, stand, stick out, stomach, support, sustain, tolerate ♦ [19] act, function, operate, perform, work ♦ *usu* **take for** [21] account, call, consider, count, esteem, hold, rate, reckon, regard

²**take** *n* **1** : the number or quantity taken; *also* : PROCEEDS, RECEIPTS **2** : an act or the action of taking **3** : a television or movie scene filmed or taped at one time; *also* : a sound recording made at one time **4** : a distinct or personal point of view **5** ♦ : a visible response or reaction (as to something unexpected)

    ♦ reaction, reply, response

take back *vb* ♦ : to make a retraction of : WITHDRAW

    ♦ abjure, recant, renounce, retract, unsay, withdraw

take down *vb* **1** ♦ : to take apart : DISASSEMBLE **2** ♦ : to lower the spirit or vanity of

    ♦ [1] disassemble, dismantle, knock down, strike ♦ [2] abase, debase, degrade, demean, discredit, disgrace, dishonor (*or* dishonour), humble, humiliate, lower, shame, smirch

take in *vb* **1** ♦ : to give shelter to **2** ♦ : to encompass within its limits **3** : to cause to accept as true or valid what is false or invalid : DECEIVE

    ♦ [1] accommodate, billet, chamber, domicile, harbor (*or* harbour), house, lodge, put up, quarter, roof, shelter ♦ [2] carry, comprehend, contain, embrace, encompass, entail, include, involve, number

take–no–prisoners *adj* ♦ : having a fierce, relentless, or merciless character

    ♦ callous, hard, heartless, inhuman, inhumane, pitiless, soulless, unfeeling, unsympathetic

take·off \'tā-,kȯf\ *n* **1** ♦ : an imitation esp. in the way of caricature **2** : an act or instance of taking off

    ♦ burlesque, caricature, parody, spoof

take off *vb* **1** ♦ : to remove (an article of wear) from the body **2** : DEDUCT **3** ♦ : to set out : go away **4** : to begin flight

    ♦ [1] doff, peel, put off, remove ♦ [3] clear out, depart, exit, get off, go, move, pull, quit, sally, shove

take on *vb* **1** ♦ : to begin to perform or deal with; *also* : to contend with as an opponent **2** ♦ : to provide occupation for : HIRE **3** : to assume or acquire as or as if one's own **4** : to make an unusual show of one's feelings esp. of grief or anger

    ♦ [1] battle, encounter, engage, face, meet ♦ [2] employ, engage, hire, retain

take out *vb* ♦ : to find release for

    ♦ loose, release, unleash, vent *Ant* bottle (up), repress, suppress

take over *vb* ♦ : to assume control or possession of or responsibility for — **take·over** \'tā-,kō-vər\ *n*

    ♦ cover, fill in, pinch-hit, stand in, sub, substitute ♦ accept, assume, bear, shoulder, undertake

take up *vb* **1** : PICK UP **2** : to begin to occupy (land) **3** : to absorb or incorporate into itself ⟨plants *taking up* nutrients⟩ **4** : to begin to engage in ⟨*took up* jogging⟩ **5** : to make tighter or shorter ⟨*take up* the slack⟩ **6** ♦ : to accept or adopt as one's own ⟨*took up* the life of a farmer⟩

    ♦ adopt, borrow, embrace

tak·ings \'tā-kiŋz\ *n pl, chiefly Brit* : receipts esp. of money

talc \'talk\ *n* : a soft mineral with a soapy feel used esp. in making a soothing powder (**tal·cum powder** \'tal-kəm-\) for the skin

tale \'tāl\ *n* **1** : a relation of a series of events **2** : a report of a confidential matter **3** : idle talk; *esp* : harmful gossip **4 ♦** : a usu. imaginative narrative **5 ♦** : an intentionally untrue report : FALSEHOOD **6** : COUNT, TALLY

♦ [4] narrative, novella, short story, story ♦ [5] fabrication, fairy tale, falsehood, falsity, fib, lie, mendacity, prevarication, story, untruth, whopper

tal·ent \'ta-lənt\ *n* **1** : an ancient unit of weight and value **2 ♦** : the natural endowments of a person **3** : a special often creative or artistic aptitude **4** : mental power : ABILITY **5** : a person of talent — **tal·ent·ed** *adj*

♦ aptitude, endowment, faculty, flair, genius, gift, knack

ta·ler \'tä-lər\ *n* : any of numerous silver coins issued by German states from the 15th to the 19th centuries

tal·is·man \'ta-ləs-mən, -ləz-\ *n, pl* **-mans** ♦ : an object thought to act as a charm

♦ amulet, charm, fetish, mascot

¹talk \'tȯk\ *vb* **1** : to express in speech : utter words : SPEAK **2** : DISCUSS ⟨~ business⟩ **3 ♦** : to influence or cause by talking ⟨~ed him into going⟩ **4** : to use (a language) for communicating **5 ♦** : to express, communicate, or exchange ideas or thoughts by means of spoken words : CONVERSE — often used with *to* or *with* **6 a ♦** : to reveal secret or confidential information **b ♦** : to relate rumor or report of an intimate nature : GOSSIP **7 ♦** : to give a talk : LECTURE **8** : to speak idly — **talk back** : to answer impertinently

♦ *usu* **talk into** [3] argue, convince, get, induce, move, persuade, prevail, satisfy, win ♦ *usu* **talk to** [5] chat, speak ♦ [6a] inform, snitch, squeal, tell ♦ [6b] blab, gossip, tattle ♦ [7] declaim, descant, discourse, harangue, lecture, orate, speak

²talk *n* **1 ♦** : the act or an instance or period of talking **2** : a way of speaking **3 ♦** : a formal discussion, negotiation, or exchange of views **4** : REPORT, RUMOR **5** : the topic of comment or gossip ⟨the ~ of the town⟩ **6 ♦** : an analysis or discussion prepared for public presentation

♦ [1] chat, chatter, chitchat, gabfest, gossip, palaver, rap ♦ [3] argument, colloquy, conference, deliberation, discourse, discussion, give-and-take, parley ♦ [6] address, declamation, harangue, oration, speech

talk·a·tive \'tȯ-kə-tiv\ *adj* ♦ : given to talking — **talk·a·tive·ly** *adv* — **talk·a·tive·ness** *n*

♦ chatty, conversational, gabby, garrulous, loquacious *Ant* close-mouthed, laconic, reserved, reticent, taciturn

talk·er \'tȯ-kər\ *n* ♦ : one that talks

♦ chatterbox, jabberer, magpie

talk·ing–to \'tȯ-kiŋ-ˌtü\ *n* : REPRIMAND, REPROOF

talk over *vb* ♦ : to review or consider in conversation

♦ argue, chew over, debate, discuss, dispute, hash, moot

talk radio *n* : radio programming consisting of call-in shows

tall \'tȯl\ *adj* **1 ♦** : high in stature; *also* : of a specified height ⟨six feet ~⟩ **2 ♦** : large or formidable in amount, extent, or degree ⟨a ~ order⟩ **3** : UNBELIEVABLE, IMPROBABLE ⟨a ~ story⟩ — **tall·ness** *n*

♦ [1] high, lofty, towering ♦ [2] arduous, demanding, difficult, exacting, formidable, grueling, hard, herculean, laborious, murderous, rough, stiff, strenuous, toilsome, tough

tal·low \'ta-lō\ *n* : a hard white fat rendered usu. from cattle or sheep tissues and used esp. in candles

¹tal·ly \'ta-lē\ *n, pl* **tallies** **1** : a device for visibly recording or accounting esp. business transactions **2** : a recorded account **3** : a corresponding part; *also* : CORRESPONDENCE

²tally *vb* **tal·lied; tal·ly·ing** **1** : to mark on or as if on a tally **2** : to make a count of : RECKON; *also* : SCORE **3 ♦** : to be in conformity or agreement : CORRESPOND

♦ accord, agree, answer, check, coincide, comport, conform, correspond, dovetail, fit, go, harmonize, jibe, square

tal·ly·ho \ˌta-lē-'hō\ *n, pl* **-hos** : a call of a huntsman at sight of the fox

Tal·mud \'täl-ˌmu̇d, 'tal-məd\ *n* : the authoritative body of Jewish tradition — **Tal·mu·dic** \tal-'mü-dik, -'myü-, -'mu̇-; täl-'mu̇-\ *adj* — **Tal·mud·ist** \'täl-ˌmu̇-dist, 'tal-mə-\ *n*

tal·on \'ta-lən\ *n* : the claw of an animal and esp. of a bird of prey

ta·lus \'tā-ləs, 'ta-\ *n* : rock debris at the base of a cliff

tam \'tam\ *n* : TAM-O'-SHANTER

ta·ma·le \tə-'mä-lē\ *n* : ground meat seasoned with chili, rolled in cornmeal dough, wrapped in corn husks, and steamed

tam·a·rack \'ta-mə-ˌrak\ *n* : a larch of northern No. America; *also* : its hard resinous wood

tam·a·rin \'ta-mə-rən\ *n* : any of several small So. American monkeys related to the marmosets

tam·a·rind \'ta-mə-rənd, -ˌrind\ *n* : a tropical tree of the legume family with hard yellowish wood and feathery leaves; *also* : its acid fruit

tam·bou·rine \ˌtam-bə-'rēn\ *n* : a small shallow drum with loose disks at the sides played by shaking or striking with the hand

¹tame \'tām\ *adj* **tam·er; tam·est** **1** : reduced from a state of native wildness so as to be useful to humans : DOMESTICATED **2** : made docile : SUBDUED **3 ♦** : lacking spirit or interest — **tame·ly** *adv* — **tame·ness** *n*

♦ dull, flat, uninteresting

²tame *vb* **tamed; tam·ing** **1** : to make or become tame; *also* : to subject (land) to cultivation **2** : HUMBLE, SUBDUE **3 ♦** : to bring under control — **tam·able** *or* **tame·able** \'tā-mə-bəl\ *adj* — **tame·less** *adj* — **tam·er** *n*

♦ bridle, check, constrain, contain, control, curb, govern, inhibit, regulate, rein, restrain

tam–o'–shan·ter \'ta-mə-ˌshan-tər\ *n* : a Scottish woolen cap with a wide flat circular crown and usu. a pom-pom in the center

tamp \'tamp\ *vb* : to drive down or in by a series of light blows

tam·per \'tam-pər\ *vb* **1** : to carry on underhand negotiations (as by bribery) ⟨~ with a witness⟩ **2 ♦** : to interfere so as to weaken or change for the worse ⟨~ with a document⟩ **3 ♦** : to try foolish or dangerous experiments

♦ *usu* **tamper with** [2, 3] fiddle, fool, mess, monkey, play, tinker

tam·pon \'tam-ˌpän\ *n* : a plug (as of cotton) introduced into a body cavity usu. to absorb secretions (as from menstruation) or to arrest bleeding

¹tan \'tan\ *vb* **tanned; tan·ning** **1** : to change (hide) into leather esp. by soaking in a liquid containing tannin **2** : to make or become brown (as by exposure to the sun) **3** : to strike with a slender lithe implement (as a lash or rod) esp. as a punishment : WHIP

²tan *n* **1** : a brown skin color induced by sun or weather **2** : a light yellowish brown color

³tan *abbr* tangent

tan·a·ger \'ta-ni-jər\ *n* : any of numerous American birds that are often brightly colored

tan·bark \'tan-ˌbärk\ *n* : bark (as of oak or sumac) that is rich in tannin and used in tanning

¹tan·dem \'tan-dəm\ *n* **1** : a 2-seated carriage with horses hitched tandem; *also* : its team **2** : a bicycle for two persons sitting one behind the other — **in tandem** : in a tandem arrangement

²tandem *adv* : one behind another

³tandem *adj* **1** : consisting of things arranged one behind the other **2** : working in conjunction with each other

tang \'taŋ\ *n* **1** : a part in a tool that connects the blade with the handle **2** : a sharp distinctive flavor; *also* : a pungent odor

¹tan·gent \'tan-jənt\ *adj* : TOUCHING; *esp* : touching a circle or sphere at only one point

²tangent *n* **1** : the trigonometric function that is the ratio between the side opposite and the side adjacent to an acute angle in a right triangle **2** : a tangent line, curve, or surface **3** : an abrupt change of course

tan·gen·tial \tan-'jen-chəl\ *adj* **1** : TANGENT **2** : touching lightly : INCIDENTAL ⟨~ involvement⟩ — **tan·gen·tial·ly** *adv*

tan·ger·ine \'tan-jə-ˌrēn, ˌtan-jə-'rēn\ *n* : a deep orange loose-skinned citrus fruit; *also* : a tree that bears tangerines

¹tan·gi·ble \'tan-jə-bəl\ *adj* **1** : perceptible esp. by the sense of touch : PALPABLE **2** : substantially real : MATERIAL ⟨~ rewards⟩ **3** : capable of being appraised — **tan·gi·bil·i·ty** \ˌtan-jə-'bi-lə-tē\ *n*

²tangible *n* : something tangible; *esp* : a tangible asset

¹tan·gle \'taŋ-gəl\ *vb* **tan·gled; tan·gling** **1 a** : to involve so as to hamper or embarrass **b ♦** : to seize or hold in or as if in a snare or net : ENTRAP **2 ♦** : to unite or knit together in intricate confusion : ENTANGLE

♦ [1b] enmesh, ensnare, entangle, entrap, mesh, snare, trap ♦ [2] entangle, interlace, intertwine, interweave, knot, snarl

²tangle *n* **1** : a tangled twisted mass **2** : a confusedly complicated state : MUDDLE

tan·go \'taŋ-gō\ *n, pl* **tangos** : a dance of Latin-American origin — **tango** *vb*

tangy \'taŋ-ē\ *adj* ♦ : having or suggestive of a tang

♦ nippy, pungent, sharp, strong

tank \'taŋk\ n **1** : a large artificial receptacle for liquids **2** : a heavily armed and armored combat vehicle that moves on tracks — **tank·ful** n

tan·kard \'taŋ-kərd\ n : a tall one-handled drinking vessel

tank·er \'taŋ-kər\ n : a vehicle equipped for transporting a liquid

tank top n : a sleeveless collarless pullover shirt with shoulder straps

tank town n : a small town

tan·ner \'ta-nər\ n : one that tans hides

tan·nery \'ta-nə-rē\ n, pl **-ner·ies** : a place where tanning is carried on

tan·nic acid \'ta-nik-\ n : TANNIN

tan·nin \'ta-nən\ n : any of various plant substances used esp. in tanning and dyeing, in inks, and as astringents

tan·sy \'tan-zē\ n, pl **tansies** : a common weedy herb related to the daisies with an aromatic odor and bitter-tasting finely divided leaves

tan·ta·lise chiefly Brit var of TANTALIZE

tan·ta·lize \'tan-tə-ˌlīz\ vb **-lized; -liz·ing** : to tease or torment by presenting something desirable but keeping it out of reach — **tan·ta·liz·er** n — **tan·ta·liz·ing·ly** adv

tan·ta·lum \'tan-tə-ləm\ n : a gray-white ductile metallic chemical element

tan·ta·mount \'tan-tə-ˌmaúnt\ adj : equivalent in value or meaning

tan·trum \'tan-trəm\ n ♦ : a fit of bad temper

♦ blowup, dudgeon, explosion, fireworks, fit, huff, scene

Tan·za·ni·an \ˌtan-zə-'nē-ən\ n : a native or inhabitant of Tanzania — **Tanzanian** adj

Tao·ism \'taú-ˌi-zəm, 'daú-\ n : a Chinese mystical philosophy; also : a religion developed from Taoist philosophy and Buddhism — **Tao·ist** \-ist\ adj or n

¹tap \'tap\ n **1** ♦ : a device consisting of a spout and valve attached to the end of a pipe to control the flow of a fluid : FAUCET, COCK **2** : liquor drawn through a tap **3** : the removing of fluid from a container or cavity by tapping **4** : a tool for forming an internal screw thread **5** : a point in an electric circuit where a connection may be made

♦ cock, faucet, gate, spigot, valve

²tap vb **tapped; tap·ping** **1** ♦ : to release or cause to flow by piercing or by drawing a plug from a container or cavity **2** : to pierce so as to let out or draw off a fluid **3** : to draw from ⟨∼ resources⟩ **4** : to cut in on (as a telephone signal) to get information **5** : to form an internal screw thread in by means of a tap **6** : to connect (as a gas or water main) with a local supply — **tap·per** n

♦ bleed, drain, draw, pump, siphon

³tap vb **tapped; tap·ping** **1** ♦ : to rap lightly **2** : to bring about by repeated light blows **3** : SELECT; esp : to elect to membership

♦ beat, drum, rap

⁴tap n **1** : a light blow or stroke; also : its sound **2** : a small metal plate for the sole or heel of a shoe

ta·pa \'tä-pə, 'ta-\ n : an hors d'oeuvre served with drinks esp. in Spanish bars — usu. used in pl

¹tape \'tāp\ n **1** : a narrow flexible band or strip (as of woven fabric) **2** : MAGNETIC TAPE; also : CASSETTE

²tape vb **taped; tap·ing** **1** : to fasten or support with tape **2** : to record on magnetic tape

tape deck n : a device used to play back cassette tapes that usu. has to be connected to an audio system

tape measure n : a tape marked off in units (as inches) for measuring

¹ta·per \'tā-pər\ n **1** : a slender wax candle; also : a long waxed wick **2** : a gradual lessening of thickness or width in a long object

²taper vb **ta·pered; ta·per·ing** **1** : to make or become gradually smaller toward one end **2** ♦ : to diminish gradually

♦ abate, decline, decrease, de-escalate, die, diminish, dwindle, ebb, fall, lessen, let up, lower, moderate, recede, relent, shrink, subside, wane

tape–re·cord \ˌtā-pri-'kȯrd\ vb : to make a recording of on magnetic tape — **tape recorder** n — **tape recording** n

taper off vb : to diminish gradually : TAPER

tap·es·try \'ta-pə-strē\ n, pl **-tries** : a heavy reversible textile that has designs or pictures woven into it and is used esp. as a wall hanging

tape·worm \'tāp-ˌwərm\ n : any of a class of long flat segmented worms parasitic esp. in vertebrate intestines

tap·i·o·ca \ˌta-pē-'ō-kə\ n : a usu. granular preparation of cassa-

va starch used esp. in puddings; also : a dish (as pudding) that contains tapioca

ta·pir \'tā-pər\ n, pl **tapirs** also **tapir** : any of a genus of large herbivorous hoofed mammals of tropical America and southeastern Asia

tap·pet \'ta-pət\ n : a lever or projection moved by some other piece (as a cam) or intended to move something else

tap·room \'tap-ˌrüm, -ˌrüm\ n : BARROOM

tap·root \-ˌrüt, -ˌrút\ n : a large main root growing straight down and giving off small side roots

taps \'taps\ n sing or pl : the last bugle call at night blown as a signal that lights are to be put out; also : a similar call blown at military funerals and memorial services

tap·ster \'tap-stər\ n : BARTENDER

¹tar \'tär\ n **1** : a thick dark sticky liquid distilled from organic material (as wood or coal) **2** ♦ : one that sails : SAILOR

♦ gob, jack, jack-tar, mariner, sailor, seaman, swab

²tar vb **tarred; tar·ring** : to cover or smear with or as if with tar

tar·an·tel·la \ˌtar-ən-'te-lə\ n : a lively folk dance of southern Italy in 6/8 time

ta·ran·tu·la \tə-'ran-chə-lə, -tə-lə\ n, pl **tarantulas** also **ta·ran·tu·lae** \-'ran-chə-ˌlē, -tə-ˌlē\ : any of a family of large hairy American spiders with a sharp bite that is not very poisonous to human beings

tar·di·ly \'tär-də-lē\ adv ♦ : in a tardy manner

♦ laggardly, slow, slowly, sluggishly

tar·dy \'tär-dē\ adj **tar·di·er; -est** **1** ♦ : moving slowly : SLUGGISH **2** ♦ : delayed beyond the expected or proper time : LATE — **tar·di·ness** \-dē-nəs\ n

♦ [1] creeping, dilatory, laggard, languid, poky, slow, sluggish ♦ [2] behind, belated, delinquent, late, overdue

¹tare \'tar\ n : a weed of grain fields

²tare n : a deduction from the gross weight of a substance and its container made in allowance for the weight of the container — **tare** vb

¹tar·get \'tär-gət\ n **1** : a mark to shoot at **2** ♦ : an object of ridicule or criticism **3** : a goal to be achieved

♦ butt, laughingstock, mark, mockery, victim

²target vb : to make a target of

tar·iff \'tar-əf\ n **1** : a schedule of duties imposed by a government esp. on imported goods; also : a duty or rate of duty imposed in such a schedule **2** : a schedule of rates or charges

tar·mac \'tär-ˌmak\ n : a surface paved with crushed stone covered with tar

tarn \'tärn\ n : a small mountain lake

tar·nish \'tär-nish\ vb **1** : to make or become dull or discolored **2** ♦ : to bring disgrace on — **tarnish** n

♦ blemish, mar, poison, spoil, stain, taint, touch, vitiate

ta·ro \'tär-ō, 'tar-\ n, pl **taros** : a large-leaved tropical plant related to the arums that is grown for its edible starchy corms; also : its corms

tar·ot \'tar-ō\ n : one of a set of usu. 78 playing cards used esp. for fortune-telling

tar·pau·lin \tär-'pȯ-lən, 'tär-pə-\ n : a piece of material (as durable plastic) used for protecting exposed objects

tar·pon \'tär-pən\ n, pl **tarpon** or **tarpons** : a large silvery bony fish often caught for sport in the warm coastal waters of the Atlantic esp. off Florida

tar·ra·gon \'tar-ə-gən\ n : a small widely cultivated perennial wormwood with aromatic leaves used as a seasoning; also : its leaves

¹tar·ry \'tar-ē\ vb **tar·ried; tar·ry·ing** **1** ♦ : to be tardy : DELAY; esp : to be slow in leaving **2** ♦ : to stay in or at a place

♦ [1] crawl, creep, dally, dawdle, delay, dillydally, drag, lag, linger, loiter, poke ♦ [2] abide, dwell, hang around, remain, stay, stick around

²tar·ry \'tär-ē\ adj : of, resembling, or smeared with tar

tar sand n : sand or sandstone that is naturally soaked with the heavy sticky portions of petroleum

tar·sus \'tär-səs\ n, pl **tar·si** \-ˌsī\ : the part of a vertebrate foot between the metatarsus and the leg; also : the small bones that support this part — **tar·sal** \-səl\ adj or n

¹tart \'tärt\ adj **1** ♦ : agreeably sharp or acid to the taste **2** ♦ : marked by a biting, acrimonious, or cutting quality : CAUSTIC ⟨∼ comments⟩ — **tart·ly** adv

♦ [1] acid, sour, vinegary ♦ [2] acrid, biting, caustic, cutting, mordant, pungent, sarcastic, satiric, scathing, sharp

²**tart** *n* **1** : a small pie or pastry shell containing jelly, custard, or fruit **2** : PROSTITUTE

tar·tan \'tärt-ᵊn\ *n* : a plaid textile design of Scottish origin usu. distinctively patterned to designate a particular clan

tar·tar \'tär-tər\ *n* **1** : a substance in the juice of grapes deposited (as in wine casks) as a reddish crust or sediment **2** : a crust on the teeth formed from plaque hardened by calcium salts

tar·tar sauce *or* **tar·tare sauce** \'tär-tər-\ *n* : mayonnaise with chopped pickles, olives, or capers

tart·ness \-nəs\ *n* ♦ : the quality or state of being tart

♦ acidity, acrimony, acuteness, asperity, bite, bitterness, edge, harshness, keenness, pungency, sharpness

¹**task** \'task\ *n* **1** ♦ : a piece of assigned work **2** ♦ : the action for which a person or thing is specially fitted or used or for which a thing exists

♦ [1] assignment, chore, duty, job, stint ♦ [2] capacity, function, job, part, place, position, purpose, role, work

²**task** *vb* : to oppress with great labor

task bar *n* : a strip of icons usu. at the bottom of a computer screen showing programs that may be used by selecting their icons

task force *n* : a temporary grouping to accomplish a particular objective

task·mas·ter \'task-ˌmas-tər\ *n* ♦ : one that imposes a task or burdens another with labor

♦ boss, captain, chief, foreman, head, headman, helmsman, kingpin, leader

¹**tas·sel** \'ta-səl, 'tä-\ *n* **1** : a hanging ornament made of a bunch of cords of even length fastened at one end **2** : something suggesting a tassel; *esp* : a male flower cluster of corn

²**tassel** *vb* **-seled** *or* **-selled; -sel·ing** *or* **-sel·ling** : to adorn with or put forth tassels

¹**taste** \'tāst\ *vb* **tast·ed; tast·ing** **1** ♦ : to become acquainted with by experience **2** : to try or determine the flavor of by taking a bit into the mouth **3** : to eat or drink esp. in small quantities : SAMPLE **4** : to have a specific flavor ⟨the milk ∼s sour⟩ **5** ♦ : to perceive or recognize as if by the sense of taste

♦ [1] endure, experience, feel, have, know, see, suffer, sustain, undergo ♦ [5] feel, perceive, scent, see, sense, smell

²**taste** *n* **1** ♦ : a small amount tasted **2** : BIT; *esp* : a sample of experience **3** : the special sense that perceives and identifies sweet, sour, bitter, or salty qualities and is mediated by taste buds on the tongue **4** : a quality perceptible to the sense of taste; *also* : the sensation obtained from a substance in the mouth : FLAVOR **5** ♦ : individual preference **6** : critical judgment, discernment, or appreciation; *also* : aesthetic quality — **tast·er** *n*

♦ [1] bite, morsel, mouthful, nibble, tidbit ♦ [5] appetite, fancy, favor (*or* favour), fondness, like, liking, love, partiality, preference, relish, shine, use

taste bud *n* : a sense organ mediating the sensation of taste

taste·ful \'tāst-fəl\ *adj* **1** : tasty **2** ♦ : having, exhibiting, or conforming to good taste — **taste·ful·ly** *adv*

♦ elegant, graceful, handsome, majestic, refined, stately

taste·less \-ləs\ *adj* **1 a** ♦ : having no taste ⟨∼ vegetables⟩ **b** : arousing no interest **2** ♦ : not having or exhibiting good taste ⟨a ∼ joke⟩ ⟨∼ clothes⟩ — **taste·less·ly** *adv*

♦ [1a] flat, flavorless (*or* flavourless), insipid ♦ [2] coarse, common, crass, crude, rough, rude, uncouth, vulgar ♦ [2] dowdy, inelegant, tacky, trashy, unfashionable, unstylish

tast·i·ness \'tā-stē-nəs\ *n* ♦ : the quality or state of being tasty

♦ lusciousness, savor

tasty \'tā-stē\ *adj* **tast·i·er; -est** ♦ : pleasing to the taste : SAVORY ⟨a very ∼ meal⟩

♦ ambrosial, appetizing, delectable, delicious, flavorful (*or* flavourful), luscious, palatable, savory, scrumptious, toothsome, yummy

tat \'tat\ *vb* **tat·ted; tat·ting** : to work at or make by tatting

¹**tat·ter** \'ta-tər\ *vb* ♦ : to make or become ragged

♦ rend, rip, rive, shred, tear

²**tatter** *n* **1** : a part torn and left hanging **2** *pl* : tattered clothing

tat·tered \'ta-tərd\ *adj* ♦ : torn into shreds

♦ ragged, ratty, seedy, shabby, threadbare, worn-out

tat·ter·sall \'ta-tər-ˌsȯl, -səl\ *n* : a pattern of colored lines forming squares on solid background; *also* : a fabric in a tattersall pattern

tat·ting \'ta-tiŋ\ *n* : a delicate handmade lace formed usu. by looping and knotting with a single thread and a small shuttle; *also* : the act or process of making such lace

tat·tle \'tat-ᵊl\ *vb* **tat·tled; tat·tling** **1** : CHATTER, PRATE **2** ♦ : to tell secrets; *also* : to inform against another

♦ blab, gossip, talk

tat·tler \'tat-lər, 'ta-tᵊl-ər\ *n* ♦ : one that tattles

♦ betrayer, blabbermouth, informer, rat, snitch, stool pigeon, tattletale

tat·tle·tale \'tat-ᵊl-ˌtāl\ *n* ♦ : one that tattles : INFORMER

♦ betrayer, blabbermouth, informer, rat, snitch, stool pigeon, tattler

¹**tat·too** \ta-'tü\ *n, pl* **tattoos** **1** : a call sounded before taps as notice to go to quarters **2** : a rapid rhythmic rapping

²**tattoo** *vb* : to mark (the skin) with tattoos

³**tattoo** *n, pl* **tattoos** : an indelible figure fixed upon the body esp. by insertion of pigment under the skin

tau \'taů, 'tȯ\ *n* : the 19th letter of the Greek alphabet — T or τ

taught *past and past part of* TEACH

¹**taunt** \'tȯnt\ *n* : a sarcastic challenge or insult

²**taunt** *vb* ♦ : to reproach or challenge in a mocking manner : jeer at ⟨the children ∼ed each other⟩

♦ bait, bug, hassle, heckle, needle, ride, tease

taunt·er \'tȯn-tər, 'tän-\ *n* ♦ : one that taunts

♦ heckler, mocker, quiz, scoffer, tease

taupe \'tōp\ *n* : a brownish gray

Tau·rus \'tȯr-əs\ *n* **1** : a zodiacal constellation between Aries and Gemini usu. pictured as a bull **2** : the 2d sign of the zodiac in astrology; *also* : one born under this sign

taut \'tȯt\ *adj* **1** : tightly drawn : not slack **2** : extremely nervous : TENSE **3** : TRIM, TIDY ⟨a ∼ ship⟩ — **taut·ly** *adv* — **taut·ness** *n*

♦ rigid, tense, tight *Ant* lax, loose, slack

tau·tol·o·gy \tȯ-'tä-lə-jē\ *n, pl* **-gies** : needless repetition of an idea, statement, or word; *also* : an instance of such repetition — **tau·to·log·i·cal** \ˌtȯt-ᵊl-'ä-ji-kəl\ *adj* — **tau·to·log·i·cal·ly** \-ji-k(ə-)lē\ *adv* — **tau·tol·o·gous** \tȯ-'tä-lə-gəs\ *adj* — **tau·tol·o·gous·ly** *adv*

tav·ern \'ta-vərn\ *n* **1** ♦ : an establishment where alcoholic liquors are sold to be drunk on the premises **2** ♦ : an establishment for the lodging and entertaining of travelers : INN

♦ [1] bar, barroom, café, pub, public house, saloon ♦ [2] hospice, hotel, inn, lodge, public house

taw \'tȯ\ *n* **1** : a marble used as a shooter **2** : the line from which players shoot at marbles

taw·dry \'tȯ-drē\ *adj* **taw·dri·er; -est** ♦ : cheap and gaudy in appearance and quality ⟨∼ decorations⟩ — **taw·dri·ly** *adv*

♦ flamboyant, flashy, garish, gaudy, glitzy, loud, ostentatious, swank

taw·ny \'tȯ-nē\ *adj* **taw·ni·er; -est** : of a brownish orange color

¹**tax** \'taks\ *vb* **1** : to levy a tax on **2** : CHARGE, ACCUSE **3** ♦ : to put under pressure — **tax·able** \'tak-sə-bəl\ *adj* — **tax·a·tion** \tak-'sā-shən\ *n*

♦ strain, stretch, test, try

²**tax** *n* **1** ♦ : a charge usu. of money imposed by authority on persons or property for public purposes **2** : a heavy charge : STRAIN

♦ assessment, duty, impost, levy

¹**taxi** \'tak-sē\ *n, pl* **tax·is** \-sēz\ *also* **tax·ies** : an automobile that carries passengers for a fare usu. based on the distance traveled : TAXICAB; *also* : a similarly operated boat or aircraft

²**taxi** *vb* **tax·ied; taxi·ing** *or* **taxy·ing; tax·is** *or* **tax·ies** **1** : to move along the ground or on the water under an aircraft's own power when starting or after a landing **2** : to go by taxicab

taxi·cab \'tak-sē-ˌkab\ *n* ♦ : an automobile that carries passengers for a fare usu. based on the distance traveled

♦ hack, taxi

taxi·der·my \'tak-sə-ˌdər-mē\ *n* : the skill or occupation of preparing, stuffing, and mounting skins of animals — **taxi·der·mist** \-mist\ *n*

tax·ing \'tak-siŋ\ *adj* ♦ : involving, imposing, or constituting a burden

♦ arduous, burdensome, challenging, demanding, exacting, grueling, laborious, onerous, toilsome

tax·on \'tak-ˌsän\ *n, pl* **taxa** \-sə\ *also* **taxons** : a taxonomic group or entity

tax·on·o·my \tak-'sä-nə-mē\ *n* : classification esp. of animals or plants according to natural relationships — **tax·o·nom·ic** \ˌtak-sə-'nä-mik\ *adj* — **tax·on·o·mist** \tak-'sä-nə-mist\ *n*

tax·pay·er \'taks-ˌpā-ər\ *n* : one who pays or is liable for a tax — **tax·pay·ing** *adj*

Tay–Sachs disease \'tā-ˌsaks-\ *n* : a hereditary disorder caused by the absence of an enzyme needed to break down fatty material, marked by buildup of lipids in nervous tissue, and causing death in childhood

tb *abbr* tablespoon; tablespoonful

Tb *symbol* terbium

TB \ˌtē-'bē\ *n* : TUBERCULOSIS

TBA *abbr, often not cap* to be announced

T–bar \'tē-ˌbär\ *n* : a ski lift with a series of T-shaped bars

tbs *or* **tbsp** *abbr* tablespoon; tablespoonful

Tc *symbol* technetium

TC *abbr* teachers college

T cell *n* : any of several lymphocytes (as a helper T cell) specialized esp. for activity in and control of immunity and the immune response

tchotch·ke \'chäch-kə, -kē\ *n* ♦ : a small object used for decoration

　♦ bauble, curiosity, gewgaw, knickknack, novelty, trinket — KNICKKNACK

TCP/IP \ˌtē-(ˌ)sē-(ˌ)pē-ˌī-'pē\ *n* : a set of communications protocols used over networks and esp. the Internet

TD *abbr* **1** touchdown **2** Treasury Department

TDD *abbr* telecommunications device for the deaf

TDY *abbr* temporary duty

Te *symbol* tellurium

tea \'tē\ *n* **1** : the cured leaves and leaf buds of a shrub grown chiefly in China, Japan, India, and Sri Lanka; *also* : this shrub **2** : a drink made by steeping tea in boiling water **3** : refreshments usu. including tea served in late afternoon; *also* : a reception at which tea is served

teach \'tēch\ *vb* **taught** \'tȯt\; **teach·ing** **1** ♦ : to cause to know something : act as a teacher **2** : to show how ⟨∼ her to swim⟩ **3** : to make to know the disagreeable consequences of an action **4** : to guide the studies of **5** : to impart the knowledge of ⟨∼ math⟩ — **teach·able** *adj*

　♦ educate, indoctrinate, instruct, school, train, tutor

teach·er \'tē-chər\ *n* ♦ : one that teaches; *esp* : one whose occupation is to instruct

　♦ educator, instructor, pedagogue, schoolteacher

teach·ing *n* **1** ♦ : the act, practice, or profession of a teacher **2** : something taught; *esp* : DOCTRINE

　♦ education, instruction, training, tutelage

tea·cup \'tē-ˌkəp\ *n* : a small cup used with a saucer for hot beverages

teak \'tēk\ *n* : the hard durable yellowish brown wood of a tall tropical Asian timber tree related to the vervains; *also* : this tree

tea·ket·tle \'tē-ˌket-ᵊl\ *n* : a covered kettle with a handle and spout for boiling water

teal \'tēl\ *n, pl* **teal** *or* **teals** **1** : any of various small short-necked wild ducks **2** : a dark greenish blue color

¹**team** \'tēm\ *n* **1** : two or more draft animals harnessed to the same vehicle or implement **2** ♦ : a number of persons associated in work or activity; *esp* : a group on one side in a match

　♦ band, company, crew, gang, outfit, party, squad

²**team** *vb* **1** : to haul with or drive a team **2** ♦ : to form a team : join forces

　♦ collaborate, concert, cooperate, join

³**team** *adj* : of or performed by a team; *also* : marked by devotion to teamwork ⟨a ∼ player⟩

team·mate \-ˌmāt\ *n* : a fellow member of a team

team·ster \'tēm-stər\ *n* : one who drives a team or truck

team·work \-ˌwərk\ *n* ♦ : the work or activity of a number of persons acting in close association as members of a unit

　♦ collaboration, cooperation, coordination

tea·pot \'tē-ˌpät\ *n* : a vessel with a spout for brewing and serving tea

¹**tear** \'tir\ *n* **1** : a drop of the salty liquid that moistens the eye and inner side of the eyelids; *also, pl* : an act of weeping or grieving

²**tear** \'tir\ *vb* : to fill with or shed tears ⟨eyes ∼ing in the wind⟩

³**tear** \'tar\ *vb* **tore** \'tȯr\; **torn** \'tȯrn\; **tear·ing** **1** ♦ : to separate parts of or pull apart by force : REND **2** : LACERATE **3** : to

disrupt by the pull of contrary forces **4** ♦ : to remove by force : WRENCH ⟨∼ down a house⟩ **5** ♦ : to move or act with violence, haste, or force

　♦ [1] rend, rip, rive, shred, tatter ♦ [4] rip, wrench, wrest ♦ [5] barrel, career, course, dash, fly, hasten, hurry, race, rip, rocket, run, rush, shoot, speed, whirl, whisk, zip, zoom

⁴**tear** \'tar\ *n* **1** : the act of tearing **2** ♦ : a hole or flaw made by tearing : RENT

　♦ gash, laceration, rent, rip, slash, slit

tear down *vb* **1 a** ♦ : to cause to decompose or disintegrate **b** : VILIFY, DENIGRATE ⟨trying to *tear down* his reputation⟩ **2** : to take apart : disassemble

　♦ demolish, desolate, destroy, devastate, do in, ruin, shatter, smash, waste, wipe out, wreck

tear·ful \'tir-fəl\ *adj* **1** : flowing with or accompanied by tears ⟨∼ entreaties⟩ **2** ♦ : causing tears ⟨a ∼ eulogy⟩ — **tear·ful·ly** *adv*

　♦ depressing, dismal, dreary, heartbreaking, melancholy, pathetic, sad, sorry

tear gas \'tir-\ *n* : a substance that on dispersion in the atmosphere blinds the eyes with tears — **tear gas** *vb*

tear·jerk·er \'tir-ˌjər-kər\ *n* : an extravagantly pathetic story, song, play, movie, or broadcast

¹**tease** \'tēz\ *vb* **teased; teas·ing** **1** : to disentangle and lay parallel by combing or carding ⟨∼ wool⟩ **2** : to scratch the surface of (cloth) so as to raise a nap **3 a** ♦ : to disturb or annoy by persistent irritating or provoking esp. in a petty or mischievous way **b** ♦ : to make fun of : KID **4** : to comb (hair) by taking a strand and pushing the short hairs toward the scalp with the comb

　♦ [3a] bait, bug, hassle, heckle, needle, ride, taunt ♦ [3b] chaff, jive, josh, kid, rally, razz, rib, ride, roast

²**tease** *n* **1** : the act of teasing or state of being teased **2** ♦ : one that teases

　♦ heckler, mocker, quiz, scoffer, taunter ♦ annoyance, bother, gadfly, nuisance, persecutor, pest

tea·sel \'tē-zəl\ *n* : a prickly herb or its flower head covered with stiff hooked bracts and used to raise the nap on cloth; *also* : an artificial device used for this purpose

tea·spoon \'tē-ˌspün\ *n* **1** : a small spoon suitable for stirring beverages **2** : a unit of measure equal to ¹/₆ fluid ounce (5 milliliters)

tea·spoon·ful \-ˌfül\ *n, pl* **-spoonfuls** *also* **-spoons·ful** \-ˌspünz-ˌfül\ : TEASPOON 2

teat \'tit, 'tēt\ *n* : the protuberance through which milk is drawn from an udder or breast

tech *abbr* **1** technical; technically; technician **2** technological; technology

tech·ne·tium \tek-'nē-shē-əm\ *n* : a radioactive metallic chemical element

tech·nic \'tek-nik, tek-'nēk\ *n* : TECHNIQUE 1

tech·ni·cal \'tek-ni-kəl\ *adj* **1** : having special knowledge esp. of a mechanical or scientific subject ⟨∼ experts⟩ **2** : of or relating to a particular and esp. a practical or scientific subject ⟨∼ training⟩ **3** : according to a strict interpretation of the rules **4** : of or relating to technique — **tech·ni·cal·ly** \-k(ə-)lē\ *adv*

tech·ni·cal·i·ty \ˌtek-nə-'ka-lə-tē\ *n, pl* **-ties** **1** : a detail meaningful only to a specialist **2** : the quality or state of being technical

technical sergeant *n* : a noncommissioned officer in the air force ranking next below a master sergeant

tech·ni·cian \tek-'ni-shən\ *n* : a person who has acquired the technique of a specialized skill or subject

tech·nique \tek-'nēk\ *n* **1** : the manner in which technical details are treated or basic physical movements are used **2** : technical methods **3** ♦ : a method of accomplishing a desired aim

　♦ approach, fashion, form, manner, method, strategy, style, system, tack, tactics, way

tech·noc·ra·cy \tek-'nä-krə-sē\ *n* : management of society by technical experts — **tech·no·crat** \'tek-nə-ˌkrat\ *n* — **tech·no·crat·ic** \ˌtek-nə-'kra-tik\ *adj*

tech·nol·o·gy \tek-'nä-lə-jē\ *n, pl* **-gies** : ENGINEERING; *also* : a manner of accomplishing a task using technical methods or knowledge — **tech·no·log·i·cal** \ˌtek-nə-'lä-ji-kəl\ *adj*

tec·ton·ics \tek-'tä-niks\ *n sing or pl* **1** : geological structural features **2** : geology dealing esp. with the faulting and folding of a planet or moon — **tec·ton·ic** \-nik\ *adj*

ted·dy bear \'te-dē-ˌbar\ *n* : a stuffed toy bear

te·dious \'tē-dē-əs\ *adj* : tiresome because of length or dullness : BORING — **te·dious·ly** *adv* — **te·dious·ness** *n*

te·di·um \'tē-dē-əm\ *n* **1** : TEDIOUSNESS **2 ♦** : the state of being weary and restless through lack of interest : BOREDOM

♦ boredom, doldrums, ennui, listlessness, restlessness, tiredness, weariness

¹tee \'tē\ *n* : a small mound or peg on which a golf ball is placed to be hit at the beginning of play on a hole; *also* : the area from which the ball is hit to begin play

²tee *vb* **teed; tee·ing** : to place (a ball) on a tee

teem \'tēm\ *vb* **♦** : to become filled to overflowing : ABOUND

♦ abound, brim, bulge, burst, crawl, swarm

teen \'tēn\ *n* : a teenage person : TEENAGER — **teen** *adj*

teen·age \'tē-ˌnāj\ *or* **teen·aged** \-ˌnājd\ *adj* : of, being, or relating to people in their teens — **teen·ag·er** \-ˌnā-jər\ *n*

teens \'tēnz\ *n pl* : the numbers 13 to 19 inclusive; *esp* : the years 13 to 19 in a person's life

tee·ny \'tē-nē\ *adj* **tee·ni·er; -est ♦** : very small or diminutive : TINY

♦ atomic, infinitesimal, microscopic, miniature, minute, tiny, wee

teepee *var of* TEPEE

tee shirt *var of* T-SHIRT

tee·ter \'tē-tər\ *vb* **1 ♦** : to move unsteadily **2 ♦** : to move backward and forward or up and down **3 a** : to shift back and forth uncertainly ⟨∼ on the brink of bankruptcy⟩ **b ♦** : to waver in mind, will, or feeling ⟨∼s between conformity and individuality⟩ — **teeter** *n*

♦ [1] career, dodder, lurch, reel, stagger, totter ♦ [2] falter, rock, seesaw, sway, totter, waver, wobble ♦ [3b] falter, hang back, hesitate, shilly-shally, vacillate

teethe \'tēth\ *vb* **teethed; teeth·ing** : to experience the rising of one's teeth through the gums : to grow teeth

teething *n* : growth of the first set of teeth through the gums with its accompanying phenomena

tee·to·tal·er *or* **tee·to·tal·ler** \'tē-ˌtō-tᵊl-ər\ *n* : a person who practices complete abstinence from alcoholic drinks — **tee·to·tal** \'tē-ˌtō-tᵊl, -ˌtō-\ *adj* — **tee·to·tal·ism** \-ᵊl-ˌi-zəm\ *n*

TEFL *abbr* teaching English as a foreign language

Te·ja·no \tā-'hä-(ˌ)nō\ *n, pl* **-nos** : a Texan of Hispanic descent

tek·tite \'tek-ˌtīt\ *n* : a glassy body of probably meteoric origin

tel *abbr* **1** telegram **2** telegraph **3** telephone

tele·cast \'te-li-ˌkast\ *vb* **-cast·ed; -cast·ing** : to broadcast by television — **telecast** *n* — **tele·cast·er** *n*

tel·e·com \'te-li-ˌkäm\ *n* : TELECOMMUNICATION; *also* : the telecommunications industry

tele·com·mu·ni·ca·tion \ˌte-li-kə-ˌmyü-nə-'kā-shən\ *n* : communication at a distance (as by telephone or radio)

tele·com·mute \'te-li-kə-ˌmyüt\ *n* : to work at home by the use of an electronic linkup with a central office

tele·con·fer·ence \'te-li-ˌkän-fə-rəns\ *n* : a conference among people remote from one another held using telecommunications — **tele·con·fer·enc·ing** *n*

teleg *abbr* telegraphy

tele·gen·ic \ˌte-lə-'je-nik, -'jē-\ *adj* : markedly attractive to television viewers

tele·gram \'te-lə-ˌgram\ *n* : a message sent by telegraph

¹tele·graph \-ˌgraf\ *n* : an electric apparatus or system for sending messages by a code over wires — **tele·graph·ic** \ˌte-lə-'gra-fik\ *adj*

²telegraph *vb* : to send or communicate by or as if by telegraph — **te·leg·ra·pher** \tə-'le-grə-fər\ *n*

te·leg·ra·phy \tə-'le-grə-fē\ *n* : the use or operation of a telegraph apparatus or system

tele·mar·ket·ing \'te-lə-'mär-kə-tiŋ\ *n* : the marketing of goods or services by telephone — **tele·mar·ket·er** \-tər\ *n*

te·lem·e·try \tə-'le-mə-trē\ *n* : the transmission esp. by radio of measurements made by automatic instruments to a distant station — **tele·me·ter** \'te-lə-ˌmē-tər\ *n*

tele·no·vela \ˌte-lə-nō-'ve-lə\ *n* : a soap opera televised in or from many Latin American countries

te·lep·a·thy \tə-'le-pə-thē\ *n* : apparent communication from one mind to another by extrasensory means — **tele·path·ic** \ˌte-lə-'pa-thik\ *adj* — **tele·path·i·cal·ly** \-thi-k(ə-)lē\ *adv*

¹tele·phone \'te-lə-ˌfōn\ *n* : an instrument for sending and receiving sounds over long distances by electricity

²telephone *vb* **-phoned; -phon·ing** **1** : to send or communicate by telephone **2 ♦** : to speak to or attempt to reach by telephone — **tele·phon·er** *n*

♦ call, dial

te·le·pho·ny \tə-'le-fə-nē, 'te-lə-ˌfō-\ *n* : use or operation of an

apparatus for transmission of sounds as electrical signals between distant points — **tel·e·phon·ic** \ˌte-lə-'fä-nik\ *adj*

tele·pho·to \ˌte-lə-'fō-tō\ *adj* : being a camera lens giving a large image of a distant object — **tele·pho·tog·ra·phy** \-fə-'tä-grə-fē\ *n*

tele·play \'te-li-ˌplā\ *n* : a story prepared for television production

tele·print·er \'te-lə-ˌprin-tər\ *n* : TELETYPEWRITER

tele·promp·ter \'te-lə-ˌprämp-tər\ *n* : a device for displaying prepared text to a speaker or performer

¹tele·scope \'te-lə-ˌskōp\ *n* **1** : a cylindrical instrument equipped with lenses or mirrors for viewing distant objects **2** : RADIO TELESCOPE

²telescope *vb* **-scoped; -scop·ing** **1** : to slide or pass or cause to slide or pass one within another like the sections of a collapsible hand telescope **2** : COMPRESS, CONDENSE

tele·scop·ic \ˌte-lə-'skä-pik\ *adj* **1** : of or relating to a telescope **2** : seen only by a telescope **3** : able to discern objects at a distance **4** : having parts that telescope — **tele·scop·i·cal·ly** \-pi-k(ə-)lē\ *adv*

tele·text \'te-lə-ˌtekst\ *n* : a system for broadcasting text over a television signal and displaying it on a decoder-equipped television

tele·thon \'te-lə-ˌthän\ *n* : a long television program usu. to solicit funds for a charity

tele·type·writ·er \ˌte-lə-'tīp-ˌrī-tər\ *n* : a printing device resembling a typewriter used to send and receive signals over telephone lines

tele·vise \'te-lə-ˌvīz\ *vb* **-vised; -vis·ing** : to broadcast by television

tele·vi·sion \'te-lə-ˌvi-zhən\ *n* : a system for transmitting images and sound by converting them into electrical or radio waves which are converted back into images and sound by a receiver; *also* : a television receiving set

¹tell \'tel\ *vb* **told** \'tōld\; **tell·ing** **1** : to indicate or name by units or groups so as to find the total number of units involved : COUNT **2 ♦** : to relate in detail : NARRATE **3** : to give utterance to : SAY **4 ♦** : to make known **5 ♦** : to report to : INFORM **6 ♦** : to give an order to : DIRECT **7** : to find out by observing **8** : to have a marked effect **9** : to serve as evidence

♦ [2] describe, narrate, recite, recount, rehearse, relate, report ♦ [4] blare, disclose, discover, divulge, expose, reveal, spill, unbosom, uncloak, uncover, unmask, unveil ♦ [5] acquaint, advise, apprise, brief, clue, enlighten, familiarize, fill in, inform, instruct, wise ♦ [6] bid, boss, charge, command, direct, enjoin, instruct, order

²tell *n* : a behavior or mannerism that reveals someone's true thoughts or emotions

tell·er \'te-lər\ *n* **1** : one that relates : NARRATOR **2** : one that counts **3** : a bank employee handling money received or paid out

tell·ing \'te-liŋ\ *adj* **♦** : producing a marked effect : EFFECTIVE

♦ cogent, compelling, conclusive, convincing, decisive, effective, forceful, persuasive, satisfying, strong

tell off *vb* : REPRIMAND, SCOLD

¹tell·tale \'tel-ˌtāl\ *n* **1** : one that informs against another : INFORMER **2** : something that serves to disclose : INDICATION

²telltale *adj* **1** : telling what one should hold secret or in confidence **2 ♦** : disclosing or indicating something often of a private or secret nature ⟨∼ crumbs on the kitchen counter⟩

♦ denotative, indicative, significant

tel·lu·ri·um \tə-'lùr-ē-əm\ *n* : a chemical element used esp. in alloys

tel·net \'tel-ˌnet\ *n* : a telecommunications protocol for accessing and using a remote computer via a local computer — **telnet** *vb*

tem·blor \'tem-blər\ *n* : EARTHQUAKE

te·mer·i·ty \tə-'mer-ə-tē\ *n, pl* **-ties ♦** : rash or presumptuous daring

♦ audacity, brass, brazenness, cheek, chutzpah, effrontery, gall, nerve, presumption, sauce, sauciness

¹temp \'temp\ *n* **1** : TEMPERATURE **2** : a temporary worker

²temp *abbr* temporary

¹tem·per \'tem-pər\ *vb* **1** : to dilute or soften by the addition of something else ⟨∼ justice with mercy⟩ **2** : to bring (as steel) to a desired hardness by reheating and cooling **3** : to toughen (glass) by gradual heating and cooling **4** : TOUGHEN **5** : TUNE

²temper *n* **1** : characteristic tone : TENDENCY **2** : the hardness or toughness of a substance ⟨∼ of a knife blade⟩ **3** : a characteristic frame of mind : DISPOSITION **4** : calmness of mind : COMPOSURE **5 ♦** : state of feeling or frame of mind at a particular time **6** : heat of mind or emotion **7 ♦** : main or essential nature esp. as strongly marked and serving to distinguish — **tem·pered** \'tem-pərd\ *adj*

♦ [5] cheer, frame, humor (*or* humour), mode, mood, spirit
♦ [7] air, atmosphere, aura, climate, flavor (*or* flavour), mood, note

tem·pera \'tem-pə-rə\ *n* : a painting process using an albuminous or colloidal medium as a vehicle; *also* : a painting done in tempera

tem·per·a·ment \'tem-prə-mənt, -pər-mənt\ *n* **1** ♦ : characteristic or habitual inclination or mode of emotional response : DISPOSITION ⟨nervous ∼⟩ **2** : excessive sensitiveness or irritability

♦ disposition, grain, nature, temper

tem·per·a·men·tal \ˌtem-prə-'ment-ᵊl, -pər-'ment-\ *adj* **1** ♦ : marked by excessive sensitivity and impulsive mood changes ⟨a ∼ child⟩ **2** ♦ : unpredictable in behavior or performance ⟨a ∼ computer⟩

♦ [1, 2] capricious, changeable, fickle, fluid, inconstant, mercurial, mutable, uncertain, unpredictable, unsettled, unstable, unsteady, variable, volatile

tem·per·ance \'tem-prəns, -pə-rəns\ *n* : habitual moderation in the indulgence of the appetites or passions; *esp* : moderation in or abstinence from the use of alcoholic beverages

tem·per·ate \'tem-prət, -pə-rət\ *adj* **1** : not extreme or excessive : MILD **2** : moderate in indulgence of appetite or desire **3** : moderate in the use of alcoholic beverages **4** ♦ : having a moderate climate

♦ balmy, clement, equable, gentle, mild, moderate

temperate zone *n, often cap T&Z* : the region between the Tropic of Cancer and the arctic circle or between the Tropic of Capricorn and the antarctic circle

tem·per·a·ture \'tem-pər-ˌchür, -prə-ˌchür, -chər\ *n* **1** : degree of hotness or coldness of something (as air, water, or the body) as shown by a thermometer **2** : FEVER 1

tem·pest \'tem-pəst\ *n* **1** : a violent storm **2** ♦ : a violent commotion or agitation

♦ cataclysm, convulsion, paroxysm, storm, tumult, upheaval, uproar

tem·pes·tu·ous \tem-'pes-chə-wəs\ *adj* ♦ : of, involving, or resembling a tempest : STORMY — **tem·pes·tu·ous·ly** *adv* — **tem·pes·tu·ous·ness** *n*

♦ explosive, ferocious, fierce, furious, hot, rabid, rough, stormy, turbulent, violent, volcanic ♦ bleak, dirty, foul, inclement, nasty, raw, rough, squally

tem·plate \'tem-plət\ *n* : a gauge, mold, or pattern that functions as a guide to the form or structure of something being made

¹**tem·ple** \'tem-pəl\ *n* **1** : a building reserved for religious practice **2** : a place devoted to a special or exalted purpose

²**temple** *n* : the flattened space on each side of the forehead esp. of humans

tem·po \'tem-pō\ *n, pl* **tem·pi** \-(ˌ)pē\ *or* **tempos** **1** : the rate of speed of a musical piece or passage **2** : rate of motion or activity : PACE

¹**tem·po·ral** \'tem-pə-rəl\ *adj* **1** : of, relating to, or limited by time ⟨∼ and spatial bounds⟩ **2** ♦ : of or relating to earthly life or secular concerns ⟨∼ power⟩

♦ carnal, earthly, fleshly, material, mundane, terrestrial, worldly ♦ nonreligious, profane, secular

²**temporal** *adj* : of or relating to the temples or the sides of the skull

¹**tem·po·rary** \'tem-pə-ˌrer-ē\ *adj* ♦ : lasting for a time only — **tem·po·rar·i·ly** \ˌtem-pə-'rer-ə-lē\ *adv*

♦ impermanent, interim, provisional, short-term *Ant* long-term, permanent

²**temporary** *n, pl* **-rar·ies** : one serving for a limited time

tem·po·rise *chiefly Brit var of* TEMPORIZE

tem·po·rize \'tem-pə-ˌrīz\ *vb* **-rized; -riz·ing** **1** : to adapt one's actions to the time or the dominant opinion : COMPROMISE **2** : to draw out matters so as to gain time — **tem·po·riz·er** *n*

tempt \'tempt\ *vb* **1** ♦ : to entice to do wrong by promise of pleasure or gain **2** : PROVOKE **3** : to risk the dangers of **4** : to induce to do something : INCITE — **tempt·er** *n* — **tempt·ing·ly** *adv*

♦ allure, beguile, decoy, entice, lead on, lure, seduce

temp·ta·tion \temp-'tā-shən\ *n* **1** ♦ : the act of tempting : the state of being tempted **2** ♦ : something that tempts

♦ enticement, lure, seduction, solicitation

tempt·ress \'temp-trəs\ *n* : a woman who tempts

ten \'ten\ *n* **1** : one more than nine **2** : the 10th in a set or series **3** : something having 10 units — **ten** *adj or pron* — **tenth** \'tenth\ *adj or adv or n*

ten·a·ble \'te-nə-bəl\ *adj* ♦ : capable of being held, maintained, or defended — **ten·a·bil·i·ty** \ˌte-nə-'bi-lə-tē\ *n*

♦ defensible, justifiable, maintainable, supportable, sustainable *Ant* indefensible, unjustifiable, insupportable, untenable

te·na·cious \tə-'nā-shəs\ *adj* **1** : not easily pulled apart : COHESIVE, TOUGH ⟨a ∼ metal⟩ **2** ♦ : holding fast ⟨∼ of his rights⟩ **3** : RETENTIVE ⟨a ∼ memory⟩ — **te·na·cious·ly** *adv*

♦ dogged, insistent, patient, persevering, persistent, pertinacious

te·nac·i·ty \tə-'na-sə-tē\ *n* ♦ : the quality or state of being tenacious

♦ hardheadedness, mulishness, obduracy, obstinacy, peevishness, pertinacity, self-will, stubbornness

ten·an·cy \'te-nən-sē\ *n, pl* **-cies** : the temporary possession or occupancy of something (as a house) that belongs to another; *also* : the period of a tenant's occupancy

ten·ant \'te-nənt\ *n* **1** ♦ : one who rents or leases (as a house) from a landlord **2** : DWELLER, OCCUPANT — **tenant** *vb* — **ten·ant·less** *adj*

♦ boarder, lodger, renter, roomer *Ant* landlord

tenant farmer *n* : a farmer who works land owned by another and pays rent either in cash or in shares of produce

Ten Commandments *n pl* : the commandments of God given to Moses on Mount Sinai

¹**tend** \'tend\ *vb* **1** : to apply oneself ⟨∼ to your affairs⟩ **2** ♦ : to take care of ⟨∼ a plant⟩ **3** : to manage the operations of ⟨∼ a machine⟩

♦ attend, care, mind, oversee, superintend, supervise ♦ crop, cultivate, culture, grow, promote, raise, rear

²**tend** *vb* **1** : to move or develop one's course in a particular direction **2** ♦ : to show an inclination or tendency

♦ incline, lean, run, trend

ten·den·cy \'ten-dən-sē\ *n, pl* **-cies** **1** ♦ : direction or approach toward a place, object, effect, or limit : TREND **2** ♦ : a proneness to or readiness for a particular kind of thought or action : PROPENSITY ⟨a ∼ to overreact⟩

♦ [1] current, drift, leaning, run, tide, trend, wind ♦ [2] aptness, bent, disposition, inclination, leaning, penchant, predilection, proclivity, proneness, propensity, way

ten·den·tious \ten-'den-chəs\ *adj* : marked by a tendency in favor of a particular point of view : BIASED ⟨∼ remarks⟩ — **ten·den·tious·ly** *adv* — **ten·den·tious·ness** *n*

¹**ten·der** \'ten-dər\ *adj* **1** : having a soft texture : easily broken, chewed, or cut **2** ♦ : physically weak : DELICATE; *also* : IMMATURE **3** ♦ : expressing or responsive to love or sympathy ⟨a ∼ smile⟩ **4** : SENSITIVE, TOUCHY **5** ♦ : delicate or soft in quality or tone — **ten·der·ly** *adv* — **ten·der·ness** *n*

♦ [2] delicate, fragile, frail, immature, sensitive *Ant* tough ♦ [3] beneficent, benevolent, compassionate, good-hearted, humane, kind, kindly, loving, sympathetic, tenderhearted, warmhearted ♦ [5] balmy, benign, bland, delicate, gentle, light, mellow, mild, soft, soothing

²**tender** *n* **1** : an offer or proposal made for acceptance; *esp* : an offer of a bid for a contract **2** ♦ : something (as money) that may be offered in payment

♦ cash, currency, dough, lucre, money, pelf

³**tender** *vb* ♦ : to present for acceptance

♦ extend, give, offer, proffer

⁴**tend·er** \'ten-dər\ *n* **1** : one that tends or takes care **2** : a boat carrying passengers and freight to a larger ship **3** : a car attached to a steam locomotive for carrying fuel and water

⁵**tender** *n* : a strip of meat (as of chicken breast) often breaded

ten·der·foot \'ten-dər-ˌfût\ *n, pl* **-feet** \-ˌfēt\ *also* **-foots** \-ˌfûts\ **1** : one not hardened to frontier or rough outdoor life **2** ♦ : an inexperienced beginner

♦ beginner, fledgling, freshman, greenhorn, neophyte, newcomer, novice, recruit, rookie, tyro

ten·der·heart·ed \ˌten-dər-'här-təd\ *adj* ♦ : easily moved to love, pity, or sorrow

♦ beneficent, benevolent, compassionate, good-hearted, humane, kind, kindly, sympathetic, tender, warmhearted

ten·der·ize \'ten-də-ˌrīz\ *vb* **-ized; -iz·ing** : to make (meat) tender — **ten·der·iz·er** \'ten-də-ˌrī-zər\ *n*

ten·der·loin \'ten-dər-ˌlöin\ *n* **1** : a tender strip of beef or pork from near the backbone **2** : a district of a city largely devoted to vice

ten·di·ni·tis *or* **ten·don·itis** \ˌten-də-'nī-təs\ *n* : inflammation of a tendon

ten·don \'ten-dən\ *n* : a tough cord of dense white fibrous tissue uniting a muscle with another part (as a bone) — **ten·di·nous** \-də-nəs\ *adj*

ten·dril \'ten-drəl\ *n* : a slender coiling organ by which some climbing plants attach themselves to a support

ten·e·brous \'te-nə-brəs\ *adj* : shut off from the light : GLOOMY, OBSCURE

ten·e·ment \'te-nə-mənt\ *n* **1** : a house used as a dwelling **2** : a building divided into apartments for rent to families; *esp* : one meeting only minimum standards of safety and comfort **3** : a room or set of rooms fitted esp. with housekeeping facilities and usu. leased as a dwelling : APARTMENT, FLAT

te·net \'te-nət\ *n* : one of the principles or doctrines held in common by members of a group (as a church or profession)

ten·fold \'ten-ˌfōld, -'fōld\ *adj* : being 10 times as great or as many — **ten·fold** \-'fōld\ *adv*

ten–gallon hat *n* : a wide-brimmed hat with a large soft crown

Tenn *abbr* Tennessee

ten·nes·sine \'te-nə-ˌsēn\ *n* : a short-lived artificially produced radioactive element

ten·nis \'te-nəs\ *n* : a game played with a ball and racket on a court divided by a net

ten·on \'te-nən\ *n* : a projecting part in a piece of material (as wood) for insertion into a mortise to make a joint

ten·or \'te-nər\ *n* **1** : the general drift of something spoken or written **2** : the highest natural adult male voice; *also* : a singer having this voice **3** : a continuing in a course, movement, or activity ⟨the ~ of my life⟩

tenpenny nail *n* : a nail three inches (about 7.6 centimeters) long

ten·pin \'ten-ˌpin\ *n* : a bottle-shaped bowling pin set in groups of 10 and bowled at in a game (**tenpins**)

¹tense \'tens\ *n* : distinction of form of a verb to indicate the time of the action or state

²tense *adj* **tens·er; tens·est 1** ♦ : stretched tight : TAUT **2 a** ♦ : feeling or showing nervous tension ⟨a ~ smile⟩ **b** ♦ : marked by strain or suspense ⟨a ~ movie⟩ — **tense·ly** *adv* — **tense·ness** *n* — **ten·si·ty** \'ten-sə-tē\ *n*

 ♦ [1] rigid, taut, tight ♦ [2a] aflutter, anxious, edgy, jittery, jumpy, nervous, nervy, perturbed, uneasy, upset, worried ♦ [2b] anxious, distressful, nervous, restless, unsettling, upsetting, worrisome

³tense *vb* **tensed; tens·ing** : to make or become tense — often used with *up*

ten·sile \'ten-səl, -ˌsīl\ *adj* : of or relating to tension ⟨~ strength⟩

ten·sion \'ten-chən\ *n* **1** : the act of straining or stretching; *also* : the condition of being strained or stretched **2** ♦ : a state of mental unrest often with signs of bodily stress **3** : a state of latent hostility or opposition

 ♦ pressure, strain, stress

ten–speed \'ten-ˌspēd\ *n* : a bicycle with a derailleur having 10 possible combinations of gears

¹tent \'tent\ *n* **1** ♦ : a collapsible shelter of material stretched and supported by poles **2** : a canopy placed over the head and shoulders to retain vapors or oxygen given for medical reasons

 ♦ canopy, ceiling, roof

²tent *vb* **1** : to lodge in tents **2** : to cover with or as if with a tent

ten·ta·cle \'ten-ti-kəl\ *n* : any of various long flexible projections about the head or mouth (as of an insect, mollusk, or fish) — **ten·ta·cled** \-kəld\ *adj* — **ten·tac·u·lar** \ten-'ta-kyə-lər\ *adj*

ten·ta·tive \'ten-tə-tiv\ *adj* **1** ♦ : not fully worked out or developed ⟨~ plans⟩ **2** : HESITANT, UNCERTAIN ⟨a ~ smile⟩ — **ten·ta·tive·ly** *adv*

 ♦ conditional, contingent, qualified

ten·u·ous \'ten-yə-wəs\ *adj* **1** : not dense : RARE ⟨a ~ fluid⟩ **2** : not thick : SLENDER ⟨a ~ rope⟩ **3** : having little substance : FLIMSY, WEAK ⟨~ influences⟩ **4** : lacking stability : SHAKY ⟨~ reasoning⟩ — **ten·u·ous·ly** \te-'nü-ə-tē, tə-, -'nyü-\ *n* — **ten·u·ous·ly** *adv* — **ten·u·ous·ness** *n*

ten·ure \'ten-yər\ *n* ♦ : the act, right, manner, or period of holding something (as a landed property, an office, or a position)

 ♦ hitch, stint, term, tour

ten·ured \'ten-yərd\ *adj* : having tenure ⟨~ faculty members⟩

te·o·sin·te \ˌtā-ō-'sin-tē\ *n* : a tall annual grass of Mexico that is closely related to and usu. considered ancestral to corn

te·pee *or* **tee·pee** \'tē-(ˌ)pē\ *n* : a conical tent usu. consisting of skins and used esp. by Indigenous people of the Great Plains

tep·id \'te-pəd\ *adj* **1** : moderately warm : LUKEWARM **2** ♦ : marked by an absence of enthusiasm or conviction : HALF-HEARTED

 ♦ halfhearted, uneager, unenthusiastic **Ant** eager, enthusiastic, hearty, keen, passionate, warm, wholehearted

te·qui·la \tə-'kē-lə, tā-\ *n* : a Mexican liquor distilled from an agave's sap

ter *abbr* **1** terrace **2** territory

tera·byte \'ter-ə-ˌbīt\ *n* : 1024 gigabytes; *also* : one trillion bytes

ter·bi·um \'tər-bē-əm\ *n* : a metallic chemical element

ter·cen·te·na·ry \ˌtər-ˌsen-'te-nə-rē, tər-'sent-ᵊn-ˌer-ē\ *n, pl* **-ries** : a 300th anniversary or its celebration — **tercentenary** *adj*

ter·cen·ten·ni·al \ˌtər-ˌsen-'te-nē-əl\ *adj or n* : TERCENTENARY

te·re·do \tə-'rē-dō, -'rā-\ *n, pl* **-dos** : SHIPWORM

ter·i·ya·ki \ˌter-ē-'yä-kē\ *n* : a Japanese dish of meat or fish soaked in a soy marinade and cooked

¹term \'tərm\ *n* **1** : END, TERMINATION **2 a** : a limited or definite extent of time : DURATION **b** ♦ : the time for which something lasts ⟨~ of office⟩ ⟨lost money in the short ~⟩ **3** : a mathematical expression connected with another by a plus or minus sign; *also* : an element (as a numerator) of a fraction or proportion **4** : a word or expression that has a precise meaning in some uses or is limited to a particular subject or field **5** *pl* : PROVISIONS, CONDITIONS ⟨~s of a contract⟩ **6** *pl* : mutual relationship ⟨on good ~s⟩ **7** : AGREEMENT, CONCORD

 ♦ hitch, stint, tenure, tour

²term *vb* ♦ : to apply a term to : CALL

 ♦ baptize, call, christen, denominate, designate, dub, entitle, label, name, style, title

ter·ma·gant \'tər-mə-gənt\ *n* ♦ : an overbearing or nagging woman : SHREW

 ♦ fury, harpy, shrew, virago

¹ter·mi·nal \'tər-mən-ᵊl\ *adj* **1** ♦ : of, relating to, or forming an end, limit, or terminus **2** : FATAL 2 ⟨~ cancer⟩; *also* : being in or relating to the final stages of a fatal disease ⟨a ~ patient⟩ — **ter·mi·nal·ly** *adv*

 ♦ final, hindmost, last, latter, ultimate

²terminal *n* **1** : EXTREMITY, END **2** : a device at the end of a wire or on electrical equipment for making a connection **3** : either end of a transportation line (as a railroad) with its offices and freight and passenger stations; *also* : a freight or passenger station **4** : a device (as in a computer system) for data entry and display

ter·mi·nate \'tər-mə-ˌnāt\ *vb* **-nat·ed; -nat·ing 1** ♦ : to bring or come to an end **2** ♦ : to serve as an ending, limit, or boundary of — **ter·mi·na·ble** \-nə-bəl\ *adj* — **ter·mi·na·tor** \'tər-mə-ˌnā-tər\ *n*

 ♦ [1] close, conclude, end, finish, round, wind up, wrap up ♦ [1] break off, break up, cease, die, discontinue, elapse, expire, halt, lapse, leave off, let up, pass, quit, stop ♦ [2] bound, circumscribe, define, delimit, demarcate, limit, mark

ter·mi·na·tion \ˌtər-mə-'nā-shən\ *n* **1** ♦ : end in time or existence **2** ♦ : the act of terminating **3** ♦ : a limit in space or extent

 ♦ [1] death, demise, expiration ♦ [2] cessation, close, closure, conclusion, end, ending, expiration, finish, halt, lapse, shutdown, stop, stoppage ♦ [3] bound, boundary, ceiling, confines, end, extent, limit, limitation, line

ter·mi·nol·o·gy \ˌtər-mə-'nä-lə-jē\ *n, pl* **-gies** ♦ : the technical or special terms used in a business, art, science, or special subject

 ♦ argot, cant, jargon, language, lingo, slang, vocabulary

ter·mi·nus \'tər-mə-nəs\ *n, pl* **-ni** \-ˌnī\ *or* **-nus·es 1** : final goal : END **2** : either end of a transportation line or travel route; *also* : the station or city at such a place

ter·mite \'tər-ˌmīt\ *n* : any of numerous pale soft-bodied social insects that feed on wood

tern \'tərn\ *n* : any of various chiefly marine birds with narrow wings and often a forked tail

ter·na·ry \'tər-nə-rē\ *adj* **1** : of, relating to, or proceeding by threes **2** : having three elements or parts

terr *abbr* territory

¹ter·race \'ter-əs\ *n* **1** : a flat roof or open platform **2** : a level area next to a building **3** : an embankment with level top **4** : a bank or ridge on a slope to conserve moisture and soil **5** : a row of houses on raised land; *also* : a street with such a row of houses **6** : a strip of park in the middle of a street

²**terrace** *vb* **ter·raced; ter·rac·ing** : to form into a terrace or supply with terraces

ter·ra–cot·ta \,ter-ə-'kä-tə\ *n* : a reddish brown earthenware

terra fir·ma \-'fər-mə\ *n* ♦ : solid ground

  ♦ dirt, dust, earth, ground, land, soil

ter·rain \tə-'rān\ *n* : the surface features of an area of land ⟨a rough ∼⟩

ter·ra in·cog·ni·ta \'ter-ə-in-ˌkäg-'nē-tə\ *n, pl* **ter·rae in·cog·ni·tae** \'ter-ˌī-in-ˌkäg-'nē-tī\ : an unexplored area or field of knowledge

ter·ra·pin \'ter-ə-pən\ *n* : any of various turtles of fresh or brackish water

ter·rar·i·um \tə-'rar-ē-əm\ *n, pl* **-ia** \-ē-ə\ *or* **-i·ums** : a usu. transparent enclosure for keeping or raising plants or small animals indoors

ter·res·tri·al \tə-'res-trē-əl\ *adj* **1** ♦ : of or relating to the earth or its inhabitants **2** : living or growing on land ⟨∼ plants⟩

  ♦ carnal, earthly, fleshly, material, mundane, temporal, worldly

ter·ri·ble \'ter-ə-bəl\ *adj* **1** ♦ : exciting terror or alarm : DREADFUL **2** : hard to bear : DISTRESSING ⟨a ∼ situation⟩ **3** : extreme in degree : INTENSE ⟨∼ heat⟩ **4** ♦ : of very poor quality : AWFUL ⟨a ∼ play⟩ **5** ♦ : strongly repulsive

  ♦ [1] dire, dreadful, fearful, fearsome, forbidding, formidable, frightful, hair-raising, horrible, redoubtable, scary, shocking, terrifying ♦ [4] atrocious, awful, cheap, execrable, lousy, punk, rotten, wretched ♦ [5] appalling, ghastly, grisly, gruesome, hideous, horrible, lurid, macabre, monstrous, nightmarish, shocking

ter·ri·bly \'ter-ə-blē\ *adv* : to an extreme degree : VERY

ter·ri·er \'ter-ē-ər\ *n* : any of various usu. small energetic dogs orig. used by hunters to drive small game animals from their holes

ter·rif·ic \tə-'ri-fik\ *adj* **1** : exciting terror ⟨a ∼ explosion⟩ **2** : EXTRAORDINARY, ASTOUNDING ⟨∼ speed⟩ **3** ♦ : unusually good ⟨makes ∼ chili⟩

  ♦ A1, excellent, fabulous, fine, marvelous, sensational, splendid, superb, superior, wonderful

ter·ri·fied \'ter-ə-ˌfīd\ *adj* ♦ : filled with fear or anxiety

  ♦ afraid, aghast, fearful, scared

ter·ri·fy \'ter-ə-ˌfī\ *vb* **-fied; -fy·ing** ♦ : to fill with terror : FRIGHTEN

  ♦ alarm, frighten, horrify, panic, scare, shock, spook, startle, terrorize

terrifying *adj* ♦ : causing terror or apprehension — **ter·ri·fy·ing·ly** *adv*

  ♦ dire, dreadful, fearful, fearsome, forbidding, formidable, frightful, hair-raising, horrible, redoubtable, scary, shocking, terrible

ter·ri·to·ry \'ter-ə-ˌtōr-ē\ *n, pl* **-ries** **1** : a geographic area belonging to or under the jurisdiction of a governmental authority **2** : a part of the U.S. not included within any state but organized with a separate legislature **3** : REGION, DISTRICT; *also* : a region in which one feels at home **4** : a field of knowledge or interest **5** : an assigned area **6** ♦ : an area occupied and defended by one or a group of animals — **ter·ri·to·ri·al** \ˌter-ə-'tōr-ē-əl\ *adj*

  ♦ habitat, home, niche, range

ter·ror \'ter-ər\ *n* **1** ♦ : a state of intense fear : FRIGHT **2** : one that inspires fear

  ♦ alarm, anxiety, apprehension, dread, fear, fright, horror, panic, trepidation

ter·ror·ism \'ter-ər-ˌi-zəm\ *n* : the systematic use of terror esp. as a means of coercion — **ter·ror·ist** \-ist\ *adj or n*

ter·ror·ize \'ter-ər-ˌīz\ *vb* **-ized; -iz·ing** **1** ♦ : to fill with terror : SCARE **2** : to coerce by threat or violence

  ♦ alarm, frighten, horrify, panic, scare, shock, spook, startle, terrify

ter·ry \'ter-ē\ *n, pl* **terries** : an absorbent fabric with a loose pile of uncut loops

terse \'tərs\ *adj* **ters·er; ters·est** ♦ : effectively brief : CONCISE

  ♦ brief, compact, compendious, concise, crisp, epigrammatic, laconic, pithy, succinct, summary

terse·ly \-lē\ *adv* ♦ : in a terse manner

  ♦ compactly, concisely, crisply, laconically, shortly, succinctly, summarily

terse·ness \-nəs\ *n* ♦ : the quality or state of being terse

  ♦ brevity, briefness, compactness, conciseness, crispness, succinctness

ter·tia·ry \'tər-shē-ˌer-ē\ *adj* **1** : of third rank, importance, or value **2** *cap* : of, relating to, or being the earlier period of the Cenozoic era **3** : occurring in or being the third stage ⟨∼ medical care⟩

Tertiary *n* : the Tertiary period

TESL *abbr* teaching English as a second language

TESOL *abbr* Teachers of English to Speakers of Other Languages

¹**test** \'test\ *n* **1** ♦ : a critical examination or evaluation **2** ♦ : a means or result of testing

  ♦ [1] experiment, trial ♦ [2] examination, quiz

²**test** *vb* **1** ♦ : to put to test : TRY **2** : to undergo or score on tests

  ♦ strain, stretch, tax, try

³**test** *adj* : relating to or used in testing ⟨a ∼ group⟩

tes·ta·ment \'tes-tə-mənt\ *n* **1** *cap* : either of two main divisions of Christian Scripture **2** ♦ : a tangible proof or tribute : EVIDENCE **3** : CREED **4** : the legal instructions for the disposition of one's property after death : WILL — **tes·ta·men·ta·ry** \ˌtes-tə-'men-tə-rē\ *adj*

  ♦ attestation, confirmation, corroboration, documentation, evidence, proof, substantiation, testimony, validation, witness

tes·tate \'tes-ˌtāt, -tət\ *adj* : having left a valid will

tes·ta·tor \'tes-ˌtā-tər, tes-'tā-\ *n* : a person who dies leaving a valid will

tes·ta·trix \tes-'tā-triks\ *n* : a woman who is a testator

¹**tes·ter** \'tēs-tər, 'tes-\ *n* : a canopy over a bed, pulpit, or altar

²**test·er** \'tes-tər\ *n* : one that tests

tes·ti·cle \'tes-ti-kəl\ *n* : TESTIS; *esp* : one of a mammal usu. with its enclosing structures — **tes·tic·u·lar** *adj*

tes·ti·fy \'tes-tə-ˌfī\ *vb* **-fied; -fy·ing** **1** : to make a statement based on personal knowledge or belief : bear witness **2** : to serve as evidence or proof **3** ♦ : to make a solemn declaration under oath for the purpose of establishing a fact (as in a court) **4** ♦ : to bear witness to : ATTEST

  ♦ [3] attest, depose, swear, witness ♦ *usu* **testify to** [4] attest, authenticate, avouch, certify, vouch, witness

tes·ti·mo·ni·al \ˌtes-tə-'mō-nē-əl\ *n* **1** : a statement testifying to benefits received; *also* : a character reference **2** : an expression of appreciation : TRIBUTE — **testimonial** *adj*

tes·ti·mo·ny \'tes-tə-ˌmō-nē\ *n, pl* **-nies** **1** ♦ : evidence based on observation or knowledge **2** : an outward sign : SYMBOL **3** : a solemn declaration made by a witness under oath esp. in a court

  ♦ attestation, confirmation, corroboration, documentation, evidence, proof, substantiation, testament, validation, witness

tes·tis \'tes-təs\ *n, pl* **tes·tes** \'tes-ˌtēz\ : a typically paired male reproductive gland that produces sperm and testosterone and that in most mammals is contained within the scrotum at sexual maturity

tes·tos·ter·one \te-'stäs-tə-ˌrōn\ *n* : a male sex hormone causing development of the male reproductive system and secondary sex characteristics

test tube *n* : a glass tube closed at one end and used esp. in chemistry and biology

tes·ty \'tes-tē\ *adj* **tes·ti·er; -est** ♦ : easily annoyed; *also* : marked by ill humor

  ♦ choleric, crabby, cranky, cross, crotchety, grouchy, grumpy, irascible, irritable, peevish, perverse, petulant, short-tempered, snappish, snappy, snippy, waspish

tet·a·nus \'tet-ᵊn-əs\ *n* : an infectious disease caused by bacterial poisons and marked by muscle stiffness and spasms esp. of the jaws — **tet·a·nal** \-ᵊl\ *adj*

tetchy \'te-chē\ *adj* **tetchi·er; -est** : irritably or peevishly sensitive

¹**tête–à–tête** \'tāt-ə-ˌtāt\ *n* : a private conversation between two persons

²**tête–à–tête** \ˌtāt-ə-'tāt\ *adv* : in private

³**tête–à–tête** \'tāt-ə-ˌtāt\ *adj* : being face-to-face : PRIVATE

¹**teth·er** \'te-thər\ *n* **1** : something (as a rope) by which an animal is fastened **2** : the limit of one's strength or resources

²**tether** *vb* : to fasten or restrain by or as if by a tether

tet·ra·eth·yl lead \ˌte-trə-'e-thəl-\ *n* : a heavy oily poisonous liquid used esp. formerly as an antiknock agent in gasoline

tet·ra·he·dron \-'hē-drən\ *n, pl* **-drons** *or* **-dra** \-drə\ : a polyhedron that has four faces — **tet·ra·he·dral** \-drəl\ *adj*
tet·ra·hy·dro·can·nab·i·nol \-‚hī-drə-kə-'na-bə-‚nól, -‚nōl\ *n* : THC
te·tram·e·ter \te-'tra-mə-tər\ *n* : a line of verse consisting of four metrical feet
Teu·ton·ic \tü-'tä-nik, tyü-\ *adj* : GERMANIC
Tex *abbr* Texas
Tex–Mex \'teks-'meks\ *adj* : characteristic of Mexican-American culture and esp. that of southern Texas
¹text \'tekst\ *n* **1** : the actual words of an author's work **2** : the main body of printed or written matter on a page **3** : a scriptural passage chosen as the subject esp. of a sermon **4** : THEME, TOPIC **5** : matter handled with a computer that is chiefly in the form of words **6** : TEXTBOOK **7** : TEXT MESSAGE — **tex·tu·al** \'teks-chə-wəl\ *adj*
²text *vb* : to communicate by text messaging — **texting** *n*
text·book \'tekst-‚búk\ *n* ♦ : a book used in the study of a subject

♦ handbook, manual, primer

tex·tile \'tek-‚stīl, 'tekst-ᵊl\ *n* : CLOTH; *esp* : a woven or knit cloth
text message *n* : a short message sent electronically usu. from one cell phone to another
text messaging *n* : the sending of short text messages electronically esp. from one cell phone to another
tex·ture \'teks-chər\ *n* **1** : the visual or tactile surface characteristics and appearance of something ⟨a coarse ∼⟩ **2** : essential part **3** : basic scheme or structure : FABRIC **4** : overall structure
TGIF *abbr* thank God it's Friday
¹Th *abbr* Thursday
²Th *symbol* thorium
²-th *or* **-eth** *adj suffix* — used in forming ordinal numbers ⟨hundred*th*⟩
³-th *n suffix* **1** : act or process **2** : state or condition ⟨dear*th*⟩
Thai \'tī\ *n, pl* **Thai** *or* **Thais** **1** : a native or inhabitant of Thailand **2** : the official language of Thailand — **Thai** *adj*
thal·a·mus \'tha-lə-məs\ *n, pl* **-mi** \-‚mī\ : a subdivision of the brain that serves as a relay station to and from the cerebral cortex and functions in arousal and the integration of sensory information
thal·as·se·mia \‚tha-lə-'sē-mē-ə\ *n* : any of a group of inherited disorders of hemoglobin synthesis
thal·as·so·ther·a·py \thə-‚la-sō-'ther-ə-pē\ *n* : the use of seawater or sea products (as seaweed) for the benefit of health or beauty
thal·li·um \'tha-lē-əm\ *n* : a poisonous metallic chemical element
¹than \'thən, 'than\ *conj* **1** — used after a comparative adjective or adverb to introduce the second part of a comparison expressing inequality ⟨older ∼ I am⟩ **2** — used after *other* or a word of similar meaning to express a difference of kind, manner, or identity ⟨adults other ∼ parents⟩
²than *prep* : in comparison with ⟨older ∼ me⟩
thane \'thān\ *n* **1** : a free retainer of an Anglo-Saxon lord **2** : a Scottish feudal lord
thank \'thaŋk\ *vb* : to express gratitude to ⟨∼ed them for the present⟩
thank·ful \'thaŋk-fəl\ *adj* **1** : conscious of benefit received **2** ♦ : expressive of thanks **3** : GLAD

♦ appreciative, grateful, obliged

thank·ful·ly \-fə-lē\ *adv* **1** : in a thankful manner **2** : as makes one thankful
thank·ful·ness \-nəs\ *n* : the quality or state of being thankful
thank·less \'thaŋ-kləs\ *adj* **1** : UNGRATEFUL **2** : UNAPPRECIATED
thanks \'thaŋks\ *n pl* ♦ : an expression of gratitude

♦ appreciation, gratefulness, gratitude *Ant* ingratitude, ungratefulness

thanks·giv·ing \thaŋks-'gi-viŋ\ *n* **1** : the act of giving thanks **2** : a prayer expressing gratitude **3** *cap* : THANKSGIVING DAY
Thanksgiving Day *n* : a day appointed for giving thanks for divine goodness: as **a** : the fourth Thursday in November observed as a legal holiday in the U.S. **b** : the second Monday in October observed as a legal holiday in Canada
¹that \'that, thət\ *pron, pl* **those** \'thōz\ **1** : the one indicated, mentioned, or understood ⟨∼ is my house⟩ **2** : the one farther away or first mentioned ⟨this is an elm, ∼'s a maple⟩ **3** : what has been indicated or mentioned ⟨after ∼, we left⟩ **4** : the one or ones : IT, THEY ⟨those who wish to leave may do so⟩
²that \thət, 'that\ *conj* **1** : the following, namely ⟨he said ∼ he would⟩; *also* : which is, namely ⟨there's a chance ∼ it may

fail⟩ **2** : to this end or purpose ⟨shouted ∼ all might hear⟩ **3** : as to result in the following, namely ⟨so heavy ∼ it can't be moved⟩ **4** : for this reason, namely : BECAUSE ⟨we're glad ∼ you came⟩
³that *adj, pl* **those** **1** : being the one mentioned, indicated, or understood ⟨∼ boy⟩ ⟨those people⟩ **2** : being the one farther away or less immediately under discussion ⟨this chair or ∼ one⟩
⁴that \thət, 'that\ *pron* **1** : WHO, WHOM, WHICH ⟨the person ∼ saw you⟩ ⟨the person ∼ you saw⟩ ⟨the money ∼ was spent⟩ **2** : in, on, or at which ⟨the way ∼ you drive⟩ ⟨the day ∼ it rained⟩
⁵that \'that\ *adv* : to such an extent or degree ⟨I like it, but not ∼ much⟩
¹thatch \'thach\ *vb* : to cover with or as if with thatch — **thatch·er** *n*
²thatch *n* **1** : plant material (as straw) for use as roofing **2** : a mat of grass clippings accumulated next to the soil on a lawn **3** : a covering of or as if of thatch ⟨a ∼ of white hair⟩
thaw \'thó\ *vb* **1** ♦ : to melt or cause to melt **2** : to become so warm as to melt ice or snow **3** : to abandon aloofness or hostility — **thaw** *n*

♦ deliquesce, flux, fuse, liquefy, melt, run

THC \‚tē-(‚)āch-'sē\ *n* : a physiologically active chemical from hemp plant resin that is the chief intoxicant in marijuana
¹the \thə, *before vowel sounds usu* thē\ *definite article* **1** : that in particular **2** — used before adjectives functioning as nouns ⟨a word to ∼ wise⟩
²the *adv* **1** : to what extent ⟨∼ sooner, the better⟩ **2** : to that extent ⟨the sooner, ∼ better⟩
theat *abbr* theater; theatrical
the·ater *or chiefly Can and Brit* **the·atre** \'thē-ə-tər\ *n* **1** ♦ : a building or area for dramatic performances; *also* : a building or area for showing motion pictures **2** : a place of enactment of significant events ⟨∼ of war⟩ **3** ♦ : a place (as a lecture room) resembling a theater **4** ♦ : dramatic literature or performance

♦ [1, 3] arena, hall ♦ [4] stage, theatricals

theater–in–the–round *n* : a theater with the stage in the center of the auditorium
the·at·ri·cal \thē-'a-tri-kəl\ *also* **the·at·ric** \-trik\ *adj* **1** : of or relating to the theater **2** ♦ : marked by artificiality of emotion : HISTRIONIC ⟨a ∼ gesture⟩ **3** : marked by extravagant display : SHOWY

♦ dramatic, histrionic, melodramatic

the·at·ri·cals \-kəlz\ *n pl* ♦ : the performance of plays

♦ stage, theater (*or* theatre)

the·at·rics \thē-'a-triks\ *n pl* **1** : THEATRICALS **2** : staged or contrived effects
thee \'thē\ *pron, archaic objective case of* THOU
theft \'theft\ *n* ♦ : the act or an instance of stealing

♦ larceny, robbery, thievery ♦ grab, rip-off

thegn \'thān\ *n* : THANE 1
their \thər, 'ther\ *adj* : of or relating to them or themselves
theirs \'therz\ *pron* : their one : their ones
the·ism \'thē-‚i-zəm\ *n* : belief in the existence of a god or gods — **the·ist** \-ist\ *n or adj* — **the·is·tic** \thē-'is-tik\ *adj*
them \thəm, 'them\ *pron, objective case of* THEY
theme \'thēm\ *n* **1** ♦ : a subject or topic of discourse or of artistic representation **2** ♦ : a written exercise : COMPOSITION **3** : a melodic subject of a musical composition or movement — **the·mat·ic** \thi-'ma-tik\ *adj*

♦ [1] content, matter, motif, motive, question, subject, topic
♦ [2] article, composition, essay, paper

them·selves \thəm-'selvz, them-\ *pron pl* : THEY, THEM — used reflexively, for emphasis, or in absolute constructions ⟨they govern ∼⟩ ⟨they ∼ came⟩ ⟨∼ busy, they sent me⟩
¹then \'then\ *adv* **1** : at that time **2** : soon after that : NEXT **3** ♦ : in addition : BESIDES **4** : in that case **5** : CONSEQUENTLY

♦ additionally, again, also, besides, further, furthermore, likewise, more, moreover, too, withal, yet

²then *n* : that time ⟨since ∼⟩
³then *adj* : existing or acting at that time ⟨the ∼ attorney general⟩
thence \'thens, 'thens\ *adv* **1** : from that place **2** *archaic* : THENCEFORTH **3** : from that fact : THEREFROM
thence·forth \-‚fōrth\ *adv* : from that time forward : THEREAFTER
thence·for·ward \thens-'fōr-wərd, thens-\ *also* **thence·for·wards** \-wərdz\ *adv* : onward from that place or time
the·oc·ra·cy \thē-'ä-krə-sē\ *n, pl* **-cies** **1** : government by officials regarded as divinely inspired **2** : a state governed by a theocracy — **the·o·crat·ic** \‚thē-ə-'kra-tik\ *adj*

theol *abbr* theological; theology

the·ol·o·gy \thē-'ä-lə-jē\ *n, pl* **-gies** **1** : the study of religious faith, practice, and experience; *esp* : the study of God and of God's relation to the world **2** : a theory or system of theology — **the·o·lo·gian** \ˌthē-ə-'lō-jən\ *n* — **the·o·log·i·cal** \-'lä-ji-kəl\ *adj*

the·o·rem \'thē-ə-rəm, 'thir-əm\ *n* **1** : a statement esp. in mathematics that has been or is to be proved **2** : an idea accepted or proposed as a demonstrable truth : PROPOSITION

the·o·ret·i·cal \ˌthē-ə-'re-ti-kəl\ *also* **the·o·ret·ic** \-'tik\ *adj* **1** : relating to or having the character of theory **2** ♦ : existing only in theory : HYPOTHETICAL — **the·o·ret·i·cal·ly** \-ti-k(ə-)lē\ *adv*

♦ conjectural, hypothetical, speculative *Ant* actual, factual, real

the·o·rise *chiefly Brit var of* THEORIZE

the·o·rize \'thē-ə-ˌrīz\ *vb* **-rized; -riz·ing** : to form a theory : SPECULATE — **the·o·rist** \-rist\ *n*

the·o·ry \'thē-ə-rē, 'thir-ē\ *n, pl* **-ries** **1** : abstract thought **2** : the general principles of a subject **3** : a plausible or scientifically acceptable general principle offered to explain observed facts **4** ♦ : a hypothesis assumed for the sake of argument or investigation : CONJECTURE

♦ conjecture, hypothesis, proposition, supposition

the·os·o·phy \thē-'ä-sə-fē\ *n* : belief about God and the world held to be based on mystical insight — **theo·soph·i·cal** \ˌthē-ə-'sä-fi-kəl\ *adj* — **the·os·o·phist** \thē-'ä-sə-fist\ *n*

ther·a·peu·tic \ˌther-ə-'pyü-tik\ *adj* : of, relating to, or dealing with healing and esp. with remedies for diseases — **ther·a·peu·ti·cal·ly** \-ti-k(ə-)lē\ *adv*

ther·a·peu·tics \ˌther-ə-'pyü-tiks\ *n* : a branch of medical or dental science dealing with the use of remedies

ther·a·py \'ther-ə-pē\ *n, pl* **-pies** : treatment of bodily, mental, or behavioral disorders — **ther·a·pist** \-pist\ *n*

¹there \'thar, 'ther\ *adv* **1** : in or at that place — often used interjectionally **2** : to or into that place ⟨went ∼ after work⟩ **3** : in that matter or respect

²there \'thar, 'ther, thər\ *pron* — used as a function word to introduce a sentence or clause ⟨∼'s a pen here⟩

³there \'thar, 'ther\ *n* **1** : that place ⟨get away from ∼⟩ **2** : that point ⟨you take it from ∼⟩

there·abouts \ˌthar-ə-'bauts, ˌther-; 'thar-ə-ˌbauts, 'ther-\ *or* **there·about** \-'baut, -ˌbaut\ *adv* **1** : near that place or time **2** : near that number, degree, or quantity

there·af·ter \thar-'af-tər, ther-\ *adv* ♦ : after that : AFTERWARD

♦ after, afterward, later, subsequently

there·at \-'at\ *adv* **1** : at that place **2** : at that occurrence : on that account

there·by \thar-'bī, ther-, 'thar-ˌbī, 'ther-ˌbī\ *adv* **1** : by that : by that means **2** : connected with or with reference to that

there·for \thar-'fȯr, ther-\ *adv* : for or in return for that

there·fore \'thar-ˌfȯr, 'ther-\ *adv* ♦ : for that reason : CONSEQUENTLY

♦ accordingly, consequently, ergo, hence, so, thus, wherefore

there·from \thar-'frəm, ther-\ *adv* : from that or it

there·in \thar-'in, ther-\ *adv* **1** : in or into that place, time, or thing **2** : in that respect

there·of \-'əv, -'äv\ *adv* **1** : of that or it **2** : from that : THEREFROM

there·on \-'ȯn, -'än\ *adv* **1** : on that **2** *archaic* : THEREUPON **3**

there·to \thar-'tü, ther-\ *adv* : to that

there·un·to \ˌthar-'ən-(ˌ)tü, ˌthar-ən-'tü, ˌther-\ *adv, archaic* : THERETO

there·upon \'thar-ə-ˌpȯn, 'ther-, -ˌpän; ˌthar-ə-'pȯn, -'pän, ˌther-\ *adv* **1** : on that matter **2** : for that reason : THEREFORE **3** : immediately after that : at once

there·with \thar-'with, ther-, -'with\ *adv* **1** : with that **2** *archaic* : THEREUPON, FORTHWITH

there·with·al \'thar-wi-ˌthȯl, 'ther-, -ˌthȯl\ *adv* **1** *archaic* : BESIDES **2** : THEREWITH

therm *abbr* thermometer

ther·mal \'thər-məl\ *adj* **1** : of, relating to, or caused by heat **2** : designed to prevent the loss of body heat ⟨∼ underwear⟩ — **ther·mal·ly** *adv*

thermal pollution *n* : the discharge of heated liquid (as waste water from a factory) into natural waters at a temperature harmful to the environment

therm·is·tor \'thər-ˌmis-tər\ *n* : an electrical resistor whose resistance varies sharply with temperature

ther·mo·cline \'thər-mə-ˌklīn\ *n* : the region in a thermally stratified body of water that separates warmer surface water from cold deep water

ther·mo·cou·ple \'thər-mə-ˌkə-pəl\ *n* : a device for measuring temperature by measuring the temperature-dependent potential difference created at the junction of two dissimilar metals

ther·mo·dy·nam·ics \ˌthər-mō-dī-'na-miks\ *n* : physics that deals with the mechanical action or relations of heat — **ther·mo·dy·nam·ic** \-mik\ *adj* — **ther·mo·dy·nam·i·cal·ly** \-mi-k(ə-)lē\ *adv*

ther·mom·e·ter \thər-'mä-mə-tər\ *n* : an instrument for measuring temperature typically by the rise or fall of a liquid (as mercury) in a thin glass tube — **ther·mo·met·ric** \ˌthər-mə-'me-trik\ *adj* — **ther·mo·met·ri·cal·ly** \-tri-k(ə-)lē\ *adv*

ther·mo·nu·cle·ar \ˌthər-mō-'nü-klē-ər, -'nyü-\ *adj* **1** : of or relating to changes in the nucleus of atoms of low atomic weight (as hydrogen) that require a very high temperature (as in the hydrogen bomb) **2** : utilizing or relating to a thermonuclear bomb ⟨∼ war⟩

ther·mo·plas·tic \ˌthər-mə-'plas-tik\ *adj* : capable of softening when heated and of hardening again when cooled ⟨∼ resins⟩ — **thermoplastic** *n*

ther·mos \'thər-məs\ *n* : a cylindrical container with a vacuum between an inner and an outer wall used to keep liquids hot or cold

ther·mo·sphere \'thər-mə-ˌsfir\ *n* : the part of the earth's atmosphere that lies above the mesosphere and that is characterized by steadily increasing temperature with height

ther·mo·stat \'thər-mə-ˌstat\ *n* : a device that automatically controls temperature — **ther·mo·stat·ic** \ˌthər-mə-'sta-tik\ *adj* — **ther·mo·stat·i·cal·ly** \-ti-k(ə-)lē\ *adv*

the·sau·rus \thi-'sȯr-əs\ *n, pl* **-sau·ri** \-'sȯr-ˌī\ *or* **-sau·rus·es** \-'sȯr-ə-səz\ : a book of words and their synonyms — **the·sau·ral** \-'sȯr-əl\ *adj*

these *pl of* THIS

the·sis \'thē-səs\ *n, pl* **the·ses** \'thē-ˌsēz\ **1** ♦ : a proposition that a person advances and offers to maintain by argument **2** : an essay embodying results of original research; *esp* : one written for an academic degree

♦ argument, assertion, contention

¹thes·pi·an \'thes-pē-ən\ *adj, often cap* : relating to the drama : DRAMATIC

²thespian *n* : ACTOR

Thess *abbr* Thessalonians

Thes·sa·lo·nians \ˌthe-sə-'lō-nyənz, -nē-ənz\ *n* : either of two books of the New Testament of Christian Scripture

the·ta \'thā-tə\ *n* : the 8th letter of the Greek alphabet — Θ or θ

thew \'thü, 'thyü\ *n* : MUSCLE, SINEW — usu. used in pl.

they \'thā\ *pron* **1** : those individuals under discussion : the ones previously mentioned or referred to **2** : unspecified persons : PEOPLE

thi·a·mine \'thī-ə-mən, -ˌmēn\ *also* **thi·a·min** \-mən\ *n* : a vitamin of the vitamin B complex essential to normal metabolism and nerve function

¹thick \'thik\ *adj* **1** ♦ : having relatively great depth or extent from one surface to its opposite ⟨a ∼ plank⟩; *also* : heavily built : THICKSET **2** ♦ : close-packed with units or individuals; *also* : NUMEROUS **3** ♦ : dense or viscous in consistency ⟨∼ syrup⟩ **4** : marked by haze, fog, or mist ⟨∼ weather⟩ **5** : measuring in thickness ⟨one meter ∼⟩ **6** : imperfectly articulated : INDISTINCT ⟨∼ speech⟩ **7** : lacking sharpness or quickness of sensibility or intellect : STUPID, OBTUSE **8** ♦ : associated on close terms : INTIMATE **9** : EXCESSIVE — **thick·ly** *adv*

♦ [1] broad, fat, thickset, wide ♦ [2] close, compact, crowded, dense, packed, serried, tight ♦ [2] flush, fraught, numerous, replete, rife ♦ [2] close, compact, crowded, dense, packed, serried, tight ♦ [3] syrupy, viscid, viscous *Ant* runny, soupy, thin, watery ♦ [8] bosom, chummy, close, familiar, friendly, intimate

²thick *n* **1** ♦ : the most crowded, intense, or active part **2** : the part of greatest thickness

♦ center, deep, depth, heart, height, middle, midst

thick and thin *n* : every difficulty and obstacle ⟨was loyal through *thick and thin*⟩

thick·en \'thi-kən\ *vb* : to make or become thick — **thick·en·er** *n*

thick·et \'thi-kət\ *n* ♦ : a dense growth of bushes or small trees

♦ brake, brushwood, chaparral, coppice, covert

thick·ness \'thik-nəs\ *n* **1** : the smallest of three dimensions ⟨length, width, and ∼⟩ **2** ♦ : the quality or state of being thick **3** : LAYER, SHEET ⟨a single ∼ of canvas⟩

♦ consistency, viscosity

thick·set \'thik-'set\ *adj* **1** : closely placed or planted **2** ♦ : having a thick body

♦ chunky, dumpy, heavyset, squat, stocky, stout, stubby, stumpy

thick–skinned \-'skind\ *adj* **1** : having a thick skin **2** ♦ : feeling no emotion or sympathy : CALLOUS **3** : not easily bothered by criticism or insult ⟨a ∼ politician⟩

♦ callous, hard, heartless, inhuman, inhumane, pitiless, soulless, unfeeling, unsympathetic

thief \'thēf\ *n, pl* **thieves** \'thēvz\ : one that steals esp. secretly
thieve \'thēv\ *vb* **thieved; thiev·ing** ♦ : to take (the property of another) wrongfully and esp. as an habitual or regular practice : STEAL

♦ appropriate, filch, hook, misappropriate, nip, pilfer, pocket, purloin, snitch, steal, swipe

thiev·ery \'thē-və-rē\ *n, pl* **-er·ies** ♦ : the act of stealing : THEFT

♦ larceny, robbery, theft

thigh \'thī\ *n* : the part of the vertebrate hind or lower limb between the knee and the hip
thigh·bone \'thī-,bōn\ *n* : FEMUR
thim·ble \'thim-bəl\ *n* : a cap or guard worn on the finger to push the needle in sewing — **thim·ble·ful** *n*
¹thin \'thin\ *adj* **thin·ner; thin·nest** **1** ♦ : having little extent from one surface through to its opposite : not thick : SLENDER **2** : not closely set or placed : SPARSE ⟨∼ hair⟩ **3** : not dense or not dense enough : more fluid or rarefied than normal ⟨∼ air⟩ ⟨∼ syrup⟩ **4** ♦ : lacking substance, fullness, or strength ⟨∼ broth⟩ **5** : FLIMSY **6** ♦ : not well fleshed : LEAN — **thin·ly** *adv* — **thin·ness** *n*

♦ [1] fine, narrow, skinny, slender, slim ♦ [4] dilute, watery, weak ♦ [6] lean, skinny, slender, slim, spare *Ant* chubby, corpulent, fat, gross, obese, overweight, plump, portly, round

²thin *vb* **thinned; thin·ning** ♦ : to make or become thin

♦ adulterate, dilute, water, weaken

thine \'thīn\ *pron, archaic* : one or the ones belonging to thee
thing \'thiŋ\ *n* **1** ♦ : a matter of concern : AFFAIR ⟨∼s to do⟩ **2** *pl* : state of affairs ⟨∼s are improving⟩ **3** : something that happens : EVENT ⟨the crime was a terrible ∼⟩ **4** : something that is done : DEED, ACT ⟨expected great ∼s of him⟩ **5** ♦ : a distinct entity : OBJECT **6** : an inanimate object distinguished from a living being **7** *pl* ♦ : movable property : EFFECTS **8** : an article of clothing **9** : DETAIL, POINT **10** : IDEA, NOTION **11** : something one likes to do : SPECIALTY ⟨doing her ∼⟩ **12** : a single human being **13 a** : a product of work or activity **b** ♦ : the end or aim of effort or activity ⟨the ∼ is to get well⟩

♦ [1] affair, business, matter ♦ [5] being, entity, individual, object, substance ♦ **things** [7] belongings, chattels, effects, holdings, paraphernalia, possessions ♦ [13b] aim, ambition, aspiration, design, dream, end, goal, intent, mark, meaning, object, objective, plan, pretension, purpose

think \'thiŋk\ *vb* **thought** \'thȯt\; **think·ing** **1** : to form or have in the mind **2** ♦ : to have as an opinion : BELIEVE **3** ♦ : to reflect on : PONDER **4** ♦ : to call to mind : REMEMBER **5** : REASON **6** : to form a mental picture of : IMAGINE **7** ♦ : to devise by thinking ⟨thought up a plan to escape⟩ — **think·er** *n*

♦ [2] believe, consider, deem, feel, figure, guess, hold, imagine, suppose ♦ *usu* **think about** *or* **think over** [3] chew over, cogitate, consider, contemplate, debate, deliberate, entertain, meditate, mull, ponder, question, ruminate, study, weigh ♦ *usu* **think of** [4] recall, recollect, remember, reminisce ♦ *usu* **think up** [7] concoct, contrive, cook up, devise, fabricate, invent, make up, manufacture

think·er \'thiŋ-kər\ *n* : one that thinks: as **a** : one that thinks in a specified way ⟨a slow ∼⟩ **b** ♦ : one that has special capacity for thinking

♦ brain, genius, intellect, whiz, wizard

think tank *n* : an institute, corporation, or group organized for interdisciplinary research (as in technological or social problems)
thin·ner \'thi-nər\ *n* : a volatile liquid (as turpentine) used to thin paint
thin–skinned \'thin-'skind\ *adj* **1** : having a thin skin or rind **2** : extremely sensitive to criticism or insult
¹third \'thərd\ *adj* : next after the second — **third** *or* **third·ly** *adv*
²third *n* **1** : one of three equal parts of something **2** : one that is number three in a countable series **3** : the 3d forward gear in an automotive vehicle

third degree *n* : the subjection of a prisoner to mental or physical torture to force a confession
third dimension *n* **1** : thickness, depth, or apparent thickness or depth that confers solidity on an object **2** : a quality that confers reality — **third–dimensional** *adj*
third world *n, often cap T&W* : the aggregate of the underdeveloped nations of the world
¹thirst \'thərst\ *n* **1** : a feeling of dryness in the mouth and throat associated with a desire to drink; *also* : a bodily condition producing this **2** ♦ : an ardent desire ⟨a ∼ for knowledge⟩

♦ appetite, craving, desire, drive, eagerness, hankering, hunger, itch, longing, lust, passion, urge, yearning, yen

²thirst *vb* **1** : to need drink : suffer thirst **2** ♦ : to have a strong desire

♦ *usu* **thirst for** ache for, covet, crave, desire, die (to *or* for), hanker for, hunger for, long for, lust (for *or* after), pine for, repine for, want, wish for, yearn for

thirsty \'thər-stē\ *adj* **thirst·i·er; -est** **1 a** : feeling thirst **b** ♦ : deficient in moisture ⟨∼ land⟩ **2** ♦ : having a strong desire : AVID

♦ [1b] arid, dry, sere ♦ [2] ardent, athirst, avid, eager, enthusiastic, keen

thir·teen \,thər-'tēn\ *n* : one more than 12 — **thirteen** *adj or pron* — **thir·teenth** \-'tēnth\ *adj or n*
thir·ty \'thər-tē\ *n, pl* **thirties** : three times 10 — **thir·ti·eth** \-tē-əth\ *adj or n* — **thirty** *adj or pron*
¹this \'this\ *pron, pl* **these** \'thēz\ **1** : the one close or closest in time or space ⟨∼ is your book⟩ **2** : what is in the present or under immediate observation or discussion ⟨∼ is a mess⟩; *also* : what is happening or being done now ⟨after ∼ we'll leave⟩
²this *adj, pl* **these** **1** : being the one near, present, just mentioned, or more immediately under observation ⟨∼ book⟩ **2** : constituting the immediate past or future ⟨friends all *these* years⟩
³this *adv* : to such an extent or degree ⟨we need a book about ∼ big⟩
this·tle \'thi-səl\ *n* : any of various tall prickly composite plants with often showy heads of tightly packed tubular flowers
this·tle·down \-,daun\ *n* : the down from the ripe flower head of a thistle
¹thith·er \'thi-thər\ *adv* : to that place
²thither *adj* : being on the farther side
thith·er·ward \-wərd\ *adv* : toward that place : THITHER
thong \'thȯŋ\ *n* **1** : a strip esp. of leather or hide **2** : a sandal held on the foot by a thong between the toes **3** : a narrow strip of swimwear or underwear that passes between the thighs
tho·rax \'thȯr-,aks\ *n, pl* **tho·rax·es** *or* **tho·ra·ces** \'thȯr-ə-,sēz\ **1** : the part of the body of a mammal between the neck and the abdomen; *also* : its cavity containing the heart and lungs **2** : the middle of the three main divisions of the body of an insect — **tho·rac·ic** \thə-'ra-sik\ *adj*
tho·ri·um \'thȯr-ē-əm\ *n* : a radioactive metallic chemical element
thorn \'thȯrn\ *n* **1** : a woody plant bearing sharp processes **2** : a sharp rigid plant process that is usu. a modified leafless branch **3** : something that causes distress

♦ aggravation, annoyance, bother, exasperation, frustration, hassle, headache, inconvenience, irritant, nuisance, peeve, pest, problem

thorny \'thȯr-nē\ *adj* **thorn·i·er; -est** **1** ♦ : full of thorns **2** ♦ : full of difficulties or controversial points

♦ [1] brambly, prickly, scratchy ♦ [2] catchy, delicate, difficult, knotty, problematic, spiny, ticklish, touchy, tough, tricky

thor·ough \'thər-ō\ *adj* **1** ♦ : testing all possibilities or considering all elements : EXHAUSTIVE ⟨a ∼ search⟩ **2** : very careful : PAINSTAKING ⟨a ∼ scholar⟩ **3** : having full mastery **4** ♦ : marked by attention to many details ⟨a ∼ description⟩ **5** ♦ : complete in all respects ⟨∼ pleasure⟩ — **thor·ough·ness** *n*

♦ [1] all-out, clean, complete, comprehensive, exhaustive, full-scale, out-and-out, thoroughgoing, total ♦ [4] circumstantial, detailed, elaborate, full, minute ♦ [5] absolute, all-out, complete, perfect, pure, total, utter

¹thor·ough·bred \'thər-ə-,bred\ *adj* **1** ♦ : bred from the best blood through a long line **2** *cap* : of or relating to the Thoroughbred breed of horses **3** : marked by high-spirited grace

♦ full-blooded, purebred

²thoroughbred *n* **1** *cap* : any of an English breed of light speedy horses kept chiefly for racing **2** : one (as a pedigreed animal) of excellent quality

thor·ough·fare \-ˌfar\ *n* ♦ : a public road or street

♦ artery, avenue, drag, drive, highway, pass, pike, road, route, row, street, trace, turnpike, way

thor·ough·go·ing \ˌthər-ə-ˈgō-iŋ\ *adj* ♦ : marked by thoroughness or zeal

♦ all-out, clean, complete, comprehensive, exhaustive, full=scale, out-and-out, thorough, total

thor·ough·ly \ˌthər-ə-lē\ *adv* ♦ : in a thorough manner or degree

♦ altogether, completely, dead, entirely, fast, flat, full, fully, perfectly, quite, well, wholly ♦ completely, exhaustively, fully, minutely, roundly, totally

¹thou \ˈthau̇\ *pron, archaic* : the person addressed
²thou \ˈthau̇\ *n, pl* **thou** : a thousand of something (as dollars)
¹though \ˈthō\ *conj* **1** ♦ : despite the fact that ⟨~ the odds are hopeless, they fight on⟩ **2** : granting that ⟨~ it may look bad, still, all is not lost⟩

♦ albeit, although, howbeit, when, while

²though *adv* ♦ : in spite of that : HOWEVER ⟨not for long, ~⟩

♦ but, howbeit, however, nevertheless, nonetheless, notwithstanding, still, withal, yet

¹thought \ˈthȯt\ *past and past part of* THINK
²thought *n* **1** : the process of thinking **2** ♦ : serious consideration **3** : reasoning power **4** : the power to imagine : CONCEPTION **5** ♦ : an individual act or product of thinking : IDEA **6** : OPINION, BELIEF

♦ [2] consideration, debate, deliberation ♦ [5] concept, idea, image, impression, notion, picture

thought·ful \ˈthȯt-fəl\ *adj* **1** ♦ : absorbed in thought **2** ♦ : marked by careful thinking ⟨a ~ essay⟩ **3** ♦ : considerate of others ⟨a ~ host⟩ — **thought·ful·ness** *n*

♦ [1] contemplative, meditative, melancholy, pensive, reflective, ruminant ♦ [2] advised, calculated, deliberate, measured, reasoned, studied, thought-out ♦ [3] attentive, considerate, kind, solicitous *Ant* heedless, inconsiderate, thoughtless, unthinking

thought·ful·ly \-fə-lē\ *adv* ♦ : in a thoughtful manner

♦ courteously, kindly, nicely, well

thought·less \-ləs\ *adj* **1** : insufficiently alert : CARELESS ⟨a ~ worker⟩ **2** : RECKLESS ⟨a ~ act⟩ **3** ♦ : lacking concern for others : INCONSIDERATE ⟨~ remarks⟩ — **thought·less·ly** *adv* — **thought·less·ness** *n*

♦ discourteous, ill-bred, ill-mannered, impertinent, impolite, inconsiderate, rude, uncivil, ungracious, unmannerly

thought–out *adj* ♦ : produced or arrived at through mental effort and esp. through careful and thorough consideration

♦ advised, calculated, deliberate, knowing, measured, reasoned, studied, thoughtful

thou·sand \ˈthau̇-ᵊnd\ *n, pl* **thousands** *or* **thousand** : 10 times 100 — **thousand** *adj* — **thou·sandth** \-ᵊnth\ *adj or n*
thousands place *n* : the place four to the left of the decimal point in an Arabic number
thrall \ˈthrȯl\ *n* **1** ♦ : an enslaved person who performs the duties of a servant : BONDMAN **2** ♦ : a state of servitude

♦ [1] bondman, chattel, slave ♦ [2] bondage, enslavement, servitude, slavery, yoke

thrall·dom *or* **thral·dom** \ˈthrȯl-dəm\ *n* : the state or condition of servitude
thrash \ˈthrash\ *vb* **1** : THRESH 1 **2** ♦ : to defeat decisively or severely : BEAT **3** : to move about violently **4** : to go over again and again ⟨~ over the matter⟩; *also* : to hammer out ⟨~ out a plan⟩ **5** ♦ : to swing, beat, or strike in the manner of a rapidly moving flail

♦ [2] beat, best, clobber, conquer, crush, defeat, drub, lick, rout, skunk, triumph, trounce, wallop, whip, win ♦ [5] flail, flog, hide, lash, scourge, slash, switch, whale, whip

¹thrash·er \ˈthra-shər\ *n* : one that thrashes or threshes
²thrasher *n* : any of various long-tailed American songbirds related to the mockingbird
¹thread \ˈthred\ *n* **1** : a thin continuous strand of spun and twisted textile fibers **2** : something resembling a textile thread **3** : the ridge or groove that winds around a screw **4** : a line of reasoning or train of thought **5** : a continuing element
²thread *vb* **1** : to pass a thread through the eye of (a needle) **2** : to pass (as film) through something **3** : to make one's way through or between **4** : to put together on or as if on a thread ⟨~ beads⟩ **5**

: to form a screw thread on or in **6** ♦ : to interweave with or as if with threads

♦ interlace, intersperse, intertwine, interweave, lace, weave, wreathe

thread·bare \-ˌbar\ *adj* **1** ♦ : worn to the point that the threads show : having the nap worn off **2** ♦ : having no interest or freshness : TRITE ⟨a ~ excuse⟩

♦ [1] ragged, ratty, seedy, shabby, tattered, worn-out ♦ [2] banal, commonplace, hackneyed, musty, stale, stereotyped, tired, trite

thready \ˈthre-dē\ *adj* **1** : consisting of or bearing fibers of filaments ⟨a ~ bark⟩ **2** : lacking in fullness, body, or vigor
threat \ˈthret\ *n* **1** : an expression of intent to do harm **2** ♦ : one that threatens

♦ danger, hazard, menace, peril, pitfall, risk, trouble

threat·en \ˈthret-ᵊn\ *vb* **1** : to utter threats against **2** : to give signs or warning of : PORTEND **3** ♦ : to hang over as a threat : MENACE **4** : to cause to feel insecure or anxious — **threat·en·ing·ly** *adv*

♦ hang, hover, menace, overhang

threat·ened *adj* : having an uncertain chance of continued survival; *esp* : likely to become an endangered species
three \ˈthrē\ *n* **1** : one more than two **2** : the 3d in a set or series **3** : something having three units — **three** *adj or pron*
3–D \ˈthrē-ˈdē\ *n* : a three-dimensional form or picture
three–dimensional *adj* **1** : relating to or having three dimensions **2** : giving the illusion of varying distances ⟨a ~ picture⟩
three·fold \ˈthrē-ˌfōld, -ˈfōld\ *adj* **1** ♦ : having three parts : TRIPLE **2** : being three times as great or as many — **three·fold** \-ˈfōld\ *adv*

♦ treble, tripartite, triple

three·pence \ˈthre-pəns, ˈthri-, ˈthrə-, *US also* ˈthrē-pens\ *n* **1** *pl* **threepence** *or* **three·penc·es** : a coin worth three pennies **2** : the sum of three British pennies
three–ring circus *n* ♦ : something wild, confusing, engrossing, or entertaining

♦ bedlam, circus, hell, madhouse

three·score \ˈthrē-ˈskōr\ *adj* : being three times twenty : SIXTY
three·some \ˈthrē-səm\ *n* ♦ : a group of three persons or things

♦ triad, trio, triple, triplet

thren·o·dy \ˈthre-nə-dē\ *n, pl* **-dies** ♦ : a song of lamentation : ELEGY

♦ dirge, elegy, lament, requiem

thresh \ˈthrash, ˈthresh\ *vb* **1** : to separate (as grain from straw) mechanically **2** : THRASH — **thresh·er** *n*
thresh·old \ˈthresh-ˌhōld\ *n* **1** : the sill of a door **2** ♦ : a point or place of beginning or entering : OUTSET **3** : a point at which a physiological or psychological effect begins to be produced ⟨a high ~ for pain⟩

♦ beginning, birth, commencement, dawn, genesis, launch, morning, onset, outset, start

threw *past of* THROW
thrice \ˈthris\ *adv* **1** : three times **2** : in a threefold manner or degree
thrift \ˈthrift\ *n* ♦ : careful management esp. of money : FRUGALITY — **thrift·i·ly** \ˈthrif-tə-lē\ *adv*

♦ economy, frugality, husbandry, providence

thrift·less \ˈthrift-ləs\ *adj* ♦ : careless, wasteful, or incompetent in handling money or resources

♦ extravagant, prodigal, profligate, spendthrift, unthrifty, wasteful

thrifty \ˈthrif-tē\ *adj* **thrift·i·er; -est** ♦ : given to or marked by economy and good management

♦ economical, frugal, provident, sparing

¹thrill \ˈthril\ *vb* **1** ♦ : to have or cause to have a sudden sharp feeling of excitement; *also* : TINGLE 1 **2** : TREMBLE, VIBRATE — **thrill·er** *n*

♦ electrify, excite, exhilarate, galvanize, intoxicate, shiver, tingle, titillate, turn on

²thrill *n* ♦ : an instantaneous excitement

♦ bang, exhilaration, kick, titillation

thrill·ing *adj* ♦ : causing an instantaneous surge of emotion — **thrill·ing·ly** *adv*

♦ breathtaking, electric, exciting, exhilarating, rousing, stirring

thrive \'thrīv\ *vb* **thrived** *or* **throve** \'thrōv\; **thrived** *also* **thriv•en** \'thri-vən\; **thriv•ing** **1** ♦ : to grow luxuriantly : FLOURISH **2** ♦ : to gain in wealth or possessions : PROSPER

♦ [1] burgeon, flourish, prosper ♦ [2] flourish, prosper, succeed

throat \'thrōt\ *n* : the part of the neck in front of the spinal column; *also* : the passage through it to the stomach and lungs — **throat•ed** *adj*

throaty \'thrō-tē\ *adj* **throat•i•er; -est** **1** ♦ : uttered or produced from low in the throat ⟨a ~ voice⟩ **2** ♦ : heavy, thick, or deep as if from the throat — **throat•i•ly** \-tə-lē\ *adv* — **throat•i•ness** \-tē-nəs\ *n*

♦ [1] bass, deep, low ♦ [2] coarse, gravelly, gruff, hoarse, husky, scratchy

¹**throb** \'thräb\ *vb* **throbbed; throb•bing** ♦ : to pulsate or pound esp. with abnormal force or rapidity : BEAT

♦ beat, palpitate, pitter-patter, pulsate, pulse

²**throb** *n* ♦ : a rhythmic pulsation or beating : BEAT, PULSE

♦ beat, palpitation, pulsation, pulse

throe \'thrō\ *n* **1** : a sudden spasm or pang **2** *pl* : a hard or painful struggle

throm•bo•sis \thräm-'bō-səs\ *n, pl* **-bo•ses** \-ˌsēz\ : the formation or presence of a clot in a blood vessel — **throm•bot•ic** \-'bä-tik\ *adj*

throm•bus \'thräm-bəs\ *n, pl* **throm•bi** \-ˌbī\ : a clot of blood formed within a blood vessel and remaining attached to its place of origin

throne \'thrōn\ *n* **1** : the chair of state of a sovereign or high dignitary **2** : royal power : SOVEREIGNTY

¹**throng** \'thròn\ *n* **1** ♦ : a multitude of assembled persons **2** : a crowding together of many persons

♦ army, crowd, crush, drove, flock, horde, host, legion, mob, multitude, press, swarm

²**throng** *vb* **thronged; throng•ing** ♦ : to crowd together in great numbers

♦ crowd, flock, mob, swarm

¹**throt•tle** \'thrät-ᵊl\ *vb* **throt•tled; throt•tling** **1** ♦ : to compress the throat of : CHOKE **2** : SUPPRESS **3** : to reduce the speed of (an engine) by closing the throttle — **throt•tler** *n*

♦ choke, garrote, strangle

²**throttle** *n* : a valve regulating the flow of steam or fuel to an engine; *also* : the lever controlling this valve

¹**through** \'thrü\ *prep* **1** : from one end or side to the other of ⟨go ~ the door⟩ **2** : by way of ⟨entered ~ a skylight⟩ **3** ♦ : in the midst of ⟨a path ~ the trees⟩ **4** ♦ : by means of ⟨succeeded ~ hard work⟩ **5** ♦ : over the whole of ⟨rumors swept ~ the office⟩ ⟨homes scattered ~ the valley⟩ **6** ♦ : during the whole of ⟨~ the night⟩ **7** : to and including ⟨Monday ~ Friday⟩

♦ [3] amid, among, midst ♦ [4] because of, due to, owing to, with ♦ [5] about, around, over, round, throughout ♦ [6] during, over, throughout

²**through** *adv* **1** ♦ : from one end or side to the other **2** : from beginning to end : to completion ⟨see it ~⟩ **3** : to the core : THOROUGHLY ⟨he was wet ~⟩ **4** : into the open : OUT ⟨break ~⟩

♦ across, over

³**through** *adj* **1** : permitting free passage ⟨a ~ street⟩ **2** : going from point of origin to destination without change or transfer ⟨a ~ train⟩ **3** : coming from or going to points outside a local area ⟨~ traffic⟩ **4** ♦ : arrived at completion or accomplishment : FINISHED ⟨~ with the job⟩

♦ complete, done, down, over, up

¹**through•out** \thrü-'aut\ *adv* **1** : in or to every part : EVERYWHERE **2** : from beginning to end

²**throughout** *prep* **1** ♦ : in or to every part of **2** ♦ : during the whole period of

♦ [1] about, around, over, round, through ♦ [2] during, over, through

through•put \'thrü-ˌput\ *n* : OUTPUT, PRODUCTION ⟨the ~ of a computer⟩

throve *past of* THRIVE

¹**throw** \'thrō\ *vb* **threw** \'thrü\; **thrown** \'thrōn\; **throw•ing** **1** ♦ : to propel through the air esp. with a forward motion of the hand and arm ⟨~ a ball⟩ **2** : to cause to fall or fall off **3** ♦ : to put suddenly in a certain position or condition ⟨~ into panic⟩ ⟨~ on a coat⟩ **4** : to put on or take off hastily ⟨~ on a coat⟩ **5** : to lose intentionally ⟨~ a game⟩ **6** : to move (a lever) so as to

connect or disconnect parts of something (as a clutch) **7** : to act as host for ⟨~ a party⟩ — **throw•er** *n*

♦ [1] cast, catapult, chuck, dash, fire, fling, heave, hurl, hurtle, launch, peg, pelt, pitch, sling, toss ♦ *usu* **throw on** [3] don, put on, slip

²**throw** *n* **1** : an act of throwing, hurling, or flinging; *also* : CAST **2** : the distance a missile may be thrown **3** : a light coverlet **4** : a woman's scarf or light wrap

throw•away \'thrō-ə-ˌwā\ *n* : something that is or is designed to be thrown away esp. after one use

throw away *vb* **1** ♦ : to get rid of as worthless or unnecessary **2** ♦ : to use in a foolish or wasteful manner

♦ [1] cast, discard, ditch, dump, fling, jettison, junk, lose, reject, scrap, shed, shuck, slough, throw out, unload ♦ [2] blow, dissipate, fritter, lavish, misspend, run through, spend, squander, waste

throw•back \-ˌbak\ *n* : reversion to an earlier type or phase; *also* : an instance or product of this

throw out *vb* **1** ♦ : to remove from a place, office, or employment usu. in a sudden or unexpected manner **2** ♦ : to get rid of as worthless or unnecessary

♦ [1] banish, boot (out), bounce, cast, chase, dismiss, drum, eject, expel, oust, rout, run off ♦ [2] cast, discard, ditch, dump, fling, jettison, junk, lose, reject, scrap, shed, shuck, slough, throw away, unload

throw up *vb* **1** : to build hurriedly **2** ♦ : to discharge the contents of the stomach through the mouth : VOMIT

♦ gag, heave, spit up, vomit

thrum \'thrəm\ *vb* **thrummed; thrum•ming** : to play or pluck a stringed instrument idly : STRUM

thrush \'thrəsh\ *n* : any of numerous small or medium-sized songbirds that are mostly of a plain color often with spotted underparts

¹**thrust** \'thrəst\ *vb* **thrust; thrust•ing** **1** ♦ : to push or drive with force : SHOVE **2** : STAB, PIERCE **3** : INTERJECT **4** : to press the acceptance of upon someone

♦ drive, propel, push, shove

²**thrust** *n* **1** : a lunge with a pointed weapon **2** : ATTACK **3** : the pressure of one part of a construction against another (as of an arch against an abutment) **4** : the force produced by a propeller or jet or rocket engine that drives a vehicle (as an aircraft) forward **5** : a violent push : SHOVE **6** : a prominent or essential element

thrust•er *also* **thrust•or** \'thrəs-tər\ *n* : one that thrusts; *esp* : a rocket engine

thru•way \'thrü-ˌwā\ *n* : EXPRESSWAY

¹**thud** \'thəd\ *n* **1** : a forcible stroke delivered with a part of the body or with an instrument : BLOW **2** : a dull sound

²**thud** *vb* **thud•ded; thud•ding** ♦ : to move or strike so as to make a thud

♦ bang, bash, bump, collide, crash, hit, impact, knock, ram, slam, smash, strike, swipe

thug \'thəg\ *n* ♦ : a brutal ruffian or assassin — **thug•gish** *adj*

♦ bully, gangster, goon, hood, hoodlum, mobster, mug, punk, rowdy, ruffian, tough

thu•li•um \'thü-lē-əm, 'thyü-\ *n* : a rare metallic chemical element

¹**thumb** \'thəm\ *n* **1** : the short thick first digit of the human hand or a corresponding digit of a lower animal **2** : the part of a glove or mitten that covers the thumb

²**thumb** *vb* **1** : to leaf through (pages) with the thumb **2** : to wear or soil with the thumb by frequent handling **3** : to request or obtain (a ride) in a passing automobile by signaling with the thumb

thumb drive *n* : FLASH DRIVE

¹**thumb•nail** \'thəm-ˌnāl\ *n* : the nail of the thumb

²**thumbnail** *adj* : BRIEF, CONCISE ⟨a ~ description⟩

thumb•print \-ˌprint\ *n* : an impression made by the thumb

thumb•screw \-ˌskrü\ *n* **1** : a screw with a head that may be turned by the thumb and forefinger **2** : a device of torture for squeezing the thumb

thumb•tack \-ˌtak\ *n* : a tack with a broad flat head for pressing with one's thumb into a board or wall

¹**thump** \'thəmp\ *vb* **1** : to strike with or as if with something thick or heavy so as to cause a dull sound **2** : to strike heavily or repeatedly : POUND

²**thump** *n* ♦ : a blow with or as if with something blunt or heavy; *also* : the sound made by such a blow

♦ blow, clout, hit, pound, punch, thud, thwack, wallop, whack

¹thun·der \'thən-dər\ *n* **1** : the sound following a flash of lightning; *also* : a noise like such a sound **2** : a loud utterance or threat

²thunder *vb* **1** : to produce thunder **2** ♦ : to utter or emit a full loud prolonged sound : ROAR ⟨jets ~ed overhead⟩

♦ bellow, boom, growl, roar

thun·der·bolt \-ˌbōlt\ *n* : a flash of lightning with its accompanying thunder

thun·der·clap \-ˌklap\ *n* **1** : a crash of thunder **2** ♦ : something sharp, loud, or sudden like a clap of thunder

♦ bang, blast, boom, clap, crack, crash, pop, report, slam, smash, snap, thwack, whack

thun·der·cloud \-ˌklau̇d\ *n* : a cloud charged with electricity and producing lightning and thunder

thun·der·head \-ˌhed\ *n* : a large cumulus or cumulonimbus cloud often appearing before a thunderstorm

thun·der·ous \'thən-də-rəs\ *adj* ♦ : producing thunder; *also* : making a noise like thunder — **thun·der·ous·ly** *adv*

♦ booming, clamorous (*or* clamourous), deafening, earsplitting, loud, piercing, resounding, ringing, roaring, sonorous, stentorian

thun·der·show·er \'thən-dər-ˌshau̇-ər\ *n* : a shower accompanied by thunder and lightning

thun·der·storm \-ˌstȯrm\ *n* : a storm accompanied by thunder and lightning

thun·der·struck \-ˌstrək\ *adj* ♦ : stunned as if struck by a thunderbolt

♦ amazed, awestruck, stunned

Thurs *or* **Thu** *abbr* Thursday

Thurs·day \'thərz-dē, -ˌdā\ *n* : the 5th day of the week

thus \'thəs\ *adv* **1** : in this or that manner **2** ♦ : to this degree or extent : SO ⟨~ far⟩ **3** ♦ : because of this or that : HENCE

♦ *usu* **thus far** [2] heretofore, hitherto, so, yet ♦ [3] accordingly, consequently, ergo, hence, so, therefore, wherefore

¹thwack \'thwak\ *vb* : to strike with or as if with something flat or heavy

²thwack *n* **1** : a heavy blow : WHACK **2** ♦ : the sound of or as if of a heavy blow

♦ bang, blast, boom, clap, crack, crash, pop, report, slam, smash, snap, whack

¹thwart \'thwȯrt\ *vb* **1** ♦ : to oppose successfully : FOIL **2** : BLOCK, DEFEAT ⟨~ed the attack⟩

♦ baffle, balk, beat, checkmate, foil, frustrate

²thwart \'thwȯrt, *naut often* 'thȯrt\ *adv* : ATHWART

³thwart *adj* : situated or placed across something else

⁴thwart \'thwȯrt\ *n* : a seat extending across a boat

thy \'thī\ *adj, archaic* : of, relating to, or done by or to thee or thyself

thyme \'tīm, 'thīm\ *n* : a garden mint with small aromatic leaves used esp. in seasoning; *also* : its leaves so used

thy·mine \'thī-ˌmēn\ *n* : a pyrimidine base that is one of the four bases coding genetic information in the molecular chain of DNA

thy·mus \'thī-məs\ *n, pl* **thy·mus·es** : a glandular organ of the neck region that is composed largely of lymphoid tissue, functions esp. in the development of the immune system, and tends to atrophy in the adult

thy·ris·tor \thī-'ris-tər\ *n* : a semiconductor device that acts as a switch, rectifier, or voltage regulator

thy·roid \'thī-ˌrȯid\ *n* : a large 2-lobed endocrine gland that lies at the base of the neck and produces several iodine-containing hormones that affect growth, development, and metabolism — **thyroid** *also* **thy·roi·dal** \thī-'rȯi-dᵊl\ *adj*

thy·rox·ine *or* **thy·rox·in** \thī-'räk-ˌsēn, -sən\ *n* : an iodine-containing hormone that is produced by the thyroid gland, increases metabolic rate, and is used to treat thyroid disorders

thy·self \thī-'self\ *pron, archaic* : YOURSELF

Ti *symbol* titanium

ti·ara \tē-'ar-ə, -'er-, -'är-\ *n* **1** : a 3-tiered crown worn by the pope **2** : a decorative headband or semicircle for formal wear by women

Ti·bet·an \tə-'bet-ᵊn\ *n* **1** : the language of the Tibetan people **2** : a native or inhabitant of Tibet — **Tibetan** *adj*

tib·ia \'ti-bē-ə\ *n, pl* **-i·ae** \-bē-ˌē\ *also* **-i·as** : the inner of the two bones of the vertebrate hind or lower limb between the knee and the ankle

tic \'tik\ *n* **1** : a local and habitual twitching of muscles esp. of the face **2** ♦ : a frequent usu. unconscious quirk of behavior or speech

♦ crotchet, eccentricity, idiosyncrasy, mannerism, oddity, peculiarity, quirk, singularity, trick

¹tick \'tik\ *n* : any of a large group of small bloodsucking arachnids

²tick *n* : the fabric case of a mattress or pillow; *also* : a mattress consisting of a tick and its filling

³tick *n* **1** : a light rhythmic audible tap or beat **2** : a small mark used to draw attention to or check something

⁴tick *vb* **1** : to make the sound of a tick or series of ticks **2** ♦ : to mark, count, or announce by or as if by ticking beats — often used with *off* **3** ♦ : to mark or check with a tick — usu. used with *off* **4** : to function as an operating mechanism : RUN

♦ *usu* **tick off** [2, 3] detail, enumerate, itemize, list, numerate, rehearse

⁵tick *n, chiefly Brit* : CREDIT; *also* : a credit account

tick·er \'ti-kər\ *n* **1** : something (as a watch) that ticks **2** : a telegraph instrument that prints information (as stock prices) on paper tape **3** *slang* : HEART

ticker tape *n* : the paper ribbon on which a telegraphic ticker prints

¹tick·et \'ti-kət\ *n* **1 a** : CERTIFICATE, LICENSE, PERMIT **b** ♦ : a certificate or token showing that a fare or admission fee has been paid **2** : a marker used for identification or classification : TAG, LABEL **3** : SLATE **4** : a summons issued to a traffic offender

♦ check, note, pass, token

²ticket *vb* **1** ♦ : to attach a ticket to **2** : to furnish or serve with a ticket

♦ label, mark, tag

tick·ing \'ti-kiŋ\ *n* : a strong fabric used in upholstering and as a mattress covering

tick·le \'ti-kəl\ *vb* **tick·led; tick·ling 1** : to excite or stir up agreeably : PLEASE, AMUSE **2** : to have a tingling sensation **3** : to touch (as a body part) lightly so as to cause uneasiness, laughter, or spasmodic movements ⟨*tickled* her under the chin⟩ — **tickle** *n* — **tick·ler** *n*

tick·lish \-kə-lish\ *adj* **1** : overly sensitive : TOUCHY **2** : UNSTABLE ⟨a ~ foothold⟩ **3** ♦ : requiring delicate handling ⟨~ subject⟩ **4** : sensitive to tickling — **tick·lish·ly** *adv* — **tick·lish·ness** *n*

♦ catchy, delicate, difficult, knotty, problematic, spiny, thorny, touchy, tough, tricky

tidal wave *n* **1** : an unusually high sea wave that sometimes follows an earthquake **2** : an unusual rise of water alongshore due to strong winds

tid·bit \'tid-ˌbit\ *n* ♦ : a choice morsel

♦ bite, morsel, mouthful, nibble, taste ♦ dainty, delicacy, goody, treat

¹tide \'tīd\ *n* **1** : the alternate rising and falling of the surface of the ocean **2** ♦ : something that fluctuates like the tides of the sea ⟨the ~ of public opinion⟩ — **tid·al** \'tīd-ᵊl\ *adj*

♦ current, drift, leaning, run, tendency, trend, wind

²tide *vb* **tid·ed; tid·ing** : to carry through or help along as if by the tide ⟨a loan to ~ us over⟩

tide·land \'tīd-ˌland, -lənd\ *n* **1** : land overflowed during flood tide **2** : land under the ocean within a nation's territorial waters — often used in pl.

tide·wa·ter \-ˌwȯ-tər, -ˌwä-\ *n* **1** : water overflowing land at flood tide **2** : low-lying coastal land

tid·ings \'tī-diŋz\ *n pl* ♦ : previously unknown information : NEWS

♦ intelligence, item, news, story, word

¹ti·dy \'tī-dē\ *adj* **ti·di·er; -est 1** ♦ : well ordered and cared for : NEAT **2 a** ♦ : exceeding most other things of like kind esp. in quantity or size : LARGE ⟨a ~ sum⟩ **b** ♦ : significantly great : SUBSTANTIAL — **ti·di·ness** \'tī-dē-nəs\ *n*

♦ [1] crisp, neat, orderly, shipshape, snug, trim, uncluttered ♦ [2a, b] considerable, good, goodly, healthy, large, respectable, significant, sizable, substantial

²tidy *vb* **ti·died; ti·dy·ing 1** : to put in order **2** : to make things tidy

³tidy *n, pl* **tidies** : a decorated covering used to protect the back or arms of a chair from wear or soil

¹tie \'tī\ *n* **1** : a line, ribbon, or cord used for fastening, uniting, or closing **2** : a structural element (as a beam or rod) holding two pieces together **3** : one of the cross supports to which railroad rails are fastened **4** ♦ : a connecting link : BOND ⟨family ~s⟩ **5**

♦ : an equality in number (as of votes or scores); *also* : an undecided or deadlocked contest   **6** : NECKTIE

♦ [4] bond, cement, knot, ligature, link   ♦ [5] dead heat, draw, stalemate, standoff

²tie *vb* **tied; ty·ing** *or* **tie·ing**   **1** ♦ : to fasten, attach, or close by means of a tie   **2** : to bring together firmly : UNITE   **3** : to form a knot or bow in ⟨~ a scarf⟩   **4** : to restrain from freedom of action : CONSTRAIN   **5 a** : to make or have an equal score with   **b** ♦ : to provide or offer something equal to

♦ [1] band, bind, gird, truss *Ant* unbind, untie   ♦ [5b] equal, match, meet

tie-back \'tī-ˌbak\ *n* : a decorative strip for draping a curtain to the side of a window

tie–dye·ing \'tī-ˌdī-iŋ\ *n* : a method of producing patterns in textiles by tying parts of the fabric so that they will not absorb the dye — **tie–dyed** \-ˌdīd\ *adj*

tie-in \'tī-ˌin\ *n* : CONNECTION

tier \'tir\ *n* : ROW, LAYER; *esp* : one of two or more rows arranged one above another — **tiered** \'tird\ *adj*

tie-rod \'tī-ˌräd\ *n* : a rod used as a connecting member or brace

tie-up \-ˌəp\ *n* **1** : a slowing or stopping of traffic or business   **2** : the act of connecting : the state of being connected : CONNECTION

tie up *vb* **1 a** : to place or invest in such a manner as to make unavailable for other purposes ⟨their money was *tied up* in stocks⟩   **b** ♦ : to restrain from normal movement, operation, or progress ⟨traffic was *tied up* for miles⟩   **2 a** : to keep busy ⟨was *tied up* in conference all day⟩   **b** : to preempt the use of ⟨*tied up* the phone for an hour⟩

♦ encumber, hamper, hinder, hold up, impede, inhibit, interfere with, obstruct

tiff \'tif\ *n* : a petty quarrel — **tiff** *vb*

Tif·fa·ny \'ti-fə-nē\ *adj* : made of pieces of stained glass ⟨a ~ lamp⟩

ti·ger \'tī-gər\ *n* : a very large tawny black-striped Asian cat — **ti·ger·ish** *adj*

¹tight \'tīt\ *adj* **1** ♦ : so close in structure as to prevent passage of a liquid or gas   **2** ♦ : strongly fixed or held : SECURE   **3** : not slack or loose : TAUT   **4** : fitting usu. too closely ⟨~ shoes⟩   **5** ♦ : set close together : COMPACT ⟨a ~ formation⟩   **6** : DIFFICULT, TRYING ⟨get in a ~ spot⟩   **7** : not liberal in giving : STINGY   **8** ♦ : evenly contested : CLOSE   **9** : INTOXICATED   **10** : low in supply : hard to get ⟨money is ~⟩ — **tight·ly** *adv*

♦ [1] impenetrable, impervious *Ant* penetrable, permeable
♦ [2] fast, firm, frozen, secure, set, snug *Ant* insecure, loose
♦ [5] close, compact, crowded, dense, packed, serried, thick
♦ [8] close, narrow, neck and neck, nip and tuck

²tight *adv* **1** : TIGHTLY, FIRMLY   **2** : SOUNDLY ⟨sleep ~⟩

tight·en \'tī-tᵊn\ *vb* : to make or become tight

tight-fist·ed \'tīt-'fis-təd\ *adj* ♦ : not liberal in giving : STINGY

♦ cheap, close, mean, niggardly, parsimonious, penurious, spare, sparing, stingy, tight, uncharitable

tight·ness \'tīt-nəs\ *n* ♦ : the quality or state of being tight

♦ cheapness, closeness, miserliness, parsimony, stinginess

tight·rope \-ˌrōp\ *n* : a taut rope or wire for acrobats to perform on

tights \'tīts\ *n pl* : skintight garments covering the body esp. below the waist; *also, Brit* : PANTY HOSE

tight·wad \'tīt-ˌwäd\ *n* ♦ : a stingy person

♦ cheapskate, miser, niggard, skinflint

ti·gress \'tī-grəs\ *n* : a female tiger

ti·la·pia \tə-'lä-pē-ə, -'lä-\ *n, pl* **tilapia** *also* **ti·la·pi·as** : any of numerous chiefly African freshwater fishes widely raised for food

til·de \'til-də\ *n* : a mark ~ placed esp. over the letter *n* (as in Spanish *señor* sir) to denote the sound \nʸ\ or over vowels (as in Portuguese *irmã* sister) to indicate nasal quality

¹tile \'tīl\ *n* **1** : a flat or curved piece of fired clay, stone, or concrete used for roofs, floors, or walls; *also* : a pipe of earthenware or concrete used for a drain   **2** : a thin piece (as of linoleum) used for covering walls or floors — **til·ing** \'tī-liŋ\ *n*

²tile *vb* **tiled; til·ing** : to cover with tiles — **til·er** *n*

¹till \'til\ *prep or conj* : UNTIL

²till *vb* : to work by plowing, sowing, and raising crops : CULTIVATE — **till·able** *adj*

³till *n* : DRAWER; *esp* : a money drawer in a store or bank

till·age \'ti-lij\ *n* **1** : the work of tilling land   **2** : cultivated land

¹til·ler \'ti-lər\ *n* : a sprout or stalk esp. from the base or lower part of a plant

²til·ler \'ti-lər\ *n* ♦ : one that tills

♦ agriculturist, cultivator, farmer, grower, planter

³til·ler \'ti-lər\ *n* : a lever used for turning a boat's rudder from side to side

¹tilt \'tilt\ *n* **1** : a contest in which two combatants charging usu. with lances try to unhorse each other : JOUST; *also* : a tournament of tilts   **2** : a verbal contest : DISPUTE   **3** ♦ : the act of tilting : the state or position of being tilted

♦ bend, cock, inclination, list, slant, tip

²tilt *vb* **1** ♦ : to move or shift so as to incline : TIP   **2** : to engage in or as if in combat with lances : JOUST, ATTACK

♦ angle, cant, cock, heel, incline, lean, list, slant, slope, tip

tilth \'tilth\ *n* **1** : TILLAGE   **2** : the state of a soil esp. in relation to the suitability of its particle size and structure for growing crops

Tim *abbr* Timothy

tim·ber \'tim-bər\ *n* **1** : growing trees or their wood — often used interjectionally to warn of a falling tree   **2** : wood for use in making something   **3** : a usu. large squared or dressed piece of wood

tim·bered \'tim-bərd\ *adj* : having walls framed by exposed timbers

tim·ber·land \'tim-bər-ˌland\ *n* ♦ : wooded land

♦ forest, woodland

tim·ber·line \'tim-bər-ˌlīn\ *n* : the upper limit of tree growth in mountains or high latitudes

timber rattlesnake *n* : a widely distributed rattlesnake of the eastern U.S.

timber wolf *n* : GRAY WOLF

tim·bre *also* **tim·ber** \'tam-bər, 'tim-\ *n* : the distinctive quality given to a sound by its overtones

tim·brel \'tim-brəl\ *n* : a small hand drum or tambourine

¹time \'tīm\ *n* **1 a** : a period during which an action, process, or condition exists or continues ⟨gone a long ~⟩   **b** : the duration of the existence of a living being (as a person or an animal) or a thing (as a star) : LIFETIME   **2** : LEISURE ⟨found ~ to read⟩   **3** : a point or period when something occurs : OCCASION ⟨the last ~ we met⟩   **4** : a set or customary moment or hour for something to occur ⟨arrived on ~⟩   **5** ♦ : a historical period : AGE, ERA   **6** : state of affairs : CONDITIONS ⟨hard ~s⟩   **7** : a rate of speed : TEMPO   **8** : a moment, hour, day, or year as indicated by a clock or calendar ⟨what ~ is it⟩   **9** : a system of reckoning time ⟨solar ~⟩   **10** : one of a series of recurring instances; *also, pl* : added or accumulated quantities or examples ⟨five ~s greater⟩   **11** ♦ : a person's experience during a particular period ⟨had a good ~⟩   **12** : the hours or days of one's work; *also* : an hourly pay rate ⟨straight ~⟩   **13** : TIME-OUT 1

♦ [5] age, epoch, era, period   ♦ [11] adventure, experience, happening

²time *vb* **timed; tim·ing**   **1** : to arrange or set the time of : SCHEDULE ⟨~s his calls conveniently⟩   **2** : to set the tempo or duration of ⟨~ a performance⟩   **3** : to cause to keep time with   **4** : to determine or record the time, duration, or rate of ⟨~ a sprinter⟩

time bomb *n* **1** : a bomb so made as to explode at a predetermined time   **2** : something with a potentially dangerous delayed reaction

time clock *n* : a clock that records the time workers arrive and depart

time frame *n* : a period of time esp. with respect to some action or project

time–hon·ored \'tīm-ˌä-nərd\ *adj* : honored because of age or long usage

time·keep·er \-ˌkē-pər\ *n* **1** : a clerk who keeps records of the time worked by employees   **2** : one appointed to mark and announce the time in an athletic game or contest

time·less \-ləs\ *adj* **1** : ETERNAL   **2** ♦ : not limited or affected by time ⟨~ works of art⟩ — **time·less·ly** *adv* — **time·less·ness** *n*

♦ abiding, ageless, continuing, dateless, enduring, eternal, everlasting, immortal, imperishable, lasting, perennial, perpetual, undying

time·li·ness \'tīm-lē-nəs\ *n* ♦ : the quality or state of being timely

♦ promptitude, punctuality

time·ly \'tīm-lē\ *adj* **time·li·er; -est**   **1** ♦ : coming early or at the right time ⟨a ~ arrival⟩   **2** : appropriate to the time ⟨a ~ book⟩

♦ immediate, prompt, punctual

time–out \'tīm-'aût\ *n* **1** : a brief suspension of activity esp. in an athletic game **2** : a quiet period used esp. as a disciplinary measure for a child

time·piece \-,pēs\ *n* ♦ : a device (as a clock) to show the passage of time

♦ watch

tim·er \'tī-mər\ *n* : one that times

times \'tīmz\ *prep* : multiplied by ⟨2 ~ 2 is 4⟩

time–shar·ing \'tīm-,shar-iŋ\ *n* **1** : simultaneous use of a computer by many users **2** *or* **time–share** \-,shar\ : joint ownership or rental of a vacation lodging by several persons with each taking turns using the place

times sign *n* : the symbol × used to indicate multiplication

time·ta·ble \'tīm-,tā-bəl\ *n* **1** : a table of the departure and arrival times (as of trains) **2** ♦ : a schedule showing a planned order or sequence

♦ agenda, calendar, docket, program, schedule

time warp *n* : an anomaly, discontinuity, or suspension held to occur in the progress of time

time·worn \-,wórn\ *adj* **1** : worn by time **2** : HACKNEYED, STALE

tim·id \'ti-məd\ *adj* ♦ : lacking in courage or self-confidence : FEARFUL — **ti·mid·i·ty** \tə-'mi-də-tē\ *n* — **tim·id·ly** *adv*

♦ fainthearted, fearful, mousy, scary, shy, skittish

tim·o·rous \'ti-mə-rəs\ *adj* ♦ : of a timid disposition : AFRAID ⟨a ~ kitten⟩ — **tim·o·rous·ly** *adv* — **tim·o·rous·ness** *n*

tim·o·thy \'ti-mə-thē\ *n* : a perennial grass with long cylindrical spikes widely grown for hay in the U.S.

Tim·o·thy \'ti-mə-thē\ *n* : either of two books of the New Testament of Christian Scripture

tim·pa·ni \'tim-pə-nē\ *n sing or pl* : a set of kettledrums played by one performer in an orchestra — **tim·pa·nist** \-nist\ *n*

¹**tin** \'tin\ *n* **1** : a soft white crystalline metallic chemical element malleable at ordinary temperatures that is used esp. in solders and alloys **2** ♦ : a container (as a can) made of metal (as tinplate)

♦ barrel, can, canister, drum

²**tin** *vb* **tinned; tin·ning** **1** : to cover or plate with tin **2** : to pack in tins

TIN *abbr* taxpayer identification number

tinct \'tiŋkt\ *n* : TINCTURE, TINGE

¹**tinc·ture** \'tiŋk-chər\ *n* **1** *archaic* : a substance that colors **2** : a slight admixture : TRACE **3** : an alcoholic solution of a medicinal substance

²**tincture** *vb* **tinc·tured; tinc·tur·ing** **1** : COLOR, TINGE **2** : AFFECT

tin·der \'tin-dər\ *n* **1** : a very flammable substance used as kindling **2** : something serving to incite or inflame

tin·der·box \'tin-dər-,bäks\ *n* **1** : a metal box for holding tinder and usu. flint and steel for striking a spark **2** : a highly flammable object or place

tine \'tīn\ *n* : a slender pointed part (as of a fork or an antler) : PRONG

tin·foil \'tin-,fóil\ *n* : a thin metal sheeting usu. of aluminum or tin-lead alloy

¹**tinge** \'tinj\ *vb* **tinged; tinge·ing** *or* **ting·ing** **1** ♦ : to color slightly : TINT **2** : to affect or modify esp. with a slight odor or taste

♦ color (*or* colour), dye, paint, stain, tint

²**tinge** *n* ♦ : a slight color, flavor, or quality

♦ cast, color (*or* colour), hue, shade, tint, tone

¹**tin·gle** \'tiŋ-gəl\ *vb* **tin·gled; tin·gling** **1** : to feel a prickling or thrilling sensation **2** : TINKLE

²**tingle** *n* ♦ : a tingling sensation or condition

♦ ache, pain, pang, prick, smart, sting, stitch, twinge

¹**tin·ker** \'tiŋ-kər\ *n* **1** : a usu. itinerant mender of household utensils **2** : an unskillful mender : BUNGLER

²**tinker** *vb* ♦ : to repair or adjust something in an unskillful or experimental manner — **tin·ker·er** *n*

♦ fiddle, fool, mess, monkey, play, tamper

¹**tin·kle** \'tiŋ-kəl\ *vb* **tin·kled; tin·kling** ♦ : to make or cause to make a tinkle

♦ chink, jingle

²**tinkle** *n* : a series of short high ringing or clinking sounds

tin·ni·tus \'ti-nə-təs, tə-'nī-təs\ *n* : a sensation of noise (as ringing or roaring) in the ears

tin·ny \'ti-nē\ *adj* **tin·ni·er; -est** **1** : abounding in or yielding

tin **2** : resembling tin; *also* : LIGHT, CHEAP **3** : thin in tone ⟨a ~ voice⟩ — **tin·ni·ly** \-nə-lē\ *adv* — **tin·ni·ness** \-nē-nəs\ *n*

tin·plate \'tin-'plāt\ *n* : thin sheet iron or steel coated with tin — **tin–plate** *vb*

tin·sel \'tin-səl\ *n* **1** : a thread, strip, or sheet of metal, paper, or plastic used to produce a glittering appearance **2** : something superficially attractive but of little worth

tin·smith \'tin-,smith\ *n* : one that works with sheet metal (as tinplate)

¹**tint** \'tint\ *n* **1** ♦ : a slight or pale coloration : HUE **2** ♦ : any of various shades of a color

♦ cast, color (*or* colour), hue, shade, tinge, tone

²**tint** *vb* ♦ : to impart a tint to : COLOR

♦ color (*or* colour), dye, paint, stain, tinge

tin·tin·nab·u·la·tion \,tin-tə-,na-byə-'lā-shən\ *n* **1** : the ringing of bells **2** : a tinkling or jingling sound as if of bells

tin·ware \'tin-,war\ *n* : articles and esp. utensils made of tinplate

ti·ny \'tī-nē\ *adj* **ti·ni·er; -est** ♦ : very small : MINUTE

♦ atomic, infinitesimal, microscopic, miniature, minute, wee *Ant* enormous, giant, gigantic, huge, immense, mammoth

¹**tip** \'tip\ *vb* **tipped; tip·ping** **1** : OVERTURN, UPSET **2** ♦ : to incline, deviate, or slant from a vertical position : LEAN; *also* : to raise and tilt forward ⟨*tipped* his hat⟩

♦ angle, cant, cock, heel, incline, lean, list, slant, slope, tilt

²**tip** *n* ♦ : the act or an instance of tipping

♦ bend, cock, inclination, list, slant, tilt

³**tip** *vb* **tipped; tip·ping** **1** : to furnish with a tip **2** : to cover or adorn the tip of

⁴**tip** *n* **1** ♦ : the usu. pointed end of something **2** : a small piece or part serving as an end, cap, or point

♦ apex, cusp, end, pike, point

⁵**tip** *n* : a light touch or blow

⁶**tip** *vb* **tipped; tip·ping** : to strike lightly : TAP

⁷**tip** *n* ♦ : a piece of advice or expert or confidential information

♦ dope, lowdown, scoop ♦ hint, lead, pointer

⁸**tip** *vb* **tipped; tip·ping** : to impart a piece of information about or to

⁹**tip** *vb* **tipped; tip·ping** : to give a gratuity to — **tip·per** *n*

¹⁰**tip** *n* ♦ : a gift or small sum given for a service performed or anticipated

♦ bonus, dividend, extra, lagniappe, perquisite

tip·off \'tip-,óf\ *n* ♦ : something that warns or serves to warn : WARNING

♦ caution, wake-up call, warning

tip·pet \'ti-pət\ *n* : a long scarf or shoulder cape

tipping point *n* : the critical point in a situation or process beyond which a significant effect takes place

tip·ple \'ti-pəl\ *vb* **tip·pled; tip·pling** : to drink intoxicating liquor esp. habitually or excessively — **tipple** *n*

tip·pler \'ti-p(ə-)lər\ *n* ♦ : one that tipples

♦ drunk, inebriate, soak, sot, souse

tip·ster \'tip-stər\ *n* : a person who gives or sells tips esp. for gambling

tip·sy \'tip-sē\ *adj* **tip·si·er; -est** ♦ : unsteady or foolish from the effects of alcohol — **tip·si·ly** \-sə-lē\ *adv*

♦ drunk, high, inebriate, intoxicated

¹**tip·toe** \'tip-,tō\ *n* : the position of being balanced on the balls of the feet and toes with the heels raised; *also* : the ends of the toes

²**tiptoe** *adv or adj* : on or as if on tiptoe

³**tiptoe** *vb* **tip·toed; tip·toe·ing** : to walk or proceed on or as if on tiptoe

¹**tip–top** \'tip-'täp\ *n* ♦ : the highest point

♦ acme, apex, climax, crown, culmination, head, height, meridian, peak, pinnacle, summit, top, zenith

²**tip–top** *adj* : very good of its kind : EXCELLENT

ti·rade \'tī-,rād\ *n* ♦ : a prolonged speech of abuse or condemnation

♦ diatribe, harangue, rant

tir·a·mi·su \,tir-ə-'mē-sü, -mē-'sü\ *n* : a dessert made with ladyfingers, mascarpone, and espresso

¹**tire** \'tīr\ *vb* **tired; tir·ing** **1** ♦ : to make or become weary **2** ♦ : to wear out the patience of : BORE

♦ [1] burn out, do in, drain, exhaust, fag, fatigue, tucker, wash out, wear, wear out, weary ♦ [2] bore, jade, weary

²**tire** *n* **1 :** a metal hoop that forms the tread of a wheel **2 :** a rubber cushion usu. containing compressed air that encircles a wheel (as of a bike)

tired \'tīrd\ *adj* **1 ♦ :** exhausted in strength, endurance, vigor, or freshness : WEARY, FATIGUED **2 ♦ :** lacking in freshness or originality : HACKNEYED **3 ♦ :** having one's patience, tolerance, or pleasure exhausted

♦ [1] beat, bushed, dead, drained, effete, jaded, limp, prostrate, spent, weary, worn-out ♦ [2] banal, commonplace, hackneyed, musty, stale, stereotyped, threadbare, trite ♦ [3] fed up, jaded, sick, weary

tired•ness *n* ♦ **:** the quality or state of being tired

♦ burnout, collapse, exhaustion, fatigue, lassitude, prostration, weariness ♦ boredom, doldrums, ennui, listlessness, restlessness, tedium, weariness

tire•less \'tīr-ləs\ *adj* ♦ **:** not tiring : UNTIRING ⟨~ workers⟩ — **tire•less•ness** *n*

♦ indefatigable, inexhaustible, unflagging, untiring

tire•less•ly *adv* ♦ **:** in a tireless manner

♦ determinedly, diligently, hard, hardly, laboriously, mightily, strenuously

tire•some \-səm\ *adj* **:** tending to bore : WEARISOME, TEDIOUS ⟨~ lecture⟩ — **tire•some•ly** *adv* — **tire•some•ness** *n*

tis•sue \'ti-shü\ *n* **1 :** a fine lightweight often sheer fabric **2 :** NETWORK, WEB **3 :** a soft absorbent paper **4 :** a mass or layer of cells forming a basic structural material of an animal or plant

¹**tit** \'tit\ *n* **:** TEAT

²**tit** *n* **:** any of various small plump Old World songbirds related to the titmice

Tit *abbr* Titus

ti•tan \'tīt-³n\ *n* **1** *cap* **:** one of a family of giants overthrown by the gods in Greek mythology **2 ♦ :** one gigantic in size or power ⟨a media ~⟩

♦ behemoth, blockbuster, colossus, giant, jumbo, leviathan, mammoth, monster, whale, whopper

ti•tan•ic \tī-'ta-nik\ *adj* ♦ **:** enormous in size, force, or power

♦ colossal, enormous, giant, gigantic, huge, mammoth, massive, prodigious, tremendous

ti•ta•ni•um \tī-'tā-nē-əm\ *n* **:** a gray light strong metallic chemical element used esp. in alloys

titbit *var of* TIDBIT

tithe \'tīth\ *n* **:** a 10th part paid or given esp. for the support of a church — **tithe** *vb* — **tith•er** *n*

tit•il•late \'ti-³l-,āt\ *vb* **-lat•ed; -lat•ing** **1 ♦ :** to excite pleasurably **2 :** TICKLE 3

♦ electrify, excite, exhilarate, galvanize, intoxicate, thrill, turn on

tit•il•la•tion \,ti-³l-'ā-shən\ *n* ♦ **:** the action of titillating or the state of being titillated

♦ bang, exhilaration, kick, thrill

ti•tle \'tīt-³l\ *n* **1 :** CLAIM, RIGHT; *esp* **:** a legal right to the ownership of property **2 ♦ :** the distinguishing name esp. of an artistic production (as a book) **3 ♦ :** an appellation of honor, rank, or office **4 :** CHAMPIONSHIP

♦ [2] heading ♦ [3] appellation, cognomen, denotation, designation, handle, name

ti•tled \'tīt-³ld\ *adj* **:** having a title esp. of nobility

title page *n* **:** a page of a book bearing the title and usu. the names of the author and publisher

tit•mouse \'tit-,maus\ *n, pl* **tit•mice** \-,mīs\ **:** any of several small long-tailed No. American songbirds related to the chickadees

ti•tra•tion \tī-'trā-shən\ *n* **:** a process of finding the concentration of a solution (as of an acid) by adding small portions of a second solution of known concentration (as of a base) to a fixed amount of the first until an expected change (as in color) occurs

¹**tit•ter** \'ti-tər\ *vb* **:** to laugh in an affected or in a nervous or half-suppressed manner : GIGGLE

²**titter** *n* ♦ **:** an act or instance of tittering

♦ cackle, chortle, laugh, laughter, snicker

tit•tle \'tit-³l\ *n* ♦ **:** a tiny piece

♦ bit, hoot, jot, lick, modicum, rap, whit

tit•tle–tat•tle \'tit-³l-,tat-³l\ *n* **:** idle talk : GOSSIP — **tittle–tattle** *vb*

tit•u•lar \'ti-chə-lər\ *adj* **1 ♦ :** existing in title only : NOMINAL ⟨~ ruler⟩ **2 :** of, relating to, or bearing a title ⟨~ role⟩

♦ formal, nominal, paper

Ti•tus \'tī-təs\ *n* **:** a book of the New Testament of Christian Scripture

tiz•zy \'ti-zē\ *n, pl* **tizzies** ♦ **:** a highly excited and distracted state of mind

♦ dither, fluster, fret, fuss, huff, lather, pother, stew, twitter

tk *abbr* **1** tank **2** truck

TKO \,tē-kā-'ō\ *n* **:** the termination of a boxing match when a boxer is declared unable to continue the fight

tkt *abbr* ticket

Tl *symbol* thallium

TLC *abbr* tender loving care

T lymphocyte *n* **:** T CELL

Tm *symbol* thulium

TM *abbr* trademark

T–man \'tē-,man\ *n* **:** a special agent of the U.S. Treasury Department

tn *abbr* **1** ton **2** town

TN *abbr* Tennessee

tng *abbr* training

tnpk *abbr* turnpike

TNT \,tē-(,)en-'tē\ *n* **:** a flammable toxic compound used as a high explosive and in chemical synthesis

¹**to** \tə, 'tü\ *prep* **1 :** in the direction of and reaching ⟨drove ~ town⟩ **2 :** in the direction of : TOWARD **3 :** ON, AGAINST ⟨apply salve ~ a burn⟩ **4 :** as far as ⟨can pay up ~ a dollar⟩ **5 :** so as to become or bring about ⟨beaten ~ death⟩ ⟨broken ~ pieces⟩ **6 ♦ :** earlier than : BEFORE ⟨it's five minutes ~ six⟩ **7 :** UNTIL ⟨from May ~ December⟩ **8 :** fitting or being a part of : FOR ⟨key ~ the lock⟩ **9 :** with the accompaniment of ⟨sing ~ the music⟩ **10 :** in relation or comparison with ⟨similar ~ that one⟩ ⟨won 10 ~ 6⟩ **11 :** in accordance with ⟨add salt ~ taste⟩ **12 :** within the range of ⟨~ my knowledge⟩ **13 :** contained, occurring, or included in ⟨two pints ~ a quart⟩ **14 :** as regards ⟨agreeable ~ everyone⟩ **15 :** affecting as the receiver or beneficiary ⟨whispered ~ her⟩ ⟨gave it ~ me⟩ **16 :** for no one except ⟨a room ~ myself⟩ **17 :** into the action of ⟨we got ~ talking⟩ **18** — used for marking the following verb as an infinitive ⟨wants ~ go⟩ and often used by itself at the end of a clause in place of an infinitive suggested by the preceding context ⟨goes to town whenever he wants ~⟩ ⟨can leave if you'd like ~⟩

♦ ahead of, before, ere, of, previous to, prior to

²**to** \'tü\ *adv* **1 :** in a direction toward ⟨run ~ and fro⟩ **2 :** into contact esp. with the frame of a door ⟨the door slammed ~⟩ **3 :** to the matter in hand ⟨fell ~ and ate heartily⟩ **4 :** to a state of consciousness or awareness ⟨came ~ hours after the accident⟩

TO *abbr* turn over

toad \'tōd\ *n* **:** any of numerous tailless leaping amphibians differing typically from the related frogs in having a shorter stockier build, rough dry warty skin, and less aquatic habits

toad•stool \-,stül\ *n* **:** MUSHROOM; *esp* **:** one that is poisonous or inedible

¹**toady** \'tō-dē\ *n, pl* **toad•ies** **:** a person who flatters in the hope of gaining favors : SYCOPHANT

²**toady** *vb* **toad•ied; toady•ing** ♦ **:** to behave as a toady

♦ fawn, fuss, kowtow

to–and–fro \,tü-ən-'frō\ *adj* **:** forward and backward — **to–and–fro** *n*

¹**toast** \'tōst\ *vb* **1 :** to warm thoroughly **2 :** to make (as bread) crisp, hot, and brown by heat **3 :** to become toasted

²**toast** *n* **1 :** sliced toasted bread **2 :** someone or something in whose honor persons drink **3 :** an act of drinking in honor of a toast

³**toast** *vb* **:** to propose or drink to as a toast

toast•er \'tō-stər\ *n* **:** an electrical appliance for toasting

toaster oven *n* **:** a portable electrical appliance that bakes, broils, and toasts

toast•mas•ter \'tōst-,mas-tər\ *n* **:** a person who presides at a banquet and introduces the after-dinner speakers

toast•mis•tress \-,mis-trəs\ *n* **:** a woman who acts as toastmaster

toasty \'tō-stē\ *adj* **toast•i•er; -est** **:** pleasantly warm

Tob *abbr* Tobit

to•bac•co \tə-'ba-kō\ *n, pl* **-cos** **1 :** a tall broad-leaved herb related to the potato; *also* **:** its leaves prepared for smoking or chewing or as snuff **2 :** manufactured tobacco products; *also* **:** smoking as a practice

to•bac•co•nist \tə-'ba-kə-nist\ *n* **:** a dealer in tobacco

To•bi•as \tō-'bī-əs\ *n* **:** TOBIT

To·bit \'tō-bət\ *n* : a book in the Roman Catholic canon of the Old Testament and in the Protestant Apocrypha

¹to·bog·gan \tə-'bä-gən\ *n* : a long flat-bottomed light sled made of thin boards curved up at one end

²toboggan *vb* **1** : to coast on or as if on a toboggan **2** : to decline suddenly (as in value) — **to·bog·gan·er** *n*

toc·sin \'täk-sən\ *n* **1** : an alarm bell **2** : a warning signal

¹to·day \tə-'dā\ *adv* **1** : on or for this day **2** ♦ : at the present time

♦ anymore, now, nowadays, presently, right now

²today *n* ♦ : the present day, time, or age

♦ moment, now, present

tod·dle \'täd-ᵊl\ *vb* **tod·dled; tod·dling** : to walk with short tottering steps in the manner of a young child — **toddle** *n* — **tod·dler** *n*

tod·dy \'tä-dē\ *n, pl* **toddies** : a drink made of liquor, sugar, spices, and hot water

to–do \tə-'dü\ *n, pl* **to–dos** \-'düz\ : excited and usu. exaggerated stir : BUSTLE, FUSS

¹toe \'tō\ *n* **1** : one of the jointed parts of the front end of the vertebrate foot **2** : the front part of a foot or hoof

²toe *vb* **toed; toe·ing** : to touch, reach, or drive with the toes

toe·hold \'tō-,hōld\ *n* **1** : a place of support for the toes **2** : a slight footing

toe·nail \-,nāl\ *n* : a nail of a toe

tof·fee *or* **tof·fy** \'tȯ-fē, 'tä-\ *n, pl* **toffees** *or* **toffies** : candy of brittle but tender texture made by boiling sugar and butter together

to·fu \'tō-(,)fü\ *n* : a soft white food product made from soybeans

tog \'täg, 'tȯg\ *vb* **togged; tog·ging** : to put togs on : DRESS

to·ga \'tō-gə\ *n* : the loose outer garment worn in public by citizens of ancient Rome — **to·gaed** \-gəd\ *adj*

¹to·geth·er \tə-'ge-thər\ *adv* **1** : in or into one place or group **2** : in or into contact or association ⟨mix ∼⟩ **3** : at one time : SIMULTANEOUSLY ⟨talk and work ∼⟩ **4** : in succession ⟨for days ∼⟩ **5** : in or into harmony or coherence ⟨get ∼ on a plan⟩ **6** ♦ : as a group : JOINTLY — **to·geth·er·ness** *n*

♦ all around, altogether, collectively, overall

²together *adj* : composed in mind or manner

tog·gery \'tä-gə-rē, 'tȯ-\ *n* : CLOTHING

tog·gle \'tä-gəl\ *vb* : to switch between two options esp. of an electronic device

tog·gle switch \'tä-gəl-\ *n* : an electric switch operated by pushing a projecting lever through a small arc

To·go·lese \,tō-gə-'lēz, -'lēs\ *n* : a native or inhabitant of Togo — **Togolese** *adj*

togs \'tägz, 'tȯgz\ *n pl* : CLOTHING; *esp* : clothes for a specified use ⟨riding ∼⟩

¹toil \'tȯil\ *n* **1** : laborious effort **2** ♦ : long fatiguing labor : DRUDGERY — **toil·ful** \-fəl\ *adj*

♦ drudgery, grind, labor (*or* labour), sweat, travail *Ant* fun, play

²toil *vb* **1** ♦ : to work hard and long **2** : to proceed with great effort : PLOD

♦ drudge, fag, grub, labor (*or* labour), sweat, travail

³toil *n* : NET, TRAP — usu. used in pl.

toil·er *n* ♦ : one that toils

♦ drudge, peon, worker

toi·let \'tȯi-lət\ *n* **1** : the act or process of dressing and grooming oneself **2** ♦ : a room furnished with a fixture for flushing body waste **3** : a fixture for use in urinating and defecating; *esp* : one consisting essentially of a water-flushed bowl and seat — **toilet** *vb*

♦ bathroom, lavatory

toilet paper *n* : an absorbent paper for drying or cleaning oneself after defecation or urination

toi·let·ry \'tȯi-lə-trē\ *n, pl* **-ries** : an article or preparation used in cleaning or grooming oneself — usu. used in pl.

toi·lette \twä-'let\ *n* **1** : TOILET 1 **2** : formal attire; *also* : a particular costume

toilet training *n* : the process of training a child to control bladder and bowel movements and to use the toilet — **toilet train** *vb*

toil·some \'tȯi-(ə)l-səm\ *adj* ♦ : marked by or full of toil or fatigue

♦ arduous, burdensome, challenging, demanding, exacting, grueling, laborious, onerous, taxing

toil·worn \'tȯil-,wȯrn\ *adj* : showing the effects of toil

To·kay \tō-'kā\ *n* : naturally sweet wine from Hungary

toke \'tōk\ *n, slang* : a puff on a marijuana cigarette or pipe

¹to·ken \'tō-kən\ *n* **1** : an outward sign **2** : SYMBOL, EMBLEM **3** ♦ : something that serves as a reminder : KEEPSAKE **4** : a small part representing the whole **5** : a piece resembling a coin issued as money or for use by a particular group on specified terms

♦ keepsake, memento, memorial, monument, remembrance, souvenir

²token *adj* **1** : done or given as a token esp. in partial fulfillment of an obligation **2** : representing only a symbolic effort : MINIMAL, PERFUNCTORY

to·ken·ism \'tō-kə-,ni-zəm\ *n* : the policy or practice of making only a symbolic effort (as to desegregate)

told *past and past part of* TELL

tole \'tōl\ *n* : sheet metal and esp. tinplate for use in domestic and ornamental wares

tol·er·a·ble \'tä-lə-rə-bəl\ *adj* **1** ♦ : capable of being borne or endured **2** ♦ : moderately good : PASSABLE

♦ [1] bearable, endurable, sufferable, supportable, sustainable
♦ [2] acceptable, adequate, all right, decent, fine, OK, passable, respectable, satisfactory

tol·er·a·bly \'tä-lə-rə-blē\ *adv* ♦ : in a tolerable manner

♦ adequately, all right, fine, good, nicely, OK, passably, satisfactorily, so-so, well

tol·er·ance \'tä-lə-rəns\ *n* **1** ♦ : the act or practice of tolerating; *esp* : sympathy or indulgence for beliefs or practices differing from one's own **2** : the allowable deviation from a standard (as of size) **3** : the body's capacity to become less responsive over time to something (as a drug used repeatedly) — **tol·er·ant·ly** *adv*

♦ forbearance, long-suffering, patience, sufferance

tol·er·ant \'tä-lə-rənt\ *adj* ♦ : inclined to tolerate; *esp* : marked by forbearance or endurance

♦ forbearing, long-suffering, patient, stoic, uncomplaining

tol·er·ate \'tä-lə-,rāt\ *vb* **-at·ed; -at·ing** **1** : to exhibit physiological tolerance for (as a drug) **2** ♦ : to allow to be or to be done without hindrance — **tol·er·a·tion** \,tä-lə-'rā-shən\ *n*

♦ abide, bear, brook, countenance, endure, meet, stand, stick out, stomach, support, sustain, take

¹toll \'tōl\ *n* **1** : a tax paid for a privilege (as for passing over a bridge) **2** : a charge for a service (as for a long-distance telephone call) **3** : the cost in life, health, loss, or suffering

²toll *vb* **1** : to cause the slow regular sounding of (a bell) esp. by pulling a rope **2** : to give signal of : SOUND **3** ♦ : to sound with slow measured strokes **4** : to announce by tolling

♦ chime, knell, peal, ring

³toll *n* : the sound of a tolling bell

toll·booth \'tōl-,büth\ *n* : a booth where tolls are paid

toll·gate \-,gāt\ *n* : a point where vehicles stop to pay a toll

toll·house \-,hau̇s\ *n* : a house or booth where tolls are paid

tol·u·ene \'täl-yə-,wēn\ *n* : a liquid hydrocarbon used esp. as a solvent

tom \'täm\ *n* : the male of various animals (as a cat or turkey)

¹tom·a·hawk \'tä-mə-,hȯk\ *n* : a light ax used as a missile and as a hand weapon esp. by Indigenous people of No. America

²tomahawk *vb* : to strike or kill with a tomahawk

to·ma·til·lo \,tä-mə-'tē-(,)yō\ *n, pl* **-los** : a small round usu. pale green edible fruit of a Mexican herb related to the tomato; *also* : this herb

to·ma·to \tə-'mā-tō, -'mä-\ *n, pl* **-toes** : a usu. large, rounded, and red or yellow pulpy edible berry of a widely grown tropical herb related to the potato; *also* : this herb

tomb \'tüm\ *n* **1** : a place of burial : GRAVE **2** : a house, chamber, or vault for the dead — **tomb** *vb*

tom·boy \'täm-,bȯi\ *n* : a girl who behaves in a manner usu. considered boyish

tom·boy·ish \-ish\ *adj* : relating to or being a tomboy

tomb·stone \'tüm-,stōn\ *n* ♦ : a stone marking a grave

♦ gravestone, headstone, monument

tom·cat \'täm-,kat\ *n* : a male domestic cat

Tom Col·lins \'täm-'kä-lənz\ *n* : a tall iced drink with a base of gin

tome \'tōm\ *n* : BOOK; *esp* : a large or weighty one

tom·fool·ery \täm-'fü-lə-rē\ *n* ♦ : playful or foolish behavior

♦ foolery, high jinks, horseplay, monkeyshines, roughhouse, shenanigans

tom·my gun \'tä-mē-,gən\ *n* : SUBMACHINE GUN — **tommy–gun** *vb*

to·mog·ra·phy \tō-'mä-grə-fē\ *n* : a method of producing a three-dimensional image of the internal structures of a solid object (as the human body or the earth) — **to·mo·graph·ic** \ˌtō-mə-ˈgra-fik\ adj

to·mor·row \tə-ˈmär-ō\ adv : on or for the day after today — **tomorrow** n

tom–tom \ˈtäm-ˌtäm\ n : a small-headed drum beaten with the hands

ton \ˈtən\ n, pl **tons** also **ton** **1 a** : a unit of weight equal to 2000 pounds in the U.S. and Canada **b** : LONG TON **2** : a unit equal to the volume of a long ton weight of seawater in reckoning the displacement of ships and equal to 35 cubic feet

to·nal·i·ty \tō-ˈna-lə-tē\ n, pl **-ties** : tonal quality

¹tone \ˈtōn\ n **1** : vocal or musical sound; esp : sound quality **2** : a sound of definite pitch **3** : WHOLE STEP **4** : accent or inflection expressive of an emotion **5** : the pitch of a word often used to express differences of meaning **6 ♦** : style or manner of expression **7 ♦** : color quality; also : SHADE **8** : the effect in painting of light and shade together with color **9** : healthy and vigorous condition of a living body or bodily part; also : the state of partial contraction characteristic of normal muscle **10 ♦** : general character, quality, or trend — **ton·al** \ˈtōn-ᵊl\ adj

    ♦ [6] fashion, locution, manner, mode, phraseology, style, vein ♦ [7] cast, color (or colour), hue, shade, tinge, tint ♦ [10] character, complexion, constitution, genius, nature, personality

²tone vb **toned; ton·ing** **1** : to give a particular intonation or inflection to **2** : to impart tone to **3** : SOFTEN, MELLOW ⟨~ down your language⟩ **4** : to harmonize in color : BLEND

tone·arm n : the movable part of a record player that carries the pickup and the needle

toney var of TONY

tong \ˈtäŋ, ˈtȯŋ\ n : a Chinese secret society in the U.S.

tongs \ˈtäŋz, ˈtȯŋz\ n pl : a grasping device consisting of two pieces joined at one end by a pivot or hinged like scissors — **tong** vb

¹tongue \ˈtəŋ\ n **1** : a fleshy movable process of the floor of the mouth used in tasting and in taking and swallowing food and in humans as a speech organ **2** : the flesh of a tongue (as of the ox) used as food **3** : the power of communication **4 ♦** : the words, their pronunciation, and the method of combining them used and understood by a community : LANGUAGE **5** : manner or quality of utterance; also : intended meaning **6** : ecstatic usu. unintelligible utterance accompanying religious excitation — usu. used in pl. **7** : something resembling an animal's tongue esp. in being elongated and fastened at one end only — **tongued** \ˈtəŋd\ adj — **tongue·less** adj

    ♦ language, lingo, speech, vocabulary

²tongue vb **tongued; tongu·ing** **1** : to touch or lick with the tongue **2** : to articulate notes on a wind instrument

tongue–in–cheek adj : characterized by insincerity, irony, or whimsical exaggeration — **tongue in cheek** adv

tongue–lash \ˈtəŋ-ˌlash\ vb : CHIDE, REPROVE — **tongue–lash·ing** \-iŋ\ n

tongue–tied \-ˌtīd\ adj : unable or disinclined to speak clearly or freely (as from shyness or a tongue impairment)

tongue twister n : an utterance that is difficult to articulate because of a succession of similar consonants

¹ton·ic \ˈtä-nik\ adj **1 ♦** : of, relating to, or producing a healthy physical or mental condition : INVIGORATING **2** : relating to or based on the 1st tone of a scale — **to·nic·i·ty** \tō-ˈni-sə-tē\ n

    ♦ bracing, invigorating, refreshing, restorative, stimulative

²tonic n **1** : something that invigorates, restores, or refreshes **2** : the 1st degree of a musical scale

tonic water n : a carbonated beverage flavored with a bit of quinine, lemon, and lime

¹to·night \tə-ˈnīt\ adv : on this present night or the coming night

²tonight n : the present or the coming night

ton·nage \ˈtə-nij\ n **1** : a duty on ships based on tons carried **2** : ships in terms of the number of tons registered or carried **3** : total weight in tons shipped, carried, or mined

ton·sil \ˈtän-səl\ n : either of a pair of oval masses of lymphoid tissue that lie one on each side of the throat at the back of the mouth

ton·sil·lec·to·my \ˌtän-sə-ˈlek-tə-mē\ n, pl **-mies** : the surgical removal of the tonsils

ton·sil·li·tis \-ˈlī-təs\ n : inflammation of the tonsils

ton·so·ri·al \tän-ˈsȯr-ē-əl\ adj : of or relating to a barber or a barber's work

ton·sure \ˈtän-chər\ n **1** : the rite of admission to the clerical state by the clipping or shaving of the head **2** : the shaven crown or patch worn by clerics (as monks) — **tonsure** vb

tony also **ton·ey** \ˈtō-nē\ adj **ton·i·er; -est** : marked by an aristocratic manner or style

too \ˈtü\ adv **1 ♦** : in addition : ALSO **2 ♦** : to an excessive degree : EXCESSIVELY ⟨the rent is ~ high⟩ **3** : to such a degree as to be regrettable **4** : to a high degree : VERY

    ♦ [1] additionally, again, also, besides, further, furthermore, likewise, more, moreover, then, withal, yet ♦ [2] devilishly, excessively, inordinately, monstrously, overly, overmuch **Ant** inadequately, insufficiently

took past of TAKE

¹tool \ˈtül\ n **1 ♦** : a hand instrument that aids in accomplishing a task **2** : the cutting or shaping part in a machine; also : a machine for shaping metal in any way **3** : something used in doing a job ⟨a scholar's books are his ~s⟩; also : a means to an end **4 ♦** : a person used by another : DUPE **5** pl : natural ability

    ♦ [1] device, implement, instrument, utensil ♦ [4] dupe, gull, pigeon, sap, sucker

²tool vb **1** : to shape, form, or finish with a tool; esp : to letter or decorate (as a book cover) by means of hand tools **2** : to equip a plant or industry with machines and tools for production **3** : DRIVE, RIDE ⟨~ing along at 60 miles per hour⟩

tool bar n : a strip of icons on a computer display providing quick access to the pictured functions

¹toot \ˈtüt\ vb **1** : to sound or cause to sound in short blasts **2** : to blow an instrument (as a horn) — **toot·er** n

²toot n : a short blast (as on a horn)

tooth \ˈtüth\ n, pl **teeth** \ˈtēth\ **1** : one of the hard bony structures borne esp. on the jaws of vertebrates and used for seizing and chewing food and as weapons; also : a hard sharp structure esp. around the mouth of an invertebrate **2** : something resembling an animal's tooth **3** : any of the projections on the edge of a wheel that fits into corresponding projections on another wheel **4** : effective means of enforcement — **toothed** \ˈtütht\ adj — **tooth·less** adj

tooth·ache \ˈtüth-ˌāk\ n : pain in or about a tooth

tooth·brush \-ˌbrəsh\ n : a brush for cleaning the teeth

tooth·paste \-ˌpāst\ n : a paste for cleaning the teeth

tooth·pick \-ˌpik\ n : a pointed instrument for removing food particles caught between the teeth

tooth powder n : a powder for cleaning the teeth

tooth·some \ˈtüth-səm\ adj **1** : AGREEABLE, ATTRACTIVE **2 ♦** : pleasing to the taste : DELICIOUS

    ♦ ambrosial, appetizing, delectable, delicious, flavorful (or flavourful), luscious, palatable, savory, scrumptious, tasty, yummy

toothy \ˈtü-thē\ adj **tooth·i·er; -est** : having or showing prominent teeth

¹top \ˈtäp\ n **1 ♦** : the highest part, point, or level of something **2** : the part of a plant with edible roots lying above the ground ⟨beet ~s⟩ **3** : the upper end, edge, or surface ⟨the ~ of a page⟩ **4 ♦** : an upper piece, lid, or covering **5** : the highest degree, pitch, or rank

    ♦ [1] acme, apex, climax, crown, culmination, head, height, meridian, peak, pinnacle, summit, tip-top, zenith ♦ [4] cap, cover, lid

²top vb **topped; top·ping** **1** : to remove or trim the top of : PRUNE ⟨~ a tree⟩ **2** : to cover with a top or on the top : CROWN, CAP **3 ♦** : to be superior to : SURPASS **4** : to go over the top of **5** : to strike (a ball) above the center **6** : to make an end or conclusion ⟨~ off a meal with coffee⟩

    ♦ beat, better, eclipse, excel, outdistance, outdo, outshine, outstrip, surpass, transcend

³top adj **1** : of, relating to, or being at the top **2** : CHIEF **3 ♦** : of the highest quality, amount, or degree

    ♦ consummate, maximum, most, nth, paramount, supreme, ultimate, utmost ♦ full, maximum, utmost

⁴top n : a toy that has a tapering point on which it is made to spin

to·paz \ˈtō-ˌpaz\ n : a hard silicate of aluminum; esp : a yellow transparent topaz used as a gem

top·coat \ˈtäp-ˌkōt\ n **1** : a lightweight overcoat **2** : a protective coating (as of paint)

top dollar n : the highest amount being paid for a commodity or service

top–dress \-ˌdres\ vb : to apply material to (as land) without working it in; esp : to scatter fertilizer over

top–dress·ing \-ˌdre-siŋ\ n : a material used to top-dress soil

top–end \ˈtäp-ˈend\ adj : TOPFLIGHT

top·flight \ˈtäp-ˈflīt\ adj : of, relating to, or being the highest level of excellence or rank — **top flight** n

top hat *n* : a tall-crowned hat usu. of beaver or silk

top–heavy \'täp-ˌhe-vē\ *adj* : having the top part too heavy for the lower part

to·pi·ary \'tō-pē-ˌer-ē\ *n, pl* **-ar·ies** : the art of training and trimming trees or shrubs with decorative shapes — **topiary** *adj*

top·ic \'tä-pik\ *n* **1** : a heading in an outlined argument **2** ♦ : the subject of a discourse or a section of it : THEME

♦ content, matter, motif, motive, question, subject, theme

top·i·cal \-pi-kəl\ *adj* **1** : designed to be applied to or to work on a part (as of the body) **2** : of, relating to, or arranged by topics ⟨a ~ outline⟩ **3** : relating to current or local events — **top·i·cal·ly** \-k(ə-)lē\ *adv*

top·knot \'täp-ˌnät\ *n* **1** : an ornament (as a knot of ribbons) forming a headdress **2** : a crest of feathers or tuft of hair on the top of the head **3** : hair worn in a knot high on the head

top·less \-ləs\ *adj* **1** : wearing no clothing on the upper body **2** : featuring topless waitresses or entertainers

top·mast \'täp-ˌmast, -məst\ *n* : the 2d mast above a ship's deck

top·most \'täp-ˌmōst\ *adj* : highest of all : UPPERMOST

top–notch \-ˈnäch\ *adj* : of the highest quality : FIRST-RATE

top–of–the–line *adj* ♦ : being or belonging to the highest or most expensive class

♦ A1, crackerjack, dandy, excellent, fine, first-rate, sensational, splendid, superb, terrific, wonderful

to·pog·ra·phy \tə-ˈpä-grə-fē\ *n* **1** : the art of showing in detail on a map or chart the physical features of a place or region **2** : the outline of the form of a place showing its relief and the position of features (as rivers, roads, or cities) — **to·pog·ra·pher** \-fər\ *n* — **top·o·graph·ic** \ˌtä-pə-ˈgra-fik\ *or* **top·o·graph·i·cal** \-fi-kəl\ *adj*

top·ping \'tä-piŋ\ *n* : a food served on top of another to make it look or taste better

top·ple \'tä-pəl\ *vb* **top·pled; top·pling** **1** ♦ : to fall from or as if from being top-heavy **2** : to push over : OVERTURN; *also* : OVERTHROW ⟨*toppled* the dictator⟩

♦ fall, slip, stumble, trip, tumble

tops \'täps\ *adj* : topmost in quality or importance ⟨~ in his field⟩

top·sail \'täp-ˌsāl, -səl\ *also* **top·s'l** \-səl\ *n* : the sail next above the lowest sail on a mast in a square-rigged ship

top secret *adj* : demanding complete secrecy among those concerned

top·side \'täp-ˈsīd\ *adv or adj* **1** : to or on the top or surface **2** : on deck

top·sides \-ˈsīdz\ *n pl* : the top portion of the outer surface of a ship on each side above the waterline

top·soil \'täp-ˌsȯil\ *n* : surface soil usu. including the organic layer in which plants have most of their roots

top·sy–tur·vy \ˌtäp-sē-ˈtər-vē\ *adj* ♦ : totally disordered — **topsy-turvy** *adv*

♦ chaotic, disheveled, disordered, disorderly, messy, untidy

toque \'tōk\ *n* : a woman's small hat without a brim

tor \'tȯr\ *n* : a high craggy hill

To·rah \'tȯr-ə\ *n* **1** : a scroll of the first five books of the Old Testament used in a synagogue; *also* : these five books **2** : the body of divine knowledge and law found in the Jewish Scriptures and tradition

torch \'tȯrch\ *n* **1** : a flaming light made of something that burns brightly and usu. carried in the hand **2** : something that resembles a torch in giving light, heat, or guidance **3** *chiefly Brit* : FLASHLIGHT **4** : a portable burner for producing a hot flame

torch *vb* : to set fire to

torch·bear·er \'tȯrch-ˌber-ər\ *n* **1** : a person who carries a torch **2** : one in the forefront (as of a political campaign)

torch·light \-ˌlīt\ *n* : light given by torches

torch song *n* : a popular sentimental song of unrequited love

tore *past of* TEAR

to·re·a·dor \'tȯr-ē-ə-ˌdȯr\ *n* : BULLFIGHTER

to·re·ro \tə-ˈrer-ō\ *n, pl* **-ros** : BULLFIGHTER

tor·ment \'tȯr-ˌment\ *n* **1** ♦ : extreme pain or anguish of body or mind **2** ♦ : a source of vexation or pain

♦ [1] affliction, agony, anguish, distress, misery, pain, torture, tribulation, woe ♦ [2] agony, hell, misery, murder, nightmare, torture

tor·ment \tȯr-ˈment\ *vb* **1** ♦ : to cause severe suffering of body or mind to **2** : DISTORT, TWIST

♦ afflict, agonize, bedevil, curse, harrow, persecute, plague, rack, torture

tor·men·tor \-ˈmen-tər\ *n* ♦ : one that torments

♦ heckler, oppressor, persecutor, taunter, torturer

torn *past part of* TEAR

tor·na·do \tȯr-ˈnā-dō\ *n, pl* **-does** *or* **-dos** : a violent destructive whirling wind accompanied by a funnel-shaped cloud that moves over a narrow path

tor·pe·do \tȯr-ˈpē-dō\ *n, pl* **-does** : a thin cylindrical self-propelled underwater weapon

torpedo *vb* **tor·pe·doed; tor·pe·do·ing** : to hit or destroy with or as if with a torpedo

torpedo boat *n* : a small very fast boat for firing torpedoes

tor·pid \'tȯr-pəd\ *adj* **1** : having lost motion or the power of exertion : DORMANT **2** : sluggish in functioning or acting **3** ♦ : lacking vigor — **tor·pid·i·ty** \tȯr-ˈpi-də-tē\ *n*

♦ dull, inactive, inert, lethargic, quiescent, sleepy, sluggish

tor·por \'tȯr-pər\ *n* **1** : DULLNESS, APATHY **2** : extreme sluggishness : STAGNATION

torque \'tȯrk\ *n* : a force that produces or tends to produce rotation or torsion

torque *vb* **torqued; torqu·ing** : to impart torque to : cause to twist (as about an axis)

tor·rent \'tȯr-ənt\ *n* **1** : a tumultuous outburst **2** ♦ : a rushing stream (as of water)

♦ cataclysm, cataract, deluge, flood, inundation, overflow, spate

tor·ren·tial \tȯ-ˈren-chəl\ *adj* : relating to or resembling a torrent ⟨~ rains⟩

tor·rid \'tȯr-əd\ *adj* **1** ♦ : parched with heat esp. of the sun : HOT **2** : ARDENT

♦ broiling, burning, fiery, hot, red-hot, scorching, sultry

torrid zone *n* : the region of the earth between the Tropic of Cancer and the Tropic of Capricorn

tor·sion \'tȯr-shən\ *n* **1** : a wrenching by which one part of a body is under pressure to turn about a longitudinal axis while the other part is held fast or is under pressure to turn in the opposite direction **2** : a twisting of a bodily organ or part on its own axis — **tor·sion·al** \'tȯr-shə-nəl\ *adj* — **tor·sion·al·ly** *adv*

tor·so \'tȯr-sō\ *n, pl* **torsos** *or* **tor·si** \'tȯr-ˌsē\ : the trunk of the human body

tort \'tȯrt\ *n* : a wrongful act which does not involve a breach of contract and for which the injured party can recover damages in a civil action

tor·ti·lla \tȯr-ˈtē-ə\ *n* : a round thin cake of unleavened cornmeal or wheat flour bread

tor·toise \'tȯr-təs\ *n* : TURTLE; *esp* : any of a family of land turtles

tor·toise·shell \-ˌshel\ *n* : the mottled horny substance of the shell of some turtles used in inlaying and in making various ornamental articles — **tortoiseshell** *adj*

tor·to·ni \tȯr-ˈtō-nē\ *n* : rich ice cream often made with minced almonds and chopped cherries and flavored with rum

tor·tu·ous \'tȯr-chə-wəs\ *adj* **1** ♦ : marked by twists or turns : WINDING ⟨a ~ path⟩ **2** : DEVIOUS, TRICKY

♦ crooked, devious, serpentine, sinuous, winding

tor·ture \'tȯr-chər\ *n* **1** ♦ : anguish of body or mind **2** ♦ : the infliction of severe pain esp. to punish or coerce — **tor·tur·ous** \'tȯrch-rəs, 'tȯr-chə-\ *adj*

♦ [1] affliction, agony, anguish, distress, misery, pain, torment, tribulation, woe ♦ [2] agony, hell, horror, misery, murder, nightmare, torment

torture *vb* **tor·tured; tor·tur·ing** **1** ♦ : to cause intense suffering to : TORMENT **2** : to punish or coerce by inflicting severe pain **3** : TWIST, DISTORT

♦ afflict, agonize, bedevil, curse, harrow, martyr, persecute, plague, rack, torment

tor·tur·er \'tȯr-chər-ər\ *n* ♦ : one that tortures

♦ heckler, oppressor, persecutor, taunter, tormentor

To·ry \'tȯr-ē\ *n, pl* **Tories** **1** : a member of a chiefly 18th century British party upholding the established church and the traditional political structure **2** : an American supporter of the British during the American Revolution **3** *often not cap* ♦ : an extreme conservative — **Tory** *adj*

♦ conservative, reactionary, rightist

toss \'tȯs, 'täs\ *vb* **1** : to fling to and fro or up and down; *also* : BANDY **2** ♦ : to throw with a quick light motion **3** : to fling or lift with a sudden motion ⟨~ed her head angrily⟩ **4** : to move restlessly or turbulently ⟨~es on the waves⟩ **5** ♦ : to twist and turn repeatedly **6** : FLOUNCE **7** : to accomplish readily ⟨~ off an article〉 **8 :** to decide an issue by flipping a coin **9 ♦ :** to consume by drinking 〈~ down a drink〉

♦ [2] cast, catapult, chuck, dash, fire, fling, heave, hurl, hurtle, launch, peg, pelt, pitch, sling, throw ♦ [5] careen, lurch, pitch, rock, roll, seesaw, sway, wobble ♦ *usu* **toss down** *or* **toss off** [9] drink, guzzle, imbibe, quaff, sup, swig

²toss *n* **:** an act or instance of tossing; *esp* **:** TOSS-UP 1

toss–up \-̦əp\ *n* **1 :** a deciding by flipping a coin **2 :** an even chance **3 :** something that offers no clear basis for choice

¹tot \'tät\ *n* **1 :** a small child **2 :** a small drink of alcoholic liquor **:** SHOT

²tot *vb* **tot·ted; tot·ting :** to add up

³tot *abbr* total

¹to·tal \'tōt-ᵊl\ *adj* **1 ♦ :** making up a whole **:** ENTIRE 〈~ amount〉 **2 :** being definitely what is stated **:** COMPLETE 〈a ~ failure〉 **3 ♦ :** involving a complete and unified effort esp. to achieve a desired effect

♦ [1] complete, comprehensive, entire, full, grand, intact, integral, perfect, plenary, whole ♦ [3] all-out, clean, complete, comprehensive, exhaustive, full-scale, out-and-out, thorough, thoroughgoing

²total *n* **1 :** SUM 4 **2 ♦ :** the entire amount

♦ aggregate, full, sum, totality, whole

³total *vb* **to·taled** *or* **to·talled; to·tal·ing** *or* **to·tal·ling 1 ♦ :** to add up **2 ♦ :** to amount to **:** NUMBER **3 :** to make a total wreck of (a car)

♦ [1] add, foot, sum ♦ [2] add up, amount, come, number, sum

to·tal·i·tar·i·an \tō-̦ta-lə-'ter-ē-ən\ *adj* **:** of, relating to, or advocating a political regime based on subordination of the individual to the state and strict control of all aspects of life esp. by coercive measures — **totalitarian** *n*

to·tal·i·tar·i·an·ism \tō-̦ta-lə-'ter-ē-ə-̦ni-zəm\ *n* **♦ :** centralized control by an autocratic authority

♦ autocracy, despotism, dictatorship, tyranny

to·tal·i·ty \tō-'ta-lə-tē\ *n, pl* **-ties 1 ♦ :** an aggregate amount **:** SUM, WHOLE **2 :** ENTIRETY, WHOLENESS

♦ aggregate, full, sum, total, whole

to·tal·iza·tor *or* **to·tal·isa·tor** \'tōt-ᵊl-ə-̦zā-tər\ *n* **:** a machine for registering and indicating the number of bets and the odds on a horse or dog race

to·tal·ly \'tō-tᵊl-ē\ *adv* **♦ :** in a total manner **:** to a total or complete degree

♦ absolutely, all, altogether, clean, completely, entirely, fully, quite, utterly, wholly ♦ completely, exhaustively, fully, minutely, roundly, thoroughly

¹tote \'tōt\ *vb* **tot·ed; tot·ing ♦ :** to carry by hand

♦ bear, carry, cart, convey, ferry, haul, lug, pack, transport

²tote *vb* **tot·ed; tot·ing :** ADD, TOTAL — usu. used with *up*

to·tem \'tō-təm\ *n* **:** an object (as an animal or plant) serving as the emblem of a family or clan and often as a reminder of its ancestry; *also* **:** something usu. carved or painted to represent such an object

totem pole *n* **:** a pole that is carved with a series of totems and is erected by Indigenous people of the northwest coast of No. America

tot·ter \'tä-tər\ *vb* **1 ♦ :** to tremble or rock as if about to fall **:** SWAY **2 ♦ :** to move unsteadily **:** STAGGER

♦ [1] falter, rock, seesaw, sway, teeter, waver, wobble ♦ [2] careen, dodder, lurch, reel, stagger, teeter

tou·can \'tü-̦kan\ *n* **:** any of a family of chiefly fruit-eating birds of tropical America with brilliant coloring and a very large bill

¹touch \'təch\ *vb* **1 :** to bring a bodily part (as the hand) into contact with so as to feel **2 ♦ :** to be or cause to be in contact **3 :** to strike or push lightly esp. with the hand or foot **4 :** DISTURB, HARM **5 :** to make use of 〈never ~es alcohol〉 **6 :** to induce to give or lend **7 :** to get to **:** REACH **8 ♦ :** to refer to in passing **:** MENTION **9 ♦ :** to affect the interest of **:** CONCERN **10 a :** to leave a mark on **b ♦ :** to harm slightly by or as if by contact **11 ♦ :** to move to sympathetic feeling **12 :** to come close **:** VERGE **13 ♦ :** to have a bearing **:** RELATE — used with *on* or *upon* **14 :** to make a usu. brief or incidental stop in port

♦ [2] abut, adjoin, border (on), flank, fringe, join, skirt, verge (on) ♦ *usu* **touch on** *or* **touch upon** [8, 13] advert (to), cite, instance, mention, name, note, notice, quote, refer (to), specify ♦ [9] affect, concern, interest, involve ♦ [10b] blemish, mar, poison, spoil, stain, taint, tarnish, vitiate ♦ [11] affect, impact, impress, influence, move, strike, sway, tell

²touch *n* **1 :** a light stroke or tap **2 :** the act or fact of touching or being touched **3 :** the sense by which pressure or traction on the skin or mucous membrane is perceived; *also* **:** a particular sensation conveyed by this sense **4 :** mental or moral sensitiveness **:** TACT **5 :** a small quantity **:** HINT 〈a ~ of spring in the air〉 **6 :** a manner of striking or touching esp. the keys of a keyboard instrument **7 :** an improving detail 〈add a few ~es to the painting〉 **8 :** distinctive manner or skill 〈the ~ of a master〉 **9 :** the state of being in contact 〈keep in ~〉

touch·down \'təch-̦dau̇n\ *n* **:** the act of scoring six points in American football by being lawfully in possession of the ball on, above, or behind an opponent's goal line

tou·ché \tü-'shā\ *interj* — used to acknowledge a hit in fencing or the success of an argument, an accusation, or a witty point

touch football *n* **:** football in which touching is substituted for tackling

touch·ing *adj* **♦ :** capable of stirring emotions

♦ affecting, emotional, impressive, moving, poignant, stirring

touch off *vb* **1 :** to describe with precision **2 ♦ :** to start by or as if by touching with fire 〈*touched off* a riot〉

♦ activate, actuate, crank, drive, move, propel, run, set off, spark, start, trigger, turn on

touch screen *n* **:** a display screen (as on a computer) on which the user selects options by touching the screen

touch·stone \'təch-̦stōn\ *n* **♦ :** a test or criterion of genuineness or quality

♦ criterion, grade, mark, measure, par, standard, yardstick

touch–tone \'təch-'tōn\ *adj* **:** of, relating to, or being a telephone having push buttons that produce tones corresponding to numbers

touch up *vb* **:** to improve or perfect by small additional strokes or alterations — **touch–up** \'təch-̦əp\ *n*

touchy \'tə-chē\ *adj* **touch·i·er; -est 1 :** easily offended **:** PEEVISH **2 ♦ :** calling for tact in treatment 〈a ~ subject〉

♦ catchy, delicate, difficult, knotty, problematic, spiny, thorny, ticklish, tough, tricky

¹tough \'təf\ *adj* **1 :** strong or firm in texture but flexible and not brittle **2 :** not easily chewed **3 :** characterized by severity and determination 〈a ~ policy〉 **4 ♦ :** capable of enduring strain or hardship **5 :** hard to influence **:** STUBBORN **6 ♦ :** difficult to accomplish, resolve, or cope with 〈a ~ problem〉 **7 :** ROWDYISH — **tough·ly** *adv* — **tough·ness** *n*

♦ [4] hard, hard-bitten, hardy, rugged, stout, strong, sturdy, vigorous ♦ [6] arduous, demanding, difficult, exacting, formidable, hard ♦ [6] catchy, delicate, difficult, knotty, problematic, spiny, thorny, ticklish, touchy, tricky

²tough *n* **♦ :** a tough person **:** ROWDY

♦ bully, gangster, goon, hood, hoodlum, mobster, mug, punk, rowdy, ruffian, thug

tough·en \'tə-fən\ *vb* **tough·ened; tough·en·ing ♦ :** to make or become tough

♦ beef, fortify, harden, steel, strengthen ♦ fortify, harden, season, steel, strengthen

tou·pee \tü-'pā\ *n* **:** a small wig for a bald spot

¹tour \'tu̇r, *1 is also* \'tau̇r\ *n* **1 ♦ :** one's turn **2 :** a journey in which one returns to the starting point

♦ hitch, stint, tenure, term

²tour *vb* **♦ :** to make a tour

♦ journey, travel, trek, voyage

tour de force \̦tu̇r-də-'fōrs\ *n, pl* **tours de force** *same*\ **:** a feat or display of strength, skill, or ingenuity

Tou·rette's syndrome \tu̇-'rets-\ *n* **:** a familial neurological disorder marked by recurrent involuntary tics and vocal sounds

tour·ism \'tu̇r-̦i-zəm\ *n* **1 :** the practice of traveling for recreation **2 :** promotion of touring **3 :** accommodation of tourists

tour·ist \'tu̇r-ist\ *n* **♦ :** one that makes a tour for pleasure or culture

♦ excursionist, sightseer, traveler

tourist class *n* **:** economy accommodations (as on a ship)

tour·ma·line \'tu̇r-mə-lən, -̦lēn\ *n* **:** a mineral that when transparent is valued as a gem

tour·na·ment \'tu̇r-nə-mənt, 'tər-\ *n* **1 :** a medieval sport in which mounted armored knights contended with blunted lances or swords **2 ♦ :** a championship series of games or athletic contests

♦ bout, competition, contest, event, game, match, meet

tour·ney \-nē\ *n, pl* **tourneys** : a championship series of games or athletic contests : TOURNAMENT

tour·ni·quet \'tùr-ni-kət, 'tər-\ *n* : a device (as a tight bandage) to check bleeding or blood flow

tou·sle \'taù-zəl\ *vb* **tou·sled; tou·sling** : to disorder by rough handling : DISHEVEL ⟨*tousled* his hair⟩

tout \'taùt, 2 *is also* 'tüt\ *vb* **1** : to give a tip or solicit bets on a racehorse **2** ♦ : to praise or publicize loudly — **tout** *n*

♦ acclaim, applaud, cheer, crack up, hail, laud, praise, salute ♦ ballyhoo, crack up, glorify, plug, promote, publicize, trumpet

¹**tow** \'tō\ *vb* ♦ : to draw or pull along behind

♦ drag, draw, hale, haul, lug, pull, tug

²**tow** *n* **1** : an act of towing or condition of being towed **2** : something (as a barge) that is towed

³**tow** *n* : short or broken fiber (as of flax or hemp) used esp. for yarn, twine, or stuffing

to·ward \'tōrd, 'tō-ərd, tə-'wòrd\ *or* **to·wards** \'tōrdz, 'tō-ərdz, tə-'wòrdz\ *prep* **1** : in the direction of ⟨heading ∼ the river⟩ **2** : along a course leading to ⟨efforts ∼ reconciliation⟩ **3** ♦ : in regard to ⟨tolerance ∼ minorities⟩ **4** : so as to face ⟨turn the chair ∼ the window⟩ **5** : close upon ⟨it was getting along ∼ sundown⟩ **6** : for part payment of ⟨here's $100 ∼ your tuition⟩

♦ about, apropos of, concerning, of, on, regarding, respecting

tow·boat \'tō-ˌbōt\ *n* : TUGBOAT

tow·el \'taù-əl\ *n* : an absorbent cloth or paper for wiping or drying

tow·el·ing *or* **tow·el·ling** *n* : a cotton or linen fabric for making towels

¹**tow·er** \'taù-ər\ *n* **1** : a tall structure either isolated or built upon a larger structure ⟨an observation ∼⟩ **2** : a towering citadel **3** : a personal computer case that stands in an upright position — **tow·ered** *adj*

²**tower** *vb* : to reach or rise to a great height

tow·er·ing *adj* **1** ♦ : impressively high or great in size or quality ⟨∼ pines⟩ **2** : reaching high intensity ⟨a ∼ rage⟩ **3** ♦ : going beyond proper bounds : EXCESSIVE ⟨∼ ambition⟩

♦ [1] high, lofty, tall ♦ [3] excessive, extreme, immoderate, inordinate, lavish, overmuch

tow·head \'tō-ˌhed\ *n* : a person having whitish blond hair — **tow·head·ed** \-ˌhe-dəd\ *adj*

to·whee \'tō-ˌhē, 'tō-(ˌ)ē, tō-'hē\ *n* : a common finch of eastern No. America having the male black, white, and reddish; *also* : any of several closely related finches

to wit *adv* : NAMELY

town \'taùn\ *n* **1** : a compactly settled area usu. larger than a village but smaller than a city **2** : a large densely populated urban area : CITY **3** : the inhabitants of a town **4** : a New England territorial and political unit usu. containing both rural and urban areas; *also* : a New England community in which matters of local government are decided by a general assembly (**town meeting**) of qualified voters

town house *n* **1** : the city residence of a person having a country home **2** : a single-family house of two or sometimes three stories connected to another house by a common wall

town·ie *or* **towny** \'taù-nē\ *n, pl* **townies** ♦ : a permanent resident of a town as distinguished from a member of another group

♦ burgher

towns·folk \'taùnz-ˌfōk\ *n pl* : TOWNSPEOPLE

town·ship \'taùn-ˌship\ *n* **1** : TOWN 4 **2** : a unit of local government in some states **3** : an unorganized subdivision of a county **4** : a division of territory in surveys of U.S. public land containing 36 square miles **5** : an area in the Republic of South Africa segregated for occupation by persons of non-European descent

towns·man \'taùnz-mən\ *n* **1** : a native or resident of a town or city **2** : a fellow citizen of a town

towns·peo·ple \-ˌpē-pəl\ *n pl* **1** : the inhabitants of a town or city **2** : town-bred persons

towns·wom·an \-ˌwù-mən\ *n* **1** : a woman who is a native or resident of a town or city **2** : a woman who is a fellow citizen of a town

tow·path \'tō-ˌpath, -ˌpath\ *n* : a path (as along a canal) traveled esp. by draft animals towing boats

tow truck *n* : a truck equipped for towing vehicles

tox·emia \täk-'sē-mē-ə\ *n* : a bodily disorder associated with the presence of toxic substances in the blood

tox·ic \'täk-sik\ *adj* : of, relating to, or caused by poison or a toxin : POISONOUS — **tox·ic·i·ty** \täk-'si-sə-tē\ *n*

tox·i·col·o·gy \ˌtäk-si-'kä-lə-jē\ *n* : a science that deals with poisons and esp. with problems of their use and control — **tox·i·co·log·i·cal** \-kə-'lä-ji-kəl\ *also* **tox·i·co·log·ic** \-kə-'lä-jik\ *adj* — **tox·i·col·o·gist** \-'kä-lə-jist\ *n*

toxic shock syndrome *n* : an acute disease that is characterized by fever, diarrhea, nausea, diffuse erythema, and shock, that is associated esp. with the presence of a bacterium, and that occurs esp. in those using tampons during menstruation

tox·in \'täk-sən\ *n* ♦ : a poisonous substance produced by metabolic activities of a living organism that is usu. unstable, very toxic when introduced into the tissues, and usu. capable of inducing antibodies

♦ bane, poison, venom

¹**toy** \'tòi\ *n* **1** : something trifling **2** : a small ornament : BAUBLE **3** : something for a child to play with

²**toy** *vb* **1** : to deal with something lightly : TRIFLE **2** : FLIRT **3** : to amuse oneself as if with a plaything

³**toy** *adj* **1** : DIMINUTIVE **2** : designed for use as a toy

tp *abbr* **1** title page **2** township

tpk *or* **tpke** *abbr* turnpike

tr *abbr* **1** translated; translation; translator **2** transpose **3** troop

¹**trace** \'trās\ *n* **1 a** ♦ : a mark (as a footprint or track) left by something that has passed **b** ♦ : a path or trail beaten by or as if by the passage of feet **2** ♦ : a minute or barely detectable amount ⟨disappeared without a ∼⟩ **3** ♦ : a sign or evidence of some past thing

♦ [1a] imprint, track, trail ♦ [1b] footpath, path, track, trail ♦ [2] glimmer, hint, particle, shadow, suspicion, touch ♦ [3] relic, shadow, vestige

²**trace** *vb* **traced; trac·ing** **1** ♦ : to mark out : SKETCH **2** : to form (as letters) carefully **3** : to copy (a drawing) by marking lines on transparent paper laid over the drawing to be copied **4** ♦ : to follow the trail of : track down **5** : to study out and follow the development of — **trace·able** *adj*

♦ [1] define, delineate, outline, silhouette, sketch ♦ [4] chase, dog, follow, hound, pursue, shadow, tag, tail, track, trail

³**trace** *n* : either of two lines of a harness for fastening a draft animal to a vehicle

trac·er \'trā-sər\ *n* **1** : one that traces **2** : ammunition containing a chemical to mark the flight of projectiles by a trail of smoke or fire

trac·ery \'trā-sə-rē\ *n, pl* **-er·ies** : ornamental work having a design with branching or interlacing lines

tra·chea \'trā-kē-ə\ *n, pl* **-che·ae** \-kē-ˌē\ *also* **-che·as** *or* **-chea** : the main tube by which air passes from the larynx to the lungs of vertebrates — **tra·che·al** \-kē-əl\ *adj*

tra·che·ot·o·my \ˌtrā-kē-'ä-tə-mē\ *n, pl* **-mies** : the surgical operation of cutting into the trachea esp. through the skin

trac·ing *n* **1** ♦ : the act of one that traces **2** : something that is traced **3** : a graphic record made by an instrument for measuring vibrations or pulsations

♦ chase, following, pursuit

¹**track** \'trak\ *n* **1** ♦ : a mark left in passing **2** ♦ : a path, trail, or road made by the passage of animals, people, or vehicles **3** : a course laid out for racing; *also* : track-and-field sports **4** : one of a series of paths along which material (as music) is recorded (as on a compact disc or magnetic tape) **5** : the course along which something moves; *esp* : a way made by two parallel lines of metal rails **6** : awareness of a fact or progression ⟨lost ∼ of time⟩ **7** : either of two endless metal belts on which a vehicle (as a bulldozer) travels

♦ [1] imprint, trace, trail ♦ [2] footpath, path, trace, trail

²**track** *vb* **1 a** ♦ : to follow the tracks or traces of : TRAIL **b** ♦ : to search for by following evidence until found — often used with *down* **2** : to observe the moving path of (as a missile) **3** : to make tracks on **4** : to carry (as mud) on the feet and deposit — **track·er** *n*

♦ [1a] chase, dog, follow, hound, pursue, shadow, tag, tail, trace, trail ♦ *usu* **track down** [1b] detect, determine, dig up, discover, ferret out, hit on, locate

track·age \'tra-kij\ *n* : lines of railway track

track–and–field *adj* : of or relating to athletic contests held on a running track or on the adjacent field

¹**tract** \'trakt\ *n* **1** ♦ : an area without precise boundaries ⟨huge ∼s of land⟩ **2** ♦ : a defined area of land **3** : a system of body parts or organs that act together to perform some function ⟨the digestive ∼⟩

♦ [1] belt, land, region, zone ♦ [2] field, ground, lot, parcel, plat, plot

²tract *n* : a pamphlet of political or religious propaganda

trac·ta·ble \'trak-tə-bəl\ *adj* ♦ : easily controlled : DOCILE

    ♦ amenable, compliant, conformable, docile, obedient, submissive

tract house *n* : any of many similar houses built on a tract of land

trac·tion \'trak-shən\ *n* **1** : the act of drawing : the state of being drawn **2** : the drawing of a vehicle by motive power; *also* : the particular form of motive power used **3** : the adhesive friction of a body on a surface on which it moves **4** : a pulling force applied to a skeletal structure (as a broken bone) by means of a special device; *also* : a state of tension created by such a pulling force ⟨a leg in ∼⟩ — **trac·tion·al** \-shə-nəl\ *adj* — **trac·tive** \'trak-tiv\ *adj*

trac·tor \'trak-tər\ *n* **1** : an automotive vehicle used esp. for drawing farm equipment **2** : a truck for hauling a trailer

¹trade \'trād\ *n* **1** ♦ : one's regular business or work : OCCUPATION **2** ♦ : an occupation requiring manual or mechanical skill **3** : the persons engaged in a business or industry **4** ♦ : the business of buying and selling or bartering commodities **5** ♦ : an act of trading

    ♦ [1] calling, employment, line, occupation, profession, vocation, work ♦ [2] craft, handicraft ♦ [4] business, commerce, marketplace, traffic ♦ [5] barter, commutation, exchange, swap, truck ♦ [5] deal, sale, transaction

²trade *vb* **trad·ed; trad·ing** **1** ♦ : to give in exchange for another commodity **2** : to engage in the exchange, purchase, or sale of goods **3** : to deal regularly as a customer — **trade on** : EXPLOIT ⟨*trades on* his family name⟩

    ♦ change, commute, exchange, shift, substitute, swap, switch

trade–in \'trād-ˌin\ *n* : an item of merchandise traded in

trade in *vb* : to turn in as part payment for a purchase

¹trade·mark \'trād-ˌmärk\ *n* **1** : a device (as a word or mark) that points distinctly to the origin or ownership of merchandise to which it is applied and that is legally reserved for the exclusive use of the owner **2** ♦ : something that identifies a person or thing

    ♦ emblem, hallmark, logo, symbol

²trademark *vb* : to secure the trademark rights for

trade name *n* : a name that is given by a manufacturer or merchant to a product to distinguish it as made or sold by that manufacturer or merchant and that may be used and protected as a trademark

trad·er \'trā-dər\ *n* **1** ♦ : a person whose business is buying or selling **2** : a ship engaged in trade

    ♦ dealer, merchant, trafficker

trades·man \'trādz-mən\ *n* **1** : one who runs a retail store **2** : a worker in a skilled trade : CRAFTSMAN

trades·peo·ple \-ˌpē-pəl\ *n pl* : people engaged in trade

trade union *n* : LABOR UNION

trade wind *n* : a wind blowing almost constantly in one direction

trading stamp *n* : a printed stamp given as a premium to a retail customer that when accumulated may be redeemed for merchandise

tra·di·tion \trə-'di-shən\ *n* **1** : an inherited, established, or customary pattern of thought or action **2** ♦ : the handing down of beliefs and customs by word of mouth or by example without written instruction; *also* : a belief or custom thus handed down

    ♦ folklore, legend, lore, myth, mythology

tra·di·tion·al \trə-ˌdi-shə-nəl\ *adj* **1** : consisting of or derived from tradition ⟨∼ history⟩ **2** ♦ : based on an order, code, or practice accepted from the past ⟨∼ morality⟩ **3** ♦ : observant of or holding to such traditions ⟨a ∼ professor⟩ — **tra·di·tion·al·ly** *adv*

    ♦ [2] classical, conventional, customary *Ant* nontraditional, unconventional, uncustomary ♦ [3] conservative, old-fashioned, orthodox, reactionary

tra·duce \trə-'düs, -'dyüs\ *vb* **tra·duced; tra·duc·ing** ♦ : to lower the reputation of : SLANDER — **tra·duc·er** *n*

    ♦ blacken, defame, libel, malign, slander, smear, vilify

¹traf·fic \'tra-fik\ *n* **1** ♦ : the business of bartering or buying and selling **2** : communication or dealings between individuals or groups **3** : the movement (as of vehicles) along a route; *also* : the vehicles, people, ships, or planes moving along a route **4** : the passengers or cargo carried by a transportation system

    ♦ business, commerce, marketplace, trade

²traffic *vb* **traf·ficked; traf·fick·ing** **1** : to carry on business dealings **2** : DEAL, TRADE ⟨*trafficked* in illegal drugs⟩

traffic circle *n* : ROTARY 2

traf·fick·er *n* ♦ : a buyer and seller of commodities for profit

    ♦ dealer, merchant, trader

traffic light *n* : a visual signal (as a system of lights) for controlling traffic

tra·ge·di·an \trə-'jē-dē-ən\ *n* **1** : a writer of tragedies **2** : an actor who plays tragic roles

tra·ge·di·enne \trə-ˌjē-dē-'en\ *n* : an actress who plays tragic roles

trag·e·dy \'tra-jə-dē\ *n, pl* **-dies** **1** : a serious drama with a sorrowful or disastrous conclusion **2** ♦ : a disastrous event : CALAMITY; *also* : MISFORTUNE **3** : tragic quality or element ⟨the ∼ of life⟩

    ♦ calamity, cataclysm, catastrophe, debacle, disaster, misfortune

trag·ic \'tra-jik\ *also* **trag·i·cal** \-ji-kəl\ *adj* **1** : of, relating to, or expressive of tragedy **2** : appropriate to tragedy **3** ♦ : that is to be regretted or lamented : LAMENTABLE, UNFORTUNATE ⟨a ∼ mistake⟩ — **trag·i·cal·ly** \-ji-k(ə-)lē\ *adv*

    ♦ deplorable, distressful, grievous, heartbreaking, lamentable, regrettable, unfortunate, unlucky, woeful

¹trail \'trāl\ *vb* **1** : to hang down so as to drag along or sweep the ground **2** : to draw or drag along behind **3** : to extend over a surface in a straggling manner **4** : to lag behind **5** ♦ : to follow the track of : PURSUE **6** : DWINDLE ⟨her voice ∼ed off⟩

    ♦ chase, dog, follow, hound, pursue, shadow, tag, tail, trace, track

²trail *n* **1** : something that trails or is trailed ⟨a ∼ of smoke⟩ **2** : a trace or mark left by something that has passed or been drawn along : TRACK ⟨a ∼ of blood⟩ **3** ♦ : a beaten path; *also* : a marked path through woods

    ♦ footpath, path, trace, track

trail bike *n* : a small motorcycle for off-road use

trail·blaz·er \-ˌblā-zər\ *n* : PATHFINDER, PIONEER — **trail·blaz·ing** *adj or n*

trail·er \'trā-lər\ *n* **1** : one that trails; *esp* : a creeping plant (as an ivy) **2** : a vehicle that is hauled by another (as a tractor) **3** ♦ : a vehicle equipped to serve wherever parked as a dwelling or place of business **4** : PREVIEW 2

    ♦ camper, caravan, motor home

trailing arbutus *n* : a creeping spring-flowering plant of the heath family with fragrant pink or white flowers

¹train \'trān\ *n* **1** : a part of a gown that trails behind the wearer **2** ♦ : a group of retainers or attendants : RETINUE **3** ♦ : a moving file of persons, vehicles, or animals **4** ♦ : a connected series ⟨a ∼ of thought⟩ **5** : AFTERMATH **6** : a connected line of railroad cars usu. hauled by a locomotive

    ♦ [2] cortege, following, retinue, suite ♦ [3] column, cue, file, line, queue, range, string ♦ [4] chain, progression, sequence, string

²train *vb* **1** : to cause to grow as desired ⟨∼ a vine on a trellis⟩ **2 a** : to form by instruction, discipline, or drill **b** ♦ : to teach so as to make fit, qualified, or proficient **3** : to make or become prepared (as by exercise) for a test of skill **4** ♦ : to aim at an object or objective ⟨∼ guns on a fort⟩ — **train·er** *n*

    ♦ [2b] educate, indoctrinate, instruct, school, teach, tutor ♦ [4] concentrate, fasten, focus, rivet ♦ [4] aim, bend, cast, direct, head, level, set

train·ee \trā-'nē\ *n* : one who is being trained esp. for a job

train·ing *n* **1** ♦ : the act, process, or method of one who trains **2** : the skill, knowledge, or experience gained by one who trains

    ♦ education, instruction, teaching, tutelage ♦ drill, exercise, practice, routine, workout

train·man \-mən\ *n* : a member of a train crew

traipse \'trāps\ *vb* **traipsed; traips·ing** **1** ♦ : to go on foot : WALK **2** ♦ : to walk or travel about without apparent plan but with or without a purpose

    ♦ [1] foot, leg, pad, step, tread, walk ♦ [2] gad, gallivant, knock, maunder, meander, mope, ramble, range, roam, rove, wander

trait \'trāt\ *n* **1** ♦ : a distinguishing quality (as of personality) : PECULIARITY **2** : an inherited characteristic

    ♦ attribute, character, characteristic, feature, mark, peculiarity, point, property, quality

trai·tor \'trā-tər\ *n* **1** ♦ : one who betrays another's trust or is false to an obligation **2** : one who commits treason

    ♦ apostate, betrayer, double-crosser, quisling, recreant, turncoat

trai·tor·ous \'trā-tə-rəs\ *adj* **1** ♦ : guilty or capable of treason **2** : constituting treason ⟨∼ activities⟩

♦ disloyal, faithless, false, fickle, inconstant, loose, perfidious, recreant, treacherous, unfaithful, untrue

tra·jec·to·ry \trə-'jek-tə-rē\ *n, pl* **-ries** : the curve that a body (as a planet in its orbit) describes in space

tram \'tram\ *n* **1** : a boxlike car running on rails (as in a mine) **2** *chiefly Brit* : STREETCAR **3** : an overhead cable car

¹tram·mel \'tra-məl\ *n* ♦ : something impeding activity, progress, or freedom — usu. used in pl.

♦ chain, encumbrance, fetter, hindrance, interference, manacle, shackle

²trammel *vb* **-meled** *or* **-melled; -mel·ing** *or* **-mel·ling** **1** : to catch and hold in or as if in a net **2** ♦ : to prevent or impede the free play of : HAMPER

♦ fetter, hamper, hinder, hobble, impede, inhibit, interfere with, manacle, shackle, tie up

¹tramp \'tramp, *1 & 3 are also* 'trämp, 'trómp\ *vb* **1** ♦ : to walk, tread, or step heavily **2** : to walk about or through; *also* : HIKE **3** ♦ : to tread on forcibly and repeatedly

♦ [1, 3] clump, lumber, pound, stamp, stomp, trample, tromp

²tramp \'tramp, *5 is also* 'trämp, 'trómp\ *n* **1** ♦ : a begging or thieving vagrant **2** : a foot traveler **3** : an immoral woman; *esp* : PROSTITUTE **4** : a walking trip : HIKE **5** : the succession of sounds made by the beating of feet on a road **6** : a ship that does not follow a regular course but takes cargo to any port

♦ bum, hobo, vagabond, vagrant

tram·ple \'tram-pəl\ *vb* **tram·pled; tram·pling** **1** : to tread heavily so as to bruise, crush, or injure **2** : to inflict injury or destruction **3** ♦ : to press down or crush by or as if by treading — **trample** *n* — **tram·pler** *n*

♦ stamp, stomp, tramp, tromp

tram·po·line \,tram-pə-'lēn, 'tram-pə-,lēn\ *n* : a resilient sheet or web (as of nylon) supported by springs in a metal frame and used as a springboard in tumbling — **tram·po·lin·ist** \-'lē-nist, -,lē-\ *n*

trance \'trans\ *n* **1** : STUPOR, DAZE **2** : a sleeplike state of altered consciousness (as of deep hypnosis) **3** ♦ : a state of very deep absorption

♦ reverie, study, woolgathering

tran·quil \'tran-kwəl, 'tran-\ *adj* ♦ : free from agitation or disturbance — **tran·quil·ly** *adv*

♦ calm, hushed, peaceful, quiet, restful, serene, still ♦ calm, collected, composed, cool, placid, self-possessed, serene, undisturbed, unperturbed, unshaken, untroubled, unworried

tran·quil·i·ty *or chiefly Brit* **tran·quil·li·ty** \tran-'kwi-lə-tē, tran-\ *n* ♦ : the quality or state of being tranquil

♦ calm, calmness, hush, peace, placidity, quiet, quietness, repose, serenity, still, stillness ♦ aplomb, calmness, composure, coolness, equanimity, placidity, self-possession, serenity

tran·quil·ize *also* **tran·quil·lize** \'tran-kwə-,līz, 'tran-\ *vb* **-ized** *also* **-lized; -iz·ing** *also* **-liz·ing** ♦ : to make or become tranquil; *esp* : to relieve of mental tension and anxiety by means of drugs

♦ allay, calm, compose, quiet, settle, soothe, still

tran·quil·iz·er *also* **tran·quil·liz·er** \-,lī-zər\ *n* : a drug used to relieve mental disturbance (as tension and anxiety)

¹trans \'tran(t)s, 'tranz\ *adj* : TRANSGENDER, TRANSSEXUAL

²trans *abbr* **1** transaction **2** transitive **3** translated; translation; translator **4** transmission **5** transportation **6** transverse

trans·act \tran-'zakt, -'sakt\ *vb* : CARRY OUT, PERFORM; *also* : CONDUCT

trans·ac·tion \-'zak-shən, -'sak-\ *n* **1** : something transacted; *esp* : a business deal **2** ♦ : an act or process of transacting **3** *pl* : the records of the proceedings of a society or organization

♦ deal, sale, trade

trans·at·lan·tic \,trans-ət-'lan-tik, ,tranz-\ *adj* : crossing or extending across or situated beyond the Atlantic Ocean

trans·ax·le \trans-'ak-səl\ *n* : a unit combining the transmission and differential gear of a front-wheel-drive automobile

trans·ceiv·er \tran-'sē-vər\ *n* : a radio transmitter-receiver that uses many of the same components for both transmission and reception

tran·scend \tran-'send\ *vb* **1** : to rise above the limits of **2** ♦ : to rise above or go beyond the limits of : SURPASS

♦ beat, better, eclipse, excel, outdistance, outdo, outshine, outstrip, surpass, top

tran·scen·dence \tran-'sen-dən(t)s\ *n* ♦ : the quality or state of being transcendent

♦ distinction, dominance, eminence, preeminence, primacy, superiority, supremacy

tran·scen·dent \-'sen-dənt\ *adj* **1** : exceeding usual limits : SURPASSING **2** : transcending material existence

tran·scen·den·tal \,tran-,sen-'dent-ᵊl, -sən-\ *adj* **1** : TRANSCENDENT **2** **2** : of, relating to, or characteristic of transcendentalism; *also* : ABSTRUSE

tran·scen·den·tal·ism \-ᵊl-,i-zəm\ *n* : a philosophy holding that ultimate reality is unknowable or asserting the primacy of the spiritual over the material and empirical — **tran·scen·den·tal·ist** \-ᵊl-ist\ *adj or n*

trans·con·ti·nen·tal \,trans-,känt-ᵊn-'ent-ᵊl\ *adj* : extending or going across a continent

tran·scribe \trans-'krīb\ *vb* **tran·scribed; tran·scrib·ing** **1** : to write a copy of **2** : to make a copy of (dictated or recorded matter) in longhand or on a typewriter **3** : to represent (speech sounds) by means of phonetic symbols; *also* : to make a musical transcription of

tran·script \'tran-,skript\ *n* **1** : a written, printed, or typed copy **2** : an official copy esp. of a student's educational record

tran·scrip·tion \tran-'skrip-shən\ *n* **1** : an act or process of transcribing **2** : COPY, TRANSCRIPT **3** : an arrangement of a musical composition for some instrument or voice other than the original

tran·scrip·tion·ist \-shə-nist\ *n* : one that transcribes; *esp* : a typist who transcribes medical reports

trans·der·mal \trans-'dər-məl, 'tranz-\ *adj* : relating to, being, or supplying a medication in a form for absorption through the skin ⟨∼ nicotine patch⟩

trans·duc·er \trans-'dü-sər, tranz-, -'dyü-\ *n* : a device that is actuated by power from one system and supplies power usu. in another form to a second system

tran·sept \'tran-,sept\ *n* : the part of a cruciform church that crosses at right angles to the greatest length; *also* : either of the projecting ends

trans fat \'tran(t)s-, 'tranz-\ *n* : a fat containing unsaturated fatty acids (**trans–fatty acids**) that have been linked to an increase in blood cholesterol

¹trans·fer \trans-'fər, 'trans-,fər\ *vb* **trans·ferred; trans·fer·ring** **1** ♦ : to pass or cause to pass from one person, place, or situation to another **2** ♦ : to make over the possession of **3** : to print or copy from one surface to another by contact **4** : to change from one vehicle or transportation line to another — **trans·fer·able** \trans-'fər-ə-bəl\ *adj* — **trans·fer·al** \-əl\ *n*

♦ [1] consign, dispatch, move, pack, send, ship, transmit, transport ♦ [1] commend, commit, consign, delegate, deliver, entrust, give, hand over, leave, pass, transmit, trust, turn over, vest ♦ [2] alienate, assign, cede, deed, make over

²trans·fer \'trans-,fər\ *n* **1** : conveyance of right, title, or interest in property from one person to another **2** : an act or process of transferring **3** : one that transfers or is transferred **4** : a ticket entitling a passenger to continue a trip on another route

trans·fer·ence \trans-'fər-əns\ *n* : an act, process, or instance of transferring

trans·fig·u·ra·tion \,trans-,fi-gyə-'rā-shən, -gə-\ *n* ♦ : a change in form or appearance

♦ changeover, conversion, metamorphosis, transformation

trans·fig·ure \trans-'fi-gyər\ *vb* **-ured; -ur·ing** **1** ♦ : to change the form or appearance of **2** : EXALT, GLORIFY

♦ convert, make over, metamorphose, transform

trans·fix \trans-'fiks\ *vb* **1** ♦ : to pierce through with or as if with a pointed weapon **2** : to hold motionless by or as if by piercing

♦ gore, harpoon, impale, lance, pierce, puncture, skewer, spear, spike, stab, stick

trans·form \trans-'fórm\ *vb* ♦ : to change in structure, appearance, or character

♦ convert, make over, metamorphose, transfigure

trans·for·ma·tion \,trans-fər-'mā-shən\ *n* ♦ : an act, process, or instance of transforming or being transformed

♦ changeover, conversion, metamorphosis, transfiguration

trans·form·er \trans-'fór-mər\ *n* : one that transforms; *esp* : a device for converting variations of current in one circuit into variations of voltage and current in another circuit

trans·fuse \trans-'fyüz\ *vb* **trans·fused; trans·fus·ing 1**
♦ : to cause to pass from one to another **2** ♦ : to diffuse into or
through **3** : to transfer (as blood) into a vein or an artery of a
person or animal — **trans·fu·sion** \-'fyü-zhən\ *n*

♦ [1] communicate, convey, impart, spread, transfer, transmit
♦ [2] percolate, permeate, suffuse

trans·gen·der \tranz-'jen-dər\ *adj* : of, relating to, or being a
person whose gender identity differs from the sex the person had
or was identified as having at birth ⟨a ∼ person⟩
trans·gen·dered \-dərd\ *adj, now usually offensive* : TRANSGENDER
trans·gen·ic \tran(t)s-'je-nik\ *adj* : being or used to produce an
organism or cell with genes introduced from another species of
organism ⟨∼ crops⟩
trans·gress \trans-'gres, tranz-\ *vb* **1** ♦ : to go beyond the limits set by ⟨∼ the divine law⟩ **2** : to go beyond : EXCEED **3** ♦ : to
violate a command or law : SIN — **trans·gres·sor** \-'gre-sər\ *n*

♦ [1] breach, break, violate ♦ [3] err, offend, sin, trespass

trans·gres·sion \trans-'gre-shən\ *n* ♦ : an act, process, or instance of transgressing

♦ breach, crime, error, malefaction, misdeed, misdoing, offense,
sin, trespass, violation, wrongdoing

¹**tran·sient** \'tran-shənt; -sē-ənt, -shē-, -zē-\ *adj* **1** ♦ : not lasting long : SHORT-LIVED **2** : passing through a place with only a
brief stay — **tran·sient·ly** *adv*

♦ ephemeral, evanescent, flash, fleeting, fugitive, impermanent,
momentary, short-lived

²**transient** *n* : one that is transient; *esp* : a transient guest
tran·sis·tor \tran-'zis-tər, -'sis-\ *n* **1** : a small electronic semiconductor device used in electronic equipment **2** : a radio having transistors
tran·sis·tor·ized \-tə-ˌrīzd\ *adj* : having or using transistors
tran·sit \'tran-sət, -zət\ *n* **1** : a passing through, across, or over
: PASSAGE **2** : conveyance of persons or things from one place to
another **3** : usu. local transportation esp. of people by public
conveyance **4** : a surveyor's instrument for measuring angles
tran·si·tion \tran-'si-shən, -'zi-\ *n* : passage from one state,
place, stage, or subject to another : CHANGE — **tran·si·tion·al**
\-'si-shə-nəl, -'zi-\ *adj*
tran·si·tive \'tran-sə-tiv, -zə-\ *adj* **1** : having or containing an
object required to complete the meaning ⟨a ∼ verb⟩ **2** : TRANSI-
TIONAL — **tran·si·tive·ly** *adv* — **tran·si·tive·ness** *n* — **tran·si·-
tiv·i·ty** \ˌtran-sə-'ti-və-tē, ˌtranz-\ *n*
tran·si·to·ry \'tran-sə-ˌtōr-ē, -zə-\ *adj* : of brief duration : SHORT-
LIVED
transl *abbr* translated; translation
trans·late \trans-'lāt, tranz-\ *vb* **trans·lat·ed; trans·lat·ing 1**
: to change from one place, state, or form to another **2** : to convey to heaven without death **3 a** : to turn into one's own or another language **b** ♦ : to express in different terms and esp. different words — **trans·lat·able** *adj* — **trans·la·tor** \-'lā-tər\ *n*

♦ paraphrase, rephrase, restate

trans·la·tion \trans-'lā-shən\ *n* **1** ♦ : an act, process, or instance of translating **2** : the process of forming a protein molecule from information in messenger RNA

♦ paraphrase

trans·lit·er·ate \trans-'li-tə-ˌrāt, tranz-\ *vb* **-at·ed; -at·ing** : to
represent or spell in the characters of another alphabet —
trans·lit·er·a·tion \ˌtrans-ˌli-tə-'rā-shən, ˌtranz-\ *n*
trans·lu·cent \trans-'lüs-ᵊnt, tranz-\ *adj* : not transparent but
clear enough to allow light to pass through — **trans·lu·cence**
\-ᵊns\ *n* — **trans·lu·cen·cy** \-ᵊn-sē\ *n* — **trans·lu·cent·ly** *adv*
trans·mi·grate \-'mi-ˌgrat\ *vb* : to pass at death from one body or
being to another — **trans·mi·gra·tion** \ˌtrans-mī-'grā-shən,
ˌtranz-\ *n* — **trans·mi·gra·to·ry** \ˌmī-grə-ˌtōr-ē\ *adj*
trans·mis·sion \-'mi-shən\ *n* **1** : an act or process of transmitting **2** : the passage of radio waves between transmitting stations
and receiving stations **3** : the gears by which power is transmitted from the engine of an automobile to the axle that propels the
vehicle **4** : something transmitted
trans·mit \-'mit\ *vb* **trans·mit·ted; trans·mit·ting 1** ♦ : to
transfer from one person or place to another **2** : to pass on by or
as if by inheritance **3** : to cause or allow to spread abroad or to
another ⟨∼ a disease⟩ **4** : to cause (as light, electricity, or force)
to pass through a medium **5** : to send out (radio or television signals) — **trans·mis·si·ble** \-'mi-sə-bəl\ *adj* —
trans·mit·tal \-'mit-ᵊl\ *n*

♦ communicate, convey, impart, spread, transfer, transfuse
♦ consign, dispatch, pack, send, ship, transfer, transport

trans·mit·ta·ble \trans-'mi-tə-bəl\ *adj* ♦ : capable of being
transmitted

♦ catching, communicable, contagious

trans·mit·ter \-'mi-tər\ *n* : one that transmits; *esp* : an apparatus
for transmitting telegraph, radio, or television signals
trans·mog·ri·fy \trans-'mä-grə-ˌfī, tranz-\ *vb* **-fied; -fy·ing** : to
change or alter often with grotesque or humorous effect —
trans·mog·ri·fi·ca·tion \-ˌmä-grə-fə-'kā-shən\ *n*
trans·mute \-'myüt\ *vb* **trans·muted; trans·mut·ing** : to change
or alter in form, appearance, or nature — **trans·mu·ta·tion** \ˌtrans-
myü-'tā-shən, ˌtranz-\ *n*
trans·na·tion·al \-'na-shə-nəl\ *adj* : extending beyond national
boundaries
trans·oce·an·ic \ˌtrans-ˌō-shē-'a-nik, ˌtranz-\ *adj* **1** : lying or
dwelling beyond the ocean **2** : crossing or extending across the
ocean
tran·som \'tran-səm\ *n* **1** : a piece (as a crossbar in the frame of
a window or door) that lies crosswise in a structure **2** : a window
above an opening (as a door) built on and often hinged to a horizontal crossbar
tran·son·ic *also* **trans–son·ic** \trans-'sä-nik\ *adj* : being or relating to speeds near that of sound in air or about 741 miles (1185
kilometers) per hour
trans·pa·cif·ic \ˌtrans-pə-'si-fik\ *adj* : crossing, extending
across, or situated beyond the Pacific Ocean
trans·par·ent \trans-'par-ənt\ *adj* **1** ♦ : clear enough to be
seen through **2** ♦ : fine or sheer enough to be seen through ⟨a
∼ fabric⟩ **3** ♦ : readily understood : CLEAR; *also* : easily detected ⟨a ∼ lie⟩ — **trans·par·en·cy** \-ən-sē\ *n* — **trans·par·-
ent·ly** *adv*

♦ [1] clear, limpid, liquid, lucent, pellucid ♦ [2] gauzy, sheer
♦ [3] apparent, broad, clear, clear-cut, distinct, evident, lucid,
manifest, obvious, palpable, patent, perspicuous, plain, unambiguous, unequivocal, unmistakable

tran·spire \trans-'pīr\ *vb* **trans·pired; trans·pir·ing 1** : to pass
or give off (as water vapor) through pores or a membrane **2** : to
become known **3** ♦ : to take place : HAPPEN — **tran·spi·ra·tion**
\ˌtrans-pə-'rā-shən\ *n*

♦ be, befall, betide, chance, come, go, happen, occur, pass

¹**trans·plant** \trans-'plant\ *vb* **1** : to dig up and plant elsewhere **2** : to remove from one place and settle or introduce elsewhere : TRANSPORT **3** : to transfer (an organ or tissue) from one
part or individual to another — **trans·plan·ta·tion** \ˌtrans-
ˌplan-'tā-shən\ *n*
²**trans·plant** \'trans-ˌplant\ *n* **1** : a person or thing transplanted **2** : the act or process of transplanting
trans·po·lar \trans-'pō-lər\ *adj* : going or extending across either of the polar regions
transponder \tran-'spän-dər\ *n* : a radio or radar set that upon
receiving a certain signal emits a radio signal and that is used to
locate and identify objects and in satellites to relay communications signals
¹**trans·port** \trans-'pōrt\ *vb* **1** ♦ : to convey from one place to
another **2** ♦ : to carry away by strong emotion : ENRAPTURE **3**
♦ : to send to a penal colony overseas — **trans·port·er** *n*

♦ [1] consign, dispatch, pack, send, ship, transfer, transmit
♦ [1] bear, carry, cart, convey, ferry, haul, lug, pack, tote ♦ [2]
carry away, enrapture, enthrall, entrance, ravish ♦ [3] banish,
deport, displace, exile, expatriate

²**trans·port** \'trans-ˌpōrt\ *n* **1** : an act of transporting **2**
♦ : strong or intensely pleasurable emotion ⟨∼s of joy⟩ **3** ♦ : a
ship used in transporting troops or supplies; *also* : a vehicle (as a
truck or plane) used to transport persons or goods

♦ [2] ecstasy, elation, euphoria, exhilaration, heaven, intoxication, paradise, rapture, rhapsody ♦ [3] conveyance, vehicle

trans·por·ta·tion \ˌtrans-pər-'tā-shən\ *n* **1** : an act, process, or
instance of transporting or being transported **2** : means of conveyance or travel from one place to another
trans·pose \trans-'pōz\ *vb* **trans·posed; trans·pos·ing 1** : to
change the position or sequence of ⟨∼ the letters in a word⟩ **2**
: to write or perform (a musical composition) in a different key —
trans·po·si·tion \ˌtrans-pə-'zi-shən\ *n*
trans·sex·u·al \(ˌ)trans-'sek-shə-wəl\ *n* : a person whose gen-
der identity is opposite the sex the person had or was identified as
having at birth
trans·ship \tran-'ship, trans-\ *vb* : to transfer for further transportation from one ship or conveyance to another —
trans·ship·ment *n*
trans·sub·stan·ti·a·tion \ˌtran-səb-ˌstan-chē-'ā-shən\ *n* : the

change in the eucharistic elements from the substance of bread and wine to the substance of the body of Christ with only the appearances of bread and wine remaining

trans·verse \trans-'vərs, tranz-\ *adj* : lying across : set crosswise — **transverse** \'trans-,vərs, 'tranz-\ *n*

trans·verse·ly *adv* ♦ : in a transverse direction or line

♦ athwart, crosswise, obliquely

trans·ves·tite \trans-'ves-,tīt, tranz-\ *n* : a person who wears clothes designed for the opposite sex — **transvestite** *adj* — **trans·ves·tism** \-,ti-zəm\ *n*

¹**trap** \'trap\ *n* **1** : a device for catching animals **2** ♦ : something by which one is caught unawares; *also* : a situation from which escape is difficult or impossible **3** : a machine for throwing clay pigeons into the air; *also* : SAND TRAP **4** : a light one-horse carriage on springs **5** : a device to allow some one thing to pass through while keeping other things out ⟨a ∼ in a drainpipe⟩ **6** *pl* : a group of percussion instruments (as in a dance orchestra)

♦ ambush, net, snare, web ♦ ambush, surprise

²**trap** *vb* **trapped; trap·ping** **1** ♦ : to catch in or as if in a trap; *also* : CONFINE **2** : to provide or set (a place) with traps **3** : to set traps for animals esp. as a business — **trap·per** *n*

♦ confine, enmesh, ensnare, entangle, entrap, mesh, snare, tangle

trap·door \'trap-'dōr\ *n* : a lifting or sliding door covering an opening in a floor or roof

tra·peze \tra-'pēz\ *n* : a gymnastic apparatus consisting of a horizontal bar suspended by two parallel ropes

trap·e·zoid \'tra-pə-,zȯid\ *n* : a 4-sided polygon with exactly two sides parallel — **trap·e·zoi·dal** \,tra-pə-'zȯid-ᵊl\ *adj*

trap·pings \'tra-piŋz\ *n pl* **1** : CAPARISON 1 **2** : outward decoration or dress; *also* : outward sign ⟨∼ of success⟩

traps \'traps\ *n pl* : personal belongings : LUGGAGE

trap·shoot·ing \'trap-,shü-tiŋ\ *n* : shooting at clay pigeons sprung from a trap into the air away from the shooter

¹**trash** \'trash\ *n* **1 a** ♦ : something of little worth : RUBBISH **b** ♦ : empty talk : NONSENSE **2 a** : a worthless person **b** ♦ : such persons as a group : RIFFRAFF

♦ [1a] chaff, deadwood, dust, garbage, junk, litter, refuse, riffraff, rubbish, scrap, waste ♦ [1b] bunk, claptrap, drivel, fiddlesticks, folly, foolishness, fudge, hogwash, humbug, nonsense, piffle, rot, silliness, slush, stupidity ♦ [2b] rabble, riffraff, scum

²**trash** *vb* **1** : VANDALIZE, DESTROY **2** : ATTACK **3** : SPOIL, RUIN **4** : to criticize or disparage harshly **5** : to dispose of : DISCARD ⟨∼ed the plans⟩

trashy \'tra-shē\ *adj* **trash·i·er; -est** ♦ : being, resembling, or containing trash : of inferior quality

♦ dowdy, inelegant, tacky, tasteless, unfashionable, unstylish ♦ cheap, common, cut-rate, inferior, junky, lousy, mediocre, miserable, poor, rotten, second-rate, shoddy, sleazy

trau·ma \'traù-mə, 'trò-\ *n, pl* **traumas** *also* **trau·ma·ta** \-mə-tə\ : a bodily or mental injury usu. caused by an external agent; *also* : a cause of trauma — **trau·mat·ic** \trə-'ma-tik, trò-, traù-\ *adj*

trau·ma·tize \-,tīz\ *vb* **-tized; -tiz·ing** : to inflict trauma upon

¹**tra·vail** \trə-'vāl, 'tra-vāl\ *n* **1** ♦ : painful work or exertion : TOIL **2** : AGONY, TORMENT **3** : CHILDBIRTH, LABOR

♦ drudgery, grind, labor (*or* labour), sweat, toil

²**travail** *vb* : to labor hard : TOIL

¹**trav·el** \'tra-vəl\ *vb* **-eled** *or* **-elled; -el·ing** *or* **-el·ling** **1** ♦ : to go on or as if on a trip or tour : JOURNEY **2** : to move as if by traveling ⟨news ∼s fast⟩ **3** : ASSOCIATE **4** : to go from place to place as a sales representative **5** : to move from point to point ⟨light waves ∼ very fast⟩ **6** ♦ : to journey over or through ⟨∼ing the highways⟩

♦ [1] journey, tour, trek, voyage ♦ [6] cover, crisscross, cross, cut, follow, go, pass, proceed, traverse

²**travel** *n* **1** : the act of traveling : PASSAGE **2** : JOURNEY, TRIP — often used in pl. **3** : the number traveling : TRAFFIC **4** : the motion of a piece of machinery and esp. when to and fro

trav·el·er \'tra-və-lər\ *or* **trav·el·ler** *n* ♦ : one that travels : one that takes a journey

♦ excursionist, sightseer, tourist

traveler's check *n* : a check paid for in advance that is signed when bought and signed again when cashed

traveling bag *n* ♦ : a portable case designed to hold a traveler's clothing and personal articles : SUITCASE

♦ carryall, grip, handbag, portmanteau, suitcase

trav·el·ogue *or* **trav·el·og** \'tra-və-,lȯg, -,läg\ *n* : a usu. illustrated lecture on travel

¹**tra·verse** \'tra-vərs\ *n* : something that crosses or lies across

²**tra·verse** \trə-'vərs, tra-'vərs, 'tra-vərs\ *vb* **tra·versed; tra·vers·ing** **1** ♦ : to go or travel across or over **2** : to move or pass along or through **3** : to extend over **4** : SWIVEL

♦ cover, crisscross, cross, cut, follow, go, pass, proceed, travel

³**tra·verse** \'tra-vərs\ *adj* : TRANSVERSE

trav·er·tine \'tra-vər-,tēn, -tən\ *n* : a crystalline mineral formed by deposition from spring waters

¹**trav·es·ty** \'tra-və-stē\ *vb* **-tied; -ty·ing** ♦ : to make a travesty of

♦ burlesque, caricature, imitate, mimic, mock, parody, take off

²**travesty** *n, pl* **-ties** ♦ : an imitation that makes crude fun of something; *also* : an inferior imitation

♦ caricature, farce, joke, mockery, parody, sham

¹**trawl** \'trȯl\ *vb* : to fish or catch with a trawl — **trawl·er** *n*

²**trawl** *n* **1** : a large conical net dragged along the sea bottom in fishing **2** : a long heavy fishing line equipped with many hooks in series

tray \'trā\ *n* : an open receptacle with flat bottom and low rim for holding, carrying, or exhibiting articles

treach·er·ous \'tre-chə-rəs\ *adj* **1** ♦ : characterized by treachery **2** : UNTRUSTWORTHY, UNRELIABLE **3** : providing insecure footing or support — **treach·er·ous·ly** *adv*

♦ disloyal, faithless, false, fickle, inconstant, loose, perfidious, recreant, traitorous, unfaithful, untrue

treach·ery \'tre-chə-rē\ *n, pl* **-er·ies** ♦ : violation of allegiance or trust

♦ betrayal, disloyalty, double cross, faithlessness, falseness, falsity, infidelity, perfidy, treason, unfaithfulness

trea·cle \'trē-kəl\ *n, chiefly Brit* : MOLASSES — **trea·cly** \-k(ə-)lē\ *adj*

¹**tread** \'tred\ *vb* **trod** \'träd\; **trod·den** \'träd-ᵊn\ *or* **trod; tread·ing** **1** : to step or walk on or over **2** ♦ : to move on foot : WALK **3** : to beat or press with the feet — **tread water** : to stay afloat and upright in water by sustaining a walking motion

♦ foot, leg, pad, step, traipse, walk

²**tread** *n* **1** : a mark made by or as if by treading **2** : the manner or sound of stepping **3** : the part of a wheel that makes contact with a road **4** : the horizontal part of a step

trea·dle \'tre-dᵊl\ *n* : a lever device pressed by the foot to drive a machine — **treadle** *vb*

tread·mill \'tred-,mil\ *n* **1** : a mill worked by persons who tread on steps around the edge of a wheel or by animals that walk on an endless belt **2** : a device with an endless belt on which a person walks or runs in place **3** ♦ : a wearisome routine

♦ groove, pattern, rote, routine, rut

treas *abbr* treasurer; treasury

trea·son \'trēz-ᵊn\ *n* **1** : the offense of attempting to overthrow the government of one's country or of assisting its enemies in war **2** ♦ : the betrayal of a trust — **trea·son·able** \-ᵊn-ə-bəl\ *adj* — **trea·son·ous** \-ᵊn-əs\ *adj*

♦ betrayal, disloyalty, double cross, faithlessness, falseness, falsity, infidelity, perfidy, treachery, unfaithfulness

¹**trea·sure** \'tre-zhər, 'trā-\ **1** : wealth stored up or held in reserve **2** ♦ : something of great value

♦ catch, gem, jewel, pearl, plum, prize

²**treasure** *vb* **trea·sured; trea·sur·ing** **1** : HOARD **2** ♦ : to keep as precious : CHERISH

♦ appreciate, cherish, love, prize, value

trea·sur·er \'tre-zhə-rər, 'trā-\ *n* : an officer of a club, business, or government who has charge of money taken in and paid out

treasure trove \-,trōv\ *n* **1** : treasure of unknown ownership found buried or hidden **2** : a valuable discovery

trea·sury \'tre-zhə-rē, 'trā-\ *n, pl* **-sur·ies** **1** : a place in which stores of wealth are kept **2** : the place where collected funds are stored and paid out **3** *cap* : a governmental department in charge of finances

¹**treat** \'trēt\ *vb* **1** : to discuss terms of accommodation or settlement **2 a** ♦ : to deal with esp. in writing — usu. used with *of* **b** ♦ : to deal with : HANDLE **3** : to pay for the food or entertainment of **4** ♦ : to behave or act toward ⟨∼ them well⟩ **5** : to regard in a specified manner ⟨∼ as inferiors⟩ **6** : to give medical or surgical care to **7** : to subject to some action ⟨∼ soil with lime⟩

♦ *usu* **treat of** [2a] concern, cover, deal, pertain ♦ [2b] contend with, cope with, grapple with, handle, manage, maneuver (*or* manoeuvre), negotiate, swing ♦ [4] act, be, deal, handle, serve, use

²**treat** *n* **1** : an entertainment given free to those invited; *also* : food, drink, or entertainment provided at another's expense **2** ♦ : a source of joy or amusement

♦ delectation, delight, joy, kick, manna, pleasure ♦ dainty, delicacy, goody, tidbit

trea•tise \'trē-təs\ *n* : a systematic written exposition or argument

treat•ment \'trēt-mənt\ *n* : the act or manner or an instance of treating someone or something; *also* : a substance or method used in treating

trea•ty \'trē-tē\ *n, pl* **treaties** ♦ : an agreement made by negotiation or diplomacy esp. between two or more states or governments

♦ accord, alliance, compact, convention, covenant, pact

¹**tre•ble** \'tre-bəl\ *n* **1** : the highest of the four voice parts in vocal music : SOPRANO **2** : a high-pitched or shrill voice or sound **3** : the upper half of the musical pitch range

²**treble** *adj* **1** ♦ : triple in number or amount **2** : relating to or having the range of a musical treble **3** ♦ : high-pitched : SHRILL — **tre•bly** *adv*

♦ [1] threefold, tripartite, triple ♦ [3] acute, sharp, shrill, squeaky

³**treble** *vb* **tre•bled; tre•bling** : to make or become three times the size, amount, or number

¹**tree** \'trē\ *n* **1** : a woody perennial plant usu. with a single main stem and a head of branches and leaves at the top **2** : a piece of wood adapted to a particular use ⟨a shoe ∼⟩ **3** : something resembling a tree ⟨a genealogical ∼⟩ — **tree•less** *adj*

²**tree** *vb* **treed; tree•ing** : to drive to or up a tree ⟨∼ a raccoon⟩

tree farm *n* : an area of forest land managed to ensure continuous commercial production

tree frog *n* : any of numerous usu. tree-dwelling amphibians with adhesive disks on the toes

tree line *n* : TIMBERLINE

tree of heaven : a Chinese ailanthus widely grown as an ornamental tree

tree surgery *n* : operative treatment of diseased trees esp. for control of decay — **tree surgeon** *n*

tre•foil \'trē-ˌfȯil, 'tre-\ *n* **1** : an herb (as a clover) with leaves that have three leaflets **2** : a decorative design with three leaflike parts

¹**trek** \'trek\ *vb* **trekked; trek•king** **1** *chiefly South Africa* : to travel or migrate by ox wagon **2** ♦ : to make one's way arduously

♦ journey, tour, travel, voyage

²**trek** *n* **1** *chiefly South Africa* : a migration esp. of settlers by ox wagon **2** ♦ : a slow or difficult journey

♦ expedition, journey, passage, peregrination, trip

¹**trel•lis** \'tre-ləs\ *n* : a frame of latticework used esp. to support climbing plants

²**trellis** *vb* : to provide with a trellis; *esp* : to train (as a vine) on a trellis

trem•a•tode \'tre-mə-ˌtōd\ *n* : any of a class of parasitic worms

¹**trem•ble** \'trem-bəl\ *vb* **trem•bled; trem•bling** **1** : to shake involuntarily (as with fear or cold) : SHIVER **2** : to move, sound, pass, or come to pass as if shaken or tremulous **3** : to be affected with fear or doubt

²**tremble** *n* ♦ : a spell of shaking or quivering

♦ quiver, shiver, shudder

tre•men•dous \tri-'men-dəs\ *adj* **1** : causing dread, awe, or terror : TERRIFYING **2** ♦ : unusually large, powerful, great, or excellent ⟨∼ strength⟩

♦ colossal, enormous, giant, gigantic, huge, mammoth, massive, monstrous, monumental, prodigious, titanic

tre•men•dous•ly *adv* ♦ : to a tremendous degree or extent

♦ broadly, considerably, greatly, hugely, largely, massively, monstrously, much, sizably, stupendously, utterly, vastly

trem•o•lo \'tre-mə-ˌlō\ *n, pl* **-los** : a rapid fluttering of a tone or alternating tones

trem•or \'tre-mər\ *n* **1** : a trembling or shaking esp. from weakness, emotional stress, or disease **2** : a quivering motion of the earth (as during an earthquake)

trem•u•lous \'trem-yə-ləs\ *adj* **1** ♦ : marked by trembling or tremors **2** : TIMOROUS, TIMID — **trem•u•lous•ly** *adv*

♦ shaky, wobbly

¹**trench** \'trench\ *n* **1** ♦ : a long narrow cut in the ground : DITCH; *esp* : a ditch protected by banks of earth and used to shelter soldiers **2** *pl* : a place or situation likened to warfare conducted from trenches **3** : a long narrow steep-sided depression in the ocean floor

♦ dike, ditch, gutter

²**trench** *vb* **1** : to cut or dig trenches in **2** : to protect (troops) with trenches **3** : to come close : VERGE

tren•chant \'tren-chənt\ *adj* **1** ♦ : vigorously effective; *also* : CAUSTIC **2** : sharply perceptive : KEEN ⟨a ∼ wit⟩ **3** : CLEAR-CUT, DISTINCT **4** : having a fine edge or point : SHARP

tren•cher \'tren-chər\ *n* : a wooden platter for serving food

tren•cher•man \'tren-chər-mən\ *n* : a hearty eater

trench foot *n* : a painful foot disorder resembling frostbite and resulting from exposure to cold and wet

trench mouth *n* : a progressive painful bacterial infection of the mouth and adjacent parts marked by ulceration, bleeding gums, and foul breath

¹**trend** \'trend\ *vb* **1** : to have or take a general direction : TEND **2** ♦ : to show a tendency : INCLINE

♦ incline, lean, run, tend

²**trend** *n* **1** : a general direction taken (as by a stream or mountain range) **2** ♦ : a prevailing tendency : DRIFT **3** ♦ : a current style or preference : VOGUE

♦ [2] current, drift, leaning, run, tendency, tide, wind ♦ [3] craze, fad, mode, rage, style, vogue

trendy \'tren-dē\ *adj* **trend•i•er; -est** ♦ : very fashionable; *also* : marked by superficial or faddish appeal or taste

♦ à la mode, chic, cool, fashionable, in, modish, sharp, smart, snappy, stylish

trep•i•da•tion \ˌtre-pə-'dā-shən\ *n* ♦ : nervous agitation : APPREHENSION

♦ alarm, anxiety, apprehension, dread, fear, fright, horror, panic, terror

¹**tres•pass** \'tres-pəs, -ˌpas\ *n* **1 a** ♦ : a violation of moral or social ethics : SIN **b** ♦ : an unwarranted infringement **2** : unlawful entry on someone else's land

♦ [1a] breach, crime, error, malefaction, misdeed, misdoing, offense, sin, transgression, violation, wrongdoing ♦ [1b] breach, infraction, infringement, transgression, violation

²**trespass** *vb* **1** ♦ : to commit an offense : ERR **2** : INTRUDE, ENCROACH; *esp* : to enter unlawfully upon the land of another — **tres•pass•er** *n*

♦ err, offend, sin, transgress

tress \'tres\ *n* : a long lock of hair — usu. used in pl.

tres•tle *also* **tres•sel** \'tre-səl\ *n* **1** : a supporting framework consisting usu. of a horizontal piece with spreading legs at each end **2** : a braced framework of timbers, piles, or steel for carrying a road or railroad over a depression

T. rex \'tē-'reks\ *n* : TYRANNOSAUR

trey \'trā\ *n, pl* **treys** : a card or the side of a die with three spots

tri•ad \'trī-ˌad, -əd\ *n* ♦ : a union or group of three usu. closely related persons or things

♦ threesome, trio, triple, triplet

tri•age \trē-'äzh, 'trē-ˌäzh\ *n* : the sorting of and allocation of treatment to patients and esp. battle or disaster victims according to a system of priorities designed to maximize the number of survivors

tri•al \'trī-əl\ *n* **1** : the action or process of trying or putting to the proof : TEST **2** : the hearing and judgment of a matter in issue before a competent tribunal **3** ♦ : a source of vexation or annoyance **4** ♦ : a tryout or experiment to test quality, value, or usefulness **5** ♦ : the act or an instance of attempting — **trial** *adj*

♦ [3] cross, gauntlet, ordeal ♦ [4] dry run, practice, rehearsal ♦ [4] experiment, test ♦ [5] attempt, crack, endeavor (*or* endeavour), essay, fling, go, pass, shot, stab, try, whack

tri•an•gle \'trī-ˌaŋ-gəl\ *n* **1** : a polygon that has three sides **2** : something shaped like a triangle — **tri•an•gu•lar** \trī-'aŋ-gyə-lər\ *adj* — **tri•an•gu•lar•ly** *adv*

tri•an•gu•la•tion \ˌ(ˌ)trī-ˌaŋ-gyə-'lā-shən\ *n* : a method using trigonometry to find the location of a point using bearings from two fixed points a known distance apart — **tri•an•gu•late** \trī-'aŋ-gyə-ˌlāt\ *vb*

Tri•as•sic \trī-'a-sik\ *adj* : of, relating to, or being the earliest period of the Mesozoic era marked by the first appearance of the dinosaurs — **Triassic** *n*

tri·ath·lon \trī-'ath-lən, -ˌlän\ *n* : an athletic contest consisting of three phases (as swimming, bicycling, and running)

trib *abbr* tributary

tribe \'trīb\ *n* **1** ♦ : a social group comprising numerous families, clans, or generations **2** : a group of persons having a common character, occupation, or interest **3** : a group of related plants or animals ⟨the cat ∼⟩ — **trib·al** \'trī-bəl\ *adj*

♦ blood, clan, family, folks, house, kin, kindred, kinfolk, line, lineage, people, race, stock

tribes·man \'trībz-mən\ *n* : a member of a tribe

trib·u·la·tion \ˌtri-byə-'lā-shən\ *n* ♦ : distress or suffering resulting from oppression or persecution; *also* : a trying experience

♦ affliction, agony, anguish, distress, misery, pain, torment, torture, woe

tri·bu·nal \trī-'byün-ᵊl, tri-\ *n* **1** : the seat of a judge **2** : a court of justice **3** : something that decides or determines ⟨the ∼ of public opinion⟩

tri·bune \'tri-ˌbyün, tri-'byün\ *n* **1** : an official in ancient Rome with the function of protecting the interests of plebeian citizens from the patricians **2** : a defender of the people

¹**trib·u·tary** \'tri-byə-ˌter-ē\ *adj* **1** : paying tribute : SUBJECT **2** : flowing into a larger stream or a lake

²**tributary** *n, pl* **-tar·ies** **1** : a ruler or state that pays tribute **2** : a tributary stream

trib·ute \'tri-(ˌ)byüt, -byət\ *n* **1** : a payment by one ruler or nation to another as an act of submission or price of protection **2** : a usu. excessive tax, rental, or levy exacted by a sovereign or superior **3 a** ♦ : a gift or service showing respect, gratitude, or affection **b** ♦ : something (as material evidence or a formal attestation) that indicates the worth, virtue, or effectiveness of the one in question

♦ [3a, b] accolade, citation, commendation, encomium, eulogy, homage, paean, panegyric, salutation

trice \'trīs\ *n* ♦ : a brief space of time : INSTANT, MOMENT

♦ flash, instant, jiffy, minute, moment, second, shake, twinkle, twinkling, wink

tri·ceps \'trī-ˌseps\ *n, pl* **triceps** : a large muscle along the back of the upper arm that is attached at its upper end by three main parts and acts to extend the forearm at the elbow joint

tri·cer·a·tops \(ˌ)trī-'ser-ə-ˌtäps\ *n, pl* **-tops** *also* **-tops·es** : any of a genus of large plant-eating Cretaceous dinosaurs with three horns, a bony crest on the neck, and hoofed toes

tri·chi·na \tri-'kī-nə\ *n, pl* **-nae** \-(ˌ)nē\ *also* **-nas** : a small slender nematode worm that in the larval state is parasitic in the striated muscles of flesh-eating mammals (as humans)

trich·i·no·sis \ˌtri-kə-'nō-səs\ *n* : infestation with or disease caused by trichinae and marked esp. by pain, fever, and swelling

¹**trick** \'trik\ *n* **1** ♦ : a crafty procedure meant to deceive **2** ♦ : a mischievous action : PRANK **3** : a childish action **4** ♦ : a deceptive or ingenious feat designed to puzzle or amuse **5** ♦ : an habitual peculiarity of behavior or manner **6** : a quick or artful way of getting a result : KNACK **7** : the cards played in one round of a card game **8** : a tour of duty : SHIFT

♦ [1] artifice, device, dodge, gimmick, jig, ploy, scheme, sleight, stratagem, wile ♦ [2] antic, caper, escapade, frolic, monkeyshine, practical joke, prank ♦ [4] deed, exploit, feat, stunt ♦ [5] crotchet, eccentricity, idiosyncrasy, mannerism, oddity, peculiarity, quirk, singularity

²**trick** *vb* **1** ♦ : to deceive by cunning or artifice **2** : to dress ornately

♦ beguile, bluff, cozen, deceive, delude, dupe, fool, gull, have, hoax, hoodwink, humbug, misinform, mislead, string along, take in

trick·ery \'tri-kə-rē\ *n* ♦ : deception by tricks and stratagems

♦ artifice, chicanery, hanky-panky, subterfuge, wile

trick·le \'tri-kəl\ *vb* **trick·led; trick·ling** **1** : to run or fall in drops **2** ♦ : to flow in a thin gentle stream — **trickle** *n*

♦ dribble, gurgle, lap, plash, ripple, slosh, splash, wash

trick·ster \'trik-stər\ *n* **1** ♦ : one who tricks or cheats **2** ♦ : one skilled at illusions

♦ [1] cheat, dodger, hoaxer, shark, sharper, swindler ♦ [2] conjurer, illusionist, magician

tricky \'tri-kē\ *adj* **trick·i·er; -est** **1** : inclined to trickery **2** ♦ : requiring skill or caution ⟨a ∼ situation to handle⟩ **3** : UNRELIABLE ⟨a ∼ lock⟩

♦ catchy, delicate, difficult, knotty, problematic, spiny, thorny, ticklish, touchy, tough

tri·col·or \'trī-ˌkə-lər\ *n* : a flag of three colors ⟨the French ∼⟩

tri·cy·cle \'trī-(ˌ)si-kəl\ *n* : a 3-wheeled vehicle usu. propelled by pedals

tri·dent \'trīd-ᵊnt\ *n* : a 3-pronged spear

tried \'trīd\ *adj* **1** ♦ : found trustworthy through testing **2** : subjected to trials

♦ dependable, good, reliable, responsible, safe, solid, steady, sure, true, trustworthy

tri·en·ni·al \trī-'e-nē-əl\ *adj* **1** : occurring or being done every three years **2** : lasting for three years — **triennial** *n*

¹**tri·fle** \'trī-fəl\ *n* **1** : something of little value or importance **2** : a dessert of cake soaked with liqueur and served with toppings (as fruit or cream)

♦ child's play, frippery, nothing, triviality

²**trifle** *vb* **tri·fled; tri·fling** **1** : to talk in a jesting or mocking manner **2** : to treat someone or something as unimportant **3** : DALLY, FLIRT **4** : to handle idly : TOY **5** : to spend or waste (as time or money) in trifling or on trifles — **tri·fler** *n*

tri·fling \'trī-fliŋ\ *adj* **1** : FRIVOLOUS **2** ♦ : lacking in significance or solid worth : TRIVIAL ⟨∼ details⟩

♦ frivolous, inconsequential, inconsiderable, insignificant, little, minor, minute, negligible, slight, small, trivial, unimportant

tri·fo·cals \trī-'fō-kəlz\ *n pl* : eyeglasses with lenses having one part for close focus, one for intermediate focus, and one for distant focus

tri·fo·li·ate \trī-'fō-lē-ət\ *adj* : having three leaves or leaflets

¹**trig** \'trig\ *adj* : stylishly trim : SMART

²**trig** *n* : TRIGONOMETRY

¹**trig·ger** \'tri-gər\ *n* : a movable lever that activates a device when it is squeezed; *esp* : the part of a firearm lock moved by the finger to fire a gun — **trigger** *adj* — **trig·gered** *adj*

²**trigger** *vb* **1** : to fire by pulling a trigger **2** ♦ : to initiate, actuate, or set off as if by a trigger

♦ activate, crank, drive, move, propel, run, set off, spark, start, touch off, turn on

tri·glyc·er·ide *n* : any of a group of lipids that are formed from glycerol and fatty acids and are widespread in animal tissue

trig·o·nom·e·try \ˌtri-gə-'nä-mə-trē\ *n* : the branch of mathematics dealing with the properties of triangles and esp. with finding unknown angles or sides given the size or length of some angles or sides — **trig·o·no·met·ric** \-nə-'me-trik\ *also* **trig·o·no·met·ri·cal** \-tri-kəl\ *adj*

trike \'trīk\ *n* : TRICYCLE

¹**trill** \'tril\ *n* **1** : the alternation of two musical tones a scale degree apart **2** : WARBLE **3** : the rapid vibration of one speech organ against another (as of the tip of the tongue against the teeth)

²**trill** *vb* : to utter as or with a trill

tril·lion \'tril-yən\ *n* **1** : a thousand billions **2** *Brit* : a million billions — **trillion** *adj* — **tril·lionth** \-yənth\ *adj or n*

tril·li·um \'tri-lē-əm\ *n* : any of a genus of spring-blooming herbs that are related to the lilies and have an erect stem bearing a whorl of three leaves and a solitary flower

tril·o·gy \'tri-lə-jē\ *n, pl* **-gies** : a series of three dramas or literary or musical compositions that are closely related and develop one theme

¹**trim** \'trim\ *vb* **trimmed; trim·ming** **1** ♦ : to put ornaments on : ADORN **2** ♦ : to defeat esp. resoundingly **3** ♦ : to make trim, neat, regular, or less bulky by or as if by cutting ⟨∼ a beard⟩ ⟨∼ a budget⟩ **4** : to cause (a boat) to assume a desired position in the water by arrangement of the load; *also* : to adjust (as a submarine or airplane) esp. for horizontal motion **5** : to adjust (a sail) to a desired position **6** : to change one's views for safety or expediency — **trim·ly** *adv* — **trim·ness** *n*

♦ [1] adorn, array, beautify, bedeck, deck, decorate, do, dress, embellish, enrich, garnish, grace, ornament ♦ [2] clobber, drub, rout, skunk, thrash, trounce, wallop, whip ♦ [3] bob, clip, crop, curtail, cut, cut back, dock, lop, nip, prune, shave, shear

²**trim** *adj* **trim·mer; trim·mest** ♦ : showing neatness, good order, or compactness ⟨a ∼ figure⟩

♦ crisp, neat, orderly, shipshape, snug, tidy, uncluttered

³**trim** *n* **1** ♦ : good condition **2** ♦ : material used for ornament or trimming; *esp* : the woodwork in the finish of a house esp. around doors and windows **3** : the position of a ship or boat esp. with reference to the horizontal; *also* : the relation between the plane of a sail and the direction of a ship **4** : the position of an airplane at which it will continue in level flight with no adjustments to the controls **5** : something that is trimmed off

♦ [1] condition, fettle, form, kilter, order, repair, shape ♦ [2]

adornment, caparison, decoration, embellishment, frill, garnish, ornament

tri·ma·ran \'trī-mə-ˌran, ˌtrī-mə-'ran\ *n* : a sailboat with three hulls

tri·mes·ter \trī-'mes-tər, 'trī-ˌmes-tər\ *n* **1** : a period of three or about three months (as in pregnancy) **2** : one of three terms into which an academic year is sometimes divided

trim·e·ter \'tri-mə-tər\ *n* : a line of verse consisting of three metrical feet

trim·mer \'tri-mər\ *n* : one that trims

trim·ming \'tri-miŋ\ *n* **1** : the loss of a contest : DEFEAT **2** : the action of one that trims **3** : something that trims, ornaments, or completes

tri·month·ly \trī-'mənth-lē\ *adj* : occurring every three months

trine \'trīn\ *adj* : THREEFOLD, TRIPLE

Trin·i·da·di·an \ˌtri-nə-'dā-dē-ən, -'dä-\ *n* : a native or inhabitant of the island of Trinidad — **Trinidadian** *adj*

Trin·i·tar·i·an \ˌtri-nə-'ter-ē-ən\ *n* : a believer in the doctrine of the Trinity — **Trin·i·tar·i·an·ism** \-ē-ə-ˌni-zəm\ *n*

Trin·i·ty \'tri-nə-tē\ *n* **1** : the unity of Father, Son, and Holy Spirit as three persons in one Godhead **2** *not cap* : TRIAD

trin·ket \'triŋ-kət\ *n* **1** ♦ : a small ornament (as a jewel or ring) **2** : TRIFLE 1

　　♦ bauble, curiosity, gewgaw, knickknack, novelty, tchotchke

trio \'trē-ō\ *n, pl* **tri·os** **1** : a musical composition for three voices or three instruments **2** : the performers of a trio **3** ♦ : a group or set of three

　　♦ threesome, triad, triple, triplet

¹trip \'trip\ *vb* **tripped; trip·ping** **1** ♦ : to move with light quick steps **2** ♦ : to catch the foot against something so as to stumble or cause to stumble **3** : to make a mistake : SLIP; *also* : to detect in a misstep : EXPOSE **4** : to release (as a spring or switch) by moving a catch; *also* : ACTIVATE **5** : to get high on a usu. hallucinatory drug

　　♦ [1] bound, hop, skip, spring ♦ [2] fall, slip, stumble, topple, tumble

²trip *n* **1** ♦ : an act or instance of traveling : JOURNEY **2** : a quick light step **3** : a false step : STUMBLE; *also* : ERROR **4** : the action of tripping mechanically; *also* : a device for tripping **5** : an intense experience; *esp* : one triggered by a hallucinatory drug **6** : absorption in an attitude or state of mind ⟨an ego ～⟩

　　♦ expedition, journey, passage, peregrination, trek

tri·par·tite \trī-'pär-ˌtīt\ *adj* **1** ♦ : divided into three parts **2** : having three corresponding parts or copies **3** : made between three parties ⟨a ～ treaty⟩

　　♦ threefold, treble, triple

tripe \'trīp\ *n* **1** : stomach tissue esp. of a ruminant (as an ox) used as food **2** : something poor, worthless, or offensive : TRASH

¹tri·ple \'tri-pəl\ *vb* **tri·pled; tri·pling** **1** : to make or become three times as great or as many **2** : to hit a triple

²triple *n* **1** : a triple quantity **2** ♦ : a group of three **3** : a hit in baseball that lets the batter reach third base

　　♦ threesome, triad, trio, triplet

³triple *adj* **1** : being three times as great or as many **2** ♦ : having three units or members **3** : repeated three times

　　♦ threefold, treble, tripartite

triple bond *n* : a chemical bond in which three pairs of electrons are shared by two atoms in a molecule

triple point *n* : the condition of temperature and pressure under which the gaseous, liquid, and solid forms of a substance can exist in equilibrium

trip·let \'tri-plət\ *n* **1** : a unit of three lines of verse **2** ♦ : a group of three of a kind **3** : one of three offspring born at one birth

　　♦ threesome, triad, trio, triple

tri·plex \'tri-ˌpleks, 'trī-\ *adj* : having three units or members : THREEFOLD

¹trip·li·cate \'tri-pli-kət\ *adj* : made in three identical copies

²trip·li·cate \-plə-ˌkāt\ *vb* **-cat·ed; -cat·ing** **1** : TRIPLE **2** : to provide three copies of ⟨～ a document⟩

³trip·li·cate \-pli-kət\ *n* : three copies all alike — used with *in* ⟨typed in ～⟩

tri·ply \'tri-plē, 'tri-pə-lē\ *adv* : in a triple degree, amount, or manner

tri·pod \'trī-ˌpäd\ *n* : something (as a caldron, stool, or camera stand) that rests on three legs — **tripod** *or* **tri·po·dal** \'trī-pəd-ᵊl, 'trī-ˌpäd-\ *adj*

trip·tych \'trip-tik\ *n* : a picture or carving in three panels side by side

tri·reme \'trī-ˌrēm\ *n* : an ancient galley having three banks of oars

tri·sect \'trī-ˌsekt, trī-'sekt\ *vb* : to divide into three usu. equal parts — **tri·sec·tion** \'trī-ˌsek-shən\ *n*

trite \'trīt\ *adj* **trit·er; trit·est** ♦ : used so commonly that the novelty is worn off : STALE

　　♦ banal, commonplace, hackneyed, musty, stale, stereotyped, threadbare, tired

tri·ti·um \'tri-tē-əm, 'tri-shē-\ *n* : a radioactive form of hydrogen with one proton and two neutrons in its nucleus and three times the mass of ordinary hydrogen

tri·ton \'trīt-ᵊn\ *n* : any of various large marine gastropod mollusks with a heavy elongated conical shell; *also* : the shell of a triton

trit·u·rate \'tri-chə-ˌrāt\ *vb* **-rat·ed; -rat·ing** : to rub or grind to a fine powder

¹tri·umph \'trī-əmf\ *n* **1** : the joy or exultation of victory or success **2** : VICTORY, CONQUEST **3** ♦ : a notable success — **tri·um·phal** \trī-'əm-fəl\ *adj*

　　♦ accomplishment, achievement, attainment, coup, success

²triumph *vb* **1** ♦ : to obtain victory : PREVAIL **2** ♦ : to celebrate victory or success exultantly

　　♦ [1] conquer, prevail, win ♦ *usu* **triumph over** [1] beat, defeat, overcome, prevail, surmount, win ♦ [2] crow, delight, exult, glory, joy, rejoice

tri·um·phant \trī-'əm-fənt\ *adj* **1** : VICTORIOUS **2** ♦ : rejoicing for or celebrating victory **3** ♦ : notably successful — **tri·um·phant·ly** *adv*

　　♦ [2] exultant, jubilant, rejoicing ♦ [3] palmy, prosperous, successful

tri·um·vir \trī-'əm-vər\ *n, pl* **-virs** *also* **-vi·ri** \-və-ˌrī\ : a member of a triumvirate

tri·um·vi·rate \-və-rət\ *n* : a ruling body of three persons

tri·une \'trī-ˌün, -ˌyün\ *adj* : being three in one ⟨the ～ God⟩

triv·et \'tri-vət\ *n* **1** : a 3-legged stand : TRIPOD **2** : a usu. metal stand with short feet for use under a hot dish

triv·ia \'tri-vē-ə\ *n sing or pl* : unimportant matters : obscure facts or details ⟨movie ～⟩

triv·i·al \'tri-vē-əl\ *adj* ♦ : of little importance

　　♦ frivolous, inconsequential, inconsiderable, insignificant, little, minor, minute, negligible, slight, small, trifling, unimportant

triv·i·al·i·ty \ˌtri-vē-'a-lə-tē\ *n* **1** : the quality or state of being trivial **2** ♦ : something trivial

　　♦ child's play, frippery, nothing, trifle

triv·i·um \'tri-vē-əm\ *n, pl* **triv·ia** \-vē-ə\ : the three liberal arts of grammar, rhetoric, and logic in a medieval university

tri·week·ly \trī-'wē-klē\ *adj* **1** : occurring or appearing three times a week **2** : occurring or appearing every three weeks — **triweekly** *adv*

tro·che \'trō-kē\ *n* : LOZENGE 2

tro·chee \'trō-(ˌ)kē\ *n* : a metrical foot of one accented syllable followed by one unaccented syllable — **tro·cha·ic** \trō-'kā-ik\ *adj*

trod *past and past part of* TREAD

trodden *past part of* TREAD

troi·ka \'troi-kə\ *n* : a group of three; *esp* : an administrative or ruling body of three

¹troll \'trōl\ *vb* **1** : to sing the parts of (a song) in succession **2** : to fish by trailing a lure or baited hook from a moving boat **3** : to sing or play jovially **4** : to deliberately antagonize (others) esp. online

²troll *n* : a lure used in trolling; *also* : the line with its lure **2** : a person who trolls others esp. online

³troll *n* ♦ : a dwarf or giant in Scandinavian folklore inhabiting caves or hills

　　♦ brownie, dwarf, elf, fairy, fay, gnome, hobgoblin, leprechaun, pixie, puck

trol·ley *also* **trol·ly** \'trä-lē\ *n, pl* **trolleys** *also* **trollies** **1** : a device (as a grooved wheel on the end of a pole) to carry current from a wire to an electrically driven vehicle **2** : a streetcar powered electrically by overhead wires **3** : a wheeled carriage running on an electrically charged overhead rail or track

trol·ley·bus \'trä-lē-ˌbəs\ *n* : a bus powered electrically by overhead wires

trolley car *n* : TROLLEY 2

trol·lop \'trä-ləp\ *n* : a disreputable woman; *esp* : one who engages in sex promiscuously

trom·bone \träm-ˈbōn, ˈträm-ˌbōn\ n : a brass wind instrument that consists of a long metal tube with two turns and a flaring end and that usu. has a movable slide to vary the pitch — **trom·bon·ist** \-ˈbō-nist, -ˌbō-\ n

tromp \ˈträmp, ˈtrȯmp\ vb 1 : to walk, tread, or step esp. heavily : TRAMP 2 : to stamp with the foot 3 : to defeat decisively 4 ♦ : to tread on forcibly and repeatedly

♦ stamp, stomp, tramp, trample

trompe l'oeil \(ˌ)trȯmp-ˈlə-ē, trōⁿp-ˈlœi\ n : a style of painting in which objects are depicted with photographic detail

¹**troop** \ˈtrüp\ n 1 : a cavalry unit corresponding to an infantry company 2 pl ♦ : the combined military, naval, and air forces of a nation : ARMED FORCES 3 : a collection of people, animals, or things 4 : a unit of Girl Scouts or Boy Scouts under an adult leader

troops ♦ armed forces, military, services

²**troop** vb : to move or gather in crowds

troop·er \ˈtrü-pər\ n 1 : an enlisted cavalryman; also : a cavalry horse 2 : a mounted or a state police officer

troop·ship \ˈtrüp-ˌship\ n : a ship or aircraft for carrying troops

trope \ˈtrōp\ n : a word or expression used in a figurative sense

tro·phy \ˈtrō-fē\ n, pl **trophies** : something gained or given in conquest or victory esp. when preserved or mounted as a memorial

trop·ic \ˈträ-pik\ n 1 : either of the two parallels of latitude approximately 23¹/₂ degrees north (**tropic of Can·cer** \-ˈkan-sər\) or south (**tropic of Cap·ri·corn** \-ˈka-prə-ˌkȯrn\) of the equator where the sun is directly overhead when it reaches its most northerly or southerly point in the sky 2 pl, often cap : the region lying between the tropics — **trop·i·cal** \-pi-kəl\ or **tropic** adj

tro·pism \ˈtrō-ˌpi-zəm\ n : an automatic movement by an organism in response to a source of stimulation; also : a reflex reaction involving this

tro·po·sphere \ˈtrō-pə-ˌsfir, ˈträ-\ n : the part of the atmosphere between the earth's surface and the stratosphere in which most weather changes occur — **tro·po·spher·ic** \ˌtrō-pə-ˈsfir-ik, ˌträ-, -ˈsfer-\ adj

¹**trot** \ˈträt\ n 1 : a moderately fast gait of a 4-footed animal (as a horse) in which the legs move in diagonal pairs 2 : a human jogging gait between a walk and a run

²**trot** vb **trot·ted; trot·ting** 1 : to ride, drive, or go at a trot 2 : to proceed briskly : HURRY — **trot·ter** n

troth \ˈträth, ˈtrȯth, ˈtrōth\ n 1 : pledged faithfulness 2 a ♦ : one's pledged word b ♦ : the act of promising to marry or the fact of being engaged to marry : BETROTHAL

♦ [2a] oath, pledge, promise, vow, word ♦ [2b] betrothal, engagement, espousal

trou·ba·dour \ˈtrü-bə-ˌdȯr\ n : any of a class of poet-musicians flourishing esp. in southern France and northern Italy during the 11th, 12th, and 13th centuries

¹**trou·ble** \ˈtrə-bəl\ vb **trou·bled; trou·bling** 1 ♦ : to feel or cause to feel mentally or spiritually agitated 2 : to produce physical disorder in 3 ♦ : to put to inconvenience 4 : RUFFLE ⟨~ the waters⟩ 5 : to make an effort

♦ [1] bother, fear, fret, stew, sweat, worry ♦ [3] discommode, disoblige, disturb, inconvenience

²**trouble** n 1 : the quality or state of being troubled esp. mentally 2 : an instance of distress or annoyance 3 ♦ : a condition of physical distress or ill health : DISEASE ⟨heart ~⟩ 4 ♦ : an effort made : EXERTION ⟨took the ~ to phone⟩ 5 ♦ : a cause of disturbance, distress, difficulty, or danger 6 ♦ : a state or condition of distress, annoyance, danger, or difficulty

♦ [3] affection, ailment, bug, complaint, complication, condition, disease, disorder, fever, ill, illness, infirmity, malady, sickness ♦ [4] effort, exertion, expenditure, labor (or labour), pains, sweat, while, work ♦ [5] case, knot, matter, problem ♦ [6] danger, distress, jeopardy, peril, risk

troubled adj ♦ : feeling worry or concern

♦ aflutter, anxious, edgy, jittery, jumpy, nervous, nervy, perturbed, tense, uneasy, upset, worried

trou·ble·mak·er \-ˌmā-kər\ n : a person who causes trouble

trou·ble·shoot·er \-ˌshü-tər\ n 1 : a worker employed to locate trouble and make repairs in equipment 2 : an expert in resolving disputes or problems — **trou·ble·shoot** vb

trou·ble·some \-səm\ adj 1 : DIFFICULT, BURDENSOME 2 ♦ : giving trouble or anxiety — **trou·ble·some·ly** adv

♦ unsettling, upsetting, worrisome Ant reassuring

trou·blous \ˈtrə-bə-ləs\ adj 1 : full of trouble 2 : causing trouble : TROUBLESOME

trough \ˈtrȯf, ˈtrȯth\ n, pl **troughs** \ˈtrȯfs, ˈtrȯvz; ˈtrȯths, ˈtrȯthz\ 1 : a long shallow open boxlike container esp. for water or feed for livestock 2 : a gutter along the eaves of a house 3 : a long channel or depression (as between waves or hills) 4 : an elongated area of low barometric pressure

trounce \ˈtrauns\ vb **trounced; trounc·ing** 1 : to thrash or punish severely 2 ♦ : to defeat decisively

♦ beat, clobber, drub, rout, skunk, thrash, trim, wallop, whip

troupe \ˈtrüp\ n : COMPANY; esp : a group of performers on the stage

troup·er \ˈtrü-pər\ n 1 ♦ : a member of a troupe 2 : a person who deals with and persists through difficulty or hardship without complaint

♦ actor, impersonator, mummer, player

trou·sers \ˈtrau-zərz\ n pl ♦ : an outer garment covering each leg separately and usu. extending from the waist to the ankle — **trouser** adj

♦ britches, pantaloons, pants, slacks

trous·seau \ˈtrü-sō, trü-ˈsō\ n, pl **trousseaux** \-sōz, -ˈsōz\ or **trousseaus** : the personal outfit of a bride

trout \ˈtraut\ n, pl **trout** also **trouts** : any of various mostly freshwater food and game fishes usu. smaller than the related salmons

trow \ˈtrō\ vb, archaic : THINK, SUPPOSE

trow·el \ˈtrau-əl\ n 1 : a hand tool used for spreading, shaping, or smoothing loose or plastic material (as mortar or plaster) 2 : a scoop-shaped tool used in gardening — **trowel** vb

troy \ˈtrȯi\ adj : expressed in troy weight ⟨~ ounce⟩

troy weight n : a system of weights based on a pound of 12 ounces and an ounce of 480 grains (31 grams)

tru·ant \ˈtrü-ənt\ n : a student who stays out of school without permission — **tru·an·cy** \-ən-sē\ n — **truant** adj

truce \ˈtrüs\ n 1 : ARMISTICE 2 : a respite esp. from something unpleasant

¹**truck** \ˈtrək\ vb 1 : EXCHANGE, BARTER 2 : to have dealings : TRAFFIC

²**truck** n 1 ♦ : the act or practice of carrying on trade by bartering : BARTER 2 : small goods or merchandise; esp : vegetables grown for market 3 : DEALINGS

♦ barter, commutation, exchange, swap, trade

³**truck** n 1 : a wheeled vehicle (as a strong heavy automobile) designed for carrying heavy articles or hauling a trailer 2 : a swiveling frame with springs and one or more pairs of wheels used to carry and guide one end of a locomotive or railroad car

⁴**truck** vb 1 : to transport on a truck ⟨~s vegetables⟩ 2 : to be employed in driving a truck — **truck·er** n

truck farm n : a farm growing vegetables for market — **truck farmer** n

truck·le \ˈtrə-kəl\ vb **truck·led; truck·ling** : to act in a subservient manner : SUBMIT

truc·u·lence \ˈtrə-kyə-ləns\ n ♦ : the quality or state of being truculent — **truc·u·len·cy** \-lən-sē\ n

♦ aggression, aggressiveness, belligerence, fight, militancy, pugnacity

truc·u·lent \ˈtrə-kyə-lənt\ adj 1 : feeling or showing ferocity : SAVAGE 2 ♦ : aggressively self-assertive : PUGNACIOUS — **truc·u·lent·ly** adv

♦ aggressive, argumentative, bellicose, belligerent, combative, contentious, discordant, disputatious, militant, pugnacious, quarrelsome, scrappy, warlike

trudge \ˈtrəj\ vb **trudged; trudg·ing** : to walk or march steadily and usu. laboriously ⟨trudged through the snow⟩

¹**true** \ˈtrü\ adj **tru·er; tru·est** 1 ♦ : faithful in allegiance 2 : free from fraud or deception 3 ♦ : agreeing with facts or reality ⟨a ~ description⟩ 4 : CONSISTENT ⟨~ to expectations⟩ 5 ♦ : properly so called ⟨~ love⟩ 6 : RIGHTFUL ⟨~ and lawful king⟩ 7 ♦ : conformable to a standard or pattern; also : placed or formed accurately

♦ [1] constant, devoted, faithful, fast, good, loyal, pious, staunch, steadfast, steady, true-blue ♦ [3] actual, concrete, existent, factual, real, very ♦ [5] authentic, bona fide, genuine, real, right ♦ [7] accurate, correct, exact, precise, proper, right, so

²**true** adv 1 : TRUTHFULLY 2 : ACCURATELY ⟨the bullet flew straight and ~⟩; also : without variation from type ⟨breed ~⟩

³**true** n 1 : TRUTH, REALITY — usu. used with the 2 : the state of being accurate (as in alignment) ⟨out of ~⟩

⁴**true** vb **trued; true·ing** also **tru·ing** : to bring or restore to a desired precision

true–blue adj ♦ : marked by unswerving loyalty

♦ constant, devoted, faithful, fast, good, loyal, pious, staunch, steadfast, steady, true

true bug *n* : BUG 2
true•heart•ed \'trü-'här-təd\ *adj* : FAITHFUL, LOYAL
truf•fle \'trə-fəl, 'trü-\ *n* **1** : the dark or light edible spore-bearing organ of any of several European fungi that grow underground; *also* : one of these fungi **2** : a candy made of chocolate, butter, and sugar shaped into balls and coated with cocoa
tru•ism \'trü-ˌi-zəm\ *n* : an undoubted or self-evident truth
tru•ly \'trü-lē\ *adv* **1** : in all sincerity ⟨is ∼ sorry⟩ **2** ♦ : in agreement with fact **3** : ACCURATELY **4** : in a proper or suitable manner **5** ♦ : without any question : INDEED

♦ [2] actually, frankly, honestly, really, truthfully, verily ♦ [5] certainly, definitely, doubtless, incontestably, indeed, indisputably, really, surely, undeniably, undoubtedly, unquestionably

¹**trump** \'trəmp\ *n* : TRUMPET
²**trump** *n* : a card of a designated suit any of whose cards will win over a card that is not of this suit; *also* : the suit itself — often used in pl.
³**trump** *vb* : to take with a trump
trumped–up \'trəmpt-'əp\ *adj* : fraudulently concocted : SPURIOUS ⟨∼ charges⟩
trum•pery \'trəm-pə-rē\ *n* **1** : NONSENSE **2** : trivial articles : JUNK
¹**trum•pet** \'trəm-pət\ *n* **1** : a wind instrument consisting of a long curved metal tube flaring at one end and with a cup-shaped mouthpiece at the other **2** : something that resembles a trumpet or its tonal quality **3** : a funnel-shaped instrument for collecting, directing, or intensifying sound
²**trumpet** *vb* **1** : to blow a trumpet **2** ♦ : to proclaim on or as if on a trumpet — **trum•pet•er** *n*

♦ ballyhoo, crack up, glorify, tout

¹**trun•cate** \'trəŋ-ˌkāt, 'trən-\ *adj* : having the end square or blunt
²**truncate** *vb* **trun•cat•ed; trun•cat•ing** ♦ : to shorten by or as if by cutting — **trun•ca•tion** \ˌtrəŋ-'kā-shən\ *n*

♦ abbreviate, abridge, curtail, cut back, dock, shorten

trun•cheon \'trən-chən\ *n* ♦ : a police officer's club

♦ bat, bludgeon, club, cudgel, staff

trun•dle \'trənd-ᵊl\ *vb* **trun•dled; trun•dling** : to roll along : WHEEL
trundle bed *n* : a low bed that can be stored under a higher bed
trunk \'trəŋk\ *n* **1** : the main stem of a tree **2** : the body of a person or animal apart from the head and limbs **3** : the main or central part of something **4** ♦ : a box or chest used to hold usu. clothes or personal effects (as of a traveler); *also* : the enclosed luggage space in the rear of an automobile **5** : the long muscular nose of an elephant **6** *pl* : men's shorts worn chiefly for sports **7** : a usu. major channel or passage

♦ box, caddy, case, casket, chest, locker

trunk line *n* : a transportation system handling long-distance through traffic
¹**truss** \'trəs\ *vb* **1** ♦ : to secure tightly : BIND **2** : to arrange for cooking by binding close the wings or legs of (a fowl) **3** : to support, strengthen, or stiffen by or as if by a truss

♦ band, bind, gird, tie

²**truss** *n* **1** : a collection of structural parts (as beams) forming a rigid framework (as in bridge or building construction) **2** : a device worn to reduce a hernia by pressure
¹**trust** \'trəst\ *n* **1** : assured reliance on the character, strength, or truth of someone or something **2** : a basis of reliance, faith, or hope **3** ♦ : confident hope **4** : financial credit **5** : a property interest held by one person for the benefit of another **6** ♦ : a combination of firms formed by a legal agreement; *esp* : one that reduces competition **7** : something entrusted to one to be cared for in the interest of another **8** ♦ : immediate charge and control exercised by a person or an authority : CUSTODY

♦ [3] confidence, credence, faith, stock *Ant* distrust, mistrust ♦ [6] cartel, combination, combine, syndicate ♦ [8] care, custody, guardianship, keeping, safekeeping, ward

²**trust** *vb* **1** : to place confidence : DEPEND **2** : to be confident : HOPE **3** ♦ : to commit or place in one's care or keeping : ENTRUST **4** : to permit to stay or go or to do something without fear or misgiving **5** ♦ : to rely on or on the truth of : BELIEVE **6** : to extend credit to

♦ [3] commend, commit, consign, delegate, deliver, entrust, give, hand over, leave, pass, transfer, transmit, turn over, vest ♦ [5] accept, believe, credit, swallow

trust•ee \ˌtrəs-'tē\ *n* **1** : a person to whom property is legally committed in trust **2** : a country charged with the supervision of a trust territory
trust•ee•ship \ˌtrəs-'tē-ˌship\ *n* **1** : the office or function of a trustee **2** : supervisory control by one or more nations over a trust territory
trust•ful \'trəst-fəl\ *adj* : full of trust : CONFIDING — **trust•ful•ly** *adv* — **trust•ful•ness** *n*
trust territory *n* : a non-self-governing territory placed under a supervisory authority by the Trusteeship Council of the United Nations
trust•wor•thi•ness \-ˌwər-thē-nəs\ *n* ♦ : the quality or state of being trustworthy

♦ dependability, reliability, solidity, sureness

trust•wor•thy \-ˌwər-thē\ *adj* ♦ : worthy of confidence : DEPENDABLE ⟨a ∼ assistant⟩

♦ dependable, good, reliable, responsible, safe, solid, steady, sure, tried, true

¹**trusty** \'trəs-tē\ *adj* **trust•i•er; -est** : worthy of confidence : DEPENDABLE
²**trusty** \'trəs-tē, ˌtrəs-'tē\ *n, pl* **trust•ies** : a trusted person; *esp* : a convict considered trustworthy and allowed special privileges
truth \'trüth\ *n, pl* **truths** \'trüthz, 'trüths\ **1** : TRUTHFULNESS, HONESTY **2** : the real state of things : FACT **3** : the body of real events or facts : ACTUALITY **4** : a true or accepted statement or proposition ⟨the ∼s of science⟩ **5** : agreement with fact or reality : CORRECTNESS
truth•er \'trü-thər\ *n* : one who believes that the truth about an important subject or event is being concealed from the public by a powerful conspiracy
truth•ful \'trüth-fəl\ *adj* : telling or disposed to tell the truth
truth•ful•ly \-fə-lē\ *adv* **1** ♦ : in reality : ACTUALLY ⟨∼, he didn't do it⟩ **2** : in a truthful manner ⟨"I didn't do it," she said ∼⟩

♦ actually, frankly, honestly, really, truly, verily

truth•ful•ness *n* ♦ : the quality or state of being truthful

♦ honesty, integrity, probity, veracity, verity

truth serum *n* : a drug held to induce a subject under questioning to talk freely
¹**try** \'trī\ *vb* **tried; try•ing** **1** : to examine or investigate judicially **2** : to conduct the trial of **3** : to put to test or trial **4** ♦ : to subject to strain, affliction, or annoyance **5** : to extract or clarify (as lard) by melting **6** ♦ : to make an effort to do something : ATTEMPT

♦ [4] strain, stretch, tax, test ♦ [6] assay, attempt, endeavor (*or* endeavour), essay, seek, strive

²**try** *n, pl* **tries** ♦ : an experimental trial

♦ attempt, crack, endeavor (*or* endeavour), essay, fling, go, pass, shot, stab, trial, whack

try•ing *adj* ♦ : severely straining the powers of endurance

♦ bitter, brutal, burdensome, cruel, excruciating, grievous, grim, hard, harsh, heavy, inhuman, murderous, onerous, oppressive, rough, rugged, severe, stiff, tough

try on *vb* : to put on (a garment) to test the fit and looks
try out *vb* : to compete for a position esp. on an athletic team or for a part in a play — **try•out** \'trī-ˌaút\ *n*
tryp•to•phan \'trip-tə-ˌfan\ *n* : a crystalline essential amino acid that is widely distributed in proteins
tryst \'trist\ *n* **1** : an agreement (as between lovers) to meet **2** : an appointed meeting or meeting place — **tryst** *vb* — **tryst•er** *n*

♦ appointment, date, engagement, rendezvous

Ts *symbol* tennessine
TSA *abbr* Transportation Security Administration
tsar *var of* CZAR
tsarina *var of* CZARINA
tset•se fly \'tset-sē-, 'tsēt-, 'tet-, 'tēt-, 'set-, 'sēt-\ *n* : any of several sub-Saharan African dipteran flies including the vector of sleeping sickness
TSgt *abbr* technical sergeant
T–shirt \'tē-ˌshərt\ *n* : a collarless short-sleeved or sleeveless cotton undershirt; *also* : an outer shirt of similar design — **T–shirt•ed** \-ˌshər-təd\ *adj*
tsk *a click; often read as* 'tisk\ *interj* — used to express disapproval
tsp *abbr* teaspoon; teaspoonful
T square *n* : a ruler with a crosspiece at one end for making parallel lines

tsu·na·mi \su̇-ˈnä-mē, tsu̇-\ *n* : a tidal wave caused esp. by an underwater earthquake or volcanic eruption

TT *abbr* Trust Territories

TTY *abbr* teletypewriter

Tu *abbr* Tuesday

tub \ˈtəb\ *n* **1** : a wide low bucketlike vessel **2** : BATHTUB; *also* : BATH **3** : the amount that a tub will hold

tu·ba \ˈtü-bə, ˈtyü-\ *n* : a large low-pitched brass wind instrument

tub·al \ˈtü-bəl, ˈtyü-\ *adj* : of, relating to, or involving a tube and esp. a fallopian tube

tube \ˈtüb, ˈtyüb\ *n* **1** ♦ : any of various usu. cylindrical structures or devices; *esp* : one to convey fluids **2** : a slender hollow anatomical part (as a fallopian tube) functioning as a channel in a plant or animal body : DUCT **3** : a soft round container from which a paste is squeezed **4** : a tunnel for vehicular or rail travel **5** *Brit* : SUBWAY **6** : INNER TUBE **7** : ELECTRON TUBE **8** : TELEVISION — **tubed** \ˈtübd, ˈtyübd\ *adj* — **tube·less** *adj*

♦ channel, conduit, duct, leader, line, penstock, pipe

tu·ber \ˈtü-bər, ˈtyü-\ *n* : a short fleshy usu. underground stem (as of a potato plant) bearing minute scalelike leaves each with a bud at its base

tu·ber·cle \ˈtü-bər-kəl, ˈtyü-\ *n* **1** : a small knobby prominence or outgrowth esp. on an animal or plant **2** : a small abnormal lump in an organ or on the skin; *esp* : one caused by tuberculosis

tubercle bacillus *n* : a bacterium that is the cause of tuberculosis

tu·ber·cu·lar \tu̇-ˈbər-kyə-lər, tyu̇-\ *adj* **1** : TUBERCULOUS **2** : of, resembling, or being a tubercle

tu·ber·cu·lin \tu̇-ˈbər-kyə-lən, tyu̇-\ *n* : a sterile liquid extracted from the tubercle bacillus and used in the diagnosis of tuberculosis esp. in children and cattle

tu·ber·cu·lo·sis \tu̇-ˌbər-kyə-ˈlō-səs, tyu̇-\ *n, pl* **-lo·ses** \-ˌsēz\ : a communicable bacterial disease that affects esp. the lungs and is typically marked by fever, cough, difficulty in breathing, and formation of tubercles — **tu·ber·cu·lous** \-ˈbər-kyə-ləs\ *adj*

tube·rose \ˈtüb-ˌrōz, ˈtyüb-\ *n* : a bulbous herb related to the agaves and often grown for its spike of fragrant waxy-white flowers

tu·ber·ous \ˈtü-bə-rəs, ˈtyü-\ *adj* : of, resembling, or being a tuber

tub·ing \ˈtü-biŋ, ˈtyü-\ *n* **1** : material in the form of a tube; *also* : a length of tube **2** : a series or system of tubes

tu·bu·lar \ˈtü-byə-lər, ˈtyü-\ *adj* : having the form of or consisting of a tube; *also* : made with tubes

tu·bule \ˈtü-byül, ˈtyü-\ *n* : a small tube

¹tuck \ˈtək\ *n* **1** : a fold stitched into cloth to shorten, decorate, or control fullness **2** : a cosmetic surgical operation for the removal of excess skin or fat ⟨a tummy ∼⟩

²tuck *vb* **1** : to pull up into a fold ⟨∼ed up her skirt⟩ **2** : to make tucks in **3** : to put into a snug often concealing place ⟨∼ a book under the arm⟩ **4** : to secure in place by pushing the edges under ⟨∼ in a blanket⟩ **5** : to cover by tucking in bedclothes

tuck·er \ˈtə-kər\ *vb* **tuck·ered; tuck·er·ing** ♦ : to tire extremely or completely : FATIGUE — often used with *out*

♦ *usu* **tucker out** burn out, do in, drain, exhaust, fag, fatigue, tire, wash out, wear, wear out, weary

Tues *or* **Tue** *abbr* Tuesday

Tues·day \ˈtüz-dē, ˈtyüz-, -dā\ *n* : the 3d day of the week

tu·fa \ˈtü-fə, ˈtyü-\ *n* : a porous rock formed as a deposit from springs or streams

tuff \ˈtəf\ *n* : a rock composed of volcanic detritus

¹tuft \ˈtəft\ *n* **1** : a small cluster of long flexible outgrowths (as hairs); *also* : a bunch of soft fluffy threads cut off short and used as ornament **2** : CLUMP, CLUSTER — **tuft·ed** *adj*

²tuft *vb* **1** : to provide or adorn with a tuft **2** : to make (as a mattress) firm by stitching at intervals and sewing on tufts — **tuft·er** *n*

¹tug \ˈtəg\ *vb* **tugged; tug·ging** **1** ♦ : to pull hard **2** : to struggle in opposition : CONTEND **3** ♦ : to move by pulling hard : HAUL **4** : to tow with a tugboat

♦ [1, 3] drag, draw, hale, haul, lug, pull, tow

²tug *n* **1** : a harness trace **2** ♦ : an act of tugging : PULL **3** : a straining effort **4** : a struggle between opposing people or forces **5** : TUGBOAT

♦ draw, haul, jerk, pluck, pull, wrench

tug·boat \-ˌbōt\ *n* : a strongly built boat used for towing or pushing

tug–of–war \ˌtəg-əv-ˈwȯr\ *n, pl* **tugs–of–war** **1** ♦ : a struggle for supremacy **2** : an athletic contest in which two teams pull against each other at opposite ends of a rope

♦ battle, combat, conflict, confrontation, contest, duel, face-off, rivalry, struggle, warfare

tu·ition \tu̇-ˈi-shən, tyu̇-\ *n* : money paid for instruction ⟨college ∼⟩

tu·la·re·mia \ˌtü-lə-ˈrē-mē-ə, ˌtyü-\ *n* : an infectious bacterial disease esp. of wild rabbits, rodents, humans, and some domestic animals that in humans is marked by symptoms (as fever) similar to those of influenza

tu·lip \ˈtü-ləp, ˈtyü-\ *n* : any of a genus of Eurasian bulbous herbs related to the lilies and grown for their large showy erect cup-shaped flowers; *also* : a flower or bulb of a tulip

tulip tree *n* : a tall No. American timber tree that is related to the magnolias and has greenish tulip-shaped flowers and soft white wood

tulle \ˈtül\ *n* : a sheer often stiffened silk, rayon, or nylon net ⟨a veil of ∼⟩

¹tum·ble \ˈtəm-bəl\ *vb* **tum·bled; tum·bling** **1 a** ♦ : to fall or cause to fall suddenly and helplessly **b** ♦ : to decline suddenly and sharply (as in price) : DROP **2** : to fall into ruin **3** : to perform gymnastic feats of rolling and turning **4** : to roll over and over : TOSS **5** : to issue forth hurriedly and confusedly **6** : to come to understand **7** ♦ : to throw together in a confused mass

♦ [1a] fall, slip, stumble, topple, trip ♦ [1b] decline, descend, dip, drop, fall, lower, plummet, plunge, sink ♦ [7] disorder, hash, jumble, mess, mix, muddle, rumple

²tumble *n* **1 a** ♦ : a disordered mass of objects or material **b** : a disorderly state **2** ♦ : an act or instance of tumbling

♦ [1a] assortment, clutter, jumble, medley, mélange, miscellany, motley, muddle, variety, welter ♦ [2] fall, slip, spill, stumble

tum·ble·down \ˈtəm-bəl-ˈdau̇n\ *adj* ♦ : fallen into partial ruin or decay : DILAPIDATED ⟨a ∼ shack⟩

♦ dilapidated, grungy, mean, neglected, ratty, seedy, shabby

tum·bler \ˈtəm-blər\ *n* **1** : one that tumbles; *esp* : ACROBAT **2** : a drinking glass without foot or stem **3** : a movable obstruction in a lock that must be adjusted to a particular position (as by a key) before the bolt can be thrown

tum·ble·weed \ˈtəm-bəl-ˌwēd\ *n* : a plant that breaks away from its roots in autumn and is driven about by the wind

tum·brel *or* **tum·bril** \ˈtəm-brəl\ *n* **1** : CART **2** : a vehicle carrying condemned persons (as during the French Revolution) to a place of execution

tu·mid \ˈtü-məd, ˈtyü-\ *adj* **1** : SWOLLEN, DISTENDED **2** : BOMBASTIC, TURGID

tum·my \ˈtə-mē\ *n, pl* **tummies** ♦ : the part of the body that contains the stomach : BELLY

♦ abdomen, belly, gut, solar plexus, stomach

tu·mor *or Can and Brit* **tu·mour** \ˈtü-mər, ˈtyü-\ *n* ♦ : an abnormal and functionless new growth of tissue that arises from uncontrolled cellular proliferation — **tu·mor·ous** *adj*

♦ excrescence, growth, lump, neoplasm

tu·mult \ˈtü-ˌməlt, ˈtyü-\ *n* **1 a** ♦ : a state of commotion, excitement, or confusion **b** ♦ : turbulent uprising **2 a** : violent agitation of mind or feelings **b** ♦ : a noisy, agitated outburst

♦ [1a] commotion, disturbance, furor, pandemonium, turmoil ♦ [1b] cataclysm, convulsion, paroxysm, storm, tempest, upheaval, uproar ♦ [2b] clamor (*or* clamour), howl, hubbub, hue and cry, hullabaloo, noise, outcry, roar, uproar

tu·mul·tu·ous \tu̇-ˈməl-chə-wəs, tyu̇-, -chəs\ *adj* **1** : marked by tumult ⟨∼ applause⟩ **2** : tending to incite a tumult **3** ♦ : marked by violent upheaval ⟨∼ war years⟩

♦ convulsive, stormy, tempestuous, turbulent, wild

tun \ˈtən\ *n* : a large cask

tu·na \ˈtü-nə, ˈtyü-\ *n, pl* **tuna** *or* **tunas** : any of several mostly large marine fishes related to the mackerels and caught for food and sport; *also* : the flesh of a tuna

tun·able \ˈtü-nə-bəl, ˈtyü-\ *adj* : capable of being tuned — **tun·abil·i·ty** \ˌtü-nə-ˈbi-lə-tē, ˌtyü-\ *n*

tun·dra \ˈtən-drə\ *n* : a treeless plain of arctic and subarctic regions

¹tune \ˈtün, ˈtyün\ *n* **1** ♦ : a succession of pleasing musical tones : MELODY **2** : correct musical pitch **3** ♦ : harmonious relationship : AGREEMENT ⟨in ∼ with the times⟩ **4** : general attitude ⟨changed his ∼⟩ **5** : AMOUNT, EXTENT ⟨in debt to the ∼ of millions⟩

♦ [1] air, lay, melody, song, strain, warble ♦ [3] accord, agreement, conformity, consonance, harmony

²tune *vb* **tuned; tun·ing** **1** : to adjust in musical pitch **2** : to bring or come into harmony : ATTUNE **3** : to put in good working order **4** : to adjust a radio or television receiver so as to receive a broadcast **5** : to adjust the frequency of the output of (a device) to a chosen frequency — **tun•er** n

tune•ful \-fəl\ adj ♦ : having a pleasing melody : MELODIOUS — **tune•ful•ly** adv — **tune•ful•ness** n

　♦ euphonious, harmonious, melodious, musical, symphonic

tune•less \-ləs\ adj **1** : UNMELODIOUS **2** : not producing music — **tune•less•ly** adv

tune out vb : to stop paying attention to what is happening or to one's surroundings

tune–up \'tün-,əp, 'tyün-\ n : an adjustment to ensure efficient functioning ⟨an engine ∼⟩

tung•sten \'tən-stən\ n : a gray-white hard heavy ductile metallic chemical element used esp. in carbide materials, electrical components, and alloys

tu•nic \'tü-nik, 'tyü-\ n **1** : a usu. knee-length belted under or outer garment worn by ancient Greeks and Romans **2** : a hiplength or longer blouse or jacket

tuning fork n : a 2-pronged metal implement that gives a fixed tone when struck and is useful for tuning musical instruments

Tu•ni•sian \tü-'nē-zhən, tyü-, -'ni-\ n : a native or inhabitant of Tunisia — **Tunisian** adj

¹**tun•nel** \'tən-ᵊl\ n : an enclosed passage (as a tube or conduit); esp : one underground (as in a mine)

²**tunnel** vb **-neled** or **-nelled; -nel•ing** or **-nel•ling** : to make a tunnel through or under — **tun•nel•er** \'tən-lər, 'tə-nᵊl-ər\ n

tun•ny \'tə-nē\ n, pl **tunnies** also **tunny** : TUNA

tuque \'tük, 'tyük\ n : a warm knitted cone-shaped cap

tur•ban \'tər-bən\ n **1** : a headdress worn esp. by Muslims and made of a cap around which is wound a long cloth **2** : a headdress resembling a turban; esp : a woman's close-fitting hat without a brim

tur•bid \'tər-bəd\ adj **1** ♦ : cloudy or discolored by suspended particles ⟨a ∼ stream⟩ **2** : CONFUSED, MUDDLED — **tur•bid•i•ty** \ˌtər-'bi-də-tē\ n

　♦ cloudy, muddy

tur•bine \'tər-bən, -ˌbīn\ n : an engine whose central driveshaft is fitted with curved vanes spun by the pressure of water, steam, or gas

tur•bo•fan \'tər-bō-ˌfan\ n : a jet engine having a fan driven by a turbine for supplying air for combustion

tur•bo•jet \-ˌjet\ n : an airplane powered by a jet engine (**turbojet engine**) having a turbine-driven air compressor supplying compressed air to the combustion chamber

tur•bo•prop \-ˌpräp\ n : an airplane powered by a jet engine (**turboprop engine**) having a turbine-driven propeller

tur•bot \'tər-bət\ n, pl **turbot** also **turbots** : a European flatfish that is a popular food fish; also : any of several similar flatfishes

tur•bu•lence \'tər-byə-ləns\ n : the quality or state of being turbulent

tur•bu•lent \-lənt\ adj **1** : causing violence or disturbance **2** ♦ : marked by agitation or tumult : TEMPESTUOUS — **tur•bu•lent•ly** adv

　♦ explosive, ferocious, fierce, furious, hot, rabid, rough, stormy, tempestuous, violent, volcanic ♦ stormy, tempestuous, tumultuous, wild

tu•reen \tə-'rēn, tyü-\ n : a deep bowl from which foods (as soup) are served at table

¹**turf** \'tərf\ n, pl **turfs** \'tərfs\ also **turves** \'tərvz\ **1** : the upper layer of soil bound by grass and roots into a close mat; also : a piece of this **2** : an artificial substitute for turf (as on a playing field) **3** : a piece of peat dried for fuel **4** : a track or course for horse racing; also : horse racing as a sport or business

²**turf** vb : to cover with turf

tur•gid \'tər-jəd\ adj **1** : being in a swollen state **2** : excessively embellished in style or language : BOMBASTIC ⟨∼ writing⟩ — **tur•gid•i•ty** \ˌtər-'ji-də-tē\ n

Turk \'tərk\ n : a native or inhabitant of Turkey

tur•key \'tər-kē\ n, pl **turkeys** **1** : a large No. American bird related to the domestic chicken and widely raised for food **2** ♦ : a complete failure **3** ♦ : a stupid, foolish, or inept person

　♦ [2] bummer, bust, catastrophe, debacle, dud, failure, fiasco, fizzle, flop, lemon, loser, washout ♦ [3] booby, fool, goose, halfwit, jackass, nitwit, simpleton

turkey buzzard n : TURKEY VULTURE

turkey vulture n : an American vulture with a red head and whitish bill

Turk•ish \'tər-kish\ n : the language of Turkey — **Turkish** adj

tur•mer•ic \'tər-mə-rik\ n : a spice or dyestuff obtained from the

large aromatic deep-yellow rhizome of an Indian perennial herb related to the ginger; also : this herb

tur•moil \'tər-ˌmȯil\ n ♦ : an extremely confused or agitated condition

　♦ disquiet, ferment, restlessness, uneasiness, unrest ♦ commotion, furor, pandemonium, storm, tumult, uproar

¹**turn** \'tərn\ vb **1** ♦ : to move or cause to move around an axis or center : ROTATE ⟨∼ a wheel⟩ **2** : to effect a desired end by turning something ⟨∼ the oven on⟩ **3** : WRENCH ⟨∼ an ankle⟩ **4** : to change or cause to change position by moving through an arc of a circle ⟨∼ed her chair to the fire⟩ **5** : to cause to move around a center so as to show another side of ⟨∼ a page⟩ **6** : to revolve mentally : PONDER **7** : to become dizzy : REEL **8** : to reverse the sides or surfaces of ⟨∼ a pancake⟩ **9** : UPSET, DISORDER ⟨things were ∼ed topsy-turvy⟩ **10** ♦ : to set in another esp. contrary direction **11** ♦ : to change one's course or direction **12** : to go around ⟨∼ a corner⟩ **13** : to undergo change or development : BECOME ⟨my hair ∼ed gray⟩ ⟨∼ed twenty-one⟩ **14** : to direct toward or away from something; also : DEVOTE, APPLY **15** ♦ : to have recourse ⟨∼ to a friend for help⟩ **16** : to become or make hostile **17** : to cause to become of a specified nature or appearance ⟨∼s the leaves yellow⟩ **18** : to make or become spoiled : SOUR **19** : to pass from one state to another ⟨water ∼s to ice⟩ **20** : CONVERT, TRANSFORM **21** : TRANSLATE, PARAPHRASE **22** : to give a rounded form to; esp : to shape by means of a lathe **23** : to gain by passing in trade ⟨∼ a quick profit⟩ — **turn color** **1** : BLUSH **2** : to become pale — **turn loose** : to set free

　♦ [1] pivot, revolve, roll, rotate, spin, swing, swirl, twirl, twist, wheel, whirl ♦ [10] divert, swerve, swing, veer, wheel, whip ♦ [11] detour, deviate, sheer, swerve, swing, turn off, veer ♦ usu **turn to** [15] go, refer, resort

²**turn** n **1** : a turning about a center or axis : REVOLUTION, ROTATION **2** : the action or an act of giving or taking a different direction ⟨make a left ∼⟩ **3** : a change of course or tendency ⟨a ∼ for the better⟩ **4** ♦ : a place at which something turns : BEND **5** ♦ : a short walk or trip round about ⟨take a ∼ around the block⟩ **6** ♦ : an act affecting another ⟨did him a good ∼⟩ **7** : a place, time, or opportunity accorded in a scheduled order ⟨waited his ∼ in line⟩ **8** : a period of duty : SHIFT **9** : a short act esp. in a variety show **10** : a special purpose or requirement ⟨the job serves his ∼⟩ **11** : a skillful fashioning ⟨neat ∼ of phrase⟩ **12** : a single round (as of rope passed around an object) **13** ♦ : natural or special aptitude **14** : a usu. sudden and brief disorder of body or spirits; esp : a spell of nervous shock or faintness

　♦ [4] angle, arc, arch, bend, bow, crook, curve, wind ♦ [5] perambulation, ramble, stroll, walk ♦ [6] boon, courtesy, favor (or favour), grace, indulgence, kindness, mercy, service ♦ [13] bent, devices, disposition, genius, inclination, leaning, partiality, penchant, predilection, proclivity, propensity, tendency

turn•about \'tər-nə-ˌbau̇t\ n **1** : a reversal of direction, trend, or policy **2** : RETALIATION

turn•buck•le \'tərn-ˌbə-kəl\ n : a link with a screw thread at one or both ends for tightening a rod or stay

turn•coat \-ˌkōt\ n ♦ : one who switches to an opposing side or party : TRAITOR

　♦ apostate, betrayer, double-crosser, quisling, recreant, traitor

turn down vb ♦ : to decline to accept : REJECT — **turn•down** \'tərn-ˌdau̇n\ n

　♦ decline, disallow, disapprove, negative, refuse, reject, repudiate, spurn

turn•er \'tər-nər\ n **1** : one that turns or is used for turning **2** : one that forms articles with a lathe

turn•ery \'tər-nə-rē\ n, pl **-er•ies** : the work, products, or shop of a turner

turn in vb **1** : to deliver up **2** : to inform on **3** : to acquit oneself of ⟨turn in a good job⟩ **4** : to go to bed

turn•ing n **1** : the act or course of one that turns **2** : a place of a change of direction

turning point n : a point at which a significant change occurs

tur•nip \'tər-nəp\ n **1** : a garden herb related to the cabbage with a thick edible usu. white root **2** : RUTABAGA **3** : the root of a turnip

turn•key \'tərn-ˌkē\ n, pl **turnkeys** : one who has charge of a prison's keys

turn•off \'tərn-ˌȯf\ n : a place for turning off esp. from an expressway

turn off vb **1** ♦ : to deviate from a straight course or a main road **2** : to stop the functioning or flow of **3** ♦ : to cause to lose interest; also : to evoke a negative feeling in

♦ [1] detour, deviate, sheer, swerve, swing, turn, veer ♦ [3] disgust, nauseate, repel, repulse, revolt, sicken

turn on *vb* **1** ♦ : to cause to flow, function, or operate **2** : to get high or cause to get high as a result of using a drug (as marijuana) **3** ♦ : to move pleasurably : EXCITE

♦ [1] activate, actuate, crank, drive, move, propel, run, set off, spark, start, touch off, trigger ♦ [3] electrify, excite, exhilarate, galvanize, intoxicate, thrill, titillate

turn•out \'tərn-ˌaút\ *n* **1** : an act of turning out **2** : the number of people who participate or attend an event **3** : a widened place in a highway for vehicles to pass or park **4** : manner of dress **5** : net yield : OUTPUT

turn out *vb* **1** : EXPEL, EVICT **2** : PRODUCE **3** : to come forth and assemble **4** : to get out of bed **5** ♦ : to prove to be in the end **6** : to cause to stop functioning by turning a switch

♦ come out, pan out, prove

¹**turn•over** \'tər-ˌnō-vər\ *n* **1** : UPSET **2** : SHIFT, REVERSAL **3** : a filled pastry made by turning half of the crust over the other half **4** : the volume of business done **5** : movement (as of goods or people) into, through, and out of a place **6** : the number of persons hired within a period to replace those leaving or dropped **7** : an instance of a team's losing possession of the ball esp. through error

²**turnover** *adj* : capable of being turned over

turn over *vb* **1** ♦ : to turn from an upright position **2** ♦ : to take and hand over to or leave for another ⟨*turn* the job *over* to her⟩

♦ [1] flip, reverse ♦ [2] commend, commit, consign, delegate, deliver, entrust, give, hand over, leave, pass, surrender, transfer, transmit, trust, vest

turn•pike \'tərn-ˌpīk\ *n* **1** : TOLLGATE; *also* : an expressway on which tolls are charged **2** ♦ : a main road

♦ highway, pike, road, route, thoroughfare, way

turn•stile \-ˌstīl\ *n* : a post with arms pivoted on the top set in a passageway so that persons can pass through only on foot one by one

turn•ta•ble \-ˌtā-bəl\ *n* : a circular platform that revolves (as for turning a locomotive or a phonograph record)

turn to *vb* : to apply oneself to work

turn up *vb* **1** ♦ : to come to light or bring to light **2** ♦ : to arrive at an appointed time or place **3** : to happen unexpectedly **4** : to raise or increase by or as if by turning a control

♦ [1] appear, come out, materialize, show up ♦ [2] arrive, come, land, show up

tur•pen•tine \'tər-pən-ˌtīn\ *n* **1** : a mixture of oil and resin obtained from various cone-bearing trees (as pines) **2** : an oil distilled from turpentine or pine wood and used as a solvent and paint thinner

tur•pi•tude \'tər-pə-ˌtüd, -ˌtyüd\ *n* : inherent baseness : DEPRAVITY

tur•quoise *also* **tur•quois** \'tər-ˌkóiz, -ˌkwóiz\ *n* **1** : a blue, bluish green, or greenish gray mineral that is valued as a gem **2** : a light greenish blue color

tur•ret \'tər-ət\ *n* **1** : a little ornamental tower often at a corner of a building **2** : a low usu. revolving structure (as on a tank or warship) in which one or more guns are mounted

¹**tur•tle** \'tərt-ᵊl\ *n, archaic* : TURTLEDOVE

²**turtle** *n, pl* **turtles** *also* **turtle** : any of an order of horny-beaked land, freshwater, or sea reptiles with the trunk enclosed in a bony shell

tur•tle•dove \'tərt-ᵊl-ˌdəv\ *n* : any of several small pigeons noted for plaintive cooing

tur•tle•neck \-ˌnek\ *n* : a high close-fitting turnover collar (as on a sweater); *also* : a sweater or shirt with a turtleneck — **tur•tle•necked** \-ˌnekt\ *adj*

turves *pl of* TURF

Tus•ca•ro•ra \ˌtəs-kə-'rōr-ə\ *n, pl* **Tuscarora** *or* **Tuscaroras** : a member of an Indigenous people orig. of No. Carolina and later of New York and Ontario; *also* : the language of the Tuscarora people

tusk \'təsk\ *n* : a long enlarged protruding tooth (as of an elephant, walrus, or boar) used esp. to dig up food or as a weapon — **tusked** \'təskt\ *adj*

tusk•er \'təs-kər\ *n* : an animal with tusks; *esp* : a male elephant with two normally developed tusks

¹**tus•sle** \'tə-səl\ *n* **1** ♦ : a physical struggle : SCUFFLE **2** : an intense argument, controversy, or struggle

♦ battle, clash, combat, conflict, contest, fight, fracas, fray, hassle, scrap, scrimmage, scuffle, skirmish, struggle

²**tussle** *vb* **tus•sled; tus•sling** ♦ : to struggle roughly

♦ grapple, scuffle, wrestle

tus•sock \'tə-sək\ *n* : a dense tuft esp. of grass or sedge; *also* : a hummock in a marsh or bog bound together by roots — **tussocky** *adj*

tu•te•lage \'tüt-ᵊl-ij, 'tyüt-\ *n* **1** : an act of guarding or protecting **2** : the state of being under a guardian or tutor **3** ♦ : instruction esp. of an individual

♦ education, instruction, teaching, training

tu•te•lary \'tüt-ᵊl-ˌer-ē, 'tyüt-\ *adj* : acting as a guardian ⟨~ deity⟩

¹**tu•tor** \'tü-tər, 'tyü-\ *n* **1** : a person charged with the instruction and guidance of another **2** : a private teacher

²**tutor** *vb* **1** : to have the guardianship of **2** ♦ : to teach or guide individually ⟨~ed her in Latin⟩ **3** : to receive instruction esp. privately

♦ educate, indoctrinate, instruct, school, teach, train ♦ coach, counsel, guide, lead, mentor, pilot, shepherd, show

tu•to•ri•al \tü-'tōr-ē-əl, tyü-\ *n* : a class conducted by a tutor for one student or a small number of students

tut•ti \'tü-tē, 'tü-, -ˌtē\ *adj or adv* : with all voices and instruments playing together — used as a direction in music

tut•ti–frut•ti \ˌtü-ti-'frü-tē, ˌtü-\ *n* : a confection or ice cream containing chopped usu. candied fruits

tu•tu \'tü-(ˌ)tü\ *n* : a short projecting skirt worn by a ballerina

tux•e•do \ˌtək-'sē-dō\ *n, pl* **-dos** *or* **-does** **1** : a usu. black or blackish blue jacket **2** : a semiformal evening suit for men

TV \'tē-'vē\ *n* : TELEVISION

TVA *abbr* Tennessee Valley Authority

TV dinner *n* : a frozen packaged dinner that needs only heating before serving

twad•dle \'twäd-ᵊl\ *n* ♦ : silly idle talk : DRIVEL — **twaddle** *vb*

♦ blarney, bunk, claptrap, drivel, fiddlesticks, folly, foolishness, fudge, hogwash, humbug, nonsense, piffle, rot, silliness, slush, stupidity, trash

twain \'twān\ *n* **1** : TWO **2** ♦ : two similar or associated things : PAIR

♦ brace, couple, duo, pair, twosome

¹**twang** \'twaŋ\ *n* **1** : a harsh quick ringing sound like that of a plucked bowstring **2** : nasal speech or resonance **3** : the characteristic speech of a region

²**twang** *vb* **twanged; twang•ing** **1** : to sound or cause to sound with a twang **2** : to speak with a nasal twang

tweak \'twēk\ *vb* **1** : to pinch and pull with a sudden jerk and twitch **2** : to make small adjustments to — **tweak** *n*

tweed \'twēd\ *n* **1** : a rough woolen fabric made usu. in twill weaves **2** *pl* : tweed clothing; *esp* : a tweed suit

tweedy \'twē-dē\ *adj* **tweed•i•er; -est** **1** : of or resembling tweed **2** : given to wearing tweeds **3** : suggestive of the outdoors in taste or habits **4** : ACADEMIC, SCHOLARLY

¹**tween** \'twēn\ *prep* : BETWEEN

²**tween** *n* : PRETEEN

¹**tweet** \'twēt\ *n* **1** : a chirping note **2** : a short message posted on the Twitter online service

²**tweet** *vb* **1** ♦ : to make a usu. repetitive short sharp sound **2** : to post a tweet

♦ cheep, chirp, peep, pipe, twitter

tweet•er \'twē-tər\ *n* : a small loudspeaker that reproduces sounds of high pitch

twee•zers \'twē-zərz\ *n pl* : a small pincerlike implement usu. held between the thumb and index finger and used for grasping something

twelve \'twelv\ *n* **1** : one more than 11 **2** : the 12th in a set or series **3** : something having 12 units — **twelfth** \'twelfth\ *adj or n* — **twelve** *adj or pron*

twelve•month \-ˌmənth\ *n* : YEAR

12–step \'twelv-ˌstep\ *adj* : of, relating to, or being a program designed esp. to help someone overcome a problem (as an addiction) by following 12 tenets

twen•ty \'twen-tē\ *n, pl* **twenties** : two times 10 — **twen•ti•eth** \-tē-əth\ *adj or n* — **twenty** *adj or pron*

twenty–twenty *or* **20/20** \ˌtwen-tē-'twen-tē\ *adj* : characterized by a visual capacity for seeing detail that is normal for the human eye ⟨~ vision⟩

twice \'twīs\ *adv* **1** : on two occasions **2** : two times ⟨~ two is four⟩

¹**twid•dle** \'twid-ᵊl\ *vb* **twid•dled; twid•dling** **1** : to be busy with trifles; *also* : to play idly with something **2** : to rotate lightly or idly

²twiddle n : TURN, TWIST

twig \'twig\ n : a small branch — **twig·gy** adj

twi·light \'twī-ˌlīt\ n **1 ♦** : the light from the sky between full night and sunrise or between sunset and full night; *also* : a time of twilight **2** : a state of imperfect clarity; *also* : a period of decline

♦ dusk, evening, gloaming, nightfall, sundown, sunset

twilight zone n **1** : TWILIGHT 2; *also* : an area just beyond ordinary legal or ethical limits **2** : a world of fantasy or unreality

twill \'twil\ n **1** : a fabric with a twill weave **2** : a textile weave that gives an appearance of diagonal lines

twilled \'twild\ adj : made with a twill weave

¹twin \'twin\ n **1** : either of two offspring produced at a birth **2 ♦** : one of two persons or things closely related to or resembling each other

♦ companion, fellow, half, match, mate

²twin vb **twinned; twin·ning 1** : to be coupled with another **2** : to bring forth twins

³twin adj **1** : born with one other or as a pair at one birth ⟨~ brother⟩ ⟨~ girls⟩ **2 ♦** : made up of two similar or related members or parts **3** : being one of a pair ⟨~ city⟩

♦ binary, bipartite, double, dual, duplex

¹twine \'twīn\ n **1** : a strong thread of two or three strands twisted together **2** : an act of entwining or interlacing — **twiny** adj

²twine vb **twined; twin·ing 1** : to twist together; *also* : to form by twisting **2** : INTERLACE, WEAVE **3** : to coil about a support **4 ♦** : to stretch or move in a sinuous manner — **twin·er** n

♦ coil, curl, entwine, spiral, twist, wind

¹twinge \'twinj\ vb **twinged; twing·ing** or **twinge·ing** : to affect with or feel a sharp sudden pain

²twinge n **♦** : a sudden sharp stab (as of pain or distress)

♦ ache, pain, pang, prick, smart, sting, stitch, tinge

¹twin·kle \'twiŋ-kəl\ vb **twin·kled; twin·kling 1 ♦** : to shine or cause to shine with a flickering or sparkling light **2** : to appear bright with merriment **3** : to flutter or flit rapidly — **twin·kler** n

♦ flame, flash, glance, gleam, glimmer, glisten, glitter, scintillate, shimmer, sparkle, wink

²twinkle n **1 a** : a wink of the eyelids **b** : the duration of a wink : TWINKLING **2** : an intermittent radiance **3** : a rapid flashing motion — **twin·kly** \'twiŋ-klē\ adj

twin·kling \'twiŋ-kliŋ\ n **♦** : the time required for a wink : INSTANT

♦ flash, instant, jiffy, minute, moment, second, shake, trice, twinkle, wink

¹twirl \'twərl\ vb **♦** : to turn or cause to turn rapidly ⟨~ a baton⟩ — **twirl·er** n

♦ pivot, revolve, roll, rotate, spin, swing, swirl, turn, twist, wheel, whirl

²twirl n **1 ♦** : an act of twirling **2** : COIL, WHORL — **twirly** \'twər-lē\ adj

♦ gyration, pirouette, reel, revolution, roll, rotation, spin, wheel, whirl

¹twist \'twist\ vb **1** : to unite by winding one thread or strand round another **2** : WREATHE, TWINE **3 ♦** : to wring or wrench so as to dislocate or distort ⟨~ed her ankle⟩ **4** : to twirl into spiral shape **5 ♦** : to subject (as a shaft) to torsion **6 ♦** : to turn from the true form or meaning **7** : to pull off or break by torsion **8 ♦** : to follow a winding course **9 ♦** : to turn around

♦ [3, 5] wrench, wrest, wring ♦ [6] color (*or* colour), distort, falsify, garble, misinterpret, misrepresent, misstate, pervert, warp ♦ [8] coil, curl, entwine, spiral, twine, wind ♦ [9] pivot, revolve, roll, rotate, spin, swing, swirl, turn, twirl, wheel, whirl

²twist n **1** : something formed by twisting or winding **2** : an act of twisting : the state of being twisted **3** : a spiral turn or curve; *also* : SPIN **4** : a turning aside **5** : ECCENTRICITY **6** : a distortion of meaning **7** : an unexpected turn or development **8** : DEVICE, TRICK **9** : a variant approach or method

twist·er \'twis-tər\ n **1** : one that twists; *esp* : a ball with a forward and spinning motion **2** : TORNADO; *also* : WATERSPOUT 2

¹twit \'twit\ n : a silly or foolish person

²twit vb **twit·ted; twit·ting** : to ridicule as a fault; *also* : TAUNT

¹twitch \'twich\ vb **1 ♦** : to move or pull with a sudden motion : JERK **2 ♦** : to move jerkily **3** : to have a twitch

♦ [1] fiddle, fidget, jerk, squirm, wiggle ♦ [2] buck, hitch, jerk, jolt

²twitch n **1** : an act or movement of twitching **2** : a brief spasmodic contraction of muscle fibers

¹twit·ter \'twi-tər\ vb **1 ♦** : to make a succession of chirping noises **2 ♦** : to talk in a chattering fashion **3** : to tremble with agitation : FLUTTER

♦ [1] cheep, chirp, peep, pipe, tweet ♦ [2] chat, converse, gab, jaw, palaver, patter, prattle, rattle, talk, visit

²twitter n **1 ♦** : a slight agitation of the nerves **2** : a small tremulous intermittent noise (as made by a swallow) **3** : a light chattering

♦ dither, fluster, fret, fuss, huff, lather, pother, stew, tizzy

twixt \'twikst\ prep : BETWEEN

two \'tü\ n, pl **twos 1** : one more than one **2** : the second in a set or series **3** : something having two units — **two** adj or pron

two cents n **1** : a sum or object of very small value **2** or **two cents worth** : an opinion offered on a topic under discussion

two–faced \'tü-ˈfāst\ adj **1 ♦** : given to or marked by duplicity : DOUBLE-DEALING **2** : having two faces

♦ artificial, double-dealing, feigned, hypocritical, insincere, left-handed, mealy, mealymouthed, unctuous

¹two·fold \'tü-ˌfōld, -ˈfōld\ adj **1** : having two units or members **2** : being twice as much or as many

²two·fold \'tü-ˈfōld\ adv : to twice as much or as many : by two times

2,4–D \ˌtü-ˌfōr-ˈdē\ n : an irritant compound used esp. as a weed killer

2,4,5–T \-ˌfīv-ˈtē\ n : an irritant compound used esp. as an herbicide and defoliant

two·pence \'tə-pəns, *US also* 'tü-ˌpens\ n : the sum of two pence

two·pen·ny \'tə-pə-nē, *US also* 'tü-ˌpe-nē\ adj : of the value of or costing twopence

two–ply \'tü-ˈplī\ adj **1** : woven as a double cloth **2** : consisting of two strands or thicknesses ⟨~ toilet paper⟩

two·some \'tü-səm\ n **1 ♦** : a group of two persons or things : COUPLE **2** : a golf match between two players

♦ brace, couple, duo, pair, twain

two–step \'tü-ˌstep\ n : a ballroom dance performed with a sliding step in march or polka time; *also* : a piece of music for this dance — **two–step** vb

two–time \'tü-ˌtīm\ vb : to betray (a spouse or lover) by secret lovemaking with another — **two–tim·er** n

two–way adj : involving two elements or allowing movement or use in two directions or manners

2WD abbr two-wheel drive

twp abbr township

TWX abbr teletypewriter exchange

TX abbr Texas

ty·coon \tī-ˈkün\ n **1 ♦** : a leader (as in politics) **2 ♦** : a powerful businessperson or magnate

♦ [1, 2] baron, czar, king, magnate, mogul, prince

tying pres part of TIE

tyke \'tīk\ n : a small child

tym·pan·ic membrane \tim-ˈpa-nik-\ n : EARDRUM

tym·pa·num \'tim-pə-nəm\ n, pl **-na** \-nə\ also **-nums** : EARDRUM; *also* : MIDDLE EAR — **tym·pan·ic** \tim-ˈpa-nik\ adj

¹type \'tīp\ n **1** : a person, thing, or event that foreshadows another to come : TOKEN, SYMBOL **2** : MODEL, EXAMPLE **3** : a distinctive stamp, mark, or sign : EMBLEM **4** : rectangular blocks usu. of metal each having a face so shaped as to produce a character when printed **5** : the letters or characters printed from or as if from type **6** : general character or form common to a number of individuals and setting them off as a distinguishable class ⟨horses of draft ~⟩ **7 ♦** : a class, kind, or group set apart by common characteristics ⟨a seedless ~ of orange⟩ *also* : something distinguishable as a variety ⟨reactions of this ~⟩

♦ breed, class, description, feather, group, ilk, kind, like, manner, nature, order, sort, species

²type vb **typed; typ·ing 1** : to produce a copy of; *also* : REPRESENT, TYPIFY **2** : to write with a typewriter or computer keyboard **3 ♦** : to identify as belonging to a type **4** : to cast (an actor or actress) repeatedly in the same type of role : TYPECAST

♦ assort, break down, categorize, class, classify, codify, grade, group, peg, place, range, rank, separate, sort

type·cast \-ˌkast\ vb **-cast; -cast·ing 1** : to cast (an actor) in a part calling for characteristics possessed by the actor **2** : to cast repeatedly in the same type of role

type·face \-ˌfās\ n : all type of a single design

type·script \'tīp-ˌskript\ n : typewritten matter

type·set \-ˌset\ *vb* **-set; -set·ting** : to set in type : COMPOSE — **type·set·ter** *n*

type·write \-ˌrīt\ *vb* **-wrote** \-ˌrōt\; **-writ·ten** \-ˌrit-ᵊn\; **-writ·ing** : TYPE 2

type·writ·er \-ˌrī-tər\ *n* **1** : a machine for writing in characters similar to those produced by printers' type by means of types striking a ribbon to transfer ink or carbon impressions onto paper **2** : TYPIST

type·writ·ing \-ˌrī-tiŋ\ *n* : the use of a typewriter ⟨teach ∼⟩; *also* : writing produced with a typewriter

¹**ty·phoid** \ˈtī-ˌfȯid, tī-ˈfȯid\ *adj* : of, relating to, or being a communicable bacterial disease (**typhoid fever**) marked by fever, diarrhea, prostration, and intestinal inflammation

²**typhoid** *n* : TYPHOID FEVER

ty·phoon \tī-ˈfün\ *n* : a hurricane occurring esp. in the region of the Philippines or the China Sea

ty·phus \ˈtī-fəs\ *n* : a severe infectious disease transmitted esp. by body lice, caused by a rickettsia, and marked by high fever, stupor and delirium, intense headache, and a dark red rash

typ·i·cal \ˈti-pi-kəl\ *adj* **1** : being or having the nature of a type **2** ♦ : exhibiting the essential characteristics of a group **3** ♦ : conforming to a type — **typ·i·cal·i·ty** \ˌti-pə-ˈka-lə-tē\ *n* — **typ·i·cal·ness** *n*

♦ [2] characteristic, classic, distinct, distinctive, individual, peculiar, proper, symptomatic ♦ [2, 3] average, characteristic, normal, regular, representative, standard *Ant* aberrant, abnormal, anomalous, atypical, deviant, irregular, nontypical

typ·i·cal·ly \-pi-k(ə-)lē\ *adv* **1** : in a typical manner **2** ♦ : in typical circumstances

♦ commonly, generally, naturally, normally, ordinarily, usually

typ·i·fy \ˈti-pə-ˌfī\ *vb* **-fied; -fy·ing** **1** : to represent by an image, form, model, or resemblance **2** : to embody the essential or common characteristics of

typ·ist \ˈtī-pist\ *n* : a person who types esp. as a job

ty·po \ˈtī-pō\ *n, pl* **typos** : an error (as of spelling) in typed or typeset material

ty·pog·ra·pher \tī-ˈpä-grə-fər\ *n* : one who designs or arranges printing

ty·pog·ra·phy \tī-ˈpä-grə-fē\ *n* : the art of printing with type; *also* : the style, arrangement, or appearance of printed matter — **ty·po·graph·ic** \ˌtī-pə-ˈgra-fik\ *or* **ty·po·graph·i·cal** \-fi-kəl\ *adj* — **ty·po·graph·i·cal·ly** *adv*

ty·ran·ni·cal \tə-ˈra-ni-kəl, tī-\ *also* **ty·ran·nic** \-nik\ *adj* ♦ : being or characteristic of a tyrant or tyranny : DESPOTIC — **ty·ran·ni·cal·ly** \-ni-k(ə-)lē\ *adv*

♦ absolute, autocratic, despotic, dictatorial, tyrannous

tyr·an·nise *chiefly Brit var of* TYRANNIZE

tyr·an·nize \ˈtir-ə-ˌnīz\ *vb* **-nized; -niz·ing** : to act as a tyrant : rule with unjust severity — **tyr·an·niz·er** *n*

ty·ran·no·saur \tə-ˈra-nə-ˌsȯr\ *n* : a massive American flesh-eating dinosaur of the Cretaceous that had small forelegs and walked on its hind legs

ty·ran·no·sau·rus \tə-ˌra-nə-ˈsȯr-əs\ *n* : TYRANNOSAUR

tyr·an·nous \ˈtir-ə-nəs\ *adj* ♦ : being or characteristic of a tyrant or tyranny; *esp* : unjustly severe : TYRANNICAL — **tyr·an·nous·ly** *adv*

♦ authoritarian, autocratic, bossy, despotic, dictatorial, domineering, imperious, overbearing, peremptory, tyrannical

tyr·an·ny \ˈtir-ə-nē\ *n, pl* **-nies** **1** : oppressive power **2** ♦ : the rule or authority of a tyrant : government in which absolute power is vested in a single ruler **3** : a tyrannical act

♦ autocracy, despotism, dictatorship, totalitarianism

ty·rant \ˈtī-rənt\ *n* **1** ♦ : an absolute ruler : DESPOT **2** ♦ : a ruler who governs oppressively or brutally **3** ♦ : one who uses authority or power harshly

♦ [1, 2, 3] autocrat, despot, dictator, oppressor

tyre *chiefly Brit var of* ²TIRE

ty·ro \ˈtī-rō\ *n, pl* **tyros** ♦ : a beginner in learning : NOVICE

♦ beginner, fledgling, freshman, greenhorn, neophyte, newcomer, novice, recruit, rookie, tenderfoot

tzar *var of* CZAR

¹**u** \ˈyü\ *n, pl* **u's** *or* **us** \ˈyüz\ *often cap* : the 21st letter of the English alphabet

²**u** *abbr, often cap* unit

¹**U** \ˈyü\ *adj* : characteristic of the upper classes

²**U** *abbr* **1** kosher certification — often enclosed in a circle **2** university **3** unsatisfactory

³**U** *symbol* uranium

UAE *abbr* United Arab Emirates

UAR *abbr* United Arab Republic

UAW *abbr* United Automobile Workers

ubiq·ui·tous \yü-ˈbi-kwə-təs\ *adj* : existing or being everywhere at the same time : constantly encountered — **ubiq·ui·tous·ly** *adv* — **ubiq·ui·ty** \-kwə-tē\ *n*

U–boat \ˈyü-ˌbōt\ *n* : a German submarine

UC *abbr* uppercase

ud·der \ˈə-dər\ *n* : an organ (as of a cow) consisting of two or more milk glands enclosed in a large hanging sac and each provided with a nipple

UFO \ˌyü-(ˌ)ef-ˈō\ *n, pl* **UFO's** *or* **UFOs** \-ˈōz\ : an unidentified flying object; *esp* : FLYING SAUCER

Ugan·dan \ü-ˈgan-dən, yü-, -ˈgän-\ *n* : a native or inhabitant of Uganda — **Ugandan** *adj*

ug·ly \ˈə-glē\ *adj* **ug·li·er; -est** **1** : FRIGHTFUL, DIRE **2** ♦ : offensive to the sight : HIDEOUS **3** : offensive or unpleasant to any sense **4** : morally objectionable : REPULSIVE **5** : likely to cause inconvenience or discomfort **6** : SURLY, QUARRELSOME ⟨an ∼ disposition⟩ — **ug·li·ness** \-glē-nəs\ *n*

♦ grotesque, hideous, unappealing, unattractive, unlovely, unsightly, vile *Ant* attractive, beauteous, beautiful, comely, cute, fair, gorgeous, handsome, lovely, pretty, stunning, taking

UHF *abbr* ultrahigh frequency

UK *abbr* United Kingdom

ukase \yü-ˈkās, -ˈkāz\ *n* : an edict esp. of a Russian emperor or government

Ukrai·ni·an \yü-ˈkrā-nē-ən\ *n* **1** : a native or inhabitant of Ukraine **2** : a slavic language of the Ukrainian people — **Ukrainian** *adj*

uku·le·le *also* **uke·le·le** \ˌyü-kə-ˈlā-lē\ *n* : a small usu. 4-stringed guitar popularized in Hawaii

ul·cer \ˈəl-sər\ *n* **1** : an open eroded sore of skin or mucous membrane often discharging pus **2** : something that festers and corrupts like an open sore — **ul·cer·ous** *adj*

ul·cer·ate \ˈəl-sə-ˌrāt\ *vb* **-at·ed; -at·ing** : to become affected with an ulcer — **ul·cer·a·tive** \ˈəl-sə-ˌrā-tiv\ *adj*

ul·cer·a·tion \ˌəl-sə-ˈrā-shən\ *n* **1** : the process of forming or state of having an ulcer **2** : ULCER 1

ul·na \ˈəl-nə\ *n* : the bone on the little-finger side of the human forearm; *also* : a corresponding bone of the forelimb of vertebrates above fishes

ul·ster \ˈəl-stər\ *n* : a long loose overcoat

ult *abbr* **1** ultimate **2** ultimo

ul·te·ri·or \ˌəl-ˈtir-ē-ər\ *adj* **1** : lying farther away : more remote **2** : situated beyond or on the farther side **3** : going beyond what is openly said or shown : HIDDEN ⟨∼ motives⟩

¹**ul·ti·mate** \ˈəl-tə-mət\ *adj* **1** ♦ : most remote in space or time : FARTHEST **2** ♦ : last in a progression : FINAL **3** ♦ : the best or most extreme of its kind **4** : arrived at as the last resort **5** : FUNDAMENTAL, ABSOLUTE, SUPREME ⟨∼ reality⟩ **6** : incapable of further analysis or division : ELEMENTAL **7** : MAXIMUM

♦ [1] extreme, outermost, utmost ♦ [2] final, hindmost, last, latter, terminal ♦ [3] consummate, maximum, most, nth, paramount, supreme, top, utmost *Ant* least, minimal, minimum

²**ultimate** *n* : something ultimate

ul·ti·mate·ly *adv* ♦ : at an unspecified later time : in the end

♦ eventually, someday, sometime, yet

ul·ti·ma·tum \ˌəl-tə-ˈmā-təm, -ˈmä-\ *n, pl* **-tums** *or* **-ta** \-tə\ : a final condition or demand whose rejection will bring about a resort to forceful action

ul·ti·mo \'əl-tə-ˌmō\ *adj* : of or occurring in the month preceding the present

¹**ul·tra** \'əl-trə\ *adj* ♦ : going beyond others or beyond due limits : EXTREME

♦ extreme, extremist, fanatic, rabid, radical, revolutionary

²**ultra** *n* : EXTREMIST

ul·tra·con·ser·va·tive \-kən-'sər-və-tiv\ *adj* : extremely conservative

ul·tra·high frequency \-'hī-\ *n* : a radio frequency between 300 and 3000 megahertz

¹**ul·tra·light** \'əl-trə-ˌlīt\ *adj* : extremely light esp. in weight

²**ultralight** *n* : a very light recreational aircraft typically carrying only one person

ul·tra·ma·rine \ˌəl-trə-mə-'rēn\ *n* **1** : a deep blue pigment **2** : a very bright deep blue color

ul·tra·mi·cro·scop·ic \-ˌmī-krə-'skä-pik\ *adj* : too small to be seen with an ordinary microscope

ul·tra·mod·ern \-'mä-dərn\ *adj* ♦ : extremely or excessively modern in idea, style, or tendency

♦ contemporary, current, hot, mod, modern, new, newfangled, red-hot, space-age, up-to-date

ul·tra·pure \-'pyu̇r\ *adj* : of the utmost purity

ul·tra·short \-'shȯrt\ *adj* **1** : having a wavelength below 10 meters **2** : very short in duration

ul·tra·son·ic \ˌəl-trə-'sä-nik\ *adj* : having a frequency too high to be heard by the human ear — **ul·tra·son·i·cal·ly** \-ni-k(ə-)lē\ *adv*

ul·tra·son·ics \-'sä-niks\ *n sing or pl* **1** : ultrasonic vibrations **2** : the science of ultrasonic phenomena

ul·tra·sound \-ˌsau̇nd\ *n* **1** : ultrasonic vibrations **2** : the diagnostic or therapeutic use of ultrasound and esp. a technique involving the formation of a two-dimensional image of internal body structures **3** : a diagnostic examination using ultrasound

ul·tra·vi·o·let \-'vī-ə-lət\ *adj* : having a wavelength shorter than those of visible light and longer than those of X-rays ⟨∼ radiation⟩; *also* : producing or employing ultraviolet radiation — **ultraviolet** *n*

ul·tra vi·res \'əl-trə-'vī-rēz\ *adv or adj* : beyond the scope of legal power or authority

ul·u·late \'əl-yə-ˌlāt\ *vb* **-lat·ed; -lat·ing** : HOWL, WAIL

uma·mi \ü-'mä-mē\ *n* : a meaty or savory taste sensation produced esp. by monosodium glutamate

um·bel \'əm-bəl\ *n* : a flat-topped or rounded flower cluster in which the individual flower stalks all arise near one point on the main stem

um·ber \'əm-bər\ *n* : a brown earthy substance valued as a pigment either in its raw state or burnt — **umber** *adj*

umbilical cord *n* : a cord containing blood vessels that connects the navel of a fetus with the placenta of its mother

um·bi·li·cus \ˌəm-'bi-li-kəs, ˌəm-bə-'lī-\ *n, pl* **um·bi·li·ci** \ˌəm-'bi-lə-ˌkī; ˌəm-bə-'lī-ˌkī, -ˌsī\ *or* **um·bi·li·cus·es** : NAVEL — **um·bil·i·cal** \ˌəm-'bi-li-kəl\ *adj*

um·bra \'əm-brə\ *n, pl* **umbras** *or* **um·brae** \-(ˌ)brē, -ˌbrī\ **1** : a shaded area : SHADE **2** : the conical part of the shadow of a celestial body from which the sun's light is completely blocked

um·brage \'əm-brij\ *n* **1** : SHADE; *also* : FOLIAGE **2** ♦ : a feeling of pique or resentment at some often fancied slight or insult : OFFENSE ⟨take ∼ at a remark⟩

♦ dudgeon, huff, offense, peeve, pique, resentment

um·brel·la \ˌəm-'bre-lə\ *n* **1** : a collapsible shade for protection against weather consisting of fabric stretched over hinged ribs radiating from a center pole **2** : something that provides protection **3** : something that covers a range of elements

umi·ak \'ü-mē-ˌak\ *n* : an open Inuit boat made of a wooden frame covered with skins

¹**um·pire** \'əm-ˌpīr\ *n* **1** ♦ : one having authority to decide finally a controversy or question between parties **2** : an official in a sport who rules on plays

♦ arbiter, arbitrator, judge, referee

²**umpire** *vb* ♦ : to supervise or decide as umpire

♦ adjudicate, arbitrate, decide, determine, judge, referee, rule, settle

ump·teen \'əmp-ˌtēn\ *adj* : very many : indefinitely numerous — **ump·teenth** \-ˌtēnth\ *adj*

UN *abbr* United Nations

un- \ˌən, 'ən\ *prefix* **1** : not : IN-, NON- **2** : opposite of : contrary to

unabated	unconquered
unabsorbed	unconsecrated
unabsorbent	unconsolidated
unacademic	unconstrained
unaccented	unconsumed
unacclimatized	unconsummated
unaccommodating	uncontaminated
unaccredited	uncontested
unacknowledged	uncontroversial
unadventurous	unconverted
unadvertised	uncooked
unaffiliated	uncooperative
unafraid	uncoordinated
unaggressive	uncorrected
unaltered	uncorroborated
unambiguously	uncreative
unambitious	uncredited
unanchored	uncrewed
unannounced	uncropped
unanswered	uncrowded
unapologetic	uncrowned
unapparent	uncrystallized
unappeased	uncured
unappreciated	uncurtained
unappreciative	undamaged
unappropriated	undamped
unapproved	undated
unarguable	undecipherable
unarguably	undeclared
unarmored	undefeated
unartistic	undefiled
unassertive	undefinable
unathletic	undemanding
unattended	undemocratic
unattested	undenominational
unauthorized	undependable
unavowed	undeserved
unawakened	undeserving
unbaked	undetected
unbeloved	undeterred
unbleached	undeveloped
unblinking	undifferentiated
unbranched	undigested
unbranded	undignified
unbreakable	undiminished
unbridgeable	undimmed
unbruised	undiplomatic
unbrushed	undirected
unburied	undisciplined
unburned	undisclosed
uncanceled	undiscovered
uncanonical	undiscriminating
uncap	undisguised
uncapitalized	undismayed
uncared-for	undisputed
uncaught	undissolved
uncensored	undistinguished
uncensured	undistributed
unchallenged	undogmatic
unchanged	undone
unchaperoned	undoubled
uncharacteristic	undramatic
unchastely	undraped
unchasteness	undreamed
unchivalrous	undrinkable
unclaimed	undulled
unclassified	undutiful
uncleaned	uneatable
uncleared	uneaten
uncoated	uneconomic
uncollected	uneconomical
uncombed	unedifying
uncombined	unedited
uncomely	unemphatic
uncommercial	unenclosed
uncompensated	unencumbered
uncompleted	unenforceable
uncomplicated	unenforced
uncompounded	unenlightened
uncomprehending	unenterprising
unconcealed	unenviable
unconfirmed	unequipped
unconformable	unessential

unexamined
unexcelled
unexcited
unexciting
unexpired
unexplained
unexploded
unexplored
unexposed
unexpurgated
unfading
unfaltering
unfashionably
unfavorably
unfeasible
unfenced
unfermented
unfertilized
unfilled
unfiltered
unfitted
unflattering
unflavored
unfocused
unfolded
unforeseeable
unforgiving
unformulated
unfortified
unframed
unfree
unfulfilled
unfunded
unfurnished
unfussy
ungentlemanly
ungerminated
unglamorous
unglazed
ungracefully
ungraded
ungrammatical
unground
ungrudging
unguided
unhackneyed
unhardened
unharmed
unharvested
unhatched
unhealed
unheated
unheeded
unhelpful
unheralded
unhesitating
unhistorical
unhonored
unhoused
unhurt
unhygienic
unidentifiable
unidiomatic
unimaginative
unimpaired
unimpassioned
unimpeded
unimposing
unimpressed
unimpressive
unimproved
unincorporated
uninfected
uninfluenced
uninformative
uninhabitable
uninhabited
uninitiated
uninjured
uninspired
uninstall
uninstructive
uninsured

unintentionally
uninviting
unjointed
unjustified
unkept
unknowable
unknowledgeable
unlabeled
unlamented
unleavened
unlicensed
unlighted
unlikable
unlined
unlit
unlivable
unlovable
unloved
unloving
unmade
unmalicious
unmanned
unmapped
unmarked
unmarketable
unmarred
unmeant
unmeasurable
unmeasured
unmentioned
unmerited
unmilitary
unmilled
unmodified
unmolested
unmotivated
unmounted
unmoved
unnameable
unnecessary
unneeded
unnewsworthy
unnoticeable
unnoticed
unobjectionable
unobservant
unobserved
unofficial
unofficially
unopened
unopposed
unorthodoxy
unostentatious
unowned
unpaged
unpaired
unpasteurized
unpatriotic
unpaved
unpeeled
unperceived
unperceptive
unperformed
unpersuaded
unpersuasive
unplanted
unplowed
unpoetic
unpolitical
unpolluted
unposed
unpractical
unpredictability
unpreparedness
unprepossessing
unpressed
unprivileged
unprofessed
unprogrammed
unpromising
unprompted
unpronounceable
unpropitious

unproven
unprovided
unprovoked
unpublished
unpunished
unquenchable
unquestioned
unraised
unrated
unratified
unreadable
unready
unrealistic
unrealized
unrecognizable
unrecognized
unreflecting
unreflective
unregulated
unrelated
unrelieved
unremembered
unremovable
unreported
unrepresentative
unrepresented
unrepressed
unresponsive
unresponsiveness
unreturnable
unrewarding
unrhymed
unrhythmic
unromantic
unromantically
unsaid
unsalable
unsalted
unsanctioned
unsanitary
unsatisfied
unscented
unscheduled
unscholarly
unsealed
unseasoned
unseaworthy
unsegmented
unself–conscious
unself–consciously
unsensational
unsentimental
unserious
unserviceable
unsexual
unshaded
unshapely
unshaven
unsifted
unsigned
unsinkable
unsold

unsoldierly
unsolved
unsorted
unspectacular
unspent
unspiritual
unspoiled
unstated
unsterile
unsubdued
unsubtle
unsuccessfully
unsuited
unsupervised
unsurprising
unsurprisingly
unsuspected
unsweetened
unsymmetrical
unsystematic
untactful
untainted
untalented
untanned
untapped
untarnished
untaxed
unteachable
untenable
untenanted
untended
untested
untilled
untraceable
untraditional
untrained
untrammeled
untranslatable
untranslated
untraveled
untraversed
untrimmed
untrod
untrodden
unvaried
unventilated
unverifiable
unverified
unversed
unvisited
unwashed
unweaned
unwearable
unwearied
unweathered
unwillingly
unwillingness
unwomanly
unworn
unwounded
unwoven

un·abashed \-ə-'basht\ *adj* ♦ : not abashed

♦ unashamed, unblushing, unembarrassed *Ant* abashed, ashamed, embarrassed, shamefaced, sheepish

un·able \-'ā-bəl\ *adj* **1** : not able **2** : UNQUALIFIED, INCOMPETENT

un·abridged \-ə-'brijd\ *adj* **1** : not abridged ⟨an ∼ edition of Shakespeare⟩ **2** : complete of its class : not based on one larger ⟨an ∼ dictionary⟩

un·ac·cept·able \-ak-'sep-tə-bəl\ *adj* ♦ : not acceptable : not pleasing or welcome

♦ bad, deficient, inferior, lousy, off, poor, punk, rotten, substandard, unsatisfactory, wanting, wretched, wrong

un·ac·com·pa·nied \-ə-'kəm-pə-nēd\ *adj* **1** ♦ : not accompanied **2** : being without instrumental accompaniment

♦ alone, lone, lonely, lonesome, solitary

un·ac·count·able \-ə-'kaůn-tə-bəl\ *adj* **1** : not to be accounted for : INEXPLICABLE **2** : not responsible — **un·ac·count·ably** \-blē\ *adv*

un·ac·count·ed \-'kau̇n-təd\ *adj* : not accounted ⟨the loss was ~ for⟩

un·ac·cus·tomed \-ə-'kəs-təmd\ *adj* **1** ♦ : not customary : not usual or common **2** ♦ : not accustomed or habituated ⟨~ to noise⟩

♦ [1] curious, extraordinary, funny, odd, peculiar, rare, strange, uncommon, uncustomary, unique, unusual, weird ♦ *usu* **unaccustomed to** [2] unadapted, unadjusted, unused

un·ac·quaint·ed \-ə-'kwān-təd\ *adj* ♦ : not having experience or knowledge

♦ ignorant, oblivious, unaware, unconscious, uninformed, unknowing, unwitting

un·adapt·ed \-ə-'dap-təd\ *adj* ♦ : not adapted

♦ unaccustomed, unadjusted, unused

un·ad·just·ed \-ə-'jəs-təd\ *adj* ♦ : not adjusted

♦ unaccustomed, unadapted, unused

un·adorned \-ə-'dȯrnd\ *adj* ♦ : not adorned : lacking embellishment or decoration

♦ bald, bare, naked, plain, simple, undecorated, unvarnished

un·adul·ter·at·ed \-ə-'dəl-tə-ˌrā-təd\ *adj* **1** ♦ : not adulterated : PURE ⟨~ meat⟩ **2** ♦ : not modified or restricted by reservations

♦ [1] absolute, fine, neat, plain, pure, refined, straight, undiluted, unmixed ♦ [2] absolute, complete, outright, perfect, profound, pure, regular, sheer, simple, total, unequivocal, unqualified, utter

un·aes·thet·ic \-es-'the-tik\ *adj* ♦ : not aesthetic

♦ grotesque, harsh

un·af·fect·ed \-ə-'fek-təd\ *adj* **1** : not influenced or changed mentally, physically, or chemically **2** ♦ : free from affectation : GENUINE

♦ artless, genuine, honest, ingenuous, innocent, naive, natural, real, simple, sincere, true, unpretentious

un·af·fect·ed·ly *adv* ♦ : in an unaffected manner

♦ artlessly, ingenuously, naively, naturally

un·aid·ed \-'ā-dəd\ *adj* ♦ : not aided : being without help

♦ alone, independently, singly, solely, unassisted

un·alien·able \-'āl-yə-nə-bəl, -'ā-lē-ə-\ *adj* : INALIENABLE

un·aligned \ˌən-ə-'līnd\ *adj* : not associated with any one of competing international blocs ⟨~ nations⟩

un·alike \-ə-'līk\ *adj* ♦ : not alike or similar

♦ different, disparate, dissimilar, distinct, distinctive, distinguishable, diverse, other, unlike

un·al·loyed \-ə-'lȯid\ *adj* : not mixed or qualified : PURE ⟨~ happiness⟩

un·al·ter·able \-'ȯl-tə-rə-bəl\ *adj* ♦ : not capable of being altered or changed ⟨an ~ rule⟩ — **un·al·ter·ably** \-blē\ *adv*

♦ fast, fixed, hard-and-fast, immutable, inflexible, unchangeable

un·am·big·u·ous \-am-'bi-gyə-wəs\ *adj* ♦ : not ambiguous : having or being a single clearly defined or stated meaning

♦ apparent, broad, clear, clear-cut, distinct, evident, lucid, manifest, obvious, palpable, patent, perspicuous, plain, transparent, unequivocal, unmistakable ♦ definite, definitive, explicit, express, specific

un–Amer·i·can \-ə-'mer-ə-kən\ *adj* : not characteristic of or consistent with American customs or principles

una·nim·i·ty \ˌyü-ə-'ni-mə-tē\ *n* ♦ : the quality or state of being unanimous

♦ accord, agreement, concurrence, consensus

unan·i·mous \yu̇-'na-nə-məs\ *adj* **1** ♦ : being of one mind **2** ♦ : formed with or indicating the agreement of all — **unan·i·mous·ly** *adv*

♦ [1, 2] agreeable, amicable, compatible, congenial, harmonious, kindred, united

un·an·swer·able \ˌən-'an-sə-rə-bəl\ *adj* ♦ : not answerable : not capable of being refuted

♦ incontestable, indisputable, indubitable, irrefutable, undeniable, unquestionable

un·an·tic·i·pat·ed \ˌən-an-'ti-sə-ˌpā-təd\ *adj* ♦ : not expected

♦ sudden, unexpected, unforeseen

un·ap·peal·ing \ˌən-ə-'pē-liŋ\ *adj* ♦ : not appealing or attractive

♦ grotesque, hideous, ugly, unattractive, unlovely, unsightly, vile

un·ap·pe·tiz·ing \ˌən-'a-pə-ˌtī-ziŋ\ *adj* ♦ : not appetizing

♦ distasteful, unsavory

un·ap·proach·able \ˌən-ə-'prō-chə-bəl\ *adj* **1** ♦ : not approachable : physically inaccessible **2** ♦ : discouraging intimacies

♦ [1, 2] inaccessible, inconvenient, unattainable, unavailable, unobtainable, unreachable, untouchable

un·arm \-'ärm\ *vb* : DISARM

un·armed \-'ärmd\ *adj* : not armed or armored

un·ashamed \-ə-'shāmd\ *adj* ♦ : not ashamed : being without guilt, self-consciousness, or doubt

♦ unabashed, unblushing, unembarrassed

un·asked \-'askt\ *adj* **1** : not being asked **2** ♦ : not requested

♦ unbidden, undesired, uninvited, unsolicited, unsought, unwanted, unwelcome

un·as·sail·able \-ə-'sā-lə-bəl\ *adj* : not liable to doubt, challenge, or attack

un·as·sist·ed \-ə-'sis-təd\ *adj* ♦ : not assisted : lacking help

♦ alone, independently, singly, solely, unaided

un·as·sum·ing \-ə-'sü-miŋ\ *adj* ♦ : neither bold nor self-assertive

♦ demure, humble, lowly, meek, modest, retiring, unpretentious

un·at·tached \-ə-'tacht\ *adj* **1** ♦ : not married or engaged **2** ♦ : not joined or united

♦ [1] single, unmarried, unwed ♦ [2] detached, disconnected, discrete, freestanding, separate, single, unconnected

un·at·tain·able \-ə-'tā-nə-bəl\ *adj* ♦ : not capable of being attained or accomplished

♦ inaccessible, inconvenient, unapproachable, unavailable, unobtainable, unreachable, untouchable ♦ hopeless, impossible, unsolvable, unworkable

un·at·trac·tive \-ə-'trak-tiv\ *adj* ♦ : not attractive : lacking beauty, interest, or charm

♦ grotesque, hideous, ugly, unappealing, unlovely, unsightly, vile

un·au·then·tic \-ȯ-'then-tik\ *adj* ♦ : not authentic

♦ bogus, counterfeit, fake, false, inauthentic, phony, sham, spurious

un·avail·able \-ə-'vā-lə-bəl\ *adj* ♦ : not available

♦ inaccessible, inconvenient, unapproachable, unattainable, unobtainable, unreachable, untouchable

un·avail·ing \-ə-'vā-liŋ\ *adj* ♦ : being of no avail — **un·avail·ing·ly** *adv*

♦ fruitless, futile, ineffective, unproductive, unsuccessful

un·avoid·able \-ə-'vȯi-də-bəl\ *adj* ♦ : not avoidable

♦ certain, inevitable, necessary, sure

un·avoid·ably \-blē\ *adv* ♦ : in a way or under a condition that is unavoidable

♦ inevitably, necessarily, needs, perforce

¹un·aware \-ə-'war\ *adv* : without warning : UNAWARES
²unaware *adj* ♦ : not aware

♦ ignorant, oblivious, unconscious, uninformed, unknowing, unwitting

un·aware·ness *n* ♦ : the state or fact of being unaware

♦ ignorance, obliviousness

un·awares \-'warz\ *adv* **1** : without knowing or intention **2** ♦ : without warning : by surprise ⟨taken ~⟩

♦ aback, suddenly, unaware

un·bal·anced \-'ba-lənst\ *adj* **1** : not in a state of balance **2** : mentally disordered **3** : not adjusted so as to make credits equal to debits

un·bap·tized \-bap-'tīzd\ *adj* **1 a** : not baptized **b** ♦ : not given a name **2** : PROFANE 2

♦ anonymous, nameless, unchristened, unidentified, unnamed, untitled

un·bar \-'bär\ *vb* : UNBOLT, OPEN

un·bear·able \-'bar-ə-bəl\ *adj* ♦ : greater than can be borne ⟨∼ pain⟩ — **un·bear·ably** \-blē\ *adv*

♦ insufferable, insupportable, intolerable, unendurable, unsupportable *Ant* endurable, sufferable, supportable, tolerable

un·beat·able \-'bē-tə-bəl\ *adj* ♦ : not capable of being defeated

♦ impregnable, indomitable, insurmountable, invincible, invulnerable, unconquerable

un·beat·en \-'bēt-ᵊn\ *adj* **1** : not pounded, beaten, or whipped **2** : UNTRODDEN **3** : UNDEFEATED

un·be·com·ing \-bi-'kə-miŋ\ *adj* ♦ : not becoming : UNSUITABLE ⟨conduct ∼ an officer⟩ — **un·be·com·ing·ly** *adv*

♦ improper, inappropriate, inapt, infelicitous, unfit, unseemly, unsuitable, wrong

un·be·knownst \-bi-'nōnst\ *also* **un·be·known** \-'nōn\ *adj* : happening or existing without one's knowledge

un·be·lief \-bə-'lēf\ *n* : the withholding or absence of belief : DOUBT — **un·be·liev·ing** \-'lē-viŋ\ *adj*

un·be·liev·able \-'lē-və-bəl\ *adj* ♦ : too improbable for belief; *also* : of such a superlative degree as to be hard to believe ⟨an ∼ catch for a touchdown⟩ — **un·be·liev·ably** \-blē\ *adv*

♦ fantastic, implausible, inconceivable, incredible, unconvincing, unimaginable, unthinkable

un·be·liev·er \-'lē-vər\ *n* **1** ♦ : one that does not believe : an incredulous person **2** : INFIDEL

♦ disbeliever, doubter, questioner, skeptic

un·bend \-'bend\ *vb* **-bent** \-'bent\; **-bend·ing** **1** : to free from being bent : make or become straight **2** : UNTIE **3** : to make or become less stiff or more affable : RELAX

un·bend·ing *adj* **1** ♦ : formal and distant in manner : INFLEXIBLE **2** : not bending

♦ adamant, hard, immovable, implacable, inflexible, pat, rigid, uncompromising, unrelenting, unyielding

un·bi·ased \-'bī-əst\ *adj* ♦ : free from bias

♦ disinterested, dispassionate, equal, equitable, fair, impartial, just, nonpartisan, objective, square, unprejudiced

un·bid·den \-'bid-ᵊn\ *also* **un·bid** \-'bid\ *adj* ♦ : not bidden : UNASKED

♦ unasked, undesired, uninvited, unsolicited, unsought, unwanted, unwelcome

un·bind \-'bīnd\ *vb* **-bound** \-'baùnd\; **-bind·ing** **1** ♦ : to remove bindings from : UNTIE **2** ♦ : to set free : RELEASE

♦ [1] undo, untie ♦ [2] discharge, emancipate, enfranchise, free, liberate, loose, loosen, manumit, release, spring, unchain, unfetter

un·blem·ished \-'ble-mishd\ *adj* ♦ : not blemished

♦ absolute, faultless, flawless, ideal, impeccable, letter-perfect, perfect

un·blessed *also* **un·blest** \-'blest\ *adj* **1** : not blessed **2** : EVIL
un·block \-'bläk\ *vb* ♦ : to free from being blocked

♦ clear, free

un·blush·ing \-'blə-shiŋ\ *adj* **1** : not blushing **2** ♦ : having no shame — **un·blush·ing·ly** *adv*

♦ unabashed, unashamed, unembarrassed

un·bod·ied \-'bä-dēd\ *adj* **1** : having no body; *also* : DISEMBODIED **2** : FORMLESS

un·bolt \-'bōlt\ *vb* : to open or unfasten by withdrawing a bolt
un·bolt·ed \-'bōl-təd\ *adj* : not fastened by bolts
un·born \-'bȯrn\ *adj* : not yet born
un·bos·om \-'bù-zəm, -'bü-\ *vb* **1** ♦ : to give expression to : REVEAL **2** : to disclose the thoughts or feelings of oneself

♦ bare, disclose, discover, divulge, expose, reveal, spill, tell, uncloak, uncover, unmask, unveil

un·bound \-'baùnd\ *adj* ♦ : not bound

♦ footloose, free, loose, unconfined, unrestrained

un·bound·ed \-'baùn-dəd\ *adj* ♦ : having no bounds or limits ⟨∼ enthusiasm⟩

♦ boundless, endless, illimitable, immeasurable, indefinite, infinite, limitless, measureless, unfathomable, unlimited

un·bowed \-'baùd\ *adj* **1** : not bowed down **2** : UNSUBDUED
un·bri·dled \-'brīd-ᵊld\ *adj* **1** ♦ : not restrained : UNRESTRAINED **2** : not confined by a bridle

♦ intemperate, rampant, unchecked, uncontrolled, ungoverned, unhampered, unhindered, unrestrained

un·bro·ken \-'brō-kən\ *adj* **1** : not damaged **2** ♦ : not subdued or tamed **3** ♦ : not interrupted : CONTINUOUS

♦ [2] feral, savage, undomesticated, untamed, wild ♦ [3] ceaseless, continual, continuous, incessant, unceasing, uninterrupted

un·buck·le \-'bə-kəl\ *vb* : to loose the buckle of : UNFASTEN ⟨∼ a belt⟩

un·budg·ing \-'bə-jiŋ\ *adj* ♦ : not budging : resisting movement or change

♦ immobile, immovable, nonmotile, unmovable

un·bur·den \-'bərd-ᵊn\ *vb* **1** ♦ : to free or relieve from a burden **2** ♦ : to relieve oneself of (as cares or worries)

♦ [1] disburden, discharge, disencumber, unload ♦ [1, 2] clear, disburden, disencumber, free, relieve, rid

un·but·ton \-'bət-ᵊn\ *vb* : to unfasten the buttons of ⟨∼ your coat⟩

un·called–for \-'kȯld-ˌfȯr\ *adj* : not called for, needed, or wanted

un·can·ny \-'ka-nē\ *adj* **1** ♦ : seeming to have a supernatural character or origin : MYSTERIOUS **2** ♦ : suggesting superhuman or supernatural powers — **un·can·ni·ly** \-'kan-ᵊl-ē\ *adv*

♦ [1] creepy, eerie, haunting, mysterious, spooky, unearthly, weird ♦ [2] magical, miraculous, phenomenal, superhuman, supernatural

un·cat·a·loged \-'kat-ᵊl-ˌȯgd\ *adj* ♦ : not cataloged

♦ unlisted, unrecorded, unregistered

un·ceas·ing \-'sē-siŋ\ *adj* ♦ : never ceasing — **un·ceas·ing·ly** *adv*

♦ ceaseless, continual, continuous, incessant, unbroken, uninterrupted

un·cer·e·mo·ni·ous \-ˌser-ə-'mō-nē-əs\ *adj* **1** : acting without or lacking ordinary courtesy : ABRUPT ⟨his ∼ dismissal⟩ **2** ♦ : marked by the absence of formality or ceremony — **un·cer·e·mo·ni·ous·ly** *adv*

♦ informal, irregular, unconventional, unorthodox

un·cer·tain \-'sərt-ᵊn\ *adj* **1** : not determined or fixed ⟨an ∼ quantity⟩ **2** ♦ : subject to chance or change : not dependable ⟨∼ weather⟩ **3** : not definitely known **4** ♦ : not sure ⟨∼ of the truth⟩ — **un·cer·tain·ly** *adv*

♦ [2] capricious, changeable, fickle, fluid, inconstant, mercurial, mutable, temperamental, unpredictable, unsettled, unstable, unsteady, variable, volatile ♦ [4] distrustful, doubtful, dubious, mistrustful, skeptical, suspicious, undecided, unsettled, unsure

un·cer·tain·ty \-'sərt-ᵊn-tē\ *n* **1** ♦ : lack of certainty : DOUBT **2** : something that is uncertain

♦ distrust, doubt, incertitude, misgiving, mistrust, skepticism, suspicion

un·chain \-'chān\ *vb* ♦ : to free by or as if by removing a chain

♦ discharge, emancipate, enfranchise, free, liberate, loose, loosen, manumit, release, spring, unbind, unfetter

un·change·able \-'chān-jə-bəl\ *adj* ♦ : not changeable : IMMUTABLE

♦ fast, fixed, hard-and-fast, immutable, inflexible, unalterable

un·chang·ing \-'chān-jiŋ\ *adj* ♦ : not changing or capable of change

♦ constant, stable, stationary, steady, unvarying

un·charged \-'chärjd\ *adj* : having no electrical charge
un·char·i·ta·ble \-'char-ə-tə-bəl\ *adj* **1** ♦ : not charitable **2** ♦ : severe in judging others — **un·char·i·ta·ble·ness** *n* — **un·char·i·ta·bly** \-blē\ *adv*

♦ [1] cheap, close, mean, niggardly, parsimonious, penurious, spare, sparing, stingy, tight, tightfisted ♦ [2] callous, hard, heartless, inhuman, inhumane, pitiless, soulless, unfeeling, unsympathetic

un·chart·ed \-'chär-təd\ *adj* **1** : not recorded on a map, chart, or plan **2** : UNKNOWN
un·chaste \-'chāst\ *adj* : not pure or modest in thought or action
un·chas·ti·ty \-'chas-tə-tē\ *n* : the quality or state of being unchaste
un·checked \-'chekt\ *adj* ♦ : not checked : not curbed or hindered

♦ intemperate, rampant, unbridled, uncontrolled, ungoverned, unhampered, unhindered, unrestrained

un·chris·tened \-'kris-ᵊnd\ *adj* ♦ : not named

♦ anonymous, nameless, unbaptized, unidentified, unnamed, untitled

un•chris•tian \-'kris-chən\ *adj* **1** : not of the Christian faith **2** : contrary to the Christian spirit

un•churched \-'chərcht\ *adj* : not belonging to or connected with a church

un•cial \'ən-shəl, -chəl; 'ən-sē-əl\ *adj* : relating to or written in a form of script with rounded letters used esp. in early Greek and Latin manuscripts — **uncial** *n*

un•cir•cu•lat•ed \-'sər-kyə-ˌlā-təd\ *adj* : issued for use as money but kept out of circulation

un•cir•cum•cised \ˌən-'sər-kəm-ˌsīzd\ *adj* **1** : not circumcised **2** : HEATHEN

un•civ•il \-'si-vəl\ *adj* **1** : not civilized : BARBAROUS **2** ♦ : lacking in courtesy : DISCOURTEOUS

♦ discourteous, ill-bred, ill-mannered, impertinent, impolite, inconsiderate, rude, thoughtless, ungracious, unmannerly

un•civ•i•lized \-'si-və-ˌlīzd\ *adj* **1** ♦ : not civilized : BARBAROUS **2** : remote from civilization : WILD

♦ barbarous, heathen, heathenish, Neanderthal, rude, savage, uncivil, uncultivated, wild

un•clad \-'klad\ *adj* ♦ : not covered or clothed

♦ bare, naked, nude, unclothed, undressed

un•clasp \-'klasp\ *vb* : to open by or as if by loosing the clasp

un•cle \'əŋ-kəl\ *n* **1** : the brother of one's father or mother **2** : the husband of one's aunt or uncle

un•clean \ˌən-'klēn\ *adj* **1** : morally or spiritually impure **2** : prohibited by ritual law for use or contact **3** ♦ : not clean or pure : DIRTY — **un•clean•ness** *n*

♦ dirty, dusty, filthy, foul, grubby, grungy, mucky, muddy, nasty, smutty, sordid

un•clean•li•ness \-'klen-lē-nəs\ *n* ♦ : the quality or state of being uncleanly

♦ dinginess, dirtiness, filthiness, foulness, grubbiness, nastiness

un•clean•ly \-'klen-lē\ *adj* : physically unclean

un•clean•ness \-'klēn-nəs\ *n* : UNCLEANLINESS

un•clear \-'klir\ *adj* **1** : difficult to grasp or understand **2** ♦ : confused or uncertain in statement or understanding

♦ bleary, dim, faint, foggy, fuzzy, hazy, indefinite, indistinct, indistinguishable, murky, nebulous, obscure, opaque, shadowy, undefined, undetermined, vague

un•clench \-'klench\ *vb* : to open from a clenched position : RELAX

Uncle Tom \-'täm\ *n, disparaging* : a Black person who is eager to win the approval of white people

un•cloak \-'klōk\ *vb* **1** : to remove a cloak or cover from **2** ♦ : to make (something secret or hidden) publicly or generally known : to reveal the true nature of

♦ bare, disclose, discover, divulge, expose, reveal, spill, tell, unbosom, uncover, unmask, unveil

un•clog \-'kläg\ *vb* ♦ : to remove an obstruction from

♦ clear, free, open, unstop ♦ ease, facilitate, loosen, smooth

un•close \-'klōz\ *vb* : OPEN — **un•closed** \-'klōzd\ *adj*

un•clothe \-'klō_th_\ *vb* ♦ : to strip of clothes or a covering

♦ strip, undress

un•clothed \-'klō_th_d\ *adj* ♦ : not clothed

♦ bare, naked, nude, unclad, undressed

un•cloud•ed \-'klau̇-dəd\ *adj* ♦ : not covered by clouds : not darkened

♦ clear, cloudless, fair, sunny, sunshiny

un•clut•tered \-'klə-tərd\ *adj* : not cluttered : having nothing extraneous or unnecessary

♦ crisp, neat, orderly, shipshape, snug, tidy, trim

un•coil \-'kȯil\ *vb* : to release or become released from a coiled state

un•col•ored *or Can and Brit* **un•col•oured** \-'kə-lərd\ *adj* ♦ : having no color

♦ colorless (*or* colourless), unpainted, white

un•com•fort•able \-'kəmf-tə-bəl, -'kəm-fər-tə-\ *adj* **1** ♦ : causing discomfort **2** : feeling discomfort : UNEASY — **un•com•fort•ably** \-blē\ *adv*

♦ awkward, disconcerting

un•com•ic \-'kä-mik\ *adj* : not funny or amusing

un•com•mit•ted \-kə-'mi-təd\ *adj* : not committed; *esp* : not pledged to a particular belief, allegiance, or program

un•com•mon \ˌən-'kä-mən\ *adj* **1** ♦ : not ordinarily encountered : UNUSUAL **2** : remarkable in character, quality, or kind : EXCEPTIONAL — **un•com•mon•ly** *adv*

♦ curious, extraordinary, funny, odd, peculiar, rare, strange, unaccustomed, unique, unusual, weird

un•com•mu•ni•ca•tive \-kə-'myü-nə-ˌkā-tiv, -ni-kə-\ *adj* ♦ : not inclined to talk or impart information

♦ closemouthed, laconic, reserved, reticent, secretive, silent, taciturn

un•com•plain•ing \-kəm-'plā-niŋ\ *adj* ♦ : not complaining

♦ forbearing, long-suffering, patient, stoic, tolerant

un•com•pli•men•ta•ry \-ˌkäm-plə-'men-t(ə-)rē\ *adj* ♦ : not complimentary : detracting from the character or standing of something

♦ contemptuous, degrading, derogatory, disdainful, scornful

un•com•pro•mis•ing \-'käm-prə-ˌmī-ziŋ\ *adj* ♦ : not making or accepting a compromise : making no concessions

♦ adamant, hard, immovable, implacable, inflexible, pat, rigid, unbending, unrelenting, unyielding

un•con•cern \-kən-'sərn\ *n* **1** : lack of care or interest : INDIFFERENCE **2** : freedom from excessive concern

un•con•cerned \-'sərnd\ *adj* **1** ♦ : not having any part or interest **2** ♦ : not anxious or upset : free of worry — **un•con•cern•ed•ly** \-'sər-nəd-lē\ *adv*

♦ [1] apathetic, casual, disinterested, indifferent, insouciant, nonchalant, perfunctory, uncurious, uninterested ♦ [2] carefree, careless, cavalier, easygoing, happy-go-lucky, insouciant, lighthearted

un•con•di•tion•al \-kən-'di-shə-nəl\ *adj* : not limited in any way : ABSOLUTE — **un•con•di•tion•al•ly** *adv*

un•con•di•tioned \-'di-shənd\ *adj* **1** : not subject to conditions **2** : not acquired or learned : NATURAL ⟨~ responses⟩ **3** : producing an unconditioned response ⟨~ stimuli⟩

un•con•fined \-kən-'fīnd\ *adj* ♦ : not kept within limits

♦ footloose, free, loose, unbound, unrestrained

un•con•ge•nial \-kən-'jē-nyəl\ *adj* **1** ♦ : not to one's taste **2** : not sympathetic

♦ bad, disagreeable, distasteful, nasty, rotten, sour, unlovely, unpleasant, unwelcome

un•con•nect•ed \-kə-'nek-təd\ *adj* ♦ : not joined or grouped together

♦ detached, disconnected, discrete, freestanding, separate, single, unattached

un•con•quer•able \-'käŋ-kə-rə-bəl\ *adj* ♦ : incapable of being conquered or overcome : INDOMITABLE

♦ impregnable, indomitable, insurmountable, invincible, invulnerable, unbeatable

un•con•scio•na•ble \-'kän-shə-nə-bəl\ *adj* **1** : not guided or controlled by conscience **2** ♦ : not in accordance with what is right or just **3** : exceeding what is usual, proper, necessary, or normal — **un•con•scio•na•bly** \-blē\ *adv*

♦ cutthroat, immoral, Machiavellian, unethical, unprincipled, unscrupulous

¹**un•con•scious** \-'kän-chəs, -shəs\ *adj* **1** ♦ : not knowing or perceiving : not aware **2** : not done consciously or on purpose **3** ♦ : having lost consciousness **4** : of or relating to the unconscious — **un•con•scious•ly** *adv* — **un•con•scious•ness** *n*

♦ [1] ignorant, oblivious, unaware, uninformed, unknowing, unwitting ♦ [3] cold, senseless *Ant* conscious

²**unconscious** *n* : the part of one's mental life of which one is not ordinarily aware but which is often a powerful force in influencing behavior

un•con•sid•ered \-kən-'si-dərd\ *adj* **1** : not resulting from consideration **2** : not considered or worth consideration

un•con•sti•tu•tion•al \-ˌkän-stə-'tü-shə-nəl, -'tyü-\ *adj* : not according to or consistent with the constitution of a state or society — **un•con•sti•tu•tion•al•i•ty** \-tü-shə-'na-lə-tē, -tyü-\ *n* — **un•con•sti•tu•tion•al•ly** \-'tü-shə-nə-lē, -'tyü-\ *adv*

un•con•trol•la•ble \ˌən-kən-'trō-lə-bəl\ *adj* ♦ : incapable of being controlled : UNGOVERNABLE — **un•con•trol•la•bly** \-blē\ *adv*

♦ froward, headstrong, intractable, recalcitrant, refractory, unmanageable, unruly, untoward, wayward, willful *Ant* tractable

un·con·trolled \-kən-'trōld\ *adj* ♦ : not being under control

♦ intemperate, rampant, unbridled, unchecked, ungoverned, unhampered, unhindered, unrestrained

un·con·ven·tion·al \-kən-'ven-chə-nəl\ *adj* ♦ : not conventional : being out of the ordinary — **un·con·ven·tion·al·i·ty** \-,ven-chə-'na-lə-tē\ *n* — **un·con·ven·tion·al·ly** \-'ven-chə-nə-lē\ *adv*

♦ dissident, heretical, heterodox, nonconforming, nonconformist, nonorthodox, unorthodox ♦ broad-minded, liberal, nontraditional, open-minded, progressive ♦ informal, irregular, unceremonious, unorthodox

un·con·vinc·ing \-kən-'vin-siŋ\ *adj* ♦ : not convincing : not likely to be believed

♦ fantastic, implausible, inconceivable, incredible, unbelievable, unimaginable, unthinkable

un·cork \-'kȯrk\ *vb* **1** : to draw a cork from **2** ♦ : to release from a sealed or pent-up state; *also* : to let go

♦ loose, loosen, release, unleash, unlock, unloosen

un·count·able \-'kaȯn-tə-bəl\ *adj* ♦ : too many to be numbered or counted : indefinitely numerous

♦ countless, innumerable, numberless, unnumbered, untold

un·count·ed \-'kaȯn-təd\ *adj* **1** : not counted **2** : too many to be numbered : INNUMERABLE
un·cou·ple \-'kə-pəl\ *vb* : to sever the connection of or between : DISCONNECT
un·couth \-'küth\ *adj* **1** : strange, awkward, and clumsy in shape or appearance **2** ♦ : vulgar in conduct or speech **3** ♦ : lacking in polish and grace

♦ [2, 3] coarse, common, crass, crude, gross, ill-bred, low, rough, rude, tasteless, uncultivated, uncultured, unpolished, unrefined, vulgar

un·cov·er \-'kə-vər\ *vb* **1** ♦ : to make known **2** : to expose to view by removing some covering **3** : to take the cover from **4** : to remove the hat from; *also* : to take off the hat as a token of respect

♦ bare, disclose, discover, divulge, expose, reveal, spill, tell, unbosom, uncloak, unmask, unveil

un·cov·ered \-vərd\ *adj* ♦ : not covered

♦ bald, bare, exposed, naked, open

un·crit·i·cal \-'kri-ti-kəl\ *adj* **1** : not critical : lacking in discrimination **2** : showing lack or improper use of critical standards or procedures — **un·crit·i·cal·ly** \-k(ə-)lē\ *adv*
un·cross \-'krȯs\ *vb* : to change from a crossed position ⟨~ed his legs⟩
unc·tion \'əŋk-shən\ *n* **1** : the act of anointing as a rite of consecration or healing **2** : exaggerated or insincere earnestness of language or manner
unc·tu·ous \'əŋk-chə-wəs\ *adj* **1** : FATTY, OILY **2** ♦ : insincerely smooth in speech and manner — **unc·tu·ous·ly** *adv*

♦ artificial, double-dealing, feigned, hypocritical, insincere, left-handed, mealy, mealymouthed, two-faced ♦ adulatory, fulsome

un·cul·ti·vat·ed \,ən-'kəl-tə-,vā-təd\ *adj* **1 a** ♦ : lacking in education or refinement **b** : not civilized : BARBAROUS **2** ♦ : not put under cultivation : not tilled

♦ [1a] coarse, common, crass, crude, gross, ill-bred, low, rough, rude, tasteless, uncouth, uncultured, unpolished, unrefined, vulgar ♦ [2] natural, untamed, wild

un·cul·tured \-'kəl-chərd\ *adj* **1** : not subjected to cultivation **2** ♦ : not improved or refined by education

♦ coarse, common, crass, crude, gross, ill-bred, low, rough, rude, tasteless, uncouth, uncultivated, unpolished, unrefined, vulgar

un·cu·ri·ous \-'kyȯr-ē-əs\ *adj* ♦ : not curious or inquisitive : having no care or interest

♦ apathetic, casual, disinterested, indifferent, insouciant, nonchalant, perfunctory, unconcerned, uninterested

un·curl \-'kərl\ *vb* : to make or become straightened out from a curled or coiled position
un·cus·tom·ary \-'kəs-tə-,mer-ē\ *adj* ♦ : not customary

♦ aberrant, abnormal, atypical, exceptional, extraordinary, freak, odd, peculiar, phenomenal, rare, singular, uncommon, unique, unusual, unwonted

un·cut \-'kət\ *adj* **1** : not cut down or into **2** : not shaped by cutting ⟨an ~ diamond⟩ **3** : not having the folds of the leaves

slit ⟨an ~ book⟩ **4** : not abridged or curtailed ⟨the ~ version of the film⟩ **5** : not diluted ⟨~ heroin⟩
un·daunt·ed \-'dȯn-təd\ *adj* ♦ : not daunted : not discouraged or dismayed — **un·daunt·ed·ly** *adv*

♦ brave, courageous, dauntless, doughty, fearless, gallant, greathearted, heroic, intrepid, lionhearted, manful, stalwart, stout, valiant, valorous

un·de·ceive \-di-'sēv\ *vb* ♦ : to free from deception, illusion, or error

♦ disenchant, disillusion

un·de·cid·ed \-di-'sī-dəd\ *adj* **1** ♦ : not yet determined **2** ♦ : uncertain how to act or proceed

♦ [1] open, pending, undetermined, unresolved, unsettled ♦ [2] distrustful, doubtful, dubious, mistrustful, skeptical, suspicious, uncertain, unsettled, unsure

un·dec·o·rat·ed \-'de-kə-,rā-təd\ *adj* ♦ : not decorated : without ornament or embellishment

♦ bald, bare, naked, plain, simple, unadorned, unvarnished

un·de·fend·ed \-di-'fen-dəd\ *adj* ♦ : not guarded or protected

♦ defenseless (*or* defenceless), exposed, helpless, susceptible, unguarded, unprotected, unresistant, vulnerable

un·de·fined \-di-'fīnd\ *adj* ♦ : not defined, determined, or distinguished

♦ bleary, dim, faint, foggy, fuzzy, hazy, indefinite, indistinct, indistinguishable, murky, nebulous, obscure, opaque, shadowy, unclear, undetermined, vague

un·de·mon·stra·tive \-di-'män-strə-tiv\ *adj* : restrained in expression of feeling : RESERVED
un·de·ni·able \-di-'nī-ə-bəl\ *adj* **1** ♦ : plainly true : INCONTESTABLE **2** : unquestionably excellent or genuine

♦ incontestable, indisputable, indubitable, irrefutable, unanswerable, unquestionable

un·de·ni·ably \-blē\ *adv* ♦ : that cannot be denied

♦ certainly, definitely, doubtless, incontestably, indeed, indisputably, really, surely, truly, undoubtedly, unquestionably

¹**un·der** \'ən-dər\ *adv* **1** ♦ : in or into a position below or beneath something **2** : below some quantity, level, or limit ⟨$10 or ~⟩ **3** : in or into a condition of subjection, subordination, or unconsciousness ⟨the ether put him ~⟩

♦ below, beneath

²**un·der** \,ən-dər, 'ən-\ *prep* **1** : lower than and overhung, surmounted, or sheltered by ⟨~ a tree⟩ **2** : subject to the authority or guidance of ⟨served ~ him⟩ ⟨was ~ contract⟩ **3** : subject to the action or effect of ⟨~ the influence of alcohol⟩ **4** : within the division or grouping of ⟨items ~ this heading⟩ **5** : less or lower than (as in size, amount, or rank) ⟨earns ~ $5000⟩
³**under** \'ən-dər\ *adj* **1** : lying below, beneath, or on the ventral side **2** : facing or protruding downward **3** ♦ : in or into a condition of subjection, subordination, or unconsciousness **4** : lower than usual, proper, or desired in amount, quality, or degree

♦ inferior, junior, less, lesser, lower, minor, subordinate

un·der·achiev·er \,ən-dər-ə-'chē-vər\ *n* : one who performs below an expected level of proficiency
un·der·act \-'akt\ *vb* : to perform feebly or with restraint
un·der·ac·tive \-'ak-tiv\ *adj* : characterized by abnormally low activity ⟨an ~ thyroid gland⟩ — **un·der·ac·tiv·i·ty** \-,ak-'ti-və-tē\ *n*
un·der·age \-'āj\ *adj* : of less than mature or legal age
un·der·arm \-'ärm\ *adj* **1** : UNDERHAND 2 ⟨an ~ throw⟩ **2** : placed under or on the underside of the arms ⟨~ seams⟩ — **underarm** *adv or n*
un·der·bel·ly \'ən-dər-,be-lē\ *n* **1** ♦ : the underside of a body or mass **2** : a vulnerable area

♦ bottom, underside

un·der·bid \,ən-dər-'bid\ *vb* **-bid; -bid·ding 1** : to bid less than another **2** : to bid too low
un·der·body \'ən-dər-,bä-dē\ *n* : the lower parts of the body of a vehicle
un·der·bred \,ən-dər-'bred\ *adj* : marked by lack of good breeding
un·der·brush \'ən-dər-,brəsh\ *n* : shrubs, bushes, or small trees growing beneath large trees
un·der·car·riage \-,kar-ij\ *n* **1** : a supporting framework (as of an automobile) **2** : the landing gear of an airplane
un·der·charge \,ən-dər-'chärj\ *vb* : to charge (as a person) too little — **undercharge** \'ən-dər-,chärj\ *n*

un·der·class \'ən-dər-ˌklas\ *n* : LOWER CLASS

un·der·class·man \ˌən-dər-'klas-mən\ *n* : a member of the freshman or sophomore class

un·der·clothes \'ən-dər-ˌklōthz\ *n pl* : UNDERWEAR

un·der·cloth·ing \-ˌklō-thiŋ\ *n* : clothing or an article of clothing worn next to the skin and under other clothing : UNDERWEAR

un·der·coat \-ˌkōt\ *n* **1** : a coat worn under another **2** : a growth of short hair or fur partly concealed by the longer and usu. coarser hairs of a mammal **3** : a coat of paint under another

un·der·coat·ing \-ˌkō-tiŋ\ *n* : a special waterproof coating applied to the underside of a vehicle

un·der·cov·er \ˌən-dər-'kə-vər\ *adj* ♦ : acting or executed in secret; *esp* : employed or engaged in secret investigation ⟨an ∼ agent⟩

♦ clandestine, covert, furtive, hugger-mugger, private, secret, sneak, sneaky, stealthy, surreptitious, underground, underhanded

un·der·croft \'ən-dər-ˌkróft\ *n* : a vaulted chamber under a church

un·der·cur·rent \-ˌkər-ənt\ *n* **1** : a current below the surface **2** : a hidden tendency of feeling or opinion

un·der·cut \ˌən-dər-'kət\ *vb* **-cut**; **-cut·ting 1** : to cut away the underpart of **2** : to offer to sell or to work at a lower rate than **3** : to strike (the ball) obliquely downward so as to give a backward spin or elevation to the shot — **un·der·cut** \'ən-dər-ˌkət\ *n*

un·der·de·vel·oped \ˌən-dər-di-'ve-ləpt\ *adj* **1** : not normally or adequately developed ⟨∼ muscles⟩ **2** : having a relatively low level of economic development ⟨the ∼ nations⟩

un·der·dog \'ən-dər-ˌdóg\ *n* : the loser or predicted loser in a struggle

un·der·done \ˌən-dər-'dən\ *adj* : not thoroughly done or cooked : RARE

un·der·draw·ers \'ən-dər-ˌdrórz, -ˌdró-ərz\ *n pl* : UNDERPANTS

un·der·em·pha·size \ˌən-dər-'em-fə-ˌsīz\ *vb* : to emphasize inadequately — **un·der·em·pha·sis** \-səs\ *n*

un·der·em·ployed \-im-'plóid\ *adj* : having less than full-time or adequate employment

un·der·es·ti·mate \-'es-tə-ˌmāt\ *vb* : to set too low a value on

un·der·ex·pose \-ik-'spōz\ *vb* : to expose (a photographic plate or film) for less time than is needed — **un·der·ex·po·sure** \-'spō-zhər\ *n*

un·der·feed \ˌən-dər-'fēd\ *vb* **-fed** \-'fed\; **-feed·ing** : to feed with too little food

un·der·foot \-'fút\ *adv* **1** : under the feet ⟨flowers trampled ∼⟩ **2** : close about one's feet : in the way

un·der·fur \'ən-dər-ˌfər\ *n* : an undercoat of fur esp. when thick and soft

un·der·gar·ment \-ˌgär-mənt\ *n* : a garment to be worn under another

un·der·gird \ˌən-dər-'gərd\ *vb* : to brace up : STRENGTHEN

un·der·go \ˌən-dər-'gō\ *vb* **-went** \-'went\; **-gone** \-'gón, -'gän\; **-go·ing 1** : to submit to : ENDURE **2** ♦ : to go through : EXPERIENCE

♦ endure, experience, feel, have, know, see, suffer, sustain, taste

un·der·grad \'ən-dər-ˌgrad\ *n* : UNDERGRADUATE

un·der·grad·u·ate \ˌən-dər-'gra-jə-wət, -jə-ˌwät\ *n* : a student at a university or college who has not taken a first degree

¹un·der·ground \ˌən-dər-'graúnd\ *adv* **1** : beneath the surface of the earth **2** : in or into hiding or secret operation

²un·der·ground \'ən-dər-ˌgraúnd\ *n* **1** : a space under the surface of the ground; *esp* : SUBWAY **2** : a secret political movement or group; *esp* : an organized body working in secret to overthrow a government or an occupying power **3** : an avant-garde group or movement that operates outside the establishment

³underground \'ən-dər-ˌgraúnd\ *adj* **1** : being, growing, operating, or located below the surface of the ground ⟨∼ stems⟩ **2** ♦ : conducted by secret means **3** : produced or published by the underground ⟨∼ publications⟩; *also* : of or relating to the avant-garde underground

♦ clandestine, covert, furtive, hugger-mugger, private, secret, sneak, sneaky, stealthy, surreptitious, undercover, underhanded

un·der·growth \'ən-dər-ˌgrōth\ *n* : low growth (as of herbs and shrubs) on the floor of a forest

¹un·der·hand \'ən-dər-ˌhand\ *adv* **1** : in a clandestine or secret manner **2** : with an underhand motion

²underhand *adj* **1** : marked by secrecy, chicanery, and deception : not honest and aboveboard : UNDERHANDED **2** : made with the hand kept below the level of the shoulder

¹un·der·hand·ed \ˌən-dər-'han-dəd\ *adv* : UNDERHAND

²underhanded *adj* ♦ : marked by secrecy and deception — **un·der·hand·ed·ly** *adv* — **un·der·hand·ed·ness** *n*

♦ clandestine, covert, furtive, hugger-mugger, private, secret, sneak, sneaky, stealthy, surreptitious, undercover, underground

♦ crooked, deceptive, dishonest, fast, fraudulent, shady, sharp, shifty

un·der·lie \-'lī\ *vb* **-lay** \-'lā\; **-lain** \-'lān\; **-ly·ing** \-'lī-iŋ\ **1** : to lie or be situated under **2** : to be at the basis of : form the foundation of

un·der·line \'ən-dər-ˌlīn\ *vb* **1** : to draw a line under **2** ♦ : to put emphasis on : EMPHASIZE — **underline** *n*

♦ accent, accentuate, emphasize, feature, highlight, play, point, stress, underscore

un·der·ling \'ən-dər-liŋ\ *n* ♦ : one who is under the orders of another : SUBORDINATE

♦ inferior, junior, subordinate *Ant* senior, superior

un·der·lip \ˌən-dər-'lip\ *n* : the lower lip

un·der·ly·ing \ˌən-dər-'lī-iŋ\ *adj* **1** : lying under or below **2** ♦ : of, relating to, or forming the base or essence : FUNDAMENTAL ⟨∼ principles⟩

♦ basic, elemental, elementary, essential, fundamental, rudimentary

un·der·mine \-'mīn\ *vb* **1** : to excavate beneath **2** : to weaken or wear away secretly or gradually ⟨∼ authority⟩

un·der·most \'ən-dər-ˌmōst\ *adj* : lowest in relative position — **undermost** *adv*

¹un·der·neath \ˌən-dər-'nēth\ *prep* **1** : directly under **2** : under subjection to

²underneath *adv* **1** : below a surface or object : BENEATH **2** : on the lower side

un·der·nour·ished \ˌən-dər-'nər-isht\ *adj* : supplied with insufficient nourishment — **un·der·nour·ish·ment** \-'nər-ish-mənt\ *n*

un·der·pants \'ən-dər-ˌpants\ *n pl* : a usu. short undergarment for the lower trunk : DRAWERS

un·der·part \-ˌpärt\ *n* : a part lying on the lower side (as of a bird or mammal)

un·der·pass \-ˌpas\ *n* : a crossing of a highway and another way (as a road) at different levels; *also* : the lower level

un·der·pay \ˌən-dər-'pā\ *vb* : to pay less than what is normal or required

un·der·pin \ˌən-dər-'pin\ *vb* : to hold up or serve as a foundation or prop for

un·der·pin·ning \'ən-dər-ˌpi-niŋ\ *n* **1** ♦ : the material and construction (as a foundation) used for support of a structure **2** ♦ : something that serves as a foundation

♦ [1] brace, bulwark, buttress, mount, shore, stay, support ♦ [2] base, basis, bedrock, footing, foundation, ground, groundwork, keystone

un·der·play \ˌən-dər-'plā\ *vb* : to treat or handle with restraint; *esp* : to play a role with subdued force

un·der·pop·u·lat·ed \ˌən-dər-'pä-pyə-ˌlā-təd\ *adj* : having a lower than normal or desirable density of population

un·der·priv·i·leged \-'priv-lijd, -'pri-və-lijd\ *adj* : having fewer esp. economic and social privileges than others

un·der·pro·duc·tion \ˌən-dər-prə-'dək-shən\ *n* : the production of less than enough to satisfy the demand or of less than the usual supply

un·der·rate \-'rāt\ *vb* : to rate or value too low

un·der·rep·re·sent·ed \-ˌre-pri-'zen-təd\ *adj* : inadequately represented

un·der·score \'ən-dər-ˌskōr\ *vb* **1** : to draw a line under : UNDERLINE **2** ♦ : to place emphasis on : EMPHASIZE — **underscore** *n*

♦ accent, accentuate, emphasize, feature, highlight, play, point, stress, underline

¹un·der·sea \ˌən-dər-'sē\ *adj* : being, carried on, or used beneath the surface of the sea

²undersea *or* **un·der·seas** \-'sēz\ *adv* : beneath the surface of the sea

un·der·sec·re·tary \ˌən-dər-'se-krə-ˌter-ē\ *n* : a secretary immediately subordinate to a principal secretary ⟨∼ of state⟩

un·der·sell \-'sel\ *vb* **-sold** \-'sōld\; **-sell·ing** : to sell articles cheaper than

un·der·sexed \-'sekst\ *adj* : deficient in sexual desire

un·der·shirt \'ən-dər-ˌshərt\ *n* : a collarless undergarment with or without sleeves

un·der·shoot \ˌən-dər-'shüt\ *vb* **-shot** \-'shät\; **-shoot·ing 1** : to shoot short of or below (a target) **2** : to fall short of (a runway) in landing an airplane

un·der·shorts \'ən-dər-ˌshȯrts\ *n pl* : underpants for men or boys

un·der·shot \'ən-dər-ˌshät\ *adj* **1** : moved by water passing beneath ⟨an ∼ waterwheel⟩ **2** : having the lower front teeth projecting beyond the upper when the mouth is closed

un·der·side \'ən-dər-ˌsīd, ˌən-dər-'sīd\ *n* ♦ : the side or surface lying underneath

  ♦ bottom, underbelly

un·der·signed \'ən-dər-ˌsīnd\ *n, pl* **undersigned** : one whose name is signed at the end of a document

un·der·sized \ˌən-dər-'sīzd\ *also* **un·der·size** \-'sīz\ *adj* ♦ : of a size less than is common, proper, or normal

  ♦ dwarf, dwarfish, fine, little, pocket, pygmy, slight, small

un·der·skirt \'ən-dər-ˌskərt\ *n* : a skirt worn under an outer skirt; *esp* : PETTICOAT

un·der·staffed \'ən-dər-'staft\ *adj* : inadequately staffed

un·der·stand \ˌən-dər-'stand\ *vb* **-stood** \-'stůd\; **-stand·ing 1** ♦ : to grasp the meaning of : COMPREHEND **2** ♦ : to have thorough or technical acquaintance with or expertness in ⟨∼ finance⟩ **3** : to have reason to believe ⟨I ∼ you are leaving tomorrow⟩ **4** : INTERPRET ⟨we ∼ this to be a refusal⟩ **5** : to have a sympathetic attitude **6** : to accept as settled ⟨it is *understood* that he will pay the expenses⟩ **7** ♦ : to believe or infer something to be the case — **un·der·stand·able** \-'stan-də-bəl\ *adj*

  ♦ [1] appreciate, apprehend, catch, catch on (to), comprehend, get, grasp, make, make out, perceive, see, seize, tumble ♦ [2] comprehend, grasp, know ♦ [7] conclude, deduce, extrapolate, gather, infer, judge, reason

un·der·stand·ably \-blē\ *adv* : as can be easily understood

¹**un·der·stand·ing** \ˌən-dər-'stan-diŋ\ *n* **1** : knowledge and ability to judge : INTELLIGENCE ⟨a person of ∼⟩ **2** : agreement of opinion or feeling **3** ♦ : a mutual agreement informally or tacitly entered into **4** ♦ : a mental grasp

  ♦ [3] accord, agreement, bargain, compact, contract, convention, covenant, deal, pact, settlement ♦ [4] appreciation, apprehension, comprehension, grasp, grip, perception

²**understanding** *adj* ♦ : endowed with understanding : SYMPATHETIC

  ♦ compassionate, humane, sympathetic

un·der·state \ˌən-dər-'stāt\ *vb* **1** : to represent as less than is the case **2** : to state with restraint esp. for effect — **un·der·state·ment** *n*

un·der·stood \ˌən-dər-'stůd\ *adj* **1** : agreed upon **2** : IMPLICIT

un·der·sto·ry \'ən-dər-ˌstōr-ē, -ˌstȯr-\ *n* : the vegetative layer between the top layer of a forest and the ground cover

un·der·study \'ən-dər-ˌstə-dē\ *n* : one who is prepared to act another's part or take over another's duties — **understudy** \'ən-dər-ˌstə-dē, ˌən-dər-'stə-dē\ *vb*

un·der·sur·face \'ən-dər-ˌsər-fəs\ *n* : the side or surface lying underneath : UNDERSIDE

un·der·take \ˌən-dər-'tāk\ *vb* **-took** \-'tůk\; **-tak·en** \-'tā-kən\; **-tak·ing 1** ♦ : to take upon oneself : set about ⟨∼ a task⟩ **2** : to put oneself under obligation **3** : GUARANTEE, PROMISE

  ♦ accept, assume, bear, shoulder, take over

un·der·tak·er \'ən-dər-ˌtā-kər\ *n* : one whose business is to prepare the dead for burial and to arrange and manage funerals

un·der·tak·ing \'ən-dər-ˌtā-kiŋ, ˌən-dər-'tā-kiŋ; *2 is* \'ən-dər-ˌtā-kiŋ *only*\ *n* **1** : the act of one who undertakes or engages in any project **2** : the business of an undertaker **3** : something undertaken **4** : PROMISE, GUARANTEE

under–the–counter *adj* : UNLAWFUL, ILLICIT ⟨∼ sale of drugs⟩

un·der·tone \'ən-dər-ˌtōn\ *n* **1** : a low or subdued tone or utterance **2** : a subdued color (as seen through and modifying another color)

un·der·tow \-ˌtō\ *n* : the current beneath the surface that flows seaward when waves are breaking upon the shore

un·der·val·ue \ˌən-dər-'val-yü\ *vb* **1** : to value or estimate below the real worth **2** : to esteem lightly

un·der·wa·ter \ˌən-dər-'wȯ-tər, -'wä-\ *adj* ♦ : lying, growing, worn, or operating below the surface of the water ⟨an ∼ camera⟩ — **un·der·wa·ter** *adv*

  ♦ submarine, sunken

under way \-'wā\ *adv* **1** : into motion from a standstill **2** : in progress

un·der·wear \'ən-dər-ˌwar\ *n* : clothing or a garment worn next to the skin and under other clothing

un·der·weight \'ən-dər-'wāt\ *adj* : weighing below what is normal, average, or necessary — **underweight** *n*

un·der·world \'ən-dər-ˌwərld\ *n* **1** : the place of departed souls : HADES **2** : the side of the world opposite to one **3** : the world of organized crime

un·der·write \'ən-dər-ˌrīt, ˌən-dər-'rīt\ *vb* **-wrote** \-ˌrōt, -'rōt\; **-writ·ten** \-ˌrit-ᵊn, -'rit-ᵊn\; **-writ·ing 1** : to write under or at the end of something else **2** : to set one's name to an insurance policy and thereby become answerable for a designated loss or damage **3** : to subscribe to : agree to **4** ♦ : to guarantee financial support of — **un·der·writ·er** *n*

  ♦ capitalize, endow, finance, fund, stake, subsidize

un·de·sign·ing \ˌən-di-'zī-niŋ\ *adj* : having no artful, ulterior, or fraudulent purpose : SINCERE

un·de·sir·able \-'zī-rə-bəl\ *adj* : not desirable — **undesirable** *n*

un·de·sired \-di-'zīrd\ *adj* ♦ : not desired : UNWANTED

  ♦ unasked, unbidden, uninvited, unsolicited, unsought, unwanted, unwelcome

un·de·ter·mined \-di-'tər-mənd\ *adj* **1** ♦ : not yet definitely or authoritatively decided, settled, or fixed **2** : not bounded by definite limits or restrictions **3** : not determinate in form or character

  ♦ open, pending, undecided, unresolved, unsettled

un·de·vi·at·ing \-'dē-vē-ˌā-tiŋ\ *adj* ♦ : keeping a true course

  ♦ steady, unchanging, uniform, unvarying, unwavering

un·dies \'ən-dēz\ *n pl* : UNDERWEAR; *esp* : women's underwear

un·di·lut·ed \ˌən-dī-'lü-təd\ *adj* ♦ : not diluted

  ♦ absolute, fine, neat, plain, pure, refined, straight, unadulterated, unmixed

un·dis·turbed \-di-'stərbd\ *adj* ♦ : not disturbed

  ♦ calm, collected, composed, cool, placid, self-possessed, serene, tranquil, unperturbed, unshaken, untroubled, unworried

un·di·vid·ed \-də-'vī-dəd\ *adj* ♦ : not divided

  ♦ all, concentrated, entire, whole

un·do \-'dü\ *vb* **-did** \-'did\; **-done** \-'dən\; **-do·ing 1** ♦ : to make or become unfastened or loosened **2** : to make null or as if not done : REVERSE **3** : to bring to ruin **4** ♦ : to disturb the composure of

  ♦ [1] unbind, untie ♦ [4] agitate, bother, concern, discompose, disquiet, distress, disturb, exercise, freak, perturb, unhinge, unsettle, upset, worry

un·doc·u·ment·ed \ˌən-'dä-kyə-ˌmen-təd\ *adj* **1** : not supported by documentary evidence **2** : lacking documents required for legal immigration

un·do·ing *n* : a cause of ruin

un·do·mes·ti·cat·ed \-də-'mes-ti-ˌkā-təd\ *adj* ♦ : not domesticated

  ♦ feral, savage, unbroken, untamed, wild

un·doubt·ed \-'daů-təd\ *adj* : not doubted or called into question : CERTAIN

un·doubt·ed·ly *adv* ♦ : in an undoubted manner

  ♦ certainly, definitely, doubtless, incontestably, indeed, indisputably, really, surely, truly, undeniably, unquestionably

¹**un·dress** \-'dres\ *vb* ♦ : to remove the clothes or covering of : STRIP

  ♦ strip, unclothe *Ant* dress, gown, robe

²**undress** *n* **1** : informal dress; *esp* : a loose robe or dressing gown **2** : ordinary dress **3** : NUDITY

un·dressed \-'dresd\ *adj* ♦ : not dressed

  ♦ crude, native, natural, raw, unprocessed, unrefined, untreated ♦ bare, naked, nude, unclad, unclothed

un·due \-'dü, -'dyü\ *adj* **1** : not due **2** : exceeding or violating propriety or fitness : EXCESSIVE

un·du·lant \'ən-jə-lənt, 'ən-də-, -dyə-\ *adj* : rising and falling in waves ⟨∼ hills⟩

undulant fever *n* : a human disease caused by bacteria from infected domestic animals or their products and marked by intermittent fever, chills, headache, weakness, and weight loss

un·du·late \-ˌlāt\ *vb* **-lat·ed; -lat·ing 1** : to have a wavelike motion or appearance **2** : to rise and fall in pitch or volume

un·du·la·tion \ˌən-jə-'lā-shən, ˌən-də-, -dyə-\ *n* **1** : wavy or wavelike motion **2** : pulsation of sound **3** : a wavy appearance or outline — **un·du·la·to·ry** \'ən-jə-lə-ˌtōr-ē, 'ən-də-, -dyə-\ *adj*

un·du·ly \-'dü-lē, 'ən-, -'dyü-\ *adv* : in an undue manner : EXCESSIVELY

un•dyed \-ˈdīd\ *adj* : not dyed
un•dy•ing \-ˈdī-iŋ\ *adj* ♦ : not dying : IMMORTAL

 ♦ ceaseless, dateless, deathless, endless, eternal, everlasting, immortal, permanent, perpetual, unending

un•ea•ger \-ˈē-gər\ *adj* ♦ : showing no eagerness

 ♦ halfhearted, tepid, unenthusiastic

un•earned \-ˈərnd\ *adj* : not earned by labor, service, or skill ⟨~ income⟩
un•earth \-ˈərth\ *vb* **1** : to dig up out of or as if out of the earth ⟨~ buried treasure⟩ **2** : to bring to light : DISCOVER ⟨~ a secret⟩
un•earth•ly \-lē\ *adj* **1** : not of or belonging to the earth **2** ♦ : departing from what is usual or normal esp. so as to appear to transcend the laws of nature

 ♦ magical, miraculous, phenomenal, superhuman, supernatural, uncanny ♦ creepy, eerie, haunting, spooky, uncanny, weird

un•eas•i•ness \-ˈē-zē-nəs\ *n* ♦ : the quality or state of being uneasy

 ♦ disquiet, ferment, restlessness, turmoil, unrest ♦ agitation, anxiety, apprehension, care, concern, disquiet, nervousness, perturbation, worry

un•easy \-ˈē-zē\ *adj* **1** ♦ : marked by lack of ease : AWKWARD ⟨~ among strangers⟩ **2** ♦ : disturbed by pain or worry **3** : lacking or denying rest **4** : UNSTABLE ⟨an ~ truce⟩ — **un•eas•i•ly** \-ˈē-zə-lē\ *adv*

 ♦ [1] awkward, clumsy, gauche, graceless, inelegant, stiff, stilted, uncomfortable, ungraceful, wooden ♦ [2] aflutter, anxious, edgy, jittery, jumpy, nervous, nervy, perturbed, tense, troubled, upset, worried

un•ed•u•cat•ed \-ˈe-jə-ˌkā-təd\ *adj* ♦ : not educated

 ♦ dark, ignorant, illiterate, simple, unlearned, untaught

un•em•bar•rassed \-im-ˈbar-əsd\ *adj* ♦ : free from embarrassment

 ♦ unabashed, unashamed, unblushing

un•emo•tion•al \-i-ˈmō-shə-nəl\ *adj* ♦ : not emotional : not easily aroused or excited

 ♦ apathetic, cold-blooded, impassive, phlegmatic, stoic, stolid

un•em•ployed \-im-ˈploid\ *adj* : not being used; *also* : having no job
un•em•ploy•ment \-ˈploi-mənt\ *n* **1** : lack of employment **2** : money paid at regular intervals (as by a government agency) to an unemployed person
un•end•ing \-ˈen-diŋ\ *adj* ♦ : having no ending : ENDLESS

 ♦ ceaseless, dateless, deathless, endless, eternal, everlasting, immortal, permanent, perpetual, undying

un•en•dur•able \-in-ˈd(y)ùr-ə-bəl\ *adj* ♦ : not endurable : UNBEARABLE

 ♦ insufferable, insupportable, intolerable, unbearable, unsupportable

un•en•thu•si•as•tic \-in-ˌthü-zē-ˈas-tik\ *adj* ♦ : lacking ardor or excitement

 ♦ halfhearted, tepid, uneager

un•equal \-ˈē-kwəl\ *adj* **1** : not alike (as in size, amount, number, or value) **2** ♦ : not uniform **3** : badly balanced or matched **4** : INADEQUATE, INSUFFICIENT ⟨~ to the task⟩ — **un•equal•ly** *adv*

 ♦ erratic, irregular, uneven, unstable, unsteady

un•equaled *or* **un•equalled** \-kwəld\ *adj* ♦ : not equaled : UNPARALLELED

 ♦ incomparable, inimitable, matchless, nonpareil, only, peerless, unmatched, unparalleled, unrivaled, unsurpassed

un•equiv•o•cal \-i-ˈkwi-və-kəl\ *adj* **1** ♦ : leaving no doubt **2** ♦ : not questionable — **un•equiv•o•cal•ly** *adv*

 ♦ [1] clear-cut, definite, definitive, explicit, express, specific, unambiguous ♦ [2] clear, distinct, evident, manifest, obvious, plain, unambiguous, unmistakable

un•err•ing \-ˈer-iŋ, ˌən-ˈer-\ *adj* : making no errors : CERTAIN, UNFAILING — **un•err•ing•ly** *adv*
UNES•CO \yü-ˈnes-kō\ *abbr* United Nations Educational, Scientific, and Cultural Organization
un•eth•i•cal \ˌən-ˈe-thi-kəl\ *adj* ♦ : not conforming to approved standards of behavior, a socially accepted code, or professionally endorsed principles and practices

 ♦ cutthroat, immoral, Machiavellian, unconscionable, unprincipled, unscrupulous

un•even \-ˈē-vən\ *adj* **1** : ODD 3 **2** ♦ : not even : not level or smooth **3** ♦ : not uniform : IRREGULAR; *also* : varying in quality **4** : varying from the straight or parallel — **un•even•ly** *adv* — **un•even•ness** *n*

 ♦ [2] broken, bumpy, coarse, irregular, jagged, lumpy, pebbly, ragged, rough, rugged *Ant* even, flat, level, plane, smooth ♦ [3] erratic, irregular, unequal, unstable, unsteady *Ant* constant, stable, steady, unchanging, unvarying

un•event•ful \-i-ˈvent-fəl\ *adj* : lacking interesting or noteworthy incidents — **un•event•ful•ly** *adv*
un•ex•am•pled \-ig-ˈzam-pəld\ *adj* : having no example or parallel : UNPARALLELED
un•ex•cep•tion•able \-ik-ˈsep-shə-nə-bəl\ *adj* : not open to exception or objection : beyond reproach
un•ex•cep•tion•al \-ik-ˈsep-shə-nəl\ *adj* **1** : open to no objection **2** : allowing no exception **3** ♦ : constituting no exception to the general rule

 ♦ average, common, commonplace, everyday, normal, ordinary, prosaic, routine, run-of-the-mill, standard, unremarkable, usual, workaday

un•ex•pect•ed \-ik-ˈspek-təd\ *adj* ♦ : not expected : UNFORESEEN

 ♦ sudden, unanticipated, unforeseen *Ant* anticipated, expected, foreseen

un•ex•pect•ed•ly *adv* : in an unexpected manner
un•ex•pressed \-ik-ˈspresd\ *adj* ♦ : not expressed : not uttered in words

 ♦ implicit, tacit, unspoken, unvoiced, wordless

un•fail•ing \-ˈfā-liŋ\ *adj* **1** ♦ : not failing, flagging, or waning **2** : INEXHAUSTIBLE **3** : incapable of error

 ♦ certain, infallible, sure

un•fail•ing•ly *adv* ♦ : in an unfailing manner : without fail

 ♦ always, constantly, continually, ever, forever, incessantly, invariably, perpetually

un•fair \-ˈfar\ *adj* **1** ♦ : marked by injustice, partiality, or deception **2** : not equitable in business dealings — **un•fair•ly** *adv* — **un•fair•ness** *n*

 ♦ dirty, foul, illegal, unsportsmanlike

un•faith•ful \-ˈfāth-fəl\ *adj* **1** ♦ : not observant of vows, allegiance, or duty : DISLOYAL **2** : INACCURATE, UNTRUSTWORTHY — **un•faith•ful•ly** *adv*

 ♦ disloyal, faithless, false, fickle, inconstant, loose, perfidious, recreant, traitorous, treacherous, untrue

un•faith•ful•ness *n* ♦ : the quality or state of being unfaithful

 ♦ disloyalty, faithlessness, falseness, falsity, inconstancy, infidelity, perfidy

un•fa•mil•iar \-fə-ˈmil-yər\ *adj* **1** ♦ : not well-known : STRANGE ⟨an ~ place⟩ **2** : not well acquainted ⟨~ with the subject⟩

 ♦ fresh, new, novel, original, strange, unknown

un•fa•mil•iar•i•ty \-ˌmi-lē-ˈar-ə-tē, -ˈyar-\ *n* : the quality or state of being unfamiliar
un•fash•ion•able \-ˈfa-shə-nə-bəl\ *adj* ♦ : not in accord with or not following current fashion : not favored socially

 ♦ dowdy, inelegant, tacky, tasteless, trashy, unstylish

un•fas•ten \-ˈfas-ᵊn\ *vb* : to make or become loose : UNDO
un•fath•om•able \-ˈfa-thə-mə-bəl\ *adj* **1** ♦ : not capable of being fathomed : IMMEASURABLE **2** ♦ : incomprehensible

 ♦ [1] boundless, endless, illimitable, immeasurable, indefinite, infinite, limitless, measureless, unbounded, unlimited ♦ [2] impenetrable, incomprehensible

un•fa•vor•able *or Can and Brit* **un•fa•vour•able** \-ˈfā-və-rə-bəl\ *adj* **1** : set or placed in opposition **2** ♦ : not propitious : DISADVANTAGEOUS

 ♦ adverse, counter, disadvantageous, hostile, inimical, negative, prejudicial, unfriendly, unsympathetic

un•feel•ing \-ˈfē-liŋ\ *adj* **1** ♦ : lacking feeling **2** ♦ : devoid of kindness or sympathy — **un•feel•ing•ly** *adv*

 ♦ [1] asleep, dead, numb ♦ [2] callous, hard, heartless, merciless, pitiless, stony, uncharitable, unsparing, unsympathetic

un•feigned \-ˈfānd\ *adj* : not feigned : not hypocritical : GENUINE

un·fem·i·nine \-'fe-mə-nən\ *adj* : not characteristic of, typical of, or appropriate for a woman : not feminine

un·fet·ter \-'fe-tər\ *vb* **1** : to free from fetters **2** ♦ : to loose from restraint : LIBERATE

♦ discharge, emancipate, enfranchise, free, liberate, loose, loosen, manumit, release, spring, unbind, unchain

un·fil·ial \-'fi-lē-əl, -'fil-yəl\ *adj* : not observing the obligations of a child to a parent : UNDUTIFUL

un·fin·ished \-'fi-nisht\ *adj* **1** : not brought to an end **2** : being in a rough or unpolished state

¹**un·fit** \-'fit\ *adj* **1** ♦ : not fit or suitable **2** : physically or mentally unsound ⟨∼ for office⟩

♦ incapable, incompetent, inept, inexpert, unqualified, unskilled, unskillful ♦ improper, inappropriate, inapt, infelicitous, unbecoming, unseemly, unsuitable, wrong

²**unfit** *vb* : to make unfit : DISQUALIFY

un·fit·ness *n* : the quality or state of being unfit

un·fix \-'fiks\ *vb* **1** : to loosen from a fastening : DETACH **2** : UNSETTLE

un·flag·ging \-'fla-giŋ\ *adj* ♦ : not flagging : continuing with vigor

♦ indefatigable, inexhaustible, tireless, untiring

un·flap·pa·ble \-'fla-pə-bəl\ *adj* ♦ : not easily upset or panicked — **un·flap·pa·bly** *adv*

♦ imperturbable, nerveless, unshakable *Ant* shakable

un·fledged \-'flejd\ *adj* **1** : not feathered or ready for flight **2** : not fully developed : IMMATURE

un·flinch·ing \-'flin-chiŋ\ *adj* ♦ : not flinching or shrinking — **un·flinch·ing·ly** *adv*

♦ determined, dogged, grim, implacable, relentless, unrelenting, unyielding

un·fold \-'fōld\ *vb* **1 a** : to open the folds of : open up **2** : to lay open to view : DISCLOSE **3** ♦ : to produce or yield flowers : BLOSSOM **4** ♦ : to open the folds of : spread or straighten out

♦ [3] bloom, blossom, blow, burgeon, flower ♦ [4] expand, extend, fan, flare, open, spread, stretch

un·fol·low \-'fä-lō\ *vb* : to stop following (someone or something) on social media

un·forced \-'fōrst\ *adj* : not forced : not compelled

un·fore·seen \-fōr-'sēn\ *adj* ♦ : not foreseen : unexpected

♦ sudden, unanticipated, unexpected

un·for·get·ta·ble \-fər-'ge-tə-bəl\ *adj* : incapable of being forgotten ⟨an ∼ event⟩ — **un·for·get·ta·bly** \-blē\ *adv*

un·for·giv·able \-fər-'gi-və-bəl\ *adj* ♦ : incapable of being forgiven

♦ indefensible, inexcusable, unjustifiable, unpardonable, unwarrantable

un·formed \-'fōrmd\ *adj* **1** : not regularly formed or ordered : UNDEVELOPED **2** ♦ : not formed

♦ amorphous, formless, shapeless, unshaped, unstructured

un·for·tu·nate \-'fōr-chə-nət\ *adj* **1** ♦ : not fortunate : UNLUCKY **2** ♦ : attended with misfortune **3** : UNSUITABLE **4** ♦ : admitting of or deserving regret : fit to be deplored — **unfortunate** *n*

♦ [1] hapless, ill-fated, ill-starred, luckless, unhappy, unlucky ♦ [2] calamitous, catastrophic, destructive, disastrous, fatal, fateful, ruinous ♦ [4] deplorable, distressful, grievous, heartbreaking, lamentable, regrettable, woeful

un·for·tu·nate·ly \-nət-lē\ *adv* **1** : in an unfortunate manner **2** : it is unfortunate

un·found·ed \-'faun-dəd\ *adj* ♦ : lacking a sound basis : GROUNDLESS

♦ baseless, groundless, invalid, unreasonable, unsubstantiated, unsupported, unwarranted

un·freeze \-'frēz\ *vb* **-froze** \-'frōz\; **-fro·zen** \-'frōz-ᵊn\; **-freez·ing** **1** : to cause to thaw **2** : to remove from a freeze ⟨∼ prices⟩

un·fre·quent·ed \-frē-'kwen-təd; ˌən-'frē-kwən-\ *adj* : seldom visited or traveled over

un·friend·ly \-'frend-lē\ *adj* **1** ♦ : not friendly or kind **2** ♦ : set or placed in opposition — **un·friend·li·ness** \-lē-nəs\ *n*

♦ [1] chill, chilly, cold, cold-blooded, cool, frigid, frosty, glacial, icy, unsympathetic, wintry ♦ [2] adverse, counter, disadvantageous, hostile, inimical, negative, prejudicial, unfavorable (*or* unfavourable), unsympathetic

un·frock \-'fräk\ *vb* : DEFROCK

un·fruit·ful \-'früt-fəl\ *adj* **1** : not producing fruit or offspring : BARREN **2** : yielding no valuable result : UNPROFITABLE — **un·fruit·ful·ness** *n*

un·fun·ny \-'fə-nē\ *adj* : not funny : failing to achieve the humor intended

un·furl \-'fərl\ *vb* : to loose from a furled state : UNFOLD

un·gain·ly \-'gān-lē\ *adj* **1** ♦ : lacking in smoothness or dexterity : CLUMSY **2** : hard to handle : UNWIELDY — **un·gain·li·ness** \-lē-nəs\ *n*

♦ awkward, clumsy, gawky, graceless, heavy-handed, lubberly, lumpish, unhandy

un·gen·er·ous \-'je-nə-rəs\ *adj* : not generous or liberal : STINGY

un·gen·tle \-'jent-ᵊl\ *adj* : lacking in softness or congeniality

un·glued \-'glüd\ *adj* : UPSET, DISORDERED

un·god·ly \-'gäd-lē, -'gȯd-\ *adj* **1** : IMPIOUS, IRRELIGIOUS **2** : SINFUL, WICKED **3** : OUTRAGEOUS ⟨an ∼ hour⟩ **4** : offensive to civilized taste — **un·god·li·ness** \-lē-nəs\ *n*

un·gov·ern·able \-'gə-vər-nə-bəl\ *adj* : not capable of being governed, guided, or restrained : UNRULY

un·gov·erned \-'gə-vərnd\ *adj* ♦ : not subjected to regulation or control

♦ intemperate, rampant, unbridled, unchecked, uncontrolled, unhampered, unhindered, unrestrained

un·grace·ful \-'grās-fəl\ *adj* ♦ : lacking in charm or felicity

♦ awkward, clumsy, gauche, graceless, inelegant, stiff, stilted, uncomfortable, uneasy, wooden

un·gra·cious \-'grā-shəs\ *adj* **1** ♦ : not courteous : RUDE **2** : not pleasing : DISAGREEABLE

♦ discourteous, ill-bred, ill-mannered, impertinent, impolite, inconsiderate, rude, thoughtless, uncivil, unmannerly

un·grate·ful \-'grāt-fəl\ *adj* **1** : not thankful for favors **2** : DISAGREEABLE; *also* : THANKLESS — **un·grate·ful·ly** *adv* — **un·grate·ful·ness** *n*

un·guard·ed \-'gär-dəd\ *adj* **1** ♦ : vulnerable to attack : UNPROTECTED **2** ♦ : free from guile or wariness : DIRECT ⟨∼ remarks⟩ **3** ♦ : marked by lack of caution : having one's guard down

♦ [1] defenseless (*or* defenceless), exposed, helpless, susceptible, undefended, unprotected, unresistant, vulnerable ♦ [2] candid, direct, forthright, foursquare, frank, honest, open, outspoken, plain, straight, straightforward, unreserved ♦ [3] careless, heedless, mindless, unsafe, unwary

un·guent \'əŋ-gwənt, 'ən-\ *n* : a soothing or healing salve : OINTMENT

¹**un·gu·late** \'əŋ-gyə-lət, 'ən-, -ˌlāt\ *adj* : having hoofs

²**ungulate** *n* : a hoofed mammal (as a cow, horse, or rhinoceros)

un·hal·lowed \ˌən-'ha-lōd\ *adj* **1** : not consecrated : UNHOLY **2** : IMPIOUS, PROFANE **3** : contrary to accepted standards : IMMORAL

un·ham·pered \-'ham-pərd\ *adj* ♦ : not held in check

♦ intemperate, rampant, unbridled, unchecked, uncontrolled, ungoverned, unhindered, unrestrained

un·hand \-'hand\ *vb* : to remove the hand from : let go

un·hand·some \-'han-səm\ *adj* **1** : not beautiful or handsome : HOMELY **2** : UNBECOMING **3** : DISCOURTEOUS, RUDE

un·handy \-'han-dē\ *adj* **1** ♦ : hard to handle **2** : lacking in skill or dexterity : AWKWARD

♦ awkward, clumsy, cranky, cumbersome, ungainly, unwieldy

un·hap·pi·ly \-'ha-pə-lē\ *adv* ♦ : in an unhappy manner : without pleasure

♦ agonizingly, bitterly, grievously, hard, hardly, sadly, sorrowfully, woefully, wretchedly

un·hap·pi·ness \-'ha-pē-nəs\ *n* : the quality or state of being unhappy

un·hap·py \-'ha-pē\ *adj* **1** ♦ : not fortunate : UNLUCKY **2** : not cheerful or glad : SAD **3** ♦ : not appropriate : INAPPROPRIATE

♦ [1] hapless, ill-fated, ill-starred, luckless, unfortunate, unlucky ♦ [3] improper, inappropriate, inapt, infelicitous, unbecoming, unfit, unseemly, unsuitable, wrong

un·har·ness \-'här-nəs\ *vb* : to remove the harness from (as a horse)

un·health·ful \-'helth-fəl\ *adj* : detrimental to good health

un·healthy \-'hel-thē\ *adj* **1** ♦ : not conducive to health : UNWHOLESOME ⟨∼ foods⟩ **2** ♦ : not in good health **3** ♦ : exposing to or involving danger

♦ [1] noisome, noxious, unwholesome *Ant* healthful, healthy

♦ [2] bad, down, ill, indisposed, peaked, punk, sick, unsound, unwell ♦ [3] dangerous, grave, grievous, hazardous, menacing, parlous, perilous, risky, serious, unsafe, venturesome

un·heard \-'hərd\ *adj* **1** : not heard **2** : not granted a hearing
unheard–of *adj* : previously unknown; *esp* : UNPRECEDENTED
un·he·ro·ic \-hi-'rō-ik\ *adj* : not heroic
un·hin·dered \-'hin-dərd\ *adj* ♦ : not hindered or restrained

♦ intemperate, rampant, unbridled, unchecked, uncontrolled, ungoverned, unhampered, unrestrained

un·hinge \-'hinj\ *vb* **1** : to take from the hinges **2** ♦ : to make unstable esp. mentally ⟨*unhinged* by grief⟩

♦ craze, derange, madden ♦ agitate, bother, concern, discompose, disquiet, distress, disturb, exercise, freak, perturb, undo, unsettle, upset, worry

un·hitch \-'hich\ *vb* : UNFASTEN, LOOSE
un·ho·ly \-'hō-lē\ *adj* **1** : not holy : PROFANE, WICKED **2** : very unpleasant ⟨an ~ mess⟩ — **un·ho·li·ness** \-lē-nəs\ *n*
un·hook \-'hůk\ *vb* : to loose from a hook
un·horse \-'hòrs\ *vb* : to dislodge from or as if from a horse
un·hur·ried \-'hər-ēd\ *adj* : not hurried : in a leisurely manner
uni·cam·er·al \ˌyü-ni-'ka-mə-rəl\ *adj* : having a single legislative house or chamber
UNI·CEF \'yü-nə-ˌsef\ *abbr* United Nations Children's Fund
uni·cel·lu·lar \ˌyü-ni-'sel-yə-lər\ *adj* : having or consisting of a single cell
uni·corn \'yü-nə-ˌkòrn\ *n* : a mythical animal with one horn in the middle of the forehead
uni·cy·cle \'yü-ni-ˌsī-kəl\ *n* : a vehicle that has a single wheel and is usu. propelled by pedals
un·iden·ti·fied \ˌən-ī-'den-tə-ˌfīd\ *adj* ♦ : not identified though not necessarily unidentifiable

♦ anonymous, certain, one, some, unnamed, unspecified

uni·di·rec·tion·al \ˌyü-ni-də-'rek-shə-nəl, -dī-\ *adj* : having, moving in, or responsive in a single direction
uni·fi·ca·tion \ˌyü-nə-fə-'kā-shən\ *n* ♦ : the act, process, or result of unifying : the state of being unified

♦ combination, connection, consolidation, coupling, junction, union

¹uni·form \'yü-nə-ˌfòrm\ *adj* **1** ♦ : not varying **2** : of the same form with others ⟨~ procedures⟩ — **uni·form·ly** *adv*

♦ steady, unchanging, undeviating, unvarying, unwavering *Ant* changing, deviating, varying

²uniform *vb* : to clothe with a uniform
³uniform *n* : distinctive dress worn by members of a particular group (as an army or a police force)
uni·for·mi·ty \ˌyü-nə-'fòr-mə-tē\ *n, pl* **-ties** : the state of being uniform
uni·fy \'yü-nə-ˌfī\ *vb* **-fied; -fy·ing** ♦ : to make into a unit or a coherent whole : UNITE

♦ associate, coalesce, combine, conjoin, connect, couple, fuse, join, link, marry, unite

uni·lat·er·al \ˌyü-nə-'la-tə-rəl\ *adj* : of, having, affecting, or done by one side only — **uni·lat·er·al·ly** *adv*
un·imag·in·able \ˌən-i-'ma-jə-nə-bəl\ *adj* ♦ : not imaginable or comprehensible

♦ fantastic, implausible, inconceivable, incredible, unbelievable, unconvincing, unthinkable

un·im·peach·able \-im-'pē-chə-bəl\ *adj* : not liable to accusation : BLAMELESS, IRREPROACHABLE
un·im·por·tant \-im-'pòrt-ᵊnt\ *adj* ♦ : lacking in importance

♦ frivolous, inconsequential, inconsiderable, insignificant, little, minor, minute, negligible, slight, small, trifling, trivial *Ant* important, major, meaningful, significant, substantial, weighty

un·in·formed \-in-'fòrmd\ *adj* ♦ : not informed; *esp* : lacking in knowledge, awareness, or information

♦ ignorant, oblivious, unaware, unconscious, unknowing, unwitting

un·in·hib·it·ed \-in-'hi-bə-təd\ *adj* ♦ : free from inhibition; *also* : boisterously informal — **un·in·hib·it·ed·ly** *adv*

♦ demonstrative, effusive, emotional, unreserved, unrestrained

un·in·struct·ed \-in-'strək-təd\ *adj* : not instructed : deficient in knowledge or enlightenment
un·in·tel·li·gent \-'te-lə-jənt\ *adj* ♦ : lacking intelligence

♦ dense, dull, dumb, fatuous, mindless, obtuse, senseless, simple, slow, stupid, thick, vacuous, witless

un·in·tel·li·gi·ble \-'jə-bəl\ *adj* : not intelligible : OBSCURE ⟨an ~ voice mail⟩ — **un·in·tel·li·gi·bly** \-blē\ *adv*
un·in·tend·ed \-in-'ten-dəd\ *adj* ♦ : not intended; *esp* : not deliberate

♦ accidental, casual, chance, fluky, fortuitous, incidental, unintentional, unplanned, unpremeditated, unwitting

un·in·ten·tion·al \-in-'ten-chə-nəl\ *adj* ♦ : not intentional

♦ involuntary, unintended

un·in·ter·est·ed \-'in-trəs-təd, -tə-rəs-, -tə-ˌres-\ *adj* ♦ : not interested : not having the mind or feelings engaged or aroused

♦ apathetic, casual, disinterested, indifferent, insouciant, nonchalant, perfunctory, unconcerned, uncurious

un·in·ter·est·ing \-'in-trəs-tiŋ, -'in-tə-rəs-tiŋ\ *adj* ♦ : not attracting interest or attention

♦ drab, dreary, dry, dull, flat, monotonous, weary

un·in·ter·rupt·ed \-ˌin-tə-'rəp-təd\ *adj* ♦ : not interrupted : CONTINUOUS

♦ ceaseless, continual, continuous, incessant, unbroken, unceasing

un·in·vit·ed \-in-'vī-təd\ *adj* ♦ : not invited

♦ unasked, unbidden, undesired, unsolicited, unsought, unwanted, unwelcome

union \'yü-nyən\ *n* **1** ♦ : an act or instance of uniting two or more things into one : the state of being so united **2** ♦ : a uniting in marriage **3** ♦ : something formed by a combining of parts or members; *esp* : a confederation of independent individuals (as nations or persons) for some common purpose **4** : an organization of workers (as a labor union or a trade union) formed to advance its members' interests esp. in respect to wages and working conditions **5** : a device emblematic of union used on or as a national flag; *also* : the upper inner corner of a flag **6** : a device for connecting parts (as of a machine); *esp* : a coupling for pipes

♦ [1] combination, connection, consolidation, coupling, junction, unification *Ant* breakup, disconnection, dissolution, division, parting, partition, schism, split ♦ [1] affiliation, association, collaboration, cooperation, hookup, liaison, partnership, relation, relationship ♦ [3] alliance, bloc, coalition, combination, combine, confederacy, confederation, federation, league

union·ism \'yü-nyə-ˌni-zəm\ *n* **1** : the principle or policy of forming or adhering to a union; *esp, cap* : adherence to the policy of a firm federal union before or during the U.S. Civil War **2** : the principles or system of trade unions — **union·ist** *n*
union·ize \'yü-nyə-ˌnīz\ *vb* **-ized; -iz·ing** : to form into or cause to join a labor union — **union·i·za·tion** \ˌyü-nyə-nə-'zā-shən\ *n*
union jack *n* **1** : a flag consisting of the part of a national flag that signifies union **2** *cap U&J* : the national flag of the United Kingdom
unique \yủ-'nēk\ *adj* **1** ♦ : being the only one of its kind **2** ♦ : very unusual — **unique·ly** *adv* — **unique·ness** *n*

♦ [1] alone, lone, only, singular, sole, solitary, special ♦ [2] aberrant, abnormal, atypical, exceptional, extraordinary, freak, odd, peculiar, phenomenal, rare, singular, uncommon, uncustomary, unusual, unwonted

uni·sex \'yü-nə-ˌseks\ *adj* : not distinguishable as male or female; *also* : suitable or designed for both males and females ⟨~ clothing⟩ — **unisex** *n*
uni·sex·u·al \ˌyü-nə-'sek-shə-wəl\ *adj* **1** : having only male or only female sex organs **2** : UNISEX
uni·son \'yü-nə-sən, -zən\ *n* **1** : sameness or identity in musical pitch **2** : the condition of being tuned or sounded at the same pitch or in octaves ⟨sing in ~⟩ **3** : harmonious agreement or union : ACCORD
unit \'yü-nət\ *n* **1** : the smallest whole number greater than zero : ONE **2** : a definite amount or quantity used as a standard of measurement **3** : a single thing, person, or group that is a constituent of a whole; *also* : a part of a military establishment that has a prescribed organization — **unit** *adj*
Uni·tar·i·an \ˌyü-nə-'ter-ē-ən\ *n* : a member of a religious denomination stressing individual freedom of belief — **Uni·tar·i·an·ism** *n*
uni·tary \'yü-nə-ˌter-ē\ *adj* **1** : of or relating to a unit **2** : not divided — **uni·tar·i·ly** \ˌyü-nə-'ter-ə-lē\ *adv*
unite \yủ-'nīt\ *vb* **unit·ed; unit·ing** **1** ♦ : to put or join together so as to make one **2 a** : to join by a legal or moral bond **b** ♦ : to join in interest or fellowship **3** ♦ : to put together to form a single unit : CONSOLIDATE **4** : to act in concert

♦ [1] associate, coalesce, combine, conjoin, connect, couple, fuse, join, link, marry, unify *Ant* break up, dissever, part, section, separate, sever, split, sunder ♦ [2b] ally, associate, band, club, confederate, conjoin, cooperate, federate, league ♦ [3] center (*or* centre), centralize, compact, concentrate, consolidate, unify

unit·ed \yü-'nī-təd\ *adj* **1** : made one : COMBINED **2** ♦ : relating to or produced by joint action **3** ♦ : being in agreement : HARMONIOUS

♦ [2] collective, common, communal, concerted, conjoint, joint, mutual, public ♦ [3] agreeable, amicable, compatible, congenial, harmonious, kindred, unanimous

unit·ize \'yü-nə-ˌtīz\ *vb* **-ized; -iz·ing** **1** : to form or convert into a unit **2** : to divide into units

uni·ty \'yü-nə-tē\ *n, pl* **-ties** **1** : the quality or state of being or being made one : ONENESS **2** : a definite quantity or combination of quantities taken as one or for which 1 is made to stand in calculation **3** ♦ : a condition of harmony **4** : continuity without change ⟨~ of purpose⟩ **5** : reference of all the parts of a literary or artistic composition to a single main idea **6** : totality of related parts

♦ balance, coherence, consonance, harmony, proportion, symmetry, symphony

univ *abbr* **1** universal **2** university

uni·valve \'yü-ni-ˌvalv\ *n* : a mollusk having a shell with only one piece; *esp* : GASTROPOD — **univalve** *adj*

uni·ver·sal \ˌyü-nə-'vər-səl\ *adj* **1** ♦ : including, covering, or affecting the whole without limit or exception ⟨a ~ rule⟩ **2** : present or occurring everywhere **3** : used or for use among all ⟨a ~ language⟩ **4** ♦ : comprehensively broad and versatile — **uni·ver·sal·ly** *adv*

♦ [1] blanket, common, general, generic, global, overall ♦ [1] compendious, complete, comprehensive, encyclopedic, full, global, inclusive, omnibus, panoramic ♦ [4] adaptable, all-around, protean, versatile

uni·ver·sal·i·ty \-vər-'sa-lə-tē\ *n* : the quality or state of being universal

uni·ver·sal·ize \-'vər-sə-ˌlīz\ *vb* **-ized; -iz·ing** : to make universal : GENERALIZE ⟨would ~ equal rights⟩ — **uni·ver·sal·i·za·tion** \-ˌvər-sə-lə-'zā-shən\ *n*

universal joint *n* : a shaft coupling for transmitting rotation from one shaft to another not in a straight line with it

Universal Product Code *n* : a combination of a barcode and numbers by which a scanner can identify a product and usu. assign a price

uni·verse \'yü-nə-ˌvərs\ *n* ♦ : the whole body of things observed or assumed : COSMOS

♦ cosmos, creation, macrocosm, nature, world

uni·ver·si·ty \ˌyü-nə-'vər-sə-tē\ *n, pl* **-ties** : an institution of higher learning authorized to confer degrees in various special fields (as theology, law, and medicine) as well as in the arts and sciences generally

un·just \ˌən-'jəst\ *adj* : characterized by injustice — **un·just·ly** *adv*

un·jus·ti·fi·able \-'jəs-tə-ˌfī-ə-bəl\ *adj* ♦ : not justifiable : lacking in propriety or justice

♦ indefensible, inexcusable, unforgivable, unpardonable, unwarrantable

un·kempt \-'kempt\ *adj* **1 a** ♦ : lacking order or neatness **b** : ROUGH, UNPOLISHED **2** : not combed : DISHEVELED

♦ chaotic, confused, disheveled, disordered, messy, muddled, sloppy, untidy

un·kind \-'kīnd\ *adj* : not kind or sympathetic ⟨an ~ remark⟩ — **un·kind·ly** *adv* — **un·kind·ness** *n*

un·kind·ly \-'kīnd-lē\ *adj* : UNKIND — **un·kind·li·ness** *n*

un·know·ing \ˌən-'nō-iŋ\ *adj* ♦ : not knowing — **un·know·ing·ly** *adv*

♦ ignorant, oblivious, unaware, unconscious, uninformed, unwitting

un·known \-'nōn\ *adj* ♦ : not known or not well-known — **unknown** *n*

♦ fresh, new, novel, original, strange, unfamiliar ♦ anonymous, nameless, obscure, unsung

un·lace \-'lās\ *vb* : to loose by undoing a lace

un·lade \-'lād\ *vb* **-lad·ed; -laded** *or* **-lad·en** \-'lād-ᵊn\; **-lad·ing** : to take the load or cargo from : UNLOAD

un·la·dy·like \-'lā-dē-ˌlīk\ *adj* : lacking the behavior, manner, or style considered proper for a lady

un·latch \-'lach\ *vb* **1** : to open or loose by lifting the latch **2** : to become loosed or opened

un·law·ful \-'lȯ-fəl\ *adj* **1** ♦ : not lawful : ILLEGAL **2** : not morally right or conventional — **un·law·ful·ly** *adv*

♦ criminal, illegal, illegitimate, illicit, wrongful

un·lead·ed \-'le-dəd\ *adj* : not treated or mixed with lead or lead compounds

un·learn \-'lərn\ *vb* : to put out of one's knowledge or memory; *also* : to discard the habit of

un·learned \-'lər-nəd *for 1;* -'lərnd *for 2*\ *adj* **1** ♦ : possessing inadequate learning or education : UNEDUCATED **2** : not gained by study or training

♦ dark, ignorant, illiterate, simple, uneducated, untaught

un·leash \-'lēsh\ *vb* ♦ : to free from or as if from a leash : let loose

♦ loose, loosen, release, uncork, unlock, unloosen

un·less \ən-'les, 'ən-ˌles\ *conj* : except on condition that ⟨won't go ~ you do⟩

un·let·tered \ˌən-'le-tərd\ *adj* : not educated : ILLITERATE

¹un·like \-'līk\ *adj* **1** ♦ : not like : DIFFERENT **2** : UNEQUAL — **un·like·ness** *n*

♦ different, disparate, dissimilar, distinct, distinctive, distinguishable, diverse, other, unalike

²unlike *prep* **1** : different from ⟨she's quite ~ her sister⟩ **2** : unusual for ⟨it's ~ you to be late⟩ **3** : differently from ⟨behaves ~ his brother⟩

un·like·li·hood \-'lī-klē-ˌhu̇d\ *n* : IMPROBABILITY

un·like·ly \-'lī-klē\ *adj* **1** ♦ : not likely : IMPROBABLE **2** : likely to fail

♦ doubtful, dubious, flimsy, improbable, questionable

un·like·ness *n* ♦ : the quality or state of being unlike

♦ contrast, difference, disagreement, discrepancy, disparity, distinction, diversity

un·lim·ber \-'lim-bər\ *vb* : to get ready for action

un·lim·it·ed \-'li-mə-təd\ *adj* **1** : lacking any controls **2** ♦ : having no bounds : without limits **3** ♦ : not bounded by exceptions

♦ [2] boundless, endless, illimitable, immeasurable, indefinite, infinite, limitless, measureless, unbounded, unfathomable ♦ [3] all-around, general, unqualified, unrestricted

un·list·ed \-'lis-təd\ *adj* **1** ♦ : not appearing on a list; *esp* : not appearing in a telephone book **2** : not listed on a stock exchange

♦ uncataloged, unrecorded, unregistered *Ant* cataloged, listed, recorded, registered

un·lit·er·ary \-'li-tə-ˌrer-ē\ *adj* : not literary

un·load \-'lōd\ *vb* **1 a** : to take away or off : REMOVE ⟨~ cargo from a hold⟩ **b** ♦ : to get rid of **2** ♦ : to take a load from ⟨~ the ship⟩; *also* : to relieve or set free : UNBURDEN ⟨~ one's mind of worries⟩ **3** : to draw the charge from ⟨~ed the gun⟩ **4** : to sell in volume

♦ [1b] cast, discard, ditch, dump, fling, jettison, junk, lose, reject, scrap, shed, shuck, slough, throw away, throw out ♦ [2] disburden, discharge, disencumber, unburden *Ant* load, pack

un·lock \-'läk\ *vb* **1** : to open or unfasten through release of a lock **2** ♦ : to free from restraints or restrictions : RELEASE ⟨~ a flood of emotions⟩ **3** : DISCLOSE, REVEAL ⟨~ nature's secrets⟩

♦ loose, loosen, release, uncork, unleash, unloosen

un·looked-for \-'lu̇kt-ˌfȯr\ *adj* : not foreseen : UNEXPECTED

un·loose \-'lüs\ *vb* **1** : UNLOOSEN **2** : UNTIE

un·loos·en \-'lüs-ᵊn\ *vb* **1** ♦ : to relax the strain of; *also* : set free **2** : UNTIE

♦ loose, loosen, release, uncork, unleash, unlock

un·love·ly \-'ləv-lē\ *adj* **1** ♦ : having no charm or appeal **2** : not amiable

♦ bad, disagreeable, distasteful, nasty, rotten, sour, uncongenial, unpleasant, unwelcome

un·luck·i·ly \-'lə-kə-lē\ *adv* : UNFORTUNATELY

un·lucky \-'lə-kē\ *adj* **1** ♦ : having or meeting with misfortune : ILL-FATED **2** : likely to bring misfortune : INAUSPICIOUS **3** : REGRETTABLE

♦ hapless, ill-fated, ill-starred, luckless, unfortunate, unhappy *Ant* fortunate, happy, lucky

un·man \-'man\ *vb* **1** ♦ : to deprive of manly courage **2** : CASTRATE

♦ demoralize, undo, unnerve ♦ daunt, demoralize, discourage, dishearten, dismay, dispirit, unnerve

un·man·age·able \-'ma-ni-jə-bəl\ *adj* ♦ : not manageable : INTRACTABLE

♦ froward, headstrong, intractable, recalcitrant, refractory, uncontrollable, unruly, untoward, wayward, willful

un·man·ly \-'man-lē\ *adj* **1** : not manly : COWARDLY **2** ♦ : having feminine qualities untypical of a man : EFFEMINATE

♦ effeminate, feminine, girlish, womanly

un·man·ner·ly \-'ma-nər-lē\ *adj* ♦ : not mannerly : IMPOLITE — **unmannerly** *adv*

♦ discourteous, ill-bred, ill-mannered, impertinent, impolite, inconsiderate, rude, thoughtless, uncivil, ungracious

un·mar·ried \-'mar-ēd\ *adj* ♦ : not married

♦ single, unattached, unwed

un·mas·cu·line \-'mas-kyə-lən\ *adj* : not characteristic of, typical of, or appropriate for a man : not masculine

un·mask \-'mask\ *vb* **1** ♦ : to strip of a mask or a disguise : EXPOSE **2** : to remove one's mask

♦ bare, disclose, discover, divulge, expose, reveal, spill, tell, unbosom, uncloak, uncover, unveil

un·matched \-'macht\ *adj* **1** ♦ : not matchable **2** : not matching

♦ incomparable, inimitable, matchless, nonpareil, only, peerless, unequaled, unparalleled, unrivaled, unsurpassed

un·mean·ing \-'mē-niŋ\ *adj* : having no meaning : SENSELESS
un·me·di·at·ed \-'mē-dē-ā-təd\ *adj* : not mediated : not communicated or transformed by an intervening agency
un·meet \-'mēt\ *adj* : not meet or fit : UNSUITABLE, IMPROPER
un·me·lo·di·ous \-mə-'lō-dē-əs\ *adj* ♦ : not melodious

♦ discordant, dissonant, inharmonious, unmusical

un·men·tion·able \-'men-chə-nə-bəl\ *adj* : not fit or proper to be talked about
un·mer·ci·ful \-'mər-si-fəl\ *adj* : not merciful : MERCILESS — **un·mer·ci·ful·ly** *adv*
un·mind·ful \-'mīnd-fəl\ *adj* : not conscientiously aware, attentive, or heedful : UNAWARE
un·mis·tak·able \-mə-'stā-kə-bəl\ *adj* ♦ : not capable of being mistaken or misunderstood : OBVIOUS — **un·mis·tak·ably** \-blē\ *adv*

♦ apparent, broad, clear, clear-cut, distinct, evident, lucid, manifest, obvious, palpable, patent, perspicuous, plain, transparent, unambiguous, unequivocal

un·mit·i·gat·ed \-'mi-tə-ˌgā-təd\ *adj* **1** : not softened or lessened **2** : being so definitely what is stated as to offer little chance of change or relief : ABSOLUTE ⟨an ~ liar⟩
un·mixed \-'mikst\ *adj* ♦ : not mixed

♦ absolute, fine, neat, plain, pure, refined, straight, unadulterated, undiluted

un·moor \-'mùr\ *vb* : to loose from or as if from moorings
un·mor·al \-'mòr-əl\ *adj* : having no moral perception or quality : AMORAL — **un·mo·ral·i·ty** \-mə-'ra-lə-tē\ *n*
un·mov·able \-'mü-və-bəl\ *adj* **1** ♦ : incapable of being moved : firmly fixed **2** ♦ : not moving or not intended to be moved

♦ [1, 2] immobile, immovable, nonmotile, stationary, unbudging

un·mu·si·cal \-'myü-zi-kəl\ *adj* ♦ : not musical

♦ discordant, dissonant, inharmonious, unmelodious

un·muz·zle \-'mə-zəl\ *vb* : to remove a muzzle from
un·named \-'nāmd\ *adj* ♦ : not named or identified

♦ anonymous, certain, one, some, unidentified, unspecified

un·nat·u·ral \-'na-chə-rəl\ *adj* **1** : contrary to or acting contrary to nature or natural instincts **2** ♦ : not being in accordance with normal human feelings or behavior : ABNORMAL — **un·nat·u·ral·ly** *adv* — **un·nat·u·ral·ness** *n*

♦ aberrant, abnormal, anomalous, atypical, deviant, irregular

un·nec·es·sar·i·ly \-ne-sə-'ser-ə-lē\ *adv* **1** : not by necessity **2** : to an unnecessary degree ⟨~ harsh⟩
un·nerve \-'nərv\ *vb* **1** ♦ : to deprive of courage, strength, or steadiness **2** : to cause to become nervous

♦ demoralize, undo, unman *Ant* nerve ♦ daunt, demoralize, discourage, dishearten, dismay, dispirit, unman

un·nil·hex·i·um \ˌyün-ᵊl-'hek-sē-əm\ *n* : the chemical element of atomic number 106

un·nil·pen·ti·um \-'pen-tē-əm\ *n* : the chemical element of atomic number 105
un·nil·qua·di·um \-'kwä-dē-əm\ *n* : the chemical element of atomic number 104
un·num·bered \ˌən-'nəm-bərd\ *adj* **1** : not numbered or counted **2** ♦ : too many to be numbered : INNUMERABLE

♦ countless, innumerable, numberless, uncountable, untold

un·ob·struct·ed \-əb-'strək-təd\ *adj* ♦ : not obstructed or hindered

♦ clear, free, open

un·ob·tain·able \-əb-'tā-nə-bəl\ *adj* ♦ : not obtainable

♦ inaccessible, inconvenient, unapproachable, unattainable, unavailable, unreachable, untouchable

un·ob·tru·sive \-əb-'trü-siv\ *adj* : not obtrusive or forward : INCONSPICUOUS — **un·ob·tru·sive·ly** *adv*
un·oc·cu·pied \-'ä-kyə-ˌpīd\ *adj* **1** : not busy : UNEMPLOYED **2** : not occupied : EMPTY, VACANT
un·or·ga·nized \-'òr-gə-ˌnīzd\ *adj* **1** : not formed or brought into an integrated or ordered whole **2** : not organized into unions ⟨~ labor⟩
un·orig·i·nal \-ə-'ri-jə-nəl\ *adj* ♦ : not original

♦ imitative, mimic

un·or·tho·dox \-'òr-thə-ˌdäks\ *adj* ♦ : not orthodox : not in accord with approved, standardized, or conventional doctrine, method, thought, custom, or opinion

♦ broad-minded, liberal, nonorthodox, nontraditional, open≈minded, progressive, radical, unconventional ♦ informal, irregular, unceremonious, unconventional

un·pack \-'pak\ *vb* **1** : to separate and remove things packed **2** : to open and remove the contents of
un·paid \-'pād\ *adj* **1** : not paid : serving without pay **2 a** : not presented as payment **b** ♦ : not cleared by payment **3** : not paying a salary

♦ outstanding, overdue, payable, unsettled

un·paint·ed \-'pān-təd\ *adj* ♦ : not painted : not having a coat of paint

♦ colorless (*or* colourless), uncolored (*or* uncoloured), white

un·pal·at·able \-'pa-lə-tə-bəl\ *adj* **1** : not palatable : DISTASTEFUL **2** : not amiable or agreeable
un·par·al·leled \-'par-ə-ˌleld\ *adj* **1** : having no parallel **2** ♦ : having no equal or match ⟨an ~ achievement⟩

♦ [1, 2] incomparable, inimitable, matchless, nonpareil, only, peerless, unequaled, unmatched, unrivaled, unsurpassed

un·par·don·able \-'pärd-ᵊn-ə-bəl\ *adj* ♦ : not worthy of pardon

♦ indefensible, inexcusable, unforgivable, unjustifiable, unwarrantable

un·par·lia·men·ta·ry \-ˌpär-lə-'men-tə-rē\ *adj* : contrary to parliamentary practice
un·peg \-'peg\ *vb* **1** : to remove a peg from **2** : to unfasten by or as if by removing a peg
un·per·son \'ən-ˌpərs-ᵊn, -ˌpərs-\ *n* : a person who usu. for political or ideological reasons is removed from recognition or consideration
un·per·turbed \ˌən-pər-'tərbd\ *adj* ♦ : not perturbed : unaffected by worry, interruption, disturbance, or disarrangement

♦ calm, collected, composed, cool, placid, self-possessed, serene, tranquil, undisturbed, unshaken, untroubled, unworried

un·pile \-'pīl\ *vb* : to take or disentangle from a pile
un·pin \-'pin\ *vb* : to remove a pin from : UNFASTEN
un·planned \-'pland\ *adj* **1** ♦ : not expected

♦ [1] ad-lib, extemporaneous, impromptu, offhand, snap, unpremeditated, unprepared, unrehearsed ♦ [2] accidental, casual, chance, fluky, fortuitous, incidental, unintended, unintentional, unpremeditated, unwitting

un·pleas·ant \-'plez-ᵊnt\ *adj* ♦ : not pleasant : DISAGREEABLE — **un·pleas·ant·ly** *adv* — **un·pleas·ant·ness** *n*

♦ bad, disagreeable, distasteful, nasty, rotten, sour, uncongenial, unlovely, unwelcome *Ant* agreeable, nice, pleasant, pleasing, pleasurable, satisfying, welcome

un·pleas·ing \-'plē-ziŋ\ *adj* : not pleasing : causing discomfort, displeasure, or repugnance
un·plug \-'pləg\ *vb* **1** : UNCLOG **2** : to remove (a plug) from a receptacle; *also* : to disconnect from an electric circuit by removing a plug

un·plumbed \-'pləmd\ adj **1** : not tested or measured with a plumb line **2** : not thoroughly explored

un·pol·ished \-'pä-lisht\ adj **1** : not made smooth by polishing **2** ♦ : not marked by refinement

♦ coarse, common, crass, crude, gross, ill-bred, low, rough, rude, tasteless, uncouth, uncultivated, uncultured, unrefined, vulgar

un·pop·u·lar \-'pä-pyə-lər\ adj : not popular : looked upon or received unfavorably — **un·pop·u·lar·i·ty** \-ˌpä-pyə-'lar-ə-tē\ n

un·prec·e·dent·ed \-'pre-sə-ˌden-təd\ adj : having no precedent : NOVEL

un·pre·dict·able \-pri-'dik-tə-bəl\ adj ♦ : not predictable

♦ capricious, changeable, fickle, fluid, inconstant, mercurial, mutable, temperamental, uncertain, unsettled, unstable, unsteady, variable, volatile

un·prej·u·diced \-'pre-jə-dəst\ adj ♦ : not prejudiced : free from undue bias

♦ disinterested, dispassionate, equal, equitable, fair, impartial, just, nonpartisan, objective, square, unbiased

un·pre·med·i·tat·ed \-pri-'me-də-ˌtā-təd\ adj ♦ : not premeditated

♦ accidental, casual, chance, fluky, fortuitous, incidental, unintended, unintentional, unplanned, unwitting

un·pre·pared \-pri-'pard\ adj **1** : not prepared **2 a** ♦ : happening without preparation **b** : arriving or taking place unexpectedly or without warning

♦ ad-lib, extemporaneous, impromptu, offhand, snap, unplanned, unpremeditated, unrehearsed

un·pre·tend·ing \-pri-'ten-diŋ\ adj : not pretending; esp : UNPRETENTIOUS

un·pre·ten·tious \-pri-'ten-chəs\ adj ♦ : not pretentious

♦ artless, genuine, honest, ingenuous, innocent, naive, natural, real, simple, sincere, true, unaffected ♦ demure, humble, lowly, meek, modest, retiring, unassuming

un·pret·ty \-'pri-tē\ adj : not pretty : lacking in beauty

un·prin·ci·pled \-'prin-sə-pəld\ adj ♦ : lacking sound or honorable principles : UNSCRUPULOUS ⟨an ~ politician⟩

♦ cutthroat, immoral, Machiavellian, unconscionable, unethical, unscrupulous Ant ethical, moral, principled, scrupulous

un·print·able \-'prin-tə-bəl\ adj ♦ : unfit to be printed; esp : too obscene or offensive to be shown in print

♦ bawdy, coarse, crude, dirty, filthy, foul, gross, indecent, lascivious, lewd, nasty, obscene, pornographic, ribald, smutty, vulgar, wanton

un·pro·cessed \-'prä-ˌsest, -'prō-\ adj ♦ : not processed; esp : not altered from an original or natural state

♦ crude, native, natural, raw, undressed, unrefined, untreated

un·pro·duc·tive \-prə-'dək-tiv\ adj ♦ : not productive

♦ barren, infertile, poor, stark, waste ♦ fruitless, futile, ineffective, unsuccessful

un·pro·fes·sion·al \-prə-'fe-shə-nəl\ adj **1** : not belonging to or gainfully employed at a particular profession **2** ♦ : not characteristic of or befitting a professional

♦ amateur, amateurish, inexperienced, inexpert, nonprofessional, unskilled, unskillful

un·prof·it·able \-'prä-fə-tə-bəl\ adj : not profitable : USELESS

un·pro·gres·sive \-prə-'gre-siv\ adj : not progressive; esp : not devoted to or showing economic, social, or political progress

un·pro·tect·ed \-prə-'tek-təd\ adj ♦ : lacking protection or defense

♦ defenseless (or defenceless), exposed, helpless, susceptible, undefended, unguarded, unresistant, vulnerable

un·qual·i·fied \-'kwä-lə-ˌfīd\ adj **1** ♦ : not having requisite qualifications **2** ♦ : not modified or restricted by reservations : COMPLETE — **un·qual·i·fied·ly** \-ˌfī-əd-lē\ adv

♦ [1] incapable, incompetent, inept, inexpert, unfit, unskilled, unskillful ♦ [2] absolute, complete, outright, total, unequivocal ♦ [2] all-around, general, unlimited, unrestricted

un·ques·tion·able \-'kwes-chə-nə-bəl\ adj ♦ : not questionable : INDISPUTABLE

♦ incontestable, indisputable, indubitable, irrefutable, unanswerable, undeniable

un·ques·tion·ably \-blē\ adv ♦ : without any question

♦ certainly, definitely, doubtless, incontestably, indeed, indisputably, really, surely, truly, undeniably, undoubtedly

un·ques·tion·ing \-chə-niŋ\ adj : not questioning : accepting without examination or hesitation ⟨~ obedience⟩ — **un·ques·tion·ing·ly** adv

un·qui·et \-'kwī-ət\ adj **1** : not quiet : AGITATED, DISTURBED **2** : physically, emotionally, or mentally restless : UNEASY

un·quote \'ən-ˌkwōt\ n — used orally to indicate the end of a direct quotation

un·rav·el \ˌən-'ra-vəl\ vb **1** ♦ : to separate the threads of **2** ♦ : to resolve the intricacy, complexity, or obscurity of : clear up ⟨~ a mystery⟩ **3** : to become unraveled

♦ [1] disentangle, untangle, untwine Ant entangle, snarl, tangle ♦ [2] answer, break, crack, dope, figure out, puzzle, resolve, riddle, solve, work, work out

un·reach·able \-'rēch-ə-bəl\ adj ♦ : incapable of being reached

♦ inaccessible, inconvenient, unapproachable, unattainable, unavailable, unobtainable, untouchable

un·read \-'red\ adj **1** : not read; also : left unexamined **2** : lacking the benefits or the experience of reading

un·re·al \-'rēl\ adj ♦ : lacking in reality, substance, or genuineness

♦ chimerical, fabulous, fanciful, fantastic, fictitious, imaginary, made-up, mythical, phantom, pretend

un·re·al·i·ty \-rē-'a-lə-tē\ n **1 a** : the quality or state of being unreal : lack of substance or validity **b** : something unreal, insubstantial, or visionary **2** : ineptitude in dealing with reality

♦ chimera, conceit, daydream, delusion, dream, fancy, fantasy, figment, hallucination, illusion, phantasm, pipe dream, vision

un·rea·son·able \-'rēz-ᵊn-ə-bəl\ adj **1 a** ♦ : not governed by or acting according to reason **b** ♦ : not conformable to reason **2** : exceeding the bounds of reason or moderation — **un·rea·son·able·ness** n — **un·rea·son·ably** adv

♦ [1a] fallacious, illogical, invalid, irrational, unsound, weak ♦ [1b] baseless, groundless, invalid, unfounded, unsubstantiated, unsupported, unwarranted

un·rea·soned \-'rēz-ᵊnd\ adj : not based on reason or reasoning

un·rea·son·ing \-'rēz-ᵊn-iŋ\ adj : not using or showing the use of reason as a guide or control

un·re·con·struct·ed \-ˌrē-kən-'strək-təd\ adj : not reconciled to some political, economic, or social change; esp : holding stubbornly to a particular belief, view, place, or style

un·re·cord·ed \-ri-'kȯr-dəd\ adj **1** ♦ : not recorded **2** : not made a matter of official record

♦ uncataloged, unlisted, unregistered

un·re·cov·er·able \-ri-'kə-və-rə-bəl\ adj **1** ♦ : incapable of being recovered, recaptured, or regained : hopelessly lost **2** : admitting of no remedy or correction

♦ irredeemable, irremediable, irreparable, unredeemable

un·re·deem·able \-ri-'dē-mə-bəl\ adj **1** : admitting of no change or release **2** ♦ : insusceptible of redemption or reform : utterly and hopelessly bad **3** : not redeemable : not recoverable on payment of what is due

♦ hopeless, incorrigible, incurable, irredeemable, irremediable, unrecoverable

un·reel \-'rēl\ vb **1** : to unwind from or as if from a reel **2** : to perform successfully

un·re·fined \-ri-'fīnd\ adj **1** ♦ : lacking moral or social cultivation or the graces of manners or speech **2** ♦ : not separated from impurity or unwanted matter

♦ [1] coarse, common, crass, crude, gross, ill-bred, low, rude, tasteless, uncouth, uncultivated, uncultured, unpolished, vulgar ♦ [2] crude, native, natural, raw, undressed, unprocessed, untreated

un·re·gen·er·ate \-ri-'je-nə-rət\ adj : not regenerated or reformed

un·reg·is·tered \-'re-jə-stərd\ adj ♦ : not registered

♦ uncataloged, unlisted, unrecorded

un·re·hearsed \-ri-'hərst\ adj **1** : not narrated **2** ♦ : not practiced or prepared

♦ ad-lib, extemporaneous, impromptu, offhand, snap, unplanned, unpremeditated, unprepared

un·re·lent·ing \-'len-tiŋ\ adj **1** ♦ : not yielding in determination ⟨~ leader⟩ **2** ♦ : not letting up or weakening in vigor or pace — **un·re·lent·ing·ly** adv

♦ [1, 2] determined, dogged, grim, implacable, relentless, unflinching, unyielding

un·re·li·able \-ri-'lī-ə-bəl\ *adj* : not reliable or trustworthy
un·re·mark·able \-ri-'mär-kə-bəl\ *adj* ♦ : lacking interest or distinction : of a kind to be expected in the normal course of events

♦ average, common, commonplace, everyday, normal, ordinary, prosaic, routine, run-of-the-mill, standard, unexceptional, usual, workaday

un·re·mit·ting \-'mi-tiŋ\ *adj* : not remitting : CONSTANT — **un·re·mit·ting·ly** *adv*
un·re·pen·tant \-ri-'pen-t²nt\ *adj* **1** : not repentant **2** : holding to a prior conviction or attitude
un·re·quit·ed \-ri-'kwī-təd\ *adj* : not reciprocated or returned in kind ⟨~ love⟩
un·re·served \-'zərvd\ *adj* **1** : not limited or partial ⟨~ enthusiasm⟩ **2** ♦ : not cautious or reticent **3** : not set aside for special use — **un·re·serv·ed·ly** \-'zər-vəd-lē\ *adv*

♦ candid, direct, forthright, foursquare, frank, honest, open, outspoken, plain, straight, straightforward, unguarded

un·re·sis·tant \-ri-'zis-tənt\ *adj* ♦ : not resistant

♦ defenseless (*or* defenceless), exposed, helpless, susceptible, undefended, unguarded, unprotected, vulnerable

un·re·sist·ing \-ri-'zis-tiŋ\ *adj* ♦ : not resistant

♦ acquiescent, passive, resigned, tolerant, unresistant, yielding

un·re·solved \-ri-'zälvd\ *adj* ♦ : not yet determined

♦ open, pending, undecided, undetermined, unsettled

un·rest \-'rest\ *n* ♦ : a disturbed or uneasy state : TURMOIL

♦ disquiet, ferment, restlessness, turmoil, uneasiness *Ant* calm, ease, peace, quiet

un·rest·ful \-'rest-fəl\ *adj* : not restful : not feeling or not conducive to repose
un·re·strained \-ri-'strānd\ *adj* **1** ♦ : not restrained **2** ♦ : free of constraint, inhibition, or timidity

♦ [1] intemperate, rampant, unbridled, unchecked, uncontrolled, ungoverned, unhampered, unhindered ♦ [2] demonstrative, effusive, emotional, spontaneous, uninhibited, unreserved

un·re·straint \-ri-'strānt\ *n* ♦ : lack of restraint

♦ abandon, abandonment, ease, lightheartedness, naturalness, spontaneity

un·re·strict·ed \-ri-'strik-təd\ *adj* ♦ : not restricted

♦ free-for-all, open, public ♦ all-around, general, unlimited, unqualified

un·rid·dle \-'rid-²l\ *vb* : to find the explanation of : SOLVE
un·righ·teous \-'rī-chəs\ *adj* **1** : not righteous : SINFUL, WICKED **2** : UNJUST — **un·righ·teous·ness** *n*
un·ripe \-'rīp\ *adj* : not ripe or fully developed : IMMATURE
un·rip·ened \-'rī-pənd\ *adj* : not ripened : not having attained maturity
un·ri·valed *or* **un·ri·valled** \-'rī-vəld\ *adj* ♦ : having no rival

♦ incomparable, inimitable, matchless, nonpareil, only, peerless, unequaled, unmatched, unparalleled, unsurpassed

un·robe \-'rōb\ *vb* : DISROBE, UNDRESS
un·roll \-'rōl\ *vb* **1** : to unwind a roll of : open out **2** : DISPLAY, DISCLOSE **3** : to become unrolled or spread out
un·roof \-'rüf, -'rúf\ *vb* : to strip off the roof or covering of
un·ruf·fled \-'rə-fəld\ *adj* **1** ♦ : not agitated or upset **2** : not ruffled : SMOOTH ⟨~ water⟩

♦ calm, collected, composed, cool, placid, self-possessed, serene, tranquil, undisturbed, unperturbed, unshaken, untroubled, unworried

un·rul·i·ness \-'rü-lē-nəs\ *n* ♦ : the quality or state of being unruly

♦ defiance, disobedience, insubordination, rebelliousness, recalcitrance, refractoriness

un·ruly \-'rü-lē\ *adj* ♦ : not readily ruled, disciplined, or managed

♦ contrary, defiant, disobedient, froward, headstrong, intractable, rebellious, recalcitrant, refractory, uncontrollable, untoward, wayward, willful

un·sad·dle \-'sad-²l\ *vb* **1** : to remove the saddle from a horse **2** : UNHORSE
un·safe \-'sāf\ *adj* ♦ : not safe : exposed or exposing to danger

♦ dangerous, grave, grievous, hazardous, menacing, parlous, perilous, risky, serious, unhealthy, venturesome

un·sat·is·fac·to·ry \-,sa-təs-'fak-tə-rē\ *adj* ♦ : not satisfactory

♦ bad, deficient, inferior, lousy, off, poor, punk, rotten, substandard, unacceptable, wanting, wretched, wrong

un·sat·u·rat·ed \-'sa-chə-,rā-təd\ *adj* **1** : capable of absorbing or dissolving more of something **2** : containing double or triple bonds between carbon atoms — ⟨~ fats⟩ — **un·sat·u·rate** \-'rət\ *n*
un·saved \-'sāvd\ *adj* : not saved; *esp* : not rescued from eternal punishment
un·sa·vory \-'sā-və-rē\ *adj* **1** : TASTELESS **2** ♦ : unpleasant to taste or smell **3** : morally offensive

♦ distasteful, unappetizing

un·say \-'sā\ *vb* **-said** \-'sed\; **-say·ing** ♦ : to take back (something said) : RETRACT

♦ abjure, recant, renounce, retract, take back, withdraw

un·scathed \-'skāthd\ *adj* : wholly unharmed : not injured
un·schooled \-'skúld\ *adj* : not schooled : UNTAUGHT
un·sci·en·tif·ic \-,sī-ən-'ti-fik\ *adj* : not scientific : not in accord with the principles and methods of science
un·scram·ble \-'skram-bəl\ *vb* **1** : RESOLVE, CLARIFY **2** : to restore (as a radio message) to intelligible form
un·screw \-'skrü\ *vb* **1** : to draw the screws from **2** : to loosen by turning
un·scru·pu·lous \-'skrü-pyə-ləs\ *adj* ♦ : not scrupulous : UNPRINCIPLED — **un·scru·pu·lous·ly** *adv* — **un·scru·pu·lous·ness** *n*

♦ cutthroat, immoral, Machiavellian, unconscionable, unethical, unprincipled

un·seal \-'sēl\ *vb* : to break or remove the seal of : OPEN
un·search·able \-'sər-chə-bəl\ *adj* : not capable of being searched or explored
un·sea·son·able \-'sēz-²n-ə-bəl\ *adj* ♦ : not seasonable : happening or coming at the wrong time : UNTIMELY

♦ early, precocious, premature, untimely

un·sea·son·ably \-'blē\ *adv* ♦ : in an unseasonable manner : at an unseasonable time

♦ beforehand, early, precociously, prematurely

un·seat \-'sēt\ *vb* **1** : to throw from one's seat esp. on horseback **2** : to remove from political office
un·seem·ly \-'sēm-lē\ *adj* **1** : not according with established standards of good form or taste ⟨~ behavior⟩ **2** ♦ : not suitable — **un·seem·li·ness** *n*

♦ improper, inappropriate, inapt, infelicitous, unbecoming, unfit, unsuitable, wrong

un·seen \-'sēn\ *adj* : not seen : INVISIBLE
un·seg·re·gat·ed \-'se-gri-,gā-təd\ *adj* : not segregated; *esp* : free from racial segregation
un·self·ish \-'sel-fish\ *adj* ♦ : not selfish : GENEROUS — **un·self·ish·ly** *adv*

♦ bountiful, charitable, free, generous, liberal, munificent, openhanded, unsparing

un·self·ish·ness *n* ♦ : the quality or state of being unselfish

♦ bounty, generosity, largesse, liberality, philanthropy

un·set·tle \-'set-²l\ *vb* **1** : to move or loosen from a settled position : DISPLACE **2** ♦ : to perturb or agitate mentally or emotionally

♦ agitate, bother, concern, discompose, disquiet, distress, disturb, exercise, freak, perturb, undo, unhinge, upset, worry

un·set·tled \-'set-²ld\ *adj* **1** ♦ : not settled : not fixed (as in position or character) **2** : not calm : DISTURBED **3** ♦ : not decided in mind **4** ♦ : not paid ⟨~ accounts⟩ **5** : not occupied by settlers

♦ [1] open, pending, undecided, undetermined, unresolved ♦ [3] distrustful, doubtful, dubious, mistrustful, skeptical, suspicious, uncertain, undecided, unsure ♦ [4] outstanding, overdue, payable, unpaid

un·set·tling \-'set-²-liŋ\ *adj* ♦ : having the effect of upsetting, disturbing, or discomposing

♦ troublesome, upsetting, worrisome

un·shack·le \-'sha-kəl\ *vb* : to free from shackles
un·shak·able \-'shā-kə-bəl\ *adj* ♦ : not shakable

♦ imperturbable, nerveless, unflappable

un·shak·en \-'shā-kən\ *adj* ♦ : not shaken

♦ calm, collected, composed, cool, placid, self-possessed, serene, tranquil, undisturbed, unperturbed, untroubled, unworried

un·shaped \-'shāpt\ *adj* ♦ : not shaped; *esp* : not being in finished, final, or perfect form ⟨∼ ideas⟩ ⟨∼ timber⟩

♦ amorphous, formless, shapeless, unformed, unstructured

un·sheathe \-'shēth\ *vb* : to draw from or as if from a sheath
un·ship \-'ship\ *vb* **1** : to remove from a ship **2** : to remove or become removed from position ⟨∼ an oar⟩
un·shod \-'shäd\ *adj* : not wearing or provided with shoes
un·shorn \-'shōrn\ *adj* **1** ♦ : not cut **2** : not harvested **3** : not diminished

♦ fleecy, furry, hairy, hirsute, rough, shaggy, woolly

un·sight·ly \-'sīt-lē\ *adj* ♦ : unpleasant to the sight : UGLY

♦ grotesque, hideous, ugly, unappealing, unattractive, unlovely, vile

un·skilled \-'skild\ *adj* **1 a** ♦ : not skilled **b** : not skilled in a specified branch of work **2** : not requiring skill

♦ amateur, amateurish, inexperienced, inexpert, nonprofessional, unprofessional, unskillful

un·skill·ful \-'skil-fəl\ *adj* ♦ : lacking in skill or proficiency — **un·skill·ful·ly** *adv*

♦ incapable, incompetent, inept, inexpert, unfit, unqualified, unskilled

un·sling \-'slin\ *vb* **-slung** \-'slən\; **-sling·ing** : to remove from being slung
un·smil·ing \-'smī-lin\ *adj* ♦ : not smiling

♦ earnest, grave, humorless (*or* humourless), serious, severe, sober, solemn, staid, weighty

un·snap \-'snap\ *vb* : to loosen or free by or as if by undoing a snap
un·snarl \-'snärl\ *vb* : to remove snarls from : UNTANGLE
un·so·cia·ble \-'sō-shə-bəl\ *adj* **1** ♦ : having or showing a disinclination for social activity **2** : not conducive to sociability

♦ aloof, antisocial, cold, cool, detached, distant, frosty, remote, standoffish

un·soiled \-'sóild\ *adj* ♦ : not soiled or dirtied : not sullied

♦ clean, immaculate, spick-and-span, spotless, stainless, unsullied

un·so·lic·it·ed \-sə-'li-sə-təd\ *adj* ♦ : not solicited : not asked for

♦ unasked, unbidden, undesired, uninvited, unsought, unwanted, unwelcome

un·solv·able \-'säl-və-bəl\ *adj* ♦ : not solvable

♦ hopeless, impossible, unattainable, unworkable

un·so·phis·ti·cat·ed \-sə-'fis-tə-,kā-təd\ *adj* **1** ♦ : not worldly-wise : lacking sophistication **2** : SIMPLE

♦ green, ingenuous, innocent, naive, simple, unknowing, unwary, unworldly

un·sought \-'sót\ *adj* ♦ : not sought : not searched for or asked for ⟨∼ honors⟩

♦ unasked, unbidden, undesired, uninvited, unsolicited, unwanted, unwelcome *Ant* desired, solicited, wanted, welcome

un·sound \-'saúnd\ *adj* **1 a** ♦ : not healthy or whole **b** : not mentally normal **2** ♦ : not valid **3** : not firmly made or fixed — **un·sound·ly** *adv*

♦ [1a] bad, down, ill, indisposed, peaked, punk, sick, unhealthy, unwell ♦ [2] fallacious, illogical, invalid, irrational, unreasonable, weak

un·sound·ness *n* ♦ : the quality or state of being unsound

♦ illness, sickness

un·spar·ing \-'spar-in\ *adj* **1** ♦ : not merciful or forbearing : HARD **2** ♦ : not frugal : LIBERAL

♦ [1] callous, hard, heartless, inhuman, inhumane, pitiless, soulless, unfeeling, unsympathetic ♦ [2] bountiful, charitable, free, generous, liberal, munificent, openhanded, unselfish

un·speak·able \-'spē-kə-bəl\ *adj* **1** ♦ : impossible to express in words **2** : extremely bad — **un·speak·ably** \-blē\ *adv*

♦ indescribable, ineffable, inexpressible, nameless, unutterable

un·spec·i·fied \-'spe-sə-,fīd\ *adj* ♦ : not specified

♦ anonymous, certain, one, some, unidentified, unnamed

un·spo·ken \-'spō-kən\ *adj* **1** ♦ : not spoken or uttered **2** : not spoken to or addressed **3** : not speaking

♦ implicit, tacit, unexpressed, unvoiced, wordless

un·sports·man·like \-'spōrts-mən-,līk\ *adj* ♦ : not sportsmanlike : not characteristic of or exhibiting good sportsmanship

♦ dirty, foul, illegal, unfair

un·spot·ted \-'spä-təd\ *adj* : not spotted or stained; *esp* : free from moral stain
un·sprung \-'sprən\ *adj* : not sprung; *esp* : not equipped with springs
un·sta·ble \-'stā-bəl\ *adj* **1 a** ♦ : not stable : not steady in action or movement **b** : lacking steadiness : apt to move, sway, or fall **2** ♦ : wavering in purpose or intent : FICKLE; *also* : lacking effective emotional control **3** : readily changing (as by decomposing) in chemical or physical composition or in biological activity ⟨an ∼ atomic nucleus⟩

♦ [1a] erratic, irregular, unequal, uneven, unsteady ♦ [2] capricious, changeable, fickle, inconstant, mercurial, temperamental, unpredictable, unsettled, unsteady, volatile

un·stained \-'stānd\ *adj* **1** : not stained or discolored : not spotted **2** : not morally blemished or stained
un·stead·i·ness \-'ste-dē-nəs\ *n* ♦ : the quality or state of being unsteady

♦ insecurity, instability, precariousness, shakiness

un·steady \-'ste-dē\ *adj* ♦ : not steady : UNSTABLE — **un·stead·i·ly** \-'sted-ªl-ē\ *adv*

♦ casual, choppy, discontinuous, erratic, fitful, intermittent, irregular, occasional, spasmodic, sporadic, spotty ♦ erratic, irregular, unequal, uneven, unstable

un·stint·ing \-'stin-tin\ *adj* **1** : not restricting or holding back **2** : giving or being given freely or generously ⟨∼ praise⟩
un·stint·ing·ly \-'stin-tin-lē\ *adv* ♦ : in an unstinting manner

♦ amply, bountifully, generously, handsomely, liberally, well

un·stop \-'stäp\ *vb* **1** ♦ : to free from any obstruction : UNCLOG **2** : to remove a stopper from

♦ clear, free, open, unclog

un·stop·pa·ble \-'stä-pə-bəl\ *adj* : incapable of being stopped
un·strap \-'strap\ *vb* : to remove or loose a strap from
un·stressed \-'strest\ *adj* : not stressed; *esp* : not bearing a stress or accent
un·struc·tured \-'strək-chərd\ *adj* ♦ : lacking structure or organization : not formally organized in a set or conventional pattern

♦ amorphous, formless, shapeless, unformed, unshaped

un·strung \-'strən\ *adj* **1** : having the strings loose or detached **2** : made weak, disordered, or unstable
un·stud·ied \-'stə-dēd\ *adj* **1** : not acquired by study **2** : NATURAL, UNFORCED ⟨moved with ∼ grace⟩
un·styl·ish \-'stī-lish\ *adj* ♦ : not stylish

♦ dowdy, inelegant, tacky, tasteless, trashy, unfashionable

un·sub·stan·tial \-səb-'stan-chəl\ *adj* ♦ : not substantial : lacking substance, firmness, or strength

♦ flimsy, gauzy, insubstantial ♦ bodiless, immaterial, incorporeal, insubstantial, nonmaterial, nonphysical, spiritual

un·sub·stan·ti·at·ed \-səb-'stan-chē-,ā-təd\ *adj* ♦ : not substantiated; *esp* : not supported or borne out by fact

♦ baseless, groundless, invalid, unfounded, unreasonable, unsupported, unwarranted

un·suc·cess·ful \-sək-'ses-fəl\ *adj* ♦ : not successful : not meeting with or producing success

♦ fruitless, futile, ineffective, unproductive

un·suit·able \-'sü-tə-bəl\ *adj* ♦ : not suitable or fitting

♦ improper, inappropriate, inapt, infelicitous, unbecoming, unfit, unseemly, wrong

un·sul·lied \-'sə-lēd\ *adj* ♦ : not sullied or stained : spotlessly clean

♦ clean, immaculate, spick-and-span, spotless, stainless, unsoiled

un·sung \-'sən\ *adj* **1** : not sung **2** ♦ : not celebrated in song or verse or otherwise praised ⟨∼ heroes⟩

♦ anonymous, nameless, obscure, unknown

un·sup·port·able \-sə-'pōr-tə-bəl\ *adj* ♦ : not supportable : hardly to be suffered or borne

♦ insufferable, insupportable, intolerable, unbearable, unendurable

un·sup·port·ed \-sə-ˈpōr-təd\ *adj* **1 a** ♦ : not supported or verified **b** : not backed up or assisted **2** : not held up or sustained

    ♦ baseless, groundless, invalid, unfounded, unreasonable, unsubstantiated, unwarranted

un·sure \-ˈshu̇r\ *adj* **1** ♦ : lacking confidence or assurance **2** : not having certain knowledge **3** ♦ : marked by lack of confidence, assurance, or certainty **4** : not steadfast or stable

    ♦ [1, 3] distrustful, doubtful, dubious, mistrustful, skeptical, suspicious, uncertain, undecided, unsettled

un·sur·passed \-sər-ˈpasd\ *adj* ♦ : not surpassed or exceeded usu. in excellence

    ♦ incomparable, inimitable, matchless, nonpareil, only, peerless, unequaled, unmatched, unparalleled, unrivaled

un·sus·pect·ing \-sə-ˈspek-tiŋ\ *adj* **1** : not suspecting : not being suspicious **2** : deficient in worldly wisdom or informed judgment

un·sus·pi·cious \-sə-ˈspi-shəs\ *adj* : UNSUSPECTING

un·swerv·ing \-ˈswer-viŋ\ *adj* **1** : not swerving or turning aside **2** : STEADY

un·sym·pa·thet·ic \-ˌsim-pə-ˈthe-tik\ *adj* ♦ : not sympathetic : not responsive

    ♦ callous, hard, heartless, merciless, pitiless, stony, uncharitable, unfeeling ♦ chill, chilly, cold, cold-blooded, cool, frigid, frosty, glacial, icy, unfriendly, wintry

un·tamed \-ˈtāmd\ *adj* ♦ : not tamed or cultivated; *esp* : WILD

    ♦ feral, savage, unbroken, undomesticated, wild

un·tan·gle \-ˈtaŋ-gəl\ *vb* **1** ♦ : to loose from tangles or entanglement : DISENTANGLE **2** : to straighten out : RESOLVE ⟨∼ a problem⟩

    ♦ disentangle, unravel, untwine ♦ clear, disengage, disentangle, extricate, free, liberate, release

un·taught \-ˈtȯt\ *adj* **1** ♦ : not instructed or taught : IGNORANT **2** : NATURAL, SPONTANEOUS ⟨∼ kindness⟩

    ♦ dark, ignorant, illiterate, simple, uneducated, unlearned

un·think·able \-ˈthiŋ-kə-bəl\ *adj* ♦ : not to be thought of or considered as possible ⟨∼ cruelty⟩

    ♦ fantastic, implausible, inconceivable, incredible, unbelievable, unconvincing, unimaginable

un·think·ing \-ˈthiŋ-kiŋ\ *adj* : not thinking; *esp* : THOUGHTLESS, HEEDLESS ⟨∼ remarks⟩ — **un·think·ing·ly** *adv*

un·thought \ˌən-ˈthȯt\ *adj* : not anticipated : UNEXPECTED — often used with *of* ⟨*unthought*-of development⟩

un·thrifty \-ˈthrif-tē\ *adj* **1** : marked by lack of thrift **2** : not thriving or prospering **3** ♦ : not given to thrift or saving

    ♦ extravagant, prodigal, profligate, spendthrift, thriftless, wasteful

un·ti·dy \-ˈtī-dē\ *adj* **1** : not fit **2 a** ♦ : not neat in appearance **b** : not neat in habits or procedure **3 a** ♦ : not neatly organized or carried out **b** ♦ : marked by or conducive to a lack of neatness

    ♦ [2a] dowdy, frowsy, sloppy, slovenly, unkempt ♦ [3a, b] chaotic, confused, disheveled, disordered, messy

un·tie \-ˈtī\ *vb* **-tied; -ty·ing** *or* **-tie·ing** **1** ♦ : to free from something that ties, fastens, or restrains : UNBIND **2** : DISENTANGLE, RESOLVE **3** : to become loosened or unbound

    ♦ unbind, undo *Ant* bind, fasten, knot, lash, tie

¹un·til \-ˈtil\ *prep* : up to the time of ⟨worked ∼ 5 o'clock⟩

²until *conj* **1** : up to the time that ⟨wait ∼ he calls⟩ **2** : to the point or degree that ⟨ran ∼ she was breathless⟩

¹un·time·ly \-ˈtīm-lē\ *adv* : at an inopportune time : UNSEASONABLY; *also* : PREMATURELY

²untimely *adj* **1** ♦ : happening, arriving, existing, or performed before the proper, usual, or intended time ⟨∼ death⟩ **2** : not convenient esp. in giving trouble or annoyance

    ♦ early, precocious, premature, unseasonable

un·tir·ing \-ˈtī-riŋ\ *adj* ♦ : not becoming tired : INDEFATIGABLE — **un·tir·ing·ly** *adv*

    ♦ indefatigable, inexhaustible, tireless, unflagging

un·ti·tled \-ˈtīt-ᵊld\ *adj* **1** : having no title or right **2** ♦ : not named **3** : not called by a title

    ♦ anonymous, nameless, unbaptized, unchristened, unidentified, unnamed

un·to \ˈən-ˌtü\ *prep* : TO

un·told \ˌən-ˈtōld\ *adj* **1** ♦ : not counted : NUMBERLESS **2** : not told : not revealed

    ♦ countless, innumerable, numberless, uncountable, unnumbered

¹un·touch·able \-ˈtə-chə-bəl\ *adj* **1 a** : forbidden to the touch **b** ♦ : exempt from criticism or control **2** ♦ : lying beyond reach **3** : disagreeable or defiling to the touch

    ♦ [1b] holy, inviolable, sacred, sacrosanct ♦ [2] inaccessible, inconvenient, unapproachable, unattainable, unavailable, unobtainable, unreachable

²untouchable *n* : a member of the lowest social class in India having in traditional Hindu belief the quality of defiling by contact a member of a higher caste

un·touched \-ˈtəcht\ *adj* **1** : not subjected to touching **2** : not described or dealt with **3** : not tasted **4** : being in a primeval state or condition **5** : UNAFFECTED

un·to·ward \ˌən-ˈtōrd, -ˈtō-ərd; ˌən-tə-ˈwȯrd\ *adj* **1** ♦ : difficult to manage : WILLFUL ⟨an ∼ child⟩ **2** : INCONVENIENT, TROUBLESOME ⟨an ∼ encounter⟩

    ♦ contrary, defiant, disobedient, froward, intractable, rebellious, recalcitrant, refractory, uncontrollable, unmanageable, unruly, wayward, willful

un·treat·ed \-ˈtrē-təd\ *adj* ♦ : not subjected to treatment

    ♦ crude, native, natural, raw, undressed, unprocessed, unrefined

un·tried \-ˈtrīd\ *adj* : not tested or proved by experience or trial; *also* : not tried in court

un·trou·bled \-ˈtrə-bəld\ *adj* **1** : marked by calm : without rough motion, storminess, or agitated activity **2** ♦ : not given trouble : not made uneasy **3** ♦ : free from agitation, excitement, or disturbance

    ♦ [2, 3] calm, collected, composed, cool, placid, self-possessed, serene, tranquil, undisturbed, unperturbed, unshaken, unworried

un·true \-ˈtrü\ *adj* **1** ♦ : not faithful : DISLOYAL **2** : not according with a standard of correctness **3** ♦ : not true : FALSE

    ♦ [1] disloyal, faithless, false, fickle, inconstant, loose, perfidious, recreant, traitorous, treacherous, unfaithful ♦ [3] erroneous, false, inaccurate, incorrect, inexact, invalid, off, unsound, wrong

un·trust·wor·thy \-ˈtrəst-ˌwər-thē\ *adj* : not to be trusted : not reliable

un·truth \ˌən-ˈtrüth, ˈən-ˌtrüth\ *n* **1** : lack of truthfulness **2** ♦ : something that is untrue; *esp* : FALSEHOOD **3** : absence of truth or accuracy

    ♦ fabrication, fairy tale, falsehood, falsity, fib, lie, mendacity, prevarication, story, tale, whopper

un·truth·ful \ˌən-ˈtrüth-fəl\ *adj* : not containing or telling the truth : FALSE

un·tune \-ˈtün, -ˈtyün\ *vb* **1** : to put out of tune **2** : DISARRANGE, DISCOMPOSE

un·tu·tored \-ˈtü-tərd, -ˈtyü-\ *adj* : having no formal learning or training : UNLEARNED

un·twine \-ˈtwīn\ *vb* ♦ : to unwind the twisted or tangled parts of : DISENTANGLE

    ♦ disentangle, unravel, untangle

un·twist \-ˈtwist\ *vb* **1** : to separate the twisted parts of : UNTWINE **2** : to become untwined

un·typ·i·cal \-ˈti-pi-kəl\ *adj* ♦ : not typical

    ♦ aberrant, abnormal, anomalous, atypical, deviant, irregular, unnatural

un·us·able \-ˈyü-zə-bəl\ *adj* ♦ : not serviceable : having or being of no use

    ♦ impractical, inoperable, unworkable, useless

un·used \for 1 -ˈyüst, -ˈyüzd; for 2 -ˈyüzd\ *adj* **1** ♦ : not habituated : UNACCUSTOMED **2** ♦ : not used

    ♦ [1] unaccustomed, unadapted, unadjusted *Ant* acclimated, accustomed, adapted, adjusted, habituated, used ♦ [2] brand-new, new, spick-and-span

un·usu·al \-ˈyü-zhə-wəl\ *adj* ♦ : not usual : UNCOMMON — **un·usu·al·ly** *adv*

    ♦ curious, exceptional, extraordinary, funny, odd, peculiar, rare, strange, unaccustomed, uncommon, unique, weird *Ant* common, ordinary, usual

un·ut·ter·able \-ˈə-tə-rə-bəl\ *adj* ♦ : being beyond the powers of description : INEXPRESSIBLE — **un·ut·ter·ably** \-blē\ *adv*

    ♦ indescribable, ineffable, inexpressible, nameless, unspeakable

un·var·nished \-'vär-nisht\ *adj* **1 :** not varnished **2 ♦ :** not embellished **:** PLAIN ⟨the ~ truth⟩

♦ bald, bare, naked, plain, simple, unadorned, undecorated

un·vary·ing \-'ver-ē-iŋ\ *adj* **♦ :** not varying

♦ constant, steady, unchanging, undeviating, uniform, unwavering

un·veil \-'vāl\ *vb* **1 ♦ :** to expose to the public **:** DISCLOSE **2 :** to present publicly for the first time

♦ bare, disclose, discover, divulge, expose, reveal, spill, tell, unbosom, uncloak, uncover, unmask

un·voiced \-'vȯist\ *adj* **1 ♦ :** not verbally expressed **:** UNSPOKEN **2 :** VOICELESS 2

♦ implicit, tacit, unexpressed, unspoken, wordless

un·want·ed \-'wȯn-təd, -'wän-təd\ *adj* **1 ♦ :** not wanted **2 :** not needed or useful **3 :** detrimental in character

♦ unasked, unbidden, undesired, uninvited, unsolicited, unsought, unwelcome

un·war·rant·able \-'wȯr-ən-tə-bəl\ *adj* **♦ :** not justifiable **:** INEXCUSABLE — **un·war·rant·ably** \-blē\ *adv*

♦ indefensible, inexcusable, unforgivable, unjustifiable, unpardonable

un·war·rant·ed \-'wȯr-ən-təd, -'wär-\ *adj* **♦ :** lacking adequate support **:** not justified

♦ baseless, groundless, invalid, unfounded, unreasonable, unsubstantiated, unsupported

un·wary \-'war-ē\ *adj* **1 ♦ :** not experienced or sophisticated **2 ♦ :** careless of consequences **:** not prudent

♦ [1] green, ingenuous, innocent, naive, simple, unknowing, unsophisticated, unworldly ♦ [2] careless, heedless, mindless, unguarded, unsafe

un·wa·ver·ing \-'wā-və-riŋ\ *adj* **♦ :** characterized by absence of fluctuation

♦ steady, unchanging, undeviating, uniform, unvarying

un·weave \-'wēv\ *vb* **-wove** \-'wōv\; **-wo·ven** \-'wō-vən\; **-weav·ing :** DISENTANGLE, RAVEL

un·wed \-'wed\ *adj* **♦ :** not married

♦ single, unattached, unmarried

un·wel·come \-'wel-kəm\ *adj* **1 ♦ :** not welcome **2 ♦ :** causing displeasure or resentment

♦ [1] unasked, unbidden, undesired, uninvited, unsolicited, unsought, unwanted ♦ [2] bad, disagreeable, distasteful, nasty, rotten, sour, uncongenial, unlovely, unpleasant

un·well \-'wel\ *adj* **♦ :** being in poor health **:** SICK

♦ bad, down, ill, indisposed, peaked, punk, sick, unhealthy, unsound

un·whole·some \-'hōl-səm\ *adj* **1 ♦ :** harmful to physical, mental, or moral well-being **2 :** CORRUPT, UNSOUND; *also* **:** offensive to the senses

♦ noisome, noxious, unhealthy

un·wieldy \-'wēl-dē\ *adj* **♦ :** not easily managed, handled, or used (as because of bulk, weight, or complexity) ⟨an ~ tool⟩

♦ awkward, clumsy, cranky, cumbersome, ungainly, unhandy

un·will·ing \-'wi-liŋ\ *adj* **:** not willing

un·wind \-'wīnd\ *vb* **-wound** \-'waund\; **-wind·ing 1 :** to undo something that is wound **:** loose from coils **2 :** to become unwound **:** be capable of being unwound **3 ♦ :** to get rid of nervous tension or anxiety **:** RELAX

♦ chill out, de-stress, relax

un·wise \-'wīz\ *adj* **♦ :** not wise **:** lacking or not showing wisdom or good sense — **un·wise·ly** *adv*

♦ foolish, ill-advised, imprudent, indiscreet, tactless

un·wit·ting \-'wi-tiŋ\ *adj* **1 ♦ :** not knowing **:** UNAWARE **2 ♦ :** not intended **:** INADVERTENT ⟨~ mistake⟩ — **un·wit·ting·ly** *adv*

♦ [1] ignorant, oblivious, unaware, unconscious, uninformed, unknowing ♦ [2] accidental, casual, chance, fluky, fortuitous, inadvertent, incidental, unintended, unintentional, unplanned, unpremeditated

un·wont·ed \-'wȯn-təd, -'wōn-\ *adj* **1 ♦ :** being out of the ordinary **:** UNUSUAL **2 :** not accustomed by experience — **un·wont·ed·ly** *adv*

♦ aberrant, abnormal, atypical, exceptional, extraordinary, freak, odd, peculiar, phenomenal, rare, singular, uncommon, uncustomary, unique, unusual

un·work·able \-'wər-kə-bəl\ *adj* **♦ :** incapable of being put into use or effect or of being accomplished successfully

♦ impractical, inoperable, unusable, useless

un·world·li·ness \-'wərld-lē-nəs\ *n* **♦ :** the quality or state of being unworldly

♦ artlessness, greenness, ingenuousness, innocence, naïveté, naturalness, simplicity

un·world·ly \-'wərld-lē\ *adj* **1 :** not of this world; *esp* **:** SPIRITUAL **2 ♦ :** deficient in worldly wisdom or informed judgment **:** NAIVE **3 :** not swayed by worldly considerations

♦ green, ingenuous, innocent, naive, simple, unknowing, unsophisticated, unwary

un·wor·ried \-'wər-ēd\ *adj* **♦ :** not worried

♦ calm, collected, composed, cool, placid, self-possessed, serene, tranquil, undisturbed, unperturbed, unshaken, untroubled

un·wor·thy \-'wər-thē\ *adj* **1 :** BASE, DISHONORABLE **2 :** not worthy **3 :** not deserved — **un·wor·thi·ly** \-thə-lē\ *adv* — **un·wor·thi·ness** \-thē-nəs\ *n*

un·wrap \-'rap\ *vb* **:** to remove the wrapping from **:** DISCLOSE

un·writ·ten \-'rit-ᵊn\ *adj* **1 ♦ :** not in writing **:** ORAL ⟨an ~ law⟩ **2 :** containing no writing **:** BLANK

♦ oral, spoken, verbal

un·yield·ing \-'yēl-diŋ\ *adj* **1 ♦ :** characterized by lack of softness or flexibility **2 ♦ :** characterized by firmness or obduracy ⟨~ opposition⟩

♦ [1] compact, firm, hard, inflexible, rigid, solid, stiff ♦ [2] determined, dogged, grim, implacable, obstinate, relentless, unflinching, unrelenting

un·yoke \-'yōk\ *vb* **1 :** to remove a yoke from **2 ♦ :** to take apart **:** SEPARATE

♦ break up, disconnect, disjoint, dissever, dissociate, disunite, divide, divorce, part, resolve, separate, sever, split, sunder

un·zip \-'zip\ *vb* **:** to zip open **:** open by means of a zipper

¹up \'əp\ *adv* **1 :** in or to a higher position or level; *esp* **:** away from the center of the earth **2 :** from beneath a surface (as ground or water) **3 :** from below the horizon **4 :** in or into an upright position; *esp* **:** out of bed **5 :** with greater intensity ⟨speak ~⟩ **6 :** in or into a better or more advanced state or a state of greater intensity or activity ⟨stir ~ a fire⟩ **7 :** into existence, evidence, or knowledge ⟨the missing book turned ~⟩ **8 :** into consideration ⟨brought the matter ~⟩ **9 :** to or at bat **10 :** into possession or custody ⟨gave himself ~⟩ **11 :** ENTIRELY, COMPLETELY ⟨eat it ~⟩ **12** — used for emphasis ⟨clean ~ a room⟩ **13 :** ASIDE, BY ⟨lay ~ supplies⟩ **14 :** so as to arrive or approach ⟨ran ~ the path⟩ **15 :** in a direction opposite to down **16 :** in or into parts ⟨tear ~ paper⟩ **17 :** to a stop ⟨pull ~ at the curb⟩ **18 :** for each side ⟨the score was 15 ~⟩

²up *adj* **1 :** risen above the horizon ⟨the sun is ~⟩ **2 :** being out of bed ⟨~ by 6 o'clock⟩ **3 ♦ :** relatively high ⟨prices are ~⟩ **4 :** RAISED, LIFTED ⟨windows are ~⟩ **5 :** BUILT, CONSTRUCTED ⟨the house is ~⟩ **6 :** grown above a surface ⟨the corn is ~⟩ **7 :** moving, inclining, or directed upward **8 :** marked by agitation, excitement, or activity **9 :** READY; *esp* **:** highly prepared **10 :** going on **:** taking place ⟨find out what is ~⟩ **11 :** come to an end **:** ENDED ⟨the time is ~⟩ **12 ♦ :** well informed ⟨~ on the news⟩ **13 :** being ahead or in advance of an opponent ⟨one hole ~ in a match⟩ **14 :** presented for or being under consideration **15 :** charged before a court ⟨~ for robbery⟩

♦ [3] advanced, high ♦ [12] abreast, conversant, familiar, informed, knowledgeable, up-to-date, versed

³up *prep* **1 :** to, toward, or at a higher point of ⟨~ a ladder⟩ **2 :** to or toward the source of ⟨~ the river⟩ **3 :** to or toward the northern part of ⟨~ the coast⟩ **4 :** to or toward the interior of ⟨traveling ~ the country⟩ **5 :** ALONG ⟨walk ~ the street⟩

⁴up *n* **1 :** an upward course or slope **2 :** a period or state of prosperity or success ⟨he had his ~s and downs⟩ **3 :** a quark with a charge of $+^2/_3$ that is one of the constituents of the proton and neutron

⁵up *vb* **upped** \'əpt\ *or in 2* **up; upped; up·ping; ups** *or in 2* **up 1 :** to rise from a lying or sitting position **2 :** to act abruptly or surprisingly ⟨she ~ and left home⟩ **3 ♦ :** to move or cause to move upward ⟨*upped* the prices⟩

♦ add, aggrandize, amplify, augment, boost, compound, enlarge, escalate, expand, extend, increase, multiply, raise, swell
♦ boost, crane, elevate, heave, heft, heighten, hike, hoist, jack, lift, pick up, raise, uphold

Upa·ni·shad \ü-ˈpän-i-ˌshäd\ *n* : one of a set of Vedic philosophical treatises

¹**up·beat** \ˈəp-ˌbēt\ *n* : an unaccented beat in a musical measure; *esp* : the last beat of the measure

²**upbeat** \ˈəp-ˈbēt\ *adj* ♦ : marked by or indicating optimism : CHEERFUL
♦ blithe, bright, buoyant, cheerful, cheery, chipper, lightsome, sunny

up·braid \ˌəp-ˈbrād\ *vb* ♦ : to criticize, reproach, or scold severely
♦ admonish, chide, lecture, rail (at *or* against), rate, rebuke, reprimand, scold

up·bring·ing \ˈəp-ˌbriŋ-iŋ\ *n* : the process of bringing up and training

UPC *abbr* Universal Product Code

up·chuck \ˈəp-ˌchək\ *vb* : VOMIT

up·com·ing \ˈəp-ˌkə-miŋ\ *adj* : coming up; *esp* : being in the near future : FORTHCOMING, APPROACHING

up–coun·try \ˈəp-ˌkən-trē\ *adj* ♦ : of, relating to, or characteristic of an inland, upland, or outlying region — **up–country** \ˈəp-ˈkən-\ *adv*
♦ backwoods, bush, frontier, hinterland, sticks

up·date \ˌəp-ˈdāt\ *vb* : to bring up to date — **update** \ˈəp-ˌdāt\ *n*

up·draft \ˈəp-ˌdraft, -ˌdrȧft\ *n* : an upward movement of gas (as air)

up·end \ˌəp-ˈend\ *vb* 1 : to set, stand, or rise on end 2 : OVERTURN

up–front \ˈəp-ˌfrənt, ˌəp-ˈfrənt\ *adj* 1 : HONEST, CANDID 2 : ADVANCE ⟨~ payment⟩
up front *adv* : in advance ⟨paid *up front*⟩

¹**up·grade** \ˈəp-ˌgrād\ *n* 1 ♦ : an upward grade or slope 2 ♦ : an increase in price, value, rate, or sum : RISE
♦ [1] cant, diagonal, grade, inclination, incline, lean, pitch, slant, slope, tilt ♦ [2] advancement, ascent, elevation, promotion, rise

²**up·grade** \ˈəp-ˌgrād, ˌəp-ˈgrād\ *vb* 1 ♦ : to raise to a higher grade or position; *esp* : to advance to a job requiring a higher level of skill 2 : to improve or replace (as software or a device) for increased usefulness
♦ advance, elevate, promote, raise

up·growth \ˈəp-ˌgrōth\ *n* : the process of growing upward : DEVELOPMENT; *also* : a product or result of this

up·heav·al \ˌəp-ˈhē-vəl\ *n* 1 : the action or an instance of uplifting esp. of part of the earth's crust 2 ♦ : a violent agitation or change
♦ cataclysm, convulsion, paroxysm, storm, tempest, tumult, uproar

¹**up·hill** \ˈəp-ˈhil\ *adv* : upward on a hill or incline; *also* : against difficulties

²**up·hill** \-ˌhil\ *adj* 1 : situated on elevated ground 2 : ASCENDING 3 ♦ : hard to do or make : DIFFICULT, LABORIOUS
♦ arduous, challenging, demanding, difficult, exacting, formidable, grueling, hard, herculean, laborious, murderous, rough, severe, stiff, strenuous, tall, toilsome, tough

up·hold \ˌəp-ˈhōld\ *vb* **-held** \-ˈheld\; **-hold·ing** 1 ♦ : to give support to 2 ♦ : to support or defend against opposition 3 a : to keep elevated b : to lift up — **up·hold·er** *n*
♦ [1] bear, bolster, brace, buttress, carry, prop, shore, stay, support ♦ [2] defend, justify, maintain, support

up·hol·ster \ˌəp-ˈhōl-stər\ *vb* : to furnish with or as if with upholstery — **up·hol·ster·er** *n*

up·hol·stery \-stə-rē\ *n, pl* **-ster·ies** : materials (as fabrics, padding, and springs) used to make a soft covering esp. for a seat

UPI *abbr* United Press International

up·keep \ˈəp-ˌkēp\ *n* ♦ : the act or cost of keeping up or maintaining; *also* : the state of being maintained
♦ conservation, maintenance, preservation

up·land \ˈəp-lənd, -ˌland\ *n* : high land esp. at some distance from the sea — **upland** *adj*

¹**up·lift** \ˌəp-ˈlift\ *vb* 1 : to lift or raise up : ELEVATE 2 : to improve the condition of esp. morally, socially, or intellectually

²**up·lift** \ˈəp-ˌlift\ *n* 1 : a lifting up; *esp* : an upheaval of the

earth's surface 2 : moral or social improvement; *also* : a movement to make such improvement

up·load \ˌəp-ˈlōd, ˈəp-ˌlōd\ *vb* : to transfer (information) from a computer to a remote computer or other device

up·mar·ket \ˌəp-ˈmär-kət\ *adj* : appealing to wealthy consumers

up·most \ˈəp-ˌmōst\ *adj* : in or into the highest or most prominent position : UPPERMOST

up·on \ə-ˈpȯn, -ˈpän\ *prep* : in or in contact with an outer surface : ON

¹**up·per** \ˈə-pər\ *adj* 1 : higher in physical position, rank, or order 2 : constituting the smaller and more restricted branch of a bicameral legislature 3 *cap* : being a later part or formation of a specific geological period 4 : being toward the interior ⟨the ~ Amazon⟩ 5 : NORTHERN ⟨~ Minnesota⟩

²**upper** *n* : one that is upper; *esp* : the parts of a shoe or boot above the sole

up·per·case \ˌə-pər-ˈkās\ *adj* : CAPITAL 1 — **uppercase** *n*

upper class *n* : a social class occupying a position above the middle class and having the highest status in a society — **up·per–class** *adj*

up·per·class·man \ˌə-pər-ˈklas-mən\ *n* : a junior or senior in a college or high school

upper crust *n* : the highest social class or group; *esp* : the highest circle of the upper class

up·per·cut \ˈə-pər-ˌkət\ *n* : a short swinging punch delivered (as in boxing) in an upward direction usu. with a bent arm

upper hand *n* ♦ : superiority of position or condition : ADVANTAGE
♦ advantage, better, drop, edge, jump, vantage

up·per·most \ˈə-pər-ˌmōst\ *adv* : in or into the highest or most prominent position — **uppermost** *adj*

up·pish \ˈə-pish\ *adj* : putting on or marked by airs of superiority : UPPITY ⟨an ~ sales clerk⟩

up·pi·ty \ˈə-pə-tē\ *adj* ♦ : putting on or marked by airs of superiority : ARROGANT
♦ arrogant, cavalier, haughty, highfalutin, high-handed, high-hat, imperious, important, lofty, lordly, overweening, peremptory, pompous, presumptuous, pretentious, supercilious, superior

up·raise \ˌəp-ˈrāz\ *vb* : to raise or lift up : ELEVATE

¹**up·right** \ˈəp-ˌrīt\ *adj* 1 ♦ : perpendicular to the plane of the horizon or to a primary axis : VERTICAL 2 : erect in carriage or posture 3 ♦ : morally correct : JUST ⟨an ~ citizen⟩ — **upright** *adv* — **up·right·ly** *adv*
♦ [1] erect, perpendicular, standing, upstanding, vertical ♦ [3] decent, ethical, good, honest, honorable (*or* honourable), just, moral, right, righteous, straight, virtuous

²**upright** *n* 1 : the state of being upright : a vertical position 2 : something that stands upright

up·right·ness *n* ♦ : the state or quality of being upright
♦ character, decency, goodness, honesty, integrity, morality, probity, rectitude, righteousness, virtue

upright piano *n* : a piano whose strings run vertically

up·ris·ing \ˈəp-ˌrī-ziŋ\ *n* ♦ : an act or instance of rising up : INSURRECTION
♦ insurrection, mutiny, rebellion, revolt, revolution

up·riv·er \ˈəp-ˈri-vər\ *adv or adj* : toward or at a point nearer the source of a river

up·roar \ˈəp-ˌrȯr\ *n* ♦ : a state of commotion, excitement, or violent disturbance
♦ commotion, disturbance, furor, hubbub, hullabaloo, pandemonium, tumult ♦ cataclysm, convulsion, paroxysm, storm, tempest, tumult, upheaval

up·roar·i·ous \ˌəp-ˈrȯr-ē-əs\ *adj* 1 : marked by uproar 2 ♦ : extremely funny — **up·roar·i·ous·ly** *adv*
♦ antic, comic, comical, droll, farcical, funny, hilarious, humorous, hysterical, laughable, ludicrous, ridiculous, riotous, risible, screaming

up·root \ˌəp-ˈrüt, -ˈru̇t\ *vb* 1 ♦ : to remove by or as if by pulling up by the roots 2 : DISPLACE 1 ⟨families were ~ed⟩
♦ extract, prize, pry, pull, root, tear, wrest

¹**up·set** \ˌəp-ˈset\ *vb* **-set**; **-set·ting** 1 : to force or be forced out of the usual upright, level, or proper position 2 ♦ : to disturb emotionally : WORRY; *also* : to make somewhat ill 3 ♦ : to throw into disorder 4 : to defeat unexpectedly
♦ [2] agitate, bother, concern, discompose, disquiet, distress, disturb, exercise, freak, perturb, undo, unhinge, unsettle, worry

♦ [3] confuse, derange, disarray, dishevel, dislocate, disorder, disrupt, jumble, mess, mix, muddle, scramble, shuffle

²**up·set** \'əp-ˌset\ *n* **1** : an upsetting or being upset; *esp* : a minor illness **2 ♦** : a derangement of plans or ideas **3** : an unexpected defeat

♦ derangement, dislocation, disruption, disturbance

³**up·set** \(ˌ)əp-'set\ *adj* ♦ : emotionally disturbed or agitated

♦ aflutter, anxious, edgy, jittery, jumpy, nervous, nervy, perturbed, tense, troubled, uneasy, worried

up·set·ting *adj* ♦ : producing an upset; *esp* : causing an emotional disturbance

♦ troublesome, unsettling, worrisome

up·shot \'əp-ˌshät\ *n* ♦ : the final result

♦ aftermath, conclusion, consequence, corollary, development, effect, issue, outcome, outgrowth, product, result, resultant, sequence

¹**up·side** \'əp-ˌsīd\ *n* **1** : the upper side **2** : a positive aspect **3** : PROMISE 2 ⟨rookies with much ∼⟩

²**up·side** \ˌəp-'sīd\ *prep* : up on or against the side of ⟨knocked him ∼ the head⟩

up·side down \ˌəp-ˌsīd-'daun\ *adv* **1** : with the upper and the lower parts reversed in position **2** : in or into confusion or disorder — **upside–down** *adj*

up·si·lon \'üp-sə-ˌlän, 'yüp-, -əp-\ *n* : the 20th letter of the Greek alphabet — Y or υ

¹**up·stage** \'əp-'stāj\ *adv or adj* : toward or at the rear of a theatrical stage

²**up·stage** \ˌəp-'stāj\ *vb* : to draw attention away from (as an actor)

¹**up·stairs** \ˌəp-'starz\ *adv* **1** : up the stairs : to or on a higher floor **2** : to or at a higher position

²**up·stairs** \'əp-'starz\ *adj* : situated above the stairs esp. on an upper floor ⟨∼ bedroom⟩

³**up·stairs** \'əp-'starz, 'əp-ˌstarz\ *n sing or pl* : the part of a building above the ground floor

up·stand·ing \ˌəp-'stan-diŋ, 'əp-\ *adj* **1** : vertical in position : ERECT **2 ♦** : marked by integrity : HONEST ⟨∼ citizens⟩

♦ decent, ethical, honest, honorable, just, noble, principled, respectable, righteous, upright

¹**up·start** \ˌəp-'start\ *vb* : to jump up suddenly

²**up·start** \'əp-ˌstart\ *n* : one that has risen suddenly; *esp* : one that claims more personal importance than is warranted — **up·start** \-'start\ *adj*

up·state \'əp-'stāt\ *adj* : of, relating to, or characteristic of a part of a state away from a large city and esp. to the north — **upstate** *adv* — **upstate** *n*

up·stream \'əp-'strēm\ *adv* : at or toward the source of a stream — **upstream** *adj*

up·stroke \'əp-ˌstrōk\ *n* : an upward stroke (as of a pen)

up·surge \-ˌsərj\ *n* : a rapid or sudden rise

up·swept \'əp-ˌswept\ *adj* : swept upward ⟨∼ hairdo⟩

up·swing \'əp-ˌswiŋ\ *n* : an upward swing; *esp* : a marked increase or rise (as in activity)

up·take \'əp-ˌtāk\ *n* **1** : UNDERSTANDING, COMPREHENSION ⟨quick on the ∼⟩ **2** : an act or instance of absorbing and incorporating esp. into a living organism, tissue, or cell

up·thrust \'əp-ˌthrəst\ *n* : an upward thrust (as of the earth's crust) — **upthrust** *vb*

up·tight \'əp-'tīt\ *adj* **1** : being tense, nervous, or uneasy : NERVOUS; *also* : INDIGNANT **2** : rigidly conventional

up–to–date *adj* **1** : extending up to the present time **2 ♦** : being, having, or involving modern techniques, methods, or information — **up–to–date·ness** *n*

♦ contemporary, current, hot, mod, modern, new, newfangled, red-hot, space-age, ultramodern ♦ abreast, conversant, familiar, informed, knowledgeable, up, versed

up·town \'əp-ˌtaun\ *n* : the upper part of a town or city; *esp* : the residential district — **up·town** \'əp-'taun\ *adj or adv*

¹**up·turn** \'əp-ˌtərn, ˌəp-'tərn\ *vb* **1** : to turn (as earth) up or over **2** : to turn or direct upward

²**up·turn** \'əp-ˌtərn\ *n* : an upward turn esp. toward better conditions or higher prices

¹**up·ward** \'əp-wərd\ *or* **up·wards** \-wərdz\ *adv* **1** : in a direction from lower to higher **2** : toward a higher or better condition **3** : toward a greater amount or higher number, degree, or rate

²**upward** *adj* : directed or moving toward or situated in a higher place or level : ASCENDING — **up·ward·ly** *adv*

upwards of *also* **upward of** *adv* : more than : in excess of ⟨they cost *upwards of* $25 each⟩

up·well \ˌəp-'wel\ *vb* : to move or flow upward

up·well·ing \-'we-liŋ\ *n* : a rising or an appearance of rising to the surface and flowing outward; *esp* : the movement of deep cold usu. nutrient-rich ocean water to the surface

up·wind \'əp-'wind\ *adv or adj* : in the direction from which the wind is blowing

ura·cil \'yur-ə-ˌsil\ *n* : a pyrimidine base that is one of the four bases coding genetic information in the molecular chain of RNA

ura·ni·um \yu-'rā-nē-əm\ *n* : a silvery heavy radioactive metallic chemical element used as a source of atomic energy

Ura·nus \'yur-ə-nəs, yu-'rā-\ *n* : the planet 7th in order from the sun

ur·ban \'ər-bən\ *adj* : of, relating to, characteristic of, or constituting a city

ur·bane \ˌər-'bān\ *adj* ♦ : very polite and polished in manner : SUAVE

♦ debonair, smooth, sophisticated, suave

ur·ban·ite \'ər-bə-ˌnīt\ *n* : a person who lives in a city

ur·ban·i·ty \ˌər-'ba-nə-tē\ *n, pl* **-ties** : the quality or state of being urbane

ur·ban·ize \'ər-bə-ˌnīz\ *vb* **-ized; -iz·ing** : to cause to take on urban characteristics — **ur·ban·i·za·tion** \ˌər-bə-nə-'zā-shən\ *n*

ur·chin \'ər-chən\ *n* ♦ : a pert or mischievous youngster

♦ devil, hellion, imp, mischief, monkey, rapscallion, rascal, rogue, scamp

Ur·du \'ur-dü, 'ər-\ *n* : a language that is the official language of Pakistan and that is widely used by Muslims in urban areas of India

urea \yu-'rē-ə\ *n* : a soluble nitrogenous compound that is the chief solid constituent of mammalian urine

ure·mia \yu-'rē-mē-ə\ *n* : accumulation in the blood of materials normally passed off in the urine resulting in a poisoned condition — **ure·mic** \-mik\ *adj*

ure·ter \'yur-ə-tər\ *n* : a duct that carries the urine from a kidney to the bladder

ure·thra \yu-'rē-thrə\ *n, pl* **-thras** *or* **-thrae** \-(ˌ)thrē\ : the canal that in most mammals carries off the urine from the bladder and in the male also serves to carry semen from the body — **ure·thral** \-thrəl\ *adj*

ure·thri·tis \ˌyur-i-'thrī-təs\ *n* : inflammation of the urethra

¹**urge** \'ərj\ *vb* **urged; urg·ing 1** : to present, advocate, or demand earnestly **2 ♦** : to try to persuade or sway ⟨∼ a guest to stay⟩ **3** : to serve as a motive or reason for **4 ♦** : to impress or impel to some course or activity ⟨*urged* him to stay⟩ ⟨the dog *urged* the sheep onward⟩

♦ [2, 4] egg on, encourage, exhort, goad, press, prod, prompt

²**urge** *n* **1** : the act or process of urging **2 ♦** : a force or impulse that urges or drives

♦ appetite, craving, desire, drive, hankering, hunger, itch, longing, lust, passion, thirst, yearning, yen

ur·gent \'ər-jənt\ *adj* **1 ♦** : calling for immediate attention : PRESSING **2** : urging insistently — **ur·gen·cy** \-jən-sē\ *n* — **ur·gent·ly** *adv*

♦ acute, critical, dire, imperative, imperious, instant, pressing

uric \'yur-ik\ *adj* : of, relating to, or found in urine

uric acid *n* : a nearly insoluble acid that is the chief nitrogenous excretory product of birds but is present in only small amounts in mammalian urine

uri·nal \'yur-ən-ᵊl\ *n* **1** : a receptacle for urine **2** : a place for urinating

uri·nal·y·sis \ˌyur-ə-'na-lə-səs\ *n* : chemical analysis of urine

uri·nary \'yur-ə-ˌner-ē\ *adj* **1** : relating to, occurring in, or being organs for the formation and discharge of urine **2** : of, relating to, or for urine

urinary bladder *n* : a membranous sac in many vertebrates that serves for the temporary retention of urine and discharges by the urethra

uri·nate \'yur-ə-ˌnāt\ *vb* **-nat·ed; -nat·ing** : to release or give off urine — **uri·na·tion** \ˌyur-ə-'nā-shən\ *n*

urine \'yur-ən\ *n* : a waste material from the kidneys that is usu. a yellowish watery liquid in mammals but is semisolid in birds and reptiles

URL \ˌyü-(ˌ)är-'el, 'ər(-ə)l\ *n* : a series of usu. alphanumeric characters that specifies the storage location of a resource on the Internet

urn \'ərn\ *n* **1** : a vessel that typically has the form of a vase on a pedestal and often is used to hold the ashes of the dead **2 :** a closed vessel usu. with a spout for serving a hot beverage

uro·gen·i·tal \ˌyu̇r-ō-ˈje-nət-ᵊl\ *adj* **:** of, relating to, or being the excretory and reproductive organs or functions

urol·o·gy \yu̇-ˈrä-lə-jē\ *n* **:** a branch of medical science dealing with the urinary or urogenital tract and its disorders — **uro·log·i·cal** \ˌyu̇r-ə-ˈlä-ji-kəl\ *also* **uro·log·ic** \-jik\ *adj* — **urol·o·gist** \yu̇-ˈrä-lə-jist\ *n*

Ur·sa Ma·jor \ˌər-sə-ˈmā-jər\ *n* **:** the northern constellation that contains the stars which form the Big Dipper

Ursa Mi·nor \-ˈmī-nər\ *n* **:** the constellation including the north pole of the heavens and the stars that form the Little Dipper with the North Star at the tip of the handle

ur·sine \ˈər-ˌsīn\ *adj* **:** of, relating to, or resembling a bear

ur·ti·car·ia \ˌər-tə-ˈkar-ē-ə\ *n* **:** HIVES

Uru·guay·an \ˌu̇r-ə-ˈgwī-ən, ˌyu̇r-ə-ˈgwä-\ *n* **:** a native or inhabitant of Uruguay — **Uruguayan** *adj*

us \ˈəs\ *pron, objective case of* WE

US *abbr* United States

USA *abbr* **1** United States Army **2** United States of America

us·able *also* **use·able** \ˈyü-zə-bəl\ *adj* ♦ **:** suitable or fit for use — **us·abil·i·ty** \ˌyü-zə-ˈbi-lə-tē\ *n*

  ♦ available, fit, functional, operable, practicable, serviceable, useful *Ant* impracticable, inoperable, nonfunctional, unavailable, unusable

USAF *abbr* United States Air Force

us·age \ˈyü-sij, -zij\ *n* **1 :** habitual or customary practice or procedure **2 :** the way in which words and phrases are actually used **3 :** the action or mode of using **4 :** manner of treating

USB \ˌyü-(ˌ)es-ˈbē\ *n* **:** a standardized computer interface for attaching peripherals

USCG *abbr* United States Coast Guard

USDA *abbr* United States Department of Agriculture

¹**use** \ˈyüs\ *n* **1** ♦ **:** the act or practice of using or employing something **:** EMPLOYMENT, APPLICATION **2 :** the fact or state of being used **3 :** the way of using **4 :** habitual or customary usage **:** USAGE, CUSTOM **5 :** the privilege or benefit of using something **6 :** the ability or power to use something (as a limb) **7 :** the legal enjoyment of property that consists in its employment, occupation, or exercise; *also* **:** the benefit or profit esp. from property held in trust **8** ♦ **:** a particular service or end **:** UTILITY **9 :** the occasion or need to employ (he had no more ∼ for it) **10** ♦ **:** a favorable attitude **:** LIKING (had no ∼ for modern art)

  ♦ [1] application, employment, exercise, operation, play ♦ [8] account, avail, service, utility *Ant* uselessness, worthlessness ♦ [10] appetite, fancy, favor (*or* favour), fondness, like, liking, love, partiality, preference, relish, shine, taste

²**use** \ˈyüz\ *vb* **used** \ˈyüzd; *"used to" usu* ˈyüs-tə\; **us·ing** **1** ♦ **:** to put into action or service **:** EMPLOY **2 :** to consume or take (as drugs) regularly **3 a :** UTILIZE (∼ tact) **b** ♦ **:** to control or play upon by artful, unfair, or insidious means esp. to one's own advantage (*used* his friends to get ahead) **4 :** to expend or consume by putting to use **5** ♦ **:** to behave toward **:** TREAT (*used* the horse cruelly) **6 :** to benefit from (house could ∼ a coat of paint) **7** — used in the past with *to* to indicate a former practice, fact, or state (we *used* to work harder)

  ♦ [1] apply, employ, exercise, exploit, harness, operate, utilize ♦ [3b] abuse, capitalize, cash in, exploit, impose, play ♦ [5] act, be, deal, handle, serve, treat

used \ˈyüzd\ *adj* **1 :** having been used by another **:** SECONDHAND (∼ cars) **2** ♦ **:** being in the habit or custom **:** ACCUSTOMED (∼ to the heat)

  ♦ accustomed, given, wont

use·ful \ˈyüs-fəl\ *adj* ♦ **:** capable of being put to use; *esp* **:** serviceable for a beneficial end — **use·ful·ly** *adv*

  ♦ applicable, functional, practicable, practical, serviceable, usable, workable, working

use·ful·ness *n* **:** the quality of having utility and esp. practical worth or applicability

use·less \-ləs\ *adj* ♦ **:** having or being of no use — **use·less·ly** *adv* — **use·less·ness** *n*

  ♦ impractical, inoperable, unusable, unworkable ♦ fruitless, futile, ineffective, unproductive, unsuccessful

us·er *n* ♦ **:** one that uses; *esp* **:** a person who regularly uses alcoholic beverages or narcotics

  ♦ addict, doper, fiend

us·er·name \ˈyü-zər-ˌnām\ *n* **:** a sequence of characters that identifies a user when logging onto a computer or website

USES *abbr* United States Employment Service

use up *vb* ♦ **:** to consume completely

  ♦ clean, consume, deplete, drain, exhaust, expend, spend

¹**ush·er** \ˈə-shər\ *n* **1 :** an officer who walks before a person of rank **2 :** one who escorts people to their seats (as in a church or theater)

²**usher** *vb* **1** ♦ **:** to conduct to a place **2 :** to precede as an usher, forerunner, or harbinger **3 :** INAUGURATE, INTRODUCE (∼ in a new era)

  ♦ conduct, direct, guide, lead, marshal, pilot, route, show, steer

ush·er·ette \ˌə-shə-ˈret\ *n* **:** a girl or woman who is an usher (as in a theater)

USIA *abbr* United States Information Agency

USMC *abbr* United States Marine Corps

USN *abbr* United States Navy

USO *abbr* United Service Organizations

USP *abbr* United States Pharmacopeia

USPS *abbr* United States Postal Service

USS *abbr* United States ship

USSR *abbr* Union of Soviet Socialist Republics

usu *abbr* usual; usually

usu·al \ˈyü-zhə-wəl\ *adj* **1 :** accordant with usage, custom, or habit **2** ♦ **:** commonly or ordinarily used **3** ♦ **:** of a kind to be expected in the normal order of events **:** ORDINARY

  ♦ [2] conventional, current, customary, popular, standard, stock ♦ [3] average, common, commonplace, everyday, normal, ordinary, prosaic, routine, run-of-the-mill, standard, unexceptional, unremarkable, workaday

usu·al·ly \ˈyü-zhə-wə-lē, ˈyü-zhə-lē\ *adv* ♦ **:** more often than not **:** as a rule

  ♦ commonly, generally, naturally, normally, ordinarily, typically

usu·fruct \ˈyü-zə-ˌfrəkt\ *n* **:** the legal right to use and enjoy the benefits and profits of something belonging to another

usu·rer \ˈyü-zhər-ər\ *n* **:** one that lends money esp. at an exorbitant rate

usu·ri·ous \yu̇-ˈzhu̇r-ē-əs\ *adj* **:** practicing, involving, or constituting usury (a ∼ rate of interest)

usurp \yu̇-ˈsərp, -ˈzərp\ *vb* ♦ **:** to seize and hold by force or without right (∼ a throne) — **usur·pa·tion** \ˌyü-sər-ˈpā-shən, -zər-\ *n* — **usurp·er** \yu̇-ˈsər-pər, -ˈzər-\ *n*

  ♦ appropriate, arrogate, commandeer, preempt

usu·ry \ˈyü-zhə-rē\ *n, pl* **-ries 1 :** the lending of money with an interest charge for its use **2 :** an excessive rate or amount of interest charged; *esp* **:** interest above an established legal rate

UT *abbr* Utah

Ute \ˈyüt\ *n, pl* **Ute** *or* **Utes :** a member of an Indigenous people orig. ranging through Utah, Colorado, Arizona, and New Mexico; *also* **:** the language of the Ute people

uten·sil \yu̇-ˈten-səl\ *n* **1 :** an instrument or vessel used in a household and esp. a kitchen **2** ♦ **:** a useful tool

  ♦ device, implement, instrument, tool

uter·us \ˈyü-tə-rəs\ *n, pl* **uter·us·es** *or* **uteri** \ˈyü-tə-ˌrī\ **:** the muscular organ of a female mammal in which the young develop before birth — **uter·ine** \-ˌrīn, -rən\ *adj*

utile \ˈyüt-ᵊl, ˈyü-ˌtīl\ *adj* **:** USEFUL

uti·lise *chiefly Brit var of* UTILIZE

¹**util·i·tar·i·an** \yu̇-ˌti-lə-ˈter-ē-ən\ *n* **:** a person who believes in utilitarianism

²**utilitarian** *adj* **1 :** of or relating to utilitarianism **2 :** of or relating to utility **:** aiming at usefulness rather than beauty; *also* **:** serving a useful purpose

util·i·tar·i·an·ism \-ē-ə-ˌni-zəm\ *n* **:** a theory that the greatest good for the greatest number should be the main consideration in making a choice of actions

¹**util·i·ty** \yu̇-ˈti-lə-tē\ *n, pl* **-ties 1** ♦ **:** fitness for some purpose or worth to some end **:** USEFULNESS **2 :** something useful or designed for use **3 :** a business organization performing a public service and subject to special governmental regulation **4 :** a public service or a commodity (as electricity or water) provided by a public utility; *also* **:** equipment to provide such or a similar service

  ♦ account, avail, service, use

²**utility** *adj* **1 :** capable of serving esp. as a substitute in various uses or positions (a ∼ outfielder) **2 :** being of a usable but poor quality (∼ beef)

utility knife *n* : a knife designed for general use; *esp* : one with a retractable blade

uti·lize \'yüt-ᵊl-ˌīz\ *vb* **-lized; -liz·ing** ♦ : to make use of : turn to profitable use — **uti·li·za·tion** \ˌyüt-ᵊl-ə-'zā-shən\ *n*

♦ apply, employ, exercise, exploit, harness, operate, use

ut·most \'ət-ˌmōst\ *adj* **1** ♦ : situated at the farthest or most distant point : EXTREME **2** ♦ : of the greatest or highest degree, quantity, number, or amount — **utmost** *n*

♦ [1] extreme, farthest, furthest, outermost, ultimate ♦ [2] consummate, maximum, most, nth, paramount, supreme, top, ultimate

uto·pia \yu̇-'tō-pē-ə\ *n* **1** *often cap* ♦ : a place of ideal perfection esp. in laws, government, and social conditions **2** : an impractical scheme for social improvement

♦ Eden, Elysium, heaven, paradise

¹**uto·pi·an** \-pē-ən\ *adj, often cap* **1** : of, relating to, or resembling a utopia **2** : proposing ideal social and political schemes that are impractical **3** : VISIONARY

²**utopian** *n* **1** ♦ : a believer in the perfectibility of human society **2** : one who proposes or advocates utopian schemes

♦ dreamer, idealist, romantic, visionary

¹**ut·ter** \'ə-tər\ *adj* : carried to the utmost point or highest degree : ABSOLUTE ⟨∼ ruin⟩

²**utter** *vb* **1** ♦ : to send forth as a sound : express in usu. spoken words **2** : to put (as currency) into circulation — **ut·ter·er** *n*

♦ articulate, say, speak, state, talk, tell, verbalize, vocalize

ut·ter·ance \'ə-tə-rəns\ *n* **1** : something uttered; *esp* : an oral or written statement **2** ♦ : the action of uttering with the voice **3** : power, style, or manner of speaking

♦ articulation, expression, formulation, statement, voice

ut·ter·ly *adv* ♦ : to the full extent

♦ absolutely, all, altogether, clean, completely, entirely, fully, quite, totally, wholly

ut·ter·most \'ə-tər-ˌmōst\ *adj* : existing in a very high degree : UTMOST ⟨the ∼ parts of the earth⟩ — **uttermost** *n*

U–turn \'yü-ˌtərn\ *n* : a turn resembling the letter U; *esp* : a 180-degree turn made by a vehicle in a road

UV *abbr* ultraviolet

uvu·la \'yü-vyə-lə\ *n, pl* **-las** *or* **-lae** \-ˌlē, -ˌlī\ : the fleshy lobe hanging at the back of the roof of the mouth — **uvu·lar** \-lər\ *adj*

UW *abbr* underwriter

ux·o·ri·ous \ˌək-'sōr-ē-əs, ˌəg-'zōr-\ *adj* : excessively devoted or submissive to a wife

¹**v** \'vē\ *n, pl* **v's** *or* **vs** \'vēz\ *often cap* : the 22d letter of the English alphabet

²**v** *abbr, often cap* **1** vector **2** velocity **3** verb **4** verse **5** versus **6** very **7** victory **8** vide **9** voice **10** voltage **11** volume **12** vowel

V *symbol* **1** vanadium **2** volt

Va *abbr* Virginia

VA *abbr* **1** Veterans Administration **2** vice admiral **3** Virginia

va·can·cy \'vā-kən-sē\ *n, pl* **-cies** **1** : a vacating esp. of an office, position, or piece of property **2** : a vacant office, position, or tenancy; *also* : the period during which it stands vacant **3** ♦ : empty space : VOID **4** ♦ : the state of being vacant

♦ [3] blank, blankness, emptiness, vacuity, void ♦ [4] emptiness, vacuity *Ant* fullness

va·cant \'vā-kənt\ *adj* **1** : not occupied ⟨∼ seat⟩ ⟨∼ room⟩ **2** ♦ : devoid of contents : EMPTY ⟨∼ space⟩ **3** ♦ : free from business or care ⟨a few ∼ hours⟩ **4** ♦ : devoid of thought, reflection, or expression ⟨a ∼ smile⟩ — **va·cant·ly** *adv*

♦ [2] bare, blank, devoid, empty, stark, void ♦ [3] dead, dormant, fallow, free, idle, inactive, inert, inoperative, latent, off ♦ [4] blank, deadpan, expressionless, impassive, inexpressive, stolid

va·cate \'vā-ˌkāt\ *vb* **va·cat·ed; va·cat·ing** **1** : to make void : ANNUL **2** ♦ : to make vacant (as an office or house); *also* : to give up the occupancy of

♦ clear, empty, evacuate, void

¹**va·ca·tion** \vā-'kā-shən, və-\ *n* ♦ : a period of rest from work

♦ break, leave, recess

²**vacation** *vb* : to take or spend a vacation — **va·ca·tion·er** *n*

va·ca·tion·ist \-shə-nist\ *n* : a person taking a vacation

va·ca·tion·land \-shən-ˌland\ *n* : an area with recreational attractions and facilities for vacationists

vac·ci·nate \'vak-sə-ˌnāt\ *vb* **-nat·ed; -nat·ing** : to administer a vaccine to usu. by injection

vac·ci·na·tion \ˌvak-sə-'nā-shən\ *n* **1** : the act of vaccinating **2** : the scar left by vaccinating

vac·cine \vak-'sēn, 'vak-ˌsēn\ *n* : material (as a preparation of killed or weakened virus or bacteria) used in vaccinating to induce immunity to a disease

vac·cin·ia \vak-'si-nē-ə\ *n* : COWPOX

vac·il·late \'va-sə-ˌlāt\ *vb* **-lat·ed; -lat·ing** **1** : SWAY, TOTTER; *also* : FLUCTUATE **2** ♦ : to incline first to one course or opinion and then to another : WAVER

♦ falter, hang back, hesitate, shilly-shally, stagger, teeter, waver, wobble

vac·il·la·tion \ˌva-sə-'lā-shən\ *n* ♦ : an act or instance of vacillating

♦ hesitancy, hesitation, indecision, irresolution

va·cu·ity \va-'kyü-ə-tē\ *n, pl* **-ities** **1** ♦ : an empty space **2** ♦ : the state, fact, or quality of being vacuous **3** : something that is vacuous

♦ [1, 2] blank, blankness, emptiness, vacancy, void ♦ [2] dopiness, mindlessness, stupidity

vac·u·ole \'va-kyə-ˌwōl\ *n* : a usu. fluid-filled cavity esp. in the cytoplasm of an individual cell — **vac·u·o·lar** \ˌva-kyə-'wō-lər, -ˌlär\ *adj*

vac·u·ous \'va-kyə-wəs\ *adj* **1** : EMPTY, VACANT, BLANK **2** ♦ : marked by or indicative of a lack of ideas or intelligence : DULL — **vac·u·ous·ly** *adv* — **vac·u·ous·ness** *n*

♦ dense, dull, dumb, mindless, simple, slow, stupid, unintelligent, witless

¹**vac·u·um** \'va-(ˌ)kyüm, -kyəm\ *n, pl* **vacuums** *or* **vac·ua** \-kyə-wə\ **1** : a space entirely empty of matter **2** : a space from which most of the air has been removed (as by a pump) **3** : VOID, GAP **4** : VACUUM CLEANER — **vacuum** *adj*

²**vacuum** *vb* : to use a vacuum device (as a vacuum cleaner) on

vacuum bottle *n* : THERMOS

vacuum cleaner *n* : a household appliance for cleaning (as floors or rugs) by suction

vacuum–packed *adj* : having much of the air removed before being hermetically sealed

vacuum tube *n* : an electron tube from which most of the air has been removed

va·de me·cum \ˌvā-dē-'mē-kəm, ˌvä-dē-'mā-\ *n, pl* **vade me·cums** : something (as a handbook or manual) regularly carried about

VADM *abbr* vice admiral

¹**vag·a·bond** \'va-gə-ˌbänd\ *adj* **1** ♦ : moving from place to place without a fixed home : WANDERING **2** : of, relating to, or characteristic of a wanderer; *esp* : of, characteristic of, or leading the life of a vagrant or tramp **3** : leading an unsettled or irresponsible life

♦ errant, itinerant, nomad, nomadic, peripatetic, roaming, vagrant

²**vagabond** *n* **1** ♦ : one leading a vagabond life **2** ♦ : an idle beggar : TRAMP

♦ [1] drifter, nomad, rambler, rover, stroller, wanderer ♦ [2] bum, hobo, tramp, vagrant

va·ga·ry \'vā-gə-rē, və-'ger-ē\ *n, pl* **-ries** ♦ : an odd or eccentric idea or action : WHIM, CAPRICE

♦ caprice, fancy, freak, notion, whim

va·gi·na \və-ˈjī-nə\ *n*, *pl* **-nae** \-(ˌ)nē\ *or* **-nas** : a canal that leads from the uterus to the external opening of the female sex organs — **vag·i·nal** \ˈva-jən-ᵊl\ *adj* — **vag·i·nal·ly** \-nᵊl-ē\ *adv*

vag·i·ni·tis \ˌva-jə-ˈnī-təs\ *n* : inflammation of the vagina

va·gran·cy \ˈvā-grən-sē\ *n*, *pl* **-cies** 1 : the quality or state of being vagrant; *also* : a vagrant act or notion 2 : the offense of being a vagrant

¹**va·grant** \ˈvā-grənt\ *n* ♦ : a person who has no job and wanders from place to place

  ♦ bum, hobo, tramp, vagabond

²**vagrant** *adj* 1 ♦ : of, relating to, or characteristic of a vagrant 2 : following no fixed course : RANDOM, CAPRICIOUS ⟨∼ thoughts⟩ — **va·grant·ly** *adv*

  ♦ errant, itinerant, nomad, nomadic, peripatetic, roaming, vagabond

vague \ˈvāg\ *adj* **vagu·er**; **vagu·est** 1 ♦ : not clear, definite, or distinct in expression or perception 2 : not clearly felt or analyzed ⟨a ∼ unrest⟩ — **vague·ly** *adv* — **vague·ness** *n*

  ♦ fuzzy, indefinite, unclear *Ant* clear, definite, explicit, specific ♦ bleary, dim, faint, foggy, fuzzy, hazy, indefinite, indistinct, indistinguishable, murky, nebulous, obscure, opaque, shadowy, unclear, undefined, undetermined

vain \ˈvān\ *adj* 1 : of no real value : IDLE, WORTHLESS 2 ♦ : marked by a lack of effectiveness or success : UNSUCCESSFUL 3 ♦ : proud of one's looks or abilities — **vain·ly** *adv*

  ♦ [2] fruitless, futile, ineffective, unproductive, unsuccessful ♦ [3] complacent, conceited, egotistic, important, overweening, pompous, prideful, proud, self-important, self-satisfied, smug, stuck-up

vain·glo·ri·ous \ˌvān-ˈglōr-ē-əs\ *adj* : marked by vainglory : being vain

vain·glo·ry \ˈvān-ˌglōr-ē\ *n* 1 ♦ : excessive or ostentatious pride esp. in one's own achievements 2 : vain display : VANITY

  ♦ complacence, conceit, ego, egotism, pride, self-conceit, self-esteem, self-importance, self-satisfaction, smugness, vanity

val *abbr* value; valued

va·lance \ˈva-ləns, ˈvā-\ *n* 1 : drapery hanging from an edge (as of an altar, table, or bed) 2 : a drapery or a decorative frame across the top of a window

vale \ˈvāl\ *n* : a low-lying country or tract usu. containing a brook or a stream : VALLEY

vale·dic·tion \ˌva-lə-ˈdik-shən\ *n* : an act or utterance of leave-taking : FAREWELL

vale·dic·to·ri·an \-ˌdik-ˈtōr-ē-ən\ *n* : the student usu. of the highest rank in a graduating class who delivers the valedictory address at commencement

vale·dic·to·ry \-ˈdik-tə-rē\ *adj* : bidding farewell : delivered as a valediction ⟨a ∼ address⟩ — **valedictory** *n*

va·lence \ˈvā-ləns\ *n* : the combining power of an atom as shown by the number of its electrons that are lost, gained, or shared in the formation of chemical bonds

Va·len·ci·ennes \və-ˌlen-sē-ˈen, ˌva-lən-sē-, -ˈenz\ *n* : a fine handmade lace

val·en·tine \ˈva-lən-ˌtīn\ *n* : a sweetheart chosen or complimented on Valentine's Day; *also* : a gift or greeting given on this day

Valentine's Day *also* **Valentine Day** *n* : February 14 observed in honor of St. Valentine and as a time for exchanging valentines

¹**va·let** \ˈva-lət, -(ˌ)lā; va-ˈlā\ *n* 1 : a male servant who takes care of a man's clothes and performs personal services 2 : an attendant in a hotel or restaurant who performs personal services (as parking cars) for customers

²**valet** *vb* : to serve as a valet

val·e·tu·di·nar·i·an \ˌva-lə-ˌtüd-ᵊn-ˈer-ē-ən, -ˌtyüd-\ *n* : a person of a weak or sickly constitution; *esp* : one whose chief concern is his or her ill health — **val·e·tu·di·nar·i·an·ism** \-ē-ə-ˌni-zəm\ *n*

val·iant \ˈval-yənt\ *adj* ♦ : having or showing valor : BRAVE — **val·iant·ly** *adv*

  ♦ brave, courageous, dauntless, doughty, fearless, gallant, great-hearted, heroic, intrepid, lionhearted, manful, stalwart, stout, undaunted, valorous

val·id \ˈva-ləd\ *adj* 1 : having legal force ⟨a ∼ contract⟩ 2 ♦ : founded on truth or fact : capable of being justified or defended ⟨∼ argument⟩ ⟨∼ reasons⟩ — **va·lid·i·ty** \və-ˈli-də-tē\ *n* — **val·id·ly** *adv*

  ♦ analytic, coherent, good, logical, rational, reasonable, sensible, sober, sound ♦ good, hard, informed, just, levelheaded, logical, reasoned, solid, well-founded

val·i·date \ˈva-lə-ˌdāt\ *vb* **-dat·ed**; **-dat·ing** 1 : to make legally valid 2 ♦ : to confirm the validity of 3 ♦ : to corroborate or support on a sound basis or authority : VERIFY

  ♦ [2] demonstrate, document, establish, prove, substantiate ♦ [3] bear out, confirm, corroborate, substantiate, support, verify, vindicate

val·i·da·tion \ˌva-lə-ˈdā-shən\ *n* ♦ : the act or an instance of validating

  ♦ attestation, confirmation, corroboration, documentation, evidence, proof, substantiation, testament, testimony, witness

va·lise \və-ˈlēs\ *n* : SUITCASE

val·ley \ˈva-lē\ *n*, *pl* **valleys** ♦ : a long depression between ranges of hills or mountains

  ♦ dale, hollow

val·or *or Can and Brit* **val·our** \ˈva-lər\ *n* ♦ : personal bravery

  ♦ bravery, courage, daring, fearlessness, gallantry, guts, hardihood, heart, heroism, nerve, stoutness

val·o·ri·za·tion \ˌva-lə-rə-ˈzā-shən\ *n* : the support of commodity prices by any of various forms of government subsidy — **val·o·rize** \ˈva-lə-ˌrīz\ *vb*

val·or·ous \ˈva-lə-rəs\ *adj* ♦ : possessing or exhibiting valor

  ♦ brave, courageous, dauntless, doughty, fearless, gallant, great-hearted, heroic, intrepid, lionhearted, manful, stalwart, stout, undaunted, valiant

val·our *chiefly Can and Brit var of* VALOR

¹**valu·able** \ˈval-yə-bəl, -yə-wə-bəl\ *adj* 1 : having money value 2 ♦ : having great money value 3 : of great use or service

  ♦ costly, dear, expensive, high, precious

²**valuable** *n* : a usu. personal possession of considerable value ⟨their ∼s were stolen⟩

val·u·ate \ˈval-yə-ˌwāt\ *vb* **-at·ed**; **-at·ing** : to place a value on : APPRAISE — **val·u·a·tor** \-ˌwā-tər\ *n*

val·u·a·tion \ˌval-yə-ˈwā-shən\ *n* 1 ♦ : the act or process of valuing; *esp* : appraisal of property 2 : the estimated or determined market value of a thing

  ♦ appraisal, assessment, estimate, estimation, evaluation, reckoning

¹**val·ue** \ˈval-yü\ *n* 1 : a fair return or equivalent in money, goods, or services for something exchanged 2 ♦ : the monetary worth of a thing; *also* : relative worth, utility, or importance ⟨nothing of ∼ to say⟩ 3 : an assigned or computed numerical quantity ⟨the ∼ of x in an equation⟩ 4 : relative lightness or darkness of a color : LUMINOSITY 5 : the relative length of a tone or note 6 : something (as a principle or ideal) intrinsically valuable or desirable ⟨human rather than material ∼s⟩

  ♦ distinction, excellence, merit, virtue ♦ account, merit, valuation, worth

²**value** *vb* **val·ued**; **valu·ing** 1 ♦ : to estimate the monetary worth of : APPRAISE 2 : to rate in usefulness, importance, or general worth 3 ♦ : to consider or rate highly : PRIZE — **val·u·er** *n*

  ♦ [1] appraise, assess, estimate, evaluate, rate, set ♦ [3] appreciate, cherish, love, prize, treasure

val·ue–add·ed tax *n* : an incremental excise tax that is levied on the value added at each stage of the processing of a raw material or the production and distribution of a commodity

val·ue·less *adj* ♦ : having no value

  ♦ chaffy, empty, junky, no-good, null, worthless

valve \ˈvalv\ *n* 1 : a structure (as in a vein) that temporarily closes a passage or that permits movement in one direction only 2 ♦ : a device by which the flow of a fluid material may be regulated by a movable part; *also* : the movable part of such a device 3 : a device in a brass wind instrument for quickly varying the tube length in order to change the fundamental tone by some definite interval 4 : one of the separate usu. hinged pieces of which the shell of some animals and esp. bivalve mollusks consists 5 : one of the pieces into which a ripe seed capsule or pod separates — **valved** \ˈvalvd\ *adj* — **valve·less** *adj*

  ♦ cock, faucet, gate, spigot, tap

val·vu·lar \ˈval-vyə-lər\ *adj* : of, relating to, or affecting a valve esp. of the heart ⟨∼ heart disease⟩

va·moose \va-ˈmüs, va-\ *vb* **va·moosed**; **va·moos·ing** : to leave or go away quickly

¹**vamp** \ˈvamp\ *vb* 1 : to provide with a new vamp 2 : to patch up with a new part 3 : INVENT, IMPROVISE ⟨∼ up an excuse⟩

²**vamp** *n* 1 : the part of a boot or shoe upper covering esp. the front

part of the foot **2** : a short introductory musical passage often repeated

³**vamp** *n* : a woman who uses her charm or wiles to seduce and exploit men

⁴**vamp** *vb* : to practice seductive wiles on : act like a vamp

vam·pire \'vam-ˌpīr\ *n* **1** : a reanimated corpse of folklore that bites and sucks the blood of the living **2** : a person who preys on other people; *esp* : a woman who exploits and ruins her lover **3** : VAMPIRE BAT

vampire bat *n* : any of various bats of Central and So. America that feed on the blood of animals; *also* : any of several other bats that do not feed on blood but are sometimes reputed to do so

¹**van** \'van\ *n* : the forefront of an action or movement : VANGUARD

²**van** *n* : a usu. enclosed wagon or motortruck for moving goods or animals; *also* : a versatile enclosed box-like motor vehicle

va·na·di·um \və-'nā-dē-əm\ *n* : a soft grayish ductile metallic chemical element used esp. to form alloys

Van Al·len belt \van-'a-lən-\ *n* : a belt of intense radiation in the magnetosphere composed of charged particles trapped by earth's magnetic field

van·dal \'vand-ᵊl\ *n* **1** *cap* : a member of a Germanic people who sacked Rome in A.D. 455 **2** : a person who willfully mars or destroys property

van·dal·ise *chiefly Brit var of* VANDALIZE

van·dal·ism \-ˌi-zəm\ *n* : willful or malicious destruction or defacement of public or private property

van·dal·ize \-ˌīz\ *vb* **-ized; -iz·ing** : to subject to vandalism : DAMAGE

Van·dyke \van-'dīk\ *n* : a trim pointed beard

vane \'vān\ *n* **1** : a movable device attached to a high object for showing wind direction **2** : a thin flat or curved object that is rotated about an axis by a flow of fluid or that rotates to cause a fluid to flow or that redirects a flow of fluid ⟨the ∼s of a windmill⟩ **3** : a feather fastened near the back end of an arrow for stability in flight

van·guard \'van-ˌgärd\ *n* **1** : the troops moving at the front of an army **2** : the forefront of an action or movement

va·nil·la \və-'ni-lə\ *n* : a flavoring extract made synthetically or obtained from the long beanlike pods (**vanilla beans**) of a tropical American climbing orchid; *also* : this orchid

van·ish \'va-nish\ *vb* ♦ : to pass from sight or existence : disappear completely — **van·ish·er** *n*

♦ disappear, dissolve, evaporate, fade, flee, go, melt

van·i·ty \'va-nə-tē\ *n, pl* **-ties** **1** : something that is vain, empty, or useless **2** : the quality or fact of being useless or futile : FUTILITY **3** ♦ : undue pride in oneself or one's appearance : CONCEIT **4** : a small case for cosmetics : COMPACT

♦ complacence, conceit, ego, egotism, pride, self-conceit, self-esteem, self-importance, self-satisfaction, smugness, vainglory

vanity plate *n* : an automobile license plate bearing distinctive letters or numbers designated by the owner

van·quish \'vaŋ-kwish, 'van-\ *vb* **1** ♦ : to overcome in battle or in a contest **2** : to gain mastery over (as an emotion)

♦ conquer, dominate, overpower, subdue, subject

van·tage \'van-tij\ *n* **1** ♦ : an advantage or superiority in a contest **2** : a position giving a strategic advantage or a commanding perspective

♦ advantage, better, drop, edge, jump, upper hand

vape \'vāp\ *vb* **vaped; vap·ing** : to inhale vapor through the mouth from a usu. battery-operated electronic device that heats up and vaporizes a liquid or solid

va·pid \'va-pəd, 'vā-\ *adj* : lacking spirit, liveliness, or zest : FLAT, INSIPID — **va·pid·i·ty** \va-'pi-də-tē\ *n* — **vap·id·ly** *adv* — **vap·id·ness** *n*

va·por *or Can and Brit* **va·pour** \'vā-pər\ *n* **1** : fine separated particles (as fog or smoke) floating in the air and clouding it **2** : a substance in the gaseous state; *esp* : one that is liquid under ordinary conditions **3** : something insubstantial or fleeting **4** *pl* : a depressed or hysterical nervous condition

va·por·ing \'vā-pə-riŋ\ *n* : an idle, boastful, or high-flown expression or speech — usu. used in pl. ⟨political ∼s⟩

va·por·ise *chiefly Brit var of* VAPORIZE

va·por·ize \'vā-pə-ˌrīz\ *vb* **-ized; -iz·ing** : to convert into vapor — **va·por·i·za·tion** \ˌvā-pə-rə-'zā-shən\ *n*

va·por·iz·er \-ˌrī-zər\ *n* : a device that vaporizes something (as a medicated liquid)

vapor lock *n* : an interruption of flow of a fluid (as fuel in an engine) caused by the formation of vapor in the feeding system

va·por·ous \'vā-pə-rəs\ *adj* **1** : full of vapor : FOGGY, MISTY **2**

: UNSUBSTANTIAL, VAGUE — **va·por·ous·ly** *adv* — **va·por·ous·ness** *n*

va·pour *chiefly Brit var of* VAPOR

va·que·ro \vä-'ker-ō\ *n, pl* **-ros** : a ranch hand : COWBOY

var *abbr* **1** variable **2** variant; variation **3** variety **4** various

¹**var·i·able** \'ver-ə-bəl\ *adj* **1** ♦ : able or apt to vary : CHANGEABLE **2** : FICKLE **3** : not true to type : ABERRANT ⟨a ∼ wheat⟩ — **var·i·abil·i·ty** \ˌver-ē-ə-'bi-lə-tē, ˌvar-\ *n* — **var·i·ably** \-blē\ *adv*

♦ adaptable, adjustable, changeable, elastic, flexible, fluid, malleable

²**variable** *n* **1** : a quantity that may take on any of a set of values; *also* : a mathematical symbol representing a variable **2** : something that is variable

var·i·ance \'ver-ē-əns\ *n* **1** : variation or a degree of variation : DEVIATION **2** ♦ : the fact or state of being in disagreement **3** : a license to do something contrary to the usual rule ⟨a zoning ∼⟩ **4** : the square of the standard deviation

♦ conflict, discord, dissension, dissent, disunity, friction, schism, strife, war, warfare

¹**var·i·ant** \'ver-ē-ənt\ *adj* **1** : differing from others of its kind or class **2** : varying usu. slightly from the standard or type

²**variant** *n* **1** : one that exhibits variation from a type or norm **2** : one of two or more different spellings or pronunciations of a word

var·i·a·tion \ˌver-ē-'ā-shən\ *n* **1** ♦ : the act, process, or an instance of varying : a change in form, position, or condition **2** : extent of change or difference **3** : divergence in the characteristics of an organism from those typical or usual for its group; *also* : one exhibiting such variation **4** : repetition of a musical theme with modifications in rhythm, tune, harmony, or key

♦ alteration, change, difference, modification, revise, revision

vari·col·ored \'ver-i-ˌkə-lərd\ *adj* : having various colors : VARIEGATED

var·i·cose \'var-ə-ˌkōs\ *adj* : abnormally swollen and dilated ⟨∼ veins⟩ — **var·i·cos·i·ty** \ˌvar-ə-'kä-sə-tē\ *n*

var·ied \'ver-ēd\ *adj* **1** ♦ : having many forms or types ⟨∼ interests⟩; *also* : composed of distinct or unlike elements or qualities **2** : VARIEGATED — **var·ied·ly** *adv*

♦ assorted, heterogeneous, miscellaneous, mixed, motley

var·ie·gat·ed \'ver-ē-ə-ˌgā-təd\ *adj* **1** ♦ : having patches, stripes, or marks of different colors ⟨∼ flowers⟩ **2** : VARIED 1 — **var·ie·gate** \-ˌgāt\ *vb* — **var·ie·ga·tion** \ˌver-ē-ə-'gā-shən\ *n*

♦ colorful (*or* colourful), multicolored (*or* multicoloured)

¹**va·ri·etal** \və-'rī-ət-ᵊl\ *adj* : of or relating to a variety; *esp* : of, relating to, or producing a varietal

²**varietal** *n* : a wine bearing the name of the principal grape from which it is made

va·ri·ety \və-'rī-ə-tē\ *n, pl* **-et·ies** **1** ♦ : the state of being varied or various : DIVERSITY **2** ♦ : a collection of different things : ASSORTMENT **3** : something varying from others of the same general kind **4** : any of various groups of plants or animals within a species distinguished by characteristics insufficient to separate species : SUBSPECIES **5** : entertainment such as is given in a stage presentation comprising a series of performances (as songs, dances, or acrobatic acts)

♦ [1] assortment, diversity ♦ [2] assortment, clutter, jumble, medley, mélange, miscellany, motley, muddle, welter

var·i·o·rum \ˌver-ē-'ōr-əm\ *n* : an edition or text of a work containing notes by various persons or variant readings of the text

var·i·ous \'ver-ē-əs\ *adj* **1** : VARICOLORED **2** : of differing kinds : MULTIFARIOUS **3** : UNLIKE ⟨animals as ∼ as the jaguar and the sloth⟩ **4** : having a number of different aspects **5** : NUMEROUS, MANY **6** : INDIVIDUAL, SEPARATE — **var·i·ous·ly** *adv*

var·let \'vär-lət\ *n* **1** : ATTENDANT **2** ♦ : a disreputable, unprincipled person : SCOUNDREL, KNAVE

♦ beast, evildoer, fiend, no-good, reprobate, rogue, villain, wretch

var·mint \'vär-mənt\ *n* **1** : an animal considered a pest; *esp* : one classed as vermin and unprotected by game law **2** : a contemptible person : RASCAL

¹**var·nish** \'vär-nish\ *n* **1** : a liquid preparation that is applied to a surface and dries into a hard glossy coating; *also* : the glaze of this coating **2** : something suggesting varnish by its gloss **3** : outside show : deceptive or superficial appearance

²**varnish** *vb* **1** : to cover with varnish **2** : to cover or conceal with something that gives a fair appearance : GLOSS

var·si·ty \'vär-sə-tē\ *n, pl* **-ties**   **1** *Brit* : UNIVERSITY   **2** : the principal team representing a college, school, or club

vary \'ver-ē\ *vb* **var·ied; vary·ing**   **1** ♦ : to make different in some attribute or characteristic : ALTER   **2** : to make or be of different kinds : introduce or have variety : DIVERSIFY, DIFFER   **3** ♦ : to exhibit or undergo change   **4** : to change in bodily structure or function away from what is usual for members of a group

     ♦ [1] alter, change, make over, modify, recast, redo, refashion, remake, remodel, revamp, revise, rework ♦ [3] change, fluctuate, mutate, shift

vas·cu·lar \'vas-kyə-lər\ *adj* : of or relating to a channel or system of channels for the conveyance of a body fluid (as blood or sap); *also* : supplied with or containing such vessels and esp. blood vessels

vascular plant *n* : a plant having a specialized system for carrying fluids that includes xylem and phloem

vas def·er·ens \'vas-'de-fə-rənz\ *n, pl* **va·sa def·er·en·tia** \'vā-zə-,de-fə-'ren-shē-ə\ : a sperm-carrying duct of the testis

vase \'vās, 'vāz\ *n* : a usu. round vessel of greater depth than width used chiefly for ornament or for flowers

va·sec·to·my \va-'sek-tə-mē, vā-'zek-\ *n, pl* **-mies** : surgical excision of all or part of the vas deferens usu. to induce sterility

va·so·con·stric·tion \,vas-ō-kən-'strik-shən, ,vāz-\ *n* : narrowing of the interior diameter of blood vessels

va·so·con·stric·tor \-tər\ *n* : an agent (as a nerve fiber or a drug) that initiates or induces vasoconstriction

vas·sal \'va-səl\ *n*   **1** : a person under the protection of a feudal lord to whom he owes homage and loyalty : a feudal tenant   **2** : one occupying a dependent or subordinate position — **vassal** *adj*

vas·sal·age \-sə-lij\ *n*   **1** : the state of being a vassal   **2** : the homage and loyalty due from a vassal   **3** : SERVITUDE, SUBJECTION

¹vast \'vast\ *adj* ♦ : very great in size, amount, degree, intensity, or esp. extent

     ♦ enormous, giant, gigantic, huge, massive, monumental, prodigious, tremendous, whopping

²vast *n* : a great expanse : IMMENSITY

vast·ly *adv* ♦ : to a vast extent or degree

     ♦ broadly, considerably, greatly, hugely, largely, massively, monstrously, much, sizably, stupendously, tremendously, utterly

vast·ness *n* ♦ : the quality or state of being vast

     ♦ enormity, hugeness, immensity, magnitude, massiveness

vasty \'vas-tē\ *adj* : VAST

vat \'vat\ *n* : a large vessel (as a tub or barrel) esp. for holding liquids in manufacturing processes

VAT *abbr* value-added tax

vat·ic \'va-tik\ *adj* : PROPHETIC, ORACULAR

Vat·i·can \'va-ti-kən\ *n*   **1** : the papal headquarters in Rome   **2** : the papal government

vaude·ville \'vòd-vəl, 'väd-, 'vōd-, -,vil\ *n* : a stage entertainment consisting of unrelated acts (as of acrobats, comedians, dancers, or singers)

¹vault \'vòlt\ *n*   **1** : an arched masonry structure usu. forming a ceiling or roof; *also* : something (as the sky) resembling a vault   **2** : a room or space covered by a vault esp. when underground   **3** : a room or compartment for the safekeeping of valuables   **4** : a burial chamber; *also* : a usu. metal or concrete case in which a casket is enclosed at burial — **vaulty** *adj*

²vault *vb* : to form or cover with a vault

³vault *vb* ♦ : to leap vigorously esp. by aid of the hands or a pole — **vault·er** *n*

     ♦ bound, hop, jump, leap, spring

⁴vault *n* : an act of vaulting : LEAP

vault·ed \'vòl-təd\ *adj*   **1** : built in the form of a vault : ARCHED   **2** : covered with a vault

vault·ing \-tiŋ\ *adj* : reaching for the heights ⟨~ ambition⟩

vaunt \'vònt\ *vb* ♦ : to boast of : BRAG — **vaunt** *n*

vaunt·ed \'vòn-təd\ *adj* : much praised or boasted of

vb *abbr* verb; verbal

V-chip \'vē-,chip\ *n* : a computer chip in a television set used to block based on content the viewing of certain programs

VCR \,vē-(,)sē-'är\ *n* : a device that records and plays back videotapes

VD *abbr* venereal disease

VDT *abbr* video display terminal

veal \'vēl\ *n* : the flesh of a young calf

vec·tor \'vek-tər\ *n*   **1** : a quantity that has magnitude and direction   **2** : an organism (as a fly or tick) that transmits a pathogen

Ve·da \'vā-də\ *n* : any of a class of Hindu sacred writings — **Ve·dic** \'vā-dik\ *adj*

Ve·dan·ta \vā-'dän-tə, və-, -'dan-\ *n* : an orthodox Hindu philosophy based on the Upanishads

vee·jay \'vē-,jā\ *n* : an announcer of a program featuring music videos

veep \'vēp\ *n* : VICE PRESIDENT

veer \'vir\ *vb* ♦ : to shift from one direction or course to another — **veer** *n*

     ♦ divert, swerve, swing, turn, wheel, whip

veg·an \'vē-gən, 'vā-; 've-jən, -,jan\ *n* : a strict vegetarian who consumes no animal food or dairy products — **veg·an·ism** \'vē-gə-,ni-zəm, 'vā-, 've-\ *n*

¹veg·e·ta·ble \'vej-tə-bəl, 've-jə-\ *adj*   **1** : of, relating to, or growing like plants ⟨the ~ kingdom⟩   **2** : made from, obtained from, or containing plants or plant products ⟨~ oils⟩   **3** : suggesting that of a plant (as in inertness) ⟨a ~ existence⟩

²vegetable *n*   **1** : PLANT 1   **2** : a usu. herbaceous plant grown for an edible part that is usu. eaten as part of a meal; *also* : such an edible part

veg·e·tal \'ve-jət-°l\ *adj*   **1** : VEGETABLE   **2** : VEGETATIVE

veg·e·tar·i·an \,ve-jə-'ter-ē-ən\ *n* : one that believes in or practices living on a diet of vegetables, fruits, grains, nuts, and sometimes animal products (as milk and cheese) — **vegetarian** *adj* — **veg·e·tar·i·an·ism** \-ē-ə-,ni-zəm\ *n*

veg·e·tate \'ve-jə-,tāt\ *vb* **-tat·ed; -tat·ing** : to live or grow in the manner of a plant; *esp* : to lead a dull inert life

veg·e·ta·tion \,ve-jə-'tā-shən\ *n*   **1** : the act or process of vegetating; *also* : inert existence   **2** ♦ : plant life or cover (as of an area) — **veg·e·ta·tion·al** \-shə-nəl\ *adj*

     ♦ flora, foliage, green, greenery, herbage, leafage, verdure

veg·e·ta·tive \'ve-jə-,tā-tiv\ *adj*   **1** : of or relating to nutrition and growth esp. as contrasted with reproduction   **2** : of, relating to, or composed of vegetation ⟨~ cover⟩   **3** : VEGETABLE 3

veg out \'vej-\ *vb* **vegged out; vegging out** : to spend time idly or passively

ve·he·mence \'vē-ə-məns\ *n* ♦ : the quality or state of being vehement

     ♦ ardor, emotion, fervency, fervor, heat, intensity, passion, warmth ♦ aggressiveness, assertiveness, emphasis, fierceness, intensity *Ant* feebleness, mildness, weakness

ve·he·ment \'vē-ə-mənt\ *adj*   **1** ♦ : marked by great force or energy   **2** : marked by strong feeling or expression ⟨~ opposition⟩ — **ve·he·ment·ly** *adv*

     ♦ [1] deep, explosive, exquisite, fearful, ferocious, fierce, furious, hard, heavy, intense, profound, terrible, vicious, violent ♦ [2] ardent, burning, charged, emotional, fervent, fiery, hot-blooded, impassioned, passionate, red-hot

ve·hi·cle \'vē-ə-kəl, 'vē-,hi-\ *n*   **1** : a medium by which a thing is applied or administered ⟨linseed oil is a ~ for pigments⟩   **2** ♦ : a medium through or by means of which something is conveyed or expressed   **3** ♦ : a means of transporting persons or goods — **ve·hic·u·lar** \vē-'hi-kyə-lər\ *adj*

     ♦ [2] agency, agent, instrument, instrumentality, machinery, means, medium, organ ♦ [3] conveyance, transport

¹veil \'vāl\ *n*   **1** : a piece of often sheer or diaphanous material used to screen or curtain something or to cover the head or face   **2** : the life of a nun ⟨take the ~⟩   **3** : something that hides or obscures like a veil

²veil *vb* ♦ : to cover with or as if with a veil

     ♦ cloak, conceal, cover, curtain, hide, mask, obscure, screen

¹vein \'vān\ *n*   **1** : a fissure in rock filled with mineral matter; *also* : a bed of useful mineral matter   **2** : any of the tubular branching vessels that carry blood from the capillaries toward the heart   **3** : any of the bundles of vascular vessels forming the framework of a leaf   **4** : any of the thickened ribs that stiffen the wings of an insect   **5** : something (as a wavy variegation in marble) suggesting veins   **6** ♦ : a distinctive style of expression   **7** : a distinctive element or quality : STRAIN   **8** : MOOD, HUMOR — **veined** \'vānd\ *adj*

     ♦ fashion, locution, manner, mode, phraseology, style, tone

²vein *vb* : to pattern with or as if with veins — **vein·ing** *n*

vel *abbr* velocity

ve·lar \'vē-lər\ *adj* : of or relating to a velum and esp. that of the soft palate

veld *or* **veldt** \'velt, 'felt\ *n* ♦ : an open grassland esp. in southern Africa usu. with scattered shrubs or trees

     ♦ down, grassland, plain, prairie, savanna, steppe

vel·lum \'ve-ləm\ *n*   **1** : a fine-grained lambskin, kidskin, or calfskin prepared for writing on or for binding books **2** : a strong cream-colored paper — **vellum** *adj*

ve·loc·i·pede \və-ˈlä-sə-ˌpēd\ *n* : an early bicycle

ve·loc·i·rap·tor \və-ˈlä-sə-ˌrap-tər\ *n* : any of a genus of agile flesh-eating bipedal dinosaurs of the Cretaceous having a sickle-shaped claw on each foot

ve·loc·i·ty \və-ˈlä-sə-tē\ *n, pl* **-ties** ♦ : quickness of motion : SPEED ⟨the ∼ of light⟩

♦ celerity, fastness, fleetness, haste, hurry, quickness, rapidity, speed, swiftness

ve·lour *or* **ve·lours** \və-ˈlu̇r\ *n, pl* **velours** \-ˈlu̇rz\ : any of various textile fabrics with pile like that of velvet

ve·lum \ˈvē-ləm\ *n, pl* **ve·la** \-lə\ : a membranous body part (as the soft palate) resembling a veil

vel·vet \ˈvel-vət\ *n* **1** : a fabric having a short soft dense warp pile **2** : something resembling or suggesting velvet (as in softness or luster) **3** : the soft skin covering the growing antlers of deer — **velvet** *adj*

vel·ve·teen \ˌvel-və-ˈtēn\ *n* **1** : a fabric woven usu. of cotton in imitation of velvet **2** *pl* : clothes made of velveteen

vel·vety \ˈvel-və-tē\ *adj* ♦ : having the character of velvet as in being soft, smooth, thick, or richly hued

♦ cottony, downy, satiny, silken, soft

Ven *abbr* venerable

ve·nal \ˈvēn-ᵊl\ *adj* ♦ : capable of being bought or bribed — **ve·nal·i·ty** \vi-ˈnal-ə-tē\ *n* — **ve·nal·ly** \ˈvēn-ᵊl-ē\ *adv*

♦ bribable, corruptible, purchasable *Ant* incorruptible

ve·na·tion \ve-ˈnā-shən, vē-\ *n* : an arrangement or system of veins ⟨the ∼ of the hand⟩ ⟨leaf ∼⟩

vend \ˈvend\ *vb* ♦ : to sell esp. as a hawker or peddler — **vend·ible** *adj*

♦ deal, market, merchandise, put up, retail, sell

vend·ee \ven-ˈdē\ *n* : one to whom a thing is sold : BUYER

ven·det·ta \ven-ˈde-tə\ *n* : a feud marked by acts of revenge

vending machine *n* : a coin-operated machine for selling merchandise

ven·dor \ˈven-dər, *for 1 also* ven-ˈdȯr\ *n* **1** ♦ : one that vends : SELLER **2** : VENDING MACHINE

♦ dealer, seller *Ant* buyer, purchaser

¹ve·neer \və-ˈnir\ *n* **1** : a thin usu. superficial layer of material ⟨brick ∼⟩; *esp* : a thin layer of fine wood glued over a cheaper wood **2** : superficial display : GLOSS **3** ♦ : a protective or ornamental facing (as of brick or stone)

♦ exterior, face, outside, skin, surface

²veneer *vb* : to overlay with a veneer

ven·er·a·ble \ˈve-nə-rə-bəl\ *adj* **1** : deserving to be venerated — often used as a religious title **2** : made sacred by association **3 a** ♦ : calling forth respect through age, character, and attainments ⟨a ∼ jazz musician⟩ **b** ♦ : impressive by reason of age ⟨under ∼ pines⟩

♦ [3a] hallowed, reverend ♦ [3b] age-old, ancient, antediluvian, antique, dateless, hoary, old

ven·er·ate \ˈve-nə-ˌrāt\ *vb* **-at·ed; -at·ing** ♦ : to regard with reverential respect — **ven·er·a·tion** \ˌve-nə-ˈrā-shən\ *n*

♦ adore, deify, glorify, revere, worship

ve·ne·re·al \və-ˈnir-ē-əl\ *adj* : of or relating to sexual intercourse or to diseases transmitted by it ⟨a ∼ infection⟩

venereal disease *n* : a contagious disease (as gonorrhea or syphilis) usu. acquired by having sexual intercourse with someone who already has it

ve·ne·tian blind \və-ˌnē-shən-\ *n* : a blind having thin horizontal parallel slats that can be adjusted to admit a desired amount of light

Ven·e·zue·lan \ˌve-nə-ˈzwā-lən\ *n* : a native or inhabitant of Venezuela — **Venezuelan** *adj*

ven·geance \ˈven-jəns\ *n* ♦ : punishment inflicted in retaliation for an injury or offense : REVENGE

♦ reprisal, requital, retaliation, retribution, revenge

venge·ful \ˈvenj-fəl\ *adj* : filled with a desire for revenge : VINDICTIVE — **venge·ful·ly** *adv*

ve·nial \ˈvē-nē-əl\ *adj* ♦ : capable of being forgiven : EXCUSABLE ⟨∼ sin⟩

♦ excusable, forgivable, pardonable *Ant* inexcusable, mortal, unforgivable, unpardonable

ve·ni·re \və-ˈnī-rē\ *n* : a panel from which a jury is drawn

ve·ni·re fa·ci·as \-ˈfā-shē-əs\ *n* : a writ summoning persons to appear in court to serve as jurors

ve·ni·re·man \və-ˈnī-rē-mən, -ˈnir-ē-\ *n* : a member of a venire

ven·i·son \ˈven-ə-sən, -zən\ *n, pl* **venisons** *also* **venison** : the edible flesh of a deer

ven·om \ˈve-nəm\ *n* **1** ♦ : poisonous material secreted by some animals (as snakes, spiders, or bees) and transmitted usu. by biting or stinging **2** ♦ : desire to cause pain, injury, or distress to another : MALEVOLENCE

♦ [1] bane, poison, toxin ♦ [2] cattiness, despite, hatefulness, malice, malignity, meanness, nastiness, spite, spleen, viciousness

ven·om·ous \ˈve-nə-məs\ *adj* **1** ♦ : full of venom : POISONOUS **2** : SPITEFUL, MALEVOLENT ⟨∼ comments⟩ **3** : secreting and using venom ⟨∼ snakes⟩ — **ven·om·ous·ly** *adv*

♦ poison, poisonous

ve·nous \ˈvē-nəs\ *adj* **1** : of, relating to, or full of veins **2** : being purplish red oxygen-deficient blood rich in carbon dioxide that is present in most veins

¹vent \ˈvent\ *vb* **1** : to provide with a vent **2** : to serve as a vent for **3** ♦ : to force out : DISCHARGE **4** ♦ : to give vigorous or emotional expression to

♦ [3] cast, discharge, emit, exhale, expel, issue, release, shoot ♦ [4] loose, release, take out, unleash ♦ [4] air, express, give, look, sound, state, voice

²vent *n* **1** : an opportunity or way of escape or passage : OUTLET **2** : an opening for the escape of a gas or liquid or for the relief of pressure

³vent *n* : a slit in a garment esp. in the lower part of a seam (as of a jacket or skirt)

ven·ti·late \ˈvent-ᵊl-ˌāt\ *vb* **-lat·ed; -lat·ing** **1** : to discuss freely and openly ⟨∼ a question⟩ **2** : to give vigorous or emotional expression to ⟨∼ one's grievances⟩ **3** : to cause fresh air to circulate through (as a room or mine) so as to replace foul air **4** : to provide with a vent or outlet — **ven·ti·la·tor** \-ᵊl-ˌā-tər\ *n*

ven·ti·la·tion \ˌvent-ᵊl-ˈā-shən\ *n* **1** : the act or process of ventilating **2** : circulation of air (as in a room) **3** : a system or means of providing fresh air

ven·tral \ˈven-trəl\ *adj* **1** : of or relating to the belly : ABDOMINAL **2** : of, relating to, or located on or near the surface of the body that in humans is the front but in most other animals is the lower surface — **ven·tral·ly** *adv*

ven·tri·cle \ˈven-tri-kəl\ *n* **1** : a chamber of the heart that receives blood from the atrium of the same side and pumps it into the arteries **2** : any of the communicating cavities of the brain that are continuous with the central canal of the spinal cord — **ven·tric·u·lar** \ven-ˈtri-kyə-lər\ *adj*

ven·tril·o·quism \ven-ˈtri-lə-ˌkwi-zəm\ *n* : the production of the voice in such a manner that the sound appears to come from a source other than the speaker — **ven·tril·o·quist** \-kwist\ *n*

ven·tril·o·quy \-kwē\ *n* : VENTRILOQUISM

¹ven·ture \ˈven-chər\ *vb* **ven·tured; ven·tur·ing** **1** ♦ : to expose to hazard : RISK **2** : to undertake the risks of : BRAVE **3** ♦ : to offer at the risk of rebuff, rejection, or censure ⟨∼ an opinion⟩ **4** : to proceed despite danger : DARE

♦ [1] adventure, compromise, gamble with, hazard, imperil, jeopardize, menace, risk ♦ [3] chance, gamble, hazard, risk

²venture *n* **1** ♦ : an undertaking involving chance or risk; *esp* : a speculative business enterprise **2** : something risked in a speculative venture : STAKE

♦ chance, enterprise, flier, gamble, speculation

ven·ture·some \ˈven-chər-səm\ *adj* **1** ♦ : involving risk : DANGEROUS **2** ♦ : inclined to venture : BOLD — **ven·ture·some·ly** *adv* — **ven·ture·some·ness** *n*

♦ [1] dangerous, grave, grievous, hazardous, menacing, parlous, perilous, risky, serious, unhealthy, unsafe ♦ [2] adventurous, audacious, bold, daring, enterprising, gutsy, hardy, nervy

ven·tur·ous \ˈven-chə-rəs\ *adj* **1** : involving risk : DANGEROUS, HAZARDOUS **2** : inclined to venture : BOLD — **ven·tur·ous·ly** *adv* — **ven·tur·ous·ness** *n*

ven·ue \ˈven-yü\ *n* : the place in which the alleged events from which a legal action arises took place; *also* : the place from which the jury is taken and where the trial is held

Ve·nus \ˈvē-nəs\ *n* : the planet 2d in order from the sun

Venus fly·trap \-ˈflī-ˌtrap\ *or* **Ve·nus's–fly·trap** \ˈvē-nə-səz-ˈflī-ˌtrap\ *n* : an insect-eating plant of the Carolina coast that has the leaf tip modified into an insect trap

Ve·nu·sian \vi-ˈnü-zhən, -ˈnyü-\ *adj* : of or relating to the planet Venus

ve·ra·cious \və-ˈrā-shəs\ *adj* **1** : TRUTHFUL, HONEST **2** ♦ : marked by truth : ACCURATE — **ve·ra·cious·ly** *adv*

♦ accurate, authentic, exact, faithful, precise, right, strict, true

ve·rac·i·ty \və-'ra-sə-tē\ *n, pl* **-ties 1 ♦** : devotion to truth : TRUTHFULNESS **2 ♦** : conformity with fact : ACCURACY **3** : something true

♦ [1] honesty, integrity, probity, truthfulness, verity ♦ [2] accuracy, closeness, delicacy, exactness, fineness, precision

ve·ran·da *or* **ve·ran·dah** \və-'ran-də\ *n* : a long open usu. roofed porch

verb \'vərb\ *n* : a word that is the grammatical center of a predicate and expresses an act, occurrence, or mode of being

¹**ver·bal** \'vər-bəl\ *adj* **1** : of, relating to, or consisting of words; *esp* : having to do with words rather than with the ideas to be conveyed **2 ♦** : expressed in usu. spoken words : ORAL ⟨a ∼ contract⟩ **3** : of, relating to, or formed from a verb **4** : LITERAL, VERBATIM — **ver·bal·ly** *adv*

♦ oral, spoken, unwritten *Ant* written

²**verbal** *n* : a word that combines characteristics of a verb with those of a noun or adjective

verbal auxiliary *n* : an auxiliary verb

ver·bal·ize \'vər-bə-ˌlīz\ *vb* **-ized; -iz·ing 1** : to speak or write in wordy or empty fashion **2 ♦** : to express something in words : describe verbally **3** : to convert into a verb — **ver·bal·i·za·tion** \ˌvər-bə-lə-'zā-shən\ *n*

♦ articulate, say, speak, state, talk, tell, utter, vocalize

verbal noun *n* : a noun derived directly from a verb or verb stem and in some uses having the sense and constructions of a verb

ver·ba·tim \(ˌ)vər-'bā-təm\ *adv or adj* : in the same words : word for word

ver·be·na \(ˌ)vər-'bē-nə\ *n* : VERVAIN; *esp* : any of several garden vervains of hybrid origin with showy spikes of bright often fragrant flowers

ver·biage \'vər-bē-ij, -bij\ *n* **1 ♦** : superfluity of words usu. of little or obscure content **2** : DICTION, WORDING

♦ circumlocution, prolixity, redundancy, wordiness

ver·bose \(ˌ)vər-'bōs\ *adj* ♦ : using more words than are needed : WORDY

♦ circuitous, diffuse, long-winded, prolix, rambling, windy, wordy

ver·bos·i·ty \(ˌ)vər-'bä-sə-tē\ *n* : the quality or state of being verbose

ver·bo·ten \vər-'bōt-ᵊn, fər-\ *adj* : forbidden usu. by dictate

ver·dant \'vərd-ᵊnt\ *adj* ♦ : green with growing plants — **ver·dant·ly** *adv*

♦ green, leafy, lush, luxuriant

ver·dict \'vər-(ˌ)dikt\ *n* **1** : the finding or decision of a jury **2 ♦** : an opinion pronounced or felt : JUDGMENT

♦ belief, conviction, eye, feeling, judgment (*or* judgement), mind, notion, opinion, persuasion, sentiment, view

ver·di·gris \'vər-də-ˌgrēs, -ˌgris\ *n* : a green or bluish deposit that forms on copper, brass, or bronze surfaces

ver·dure \'vər-jər\ *n* **1** : the greenness of growing vegetation **2 ♦** : a growth or expanse of vegetation

♦ flora, foliage, green, greenery, herbage, leafage, vegetation

¹**verge** \'vərj\ *n* **1** : a staff carried as an emblem of authority or office **2 ♦** : something that borders or bounds : EDGE **3** : BRINK, THRESHOLD

♦ border, bound, boundary, circumference, compass, confines, edge, end, fringe, margin, perimeter, periphery, rim, skirt

²**verge** *vb* **verged; verg·ing 1 ♦** : to be next to — often used with *on* **2** : to be on the verge

♦ *often* verge on abut, adjoin, border (on), flank, fringe, join, skirt, touch

³**verge** *vb* **verged; verg·ing 1** : to move or extend in some direction or toward some condition : INCLINE **2** : to be in transition or change

verg·er \'vər-jər\ *n* **1** *chiefly Brit* : an attendant who carries a verge (as before a bishop) **2** : SEXTON

ve·rid·i·cal \və-'ri-di-kəl\ *adj* **1** : TRUTHFUL **2** : not illusory : GENUINE

ver·i·fi·able \ˌver-ə-'fī-ə-bəl\ *adj* ♦ : capable of being verified

♦ demonstrable, provable, supportable, sustainable *Ant* insupportable, unsupportable

ver·i·fy \'ver-ə-ˌfī\ *vb* **-fied; -fy·ing 1** : to confirm in law by oath **2 ♦** : to establish the truth, accuracy, or reality of — **ver·i·fi·ca·tion** \ˌver-ə-fə-'kā-shən\ *n*

♦ bear out, confirm, corroborate, substantiate, support, validate, vindicate

ver·i·ly \'ver-ə-lē\ *adv* ♦ : in truth : in actual fact

♦ actually, frankly, honestly, really, truly, truthfully

veri·si·mil·i·tude \ˌver-ə-sə-'mi-lə-ˌtüd, -ˌtyüd\ *n* : the quality or state of appearing to be true or real

ver·i·ta·ble \'ver-ə-tə-bəl\ *adj* : ACTUAL, GENUINE, TRUE

ver·i·ta·bly \'ver-ə-tə-blē\ *adv* ♦ : in a way that is genuine or true

♦ actually, authentically, genuinely, really, very

ver·i·ty \'ver-ə-tē\ *n, pl* **-ties 1** : the quality or state of being true or real : TRUTH, REALITY **2** : something (as a statement) that is true **3 ♦** : the quality or state of being truthful or honest : HONESTY

♦ honesty, integrity, probity, truthfulness, veracity

ver·meil *n* **1** \'vər-məl, -ˌmāl\ : VERMILION **2** \ver-'mā\ : gilded silver

ver·mi·cel·li \ˌvər-mə-'che-lē, -'se-\ *n* : a pasta made in thinner strings than spaghetti

ver·mic·u·lite \ˌvər-'mi-kyə-ˌlīt\ *n* : any of various lightweight water-absorbent minerals derived from mica

ver·mi·form appendix \'vər-mə-ˌform-\ *n* : APPENDIX 2

ver·mil·ion *also* **ver·mil·lion** \vər-'mil-yən\ *n* : a bright reddish orange color; *also* : any of various red pigments

ver·min \'vər-mən\ *n, pl* **vermin 1** : small common harmful or objectionable animals (as lice or mice) that are difficult to get rid of **2** : birds and mammals that prey on game — **ver·min·ous** *adj*

ver·mouth \vər-'müth\ *n* : a dry or sweet wine flavored with herbs and often used in mixed drinks

¹**ver·nac·u·lar** \vər-'na-kyə-lər\ *adj* **1** : of, relating to, or being a language or dialect native to a region or country rather than a literary, cultured, or foreign language **2** : of, relating to, or being the normal spoken form of a language **3** : applied to a plant or animal in common speech as distinguished from biological nomenclature ⟨∼ names⟩

♦ colloquial, conversational, informal, nonliterary, vulgar

²**vernacular** *n* **1** : a vernacular language **2** : the mode of expression of a group or class **3** : a vernacular name of a plant or animal

ver·nal \'vərn-ᵊl\ *adj* : of, relating to, or occurring in the spring ⟨∼ equinox⟩

ver·ni·er \'vər-nē-ər\ *n* : a short scale made to slide along the divisions of a graduated instrument to indicate parts of divisions

ve·ron·i·ca \və-'rä-ni-kə\ *n* : any of a genus of herbs related to the snapdragons that have small usu. bluish flowers

ver·sa·tile \'vər-sət-ᵊl\ *adj* **1** : turning with ease from one thing or position to another **2 ♦** : having many aptitudes — **ver·sa·til·i·ty** \ˌvər-sə-'ti-lə-tē\ *n*

♦ adaptable, all-around, protean, universal

¹**verse** \'vərs\ *n* **1** : a line of poetry; *also* : STANZA **2** : metrical writing distinguished from poetry esp. by its lower level of intensity **3 ♦** : writing that creates a specific emotional response through the intentional use of meaning, sound, and rhythm : POETRY **4** : a composition in verse : POEM **5** : one of the short divisions of a chapter in the Bible

♦ poetry, song

²**verse** *vb* **versed; vers·ing** : to familiarize by experience, study, or practice ⟨well *versed* in the theater⟩

versed *adj* ♦ : acquainted or familiar from experience, study, or practice

♦ abreast, conversant, familiar, informed, knowledgeable, up, up-to-date

ver·si·cle \'vər-si-kəl\ *n* : a verse or sentence said or sung by a leader in public worship and followed by a response from the people

ver·si·fi·ca·tion \ˌvər-sə-fə-'kā-shən\ *n* **1** : the making of verses **2** : metrical structure

ver·si·fi·er \'vər-sə-ˌfī-ər\ *n* ♦ : one that versifies

♦ bard, minstrel, poet

ver·si·fy \'vər-sə-ˌfī\ *vb* **-fied; -fy·ing 1** : to write verse **2** : to turn into verse

ver·sion \'vər-zhən\ *n* **1** : TRANSLATION; *esp* : a translation of the Bible **2** : an account or description from a particular point of view esp. as contrasted with another **3** : a form or variant of a type or original

vers li·bre \ˌver-'lēbrᵊ\ *n, pl* **vers li·bres** *same*\ : FREE VERSE

ver·so \'vər-sō\ *n, pl* **versos** : a left-hand page

ver·sus \'vər-səs\ *prep* **1** : AGAINST 1 ⟨the champion ～ the challenger⟩ **2** : in contrast or as an alternative to ⟨free trade ～ protection⟩

vert *abbr* vertical

ver·te·bra \'vər-tə-brə\ *n, pl* **-brae** \-ˌbrā, -ˌbrē\ *or* **-bras** : one of the segments of bone or cartilage making up the backbone

ver·te·bral \(ˌ)vər-'tē-brəl, 'vər-tə-\ *adj* : of, relating to, or made up of vertebrae : SPINAL

vertebral column *n* ♦ : the bony column in the back of a vertebrate that is the chief support of the trunk and consists of a jointed series of vertebrae enclosing and protecting the spinal cord : BACKBONE

   ♦ backbone, spine

¹**ver·te·brate** \'vər-tə-brət, -ˌbrāt\ *adj* **1** : having a backbone **2** : of or relating to the vertebrates

²**vertebrate** *n* : any of a large group of animals (as mammals, birds, reptiles, amphibians, or fishes) that have a backbone or in some primitive forms (as a lamprey) a flexible rod of cells and that have a tubular nervous system arranged along the back and divided into a brain and spinal cord

ver·tex \'vər-ˌteks\ *n, pl* **ver·ti·ces** \'vər-tə-ˌsēz\ *also* **ver·tex·es** **1** : the point opposite to and farthest from the base of a geometrical figure **2** : the point where the sides of an angle or three or more edges of a polyhedron (as a cube) meet **3** : the highest point : TOP, SUMMIT

ver·ti·cal \'vər-ti-kəl\ *adj* **1** : of, relating to, or located at the vertex : directly overhead **2** ♦ : rising perpendicularly from a level surface : UPRIGHT — **vertical** *n* — **ver·ti·cal·i·ty** \ˌvər-tə-'ka-lə-tē\ *n* — **ver·ti·cal·ly** \-k(ə-)lē\ *adv*

   ♦ erect, perpendicular, standing, upright, upstanding

ver·tig·i·nous \(ˌ)vər-'ti-jə-nəs\ *adj* : marked by, affected with, or tending to cause dizziness

ver·ti·go \'vər-ti-ˌgō\ *n, pl* **-goes** *or* **-gos** : DIZZINESS, GIDDINESS

vertu *var of* VIRTU

ver·vain \'vər-ˌvān\ *n* : any of a genus of chiefly American herbs or low woody plants with often showy heads or spikes of tubular flowers

verve \'vərv\ *n* **1** : liveliness of imagination **2** ♦ : the quality or state of being lively in temper, conduct, or spirit

   ♦ bounce, dash, drive, esprit, pep, punch, snap, spirit, vim, zing, zip

¹**very** \'ver-ē\ *adj* **veri·er; -est** **1** : EXACT, PRECISE ⟨the ～ heart of the city⟩ **2** : exactly suitable ⟨the ～ tool for the job⟩ **3** : ABSOLUTE, UTTER ⟨the *veriest* nonsense⟩ **4** — used as an intensive esp. to emphasize identity ⟨before my ～ eyes⟩ **5** : MERE, BARE ⟨the ～ idea scared him⟩ **6** ♦ : being the same one : IDENTICAL ⟨the ～ man I saw⟩ **7** ♦ : existing in fact or reality : ACTUAL

   ♦ [6] identical, same, selfsame ♦ [7] actual, concrete, existent, factual, real, true

²**very** *adv* **1** ♦ : in actual fact **2** ♦ : to a high degree : EXTREMELY

   ♦ [1] actually, authentically, genuinely, really, veritably *Ant* professedly, supposedly ♦ [2] extra, extremely, greatly, highly, hugely, mightily, mighty, mortally, most, much, real, right, so *Ant* little, nominally, slightly

very high frequency *n* : a radio frequency of between 30 and 300 megahertz

ves·i·cant \'ve-si-kənt\ *n* : an agent that causes blistering — **vesicant** *adj*

ves·i·cle \'ve-si-kəl\ *n* : a membranous and usu. fluid-filled cavity in a plant or animal; *also* : BLISTER — **ve·sic·u·lar** \və-'si-kyə-lər\ *adj*

¹**ves·per** \'ves-pər\ *n* **1** *cap, archaic* : EVENING STAR **2** : a vesper bell **3** *archaic* : EVENING, EVENTIDE

²**vesper** *adj* : of or relating to vespers or the evening

ves·pers \-pərz\ *n pl, often cap* : a late afternoon or evening worship service

ves·sel \'ve-səl\ *n* **1** ♦ : a container (as a barrel, bottle, bowl, or cup) for holding something **2** : a person held to be the recipient of a quality (as grace) **3** ♦ : a craft bigger than a rowboat **4** : a tube in which a body fluid (as blood or sap) is contained and circulated

   ♦ [1] container, holder, receptacle ♦ [3] boat, bottom, craft

¹**vest** \'vest\ *vb* **1** ♦ : to place or give into the possession or discretion of some person or authority **2** : to grant or endow with a particular authority, right, or property **3** : to become legally vested **4** : to clothe with or as if with a garment; *esp* : to garb in ecclesiastical vestments

   ♦ commend, commit, consign, delegate, deliver, entrust, give, hand over, leave, pass, transfer, transmit, trust, turn over

²**vest** *n* **1** : a sleeveless garment for the upper body usu. worn over a shirt **2** *chiefly Brit* : a man's sleeveless undershirt **3** : a front piece of a dress resembling the front of a vest

¹**ves·tal** \'vest-ᵊl\ *adj* : CHASTE

²**vestal** *n* : VESTAL VIRGIN

vestal virgin *n* **1** : a virgin consecrated to the Roman goddess Vesta and to the service of watching the sacred fire perpetually kept burning on her altar **2** : a chaste woman

vest·ed \'ves-təd\ *adj* : fully and unconditionally guaranteed as a legal right, benefit, or privilege

vested interest *n* : an interest (as in an existing political, economic, or social arrangement) to which the holder has a strong commitment; *also* : one (as a corporation) having a vested interest

ves·ti·bule \'ves-tə-ˌbyül\ *n* **1** : any of various bodily cavities forming or suggesting an entrance to some other cavity or space **2** ♦ : a passage or room between the outer door and the interior of a building — **ves·tib·u·lar** \ve-'sti-byə-lər\ *adj*

   ♦ entry, foyer, hall, lobby

ves·tige \'ves-tij\ *n* ♦ : a trace or visible sign left by something lost or vanished; *also* : a minute remaining amount — **ves·ti·gial** \ve-'sti-jē-əl, -jəl\ *adj* — **ves·ti·gial·ly** *adv*

   ♦ relic, shadow, trace

vest·ing \'ves-tiŋ\ *n* : the conveying to an employee of inalienable rights to share in a pension fund; *also* : the right so conveyed

vest·ment \'vest-mənt\ *n* **1** : an outer garment; *esp* : a ceremonial or official robe **2** *pl* : CLOTHING, GARB **3** : a garment or insignia worn by a cleric when officiating or assisting at a religious service

vest–pocket *adj* : very small ⟨a ～ park⟩

ves·try \'ves-trē\ *n, pl* **vestries** **1** : a room in a church for vestments, altar linens, and sacred vessels **2** : a room used for church meetings and classes **3** : a body administering the temporal affairs of an Episcopal parish

ves·try·man \-mən\ *n* : a member of a vestry

ves·ture \'ves-chər\ *n* **1** : a covering garment **2** : CLOTHING, APPAREL

¹**vet** \'vet\ *n* : VETERINARIAN

²**vet** *adj or n* : VETERAN

³**vet** *vb* : to evaluate for appraisal or acceptance ⟨～ a manuscript⟩

vetch \'vech\ *n* : any of a genus of twining leguminous herbs including some grown for fodder and green manure

¹**vet·er·an** \'ve-trən, -tə-rən\ *n* **1** : an old soldier of long service **2** : a former member of the armed forces **3** : a person of long experience usu. in an occupation or skill

²**veteran** *adj* : of, relating to, or characteristic of a veteran

Veterans Day *n* : November 11 observed as a legal holiday in commemoration of the end of hostilities in 1918 and 1945

vet·er·i·nar·i·an \ˌve-trə-'ner-ē-ən, ˌve-tə-rə-\ *n* : one qualified and authorized to practice veterinary medicine

¹**vet·er·i·nary** \'ve-trə-ˌner-ē, 've-tə-rə-\ *adj* : of, relating to, or being the medical care of animals and esp. domestic animals

²**veterinary** *n, pl* **-nar·ies** : VETERINARIAN

¹**ve·to** \'vē-tō\ *n, pl* **vetoes** **1** ♦ : an authoritative prohibition **2** : a power of one part of a government to forbid the carrying out of projects attempted by another part; *esp* : a power vested in a chief executive to prevent the carrying out of measures adopted by a legislature **3** : the exercise of the power of veto

   ♦ ban, embargo, interdict, interdiction, prohibition, proscription

²**veto** *vb* **1** ♦ : to refuse to admit or approve **2** ♦ : to refuse assent to (a legislative bill) so as to prevent enactment or cause reconsideration — **ve·to·er** *n*

   ♦ [1, 2] blackball, kill, negative

vex \'veks\ *vb* **vexed** *also* **vext; vex·ing** **1** : to bring trouble, distress, or agitation to **2** ♦ : to annoy continually with little irritations

   ♦ aggravate, annoy, bother, bug, chafe, exasperate, gall, get, grate, irk, irritate, nettle, peeve, persecute, pique, put out, rasp, rile

vex·a·tion \vek-'sā-shən\ *n* **1** ♦ : the act of vexing **2** : the quality or state of being vexed : IRRITATION **3** : a cause of trouble or annoyance

   ♦ aggravation, annoyance, disturbance, harassment

vex·a·tious \-shəs\ *adj* **1** ♦ : causing vexation : ANNOYING **2** : full of distress or annoyance : TROUBLED — **vex·a·tious·ly** *adv* — **vex·a·tious·ness** *n*

♦ aggravating, annoying, bothersome, frustrating, galling, irksome, irritating, pesty

vexed \'vekst\ *adj* : fully debated or discussed ⟨a ~ question⟩
vexing *adj* : causing or likely to cause vexation
VF *abbr* **1** video frequency   **2** visual field
VFD *abbr* volunteer fire department
VFW *abbr* Veterans of Foreign Wars
VG *abbr* **1** very good   **2** vicar-general
VHF *abbr* very high frequency
VI *abbr* Virgin Islands
via \'vī-ə, 'vē-ə\ *prep* **1** : by way of   **2** : by means of
vi·a·ble \'vī-ə-bəl\ *adj* **1** : capable of living; *esp* : sufficiently developed as to be capable of surviving outside the mother's womb ⟨a ~ fetus⟩   **2** : capable of growing and developing ⟨~ seeds⟩   ♦ : capable of being put into practice : WORKABLE   **4** : having a reasonable chance of succeeding ⟨a ~ candidate⟩ — **vi·a·bil·i·ty** \ˌvī-ə-'bi-lə-tē\ *n* — **vi·a·bly** \'vī-ə-blē\ *adv*

♦ achievable, attainable, doable, feasible, possible, practicable, realizable, workable

vi·a·duct \'vī-ə-ˌdəkt\ *n* : a long elevated roadway usu. consisting of a series of short spans supported on arches, piers, or columns
vi·al \'vī-əl\ *n* : a small vessel for liquids
vi·and \'vī-ənd\ *n* **1** : an article of food   **2** ♦ : a stock of food — usu. used in pl.

♦ *usu* **viands** chow, fare, food, grub, meat, provender, provisions

vi·at·i·cum \vī-'a-ti-kəm, vē-\ *n, pl* **-cums** *or* **-ca** \-kə\ **1** : the Christian Eucharist given to a person in danger of death   **2** : an allowance esp. in money for traveling needs and expenses
vibes \'vībz\ *n pl* **1** : VIBRAPHONE   **2** : VIBRATIONS
vi·bran·cy \'vī-brən-sē\ *n* ♦ : the quality or state of being vibrant

♦ animation, briskness, exuberance, liveliness, lustiness, robustness, sprightliness, vitality

vi·brant \'vī-brənt\ *adj* **1** : VIBRATING, PULSATING   **2** ♦ : pulsating with vigor or activity   **3** : readily set in vibration : RESPONSIVE   **4** ♦ : sounding from vibration : RESONANT; *also* : intensified and enriched by or as if by resonance   **5** : BRIGHT ⟨~ colors⟩

♦ [2] alive, animated, astir, busy, lively ♦ [4] golden, resonant, resounding, ringing, round, sonorous

vi·bra·phone \'vī-brə-ˌfōn\ *n* : a percussion instrument like the xylophone but with metal bars and motor-driven resonators
vi·brate \'vī-ˌbrāt\ *vb* **vi·brat·ed; vi·brat·ing** **1** : OSCILLATE   **2** : to set in vibration   **3** ♦ : to be in vibration : QUIVER   **4** : WAVER, FLUCTUATE   **5** : to respond sympathetically : THRILL

♦ agitate, convulse, jolt, jounce, quake, quiver, shake, shudder, wobble

vi·bra·tion \vī-'brā-shən\ *n* **1** : a rapid to-and-fro motion of the particles of an elastic body or medium (as a stretched cord) that produces sound   **2** ♦ : an act of vibrating : OSCILLATION   **3** : a trembling motion   **4** : VACILLATION   **5** : a feeling or impression that someone or something gives off — usu. used in pl. ⟨good ~s⟩ — **vi·bra·tion·al** \-shə-nəl\ *adj*

♦ oscillation, quivering

vi·bra·to \vi-'brä-tō\ *n, pl* **-tos** : a slightly tremulous effect imparted to vocal or instrumental music
vi·bra·tor \'vī-ˌbrā-tər\ *n* : one that vibrates or causes vibration; *esp* : a vibrating electrical device used in massage or for sexual stimulation
vi·bra·to·ry \'vī-brə-ˌtōr-ē\ *adj* : consisting of, capable of, or causing vibration
vi·bur·num \vī-'bər-nəm\ *n* : any of a genus of widely distributed shrubs or small trees related to the honeysuckle and bearing small usu. white flowers in broad clusters
vic *abbr* vicinity
Vic *abbr* Victoria
vic·ar \'vi-kər\ *n* **1** : an administrative deputy   **2** : a minister in charge of a church who serves under the authority of another minister — **vi·car·i·ate** \vī-'ker-ē-ət\ *n*
vic·ar·age \'vi-kə-rij\ *n* : a vicar's home
vicar–general *n, pl* **vicars–general** : an administrative deputy (as of a Roman Catholic or Anglican bishop)
vi·car·i·ous \vī-'ker-ē-əs, -'kar-\ *adj* **1** : acting for another   **2** : done or suffered by one person on behalf of another or others ⟨a ~ sacrifice⟩   **3** : sharing in someone else's experience through the use of the imagination or sympathetic feelings — **vi·car·i·ous·ly** *adv* — **vi·car·i·ous·ness** *n*
¹**vice** \'vīs\ *n* **1** ♦ : moral depravity or corruption   **2** ♦ : a moral fault or failing   **3** : an habitual usu. trivial fault   **4** : an undesirable behavior pattern in a domestic animal

♦ [1] corruption, debauchery, depravity, immorality, iniquity, licentiousness, sin *Ant* morality, virtue ♦ [2] demerit, failing, fault, foible, frailty, shortcoming, weakness

²**vice** *chiefly Brit var of* VISE
³**vice** *prep* : in the place of; *also* : rather than
vice admiral *n* : a commissioned officer in the navy or coast guard ranking above a rear admiral
vice·ge·rent \'vīs-'jir-ənt\ *n* : an administrative deputy of a king or magistrate — **vice·ge·ren·cy** \-ən-sē\ *n*
vi·cen·ni·al \vī-'se-nē-əl\ *adj* : occurring once every 20 years
vice presidency *n* : the office of vice president
vice president *n* **1** : an officer ranking next to a president and usu. empowered to act for the president during an absence or disability   **2** : any of several of a president's deputies
vice·re·gal \'vīs-'rē-gəl\ *adj* : of or relating to a viceroy
vice·roy \'vīs-ˌrȯi\ *n* : the governor of a country or province who rules as representative of the sovereign — **vice·roy·al·ty** \-əl-tē\ *n*
vice ver·sa \ˌvī-si-'vər-sə, 'vīs-'vər-\ *adv* : with the order reversed
vi·chys·soise \ˌvi-shē-'swäz, ˌvē-\ *n* : a soup made esp. from leeks or onions and potatoes, cream, and chicken stock and usu. served cold
vic·i·nage \'vis-ə-nij\ *n* : a neighboring or surrounding district : VICINITY
vi·cin·i·ty \və-'si-nə-tē\ *n, pl* **-ties** **1** : NEARNESS, PROXIMITY   **2** : a surrounding area : NEIGHBORHOOD
vi·cious \'vi-shəs\ *adj* **1** ♦ : having the quality of vice : WICKED   **2** : DEFECTIVE, FAULTY; *also* : INVALID   **3** : IMPURE, FOUL   **4** ♦ : having a savage disposition; *also* : marked by violence or ferocity ⟨a ~ attack⟩   **5** : MALICIOUS, SPITEFUL   **6** : worsened by internal causes that augment each other ⟨~ wage-price spiral⟩

♦ [1] bad, evil, immoral, iniquitous, nefarious, rotten, sinful, unethical, unsavory, vile, villainous, wicked, wrong ♦ [4] barbarous, brutal, cruel, heartless, inhumane, sadistic, savage, wanton ♦ [4] fell, ferocious, fierce, grim, savage

vi·cious·ly *adv* ♦ : in a vicious manner

♦ hatefully, maliciously, meanly, nastily, spitefully, wickedly

vi·cious·ness *n* ♦ : the quality or state of being vicious

♦ cattiness, despite, hatefulness, malice, malignity, meanness, nastiness, spite, spleen, venom

vi·cis·si·tude \və-'si-sə-ˌtüd, vī-, -ˌtyüd\ *n* : an irregular, unexpected, or surprising change ⟨the ~s of business⟩
vic·tim \'vik-təm\ *n* **1** : a living being offered as a sacrifice in a religious rite   **2** ♦ : an individual injured or killed (as by disease or accident)   **3** ♦ : a person cheated, fooled, or injured ⟨a ~ of circumstances⟩

♦ [2] casualty, fatality, loss ♦ [3] butt, mark, target

vic·tim·ise *chiefly Brit var of* VICTIMIZE
vic·tim·ize \'vik-tə-ˌmīz\ *vb* **-ized; -iz·ing** ♦ : to make a victim of — **vic·tim·i·za·tion** \ˌvik-tə-mə-'zā-shən\ *n* — **vic·tim·iz·er** \'vik-tə-ˌmī-zər\ *n*

♦ bleed, cheat, chisel, cozen, defraud, fleece, hustle, mulct, rook, shortchange, skin, squeeze, stick, sting, swindle

vic·tim·less \'vik-təm-ləs\ *adj* : having no victim ⟨considered gambling to be a ~ crime⟩
vic·tor \'vik-tər\ *n* ♦ : one that defeats an enemy or opponent : WINNER

♦ conqueror, master, winner *Ant* loser

vic·to·ria \vik-'tōr-ē-ə\ *n* : a low 4-wheeled carriage with a folding top and a raised driver's seat in front
¹**Vic·to·ri·an** \vik-'tōr-ē-ən\ *adj* **1** : of or relating to the reign of Queen Victoria of England or the art, letters, or tastes of her time   **2** : typical of the standards, attitudes, or conduct of the age of Victoria esp. when considered prudish or narrow
²**Victorian** *n* **1** : a person and esp. an author of the Victorian period   **2** : a typically large ornate house built during Queen Victoria's reign
vic·to·ri·ous \vik-'tōr-ē-əs\ *adj* **1** : having won a victory   **2** : of, relating to, or characteristic of victory — **vic·to·ri·ous·ly** *adv*
vic·to·ry \'vik-tə-rē\ *n, pl* **-ries** **1** : the overcoming of an enemy or an antagonist   **2** : achievement of mastery or success in a struggle or endeavor
¹**vict·ual** \'vit-ᵊl\ *n* **1** : food fit for humans   **2** *pl* ♦ : food supplies

victuals ♦ chow, fare, food, grub, meat, provender, provisions, viands

²victual vb **-ualed** or **-ualled; -ual·ing** or **-ual·ling**   **1** ♦ : to supply with food   **2** : to store up provisions

♦ board, cater, provision

vict·ual·ler or **vict·ual·er** \'vit-ᵊl-ər\ n : one that supplies provisions (as to an army or a ship)

vi·cu·ña or **vi·cu·na** \vi-'kün-yə, vī-; vī-'kü-nə, -'kyü-\ n   **1** : a So. American wild mammal related to the llama and alpaca; also : its wool   **2** : a soft fabric woven from the wool of the vicuña; also : a sheep's wool imitation of this

vi·de \'vī-dē, 'vē-ˌdā\ vb imper : SEE — used to direct a reader to another item

vi·de·li·cet \və-'de-lə-ˌset, vī-; vi-'dā-li-ˌket\ adv : that is to say : NAMELY

¹vid·eo \'vi-dē-ˌō\ n   **1** : TELEVISION   **2** : VIDEOTAPE; also : a recording similar to a videotape but stored in digital form   **3** : a videotaped performance ⟨music ∼s⟩

²video adj   **1** : relating to or used in transmission or reception of the television image   **2** : relating to or being images on a television screen or computer display ⟨a ∼ terminal⟩

video camera n : a camera that records visual images and usu. sound; esp : CAMCORDER

vid·eo·cas·sette \ˌvi-dē-ō-kə-'set\ n   **1** : a case containing videotape for use with a VCR   **2** : a recording (as of a movie) on a videocassette

videocassette recorder n : VCR

vid·eo·con·fer·enc·ing \-'kän-f(ə-)rən-siŋ\ n : the holding of a conference among people at remote locations by means of transmitted audio and video signals

vid·eo·disc or **vid·eo·disk** \'vi-dē-ō-ˌdisk\ n   **1** : OPTICAL DISK   **2** : a recording (as of a movie) on a videodisc

video game n : an electronic game played on a video screen

vid·e·o·gen·ic \ˌvi-dē-ō-'je-nik\ adj : TELEGENIC

vid·eo·phone \'vid-ə-ˌfōn\ n : a telephone for transmitting both audio and video signals

¹vid·eo·tape \'vid-ē-ō-ˌtāp\ n : a recording of visual images and sound made on magnetic tape; also : the magnetic tape used for such a recording

²videotape vb : to make a videotape of

videotape recorder n : a device for recording and playing back videotapes

vie \'vī\ vb **vied; vy·ing** \'vī-iŋ\ ♦ : to compete for superiority : CONTEND — **vi·er** \'vī-ər\ n

♦ battle, compete, contend, fight, race

Viet·cong \vē-et-'käŋ, ˌvē-ət-, -'kȯŋ\ n, pl **Vietcong** : a guerrilla member of the Vietnamese communist movement

Viet·nam·ese \vē-ˌet-nə-'mēz, ˌvē-ət-, -'mēs\ n, pl **Vietnamese** : a native or inhabitant of Vietnam — **Vietnamese** adj

¹view \'vyü\ n   **1 a** ♦ : the act of seeing or examining   **b** : SURVEY   **2** : a way of looking at or regarding something   **3** ♦ : an opinion or judgment colored by the feeling or bias of its holder ⟨stated his ∼s⟩   **4** ♦ : a sight (as of a landscape) regarded for its pictorial quality   **5** : extent or range of vision ⟨within ∼⟩   **6** : OBJECT, PURPOSE ⟨done with a ∼ to promotion⟩   **7** : a picture of a scene

♦ [1a] cast, eye, gander, glance, glimpse, look, peek, peep, regard, sight ♦ [3] belief, conviction, eye, feeling, judgment (or judgement), mind, notion, opinion, persuasion, sentiment, verdict ♦ [4] lookout, outlook, panorama, prospect, vista

²view vb   **1** : to look at attentively : EXAMINE   **2** : to perceive by the eye : SEE   **3** : to examine mentally : CONSIDER ⟨∼ a problem⟩ — **view·er** n

view·er·ship \'vyü-ər-ˌship\ n : a television audience esp. with respect to size or makeup

view·find·er \'vyü-ˌfīn-dər\ n : a device on a camera for showing the view to be included in the picture

view·point \-ˌpȯint\ n ♦ : a position or perspective from which something is considered or evaluated : POINT OF VIEW

♦ angle, outlook, perspective, point of view, slant, standpoint

vi·ges·i·mal \vī-'je-sə-məl\ adj : based on the number 20

vig·il \'vi-jəl\ n   **1** : a religious observance formerly held on the night before a religious feast   **2** : the day before a religious feast observed as a day of spiritual preparation   **3** : evening or nocturnal devotions or prayers — usu. used in pl.   **4** : an act or a time of keeping awake when sleep is customary; esp : WATCH 1

vig·i·lance \'vi-jə-ləns\ n ♦ : the quality or state of being vigilant

♦ alertness, attentiveness, lookout, watch

vigilance committee n : a committee of vigilantes

vig·i·lant \'vi-jə-lənt\ adj ♦ : alertly watchful esp. to avoid danger — **vig·i·lant·ly** adv

♦ alert, attentive, awake, watchful, wide-awake

vig·i·lan·te \ˌvi-jə-'lan-tē\ n : a member of a volunteer committee organized to suppress and punish crime summarily (as when the processes of law are viewed as inadequate); also : a self-appointed doer of justice — **vig·i·lan·tism** \-'lan-ˌti-zəm\ n

¹vi·gnette \vin-'yet\ n   **1** : a small decorative design   **2** : a picture (as an engraving or a photograph) that shades off gradually into the surrounding ground   **3** ♦ : a short descriptive literary sketch

♦ delineation, depiction, description, picture, portrait, portrayal, sketch

²vignette vb **vi·gnett·ed; vi·gnett·ing**   **1** : to finish (as a photograph) like a vignette   **2** : to describe briefly

vig·or or Can and Brit **vig·our** \'vi-gər\ n   **1** ♦ : active strength or energy of body or mind   **2** : INTENSITY, FORCE

♦ dash, drive, energy, ginger, hardihood, life, pep, sap, snap, vim, vitality, zing, zip Ant lethargy, listlessness, sluggishness ♦ energy, force, main, might, muscle, potency, power, sinew, strength

vig·or·ous \'vi-gə-rəs\ adj   **1** ♦ : having vigor   **2** ♦ : done with force and energy ⟨a ∼ debate⟩

♦ [1] hard, hard-bitten, hardy, rugged, stout, strong, sturdy, tough ♦ [1] dynamic, energetic, flush, lusty, peppy, robust, strenuous, vital Ant lethargic, listless, sluggish, torpid ♦ [2] aggressive, assertive, dynamic, emphatic, energetic, forceful, resounding, strenuous, vehement ♦ [2] firm, forceful, hearty, lusty, robust, solid, stout, strong, sturdy

vig·or·ous·ly adv ♦ : in a vigorous manner

♦ energetically, firmly, forcefully, forcibly, hard, mightily, powerfully, stiffly, stoutly, strenuously, strongly, sturdily

vig·or·ous·ness n : the quality or state of being vigorous

vig·our chiefly Brit var of VIGOR

Vi·king \'vī-kiŋ\ n : any of the pirate Norsemen who raided or invaded the coasts of Europe in the 8th to 10th centuries

vile \'vīl\ adj **vil·er; vil·est**   **1** ♦ : morally despicable   **2** : physically repulsive : FOUL   **3** : of little worth   **4** : DEGRADING, IGNOMINIOUS   **5** : utterly bad or contemptible ⟨∼ weather⟩ — **vile·ly** \'vīl-lē\ adv

♦ bad, evil, immoral, iniquitous, nefarious, rotten, sinful, unethical, unsavory, vicious, villainous, wicked, wrong ♦ base, contemptible, despicable, detestable, dirty, dishonorable (or dishonourable), ignoble, low, mean, snide, sordid, wretched

vile·ness n ♦ : the quality or state of being vile

♦ atrociousness, atrocity, depravity, enormity, heinousness, monstrosity, wickedness

vil·i·fi·ca·tion \ˌvi-lə-fə-'kā-shən\ n ♦ : an instance of vilifying : a defamatory utterance

♦ defamation, libel, slander

vil·i·fy \'vi-lə-ˌfī\ vb **-fied; -fy·ing** ♦ : to utter slanderous and abusive statements against : DEFAME — **vil·i·fi·er** \'vi-lə-ˌfī-ər\ n

♦ blacken, defame, libel, malign, slander, smear, traduce

vil·la \'vi-lə\ n   **1** : a country estate   **2** ♦ : the rural or suburban residence of a wealthy person

♦ castle, estate, hall, manor, mansion, palace

vil·lage \'vi-lij\ n   **1** : a settlement usu. larger than a hamlet and smaller than a town   **2** : an incorporated minor municipality   **3** : the people of a village

vil·lag·er \'vi-li-jər\ n : an inhabitant of a village

vil·lain \'vi-lən\ n   **1** : VILLEIN   **2** ♦ : an evil person : SCOUNDREL

♦ beast, devil, evildoer, fiend, heavy, knave, no-good, rapscallion, rascal, reprobate, rogue, scalawag, scamp, scoundrel, varlet, wretch

vil·lain·ess \-lə-nəs\ n : a woman who is a villain

vil·lain·ous \-lə-nəs\ adj   **1** ♦ : befitting a villain : WICKED   **2** : highly objectionable : DETESTABLE — **vil·lain·ous·ness** n

♦ bad, evil, immoral, iniquitous, nefarious, rotten, sinful, unethical, unsavory, vicious, vile, wicked, wrong

vil·lain·ous·ly adv : in a villainous manner

vil·lainy \-lə-nē\ n, pl **-lain·ies** ♦ : villainous conduct; also : a villainous act   **2** : villainous character or nature

♦ bad, evil, ill, immorality, iniquity, sin, wrong

vil·lein \'vi-lən, -ˌlān\ n   **1** : a free villager of Anglo-Saxon times   **2** : an unfree peasant enslaved to a feudal lord

vil·lous \'vi-ləs\ adj : covered with fine hairs or villi

vil·lus \'vi-ləs\ n, pl **vil·li** \-ˌlī, -(ˌ)lē\ : a slender usu. vascular process; *esp* : one of the tiny projections of the mucous membrane of the small intestine that function in the absorption of food

vim \\'vim\\ *n* ♦ : robust energy and enthusiasm

♦ dash, energy, life, pep, vigor (*or* vigour), vitality

VIN *abbr* vehicle identification number

vin·ai·grette \\ˌvi-ni-'gret\\ *n* : a sauce made typically of oil, vinegar, and seasonings

vin·ci·ble \\'vin-sə-bəl\\ *adj* : capable of being overcome or subdued

vin·di·cate \\'vin-də-ˌkāt\\ *vb* **-cat·ed; -cat·ing 1** : AVENGE **2** ♦ : to free from allegation or blame : EXONERATE **3** ♦ : to establish by proof or competent evidence : CONFIRM **4** : to provide defense for : JUSTIFY **5** : to maintain a right to : ASSERT — **vin·di·ca·tor** \\-ˌkā-tər\\ *n*

♦ [2] absolve, acquit, clear, exculpate, exonerate ♦ [3] bear out, confirm, corroborate, substantiate, support, validate, verify

vin·di·ca·tion \\ˌvin-də-'kā-shən\\ *n* ♦ : the act of vindicating or the state of being vindicated; *esp* : justification against denial or censure : DEFENSE

♦ acquittal, exculpation, exoneration

vin·dic·tive \\vin-'dik-tiv\\ *adj* **1** : disposed to revenge **2** : intended for or involving revenge **3** : VICIOUS, SPITEFUL — **vin·dic·tive·ly** *adv* — **vin·dic·tive·ness** *n*

vine \\'vīn\\ *n* **1** : GRAPE 2 **2** ♦ : a plant whose stem requires support and which climbs (as by tendrils) or trails along the ground; *also* : the stem of such a plant

vin·e·gar \\'vi-ni-gər\\ *n* : a sour liquid obtained by fermentation (as of cider, wine, or malt) and used to flavor or preserve foods

vin·e·gary \\-gə-rē\\ *adj* **1** ♦ : resembling vinegar : SOUR **2** : disagreeable in manner or disposition : CRABBED

♦ acid, sour, tart

vine·yard \\'vin-yərd\\ *n* **1** : a field of grapevines esp. to produce grapes for wine production **2** : a sphere of activity : field of endeavor

vi·nous \\'vī-nəs\\ *adj* **1** : of, relating to, or made with wine ⟨∼ medications⟩ **2** : showing the effects of the use of wine ⟨∼ bloodshot eyes⟩

1vin·tage \\'vin-tij\\ *n* **1** : a season's yield of grapes or wine **2** : WINE; *esp* : a usu. superior wine which comes from a single year **3** : the act or period of gathering grapes or making wine **4** : a period of origin ⟨clothes of 1890 ∼⟩

2vintage *adj* **1** : of, relating to, or produced in a particular vintage **2** : of old, recognized, and enduring interest, importance, or quality : CLASSIC ⟨∼ cars⟩ **3** : of the best and most characteristic — used with a proper noun

vint·ner \\'vint-nər\\ *n* : a dealer in wines

vi·nyl \\'vīn-ᵊl\\ *n* **1** : a chemical derived from ethylene by the removal of one hydrogen atom **2** : a polymer of a vinyl compound or a product (as a textile fiber) made from one

vinyl chloride *n* : a flammable gaseous carcinogenic compound used esp. to make vinyl resins

vi·ol \\'vī-əl\\ *n* : a bowed stringed instrument chiefly of the 16th and 17th centuries having a fretted neck and usu. six strings

1vi·o·la \\vī-'ō-lə, 'vī-ə-lə\\ *n* : VIOLET 1; *esp* : any of various hybrid garden plants with white, yellow, purple, or variously colored flowers that resemble but are smaller than those of the related pansies

2vi·o·la \\vē-'ō-lə\\ *n* : an instrument of the violin family slightly larger and tuned lower than a violin — **vi·o·list** \\-list\\ *n*

vi·o·la·ble \\'vī-ə-lə-bəl\\ *adj* : capable of being violated

vi·o·late \\'vī-ə-ˌlāt\\ *vb* **-lat·ed; -lat·ing 1** ♦ : to go beyond limits set or prescribed by : BREAK ⟨∼ a law⟩ ⟨∼ a frontier⟩ **2** : RAPE **3** ♦ : to fail to show proper respect for : DESECRATE **4** : INTERRUPT, DISTURB ⟨*violated* his privacy⟩ — **vi·o·la·tor** \\-ˌlā-tər\\ *n*

♦ [1] breach, break, transgress *Ant* comply (with), conform (to), follow, mind, obey, observe ♦ [3] defile, desecrate, profane

vi·o·la·tion \\ˌvī-ə-'lā-shən\\ *n* ♦ : an act or instance of violating : the state of being violated

♦ breach, crime, error, infraction, malefaction, misdeed, misdoing, offense, sin, transgression, trespass, wrongdoing

vi·o·lence \\'vī-ləns, 'vī-ə-\\ *n* **1** : exertion of physical force so as to injure or abuse **2** : injury by or as if by infringement or profanation **3** : intense or furious often destructive action or force **4** : vehement feeling or expression : INTENSITY **5** : jarring quality : a state of discord

vi·o·lent \\-lənt\\ *adj* **1** ♦ : marked by extreme force or sudden intense activity **2** : caused by or showing strong feeling ⟨∼

words⟩ **3** ♦ : existing in an extreme degree : INTENSE **4** : emotionally agitated to the point of loss of self-control **5** : caused by force : not natural ⟨∼ death⟩ — **vi·o·lent·ly** *adv*

♦ [1] explosive, ferocious, fierce, furious, hot, rabid, rough, stormy, tempestuous, turbulent, volcanic *Ant* nonviolent, peaceable, peaceful ♦ [3] deep, exquisite, fearful, hard, heavy, intense, profound, terrible, vehement, vicious

vi·o·let \\'vī-ə-lət\\ *n* **1** : any of a genus of herbs or small shrubs usu. with heart-shaped leaves and both aerial and underground flowers; *esp* : one with small usu. solid-colored flowers **2** : a reddish blue color

vi·o·lin \\ˌvī-ə-'lin\\ *n* : a bowed stringed instrument with four strings that has a shallow body, a fingerboard without frets, and a curved bridge — **vi·o·lin·ist** \\-'li-nist\\ *n*

vi·o·lon·cel·lo \\ˌvī-ə-lən-'che-lō\\ *n* : CELLO — **vi·o·lon·cel·list** \\-list\\ *n*

VIP \\ˌvē-ˌī-'pē\\ *n, pl* **VIPs** \\-'pēz\\ ♦ : a person of great influence or prestige; *esp* : a high official with special privileges

♦ celebrity, figure, light, luminary, notable, personage, personality, somebody, standout, star, superstar

vi·per \\'vī-pər\\ *n* **1** : a common stout-bodied Eurasian venomous snake having a bite only rarely fatal to humans; *also* : any snake (as a pit viper) of the same family as the viper **2** : any venomous or reputedly venomous snake **3** : a vicious or treacherous person — **vi·per·ine** \\-pə-ˌrīn\\ *adj*

vi·ra·go \\və-'rä-gō, -'rā-\\ *n, pl* **-goes** *or* **-gos 1** ♦ : a loud overbearing woman **2** : a woman of great strength and courage

♦ fury, harpy, shrew, termagant

vi·ral \\'vī-rəl\\ *adj* **1** : of, relating to, or caused by a virus ⟨a ∼ infection⟩ **2** : quickly and widely spread or popularized esp. by means of social media ⟨a ∼ video⟩ — **vi·ral·ly** *adv*

vir·eo \\'vir-ē-ˌō\\ *n, pl* **-e·os** : any of various small insect-eating American songbirds mostly olive green and grayish in color

1vir·gin \\'vər-jən\\ *n* **1** : an unmarried woman devoted to religion **2** : an unmarried girl or woman **3** *cap* : the mother of Jesus **4** : a person who has not had sexual intercourse

2virgin *adj* **1** : free from stain : PURE, SPOTLESS **2** : CHASTE **3** : befitting a virgin : MODEST **4** ♦ : having its original qualities unimpaired : FRESH; *esp* : not altered by human activity ⟨∼ forest⟩ **5** : INITIAL, FIRST

♦ brand-new, fresh, pristine

1vir·gin·al \\'vər-jən-ᵊl\\ *adj* : of, relating to, or characteristic of a virgin or virginity — **vir·gin·al·ly** *adv*

2virginal *n* : a small rectangular spinet without legs popular in the 16th and 17th centuries

Vir·gin·ia creeper \\vər-'jin-yə-\\ *n* : a No. American vine related to the grapes that has leaves with five leaflets and bluish-black berries

Virginia reel *n* : an American country-dance

vir·gin·i·ty \\vər-'ji-nə-tē\\ *n, pl* **-ties 1** : the quality or state of being virgin; *esp* : MAIDENHOOD **2** : the unmarried life : CELIBACY

Vir·go \\'vər-ˌgō\\ *n* **1** : a zodiacal constellation between Leo and Libra usu. pictured as a young woman **2** : the 6th sign of the zodiac in astrology; *also* : one born under this sign

vir·gule \\'vər-gyül\\ *n* : ²SLASH 3

vir·i·des·cent \\ˌvir-ə-'des-ᵊnt\\ *adj* : slightly green : GREENISH

vir·ile \\'vir-əl\\ *adj* **1** : having the nature, properties, or qualities of a man **2** ♦ : characteristic of or associated with men : MASCULINE **3** : MASTERFUL, FORCEFUL

♦ male, manly, mannish, man-size, masculine

vi·ril·i·ty \\və-'ri-lə-tē\\ *n* ♦ : the quality or state of being virile

♦ manhood, manliness, masculinity *Ant* femininity

vi·ri·on \\'vī-rē-ˌän, 'vir-ē-\\ *n* : a complete virus particle consisting of an RNA or DNA core with a protein coat

vi·rol·o·gy \\vī-'rä-lə-jē\\ *n* : a branch of science that deals with viruses and viral diseases — **vi·rol·o·gist** \\-jist\\ *n*

vir·tu \\ˌvər-'tü, vir-\\ *or* **ver·tu** \\ˌvər-, ˌvert-\\ *n* **1** : a love of or taste for objects of art **2** : objects of art (as curios and antiques)

vir·tu·al \\'vər-chə-wəl\\ *adj* **1** : being in essence or in effect though not formally recognized or admitted ⟨a ∼ dictator⟩ **2** : being on or simulated on a computer or computer network ⟨∼ shopping⟩

vir·tu·al·ly \\'vər-chə-wə-lē\\ *adv* **1** ♦ : almost entirely : NEARLY **2** : for all practical purposes

♦ about, almost, most, much, near, nearly, next to, nigh, practically, some, well-nigh

virtual reality *n* : an artificial environment that is experienced through sensory stimuli (as sights and sounds) provided by an interactive computer program; *also* : the technology used to create or access a virtual reality

vir·tue \'vər-chü\ *n* **1** ♦ : conformity to a standard of right : MORALITY **2** : a particular moral excellence **3** : manly strength or courage : VALOR **4** ♦ : a commendable quality : MERIT **5** : active power to accomplish a given effect : POTENCY, EFFICACY **6** : chastity esp. in a woman

♦ [1] character, decency, goodness, honesty, integrity, morality, probity, rectitude, righteousness, uprightness ♦ [4] distinction, excellence, merit, value

vir·tu·os·i·ty \,vər-chə-'wä-sə-tē\ *n, pl* **-ties** : great technical skill in the practice of a fine art

¹**vir·tu·o·so** \,vər-chə-'wō-sō, -zō\ *n, pl* **-sos** *or* **-si** \-sē, -zē\ **1** : one skilled in or having a taste for the fine arts **2** ♦ : one who excels in the technique of an art; *esp* : a highly skilled musical performer **3** ♦ : a person who has great skill at some endeavor

♦ [2, 3] ace, adept, artist, authority, crackerjack, expert, maestro, master, scholar, shark, whiz, wizard

²**virtuoso** *adj* ♦ : of, relating to, or characteristic of a virtuoso

♦ accomplished, adept, consummate, crack, crackerjack, expert, good, great, master, masterful, masterly, proficient, skilled, skillful

vir·tu·ous \'vər-chə-wəs\ *adj* **1** ♦ : having or showing virtue and esp. moral virtue **2** : CHASTE

♦ decent, ethical, good, honest, honorable (*or* honourable), just, moral, right, righteous, straight, upright

vir·tu·ous·ly *adv* ♦ : in a virtuous manner

♦ chastely, modestly, purely, righteously

vir·u·lence \'vir-ə-ləns, 'vir-yə-\ *n* ♦ : the quality or state of being virulent

♦ acidity, acrimony, asperity, bitterness, cattiness, tartness, vitriol

vir·u·lent \'vir-ə-lənt, 'vir-yə-\ *adj* **1** : highly infectious ⟨a ~ germ⟩; *also* : marked by a rapid, severe, and often deadly course ⟨a ~ disease⟩ **2** : extremely poisonous or venomous : NOXIOUS **3** ♦ : full of malice : MALIGNANT

♦ catty, cruel, hateful, malevolent, malicious, malign, malignant, mean, nasty, spiteful

vir·u·lent·ly *adv* : in a virulent manner

vi·rus \'vī-rəs\ *n, pl* **vi·rus·es 1** : any of a large group of submicroscopic infectious agents that have an outside coat of protein around a core of RNA or DNA, that can grow and multiply only in living cells, and that cause important diseases in human beings, lower animals, and plants; *also* : a disease caused by a virus **2** : something (as a corrupting influence) that poisons the mind or spirit **3** : a computer program that is usu. hidden within another program and that reproduces itself and inserts the copies into other programs and usu. performs a malicious action (as destroying data)

vis *abbr* **1** visibility **2** visual

¹**vi·sa** \'vē-zə, -sə\ *n* **1** : an endorsement by the proper authorities on a passport to show that it has been examined and the bearer may proceed **2** : a signature by a superior official signifying approval of a document

²**visa** *vb* **vi·saed** \-zəd, -səd\; **vi·sa·ing** \-zə-iŋ, -sə-\ : to give a visa to (a passport)

vis·age \'vi-zij\ *n* ♦ : the face or countenance of a person or sometimes an animal; *also* : LOOK

♦ cast, countenance, expression, face, look

¹**vis-à-vis** \,vēz-ə-'vē, ,vēs-\ *prep* **1** : face-to-face with : OPPOSITE **2** : in relation to **3** : as compared with

²**vis-à-vis** *n, pl* **vis-à-vis** *same or* -'vēz\ **1** : one that is face-to-face with another **2** : ESCORT **3** : COUNTERPART **4** : TÊTE-À-TÊTE

³**vis-à-vis** *adv* : in company : TOGETHER

viscera *pl of* VISCUS

vis·cer·al \'vi-sə-rəl\ *adj* **1** : felt in or as if in the viscera **2** : not intellectual : INSTINCTIVE **3** : of or relating to the viscera — **vis·cer·al·ly** *adv*

vis·cid \'vi-səd\ *adj* **1** ♦ : having an adhesive quality **2** : having a glutinous consistency : VISCOUS — **vis·cid·i·ty** \vi-'si-də-tē\ *n*

♦ adhesive, gelatinous, gluey, glutinous, gooey, gummy, sticky, viscous

vis·cos·i·ty \vis-'kä-sə-tē\ *n, pl* **-ties** ♦ : the quality of being viscous; *esp* : the property of resistance to flow in a fluid

♦ consistency, thickness

vis·count \'vī-,kau̇nt\ *n* : a member of the British peerage ranking below an earl and above a baron

vis·count·ess \-,kau̇n-təs\ *n* **1** : the wife or widow of a viscount **2** : a woman who holds the rank of viscount in her own right

vis·cous \'vis-kəs\ *adj* **1** : having the sticky consistency of glue : VISCID **2** ♦ : having or characterized by viscosity

♦ syrupy, thick, viscid

vis·cus \'vis-kəs\ *n, pl* **vis·cera** \'vi-sə-rə\ : an internal organ of the body; *esp* : one (as the heart or liver) located in the cavity of the trunk

vise \'vīs\ *n* : a tool with two jaws for holding work that typically close by a screw or lever

vis·i·bil·i·ty \,vi-zə-'bi-lə-tē\ *n, pl* **-ties 1** : the quality, condition, or degree of being visible **2** : the degree of clearness of the atmosphere

vis·i·ble \'vi-zə-bəl\ *adj* ♦ : capable of being seen ⟨~ stars⟩; *also* : APPARENT ⟨has no ~ means of support⟩ — **vis·i·bly** \-blē\ *adv*

♦ apparent, observable, visual *Ant* invisible

¹**vi·sion** \'vi-zhən\ *n* **1** : something seen otherwise than by ordinary sight (as in a dream or trance) **2** ♦ : a vivid picture created by the imagination ⟨~s of fame and fortune⟩ **3** : the act or power of imagination **4** : unusual wisdom in foreseeing what is going to happen **5** ♦ : the act or power of seeing : SIGHT **6** : something seen; *esp* : a lovely sight **7** : the apparition of a person : PHANTOM

♦ [2] chimera, conceit, daydream, delusion, dream, fancy, fantasy, figment, hallucination, illusion, phantasm, pipe dream, unreality ♦ [5] eye, sight

²**vision** *vb* ♦ : to picture to oneself : IMAGINE

♦ conceive, dream, envisage, fancy, imagine, picture, visualize

¹**vi·sion·ary** \'vi-zhə-,ner-ē\ *adj* **1** : of the nature of a vision : ILLUSORY, UNREAL **2** : not practical : UTOPIAN **3** : seeing or likely to see visions : given to dreaming or imagining **4** ♦ : having or marked by foresight and imagination

♦ farsighted, forehanded, foresighted, prescient, proactive, provident

²**visionary** *n, pl* **-ar·ies 1** ♦ : one whose ideas or projects are impractical : DREAMER **2** : one who sees visions

♦ dreamer, idealist, romantic, utopian

¹**vis·it** \'vi-zət\ *vb* **1** : to go to see in order to comfort or help **2** : to call on either as an act of courtesy or friendship **3** ♦ : to dwell with for a time as a guest **4** : to come to or upon as a reward, affliction, or punishment **5** : INFLICT **6** ♦ : to make a visit or regular or frequent visits **7** ♦ : to talk in an informal or familiar manner : CHAT — **vis·it·able** *adj*

♦ [3] sojourn, stay, tarry ♦ [6] call, drop (by *or* in), pop (in), stop (by *or* in) ♦ [7] chat, converse, gab, jaw, palaver, patter, prattle, rattle, talk

²**visit** *n* **1** : a short stay : CALL **2** ♦ : a brief residence as a guest **3** : a journey to and stay at a place **4** : a formal or professional call (as by a doctor)

♦ sojourn, stay

vis·i·tant \'vi-zə-tənt\ *n* : VISITOR

vis·i·ta·tion \,vi-zə-'tā-shən\ *n* **1** : an instance of visiting : VISIT; *esp* : an official visit **2** : a special dispensation of divine favor or wrath; *also* : a severe trial

visiting nurse *n* : a nurse employed to visit sick persons or perform public health services in a community

vis·i·tor \'vi-zə-tər\ *n* ♦ : one that visits

♦ caller, guest

vi·sor \'vī-zər\ *n* **1** : the front piece of a helmet; *esp* : a movable upper piece **2** : VIZARD **3** ♦ : a projecting part (as on a cap) to shade the eyes — **vi·sored** \-zərd\ *adj*

♦ bill, peak

vis·ta \'vis-tə\ *n* **1** ♦ : a distant view through or along an avenue or opening **2** : an extensive mental view over a series of years or events

♦ lookout, outlook, panorama, prospect, view

VISTA *abbr* Volunteers in Service to America

¹**vi·su·al** \'vi-zhə-wəl\ *adj* **1** ♦ : of, relating to, or used in vision ⟨~ organs⟩ **2** : perceived by vision ⟨a ~ impression⟩ **3** ♦ : capable of being seen : VISIBLE **4** : done by sight only ⟨~ navigation⟩ **5** : of or relating to instruction by means of sight ⟨~ aids⟩ — **vi·su·al·ly** *adv*

♦ [1] ocular, optical *Ant* nonvisual ♦ [3] apparent, observable, visible

²visual *n* : something (as a picture, chart, or film) that appeals to the sight and is used for illustration, demonstration, or promotion — usu. used in pl.

vi·su·al·ize \'vi-zhə-wə-ˌlīz\ *vb* **-ized; -iz·ing** ♦ : to make visible; *esp* : to form a mental image of — **vi·su·al·i·za·tion** \ˌvi-zhə-wə-lə-'zā-shən\ *n* — **vi·su·al·iz·er** *n*

♦ conceive, dream, envisage, fancy, imagine, picture, vision

vi·ta \'vē-tə, 'vī-\ *n, pl* **vi·tae** \'vē-ˌtī, 'vī-ˌtē\ : a brief autobiographical sketch

vi·tal \'vīt-ᵊl\ *adj* **1** : concerned with or necessary to the maintenance of life ⟨∼ organs⟩ **2** ♦ : full of life and vigor **3** : of, relating to, or characteristic of life or living beings **4** ♦ : destructive to life : FATAL ⟨∼ wound⟩ **5** ♦ : of the utmost importance — **vi·tal·ly** *adv*

♦ [2] active, animate, animated, brisk, energetic, lively, peppy, spirited, sprightly, springy, vigorous, vivacious ♦ [4] baleful, deadly, deathly, fatal, fell, lethal, mortal, murderous, pestilent ♦ [5] essential, imperative, indispensable, integral, necessary, needful, requisite ♦ [5] critical, crucial, key, pivotal

vi·tal·i·ty \vī-'ta-lə-tē\ *n, pl* **-ties** **1** : the property distinguishing the living from the nonliving **2** ♦ : mental and physical vigor **3** : enduring quality **4** ♦ : lively and animated character ⟨the ∼ of youth⟩

♦ [2] dash, energy, life, pep, vigor (*or* vigour), vim ♦ [4] animation, briskness, exuberance, liveliness, lustiness, robustness, sprightliness, vibrancy *Ant* inactivity

vi·tal·ize \'vīt-ᵊl-ˌīz\ *vb* **-ized; -iz·ing** ♦ : to impart life or vigor to : ANIMATE — **vi·tal·i·za·tion** \ˌvīt-ᵊl-ə-'zā-shən\ *n*

♦ animate, brace, energize, enliven, fire, invigorate, jazz up, liven up, pep up, quicken, stimulate, vivify, zip (up)

vi·tals \'vīt-ᵊlz\ *n pl* **1** : vital organs (as the heart and brain) **2** : essential parts

vital signs *n pl* : the pulse rate, respiratory rate, body temperature, and often blood pressure of a person

vital statistics *n pl* : statistics dealing with births, deaths, marriages, health, and disease

vi·ta·min \'vī-tə-mən\ *n* : any of various organic substances that are essential in tiny amounts to the nutrition of most animals and some plants and are mostly obtained from foods

vitamin A *n* : any of several vitamins (as from egg yolk or fish-liver oils) required esp. for good vision

vitamin B *n* **1** : VITAMIN B COMPLEX **2** *or* **vitamin B₁** : THIAMINE

vitamin B complex *n* : a group of vitamins that are found widely in foods and are essential for normal function of certain enzymes and for growth

vitamin B₆ \-'bē-'siks\ *n* : any of several compounds that are considered essential to vertebrate nutrition

vitamin B₁₂ \-'bē-'twelv\ *n* : a complex cobalt-containing compound that occurs esp. in liver and is essential to normal blood formation, neural function, and growth; *also* : any of several compounds of similar action

vitamin C *n* : a vitamin found esp. in fruits and vegetables that is needed by the body to prevent scurvy

vitamin D *n* : any or all of several vitamins that are needed for normal bone and tooth structure and are found esp. in fish-liver oils, egg yolk, and milk or are produced by the body in response to ultraviolet light

vitamin E *n* : any of various oily fat-soluble liquid vitamins whose absence in the body is associated with such ailments as infertility, the breakdown of muscles, and vascular problems and which are found esp. in leaves and in seed germ oils

vitamin K *n* : any of several vitamins needed for blood to clot properly

vi·ti·ate \'vi-shē-ˌāt\ *vb* **-at·ed; -at·ing** **1** ♦ : to make faulty or defective : IMPAIR **2** : to make legally ineffective : INVALIDATE **3** ♦ : to debase in moral or aesthetic status — **vi·ti·a·tion** \ˌvi-shē-'ā-shən\ *n* — **vi·ti·a·tor** \'vi-shē-ˌā-tər\ *n*

♦ [1] blemish, break, cripple, damage, deface, disfigure, flaw, harm, hurt, injure, mar, spoil ♦ [3] blemish, mar, poison, spoil, stain, taint, tarnish, touch

vi·ti·cul·ture \'vi-tə-ˌkəl-chər\ *n* : the growing of grapes — **vi·ti·cul·tur·al** \ˌvi-tə-'kəl-chə-rəl\ *adj* — **vi·ti·cul·tur·ist** \-rist\ *n*

vit·re·ous \'vi-trē-əs\ *adj* **1** : of, relating to, or resembling glass : GLASSY ⟨∼ rocks⟩ **2** : of, or being the clear colorless transparent jelly (**vitreous humor**) behind the lens in the eyeball

vit·ri·ol \'vi-trē-əl\ *n* ♦ : something resembling acid in being caustic, corrosive, or biting — **vit·ri·ol·ic** \ˌvi-trē-'ä-lik\ *adj*

♦ acidity, acrimony, asperity, bitterness, cattiness, tartness, virulence ♦ abuse, fulmination, invective, vituperation

vit·tles \'vit-ᵊlz\ *n pl* : supplies of food : VICTUALS

vi·tu·per·ate \vī-'tü-pə-ˌrāt, və-, -'tyü-\ *vb* **-at·ed; -at·ing** ♦ : to abuse in words — **vi·tu·per·a·tive** \-'tü-pə-rə-tiv, -'tyü-, -ˌrā-\ *adj* — **vi·tu·per·a·tive·ly** *adv*

♦ abuse, assail, attack, belabor, blast, castigate, excoriate, jump, lambaste, slam

vi·tu·per·a·tion \(ˌ)vī-tü-pə-'rā-shən, və-, -tyü-\ *n* ♦ : lengthy harsh criticism or abuse

♦ abuse, fulmination, invective, vitriol

vi·va \'vē-və\ *interj* — used to express goodwill or approval

vi·va·ce \vē-'vä-chā\ *adv or adj* : in a brisk spirited manner — used as a direction in music

vi·va·cious \və-'vā-shəs, vī-\ *adj* ♦ : lively in temper, conduct, or spirit ⟨a ∼ personality⟩ — **vi·va·cious·ness** *n*

♦ active, animate, animated, brisk, energetic, frisky, jaunty, jazzy, lively, peppy, perky, pert, racy, snappy, spirited, sprightly, springy, vital

vi·va·cious·ly *adv* ♦ : in a vivacious manner

♦ gaily, jauntily, sprightly

vi·vac·i·ty \-'va-sə-tē\ *n* : the quality or state of being vivacious

vi·va vo·ce \ˌvī-və-'vō-sē, ˌvē-və-'vō-ˌchā\ *adj* : expressed or conducted by word of mouth : ORAL — **viva voce** *adv*

viv·id \'vi-vəd\ *adj* **1** : having the appearance of vigorous life **2** : BRILLIANT, INTENSE ⟨a ∼ red⟩ **3** : producing a strong impression on the senses; *esp* : producing distinct mental pictures : GRAPHIC ⟨a ∼ description⟩ — **viv·id·ly** *adv* — **viv·id·ness** *n*

viv·i·fy \'vi-və-ˌfī\ *vb* **-fied; -fy·ing** **1** ♦ : to put life into : ANIMATE **2** : to make vivid ⟨details that ∼ a story⟩ — **viv·i·fi·ca·tion** \ˌvi-və-fə-'kā-shən\ *n* — **viv·i·fi·er** *n*

♦ animate, brace, energize, enliven, fire, invigorate, jazz up, liven up, pep up, quicken, stimulate, vitalize, zip (up)

vi·vip·a·rous \vī-'vi-pə-rəs, və-\ *adj* : producing living young from within the body rather than from eggs — **vi·vi·par·i·ty** \ˌvī-və-'par-ə-tē, ˌvi-\ *n*

viv·i·sec·tion \ˌvi-və-'sek-shən, 'vi-və-ˌsek-\ *n* : the cutting of or operation on a living animal; *also* : animal experimentation esp. if causing distress to the subject

vix·en \'vik-sən\ *n* **1** : an angry and unpleasant woman **2** : a female fox

viz *abbr* videlicet

viz·ard \'vi-zərd\ *n* : a mask for disguise or protection

vi·zier \və-'zir\ *n* : a high executive officer of many Muslim countries

VJ *abbr* veejay

vlog \'vlóg, 'vläg\ *n* : a blog that contains video material — **vlog** *vb* — **vlog·ger** *n*

VOA *abbr* Voice of America

voc *abbr* **1** vocational **2** vocative

vocab *abbr* vocabulary

vo·ca·ble \'vō-kə-bəl\ *n* : TERM, NAME; *esp* : a word as such without regard to its meaning

vo·cab·u·lary \vō-'ka-byə-ˌler-ē\ *n, pl* **-lar·ies** **1** : a list or collection of words usu. alphabetically arranged and defined or explained : LEXICON **2** ♦ : a stock of words in a language used by a class or individual or in relation to a subject

♦ argot, cant, jargon, language, lingo, slang, terminology

vocabulary entry *n* : a word (as the noun *book*), hyphened or open compound (as the verb *cross-refer* or the noun *boric acid*), word element (as the affix *-an*), abbreviation (as *agt*), verbalized symbol (as *Na*), or term (as *master of ceremonies*) entered alphabetically in a dictionary for the purpose of definition or identification or expressly included as an inflected form (as the noun *mice* or the verb *saw*) or as a derived form (as the noun *godlessness* or the adverb *globally*) or related phrase (as *in spite of*) run on at its base word and usu. set in a type (as boldface) readily distinguishable from that of the lightface running text which defines, explains, or identifies the entry

¹vo·cal \'vō-kəl\ *adj* **1** ♦ : uttered by the voice : ORAL **2** : relating to, composed or arranged for, or sung by the human voice ⟨∼ music⟩ **3** : given to expressing oneself freely or insistently : OUTSPOKEN ⟨a ∼ critic⟩ **4** : of or relating to the voice

♦ oral, voiced *Ant* nonvocal

²vocal *n* **1** : a vocal sound **2** ♦ : a vocal composition or its performance

♦ jingle, lay, lyric, song

vocal cords *n pl* : either of two pairs of elastic folds of mucous membrane that project into the cavity of the larynx and function in the production of vocal sounds

vo•cal•ic \vō-'ka-lik\ *adj* : of, relating to, or functioning as a vowel

vo•cal•ise *chiefly Brit var of* VOCALIZE

vo•cal•ist \'vō-kə-list\ *n* ♦ : one that sings : SINGER

♦ caroler, singer, songster, voice

vo•cal•ize \-ˌlīz\ *vb* **-ized; -iz•ing** **1** ♦ : to give vocal expression to : UTTER; *esp* : SING **2** : to make voiced rather than voiceless

♦ articulate, say, speak, state, talk, tell, utter, verbalize ♦ carol, chant, descant, sing

vo•cal•iz•er \'vō-kə-ˌlī-zər\ *n* : one that vocalizes

vo•ca•tion \vō-'kā-shən\ *n* **1** : a summons or strong inclination to a particular state or course of action ⟨religious ∼⟩ **2** ♦ : regular employment : OCCUPATION — **vo•ca•tion•al** \-shə-nəl\ *adj*

♦ calling, employment, line, occupation, profession, trade, work

vo•ca•tion•al•ism \-shə-nə-ˌli-zəm\ *n* : emphasis on vocational training in education

voc•a•tive \'vä-kə-tiv\ *adj* : of, relating to, or constituting a grammatical case marking the one addressed — **vocative** *n*

vo•cif•er•ate \vō-'si-fə-ˌrāt\ *vb* **-at•ed; -at•ing** : to cry out loudly : SHOUT — **vo•cif•er•a•tion** \-ˌsi-fə-'rā-shən\ *n*

♦ bawl, call, cry, holler, shout, yell

vo•cif•er•ous \vō-'si-fə-rəs\ *adj* ♦ : making or given to loud outcry — **vo•cif•er•ous•ly** *adv* — **vo•cif•er•ous•ness** *n*

♦ blatant, boisterous, clamorous, obstreperous

vod•ka \'väd-kə\ *n* : a colorless liquor distilled from a mash (as of rye or wheat)

vogue \'vōg\ *n* **1** ♦ : popular acceptance or favor : POPULARITY **2** : a period of popularity **3** ♦ : one that is in fashion at a particular time

♦ [1] favor, modishness, popularity ♦ [3] craze, fad, mode, rage, style, trend

vogu•ish \'vō-gish\ *adj* **1** : FASHIONABLE, SMART **2** : suddenly or temporarily popular ⟨∼ expressions⟩

¹**voice** \'vȯis\ *n* **1** : sound produced through the mouth by vertebrates and esp. by human beings (as in speaking or singing) **2** : musical sound produced by the vocal cords : the power to produce such sound; *also* : one of the melodic parts in a vocal or instrumental composition **3** : the vocal organs as a means of tone production ⟨train the ∼⟩ **4** : sound produced by vibration of the vocal cords as heard in vowels and some consonants **5** : the power of speaking **6** : a sound suggesting a voice ⟨the ∼ of the sea⟩ **7** : an instrument or medium of expression **8** ♦ : a choice, opinion, or wish openly expressed; *also* : right of expression **9** : distinction of form of a verb to indicate the relation of the subject to the action expressed by the verb **10** : one that sings : SINGER

♦ articulation, expression, formulation, statement, utterance

²**voice** *vb* **voiced; voic•ing** ♦ : to give voice or expression to ⟨∼ a complaint⟩

♦ air, express, give, look, sound, state, vent

voice box *n* : LARYNX

voiced \'vȯist\ *adj* **1** : having a voice ⟨soft-*voiced*⟩ **2** ♦ : uttered with voice ⟨a ∼ consonant⟩ — **voiced•ness** \'vȯist-nəs, 'vȯi-səd-nəs\ *n*

♦ oral, vocal

voice•less \'vȯis-ləs\ *adj* **1** ♦ : having no voice **2** : not pronounced with voice — **voice•less•ly** *adv* — **voice•less•ness** *n*

♦ dumb, inarticulate, mute, speechless

voice mail *n* : an electronic communication system in which spoken messages are recorded for later playback to the intended recipient; *also* : such a message

voice–over *n* : the voice in a film or television program of a person who is heard but not seen or not seen talking

voice•print \'vȯis-ˌprint\ *n* : an individually distinctive pattern of voice characteristics that is spectrographically produced

¹**void** \'vȯid\ *adj* **1** : UNOCCUPIED, VACANT **2** ♦ : containing nothing : EMPTY **3** ♦ : being without something specified : DEVOID ⟨proposals ∼ of sense⟩ **4** : VAIN, USELESS **5** ♦ : of no legal force or effect : NULL

♦ [2] bare, blank, devoid, empty, stark, vacant ♦ [3] bereft, destitute, devoid ♦ [5] invalid, null

²**void** *n* **1** ♦ : empty space : EMPTINESS **2** : a feeling of want or hollowness

♦ blank, blankness, emptiness, vacancy, vacuity

³**void** *vb* **1** ♦ : to make or leave empty; *also* : VACATE **2** : DISCHARGE, EMIT ⟨∼ urine⟩ **3** ♦ : to render void : ANNUL ⟨∼ a contract⟩ — **void•able** *adj* — **void•er** *n*

♦ [1] clear, empty, evacuate, vacate ♦ [3] abolish, abrogate, annul, cancel, dissolve, invalidate, negate, nullify, quash, repeal, rescind

voi•là \vwä-'lä\ *interj* — used to call attention or to express satisfaction or approval

voile \'vȯil\ *n* : a sheer fabric used esp. for women's clothing and curtains

vol *abbr* **1** volume **2** volunteer

vol•a•tile \'vä-lət-ᵊl\ *adj* **1** : readily becoming a vapor at a relatively low temperature ⟨a ∼ liquid⟩ **2** ♦ : likely to change suddenly ⟨a ∼ temper⟩ — **vol•a•til•i•ty** \ˌvä-lə-'ti-lə-tē\ *n* — **vol•a•til•ize** \'vä-lət-ᵊl-ˌīz\ *vb*

♦ capricious, changeable, fickle, fluid, inconstant, mercurial, mutable, temperamental, uncertain, unpredictable, unsettled, unstable, unsteady, variable

vol•ca•nic \väl-'ka-nik\ *adj* **1** : of, relating to, or produced by a volcano **2** ♦ : explosively violent

♦ explosive, ferocious, fierce, furious, hot, rabid, rough, stormy, tempestuous, turbulent, violent

vol•ca•nism \'väl-kə-ˌni-zəm\ *n* : volcanic action or activity

vol•ca•no \väl-'kā-nō\ *n, pl* **-noes** *or* **-nos** : an opening in the crust of the earth, a planet, or a moon from which molten rock and steam issue; *also* : a hill or mountain composed of the ejected material

vol•ca•nol•o•gy \ˌväl-kə-'nä-lə-jē\ *n* : a branch of geology that deals with volcanic phenomena — **vol•ca•nol•o•gist** \-kə-'nä-lə-jist\ *n*

vole \'vōl\ *n* : any of various small rodents that are closely related to the lemmings and muskrats

vo•li•tion \vō-'li-shən\ *n* **1** ♦ : the act or the power of making a choice or decision : WILL **2** : a choice or decision made

♦ accord, choice, free will, option, self-determination, will

vo•li•tion•al \vō-'li-shə-nəl\ *adj* : of, relating to, or of the nature of volition : possessing or exercising volition

¹**vol•ley** \'vä-lē\ *n, pl* **volleys** **1** : a flight of missiles (as arrows) **2** : simultaneous discharge of a number of missile weapons **3** : an act of volleying **4** ♦ : a burst of many things at once ⟨a ∼ of angry letters⟩

♦ barrage, bombardment, cannonade, fusillade, hail, salvo, shower, storm

²**volley** *vb* **vol•leyed; vol•ley•ing** **1** : to discharge or become discharged in or as if in a volley **2** : to hit an object of play (as a ball) in the air before it touches the ground

vol•ley•ball \-ˌbȯl\ *n* : a game played by volleying an inflated ball over a net; *also* : the ball used in this game

volt \'vōlt\ *n* : the meter-kilogram-second unit of electrical potential difference and electromotive force equal to the difference in potential between two points in a wire carrying a constant current of one ampere when the power dissipated between the points is equal to one watt

volt•age \'vōl-tij\ *n* : potential difference measured in volts

vol•ta•ic \väl-'tā-ik, vōl-\ *adj* : of, relating to, or producing direct electric current by chemical action

volte–face \ˌvȯlt-'fäs, ˌvȯl-tə-\ *n* : a reversal in policy : ABOUT= FACE

volt•me•ter \'vōlt-ˌmē-tər\ *n* : an instrument for measuring in volts the difference in potential between different points of an electrical circuit

vol•u•ble \'väl-yə-bəl\ *adj* : fluent and smooth in speech : GLIB — **vol•u•bil•i•ty** \ˌväl-yə-'bi-lə-tē\ *n* — **vol•u•bly** \'väl-yə-blē\ *adv*

vol•ume \'väl-yəm\ *n* **1** : a series of printed sheets bound typically in book form; *also* : an arbitrary number of issues of a periodical **2** : space occupied as measured by cubic units ⟨the ∼ of a cylinder⟩ **3** : sufficient matter to fill a book ⟨her glance spoke ∼s⟩ **4 a** : the total number or quantity : AMOUNT ⟨increasing ∼ of business⟩ **b** : considerable quantity **5** : the degree of loudness of a sound

vo•lu•mi•nous \və-'lü-mə-nəs\ *adj* ♦ : having or marked by great volume or bulk : LARGE — **vo•lu•mi•nous•ly** *adv*

♦ big, grand, great, large, sizable, substantial

vo•lu•mi•nous•ness *n* : the quality or state of being voluminous

¹**vol·un·tary** \'vä-lən-ˌter-ē\ *adj* **1 ♦** : done, made, or given freely and without compulsion ⟨a ~ sacrifice⟩ **2** : done on purpose : INTENTIONAL ⟨~ manslaughter⟩ **3 ♦** : of, relating to, or regulated by the will ⟨~ behavior⟩ **4** : having power of free choice **5** : provided or supported by voluntary action ⟨a ~ organization⟩ — **vol·un·tar·i·ly** \ˌvä-lən-'ter-ə-lē\ *adv*

♦ [1] deliberate, freewill, intentional, purposeful, willful, willing ♦ [3] discretionary, elective, optional

²**voluntary** *n, pl* **-tar·ies** : an organ solo played in a religious service

voluntary muscle *n* : muscle (as most striated muscle) under voluntary control

¹**vol·un·teer** \ˌvä-lən-'tir\ *n* **1** : a person who voluntarily undertakes a service or duty **2** : a plant growing spontaneously esp. from seeds lost from a previous crop

²**volunteer** *vb* **1 ♦** : to offer or give voluntarily **2** : to offer oneself as a volunteer

♦ bestow, contribute, donate, give, present

vo·lup·tu·ary \və-'ləp-chə-ˌwer-ē\ *n, pl* **-ar·ies** : a person whose chief interest in life is the indulgence of sensual appetites

vo·lup·tu·ous \-chə-wəs\ *adj* **1 ♦** : giving sensual gratification **2** : given to or spent in enjoyment of luxury or pleasure — **vo·lup·tu·ous·ly** *adv* — **vo·lup·tu·ous·ness** *n*

♦ carnal, fleshly, luscious, sensual, sensuous

vo·lute \və-'lüt\ *n* : a spiral or scroll-shaped decoration

¹**vom·it** \'vä-mət\ *n* : an act or instance of throwing up the contents of the stomach through the mouth; *also* : the matter thrown up

²**vomit** *vb* **1 ♦** : to throw up the contents of the stomach through the mouth **2** : to belch forth : GUSH

♦ gag, heave, spit up, throw up

voo·doo \'vü-dü\ *n, pl* **voodoos** **1** : a religion that is derived from African polytheism and is practiced chiefly in Haiti **2 ♦** : a person who deals in spells and necromancy **3** : a charm used in voodoo; *also* : ²SPELL 1 — **voodoo** *adj*

♦ conjurer, enchanter, magician, necromancer, sorcerer, witch, wizard

voo·doo·ism \-ˌi-zəm\ *n* **1** : VOODOO 1 **2** : the practice of witchcraft

vo·ra·cious \vȯ-'rā-shəs, və-\ *adj* **1 ♦** : having a huge appetite : RAVENOUS **2 ♦** : very eager ⟨a ~ reader⟩ — **vo·ra·cious·ly** *adv* — **vo·ra·cious·ness** *n* — **vo·rac·i·ty** \-'ra-sə-tē\ *n*

♦ [1] gluttonous, greedy, hoggish, piggish, rapacious, ravenous ♦ [2] ardent, avid, eager, enthusiastic, keen

vor·tex \'vȯr-ˌteks\ *n, pl* **vor·ti·ces** \'vȯr-tə-ˌsēz\ *also* **vor·tex·es** \'vȯr-ˌtek-səz\ : WHIRLPOOL; *also* : something resembling a whirlpool

vo·ta·ry \'vō-tə-rē\ *n, pl* **-ries** **1 a** : ENTHUSIAST, DEVOTEE **b ♦** : a devoted adherent or admirer **2 ♦** : a devout or zealous worshiper

♦ [1b, 2] adherent, convert, disciple, follower, partisan, pupil

¹**vote** \'vōt\ *n* **1** : a choice or opinion of a person or body of persons expressed usu. by a ballot, spoken word, or raised hand; *also* : the ballot, word, or gesture used to express a choice or opinion **2** : the decision reached by voting **3 ♦** : the right or privilege of voting in political matters **4** : a group of voters with some common characteristics ⟨the big city ~⟩ — **vote·less** *adj*

♦ enfranchisement, franchise, suffrage *Ant* disenfranchisement

²**vote** *vb* **vot·ed; vot·ing** **1** : to cast a vote **2** : to elect, decide, pass, defeat, grant, or make legal by a vote **3** : to declare by general agreement **4 ♦** : to offer as a suggestion : PROPOSE **5** : to cause to vote esp. in a given way — **vot·er** *n*

♦ advance, offer, pose, proffer, propose, propound, suggest

vo·tive \'vō-tiv\ *adj* : consisting of or expressing a vow, wish, or desire

vou *abbr* voucher

vouch \'vau̇ch\ *vb* **1** : to give tangible support to : PROVE **2** : to verify by examining documentary evidence **3** : to give a guarantee **4 ♦** : to supply supporting evidence or testimony; *also* : to give personal assurance

♦ attest, authenticate, avouch, certify, testify, witness

vouch·er \'vau̇-chər\ *n* **1** : an act of vouching **2** : one that vouches for another **3** : a documentary record of a business transaction **4** : a written affidavit or authorization **5** : a form indicating a credit against future purchases or expenditures

vouch·safe \vau̇ch-'sāf\ *vb* **vouch·safed; vouch·saf·ing** : to grant or give as or as if a privilege or a special favor

¹**vow** \'vau̇\ *n* **♦** : a solemn promise or statement; *esp* : one by which a person is bound to an act, service, or condition ⟨marriage ~s⟩

♦ oath, pledge, promise, troth, word

²**vow** *vb* **1 ♦** : to make a vow or as a vow **2** : to bind or commit by a vow — **vow·er** *n*

♦ covenant, pledge, promise, swear

vow·el \'vau̇-əl\ *n* **1** : a speech sound produced without obstruction or friction in the mouth **2** : a letter representing such a sound

vox po·pu·li \'väks-'pä-pyə-ˌlī\ *n* : popular sentiment

¹**voy·age** \'vȯi-ij\ *n* **♦** : a journey esp. by water from one place or country to another

♦ crossing, cruise, passage, sail

²**voyage** *vb* **voy·aged; voy·ag·ing ♦** : to take or make a voyage — **voy·ag·er** *n*

♦ journey, tour, travel, trek ♦ boat, cruise, navigate, sail

voya·geur \ˌvȯi-ə-'zhər, ˌvwä-yä-\ *n* : a person employed by a fur company to transport goods to and from remote stations esp. in the Canadian Northwest

voy·eur \vwä-'yər, vȯi-'ər\ *n* **1** : one who obtains sexual pleasure from viewing esp. covertly the nudity or sexual activity of others **2** : an observer of the sordid — **voy·eur·is·tic** \ˌvwä-(ˌ)yər-'is-tik, ˌvȯi-ər-\ *adj* — **voy·eur·ism** \-ˌi-zəm\ *n*

VP *abbr* **1** verb phrase **2** vice president

vs *abbr* **1** verse **2** versus

vss *abbr* **1** verses **2** versions

V/STOL *abbr* vertical or short takeoff and landing

Vt *or* **VT** *abbr* Vermont

VTOL *abbr* vertical takeoff and landing

VTR *abbr* videotape recorder

vul·ca·nize \'vəl-kə-ˌnīz\ *vb* **-nized; -niz·ing** : to treat rubber or rubberlike material chemically to give useful properties (as elasticity and strength)

Vulg *abbr* Vulgate

vul·gar \'vəl-gər\ *adj* **1** : of or relating to common speech : VERNACULAR **2 ♦** : of or relating to the common people : COMMON **3 a ♦** : lacking cultivation or refinement **b** : offensive to good taste or refined feelings : OBSCENE ⟨~ language⟩ — **vul·gar·ly** *adv*

♦ [2] common, humble, ignoble, inferior, low, lowly, mean, plebeian ♦ [3a] coarse, common, crass, crude, gross, ill-bred, low, rough, rude, tasteless, uncouth, uncultivated, uncultured, unpolished, unrefined

vul·gar·i·an \ˌvəl-'gar-ē-ən\ *n* : a vulgar person

vul·gar·ism \'vəl-gə-ˌri-zəm\ *n* **1** : VULGARITY **2** : a word or expression originated or used chiefly by illiterate persons **3** : a coarse expression : OBSCENITY

vul·gar·i·ty \ˌvəl-'gar-ə-tē\ *n, pl* **-ties** **1** : something vulgar **2 ♦** : the quality or state of being vulgar

♦ bawdiness, grossness, indecency, lewdness, nastiness, obscenity, ribaldry, smut ♦ coarseness, grossness, indelicacy, lowness, rudeness

vul·gar·ize \'vəl-gə-ˌrīz\ *vb* **-ized; -iz·ing** : to make vulgar — **vul·gar·i·za·tion** \ˌvəl-gə-rə-'zā-shən\ *n* — **vul·gar·iz·er** \'vəl-gə-ˌrī-zər\ *n*

Vul·gate \'vəl-ˌgāt\ *n* : a Latin version of the Bible used by the Roman Catholic Church

vul·ner·a·bil·i·ty \ˌvəl-nə-rə-'bi-lə-tē\ *n* **♦** : the quality or state of being vulnerable

♦ exposure, liability, openness

vul·ner·a·ble \'vəl-nə-rə-bəl\ *adj* **1 ♦** : capable of being wounded : susceptible to wounds **2 ♦** : open to attack **3** : liable to increased penalties in contract bridge — **vul·ner·a·bly** \'vəl-nə-rə-blē\ *adv*

♦ [1] exposed, liable, open, sensitive, subject, susceptible ♦ [2] defenseless (*or* defenceless), exposed, helpless, susceptible, undefended, unguarded, unprotected, unresistant

vul·pine \'vəl-ˌpīn\ *adj* : of, relating to, or resembling a fox esp. in cunning

vul·ture \'vəl-chər\ *n* **1** : any of various large birds (as a turkey vulture) related to the hawks, eagles, and falcons but having weaker claws and the head usu. naked and living chiefly on carrion **2** : a rapacious person

vul·va \'vəl-və\ *n, pl* **vul·vae** \-ˌvē\ : the external parts of the female genital organs — **vul·val** \'vəl-vəl\ *or* **vul·var** \-vər, -ˌvär\ *adj*

vv *abbr* **1** verses **2** vice versa

vying *pres part of* VIE

¹w \'də-bəl-(ˌ)yü\ *n, pl* **w's** *or* **ws** *often cap* : the 23d letter of the English alphabet

²w *abbr, often cap* **1** water **2** watt **3** week **4** weight **5** west; western **6** wide; width **7** wife **8** with

W *symbol* tungsten

WA *abbr* **1** Washington **2** Western Australia

wacky \'wa-kē\ *adj* **wack·i·er; -est** ♦ : eccentric or irrational esp. in an amusing, absurd, or fantastic manner; *also* : CRAZY

♦ far-out, funny, odd, quirky, screwy, strange, wild ♦ absurd, cockeyed, cuckoo, daft, foolish, harebrained, nutty, preposterous, sappy, screwball, silly, zany

¹wad \'wäd\ *n* **1** ♦ : a little mass, bundle, or tuft ⟨~s of clay⟩ **2** : a soft mass of usu. light fibrous material **3** : a pliable plug (as of felt) used to retain a powder charge (as in a cartridge) **4** ♦ : a considerable amount (as of money) **5** : a roll of paper money

♦ [1] blob, chunk, clod, clump, glob, gob, hunk, lump, nub ♦ [4] fortune, mint

²wad *vb* **wad·ded; wad·ding** **1** : to push a wad into ⟨~ a gun⟩ **2** ♦ : to form into a wad **3** : to hold in by a wad ⟨~ a bullet in a gun⟩ **4** : to stuff or line with a wad : PAD

♦ agglomerate, ball, conglomerate, roll, round *Ant* unroll

wad·ding \'wä-diŋ\ *n* **1** : WADS; *also* : material for making wads **2** : a soft mass or sheet of short loose fibers used for stuffing or padding

wad·dle \'wäd-ᵊl\ *vb* **wad·dled; wad·dling** : to walk with short steps swaying from side to side like a duck — **waddle** *n*

wade \'wād\ *vb* **wad·ed; wad·ing** **1** : to step in or through a medium (as water) more resistant than air **2** : to move or go with difficulty or labor and often with determination ⟨~ through a dull book⟩ **3** : to set to work or attack with determination or vigor — used with *in* or *into* — **wad·able** *or* **wade·able** \'wā-də-bəl\ *adj* — **wade** *n*

wad·er \'wā-dər\ *n* **1** : one that wades **2** : SHOREBIRD; *also* : WADING BIRD **3** *pl* : a waterproof garment consisting of pants with attached boots for wading

wa·di \'wä-dē\ *n* : a streambed of southwest Asia and northern Africa that is dry except in the rainy season

wading bird *n* : any of an order of long-legged birds (as sandpipers, cranes, or herons) that wade in water in search of food

wa·fer \'wā-fər\ *n* **1** : a thin crisp cake or cracker **2** : a thin round piece of unleavened bread used in the Eucharist **3** : something (as a piece of candy) that resembles a wafer

¹waf·fle \'wä-fəl\ *n* : a soft but crisped cake of batter cooked in a special hinged metal utensil (**waffle iron**)

²waffle *vb* **waf·fled; waf·fling** \-f(ə)liŋ\ : to speak or write in a vague or evasive manner ⟨*waffled* on the issue⟩

¹waft \'wäft, 'waft\ *vb* ♦ : to cause to move or go lightly by or as if by the impulse of wind or waves

♦ drift, float, glide, hang, hover, poise, ride, sail

²waft *n* **1** ♦ : a slight breeze : PUFF **2** : the act of waving

♦ air, breath, breeze, puff, zephyr

¹wag \'wag\ *vb* **wagged; wag·ging** **1** : to sway or swing shortly from side to side or to-and-fro ⟨the dog *wagged* his tail⟩ **2** : to move in chatter **3** : GOSSIP ⟨scandal caused tongues to ~⟩

²wag *n* : an act of wagging : a wagging movement

³wag *n* ♦ : a person full of sport and humor : JOKER

♦ card, comedian, comic, humorist, jester, joker, wit

¹wage \'wāj\ *n* **1** ♦ : payment for labor or services usu. according to contract — often used in pl. **2** *pl* : an equivalent or a return for something done, suffered, or given : RECOMPENSE

♦ *usu* **wages** pl emolument, hire, pay, payment, salary, stipend

²wage *vb* **waged; wag·ing** **1** : to engage in : CARRY ON ⟨~ a war⟩ **2** : to be in process of being waged

¹wa·ger \'wā-jər\ *n* **1** : something (as a sum of money) risked on an uncertain event : BET, STAKE **2** : something on which bets are laid : GAMBLE

²wager *vb* ♦ : to make a bet

♦ bet, gamble, go, lay, stake

wa·ger·er *n* : one that makes a wager

wag·gery \'wa-gə-rē\ *n, pl* **-ger·ies** **1** ♦ : playfulness and mischievous merriment **2** ♦ : something done or said in fun : JEST

♦ [1] devilishness, impishness, knavery, mischief, mischievousness, rascality, shenanigans, wickedness ♦ [2] crack, gag, jest, joke, laugh, pleasantry, quip, sally, wisecrack, witticism

wag·gish \'wa-gish\ *adj* **1** ♦ : resembling or characteristic of a wag : MISCHIEVOUS **2** : done or made for fun : HUMOROUS

♦ devilish, impish, knavish, mischievous, rascally, roguish, sly, wicked

¹wag·gle \'wa-gəl\ *vb* **wag·gled; wag·gling** : to move backward and forward or from side to side : WAG

²waggle *n* : a jerky motion back and forth or up and down

wag·gon *chiefly Brit var of* WAGON

wag·on \'wa-gən\ *n* **1** : a 4-wheeled vehicle; *esp* : one drawn by animals and used for freight or merchandise **2** : PADDY WAGON **3** : a child's 4-wheeled cart **4** : STATION WAGON

wag·on·er \'wa-gə-nər\ *n* : the driver of a wagon

wag·on·ette \ˌwa-gə-'net\ *n* : a light wagon with two facing seats along the sides behind a cross seat in front

wa·gon–lit \ˌvá-gōⁿ-'lē\ *n, pl* **wagons–lits** *or* **wagon–lits** *same or* -'lēz\ : a railroad sleeping car

wagon train *n* : a column of wagons traveling overland

wag·tail \'wag-ˌtāl\ *n* : any of various slender-bodied mostly Old World birds with a long tail that jerks up and down

wa·hi·ne \wä-'hē-nē, -ˌnä\ *n* **1** : a Polynesian woman **2** : a female surfer

wa·hoo \'wä-ˌhü\ *n, pl* **wahoos** : a large vigorous food and sport fish related to the mackerel and found in warm seas

waif \'wāf\ *n* **1** : something found without an owner and esp. by chance **2** : a stray person or animal; *esp* : a homeless child

¹wail \'wāl\ *vb* **1** ♦ : to express sorrow audibly : make a mournful outcry **2** : to make a sound suggestive of a mournful cry **3** : to express dissatisfaction in a manner suggestive of sadness : COMPLAIN

♦ bay, howl, keen, yowl ♦ *usu* **wail for** bemoan, bewail, deplore, grieve, lament, mourn

²wail *n* ♦ : a usu. prolonged cry or sound expressing grief or pain

♦ groan, howl, keen, lament, moan, plaint

wail·ful \-fəl\ *adj* : SORROWFUL, MOURNFUL — **wail·ful·ly** *adv*

wain \'wān\ *n* : a large heavy farm wagon

wain·scot \'wān-skət, -ˌskōt, -ˌskät\ *n* **1** : a usu. paneled wooden lining of an interior wall of a room **2** : the lower part of an interior wall when finished differently from the rest — **wainscot** *vb*

wain·scot·ing *or* **wain·scot·ting** \-ˌskō-tiŋ, -ˌskä-, -skə-\ *n* : material for a wainscot; *also* : WAINSCOT

waist \'wāst\ *n* **1** : the narrowed part of the body between the chest and hips **2** : a part resembling the human waist esp. in narrowness or central position ⟨the ~ of a ship⟩ **3** : a garment or part of a garment (as a blouse or bodice) for the upper part of the body

♦ middle, midriff

waist·band \-ˌband\ *n* : a band (as on pants or a skirt) that fits around the waist

waist·coat \'wes-kət, 'wāst-ˌkōt\ *n, chiefly Brit* : VEST 1

waist·line \'wāst-ˌlīn\ *n* : an arbitrary usu. imaginary line around the waist at its narrowest part; *also* : the length of this **2** : the line at which the bodice and skirt of a dress meet

¹wait \'wāt\ *vb* **1** ♦ : to remain inactive in readiness or expectation ⟨~ for orders⟩ **2** : to delay serving (a meal) **3** : to act as attendant or servant ⟨~ on customers⟩ **4** : to attend as a waiter : SERVE ⟨~ tables⟩ ⟨~ at a banquet⟩ **5** ♦ : to be ready ⟨a letter ~ing for you⟩

♦ [1, 5] await, bide, hold on, stay

²wait *n* **1** : a position of concealment usu. with intent to attack or surprise ⟨lie in ~⟩ **2** : an act or period of waiting

wait·er \'wā-tər\ *n* **1** : one that waits on another; *esp* ♦ : a person who waits tables **2** : TRAY

♦ server, waitperson, waitress

waiting game *n* : a strategy in which one or more participants withhold action in the hope of an opportunity for more effective action later

waiting room *n* : a room (as at a doctor's office) for the use of persons who are waiting

wait·per·son \'wāt-ˌpər-sən\ *n* ♦ : a waiter or waitress

   ♦ server, waiter, waitress

wait·ress \'wā-trəs\ *n* ♦ : a woman who waits tables

   ♦ server, waiter, waitperson

waive \'wāv\ *vb* **waived; waiv·ing** **1** : to give up claim to ⟨*waived* his right to a trial⟩ **2** : POSTPONE

waiv·er \'wā-vər\ *n* **1** : the act of waiving right, claim, or privilege **2** : a document containing a declaration of a waiver

¹**wake** \'wāk\ *vb* **woke** \'wōk\ *also* **waked** \'wākt\; **wo·ken** \'wō-kən\ *or* **waked** *also* **woke; wak·ing** **1** : to be or remain awake; *esp* : to keep watch (as over a corpse) **2** ♦ : to become awake : AWAKEN ⟨the baby *woke* up early⟩ **3** : to rouse from sleep : AWAKEN

   ♦ arouse, awake, rouse

²**wake** *n* **1** : the state of being awake **2** : a watch held over the body of a dead person prior to burial

³**wake** *n* : the track left by a ship in the water; *also* : a track left behind

wake·board \'wāk-ˌbȯrd\ *n* : a short board with foot bindings on which a rider is towed by a motorboat across its wake — **wake·board·er** *n* — **wake·board·ing** *n*

wake·ful \'wāk-fəl\ *adj* ♦ : not sleeping or able to sleep : SLEEPLESS — **wake·ful·ness** *n*

   ♦ awake, sleepless, wide-awake *Ant* asleep, dormant, dozing, napping, resting, sleeping, slumbering

wak·en \'wā-kən\ *vb* **1** : to cause to come awake : WAKE **2** : to cease to be asleep : WAKE

wake–rob·in \'wāk-ˌrä-bən\ *n* : TRILLIUM

wake–up call *n* ♦ : something that serves to alert a person to a problem, danger, or need

   ♦ caution, tip-off, tocsin, warning

wak·ing \'wā-kiŋ\ *adj* : passed in a conscious or alert state ⟨every ∼ hour⟩

wale \'wāl\ *n* : a ridge esp. on cloth; *also* : the texture esp. of a fabric

¹**walk** \'wȯk\ *vb* **1** ♦ : to move or cause to move on foot usu. at a natural unhurried gait ⟨∼ to town⟩ ⟨∼ a horse⟩ **2** : to pass over, through, or along by walking ⟨∼ the streets⟩ **3** : to perform or accomplish by walking ⟨∼ guard⟩ **4** : to follow a course of action or way of life ⟨∼ humbly in the sight of God⟩ **5** : WALK OUT **6** : to receive a base on balls; *also* : to give a base on balls to — **walk·er** *n*

   ♦ foot, leg, pad, step, traipse, tread

²**walk** *n* **1** ♦ : a going on foot ⟨go for a ∼⟩ **2** : a place, path, or course for walking **3** : distance to be walked ⟨a quarter-mile ∼ from here⟩ **4** : manner of living : CONDUCT, BEHAVIOR **5** : social or economic status ⟨various ∼s of life⟩ **6** : manner of walking : GAIT; *esp* : a slow 4-beat gait of a horse **7** : BASE ON BALLS

   ♦ perambulation, ramble, stroll, turn

walk·away \'wȯ-kə-ˌwā\ *n* : an easily won contest

walk·ie–talk·ie \ˌwȯ-kē-'tȯ-kē\ *n* : a small portable radio transmitting and receiving set

¹**walk–in** \'wȯk-ˌin\ *adj* : large enough to be walked into ⟨a ∼ refrigerator⟩

²**walk–in** *n* **1** : an easy election victory **2** : one that walks in

walking papers *n pl* : DISMISSAL, DISCHARGE

walking stick *n* **1** : a stick used in walking **2** : STICK INSECT; *esp* : one of the U.S. and Canada

walk·on \'wȯk-ˌȯn, -ˌän\ *n* : a small part in a dramatic production

walk·out \-ˌaut\ *n* **1** : a labor strike **2** : the action of leaving a meeting or organization as an expression of disapproval

walk out *vb* **1** : to leave suddenly often as an expression of disapproval **2** : to go on strike

walk·over \-ˌō-vər\ *n* : a one-sided contest : an easy victory

walk–up \'wȯk-ˌəp\ *n* : a building or apartment house without an elevator — **walk–up** *adj*

walk·way \-ˌwā\ *n* : a passage for walking

¹**wall** \'wȯl\ *n* **1 a** ♦ : a structure (as of stone or brick) intended for defense or security or for enclosing something **b** ♦ : something that resembles a wall in function esp. by establishing limits or providing defense **2** : one of the upright enclosing parts of a building or room **3** : the inside surface of a cavity or container

⟨the ∼ of a boiler⟩ **4** : something like a wall in appearance, function, or effect ⟨a tariff ∼⟩ — **walled** \'wȯld\ *adj*

   ♦ [1a] barrier, fence, hedge ♦ [1b] aegis, armor, cover, defense (*or* defence), guard, protection, safeguard, screen, security, shield, ward

²**wall** *vb* **1** ♦ : to provide, separate, or surround with or as if with a wall ⟨∼ in a garden⟩ **2** : to close (an opening) with or as if with a wall ⟨∼ up a door⟩

   ♦ *usu* **wall in** cage, closet, coop, corral, encase, enclose, envelop, fence, hedge, hem, house, immure, pen

wal·la·by \'wä-lə-bē\ *n, pl* **wallabies** *also* **wallaby** : any of various small or medium-sized kangaroos

wall·board \'wȯl-ˌbȯrd\ *n* : a structural material (as of wood pulp or plaster) made in large sheets and used for sheathing interior walls and ceilings

wal·let \'wä-lət\ *n* **1** : a bag or sack for carrying things on a journey **2** : a pocketbook with compartments (as for personal papers and usu. unfolded money) : BILLFOLD

wall·eye \'wȯ-ˌlī\ *n* **1** : an eye with a whitish iris or an opaque white cornea **2** : a large vigorous No. American food and sport fish related to the perches — **wall·eyed** \-ˌlīd\ *adj*

wall·flow·er \'wȯl-ˌflau̇-ər\ *n* **1** : any of several Old World herbs related to the mustards; *esp* : one with showy fragrant flowers **2** : a person who usu. from shyness or unpopularity remains alone (as at a dance)

Wal·loon \wä-'lün\ *n* : a member of a people of southern and southeastern Belgium and adjacent parts of France — **Walloon** *adj*

¹**wal·lop** \'wä-ləp\ *vb* **1** ♦ : to beat soundly : TROUNCE **2** ♦ : to hit hard and often repeatedly

   ♦ [1] clobber, drub, rout, skunk, thrash, trim, trounce, whip
   ♦ [2] bash, bat, batter, beat, belt, bludgeon, buffet, club, drub, flog, hammer, hide, lace, lambaste, lick, maul, pelt, pound, thrash, thump, whale, whip

²**wallop** *n* **1** : a powerful blow or impact **2** : the ability to hit hard **3** : emotional, sensory, or psychological force : IMPACT

wal·lop·ing \'wä-lə-piŋ\ *adj* **1** : LARGE, WHOPPING ⟨a ∼ storm⟩ **2** : exceptionally fine or impressive ⟨a ∼ fun party⟩

¹**wal·low** \'wä-lō\ *vb* **1** : to roll oneself about sluggishly in or as if in deep mud ⟨hogs ∼ing in the mire⟩ **2** : to indulge oneself excessively ⟨∼ in luxury⟩ **3** : to become or remain helpless ⟨∼ in ignorance⟩

²**wallow** *n* : a muddy or dust-filled area where animals wallow

wall·pa·per \'wȯl-ˌpā-pər\ *n* **1** : decorative paper for the walls of a room **2** : the background image or set of images displayed on a computer screen — **wallpaper** *vb*

wall–to–wall *adj* **1** : covering the entire floor ⟨*wall-to-wall* carpeting⟩ **2** : covering or filling one entire space or time ⟨crowds of *wall-to-wall* people⟩

wal·nut \'wȯl-(ˌ)nət\ *n* **1** : a nut with a furrowed usu. rough shell and an adherent husk from any of a genus of trees related to the hickories; *esp* : the large edible nut of a Eurasian tree **2** : a tree that bears walnuts **3** : the usu. reddish to dark brown wood of a walnut used esp. in cabinetwork and veneers

wal·rus \'wȯl-rəs, 'wäl-\ *n, pl* **walrus** *or* **wal·rus·es** : a large mammal of arctic waters that is related to the seals and has long ivory tusks

¹**waltz** \'wȯlts\ *n* **1** : a gliding dance done to music having three beats to the measure **2** : music for or suitable for waltzing

²**waltz** *vb* **1** : to dance a waltz **2** : to move or advance easily, successfully, or conspicuously ⟨he ∼ed off with the championship⟩

wam·ble \'wäm-bəl\ *vb* **wam·bled; wam·bling** : to progress unsteadily or with a lurching shambling gait

Wam·pa·no·ag \ˌwäm-pə-'nō-(ˌ)ag, ˌwȯm-\ *n, pl* **Wampanoag** *or* **Wampanoags** : a member of an Indigenous people of parts of Rhode Island and Massachusetts

wam·pum \'wäm-pəm\ *n* **1** : beads made of shells strung in strands, belts, or sashes and used by No. American Indigenous people as money and ornaments **2** : MONEY

wan \'wän\ *adj* **wan·ner; wan·nest** **1** : having a sickly, pale color suggestive of ill health : PALLID; *also* : FEEBLE **2** : DIM, FAINT **3** : LANGUID ⟨a ∼ smile⟩ — **wan·ly** *adv* — **wan·ness** *n*

wand \'wänd\ *n* **1** : a slender staff carried in a procession **2** : the staff of a fairy, diviner, or magician

wan·der \'wän-dər\ *vb* **1** ♦ : to move about aimlessly or without a fixed course or goal : RAMBLE **2** : to go astray in conduct or thought; *esp* : to become delirious

   ♦ gad, gallivant, knock, maunder, meander, mope, ramble, range, roam, rove, traipse

wan·der·er *n* ♦ : one that wanders

♦ drifter, nomad, rambler, rover, stroller, vagabond

wandering Jew *n* : either of two trailing or creeping plants cultivated for their showy and often white-striped foliage

wan·der·lust \'wän-dər-ˌləst\ *n* : strong longing for or impulse toward wandering

¹**wane** \'wān\ *vb* **waned; wan·ing** **1** ♦ : to grow gradually smaller or less ⟨the full moon ⟨~s to new⟩ ⟨his strength *waned*⟩ **2** : to lose power, prosperity, or influence **3** : to draw near an end ⟨summer is *waning*⟩

♦ abate, decline, decrease, de-escalate, die, diminish, dwindle, ebb, fall, lessen, let up, lower, moderate, recede, relent, shrink, subside, taper

²**wane** *n* : a waning (as in size or power); *also* : a period in which something is waning

wan·gle \'waŋ-gəl\ *vb* **wan·gled; wan·gling** **1** ♦ : to obtain by sly or devious means; *also* : to use trickery or questionable means to achieve an end **2** ♦ : to adjust or manipulate esp. for personal or fraudulent ends; *also* : FINAGLE

♦ [1, 2] contrive, finagle, finesse, frame, machinate, maneuver (*or* manoeuvre), mastermind, negotiate

wan·na·be *also* **wan·na·bee** \'wä-nə-ˌbē\ *n* : a person who wants or aspires to be someone or something else or who tries to look or act like someone else

¹**want** \'wȯnt, 'wänt\ *vb* **1** : to fail to possess : LACK ⟨they ~ the necessities of life⟩ **2** ♦ : to feel the need of ⟨~ed a chance to rest⟩ **3** ♦ : to be in need of : REQUIRE ⟨the house ~s painting⟩ **4** ♦ : to desire earnestly : WISH

♦ [2, 3] demand, necessitate, need, require, take, warrant ♦ [4] ache for, covet, crave, desire, die (to *or* for), hanker (for *or* after), hunger for, long for, lust (for *or* after), pine for, repine for, thirst for, wish for, yearn for

²**want** *n* **1** ♦ : a lack of a required or usual amount **2** ♦ : dire need : DESTITUTION **3** : something wanted : DESIRE **4** : personal defect : FAULT

♦ [1] dearth, deficiency, deficit, failure, famine, inadequacy, insufficiency, lack, paucity, poverty, scantiness, scarcity, shortage ♦ [1] absence, lack, need ♦ [2] beggary, destitution, impecuniousness, impoverishment, indigence, need, pauperism, penury, poverty

¹**want·ing** \'wȯn-tiŋ, 'wän-\ *adj* **1** ♦ : not present or in evidence : ABSENT **2** ♦ : falling below standards or expectations **3** ♦ : lacking in ability or capacity : DEFICIENT ⟨~ in common sense⟩

♦ [1] absent, missing, nonexistent ♦ [2, 3] deficient, inadequate, insufficient, scarce, short, shy

²**wanting** *prep* **1** : LESS, MINUS ⟨a month ~ two days⟩ **2** : not having : WITHOUT ⟨a book ~ a cover⟩

¹**wan·ton** \'wȯnt-ᵊn, 'wänt-\ *adj* **1** ♦ : having, expressing, or inciting sensual desire or imagination **2** ♦ : having no regard for justice or for other persons' feelings, rights, or safety : INHUMANE ⟨~ cruelty⟩ **3** : having no just cause ⟨a ~ attack⟩ — **wan·ton·ly** *adv*

♦ [1] lascivious, lewd, lustful, passionate ♦ [2] barbarous, brutal, cruel, heartless, inhumane, sadistic, savage, vicious

²**wanton** *n* : a wanton individual; *esp* : a lewd or immoral person

³**wanton** *vb* **1** : to be wanton : act wantonly **2** : to pass or waste wantonly

wan·ton·ness *n* ♦ : the quality or state of being wanton

♦ barbarity, brutality, cruelty, inhumanity, sadism, savagery, viciousness

wa·pi·ti \'wä-pə-tē\ *n, pl* **wapiti** *or* **wapitis** : ELK 2

¹**war** \'wȯr\ *n* **1** ♦ : a state or period of usu. open and declared armed fighting between states or nations **2** : the art or science of warfare **3** ♦ : a state of hostility, conflict, or antagonism **4** : a struggle between opposing forces or for a particular end ⟨~ against disease⟩ — **war·less** \-ləs\ *adj*

♦ [1] combat, conflict, warfare *Ant* peace ♦ [3] conflict, discord, dissension, dissent, disunity, friction, schism, strife, variance, warfare

²**war** *vb* **warred; war·ring** ♦ : to engage in warfare : be in conflict

♦ *usu* **war against** battle, clash, combat, fight, scrimmage, skirmish

³**war** *abbr* warrant

¹**war·ble** \'wȯr-bəl\ *n* **1** ♦ : a melodious succession of low pleasing sounds **2** : a musical trill

♦ air, lay, melody, song, strain, tune

²**warble** *vb* **war·bled; war·bling** **1** : to sing or utter in a trilling manner or with variations **2** : to express by or as if by warbling

³**warble** *n* : a swelling under the skin esp. of the back of cattle, horses, and wild mammals caused by the maggot of a fly (**warble fly**); *also* : its maggot

war·bler \'wȯr-blər\ *n* **1** : SONGSTER **2** : any of various small slender-billed chiefly Old World songbirds related to the thrushes and noted for their singing **3** : any of numerous small bright-colored insect-eating American birds with a usu. weak and unmusical song

war·bon·net \'wȯr-ˌbä-nət\ *n* : a feathered ceremonial headdress worn mainly by Indigenous people of the Great Plains

war crime *n* : a crime (as genocide) committed during or in connection with war

war cry *n* **1** : a cry used by fighters in war **2** : a slogan used esp. to rally people to a cause

¹**ward** \'wȯrd\ *n* **1** ♦ : a guarding or being under guard or guardianship; *esp* : CUSTODY **2** : a body of guards **3** : a division of a prison **4** : a division in a hospital **5** : a division of a city for electoral or administrative purposes **6** : a person (as a child) under the protection of a guardian or a law court **7** : a person or body of persons under the protection or tutelage of a government **8** ♦ : a means of defense : PROTECTION

♦ [1] care, custody, guardianship, keeping, safekeeping, trust ♦ [8] aegis, armor, cover, defense (*or* defence), guard, protection, safeguard, screen, security, shield, wall

²**ward** *vb* : to turn aside : DEFLECT — usu. used with *off* ⟨~ off a blow⟩

¹**-ward** \wərd\ *also* **-wards** \wərdz\ *adj suffix* **1** : that moves, tends, faces, or is directed toward ⟨wind*ward*⟩ **2** : that occurs or is situated in the direction of ⟨sea*ward*⟩

²**-ward** *or* **-wards** *adv suffix* **1** : in a (specified) direction ⟨up*wards*⟩ ⟨after*ward*⟩ **2** : toward a (specified) point, position, or area ⟨sky*ward*⟩

war dance *n* : a dance performed by members of tribal societies before going to war or in celebration of victory

war·den \'wȯrd-ᵊn\ *n* **1** ♦ : one having care or charge of something : GUARDIAN **2** : the governor of a town, district, or fortress **3** : an official charged with special supervisory or enforcement duties ⟨game ~⟩ ⟨air raid ~⟩ **4** : an official in charge of the operation of a prison **5** : one of two ranking lay officers of an Episcopal parish **6** : any of various British college officials

♦ caretaker, custodian, guardian, janitor, keeper, watchman

ward·er \'wȯr-dər\ *n* ♦ : one that keeps guard esp. at a tower, gate, or door : WATCHMAN

♦ custodian, guard, guardian, keeper, lookout, picket, sentry, warden, watch, watchman

ward heel·er \-ˌhē-lər\ *n* : a local worker for a political boss

ward·robe \'wȯr-ˌdrōb\ *n* **1** : a room or closet where clothes are kept; *also* : CLOTHESPRESS **2** : a collection of wearing apparel ⟨his summer ~⟩

ward·room \-ˌdrüm, -ˌdrùm\ *n* : the dining area for officers aboard a warship

ward·ship \'wȯrd-ˌship\ *n* **1** : GUARDIANSHIP **2** : the state of being under care of a guardian

ware \'war\ *n* **1** : manufactured articles or products of art or craft : GOODS ⟨glass*ware*⟩ **2** ♦ : an article of merchandise — often used in pl. ⟨a peddler hawking his ~s⟩ **3** : items (as dishes) of fired clay : POTTERY

wares ♦ commodities, merchandise

ware·house \-ˌhaús\ *n* ♦ : a place for the storage of merchandise or commodities : STOREHOUSE — **warehouse** *vb* — **warehouse·man** \-mən\ *n* — **ware·hous·er** \-ˌhaú-zər, -sər\ *n*

♦ depository, depot, magazine, repository, storage, storehouse

ware·room \'war-ˌrüm, -ˌrùm\ *n* : a room in which goods are exhibited for sale

war·fare \'wȯr-ˌfar\ *n* **1** : military operations between enemies : WAR; *also* : an activity undertaken by one country to weaken or destroy another ⟨economic ~⟩ **2** ♦ : the process of struggle between competing entities : STRUGGLE, CONFLICT

♦ battle, combat, conflict, confrontation, contest, duel, face-off, rivalry, struggle, tug-of-war

war·fa·rin \'wȯr-fə-rən\ *n* : an anticoagulant compound used as a rodent poison and in medicine

war·head \'wȯr-ˌhed\ *n* : the section of a missile containing the charge

war·horse \-ˌhȯrs\ *n* **1** : a horse for use in war **2** : a veteran soldier or public person (as a politician) **3** : a musical composition that is often performed

war·like \-ˌlīk\ *adj* **1** ◆ : fond of war ⟨~ peoples⟩ **2** : of, relating to, or useful in war : MILITARY, MARTIAL ⟨~ supplies⟩ **3** ◆ : befitting or characteristic of war or of soldiers ⟨~ attitudes⟩

◆ [1, 3] aggressive, argumentative, bellicose, belligerent, combative, contentious, discordant, disputatious, militant, pugnacious, quarrelsome, scrappy, truculent

war·lock \-ˌläk\ *n* : SORCERER, WIZARD

war·lord \-ˌlȯrd\ *n* **1** : a high military leader **2** : a military commander exercising local civil power by force ⟨former Chinese ~s⟩

¹**warm** \ˈwȯrm\ *adj* **1** ◆ : having or giving out heat to a moderate or adequate degree ⟨~ milk⟩ ⟨a ~ stove⟩ **2** : serving to retain heat ⟨~ clothes⟩ **3** : feeling or inducing sensations of heat ⟨~ from exercise⟩ ⟨a ~ climb⟩ **4 a** : showing or marked by strong feeling : ARDENT ⟨~ support⟩ **b** ◆ : demonstratively genial, cordial, or sympathetic ⟨~ to the idea⟩ **5** : marked by tense excitement or hot anger ⟨a ~ campaign⟩ **6** : giving a pleasant impression of warmth, cheerfulness, or friendliness ⟨~ colors⟩ ⟨a ~ tone of voice⟩ **7** : marked by or tending toward injury, distress, or pain ⟨made things ~ for the enemy⟩ **8** : newly made : FRESH ⟨a ~ scent⟩ **9** : near to a goal ⟨getting ~ in a search⟩ — **warm·ly** *adv*

◆ [1] heated, tepid *Ant* chilled, cool, cooled ◆ [4b] amicable, companionable, comradely, cordial, friendly, genial, hearty, neighborly (*or* neighbourly), warmhearted ◆ [4b] affirmative, favorable, good, positive

²**warm** *vb* **1** : to make or become warm **2** : to give a feeling of warmth or vitality to **3** : to experience feelings of affection or pleasure ⟨she ~ed to her guest⟩ **4** : to reheat for eating ⟨~ed over the roast⟩ **5** : to make ready for operation or performance by preliminary exercise or operation ⟨~ up the motor⟩ **6** : to become increasingly ardent, interested, or competent ⟨the speaker ~ed to his topic⟩ — **warm·er** *n*

warm–blood·ed \-ˈblə-dəd\ *adj* **1** : able to maintain a relatively high and constant body temperature relatively independent of that of the surroundings **2** : ardent in spirit : expressing great feeling

warmed–over \ˈwȯrmd-ˌō-vər\ *adj* **1** : REHEATED ⟨~ cabbage⟩ **2** : not fresh or new ⟨~ ideas⟩

warm front *n* : an advancing edge of a warm air mass

warm·heart·ed \ˈwȯrm-ˈhär-təd\ *adj* : marked by or indicative of ready affection, generosity, cordiality, sympathy, or compassion — **warm·heart·ed·ness** *n*

◆ beneficent, benevolent, compassionate, good-hearted, humane, kind, kindly, sympathetic, tender, tenderhearted ◆ amicable, companionable, comradely, cordial, friendly, genial, hearty, neighborly (*or* neighbourly), warm

warming pan *n* : a long-handled covered pan filled with live coals and formerly used to warm a bed

war·mon·ger \ˈwȯr-ˌmən-gər, -ˌmäŋ-\ *n* ◆ : one who urges or attempts to stir up war — **war·mon·ger·ing** \-g(ə-)riŋ\ *n*

◆ agitator, firebrand, militant, rabble-rouser *Ant* dove, pacifist

warmth \ˈwȯrmth\ *n* ◆ : the quality or state of being warm in temperature or feeling

◆ ardor, emotion, fervency, fervor, heat, intensity, passion, vehemence

warm up *vb* : to engage in exercise or practice esp. before entering a game or contest — **warm–up** \ˈwȯrm-ˌəp\ *n*

warn \ˈwȯrn\ *vb* **1 a** ◆ : to put on guard : CAUTION **b** : to give supportive advice to : ADMONISH **2** ◆ : to notify esp. in advance **3** : to order to go or keep away

◆ [1a, 2] alert, caution, forewarn

¹**warn·ing** \ˈwȯr-niŋ\ *n* **1** ◆ : the act of warning : the state of being warned **2** : something that warns or serves to warn

◆ admonition, alarm, alert, caution, notice

²**warning** *adj* ◆ : serving as an alarm, signal, summons, or admonition ⟨a ~ bell⟩ — **warn·ing·ly** *adv*

◆ cautionary

¹**warp** \ˈwȯrp\ *n* **1** : the lengthwise threads on a loom or in a woven fabric **2** : a twist out of a true plane or straight line ⟨a ~ in a board⟩

²**warp** *vb* **1** ◆ : to turn or twist out of shape; *also* : to become so twisted **2** ◆ : to falsify, misinterpret, or give a false impression of : DISTORT **3** : to lead astray

◆ [1] contort, deform, distort, screw ◆ [2] color (*or* colour), dis-

tort, falsify, garble, misinterpret, misrepresent, misstate, pervert, twist

war paint *n* : paint put on the face and body by American Indigenous communities as a sign of going to war

war·path \ˈwȯr-ˌpath, -ˌpȧth\ *n* : the course taken by a party of Indigenous warriors going on a hostile expedition — **on the warpath** : ready to fight or argue

warped \ˈwȯrpt\ *adj* : affected by warping : having become distorted or perverted

war·plane \-ˌplān\ *n* : a military airplane; *esp* : one armed for combat

warp speed *n* : the highest possible speed

¹**war·rant** \ˈwȯr-ənt, ˈwär-\ *n* **1** : AUTHORIZATION; *also* : JUSTIFICATION, GROUND **2** : evidence (as a document) of authorization; *esp* : a legal writ authorizing an officer to take action (as in making an arrest, seizure, or search) **3** : a certificate of appointment issued to an officer of lower rank than a commissioned officer

²**warrant** *vb* **1** : to guarantee security or immunity to : SECURE **2** ◆ : to declare or maintain positively ⟨I ~ this is so⟩ **3** : to assure (a person) of the truth of what is said **4** : to guarantee to be as it appears or as it is represented ⟨~ goods as of the first quality⟩ **5** ◆ : to give authority or power to for doing or forbearing to do something : SANCTION **6** : to give proof of : ATTEST **7** : JUSTIFY ⟨his need ~s the expenditure⟩

◆ [2] affirm, allege, assert, aver, avouch, avow, claim, contend, declare, insist, maintain, profess, protest ◆ [5] approve, authorize, clear, OK, ratify, sanction

warrant officer *n* **1** : an officer in the armed forces ranking next below a commissioned officer **2** : a commissioned officer ranking below an ensign in the navy or coast guard and below a second lieutenant in the marine corps

war·ran·ty \ˈwȯr-ən-tē, ˈwär-\ *n, pl* **-ties** ◆ : an expressed or implied statement that some situation or thing is as it appears to be or is represented to be; *esp* : a usu. written guarantee of the integrity of a product and of the maker's responsibility for the repair or replacement of defective parts

◆ bond, contract, covenant, guarantee, guaranty, surety

war·ren \ˈwȯr-ən, ˈwär-\ *n* **1** : an area where rabbits breed; *also* : a structure where rabbits are bred or kept **2** : a crowded tenement or district

war·rior \ˈwȯr-yər; ˈwȯr-ē-ər, ˈwär-\ *n* ◆ : a person engaged or experienced in warfare

◆ fighter, legionnaire, man-at-arms, regular, serviceman, soldier

war·ship \ˈwȯr-ˌship\ *n* : a naval vessel

wart \ˈwȯrt\ *n* **1** : a small usu. horny projecting growth on the skin; *esp* : one caused by a virus **2** : a protuberance resembling a wart (as on a plant) — **warty** *adj*

wart·hog \ˈwȯrt-ˌhȯg, -ˌhäg\ *n* : a wild African hog that has large tusks and in the male two pairs of rough warty protuberances below the eyes

war·time \ˈwȯr-ˌtīm\ *n* : a period during which a war is in progress

wary \ˈwar-ē\ *adj* **war·i·er; -est** ◆ : very cautious; *esp* : careful in guarding against danger or deception — **war·i·ly** \ˈwer-ə-lē\ *adv* — **war·i·ness** \ˈwer-ē-nəs\ *n*

◆ alert, careful, cautious, circumspect, considerate, gingerly, guarded, heedful, safe

was *past 1st & 3d sing of* BE

wa·sa·bi \ˈwä-sə-bē; wä-ˈsä-\ *n* : a condiment prepared from the ground greenish root of an Asian herb and similar in flavor and use to horseradish; *also* : the herb or its root

¹**wash** \ˈwȯsh, ˈwäsh\ *vb* **1** : to clean with water and usu. soap or detergent ⟨~ clothes⟩ ⟨~ your hands⟩ **2** ◆ : to wet thoroughly : DRENCH **3** ◆ : to flow along the border of ⟨waves ~ the shore⟩ **4** : to pour or flow in a stream or current **5** : to move or remove by or as if by the action of water **6** : to cover or daub lightly with a liquid (as whitewash) **7** ◆ : to run water over (as gravel or ore) in order to separate valuable matter from refuse ⟨~ sand for gold⟩ **8** : to undergo laundering ⟨a dress that doesn't ~ well⟩ **9** : to stand a test ⟨that story will not ~⟩ **10** : to be worn away by water **11** : to pour, sweep, or flow in a stream or current

◆ [2] bathe, douse, drench, soak, sop, souse, water, wet ◆ [3] lap, lave, splash ◆ [7] flush, irrigate, rinse, sluice

²**wash** *n* **1** : the act or process or an instance of washing or being washed **2** : articles to be washed or being washed **3** : the flow or action of a mass of water (as a wave) **4** : erosion by waves (as of the sea) **5** *West* : the dry bed of a stream **6** : worthless esp. liquid waste : REFUSE, SWILL **7** : a thin coat of paint (as water-

color) **8** : a disturbance in a fluid (as water or the air) caused by the passage of a wing or propeller

³wash *adj* : WASHABLE

Wash *abbr* Washington

wash·able \'wȯ-shə-bəl, 'wä-\ *adj* : capable of being washed without damage

wash–and–wear *adj* : of, relating to, or being a fabric or garment that needs little or no ironing after washing

wash·ba·sin \'wȯsh-ˌbās-ᵊn, 'wäsh-\ *n* : WASHBOWL

wash·board \-ˌbȯrd\ *n* : a grooved board to scrub clothes on

wash·bowl \-ˌbōl\ *n* : a large bowl for water for washing hands and face

wash·cloth \-ˌklȯth\ *n* : a cloth used for washing one's face and body

washed–out \'wȯsht-'aút, 'wäsht-\ *adj* **1** ♦ : faded in color **2** : EXHAUSTED ⟨felt ~ after working all night⟩

♦ dull, light, pale, pastel

washed–up \-'əp\ *adj* : no longer successful, popular, skillful, or needed

wash·er \'wȯ-shər, 'wä-\ *n* **1** : a ring or perforated plate used around a bolt or screw to ensure tightness or relieve friction **2** : one that washes; *esp* : a machine for washing

wash·er·wom·an \-ˌwu̇-mən\ *n* : a woman whose occupation is washing clothes

wash·ing \'wȯ-shiŋ, 'wä-\ *n* **1** : material obtained by washing **2** : articles washed or to be washed

washing soda *n* : SODIUM CARBONATE

Wash·ing·ton's Birthday \'wȯ-shiŋ-tənz-, 'wä-\ *n* : the 3d Monday in February observed as a legal holiday

wash·out \'wȯsh-ˌaút, 'wäsh-\ *n* **1** : the washing away of earth (as from a road); *also* : a place where earth is washed away **2** ♦ : a complete failure

♦ bummer, bust, catastrophe, debacle, dud, failure, fiasco, fizzle, flop, lemon, loser, turkey

wash out *vb* **1** : to wash free of an extraneous substance (as dirt) **2** : to drain of color in laundering **3** : to eliminate as useless or unsatisfactory : REJECT **4** : to destroy or render useless by the force or action of water **5** : to deplete of strength or vitality : EXHAUST **6** ♦ : to fail to meet requirements or measure up to a standard

♦ collapse, fail, flop, flunk, fold

wash·room \-ˌrüm, -ˌru̇m\ *n* : a room (as in a public building) equipped with washing and toilet facilities : BATHROOM

wash·stand \-ˌstand\ *n* **1** : a stand holding articles needed for washing face and hands **2** : LAVATORY 1

wash·tub \-ˌtəb\ *n* : a tub for washing or soaking clothes

wash·wom·an \'wȯsh-ˌwu̇-mən, 'wäsh-\ *n* : WASHERWOMAN

washy \'wȯ-shē, 'wä-\ *adj* **wash·i·er; -est** **1** ♦ : WEAK, WATERY **2** : PALLID ⟨a ~ yellow⟩ **3** : lacking in vigor, individuality, or definiteness

wasp \'wäsp, 'wȯsp\ *n* : any of numerous social or solitary winged insects related to the bees and ants with biting mouthparts and in females and workers an often formidable sting

WASP *or* **Wasp** *n, sometimes disparaging* : an American of northern European and esp. British ancestry and of Protestant background

wasp·ish \'wäs-pish, 'wȯs-\ *adj* **1** ♦ : easily irritated : IRRITABLE **2** : resembling a wasp in form; *esp* : slightly built

♦ choleric, crabby, cranky, cross, crotchety, grouchy, grumpy, irascible, irritable, peevish, perverse, petulant, short-tempered, snappish, snappy, snippy, testy

wasp waist *n* : a very slender waist

¹was·sail \'wä-səl, wä-'sāl\ *n* **1** : an early English toast to someone's health **2** : a hot drink made with wine, beer, or cider, spices, sugar, and usu. baked apples and traditionally served at Christmas **3** : a period of riotous drinking

²wassail *vb* **1** : CAROUSE **2** : to drink to the health of — **was·sail·er** *n*

wast·age \'wā-stij\ *n* ♦ : loss, decrease, or destruction of something (as by use, decay, erosion, or leakage)

♦ annihilation, demolition, desolation, destruction, devastation, havoc, loss, obliteration, ruin, wreckage

¹waste \'wāst\ *n* **1** ♦ : a sparsely settled or barren region : DESERT; *also* : uncultivated land **2 a** : the act or an instance of wasting : the state of being wasted **b** : useless or profitless consumption or expenditure **3** : gradual loss or decrease by use, wear, or decay **4** ♦ : material left over, rejected, or thrown away; *also* : an unwanted by-product of a manufacturing or chemical process **5** : refuse (as garbage) that accumulates about habitations **6** ♦ : material (as feces) produced but not used by a living organism

♦ [1] barren, desert, desolation, wasteland ♦ [4] chaff, deadwood, dust, garbage, junk, litter, refuse, riffraff, rubbish, scrap, trash ♦ [6] droppings, slops

²waste *vb* **wast·ed; wast·ing** **1** ♦ : to damage or destroy gradually and progressively : DEVASTATE **2** : to wear away or diminish gradually : CONSUME **3** ♦ : to spend or use carelessly or uselessly : SQUANDER **4** ♦ : to lose or cause to lose weight, strength, or energy ⟨*wasting* away from fever⟩ **5** : to become diminished in bulk or substance : DWINDLE

♦ [1] annihilate, blot out, demolish, desolate, destroy, devastate, do in, exterminate, extinguish, obliterate, pulverize, ruin, shatter, smash, tear down, wipe out, wreck ♦ [3] blow, dissipate, fritter, lavish, misspend, run through, spend, squander, throw away *Ant* conserve ♦ [4] debilitate, enervate, enfeeble, prostrate, sap, soften, tire, weaken ♦ *usu* **waste away** [4] decay, droop, fail, flag, go, lag, languish, sag, weaken, wilt

³waste *adj* **1** : being wild and uninhabited : BARREN; *also* : UNCULTIVATED **2** : being in a ruined condition **3** : discarded as worthless after being used ⟨~ water⟩ **4** : excreted from or stored in inert form in a living organism as a by-product of vital activity ⟨~ matter from birds⟩

waste·bas·ket \'wāst-ˌbas-kət\ *n* : a receptacle for refuse

wast·ed *adj* ♦ : showing or feeling the effects of wasting

♦ cadaverous, gaunt, haggard, skeletal

waste·ful \-fəl\ *adj* ♦ : given to or marked by lack of thrift or careful use — **waste·ful·ly** *adv*

♦ extravagant, prodigal, profligate, spendthrift, thriftless, unthrifty

waste·ful·ness *n* ♦ : the quality of fact of being wasteful

♦ extravagance, lavishness, prodigality

waste·land \-ˌland, -lənd\ *n* ♦ : land that is barren or unfit for cultivation

♦ barren, desert, desolation, waste

waste·pa·per \-'pā-pər\ *n* : paper thrown away as used, not needed, or not fit for use

wast·er *n* : one that wastes

wast·rel \'wā-strəl\ *n* ♦ : one that wastes : SPENDTHRIFT

♦ prodigal, profligate, spendthrift

¹watch \'wäch, 'wȯch\ *vb* **1** : to be or stay awake intentionally : keep vigil ⟨~ed by the patient's bedside⟩ ⟨~ and pray⟩ **2** : to be on the lookout for danger : be on one's guard **3** : to keep guard ⟨~ outside the door⟩ **4 a** : OBSERVE ⟨~ a game⟩ **b** : to take care of **5 a** ♦ : to observe closely in order to check on action or change **b** : to keep in view so as to prevent harm or warn of danger ⟨~ a brush fire carefully⟩ **6** : to keep oneself informed about ⟨~ his progress⟩ **7** : to lie in wait for esp. so as to take advantage of ⟨~ed her opportunity⟩ **8** ♦ : to be expectant : wait for something

♦ [5a] follow, heed, listen, mind, note, observe, regard ♦ *usu* **watch for** [8] anticipate, await, expect, hope

²watch *n* **1** ♦ : the act of keeping awake to guard, protect, or attend; *also* : a state of alert and continuous attention **2** : a public weather alert ⟨a winter storm ~⟩ **3** : close observation **4** ♦ : a person who watches : LOOKOUT; *also* : the office or function of a sentinel or guard **5** : a period during which a part of a ship's crew is on duty; *also* : the part of a crew on duty during a watch **6** : a portable timepiece carried on the person

♦ [1] alertness, attentiveness, lookout, surveillance, vigilance ♦ [4] custodian, guard, guardian, keeper, lookout, picket, sentry, warden, warder, watchman

watch·band \'wäch-ˌband, 'wȯch-\ *n* : the bracelet or strap of a wristwatch

watch·dog \-ˌdȯg\ *n* **1** : a dog kept to guard property **2** : one that guards or protects

watch·er \'wäch-ər, 'wȯch-\ *n* ♦ : one that watches

♦ custodian, guard, guardian, keeper, lookout, picket, sentinel, sentry, warden, warder, watch, watchman

watch·ful \-fəl\ *adj* ♦ : steadily attentive and alert esp. to danger : VIGILANT — **watch·ful·ly** *adv*

♦ alert, attentive, awake, vigilant, wide-awake

watch·ful·ness *n* : the act or state of being watchful

watch·mak·er \-ˌmā-kər\ *n* : a person who makes or repairs watches — **watch·mak·ing** \-ˌmā-kiŋ\ *n*

watch·man \-mən\ *n* **1** ♦ : a person assigned to watch : GUARD **2** ♦ : one who is employed to patrol property for the purpose of protecting it against theft, fire, or other damage

♦ [1, 2] custodian, guard, guardian, keeper, lookout, picket, sentry, warden, warder, watch

watch night *n* : a devotional service lasting until after midnight esp. on New Year's Eve

watch out *vb* ♦ : to be vigilant or alert : be on the lookout — often used with *for*

    ♦ *usu* **watch out for** beware (of), guard (against), mind

watch·tow·er \'wäch-ˌtaú-ər, 'wóch-\ *n* : a tower for a lookout
watch·word \-ˌwərd\ *n* **1** : a secret word used as a signal or sign of recognition **2** ♦ : a word or motto used as a slogan or rallying cry

    ♦ cry, shibboleth, slogan

¹wa·ter \'wó-tər, 'wä-\ *n* **1** : the liquid that descends as rain and forms rivers, lakes, and seas **2** : a natural mineral water — usu. used in pl. **3** *pl* : the water occupying or flowing in a particular bed; *also* : a band of seawater bordering on and under the control of a country **4** : any of various liquids containing or resembling water; *esp* : a watery fluid (as tears, urine, or sap) formed or circulating in a living organism **5** : a specified degree of thoroughness or completeness ⟨a scoundrel of the first ∼⟩
²water *vb* **1 a** ♦ : to moisten, sprinkle, or soak with water **b** : to supply with or get or take water ⟨∼ horses⟩ ⟨the ship ∼ed at each port⟩ **2** : to treat (as cloth) so as to give a lustrous appearance in wavy lines **3** ♦ : to dilute by or as if by adding water to — often used with *down* **4** : to form or secrete water or watery matter ⟨her eyes ∼ed⟩ ⟨my mouth ∼ed⟩

    ♦ [1a] bathe, douse, drench, soak, sop, souse, wash, wet ♦ *usu* **water down** [3] adulterate, dilute, thin, weaken

wa·ter·bed \-ˌbed\ *n* : a bed whose mattress is a watertight bag filled with water
wa·ter·borne \-ˌbōrn\ *adj* : supported, carried, or transmitted by water
water buffalo *n* : a common oxlike often domesticated Asian bovine
water chestnut *n* : a whitish crunchy vegetable used esp. in Chinese cooking that is the peeled tuber of a widely cultivated Asian sedge; *also* : the tuber or the sedge itself
water closet *n* : a compartment or room with a toilet bowl : BATHROOM; *also* : a toilet bowl along with its accessories
wa·ter·col·or \'wó-tər-ˌkə-lər, 'wä-\ *n* **1** : a paint whose liquid part is water **2** : the art of painting with watercolors **3** : a picture made with watercolors
wa·ter·course \-ˌkōrs\ *n* ♦ : a stream of water; *also* : the bed of a stream

    ♦ aqueduct, canal, channel, conduit, flume, raceway

wa·ter·craft \-ˌkraft\ *n* : a craft for water transport : BOAT
wa·ter·cress \-ˌkres\ *n* : an aquatic perennial Eurasian cress that is naturalized in the U.S. and has edible leaves used esp. in salads
wa·ter·fall \-ˌfól\ *n* ♦ : a very steep descent of the water of a stream

    ♦ cascade, cataract, falls

wa·ter·fowl \'wó-tər-ˌfaú(-ə)l, 'wä-\ *n, pl* **-fowl** *also* **-fowls** : a bird that frequents water; *esp* : a swimming bird (as a duck) hunted as game
wa·ter·front \-ˌfrənt\ *n* : land or a section of a town fronting or abutting on a body of water
water gap *n* : a pass in a mountain ridge through which a stream runs
water glass *n* : a drinking glass
water hyacinth *n* : a showy floating aquatic plant of tropical America that often clogs waterways (as in the southern U.S.)
watering hole *n* : a place (as a bar) where people gather socially
watering place *n* : a resort that features mineral springs or bathing
water lily *n* : any of various aquatic plants with floating roundish leaves and showy solitary flowers
wa·ter·line \'wó-tər-ˌlīn, 'wä-\ *n* : a line that marks the level of the surface of water on something (as a ship or the shore)
wa·ter·logged \-ˌlógd, -ˌlägd\ *adj* ♦ : so filled or soaked with water as to be heavy or unmanageable ⟨a ∼ boat⟩

    ♦ saturated, sodden, soggy, watery, wet

wa·ter·loo \ˌwó-tər-'lü, ˌwä-\ *n, pl* **-loos** : a decisive or final defeat or setback
¹wa·ter·mark \'wó-tər-ˌmärk, 'wä-\ *n* **1** : a mark indicating the height to which water has risen **2** : a marking in paper visible when the paper is held up to a light
²watermark *vb* : to mark (paper) with a watermark
wa·ter·mel·on \-ˌme-lən\ *n* : a large roundish or oblong fruit with

sweet juicy usu. red pulp; *also* : a widely grown African vine related to the squashes that produces watermelons
water moccasin *n* : a venomous pit viper chiefly of the southeastern U.S. that is related to the copperhead
water ou·zel \-'ü-zəl\ *n* : DIPPER 1
water park *n* : an amusement park with a pool and wetted slides
water pipe *n* : a pipe for smoking that has a long flexible tube whereby the smoke is cooled by passing through water
water polo *n* : a team game played in a swimming pool with a ball resembling a soccer ball
wa·ter·pow·er \'wó-tər-ˌpaú-ər, 'wä-\ *n* : the power of moving water used to run machinery
¹wa·ter·proof \'wó-tər-ˌprüf, 'wä-\ *adj* : not letting water through; *esp* : covered or treated with a material to prevent permeation by water — **wa·ter·proof·ing** *n*
²waterproof *n* **1** : a waterproof fabric **2** *chiefly Brit* : RAINCOAT
³waterproof *vb* : to make waterproof
wa·ter–re·pel·lent \ˌwó-tər-ri-'pe-lənt, ˌwä-\ *adj* : treated with a finish that is resistant to water penetration
wa·ter–re·sis·tant \-ri-'zis-tənt\ *adj* : WATER-REPELLENT
wa·ter·shed \'wó-tər-ˌshed, 'wä-\ *n* **1** : a dividing ridge between two drainage areas **2** : the region or area drained by a particular body of water
wa·ter·side \-ˌsīd\ *n* : the land bordering a body of water
water ski *n* : a ski used on water when the wearer is towed — **wa·ter–ski** *vb* — **wa·ter–ski·er** \-ˌskē-ər\ *n*
water snake *n* : any of various snakes found in or near freshwater and feeding largely on aquatic animals
wa·ter·spout \'wó-tər-ˌspaút, 'wä-\ *n* **1** : a pipe for carrying water **2** : a funnel-shaped cloud extending from a cloud down to a spray torn up by whirling winds from an ocean or lake
water strider *n* : any of various long-legged bugs that move about swiftly on the surface of water
water table *n* : the upper limit of the portion of the ground wholly saturated with water
wa·ter·tight \ˌwó-tər-'tīt, ˌwä-\ *adj* **1** : constructed so as to keep water out **2** : allowing no possibility for doubt or uncertainty ⟨a ∼ case against the accused⟩
wa·ter·way \'wó-tər-ˌwā, 'wä-\ *n* : a navigable body of water
wa·ter·wheel \-ˌhwēl, -ˌwēl\ *n* : a wheel made to turn by water flowing against it
water wings *n pl* : an air-filled device to give support to a person's body esp. when learning to swim
wa·ter·works \'wó-tər-ˌwərks, 'wä-\ *n pl* : a system for supplying water (as to a city)
wa·tery \'wó-tə-rē, 'wä-\ *adj* **1** ♦ : containing, full of, or giving out water ⟨∼ clouds⟩ **2** ♦ : resembling water or watery matter esp. in thin fluidity, soggy texture, paleness, or lack of flavor : THIN ⟨∼ lemonade⟩; *also* : being soft and soggy ⟨∼ turnips⟩

    ♦ [1] saturated, sodden, soggy, waterlogged, wet ♦ [2] dilute, thin, weak

WATS \'wäts\ *abbr* Wide-Area Telecommunications Service
watt \'wät\ *n* : the metric unit of power equal to the work done at the rate of one joule per second or to the power produced by a current of one ampere across a potential difference of one volt
watt·age \'wä-tij\ *n* : amount of power expressed in watts
wat·tle \'wät-ᵊl\ *n* **1** : a framework of rods with flexible branches or reeds interlaced used esp. formerly in building; *also* : material for this framework **2** : a naked fleshy process hanging usu. from the head or neck (as of a bird) — **wat·tled** \-ᵊld\ *adj*
W Aust *abbr* Western Australia
¹wave \'wāv\ *vb* **waved; wav·ing** **1** : FLUTTER ⟨flags *waving* in the breeze⟩ **2** ♦ : to motion with the hands or with something held in them in signal or salute; *also* : to convey by waving ⟨*waved* farewell⟩ **3** : to become moved or brandished to-and-fro; *also* : BRANDISH, FLOURISH ⟨∼ a sword⟩ **4** : to move before the wind with a wavelike motion ⟨fields of *waving* grain⟩ **5** : to curve up and down like a wave : UNDULATE

    ♦ flag, gesture, motion, signal

²wave *n* ♦ : a moving ridge or swell on the surface of water **2** : a wavelike formation or shape ⟨a ∼ in the hair⟩ **3** : the action or process of making wavy or curly **4** : a waving motion; *esp* : a signal made by waving something **5** : FLOW, GUSH ⟨a ∼ of anger swept over her⟩ **6** : a peak of activity ⟨a ∼ of selling⟩ **7** : a disturbance that transfers energy progressively from point to point in a medium ⟨light travels in ∼s⟩ ⟨a sound ∼⟩ **8** : a period of hot or cold weather — **wave·like** *adj*

    ♦ billow, curl, surge, swell

wave·length \'wāv-ˌleŋth\ *n* **1** : the distance in the line of advance of a wave from any one point (as a crest) to the next corresponding point **2** : a line of thought that reveals a common understanding

wave·let \-lət\ *n* : a little wave : RIPPLE

wa·ver \'wā-vər\ *vb* **1** ◆ : to fluctuate in opinion, allegiance, or direction **2** ◆ : to weave or sway unsteadily to and fro : TOTTER; *also* : FLICKER ⟨~*ing* flames⟩ **3** : FALTER **4** : to give an unsteady sound : QUAVER — **waver** *n* — **wa·ver·er** *n* — **wa·ver·ing·ly** *adv*

◆ [1] falter, hang back, hesitate, shilly-shally, stagger, teeter, vacillate, wobble ◆ [2] falter, rock, seesaw, sway, teeter, totter, wobble

wavy \'wā-vē\ *adj* **wav·i·er; -est** : having waves : moving in waves

¹**wax** \'waks\ *n* **1** : a yellowish plastic substance secreted by bees for constructing the honeycomb **2** : any of various substances like beeswax

²**wax** *vb* : to treat or rub with wax

³**wax** *vb* **1** ◆ : to increase in size, numbers, strength, volume, or duration **2** : to increase in apparent size ⟨the moon ~*es* toward the full⟩ **3** ◆ : to take on a quality or state : BECOME ⟨~*ed* in-dignant⟩ ⟨the party ~*ed* merry⟩

◆ [1] accumulate, appreciate, balloon, build, burgeon, enlarge, es-calate, expand, increase, mount, multiply, mushroom, proliferate, rise, snowball, swell ◆ [3] become, come, get, go, grow, run, turn

wax bean *n* : a kidney bean with pods that turn creamy yellow to bright yellow when mature enough to use as snap beans

wax·en \'wak-sən\ *adj* **1** : made of or covered with wax **2** : re-sembling wax (as in color or consistency)

wax museum *n* : a place where wax effigies are exhibited

wax myrtle *n* : any of a genus of shrubs or trees with aromatic leaves; *esp* : an evergreen shrub or small tree of the eastern U.S. that produces small hard berries with a thick coating of bluish≠white wax used for candles

wax·wing \'waks-ˌwiŋ\ *n* : any of a genus of chiefly brown to gray singing birds with a showy crest and red waxy material on the tips of some wing feathers

wax·work \-ˌwərk\ *n* **1** : an effigy usu. of a person in wax **2** *pl* : an exhibition of wax figures

waxy \'wak-sē\ *adj* **wax·i·er; -est** **1** : made of or full of wax **2** : WAXEN 2

way \'wā\ *n* **1** ◆ : a thoroughfare for travel or passage **2** : the course of travel from one place to another : ROUTE **3 a** ◆ : a course of action ⟨chose the easy ~⟩ **b** ◆ : opportunity, capabil-ity, or fact of doing as one pleases ⟨always had your own ~⟩ **4** : a possible course : POSSIBILITY ⟨no two ~s about it⟩ **5** ◆ : a characteristic or habitual manner of acting ⟨this ~ of thinking⟩ ⟨a new ~ of painting⟩ **6** : FEATURE, RESPECT ⟨a good worker in many ~s⟩ **7** : the usual or characteristic state of affairs ⟨as is the ~ with old people⟩; *also* : individual characteristic or pecu-liarity ⟨used to her ~s⟩ **8 a** : the length of a course : DISTANCE ⟨a short ~ from here⟩ ⟨a long ~ from success⟩ **b** ◆ : room for moving, passing, or occupying — often used in the phrase *make way* **9** : progress along a course ⟨working my ~ through col-lege⟩ **10** : a direction of motion, facing, pointing, or nonspatial advance or tendency ⟨turn this ~⟩; *also* : LOCALITY ⟨out our ~⟩ **11** : STATE, CONDITION ⟨the ~ things are⟩ **12** *pl* : an in-clined structure upon which a ship is built or is supported in launching **13** : CATEGORY, KIND ⟨get what you need in the ~ of supplies⟩ **14** : motion or speed of a boat through the water — **by the way** : by way of interjection or digression — **by way of** **1** : for the purpose of ⟨*by way of* illustration⟩ **2** : by the route through : VIA — **out of the way** **1** : WRONG, IMPROPER **2** : SE-CLUDED, REMOTE

◆ [1] artery, avenue, drag, drive, highway, pass, pike, road, route, row, street, thoroughfare, trace, turnpike ◆ [3a] approach, fashion, form, manner, method, strategy, style, system, tack, tac-tics, technique ◆ [3b] alternative, choice, discretion, option, pick, preference ◆ [5] custom, fashion, habit, pattern, practice, trick, wont ◆ [8b] place, room, space

way·bill \'wā-ˌbil\ *n* : a paper that accompanies a freight ship-ment and gives details of goods, route, and charges

way·far·er \'wā-ˌfar-ər\ *n* : a traveler esp. on foot — **way·far·ing** \-ˌfar-iŋ\ *adj*

way·lay \'wā-ˌlā\ *vb* **-laid** \-ˌlād\; **-lay·ing** ◆ : to lie in wait for or attack from ambush

◆ ambush, surprise

way–out \'wā-'aut\ *adj* : marked by a considerable departure from the conventional or traditional : FAR-OUT

-ways \ˌwāz\ *adv suffix* : in (such) a way, course, direction, or manner ⟨side*ways*⟩

ways and means *n pl* : methods and resources esp. for raising revenues needed by a state; *also* : a legislative committee con-cerned with this function

way·side \'wā-ˌsīd\ *n* : the side of or land adjacent to a road or path

way station *n* : an intermediate station on a line of travel (as a railroad)

way·ward \'wā-wərd\ *adj* **1** ◆ : following one's own capricious or wanton inclinations ⟨~ children⟩ **2** : UNPREDICTABLE, IR-REGULAR ⟨a ~ act⟩

◆ contrary, defiant, disobedient, froward, intractable, rebellious, recalcitrant, refractory, unruly, untoward, willful

way·ward·ness *n* ◆ : the quality or state of being wayward

◆ contrariness, defiance, disobedience, frowardness, insubordi-nation, intractability, rebelliousness, recalcitrance, refractori-ness, unruliness

WBC *abbr* white blood cells

WC *abbr* **1** water closet **2** without charge

WCTU *abbr* Women's Christian Temperance Union

we \'wē\ *pron* **1** — used of a group that includes the speaker or writer **2** — used for the singular *I* by a monarch, editor, or writer

weak \'wēk\ *adj* **1** ◆ : lacking strength or vigor : FEEBLE **2** : not able to sustain or resist much weight, pressure, or strain **3** ◆ : deficient in vigor of mind or character; *also* : resulting from or indicative of such deficiency ⟨a ~ policy⟩ ⟨a ~ will⟩ **4** ◆ : not supported by truth or logic ⟨a ~ argument⟩ **5** : lacking skill or proficiency; *also* : indicative of a lack of skill or apti-tude **6** ◆ : lacking vigor of expression or effect **7** ◆ : of less than usual strength ⟨~ tea⟩ **8** : not having or exerting authority ⟨~ government⟩; *also* : INEFFECTIVE, IMPOTENT **9** : of, relating to, or constituting a verb or verb conjugation that forms the past tense and past participle by adding *-ed* or *-d* or *-t* — **weak·ly** *adv*

◆ [1] delicate, enervated, faint, feeble, frail, infirm, languid, low, prostrate, slight, soft, tender, torpid, unsubstantial, wasted *Ant* mighty, powerful, rugged, stalwart, stout, strong ◆ [3] ef-fete, frail, ineffective, nerveless, soft, spineless, wimpy, wishy≠washy *Ant* firm, strong, tough ◆ [4] fallacious, illogical, invalid, irrational, unreasonable, unsound ◆ [6] helpless, impotent, pow-erless ◆ [7] dilute, thin, watery *Ant* full-bodied, rich, strong

weak·en \'wē-kən\ *vb* ◆ : to make or become weak

◆ adulterate, dilute, thin, water ◆ debilitate, enervate, enfeeble, prostrate, sap, soften, tire, waste *Ant* beef (up), fortify, recruit, strengthen ◆ decay, droop, fail, flag, go, lag, languish, sag, waste, wilt

weak·fish \'wēk-ˌfish\ *n* : a common marine fish of the Atlantic coast of the U.S. caught for food and sport; *also* : any of several related food fishes

weak force *n* : the physical force responsible for particle decay processes in radioactivity

weak–kneed \'wēk-'nēd\ *adj* : lacking willpower or resolution ⟨~ appeasers⟩

weak·ling \'wē-kliŋ\ *n* : a person who is physically, mentally, or morally weak

weak·ly \'wē-klē\ *adj* ◆ : not strong or robust in health

◆ invalid, sickly

weak·ness \'wēk-nəs\ *n* **1 a** ◆ : the quality or state of being weak : lack of strength or vigor **b** : an instance or period of be-ing weak ⟨in a moment of ~ he agreed to go⟩ **2** ◆ : something that is a mark of lack of strength or resolution **3** : an object of special desire or fondness ⟨chocolate is her ~⟩

◆ [1a] debility, delicacy, enfeeblement, faintness, feebleness, frailty, infirmity, languor, lowness *Ant* hardihood, hardiness, ro-bustness, strength, vigor ◆ [2] demerit, failing, fault, foible, frailty, shortcoming, vice

¹**weal** \'wēl\ *n* ◆ : a sound, healthy, or prosperous state : WELL-BEING

◆ good, interest, welfare, well-being

²**weal** *n* : WELT

weald \'wēld\ *n* **1** : FOREST **2** : WOLD

wealth \'welth\ *n* **1** : abundance of possessions or resources **2** ◆ : abundant supply ⟨a ~ of detail⟩ **3** ◆ : all property that has a money or an exchange value; *also* : all objects or resources that have economic value

◆ [2] abundance, plenty, superabundance ◆ [3] assets, capital, fortune, means, opulence, riches, substance, wherewithal

wealthy \'wel-thē\ *adj* **wealth·i·er; -est** ◆ : having wealth : RICH

◆ affluent, flush, loaded, moneyed, opulent, rich, well-fixed, well≠heeled, well-off, well-to-do

wean \'wēn\ *vb* **1 :** to accustom (a young mammal) to take food by means other than nursing **2 :** to free from a source of dependence; *also* **:** to free from a usu. unwholesome habit or interest

weap·on \'we-pən\ *n* **1 :** something (as a gun, knife, or club) used to injure, defeat, or destroy **2 :** a means of contending against another — **weap·on·less** \-ləs\ *adj*

weap·on·ry \-rē\ *n* **:** WEAPONS

¹**wear** \'war\ *vb* **wore** \'wōr\; **worn** \'wōrn\; **wear·ing** **1 :** to use as an article of clothing or adornment ⟨~ a coat⟩ ⟨~s earrings⟩; *also* **:** to carry on the person ⟨~ a gun⟩ **2 :** EXHIBIT, PRESENT ⟨~ a smile⟩ **3 ♦ :** to impair, diminish, or decay by use or by scraping or rubbing ⟨clothes *worn* to shreds⟩; *also* **:** to produce gradually by friction, rubbing, or wasting away ⟨~ a hole in the rug⟩ **4 ♦ :** to exhaust or lessen the strength of **:** FATIGUE ⟨*worn* by care and toil⟩ **5 :** to endure use **:** last under use or the passage of time ⟨this cloth ~s well⟩ **6 :** to diminish or fail with the passage of time ⟨the day ~s on⟩ ⟨the effect of the drug *wore* off⟩ **7 :** to grow or become affected in some way by attrition, use, or age ⟨the coin was *worn* thin⟩ — **wear·able** \'war-ə-bəl\ *adj* — **wear·er** *n*

  ♦ [3] abrade, chafe, erode, fray, fret, gall, rub ♦ [4] burn out, do in, drain, exhaust, fag, fatigue, tire, tucker, wash out, weary

²**wear** *n* **1 :** the act of wearing **:** the state of being worn ⟨clothes for everyday ~⟩ **2 :** clothing usu. of a particular kind or for a special occasion or use ⟨children's ~⟩ **3 :** wearing or lasting quality ⟨the coat still has lots of ~ in it⟩ **4 :** the result of wearing or use **:** impairment due to use ⟨the suit shows ~⟩

wear and tear *n* **:** the loss, injury, or stress to which something is subjected in the course of use; *esp* **:** normal depreciation

wear down *vb* **:** to weary and overcome by persistent resistance or pressure

wea·ri·ness \-ē-nəs\ *n* ♦ **:** the quality or state of being weary

  ♦ burnout, collapse, exhaustion, fatigue, lassitude, prostration, tiredness

wea·ri·some \'wir-ē-səm\ *adj* **:** causing weariness **:** TIRESOME — **wea·ri·some·ly** *adv* — **wea·ri·some·ness** *n*

wear out *vb* **1 ♦ :** to exhaust or lessen the strength of **:** TIRE **2 :** to make or become useless by wear

  ♦ burn out, do in, drain, exhaust, fag, fatigue, tire, tucker, wash out, wear, weary

¹**wea·ry** \'wir-ē\ *adj* **wea·ri·er; -est** **1 ♦ :** worn out in strength, energy, or freshness **2 :** expressing or characteristic of weariness ⟨a ~ sigh⟩ **3 ♦ :** having one's patience, tolerance, or pleasure exhausted ⟨~ of war⟩ **4 :** causing weariness of body or spirit **:** TIRESOME ⟨a long, ~ drive home⟩ — **wea·ri·ly** \'wir-ə-lē\ *adv*

  ♦ [1] beat, bushed, dead, drained, effete, jaded, limp, prostrate, spent, tired, worn-out ♦ [3] fed up, jaded, sick, tired **Ant** absorbed, engaged, engrossed, gripped, interested, intrigued

²**weary** *vb* **wea·ried; wea·ry·ing** ♦ **:** to become or make weary **:** TIRE

  ♦ burn out, do in, drain, exhaust, fag, fatigue, tire, tucker, wash out, wear, wear out

¹**wea·sel** \'wē-zəl\ *n, pl* **weasels :** any of various small slender flesh-eating mammals related to the minks — **wea·sel·ly** *also* **wea·sely** \'wēz-lē, 'wē-zə-lē\ *adj*

²**weasel** *vb* **wea·seled; wea·sel·ing** **1 :** to use weasel words **:** EQUIVOCATE **2 :** to escape from or evade a situation or obligation — often used with *out*

weasel word *n* **:** a word used to avoid a direct or forthright statement or position

¹**weath·er** \'we-thər\ *n* **1 :** the state of the atmosphere with respect to heat or cold, wetness or dryness, calm or storm, clearness or cloudiness **2 :** a particular and esp. a disagreeable atmospheric state **:** RAIN, STORM

²**weather** *vb* **1 :** to expose to or endure the action of weather; *also* **:** to alter (as in color or texture) by such exposure **2 :** to bear up against successfully ⟨~ a storm⟩ ⟨~ troubles⟩

³**weather** *adj* **:** WINDWARD

weath·er–beat·en \'we-thər-ˌbēt-ᵊn\ *adj* **:** worn or damaged by exposure to the weather; *also* **:** toughened or tanned by the weather ⟨~ face⟩

weath·er·cock \-ˌkäk\ *n* **:** a weather vane shaped like a rooster

weath·er·ing \'we-thə-riŋ\ *n* **:** the action of the weather in altering the color, texture, composition, or form of exposed objects; *also* **:** alteration thus effected

weath·er·ize \'we-thə-ˌrīz\ *vb* **-ized; -iz·ing :** to make (as a house) better protected against winter weather (as by adding insulation)

weath·er·man \-ˌman\ *n* **:** one who reports and forecasts the weather **:** METEOROLOGIST

weath·er·per·son \-ˌpər-sən\ *n* **:** a person who reports and forecasts the weather **:** METEOROLOGIST

weath·er·proof \'we-thər-ˌprüf\ *adj* **:** able to withstand exposure to weather — **weatherproof** *vb*

weath·er·strip·ping \'we-thər-ˌstri-piŋ\ *n* **:** material used to seal a door or window at the edges — **weath·er–strip** *vb* — **weather strip** *n*

weather vane *n* **:** VANE 1

weath·er·worn \'we-thər-ˌwōrn\ *adj* **:** worn by exposure to the weather

¹**weave** \'wēv\ *vb* **wove** \'wōv\ *or* **weaved; wo·ven** \'wō-vən\ *or* **weaved; weav·ing** **1 :** to form by interlacing strands of material; *esp* **:** to make on a loom by interlacing warp and filling threads ⟨~ cloth⟩ **2 :** to interlace (as threads) into a fabric and esp. cloth **3 :** SPIN 2 **4 :** to make as if by weaving together parts **5 ♦ :** to insert as a part **:** work in **6 :** to move in a winding or zigzag course esp. to avoid obstacles ⟨we *wove* our way through the crowd⟩ — **weav·er** *n*

  ♦ interlace, intersperse, intertwine, interweave, lace, thread, wreathe

²**weave** *n* **:** something woven; *also* **:** a pattern or method of weaving ⟨a loose ~⟩

¹**web** \'web\ *n* **1 :** a fabric on a loom or coming from a loom **2 a :** COBWEB **b ♦ :** something by which one is entangled, involved in difficulties, held fast, or impeded in one's progress ⟨caught in a ~ of deceit⟩ **3 :** an animal or plant membrane; *esp* **:** one uniting the toes (as in many birds) **4 :** NETWORK ⟨a ~ of highways⟩ **5 :** the series of barbs on each side of the shaft of a feather **6 :** WORLD WIDE WEB — **webbed** \'webd\ *adj*

  ♦ entanglement, net, snare, trap

²**web** *vb* **webbed; web·bing** **1 :** to make a web **2 :** to cover or provide with webs or a network **3 :** ENTANGLE, ENSNARE

web·bing \'we-biŋ\ *n* **:** a strong closely woven tape designed for bearing weight and used esp. for straps, harnesses, or upholstery

web·cam \'web-ˌkam\ *n* **:** a camera used in transmitting live images over the World Wide Web

web·cast \'web-ˌkast\ *n* **:** a transmission of sound and images via the World Wide Web — **webcast** *vb*

web–foot·ed \'web-'fu̇-təd\ *adj* **:** having webbed feet

web·i·nar \'we-bə-ˌnär\ *n* **:** a live online educational presentation during which participating viewers can submit questions and answers

web·log \'web-ˌlȯg, -ˌläg\ *n* **:** BLOG

web·mas·ter \'web-ˌmas-tər\ *n, often cap* **:** a person responsible for the creation or maintenance of a website

web page *n* **:** ³PAGE 2

web·site \'web-ˌsīt\ *or* **Web site** *n* **:** a group of World Wide Web pages made available online (as by an individual or business)

wed \'wed\ *vb* **wed·ded** *also* **wed; wed·ding** **1 :** to take, give, enter into, or join in marriage **:** MARRY **2 :** to unite firmly

Wed *abbr* Wednesday

wed·ding \'we-diŋ\ *n* **1 ♦ :** a marriage ceremony usu. with accompanying festivities **:** NUPTIALS **2 :** a joining in close association **3 :** a wedding anniversary or its celebration

  ♦ espousal, marriage

¹**wedge** \'wej\ *n* **1 :** a piece of wood or metal that tapers to a thin edge and is used to split logs or rocks or to raise heavy weights **2 :** something (as an action or policy) that serves to open up a way for a breach, change, or intrusion **3 :** a wedge-shaped object or part ⟨a ~ of pie⟩

²**wedge** *vb* **wedged; wedg·ing** **1 :** to hold firm by or as if by driving in a wedge **2 ♦ :** to force (something) into a narrow space

  ♦ cram, crowd, jam, ram, sandwich, squeeze, stuff

wed·lock \'wed-ˌläk\ *n* **:** the state of being married **:** MARRIAGE

Wednes·day \'wenz-(ˌ)dā, -dē\ *n* **:** the 4th day of the week

wee \'wē\ *adj* **1 ♦ :** very small **:** TINY **2 :** very early ⟨~ hours of the morning⟩

  ♦ atomic, infinitesimal, microscopic, miniature, minute, teeny, tiny

¹**weed** \'wēd\ *n* **1 :** a plant that tends to grow thickly where it is not wanted and to choke out more desirable plants **2 :** MARIJUANA

²**weed** *vb* **1 :** to clear of or remove weeds or something harmful, inferior, or superfluous ⟨~ a garden⟩ **2 :** to get rid of ⟨~ out the troublemakers⟩ — **weed·er** *n*

³**weed** *n* **:** mourning clothes — usu. used in pl. ⟨widow's ~s⟩

weedy \'wē-dē\ *adj* **1 :** full of weeds **2 ♦ :** resembling a weed esp. in vigor of growth or spread **3 :** noticeably lean and scrawny **:** LANKY ⟨a ~ young man⟩

  ♦ lush, luxuriant, prosperous, rampant, rank

week \'wēk\ *n* **1 :** seven successive days; *esp* : a calendar period of seven days beginning with Sunday and ending with Saturday **2 :** the working or school days of the calendar week

week·day \'wēk-ˌdā\ *n* **:** a day of the week except Sunday or sometimes except Saturday and Sunday

¹**week·end** \-ˌend\ *n* **:** the period between the close of one working or business or school week and the beginning of the next

²**weekend** *vb* **:** to spend the weekend

¹**week·ly** \'wē-klē\ *adj* **1 :** occurring, appearing, or done every week **2 :** computed in terms of one week — **weekly** *adv*

²**weekly** *n, pl* **weeklies :** a weekly publication

ween \'wēn\ *vb, archaic* **:** SUPPOSE 3

wee·ny \'wē-nē\ *also* **ween·sy** \'wēn-sē\ *adj* **:** exceptionally small

weep \'wēp\ *vb* **wept** \'wept\; **weep·ing 1 ♦ :** to express emotion and esp. sorrow by shedding tears **:** CRY **2 ♦ :** to give off fluid slowly **:** OOZE — **weep·er** *n*

   ♦ [1] bawl, blubber, cry, sob ♦ [2] bleed, exude, ooze, percolate, seep, strain, sweat

weep·ing *adj* **1 ♦ :** expressing or showing emotion by shedding tears **2 :** having slender drooping branches

   ♦ dolorous, funeral, lugubrious, mournful, plaintive, regretful, rueful, sorrowful, woeful

weeping willow *n* **:** a willow with slender drooping branches

weepy \'wē-pē\ *adj* **:** inclined to weep

wee·vil \'wē-vəl\ *n* **:** any of a large group of beetles having a long head usu. curved into a snout and including many whose larvae are destructive plant-feeding pests — **wee·vily** *or* **wee·vil·ly** \'wē-və-lē\ *adj*

weft \'weft\ *n* **1 :** a filling thread or yarn in weaving **2 :** WEB, FABRIC; *also* **:** something woven

¹**weigh** \'wā\ *vb* **1 :** to find the heaviness of **2 :** to have weight or a specified weight **3 ♦ :** to consider carefully **:** PONDER **4 :** to merit consideration as important **:** COUNT ⟨evidence *∼ing* against him⟩ **5 :** to raise before sailing ⟨∼ anchor⟩ **6 ♦ :** to press down with or as if with a heavy weight

   ♦ [3] chew over, cogitate, consider, contemplate, debate, deliberate, entertain, meditate, mull, ponder, question, ruminate, study, think ♦ *usu* **weigh on** *or* **weigh upon** [6] bear, depress, press, shove

²**weigh** *n* **:** WAY — used in the phrase *under weigh*

¹**weight** \'wāt\ *n* **1 :** the amount that something weighs; *also* **:** the standard amount that something should weigh **2 ♦ :** a quantity or object weighing a usu. specified amount **3 :** a unit (as a pound or kilogram) of weight or mass; *also* **:** a system of such units **4 :** a heavy object for holding or pressing something down; *also* **:** a heavy object for throwing or lifting in an athletic contest **5 :** a mental or emotional burden **6 a ♦ :** the relatively great importance or authority accorded something **b ♦ :** measurable influence esp. in determining the acts of others ⟨threw his ∼ around⟩ **7 :** overpowering force **8 :** relative thickness (as of a textile) ⟨summer-*weight* clothes⟩

   ♦ [2] burden, cargo, draft, freight, haul, lading, load, payload ♦ [6a] consequence, import, magnitude, moment, significance ♦ [6b] authority, clout, influence, pull, sway

²**weight** *vb* **1 :** to load with or as if with a weight **2 ♦ :** to oppress with a burden ⟨∼ed down with cares⟩

   ♦ burden, encumber, load, lumber, saddle

weight·less \'wāt-ləs\ *adj* **♦ :** having little weight **:** lacking apparent gravitational pull ⟨a ∼ environment⟩ — **weight·less·ly** *adv* — **weight·less·ness** *n*

   ♦ airy, feathery, light

weighty \'wā-tē\ *adj* **weight·i·er; -est 1 ♦ :** of much importance or consequence **:** SERIOUS ⟨∼ problems⟩ **2 ♦ :** expressing or characterized by seriousness or gravity ⟨a ∼ manner⟩ **3 ♦ :** weighing a considerable amount **:** HEAVY **4 ♦ :** having much force, influence, or authority ⟨∼ arguments⟩

   ♦ [1] grave, heavy, serious ♦ [1, 2] big, consequential, eventful, important, major, material, meaningful, momentous, significant, substantial ♦ [3] heavy, hefty, massive, ponderous ♦ [4] authoritative, forceful, influential

weiner *var of* WIENER

weir \'war, 'wir\ *n* **1 :** a fence set in a waterway for catching fish **2 :** a dam in a stream to raise the water level or divert its flow

weird \'wird\ *adj* **1 ♦ :** caused by or suggesting magical influence **:** MAGICAL **2 ♦ :** passing beyond natural limits **:** UNEARTH-

LY **3 ♦ :** curious in nature or appearance **:** of strange or extraordinary character — **weird·ly** *adv* — **weird·ness** *n*

   ♦ [1] magic, magical, mystic, occult ♦ [2] creepy, eerie, haunting, spooky, uncanny, unearthly ♦ [3] bizarre, curious, far-out, funny, kinky, odd, outlandish, outré, peculiar, quaint, quirky, remarkable, screwy, strange, unusual, wacky, wild

weirdo \'wir-(ˌ)dō\ *n, pl* **weird·os ♦ :** a person who is extraordinarily strange or eccentric

   ♦ character, crackpot, crank, eccentric, kook, nut, oddball, screwball

Welch *var of* WELSH

¹**wel·come** \'wel-kəm\ *vb* **wel·comed; wel·com·ing 1 :** to greet cordially or courteously **2 :** to accept, meet, or face with pleasure ⟨he ∼s criticism⟩

²**welcome** *adj* **1 :** received gladly into one's presence ⟨a ∼ visitor⟩ **2 :** giving pleasure **:** PLEASING ⟨∼ news⟩ **3 :** willingly permitted or admitted ⟨all are ∼ to use the books⟩ **4 :** used in the phrase "You're welcome" as a reply to an expression of thanks

³**welcome** *n* **1 :** a cordial greeting or reception **2 :** the state of being welcome ⟨overstayed their ∼⟩

¹**weld** \'weld\ *vb* **1 :** to unite (metal or plastic parts) either by heating and allowing the parts to flow together or by hammering or pressing together **2 :** to unite closely or intimately ⟨∼ed together in friendship⟩ — **weld·er** *n*

²**weld** *n* **1 :** a welded joint **2 :** union by welding

wel·fare \'wel-ˌfar\ *n* **1 ♦ :** the state of doing well esp. in respect to happiness, well-being, or prosperity **2 :** aid in the form of money or necessities for those in need; *also* **:** the agency through which the aid is given

   ♦ good, interest, weal, well-being

welfare state *n* **:** a nation or state that assumes primary responsibility for the individual and social welfare of its citizens

wel·kin \'wel-kən\ *n* **:** SKY; *also* **:** AIR

¹**well** \'wel\ *n* **1 :** a spring with its pool **:** FOUNTAIN; *also* **:** a source of supply ⟨a ∼ of information⟩ **2 :** a hole sunk in the earth to obtain a natural deposit (as of water, oil, or gas) **3 :** an open space (as for a staircase) extending vertically through floors of a structure **4 :** something suggesting a well

²**well** *vb* **:** to rise up and flow out

³**well** *adv* **bet·ter** \'be-tər\; **best** \'best\ **1 a :** in a good or proper manner **:** RIGHTLY **b ♦ :** in a skillful or expert manner **:** SKILLFULLY **2 ♦ :** in a satisfactory manner **:** SATISFACTORILY ⟨the party turned out ∼⟩ **3 ♦ :** in a prosperous, affluent, or generous manner ⟨eat ∼⟩ ⟨was ∼ rewarded⟩ **4 ♦ :** with reason or courtesy ⟨I cannot ∼ refuse⟩ **5 :** to the full degree or extent **:** FULLY ⟨∼ worth the price⟩ ⟨*well*-hidden⟩ **6 :** INTIMATELY, CLOSELY ⟨I know him ∼⟩ **7 :** CONSIDERABLY, FAR ⟨∼ over a million⟩ ⟨∼ ahead⟩ **8 :** without trouble or difficulty ⟨we could ∼ have gone⟩ **9 :** EXACTLY, DEFINITELY ⟨remember it ∼⟩ **10 :** with spirit and courage **:** with equanimity or good nature ⟨took the news ∼⟩

   ♦ [1b] ably, adeptly, capably, expertly, masterfully, proficiently, skillfully *Ant* inefficiently, ineptly, inexpertly, poorly, unskillfully ♦ [2] adequately, all right, fine, good, nicely, OK, passably, satisfactorily, so-so, tolerably *Ant* bad, badly, inadequately, intolerably, poorly ♦ [3] bountifully, generously, handsomely, liberally ♦ [4] courteously, kindly, nicely, thoughtfully

⁴**well** *adj* **1 :** PROSPEROUS; *also* **:** being in satisfactory condition or circumstances **2 :** SATISFACTORY, PLEASING ⟨all is ∼⟩ **3 :** ADVISABLE, DESIRABLE ⟨it is not ∼ to anger him⟩ **4 ♦ :** free or recovered from ill health **:** HEALTHY **5 :** FORTUNATE ⟨it is ∼ that this has happened⟩

   ♦ able-bodied, chipper, fit, hale, healthy, hearty, robust, sound, whole, wholesome

well–ad·just·ed \ˌwel-ə-'jəs-təd\ *adj* **:** WELL-BALANCED 2

well–ad·vised \-əd-'vīzd\ *adj* **1 :** PRUDENT **2 :** resulting from, based on, or showing careful deliberation or wise counsel ⟨∼ plans⟩

well–ap·point·ed \-ə-'pȯin-təd\ *adj* **:** properly fitted out

well–ba·lanced \'wel-'ba-lənst\ *adj* **1 :** nicely or evenly balanced or arranged ⟨a ∼ meal⟩ **2 :** emotionally or psychologically untroubled

well–be·ing \-'bē-iŋ\ *n* **♦ :** the state of being happy, healthy, or prosperous

   ♦ good, interest, weal, welfare

well·born \-'bȯrn\ *adj* **♦ :** born of noble or wealthy lineage

   ♦ aristocratic, genteel, gentle, grand, highborn, noble, patrician

well–bred \-'bred\ *adj* ♦ : having or indicating qualities or characteristics associated with good breeding

♦ civil, courteous, genteel, gracious, mannerly, polite

well–de·fined \-di-'fīnd\ *adj* : having clearly distinguishable limits or boundaries

well–dis·posed \-di-'spōzd\ *adj* ♦ : disposed to be friendly, favorable, or sympathetic ⟨∼ to the idea⟩

♦ affable, agreeable, amiable, genial, good-natured, gracious, nice, sweet

well–done \'wel-'dən\ *adj* **1** : rightly or properly performed **2** : cooked thoroughly

well-en·dowed \'wel-in-'daùd\ *adj* **1** : having plenty of money or property **2** : having large breasts **3** : having a large penis

well–fa·vored \-'fā-vərd\ *adj* : GOOD-LOOKING, HANDSOME

well–fixed \-'fikst\ *adj* ♦ : financially well-off : WELL-HEELED

♦ affluent, flush, loaded, moneyed, opulent, rich, wealthy, well= heeled, well-off, well-to-do

well–found·ed \-'faùn-dəd\ *adj* ♦ : based on good reasons

♦ good, hard, informed, just, levelheaded, logical, rational, reasonable, reasoned, sensible, sober, solid, valid

well–groomed \-'grümd, -'grùmd\ *adj* : neatly dressed or cared for

well–ground·ed \-'graùn-dəd\ *adj* **1** : having a firm foundation **2** : WELL-FOUNDED

well·head \-,hed\ *n* **1** : the source of a spring or a stream **2** : principal source **3** : the top of or a structure built over a well

well–heeled \-'hēld\ *adj* ♦ : financially well-off

♦ affluent, flush, loaded, moneyed, opulent, rich, wealthy, well= fixed, well-off, well-to-do

well–known \-'nōn\ *adj* ♦ : fully or widely known

♦ celebrated, famed, famous, noted, notorious, prominent, renowned, star

well–mean·ing \-'mē-niŋ\ *adj* : having or based on good intentions

well·ness \-nəs\ *n* ♦ : good health esp. as an actively sought goal ⟨∼ clinics⟩ ⟨lifestyles that promote ∼⟩

♦ fitness, health, heartiness, robustness, soundness, wholeness, wholesomeness

well–nigh \-'nī\ *adv* ♦ : very nearly : ALMOST

♦ about, almost, most, much, near, nearly, next to, nigh, practically, virtually

well–off \-'òf\ *adj* : being in good condition or circumstances; *esp* ♦ : having more than adequate financial resources : WELL-TO-DO

♦ affluent, flush, loaded, moneyed, opulent, rich, wealthy, well= fixed, well-heeled, well-to-do

well–or·dered \-'òr-dərd\ *adj* : having an orderly procedure or arrangement

well–placed \-'plāst\ *adj* : appropriately or advantageously directed or positioned

well–read \-'red\ *adj* ♦ : well-informed through reading

♦ educated, erudite, knowledgeable, learned, literate, scholarly

well–round·ed \-'raùn-dəd\ *adj* **1** : broadly trained, educated, and experienced **2** : COMPREHENSIVE ⟨a ∼ program of activities⟩

well–spo·ken \'wel-'spō-kən\ *adj* **1** ♦ : speaking well and esp. courteously **2** : spoken with propriety ⟨∼ words⟩

♦ articulate, eloquent, fluent

well·spring \-,spriŋ\ *n* : a source of continuous supply

well·timed \-'tīmd\ *adj* : TIMELY

well–to–do \,wel-tə-'dü\ *adj* ♦ : having more than adequate financial resources

♦ affluent, flush, loaded, moneyed, opulent, rich, wealthy, well= fixed, well-heeled, well-off

well–turned \'wel-'tərnd\ *adj* **1** : pleasingly shaped ⟨a ∼ ankle⟩ **2** : pleasingly expressed ⟨a ∼ phrase⟩

well–wish·er \'wel-,wi-shər\ *n* : an admiring supporter or fan — **well–wish·ing** *adj or n*

welsh \'welsh, 'welch\ *also* **welch** \'welch\ *vb* **1** *now sometimes offensive* : to avoid payment **2** *now sometimes offensive* : to break one's word ⟨∼ed on their promises⟩

Welsh \'welsh\ *n* **1** *Welsh pl* : the people of Wales **2** : the Celtic language of Wales — **Welsh** *adj* — **Welsh·man** \-mən\ *n*

Welsh cor·gi \-'kòr-gē\ *n* : a short-legged long-backed dog with foxy head of either of two breeds of Welsh origin

Welsh rabbit *n* : melted often seasoned cheese served over toast or crackers

Welsh rare·bit \-'rar-bət\ *n* : WELSH RABBIT

¹**welt** \'welt\ *n* **1** : the narrow strip of leather between a shoe upper and sole to which other parts are stitched **2** : a doubled edge, strip, insert, or seam for ornament or reinforcement **3** : a ridge or lump raised on the skin usu. by a blow; *also* : a heavy blow

²**welt** *vb* **1** : to furnish (as a shoe) with a welt **2** : to hit hard

¹**wel·ter** \'wel-tər\ *vb* **1** : WRITHE, TOSS; *also* : WALLOW **2** : to rise and fall or toss about in or with waves **3** : to become deeply sunk, soaked, or involved **4** : to be in turmoil

²**welter** *n* **1** : a state of wild disorder : TURMOIL **2** ♦ : a chaotic mass or jumble ⟨a ∼ of data⟩

♦ clutter, hash, hodgepodge, jumble, miscellany, motley, muddle, potpourri

wel·ter·weight \'wel-tər-,wāt\ *n* : a boxer weighing more than 135 but not over 147 pounds

wen \'wen\ *n* : an abnormal growth or a cyst protruding from a surface esp. of the skin

wench \'wench\ *n* **1** : a young woman **2** : a female servant

wend \'wend\ *vb* : to direct one's course : proceed on (one's way)

went *past of* GO

wept *past and past part of* WEEP

were *past 2d sing, past pl, or past subjunctive of* BE

were·wolf \'wer-,wùlf, 'wir-, 'wər-\ *n, pl* **were·wolves** \-,wùlvz\ : a person who in stories is transformed into a wolf or is capable of assuming a wolf's form

wes·kit \'wes-kət\ *n* : VEST 1

¹**west** \'west\ *adv* : to or toward the west

²**west** *adj* **1** : situated toward or at the west **2** : coming from the west

³**west** *n* **1** : the general direction of sunset **2** : the compass point directly opposite to east **3** *cap* : regions or countries west of a specified or implied point **4** *cap* : Europe and the Americas — **west·er·ly** \'wes-tər-lē\ *adv or adj* — **west·ward** *adv or adj* — **west·wards** *adv*

¹**west·ern** \'wes-tərn\ *adj* **1** : lying toward or coming from the west **2** *cap* : of, relating to, or characteristic of a region conventionally designated West **3** *cap* : of or relating to the Roman Catholic or Protestant segment of Christianity — **West·ern·er** *n*

²**western** *n, often cap* : a novel, story, film, or radio or television show about life in the western U.S. during the latter half of the 19th century

west·ern·ize \'wes-tər-,nīz\ *vb* **-ized; -iz·ing** : to give western characteristics to ⟨wanted to ∼ the country⟩ — **west·ern·i·za·tion** \,wes-tər-nə-'zā-shən\ *n*

West Nile virus \-'nī-(ə)l-\ *n* : a virus that is transmitted to humans by mosquitoes and causes an illness marked by fever, headache, muscle ache, and sometimes encephalitis or meningitis; *also* : this illness

¹**wet** \'wet\ *adj* **wet·ter; wet·test** **1** ♦ : consisting of or covered or soaked with liquid (as water) **2** : having frequent rains : RAINY **3** : not dry ⟨∼ paint⟩ **4** : permitting or advocating the manufacture and sale of alcoholic beverages ⟨a ∼ town⟩ ⟨a ∼ candidate⟩ — **wet·ly** *adv* — **wet·ness** *n*

♦ saturated, sodden, soggy, waterlogged, watery *Ant* arid, dry

²**wet** *n* **1** : WATER; *also* : WETNESS, MOISTURE **2** : rainy weather : RAIN **3** : an advocate of a wet liquor policy

³**wet** *vb* **wet** *or* **wet·ted; wet·ting** ♦ : to make or become wet — **wet·ter** *n*

♦ bathe, douse, drench, soak, sop, souse, wash, water *Ant* dry

wet blanket *n* ♦ : one that quenches or dampens enthusiasm or pleasure

♦ drag, killjoy, spoilsport

weth·er \'we-thər\ *n* : a castrated male sheep or goat

wet·land \'wet-,land, -lənd\ *n* : land or areas (as swamps) containing much soil moisture — usu. used in pl.

wet nurse *n* : a woman who cares for and breastfeeds children not her own

wet suit *n* : a rubber suit for swimmers that acts to retain body heat by keeping a layer of water against the body as insulation

wh *abbr* **1** which **2** white

¹**whack** \'hwak\ *vb* **1** : to strike with a smart or resounding blow **2** : to cut with or as if with a whack

²**whack** *n* **1 a** ♦ : a smart or resounding blow **b** ♦ : the sound of or like that of a blow **2** : PORTION, SHARE **3** : CONDITION, STATE ⟨the machine is out of ∼⟩ **4** ♦ : an opportunity or attempt to do something **5** : a single action or occasion ⟨made three pies at a ∼⟩

♦ [1b] bang, blast, boom, clap, crack, crash, pop, report, slam, smash, snap, thwack ♦ [4] attempt, crack, endeavor (or endeavour), essay, fling, go, pass, shot, stab, trial, try

¹whale \'hwāl\ *n, pl* **whales 1** *or pl* **whale :** CETACEAN; *esp* : one (as a sperm whale or killer whale) of large size **2** ♦ : a person or thing impressive in size or quality ⟨a ∼ of a story⟩

♦ behemoth, blockbuster, colossus, giant, jumbo, leviathan, mammoth, monster, titan, whopper

²whale *vb* **whaled; whal·ing :** to fish or hunt for whales
³whale *vb* **whaled; whal·ing 1** : to defeat soundly : THRASH **2** : to strike or hit vigorously
whale·boat \-ˌbōt\ *n* : a long narrow rowboat originally used by whalers
whale·bone \-ˌbōn\ *n* : BALEEN
whal·er \'hwā-lər\ *n* **1** : a person or ship that hunts whales **2** : WHALEBOAT
whale shark *n* : a shark of warm waters that is the largest known fish
wham·my \'hwa-mē\ *n, pl* **wham·mies :** JINX, HEX
wharf \'hwȯrf\ *n, pl* **wharves** \'hwȯrvz\ *also* **wharfs** ♦ : a structure alongside which ships lie to load and unload

♦ dock, float, jetty, landing, levee, pier, quay

¹what \'hwät, 'hwət\ *pron* **1** — used to inquire about the identity or nature of a being, an object, or some matter or situation ⟨∼ is he, a salesman⟩ ⟨∼'s that⟩ ⟨∼ happened⟩ **2** : that which ⟨I know ∼ you want⟩ **3** : WHATEVER 1 ⟨take ∼ you want⟩
²what *adv* **1** : in what respect : HOW ⟨∼ does he care⟩ **2** — used with *with* to introduce a prepositional phrase that expresses cause ⟨kept busy ∼ with school and work⟩
³what *adj* **1** — used to inquire about the identity or nature of a person, object, or matter ⟨∼ books do you read⟩ **2** : how remarkable or surprising ⟨∼ an idea⟩ **3** : WHATEVER
¹what·ev·er \hwät-'e-vər\ *pron* **1** : anything or everything that ⟨does ∼ he wants to⟩ **2** : no matter what ⟨∼ you do, don't cheat⟩ **3** : WHAT 1 — used as an intensive ⟨∼ do you mean⟩
²whatever *adj* : of any kind at all ⟨no food ∼⟩
³whatever *adv* : in any case : whatever the case may be — often used to suggest the unimportance of an issue or choice ⟨see a movie, watch TV,—∼⟩
¹what·not \'hwät-ˌnät\ *pron* : any of various other things that might also be mentioned ⟨needles, pins, and ∼⟩
²whatnot *n* : a light open set of shelves for small ornaments
what·so·ev·er \ˌhwät-sō-'e-vər\ *pron or adj* : WHATEVER
wheal \'hwēl\ *n* : a rapidly formed flat slightly raised itching or burning patch on the skin; *also* : WELT
wheat \'hwēt\ *n* : a cereal grain that yields a fine white flour used chiefly in breads, baked goods, and pastas; *also* : any of several widely grown grasses yielding wheat — **wheat·en** *adj*
wheat germ *n* : the vitamin-rich wheat embryo separated in milling
whee·dle \'hwēd-ᵊl\ *vb* **whee·dled; whee·dling 1** ♦ : to entice by flattery **2** : to gain or get by wheedling

♦ blarney, cajole, coax

¹wheel \'hwēl\ *n* **1** : a disk or circular frame that turns on a central axis **2** : a device whose main part is a wheel **3** : something resembling a wheel in shape or motion **4** ♦ : a curving or circular movement : a rotation or turn usu. about an axis or center **5** : machinery that imparts motion : moving power ⟨the ∼s of government⟩ **6** : a person of importance **7** *pl, slang* : AUTOMOBILE — **wheeled** \'hwēld\ *adj* — **wheel·less** *adj*

♦ gyration, pirouette, reel, revolution, roll, rotation, spin, twirl, whirl

²wheel *vb* **1** ♦ : to move or turn like a wheel on or as if on an axis : REVOLVE **2** ♦ : to change direction as if turning on a pivot : to cause to move as if turning on a pivot **3** : to convey or move on wheels or in a vehicle

♦ [1] gyrate, pirouette, revolve, roll, rotate, spin, turn, twirl, whirl ♦ [2] divert, pivot, swerve, swing, turn, veer, whip

wheel·bar·row \-ˌbar-ō\ *n* : a vehicle with handles and usu. one wheel for carrying small loads
wheel·base \-ˌbās\ *n* : the distance in inches between the front and rear axles of an automotive vehicle
wheel·chair \-ˌcher\ *n* : a chair mounted on wheels esp. for the use of disabled persons
wheel·er \'hwē-lər\ *n* **1** : one that wheels **2** : WHEELHORSE **3** : something that has wheels — used in combination ⟨a side-*wheel-er*⟩
wheel·er–deal·er \ˌhwē-lər-'dē-lər\ *n* : a shrewd operator esp. in business or politics

wheel·horse \'hwēl-ˌhȯrs\ *n* **1** : a horse in a position nearest the front wheels of a wagon **2** : a steady and effective worker esp. in a political body
wheel·house \-ˌhaus\ *n* : PILOTHOUSE
wheel–thrown \'hwēl-ˌthrōn\ *adj* : made on a potter's wheel
wheel·wright \-ˌrīt\ *n* : a maker and repairer of wheels and wheeled vehicles
¹wheeze \'hwēz\ *vb* **wheezed; wheez·ing** ♦ : to breathe with difficulty usu. with a whistling sound

♦ blow, gasp, pant, puff

²wheeze *n* **1** : a sound of wheezing **2** : an often repeated and well-known joke **3** : a trite saying
wheezy \'hwē-zē\ *adj* **wheez·i·er; -est 1** : inclined to wheeze **2** : having a wheezing sound — **wheez·i·ly** \-zə-lē\ *adv* — **wheez·i·ness** \-zē-nəs\ *n*
whelk \'hwelk\ *n* : a large sea snail; *esp* : one much used as food in Europe
whelm \'hwelm\ *vb* : to overcome or engulf completely : OVERWHELM
¹whelp \'hwelp\ *n* **1** : any of the young of various carnivorous mammals (as a dog) **2** ♦ : a young boy or girl

♦ child, cub, juvenile, kid, kiddo, moppet, youngster, youth

²whelp *vb* : to give birth to (whelps); *also* : bring forth young
¹when \'hwen\ *adv* **1** : at what time ⟨∼ will you return⟩ **2** : at or during which time ⟨a time ∼ things were better⟩
²when *conj* **1** : at or during the time that ⟨leave ∼ I do⟩ **2** : every time that ⟨they all clapped ∼ he sang⟩ **3** : in the event that : IF ⟨disqualified ∼ you cheat⟩ **4** ♦ : in spite of the fact that : ALTHOUGH ⟨quit politics ∼ he might have had a great career in it⟩

♦ albeit, although, howbeit, though, while

³when *pron* : what or which time ⟨since ∼ have you been the boss⟩
⁴when *n* : the time of a happening
whence \'hwens\ *adv or conj* : from what place, source, or cause
when·ev·er \hwe-'ne-vər, hwə-\ *conj or adv* : at whatever time
when·so·ev·er \'hwen-sō-ˌe-vər\ *conj* : at any or every time that
¹where \'hwer\ *adv* **1** : at, in, or to what place ⟨∼ is it⟩ ⟨∼ will we go⟩ **2** : at, in, or to what situation, position, direction, circumstances, or respect ⟨∼ does this road lead⟩
²where *conj* **1** : at, in, or to what place ⟨knows ∼ the house is⟩ **2** : at, in, or to what situation, position, direction, circumstances, or respect ⟨shows ∼ the road leads⟩ **3** : WHEREVER ⟨goes ∼ she likes⟩ **4** : at, in, or to which place ⟨the town ∼ we live⟩ **5** : at, in, or to the place at, in, or to which ⟨stay ∼ you are⟩ **6** : in a case, situation, or respect in which ⟨outstanding ∼ endurance is called for⟩
³where *n* : PLACE, LOCATION ⟨the ∼ and how of the accident⟩
¹where·abouts \-ə-ˌbauts\ *also* **where·about** \-ˌbaut\ *adv* : about where : near what place ⟨∼ does he live⟩
²whereabouts *n sing or pl* : the place where a person or thing is ⟨his present ∼ are unknown⟩
where·as \hwer-'az\ *conj* **1** : while on the contrary; *also* : ALTHOUGH **2** ♦ : in view of the fact that : SINCE

♦ because, for, now, since

where·at \-'at\ *conj* **1** : at or toward which **2** : in consequence of which : WHEREUPON
where·by \-'bī\ *conj* : by, through, or in accordance with which ⟨the means ∼ we achieved our goals⟩
¹where·fore \'hwer-ˌfȯr\ *adv* **1** : for what reason or purpose : WHY **2** ♦ : because of that : THEREFORE

♦ accordingly, consequently, ergo, hence, so, therefore, thus

²wherefore *n* ♦ : an answer or statement giving an explanation : REASON

♦ grounds, motive, reason, why

¹where·in \hwer-'in\ *adv* : in what : in what respect ⟨∼ was I wrong⟩
²wherein *conj* **1** : in which : WHERE ⟨the city ∼ we live⟩ **2** : during which **3** : in what way : HOW ⟨showed me ∼ I was wrong⟩
where·of \-'əv, -'äv\ *conj* **1** : of what ⟨knows ∼ he speaks⟩ **2** : of which or whom ⟨books ∼ the best are lost⟩
where·on \-'ȯn, -'än\ *conj* : on which ⟨the base ∼ it rests⟩
where·so·ev·er \'hwer-sō-ˌe-vər\ *conj* : WHEREVER
where·to \'hwer-ˌtü\ *conj* : to which
where·up·on \'hwer-ə-ˌpȯn, -ˌpän\ *conj* **1** : on which **2** : closely following and in consequence of which
¹wher·ev·er \hwer-'e-vər\ *adv* : where in the world ⟨∼ did he get that tie⟩

²wherever *conj* **1** : at, in, or to whatever place **2** : in any circumstance in which

where·with \'hwer-ˌwith, -ˌwith\ *conj* : with or by means of which

where·with·al \'hwer-wi-ˌthȯl, -ˌthȯl\ *n* ♦ : means or resources for purchasing or doing something; *esp* : MONEY

♦ finances, fund, pocket, resources

wher·ry \'hwer-ē\ *n, pl* **wherries** : a long light rowboat sharp at both ends

whet \'hwet\ *vb* **whet·ted; whet·ting** **1** ♦ : to sharpen by rubbing on or with something abrasive (as a whetstone) **2** : to make keen : STIMULATE ⟨∼ the appetite⟩

♦ edge, grind, hone, sharpen, strop

wheth·er \'hwe-thər\ *conj* **1** : if it is or was true that ⟨ask ∼ he is going⟩ **2** : if it is or was better ⟨uncertain ∼ to go or stay⟩ **3** : whichever is or was the case, namely that ⟨∼ we succeed or fail, we must try⟩ **4** : EITHER ⟨turned out well ∼ by accident or design⟩

whet·stone \'hwet-ˌstōn\ *n* : a stone for sharpening blades

whey \'hwā\ *n* : the watery part of milk that separates after the milk sours and thickens

¹which \'hwich\ *adj* **1** : being what one or ones out of a group ⟨∼ shirt should I wear⟩ **2** : WHICHEVER

²which *pron* **1** : which one or ones ⟨∼ is yours⟩ ⟨∼ are his⟩ ⟨it's in May or June, I'm not sure⟩ **2** : WHICHEVER ⟨we have all kinds; take ∼ you like⟩ **3** — used to introduce a relative clause and to serve as a substitute therein for the noun modified by the clause ⟨the money ∼ is coming to me⟩

¹which·ev·er \hwich-'e-vər\ *adj* : no matter which ⟨∼ way you go⟩

²whichever *pron* : whatever one or ones

which·so·ev·er \ˌhwich-sō-'e-vər\ *pron or adj* : WHICHEVER

whick·er \'hwi-kər\ *vb* : NEIGH, WHINNY — **whicker** *n*

¹whiff \'hwif\ *n* **1** : a quick puff or slight gust (as of air) **2** : an inhalation of odor, gas, or smoke **3** : a slight trace **4** : STRIKE-OUT

²whiff *vb* **1** : to expel, puff out, or blow away in or as if in whiffs **2** ♦ : to inhale an odor **3** : STRIKE OUT 3

♦ nose, scent, smell, sniff

Whig \'hwig\ *n* **1** : a member or supporter of a British political group of the late 17th through early 19th centuries seeking to limit royal authority and increase parliamentary power **2** : an American favoring independence from Great Britain during the American Revolution **3** : a member or supporter of an American political party formed about 1834 to oppose the Democrats

¹while \'hwīl\ *n* **1** : a period of time ⟨stay a ∼⟩ **2** ♦ : the time and effort used : TROUBLE ⟨worth your ∼⟩

♦ [1] bit, space, spell, stretch ♦ [2] effort, exertion, expenditure, labor (*or* labour), pains, sweat, trouble, work

²while *conj* **1** : during the time that ⟨she called ∼ you were out⟩ **2** : AS LONG AS ⟨∼ there's life there's hope⟩ **3** ♦ : in spite of the fact that : ALTHOUGH ⟨∼ he's respected, he's not liked⟩

♦ albeit, although, howbeit, though, when

³while *vb* **whiled; whil·ing** : to cause to pass esp. pleasantly ⟨∼ away an hour⟩

¹whi·lom \'hwī-ləm\ *adv, archaic* : FORMERLY

²whilom *adj* ♦ : at a time in the past : FORMER ⟨his ∼ friends⟩

♦ erstwhile, former, late, old, onetime, past, sometime

whilst \'hwīlst\ *conj, chiefly Brit* : WHILE

whim \'hwim\ *n* ♦ : a sudden wish, desire, or change of mind

♦ caprice, fancy, freak, notion, vagary

whim·per \'hwim-pər\ *vb* : to make a low whining plaintive or broken sound — **whimper** *n*

whim·si·cal \'hwim-zi-kəl\ *adj* **1** ♦ : full of whims : CAPRICIOUS **2** : resulting from or characterized by whim or caprice ⟨∼ notions⟩ — **whim·si·cal·i·ty** \ˌhwim-zə-'ka-lə-tē\ *n* — **whim·si·cal·ly** \'hwim-zi-k(ə-)lē\ *adv*

♦ capricious, impulsive

whim·sy *also* **whim·sey** \'hwim-zē\ *n, pl* **whim·sies** *also* **whimseys** **1** : a sudden impulsive apparently unmotivated change of mind : WHIM **2** : a fanciful or fantastic device, object, or creation esp. in writing or art ⟨decorative ∼⟩

whine \'hwīn\ *vb* **whined; whin·ing** **1** : to utter a usu. high-pitched plaintive or distressed cry; *also* : to make a sound similar to such a cry **2** ♦ : to complain with or as if with a whine — **whine** *n* — **whiny** *also* **whin·ey** \'hwī-nē\ *adj*

♦ beef, bellyache, carp, complain, crab, croak, fuss, gripe, grouse,

growl, grumble, kick, moan, murmur, mutter, repine, squawk, wail

whin·er *n* ♦ : one that whines

♦ bear, complainer, crab, crank, grouch, grumbler

¹whin·ny \'hwi-nē\ *vb* **whin·nied; whin·ny·ing** : to neigh usu. in a low or gentle manner

²whinny *n, pl* **whinnies** : NEIGH

¹whip \'hwip\ *vb* **whipped; whip·ping** **1** : to move, snatch, or jerk quickly or forcefully ⟨∼ out a gun⟩ ⟨*whipped* the car around and sped off⟩ **2** ♦ : to strike with a slender lithe implement (as a lash) esp. as a punishment; *also* : SPANK **3** : to drive or urge on by or as if by using a whip **4** : to bind or wrap (as a rope or rod) with cord in order to protect and strengthen; *also* : to wind or wrap around something **5** ♦ : to thoroughly overcome : DEFEAT **6** ♦ : to stir up : INCITE ⟨∼ up enthusiasm⟩ **7** : to produce in a hurry ⟨∼ up a meal⟩ **8** : to beat (as eggs or cream) into a froth **9 a** : to proceed nimbly or briskly **b** : to flap about forcefully ⟨flags *whipping* in the wind⟩ — **whip·per** *n* — **whip into shape** : to bring forcefully to a desired state or condition

♦ [2] beat, flog, hide, thrash ♦ [5] beat, best, clobber, conquer, crush, defeat, drub, lick, master, overcome, rout, skunk, subdue, trim, triumph, trounce, wallop, win ♦ *usu* **whip up** [6] abet, ferment, foment, incite, instigate, provoke, raise, stir

²whip *n* **1** ♦ : a flexible instrument used for whipping **2** : a stroke or cut with or as if with a whip **3** : a dessert made by whipping a portion of the ingredients ⟨prune ∼⟩ **4** : a person who handles a whip **5** : a member of a legislative body appointed by a party to enforce party discipline **6** : a whipping or thrashing motion

♦ lash, scourge, switch

whip·cord \-ˌkȯrd\ *n* **1** : a thin tough braided cord **2** : a strong cloth with fine diagonal cords or ribs

whip hand *n* : positive control : ADVANTAGE

whip·lash \'hwip-ˌlash\ *n* **1** : the lash of a whip **2** : injury resulting from a sudden sharp movement of the neck and head (as of a person in a vehicle that is struck from the rear)

whip·per·snap·per \'hwi-pər-ˌsna-pər\ *n* ♦ : a small, insignificant, or presumptuous person

♦ nobody, nonentity, nothing, zero

whip·pet \'hwi-pət\ *n* : any of a breed of small swift slender dogs that are used for racing

whipping boy *n* : one who is receives criticism or blame instead of the ones deserving it : SCAPEGOAT

whip·poor·will \'hwi-pər-ˌwil\ *n* : an American insect-eating bird with dull variegated plumage whose call at nightfall and just before dawn is suggestive of its name

whip·saw \'hwip-ˌsȯ\ *vb* : to beset with two or more adverse conditions or situations at once

¹whir *also* **whirr** \'hwər\ *vb* **whirred; whir·ring** ♦ : to move, fly, or revolve with a whir

♦ buzz, drone, hum, whish, whiz, zip, zoom

²whir *also* **whirr** *n* : a continuous fluttering or vibratory sound made by something in rapid motion

¹whirl \'hwərl\ *vb* **1** ♦ : to move or drive in a circle or curve esp. with force or speed **2** ♦ : to turn or cause to turn rapidly in circles **3** : to turn abruptly **4** ♦ : to move or go quickly **5** ♦ : to become dizzy or giddy : REEL

♦ [1, 2] pivot, revolve, roll, rotate, spin, swing, swirl, turn, twirl, twist, wheel ♦ [4] breeze, career, course, dash, fly, hasten, hurry, race, rip, rocket, run, rush, shoot, speed, step, tear, zip, zoom ♦ [5] reel, spin

²whirl *n* **1** ♦ : a rapid rotating or circling movement; *also* : something whirling **2** : COMMOTION, BUSTLE ⟨the social ∼⟩ **3** ♦ : a state of mental confusion **4** : TRY ⟨gave it a ∼⟩

♦ [1] gyration, pirouette, reel, revolution, roll, rotation, spin, twirl, wheel ♦ [3] bafflement, bewilderment, confusion, distraction, muddle, mystification, perplexity, puzzlement

whirl·i·gig \'hwər-li-ˌgig\ *n* **1** : a child's toy having a whirling motion **2** : something that continuously whirls or changes

whirl·pool \'hwərl-ˌpül\ *n* : water moving rapidly in a circle so as to produce a depression in the center into which floating objects may be drawn

whirl·wind \-ˌwind\ *n* **1** : a small whirling windstorm **2** : a confused rush **3** : a violent or destructive force

whirly·bird \'hwər-lē-ˌbərd\ *n* : HELICOPTER

¹whish \'hwish\ *vb* **1** : to move with a whish or swishing sound **2** ♦ : to have or make a sound like that of a long \s\ or \sh\

♦ fizz, hiss, sizzle, swish

²whish n : a rushing sound : SWISH

¹whisk \'hwisk\ n **1** : a quick light sweeping or brushing motion **2** : a usu. wire kitchen implement for beating food by hand **3** : WHISK BROOM

²whisk vb **1** ♦ : to move nimbly and quickly **2** ♦ : to move or convey briskly ⟨~ed the children off to bed⟩ **3** : to beat or whip lightly ⟨~ eggs⟩ **4** : to brush or wipe off lightly ⟨~ a coat⟩

♦ [1] bowl, breeze, coast, drift, flow, glide, roll, sail, skim, slide, slip, stream, sweep ♦ [2] accelerate, hasten, hurry, quicken, rush, speed, step up

whisk broom n : a small broom with a short handle used esp. as a clothes brush

whis·ker \'hwis-kər\ n **1** : one hair of the beard **2** pl : the part of the beard that grows on the sides of the face or on the chin **3** : one of the long bristles or hairs growing near the mouth of an animal (as a cat or mouse) — **whis·kered** \-kərd\ adj

whis·key or **whis·ky** \'hwis-kē\ n, pl **whiskeys** or **whiskies** : a liquor distilled from fermented wort (as that obtained from rye, corn, or barley mash)

¹whis·per \'hwis-pər\ vb **1 a** : to speak very low or under the breath **b** ♦ : to tell or utter by or as if by whispering ⟨~ a secret⟩ **2** : to make a low rustling sound ⟨~ing leaves⟩ — **whis·per·er** \-pər-ər\ n

♦ circulate, noise, rumor

²whisper n **1** : something communicated by or as if by whispering : HINT, RUMOR **2** : an act or instance of whispering

whist \'hwist\ n : a card game played by four players in two partnerships with a deck of 52 cards

¹whis·tle \'hwi-səl\ n **1** : a device by which a shrill sound is produced ⟨steam ~⟩ ⟨tin ~⟩ **2** : a shrill clear sound made by forcing breath out or air in through the puckered lips **3** : the sound or signal produced by a whistle or as if by whistling **4** : the shrill clear note of an animal (as a bird)

²whistle vb **whis·tled; whis·tling 1** : to utter a shrill clear sound by blowing or drawing air through the puckered lips **2** : to utter a shrill note or call resembling a whistle **3** : to make a shrill clear sound esp. by rapid movements ⟨the wind whistled⟩ **4** : to blow or sound a whistle **5** : to signal or call by a whistle **6** : to produce, utter, or express by whistling ⟨~ a tune⟩ — **whis·tler** n

whis·tle-blow·er \'hwi-səl-ˌblō-ər\ n : INFORMER

whis·tle-stop \-ˌstäp\ n : a brief personal appearance by a political candidate orig. on the rear platform of a touring train

whit \'hwit\ n ♦ : the smallest part or particle

♦ hoot, jot, lick, modicum, rap, tittle

¹white \'hwīt\ adj **whit·er; whit·est 1** ♦ : free from color **2** : of the color of new snow or milk; esp : of the color white **3** : light or pallid in color ⟨lips ~ with fear⟩ **4** : SILVERY; also : made of silver **5** often cap : of or relating to any of various population groups considered as having light pigmentation of the skin **6** : free from spot or blemish : PURE, INNOCENT **7** : BLANK 2 ⟨~ space in printed matter⟩ **8** ♦ : not intended to cause harm ⟨a ~ lie⟩ **9** : wearing white ⟨~ friars⟩ **10** : marked by snow ⟨~ Christmas⟩ **11** : consisting of a wide range of frequencies ⟨~ light⟩ — **white·ness** \-nəs\ n — **whit·ish** \'hwī-tish\ adj

♦ [1] colorless (or colourless), uncolored (or uncoloured), unpainted ♦ [8] harmless, innocent, innocuous, safe

²white n **1** : the color of maximal lightness that characterizes objects which both reflect and transmit light : the opposite of black **2** : a white or light-colored part or thing ⟨the ~ of an egg⟩; also, pl : white garments **3** : the light-colored pieces in a 2-player board game; also : the person by whom these are played **4** : one that is or approaches the color white **5** : a person belonging to any of various population groups considered as having light pigmentation of the skin — usu. used in pl.

white ant n : TERMITE

white blood cell n : any of the colorless blood cells (as lymphocytes) that do not contain hemoglobin but do have a nucleus

white–bread \'hwīt-'bred\ adj : being, typical of, or having qualities (as blandness) associated with the white middle class ⟨~ values⟩

white·cap \'hwīt-ˌkap\ n : a wave crest breaking into white foam

white chocolate n : a whitish confection chiefly of cocoa butter, milk, and sugar

white–col·lar \'hwīt-'kä-lər\ adj : of, relating to, or constituting the class of salaried workers whose duties do not require the wearing of work clothes or protective clothing ⟨~ jobs⟩

white dwarf n : a small very dense whitish star of low luminosity

white elephant n **1** : an Indian elephant of a pale color that is sometimes venerated in India, Sri Lanka, Thailand, and Myan-

mar **2** : something requiring much care and expense and giving little profit or enjoyment

white feather n : a mark or symbol of cowardice

white·fish \'hwīt-ˌfish\ n : any of various freshwater food fishes related to the salmons and trouts

white flag n : a flag of pure white used to signify truce or surrender

white gold n : a pale alloy of gold resembling platinum in appearance

white goods n pl : white fabrics or articles (as sheets or towels) typically made of cotton or linen

White·hall \'hwīt-ˌhȯl\ n : the British government

white hat n **1** : an admirable and honorable person **2** : a mark or symbol of goodness

white·head \-ˌhed\ n : a small whitish lump in the skin due to retention of secretion in an oil gland duct

white heat n : a temperature higher than red heat at which a body becomes brightly incandescent

white–hot adj **1** : being at or radiating white heat **2** : FERVID

White House \-ˌhaus\ n **1** : the executive department of the U.S. government **2** : a residence of the president of the U.S.

white lead n : a heavy white poisonous carbonate of lead used esp. formerly as a pigment in exterior paints

white matter n : whitish nerve tissue esp. of the brain and spinal cord that consists largely of neuron processes enclosed in a fatty material and that typically lies under the cortical gray matter

whit·en \'hwīt-ᵊn\ vb ♦ : to make or become white — **whit·en·er** n

♦ blanch, bleach, blench, dull, fade, pale, wash out

white pepper n : a spice that consists of the berry of a pepper plant ground after removal of its black husk

white pine n : a tall-growing pine of eastern No. America with needles in clusters of five; also : its wood

white sale n : a sale on white goods

white shark n : GREAT WHITE SHARK

white slave n, dated : a woman or girl held unwillingly for purposes of prostitution — **white slavery** n

white supremacy n **1** : the belief that the white race is inherently superior to other races **2** : the social, economic, and political systems that enable white people to maintain power over people of other races

white·tail \'hwīt-ˌtāl\ n : WHITE-TAILED DEER

white–tailed deer n : a No. American deer with a rather long tail white on the underside and the males of which have forward-arching antlers

white–tie \-ˌtī\ adj : characterized by or requiring formal evening clothes consisting of usu. white tie and tailcoat for men and a formal gown for women

white·wall \'hwīt-ˌwȯl\ n : an automobile tire having a white band on the sidewall

¹white·wash \-ˌwȯsh, -ˌwäsh\ vb **1** : to whiten with whitewash **2** ♦ : to clear of a charge of wrongdoing by offering excuses, hiding facts, or conducting a perfunctory investigation **3** : SHUT OUT 2

♦ excuse, gloss, palliate

²whitewash n **1** : a liquid mixture (as of lime and water) for whitening a surface **2** : a clearing of wrongdoing by whitewashing

white water n : frothy water (as in breakers, rapids, or falls)

white·wood \-ˌwud\ n : any of various trees and esp. a tulip tree having light-colored wood; also : such wood

¹whith·er \'hwi-thər\ adv **1** : to what place **2** : to what situation, position, degree, or end ⟨~ will this drive him⟩

²whither conj **1** : to the place at, in, or to which; also : to which place **2** : to whatever place

whith·er·so·ev·er \ˌhwi-thər-sō-'e-vər\ conj : to whatever place

¹whit·ing \'hwī-tiŋ\ n, pl **whiting** also **whit·ings** : any of several usu. light or silvery food fishes (as a hake) found mostly near seacoasts

²whiting n : calcium carbonate in powdered form used esp. as a pigment and in putty

whit·low \'hwit-ˌlō\ n : a deep inflammation of a finger or toe with pus formation

Whit·sun·day \'hwit-'sən-dē, -sən-ˌdā\ n : PENTECOST

whit·tle \'hwit-ᵊl\ vb **whit·tled; whit·tling 1** : to pare or cut off chips from the surface of (wood) with a knife; also : to cut or shape by such paring **2** : to reduce as if by paring down ⟨~ down expenses⟩

¹whiz or **whizz** \'hwiz\ vb **whizzed; whiz·zing 1** ♦ : to hum, whir, or hiss like a speeding object (as an arrow or ball) passing through air **2** ♦ : fly or move swiftly with a hissing or buzzing sound

♦ [1, 2] buzz, drone, hiss, hum, whir, whish, zip, zoom

whiz • wickedness

²whiz *or* **whizz** *n, pl* **whiz·zes ♦** : a hissing, buzzing, or whizzing sound

♦ buzz, drone, hiss, hum, purr, whir, zoom

³whiz *n, pl* **whiz·zes ♦** : a person notably qualified or able usu. in a specified field of interest : WIZARD 2

♦ ace, adept, artist, authority, crackerjack, expert, maestro, master, scholar, shark, virtuoso, wizard ♦ brain, genius, intellect, thinker, wizard

who \'hü\ *pron* **1** : what or which person or persons ⟨~ did it⟩ ⟨~ is he⟩ ⟨~ are they⟩ **2** : the person or persons that ⟨knows ~ did it⟩ **3** — used to introduce a relative clause and to serve as a substitute therein for the substantive modified by the clause ⟨the man ~ lives there is rich⟩

WHO *abbr* World Health Organization

whoa \'wō, 'hwō, 'hō\ *vb imper* — a command to an animal to stand still

who·dun·it *also* **who·dun·nit** \hü-'də-nət\ *n* : a detective or mystery story

who·ev·er \hü-'e-vər\ *pron* : whatever person : no matter who

¹whole \'hōl\ *adj* **1 ♦** : being in healthy or sound condition : free from defect or damage **2 ♦** : having all its proper parts or elements ⟨~ milk⟩ **3** : constituting the total sum of : ENTIRE ⟨owns the ~ island⟩ **4** : each or all of the ⟨the ~ family⟩ **5 ♦** : not scattered or divided : CONCENTRATED ⟨gave me his ~ attention⟩ **6** : seemingly complete or total ⟨the ~ idea is to help, not hinder⟩

♦ [1] able-bodied, chipper, fit, hale, healthy, hearty, robust, sound, well, wholesome ♦ [2] complete, comprehensive, entire, full, grand, intact, integral, perfect, plenary, total ♦ [5] all, concentrated, entire, undivided *Ant* diffuse, divided, scattered

²whole *n* **1 ♦** : a complete amount or sum **2** : something whole or entire — **on the whole 1** : in view of all the circumstances or conditions **2** : in general

♦ aggregate, full, sum, total, totality

³whole *adv* : COMPLETELY, ENTIRELY ⟨a ~ new team⟩

whole food *n* : a food eaten in its natural state with little or no artificial additives

whole·heart·ed \'hōl-'här-təd\ *adj* : undivided in purpose, enthusiasm, will, or commitment

whole hog *adv* : to the fullest extent : COMPLETELY ⟨accepted the proposals *whole hog*⟩

whole·ness *n* **♦** : the quality or state of being whole : an unreduced or unbroken completeness or totality

♦ fitness, health, heartiness, robustness, soundness, wellness, wholesomeness

whole note *n* : a musical note equal to one measure of four beats

whole number *n* **1** : any of the set of nonnegative integers **2 ♦** : any of the natural numbers that do not include fractions : INTEGER

♦ digit, figure, integer, number, numeral

¹whole·sale \'hōl-,sāl\ *n* : the sale of goods in quantity usu. for resale by a retail merchant

²wholesale *adj* **1** : performed on a large scale without discrimination ⟨~ slaughter⟩ **2** : of, relating to, or engaged in wholesaling — **wholesale** *adv*

³wholesale *vb* **whole·saled; whole·sal·ing** : to sell at wholesale — **whole·sal·er** *n*

whole·some \'hōl-səm\ *adj* **1 ♦** : promoting mental, spiritual, or bodily health or well-being ⟨a ~ environment⟩ **2 ♦** : sound in body, mind, or morals : HEALTHY **3** : PRUDENT ⟨~ respect for the law⟩

♦ [1] healthful, healthy, restorative, salubrious, salutary ♦ [2] able-bodied, chipper, fit, hale, healthy, hearty, robust, sound, well, whole

whole·some·ness *n* **♦** : the quality, fact, or state of being wholesome

♦ fitness, health, heartiness, robustness, soundness, wellness, wholeness

whole step *n* : a musical interval comprising two half steps (as C–D or F♯–G♯)

whole wheat *adj* : made of ground entire wheat kernels

whol·ly \'hōl-lē\ *adv* **1 ♦** : to the full or entire extent : COMPLETELY **2** : SOLELY, EXCLUSIVELY

♦ absolutely, all, altogether, clean, completely, entirely, fully, quite, totally, utterly

whom \'hüm\ *pron, objective case of* WHO

whom·ev·er \hü-'me-vər\ *pron, objective case of* WHOEVER

whom·so·ev·er \,hüm-sō-'e-vər\ *pron, objective case of* WHOSOEVER

¹whoop \'hwüp, 'hwu̇p, 'hüp, 'hu̇p\ *vb* **1** : to shout or call loudly and vigorously **2** : to make the characteristic whoop of whooping cough **3** : to go or pass with a loud noise **4** : to utter or express with a whoop; *also* : to urge, drive, or cheer with a whoop

²whoop *n* **1 ♦** : a whooping sound or utterance : SHOUT **2** : a crowing intake of breath after a fit of coughing in whooping cough

♦ cry, holler, hoot, howl, shout, yell, yowl

¹whoop·ee \'hwu̇-(,)pē, 'hwü-\ *interj* — used to express exuberance

²whoopee *n* **1** : boisterous fun **2** : sexual play — usu. used with *make*

whooping cough *n* : an infectious bacterial disease esp. of children marked by convulsive coughing fits often followed by a shrill gasping intake of breath

whooping crane *n* : a large white nearly extinct No. American crane noted for its loud whooping call

whoop·la \'hwu̇p-,lä, 'hwüp-\ *n* **1** : HOOPLA **2** : boisterous merrymaking

whop·per \'hwä-pər\ *n* **1 ♦** : something unusually large or extreme of its kind **2 ♦** : a monstrous lie

♦ [1] behemoth, blockbuster, colossus, giant, jumbo, leviathan, mammoth, monster, titan, whale ♦ [2] fabrication, fairy tale, falsehood, falsity, fib, lie, mendacity, prevarication, story, tale, untruth

whop·ping \'hwä-piŋ\ *adj* **♦** : extremely large

♦ colossal, enormous, giant, gigantic, grand, huge, jumbo, mammoth, massive, outsize, oversize, prodigious, titanic, tremendous

whore \'hōr\ *n* : PROSTITUTE

whorl \'hwȯrl, 'hwərl\ *n* **1** : a group of parts (as leaves or petals) encircling an axis and esp. a plant stem **2** : something that whirls or coils around a center : COIL, SPIRAL **3** : one of the turns of a snail shell

whorled \'hwȯrld, 'hwərld\ *adj* : having or arranged in whorls

¹whose \'hüz\ *adj* : of or relating to whom or which esp. as possessor or possessors, agent or agents, or object or objects of an action ⟨asked ~ bag it was⟩

²whose *pron* : whose one or ones ⟨~ is this car⟩ ⟨~ are those books⟩

who·so \'hü-,sō\ *pron* : WHOEVER

who·so·ev·er \,hü-sō-'e-vər\ *pron* : WHOEVER

whs *or* **whse** *abbr* warehouse

whsle *abbr* wholesale

¹why \'hwī\ *adv* : for what reason, cause, or purpose ⟨~ did you do it?⟩

²why *conj* **1** : the cause, reason, or purpose for which ⟨that is ~ you did it⟩ **2** : for which : on account of which ⟨knows the reason ~ you did it⟩

³why *n, pl* **whys ♦** : the reason or cause of something ⟨wants to know the ~s and wherefores⟩

♦ grounds, motive, reason, wherefore

⁴why \'wī, 'hwī\ *interj* — used to express surprise, hesitation, approval, disapproval, or impatience ⟨~, here's what I was looking for⟩

WI *abbr* **1** West Indies **2** Wisconsin

WIA *abbr* wounded in action

Wic·ca \'wi-kə\ *n* : a religion that affirms the existence of supernatural power (as magic) and of deities who inhere in nature and that ritually observes seasonal and life cycles

wick \'wik\ *n* : a loosely bound bundle of soft fibers that draws up oil, tallow, or wax to be burned in a candle, oil lamp, or stove

wick·ed \'wi-kəd\ *adj* **1 ♦** : morally bad : EVIL, SINFUL **2** : FIERCE, VICIOUS **3 a ♦** : playfully or engagingly mischievous : ROGUISH ⟨a ~ glance⟩ **b** : showing or expressing ill will : MALICIOUS **4** : REPUGNANT, VILE ⟨a ~ odor⟩ **5** : HARMFUL, DANGEROUS ⟨a ~ attack⟩ **6** : impressively excellent ⟨throws a ~ fastball⟩

♦ [1] bad, evil, immoral, iniquitous, nefarious, rotten, sinful, unethical, unsavory, vicious, vile, villainous, wrong ♦ [3a] devilish, impish, knavish, mischievous, rascally, roguish, sly, waggish

wick·ed·ly *adv* **♦** : in a wicked manner

♦ hatefully, maliciously, meanly, nastily, spitefully, viciously

wick·ed·ness *n* **♦** : the quality or state of being wicked

♦ devilishness, impishness, knavery, mischief, mischievousness, rascality, shenanigans, waggery ♦ atrociousness, atrocity, depravity, enormity, heinousness, monstrosity, vileness

wick·er \'wi-kər\ n **1** : a small pliant branch (as an osier or a withe) **2** : WICKERWORK — **wicker** adj

wick·er·work \-ˌwərk\ n : work made of osiers, twigs, or rods : basket weaving

wick·et \'wi-kət\ n **1** : a small gate or door; esp : one forming a part of or placed near a larger one **2** : a windowlike opening usu. with a grille or grate (as at a ticket office) **3** : a set of three upright rods topped by two crosspieces bowled at in cricket **4** : an arch or hoop in croquet

wick·i·up \'wi-kē-ˌəp\ n : a hut used by nomadic Indigenous Americans of the western and southwestern U.S. with a usu. oval base and a rough frame covered with reed mats, grass, or brushwood

wid abbr widow, widower

¹**wide** \'wīd\ adj **wid·er; wid·est 1** ♦ : covering a vast area **2** : measured across or at right angles to the length **3** ♦ : not narrow : BROAD; also : ROOMY **4** : opened to full width ⟨eyes ∼ with wonder⟩ **5** : not limited : EXTENSIVE ⟨∼ experience⟩ **6** : far from the goal, mark, or truth ⟨a ∼ guess⟩ — **wide·ly** adv

♦ [1] broad, expansive, extended, extensive, far-flung, far-reaching, widespread ♦ [3] broad, commodious, expansive, extensive, roomy, spacious, thick Ant narrow, skinny, slender, slim, thin

²**wide** adv **wid·er; wid·est 1** : over a great distance or extent : WIDELY ⟨searched far and ∼⟩ **2** : over a specified distance, area, or extent **3** : so as to leave a wide space between ⟨∼ apart⟩ **4** : so as to clear by a considerable distance ⟨ran ∼ around left end⟩ **5** : COMPLETELY, FULLY ⟨opened her eyes ∼⟩

wide–awake \ˌwīd-ə-'wāk\ adj **1** ♦ : fully awake **2** ♦ : marked by careful watchfulness and promptness to cope with emergencies : ALERT

♦ [1] awake, sleepless, wakeful ♦ [2] alert, attentive, awake, vigilant, watchful

wide–body \'wīd-ˌbä-dē\ n : a large jet aircraft having a wide cabin

wide–eyed \'wīd-'īd\ adj **1** : having the eyes wide open esp. with wonder or astonishment **2** : marked by unsophisticated or uncritical acceptance or admiration : NAIVE

wide·mouthed \-'mau̇thd, -'mau̇tht\ adj **1** : having one's mouth opened wide (as in awe) **2** : having a wide mouth ⟨∼ jars⟩

wid·en \'wīd-ᵊn\ vb : to increase in width, scope, or extent

wide·spread \'wīd-'spred\ adj **1** : widely scattered or prevalent **2** ♦ : widely extended or spread out

♦ broad, expansive, extended, extensive, far-flung, far-reaching, wide

widgeon var of WIGEON

¹**wid·ow** \'wi-dō\ n : a woman who has lost her spouse or partner by death and has not married again — **wid·ow·hood** n

²**widow** vb : to cause to become a widow or widower

wid·ow·er \'wi-də-wər\ n : a man who has lost his spouse or partner by death and has not married again

width \'width\ n **1** : a distance from side to side : the measurement taken at right angles to the length : BREADTH **2** ♦ : largeness of extent or scope; also : FULLNESS **3** : a measured and cut piece of material ⟨a ∼ of calico⟩

♦ amplitude, breadth, compass, extent, range, reach, realm, scope, sweep

wield \'wēld\ vb **1** : to use or handle esp. effectively ⟨∼ a broom⟩ **2** ♦ : to exert authority by means of ⟨∼ influence⟩ — **wield·er** n

♦ apply, exercise, exert, put out

wie·ner also **wei·ner** \'wē-nər\ n : FRANKFURTER

wife \'wīf\ n, pl **wives** \'wīvz\ **1** dial : WOMAN **2** : a woman acting in a specified capacity — used in combination ⟨fishwife⟩ **3** ♦ : a female partner in a marriage — **wife·hood** n — **wife·less** adj — **wife·ly** adj

♦ consort, helpmate, lady, mate, partner, spouse

wig \'wig\ n : a manufactured covering of natural or synthetic hair for the head; also : TOUPEE

wi·geon or **wid·geon** \'wi-jən\ n, pl **wigeon** or **wigeons** or **widgeon** or **widgeons** : any of several medium-sized freshwater ducks

wig·gle \'wi-gəl\ vb **wig·gled; wig·gling 1** ♦ : to move to and

fro with quick jerky or shaking movements **2** : to proceed with twisting and turning movements ⟨wiggled his toes⟩ — **wiggle** n

♦ fiddle, fidget, jerk, squirm, twitch

wig·gler \'wi-glər, -gə-lər\ n **1** : a larva or pupa of a mosquito **2** : one that wiggles

wig·gly \'wi-glē, -gə-lē\ adj **1** : tending to wiggle ⟨a ∼ worm⟩ **2** : WAVY ⟨∼ lines⟩

wight \'wīt\ n : a living being : CREATURE

wig·let \'wi-glət\ n : a small wig used esp. to enhance a hairstyle

¹**wig·wag** \'wig-ˌwag\ vb **1** : to signal by or as if by a flag or light waved according to a code **2** : to make or cause to make a signal (as with the hand or arm)

²**wigwag** n : the art or practice of wigwagging

wig·wam \'wig-ˌwäm\ n : a hut used by Indigenous peoples of the eastern U.S. having typically an arched framework of poles overlaid with bark, rush mats, or hides

¹**wild** \'wīld\ adj **1** : living in a state of nature and not ordinarily tamed ⟨∼ ducks⟩ **2** : growing or produced without human aid or care ⟨∼ honey⟩ ⟨∼ plants⟩ **3** : WASTE, DESOLATE ⟨∼ country⟩ **4** : not subjected to restraint or regulation : UNCONTROLLED, UNRULY ⟨∼ passions⟩ ⟨a ∼ young stallion⟩ **5** ♦ : marked by turbulent violent agitation ⟨a ∼ night⟩ **6** ♦ : exceeding normal or conventional bounds in thought, design, conception, or nature ⟨∼ ideas⟩ **7** : indicative of strong passion, desire, or emotion ⟨a ∼ stare⟩ **8** ♦ : not acculturated to an advanced civilization : SAVAGE **9 a** ♦ : deviating from the natural or expected course, goal, or practice : acting, appearing, or being in an unexpected, undesired, or unpredictable manner ⟨a ∼ throw⟩ **b** ♦ : having no basis in known or surmised fact **10** : able to represent any playing card designated by the holder ⟨deuces ∼⟩ — **wild** adv — **wild·ness** n

♦ [1] feral, savage, unbroken, undomesticated, untamed Ant broken, busted, domestic, domesticated, tame, tamed ♦ [1, 2] natural, uncultivated, undomesticated, untamed Ant cultivated, tamed ♦ [5] blustery, rough, stormy, tempestuous, tumultuous, turbulent, violent ♦ [6, 9a] bizarre, curious, far-out, funny, kinky, odd, outlandish, outré, peculiar, quaint, quirky, remarkable, screwy, strange, wacky, weird ♦ [8] barbarous, heathen, heathenish, Neanderthal, rude, savage, uncivil, uncivilized, uncultivated ♦ [9b] absurd, bizarre, fanciful, fantastic, foolish, nonsensical, preposterous, unreal

²**wild** adv **1** ♦ : in a wild manner : WILDLY **2** ♦ : without regulation or control ⟨running ∼⟩

♦ amok, berserk, frantically, harum-scarum, hectically, helter-skelter, madly, pell-mell, wildly

³**wild** n **1** : a region or tract that is sparsely inhabited or uncultivated : WILDERNESS **2** : a natural or undomesticated state or existence

wild boar n : an Old World wild hog from which most domestic swine have been derived

wild card n **1** : an unknown or unpredictable factor **2** : one picked to fill a leftover play-off or tournament position **3** usu **wild·card** : a symbol (as ? or *) used in a keyword search to represent the presence of unspecified characters

wild carrot n : QUEEN ANNE'S LACE

¹**wild·cat** \'wīld-ˌkat\ n, pl **wildcats 1** : any of various small or medium-sized cats (as a lynx or ocelot) **2** : a quick-tempered hard-fighting person

²**wildcat** adj **1** : not sound or safe ⟨∼ schemes⟩ **2** : initiated by a group of workers without formal union approval ⟨∼ strike⟩

³**wildcat** vb **wild·cat·ted; wild·cat·ting** : to drill an oil or gas well in a region not known to be productive

wil·de·beest \'wil-də-ˌbēst\ n, pl **wildebeests** also **wildebeest** : either of two large African antelopes with an oxlike head and horns and a horselike mane and tail

wil·der·ness \'wil-dər-nəs\ n ♦ : an uncultivated and uninhabited region

♦ nature, open, outdoors, wild

wild·fire \'wīld-ˌfīr\ n : an uncontrollable fire — **like wildfire** : very rapidly

wild·flow·er \-ˌflau̇(-ə)r\ n : the flower of a wild or uncultivated plant or the plant bearing it

wild·fowl \-ˌfau̇l\ n : a bird and esp. a waterfowl hunted as game

wild–goose chase n : the pursuit of something unattainable

wild·life \'wīld-ˌlīf\ n : nonhuman living things and esp. wild animals living in their natural environment

wild·ly adv ♦ : in a wild manner

♦ amok, berserk, frantically, harum-scarum, hectically, helter-skelter, madly, pell-mell, wild

wild oat *n* **1** : any of several Old World wild grasses **2** *pl* : offenses and indiscretions attributed to youthful exuberance — usu. used in the phrase *sow one's wild oats*

wild rice *n* : a No. American aquatic grass; *also* : its edible seed

wild•wood \'wīld-ˌwu̇d\ *n* : a wood unaltered or unfrequented by humans

¹wile \'wīl\ *n* **1** ♦ : a trick or stratagem intended to ensnare or deceive; *also* : a playful trick **2** ♦ : the use of deceitfulness and trickery

    ♦ [1] artifice, device, dodge, gimmick, jig, ploy, scheme, sleight, stratagem, trick ♦ [2] artifice, chicanery, hanky-panky, subterfuge, trickery

²wile *vb* **wiled; wil•ing** ♦ : to lure by or as if by a magic spell

    ♦ allure, beguile, bewitch, captivate, charm, enchant, fascinate

wil•i•ness \-lē-nəs\ *n* ♦ : the quality or state of being wily

    ♦ artfulness, artifice, caginess, canniness, craft, craftiness, cunning, guile, slyness ♦ artifice, craft, craftiness, crookedness, cunning, deceit, deceitfulness, dishonesty, dissimulation, double-dealing, duplicity, guile

¹will \'wil\ *vb, past* **would** \'wu̇d\ *pres sing & pl* **will** **1** : WISH, DESIRE ⟨call it what you ∼⟩ **2** — used as an auxiliary verb to express (1) desire, willingness, or in negative constructions refusal ⟨∼ you have another⟩ ⟨he *won't* do it⟩, (2) customary or habitual action ⟨∼ get angry over nothing⟩, (3) simple futurity ⟨tomorrow we ∼ go shopping⟩, (4) capability or sufficiency ⟨the back seat ∼ hold three⟩, (5) determination or willfulness ⟨I ∼ go despite them⟩, (6) probability ⟨that ∼ be the mailman⟩, (7) inevitability ⟨accidents ∼ happen⟩, or (8) a command ⟨you ∼ do as I say⟩

²will *n* **1** : wish or desire often combined with determination ⟨the ∼ to win⟩ **2** : something desired; *esp* : a choice or determination of one having authority or power **3** : the act, process, or experience of willing : VOLITION **4** ♦ : the mental powers manifested as wishing, choosing, desiring, or intending **5** : a disposition to act according to principles or ends **6** ♦ : power of controlling one's own actions or emotions ⟨a leader of iron ∼⟩ **7** : a legal document in which a person declares to whom his or her possessions are to go after death

    ♦ [4] accord, choice, free will, option, self-determination, volition ♦ [6] restraint, self-control, self-discipline, self-government, self-possession, self-restraint, willpower

³will *vb* **1** : to dispose of by or as if by a will : BEQUEATH **2** : to determine by an act of choice **3** ♦ : to have the intention of : CHOOSE

    ♦ choose, like, want, wish

will•ful *or* **wil•ful** \'wil-fəl\ *adj* **1** ♦ : governed by will without regard to reason : obstinately or perversely doing what one wants without regard to others **2** ♦ : done deliberately : INTENTIONAL ⟨∼ murder⟩

    ♦ [1] contrary, defiant, disobedient, froward, intractable, rebellious, recalcitrant, refractory, uncontrollable, unruly, untoward, wayward ♦ [1] dogged, hardheaded, headstrong, mulish, obdurate, obstinate, opinionated, peevish, pertinacious, perverse, pigheaded, stubborn, unyielding ♦ [2] deliberate, freewill, intentional, purposeful

will•ful•ly *adv* ♦ : in a willful manner

    ♦ consciously, deliberately, intentionally, knowingly, purposely

wil•lies \'wi-lēz\ *n pl* ♦ : a fit of nervousness : JITTERS — used with *the*

    ♦ dither, jitters, shakes, shivers

will•ing \'wi-liŋ\ *adj* **1** ♦ : inclined or favorably disposed in mind : READY ⟨∼ to go⟩ **2** ♦ : prompt to act or respond ⟨∼ workers⟩ **3** ♦ : done, borne, or accepted voluntarily or without reluctance **4** : of or relating to the will

    ♦ [1] amenable, disposed, game, glad, inclined, ready *Ant* disinclined, unwilling ♦ [2] alert, expeditious, prompt, quick, ready ♦ [3] freewill, voluntary

will•ing•ly *adv* : in a willing manner

will•ing•ness *n* ♦ : the quality or state of being willing

    ♦ alacrity, gameness, goodwill

wil•li•waw \'wi-lē-ˌwȯ\ *n* ♦ : a sudden violent gust of cold land air common along mountainous coasts of high latitudes

    ♦ blast, blow, flurry, gust

will–o'–the–wisp \ˌwil-ə-thə-'wisp\ *n* **1** : a light that appears at night over marshy grounds **2** : a misleading or elusive goal or hope

wil•low \'wi-lō\ *n* **1** : any of a genus of quick-growing shrubs and trees with tough pliable shoots **2** : an object made of willow wood

wil•low•ware \-ˌwar\ *n* : dinnerware that is usu. blue and white and that is decorated with a story-telling design featuring a large willow tree by a little bridge

wil•lowy \'wi-lə-wē\ *adj* **1** : pliant, soft, and yielding in texture **2** : gracefully tall and slender

    ♦ flexible, limber, lissome, lithe, pliable, supple *Ant* inflexible, rigid, stiff

will•pow•er \'wil-ˌpau̇-ər\ *n* ♦ : the power to control one's actions or emotions : energetic determination

    ♦ restraint, self-control, self-discipline, self-government, self-possession, self-restraint, will

wil•ly–nil•ly \ˌwi-lē-'ni-lē\ *adv or adj* **1** : without regard for one's choice : by compulsion ⟨they rushed us along ∼⟩ **2** ♦ : in a haphazard or spontaneous manner

    ♦ aimlessly, anyhow, anyway, anywise, desultorily, erratically, haphazard, haphazardly, helter-skelter, irregularly, randomly

¹wilt \'wilt\ *vb* **1** ♦ : to lose or cause to lose freshness and become limp esp. from lack of water : DROOP ⟨the roses were ∼ing⟩ **2** ♦ : to grow weak or faint : LANGUISH

    ♦ decay, droop, fail, flag, go, lag, languish, sag, waste, weaken

²wilt *n* : any of various plant disorders marked by wilting and often shriveling

wily \'wī-lē\ *adj* **wil•i•er; -est** ♦ : full of guile : TRICKY

    ♦ artful, cagey, crafty, cunning, devious, foxy, guileful, slick, sly, subtle, tricky

wimp \'wimp\ *n* : a weak, cowardly, or ineffectual person

¹wim•ple \'wim-pəl\ *n* : a cloth covering worn over the head and around the neck and chin by women esp. in the late medieval period and by some nuns

²wimple *vb* **wim•pled; wim•pling** **1** : to cover with or as if with a wimple **2** : to ripple or cause to ripple

wimpy \'wim-pē\ *adj* ♦ : being a wimp

    ♦ effete, frail, nerveless, soft, spineless, weak, wishy-washy

¹win \'win\ *vb* **won** \'wən\; **win•ning** **1 a** : to get possession of esp. by effort : GAIN **b** ♦ : to obtain by work : EARN **2 a** : to gain in or as if in battle or contest **b** ♦ : to be the victor in ⟨won the war⟩ **3** ♦ : to solicit and gain the favor of — often used with *over*; *esp* : to induce to accept oneself in marriage

    ♦ [1b] achieve, acquire, attain, capture, carry, draw, earn, gain, garner, get, land, make, obtain, procure, realize, secure ♦ [2b] conquer, prevail, triumph *Ant* lose ♦ *usu* **win over** [3] argue, convince, get, induce, move, persuade, prevail, satisfy, talk

²win *n* : VICTORY; *esp* : 1st place at the finish (as of a horse race)

wince \'wins\ *vb* **winced; winc•ing** ♦ : to shrink back involuntarily (as from pain) : FLINCH — **wince** *n*

    ♦ blench, flinch, quail, recoil, shrink

winch \'winch\ *n* : a machine that has a drum on which is wound a rope or cable for hauling or hoisting — **winch** *vb*

¹wind \'wind\ *n* **1** : a movement of the air **2** ♦ : a prevailing force or influence : TENDENCY **3** : BREATH ⟨he had the ∼ knocked out of him⟩ **4** : gas produced in the stomach or intestines **5** ♦ : idle talk as insubstantial as air **6** : air carrying a scent (as of game) **7** : INTIMATION ⟨they got ∼ of our plans⟩ **8** *pl* : WIND INSTRUMENTS; *also* : players of wind instruments

    ♦ [2] current, drift, leaning, run, tendency, tide, trend ♦ [5] bombast, gas, grandiloquence, hot air, rhetoric

²wind *vb* **1** : to get a scent of ⟨the dogs ∼ed the game⟩ **2** : to cause to be out of breath ⟨he was ∼ed from the climb⟩ **3** : to allow (as a horse) to rest so as to recover breath

³wind \'wīnd, 'wind\ *vb* **wind•ed** \'wīn-dəd, 'win-\ *or* **wound** \'wau̇nd\; **wind•ing** : to sound by blowing ⟨∼ a horn⟩

⁴wind \'wīnd\ *vb* **wound** \'wau̇nd\ *also* **wind•ed; wind•ing** **1** : ENTANGLE, INVOLVE **2** ♦ : to introduce stealthily : INSINUATE **3** : to encircle or cover with something pliable : WRAP, COIL, TWINE ⟨∼ a bobbin⟩ **4** : to hoist or haul by a rope or chain and a winch **5** : to tighten the spring of; *also* : CRANK **6** : to raise to a high level (as of excitement) **7** : to cause to move in a curving line or path **8** ♦ : to have a curving course or shape ⟨a river ∼ing through the valley⟩ **9** : to move or lie so as to encircle

    ♦ bend, coil, curl, curve, entwine, spiral, twine, twist

⁵wind \'wīnd\ *n* ♦ : something having a curving or twisting form : TURN

    ♦ angle, arc, arch, bend, bow, crook, curve, turn

wind·age \'win-dij\ *n* : the influence of the wind in deflecting the course of a projectile through the air; *also* : the amount of such deflection

wind·bag \'wind-ˌbag\ *n* ♦ : an overly talkative person
   ♦ babbler, cackler, chatterbox, chatterer, conversationalist, gabbler, jabberer, magpie, prattler, talker

wind·blown \-ˌblōn\ *adj* : blown by the wind; *also* : having the appearance of being blown by the wind ⟨∼ hair⟩

wind·break \-ˌbrāk\ *n* : a growth of trees or shrubs serving to break the force of the wind; *also* : a shelter from the wind

wind·burned \-ˌbərnd\ *adj* : irritated and inflamed by exposure to the wind — **wind·burn** \-ˌbərn\ *n*

wind·chill \-ˌchil\ *n* : a still-air temperature that would have the same cooling effect on exposed human skin as a given combination of temperature and wind speed

windchill factor *n* : WINDCHILL

wind down *vb* **1** : to draw toward an end **2** : RELAX, UNWIND

wind·er \'wīn-dər\ *n* : one that winds

wind·fall \'wind-ˌfȯl\ *n* **1** : something (as a tree or fruit) blown down by the wind **2** ♦ : an unexpected or sudden gift, gain, or advantage ⟨won a ∼ from the lottery⟩
   ♦ benefit, blessing, boon, felicity, godsend, good, manna

wind·flow·er \-ˌflau̇-ər\ *n* : ANEMONE

¹**wind·ing** \'wīn-diŋ\ *n* : material (as wire) wound or coiled about an object

²**winding** *adj* **1** ♦ : having a pronounced curve or spiral ⟨∼ stairs⟩ **2** ♦ : having a course that winds ⟨a ∼ road⟩
   ♦ [1] helical, spiral ♦ [2] crooked, devious, serpentine, sinuous, tortuous

wind·ing–sheet \-ˌshēt\ *n* : SHROUD

wind instrument *n* : a musical instrument (as a flute or horn) sounded by wind and esp. by the breath

wind·jam·mer \'wind-ˌja-mər\ *n* : a sailing ship; *also* : one of its crew

wind·lass \'wind-ləs\ *n* : a winch used esp. on ships for hoisting or hauling

wind·mill \'wind-ˌmil\ *n* : a mill or machine worked by the wind turning sails or vanes that radiate from a central shaft

win·dow \'win-dō\ *n* **1** : an opening in the wall of a building to let in light and air; *also* : the framework with fittings that closes such an opening **2** : WINDOWPANE **3** : an opening resembling or suggesting that of a window in a building **4** : an interval of time during which certain conditions or an opportunity exists **5** : a rectangular box appearing on a computer screen on which information (as files or program output) is displayed — **win·dow·less** *adj*

window box *n* : a box for growing plants in or by a window

window dressing *n* **1** : display of merchandise in a store window **2** : a showing made to create a deceptively favorable impression

win·dow·pane \'win-dō-ˌpān\ *n* : a pane in a window

win·dow–shop \-ˌshäp\ *vb* : to look at the displays in store windows without going inside the stores to make purchases — **win·dow–shop·per** *n*

win·dow·sill \-ˌsil\ *n* : the horizontal member at the bottom of a window

wind·pipe \'wind-ˌpīp\ *n* : TRACHEA

wind·proof \-'prüf\ *adj* : impervious to wind ⟨a ∼ jacket⟩

wind·row \'wind-ˌrō\ *n* **1** : hay raked up into a row to dry **2** : a row of something (as dry leaves) swept up by or as if by the wind

wind shear *n* : a radical shift in wind speed and direction that occurs over a very short distance

wind·shield \'wind-ˌshēld\ *n* : a transparent screen (as of glass) in front of the occupants of a vehicle

wind sock *n* : an open-ended truncated cloth cone mounted in an elevated position to indicate wind direction

wind·storm \-ˌstȯrm\ *n* : a storm with high wind and little or no rain

wind·surf·ing \-ˌsər-fiŋ\ *n* : the sport or activity of riding a sailboard — **wind·surf** \-ˌsərf\ *vb* — **wind·surf·er** *n*

wind·swept \'wind-ˌswept\ *adj* : swept by or as if by wind ⟨∼ plains⟩

wind tunnel *n* : an enclosed passage through which air is blown to investigate air flow around an object

wind·up \'wīn-ˌdəp\ *n* **1** ♦ : a concluding act or part : CONCLUSION **2** : a series of regular and distinctive motions made by a pitcher preliminary to delivering a pitch
   ♦ close, conclusion, consummation, end, ending, finale, finis, finish

wind up *vb* **1** ♦ : to bring or come to a conclusion : END ⟨wind

up the meeting⟩ **2** : to put in order for the purpose of bringing to an end **3** : to arrive in a place, situation, or condition at the end or as a result of a course of action ⟨wound up as paupers⟩ **4** : to make a pitching windup
   ♦ close, conclude, end, finish, round, terminate, wrap up

¹**wind·ward** \'win-dwərd\ *n* : the side or direction from which the wind is blowing

²**windward** *adj* : being in or facing the direction from which the wind is blowing

windy \'win-dē\ *adj* **wind·i·er; -est 1** ♦ : having wind : exposed to winds ⟨a ∼ day⟩ ⟨a ∼ prairie⟩ **2** : STORMY **3** : FLATULENT **4** ♦ : indulging in or characterized by useless talk
   ♦ [1] blowy, blustery, breezy, gusty ♦ [4] bombastic, gaseous, grandiloquent, oratorical, rhetorical ♦ [4] circuitous, diffuse, long-winded, prolix, rambling, verbose, wordy

¹**wine** \'wīn\ *n* **1** : fermented grape juice used as a beverage **2** : the usu. fermented juice of a plant product (as fruit) used as a beverage ⟨rice ∼⟩

²**wine** *vb* **wined; win·ing** : to treat to or drink wine

wine cellar *n* : a room for storing wines; *also* : a stock of wines

wine·grow·er \-ˌgrō-ər\ *n* : one that cultivates a vineyard and makes wine

wine·press \-ˌpres\ *n* : a vat in which juice is pressed from grapes

win·ery \'wī-nə-rē, 'wīn-rē\ *n, pl* **-eries** : a wine-making establishment

¹**wing** \'wiŋ\ *n* **1** : one of the movable feathered or membranous paired appendages by means of which a bird, bat, or insect flies **2** : something suggesting a wing; *esp* : an airfoil that develops the lift which supports an aircraft in flight **3** : a plant or animal appendage or part likened to a wing **4** : a turned-back or extended edge on an article of clothing **5** : a means of flight or rapid progress **6** : the act or manner of flying : FLIGHT **7** *pl* : the area at the side of the stage out of sight **8** : one of the positions or players on either side of a center position or line **9** : either of two opposing groups within an organization : FACTION **10** : a unit in military aviation consisting of two or more squadrons — **wing·less** *adj* — **on the wing** : in flight : FLYING — **under one's wing** : in one's charge or care
   ♦ bloc, body, coalition, combination, combine, faction, party, sect, set, side

²**wing** *vb* **1** : to fit with wings; *also* : to enable to fly easily **2** ♦ : to pass through in flight : FLY ⟨∼ the air⟩ ⟨swallows ∼ing southward⟩ **3** : to let fly : DISPATCH **4** : to wound in the wing ⟨∼ a bird⟩; *also* : to wound without killing **5** : to perform without preparation : IMPROVISE ⟨∼ing it⟩
   ♦ fly, glide, plane, soar

wing–ding \'wiŋ-ˌdiŋ\ *n* : a wild, lively, or lavish party

winged \'wiŋd, 'wiŋ-əd, *in compounds* 'wiŋd\ *adj* **1** : having wings esp. of a specified character **2** : soaring with or as if with wings : ELEVATED **3** : SWIFT, RAPID

wing nut *n* : a nut with winglike extensions that can be gripped with the thumb and finger

wing·span \'wiŋ-ˌspan\ *n* : the distance between the tips of a pair of wings

wing·spread \-ˌspred\ *n* : the spread of the wings; *esp* : the distance between the tips of the fully extended wings of a winged animal

¹**wink** \'wiŋk\ *vb* **1** : to close and open one eye quickly as a signal or hint **2** : to close and open the eyes quickly : BLINK **3** ♦ : to avoid seeing or noticing something — often used with *at* ⟨∼ at a traffic violation⟩ **4** ♦ : to gleam or flash fitfully or intermittently : TWINKLE — **wink·er** \'wiŋ-kər\ *n*
   ♦ *usu* **wink at** [3] brush (off), condone, disregard, excuse, gloss, ignore, pardon, pass over, shrug off ♦ [4] blink, flame, flash, glance, gleam, glimmer, glisten, glitter, scintillate, shimmer, sparkle, twinkle

²**wink** *n* **1** ♦ : a brief period of sleep : NAP **2** : an act of winking; *esp* : a hint or sign given by winking **3** ♦ : an exceedingly brief period : INSTANT ⟨dries in a ∼⟩
   ♦ [1] catnap, doze, drowse, forty winks, nap, siesta, snooze
   ♦ [3] flash, instant, jiffy, minute, moment, second, shake, trice, twinkle, twinkling

win·ner \'wi-nər\ *n* ♦ : one that wins or is successful
   ♦ blockbuster, hit, smash, success ♦ champ, champion, victor

¹**win·ning** \'wi-niŋ\ *n* **1** : VICTORY **2** : something won; *esp* : money won at gambling ⟨large ∼s⟩

²**winning** *adj* **1** : successful esp. in competition **2 ♦** : having an attractive, captivating, and charming nature

♦ adorable, darling, dear, endearing, lovable, precious, sweet

win•now \'wi-nō\ *vb* **1** : to remove (as chaff) by a current of air; *also* : to free (as grain) from waste in this manner **2** : to sort or separate as if by winnowing

wino \'wī-nō\ *n, pl* **win•os** : one who is addicted to drinking wine

win•some \'win-səm\ *adj* **1 ♦** : generally pleasing and engaging ⟨a ~ smile⟩ **2** : CHEERFUL, LIGHTHEARTED — **win•some•ly** *adv* — **win•some•ness** *n*

♦ endearing, ingratiating, winning

¹**win•ter** \'win-tər\ *n* : the season of the year in any region in which the noonday sun shines most obliquely : the coldest period of the year

²**winter** *vb* **1** : to pass the winter ⟨~ed in Florida⟩ **2** : to feed or find food during the winter ⟨~ed on hay⟩

³**winter** *adj* : sown in autumn for harvesting in the following spring or summer ⟨~ wheat⟩

win•ter•green \'win-tər-ˌgrēn\ *n* **1** : a low evergreen plant of the heath family with white bell-shaped flowers and spicy red berries **2** : an aromatic oil or its flavor from the wintergreen

win•ter•ize \'win-tə-ˌrīz\ *vb* **-ized; -iz•ing** : to make ready for winter

win•ter•kill \'win-tər-ˌkil\ *vb* : to kill or die by exposure to winter weather

winter squash *n* : any of various hard-shelled squashes that keep well in storage

win•ter•tide \-ˌtīd\ *n* : WINTER

win•ter•time \-ˌtīm\ *n* : WINTER

win•try \'win-trē\ *also* **win•tery** \'win-tə-rē\ *adj* **win•tri•er; -est 1 ♦** : of, relating to, or characteristic of winter ⟨~ weather⟩ **2** : lacking qualities that cheer ⟨a ~ welcome⟩

♦ arctic, bitter, chill, chilly, cold, cool, freezing, frigid, frosty, glacial, icy, nippy, polar, raw, snappy

¹**wipe** \'wīp\ *vb* **wiped; wip•ing 1** : to clean or dry by rubbing ⟨~ dishes⟩ **2** : to remove by or as if by rubbing ⟨~ away tears⟩ **3** : to erase completely : OBLITERATE **4** : to pass or draw over a surface ⟨wiped his hand across his face⟩ — **wip•er** *n*

²**wipe** *n* **1** : an act or instance of wiping; *also* : BLOW, STRIKE, SWIPE **2** : something used for wiping ⟨disposable ~s⟩

wipe out *vb* **♦** : to destroy completely

♦ annihilate, blot out, demolish, destroy, eradicate, exterminate, liquidate, obliterate, root, rub out, snuff, stamp

¹**wire** \'wī(-ə)r\ *n* **1 ♦** : metal in the form of a thread or slender rod; *also* : a thread or rod of metal **2** : hidden or secret influences controlling the action of a person or organization — usu. used in pl. ⟨pull ~s⟩ **3** : a line of wire for conducting electric current **4** : a telegraph or telephone wire or system **5** : TELEGRAM, CABLEGRAM **6** : the finish line of a race

♦ cable, cord, lace, line, rope, string

²**wire** *vb* **wired; wir•ing 1** : to provide or equip with wire ⟨~ a house⟩ **2** : to bind, string, or mount with wire **3** : to send or send word to by telegraph

wired *adj* **1** : furnished with wires **2** : connected to the Internet **3** : feverishly excited

wire•hair \'wī(-ə)r-ˌhar\ *n* : a wirehaired dog or cat

wire•haired \-'hard\ *adj* : having a stiff wiry outer coat of hair

¹**wire•less** \-ləs\ *adj* **1** : having no wire or wires **2** : RADIO **3** : of or relating to data communications using radio waves

²**wireless** *n* **1** : telecommunication involving signals transmitted by radio waves; *also* : the technology used in radio telecommunication **2** *chiefly Brit* : RADIO

wire service *n* : a news agency that sends out syndicated news copy to subscribers by wire or satellite

wire•tap \-ˌtap\ *n* : the act or an instance of tapping a telephone or telegraph wire to get information; *also* : an electrical connection used for such tapping — **wiretap** *vb* — **wire•tap•per** \-ˌta-pər\ *n*

wire•worm \-ˌwərm\ *n* : any of various slender hard-coated beetle larvae esp. destructive to plant roots

wir•ing \'wīr-iŋ\ *n* : a system of wires

wiry \'wīr-ē\ *adj* **wir•i•er** \-wī-rē-ər\; **-est 1** : made of or resembling wire **2** : slender yet strong and sinewy ⟨~ arms⟩ — **wir•i•ness** \'wī-rē-nəs\ *n*

Wis *or* **Wisc** *abbr* Wisconsin

Wisd *abbr* Wisdom

wis•dom \'wiz-dəm\ *n* **1 ♦** : accumulated philosophic or scientific learning : KNOWLEDGE; *also* : INSIGHT **2 ♦** : good sense : JUDGMENT **3** : a wise attitude or course of action

♦ [1] knowledge, lore, science ♦ [2] discernment, insight, judgment, perception, sagacity, sapience, sense, wit

Wisdom *n* : a book included in the Roman Catholic canon of the Old Testament and corresponding to the Wisdom of Solomon in the Protestant Apocrypha

wisdom tooth *n* : the last tooth of the full set on each side of the upper and lower jaws of humans

¹**wise** \'wīz\ *n* : WAY, MANNER, FASHION ⟨in no ~⟩ ⟨in this ~⟩

²**wise** *adj* **wis•er; wis•est 1 ♦** : having wisdom : SAGE **2** : having or showing good sense or good judgment **3 ♦** : aware of what is going on : KNOWING; *also* : CRAFTY, SHREWD **4 ♦** : possessing inside information **5** : INSOLENT, FRESH ⟨a ~ retort⟩ — **wise•ly** *adv*

♦ [1] discerning, insightful, perceptive, sagacious, sage, sapient *Ant* unperceptive, unwise ♦ [3, 4] aware, informed, knowing, ready *Ant* unknowing

³**wise** *vb* **wised; wis•ing; wis•es ♦** : to supply with information — often used with *up*

♦ *usu* **wise up** acquaint, advise, apprise, brief, clue, enlighten, familiarize, fill in, inform, instruct, tell

-wise \-ˌwīz\ *adv comb form* : in the manner or direction of ⟨slant*wise*⟩

wise•acre \'wī-zā-kər\ *n* : SMART ALECK

¹**wise•crack** \'wīz-ˌkrak\ *n* **♦** : a clever, smart, or flippant remark

♦ crack, gag, jest, joke, laugh, pleasantry, quip, sally, waggery, witticism

²**wisecrack** *vb* **♦** : to make a wisecrack

♦ banter, fool, fun, jest, jive, joke, josh, kid, quip

wise guy *n* : SMART ALECK

¹**wish** \'wish\ *vb* **1 ♦** : to have a desire : long for ⟨~ you were here⟩ ⟨~ for a puppy⟩ **2** : to form or express a wish concerning ⟨~ed him a happy birthday⟩ **3** : BID ⟨he ~ed me good morning⟩ **4** : to request by expressing a desire ⟨I ~ you to go now⟩ **5 ♦** : to have the intention of ⟨I don't ~ to impose⟩

♦ *usu* **wish for** [1] ache for, covet, crave, desire, die (to *or* for), hanker (for *or* after), hunger for, long for, lust (for *or* after), pine for, repine for, thirst for, want, yearn for ♦ [5] choose, like, want, will

²**wish** *n* **1** : an act or instance of wishing or desiring : WANT; *also* : GOAL **2** : an expressed will or desire

wish•bone \-ˌbōn\ *n* : a forked bone in front of the breastbone in most birds

wish•ful \'wish-fəl\ *adj* **1** : expressive of a wish; *also* : having a wish **2** : according with wishes rather than fact ⟨~ thinking⟩

wishy–washy \'wi-shē-ˌwȯ-shē, -ˌwä-\ *adj* **♦** : lacking in character or determination; *also* : morally feeble

♦ banal, flat, insipid ♦ effete, frail, nerveless, soft, spineless, weak, wimpy

wisp \'wisp\ *n* **1** : a small handful (as of hay or straw) **2** : a thin strand, strip, or fragment ⟨a ~ of hair⟩; *also* : a thready streak ⟨a ~ of smoke⟩ **3** : something frail, slight, or fleeting ⟨a ~ of a smile⟩ — **wispy** *adj*

wis•te•ria \wis-'tir-ē-ə\ *also* **wis•tar•ia** \-'tir-ē-ə *also* -'ter-\ *n* : any of a genus of chiefly Asian mostly woody vines related to the peas and widely grown for their long showy clusters of blue, white, purple, or rose flowers

wist•ful \'wist-fəl\ *adj* : feeling or showing a yearning tinged with melancholy — **wist•ful•ly** *adv* — **wist•ful•ness** *n*

wit \'wit\ *n* **1** : reasoning power : INTELLIGENCE **2 ♦** : mental soundness : SANITY — usu. used in pl. **3 ♦** : resourcefulness and creative imagination; *esp* : quickness and cleverness in handling words and ideas **4 a** : a talent for making clever remarks **b ♦** : a person noted for making witty remarks — **wit•ted** \'wi-təd\ *adj* — **at one's wit's end** : at a loss for a means of solving a problem

♦ [2] head, mind, reason, sanity ♦ [3] common sense, horse sense, sense, wisdom ♦ [4b] card, comedian, comic, humorist, jester, joker, wag

¹**witch** \'wich\ *n* **1 ♦** : a person believed to have magic power; *esp* : SORCERESS **2 ♦** : an ugly old woman : HAG **3** : a charming or alluring girl or woman **4** : an adherent of Wicca

♦ [1] conjurer, enchanter, magician, necromancer, sorcerer, voodoo, wizard ♦ [1] enchantress, hag, hex ♦ [2] crone, hag

²**witch** *vb* : BEWITCH

witch•craft \'wich-ˌkraft\ *n* **1 ♦** : the power or practices of a witch : SORCERY **2** : WICCA

♦ bewitchment, enchantment, magic, necromancy, sorcery, wizardry

witch doctor *n* : a person in a primitive society who uses magic to treat sickness and to fight off evil spirits

witch·ery \'wi-chə-rē\ *n, pl* **-er·ies** **1** : the practice of witchcraft : SORCERY **2** : an irresistible fascination : CHARM

witch·grass \'wich-ˌgras\ *n* : any of several grasses that are weeds in cultivated areas

witch ha·zel \'wich-ˌhā-zəl\ *n* **1** : a shrub of eastern No. America bearing small yellow flowers in the fall **2** : a soothing alcoholic lotion made from witch hazel bark

witch–hunt \'wich-ˌhənt\ *n* **1** : a searching out and persecution of persons accused of witchcraft **2** : the searching out and deliberate harassment esp. of political opponents

witch·ing \'wi-chiŋ\ *adj* : of, relating to, or suitable for sorcery or supernatural occurrences

with \'with, 'with\ *prep* **1** : AGAINST ⟨a fight ~ his brother⟩ **2** : FROM ⟨parting ~ friends⟩ **3** : in mutual relation to ⟨talk ~ a friend⟩ **4** : in the company of ⟨went there ~ her⟩ **5** : AS REGARDS, TOWARD ⟨is patient ~ children⟩ **6** : compared to ⟨on equal terms ~ another⟩ **7** : in support of ⟨I'm ~ you all the way⟩ **8** : in the presence of : CONTAINING ⟨tea ~ sugar⟩ **9** : in the opinion of : as judged by ⟨their arguments had weight ~ her⟩ **10 a** ♦ : by reason of : BECAUSE OF ⟨pale ~ anger⟩ **b** : by means of ⟨hit him ~ a club⟩ **11** : in a manner indicating ⟨work ~ a will⟩ **12** : GIVEN, GRANTED ⟨~ your permission I'll leave⟩ **13** : HAVING ⟨came ~ good news⟩ ⟨stood there ~ his mouth open⟩ **14** : at the time of : right after ⟨~ that we left⟩ **15** ♦ : in spite of : DESPITE ⟨~ all her cleverness, she failed⟩ **16** : in the direction of ⟨swim ~ the tide⟩

♦ [10a] because of, due to, owing to, through ♦ [15] despite, notwithstanding, regardless of

with·al \wi-'thȯl, -'thäl\ *adv* **1** ♦ : together with this : BESIDES **2** ♦ : on the other hand : NEVERTHELESS

♦ [1] additionally, again, also, besides, further, furthermore, likewise, more, moreover, then, too, yet ♦ [2] but, howbeit, however, nevertheless, nonetheless, notwithstanding, still, though, yet

with·draw \with-'drȯ, with-\ *vb* **-drew** \-'drü\; **-drawn** \-'drȯn\; **-draw·ing** \-'drȯ-iŋ\ **1** ♦ : to take back or away : REMOVE **2** ♦ : to call back (as from consideration); *also* : RETRACT **3** : to go away : RETREAT, LEAVE **4** : to terminate one's participation in or use of something **5** ♦ : to remove or draw out from a place or position

♦ [1] clear, draw, remove ♦ [2] abjure, recant, renounce, retract, take back, unsay ♦ [5] back, fall back, recede, retire, retreat

with·draw·al \-'drȯ-əl\ *n* **1** ♦ : an act or instance of withdrawing **2** : the discontinuance of the use or administration of a drug and esp. an addicting drug; *also* : the period following such discontinuance marked by often painful physiological and psychological symptoms **3** : a pathological retreat from the real world (as in some schizophrenic states)

♦ retreat, revulsion

with·drawn \with-'drȯn\ *adj* **1** : ISOLATED, SECLUDED **2** ♦ : socially detached and unresponsive

♦ bashful, coy, demure, diffident, introverted, modest, retiring, sheepish, shy

withe \'with\ *n* : a slender flexible twig or branch

with·er \'wi-thər\ *vb* **1** : to shrivel from or as if from loss of bodily moisture and esp. sap **2** : to lose or cause to lose vitality, force, or freshness **3** : to cause to feel shriveled ⟨~ed him with a glance⟩

with·ers \'wi-thərz\ *n pl* : the ridge between the shoulder bones of a horse; *also* : the corresponding part in other 4-footed animals

with·hold \with-'hōld, with-\ *vb* **-held** \-'held\; **-hold·ing 1 a** : to hold back **b** ♦ : keep in one's possession or control : RETAIN **2** ♦ : to refrain from granting, giving, or allowing ⟨~ permission⟩ ⟨~ names⟩

♦ [1b] hang on, hold, keep, reserve, retain ♦ [2] decline, deny, disallow, refuse, reject

withholding tax *n* : a tax on income withheld at the source

¹with·in \wi-'thin, -'thin\ *adv* **1** : in or into the interior : INSIDE **2** : inside oneself : INWARDLY

²within *prep* **1** : inside the limits or influence of ⟨~ call⟩ **2** : in the limits or compass of ⟨~ a mile⟩ **3** : in or to the inner part of ⟨~ the room⟩

with-it \'wi-thət, -thət\ *adj* : socially or culturally up-to-date

¹with·out \wi-'thaut, -'thaut\ *prep* **1** : at, to, or on the outside of : OUTSIDE **2** ♦ : not having : LACKING ⟨~ hope⟩; *also* : not accompanied by or showing ⟨spoke ~ thinking⟩

♦ lacking, minus, sans, wanting

²without *adv* **1** : on the outside : EXTERNALLY **2** : with something lacking or absent ⟨has learned to do ~⟩

with·stand \with-'stand, with-\ *vb* **-stood** \-'stud\; **-stand·ing** ♦ : to stand against : RESIST; *esp* : to oppose (as an attack) successfully

♦ buck, defy, fight, oppose, repel, resist

wit·less \'wit-ləs\ *adj* ♦ : lacking wit or understanding — **wit·less·ly** *adv*

♦ absurd, asinine, balmy, cockeyed, foolish, harebrained, nonsensical, nutty, preposterous, sappy, screwball, senseless, silly, stupid, unwise, wacky, zany

wit·less·ness *n* : the quality or state of being witless

¹wit·ness \'wit-nəs\ *n* **1** : TESTIMONY ⟨bear ~ to the fact⟩ **2** : one that gives evidence; *esp* : one who testifies in a cause or before a court **3** : one present at a transaction so as to be able to testify that it has taken place **4** : one who has personal knowledge or experience of something **5** ♦ : something serving as evidence or proof

♦ attestation, confirmation, corroboration, documentation, evidence, proof, substantiation, testament, testimony, validation

²witness *vb* **1** ♦ : to furnish evidence or proof such as to establish : TESTIFY **2** : to act as legal witness of **3** : to furnish proof of : BETOKEN **4** ♦ : to see or know by reason of personal presence : to be a witness of **5** : to be the scene of ⟨this region has ~ed many wars⟩

♦ [1] attest, authenticate, avouch, certify, testify, vouch ♦ [4] behold, descry, discern, distinguish, espy, eye, look, note, notice, observe, perceive, regard, remark, see, sight, spy, view

wit·ti·cism \'wi-tə-ˌsi-zəm\ *n* ♦ : a witty saying or phrase

♦ crack, gag, jest, joke, laugh, pleasantry, quip, sally, waggery, wisecrack

wit·ting \'wi-tiŋ\ *adj* **1** : cognizant or aware of something **2** : done knowingly

♦ alive, aware, cognizant, conscious, mindful, sensible, sentient

wit·ting·ly *adv* : with knowledge or awareness of what one is doing

wit·ty \'wi-tē\ *adj* **wit·ti·er; -est** ♦ : marked by or full of wit ⟨a ~ writer⟩ ⟨a ~ remark⟩ — **wit·ti·ly** \-tə-lē\ *adv* — **wit·ti·ness** \-tē-nəs\ *n*

♦ clever, facetious, humorous, jocular, smart

wive \'wīv\ *vb* **wived; wiv·ing** : to take a wife

wives *pl of* WIFE

wiz·ard \'wi-zərd\ *n* **1** ♦ : one skilled in the knowledge and practice of the magic arts : MAGICIAN **2** ♦ : a very clever or skillful person ⟨a ~ at chess⟩

♦ [1] conjurer, enchanter, magician, necromancer, sorcerer, voodoo, witch ♦ [2] ace, adept, artist, authority, crackerjack, expert, maestro, master, scholar, shark, virtuoso, whiz ♦ [2] brain, genius, intellect, thinker

wiz·ard·ry \'wi-zər-drē\ *n, pl* **-ries** **1** ♦ : magic skill : SORCERY **2** : great skill or cleverness in an activity

♦ bewitchment, enchantment, magic, necromancy, sorcery, witchcraft

wiz·en \'wiz-ᵊn, 'wēz-\ *vb* : to become or cause to become dry, shrunken, or wrinkled

wk *abbr* **1** week **2** work

WL *abbr* wavelength

wmk *abbr* watermark

WNW *abbr* west-northwest

WO *abbr* warrant officer

w/o *abbr* without

woad \'wōd\ *n* : a European herb related to the mustards; *also* : a blue dyestuff made from its leaves

wob·ble \'wä-bəl\ *vb* **wob·bled; wob·bling 1** ♦ : to move or cause to move with an irregular rocking or side-to-side motion **2** ♦ : to shake unsteadily **3** ♦ : to show indecision : WAVER — **wobble** *n*

♦ [1] falter, rock, seesaw, sway, teeter, totter, waver ♦ [2] agitate, convulse, jolt, jounce, quake, quiver, shake, shudder, vibrate ♦ [3] falter, hang back, hesitate, shilly-shally, stagger, teeter, vacillate, waver

wob·bly \-bə-lē\ *adj* ♦ : inclined to shake, sway, or quaver unsteadily

♦ shaky, tremulous

woe \'wō\ *n* **1** ♦ : deep suffering from misfortune, affliction, or grief **2** : TROUBLE, MISFORTUNE ⟨economic ∼s⟩

♦ affliction, agony, anguish, distress, misery, pain, torment, torture, tribulation ♦ dolor, grief, heartache, sorrow

woe·be·gone \'wō-bi-ˌgȯn\ *adj* ♦ : exhibiting woe, sorrow, or misery ⟨∼ faces⟩; *also* : being in a sorry condition

♦ bad, blue, dejected, depressed, despondent, disconsolate, down, downcast, droopy, forlorn, low, melancholy, miserable, mournful, sad, sorrowful, sorry, unhappy, woeful, wretched

woe·ful *also* **wo·ful** \'wō-fəl\ *adj* **1** ♦ : full of woe : distressed with grief or sadness **2** : involving, bringing, or relating to woe **3** ♦ : to be regretted or lamented : DEPLORABLE

♦ [1] anguished, dolorous, lamentable, mournful, plaintive, sad, sorrowful, sorry ♦ [3] deplorable, distressful, grievous, heartbreaking, lamentable, regrettable, unfortunate

woe·ful·ly *adv* ♦ : in a woeful manner

♦ agonizingly, bitterly, grievously, hard, hardly, sadly, sorrowfully, unhappily, wretchedly

wok \'wäk\ *n* : a bowl-shaped cooking utensil used esp. in stir-frying

¹**woke** *past and past part of* WAKE

²**woke** \'wōk\ *adj* **wok·er; wok·est** *slang* : aware of and actively attentive to important facts and issues (esp. issues of racial and social justice)

woken *past part of* WAKE

wold \'wōld\ *n* : an upland plain or stretch of rolling land without woods

¹**wolf** \'wu̇lf\ *n, pl* **wolves** \'wu̇lvz\ **1** : any of several large erect-eared bushy-tailed doglike predatory mammals that live and hunt in packs; *esp* : GRAY WOLF **2** : a fierce or destructive person — **wolf·ish** *adj*

²**wolf** *vb* ♦ : to eat greedily : DEVOUR

♦ bolt, devour, gobble, gorge, gormandize, gulp, scarf, scoff

wolf·hound \-ˌhau̇nd\ *n* : any of several large dogs orig. used in hunting wolves

wol·fram \'wu̇l-frəm\ *n* : TUNGSTEN

wol·ver·ine \ˌwu̇l-və-'rēn\ *n, pl* **wolverines** *also* **wolverine** : a dark shaggy-coated flesh-eating mammal of northern forests and associated tundra that is related to the weasels

wom·an \'wu̇-mən\ *n, pl* **wom·en** \'wi-mən\ **1** ♦ : an adult female person **2** : WOMANKIND **3** : feminine nature : WOMANLINESS **4** : an adult female servant

♦ dame, female, gentlewoman, lady

wom·an·hood \'wu̇-mən-ˌhu̇d\ *n* **1** : the state of being a woman **2** : qualities associated with women **3** : WOMEN, WOMANKIND

wom·an·ish \'wu̇-mə-nish\ *adj* **1** : associated with or characteristic of women rather than men **2** : suggestive of a weak character : EFFEMINATE ⟨a ∼ voice⟩

wom·an·ize \'wu̇-mə-ˌnīz\ *vb* : to pursue casual sexual relationships with numerous women — **wom·an·iz·er** *n*

wom·an·kind \'wu̇-mən-ˌkīnd\ *n* : female human beings : women esp. as distinguished from men

wom·an·like \-ˌlīk\ *adj* : WOMANLY

wom·an·ly \-lē\ *adj* **1** ♦ : having qualities generally associated with a woman **2** : appropriate in character to a woman — **wom·an·li·ness** \-lē-nəs\ *n*

♦ female, feminine

woman suffrage *n* : possession and exercise of suffrage by women

womb \'wüm\ *n* **1** : UTERUS **2** : a place where something is generated

wom·bat \'wäm-ˌbat\ *n* : any of several stocky burrowing Australian marsupials that resemble small bears

wom·en·folk \'wi-mən-ˌfōk\ *also* **wom·en·folks** \-ˌfōks\ *n pl* : WOMEN

won \'wən\ *past and past part of* WIN

¹**won·der** \'wən-dər\ *n* **1** ♦ : a cause of astonishment or surprise : MARVEL **2** : the quality of exciting wonder ⟨the charm and ∼ of the scene⟩ **3** ♦ : a feeling (as of awed astonishment or uncertainty) aroused by something extraordinary or affecting

♦ [1] caution, flash, marvel, miracle, phenomenon, portent, prodigy, sensation ♦ [3] admiration, amazement, astonishment, awe, wonderment

²**wonder** *vb* **1** : to feel surprise or amazement **2** : to feel curiosity or doubt

wonder drug *n* : MIRACLE DRUG

won·der·ful \'wən-dər-fəl\ *adj* **1** ♦ : exciting wonder : MAR-

VELOUS **2** : unusually good : ADMIRABLE — **won·der·ful·ly** \-f(ə-)lē\ *adv* — **won·der·ful·ness** *n*

♦ amazing, astonishing, astounding, awesome, awful, eye-opening, fabulous, marvelous, miraculous, portentous, prodigious, stunning, stupendous, sublime, surprising

won·der·land \-ˌland, -lənd\ *n* **1** : an imaginary place of delicate beauty or magical charm **2** : a place that excites admiration or wonder

won·der·ment \-mənt\ *n* **1** ♦ : a state or feeling of wonder : ASTONISHMENT **2** : a cause of or occasion for wonder **3** : curiosity about something

♦ admiration, amazement, astonishment, awe, wonder

won·drous \'wən-drəs\ *adj* : exciting wonder or surprise : MARVELOUS, WONDERFUL — **won·drous·ly** *adv* — **won·drous·ness** *n*

wonk \'wäŋk, 'wȯŋk\ *n* : one who works in a specialized usu. intellectual field ⟨computer ∼s⟩

¹**wont** \'wȯnt, 'wōnt\ *adj* **1** ♦ : in the habit or custom : ACCUSTOMED ⟨as we are ∼ to do⟩ **2** : INCLINED, APT

♦ accustomed, given, used

²**wont** *n* ♦ : a usage or practice that is common : CUSTOM ⟨according to her ∼⟩

♦ custom, fashion, habit, pattern, practice, trick, way

won't \'wōnt\ : will not

wont·ed \'wȯn-təd, 'wōn-\ *adj* : ACCUSTOMED, CUSTOMARY ⟨his ∼ courtesy⟩

woo \'wü\ *vb* **1** : to try to gain the love of : COURT **2** : SOLICIT, ENTREAT **3** ♦ : to try to gain or bring about ⟨∼ public favor⟩

♦ ask, court

¹**wood** \'wu̇d\ *n* **1** : a dense growth of trees usu. larger than a grove and smaller than a forest — often used in pl. **2** : a hard fibrous substance that is basically xylem and forms the bulk of trees and shrubs beneath the bark; *also* : this material fit or prepared for some use (as burning or building) **3** : something made of wood **4** : the trunks or large branches of trees sawed or prepared for commercial use

²**wood** *adj* **1** : WOODEN **2** : suitable for holding, cutting, or working with wood **3** *or* **woods** \'wu̇dz\ : living or growing in woods

³**wood** *vb* **1** : to supply or load with wood esp. for fuel **2** : to cover with a growth of trees

wood alcohol *n* : METHANOL

wood·bine \'wu̇d-ˌbīn\ *n* : any of several honeysuckles; *also* : VIRGINIA CREEPER

wood·block \-ˌbläk\ *n* : WOODCUT

wood·chop·per \-ˌchä-pər\ *n* : one engaged esp. in chopping down trees

wood·chuck \-ˌchək\ *n* : a thickset grizzled marmot of Alaska, Canada, and the northeastern U.S.

wood·cock \'wu̇d-ˌkäk\ *n, pl* **woodcocks** : a brown eastern No. American game bird with a short neck and long bill that is related to the snipe; *also* : a related and similar Old World bird

wood·craft \-ˌkraft\ *n* **1** : skill and practice in matters relating to the woods and esp. in how to take care of oneself in them **2** : skill in shaping or constructing articles from wood

wood·cut \-ˌkət\ *n* **1** : a relief printing surface engraved on a block of wood **2** : a print from a woodcut

wood·cut·ter \-ˌkə-tər\ *n* : a person who cuts wood

wood duck *n* : a showy crested American duck of which the male has iridescent multicolored plumage

wood·ed \'wu̇-dəd\ *adj* : covered with woods or trees ⟨∼ slopes⟩

wood·en \'wu̇d-ᵊn\ *adj* **1** : made of wood **2** ♦ : lacking in ease, grace, or flexibility : awkwardly stiff ⟨∼ acting⟩ — **wood·en·ly** *adv* — **wood·en·ness** *n*

♦ awkward, clumsy, gauche, graceless, inelegant, stiff, stilted, uncomfortable, uneasy, ungraceful

wood·en·ware \'wu̇d-ᵊn-ˌwar\ *n* : articles made of wood for domestic use

wood·land \'wu̇d-lənd, -ˌland\ *n* ♦ : land covered with trees : FOREST — **woodland** *adj*

♦ forest, timberland

wood·lot \'wu̇d-ˌlät\ *n* : a restricted area of woodland usu. privately kept to meet fuel and timber needs

wood louse *n* : any of various small flat crustaceans that live esp. in ground litter and under stones and bark

wood·man \'wu̇d-mən\ *n* : WOODSMAN

wood·note \-ˌnōt\ *n* : verbal expression that is natural and artless

wood nymph *n* : a nymph living in the woods

wood·peck·er \'wùd-ˌpe-kər\ n : any of numerous usu. brightly marked climbing birds with stiff spiny tail feathers and a chisel-like bill used to drill into trees for insects

wood·pile \-ˌpīl\ n : a pile of wood and esp. firewood

wood·shed \-ˌshed\ n : a shed for storing wood and esp. firewood

woods·man \'wùdz-mən\ n : a person who frequents or works in the woods; esp : one skilled in woodcraft

woodsy \'wùd-zē\ adj **woods·i·er; -est** : relating to or suggestive of woods

wood·wind \'wùd-ˌwind\ n : one of a group of wind instruments including flutes, clarinets, oboes, bassoons, and sometimes saxophones

wood·work \-ˌwərk\ n : work made of wood; esp : interior fittings (as moldings or stairways) of wood

woody \'wù-dē\ adj **wood·i·er; -est** **1** : abounding or overgrown with woods **2** : of or containing wood or wood fibers **3** : characteristic or suggestive of wood ⟨a ∼ flavor⟩ — **wood·i·ness** \'wù-dē-nəs\ n

woo·er n ♦ : one that woos : one that courts a woman or seeks to marry her

  ♦ gallant, suitor, swain

woof \'wùf\ n **1** : WEFT 1 **2** : a woven fabric; also : its texture

woof·er \'wù-fər\ n : a loudspeaker that reproduces sounds of low pitch

wool \'wùl\ n **1** ♦ : the soft wavy or curly hair of some mammals and esp. the domestic sheep; also : something (as a textile or garment) made of wool **2** : material that resembles a mass of wool — **wooled** \'wùld\ adj

  ♦ coat, fleece, fur, hair, pelage, pile

¹wool·en or **wool·len** \'wù-lən\ adj **1** : made of wool **2** : of or relating to the manufacture or sale of woolen products ⟨∼ mills⟩

²woolen or **woollen** n **1** : a fabric made of wool **2** : garments of woolen fabric — usu. used in pl.

wool·gath·er·ing \-ˌga-thə-riŋ\ n ♦ : idle daydreaming

  ♦ reverie, study, trance

¹wool·ly also **wooly** \'wù-lē\ adj **wool·li·er; -est** **1** : of, relating to, or bearing wool **2 a** ♦ : consisting of or resembling wool **b** ♦ : thickly covered with long hair or fuzz **3** : mentally confused ⟨∼ thinking⟩ **4** : marked by a lack of order or restraint ⟨the wild and ∼ West⟩

  ♦ [2a, 2b] furry, fuzzy, hairy, rough, shaggy

²wool·ly also **wool·ie** or **wooly** \'wù-lē\ n, pl **wool·lies** : a garment made from wool; esp : underclothing of knitted wool — usu. used in pl.

woolly bear n : any of numerous very hairy moth caterpillars

woolly mammoth n : a heavy-coated mammoth formerly inhabiting colder parts of the northern hemisphere

woo·zy \'wü-zē\ adj **woo·zi·er; -est** **1** : BEFUDDLED **2** : somewhat dizzy, nauseated, or weak ⟨∼ from fatigue⟩ — **woo·zi·ness** \'wü-zē-nəs\ n

¹word \'wərd\ n **1** : something that is said; esp : a brief remark **2** ♦ : a speech sound or series of speech sounds that communicates a meaning; also : a graphic representation of such a sound or series of sounds **3** ♦ : an instruction, authorization, or direction for action or behavior : COMMAND **4** often cap : the 2d person of the Trinity; also : GOSPEL **5** ♦ : a report of a recent event or of new information : NEWS, INFORMATION **6** ♦ : a declaration that one will do or refrain from doing something : PROMISE **7** pl : QUARREL, DISPUTE **8** : a verbal signal : PASSWORD

  ♦ [2] expression, term ♦ [3] behest, charge, command, commandment, decree, dictate, direction, directive, edict, instruction, order ♦ [5] information, intelligence, item, news, story, tidings ♦ [6] oath, pledge, promise, troth, vow

²word vb ♦ : to express in words : PHRASE

  ♦ articulate, clothe, couch, express, formulate, phrase, put, say, state

word·age \'wər-dij\ n **1** : WORDS **2** : number of words **3** : WORDING

word·book \'wərd-ˌbùk\ n : a book containing a collection of words : DICTIONARY

word for word adv ♦ : in the exact words : VERBATIM

  ♦ directly, exactly, verbatim

word·i·ness \-dē-nəs\ n ♦ : the quality or state of being wordy

  ♦ circumlocution, prolixity, redundancy, verbiage

word·ing \'wər-diŋ\ n ♦ : verbal expression : PHRASEOLOGY

  ♦ diction, language, phraseology, phrasing

word·less adj **1** : not expressed or not expressible in words **2** ♦ : involving no use of words

  ♦ implicit, tacit, unexpressed, unspoken, unvoiced

word of mouth n : oral communication

word·play \'wərd-ˌplā\ n : playful use of words

word processing n : the production of typewritten documents with automated and usu. computerized text-editing equipment — **word process** vb

word processor n : a keyboard-operated terminal for use in word processing; also : software to perform word processing

wordy \'wər-dē\ adj **word·i·er; -est** ♦ : using or having too many words : VERBOSE ⟨∼ sentences⟩

  ♦ circuitous, diffuse, long-winded, prolix, rambling, verbose, windy **Ant** compact, concise, crisp, pithy, succinct, terse

wore past of WEAR

¹work \'wərk\ n **1** ♦ : activity in which one exerts strength or faculties to do or perform something : LABOR **2 a** : something that needs to be done or accomplished : TASK, JOB ⟨have ∼ to do⟩ **b** ♦ : the labor, task, or duty that affords one his accustomed means of livelihood : EMPLOYMENT ⟨out of ∼⟩ **3** : the energy used when a force is applied over a given distance **4** ♦ : something produced or accomplished by effort, exertion, or exercise of skill **5** : a fortified structure **6** pl : engineering structures **7** pl ♦ : a place where industrial labor is done : FACTORY **8** pl : the moving parts of a mechanism **9** ♦ : something produced by mental effort or physical labor; esp : an artistic production (as a book or needlework) **10** : WORKMANSHIP ⟨careless ∼⟩ **11** : material in the process of manufacture **12** pl : everything possessed, available, or belonging ⟨the whole ∼s went overboard⟩; also : drastic treatment ⟨gave him the ∼s⟩ — **in the works** : in process of preparation

  ♦ [1] effort, exertion, expenditure, labor (or labour), pains, sweat, trouble, while ♦ [2b] calling, employment, line, occupation, profession, trade, vocation ♦ [4, 9] affair, fruit, handiwork, output, produce, product, thing, yield ♦ usu **works** [7] factory, mill, plant, shop, workshop ♦ [9] composition, opus, piece

²work adj **1** : used for work ⟨∼ elephants⟩ **2** : suitable or styled for wear while working ⟨∼ clothes⟩

³work vb **worked** \'wərkt\ or **wrought** \'ròt\; **work·ing** **1** ♦ : to bring to pass : EFFECT **2** ♦ : to fashion or create a useful or desired product through labor or exertion **3** : to prepare for use (as by kneading) **4** : to bring into a desired form by a manufacturing process ⟨∼ cold steel⟩ **5** ♦ : to set or keep in operation ⟨a pump ∼ed by hand⟩ **6** ♦ : to solve by reasoning or calculation ⟨∼ out a problem⟩ **7** : to cause to toil or labor ⟨∼ed the team hard⟩; also : to make use of ⟨∼ a mine⟩ **8** : to pay for with labor or service ⟨∼ off a debt⟩ **9** : to bring or get into some position or condition by stages ⟨the stream ∼ed itself clear⟩ ⟨the knot ∼ed loose⟩ **10** : CONTRIVE, ARRANGE ⟨∼ it so you can leave early⟩ **11** : to practice trickery or cajolery on ⟨∼ed the management for a free ticket⟩ **12** : EXCITE, PROVOKE ⟨∼ed himself into a rage⟩ **13** ♦ : to exert oneself physically or mentally; esp : to perform work regularly for wages **14** : to function according to plan or design **15** : to produce a desired effect : SUCCEED ⟨the plan ∼ed⟩ **16** : to make way slowly and with difficulty ⟨he ∼ed forward through the crowd⟩ **17** : to permit of being worked ⟨this wood ∼s easily⟩ **18** : to be in restless motion; also : FERMENT 1 — **work on 1** : AFFECT **2** : to try to influence or persuade — **work upon** : to have effect upon : operate on : INFLUENCE

  ♦ [1] bring about, cause, create, effect, effectuate, generate, induce, make, produce, prompt, result, yield ♦ [5] handle, operate, run ♦ [5] actuate, drive, impel, move, propel ♦ [6] answer, break, crack, dope, figure out, puzzle, resolve, riddle, solve, unravel, work out ♦ [13] drudge, endeavor, fag, grub, hustle, labor, peg, plod, plug, slog, strain, strive, struggle, sweat, toil, travail

work·able \'wər-kə-bəl\ adj **1** : capable of being worked **2** ♦ : capable of being put into successful operation : PRACTICABLE — **work·able·ness** n

  ♦ achievable, attainable, doable, feasible, possible, practicable, realizable, viable

work·a·day \'wər-kə-ˌdā\ adj **1** ♦ : relating to or suited for working days as distinguished from special occasions **2** ♦ : being ordinary and unexceptional

  ♦ [1] casual, everyday, informal ♦ [2] average, common, commonplace, everyday, normal, ordinary, prosaic, routine, run-of-the-mill, standard, unexceptional, unremarkable, usual

work·a·hol·ic \ˌwər-kə-'hò-lik, -'hä-\ n : a compulsive worker

work·bench \-,bench\ n : a bench on which work esp. of mechanics, machinists, and carpenters is performed

work·book \-,bu̇k\ n **1** : a worker's manual **2** : a student's book of problems to be answered directly on the pages

work·day \'wərk-,dā\ n **1** : a day on which work is done as distinguished from a day off **2** : the period of time in a day when work is performed

work·er \'wər-kər\ n **1** ♦ : onc that works; *esp* : a person who works for wages **2** : any of the sexually undeveloped individuals of a colony of social insects (as bees, ants, or termites) that perform the work of the community

  ♦ drudge, peon, toiler ♦ employee, hand, hireling, jobholder

workers' compensation n : a system of insurance that reimburses an employer for damages paid to an employee who was injured while working

work ethic n : belief in work as a moral good

work farm n : a farm on which persons guilty of minor law violations are confined

work·force \'wərk-,fȯrs\ n **1** ♦ : the workers engaged in a specific activity or enterprise **2** ♦ : the number of workers potentially available for any purpose

  ♦ [1, 2] force, help, manpower, personnel, pool, staff

work·horse \'wərk-,hȯrs\ n **1** : a horse used for hard work **2** : a person who does most of the work of a group task **3** : something that is useful, durable, or dependable

work·house \-,hau̇s\ n **1** *Brit* : POORHOUSE **2** : a house of correction for persons guilty of minor law violations

work in vb **1** : to insert or cause to penetrate by repeated or continued effort **2** ♦ : to interpose or insinuate gradually or unobtrusively

  ♦ infiltrate, insinuate, slip, sneak, worm

¹**work·ing** \'wər-kiŋ\ n **1** : manner of functioning — usu. used in pl. **2** *pl* : an excavation made in mining or tunneling

²**working** adj **1** : engaged in work ⟨a ∼ journalist⟩ **2** : adequate to allow work to be done ⟨a ∼ majority⟩ ⟨a ∼ knowledge of French⟩ **3** ♦ : adopted or assumed to help further work or activity ⟨a ∼ draft⟩ **4** : spent at work ⟨∼ life⟩

  ♦ applicable, functional, practicable, practical, serviceable, usable, useful, workable

work·ing·man \'wər-kiŋ-,man\ n : WORKER 1

work·man \'wərk-mən\ n **1** : WORKER 1 **2** : ARTISAN, CRAFTSMAN

work·man·like \-,līk\ adj : worthy of a good workman : SKILLFUL

work·man·ship \-,ship\ n : the art or skill of a workman : CRAFTSMANSHIP; *also* : the quality of a piece of work ⟨a vase of exquisite ∼⟩

work·out \'wərk-,au̇t\ n **1** ♦ : a practice or exercise to test or improve one's fitness, ability, or performance **2** : a test or trial to determine ability or capacity or suitability

  ♦ drill, exercise, practice, routine, training

work out vb **1 a** ♦ : to bring about esp. by resolving difficulties **b** ♦ : to create or cause by labor and exertion **2** : to expand, develop, or perfect esp. by analysis or reasoning : DEVELOP, ELABORATE **3** ♦ : to prove effective, practicable, or suitable ⟨I think this plan will *work out*⟩ **4 a** : to amount to a total or calculated figure — used with *at* **b** ♦ : to solve (as a problem) by a process of reasoning or calculation **5** : to engage in a workout

  ♦ [1a, b] build, carve, forge, grind, hammer ♦ [3] click, deliver, go over, pan out, succeed ♦ [4b] calculate, compute, figure, reckon ♦ [4b] answer, break, crack, dope, figure out, puzzle, resolve, riddle, solve, unravel, work

work·place \'wərk-,plās\ n : a place (as an office) where work is done

work·room \'wərk-,rüm, -,ru̇m\ n : a room used for work

work·shop \-,shäp\ n **1** : a shop where manufacturing or handicrafts are carried on **2** : a seminar emphasizing exchange of ideas and practical methods

  ♦ factory, mill, plant, shop, works

work·sta·tion \-,stā-shən\ n : an area with equipment for the performance of a specialized task; *also* : a personal computer usu. connected to a computer network

world \'wərld\ n **1** ♦ : the earth with its inhabitants and all things upon it **2** ♦ : people in general **3** : human affairs ⟨withdraw from the ∼⟩ **4** ♦ : the entire system of created things : UNIVERSE, CREATION **5** : a state of existence : scene of life and action ⟨the ∼ of the future⟩ **6** : a distinctive class of persons or their sphere of interest ⟨the musical ∼⟩ **7** : a part or section of the earth or its inhabitants by itself **8** : a great number or quantity ⟨a ∼ of troubles⟩ **9** : a celestial body

  ♦ [1] earth, planet ♦ [2] folks, humanity, humankind, people, persons, public, society ♦ [4] cosmos, creation, macrocosm, nature, universe

world–beat·er \-,bē-tər\ n : one that excels all others of its kind : CHAMPION

world–class adj : of the highest caliber in the world ⟨a ∼ athlete⟩

world·ling \-liŋ\ n : a person absorbed in the concerns of the present world

world·ly \-lē\ adj **1** ♦ : of, relating to, or devoted to this world and its pursuits rather than to religion or spiritual affairs ⟨∼ pleasures⟩ **2** : experienced or knowledgeable in things and ways of this world : WORLDLY-WISE — **world·li·ness** \-lē-nəs\ n

  ♦ carnal, earthly, fleshly, material, mundane, temporal, terrestrial

world·ly–wise \-,wīz\ adj ♦ : possessing a practical and often shrewd understanding of human affairs

  ♦ cosmopolitan, smart, sophisticated, worldly *Ant* ingenuous, innocent, naive, unsophisticated, unworldly, wide-eyed

world·wide \'wərld-'wīd\ adj : extended throughout the entire world ⟨attracted ∼ attention⟩ — **worldwide** adv

World Wide Web n : a part of the Internet usu. accessed through a browser and containing files connected by hyperlinks

¹**worm** \'wərm\ n **1** : any of various small long usu. naked and soft-bodied round or flat invertebrate animals (as an earthworm, nematode, tapeworm, or maggot) **2** : a human being who is an object of contempt, loathing, or pity : WRETCH **3** : something that inwardly torments or devours **4** *pl* : infestation with or disease caused by parasitic worms **5** : a spiral or wormlike thing (as the thread of a screw) — **wormy** adj

²**worm** vb **1** ♦ : to move or cause to move or proceed slowly and deviously or as if in the manner of a worm **2** ♦ : to insinuate or introduce (oneself) by devious or subtle means **3** : to obtain or extract by artful or insidious pleading, asking, or persuading ⟨∼ed the truth out of him⟩ **4** : to treat (an animal) with a drug to destroy or expel parasitic worms

  ♦ [1] crawl, creep, grovel, slither, snake ♦ [2] infiltrate, insinuate, slip, sneak, work in

worm–eat·en \'wərm-,ēt-ᵊn\ adj : eaten or burrowed by worms

worm gear n : a mechanical linkage consisting of a short rotating screw whose threads mesh with the teeth of a gear wheel

worm·hole \'wərm-,hōl\ n : a hole or passage burrowed by a worm

worm·wood \-,wu̇d\ n **1** : any of a genus of aromatic woody plants (as a sagebrush); *esp* : one of Europe used in absinthe **2** : something bitter or grievous : BITTERNESS

worn past part of WEAR

worn–out \'wōrn-'au̇t\ adj ♦ : damaged, used up, or exhausted by or as if by wear

  ♦ beat, bushed, dead, drained, effete, jaded, limp, prostrate, spent, tired, weary ♦ ragged, ratty, seedy, shabby, tattered, threadbare

wor·ried adj ♦ : mentally troubled or concerned

  ♦ aflutter, anxious, edgy, jittery, jumpy, nervous, nervy, perturbed, tense, troubled, uneasy, upset

wor·ri·some \'wər-ē-səm\ adj **1** ♦ : causing distress or worry **2** : inclined to worry or fret

  ♦ troublesome, unsettling, upsetting

¹**wor·ry** \'wər-ē\ vb **wor·ried; wor·ry·ing 1** : to shake and mangle with the teeth ⟨a terrier ∼ing a rat⟩ **2** ♦ : to make anxious or upset ⟨her poor health *worries* me⟩ **3** ♦ : to feel or express great care or anxiety : FRET — **wor·ri·er** n

  ♦ [2] agitate, bother, concern, discompose, disquiet, distress, disturb, exercise, freak, perturb, undo, unhinge, unsettle, upset ♦ [3] bother, fear, fret, stew, sweat, trouble

²**worry** n, pl **worries 1** ♦ : mental distress or agitation resulting from concern usu. for something impending or anticipated : ANXIETY **2** : a cause of anxiety : TROUBLE

  ♦ agitation, anxiety, apprehension, care, concern, disquiet, nervousness, perturbation, uneasiness

wor·ry·wart \'wər-ē-,wȯrt\ n : one who is inclined to worry unduly

¹**worse** \'wərs\ adj, *comparative of* BAD *or of* ILL **1** : bad or evil in a greater degree : less good **2** : more unfavorable, unpleasant, or painful; *also* : SICKER

²**worse** *n* **1** : one that is worse **2** : a greater degree of ill or badness ⟨a turn for the ∼⟩

³**worse** *adv, comparative of* BAD *or of* ILL : in a worse manner : to a worse extent or degree

wors·en \ˈwərs-ᵊn\ *vb* ♦ : to make or become worse

♦ decay, decline, degenerate, descend, deteriorate, ebb, rot, sink

¹**wor·ship** \ˈwər-shəp\ *n* **1** *chiefly Brit* : a person of importance — used as a title for officials **2** : reverence toward a divine being or supernatural power; *also* : the expression of such reverence **3** ♦ : extravagant respect or admiration or devotion ⟨∼ of the dollar⟩

♦ adulation, deification, idolatry

²**worship** *vb* **-shipped** *also* **-shiped; -ship·ping** *also* **-ship·ing** **1** ♦ : to honor or reverence as a divine being or supernatural power **2** ♦ : to regard with respect, honor, or devotion **3** : to perform or take part in worship — **wor·ship·er** *or* **wor·ship·per** *n*

♦ [1] adore, deify, glorify, revere, venerate ♦ [2] adore, canonize, deify, dote, idolize, love

wor·ship·ful \ˈwər-shəp-fəl\ *adj* **1** *archaic* : NOTABLE, DISTINGUISHED **2** *chiefly Brit* — used as a title for various persons or groups of rank or distinction **3** ♦ : giving or expressing adoration or reverence ⟨∼ fans⟩

♦ adulatory

¹**worst** \ˈwərst\ *adj, superlative of* BAD *or of* ILL **1** : most bad, evil, ill, or corrupt **2** : most unfavorable, unpleasant, or painful; *also* : most unsuitable, faulty, or unattractive **3** : least skillful or efficient

²**worst** *adv, superlative of* ILL *or of* BAD *or* BADLY **1** : to the extreme degree of badness or inferiority : in the worst manner **2** : MOST ⟨those who need help ∼⟩

³**worst** *n* : one that is worst

⁴**worst** *vb* : to get the better of in a fight, conflict, or contest : DEFEAT

wor·sted \ˈwu̇s-təd, ˈwər-stəd\ *n* : a smooth compact yarn from long wool fibers; *also* : a fabric made from such yarn

wort \ˈwərt, ˈwȯrt\ *n* : a sweet liquid drained from mash and fermented to form beer and whiskey

¹**worth** \ˈwərth\ *n* **1** : monetary value; *also* : the equivalent of a specified amount or figure ⟨$5 ∼ of gas⟩ **2** ♦ : the value of something measured by its qualities **3** : MERIT, EXCELLENCE

♦ account, merit, valuation, value

²**worth** *prep* **1** : equal in value to; *also* : having possessions or income equal to **2** : deserving of ⟨well ∼ the effort⟩

worth·less \ˈwərth-ləs\ *adj* **1** ♦ : lacking use, value, or profit **2** : LOW, DESPICABLE — **worth·less·ness** *n*

♦ chaffy, empty, junky, no-good, null, valueless *Ant* useful, valuable, worthy

worth·while \ˈwərth-ˈhwīl\ *adj* : being worth the time or effort spent

¹**wor·thy** \ˈwər-thē\ *adj* **wor·thi·er; -est** **1** : having worth or value **2** ♦ : marked by personal qualities warranting honor, respect, or esteem : MERITORIOUS **3** : having sufficient worth ⟨∼ of the honor⟩ — **wor·thi·ly** \ˈwər-thə-lē\ *adv* — **wor·thi·ness** \-thē-nəs\ *n*

♦ deserving, good, meritorious *Ant* no-good, undeserving, valueless, worthless

²**worthy** *n, pl* **worthies** : a worthy person

would \ˈwu̇d\ *past of* WILL **1** *archaic* : wish for : WANT **2** : strongly desire : WISH ⟨I ∼ I were young again⟩ **3** — used as an auxiliary to express (1) preference ⟨∼ rather run than fight⟩, (2) wish, desire, or intent ⟨those who ∼ forbid gambling⟩, (3) habitual action ⟨we ∼ meet often for lunch⟩, (4) a contingency or possibility ⟨if he were coming, he ∼ be here by now⟩, (5) probability ⟨∼ have won if he hadn't tripped⟩, or (6) a request ⟨∼ you help us⟩ **4** : COULD **5** : SHOULD

would–be \ˈwu̇d-ˈbē\ *adj, disparaging* : desiring or pretending to be ⟨a ∼ artist⟩

¹**wound** \ˈwünd\ *n* **1** : an injury involving cutting or breaking of bodily tissue (as by violence, accident, or surgery) **2** ♦ : an injury or hurt to feelings or reputation

♦ affront, barb, dart, dig, indignity, insult, name, offense, outrage, put-down, sarcasm, slight, slur

²**wound** *vb* ♦ : to inflict a wound to or in

♦ damage, harm, hurt, injure ♦ affront, insult, offend, outrage, slight

³**wound** \ˈwau̇nd\ *past and past part of* WIND

wove *past of* WEAVE

woven *past part of* WEAVE

¹**wow** \ˈwau̇\ *n* : a striking success : HIT

²**wow** *vb* : to arouse enthusiastic approval

WP *abbr* word processing; word processor

WPM *abbr* words per minute

wpn *abbr* weapon

wrack \ˈrak\ *n* : violent or total destruction

wraith \ˈrāth\ *n, pl* **wraiths** \ˈrāths, ˈrāthz\ **1** ♦ : a visible appearance of a dead person : GHOST **2** : an insubstantial appearance : SHADOW

♦ apparition, bogey, ghost, phantasm, phantom, poltergeist, shade, shadow, specter, spirit, spook, vision

¹**wran·gle** \ˈraŋ-gəl\ *vb* **wran·gled; wran·gling** **1** ♦ : to quarrel angrily or peevishly : BICKER **2** : ARGUE ⟨they *wrangled* about money⟩ **3** : to obtain by persistent arguing **4** : to herd and care for (livestock) on the range — **wran·gler** *n*

♦ argue, bicker, brawl, dispute, fall out, fight, hassle, quarrel, row, scrap, spat, squabble

²**wrangle** *n* ♦ : an angry, noisy, or prolonged dispute; *also* : CONTROVERSY

♦ altercation, argument, bicker, brawl, controversy, disagreement, dispute, fight, hassle, misunderstanding, quarrel, row, scrap, spat, squabble

¹**wrap** \ˈrap\ *vb* **wrapped; wrap·ping** **1** : to cover esp. by winding or folding **2** : to envelop and secure for transportation or storage **3** ♦ : to enclose wholly **4** : to coil, fold, draw, or twine about something **5** : SURROUND, ENVELOP ⟨*wrapped* in mystery⟩ **6** : INVOLVE, ENGROSS ⟨*wrapped* up in a hobby⟩ **7** : to complete filming or recording

♦ embrace, enclose, encompass, enfold, enshroud, envelop, invest, lap, mantle, shroud, swathe, veil

²**wrap** *n* **1** : WRAPPER, WRAPPING **2** : an article of clothing that may be wrapped around a person **3** *pl* : SECRECY ⟨kept under ∼s⟩ **4** : completion of filming or recording **5** : a thin piece of bread that is rolled around a filling

wrap·around \ˈra-pə-ˌrau̇nd\ *n* : a garment (as a dress) adjusted to the figure by wrapping around

wrap·per \ˈra-pər\ *n* **1** : that in which something is wrapped **2** : one that wraps **3** : an article of clothing worn wrapped around the body

wrap·ping \ˈra-piŋ\ *n* : something used to wrap an object : WRAPPER

wrap–up \ˈrap-ˌəp\ *n* ♦ : a concise statement of the main points : SUMMARY

♦ abstract, digest, encapsulation, epitome, outline, précis, recap, recapitulation, résumé (*or* resume), roundup, sum, summarization, summary, synopsis

wrap up *vb* **1** ♦ : to make a single comprehensive report from : SUMMARIZE **2** ♦ : to bring to a usu. successful conclusion

♦ [1] abstract, digest, encapsulate, epitomize, outline, recapitulate, summarize, sum up ♦ [2] close, conclude, end, finish, round, terminate, wind up

wrasse \ˈras\ *n* : any of a large family of usu. brightly colored marine fishes including many food fishes

wrath \ˈrath\ *n* **1** ♦ : violent anger : RAGE **2** ♦ : condemnation esp. of a deity or sovereign; *esp* : divine punishment

♦ [1] anger, furor, fury, indignation, ire, outrage, rage, spleen, wrathfulness ♦ [2] castigation, chastisement, correction, desert, discipline, nemesis, penalty, punishment

wrath·ful \-fəl\ *adj* **1** ♦ : filled with wrath : very angry **2** ♦ : showing, marked by, or arising from anger ⟨a ∼ assault⟩ — **wrath·ful·ly** *adv*

♦ [1, 2] angry, boiling, enraged, furious, irate, mad, rabid, sore

wrath·ful·ness *n* ♦ : the quality or fact of being wrathful

♦ anger, furor, fury, indignation, ire, outrage, rage, spleen, wrath

wreak \ˈrēk\ *vb* **1** : to exact as a punishment : INFLICT ⟨∼ vengeance on an enemy⟩ **2** : to give free scope or rein to ⟨∼ed his wrath⟩ **3** : BRING ABOUT, CAUSE ⟨∼ havoc⟩

wreath \ˈrēth\ *n, pl* **wreaths** \ˈrēthz, ˈrēths\ : a circular band of flowers or leaves usu. for decoration; *also* : something having a circular or coiling form ⟨a ∼ of smoke⟩

wreathe \ˈrēth\ *vb* **wreathed; wreath·ing** **1** : to shape or take on the shape of a wreath **2** : to crown, decorate, or cover with or as if with a wreath ⟨a face *wreathed* in smiles⟩ **3** ♦ : to interweave or blend together

♦ interlace, intersperse, intertwine, interweave, lace, thread, weave

¹wreck \'rek\ *n* **1** : something (as goods) cast up on the land by the sea after a shipwreck **2** : the injury, destruction, or sinking of a vessel esp. by being cast on rocks or affected by the force of winds or waves : SHIPWRECK **3** ♦ : the action or an instance of crashing, breaking up, or destroying something **4** ♦ : broken remains (as of a vehicle after a crash) **5** : something disabled or in a state of ruin; *also* : an individual broken in health, strength, or spirits

♦ [3] collision, crack-up, crash, smash ♦ [4] debris, remains, residue, rubble, ruins, wreckage

²wreck *vb* **1** : SHIPWRECK **2** ♦ : to ruin or damage by breaking up ⟨~ed their marriage⟩ : involve in disaster or ruin

♦ annihilate, blot out, demolish, desolate, destroy, devastate, do in, exterminate, extinguish, obliterate, pulverize, ruin, shatter, smash, tear down, waste, wipe out

wreck·age \'re-kij\ *n* **1** ♦ : the act of wrecking : the state of being wrecked **2** ♦ : the remains of a wreck

♦ [1] annihilation, demolition, desolation, destruction, devastation, havoc, loss, obliteration, ruin, wastage ♦ [2] debris, remains, residue, rubble, ruins, wreck

wreck·er \'re-kər\ *n* **1** : one that searches for or works upon the wrecks of ships **2** : TOW TRUCK **3** : one that wrecks; *esp* : one whose work is the demolition of buildings

wren \'ren\ *n* : any of a family of small mostly brown singing birds with short wings and often a tail that points upward

¹wrench \'rench\ *vb* **1** : to move with a violent twist **2** ♦ : to pull, strain, or tighten with violent twisting or force **3** ♦ : to injure or disable by a violent twisting or straining **4** ♦ : to snatch forcibly : WREST

♦ [2] twist, wrest, wring ♦ [3] pull, rack, strain, stretch ♦ [4] rip, tear, wrest

²wrench *n* **1** : a forcible twisting; *also* : an injury (as to one's ankle) by twisting **2** : a tool for holding, twisting, or turning (as nuts or bolts)

¹wrest \'rest\ *vb* **1** ♦ : to pull or move by a forcible twisting movement **2** ♦ : to gain with difficulty by or as if by coercion, force, or violence ⟨~ed the book from her hands⟩ ⟨~ control of the government from the dictator⟩

♦ [1] extract, prize, pry, pull, root, tear, uproot ♦ [1, 2] rip, tear, wrench ♦ [2] exact, extort, wring

²wrest *n* : a forcible twist : WRENCH

¹wres·tle \'re-səl, 'ra-\ *vb* **wres·tled; wres·tling 1** ♦ : to grapple with and try to throw down an opponent **2** ♦ : to compete against in wrestling **3** : to struggle for control (as of something difficult) ⟨~ with a problem⟩ — **wres·tler** \'res-lər, 'ras-\ *n*

♦ [1, 2] grapple, scuffle, tussle

²wrestle *n* : the action or an instance of wrestling : STRUGGLE

wres·tling \'res-liŋ\ *n* : the sport in which two opponents wrestle each other

wretch \'rech\ *n* **1** : a miserable unhappy person **2** : a base, despicable, or vile person

♦ beast, devil, evildoer, fiend, heavy, knave, no-good, rapscallion, rascal, reprobate, rogue, scalawag, scamp, varlet, villain

wretch·ed \'re-chəd\ *adj* **1** ♦ : deeply afflicted, dejected, or distressed : extremely sad and depressed **2** ♦ : characterized by or tending to produce discomfort, distress, or misery ⟨~ living conditions⟩ **3** ♦ : having a mean or contemptible nature or appearance ⟨a ~ trick⟩ **4** ♦ : poor in quality or ability : INFERIOR ⟨~ workmanship⟩ — **wretch·ed·ness** *n*

♦ [1] dejected, depressed, despondent, disconsolate, heartsick, miserable, mournful, sad, sorrowful, sorry, unhappy, woebegone, woeful ♦ [3] contemptible, despicable, lousy, nasty, pitiful, scabby, scurvy, sorry ♦ [4] atrocious, awful, execrable, inferior, lousy, punk, rotten, terrible *Ant* great, marvelous, wonderful

wretch·ed·ly *adv* **1** ♦ : in a wretched state or manner

♦ agonizingly, bitterly, grievously, hard, hardly, sadly, sorrowfully, unhappily, woefully

wrig·gle \'ri-gəl\ *vb* **wrig·gled; wrig·gling 1** : to twist or move to and fro like a worm ⟨wriggled in his chair⟩ ⟨~ your toes⟩; *also* : to move along by twisting and turning ⟨a snake wriggled along the path⟩ **2** : to extricate oneself as if by wriggling ⟨~ out of difficulty⟩ — **wriggle** *n*

wrig·gler *n* **1** : one that wriggles **2** : WIGGLER 1

wring \'riŋ\ *vb* **wrung** \'rəŋ\; **wring·ing 1** : to squeeze or twist esp. so as to make dry or to extract moisture or liquid ⟨~ wet clothes⟩ **2** : to get by or as if by twisting or pressing ⟨~ the truth out of him⟩ **3** : to twist so as to strain or sprain ⟨~ his neck⟩ **4** : to twist together as a sign of anguish ⟨wrung her hands⟩ **5** : to affect painfully as if by wringing : TORMENT ⟨her plight wrung my heart⟩

♦ twist, wrench, wrest

wring·er \'riŋ-ər\ *n* : one that wrings; *esp* : a device for squeezing out liquid or moisture ⟨clothes ~⟩

¹wrin·kle \'riŋ-kəl\ *n* **1** ♦ : a crease or small fold on a smooth surface (as in the skin or in cloth) **2** ♦ : a clever or new method, trick, or idea — **wrin·kly** \-k(ə-)lē\ *adj*

♦ [1] crease, crimp, crinkle, furrow ♦ [2] coinage, concoction, contrivance, creation, innovation, invention

²wrinkle *vb* **wrin·kled; wrin·kling** ♦ : to develop or cause to develop wrinkles

♦ crease, crinkle, furrow, rumple

wrist \'rist\ *n* : the joint or region between the hand and the arm; *also* : a corresponding part in a lower animal

wrist·band \-ˌband\ *n* : a band or the part of a sleeve encircling the wrist

wrist·let \-lət\ *n* : WRISTBAND; *esp* : a close-fitting knitted band attached to a glove or the end of a sleeve

wrist·watch \-ˌwäch\ *n* : a small watch attached to a bracelet or strap to fasten about the wrist

writ \'rit\ *n* **1** : something written **2** : a written legal order signed by a court officer

write \'rit\ *vb* **wrote** \'rōt\; **writ·ten** \'rit-ᵊn\ *also* **writ** \'rit\; **writ·ing** \'rī-tiŋ\ **1** : to form characters, letters, or words on a surface ⟨learn to read and ~⟩ **2** : to form the letters or the words of ⟨~ your name⟩ ⟨~ a check⟩ **3** ♦ : to put down on paper : express in writing **4** : to make up and set down for others to read ⟨~ a book⟩ ⟨~ music⟩ **5** : to write a letter to **6** : to communicate by letter : CORRESPOND

♦ author, pen, scratch, scribble

write–in \'rīt-ˌin\ *n* : a vote cast by writing in the name of a candidate; *also* : a candidate whose name is written in

write in *vb* : to insert (a name not listed on a ballot) in an appropriate space; *also* : to cast (a vote) in this manner

write off *vb* **1 a** ♦ : to reduce the estimated value of : DEPRECIATE **b** ♦ : to disparage or deny the worth of **2** : CANCEL ⟨write off a bad debt⟩

♦ [1a] cheapen, depreciate, depress, mark down ♦ [1b] belittle, cry down, decry, deprecate, depreciate, diminish, discount, disparage, minimize, put down

writ·er \'rī-tər\ *n* : one that writes esp. as a business or occupation : AUTHOR

writer's cramp *n* : a painful spasmodic contraction of muscles of the hand or fingers brought on by excessive writing

write–up \'rīt-ˌəp\ *n* : a written account (as in a newspaper); *esp* : a flattering article

writhe \'rīth\ *vb* **writhed; writh·ing 1** : to twist and turn this way and that ⟨~ in pain⟩ **2** : to suffer with shame or confusion

writ·ing *n* **1** : the act of one that writes; *also* : HANDWRITING **2** : something that is written or printed **3** : a style or form of composition **4** : the occupation of a writer

Writings \'rī-tiŋz\ *n pl* : the third part of the Jewish scriptures

wrnt *abbr* warrant

¹wrong \'rȯŋ\ *n* **1** ♦ : an injurious, unfair, or unjust act **2** : a violation of the legal rights of another person **3** ♦ : something that is wrong : wrong principles, practices, or conduct ⟨know right from ~⟩ **4** : the state, position, or fact of being wrong ⟨was in the ~⟩

♦ [1] disservice, injury, injustice, raw deal ♦ [3] bad, evil, ill, immorality, iniquity, sin, villainy

²wrong *adj* **wrong·er** \'rȯŋ-ər\; **wrong·est** \'rȯŋ-əst\ **1** ♦ : lacking in moral behavior and integrity : IMMORAL **2** ♦ : not right according to a standard or code : IMPROPER **3** ♦ : not agreeing with or conforming to facts : INCORRECT ⟨a ~ solution⟩ **4** ♦ : being at variance with what is generally acceptable or preferable : UNSATISFACTORY **5** : not fitted or qualified for a particular intention or purpose : UNSUITABLE, INAPPROPRIATE **6** : constituting a surface that is considered the back, bottom, inside, or reverse of something ⟨iron only on the ~ side of the fabric⟩

♦ [1] bad, evil, immoral, iniquitous, nefarious, rotten, sinful, unethical, unsavory, vicious, vile, villainous ♦ [2] graceless, improper, inapt, incongruous, incorrect, indecorous, inept, infelicitous, unbecoming, unfit, unhappy, unseemly, unsuitable ♦ [3]

erroneous, false, inaccurate, incorrect, inexact, invalid, off, unsound, untrue ♦ [4] bad, deficient, inferior, lousy, off, poor, punk, rotten, substandard, unacceptable, unsatisfactory, wanting, wretched

³**wrong** *adv* **1** : in a mistaken or erroneous manner **2** ♦ : in a wrong direction, manner, or relation

♦ afield, amiss, astray, awry *Ant* aright, right, well

⁴**wrong** *vb* **wronged; wrong•ing** \'rȯŋ-iŋ\ **1** : to do wrong to : INJURE, HARM **2** : to treat unjustly : DISHONOR, MALIGN
wrong•do•er \'rȯŋ-ˌdü-ər\ *n* ♦ : a person who does wrong and esp. moral wrong

♦ evildoer, malefactor, sinner

wrong•do•ing \-ˌdü-iŋ\ *n* ♦ : the act or action of doing wrong

♦ breach, crime, error, malefaction, misdeed, misdoing, offense, sin, transgression, trespass, violation ♦ malfeasance, misbehavior, misconduct, misdoing

wrong•ful \'rȯŋ-fəl\ *adj* **1** : WRONG, UNJUST **2** ♦ : having no legal sanction : UNLAWFUL ⟨~ conduct⟩ — **wrong•ful•ly** *adv* — **wrong•ful•ness** *n*

♦ criminal, illegal, illegitimate, illicit, unlawful

wrong•head•ed \-'he-dəd\ *adj* : stubborn in clinging to wrong opinion or principles — **wrong•head•ed•ly** *adv* — **wrong•head•ed•ness** *n*
wrong•ly *adv* ♦ : in a bad, incorrect, inappropriate, or unsuitable manner

♦ amiss, erroneously, faultily, improperly, inaptly, incorrectly,

mistakenly *Ant* appropriately, aptly, correctly, fittingly, properly, right, rightly, suitably

wrote *past of* WRITE
wroth \'rȯth, 'rōth\ *adj* : filled with wrath : ANGRY
wrought \'rȯt\ *adj* **1** : FASHIONED, FORMED ⟨carefully ~ essays⟩ **2** : ORNAMENTED **3** : beaten into shape by tools : HAMMERED ⟨~ metals⟩ **4** : deeply stirred : EXCITED ⟨gets easily ~ up⟩
wrung *past and past part of* WRING
wry \'rī\ *adj* **wry•er** \'rī-ər\; **wry•est** \'rī-əst\ **1** : having a bent or twisted shape ⟨a ~ smile⟩; *also* : turned abnormally to one side : CONTORTED ⟨a ~ neck⟩ **2** : cleverly and often ironically humorous — **wry•ly** *adv* — **wry•ness** *n*
wry•neck \'rī-ˌnek\ *n* **1** : either of two Old World woodpeckers that differ from typical woodpeckers in having a peculiar manner of twisting the head and neck **2** : an abnormal twisting of the neck and head to one side caused by muscle spasms
WSW *abbr* west-southwest
wt *abbr* weight
wurst \'wərst, 'wu̇rst\ *n* : SAUSAGE
wu•shu \'wü-'shü\ *n* : Chinese martial arts
wuss \'wu̇s\ *n* : WIMP — **wussy** \'wu̇-sē\ *adj*
WV *or* **W Va** *abbr* West Virginia
WW *abbr* World War
w/w *abbr* wall-to-wall
WY *or* **Wyo** *abbr* Wyoming
WYS•I•WYG \'wi-zē-ˌwig\ *adj* : of, relating to, or being a computer display that shows a document exactly as it will appear when printed out

¹**x** \'eks\ *n, pl* **x's** *or* **xs** \'ek-səz\ *often cap* **1** : the 24th letter of the English alphabet **2** : an unknown quantity
²**x** *vb* **x-ed** *also* **x'd** *or* **xed** \'ekst\; **x-ing** *or* **x'ing** \'ek-siŋ\ : to cancel or obliterate with a series of *x*'s — usu. used with *out*
³**x** *abbr* **1** ex **2** experimental **3** extra
⁴**x** *symbol* **1** times ⟨3 x 2 is 6⟩ **2** by ⟨a 3 x 5 index card⟩ **3** *often cap* power of magnification
Xan•a•du \'za-nə-ˌdü, -ˌdyü\ *n* : an idyllic, exotic, or luxurious place
Xan•thip•pe \zan-'thi-pē, -'ti-\ *or* **Xan•tip•pe** \-'ti-pē\ *n* : an ill-tempered woman
x–ax•is \'eks-ˌak-səs\ *n* : the axis of a graph or of a system of coordinates in a plane parallel to which abscissas are measured
X–C *abbr* cross-country
X chromosome *n* : a sex chromosome that usu. occurs paired in each female cell and single in each male cell in organisms (as humans) in which the male normally has two unlike sex chromosomes
Xe *symbol* xenon
xe•non \'zē-ˌnän, 'ze-\ *n* : a heavy gaseous chemical element occurring in minute quantities in air
xe•no•pho•bia \ˌze-nə-'fō-bē-ə, ˌzē-\ *n* : fear and hatred of strangers or foreigners or of what is strange or foreign — **xe•no•phobe** \'ze-nə-ˌfōb, 'zē-\ *n* — **xe•no•pho•bic** \ˌze-nə-'fō-bik, ˌzē-\ *adj*
xe•ric \'zir-ik, 'zer-\ *adj* : characterized by or requiring only a small amount of moisture ⟨a ~ habitat⟩
xeri•scape \'zir-ə-ˌskāp, 'zer-\ *n, often cap* : a landscaping method utilizing water-conserving techniques

xe•rog•ra•phy \zə-'rä-grə-fē\ *n* : a process for copying printed matter by the action of light on an electrically charged surface in which the latent image is developed with a powder — **xe•ro•graph•ic** \ˌzir-ə-'gra-fik\ *adj*
xe•ro•phyte \'zir-ə-ˌfīt\ *n* : a plant adapted for growth with a limited water supply — **xe•ro•phyt•ic** \ˌzir-ə-'fi-tik\ *adj*
xi \'zī, 'ksī\ *n* : the 14th letter of the Greek alphabet — Ξ *or* ξ
XL *abbr* **1** extra large **2** extra long
Xmas \'kris-məs *also* 'eks-məs\ *n* : CHRISTMAS
XML \ˌeks-(ˌ)em-'el\ *n* : a markup language that indicates the structural type of data
XO *abbr* executive officer
x–ra•di•a•tion \ˌeks-ˌrā-dē-'ā-shən\ *n, often cap* **1** : exposure to X-rays **2** : radiation consisting of X-rays
x–ray \'eks-ˌrā\ *vb, often cap* : to examine, treat, or photograph with X-rays
X–ray \'eks-ˌrā\ *n* **1** : a radiation with an extremely short wavelength of less than 100 angstroms that is able to penetrate through various thicknesses of solids and to act on photographic film **2** : a photograph taken with X-rays — **X–ray** *adj*
XS *abbr* extra small
xy•lem \'zī-ləm, -ˌlem\ *n* : a woody tissue of vascular plants that transports water and dissolved materials upward, functions in support and storage, and lies central to the phloem
xy•lo•phone \'zī-lə-ˌfōn\ *n* : a musical instrument consisting of a series of wooden bars graduated in length to produce the musical scale, supported on belts of straw or felt, and sounded by striking with two small wooden hammers — **xy•lo•phon•ist** \-ˌfō-nist\ *n*

¹y \'wī\ *n, pl* **y's** *or* **ys** \'wīz\ *often cap* : the 25th letter of the English alphabet

²y *abbr* **1** yard **2** year

¹Y \'wī\ *n* : YMCA, YWCA

²Y *symbol* yttrium

¹-y *also* **-ey** \ē\ *adj suffix* **1** : characterized by : full of ⟨dirty⟩ ⟨clayey⟩ **2** : having the character of : composed of ⟨icy⟩ **3** : like : like that of ⟨homey⟩ ⟨wintry⟩ ⟨stagy⟩ **4** : tending or inclined to ⟨sleepy⟩ ⟨chatty⟩ **5** : giving occasion for (specified) action ⟨teary⟩ **6** : performing (specified) action ⟨curly⟩

²-y \ē\ *n suffix, pl* **-ies** **1** : state : condition : quality ⟨beggary⟩ **2** : activity, place of business, or goods dealt with ⟨laundry⟩ **3** : whole body or group ⟨soldiery⟩

³-y *n suffix, pl* **-ies** : instance of a (specified) action ⟨entreaty⟩ ⟨inquiry⟩

YA *abbr* young adult

¹yacht \'yät\ *n* : a usu. large recreational watercraft; *also* : sailboat

²yacht *vb* : to race or cruise in a yacht

yacht·ing \'yä-tiŋ\ *n* : the sport of racing or cruising in a yacht

yachts·man \'yäts-mən\ *n* : a person who owns or sails a yacht

ya·hoo \'yā-hü, 'yä-\ *n, pl* **yahoos** : a boorish, crass, or stupid person

Yah·weh \'yä-ˌwä\ *also* **Yah·veh** \-ˌvä\ *n* : GOD 1 — used esp. by the Hebrews

¹yak \'yak\ *n, pl* **yaks** *also* **yak** : a large long-haired wild or domesticated ox of Tibet and adjacent Asian uplands

²yak *also* **yack** \'yak\ *n* : persistent or voluble talk — **yak** *also* **yack** *vb*

yam \'yam\ *n* **1** : the edible starchy root of various twining plants used as a staple food in tropical areas; *also* : a plant that produces yams **2** : a usu. deep orange sweet potato

yam·mer \'ya-mər\ *vb* **1** : to utter repeated cries of distress or sorrow : WHIMPER **2** : CHATTER — **yammer** *n*

¹yank \'yaŋk\ *n* : a strong sudden pull : JERK

²yank *vb* : to pull with a quick vigorous movement

Yank \'yaŋk\ *n* : YANKEE

Yan·kee \'yaŋ-kē\ *n* **1** : a native or inhabitant of New England; *also* : a native or inhabitant of the northern U.S. **2** : AMERICAN 2

yan·qui \'yän-kē\ *n, often cap* : a citizen of the U.S. as distinguished from a Latin American

¹yap \'yap\ *vb* **yapped; yap·ping** **1** : BARK, YELP **2** : GAB

²yap *n* **1** : a quick sharp bark **2** : CHATTER

¹yard \'yärd\ *n* **1** ♦ : a small enclosed area open to the sky and adjacent to a building **2** ♦ : the grounds of a building **3** : the grounds surrounding a house usu. covered with grass **4** : an enclosure for livestock **5** : an area set aside for a particular business or activity **6** : a system of railroad tracks for storing cars and making up trains

   ♦ [1] close, court, courtyard, quadrangle ♦ [2] demesne, grounds, park, premises

²yard *n* **1** : a unit of length equal to three feet **2** : a long spar tapered toward the ends that supports and spreads the head of a sail — **the whole nine yards** : all of a set of circumstances, conditions, or details

yard·age \'yär-dij\ *n* : an aggregate number of yards; *also* : the length, extent, or volume of something as measured in yards

yard·arm \'yärd-ˌärm\ *n* : either end of the yard of a square-rigged ship

yard·man \-mən, -ˌman\ *n* **1** : a person employed to do outdoor work (as mowing lawns) **2** : a person employed in or about a yard (as a lumberyard or railroad yard)

yard·mas·ter \-ˌmas-tər\ *n* : the person in charge of a railroad yard

yard sale *n* : GARAGE SALE

yard·stick \-ˌstik\ *n* **1** : a graduated measuring stick three feet long **2** ♦ : a standard for making a critical judgment : CRITERION

   ♦ criterion, grade, mark, measure, par, standard, touchstone

yar·mul·ke \'yä-mə-kə, 'yär-, -məl-\ *n* : a skullcap worn esp. by Jewish males in the synagogue and the home

yarn \'yärn\ *n* **1** : a continuous often plied strand composed of fibers or filaments and used in weaving and knitting to form cloth **2** : an entertaining narrative of adventures : STORY; *esp* : a tall tale

yar·row \'yar-ō\ *n* : a strong-scented herb related to the daisies that has white or pink flowers in flat clusters

yaw \'yȯ\ *vb* ♦ : to deviate erratically from a course ⟨the ship ∼ed in the heavy seas⟩ — **yaw** *n*

   ♦ sheer, swerve, veer

yawl \'yȯl\ *n* : a 2-masted sailboat with the shorter mast aft of the rudder

¹yawn \'yȯn\ *vb* : to open wide; *esp* : to open the mouth wide and take a deep breath usu. as an involuntary reaction to fatigue or boredom — **yawn·er** *n*

²yawn *n* : the act of yawning

yawp *or* **yaup** \'yȯp\ *vb* **1** : to make a raucous noise : SQUAWK **2** : CLAMOR, COMPLAIN — **yawp·er** *n*

yaws \'yȯz\ *n pl* : a contagious tropical disease caused by a spirochete closely resembling the causative agent of syphilis and marked by skin lesions

y–ax·is \'wī-ˌak-səs\ *n* : the axis of a graph or of a system of coordinates in a plane parallel to which the ordinates are measured

Yb *symbol* ytterbium

YB *abbr* yearbook

Y chromosome *n* : a sex chromosome that is characteristic of male cells in organisms (as humans) in which the male typically has two unlike sex chromosomes

yd *abbr* yard

¹ye \'yē\ *pron* : YOU 1

²ye \yē, yə, *originally same as* THE\ *definite article, archaic* : THE — used by early printers to represent the manuscript word *þe* (*the*)

¹yea \'yā\ *adv* **1** ♦ — used as a function word esp. to express assent or agreement esp. in oral voting **2** ♦ : not only so but : INDEED

   ♦ [1] all right, alright, OK, yes ♦ [2] even, indeed, nay, truly, verily

²yea *n* : an affirmative vote; *also* : a person casting such a vote

yeah \'yeə, 'yaə\ *adv* : YES

year \'yir\ *n* **1** : the period of about 365¼ solar days required for one revolution of the earth around the sun; *also* : the time in which a planet completes a revolution about the sun **2** : a cycle of 365 or 366 days beginning with January 1; *also* : a calendar year specified usu. by a number **3** *pl* : a time of special significance ⟨their glory ∼s⟩ **4** *pl* : AGE ⟨advanced in ∼s⟩ **5** : a period of time other than a calendar year ⟨the school ∼⟩

year·book \-ˌbu̇k\ *n* **1** : a book published annually esp. as a report **2** : a school publication recording the history and activities of a graduating class

year·ling \'yir-liŋ, 'yər-lən\ *n* **1** : one that is a year old **2** : a racehorse between January of the year after the year in which it was born and the next January

year·long \'yir-ˌlȯŋ\ *adj* : lasting through a year

¹year·ly \'yir-lē\ *adj* : ANNUAL

²yearly *adv* : every year

yearn \'yərn\ *vb* **1** ♦ : to feel a longing or craving ⟨∼ing for freedom⟩ **2** : to feel tenderness or compassion

   ♦ *usu* yearn for ache for, crave, desire, die for, hanker for, hunger for, long for, lust (for *or* after), pine for, repine for, thirst for, want, wish for

yearn·ing *n* ♦ : a tender or urgent longing

   ♦ appetite, craving, desire, drive, hankering, hunger, itch, longing, lust, passion, thirst, urge, yen

year–round \'yir-ˈrau̇nd\ *adj* : effective, employed, or operating for the full year : not seasonal ⟨a ∼ resort⟩

yeast \'yēst\ *n* **1** : a surface froth or a sediment in sugary liquids (as fruit juices) that consists largely of cells of a tiny fungus and is used in making alcoholic liquors and as a leaven in baking **2** : a commercial product containing yeast fungi in a moist or dry medium **3** : a minute one-celled fungus present and functionally active in yeast that reproduces by budding; *also* : any of several similar fungi **4** *archaic* : the foam of waves : SPUME **5** ♦ : something that causes ferment or activity

   ♦ boost, encouragement, goad, impetus, impulse, incentive, incitement, instigation, momentum, motivation, provocation, spur, stimulus

yeast infection *n* : infection of the vagina with an excess growth of a normally present fungus that resembles a yeast

yeasty \'yē-stē\ *adj* **yeast·i·er; -est** **1** : of, relating to, or resembling yeast **2** : UNSETTLED **3** : full of vitality ⟨∼ youths⟩; *also* : FRIVOLOUS

¹yell \'yel\ *vb* **1** ♦ : to utter a loud cry or scream **2** ♦ : to speak or call out in a loud voice : SHOUT — **yell·er** *n*

♦ [1] howl, scream, shriek, shrill, squeal, yelp ♦ [2] bawl, call, cry, holler, shout, vociferate

²yell *n* **1** ♦ : a loud or sudden outcry : SHOUT **2** : a cheer used esp. to encourage an athletic team (as at a college)

♦ cry, holler, hoot, shout, whoop

¹yel·low \'ye-lō\ *adj* **1** : of the color yellow **2** *sometimes offensive* : having a yellow complexion or skin **3** : SENSATIONAL ⟨∼ journalism⟩ **4** ♦ : showing or marked by an utter lack of courage : COWARDLY — **yel·low·ish** \'ye-lə-wish\ *adj*

♦ chicken, cowardly, craven, dastardly, pusillanimous, recreant, spineless

²yellow *n* **1** : a color between green and orange in the spectrum : the color of ripe lemons or sunflowers **2** : something yellow; *esp* : the yolk of an egg **3** *pl* : any of several plant diseases marked by stunted growth and yellowing of foliage

³yellow *vb* : to make or turn yellow

yellow birch *n* : a No. American birch with thin lustrous gray or yellow bark; *also* : its strong hard wood

yellow fever *n* : an acute infectious viral disease marked by prostration, jaundice, fever, and often hemorrhage and transmitted by a mosquito

yellow jack *n* : YELLOW FEVER

yellow jacket *n* : any of various small social wasps having the body barred with bright yellow

yel·low·tail \'ye-lō-ˌtāl\ *n* : any of various fishes with a yellow or yellowish tail including several valuable food fishes

yelp \'yelp\ *vb* ♦ : to utter a sharp quick shrill cry — **yelp** *n*

♦ howl, scream, shriek, shrill, squeal, yell

Ye·me·ni \'ye-mə-nē\ *n* : YEMENITE — **Yemeni** *adj*

Ye·men·ite \'ye-mə-ˌnīt\ *n* : a native or inhabitant of Yemen — **Yemenite** *adj*

¹yen \'yen\ *n, pl* **yen** : the basic monetary unit of Japan

²yen *n* ♦ : a strong desire : LONGING ⟨a ∼ to travel⟩

♦ appetite, craving, desire, drive, hankering, hunger, itch, longing, lust, passion, thirst, urge, yearning

yeo·man \'yō-mən\ *n* **1** : an attendant or officer in a royal or noble household **2** : a naval petty officer who performs clerical duties **3** : a person who owns and cultivates a small farm; *esp* : one of a class of English freeholders below the gentry — **yeo·man·ly** \-lē\ *adj*

yeo·man·ry \-rē\ *n* : the body of yeomen and esp. of small landed proprietors

¹yes \'yes\ *adv* ♦ — used as a function word esp. to express assent or agreement or to introduce a more emphatic or explicit phrase

♦ all right, alright, OK, yea *Ant* nay, no

²yes *n* : an affirmative reply

ye·shi·va *also* **ye·shi·vah** \yə-'shē-və\ *n, pl* **yeshivas** *or* **ye·shi·voth** \-ˌshē-'vōt, -'vōth\ : a Jewish school esp. for religious instruction

yes–man \'yes-ˌman\ *n* : a person who endorses uncritically every opinion or proposal of a superior

¹yes·ter·day \'yes-tər-dē, -ˌdā\ *adv* **1** : on the day preceding today **2** : only a short time ago

²yesterday *n* **1** : the day last past **2** : time not long past

yes·ter·year \'yes-tər-ˌyir\ *n* **1** : last year **2** ♦ : the recent past

♦ history, past, yore

¹yet \'yet\ *adv* **1** ♦ : in addition : BESIDES; *also* : EVEN **6** **2** ♦ : up to now; *also* : STILL **3** : so soon as now ⟨not time to go ∼⟩ **4** ♦ : at an unspecified later time : EVENTUALLY **5** : in spite of that : NEVERTHELESS

♦ [1] additionally, again, also, besides, even, further, furthermore, likewise, more, moreover, then, too, withal ♦ [2] heretofore, hitherto, still ♦ [4] eventually, someday, sometime, ultimately

²yet *conj* ♦ : but nevertheless : BUT

♦ but, except, only

ye·ti \'ye-tē, 'yā-\ *n* : ABOMINABLE SNOWMAN

yew \'yü\ *n* **1** : any of a genus of evergreen trees and shrubs with dark stiff poisonous needles and fleshy fruits **2** : the wood of a yew; *esp* : that of an Old World yew

Yid·dish \'yi-dish\ *n* : a language derived from medieval German and spoken by Jews esp. of eastern European origin — **Yiddish** *adj*

¹yield \'yēld\ *vb* **1** : to give as fitting, owed, or required **2** ♦ : to surrender or relinquish to the physical control of another : GIVE UP; *esp* : to give up possession of on claim or demand **3** ♦ : to bear as a natural product **4** : to bear or bring forth as a natural result of effort or cultivation : PRODUCE **5** ♦ : to bring in : RETURN **6** ♦ : to give way (as to force, influence, or temptation) **7** : to give place

♦ [2] cede, deliver, give up, hand over, leave, relinquish, render, surrender, turn over ♦ [5] give, pay, return ♦ [6] blink, bow, budge, capitulate, concede, give in, knuckle under, quit, submit, succumb, surrender *Ant* resist

²yield *n* ♦ : something yielded; *esp* : the amount or quantity produced or returned

♦ earnings, income, proceeds, profit, return, revenue ♦ affair, fruit, handiwork, output, produce, product, thing, work

yield·ing \'yēl-diŋ\ *adj* **1** ♦ : not rigid or stiff **2** ♦ : having a tendency to give in, surrender, or agree

♦ [1] droopy, flaccid, floppy, lank, limp, slack ♦ [2] acquiescent, passive, resigned, tolerant, unresistant, unresisting

yikes \'yīks\ *interj* — used to express fear or astonishment

yip \'yip\ *vb* **yipped; yip·ping** : YAP

YK *abbr* Yukon; Yukon Territory

YMCA \ˌwī-ˌem-(ˌ)sē-'ā\ *n* : Young Men's Christian Association

YMHA \ˌwī-ˌem-ˌāch-'ā\ *n* : Young Men's Hebrew Association

yo \'yō\ *interj* — used to call attention, indicate attentiveness, or express affirmation

YOB *abbr* year of birth

yo·del \'yōd-ᵊl\ *vb* **yo·deled** *or* **yo·delled; yo·del·ing** *or* **yo·del·ling** : to sing by suddenly changing from chest voice to falsetto and back; *also* : to shout or call in this manner — **yodel** *n* — **yo·del·er** *n*

yo·ga \'yō-gə\ *n* **1** *cap* : a Hindu theistic philosophy teaching the suppression of all activity of body, mind, and will in order that the self may realize its distinction from them and attain liberation **2** : a system of exercises for attaining bodily or mental control and well-being — **yo·gic** \-gik\ *adj, often cap*

yo·gi \'yō-gē\ *also* **yo·gin** \-gən, -ˌgin\ *n* : a person who practices yoga **2** *cap* : an adherent of Yoga philosophy

yo·gurt *also* **yo·ghurt** \'yō-gərt\ *n* : a soured slightly acid often flavored semisolid food made of milk and milk solids to which cultures of bacteria have been added

¹yoke \'yōk\ *n, pl* **yokes** **1** : a wooden bar or frame by which two draft animals (as oxen) are coupled at the heads or necks for working together; *also* : a frame fitted to a person's shoulders to carry a load in two equal portions **2** : a clamp that embraces two parts to hold or unite them in position **3** *pl usu* **yoke** : two animals yoked together **4** ♦ : an oppressive state of subjection, submission, or servitude : BONDAGE **5** : TIE, LINK ⟨the ∼ of matrimony⟩ **6** : a fitted or shaped piece esp. at the shoulder of a garment

♦ bondage, enslavement, servitude, slavery, thrall

²yoke *vb* **yoked; yok·ing** **1** : to put a yoke on : couple with a yoke **2** : to attach a draft animal to ⟨∼ a plow⟩ **3** ♦ : to couple, join, or associate as if by a yoke; *esp* : MARRY

♦ chain, compound, connect, couple, hitch, hook, join, link

yo·kel \'yō-kəl\ *n* ♦ : a naive or gullible country person

♦ bumpkin, clodhopper, hick, rustic

yolk \'yōk\ *n* **1** : the yellow rounded inner mass of the egg of a bird or reptile **2** : the stored food material of an egg that supplies nutrients (as proteins and cholesterol) to the developing embryo — **yolked** \'yōkt\ *adj*

Yom Kip·pur \ˌyōm-ki-'pùr, ˌyäm-, -'ki-pər\ *n* : a Jewish holiday observed in September or October with fasting and prayer as a day of atonement

¹yon \'yän\ *adj* : YONDER

²yon *adv* **1** : YONDER **2** : THITHER ⟨ran hither and ∼⟩

¹yon·der \'yän-dər\ *adv* ♦ : at or to that place

♦ beyond, farther, further

²yonder *adj* **1** : more distant ⟨the ∼ side of the river⟩ **2** : being at a distance within view ⟨∼ hills⟩

yore \'yōr\ *n* ♦ : time long past ⟨in days of ∼⟩

♦ history, past, yesteryear

York·ie \'yȯr-kē\ *n* : YORKSHIRE TERRIER

York·shire terrier \'yȯrk-ˌshir-, -shər-\ *n* : any of a breed of compact toy terriers with long straight silky hair

you \'yü\ *pron* **1** : the person or persons addressed ⟨∼ are a nice person⟩ ⟨∼ are nice people⟩ **2 :** ONE 2 ⟨∼ turn this knob to open it⟩

¹young \'yəŋ\ *adj* **youn·ger** \'yəŋ-gər\; **youn·gest** \'yəŋ-gəst\ **1 ♦ :** being in the first or an early stage of life, growth, or development **2 :** having little experience **3 :** recently come into being **4 :** YOUTHFUL **5** *cap* **:** belonging to or representing a new or revived usu. political group or movement

   ♦ adolescent, immature, juvenile, youthful **Ant** adult, mature, matured

²young *n, pl* **young :** young persons; *also* **:** young animals
young·ish \'yəŋ-ish\ *adj* **:** somewhat young
young·ling \'yəŋ-liŋ\ *n* **:** one that is young — **youngling** *adj*
young·ster \-stər\ *n* **♦ :** a young person **:** CHILD

   ♦ child, cub, juvenile, kid, youth

your \'yùr, 'yôr, yər\ *adj* **:** of or relating to you or yourself
yours \'yùrz, 'yōrz\ *pron* **:** one or the ones belonging to you
your·self \yər-'self\ *pron, pl* **yourselves** \-'selvz\ **:** YOU — used reflexively, for emphasis, or in absolute constructions ⟨you'll hurt ∼⟩ ⟨do it ∼⟩
youth \'yüth\ *n, pl* **youths** \'yüthz, 'yüths\ **1 :** the period of life between childhood and maturity **2 ♦ :** a young person; *esp* **:** a young male **3 :** YOUTHFULNESS

   ♦ boy, lad, nipper, shaver, stripling ♦ child, cub, juvenile, kid, youngster

youth·ful \'yüth-fəl\ *adj* **1 :** of, relating to, or appropriate to youth **2 ♦ :** being young and not yet mature **3 :** FRESH, VIGOROUS — **youth·ful·ly** *adv* — **youth·ful·ness** *n*

   ♦ adolescent, immature, juvenile, young

youth hostel *n* **:** HOSTEL 2
¹yowl \'yaùl\ *vb* **♦ :** to utter a loud long mournful cry **:** WAIL

   ♦ bay, howl, keen, wail

²yowl *n* **:** a loud long mournful wail or howl
yo–yo \'yō-(ˌ)yō\ *n, pl* **yo–yos :** a thick grooved double disk with a string attached to its center that is made to fall and rise to the hand by unwinding and rewinding on the string — **yo–yo** *vb*

yr *abbr* **1** year **2** your
yrbk *abbr* yearbook
YT *abbr* Yukon Territory
yt·ter·bi·um \i-'tər-bē-əm\ *n* **:** a rare metallic chemical element
yt·tri·um \'i-trē-əm\ *n* **:** a rare metallic chemical element
yu·an \'yü-ən, yü-'än\ *n, pl* **yuan :** the basic monetary unit of China
yuc·ca \'yə-kə\ *n* **:** any of a genus of plants related to the agaves that grow esp. in warm dry regions and bear large clusters of white cup-shaped flowers atop a long stiff stalk
yuck *also* **yuk** \'yək\ *interj* — used to express rejection or disgust
yucky \'yə-kē\ *adj* **♦ :** causing distaste or aversion **:** REPUGNANT; *also* **:** causing discomfort **:** UNPLEASANT

   ♦ bad, disagreeable, displeasing, distasteful, nasty, rotten, sour, uncongenial, unlovely, unpleasant, unpleasing, unsatisfying, unwelcome

yule \'yül\ *n, often cap* **:** CHRISTMAS
Yule log *n* **:** a large log formerly put on the hearth on Christmas Eve as the foundation of the fire
yule·tide \'yül-ˌtīd\ *n, often cap* **♦ :** CHRISTMASTIDE

   ♦ Christmastide, Christmastime, Noel

yum·my \'yə-mē\ *adj* **yum·mi·er; -est ♦ :** highly attractive or pleasing

   ♦ ambrosial, appetizing, delectable, delicious, flavorful, luscious, palatable, savory, scrumptious, tasty, toothsome

Yu·pik \'yü-pik\ *n pl* **Yupik** *also* **Yu·piks** *or* **Yu·piit** \-ˌpēt\ **:** a member of a group of Indigenous peoples of chiefly southwestern Alaska and eastern Siberia; *also* **:** the languages of the Yupik people
yup·pie \'yə-pē\ *n* **:** a young college-educated adult employed in a well-paying profession and living and working in or near a large city — **yup·pie·dom** \-dəm\ *n*
yurt \'yùrt\ *n* **:** a light round tent of skins or felt stretched over a lattice framework used by pastoral peoples of inner Asia
YWCA \ˌwī-ˌdə-bəl-yù-(ˌ)sē-'ā\ *n* **:** Young Women's Christian Association
YWHA \-ˌāch-'ā\ *n* **:** Young Women's Hebrew Association

Z

¹z \'zē\ *n, pl* **z's** *or* **zs** *often cap* **:** the 26th letter of the English alphabet
²z *abbr* **1** zero **2** zone
Z *symbol* atomic number
Zach *abbr* Zacharias
Zach·a·ri·as \ˌza-kə-'rī-əs\ *n* **:** ZECHARIAH
Zair·ian \zä-'ir-ē-ən\ *n* **:** a native or inhabitant of Zaire — **Zairian** *adj*
Zam·bi·an \'zam-bē-ən\ *n* **:** a native or inhabitant of Zambia — **Zambian** *adj*
za·ni·ness \'zā-nē-nəs\ *n* **♦ :** the quality or state of being absurd or foolish

   ♦ absurdity, asininity, balminess, daftness, foolishness, inanity, silliness

¹za·ny \'zā-nē\ *n, pl* **zanies 1 :** a person who acts in a comical manner to amuse others **:** CLOWN **2 :** a silly or foolish person
²zany *adj* **za·ni·er; -est 1 :** characteristic of a zany **2 ♦ :** having an absurd or foolish manner or nature **:** CRAZY — **za·ni·ly** \'zā-nə-lē, 'zān-ᵊl-ē\ *adv*

   ♦ absurd, asinine, balmy, cuckoo, daft, fatuous, foolish, nutty, sappy, screwball, silly, wacky

zap \'zap\ *vb* **zapped; zap·ping 1 :** to hit with or as if with a sudden powerful and usu. harmful force or energy; *esp* **:** DESTROY, KILL **2 :** to heat or cook in a microwave oven ⟨*zapped* the soup⟩
zeal \'zēl\ *n* **:** eager and ardent interest in the pursuit of something **:** FERVOR
zeal·ot \'ze-lət\ *n* **♦ :** a zealous person; *esp* **:** a fanatical partisan

   ♦ crusader, fanatic, militant, partisan

zeal·ous \'ze-ləs\ *adj* **:** filled with, characterized by, or due to zeal — **zeal·ous·ly** *adv* — **zeal·ous·ness** *n*
ze·bra \'zē-brə\ *n, pl* **zebras** *also* **zebra :** any of several African

mammals related to the horse but conspicuously striped with black or dark brown and white or buff
ze·bu \'zē-bü, -byü\ *n* **:** any of various breeds of domestic oxen developed in India that have a large fleshy hump over the shoulders, a dewlap, drooping ears, and marked resistance to heat and to insect attack
Zech *abbr* Zechariah
Zech·a·ri·ah \ˌze-kə-'rī-ə\ *n* **:** a book of Jewish and Christian Scripture
zed \'zed\ *n, chiefly Brit* **:** the letter z
zeit·geist \'tsīt-ˌgīst, 'zīt-\ *n* **:** the general intellectual, moral, and cultural state of an era
Zen \'zen\ *n* **:** a Japanese Buddhist sect that teaches self-discipline, meditation, and attainment of enlightenment through direct intuitive insight
ze·na·na \zə-'nä-nə\ *n* **:** HAREM
ze·nith \'zē-nəth\ *n* **1 :** the point in the heavens directly overhead **2 ♦ :** the highest point **:** ACME

   ♦ acme, apex, climax, crown, culmination, head, height, meridian, peak, pinnacle, summit, tip-top, top

ze·o·lite \'zē-ə-ˌlīt\ *n* **:** any of various feldsparlike silicates used esp. as water softeners
Zeph *abbr* Zephaniah
Zeph·a·ni·ah \ˌze-fə-'nī-ə\ *n* **:** a book of canonical Jewish and Christian Scripture
zeph·yr \'ze-fər\ *n* **1 :** a breeze from the west **2 ♦ :** a gentle breeze

   ♦ air, breath, breeze, puff, waft

zep·pe·lin \'ze-plən, -pə-lən\ *n* **:** a cylindrical rigid blimplike airship
¹ze·ro \'zē-rō, 'zir-ō\ *n, pl* **zeros** *also* **zeroes 1 ♦ :** the numeri-

cal symbol 0   **2** ♦ : the number represented by the symbol 0   **3** : the point at which the graduated degrees or measurements on a scale (as of a thermometer) begin   **4** : the lowest point   **5** ♦ : a person or thing that has no importance, influence, or independent existence

♦ [1, 2] aught, cipher, naught, nil, nothing, zip ♦ [5] nobody, nonentity, nothing, whippersnapper

²ze·ro *adj* **1** : of, relating to, or being a zero   **2** : having no magnitude or quantity   **3** : ABSENT, LACKING; *esp* : having no modified inflectional form

³zero *vb* : to adjust the sights of a firearm to hit the point aimed at — usu. used with *in*

zero hour *n* **1** : the time at which an event (as a military operation) is scheduled to begin   **2** : a time when a vital decision or decisive change must be made

zest \'zest\ *n* **1** : a quality of enhancing enjoyment : PIQUANCY   **2** : keen enjoyment : GUSTO — **zest·ful** \-fəl\ *adj* — **zest·ful·ly** *adv* — **zest·ful·ness** *n* — **zesty** \'zes-tē\ *adj*

ze·ta \'zā-tə, 'zē-\ *n* : the 6th letter of the Greek alphabet — Z or ζ

zi·do·vu·dine \zī-'dō-vyü-ˌdēn\ *n* : AZT

¹zig·zag \'zig-ˌzag\ *n* : one of a series of short sharp turns, angles, or alterations in a course; *also* : something marked by such a series

²zigzag *adv* : in or by a zigzag path

³zigzag *adj* : having short sharp turns or angles

⁴zigzag *vb* **zig·zagged; zig·zag·ging** : to form into or proceed along a zigzag

zil·lion \'zil-yən\ *n* : a large indeterminate number

Zim·ba·bwe·an \zim-'bä-bwē-ən\ *n* : a native or inhabitant of Zimbabwe — **Zimbabwean** *adj*

zinc \'ziŋk\ *n* : a bluish-white metallic chemical element that is commonly found in minerals and is used esp. in alloys and as a protective coating for iron and steel

zinc oxide *n* : a white solid used esp. as a pigment, in compounding rubber, and in ointments and sunblocks

zine \'zēn\ *n* : a noncommercial publication usu. devoted to specialized subject matter

zin·fan·del \'zin-fən-ˌdel\ *n, often cap* : a dry red table wine made chiefly in California

zing \'ziŋ\ *n* **1** : a shrill humming noise   **2** ♦ : the energy and vigor characteristic of a healthy life : VITALITY   **3** ♦ : the quality of having activity, drive, and enthusiasm — **zing** *vb*

♦ [2, 3] dash, drive, energy, ginger, go, hardihood, life, pep, sap, snap, vigor (*or* vigour), vim, vitality, zip ♦ [3] bounce, esprit, punch, spirit, verve

zing·er \'ziŋ-ər\ *n* : a pointed witty remark or retort

zin·nia \'zi-nē-ə, 'zēn-yə\ *n* : any of a genus of tropical American herbs or low shrubs related to the daisies and widely grown for their showy long-lasting flowers

Zi·on \'zī-ən\ *n* **1** : the Jewish people   **2** : the Jewish homeland as a symbol of Judaism or of Jewish national aspiration   **3** : HEAVEN   **4** : UTOPIA

Zi·on·ism \'zī-ə-ˌni-zəm\ *n* : an international movement orig. for the establishment of a Jewish national or religious community in Palestine and later for the support of modern Israel — **Zi·on·ist** \-nist\ *adj or n*

¹zip \'zip\ *vb* **zipped; zip·ping** **1** ♦ : to move, act, or function with speed or vigor   **2** : to travel with a sharp hissing or humming sound   **3** ♦ : to add zest, interest, or life to — often used with *up*

♦ [1] barrel, career, course, dash, fly, hurry, race, rip, rocket, run, rush, shoot, speed, whirl, whisk, zoom ♦ *or* **zip up** [3] brace, energize, enliven, fire, invigorate, jazz up, liven up, pep up, quicken, stimulate, vitalize, vivify

²zip *n* **1** : a sudden sharp hissing sound   **2** ♦ : the quality of being active, enthusiastic, or motivated : VIM

♦ bounce, dash, drive, esprit, ginger, pep, punch, snap, spirit, verve, vim, zing

³zip *n* ♦ : the absence of any significant quality or amount : NOTHING, ZERO

♦ aught, cipher, naught (*also* nought), nil, nothing, oh, zero

⁴zip *vb* **zipped; zip·ping** : to close or open with a zipper

zip code *n, often cap Z&I&P* : a number that identifies each postal delivery area in the U.S.

zip file *n* : a computer file in which a large amount of repeated information has been removed to make it smaller

zip line *n* : a cable suspended usu. over an incline to which a rider is harnessed

zip·per \'zi-pər\ *n* : a fastener consisting of two rows of metal or plastic teeth on strips of tape and a sliding piece that closes an opening by drawing the teeth together

zip·py \'zi-pē\ *adj* **zip·pi·er; -est** **1** : very speedy ⟨a ~ car⟩   **2** : strikingly appealing ⟨~ clothes⟩

zir·con \'zər-ˌkän\ *n* : a zirconium-containing mineral transparent varieties of which are used as gems

zir·co·ni·um \ˌzər-'kō-nē-əm\ *n* : a gray corrosion-resistant metallic chemical element used esp. in alloys and ceramics

zit \'zit\ *n* : PIMPLE

zith·er \'zi-thər, -thər\ *n* : a musical instrument having 30 to 40 strings played with plectrum and fingers

zi·ti \'zē-tē\ *n, pl* **ziti** : medium-size tubular pasta

Zn *symbol* zinc

zo·di·ac \'zō-dē-ˌak\ *n* **1** : an imaginary belt in the heavens that encompasses the paths of most of the planets and that is divided into 12 constellations or signs   **2** : a figure representing the signs of the zodiac and their symbols — **zo·di·a·cal** \zō-'dī-ə-kəl\ *adj*

zom·bie *also* **zom·bi** \'zäm-bē\ *n* : a person who is believed to have died and been brought back to life without speech or free will

zon·al \'zōn-əl\ *adj* : of, relating to, or having the form of a zone — **zon·al·ly** *adv*

¹zone \'zōn\ *n* **1** : any of five great divisions of the earth's surface made according to latitude and temperature including the torrid zone, two temperate zones, and two frigid zones   **2** : something that forms an encircling band ⟨a ~ of tissue⟩   **3 a** ♦ : an area that is distinguished in some way from neighboring areas   **b** : a section of an area or territory created for a particular purpose ⟨business ~⟩ ⟨postal ~⟩

♦ area, belt, land, region, tract

²zone *vb* **zoned; zon·ing** **1** : ENCIRCLE   **2** : to arrange in or mark off into zones; *esp* : to divide (as a city) into sections reserved for different purposes

zonked \'zäŋkt\ *adj* : being or acting as if under the influence of alcohol or a drug : HIGH

zoo \'zü\ *n, pl* **zoos** : a park where wild animals are kept for exhibition

zoo·ge·og·ra·phy \ˌzō-ə-jē-'ä-grə-fē\ *n* : a branch of biogeography concerned with the geographic distribution of animals — **zoo·ge·og·ra·pher** \-fər\ *n* — **zoo·geo·graph·ic** \-ˌjē-ə-'gra-fik\ *also* **zoo·geo·graph·i·cal** \-fi-kəl\ *adj*

zoo·keep·er \'zü-ˌkē-pər\ *n* : a person who cares for animals in a zoo

zool *abbr* zoological; zoology

zoological garden *n* : ZOO

zo·ol·o·gy \zō-'ä-lə-jē\ *n* : a branch of biology that deals with the classification and the properties and vital phenomena of animals — **zo·o·log·i·cal** \ˌzō-ə-'lä-ji-kəl\ *adj* — **zo·ol·o·gist** \zō-'ä-lə-jist\ *n*

¹zoom \'züm\ *vb* **1 a** ♦ : to move with a loud hum or buzz   **b** : to move or increase suddenly or rapidly : ZIP   **2** ♦ : to gain altitude quickly   **3** : to focus a camera or microscope using a special lens that permits the apparent distance of the object to be varied

♦ [1a] buzz, drone, hum, whir, whish, whiz, zip ♦ [2] rocket, shoot, skyrocket, soar

²zoom *n* **1** : the act or process of zooming   **2** ♦ : the sound of something that zooms

♦ buzz, drone, hum, purr, whir, whiz

zoom lens *n* : a camera lens in which the image size can be varied continuously while the image remains in focus

zoo·mor·phic \ˌzō-ə-'mòr-fik\ *adj* **1** : having the form of an animal   **2** : of, relating to, or being the representation of a deity in the form or with the attributes of an animal

zoo·plank·ton \ˌzō-ə-'plaŋk-tən, -ˌtän\ *n* : plankton composed of animals

zoo·spore \'zō-ə-ˌspòr\ *n* : a motile spore

zoot suit \'züt-\ *n* : a flashy suit of extreme cut typically consisting of a thigh-length jacket with wide padded shoulders and pants that are wide at the top and narrow at the bottom — **zoot·suit·er** \-ˌsü-tər\ *n*

Zo·ro·as·tri·an·ism \ˌzòr-ə-'was-trē-ə-ˌni-zəm\ *n* : a religion founded by the Persian prophet Zoroaster — **Zo·ro·as·tri·an** \-trē-ən\ *adj or n*

zounds \'zaùndz\ *interj* — used as a mild oath

zoy·sia \'zòi-shə, -zhə, -sē-ə, -zē-ə\ *n* : any of a genus of creeping perennial grasses having fine wiry leaves and including some used as lawn grasses

ZPG *abbr* zero population growth

Zr *symbol* zirconium

zuc·chet·to \zü-'ke-tō, tsü-\ *n, pl* **-tos** : a small round skullcap worn by Roman Catholic ecclesiastics

zuc·chi·ni \zù-'kē-nē\ *n, pl* **-ni** *or* **-nis** : a smooth cylindrical usu. dark green summer squash; *also* : a plant that bears zucchini

Zu·lu \'zü-ˌlü\ *n, pl* **Zulu** *or* **Zulus** : a member of a Bantu-speaking people of South Africa; *also* : the Bantu language of the Zulus

Zu·ni \'zü-nē\ *or* **Zu·ñi** \-nyē\ *n, pl* **Zuni** *or* **Zunis** *or* **Zuñi** *or* **Zuñis** : a member of an Indigenous people of western New Mexico; *also* : the language of the Zuni people

zwie·back \'swē-ˌbak, 'swī-, 'zwē-, 'zwī-, -ˌbäk\ *n* : a usu. sweetened bread that is baked and then sliced and toasted until dry and crisp

Zwing·li·an \'zwiŋ-glē-ən, 'swiŋ-, -lē-; 'tsfiŋ-lē-\ *adj* : of or relating to the Swiss religious reformer Ulrich Zwingli or his teachings — **Zwinglian** *n*

zy·de·co \'zī-də-ˌkō\ *n* : popular music of southern Louisiana that combines tunes of French origin with elements of Caribbean music and the blues

zy·gote \'zī-ˌgōt\ *n* : a cell formed by the union of two sexual cells; *also* : the developing individual produced from such a cell — **zy·got·ic** \zī-'gä-tik\ *adj*